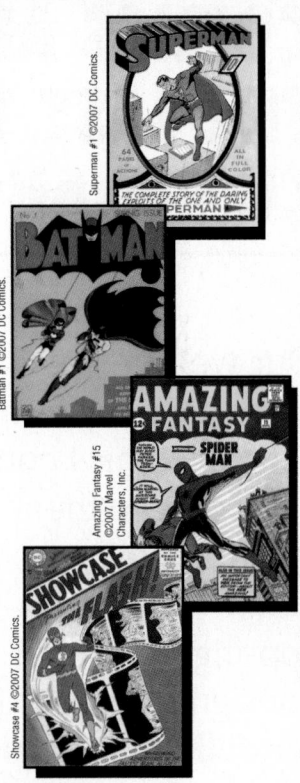

HERE'S WHY SELLERS CHOOSE HERITAGE:

$18 MILLION WORTH OF COMICS AND COMIC ART SOLD IN THE LAST YEAR, <u>TRIPLE</u> ALL OTHER COMIC AUCTIONEERS <u>COMBINED</u>!

Our website receives **over 20 times as many visitors** as our nearest comics competitor according to the independent tracking site <u>compete.com</u>.

Top-flight material that's consigned to us is featured in our **full-color catalogs** that are distributed to thousands of bidders worldwide.

Our **heavily advertised** Signature auctions are among the biggest events in the comic book hobby. The live sessions have bidders participating by phone, in person, and over the Internet.

WE HAVE PAID CASH ADVANCES AS HIGH AS $4.25 MILLION EACH AGAINST SINGLE CONSIGNMENTS

OFFICIAL OVERSTREET COMIC BOOK PRICE GUIDE

38th Edition
COMICS FROM THE 1500s–PRESENT INCLUDED
FULLY ILLUSTRATED CATALOGUE & EVALUATION GUIDE

by ROBERT M. OVERSTREET

GEMSTONE PUBLISHING

J.C. Vaughn, Executive Editor & Associate Publisher
Brenda Busick, Creative Director • **Lindsay Dunn**, Editor
Tom Gordon III, Managing Editor • **Mark Huesman**, Production Coordinator
Diana Hundt, Advertising Assistant • **Courtney Jenkins**, Marketing Manager
Amanda Sheriff, Editorial Coordinator • **Heather Winter**, Office Manager

SPECIAL CONTRIBUTORS TO THIS EDITION

Robert L. Beerbohm • Dr. Arnold T. Blumberg • Steve Borock • Eric C. Caren • Michael Eury • Gene Gonzales • John Jackson Miller
Richard D. Olson, Ph.D. • J.C. Vaughn • Richard Samuel West • Mark Zaid

SENIOR OVERSTREET ADVISORS FOR OVER 25 YEARS

Dave Alexander • Gary M. Carter • Bill Cole • Steve Geppi • Stan Gold • M. Thomas Inge • Phil Levine • Paul Levitz • Michelle Nolan
Richard D. Olson, Ph.D. • Ron Pussell • Gene Seger • Rick Sloane • David R. Smith • John K. Snyder Jr. • Doug Sulipa • Harry B. Thomas
Raymond S. True • Frank Verzyl • John Verzyl

SENIOR OVERSTREET ADVISORS FOR OVER 20 YEARS

Jon Berk • Gary Colabuono • Stephen Fishler • James Payette • Joe Vereneault • Jerry Weist

SPECIAL ADVISORS

Weldon Adams • David Alexander • Tyler Alexander • Lon Allen • Dave Anderson • David J. Anderson, DDS • Stephen Barrington • Lauren Becker
Robert L. Beerbohm • Jon Berk • Peter J. Bilelis • Brian Block • Dr. Arnold T. Blumberg • Steve Borock • Kevin Boyd • Mike Broder
Michael Browning • Michael Carbonaro • Gary M. Carter • John Chruscinski • Russ Cochran • Gary Colabuono • Bill Cole • Tim Collins • Jack Copley
Dan Cusimano • Carl De La Cruz • Peter Dixon • Gary Dolgoff • Joe Duncan • Bruce Ellsworth • Conrad Eschenberg • Michael Eury • Richard Evans
D'Arcy Farrell • Stephen Fishler • Dan Fogel • Chris Foss • Philip J. Gaudino • Steven Gentner • Steve Geppi • Stan Gold • Michael Goldman
Tom Gordon III • Jamie Graham • Daniel Greenhalgh • Eric Groves • Gary Guzzo • John Grasse • John Haines • Jim Halperin • Mark Haspel
John Hauser • Jef Hinds • Greg Holland • John Hone • George Huang • Bill Hughes • Rob Hughes • M. Thomas Inge • William Insignares • Ed Jaster
Brian Ketterer • Dennis Keum • Tim Kupin • Phil Levine • Paul Levitz • Larry Lowery • Joe Mannarino • Nadia Mannarino • Rick Manzella
Harry Matetsky • Dave Matteini • Jon McClure • Todd McDevitt • Michael McKenzie • Fred McSurley • Pete Merolo • John Jackson Miller
Steve Mortensen • Michael Naiman • Marc Nathan • Josh Nathanson • Matt Nelson • Michelle Nolan • Charlie Novinski • Richard D. Olson, Ph.D.
Terry O'Neill • George Pantela • James Payette • Chris Pedrin • John Petty • Jim Pitts • Bill Ponseti • Ron Pussell • Yolanda Ramirez • Jo Ann Reisler
Stephen Ritter • Dave Robie • "Doc" Robinson • Israel Rodriguez • Robert Rogovin • Marnin Rosenberg • Chuck Rozanski • Gene Seger
Matt Schiffman • Doug Schmell • Rich Slone • David R. Smith • John K. Snyder, Jr. • Laura Sperber • Tony Starks • West Stephan • Al Stoltz
Bob Storms • Ken Stribling • Doug Sulipa • Joel Thingvall • Harry B. Thomas • Maggie Thompson • Michael Tierney • Raymond S. True
Ted Van Liew • Joe Verenault • Frank Verzyl• John Verzyl • Rose Verzyl • Bob Wayne • Lon Webb • Jerry Weist • Mark Wilson
Alex Winter • Anthony Yamada • Harley Yee • Mark Zaid • Vincent Zurzolo, Jr.

THE OFFICIAL OVERSTREET COMIC BOOK PRICE GUIDE. Copyright © 1992, 1993, 1994, 1995, 1996, 1997, 1998, 1999, 2000, 2001, 2002, 2003, 2004, 2005, 2006, 2007, 2008 by Gemstone Publishing, Inc. All rights reserved. Printed in China. No part of this book may be used or reproduced in any manner whatsoever without written permission except in the case of brief quotations embodied in critical articles and reviews. For information, write to: Gemstone Publishing, 3679 Concord Rd., York, PA 17402

Superman [Random House] (*Superman* #14) cover recreation by Murphy Anderson. Superman and *Superman* #14 image ©2007 DC Comics. All rights reserved.
Marvel Villains [Direct Market] cover by Mark Sparacio. Doctor Doom, Red Skull, Madame Hydra, Magneto & Titanium Man ©2007 Marvel Characters, Inc. All rights reserved.
Star Wars [Direct Market] cover art by Douglas Wheatley. *Star Wars* ©2007 Lucasfilm Ltd. & ™. All rights reserved. Used under authorization.

Spine, Direct Market Editions: Iron Man and *Iron Man* #1 image © Marvel Characters, Inc. Green Lantern and *Green Lantern* #76 image © DC Comics. All rights reserved.

THE OFFICIAL OVERSTREET COMIC BOOK PRICE GUIDE (38th Edition) is an original publication of Gemstone Publishing, Inc. and House of Collectibles. Distributed by The Random House Information Group, a division of Random House, Inc., New York and simultaneously in Canada by Random House of Canada Limited, Toronto. This edition has never before appeared in book form.

House of Collectibles
Random House Information Group
1745 Broadway
New York, New York 10019

 www.houseofcollectibles.com

Overstreet is a registered trademark of Gemstone Publishing, Inc.

House of Collectibles is a registered trademark and the colophon is a trademark of Random House, Inc.

Published by arrangement with Gemstone Publishing, Inc.

ISBN: 978-0-375-72239-4
ISSN: 0891-8872

Printed in China

10 9 8 7 6 5 4 3 2 1

Thirty-Eighth Edition: May 2008

Table of Contents

Acknowledgements

Lon Allen (Golden Age data); Mark Arnold (Harvey data); Larry Bigman (Frazetta-Williamson data); Glenn Bray (Kurtzman data); Gary Carter (DC data); J. B. Clifford Jr. (EC data); Gary Coddington (Superman data); Gary Colabuono (Golden Age ashcan data); Wilt Conine (Fawcett data); Chris Cormier (Miracleman data); Dr. S. M. Davidson (Cupples & Leon data); Al Dellinges (Kubert data); Chris Friesen (Glossary additions); David Gerstein (Walt Disney Comics data); Gene Gonzales (introduction illustrations); Kevin Hancer (Tarzan data); Charles Heffelfinger and Jim Ivey (March of Comics listing); R. C. Holland and Ron Pussell (Seduction and Parade of Pleasure data); Grant Irwin (Quality data); Richard Kravitz (Kelly data); Phil Levine (giveaway data); Paul Litch (Copper & Modern Age data); Dan Malan & Charles Heffelfinger (Classic Comics data); Jon McClure (Whitman data); Fred Nardelli (Frazetta data); Michelle Nolan (love comics); Mike Nolan (MLJ, Timely, Nedor data); George Olshevsky (Timely data); Chris Pedrin (DC War data); Scott Pell ('50s data); Greg Robertson (National data); Don Rosa (Late 1940s to 1950s data); Matt Schiffman (Bronze Age data); Frank Scigliano (Little Lulu data); Gene Seger (Buck Rogers data); Rick Sloane (Archie data); David R. Smith, Archivist, Walt Disney Productions (Disney data); Tony Starks (Silver and Bronze Age data); Al Stoltz (Golden Age & Promo data); Don and Maggie Thompson (Four Color listing); Mike Tiefenbacher & Jerry Sinkovec (Atlas and National data); Raymond True & Philip J. Gaudino (Classic Comics data); Jim Vadeboncoeur Jr. (Williamson and Atlas data); Kim Weston (Disney and Barks data); Cat Yronwode (Spirit data); Andrew Zerbe and Gary Behymer (M. E. data).

Thanks to Mark "Sparky" Sparacio for his Marvel Villains cover (a great bookend to last year's *New Avengers* piece), Doug Wheatley for the inspired *Star Wars* cover, and the great Murphy Anderson for his wonderful *Superman* #14 recreation featured on the traditional book market version of this edition.Credit is due my two grading advisors, Steve Borock and Mark Haspel of Comics Guaranty Corp., for their ongoing input on grading.

Thanks again to Doug Sulipa, Jon McClure, Fred McSurley and Tony Starks for continuing to provide detailed Bronze Age data. To Dave Alexander, Tyler Alexander, Lon Allen, Dave Anderson (Oklahoma), Dave Anderson (Virginia), Stephen Barrington, Lauren Becker, Peter J. Bilelis, Kevin Boyd, Michael Browning, Dan Cusimano, Peter Dixon, Gary Dolgoff, Bruce Ellsworth, Conrad Eschenberg, D'Arcy Farrell, Dan Fogel, Stephen Gentner, Jamie Graham, Dan Greenhalgh, Eric Groves, John Haines, John Hauser, Jef Hinds, Greg Holland, Bill Hughes, William Insignares, Brian Ketterer, Dennis Keum, Nadia Mannarino, Joe Mannarino, Frédéric Manzano, Dave Mattenini, Todd McDevitt, Steve Mortensen, Josh Nathanson, Matt Nelson, Terry O'Neill, Jim Payette, John Petty, Jim Pitts, Ron Pussell, Stephen Ritter, Dave Robie, Rob Rogovin, Marnin Rosenberg, Chuck Rozanski, Barry Sandoval, Matt Schiffman, Doug Schmell, Doug Simpson, Ben Smith, West Stephan, Al Stoltz, Harry B. Thomas, Maggie Thompson, Michael Tierney, John Verzyl, Frank Verzyl, Lon Webb, Alex Winter, Harley Yee, Mark Zaid and Vincent Zurzolo Jr., who supplied detailed pricing data, market reports or other material in this edition.

My gratitude is given to Chris Pedrin for his advice on DC war comics data; to Stephen Fishler for inspiring and helping develop the 10-point grading system adopted in the 30th Edition; to Dr. Richard Olson for grading and Yellow Kid information; to Dr. Arnold T. Blumberg for his introduction to the Promotional Comics section; to Bill Blackbeard of the San Francisco Academy of Comic Art for his Platinum Age cover photos; to Bill Spicer and Zetta DeVoe (Western Publishing Co.) for their contribution of data; to Ted Hake for pricing the Big Little Book section; and especially to Bill for his kind permission to reprint portions of his and Jerry Bails' America's Four Color Pastime.

Special recognition is due Bob Beerbohm, Richard Samuel West and Richard Olson for researching the Victorian and Platinum sections. Thanks to Eric C. Caren for providing the Pioneer Age article, John Jackson Miller for the *Star Wars* article, and Gary Colabuono and Mark Zaid for the ashcans feature.

Acknowledgement is also due to the following people who generously contributed much needed data for this edition, including but not limited to Stephen Baer, Jonathan Calure, Dave Frost, Jason Lohr, John Mlachnik, James Pender, Mark Squirek, Dennis Ray, Geoff Steel, Timothy M. Walters, Mike Wilbur and Neil Young.

Finally, special credit is due our talented production staff for their assistance with this edition: Mark Huesman (Production Coordinator), Brenda Busick (Creative Director), Tom Gordon III (Managing Editor), Lindsay Dunn (Editor), Courtney Jenkins (Marketing Manager), Diana Hundt (Advertising Assistant), Amanda Sheriff (Editorial Coordinator), and Heather Winter (Office Manager), and J.C. Vaughn (Executive Editor and Associate Publisher). Thanks to my wife, Caroline, for her encouragement and support on such a tremendous project, and to all who placed ads in this edition.

Comic Book Collecting
Redefined

A Proven Standard of Integrity

CGC has made a commitment to exceed the market's unique requirements by applying its graders' experience and reputation for integrity in certification. And since CGC's employees are not allowed to commercially buy or sell comics, CGC can remain completely impartial and committed to serving clients through accurate and consistent grading and professional, courteous customer service.

CGC's attractive, and durable, tamper-evident holder utilizes cutting-edge technologies to provide the best protection for your books. The holder is slim and lightweight, making for easy storage and transportation. Its front and top labels display comprehensive information about the book and its grade.

Benefits of CGC Grading

▌ **CGC has an established and trusted grading standard.** CGC's grading team includes the most experienced, knowledgeable and recognized experts in the field, with over 150 years of combined grading experience.

▌ **CGC provides a restoration check for each book submitted.** When detected by our restoration experts, a description of the restoration is noted on our CGC purple label.

▌ **Better protection for your comic books.** The CGC holder is made with state-of-the-art materials and is designed to meet the needs and demands of comic book collectors.

▌ **Buying comic books on the Internet has never been safer.** Each comic book certified by CGC has been reviewed by the hobby's most expert team, and is then encapsulated with a detailed grading label inside our tamper-evident holder. Collectors know what they are getting when buying a CGC-certified comic book.

▌ **Access to the Message Boards.** Talk to the experts and collectors who have similar interests to yours. Do you have a question about a rare piece? Ever wondered who's collecting what? Maybe you want to share a bit of interesting information? Speak out on the Message Boards, get your answers and become a more knowledgeable collector today!

▌ **Access to the Comic Population Reports.** A comprehensive database lists comic books graded by CGC. Watch for updates and see the trend shift month-by-month.

"...probably the most important event [in our hobby] to date was the arrival of comic book certification with CGC. The technical grade applied to each comic has become the standard used for buying and selling."

Robert M. Overstreet
Overstreet Comic Book Price Guide
36th Edition

22

COLLECTORS:

Make Your Next Big Find a Great Comics Shop!

COMIC SHOP LOCATOR SERVICE

COMICS

888-COMIC-BOOK
comicshoplocator.com

By phone and online, millions of people around the world have used the Comic Shop Locator Service to find comic book specialty stores in their areas!

Sponsored By

Don't forget!

FREE COMIC BOOK DAY
1st Saturday In May
www.freecomicbookday.com

Save the date!

MARVEL™
minimates

The powerhouse Marvel Minimates line expands to include the very best heroes and villains the Marvel Universe has to offer!

Series 19 features Amazing Fantasy Spider-Man & Mysterio, Ms. Marvel & Ultron, Apocalypse & Death Archangel and the limited Archangel variant!

Series 20 features
Professor Hulk & Abomination,
Havok & Polaris, Hawkeye & Vision
and the limited Vision 2.0!

MARVEL™

DIAMOND
SELECT TOYS™

ART ASYLUM

COMIC SHOP LOCATOR SERVICE
888-COMIC-BOOK
comicshoplocator.com

www.marvel.com

www.diamondselecttoys.com

www.artasylum.com

41

45

A Gem

pop culture with character

GEPPI'S
entertainment
MUSEUM

It's a nostalgic treasure trove,
a time capsule of media and memories . . .

AT CAMDEN YARDS!

From the silver screen to the TV screen,
from cartoons to comics strips, visit all your
beloved characters at Geppi's Entertainment Museum!

Geppi's Entertainment Museum also features toys and collectibles from over
340 categories, starring hundreds of your favorite comic, cartoon, newspaper strip,
radio, television and film stars. It's a nostalgic treasure trove, a time capsule of
media and memories, and it's all here at Geppi's Entertainment Museum!

GEPPI'S entertainment MUSEUM
301 W. Camden Street • Baltimore, Maryland 21201

# of a Comic Book Collection!

Geppi's Entertainment Museum offers a one-of-a-kind journey through over 230 years of American pop culture! In just one of its galleries, **"A Story in Four Colors,"** you'll see an amazing comic book library showcasing some of the finest examples of key books from the Pioneer to the Modern Age, from *The Adventures of Obadiah Oldbuck* through Action Comics and Walt Disney's Comics and Stories to The Amazing Spider-Man and Spawn! The gallery also features Big Little Books, pulps, and original art including some of the most memorable past covers of *The Overstreet Comic Book Price Guide!* You can page through 'virtual' reprints of classic comic stories like the origins of Batman and the Fantastic Four, answer trivia questions, and learn more about EC Comics and the censorship controversy of the 1950s. And all of that is in just one room!

STARRING HUNDREDS OF YOUR FAVORITE COMIC CHARACTERS!

INVEST IN THE BEST.

The long-standing leader in high-quality archival supplies, E. Gerber Supply Products understands why every one of its valued customers is serious about this deceptively simple sentiment. Why else would they choose its archival products – the finest preservation and storage supply products on the market – to keep their collectibles pristine and resistant to the ravages of age?

Top of the Line Preservation And Storage Supplies

E. Gerber
PRODUCTS
...At The Lowest Prices

The answer is simple:
E. Gerber Supply Products offers serious protection for the serious collector. And its customers only demand the best. **Shouldn't you?**

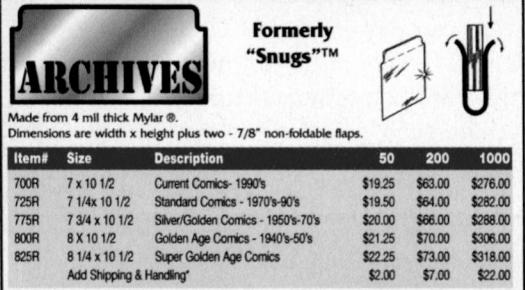

ARCHIVES
Formerly "Snugs"™

Made from 4 mil thick Mylar ®.
Dimensions are width x height plus two - 7/8" non-foldable flaps.

Item#	Size	Description	50	200	1000
700R	7 x 10 1/2	Current Comics- 1990's	$19.25	$63.00	$276.00
725R	7 1/4 x 10 1/2	Standard Comics - 1970's-90's	$19.50	$64.00	$282.00
775R	7 3/4 x 10 1/2	Silver/Golden Comics - 1950's-70's	$20.00	$66.00	$288.00
800R	8 X 10 1/2	Golden Age Comics - 1940's-50's	$21.25	$70.00	$306.00
825R	8 1/4 x 10 1/2	Super Golden Age Comics	$22.25	$73.00	$318.00
		Add Shipping & Handling*	$2.00	$7.00	$22.00

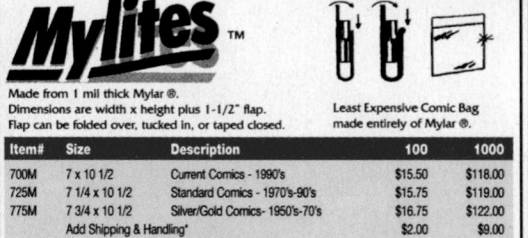

Mylites™
Made from 1 mil thick Mylar ®.
Dimensions are width x height plus 1-1/2" flap.
Flap can be folded over, tucked in, or taped closed.

Least Expensive Comic Bag made entirely of Mylar ®.

Item#	Size	Description	100	1000
700M	7 x 10 1/2	Current Comics - 1990's	$15.50	$118.00
725M	7 1/4 x 10 1/2	Standard Comics - 1970's-90's	$15.75	$119.00
775M	7 3/4 x 10 1/2	Silver/Gold Comics- 1950's-70's	$16.75	$122.00
		Add Shipping & Handling*	$2.00	$9.00

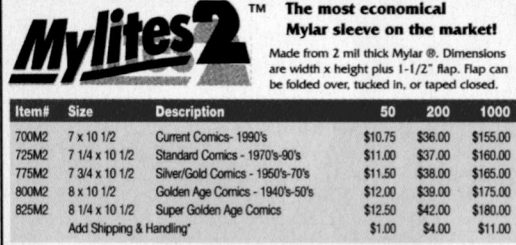

Mylites2™
The most economical Mylar sleeve on the market!
Made from 2 mil thick Mylar ®. Dimensions are width x height plus 1-1/2" flap. Flap can be folded over, tucked in, or taped closed.

Item#	Size	Description	50	200	1000
700M2	7 x 10 1/2	Current Comics - 1990's	$10.75	$36.00	$155.00
725M2	7 1/4 x 10 1/2	Standard Comics - 1970's-90's	$11.00	$37.00	$160.00
775M2	7 3/4 x 10 1/2	Silver/Gold Comics- 1950's-70's	$11.50	$38.00	$165.00
800M2	8 x 10 1/2	Golden Age Comics - 1940's-50's	$12.00	$39.00	$175.00
825M2	8 1/4 x 10 1/2	Super Golden Age Comics	$12.50	$42.00	$180.00
		Add Shipping & Handling*	$1.00	$4.00	$11.00

DON'T FORGET OUR TOP-QUALITY BACKING BOARDS!
We can provide any custom size to fit your needs! Boards are genuine acid-free, virgin wood, cellular fiber that meets strict U.S. Government standards for archival storage. Both styles are white on both sides, and contain 3% calcium carbonate buffer throughout, maintains ph of 8.0

FULL-BACK
- 42 mil, Acid-free,
- 3% Buffered Backing Board

HALF-BACK
- 24 mil, Acid-free
- 3% Buffered Backing Board

CGC Storage Box
The official storage box of the CGC!

Holds up to 30 CGC- "slabbed" comics
Durable construction withstands
200 pounds of pressure

Item#	Size	Description	Price per:	1-10	11-50	51+
514	15x8 1/2x13	CGC Storage Box		$4.50	$3.30	$2.75
545	15 1/4x9 7/8x14 1/4	CGC Magazine Storage Box		$4.50	$3.30	$2.75
		Add Shipping & Handling*		$8.00	$20.00	$40.00

Corrugated Comic Carton
ACID FREE BOXES

Grey corrugated. Acid-free,
3% buffered, 200 lb strength. Min. ph of 8.5 throughout.
Life time acid-free storage. Box plus separate lid.

The boxes have had a **3% calcium carbonate buffer** added, which maintains an acid-free alkaline ph content of 8.0-8.5 throughout, not just on the surface.

All boxes fold flat for shipping. Easy snap up assembly. Does not require glue nor tape.

Sold in Packs of 5 Boxes

Item#	Size	Description	Price per:	5	20	50
13	15 x 8 x 11 1/2	Silver/Golden Comics		$45.00	$175.00	$400.00
15	15 x 9 1/4 x 12 1/2	Super Golden/Magazines		$47.50	$185.00	$450.00
		Add Shipping & Handling*		$8.00	$24.00	$49.00

For a complete list of our affordable archival products, please call us toll-free at

1-800-79-MYLAR

Top of the Line Preservation And Storage Supplies

E. Gerber
PRODUCTS
...At The Lowest Prices

from 8:00 a.m. to 5:00 p.m. EST,
or mail your request to:

E. Gerber Products ● 1720 Belmont Avenue
Suite C ● Baltimore, MD 21244
Fax: 1-410-944-9363
e-mail: archival@egerber.com

The Best Protection at the Best Price!

www.egerber.com

* Minimum Shipping Charge $7.00   Mylar® by Dupont Co. or approved equivalent.

PLEASE NOTE: All returns are subject to a 10% restock fee. Returned items must be undamaged and unopened unless otherwise approved.

SOLD $414,000

WHY CONSIGN with MORPHY AUCTIONS?

- All items are on display at Morphy Auctions two months prior to the sale.

- Your collection is securely housed and insured to guarantee ultimate protection and safekeeping.

- All items are available to view online at www.morphyauctions.com and www.liveauctioneers.com one month prior to the sale.

SOLD $287,500

- Consignors are paid within 30 days.

- Over 85,000 full-color brochures and 10,000 hardbound catalogs are printed.

- Morphy Auctions promotes its sales at the top antique shows in the country.

- A well-planned marketing and advertising campaign is launched to maximize exposure.

53

WANTED!
AUCTION CONSIGNMENTS
Now Accepting Consignments from Film, Television and Music

Get the Best Prices for Your Hollywood Collectibles

Original Robert McGinnis Poster
Artwork for *Thunderball*

SOLD for
$63,250.00

Hugh Jackman "Wolverine" Hero Claws
from *X2: X-Men United*

SOLD for
$40,250.00

Profiles
IN HISTORY

ABOUT THIS BOOK

BY J.C. VAUGHN

ILLUSTRATED BY GENE GONZALES

HI THERE!

WELCOME TO THE 38TH EDITION OF THE OFFICIAL OVERSTREET COMIC BOOK PRICE GUIDE.

SINCE THE PRICE GUIDE DEBUTED IN 1970, A LOT HAS CHANGED. COVER PRICES FOR NEW ISSUES HAVE GONE UP...

CHARACTERS AND EVEN PUBLISHERS HAVE COME AND GONE...

AND THE BACK ISSUE MARKET HAS HAD ITS UPS AND DOWNS... MOSTLY UPS, OF COURSE.

BUT SOME THINGS HAVEN'T CHANGED AT ALL.

NO MATTER HOW MUCH MONEY WE'RE TALKING ABOUT...

MOST OF US ARE STILL COLLECTING COMICS FOR FUN.

BUT "FUN" ALSO MEANS WE'D LIKE TO KNOW WHAT THEY'RE REALISTICALLY SELLING FOR, RIGHT?

THAT'S WHAT THIS BOOK IS ABOUT.

AND WE'RE GLAD YOU ARE HERE.

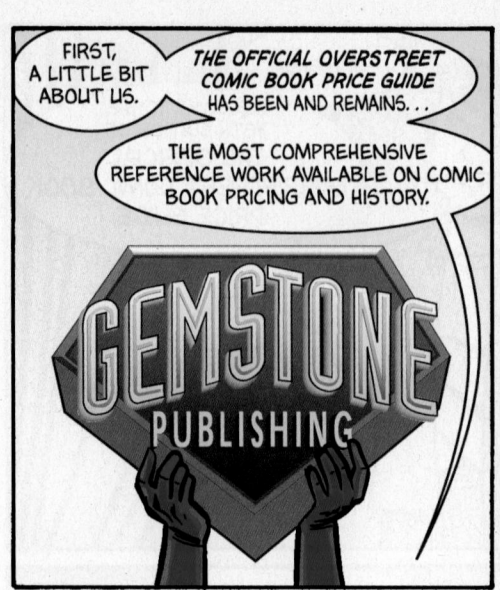

FIRST, A LITTLE BIT ABOUT US.

THE OFFICIAL OVERSTREET COMIC BOOK PRICE GUIDE HAS BEEN AND REMAINS...

THE MOST COMPREHENSIVE REFERENCE WORK AVAILABLE ON COMIC BOOK PRICING AND HISTORY.

GEMSTONE PUBLISHING

IT'S RESPECTED AND USED BY DEALERS AND COLLECTORS EVERYWHERE.

OVERSTREET PRICING AND GRADING STANDARDS ARE THE ACCEPTED FOUNDATIONS OF THE COMIC BOOK MARKETPLACE AROUND THE WORLD.

THROUGH HARD WORK, DILIGENCE AND CONSTANT CONTACT WITH THE MARKET FOR DECADES, OVERSTREET HAS BECOME THE MOST TRUSTED NAME IN COMICS.

OUR BOOK IS A DETAILED ALPHABETICAL LIST OF COMIC BOOKS AND THEIR MARKET VALUES.

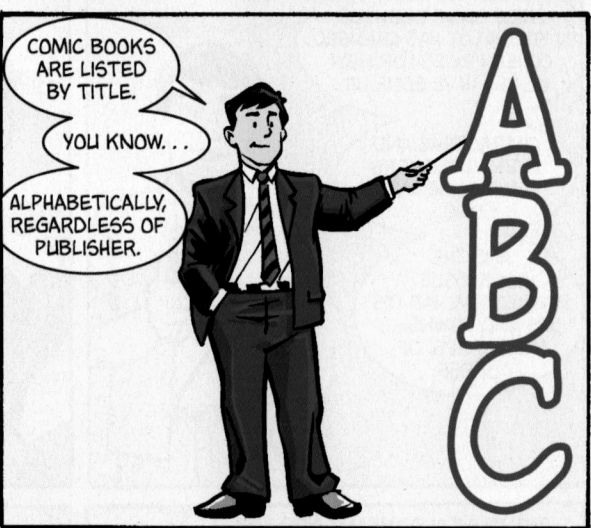

COMIC BOOKS ARE LISTED BY TITLE.

YOU KNOW...

ALPHABETICALLY, REGARDLESS OF PUBLISHER.

This book includes...
Big Little Books
Promotional Comics
Pioneer Age Comics
Victorian Age Comics
Platinum Age Comics

WHOA!

THE MAIN PRICING SECTION FEATURES COMICS FROM 1938 THROUGH THE PRESENT!

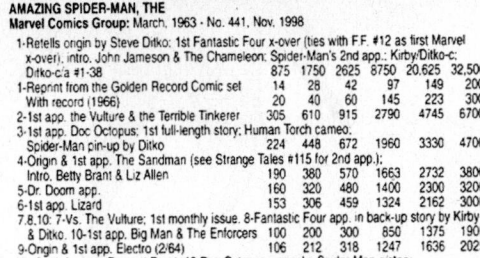

9.2
9.0
8.5
8.0
7.5
7.0
6.5
6.0
5.5
5.0
4.5
4.0
3.5
3.0
2.5
2.0

PRICES ARE LISTED IN SIX GRADES, RANGING FROM 2.0 TO 9.2 ON A 10.0 SCALE.

THERE ARE MORE GRADES THAN THE SIX WE HAVE LISTED, BUT THESE WILL GIVE YOU THE KEYS TO UNDERSTANDING THE MARKET.

WHILE PRICES BELOW 9.2 ARE FAIRLY STEADY, IT'S IMPORTANT TO NOTE THAT PRICES ABOVE 9.2 ARE FREQUENTLY CONSIDERED EXTREMELY VOLATILE.

AMAZING SPIDER-MAN, THE
Marvel Comics Group: March, 1963 - No. 441. Nov. 1998

1-Retells origin by Steve Ditko: 1st Fantastic Four x-over (ties with F.F. #12 as first Marvel x-over), intro. John Jameson & The Chameleon; Spider-Man's 2nd app.; Kirby/Ditko-c; Ditko-c/a #1-38   875 1750 2625 8750 20,625 32,500
1-Reprint from the Golden Record Comic set   14 28 42 97 149 200
With record (1966)   20 40 60 145 223 300
2-1st app. the Vulture & the Terrible Tinkerer   305 610 915 2790 4745 6700
3-1st app. Doc Octopus: 1st full-length story; Human Torch cameo. Spider-Man pin-up by Ditko   224 448 672 1960 3330 4700
4-Origin & 1st app. The Sandman (see Strange Tales #115 for 2nd app.); Intro. Betty Brant & Liz Allen   190 380 570 1663 2732 3800
5-Dr. Doom app.   160 320 480 1400 2300 3200
6-1st app. Lizard   153 306 459 1324 2162 3000
7,8,10: 7-Vs. The Vulture; 1st monthly issue. 8-Fantastic Four app. in back-up story by Kirby & Ditko. 10-1st app. Big Man & The Enforcers   100 200 300 850 1375 1900
9-Origin & 1st app. Electro (2/64)   106 212 318 1247 1636 2025
11,12: 11-1st app. Bennett Brant. 12-Doc Octopus unmasks Spider-Man-c/story   67 134 201 570 923 1275

- Many of the comic books are listed in groups, such as 11-20, 21-30, 31-50, and so on.
- The prices listed along with such groupings represent the value of each issue in that group, not the group as a whole.
- It's difficult to overstate how much accurate grading plays into getting a good price for your sales or purchases.

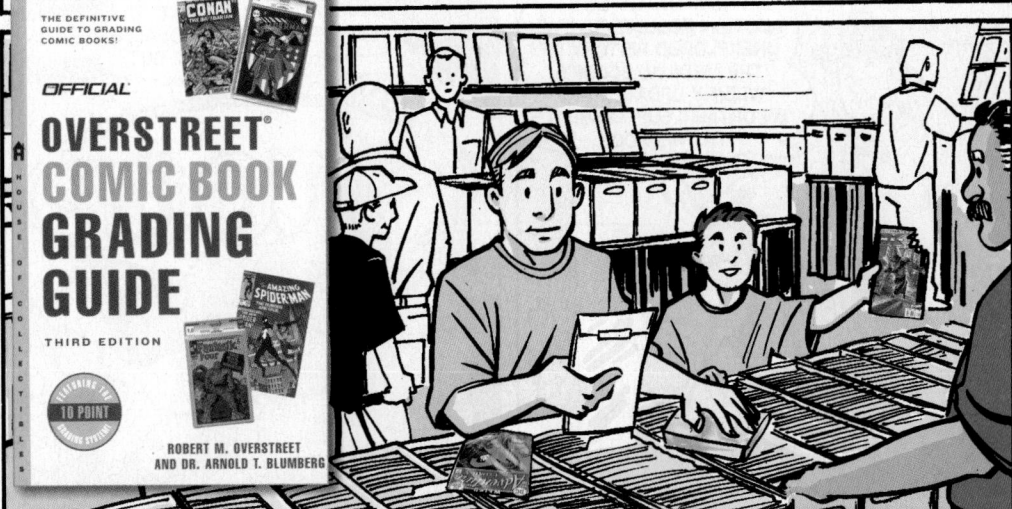

THE DEFINITIVE GUIDE TO GRADING COMIC BOOKS!

OFFICIAL
OVERSTREET
COMIC BOOK
GRADING GUIDE

THIRD EDITION

FEATURING THE 10 POINT GRADING SYSTEM

ROBERT M. OVERSTREET AND DR. ARNOLD T. BLUMBERG

LIKE ANY OTHER PART OF LIFE, IN COMICS INFORMATION IS KING. THERE ARE ALL SORTS OF PUBLICATIONS ABOUT COLLECTING.

THEY COVER WHAT'S GOING ON IN THE BUSINESS NOW AS WELL AS WHAT HAPPENED IN THE PAST AND WHAT'S COMING UP IN THE FUTURE.

THERE ARE LOTS OF INTERESTING WEBSITES AND CHATROOMS DEVOTED TO COMIC BOOKS, TOO.

OUR OWN FREE WEEKLY NEWSLETTER, SCOOP, COVERS COMICS AND COMIC CHARACTERS.

FROM THE LATEST AUCTION RESULTS TO THE UNEXPLORED HISTORY OF THE MEDIUM, SCOOP'S WEEKLY UPDATES ARE IMPORTANT SUPPLEMENTS TO THIS BOOK.

JUST VISIT HTTP://SCOOP.DIAMONDGALLERIES.COM TO CHECK IT OUT.

WHAT'S THE FIRST APPEARANCE OF WOLVERINE?

I THINK IT WAS INCREDIBLE HULK #181, BUT LET'S LOOK IT UP IN OVERSTREET.

DID JOSS WHEDON OR JIMMY PALMIOTTI WRITE IT?

NO, THAT WAS BEFORE THEY WROTE EVERYTHING.

HERE IT IS. WOLVERINE HAD A BRIEF APPEARANCE AT THE END OF #180 AND SHOWED UP FOR REAL IN #181.

MANY FIRST APPEARANCES AND OTHER IMPORTANT ISSUES ARE NOTED.

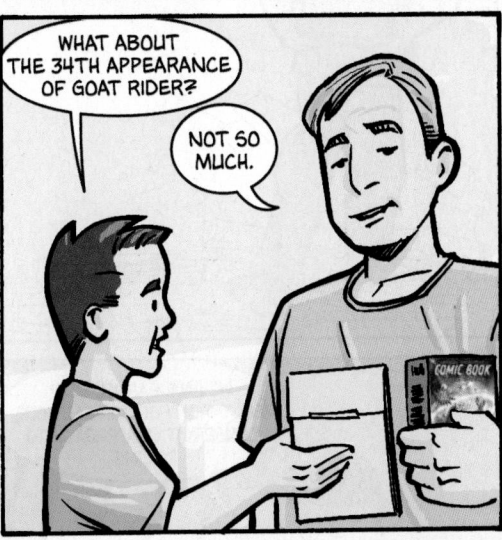

WHAT ABOUT THE 34TH APPEARANCE OF GOAT RIDER?

NOT SO MUCH.

IT IS IMPORTANT TO UNDERSTAND THAT VALUES LISTED IN THIS BOOK ARE APPROXIMATIONS OR GUIDELINES, PRESENTING AN AVERAGE RANGE OF WHAT ONE MIGHT EXPECT TO PAY FOR THE CORRESPONDING ITEMS.

THAT'S A COMPLICATED WAY OF SAYING "IT'S A GUIDE, NOT A PRICE LIST." IN THE MARKETPLACE, BUYERS AND SELLERS DETERMINE PRICES ASKED AND PRICES PAID.

ACROSS THE BOARD!
2007 IN REVIEW

by Robert M. Overstreet

In spite of gold reaching its highest level in decades and the stock market's volatile swings, the collectable markets, including comic books, have enjoyed yet another banner year. The 11,000-issue "D Copy" Davis Crippin collection of Golden Age books came out in late 2005 and was offered over the past two years in several auctions by Heritage Auction Galleries to anxious buyers. Just as in the past, whenever large collections of this type emerge, collectors seem to always be there to absorb the books.

Comic books, of course, are not only sold to the public through the old traditional channels such as comic book stores and convention and mail order dealers, but today are also sold on the internet through auctions and sites such as eBay. As dealer Harley Yee observed, "2007 was one of my best years ever with the internet playing an important part. I am completely astounded by the hundreds of new buyers I am finding."

After handing the responsibility of grading to third party certification companies, auction houses can now sell certified (or "slabbed") comic books to their customers. This has certainly been a factor in record prices, but the demand for certified comics is still mixed. Many collectors want uncertified (or "raw") issues, others accept raw and slabbed copies, while still others only want the slabbed comics.

As experienced collectors and dealers detected some time back, there is definitely a phenomenon with certification in that certain collectors are willing to pay multiples of *Guide* prices for books that are listed in the CGC Census as the highest graded copies. Some collector-investors are betting that these copies will not be out-ranked.

Additionally, near perfect to perfect copies in 9.9 or 10.0 have become sought-after as well, and this clearly includes even the more recent comics. While the vast majority of recent releases – and indeed, many books available

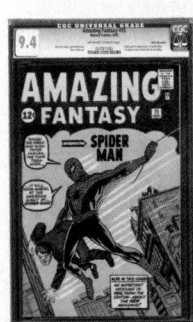

© MAR

Amazing Fantasy #15
9.4 White Mountain pedigree copy sold for a record $227,000

from the past two decades – have values too low to be slabbed economically, the wise investor of this kind of material should be aware that the published population reports are only for copies that have been submitted and do not include the larger quantity of those yet to be certified.

The reasons for the impressive growth in independent certification have a lot to do with the comic book grading as a balance of science and art. Grades on raw books can vary considerably from dealer to dealer (or from collector to collector). Correspondingly, so would the prices realized from their sales. The results of these disparities are obvious.

The inconsistency in grades between different parties lends itself to restraining consumer confidence. For instance, take a raw book that has been designated with a high grade. If it was not graded accurately and then was submitted to a grading company, it could very well come back with a lower grade than expected, disappointing the purchaser. The benefit of a third-party grading service using consistent and accepted benchmarks has instead increased confidence in the grade and therefore the price. For this reason we have seen many slabbed books sell for prices much higher than their raw counterparts.

This has produced a certain volatility in the marketplace (this is particularly true of Silver Age and later comics). Along with other industry veterans, we have noticed when particular books are sold and then later resold at auction with widely varied results.

In the Golden Age, for instance, a CGC-certified Denver copy of *Special Edition Comics* #1 (9.4) sold in 2001 for $26,450 and again in 2005 for $15,525. If the *Guide* had raised the list price too much based just on the 2001 sale, it would later have to lower the price in 2005 when it sold for much less. Indeed, special issues and pedigree books can become very volatile at any time selling for prices way over the listed values.

Warehouse finds can also affect the sales price realized. A case in point is the recent warehouse of Gold Key books from Random House released into the market in 2007 as noted by advisor Lon Webb: "Gold Keys and Dells are slowing with the Random House file copies that flooded the market and buyers are picking and choosing among high (grade) copies at small to large price reductions."

During 2007, we saw thousands of changes in values – both up and down – which are reflected in this volume. Many titles and individual issues have enjoyed increased demand forcing prices higher while other titles have been selling for under *Guide* list with prices adjusted accordingly. **Platinum Age:** Steady and sometimes surprising growth in this market has been witnessed throughout 2007 in auctions from Heritage Auction Galleries, Hake's Americana & Collectibles and eBay. There have been record prices, to be sure, but it is more impressive to note the wider and stronger support of this particular part of the overall comic market. As collectors continue to seek out the history of the comic book medium, they are increasingly drawn past the artificial limits and into this early realm.

Golden Age: Early Archie books remained scarce with copies selling at above *Guide*. A 3.0 copy of #1 brought $6,500, a good/very good #1 sold for $5,748. A CGC-certified *Pep Comics* #22, the first Archie, in 7.5 sold for $70,000 ("Archie titles have always sold well over many generations" noted Harley Yee).

Among the successes reported to us in 2007: Timely comics as a group sold briskly, a CGC-certified *Detective Comics* #27 in brought $190,000, early *Action Comics* seemed impossible to find, Centaur and Fiction House titles – always hard to find – became hot books. A Good copy of *Action Comics* #1 sold for $85,000. *All-Negro* continued to outpace the *Guide* as a Good+ copy sold for $3,720 and Very Fine- copy sold for $10,063. Matt Baker books such as *Giant Comics Edition* #12, *Teenage Diary Secrets*, etc. were in very high demand along with *Reform School Girl* and *Phantom Lady*. A *Phantom Lady* #17 in fine sold for $3227 while a copy of *Daring Love* #1 (Ditko's first published story) sold for a record $1,793!

The Atlas superhero revival books that occurred between the Golden and Silver Ages in 1954 continue to set record prices as they have in years past. An uncertified *Captain America* #78 in NM- sold for $4,182. It is difficult to say for certain, but we can't help but wonder if Marvel's *Agents of Atlas* mini-series and the beautiful hardcover collection of the same with its glorious reproductions of key Atlas issues helped fuel awareness of this material.

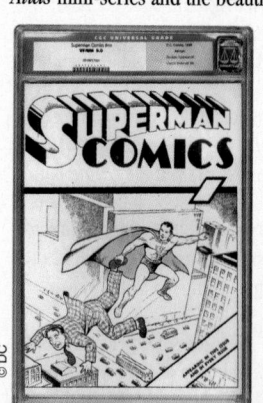

© DC

Superman Comics *ashcan CGC-certified 9.0 sold for $90,000 in a private transaction in 2007.*

Due at least in part to the continued availability of the Gerber *Photo-Journal* reference books, more and more covers are being singled out and collected. Because of the high value of Golden Age runs in today's market, most collectors can't afford to collect entire runs. Therefore, collectors are picking the best covers and are willing to pay more to get that "special" issue for their collections. As Heritage's Lon Allen and Barry Sandoval reported, "*Superman* #14 (Fred Ray Patriotic cover) sells for at least double what a #15 sells for." They also suggested that *Exciting Comics* #39 (the one with Nazis giving poisoned candy to kids on the cover), "should be doubled."

EC Gaines file copies continued to sell at multiples of *Guide* during the year while non-Gaines copies in high grade remained scarce. Vincent Zurzolo wrote, "Of particular note is the returning strength of pre-code horror and the ever-present popularity of ECs. ECs sell because people love quality art and story-telling."

In the past few years early issues of *Walt Disney's Comics & Stories*, *Uncle Scrooge* and the duck one-shots have been scarce in high-grade selling at significant prices whenever they do appear on the market. A CGC-certified *Uncle Scrooge* #386 in 9.4 sold for $8,000 in 2003. In 2006 that copy sold again for $26,290 and then another certified 9.4 brought $28,680 which is over 10 times current *Guide*. A CGC-certified *WDC&S* #2 in 9.0 sold for $16,100 and $13,145 in Very Fine. When it comes to high-grade copies of this title, early issues remained scarce to non-existent. A *Four Color Comics* #4 Donald Duck in VG-F went for $6,573, two and one half times *Guide*.

This has not been a casual blip or anomaly. Rather it has been a sustained interest in high-grade Disneyana reaching far beyond comics. By setting its various benchmarks (and including Overstreet pricing on its selected comics), *The Official Price Guide to Disney Collectibles* may have been all the encouragement consumer confidence in this area needed. Its second edition is now available. We should also note that numerous other duck one-shots were consistently selling for over *Guide* in Very Fine and better. CGC-certified issues in 9.4 or better can really get crazy, selling for up to 10 times *Guide*.

"Significant amounts of quality material became available to the market as a result of individual collectors deciding to part with portions of their collections." noted Dave Anderson. "There are currently more options for selling material of any value level than ever before. Auction options include Heritage, ComicLink, Hake, and of course, eBay."

Many of our advisors have reported a pick-up in sales for restored books. Collectors are discovering that books with slight restoration such as minor color touch or glue repairs can be bought at a discount. "While they categorically sell for prices well under *Guide*, hobbyists are realizing that a few dots of glue are not equivalent to more extensive treatments," wrote collector Peter Bilelis.

Silver Age: There is a big disparity in the perceived value between Silver Age comics that are uncertified and those that are certified. The certified copies tend to sell for much higher prices generally even though there are numerous raw copies that might grade exactly the same.

Given our continued focus on consumer confidence, this discrepancy is logical since collectors can't be certain of what the "official" grade of an uncertified issue might be if later submitted to CGC for grading. Correspondingly then, even though we raise many of the prices for these issues graded 9.2 each year in the *Guide* – and there continue to be many examples sold in this grade – our top price listed may well fall short of what these issues bring when certified.

Silver Age keys such as *Tales of Suspense* #39, *Journey Into Mystery* #83, *Incredible Hulk* #1, *Amazing Fantasy* #15, *Fantastic Four* #1, *Amazing Spider-Man* #1 all sold for record prices during the year, and some broke records more than once. Marvel's success at the movie box office (and with subsequent DVD sales) certainly doesn't hurt this.

Two CGC-certified copies of *Amazing Fantasy* #15 (the first Spider-Man story) sold in 9.4 for $210,000 and $227,000, respectively, and another in 7.5 went for $23,200. Other amazing sales included *Amazing Spider-Man* #1, which brought $100,000 in 9.6 and another copy sold for $34,000 in 9.0. Others: a *Fantastic Four* #1 went for $23,500 in VF and another copy sold for $13,384 in Fine+, *Incredible Hulk* #1 fetched $82,500 in 9.2 while another copy in 9.0 went for $50,000; a *Tales of Suspense* #39 got $25,000 in 9.2, $11,950 in 9.0 and $1,600 in Fine-Very Fine. DC war books have enjoyed a marked increase in prices realized this year.

Bronze Age: "1970s' comics are now out-selling all other eras by volume," wrote dealer John Haines. The level of enthusiasm for this period was seconded by Heritage, which reported getting multiples of *Guide* for copies of *Green Lantern* #76 and *Detective Comics* #400, among others.

Further confirmation comes from Valiant expert Greg Holland, who hosts an analysis of the CGC Census on his site at www.valiantcomics.com/cgc/. Through this evaluation, we are able to observe that the Bronze Age comics clearly make up the largest percentage of comic books certified by CGC with over 205,861 books as of October, 2007. While facing only grudging acknowledgment from certain quarters, the comics of this era are over thirty years old.

While the typical Bronze Age keys including *Amazing Spider-Man* #129, *Giant-Size X-Men* #1, *Incredible Hulk* #181, and *X-Men* #94 have performed for a protracted period, the aforementioned *Green Lantern* #76 has also seen new records. A CGC-certified copy graded 9.4 sold for $8,365.00 (Spring '07) was followed another 9.4, which realized $9,030 (Fall '07). Copies in 9.0 and 9.2 have repeatedly sold in the $700-$2,000+ range.

For specialty comics within this category, historian Jon McClure reported "The Holy Grail of 35¢ variants, *Iron Fist* #14, sold in three notable transactions," and nominated it for the top spot in Bronze Age books, listing at 9.2 for $2,000."

Copper Age: With *Transformers* #1 in 9.8 bringing in $500+, *Amazing Spider-Man* #300 selling over $800, this is an area of the market that will warrant continued reevaluation. Many of those predisposed to dismiss Bronze Age comics will doubly miss out on the growth of this market sector. The prices in higher grades are significantly more volatile than in lower grades, but don't underestimate the market for the keys. Be sure to check out our top sales lists for more.

Modern Age: Last year Marvel killed off one of their main characters, Captain America. Even in this media-savvy age of marketing, the national and international reaction was some-

what surprising.

Retailer D'Arcy Farrel wrote, "Marvel then supposedly kills Cap off in an unexpected issue, *Captain America* #25. That had a lot of real press. So much that it reminded me of Superman's death in the early 1990s."

Regardless of the comparisons, Lauren Becker of Warp 9 Comics reported, "Prices soared...a lot! eBay had first printing sets (two covers) from low $25 to $200+ within 24 hours of release."

Prices, of course, dropped significantly afterward then stabilized. This has not slowed the flood of variant or retailer incentive

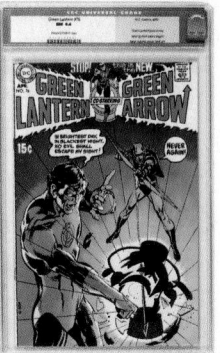

Green Lantern #76 continues to be a popular book with collectors, as copies sold for record prices in high-grade condition.

covers. The market has fluctuated on these often and rapidly, and the pricing of such issues (including second printings, sketch covers, logo-free editions and numerous other gimmicks) remains anything but consistent. We have seen everything from the most egalitarian offerings to price gouging when it comes to these novelties. The best advice when collecting these remains "Collect what you like," because this particular niche market continues to flip-flop.

The impact of the rapid publishing cycles that release trade paperbacks and hard covers soon after original individual issues are published has yet to be fully understood in the recent back issue marketplace. Large scale "events," such as *Civil War*, *World War Hulk*, and *Infinite Crisis* continue to dominate the marketing of new material from Marvel and DC.

In summary, 2007 has been a very good year for comic books as the market continues to grow. Most would agree with our Advisor Mark Zaid, who wrote, "...within the Golden Age market, I do not envision a significant slowdown for sales in the coming year. Indeed, I believe the opposite will happen as a new wave of collectors continue to enter the marketplace."

We would like to personally salute our friends at CGC, who certified their one millionth comic just as we were in the final editing stages of this market report. Congratulations to Steve Eichenbaum, Steve Borock, Mark Haspel, Paul Litch and everyone at CGC on this monumental accomplishment.

Additional congratulations to Jamie Graham, whose Graham Crackers chain reached its twenty-fifth anniversary and to all of our other contributors who celebrated important events this past year.

The following market reports were submitted from some of our many advisors and are published here for your information only. The opinions in these reports belong to each contributor and do not necessarily reflect the views of the publisher or the staff of *The Official Overstreet Comic Book Price Guide* or Gemstone Publishing.

Have a great 2008 everyone!

David T. Alexander and Tyler Alexander
www.cultureandthrills.com

After 39 years of continuous operations we have seen an increase in collector enthusiasm in 2007. More fans are entering the field of hard core collecting and lots of collections have hit the marketplace. There does not seem to be any lack of interest in the items that have come into our hands in 2007. A lot of collections are being released by older collectors or the estates of deceased collectors. Many books that have been hidden away for decades are available again. Generally there is only one copy per item and the scramble is often quite fierce to get that elusive copy. When a rare book goes into another collection it probably will be decades before it hits the market again.

Internet Sales: We have been continually producing and mailing catalogs since 1969. Many of our past catalogs are considered by prominent comic book historians to be ground breaking reference works in the field of comic book collecting.

During the 1970s thru the mid 1980s, under our retail store name – The American Comic Book Company of California, we produced many tabloid catalogs that were distributed as supplements to Alan Light's original fanzine, *The Buyer's Guide For Comic Fandom*, which today is the monthly *Comic Buyer's Guide*. A number of these catalogs were 80-90 pages in length and heavily photo illustrated. In total we have produced over 200 catalogs of various sizes. As far as we can determine no other dealer or store has produced a larger volume of original material. Sadly, in 2007 we did not issue a single new catalog, devoting all our energy and man power to our website. The internet has changed daily activities for all of us and we sincerely hope it is for the better. As we write this our site has around 30,000 individually scanned and described items and we anticipate that we will have around 50,000 items on site when this sees print. Check our site when you get a chance. We'll have lots of original material, unique descriptions, and important comments.

Collections: The best original owner collection that we acquired in 2007 came out of Florida. The owner bought the books as a child in Egypt at an American military base PX store and various newsstands that carried American material. Made up of almost 600 books from 1945 to 1954, the collection is characterized by the white and bright off-white page quality that is present in every book. For several decades this collection was stored near the pyramids in the arid desert climate that is so well known in Egypt. The books did show some wear as they were accumulated by a child, but they were well taken care of and the average grade is in the Fine/Fine+ range. We did buy them from the original owner who had moved to the US and had retired in Florida. Several of the books have distinct distributor marks on them and a few have Arabic writing. We were quite thrilled to get an original owner collection that is entirely made up of pre-code comic book issues.

Highlights of the collection were: *Catman Comics* (how often do you see even a small run of this title?) and long runs of Fawcett titles – *Captain Marvel*, *Whiz*, *Marvel Family*, *Mary Marvel*, *Lash LaRue*, *Hopalong Cassidy*, and *Nyoka*. Fiction House was represented by *Jungle*, *Jumbo* and *Planet*. *Action*, *Superman* and *Adventure* were the predominant DC titles, with a handful of war titles mixed in. There was a small stack of pre-code horror issues, which was a surprise to us, as we had always heard that foreign censors would not tolerate horror and terror publications into their countries. The highlights of this group were the Fox titles, most of which were sold before we could get them on our web site. That should not come as a surprise to anyone. As you might anticipate, we have elected to call this The Egyptian Collection.

We thought 2006 was our biggest year for acquisitions, but clearly 2007 has topped last year. We were surprised by the sheer volume of Golden Age books that were made available to us, and we did not turn down a single collection. Timely Comics normally trickle into our inventory, but in 2007 there was a constant flow of the top titles including: *Captain America*, *Human Torch*, *Sub-Mariner*, *Marvel Mystery*, *Young Allies*, *All-Winners*, and *All-Select*. Not many of the Timely issues were long term residents of our vault. They went out faster than they came in and at this instant we only have a couple dozen Timelys in stock.

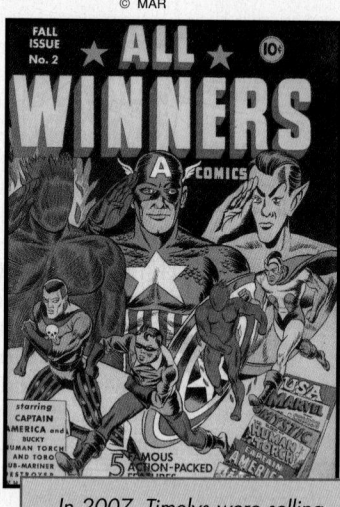

© MAR

FALL ISSUE No. 2

★ ALL ★ WINNERS COMICS 10¢

In 2007, Timelys were selling faster than they came in.
(All Winners Comics *#2 shown)*

Our biggest volume seller in Golden Age has been DC Comics followed by Fawcett titles. This should not be a shock to anyone. The average Fawcett super-hero issue is inexpensive compared to most other publishers. Most collectors can complete collections of most Fawcett titles without the threat of divorce or bankruptcy and the comics have a nostalgic quality about them that will transport you back to the Golden Age.

DC Golden Age issues are automatic sellers. So many people have enjoyed them over the decades that they will never lose their popularity. Early *Batman*, *Superman*, *Action*, *Adventure*, *Detective*, *More Fun* and *All-American* issues are always in demand. Some of these issues are so much fun to read that it breaks our hearts when we have to ship them out.

Sales: We have experienced more material selling above

Guide estimates than any other year in recent memory. Titles from the Golden Age that have been bringing 10% - 25% above 2006 *Guide* listings include: *Black Terror, Blonde Phantom, Phantom Lady*, anything with a Matt Baker cover – and lots of issues with Matt Baker stories, *Jumbo, Sensation, Wonder Woman, Red Ryder-Victory Patrol, Captain Video, Tim Holt* – issues featuring The Ghost Rider, *Rulah* and the other Fox jungle girl titles, *Gene Autry* – Fawcett issues, Avon – one shot issues, *Shadow, Doc Savage*, photo cover westerns, any comic book with the American flag on the cover and most pre-code horror issues.

1950s Comics: Pre-code leads the way here. Horror and science fiction titles bring the most money followed closely by Good Girl Art and Esoteric issues. EC Comics continue to have an appeal to collectors. The originals always find homes and the Russ Cochran reprint sets in slipcases have become hot sellers. We recently received 22 sets and sold 18 of them in one week. *Tales From The Crypt*, horror titles, *Mad*, science-fiction titles, crime, westerns, and everything else is the pecking order of the original EC Comics. Western and crime comics have been steady sellers. As was the case last year, romance comics have been in high demand. The most popular issues have been those with art by Matt Baker, Wally Wood, L.B. Cole or issues with lingerie panels, lurid stories, and off beat themes.

Walt Disney and Humor Comics: The Disney titles that Carl Barks was involved with are very popular. Most of our sales on these are to collectors who live outside the US. This trend has been building for 3 years. Non-Barks issues end up in with the piles of *Looney Tunes*. Archie and Harvey titles have a consistent and constant demand. Although they are a couple of decades apart, the first 10 issues of each of the major series are not easy to locate and will sell quickly. *Katy Keene* continues to be the most widely sought after Archie series title, while *Richie Rich* gets the honor in the Harvey camp. If you are a comic book investor, you will not get hurt when you add any of these early issues to your selection. Pre-code humor comics from the off trail publishers have had an extreme increase in demand.

Silver Age Comics: They are never going to stop. They are never going away. Too many people love Spider-Man, the Fantastic Four, and the X-Men. People like to collect them and kids like to read them. Even with the appeal of video games and sports, kids like Spidey. When the kids grow up and have money to spend, they want to buy the old comics. Is it any surprise that the prices go higher and higher? The demand will never stop. Collecting is fun.

Pulp Magazines: The Pulp Magazines were forerunners of modern comic books and any of them with a comic book connection has had a constant if not increased demand during 2007. The most popular comic book related pulps were: *Lone Ranger, Phantom Detective, Masked Rider, Shadow, Doc Savage, Nick Carter, Hopalong Cassidy, Thrilling Wonder Stories* – published by Nedor who produced *Thrilling Comics, Dan Dunn* – which was based on the newspaper comic strip, *Flash Gordon Strange Adventures,*

and any issues with Tarzan or John Carter of Mars stories. *All-Story* Oct 1912, which features the first appearance of Tarzan, is selling well into the five figure range – when a copy can be found. Also popular were: *Don Winslow, Ka-Zar, Jungle Stories* (the pulp version of *Jungle Comics,*) *Planet Stories* (*Planet Comics* pulp twin,) *Out Of This World Adventures* (which had full color Avon comic book inserts,) *Black Book Detective* featuring the Black Bat (who looks just like Batman,) *The Angel Detective* (whose original appearance was in *Marvel Mystery Comics,*) *Black Hood Detective, Sheena – Queen Of The Jungle, Strange Tales* and *Wings*.

Non-comic related pulps also had a banner year. Top movers were: *Weird Tales* (the first issue is pushing five figures,) *Spicy Mystery, Spicy Detective, Spicy Adventure, Horror Stories, G-8 And His Battle Aces, Dusty Ayres, Ace G-Man, Medical Horrors, Popular Stories, Famous Fantastic Mysteries, Amazing Stories, Science and Invention* (one of the first pulp format magazines to carry science fiction stories,) *The Spider*, and *Unknown*. Don't hesitate to add pulps to your collection. This is a wide open area and there are many rare items waiting for you.

Conventions and the Future of Collecting: Comic-Con International: San Diego has slowly pushed Golden & Silver Age dealers and collectors into the background. The original focus of the convention has been changed. Fewer dealers of vintage material arrive each year. Collectors complain about parking 15 blocks from the convention center. Now would be a good time for the convention promoters to rent a hotel ballroom several blocks away from the convention center and set up a Golden & Silver Age dealers room. Promote it along with the rest of the show, just make it easy for people to get to see what they came for. San Diego is way too crowded. We have been at the show since the first one in 1970 and have never made a sale to any one in a costume.

Conventions still provide an important aspect of collecting that is not found on the internet. Hanging out with other collectors for a day or two is a lot of fun, and aren't we all looking for fun when we collect comic books?

Lon Allen & Barry Sandoval Heritage Auction Galleries

If you needed proof that the vintage comic market is very strong across the board, look no further than the fact that we were able to hit $4.7 million with a comic and comic art auction held the week after ComicCon International, the hobby's biggest annual spending spree!

Our observations on the past 12 months:

Personal collections: As we write this, we are just grading the last few comics from the Davis Crippen ("D" Copy) collection, having sold some 11,000 comics and sent Mr. Crippen's heirs checks totaling more than $1.5 million. Fortunately, this isn't the only superb personal collection that has come our way lately– a couple of other highlights are the Janowicz collection ($300,000 sold to date for a collection with some of the nicest Silver Age Marvels we've seen) and the Warren Hall Collection ($200,000 sold to date, featuring exceptional DC Silver Age.)

Also, if you enjoy paging through *Overstreet Guides* of yore as much as we do you, may recall the ads for the Fantasy Mail Company – the collection of that firm's owner, "Fantastic Frank" Johnson, may well rank with Hall and Janowicz before all is said and done, stay tuned.

Atlas "superhero revival": The Hall collection we mentioned above featured the best copies we've seen of the Atlas revival books, and we wondered if this isn't a category with more room to grow.

The demand for Mr. Hall's books was very strong with results far above *Guide* (*Captain America Comics* #78 in unslabbed NM- for $4,182), but the *Guide* prices for these Cap/Human Torch/Sub-Mariner issues seem to be about right in the lower grades for now. Perhaps more collectors will start comparing *Young Men* #24 to *Showcase* #4 in terms of significance and begin snapping up available copies… and it would be so very tempting to try and put together the whole "Atlas revival" set, since there are only 23 comics total.

Vancouver pedigree: As of this writing, we have sold 205 of the Vancouver books for a total of $145,000. To put that $700 per book average in perspective, consider that many of the titles were fairly obscure books like *Funny Book*, *It Really Happened*, *Kiddie Kapers*, etc. Yet the whiteness of the pages and the absence of any dust shadows or the like makes these copies incredible to behold. It's tough to compare this collection with the Mile High hoard since the latter is 100 times as large and has all of the keys, but on a book for book basis the condition equals or tops that of the Mile Highs.

Hot Covers: The Golden Age issues with the best covers are simply running away from the others in terms of value. Take the Lev Gleason books as an example: the first appearance of the Little Wise Guys in *Daredevil Comics* #13, a significant story moment, not only fails to command a special premium, it sells for less than *Guide* – nothing against Charles Biro's characters, but nobody born after 1950 has had any exposure to them. But while #13 languishes, there are countless takers for #11 of that same series (a bizarre bondage cover) which now stands as the second most-desirable cover of the series behind only the immortal *Daredevil Battles Hitler* (#1.) The brutal cover of #27 would probably give #11 a run for its money if it came up for sale a bit more often. *Crime Does Not Pay* is similar: even the collector who has no interest in this series will still

bid on the bizarre #33.

More Top Covers: *Superman* #14 (Fred Ray patriotic cover) sells for at least double what #15 sells for, usually closer to triple, and was too low in last year's *Guide* in all grades except perhaps GD. Another issue you'll pay a premium for if you can find one is *Exciting Comics* #39 (the one with Nazis giving poisoned candy to kids on the cover, with art by Schomburg), here again the value from *Guide* #37 should be doubled.

Low-Grade Keys: Not that we are scouring the country for beaters, but a *Batman* #1 is always welcome in any grade -- we have offered two PR copies lately that sold for over $4,000 each. Meanwhile, a *Human Torch* #2 with three wraps missing brought $1,400! The lesson here is, the top 25 Golden Age books have gotten so expensive that any chance to get any copy is pounced on.

Disney Ducks: We all know the Uncle Scrooge keys are not rare… if condition isn't a factor. Strict NM copies, on the other hand, are among the most fought-over books out there, especially now that the CGC census has shown just how tough these are in grade. Case in point: in 2003 we auctioned *Four Color* #386 in CGC 9.4 for $8,000, a very pleasing six times 2003 *Guide*. Three years later (after the census made it apparent how tough the book is in NM) that same

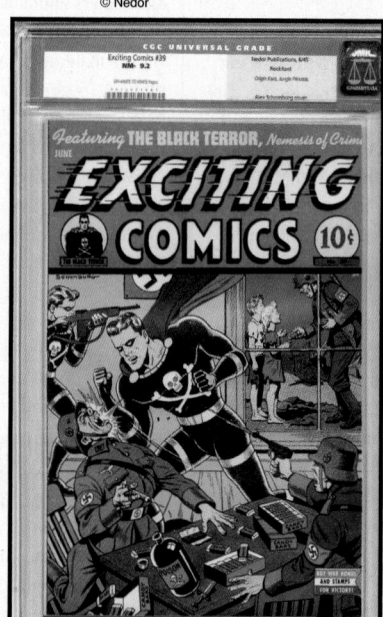

© Nedor

*If you can find one, you'll pay a premium for **Exciting Comics #39** with its classic cover. (the Rockford copy shown)*

copy was consigned to us again and brought $26,290… then another consignor sent us the only other 9.4 copy, and it sold for $28,680! That's about 200 times what an average VG-type copy is worth, one of the bigger disparities we've seen for a vintage comic.

Scarcity in the Internet era: We don't doubt that Bob Overstreet and his able aides will be going through the books designated as "scarce" or "rare" in *The Guide* as more data is accumulated in the CGC census and our own online Permanent Auction Archives, both of which are free for all to use for research. One nominee: *Eerie #1* (1947) should probably lose its "scarce" designation – though an intriguing book, it's one we come across quite often, and indeed, there are 37 copies on the CGC census as we write this. A candidate to be awarded the "scarce" rating: as tough as *All-American #16* is, we dare say you'd have an easier time finding that than #18 or #25!

Ice-cold: Alas, those non-fiction series like *Real Life Comics*, *True Comics* et al. are easily the lowest-demand Golden Age books, and some of the few Golden Age comics whose *Guide* value is too high even in 9.2. Only the Mile High copies would have a chance to surpass (or even equal?) 9.2 *Guide*, and even the Schomburg covers boasted by the former title don't help much.

Peanuts: Since we tend to sell – and write about – the established megahit-type books, it gives us great pleasure to reveal a sleeper in the form of United Feature Syndicate's 1953 *Peanuts* #1. Not the first comic book appearance of the Peanuts, but their first solo/headlining comic book, published some five years before *Four Color* #878. We surprised even ourselves by auctioning the Crippen copy (a VF-) for $1,454! Speaking of surprises, the original art for the Charles Schulz *Peanuts* strips has always done very well for us, but we just topped ourselves by selling a 1959 Sunday for $77,675.

Spirit Sections: Demand for these has gone up considerably in a year's time, perhaps because of the whisperings about a Frank Miller-scripted movie or because of Darwyn Cooke's excellent new series. At any rate, the June 2, 1940 issue (which is #1) sold for $448, or 6 times *Guide* in CGC 3.0 condition. Others from as late as 1947 have fetched double or triple *Guide*, and the result above notwithstanding seem to sell better in unslabbed form.

DC Silver Age: Another area where the CGC census has been very helpful. In the case of many 1950s DCs, a VF+ or VF/NM is the finest known copy, and while multiples of *Guide* have been paid for the "sole highest-graded" certified copy of superhero mags for some years now, the past year has seen this trend spread to the likes of *Brave and the Bold* #31 (Cave Carson) and *Rip Hunter* #1. We are no longer shocked by the likes of *Metamorpho* #12 selling for $425 in 9.4 – sorry Metamorpho, but in VG nobody even wants you for the $10 *Guide* price!

DC 80-Pagers: When we offer a strictly graded NM- 9.2, it often creates the same excitement as a 9.6 might for a staple-bound issue. The likes of *Batman* #203 and 208 still *Guide* for under $100 in NM- as we write this, that shouldn't last long.

DC War: Having auctioned off runs of DC's "Big Five" titles courtesy of collector Keith Marlow, we now have a better handle on the values of some of the keys in high grade, and just as we expected, they commanded top prices. Frustratingly enough, the best Big Five covers seem to grace non-key issues, but one major exception to that is *G.I. Combat* #87, with an absolutely awesome Russ Heath cover outside and the first appearance of the Haunted Tank inside; a CGC 8.0 copy sold for $2,868. Meanwhile issues #44 (the first DC issue) in VF/NM and #68 (featuring "the Rock" who may or may not be the Rock) in VF- both brought $2,600 and change.

Hawkman: Issue #4 (the first Zatanna) has "flown" under the radar – it should be second only to #1 in value, and already is, at least for our bidders.

VG Comics: Many Silver Age books still *Guide* too high in VG in our estimation, for example *Showcase* #9 (not worth $1,000) and *Tales to Astonish* #35 (not worth $310.) The true keys that people are passionate about will be fought over

even in low-grade, but when it comes to second appearances and the like, it's different. To put it another way, *Journey Into Mystery* #83 in lower grades is great, but *JIM* 84… we don't see people paying $155 for GD or $310 for VG.

9.2 Marvels: While *The Guide* seems to put the NM- price at about 130% of VF/NM, our experience is that – for certified copies of Silver Age Marvels – the range is 180% to 200%. This, despite the fact that for many issues in this category, the census numbers for 9.0 or 9.2 are about the same. It's evident that for many collectors "high grade" begins at 9.2 – a policy you'd have a hard time adhering to with DCs (see above) but can be done with Marvels (though not inexpensively!)

Marvel Silver Age Odds and Ends: The aforementioned *Journey Into Mystery* #83 is the key book that has heated up the most since our last market report! Also, we're pretty sure our $5,228 sale of *Tales of Suspense* #57 is a record for that book. Hawkeye's hot, who knew?

Bronze Age DC: We think it's safe to say *Green Lantern* #76 is hot – Heritage results from the last year (all CGC-certified): NM $8,365, NM- $2,031, VF/NM $717! Another very strong book (also with an Adams cover) is *Detective Comics* #400: CGC NM $1,195 and NM- $388.

Again, we are bullish on the vintage comic market. And while we are proud of the high prices that intense bidder competition has produced, it also gives us no small measure of satisfaction to talk to the collectors who have helped put their kids through college, made a down payment on a house, or accomplished other long-held goals with the proceeds from a consignment of old comic books. We look forward to helping more collectors maximize the value of their four-color treasures.

David J. Anderson, DDS
Collector

2007 was an outstanding year in the comic collecting community. Significant amounts of quality material became available to the market as a result of individual collectors deciding to part with portions of their collections. The money generated from these sales was in turn put back into the market buying different available items. This is a trend we can expect to see for years to come as fewer and fewer original collections turn up. There are currently more options for selling material of any value level than ever before. Auction options include Heritage, ComicLink, Hake's, and of course eBay. Recognizing this, dealers are forced to offer higher prices for quality material in order to maintain a healthy inventory, and most will eagerly accept consignments to include in their catalogs and convention stock. Although many of us sometimes complain about the prices listed in *The Guide* as either being too high or too low, we should all stop to reflect and realize that the comic book market remains healthy in large part due to the fact that Bob Overstreet and his staff have consistently done an outstanding job in putting out a price guide that accurately reflects market conditions.

When it comes to new comic sales for the past year, it has been a giant wrestling match between DC and Marvel for the top spot. Both companies have been doing extremely well.

DC's Sinestro War series exploded last summer catching quite a few shop owners by surprise. *Green Lantern* and *Green Lantern Corps* sales went up 200 percent. Sales of *Superman*, *Action*, *Batman*, *Justice League of America*, *Justice Society of America* and *Superman/Batman* were very strong. *All-Star Batman* sales are also up. DC's *Countdown* series is a consistently good seller following in the footsteps of *52*.

Marvel's *Civil War* issues were very popular as well as the death of Captain America storyline. Demand for *Civil War* and the *Marvel Zombies* issues have been strong. Prices for a first print *Captain America* #25 spiked at around $20 but are about half that now. World War Hulk comics have sold very well with demand for the Planet Hulk comics also selling well. Pre-#25 *Captain America* comics are hard to keep in stock.

New Avengers leads the pack for Marvel with *Amazing Spider-Man* right behind. *Uncanny X-Men* and *X-Men* always do well but the other X-titles aren't nearly as strong. The re-launching of *Thor* was a big success. The Ultimate titles sell consistently at a good pace.

Back Issue Sales: Golden Age sales are very weak in the Alabama region unless they are Batman or Superman and even then they are slow to move. Silver Age sales are much better with *Batman* and *Amazing Spider-Man* leading the way. Early *X-Men* can be difficult to sell. However, the vast majority of main DC and Marvel titles from this period do not bring *Guide* prices; this area seems to show a lot of resistance to moderate to high prices. Lower grade Silver Age move somewhat at 50 percent off. CGC comics are virtually ignored here; no interest whatsoever.

Bronze Age sales are flat to weak. The abundance of copies from this period makes it hard to get even *Guide* prices. Dollar back issues and 25-cent comics do well for the bargain hunters. Back issues of newer comics do very well until they reach about a year old and then they fall off dramatically. If a title gets cancelled after running a few years, the back issues are doomed to reside in the cheap boxes.

More obscure titles from the 1940s and 1950s (crime, horror, and war) and *Classics Illustrated* occasionally sell to out-of-town collectors passing through but at well below *Guide* prices. Archie titles from the 1970s on up sell moderately, mostly to parents and grandparents.

Dell Comics are terrible sellers with maybe the exception of *Little Lulu*. Duck titles scarcely move; the same with Gold Key issues. Movie cowboy titles are not only dead in the water, they are at the bottom of the harbor.

Conan black and white magazines in average condition are impossible to keep in stock. We are constantly out of them. Cheap regular four-color *Conan's* sell well. Warren's

Creepy and *Eerie* are requested frequently but are hard to come by.

On eBay, Duck books fetch maybe 20 percent of *Guide*. Silver Age Marvels do better but non-key issues, even CGC 8.0 or above don't bring great prices. The eBay market for comics is a crap-shoot with too many novices testing the field with outlandish prices on common comics (i.e. *Superman* #75, black bag edition, $500 "Buy-It-Now".) Many of the new sellers have no comic book marketing experience and with grading all over the map. Overall, the eBay market is very soft but with a little searching, big bargains can be found (i.e. *Superman* #20, very good+ $145.) It seems too many sellers want way too much for opening bids. Established dealers are the best to do business with.

The Official Overstreet Comic Book Price Guide sells well in the Spring but falls off after that. The real hard-core collectors have to have this book because of the tremendous data it contains. Since it is a guide, it is a great selling tool. The history of the different periods of comics plus the Big Little Book listings as well as Promotional Comics section makes *The Guide* the most comprehensive on the market.

Wizard World Chicago: It seems it was slim pickings at this convention for 2007. Some dealers said it was too soon after the San Diego Comic-Con (two weeks before) and they didn't have time to restock. Golden Age Superman comics were hard to find as were many Timely titles. Still, it was a well-attended show with many great attractions for those attending.

The convention was a buyers' paradise for many with discounts of up to 60 percent even on some Golden Age and a lot of non-key Silver Age from many smaller sellers. The bigger dealers had nice selections including Bedrock Comics, Graham Crackers, JHV Associates, Metropolis Comics, Motor City Comics, Terry's Comics and Harley Yee.

What Prices Should Go Up?: If I read my clientele correctly, no prices should go up. I tend to agree with them since my region is not very competitive when compared to the markets on the East coast, the West coast and Chicago area. There are only two comic shops in a metropolitan area of over 400,000 in south Alabama and one of them is only part-time.

What Prices Should Go Down?: Almost all prices on non-key mid-grade Silver Age comics seem over-priced. All 1950s Dells, including Duck titles, are too bloated. Silver Age DCs and Marvels have leveled off quite a bit and may need to come down in lower grades. The prices on lesser-known titles from the 1950s through the 70s seem too high. Humor comics from the 1940s and 50s do not come close to *Guide* prices and should have their prices reevaluated.

Marvel: *Spider-Man 3*, *Ghost Rider* and *Fantastic Four 2* had virtually **zero** presence for in-store sales. Instead, Marvel's two main titles for this year were both non-Marvel properties (almost). Stephen King's *Dark Tower* was our most-ordered and best-selling series! People came in droves to get the first issue of this series and surprisingly came back every month for the next installment. And, as well as the series did in-store, it did better online, as prices for sets reached $5 to $8 per issue. Marvel's second best series was *Army of Darkness Vs. Marvel Zombies*, which starred a non-Marvel character (Ash) even though most bought it for the Marvel zombies. Although not as great a seller as *Dark Tower*, orders on this book exceeded many other titles and did quite well.

O.K., so a non-Marvel property dominated the Marvel line, at least by our standards. Because of this and because of the press that this title received, how long will it be until Marvel (and DC) begin their trek back into the licensing world? Marvel's got a pretty good head start, as there may be another *Dark Tower* series coming, as well as picking up the über-popular *Halo* line (which they published last year as a hardcover.) DC on the low end have the "horror" licenses (Freddy Krueger, Jason, *Texas Chainsaw Massacre*) but these properties have been more of a loss than a gain, as readers here are just kinda "ehh." Even the indies are getting more into licensed properties. IDW is one of the leaders with *Angel, Transformers*, and even *Scarface*. Dark Horse has one of the heavy hitters with *Buffy the Vampire Slayer*. Now of course the big buzz on this book was series creator Joss Whedon writing the book. It sold out the first issue in 3 printings with spiked up prices (#1 1st printing at $10, #2 1st printing at $7.) Will the book do just as well without

© 20th Century Fox

Dark Horse had a heavy hitter in ***Buffy the Vampire Slayer***, written by Joss Whedon. (#1 shown)

Whedon's writing after issue #5? We'll just have to see. When will we see comics of *Lost, Grey's Anatomy, Prison Break* or even *Heroes?*... Wait, DC just got the license. Looks like someone's been paying attention.

Even excluding the licensing phenomenon, Marvel sales have been steady, even climbing in certain titles. Most notably *Captain America*. The infamous issue #25, which no one really knew about (except for *Wizard*.) Prices soared... high! eBay had 1st printing sets (2 covers) from low $25 to $200+ within 24 hours of release. People showed up alright, mostly to buy multiples to sell on eBay themselves. Many stores dropped the ball on ordering this, but to be fair, no info was provided by Marvel (only hints on the retailer site saying "Retailers might want to consider ordering *Civil War* numbers"). Prices have steadied out at $15-$20 each.

DC: DC's biggest hit of the year, bar none was *Green Lantern: Sinestro Corps*. This one-shot sold 1-1/2 times *Green Lantern* numbers and has 3 printings. 1st prints sold for $15, and 2nd prints with the variant cover go for about the same. The story crossed into *Green Lantern, Green Lantern Corps* and even *Blue Beetle* (which should boost numbers). Unfortunately, unlike Marvel, DC's titles have been inconsistent in sales. For example, *Superman/Batman* was once a 100 copy seller for us, but has dropped 40%. When *Flash* was re-launched, sales dropped mainly due to horrible storylines, weak & trite characters, and mediocre art. It took Bart (The Flash) Allen's death and Mark Waid's return as writer to make people pick up this title.

By the way, when did DC become Image? They have the big talent (Frank Miller, Jim Lee, Richard Donner) but the titles they work on take sooooo long to come out. Example? As of this writing, *All Star Batman* came out twice this year, unlike last year with only one issue. It's been a year and a half... where's *Wildcats* #2? It's ironic... people asked this 10 years ago... same question. DC makes the late titles returnable, but I spend more money on return postage than I do on regular postage. To be fair though, *Ultimate Hulk Vs. Wolverine* is two years late. Why do Marvel & DC drop the publishing ball on the stuff people want, yet the dreck continues to come in on time?

Independents: One of the most anticipated titles coming from Dark Horse is *Umbrella Academy*. Written by Gerald Way from the band "My Chemical Romance," I guarantee people will be asking for this title. Way had produced a *My Chemical Romance* comic 3 years ago, and when it's offered, goes for $50-$100 and up. The Free Comic Book Day version of *Umbrella Academy* goes for $5-$10, and that's a preview book. Not to be outdone, the band Gorillaz has a graphic novel coming out in November 2007. Alternative band comics are picking up steam, but the same can't be said of old rock or rap. *KISS 4K* and *Public Enemy* are pretty bad and are passed over even by the most avid fan.

Overall, sales are steady, and rising slowly in certain genres. We are seeing newer collectors, and more importantly, newer readers everyday.

Peter J. Bilelis, Esq. Collector

Just back from the Advisors' meeting. Many topics were discussed, but one vaulted to the top of the list: a need for *The Guide*'s on-line presence. The hobby is demanding such access to *The Guide*'s data, and various quality solutions are being considered. My market report primarily discusses the Golden Age (GA) and Bronze Age (BA) hobby segments.

Sales /Acquisitions: The last year or so has been very satisfying for me as a GA aficionado. Through eBay, I acquired a nice copy of *Daredevil Battles Hitler* #1 for 60% of *Guide* and a gorgeous copy of *More Fun Comics* #53 for 55% of *Guide*. And eBay was the stepping stone for my acquisition of a beautifully preserved original owner collection that spans 1936 – 1942. My eBay experience is far from unique, as many scarce books were auctioned via eBay this year (including *Amazing-Man* #22, *Wow* #1 and some ashcans). I also acquired the remaining books from Leonard Brown's collection. For those who didn't know Leonard, he was a true hobby pioneer and the herald for the successful comic book-based business. While he sold the bulk of his collection years ago, he held onto the cream until the end. I was glad to acquire these jewels.

Material Availability: Availability of top GA material could have been better. There were a lot of GA books for sale, but few, if any, were unrestored F/VF or better copies of *Action Comics* (through #40), pre-Robin *Detective Comics* (except for #15, 29, and 31), big logo *More Fun Comics*, or early issues of *Captain America Comics* and *Marvel Mystery Comics*. Similarly, *Master Comics* that feature Mac Raboy artwork were very difficult, if not impossible, to locate. Finally, many MLJ, Fiction House, Fox, and Centaur books (including *Pep* #20 – 34 and several issues of *Jumbo* and *Science*) rarely appeared, and when they did, they were typically beater copies. Books like *All-Select* #1, and *Captain America Comics* #1, however, were much more common, as were *Human Torch* #2 (#1), *Green Lantern* #1, *Batman* #1, *Sub-Mariner* #1, *Wings* #1, and most other issues from these titles. Thus, respective sale prices for this more common material were often well below *Guide*.

Market – Performance: I see a trend of growing interest in the hobby, evident by the number or auction bidders, the level of interest in the books I sold this year, and the growing number of newer collectors with whom I correspond. Sales of super high-grade copies of BA books like *Silver Surfer* #1 –18, *Amazing Spider-Man* #252 and *Marvel Spotlight* #5 were brisk, presumably because of this year's related Hollywood films. GA books with classic covers and WWII propaganda covers also did very well. And, competition over most other quality material confirms continuing hobby interest.

Market – Trends: Once again, the word that best describes the hobby is bifurcation. First, *Guide* values and respective sale prices for many key GA books continue to rise, as do sale prices for many so-called pedigree copies and pricier GA run books in top-grade. Economics, therefore, dictate a shrinking market for this material, as few have the disposable income to support such purchases. While this didn't affect respective sales (although some $50K+ books experienced resistance), it meant that two discrete markets continued to emerge – the market for museum-piece type books and the market for less lofty material, comprising 98% of the remaining books. And, while there is still a distinction between "non-museum" top-graded books (those that do not command thousands of dollars unless they are in top grade) and the rest, it is eroding. I see this as a market correction due to several factors: (a) people realizing that if there are multiple highest graded copies of a book, it isn't rare in the given grade; (b) a top-graded non-descript run book isn't necessarily worth 2X (or more) another copy that

is slightly inferior, especially if the top-graded copy leaves sufficient room to be bested or its grade is its only distinguishing feature; and (c) the dispelled perception that virtually any GA book in VF or any BA book in NM+ is a rarity (obviously, there are exceptions).

Second, there is a continuing distinction between the unencapsulated book (raw) market and the market for books encapsulated by third-party grading services (slabs). Many people slab when they decide to sell either a book that is expensive irrespective of grade or an inexpensive book that commands real money because it is in super high-grade. In these instances, slabs often result in higher sale prices. Others, however, will not slab books as grading is not a science and an overly strict assigned grade could mean the loss of thousands of dollars upon resale. And others will not buy slabbed books for reasons that include: (a) a priority on owning a copy for its content rather than its grade; and (b) no immediate intention to resell. These differing positions illustrate the slab's strengths and limitations.

Another continuing trend is the shift in avenues through which to acquire quality material. Dealers used to be the portal to your collecting needs. Today, most quality material is available through eBay and the auction houses. In fact, the auction-style sale was so hot this year, people also increasingly opted to sell via auction, forcing dealers to compete with collectors for the material. These dynamics resulted in some dealers being light in quality material and being relegated to consignment services, allowing hobbyists to auction books on their websites in return for being paid a fraction of the hammer price as the consignment fee. I like the traditional sales model, but believe the auction-style sale represents evolution. It ensures the seller a wider audience and lower costs than other selling methods, and it ensures that the purchaser will pay only one increment over anyone else at that moment (versus an arbitrary fixed dealer price).

Yet another development (not yet enough data to call it a trend) is that very low-grade copies of some key GA and Silver Age (SA) books sold at, or over, respective *Guide* value. This defies the general rule that low and mid-grade books sell at under *Guide* and that high-grade books sell at, or over, *Guide*. Presumably, this development is a function of either: (a) collecting desires competing with prohibitive prices for higher grade copies; or (b) simple business acumen, as a low-grade copy doesn't necessarily offer less investment potential (on a percentage basis) than a mid-grade copy of a given book, yet the low-grade copy requires a much smaller monetary commitment and will likely appeal to a wider audience upon resale.

Market – Other Developments:

Intact Pressing – A year ago, some wanted pressing classified as restoration and claimed that it is harmful. Clearly, the market does not believe pressing to be restoration, as restored books do not sell at unrestored prices, yet books known to be pressed sell at unrestored market value for the attained grades. And harmful effects specific to pressing have yet to be reported. As such, improving a book's aesthetics via

© MARVEL

Of all the Modern Age books submitted to CGC, **Captain America #25** *was one of the top.*

pressing seems perfectly acceptable.

Restored Books – While they categorically sell for prices well under *Guide*, hobbyists are realizing that a few dots of glue are not equivalent to more extensive treatments. The fall-out is a growing linear relationship (on a scaled basis) between degree of restoration and prices realized.

Based on the foregoing, 2007 can be summarized as a year of continued growth and appreciation. High-grade did well, as did some low-grade key GA and SA books. Market corrections continued for material that had previously achieved untenably high sale prices. Finally, many thanks to Karen and Ruben who introduced me to the Golden Age of comic books all those years ago, as collecting these treasures continues to be an enriching experience. Good luck hunting in 2008.

Steve Borock
CGC

This is our second market report for *The Overstreet Comic Book Price Guide*, and it will have the same tone and feel of the past one. This report is different from the others here because CGC does not buy or sell comic books. In fact, our full-time employees are prohibited from commercially trading comic books in order to ensure our impartiality. As a result, we really don't have a great sense of market values and pricing.

However, we do know something about the market from the books that are being submitted to us for certification. So, in our "market report," we can tell you what books are hot based on the past year's submissions. CGC submission numbers for a particular book are a great gauge of both collector and dealer interest because, to top our list, a book has to be submitted from both groups. That means collectors want to put copies away, and dealers are doing well selling high-grade certified copies. The other thing that our submission numbers can tell is what quality of books exists in the marketplace. These figures are regularly updated and available for free in our online census. Here, we'll take a close look at some of these numbers.

As of this writing, the top 2007 modern submissions are *Captain America, World War Hulk* titles, *Wolverine: Origins, Aspen Splash: 2007* swimsuit spectacular, *Ultimate*

Spider-Man, Justice League of America, Thor, and *Batman*. The top submissions of books from the 1980s and 1990s include: *Amazing Spider-Man, Spider-Man, Wolverine* Limited Series, *Watchmen, Superman* and *Daredevil*.

In 2006 we saw a surge of submission of comics from the 1970s, this continues in 2007 as well. The four that still stand out above the rest are *Incredible Hulk* #181, *Amazing Spider-Man* #129, *X-Men* #94 and *Giant-Size X-Men* #1. Submissions of books from the 1960s: *Amazing Spider-Man* is still king! Besides *ASM*, we receive healthy numbers of other mainstay Marvel titles, such as *Fantastic Four, Journey Into Mystery/Thor*, and *Avengers*. DCs are submitted quite often as well, but by looking at the CGC census, you can note that the ones from the early to mid 1960s are much harder to find in high grades than the Marvels from that time period.

For the 1950s, just like last year, EC comics are still submitted in the greatest numbers.

The top Golden Age titles by submission are still *Batman, Superman, Detective, Action*, and any Timely, though we are now seeing a "next generation" of Golden Age collectors focusing not only on those titles. Fawcetts are on the rise as well as many under rated titles from the 1940s such as *Smash, Top-Notch, Archie*, and other such titles. Duck books are back in fashion and we see more and more submitted every day.

The above lists show the most sought-after or actively traded comics. An analysis of CGC submissions of "hot titles" also reveals some alarming trends. It seems that the most popular books submitted for grading are also among the most frequently restored. People use CGC for our impartial grading, and also for our expert restoration check that is performed on each book during the certification process. When restoration is detected, we encapsulate the comic book with a purple restored CGC label, and clearly describe the restoration. From the many phone calls we get after comic books were given the purple restored CGC label, we can tell you that most submitters believed that their comic books were unrestored. The statistics are staggering and show how one must be careful buying any uncertified book. Regardless of how honest and well-intentioned they are, few sellers have the eyes for detection that we do.

One of the best examples that illustrates this phenomenon is the number of restored *Amazing Fantasy* #15s. As we write this, CGC has certified 584 unrestored Universal copies and 317 restored copies. (Universal is CGC's terminology for an unrestored, unqualified grade.) That means almost 1 out of every 3 copies submitted is restored, which is the same ratio as last year. The ratio of restored copies increases when you get to the top grades, where the book sells for "big money" (8.0 and higher) to some, this percentage will be scary! Out of 75 *Amazing Fantasy* #15s certified 8.0 and higher, there are 25 unrestored copies and 50 restored copies; 2 out of every 3 copies submitted have had some form of restoration. This is also the same ratio as last year.

Here are a few more statistics (not including the

Qualified or Signature Series labels) that show how much restoration we are finding. We are using many of the same comic book examples as last year to show whether the ratio of restored comic books compared to unrestored is consistent or not. Just like last year, we think they may surprise many readers. Note that newer comics are on this list, as well as old:

Marvel Team-Up #1 (1972): Unrestored 292; Restored 36; more than 1 in 9 copies is restored. The ratio of restored copies has gone up from last year.

X-Men #94 (1975): Unrestored 2005; Restored 222; more than 1 in 10 copies is restored. Same ratio as last year.

Batman #9 (1942): Unrestored 46; Restored 18; more than 1 in 3 copies is restored. The ratio of restored copies has gone up from last year.

Amazing Spider-Man #13 (1964): Unrestored 400; Restored 72; more than 1 in 5 copies is restored. Same ratio as last year.

Amazing Spider-Man #300 (1988): Unrestored 4053; Restored 99; more than 1 in 40 copies is restored. The ratio of restored copies has gone up from last year.

Mystery in Space #53 (1959): Unrestored 41; Restored 9; about 1 in 4 copies is restored. Just a touch less than last year's ratio.

Fantastic Four #49 (1966): Unrestored 364; Restored 44; more than 1 in 9 copies is restored. Same ratio as last year.

Superman #100 (1955): Unrestored 53; Restored 14; almost 1 in 5 copies restored. The ratio of restored copies has gone up from last year.

Some collectors don't expect to encounter restoration. The numbers above tell a different story. If you buy uncertified books, you're highly likely to come across a restored book. Will it be disclosed?

After all this scary news, just as we did last year, we should talk about the best part of this wonderful hobby: the friendships we make and the knowledge we gain from them. For many collectors this is centered around the CGC chat board. It has become, for many comic books enthusiasts, the hobby's "water cooler." This is where some of the most knowledgeable veteran collectors and sellers talk with each other, and where novice collectors go to learn more about the hobby. Many new friendships have been created on the chat boards, and the "CGC forum dinners" are the talk of conventions the day after they happen. We have had as many as 75 collectors, dealers, CGC employees, and special guests attend including: Bob Overstreet, Neal Adams, Jason Spyda Adams, Michelle Nolan, Rich Koslowski, Dave Sim, J.C. Vaughn, Paul Litch, Don Rosa, Maggie Thompson, Jim Starlin, Mark Haspel, Michael Bair, Lamont Larson, John Dolmayan, Frank Brunner, Stephen "Buzz" Sadowski, Tom Gordon, Richard Henn and Jim McLauchlin. We spend the evening eating a good meal, talking comics, then talking everything related to comics, and always, by the end of the evening, we just get to know each other.

From what we have heard, the market for comic books has been very strong. That is great for everyone! ComicLink even set a new record for our hobby, by breaking the $200,000 mark with a CGC'd 9.4 *Amazing Fantasy* #15 selling for $210,000! Geppi's Entertainment Museum has been gaining attendance and adulation every day and for those of you who have not been there, comic book fan or not, it is a must see. Steve Geppi has really gone out of his way building this museum to keep the future looking bright for our beloved hobby. Many blockbuster comic book movies are coming out more often and have been just great, such as, *Fantastic Four: Rise of the Silver Surfer*, *Stardust* (Gaiman/Vess llustrated novel), and *300*. Every time one of these movies is announced, we get an abundance of submissions of those titles. Some of the writing and art in the newly published titles this year was outstanding! Some of the best this hobby has seen in years for kids and adults alike.

So, until our next year's *Overstreet* market report, HAPPY COLLECTING!

Kevin A. Boyd
Collector/Dealer
& CGC Signature Series Director

This has been an interesting year, with plenty of personal and professional upheavals in my life. Shortly after I submitted by last report I had a life-threatening encounter with a shrimp! Aside from a bit of a wake-up call, it definitely helped put some things into perspective, including comics.

As I always point out at the start of each of my market reports, I am not a dealer, although I do dabble in eBay sales of original art and other items, and occasionally sell at local shows. I am an involved collector and fan, one who has been involved in different ways to promote comic books to new audiences. That promotion has included running and working on Toronto area conventions, working on the Joe Shuster Canadian Comic Book Creator Awards and going to a lot of different conventions across North America working for CGC as their Signature Series Director.

Toronto Conventions: The Toronto market is still a vibrant one for convention sales and attendance. This past year, 2007, saw four major comic book weekend events between April and August: Toronto ComiCon Fan Appreciation Show, The Paradise Toronto Comicon, the Toronto Comic Arts Festival and Fan Expo Canada.

I started out the year working for Paradise Conventions on their Fan Supershows and the big Toronto ComiCon event in June. After the completion of the June event it became evident that I could no longer continue working on the Paradise shows. Running a show of that size had became too much of a strain of time, health and effort to continue as is.

In July 2007, I was invited by HobbyStar Marketing to work on some of their comic book event programming at Fan Expo Canada (late August) and accepted. As I write this, it appears that this relationship is continuing as I am now working on some of their one-day events for October 2007, February 2008 and April 2008 – all of which will have happened by the time you read this report.

The only event I got to enjoy as a fan was the Toronto

Comic Arts Festival, which was an exceptional time and one of the most exciting comic events I've attended in many years.

The Joe Shuster Awards: The awards were handed out at a special ceremony held on the same weekend as the Paradise Toronto Comicon. This was the third year of the awards and it has been amazing to watch as they have grown in importance and how the awards show itself has progressed. It is a long process, and we start working on the next year's awards almost right after we hand out our previous year's awards.

You would be amazed and surprised at the number of talented individuals working in comics who are Canadian. The purpose of the Joe Shuster Awards, named in honor of the Canadian born co-creator of Superman, is to raise the visibility of, and honor the accomplishments of Canadian creators, retailers and publishers. The winners this year included: Outstanding Canadian Comic Book Cartoonist (Writer/Artist) - Darwyn Cooke, *The Spirit*; Outstanding Canadian Comic Book Writer - Darwyn Cooke, *Superman Confidential*; Outstanding Canadian Comic Book Artist - Darwyn Cooke & J. Bone, *Batman/The Spirit* #1; and Outstanding International Comic Book - Brian K. Vaughan, *Y the Last Man*, *Ex Machina*, *Pride of Baghdad*, *Runaways* & *Doctor Strange: The Oath*. The four inductees into the Canadian Comic Book Creator Hall of Fame were: Albert Chartier, Gene Day, Jacques Hurtubise aka Zyx, and Gerald Lazarre

Congratulations to all the nominees and winners, and thanks to everyone who participated this year – from the nomination committees, to the administrative committee, to our sponsors (CGC, Lionshead, Paradise Conventions, Visions of Utopia, Diamond Comic Distributors, Sips Publishing and Quebecor World), to the amazing Canadian artists that contributed to our jam poster and Hall of Fame print, to lastly, show producer & writer Liana K.

CGC Signature Series: This was another record year for submissions to CGC's prestigious Signature Series service. We were proud to offer this service to fans and collectors and almost every major convention or comics related event in 2007 and hope to continue to do so in 2008.

The prestigious CGC Signature Series label (yellow) is applied to comic books that have been signed by someone of significance to the comic, under the direct observation of a CGC employee or select CGC authorized Witness. The signatures are then authenticated by CGC with the labels indicating who signed the book, the date it was signed, and in some cases, the location of where it was signed. The Signature

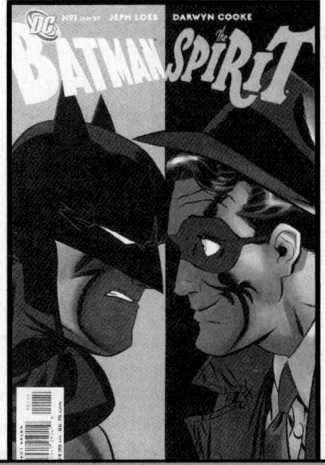

© DC & Will Eisner Studios

Canadian creators like Darwyn Cooke produce award-winning material. **(Batman/The Spirit** #1 shown)

Series service is the hobby's only 100% Authenticated Signature service.

In 2007 we added a new option, Restored Signature Series (a yellow label with a purple stripe) so that restored books can also be submitted for the Signature Series service. The degree of restoration and details of the work performed are noted on the label.

In 2007, I attended the following events for CGC: New York Comic-Con, WonderCon, Wizard World Los Angeles, the Pittsburgh Comicon, the Motor City Comic-Con, Wizard World Philadelphia, San Diego Comic-Con, Wizard World Chicago, the Baltimore Comic-Con, FallCon, the National and the Mid-Ohio Con. The remaining cons: MegaCon, Emerald City ComiCon and Wizard World Dallas were covered by other CGC employees.

I can say, without a doubt, that the most popular creator for Signature Series remains the previous year's champ: Michael Turner. Other creators in high demand for Signature Series in 2007 were: Steve McNiven, Mark Millar, Greg Pak, Ed Brubaker, Joe Quesada, Todd McFarlane, Jim Lee, John Cassaday, Stan Lee, the Romitas (Sr. and Jr.), the Kuberts (Joe, Adam, Andy) and David Finch. Grant Morrison, Neil Gaiman and Joss Whedon would be in there as well if they did more public appearances! *Civil War* remains *the* Signature Series title of 2007. Other titles that were popular submissions in 2007 were *World War Hulk*, *Thor*, and *Buffy the Vampire Slayer: Season Eight*. If you have any questions about Signature Series, you can e-mail us directly at signature@cgccomics.com.

General Observations: There are way too many comic book conventions! Seriously, as much as I love comic book conventions, there are simply way too many of these in a given year, and the 2008 schedule is downright scary. Between April and June there's almost a con every weekend. I fear for the survival of some of these smaller cons in a season where the monster conventions dominate. While I'm certain there is a sustainable minimum amount of attendance required to maintain them, are there enough consumer dollars out there to continue supporting all of these dealers and creators? We are not a large market, and I fear we won't, though I may be proven wrong.

Shows seem to gravitate in different directions – art collectors have their favorites, back issue collectors have theirs, and everyone else falls somewhere in between.

Marvel Comics: *Civil War* fed right into the Initiative and the Death of Captain America, which led into *World War Hulk* and the discovery that certain heroes had been replaced by Skrulls. Another intriguing year for the House of

Ideas. Certainly my personal favourites were Brubaker's *Captain America* and *Daredevil*. There are way too many "throw them at the wall and see if they will stick" theme books – magic, monsters, etc.

Marvel continues to do an excellent job with keeping their older material out there in many different formats such as Masterworks, Omnibuses and Essentials.

DC Comics: *52* and *Countdown* proved that the weekly comic can exist and thrive. I fear that DC's momentum post-*Infinite Crisis* and One Year Later is still in decline. *Final Crisis* is not igniting a lot of interest among the people that I talk to, however we are still months away from getting a sense of it. The Sinestro Corps War, however, was very well received and has done well for many stores. *Justice League* and *Justice Society* continue to do very well, and despite some artistic setbacks, the Batman and Superman titles still do well. Bringing Eric Powell onto *Action Comics* was an inspired choice and will lead right into Gary Frank's debut on the title. My personal favorite DC titles include: Darwyn Cooke's amazing interpretation of Will Eisner's *The Spirit*, *All Star Superman*, *Y: the Last Man*, *Fables* and *Ex Machina*.

As with Marvel, there seems to be a lot of "throw them at the wall and see if they will stick" comics being published by DC, and they take attention and dollars away from other titles.

Image Comics: The home of my three favorite series: *Invincible*, *The Walking Dead* and the *Astounding Wolf-Man*. I love Kirkman! As well, titles like *After the Cape*, *Mice Templar* and *Casanova* continue to push the boundaries.

Dark Horse Comics: *Buffy* was a huge hit in 2007, bigger than I would have thought. Dark Horse continues to do well with their other properties such as *Star Wars* and *Conan*. *Fear Agent*, *The Umbrella Academy* and *Hellboy* are all great comics and deserve looking into.

Other: As with my retailer friends, the *other* part of the catalogue is a rather scary place to look from time to time. There is a lot of product out there and it is not easy to discern good from okay. David Petersen's *Mouse Guard* is a great book, in any format. As was *Strangers in Paradise*, although it finished up in the spring of 2007. Dynamite, Drawn & Quarterly, Fantagraphics... I've sampled many different titles and graphic novels from these companies, and I highly recommend Joe Matt's *Spent* (D+Q) and the *Popeye: I Yam What I Yam* collection (Fantagraphics).

General: With the quick reprinting of most modern comics, recent back issues are becoming less saleable. The only items that seem to hold longer interest are variants, and my concerns about the plethora of variant editions have been addressed in previous reports.

Overall, I see a lot of interest in comic books and comic book properties, and we need to make sure that we are able to address the needs of new collectors and fans that these properties are bringing to comics and graphic novels. The audience is shifting and we need to be prepared to cater to their needs as well as maintain our existing collector/reader base. Not an easy task.

Michael Browning
Collector

Big events have meant big bucks for comic companies and comic sellers in my area of West Virginia, Kentucky, southeastern Virginia and east Tennessee.

Tie-ins have sold for premiums this year, including *She-Hulk* #8, which tied into Marvel's Civil War event. *What If?* #51 from 1993, which was an imaginary story where the Punisher became Captain America, mirrored what was really happening with the Punisher after Cap died. *She-Hulk* #8 stayed strong at $20 for most of the year. *What If?* #51 went as high as $50 at some shops and settled around $20 after all the hype wore off.

I traveled around to several comics shops in West Virginia, Kentucky, Virginia, Tennessee and South Carolina and saw last issues in high demand. One shop had many Marvel last issues, such as *X-Factor* #149 and *Excalibur* #125 for $20 each. One shop even had the last issue of the *Flash*, issue #230, from the Wally West series, selling for $10! *Jonah Hex* #92 was selling in two stores for $20 each, while *Flash* #350 was going for $20 in one. *Flash* #323 in NM has to be one of the most elusive comics I've ever searched for and I still haven't found a copy. There have only been four copies graded by CGC and those are a single 9.4, a lone 9.2 and two 9.0s. That black cover, which deserves the classic designation in my opinion, is easily smudged and fingerprints can be seen on every copy I've found. Of course, the whole "Trial of the Flash" storyline, which began an issue earlier in *Flash* #322, with the return of the Reverse Flash, is tough to find in really high grade. Trust me, I know, because I've been trying to put together a high grade set for years.

I think 1980s comics are to current collectors what 1970s and 1960s comics were to me many years ago: hot, hot, hot. I see fewer and fewer stores with 1980s issues in their back issue bins. Byrne *Fantastic Four*, Paul Smith *X-Men*, Gene Day *Master of Kung Fu* are all in high demand here. Those last few issues of *Ghost Rider*, with the Bob Budiansky art, are seldom, if ever, found in high grade in any of the shops I visit each year. One shop in Pikeville, KY always has an amazing backstock and there are numerous 1980s comics that I can't find even there!

There were a lot of big events in the 1980s, including *Dark Knight*, *Watchmen* and *Batman: The Killing Joke*, not forgetting *Man of Steel* and the revitalization of Superman. *Ronin* #6 has been elusive all year. Those later *What Ifs* are tough to find, too. Sets of the Shan-Lon comics that came with cassette tapes were selling for high dollars. A set of the *Captain America* Shan-Lons sold for $78, while a set of the *Spider-Mans* sold for more than $100. Others that Shan-Lon produced were the *Untold Legend of the Batman* miniseries and three *Archie Comics* with cassettes. These are almost as hot as the SoMuchFun! variants that I discovered and wrote about a few years back.

A set of the Marvel Comics movie comic, *Labyrinth*, sold for $102! A last issue, *Transformers* #80 sold for $50 and *G.I. Joe, A Real American Hero* #155 from Marvel (also the last issue) sold for $150. These books all had low print runs and are highly collectible today, especially with the *Transformers* movie being so hot and a *G.I. Joe* movie in the works.

But, it's the 1990s that have surprised me. What's the deal with *Cosmic Powers* being a hot comic? The last issue of *Silver Surfer* I know was underordered, but I never expected it to be a $20 book. It is, though. On eBay, sets of *Indiana Jones and the Spear of Destiny* were selling for $70 each.

The last few issues of *Conan the Barbarian* and the miniseries that Marvel produced into 2000 are all hot and some of those are really tough to find. Most Marvels from 1999 to 2001 are tough to locate because of Marvel's no overprint policy. That meant many comics were made to order and only those who were actually reading and collecting the series were buying them. Nowadays, when someone wants to fill a hole in his *Deadpool* collection, finding some of those, like #54 & #55 (the Punisher crossover,) you've got to pay a premium.

In South Carolina, I saw Grant Morrison's *New X-Men* and Michael Allred's *X-Force* getting double cover for issues I thought were fairly common. The newstand edition of *X-Force* #116 sells for $10. *What If* #44 with the Venom Punisher has been selling for upwards of $10.

What's going on with these 1990s titles being so hot? A *Superman* #75 Platinum in 9.8 sold for more than $1,000 this year. One dealer was asking $1,200 for a *Killing Joke* in 10.0. Are these comics worth that? The *Superman* #75 was worth it to the collector who bought that copy.

Last issues of *Guy Gardner*, *Teen Titans*, *New Gods*, *Justice League America* and *Mister Miracle* were all selling for around $10 each. *Justice League America* #113 is especially hard to find here in the West Virginia-Kentucky-Virginia-Tennessee region. I've yet to find a single copy at any of the stores I checked.

The last issue of *Savage Sword of Conan* was impossible to find in the stores here and on many online shops. This one must have had a very low print run, just like *Conan the Barbarian* #275. Another last issue, *Ghost Rider* #93, is a $25 comic.

Many hard-to-find trade paperbacks and hardcovers have been reaching record prices. It almost reminds me of when the *Miracleman* trades and hardcovers were so hot. *Deadpool: Mission Improbable* is impossible to find for cheap. The *Conan Essential* is tough to find and expensive when you do locate one. The *Wonder Woman: The Challenge of Artemis* trade paperback sold for $36 on eBay. And a *Fatale: Inherit the Earth* trade sold for $50. *Buffy the Vampire Slayer: Tales of the Slayer* sells anywhere from $20-$40 a copy. Trade paperbacks used to be throwaway

comics and now collectors are starting to realize that, hey, these are comics, too.

Some of the hardcovers Marvel released early in this decade are tough to find, such as the Bruce Jones' *Incredible Hulk* Vol. 2 and Grant Morrison's *New X-Men* Vol. 2-3. I very rarely see the *Ultimate Spider-Man Collection* hardcover released by Barnes and Noble. It was as big as those really great omnibuses Marvel's putting out now.

The *Cable and Deadpool* trade paperbacks were hitting some high prices until Marvel released a load of first prints onto the market which brought the prices down considerably. *The Punisher: Army of One* trade paperback sold for more than $20 every time I saw it up for sale. The *House of M Prelude Excalibur* trade paperback is tough to find and sells for $26.

People were looking for the *Man of Steel* raffle edition, which is one of the rarest Superman collectibles ever published. This edition was given away to raffle winners and select retailers and is extremely hard to find. To my knowledge, only about 20 copies have surfaced and very few of those have the congratulatory letters that came with them when they were mailed out. The *Blind Justice* Diamond Comic Distributors Seminar trade paperback from the early 1990s has been very elusive this year, too. One copy sold for $100 and it was only in Fine condition.

As far as current comics go, *Mouse Guard* has been hot all year, with NM copies of issue 1 selling for nearly $100. The Comics XPress copy of No. 1 has sold for $250 and one seller with a slabbed copy was asking $1,300.

Any Civil War, Planet Hulk and World War Hulk tie-in was hot and shops sold out immediately of the *Green Lantern: Sinestro Corps Special*. That one went to a second printing a day or two after the first printing was released and sold out and many retailers in my area weren't even able to get second printings, because they, too, were sold out at Diamond. One shop had the *Sinestro Corps Special* on its "hot" wall for $20 with appearances in Green Lantern selling for $10 each.

The variant editions for Steven King's *The Dark Tower: A Gunslinger Born* were hot here with copies of the Jae Lee sketch edition selling for $95. A week after the first issue was released, one shop here was selling first prints of the first issue for $9 each.

Valiants sales are getting healthier and healthier as time goes on. People who read these great comics in the early- to mid-1990s are rediscovering them all over again and prices on the pre-Unity Valiants are rising once again. The last issues have stayed hot for the past few years and continue to be in high demand. A last issue of *Shadowman* V3 and the last issue of *Armorines* V2 sells for upwards of $30 each. At

© MAR

Tie-ins to Civil War were hot and sold out immediately.
(New Avengers: Illuminati #1 shown)

one time, I was finding these in quarter boxes and now they're nowhere to be found! The *Harbinger Blue Bird* trade paperback still sells for $25 and the *Magnus Robot Fighter Steel Nation* trade paperback is all but impossible to find. A *Magnus Robot Fighter* #0 with the card sold on eBay for $49. A *Shadowman* V3 No. 1 Special Edition sold on eBay for $153 and a *Shadowman* #0 Gold sold for $26. A *Harbinger* #0 pink edition sold for $71 and another copy sold for $65.

Miracleman still has a solid following. The *Olympus* trade paperback still sells for $150 in nice shape. A complete set of *Miracleman*s sold for $630, while an *Olympus* hardcover sold for $338. I still haven't seen a *Miracleman 3D* 2D edition sold anywhere online or in shops. Miracleman stuff very rarely comes into the shops I frequent, but, when it does, they almost always blow off the shelves and out of boxes within a couple of days.

© DC

Nice variant covers on **Justice League of America** #1 made extra dough for comic shops.

In Huntington, W.Va., older back issues were hot. The shop there, which has been in business since the 1970s and is one of the best shops in the eastern United States in my opinion, had a showcase full of really nice Silver Age comics for sale and thousands of back issues that were all priced to move. The shop stays busy year round and there's regularly back issue collectors flipping through the long boxes looking for those issues they need to fill in their collections.

The shop in Pikeville, KY sells a lot of hot comics and a good number of back issues. The wall was always filled with the hot comics of the week and many people were paying premiums for the issues they'd missed. The shop there also sold a lot of comic-related toys.

Variants sold well in Charleston, W.Va. *New Avengers*, *Dark Tower*, *Justice League of America*, *Red Sonja* and the *Lone Ranger* were some of the comics that had nice variants that made a lot of extra dough for the shop there.

In Myrtle Beach, *Civil War* and last issues reigned supreme.

In east Tennessee, Bronze and Copper Age keys were big sellers.

In Wise, VA, Silver Age keys and the occasional Golden Age comic that came into the shop sold well, as did variants and hot books like *Civil War* and Planet Hulk.

DC Comics' weekly series *52* sold well in every shop I visited, but back issues of *52* in many of the stores were found in the dollar boxes only a few weeks after their release.

Many comics collectors are branching off into original art. I've only been collecting original covers and pages for a decade now and I've seen pieces sell for hundreds of dollars, then, a year later, sell for thousands, so I know firsthand that the original art community is growing. Original art is one of a kind, so it becomes very personal when a collector puts a piece into his collection. Many of us original art collectors have "grails" that we are searching for and the chase can be as fun as acquiring those pieces we believe we just can't live without.

Now is definitely the time to get in on the original art market because prices are still at an affordable level and there is so much great art out there for sale.

Peter Dixon and Doug Simpson Paradise Comics

2007 was an amazing year for Paradise Comics because our sales were through the roof; our in-store business grew by 8% while our internet sales were up close to 15%. I predict that sales will continue to grow in 2008 and the release of *Iron Man* can only increase interest in the hobby.

The greatest area of growth in-store came from our sales of graphic novels; this format is definitely the direction the hobby is going and I hope the major companies take notice. I had more regular customers change their collecting habits from picking up the regular monthly issues to graphic novels that I had to do a major renovation in order to make room for more stock.

Key issues from the Silver and Bronze Age are still selling incredibly well and don't seem to be slowing down at all. I simply can't keep up with the demand for high-grade Silver and Bronze Age books – from *Action* to *X-Men*, people want them in the highest grades and as fast as possible. I would need a full-time employee just to keep up with the want lists. The usual suspects are always involved: *Amazing Fantasy* #15, *Fantastic Four* #1, *Daredevil* #1, *Giant-Size X-Men* #1, *Incredible Hulk* #181, and *X-Men* #94, but I'm also seeing some new ones, *Fantastic Four* #48, *Tales of Suspense* #39, *Batman* #232 & 234 and *Marvel Premiere* #2 are just a few examples.

Golden Age sales are still very sluggish and, with so many collectors only pursuing Timely issues and high-grade Silver Age, sales have been exceptionally slow. There is always a market for Golden Age Hero comics, but never at *Guide*, and usually well below. I really can't see this trend changing in the near future.

Silver Age sales are definitely continuing to grow, and high-grade copies are continuing to sell as fast as I can get them in. For DC Silver Age, Hero and Horror comics have seen the greatest growth in sales, especially the horror tandem of *House of Mystery* and *House of Secrets*, while Romance has slowed right down. It could just be the affordability but DC bin stock sells way more in volume than its Marvel counterpart.

Marvel Silver Age is selling very well, with *Amazing Spider-Man* and *X-Men* leading the way, and demand for

90

Captain America and *Iron Man* increasing. The Marvel Silver Age market is always strong and doesn't look to be slowing down anytime soon.

Bronze Age comic sales are through the roof in high grade, and demand for mid-grade copies have increased as well. Marvel leads the way in this category because of Byrne *X-Men* (#108-143) and all *Amazing Spider-Man* issues between #100 and #200. These issues are on almost everyone's list and, if I had an entire box of each, they would be gone within a week. I have also noticed an increase in demand for Marvel Horror comics; *Tomb of Dracula* and *Werewolf by Night* lead the pack followed by *Ghost Rider* and *Monster of Frankenstein*.

Modern books still have a following and a new market of younger readers is coming into the shop looking for titles that they can pick up and enjoy without knowing any of the history of the characters. *New Avengers*, *JLA*, and the entire Ultimate line fill this niche. *Astonishing X-Men* is consistently our best selling X-book, selling double what the original title sells. *Ultimate Spider-Man* now sells equal numbers to *Amazing Spider-Man* in our shop.

Mid-2007 seemed to spell the end of the variant craze. Whether it was 10 to 1 or 75 to 1, the demand was down and we started selling them at a discounted rate.

CGC continues to be the standard in grading and we are continually submitting more and more books to their great service every year. I would like to mention that CGC is the exclusive grading company for Paradise Comics and Paradise Conventions.

Some recent CGC sales include:
All Star Comics #22 CGC 6.5 Classic Flag Cover $600
Amazing Spider-Man #129 CGC 9.4 1st Punisher $914
Batman #234 CGC 9.6 1st Silver Age Two-Face $1,199.99
Tales Of Suspense #39 CGC 4.5 Origin & 1st Iron Man $1,224.99
Fantastic Comics #1 CGC 1.5 $479.99
CGC Signature Series *Captain America* #25 9.8 Ww La 2007 $218.50
CGC Signature Series *Cerebus* #1 3.0 $396.77
CGC Signature Series *Cerebus* #5 9.8 Dave Sim File Copy $228.50
CGC Signature Series *Cerebus* #55 9.8 Dave Sim File Copy $224.50

As mentioned above, our on-line sales were dynamite and continued to grow all year, our eBay store has been a wonderful addition to business and simply put, you must get one. Customers really like the buy-it-now option of the store, and I like the simplicity of the set-up and listing services. As a result, our sales continued to grow all throughout 2007. Our new website will hopefully continue our on-line sales growth in 2008.

I can't fail to mention our 5th annual Paradise Toronto Comicon, held June 8 – June 10 2007. We would like to thank our guests, dealers, volunteers and the over 5,800 attendees at the 2007 Paradise Toronto Comicon at the National Trade Centre in Toronto. Highlights of the event included the return of Golden Age great Jerry Robinson to Toronto, and the appearance of Terry Moore as a guest of honour with his *Strangers in Paradise* Farewell Tour.

Come join us for our 6th year and let's make it more successful then ever. For more information visit www.toronto-comicon.com

Gary Dolgoff
Gary Dolgoff Comics

2007… 'The Beat Goes On'!... First of all, I'm happy to say that I've been attending more conventions than I have in past years… and the crowds do look like they're getting younger (as well as the 're-tread' folks, 'natch'); and I say, "Welcome aboard!"

I've bought some interesting & varied collections and dealers' stocks since my last *Price Guide* write-up… and I have done well-enough with all of them essentially. One collection from Wisconsin (I paid about $50,000) had over 10,000 comics from the 1940s thru the 1970s – very little Marvels unfortunately, but a lot of DCs, plus some interesting miscellaneous oldies (Charlton, Fiction House, Fawcett, A.C.G., etc.), which I like (as well as the 'mainline' 1940s DCs and Timelys, of course.) One other comic dealer who knew of this collection said to me, "Why do you even want these? Who cares about these books?" Well, I cared, and still care; so I bought the collection, and let him buy from me (at a fair markup for G.D.C.); essentially, they bought from me 'the best'- and I put into inventory, 'the rest'!

I've done well with that collection, as I get want lists from fellow dealers as well as collectors (although I have over 800,000 comic books and magazines: over 50,000 '50s/'60s; over 200,000 '70s; plus a few thousand '40s, only about 1/3 of them are in order, so new inventory, always helps to 'fill-in the gaps.)

Another collection I did quite well with was a $95,000 collection out of Tennessee. It contained runs of DCs from the mid '50s thru about 1972, and Marvels from #1-up for *Avengers*, *Daredevil*, *Fantastic Four*, *X-Men*, etc. I sold them as sets to happy buyers (who are quite familiar and happy with my grading).

March of 2007, I spent tens of thousands on a nice collection of Golden Age *Superman*, *Batman* and early *Human Torch* – plus a stack of ECs, *Hulk* #1, #181 and others. I kept the early *Torch*es for me. [Note: I always will pay more for oldies that will end up being my "keepsies."] Then, a couple of weeks later, (after a sunny vacation in Florida with my beloved) I flew home and picked up a large value of bank teller's checks… and then the very next morning flew back down to (another part of) Florida to buy the books!

This poor lady had given some valuable comics (*Amazing Spider-Man* #1, '60s, etc) to some auctioneer who had no real comic-selling experience and knowledge. After 4 months, she couldn't seem to get them back from him! She had also sold some other books to some "primitive dealer" who had only paid her $250 for an *Incredible Hulk* #1 and so forth (he "cherry-picked" her of some prime-oldies and then "paid her dirt" in so many words, according to the seller.) Well, I looked over the collection for several hours and then offered and paid her a very fair price of $55,000 for the collection. The conclusion here: When selling your collection, make sure that the seller is a comic book specialist and will offer you an honest price for your goods and not try to take advantage of you, the seller. (I – G.D. – must immodestly say that I offer a fair price… whether you know your stuff on comic books or not – and whether you're a millionaire, middle-class… or a pauper!)

In other books, I got a kick out of buying a big batch of pulps (mostly '40s, early '50s, with some '30s) that contained sometimes 5 to 20 of a single pulp. This eclectic batch also included a 1954 *Playboy* #2 (quite rare!,) some 1940s "Strength & Health" magazines, etc… a real warehouse find, I'd say (although I hunger to buy the more expensive, more exotic Pulp collections as well: *Operator 5, The Spider, The Shadow, Terror Tales, Wu Fang, Thrill Book,* etc.) "Pulps are boss!"

I was also quite happy to obtain *Action Comics* #7 (2nd Superman cover) and I happily paid 90% of *Guide* for that one, plus a near complete run of *Wonder Woman* #2-200. I also bought a collection of Western titles (with another "dealer-fellow" that I get along with)- which included the 1938-1939 *Lone Ranger Ice Cream* Giveaway comic!

The following is a brief summary, of how I find various categories of comics to be selling:

Golden Age (1930s – early '50s): They're still, basically… "the best!" For most Timely (*Captain America, Human Torch, Marvel Mystery, Sub-Mariner,* etc.) I can safely pay 75% to 100% of *Guide* in all grades knowing that I can get at least *Guide*, often more!

DC Golden Age is quite solid, with the very early (pre - 1940) appearances of Superman and Batman, often going for over *Guide*. I find the market is very strong for low-grade DCs, as well as Fair/Poor to Good. And, of course, higher-grade (Fine to Mint) "Goldies" are always welcome!

MLJ, Fox, Centaur, Fiction House, etc. – all move well, although some miscellaneous mid to late '40s must now be sold a bit under *Guide*.

CGC'd Golden Age, unless it's a particularly "hot" book, don't seem to be nearly as well received at full *Guide* and often must be slightly discounted. By comparison, 1960s Marvels are generally the best-selling CGC books, especially early '60s *Spider-Man, Fantastic Four, X-Men, Hulk #1-6,* etc., in almost any grade. Also popular are any Silver Age Marvel Superhero in 9.4 or better. In these grades, they of course go well over *Guide*.

Non-Superhero Golden Age from the late '30s and early '40s sells well. I get strictly-graded *Guide* prices for them, every time. I love getting large collections of these, and ogling the covers, before keeping a few.

Funny Animal Dells have always been the bleakest of sellers, but just recently, sales on these (much to my surprise) have been picking up. I recently sold a 're-saler' 100 of 1950s-'61 10¢-cover Disneys for $3 each.

Sci-Fi, Crime, and Misc. sell well enough, and I'm surprised that they don't sell better, as of now. Those crime covers are often "real gripping and cool."

Silver Age (1960s-1971, later 10¢ cover thru 15¢-cover, plus 25¢-cover Giants):

Marvel Comics: Early Marvels are the "Gold Standard" here, in all grades (especially early *Fantastic Four*s and *Amazing Spider-Man*s). I can get *Guide* for most of 'em, (pretty much) with a snap of my fingers. Mid/late '60s Marvels also sell solidly. In general, I love buying Marvel collections (1960s in general as well but especially Marvel stuff.) Over the last year, I have sold at "*Guide* by my grading" runs (sold as sets) of *Amazing Spider-Man* #1-100, *Daredevil* #1-200, *Fantastic Four* #1-100, *X-Men* #1-66… even *Strange Tales* #101-168! *Sgt. Fury*s, unfortunately, still move very slowly, except for the elusive #1. I enjoy the title, but "whaddaya gonna do!" like they'd say in N.Y.C.

DC Comics: With the exception of *Batman*, 1960s DCs generally don't sell as well as their Marvel counterparts, though they're "O.K enough" that I like to buy 'em.

Bronze Age (1970's; 20¢ to 40¢ 'cover price'): I find that sales are picking up on these from time-to-time, and the variety of them that we have at our humble warehouse, is definitely appreciated. One fellow dealer asked for 3 each of a large variety of '70s comics (he had a "list of wants"). The guy ended up getting over 10,000 comics! That's more than 3,000 different '70s, folks. Some of my favorite '70s sellers are *Batman, Tomb of Dracula, Amazing Spider-Man* #150 & earlier, *X-Men* #142 and earlier, plus mainline titles of 20¢-cover price. Folks also like my "batches of bargain '70s" at 75¢-$1.00 each.

Magazines '60s-'70s (Comic book related): Yes, folks are "diggin' them, for sure!" I have over 600 boxes of this cool stuff (Marvel, Warren, Misc., Horror, etc.) and I'm here to say that, "I'm starting to release 'em at last!" Magazines, which have been pretty much ignored, are now being snatched-up by dealers and collectors alike. They are selling almost as fast as I can "price n' process" them. Basically, I divide them up by wholesale prices - $1, $2, $3, $5, & over $5. In Chicago, I sold approximately 38% of the wholesale magazine boxes that I brought there. If I have books at San Diego Comic Convention this summer, I might ship a few dozen out there. Folks also love seeing early *Creepy*s and *Eerie*s, *Foom* magazines, *Mad*s, *Horror Tales, Epic*s, *Savage Swords, Dracula Lives,* etc.

Modern Age (1980s-Present): These, generally are my least compelling sellers, though McFarlane's *Amazing Spider-Man*s and early *Wolverine*s (the Miller '82 mini-series) have recently gotten more popular. I don't know if it's a fluke, but I recently sold a CGC 9.4 *Wolverine* '82 #1 for $127! Most of the time, I wholesale them to everybody for 50¢ each or less in bigger batches, and I'm happy to get 25% to 1/3 of NM *Guide* for the most popular Marvel and DC titles. Sometimes, sellers with a lot of "1980s and up" comics are quite disappointed when they're offered 25¢ or less for those books from the last 25 years or so… but I always say, "Age is Absolute!" Give me a bunch of "rag-tag" '50s & '60s anyday over a collection of shiny '90s books!

The 6-Point Price Spread in the Guide: I think it inadvertently creates confusion for sellers "not in the know." I am one of the biggest fans of the *Guide* (I'll say that Bob O. genuinely cares about the comic book market greatly, and we in comicdom are very lucky to have him in our industry. He's very fair and competent, I'd say.) However, his "6-price spread" of recent years (GD, VG, FN, VF, VF/NM, NM-) seriously needs a large disclaimer that says something like: "Please note, sellers and buyers, that the top 3 grades (VF, VF/NM, NM-) are very close in appearance. Unless a book looks "practically new" to the untrained eye, it's most likely GD or VG (the lowest two prices, on the far left of each price column) as are about 80-90% of 1930s to 1960s comics." Bob Overstreet, to my mind, should make the above blurb a full-page one, perhaps on the page before the main prices begin. It would greatly enhance the knowledge of "rookie" buyers and sellers, making it easier and more equitable for everyone.

So, that's all for now. Have a happy and healthy "Comic book year!"

Bruce Ellsworth
Gold Coast Comics

G'Day from the Gold Coast, Australia.

My wife and I moved to Australia in September 2005 and I instantly started looking for comic books. Comic books in Australia are very hard to find, the main problem being the condition. Most Australian comics are printed on non-gloss paper unlike most American comic books. This makes them deteriorate faster.

I found that by putting ads nationwide that I am starting to receive some offers on comic books. Most of the comics that I have found here are of the Humour variety with a smattering of *Captain Atom* and *The Phantom*. I have been able to find some American comics with the occasional Marvel or DC from the '60s and a few *Classics Illustrated*. All in all, sales were good in the Science Fiction and Horror genres with Atlas Horror and Sci-Fi and EC comics being at the top. I was surprised to find people calling me for CGC graded American Silver Age comics in 9.2 or better. If anyone has some, please send them to me.

Silver Surfer issues are popular in Australia too. (#5 shown)

Seriously though, life in Australia is just like America in many respects. You get the same TV programs, sports and conveniences. It's not all outback, you know. It is hard to drive on the left side of the road and go through roundabouts, but I love surfing and living in the Orlando of Australia on the Gold Coast.

Here is a short history of Australian comic books: The first Australian comic book published was *The Kookaburra* in 1931. Australian comics were not a significant industry until after the government put a ban on American publications in 1940. Despite paper shortages, the industry flourished until 1950. In 1950 the Australian publications were affected by censorship and the introduction of television, and then the return of American comics to Australia in 1959. The most popular Australian comic books are *The Phantom* and *Captain Atom*. One of the top comic book publishers, Frank Johnson Publications, started in July 1941 and was releasing four titles a month. Unlike American comic books, the Australian comics were not numbered consecutively. They were one shot titles because of war restrictions. The first of the Frank Johnson comics, *Amazing Comics* came out in 1941 and consisted of adventure stories. My favourite comic book from this period and probably the best drawn is *Silver Starr*. It was drawn by Stanley Pitt, who also drew a version of Tarzan called *Yarmak*.

Australian comic books covered all genres and walks of life from Western to Romance. Some artwork and stories from Australian comics made it to America. *Felix* by Pat Sullivan and *Kazanda* were reprinted in 1940s issues of *Rangers Comics*.

Other than *The Phantom*, the best selling Australian comic was *Captain Atom*, which was published between 1948 and 1954 by Atlas Publications. This title sold 180,000 copies every month and was the only Australian superhero apart from the Phantom that sold well. Humour and Westerns sold better than any other comic in that era.

In conclusion, most Australian comic books were successful because they mixed local humour and the Australian way of life into their stories, thus making them quite a different read from their American counterparts. The most popular back issues in Australia are *Phantom*, *Spider-Man*, *Silver Surfer*, *Superman* and *Batman*. I would like to thank Mick Stone of Camberwell Books & Collectables for all his help and advice on this information.

Sales this year included *Phantom* #10 for $800(AU), *Silver Surfer* #1 in Fine condition for $200(AU) and *Popeye Thimble Theatre* #1 for $700(AU).

I am looking forward to a great year in 2007/2008.

D'Arcy Farrell
Pendragon Comics

What a MARVELous year! If "Civil War" didn't bring old heroes and villains to life, as well as a refreshing apocalyptic storyline, "World War Hulk" did. Who does not like the Hulk? WWH is 4+ decades in the making. Way back in the 1960s, General Ross warned everyone about the Hulk. Ross did everything in his power to bring Hulk down, dirty and fair, using the US military machine at his disposal. Most readers thought, "what a bad dude" and "how dare someone with such authority abuse it for his own end(hatred)"? Well so far it appears Ross was right all along, though for the wrong reasons. I think only Betty can stop Hulk now(but she's dead!). By the time you read this, we should know the ending, and this rant has no bearing. But it does represent the excitement Marvel has caused in comic stores everywhere. My only beef about Civil War and WWH is The Sentry. Does anyone like this character? I certainly do not, nor do my customers. I will dislike any conclusion with him involved. I had hoped Thor would show up in *Civil War*'s conclusion, but alas, it was not to be. Instead, Cap gives up for everyone's sake. Marvel then supposedly kills Cap off in an unexpected issue of *Captain America* #25. That had a lot of real press. So much that it reminded me of Superman's death in early 1990s(nowhere near that news, but still noticed). I do not think he died. Perhaps Cap was impersonated to deceive The Red Skull or others? A clone created by Reed(remember the cloned Thor in *Civil War* #3.) Perhaps Nick did a switcheroo(though he said nothing to Winter Soldier). I hope it is something smart and twisted to keep readers puzzled for some time. As a note, expect Nick Fury to save the day at some point. That soldier is as old as Cap, but very wily with plenty of connections and allies to pull anything off! I hazard to guess that you will see Steve show up near WWH's end, or at least within 1-2 years.

Other nice surprises? The crossover *Annihilation*, anything with Winter Soldier(Bucky?), the company Zenescope (*Grimm's Fairy Tales*.) What to watch for in 2008? The "Green Lantern - Sinestro Corps" duel may have ended, but even if it did by this review's printing, I'm sure we will see repercussions. Superboy Prime being loose and Ion-Parallax with him is scary for the DC universe. Expect the last Crisis to occur from this (it already is if Superboy-Prime is loose!) I love seeing DC bringing old great villains from yesteryear. Sinestro is the all-time great baddie for GL/Hal. It should be exciting. Here's hoping Barry finally makes it back to save the day, once and for all (though I expect DC would maintain his death in saving the universe once again like in 1986.) Hope Pérez does it all as that fantastic pencilling is awesome! Last note.... *JSA* #10. The beginning of "Thy Kingdom Come" by Alex Ross(covers) and Geoff Johns (main writer.) Sequel to *Kingdom Come*, this should be awesome. Kudos to DC. You all should realize DC could have made a prestige $6-$9 formatted maxi-series, even without Ross, and it would have sold huge. Instead, a reasonable $3 per issue. To non-DC buyers, buy the trade and the 2 prequel trades as well. This being said before *JSA* #10's release, the original *Kingdom Come* is always in print, great art and story. So buy it! You will not be disappointed.

Trades, Graphic Novels and Hardcovers: I am seeing more independent trades, and for that I'm glad. Indies are a tougher sell on the classic Marvel/DC older collector. But when they put their wares into a tidy package, with no issues missing, no delays in publishing, and at a fair price, they will grab it. The best indie seller for me would be *Grimm's Fairy Tales* Vol 1, and soon to be Vol 2. Boom! Studios is doing better as well. Marvel still, and always will, lag behind DC

(king of trades!). Every year, week to week, DC rules in trades! Manga appears to be slowing for me, but I'm sure it's just my area. I cannot imagine Manga ever slowing down with the younger collectors. *Naruto* and *Fruits Baskets* leads titles with Tokyopop the best selling publisher.

Current Comics This Year: Best in sales would be as follows: all *Civil War* and crossovers, all *World War Hulk* and crossovers, *Annihilation*, *Captain America* #25, *Grimm's Fairy Tales*, *Dark Tower*, *Omega Flight* mini, *Sinestro Corps* and its crossovers (excellent story). Continous titles that sell excellent year after year would be: *Astonishing X-Men*, *JLA*, *Batman*, *X-Men*, all *Marvel Zombies*, *Uncanny X-Men*, *Wolverine* (and *Origins*), and any *Avengers*. Surprises in sales would be: the continued sales of *Daredevil*(after Bendis left in #81, no one expected same sales, and they actually increased with Brubaker's great writing!), crossover event *Annihilation* (underrated, get the 3 volume hardcovers, but realize the volumes are out of chronological order), both *Shazam* minis(definitely a surprise), *Silver Surfer: Requiem*, many main-

World War Hulk #1 *was one of the year's best in sales.*

stream and independent horrors (especially from IDW and *Marvel Zombies*), *Countdown* and *52* (I expected readers to give up after 1-2 months, but they held on for a great Black Adam and Isis story), *Black Adam* maxiseries. For my list of disappointments, there are plenty, but I'll minimize it perferring not to be reminded of these follies of the past year. Worst things to happen in 2006/07: Anything Black Panther, especially the wedding; the main Image titles (like *Spawn*); and the ending of *Comic Book Marketplace* (great mag for the experienced collector.) Finally, my list of undersold that deserves mentioning: *The Programme*(Wildstorm/DC), *Fallen Angel* (IDW), *Flash* (death of Impulse as the new Flash), *Savage Tales* (and other Dynamite Entertainment books like *Red Sonja* and *The Boys*), *Sgt.Rock* mini, *Elephantmen* (Image), *Walking Dead* (Image, get the trades!), *Lone Ranger*(DE), *Zombies* (IDW). Movies were a disappointment, with the *Fantastic Four* sequel and *Spiderman 3*. Higher sales were definitely noticed for Venom and Surfer issues. Especially for *AMS* #300(1st full Venom). Hard to believe what it was going for pre-movie. I expect an increase, but nowhere near early 2007 levels.

Modern Back Issue Sales (1986-2004): Sales slipped in this area due to increased trade awareness. For example, why spend money on back issues of *Hellblazer*? That's 200+ issues!!! Get the trades. You miss nothing. Cost is far less and it's easier. This trend will continue, and you will see more dumping of recent period books at conventions for this reason. But it is a good reason. Trades are a good way to go. Maintain your existing long runs, and look to the trades section of your local store.

Copper-Late Bronze Age Back Issues (1976-1985): Low print mainstream titles are picking up steam! *Wonder Woman*, *Flash*, *GL*, *JLA*, and *Daredevil* are my best sellers for this age. Around 5-10 years ago, Bronze Age books were so affordable. Now we find what were $5-$20 books are all $50-$200 such as *Marvel Spotlight* #5, *Tomb of Dracula* #1 and so on. Well, not so many early Bronze are that cheap and key anymore. You have to look in this era. The problem is less obvious keys to go for. Certain *JLA* issues after #160 come to mind, and other items like *Fury of Firestorm* #1, *Ms. Marvel* #1,16-18, various *Defender* issues just to name some with potential. Go ahead, try and find a *Fury of Firestorm* #1 that is a true 9.6 or better. Or a *Teen Titans* #1 or #2 (1st Deathstroke). You may get lucky, but most people will fail. It's those useful *Overstreet* notations that are placed in your *Guide* that will help you discover the future big books. All those minor key issue notes. Refer to JLA for example. Issue #'s 161,192,193,244,245,137(wow! really low to me),144, and 145. All somewhat important. The *Teen Titans* #2 I mentioned earlier (1st Deathstroke) has always been important. Deathstroke has always been a fan-fave. He slowed down a bit in the 90s, but now is in the midst of this big DC event. This book definetely is going up.

Early Bronze Age Back Issues (1970-1975): A very volatile area. Any high grade keys, even minor, sell at full *Guide* or better. Most books are still reasonable compared to the Silver Age, easier to find in a higher grade, and prove to give a greater return by percentage. Percentage? How does that factor? Well if you take a $1000 comic from the Silver or Golden Age, compare it to 10 reasonably popular Bronze Age books(such as *Marvel Spotlight* #2,28,29, *Tomb of Dracula* #1, *Ms. Marvel* #16-18 and so many more choices) that also add up to $1000, you would notice from last year or even 5 years ago, your gain is greater with the Bronze Age selection. There are exceptions. Not everything goes up year to year in any age. But overall, it is the better bet. My best selling titles of this age would be *Batman*, *Amazing Spider-Man*, *Our Army At War*, various DC/Marvel original horrors (not reprints, Marvel has too many), *Incredible Hulk* (especially #141,162). My poorest selling titles, and least favored for investment, would be *Sgt. Fury*, *MAD* magazines, Romance, Charltons, Marvel reprint horrors (not *Werewolf By Night* or *Tomb of Dracula* as these are original and excellent!) .

1960s Marvel: This year I noticed a huge surge for anything Silver Surfer and Hulk. *Fantastic Four* #48,49,50 and *Silver Surfer* #1-4 actually sold well. Of course, this is due to the (again) disappointing *Fantastic Four* movie sequel. I do not think these books should increase in value this year, as they are already too high, but the rest of Surfer's appear-ances should (such as later *FF* issues). Surfer is a great "appearance" character, and he generates excitement even in the modern age. I would go after the more affordable appearances he made for investment and reading. Hulk is and always will be a fan favorite. The current WWHulk story is fueling all levels of sales for the green behemoth, and deservedly so. Aside from *Hulk* #1-6,102,181 issues, everything else to me is undervalued and in high demand. Not to mention the numerous appearances all over the Marvel universe where he bounces in, and bounces out with the title's hero thrashed. Tops in demand is always *FF*#12. This book is very pricey, but if you look hard, you will find battles against the Thing, Thor, Spidey (just try to find *AMS* #119,120 at *Guide*!) Hulk is great and popular in all ages from Silver-Bronze-Modern-Current. You cannot go wrong collecting his issues. This section of my sales report always has the most activity by dollar and volume. Needless to say practically everything sells(even early *Sgt. Fury*). Remember that DC and Timely (1938-1945) created the first Super Heroes(still kicking to this day, such as Superman, Batman, Cap.) Marvel did it for the Silver Age. DC did as well, but much less so (they already were well established 25 years earlier). Marvel mostly did new creations and ideas. Most heroes had some problems, politically, economically, or just at school (Peter Parker). DC maintained the old guard (WW, Sup, Bat) and reinvented old heroes (Flash, GL and many more), but the ideas were stale and campy. You have to get into the late Silver Age and into Bronze for cool and unique writing/art (for example *Swamp Thing*). So in a nutshell, if you can afford it, buying anything Marvel in this key area is worth every penny. For the art, stories, investment and Americana value, you can't go wrong!

1960s DC: Nothing can compare to Marvel in the 1960s, though DC tries. The only titles that come close to Marvel in importance and value would be *Showcase* (many heroes like GL, Flash, Atom, Aquaman start in this expensive title), *Batman*, *Detective*, *Adventure*, *Brave and the Bold*, *Action* and *Superman*. Maybe DC can field these and maybe 5-10 more top titles for the 1960s. Marvel would have multiples more! Even said, sales is always #1 for me with Batman(anything with him!). Especially beginning in mid 1960s with Neal Adams issues in *Detective*. Nothing outsells Neal Adams' Batman. For you younger generation collectors, Alex Ross, Jim Lee and McFarlane are great artists, but who do you think they got some of their inspriations from? Neal Adams, Wrightson, Kirby, Ditko, Romita(s), Kubert(sorry if I missed someone) and Crumb (he is most unique!). And those greats had inspiration from the likes of Evans, Schomburg, Williams, Frazetta and plenty more. But for every name I mentioned, Neal Adams is the quintessential artist for the human body (especially in tights!). This is why whenever Adams pencilled any Batman, it is an instant seller! What do you think would sell faster? A high grade *Detective* #400 or an Amazing Spider-Man #100? Both have similar value, age and relative keyness. I would bet on the *Detective*. Fewer high grade copies available and far more important with Adams. Sales were outstanding this year for my DCs, even though the current titles lagged after *Crisis*. No surprise, as I had large influxes of vintage collections come my way. Typical top sellers were *Batman*, *Detective*, *Showcase*, *Action*, *Superman*, *Adventure*, *WW*, and anything *Sgt. Rock*. Slow sellers would be *Lois Lane*, *Jimmy Olsen*, *Hawkman*, *Atom*, *Aquaman*.

1960s Other: Gold Key is my best in sales with *Solar*, *Magnus* and *Star Trek* tops. Charlton is slower this year. Romance for me is dead except DC. Horror moves best after TV/movie related books, especially Warren mags like *Vampirella*, *Creepy* and *Eerie*. Archie is OK this year, and Harvey is hot, especially *Hot Stuff* and *Casper*.

Golden-Atomic-Early DC Silver (1939-1962): As mentioned earlier, DC and Timely rule this era. With all the innovation that has carried into the current age, it hardly is a surprise. The main stickler to this early period is availability, grades and cost. Timelys are near impossible in quantity, and sell quite fast even if over *Guide* (especially *Cap* and *Marvel Mystery*). *Sub-Mariner* is slower, but being a Timely alone sells it. As per DC, Batman and Superman titles are always out in front. These books are more available in quantity, and prices can be quite high as well. I find early *Detective* and *Action* go over *Guide*, and *Batman* and *Superman* sell at *Guide*. I have sold some of all above, most noteworthy would be some *Detective*s falling in from #45-65, *Superman* #6 and four high grade Timelys. Unfortunately, not much in the way of collections came my way (except Silver and Bronze, which was abundant), so my report is less than normal in the era. The non super-hero titles (Disneys by Dell for example) I found slower than normal across the board.

Conventions: Hobbystar yet again provided an exciting convention in Toronto last August. This convention showcased many venues and guests, providing 46,000+ attendees with many signings, merchandise and social events. It was a great mixture of all the genres of our hobby. The comic industry was well represented with advisors such as Harley Yee and Graham Crackers. I noticed a greater increase on the floor for vintage books. Nothing big appeared to have sold, but plenty of mid-range Silver and Golden Age books valued under $1,000 were sold. As usual the bulk dealers did their share, and I noticed a *much* greater interest in early Copper Age. I have mentioned in a few articles previously that this age will become very hot soon, approaching 30+ years of age. The low print runs of DC such as *Wonder Woman*, *Flash*, *Green Lantern*, *Brave and the Bold*, *JLA* and so on certainly help. The 2008 show Aug. 22-24 should increase to over 50,000 attendees. I hope to see you there.

Conclusion: New comic sales this year were fantastic thanks to Marvel. Civil War and World War Hulk made for great reading. Most of my customers are beginning to ignore movie hype, leaving increased demand and cost to non-regular collectors. Too much recent disappointment. We hope the *Batman: The Dark Knight* movie does well (it should from what I read). I don't expect better sales, but perhaps younger collectors may spend on DC more than Marvel. A bit too much Spidey I think. The new *Iron Man* movie and *Hulk*

may bring new people in though, especially *Hulk*. For you investors of vintage pricey books, be wary of online purchases. I am getting more and more customer feedback on eBay and CGC sales. Pictures are being doctored, and CGC serial #'s are being used on books not owned. Anyone can cut and paste a picture on the net. So when an expensive 9.8 is posted, you can cut and paste the item's picture, list this item later on with the pic (maybe cropped, resized and doctored a bit). Other tricks can be making the pic a bit blurry so the serial # cannot be seen. Whatever the way, someone always discovers how to take your money. So be wary, buy in person when possible, or at least from someone well known, a store, an Overstreet advisor, a convention. If on the net, look at feedback, their recent history, return policy, if any, and clear pictures. What we do for example for bigger purchase buyers, is either send a DVD with closeups of whatever is wanted, or offer to have them fly in to Toronto. Never a guarantee, but usually we subsidize the trip with the comics purchased (they get a deal on the trip and make a holiday of it). Seems excessive, but I truly believe in buying in person at all costs if possible.

Dan Fogel
Hippy Comix, Inc.

2008 marks my 30th year in comics and collectibles retailing, and I honestly feel that I'm learning more with every passing year and my enthusiasm keeps growing! Most of my friends are people in every facet of our industry and art form, and the level of positive networking and spirit of cooperation has never been higher.

It's been no secret that most of my sales have been mainly focusing on Underground, Adult, and Alternative Comix, an area showing rapid growth following the 2006 release of (insert shameless plug) my book *Fogel's Underground Comix Price Guide*. Although Overstreet's *Guide* has thus far not included the vast majority of these titles, perhaps Uncle Bob and Mr. Geppi may soon change that policy, starting with buying me out? (end shameless plug.)

Bulk sales were most of my mainstream comics transactions, including: complete sets of the "pro-zines" *Amazing World of DC Comics* and *FOOM* (along with a membership kit), and DC digests and treasuries, and a near-complete set of Marvel treasuries. Also sold were miscellaneous Marvel, Archie, and Disney digests, DC and Marvel reprint and prose paperbacks, and hard-and-softcover graphic novels. In addition, I moved dozens of short boxes of *Mad* and *Cracked* magazine, Marvel black and white mags, the color series *Epic Illustrated* and *Hulk*, and the Warren titles *Creepy*, *Eerie*, *Famous Monsters* and *Vampirella*.

A growing trend has been vast single-owner collections of later Silver Age, Bronze Age, and Modern Age books hitting the market. Most of these have been the remaindered stock of stores that closed for a variety of reasons, although some have been the accumulations of dedicated or over-eager collectors. Far from breaking sales records, the late Silver and Bronze transactions are mostly bought at steep *Guide* price discounts, and resold for higher but still wholesale value.

Post-1980 collections are literally bought either by the pound or longbox, at pennies or dimes per book. Sellers especially need to be aware of these facts, because it's definitely a buyer's market for what I like to call "macro-sales."

As always, collectors should only buy what they like, and please take the time to read at least some of them for pleasure and not with only dollar signs in their eyes!

John Haines
John Haines Rare Comics

Bronze Age: For us, 1970s comics are now outselling all other eras by volume. Over half of the collectible comics that we sold during the year were published during the Bronze Age. Collectors are all looking for the best available copies, therefore very good and lower must be discounted or packaged together to make them attractive. Bronze Age graded above Very Good needs no special marketing. Collectors are looking to complete their runs and are aggressively searching for missing issues. To our surprise, our records show that for the first time, Marvel horror comics like *Tomb of Dracula*, *Creatures on the Loose*, and *Werewolf by Night* are selling just as well as Super-Hero titles. As for DC, please send us all your high grade *House of Secrets* and *House of Mystery* issues with Neal Adams, Jeff Jones or Bernie Wrightson artwork in them – we are scrambling to keep our regular customers satisfied. Got Super-Hero books? Good, 'cause collectors want them too. We have sold through multiple runs of *Iron Fist*, *Marvel Team-Up*, *Black Lightning*, *Ghost Rider*, *Flash*, and most requested of all: *Wonder Woman*. Square bound books are selling well above *Guide* and are heavily requested, including: Marvel's *Giant-Size* series, Atlas' *Vicki* series, and DC's 100 pagers.

ONLY A STRONG AMERICA CAN PREVENT
ATOMIC WAR!

©ACE

That most interesting era, the Atom Age, gave us popular gems like **Atomic War!** *#1.*

Silver Age: 2007 continued trends established over the past several years. Collectors want high grade copies of Super-Hero titles at mid-grade prices, and you have to be creative to get mid/low grade issues to move – no surprises here. We have been actively accumulating movie/TV comics in all grades for a long time now and the collectors that we know are loving it – drawn covers do just as well as photo covers. Gold Key and Charlton continue to keep up their end of the bargain with *Turok*, *Star Trek*, *The Phantom*, *Many Ghosts of Dr. Graves,* and the like selling quite briskly.

Atom Age: By far the most interesting era – newly re-discovered gems are being snapped up as fast as collectors can be shown them, especially in higher grades. Like what? Well, pay attention now 'cause we're gonna do this fast: *Atomic Comics* #4, *Atomic War* #1, *Thing* #12 and #15, all Timely/Atlas good girl titles (*Millie*, *Patsy*, *Cindy*, etc.),

Thrilling airbrush covers, *Teenage Diary Secrets*, *Giant Comics Edition* #12, *Reform School Girl*, *Wings* #90, #91, #94, and #112, *Planet* #66, #71, and #72, *Cannonball* #1 and #2, *My Desire* #4, *Intimate Confessions* #1, *Captain America Comics* #76 - #78, *It's Game Time*, *Little Dot*, *Four Color* (that's right, I said *Four Color*), *My Confession* #7, *Dollman* #42, *Plastic Man* #33, *Ken Shannon*, and on and on – if you can find it, someone will probably be looking for it.

Golden Age: Since the advent of *The Gerber Photo Journal*, and the ascendancy of eBay, all Golden Age titles are selling well. The combination of visibility and availability have inspired collectors to go for it. Unlike other eras, Golden Age collectors search all grades and all titles with equal gusto. Over the year we were happy to have found collectors looking for previously slow titles like *Daredevil*, *Air Boy*, *Popular*, *King*, *Tip Top*, and *Crime Does Not Pay*. What sells the most? For us, it's Dell far and away. Makes sense since Dell out-produced all the other publishers during the '40s anyway. We have several collectors looking for *Four Color*, *Looney Tunes*, *Walt Disney's Comics and Stories*, *Raggedy Ann and Andy*, etc. What sells fastest? First and foremost all Timely Super-Hero issues, classic Fiction House Good Girl issues, DC's *Flash*, *More Fun*, *Wonder Woman*, and *Sensation*. Bottom line though – we'll tell you what we tell our regulars: ignore what the other guy is doing, buy what you like best and you'll never be unhappy with your collection.

Conventions: We enjoy seeing old friends and meeting new collectors over the course of the convention season. Conventions continue to be the best venues for collectors since they can physically handle and inspect more comics in a single day at a quality convention than they can just look at in a week on eBay. Know what we're asked for the most at cons? Sit down, 'cause you'll be surprised to hear that it is for *Sonic the Hedgehog*. Who knew?

Restoration: We sell restored and unrestored comics with equal ease due to the fact that we are willing to buy vintage restored comics without giving the seller a big song and dance. Our customer base is comfortable with the fact that they will always be able to sell their restored books to us at the end of the day since we do not hesitate to buy them back. During the course of the year, we have again overheard professional dealers publicly trashing restoration in front of collectors and then privately complaining to other dealers that they cannot sell restored books – you don't need to wonder why. All vintage, collectible comics will find a home with a collector if they are accurately graded, reasonably priced, and any known restoration/conservation has been disclosed.

John Hauser
JMHComics

Comics shows have been slowing down for mid-grade Silver Age. This material is plentiful and cheap on eBay. So many comic collectors are just saving the gas money and shopping on-line. 50-cent comics still sell very well at the local shows. The collectors of these comics find it's better to buy in person. Buying on eBay just adds too much cost for postage. Sets and runs of comics continue to sell well at all the local shows. The readers are alive and well.

Golden Age and high grade comics sell steady wherever I am. Sales at shows, on eBay and to friends maintain steady sales for the business. Recently, I have been doing a lot more consignment sales. This works well for sellers that aren't in a hurry and want to receive the maximum amount for their collections. I've had great success deciding the best ways to sell their valuable comics.

Golden Age: These are all steady sellers at current *Guide* prices. This year I bought a large collection of pre-code horror, ECs, Fawcett Super-hero comics, strip reprint comics, DC Golden Age, plus a lot more. Everything has been selling at a very steady pace regardless of the grade. Esoteric and horror comics lead the pack, followed closely by Golden Age Captain Marvel comics. The rest have been selling, but at a much slower pace.

Silver Age: Nice clean Silver Age sells very well. Marvel always sell the best. At the moment, my supply of Marvels is getting thin. The supply of Marvel Silver Age collections seems to be drying up. DCs sell well in nice shape. Average very good copies of Silver Age are becoming increasingly tougher to sell. The collectors are not turning out and trying to fill in their runs like they did in the good old days.

Bronze Age: Continues to be one of the best selling time periods of comics. Prices are still relatively low on this kind of material. There seems to be plenty of collectors trying to fill in their runs.

Modern Age: 1980s comics are finally picking up some steam. Many buyers have been turning up at the shows trying to fill in their runs from my 50 cent boxes. Many of these comics sell for multiples of *Guide* if certified by CGC in 9.8.

Greg Holland
ValiantFans.com

Valiant RETURNS! As predicted in last year's market report, Valiant Entertainment, Inc., (VEI) has brought the Valiant universe back to life. The first product, *Harbinger: The Beginning* hardcover was released in August 2007. In addition to reprinting the first eight issues of *Harbinger* (1992) in digital color for 200 pages at $24.95 retail, a short "Origin of Harada" story was newly written by Jim Shooter and illustrated by Bob Hall.

VEI now owns the copyrights to all of Valiant universe from the 1990s. That's everything from over 1,000 comics produced by Valiant and Acclaim, excluding the Gold Key properties (Magnus, Solar, and Turok). Some of the Valiant trademarks are in the process of finalizing, and the copy-

rights now completely belong to VEI. As a fan of the Valiant line since 1992, I can say that I'm definitely excited to have Valiant back. I wish VEI the best of luck in their endeavors with this comic universe.

Not surprisingly, the return to publishing for *Harbinger* had an effect on the back issue market for the original books. CGC 9.6 graded copies of *Harbinger* #1 trade regularly in the $85 range, which is fairly significant for a regular issue from 1992. Most collectors who follow CGC prices on modern issues recognize that there is rarely much value in regular issues graded 9.6 or below. *Harbinger* #1 has production flaws that have given 9.8s a very low population. With 300 copies submitted to CGC, only 12 have received 9.8 grading. The most recent public sale (as of this writing) of a 9.8 *Harbinger* #1 was $1,000 on ComicLink in May 2007.

Though lower printed, the *Harbinger* #0 Pink (sendaway) edition is often found in top condition, and prices for CGC graded copies seem fairly stable around $125 for 9.8, and $60 for 9.6. Fewer copies have been graded for *Harbinger* #2 through #7, so prices tend to fluctuate between $50 and $150 when 9.8 examples are sold.

Besides the *Harbinger* title, Valiant books in general seem a little more popular than in recent years, however, it is a small (but loyal) fanbase which is responsible for much of the market activity.

Current demand for a few Valiant books should not be interpreted as demand for all Valiant books. Though a complete Valiant collection (1991-1996) consists of just over 800 issues, half of the eighty-million total Valiant books in print were printed in 1993. As a result, Valiant regular issues from 1993 are nearly impossible to sell for more than a few cents each, which is true of most 1993 Marvel, DC, and Image comic books as well.

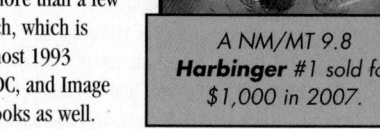

A NM/MT 9.8 ***Harbinger*** *#1 sold for $1,000 in 2007.*

Less than 10% of the 1990s Valiant books in print sell consistently for even cover price, while fewer than 5% of the books are consistent sellers for $5 or more. Many Valiant longboxes sit idly in comic shops around the country because the contents are simply too common. At these low price levels, the cost of shipping is a major factor in the final auction prices realized. Sellers who attempt to increase profit through higher shipping charges generally see lower auction prices as bidders compensate. Some bidders now avoid shipping-profiteers altogether.

Though Valiant's time in the market spotlight of the 1990s was brief, the impact appears to have been significant enough that many 25-to-40-year-olds consider Valiant as the comic universe for their generation. The results of nostalgia are well-documented in this industry, with both Marvel and DC's "first years" considered the most prized. It remains to be seen how much the combination of nostalgia and Valiant's return by VEI will contribute to the back issue market. At this point it's anyone's guess, but it is already clear from the significant internet presence of Valiant fans that the Valiant universe will be closely watched in whatever forms it might take in the future.

William Insignares
Demolition Comics

2007 was another busy and successful year for the comic book industry. Comic book related movies dominated and continue to dominate the box office: *Fantastic Four*, *300*, *Transformers*, *30 Days Of Night* and *The Simpsons* all played to sold out screenings. Comics fans packed the theaters and so did future comic fans. Many were curious about what all the fuss is about in our neck of the woods. Some of these new comic fans are people you know, or you may even be one of them, now wondering why they didn't pick up a comic or graphic novel sooner. We just have to smile and say: "Welcome, come on in and enjoy the ride!" – and it should be a ride, a wonderful kaleidoscope of twists and turns. Discovering wild and intricate new worlds where incredible heroes clash against sinister villains in the ultimate on-going battles of good vs. evil, man vs. machine, Romance, Adventure, Science Fiction, Adult themes, Animation, Horror, and Crime. But there's more, because there always is. Our industry is one that has evolved for the better through the ages, through good times and bad. As our country went through some trying times this past year with the dreaded collapse of the booming house market, to the reality check of the bridge collapse in Minnesota, to the panic when Mattel recalled millions of children's toys, to some scary stock market days – everyone was touched in some way or had someone close to them affected either emotionally or financially or both, by these pitfalls and tragedies.

After each event we are forced to pick up the pieces, comfort our loved ones and look ahead to a new day. At least we know that in the thick of it all, in between emails, meetings, the drive thru and all the hustle and bustle, a plethora of fantastic tales awaits us between two glossy color covers, or two cardboard covers. Even though we never seem to have time, and we grow older, the characters we read about never get old, and never tire. They wait for us whenever we can make time for them. They wait to captivate and entertain us because ultimately that's what the comic medium is all about: Intelligent Entertainment.

Demolition Comics was in Heaven in 2007! We did some promising promotions, including a brand new commercial featuring yours truly fantasizing about Wonder Woman, as she appears next to me in all her Amazonian glory much to my absolute bewilderment. We snagged quite a few new customers with that advertisement. We gave out free comics and prizes at a dozen different movie events. Chances are that if you went to see a movie in Tampa, Clearwater, St. Pete, or Largo in Florida in 2007 you saw us at least once, and you always walked away with a gift. It's awesome to be at the opening or special screening of comic book movies and see the expressions of awe on everyone's faces.

While our local business was very good, our sales abroad were also positive. That's another great thing about comic book movies; they are also making new comic fans abroad, and those new international readers need to find a reliable connection in the states to supply them with fresh product. Our website, www.demolitioncomics.com, continues to upgrade with constantly evolving technology so that we may better serve local and international customers.

We sold thousands of regularly priced comics, toys, posters, apparel, trading cards, gaming, and even thousands of moderately priced back issues. When Transformers customers came in looking for merchandise, we fixed them up with a T-shirt, poster, new comics and back issues. *30 Days of Night* vampire fans? No problem. We have tons of back issues. "How about the first trade paperback?" Borders forgot to stock it, because they were busy putting in orders for the O. J. book, but we have it. Sold. Again, and again. No sales of *Detective Comics* #37, so sorry to disappoint. They were working on a Trump Towers in downtown Tampa, but unfortunately the Donald never happened to drop by one of our stores asking for *Superman* #1. If he had we would have suggested maybe Donald Duck, whatever the latest issue was from Gemstone Publishing, as it is a great read and he probably could use a good laugh. If that had happened, we would probably have had a return customer.

As local business was very good and sales abroad were increasing, we decided to expand our store fronts. We made a daring leap into another town, over an hour away and opened our fourth location in Largo. Our latest store is over 2,200 square ft. and almost twice the size of our other locations. We worked tirelessly day and night to open the best store we possibly could and the end result was spectacular. It is a one stop shop for all comic book and related pop culture merchandise. We carry full lines of many different publishers and stock almost 40,000 back issues, hundreds of action figures, dozens of nice looking posters, a large assortment of apparel and whatever else we can fit in (still no *Action Comics* #1). You know, I make humorous reference to the stocking of key Golden Age books not because I think they are not note worthy, but because I wanted to make a point that it's not all about just the buying and selling of "those" books. In fact, we learned from the housing market downfall and stock market uneasiness that those types of investments can be very risky, yet consistently key Silver Age and Golden Age books continue to rise in value, as you may have witnessed in years past and present. As with any investment it's important not to go beyond your means. We want to keep you as a customer and enthusiast and not another negative statistic of someone who got burned in this industry because they bought into something they could not afford and it hurt them financially later. Entertainment first.

Investment second. Why save for a possibly fruitful future by giving up an otherwise enjoyable today?

Brian Ketterer
Collector

I have just returned from the 2007 Chicago and Baltimore shows and am happy to report that the vintage comic book market is strong and healthy. Reports from dealers I spoke to reported incredibly strong sales at the San Diego Comic-Con. While Chicago started slow for many dealers, it slowly picked up steam over the weekend. Baltimore, a well-run show but with lesser expectations in terms of sales for most dealers, was also a decent show for most. While I do sell books from time to time on eBay, other internet outlets and to comic book dealers, I do not view the market from a sales perspective but rather from a collector's standpoint. Even though the market was strong in many areas, there were still some down trends on certain books during the course of this year.

As has been the case for many, many years, prices on books VF and below continue to fall in the market in relationship to their high grade counterparts. Most dealers are aware and have known this for many years, yet some collectors are still paying high prices (meaning at or near *Guide* prices) for low and mid-grade common run non-keys. Even top line titles like *Amazing Spider-Man*, *Avengers*, *X-Men* and *Batman* have scores of copies available of almost every book in mid/low grade. So many copies exist that there is far more supply than demand for these books. For now, high grade copies continue to have demand outpacing supply and so prices have remained strong. It is clear right now that collectors need to take their time to explore many other buying options such as eBay, where common run books in mid/low grade are often available for purchase at 50% off *Guide* or far less. While many people will try to scare you off of eBay and the grading problems, the truth is that when you are talking about books in that grade, they are often available for extremely reasonable prices and you can still have confidence in the stated product.

This widening gulf has produced a continuing disparity in prices where a VF copy can obtain 10% of what a copy of the book in CGC graded 9.6 does. While this is not new news, I state it again to remind collectors who are reading this to exercise patience when buying lower/mid grade copies. Also, do not be deceived by those dealers who promise "50% off discounts" but have raised the prices to almost double the *Guide* price. Thus there is no real discount. There are often several dealers at shows who are offering deals at 50% off and it is a legitimate deal. Be patient when buying. If you see a book offered to you, check all of the available outlets to determine whether or not the price you are buying is the most reasonable deal. It is important for collectors both new and experienced to be patient and not jump at the first available deal unless it is a rare or key piece. Since quantities of most mainstream titles are readily available, it is unnecessary to overpay given the current market conditions.

Once again, let me make a push for every collector to support their local comic book stores. While I hear more than my fair share of horror stories from people going to a comic book shop and seeing wildly over-priced back issues and grousing employees, many local comic book shops still carry a wonderful supply of back issues. I encourage supporting them because eventually, they won't be around without our support. While I think eBay is wonderful, I still love showing up at the store and checking out the books myself. Additionally, there are many wonderful deals out there to be found in the stores. Many have high grade, low grade, mid grade and wide runs of material. Just because you have a bad experience at one store, don't let that stop you

Silver & Bronze Age Marvels are still "King of the Mountain" in sales. (**Amazing Spider-Man** #185 shown)

from exploring other stores. Once you find a good solid local shop, support it! Zapp Comics in Wayne, NJ, JC Comics in Plainfield, NJ and Comic Universe in Folsom, PA are just a few of the incredible standout stores that exist in my general area. If you cultivate a relationship with these individuals you will find a wonderful resource for discovering vintage books at fair prices and you will be helping to support your local business.

I think anyone reading or writing in *The Guide* knows that Silver/Bronze Age Marvels are still the king of the mountain. *Amazing Spider-Man* is unquestionably the blue chip of all Marvels and high grade copies remain the most liquid Silver Age book. Even low/mid grade copies of *ASM* sell briskly at a discount. Other hot titles are the *Avengers*, *Fantastic Four* (especially #1-50, 72), *Incredible Hulk* #181 (surprise, surprise), *X-Men* #1-10, 94-101, *Giant-Size X-Men* #1, *Iron Man* #1 (movie hype reaching huge proportions given that this book is not rare in high grade) and *Marvel Spotlight* #5. While these books are the same that have been appearing for many years, some "sleepers" are *Conan* #24 (1st Red Sonja), *Iron Man* #128 (Classic Alcoholism cover), *ASM* #229, 230 (tough in high grade, great story), *Incredible Hulk* #180 (the actual first appearance of Wolverine), *Captain America* #117 (1st Falcon) and *Thor* #225 (1st Firelord). All are books that sell well above the *Guide* price and if you track down high grade copies, snap them up when you see them at bargains!

DCs are wonderful books and while they have far less demand, they also appear to be available in lesser quantity. Neal Adams' covers and interiors are white hot right now. *Green Lantern* #76 in all grades is selling briskly, but in high grade it continues to sell for record highs. While *Green Lantern* #76 often gets a lot of the attention, *Green Lantern* #79 is actually more difficult to find in high grade. *Green Lantern* #87, the first appearance of John Stewart, is also very hot in high grade. Of course, Adams' legendary run on Batman is what brought him the most notoriety and books like *Detective Comics* #400, 402 and 405 are all highly sought after Neal Adams covers. In addition, *Batman* #227, 232, 234, 244, 245 and 251 remain extremely sought after books. Neal Adams' *Tomahawk* books and his Superman covers are also very desirable. We haven't even mentioned his horror work, Spectre and Phantom Stranger work – it's all in demand! Adams is clearly the driving force behind many Bronze Age DCs, with his incredible covers and revolutionary artwork. Beyond Neal Adams' work, ten cent DCs from 1956-1962 are unbelievably tough to find in high grade with many books including *Batman* #121, *Adventure Comics* #210 and *Action Comics* #242 nearly impossible to find even in grades of 6.0 and better. Just astonishing! Those are just a few of the very tough to find ten cent DCs that are out there. Many DCs would be considered "high grade" in 8.0 from that time period because they simply cannot be found in better shape. There's only one 8.5 copy of *Action Comics* #242 on the CGC census and that's the top grade! As more people continue to discover the wonder of DC, expect these books to climb in value.

This year, while there have been many variant and sketch covers, I have not seen a lot of sustained high prices for moderns. Most have had quick runs like the *Civil War* #1 sketch cover that quickly lose their value in 60 or fewer days. Again, I caution my fellow collectors NOT to invest in such quick dollars. If you are patient and wait a few months, you will pay far less in most cases for these new, hot sketch covers that will have no staying power. Consider that in the last 7 or 8 years, very few moderns have had the kind of sustained value that a book like *Ultimate Spider Man* #1 has had. *Marvel Zombies* #1, *Batman* #608 (2nd print) and a few other books have been able to have moderate growth that is sustained. Sketch covers are simply gimmicks and when a store or an online dealer attempts to pump up the hype for a "rare" copy of something, be very careful about rushing out and spending money right away. Wait and see if there is going to be sustained value behind the collectible. The way most new comics are published today, the sketch cover is reprinted and the original loses its value quickly (for example, *Civil War* #1 sketch cover is not worth $75 anymore). One of the prime examples from this past year is *Captain America* #25 (his "death"), which for the first two days on eBay was white hot with people paying $25 to get a copy and individual retailers charging high, high prices. Two weeks later, copies were struggling to sell for $10 a copy. Modern hot books are the most volatile market with very little upside for speculation and collectors who get burned when they pay top of the market prices.

I'd like to mention that one of the other things that has contributed to recently strong sales is that the foreign market, including Great Britain and Europe, and the weak dollar has led to many collectors abroad to feel that "aggressive pricing" in the U.S. is really moderate to them. In the future, it's important to monitor and listen to the voice of this segment of the market as I feel it will have increasing influence moving forward.

Overall, the vintage market continues to be strong for high grade and the volume of sales for other grades is still strong. I look forward to the rest of 2007 and 2008 where I anticipate continued strong sales in a variety of areas.

Dennis Keum
Fantasy-comics.com

2007 was a tremendous year for us. It marked our second full year of operation since we started our website and sales really took off this past year. We are an internet-based buy and bid site and also maintain an eBay store and run weekly auctions. We mainly try to present new material to the market so we focus on acquiring original owner collections rather than buying from other dealers or at conventions. The following are some specific observations over the past year:

Silver Age: Marvel keys are the story here. With constant exposure from film and mainstream media, it seems everybody wants to own an *Amazing Fantasy* #15, *Amazing Spider-Man* #1 and *Fantastic Four* #1. Every copy we were able to acquire sold immediately at prices above *Guide*. Good to Very Good grade copies of these keys were particularly quick to sell. From the Silver Age, there seems to be an endless demand for *Amazing Spider-Man* comics followed by *X-Men*. DC titles such as *Batman*, *Superman*, *Justice League*, and *Green Lantern* were also strong sellers.

Bronze Age: This area of the market is where the largest part of sales volume has been this past year. Bronze Age books are easy to find and easy to sell. More and more collectors are coming into this market and rediscovering comics from their youth. If I were looking to buy comics as an investor, I would put my money on high grade '70s Marvel comics. Even though there are many high grade copies available in the market and in collections, this is being offset by constantly increasing demand for these issues driving prices higher. While every mainstream Marvel title was in strong demand, it was especially difficult to keep *X-Men* #94 -143 in stock due to strong demand from collectors in both the U.S. and Europe. DC titles such as *Weird War Tales*, *The Unexpected*, and *The Witching Hour* sold very well. Also all Charlton horror titles in high grade were in strong demand throughout the year.

Golden Age: We were able to find one original owner collection this past year of around 500 early 1940s books. These books were mainly in the Good to Very Good range with a mix of superhero and non-superhero books. Timely books from this collection sold at 1.5 times *Guide* within a week of being listed on our eBay store. The mainstream DC titles such as *Superman* and *Batman* were surprisingly slower to sell at *Guide* prices.

Copper/Modern Age: The big news for us in this area of the market was the acquisition of a collection of 100,000 books. We selected 1,700 of the best books and sent these to CGC for certification. Of the 1,700 books, nearly 1,200 were certified as 9.8s with 14 being graded a 9.9, and the rest graded as 9.6. As of this writing we have just started selling these issues and are seeing tremendous demand for high grade CGC graded modern comics with astounding multiples being paid. This can be attributed to market confidence in CGC graded comics and increased demand for early '80s books. With more and more collectors that read and collected comics from their childhood re-entering this hobby, we should see increasing prices for high grade books in this area of the market.

Conventions: We set up a few times a year at the Big Apple Convention to sell discounted low grade Silver/Bronze Age and Modern books and have to say this show is a lot of fun. It is especially great to see young collectors buying stacks of low grade reading copies of '60s and '70s books.

Nadia Mannarino
All Star Auctions

2006 was the banner year for museum openings and showings, and the trend continued into 2007 with more thematic exhibits highlighting the best of comic art and newspaper strip art. As we write this recap of 2007, we are looking forward to the opening September 15, at the Montclair Art Museum (www.montclairartmuseum.org). There are 4 exhibitions, *Reflecting Culture: The Evolution of American Comic Book Superheroes*; *Comic Book Legends: Joe, Adam and Andy Kubert*; *Dulce Pinzon: The Real Story of The Superheroes* and *Greg Hildebrandt: Golden and Silver Age Superheroes*.

It is extremely important that this type of exposure continue as it elevates the medium to a new level. For the past several years, attention has been paid to our industry as Hollywood adapted comic books and their heroes for movies. Now with all this increased attention in the form of museum opening and showings, we are even further poised for takeoff!

As a result of this heightened awareness, prices have risen sharply, and we have been approached for interviews by various publications to explain the continued rise in popularity as well as the steady growth and increase in prices seen in the Comic Character Collectibles arena. It is easy enough to cite Hollywood's influence but there are other factors contributing as well.

Historically, in uncertain times, collectibles do enjoy resurgence. There is a need for a comfort zone which these items provide, bringing us back to our childhood and simpler times; many of these items are "feel good" purchases. We have seen the resurrection of the toy market, the animation market and the premium market. The other areas of Comic Character Collectibles are still extremely solid, with the original comic book and newspaper strip art market leading the way.

With record prices being established, a need arises for more information about caring for, storing and insuring collectibles. Appraisals are becoming a necessity rather than a luxury as most insurance companies will not insure items valued at $5,000 or above without proof of authenticity and proof of ownership. Mark your calendars, review your collection and remember it is our responsibility to be caretakers of these precious items! Let your motto be: Collect and Protect, what you like!

San Diego Comic Con 2007 was yet another incredible event! With the final attendance numbers coming in at over 125,000 attendees, plus 9,000 exhibitors and their staff, this has become the "must exhibit" and "must attend" show of the year. The Con has become a launching pad for TV and movie projects, and with so many stars in attendance, the media once again covered the Con throughout the country.

Auctions and auction concerns are popping up all over. The lure of auctions does bring out collections and items which have been in hiding, as the auction route is the best way to maximize results. And of course, eBay remains a very strong presence in the field.

We ran thousands of eBay and Internet sales as well as catalogue sales throughout 2007 and we noticed the increased demand for CGC graded comic books from the Silver and Bronze Age. We also noticed that in the arena of comic and newspaper strip art, European buyers are certainly impacting prices once again, with their currency enjoying a healthy run against the dollar.

2008 promises to be another banner year as far as comic character themed movies are concerned, with many movies scheduled for release.

Following are some highlights and results from 2007:

Golden Age: CGC graded Golden Age comic books in the 8.0 to 9.0 range continue their upward climb, with copies graded higher obviously realizing higher prices. It seems selling Golden Age comic books is not the problem, but securing these individual books and collections is certainly the issue. Another area within Golden Age comics is the Bound volume, these are copies bound by the publisher (publisher file copies), and in some instances by collectors. These bound volumes are such a great resource because the books can be read and enjoyed and still maintain their condition. Dell Bound volumes, Harvey Bound volumes, Timely Bound volumes etc., exist and we are seeing an increased interest.

Silver Age: CGC graded Silver Age comics in the 9.4 to 9.8 ranges continue to exceed expectations. The frenzy for high grade Silver Age books seems to have subsided a bit, but for the high grade (9.6 to 9.8) key Silver Age issues, demand is still strong.

Newspaper strip art: This uniquely American art form continues to gain in popularity. Europeans appreciate this art form and continue their unabashed enthusiasm. The seminal artists: Raymond, Herriman, McCay, Foster, Frazetta, Caniff, Gould, Sickles, Capp, Schulz, Kelly etc. remain sought after and prices certainly reflect that. We are also seeing a rising trend in the "newer" comic strip artists: Jim Davis (Garfield), Russell Myers (Broom Hilda), Scott Adams (Dilbert) etc. While these artists have been toiling and producing their dailies and Sundays for years, we are now seeing more demand for their art.

During 2007, we sold many examples of Winsor McCay's art, including *Little Nemo In Slumberland*, *Sammy Sneeze*, as well as editorial cartoons and the very popular feature, *Dreams of the Rarebit Fiend*. We also sold examples of Herriman, Schulz, Raymond, Capp, Caniff and Frazetta newspaper strip art.

Original Comic art: Covers and splash pages, whether DC or Marvel, still continue to be the items of interest to most collectors. Throughout 2007 we offered and sold many DC splash pages by the masters: Carmine Infantino and Murphy Anderson. At the 2007 San Diego Comic Convention, we sold the masterpiece cover to *Mystery in Space* #90, *the* classic image of Adam Strange. During 2007, we also sold the cover art to *Hawkman* #1. Other examples of DC art covers and splashes, included *Justice League of America*, *Brave and the Bold*, *The Flash* and *Mystery in Space*. As always, the mainstay artists: Kirby, Ditko, Steranko, Wood, Infantino, etc. continue in popularity, with prices reflecting this.

Animation Art: This market is enjoying resurgence and with proper guidance and nurturing should once again become a dominant market. With the majority of studios going to computer generated animation, these hand drawn examples by the masters should once again gain strength. Look to this market to continue to rebound in 2008 due to increased attention.

Toys and premiums: Another area of Comic Character collectibles that seems to be enjoying a comeback. A great and educational way to link with the past while building a collection.

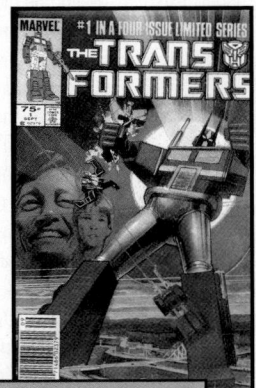

Transformers was the comic book movie success story of 2007. © Hasbro *(Transformers #1 shown)*

These are very exciting times to be in our business. Increased awareness along with integrity should be the focus in 2008!

For all prices realized for 2007 events and earlier, please visit our web site at:
http://allstarauc.com/asonline/realized.htm.

Dave Matteini
Collector

Greetings, comic collectors! This year I wanted to comment on three key themes. First, the success of comic related movies (particularly of second tier characters); second, the continued popularity of conventions and third, the relative scarcity of high grade DC Golden Age material relative to the most recent past.

Dare I say that 2007 confirmed the acceptance of comic books and comic characters throughout pop culture? It was a very positive development that some arguably lesser tier (or certainly, lesser promoted) characters were able to have movies that were wildly successful both through the story

telling and financially. Without question, the comic book movie success story of 2007 was *Transformers*. At the time of this writing, as per Boxofficemojo.com, *Transformers* grossed $310.5 million domestically. Also worth mentioning, Frank Miller's *300* grossed $210.6 million in 2007. By comparison, *Spider-Man 3* grossed $336.5 million! Clearly, comic characters are hot in our mainstream, and not just the "A" list heroes like Spider-Man.

I would also like to take a minute and congratulate the organizers of the New York Comic Con, which was held at the Jacob Javits Center this past February. I think that the second show was even better than the first with tons of dealers, exhibits, and guest appearances (including Stan Lee himself!) Shows like the New York Comic Con, and of course the San Diego Comic-Con, have transcended the medium and have become pop culture events in and of themselves.

The key challenge is how the comic community can continue to build upon the successes of the movies and events to attract the next generation of readers. There are no easy answers. I truly worry about the future of this hobby when it appears to me, and I say this purely anecdotally, that the average age of people frequenting comic conventions is north of 30, and that there exists a very clear gap amongst the under 21 collector, both male and female.

From a collector side, I am constantly amazed at some of the deals to be had on eBay. From my experiences this year purchasing some SA Marvels and DCs, there seems to be no distinction between a solid reader in the G/VG through the FN+ to even the FN/VF category. The comic reader can find some great deals on eBay in these grades – but of course buyer beware!

On the Golden Age *Batman* front, it seems that the availability of high grade (here 8.0 or better) *Batman* books from #2-20 has dried up materially. In years past, it always seemed that you could get a nice copy and perhaps even a pedigree if you were willing to pay for it. This year the quality material seems to be off the market as perhaps these books have found more permanent homes.

Looking ahead to next year, I am very excited for *The Dark Knight* movie and the New York Comic-Con of 2008. In terms of new offerings, I hope that DC and Marvel continue to bulk up their Archives and Masterworks series, which are the best value in the hobby IMHO.

Happy Collecting!

Jon McClure
Collector/Dealer

2007 continues the trend of increasing demand for Bronze Age books. Horror remains popular in all grades, selling over *Guide*, but not double *Guide* like last year. Bronze keys continue to set records with no end in sight. Even minor keys from the 1970s are heavily sought after. High grade Copper is still in demand for long term investors, as most in the hobby recognize the relative scarcity of true 9.4 or better copies. High grade Silver Age DC is heating up, with some CGC books in 9.2 and 9.4 bringing unbelievable percentages of *Guide*, or 10-20 times the 9.2 value, as collectors realize how rare these gems truly are. Even 8.0 graded DCs are now moving well, as hobbyists realize the impossibility of acquiring 9.0 or higher, and can buy them at a fraction of the price of those only slightly higher in grade. Bronze Age price variants, especially the 35¢ issues, continue to be requested, with demand far outstripping the supply. The Holy Grail of 35 cent variants, *Iron Fist* #14, has sold in three notable transactions this summer: a CGC 8.5 for $1700 on ComicLink; a Fine Minus for $885 on eBay; and a G/VG for $185 also on eBay. As I stated last year, I believe this Bronze Age key should hold the top spot in Bronze Age books, listing at 9.2 for $2,000.

Todd McDevitt
New Dimension Comics

I have the exciting extra insight this year of having just come off of my first Overstreet advisors meeting. It's kept me thinking a lot of about the marketplace for this crazy hobby and where it will go from here. Where *can* it go from here? So much has passed that has shaped where we are now. With that in mind, I always make a promise to myself and to readers that I won't go on and on about typical stuff. I end up being pretty random, but I think it's better than telling you for the 47th time how hot *Hulk* #181 is…

I'm lucky to have the chance to contribute to the *Guide*. Here's a little history on me and my business that helps to shed light on my specific perspective of the market. I started New Dimension Comics in 1986 while still in high school. I have grown to 5 stores surrounding the Pittsburgh area. I have been blessed with many adventures, some of which I have chronicled in my own comic, which I will be happy to send to any curious reader. I have always been fascinated by the difference in market conditions between my area and when I travel. Things that collect dust here, fly for me on the road. And vice versa. I often find treasures at other stores/conventions that get gobbled up by my local clientele. Part of the fun…

Golden Age: The good stuff sells fast. Period. I get asked what my Golden Age selection is like all the time and I have to say it's next to nothing. I just don't get them fast enough. But I think most guys will tell you that of course… I get stuck with the oddballs. My new resolve is not let them collect dust in my stores, but instead put them on eBay and let the world see them. We recently had a guy from Australia crazy for our Tom Mix comics. Happy to oblige…

Silver Age: High grade rules again. This is the year for Iron Man. *Iron Man* #1 has always been an affordable key book. I think I'd compare it to the spike we all saw for *Amazing Spider-Man* #300 with Venom in the 3rd movie. Unlike other key movie tie-ins, it's actually possible for the average collec-

tor to afford one. Speaking of the effect of movies on the price of comics, it seems the time to sell them is when they are first announced. The hype and speculation are high and there's a scramble to "get it before it goes up." I haven't seen this work. They are in high demand during this window, but right now (as I write this it's months after *Fantastc Four* 2 with the Silver Surfer), it's harder sell a *FF* #48 than it was a year ago. Varying reviews might have done that, but that just means that the pre-release hype phase is even more important to move books like this. *Iron Man* is almost a year away and I'm selling his comics well now. Another one to watch is *Iron Man & Sub-Mariner* #1. Still very affordable.

Modern Age: The bar of the quality of new comics is raised higher every year. Better stories, better art, better formats. And the fans love it. I'm sure if you went back 20 years and told a comic retailer that the standard price for comics would one day be $2.99, they would predict the end of the hobby. Who would ever pay $2.99 for a comic book? Well, apparently lots of people. And even after that, some still become MORE valuable as collectibles. No matter what, there is always a surprise that catches the market off guard. It's the classic if popularity (demand) exceeds the print run (supply), then the price of the existing copies goes up. Titles like *Incredible Hulk* (Planet Hulk storyline,) *Marvel Zombies* and *Fallen Son: Death of Captain America*. Speaking of…one odd book that seems to be catching on is *Captain America* #360. It's the first appearance of Crossbones, who is the bad guy who shot Cap!

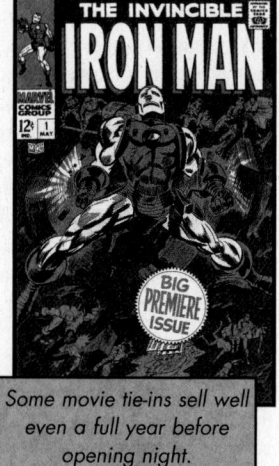

© MAR

Some movie tie-ins sell well even a full year before opening night.
(Iron Man #1 shown)

What's Next?: Kudos and credits to ace collector Josh Hvizdos for a lengthy, insightful conversation on this topic. Many ideas here sprang from there. It starts with…. Who will be collecting comics in the future? I don't think Spider-Man is going to go anywhere, but who's going to be chasing down Rex the Wonder Dog in 40 years? There won't be folks around anymore who remember Rex since there won't really be a mechanism in place for him to have any exposure at all. And the thing that store owners fear the most right now is that there aren't a lot of new people entering this hobby. Kids now-a-days (I've been waiting to be old enough to use that expression) have enough other distractions. Reading funny books isn't high on their list. And even if it is, they won't really have a desire for old, obscure characters. What will drive the demand for these old comics when all the people who remember them fondly are gone? Assuming no new memories are being generated of course. I guess a good parallel would be Platinum Age books. Sure they have some value, but I've never run across a guy looking to collect them. Anyone who's ever bought them—and I admit it's not my focus—has also collected a lot of other things. No one is beating down my door for the *Mutt and Jeff* I have from 1911. So what are the *Mutt and Jeff*s of the future? Sorry to bring you down, but it's kinda scary to think about who will still want certain titles in the next generation.

Steve Mortensen
Colossus Comics and Micurio

The graded modern market remains strong, especially in the signature series market. Collectors love to have their comics signed by creators and having CGC certification service guarantees that the signatures have been witnessed by someone approved by CGC. Popular signature series books usually contain key appearances, special cover artists, new storylines and other memorable events. The collectors of common issues still prefer non-signed books to complete their runs and save the signature series for comics that are extra special.

Making money with CGC moderns is hard. 2006/2007 saw the demise of a few of my competitors due to the fact they were selling books at or below their cost. Unfortunately eBay buyers became used to these prices and it has since made it difficult to sell common issues for more than $20. For a dealer, the minimum cost of grading a modern comic is $18 when you factor in shipping back and forth to CGC, grading fees and the cost of the comic. If a seller sells their books through their eBay store, eBay takes 10% of the sale so at $20 dealers are just breaking even. Many of my competitors last year were selling their books for under $20 and they eventually went out of business.

CGC Modern collectors need to be in it for the long haul. Many of their common issue books won't show appreciation for perhaps years but a complete graded collection of a title may be worth more as a whole than as individual issues. Many times, the titles I submit are the only issues being graded. Each year that passes makes these titles rarer, as more copies fall into the hands of people that aren't careful in the handling of comics and the chances of getting a CGC 9.8 grade diminish.

Colossus Comics' most popular CGC 9.8 subscriptions this year have been: *Ultimate Spider-Man, Amazing Spider-Man, Dark Tower, Civil War, Batman, All Star Batman, Astonishing X-Men, Green Lantern, Justice, Justice League of America, New Avengers, Superman/Batman, Moon Knight, Wolverine Origins, X-23: Target X* and *Y: The Last Man*. Our subscription service continues strong for those who want the convenience and assurance of receiving a 9.8 book of their favorite series each month.

Early in 2007, we did a big marketing push pre-selling copies of *Amazing Spider-Man* #539. I think we ended up selling about 125 preorders for the books which was a pretty good number for us. Turned out that the first reappearance of the black costume was in *Friendly Neighborhood Spider-Man* #17 not *ASM* #539. Many dealers/collectors were sur-

prised when that book came out first and quickly *FNS* #17 sold out and went to a 2nd printing.

Transformers comics began heating up about this time in anticipation of the movie. CGC-certified 9.8 issues of the first Marvel series sold very well at many multiple times guide. *Tomb of Dracula, Werewolf by Night, Frankenstein* and other Bronze Age Marvel horror books also sold well and continue to sell well. Early issues of *G.I. Joe* in 9.8 are also hot and command multiple *Guide* prices.

Stephen King's *Dark Tower* was a very popular series in 2007. Most issues sold out and all covers were popular. The sketch variants in particular fetch high prices. The 9.9/10.0 market remains very strong with most books selling for 5 or 10 times the price of 9.8s. I've found that about 1-2 of every 500 Modern CGC books I graded gets a 9.9/10 grade. It's very difficult and impossible to preorder. Some books will never reach beyond a 9.8 because of some inherent printing flaw.

Back issues of *Amazing Spider-Man* from the 80s sell great and are in hot demand. 1980s books are somewhat difficult to grade in 9.8 due to the newsprint paper and overall production quality in comparison to modern day comics.

The *Heroes* TV show became very popular among comic fans. Wizard created a special edition comic that became a hot commodity in the Spring of '07. *Captain America* #25 was Marvel's big book of the year with the surprise death of Steve Rogers. Most retailers were taken by surprise and vastly under ordered the book. Even after Marvel announced that more copies were available for reorder many retailers only ordered a small quantity the second time around and were again left without enough copies to fill demand. Marvel received many complaints from retailers who lost out on the profits of the book because they lacked inventory to fill orders. Since then Marvel has promised to inform retailers ahead of time of significant storylines.

In April, we shipped out over 450 copies of *Captain America* #25 in 9.8. Out of 500 copies graded we received 3 9.9s and no 10.0s. It was our biggest pre-order ever. In order to meet demand we drove the raw copies to LA and had them graded on site by CGC at Wizard World LA.

Every few months we encounter a couple troublesome books to grade. We were unable to grade *Ultimate Spider-Man* #93 and *Incredible Hulk* #95 in 9.8. In fact as of this writing only one copy of *USM* #93 has been graded in 9.8 and no copies exist of *Incredible Hulk* #95 in 9.8. We have been selling *Incredible Hulk* #95s in 9.6s for $70. If I owned either one in 9.8, I would price it at $300+. This shows that 9.8s are not a given with modern comics and the books with poor production quality command a premium when you can find them in high grade.

We found a stash of late Bronze Age super-hero books including *Spider-Woman* #1, a book that has sold well for the past couple years since Marvel has brought back the character in a mainstream role in *New Avengers*.

In May, *Web of Spider-Man* #18 was heating up due to the movie. It's the first appearance of Venom in the shadows. It pre-dates *Amazing Spider-Man* #300 by almost 2 years.

Only one CGC-certified 9.8 exists and it last sold in April 2007 for $575; 9.6 copies sell for around $50-75. As a whole I think *Web of Spider-Man* is an undervalued title. It has great stories/covers/art and many early appearances of the black costume – besides it's a personal favorite of mine since I remember buying each issue off the newsstand beginning with issue #1.

There's been much talk about who will be the new Captain America. At the end of *Civil War*, it was the Punisher who picked up Cap's mask and later in *Punisher War Journal* #7 he created a new costume which was sort of a blend between the Punisher logo and Captain America's costume. This idea first appeared in *What If* vol. 2 #51: "What if Punisher Became Captain America." This issue went from the quarter bins to $25 in less than a month. The price has held at $25 for raw copies and CGC-certified 9.8s sell for around $125 (so far only one has been graded in 9.8.)

We've had several subscribers request back issues of *Captain America* (new series) and have had trouble locating quality copies. It's very difficult to find 9.8 worthy comics once they've hit the back issue bins. This is one of the reasons why we started our 9.8 subscription service where a collector can choose a title and receive each month's issue certified in CGC 9.8 with a reader copy. Our books come directly from the distributor and we carefully prescreen them before sending them to CGC for grading. It's one way to insure that you'll be able to keep your ongoing series in 9.8.

The new *Jonah Hex* series has been a sleeper hit. Collectors are now seeking out the early issues in 9.8. It's been a personal favorite of mine and I'm glad to see it do well. *Walking Dead* continues to be a strong title also. Robert Kirkman has the Midas touch and this series has been gold for him. We were lucky to score a couple 9.9s on the title this month. *Marvel Two-In-One* and *Marvel Team-Up* have been great back issue sellers in 9.6+. The new series *Conan* from Dark Horse has been a smash hit and the Linsner cover of #1 sells very well. Each sale we inch the price higher and the book still sells. Note also *Red Sonja* #1 Linsner cover is a great cover and is also a good seller.

I'm trying to get my hands on back issues of *Iron Man* because the movie is approaching and I expect the title to heat up – especially #128 the alcohol issue which I hear is a theme in the upcoming film. So far only one copy has been graded in CGC 9.8 but I would expect many collectors will begin pulling that one out of the closet before the film and getting it graded. The cast of the movie sounds great and Robert Downey Jr. should make for a terrific Tony Stark. Iron Man was my favorite character as a child. I had issues #1-200 but the value always paled in comparison to my Cockrum/Byrne run on *X-Men*. Bob Layton's covers still remain some of my favorites.

There's lots to look forward to in 2008. The movie business has brought new life to the comics market – especially the back issues. Comics as an investment may be one of the best places to place your money if you know the right books to buy. In general, buy the best quality books you can afford; this generally means staying in the 9.4+ category for Silver Age, 9.6+ category for Bronze Age and 9.8+ for Moderns.

The community of collectors who buy, sell, meet and swap information online is increasing all the time. Auction houses and other comic-selling sites are offering online auctions to compete with eBay, who is turning off some collectors with increasing fees and little-to-no access to customer service for the individual collector.

About a year ago, I began building a site that I thought would fill another online need/want for collectors — a central place where collectors of any category could easily display, buy, sell, trade and talk about all their collections in one place. There are already sites to display your graded comic collection, and some great message boards about comics. But I wanted to meet the need/want for an online community where you can show off graded and ungraded comics, plus your statues, toys, cards, Pez, antiques, costumes, Grandma's china, Grandpa's guns, or whatever other collectibles a person might have – all under one ID.

This new site, Micurio (www.micurio.com), is being built out with new collections every day, along with features like a collection gallery, personal comments, message boards, personal/vendor pages, classifieds and a buy/sell function. Current users are having fun posting and talking about the widest range of collectibles, like Star Wars statues, Asian antiquities, Transformers, Louis Vuitton dice, classic cars, medieval manuscripts, elongated coins, taxidermy and, of course, plenty of comics. Hope you'll sign up to join the fun (it's free,) and drop me an email at steve@micurio.com to let me know what you think.

Josh Nathanson
ComicLink.com

ComicLink had a banner year in 2007, with sellers achieving record prices for items from many different areas within the comic book market. Of course, Silver and Bronze Age Marvels were the usual standouts (our record auction sales of *Amazing Fantasy* #15 in 9.4 for $210,000 and 8.5 for $62,000 are cases in point.) Silver and Bronze Age DC comics in high-grade have also come into their own, with collectors recognizing the true scarcity of these issues. *Showcase* #4 in 8.0 sold for $17,000 within mere hours of being listed on ComicLink! Golden Age also surged, led by the Superman and Batman titles, but fanning out into many different titles and esoteric genres. The *Action Comics* #1 sale on ComicLink in 2.0 for $85,000 and the *All Star Comics* #8 sale of a 8.5 for $62,000 are examples of record Golden Age sales realized on ComicLink.

Collection owners are still coming out of the woodwork, and it is always exciting to inform them of how much their comic books and comic art are really worth in today's market. The excitement in a collector's voice when he finds out his 10 cent investment is worth $10,000, and when he realizes top dollar on the Exchange or at Auction will always be priceless. On the other side of the equation, collector-investors continue to appear out of nowhere, nostalgic for their childhood and seeking out new ways to spend their money. Thanks largely to CGC, Baby Boomers continue to see comic books and comic art as undervalued investments, with little risk relative to their stock market alternatives. Now in their mid-30s and spending, Generation Xers are now also a force to be reckoned with. It is simply mind-blowing what *Amazing Spider-Man* #252's and #300's are going for, not to mention *Teenage Mutant Ninja Turtles* #1, but people buy what they are nostalgic for and then the price goes up.

Those of us that have been around for awhile find the current price levels somewhat hard to believe. But when compared to other scarce and highly demanded pieces of history and art, the comic books and comic art still look inexpensive, with legs to run. A dealer friend of mine likes to say, "sell high, buy higher," which on the surface is counter-intuitive. However, the reality is, whether you are a dealer or a collector, that is the only way to get good stuff nowadays. You just need to add "then sell higher still" to the end of it, and that is how to make money in a rising market. We are constantly advising buyers and sellers using our Auction and Exchange services how to do this.

So what does the future hold? Well, the Silver Surfer looked great! Venom was semi-believable! The upcoming Batman, Iron Man and Hulk movies showcase strong acting and directing talent, and I can't wait to see them. The blockbusters keep on coming and coming! The ever-increasing Hollywood interest, constant advancement of special effects, and insertion of comic book characters into the minds, consciousness and living rooms all over the world bodes very well for comic book prices. So does exposure and support given to this market through such venues as Geppi's Entertainment Museum -- a wonderful project that should be emulated throughout the country.

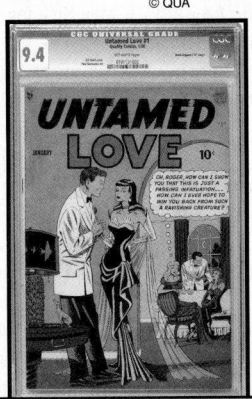

The diversity of the Crippen Pedigree offered something for everyone.
(Untamed Love #1 shown)

Matt Nelson and Stephen Ritter Focused on Pedigree comics

As you read this, we hope you're also reading a copy of our long-awaited book on the greatest Golden Age pedigreed collections ever discovered. This full-color book covers nearly 50 famous pedigree collections ranging from the über-famous (Mile High, Larson, San Francisco) to the little known (Toledo, Van Buren, Cookeville.) In addition to the stories behind the discovery and disbursement of these collections, the book includes the existing original lists, loads of pictures and CGC grade averages for each. We even broke down their content by genre, company, and year, displaying the data in color charts and graphs. Ultimately, all of this information was combined to rank the collections in order of greatness, with #1 of course being the incomparable Edgar Church/Mile High pedigree.

If you are a fan of the Golden Age, even if not necessarily of pedigreed comics, you'll absolutely enjoy reading how these collections came about. More than just a book about the greatest existing specimens of our hobby, it's also an examination of 45 different collecting mentalities among a culture of millions who made comic books a part of their everyday lives. It provides a glimpse into the life of a comic book fan from the '30s, '40s, and '50s, long before comics were ever considered collectible or valuable.

Our idea originally encompassed both Silver and Golden Age pedigrees in one volume, but after a point we realized that such an endeavor would take several more years to complete, and produce quite an unwieldy book. So the decision was made to break it up into two volumes, starting with the Golden Age. The Silver Age volume is already in the works, and will follow soon.

A debt of gratitude is owed to the dealers and collectors who were gracious enough to share their knowledge and experience with us to make this book whole. A lot of them have spent the past decades buying and selling pedigrees, and their intimate, and sometimes exclusive knowledge will certainly benefit anyone who reads the book. We plan on continuing this ongoing stream of knowledge, both past and future, through market reports and our website, comicpedigrees.com, which covers current events in the pedigree comic world. And now, on to our first Overstreet report!

Pedigrees of Note This Year:

Pedigreed comic books are circulating through the market more today than ever before. We've come a long way since the '80s, a time when pedigrees were nowhere to be found, and knowledge could only be gained through word-of-mouth. As they represent the best this hobby has to offer, this shouldn't come as a surprise to anyone who has spent their time searching out high grade gems for their own collection.

The influx of pedigrees during the '90s filled collections until the seams were about to burst. Then along came the internet and CGC, which opened the floodgates for buying and selling, and coaxed scores of pedigrees back into the market. The past two years have seen some amazing activity in an already amazing decade for these special comics.

Crippen/"D" Pedigree: Heritage made a splash when it landed the giant 11,000 comic collection of David Crippen in late 2005, the biggest pedigree to surface in over a decade. It's taken over a year to sell all of them, but the market has held up well. The immense size and scope of the collection, which covered the most diverse period in comic history, was spread over practically every genre of the Golden Age. This diversity meant something for everyone, and the avoidance of a glut in the market. Crippen grades varied greatly, but most copies present well with unblemished spines and sharp corners. Foxing and average page quality seemed to be the only detractors. Many became the highest graded copy on CGC's census, brought record prices when sold, and will not see the light of day again for several years. Even though 11,000

Crippens entered the market in only 13 months, many will vanish into collections.

Vancouver Pedigree: When the Vancouvers first surfaced for sale in 1996, Steve Geppi bought them all, only releasing a few into the wild starting in 2003. The polar opposite of the Crippen pedigree, Vancouvers number just less than 350, and are best known for their blinding white pages (ranked #1 over all the Golden Age pedigrees). The collection is mainly humor, with only snapshots of more collectible titles and genres mixed among its small numbers. Despite the lack of strong titles and demand issues, this collection received a warm welcome at auction in 2007, most selling for over two to three times top *Guide*. Eclectic yes, but few in number and high in grade – factors which will ultimately lead to a shortage of supply as demand for pedigrees continue to rise each year.

Central Valley Pedigree: Like the Vancouvers, the Central Valley pedigree is known for its snow white pages and small size. They're a bit earlier than Vancouvers though, focusing more on the early to mid '40s, and representing the strip reprint genre first and foremost. Out of it came some of the prettiest early Batmans and Supermans we've seen in a long time, and a smoking copy of *Fantastic Comics* #3. Brian Peets, the lucky dog who bought the collection, put the second half up for sale at this year's San Diego Comic-Con. Sales were strong.

MacLaughlin Mile High Collection: As thousands of Crippen books rained from the sky in late 2006, John MacLaughlin's huge collection of Mile Highs hit like a thunderbolt, and some wondered if the market could weather the storm. It did, as a handful of heavy hitters duked it out during auction, pushing many prices to nosebleed level. Astonishingly, few of these books were CGC graded, a testament to the potency of the Mile High pedigree and the appeal of "fresh" material that has been off the market for decades.

Geppi Pedigrees for Auction: To stir up the mix, Steve Geppi dipped deep into his vaults in 2007and auctioned many other pedigrees in sizeable numbers, including Carson City, Cape Cod, Cookeville and New Hampshire. The last three are not currently recognized by CGC, but all have clear identifying marks and share a number of pedigree attributes. The New Hampshires came from the Western portion of Bob Overstreet's collection, which Geppi had purchased lock stock and barrel over a decade ago. Many of Bob's non-pedigree books were auctioned this past year as well, particularly Western, Horror and War.

Lloyd Jacquet File Copies: Even though not usually considered a pedigree, an industry professional's collection always demands respect, especially from someone as illustrious and influential as Lloyd Jacquet. His studio had a hand in many of the best comics to see print in the '30s and '40s, including *Marvel Comics* #1. Ironically, the *Marvel* #1 he saved is one of the best in existence.

It was no surprise when Jacquet's personal file copies sold well in auction this past year. David Anderson in Virginia sold many of Geppi's bound volumes from Jacquet's estate, which Geppi had been holding for over a decade. Jerry Weist

also sold many Jacquet file copies and personal items in a one-day eBay auction. Prices were strong across the board as collectors snapped up these pieces of history.

Even before the occurrence of these recent events, there's no denying that Mile Highs (and pedigrees in general) are more available now than at any given time in the past. Years ago, the average collector's best hope was to pick from the crumbs. Now he can feast on whatever catches his fancy.

THE PEDIGREE MARKET

Golden Age: Starting at the top, Mile Highs are harder to price than ever before. Back in the day, you could price a Mile High for 3x-5x top *Overstreet Guide* and get that. But since CGC has sharpened focus on individual grades, prices can run as high as 20x *Guide*, or as low as whatever *Guide* value is in that particular grade. With so many Mile Highs on the market, buyers can afford to be choosy. Ultra-cool covers and in-demand titles and characters still demand crazy money, and typically vanish as soon as they appear for sale. This trend never changes.

There doesn't ever seem to be many San Francisco/Tom Reilly books for sale. The true size of this collection seems to be in question, but there's no denying the seductiveness of this pedigree. Its powerful combination of ultra-high grade, white pages, and high demand titles has always placed San Franciscos at the front of the class. Which leaves pedigree collectors wondering…where are the rest of them?

Crowleys are abundant thanks to heavy auction activity of late. Sales are a bit flat, probably since most of the books are from one publisher, and the page quality is average. But many of these are the highest grade on CGC's census, and eventually the market will fully absorb them all, leaving the slower Fawcett collectors scratching their heads.

Golden Age pedigrees that seldom come up for sale: Allentown, Chicago, Denver, Hawkeye, Kansas City, New Hampshire, Nova Scotia, Recil Macon, Toledo, Twilight and Windy City.

Golden Age pedigrees that often have large number of issues available in the market: Bethlehem, Big Apple, Cookeville, Crowley, Gaines, Mile High, Northford, Rockford and White Mountain.

Golden Age pedigrees that frequently surface, but generally not in large numbers: Aurora, Cape Cod, Carson City, Circle 8, Cosmic Aeroplane, Lamont Larson, Lost Valley, Ohio, Okajima, Palo Alto, Pennsylvania, River City, Spokane, and Tom Reilly/San Fran.

Silver Age: Silver Age pedigrees play by a different rulebook. For one, most interest is focused on only a handful of companies, Marvel and DC, with superhero titles dominating the period. This is a dramatic departure from the vast landscape of the Golden Age. The best Silver Age collections usually contain the same books, such as classic Marvel titles like *Amazing Spider-Man* #1-up or *Fantastic Four* #1-up. They may also represent the ultra-rare 10 cent DCs of the late '50s, or possibly Dell and Richie Rich.

Because of this more narrow (and currently red hot) period in collecting, it is grade that rules the world of Silver Age pedigrees. With so much attention focused on a considerably smaller sampling of books, the ranking of collections comes down to only grade comparisons. How does the Curator copy of *Amazing Fantasy* #15 compare to the White Mountain or Ohio copies? This approach also affects the prices Silver Age pedigrees bring. Because demand is so closely tied to grade, pedigreed Silver Age can sometimes sell for the same as non-pedigrees in the same grade, a phenomenon that rarely occurs in the Golden Age pedigree market. Otherwise, pedigreed Silver Age can bring 20% more than non-pedigreed copies in the same grade.

This year has seen a varied range of Silver Age pedigrees come to market, including White Mountain, Northland, Massachusetts, and Pacific Coast. Besides the strong following these collections already have, the fact that Silver Age superhero comics are hotter than ever have led to incredible sales across the board.

Though a few collections that were auctioned by Heritage and found in California came close, no new Silver Age pedigrees surfaced in 2007. The requirements for Silver Age pedigree status have become more stringent of late due to their prevalence. In fact, many accepted pedigrees containing large numbers of Silver Age issues would not rate a pedigree status if not for their Golden Age content (examples include Bethlehem, Big Apple, Circle 8 and Ohio). Others were grandfathered in (Mohawk Valley), or passed based on more lenient standards from several years ago. It doesn't mean these collections do not have exceptional copies, but as a whole they may lack in average quality or overall quantity.

Silver Age Pedigrees that seldom come up for sale: Circle 8, Cleveland, Don & Maggie, Edenwald, Mohawk Valley, Newsboy, Ohio-Fairborn, Salida and Slabodian.

Silver Age pedigrees that often have large number of issues available in the market: Boston, Don Rosa, Northland, Oakland, Pacific Coast, Western Penn and Winnipeg.

Silver Age pedigrees that frequently surface, but generally not in large numbers: Bethlehem, Big Apple, Bowling Green, Curator, Green River, Massachusetts, Ohio and White Mountain.

The Future of Pedigree Comic Books: Collectors have a better understanding of their comic books now more than ever. As CGC continues to grade and track every vintage comic book passing through their doors, they are slowly pulling back the veil to reveal the true quality of pedigreed collections, and how they compare to each other in grade. Online trading has opened the door to a hoard of new collectors and collections, as Overstreet and GPAnalysis do real-time tracking of sales for more sound investment decision making.

Comicpedigrees.com adds to this information flow, allowing anyone to post pictures of their pedigree comics to the permanent archive. Ultimately, visitors to the site can view the story and scans of any pedigree collection, check original lists, and follow real-time market trends and grade averages for each. As pedigreed comics surface each year, their addition to the website's database will gradually bring each collection back to its whole, allowing us to envision how they

looked upon discovery all those years ago. It will be interesting to see how rankings may change as data flows in, especially when newly discovered collections are added.

Terry O'Neill
Terry's Comics/Nationwide Comics

Sales from 2006 to 2007 have been great; they are up from previous years. Most conventions had higher attendance, with corresponding higher sales. Catalog orders have increased, and sales per order have increased. Despite the competition from auction houses and consignment websites, we have been able to purchase many collections with quality material. It seems that many people still prefer the one-on-one attention that they get when selling their collection. We use the *Overstreet Comic Book Grading Guide* to explain how comics are graded. We also show equivalent books graded by CGC. We explain the market as to what is going to be a good seller so we can pay more for them and explain what will need to be discounted so we have to pay less in order to sell them at a discount.

Golden Age: Golden Age sales have been great for all the major super hero titles. We purchased comics by all the major publishing houses and many esoteric publishers. Most scarce and high grade super heroes sell well at and above *Guide*. Early DC and Timely were our best sellers with *Captain America Comics* and *Superman* being most requested. Even restored books sold well when priced reasonably. Fiction House titles like *Planet*, *Fight* and *Rangers* as well as early Disney titles like *Walt Disney's Comics and Stories* and *Four Color* titles are in demand.

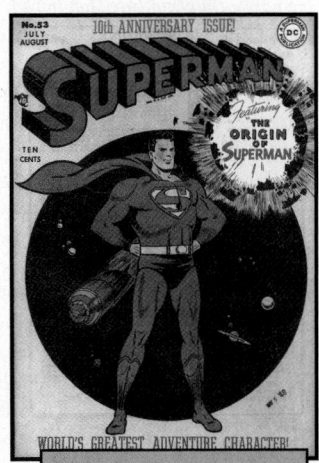

Atom Age: We acquired a run of Fox good girl titles like *Phantom Lady*, *Rulah*, *Zoot* and *Women Outlaws*. We had to pay rather high for them but we were able to sell them above *Guide*. Crime titles are starting to

Superman is one of the most requested titles of the Golden Age. (#53 shown)

move a little better with Fox titles doing best. Some obscure titles like *Saddle Justice*, *Moon Girl* and *Murder Inc.* are being collected. Western titles are selling well from most publishers. Early *Tarzan* still sells if the selection is good. Romance comics are picking up with ACG titles like *Confessions of the Lovelorn* and *My Romantic Adventure* selling quickly. War comics are a little mixed with Atlas and DC titles selling well, but small publishers are a little cool. Horror and Sci-Fi titles are moving with ECs still leading the pack with titles like *Tales From The Crypt* and *Weird Science* selling at around *Guide*, despite being reprinted many times.

Silver Age: Super-hero titles still lead in this group with Marvel out-selling DC titles about two to one. *Amazing Spider-Man* has had a great year, probably because of the huge success of the *Spider-Man 3* movie. Early Silver Age keys in mid to high grade are getting a little harder to come by, causing us to pay a higher percentage for these than in previous years. We don't make as much money when we sell them but it is important to have them on the board when we do shows. Humor titles of this era sell well with Harvey titles like *Sad Sack* and *Richie Rich* selling best, (probably because they are all still quite affordable for those just wanting to read them) and Archie titles have picked up again. Movie titles are still selling well with many non-comic collectors crossing over to buy actor-specific titles.

Bronze Age: Keys from this era are not as plentiful as they used to be, so we are always looking to buy them. The exceptions are Kirby DC titles like *New Gods*, *Kamandi* and *Mister Miracle* that are in great supply due to speculation. Most other comics from this era are in great supply, but are being collected by many people due to their affordability. Super hero, Monster and Mystery titles with Bernie Wrightson, Mike Kaluta and Neal Adams are always in demand. Most superhero titles from this era sell well, with *Adventure*, *Green Lantern*, *Justice League*, *Avengers*, *Incredible Hulk* and *Iron Man* in high demand.

Magazines: We are one of only a few exhibitors to have a large selection of Comic Magazines in stock and as a result, we had many collectors thank us for providing them a source for this type of material. Most titles sell well at around *Guide*, with Warren titles always in demand. *Savage Sword of Conan* is our best selling Marvel magazine. *Mad Magazine* has been selling better this year than in the past.

Modern Age & Independents: We only stock the titles that collectors of vintage books seem to ask about. High grade *X-Men* and *Amazing Spider-Man* sell well but most other titles go to the dollar box. Some better selling independent titles are *Xenozoic Tales* and *Cadillacs and Dinosaurs*.

Graded Books: Graded books are selling well and they often get a premium price in high grade. They seem to be the best way to sell comics on auction sites.

Internet Sales: As time goes on, more and more of our business is coming from our web-site. Many people want scans of listed items but with over 40,000 items in our inventory it is not possible to scan all of them. We put some items on eBay for auction but had disappointing results with most of them. We opened up an eBay store to highlight some of our CGC books and were much happier with the results.

In summary, despite the many factors against selling vintage comics at conventions and by catalog, we are on course to have one of our best years ever. Buying has been good and sales are steady. As long as people keep collecting, we should be able provide them with those missing pieces for their collections.

Jim Pitts
Surf City Comix

Is it time already for another market report?!? In my 23rd year as an Overstreet contributor/Advisor, the date always seems to creep up quickly. This year saw the expansion of many show promoters, and more comic movie tie-ins than in past years. This brought in new fans, but in some cases not a lot of dollars. The end of 2006, and most of 2007, have been a year of "ups and downs." Let's take a peek at the action I saw.

Golden Age: Always a great seller for me, in nearly any condition, as long as the books aren't restored. Restored books have slowed for me in the past year. Later printing *Classics* did well and I sold every EC that I could get, and sell, in the $20 to $50 range. While I didn't have any Golden Age "Keys" this year, some sales of note were: *The Spirit* #3 (Crippen) VG- $150, *Batman* #5 Fr/GD $400, *Walt Disney's Comics & Stories* #5 GD/VG $225, *Captain Marvel Jr.* #4 GD- $125, *Four Color* #38 GD+ $250, *Four Color* #178 VG/FN $300, *Captain Marvel Adventures* #10 GD+ $200, #16 VG $200 and *Whiz Comics* #5 GD+ $375.

Silver Age: Always a strong seller, in almost every grade. Mid-grade Marvel titles from this period remain slow as they are too pricey for the "readers", and not nice enough for the "graders". Though demand for DC has been stronger than Marvel for me in the past year, Marvel "keys" remain in high demand. Sales worth noting in this area were: *Adventure Comics* #247 GD $400, *Atom* #1 GD $90, *Avengers* #1 FR/GD $200, *Captain America* #100 FN $80, #109 VF/NM $100, *Captain Marvel* #1 VF+ $100, *Strange Tales* #102 VG/FN $100, #107 FN $100, #115 FN $150, *Superman's Girlfriend Lois Lane* #70 FN/VF $125 and *Tales of Suspense* #40 VG $300.

Bronze Age: An area that has just been blazing these last few years. Conan remains the big seller for me, with '70s Jack Kirby books close behind. Whether Marvel or DC the "King's" books just keep on selling. DC War books from the 1970s have really picked up in the past year or so as well. Spider-Man books from this time period have seemed to slow up some. Even though the new *Fantastic Four* movie was only a moderate success, all Silver Surfer books from the Bronze Age don't stick around for long.

Modern Age: What's hot in the Modern Age seems to change on a whim, depending on grade, artist, sketch cover, etc. One thing that seems to stay as reliable as IBM stock........X-Men and Wolverine. You can be at the biggest show in the country, or a small local show, and the muties will always be in demand.

Undergrounds: An area that has really exploded in the last 18 months. A great deal of interest has been generated thanks to Dan Fogel's new and long overdue price guide. Titles that seem to be in perpetual demand include *Bogeyman*, *Tales of Toad*, *Death Rattle*, *Yellow Dog*, *Freak Brothers* (almost any printing), *Zap Comics* (almost any printing). Many people are collecting different printings due to differences in the books from printing to printing (some changed stories.) These days, nearly any older Underground that has art by Robert Crumb, Rick Griffin, Vaughn Bode, Victor Moscoso, Joel Beck, Greg Irons, Gilbert Shelton or Rory Hayes seems to be desirable.

Rock Posters: Another area that has "blown up" in the last year. As many collectors of Underground Comix seem to expand into wanting posters by Irons, Crumb, Shelton, and others. With super-limited printings on many of these posters, this is an area that will continue to grow!

Thanks to everyone I saw, sold to, bought from, or traded with this year!

Matt Schiffman
Collector

Big Little Books: Most of the key and high value BLB titles are centered around Disney titles, and therefore this genre has a difficult time bringing the Superhero collector into the fold. Rarity drives the hobby, and therefore the difficulty of bringing open auction and sale results to the comic collector stifles new interest. Perhaps a few more years of exposure from *The Guide* will convert comic collectors into the BLB market.

Pulps: With scarce availability and increasing interest, the high grade and key pulps did not surface much in 2007. The previous shift in interest from *Shadow* and *Weird Tales* into

© DC

Prices on Silver Age
Brave and the Bold
show much movement.
(#59 shown)

Horror and other gothic covers still continues, but not many books make it to the open marketplace. The Pulp market still remains one of the most closed and insular niches in our hobby, with new collections and high-grade books, more often than not, privately trading hands. **Platinum Comics:** Historically interesting. Visually groundbreaking. And quite expensive if you are in the market for a high-grade copy. But finding their place in the comic medium has been a struggle. A loyal and often vocal pool of collectors are huge fans, but getting the message out has been difficult. Low auction results for the mid to low grade books do not always represent the true difficulty in finding high-grade material, and therefore a PR problem exists. Again, as with the BLB books, continued exposure can only help bring the importance of the hobby to the forefront.

Golden Age Comics: A shift in the perception of Golden Age has been underway over the past two years. Incredible collections have been brought to the marketplace, and not many of these have been from noted collectors or collections. Rewriting of the available supply of these books has kept the discussion boards, comic dinners, and blogs very busy. Never has such a supply of high grade and spectacular Timely books been brought to the market in the past twenty years. Heritage has unearthed some of the most amazing runs of mainline DC and Timely for collectors to see, and interest in the Golden Age has ignited. No longer does a collector have to wonder if a run of *All Select* could be completed in their lifetime. That was the case for so long, that new doors have opened and that quandary has been shifted to the Silver Age for now. The advent of change is upon the Golden Age and more collections of high quality and interesting books are going to come to the market with increasing frequency. What this does for prices and the overall growth of relevance of these books will be interesting to track.

Atomic Age: *Comic Book Marketplace* did more for the exposure and growth of this market; its demise seems to have a direct correlation to the pullback of the Atomic Age. Matt Baker, Horror, Sci-Fi and late Timely and DC issues drive the hobby, with Fiction House, Fox, and Standard-Nedor holding its own. Quality material always brings high prices, while mid-grade and slower titles continue to slow down. Spikes in the Western market are purely driven by forces outside the comic hobby, while the *Peanuts* collector has discovered the comic and original art market for Schulz and driven it into the stratosphere.

Silver Age: Should we be surprised? Should we be shocked? I guess we are supposed to be, but when looking at the past four years of this market, there really is no reason. High grade Marvel and DC continue to dominate, but there are the introductions to the record books from other publishers, although no trend could be called this year. The only real new introduction to the market was the increased interest in the 8.0 to 9.2 Marvels. For years, it had been predicted that these books would begin to come alive, but only this year did they really begin to show upward momentum and carrying strong at the time of this report. Prohibitive prices of the 9.4 and up books and those looking for a very, very high grade 9.2 have collectors searching for these books. *Brave and the Bold* showed some of the highest DC movement on a percentage basis, and *Detective* and *Batman* lead the way with price increases.

Bronze: The health of the Bronze Age market was called into question last year when the volume of high-grade new material continued to find its way onto the market. The predicted pull back on prices did not materialize in the way predicted by some and even the continued growth rate and absorption of these keys ran unabated. While the understood keys held strong, the depth of the Bronze Age showed that in 9.4 or better, quality books will find a home. Neal Adams remains the icon of the era and coupled with Batman, prices still set records. As rarity vs. popularity continues to be defined, the shifting of prices makes this the least understood and most exciting segment of the market over the past five years. Close cross-over toy and paper ephemera in the

Bronze Age has allowed collectors to participate in the Mego/Aurora/Fireside/Ideal/Third-Eye marketplace and has only served to enhance the overall interest in the Bronze Age.

Copper Age: As more and more key issues are discovered and more collectors begin to covet these issues, prices are climbing for the established books and new discoveries. The Graphic Novel and collected Hardcover market has its genesis here, and prices for these books often outpace the growth rate of the true first printings. Low print runs, quality packaging from Graphitti, among others, and icon titles make for a potent combination and record prices. Getting a handle on the true print runs for these books has collectors scrambling to unearth the still lingering hidden gems out there. An interesting facet to this genre is the price escalation of the last issue in the print run and also the sheer volume of collectors interested in these last issues. Slight interest has always been the case for these last issues, but the Modern Age has ten-fold the demand on these books. *G.I. Joe*, *Star Wars*, *Transformers*, and the small press books all share this demand. As we only begin to discover the last issue on some of these small press books, it is a fun route for collectors to actually find a piece of evolving comic history in their local shop. Try that with Golden Age.

Doug Schmell
Pedigree Comics, Inc.

Greetings to everyone reading this report from Pedigree Comics, Inc. 2007 is now two-thirds over (this report was made at the end of August) and we have already eclipsed our record sales totals from 2006 (over $2,000,000 in internet sales!) We only sell CGC certified comics and magazines online (www.PedigreeComics.com) and the CGC Marvel back issue market continues to exceed all of our wildest expectations. High grade Marvels sell like hot cakes off of our website and it would take a significant portion of this price guide to list all of our sales this past year. Instead, I will comment on a few significant trends/collections/segments of the market, focusing solely on CGC certified Marvel (and DC) Silver and Bronze Age comic books (our area of expertise).

As new collectors and consignors find and register onto my website, I notice that a large percentage are baby boomers in their late 30s and, more so, 40s and 50s who have re-entered the comic book market. Almost all of these new registrants are men who collected Marvels in their adolescent years, broke away from comics in their high school and college days (due to girls, sports, lack of funds, etc.) and came back to comics because they now realize how cool they really are and how much they loved collecting them in the first place. The coup de grace is CGC, which has created a trusted and unbiased grading service, as well as a forum for new collectors to meet and exchange comic-related ideas and interests. Comic books are now in the limelight once again (all the recent motion pictures are to thank) and the days of buying over-graded and/or undisclosed restored raw comic books are almost over. Only a fool would make an expensive purchase of a key or signifi-

cant comic without it being CGC'd, as the experts there check each comic for page content, restoration etc. Collector (and seller) confidence is a wonderful thing in a collectibles market and certification is here to stay (as in sports card, coins and now stamps).

All it takes is a few or even one new collector to re-fuel interest in a genre, title or issue. A perfect example of this has occurred in 2007. In the beginning of the year, a passionate Spidey lover, who wanted only ultra-high grade *Amazing Spider-Man*s from the '60s, began buying as many 9.4 or better *ASM*'s as he could find, many from pedigreed collections. He purchased a significant number of *Spidey*s off of my web site, as well as a few other ones, and in doing so, set new sales records and created a buzz that is still reverberating in our industry. Outrageous multiples of *Guide* were paid to secure these early Silver Age treasures. I'll just give you a few examples of Pedigree Comics' sales so you will see what I mean: *Amazing Spider-Man* #10 (9.6) (Curator) for $12,500; #12 (9.6) (Pacific Coast) for $16,500; #14 (9.6) (Pacific Coast) for $37,500; #21 (9.6) (Pacific Coast) for $6,600; #23 (9.6) (Pacific Coast) for $7,000; #27 (9.6) (Pacific Coast) for $6,000; #28 (9.6) (Pacific Coast) for $15,000; #29 (9.6) (Pacific Coast) for $3,250; #30 (9.6) (Boston) for $3,400; #32 (9.6) (Massachusetts) for $3,250; #38 (9.6) (Golden State) for $2,800; #40 (9.6) (Pacific Coast) for $6,400; #52 (9.6) for $7,000 and #55 (9.6) (Hollywood Hills) for $1,800. This same collector also purchased from us the Curator copy of *Amazing Fantasy* #15 for $60,000 in June.

I have noticed the after-effects of all of these record purchases as sales of *Amazing Spider-Man* issues have been incredibly brisk throughout 2007. Sure, *Amazing Spider-Man* has always been a consistent top seller, but the multiples we have been seeing in 2007 has been ridiculous, a direct result of the almost crazed spending of our new customer. This same scenario occurred in the latter part of the year when a new Fantastic Four lover entered the market. His entrance mirrored the release of the second FF motion picture (*"Rise of the Silver Surfer"*) and he only wanted the highest or second highest CGC-rated copies. Sales of ultra high grade early *Fantastic Four*s have not, historically, been as brisk as other mainstream titles (high *Guide* values are to blame) but that all changed when this frenzied collector/investor hit my site. The evidence is as follows: *Fantastic Four* #11 (9.4) for $11,200; #17 (9.4) for $4,850; #27 (9.6) for $5650; #29 (9.4) for $2,800; #34 (9.4) for $900; #53 (9.6) for $1050; #66 (9.6) (Hollywood Hills) for $1400; #70 (9.6) for $500; #84 (9.6) for $375; #87 (9.6) for $350 and #95 (9.6) for $300. Other strong *Fantastic Four* sales were a function of this new customer's record purchases: #1 (8.0) for $22,500; #14 (9.6) for $6,000; #15 (9.6) for $5,250; #20 (9.4) for $5,000; #22 (9.4) for $1,700; #30 (9.4) for $1,250; #32 (9.4) (Massachusetts) for $1,325; #44 (9.6) for $900; #48 (9.6) for $3,800; #48 (9.6) for $3,600; #55 (9.6) for $2,250; #67 (9.4) (White Mountain) for $650; #73 (9.6) (Massachusetts) for $700 and many more.

It doesn't necessarily take a new collector to push sales into the stratosphere. One of our best customers, an across the board CGC Silver Age collector, turned his attention in 2007 toward the early *Tales to Astonish* issues and the results have been, well, astonishing. He only likes certified 9.4s (good luck finding 9.6s on these early Ant-Man/Giant-Man books!) but will settle for a 9.2 if a Near-Mint isn't available. Pedigrees are favored too as these recent sales exhibit: *Tales to Astonish* #37 (9.4) for $2,700; #38 (9.4) for $2,300; #39 (9.4) for $1,900; #41 (9.2) for $580; #41 (9.4) for $1,600; #42 (9.4) (Western Penn) for $1,900; #43 (9.4) (Massachusetts) for $2,750; #44 (9.4) for $2,900; #45 (9.4) for $1,300; #47 (9.4) (Northland) for $1,250; #48 (9.4) for $1,200; #50 (9.4) for $750; #54 (9.4) for $500; #55 (9.4) (Northland) for $500; #56 (9.4) for $650; #58 (9.4) (Northland) for $900.

Other early *Tales to Astonish* issues achieved remarkable prices as well, spurred by the aforementioned customer. Some of these include: #27 (9.2) for $17,000; #38 (9.4) for $2,175; #39 (9.6) (White Mountain) for $4,500; #47 (9.4) for $750; #51 (9.4) for $650; #53 (9.4) for $500; #57 (9.6) (White Mountain) for $2,650 and another #57 (9.6) for $2,750.

Some flagship Marvel Silver Age titles needed no new collectors or customers to spark interest. *Tales of Suspense* continued to sell incredibly well in high grade. A few choice sales include *Tales of Suspense* #39 (9.2) for $25,000; #41 (9.4) for $7,000; #42 (9.4) for $2,800; #43 (9.4) for $4,200; #44 (9.4) for $4,200; #45 (9.4) for $4,200; #46 (9.4) for $2,600; #47 (9.4) (Northland) for $2,700; #49 (9.4) for $3,300; #52 (9.4) for $4,000; #61 (9.4) for $700; #63 (9.6) for $1,900; #65 (9.4) for $900 and #66 (9.4) for $1,000. *Journey Into Mystery* is another automatic sell. Although not as hot as in its ground-breaking years of 2003 and 2004, the Thunder God still commands a ton of respect here in South Florida, especially the issues in 9.2 and above: *Journey Into Mystery* #85 (9.2) for $6,000; #86 (9.6) (Massachusetts) for $9,500; #88 (9.4) for $5,100; #91 (9.2) for $1,300; #93 (9.4) (Pacific Coast) for $3,200; #96 (9.6) for $2,600; #96 (9.4) (Massachusetts) for $2,000; #99 (9.6) for $3,000; #100 (9.4) (Massachusetts) for $2,000; #100 (9.4) for $1,900; #101 (9.4) for $1,400; #102 (9.4) for $1,550; #104 (9.6) (Massachusetts) for $4,250; #104 (9.4) (Northland) for $2,400; #104 (9.2) for $1,050; #105 (9.4) for $1,100; #106 (9.4) for $1,800; #111 (9.4) for $1,600; #112 (9.6) (Massachusetts) for $14,500 and #112 (9.6) (Circle 8) for $12,500.

Strange Tales, X-Men, Daredevil, Thor, Silver Surfer, Avengers, Incredible Hulk, Captain America and *Iron Man* lead the rest of the pack in Silver Age sales. *Nick Fury, Agent of S.H.I.E.L.D., Sub-Mariner, Sgt. Fury and His Howling Commandos* and *Captain Marvel* also sell at multiples of *Guide* off of our website. A few key issues from these titles created record sales for us in 2007: *Sgt. Fury* #1 (9.4) for $21,500; *Strange Tales* #101 (9.4) for $10,000; *Strange Tales* Annual #2 (9.8) (Pacific Coast) for $25,000; *Nick Fury* #1 (9.8) for $1,500; *Incredible Hulk* #1 (6.5)

for $5,850; *Incredible Hulk* #102 (9.6) for $1,425; *Avengers* #3 (9.6) for $4,900 and *Avengers* #11 (9.6) (Curator) for $3,300.

Overall, the CGC Silver Age Marvel market is stronger than ever. The demand increases almost daily as new collectors learn about CGC, witness the high prices these old funny books are fetching and are more enthusiastic than ever about the hobby due to the influx of new major motion pictures starring household names depicting these characters (i.e. Robert Downey, Jr. as Iron Man). With more and more information at their fingertips (CGC, CGC Registry, CGC chat boards, GPA, Scoop, *Overstreet Comic Book Price Guide*, etc.), these born again comic lovers with disposable income are getting back into comic collecting fully armed and ready to spend. The supply will never go up so it does not take a genius to figure out that this vibrant section of the hobby should stay vibrant for a long time.

As for the CGC Marvel Bronze Age, I will keep it short as my past few market reports have centered on this section of the market. I can pretty much sum up how hot Bronze Marvels are with one word: Winnipeg. I purchased almost all of the Bronze (and Copper) Age Marvels from the Winnipeg pedigree, founded in late 1996 and early 1997, and I have been getting them graded by the CGC and selling them on my website for the past 3 years. The results have been beyond description. Whereas some non-pedigreed titles do not sell at high multiples, Winnipeg books smash all GPA sales figures and consistently sell as soon as we list

Early **Tales to Astonish** achieved remarkable prices. (#38 shown)

them in the new arrivals section of the Pedigree Comics Website. This is not an exaggeration. The predominance of titles listed sell at the ask price, issue by issue, within moments of their listing. When these Winnipeg collectors read the "Latest News" portion of the site and find out when new Winnipegs are going to be uploaded, they are ready! What makes Winnipegs so enticing and attractive are the bone white pages (over 95% of Winnipegs have strict white pages) incredible cover gloss, perfect structure and an amazing, just-printed look and feel from having been meticulously stored by the original owners in the cool and dry climate of Western Canada.

We started listing the Bronze Age Winnipegs in 2004 and have never stopped. Almost all the major titles from the '70s and '80s have already been listed with amazing results. In 2007, the following titles were met with the same unbridled enthusiasm: *Fantastic Four, Captain Marvel, Creatures on the Loose, Iron Man, Master of Kung Fu, Marvel Team-Up, Marvel Two-In-One, Incredible Hulk, Doctor Strange, Spectacular Spider-Man, Web of Spider-Man, Defenders, Ghost Rider, Thor, Dazzler, Daredevil, Official Index to the Marvel Universe, Doc Savage, Amazing Spider-Man, Spider-Woman, Skull the Slayer, Nova, Ka-zar the Savage* and more. Unbelievably, almost every Winnipeg sale constituted a record one according to the sales figures maintained by the GPA. We anticipate this trend to continue as we have hundreds more Winnipeg Bronze and Copper Marvels to list in 2008.

The final area of the market I will comment on is, surprisingly, the DC one (1960s, '70s and '80s *The Flash* in particular). Although we are associated most frequently with high grade Marvels (most likely by design as I have always collected Marvels as opposed to DCs), the biggest spark from our site (and from the entire hobby for that matter) in 2007 came from the incredible, near-complete *Flash* run (issues #105-350) of noted collector Steve Rubin that he consigned to us in August. In fact, the listing of this #1 CGC Registry set constituted the most significant sale of any run in many, many years. An amazing 231 out of the possible 247 issues of the title were present in the collection (a whopping 93%), and almost all of the books were 9.4 or higher with most being the top certified copy. The reaction to the listing was unbelievable, as over two-thirds of the run has sold as of late August 2007 (with many other anticipated sales not finalized as of this writing). There were dozens of interested collectors bidding and buying these books at a rapid pace. Many of the top certified issues were gobbled up within seconds of their respective listings even though none were pre-sold or listed as pending before being uploaded. I found myself scratching my head thinking "Make Mine DC!".

What made the sales even more amazing was the fact that two other significant (but not as voluminous or as high of grade) *Flash* collections were sold by the same auction house within 9 months of our listing, the second one only a few days prior to ours. With that many 9.4 or better *Flash* issues on the market within months, I was not sure if the *Flash* collectors out there had had their fill. Obviously, and to Steve's and my delight, they had not. It goes to show that quality comic books in superior certified condition will always attract attention and find new homes. Another factor in our favor was that a bunch of the issues in the #100s were from Pedigree collections (mostly Pacific Coast and Western Penn.) *The Flash* has always been one of DC's best and biggest Silver Age sellers, but there were just as many

© DC

A CGC Registry **Flash** set sold at a rapid pace. (#106 shown)

Bronze Age collectors looking to buy these books. A special thanks is due to Mr. Rubin for bringing his amazing *Flash* run to market. In Marvel terms, it is almost the equivalent of the highest graded *Journey Into Mystery/Thor* run (issues #83-300) being offered for sale. Just mind-boggling stuff when you consider how many 9.6s were present in the first 100 issues!

As follows are some highlighted sales from the #1 CGC Registry *Flash* set: #106 (8.5) $4,000; #109 (9.0) $2,500; #111 (8.5) $1,300; #113 (9.0) $2,850; #114 (8.5) $1,025; #121 (9.2) $4,500; #124 (9.2)(Western Penn) $1,700; #131 (9.4)(Dallas Stephens) $1,250; #133 (9.4) $1,175; #136 (9.4)(Western Penn) $1,750; #138 (9.4) $800; #140 (9.4)(Pacific Coast) $1,200; #141 (9.4)(Pacific Coast) $1,100; #142 (9.6)(Pacific Coast) $1,500; #143 (9.6)(Pacific Coast) $2,200; #144 (9.4)(Western Penn) $800; #146 (9.6)(Pacific Coast) $1,650; #147 (9.6)(Pacific Coast) $1,350; #151 (9.6) $1,550; #153 (9.8)(Pacific Coast) $1,995; #158 (9.6) $975; #160 (9.6) $1,575; #163 (9.6) $900; #164 (9.6) $900; #166 (9.6)(Boston) $900; #169 (9.6) $1,000; #171 (9.8)(Pacific Coast) $1,500; #173 (9.6)(Pacific Coast) $1,500; #175 (9.6) $2,300; #179 (9.6) $850; #180 (9.8) $1,100; #181 (9.6)(Massachusetts) $650; #187 (9.6)(Pacific Coast) $650; #196 (9.6) $600; #200 (9.6) $500; #205 (9.6) $450; #214 (9.6) $600; #229 (9.8) $750; #232 (9.6) $375; #241 (9.8) $200; #275 (9.8) $200 and #300 (9.6) $55. Thanks in part to this run, a few other *Flash* consignors asked us to list their top-graded early issues and these too were met with very little resistance: *Flash* #109 (9.2) for $6,000 and *Flash* #131 (9.6)(Pacific Coast) for $3,000.

In retrospect, 2007 has been a record-breaking year for our hobby and for my company in particular. More and more collectors and consignors are utilizing our non time-based auction services to buy and sell their prized high grade CGC certified comics and magazines. Collecting comic books can be such an amazing thing. We hope we have made it more informative, interesting and enjoyable for everyone.

See you next year!

Ben Smith
ComicConnect.com

2007 marked the beginning of an experiment called ComicConnect.com. More and more, we've recognized a growing disenfranchisement among comic collectors with the skyrocketing fees of eBay and auction houses. These rising costs don't make sense to us, especially now in our Internet Age when these businesses have less leverage, and provide less added-value than ever before. This provided the inspiration to build a site that gives comic collectors an alternative and safe place to buy and sell comics. For sellers, we sought to provide a place for them to showcase their comics to other collectors with no financial impediments such as listing fees or time limits. In short, we wanted to provide members with complete control over selling their comics. For buyers, we sought to provide a more secure method of transactoin by ensuring the comics they buy are from legitimate sellers, and guaranteeing that they receive the merchandise. The site was launched in June and here are the results:

At the time of writing this report (September 2007), members of ComicConnect have listed a cumulative total of just over $3 million dollars worth of material on the website. The system of making offers, and counter-offers, on "Fixed Price" listings has attracted a lot of activity, especially on high-grade Golden, Silver & Bronze Age material. The site also maintains a steady stream of "Daily Auctions," which to date, have seen a lot of Bronze and Modern CGC graded material, as well as reader copies of older comics. In the coming months, ComicConnect plans to host an "Event Auction" coordinating and heavily promoting high-grade material. The development of this Event Auction comes largely at the request of users of the site as a suggestion to further elevate the profile of some of their best material. To date, the feedback we've received from both buyers and sellers has been very positive, and also very helpful in suggesting future initiatives as ways to improve the site.

Listed below are some sales on ComicConnect from its first 3 months. We believe the prices realized compare very favorably to previous online sites and auction houses that sellers have used in the past. The "net amount" received by sellers has also played an important role, as not levying "buyer premiums" was a founding principle, and the consignment rate is only 10%, charged only when an item sells. The site is very easy to use and extremely safe – two major components collectors expressed as a must for an online comics community. (The site was initially free for the first 5 months as a courtesy to all those involved who helped get ComicConnect started.)

Sales included the following CGC-certified comics: *Action Comics* #40 (6.5) $1000, *Action Comics* #432 (9.8 Oakland Copy) $300, *All-Star Western* #4 (9.6) $160, *Amazing Fantasy* #15 (2.5) $2700, *Amazing Spider-Man* #2 (4.5) $640, #8 (8.5) $900, #9 (9.4) $7500, #39 (9.6) $4350, #52 (9.4) $1100, #106 (9.6) $750, #122 (9.6) $1200, #129 (9.2) $645, #144 (9.6) $300, #149 (9.6) $500, #157 (9.4) $125, #252 (9.8) $350, *Giant-Size Amazing Spider-Man* #1 (9.6) $290, *Avengers* #4 (8.0) $1200, #6 (8.0) $178, #11 (9.2) $600, *Batman* #227 (9.0) $215, *Beware the Creeper* #1 (9.6) $260, *Captain America* #100 (9.6 Boston Copy) $1800, *Captain America Comics* #9 (6.5) $2550, *Captain Marvel Adventures* #11 (9.4 Edgar Church/Mile High Copy) $5000, *Crime Does Not Pay* #24 (7.0) $2200, *Daredevil* #9 (9.4) $600, *Daredevil* #57 (9.6) $255, *Detective Comics* #65 (8.0) $2250, #72 (8.5 Rockford Copy) $1300, #408 (9.4) $265, *Doctor Strange* #169 (9.6) $754, *Fantastic Four* #2 (9.0) $8400, #11 (9.4) $10,400, #44 (9.4 Cleveland Copy) $525, *Flash Comics* #71 (9.4 Big Apple Copy) $2650, *Frankenstein Jr.*

#1 (9.6 File Copy) $374, *Green Lantern* (SA) #41 (9.4) $400, *Hawkman* #1 (9.4) $3795, *Hero For Hire* #1 (9.4) $865, *House of Mystery* #174 (9.4) $875, *House of Secrets* #89 (9.4) $200, *Incredible Hulk* #161 (9.6) $225, #181 (7.5) $625, *Iron Man* #1 (9.8) $6000, *Iron Man* #2 (9.6) $550, #55 (8.0) $145, *Marvel Team-Up* #23 (9.8) $225, *Master Comics* #21 (6.5 Crowley Copy) $3000, *Master Comics* #43 (9.0 Crowley Copy) $450, *The Ringo Kid* #27 (8.0) $175, *Silver Surfer* #5 (9.4) $595, *Spectacular Spider-Man Annual* #1 (9.8) $225, *Spectre* #5 (9.6) $500, *Super DC Giant* #13 (9.4) $300, *Superman* #13 (5.5) $749, *Tales of Suspense* #39 (2.0) $650, *Thor* #246 (9.4) $131, *X-Men* #7 (8.0) $485, #29 (9.6) $750, #55 (9.6) $725 and #104 (9.6) $250.

At present, the forecast for ComicConnect.com seems very favorable, as the user-base and listings continue to grow at a near exponential rate. We thank everybody who has used ComicConnect.com or told a friend about the site for their continued support. We also would like to welcome comic collectors who may be hearing about the site for the first time. To become a member, and to get started buying or selling, visit ComicConnect.com. Please also feel free to call our knowledgeable staff at (212) 895-3999 or email support@ComicConnect.com with questions.

Al Stoltz
Basement Comics

The comic market was alive and strong for 2007 and while we write this report before the last quarter of the year, we feel it will finish just as strong at the end of the year. Sales were steady at the major shows that we attended and were equally impressed by the amount of material we sold thru our eBay online store. If I had to comment at all, it would be that we seemed to sell a great amount of material that we have had in stock for a long while, and most were non-hero comics. It seemed that customers had moved to collecting comics that were not the targets of the high grade hawks that look to pump them up to multiples of *Guide*, they are looking for bargains. Nothing wrong with that at all actually, the public will find trends and titles that have not been mined and enjoy them while they can and get the most out of their money.

It was recently discussed as to what market should influence *The Guide*, perhaps a blend or use of all markets are needed to reflect realized prices for comics and material. Its time to jump to the 21st century and get *all* available info online for buyers of *The Overstreet Guide* to use. Sources such as "brick and mortar" stores, E-sales, shows and auctions, while each a separate market, all could provide great info for a future online *Guide* that could be very helpful to buyers.

eBay: We set up a E-Store thru eBay almost two years ago and have been amazed at its growth and the power of selling your comics to buyers outside the USA. Our international sales have more than tripled in the last year and that means lots of material leaving the country that may never get back here to be sold in the USA again. Buyers seemed to be very interested in titles such as *Aquaman*, *Plop*, *THUNDER Agents*, *Rip Hunter*, CGC Graded items, *Creepy*, *Eerie* and lots of *Conan* magazines shipped across the Atlantic this year. As long as items are strictly graded and priced at *Guide*, repeat buyers line up to get more of the items after they establish a relationship with the seller. I never knew there were so many comic collectors in Portugal looking for CGC graded books until I opened this online store.

We also have found our niche and aggressively purchase and list items such as strip reprints of all kinds including *Comic Review Magazine*, Warren magazines, *Fangoria*, specialized trade paperbacks and graphic novels. It seems that esoteric items that we could never sell at any show eventually sell within a year if we take the time to list them and describe them accurately.

Books of note that have sold through our E-Store include: *Funny Pages* #6-12 Lost Valley Copies $9,000 for the group, three Ken Kelly paintings that averaged $1,200 each, *Air Pirates Funnies* #2 VF+ $120, *Whiz Comics* 10 VG $435, a Bill Gaines Rejection Letter $90, *Exciting Comics* #59 VF $500, Sign of Zorro Exhibitor's Campaign Book $50, large amounts of *Spirit* sections and Warren magazines that are to numerous to list. I can say that our online store is not a bargain bin looking to dump at deep discount levels, we instead take the time to list interesting items and have no problem selling them at *Guide* prices. **Good Old Fashioned Comic Conventions:** I have been attending comic shows first as a helper for Bob Cook (a local comic legend) since 1975 and have graduated to having my own booths and "winged monkeys" of my own to help me sell my wares now. The excitement of getting to the show and running around on the floor trying to score material for future sales still excites me just as much now as then, but times are changing.

While the San Diego Comic-Con is by far the largest event, I saw even less old time sellers and old comic booths than the year before! Cost of gasoline, hotels and shipping of inventory puts many of us retailers deep in the hole before we make our first dollar at the show. So doing shows far from home may just be replaced with E-Selling. I was amazed by many of the top end buyers saying that they may not brave the huge crowds next year for the show. Sales were decent but a week long event just seems to tire me out and it takes another week just to recover.

However, I can say that Wizard World Chicago for us is still the best buying show of the entire season. Sure, we sold a good amount to make it worth the day long ride as well. We had a phenomenal year at shows and sold lots of oddball material along with the usual issues that are asked for endlessly. NY Comic Con, Pittsburgh, FX were all pretty decent and we had a great chance to sell, buy and push the online store to as many customers that we can while out on the road.

Many books change hands at these mega-shows and do in the end affect trends, and more importantly, mold hopefully new buyers of older material for the future. Some good-ies sold at conventions this year: *King Kong* Movie Program 1933 $1,000, *Weird Suspenstories* #1 Rare Canadian version CGC 6.5 $1,300, *Incredible Hulk* #1 FN+ $3,000, *Avengers* #1 VG $500, *Daredevil* #1 VG $515, *Tales of Suspense* #39 FN $2850, *Journey into Mystery* #83 FN+ $1455, *Tarzan* #3 Dell File Copy $350, *Incredible Hulk* #181 FN+ $675, *WOW What a Magazine* #1-4 avg GD Condition $5,000 for set, *Showcase* #1 GD- $160, *Pussycat* #1 magazine $250, *Hit Comics* #6 G-GD+ $375, *Slow Death* #1 VF+ $55, *Phantom Lady* #22 GD+ $240, *Star Studded* fanzine #1 VF $100.

We were glad to see lots of new faces at shows and lots of new customers eagerly looking for all types of comics this year. Seemed like Dell and Charlton and Undergrounds were finally getting some attention again and it seemed like Funny Animal titles were being sought after just a little more this year. DC Digest, Treasury Editions, Magazines and Fanzines still are constant sellers and we always are quick to pull the trigger on a collection full of these items.

I guess in closing I will say the same old thing I say to all my customers, "Buy what you like, you may own it a long time!"

Doug Sulipa
Doug Sulipa's Comic World

We bought and sold a lot of comics in the last year. There was the usual relentless demand for popular key issues, in almost all grades. High Grade Marvel and DC comics were the most requested, but we were only able to supply about 20% of the issues requested in these grades. Most of the 9.0 thru 9.8 graded raw comics we sold were from the 1975 thru 1987 era. If we had more 9.0 and up copies from 1974 and older, we would have sold a lot of them. We also had a lot of requests for GD to VF Comics from the 1960 thru 2006 era from all publishers and were able to fill about 90% of those orders. About 50% of 1960s comics we did not have in VF or better, otherwise we would have fulfilled about 95% of want lists. We sold a lot of 1950s comics, but especially Dell comics. I specialize in trying to carry all comics printed from 1960 to 2006 in the $100 and under price range. Although we do have a decent selection of "Over-$100" comics and probably 50,000 comics from the 1950s and perhaps 2,000 comics from the 1940s. The great majority of collectors buy only the more affordable under-$100 comics. If at one point in their lives, they have more disposable income, collectors might graduate to the more expensive items they have always dreamed about. In the late 1980s, I was still dealing in a lot of high end items but made the decision to instead try to stock everything (in the under $100 price range) from all publishers. I have never regretted the decision and have since handled almost everything printed in North American comics related items from the last 50 years, most items many many times. In addition I got into everything comics-related and also into all types of non-comic magazines, books, records and posters. I have a very loyal group of buyers who constantly thank me for carrying 1000s of items almost no one else can be bothered with. It was, and still is, an amazing experience. For me, *Sad Sack* and *Jughead* comics outsell both *Wolverine* and *X-Men* comics, mainly because the latter are carried by almost every back issue dealer nationwide, so why bother ordering by mail. How many dealers have a decent selection of Harvey and Archie comics? Superhero comic sales have been strong in the last year (to investors, in part because of all the films, but also to buyers wanting to fill in runs and get a lot of books all in one place, with good grading). But the oddball comics that most dealers do not carry are much more notable, because they tend to sell well in all grades, at higher percentages of *Guide* and at a much better turnover rate. As in any collectible field, dealers who specialize and excel in one area of collecting obtain better prices and have a strong repeat clientele and that has been our aim. eBay sellers will usually tell you that it is hard to convert one-time buyers into new long-term clients. The presence of the *Overstreet Comic Book Price Guide* since 1970 has done a superior job of stablizing prices, far beyond what we see in most other hobbies. Many would say it has over-inflated superhero comics, but that is not so, because if you take into account strict grading, you will find the majority of items that sell are within the 50% to 150% of *Guide* price range, which it relatively stable for a collectibles hobby. Without *The Guide*, we would see wildly erratic pricing (as with the used paperback market, where books that should sell for $2 can bring $50, and books that should sell for $50 can he had for $10.) For example, *Richie Rich Digest Magazine* (10/1986-10/1994) #11-42 are near impossible to find for collectors who need them, and low *Guide* prices make them sell instantly when they do show up. Demand is 5-10 times bigger than supply, and in another marketplace one would expect them to sell for $25-$50 each range, but they simply remain sold out everywhere in the $5 and under range. Just a few lesser known items that consistesntly sell for 200% or more include: *Josie* #45, 106, *Transformers* #80, *Savage Sword* #235, *Katy Keene Digests*, *Creepshow*, *Betty and Veronica* #320, many giveaway comics, *Dennis and the Bible Kids*, *Masters of the Universe* #12, 13, Moebius Graphic Novels, *Hunger Dogs* GN, *Squadron Supreme: Death of a Universe* GN, *Conan* GNs, Charlton Comic Digests, and many more. Many investors try hard to make money in comics and do not succeed, while many collectors who do not follow the trend and buy what they like, do make good money when selling their collections. It is always recommended that you go after the items that you enjoy. Once there, learn about them and use that knowledge to guide your buying decisions.

Alternative/Independant Comics: We have managed to sell to the "Book Reading Crowd" (normally non-comic collectors), quite a lot of alternative comics from popular media, at a much faster rate than to comic collectors, including; (*Doc Savage*, *Shadow*, most horror, *Aliens*, *Predator*, *Star Wars*, *Crow*, Vampires, Werewolf, Zombies, Anne Rice, H.P. Lovecraft, Adult, Underground, *Planet of the Apes*, *Green Hornet*, Westerns, Vietnam War, WW2, Animated Cartoons, *Bone*, *Buffy*, *Classics*, Religious, all EC

Reprints, *Indiana Jones*, *Elric*, *Phantom*, *Sherlock Holmes*, 1990s *Robotech*, *James Bond*, Personality, *Simpsons*, top comic artists, much TV related, *Tarzan*, Robert E. Howard, movie adaptations, SF and other author book adaptations, comic strips, *Dick Tracy*, etc. These buyers appreciate them for what they are, good reading and are not particularly concerned about condition.

Comic collectors are fascinated with all 1980 and older comics, including: "Ground-Level" Comics, Underground Comics, Ditto-Zines and Fanzines. Most of these have small print runs and are never seen by the average collector. When you add to that the challenge of locating these scarce and cool items, and at still reasoanble price levels, it is easy to see why many fans get hooked. These sell in any and all grades, with most attempts at price guides being futile, as pure supply and demand is the rule. Record prices and demand continue for the best known of the "Investment Alternate" comics (at 150-300% *Guide*,) including: *Albedo* #1,2, *Cerebus* #1-21, *Elflord* (Nightwind: 1980-82) #1-15, *Orb* #1, *TMNT* #1, etc.

We have over 50,000 different Independent comics from the 1980-2006 era in stock, surely the biggest selection anywhere, with well over 1/3 not listed in the *Guide*. Probably only about 10% of them were overprinted, giving the false impression that they are all common and worthless. Millions of these comics were dumped in bargain bins and many are no longer common in high grade, because of over-handling. Many had small print runs of only 1000-5000 copies, making them among the scarcest comics of the last 30 years. Yet about 95% can be had for under $5.00. So if you

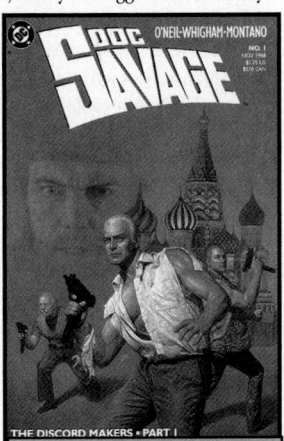

The "Book Reading Crowd" finds titles like **Doc Savage** popular, regardless of condition. (#1 from the 1988 series shown)

want an affordable area to collect, with endless variety and lots of surprises, this is for you.

Some of the bestsellers (at 120-175% *Guide*) include: *Alien Encounters*, *Aliens* (1988 mini), *Alien Worlds*, all Alan Moore tites, *Armour*, *Army of Darkness* ($20 ea), *Berni Wrightson Master of Macabre*, Big Apple, Blackthorne, *3-D Zone* and other 3-D comics (*G.I. Joe*, *Star Wars*, *Transformers*, Harvey, TV etc), *Blazing Combat* (Apple), *Blood of Dracula* (Wrightson issues), *Bone*, *Cody Starbuck* (1978), 1980s Continuity Comics (Adams, etc), *Cobalt Blue* (1977), *Crow* #1-3, *Critters* #1-5,48-50 (scarce), *Crow* (1st series), *Crusaders* #1 (Southern Knights), *Deadworld*, *Dick Tracy* (Blackthorne) #71-99, *Dick Tracy* Reuben Award series, *Echo of Futurepast*, *Eddie*

Campbell's Bacchus, Eightball, Elfquest, Fantasy Quarterly #1, Faust, Femforce, Flaming Carrot #1-5, Galaxia, Gasm, Gobbledygook (1984), Grendel (Comico), Hate, Hobbit, Hot Stuf (Sal Q), How to Draw series (Transformers and G.I. Joe), Imagine(Star Reach), John Byrne's Next Men #21, Judge Dredd, Justice Machine (Noble) #1-3 and Annual #1, Leather & Lace, Lone Wolf & Cub #1,41-45; Love and Rockets #1-20, Macross #1(1984), Mage (1984) #1-7, Magnus #1-12, Magazine #1-4, Mr. A series (Ditko), Miracleman #11-24 (Red Hot), Nexus (Capital) #1-3, Ninja High School (1986/87), Nucleus, Oktoberfest, Omaha Cat Dancer, Omen (Vigil), ORB, all Paragon Pub (pre-1982 titles, Femzine etc.,) Phantacea, Planet of the Apes(all), Power Comics(1970s), Primer (Comico), Quadrant, Quack (Star Reach), Rai #1-10, Rock Comics (Adams-a), Solar #1-10, Spirit, Star Reach, Tales Too Terrible to Tell (hot and scarce), Tank Girl, Tarzan(all), Tick, Transit, Twisted Tales, Uncensored Mouse, Untamed Love, Usagi Yojimbo #1-5, Vortex, Wally Wood's Thunder Agents, Weird Romance, World of Wood, Xenozoic Tales, Yummy Fur, Zen (1987), Zot and more.

Archie Comics: We have a giant selection of 35,000 Archie Comics and 10,000 Digests, thus they are a specialty and one of our bestsellers. Since there are so many to choose from, collectors have seemed focused on their favorite characters, and/or anything that could be considered a key issue including Giants, #100s, last issues, X-overs, monster covers, origins, all 1980s appearances of Cheryl Blossom/Josie/Sabrina, etc. The High-Grade collectors mainly seem interested in

Early issues of **Archie's Girls Betty and Veronica** are best sellers by far. (#1 shown)

Betty and Veronica, Red Circle Horror and key issues, but most of these are scarce in better than VF, so we mainly had and sold only 1980s and newer issues in 9.0 or better. The only exceptions were the Archie digests of the 1974-1985 era, as we bought and sold over 100 high grade 9.0-9.6 copies from the Manitoba Collection at 125-300% Guide. Most buyers were just happy to find someone who had what they needed in any grade, thus we sold mainly GD thru FN copies all through the year. Archie's Betty and Veronica was by far the best seller, with #1-30, 320-347 being hot sellers and very hard to keep in stock. B&V #320(1st Cheryl Blossom) is the #1 most requested Archie and when we can locate it at all it is worth 200% Guide. 1950 and older Golden Age Archies are in very low supply and have big demand, bringing 120-150% Guide. 1951-1960 Archies are

even getting scarcer as more disappear into permanent collections. It is getting more commonplace for overgraded scarce and key issue Archies to sell on eBay for 150-300% Guide in actual grade, especially on lower graded and more affordable copies. All Dan DeCarlo art comics are in high demand, including all his non-Archie comics and even his Adult cartoon digests.

With the last Teenage Mutant Ninja Turtles movie came an unexpected demand for the Archie comics, but not the Mirage Pub. ones. Presumably it is because the Archie editions had widespread newsstand distribution. The 1988-1990 titles are mostly still relatively common, but the 1991-up issues are scarce. Teenage Mutant Ninja Turtles Adventures #50-72, Specials #6-10 and Digests all had low print runs and are now quite scarce, and are suddenly in big demand, bringing 200-400% Guide, with virtually every dealer everywhere sold out (#72 in VF/NM brings $30.) The Mighty Mutanimals in Teenage Mutant Ninja Turtles Adventures are extra hot (1st app. in #19, and #51-54.) The Mighty Mutanimals (4/1992-6/1993) is a hot title (current VF/NM values are: #1=$6; #2-4=$4; #5-7=$6; #8=$8; #9=$12.) Teenage Mutant Ninja Turtles Adventures Special (1992-1994) is a hot title (current VF/NM values are: #1,2,4-6=$6; #7-9=$12; #10=$20.) TMNT Mutant Universe Sourcebook is a hot title (current VF/NM values are: #1,2=$10; Update=$15.)

This year's bestsellers include (with percentage of Guide they sell at in brackets): Archie Comics #1-100(120-150%), 300,322,326,400,429(125-150%), Archie All-Star Special - Series; (Winter/1975; 164 Pages, 4 different = 200%), Archie as Pureheart(120%), Archie at Riverdale High (early appearances of Cheryl Blossom in #89,90,92,96,99,103 = 150%), #113(200%), Archie Giant #26, 32(150%), Archie Giant Series (B&V, Josie and Sabrina issues = 125-150%), Archie's Girls Betty and Veronica #1-30(125-150%), #31-200(120-135%), (#320-322,327,328 Cheryl Blossom = 200%), Archie and Big Ethyl (150%), Archie and Mr. Weatherbee(150%), Archie's Circus(200%), Archie's Date Book(150%), Archie's Festival(150%), Archie's Roller Coaster(200%), Archie's Roller Sports Scene (200%), Christmas with Archie (Giant; Spire Edition 250%), Archie's Jokebook #44-48(Neal Adams = 125-135%), #288(200%), Archie's Madhouse #22(150%), Sabrina issues(125-135%), Archie's Mechanics(135%), Archie's Pal Jughead #79(Creature-c 150%), #77,78,80-82,85,86,88(125-135%), Archie's Pals N Gals #1-20(125%), #23(1st Josie = 200%), #29(Beatles 150%), #161(1st Cheryl Blossom solo 200%), Archie's Ten Issue Collectors Set #1-10(giveaway 125-150%), Archie's TV Laughout #1-23(125%), #91(200%), #92-106(120-150%), Betty and Me #1-10(125%), #16(200%), #23(150%), #40(125%), #79-86(125%), #200(150%), Black Hood (1983 = 150%), Cartoon Network presents Space Ghost #1(200%), Cheryl Blossom Mini-Series (13 issues total from 1995-1996 = 150-200%), Chilling Adv. in Sorcery (150%), Christmas with Archie Treasury(200%),

Cosmo the Merry Martian (125%), *Flintstones* #1-10(150%), #11-22(200%), *The Fly* (1983-84 = 150%), Horror/Science Fiction covers issues (circa 1962 = 125-135%), *Ginger* (120-135%), *Hanna-Barbera All Stars* (200%), *Hanna-Barbera Presents* (200%), *Jetsons* (200%), *Josie* #1(150%), #2-20(125%), #45(150%), #46-74(125-150%), #100-106(150%), *JCP Presents Thunder Agents* (200%), *Jughead* #325 (Cheryl Blossom = 300%), #352(200%), *Jughead as Capt Hero* (125%), *Jughead's Folly* #1(1st Elvis in comics = 125%), *Jughead Soul Food* (150%), *Katy Keene* (1983-1990 = 150%), *Laugh Comics* #20-168 (120-150%), *Life with Archie* #1-20, 45-66(125%), *Little Archie* #1-66(125%), *Madhouse* #95-97(Horror 150%), *Mighty Crusaders* (1983-85 = 150%), *Pep Comics* #22-180(120-135%), *Red Circle Sorcery* (150%), *Riverdale Rambling* (Archie fanzine = $5-12 ea.,) *Sabrina* #1-17, 71-77 (135-150%), *Scooby-Doo* (200%), *SHIELD* (1983-84 = 150%); *Sonic the Hedgehog* #1-50(120-150%), *Suzie* (120-135%), *Tales Calculated to Drive you Bats* (120%), *That Wilkin Boy* (150%), *Thunder Agents* (Archie; 150%), *Whiz Kids* (Archie and Radio Shack $5 ea.,) *Wilbur* (Katy Keene #5-56,58-69 and DeCarlo art in later issues = 120%.)

Atlas/Marvel Comics: We had a lot of requests for the pre-Marvel horror/SF prototype issues and have virtually sold out (120-135% *Guide*). *Millie the Model* #18-93(Dan DeCarlo) were in huge demand and we nearly sold out (125-150% *Guide*). All the Western titles sold well, but especially those that became Marvel (*Gunsmoke Western, Kid Colt, Rawhide Kid, Ringo Kid, Two Gun Kid*) at 110-125% *Guide*. We sold every $50 and under Atlas in stock that had Dan DeCarlo art (120-135% *Guide*.) The most popular genre this year was the Teenage titles at 125-150% *Guide*, including: *Cindy, Frankie, Georgie, Hedy Devine, Jeannie, Kathy, Linda Carter, Millie the Model* (all titles), *Miss America, Mitzi, My Friend Irma, Nellie the Nurse, Patsy Walker* (all titles), *Tessie the Typist, Teen* and *Wendy Parker*. All Horror/SF and War titles were steady sellers (115-125% *Guide*). The other genres sold slower (but still better than many other publishers of same vintage) through the year (at 100-120% *Guide*) including: Crime/Mystery, Funny Animal, Humor /Parody, Romance, Sports, Spy titles.

Atlas/Seaboard Comics: We sold more 9.0 and up High Grade copies this year than any other, mainly from the Manitoba collection (125-200%+ *Guide*.) There are 61 different color comics from this publisher and they are one of the most sought of all publishers for Bronze Age completionists, as the number is so finite and they are historically interesting. *Vicki* is by far the toughest of the color comics to find, especially the low print #3,4. The titles with art by Adams, Chaykin, Ditko, Toth, Wood, and Wrightson sold fastest as usual. We sold a lot of GD-FN copies also (125-150% *Guide*.) Most also pick from the 6 comics related mags: *Devilina, Thrilling Adventure* and *Weird Tales of the Macabre* sold in all grades, with the scarcer #2s at 150% *Guide*, and #1s at 125% *Guide*. Getting a complete set of the 7 non-comic B&W magazines is a great challenge. *My Secrets* #1(2/1975) is very rare. We sold a GD/VG copy for $50. *Sea Monsters* #1(1976) is rare (VG $50.) *Movie Monsters* are harder to find #1(VF$30; FN$20; VG$14); #2-4(VF=$40; FN$=30; VG=$20.) *Gothic Romances* #1 is rare in any grade and sells instantly in the 300% *Guide* range.

Charlton Comics: With our 35,000 Charlton comics, we have the world's biggest selection, thus we always do well with them. These comics sell well in all grades, but easily 85% of sales are in the G to FN/VF condition ranges, mainly because most are tough in VF or better. We sold over 100 issues from the Manitoba collection (almost entirely Horror and SF) in 9.0-9.6 grades at 125-200%+ *Guide*. In addition we sold a lot of Horror/SF and Superhero/Hero comics in VF or better. The other genres actually sell better in FN or lower. The Hanna-Barbera titles were easily the bestsellers in mid-to-lower grades, followed by the TV related titles. All 1960 and older titles were way up in demand, but especially the more obscure titles. By far the most popular hero title was *The Phantom*, especially #67-74 (Don Newton art issues); *Hercules* and other titles with Jim Aparo art are up in demand. This year was notable in that we had far more buyers filling in sets, rather than key issue buyers. Collectors who enjoy the hard to find and unusual love the Charlton magazines and odd related items including: Adult Cartoon Titles (*Cartoon Carnival, Comedy Capers, Good Humor, 150 Cartoons*), *Charlton Bullseye*, Charlton/Xerox Comic Digests (12+ Different), *CPL* (Fanzine), *Horror Monsters, Mad Monsters, Monsters Attack, Sick* magazine, and other non-comic mags by Charlton (*True Western*, Romance, Movie/TV, Puzzle, etc.).

Our bestsellers (at 120% to 150% *Guide*) included most 1950-1970 War comics, *Abbott and Costello, Barney and Betty, Beetle Bailey, Beyond the Grave, Bionic Woman, Blondie, Blue Beetle, Bobby Sherman, Bugaloos, Bullwinkle, Capt. Atom, Charlton Bullseye* (comic and mag), *Charlton Premiere, Cheyenne Kid, Cowboy Western, David Cassidy, Dino, Doomsday+1* (Byrne), *Dudley Do-Right, EH!, E-Man, Emergency, Flash Gordon, Flintstones, Ghostly Haunts, Ghostly Tales, Ghost Manor, Go-Go, Gorgo, Great Gazoo, Gunfighters, Hanna-Barbera Parade, Haunted, Haunted Love, Hercules* (hot), *Hong Kong Phooey, Huckleberry Hound, Jetsons, Judo Master, Jungle Jim, Jungle Tales of Tarzan, Kid Montana, Konga, Korg, Magilla Gorilla, Many Ghosts of Dr. Graves, Masked Raider, Midnight Tales, Monster Hunters, Mysterious Suspense, Outer Space, Outlaws of the West, Partridge Family, Pebbles, Phantom, Ponytail, Popeye, Primus, Ronald McDonald, Quick Draw McGraw, Reptisaurus, Ronald McDonald, Sarge Steel, Scary Tales, Scooby Doo, Six Million Dollar Man, Soap Opera Love/Romances, Son of Vulcan, Space Adv., Space 1999, Space War, Speed Buggy, Static, Strange Suspense, Thane, Thunderbolt, Top Cat, Underdog, Unusual Tales, Valley of Dinosaurs, Vengeance Squad, War, Wheelie and the Chopper Bunch, Wyatt Earp, Yang* and *Yogi Bear.*

Christian and Religious Comics: We sell a lot of religious comics, because we have the biggest selection around. The Spire titles are by far the most collected of the genre. These 19 Archie titles are always in the highest demand at 125-150% *Guide*. Scarce Archie Spires titles (200%+ *Guide*) include: *Archie and Mr. Weatherbee, Archie's Circus, Archie's Date Book, Archie's Festival, Archie's Roller Coaster, Archie's Sports Scene* and *Christmas with Archie*. There are about 38 non-Archie Spire titles and many completionists that want them all (at 125-150% *Guide*). Spire comics are typically found in G or VG condition, with FN copies being uncommon and VF or better copies being scarce. The bestsellers (at 150-200% *Guide*) are *Hansi the Girl Who Loved the Swastika, Hello I'm Johnny Cash*, and *Tom Landry and the Dallas Cowboys. Life of Pope John Paul II* #1 is the bestselling of all Christian comics at 200-300% *Guide*. Other consistent DC and Marvel sellers include *Easter Story, Francis Brother of the Universe* #1, *Life of Christ, Limited Collectors Edition C-36* (Bible), *Mother Teresa and Life of Christ, Pilgrims Progress* and *Screwtape Letters*.

Classics Illustrated and Related: This year was the opposite of last year, as we sold mostly GD-FN range cheaper editions in the $5-$50 price range. We helped fill in some reading copy runs, with the scarce issues and issues with less printings still being the usual obstacles. First appearance of new art and new cover issues were in even higher demand, as they are a different type of original. Many collectors are just as satisfied with any printings, but want both the old and new cover and art editions. Canadian variant editions (not in *Guide*) of #1-74 are in high demand, especially those with new illustrated text stories that do not appear in US editions (150-400% of equivalent US edition.) The scarcer *Classics Illustrated Junior* issues are; #506, 514, 525-529, 532-534,537,540,542,543,547,553,555, 556,558-565,568,571-573,575-577 (FA-VG = 200-300% *Guide*; FN-VF = 150-200% *Guide*.) In constant demand are all the scarcer issues of *Classics Illustrated* (in any printing and in all grades = 120-150% *Guide*) #8,14,20,21,33,40,43,44,53,66,71,73, 74,84,110,113-118,129,161-169. Once they finish their main sets, many buyers then go out to complete *World Around Us, Classics Special Issue, Classics Junior, Famous Authors, Picture Progress, Boys Life*, etc. I do well with and carry a large selection of non-Gilberton *Classics* related items, including: Berklet/*First Classics* #1-27(#14 up = low print and scarcer), *Marvel Classics* #1-36, Moby Books BLB Classics (36 Diff), *Pocket Classics* (72 diff), *Clasicos Infantiles* (Mexican Juniors), *Jack Lake* (30+ diff, Modern Junior-r), *King Classics, Golden Legacy, Golden Picture Classics, Power Records, Tele-Guide*, Marvel-UK Digests, Acclaim Classics, and more. The UK *Classics Illustrated* with all-new stories and covers never seen in USA are in very high demand in the $25-$150 each range (#158A James Bond *Dr. No* brings $500 in high grade and became DC's *Showcase* #43.)

Comic Digests: We have about 15,000 comic digests in stock, thus we are the #1 destination for fans who want to complete sets. Over 85% of what we sold this year were in the GD to FN/VF ranges, going to fans trying to complete various sets. Most of the pre-1994 comics digests were never bagged, as nothing was commonly available to collectors, thus rubbing and handling wear is present on almost all still existing copies. High grade begins at VF on pre-1995 comic digests. Most sets are tough to assemble in even VF, never mind VF/NM or better. Most digests have zero copies graded by CGC, with even the most popular issues have only 1-3 copies each slabbed. In the last 5 years, we managed to buy several collections, especially those from the Manitoba Collection and we have sold over 300 in strict 9.0 or better. But now all the sources have dried up and we will again find it tough to stock even VF or better copies.

The rare Charlton/Xerox Comic Digests bring 200-300% *Guide*, including *Barney and Betty, Bugs Bunny, Dino, Flintstones, Jetsons, Pebbles and Bamm-Bamm, Road Runner, Scooby Doo, Space: 1999, Tweety and Sylvester, Woody Woodpecker* and *Yogi Bear*. The Marvel digests are often requested in high grade, but sell in all grades (135-175% *Guide*) including *Alf, Dennis, G.I. Joe, Haunt of Horror, Spider-Man, Star* and *Transformers*. The DC Digests are most requested in high grade, but sell in all grades (125-150% *Guide*) including *Adventure* #491-503, *Best of DC* #1-71(with 41-71 low print), *DC Special Blue Ribbon* #1-24, *DC Special Series* #18,19,23,24, *Jonah Hex and other Western Tales* 1-3, *Tarzan Digest* #1. The 1979 Skylark Digests of *Doc Savage* and *Stories from the Twilight Zone* are scarce and sell instantly at 200% *Guide*. *Dennis the Menace Pocket Full of Fun* #1-50 and *Dennis and His Friends* #38-46 digests are undervalued and getting scarcer (150-200% *Guide*). The Gold Key comic digests started it all, with the 1960s issues being the most desirable of all digests (*Golden, Mystery, Walt Disney*, plus the even scarcer *Story Digests of Boris Karloff, Dark Shadows, Ripleys, Tarzan*.) They are always regular bestsellers (at 125%-150% *Guide* in any grade). High grade 9.0 and better GK digests are nearly non-existent.

The Harvey digests were in big demand (1977-1985 = 120-135% *Guide*; 1986-1993= 150-500% *Guide*). These Harvey digests had low print runs, are extra scarce, dealers are sold out everywhere. They are on most wantlists (bringing 200-500% *Guide* in ANY grade.) *Casper Adventure Digest* #6-8, *Casper Digest* (10/86-1991) #11-18, *Casper Digest* (V2; 9/91-11/94) #6-14, *Casper Enchanted Tales* #6-10, *Harvey Wiseguys* #3,4, *Hot Stuff Digest* #2-5, *Million Dollar Digest* (11/86-11/94) #11-34, *New Kids on the Block Digest* #1-5, *Richie Rich Adventure Digest* #4-7, *Richie Rich Digest* (10/86-10/94) #11-42, *Richie Rich Digest Stories* #11-17, *Richie Rich Digest Winners* #11-16, *Richie Rich Gold Nuggets* #1-4, *Richie Rich Million Dollar Digest* #6-10, *Richie Rich Money World Digest* #1-8, *Richie Rich Digest* (11/77-8/82) #7-9, *Wendy Digest* #2-5.

DC Comics: For the Silver, Bronze Age and on, Batman is seen as the main character to buy from DC. Perhaps only in the Golden Age does Superman become more important to collectors. Especially in the Bronze Age, we see 2-3 times the demand for Batman over Superman. Wonder Woman is hands down the most important female superhero of all time. JLA and JSA are incredibly popular teams, and along with the 3 previous characters, they form the backbone of collectible DC Comics. It is hard to recall that in the 1981-1985 period, that all the above were all slower sellers and had smaller print runs, because Marvel dominated the marketplace. If you check around, you will find no one is heavily stocked on the above in the 1981-1986 era. Perhaps inspired by the success of the new X-Men, Pérez's *New Teen Titans* hit the market in late 1980 and became a bestseller. *Crisis* hit the market in 1986 to revamp the entire roster at DC Comics, perhaps the best move they ever made. The *Man of Steel* 6 issue mini-series in 1986 turned Superman back into the top seller it should have always been. Frank Miller blew away fans and breathed new life into Batman in *Dark Knight Returns* in 1986. The 1987 *Justice League* series was the starting point for entrenching their popularity near the top. Pérez's 1987 *Wonder Woman* series finally restored her to glory. The 1986 *Secret Origins* series, featured all-new post-*Crisis* origins for most of the main characters. The 1989 *Batman* movie blew it into the stratosphere. As a result, most 1989-1990 Batman comics were overprinted. All these 1985 and newer comics form most of the important DC comics that started the Copper Age of comics. The *Overstreet Comic Book Price Guide* glossary now officially defines the Bronze Age as 1970-1984. The above 1985-1989 era comics are good long-term investments in strict 9.0 or better. But take note that the lower print run 1981-1985 era books might outperform them.

Many fans are assembling sets of DCs with Neal Adams covers. The *Tomahawk*s with Adams' covers remain the most elusive in high grades. If you check the CGC Census, you will see only 1-3 copies each exist in 9.0 or better. CGC 9.4 copies would easily bring $500 each, with #116 (the 1st and most wanted issue) probably worth closer to $1000. Up in demand are the classic 1960s covers by Nick Cardy, thus *Aquaman* and *Bat Lash* are a bit up in demand. But the most requested Cardy covers are the *Teen Titans* issues and Romance comics. High Grade CGC copies are still rare.

DC comics seem to attract more readers than Marvel, thus they sell well in all grades. Perhaps it is simply because

Oddball comics sold better in 2007 than in the last 3 years. (**FOOM** #22 shown)

there are usually more than double the Marvel comics in dealer inventories as compared to DC. There most certainly is a lot of demand for high grade copies, but lower grades are perhaps even more popular, as most buyers seemed to be filling in runs this year, rather than just chasing key issues. Silver and Bronze Age DC have far less copies, and are also much scarcer in high grades, as compared to their Marvel counterparts, yet on average, the Marvels are far more expensive. The sales of new comics from DC often rival and surpass the new Marvels, thus the 1960s-1970s DC seem to be a relative bargain. This year we sold over 700 raw high grade Manitoba collection comics in the 9.0 to 9.8 range from the 1975-1985 era at 125-300% *Guide*. DC War comics were the most requested and bestsellers in high grade. DC Horror would have rivaled them, if we had not previously sold most of the high grade Manitoba copies. High Grade collectors have started realizing that 1960s DC comics are quite scarce in even VF and I have noticed a sharp increase in sales of VF range copies. Oddball comics sold better than the last 3 years at 120-135% *Guide*, mostly in GD-FN grades, including *Amazing World of DC*, Cartoon/Humor, Digests, Fanzines, Fireside Books, Giveaways, Magazines, Paperbacks, Posters, Promo items, Romance, Teenage, Treasuries, TV, War and Western. All DC Horror titles were again top sellers in all grades, especially 1968-1974 era, Giants, Neal Adams and Wrightson art issues. DC Horror and War comics have been getting harder to re-stock, as supplies continue to dry up.

The bestsellers for us this year (at 110% to 135% *Guide*) included *Action* #252-300, 347, 360, 373(Giants), 377-392(Legion), 401-440, *Adventure* #267-320, 381-400, 428-440, 459-467, 461-466, 491-503, *All-American Men of War* #82-117, *All-New Collectors Edition* C-54-56,58, *All-Out War*, *All Star Comics* #58-74, *Aquaman* #50-52, *All-Star Comics* #59-74, *All-Star Western* #1-11, *Amazing World of DC* #1-4,9,14-17, *Bat Lash*, *Batman* #121-429, *Batman Family* #11-20; *Best of DC Digest* #1-71, *Black Magic*, *Blitzkrieg*, *Brave and the Bold* #59-200, *Challengers* #74, *Crisis* #1-12, *Dark Mansion* #1-4, *DC Comics Presents* #1,2,26,47,56,77,78,85-88,94,97 and Annual #1, *DC 100 Page Super Spectacular* #4-22, *DC Special* #2-4,6,11,28,29, *DC Special Series* #1,3-13,15,16,18-24,27, *DC Special Blue Ribbon Digest* #1-24, *DC Superstars* #17, *Detective* #311,318, 325, 327,328,355,359,362-364,369-372,385,387, 389,391,392, 394-495, *Doorway to Nightmare*, *1st Issue Special* #1,3,5,7-9,12,13, *Flash* #105-130, 201-250, 275-313, 340- 350, *Flex Mentallo*, *Fox and Crow*, *Freedom Fighters*, *Ghosts* #1-40, *GI Combat* #66-68,83,87-154,200-210, *Girls' Love* #84-180, *Girls' Romances* #81-160, *Green Lantern* (1960-1986) #40,45,59,61,76-123,181-200, *Heart Throbs* #75-146, *Hot Wheels*, *House of Mystery* #174-259,291-300,321, *House of Secrets* #81-154, *Isis* #1-8, *Joker* #1-9, *Jonah Hex* #1-20,81-92 and Digest #1-3, *Justice League of America* #91-261, *Kamandi* #50-59, *Legion* #259-300, *Limited Collectors' Edition* C#23-25,32-34,37,39,41,43-46,48-52,57, *Men of*

War, Our Army at War #83-301, *Our Fighting Forces* #123-162, *Plop* #1-5, 21-24, *New Teen Titans* #1-20, *Real Screen, Our Army at War* #83-250, *Our Fighting Forces* #123-181, *Phantom Stranger* #1-41, *Rima* #1-7, *Secret Society of Super-Villains* #1-15, *Secrets of Haunted House* #1-20,41,44, *Sgt Rock* #302-350,400-422, *Shazam!* #1,8,12-17, 25-35, *Showcase* #55,57,60,61,64,70,79-81,83,84, 97-99, *Sinister House* #1-4, *Spectre* #1-5, 9, *Star Spangled War* #84-183, *Strange Advs.* #205-236, *Superboy* #80-100, 197-245, *Super DC Giant* #S-13 thru S-26, *Super Friends* #1-20, *Supergirl* (1972) #1-10, *Superman* #150-200, 233-300, 400-423, *Superman's GF Lois Lane* #79-137, *Superman's Pal Jimmy Olsen* #100-150, *Superman Family* #164-190, *Swamp Thing* (1982) #20-40, *Tales of New Teen Titans* #42-44 and Annual #3, *Tarzan* #207-258, *Tarzan Family, Teen Titans* (1966) #1-25, 46-53, *Time Masters* #1-8, *Time Warp, Tomahawk* #116-119,121,123-130, *Unexpected* #105-162, *Unknown Soldier* #205-219,248-268, *V for Vendetta, Watchmen, Warlord* #1-10, 37-50, *Weird Mystery* #1-10, *Weird War* #1-30,64, 68, 93-101, *Weird Western* #12-39, *Weird Worlds, Witching Hour* #1-85, *Wonder Woman* (1942-86) #51-130,171-220, 267-329, *Wonder Woman* (1987-2007) #51-63, 85-96, 120-200, *World's Finest* #81-120, 169,173-179, 198-212, 244-282, 320-323, *Young Love* #39-126 and *Young Romance* #125-208.

Dell Comics: We have a large selection of 20,000+ Dell comics, thus they always do very well for us. Tarzan comics were the #1 Dell/GK seller of the year, followed not far behind by Turok. TV comics and Western comics were the next most requested this time around. Those with photo covers sell fastest. Next most popular were animated titles from TV cartoons, especially those from Hanna-Barbera. After a period of being moderate to slow, the *Movie Classics* have again picked up in demand, especially those with photo covers, Horror/SF themes, good art (Manning, Toth, etc.) or John Wayne appearances. Newspaper strip reprint titles have slowed again in sales. Over 90% of Dell buyers purchaed GD-FN copies; FN/VF and better copies were slow sellers. The *Guide* is low on GD-FN copies, and at the same time high on VF to NM-copies. The wide condition/price spread that works for superhero comics, just does not work as well on other comic genres and especially with Dell. Most investors do not think of Dell

Movie Classics *issues with photo covers have picked up in demand.* (**El Dorado** *shown*)

when looking for their high grade investments, except perhaps the key issues. Easily over 50% of the pre-1970 Comics we sell to overseas customers are Dell Comics.

The bestselling titles (115-135% guide for GD-FN copies) included *Annie Oakley, Bat Masterson, Beetle Bailey, Ben Bowie, Beverly Hillbillies, Bewitched, Big Valley, Brain Boy, Brave Eagle, Bugs Bunny, Bullwinkle, Cheyenne, Chilly Willy, Cisco Kid, Colt 45, Combat, Creature, Dick Tracy, Dracula, Felix the Cat, Flintstones, Flying Nun, Flying Saucers, Four Color* (most photo-c), *Frankenstein, Fritzi Ritz* (with Peanuts), *F-Troop, Gene Autry, Get Smart, Ghost Stories, Have Gun Will Travel, Hogan's Heroes, Howdy Doody, Huckleberry Hound, I Love Lucy, Indian Chief, Jetsons,* John Wayne(all), *King of Royal Mounted, Kookie, Laramie, Lawman, Leave It To Beaver, Little Lulu, Lone Ranger, Looney Tunes, Maverick, Melvin Monster, Mighty Mouse, Monkees, Movie Classics* (Western, SF and Horror), *Mummy, Nancy* (Stanley-a), *Outer Limits, Peanuts, Ponytail, Popeye, Rawhide, Real McCoys, Red Ryder, Ricky Nelson, Rifleman, Roy Rogers, Sea Hunt, Sgt. Preston, Smokey Stover, Sugarfoot, Tales of Wells Fargo, Tarzan, Thirteen, Tonto, Turok, Twilight Zone, Voyage to the Bottom of Sea, Western Roundup, Wolfman, Wyatt Earp, Woody Woodpecker* and *Yogi Bear*.

Fanzines, Misc. Comic and Cartoon Magazines: We have a giant selection of 10,000 different (non-Marvel/DC), assorted comic and cartoon related magazines, fanzines and related items. I have bought and sold literally 100s of items that I have only seen once in the last 40 years. I really enjoy dealing in "oddball" items, and they certainly abound among these. These are loaded with early and obscure works of now famous artists, and writers (much never reprinted), plus have in-depth articles, pinup covers and art on all the popular characters, through all the way to totally obscure and "the very bad." These can be exciting to collect, as you run across endless things of interest, that most collectors will never see in a lifetime. The majority of these items sell in the $5 to $25 each price range. Most customers are not overly concerned about condition, most are focused on finding any copy of the item of interest.

Giveaway and Promotional Comics: Giveaway comics are fascinating. Less than 25% of those existing are listed in the *Guide*, but most of the important ones are in fact listed. The Marvel, DC, Popular Character and Popular Artist issues, are just an extension of the collecting the regular series of those titles. Some Promo comics are so rare that it is not unusual to see them sell for 2 times to 100 times *Guide* prices at auction. Most of those that go for the highest multiples, are the ones not listed in the *Guide* and usually involve a highly collectible character, especially Spider-Man. When you take into account regional giveaways, pamphlets, flyers, Marvel shareholder items and titles with 10 or more variant printings, Spider-Man collectors will tell you that under 25% are listed in the *Guide*. If you collect promo items with Spider-Man on the cover, the number suddenly explodes ten-fold into hundreds and perhaps thousands of items. Marvel and

DC related promo and ephemera items are in the biggest demand by the fans who love scarcer and oddball items, including these titles: *Marvel Age*, *Marvel Comics Preview* (Distributor ashcan promo), *Marvel Monthly Catalog*, *Marvel Quarterly Report*, *Marvel Requirer*, *Marvel Spotlight* (Retailer promo giveaway from Marvel on slick paper), *Marvel Spotlight* (Retailer promo giveaway on newsprint), *Mega Marvel* and *Sales to Astonish*, handouts, flyers, displays, posters, advance news items, distributor books, shareholder items, *Previews* items, insert items, sendaway items, toy items, *Direct Currents*(DC), store and restaraunt promos, and more. Most of these items sell in the $3 to $20 each price ranges, to very active buyers. *Supergear Comics* (Superman) and Boston Pops' *Biff Bam Pops* (Spider-Man) are $500-$1000 items in high grade, but impossible to find.

There are over 35 titles of *He-Man/Masters of the Universe* and over 12 titles of *She-Ra/Princess of Power* mini-comics that came with the action figures, and if you include variants, it might be double that. These are among the most collected giveaways. The DC comic booklets from Atari video games are in high demand: *Atari Force*, *Centipede* and *Swordquest*. *Super Power Collection* #1-25, those Kenner Color Gum card size mini-comics (2-3/4" x 4-1/4") are fast sellers (VF $10 ea.) *March of Comics* are top sellers, but can be extremely elusive. I have many customers who have searched for many years for select issues (125-200% *Guide*.)

Literally 1000s of non-character giveaways, especially post-1980 titles remain unlisted. Many of these are regional items, which makes them even scarcer. Most collectors collect by: (1) the comic's age, (2) its scarcity and (3) its theme. The most commonly collected themes are: Unknown Superheroes, Politics, Health, Restaurants, Christmas, Foreign Country, Job-Related, Environmental, Educational, Substance Abuse, Sex-related, Institutional, Cartoon, Science, etc. Our #1 best sellers are any and all titles published in Canada, as we have many Canadian comic completionists. The majority of Promo comics are in the $5-$15 price range, with scarce and desirable titles widely varied from $20 to $100 each.

Gold Key Comics (non-Disney): *Tarzan* was our #1 best-selling Gold Key (and Dell) this year, with VF or better copies the most requested. Reading copies were the next most requested, and finally even mid-grade copies moved well, as many people seemed to want to complete their runs. The scarce Photo Back Cover Variants are selling in all grades (at 125-150% *Guide*) including: *Avengers*(TV) #1, *Star Trek* #1-3, and *Wild Wild West* #1-2. Demand for *Dark Shadows* virtually doubled this year, presumably due to the 40th anniversary and the release of seasons on DVD. Demand for *Dark Shadows* paperbacks was even higher.

Whitman variants of the Gold Key comics and digests published from 11/1971 thru 3/1980 sell moderately well at 125-200% of GK issue values. 1968 Canadian Newsstand Variant cover price issues are still selling to completionists

and variant collectors at 115-125% *Guide*. The 1972-1974 era Gold Keys with 16-page Bonus Fun Catalogues (advertising) make the standard 36 page comics into 52 pagers. These 52 pg. Fun Catalogue issues seem to have a slightly smaller survival rate and tend to be about a grade lower than surrounding issues. It is perhaps time they got identified and had a premium of about 20% added in the *Guide*.

Demand for high grade copies was up by almost 50%, with these titles bringing 125-150% *Guide* (for VF or better copies) including: *Boris Karloff*, *Dark Shadows*, *Dr. Solar*, *Grimm's Ghost*, *Korak*, *John Carter*, *Magnus Robot Fighter*, *Mars Patrol*, *Mighty Samson*, *Munsters*, *Occult Files of Dr. Spector*, *Phantom*, *Ripley's Believe it or Not*, *Scooby Doo*, *Space Family Robinson*, *Spine Tingling Tales*, *Star Trek* #1-10, *Tarzan*, *Turok*, *Twilight Zone*, *Wild Wild West* and all Hanna-Barbera #1 and key issues.

These issues are among the bestsellers (selling in all grades at 115-135% *Guide*) including: *Adam-12*, *Addams Family*, *Amazing Chan*, *Auggie Doggie*, *Banana Splits*, *Battle of the Planets*, *Beatles Yellow Submarine*, *Beetle Bailey*, *Beneath the Planet of the Apes*, *Bullwinkle*, *Close Shaves of Pauline Peril*, *Dagar*, Dan Curtis (Giveaways) #1-9, *Family Affair*, *Fat Albert*, *Flash Gordon*, *Flintstones*, *Fun-In*, *Funky Phantom*, *George of the Jungle*, *Gold Key Spotlight*, *Gomer Pyle*, *Hair Bear Bunch*, *Hanna-Barbera Bandwagon*, *Happy Days*, *H.R. Pufnstuf*, *Huckleberry Hound*, *Inspector*, *Jetsons*, *Kroft Supershow*, *Lancelot Link*, *Land of the Giants*, *Laredo*, *Lidsville*, *Little Lulu*, *Little Monsters*, *Lone Ranger*, *Looney Tunes*, *Lucy Show*, *Magilla Gorilla*, *Mighty Mouse*, *Milton Monster*, *Mr. Ed*, *Mr. and Mrs. J. Evil Scientist*, *My Favorite Martian*, *Nancy and Sluggo*, *Peanuts*, *Peter Potomus*, *Phantom*, *Pink Panther*, *Popeye*, *Quick Draw McGraw*, *Rifleman*, *Smokey Bear*, *Snagglepuss*, *Snooper and Blabber*, *Space Ghost*, *Super TV Heroes*, *Three Stooges*, *UFO Flying Saucers*, *Underdog*, *Wacky Races*, *Wacky Witch*, *Wagon Train*, *Yakkey Doodle*, and *Zody the Mod Rob*.

Harvey Comics: 1950s and 1960s Harvey cartoon comics are among our best sellers in any grade, with the biggest problem being trying to re-stock them once sold. The only Harvey comics that seem a bit more plentiful are the Richie Rich, Sad Sack and Casper issues from the 1977-1984 period, otherwise everything else is uncommon to scarce. These comics were traditionally not saved by collectors, thus most copies on the market are "Used" copies from childhood days and casual readers, so high grade copies are scarce to rare. Most of the Harvey cartoons have been around longer than the Marvel superheroes and those generations remember them well. Completing any of the 50+ issues runs can actually be very difficult, as most dealers have only tiny selections. We have 30,000 Harveys, so we help many fans fill in gaps in their sets. High grade copies are hard to find and continue to bring record prices. We managed to get in a batch of about 75 Sad Sack File Copies from the 1960s in 9.0 to 9.4 and sold over 50% of them within the first week at 150-250% *Guide*. We also sold over 50 more 1976-1984 Richie Rich comics from the Manitoba Collection (9.0-9.6 at 150-300% *Guide*).

The 1988-1994 Hanna-Barbera and other Harvey cartoon titles had low print runs, but at least can be more easily found in VF. They remain undervalued (VF copies bring $4-$8 ea.). The non-cartoon Harveys are actually good solid sellers and often get forgotten. All 1960s comics with a Richie Rich backup story are more sought, as collectors with near-complete Richie sets are now moving on to these, thus titles like *Mutt and Jeff* are up in demand. Scooby Doo is hot from all publishers and the Harvey ones are getting scarcer (bringing 200% *Guide*). All Richie Rich issues #1-10 (over 50 titles of comics and digests) sell 50-150% faster than later issues. Richie Rich is by far the most important and collected character from this publisher and should be a great long-term investment for decades to come.

Bestselling titles (at 130-160% *Guide*) include *Baby Huey*, *Blondie* (undervalued), *Casper's Ghostland*, *Casper and Nightmare*, *Dagwood*, *Devil Kids*, *Flintstones*, *Fruitman*, *Hanna-Barbera Giant Size*, *Harvey Hits*, *Hot Stuff*, *Jetsons*, *Little Dot*, *Little Dot's Uncles and Aunts*, *Little Lotta*, *Playful Little Audrey*, *Pebbles and Bamm-Bamm*, Richie Rich (all 1975 and older,) Sad Sack (all pre-1965,) *Spooky*, *Stumbo Tinytown*, *Tuff Ghosts*, *TV Casper and Co.*, *Underdog*, *Unearthly Spectacular*, *Wendy* and *Yogi Bear*. Other good sellers (at 115-125% *Guide*) include *Alarming Tales*, *Alarming Adventures*, *Astro Comics* (give-away with 15+ variations,) *Black Cat*, *Blast-Off*, *Casper the Friendy Ghost*, *Dick Tracy*, *Felix the Cat*, *First Love*, *First Romance*, *Friendly Ghost Casper*, *Joe Palooka*, *Kerry Drake*, *Little Max*, *Man in Black*, *Mazie*, *Mutt and Jeff*, Richie Rich (all 1976 up), Sad Sack(all 1965 up) and *Warfront*.

IW and Super Reprints: There are a lot of completionists for these publishers, thus they all sell. About 1/3 are common, 1/3 are uncommon, with 1/3 being scarce to rare. Our minimum prices are: (GD=$4; VG=$7; FN=$10; VF=$18), with better titles selling for about 50-100% higher. Those who like old cheap books usually buy reading copies. Completionists usually prefer the higher graded copies. Scarcer titles sell instantly when listed, with many still undervalued in the *Guide*. Many have Pre-Code reprints at much lower prices than the slightly earlier vintage originals. None of these comics carry the Comics Code, but should have. Superhero, Jungle, Horror/SF, and War titles being the best-sellers. Western, Teenage, Humor, Funny Animal and Cartoon and Romance titles are are all moderate sellers. Top artists include Cole, Crandall, Davis, DeCarlo, Fine, Frazetta, Heath, Kinstler, Kirby, Krigstein, Powell, Severin, Ward, Wood and others. Most of these books are 40-50+ years old, yet reading copies are only in the $5-$10 range.

Liquidity and Beyond: The backbone of the comics back issue market is the Superhero comic. In the pre-1970 years, it was Golden Age superheroes that transformed readers into collectors. From the 1970s to date, it has become the Marvel and DC Silver Age superheroes that dominate the market. Many of us started as younger readers with cartoon, Archie or other comics and drifted into reading superheroes, but it is the Marvel superheroes of the Silver Age in particular and beyond that have driven the Market to the lofty heights we know today. The superhero Universe was a world most of us got hooked on, usually in our pre-teen to teenage years. The quest to read and enjoy more of these classic tales has made many readers into lifetime collectors. As we delve more into the world of comics, many of us tried out other genres of comics: Horror, Sci-Fi, Western, War, TV, Cartoon, etc. A very large portion stayed with Superheroes, but perhaps moved on to try and enjoy those of other publishers too. Naturally the GA superheroes are the rarest, most valuable and are extremely important, but likely over 90% of today's collectors will never purchase a single GA back issue. Most of the comics currently available for sale in dealer inventories are Marvel comics. Well over 50% of the comics currently available for sale are 1981-2007, about 1/3 are Silver thru Bronze Age, about 15% are comic-related items and only about 3% are Golden Age. The vast majority of existing back issues are in collections. In my 36 years as a dealer I estimate I purchased 6 million comics and sold 5 million of them, thus my remaining current stock of just over 1 million comics. When collectors buy these items, few of them worry about future liquidity. If you are buying them to enjoy, this is not a concern. If you are spending large amounts, or a substantial portion of your income, this should be a concern. Currently the biggest gluts in the Market are the 1981-1995 Marvel and DC superhero comics in strict 8.5 Very Fine+ or lower grades, especially those from 1988-1995. Many dealer inventories are loaded with these slow sellers (including about 40% of my own inventory). It needs to be duly noted that for us, 1981-1987 Marvel and DC superhero comics in strict 9.0 or better (especially 9.4 up) are currently among our hottest sellers. Most of the collections we have been offered in the last few years are heavily loaded with average graded 1981-1995 Marvel and DC superhero comics, thus would be yet more overstock for us and of no value (in fact they would take up more valuable space and cost more for labour to process them. Collections like these, if one is able to find a dealer-buyer at all, typically garner offers of 5% to 15% of *Guide* value (often only 10 cents per book). Meanwhile, the TNC comics (Traditionally Non-Collected) from the 1981-1995 period are uncommon to scarce, including Archie, Harvey, Cartoon, Charlton, Gold Key/Whitman, Western, War, Horror, Digests, Magazines, Fanzines, *Mad* and *Cracked*. These TNC comics are low in stock in most dealer inventories and tend to have a higher wholesale value per unit, as they are harder to re-stock. Yes, most dealers do not care about Harvey and Archie comics, but how many dealers have a decent stock of these collectible items? TNC comics tend to sell well in all grades, for us with a turnover rate of 300% to 1000% better then average graded Superhero comics of the 1981-1995 period. This is the year that I have finally decided to begin clearance sales on our overstock of 1981-1995 Marvel and DC superhero comics, with most being sold in lots of 25-100 comics each in the 50 cents to $1 each wholesale price range. Some sell to dealers, but most sell to fans who just want to READ THEM (Gasp!) So far they have sold quite well and we hope to clear out 300,000+ comics from our warehouse in the next few years. We added in some TNC comic sets to the mix and on average we have yielded about double the average prices as compared to Superhero comics of the period.

Supply and demand plays a large role in the market. If you buy all the same comics as everybody else, you might end up with common and thus slow selling material. If you buy items that are scarce in any condition, you will find a lot more buyers and at better percentages of retail. If you decide to collect the most popular and common characters, and want them saleable at a good price in the future, you will need to buy high grade items that are scarce in condition. These high grade comics need to be able to withstand the strict grading standards of CGC and not just wishful thinking. High grade comics (even those from the 1980s) can be sold successfully in many ways: (1) let CGC grade them and then auction them; (2) sell them to a knowledgeable high grade dealer; (3) sell them to fellow collectors; (4) sell them raw on eBay with large scans to show you know how to grade; (5) display them on the CGC Chat Boards. On the flip side, older comics in low grade sell quite well to readers on eBay and for a decent percentage of *Guide*.

Many collectors bought a lot of comics in the 1980s, only to realize today that they did not hand-select them by today's CGC standards, they did NOT bag and board them on the day of release and they made the mistake of reading them, thus the collection they thought was "Pristine Mint" is now in fact only a bunch of common Very Fine average comics and thus hard to sell.

Marvel Comics: Marvel Superhero comics from the 1961-1964 era are by far the most wanted comics of the Silver Age comics. Yes we all dream about those rare Golden Age comics, but as most collectors today grew up on Marvel Comics, they have become the holy grails of the hobby for many, or even most, fans. This explains the staggering prices received on high grade issues and since most of them are still issued today as new comics, it seems there is no end in sight. Thus the 1961-1964 Marvel Superhero comics sell in every grade. For the 1965-1969 era, low grade and high grade copies sell the fastest, but because even 9.0 copies are getting expensive, I have seen increased demand for nice VF copies. The 1970-1974 era Marvels had small print runs and are scarcer than most of the 1965-1969 issues and are more affordable, so they sell about 2-3 times faster and moving well in all

grades. The 1975-1980 era are in high demand, mainly in VF or better. The 1981-1987 Late Bronze to Copper Age comics were in very high demand, but mainly only in strict VF/NM 9.0 or better grades. 1981-1995 Marvel Superhero issues in VG to VF are perhaps the most overstocked comics of all time, and mainly sell in investment grades and as reading copies. Most 1996-2007 Marvels had lower print runs and fetch better prices than 1988-1995 era comics, and they might even be good long-term investments. All good Bronze Age key issues were selling in all grades, but non-key issues of lesser titles were slower. We had a lot of Bronze and Copper Age issues in 9.0 and better from the Manitoba Collection and they sold about three times faster than the more common VG-VF grades. As usual, I sold a lot of odd-ball comics and other format items, mainly because of our huge selection, including: Cartoon, Humor and Parody, TV/Movie, Romance, Teenage, Toy Related, TV, War, Western, etc, at 125-200% *Guide*. I also sold more than usual odd-ball format items, including: Digests, Fanzines, Giveaway/Promo items, Memorabilia, Paperbacks, Posters, Treasuries, Slurpee Cups, Calendars, Portfolios, etc. Many of these odd items are getting harder to restock once sold out.

All Marvel Horror comics and all pre-1985 Marvel magazines (all types) were top sellers in all grades, with high grade the most wanted. Reading copies are always in high demand, and in fact I have sold out on lower graded copies (GD, VG) on many many issues and often have only FN or even VF as my cheapest copies. We have more people trying to fill out the Marvel magazine runs than anything else from this publisher this year. *Savage Sword of Conan* is a set everyone wanted to complete this year, with the biggest obstacle being the lower printed #200-235 for most buyers. Issues #200-235 are hard to keep in stock even at 150-250% *Guide*. This year *Savage Sword* #235 was our bestselling Marvel and constantly sold out (NM=$125; VF/NM=$60; VF=$45; FN=$30; VG=$20; G=$12). If you check out the CGC Census, you will see that the

© Conan Props.

Savage Sword of Conan is a set everyone wanted to complete. (#204 shown)

1970s Marvel Magazines are much 2-10 times scarcer in high grade than their color comic counterparts. From the Manitoba Collection, we had another great year, selling over 900+ raw 1976-1985 era high grade 9.0 to 9.8 Marvel comics, magazines and Treasuries at 125-300% of *Guide*. The most undervalued comic of the Silver Age is probably *Strange Tales Annual* #2(7/1973; 4th app. Spider-Man) which precedes *Amazing Spider-Man* #3 yet lists at 25% of the value. *Tales of Suspense* #49(1st X-Men x-over) is undervalued too.

The bestsellers for us this year (at 115%-150% *Guide*)

included: *Amazing Adventures* #1,5-8,11-18, *Amazing Spider-Man* #1-30, 101-150, 252, 298-300, *Astonishing Tales* #1-6, 12,13, 21-25, *Avengers* #1-11, 47-250, *Beware, Bizarre Advs., Capt. America* #100, 109-113, 131-300, *Capt. Marvel* #1,14, 21-36, *Cat, Chamber of Chills, Champions, Chili, Conan* #1, 25-50, 261-275, *Conan the King* #51-55, *Creatures on the Loose* #10-16, 21, 22, 30-37, *Crypt of Shadows, Daredevil* #1-7, 50-168, *Dazzler* #6-7(Hulk) and Mystique/Rogue issues, *Dead of Night, Deadly Hands of Kung-Fu, Defenders* #1-11, *Doc Savage Mag, Dr. Strange* (1974) #1,2 14, 48-53(Rogers-a), 58-62(Dracula), *Dracula Lives, Electric Company Mag* (with Spider-Man), *Fear* #1-31, *Fantastic Four* #1-30, 110-200, *Foom* #1-15, 22, *Frankenstein, Ghost Rider* #1-20, *Giant-Size X-Men* #1, *G.I. Joe* #1-21, 91-100, 138-155, *G.I. Joe Digest, Godzilla* #1-3, 25, *Gothic Tales of Love* #1-3, *Haunt of Horror, Hero For Hire* #1-10, *Hulk* mag, *Incredible Hulk* #121-250, *Invaders* #1-20, 31-33, *Iron Fist, Iron Man* #1, 21-150, *John Carter, Journey into Mystery* #83-112, *Journey into Mystery* (1972-75 all), *Jungle Action* #5-23, *Lil Kids, Lil Pals, Kull and the Barbarians, Kull* (1971) #1-5, *Man-Thing, Marvel Comics Presents* #72-84(Weapon X), *Marvel Comics Super Special* #1,2,4,5,9, *M.Fanfare* #45(all Pinup), *M. Feature*(1971) #1-4,11,12, *M.Feature* (1975) #1-7, *Marvel Novel* series #1-11, *M. Premiere* #1,3,7,8,15, 45-50, *M. Preview* #1-10, *Marvel Spotlight* #1-12, 26-32, *MSH Contest of Champions, MSH Secret Wars* #8, *Marvel Team-Up* #1-15 and John Byrne issues, *M. Treasury* #1-28, *M.Two-in-One* #1-10 and all Byrne/Perez/Miller art issues, *Master of Kung Fu* #15-50, *Masters of the Universe* #12-13, *Micronauts* #1-10 (Golden-a), *Mighty Marvel Western* #1-15, *Monsters of the Prowl, Monsters Unleashed, Moon Knight* #29,30, *Ms. Marvel* #1,16-18, *My Love* #1-39, *Nick Fury* #1-7, *Night Nurse, Night Rider, Nova* #1,12,25, *Our Love Story* #1-38(esp #5), *Pete the Pest, Planet of the Apes* mag #21-29, *Powerman* #17-50, prototypes (Atlas 1961 and older), *Punisher* (1986 mini), *Pussycat* #1, *Rampaging Hulk, Red Wolf, Savage Sword of Conan* #1-30, 200-235, *Savage Tales* #1, *Savage She-Hulk* #1,6,8,25, *Sgt. Fury* #1-13, *Shanna, Silver Surfer*(1968) #1,3,4,12, *Spidey Super Stories* #1-30, *Spider-Man Digest, Spider-Woman* #6, 19, 32, *Star Digest, Strange Tales* #101-115, 169-181, *Sub-Mariner* #1, 8, 14, 34-50, 59, 69, *Superman vs Spider-Man* #1, *Supernatural Thrillers, Super Villian Team-Up, Tales of the Zombie, Tales of Suspense* #39-60, *Tales to Astonish* #27, 35-60, *Thor* #181-250, 332,333,337, *Tomb of Darkness, Tomb of Dracula* #1-30, *Transformers* #1-10, 61-80, *Transformers Digest, Uncanny Tales, Unknown Worlds of Science Fiction, Vampire Tales, Vault of Evil, War is Hell, Werewolf by Night* #1-20,32,33, *Western Gunfighters* #1-15, *Western Kid, What If* (1977) #1-20, *Worlds Unknown* and *X-Men* #1-20, 50-66, 94-121.

National Lampoon Magazines: *National Lampoon* are loaded with great material that is unknown or forgotten. In the 1950s and 1960s *Mad* was arguably the greatest parody magazine of them all, but in the 1970s *National Lampoon*

took that position. 90% of the issues we sell are in the GD-FN range. We had about 100+ high grade 1970s issues from the Manitoba collection and sold about 50% of them at 150-200%+ our normal VF range prices.

Included in the title is great art by Adams, Bode, Frazetta, Jeff Jones, Kaluta, Morrow, Romita, Arnold Roth, Barry Windsor-Smith, Gahan Wilson, Berni Wrightson and many others.

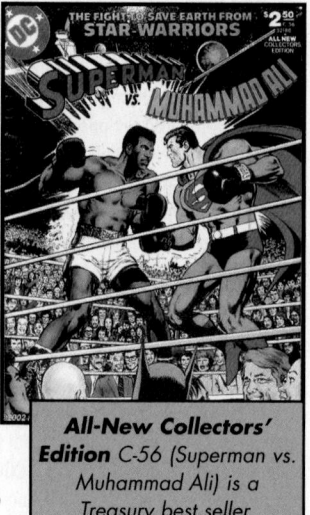

All-New Collectors' Edition C-56 (Superman vs. Muhammad Ali) is a Treasury best seller.

Treasury Editions: Treasury Editions are steady good sellers, with the Marvel and DC titles the best sellers. The majority sell best in affordable GD to FN/VF grades. We sold about 75 Manitoba collection high grade 9.0-9.6 range copies (120-300% *Guide*). All are now scarce in strict 9.0 or better. Bestsellers (at 120-135% *Guide*) included: *All-New Collectors' Edition* C-54 (Superman vs. Wonder Woman), C-55(Legion), C-56 (Superman vs. Muhammad Ali), *Captain America's Bicentennial Battles* (Kirby/Smith-a), *DC Special Series* #27(Batman vs. Hulk), *Funtastic World of Hanna Barbera* #1-3(New-s), *Limited Collectors' Edition* C-23 (House of Mystery), (Batman issues = C-25, C-37, C-44, C-51), C-32 (Ghosts), C-34 (Christmas w/Super-Heroes), C-46(JLA), C-48(Superman vs. Flash), *Marvel Treasury* #24-28(with new material), #1-10(reprints), *Superman vs. Spider-Man* #1. The *Annie, G.I. Joe* and *Smurfs* Treasuries all had small print runs and are scarcer (150% *Guide*). Rudolph #NN(1972) is one of the rarest Bronze Age comics and the *Christmas & Archie* Treasury is rare too (both bring 200% *Guide*). *Amazing World of Superman* is getting scarcer, but especially in high grade (due to its black-c). The oddball titles are scarce and bring 125% *Guide*, including: *Golden Picture Story Book* (1961) ST#1-4, *Modern Promotions* (1972/73; Beetle Bailey, Flash Gordon, Katzenjammer Kids, Mandrake) and *Walt Disney Paint Book* series (6 different circa 1975). A forgotten rarity was uncovered this year: a Famous First Edition C-61 Signature Edition (Silver Stone Graphics Pub., 1979, *Superman* #1 softcover in a portfolio type slipcase; Serial Numbered Edition of 250 copies; signed by Jerry Siegel and Joe Shuster; NM- value estimated at $500.)

Tower Comics: *Dynamo, Fight the Enemy, Go-Go, Noman, Thunder Agents, Tippy Teen,* and *Undersea Agents* were all great sellers thru the year, selling mostly to readers and fans filling out sets in GD-FN grades (at 110-125%

Guide). We did fill a few want lists for VF or better copies, but these are becoming tougher to find in higher grades and very few exist in CGC 9.0 or better. These gems remain undervalued in high grades, considering they contain the talents of Crandall, Ditko, Kane, Wood, etc. They published *Good Old Days* magazine (1964-1981; $5-$20 ea.) Tower was also a vintage paperback publisher (related to Belmont and Midwood books) with many highly collectible titles.

Variants and Premium Editions: Marvel's 30 and 35 cent Variants are the ones that started the Variant craze. These are some of the highest demand comics of the entire Bronze Age. *Guide* values are still well below market and even wholesale values, but are finally beginning to creep up. The 30 cent Variants are about 50-200 times scarcer than regular 25 cent printings and should *Guide* at a minimum of 300% of the 25 cent edition prices (better and scarcer titles bring 500-1000%). The 35 cent Variants are about 200-1000 times scarcer than regular 30 cent printings and should guide at a minimum of 600% the 30 cent edition prices (better and scarcer titles at 800-2000%). *Iron Fist* #14(35 cent Variant) is the most desirable of the Marvel Variants. The Western, War, Horror and Reprint title issues turn out to be some of the rarest, with raw copies sometimes bringing $50-$200 for 30 Cent Variants in mid-grades and $100-$800 for 35 Cent Variants in mid-grades. Spider-Man titles bring top premiums and should be priced at about 50-100% higher than other Superhero titles. *Star Wars* #1 (35 cent Variant) still brings top premiums and although it is one of the most common Variants, it has gone unfilled on hundreds of Marvel want lists for up to 25 years (which is strange because regular printings of *Star Wars* #1 are slow to dead sellers).

Limited Edition Modern Variants (mainly 1990-2007) including Gold Editions, Multiple Cover Variants, Convention Editions, Dynamic Forces, Signed Copies, Hologram covers, Platinum, Polybagged specials, Signed and Numbered, are often red hot upon release. However, most do not perform well in the long-term, because as soon the the newest "hot" Limited Edition Variant gets released, the previous one tends to get forgotten. Unfortunately, this is what happened to Limited Edition Sports Cards, one can always make more new limited editions and the old ones get more and more diluted in value. The ones that seem to hold value and demand, are those in which there is constant demand for the regular editions.

Canadian Newsstand Variant cover price editions sold better than ever before, as awareness spreads. There are *far* too many of them (5000++) to ever be listed in the main part of the *Guide*. Many times this year I saw them both intentionally and mistakenly sold as "Rare Price Variants, *not* listed in *Overstreet*." Just two examples of many: a FR/GD *Transformers* #1 and a *G.I. Joe* #21 in VG, both sold for over $50 on eBay. In general, these are about 50 to 100 times scarcer than a USA Direct Edition printing. To make matters more difficult, about 90% of them are only FR/GD thru FN/VF, with about 9% in VF or VF+, and perhaps 1% are

in VF/NM or better. Dates for existing Canadian Newsstand Cover Price Variants include: Archie comics and digests (1/1984-12/1997); Charlton (2/1983-8/1984); DC (all newsstand comics, magazines and digests from 10/1982-9/1988); Dell (random 1960-1962, plus back cover variants and assorted 1950s cover price variants = regular issues with 15 Cent covers and Giants with 30 cent covers), Gold Key (5-8/1968, and 4/1972-4/1973), Harvey (1960s Giants with 35 Cent cover prices), *Mad* (some 1964 and 7/1978-7/1979), Marvel (all newsstand comics, magazines and digests from 10/1982-8/1986), Warren (3/1977-3/1983), Whitman (mainly early 1981, and 1983-1984.) We sell these Variants at 135-200% *Guide*. High grade copies have been known to change hands at 300% or more of *Guide*. Very few of these Variants have been graded by CGC. For example, *Secret Wars* #8 has 1885 copies graded, but only one Canadian Variant (in FN) on their Census. One day I expect that Variant collectors will regret not buying these sooner.

Early 1977-1979 Marvel Direct Editions were both intentionally and mistakenly sold as "Whitman Variants of Marvel" comics, all through the year. Only a few Treasuries were actual Whitman editions. Otherwise only the outer plastic bags were actually "Whitman." See *Guide* #36 on page 125 for full details, or email me. I have witnessed sellers who know they have early Marvel Direct Editions, intentionally sell them as "rare Whitman Variants" in a quest for more money and are often indeed getting rewarded with 200%-1000% selling prices for their efforts. Early Marvel Direct Editions have a Black Diamond on the cover, no "cc" on the cover, and no UPC or obscured UPC Codes etc.) The 1977 issues are most desirable and sell at 120-150% *Guide* to Variant collectors. For 7/1978 and 3-4/1979, there were only Newsstand Editions printed (with the exceptions of *Micronauts* and *Shogun Warriors*, which are often mistaken as reprints, but are actually uncommon Direct 1st printings). Strangely enough, I am told by Variant Completionists, a few 1978-1979 Direct issues are very elusive and scarce, but it's too early to identify and price these in this newer segment of the collecting market.

A new trend in Variants is the quest for scarce 2nd, 3rd and beyond printings (mostly from Marvel and DC comics in the 1980s to early 1990s). *Batman: The Killing Joke* (1988) had at least 11 printings, of which typically 65% of the copies on the for-sale market are First Printings, thus gathering a complete set of 11 printings is a very difficult task. *Batman* #397-399, 401-403, 408-416, 421-425, 430-432 all had at least 2 printings, with some issues having 6 or more printings. About 50% have the printings noted in the indicia inside. The other printings, one can only tell apart by comparing the ads on the back cover. At least 75 different printings exist for these 23 different issues, but most likely the actual number exceeds 100 different. This "*Batman* Variants" set would be extremely difficult to assemble, as no one knows what exists and many are rare. Other early 1990s and older second printings include *X-Men* #248,270,275, 282, *New Mutants* #87, 100, *New Warriors* #1, *G.I. Joe* #1-

30, *Amazing Spider-Man* #361, *Silver Surfer* #34, many assorted other Marvel and DC comics. The strange part is that most later printings are scarcer than First Printings and it would not suprise me to see Variant collectors pay multiples to complete their sets.

Warren, Skywald, Eerie/Stanley and other Horror Comic Mags: Warren magazines are one of the bestselling and fastest turnover items in my entire inventory. They sell in every grade, but the Reading Copies (VG and Lower) are the toughest grades to keep in stock. When Warren folded circa 1983, their back issue department copies got dumped on the market in quantities of about 1000-5000 copies each (more of the low numbers and less of the high numbers). By about 2002, over 95% finally got absorbed by the market, as most of the final copies got dumped on eBay. Suddenly, Horror comics became hot, and literally thousands of collectors found themselves having half to nearly-completed sets of *Creepy*, *Eerie* and *Vampirella*, so they all decided to start filling in these sets. These are by far the most collected titles. This resulted in dramatic price increases and constant demand. Most of our buyers buy groups of 20, 50 or even 100 mags at a time. We have discovered that some issues seem to be much scarcer than others, so the theory is that some issues were initially sold out, and others only available in low quantities, from the Warren Warehouse. It is only the Warehouse that has held back the values of these amazing mags, otherwise under regular market conditions, they would be 200% to 600% higher in price. *Blazing Combat* #1 and the *Anthology* (Mail Order only) are scarce in any grade, but rare in 9.0 or better and sell instantly at 200% *Guide*. The scarcity of *Eerie* #17 is now legendary (90% of existing copies have chipped interior upper and lower right corners, caused by a dull blade at the factory), with most copies bringing 300%-500% *Guide* on eBay. Recently a raw FN/VF copy sold for $548.99. I sold the best copy I ever owned 3 years ago for $500. This book's value needs to triple in the *Guide* and it would still be low. We sold hundreds of high grade copies of Warren mags in the 1975-1983 era from the Manitoba Collection (9.0 to 9.6 copies) at 125-300% *Guide*.

The scarce and/or high demand Warren magazines include: *After Hours* #1 (1957; 1st Warren mag; Bettie Page) *Blazing Combat* #1 and *Anthology*, *Comix International*, *Creepy*, *Best of Creepy* paperback, *Dracula* (TPB & UK New English Library mag editions,) *Edgar Allan Poe's Fall of the House of Usher* HC, *Eerie*, *Famous Monsters*, *FM Convention Books and Paperbacks*, *Flintstones at New York World's Fair 1964*, *HELP*, *Heidi Saha* (500 printed? Very RARE,) *Monsterland/Forrest J. Ackerman's Monsterland*, *Monster World* (replaces *Famous Monsters* #70-79), *Odd World of Richard Corben*, *On The Scene Presents Freak-Out, USA*, *Screen Thrills* (1962-1965,) *Spacemen*, *Spirit Special* (Mail only, approx. 1500 printed). *Teen Love Stories*, *Tiny Tim*, *Vampirella*, *Warren Presents* and *Wildest Westerns/Favorite Westerns of Filmland*.

The Comics Horror mags by Eerie Pub, Globe, Hamilton,

Major, Modern Day, Stanley, Tempest Pub, and World Famous are never hot, but are always consistent sellers. Reading copies are in highest demand and we have started to sell out of everything in less than FN Condition. The Eerie and Stanley titles, with their gloriously colorful "Violent Torture, Bondage and Gore" covers and contents, have what everyone remembers and that's why collectors want them. *Weird Vampire Tales* and *Terrors of Dracula* are uncommon to scarce and bring 135-150% *Guide*. The rest sell in all grades in the 120-135% *Guide* price range, including: *Chilling Tales of Horror*, *Horror Tales*, *Murder Tales*, *Shock*, *Strange Galaxy*, *Tales from the Tomb*, *Tales of Killers*, *Tales of Voodoo*, *Terror Tales*, *Web of Horror*, *Weird*, *Weird Worlds*, and *Witches Tales*.

The Skywald magazines (*Nightmare*, *Psycho* and *Scream*) are about three to six times scarcer than the average Warren magazine, with the last four issues of each title being the scarcest issues. They sell in all grades bringing at 140-160% *Guide*. They are very hard to restock once sold, and VF or better copies are getting very hard to find all the time. *King* magazines (3-7/1971; Boris-a) are rare. *Crime-Machine* and *Hell-Rider* are also decent sellers.

Whitman Comics: The 8-12/1980 Whitman issues of former Gold Key titles are finally understood to be scarce and still bring 150-500% *Guide* prices. The 1983-1984 issues are uncommon and bring 120-200% *Guide* prices. The Whitman Variants (not yet listed in the *Guide*) of Gold Keys published from 11/1971 thru 2/1980 are uncommon to scarce, with some rare, depending of the popularity of the character bringing 125-200% of GK issue values. The better non-Cartoon titles (*Star Trek*, *Tarzan*, *Twilight Zone* etc.) approach the high end in pricing. Marvel Whitmans do not exist (see Variants in this report).

We got the most requests ever for the Whitman Variants of DC comics, with most buyers wanting FN or better (but we sold VG and lower to a few buyers completing their runs). We sell most DC Whitmans from this price range (and up): VF/NM=$16; VF=$12; FN=$9; VG=$6; GD=$4.

Maggie Thompson
Comics Buyer's Guide

Overview of the Market: Attendees I saw at 2007 conventions demonstrated (along with comics-shop sales) that it has been another growth year for the comics market. Mind you, the feeding frenzy at Wizard World Chicago seemed based to a large extent on dealers' cutting prices. On the other hand, the top end of the top end of comics collectibles is also seeing big bucks.

And media attention always seems to draw the curious to pay increased attention to the comics from which they came – though minor successes (or downright failures) don't lead to high profits for "investing" in, say, *Painkiller Jane* (on- and off-screen so quickly that there seemed to be little if any movement) or *Ghost Rider* (with a little more interest, but …) back issues. On the other hand, the third film outing for

Spider-Man and the second for Fantastic Four provided better box-office results and more back-issue performance.

Nevertheless, even cautious collectors are looking ahead already to the "dark" version of Batman. Based on fan reaction at Wizard World Chicago to a preview panel for *Batman: The Dark Knight*, it's not hard to anticipate a wave of collecting nostalgia that a reimagined franchise could bring. Moreover, younger viewers of the 1989 film are now entering the prime "disposable income" demographic and may be looking for support for nostalgia that older collectors don't even feel.

Moving away from super-heroes: Neil Gaiman's and Charles Vess' fantasy series *Stardust* was brought to the big screen in late summer with Gaiman fans eagerly picking up the movie adaptation, the original comics, and DC's special-edition hardcover collection. However, as back-issue properties, they're still easy to find – which is what fuels collectibles down the line. If everyone takes them for granted today, they may be hard to find when the film is declared a classic a decade from now (which will be 20 years after the first release of #1).

© Gaiman & Vess

Neil Gaiman's fans flocked to **Stardust** in theaters. (#1 shown)

In fact, it's never too late to scout out items that could pay off. Here's the thing: As this is written, the stock market is spitting up blood from an ulcer that threatens to throw the U.S. economy into the hospital. Abandoning the metaphor: When stocks and bonds are questionable investment, investors often look to collectibles as a hedge. If people continue to be nervous about their portfolios, it's almost a tradition that they'll start paying high prices for high-quality rarities.

In the meantime, prices for run-of-the-mill 1940s and 1950s reading copies aren't uncommonly found at what you'd pay for a new comic book you'd find on comics racks today.

Michael Tierney
Collector's Edition

At the turn of the new Millennium, things looked pretty grim for the comics industry, especially while new comic sales continued to plummet. But the turnaround that began a few years ago continued on into 2007, and what sells new affects what sells old.

The year started with a duel over the Number One new comics sales spot being fought each month between Marvel and DC. At first the contest was like an old fight movie, with each company taking turns delivering dominating blows. But by the middle of the year, titles with high mainstream recognition like Stephen King's *Dark Tower: The Gunslinger* and Laurell K. Hamilton's *Anita Blake*, along with numerous

crossover events like World War Hulk, Fallen Son and the X-Men's Endangered Species, placed Marvel firmly in the top spot. And no event in 2007 was bigger than the epilogue to last year's Civil War crossover, when Captain America was assassinated. Retailers had no idea about Cap's death until customers heard it on the news. *Captain America* #25 sold out instantly and its value shot through the roof. The highest I've sold a copy for was $16, and it always sells very quickly at that price. Could I have sold them for more? Most certainly. But I've always held the line on pricing books that see a lot of short-term speculation, because I don't want someone with 20/20 hindsight to say years later that I ripped them off. Giving customers a good deal that they'll always remember is more important that a quick profit, and hopefully ensures that I'll keep them around for the long term. I've heard many stories of astounding prices on eBay, but more about the online facet of the industry later.

Even though DC's grip on the top spot was eventually broken by Marvel, the impact caused by their new comics dominance over the last few years is still very evident in the back issue department. The demand for Golden and Silver Age DCs is dramatically different from when I first started retailing comic books over 25 years ago. Back then Marvel was the market. Whenever I'd buy a collection, it was mainly for the Marvel back issues, and I'd dump the DCs cheap just to be rid of them. In 2007, the demand for DC back issues was the greatest that I've ever seen. A Fine Minus copy of the *Adventures of Dean Martin & Jerry Lewis* #1 sold instantly for $275. A Very Good copy of *Challengers of the Unknown* #3 went for $120. The first Catwoman cover on *Detective Comics* #122 went quickly in Very Good Minus for $240. The first appearance of Lana Lang in *Superboy* #10 went for $350 in Fine Minus. And a rare copy of *The Phantom Stranger* #6 from the 1950s sold for $110 in Good Plus.

Obviously, key issues are always hot. But DC was in demand across the board. *Detective Comics* #181 sold in Fine Plus for $200, and #193 in Fine Minus for $120. *Whiz Comics* #117 went for $64 in Fine Minus, and *Wow Comics* #10 for $110 in Very Good Minus. By contrast, my biggest Marvel sale was the *Amazing Spider-Man* Annual #2 in Fine Plus for $88. That's a huge change from previous years, where Marvel was once the dominant force in back issue sales.

One of the smart things Marvel did during their journey back to the top was a return to producing All Ages material. Not kiddie pabulum like they did with the Marvel Age line, but true All Ages material that any reader of any age could enjoy. With the new Marvel Adventures line, Marvel also created yet another continuity that runs separate from those of the old time Marvel Universe, the M2 Universe, and the Ultimate Universe. Yep. Marvel has four continuities all running simultaneously. While it might seem daunting for new readers to find their way into reading Marvels these days, the important thing is that they are producing entry material for youth. This is where the next generation of comic readers is being developed today. And the Marvel Adventures line outsells the DC mature Vertigo line, with the exception of the excellent *Fables*. So, for me at least, sales to youth are more important than mature sales.

There are, however, three big laments that I hear from customers on a regular basis. While big crossovers and event books have created much of the popularity for whichever company is on top at the time, self-contained issues have become a rarity. I hear more and more requests for stand alone stories, that don't require reading half of a publisher's monthly line. Big crossovers are another barrier to entry level readers. The flip side of this is that customers who're demanding stand alone stories can still find them in my back issues bins. And many comics from the '80s, and even the '70s, sell for less than what a new comic costs.

Also a concern for customers is the seemingly unending problem of late shipping. While the impact on the sales for a late shipping mini-series like *Civil War* or *Infinite Crisis* might not be evident, for a supposedly monthly title it can be devastating. *Wonder Woman* was a perfect example of this. The new series launched to big numbers, but after only four issues in a year's time, when DC finally jumped over the missing last issue of the story arc and went on to the new writer, sales suffered. This probably reflected more than it should have on the performance by the new writer, who was quickly replaced. Late shipping is what killed the sales on *Wonder Woman*. An independent example is *Hunter-Killer*, which was doing solid numbers until sporadic shipping killed interest. The most glaring effect of late shipping was on *Captain America*, who reached new heights of popularity when he died, but it took two months for the next issue to ship. By then, the momentum was lost. In contrast, the five part followup of *Fallen Son: Death of Captain America* mini-series arrived on time and sold very well. I went through several reorders just to keep the book stocked on the shelves. That Marvel did a large overprint is a welcome change from the old days, when their reaction to declining sales was to short print hot titles.

The other lament I heard is concern about

The relaunch of **Brave and the Bold** performed well. (#1 shown)

the bottom dollar prices often brought on the back issue market on eBay. While high grade, key books always sell well, just about everything else often sells at bargain basement prices. I currently do a lot of buying for my stores off of eBay, but for now have stopped selling there. The reason for this is because literally thousands of comic stores failed during the late '90s and early part of the new Millennium. All of their inventory, primarily from the last 40 years, is being dumped onto the online market. Add to this that every collector who has an urge to sell is also dumping their collections on eBay at the same time, and you get a flooded market that still shows the repercussions of the new comics glut from the '90s. It will take a while for all of this excess inventory to be absorbed. So... now is the time to buy. Eventually the online marketplace will reach equilibrium, and return to the lucrative early days when there were more buyers than sellers. Once this happens, that'll be the time to sell online.

Given enough time, everything goes through cycles. In new comics, long dormant titles like *Thor* and *The Brave and The Bold* returned in 2007 and performed very well. Plus, the independent publishers were not to be over looked. Dynamite had a bona fide hit when *The Lone Ranger* galloped off the shelves even faster with each successive month. *Buffy the Vampire Slayer* by Dark Horse saw monster sales with Josh Whedon doing the story work, helped by constant reprints that kept each issue available. And *Classics Illustrated* returned with both old and new material. Everything old is new again.

Lon Webb
Dark Adventure Comics

In the last handful of years there has been a kind of marketplace disparity between product and price results between online selling, conventions, auctions, eBay, mail order and "brick and mortar" retail. This looked to be a fracturing and possible herald of implosion in the overall market in general that was starting in the middle grades and spreading outwards, halting at high grade slabbed. To paraphrase one dealer, what was once the foundation of base sales was now a levy of discounted sand. I have come to see it as market correction.

The one predominant factor I have noticed in the past year is that the 21st Century comics market is beginning to achieve a sense of balance in the sales venues noted above, as all are exhibiting some similarities of sales patterns. The overall market has not fractured so much into niche markets of selling but has been directed into niche markets of buying that are barking loudly. The industry that exists today is not the one we originally created or grew up with. The platforms of sales have changed and along with it the rules of inventory and vagaries of buying. The comic animal has been changing for a long time and is now possibly settling down and achieving definition again now that the analog sales mind of the past has become the digital future set down by the consumer.

Product is everywhere, not just in the hands of the dealer and the dusty boxes in the back room. There is more material available currently than at anytime I can remember. The only difference is it just isn't as readily available anymore to the industry dealer to fit into the industry discipline to create a stable across the board industry market model based on availability, grade and pricing. It is a buyer's market that has a chaotic discipline of its own and the challenge is to continue to define it so the long term market is durable, the business of the industry is balanced and the *Guide* still relevant. And also so that the collectors are happy, the participants make money and read well and the business of comics goes on, even without a new generation of comic readers.

What is true today and most obvious is that key issues are the dominant sellers and high-grade slabbed 9.4+ copies are and will remain the crux of the investment portfolio and high-end collector market which accounts for a huge portion of the overall back-issue industry sales figures. The present and future is high-grade pre-1975 comics, pedigree issues and memorabilia for the top-end money. The only flaw here is the lower percentage of buyers who can afford the price tag which now separates this segment completely from the rest of the overall market with its day trading aura. Key 9.8 Silver and Bronze brings staggering multiples – it is still way cheaper than key Gold and is bought by the Memory-Laners who remember them and who are now popping in career earnings and riding the tail of this segment while reaching for the bridle.

Another large sales segment is affordable lower grade buyers which, strangely enough, push prices on low-grade keys almost into mid-grade territory, so there is more equity on a low-grade key than a mid-grade. Sales on filling title runs are an even larger segment, as both high and low-grade buyers are active in doing this. The remaining market is all collectors and readers looking for the best deal possible in the heady boom or bust buyer's climate that is comics.

What is painfully obvious is that a great deal of comics material is, has and will become nothing more than cultural box filler in a search of a buyer. This needs to be recognized, as there is more product than there are buyers or readers on many items. Look at the large amounts of non-key Silver Age comics that are not affordable low grade or investment high grade. The buyer's market dictates 30-60% reductions in *Guide* prices for any movement. The same can also be said for Bronze and later books but the lower prices have not made them so apparent. For years the buyers have spoken and the market has corrected & this is the plain truth and nothing other than a sudden one hundred thousand more active buyers in the market is going to change this anytime soon.

There's low-end, high-end and everything else is a crapshoot, though saleable at some price – a new rule of thumb for us all. There are always a few exceptions, but this is our current state of affairs that will be here indefinitely until pricing spreads are realistic to buying realities. It isn't the market of 20 years ago with moderate 1-2-3 spreads for affordable money and stable sales across the board at *Guide*. The great news is that these buying patterns are present in all selling venues and to me that means a stable and balanced market (though one for buyers) that has changed, settled and which I can do business in.

So, speaking of business (and ending the soapboxing on the obvious) – we haven't dropped off the earth the last couple of years. I was hit by a drunk driver and sustained enough injury to seriously curtail my running around the country so I apologize to all our national convention customers. We have been very active locally and moving warehouse material online and with eBay and wholesaling to other dealers (as always) and wish to thank all of our longtime customers.

This is actually a nice time for the industry. There is more in-depth information on the hobby than ever before in this *Guide* and online with ever-increasing websites, chatrooms, info boards and collector's associations and tons more areas in which to acquire material. CGC has become indispensable and offers great resources to the collector in addition to their third party grading service and there are more quality comic-related movies in the theaters seeping into the public consciousness. It would be great if the publishers could finally figure out how to better market new comics material to readers outside the existing buying group to create a new crop of collectors.

I will leave it to the other advisors who have hit the pavement hard to examine the year in minutiae while I note my current observations on the scene.

Golden Age: Superman, Batman and Captain America have all sold well this past year and we have noticed an upswing in Good Girl art and sales of issues mentioned in *Seduction Of The Innocent*. Timelys are still the hottest ticket but have slowed and perhaps reached their price wall for the present with the exception of 9.2+ slabbed copies. Nedor has had some action and Fawcetts overall are weak. The large amount of books pushed into the market from a few major collections over the past year have sated the esoteric and key book buyers, but have created price reductions in many regular titles and non-key character issues.

Atom Age: Clearly the only market segment that has blanket sales in all grades in all genres and categories. Horror and resurgent superhero titles are much in demand and high grades are setting record prices as many books in this age are scarce in any condition. ECs are hitting a wall in high-end price but I have noticed a few exceptions. Most other horror titles are still the best bargain in this era.

Silver Age: Key issues in high grade dominate sales with low grade affordable issues following and as stated previously, mid-grades are searching aimlessly for a market. DCs in high grade CGC 9.4+ are exploding in value, especially on high end superhero and war with Marvels following closely. I notice most of the important sales are of CGC 9.6+ only representation. Archies and Harveys like *Richie Rich* are of increasing interest and moving well and getting above *Guide* in high grades with lesser grades still moving well at slight reductions. Gold Keys and Dells are slowing with the Random House File Copies that flooded the market and buyers are picking and choosing among high grades at small to large price reductions.

Bronze Age: All mainstream titles and characters are selling in various grades at reduced pricing but clearly, high grade is ruling with 9.8 key copies bringing unbelievable results. Giants, romance and westerns have slowed considerably and war and horror are moving nicely in upward gains.

Modern Age: With the exception of reading and enjoying, key issues only in exemplary grade are the rule. Current hot titles like *Walking Dead* have shown impressive movement but it is always important to note new books spark interest, get hot, their prices rise rapidly and then cools to overall small gains. Even though there are smaller print runs today it still doesn't change the fact they are readily available in grade.

Everything Else: Fanzines, high grade Marvel and DC magazines, *Vampirella*, Skywald and Atlas magazines are still showing growing interest and I've seen CGC high-end slowing somewhat, though still strong. Memorabilia sales on most comic-related characters pre-1970 are hot and heavy and the Seventies memorabilia is starting to plateau. Figures, statues and toys show no major change other than a slight downward dip.

It is becoming more and more apparent that slabbing should only be done for high grade books pre-1975 and most grades pre-1955 for the conservation aspect. I've seen tons of unsold later CGC'd books languishing because it simply isn't cost effective for non-keys and lower grades. Plus comics are there to hopefully be read and enjoyed. Thanks to all and I hope everyone has a fun and productive year and finds a true gem in the dust of antiquity.

Alex Winter
Hake's Americana & Collectibles

Comic books and original comic book and comic strip art continue to play a large role in our auctions, and we have seen a number of record prices for them as they are combined with our traditional strengths in other comic character items and political collectibles.

In our January 2007 auction, we sold the Alex Toth-illustrated splash page from the Black Canary story in *Adventure Comics* #418 for $15,181. Toth, of course, is considered one of the masters of comic book illustration. His line work and the distinctive use of shadowing in his work is as appealing as when it was first conceived. Widely known as the designer of cult favorites Space Ghost and Harvey Birdman: Attorney at Law, Toth also did design work for Hanna-Barbera and illustrated several non-superhero comic books, Disney's *Zorro* being one of the most fondly remembered. Toth also drew the Golden Age Flash, Green Lantern, Atom and Dr. Mid-Nite. While many of us were saddened when he passed away in May 2006, there was something fitting to the fact that he was still at his drawing board when it happened.

In another of our auctions, just two weeks before *Fantastic Four: Rise of the Silver Surfer* opened, we saw record prices on three *Fantastic Four* comics: a CGC-certified *Fantastic Four* #1 graded 7.5 with off-white to white pages sold for a record $19,898, a CGC-certified *Fantastic Four* #2 graded 9.2 with off-white to white pages brought in $11,638, and a CGC-certified *Fantastic Four* #4 graded 9.0 sold for $4,495.

We have also seen continued strength in a number of genres, particularly in Westerns, space-themed heroes, and Disneyana, and this has applied to a number of different categories in addition to comics. Watches, play sets, and tin toys specifically have performed well in our auctions. It's important to note that both the Disneyana and watch categories are have witnessed sustained upsurges over protracted periods.

A few examples of these successful areas include Major Robertson's (actor Ken Mayer) original uniform from the science fiction show *Space Patrol* ($16,675), a Walt Disney US Time-Ingersoll Birthday Watches Retailers Complete Display ($12,650), a rarely seen Boxed Windup Toy "Mickey and Minnie Mouse Playland" ($4,600), the Strange World Adventure Club Buck Rogers pinback ($3,749), a rare Hopalong Cassidy Pocket Watch by U.S. Time, boxed ($2,625), a Hopalong Cassidy Film Festival autographed poster with numerous signatures including Ronald Reagan, John Wayne, Roy Rogers, Dale Evans, and others ($1,782), an Official Hopalong Cassidy Holster Set by All Metal Products Co. ($1,544), The Lone Ranger And His Great Horse Silver boxed Hartland set ($1,786), the Marx Alamo Playset No. 3546 ($1,581), a Gene Autry Watch by Wilane Watch Company, boxed ($1,265), the Toreador on Horseback from *Ferdinand* ceramic figurine by Zaccagnini ($4,025), Hobo Mickey Seated On "London Xii Miles" Marker glazed ceramic figure by Wadeheath ($2,981), and the complete Spanish edition of the always popular *Mickey Mouse Waddle Book* ($2,788).

Also highlighting this success were a Queen of the West/Dale Evans Official Autographed Deluxe Wrist Watch and accessories set ($3,162), a Howdy Doody Wrist Watch with rare packaging and box ($1,626), a complete Orphan Annie Miracle Compass Sun-Watch ($1,518), a Buck Rogers Rare Strip Card Set ($4,427), the Space Patrol Magic Space Pictures, Membership Kit Letter and Out Of Stock Postcard ($3,289), and a Flash Gordon Sparkling Rocket Fighter Ship, boxed Marx Windup ($2,713).

This is not the venue to detail successes in the political collectibles arena, I would be remiss if I did not point out the spectacular sales this niche has experienced. While they certainly don't have superpowers, there are definitely *characters* involved, if you know what I mean.

Harley Yee
Harley Yee Comics

2007 was one of my best years ever, with the Internet playing an important part. As most people know, I have been traveling to shows for over 20 years, and I've also had a catalog for most of those years. However, either through my website or eBay store, I am completely astounded by the hundreds of new buyers I am finding.

As with 2006, my best seller was again *Amazing Spider-*

Man leading the way. Again, some of the current and future movies have influenced the market with a record price for a *Silver Surfer* #1. Also, the future *Iron Man* movie has made *Tales of Suspense* #39 and *Iron Man* #1 hard to keep in stock.

Timelys again were my fastest selling Golden Age group. *Captain America Comics* and related titles were hard to keep in stock. Many new collectors have entered the market and the demand will only grow in 2008.

Golden Age DC have continued their resurgence with the Superman titles leading the way. Early *Action*s were impossible to find and prices have hit the multiples of *Guide*. The Batman titles and Wonder Woman titles have remained strong with all DC titles selling at an above average pace.

I see Silver Age DCs as the big growth area, as long-time collectors seem to be releasing some of their books or whole collections into the market. The grades will never be Marvel-like, but you will see some of the old Marvel multiples if the books are 9.2 or better. Batman titles still remain the most popular Silver Age title.

DC 1950s titles have always sold well for me, but I have seen a surge in demand for *Mystery in Space*, *Strange Adventures*, *Brave and the Bold*, *Showcase* and *Phantom Stranger*. This group of books has some real quality material in them and I think collectors have come to realize this.

Bronze Age Marvels and DCs has been a growth area for many years now. Younger collectors may not buy an *Amazing Fantasy* #15 or *Batman* #1, but they may buy an *Incredible Hulk* #181 or *House of Secrets* #92 instead.

Archie titles have always sold well over many generations and collectors. There is something about the character that appeals to collectors who mainly collect DC, Timely, Marvel and just about anything else. Maybe a lot of us want to be a little like Archie in real life.

Some of the other Golden Age groups like Centaurs and Fiction House have always been hard to find but have recently become hot books. I can only credit this increase to Internet discussion boards where books are displayed and discussed and some of the classic artists' covers are displayed.

Good Girl and Horror books have been a little soft the last few years. Collectors still want the key books or classic covers but seem to hold off buying the entire title run.

2008 will see those trends continue as the internet, CGC, and discussion boards continue to influence the market in a positive way by spreading the words and pictures to more and more collectors.

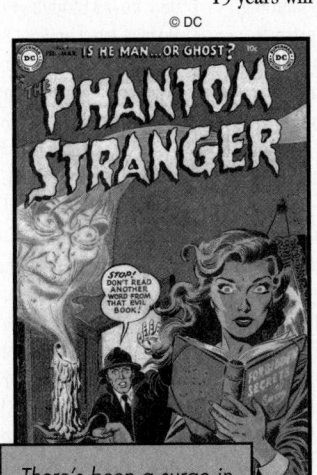

© DC

There's been a surge in demand for 1950s DC titles like **The Phantom Stranger**. (#4 shown)

Mark S. Zaid, Esq. EsquireComics.com

EsquireComics.com enjoyed yet another incredible year for 2007, especially as I attempt to balance my time between comics and my full-time national security law practice. I primarily specialize in investment quality, high-grade Golden Age, as well as Platinum Age, and particularly rare or esoteric books such as promotional anti-communism or political issues.

Within the Golden Age market, absent a market crash overall with the U.S. or world economy, I do not envision a significant slow-down for sales in the coming year. Indeed, I believe the opposite will happen, as a new wave of collectors continues to enter the marketplace. These investors are primarily old collectors who have finally matured into their place of life. Their careers have solidified and their family lives have stabilized. A perfect combination for the brand new investor-collector! Added to the fact that I feel the next 15 years will continue to see new and amazing original owner collections coming to light as those from the depression/WWII era sadly pass on, we are actually poised to witness one of the most exciting eras of Platinum and Golden Age collecting.

The Internet, of course, continues to be buck all trends by reducing our previously held notions of rarity by constantly bringing to light some of the most difficult and seldom-seen copies of [FILL-IN-THE-NAME-HERE]. Without a doubt, the scarcity ratings we have come to love within both *The Overstreet Price Guide* and Gerber *Photo-Journals* are continually being redefined. While on many levels, I love the ability of the Internet to help me find those issues that simply never show up at conventions or in dealer's inventories, I must also admit a breath of disappointment at how easy it often becomes to locate books I thought I would spend years having to search for across the globe yet simply find through Internet searches or unsolicited solicitations. The only true factor that always matters nowadays is just simply how much money you are willing to spend to own that key book. And while on the topic of the Internet, I was honored to serve as an expert commentator for an educational website designed to teach primarily new collectors about comic books and collecting: http://www.videojug.com/tag/comic-books.

As far as some financial data, on all levels during the last year I continued to see significant sales/purchases such as the following CGC certified comics: *Green Lantern* #1 9.0 (GA) - $35,000.00; *Green Lantern* #2 9.0 (GA) - $7,000.00; *Mad* #17 9.6 Gaines - $2,900.00; *All Star* #7 9.0 - $3,300.00; ; *Superman* #48 9.4 Toledo - $5,100.00; along with *Cancelled Comic Cavalcade* #1 & #2 - $2,800.00 and *More Fun* #94 Church - $4,500.00.

I have also continued to expand my involvement in

obtaining legal related comic book items such as "ashcans" (comics submitted to secure trademarks) (please see my article co-authored with fellow advisor Gary Colabuono that appears in this edition of the *Guide*), copyright deposits copies submitted to the Library of Congress, and trial exhibits (issues submitted during litigation such as between DC and Fawcett in 1948). An amazing piece of history surfaced this past year when I had consigned to me a collection of documents (both original and vintage copies) from the 1947 litigation between Superman's creators Jerry Siegel and Joseph Shuster and DC Comics. The collection included legal briefs and correspondence that had never publicly surfaced before and, in my opinion, helped rewrite what we thought we knew about Superman's creators and publisher.

The past year also witnessed growth in an area that means a great deal to me, and that is educating the public on matters that relate to the integrity of the hobby. The Network of Disclosure (www.networkofdisclosure.com), of which I am now in my second term as a Committee Member, continues to expand its membership and includes long-standing dealers and collectors. Together, those who comprise the NOD seek to ensure buyers and sellers engage in fair transactions that involves complete disclosure of all known enhancements that any comic book has undergone. I encourage collectors and dealers, both new and old alike, to take a few minutes to review the NOD's website and consider adding your voice to the effort.

At the end of the day, collecting as an adult is not that different from when we were kids. To be sure, the amount of money involved has changed significantly, though perhaps it is relative given we spent probably 75% of our allowances on comics (could you imagine doing that today with your income!) But no matter the extent to which your foray into comics is to enjoy a healthy return on your investment, comic collecting should remain fun. When the enjoyment from the time I spend through EsquireComics.com disappears, that is when I will also close shop. Fortunately, that time has not yet come!

Vincent Zurzolo
Metropolis Comics

Twelve years ago the 26th edition of *The Overstreet Price Guide* hit the stores. This was the first *Guide* in which I would be listed as an Overstreet Advisor and I was excited to say the least. I had already been in the business for about 9 years and had been collecting practically my whole life (even before I could read – as a wee lad I was literally drooling over copies of *Ghost Rider* and *Marvel Team-Up* much to the dismay of my older brothers who tried to keep their comics in Mint condition). I remember conversations with Bob Overstreet, who was very kind and spent time talking to me about comics and treated me like I was a Senior Advisor. I collected sales data as best I could for Bob to utilize in his annual assessment of the market. I didn't even have a computer let alone a database at the time so I faxed pages upon pages of sales to his office. My "lightning bolt" ad for my old

company, Vincent's Collectibles, graced the second page of the *Guide* and my picture was right there with the rest of the advisors on page A-65. Life was good. I was starting to move up the ranks, get my name out there and carry out my goals in the comic book biz.

It is hard to believe a dozen years have gone by. So much has changed in comics. The advent of the internet, eBay and third party grading has made an immense impact on the way we view, buy, sell and trade comics. But as much as things have changed there has been one constant for me, and that is my love of comic books. I still get excited walking into a comic store, picking up the latest copy of *Superman*, *Hulk*, *Batman* or *Spider-Man* and seeing how my favorite good guys are doing in their never-ending battle against the forces of evil. When I buy a Silver Age key, Golden Age collection or a hoard of high grade Bronze Age comics I still get a kick out of it. I never imagined as a kid that I would ever have an *Action Comics* #1, *Batman* #1 or *Spider-Man* #1. I still read, collect and invest in comics and I think I always will. People often tell me I am very fortunate to have been able to turn my passion into a business. I have to agree. I am very fortunate and blessed to be doing something I love and believe in.

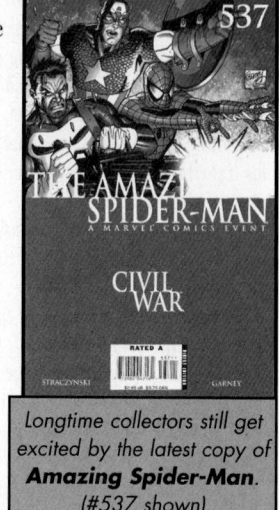

© MAR

Longtime collectors still get excited by the latest copy of **Amazing Spider-Man**. *(#537 shown)*

On behalf of my partner Stephen Fishler and my entire staff I would like to thank all of the customers, dealers, creators, historians, and fans who have helped us have such an amazing year. Sales for our company are at an all time high due to increased interest at conventions, our gallery, through the mail and of course, online. We will continue to strive to bring you the best selection of vintage comics and customer service in the business. Thanks so very much. And now, on to the market report…

Golden Age: Many comic fans collect Silver Age, as they can more easily connect to the characters they grew up with or because they are not too familiar with many of the Golden Age heroes/titles. I think this is a mistake and can limit the enjoyment one gets from comic collecting. A great reference tool that every avid comic collector should have is the Gerber *Photo Journals*. There are four volumes, two Golden Age and two Marvel, the DCs were never completed. In the Golden Age volumes you will find pictures of the covers of almost every Golden Age comics published. Astounding? Yes, it is! If you really want to have fun as a collector you should own these. I can not count how many times I have spoken to collectors who have been looking for something new or different to collect and had no idea about the *Gerbers*. As soon as they had them it was like a whole new world opened up to them. Titles like *Red Dragon, Tip Top, Captain Battle, Mystery Men, Blue Ribbon, The Arrow, Blue Bolt, Master Comics* and *Keen Detective Funnies* become exciting new titles to collect. Ask your local dealer or give me a call if you are interested in picking up a set!

The desire for quality Golden Age comics is very strong. To say it is a robust market would be an understatement. This past year we have moved big keys like *Detective* #27 F/VF w/light restoration, *Batman* #1s from Fair to FN+, the highest grade October copy of *Marvel Comics* #1 CGC 5.0, *Human Torch* #2 (#1) CGC 9.0, *Marvel Mystery* #9 VF-, *Superman* #1 CGC 5.50 w/slight professional restoration, *All-American* #16 CGC 5.0 and *Captain America* #1 VG. We also sold an outstanding run of *All Star Comics* that averaged about VF 8.0 with highlights like #1 CGC 9.0, 2 CGC 9.2 Edgar Church Copy, 3 F/VF, 4 CGC 9.0 Edgar Church and #8 VF.

Thousands of copies of low and moderately priced comics have also been scooped up by avid collectors including titles like *Action, Adventure, Batman, All Top, All Winners, Archie Comics, Captain Marvel Adventures, Catman, Classics Illustrated, Crime Does Not Pay, Detective, Famous Funnies, Fantastic, Fight, Flash Comics, Four Color* Disneys, *Human Torch, Little Lulu, March of Comics, Marvel Mystery, Modern, More Fun, New Adventure, Phantom Lady, Planet, Plastic Man, Police, Popeye, Popular, Red Dragon, Sensation, Seven Seas, Shadow, Spirit* sections, *Stamp, Star Spangled Comics, Superman, Tarzan, Terry & The Pirates, Tip Top, True Crime, Uncle Scrooge, Walt Disney Comics & Stories, Western, Whiz, Wings, Wonder Woman, World's Finest, Wow, Zip* and *Zoot.*

Of particular note is the returning strength of Pre-code horror and the ever-present popularity of ECs. Pre-code horror was very cheap and popular about 10-15 years ago but then jumped. Now with the appreciation of other genres in recent years Pre-code horror is beginning to look somewhat affordable again. ECs sell because people love quality art and story-telling. Creators like Wood, Craig, Kamen, Davis, Feldstein, Ingles and Frazetta will always be valued by comic fans. Speaking of Frazetta, Sci-Fi, Adventure, Western and Horror comics featuring art and covers by the legend have also been increasing in collectability over the last year. Issues #209-216 of *Famous Funnies* feature fantastic covers by Frazetta and are popular. Even though they are all listed at the same price in the *Guide,* an educated comic collector knows that there are common issues (209-212) and tougher issues (213-216) and the books are priced accordingly in the market.

Silver Age: The ruler of the roost is once again Marvel. I

realize this is no big surprise. As I mentioned last year, look out for *Iron Man,* as he is coming on strong due to the anticipation of the movie. The trailer was received with a very positive reaction at the SD Comic Con last summer and prices have been skyrocketing on *Tales of Suspense* #39 and *Iron Man* #1 ever since. This has been the trend over the years with many of the comic to movie Silver Age Marvel characters. I know we are all purist collectors but for those entrepreneurs out there, the key to making money on these comics is to buy early (when you first hear the project has been green lit and there is a good name attached to the lead and supporting characters), and then sell at the peak which is about 2-3 months before the movie debuts. However, there is also plenty of excitement after the movie hits screens across the country... if it's a hit!

Amazing Spider-Man is still by far the best selling Silver Age title, no, make that best selling title – period. No other title comes close. We sold over 30 copies of *Amazing Fantasy* #15 and *Amazing Spider-Man* #1 and at the time of this writing it is only September '07. The 1960s keys from Marvel and the mid 1950s and early 60s DC keys are prime movers. While a major focus is usually placed on Marvel here are some recent sales on DCs from this past year: *Action* #242 VF- sold for $2400, *Green Lantern* #76 CGC 9.0 $1150, *Aquaman* #1 CGC 9.2 $2700, *Batman* #181 CGC 9.6 $3600 and *Showcase* #30 CGC 9.0 $1500. Gold Key titles like *Magnus, Turok* and *Dr. Solar* have also been selling well, especially the File copy collection we have.

Bronze Age: *Conan, Daredevil, Defenders, Batman, House of Mystery, House of Secrets, Incredible Hulk, Inhumans, Iron Fist, The Joker, Justice League of America, Mr. Miracle* and *Swamp Thing* have all been steady sellers. Though it was a little slow for some time, *Incredible Hulk* #181 has been coming back strong. Keep investing in Bronze Age as it is still cheap and it has a lot of room to appreciate.

The Future: For the last four years I have been hosting the *Comic Zone* radio show. You can listen to over 150 interviews for free at www.comiczoneradio.com. This has been a great joy for me. Being able to interview legends like Stan Lee, Neal Adams, Frank Miller and Todd McFarlane has been a blast. Being able to spread the word about comics, a true American art form, has been tremendously rewarding. As a fan, collector, creator, dealer, promoter or whatever, you can help too. Turning the next generation of potential fans on to the modern-day mythology and folklore known as comics is our job. Give a comic to a son, daughter, nephew, niece, cousin, parent, grandparent or heck even a complete stranger. In closing, I wish you all the best in your collecting endeavors!

	In the inaugural edition of *The Overstreet Comic Book Price Guide* in 1970, the top five Golden Age keys were valued at the following.		
		Mint 1970	9.2 2008
	Action Comics #1	$300	$675,000
	Detective Comics #27	$275	$525,000
	Marvel Comics #1	$250	$440,000
	Superman #1	$250	$400,000
	All-American Comics #16	$50	$245,000

Key Comics Sold in 2007

The following lists of sales were reported to Gemstone during the year and represent only a small portion of the total amount of important books that have sold.

PLATINUM AGE SALES

Alphonse And Gaston And Their Friend Leon VG/FN $1,270.50

Banana Oil FN $330

Bringing Up Father #18 VF $126.50

Bringing Up Father #20 VG/FN $126.50

Bringing Up Father #24 FN $210.47

Buster Brown And His Dog Tige And Their Troubles FN/FN+ $460

Buster Brown and His Resolutions FR $334.60

Buster Brown And His Resolutions FN $1,250

Charlie Chaplin Tn The Army #318 FN/VF $358.50

Clancy The Cop VF $399.30

Comic Monthly #1 FN+ $2,136.99

Comic Monthly #2 FN $368.50

Comic Monthly #5 FN- $242

Comic Monthly #6 FN/VF $297

Comic Monthly #10 FN $398.20

Comic Monthly #11 FN/VF $368.50

Comic Monthly #12 FN+ $500

Dreams Of The Rarebit Fiend Appt. VG $4,481.25

Foxy Grandpa And Flip-Flaps VG $131.45

Funny Larks of Hans Und Fritz, The 1917 Edition VG $68.12

Gumps, The #3 VF/NM $388.38

Gumps, The # 4 FN/VF $388.38

Happy Hooligan Home Again FN+ $825

Harold Teen FN $115

Henry #1 VF $166.38

Joe Palooka GD $173.03

Latest Larks Of Foxy Grandpa, The GD/VG $100

Life's Little Jokes FN+ $230

Little Sammy Sneeze FN $3,000

Moon Mullins Big Book FN+ $275

Naughty Adventures of Vivacious Mr. Jack, The PR $569.25

Popeye #1 VG/FN $239

Pore Lil Mose PR $1,912

Pore Lil Mose: FR/GD $507.88

Pore Lil Mose GD/VG $750

Tillie The Toiler #3 $200

GOLDEN AGE - ATOM AGE SALES

Action Comics #1 VF (restored) $60,000

Action Comics #1 FN- (restored) $60,000

Action Comics #40 F/VF $825

Action Comics #133 GD- $26

Adventure Comics #208 VG+ $95

Adventures of Bob Hope #26 GD $16

Adventures of Dean Martin & Jerry Lewis #1 FN- $275

Adventures of Dean Martin & Jerry Lewis #13 VG+ $45

Air Pirates Funnies #2 VF+ $120

Al Capp's Wolf Gal #1 VG $33

All-American Comics #56 VG- $150

All-Star Comics #52 VG+ $295

Batman #5 FR/GD $400

Batman #11 VG $1,100

Batman #45 VG $120

Batman #48 VG+ $175

Batman #53 VG+ $171

Batman #68 VF/NM $1,600

Batman #68 VF $1500

Blackhawk #63 GD $18

Blue Beetle #30 VG $25.75

Boy Comics #11 VF $1,150

Captain America Comics #28 VF+ $3,850

Captain America Comics #53 VG $375

Captain America Comics #57 G/VG $300

Captain America Comics #78 NM- $4,182

Captain Marvel Adventures #10 GD+ $200

Captain Marvel Adventures #16 VG $200

Captain Marvel Jr. #4 GD- $125

Captain Marvel Jr. #79 FN $50

Comic Cavalcade #25 FR $19.50

Crime & Justice #26 VG/FN $59

Crime Suspenstories #11 VG $42

Dell Giant Peter Pan Treaure Chest #1 G/VG $190

Detective Comics #121 VG/FN $152

Detective Comics #122 VG- $240

Detective Comics #151 GD/VG $72

Detective Comics #152 VG $116

Detective Comics #159 GD- $50
Detective Comics #181 FN+ $200
Detective Comics #193 FN- $120
Detective Comics #209 GD- #32
Dick Tracy #36 VG $28
Exciting Comics #59 VF $500
Flash Comics #77 FN+ (restored) $174
Four Color #16 F/VF $5,400
Four Color #38 GD+ $250
Four Color #178 VG/FN $300
Gift Comics #4 VG+ $165
Hit Comics #6 GD+ $375
Hopalong Cassidy #95 GD $14
House of Mystery #14 VG $48
Human Torch #15 VG $400
Lone Ranger (v1) #12 VG $15
Marvel Comics #1 VF/NM (restored) $75,000
Master Comics #22 F/VF $2,500
Master Comics #42 VF $580
Master Comics #48 VF $595
Marvel Family #42 VG+ $42
Marvel Family #46 VG $39.50
Marvel Family #47 VG+ $64
Marvel Family #64 FN- $39.50
More Fun Comics #72 VG $680
More Fun Comics #84 FN $400
Mystic #61 GD+ $28
Panic #1 GD- $25
Phantom Lady #22 GD+ $240
Phantom Stranger #6 GD+ $110
Planet Comics #23 VF $1,000

Police Comics #1 VG $1,500
Popeye #1 (file copy) VF+ $200
Roy Rogers #24 GD $15
Showcase #1 GD- $160
Showgirls #2 (v1#1) GD+ $15
Spirit #3 (Crippen) VG- $150
Startling Comics #49 VG (Restored) $1,000
Strange Adventures #7 GD+ $88
Superboy #6 VG- $100
Superboy #10 FN- $350
Superman #1 FN (restored) $20,000
Superman #2 GD- $1100
Superman #8 VG- (no centerfold) $200
Superman #18 VF- $1,425
Superman #22 VG $350
Superman #93 VG+ $110
Tarzan #3 Dell File Copy $350
Tarzan #20 GD $14.25
Tomahawk #11 GD- $25
USA Comics #1 VG $1,900
Walt Disney's Comics & Stories #5 GD/VG $225
Walt Disney's Comics & Stories #13 F/VF $2,200
War Comics #36 VG $15
Whiz Comics #2 (#1) VF (restored) $8,500
Whiz Comics #5 GD+ $375
Whiz Comics #10 VG $435
Whiz Comics #117 FN- $65
World's Finest Comics #45 GD $60
Wow #10 VG- $110
Wow #53 VG+ $54
Young Allies Comics #1 $2,200

SILVER AGE SALES

Action Comics #257 FN $69
Action Comics #294 FN/VF $53
Adventure Comics #244 VF- $162
Adventure Comics #247 GD $400
Adventure Comics #258 VF/NM $189
Adventure Comics #278 FN $48
Adventure Comics #286 FN/VF $86
Adventure Comics #291 VF $74
Adventure Comics #300 VF- $243
Adventure Comics #304 FN $36
Adventure Comics #306 FN/VF $54
Amazing Spider-Man #1 VF/NM $29,000
Amazing Spider-Man #27 GD $22.25
Amazing Spider-Man #28 GD $22
Amazing Spider-Man #50 NM- $800
Amazing Spider-Man Annual #2 FN+ $88
Aquaman #9 VF $90
Archie Comic Digest #1 VF $125
Archie Giant Series #26 FN $75
Archie's Girls Betty & Veronica #4 G/VG $120

Archie's Madhouse #22 VG $95
Archie's Pals N Gals #23 VF $200
Atom #1 GD $90
Atom #4 VF+ $160
Atom #7 VF $214
Atom #8 VF+ $118
Atom #10 VF/NM $138
Avengers #1 VG $500
Avengers #1 VG $450
Avengers #1 FR/GD $200
Avengers #4 FN/VF $500
Avengers #4 FN- $200
Avengers #6 GD- $16.50
Avengers #44 FN $18.50
Batman #130 FN/VF $132
Batman #135 VF- $114
Batman #146 FN/VF $66
Batman #152 FN+ $40
Batman #154 FN/VF $54
Batman #156 GD+ $15.75

Batman #158 GD+ $15
Batman #167 FN/VF $54
Batman #170 VG- $17.75
Batman #200 GD+ $12
Blackhawk #136 VG $14.50
Blazing Combat (Warren) #1 VG/FN $125
Blazing Combat Anthology FN $75
Brave and the Bold #28 VG $700
Brave and the Bold #42 VF+ $290
Captain America #100 FN $80
Captain America #100 FN- $95
Captain America #109 VF/NM $100
Captain Marvel #1 VF+ $100
Captain Marvel #1 GD $12.50
Challengers of the Unknown #3 VG $120
Challengers of the Unknown #3 GD $39.50
Challengers of the Unknown #9 VG $27.50
Classics Illustrated Special: The Atomic Age FN $26
Classics Ill. Special - The United Nations FN/VF $200
Creepy #32 VF $75
Daredevil #1 VG $515
Daredevil #1 VG $350
Dennis The Menace Pocket Full Of Fun #1 FN $50
Eerie (Warren) #17 VF/NM $500
Eerie (Warren) #23 VF $75
Fantastic Four #1 VG $3,200
Fantastic Four #1 VG $2,200
Fantastic Four #32 VG $38
Fantastic Four #55 VG $22
Fantastic Four #58 VG $19
Fantastic Four #72 GD+ $22.75
Fantastic Four #75 FN- $28
Flash #116 FN+ $105
Flash #126 FN+ $61
Flash #129 VF/NM $330
Flash #130 FN/VF $105
Flash Annual #1 VF $293
Flintstones on the Rocks VG/FN $125
Fox & Crow #1 VG $300
Green Lantern #7 FN+ $132
Hero For Hire #1 FN/VF $68
Hot Stuff the Little Devil #1 VG $200
Incredible Hulk #1 VF- $10,000
Incredible Hulk #1 FN+ $3,000
Incredible Hulk #1 GD $600
Incredible Hulk #1 F/VF $4,500
Incredible Hulk #2 VG $650
Incredible Hulk #5 VG+ $480
Iron Man #1 VG/FN $105
Iron Man #1 FN+ (Color Touch) $125
Iron Man #1 VF/NM $600
Jetta of the 21st Century #6 FN $75
Josie & the Pussycats #45 FN/VF $100
Journey Into Mystery #83 VF- $4,500
Journey into Mystery #83 FN+ $1455
Journey into Mystery #83 G/VG $650

Justice League of America #6 FN $105
Justice League of America #13 FN/VF $116
Justice League of America #18 FN/VF $98
Justice League of America #29 VG $25
Justice League of America #45 VG+ $17.75
Magnus Robot Fighter #1 VF+ $350
Millie the Model #18 VG $50
My Greatest Adventure #52 VG+ $22
Mystery in Space #79 FN- $27
New Advs. of Sherlock Holmes FC #1169 NM- $600
Our Army at War #81 VG $550
Our Army at War #82 VG $250
Our Army at War #83 VG/FN $480
Our Army At War #146 VG $14.75
Outer Limits #1 VF/NM (Northland Copy) $145
Pussycat Magazine $250
Rawhide Kid #59 FN $18
Sad Sad Sack World #16 NM $79
Sad Sad Sack World #18 NM $79
Sad Sad Sack World #21 NM $59
Showcase #8 G/VG $600
Showcase #35 FN/VF $345
Showcase #36 VF- $338
Silver Surfer #1 G/VG $95
Star Spangled War Stories #105 VG $59
Strange Tales #101 VG $100
Strange Tales #102 VG/FN $100
Strange Tales #115 FN $150
Strange Tales Annual #2 FN $275
Superman #139 FN/VF $108
Superman's Girlfriend Lois Lane #70 FN/VF $125
Superman's Girlfriend Lois Lane #79 FN+ $19.25
Superman's Pal Jimmy Olsen #64 FN/VF $32
Tales of Suspense #30 GD $400
Tales of Suspense #39 FN $2850
Tales of Suspense #39 VG $800
Tales of Suspense #40 VG $300
Tales of Suspense #74 FN- $18.75
Tales of the Unexpected #43 FN+ $280
Teen Titans #2 GD $15
Thor #144 VG $15
Three Stooges #6 VG $21
Tomahawk #116 FN/VF $45
Turok, Son of Stone #62 VF $21.25
Wild Wild West #1 (Photo Back-c Variant) FN/VF $99
Wonder Woman #107 GD $75
X-Men #1 NM $25,000
X-Men #1 VG $1300
X-Men #1 GD $600
X-Men #43 VF- $39.25
X-Men #68 VG+ $17
X-Men #69 VG $13.50
X-Men #75 VG $14.50
X-Men #76 VG $14.50
X-Men #77 FN- $17.25
X-Men #81 VG $14.50

Bronze Age Sales:

Action #484(with 3-D insert) VF $35
All-New Collectors' Edition C-56 NM $150
Amazing Spider-Man #121 VF/NM $300
Amazing Spider-Man #122 VG $37
Amazing Spider-Man #122 GD+ $38
Amazing Spider-Man #129 VF $425
Amazing Spider-Man #129 VF $275
Amazing Spider-Man #252 NM- $250
Amazing Spider-Man #252 VF+ $32.50
Batman #234 (1st Modern Two-Face) VG $27
Batman #244 FN+ $25
Batman #261 FN- $15
Batman #300 VF $13.50
Captain America #158 NM $25
Cerebus the Aadrvark #1 FN/VF $400
Christmas & Archie Treasury #1 FN $50
Creepshow GN NM $75
Daredevil #108 NM $45
Dennis & the Bible Kids #10 VF $125
Detective Comics #400 NM ($1,195
Detective Comics #400 NM- $388
Detective Comics #467 VF+ $25
Fantastic Four #110 (Green/Pink Error-c) FN/VF $60
Fantastic Four #112 VF- $47
Fantastic Four #125 NM $65
Giant-Size Avengers #3 VF+ $19
Giant-Size X-Men #1 VF- $800
Giant-Size X-Men #1 VG/FN $450
Giant-Size X-Men #1 VG $300
Giant-Size X-Men #1 G/VG $150
Golden Comics Digest #1 NM $150.00
Green Lantern #76 NM $8,365
Green Lantern #76 NM- $2,031
Green Lantern #76 VF/NM $717
Green Lantern #76 FN+ $167.30
Hansi, the Girl who Loved the Swastika VF $50
Haunt of Horror (Marvel Mag) #5 VF/NM $35
Hot Wheels #1 NM- $100
Hot Wheels #2 VF/NM $50
House of Secrets #92 VF $450
Incredible Hulk #181 VF/NM $2,500
Incredible Hulk #181 VF $1,500
Incredible Hulk #181 FN/VF $340
Incredible Hulk #181 FN+ $675
Incredible Hulk #181 FN $350
Incredible Hulk #181 VG $180
Iron Fist #14 (35¢-c variant) FN- $885
Iron Fist #14 (35¢-c variant) GD/VG $185
Iron Fist #14 (30¢-c) VF/NM $250
Iron Man #55 VF/NM $200
Iron Man #57 NM $35
Limited Collectors' Edition C-25 NM+ $180

Marvel Spotlight #5 VF/NM $525
Ms. Marvel #18 NM $120
Nova #1 VF- $10
Planet of the Apes (Mag) #29 VF+ $90
Power Records #PR-30 NM $110
Rudolph Treasury #NN (1972) G/VG $99
Sabrina (1971) #1 FN/VF $88
Scooby Doo Digest (Charlton) #1 FN $50
Space 1999 Digest (Charlton) #1 VG $35
Tarzan of the Apes Story Digest Mag. #1 NM $250
Twilight Zone #84 VF/NM $90
Vampirella #1 VF/NM $675
Werewolf By Night #32 VF/NM $175
Wonder Woman #219 NM- $15
X-Men #94 VG $155
X-Men #103 VF $28
X-Men #106 FN+ $24
X-Men #201 VF $17

Copper Age Sales:

Archie's Girls Betty & Veronica #320 FN/VF $75
Albedo #1 FN/VF $79
Amazing Spider-Man #252 (Canadian Var.) VF/NM $70
Amazing Spider-Man #300 VF/NM $125
Amazing Spider-Man #300 NM- $153
Batman #404 NM $19.50
Batman: The Killing Joke #1 NM $35
Batman: The Killing Joke #1 (11th Printing) VF/NM $15
DC Graphic Novel #4 (Hunger Dogs) VF/NM $75
G.I. Joe, A Real American Hero #21 NM $90
Hot Stuff Digest #1 NM $25
Jughead #325 VF $75
Masters of the Universe #12 NM $25
Miracleman #15 NM $200
Miracleman #24 NM $75
Richie Rich Digest #42 VF $25

Modern Age Sales:

Conan the Barbarian #275 NM $75
Conan the Barbarian #275 VF/NM $35
Ghost Rider #93 NM $65
Ghost Rider #93 VF/NM $35
G.I. Joe, A Real American Hero #155 VF/NM $65
Mighty Mutanimals #9 VF/NM $20
Savage Sword of Conan #235 VF+ $49
Savage Sword of Conan #235 NM $100
Serenity #1 NM- $12
Spawn #1 VF/NM $20
Teenage Mutant Ninja Turtles Advs. #72 NM $30
Transformers #80 VF/NM $90
Transformers #80 FN/VF $50

Adventures of Dick Tracy and Dick Tracy Jr. VF+ $500
Betty Boop in Snow White FN $200
Bringing Up Father VF $110
Buck Rogers and the Planetoid Plot FN $110
Dan Dunn on the Trail of the Counterfeiters NM $90
Flash Gordon on the Planet Mongo NM $480.50
Flash Gordon and the Forest Kingdom of Mongo NM $635
Flash Gordon and the Forest Kingdom of Mongo VF $175.50
Flash Gordon and the Red Sword Invaders NM $237.50
Flash Gordon and the Witch Queen of Mongo NM $490
Flash Gordon and the Tyrant of Mongo NM $480.50
Green Hornet Cracks Down, The NM $325
Green Hornet Cracks Down, The VF $84
Green Hornet Strikes!, The NM $350
Green Hornet Strikes!, The VG+ $105
Jack Armstrong and the Mystery of the Iron Key NM $99
Just Kids, The Adventures of VF $95
Laughing Dragon of Oz, The VG $149.95
Li'l Abner Among The Millionaires NM $279
Little Orphan Annie 1933 FN $150
Little Orphan Annie and Chizzler VF+ $130
Little Orphan Annie and the $1,000,000 Formula NM $125
Mickey Mouse #731 VG+ $225

Mickey Mouse and the 7 Ghosts NM $212.50
Mickey Mouse and the 7 Ghosts FN $99
Mickey Mouse the Mail Pilot #731 FA/GD $2,500
Nancy and Sluggo NM $100
Og Son of Fire NM- $100
Phantom, The NM $250
Phantom and the Girl of Mystery, The VF $100
Phantom and the Sign of the Skull, The NM $145
Phantom and the Sign of the Skull, The FN $100
Popeye and the Deep Sea Mystery NM $280.50
Porky Pig and Petunia VF $100
Red Ryder in War on the Range NM $100
Red Ryder Brings Law to Devil's Hole FN $125
Shadow and the Living Death, The NM- $390
Shadow and the Master of Evil, The NM $380
Shadow and the Master of Evil, The VF $175
Shadow and the Ghost Makers, The VF $300
Shadow and the Ghost Makers, The FN $200
Tarzan Escapes NM $325
Texas Ranger, The VF $75
Tom Mix in the Fighting Cowboy NM $200
Tom Swift and His Magnetic Silencer VF $95
Union Pacific NM $100

GOLDEN AGE · SALES OF CGC-CERTIFIED COMICS

Action Comics #1 VF (8.0) Moderate (P) $65,725
Action Comics #1 VG/FN (5.0) Extensive (P) $56,762.50
Action Comics #1 GD (2.0) $85,000
Action Comics #4 GD/VG (3.0) $2,950
Action Comics #13 VG (4.0) $6,000
Action Comics #13 VG (4.0) $3,600
Adventure Comics #72 NM- (9.2) $16,730
Adventure Comics #72 VF+ (8.5) $5,975 Rockford
Adventure Comics #72 VF- (7.5) $3,107
Adventure Comics #147 NM+ (9.6) $2,390
All American Comics #16 GD/VG (3.0) Slight (A) $8,962.50
All American Comics #28 NM (9.4) $7,767.50
All American Comics #61 FN (6.0) $2,270.50
All Negro Comics #1 FN+ (6.5) $5,078.75 Crowley
All Select Comics #11 VF/NM (9.0) $2,270.50
All Star Comics #1 VG/FN (5.0) $2,091.25
All Star Comics #3 GD (2.0) $3,150
All Star Comics #5 NM (9.4) $16,750 Mile High
All Star Comics #7 NM (9.4) $15,535 Hawkeye
All Star Comics #8 VF+ (8.5) $62,000
All Star Comics #8 VF- (7.5) $20,000
All Star Comics #21 NM+ (9.6) $7,170 Hawkeye
All Star Comics #22 FN+ (6.5) $600

All Star Comics #56 NM (9.4) $2,390
All Top Comics #8 VF (8.0) $1,195
All Winners Comics #1 FN/VF (7.0) $8,455
Amazing-Man Comics #5 CGC 3.5 $3,883.75
Archie Comics #1 GD/VG (3.0) $6,500
Batman #1 VF+ (8.5) $107,000 Kansas City
Batman #1 FN+ (6.5) $38,837.50
Batman #3 FN/VF (7.0) $3,107
Batman #27 VF/NM (9.0) $2,031.50
Batman #32 NM- (9.2) $2,390
Batman #41 NM (9.4) $2,031.50
Captain America Comics #1 VG/FN (5.0) $15,250
Captain America Comics #1 GD+ (2.5) (restored) $7,500
Captain America Comics #9 FN+ (6.5) $2,550
Captain America Comics #9 FN+ (6.5) $2,473.50
Captain America Comics #59 NM- (9.2) $5,377.50
Captain Midnight #3 NM (9.4) $3,883.75 Mile High
Captain Midnight #5 NM+ (9.6) $3,346.00 Pennsylvania
Clue Comics #2 NM/MT (9.8) $3,585 Mile High
Comedy Comics #10 VF/NM (9.0) $2,031.50
Contact Comics #12 NM- (9.2) $3,107 Vancouver
Crack Comics #1 NM- (9.2) $7,500 Denver
Cyclone Comics #3 NM- (9.2) $1,195 Larson
Daring Mystery Comics #3 VF (8.0) $2,868

Daredevil Battles Hitler #1 NM (9.4) $41,825 Mile High
Desert Dawn #nn FR (1.0) $657.25
Detective Comics #1 FN/VF FN/VF (7.0) Extensive (P) $17,925
Detective Comics #1 GD/VG (3.0) $23,900
Detective Comics #27 FN/VF (7.0) $190,000
Detective Comics #27 FN/VF FN/VF (7.0) Moderate (P) $50,787.50
Detective Comics #27 Apparent VF+ VF+ (8.5) Extensive (P) $47,000
Detective Comics #38 FN+ (6.5) $20,000
Detective Comics #168 VF- (7.5) $4,780 Davis Crippen
Doc Savage Comics #5 NM (9.4) $2,987.50 Mile High
Fantastic Comics #1 FR/GD (1.5) $479.99
Feature Comics #27 VF/NM (9.0) $11,352.50
Flash #51 NM (9.4) $2,390 Davis Crippen
Flash #104 VG/FN (5.0) $1,553.50
Four Color Series 1 #4 FN- (5.5) $9,560
Four Color Series 1 #4 FN- (5.5) $6,100
Four Color Series 1 #16 FN+ (6.5) $3,883.75
Four Color #9 VF- (7.5) $4,481.25
Four Color #108 VF+ (8.5) $1,673
Four Color #170 VF+ (8.5) $1,314.50
Four Color #194 NM+ (9.6) $4,481.25
Four Color #199 VF+ (8.5) $1,673
Four Color #386 NM (9.4) $28,680
Four Color #386 VF (8.0) $1,553.50
Green Giant Comics #1 VF (8.0) $8,484.50
Green Lantern #1 Apparent VF+ (8.5) Slight (A) $44,812.50 Mile High
Green Lantern #2 Apparent VF+ (8.5) Slight (P) $6,572.50 Mile High
Green Lantern #3 NM (9.4) $50,787.50 Mile High
Green Lantern #4 NM- (9.2) $22,705 Mile High
Green Lantern #6 NM (9.4) $19,120 Mile High
Green Lantern #7 VF/NM (9.0) $8,962.50 Mile High
Green Lantern #8 NM+ (9.6) $20,315 Mile High
Green Lantern #9 NM- (9.2) $19,120 Mile High
Green Lantern #10 NM (9.4) $15,535 Mile High
Green Lantern #12 NM+ (9.6) $14,340 Mile High
Green Lantern #13 NM (9.4) $11,352.50 Mile High
Green Lantern #14 NM (9.4) $10,157.50 San Francisco
Green Lantern #16 NM+ (9.6) $14,340 Mile High
Human Torch #1 GD/VG (3.0) $225
Human Torch #2 (#1) VF- (7.5) $11,650
Human Torch #4 (#3) VF/NM (9.0) $5,078.75
Looney Tunes and Merry Melodies #9 NM+ (9.6) $2,629
March of Comics #20 NM+ (9.6) $11,950
March of Comics #20 VF/NM (9.0) $4,182.50 File Copy
March of Comics #41 VF (8.0) $1,912
Marvel Comics #1 VF/NM (9.0) $204,999.99 Pay Copy
Marvel Comics #1 FN (6.0) $75,000
Marvel Mystery Comics #82 NM+ (9.6) $10,200 Ohio
Marvel Mystery Comics #82 NM+ (9.6) $7,170 Ohio
Mary Marvel Comics #1 NM+ (9.6) $7,767.50

Master Comics #21 FN+ (6.5) (Crowley) $3,000
Master Comics #36 VF/NM (9.0) (Mile High) $1,135.25
Master Comics #36 VF/NM (9.0) $1,135.25 Mile High
Military Comics #22 NM (9.4) $1,434 San Francisco
More Fun Comics #55 VF+ (8.5) (restored) $4,000
More Fun Comics #56 FN (6.0) (restored) $2,000
More Fun Comics #57 FN (6.0) (restored) $1,000
More Fun Comics #58 VF- (7.5) (restored) $1,000
More Fun Comics #59 VF (8.0) (restored) $1,000
More Fun Comics #61 VF/NM (9.0) (restored) $1,000
More Fun Comics #63 FN+ (6.5) (restored) $1,000
More Fun Comics #66 FN/VF (7.0) (restored) $1,000
More Fun Comics #69 NM- (9.2) $3,883.75
More Fun Comics #69 VF/NM (9.0) $2,031.50
More Fun Comics #84 NM+ (9.6) $6,572.50 Mile High
More Fun Comics #93 NM+ (9.6) $5,078.75 Mile High
More Fun Comics #101 VF/NM (9.0) $11,352.50
New York World's Fair Comics #1940 VF- (7.5) $5,676.25
Nickel Comics #1 NM (9.4) $14,340 Mile High
Pep Comics #22 VF- (7.5) $70,000
Red Raven Comics #1 FN- (5.5) $8,400
Reform School Girl! nn VF (8.0) $8,962.50
Reform School Girl! nn VF- (7.5) $11,001
Roy Rogers Comics #1 VF/NM (9.0) $1,135.25
Sensation Comics #1 VF+ (8.5) $25,250
Strange Adventures #9 NM+ (9.6) $5,975.
Sub-Mariner Comics #1 VF+ (8.5) $31,000
Sub-Mariner Comics #21 NM (9.4) $3,346 Ohio
Superman Comics #nn VF/NM (9.0) $90,000 Ashcan
Superman #1 Apparent VG + VG+ (4.5) Slight (P) $18,100
Superman #1 Apparent G/VG GD/VG (3.0) Extensive (P) $17,000
Superman #1 CGC 1.0 $22,000
Superman #9 FR/GD (1.5) $225
Superman #13 VF/NM (9.0) $6,572.50
Superman #27 NM+ (9.6) $14,340 Pennsylvania Double-c
Superman #28 NM+ (9.6) $14,340 Pennsylvania
Suspense Comics #1 VF+ (8.5) $9,560 Mile High
Suspense Comics #3 Apparent FN/VF FN/VF (7.0) Moderate (P) $6,076.58
Suspense Comics #3 CGC 1.5 $4,494
Tales From The Crypt #20 (#1) NM/MT (9.8) $7,767.50 Gaines File Copy
Target Comics #2 NM (9.4) $7,170 Mile High
Top-Notch Comics #4 NM- (9.2) $4,780 Mile High
Top-Notch Comics #5 NM (9.4) $7,111 Mile High
Top-Notch Comics #8 NM+ (9.6) $5,377.50 Mile High
Tough Kid Squad #1 VF+ (8.5) $6,572.50 Kansas City
USA Comics #1 VF/NM (9.0) $11,352.50 Larson
Walt Disney's Comics & Stories #2 VF (8.0) $13,145 File Copy
Walt Disney's Comics & Stories #29 NM- (9.2) $5,975
Walt Disney's Comics & Stories #31 VF+ (8.5) $3,585
Walt Disney's Comics & Stories #36 VF+ (8.5) $836.50
Witness #1 NM (9.4) $5,975 Vancouver
Wonder Woman #1 VF- (7.5) $13,145 Rockford

Amazing Fantasy #15 NM (9.4) $227,000 White Mountain
Amazing Fantasy #15 NM (9.4) $210,000
Amazing Fantasy #15 VF/NM (9.0) $60,000 Curator
Amazing Fantasy #15 GD (2.0) $1,673.00
Amazing Spider-Man #1 VF/NM (9.0) $34,000
Amazing Spider-Man #1 VF/NM (9.0) $30,000
Amazing Spider-Man #1 VF (8.0) $12,500
Amazing Spider-Man #2 NM+ (9.6) $72,000
Amazing Spider-Man #3 NM+ (9.6) $57,000
Amazing Spider-Man #4 FN/VF (7.0) $1,050
Amazing Spider-Man #6 NM+ (9.6) Curator $24,100
Amazing Spider-Man #7 VF/NM (9.0) $1,830
Amazing Spider-Man #7 VG+ (4.5) $205
Amazing Spider-Man #8 VF+ (8.5) $900
Amazing Spider-Man #9 NM (9.4) $7,550
Amazing Spider-Man #10 NM+ (9.6) Curator $12,500
Amazing Spider-Man #12 NM+ (9.6) Pacific Coast $16,500
Amazing Spider-Man #14 NM+ (9.6) Pacific Coast $37,500
Amazing Spider-Man #14 NM (9.4) $8,500
Amazing Spider-Man #18 NM+ (9.6) $4,558
Amazing Spider-Man #20 NM+ (9.6) $6,789
Amazing Spider-Man #21 NM+ (9.6) Pacific Coast $6,600
Amazing Spider-Man #23 NM+ (9.6) Pacific Coast $7,000
Amazing Spider-Man #26 NM+ (9.6) $5,700
Amazing Spider-Man #27 NM+ (9.6) Pacific Coast $6,000
Amazing Spider-Man #28 NM+ (9.6) Pacific Coast $15,000
Amazing Spider-Man #29 NM+ (9.6) Pacific Coast $3,250
Amazing Spider-Man #30 NM+ (9.6) Boston $3,400
Amazing Spider-Man #32 NM+ (9.6) Massachusetts $3,250
Amazing Spider-Man #36 NM (9.4) $1,700
Amazing Spider-Man #38 NM+ (9.6) Golden State $2,800
Amazing Spider-Man #40 NM+ (9.6) Pacific Coast $6,400
Amazing Spider-Man #39 NM+ (9.6) $5,334
Amazing Spider-Man #46 NM+ (9.6) $2,909
Amazing Spider-Man #49 NM+ (9.6) Northland $2,500
Amazing Spider-Man #51 NM+ (9.6) $2,750
Amazing Spider-Man #52 NM+ (9.6) $7,000
Amazing Spider-Man #55 NM+ (9.6) Hollywood Hills $1,800
Amazing Spider-Man #59 NM (9.4) $165
Avengers #3 NM+ (9.6) $4,900
Avengers #4 VF (8.0) $1200
Avengers #11 NM+ (9.6) Curator $3,300.
Brave and the Bold #28 VF/NM (9.0) $10,755
Brave and the Bold #28 VF+ (8.5) $5,258
Brave and the Bold #28 VF+ (8.5) $5,377.50
Challengers of the Unknown #1 NM (9.4) $8,977
Daredevil #7 NM- (9.2) $6,460
Fantastic Four #1 VF+ (8.5) $52,000
Fantastic Four #1 VF (8.0) $22,500
Fantastic Four #1 FN (6.0) $6,150
Fantastic Four #2 NM (9.4) $33,000

Fantastic Four #2 GD (2.0) $325
Fantastic Four #4 NM (9.4) $16,730
Fantastic Four #11 NM (9.4) $11,200
Fantastic Four #14 NM+ (9.6) $6,000
Fantastic Four #15 NM+ (9.6) $5,250
Fantastic Four #17 NM (9.4) $4,850
Fantastic Four #20 NM (9.4) $5,000
Fantastic Four #22 NM (9.4) $1,700
Fantastic Four #27 NM+ (9.6) $5650
Fantastic Four #29 NM (9.4) $2,800
Fantastic Four #30 NM (9.4) $1,250
Fantastic Four #32 NM (9.4) Massachusetts $1,325
Fantastic Four #34 NM (9.4) $900
Fantastic Four #44 NM+ (9.6) $900
Fantastic Four #48 NM+ (9.6) $3,800
Fantastic Four #48 NM+ (9.6) $3,600
Fantastic Four #48 NM+ (9.6) $3,450
Fantastic Four #50 NM (9.4) $6,600
Fantastic Four #53 NM+ (9.6) $1050
Fantastic Four #55 NM+ (9.6) $2,250
Fantastic Four #66 NM+ (9.6) Hollywood Hills $1400
Fantastic Four #67 NM (9.4) White Mountain $650
Fantastic Four #70 NM+ (9.6) $500
Fantastic Four #73 NM+ (9.6) Massachusetts $700
Fantastic Four #84 NM+ (9.6) $375
Fantastic Four #87 NM+ (9.6) $350
Fantastic Four #95 NM+ (9.6) $300
Flash #105 FN+ (6.5) $1,314.50
Flash #106 VF+ (8.5) $4,000
Flash #109 NM- (9.2) $6,000
Flash #109 VF/NM (9.0) $2,500
Flash #110 VF/NM (9.0) $8,962.50
Flash #111 VF+ (8.5) $1,300
Flash #113 VF/NM (9.0) $2,850
Flash #114 VF+ (8.5) $1,025
Flash #121 NM- (9.2) $4,500
Flash #124 NM- (9.2) Western Penn $1,700
Flash #131 NM+ (9.6) Pacific Coast $3,000
Flash #131 NM (9.4) Dallas Stephens $1,250
Flash #133 NM (9.4) $1,175
Flash #136 NM (9.4) Western Penn $1,750
Flash #138 NM (9.4) $800
Flash #140 NM (9.4) Pacific Coast $1,200
Flash #141 NM (9.4) Pacific Coast $1,100
Flash #142 NM+ (9.6) Pacific Coast $1,500
Flash #143 NM+ (9.6) Pacific Coast $2,200
Flash #144 NM (9.4) Western Penn $800
Flash #146 NM+ (9.6) Pacific Coast $1,650
Flash #147 NM+ (9.6) Pacific Coast $1,350
Flash #151 NM+ (9.6) $1,550
Flash #153 NM/MT (9.8) Pacific Coast $1,995

Flash #155 NM+ (9.6) $350

Flash #158 NM+ (9.6) $975

Flash #160 NM+ (9.6) $1,575

Flash #163 NM+ (9.6) $900

Flash #164 NM+ (9.6) $900

Flash #166 NM+ (9.6) Boston $900

Flash #169 NM+ (9.6) $1,000

Flash #171 NM/MT (9.8) Pacific Coast $1,500

Flash #173 NM+ (9.6) Pacific Coast $1,500

Flash #175 NM+ (9.6) $2,300

Flash #179 NM+ (9.6) $850

Flash #180 NM/MT (9.8) $1,100

Flash #181 NM+ (9.6) Massachusetts $650

Flash #187 NM+ (9.6) Pacific Coast $650

Flash #196 NM+ (9.6) $600

Flash #200 NM+ (9.6) $500

G.I. Combat #44 VF/NM (9.0) $2,629

G.I. Combat #68 VF- (7.5) $2,629

G.I. Combat #87 VF (8.0) $2,868

Green Lantern #1 VF+ (8.5) $4,182.50

Incredible Hulk #1 VF (8.0) $25,000

Incredible Hulk #1 FN+ (6.5) $5,850

Incredible Hulk #1 VG/FN (5.0) $3,250

Incredible Hulk #102 NM+ (9.6) $1,425

Journey Into Mystery #85 NM- (9.2) $6,000

Journey Into Mystery #86 NM+ (9.6) Massachusetts $9,500

Journey Into Mystery #88 NM (9.4) $5,100

Journey Into Mystery #91 NM- (9.2) $1,300

Journey Into Mystery #93 NM (9.4) Pacific Coast $3,200

Journey Into Mystery #96 NM+ (9.6) $2,600

Journey Into Mystery #96 NM (9.4) Massachusetts $2,000

Journey Into Mystery #99 NM+ (9.6) $3,000

Journey Into Mystery #100 NM (9.4) Massachusetts $2,000

Journey Into Mystery #100 NM (9.4) $1,900

Journey Into Mystery #101 NM (9.4) $1,400

Journey Into Mystery #102 NM (9.4) $1,550

Journey Into Mystery #104 NM+ (9.6) Massachusetts $4,250

Journey Into Mystery #104 NM (9.4) Northland $2,400

Journey Into Mystery #104 NM- (9.2) $1,050

Journey Into Mystery #105 NM (9.4) $1,100

Journey Into Mystery #106 NM (9.4) $1,800

Journey Into Mystery #111 NM (9.4) $1,600

Journey Into Mystery #112 NM+ (9.6) Massachusetts $14,500

Journey Into Mystery #112 NM+ (9.6)(Circle 8) $12,500

Nick Fury #1 NM/MT (9.8) $1,500

Our Army At War #81 FN (6.0) $1,195

Our Army At War #83 6.5 CGC $1,912

Sgt. Fury #1 NM (9.4) $21,500

Showcase #8 VF (8.0) $6,990.75

Showcase #14 VF+ (8.5) $3,927.88

Showcase #22 VF/NM (9.0) $20,250

Showcase #23 NM (9.4) $15,928

Silver Surfer #1 NM/MT (9.8) Boston $25,000

Silver Surfer #1 NM+ (9.6) $6,000

Silver Surfer #1 VF/NM (9.0) $750

Strange Tales #101 NM (9.4) $10,000

Strange Tales Annual #2 NM/MT (9.8) Pacific Coast $25,000

Sub-Mariner #8 NM- (9.2) $150

Superman #128 VF/NM (9.0) $2,629

Tales Of Suspense #39 NM- (9.2) $25,000

Tales of Suspense #39 VF- (7.5) $5,676.25

Tales Of Suspense #39 VG+ (4.5) $1,224.99

Tales Of Suspense #41 NM (9.4) $7,000

Tales Of Suspense #42 NM (9.4) $2,800

Tales Of Suspense #43 NM (9.4) $4,200

Tales Of Suspense #44 NM (9.4) $4,200

Tales Of Suspense #45 NM (9.4) $4,200

Tales Of Suspense #46 NM (9.4) $2,600

Tales Of Suspense #47 NM (9.4) Northland $2,700

Tales Of Suspense #49 NM (9.4) $3,300

Tales Of Suspense #52 NM (9.4) $4,000

Tales of Suspense #57 NM (9.4) $5,228.13

Tales Of Suspense #61 NM (9.4) $700

Tales Of Suspense #63 NM+ (9.6) $1,900

Tales Of Suspense #65 NM (9.4) $900

Tales Of Suspense #66 NM (9.4) $1,000

Tales To Astonish #27 NM- (9.2) $17,000

Tales To Astonish #35 GD+ (2.5) $150

Tales To Astonish #37 NM (9.4) $2,700

Tales To Astonish #38 NM (9.4) $2,300

Tales To Astonish #38 NM (9.4) $2,175

Tales To Astonish #39 NM+ (9.6) White Mountain $4,500

Tales To Astonish #39 NM (9.4) $1,900

Tales To Astonish #41 NM (9.4) $1,600

Tales To Astonish #41 NM- (9.2) $580

Tales To Astonish #42 NM (9.4) Western Penn $1,900

Tales To Astonish #43 NM (9.4) Massachusetts $2,750

Tales To Astonish #44 NM (9.4) $2,900

Tales To Astonish #45 NM (9.4) $1,300

Tales To Astonish #47 NM (9.4) Northland $1,250

Tales To Astonish #47 NM (9.4) $750

Tales To Astonish #48 NM (9.4) $1,200

Tales To Astonish #50 NM (9.4) $750

Tales To Astonish #51 NM (9.4) $650

Tales To Astonish #53 NM (9.4) $500

Tales To Astonish #54 NM (9.4) $500

Tales To Astonish #55 NM (9.4) Northland $500

Tales To Astonish #56 NM (9.4) $650

Tales To Astonish #57 NM+ (9.6) White Mountain $2,650

Tales To Astonish #57 NM+ (9.6) $2,750

Tales To Astonish #58 NM (9.4) Northland $900

X-Men #1 VF+ (8.5) $11,950

X-Men #1 FN/VF (7.0) $4,800

X-Men #4 NM (9.4) $6,500

X-Men #14 NM- (9.2) $1,200

Adventure Comics #433 NM+ (9.6) $80
Amazing Spider-Man #129 NM (9.4) $914
Amazing Spider-Man #234 NM/MT (9.8) $125
Amazing Spider-Man #234 NM/MT (9.8) $125
Astonishing Tales #27 NM+ (9.6) $75
Batman #234 NM+ (9.6) $1,199.99
Captain Marvel #48 NM/MT (9.8) $150
Cerebus #1 GD/VG (3.0) Sig. Series $396.77
Cerebus #5 NM/MT (9.8) Dave Sim File Copy Sig. Series $228.50
Cerebus #55 NM/MT (9.8) Dave Sim File Copy Sig. Series $224.50
Conan the Barbarian #1 NM (9.4) $600
Conan The Barbarian #15 NM+ (9.6) $170
Dark Shadows Story Digest Magazine #1 NM+ (9.6) $360
DC Comics Presents #26 NM+ (9.6) $129
DC Comics Presents #29 NM/MT (9.8) $51
DC Comics Presents #58 NM/MT (9.8) $51
DC Comics Presents #65 NM/MT (9.8) $51
DC Comics Presents #85 NM/MT (9.8) $51
DC Comics Presents #87 NM- (9.2) $50
Deadly Hands of Kung-Fu #1 NM (9.4) $150
Deadly Hands of Kung-Fu #28 VF/NM (9.0) $100
Flash #205 NM+ (9.6) $450
Flash #214 NM+ (9.6) $600
Flash #229 NM+ (9.6) $750
Flash #232 NM+ (9.6) $375
Flash #241 NM/MT (9.8) $200
Flash #275 NM/MT (9.8) $200
Flash #300 NM+ (9.6) $55
Freedom Fighters #8 NM+ (9.6) $50
Green Lantern #76 NM (9.4) $9,030
Green Lantern #76 NM (9.4) $8,365
Green Lantern #76 NM- (9.2) $2,031.50
Howard The Duck #13 NM/MT (9.8) $150
Incredible Hulk #181 NM/MT (9.8) $18,027
Invaders #14 NM+ (9.6) $55

Invaders #16 NM+ (9.6) $50
Invaders #24 NM+ (9.6) $55
Invaders #30 NM+ (9.6) $45
Invaders #37 NM+ (9.6) $59
Iron Fist #14 (35¢-c variant) VF+ (8.5) $1700
Jonah Hex (1977 series) #1 NM- (9.2) $100
Marvel Premiere #26 NM/MT (9.8) $150
Marvel Preview #3 NM (9.4) $60
Marvel Preview #10 NM (9.4) $55
Marvel Spotlight #24 NM+ (9.6) $50
Marvel Treasury #1 NM/MT (9.8) $280
Marvel Treasury #2 NM+ (9.6) $84
Marvel Treasury #3 NM+ (9.6) $84
Marvel Treasury #10 NM/MT (9.8) $112
Marvel Treasury #28 NM (9.4) $99
Marvel Two-In-One #54 NM+ (9.6) $83
Marvel Two-In-One #65 NM/MT (9.8) $76
Marvel Two-In-One #78 NM/MT (9.8) $50
Marvel Two-In-One #84 NM/MT (9.8) $70
Moon Knight #27 NM/MT (9.8) $45
Primer #2 NM- (9.2) $200
Rampaging Hulk #1 NM (9.4) $75
Richie Rich & Timmy Time #1 NM+ (9.6) $60
Savage Tales #1 VF/NM(9.0) $295
Scream #11 NM- (9.2) $110
Spider-Woman #2 NM/MT (9.8) $50
Spider-Woman #4 NM/MT (9.8) $50
Spider-Woman #7 NM/MT (9.8) $50
Spider-Woman #16 NM/MT (9.8) $50
Tales of the Zombie #1 NM-(9.2) $100
Thor #333 NM/MT (9.8) $50
Thor #337 NM/MT (9.8) $60
Tomb Of Dracula #19 NM+ (9.6) $115
Tomb Of Dracula #19 NM/MT (9.8) $275
Vampirella #112 NM- (9.2) $175
X-Men #94 NM+ (9.6) $5,860.80
X-Men #97 NM/MT (9.8) $3,505

Amazing Spider-Man #260 NM/MT (9.8) $200
Amazing Spider-Man #260 NM/MT (9.8) $200
Amazing Spider-Man #282 NM/MT (9.8) $65
Amazing Spider-Man #282 NM/MT (9.8) $65
Amazing Spider-Man #297 NM/MT (9.8) $55
Amazing Spider-Man #300 NM+ (9.6) $328
Amazing Spider-Man #303 NM/MT (9.8) $140
Amazing Spider-Man #303 NM/MT (9.8) $140
Amazing Spider-Man #312 NM/MT (9.8) $120
Amazing Spider-Man #312 NM/MT (9.8) $120
Amazing Spider-Man #316 NM/MT (9.8) $195
Amazing Spider-Man #316 NM/MT (9.8) $195

Amazing Spider-Man #320 NM/MT (9.8) $65
G.I. Joe, A Real American Hero #21 NM/MT (9.8) $860
G.I. Joe A Real American Hero #85 NM/MT (9.8) $46
Incredible Hulk #340 NM/MT (9.8) $265
Infinity Gauntlet #1 NM/MT (9.8) $50
Marvel Super-Heroes Secret Wars #8 NM/MT (9.8) $120
Marvel Super-Heroes Secret Wars #8 NM (9.4) $60
Miracleman #1 NM/MT (9.8) $100
Punisher (mini) #1 NM+ (9.6) $99.75
Sandman #8 NM/MT (9.8) $227
Spider-Man #1 NM/MT (9.8) Gold Ed. $100
Star Trek #16 NM/MT (9.8) $50

Superman #423 NM (9.4) $30
Superman (2nd) #1 NM/MT (9.8) $105
Superman #1 NM/MT (9.8) $125
Swamp Thing #20 NM+ (9.6) $90
Tales of the New Teen Titans #44 NM+ (9.6) $36
Teenage Mutant Ninja Turtles #1 NM- (9.2) $2,500
Transformers #1 NM/MT (9.8) $450
Transformers #1 NM/MT (9.8) $350
Transformers #1 NM+ (9.6) $160
Transformers #1 NM+ (9.6) $100
Transformers #1 NM+ (9.6) $175
Transformers #4 NM/MT (9.8) $150

Transformers #8 NM/MT (9.8) $150
Transformers #11 NM/MT (9.8) $95
Transformers #12 NM/MT (9.8) $100
Transformers #14 NM/MT (9.8) $130
Uncanny X-Men #205 NM/MT (9.8) $100
Uncanny X-Men #205 NM/MT (9.8) $100
Uncanny X-Men #244 NM+ (9.6) $50
Unknown Soldier #268 NM (9.4) $50
V For Vendetta #1 NM/MT (9.8) $82
V For Vendetta #1 NM/MT (9.8) $92
Weird War #64 NM- (9.2) $75
X-Factor #1 NM/MT (9.8) $75

MODERN AGE - SALES OF CGC-CERTIFIED COMICS

All Star Batman and Robin #1 NM+ (9.6) RRP $200
All Star Batman and Robin #1 NM/MT (9.8) RRP $350
All Star Batman and Robin #2 NM/MT (9.8) Lee-c $52
All Star Batman and Robin #2 NM/MT (9.8) Lee-c $70
All Star Batman and Robin #3 NM/MT (9.8) Sig. Series $70
All Star Batman and Robin #3 NM/MT (9.8) Sig. Series $90
Amazing Spider-Man #361 NM/MT (9.8) $150
Amazing Spider-Man #362 NM/MT (9.8) $55
Army of Darkness Vs. Marvel Zombies #1 (DF variant)
NM/MT (9.8) $99.95
Batman #608 (RRP) NM+ (9.6) $800
Captain America #25 WWLA 2007 NM/MT (9.8) Sig. Series
$218.50
Civil War #1 NM+ (9.6) Sketch-c $200
Civil War #1 NM/MT (9.8) Aspen Var. Signed Turner $125
Civil War #1 NM/MT (9.8) Aspen Var. Signed Turner $160
Civil War #1 NM/MT (9.8) Sketch Cover $200
Civil War #1 NM/MT (9.8) Turner Variant $77
Civil War #2 NM/MT (9.8) Spider-Man Turner Variant $112
Civil War #3 NM/MT (9.8) Signed Turner Variant $150
Civil War: X-Men #1 NM/MT (9.8) Signed Turner Var. $135
Conan #1 NM/MT (9.8) $90
Conan #1 NM/MT (9.8) Linsner Cover $150
Conan #1 NM/MT (9.8) Linsner Cover $90
Conan #24 NM/MT (9.8) Variant Cover $92
Conan #24 NM/MT (9.8) Variant Cover $95
Flash #92 NM/MT (9.8) $160
Flash: Fastest Man Alive #1 NM/MT (9.8) Variant Cover $80
Friday The 13th #1 NM/MT (9.8) Variant Cover $60
Friendly Neighborhood Spider-Man #1 NM/MT (9.8) $72
Futurama #1 NM/MT (9.8) $70
G.I. Joe: Special #1 NM- (9.2) $100
Green Lantern #5 MT (9.9) $112
Heroes #1 NM/MT (9.8) NBC Studios Wizard Edition $215
Incredible Hulk #100 NM/MT (9.8) Turner Signed Var. $80
Incredible Hulk #100 NM/MT (9.8) Turner Signed Var. $90
Incredible Hulk #100 NM/MT (9.8) Turner Signed Var. $140
Incredible Hulk #100 NM/MT (9.8) Var. Gray Turner-c $250
JSA Classified #1 GM (10.0) Sketch Cover $225

JSA Classified #1 NM/MT (9.8) Hughes-c $90
Justice #7 MT (9.9) $200
Justice #7 MT (9.9) $150
Justice League Of America #1 NM/MT (9.8) Variant $80
Justice League Of America #1 NM/MT (9.8) Variant $75
Marvel Zombies #1 NM+ (9.6) Sig. Series $150
Marvel Zombies #1 NM+ (9.6) Signed Suydam $120
Marvel Zombies #1 NM+ (9.6) Signed Suydam $150
Marvel Zombies #3 NM/MT (9.8) (Hulk #340-c) $50
Moon Knight #1 NM/MT (9.8) Finch Signed Sketch-c $70
Mouse Guard #1 NM/MT (9.8) $250
NYX #3 NM/MT (9.8) $125
Radioactive Man #1000 NM/MT (9.8) $60
Red Sonja #1 NM/MT (9.8) Signed Turner $60
Secret War #1 MT (9.9) $150
Simpsons Comics #1 NM/MT (9.8) $120
Simpsons Comics #1 NM/MT (9.8) $125
Spawn #1 NM/MT (9.8) $60
Spider-Man/Black Cat: Evil That Men Do #4 MT (9.9) $52
Superman #202 MT (9.9) $52
Superman/Batman #9 NM/MT (9.8) Signed Turner $60
Superman Returns Prequel #1 NM/MT (9.8) $60
Thunderbolts #1 NM/MT (9.8) $70
Ultimate Fantastic Four #3 MT (9.9) $75
Ultimate Fantastic Four #22 NM/MT (9.8) $110
Ultimates #5 NM/MT (9.8) $100
Ultimate Wolverine Vs. Hulk #1 MT (9.9) $225
Ultimate Wolverine Vs. Hulk #1 NM+ (9.6) Ltd Sketch $120
Ultimate Wolverine Vs. Hulk #1 NM+ (9.6) Ltd Sketch $100
Ultimate Wolverine Vs. Hulk #1 NM/MT (9.8) Signed $75
Ultimate Wolverine Vs. Hulk #2 NM/MT (9.8) Sketch $95
Walking Dead #32 MT (9.9) $110
Walking Dead #32 MT (9.9) $150
Walking Dead #34 MT (9.9) $105
Walking Dead #34 MT (9.9) $110
Wolverine #1/2 MT (9.9) Wizard $102
Wolverine: Origins #2 NM/MT (9.8) Canada Variant $160
Wolverine: Origins #3 NM/MT (9.8) Hidden Text Var. $70
X-O Manowar #1 NM/MT (9.8) $80

Top Books

The following tables denote the rate of appreciation of the top Golden Age, Platinum Age, Silver Age and Bronze Age books, as well as selected genres over the past year. The retail value for a Near Mint- copy of each book (or VF where a Near Mint- copy is not known to exist) in 2008 is compared to its Near Mint- value in 2007. The rate of return for 2008 over 2007 is given. The place in rank is given for each comic by year, with its corresponding value in highest known grade. These tables can be very useful in forecasting trends in the market place. For instance, the investor might want to know which book is yielding the best dividend from one year to the next, or one might just be interested in seeing how the popularity of books changes from year to year. For instance, *All Star Comics* #8 was in 22nd place in 2007 and has increased to 19th place in 2008. Premium books are also included in these tables and are denoted with an asterisk(*).

The following tables are meant as a guide to the investor. However, it should be pointed out that trends may change at anytime and that some books can meet market resistance with a slowdown in price increases, while others can develop into real comers from a presently dormant state. In the long run, if the investor sticks to the books that are appreciating steadily each year, he shouldn't go very far wrong.

Top 100 Golden Age Books

TITLE/ISSUE#	2008 RANK	2008 NM- PRICE	2007 RANK	2007 NM- PRICE	$ INCR.	% INCR.
Action Comics #1	1	$675,000	1	$600,000	$75,000	13%
Detective Comics #27	2	$525,000	2	$485,000	$40,000	8%
Marvel Comics #1	3	$440,000	3	$420,000	$20,000	5%
Superman #1	4	$400,000	4	$360,000	$40,000	11%
All -American Comics #16	5	$245,000	5	$220,000	$25,000	11%
Batman #1	6	$185,000	6	$165,000	$20,000	12%
Captain America Comics #1	7	$175,000	7	$160,000	$15,000	9%
Flash Comics #1	8	$130,000	8	$125,000	$5,000	4%
More Fun Comics #52	9	$115,000	9	$105,000	$10,000	10%
Adventure Comics #40	10	$95,000	11	$85,000	$10,000	12%
Whiz Comics #2 (#1)	10	$95,000	10	$92,000	$3,000	3%
Detective Comics #33	12	$80,000	12	$75,000	$5,000	7%
All Star Comics #3	13	$75,000	13	$70,000	$5,000	7%
Detective Comics #38	13	$75,000	13	$70,000	$5,000	7%
Detective Comics #31	15	$70,000	16	$62,000	$8,000	13%
Detective Comics #1	16	VF $68,000	15	VF $64,000	$4,000	6%
Action Comics #2	17	$66,000	17	$60,000	$6,000	10%
Detective Comics #29	17	$66,000	17	$60,000	$6,000	10%
All Star Comics #8	19	$60,000	22	$56,000	$4,000	7%
Green Lantern #1	19	$60,000	19	$59,000	$1,000	2%
Human Torch #2 (#1)	19	$60,000	20	$58,000	$2,000	3%
More Fun Comics #53	19	$60,000	23	$54,000	$6,000	11%
Sensation Comics #1	19	$60,000	23	$54,000	$6,000	11%
Sub-Mariner Comics #1	19	$60,000	20	$58,000	$2,000	3%
Action Comics #7	25	$57,000	25	$50,000	$7,000	14%
Marvel Mystery Comics #2	26	$55,000	25	$50,000	$5,000	10%
Marvel Mystery Comics #9	27	$52,000	28	$47,500	$4,500	9%
Captain Marvel Adventures #1	28	$50,000	27	$48,000	$2,000	4%
New Fun Comics #1	29	VF $49,000	28	VF 47,500	$1,500	3%
Adventure Comics #48	30	$47,500	30	$44,000	$3,500	8%
Wonder Woman #1	31	$47,000	30	$44,000	$3,000	7%
Marvel Mystery Comics #5	32	$46,000	32	$42,000	$4,000	10%
Action Comics #3	33	$44,000	33	$40,000	$4,000	10%
All Winners Comics #1	34	$40,000	33	$40,000	$0	0%
Detective Comics #28	34	$40,000	35	$36,000	$4,000	11%
Action Comics #10	36	$36,000	37	$32,000	$4,000	13%
Daring Mystery Comics #1	36	$36,000	36	$35,000	$1,000	3%
Archie Comics #1	38	$34,200	45	$27,500	$6,700	24%
Pep Comics #22	39	$33,000	45	$27,500	$5,500	20%
Walt Disney's Comics & Stories #1	39	$33,000	39	$30,000	$3,000	10%

TITLE/ISSUE#	2008 RANK	2008 NM- PRICE	2007 RANK	2007 NM- PRICE	$ INCR.	% INCR.
All-American Comics #19	41	$31,000	42	$28,000	$3,000	11%
New York World's Fair 1939	41 VF/NM	$31,000	38 VF/NM	$31,000	$0	0%
Marvel Mystery Comics #3	43	$30,000	45	$27,500	$2,500	9%
*Marvel Mystery Comics 132 pg.	43 VF	$30,000	42VF	$28,000	$2,000	7%
Suspense Comics #3	43	$30,000	51	$25,000	$5,000	20%
Famous Funnies-Series 1 #1	46 VF	$29,000	40 VF	$29,000	$0	0%
*Motion Picture Funn. Wkly #1	46	$29,000	42	$28,000	$1,000	4%
New Book of Comics #1	46 VF	$29,000	41 VF	$28,500	$500	2%
Captain AmericaCom132 pg.	49 VF	$28,000	48 VF	$26,000	$2,000	8%
Amazing Man Comics #5	50	$27,000	48	$26,000	$1,000	4%
Batman #2	50	$27,000	51	$25,000	$2,000	8%
Captain America Comics #2	50	$27,000	51	$25,000	$2,000	8%
More Fun Comics #55	50	$27,000	58	$24,500	$2,500	10%
Superman #2	50	$27,000	60	$24,000	$3,000	13%
All Flash #1	55	$26,500	48	$26,000	$500	2%
All-American Comics #17	56	$26,000	51	$25,000	$1,000	4%
More Fun Comics #54	56	$26,000	64	$23,000	$3,000	13%
More Fun Comics #73	56	$26,000	60	$24,000	$2,000	8%
Wonder Comics #1	56	$26,000	51	$25,000	$1,000	4%
Wow Comics (FAW) #1	56	$26,000	60	$24,000	$2,000	8%
Mystic Comics #1	61	$25,500	58	$24,500	$1,000	4%
Young Allies Comics #1	61	$25,500	51	$25,000	$500	2%
Action Comics #4	63	$25,000	64	$23,000	$2,000	9%
Action Comics #5	63	$25,000	64	$23,000	$2,000	9%
Action Comics #6	63	$25,000	64	$23,000	$2,000	9%
*Century of Comics	63 VF	$25,000	51 VF	$25,000	$0	0%
Adventure Comics #73	67	$24,000	64	$23,000	$1,000	4%
All-Select Comics #1	67	$24,000	70	$22,500	$1,500	7%
Detective Comics #35	67	$24,000	74	$21,500	$2,500	12%
Marvel Mystery Comics #4	67	$24,000	74	$21,500	$2,500	12%
Silver Streak Comics #6	67	$24,000	64	$23,000	$1,000	4%
World's Best Comics #1	67	$24,000	60	$24,000	$0	0%
New Fun Comics #6	73 VF	$23,000	72 VF	$22,000	$1,000	5%
Daredevil Comics #1	74	$22,500	70	$22,500	$0	0%
Adventure Comics #61	75	$22,000	80	$21,000	$1,000	5%
All Star Comics #1	75	$22,000	74	$21,500	$500	2%
Captain America Comics #3	75	$22,000	80	$20,000	$2,000	10%
Famous Funnies #1	75 VF	$22,000	72 VF	$22,000	$0	0%
Planet Comics #1	75	$22,000	80	$21,000	$1,000	5%
Red Raven Comics #1	75	$22,000	74	$21,500	$500	2%
USA Comics #1	75	$22,000	74	$21,500	$500	2%
Four Color Ser. 1 (Donald Duck) #4	82	$21,500	84	$19,000	$2,500	13%
Jumbo Comics #1	82 VF	$21,500	74 VF	$21,500	$0	0%
New Fun Comics #2	84 VF	$21,000	80 VF	$20,000	$1,000	5%
Looney Tunes and Merrie Melodies #1	85	$20,000	84	$19,000	$1,000	5%
Marvel Mystery Comics #8	85	$20,000	87	$18,500	$1,500	8%
Adventure Comics #72	87	$19,000	84	$19,000	$0	0%
Detective Comics #2	87 VF	$19,000	91 VF	$17,600	$1,400	8%
Green Giant Comics #1	87	$19,000	87	$18,500	$500	3%
New Comics #1	87 VF	$19,000	87 VF	$18,500	$500	3%
All-American Comics #18	91	$18,500	95	$17,000	$1,500	9%
Double Action Comics #2	91	$18,500	87	$18,500	$0	0%
Action Comics #13	93	$18,000	100	$16,000	$2,000	13%
Daring Mystery Comics #2	93	$18,000	92	$17,500	$500	3%
Mickey Mouse Magazine #1 (1935)	93 VF/NM	$18,000	92 VF/NM	$17,500	$500	3%
Silver Streak Comics #1	93	$18,000	94	$17,300	$700	4%
Mystery Men Comics #1	97	$17,500	95	$17,000	$500	3%
All-American Comics #25	98	$17,000	100	$16,000	$1,000	6%
Four Color Ser. 2 (Donald Duck) #9	98	$17,000	100	$16,000	$1,000	6%
Pep Comics #1	98	$17,000	98	$16,500	$500	3%

Top 20 Silver Age Books

TITLE/ISSUE#	2008 RANK	2008 NM- PRICE	2007 RANK	2007 NM- PRICE	$ INCR.	% INCR.
Amazing Fantasy #15	1	$50,000	1	$44,000	$6,000	14%
Showcase #4 (The Flash)	2	$45,000	2	$43,000	$2,000	5%
Fantastic Four #1	3	$41,000	3	$37,000	$4,000	11%
Amazing Spider-Man #1	4	$40,000	4	$34,000	$6,000	18%
Incredible Hulk #1	5	$32,000	5	$28,500	$3,500	12%
X-Men #1	6	$19,000	7	$16,500	$2,500	15%
Showcase #8 (The Flash)	7	$18,000	6	$18,000	$0	0%
Journey Into Mystery #83 (Thor)	8	$15,000	8	$12,500	$2,500	20%
Showcase #9 (Lois Lane)	9	$13,000	9	$11,700	$1,300	11%
The Flash #105	10	$12,500	10	$10,500	$2,000	19%
Tales of Suspense #39 (Iron Man)	10	$12,500	10	$10,500	$2,000	19%
Brave and the Bold #28	12	$11,500	10	$10,500	$1,000	10%
Adventure Comics #247 (Legion)	13	$10,000	14	$9,000	$1,000	11%
Justice League of America #1	13	$10,000	13	$9,200	$800	9%
Showcase #22 (Green Lantern)	15	$9,300	15	$8,700	$600	7%
Fantastic Four #5	16	$9,200	16	$8,400	$800	10%
Tales To Astonish #27 (Ant-Man)	16	$9,200	19	$8,200	$1,000	12%
Fantastic Four #2	18	$9,000	17	$8,300	$700	8%
Green Lantern #1	19	$8,700	17	$8,300	$400	5%
Amazing Spider-Man #2	20	$8,500	21	$7,800	$700	9%

Top 10 Bronze Age Books

TITLE/ISSUE#	2008 RANK	2008 NM- PRICE	2007 RANK	2007 NM- PRICE	$ INCR.	% INCR.
Star Wars #1 (35¢ price variant)	1	$2,000	1	$1,700	$300	18%
Incredible Hulk #181	2	$1,450	2	$1,400	$50	4%
Giant-Size X-Men #1	3	$1,200	3	$1,175	$25	2%
Iron Fist #14 (35¢ price variant)	3	$1,200	5	$950	$250	26%
X-Men #94	5	$1,150	4	$1,080	$70	6%
House of Secrets #92	6	$1,000	5	$950	$50	5%
DC 100 Page Super Spectacular #5	7	$925	7	$850	$75	9%
Cerebus #1	8	$900	8	$750	$150	20%
Uncle Scrooge #179 (Whitman)	9	$725	10	$675	$50	7%
All-Star Western #10	10	$700	9	$700	$0	0%
Amazing Spider-Man #129	10	$700	10	$625	$75	12%
Green Lantern #76	10	$700	10	$550	$150	27%

Top 10 Copper Age Books

TITLE/ISSUE#	2008 RANK	2008 NM- PRICE	2007 RANK	2007 NM- PRICE	$ INCR.	% INCR.
Miracleman #1 Gold Edition	1	$1,500	1	$1,500	$0	0%
Gobbledygook #1	2	$1,000	2	$950	$50	5%
Miracleman #1 Blue Edition	3	$800	3	$800	$0	0%
Gobbledygook #2	4	$650	4	$600	$50	8%
Albedo #2	5	$550	6	$450	$100	22%
Vampirella #113	6	$485	5	$475	$10	2%
Grendel #1	7	$175	7	$170	$5	3%
Primer #2	8	$130	8	$130	$0	0%
Spider-Man #1 (Platinum)	9	$130	9	$130	$0	0%
Spider-Man #1 (2nd pr. w/Gold UPC)	10	$120	10	$120	$0	0%

*Teenage Mutant Ninja Turtles #1 - Recent sales of this book include a CGC 9.2 for $1,713

Top 20 Big Little Books

BOOK #	TITLE	2008 RANK	2008 VF/NM PRICE	2007 RANK	2007 VF/NM PRICE	$ INCR.	% INCR.
731	Mickey Mouse the Mail Pilot						
	(variant version of Mickey Mouse #717) (Fine copy sold at auction for $5,090)						
nn	Mickey Mouse and Minnie Mouse at Macy's	2	$3,200	2	$3,150	$50	2%
717	Mickey Mouse (skinny Mickey on-c)	3	$2,850	3	$2,730	$120	4%
nn	Mickey Mouse and Minnie March to Macy's	4	$2,200	4	$2,150	$50	2%
W-707	Dick Tracy The Detective	5	$2,100	5	$2,000	$100	5%
725	Big Little Mother Goose HC	6	$1,850	6	$1,825	$25	1%
717	Mickey Mouse (reg. Mickey on-c)	7	$1,500	8	$1,400	$100	7%
4063	Popeye Thimble Theater Starring... (2nd printing)	8	$1,470	7	$1,470	$0	0%
721	Big Little Paint Book	9	$1,400	9	$1,350	$50	4%
725	Big Little Mother Goose SC	10	$1,350	10	$1,300	$50	4%
nn	Mickey Mouse (Great Big Midget Book)	10	$1,350	11	$1,260	$90	7%
4062	Mickey Mouse and the Smugglers	12	$1,300	14	$1,200	$100	8%
2070	Big Big Paint Book	13	$1,275	11	$1,260	$15	1%
4063	Popeye Thimble Theater Starring...(1st pr.)	14	$1,260	11	$1,260	$0	0%
nn	Buck Rogers	15	$1,200	15	$1,050	$150	14%
nn	Mickey Mouse Silly Symphonies	15	$1,200	15	$1,050	$150	14%
4062	Mickey Mouse, The Story of...	17	$1,100	15	$1,050	$50	5%
nn	Mickey Mouse Sails For Treasure Island (Great Big Midget Book)	18	$1,050	15	$1,050	$0	0%
nn	Tarzan	19	$980	19	$970	$10	1%
4057	Buck Rogers, The Adventures of...	20	$975	20	$950	$25	3%

Top 10 Platinum Age Books

TITLE/ISSUE#	2008 RANK	2008 PRICE	2007 RANK	2007 PRICE	$ INCR.	% INCR.
Yellow Kid in McFadden Flats	1	FN $13,000	1	FN $12,000	$1,000	8%
Mickey Mouse Book (2nd printing)-variant	2	FN $12,000	1	FN $12,000	$0	0%
Mickey Mouse Book (1st printing)	2	VF $12,000	1	VF $12,000	$0	0%
Mickey Mouse Book (2nd printing)	4	VF $10,000	4	VF $10,000	$0	0%
Buster Brown and His Resolutions 1903	5	FN $5,500	5	FN $5,500	$0	0%
Pore Li'l Mose	5	FN $5,500	5	FN $5,500	$0	0%
Little Sammy Sneeze	7	FN $5,000	7	FN $4,800	$200	4%
Little Nemo 1906	8	FN $4,500	8	FN $4,000	$500	13%
Little Nemo 1909	9	FN $3,500	10	FN $3,000	$500	17%
Yellow Kid #1	9	FN $3,500	9	FN $3,300	$200	6%

Top 10 Crime Books

TITLE/ISSUE#	2008 RANK	2008 NM- PRICE	2007 RANK	2007 NM- PRICE	$ INCR.	% INCR.
Crime Does Not Pay #22	1	$4,500	1	$4,000	$500	13%
Crime Does Not Pay #23	2	$2,400	3	$2,000	$400	20%
True Crime Comics #2	3	$2,300	2	$2,100	$200	10%
Crime Does Not Pay #24	4	$2,000	5	$1,550	$450	29%
Crimes By Women #1	5	$1,750	4	$1,700	$50	3%
The Killers #1	6	$1,650	6	$1,540	$110	7%
True Crime Comics #3	6	$1,650	7	$1,525	$125	8%
True Crime Comics #4	8	$1,425	8	$1,325	$100	8%
The Killers #2	9	$1,350	9	$1,260	$90	7%
True Crime Comics V2 #1	10	$1,300	10	$1,200	$100	8%

Top 10 Horror Books

TITLE/ISSUE#	2008 RANK	2008 NM- PRICE	2007 RANK	2007 NM- PRICE	$ INCR.	% INCR.
Vault of Horror #12 1		$8,000	1	$7,700	$300	4%
Eerie #1 2		$7,300	2	$6,800	$500	7%
Tales of Terror Annual #1 3		VF $5,200	3	VF $5,000	$200	4%
Journey into Mystery #1 4		$5,000	4	$4,800	$200	4%
Crypt of Terror #17 5		$4,800	5	$4,600	$200	4%
Strange Tales #1 5		$4,800	5	$4,600	$200	4%
Haunt of Fear #15 7		$4,750	5	$4,600	$150	3%
Crime Patrol #15 8		$4,400	8	$4,200	$200	5%
House of Mystery #1 9		$3,500	9	$3,400	$100	3%
Tales to Astonish #1 10		$3,300	10	$3,000	$300	10%

Top 10 Romance Books

TITLE/ISSUE#	2008 RANK	2008 NM- PRICE	2007 RANK	2007 NM- PRICE	$ INCR.	% INCR.
Giant Comics Edition #12 1		$2,500	1	$1,850	$650	35%
Intimate Confessions #1 2		$1,250	2	$1,100	$150	14%
A Moon, A Girl...Romance #9 3		$1,100	3	$1,010	$90	9%
A Moon, A Girl...Romance #12 3		$1,100	3	$1,010	$90	9%
Modern Love #1 5		$1,075	5	$1,000	$75	8%
Giant Comics Edition #9 6		$950	9	$800	$150	19%
DC 100 Page Super Spectacular #5 .7		$925	6	$850	$75	9%
Giant Comics Edition #15 8		$900	9	$800	$100	13%
A Moon, A Girl...Romance #10 8		$900	7	$820	$80	10%
A Moon, A Girl...Romance #11 8		$900	7	$820	$80	10%

Top 10 Sci-Fi Books

TITLE/ISSUE#	2008 RANK	2008 NM- PRICE	2007 RANK	2007 NM- PRICE	$ INCR.	% INCR.
Mystery In Space #1 1		$5,700	1	$5,500	$200	4%
Strange Adventures #1 2		$5,400	2	$5,250	$150	3%
Showcase #17 (Adam Strange) 3		$4,400	3	$4,200	$200	5%
Journey Into Unknown Worlds #36 . .4		$3,700	4	$3,600	$100	3%
Weird Science-Fantasy Annual 1952 .4		$3,700	6	$3,400	$300	9%
Showcase #15 (Space Ranger) 6		$3,600	5	$3,450	$150	4%
Fawcett Movie #15 (Man From Planet X) .7		$3,500	7	$3,300	$200	6%
Weird Fantasy #13 (#1) 8		$3,350	8	$3,215	$135	4%
Weird Science #12 (#1) 8		$3,350	8	$3,215	$135	4%
Strange Adventures #9 10		$3,250	10	$3,200	$50	2%

Top 10 Western Books

TITLE/ISSUE#	2008 RANK	2008 NM- PRICE	2007 RANK	2007 NM- PRICE	$ INCR.	% INCR.
Gene Autry Comics #1 1		$12,000	1	$13,500	-$1,500	-11%
Hopalong Cassidy #1 2		$8,300	2	$8,200	$100	1%
*Lone Ranger Ice Cream 1939 2nd . .3		VF $7,000	3	VF $7,300	-$300	-4%
*Lone Ranger Ice Cream 1939 4		VF $6,400	4	VF $6,800	-$400	-6%
*Red Ryder Victory Patrol '42 5		$4,800	5	$5,300	-$500	-9%
*Red Ryder Victory Patrol '43 6		$4,400	6	$4,900	-$500	-10%
*Red Ryder Victory Patrol '44 6		$4,400	6	$4,900	-$500	-10%
Red Ryder Comics #1 8		$4,000	8	$4,500	-$500	-11%
Roy Rogers Four Color #38 8		$4,000	10	$4,000	$0	0%
*Tom Mix Ralston #1 8		$4,000	9	$4,300	-$300	-7%

Grading Definitions

10.0 GEM MINT (GM): This is an exceptional example of a given book - the best ever seen. The slightest bindery defects and/or printing flaws may be seen only upon very close inspection. The overall look is "as if it has never been handled or released for purchase." Only the slightest bindery or printing defects are allowed, and these would be imperceptible on first viewing. No bindery tears. Cover is flat with no surface wear. Inks are bright with high reflectivity. Well centered and firmly secured to interior pages. Corners are cut square and sharp. No creases. No dates or stamped markings allowed. No soiling, staining or other discoloration. Spine is tight and flat. No spine roll or split allowed. Staples must be original, centered and clean with no rust. No staple tears or stress lines. Paper is white, supple and fresh. No hint of acidity in the odor of the newsprint. No interior autographs or owner signatures. Centerfold is firmly secure. No interior tears.

9.9 MINT (MT): Near perfect in every way. Only subtle bindery or printing defects are allowed. No bindery tears. Cover is flat with no surface wear. Inks are bright with high reflectivity. Generally well centered and firmly secured to interior pages. Corners are cut square and sharp. No creases. Small, inconspicuous, lightly penciled, stamped or inked arrival dates are acceptable as long as they are in an unobtrusive location. No soiling, staining or other discoloration. Spine is tight and flat. No spine roll or split allowed. Staples must be original, generally centered and clean with no rust. No staple tears or stress lines. Paper is white, supple and fresh. No hint of acidity in the odor of the newsprint. Centerfold is firmly secure. No interior tears.

9.8 NEAR MINT/MINT (NM/MT): Nearly perfect in every way with only minor imperfections that keep it from the next higher grade. Only subtle bindery or printing defects are allowed. No bindery tears. Cover is flat with no surface wear. Inks are bright with high reflectivity. Generally well centered and firmly secured to interior pages. Corners are cut square and sharp. No creases. Small, inconspicuous, lightly penciled, stamped or inked arrival dates are acceptable as long as they are in an unobtrusive location. No soiling, staining or other discoloration. Spine is tight and flat. No spine roll or split allowed. Staples must be original, generally centered and clean with no rust. No staple tears or stress lines. Paper is off-white to white, supple and fresh. No hint of acidity in the odor of the newsprint. Centerfold is firmly secure. Only the slightest interior tears are allowed.

9.6 NEAR MINT+ (NM+): Nearly perfect with a minor additional virtue or virtues that raise it from Near Mint. The overall look is "as if it was just purchased and read once or twice." Only subtle bindery or printing defects are allowed. No bindery tears are allowed, although on Golden Age books bindery tears of up to 1/8" have been noted. Cover is flat with no surface wear. Inks are bright with high reflectivity. Well centered and firmly secured to interior pages. One corner may be almost imperceptibly blunted, but still almost sharp and cut square. Almost imperceptible indentations are permissible, but no creases, bends, or color break. Small, inconspicuous, lightly penciled, stamped or inked arrival dates are acceptable as long as they are in an unobtrusive location. No soiling, staining or other discoloration. Spine is tight and flat. No spine roll or split allowed. Staples must be original, generally centered, with only the slightest discoloration. No staple tears, stress lines, or rust migration. Paper is off-white, supple and fresh. No hint of acidity in the odor of the newsprint. Centerfold is firmly secure. Only the slightest interior tears are allowed.

9.4 NEAR MINT (NM): Nearly perfect with only minor imperfections that keep it from the next higher grade. The overall look is "as if it was just purchased and read once or twice." Subtle bindery defects are allowed. Bindery tears must be less than 1/16" on Silver Age and later books, although on Golden Age books bindery tears of up to 1/4" have been noted. Cover is flat with no surface wear. Inks are bright with high reflectivity. Generally well centered and secured to interior pages. Corners are cut square and sharp with ever-so-slight blunting permitted. A 1/16" bend is permitted with no color break. No creases. Small, inconspicuous, lightly penciled, stamped or inked arrival dates are acceptable as long as they are in an unobtrusive location. No soiling, staining or other discoloration apart from slight foxing. Spine is tight and flat. No spine roll or split allowed. Staples are generally centered; may have slight discoloration. No staple tears are allowed; almost no stress lines. No rust migration. In rare cases, a comic was not stapled at the bindery and therefore has a missing staple; this is not considered a defect. Any staple can be replaced on books up to Fine, but only vintage staples can be used on books from Very Fine to Near Mint. Mint books must have original staples. Paper is cream to off-white, supple and fresh. No hint of acidity in the odor of the newsprint. Centerfold is secure. Slight interior tears are allowed.

9.2 NEAR MINT– (NM–): Nearly perfect with only a minor additional defect or defects that keep it from Near Mint. A limited number of minor bindery defects are allowed. Cover is flat with no surface wear. Inks are bright with only the slightest dimming of reflectivity. Generally well centered and secured to interior pages. Corners are cut square and sharp with ever-so-slight blunting permitted. A 1/16"-1/8" bend is permitted with no color break. No creases. Small, inconspicuous, lightly penciled, stamped or inked arrival dates are acceptable as long as they are in an unobtrusive location. No soiling, staining or other discoloration apart from slight foxing. Spine is tight and flat. No spine roll or split allowed. Staples may show some discoloration. No staple tears are allowed; almost no stress lines. No rust migration. In rare cases, a comic was not stapled at the bindery and therefore has a missing staple; this is not considered a defect. Any staple can be replaced on books up to Fine, but only vintage staples can be used on books from Very Fine to Near Mint. Mint books must have original staples. Paper is cream to off-white, supple and fresh. No hint of acidity in the odor of the newsprint. Centerfold is secure. Slight interior tears are allowed.

9.0 VERY FINE/NEAR MINT (VF/NM): Nearly perfect with outstanding eye appeal. A limited number of bindery defects are allowed. Almost flat cover with almost imperceptible wear. Inks are bright with slightly diminished reflectivity. An 1/8" bend is allowed if color is not broken. Corners are cut square and sharp with ever-so-slight blunting permitted but no creases. Several lightly penciled, stamped or inked arrival dates are acceptable. No obvious soiling, staining or other discoloration, except for very minor foxing. Spine is tight and flat. No spine roll or split allowed. Staples may show some discoloration. Only the slightest staple tears are allowed. A very minor accumulation of stress lines may be present if they are nearly imperceptible. No rust migration. In rare cases, a comic was not stapled at the bindery and therefore has a missing staple; this is not considered a defect. Any staple can be replaced on books up to Fine, but only vintage staples can be used on books from Very Fine to Near Mint. Mint books must have original staples. Paper is cream to off-white and supple. No hint of acidity in the odor of the newsprint. Centerfold is secure. Very minor interior tears may be present.

8.5 VERY FINE+ (VF+): Fits the criteria for Very Fine but with an additional virtue or small accumulation of virtues that improves the book's appearance by a perceptible amount.

8.0 VERY FINE (VF): An excellent copy with outstanding eye appeal. Sharp, bright and clean with supple pages. A comic book in this grade has the appearance of having been carefully handled. A limited accumulation of minor bindery defects is allowed. Cover is relatively flat with minimal surface wear beginning to show, possibly including some minute wear at corners. Inks are generally bright with moderate to high reflectivity. A 1/4" crease is acceptable if color is not broken. Stamped or inked arrival dates may be present. No obvious soiling, staining or other discoloration, except for minor foxing. Spine is almost flat with no roll. Possible minor color break allowed. Staples may show some discoloration. Very slight staple tears and a few almost very minor to minor stress lines may be present. No rust migration. In rare cases, a comic was not stapled at the bindery and therefore has a missing staple; this is not considered a defect. Any staple can be replaced on books up to Fine, but only vintage staples can be used on books from Very Fine to Near Mint. Mint books must have original staples. Paper is tan to cream and supple. No hint of acidity in the odor of the newsprint. Centerfold is mostly secure. Minor interior tears at the margin may be present.

7.5 VERY FINE– (VF–): Fits the criteria for Very Fine but with an additional defect or small accumulation of defects that detracts from the book's appearance by a perceptible amount.

7.0 FINE/VERY FINE (FN/VF): An above-average copy that shows minor wear but is still relatively flat and clean with outstanding eye appeal. A small accumulation of minor bindery defects is allowed. Minor cover wear beginning to show with interior yellowing or tanning allowed, possibly including minor creases. Corners may be blunted or abraded. Inks are generally bright with a moderate reduction in reflectivity. Stamped or inked arrival dates may be present. No obvious soiling, staining or other discoloration, except for minor foxing. The slightest spine roll may be present, as well as a possible moderate color break. Staples may show some discoloration. Slight staple tears and a slight accumulation of light stress lines may be present. Slight rust migration. In rare cases, a comic was not stapled at the bindery and therefore has a missing staple; this is not considered a defect. Any staple can be replaced on books up to Fine, but only vintage staples can be used on books from Very Fine to Near Mint. Mint books must have original staples. Paper is tan to cream, but not brown. No hint of acidity in the odor of the newsprint. Centerfold is mostly secure. Minor interior tears at the margin may be present.

6.5 FINE+ (FN+): Fits the criteria for Fine but with an additional virtue or small accumulation of virtues that improves the book's appearance by a perceptible amount.

6.0 FINE (FN): An above-average copy that shows minor wear but is still relatively flat and clean with no significant creasing or other serious defects. Eye appeal is somewhat reduced because of slight surface wear and the accumulation of small defects, especially on the spine and edges. A FINE condition comic book appears to have been read a few times and has been handled with moderate care. Some accumulation of minor bindery defects is allowed. Minor cover wear apparent, with minor to moderate creases. Inks show a major reduction in reflectivity. Blunted or abraded corners are more common, as is minor staining, soiling, discoloration, and/or foxing. Stamped or inked arrival dates may be present. A minor spine roll is allowed. There can also be a 1/4" spine split or severe color break. Staples show minor discoloration. Minor staple tears and an accumulation of stress lines may be present, as well as minor rust migration. In rare cases, a comic was not stapled at

the bindery and therefore has a missing staple; this is not considered a defect. Any staple can be replaced on books up to Fine, but only vintage staples can be used on books from Very Fine to Near Mint. Mint books must have original staples. Paper is brown to tan and fairly supple with no signs of brittleness. No hint of acidity in the odor of the newsprint. Minor interior tears at the margin may be present. Centerfold may be loose but not detached.

5.5 FINE– (FN–): Fits the criteria for Fine but with an additional defect or small accumulation of defects that detracts from the book's appearance by a perceptible amount.

5.0 VERY GOOD/FINE (VG/FN): An above-average but well-used comic book. A comic in this grade shows some moderate wear; eye appeal is somewhat reduced because of the accumulation of defects. Still a desirable copy that has been handled with some care. An accumulation of bindery defects is allowed. Minor to moderate cover wear apparent, with minor to moderate creases and/or dimples. Inks have major to extreme reduction in reflectivity. Blunted or abraded corners are increasingly common, as is minor to moderate staining, discoloration, and/or foxing. Stamped or inked arrival dates may be present. A minor to moderate spine roll is allowed. A spine split of up to 1/2" may be present. Staples show minor discoloration. A slight accumulation of minor staple tears and an accumulation of minor stress lines may also be present, as well as minor rust migration. In rare cases, a comic was not stapled at the bindery and therefore has a missing staple; this is not considered a defect. Any staple can be replaced on books up to Fine, but only vintage staples can be used on books from Very Fine to Near Mint. Mint books must have original staples. Paper is brown to tan with no signs of brittleness. May have the faintest trace of an acidic odor. Centerfold may be loose but not detached. Minor tears may also be present.

4.5 VERY GOOD+ (VG): Fits the criteria for Very Good but with an additional virtue or small accumulation of virtues that improves the book's appearance by a perceptible amount.

4.0 VERY GOOD (VG): The average used comic book. A comic in this grade shows some significant moderate wear, but still has not accumulated enough total defects to reduce eye appeal to the point that it is not a desirable copy. Cover shows moderate to significant wear, and may be loose but not completely detached. Moderate to extreme reduction in reflectivity. Can have an accumulation of creases or dimples. Corners may be blunted or abraded. Store stamps, name stamps, arrival dates, initials, etc. have no effect on this grade. Some discoloration, fading, foxing, and even minor soiling is allowed. As much as a 1/4" triangle can be missing out of the corner or edge; a missing 1/8" square is also acceptable. Only minor unobtrusive tape and other amateur repair allowed on otherwise high grade copies. Moderate spine roll may be present and/or a 1" spine split. Staples discolored. Minor to moderate staple tears and stress lines may be present, as well as some rust migration. Paper is brown but not brittle. A minor acidic odor can be detectable. Minor to moderate tears may be present. Centerfold may be loose or detached at one staple.

3.5 VERY GOOD– (VG–): Fits the criteria for Very Good but with an additional defect or small accumulation of defects that detracts from the book's appearance by a perceptible amount.

3.0 GOOD/VERY GOOD (GD/VG): A used comic book showing some substantial wear. Cover shows significant wear, and may be loose or even detached at one staple. Cover reflectivity is very low. Can have a book-length crease and/or dimples. Corners may be blunted or even rounded. Discoloration, fading, foxing, and even minor to moderate soiling is allowed. A triangle from 1/4" to 1/2" can be missing out of the corner or edge; a missing 1/8" to 1/4" square is also acceptable. Tape and other amateur repair may be present. Moderate spine roll likely. May have a spine split of any-where from 1" to 1-1/2". Staples may be rusted or replaced. Minor to moderate staple tears and moderate stress lines may be present, as well as some rust migration. Paper is brown but not brittle. Centerfold may be loose or detached at one staple. Minor to moderate interior tears may be present.

2.5 GOOD+ (GD+): Fits the criteria for Good but with an addi-tional virtue or small accumulation of virtues that improves the book's appearance by a perceptible amount.

2.0 GOOD (GD): Shows substantial wear; often considered a "read-ing copy." Cover shows significant wear and may even be detached. Cover reflectivity is low and in some cases completely absent. Book-length creases and dimples may be present. Rounded corners are more common. Moderate soiling, staining, discoloration and foxing may be present. The largest piece allowed missing from the front or back cover is usually a 1/2" triangle or a 1/4" square, although some Silver Age books such as 1960s Marvels have had the price corner box clipped from the top left front cover and may be considered Good if they would otherwise have graded higher. Tape and other forms of amateur repair are common in Silver Age and older books. Spine roll is likely. May have up to a 2" spine split. Staples may be degraded, replaced or missing. Moderate staple tears and stress lines may be present, as well as rust migration. Paper is brown but not brittle. Centerfold may be loose or detached. Moderate interior tears may be present.

1.8 GOOD– (GD–): Fits the criteria for Good but with an addi-tional defect or small accumulation of defects that detracts from the book's appearance by a perceptible amount.

1.5 FAIR/GOOD (FR/GD): A comic showing substantial to heavy wear. A copy in this grade still has all pages and covers, although there may be pieces missing. Books in this grade are commonly creased, scuffed, abraded, soiled, and possibly unattractive, but still generally readable. Cover shows considerable wear and may be detached. Nearly no reflectivity to no reflectivity remaining. Store stamp, name stamp, arrival date and initials are permitted. Book-length creases, tears and folds may be present. Rounded corners are increasingly common. Soiling, staining, discoloration and foxing is generally present. Up to 1/10 of the back cover may be missing. Tape and other forms of amateur repair are increas-ingly common in Silver Age and older books. Spine roll is com-mon. May have a spine split between 2" and 2/3 the length of the book. Staples may be degraded, replaced or missing. Staple tears and stress lines are common, as well as rust migration. Paper is brown and may show brittleness around the edges. Acidic odor

may be present. Centerfold may be loose or detached. Interior tears are common.

1.0 FAIR (FR): A copy in this grade shows heavy wear. Some col-lectors consider this the lowest collectible grade because comic books in lesser condition are usually incomplete and/or brittle. Comics in this grade are usually soiled, faded, ragged and possi-bly unattractive. This is the last grade in which a comic remains generally readable. Cover may be detached, and inks have lost all reflectivity. Creases, tears and/or folds are prevalent. Corners are commonly rounded or absent. Soiling and staining is present. Books in this condition generally have all pages and most of the covers, although there may be up to 1/4 of the front cover miss-ing or no back cover, but not both. Tape and other forms of ama-teur repair are more common. Spine roll is more common; spine split can extend up to 2/3 the length of the book. Staples may be missing or show rust and discoloration. An accumulation of sta-ple tears and stress lines may be present, as well as rust migra-tion. Paper is brown and may show brittleness around the edges but not in the central portion of the pages. Acidic odor may be present. Accumulation of interior tears. Chunks may be missing. The center-fold may be missing if readability is generally preserved (although there may be difficulty). Coupons may be cut.

0.5 POOR (PR): Most comic books in this grade have been suffi-ciently degraded to the point where there is little or no collector value; they are easily identified by a complete absence of eye appeal. Comics in this grade are brittle almost to the point of turning to dust with a touch, and are usually incomplete. Extreme cover fading may render the cover almost indiscernible. May have extremely severe stains, mildew or heavy cover abrasion to the point that some cover inks are indistinct/absent. Covers may be detached with large chunks missing. Can have extremely ragged edges and extensive creasing. Corners are rounded or virtually absent. Covers may have been defaced with paints, varnishes, glues, oil, indelible markers or dyes, and may have suffered heavy water damage. Can also have extensive amateur repairs such as lami-nated covers. Extreme spine roll present; can have extremely ragged spines or a complete, book-length split. Staples can be missing or show extreme rust and discoloration. Extensive staple tears and stress lines may be present, as well as extreme rust migration. Paper exhibits moderate to severe brittleness (where the comic book literally falls apart when examined). Extreme acidic odor may be present. Extensive interior tears. Multiple pages, including the centerfold, may be missing that affect read-ability. Coupons may be cut.

Publishers' Codes

The following abbreviations are used with cover reproductions throughout the book for copyright purposes:

ABC-America's Best Comics
AC-AC Comics
ACE-Ace Periodicals
ACG-American Comics Group
AJAX-Ajax-Farrell
AP-Archie Publications
ATLAS-Atlas Comics (see below)
AVON-Avon Periodicals
BP-Better Publications
C & L-Cupples & Leon
CC-Charlton Comics
CEN-Centaur Publications
CCG-Columbia Comics Group
CG-Catechetical Guild
CHES-Harry 'A' Chesler
CLDS-Classic Det. Stories
CM-Comics Magazine
CN-Condé Nast
DC-DC Comics, Inc.

DEF-Defiant Comics
DELL-Dell Publishing Co.
DH-Dark Horse
DIS-Disney Enterprises, Inc.
DMP-David McKay Publishing
DS-D. S. Publishing Co.
EAS-Eastern Color Printing Co.
EC-E. C. Comics
ECL-Eclipse Comics
ENWIL-Enwil Associates
EP-Elliott Publications
ERB-Edgar Rice Burroughs
FAW-Fawcett Publications
FC-First Comics
FF-Famous Funnies
FH-Fiction House Magazines
FOX-Fox Features Syndicate
GIL-Gilberton
GK-Gold Key

GP-Great Publications
HARV-Harvey Publications
H-B-Hanna-Barbera
HILL-Hillman Periodicals
HOKE-Holyoke Publishing Co.
IM-Image Comics
KING-King Features Syndicate
LEV-Lev Gleason Publications
MAL-Malibu Comics
MAR-Marvel Characters, Inc.
ME-Magazine Enterprises
MLJ-MLJ Magazines
MS-Mirage Studios
NOVP-Novelty Press
NYNS-New York News Syndicate
PG-Premier Group
PINE-Pines
PMI-Parents' Magazine Institute
PRIZE-Prize Publications
QUA-Quality Comics Group
REAL-Realistic Comics
RH-Rural Home

S & S-Street and Smith Publishers
SKY-Skywald Publications
STAR-Star Publications
STD-Standard Comics
STJ-St. John Publishing Co.
SUPR-Superior Comics
TC-Tower Comics
TM-Trojan Magazines
TMP-Todd McFarlane Prods.
TOBY-Toby Press
TOPS-Tops Comics
UFS-United Features Syndicate
VAL-Valiant
VITL-Vital Publications
WB-Warner Brothers.
WEST-Western Publishing Co.
WHIT-Whitman Publishing Co.
WHW-William H. Wise
WMG-William M. Gaines (E. C.)
WP-Warren Publishing Co.
YM-Youthful Magazines
Z-D-Ziff-Davis Publishing Co.

Overstreet Advisors

Even before the first edition of *The Official Overstreet Comic Book Price Guide* was printed, author Robert M. Overstreet solicited pricing data, historical notations, and general information from a variety of sources. What was initially an informal group offering input quickly became an organized field of comic book collectors, dealers and historians whose opinions are actively solicited in advance of each edition of this book. Some of these Overstreet Advisors are specialists who deal in particular niches within the comic book world, while others are generalists who are interested in commenting on the broader marketplace. Each advisor provides information from their respective areas of interest and expertise, spanning the history of American comics.

While some choose to offer pricing and historical information in the form of annotated sales catalogs, auction catalogs, or documented private sales, assistance from others comes in the form of the market reports such as those beginning on page 75 in this book. In addition to those who have served as Overstreet Advisors almost since *The Guide*'s inception, each year new contributors are sought.

With that in mind, we are pleased to present our newest Overstreet Advisors:

THE CLASS OF 2007

LAUREN BECKER
Dealer
Clawson, MI

MIKE BRODER
Dealer
Fort Lauderdale, FL

DENNIS KEUM
Dealer
Goldens Bridge, NY

TIM KUPIN
Dealer
Waldorf, MD

JOHN JACKSON MILLER
Historian, Writer
Waupaca, WI

BILL PONSETI
Collector
Saucier, MS

LON WEBB
Dealer
Norcross, GA

A complete listing of our Overstreet Advisors can be found on our title page and beginning on page 1,104.

www.comiclink.com

The ultimate site for buyers and sellers of investment quality comic books and comic art.

SIX CENTS PER COPY.

SERIES OF COMICAL DESIGNS,
EXECUTED FOR THIS BOSTON EDITION,
D. C. JOHNSTON,
THE CRUIKSHANK OF THE NEW WORLD.

No. 11.

RARE AND HISTORICAL
NEWSPAPERS BOUGHT AND SOLD

(16th Century-20th Century)

BUYING:

Bound Volumes and Rare Individual Issues of Newspapers,
Harper's Weekly, Leslie's, Gentleman's Magazine (18th century),
Police Gazettes (19th century only), The Daily Graphic, etc.

SELLING:

Major Events in U.S. and World History, European 16th-17th
century, Colonial and Rev. War, Civil War, Wild West,
20th century big headlines, etc.

**Contact Eric C. Caren 914-248-8038 or
Stephen A. Goldman toll free at 888-228-8755
or in PA. 717-846-5120**

OldNews, Inc. The Caren Archive and
Stephen A. Goldman Historical Newspapers
P.O. Box 359, Parkton, MD 21120

CREDENTIALS:

Both Members- American
Antiquarian Society, Consultants-
The Freedom Forum Newseum, etc.
Author, *Pioneer Age*

NEW YORK
ILLUSTRATED NEWS.

COMIC ALMANAC.

ANTI-AMALGAMATIONIST.
NATIONAL UNION.

THE FOLLOWING IS A TRUE STORY...

METROPOLIS

WE'RE CONFUSED!

We hope that someone who reads this will be able to explain
why this kind of thing happens, because
we don't get it!

At the biggest convention of the year, a dealer who traveled
hundreds of miles to set up bought a high-grade **Fantastic Four #1** for
roughly **1/2 the price** that we would have paid. After that comic passed
through the hands of several dealers, Metropolis did in fact buy it. The fellow
who had initially sold it at the convention could easily have made
seven thousand dollars more if he had sold it to us.

SHOULDN'T THESE GUYS KNOW BETTER?

SHOULDN'T EVERYONE? IS IT STILL BETTER TO GET MORE
MONEY FOR YOUR COMICS THAN LESS? DOES THE EARTH STILL
REVOLVE AROUND THE SUN? ARE THERE STILL PEOPLE OUT
THERE WHO ARE NOT OFFERING THEIR BOOKS TO METROPOLIS
AND LOSING MONEY SELLING TO THE WRONG GUY?

If anyone out there can shed some light on why this still happens
in this day and age, could you please let us know?

METROPOLISCOMICS.COM, 873 BROADWAY SUITE 201, NEW YORK, NY 10003
PH: 212.260.4147 FX: 212.260.4304 BUYING@METROPOLISCOMICS.COM

THE NATION'S LARGEST COMIC DEALER

METROPOLIS

172

THE PROBLEM :
What is wrong with public auctions ?
Long wait until results

Sometimes six months or more. Then if the item does not sell more waiting. *You only get one chance per auction!*

Advance Squeeze

They give money so you do not have to wait for funds, you spend the money, the item comes up for sale and fails to meet reserve, *you let it sell for less because you do not want to pay back the advance,* or they negotiate to buy the piece out from you.

Price Games

Items not protected by reserves or by illegal shill bidding will sell for far less that other ways of personal selling. Think about it! An auction is a wholesale marketplace attended largely by professional dealers. You collect, how often do you go ? So dealers buy your stuff and then sell it for a profit. You wind up waiting months to pay the auctioneer 30% for wholesaling your item. Also big auctions report millions in sales. There are only a handful of firms who can report millions in revenue per year, so how does so much stuff get absorbed in one day of selling, in one physical location, answer, *it either sells wholesale, or it never really sold.*

Multiple Rarity Dilution

Seven Batman #1's available all at once in one auction will not perform as well as selling one .... *The perception of scarcity creates value.*

Selling myths

Buyers assume auction is the cheapest way to buy items, Sellers think its often the place to get the best price, how can both be right? Most items are from dealers placing things in auction or the auction house themselves. Very often it is not disclosed in the realized prices that they bought back their own material as no outside buyer stepped up to meet the price, many fantastic prices you see reported are dealers trying to seed records so they can sell the items in the open market after for less….. so your stuff sells for less creating the myth of bargains, the house stuff does not sell or sells for run up prices, nobody really knows.

No special attention

Your stuff is offered among many other things with no special attention. All you get is a photo and bland description.No professional sales copy. There is no sales department to contact with questions. *No personal salesmanship at all.*

No personal or phone selling

Many serious buyers have questions or require a personal touch when spending their fortunes. The current options of websites and auction houses offer no personal touch.

Hidden fee's

You truly receive only about 70% of the final realized price. Auction's charge a buyers fee of 15-20% and the consignor at least 5%, sometimes 15% also. This means that you are actually giving up 15% - 35% of the sale price, so you cannot go by just sellers fees. Also, there is usually buyback fee if you try to protect your items, sort of like paying rent on a property you own.

Rings, shills, and other illegal games

Rings are buyers that control auctions, make non-compete deals. This is done in order to get yours and others items cheap so they can have another auction amongst themselves and split the difference between what they paid for the auction and the real price. Shills are used when an auction house has a bid of lets say $4,000 for an item on the book or called in, and on the floor the item is $2,000, the shill is used to raise to the book so the item does not sell for $2,200, but $4,000 to the unfortunate trusting buyer. Although this might seem helpful to sellers, they usually only do it for their own items because they do want some bargains to go through to please buyers. *It is just another unethical thing that goes on and both are well documented with many lawsuits and criminal records.*

178

FOLLOW the LEADER

...To the Very Finest Selection in Rare Comic Books Today!

Harley Yee has been Servicing his Clientele All Over the World for Over 15 years, traveling to more than 30 Comic Conventions in the United States, Canada, England, Australia and New Zealand year end and year out. Because of this, we have the Golden Opportunity to Purchase and Offer one of the Most Vast Selections of Golden-Age, Silver-Age and Bronze-Age comics in the marketplace today. Our Material is Special and quite Diverse, just like our Client Base, Catering to Every Kind of Collector's "Wish-List" Worldwide; From Very Rare and Unique Items to Super High-Grade, Investment books to the lower and mid-grade "collector copies" that complete those "missing run issues." We also offer our quarterly Catalog which features well over One Million Dollars in Rare Comic Books. So, whatever type of comics you might be looking for, whether certified or uncertified, Give Us a Try! Our Reputation Speaks for Itself:

- Accurate Grading
- Great Selection of certified (CGC) and uncertified Comics
- Competitive Pricing
- Prompt and Professional Service
- Want-Lists Always Welcome
- Complete Customer Satisfaction

Selling your Comics?

Make Sure to Give Us a Call **FIRST**. We Will travel Anywhere to View Collections and Pay the **Highest Prices** with **Immediate Cash**. No Collection to is too Large or too Small for Us.

GOLDEN-AGE

SILVER-AGE

TEMPTATION HAS A PRICE

IRRESISTABLE!

THE SELLER'S GUIDE

Yes, here are the pages you're looking for. These percentages will help you determine the sale value of your collection. If you do not find your title, call with any questions. We have purchased many of the major well-known collections. We are serious about buying your comics and paying you the most for them.

If you have comics or related items for sale call or send your list for a quote. No collection is too large or small. Immediate funds available of 500K and beyond.

These are some of the high prices we will pay. Percentages stated will be paid for any grade unless otherwise noted. All percentages based on this Overstreet Guide.

—*JAMES PAYETTE*

We are paying 100% of Guide for the following:

All Select	1-up	Marvel Mystery	11-up
All Winners	6-up	Pep	22-45
America's Best	1-up	Prize	2-50
Black Terror	1-25	Reform School Girl	1
Captain Aero	3-25	Speed	10-30
Captain America	11-up	Startling	2-up
Catman	1-up	Sub-Mariner	3-32
Dynamic	2-15	Thrilling	2-52
Exciting	3-50	U.S.A.	6-up
Human Torch	6-35	Wonder (Nedor)	1-up

We are paying 75% of Guide for the following:

Action 1-15	Detective 2-26	Keen Detective Funnies all
Adventure 247	Detective Eye all	Marvel Mystery 1-10
All New 2-13	Detective Picture Stories all	Mystery Men all
All Winners 1-5	Fantastic Four 1-2	Showcase 4
Amazing Man all	Four Favorites 3-27	Spiderman 1-2
Amazing Mystery Funnies all	Funny Pages all	Superman 1
Andy Devine	Funny Picture Stories all	Superman's Pal 1
Arrow all	Hangman all	Tim McCoy all
Captain America 1-10	Jumbo 1-10	Wonder (Fox)
Daredevil (2nd) 1	Journey into Mystery 83	Young Allies all

DISCOVER THE MISS NG L NK

pop culture with character

GEPPI'S entertainment MUSEUM

Find out what's missing from your collection!

At Geppi's Entertainment Museum, expect the unexpected! If you're looking to discover something unusual or offbeat in your quest to fill the gaps in your comic book collection, GEM will give you a glimpse of many more comics than just the well-known classics. You'll see the history of comics unfold before your eyes, with everything from rare premiums to Atom Age horror to Silver Age romance and beyond. Find these GEMs and many more in the museum's "A Story in Four Colors" comic book gallery!

GEPPI'S ENTERTAINMENT MUSEUM AT CAMDEN YARDS

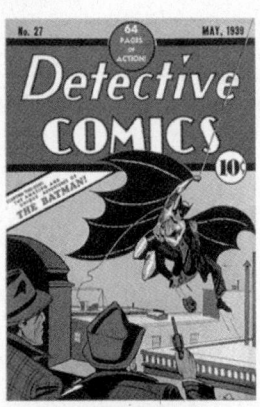

DON'T BUY OR SELL ANOTHER

This X-men #66 had previously graded CGC 9.2. Utilizing the **pressing service**, the book obtained a CGC 9.6 grade upon resubmission. Cost for pressing: $35.

A Batman #1 with an ugly sticker on the front cover, dying to be removed using the **conservation service**. Cost for conservation: $90.

WHAT WE DO

For over a decade, Classics Incorporated has been helping collectors preserve their treasures. Given the advanced state of the hobby these days, it's imperative that you make the right decisions whether you're buying or selling one comic, or an entire collection. Classics Incorporated is an expert in all aspects of the marketplace, from third-party grading and auctions, to pedigreed comics, restoration, and investment consulting. Our accuracy in CGC grading, pressing and valuation is unparalleled. Using our unique combination of services and advice will ensure that you make the best decision for your comics.

The process is easy. Our website classicsincorporated.com will answer any questions you have about our services, and guide you through the easy process of submission. In addition, the website offers many insights into the marketplace, including published articles, comic valuation tables, before and after pictures of our work, and links to helpful sites that delve deeper into the nuances of comic collecting. You will not find such a complete accumulation of crucial information anywhere else.

A quick look at a few of the many services we offer:

PRESSING

One of the most popular services used by our clients today, pressing is best utilized for **high grade, unrestored comics**. Pressing is not considered restoration, and is used to remove light defects to make a high grade even higher (for example, pressing a Spider-man #20 from CGC 9.0 to 9.2). The age of the comic does not matter, and because of the low cost of pressing (as low as $15 per book), the comic's value does not have to be high for the service to be beneficial. But it takes practice to find the right candidates for pressing. Many factors must be considered for each book, such as how to spot "bad" and "good" defects. Guidelines are set forth on classicsincorporated.com so you can make informed decisions before sending us your books for review.

CONSERVATION

Another low-cost service, conservation best suits **lower to mid grade comics in the GD to VF range**. Its main goal is to rid a comic book of harmful agents (tape, glue, stains, mold), and/or improve the appearance and

(972) 980-8040 • 1440 Halsey Way, Suite 114 • Carrollton, TX 75007 • www.classicsincorporated.com

COMIC UNTIL YOU CALL US!

desirability through light restorative techniques. Comics older than 1964 are the best candidates for conservation, although there are exceptions. Value is not a significant factor due to the low cost of conservation, which starts at $30. Conservation can include water, dry, and solvent cleaning, tear seals, support, staple cleaning/replacement and pressing. A breakdown of costs can be found on classicsincorporated.com.

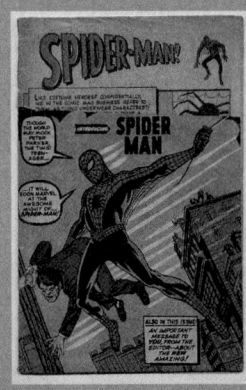

RESTORATION

The eldest of the services offered, restoration targets **low grade comics in the FA to GD+ range**. It utilizes every weapon in our arsenal to maximize the grade of a comic, including piece replacement, grafting and color matching. The best candidates for restoration are pre-1960 comics with a current value of $1000 or more. The truth is as many as 50% of comics submitted to us for restoration are turned down because the work is either unnecessary or detrimental to its value. But restoring the right candidates can produce eye-popping results. Classicsincorporated.com offers guidelines that will aid you in finding the right books for this service. We also offer free appraisals on emailed scans and online auctions.

This Amazing Fantasy #15 is a prime **restoration** candidate. Other than the torn off logo area, the book is in VF. Current value is $750.

RE-CREATION

This service is strictly for coverless comics, particularly the key issues like Spider-man #1, Superman #1, and Marvel Comics #1. We attach exact replicas of covers onto these **coverless comics**, each cut to fit the comic perfectly. Many collectors purchase coverless key issues because of their affordability. This service allows the comic to appear complete without the collector having to pay thousands of dollars more for a real cover. Cost is $150 per cover, and includes any necessary interior support, tear seals, assembly and pressing. Check classicsincorporated. com for more information and a complete list of available covers.

RESTORATION REMOVAL

On occasion, you may find minor unnecessary restoration on one of your books. Is removal feasible? Minor professional restoration, such as tear seals and support using rice paper and water-soluble adhesive, and acrylic and water-based color touch are the safest to remove. In some cases a book's value can significantly increase with this service, but great care must be taken in choosing the right candidates. Check classicsincorporated.com if you think you have a book that can benefit from restoration removal.

The same Amazing Fantasy #15 after restoration. Its new grade is VF, with a value of $2000. Cost of restoration: $500.

Time Machine!

POP CULTURE *with* **CHARACTER**

a look inside GEPPI'S ENTERTAINMENT MUSEUM

by DR. ARNOLD T. BLUMBERG

GEMSTONE PUBLISHING

Hundreds of photos
Full Color
Hardcover
272 Pages
$24.95

Geppi's Entertainment Museum is popular culture in the setting it deserves and now you can take the walk through time yourself in the pages of this new book!

Available at your local book stop or call
888-375-9800 ext. 1612 to order

Hear what Collectors are saying about CGC.

"CGC is a GREAT organization and the staff and company are simply the best out there. I believe that CGC is going to stay the industry leader of which the other small timers will try to strive for, but never even come close to reaching."
Michael Gray • Collector

"I want to say that the level of service that your company has provided so far has been first rate. On my family's vacation to Florida in August, Scott agreed on short notice to accept my books for grading in person. What a terrific experience. Friendly reception, great communication and consistent grading among all of my books. You guys do a terrific job. Despite the heated discussions going around regarding grading consistency (I suppose everyone thinks their books are NM!!) I understand your position and the pressure involved to perform. I commend you on your ability to remain consistent, as far as I can see, in your grading standards."
Roy Delic • Collector

"Thanks for the excellent service I consistently receive from you! I have been in this field for over 40 years, and appreciate the important role that third party grading can have in facilitating the wonderful world of rare comic books. Over time I have personally developed a tremendous respect for all of the effort that CGC puts into its operation. There are very few people I will let handle my best comics, but I have met CGC's Steve Borock and Mark Haspel and trust them with my books. Doing business with CGC has been a real pleasure. Thanks CGC!"
Charles Wooley • Collector and Dealer • Former Co-Owner "Million Year Picnic"

"Thank you for your professional service during my visit to your operations. I am now more confident your abilities to be the best grading service in comics for the collector, investor or dealer. After seeing every aspect of the operation, one could see that CGC will be the main player in securing high grade comics for all of us!"
Dan Davis • Collector

"With CGC, buying through the post office is no longer Russian roulette"
Frédéric Manzano • Editions Déesse Paris, France

"Steve Borock and his team are real professionals. The service you provide fills the credibility gap in comic book collection which private collectors (like me) have been searching for. Your service has further legitimized this collectible."
Michael Katz • Collector

"I recently sold a several hundred comic book collection book by book for $12,000 on eBay. Unfortunately, I only submitted a few books to CGC. What a mistake! Were I to do it again, I would have submitted everything. The graded books went at guide or much better every time. The ungraded books went at a discount to guide, simply because one person's grading standards vary from another. The CGC grade was one that everyone trusted."
Mike Finn • Collector

"I've been a collector since 1974....I have certainly seen this hobby mature through the years. I truly feel that CGC has been the catalyst to finally bring a standard structure to our hobby – no small feat! CGC has carried our hobby to a new level of integrity and safety."
Jon Lindstrom • Collector

"CGC has taken the guessing game out of the comic business for me. I can't imagine going back to the days of over graded comics and undisclosed restoration."
Jeff Williams • Collector

"CGC has added real value to collections. I am very excited that Overstreet has recognized CGC's expertise and I hope that the result will be a new price guide which reflects the true marketplace."
Scott Collins • Collector

"My opinion of CGC's grading has been verified. Steve, I want to thank you and CGC for your honesty and your accuracy and look forward to many many years of future grading."
Kennith M. Basteiro • Collector

"I have been happily following CGC's impact on the marketplace. Speaking as a collector that has been into comics for over 30 years, and the founder of the Western PA collection, I believe such a service is long overdue in this hobby."
Michael Friedlander • Collector

"I have been a part of comic fandom since 1963. Since having my first comics graded in 2002, I have had nothing but good things to say about my experience with CGC. Mr. Borock and his staff have been consistent with their grading and turn around times. I know I am one of the few "underground" comics collectors around and I really appreciate the extra time and effort Mark Haspel has put into the analysis of each book to verify its proper printing and grade."
Howard Gerber • Collector

"Steve, I must say if it wasn't for your advice and help, I wouldn't have known about the alterations to the book. I can only imagine the horror and disappointment in finding out later. I really appreciate all your extra efforts and taking the time to help me. You've been great. CGC provides an invaluable resource to collectors. I'm glad you guys are around to make a new era of collecting a better place."
Rob Gonzalez • Collector

"The Gaines estate is thrilled with the results. You know what? We'd be mad NOT to use CGC's services!"
Grant Geissman • Author, "Foul Play!" & "Tales of Terror! The EC Companion"

Advertise!

 is your ticket to the comics and collectibles market!

OFFICIAL OVERSTREET COMIC BOOK PRICE GUIDE #38

ROBERT M. OVERSTREET

Would you like to advertise in a future edition of one of our publications?

Let our line of publications, including *The Overstreet Comic Book Price Guide*, *The Overstreet Comic Book Grading Guide*, and *Hake's Price Guide To Character Toys*, be your vehicle for reaching out to an audience comprised entirely of serious collectors, dealers, manufacturers and other comic character enthusiasts!

Just call toll free (888)375-9800 ext 1625 or e-mail hdiana@gemstonepub.com for details!

Visit us on the web at www.gemstonepub.com

215

221

I BUY OLD COMICS
1930 to 1975

Any Title
Any Condition
Any Size Collection

Can Easily Travel to:

Atlanta
Chicago
Cincinnati
Dallas
Little Rock
Louisvillle
Memphis
St. Louis

Paducah, KY

I want your comics:

Superhero
Western
Horror
Humor
Romance

Leroy Harper
PO BOX 212
WEST PADUCAH, KY 42086

PHONE 270-748-9364
EMAIL LHCOMICS@hotmail.com

Over 20 years of experience

225

228

Why consign to a Heritage auction instead of selling to a dealer?

The dealers in this guide bid in our auctions! If you sell outright to a comic dealer, you will never know how much he might have been willing to pay. In a Heritage auction, that same dealer will have to bid against all of the other major dealers, as well as thousands of retail collectors, driving the auction price higher and higher. You'll know each and every item was sold to the one buyer willing to pay the highest price for it.

SATISFIED SELLERS:

"Far as I'm concerned, the real superheroes are those great guys at Heritage. I really lucked out when I met' em 'cause they got me prices that exceeded my wildest expectations, plus it was a real kick to work with them. I don't want this to sound like a TV commercial but, so help me Spidey, there's no one I'd rather entrust with my collection. Excelsior!"

– Stan Lee

"We have been very pleased with our decision to consign our extensive comic book collection to Heritage Auction Galleries. It was Heritage's promised professionalism that attracted us. We have not been disappointed... It's an exciting, slightly unnerving venture for us, but we are comforted that Heritage is running our show."

– Cynthia Crippen
Executor of the Davis Crippen Estate

234

235

GARY DOLGOFF COMICS

WANTS:
YOUR 'COLLECTION ENTIRE'!

'THE GOOD, THE BAD, & THE UGLY'...
...1930's - 1970's

All Grades Wanted (Poor to Mint!)

Superman ©DC Comics

We <u>travel</u> (*anywhere, anytime*) for 'more valuable collections'...

CALL NOW, TOLL FREE: 1-866-830-4367

SOME COMICS I OFTEN PAY 50%-100%+ OF GUIDE FOR:

ACE 1-50	DAREDEVIL (LEV GLEASON; 40s)	JUSTICE LEAGUE 1-100
ACTION 1-400	DAREDEVIL (MARVEL) 1-100	KING 1-100
ADVENTURE 1-400	DARING MYSTERY	KID COLT 1-100
ALL-AMERICAN	DETECTIVE 1-450	LARGE FEATURE COMICS
ALL FLASH	FAMOUS MONSTERS MAG. 1-40	LOIS LANE 1-50
ALL STAR	FAMOUS FUNNIES 1-100	MAD 1-50
AM. SPIDERMAN 1-200	FANTASTIC FOUR 1-150	MARGE'S LITTLE LULU 1-100
AMAZING FANTASY 15	FIGHT COMICS	MARVEL COMICS 1
ARCHIE 1-100	FLASH 1-200	MARVEL MYSTERY
AVENGERS 1-150	FOUR COLOR 1-300	MASTER COMICS
BATMAN 1-300	FORBIDDEN WORLDS 1-80	MICKEY MOUSE MAGAZINE
BETTY & VERONICA 1-50	GIRLS LOVE STORIES	MILLIE THE MODEL
BATTLE	GREEN LANTERN (40's)	MILITARY
BLACKHAWK 9(#1) - 100	GREEN LANTERN (60's) 1-40	MODERN
BLACK TERROR	HIT COMICS	MR. MYSTERY
BLUE RIBBON	HOUSE OF MYSTERY 1-100	MORE FUN
BRAVE & BOLD 1-100	HOUSE OF SECRETS 1-61	MYSTERY IN SPACE 1-110
CAPTAIN AMERICA (40's)	HUMAN TORCH	MYSTIC COMICS
CAPTAIN MARVEL	INCREDIBLE HULK 1-6, 102-182	NATIONAL
CAPTAIN MARVEL JR.	IRON MAN 1-60	OUR ARMY AT WAR 1-200
COMIC CAVALCADE	JIMMY OLSEN 1-75	PEP COMICS 1-100
CRACKAJACK FUNNIES	JOURNEY INTO MYSTERY	PERFECT CRIME
CRACK COMICS	JUGHEAD 1-50	PLANET COMICS
CRIME DOES NOT PAY	JUMBO COMICS	PLASTIC MAN
CRIME SUSPENSE	JUNGLE COMICS	POLICE COMICS

STEP BACK IN TIME
TO AN ERA OF SUPERB ARTISTRY AND IMAGINATION

249

255

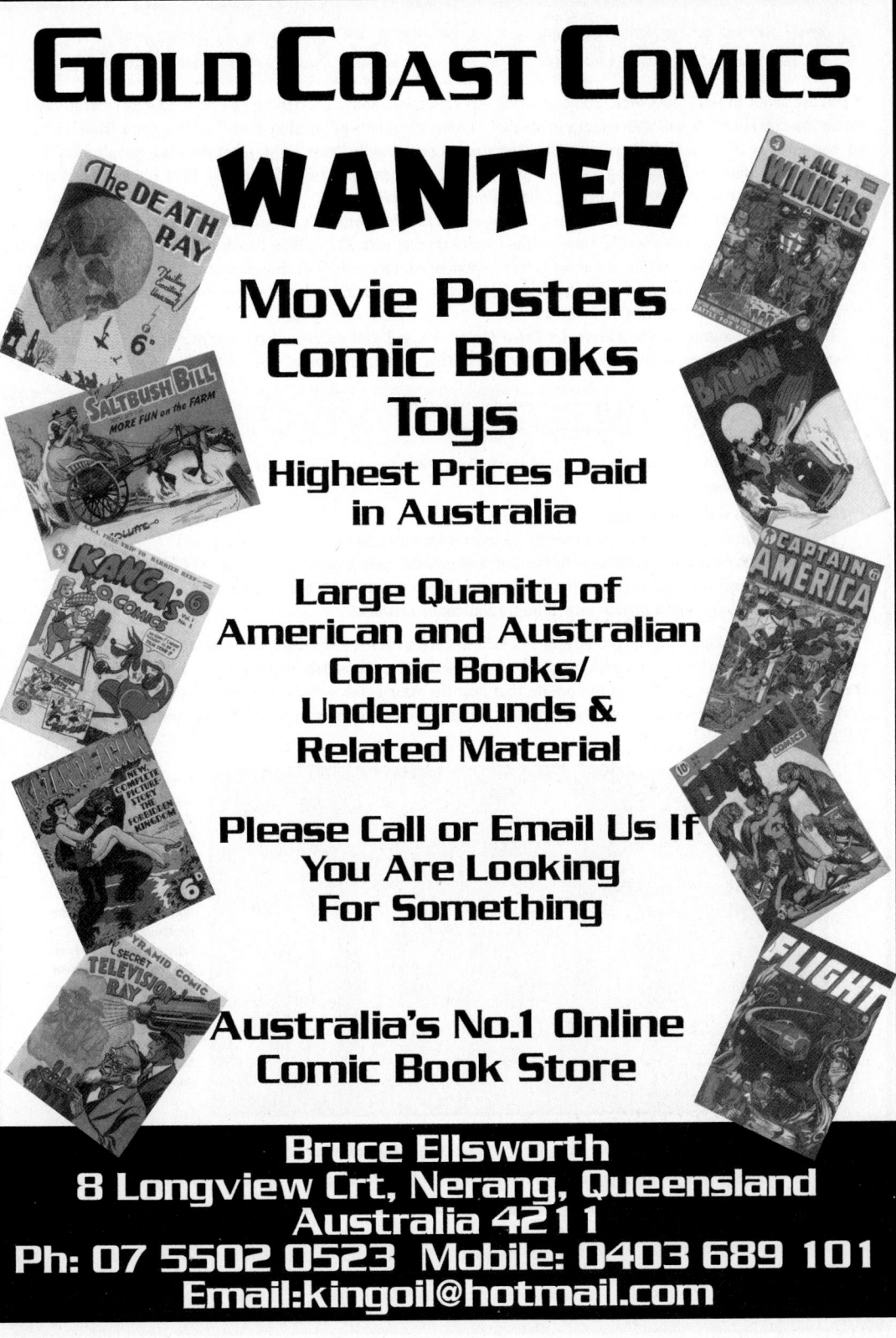

MY HISTORY IN COMICS:

If you are about to sell your Comic Book or Comic Art collection, above everything else seek an *experienced dealer whom you can trust.* I began with comics in the early 1960s, eventually publishing the EC fanzine *Squa Tront.* I attended conventions (even before there was *The Overstreet Comic Book Price Guide*), introducing people like Bruce Hamilton to fandom and becoming friends with *MAD Magazine* publisher Bill Gaines. By 1974 I had opened one of the first specialty comic stores in America, *The Million Year Picnic.*

Two partnerships and twenty years later, I inaugurated the first *Sotheby's Comic Book and Comic Art Auctions* in the fall of 1991. The auctions set the tone for the comics market with $12 million in sales and brought national press coverage and respect that comics had never before experienced. I recently have moved onto *eBay* with special "event" auctions that have sold over $1.5 million during the past two years and made me one of the leading *PowerSellers* in America for rare *Comic Art and Comic Books.*

I am also the author of *The Comic Art Price Guide*, 1st and 2nd editions, have recently finished Bradbury: An Illustrated Life for William Morrow, and also wrote The 100 Greatest Comic Books, just out this year from Whitman Press.

MY PROMISE TO YOU:

What all this means to you the seller is that in Jerry Weist you have one of the most experienced and capable people in comics at your disposal.

** Do you want to sell your comics?

I can give you the best price, and honestly appraise your collection before you sell.

** Do you want to bring your collection to auction, and possibly gain a better percentage of Guide value?

I have been bringing people to auction for the past fifteen years – with outstanding results!

** Do you want to consider a private sale of important comic artwork?

I have been working with the top buyers and VIP clients for over twenty years, and I wrote the book on comic art prices. My promise to you is that with my years of experience, I can honestly evaluate your collectibles and give you the assurance that you can choose the option that best fits your needs — Private Sales, Auction Sales or Individual Purchase. I have the flexibility to act as a consult, helping you decide how to best sell your collection and gain top dollar.

Jerry Weist, Ray Bradbury and Al Feldstein during filming for Tales From The Crypt: From Comic Books To Television, produced by Chip Selby in the fall of 2003. This photo was taken during the filming for the special DVD release interview where Bradbury and Feldstein met for the first time on film to discuss their experiences working together on EC's Bradbury adaptations.

You may contact me at jerryweist@adelphia.net, my home phone (978) 283-1419, or my home office at Jerry Weist, 18 Edgemoor Road, Gloucester, Massachusetts, 10930, USA.

Senior Overstreet Advisor since the 1970s, Charter CGC Member, Sotheby's Comic Art and Comic Book Consultant, eBay seller of the month and Power Seller with over 400 100% positive feedbacks, author of *The Comic Art Price Guide*, with over 40 years experience in the comic field.

COMIC
BUY

- Timelys
- MLJs
- Golden Age DCs
- "Mile High" Copies (Church Collection)
- "San Francisco," "Bethlehem" and "Chicago" Copies
- 1950s Horror and Sci-Fi Comics
- Fox/Quality/ECs
- Silver Age Marvels and DCs
- Most other brands and titles from the Golden and Silver Age

Specializing In Large Silver And Golden Age Collections

JOHN VERZYL AND DAUGHTER ROSE, "HARD AT WORK."

John Verzyl started collecting comic books in 1965, and within ten years he had amassed thousands of Golden and Silver Age comic books. In 1979, with his wife Nanette, he opened "COMIC HEAVEN," a retail store devoted entirely to the buying and selling of comic books.

Over the years, John Verzyl has come to be recognized as an authority in the field of comic books. He has served as a special advisor to the "Overstreet Comic Book Price Guide" for the last 25 years. Thousands of his "mint" comics were photographed for Ernst Gerber's "Photo-Journal Guide to Comic Books." His tables and displays at the annual San Diego Comic Convention and the Chicago Comic Convention draw customers from all over the country.

The first COMIC HEAVEN AUCTION was held in 1987, and today his Auction Catalogs are mailed out to more than ten thousand interested collectors and dealers.

Comic Heaven
John and Nanette Verzyl
P.O. Box 900
Big Sandy, TX 75755
www.comicheaven.net
1-903-636-5555

YOU
CAN MAKE A
DIFFERENCE!

  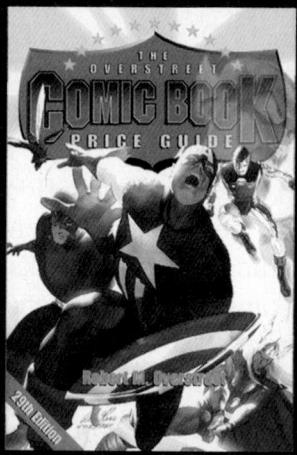

The Overstreet Comic Book Price Guide doesn't happen by magic. A network of advisors - made up of experienced dealers, collectors and comic historians - gives us input for every edition we publish. If you spot an error or omission in this or any of our publications, let us know!

Write to us at Gemstone Publishing, Inc., P.O. Box 12001, York, PA 17402
Or e-mail feedback@gemstonepub.com

We want your help!

Big Little Books

INTRODUCTION

In 1932, at the depths of the Great Depression, comic books were not selling despite their successes in the previous two decades. Desperate publishers had already reduced prices to 25¢, but this was still too much for many people to spend on entertainment.

Comic books quickly evolved into two newer formats, the comics magazine and the Big Little Book. Both types retailed for 10¢.

Big Little Books began by reprinting the art (and adapting the stories) from newspaper comics. As their success grew and publishers began commissioning original material, movie adaptations and other entertainment-derived stories became commonplace.

GRADING

Before a Big Little Book's value can he assessed, its condition or state of preservation must be determined. A book in **Near Mint** condition will bring many times the price of the same book in **Poor** condition. Many variables influence the grading of a Big Little Book and all must be considered in the final evaluation. Due to the way they are constructed, damage occurs with very little use - usually to the spine, book edges and binding. More important defects that affect grading are: Split spines, pages missing, page browning or brittleness, writing, crayoning, loose pages, color fading, chunks missing, and rolling or out of square. The following grading guide is given to aid the novice:

9.4 Near Mint: The overall look is as if it was just purchased and maybe opened once; only subtle defects are allowed; paper is cream to off-white, supple and fresh; cover is flat with no surface wear or creases; inks and colors are bright; small penciled or inked arrival dates are acceptable; very slight blunting of corners at top and bottom of spine are common; outside corners are cut square and sharp. Books in this grade could bring prices of guide and a half or more.

9.0 Very Fine/Near Mint: Limited number of defects; full cover gloss with only very slight wear on book corners and edges; very minor foxing; very minor tears allowed, binding still square and tight with no pages missing; paper quality still fresh from cream to off-white. Dates, stamps or initials allowed on cover or inside.

8.0 Very Fine: Most of the cover gloss retained with minor wear appearing at corners and around edges; spine tight with no pages missing; cream/tan paper allowed if still supple; up to 1/4" bend allowed on covers with no color break; cover relatively flat; minor tears allowed.

6.0 Fine: Slight wear beginning to show; cover gloss reduced but still clean, pages tan/brown but still supple (not brittle); up to 1/4" split or color break allowed; minor discoloration and/or foxing allowed.

4.0 Very Good: Obviously a read copy with original printing luster almost gone; some fading and discoloration, but not soiled; some signs of wear such as corner splits and spine rolling; paper can be brown but not brittle; a few pages can be loose but not missing; no chunks missing; blunted corners acceptable.

2.0 Good: An average used copy complete with only minor pieces missing from the spine, which may be partially split; slightly soiled or marked with spine rolling; color flaking and wear around edges, but perfectly sound and legible; could have minor tape repairs but otherwise complete.

1.0 Fair: Very heavily read and soiled with small chunks missing from cover; most or all of spine could be missing; multiple splits in spine and loose pages, but still sound and legible, bringing 50 to 70 percent of good price.

0.5 Poor: Damaged, heavily weathered, soiled or otherwise unsuited for collecting purposes.

IMPORTANT

Most BLBs on the market today will fall in the **Good** to **Fine** grade category. When **Very Fine** to **Near Mint** BLBs are offered for sale, they usually bring premium prices.

A WORD ON PRICING

The prices are given for **Good, Fine** and **Very Fine/Near Mint** condition. A book in **Fair** would be 50-70% of the **Good** price. **Very Good** would be halfway between the **Good** and **Fine** price, and **Very Fine** would be halfway between the **Fine** and **Very Fine/**

Near Mint price. The prices listed were averaged from convention sales, dealers' lists, adzines, auctions, and by special contact with dealers and collectors from coast to coast. The prices and the spreads were determined from sales of copies in available condition or the highest grade known. Since most available copies are in the **Good** to **Fine** range, neither dealers nor collectors should let the **Very Fine/Near Mint** column influence the prices they are willing to charge or pay for books in less than near perfect condition.

The prices listed reflect a six times spread from **Good** to **Very Fine/ Near Mint** (1 - 3 - 6). We feel this spread accurately reflects the current market, especially when you consider the scarcity of books in **Very Fine/Near Mint** condition. When one or both end sheets are missing, the book's value would drop about a half grade.

Books with movie scenes are of double importance due to the high crossover demand by movie collectors.

Abbreviations: a-art; c-cover; nn-no number; p-pages; r-reprint.

Publisher Codes: BRP-Blue Ribbon Press; **ERB**-Edgar Rice Burroughs; **EVW**-Engel van Wiseman; **FAW**-Fawcett Publishing Co.; **Gold**-Goldsmith Publishing Co.; **Lynn**-Lynn Publishing Co.; **McKay**-David McKay Co.; **Whit**-Whitman Publishing Co.; **World**-World Syndicate Publishing Co.

Terminology: *All Pictures Comics*-no text, all drawings; *Fast-Action*-A special series of Dell books highly collected; *Flip Pictures*-upper right corner of interior pages contain drawings that are put into motion when rifled; *Movie Scenes*-book illustrated with scenes from the movie. *Soft Cover*-A thin single sheet of cardboard used in binding most of the giveaway versions.

"Big Little Book" and "Better Little Book" are registered trademarks of Whitman Publishing Co. "Little Big Book" is a registered trademark of the Saalfield Publishing Co.

"Pop-Up" is a registered trademark of Blue Ribbon Press. "Little Big Book" is a registered trademark of the Saalfield Co.

Top 20 Big Little Books and related size books*

Issue#	Rank	Title	Price
731	1	Mickey Mouse the Mail Pilot (variant version of Mickey Mouse #717) (Fine copy sold at auction for $5,090)	
nn	2	Mickey Mouse and Minnie Mouse at Macy's	$3,200
717	3	Mickey Mouse (skinny Mickey on-c)	$2,850
nn	4	Mickey Mouse and Minnie March to Macy's	$2,200
W-707	5	Dick Tracy The Detective	$2,100
725	6	Big Little Mother Goose HC	$1,850
717	7	Mickey Mouse (reg. Mickey on-c)	$1,500
4063	8	Popeye Thimble Theater Starring... (2nd printing)	$1,470
721	9	Big Little Paint Book	$1,400
725	10	Big Little Mother Goose SC	$1,350
nn	10	Mickey Mouse (Great Big Midget Book)	$1,350
4062	12	Mickey Mouse and the Smugglers	$1,300
2070	13	Big Big Paint Book	$1,275
4063	14	Popeye Thimble Theater Starring... (1st printing)	$1,260
nn	15	Buck Rogers	$1,200
nn	15	Mickey Mouse Silly Symphonies	$1,200
4062	17	Mickey Mouse, The Story of...	$1,100
nn	18	Mickey Mouse Sails For Treasure Island (Great Big Midget Book)	$1,050
nn	19	Tarzan	$980
4057	20	Buck Rogers, The Adventures of...	$975

*Includes only the various sized BLBs; no premiums, giveaways or other divergent forms are included.

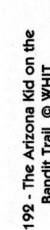

1058 - The Adventures of Tom Sawyer © Saalfield

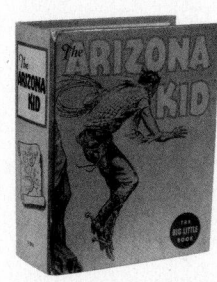

1192 - The Arizona Kid on the Bandit Trail © WHIT

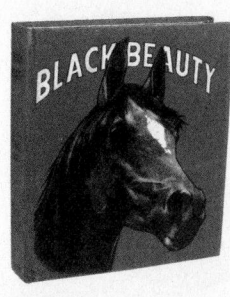

1057 - Black Beauty © Saalfield

	GD	FN	VF/NM
1175-0- Abbie an' Slats, 1940, Saalfield, 400 pgs.	11.00	33.00	72.00
1182- Abbie an' Slats-and Becky, 1940, Saalfield, 400 pgs.	11.00	33.00	72.00
1177- Ace Drummond, 1935, Whitman, 432 pgs.	12.00	36.00	80.00
Admiral Byrd (See Paramount Newsreel ...)			
nn- Adventures of Charlie McCarthy and Edgar Bergen, The, 1938, Dell, 194 pgs., Fast-Action Story, soft-c	24.00	72.00	170.00
1422- Adventures of Huckleberry Finn, The, 1939, Whitman, 432 pgs., Henry E. Vallely-a	10.00	30.00	62.00
1648- Adventures of Jim Bowie (TV Series), 1958, Whitman, 280 pgs.	5.00	15.00	30.00
1056- Adventures of Krazy Kat and Ignatz Mouse in Koko Land, 1934, Saalfield, 160 pgs., oblong size, hard-c, Herriman-c/a	65.00	195.00	460.00
1306- Adventures of Krazy Kat and Ignatz Mouse in Koko Land, 1934, Saalfield, 164 pgs., oblong size, soft-c, Herriman-c/a	65.00	195.00	460.00
1082- Adventures of Pete the Tramp, The, 1935, Saalfield, hard-c, by C. D. Russell	10.00	30.00	68.00
1312- Adventures of Pete the Tramp, The, 1935, Saalfield, soft-c, by C. D. Russell	10.00	30.00	68.00
1053- Adventures of Tim Tyler, 1934, Saalfield, hard-c, oblong size, by Lyman Young	24.00	72.00	165.00
1303- Adventures of Tim Tyler, 1934, Saalfield, soft-c, oblong size, by Lyman Young	24.00	72.00	165.00
1058- Adventures of Tom Sawyer, The, 1934, Saalfield, 160 pgs., hard-c, Park Sumner-a	10.00	30.00	68.00
1308- Adventures of Tom Sawyer, The, 1934, Saalfield, 160 pgs., soft-c, Park Sumner-a	10.00	30.00	68.00
1448- Air Fighters of America, 1941, Whitman, 432 pgs., flip picture	12.00	36.00	80.00
Alexander Smart, ESQ. (See Top Line Comics)			
759- Alice in Wonderland, 1933, Whitman, 160 pgs., hard-c, photo-c, movie scenes	27.00	81.00	190.00
1481- Allen Pike of the Parachute Squad U.S.A., 1941, Whitman, 432 pgs.	12.00	36.00	78.00
763- Alley Oop and Dinny, 1935, Whitman, 384 pgs., V. T. Hamlin-a	19.00	57.00	130.00
1473- Alley Oop and Dinny in the Jungles of Moo, 1938, Whitman, 432 pgs., V. T. Hamlin-a	19.00	57.00	130.00
nn- Alley Oop and the Missing King of Moo, 1938, Whitman, 36 pgs., 2 1/2" x 3 1/2", Penny Book	12.00	36.00	80.00
nn- Alley Oop in the Kingdom of Foo, 1938, Whitman, 68 pgs., 3 1/4" x 3 1/2", Pan-Am premium	26.00	78.00	180.00
nn- "Alley Oop the Invasion of Moo," 1935, Whitman, 260 pgs., Cocomalt premium, soft-c; V. T. Hamlin-a	20.00	60.00	140.00
Andy Burnette (See Walt Disney's...)			
Andy Panda (Also see Walter Lantz ...)			
531- Andy Panda, 1943, Whitman, 3 3/4x6 3/4", Tall Comic Book, All Pictures Comics	24.00	72.00	165.00
1425- Andy Panda and Tiny Tom, 1944, Whitman, All Pictures Comics	12.00	36.00	78.00
1431- Andy Panda and the Mad Dog Mystery, 1947, Whitman, 288 pgs., by Walter Lantz	11.00	33.00	72.00
1441- Andy Panda in the City of Ice, 1948, Whitman, All Picture Comics, by Walter Lantz	12.00	36.00	78.00
1459- Andy Panda and the Pirate Ghosts, 1949, Whitman, 88 pgs., by Walter Lantz	11.00	33.00	72.00
1485- Andy Panda's Vacation, 1946, Whitman, All Pictures Comics, by Walter Lantz	12.00	36.00	78.00
15- Andy Panda (The Adventures of), 1942, Dell, Fast-Action Story	24.00	72.00	165.00
707-10- Andy Panda and Presto the Pup, 1949, Whitman	11.00	33.00	72.00
1130- Apple Mary and Dennie Foil the Swindlers, 1936, Whitman, 432 pgs. (Forerunner to Mary Worth)	11.00	33.00	72.00
1403- Apple Mary and Dennie's Lucky Apples, 1939, Whitman, 432 pgs.	11.00	33.00	72.00
2017-(#17)-Aquaman-Scourge of the Sea, 1968, Whitman, 260 pgs., 39 cents, hard-c, color illos	4.00	12.00	25.00
1192- Arizona Kid on the Bandit Trail, The, 1936, Whitman, 432 pgs.	10.00	30.00	62.00
1469- Bambi (Walt Disney's), 1942, Whitman, 432 pgs.	24.00	72.00	165.00
1497- Bambi's Children (Disney), 1943, Whitman, 432 pgs., Disney Studios-a	24.00	72.00	165.00
1138- Bandits at Bay, 1938, Saalfield, 400 pgs.	9.00	29.00	58.00
1459- Barney Baxter in the Air with the Eagle Squadron, 1938, Whitman, 432 pgs.	11.00	33.00	72.00
1083- Barney Google, 1935, Saalfield, hard-c	19.00	57.00	130.00
1313- Barney Google, 1935, Saalfield, soft-c	19.00	57.00	130.00
2031-(#31)- Batman and Robin in the Cheetah Caper, 1969, Whitman, 258 pgs.	4.00	12.00	25.00
5771- Batman and Robin in the Cheetah Caper, 1974, Whitman, 258 pgs., 49 cents	2.00	5.00	10.00
5771-1- Batman and Robin in the Cheetah Caper, 1974, Whitman, 258 pgs., 69 cents	2.00	5.00	10.00
5771-2- Batman and Robin in the Cheetah Caper, 1975?, Whitman, 258 pgs.	2.00	5.00	10.00
nn- Beauty and the Beast, nd (1930s), np (Whitman), 36 pgs., 3" x 3 1/2" Penny Book	4.00	12.00	25.00
760- Believe It or Not!, 1933, Whitman, 160 pgs., by Ripley (c. 1931)	11.00	33.00	85.00
Betty Bear's Lesson (See Wee Little Books)			
1119- Betty Boop in Snow White, 1934, Whitman, 240 pgs., hard-c; adapted from Max Fleischer Paramount Talkartoon	62.00	186.00	435.00
1119- Betty Boop in Snow White, 1934, Whitman, 240 pgs., soft-c; same contents as hard-c	50.00	150.00	350.00
1158- Betty Boop in "Miss Gullivers Travels," 1935, Whitman, 288 pgs., hard-c	54.00	162.00	375.00
2070- Big Big Paint Book, 1936, Whitman, 432 pgs., 8 1/2" x 11 3/8", B&W pages to color	159.00	477.00	1275.00
1432- Big Chief Wahoo and the Lost Pioneers, 1942, Whitman, 432 pgs., Elmer Woggon-a	11.00	33.00	72.00
1443- Big Chief Wahoo and the Great Gusto, 1938, Whitman, 432 pgs., Elmer Woggon-a	11.00	33.00	72.00
1483- Big Chief Wahoo and the Magic Lamp, 1940, Whitman, 432 pgs., flip pictures, Woggon-c/a	11.00	33.00	72.00
725- Big Little Mother Goose, The, 1934, Whitman, 580 pgs. (Rare) Hardcover	231.00	693.00	1850.00
725- Big Little Mother Goose, The, 1934, Whitman, 580 pgs. (Rare) Softcover	169.00	507.00	1350.00
1005- Big Little Nickel Book, 1935, Whitman, 144 pgs., Blackie Bear stories and Donna the Donkey	10.00	30.00	62.00
1006- Big Little Nickel Book, 1935, Whitman, 144 pgs., Blackie Bear stories, folk tales in primer style	10.00	30.00	62.00
1007- Big Little Nickel Book, 1935, Whitman, 144 pgs., Wee Wee Woman, etc.	10.00	30.00	62.00
1008- Big Little Nickel Book, 1935, Whitman, 144 pgs., Peter Rabbit, etc.	10.00	30.00	62.00
721- Big Little Paint Book, The, 1933, Whitman, 336 pgs., 3 3/4" x 8 1/2", for crayoning (Rare)	175.00	525.00	1400.00
1178- Billy of Bar-Zero, 1940, Saalfield, 400 pgs.	10.00	30.00	62.00
773- Billy the Kid, 1935, Whitman, 432 pgs., Hal Arbo-a	11.00	33.00	72.00
1159- Billy the Kid on Tall Butte, 1939, Saalfield, 400 pgs.	10.00	30.00	62.00
1174- Billy the Kid's Pledge, 1940, Saalfield, 400 pgs.	10.00	30.00	62.00
nn- Billy the Kid, Western Outlaw, 1935, Whitman, 260 pgs., Cocomalt premium, Hal Arbo-a, soft-c	12.00	36.00	78.00
1057- Black Beauty, 1934, Saalfield, hard-c	9.00	27.00	57.00
1307- Black Beauty, 1934, Saalfield, soft-c	9.00	27.00	57.00
1414- Black Silver and His Pirate Crew, 1937, Whitman, 300 pgs.	10.00	30.00	68.00
1447- Blaze Brandon with the Foreign Legion, 1938, Whitman, 432 pgs.	10.00	30.00	68.00
1410- Blondie and Dagwood in Hot Water, 1946, Whitman, 352 pgs., by Chic Young	11.00	33.00	72.00

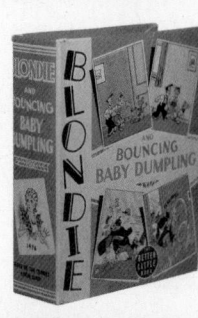

1476 - Blondie and Bouncing Baby Dumpling © WHIT

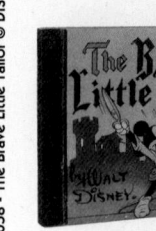

1058 - The Brave Little Tailor © DIS

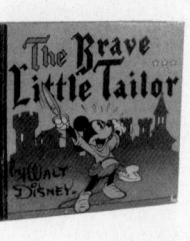

4069 - Buck Jones and the Night Riders © WHIT

	GD	FN	VF/NM

1415- Blondie and Baby Dumpling, 1937, Whitman, 432 pgs., by Chic Young — 12.00 / 36.00 / 78.00

1419- Oh, Blondie the Bumsteads Carry On, 1941, Whitman, 432 pgs., flip pictures, by Chic Young — 12.00 / 36.00 / 78.00

1423- Blondie Who's Boss?, 1942, Whitman, 432 pgs., flip pictures, by Chic Young — 12.00 / 36.00 / 78.00

1429- Blondie with Baby Dumpling and Daisy, 1939, Whitman, 432 pgs., by Chic Young — 10.00 / 36.00 / 78.00

1430- Blondie Count Cookie in Too!, 1947, Whitman, 288 pgs., by Chic Young — 11.00 / 33.00 / 72.00

1438- Blondie and Dagwood Everybody's Happy, 1948, Whitman, 288 pgs., by Chic Young — 11.00 / 33.00 / 72.00

1450- Blondie No Dull Moments, 1948, Whitman, 288 pgs., by Chic Young — 11.00 / 33.00 / 72.00

1463- Blondie Fun For All, 1949, Whitman, 288 pgs., by Chic Young — 11.00 / 33.00 / 72.00

1466- Blondie or Life Among the Bumsteads, 1944, Whitman, 352 pgs., by Chic Young — 12.00 / 36.00 / 78.00

1476- Blondie and Bouncing Baby Dumpling, 1940, Whitman, 432 pgs., by Chic Young — 10.00 / 36.00 / 78.00

1487- Blondie Baby Dumpling and All!, 1941, Whitman, 432 pgs. flip pictures, by Chic Young — 10.00 / 36.00 / 78.00

1490- Blondie Papa Knows Best, 1945, Whitman, 352 pgs., by Chic Young — 11.00 / 33.00 / 72.00

1491- Blondie-Cookie and Daisy's Pups, 1943, Whitman, 1st printing, 432 pgs. — 10.00 / 36.00 / 78.00

1491- Blondie-Cookie and Daisy's Pups, 1943, Whitman, 2nd printing with different back-c & 352 pgs. — 10.00 / 30.00 / 68.00

703-10- Blondie and Dagwood Some Fun!, 1949, Whitman, by Chic Young — 9.00 / 27.00 / 57.00

21- Blondie and Dagwood, 1936, Lynn, by Chic Young — 19.00 / 57.00 / 135.00

1108- Bobby Benson on the H-Bar-O Ranch, 1934, Whitman, 300 pgs., based on radio serial — 12.00 / 36.00 / 87.00

Bobby Thatcher and the Samarang Emerald (See Top-Line Comics)

1432- Bob Stone the Young Detective, 1937, Whitman, 240 pgs., movie scenes — 12.00 / 36.00 / 78.00

2002- (#2)-Bonanza-The Bubble Gum Kid, 1967, Whitman, 260 pgs., 39 cents, hard-c, color illos — 4.00 / 12.00 / 25.00

1139- Border Eagle, The, 1938, Saalfield, 400 pgs. — 9.00 / 27.00 / 57.00

1153- Boss of the Chisholm Trail, 1939, Saalfield, 400 pgs. — 9.00 / 27.00 / 57.00

1425- Brad Turner in Transatlantic Flight, 1939, Whitman, 432 pgs. — 10.00 / 30.00 / 62.00

1058- Brave Little Tailor, The (Disney), 1939, Whitman, 5" x 5 1/2", 68 pgs., hard-c (Mickey Mouse) — 15.00 / 45.00 / 105.00

1427- Brenda Starr and the Masked Impostor, 1943, Whitman, 352 pgs., Dale Messick-a — 14.00 / 42.00 / 100.00

1426- Brer Rabbit (Walt Disney's ...), 1947, Whitman, All Picture Comics, from "Song Of The South" movie — 20.00 / 60.00 / 140.00

704-10- Brer Rabbit, 1949, Whitman — 17.00 / 51.00 / 120.00

1059- Brick Bradford in the City Beneath the Sea, 1934, Saalfield, hard-c, by William Ritt & Clarence Gray — 16.00 / 48.00 / 115.00

1309- Brick Bradford in the City Beneath the Sea, 1934, Saalfield, soft-c, by Ritt & Gray — 16.00 / 48.00 / 115.00

1468- Brick Bradford with Brocco the Modern Buccaneer, 1938, Whitman, 432 pgs., by Wrn. Ritt & Clarence Gray — 11.00 / 33.00 / 72.00

1133- Bringing Up Father, 1936, Whitman, 432 pgs., by George McManus — 15.00 / 45.00 / 105.00

1100- Broadway Bill, 1935, Saalfield, photo-c, 4 1/2" x 5 1/4", movie scenes (Columbia Pictures, horse racing) — 12.00 / 36.00 / 78.00

1580- Broadway Bill, 1935, Saalfield, soft-c, photo-c, movie scenes — 12.00 / 36.00 / 78.00

1181- Broncho Bill, 1940, Saalfield, 400 pgs. — 10.00 / 30.00 / 62.00

nn- Broncho Bill, 1935, Whitman, 148 pgs., 3 1/2" x 4", Tarzan Ice Cream cup lid premium — 33.00 / 99.00 / 230.00

nn- Broncho Bill in Suicide Canyon (See Top-Line Comics)

1417- Bronc Peeler the Lone Cowboy, 1937, Whitman, 432 pgs., by Fred Harman, forerunner of Red Ryder (also see Red Death on the

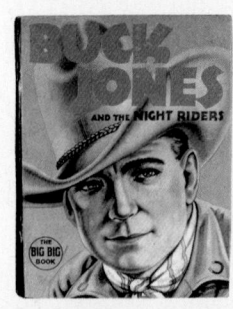

	GD	FN	VF/NM

Range) — 11.00 / 33.00 / 72.00

nn- Brownies' Merry Adventures, The, 1993, Barefoot Books, 202 pgs., reprints from Palmer Cox's late 1800s books — 2.00 / 6.00 / 15.00

1470- Buccaneer, The, 1938, Whitman, 240 pgs., photo-c, movie scenes — 12.00 / 36.00 / 85.00

1646- Buccaneers, The (TV Series), 1958, Whitman, 4 1/2" x 5 1/4", 280 pgs., Russ Manning-a — 5.00 / 15.00 / 30.00

1104- Buck Jones in the Fighting Code, 1934, Whitman, 160 pgs., hard-c, movie scenes — 17.00 / 51.00 / 120.00

1116- Buck Jones in Ride 'Em Cowboy (Universal Presents), 1935, Whitman, 240 pgs., photo-c, movie scenes — 17.00 / 51.00 / 120.00

1174- Buck Jones in the Roaring West (Universal Presents), 1935, Whitman, 240 pgs., movie scenes — 17.00 / 51.00 / 120.00

1188- Buck Jones in the Fighting Rangers (Universal Presents), 1936, Whitman, 240 pgs., photo-c, movie scenes — 17.00 / 51.00 / 120.00

1404- Buck Jones and the Two-Gun Kid, 1937, Whitman, 432 pgs. — 12.00 / 36.00 / 85.00

1451- Buck Jones and the Killers of Crooked Butte, 1940, Whitman, 432 pgs. — 12.00 / 36.00 / 85.00

1461- Buck Jones and the Rock Creek Cattle War, 1938, Whitman, 432 pgs. — 12.00 / 36.00 / 85.00

1486- Buck Jones and the Rough Riders in Forbidden Trails, 1943, Whitman, flip pictures, based on movie; Tim McCoy app. — 16.00 / 48.00 / 110.00

3- Buck Jones in the Red Ryder, 1934, EVW, 160 pgs., movie scenes — 21.00 / 63.00 / 150.00

8- Buck Jones Cowboy Masquerade, 1938, Whitman, 132 pgs., soft-c, 3 3/4" x 3 1/2", Buddy Book premium — 39.00 / 117.00 / 275.00

15- Buck Jones in Rocky Rhodes, 1935, EVW, 160 pgs., photo-c, movie scenes — 21.00 / 63.00 / 150.00

4069- Buck Jones and the Night Riders, 1937, Whitman, 7" x 9", 320 pgs., Big Big Book — 71.00 / 213.00 / 500.00

nn- Buck Jones on the Six-Gun Trail, 1939, Whitman, 36 pgs., 2 1/2" x 3 1/2", Penny Book — 11.00 / 33.00 / 70.00

nn- Buck Jones Big Thrill Chewing Gum, 1934, Whitman, 8 pgs., 2 1/2" x 3 1/2" (6 diff.) each... — 18.00 / 54.00 / 125.00

742- Buck Rogers in the 25th Century A.D., 1933, Whitman, 320 pgs., Dick Calkins-a — 43.00 / 129.00 / 300.00

nn- Buck Rogers in the 25th Century A.D., 1933, Whitman, 204 pgs.,Cocomalt premium, Calkins-a — 27.00 / 81.00 / 190.00

765- Buck Rogers in the City Below the Sea, 1934, Whitman, 320 pgs., Dick Calkins-a — 33.00 / 99.00 / 230.00

765- Buck Rogers in the City Below the Sea, 1934, Whitman, 324 pgs., soft-c, Dick Calkins-c/a — 58.00 / 174.00 / 410.00

1143- Buck Rogers on the Moons of Saturn, 1934, Whitman, 320 pgs., Dick Calkins-a — 34.00 / 102.00 / 240.00

nn- Buck Rogers on the Moons of Saturn, 1934, Whitman, 324 pgs., premium w/no ads, soft 3-color-c, Dick Calkins-a — 58.00 / 174.00 / 410.00

1169- Buck Rogers and the Depth Men of Jupiter, 1935, Whitman, 432 pgs., Calkins-a — 33.00 / 99.00 / 230.00

1178- Buck Rogers and the Doom Comet, 1935, Whitman, 432 pgs., Calkins-a — 31.00 / 93.00 / 220.00

1197- Buck Rogers and the Planetoid Plot, 1936, Whitman, 432 pgs., Calkins-a — 31.00 / 93.00 / 220.00

1409- Buck Rogers Vs. the Fiend of Space, 1940, Whitman, 432 pgs., Calkins-a — 31.00 / 93.00 / 220.00

1437- Buck Rogers in the War with the Planet Venus, 1938, Whitman, 432 pgs., Calkins-a — 31.00 / 93.00 / 220.00

1474- Buck Rogers and the Overturned World, 1941, Whitman, 432 pgs., flip pictures, Calkins-a — 32.00 / 96.00 / 225.00

1490- Buck Rogers and the Super-Dwarf of Space, 1943, Whitman, 11 Pictures Comics, Calkins-a — 31.00 / 93.00 / 220.00

4057- Buck Rogers, The Adventures of, 1934, Whitman, 7" x 9 1/2", 320 pgs., Big Big Book, "The Story of Buck Rogers on the Planet Eros," Calkins-c/a — 124.00 / 372.00 / 975.00

nn- Buck Rogers, 1935, Whitman, 4" x 3 1/2", Tarzan Ice Cream cup premium (Rare) — 150.00 / 450.00 / 1200.00

nn- Buck Rogers in the City of Floating Globes, 1935, Whitman, 258 pgs., Cocomalt premium, soft-c, Dick Calkins-a

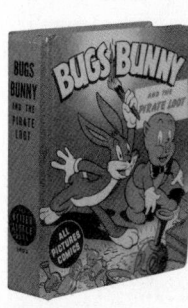

1403 - Bugs Bunny and the Pirate Loot © W/B

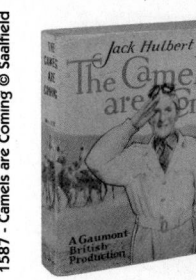

1587 - Camels are Coming © Saalfield

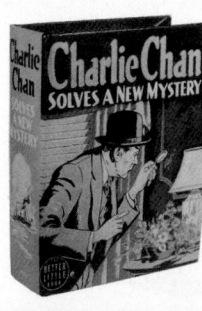

1459 - Charlie Chan Solves a New Mystery © WHIT

	GD	FN	VF/NM
	104.00	312.00	725.00
nn- **Buck Rogers Big Thrill Chewing Gum**, 1934, Whitman,			
8 pgs., 2 1/2" x 3 " (6 diff.) each...	24.00	72.00	170.00
1135- **Buckskin and Bullets**, 1938, Saalfield, 400 pgs.			
	10.00	30.00	62.00
Buffalo Bill (See Wild West Adventures of ...)			
nn- **Buffalo Bill**, 1934, World Syndicate, All pictures, by J. Carroll Mansfield			
	10.00	30.00	62.00
713- **Buffalo Bill and the Pony Express**, 1934, Whitman, hard-c, 384 pgs.,			
Hal Arbo-a	11.00	33.00	72.00
nn- **Buffalo Bill and the Pony Express**, 1934, Whitman, soft-c, 384 pgs.,			
Hal Arbo-a; three-color premium	33.00	99.00	230.00
1194- **Buffalo Bill Plays a Lone Hand**, 1936, Whitman, 432 pgs.,			
Hal Arbo-a	10.00	30.00	62.00
530- **Bugs Bunny**, 1943, Whitman, All Pictures Comics, Tall Comic Book,			
3 1/4" x 8 1/4", reprints/Looney Tunes 1 & 5	28.00	84.00	195.00
1403- **Bugs Bunny and the Pirate Loot**, 1947, Whitman, All Pictures Comics			
	11.00	33.00	72.00
1435- **Bugs Bunny**, 1944, Whitman, All Pictures Comics			
	12.00	36.00	78.00
1440- **Bugs Bunny in Risky Business**, 1948, Whitman, All Pictures & Comics			
	11.00	33.00	72.00
1455- **Bugs Bunny and Klondike Gold**, 1948, Whitman, 288 pgs.			
	11.00	33.00	72.00
1465- **Bugs Bunny The Masked Marvel**, 1949, Whitman, 288 pgs.			
	11.00	33.00	72.00
1496- **Bugs Bunny and His Pals**, 1945, Whitman, All Pictures Comics; r/Four Color Comics #33	12.00	36.00	82.00
13- **Bugs Bunny and the Secret of Storm Island**, 1942, Dell,194 pgs.,			
Fast-Action Story	33.00	99.00	230.00
706-10- **Bugs Bunny and the Giant Brothers**, 1949, Whitman			
	10.00	30.00	62.00
2007- (#7)-**Bugs Bunny-Double Trouble on Diamond Island**, 1967, Whitman, 260 pgs., 39 cents, hard-c, color illos			
	5.00	15.00	30.00
2029-(#29)- **Bugs Bunny, Accidental Adventure**, 1969, Whitman, 256 pgs., hard-c, color illos.	3.00	9.00	20.00
2952- **Bugs Bunny's Mistake**, 1949, Whitman, 3 1/4" x 4", 24 pgs., Tiny Tales, full color (5 cents) (1030-5 on back-c)	10.00	30.00	62.00
5757-2- **Bugs Bunny in Double Trouble on Diamond Island**,1967, (1980-reprints #2007), Whitman, 260 pgs., soft-c, 79 cents, B&W			
	2.00	5.00	10.00
5758- **Bugs Bunny, Accidental Adventure**, 1973, Whitman, 256 pgs., soft-c, B&W illos.	2.00	5.00	10.00
5758-1- **Bugs Bunny, Accidental Adventure**, 1973, Whitman, 256 pgs., soft-c, B&W illos.	2.00	5.00	10.00
5772- **Bugs Bunny the Last Crusader**, 1975, Whitman, 49 cents, flip-it book	2.00	5.00	10.00
5772-2- **Bugs Bunny the Last Crusader**, 1975, Whitman, $1.50, flip-it book	1.00	3.00	6.00
1169- **Bullet Benton**, 1939, Saalfield, 400 pgs.	10.00	30.00	62.00
nn- **Bulletman and the Return of Mr. Murder**, 1941, Fawcett, 196 pgs., Dime Action Book	48.00	144.00	340.00
1142- **Bullets Across the Border** (A Billy The Kid story), 1938, Saalfield, 400 pgs.	10.00	30.00	62.00
Bunky (See Top-Line Comics)			
837- **Bunty** (Punch and Judy), 1935, Whitman, 28 pgs., Magic-Action with 3 pop-ups	15.00	45.00	105.00
1091- **Burn 'Em Up Barnes**, 1935, Saalfield, hard-c, movie scenes			
	14.00	42.00	95.00
1321- **Burn 'Em Up Barnes**, 1935, Saalfield, soft-c, movie scenes			
	14.00	42.00	95.00
1415- **Buz Sawyer and Bomber 13**,1946, Whitman, 352 pgs., Roy Crane-a			
	14.00	42.00	95.00
1412- **Calling W-1-X-Y-Z, Jimmy Kean and the Radio Spies**, 1939, Whitman, 300 pgs.	11.00	33.00	72.00
Call of the Wild (See Jack London's...)			
1107- **Camels are Coming**, 1935, Saalfield, movie scenes			
	10.00	30.00	68.00
1587- **Camels are Coming**, 1935, Saalfield, movie scenes			

	GD	FN	VF/NM
	10.00	30.00	68.00
nn- **Captain and the Kids, Boys Vill Be Boys, The**, 1938, 68 pgs., Pan-Am Oil premium, soft-c	14.00	42.00	95.00
1128- **Captain Easy Soldier of Fortune**, 1934, Whitman, 432 pgs., Roy Crane-a	14.00	42.00	95.00
nn- **Captain Easy Soldier of Fortune**, 1934, Whitman, 436 pgs., Premium, no ads, soft 3-color-c, Roy Crane-a	24.00	72.00	165.00
1474- **Captain Easy Behind Enemy Lines**, 1943, Whitman, 352 pgs., Roy Crane-a	12.00	36.00	85.00
nn- **Captain Easy and Wash Tubbs**, 1935, 260 pgs., Cocomalt premium, Roy Crane-a	12.00	36.00	85.00
1444- **Captain Frank Hawks Air Ace and the League of Twelve**, 1938, Whitman, 432 pgs.	11.00	33.00	72.00
nn- **Captain Marvel**, 1941, Fawcett, 196 pgs., Dime Action Book	60.00	180.00	420.00
1402- **Captain Midnight and Sheik Jomak Khan**, 1946, Whitman, 352 pgs.	24.00	72.00	165.00
1452- **Captain Midnight and the Moon Woman**, 1943, Whitman, 352 pgs.	25.00	75.00	175.00
1458- **Captain Midnight Vs. The Terror of the Orient**, 1942, Whitman, 432 pgs., flip pictures, Hess-a	25.00	75.00	175.00
1488- **Captain Midnight and the Secret Squadron**, 1941, Whitman, 432 pgs.	25.00	75.00	175.00
Captain Robb of. (See Dirigible ZR90 ...)			
nn- **Cauliflower Catnip Pearls of Peril**, 1981, Teacup Tales, 290 pgs., Joe Wehrle Jr.-s/a; deliberately printed on aged-looking paper to look like an old BLB	4.00	12.00	25.00
20- **Ceiling Zero**, 1936, Lynn, 128 pgs., 7 1/2" x 5", hard-c, James Cagney, Pat O'Brien photos on-c, movie scenes, Warner Bros. Pictures			
	11.00	33.00	72.00
1093- **Chandu the Magician**, 1935, Saalfield, 5" x 5 1/4", 160 pgs., hard-c, Bela Lugosi photo-c, movie scenes	15.00	45.00	105.00
1323- **Chandu the Magician**, 1935, Saalfield, 5" x 5 1/4", 160 pgs., soft-c, Bela Lugosi photo-c	16.00	48.00	115.00
Charlie Chan (See Inspector ...)			
1459- **Charlie Chan Solves a New Mystery** (See Inspector..), 1940, Whitman, 432 pgs., Alfred Andriola-a	14.00	42.00	100.00
1478- **Charlie Chan of the Honolulu Police, Inspector**, 1939, Whitman, 432 pgs., Andriola-a	14.00	42.00	100.00
Charlie McCarthy (See Story Of ...)			
734- **Chester Gump at Silver Creek Ranch**, 1933, Whitman, 320 pgs., Sidney Smith-a	14.00	42.00	95.00
nn- **Chester Gump at Silver Creek Ranch**, 1933, Whitman, 204 pgs., Cocomalt premium, soft-c, Sidney Smith-a	16.00	48.00	115.00
nn- **Chester Gump at Silver Creek Ranch**, 1933, Whitman, 52 pgs., 4" x 5 1/2", premium-no ads, soft-c, Sidney Smith-a			
	24.00	72.00	165.00
766- **Chester Gump Finds the Hidden Treasure**, 1934, Whitman, 320 pgs., Sidney Smith-a	14.00	42.00	100.00
nn- **Chester Gump Finds the Hidden Treasure**, 1934, Whitman, 52 pgs., 3 1/2" x 5 3/4", premium-no ads, soft-c, Sidney Smith-a			
	24.00	72.00	165.00
nn- **Chester Gump Finds the Hidden Treasure**, 1934, Whitman, 52 pgs., 4" x 5 1/2", premium-no ads, Sidney Smith-a			
	24.00	72.00	165.00
1146- **Chester Gump in the City Of Gold**, 1935, Whitman, 432 pgs., Sidney Smith-a	14.00	42.00	95.00
nn- **Chester Gump in the City Of Gold**, 1935, Whitman, 436 pgs., premium-no ads, 3-color, soft-c, Sidney Smith-a			
	27.00	81.00	190.00
1402- **Chester Gump in the Pole to Pole Flight**, 1937, Whitman, 432 pgs.	12.00	36.00	85.00
5- **Chester Gump and His Friends**, 1934, Whitman, 132 pgs., 3 1/2" x 3 1/2", soft-c, Tarzan Ice Cream cup lid premium			
	26.00	78.00	180.00
nn- **Chester Gump at the North Pole**, 1938, Whitman, 68 pgs. soft-c, 3 3/4" x 3 1/2", Pan-Am giveaway	26.00	78.00	180.00
nn- **Chicken Greedy**, nd(1930s), np (Whitman), 36 pgs., 3" x 2 1/2", Penny Book	3.00	9.00	20.00
nn- **Chicken Licken**, nd (1930s), np (Whitman), 36 pgs., 3" x 2 1/2",			

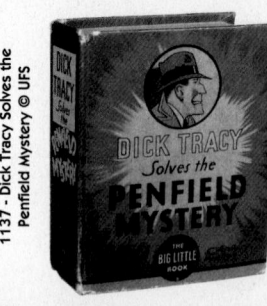

	GD	FN	VF/NM
Penny Book	3.00	9.00	20.00
1101- Chief of the Rangers, 1935, Saalfield, hard-c, Tom Mix photo-c, movie scenes from "The Miracle Rider"	19.00	57.00	135.00
1581- Chief of the Rangers, 1935, Saalfield, soft-c, Tom Mix photo-c, movie scenes	19.00	57.00	135.00
Child's Garden of Verses (See Wee Little Books)			
L14- Chip Collins' Adventures on Bat Island, 1935, Lynn, 192 pgs.	12.00	36.00	78.00
2025- Chitty Chitty Bang Bang, 1968, Whitman, movie photos	4.00	12.00	22.00
Chubby Little Books, 1935, Whitman, 3" x 2 1/2", 200 pgs.			
W803- Golden Hours Story Book, The	6.00	18.00	35.00
W803- Story Hours Story Book, The	6.00	18.00	35.00
W804- Gay Book of Little Stories, The	6.00	18.00	35.00
W804- Glad Book of Little Stories, The	6.00	18.00	35.00
W804- Joy Book of Little Stories, The	6.00	18.00	35.00
W804- Sunny Book of Little Stories, The	6.00	18.00	35.00
1453- Chuck Malloy Railroad Detective on the Streamliner,1938, Whitman, 300 pgs.	10.00	30.00	68.00
Cinderella (See Walt Disney's...)			
Clyde Beatty (See The Steel Arena)			
1410- Clyde Beatty Daredevil Lion and Tiger Tamer, 1939, Whitman, 300 pgs.	13.00	39.00	90.00
1480- Coach Bernie Bierman's Brick Barton and the Winning Eleven, 1938, 300 pgs.	10.00	30.00	62.00
1446- Convoy Patrol (A Thrilling U.S. Navy Story), 1942, Whitman, 432 pgs., flip pictures	10.00	30.00	62.00
1127- Corley of the Wilderness Trail, 1937, Saalfield, hard-c	10.00	30.00	62.00
1607- Corley of the Wilderness Trail, 1937, Saalfield, soft-c	10.00	30.00	62.00
1- Count of Monte Cristo, 1934, EVW, 160 pgs., (Five Star Library), movie scenes, hard-c	18.00	54.00	125.00
1457- Cowboy Lingo Boys' Book of Western Facts, 1938, Whitman, 300 pgs., Fred Harman-a	10.00	30.00	68.00
1171- Cowboy Malloy, 1940, Saalfield, 400 pgs.	9.00	27.00	57.00
1106- Cowboy Millionaire, 1935, Saalfield, movie scenes with George O'Brien, photo-c, hard-c	14.00	42.00	95.00
1586- Cowboy Millionaire, 1935, Saalfield, movie scenes with George O'Brien, photo-c, soft-c	14.00	42.00	95.00
724- Cowboy Stories, 1933, Whitman, 300 pgs., Hal Arbo-a	12.00	36.00	78.00
nn- Cowboy Stories, 1933, Whitman, 52 pgs., soft-c, premium-no ads, 4" x 5 1/2" Hal Arbo-a	14.00	42.00	95.00
1161- Crimson Cloak, The, 1939, Saalfield, 400 pgs.	10.00	30.00	62.00
L19- Curley Harper at Lakespur, 1935, Lynn, 192 pgs.	10.00	30.00	62.00
5785-2- Daffy Duck in Twice the Trouble, 1980, Whitman, 260 pgs., 79 cents soft-c	1.00	2.00	5.00
2018-(#18)-Daktari-Night of Terror, 1968, Whitman, 260 pgs., 39 cents, hard-c, color illos	4.00	12.00	22.00
1010- Dan Dunn And The Gangsters' Frame-Up, 1937, Whitman, 7 1/4" x 5 1/2", 64 pgs., Nickel Book	41.00	123.00	290.00
1116- Dan Dunn "Crime Never Pays," 1934, Whitman, 320 pgs., by Norman Marsh	12.00	36.00	85.00
1125- Dan Dunn on the Trail of the Counterfeiters, 1936, Whitman, 432 pgs., by Norman Marsh	12.00	36.00	85.00
1171- Dan Dunn and the Crime Master, 1937, Whitman, 432 pgs., by Norman Marsh	12.00	36.00	85.00
1417- Dan Dunn and the Underworld Gorillas, 1941, Whitman, All Pictures Comics, flip pictures, by Norman Marsh	12.00	36.00	85.00
1454- Dan Dunn on the Trail of Wu Fang, 1938, Whitman, 432 pgs., by Norman Marsh	15.00	45.00	105.00
1481- Dan Dunn and the Border Smugglers, 1938, Whitman, 432 pgs., by Norman Marsh	12.00	36.00	85.00
1492- Dan Dunn and the Dope Ring, 1940, Whitman, 432 pgs., by Norman Marsh	12.00	36.00	78.00
nn- Dan Dunn and the Bank Hold-Up, 1938, Whitman, 36 pgs.,			

	GD	FN	VF/NM
2 1/2" x 3 1/2", Penny Book	10.00	30.00	62.00
nn- Dan Dunn and the Zeppelin Of Doom, 1938, Dell, 196 pgs., Fast-Action Story, soft-c	30.00	90.00	210.00
nn- Dan Dunn Meets Chang Loo, 1938, Whitman, 66 pgs., Pan-Am premium, by Norman Marsh	26.00	78.00	180.00
nn- Dan Dunn Plays a Lone Hand, 1938, Whitman, 36 pgs., 2 1/2" x 3 1/2", Penny Book	10.00	30.00	62.00
3 3/4" x 3 1/2", Buddy book	36.00	108.00	250.00
6- Dan Dunn Secret Operative 48 and the Counterfeiter Ring, 1938, Whitman, 132 pgs., soft-c, 3 3/4" x 3 1/2", Buddy Book premium	36.00	108.00	250.00
9- Dan Dunn's Mysterious Ruse, 1936, Whitman, 132 pgs., soft-c, 3 1/2" x 3 1/2", Tarzan Ice Cream cup lid premium	36.00	108.00	250.00
1177- Danger Trail North, 1940, Saalfield, 400 pgs.	10.00	30.00	62.00
1151- Danger Trails in Africa, 1935, Whitman, 432 pgs.	16.00	48.00	115.00
nn- Daniel Boone, 1934, World Syndicate, High Lights of History Series, hard-c, All in Pictures	10.00	30.00	62.00
1160- Dan of the Lazy L, 1939, Saalfield, 400 pgs.	10.00	30.00	62.00
1148- David Copperfield, 1934, Whitman, hard-c, 160 pgs., photo-c, movie scenes (W. C. Fields)	18.00	54.00	125.00
nn- David Copperfield, 1934, Whitman, soft-c, 164 pgs., movie scenes	18.00	54.00	125.00
1151- Death by Short Wave, 1938, Saalfield	10.00	30.00	68.00
1156- Denny the Ace Detective, 1938, Saalfield, 400 pgs.	9.00	27.00	57.00
1431- Desert Eagle and the Hidden Fortress, The, 1941, Whitman, 432 pgs., flip pictures	10.00	30.00	68.00
1458- Desert Eagle Rides Again, The, 1939, Whitman, 300 pgs.	10.00	30.00	68.00
1136- Desert Justice, 1938, Saalfield, 400 pgs.	9.00	27.00	57.00
1484- Detective Higgins of the Racket Squad, 1938, Whitman, 432 pgs.	10.00	30.00	68.00
1124- Dickie Moore in the Little Red School House, 1936, Whitman, 240 pgs., photo-c, movie scenes (Chesterfield Motion Picts. Corp)	12.00	36.00	90.00
W-707- Dick Tracy the Detective, The Adventures of, 1933, Whitman, 320 pgs. (The 1st Big Little Book), by Chester Gould (Scarce)	263.00	789.00	2100.00
nn- Dick Tracy Detective, The Adventures of, 1933, Whitman, 52 pgs., 4" x 5 1/2", premium-no ads, soft-c, by Chester Gould	89.00	267.00	630.00
nn- Dick Tracy Detective, The Adventures of, 1933, Whitman, 52 pgs., 4" x 5 1/2", inside back-c & back-c ads for Sundial Shoes, soft-c, by Chester Gould	96.00	288.00	680.00
710- Dick Tracy and Dick Tracy, Jr. (The Advs. of ...), 1933, Whitman, 320 pgs., by Chester Gould	71.00	213.00	495.00
nn- Dick Tracy and Dick Tracy, Jr. (The Advs. of ...), 1933, Whitman, 52 pgs., premium-no ads, soft-c, 4" x 5 1/2", by Chester Gould	71.00	213.00	495.00
nn- Dick Tracy the Detective and Dick Tracy, Jr., 1933, Whitman, 52 pgs., premium-no ads, 3 1/2"x 5 1/4", soft-c, by Chester Gould	71.00	213.00	495.00
723- Dick Tracy Out West, 1933, Whitman, 300 pgs., by Chester Gould	45.00	135.00	315.00
749- Dick Tracy from Colorado to Nova Scotia, 1933, Whitman, 320 pgs., by Chester Gould	40.00	120.00	280.00
nn- Dick Tracy from Colorado to Nova Scotia, 1933, Whitman, 204 pgs., premium-no ads, soft-c, by Chester Gould	45.00	135.00	315.00
1105- Dick Tracy and the Stolen Bonds, 1934, Whitman, 320 pgs., by Chester Gould	24.00	72.00	170.00
1112- Dick Tracy and the Racketeer Gang, 1936, Whitman, 432 pgs., by Chester Gould	19.00	57.00	135.00
1137- Dick Tracy Solves the Penfield Mystery, 1934, Whitman, 320 pgs., by Chester Gould	24.00	72.00	170.00
nn- Dick Tracy Solves the Penfield Mystery, 1934, Whitman, 324 pgs., premium-no ads, 3-color, soft-c, by Chester Gould	48.00	144.00	340.00
1163- Dick Tracy and the Boris Arson Gang, 1935, Whitman,			

3 - Dick Tracy Meets a New Gang © UFS

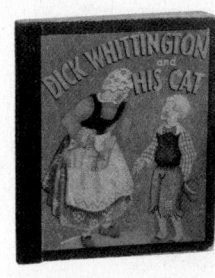

Dick Whittington and His Cat © WHIT

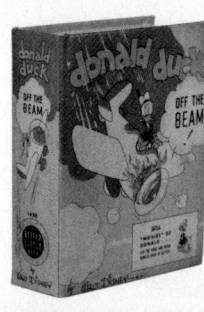

1438 - Donald Duck Off the Beam © DIS

	GD	FN	VF/NM
432 pgs., by Chester Gould	21.00	63.00	145.00
1170- Dick Tracy on the Trail of Larceny Lu, 1935, Whitman,			
432 pgs., by Chester Gould	19.00	57.00	135.00
1185- Dick Tracy in Chains of Crime, 1936, Whitman, 432 pgs.,			
by Chester Gould	21.00	63.00	145.00
1412- Dick Tracy and Yogee Yamma, 1946, Whitman, 352 pgs.,			
by Chester Gould	19.00	57.00	135.00
1420- Dick Tracy and the Hotel Murders, 1937, Whitman, 432 pgs.,			
by Chester Gould	21.00	63.00	145.00
1434- Dick Tracy and the Phantom Ship, 1940, Whitman, 432 pgs.,			
by Chester Gould	21.00	63.00	145.00
1436- Dick Tracy and the Mad Killer, 1947, Whitman, 288 pgs., by			
Chester Gould	16.00	48.00	115.00
1439- Dick Tracy and His G-Men, 1941, Whitman, 432 pgs., flip pictures,			
by Chester Gould	21.00	63.00	145.00
1445- Dick Tracy and the Bicycle Gang, 1948, Whitman, 288 pgs.,			
by Chester Gould	16.00	48.00	115.00
1446- Detective Dick Tracy and the Spider Gang, 1937, Whitman, 240 pgs.,			
movie scenes from "Adventures of Dick Tracy" (Republic serial)	26.00	78.00	185.00
1449- Dick Tracy Special F.B.I. Operative, 1943, Whitman, 432 pgs.			
by Chester Gould	21.00	63.00	145.00
1454- Dick Tracy on the High Seas, 1939, Whitman, 432 pgs.,			
by Chester Gould	21.00	63.00	145.00
1460- Dick Tracy and the Tiger Lilly Gang, 1949, Whitman,			
288 pgs., by Chester Gould	16.00	48.00	115.00
1478- Dick Tracy on Voodoo Island, 1944, Whitman, 352 pgs.,			
by Chester Gould	16.00	48.00	115.00
1479- Detective Dick Tracy Vs. Crooks in Disguise, 1939, Whitman,			
432 pgs., flip pictures, by Chester Gould	21.00	63.00	145.00
1482- Dick Tracy and the Wreath Kidnapping Case, 1945,			
Whitman, 352 pgs.	18.00	54.00	125.00
1488- Dick Tracy the Super-Detective, 1939, Whitman, 432 pgs.,			
by Chester Gould	21.00	63.00	145.00
1491- Dick Tracy the Man with No Face, 1938, Whitman, 432 pgs.			
	21.00	63.00	145.00
1495- Dick Tracy Returns, 1939, Whitman, 432 pgs., based on Republic			
Motion Picture serial, Chester Gould-a	21.00	63.00	145.00
2001- (#1)-Dick Tracy-Encounters Facey, 1967, Whitman, 260 pgs.,			
39 cents, hard-c, color illos	4.00	12.00	25.00
4055- Dick Tracy, The Adventures of, 1934, Whitman, 7" x 9 1/2", 320 pgs.,			
Big Big Book, by Chester Gould	96.00	288.00	680.00
4071- Dick Tracy and the Mystery of the Purple Cross, 1938,			
7" x 9 1/2", 320 pgs., Big Big Book, by Chester Gould			
(Scarce)	124.00	372.00	945.00
nn- Dick Tracy and the Invisible Man, 1939, Whitman,			
3 1/4" x 3 3/4", 132 pgs., stapled, soft-c, Quaker Oats premium;			
NBC radio play script, Chester Gould-a	37.00	111.00	260.00
Vol. 2- Dick Tracy's Ghost Ship, 1939, Whitman, 3 1/2" x 3 1/2", 132 pgs.,			
soft-c, stapled, Quaker Oats premium; NBC radio play script episode			
from actual radio show; Gould-a	37.00	111.00	260.00
3- Dick Tracy Meets a New Gang, 1934, Whitman, 3" x 3 1/2", 132 pgs.,			
soft-c, Tarzan Ice Cream cup lid premium	63.00	189.00	445.00
11- Dick Tracy in Smashing the Famon Racket, 1938, Whitman,			
3 3/4" x 3 1/2", Buddy Book-ice cream premium, by Chester Gould	63.00	189.00	445.00
nn- Dick Tracy Gets His Man, 1938, Whitman, 36 pgs., 2 1/2" x 3 1/2",			
Penny Book	10.00	30.00	68.00
nn- Dick Tracy the Detective, 1938, Whitman, 36 pgs., 2 1/2" x 3 1/2"			
Penny Book	10.00	30.00	68.00
9- Dick Tracy and the Frozen Bullet Murders, 1941, Dell, 196 pgs.,			
Fast-Action Story, soft-c, by Gould	37.00	111.00	260.00
6833- Dick Tracy Detective and Federal Agent, 1936, Dell, 244 pgs.,			
Cartoon Story Books, hard-c, by Gould	45.00	135.00	315.00
nn- Dick Tracy Detective and Federal Agent, 1936, Dell, 244 pgs.,			
Fast-Action Story, soft-c, by Gould	41.00	123.00	290.00
nn- Dick Tracy and the Blackmailers, 1939, Dell, 196 pgs.,			
Fast-Action Story, soft-c, by Gould	41.00	123.00	290.00
nn- Dick Tracy and the Chain of Evidence, Detective, 1938, Dell,			
196 pgs., Fast-Action Story, soft-c, by Chester Gould			

	GD	FN	VF/NM
	41.00	123.00	290.00
nn- Dick Tracy and the Crook Without a Face, 1938, Whitman, 68 pgs.,			
3 1/4" x 3 1/2", Pan-Am giveaway, Gould-c/a	45.00	135.00	315.00
nn- Dick Tracy and the Maroon Mask Gang, 1938, Dell, 196 pgs.,			
Fast-Action Story, soft-c, by Gould	41.00	123.00	290.00
nn- Dick Tracy Cross-Country Race, 1934, Whitman, 8 pgs., 2 1/2" x 3",			
Big Thrill chewing gum premium (4 diff.)	16.00	48.00	110.00
nn- Dick Whittington and his Cat, nd(1930s), np(Whitman),			
36 pgs., Penny Book	5.00	15.00	30.00
Dinglehoofer und His Dog Adolph (See Top-Line Comics)			
Dinky (See Jackie Cooper in ...)			
1464- Dirigible ZR90 and the Disappearing Zeppelin (Captain Robb of ...),			
1941, Whitman, 300 pgs., Al Lewin-a	18.00	54.00	125.00
1167- Dixie Dugan Among the Cowboys, 1939, Saalfield, 400 pgs.	12.00	30.00	68.00
1188- Dixie Dugan and Cuddles, 1940, Saalfield, 400 pgs.,			
by Striebel & McEvoy	12.00	30.00	68.00
Doctor Doom (See Foreign Spies... & International Spy...)			
Dog of Flanders, A (See Frankie Thomas in ...)			
1114- Dog Stars of Hollywood, 1936, Saalfield, photo-c, photo-illos	15.00	45.00	105.00
1594- Dog Stars of Hollywood, 1936, Saalfield, photo-c, soft-c,			
photo-illos	15.00	45.00	105.00
Donald Duck (See Silly Symphony... & Walt Disney's ...)			
800- Donald Duck in Bringing Up the Boys, 1948, Whitman,			
hard-c, Story Hour series	12.00	36.00	78.00
1404- Donald Duck (Says Such a Life) (Disney), 1939, Whitman,			
432 pgs., Taliaferro-a	29.00	87.00	200.00
1411- Donald Duck and Ghost Morgan's Treasure (Disney), 1946,			
Whitman, All Pictures Comics, Barks-a; reprints Four Color #9	34.00	102.00	240.00
1422- Donald Duck Sees Stars (Disney), 1941, Whitman, 432 pgs.,			
flip pictures, Taliaferro-a	28.00	84.00	195.00
1424- Donald Duck Says Such Luck (Disney), 1941, Whitman,			
432 pgs., flip pictures, Taliaferro-a	28.00	84.00	195.00
1430- Donald Duck Headed For Trouble (Disney), 1942, Whitman,			
432 pgs., flip pictures, Taliaferro-a	28.00	84.00	195.00
1432- Donald Duck and the Green Serpent (Disney), 1947, Whitman,			
All Pictures Comics, Barks-a; reprints Four Color #108	31.00	93.00	220.00
1434- Donald Duck Forgets To Duck (Disney), 1939, Whitman,			
432 pgs., Taliaferro-a	28.00	84.00	195.00
1438- Donald Duck Off the Beam (Disney), 1943, Whitman,			
352 pgs., flip pictures, Taliaferro-a	28.00	84.00	195.00
1438- Donald Duck Off the Beam (Disney), 1943, Whitman,			
432 pgs., flip pictures, Taliaferro-a	28.00	84.00	195.00
1449- Donald Duck Lays Down the Law, 1948, Whitman, 288 pgs.,	28.00	84.00	195.00
1457- Donald Duck in Volcano Valley (Disney), 1949, Whitman,			
288 pgs., Barks-a	28.00	84.00	195.00
1462- Donald Duck Gets Fed Up (Disney), 1940, Whitman,			
432 pgs.,Taliaferro-a	28.00	84.00	195.00
1478- Donald Duck-Hunting For Trouble (Disney), 1938,			
Whitman, 432 pgs., Taliaferro-a	28.00	84.00	195.00
1484- Donald Duck is Here Again!, 1944, Whitman, All Pictures Comics,			
Taliaferro-a	28.00	84.00	195.00
1486- Donald Duck Up in the Air (Disney), 1945, Whitman,			
352 pgs., Barks-a	31.00	93.00	220.00
705-10- Donald Duck and the Mystery of the Double X,			
(Disney), 1949, Whitman, Barks-a	15.00	45.00	105.00
2033-(#33)- Donald Duck, Luck of the Ducks, 1969, Whitman, 256 pgs.,			
hard-c, 39 cents, color illos.	3.00	9.00	20.00
2009-(#9)-Donald Duck-The Fabulous Diamond Fountain,			
(Walt Disney), 1967, Whitman, 260 pgs., 39 cents, hard-c,			
color illos	4.00	12.00	25.00
5756- Donald Duck-The Fabulous Diamond Fountain,			
(Walt Disney), 1973, Whitman, 260 pgs., 79 cents, soft-c,			
color illos	3.00	9.00	18.00
5756-1- Donald Duck-The Fabulous Diamond Fountain,			
(Walt Disney), 1973, Whitman, 260 pgs., 79 cents, soft-c,			

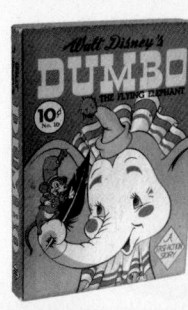

10 - Dumbo the Flying Elephant © DIS

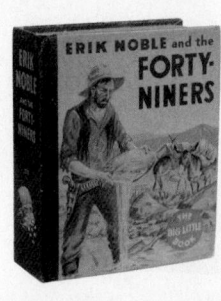

722 - Erik Noble and the Forty-Niners © WHIT

22 - Flaming Guns © EVW

	GD	FN	VF/NM
color illos	3.00	9.00	18.00

5756-2- Donald Duck-The Fabulous Diamond Fountain,
(Walt Disney), 1973, Whitman, 260 pgs., 79 cents, soft-c,
color illos — 3.00 / 9.00 / 18.00

5760- Donald Duck in Volcano Valley (Disney), 1973, Whitman,
39 cents, flip-it book — 3.00 / 9.00 / 18.00

5760-2- Donald Duck in Volcano Valley (Disney), 1973, Whitman,
79 cents, flip-it book — 2.00 / 6.00 / 12.00

5764- Donald Duck, Luck of the Ducks, 1969, Whitman, 256 pgs.,
soft-c, 49 cents, color illos. — 3.00 / 9.00 / 18.00

5773- Donald Duck - The Lost Jungle City, 1975, Whitman,
49 cents, flip-it book; 6 printings through 1980 2.00 / 5.00 / 10.00

nn- Donald Duck and the Ducklings, 1938, Dell, 194 pgs.,
Fast-Action Story, soft-c, Taliaferro-a — 54.00 / 162.00 / 380.00

nn- Donald Duck Out of Luck (Disney), 1940, Dell, 196 pgs.,
Fast-Action Story, has Four Color #4 on back-c, Taliaferro-a
— 54.00 / 162.00 / 380.00

8- Donald Duck Takes It on the Chin (Disney), 1941, Dell, 196 pgs.,
Fast-Action Story, soft-c, Taliaferro-a — 54.00 / 162.00 / 380.00

L13- Donnie and the Pirates, 1935, Lynn, 192 pgs.
— 12.00 / 36.00 / 78.00

1438- Don O'Dare Finds War, 1940, Whitman, 432 pgs.
— 10.00 / 30.00 / 62.00

1107- Don Winslow, U.S.N., 1935, Whitman, 432 pgs.
— 18.00 / 54.00 / 125.00

nn- Don Winslow, U.S.N., 1935, Whitman, 436 pgs., premium-no ads,
3-color, soft-c — 29.00 / 87.00 / 200.00

1408- Don Winslow and the Giant Girl Spy, 1946, Whitman,
352 pgs. — 12.00 / 36.00 / 85.00

1418- Don Winslow Navy Intelligence Ace, 1942, Whitman,
432 pgs., flip pictures — 16.00 / 48.00 / 115.00

1419- Don Winslow of the Navy Vs. the Scorpion Gang,
1938, Whitman, 432 pgs. — 16.00 / 48.00 / 115.00

1453- Don Winslow of the Navy and the Secret Enemy Base,
1943, Whitman, 352 pgs. — 16.00 / 48.00 / 115.00

1489- Don Winslow of the Navy and the Great War Plot,
1940, Whitman, 432 pgs. — 16.00 / 48.00 / 115.00

nn- Don Winslow U.S. Navy and the Missing Admiral, 1938, Whitman,
36 pgs., 2 1/2" x 3 1/2", Penny Book — 10.00 / 30.00 / 62.00

1137- Doomed To Die, 1938, Saalfield, 400 pgs. — 10.00 / 30.00 / 62.00

1140- Down Cartridge Creek, 1938, Saalfield, 400 pgs.
— 10.00 / 30.00 / 62.00

1416- Draftie of the U.S. Army, 1943, Whitman, All Pictures Comics
— 10.00 / 30.00 / 68.00

1100B- Dreams (Your dreams & what they mean), 1938, Whitman,
36 pgs., 2 1/2" x 3 1/2", Penny Book — 4.00 / 12.00 / 25.00

24- Dumb Dora and Bing Brown, 1936, Lynn — 13.00 / 39.00 / 90.00

1400- Dumbo, of the Circus - Only His Ears Grew! (Disney), 1941,
Whitman, 432 pgs., based on Disney movie 25.00 / 75.00 / 175.00

10- Dumbo the Flying Elephant (Disney), 1944, Dell,
194 pgs., Fast-Action Story, soft-c — 41.00 / 123.00 / 285.00

nn- East O' the Sun and West O' the Moon, nd (1930s), np (Whitman),
36 pgs., 3" x 2 1/2", Penny Book — 4.00 / 12.00 / 25.00

774- Eddie Cantor in an Hour with You, 1934, Whitman, 154 pgs.,
4 1/4" x 5 1/4", photo-c, movie scenes — 15.00 / 45.00 / 105.00

nn- Eddie Cantor in Laughland, 1934, Goldsmith, 132 pgs., soft-c,
photo-c, Vallely-a — 15.00 / 45.00 / 105.00

1106- Ella Cinders and the Mysterious House, 1934, Whitman,
432 pgs. — 14.00 / 42.00 / 95.00

nn- Ella Cinders and the Mysterious House, 1934, Whitman, 52 pgs.,
premium-no ads, soft-c, 3 1/2" x 5 3/4" — 20.00 / 60.00 / 140.00

nn- Ella Cinders, 1935, Whitman, 148 pgs., 3 1/4" x 4", Tarzan Ice Cream
cup lid premium — 33.00 / 99.00 / 230.00

nn- Ella Cinders Plays Duchess, 1938, Whitman, 68 pgs., 3 3/4" x 3 1/2",
Pan-Am Oil premium — 15.00 / 45.00 / 105.00

nn- Ella Cinders Solves a Mystery, 1938, Whitman, 68 pgs., Pan-Am Oil
premium, soft-c — 15.00 / 45.00 / 105.00

11- Ella Cinders' Exciting Experience, 1934, Whitman, 3 1/2" x 3 1/2",
132 pgs., Tarzan Ice Cream cup lid giveaway
— 33.00 / 99.00 / 230.00

1406- Ellery Queen the Adventure of the Last Man Club,
1940, Whitman, 432 pgs. — 14.00 / 42.00 / 95.00

1472- Ellery Queen the Master Detective, 1942, Whitman, 432 pgs.,
flip pictures — 14.00 / 42.00 / 95.00

1081- Elmer and his Dog Spot, 1935, Saalfield, hard-c
— 10.00 / 30.00 / 62.00

1311- Elmer and his Dog Spot, 1935, Saalfield, soft-c
— 10.00 / 30.00 / 62.00

722- Erik Noble and the Forty-Niners, 1934, Whitman, 384 pgs.
— 10.00 / 30.00 / 68.00

nn- Erik Noble and the Forty-Niners, 1934, Whitman, 386 pgs.,
3-color, soft-c — 15.00 / 45.00 / 105.00

2019-(#19)- Fantastic Four in the House of Horrors, 1968, Whitman,
256 pgs., hard-c, color illos. — 4.00 / 12.00 / 22.00

5775- Fantastic Four in the House of Horrors, 1976, Whitman,
256 pgs., soft-c, color illos. — 3.00 / 9.00 / 18.00

5775-1 - Fantastic Four in the House of Horrors, 1976, Whitman,
256 pgs., soft-c, color illos. — 3.00 / 9.00 / 18.00

1058- Farmyard Symphony, The (Disney), 1939, 5" X 5 1/2",
68 pgs., hard-c — 14.00 / 42.00 / 95.00

1129- Felix the Cat, 1936, Whitman, 432 pgs., Messmer-a
— 30.00 / 90.00 / 210.00

1439- Felix the Cat, 1943, Whitman, All Pictures Comics,
Messmer-a — 24.00 / 72.00 / 170.00

1465- Felix the Cat, 1945, Whitman, All Pictures Comics,
Messmer-a — 21.00 / 63.00 / 150.00

nn- Felix (Flip book), 1967, World Retrospective of Animation Cinema,
188 pgs., 2 1/2" x 4" by Otto Messmer — 4.00 / 12.00 / 25.00

nn- Fighting Cowboy of Nugget Gulch, The, 1939, Whitman,
2 1/2" x 3 1/2", Penny Book — 7.00 / 20.00 / 40.00

1401- Fighting Heroes Battle for Freedom, 1943, Whitman, All Pictures
Comics, from "Heroes of Democracy" strip, by Stookie Allen
— 10.00 / 30.00 / 62.00

6- Fighting President, The, 1934, EVW (Five Star Library), 160 pgs.,
photo-c, photo ill., F. D. Roosevelt — 12.00 / 36.00 / 78.00

nn- Fire Chief Ed Wynn and "His Old Fire Horse," 1934, Goldsmith,
132 pgs., H. Vallely-a, photo, soft-c — 12.00 / 36.00 / 78.00

1464- Flame Boy and the Indians' Secret, 1938, Whitman, 300 pgs.,
Sekakuku-a (Hopi Indian) — 10.00 / 30.00 / 62.00

22- Flaming Guns, 1935, EVW, with Tom Mix, movie scenes
— 18.00 / 54.00 / 125.00

1110- Flash Gordon on the Planet Mongo, 1934, Whitman,
320 pgs., by Alex Raymond — 45.00 / 135.00 / 315.00

1166- Flash Gordon and the Monsters of Mongo, 1935, Whitman,
432 pgs., by Alex Raymond — 38.00 / 114.00 / 265.00

nn- Flash Gordon and the Monsters of Mongo, 1935, Whitman, 436 pgs.,
premium-no ads, 3-color, soft-c, by Alex Raymond
— 57.00 / 171.00 / 395.00

1171- Flash Gordon and the Tournaments of Mongo, 1935, Whitman,
432 pgs., by Alex Raymond — 39.00 / 117.00 / 275.00

1190- Flash Gordon and the Witch Queen of Mongo, 1936,
Whitman, 432 pgs., by Alex Raymond — 39.00 / 117.00 / 275.00

1407- Flash Gordon in the Water World of Mongo, 1937,
Whitman, 432 pgs., by Alex Raymond — 35.00 / 105.00 / 245.00

1423- Flash Gordon and the Perils of Mongo, 1940, Whitman,
432 pgs., by Alex Raymond — 30.00 / 90.00 / 210.00

1424- Flash Gordon in the Jungles of Mongo, 1947, Whitman,
352 pgs., by Alex Raymond — 22.00 / 66.00 / 155.00

1443- Flash Gordon in the Ice World of Mongo, 1942, Whitman,
432 pgs., flip pictures, by Alex Raymond — 32.00 / 96.00 / 225.00

1447- Flash Gordon and the Fiery Desert of Mongo, 1948,
Whitman, 288 pgs., Raymond-a — 22.00 / 66.00 / 155.00

1469- Flash Gordon and the Power Men of Mongo, 1943,
Whitman, 352 pgs., by Alex Raymond — 32.00 / 96.00 / 225.00

1479- Flash Gordon and the Red Sword Invaders, 1945,
Whitman, 352 pgs., by Alex Raymond — 31.00 / 93.00 / 220.00

1484- Flash Gordon and the Tyrant of Mongo, 1941, Whitman,
432 pgs., flip pictures, by Alex Raymond — 32.00 / 96.00 / 225.00

1492- Flash Gordon in the Forest Kingdom of Mongo, 1938,
Whitman, 432 pgs., by Alex Raymond — 41.00 / 123.00 / 290.00

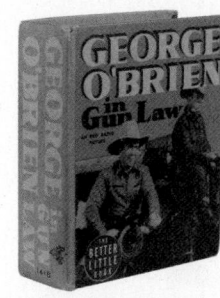

1492 - Flash Gordon in the Forest Kingdom of Mongo © KING

1437 - Gang Busters Smash Through © WHIT

1418 - George O'Brien in Gun Law © WHIT

	GD	FN	VF/NM
12- Flash Gordon and the Ape Men of Mor, 1942, Dell, 196 pgs., Fast-Action Story, by Alex Raymond	58.00	174.00	410.00
6833- Flash Gordon Vs. the Emperor of Mongo, 1936, Dell, 244 pgs., Cartoon Story Books, hard-c, Alex Raymond-c/a	71.00	213.00	500.00
nn- Flash Gordon Vs. the Emperor of Mongo, 1936, Dell, 244 pgs., Fast-Action Story, soft-c, Alex Raymond-c/a	57.00	171.00	400.00
1467- Flint Roper and the Six-Gun Showdown, 1941, Whitman, 300 pgs.	10.00	30.00	62.00
2014-(#14)- Flintstones-The Case of the Many Missing Things, 1968, Whitman, 260 pgs., 39 cents, hard-c, color illos	4.00	12.00	22.00
nn- Flintstones: A Friend From the Past, 1977, Modern Promotions, 244 pgs., 49 cents, soft-c, flip pictures	2.00	5.00	10.00
nn- Flintstones: It's About Time, 1977, Modern Promotions, 244 pgs., 49 cents, soft-c, flip pictures	2.00	5.00	10.00
nn- Flintstones: Pebbles & Bamm-Bamm Meet Santa Claus, 1977, Modern Promotions, 244 pgs., 49 cents, soft-c, flip pictures	2.00	5.00	10.00
nn- Flintstones: The Great Balloon Race, 1977, Modern Promotions, 244 pgs., 49 cents, soft-c, flip pictures	2.00	5.00	10.00
nn- Flintstones: The Mystery of the Many Missing Things, 1977, Modern Promotions, 244 pgs., 49 cents, soft-c, flip pictures	2.00	5.00	10.00
2003-(#3)- Flipper-Killer White Trouble, 1967, Whitman, 260 pgs., hard-c, 39 cents, color illos	3.00	9.00	18.00
2032-(#32)- Flipper, Deep-Sea Photographer, 1969, Whitman, 256 pgs., hard-c, color illos.	3.00	9.00	18.00
1108- Flying the Sky Clipper with Winsie Atkins, 1936, Whitman, 432 pgs.	10.00	30.00	68.00
1460- Foreign Spies Doctor Doom and the Ghost Submarine, 1939, Whitman, 432 pgs., Al McWilliams-a	12.00	36.00	85.00
1100B- Fortune Teller, 1938, Whitman, 36 pgs., 2 1/2" x 3 1/2", Penny Book	5.00	15.00	30.00
1175- Frank Buck Presents Ted Towers Animal Master, 1935, Whitman, 432 pgs.	11.00	33.00	72.00
2015-(#15)- Frankenstein, Jr. - The Menace of the Heartless Monster, 1968, Whitman, 260 pgs., 39 cents, hard-c, color illos.	4.00	12.00	22.00
16- Frankie Thomas in A Dog of Flanders, 1935, EVW, movie scenes	14.00	42.00	100.00
1121- Frank Merriwell at Yale, 1935, 432 pgs.	10.00	30.00	68.00
Freckles and His Friends in the North Woods (See Top-Line Comics)			
nn- Freckles and His Friends Stage a Play, 1938, Whitman, 36 pgs., 2 1/2" x 3 1/2", Penny Book	10.00	30.00	68.00
1164- Freckles and the Lost Diamond Mine, 1937, Whitman, 432 pgs., Merrill Blosser-a	12.00	36.00	80.00
nn- Freckles and the Mystery Ship, 1935, Whitman, 66 pgs., Pan-Am premium	15.00	45.00	105.00
1100B- Fun, Puzzles, Riddles, 1938, Whitman, 36 pgs., 2 1/2" x 3 1/2", Penny Book	4.00	12.00	25.00
1433- Gang Busters Step In, 1939, Whitman, 432 pgs., Henry E. Vallely-a	12.00	36.00	85.00
1437- Gang Busters Smash Through, 1942, Whitman, 432 pgs.	12.00	36.00	85.00
1451- Gang Busters in Action!, 1938, Whitman, 432 pgs.	12.00	36.00	85.00
nn- Gang Busters and Guns of the Law, 1940, Dell, 4" x 5", 194 pgs., Fast-Action Story, soft-c	37.00	111.00	260.00
nn- Gang Busters and the Radio Clues, 1938, Whitman, 36 pgs., 2 1/2" x 3 1/2", Penny Book	10.00	30.00	62.00
1409- Gene Autry and Raiders of the Range, 1946, Whitman, 352 pgs.	14.00	42.00	95.00
1425- Gene Autry and the Mystery of Paint Rock Canyon, 1947, Whitman, 288 pgs.	14.00	42.00	95.00
1428- Gene Autry Special Ranger, 1941, Whitman, 432 pgs., Erwin Hess-a	18.00	54.00	125.00
1433- Gene Autry in Public Cowboy No. 1, 1939, Whitman, 240 pgs., photo-c, movie scenes (1st Autry BLB)	34.00	102.00	235.00
1434- Gene Autry and the Gun-Smoke Reckoning, 1943, Whitman, 352 pgs.	17.00	51.00	120.00

	GD	FN	VF/NM
1439- Gene Autry and the Land Grab Mystery, 1948, Whitman, 290 pgs.	13.00	39.00	90.00
1456- Gene Autry in Special Ranger Rule, 1945, Whitman, 352 pgs., Henry E. Vallely-a	17.00	51.00	120.00
1461- Gene Autry and the Red Bandit's Ghost, 1949, Whitman, 288 pgs.	12.00	36.00	85.00
1483- Gene Autry in Law of the Range, 1939, Whitman, 432 pgs.	17.00	51.00	120.00
1493- Gene Autry and the Hawk of the Hills, 1942, Whitman, 428 pgs., flip pictures, Vallely-a	17.00	51.00	120.00
1494- Gene Autry Cowboy Detective, 1940, Whitman, 432 pgs., Erwin Hess-a	17.00	51.00	120.00
700-10- Gene Autry and the Bandits of Silver Tip, 1949, Whitman	11.00	33.00	70.00
714-10- Gene Autry and the Range War, 1950, Whitman	11.00	33.00	70.00
nn- Gene Autry in Gun-Smoke, 1938, Dell, 196 pgs., Fast-Action story, soft-c	41.00	123.00	290.00
2035-(#35)- Gentle Ben, Mystery of the Everglades, 1969, Whitman, 256 pgs., hard-c, color illos.	3.00	9.00	18.00
1176- Gentleman Joe Palooka, 1940, Saalfield, 400 pgs.	15.00	45.00	105.00
George O'Brien (See The Cowboy Millionaire)			
1101- George O'Brien and the Arizona Badman, 1936?, Whitman	14.00	42.00	95.00
1418- George O'Brien in Gun Law, 1938, Whitman, 240 pgs., photo-c, movie scenes, RKO Radio Pictures	14.00	42.00	95.00
1457- George O'Brien and the Hooded Riders, 1940, Whitman, 432 pgs., Erwin Hess-a	10.00	30.00	68.00
nn- George O'Brien and the Arizona Bad Man, 1939, Whitman, 36 pgs., 2 1/2" x 3 1/2", Penny Book	10.00	30.00	62.00
1462- Ghost Avenger, 1943, Whitman, 432 pgs., flip pictures, Henry Vallely-a	10.00	30.00	62.00
nn- Ghost Gun Gang Meet Their Match, The, 1939. Whitman, 2 1/2" x 3 1/2", Penny Book	9.00	27.00	57.00
nn- Gingerbread Boy, The, nd(1930s), np(Whitman), 36 pgs., Penny Book	3.00	9.00	20.00
1118- G-Man on the Crime Trail, 1936, Whitman, 432 pgs.	12.00	36.00	72.00
1147- G-Man Vs. the Red X, 1936, Whitman, 432 pgs.	13.00	39.00	90.00
1162- G-Man Allen, 1939, Saalfield, 400 pgs.	10.00	30.00	62.00
1173- G-Man in Action, A, 1940, Saalfield, 400 pgs., J.R. White-a	10.00	30.00	62.00
1434- G-Man and the Radio Bank Robberies, 1937, Whitman, 432 pgs.	12.00	36.00	85.00
1469- G-Man and the Gun Runners, The, 1940, Whitman, 432 pgs.	12.00	36.00	85.00
1470- G-Man vs. the Fifth Column, 1941, Whitman, 432 pgs., flip pictures	12.00	36.00	85.00
1493- G-Man Breaking the Gambling Ring, 1938, Whitman, 432 pgs., James Gary-a	12.00	36.00	85.00
4- G-Men Foil the Kidnappers, 1936, Whitman, 132 pgs., 3 1/2" x 3 1/2", soft-c, Tarzan Ice Cream cup lid premium	33.00	99.00	230.00
nn- G-Man on Lightning Island, 1936, Dell, 244 pgs., Fast-Action Story, soft-c, Henry E. Vallely-a	30.00	90.00	210.00
6833- G-Man on Lightning Island, 1936, Dell, 244 pgs., Cartoon Story Book, hard-c, Henry E. Vallely-a	26.00	78.00	185.00
1157- G-Men on the Trail, 1938, Saalfield, 400 pgs.	10.00	30.00	62.00
1168- G Men on the Job, 1935, Whitman, 432 pgs.	12.00	36.00	78.00
nn- G-Men on the Job Again, 1938, Whitman, 36 pgs., 2 1/2" x 3 1/2", Penny Book	10.00	30.00	62.00
nn- G-Men and Kidnap Justice, 1938, Whitman, 68 pgs., Pan-Am premium, soft-c	12.00	36.00	78.00
nn- G-Men and the Missing Clues, 1938, Whitman, 36 pgs., 2 1/2"x 3 1/2", Penny Book	10.00	30.00	62.00
1097- Go Into Your Dance, 1935, Saalfield, 160 pgs.. photo-c, movie scenes with Al Jolson & Ruby Keeler	14.00	42.00	95.00
1577- Go Into Your Dance, 1935, Saalfield, 160 pgs., photo-c, movie scenes, soft-c	14.00	42.00	95.00

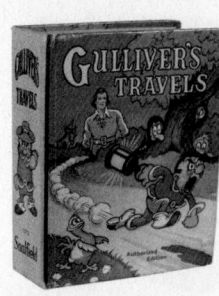

1172 - Gulliver's Travels © Saalfield

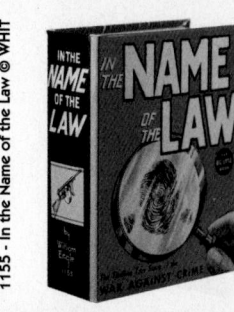

1155 - In the Name of the Law © WHIT

1498 - Jane Arden the Vanished Princess © WHIT

	GD	FN	VF/NM

2021- Goofy in Giant Trouble (Walt Disney's ...), 1968, Whitman, hard-c, 260 pgs., 39 cents, color illos. 3.00 9.00 18.00

5751- Goofy in Giant Trouble (Walt Disney's ...), 1968, Whitman, soft-c, 260 pgs., 39 cents, color illos. 3.00 9.00 18.00

5751-2- Goofy in Giant Trouble, 1968 (1980-reprint of '67 version), Whitman, soft-c, 260 pgs., 79 cents, B&W 1.00 2.00 5.00

8- Great Expectations, 1934, EVW, (Five Star Library), 160 pgs., photo-c, movie scenes 18.00 54.00 125.00

1453- Green Hornet Strikes!, The, 1940, Whitman, 432 pgs., Robert Weisman-a 45.00 135.00 315.00

1480- Green Hornet Cracks Down, The, 1942, Whitman, 432 pgs., flip pictures, Henry Vallely-a 41.00 123.00 290.00

1496- Green Hornet Returns, The, 1941, Whitman, 432 pgs., flip pictures 45.00 135.00 315.00

5778- Grimm's Ghost Stories, 1976, Whitman, 256 pgs., Laura French-s adapted from fairy tales; blue spine & back-c 2.00 6.00 12.00

5778-1- Grimm's Ghost Stories, 1976, Whitman, 256 pgs., reprint of #5778; yellow spine & back-c 2.00 6.00 12.00

1172- Gullivers' Travels, 1939, Saalfield, 320 pgs., adapted from Paramount Pict. Cartoons 18.00 54.00 125.00

nn- Gumps In Radio Land, The (Andy Gump and the Chest of Gold), 1937, Lehn & Fink Prod. Corp., 100 pgs., 3 1/4" x 5 1/2", Pebeco Tooth Paste giveaway, by Gus Edson 21.00 63.00 145.00

nn- Gunmen of Rustlers' Gulch, The, 1939, Whitman, 36 pgs., 2 1/2" x 3 1/2", Penny Book 10.00 30.00 62.00

1426- Guns in the Roaring West, 1937, Whitman, 300 pgs. 10.00 30.00 62.00

1647- Gunsmoke (TV Series), 1958, Whitman, 280 pgs., 4 1/2" x 5 3/4" 7.00 20.00 40.00

1101- Hairbreath Harry in Department QT, 1935, Whitman, 384 pgs., by J. M. Alexander 12.00 36.00 78.00

1413- Hal Hardy in the Lost Land of Giants, 1938, Whitman, 300 pgs., "The World 1,000,000 Years Ago" 12.00 36.00 75.00

1159- Hall of Fame of the Air, 1936, Whitman, 432 pgs., by Capt. Eddie Rickenbacker 10.00 30.00 62.00

nn- Hansel and Grethel, The Story of, nd (1930s), no publ., 36 pgs., Penny Book 3.00 9.00 20.00

1145- Hap Lee's Selection of Movie Gags, 1935, Whitman, 160 pgs., photos of stars 14.00 42.00 95.00

Happy Prince, The (See Wee Little Books)

1111- Hard Rock Harrigan-A Story of Boulder Dam, 1935, Saalfield, hard-c, photo-c, photo illos. 10.00 30.00 62.00

1591- Hard Rock Harrigan-A Story of Boulder Dam, 1935, Saalfield, soft-c, photo-c, photo illos. 10.00 30.00 62.00

1418- Harold Teen Swinging at the Sugar Bowl, 1939, Whitman, 432 pgs., by Carl Ed 11.00 33.00 72.00

nn- Hercules - The Legendary Journeys, 1998, Chronicle Books, 310 pgs., based on TV series, 1-color (brown) illos 1.00 3.00 8.00

1100B- Hobbies, 1938, Whitman, 36 pgs., 2 1/2" x 3 1/2", Penny Book 3.00 9.00 20.00

1125- Hockey Spare, The, 1937, Saalfield, sports book 7.00 22.00 45.00

1605- Hockey Spare, The, 1937, Saalfield, soft-c 7.00 22.00 45.00

728- Homeless Homer, 1934, Whitman, by Dee Dobbin, for young kids 5.00 15.00 30.00

17- Hoosier Schoolmaster, The, 1935, EVW, movie scenes 14.00 42.00 95.00

715- Houdini's Big Little Book of Magic, 1927 (1933), 300 pgs. 15.00 45.00 105.00

nn- Houdini's Big Little Book of Magic, 1927 (1933), 196 pgs., American Oil Co. premium, soft-c 15.00 45.00 105.00

nn- Houdini's Big Little Book of Magic, 1927 (1933), 204 pgs., Cocomalt premium, soft-c 15.00 45.00 105.00

Huckleberry Finn (See The Adventures of...)

nn- Huckleberry Hound Newspaper Reporter, 1977, Modern Promotions, 244 pgs., 49 cents, soft-c, flip pictures 2.00 6.00 12.00

1644- Hugh O'Brian TV's Wyatt Earp (TV Series), 1958, Whitman, 280 pgs. 7.00 20.00 40.00

5782-2- Incredible Hulk Lost in Time, 1980, 260 pgs., 79¢-c, soft-c, B&W 1.00 3.00 8.00

1424- Inspector Charlie Chan Villainy on the High Seas, 1942, Whitman, 432 pgs., flip pictures 15.00 45.00 105.00

1186- Inspector Wade of Scotland Yard, 1940, Saalfield, 400 pgs. 10.00 30.00 62.00

1448- Inspector Wade and The Feathered Serpent, 1939, Saalfield, 400 pgs. 10.00 30.00 62.00

1448- Inspector Wade Solves the Mystery of the Red Aces, 1937, Whitman, 432 pgs. 10.00 30.00 62.00

1148- International Spy Doctor Doom Faces Death at Dawn, 1937, Whitman, 432 pgs., Arbo-a 12.00 36.00 78.00

1155- In the Name of the Law, 1937, Whitman, 432 pgs., Henry E. Vallely-a 10.00 30.00 68.00

2012-(#12)-Invaders, The-Alien Missile Threat (TV Series), 1967, Whitman, 260 pgs., hard-c, 39 cents, color illos. 4.00 12.00 22.00

1403- Invisible Scarlet O'Neil, 1942, Whitman, All Pictures Comics, flip pictures 12.00 36.00 78.00

1406- Invisible Scarlet O'Neil Versus the King of the Slums, 1946, Whitman, 352 pgs. 10.00 30.00 62.00

1098- It Happened One Night, 1935, Saalfield, 160 pgs., Little Big Book, Clark Gable, Claudette Colbert photo-c, movie scenes from Academy Award winner 19.00 57.00 130.00

1578- It Happened One Night, 1935, Saalfield, 160 pgs., soft-c 19.00 57.00 130.00

Jack and Jill (See Wee Little Books)

1432- Jack Armstrong and the Mystery of the Iron Key, 1939, Whitman, 432 pgs., Henry Vallely-a 12.00 36.00 78.00

1435- Jack Armstrong and the Ivory Treasure, 1937, Whitman, 432 pgs., Henry Vallely-a 12.00 36.00 78.00

Jackie Cooper (See Story Of..)

1084- Jackie Cooper in Peck's Bad Boy, 1934, Saalfield, 160 pgs., hard, photo-c, movie scenes 14.00 42.00 95.00

1314- Jackie Cooper in Peck's Bad Boy, 1934, Saalfield, 160 pgs., soft, photo-c, movie scenes 14.00 42.00 95.00

1402- Jackie Cooper in "Gangster's Boy," 1939, Whitman, 240 pgs., photo-c, movie scenes 14.00 42.00 95.00

13- Jackie Cooper in Dinky, 1935, EVW, 160 pgs., movie scenes 14.00 42.00 100.00

nn- Jack King of the Secret Service and the Counterfeiters, 1939, Whitman, 36 pgs., 2 1/2" x 3 1/2", Penny Book, by John G. Gray 10.00 30.00 62.00

L11- Jack London's Call of the Wild, 1935, Lynn, 20th Cent. Pic., movie scenes with Clark Gable 14.00 42.00 100.00

nn- Jack Pearl as Detective Baron Munchausen, 1934, Goldsmith, 132 pgs., soft-c 12.00 36.00 78.00

1102- Jack Swift and His Rocket Ship, 1934, Whitman, 320 pgs. 21.00 63.00 150.00

1498- Jane Arden the Vanished Princess, Whitman, 300 pgs. 10.00 30.00 68.00

1179- Jane Withers in This is the Life (20th Century-Fox Presents...), 1935, Whitman, 240 pgs., photo-c, movie scenes 13.00 39.00 95.00

1463- Jane Withers in Keep Smiling, 1938, Whitman, 240 pgs., photo-c, movie scenes 13.00 39.00 95.00

Jaragu of the Jungle (See Rex Beach's ...)

1447- Jerry Parker Police Reporter and the Candid Camera Clue, 1941, Whitman, 300 pgs. 10.00 30.00 62.00

Jim Bowie (See Adventures of ...)

nn- Jim Brant of the Highway Patrol and the Mysterious Accident, 1939, Whitman, 36 pgs., 2 1/2" x 3 1/2", Penny Book 9.00 27.00 57.00

1466- Jim Craig State Trooper and the Kidnapped Governor, 1938, Whitman, 432 pgs. 10.00 30.00 62.00

nn- Jim Doyle Private Detective and the Train Hold-Up, 1939, Whitman, 36 pgs., 2 1/2" x 3 1/2", Penny Book 10.00 30.00 68.00

1180- Jim Hardy Ace Reporter, 1940, Saalfield, 400 pgs., Dick Moores-a 10.00 30.00 68.00

1143- Jimmy Allen in the Air Mail Robbery, 1936, Whitman, 432 pgs. 10.00 30.00 68.00

27- Jimmy Allen in The Sky Parade, 1936, Lynn, 130 pgs., 5 x 7 1/2", Paramount Pictures, movie scenes 12.00 36.00 85.00

L15- Jimmy and the Tiger, 1935, Lynn, 192 pgs. 10.00 30.00 68.00

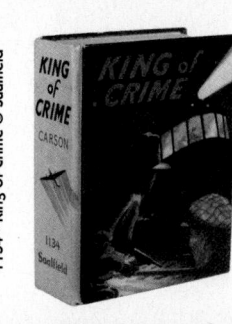

1470 - Junior Nebb Joins the Circus © WHIT

1134 - King of Crime © Saalfield

1316 - Laurel and Hardy © Saalfield

	GD	FN	VF/NM
1428- Jim Starr of the Border Patrol, 1937, Whitman, 432 pgs.			
	10.00	30.00	68.00
Joan of Arc (See Wee Little Books)			
1105- Joe Louis the Brown Bomber, 1936, Whitman, 240 pgs.,			
photo-c, photo-illos.	22.00	66.00	155.00
Joe Palooka (See Gentleman ...)			
1123- Joe Palooka the Heavyweight Boxing Champ, 1934,			
Whitman, 320 pgs., Ham Fisher-a	20.00	60.00	140.00
1168- Joe Palooka's Great Adventure, 1939, Saalfield			
	16.00	48.00	115.00
nn- Joe Penner's Duck Farm, 1935, Goldsmith, Henry Vallely-a			
	12.00	36.00	78.00
1402- John Carter of Mars, 1940, Whitman, 432 pgs., John Coleman			
Burroughs-a	76.00	228.00	530.00
nn- John Carter of Mars, 1940, Dell, 194 pgs., Fast-Action Story,			
soft-c	76.00	228.00	530.00
1164- Johnny Forty Five, 1938, Saalfield, 400 pgs.	10.00	30.00	62.00
John Wayne (See Westward Ho!)			
1100B- Jokes (A book of laughs galore), 1938, Whitman, 36 pgs.,			
2 1/2" x 3 1/2", Penny Book, laughing guy-c	3.00	9.00	20.00
1100B- Jokes (A book of side-splitting funny stories), 1938, Whitman, 36 pgs.,			
2 1/2" x 3 1/2", Penny Book, clowns on-c	3.00	9.00	20.00
2026-(#26)- Journey to the Center of the Earth, The Fiery Foe,			
1968, Whitman	4.00	12.00	22.00
Jungle Jim (See Top-Line Comics)			
1138- Jungle Jim, 1936, Whitman, 432 pgs., Alex Raymond-a			
	20.00	60.00	140.00
1139- Jungle Jim and the Vampire Woman, 1937, Whitman,			
432 pgs., Alex Raymond-a	20.00	60.00	140.00
1442- Junior G-Men, 1937, Whitman, 432 pgs., Henry E. Vallely-a			
	11.00	33.00	72.00
nn- Junior G-Men Solve a Crime, 1939, Whitman, 36 pgs., 2 1/2" x 3 1/2",			
Penny Book	11.00	33.00	72.00
1422- Junior Nebb on the Diamond Bar Ranch, 1938, Whitman,			
300 pgs., by Sol Hess	11.00	33.00	72.00
1470- Junior Nebb Joins the Circus, 1939, Whitman, 300 pgs. by			
Sol Hess	11.00	33.00	72.00
nn- Junior Nebb Elephant Trainer, 1939, Whitman, 68 pgs., Pan-Am Oil			
premium, soft-c	14.00	42.00	95.00
1052- "Just Kids" (Adventures of ...), 1934, Saalfield, oblong size,			
by Ad Carter	20.00	60.00	140.00
1094- Just Kids and the Mysterious Stranger, 1935, Saalfield, 160 pgs.,			
by Ad Carter	14.00	42.00	95.00
1184- Just Kids and Deep-Sea Dan, 1940, Saalfield, 400 pgs., by Ad Carter			
	12.00	36.00	78.00
1302- Just Kids, The Adventures of, 1934, Saalfield, oblong size,			
soft-c, by Ad Carter	20.00	60.00	140.00
1324- Just Kids and the Mysterious Stranger, 1935, Saalfield,			
160 pgs., soft-c, by Ad Carter ,	14.00	42.00	95.00
1401- Just Kids, 1937, Whitman, 432 pgs., by Ad Carter			
	14.00	42.00	95.00
1055- Katzenjammer Kids in the Mountains, 1934, Saalfield, hard-c, oblong,			
H. H. Knerr-a	19.00	57.00	135.00
1305- Katzenjammer Kids in the Mountains, 1934, Saalfield, soft-c, oblong,			
H. H. Knerr-a	19.00	57.00	135.00
14- Katzenjammer Kids, The, 1942, Dell, 194 pgs., Fast-Action Story,			
H. H. Knerr-a	21.00	63.00	145.00
1411- Kay Darcy and the Mystery Hideout, 1937, Whitman,			
300 pgs., Charles Mueller-a	12.00	36.00	85.00
1180- Kayo in the Land of Sunshine (With Moon Mullins),			
1937, Whitman, 432 pgs., by Willard	14.00	42.00	95.00
1415- Kayo and Moon Mullins and the One Man Gang, 1939, Whitman,			
432 pgs., by Frank Willard	12.00	36.00	78.00
7- Kayo and Moon Mullins 'Way Down South, 1938, Whitman,			
132 pgs., 3 1/2" x 3 1/2", Buddy Book	29.00	87.00	200.00
1105- Kazan in Revenge of the North (James Oliver Curwood's...),			
1937, Whitman, 432 pgs., Henry E. Vallely-a	10.00	30.00	62.00
1471- Kazan, King of the Pack (James Oliver Curwood's...),			
1940, Whitman, 432 pgs.	9.00	27.00	57.00
1420- Keep 'Em Flying! U.S.A. for America's Defense, 1943, Whitman,			

	GD	FN	VF/NM
432 pgs., Henry E. Vallely-a, flip pictures	10.00	30.00	62.00
1133- Kelly King at Yale Hall, 1937, Saalfield	9.00	27.00	57.00
Ken Maynard (See Strawberry Roan, Western Frontier & Wheels of Destiny)			
776- Ken Maynard in "Gun Justice," 1934, Whitman, 160 pgs., hard-c,			
movie scenes (Universal Pic.)	19.00	57.00	135.00
776- Ken Maynard in "Gun Justice," 1934, Whitman, 160 pgs., soft-c,			
movie scenes (Universal Pic.)	19.00	57.00	135.00
1430- Ken Maynard in Western Justice, 1938, Whitman, 432 pgs.,			
Irwin Myers-a	12.00	36.00	78.00
1442- Ken Maynard and the Gun Wolves of the Gila, 1939,			
Whitman, 432 pgs.	12.00	36.00	78.00
nn- Ken Maynard in Six-Gun Law, 1938, Whitman, 36 pgs.,			
2 1/2" x 3 1/2", Penny Book	9.00	27.00	57.00
1134- King of Crime, 1938, Saalfield, 400 pgs.	10.00	30.00	62.00
King of the Royal Mounted (See Zane Grey)			
nn- Kit Carson, 1933, World Syndicate, by J. Carroll Mansfield, High Lights			
Of History Series, hard-c	10.00	30.00	62.00
nn- Kit Carson, 1933, World Syndicate, same as hard-c above but			
with a black cloth-c	10.00	30.00	62.00
1105- Kit Carson and the Mystery Riders, 1935, Saalfield, hard-c,			
Johnny Mack Brown photo-c, movie scenes	16.00	48.00	115.00
1585- Kit Carson and the Mystery Riders, 1935, Saalfield, soft-c,			
Johnny Mack Brown photo-c, movie scenes	16.00	48.00	115.00
Krazy Kat (See Adventures of...)			
2004- (#4)-Lassie-Adventure in Alaska (TV Series), 1967, Whitman,			
hard-c, 260 pgs., 39 cents, color illos	4.00	12.00	22.00
5754- Lassie-Adventure in Alaska (TV Series), 1973, Whitman,			
soft-c, 260 pgs., 49 cents, color illos	2.00	6.00	12.00
2027- Lassie and the Shabby Sheik (TV Series), 1968, Whitman,			
hard-c, 260 pgs., 39 cents	4.00	12.00	22.00
5762- Lassie and the Shabby Sheik (TV Series), 1972, Whitman,			
soft-c, 260 pgs., 39 cents	2.00	6.00	12.00
5769- Lassie, Old One-Eye (TV Series), 1975, Whitman, soft-c,			
260 pgs., 49 cents, three printings	2.00	6.00	12.00
1132- Last Days of Pompeii, The, 1935, Whitman, 5 1/4" x 6 1/4",			
260 pgs., photo-c, movie scenes	14.00	42.00	95.00
1128- Last Man Out (Baseball), 1937, Saalfield, hard-c			
	10.00	30.00	62.00
L30- Last of the Mohicans, The, 1936, Lynn, 192 pgs., movie scenes with			
Randolph Scott, United Artists Pictures	15.00	45.00	105.00
1126- Laughing Dragon of Oz, The, 1934, Whitman 432 pgs., by			
Frank Baum (scarce)	93.00	279.00	650.00
1086- Laurel and Hardy, 1934, Saalfield, 160 pgs., hard-c, photo-c,			
movie scenes	19.00	57.00	135.00
1316- Laurel and Hardy, 1934, Saalfield, 160 pgs. soft-c, photo-c,			
movie scenes	19.00	57.00	135.00
1092- Law of the Wild, The, 1935, Saalfield, 160 pgs., photo-c, movie scenes			
of Rex, The Wild Horse & Rin-Tin-Tin Jr.	12.00	36.00	78.00
1322- Law of the Wild, The, 1935, Saalfield, 160 pgs., photo-c, movie scenes,			
soft-c	12.00	36.00	78.00
1100B- Learn to be a Ventriloquist, 1938, Whitman, 36 pgs.			
2 1/2" x 3 1/2", Penny Book	3.00	9.00	20.00
1149- Lee Brady Range Detective, 1938, Saalfield, 400 pgs.			
	9.00	27.00	57.00
L10- Les Miserables (Victor Hugo's ...), 1935, Lynn, 192 pgs.,			
movie scenes	14.00	42.00	95.00
1441- Lightning Jim U.S. Marshal Brings Law to the West, 1940, Whitman,			
432 pgs., based on radio program	12.00	42.00	78.00
nn- Lightning Jim Whipple U.S. Marshal in Indian Territory, 1939,			
Whitman, 36 pgs., 2 1/2" x 3 1/2", Penny Book	10.00	30.00	62.00
653- Lions and Tigers (With Clyde Beatty), 1934, Whitman, 160 pgs.,			
photo-c movie scenes	14.00	42.00	95.00
1187- Li'l Abner and the Ratfields, 1940, Saalfield, 400 pgs., by Al Capp			
	18.00	54.00	125.00
1193- Li'l Abner and Sadie Hawkins Day, 1940, Saalfield, 400 pgs.,			
by Al Capp	17.00	51.00	125.00
1198- Li'l Abner in New York, 1936, Whitman, 432 pgs., by Al Capp			
	19.00	57.00	135.00
1401- Li'l Abner Among the Millionaires, 1939, Whitman, 432 pgs.,			
by Al Capp	19.00	57.00	135.00

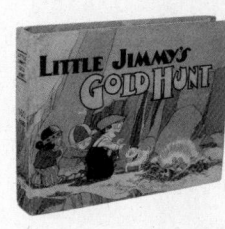

1087 - Little Jimmy's Gold Hunt © Saalfield

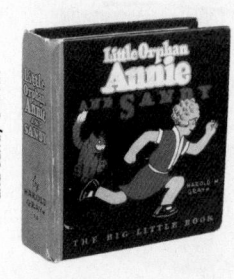

716 - Little Orphan Annie and Sandy © WHIT

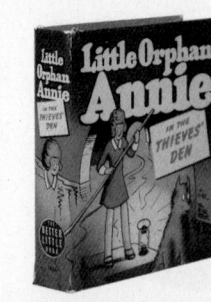

1446 - Little Orphan Annie in the Thieves' Den © WHIT

	GD	FN	VF/NM
1054- Little Annie Rooney, 1934, Saalfield, oblong - 4" x 8", All Pictures			
Comics, hard-c	18.00	54.00	125.00
1304- Little Annie Rooney, 1934, Saalfield, oblong - 4" x 8", All Pictures,			
soft-c	18.00	54.00	125.00
1117- Little Annie Rooney and the Orphan House, 1936,			
Whitman, 432 pgs.	11.00	33.00	72.00
1406- Little Annie Rooney on the Highway to Adventure, 1938,			
Whitman, 432 pgs.	11.00	33.00	72.00
1149- Little Big Shot (With Sybil Jason), 1935, Whitman, 240 pgs.,			
photo-c, movie scenes	14.00	42.00	95.00
nn- Little Black Sambo, nd (1930s), np (Whitman), 36 pgs.,			
3" x 2 1/2", Penny Book	12.00	36.00	78.00
Little Bo-Peep (See Wee Little Books)			
Little Colonel, The (See Shirley Temple)			
1148- Little Green Door, The, 1938, Saalfield, 400 pgs.			
	10.00	30.00	68.00
1112- Little Hollywood Stars, 1935, Saalfield, movie scenes			
(Little Rascals, etc.), hard-c	14.00	42.00	95.00
1592- Little Hollywood Stars, 1935, Saalfield, movie scenes,			
soft-c	14.00	42.00	95.00
1087- Little Jimmy's Gold Hunt, 1935, Saalfield, 160 pgs., hard-c,			
Little Big Book, by Swinnerton	18.00	54.00	125.00
1317- Little Jimmy's Gold Hunt, 1935, Saalfield, 160 pgs., 4 1/4" x 5 3/4",			
soft-c, by Swinnerton	18.00	54.00	125.00
Little Joe and the City Gangsters (See Top-Line Comics)			
Little Joe Otter's Slide (See Wee Little Books)			
1118- Little Lord Fauntleroy, 1936, Saalfield, movie scenes, photo-c,			
4 1/2" x 5 1/4", starring Mickey Rooney & Freddie Bartholomew,			
hard-c	12.00	36.00	78.00
1598- Little Lord Fauntleroy, 1936, Saalfield, photo-c, movie scenes,			
soft-c	12.00	36.00	78.00
1192- Little Mary Mixup and the Grocery Robberies, 1940, Saalfield			
	10.00	30.00	62.00
8- Little Mary Mixup Wins A Prize, 1936, Whitman, 132 pgs.,			
3 1/2" x 3 1/2", soft-c, Tarzan Ice Cream cup lid premium			
	33.00	99.00	230.00
1150- Little Men, 1934, Whitman, 4 3/4" x 5 1/4", movie scenes			
(Mascot Prod.), photo-c, hard-c	11.00	33.00	72.00
9- Little Minister, The,-Katharine Hepburn, 1935, 160 pgs., 4 1/4" x 5 1/2",			
EVW (Five Star Library), movie scenes (RKO)			
	15.00	45.00	105.00
1120- Little Miss Muffet, 1936, Whitman, 432 pgs., by Fanny Y. Cory			
	11.00	33.00	72.00
708- Little Orphan Annie, 1933, Whitman, 320 pgs., by Harold Gray,			
the 2nd Big Little Book	64.00	192.00	450.00
nn- Little Orphan Annie, 1928('33), Whitman, 52 pgs.,			
4" x 5 1/2", premium-no ads, soft-c, by Harold Gray			
	36.00	108.00	250.00
716- Little Orphan Annie and Sandy, 1933, Whitman, 320 pgs.,			
by Harold Gray	30.00	90.00	210.00
716- Little Orphan Annie and Sandy, 1933, Whitman, 300 pgs.,			
by Harold Gray	30.00	90.00	210.00
nn- Little Orphan Annie and Sandy, 1933, Whitman, 52 pgs.,			
premium-no ads, 4" x 5 1/2", soft-c by Harold Gray			
	36.00	108.00	250.00
748- Little Orphan Annie and Chizzler, 1933, Whitman, 320 pgs.,			
by Harold Gray	24.00	72.00	170.00
1010- Little Orphan Annie and the Big Town Gunmen, 1937,			
7 1/4" x 5 1/2", 64 pgs., Nickel Book	14.00	42.00	95.00
nn- Little Orphan Annie with the Circus, 1934, Whitman, 320 pgs., same			
cover as L.O.A. 708 but with blue background, Ovaltine giveaway			
stamp inside front-c, by Harold Gray	54.00	162.00	375.00
1140- Little Orphan Annie and the Big Train Robbery,			
1934, Whitman, 300 pgs., by Gray	18.00	54.00	125.00
1140- Little Orphan Annie and the Big Train Robbery, 1934, Whitman,			
300 pgs., premium-no ads, soft-c, by Harold Gray			
	33.00	99.00	230.00
1154- Little Orphan Annie and the Ghost Gang, 1935, Whitman,			
432 pgs. by Harold Gray	18.00	54.00	125.00
nn- Little Orphan Annie and the Ghost Gang, 1935, Whitman, 436 pgs.,			

	GD	FN	VF/NM
premium-no ads, 3-color, soft-c, by Harold Gray			
	33.00	99.00	230.00
1162- Little Orphan Annie and Punjab the Wizard, 1935,			
Whitman, 432 pgs., by Harold Gray	18.00	54.00	125.00
1186- Little Orphan Annie and the $1,000,000 Formula,			
1936, Whitman, 432 pgs., by Gray	16.00	48.00	115.00
1414- Little Orphan Annie and the Ancient Treasure of Am,			
1939, Whitman, 432 pgs., by Gray	15.00	45.00	105.00
1416- Little Orphan Annie in the Movies, 1937, Whitman, 432 pgs.,			
by Harold Gray	15.00	45.00	105.00
1417- Little Orphan Annie and the Secret of the Well,			
1947,Whitman, 352 pgs., by Gray	12.00	36.00	78.00
1435- Little Orphan Annie and the Gooneyville Mystery,			
1947, Whitman, 288 pgs., by Gray	12.00	36.00	85.00
1446- Little Orphan Annie in the Thieves' Den, 1949, Whitman,			
288 pgs., by Harold Gray	12.00	36.00	85.00
1449- Little Orphan Annie and the Mysterious Shoemaker,			
1938, Whitman, 432 pgs., by Harold Gray	13.00	39.00	95.00
1457- Little Orphan Annie and Her Junior Commandos,			
1943, Whitman, 352 pgs., by H. Gray	12.00	36.00	78.00
1461- Little Orphan Annie and the Underground Hide-Out,			
1945, Whitman, 352 pgs., by Gray	12.00	36.00	78.00
1468- Little Orphan Annie and the Ancient Treasure of Am,			
1949 (Misdated 1939), 288 pgs., by Gray	12.00	36.00	78.00
1482- Little Orphan Annie and the Haunted Mansion, 1941, Whitman,			
432 pgs., flip pictures, by Harold Gray	15.00	45.00	105.00
3048- Little Orphan Annie and Her Big Little Kit, 1937, Whitman,			
384 pgs., 4 1/2" x 6 1/2" box, includes miniature box of 4 crayons-			
red, yellow, blue and green	86.00	258.00	600.00
4054- Little Orphan Annie, The Story of, 1934, Whitman, 7" x 9 1/2",			
320 pgs., Big Big Book, Harold Gray-c/a	93.00	279.00	650.00
nn- Little Orphan Annie Gets into Trouble, 1938, Whitman,			
36 pgs., 2 1/2" x 3 1/2", Penny Book	10.00	30.00	62.00
nn- Little Orphan Annie in Hollywood, 1937, Whitman,			
3 1/2" x 3 1/4", Pan-Am premium, soft-c	26.00	78.00	185.00
nn- Little Orphan Annie in Rags to Riches, 1939, Dell,			
194 pgs., Fast-Action Story, soft-c	36.00	108.00	250.00
nn- Little Orphan Annie Saves Sandy, 1938, Whitman, 36 pgs.,			
2 1/2" x 3 1/2", Penny Book	10.00	30.00	62.00
nn- Little Orphan Annie Under the Big Top, 1938, Dell,			
194 pgs., Fast-Action Story, soft-c	35.00	105.00	245.00
nn- Little Orphan Annie Wee Little Books (In open box)			
nn, 1934, Whitman, 44 pgs., by H. Gray			
L.O.A. And Daddy Warbucks	8.00	25.00	50.00
L.O.A. And Her Dog Sandy	8.00	25.00	50.00
L.O.A. And The Lucky Knife	8.00	25.00	50.00
L.O.A. And The Pinch-Pennys	8.00	25.00	50.00
L.O.A. At Happy Home	8.00	25.00	50.00
L.O.A. Finds Mickey	8.00	25.00	50.00
Complete set with box	45.00	135.00	315.00
nn- Little Polly Flinders, The Story of, nd (1930s), no publ.,			
36 pgs., 2 1/2" x 3", Penny Book	3.00	9.00	20.00
nn- Little Red Hen, The, nd(1930s), np(Whitman), 36 pgs., Penny Book			
	3.00	9.00	20.00
nn- Little Red Riding Hood, nd(1930s), np(Whitman), 36 pgs.,			
3" x 2 1/2", Penny Book	3.00	9.00	20.00
nn- Little Red Riding Hood and the Big Bad Wolf			
(Disney), 1934, McKay, 36 pgs., stiff-c, Disney Studio-a			
	30.00	90.00	210.00
757- Little Women, 1934, Whitman, 4 3/4" x 5 1/4", 160 pgs., photo-c,			
movie scenes, starring Katharine Hepburn	19.00	57.00	135.00
Littlest Rebel, The (See Shirley Temple)			
1181- Lone Ranger and his Horse Silver, 1935, Whitman, 432 pgs.,			
Hal Arbo-a	26.00	78.00	180.00
1196- Lone Ranger and the Vanishing Herd, 1936, Whitman,			
432 pgs.	21.00	63.00	150.00
1407- Lone Ranger and Dead Men's Mine, The, 1939, Whitman,			
432 pgs.	20.00	60.00	140.00
1421- Lone Ranger on the Barbary Coast, The, 1944, Whitman,			
352 pgs., Henry Vallely-a	17.00	51.00	120.00

1468 - Lone Ranger Follows Through © Lone Ranger Inc.

1400 - Mac of the Marines in China © WHIT

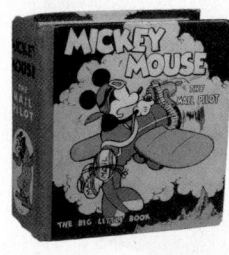

731 - Mickey Mouse the Mail Pilot © WDC

	GD	FN	VF/NM

1428- Lone Ranger and the Secret Weapon, The, 1943, Whitman, — 17.00 51.00 120.00

1431- Lone Ranger and the Secret Killer, The, 1937, Whitman 432 pgs., H. Anderson-a — 21.00 63.00 150.00

1450- Lone Ranger and the Black Shirt Highwayman, The, 1939, Whitman, 432 pgs. — 20.00 60.00 140.00

1465- Lone Ranger and the Menace of Murder Valley, The, 1938, Whitman, 432 pgs., Robert Wiseman-a — 19.00 57.00 135.00

1468- Lone Ranger Follows Through, The, 1941, Whitman, 432 pgs., H.E. Vallely-a — 19.00 57.00 135.00

1477- Lone Ranger and the Great Western Span, The, 1942, Whitman, 424 pgs., H. E. Vallely-a — 17.00 51.00 120.00

1489- Lone Ranger and the Red Renegades, The, 1939, Whitman, 432 pgs. — 21.00 63.00 150.00

1498- Lone Ranger and the Silver Bullets, 1946, Whitman, 352 pgs., Henry E. Vallely-a — 17.00 51.00 120.00

712-10- Lone Ranger and the Secret of Somber Cavern, The, 1950, Whitman — 11.00 33.00 70.00

2013- (#13)-Lone Ranger Outwits Crazy Cougar, The, 1968, Whitman, 260 pgs., 39 cents, hard-c, color illos — 4.00 12.00 22.00

5774- Lone Ranger Outwits Crazy Cougar, The, 1976, Whitman, 260 pgs., 49 cents, soft-c, color illos — 3.00 9.00 20.00

5774-1- Lone Ranger Outwits Crazy Cougar, The, 1979, Whitman, 260 pgs., 69 cents, soft-c, color illos — 3.00 9.00 18.00

nn- Lone Ranger and the Lost Valley, The, 1938, Dell, 196 pgs., Fast-Action Story, soft-c — 39.00 117.00 275.00

1405- Lone Star Martin of the Texas Rangers, 1939, Whitman, 432 pgs. — 16.00 48.00 115.00

19- Lost City, The, 1935, EVW, movie scenes — 14.00 42.00 95.00

1103- Lost Jungle, The (With Clyde Beatty), 1936, Saalfield, movie scenes, hard-c — 14.00 42.00 95.00

1583- Lost Jungle, The (With Clyde Beatty), 1936, Saalfield, movie scenes, soft -c — 12.00 36.00 85.00

753- Lost Patrol, The, 1934, Whitman, 160 pgs., photo-c, movie scenes with Boris Karloff — 14.00 42.00 95.00

nn- Lost World, The - Jurassic Park 2, 1997, Chronicle Books, 312 pgs., adapts movie, 1-color (green) illos — 3.00 9.00 18.00

1189- Mac of the Marines in Africa (1936), Whitman, 432 pgs. — 11.00 33.00 72.00

1400- Mac of the Marines in China, 1938, Whitman, 432 pgs. — 11.00 33.00 72.00

1100B- Magic Tricks (With explanations), 1938, Whitman, 36 pgs., 2 1/2" x 3 1/2", Penny Book, rabbit in hat-c — 3.00 9.00 20.00

1100B- Magic Tricks (How to do them), 1938, Whitman, 36 pgs., 2 1/2" x 3 1/2", Penny Book, genie-c — 3.00 9.00 20.00

Major Hoople (See Our Boarding House)

2022- (#22)- Major Matt Mason, Moon Mission, 1968, Whitman, 256 pgs., hard-c, color illos — 4.00 12.00 25.00

1167- Mandrake the Magician, 1935, Whitman, 432 pgs., by Lee Falk & Phil Davis — 22.00 66.00 155.00

1418- Mandrake the Magician and the Flame Pearls, 1946, Whitman, 352 pgs., by Lee Falk & Phil Davis — 14.00 42.00 95.00

1431- Mandrake the Magician and the Midnight Monster, 1939, Whitman, 432 pgs., by Lee Falk & Phil Davis — 15.00 45.00 105.00

1454- Mandrake the Magician Mighty Solver of Mysteries, 1941, Whitman, 432 pgs., by Lee Falk & Phil Davis, flip pictures — 15.00 45.00 105.00

2011- (#11)-Man From U.N.C.L.E., The-The Calcutta Affair (TV Series), 1967, Whitman, 260 pgs., 39 cents, hard-c, color illos — 4.00 12.00 25.00

1429- Marge's Little Lulu Alvin and Tubby, 1947, Whitman, All Pictures Comics, Stanley-a — 28.00 84.00 195.00

1438- Mary Lee and the Mystery of the Indian Beads, 1937, Whitman, 300 pgs. — 20.00 60.00 62.00

1165- Masked Man of the Mesa, The, 1939, Saalfield, 400 pgs. — 9.00 27.00 57.00

nn- Mask of Zorro, The, 1998, Chronicle Books, 312 pgs., adapts movie, 1-color (yellow-green) illos — 1.00 3.00 8.00

1436- Maximo the Amazing Superman, 1940, Whitman, 432 pgs., Henry E. Vallely-a — 14.00 42.00 95.00

1444- Maximo the Amazing Superman and the Crystals of Doom, 1941, Whitman,432 pgs., Henry E. Vallely-a — 14.00 42.00 95.00

1445- Maximo the Amazing Superman and the Supermachine, 1941, Whitman, 432 pgs. — 14.00 42.00 95.00

755- Men of the Mounted, 1934, Whitman, 320 pgs. — 14.00 42.00 95.00

nn- Men of the Mounted, 1933, Whitman, 52 pgs., 3 1/2" x 5 3/4", premium-no ads; other versions with Poll Parrot & Perkins ad; soft-c — 19.00 57.00 135.00

nn- Men of the Mounted, 1934, Whitman, Cocomalt premium, soft-c, by Ted McCall — 12.00 36.00 78.00

1475- Men With Wings, 1938, Whitman, 240 pgs., photo-c, movie scenes (Paramount Pics.) — 12.00 36.00 78.00

1170- Mickey Finn, 1940, Saalfield, 400 pgs., by Frank Leonard — 12.00 36.00 78.00

717- Mickey Mouse (Disney), (1st printing) 1933, Whitman, 320 pgs., Gottfredson-a, skinny Mickey on cover — 356.00 1068.00 2850.00

717- Mickey Mouse (Disney), (2nd printing)1933, Whitman, 320 pgs., Gottfredson-a, regular Mickey on cover — 188.00 564.00 1500.00

nn- Mickey Mouse (Disney), 1933, Dean & Son, Great Big Midget Book, 320 pgs. — 168.00 504.00 1350.00

731- Mickey Mouse the Mail Pilot (Disney), 1933, Whitman, (This is the same book as the 1st Mickey Mouse BLB #717(2nd printing) but with "The Mail Pilot" printed on the front. Lower left of back cover has a small box printed over the existing "No. 717." "No. 731" is printed next to it.) (sold at auction in 2001 in Fine condition for $5,090)

726- Mickey Mouse in Blaggard Castle (Disney), 1934, Whitman, 320 pgs., Gottfredson-a — 43.00 129.00 300.00

731- Mickey Mouse the Mail Pilot (Disney), 1933, Whitman, 300 pgs., Gottfredson-a — 43.00 129.00 300.00

nn- Mickey Mouse the Mail Pilot (Disney), 1933, Whitman, 292 pgs., American Oil Co. premium, soft-c, Gottfredson-a; another version 3 1/2" x 4 3/4" — 43.00 129.00 300.00

750- Mickey Mouse Sails for Treasure Island (Disney), 1933, Whitman, 320 pgs., Gottfredson-a — 43.00 129.00 300.00

nn- Mickey Mouse Sails for Treasure Island (Disney), 1935, Whitman, 196 pgs., premium-no ads, soft-c, Gottfredson-a (Scarce) — 51.00 153.00 360.00

nn- Mickey Mouse Sails for Treasure Island (Disney), 1935, Whitman, 196 pgs., Kolynos Dental Cream premium (Scarce) — 51.00 153.00 360.00

nn- Mickey Mouse Sails for Treasure Island (Disney), 1933, Dean & Son, Great Big Midget Book, 320 pgs. — 131.00 393.00 1050.00

756- Mickey Mouse Presents a Walt Disney Silly Symphony (Disney), 1934, Whitman, 240 pgs., Bucky Bug app. — 39.00 117.00 275.00

801- Mickey Mouse's Summer Vacation, 1948, Whitman, hard-c, Story Hour series — 12.00 36.00 78.00

1111- Mickey Mouse Presents Walt Disney's Silly Symphonies Stories, 1936, Whitman, 432 pgs., Donald Duck app. — 39.00 117.00 275.00

1128- Mickey Mouse and Pluto the Racer (Disney), 1936, Whitman, 432 pgs., Gottfredson-a — 34.00 102.00 235.00

1139- Mickey Mouse the Detective (Disney), 1934, Whitman, 300 pgs., Gottfredson-a — 39.00 117.00 275.00

1139- Mickey Mouse the Detective (Disney), 1934, Whitman, 304 pgs., premium-no ads, soft-c, Gottfredson-a (Scarce) — 58.00 174.00 410.00

1153- Mickey Mouse and the Bat Bandit (Disney), 1935, Whitman, 432 pgs., Gottfredson-a — 36.00 108.00 255.00

nn- Mickey Mouse and the Bat Bandit (Disney), 1935, Whitman, 436 pgs., premium-no ads, 3-color, soft-c, Gottfredson-a (Scarce) — 58.00 174.00 410.00

1160- Mickey Mouse and Bobo the Elephant (Disney), 1935, Whitman, 432 pgs., Gottfredson-a — 36.00 108.00 255.00

1187- Mickey Mouse and the Sacred Jewel (Disney), 1936, Whitman, 432 pgs., Gottfredson-a — 33.00 99.00 230.00

1401- Mickey Mouse in the Treasure Hunt (Disney), 1941, Whitman, 430 pgs., flip pictures of Pluto, Gottfredson-a — 31.00 93.00 220.00

1409- Mickey Mouse Runs His Own Newspaper (Disney), 1937, Whitman, 432 pgs., Gottfredson-a — 31.00 93.00 220.00

1413- Mickey Mouse and the 'Lectro Box (Disney), 1946,

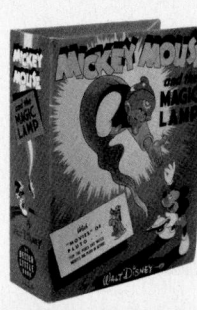

1429 - Mickey Mouse and the Magic Lamp © DIS

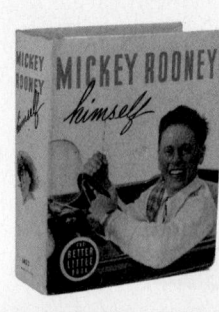

1427 - Mickey Rooney Himself © WHIT

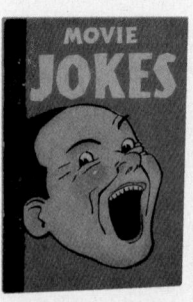

1100B - Movie Jokes © WHIT

	GD	FN	VF/NM
Whitman, 352 pgs., Gottfredson-a	21.00	63.00	145.00
1417- Mickey Mouse on Sky Island (Disney), 1941, Whitman, 432 pgs., flip pictures, Gottfredson-a; considered by Gottfredson to be his best Mickey story	31.00	93.00	220.00
1428- Mickey Mouse in the Foreign Legion (Disney), 1940, Whitman, 432 pgs., Gottfredson-a	31.00	93.00	220.00
1429- Mickey Mouse and the Magic Lamp (Disney), 1942, Whitman, 432 pgs., flip pictures	31.00	93.00	220.00
1433- Mickey Mouse and the Lazy Daisy Mystery (Disney), 1947, Whitman, 288 pgs.	21.00	63.00	145.00
1444- Mickey Mouse in the World of Tomorrow (Disney), 1948, Whitman, 288 pgs., Gottfredson-a	33.00	99.00	230.00
1451- Mickey Mouse and the Desert Palace (Disney), 1948, Whitman, 288 pgs.	21.00	63.00	145.00
1463- Mickey Mouse and the Pirate Submarine (Disney), 1939, Whitman, 432 pgs., Gottfredson-a	31.00	93.00	220.00
1464- Mickey Mouse and the Stolen Jewels (Disney), 1949, Whitman, 288 pgs.	30.00	90.00	210.00
1471- Mickey Mouse and the Dude Ranch Bandit (Disney), 1943, Whitman, 432 pgs., flip pictures	31.00	93.00	220.00
1475- Mickey Mouse and the 7 Ghosts (Disney), 1940, Whitman, 432 pgs., Gottfredson-a	31.00	93.00	220.00
1476- Mickey Mouse in the Race for Riches (Disney), 1938, Whitman, 432 pgs., Gottfredson-a	31.00	93.00	220.00
1483- Mickey Mouse Bell Boy Detective (Disney), 1945, Whitman, 352 pgs.	30.00	90.00	210.00
1499- Mickey Mouse on the Cave-Man Island (Disney), 1944, Whitman, 352 pgs.	30.00	90.00	210.00
2004- Mickey Mouse, Here Comes (Disney), 1936, Whitman, (Very Rare), 224 pgs., 12" x 8 1/4" box, with red, yellow and blue crayons, contains 224 loose pages to color, reprinted from early Mickey Mouse related movie and strip reprints	431.00	1293.00	3450.00
2020-(#20)- Mickey Mouse, Adventure in Outer Space, 1968, Whitman, 256 pgs.,hard-c, color illos.	4.00	12.00	22.00
5750- Mickey Mouse, Adventure in Outer Space, 1973, Whitman, 256 pgs.,soft-c, color illos.	2.00	6.00	12.00
3049- Mickey Mouse and His Big Little Kit (Disney) 1937, Whitman, 384 pgs., 4 1/2" x 6 1/2" box, includes miniature box of 4 crayons-red, yellow, blue and green	138.00	414.00	1100.00
3061- Mickey Mouse to Draw and Color (The Big Little Set), nd (early 1930s), Whitman, with crayons; box contains 320 loose pages to color, reprinted from early Mickey Mouse BLBs	114.00	342.00	800.00
4062- Mickey Mouse, The Story Of, 1935, Whitman, 7" x 9 1/2", 320 pgs., Big Big Book, Gottfredson-a	138.00	414.00	1100.00
4062- Mickey Mouse and the Smugglers, The Story Of, 1935, Whitman, (Scarce) 7" x 9 1/2", 320 pgs., Big Big Book, same contents as above version; Gottfredson-a	163.00	489.00	1300.00
708-10- Mickey Mouse on the Haunted Island (Disney), 1950, Whitman, Gottfredson-a	14.00	42.00	95.00
nn- Mickey Mouse and Minnie at Macy's, 1934 Whitman, 148 pgs., 3 1/4" x 3 1/2", soft-c, R. H. Macy & Co. Christmas giveaway (Rare, less than 20 known copies)	400.00	1200.00	3200.00
nn- Mickey Mouse and Minnie March to Macy's, 1935, Whitman, 148 pgs., 3 1/2" x 3 1/2", soft-c, R. H. Macy & Co. Christmas giveaway (scarce)	275.00	825.00	2200.00
nn- Mickey Mouse and the Magic Carpet, 1935, Whitman, 148 pgs., 3 1/2"x 4", soft-c, giveaway, Gottfredson-a, Donald Duck app.	114.00	342.00	800.00
nn- Mickey Mouse Silly Symphonies, 1934, Dean & Son, Ltd (England), 48 pgs., with 4 pop-ups, Babes In The Woods, King Neptune			
With dust jacket	150.00	450.00	1200.00
Without dust jacket	108.00	324.00	760.00
nn- Mickey Mouse the Sheriff of Nugget Gulch (Disney) 1938, Dell, 196 pgs., Fast-Action Story, soft-c, Gottfredson-a	51.00	153.00	360.00
nn- Mickey Mouse Waddle Book, 1934, BRP, 20 pgs., 7 1/2" x 10", forerunner of the Blue Ribbon Pop-Up books; with 4 removable articulated cardboard characters (a file copy sold for $30,000 in 2004)			

	GD	FN	VF/NM
(an incomplete copy sold for $4,600 in 2005)			
nn- Mickey Mouse with Goofy and Mickey's Nephews, 1938, Dell, Fast-Action Story, Gottfredson-a	51.00	153.00	360.00
16- Mickey Mouse and Pluto (Disney), 1942, Dell, 196 pgs., Fast-Action story	51.00	153.00	360.00
512- Mickey Mouse Wee Little Books (In open box), nn, 1934, Whitman, 44 pgs., small size, soft-c			
Mickey Mouse and Tanglefoot	12.00	36.00	85.00
Mickey Mouse at the Carnival	12.00	36.00	85.00
Mickey Mouse Will Not Quit!	12.00	36.00	85.00
Mickey Mouse Wins the Race!	12.00	36.00	85.00
Mickey Mouse's Misfortune	12.00	36.00	85.00
Mickey Mouse's Uphill Fight	12.00	36.00	85.00
Complete set with box	83.00	249.00	580.00
1493- Mickey Rooney and Judy Garland and How They Got into the Movies, 1941, Whitman, 432 pgs., photo-c	14.00	42.00	95.00
1427- Mickey Rooney Himself, 1939, Whitman, 240 pgs., photo-c, movie scenes, life story	14.00	42.00	95.00
532- Mickey's Dog Pluto (Disney), 1943, Whitman, All Picture Comics, A Tall Comic Book , 3 3/4" x 8 3/4"	37.00	111.00	260.00
2113- Midget Jumbo Coloring Book, 1935, Saalfield	37.00	111.00	260.00
21- Midsummer Night's Dream, 1935, EVW, movie scenes	14.00	42.00	95.00
nn- Minute-Man (Mystery of the Spy Ring), 1941, Fawcett, Dime Action Book	52.00	156.00	365.00
710- Moby Dick the Great White Whale, The Story of, 1934, Whitman, 160 pgs., photo-c, movie scenes from "The Sea Beast"	14.00	42.00	95.00
746- Moon Mullins and Kayo (Kayo and Moon Mullins-inside), 1933, Whitman, 320 pgs., Frank Willard-c/a	15.00	45.00	105.00
nn- Moon Mullins and Kayo, 1933, Whitman, Cocomalt premium, soft-c, by Willard	15.00	45.00	105.00
1134- Moon Mullins and the Plushbottom Twins, 1935, Whitman, 432 pgs., Willard-c/a	15.00	45.00	105.00
nn- Moon Mullins and the Plushbottom Twins, 1935, Whitman, 436 pgs., premium-no ads, 3-color, soft-c, by Willard	26.00	78.00	185.00
1058- Mother Pluto (Disney), 1939, Whitman, 68 pgs., hard-c	12.00	36.00	85.00
1100B- Movie Jokes (From the talkies), 1938, Whitman, 36 pgs., 2 1/2" x 3 1/2", Penny Book	3.00	9.00	20.00
1408- Mr. District Attorney on the Job, 1941, Whitman, 432 pgs., flip pictures	10.00	30.00	68.00
nn- Musicians of Bremen, The, nd (1930s), np (Whitman), 36 pgs., 3" x 2 1/2", Penny Book	3.00	9.00	20.00
1113- Mutt and Jeff, 1936, Whitman, 300 pgs., by Bud Fisher	24.00	72.00	165.00
1116- My Life and Times (By Shirley Temple), 1936, Saalfield, Little Big Book, hard-c, photo-c/illos	15.00	45.00	105.00
1596- My Life and Times (By Shirley Temple), 1936, Saalfield, Little Big Book, soft-c, photo-c/illos	15.00	45.00	105.00
1497- Myra North Special Nurse and Foreign Spies, 1938, Whitman, 432 pgs.	12.00	36.00	78.00
1400- Nancy and Sluggo, 1946, Whitman, All Pictures Comics, Ernie Bushmiller-a	12.00	36.00	85.00
1487- Nancy Has Fun, 1946, Whitman, All Pictures Comics	12.00	36.00	85.00
1150- Napoleon and Uncle Elby, 1938, Saalfield, 400 pgs., by Clifford McBride	12.00	36.00	78.00
1166- Napoleon Uncle Elby And Little Mary, 1939, Saalfield, 400 pgs., by Clifford McBride	12.00	36.00	78.00
1179- Ned Brant Adventure Bound, 1940, Saalfield, 400 pgs.	10.00	30.00	62.00
1146- Nevada Rides The Danger Trail, 1938, Saalfield, 400 pgs., J.R. White-a	10.00	30.00	62.00
1147- Nevada Whalen, Avenger, 1938, Saalfield, 400 pgs.	10.00	30.00	62.00
Nicodemus O'Malley (See Top-Line Comics)			
1115- Og Son of Fire, 1936, Whitman, 432 pgs.	15.00	45.00	105.00

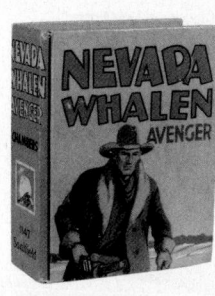

1147 - Nevada Whalen © Saalfield

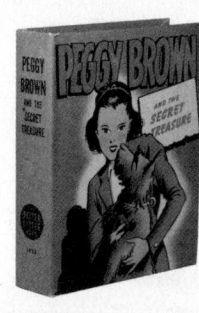

1423 - Peggy Brown and the Secret Treasure © WHIT

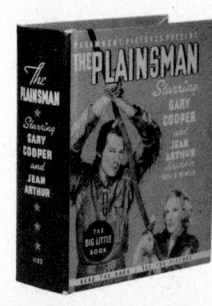

1123 - The Plainsman © WHIT

	GD	FN	VF/NM
1419- Oh, Blondie the Bumsteads (See Blondie)			
11- Oliver Twist, 1935, EVW (Five Star Library), movie scenes, starring Dickie Moore (Monogram Pictures)	14.00	42.00	95.00
718- Once Upon a Time, 1933, Whitman, 364 pgs., soft-c	14.00	42.00	95.00
712- 100 Fairy Tales for Children, The, 1933, Whitman, 288 pgs., Circle Library	10.00	30.00	62.00
1099- One Night of Love, 1935, Saalfield, 160 pgs., hard-c, photo-c, movie scenes, Columbia Pictures, starring Grace Moore	14.00	42.00	95.00
1579- One Night of Love, 1935, Sat, 160 pgs., soft-c, photo-c, movie scenes, Columbia Pictures, starring Grace Moore	14.00	42.00	95.00
1155- $1000 Reward, 1938, Saalfield, 400 pgs.	10.00	30.00	62.00
Orphan Annie (See Little Orphan ...)			
L17- O'Shaughnessy's Boy, 1935, Lynn, 192 pgs., movie scenes, w/Wallace Beery & Jackie Cooper (Metro-Goldwyn-Mayer)	12.00	36.00	78.00
1109- Oswald the Lucky Rabbit, 1934, Whitman, 288 pgs.	19.00	57.00	135.00
1403- Oswald Rabbit Plays G-Man, 1937, Whitman, 240 pgs., movie scenes by Walter Lantz	20.00	60.00	140.00
1190- Our Boarding House, Major Hoople and his Horse, 1940, Saalfield, 400 pgs.	12.00	36.00	78.00
1085- Our Gang, 1934, Saalfield, 160 pgs., photo-c, movie scenes, hard-c	14.00	42.00	95.00
1315- Our Gang, 1934, Saalfield, 160 pgs., photo-c, movie scenes, soft-c	14.00	42.00	95.00
1451- "Our Gang" on the March, 1942, Whitman, 432 pgs., flip pictures, Vallely-a	14.00	42.00	95.00
1456- Our Gang Adventures, 1948, Whitman, 288 pgs.	12.00	36.00	78.00
nn- Paramount Newsreel Men with Admiral Byrd in Little America, 1934, Whitman, 96 pgs., 6 1/4" x 6 1/4", photo-c, photo ill.	15.00	45.00	105.00
nn- Patch, nd (1930s), np (Whitman), 36 pgs., 3" x 2 1/2", Penny Book	3.00	9.00	20.00
1445- Pat Nelson Ace of Test Pilots, 1937, Whitman, 432 pgs.	10.00	30.00	62.00
1411- Peggy Brown and the Mystery Basket, 1941, Whitman, 432 pgs., flip pictures, Henry E. Vallely-a	10.00	30.00	68.00
1423- Peggy Brown and the Secret Treasure, 1947, Whitman, 288 pgs., Henry E. Vallely-a	10.00	30.00	68.00
1427- Peggy Brown and the Runaway Auto Trailer, 1937, Whitman, 300 pgs., Henry E. Vallely-a	10.00	30.00	68.00
1463- Peggy Brown and the Jewel of Fire, 1943, Whitman, 352 pgs., Henry E. Vallely-a	10.00	30.00	68.00
1491- Peggy Brown in the Big Haunted House, 1940, Whitman, 432 pgs., Vallely-a	10.00	30.00	68.00
1143- Peril Afloat, 1938, Saalfield, 400 pgs.	10.00	30.00	62.00
1199- Perry Winkle and the Rinkeydinks, 1937, Whitman, 432 pgs., by Martin Branner	14.00	42.00	95.00
1487- Perry Winkle and the Rinkeydinks get a Horse, 1938, Whitman, 432 pgs., by Martin Branner	14.00	42.00	95.00
Peter Pan (See Wee Little Books)			
nn- Peter Rabbit, nd(1930s), np(Whitman), 36 pgs., Penny Book, 3" x 2 1/2"	5.00	15.00	30.00
Peter Rabbit's Carrots (See Wee Little Books)			
1100- Phantom, The, 1936, Whitman, 432 pgs., by Lee Falk & Ray Moore	43.00	129.00	300.00
1416- Phantom and the Girl of Mystery, The, 1947, Whitman, 352 pgs. by Falk & Moore	19.00	57.00	130.00
1421- Phantom and Desert Justice, The, 1941, Whitman, 432 pgs., flip pictures, by Falk & Moore	25.00	75.00	175.00
1468- Phantom and the Sky Pirates, The, 1945, Whitman, 352 pgs., by Falk & Moore	22.00	66.00	155.00
1474- Phantom and the Sign of the Skull, The, 1939, Whitman, 432 pgs., by Falk & Moore	26.00	78.00	185.00
1489- Phantom, Return of the..., 1942, Whitman, 432 pgs., flip pictures, by Falk & Moore	25.00	75.00	175.00

	GD	FN	VF/NM
1130- Phil Barton, Sleuth (Scout Book), 1937, Saalfield, hard-c	8.00	25.00	50.00
Pied Piper of Hamlin (See Wee Little Books)			
1466- Pilot Pete Dive Bomber, 1941, Whitman, 432 pgs., flip pictures	10.00	50.00	62.00
5776- Pink Panther Adventures in Z-Land, The, 1976, Whitman, 260 pgs., soft-c, 49 cents, B&W	1.00	3.00	7.00
5776-2- Pink Panther Adventures in Z-Land, The, 1980, Whitman, 260 pgs., soft-c, 79 cents, B&W	1.00	3.00	6.00
5783-2- Pink Panther at Castle Kreep, The, 1980, Whitman, 260 pgs., soft-c, 79 cents, B&W	1.00	3.00	6.00
Pinocchio and Jiminy Cricket (See Walt Disney's ...)			
nn- Pioneers of the Wild West (Blue-c), 1933, World Syndicate, High Lights of History Series	9.00	27.00	57.00
nn- Pioneers of the Wild West (Red-c), 1933, World Syndicate, High Lights of History Series	9.00	27.00	57.00
1123- Plainsman, The, 1936, Whitman, 240 pgs., photo-c, movie scenes with Gary Cooper (Paramount Pics.)	24.00	72.00	165.00
Pluto (See Mickey's Dog ... & Walt Disney's ...)			
2114- Pocket Coloring Book, 1935, Saalfield	35.00	105.00	245.00
1060- Polly and Her Pals on the Farm, 1934, Saalfield, 164 pgs., hard-c, by Cliff Sterrett	14.00	42.00	95.00
1310- Polly and Her Pals on the Farm, 1934, Saalfield, soft-c	14.00	42.00	95.00
1051- Popeye, Adventures of..., 1934, Saalfield, oblong-size, E.C. Segar-a, hard-c	54.00	162.00	380.00
1088- Popeye in Puddleburg, 1934, Saalfield, 160 pgs., hard-c, E. C. Segar-a	20.00	60.00	140.00
1113- Popeye Starring in Choose Your Weppins, 1936, Saalfield, 160 pgs., hard-c, Segar-a	41.00	123.00	285.00
1117- Popeye's Ark, 1936, Saalfield, 4 1/2" x 5 1/2", hard-c, Segar-a	21.00	63.00	145.00
1163- Popeye Sees the Sea, 1936, Whitman, 432 pgs., Segar-a	22.00	66.00	155.00
1301- Popeye, Adventures of..., 1934, Saalfield, oblong-size, Segar-a	54.00	162.00	380.00
1318- Popeye in Puddleburg, 1934, Saalfield, 160 pgs., soft-c, Segar-a	21.00	63.00	145.00
1405- Popeye and the Jeep, 1937, Whitman, 432 pgs., Segar-a	22.00	66.00	155.00
1406- Popeye the Super-Fighter, 1939, Whitman, All Pictures Comics, flip pictures, Segar-a	21.00	63.00	145.00
1422- Popeye the Sailor Man, 1947, Whitman, All Pictures Comics	15.00	45.00	105.00
1450- Popeye in Quest of His Poopdeck Pappy, 1937, Whitman, 432 pgs., Segar-c/a	22.00	66.00	155.00
1458- Popeye and Queen Olive Oyl, 1949, Whitman, 288 pgs., Sagendorf-a	15.00	45.00	105.00
1459- Popeye and the Quest for the Rainbird, 1943, Whitman, Winner & Zaboly-a	16.00	48.00	115.00
1480- Popeye the Spinach Eater, 1945, Whitman, All Pictures Comics	15.00	45.00	105.00
1485- Popeye in a Sock for Susan's Sake, 1940, Whitman, 432 pgs., flip pictures	16.00	48.00	115.00
1497- Popeye and Caster Oyl the Detective, 1941, Whitman, 432 pgs. flip pictures, Segar-a	19.00	57.00	135.00
1499- Popeye and the Deep Sea Mystery, 1939, Whitman, 432 pgs., Segar-c/a	19.00	57.00	135.00
1593- Popeye Starring in Choose Your Weppins, 1936, Saalfield, 160 pgs., soft-c, Segar-a	19.00	57.00	135.00
1597- Popeye's Ark, 1936, Saalfield, 4 1/2" x 5 1/2", soft-c, Segar-a	19.00	57.00	135.00
2008-(#8)- Popeye-Ghost Ship to Treasure Island, 1967, Whitman, 260 pgs., 39 cents, hard-c, color illos	4.00	12.00	22.00
5755- Popeye-Ghost Ship to Treasure Island, 1973, Whitman, 260 pgs., soft-c, color illos	2.00	5.00	10.00
2034-(#34)- Popeye, Danger Ahoy!, 1969, Whitman, 256 pgs., hard-c, color illos.	4.00	12.00	22.00
5768- Popeye, Danger Ahoy!, 1975, Whitman, 256 pgs.,			

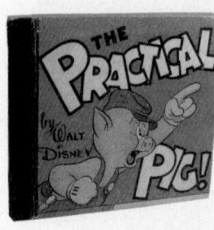

1058 - The Practical Pig! © DIS

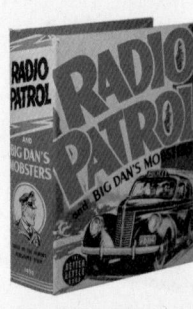

1498 - Radio Patrol and Big Dan's Mobsters © WHIT

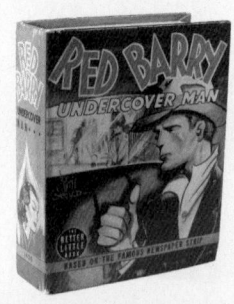

1426 - Red Barry Undercover Man © WHIT

	GD	FN	VF/NM
soft-c, color illos.	2.00	5.00	10.00
4063- Popeye, Thimble Theatre Starring, 1935, Whitman, 7" x 9 1/2", 320 pgs., Big Big Book, Segar-c/a; (Cactus cover w/yellow logo)	157.00	471.00	1260.00
4063- Popeye, Thimble Theatre Starring, 1935, Whitman, 7" x 9 1/2", 320 pgs., Big Big Book, Segar-c/a; (Big Balloon-c with red logo), (2nd printing w/same contents as above)	184.00	552.00	1470.00
5761- Popeye and Queen Olive Oyl, 1973, 260 pgs., B&W, soft-c	4.00	12.00	22.00
5761-2- Popeye and Queen Olive Oyl, 1973 (1980-reprint of 1973 version), 260 pgs., 79 cents, B&W, soft-c	2.00	5.00	10.00
103- "Pop-Up" Buck Rogers in the Dangerous Mission (with Pop-Up picture), 1934, BRP, 62 pgs., The Midget Pop-Up Book w/Pop-Up in center of book, Calkins-a	157.00	471.00	1260.00
206- "Pop-Up" Buck Rogers - Strange Adventures in the Spider Ship, The, 1935, BRP, 24 pgs., 8" x 9", 3 Pop-Ups, hard-c, by Dick Calkins	157.00	471.00	1260.00
nn- "Pop-Up" Cinderella, 1933, BRP, 7 1/2" x 9 3/4", 4 Pop-Ups, hard-c			
With dustjacket ($2.00)	107.00	321.00	750.00
Without dustjacket	82.00	246.00	575.00
207- "Pop-Up" Dick Tracy-Capture of Boris Arson, 1935, BRP, 24 pgs., 8" x 9", 3 Pop-Ups, hard-c, by Gould	105.00	315.00	735.00
210- "Pop-Up" Flash Gordon Tournament of Death, The, 1935, BRP, 24 pgs., 8" x 9", 3 Pop-Ups, hard-c, by Alex Raymond	157.00	471.00	1260.00
202- "Pop-Up" Goldilocks and the Three Bears, The, 1934, BRP, 24 pgs., 8" x 9", 3 Pop-Ups, hard-c	41.00	123.00	285.00
nn- "Pop-Up" Jack and the Beanstalk, 1933, BRP, hard-c (50 cents), 1 Pop-Up	41.00	123.00	285.00
nn- "Pop-Up" Jack the Giant Killer, 1933, BRP, hard-c (50 cents), 1 Pop-Up	41.00	123.00	285.00
nn- "Pop-Up" Jack the Giant Killer, 1933, BRP, 4 Pop-Ups, hard-c			
With dust jacket ($2.00)	107.00	321.00	750.00
Without dust jacket	82.00	246.00	575.00
nn- "Pop-Up" Little Black Sambo, (with Pop-Up picture), 1934, BRP, 62 pgs., The Midget Pop-Up Book, one Pop-Up in center of book	67.00	201.00	470.00
208- "Pop-Up" Little Orphan Annie and Jumbo the Circus Elephant, 1935, BRP, 24 pgs., 8" x 9 1/2", 3 Pop-Ups, hard-c, by H. Gray	108.00	324.00	760.00
nn- "Pop-Up" Little Red Ridinghood, 1933, BRP, hard-c (50 cents), 1 Pop-Up	52.00	156.00	365.00
nn- "Pop-Up" Mickey Mouse, The, 1933, BRP, 34 pgs., 6 1/2" x 9", 3 Pop-Ups, hard-c, Gottfredson-a (75 cents)	101.00	303.00	705.00
nn- "Pop-Up" Mickey Mouse in King Arthur's Court, The, 1933, BRP, 56 pgs., 7 1/2" x 9 1/4", 4 Pop-Ups, hard-c, Gottfredson-a			
With dust jacket ($2.00)	275.00	825.00	2200.00
Without dustjacket	170.00	510.00	1365.00
101- "Pop-Up" Mickey Mouse in "Ye Olden Days" (with Pop-Up picture), 1934, 62 pgs., BRP, The Midget Pop-Up Book, one Pop-Up in center of book, Gottfredson-a	124.00	372.00	945.00
nn- "Pop-Up" Minnie Mouse, The, 1933, BRP, 36 pgs., 6 1/2" x 9", 3 Pop-Ups, hard-c (75 cents), Gottfredson-a	101.00	303.00	705.00
203- "Pop-Up" Mother Goose, The, 1934, BRP, 24 pgs., 8" x 9 1/4", 3 Pop-Ups, hard-c	71.00	213.00	500.00
nn- "Pop-Up" Mother Goose Rhymes, The, 1933, BRP, 96 pgs., 7 1/2" x 9 1/4", 4 Pop-Ups, hard-c			
With dustjacket ($2.00)	96.00	288.00	675.00
Without dustjacket	75.00	225.00	525.00
209- "Pop-Up" New Adventures of Tarzan, 1935, BRP, 24 pgs., 8" x 9", 3 Pop-Ups, hard-c	124.00	372.00	945.00
104- "Pop-Up" Peter Rabbit, The (with Pop-Up picture), 1934, BRP, 62 pgs., The Midget Pop-Up Book, one Pop-Up in center of book	67.00	201.00	470.00
nn- "Pop-Up" Pinocchio, 1933, BRP, 7 1/2" x 9 3/4", 4 Pop-Ups, hard-c			
With dustjacket ($2.00)	107.00	321.00	750.00
Without dust jacket	82.00	246.00	575.00
102- "Pop-Up" Popeye among the White Savages (with Pop-Up picture), 1934, BRP, 62 pgs., The Midget Pop-Up Book, one Pop-Up in center			

	GD	FN	VF/NM
of book, E. C. Segar-a	105.00	315.00	735.00
205- "Pop-Up" Popeye with the Hag of the Seven Seas, The, 1935, BRP, 24 pgs., 8" x 9", 3 Pop-Ups, hard-c, Segar-a	122.00	366.00	865.00
201- "Pop-Up" Puss In Boots, The, 1934, BRP, 24 pgs., 3 Pop-Ups, hard-c	41.00	123.00	285.00
nn- "Pop-Up" Silly Symphonies, The (Mickey Mouse Presents His ...), 1933, BRP, 56 pgs., 9 3/4" x 7 1/2", 4 Pop-Ups, hard-c			
With dust jacket ($2.00)	156.00	468.00	1250.00
Without dust jacket	112.00	336.00	785.00
nn- "Pop-Up" Sleeping Beauty, 1933, BRP, hard-c, (50 cents), 1 Pop-up	47.00	141.00	330.00
212- "Pop-Up" Terry and the Pirates in Shipwrecked, The, 1935, BRP, 24 pgs., 8" x 9", 3 Pop-Ups, hard-c	101.00	303.00	705.00
211- "Pop-Up" Tim Tyler in the Jungle, The, 1935, BRP, 24 pgs., 8" x 9", 3 Pop-Ups, hard-c	75.00	225.00	525.00
1404- Porky Pig and His Gang, 1946, Whitman, All Pictures Comics, Barks-a, reprints Four Color #48	21.00	63.00	150.00
1408- Porky Pig and Petunia, 1942, Whitman, All Pictures Comics, flip pictures, reprints Four Color #16 & Famous Gang Book of Comics	15.00	45.00	105.00
1176- Powder Smoke Range, 1935, Whitman, 240 pgs., photo-c, movie scenes, Hoot Gibson, Harey Carey app. (RKO Radio Pict.)	13.00	39.00	90.00
1058- Practical Pig!, The (Disney), 1939, Whitman, 68 pgs., 5" x 5 1/2", hard-c	12.00	36.00	78.00
758- Prairie Bill and the Covered Wagon, 1934, Whitman, 384 pgs., Hal Arbo-a	12.00	36.00	78.00
nn- Prairie Bill and the Covered Wagon, 1934, Whitman, 390 pgs., premium-no ads, 3-color, soft-c, Hal Arbo-a	16.00	48.00	115.00
1440- Punch Davis of the U.S. Aircraft Carrier, 1945, Whitman, 352 pgs.	9.00	27.00	57.00
nn- Puss in Boots, nd(1930s), np(Whitman), 36 pgs., Penny Book	3.00	9.00	20.00
1100B- Puzzle Book, 1938, Whitman, 36 pgs., 2 1/2" x 3 1/2", Penny Book	4.00	12.00	24.00
1100B- Puzzles, 1938, Whitman, 36 pgs., 2 1/2" x 3 1/2", Penny Book	4.00	12.00	24.00
1100B- Quiz Book, The, 1938, Whitman, 36 pgs., 2 1/2" x 3 1/2", Penny Book	4.00	12.00	24.00
1142- Radio Patrol, 1935, Whitman, 432 pgs., by Eddie Sullivan & Charlie Schmidt (#1)	12.00	36.00	78.00
1173- Radio Patrol Trailing the Safeblowers, 1937, Whitman, 432 pgs.	10.00	30.00	62.00
1496- Radio Patrol Outwitting the Gang Chief, 1939, Whitman, 432 pgs.	10.00	30.00	62.00
1498- Radio Patrol and Big Dan's Mobsters, 1937, Whitman, 432 pgs.	10.00	30.00	62.00
nn- Raiders of the Lost Ark, 1998, Chronicle Books, 304 pgs., adapts movie, 1-color (green) illos	3.00	9.00	20.00
1441- Range Busters, The, 1942, Whitman, 432 pgs., Henry E. Vallely-a	10.00	30.00	62.00
1163- Ranger and the Cowboy, The, 1939, Saalfield, 400 pgs.	10.00	30.00	62.00
1154- Rangers on the Rio Grande, 1938, Saalfield, 400 pgs.	10.00	30.00	62.00
1447- Ray Land of the Tank Corps, U.S.A., 1942, Whitman, 432 pgs., flip pictures, Hess-a	10.00	30.00	62.00
1157- Red Barry Ace-Detective, 1935, Whitman, 432 pgs., by Will Gould	14.00	42.00	95.00
1426- Red Barry Undercover Man, 1939, Whitman, 432 pgs., by Will Gould	12.00	36.00	85.00
20- Red Davis, 1935, EVW, 160 pgs.	12.00	36.00	78.00
1449- Red Death on the Range, The, 1940, Whitman, 432 pgs., Fred Harman-a (Bronc Peeler)	12.00	36.00	78.00
nn- Red Falcon Adventures, The, 1937, Seal Right Ice Cream, 8 pgs., set of 50 books, circular in shape			
Issue #1	79.00	237.00	550.00
Issue #2-5	55.00	165.00	390.00
Issue #6-10	45.00	135.00	315.00

1424 - Rex Beach's Jaragu of the Jungle © WHIT

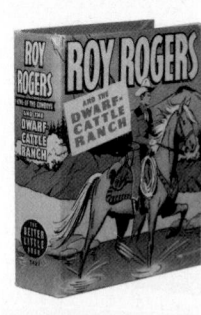

1421 - Roy Rogers and the Dwarf-Cattle Ranch © WHIT

1472 - Secret Agent X-9 and the Mad Assassin © WHIT

	GD	FN	VF/NM
Issue #11-50	29.00	87.00	200.00
nn- Red Hen and the Fox, The, nd(1930s), np(Whitman), 36 pgs.,			
3" x 2 1/2", Penny Book	3.00	9.00	20.00
1145- Red-Hot Holsters, 1938, Saalfield, 400 pgs.	10.00	30.00	62.00
1400- Red Ryder and Little Beaver on Hoofs of Thunder,			
1939, Whitman, 432 pgs., Harman-c/a	18.00	54.00	125.00
1414- Red Ryder and the Squaw-Tooth Rustlers, 1946, Whitman,			
352 pgs., Fred Harman-a	14.00	42.00	100.00
1427- Red Ryder and the Code of the West, 1941, Whitman,			
432 pgs., flip pictures, by Harman	17.00	51.00	120.00
1440- Red Ryder the Fighting Westerner, 1940, Whitman,			
Harman-a	17.00	51.00	120.00
1443- Red Ryder and the Rimrock Killer, 1948, Whitman, 288 pgs.,			
Harman-a	13.00	39.00	90.00
1450- Red Ryder and Western Border Guns, 1942, Whitman,			
432 pgs., flip pictures, by Harman	17.00	51.00	120.00
1454- Red Ryder and the Secret Canyon, 1948, Whitman, 288 pgs.,			
Harman-a	13.00	39.00	90.00
1466- Red Ryder and Circus Luck, 1947, Whitman, 288 pgs.,			
by Fred Harman	13.00	39.00	90.00
1473- Red Ryder in War on the Range, 1945, Whitman, 352 pgs.,			
by Fred Harman	14.00	42.00	100.00
1475- Red Ryder and the Outlaw of Painted Valley, 1943,			
Whitman, 352 pgs., by Harman	13.00	39.00	90.00
702-10- Red Ryder Acting Sheriff, 1949, Whitman, by Fred Hannan			
	12.00	36.00	75.00
nn- Red Ryder Brings Law to Devil's Hole, 1939, Dell, 196 pgs.,			
Fast-Action Story, Harman-c/a	40.00	120.00	280.00
nn- Red Ryder and the Highway Robbers, 1938, Whitman,			
36 pgs., 2 1/2" x 3 1/2", Penny Book	12.00	36.00	80.00
754- Reg'lar Fellers, 1933, Whitman, 320 pgs., by Gene Byrnes			
	12.00	36.00	87.00
nn- Reg'lar Fellers, 1933, Whitman, 202 pgs., Cocomalt premium,			
by Gene Byrnes	12.00	36.00	87.00
1424- Rex Beach's Jaragu of the Jungle, 1937, Whitman, 432 pgs.			
	10.00	30.00	62.00
12- Rex, King of Wild Horses in "Stampede", 1935, EVW, 160 pgs.,			
movie scenes, Columbia Pictures	10.00	30.00	67.00
1100B- Riddles for Fun, 1938, Whitman, 36 pgs., 2 1/2" x 3 1/2",			
Penny Book	4.00	12.00	24.00
1100B- Riddles to Guess, 1938, Whitman, 36 pgs., 2 1/2" x 3 1/2",			
Penny Book	4.00	12.00	24.00
1425- Riders of Lone Trails, 1937, Whitman, 300 pgs.			
	10.00	30.00	67.00
1141- Rio Raiders (A Billy The Kid Story), 1938, Saalfield, 400 pgs.			
	10.00	30.00	67.00
2023-(#23)- The Road Runner, The Super Beep Catcher, 1968, Whitman,			
256 pgs., hard-c, color illos.	1.00	3.00	8.00
5759- The Road Runner, The Super Beep Catcher, 1973, Whitman, 256 pgs.,			
soft-c, 39 cents, B&W illos., and flip pictures	1.00	2.00	5.00
5767-2- Road Runner, The Lost Road Runner Mine, The,			
1974 (1980), 260 pgs., 79 cents, B&W, soft-c	1.00	2.00	5.00
5784- The Road Runner and the Unidentified Coyote, 1974, Whitman,			
260 pgs., soft-c, flip pictures	1.00	2.00	5.00
5784-2- The Road Runner and the Unidentified Coyote, 1980, Whitman,			
260 pgs., soft-c, flip pictures	1.00	2.00	5.00
nn- Road To Perdition, 2002, Dreamworks, screenplay from movie, hard-c			
(Dreamworks and 20th Century Fox)	1.00	3.00	8.00
Robin Hood (See Wee Little Books)			
10- Robin Hood, 1935, EVW, 160 pgs., movie scenes w/Douglas Fairbanks			
(United Artists), hard-c	16.00	48.00	115.00
719- Robinson Crusoe (The Story of...), nd (1933), Whitman,			
364 pgs., soft-c	12.00	36.00	87.00
1421- Roy Rogers and the Dwarf-Cattle Ranch, 1947, Whitman,			
352 pgs., Henry E. Vallely-a	16.00	48.00	115.00
1437- Roy Rogers and the Deadly Treasure, 1947, Whitman,			
288 pgs.	16.00	48.00	115.00
1448- Roy Rogers and the Mystery of the Howling Mesa,			
1948, Whitman, 288 pgs.	16.00	48.00	115.00

	GD	FN	VF/NM
1452- Roy Rogers in Robbers' Roost, 1948, Whitman, 288 pgs.			
	16.00	48.00	115.00
1460- Roy Rogers Robinhood of the Range, 1942, Whitman,			
432 pgs., Hess-a (1st)	19.00	57.00	130.00
1462- Roy Rogers and the Mystery of the Lazy M, 1949,			
Whitman	14.00	42.00	100.00
1476- Roy Rogers King of the Cowboys, 1943, Whitman, 352 pgs.,			
Irwin Myers-a, based on movie	20.00	60.00	140.00
1494- Roy Rogers at Crossed Feathers Ranch, 1945, Whitman,			
320 pgs., Erwin Hess-a , 3 1/4" x 5 1/2"	16.00	48.00	115.00
701-10- Roy Rogers and the Snowbound Outlaws, 1949,			
3 1/4" x 5 1/2"	12.00	36.00	75.00
715-10- Roy Rogers Range Detective, 1950, Whitman, 2 1/2" x 5"			
	12.00	36.00	75.00
nn- Sandy Gregg Federal Agent on Special Assignment, 1939, Whitman,			
36 pgs., 2 1/2" x 3 1/2", Penny Book	10.00	30.00	62.00
Sappo (See Top-Line Comics)			
1122- Scrappy, 1934, Whitman, 288 pgs.	18.00	54.00	125.00
L12- Scrappy (The Adventures of...), 1935, Lynn, 192 pgs.,			
movie scenes	18.00	54.00	125.00
1191- Secret Agent K-7,1940, Saalfield, 400 pgs., based on radio show			
	10.00	30.00	62.00
1144- Secret Agent X-9, 1936, Whitman, 432 pgs., Charles Flanders-a			
	14.00	42.00	95.00
1472- Secret Agent X-9 and the Mad Assassin, 1938, Whitman,			
432 pgs., Charles Flanders-a	14.00	42.00	95.00
1161- Sequoia, 1935, Whitman, 160 pgs., photo-c, movie scenes			
	12.00	36.00	78.00
1430- Shadow and the Living Death, The, 1940, Whitman,			
432 pgs., Erwin Hess-a	60.00	180.00	420.00
1443- Shadow and the Master of Evil, The, 1941, Whitman,			
432 pgs., flip pictures, Hess-a	60.00	180.00	420.00
1495- Shadow and the Ghost Makers, The, 1942, Whitman,			
432 pgs., John Coleman Burroughs-c	60.00	180.00	420.00
2024- Shazzan, The Glass Princess, 1968, Whitman			
	4.00	12.00	25.00
Shirley Temple (See My Life and Times & Story of..)			
1095- Shirley Temple and Lionel Barrymore Starring In "The Little Colonel,"			
1935, Saalfield, photo hard-c, movie scenes 18.00		54.00	125.00
1115- Shirley Temple in "The Littlest Rebel," 1935, Saalfield, photo-c,			
movie scenes, hard-c	18.00	54.00	125.00
1575- Shirley Temple and Lionel Barrymore Starring In "The Little Colonel,"			
1935, Saalfield, photo soft-c, movie scenes 18.00		54.00	125.00
1595- Shirley Temple in "The Littlest Rebel," 1935, Saalfield, photo-c,			
movie scenes, soft-c	18.00	54.00	125.00
1195- Shooting Sheriffs of the Wild West, 1936, Whitman, 432 pgs.			
	10.00	30.00	62.00
1169- Silly Symphony Featuring Donald Duck (Disney),			
1937, Whitman, 432 pgs., Taliaferro-a	34.00	102.00	240.00
1441- Silly Symphony Featuring Donald Duck and His (MIS) Adventures			
(Disney), 1937, Whitman, 432 pgs., Taliaferro-a			
	34.00	102.00	240.00
1155- Silver Streak, The, 1935, Whitman, 160 pgs., photo-c, movie scenes			
(RKO Radio Pict.)	10.00	30.00	67.00
Simple Simon (See Wee Little Books)			
1649- Sir Lancelot (TV Series), 1958, Whitman, 280 pgs.			
	7.00	20.00	40.00
1112- Skeezix in Africa, 1934, Whitman, 300 pgs., Frank King-a			
	12.00	36.00	87.00
1408- Skeezix at the Military Academy, 1938, Whitman, 432 pgs.,			
Frank King-a	12.00	36.00	87.00
1414- Skeezix Goes to War, 1944, Whitman, 352 pgs., Frank King-a			
	12.00	36.00	87.00
1419- Skeezix on His Own in the Big City, 1941, Whitman, All Pictures			
Comics, flip pictures, Frank King-a	12.00	36.00	87.00
761- Skippy, 1934, Whitman, 320 pgs., by Percy Crosby			
	12.00	36.00	87.00
4056- Skippy, The Story of, 1934, Whitman, 320 pgs., 7" x 9 1/2",			
Big Big Book, Percy Crosby-a	63.00	189.00	445.00

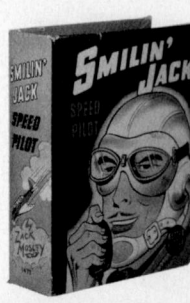

1473 - Smilin' Jack Speed Pilot © WHIT

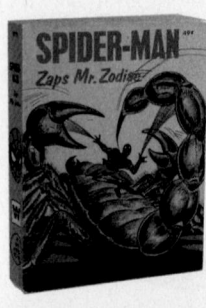

5779 - Spider-Man Zaps Mr. Zodiac © MAR

.1110 - The Story of Freddie Bartholomew © Saalfield

nn- **Skippy, The Story of**, 1934, Whitman, Phillips Dental Magnesia premium, soft-c, by Percy Crosby   12.00   36.00   87.00

1439- **Skyroads with Clipper Williams of the Flying Legion**, 1938, Whitman, 432 pgs., by Lt. Dick Calkins, Russell Keaton-a   12.00   36.00   78.00

1127- **Skyroads with Hurricane Hawk**, 1936, Whitman, 432 pgs., by Lt. Dick Calkins, Russell Keaton-a   11.00   33.00   72.00

Smilin' Jack and his Flivver Plane (See Top-Line Comics)

1152- **Smilin' Jack and the Stratosphere Ascent**, 1937, Whitman, 432 pgs., Zack Mosley-a   15.00   45.00   105.00

1412- **Smilin' Jack Flying High with "Downwind,"** 1942, Whitman, 432 pgs., Zack Mosley-a   14.00   42.00   95.00

1416- **Smilin' Jack in Wings over the Pacific**, 1939, Whitman, 432 pgs., Zack Mosley-a   14.00   42.00   95.00

1419- **Smilin' Jack and the Jungle Pipe Line**, 1947, Whitman, 352 pgs., Zack Mosley-a   12.00   36.00   78.00

1445- **Smilin' Jack and the Escape from Death Rock**, 1943, Whitman, 352 pgs., Mosley-a   12.00   36.00   78.00

1464- **Smilin' Jack and the Coral Princess**, 1945, Whitman, 352 pgs., Zack Mosley-a   12.00   36.00   78.00

1473- **Smilin' Jack Speed Pilot**, 1941, Whitman, 432 pgs., Zack Mosley-a   14.00   42.00   95.00

2- **Smilin' Jack and his Stratosphere Plane**, 1938, Whitman, 132 pgs., Buddy Book, soft-c, Zack Mosley-a   36.00   108.00   250.00

nn- **Smilin' Jack Grounded on a Tropical Shore**, 1938, Whitman, 36 pgs., 2 1/2" x 3 1/2", Penny Book   10.00   30.00   62.00

11- **Smilin' Jack and the Border Bandits**, 1941, Dell, 196 pgs., Fast-Action Story, soft-c, Zack Mosley-a   33.00   99.00   230.00

745- **Smitty Golden Gloves Tournament**, 1934, Whitman, 320 pgs., Walter Berndt-a   14.00   42.00   95.00

nn- **Smitty Golden Gloves Tournament**, 1934, Whitman, 204 pgs., Cocomalt premium, soft-c, Walter Berndt-a   15.00   45.00   105.00

1404- **Smitty and Herby Lost Among the Indians**, 1941, Whitman, All Pictures Comics   10.00   30.00   67.00

1477- **Smitty in Going Native**, 1938, Whitman, 300 pgs., Walter Berndt-a   10.00   30.00   67.00

2- **Smitty and Herby**, 1936, Whitman, 132 pgs., 3 1/2" x 3 1/2", soft-c, Tarzan Ice Cream cup lid premium   33.00   99.00   230.00

9- **Smitty's Brother Herby and the Police Horse**, 1938, Whitman, 132 pgs., 3 1/4" x 3 1/2", Buddy Book-ice cream premium, by Walter Berndt   33.00   99.00   230.00

1010- **Smokey Stover Firefighter of Foo**, 1937, Whitman, 7 1/4" x 5 1/2", 64 pgs., Nickel Book, Bill Holman-a   15.00   45.00   105.00

1413- **Smokey Stover**, 1942, Whitman, All Pictures Comics, flip pictures, Bill Holman-a   13.00   39.00   90.00

1421- **Smokey Stover the Foo Fighter**, 1938, Whitman, 432 pgs., Bill Holman-a   13.00   39.00   90.00

1481- **Smokey Stover the Foolish Foo Fighter**, 1942, Whitman, All Pictures Comics   13.00   39.00   90.00

1- **Smokey Stover the Fireman of Foo**, 1938, Whitman, 3 3/4" x 3 1/2", 132 pgs., Buddy Book-ice cream premium, by Bill Holman   37.00   111.00   260.00

1100A- **Smokey Stover**, 1938, Whitman, 36 pgs., 2 1/2" x 3 1/2", Penny Book   11.00   33.00   70.00

nn- **Smokey Stover and the Fire Chief of Foo**, 1938, Whitman, 36 pgs., 2 1/2" x 3 1/2", Penny Book, yellow shirt on-c   11.00   33.00   70.00

nn- **Smokey Stover and the Fire Chief of Foo**, 1938, Whitman, 36 pgs., Penny Book, green shirt on-c   11.00   33.00   70.00

1460- **Snow White and the Seven Dwarfs** (The Story of Walt Disney's ...), 1938, Whitman, 288 pgs.   26.00   78.00   180.00

1136- **Sombrero Pete**, 1936, Whitman, 432 pgs.   10.00   30.00   62.00

1152- **Son of Mystery**, 1939, Saalfield, 400 pgs.   10.00   30.00   62.00

1191- **SOS Coast Guard**, 1936, Whitman, 432 pgs., Henry E. Vallely-a   10.00   30.00   67.00

2016-(#16)- **Space Ghost-The Sorceress of Cyba-3** (TV Cartoon), 1968, Whitman, 260 pgs., 39¢-c, hard-c, color illos   9.00   27.00   55.00

1455- **Speed Douglas and the Mole Gang-The Great Sabotage Plot**, 1941, Whitman, 432 pgs., flip pictures   10.00   30.00   62.00

5779- **Spider-Man Zaps Mr. Zodiac**, 1976, 260 pgs.,

soft-c, B&W   1.00   3.00   8.00

5779-2- **Spider-Man Zaps Mr. Zodiac**, 1980, 260 pgs., 79¢-c, soft-c, B&W   1.00   2.00   5.00

1467- **Spike Kelly of the Commandos**, 1943, Whitman, 352 pgs.   10.00   30.00   62.00

1144- **Spook Riders on the Overland**, 1938, Saalfield, 400 pgs.   10.00   30.00   62.00

768- **Spy, The**, 1936, Whitman, 300 pgs.   12.00   35.00   85.00

nn- **Spy Smasher and the Red Death**, 1941, Fawcett, 4" x 5 1/2", Dime Action Book   54.00   162.00   375.00

1120- **Stan Kent Freshman Fullback**, 1936, Saalfield, 148 pgs., hard-c   8.00   25.00   50.00

1132- **Stan Kent, Captain**, 1937, Saalfield   8.00   25.00   50.00

1600- **Stan Kent Freshman Fullback**, 1936, Saalfield, 148 pgs., soft-c   8.00   25.00   50.00

1123- **Stan Kent Varsity Man**, 1936, Saalfield, 160 pgs., hard-c   8.00   25.00   50.00

1603- **Stan Kent Varsity Man**, 1936, Saalfield, 160 pgs., soft-c   8.00   25.00   50.00

nn- **Star Wars - A New Hope**, 1997, Chronicle Books, 320 pgs., adapts movie, 1-color (blue) illos   3.00   9.00   18.00

nn- **Star Wars - Empire Strikes Back, The**, 1997, Chronicle Books, 296 pgs., adapts movie, 1-color (blue) illos   3.00   9.00   18.00

nn- **Star Wars - Episode 1 - The Phantom Menace**, 1999, Chronicle Books, 344 pgs., adapts movie, 1-color (blue) illos   1.00   3.00   8.00

nn- **Star Wars - Episode 2 - Attack of the Clones**, 2002, Chronicle Books, 340 pgs., adapts movie, 1-color (blue) illos   1.00   3.00   8.00

nn- **Star Wars - Return of the Jedi**, 1997, Chronicle Books, 312 pgs., adapts movie, 1-color (blue) illos   3.00   9.00   18.00

1104- **Steel Arena, The** (With Clyde Beatty), 1936, Saalfield, hard-c, movie scenes adapted from "The Lost Jungle" 12.00   36.00   78.00

1584- **Steel Arena, The** (With Clyde Beatty), 1936, Saalfield, soft-c, movie scenes   12.00   36.00   78.00

1426- **Steve Hunter of the U.S. Coast Guard Under Secret Orders**, 1942, Whitman, 432 pgs.   10.00   30.00   62.00

1456- **Story of Charlie McCarthy and Edgar Bergen, The**, 1938, Whitman, 288 pgs.   14.00   42.00   95.00

Story of Daniel, The (See Wee Little Books)

Story of David, The (See Wee Little Books)

1110- **Story of Freddie Bartholomew, The**, 1935, Saalfield, 4 1/2" x 5 1/4", hard-c, movie scenes (MGM)   10.00   30.00   67.00

1590- **Story of Freddie Bartholomew, The**, 1935, Saalfield, 4 1/2" x 5 1/4", soft-c, movie scenes (MGM)   10.00   30.00   67.00

Story of Gideon, The (See Wee Little Books)

W714- **Story of Jackie Cooper, The**, 1933, Whitman, 240 pgs., photo-c, movie scenes, "Skippy" & "Sooky" movie   14.00   42.00   95.00

Story of Joseph, The (See Wee Little Books)

Story of Moses, The (See Wee Little Books)

Story of Ruth and Naomi (See Wee Little Books)

1089- **Story of Shirley Temple, The**, 1934, Saalfield, 160 pgs., hard-c, photo-c, movie scenes   12.00   36.00   85.00

1319- **Story of Shirley Temple, The**, 1934, Saalfield, 160 pgs., soft-c, photo-c, movie scenes   12.00   36.00   85.00

1090- **Strawberry-Roan**, 1934, Saalfield, 160 pgs., hard-c, Ken Maynard photo-c, movie scenes   12.00   36.00   85.00

1320- **Strawberry-Roan**, 1934, Saalfield, 160 pgs., soft-c, Ken Maynard photo-c, movie scenes   12.00   36.00   85.00

Streaky and the Football Signals (See Top-Line Comics)

5780-2- **Superman in the Phantom Zone Connection**, 1980, 260 pgs., 79¢-c, soft-c, B&W   1.00   3.00   8.00

582- **"Swap It" Book, The**, 1949, Samuel Lowe Co., 260 pgs., 3 1/2" x 4 1/2"
1. Little Tex in the Midst of Trouble   7.00   20.00   40.00
2. Little Tex's Escape   7.00   20.00   40.00
3. Little Tex Comes to the XY Ranch   7.00   20.00   40.00
4. Get Them Cowboy   7.00   20.00   40.00
5. The Mail Must Go Through! A Story of the Pony Express
                                         7.00   20.00   40.00
6. Nevada Jones, Trouble Shooter   7.00   20.00   40.00
7. Danny Meets the Cowboys   7.00   20.00   40.00

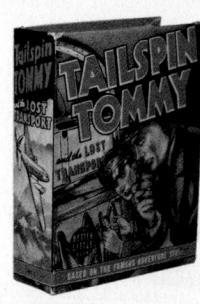

1413 - Tailspin Tommy and the Lost Transport © WHIT

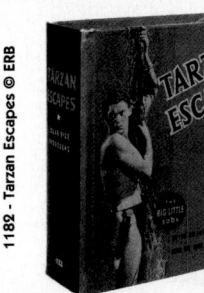

1182 - Tarzan Escapes © ERB

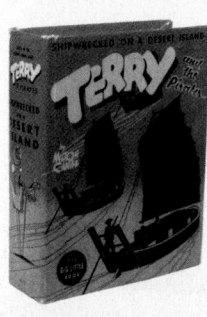

1412 - Terry and the Pirates Shipwrecked on a Desert Island © WHIT

	GD	FN	VF/NM
8. Flint Adams and the Stage Coach	7.00	20.00	40.00
9. Bud Shinners and the Oregon Trail	7.00	20.00	40.00
10. The Outlaws' Last Ride	7.00	20.00	40.00
Sybil Jason (See Little Big Shot)			
747- **Tailspin Tommy in the Famous Pay-Roll Mystery**, 1933, Whitman, hard-c, 320 pgs., Hal Forrest-a (# 1)	14.00	42.00	95.00
747- **Tailspin Tommy in the Famous Pay-Roll Mystery**, 1933, Whitman, soft-c, 320 pgs., Hal Forrest-a (# 1)	14.00	42.00	95.00
nn- **Tailspin Tommy the Pay-Roll Mystery**, 1934, Whitman, 52 pgs., 3 1/2" x 5 1/4", premium-no ads, soft-c; another version with Perkins ad, Hal Forrest-a	24.00	72.00	170.00
1110- **Tailspin Tommy and the Island in the Sky**, 1936, Whitman, 432 pgs., Hal Forrest-a	12.00	36.00	85.00
1124- **Tailspin Tommy the Dirigible Flight to the North Pole**, 1934, Whitman, 432 pgs., H. Forrest-a	14.00	42.00	95.00
nn- **Tailspin Tommy the Dirigible Flight to the North Pole**, 1934, Whitman, 436 pgs., 3-color, soft-c, premium-no ads, Hal Forrest-a	33.00	99.00	230.00
1172- **Tailspin Tommy Hunting for Pirate Gold**, 1935, Whitman, 432 pgs., Hal Forrest-a	12.00	36.00	85.00
1183- **Tailspin Tommy Air Racer**, 1940, Saalfield, 400 pgs., hard-c	12.00	36.00	85.00
1184- **Tailspin Tommy in the Great Air Mystery**, 1936, Whitman, 240 pgs., photo-c, movie scenes	14.00	42.00	95.00
1410- **Tailspin Tommy the Weasel and His "Skywaymen,"** 1941, Whitman, All Pictures Comics, flip pictures	11.00	33.00	72.00
1413- **Tailspin Tommy and the Lost Transport**, 1940, Whitman, 432 pgs., Hal Forrest-a	11.00	33.00	72.00
1423- **Tailspin Tommy and the Hooded Flyer**, 1937, Whitman, 432 pgs., Hal Forrest-a	12.00	36.00	85.00
1494- **Tailspin Tommy and the Sky Bandits**, 1938, Whitman 432 pgs., Hal Forrest-a	12.00	36.00	85.00
nn- **Tailspin Tommy and the Airliner Mystery**, 1938, Dell, 196 pgs., Fast-Action Story, soft-c, Hal Forrest-a	43.00	129.00	300.00
nn- **Tailspin Tommy in Flying Aces**, 1938, Dell, 196 pgs., Fast-Action Story, soft-c, Hal Forrest-a	43.00	129.00	300.00
nn- **Tailspin Tommy in Wings Over the Arctic**, 1934, Whitman, Cocomalt premium, Forrest-a	18.00	54.00	125.00
nn- **Tailspin Tommy Big Thrill Chewing Gum**, 1934, Whitman, 8 pgs., 2 1/2" x 3 " (6 diff.) each..	12.00	36.00	85.00
3- **Tailspin Tommy on the Mountain of Human Sacrifice**, 1938, Whitman, soft-c, Buddy Book	39.00	117.00	275.00
7- **Tailspin Tommy's Perilous Adventure**, 1934, Whitman, 132 pgs., 3 1/2" x 3 1/2" soft-c, Tarzan Ice Cream cup premium	39.00	117.00	275.00
nn- **Tailspin Tommy**, 1935, Whitman, 148 pgs., 3 1/2" x 4", Tarzan Ice Cream cup premium	50.00	150.00	355.00
L16- **Tale of Two Cities, A**, 1935, Lynn, movie scenes	14.00	42.00	95.00
744- **Tarzan of the Apes**, 1933, Whitman, 320 pgs., by Edgar Rice Burroughs (1st)	42.00	126.00	295.00
nn- **Tarzan of the Apes**, 1935, Whitman, 52 pgs., 3 1/2" x 5 1/4", soft-c, stapled, premium, no ad; another version with a Perkins ad	54.00	162.00	375.00
769- **Tarzan the Fearless**, 1934, Whitman, 240 pgs., Buster Crabbe photo-c, movie scenes, ERB	30.00	90.00	210.00
770- **Tarzan Twins, The**, 1934, Whitman, 432 pgs., ERB	107.00	321.00	750.00
770- **Tarzan Twins, The**, 1935, Whitman, 432 pgs., ERB	54.00	162.00	380.00
nn- **Tarzan Twins, The**, 1935, Whitman, 52 pgs., 3 1/2" x 5 3/4", premium-no ads, soft-c, ERB	71.00	213.00	500.00
nn- **Tarzan Twins, The**, 1935, Whitman, 436 pgs., 3-color, soft-c, premium-no ads, ERB	75.00	225.00	525.00
778- **Tarzan of the Screen** (The Story of Johnny Weissmuller), 1934, Whitman, 240 pgs., photo-c, movie scenes, ERB	31.00	93.00	220.00
1102- **Tarzan, The Return of**, 1936, Whitman, 432 pgs., Edgar Rice Burroughs	22.00	66.00	155.00

	GD	FN	VF/NM
1180- **Tarzan, The New Adventures of**, 1935, Whitman, 160 pgs., Herman Brix photo-c, movie scenes, ERB	25.00	75.00	175.00
1182- **Tarzan Escapes**, 1936, Whitman, 240 pgs., Johnny Weissmuller photo-c, movie scenes, ERB	31.00	93.00	220.00
1407- **Tarzan Lord of the Jungle**, 1946, Whitman, 352 pgs., ERB	16.00	48.00	115.00
1410- **Tarzan, The Beasts of**, 1937, Whitman, 432 pgs., Edgar Rice Burroughs	19.00	57.00	135.00
1442- **Tarzan and the Lost Empire**, 1948, Whitman, 288 pgs., ERB	16.00	48.00	115.00
1444- **Tarzan and the Ant Men**, 1945, Whitman, 352 pgs., ERB	16.00	48.00	115.00
1448- **Tarzan and the Golden Lion**, 1943, Whitman, 432 pgs., ERB	20.00	60.00	140.00
1452- **Tarzan the Untamed**, 1941, Whitman, 432 pgs., flip pictures, ERB	20.00	60.00	140.00
1453- **Tarzan the Terrible**, 1942, Whitman, 432 pgs., flip pictures, ERB	20.00	60.00	140.00
1467- **Tarzan in the Land of the Giant Apes**, 1949, Whitman, ERB	16.00	48.00	115.00
1477- **Tarzan, The Son of**, 1939, Whitman, 432 pgs., ERB	20.00	60.00	140.00
1488- **Tarzan's Revenge**, 1938, Whitman, 432 pgs., ERB	20.00	60.00	140.00
1495- **Tarzan and the Jewels of Opar**, 1940, Whitman, 432 pgs.	20.00	60.00	140.00
4056- **Tarzan and the Tarzan Twins with Jad-Bal-Ja the Golden Lion**, 1936, Whitman, 7" x 9 1/2", 320 pgs., Big Big Book	105.00	315.00	735.00
709-10- **Tarzan and the Journey of Terror**, 1950, Whitman, 2 1/2" x 5", ERB, Marsh-a	10.00	30.00	67.00
2005- **(#5)-Tarzan: The Mark of the Red Hyena**, 1967, Whitman, 260 pgs., 39 cents, hard-c, color illos	4.00	12.00	25.00
nn- **Tarzan**, 1935, Whitman, 148 pgs., soft-c, 3 1/2" x 4", Tarzan Ice Cream cup premium, ERB (scarce)	124.00	372.00	980.00
nn- **Tarzan and a Daring Rescue**, 1938, Whitman, 68 pgs., Pan-Am premium, soft-c, ERB (blank back-c version also exists)	43.00	129.00	300.00
nn- **Tarzan and his Jungle Friends**, 1936, Whitman, 132 pgs., soft-c, 3 1/2" x 3 1/2", Tarzan Ice Cream cup premium, ERB (scarce)	102.00	306.00	715.00
nn- **Tarzan in the Golden City**, 1938, Whitman, 68 pgs., Pan-Am premium, soft-c, ERB	30.00	90.00	210.00
nn- **Tarzan The Avenger**, 1939, Dell, 194 pgs., Fast-Action Story, ERB, soft-c	43.00	129.00	300.00
nn- **Tarzan with the Tarzan Twins in the Jungle**, 1938, Dell, 194 pgs., Fast-Action Story, ERB	43.00	129.00	300.00
1100B- **Tell Your Fortune**, 1938, Whitman, 36 pgs., 2 1/2" x 3 1/2", Penny Book	5.00	15.00	30.00
nn- **Terminator 2: Judgment Day**, 1998, Chronicle Books, 310 pgs., adapts movie, 1-color (blue-gray) illos	1.00	3.00	8.00
1156- **Terry and the Pirates**, 1935, Whitman, 432 pgs., Milton Caniff-a (#1)	16.00	48.00	115.00
nn- **Terry and the Pirates**, 1935, Whitman, 52 pgs., 3 1/2" x 5 1/4", soft-c, premium, Milton Caniff-a; 3 versions: No ad, Sears ad & Perkins ad	29.00	87.00	200.00
1412- **Terry and the Pirates Shipwrecked on a Desert Island**, 1938, Whitman, 432 pgs., Milton Caniff-a	14.00	42.00	95.00
1420- **Terry and War in the Jungle**, 1946, Whitman, 352 pgs., Milton Caniff-a	12.00	36.00	85.00
1436- **Terry and the Pirates the Plantation Mystery**, 1942, Whitman, 432 pgs., flip pictures, Milton Caniff-a	14.00	42.00	95.00
1446- **Terry and the Pirates and the Giant's Vengeance**, 1939, Whitman, 432 pgs., Caniff-a	14.00	42.00	95.00
1499- **Terry and the Pirates in the Mountain Stronghold**, 1941, Whitman, 432 pgs., Caniff-a	14.00	42.00	95.00
4073- **Terry and the Pirates, The Adventures of**, 1938, Whitman, 7" x 9 1/2", 320 pgs., Big Big Book, Milton Caniff-a	79.00	237.00	550.00
4- **Terry and the Pirates Ashore in Singapore**, 1938, Whitman, 132 pgs.,			

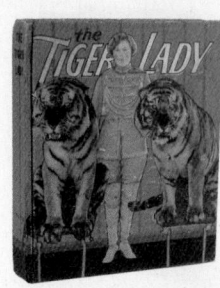

1588 - The Tiger Lady © Saalfield

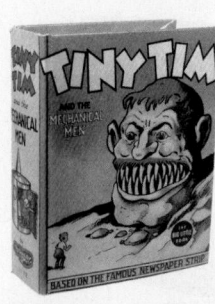

1172 - Tiny Tim and the Mechanical Men © WHIT

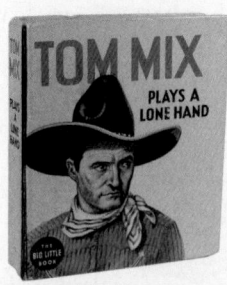

1173 - Tom Mix Plays a Lone Hand © WHIT

	GD	FN	VF/NM

3 1/2" x 3 3/4", soft-c, Buddy Book premium 34.00 102.00 235.00
10- **Terry and the Pirates Meet Again**, 1936, Whitman, 132 pgs.,
3 1/2" x 3 1/2", soft-c, Tarzan Ice Cream cup lid premium
54.00 162.00 380.00
nn- **Terry and the Pirates, Adventures of**, 1938, 36 pgs.,
2 1/2" x 3 1/2", Penny Book, Caniff-a 10.00 30.00 62.00
nn- **Terry and the Pirates and the Island Rescue**, 1938, Whitman,
68 pgs., 3 1/4" x 3 1/2", Pan-Am premium 26.00 78.00 180.00
nn- **Terry and the Pirates on Their Travels**, 1938, 36 pgs.,
2 1/2" x 3 1/2", Penny Book, Caniff-a 10.00 30.00 62.00
nn- **Terry and the Pirates and the Mystery Ship**, 1938, Dell,
194 pgs., Fast-Action Story, soft-c 36.00 108.00 250.00
1492- **Terry Lee Flight Officer U.S.A.**, 1944, Whitman, 352 pgs.,
Milton Caniff-a 12.00 36.00 78.00
7- **Texas Bad Man, The** (Tom Mix), 1934, EVW, 160 pgs.,
(Five Star Library) movie scenes 21.00 63.00 145.00
1429- **Texas Kid, The**, 1937, Whitman, 432 pgs. 10.00 30.00 62.00
1135- **Texas Ranger, The**, 1936, Whitman, 432 pgs., Hal Arbo-a
10.00 30.00 62.00
nn- **Texas Ranger, The**, 1935, Whitman, 260 pgs., Cocomalt premium,
soft-c 12.00 36.00 78.00
nn- **Texas Ranger and the Rustler Gang, The**, 1936, Whitman,
Pan-Am giveaway 26.00 78.00 180.00
nn- **Texas Ranger in the West, The**, 1938, Whitman, 36 pgs.,
2 1/2" x 3 1/2", Penny Book 9.00 27.00 57.00
nn- **Texas Ranger to the Rescue, The**, 1938, Whitman, 36 pgs.,
2 1/2" x 3 1/2", Penny Book 9.00 27.00 57.00
12- **Texas Ranger in Rustler Strategy, The**, 1936, Whitman, 132 pgs.,
3 1/2" x 3 1/2", soft-c, Tarzan Ice Cream cup lid premium
33.00 99.00 230.00

Tex Thorne (See Zane Grey)
Thimble Theatre (See Popeye)

26- **13 Hours By Air**, 1936, Lynn, 128 pgs., 5" x 7 1/2", photo-c,
movie scenes (Paramount Pictures) 12.00 36.00 87.00
nn- **Three Bears, The**, nd (1930s), np (Whitman), 36 pgs.,
3" x 2 1/2", Penny Book 3.00 9.00 20.00
1129- **Three Finger Joe** (Baseball), 1937, Saalfield, Robert A. Graef-a
9.00 27.00 57.00
nn- **Three Little Pigs, The**, nd (1930s), np (Whitman), 36 pgs.,
3" x 2 1/2", Penny Book 3.00 9.00 20.00
1131- **Three Musketeers**, 1935, Whitman, 182 pgs., 5 1/4" x 6 1/4",
photo-c, movie scenes 16.00 48.00 115.00
1409- **Thumper and the Seven Dwarfs** (Disney), 1944, Whitman,
All Pictures Comics 21.00 63.00 145.00
1108- **Tiger Lady, The** (The life of Mabel Stark, animal trainer), 1935,
Saalfield, photo-c, movie scenes, hard-c 10.00 30.00 67.00
1588- **Tiger Lady, The**, 1935, Saalfield, photo-c, movie scenes,
soft-c 10.00 30.00 67.00
1442- **Tillie the Toiler and the Wild Man of Desert Island**, 1941,
Whitman, 432 pgs., Russ Westover-a 12.00 36.00 78.00
1058- **"Timid Elmer"** (Disney), 1939, Whitman, 5" x 5 1/2", 68 pgs.,
hard-c 12.00 36.00 78.00
1152- **Tim McCoy in the Prescott Kid**, 1935, Whitman, 160 pgs.,
hard-c, photo-c, movie scenes 18.00 54.00 125.00
1193- **Tim McCoy in the Westerner**, 1936, Whitman, 240 pgs.,
photo-c, movie scenes 16.00 48.00 115.00
1436- **Tim McCoy on the Tomahawk Trail**, 1937, Whitman,
432 pgs., Robert Weisman-a 12.00 36.00 78.00
1490- **Tim McCoy and the Sandy Gulch Stampede**, 1939,
Whitman, 424 pgs. 10.00 30.00 67.00
2- **Tim McCoy in Beyond the Law**, 1934, EVW, Five Star Library,
photo-c, movie scenes (Columbia Pictures) 19.00 57.00 135.00
10- **Tim McCoy in Fighting the Redskins**, 1938, Whitman, 130 pgs.,
Buddy Book, soft-c 31.00 93.00 220.00
14- **Tim McCoy in Speedwings**, 1935, EVW, Five Star Library, 160 pgs.,
photo-c, movie scenes (Columbia Pictures) 21.00 63.00 145.00
nn- **Tim the Builder**, nd (1930s), np (Whitman), 36 pgs., 3" x 2 1/2",
Penny Book 3.00 9.00 20.00
Tim Tyler (Also see Adventures of ...)

1140- **Tim Tyler's Luck Adventures in the Ivory Patrol**, 1937,
Whitman, 432 pgs., by Lyman Young 12.00 36.00 85.00
1479- **Tim Tyler's Luck and the Plot of the Exiled King**, 1939,
Whitman, 432 pgs., by Lyman Young 11.00 33.00 72.00
767- **Tiny Tim, The Adventures of**, 1935, Whitman, 384 pgs., by
Stanley Link 14.00 42.00 95.00
1172- **Tiny Tim and the Mechanical Men**, 1937, Whitman, 432 pgs.,
by Stanley Link 12.00 36.00 85.00
1472- **Tiny Tim in the Big, Big World**, 1945, Whitman, 352 pgs., by
Stanley Link 12.00 36.00 78.00
2006- (#6)-**Tom and Jerry Meet Mr. Fingers**, 1967, Whitman, 39¢-c
260 pgs., hard-c, color illos. 4.00 12.00 22.00
5752- **Tom and Jerry Meet Mr. Fingers**, 1973, Whitman, 39¢-c
260 pgs., soft-c, color illos., 5 printings 2.00 5.00 10.00
2030-(#30)- **Tom and Jerry, The Astro-Nots**, 1969, Whitman, 256 pgs.,
hard-c, color illos. 3.00 9.00 18.00
5765- **Tom and Jerry, The Astro-Nots**, 1974, Whitman, 256 pgs.,
soft-c, color illos. 2.00 5.00 10.00
5787-2- **Tom and Jerry Under the Big Top**, 1980, Whitman, 79¢-c,
260 pgs., soft-c, B&W 2.00 5.00 10.00
723- **Tom Beatty Ace of the Service**, 1934, Whitman, 256 pgs.,
George Taylor-a 12.00 36.00 85.00
nn- **Tom Beatty Ace of the Service**, 1934, Whitman, 260 pgs.,
soft-c 12.00 36.00 85.00
1165- **Tom Beatty Ace of the Service Scores Again**, 1937, Whitman,
432 pgs., Weisman-a 11.00 33.00 72.00
1420- **Tom Beatty Ace of the Service and the Big Brain Gang**,
1939, Whitman, 432 pgs. 11.00 33.00 72.00
nn- **Tom Beatty Ace Detective and the Gorgon Gang**, 1938?, Whitman,
36 pgs., 2 1/2" x 3 1/2", Penny Book 10.00 30.00 62.00
nn- **Tom Beatty Ace of the Service and the Kidnapers**, 1938?, Whitman,
36 pgs., 2 1/2" x 3 1/2", Penny Book 10.00 30.00 62.00
1102- **Tom Mason on Top**, 1935, Saalfield, 160 pgs., Tom Mix photo-c,
from Mascot serial "The Miracle Rider," movie scenes,
hard-c 18.00 54.00 125.00
1582- **Tom Mason on Top**, 1935, Saalfield, 160 pgs., Tom Mix photo-c,
movie scenes, soft-c 18.00 54.00 125.00
Tom Mix (See Chief of the Rangers, Flaming Guns & Texas Bad Man)
762- **Tom Mix and Tony Jr. in "Terror Trail,"** 1934, Whitman,
160 pgs., movie scenes 18.00 54.00 125.00
1144- **Tom Mix in the Fighting Cowboy**, 1935, Whitman, 432 pgs.,
Hal Arbo-a 14.00 42.00 95.00
nn- **Tom Mix in the Fighting Cowboy**, 1935, Whitman, 436 pgs.,
premium-no ads, 3 color, soft-c, Hal Arbo-a 26.00 78.00 185.00
1166- **Tom Mix in the Range War**, 1937, Whitman, 432 pgs., Hal Arbo-a
12.00 36.00 78.00
1173- **Tom Mix Plays a Lone Hand**, 1935, Whitman, 288 pgs., hard-c,
Hal Arbo-a 12.00 36.00 78.00
1183- **Tom Mix and the Stranger from the South**, 1936,
Whitman, 432 pgs. 12.00 36.00 78.00
1462- **Tom Mix and the Hoard of Montezuma**, 1937, Whitman,
H. E. Vallely-a 12.00 36.00 78.00
1482- **Tom Mix and His Circus on the Barbary Coast**,
1940, Whitman, 432 pgs., James Gary-a 12.00 36.00 78.00
3047- **Tom Mix and His Big Little Kit**, 1937, Whitman,
384 pgs., 4 1/2" x 6 1/2" box, includes miniature box of 4 crayons-
red, yellow, blue and green 89.00 267.00 630.00
4068- **Tom Mix and the Scourge of Paradise Valley**, 1937, Whitman,
7" x 9 1/2", 320 pgs., Big Big Book, Vallely-a 63.00 189.00 445.00
6833- **Tom Mix in the Riding Avenger**, 1936, Dell, 244 pgs.,
Cartoon Story Book, hard-c 29.00 87.00 200.00
nn- **Tom Mix Rides to the Rescue**, 1939, 36 pgs., 2 1/2" x 3",
Penny Book 10.00 30.00 62.00
nn- **Tom Mix Avenges the Dry Gulched Range King**, 1939, Dell,
196 pgs., Fast-Action Story, soft-c 30.00 90.00 210.00
nn- **Tom Mix in the Riding Avenger**, 1936, Dell, 244 pgs.,
Fast-Action Story 30.00 90.00 210.00
nn- **Tom Mix the Trail of the Terrible 6**, 1935, Ralston Purina Co.,
84 pgs., 3" x 3 1/2", premium 20.00 60.00 140.00

1141 - Treasure Island © WHIT

1411 - Union Pacific © WHIT

1066 - Walt Disney's Story of Clarabelle Cow © DIS

	GD	FN	VF/NM
4- **Tom Mix and Tony in the Rider of Death Valley,**			
1934, EVW, Five Star Library, 160 pgs., movie scenes			
(Universal Pictures), hard-c	21.00	63.00	145.00
7- **Tom Mix in the Texas Bad Man,** 1934, EVW, Five Star Library,			
160 pgs., movie scenes	21.00	63.00	145.00
10- **Tom Mix in the Tepee Ranch Mystery,** 1938, Whitman,			
132 pgs., Buddy Book, soft-c	31.00	93.00	220.00
1126- **Tommy of Troop Six** (Scout Book), 1937, Saalfield, hard-c			
	9.00	27.00	57.00
1606- **Tommy of Troop Six** (Scout Book), 1937, Saalfield, soft-c			
	9.00	27.00	57.00
Tom Sawyer (See Adventures of ...)			
1437- **Tom Swift and His Magnetic Silencer,** 1941, Whitman,			
432 pgs., flip pictures	18.00	54.00	125.00
1485- **Tom Swift and His Giant Telescope,** 1939, Whitman,			
432 pgs., James Gary-a	18.00	54.00	125.00
540- **Top-Line Comics** (In Open Box), 1935, Whitman, 164 pgs.,			
3 1/2" x 3 1/2", 3 books in set, all soft-c:			
Bobby Thatcher and the Samarang Emerald	16.00	48.00	110.00
Broncho Bill in Suicide Canyon	16.00	48.00	110.00
Freckles and His Friends in the North Woods	16.00	48.00	110.00
Complete set with box	57.00	171.00	400.00
541- **Top-Line Comics** (In Open Box), 1935, Whitman, 164 pgs.,			
3 1/2" x 3 1/2", 3 books in set; all soft-c:			
Little Joe and the City Gangsters	16.00	48.00	110.00
Smilin' Jack and His Flivver Plane	16.00	48.00	110.00
Streaky and the Football Signals	16.00	48.00	110.00
Complete set with box	57.00	171.00	400.00
542- **Top-Line Comics** (In Open Box), 1935, Whitman, 164 pgs.,			
3 1/2" x 3 1/2", 3 books in set; all soft-c:			
Dinglehoofer Und His Dog Adolph by Knerr	16.00	48.00	110.00
Jungle Jim by Alex Raymond	20.00	60.00	140.00
Sappo by Segar	20.00	06.00	140.00
Complete set with box	71.00	213.00	500.00
543- **Top-Line Comics** (In Open Box), 1935, Whitman, 164 pgs.,			
3 1/2" x 3 1/2", 3 books in set; all soft-c:			
Alexander Smart, ESQ by Winner	16.00	48.00	110.00
Bunky by Billy de Beck	16.00	48.00	110.00
Nicodemus O'Malley by Carter	16.00	48.00	110.00
Complete set with box	57.00	171.00	400.00
1158- **Tracked by a G-Man,** 1939, Saalfield, 400 pgs.			
	9.00	27.00	57.00
25- **Trail of the Lonesome Pine, The,** 1936, Lynn, movie scenes			
	15.00	45.00	105.00
nn- **Trail of the Terrible 6** (See Tom Mix ...)			
1185- **Trail to Squaw Gulch, The,** 1940, Saalfield, 400 pgs.			
	10.00	30.00	62.00
720- **Treasure Island,** 1933, Whitman, 362 pgs.	19.00	57.00	135.00
1141- **Treasure Island,** 1934, Whitman, 164 pgs., hard-c, 4 1/4" x 5 1/4",			
Jackie Cooper photo-c, movie scenes	15.00	45.00	105.00
1141- **Treasure Island,** 1934, Whitman, 164 pgs., soft-c, 4 1/4" x 5 1/4",			
Jackie Cooper photo-c, movie scenes	15.00	45.00	105.00
1018- **Trick and Puzzle Book,** 1939, Whitman, 100 pgs.,			
soft-c	3.00	9.00	20.00
1100B- **Tricks Easy to Do** (Slight of hand & magic), 1938, Whitman,			
36 pgs., 2 1/2" x 3 1/2", Penny Book	3.00	9.00	20.00
1100B- **Tricks You Can Do,** 1938, Whitman, 36 pgs., 2 1/2" x 3 1/2",			
Penny Book	3.00	9.00	20.00
5777- **Tweety and Sylvester, The Magic Voice,** 1976, Whitman, 260 pgs.,			
soft-c, flip-it feature; 5 printings	2.00	5.00	10.00
1104- **Two-Gun Montana,** 1936, Whitman, 432 pgs., Henry E. Vallely-a			
	10.00	30.00	62.00
nn- **Two-Gun Montana Shoots it Out,** 1939, Whitman, 36 pgs.,			
2 1/2" x 3 1/2", Penny Book	10.00	30.00	62.00
1058- **Ugly Duckling, The** (Disney), 1939, Whitman, 68 pgs.,			
5" x 5 1/2", hard-c	12.00	36.00	87.00
nn- **Ugly Duckling, The,** nd (1930s), np (Whitman), 36 pgs.,			
3" x 2 1/2", Penny Book	3.00	9.00	20.00
Unc' Billy Gets Even (See Wee Little Books)			

	GD	FN	VF/NM
1114- **Uncle Don's Strange Adventures,** 1935, Whitman, 300 pgs.,			
radio star-Uncle Don Carney	10.00	30.00	67.00
722- **Uncle Ray's Story of the United States,** 1934, Whitman,			
300 pgs.	10.00	30.00	67.00
1461- **Uncle Sam's Sky Defenders,** 1941, Whitman, 432 pgs., flip pictures			
	10.00	30.00	62.00
1405- **Uncle Wiggily's Adventures,** 1946, Whitman, All Pictures Comics			
	15.00	45.00	105.00
1411- **Union Pacific,** 1939, Whitman, 240 pgs., photo-c, movie scenes			
	12.00	36.00	78.00
1189- **Up Dead Horse Canyon,** 1940, Saalfield, 400 pgs.			
	9.00	27.00	57.00
1455- **Vic Sands of the U.S. Flying Fortress Bomber Squadron,**			
1944, Whitman, 352 pgs.	12.00	36.00	78.00
1645- **Walt Disney's Andy Burnett on the Trail** (TV Series),			
1958, Whitman, 280 pgs.	4.00	12.00	25.00
803- **Walt Disney's Bongo,** 1948, Whitman,			
hard-c, Story Hour Series	12.00	36.00	78.00
711-10-**Walt Disney's Cinderella and the Magic Wand,** 1950, Whitman,			
2 1/2" x 5", based on Disney movie	10.00	30.00	67.00
845- **Walt Disney's Donald Duck and his Cat Troubles** (Disney), 1948,			
Whitman, 100 pgs., 5" x 5 1/2", hard-c	12.00	36.00	78.00
845- **Walt Disney's Donald Duck and the Boys,** 1948, Whitman, 100 pgs.,			
5" x 5 1/2", hard-c, Barks-a	25.00	75.00	175.00
2952- **Walt Disney's Donald Duck in the Great Kite Maker,**			
1949, Whitman, 24 pgs., 3 1/4" x 4", Tiny Tales, full color (5 cents)			
	10.00	30.00	62.00
804- **Walt Disney's Mickey and the Beanstalk,** 1948, Whitman,			
hard-c, Story Hour Series	12.00	36.00	78.00
845- **Walt Disney's Mickey Mouse and the Boy Thursday,**			
194 pgs., Whitman, 5" x 5 1/2", 100 pgs.	12.00	36.00	78.00
845- **Walt Disney's Mickey Mouse the Miracle Maker,**			
1948, Whitman, 5" x 5 1/2", 100 pgs.	12.00	36.00	78.00
2952- **Walt Disney's Mickey Mouse and the Night Prowlers,** Whitman, 1949,			
24 pgs., 3 1/4" x 4", Tiny Tales, full color (5 ¢)	10.00	30.00	62.00
5770- **Walt Disney's Mickey Mouse - Mystery at Disneyland,** Whitman, 1975,			
260 pgs., four printings	2.00	6.00	12.00
5781-2- **Walt Disney's Mickey Mouse - Mystery at Dead Man's Cove,** Whitman,			
1980, 260 pgs., two printings	2.00	5.00	10.00
845- **Walt Disney's Minnie Mouse and the Antique Chair,**			
1948, Whitman, 5" x 5 1/2", 100 pgs.	12.00	36.00	78.00
1435- **Walt Disney's Pinocchio and Jiminy Cricket,** 1940,			
Whitman, 432 pgs.	19.00	57.00	130.00
845- **Walt Disney's Poor Pluto,** 1948, Whitman, 5" x 5 1/2",			
100 pgs., hard-c	12.00	36.00	78.00
1467- **Walt Disney's Pluto the Pup** (Disney), 1938, Whitman,			
432 pgs., Gottfredson-a	16.00	48.00	115.00
1066- **Walt Disney's Story of Clarabelle Cow** (Disney),			
1938, Whitman, 100 pgs.	12.00	36.00	78.00
66- **Walt Disney's Story of Dippy the Goof** (Disney),			
1938, Whitman, 100 pgs.	12.00	36.00	78.00
1066- **Walt Disney's Story of Donald Duck** (Disney), 1938,			
Whitman, 100 pgs., hard-c, Taliaferro-a	12.00	36.00	78.00
1066- **Walt Disney's Story of Mickey Mouse** (Disney), 1938, Whitman,			
100 pgs., hard-c, Gottfredson-a, Donald Duck app.			
	12.00	36.00	78.00
1066- **Walt Disney's Story of Minnie Mouse** (Disney),			
1938, Whitman, 100 pgs., hard-c	12.00	36.00	78.00
1066- **Walt Disney's Story of Pluto the Pup,** (Disney),			
1938, Whitman, 100 pgs., hard-c	12.00	36.00	78.00
2952- **Walter Lantz Presents Andy Panda's Rescue,** 1949, Whitman, Tiny			
Tales, full color (5 cents) (1030-5 on back-c)	10.00	30.00	62.00
751- **Wash Tubbs in Pandemonia,** 1934, Whitman, 320 pgs., Roy Crane-a			
	12.00	36.00	78.00
nn- **Wash Tubbs in Pandemonia,** 1934, Whitman, 52 pgs., 4" x 5 1/2",			
premium-no ads, soft-c, Roy Crane-a	18.00	54.00	125.00
1455- **Wash Tubbs and Captain Easy Hunting For Whales,**			
1938, Whitman, 432 pgs., Roy Crane-a	12.00	36.00	78.00
6- **Wash Tubbs in Foreign Travel,** 1934, Whitman, soft-c, 3 1/2" x 3 1/2",			

1164 - West Point of the Air © WHIT

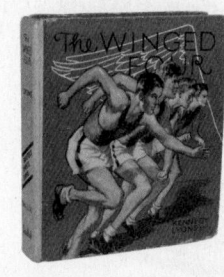

1131 - The Winged Four © Saalfield

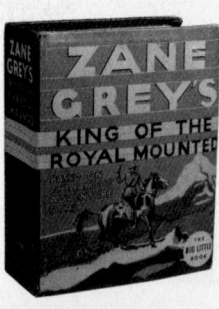

1103 - Zane Grey's King of the Royal Mounted © WHIT

	GD	FN	VF/NM
Tarzan Ice Cream cup premium	31.00	93.00	220.00
513- Wee Little Books (In Open Box), 1934, Whitman, 44 pgs., small size, 6 books in set			
Child's Garden of Verses	4.00	12.00	25.00
The Happy Prince (The Story of)	4.00	12.00	25.00
Joan of Arc (The Story of)	4.00	12.00	25.00
Peter Pan (The Story of)	4.00	12.00	25.00
Pied Piper Of Hamlin	4.00	12.00	25.00
Robin Hood (A Story of...)	4.00	12.00	25.00
Complete set with box	30.00	90.00	210.00
514- Wee Little Books (In Open Box), 1934, Whitman, 44 pgs., small size, 6 books in set			
Jack And Jill	4.00	12.00	25.00
Little Bo-Peep	4.00	12.00	25.00
Little Tommy Tucker	4.00	12.00	25.00
Mother Goose	4.00	12.00	25.00
Old King Cole	4.00	12.00	25.00
Simple Simon	4.00	12.00	25.00
Complete set with box	30.00	90.00	210.00
518- Wee Little Books (In Open Box), 1933, Whitman, 44 pgs., small size, 6 books in set, written by Thornton Burgess			
Betty Bear's Lesson-1930	4.00	12.00	25.00
Jimmy Skunk's Justice-1933	4.00	12.00	25.00
Little Joe Otter's Slide-1929	4.00	12.00	25.00
Peter Rabbit's Carrots-1933	4.00	12.00	25.00
Unc' Billy Gets Even-1930	4.00	12.00	25.00
Whitefoot's Secret-1933	4.00	12.00	25.00
Complete set with box	30.00	90.00	210.00
519- Wee Little Books (In Open Box) (Bible Stories), 1934, Whitman, 44 pgs., small size, 6 books in set, Helen Janes-a			
The Story of David	4.00	12.00	25.00
The Story of Gideon	4.00	12.00	25.00
The Story of Daniel	4.00	12.00	25.00
The Story of Joseph	4.00	12.00	25.00
The Story of Ruth and Naomi	4.00	12.00	25.00
The Story of Moses	4.00	12.00	25.00
Complete set with box	30.00	90.00	210.00
1471- Wells Fargo, 1938, Whitman, 240 pgs., photo-c, movie scenes			
	12.00	36.00	87.00
L18- Western Frontier, 1935, Lynn, 192 pgs., starring Ken Maynard, movie scenes	19.00	57.00	130.00
1121- West Pointers on the Gridiron, 1936, Saalfield, 148 pgs., hard-c, sports book	9.00	27.00	57.00
1601- West Pointers on the Gridiron, 1936, Saalfield, 148 pgs., soft-c, sports book	9.00	27.00	57.00
1124- West Point Five, The, 1937, Saalfield, 4 3/4" x 5 1/4", sports book, hard-c	9.00	27.00	57.00
1604- West Point Five, The, 1937, Saalfield, 4 1/4" x 5 1/4", sports book, soft-c	9.00	27.00	57.00
1164- West Point of the Air, 1935, Whitman, 160 pgs., photo-c, movie scenes	16.00	38.00	78.00
18- Westward Ho!, 1935, EVW, 160 pgs., movie scenes, starring John Wayne (Scarce)	45.00	135.00	315.00
1109- We Three, 1935, Saalfield, 160 pgs., photo-c, movie scenes, by John Barrymore, hard-c	10.00	30.00	62.00
1589- We Three, 1935, Saalfield, 160 pgs., photo-c, movie scenes, by John Barrymore, soft-c	10.00	30.00	62.00
5- Wheels of Destiny, 1934, EVW, 160 pgs., movie scenes, starring Ken Maynard	19.00	57.00	135.00
Whitefoot's Secret (See Wee Little Books)			
nn- Who's Afraid of the Big Bad Wolf, "Three Little Pigs" (Disney), 1933, McKay, 36 pgs., 6" x 8 1/2", stiff-c, Disney studio-a	36.00	108.00	250.00
nn- Wild West Adventures of Buffalo Bill, 1935, Whitman, 260 pgs., Cocomalt premium, soft-c, Hal Arbo-a	14.00	42.00	95.00
1096- Will Rogers, The Story of, 1935, Saalfield, photo-hard-c	10.00	30.00	67.00
1576- Will Rogers, The Story of, 1935, Saalfield, photo-soft-c	10.00	30.00	67.00

	GD	FN	VF/NM
1458- Wimpy the Hamburger Eater, 1938, Whitman, 432 pgs., E.C. Segar-a	21.00	63.00	145.00
1433- Windy Wayne and His Flying Wing, 1942, Whitman, 432 pgs., flip pictures	10.00	30.00	62.00
1131- Winged Four, The, 1937, Saalfield, sports book, hard-c	10.00	30.00	62.00
1407- Wings of the U.S.A., 1940, Whitman, 432 pgs., Thomas Hickey-a	10.00	30.00	62.00
nn- Winning of the Old Northwest, The, 1934, World Syndicate, High Lights of History Series, full color-c	10.00	30.00	62.00
nn- Winning of the Old Northwest, The, 1934, World Syndicate, High Lights of History Series; red & silver-c	10.00	30.00	62.00
1122- Winning Point, The, 1936, Saalfield, (Football), hard-c	8.00	25.00	52.00
1602- Winning Point, The, 1936, Saalfield, soft-c	8.00	25.00	52.00
nn- Wizard of Oz Waddle Book, 1934, BRP, 20 pgs., 7 1/2" x 10", forerunner of the Blue Ribbon Pop-Up books; with 6 removable articulated cardboard characters. Book only	48.00	144.00	340.00
Dust jacket only	63.00	189.00	445.00
Near Mint Complete - $11,500			
710-10-Woody Woodpecker Big Game Hunter, 1950, Whitman, by Walter Lantz	9.00	27.00	57.00
2010-(#10)-Woody Woodpecker-The Meteor Menace, 1967, Whitman, 260 pgs., 39¢-c, hard-c, color illos.	4.00	12.00	25.00
5753- Woody Woodpecker-The Meteor Menace, 1973, Whitman, 260 pgs., no price, soft-c, color illos.	1.00	2.00	5.00
2028- Woody Woodpecker-The Sinister Signal, 1969, Whitman	3.00	9.00	20.00
5763- Woody Woodpecker-The Sinister Signal, 1974, Whitman, 1st printing-no price; 2nd printing-39¢-c	1.00	2.00	5.00
23- World of Monsters, The, 1935, EVW, Five Star Library, movie scenes	15.00	45.00	105.00
779- World War in Photographs, The, 1934, Whitman, photo-c, photo illus.	10.00	30.00	62.00
Wyatt Earp (See Hugh O'Brian ...)			
nn- Xena - Warrior Princess, 1998, Chronicle Books, 310 pgs., based on TV series, 1-color (purple) illos	1.00	3.00	8.00
nn- Yogi Bear Goes Country & Western, 1977, Modern Promotions, 244 pgs., 49 cents, soft-c, flip pictures	2.00	6.00	12.00
nn- Yogi Bear Saves Jellystone Park, 1977, Modern Promotions, 244 pgs., 49 cents, soft-c, flip pictures	2.00	6.00	12.00
nn- Zane Grey's Cowboys of the West, 1935, Whitman, 148 pgs., 3 3/4" x 4", Tarzan Ice Cream Cup premium, soft-c, Arbo-a	36.00	108.00	250.00
Zane Grey's King of the Royal Mounted (See Men of the Mounted)			
1010- Zane Grey's King of the Royal Mounted in Arctic Law, 1937, Whitman, 7 1/4" x 5 1/2", 64 pgs., Nickel Book	14.00	42.00	95.00
1103- Zane Grey's King of the Royal Mounted, 1936, Whitman, 432 pgs.	12.00	36.00	87.00
nn- Zane Grey's King of the Royal Mounted, 1935, Whitman, 260 pgs., Cocomalt premium, soft-c	16.00	48.00	115.00
1179- Zane Grey's King of the Royal Mounted and the Northern Treasure, 1937, Whitman, 432 pgs.	12.00	36.00	87.00
1405- Zane Grey's King of the Royal Mounted the Long Arm of the Law, 1942, Whitman, All Pictures Comics	12.00	36.00	87.00
1452- Zane Grey's King of the Royal Mounted Gets His Man, 1938, Whitman, 432 pgs.	12.00	36.00	87.00
1486- Zane Grey's King of the Royal Mounted and the Great Jewel Mystery, 1939, Whitman, 432 pgs.	12.00	36.00	87.00
5- Zane Grey's King of the Royal Mounted in the Far North, 1938, Whitman, 132 pgs., Buddy Book, soft-c	33.00	99.00	230.00
nn- Zane Grey's King of the Royal Mounted in Law of the North, 1939, Whitman, 36 pgs., 2 1/2" x 3 1/2", Penny Book	8.00	25.00	52.00
nn- Zane Grey's King of the Royal Mounted Policing the Frozen North, 1938, Dell, 196 pgs., Fast-Action Story, soft-c	24.00	72.00	165.00
1440- Zane Grey's Tex Thorne Comes Out of the West, 1937, Whitman, 432 pgs.	10.00	30.00	62.00
1465- Zip Saunders King of the Speedway, 1939, 432 pgs., Weisman-a	10.00	30.00	62.00

THE MARKETING OF A MEDIUM

by Dr. Arnold T. Blumberg, DCD

with new material and additional research by Sol M. Davidson, PhD, and Robert L. Beerbohm

Everyone wants something for free. It's in our nature to look for the quick fix, the good deal, the complimentary gift. We long to hit the lottery and quit our job, to win the trip around the world, or find that pot of gold at the end of the proverbial rainbow. Collectors in particular are certainly built to appreciate the notion of the "free gift," since it not only means a new item to collect and enjoy, but no risk or obligation in order to acquire it.

Ah, but there's the rub. Because things are not always what they seem, and "free gifts" usually come with a price. As the saying goes, "there's no such thing as a free lunch," so if it seems too good to be true, it probably is. This is the case even in the world of comics, where premiums and giveaways have a familiar agenda hidden behind the bright colors and fanciful stories. But where did it all begin?

EXTRA EXTRA

As we learn more about the early history of the comic book industry through continual investigation and the publishing of articles like those regularly featured in this book, we gain a much greater understanding of the financial and creative forces at work in shaping the medium,

Some of the earliest characters that were used as successful tools in promotional comics were Palmer Cox's creation "The Brownies." The illustration shown here showcases them drinking and endorsing Seal Brand Coffee.

but perhaps one of the most intriguing and least recognized factors that influenced the dawn of comics is the concept of the premium or giveaway. (Note: Some of the historical information referenced in this article is derived from material also presented in Robert L. Beerbohm's introductory articles to the Platinum Age and Modern Age sections.)

The birth of the comic book as we know it today is intimately connected with the development of the comic strip in American newspapers and their use as an advertising and marketing tool for staple products such as bread, milk, and cereal. From the very beginning, comic characters have played several roles in pop culture, entertaining the youth of the country while also (sometimes none too subtly) acting as hucksters for whatever corporation foots the bill. From important staples to frivolous material produced simply to make a buck, these products have utilized the comics medium to sell, sell, sell. And what better way to hook a prospective customer than to give them "something for nothing?"

Starting in the 1850s, comics were being used in free almanacs such as **Elton's**, **Hostetter's** and **Wright's** to lure readers for the little booklets to sell patent medicine, farm products, tobacco, shoe polish, etc. Most of these are exceedingly rare today, hence it is difficult to compile an accurate history. More mention of these early precursors can be found in the Victorian Comics Era essay following this one. But although comic characters themselves were already being aggressively merchandised all around the world by the mid-1890s--as with, for example, Palmer Cox's **The Brownies**--the real starting point for the success of comics as a giveaway marketing mechanism can be traced to the introduction of **The Yellow Kid**, Richard Outcault's now legendary newspaper strip.

Newspaper publishers had already recognized that comic strips could boost circulation as well as please sponsors and advertisers by drawing more eyes to the page, so Sunday "supplements" were introduced to entice fans. Outcault's creation cemented the theory with proof of comic characters' marketing and merchandising power.

This unused cover was designed as the second cover for "Motion Picture Funnies Weekly." While the concept for this promotional comic title never caught on, the inaugural issue did feature the origin and first printed appearance of the Sub-Mariner.

Soon after, Outcault (who had most likely been inspired by Cox's merchandising success with **The Brownies** in the first place) caught lightning in a bottle once more with **Buster Brown**, who has the distinction of being America's first nationally licensed comic strip character. Soon, comic strips proliferated throughout the nation's newspapers as tycoons like Hearst and Pulitzer recognized the drawing power of the new medium and fought circulation wars to capture the pennies of the nouveau readership. They paid exorbitant salaries to comic strip artists such as Rudolph Dirks (**Katzenjammer Kids**), and used the funnies as newspaper supplements and as premiums to attract readers. Corporations soon had the chance to license recognizable personas as their own personal pitchmen (or women or animals...). Comic character merchandise wasn't far behind, resulting in a boom of future collectibles now catalogued in volumes like **Hake's Price Guide to Character Toys**.

TWO BIRTHS FOR THE PRICE OF ONE

Comic books themselves were at the heart of this movement, and giveaway and premium collections of comic strips not only appealed to children and adults alike, but provided the impetus for the birth of the modern comic book format itself. It could be said that without the concept of the giveaway comic or the marketing push behind it, there would be no comic book industry as we have it today. Well-known now is the story of how in spring 1933 Harry Wildenberg of Eastern Color Printing Company convinced Proctor & Gamble to sponsor the first modern comic book, **Funnies on Parade**, as a premium. Its success led to the first continuing comic book, **Famous Funnies**, and the rest, as they say, is history.

In 1935, while working on the printing presses of Eastern Color developing how modern comic books get printed,

Juliun J. Proskauer came up with an idea for printing "Comic-Books-For-Industry." In July 1936 he made his first sale through his newly formed William C. Popper & Co. to David M. Davies, then advertising manager for Seagram's Distillers Corp. for three million copies of **Seagram's Merrymakers** in time for the 1936-37 Christmas season. "Thus was a new industry born," wrote **Printing News** in August 1945.

Even a casual perusal of the listings in this section of the Guide will dazzle the reader with the endless variety of purposes that this medium has served. Yes, promos have been used to hawk products from athletic equipment to zithers and zip codes, but comics are too versatile an art form to be confined to a few uses. They've swayed elections in cities (**The O'Dwyer Story**, 1949), in states (**Giant for a Day**: Jacob Javits, 1946) and nationwide (**The Story of Harry Truman**, 1948); solicited for charities (**Donald Duck and the Red Feather**, 1948); addressed health issues (**Blondie**, 1949, mental hygiene); discouraged kids from smoking (**Captain America Meets the Asthma Monster**, 1987); coached youngsters in sports skills (**Circling the Bases**, 1947, A.G. Spaulding); explained scientific complexities (**Adventures in Science**, 1946-61, GE); pleaded for social justice (**Consumer Comics**, 1975); espoused religious causes (**Oral Roberts' True Stories**, 1950s); protected the environment (**Our Spaceship Earth**, 1947); encouraged tourism (**Wyoming, The Cowboy State**, 1954); conveyed a sense of history (**Louisiana Purchase**, 1953); taught about computers (**Superman Radio Shack Giveaway**, 1980); trained employees (**Dial Finance Dialogues**, 1961-70) and executives (**Beneficial Finance System, Managing New Employees**, 1950s); cautioned safety (**Willy Wing Flap**, 1944(?)); announced corporate annual results (**Motorola Annual Report**, 1952); defended free enterprise (**Steve Merritt**, 1949); hammered communism (**How Stalin Hopes to Destroy America**, 1951); fought discrimination (**Mammy Yokum & the Great Dogpatch Mystery**, 1956, B'nai Brith); aided young workers in job-hunting (**The Job Scene**, 1969); battled the scourge of sickle cell anemia (**Where's Herbie**, 1972, U.S. H.E.W.); inspired the overcoming of adversity (**Al Capp by Li'l Abner**, 1946); fostered reading (**Linus Gets a Library Card**, 1960); recruited for the armed forces (**Li'l Abner Joins the Navy**, 1950); beguiled readers into

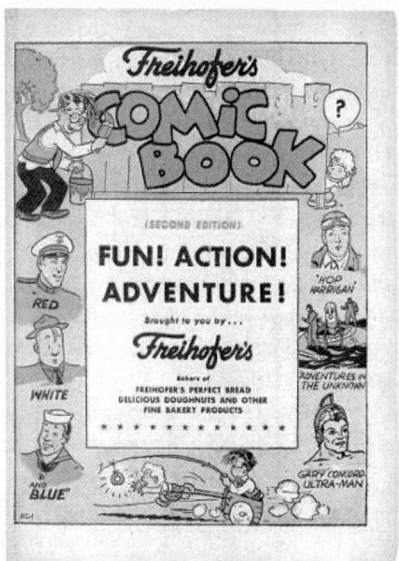

Every market and product has been on the promotional comic book bandwagon. Freihofer's Baking Company distributed a comic in the 1940s that featured reprinted pages from "All-American Comics."

learning languages (**Blondie**, 1949, Philadelphia public schools); and even instructed in such delicate matters as birth control (**Escape from Fear**, 1950 (revised 1959, etc.), for Planned Parenthood).

READ ALL ABOUT IT

The impact of this new approach to advertising was not lost on the business world. Contrary to modern belief, comic books were hardly discounted by the adults of the time...at least not those who had the marketing savvy to recognize an opportunity - or a threat - when they saw one. In the April 1933 issue of **Fortune** magazine, an article titled "The Funny Papers" trumpeted the arrival of comics as a force to be reckoned with in the world of advertising and business, and what's more, a force to fear as well. At first providing a brief survey of the newspaper comic strip business (which for many of the magazine's readers must have seemed a foreign topic for serious discussion), the article goes on to examine the incredible financial draw of comics and their characters:

"Between 70 and 75 per cent {sic} of the readers of any newspaper follow its comic sections regularly...Even the advertiser has succumbed to the comic, and in 1932 spent well over $1,000,000 for comic-paper space."

"**Comic Weekly** is the comic section of seventeen Hearst Sunday papers...Advertisers who market their wares through balloon-speaking manikins {sic} may enjoy the proximity of Jiggs, Maggie, Barney Google, and other funny Hearst headliners."

Although the article continues to cast the notion of relying on comic strip material to sell product in a negative light, actually suggesting that advertisers who utilize comics are violating unspoken rules of "advertising decorum" and bringing themselves "down to the level" of comics (and since when have advertisers been stalwart preservers of good taste and high moral standards), there is no doubt that they are viewing comics in a new light. The comic characters have arrived by 1933...and they're ready to help sell your merchandise too.

Fortune wasn't the only one to take notice as World War II came and went. In 1948, Louis P. Birk, the head of Brevity, Inc., an important promotional comics publisher said, "Comics are serious business." In an article in **Printers' Ink** magazine, he estimated that more than 80 different "comic booklets" had been produced and more than 45,000,000 million copies distributed in the five years before 1948. But of course, comics were serious business long before businessman/historian Birk noted the fact for posterity.

THE MARCH OF WAR AND BEYOND

Through the relentless currents of time, comic strips, books, and the characters that starred in them became more and more an intrinsic part of American culture. During the turmoil of the Great Depression and World War II, comic characters in print and celluloid form entertained while informing and selling at the same time, and premium and giveaway comics came well and truly into their own, pushing everything from loaves of bread to war bonds.

In the 1950s and '60s, there was a shift in focus as the power of giveaway and premium comics was applied to more altruistic endeavors than simply selling something. Comic book format pamphlets, fully illustrated and often inventively written, taught children about banking, money, the dangers of poison and other household products, and even chronicled moments in

The promotional title "March of Comics" was a prolific comic that ran for 36 years and 488 issues featuring a variety of subjects and characters. (#25 shown)

American history. The comic book as giveaway was now not only a marketing gimmick--it was a tool for educating as well.

The 1970s and '80s saw another boom in premium and giveaway comics. Every product imaginable seemed to have a licensing deal with a comic book character, usually one of the prominent flag bearers of the Big Two, Marvel or DC. Spider-Man fought bravely against the Beetle for the benefit of All Detergent; Captain America allied himself with the Campbell Kids; and Superman helped a class of computer students beat a disaster-conjuring foe at his own game with the help of Radio Shack Tandy computers.

Newspapers rediscovered the power of comics, not just with enlarged strip supplements but with actual comic books. Spider-Man, the Hulk, and others turned up as giveaway comic extras in various American newspapers (including Chicago and Dallas publications), while a whole series of public information comics like those produced decades earlier used superheroes to caution children about the dangers of smoking, drugs, and child abuse.

Comics also turned up in a plethora of other toy products as the 1980s introduced kids to the joy of electronic games and action figures. Supplementary comics provided "free" with action figure and video game packages told the backstory about the product, adding depth to the play experience while providing an extra incentive to buy. Comics became an intrinsic part of the Atari line of video cartridges, for example, eventually spawning its own full-blown newsstand series as well.

As the twentieth century gave way to the twenty-first, giveaway comics were still being produced for inclusion in action figure and video game packages,

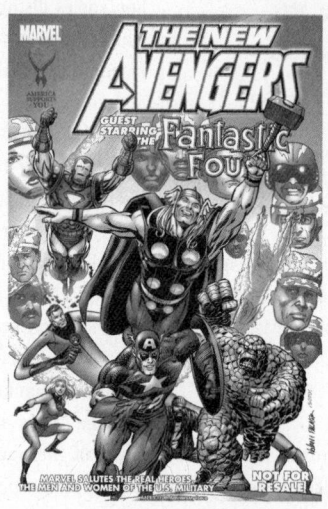

Today, promotional comics continue to be used as a marketing tool to reach both children and adults alike. This 2005 comic was produced by Marvel Comics as a salute to the men and women of the armed forces.

as well as in conjunction with countless consumer items and corporations. It seems that the medium still has a lot to offer for all those companies desperate to make the most of their market share.

A COMIC BY ANY OTHER NAME

One of the earliest names for promotional comics was "special purpose comics." In their pursuit of superheroes, collectors have allowed promotional comics to lie fallow - underappreciated and uncollected. Without a legitimate name, these products were given sundry other appellations - industrial comics, promos, giveaways, premiums, promics - each accurate but only for a small segment of the unorganized but lusty and lively medium. Perhaps no one name can cover all the

variations and purposes of this branch of comic art, but for practical reasons if we accept the general premise that these comics were created to promote an idea, a product or a person, then "Promotional Comics" is probably as convenient a catch-all title as we can come up with.

We used the phrase "for practical reasons" because the word "practical" goes to the heart of promotional comics more than it does for any other comics product. What greater testimony is there to the medium's impact on American culture than to note their use by hard-headed, profit-minded business people and corporations? They invest their money and they expect results.

Today, premium comics continue to thrive and are still utilized as a valuable marketing and promotional tool. "Free" comics are still packaged with action figures and video games, and offered as mail-away premiums from a variety of product manufacturers. The comic industry itself has expanded its use of giveaway comics to self-promote as well, with "ashcan" and other giveaway editions turning up at conventions and comic shops to advertise upcoming series and special events. Many of these function as old-fashioned premiums, with a coupon or other response required from the reader to receive the comic.

As for the supplements and giveaways printed all those years ago, they have spawned a collectible fervor all their own, thanks to their atypical distribution and frequent rarity. For that and the desire to delve deeper into comics history, we hope that by focusing more directly on this genre, we can enhance our understanding of this vital component in the development and history of the modern comic book.

Whether you're a collector or not, we're all motivated by that desire to get something for nothing. For as long as consumers are enticed by the notion of the "free gift," promotional comics will remain a vital marketing component in many business models, but they will also continue to fight the stigma that has long been associated with the industry as a whole. "Respectable" sources like **Fortune** may have taken notice of the power of comic-related advertising 71 years ago, but after all this time comics still fight an uphill battle to establish some measure of dignity for the medium. Perhaps the higher visibility of promotional comics will eventually prove to be a deciding factor in that intellectual war.

See ya in the funny papers.

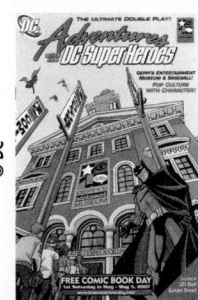

Adventures of Big Boy #274 © Shoney's

Adventures with the DC Super Heroes © DC

Amazing Spider-Man All Detergent Giveaway © MAR

	GD 2.0	VG 4.0	FN 6.0	VF 8.0	VF/NM 9.0	NM- 9.2

ACTION COMICS
DC Comics: 1947 - 1998 (Giveaway)

	GD	VG	FN	VF	VF/NM	NM-
1 (1976) paper cover w/10¢ price, 16 pgs. in color; reprints complete Superman story from #1 ('38)	3	6	9	18	27	35
1 (1976) Safeguard Giveaway; paper cover w/"free", 16 pgs. in color; reprints complete Superman story from #1 ('38)	3	6	9	18	27	35
1 (1983) paper cover w/10¢ price, 16 pgs. in color; reprints complete Superman story from #1 ('38)	3	6	9	15	20	25
1 (1987 Nestle Quik; 1988, 50¢)	1	2	3	5	7	9
1 (1993)-Came w/Reign of Superman packs						4.00
1 (1998 U.S. Postal Service, $7.95) Reprints entire issue; extra outer half-cover contains First Day Issuance of 32¢ Superman stamp with Sept. 10, 1998 Cleveland, OH postmark						8
Theater (1947, 32 pgs., 5" x 7", nn)-Vigilante story based on Columbia Vigilante serial; no Superman-c or story	66	132	198	413	682	950

ACTION ZONE
CBS Television: 1994 (Promotes CBS Saturday morning cartoons)

1-WildC.A.T.s, T.M.N.Turtles, Skeleton Warriors stories; Jim Lee-c   2.25

ADVENTURE COMICS
IGA: No date (early 1940s) (Paper-c, 32 pgs.)

	GD	VG	FN	VF	VF/NM	NM-
Two diff. issues; Super-Mystery-r from 1941	23	46	69	132	209	285

ADVENTURE IN DISNEYLAND
Walt Disney Productions (Dist. by Richfield Oil): May, 1955 (Giveaway, soft-c, 16 pgs)

	GD	VG	FN	VF	VF/NM	NM-
nn	10	20	30	56	76	95

ADVENTURES @ EBAY
eBay: 2000 (6 3/4" x 4 1/2", 16 pgs.)

1-Judd Winick-a/Rucka & Van Meter-s; intro to eBay comic buying   2.25

ADVENTURES OF BARRY WEEN, BOY GENIUS, THE
Oni Press: July, 2004 (Free Comic Book Day giveaway)

...: Secret Crisis Origin Files -Judd Winick-s/a   2.25

ADVENTURES OF BIG BOY
Timely Comics/Webs Adv. Corp./Illus. Features: 1956 - Present (Giveaway) (East & West editions of early issues)

	GD	VG	FN	VF	VF/NM	NM-
1-Everett-a	97	194	291	606	1003	1400
2-Everett-a	36	72	108	208	329	450
3-5: 4-Robot-c	17	34	51	98	154	210
6-10: 6-Sci/fic issue	10	20	30	68	119	170
11-20	6	12	18	41	66	90
21-30	4	8	12	22	34	45
31-50	3	6	9	16	23	30
51-100	2	4	6	10	12	15
101-150	2	4	6	8	10	12
151-240	1	2	3	5	7	9
241-265,267-269,271-300:						6.00
266-Superman x-over	3	6	9	18	27	35
270-TV's Buck Rogers-c/s	3	6	9	14	20	25
301-400						4.00
401-500						3.00
1-(2nd series - '76-'84,Paragon Prod.) (...Shoney's Big Boy)	1	3	4	6	8	10
2-20						5.00
21-50						3.00
Summer, 1959 issue, large size	7	14	21	47	76	105

ADVENTURES OF G. I. JOE
1969 (3-1/4x7") (20 & 16 pgs.)

First Series: 1-Danger of the Depths. 2-Perilous Rescue. 3-Secret Mission to Spy Island. 4-Mysterious Explosion. 5-Fantastic Free Fall. 6-Eight Ropes of Danger. 7-Mouth of Doom. 8-Hidden Missile Discovery. 9-Space Walk Mystery. 10-Fight for Survival. 11-The Shark's Surprise.
Second Series: 2-Flying Space Adventure. 4-White Tiger Hunt. 7-Capture of the Pygmy Gorilla. 12-Secret of the Mummy's Tomb.
Third Series: Reprinted surviving titles of First Series. Fourth Series: 13-Adventure Team Headquarters. 14-Search For the Stolen Idol.

	GD	VG	FN	VF	VF/NM	NM-
each....	3	6	9	16	22	28

ADVENTURES OF KOOL-AID MAN
Marvel Comics: 1983 - No. 3, 1985 (Mail order giveaway)

	GD	VG	FN	VF	VF/NM	NM-
1-3	1	2	3	4	5	7

ADVENTURES OF MARGARET O'BRIEN, THE
Bambury Fashions (Clothes): 1947 (20 pgs. in color, slick-c, regular size) (Premium)

	GD	VG	FN	VF	VF/NM	NM-
In "The Big City" movie adaptation (scarce)	18	36	54	107	169	230

ADVENTURES OF QUIK BUNNY
Nestle's Quik: 1984 (Giveaway, 32 pgs.)

	GD	VG	FN	VF	VF/NM	NM-
nn-Spider-Man app.	2	4	6	8	11	14

ADVENTURES OF STUBBY, SANTA'S SMALLEST REINDEER, THE
W. T. Grant Co.: nd (early 1940s) (Giveaway, 12 pgs.)

	GD	VG	FN	VF	VF/NM	NM-
nn	7	14	21	37	46	50

ADVENTURES OF VOTEMAN, THE
Foundation For Citizen Education Inc.: 1968

	GD	VG	FN	VF	VF/NM	NM-
nn	4	8	12	28	44	60

ADVENTURES WITH SANTA CLAUS
Promotional Publ. Co. (Murphy's Store): No date (early 50's) (9-3/4x 6-3/4", 24 pgs., giveaway, paper-c)

	GD	VG	FN	VF	VF/NM	NM-
nn-Contains 8 pgs. ads	6	12	18	28	34	40
16 pg. version	6	12	18	31	38	45

ADVENTURES WITH THE DC SUPER HEROES (Interior also inserted into some DC issues)
DC Comics/Geppi's Entertainment Museum: 2007 Free Comic Book Day giveaway

"The Batman and Cal Ripken, Jr. Hall of Fame Edition "A Rare Catch" " in indicia   2.25

AIR POWER (CBS TV & the U.S. Air Force Presents)
Prudential Insurance Co.: 1956 (5-1/4x7-1/4", 32 pgs., giveaway, soft-c)

	GD	VG	FN	VF	VF/NM	NM-
nn-Toth-a? Based on 'You Are There' TV program by Walter Cronkite	10	20	30	56	76	95

ALASKA BUSH PILOT
Jan Enterprises: 1959 (Paper cover)

1-Promotes Bush Pilot Club   (Value will be based on sale)
NOTE: A CGC certified 9.9 Mint sold for $632.50 in 2005.

ALICE IN BLUNDERLAND
Industrial Services: 1952 (Paper cover, 16 pgs. in color)

	GD	VG	FN	VF	VF/NM	NM-
nn-Facts about government waste and inefficiency	14	28	42	76	108	140

ALICE IN WONDERLAND
Western Printing Company/Whitman Publ. Co.: 1965; 1969; 1982

	GD	VG	FN	VF	VF/NM	NM-
Meets Santa Claus(1950s), nd, 16 pgs.	6	12	18	28	34	40
Rexall Giveaway(1965, 16 pgs., 5x7-1/4) Western Printing (TV, Hanna-Barbera)	3	6	9	16	23	30
Wonder Bakery Giveaway(1969, 16 pgs, color, nn, nd) (Continental Baking Company)	3	6	9	16	22	28

ALICE IN WONDERLAND MEETS SANTA
No publisher: nd (6-5/8x9-11/16", 16 pgs., giveaway, paper-c)

	GD	VG	FN	VF	VF/NM	NM-
nn	9	18	27	50	65	80

ALL ABOARD, MR. LINCOLN
Assoc. of American Railroads: Jan, 1959 (16 pgs.)

	GD	VG	FN	VF	VF/NM	NM-
nn-Abraham Lincoln and the Railroads	6	12	18	28	34	40

ALL NEW COMICS
Harvey Comics: Oct, 1993 (Giveaway, no cover price, 16 pgs.)(Hanna-Barbera)

1-Flintstones, Scooby Doo, Jetsons, Yogi Bear & Wacky Races previews for upcoming Harvey's new Hanna-Barbera line-up   5.00
NOTE: Material previewed in Harvey giveaway was eventually published by Archie.

AMAZING SPIDER-MAN, THE
Marvel Comics Group

	GD	VG	FN	VF	VF/NM	NM-
Acme & Dingo Children's Boots (1980)-Spider-Woman app.	2	4	6	10	14	18
Adventures in Reading Starring... (1990,1991) Bogdanove & Romita-c/a						4.00
Aim Toothpaste Giveaway (36 pgs., reg. size)-1 pg. origin recap; Green Goblin-c/story	2	4	6	8	11	14
Aim Toothpaste Giveaway (16 pgs., reg. size)-Dr. Octopus app.	2	4	6	9	12	15
All Detergent Giveaway (1979, 36 pgs.), nn-Origin-r	2	4	6	9	13	16
Amazing Fantasy #15 (8/02) reprint included in Spider-Man DVD Collector's Gift Set						3.00
Amazing Fantasy #15 (2006) News America Marketing newspaper giveaway						2.50
Amazing Spider-Man nn (1990, 6-1/8x9", 28 pgs.)-Shan-Lon giveaway; reprints Amazing Spider-Man #303 w/McFarlane-c/a	2	3	5	7		9
Amazing Spider-Man #1 Reprint (1990, 4-1/4x6-1/4", 28 pgs.)-Packaged with the book "Start Collecting Comic Books" from Running Press						4.00
Amazing Spider-Man #3 Reprint (2004)-Best Buy/Sony giveaway						2.50
Amazing Spider-Man #50 (Sony Pictures Edition) (8/04)-mini-comic included in Spider-Man 2 movie DVD Collector's Gift Set; r/#50 & various ASM covers with Dr. Octopus						2.50
Amazing Spider-Man #129 (Lion Gate Films) (6/04)-promotional comic given away at movie theaters on opening night for The Punisher						2.50

...& Power Pack (1984, nn)(Nat'l Committee for Prevention of Child Abuse) (two versions, mail offer & store giveaway)-Mooney-a; Byrne-c

	GD	VG	FN	VF	VF/NM	NM-
Mail offer	2	4	6	8	10	12
Store giveaway						4.00

Archie Shoe-Store Giveaway 5/49 © AP

Aurora Comic Scenes Instruction Booklet - Captain America © MAR

Batman and Robin Movie Preview © DC

	GD 2.0	VG 4.0	FN 6.0	VF 8.0	VF/NM 9.0	NM- 9.2

...& The Hulk (Special Edition)(6/8/80; 20 pgs.)-Supplement to Chicago Tribune

| | | 3 | 6 | 9 | 13 | 16 |

...& The Incredible Hulk (1981, 1982; 36 pgs.)-Sanger Harris or May D&F supplement to Dallas Times, Dallas Herald, Denver Post, Kansas City Star, Tulsa World; Foley's supplement to Houston Chronicle (1982, 16 pgs.)- "Great Rodeo Robbery"; The Jones Store-giveaway (1983, 16 pgs.)

| | 2 | 4 | 6 | 11 | 16 | 20 |

...and the New Mutants Featuring Skids nn (National Committee for Prevention of Child Abuse/K-Mart giveaway)-Williams-c(i)

| | | | | | | 5.00 |

...Battles Ignorance (1992)(Sylvan Learning Systems) giveaway; Mad Thinker app. Kupperberg-a

| | 1 | 2 | 3 | 5 | 6 | 8 |

...Captain America, The Incredible Hulk, & Spider-Woman (1981) (7-11 Stores giveaway; 36 pgs.)

| | 2 | 4 | 6 | 9 | 12 | 15 |

...: Christmas in Dallas (1983) (Supplement to Dallas Times Herald) giveaway

| | 2 | 4 | 6 | 9 | 12 | 15 |

...: Danger in Dallas (1983) (Supplement to Dallas Times Herald) giveaway

| | 2 | 4 | 6 | 9 | 12 | 15 |

...: Danger in Denver (1983) (Supplement to Denver Post) giveaway for May D&F stores

| | 2 | 4 | 6 | 9 | 12 | 15 |

..., Fire-Star, And Ice-Man at the Dallas Ballet Nutcracker (1983; supplement to Dallas Times Herald)-Mooney-p

| | 2 | 4 | 6 | 9 | 12 | 15 |

Giveaway-Esquire Magazine (2/69)-Miniature-Still attached (scarce)

| | 12 | 24 | 36 | 82 | 146 | 210 |

Giveaway-Eye Magazine (2/69)-Miniature-Still attached

| | 9 | 18 | 27 | 60 | 100 | 140 |

...: Riot at Robotworld (1991; 16 pgs.)(National Action Council for Minorities in Engineering, Inc.) giveaway; Saviuk-c

| | | | | | | 6.00 |

..., Storm & Powerman (1982; 20 pgs.)(American Cancer Society) giveaway; also a 1991 2nd printing and a 1994 printing

| | 1 | 2 | 3 | 5 | 6 | 8 |

...: Swing Shift (2007 FCBD Edition) Jimenez-c/a; Slott-s

| | | | | | | 2.25 |

...Vs. The Hulk (Special Edition; 1979, 20 pgs.)(Supplement to Columbus Dispatch)

| | 2 | 4 | 6 | 11 | 16 | 20 |

...Vs. The Prodigy (Giveaway, 16 pgs. in color (1976, 5x6-1/2")-Sex education; (1 million printed; 35-50¢)

| | 3 | 6 | 9 | 14 | 19 | 24 |

Spidey & The Mini-Marvels Halloween 2003 Ashcan (12/03, 8 1/2"x 5 1/2") Giarusso-s/a; Venom and Green Goblin app.

| | | | | | | 2.00 |

AMERICA MENACED!
Vital Publications: 1950 (Paper-c)

nn-Anti-communism

| | 32 | 64 | 96 | 186 | 293 | 400 |

AMERICAN COMICS
Theatre Giveaways (Liberty Theatre, Grand Rapids, Mich. known): 1940's

Many possible combinations. "Golden Age" superhero comics with new cover added and given away at theaters. Following known: Superman #59, Capt. Marvel #20, Capt. Marvel Jr. #5, Action #33, Classics Comics #8, Whiz #39. Value would vary with book and should be 70-80 percent of the original.

ANDY HARDY COMICS
Western Printing Co.:

...& the New Automatic Gas Clothes Dryer (1952, 5x7-1/4", 16 pgs.) Bendix Giveaway (soft-c)

| | 6 | 12 | 18 | 31 | 38 | 45 |

ANIMANIACS EMERGENCY WORLD
DC Comics: 1995

nn-American Red Cross

| | | | | | | 4.00 |

APACHE HUNTER
Creative Pictorials: 1954 (18 pgs. in color) (promo copy) (saddle stitched)

nn-Severin, Heath stories

| | 15 | 30 | 45 | 85 | 130 | 175 |

AQUATEERS MEET THE SUPER FRIENDS
DC Comics: 1979

nn

| | 2 | 4 | 6 | 9 | 12 | 15 |

ARCHIE AND HIS GANG (Zeta Beta Tau Presents...)
Archie Publications: Dec. 1950 (St. Louis National Convention giveaway)

nn-Contains new cover stapled over Archie Comics #47 (11-12/50) on inside; produced for Zeta Beta Tau

| | 15 | 30 | 45 | 88 | 137 | 185 |

ARCHIE COMICS (Also see Sabrina)
Archie Publications

... And Friends and the Shield (10/02, 8 1/2"x 5 1/2") Diamond Comic Dist.

| | | | | | | 3.00 |

... And Friends - A Halloween Tale (10/98, 8 1/2"x 5 1/2") Diamond Comic Dist.; Sabrina and Sonic app.; Dan DeCarlo-a

| | | | | | | 3.00 |

... And Friends - A Timely Tale (10/01, 8 1/2"x 5 1/2") Diamond Comic Dist.

| | | | | | | 3.00 |

... And Friends Monster Bash 2003 (8 1/2"x 5 1/2") Diamond Comic Dist. Halloween

| | | | | | | 3.00 |

...And His Friends Help Raise Literacy Awareness In Mississippi nn (3/94)

| | | | | | | 6.00 |

...And His Pals in the Peer Helping Program nn (2/91, 7"x4 1/2") produced by the FBI

| | | | | | | 6.00 |

...And the History of Electronics nn (5/90, 36 pgs.)-Radio Shack giveaway; Bender-c/a

| | | | | | | 6.00 |

Fairmont Potato Chips Giveaway-Mini comics 1970 (8 issues-nn's., 8 pgs. each)

| | 3 | 6 | 9 | 16 | 22 | 28 |

Fairmont Potato Chips Giveaway-Mini comics 1970 (6 issues-nn's.,6 7/8" x 2 1/4", 8 pgs. each)

| | 3 | 6 | 9 | 16 | 22 | 28 |

Fairmont Potato Chips Giveaway-Mini comics 1971 (4 issues-nn's.,6 7/8" x 5", 8 pgs. each)

| | 3 | 6 | 9 | 16 | 22 | 28 |

... Free Comic Book Day Edition 1,2: 1-(7/03). 2-(9/04)

| | | | | | | 2.50 |

Little Archie "The Legend of the Lost Lagoon FCBD Edition (5/07) Bolling-s/a

| | | | | | | 2.25 |

Official Boy Scout Outfitter (1946, 9-1/2x6-1/2, 16 pgs.)-B. R. Baker Co. (Scarce)

| | 46 | 92 | 138 | 281 | 466 | 650 |

...'s Ham Radio Adventure (1997) Morse code instruction; Goldberg-a

| | | | | | | 5.00 |

...'s 65th Anniversary Bash ('06) Free Comic Book Day giveaway

| | | | | | | 2.50 |

...'s Weird Mysteries (9/99, 8 1/2"x 5 1/2") Diamond Comic Dist. Halloween giveaway

| | | | | | | 2.50 |

Tales From Riverdale (2006, 8 1/2"x 5 1/2") Diamond Comic Dist. Halloween giveaway

| | | | | | | 2.50 |

ARCHIE SHOE-STORE GIVEAWAY
Archie Publications: 1944-49 (12-15 pgs. of games, puzzles, stories like Superman-Tim books, No nos. - came out monthly)

	GD 2.0	VG 4.0	FN 6.0	VF 8.0	VF/NM 9.0	NM- 9.2
(1944-47)-issues	14	28	42	82	121	160
2/48-Peggy Lee photo-c	14	28	42	82	121	160
3/48-Marylee Robb photo-c	14	28	42	78	112	145
4/48-Gloria De Haven photo-c	14	28	42	82	121	160
5/48,6/48,7/48	14	28	42	78	112	145
8/48-Story on Shirley Temple	14	30	45	83	124	165
10/48-Archie as Wolf on cover	14	28	42	81	118	155
5/49-Kathleen Hughes photo-c	12	24	36	69	97	125
7/49	12	24	36	67	94	120
8/49-Archie photo-c from radio show	15	30	45	90	140	190
10/49-Gloria Mann photo-c from radio show	14	28	42	81	118	155
11/49,12/49	12	24	36	67	94	120

ARCHIE'S JOKE BOOK MAGAZINE (See Joke Book ...)
Archie Publications

Drug Store Giveaway (No. 39 w/new-c)

| | 7 | 14 | 21 | 35 | 43 | 50 |

ARCHIE'S TEN ISSUE COLLECTOR'S SET (Title inside of cover only)
Archie Publications: June, 1997 - No. 10, June, 1997 ($1.50, 20 pgs.)

1-10: 1,7-Archie. 2,8-Betty & Veronica. 3,9-Veronica. 4-Betty. 5-World of Archie. 6-Jughead. 10-Archie and Friends each...

| | | | | | | 4.00 |

ASTRO COMICS
American Airlines (Harvey): 1968 - 1979 (Giveaway)(Reprints of Harvey comics)

1968-Richie Rich, Hot Stuff, Casper, Wendy on-c only; Spooky and Nightmare app. inside

| | 4 | 8 | 12 | 22 | 34 | 45 |

1970-Casper, Spooky, Hot Stuff, Stumbo the Giant, Little Audrey, Little Lotta, & Richie Rich reprints. Five different versions

| | 3 | 6 | 9 | 19 | 29 | 38 |

1973,1975,1976: 1973-Three different versions

| | 3 | 6 | 9 | 16 | 23 | 30 |

1977-r/Richie Rich & Casper #20. 1978-r/Richie Rich & Casper #25. 1979-r/Richie Rich & Casper #30 (scarce)

| | 3 | 6 | 9 | 16 | 23 | 28 |

ATARI FORCE
DC Comics: 1982 - No. 5, 1983

1-3 (1982, 5X7", 52 pgs.)-Given away with Atari games

| | 1 | 2 | 3 | 4 | 5 | 7 |

4,5 (1982-1983, 52 pgs.)-Given away with Atari games (scarcer)

| | 2 | 4 | 6 | 8 | 10 | 12 |

AURORA COMIC SCENES INSTRUCTION BOOKLET (Included with superhero model kits)
Aurora Plastics Co.: 1974 (6-1/4x9-3/4", 8 pgs., slick paper)

181-140-Tarzan; Neal Adams-a

| | 3 | 6 | 9 | 18 | 27 | 36 |

182-140-Spider-Man.

| | 4 | 8 | 12 | 24 | 37 | 50 |

183-140-Tonto(Gil Kane art). 184-140-Hulk. 185-140-Superman. 186-140-Superboy. 187-140-Batman. 188-140-The Lone Ranger(1974-by Gil Kane). 192-140-Captain America(1975). 193-140-Robin

| | 3 | 6 | 9 | 16 | 23 | 30 |

BACK TO THE FUTURE
Harvey Comics

Special nn (1991, 20 pgs.)-Brunner-c; given away at Universal Studios in Florida

| | | | | | | 5.00 |

BALTIMORE COLTS
American Visuals Corp.: 1950 (Giveaway)

nn-Eisner-a

| | 45 | 90 | 135 | 275 | 450 | 625 |

BAMBI (Disney)
K. K. Publications (Giveaways): 1941, 1942

1941-Horlick's Malted Milk & various toy stores; text & pictures; most copies mailed out with store stickers on-c

| | 41 | 82 | 123 | 250 | 400 | 550 |

1942-Same as 4-Color #12, but no price (Same as '41 issue?) (Scarce)

| | 66 | 132 | 198 | 413 | 682 | 950 |

BATMAN
DC Comics: 1966 - Present

Act II Popcorn mini-comic(1998)

| | | | | | | 3.00 |

Batman #121 Toys R Us edition (1997) r/1st Mr. Freeze

| | | | | | | 3.00 |

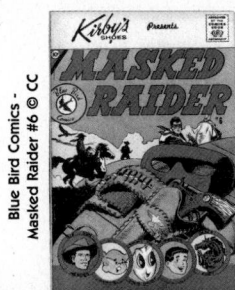

Beetle Bailey Cerebral Palsy Assn. V2 #73 © CC

Blue Bird Comics - Masked Raider #6 © CC

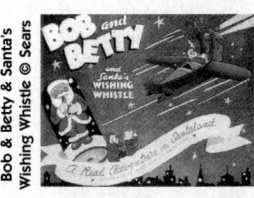

Bob & Betty & Santa's Wishing Whistle © Sears

	GD 2.0	VG 4.0	FN 6.0	VF 8.0	VF/NM 9.0	NM- 9.2

Batman #362 Mervyn's edition (1989) — 4.00
Batman #608 New York Post edition (2002) — 3.00
Batman Adventures #1 Free Comic Book Day edition (6/03) Timm-c — 3.00
Batman Adventures #25 Best Western edition (1997) — 3.00
Batman and Other DC Classics 1 (1989, giveaway)-DC Comics/Diamond Comic Distributors;
  Batman origin-r/Batman #47, Camelot 3000-r, Justice League-r('87), New Teen Titans-r — 4.00
Batman and Robin movie preview (1997, 8 pgs.) Kellogg's Cereal promo — 2.50
Batman Beyond Six Flags edition — 6.00
Batman: Canadian Multiculturalism Custom (1992) — 4.00
Batman Claritan edition (1999) — 2.50
Kellogg's Poptarts comics (1966, Set of 6, 16 pgs.); All were folded and placed in
  Poptarts boxes. Infantino art on Catwoman and Joker issues.
"The Man in the Iron Mask", "The Penguin's Fowl Play", "The Joker's Happy Victims", "The Catwoman's
  Catnapping Caper", "The Mad Hatter's Hat Crimes", "The Case of the Batman II"

| each.... | 4 | 8 | 12 | 28 | 44 | 60 |

Mask of the Phantasm (1993) Mini-comic released w/video

| | 1 | 2 | 3 | 4 | 5 | 7 |

Onstar - Auto Show Special Edition (OnStar Corp., 2001, 8 pgs.) Riddler app. — 2.50
Pizza Hut giveaway (12/77)-exact-r of #122,123; Joker-c/story

| | 2 | 4 | 6 | 8 | 10 | 12 |

Prell Shampoo giveaway (1966, 16 pgs.) - "The Joker's Practical Jokes"
  (6-7/8x3-3/8")

| | 4 | 8 | 12 | 28 | 44 | 60 |

Revell in pack (1995) — 3.00
The Batman Strikes #1 Free Comic Book Day edition (6/05) Penguin app. — 2.50
...: The 10-Cent Adventure (3/02, 10¢) intro. to the "Bruce Wayne: Murderer" x-over; Rucka-s/
  Burchett & Janson-a/Dave Johnson-c; these are alternate copies with special outer half-
  covers (at least 10 different) promoting comics, toys and games shops — 2.50

BATMAN RECORD COMIC
National Periodical Publications: 1966 (one-shot)

| 1-With record (still sealed) | 14 | 28 | 42 | 102 | 181 | 260 |
| Comic only | 8 | 16 | 24 | 58 | 97 | 135 |

BATTLESTAR GALACTICA SEASON ZERO/THE LONE RANGER #0
Dynamite Entertainment: 2007 Free Comic Book Day Edition

nn-Flip book with Cassaday Lone Ranger-c — 2.25

BEETLE BAILEY
Charlton Comics: 1969-1970 (Giveaways)

Armed Forces ('69)-same as regular issue (#68)	2	4	6	10	14	18
Bold Detergent ('69)-same as regular issue (#67)	2	4	6	10	14	18
Cerebral Palsy Assn. V2#71('69) - V2#73(#1,1/70)	2	4	6	10	14	18
Red Cross (1969, 5x7", 16 pgs., paper-c)	2	4	6	10	14	18

BEST WESTERN GIVEAWAY
DC Comics: 1999

nn-Best Western hotels — 2.50

BETTER LIFE FOR YOU, A
Harvey Publications Inc.: (16 pgs., paper cover)

| nn-Better living through higher productivity | 3 | 6 | 9 | 16 | 22 | 28 |

BETTY AND VERONICA
Archie Comic Publications: 2005

... Free Comic Book Day Edition #1 (6/05) Katy Keene-c/app.; Cheryl Blossom app. — 2.50

BEWARE THE BOOBY TRAP
Malcolm Alter: 1970 (5" x 7")

| nn-Deals with drug abuse | 4 | 8 | 12 | 24 | 37 | 50 |

B-FORCE (Milwaukee Brewers and Wisconsin Dental Asso.)
Dark Horse Comics: 2001 (School and stadium giveaway)

nn-Brewers players combat the evils of smokeless tobacco — 3.00

BIG BOY (see Adventures of...)

BIG JIM'S P.A.C.K.
Mattel, Inc. (Marvel Comics): No date (1975) (16 pgs.)

| nn-Giveaway with Big Jim doll; Buscema/Sinnott-c/a | 4 | 8 | 12 | 22 | 34 | 45 |

"BILL AND TED'S EXCELLENT ADVENTURE" MOVIE ADAPTATION
DC Comics: 1989 (No cover price)

nn-Torres-a — 4.00

BIONICLE (LEGO robot toys)
DC Comics: Jun, 2001 - No. 18 ($2.25/$3.25, 16 pages, available to LEGO club members)

1	1	2	3	5	6	8
2-5						6.00
6-13						4.00
14-18						3.00
The Legend of Bionicle (McDonald's Mini-comic, 4-1/4 x 7")						4.00
Special Edition #0 (Six Heroes...One Destiny) '03 San Diego Comic Con; Ashley Wood-c						6.00

BLACK GOLD
Esso Service Station (Giveaway): 1945? (8 pgs. in color)

| nn-Reprints from True Comics | 6 | 12 | 18 | 27 | 33 | 38 |

BLAZING FOREST, THE (See Forest Fire and Smokey Bear)
Western Printing: 1962 (20 pgs., 5x7", slick-c)

| nn-Smokey The Bear fire prevention | 2 | 4 | 6 | 12 | 16 | 20 |

BLESSED PIUS X
Catechetical Guild (Giveaway): No date (Text/comics, 32 pgs., paper-c)

| nn | 6 | 12 | 18 | 28 | 34 | 40 |

BLIND JUSTICE (Also see Batman: Blind Justice)
DC Comics/Diamond Comic Distributors: 1989 (Giveaway, squarebound)

nn-Contains Detective #598-600 by Batman movie writer Sam Hamm, w/covers; published
  same time as originals? — 6.00

BLONDIE COMICS
Harvey Publications: 1950-1964

1950 Giveaway	7	14	21	37	46	55
1962,1964 Giveaway	3	6	9	16	22	28
N. Y. State Dept. of Mental Hygiene Giveaway-(1950) Regular size;						
16 pgs.; no #	4	8	12	22	34	45
N. Y. State Dept. of Mental Hygiene Giveaway-(1956) Regular size;						
16 pgs.; no #	3	6	9	16	23	30
N. Y. State Dept. of Mental Hygiene Giveaway-(1961) Regular size;						
16 pgs.; no #	3	6	9	15	21	26

BLOOD IS THE HARVEST
Catechetical Guild: 1950 (32 pgs., paper-c)

(Scarce)-Anti-communism (13 known copies)	166	332	498	1038	1719	2400
Black & white version (5 known copies), saddle stitched						
	86	174	258	538	894	1250

Untrimmed version (only one known copy); estimated value - $1000
NOTE: In 1979 nine copies of the color version surfaced from the old Guild's files plus the five black & white copies.

BLUE BIRD CHILDREN'S MAGAZINE, THE
Graphic Information Service: V1#2, 1957 - No. 10 1958 (16 pgs., soft-c, regular size)

| V1#2-10: Pat, Pete & Blue Bird app. | 2 | 4 | 6 | 8 | 11 | 14 |

BLUE BIRD COMICS
Various Shoe Stores/Charlton Comics: Late 1940's - 1964 (Giveaway)

nn(1947-50)(36 pgs.)-Several issues; Human Torch, Sub-Mariner app. in some						
	17	34	51	98	154	210
1959-Li'l Genius, Timmy the Timid Ghost, Wild Bill Hickok (All #1)						
	3	6	9	16	21	26
1959-(6 titles; all #2) Black Fury #1,4,5, Freddy #4, Li'l Genius, Timmy the Timid Ghost #4,						
Masked Raider #4, Wild Bill Hickok (Charlton)	3	6	9	14	20	25
1959-(#5) Masked Raider #21	3	6	9	16	22	28
1960-(6 titles)(All #4) Black Fury #6,8,9, Masked Raider #6, Freddy #8,9, Timmy the Timid						
Ghost #6,9, Li'l Genius #7,9 (Charlt.)	3	6	9	14	19	24
1961,1962-(All 10's) Black Fury #12,13,16, Black Fury #11,12, Freddy, Li'l Genius,						
Masked Raider, Six Gun Heroes, Texas Rangers in Action, Timmy the Ghost, Wild Bill						
Hickok, Wyatt Earp #3,11-13,16-18 (Charlton)	2	4	6	13	18	22
1963-Texas Rangers #17 (Charlton)	2	4	6	9	13	16
1964-Mysteries of Unexplored Worlds #18, Teenage Hotrodders #18, War Heroes #18						
(Charlton)	2	4	6	8	13	16
1965-War Heroes #18	2	4	6	8	10	12

NOTE: More than one issue of each character could have been published each year. Numbering is sporadic.

BOB & BETTY & SANTA'S WISHING WHISTLE
Sears Roebuck & Co.: 1941 (Christmas giveaway, 12 pgs.)

| nn | 12 | 24 | 36 | 67 | 94 | 120 |

BOBBY BENSON'S B-BAR-B RIDERS (Radio)
Magazine Enterprises/AC Comics

...in the Tunnel of Gold-(1936, 5-1/4x8"; 100 pgs.) Radio giveaway by Hecker-H.O. Company
  (H.O. Oats); contains 22 color pgs. of comics, rest in novel form

| | 11 | 22 | 33 | 60 | 83 | 105 |
| ...And The Lost Herd-same as above | 11 | 22 | 33 | 60 | 83 | 105 |

BOBBY SHELBY COMICS
Shelby Cycle Co./Harvey Publications: 1949

| nn | 5 | 10 | 14 | 20 | 24 | 28 |

BONGO COMICS ...
Bongo Comics: 2005; 2006; 2007 (Free Comic Book Day giveaways)

Gimme Gimme Giveaway! (2005) - Short stories from Simpsons Comics, Futurama Comics
  and Radioactive Man — 2.50
Free-For-All! (2006, 2007) - Short stories in each — 2.50

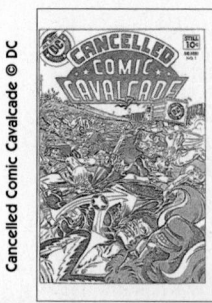
	GD 2.0	VG 4.0	FN 6.0	VF 8.0	VF/NM 9.0	NM- 9.2

BOY SCOUT ADVENTURE
Boy Scouts of America: 1954 (16 pgs., paper cover)
nn — 5, 10, 14, 20, 24, 28

BOYS' RANCH
Harvey Publications: 1951
Shoe Store Giveaway #5,6 (Identical to regular issues except Simon & Kirby centerfold replaced with ad) — 14, 28, 42, 80, 115, 150

BOZO THE CLOWN (TV)
Dell Publishing Co.: 1961
Giveaway-1961, 16 pgs., 3-1/2x7-1/4", Apsco Products — 5, 10, 15, 32, 51, 70

BRER RABBIT IN "ICE CREAM FOR THE PARTY"
American Dairy Association: 1955 (5x7-1/4", 16 pgs., soft-c) (Walt Disney) (Premium)
nn-(Scarce) — 38, 76, 114, 219, 347, 475

BUCK ROGERS (In the 25th Century)
Kelloggs Corn Flakes Giveaway: 1933 (6x8", 36 pgs)
370A-By Phil Nowlan & Dick Calkins; 1st Buck Rogers radio premium & 1st app. in comics (tells origin) (Reissued in 1995) — 110, 220, 330, 800, -, -
with envelope — 130, 260, 390, 950, -, -

BUGS BUNNY (Puffed Rice Giveaway)
Quaker Cereals: 1949 (32 pgs. each, 3-1/8x6-7/8")
A1-Traps the Counterfeiters, A2-Aboard Mystery Submarine, A3- Rocket to the Moon, A4-Lion Tamer, A5-Rescues the Beautiful Princess, B1-Buried Treasure, B2-Outwits the Smugglers, B3-Joins the Marines, B4-Meets the Dwarf Ghost, B5-Finds Aladdin's Lamp, C1-Lost in the Frozen North, C2-Secret Agent, C3-Captured by Cannibals, C4-Fights the Man from Mars, C5-And the Haunted Cave
each.... — 9, 18, 27, 50, 65, 80
Mailing Envelope (has illo of Bugs on front)(Each envelope designates what set it contains, A,B or C on front) — 9, 18, 27, 50, 65, 80

BUGS BUNNY (3-D)
Cheerios Giveaway: 1953 (Pocket size) (15 titles)
each.... — 11, 22, 33, 60, 83, 105
Mailing Envelope (has Bugs drawn on front) — 11, 22, 33, 60, 83, 105

BUGS BUNNY
DC Comics: May, 1997 ($4.95, 24 pgs., comic-sized)
1-Numbered ed. of 100,000; "1st Day of Issue" stamp cancellation on-c — 6.00

BUGS BUNNY POSTAL COMIC
DC Comics: 1997 (64 pgs., 7.5" x 5")
nn -Mail Fan; Daffy Duck app. — 4.50

BULLETMAN
Fawcett Publications
Well Known Comics (1942)-Paper-c, glued binding; printed in red (Bestmaid/Samuel Lowe giveaway) — 15, 30, 45, 85, 130, 175

BULLS-EYE (Cody of The Pony Express No. 8 on)
Charlton: 1955
Great Scott Shoe Store giveaway-Reprints #2 with new cover — 18, 36, 54, 103, 162, 220

BUSTER BROWN COMICS (Radio)(Also see My Dog Tige in Promotional sec.)
Brown Shoe Co: 1945 - No. 43, 1959 (No. 5: paper-c)
nn, nd (#1,scarce)-Featuring Smilin' Ed McConnell & the Buster Brown gang "Midnight" the cat, "Squeaky" the mouse & "Froggy" the Gremlin; covers mention diff. shoe stores.
Contains adventure stories — 61, 122, 183, 381, 633, 885
2 — 18, 36, 54, 105, 165, 225
3,5-10 — 12, 24, 36, 69, 97, 125
4 (Rare)-Low print run due to paper shortage — 15, 30, 45, 90, 140, 190
11-20 — 9, 18, 27, 47, 61, 75
21-24,26-28 — 6, 12, 18, 31, 38, 45
25,33-37,40,41-Crandall-a in all — 10, 20, 30, 56, 76, 95
29-32-"Interplanetary Police Vs. the Space Siren" by Crandall (pencils only #29) — 10, 20, 30, 58, 79, 100
38,39,42,43 — 6, 12, 18, 31, 38, 45

BUSTER BROWN COMICS (Radio)
Brown Shoe Co: 1950s
...Goes to Mars (2/58-Western Printing), slick-c, 20 pgs., reg. size — 11, 22, 33, 64, 90, 115
...In "Buster Makes the Team!" (1959-Custom Comics) — 8, 16, 24, 44, 57, 70
...In The Jet Age ('50s), slick-c, 20 pgs., 5x7-1/4" — 10, 20, 30, 58, 79, 100
...Of the Safety Patrol ('60-Custom Comics) — 3, 6, 9, 18, 27, 35
...Out of This World ('59-Custom Comics) — 7, 14, 21, 35, 43, 50
...Safety Coloring Book ('58, 16 pgs.)-Slick paper — 7, 14, 21, 35, 43, 50

CALL FROM CHRIST
Catechetical Educational Society: 1952 (Giveaway, 36 pgs.)
nn — 6, 12, 18, 28, 34, 40

CANCELLED COMIC CAVALCADE
DC Comics, Inc.: Summer, 1978 - No. 2, Fall, 1978 (8-1/2x11", B&W)
(Xeroxed pgs. on one side only w/blue cover and taped spine)(Only 35 sets produced)
1-(412 pgs.) Contains xeroxed copies of art for: Black Lightning #12, cover to #13; Claw #13,14; The Deserter #1; Doorway to Nightmare #6; Firestorm #6; The Green Team #2,3.
2-(532 pgs.) Contains xeroxed copies of art for: Kamandi #60 (including Omac), #61; Prez #5; Shade #9 (including The Odd Man); Showcase #105 (Deadman), 106 (The Creeper); Secret Society of Super Villains #16 & 17; The Vixen #1; and covers to Army at War #2, Battle Classics #3, Demand Classics #1 & 2, Dynamic Classics #3, Mr. Miracle #26, Ragman #6, Weird Mystery #25 & 26, & Western Classics #1 & 2.
(A FN set of Number 1 & 2 was sold in 2005 for $3680; a VG set sold in 2007 for $2629)
NOTE: In June, 1978, DC cancelled several of their titles. For copyright purposes, the unpublished original art for these titles was xeroxed, bound in the above books, published and distributed. Only 35 copies were made. Beware of bootleg copies.

CAP'N CRUNCH COMICS (See Quaker Oats)
Quaker Oats Co.: 1963; 1965 (16 pgs.; miniature giveaways; 2-1/2x6-1/2")
(1963 titles)- "The Picture Pirates", "The Fountain of Youth", "I'm Dreaming of a Wide Isthmus". (1965 titles)- "Bewitched, Betwitched, & Betweaked", "Seadog Meets the Witch Doctor", "A Witch in Time" — 5, 10, 15, 35, 55, 75

CAPTAIN ACTION (Toy)
National Periodical Publications
...& Action Boy('67)-Ideal Toy Co. giveaway (1st app. Captain Action) — 12, 24, 36, 84, 150, 215

CAPTAIN AMERICA
Marvel Comics Group
...& The Campbell Kids (1980, 36pg. giveaway, Campbell's Soup/U.S. Dept. of Energy) — 2, 4, 6, 8, 10, 12
...Goes To War Against Drugs(1990, no #, giveaway)-Distributed to direct sales shops; 2nd printing exists — 6.00
...Meets The Asthma Monster (1987, no #, giveaway, Your Physician and Glaxo, Inc.) — 6.00
Return of the Asthma Monster Vol. 1 #2 (1992, giveaway, Your Physician & Allen & Hanbury's) — 6.00
...Vs. Asthma Monster (1990, no #, giveaway, Your Physician & Allen & Hanbury's) — 6.00

CAPTAIN AMERICA COMICS
Timely/Marvel Comics: 1954
Shoestore Giveaway #77 — 68, 136, 204, 425, 705, 985

CAPTAIN ATOM
Nationwide Publishers
...- Secret of the Columbian Jungle (16 pgs. in color, paper-c, 3-3/4x5-1/8")- Fireside Marshmallow giveaway — 6, 12, 18, 28, 34, 40

CAPTAIN BEN DIX
Bendix Aviation Corporation: 1943 (Small size)
nn — 8, 16, 24, 42, 54, 65

CAPTAIN BEN DIX IN ACTION WITH THE INVISIBLE CREW
Bendix Aviation Corp.: 1940s (nd), (20 pgs, 8-1/4"x11", heavy paper)
nn-WWII bomber-c; Jap app. — 7, 14, 21, 35, 43, 50

CAPTAIN BEN DIX IN SECRETS OF THE INVISIBLE CREW
Bendix Aviation Corp.: 1940s (nd), (32 pgs, soft-c)
nn — 6, 12, 18, 31, 38, 45

CAPTAIN FORTUNE PRESENTS
Vital Publications: 1955 - 1959 (Giveaway, 3-1/4x6-7/8", 16 pgs.)
"Davy Crockett in Episodes of the Creek War", "Davy Crockett at the Alamo", "In Sherwood Forest Tells Strange Tales of Robin Hood" ('57), "Meets Bolivar the Liberator" ('59), "Tells How Buffalo Bill Fights the Dog Soldiers" ('57), "Young Davy Crockett" — 4, 7, 9, 14, 17, 20

CAPTAIN GALLANT (...of the Foreign Legion) (TV)
Charlton Comics
Heinz Foods premium (#1?)(1955; regular size)-U.S. Pictorial; contains Buster Crabbe photos; Don Heck-a — 1, 3, 4, 6, 8, 10
Mailing Envelope — 20.00

CAPTAIN MARVEL ADVENTURES
Fawcett Publications
Bond Bread Giveaways-(24 pgs.; pocket size-7-1/4x3-1/2"; paper cover): "...& the Stolen City" ('48), "The Boy Who Never Heard of Capt. Marvel", "Meets the Weatherman" (1950) (reprint) each.... — 23, 46, 69, 135, 213, 290
...Well Known Comics (1944; 12 pgs.; 8-1/2x10-1/2")-printed in red & in blue; soft-c; glued binding - (Bestmaid/Samuel Lowe Co. giveaway) — 16, 32, 48, 94, 147, 200

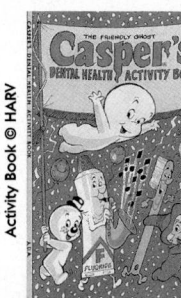
Casper's Dental Health Activity Book © HARV

Cheerios Premium W3 © DIS

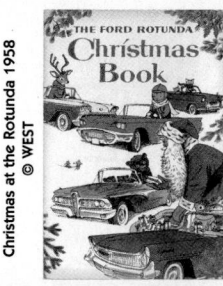
Christmas at the Rotunda 1958 © WEST

	GD 2.0	VG 4.0	FN 6.0	VF 8.0	VF/NM 9.0	NM- 9.2

CAPTAIN MARVEL ADVENTURES (Also see Flash and Funny Stuff)
Fawcett Publications (Wheaties Giveaway): 1945 (6x8", full color, paper-c)

	GD 2.0	VG 4.0	FN 6.0	VF 8.0	VF/NM 9.0	NM- 9.2
nn- "Captain Marvel & the Threads of Life" plus 2 other stories (32 pgs.)						
	110	275	450	700	-	-

NOTE: All copies were taped at each corner to a box of Wheaties and are never found in Fine or Mint condition. Prices listed for each grade include tape.

CAPTAIN MARVEL AND THE LTS. OF SAFETY
Ebasco Services/Fawcett Publications: 1950 - 1951 (3 issues - no No.'s)

	GD	VG	FN	VF	VF/NM	NM-
nn (#1) "Danger Flies a Kite" ('50, scarce),	110	220	330	688	1144	1600
nn (#2) "Danger Takes to Climbing" ('50),	86	172	258	538	894	1250
nn (#3) "Danger Smashes Street Lights" ('51)	86	172	258	538	894	1250

CAPTAIN MARVEL, JR.
Fawcett Publications: (1944; 12 pgs.; 8-1/2x10-1/2")

	GD	VG	FN	VF	VF/NM	NM-
...Well Known Comics (Printed in blue; paper-c, glued binding)-Bestmaid/Samuel Lowe Co. giveaway	14	28	42	76	108	140

CARDINAL MINDSZENTY (The Truth Behind the Trial of...)
Catechetical Guild Education Society: 1949 (24 pgs., paper cover)

	GD	VG	FN	VF	VF/NM	NM-
nn-Anti-communism	10	20	30	56	76	95
Press Proof-(Very Rare)-(Full color, 7-1/2x11-3/4", untrimmed) Only two known copies						275.00
Preview Copy (B&W, stapled), 18 pgs.; contains first 13 pgs. of Cardinal Mindszenty and was sent out as an advance promotion. Only one known copy					275.00 - 375.00	

NOTE: Regular edition also printed in French. There was also a movie released in 1949 called "Guilty of Treason" which is a fact-based account of the trial and imprisonment of Cardinal Mindszenty by the Communist regime in Hungary.

CARNIVAL OF COMICS
Fleet-Air Shoes: 1954 (Giveaway)

	GD	VG	FN	VF	VF/NM	NM-
nn-Contains a comic bound with new cover; several combinations possible; Charlton's Eh! known	5	10	15	24	30	35

CARTOON NETWORK
DC Comics: 1997 (Giveaway)

nn-reprints Cow and Chicken, Scooby-Doo, & Flintstones stories						4.00

CARVEL COMICS (Amazing Advs. of Capt. Carvel)
Carvel Corp. (Ice Cream): 1975 - No. 5, 1976 (25¢; #3-5: 35¢) (#4,5: 3-1/4x5")

	GD	VG	FN	VF	VF/NM	NM-
1-3	1	2	3	5	6	8
4,5(1976)-Baseball theme	2	4	6	8	10	12

CASE OF THE WASTED WATER, THE
Rheem Water Heating: 1972? (Giveaway)

	GD	VG	FN	VF	VF/NM	NM-
nn-Neal Adams-a	4	8	12	26	41	55

CASPER SPECIAL
Target Stores (Harvey): nd (Dec, 1990) (Giveaway with $1.00 cover)

Three issues-Given away with Casper video						6.00

CASPER, THE FRIENDLY GHOST (Paramount Picture Star...)(2nd Series)
Harvey Publications
American Dental Association (Giveaways):

	GD	VG	FN	VF	VF/NM	NM-
...'s Dental Health Activity Book-1977	2	4	6	8	10	12
...Presents Space Age Dentistry-1972	2	4	6	8	11	14
..., His Den, & Their Dentist Fight the Tooth Demons-1974						
	2	4	6	8	11	14

CELEBRATE THE CENTURY SUPERHEROES STAMP ALBUM
DC Comics: 1998 - No. 5, 2000 (32 pgs.)

1-5: Historical stories hosted by DC heroes						3.00

CENTIPEDE
DC Comics: 1983

	GD	VG	FN	VF	VF/NM	NM-
1-Based on Atari video game	1	3	4	6	8	10

CENTURY OF COMICS
Eastern Color Printing Co.: 1933 (100 pgs.)
Bought by Wheatena, Malt-O-Milk, John Wanamaker, Kinney Shoe Stores, & others to be used as premiums and radio giveaways. No publisher listed.

	GD	VG	FN	VF	VF/NM	NM-
nn-Mutt & Jeff, Joe Palooka, etc. reprints	3670	7335	11,000	25,000	-	-

CHEERIOS PREMIUMS (Disney)
Walt Disney Productions: 1947 (16 titles, pocket size, 32 pgs.)

	GD	VG	FN	VF	VF/NM	NM-
Mailing Envelope for each set "W,X,Y & Z" (has Mickey illo on front)(each envelope designates the set it contains on the front)	11	22	33	60	83	105
Set "W"						
W1-Donald Duck & the Pirates	11	22	33	60	83	105
W2-Bucky Bug & the Cannibal King	7	14	21	37	46	55
W3-Pluto Joins the F.B.I.	7	14	21	37	46	55
W4-Mickey Mouse & the Haunted House	8	16	24	42	54	65
Set "X"						

	GD	VG	FN	VF	VF/NM	NM-
X1-Donald Duck, Counter Spy	11	22	33	60	83	105
X2-Goofy Lost in the Desert	7	14	21	37	46	55
X3-Br'er Rabbit Outwits Br'er Fox	7	14	21	37	46	55
X4-Mickey Mouse at the Rodeo	8	16	24	42	54	65
Set "Y"						
Y1-Donald Duck's Atom Bomb by Carl Barks. Disney has banned reprinting this book						
	88	176	264	550	913	1275
Y2-Br'er Rabbit's Secret	7	14	21	37	46	55
Y3-Dumbo & the Circus Mystery	7	14	21	37	46	55
Y4-Mickey Mouse Meets the Wizard	8	16	24	42	54	65
Set "Z"						
Z1-Donald Duck Pilots a Jet Plane (not by Barks)	11	22	33	60	83	105
Z2-Pluto Turns Sleuth Hound	7	14	21	37	46	55
Z3-The Seven Dwarfs & the Enchanted Mtn.	8	16	24	42	54	65
Z4-Mickey Mouse's Secret Room	8	16	24	42	54	65

CHEERIOS 3-D GIVEAWAYS (Disney)
Walt Disney Productions: 1954 (24 titles, pocket size) (Glasses came in envelopes)

	GD	VG	FN	VF	VF/NM	NM-
Glasses only...	8	16	24	40	50	60
Mailing Envelope (no art on front)	9	18	27	47	61	75
(Set 1)						
1-Donald Duck & Uncle Scrooge, the Firefighters	9	18	27	52	69	85
2-Mickey Mouse & Goofy, Pirate Plunder	9	18	27	47	61	75
3-Donald Duck's Nephews, the Fabulous Inventors	9	18	27	52	69	85
4-Mickey Mouse, Secret of the Ming Vase	9	18	27	47	61	75
5-Donald Duck with Huey, Dewey, & Louie; ...the Seafarers (title on 2nd page)						
	9	18	27	52	69	85
6-Mickey Mouse, Moaning Mountain	9	18	27	47	61	75
7-Donald Duck, Apache Gold	9	18	27	52	69	85
8-Mickey Mouse, Flight to Nowhere	9	18	27	47	61	75
(Set 2)						
1-Donald Duck, Treasure of Timbuktu	9	18	27	52	69	85
2-Mickey Mouse & Pluto, Operation China	9	18	27	47	61	75
3-Donald Duck and the Magic Cows	9	18	27	52	69	85
4-Mickey Mouse & Goofy, Kid Kokonut	9	18	27	47	61	75
5-Donald Duck, Mystery Ship	9	18	27	52	69	85
6-Mickey Mouse, Phantom Sheriff	9	18	27	47	61	75
7-Donald Duck, Circus Adventures	9	18	27	52	69	85
8-Mickey Mouse, Arctic Explorers	9	18	27	47	61	75
(Set 3)						
1-Donald Duck & Witch Hazel	9	18	27	52	69	85
2-Mickey Mouse in Darkest Africa	9	18	27	47	61	75
3-Donald Duck & Uncle Scrooge, Timber Trouble	9	18	27	52	69	85
4-Mickey Mouse, Rajah's Rescue	9	18	27	47	61	75
5-Donald Duck in Robot Reporter	9	18	27	52	69	85
6-Mickey Mouse, Slumbering Sleuth	9	18	27	47	61	75
7-Donald Duck in the Foreign Legion	9	18	27	52	69	85
8-Mickey Mouse, Airwalking Wonder	9	18	27	47	61	75

CHESTY AND COPTIE (Disney)
Los Angeles Community Chest: 1946 (Giveaway, 4pgs.)

	GD	VG	FN	VF	VF/NM	NM-
nn-(One known copy) by Floyd Gottfredson	83	162	249	519	860	1200

CHESTY AND HIS HELPERS (Disney)
Los Angeles War Chest: 1943 (Giveaway, 12 pgs., 5-1/2x7-1/4")

	GD	VG	FN	VF	VF/NM	NM-
nn-Chesty & Coptie	55	110	165	336	543	750

CHOCOLATE THE FLAVOR OF FRIENDSHIP AROUND THE WORLD
The Nestle Company: 1955

	GD	VG	FN	VF	VF/NM	NM-
nn	4	8	12	21	30	40

CHRISTMAS ADVENTURE, THE
S. Rose (H. L. Green Giveaway): 1963 (16 pgs.)

	GD	VG	FN	VF	VF/NM	NM-
nn	2	4	6	10	13	16

CHRISTMAS AT THE ROTUNDA (Titled Ford Rotunda Christmas Book 1957 on) (Regular size)
Ford Motor Co. (Western Printing): 1954 - 1961 (Given away every Christmas at one location)

	GD	VG	FN	VF	VF/NM	NM-
1954-56 issues (nn's)	5	10	15	24	30	35
1957-61 issues (nn's)	5	10	14	20	24	28

CHRISTMAS CAROL, A
Sears Roebuck & Co.: No date (1942-43) (Giveaway, 32 pgs., 8-1/4x10-3/4", paper cover)

	GD	VG	FN	VF	VF/NM	NM-
nn-Comics & coloring book	17	34	51	98	154	210

CHRISTMAS CAROL, A
Sears Roebuck & Co.: 1940s ? (Christmas giveaway, 20 pgs.)

	GD	VG	FN	VF	VF/NM	NM-
nn-Comic book & animated coloring book	15	30	45	88	137	185

CHRISTMAS CAROLS
Hot Shoppes Giveaway: 1959? (16 pgs.)

297

The Christophers © CG

Cinema Comics Herald - Thunder Birds © 20th Century Fox

Classics Giveaways - 12/69 Stacey's

	GD 2.0	VG 4.0	FN 6.0	VF 8.0	VF/NM 9.0	NM- 9.2
nn	4	8	11	16	19	22
CHRISTMAS COLORING FUN H. Burnside: 1964 (20 pgs., slick-c, B&W)						
nn	2	4	6	11	16	20
CHRISTMAS DREAM, A Promotional Publishing Co.: 1950 (Kinney Shoe Store Giveaway, 16 pgs.)						
nn	5	10	15	23	28	32
CHRISTMAS DREAM, A J. J. Newberry Co.: 1952? (Giveaway, paper cover, 16 pgs.)						
nn	4	8	12	18	22	25
CHRISTMAS DREAM, A Promotional Publ. Co.: 1952 (Giveaway, 16 pgs., paper cover)						
nn	4	8	12	18	22	25
CHRISTMAS FUN AROUND THE WORLD No publisher: No date (early 50's) (16 pgs., paper cover)						
nn	5	10	15	22	26	30
CHRISTMAS IS COMING! No publisher: No date (early 50's?) (Store giveaway, 16 pgs.)						
nn	4	8	12	18	22	25
CHRISTMAS JOURNEY THROUGH SPACE Promotional Publishing Co.: 1960						
nn-Reprints 1954 issue Jolly Christmas Book with new slick cover	3	6	9	16	23	30
CHRISTMAS ON THE MOON W. T. Grant Co.: 1958 (Giveaway, 20 pgs., slick cover)						
nn	8	16	24	44	57	70
CHRISTMAS PLAY BOOK Gould-Stoner Co.: 1946 (Giveaway, 16 pgs., paper cover)						
nn	8	16	24	44	57	70
CHRISTMAS ROUNDUP Promotional Publishing Co.: 1960						
nn-Marv Levy-c/a	2	4	6	9	13	16
CHRISTMAS STORY CUT-OUT BOOK, THE Catechetical Guild: No. 393, 1951 (15¢, 36 pgs.)						
393-Half text & half comics	8	16	24	42	54	65
CHRISTMAS USA (Through 300 Years) (Also see Uncle Sam's...) Promotional Publ. Co.: 1956 (Giveaway)						
nn-Marv Levy-c/a		7	9	14	16	18
CHRISTMAS WITH SNOW WHITE AND THE SEVEN DWARFS Kobackers Giftstore of Buffalo, N.Y.: 1953 (16 pgs., paper-c)						
nn	8	16	24	42	54	65
CHRISTOPHERS, THE Catechetical Guild: 1951 (Giveaway, 36 pgs.) (Some copies have 15¢ sticker)						
nn-Stalin as Satan in Hell	23	46	69	130	205	280
CINDERELLA IN "FAIREST OF THE FAIR" American Dairy Association (Premium): 1955 (5x7-1/4", 16 pgs., soft-c) (Walt Disney)						
nn	10	20	30	56	76	95
CINEMA COMICS HERALD Paramount Pictures/Universal/RKO/20th Century Fox/Republic: 1941 - 1943 (4-pg. movie "trailers", paper-c, 7-1/2x10-1/2")(Giveaway)						
"Mr. Bug Goes to Town" (1941)	15	30	45	84	127	170
"Bedtime Story"	10	20	30	58	79	100
"Lady For A Night", John Wayne, Joan Blondell ('42)	17	34	51	98	154	210
"Reap The Wild Wind" (1942)	11	22	33	62	86	110
"Thunder Birds" (1942)	10	20	30	58	79	100
"They All Kissed the Bride"	10	20	30	58	79	100
"Arabian Nights" (nd)	11	22	33	62	86	110
"Bombardie" (1943)	10	20	30	58	79	100
"Crash Dive" (1943)-Tyrone Power	11	22	33	62	86	110

NOTE: *The 1941-42 issues contain line art with color photos. 1943 issues are line art.*

	GD 2.0	VG 4.0	FN 6.0	VF 8.0	VF/NM 9.0	NM- 9.2
CLASSICS GIVEAWAYS (Classic Comics reprints)						
12/41–Walter Theatre Enterprises (Huntington, WV) giveaway containing #2 (orig.) w/new generic-c (only 1 known copy)	76	152	228	475	788	1100
1942–Double Comics containing CC#1 (orig.) (diff. cover) (not actually a giveaway) (very rare) (also see Double Comics) (only one known copy)	145	290	435	906	1503	2100

	GD 2.0	VG 4.0	FN 6.0	VF 8.0	VF/NM 9.0	NM- 9.2
12/42–Saks 34th St. Giveaway containing CC#7 (orig.) (diff. cover) (very rare; only 6 known copies)	300	600	900	1970	3485	5000
2/43–American Comics containing CC#8 (orig.) (Liberty Theatre giveaway) (different cover) (only one known copy) (see American Comics)	103	206	309	644	1072	1500
12/44–Robin Hood Flour Co. Giveaway - #7-CC(R) (diff. cover) (rare) (edition probably 5 [22])	166	332	498	1038	1719	2400

NOTE: How are above editions determined without CC covers? 1942 is dated 1942, and CC#1-first reprint did not come out until 5/43. 12/42 and 2/43 are determined by blue note at bottom of first text page only in original edition. 12/44 is estimated from page width each reprint edition had progressively slightly smaller page width.

	GD 2.0	VG 4.0	FN 6.0	VF 8.0	VF/NM 9.0	NM- 9.2
1951–Shelter Thru the Ages (C.I. Educational Series) (actually Giveaway by the Ruberoid Co.) (16 pgs.) (contains original artwork by H. C. Kiefer) (there are 5 diff. back cover ad variations: "Ranch" house ad, "Igloo" ad, "Doll House" ad, "Tree House" ad & blank) (scarce)	55	110	165	344	572	800
1952–George Daynor Biography Giveaway (CC logo) (partly comic book/pictures/newspaper articles) (story of man who built Palace Depression out of junkyard swamp in NJ) (64 pgs.) (very rare; only 3 known copies, one missing back-c)	382	764	1146	2483	4392	6300
1953–Westinghouse/Dreams of a Man (C.I. Educational Series) (Westinghousebio./ Westinghouse Co. giveaway) (contains original artwork by H. C. Kiefer) (16 pgs.) (also French/Spanish/Italian versions) (scarce)	50	100	150	305	503	700

NOTE: Reproductions of 1951, 1952, and 1953 exist with color photocopy covers and black & white photocopy interior ("W.C.N. Reprint")

	GD 2.0	VG 4.0	FN 6.0	VF 8.0	VF/NM 9.0	NM- 9.2
	2	4	5	7	8	10
1951-53–Coward Shoe Giveaways (all editions very rare); 2 variations of back-c ad exist: With back-c photo ad: 5 (87), 12 (89), 22 (85), 32 (85), 49 (85), 69 (87), 72 (no HRN), 80 (0), 91 (0), 92 (0), 96 (0), 98 (0), 100 (0), 101 (0), 103-105 (all Os)	31	62	93	178	282	385
With back-c cartoon ad: 106-109 (all Os), 110 (111), 112 (0)	34	68	102	195	308	420
1956–Ben Franklin 5-10 Store Giveaway (#65-PC with back cover ad) (scarce)	26	52	78	152	239	325
1956–Ben Franklin Insurance Co. Giveaway (#65-PC with diff. back cover ad) (very rare)	50	100	150	305	503	700
11/56–Sealtest Co. Edition - #4 (135) (identical to regular edition except for Sealtest logo printed, not stamped, on front cover) (only two copies known to exist)	30	60	90	174	275	375
1958–Get-Well Giveaway containing #15-CI (new cartoon-type cover) (Pressman Pharmacy) (only one copy known to exist)	28	56	84	162	256	350
1967-68–Twin Circle Giveaway Editions - all HRN 166, with back cover ad for National Catholic Press.						
2(R68), 4(R67), 10(R68), 13(R68)	3	6	9	18	27	35
48(R67), 128(R68), 535(576-R68)	3	6	9	20	30	40
16(R68), 68(R67)	4	8	12	26	41	55
12/69–Christmas Giveaway ("A Christmas Adventure") (reprints Picture Parade #4-1953, new cover) (4 ad variations)						
Stacey's Dept. Store	3	6	9	18	27	35
Anne & Hope Store	4	8	12	28	44	60
Gibson's Dept. Store (rare)	4	8	12	28	44	60
"Merry Christmas" & blank ad space	3	6	9	18	27	35
CLIFF MERRITT SETS THE RECORD STRAIGHT Brotherhood of Railroad Trainsmen: Giveaway (2 different issues)						
...and the Very Candid Candidate by Al Williamson	1	3	4	6	8	10
...Sets the Record Straight by Al Williamson (2 different-c: one by Williamson, the other by McWilliams)	1	3	4	6	8	10
CLYDE BEATTY COMICS (Also see Crackajack Funnies) Commodore Productions & Artists, Inc.						
...African Jungle Book('56)-Richfield Oil Co. 16 pg. giveaway, soft-c	10	20	30	54	72	90
C-M-O COMICS Chicago Mail Order Co.(Centaur): 1942 - No. 2, 1942 (68 pgs.), full color)						
1-Invisible Terror, Super Ann, & Plymo the Rubber Man app. (all Centaur costume heroes)	88	176	264	550	913	1275
2-Invisible Terror, Super Ann app.	53	106	159	323	529	735
COCOMALT BIG BOOK OF COMICS Harry 'A' Chesler (Cocomalt Premium): 1938 (Reg. size, full color, 52 pgs.)						
1-(Scarce)-Biro-c/a; Little Nemo by Winsor McCay Jr., Dan Hastings; Jack Cole, Guardineer, Gustavson, Bob Wood-a	214	428	642	1338	2219	3100
COMIC BOOK (Also see Comics From Weatherbird) American Juniors Shoe: 1954 (Giveaway)						

Contains a comic rebound with new cover. Several combinations possible. Contents determine price.

	GD 2.0	VG 4.0	FN 6.0	VF 8.0	VF/NM 9.0	NM- 9.2
COMIC BOOK MAGAZINE Chicago Tribune & other newspapers: 1940 - 1943 (Similar to Spirit sections) (7-3/4x10-3/4"; full color; 16-24 pgs. ea.)						
1940 issues	7	14	21	37	46	55
1941, 1942 issues	6	12	18	28	34	40

Comic Cavalcade - One Hundred Years of Co-operation © DC

Daisy Comics © EAS

Dan Curtis Giveaways #4 © Ripley's

	GD 2.0	VG 4.0	FN 6.0	VF 8.0	VF/NM 9.0	NM- 9.2

1943 issues ... 5 10 15 24 30 35

NOTE: Published weekly. Texas Slim, Kit Carson, Spooky, Josie, Nuts & Jolts, Lew Loyal, Brenda Starr, Daniel Boone, Captain Storm, Rocky, Smokey Stover, Tiny Tim, Little Joe, Fu Manchu appear among others. Early issues had photo stories with pictures from the movies; later issues had comic art.

COMIC BOOKS (Series 1)
Metropolitan Printing Co. (Giveaway): 1950 (16 pgs.; 5-1/4x8-1/2"; full color; bound at top; paper cover)

	GD	VG	FN	VF	VF/NM	NM-
1-Boots and Saddles; intro The Masked Marshal	6	12	18	31	38	45
1-The Green Jet; Green Lama by Raboy	24	48	72	139	220	300
1-My Pal Dizzy (Teen-age)	5	10	15	22	26	30
1-New World; origin Atomaster (costumed hero)	10	20	30	56	76	95
1-Talulah (Teen-age)	5	10	15	22	26	30

COMIC CAVALCADE
All-American/National Periodical Publications
Giveaway (1944, 8 pgs., paper-c, in color)-One Hundred Years of Co-operation-
r/Comic Cavalcade #9 ... 59 118 177 369 610 850
Giveaway (1945, 16 pgs., paper-c, in color)-Movie "Tomorrow The World" (Nazi theme);
r/Comic Cavalcade #10 ... 76 152 228 475 788 1100
Giveaway (c. 1944-45; 8 pgs, paper-c, in color)-The Twain Shall Meet-r/Comic Cavalcade #8 ... 59 118 177 369 610 850

COMIC SELECTIONS (Shoe store giveaway)
Parents' Magazine Press: 1944-46 (Reprints from Calling All Girls, True Comics, True Aviation, & Real Heroes)

	GD	VG	FN	VF	VF/NM	NM-
1	5	10	15	22	26	30
2-5	4	8	11	16	19	22

COMICS FROM WEATHER BIRD (Also see Comic Book, Edward's Shoes, Free Comics to You & Weather Bird)
Weather Bird Shoes: 1954 - 1957 (Giveaway)
Contains a comic bound with new cover. Many combinations possible. Contents would determine price. Some issues do not contain complete comics, but only parts of comics. Value equals 40 to 60 percent of contents.

COMICS READING LIBRARIES (Educational Series)
King Features (Charlton Publ.): 1973, 1977, 1979 (36 pgs. in color) (Giveaways)

	GD	VG	FN	VF	VF/NM	NM-
R-01-Tiger, Quincy	2	4	6	8	10	12
R-02-Beetle Bailey, Blondie & Popeye	2	4	6	9	13	16
R-03-Blondie, Beetle Bailey	2	4	6	8	10	12
R-04-Tim Tyler's Luck, Felix the Cat	3	6	9	16	22	28
R-05-Quincy, Henry	2	4	6	8	10	12
R-06-The Phantom, Mandrake	3	6	9	16	22	28
1977 reprint(R-04)	2	4	6	9	11	14
R-07-Popeye, Little King	2	4	6	11	16	20
R-08-Prince Valiant (Foster), Flash Gordon	3	6	9	17	26	34
1977 reprint	2	4	6	10	14	18
R-09-Hagar the Horrible, Boner's Ark	2	4	6	9	13	16
R-10-Redeye, Tiger	2	4	6	8	10	12
R-11-Blondie, Hi & Lois	2	4	6	8	10	12
R-12-Popeye-Swee'pea, Brutus	2	4	6	11	16	20
R-13-Beetle Bailey, Little King	2	4	6	8	10	12
R-14-Quincy-Hamlet	2	4	6	8	10	12
R-15-The Phantom, The Genius	2	4	6	11	16	20
R-16-Flash Gordon, Mandrake	3	6	9	17	26	34
1977 reprint	2	4	6	9	13	16
Other 1977 editions....	1	2	3	5	7	9
1979 editions (68 pgs.)	1	2	3	5	7	9

NOTE: Above giveaways available with purchase of $45.00 in merchandise. Used as a reading skills aid for small children.

COMMANDMENTS OF GOD
Catechetical Guild: 1954, 1958
300-Same contents in both editions; diff-c ... 5 10 15 23 28 32

COMPLIMENTARY COMICS
Sales Promotion Publ.: No date (1950's) (Giveaway)
1-Strongman by Powell, 3 stories ... 8 16 24 40 50 60

CONAN
Dark Horse Comics: May, 2006 (Free Comic Book Day giveaway)
...: FCBD 2006 Special (5/06) Paul Lee-a; flip book with Star Wars FCBD 2006 Special ... 2.50

COURTNEY CRUMRIN & THE NIGHT THINGS
Oni Press: 2003
Free Comic Book Day Edition (5/03) Naifeh-s/a ... 2.50

CRACKAJACK FUNNIES (Giveaway)
Malto-Meal: 1937 (Full size, soft-c, full color, 32 pgs.)(Before No. 1?)
nn-Features Dan Dunn, G-Man, Speed Bolton, Buck Jones, The Nebbs, Clyde Beatty, Freckles, Major Hoople, Wash Tubbs ... 86 172 258 538 894 1250

CROSLEY'S HOUSE OF FUN (Also see Tee and Vee Crosley...)

Crosley Div. AVCO Mfg. Corp.: 1950 (Giveaway, paper cover, 32 pgs.)
nn-Strips revolve around Crosley appliances ... 5 10 15 22 26 30

CSI: CRIME SCENE INVESTIGATION
IDW Publishing: July, 2004 (Free Comic Book Day edition)
Previews CSI: Bad Rap; The Shield: Spotlight; 24: One Shot; and 30 Days of Night ... 2.50

DAGWOOD SPLITS THE ATOM (Also see Topix V8#4)
King Features Syndicate: 1949 (Science comic with King Features characters) (Giveaway)
nn-Half comic, half text; Popeye, Olive Oyl, Henry, Mandrake, Little King, Katzenjammer Kids app. ... 9 18 27 50 65 80

DAISY COMICS (Daisy Air Rifles)
Eastern Color Printing Co.: Dec, 1936 (5-1/4x7-1/2")
nn-Joe Palooka, Buck Rogers (2 pgs. from Famous Funnies No. 18, 1st full cover app.), Napoleon Flying to Fame, Butty & Fally ... 34 68 102 197 311 425

DAISY LOW OF THE GIRL SCOUTS
Girl Scouts of America: 1954, 1965 (16 pgs., paper-c)

	GD	VG	FN	VF	VF/NM	NM-
1954-Story of Juliette Gordon Low	5	10	15	22	26	30
1965	2	4	6	9	12	15

DAN CURTIS GIVEAWAYS
Western Publishing Co.: 1974 (3x6", 24 pgs., reprints)

	GD	VG	FN	VF	VF/NM	NM-
1-Dark Shadows	3	6	9	16	22	28
2,6-Star Trek	3	6	9	16	22	28
3,4,7-9: 3-The Twilight Zone. 4-Ripley's Believe It or Not! 7-The Occult Files of Dr. Spektor. 8-Dagar the Invincible. 9-Grimm's Ghost Stories	2	4	6	10	14	18
5-Turok, Son of Stone (partial-r/Turok #78)	3	6	9	16	22	28

DANNY KAYE'S BAND FUN BOOK
H & A Selmer: 1959 (Giveaway)
nn ... 7 14 21 35 43 50

DAREDEVIL
Marvel Comics Group: 1993
...Vs. Vapora 1 (Engineering Show Giveaway, 16 pg.) - Intro Vapora ... 6.00

DAVY CROCKETT (TV)
Dell Publishing Co.
...Christmas Book (no date, 16 pgs., paper-c)-Sears giveaway ... 6 12 18 31 38 45
...Safety Trails (1955, 16pgs, 3-1/4x7")-Cities Service giveaway ... 8 16 24 40 50 60

DAVY CROCKETT
Charlton Comics
Hunting With... nn ('55, 16 pgs.)-Ben Franklin Store giveaway (Publ.-S. Rose) ... 5 10 15 24 30 35

DAVY CROCKETT
Walt Disney Prod.: (1955, 16 pgs., 5x7-1/4", slick, photo-c)
...In the Raid at Piney Creek-American Motors giveaway ... 8 16 24 40 50 60

DC SAMPLER
DC Comics: nn (#1) 1983 - No. 3, 1984 (36 pgs.; 6 1/2" x 10", giveaway)
nn(#1) -3: nn-Wraparound-c, previews upcoming issues. 3-Kirby-a ... 6.00

DC SPOTLIGHT
DC Comics: 1985 (50th anniversary special) (giveaway)
1-Includes profiles on Batman:The Dark Knight & Watchmen ... 5.00

DEATH JR. HALLOWEEN SPECIAL
Image Comics: Oct, 2006 (8-1/2"x 5-1/2", Halloween giveaway)
nn-Guy Davis-a/Joe Morrisey-s; wraparound-c ... 2.50

DENNIS THE MENACE
Hallden (Fawcett)
...& Dirt ('59)-Soil Conservation giveaway; r-# 36; Wiseman-c/a ... 2 4 6 13 18 22
...& Dirt ('68)-reprints '59 edition ... 2 4 6 8 10 12
...Away We Go('70)-Caladryl giveaway ... 1 3 4 6 8 10
...Coping with Family Stress-giveaway ... 1 3 4 6 8 10
...Takes a Poke at Poison('61)-Food & Drug Admin. giveaway; Wiseman-c/a ... 2 4 6 8 10 12
...Takes a Poke at Poison-Revised 1/66, 11/70 ... 1 2 3 5 6 8
...Takes a Poke at Poison-Revised 1972, 1974, 1977, 1981 ... 1 2 3 4 5 7

DESERT DAWN
E.C./American Museum of Natural History: 1935 (paper-c)
nn-Johnny Jackrabbit stars (rare) ... 50 100 150 305 503 700

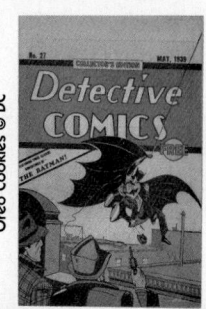

Detective Comics #27 - Oreo Cookies © DC

Dick Tracy Shoe Store Giveaway © NYNS

Evel Knievel © Ideal Toy Corp.

	GD 2.0	VG 4.0	FN 6.0	VF 8.0	VF/NM 9.0	NM- 9.2

DETECTIVE COMICS (Also see other Batman titles)
National Periodical Publications/DC Comics

27 (1984)-Oreo Cookies giveaway (32 pgs., paper-c) r-/Det. #27,#38 & Batman #1 (1st Joker)

	GD 2.0	VG 4.0	FN 6.0	VF 8.0	VF/NM 9.0	NM- 9.2
	4	8	12	28	44	60

38 (1995) Blockbuster Video edition; reprints 1st Robin app. — 3.00
38 (1997) Toys R Us edition — 3.00
359 (1997) Toys R Us edition; reprints 1st Batgirl app. — 3.00
373 (1997, 6 1/4" x 4") Warner Brothers Home Video — 3.00

DEVIL'S DUE FREE COMIC BOOK DAY
Devil's Due Publ.: May, 2005 (Free Comic Book Day giveaway)
nn-Short stories of G.I. Joe, Defex and Darkstalkers; Darkstalkers flip cover — 2.50

DICK TRACY GIVEAWAYS
1939 - 1958; 1990
Buster Brown Shoes Giveaway (1940s?, 36 pgs. in color); 1938-39-r by Gould

	GD 2.0	VG 4.0	FN 6.0	VF 8.0	VF/NM 9.0	NM- 9.2
Buster Brown Shoes Giveaway	31	62	93	178	282	385
Gillmore Giveaway (See Superbook)						
…Hatful of Fun (No date, 1950-52, 32pgs.; 8-1/2x10")-Dick Tracy hat promotion; Dick Tracy games, magic tricks. Miller Bros. premium	15	30	45	90	140	190
Motorola Giveaway (1953)-Reprints Harvey Comics Library #2; "The Case of the Sparkle Plenty TV Mystery"	7	14	21	37	46	55
Original Dick Tracy by Chester Gould, The (Aug, 1990, 16 pgs., 5-1/2x8-1/2")-Gladstone Publ.; Bread Giveaway	1	3	4	6	8	10
Popped Wheat Giveaway (1947, 16 pgs. in color)-1940-r; Sig Feuchtwanger Publ.; Gould-a	4	8	12	18	22	25
…Presents the Family Fun Book; Tip Top Bread Giveaway, no date or number (1940, Fawcett Publ., 16 pgs. in color)-Spy Smasher, Ibis, Lance O'Casey app.	46	92	138	281	466	650
Same as above but without app. of heroes & Dick Tracy on cover only	14	28	42	82	121	160
Service Station Giveaway (1958, 16 pgs. in color)(regular size, slick cover)-Harvey Info. Press	5	10	14	20	24	28
Shoe Store Giveaway (Weatherbird and Triangle Stores)(1939, 16 pgs.)-Gould-a	14	28	42	76	108	140

DICK TRACY SHEDS LIGHT ON THE MOLE
Western Printing Co.: 1949 (16 pgs.) (Ray-O-Vac Flashlights giveaway)

	GD	VG	FN	VF	VF/NM	NM-
nn-Not by Gould	8	16	24	40	50	60

DICK WINGATE OF THE U.S. NAVY
Superior Publ./Toby Press: 1951; 1953 (no month)

	GD	VG	FN	VF	VF/NM	NM-
nn-U.S. Navy giveaway	5	10	15	24	30	35
1(1953, Toby)-Reprints nn issue? (same-c)	5	10	14	20	24	28

DIG 'EM
Kellogg's Sugar Smacks Giveaway: 1973 (2-3/8x6", 16 pgs.)

	GD	VG	FN	VF	VF/NM	NM-
nn-4 different issues	1	3	4	6	8	10

DOC CARTER VD COMICS
Health Publications Institute, Raleigh, N. C. (Giveaway): 1949 (16 pgs. in color) (Paper-c)

	GD	VG	FN	VF	VF/NM	NM-
nn	18	36	54	103	162	220

DONALD AND MICKEY MERRY CHRISTMAS (Formerly Famous Gang Book Of Comics)
K. K. Publ./Firestone Tire & Rubber Co.: 1943 - 1949 (Giveaway, 20 pgs.)
Put out each Christmas; 1943 issue titled "Firestone Presents Comics" (Disney)

	GD	VG	FN	VF	VF/NM	NM-
1943-Donald Duck-r/WDC&S #32 by Carl Barks	79	158	237	494	822	1150
1944-Donald Duck-r/WDC&S #35 by Barks	76	152	228	475	788	1100
1945- "Donald Duck's Best Christmas", 8 pgs. Carl Barks; intro. & 1st app. Grandma Duck in comic books	114	228	342	713	1182	1650
1946-Donald Duck in "Santa's Stormy Visit", 8 pgs. Carl Barks	78	156	234	488	807	1125
1947-Donald Duck in "Three Good Little Ducks", 8 pgs. Carl Barks	78	156	234	488	807	1125
1948-Donald Duck in "Toyland", 8 pgs. Carl Barks	78	156	234	488	807	1125
1949-Donald Duck in "New Toys", 8 pgs. Barks	72	144	216	450	750	1050

DONALD DUCK
K. K. Publications: 1944 (Christmas giveaway, paper-c, 16 pgs.)(2 versions)

	GD	VG	FN	VF	VF/NM	NM-
nn-Kelly cover reprint	88	176	264	550	913	1275

DONALD DUCK AND THE RED FEATHER
Red Feather Giveaway: 1948 (8-1/2x11", 4 pgs., B&W)

	GD	VG	FN	VF	VF/NM	NM-
nn	18	36	54	107	169	230

DONALD DUCK IN "THE LITTERBUG"
Keep America Beautiful: 1963 (5x7-1/4", 16 pgs., soft-c) (Disney giveaway)

	GD	VG	FN	VF	VF/NM	NM-
nn	4	8	12	26	41	55

DONALD DUCK "PLOTTING PICNICKERS" (See Frito-Lay Giveaway)
DONALD DUCK'S SURPRISE PARTY

Walt Disney Productions: 1948 (16 pgs.) (Giveaway for Icy Frost Twins Ice Cream Bars)

	GD	VG	FN	VF	VF/NM	NM-
nn-(Rare)-Kelly-c/a	262	524	786	1638	2719	3800

DOT AND DASH AND THE LUCKY JINGLE PIGGIE
Sears Roebuck Co.: 1942 (Christmas giveaway, 12 pgs.)

	GD	VG	FN	VF	VF/NM	NM-
nn-Contains a war stamp album and a punch out Jingle Piggie bank	11	22	33	62	86	110

DOUBLE TALK (Also see Two-Faces)
Feature Publications: No date (1962?) (32 pgs., full color, slick-c)
Christian Anti-Communism Crusade (Giveaway)

	GD	VG	FN	VF	VF/NM	NM-
nn-Sickle with blood-c	15	30	45	86	133	180

DRUMMER BOY AT GETTYSBURG
Eastern National Park & Monument Association: 1976

	GD	VG	FN	VF	VF/NM	NM-
nn-Fred Ray-a	3	6	9	14	20	25

DUEL MASTERS (Based on a trading card game)
Dreamwave Productions: July, 2004 (Free Comic Book Day giveaway)
1-Augustyn-s — 2.50

DUMBO (Walt Disney's…, The Flying Elephant)
Weatherbird Shoes/Ernest Kern Co.(Detroit)/ Wieboldt's (Chicago): 1941 (K.K. Publ. Giveaway)

	GD	VG	FN	VF	VF/NM	NM-
nn-16 pgs., 9x10" (Rare)	45	90	135	275	450	625
nn-52 pgs., 5-1/2x8-1/2", slick cover in color; B&W interior; half text, half reprints 4-Color No. 17 (Dept. store)	24	48	72	139	220	300

DUMBO WEEKLY
Walt Disney Prod.: 1942 (Premium supplied by Diamond D-X Gas Stations)

	GD	VG	FN	VF	VF/NM	NM-
1	53	106	159	323	537	750
2-16	17	34	51	98	154	210
Binder only						350

NOTE: *A cover and binder came separate at gas stations. Came with membership card.*

EAT RIGHT TO WORK AND WIN
Swift & Company: 1942 (16 pgs.) (Giveaway)
Blondie, Henry, Flash Gordon by Alex Raymond, Toots & Casper, Thimble Theatre(Popeye), Tillie the Toiler, The Phantom, The Little King, & Bringing up Father - original strips just for this book -(in daily strip form which shows what foods we should eat and why)

	GD	VG	FN	VF	VF/NM	NM-
	39	78	117	224	355	485

EDWARD'S SHOES GIVEAWAY
Edward's Shoe Store: 1954 (Has clown on cover)
Contains comic with new cover. Many combinations possible. Contents determines price, 50-60 percent of original. (Similar to Comics From Weatherbird & Free Comics to You)

ELSIE THE COW
D. S. Publishing Co.

	GD	VG	FN	VF	VF/NM	NM-
Borden's cheese comic picture bk ("40, giveaway)	19	38	57	112	176	240
Borden Milk Giveaway-(16 pgs., nn) (3 ishs, 1957)	14	28	42	80	115	150
Elsie's Fun Book(1950; Borden Milk)	14	28	42	80	115	150
Everyday Birthday Fun With… (1957; 20 pgs.)(100th Anniversary); Kubert-a	14	28	42	80	115	150

ESCAPE FROM FEAR
Planned Parenthood of America: 1956, 1962, 1969 (Giveaway, 8 pgs., color) (On birth control)

	GD	VG	FN	VF	VF/NM	NM-
1956 edition	10	20	30	58	79	100
1962 edition	4	8	12	24	37	50
1969 edition	3	6	9	14	20	25

EVEL KNIEVEL
Marvel Comics Group (Ideal Toy Corp.): 1974 (Giveaway, 20 pgs.)

	GD	VG	FN	VF	VF/NM	NM-
nn-Contains photo on inside back-c	4	8	12	26	41	55

FAMOUS COMICS (Also see Favorite Comics)
Zain-Eppy/United Features Syndicate: No date; Mid 1930's (24 pgs., paper-c)

	GD	VG	FN	VF	VF/NM	NM-
nn-Reprinted from 1933 & 1934 newspaper strips in color; Joe Palooka, Hairbreadth Harry, Napoleon, The Nebbs, etc. (Many different versions known)	62	124	186	388	644	900

FAMOUS FAIRY TALES
K. K. Publ. Co.: 1942; 1943 (32 pgs.); 1944 (16 pgs.) (Giveaway, soft-c)

	GD	VG	FN	VF	VF/NM	NM-
1942-Kelly-a	40	80	120	239	380	520
1943-r/Fairy Tale Parade No. 2,3; Kelly-a	27	54	81	158	249	340
1944-Kelly-a	24	48	72	139	220	300

FAMOUS FUNNIES -A CARNIVAL OF COMICS
Eastern Color: 1933
36 pgs., no date given, no publisher, no number; contains strip reprints of The Bungle Family, Dixie Dugan, Hairbreadth Harry, Joe Palooka, Keeping Up With the Jones, Mutt & Jeff, Reg'lar Fellers, S'Matter Pop, Strange As It Seems, and others. This book was sold by M. C. Gaines to Wheatena, Malt-O-Milk, John Wanamaker, Kinney Shoe Stores, & others to be given away as premiums and radio giveaways (1933). Originally came with a mailing enve-lope.

	GD	VG	FN	VF	VF/NM	NM-
	800	1600	2400	4800	8900	13,000

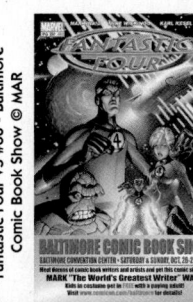
Fantastic Four V3 #60 - Baltimore Comic Book Show © MAR

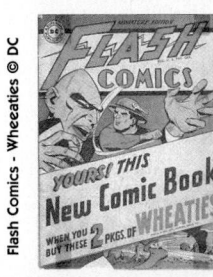
Flash Comics - Wheeaties © DC

The Fork in the Road © U.S. Army

	GD 2.0	VG 4.0	FN 6.0	VF 8.0	VF/NM 9.0	NM- 9.2

FAMOUS GANG BOOK OF COMICS (Becomes Donald & Mickey Merry Christmas 1943 on)
Firestone Tire & Rubber Co.: Dec, 1942 (Christmas giveaway, 32 pgs., paper-c)
nn-(Rare)-Porky Pig, Bugs Bunny, Mary Jane & Sniffles, Elmer Fudd; r/Looney Tunes
| | 66 | 132 | 198 | 413 | 682 | 950 |

FANTASTIC FOUR
Marvel Comics
nn (1981, 32 pgs.) Young Model Builders Club
| | 2 | 4 | 6 | 8 | 10 | 12 |
Vol. 3 #60 Baltimore Comic Book Show (10/02, newspaper supplement) 200,000 copies were distributed to Baltimore Sun home subscribers to promote Baltimore Comic Con 3.00

FATHER OF CHARITY
Catechetical Guild Giveaway: No date (32 pgs.; paper cover)
nn
| | 5 | 10 | 15 | 23 | 28 | 32 |

FAVORITE COMICS (Also see Famous Comics)
Grocery Store Giveaway (Diff. Corp.) (detergent): 1934 (36 pgs.)
Book 1-The Nebbs, Strange As It Seems, Napoleon, Joe Palooka, Dixie Dugan, S'Matter Pop, Hairbreadth Harry, etc. reprints
| | 97 | 194 | 291 | 606 | 1003 | 1400 |
Book 2,3
| | 62 | 124 | 186 | 388 | 644 | 900 |

FAWCETT MINIATURES (See Mighty Midget)
Fawcett Publications: 1946 (3-3/4x5", 12-24 pgs.) (Wheaties giveaways)
Captain Marvel "And the Horn of Plenty"; Bulletman story
| | 16 | 32 | 48 | 94 | 147 | 200 |
Captain Marvel "& the Raiders From Space"; Golden Arrow story
| | 16 | 32 | 48 | 94 | 147 | 200 |
Captain Marvel Jr. "The Case of the Poison Press!" Bulletman story
| | 16 | 32 | 48 | 94 | 147 | 200 |
Delecta of the Planets; C. C. Beck art; B&W inside; 12 pgs.; 3 printing variations (coloring) exist
| | 22 | 44 | 66 | 128 | 202 | 275 |

FEARLESS FOSDICK
Capp Enterprises Inc.: 1951
...& The Case of The Red Feather
| | 6 | 12 | 18 | 27 | 33 | 38 |

FIGHT FOR FREEDOM
National Assoc. of Mfgrs./General Comics: 1949, 1951 (Giveaway, 16 pgs.)
nn-Dan Barry-c/a; used in POP, pg. 102
| | 6 | 12 | 18 | 31 | 38 | 45 |

FIRE AND BLAST
National Fire Protection Assoc.: 1952 (Giveaway, 16 pgs., paper-c)
nn-Mart Baily A-Bomb-c; about fire prevention
| | 14 | 28 | 42 | 82 | 121 | 160 |

FIRE CHIEF AND THE SAFE OL' FIREFLY, THE
National Board of Fire Underwriters: 1952 (16 pgs.) (Safety brochure given away at schools) (produced by American Visuals Corp.)(Eisner)
nn-(Rare) Eisner-c/a
| | 43 | 86 | 129 | 262 | 431 | 600 |

FLASH, THE
DC Comics
nn-(1990) Brochure for CBS TV series 4.00
The Flash Comes to a Standstill (1981, General Foods giveaway, 8 pages, 3-1/2 x 6-3/4", oblong)
| | 2 | 4 | 6 | 9 | 12 | 15 |

FLASH COMICS (Also see Captain Marvel and Funny Stuff)
National Periodical Publications: 1946 (6-1/2x8-1/4", 32 pgs.) (Wheaties Giveaway)
nn-Johnny Thunder, Ghost Patrol, The Flash & Kubert Hawkman app.; Irwin Hasen-c/a
| | 350 | 975 | 1600 | - | - | - |
NOTE: All known copies were taped to Wheaties boxes and are never found in mint condition. Copies with light tape residue bring the listed prices in all grades.

FLASH FORCE 2000
DC Comics: 1984
1-5 5.00

FLASH GORDON
Dell Publishing Co.: 1943 (20 pgs.)
Macy's Giveaway-(Rare); not by Raymond
| | 60 | 120 | 180 | 375 | 625 | 875 |

FLASH GORDON
Harvey Comics: 1951 (16 pgs. in color, regular size, paper-c) (Gordon Bread giveaway)
1,2; 1- r/strips 10/24/37 - 2/6/38. 2- r/strips 7/14/40 - 10/6/40; Reprints by Raymond
each....
| | 2 | 4 | 6 | 10 | 14 | 18 |
NOTE: Most copies have brittle edges.

FLOOD RELIEF
Malibu Comics (Ultraverse): Jan, 1994 (36 pgs.)(Ordered thru mail w/$5.00 to Red Cross)
1-Hardcase, Prime & Prototype app. 6.00

FOREST FIRE (Also see The Blazing Forest and Smokey Bear)
American Forestry Assn.(Commerical Comics): 1949 (dated-1950) (16 pgs., paper-c)

nn-Intro/1st app. Smokey The Forest Fire Preventing Bear; created by Rudy Wendelein; Wendelein/Sparling-a; 'Carter Oil Co.' on back-c of original
| | 16 | 32 | 48 | 94 | 147 | 200 |

FOREST RANGER HANDBOOK
Wrather Corp.: 1967 (5x7", 20 pgs., slick-c)
nn-With Corey Stuart & Lassie photo-c
| | 2 | 4 | 6 | 13 | 18 | 22 |

FORGOTTEN STORY BEHIND NORTH BEACH, THE
Catechetical Guild: No date (8 pgs., paper-c)
nn
| | 5 | 10 | 15 | 22 | 26 | 30 |

FORK IN THE ROAD
U.S. Army Recruiting Service: 1961 (16 pgs., paper-c)
nn
| | 2 | 4 | 6 | 11 | 16 | 20 |

48 FAMOUS AMERICANS
J. C. Penney Co. (Cpr. Edwin H. Stroh): 1947 (Giveaway) (Half-size in color)
nn - Simon & Kirby-a
| | 12 | 24 | 36 | 69 | 97 | 125 |

FOXHOLE ON YOUR LAWN
No Publisher: No date
nn-Charles Biro art
| | 4 | 7 | 10 | 14 | 17 | 20 |

FRANKIE LUER'S SPACE ADVENTURES
Luer Packing Co.: 1955 (5x7", 36 pgs., slick-c)
nn - With Davey Rocket
| | 4 | 8 | 12 | 17 | 21 | 24 |

FREDDY
Charlton Comics
Schiff's Shoes Presents... #1 (1959)-Giveaway
| | 4 | 7 | 10 | 14 | 17 | 20 |

FREE COMICS TO YOU FROM... (name of shoe store) (Has clown on cover & another with a rabbit) (Like comics from Weather Bird & Edward's Shoes)
Shoe Store Giveaway: Circa 1956, 1960-61
Contains a comic bound with new cover - several combinations possible; some Harvey titles known. Contents determine price.

FREEDOM TRAIN
Street & Smith Publications: 1948 (Giveaway)
nn-Powell-c w/mailer
| | 18 | 36 | 54 | 103 | 162 | 220 |

FREIHOFER'S COMIC BOOK
All-American Comics: 1940s (7 1/2 x 10 1/4")
2nd edition-(Scarce) Cover features All-American Comics characters Ultra-Man, Hop Harrigan, Red, White and Blue and others
| | 57 | 114 | 171 | 356 | 591 | 825 |

FRIENDLY GHOST, CASPER, THE
Harvey Publications: 1967 (16 pgs.)
American Dental Assoc. giveaway-Small size
| | 3 | 6 | 9 | 17 | 25 | 32 |

FRITO-LAY GIVEAWAY
Frito-Lay: 1962 (3-1/4x7", soft-c, 16 pgs.) (Disney)
nn-Donald Duck "Plotting Picnickers"
| | 5 | 10 | 15 | 32 | 51 | 70 |
nn-Ludwig Von Drake "Fish Stampede"
| | 3 | 6 | 9 | 20 | 30 | 40 |
nn- Mickey Mouse & Goofy "Bicep Bungle"
| | 4 | 8 | 12 | 22 | 34 | 45 |

FRONTIER DAYS
Robin Hood Shoe Store (Brown Shoe): 1956 (Giveaway)
1
| | 4 | 7 | 10 | 14 | 17 | 20 |

FUNNIES ON PARADE (Premium)(See Toy World Funnies)
Eastern Color Printing Co.: 1933 (36 pgs., slick cover)
No date or publisher listed
nn-Contains Sunday page reprints of Mutt & Jeff, Joe Palooka, Hairbreadth Harry, Reg'lar Fellers, Skippy, & others (10,000 print run). This book was printed for Proctor & Gamble to be given away & came out before Famous Funnies or Century of Comics.
| | 1000 | 2000 | 3000 | 6000 | 10,500 | 15,000 |

FUNNY PICTURE STORIES (Comic Pages V3#4 on)
Comics Magazine Co./Centaur Publications
Laundry giveaway (16-20 pgs., 1930s)-slick-c
| | 26 | 52 | 78 | 154 | 242 | 330 |

FUNNY STUFF (Also see Captain Marvel & Flash Comics)
National Periodical Publications (Wheaties Giveaway): 1946 (6-1/2x8-1/4")
nn-(Scarce)-Dodo & the Frog, Three Mouseketeers, etc.; came taped to Wheaties box; never found in better than fine
| | 170 | 340 | 500 | – | – | – |

FUTURE COP: L.A.P.D. (Electronic Arts video game)
DC Comics (WildStorm): 1998
nn-Ron Lim-a/Dave Johnson-c 2.50

FUTURE SHOCK
Image Comics: 2006 (Free Comic Book Day giveaway)
...: FCBD 2006 Edition; Spawn, Invincible, Savage Dragon & others short stories 2.50

Golden Arrow
Well Known Comics © FAW

Gulf Funny Weekly #357 © Gulf Oil

Hoods Up #1 © Fram Corp.

	GD 2.0	VG 4.0	FN 6.0	VF 8.0	VF/NM 9.0	NM- 9.2		GD 2.0	VG 4.0	FN 6.0	VF 8.0	VF/NM 9.0	NM- 9.2

GABBY HAYES WESTERN (Movie star)
Fawcett Publications
Quaker Oats Giveaway nn's(#1-5, 1951, 2-1/2x7") (Kagran Corp.)-...In Tracks of Guilt, ...In the
  Fence Post Mystery, ...In the Accidental Sherlock, ...In the Frame-Up, ...In the Double
  Cross Brand known   10   20   30   54   72   90
Mailing Envelope (has illo of Gabby on front)   10   20   30   54   72   90

GARY GIBSON COMICS (Donut club membership)
National Dunking Association: 1950 (Included in donut box with pin and card)
1-Western soft-c, 16 pgs.; folded into the box   5   10   14   20   24   28

GENE AUTRY COMICS
Dell Publishing Co.
...Adventure Comics And Play-Fun Book ('47)-32 pgs., 8x6-1/2"; games, comics, magic
  (Pillsbury premium)   37   74   111   213   337   460
Quaker Oats Giveaway(1950)-2-1/2x6-3/4"; 5 different versions; "Death Card Gang", "Phantoms
  of the Cave", "Riddle of Laughing Mtn.", "Secret of Lost Valley", "Bond of the Broken Arrow"
  (came in wrapper)   each...   14   28   42   82   121   160
Mailing Envelope (has illo. of Gene on front)   14   28   42   82   121   160
3-D Giveaway(1953)-Pocket-size; 5 different   14   28   42   82   121   160
  Mailing Envelope (no art on front)   10   20   30   58   79   100

GENE AUTRY TIM (Formerly Tim) (Becomes Tim in Space)
Tim Stores: 1950 (Half-size) (B&W Giveaway)
nn-Several issues (All Scarce)   19   38   57   109   172   235

GENERAL FOODS SUPER-HEROES
DC Comics: 1979, 1980
1-4 (1979), 1-4 (1980)   each...   12.00

G. I. COMICS (Also see Jeep & Overseas Comics)
Giveaways: 1945 - No. 73?, 1946 (Distributed to U. S. Armed Forces)
1-73-Contains Prince Valiant by Foster, Blondie, Smilin' Jack, Mickey Finn, Terry & the
  Pirates, Donald Duck, Alley Oop, Moon Mullins & Capt. Easy strip reprints
  (at least 73 issues known to exist)   8   16   24   42   54   65

GOLDEN ARROW
Fawcett Publications
...Well Known Comics (1944; 12 pgs.; 8-1/2x10-1/2"; paper-c; glued binding)- Bestmaid/
  Samuel Lowe giveaway; printed in green   10   20   30   54   72   90

GOLDILOCKS & THE THREE BEARS
K. K. Publications: 1943 (Giveaway)
nn   13   26   39   74   106   135

GREAT PEOPLE OF GENESIS, THE
David C. Cook Publ. Co.: No date (Religious giveaway, 64 pgs.)
nn-Reprint/Sunday Pix Weekly   5   10   15   23   28   32

GREAT SACRAMENT, THE
Catechetical Guild: 1953 (Giveaway, 36 pgs.)
nn   5   10   15   22   26   30

GRENADA
Commercial Comics Co.: 1983 (Giveaway produced by the CIA)
1-Air dropped over Grenada during the 1983 invasion   30.00

GRIT (YOU'VE GOT TO HAVE...)
GRIT Publishing Co.: 1959
nn-GRIT newspaper sales recruitment comic; Schaffenberger-a. Later version has altered
  artwork   5   10   15   22   26   30

GULF FUNNY WEEKLY (Gulf Comic Weekly No. 1-4)(See Standard Oil Comics)
Gulf Oil Company (Giveaway): 1933 - No. 422, 5/23/41 (in full color; 4 pgs.; tabloid size to
  2/3/39; 2/10/39 on, regular comic book size)(early issues undated)
1   59   118   177   369   610   850
2-5   26   52   78   152   239   325
6-30   15   30   45   86   133   180
31-100   13   26   39   72   101   130
101-196   9   18   27   50   65   80
197-Wings Winfair begins(1/29/37); by Fred Meagher beginning in 1938
                                                             22   44   66   128   202   275
198-300 (Last tabloid size)   14   28   42   76   108   140
301-350 (Regular size)   9   18   27   47   61   75
351-422   7   14   21   37   46   55

GULLIVER'S TRAVELS
Macy's Department Store: 1939, small size
nn-Christmas giveaway   14   28   42   76   108   140

GUN THAT WON THE WEST, THE
Winchester-Western Division & Olin Mathieson Chemical Corp.: 1956 (Giveaway, 24 pgs.)
nn-Painted-c   5   10   15   24   30   35

HAPPINESS AND HEALING FOR YOU (Also see Oral Roberts'...)
Commercial Comics: 1955 (36 pgs., slick cover) (Oral Roberts Giveaway)
nn   9   18   27   52   69   85
NOTE: *The success of this book prompted Oral Roberts to go into the publishing business himself to produce his own material.*

HAPPY TOOTH
DC Comics: 1996
1   3.00

HAWKMAN - THE SKY'S THE LIMIT
DC Comics: 1981 (General Foods giveaway, 8 pages, 3-1/2 x 6-3/4", oblong)
nn   2   4   6   9   12   15

HAWTHORN-MELODY FARMS DAIRY COMICS
Everybody's Publishing Co.: No date (1950's) (Giveaway)
nn-Cheerie Chick, Tuffy Turtle, Robin Koo Koo, Donald & Longhorn Legends
                                                              2   4   6   8   11   14

HENRY ALDRICH COMICS (TV)
Dell Publishing Co.
Giveaway (16 pgs., soft-c, 1951)-Capehart radio   3   6   9   17   25   32

HERE IS SANTA CLAUS
Goldsmith Publishing Co. (Kann's in Washington, D.C.): 1930s (16 pgs., 8 in color) (stiff
paper covers)
nn   12   24   36   67   94   120

HERE'S HOW AMERICA'S CARTOONISTS HELP TO SELL U.S. SAVINGS BONDS
Harvey Comics: 1950? (16 pgs., giveaway, paper cover)
Contains: Joe Palooka, Donald Duck, Archie, Kerry Drake, Red Ryder, Blondie
  & Steve Canyon   19   38   57   112   176   240

HISTORY OF GAS
American Gas Assoc.: Mar, 1947 (Giveaway, 16 pgs.)
nn-Miss Flame narrates   6   12   18   29   36   42

HOME DEPOT, SAFETY HEROES
Marvel Comics.: Oct, 2005 (Giveaway)
nn-Spider-Man and the Fantastic Four on the cover; Olliffe-a/c; Roseman-s   2.50

HONEYBEE BIRDWHISTLE AND HER PET PEPI (Introducing...)
Newspaper Enterprise Assoc.: 1969 (Giveaway, 24 pgs., B&W, slick cover)
nn-Contains Freckles newspaper strips with a short biography of Henry Fornhals (artist)
  & Fred Fox (writer) of the strip   4   8   12   28   44   60

HOODS UP
Fram Corp.: 1953 (15¢, distributed to service station owners, 16 pgs.)
1-(Very Rare; only 2 known); Eisner-c/a in all.   50   100   150   305   503   700
2-6-(Very Rare; only 1 known of #3, 2 known of #2,4)
                                                             48   96   144   293   484   675
NOTE: *Convertible Connie gives tips for service stations, selling Fram oil filters.*

HOPALONG CASSIDY
Fawcett Publications
Grape Nuts Flakes giveaway (1950,9x6")   14   28   42   82   121   160
...& the Mad Barber (1951 Bond Bread giveaway)-7x5"; used in SOTI, pgs. 308,309
                                                             20   40   60   117   184   250
...Meets the Brend Brothers Bandits (1951 Bond Bread giveaway, color, paper-c,
  16 pgs., 3-1/2x7")- Fawcett Publ.   10   20   30   58   79   100
...Strange Legacy (1951 Bond Bread giveaway)   10   20   30   58   79   100
White Tower Giveaway (1946, 16pgs., paper-c)   11   22   33   62   86   110

HOPELESS SAVAGES
Oni Press: May, 2002 (B&W)
Free Comic Book Day giveaway-Reprints #1 with "Free Comic Book Day" banner on-c   2.50

HOPPY THE MARVEL BUNNY (WELL KNOWN COMICS)
Fawcett Publications: 1944 (8-1/2x10-1/2", paper-c)
Bestmaid/Samuel Lowe (printed in red or blue)   10   20   30   56   76   95

HOT STUFF, THE LITTLE DEVIL
Harvey Publications (Illustrated Humor):1963
Shoestore Giveaway   4   8   12   22   34   45

HOW KIDS ENJOY NEW YORK
American Airlines: 1966 (Giveaway, 40 pgs., 4x9")
nn-Includes 8 color pages by Bob Kane featuring a tour of New York and his studio
  (a VG copy sold for $180 and a FN+ sold for $250 in 2004)

HOW STALIN HOPES WE WILL DESTROY AMERICA
Joe Lowe Co. (Pictorial Media): 1951 (Giveaway, 16 pgs.)
nn   50   100   150   305   503   700

302

The Iron Giant © WB

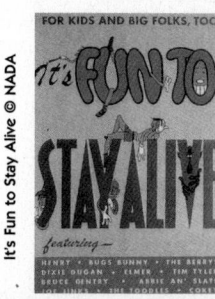

It's Fun to Stay Alive © NADA

Justice League of America #0 FCBD Edition © DC

	GD 2.0	VG 4.0	FN 6.0	VF 8.0	VF/NM 9.0	NM- 9.2		GD 2.0	VG 4.0	FN 6.0	VF 8.0	VF/NM 9.0	NM- 9.2

HURRICANE KIDS, THE (Also See Magic Morro, The Owl, Popular Comics #45)
R.S. Callender: 1941 (Giveaway, 7-1/2x5-1/4", soft-c)

nn-Will Ely-a.   10   20   30   56   76   95

IF THE DEVIL WOULD TALK
Roman Catholic Catechetical Guild/Impact Publ.: 1950; 1958 (32 pgs.; paper cover; in full color)

nn-(Scarce)-About secularism (20-30 copies known to exist); very low distribution
   81   162   243   506   841   1175

1958 Edition-(Impact Publ.); art & script changed to meet church criticism of earlier edition; 80 plus copies known to exist   26   52   78   152   239   325

Black & White version of nn edition; small size; only 4 known copies exist
   32   64   96   183   289   395

NOTE: The original edition of this book was printed and killed by the Guild's board of directors. It is believed that a very limited number of copies were distributed. The 1958 version was a complete bomb with very limited, if any, circulation. In 1979, 11 original, 4 1958 reprints, and 4 B&W's surfaced from the Guild's old files in St. Paul, Minnesota.

IMAGE COMICS SUMMER SPECIAL
Image Comics: July, 2004 (Free Comic Book Day giveaway)

1-New short stories of Spawn, Invincible, Savage Dragon and Witchblade   2.50

IN LOVE WITH JESUS
Catechetical Educational Society: 1952 (Giveaway, 36 pgs.)

nn   6   12   18   31   38   45

INTERSTATE THEATRES' FUN CLUB COMICS
Interstate Theatres: Mid 1940's (10¢ on cover) (B&W cover) (Premium)

Cover features MLJ characters looking at a copy of Top-Notch Comics, but contains an early Detective Comic on inside; many combinations possible
   10   20   30   56   76   95

IN THE GOOD HANDS OF THE ROCKEFELLER TEAM
Country Art Studios: No date (paper cover, 8 pgs.)

nn-Joe Simon-a   8   16   24   42   54   65

IRON GIANT
DC Comics: 1999 (4 pages, theater giveaway)

1-Previews movie   3.00

IRON HORSE GOES TO WAR, THE
Association of American Railroads: 1960 (Giveaway, 16 pgs.)

nn-Civil War & railroads   3   6   9   14   20   25

IS THIS TOMORROW?
Catechetical Guild: 1947 (One Shot) (3 editions) (52 pgs.)

1-Theme of communists taking over the USA; (no price on cover) Used in POP, pg. 102   18   36   54   105   165   225

1-(10¢ on cover)   24   48   72   139   220   300

1-Has blank circle with no price on cover   26   52   78   152   239   325

Black & White advance copy titled "Confidential" (52 pgs.)-Contains script and art edited out of the color edition, including one page of extreme violence showing mob nailing a Cardinal to a door; (only two known copies)   117   234   351   731   1216   1700

NOTE: The original color version first sold for 10 cents. Since sales were good, it was later printed as a giveaway. Approximately four million in total were printed. The two black and white copies listed plus two other versions as well as a full color untrimmed version surfaced in 1979 from the Guild's old files in St. Paul, Minnesota.

IT'S FUN TO STAY ALIVE
National Automobile Dealers Association: 1948 (Giveaway, 16 pgs., heavy stock paper)

Featuring: Bugs Bunny, The Berrys, Dixie Dugan, Elmer, Henry, Tim Tyler, Bruce Gentry, Abbie & Slats, Joe Jinks, The Toodles, & Cokey; all art copyright 1946-48 drawn especially for this book   16   32   48   92   144   195

JACK & JILL VISIT TOYTOWN WITH ELMER THE ELF
Butler Brothers (Toytown Stores): 1949 (Giveaway, 16 pgs., paper cover)

nn   5   10   15   22   26   30

JACK ARMSTRONG (Radio)(See True Comics)
Parents' Institute: 1949

12-Premium version (distr. in Chicago only); Free printed on upper right-c; no price (Rare)   17   34   51   98   154   210

JACKIE JOYNER KERSEE IN HIGH HURDLES (Kellogg's Tony's Sports Comics)
DC Comics: 1992 (Sports Illustrated)

nn   3.00

JACKPOT OF FUN COMIC BOOK
DCA Food Ind.: 1957, giveaway

nn-Features Howdy Doody   11   22   33   62   86   110

JEEP COMICS
R. B. Leffingwell & Co.: 1945 - 1946

1-46 (Giveaways)-Strip reprints in all; Tarzan, Flash Gordon, Blondie, The Nebbs, Little Iodine,

---

Red Ryder, Don Winslow, The Phantom, Johnny Hazard, Katzenjammer Kids; distr. to U.S. Armed Forces from 1945-1946   6   12   18   31   38   45

JINGLE BELLS CHRISTMAS BOOK
Montgomery Ward (Giveaway): 1971 (20 pgs., B&W inside, slick-c)

nn   6.00

JOAN OF ARC
Catechetical Guild (Topix) (Giveaway): No date (28 pgs., blank back-c)

nn-Ingrid Bergman photo-c; Addison Burbank-a   11   22   33   62   86   110
NOTE: Unpublished version exists which came from the Guild's files.

JOE PALOOKA (2nd Series)
Harvey Publications

...Body Building Instruction Book (1958 B&M Sports Toy giveaway, 16pgs., 5-1/4x7")-Origin   9   18   27   47   61   75

...Fights His Way Back (1945 Giveaway, 24 pgs.) Family Comics   15   30   45   85   130   175

...in Hi There! (1949 Red Cross giveaway, 12 pgs., 4-3/4x6")   9   18   27   50   65   80

...in It's All in the Family (1945 Red Cross giveaway, 16 pgs., regular size)   11   22   33   60   83   105

JOE THE GENIE OF STEEL
U.S. Steel Corp., Pittsburgh, PA: 1950 (16 pgs.)

nn   5   10   15   22   26   30

JOHNNY JINGLE'S LUCKY DAY
American Dairy Assoc.: 1956 (16 pgs.; 7-1/4x5-1/8") (Giveaway) (Disney)

nn   5   10   15   24   30   35

JO-JOY (The Adventures of...)
W. T. Grant Dept. Stores: 1945 - 1953 (Christmas gift comic, 16 pgs., 7-1/16x10-1/4")

1945-53 issues   6   12   18   29   36   42

JOLLY CHRISTMAS BOOK (See Christmas Journey Through Space)
Promotional Publ. Co.: 1951; 1954; 1955 (36 pgs.; 24 pgs.)

1951-(Woolworth giveaway)-slightly oversized; no slick cover; Marv Levy-c/a   7   14   21   37   46   55

1954-(Hot Shoppes giveaway)-regular size-reprints 1951 issue; slick cover added; 24 pgs.; no ads   6   12   18   31   38   45

1955-(J. M. McDonald Co. giveaway)-reg. size   6   12   18   28   34   40

JOURNEY OF DISCOVERY WITH MARK STEEL (See Mark Steel)

JUMPING JACKS PRESENTS THE WHIZ KIDS
Jumping Jacks Stores giveaway: 1978 (In 3-D) with glasses (4 pgs.)

nn   6.00

JUNGLE BOOK FUN BOOK, THE (Disney)
Baskin Robbins: 1978

nn-Ice Cream giveaway   2   4   6   9   12   15

JUSTICE LEAGUE ADVENTURES (Based on Cartoon Network series)
DC Comics: May, 2002

Free Comic Book Day giveaway-Reprints #1 with "Free Comic Book Day" banner on-c   2.50

JUSTICE LEAGUE OF AMERICA
DC Comics: 1999 (included in Justice League of America Monopoly game); 2007

nn - Reprints 1st app. in Brave and the Bold #28   2.50
Free Comic Book Day giveaway-Reprints #0 with "Free Comic Book Day" banner on-c   2.50

JUSTICE LEAGUE UNLIMITED (Based on Cartoon Network series)
DC Comics: May, 2006

Free Comic Book Day giveaway-Reprints #1 with "Free Comic Book Day" banner on-c   2.25

KASCO KOMICS
Kasko Grainfeed (Giveaway): 1945; No. 2, 1949 (Regular size, paper-c)

1(1945)-Similar to Katy Keene; Bill Woggon-a; 28 pgs.; 6-7/8x9-7/8"   16   32   48   92   144   195

2(1949)-Woggon-c/a   13   26   39   74   105   135

KATY AND KEN VISIT SANTA WITH MISTER WISH
S. S. Kresge Co.: 1948 (Giveaway, 16 pgs., paper-c)

nn   6   12   18   29   36   42

KELLOGG'S CINNAMON MINI-BUNS SUPER-HEROES
DC Comics: 1993 (4 1/4" x 2 3/4")

4 editions: Flash, Justice League America, Superman, Wonder Woman and the Star Riders each.....   4.00

KERRY DRAKE DETECTIVE CASES
Publisher's Syndicate

...in the Case of the Sleeping City-(1951)-16 pg. giveaway for armed forces; paper cover

King James © DC

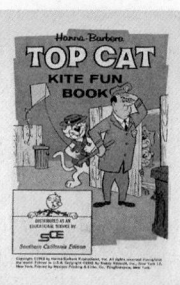
Kite Fun Book 1963 - Top Cat © H-B

Legion of Super-Heroes in the 31st Century #1 FCBD Edition © DC

	GD 2.0	VG 4.0	FN 6.0	VF 8.0	VF/NM 9.0	NM- 9.2

KEY COMICS
Key Clothing Co./Peterson Clothing: 1951 - 1956 (32 pgs.) (Giveaway)

	6	12	18	29	36	42

Contains a comic from different publishers bound with new cover. Cover changed each year. Many combinations possible. Distributed in Nebraska, Iowa, & Kansas. Combinations would determine price, 40-60 percent of original.

KING JAMES "THE KING OF BASKETBALL"
DC Comics: 2004 (Promo comic for LeBron James and Powerade Flava23 sports drink)

nn - Ten different covers by various artists; 4 covers for retail, 4 for mail-in, 1 for military commissaries, and 1 general market; Damion Scott-a/Gary Phillips-s ... 2.50

KIRBY'S SHOES COMICS
Kirby's Shoes: 1959 (8 pgs., soft-c)

nn-Features Kirby the Golden Bear	3	5	7	10	12	14

KITE FUN BOOK
Pacific, Gas & Electric/Sou. California Edison/Florida Power & Light/ Missouri Public Service Co.: 1952 - 1998 (16 pgs, 5x7-1/4", soft-c)

1952-Having Fun With Kites (P.G.&E.)	12	24	36	69	97	125
1953-Pinocchio Learns About Kites (Disney)	43	86	129	262	431	600
1954-Donald Duck Tells About Kites-Fla. Power, S.C.E. & version with label issues						
-Barks pencils-8 pgs.; inks-7 pgs. (Rare)	276	552	828	1725	2863	4000
1954-Donald Duck Tells About Kites-P.G.&E. issue -7th page redrawn changing middle 3 panels to show P.G.&E. in story line; (All Barks-a) Scarce						
	221	442	663	1381	2291	3200
1955-Brer Rabbit in "A Kite Tail" (Disney)	28	56	84	162	256	350
1956-Woody Woodpecker (Lantz)	14	28	42	80	115	150
1957-Ruff and Reddy (exist?)						
1958-Tom And Jerry (M.G.M.)	10	20	30	54	72	90
1959-Bugs Bunny (Warner Bros.)	5	10	15	30	48	65
1960-Porky Pig (Warner Bros.)	5	10	15	32	51	70
1960-Bugs Bunny (Warner Bros.)	5	10	15	32	51	70
1961-Huckleberry Hound (Hanna-Barbera)	6	12	18	37	59	80
1962-Yogi Bear (Hanna-Barbera)	4	8	12	28	44	60
1963-Rocky and Bullwinkle (TV)(Jay Ward)	9	18	27	60	100	140
1963-Top Cat (TV)(Hanna-Barbera)	5	10	15	32	51	70
1964-Magilla Gorilla (TV)(Hanna-Barbera)	5	10	15	30	48	65
1965-Jinks, Pixie and Dixie (TV)(Hanna-Barbera)	4	8	12	22	34	45
1965-Tweety and Sylvester (Warner); S.C.E. version with Reddy Kilowatt app.						
	3	6	9	16	22	28
1966-Secret Squirrel (Hanna-Barbera); S.C.E. version with Reddy Kilowatt app.						
	7	14	21	45	73	100
1967-Beep! Beep! The Road Runner (TV)(Warner)	3	6	9	17	25	32
1968-Bugs Bunny (Warner Bros.)	3	6	9	18	27	35
1969-Dastardly and Muttley (TV)(Hanna-Barbera)	5	10	15	30	48	65
1970-Rocky and Bullwinkle (TV)(Jay Ward)	6	12	18	43	69	95
1971-Beep! Beep! The Road Runner (TV)(Warner)	3	6	9	16	23	30
1972-The Pink Panther (TV)	3	6	9	15	21	26
1973-Lassie (TV)	4	8	12	22	34	45
1974-Underdog (TV)	3	6	9	17	25	32
1975-Ben Franklin	2	4	6	10	14	18
1976-The Brady Bunch (TV)	4	8	12	24	37	50
1977-Ben Franklin (exist?)	2	4	6	10	14	18
1977-Popeye	3	6	9	16	23	30
1978-Happy Days (TV)	3	6	9	18	27	35
1979-Eight is Enough (TV)	3	6	9	16	23	30
1980-The Waltons (TV, released in 1981)	3	6	9	16	23	30
1982-Tweety and Sylvester	2	4	6	13	18	22
1984-Smokey Bear	2	4	6	9	13	16
1986-Road Runner	2	4	6	8	11	14
1997-Thomas Edison						4.00
1998-Edison Field (Anaheim Stadium)						3.00

KNOW YOUR MASS
Catechetical Guild: No. 303, 1958 (35¢, 100 Pg. Giant) (Square binding)

303-In color	7	14	21	35	43	50

KOLYNOS PRESENTS THE WHITE GUARD
Whitehall Pharmacal Co.: 1949 (paper cover, 8 pgs.)

nn	6	12	18	27	33	38

K. O. PUNCH, THE (Also see Lucky Fights It Through)
E. C. Comics: 1948 (Educational giveaway)

nn-Feldstein-splash; Kamen-a	85	170	255	531	878	1225

KOREA MY HOME (Also see Yalta to Korea)
Johnstone and Cushing: nd (1950s)

nn-Anti-communist; Korean War	21	42	63	120	188	255

KRIM-KO KOMICS
Krim-ko Chocolate Drink: 5/18/35 - No. 6, 6/22/35; 1936 - 1939 (weekly)

1-(16 pgs., soft-c, Dairy giveaways)-Tom, Mary & Sparky Advs. by Russell Keaton, Jim Hawkins by Dick Moores, Mystery Island! by Rick Yager begin

	14	28	42	76	108	140
2-6 (6/22/35)	10	20	30	56	76	95

Lola, Secret Agent; 184 issues, 4 pg. giveaways - all original stories

each....	7	14	21	37	46	55

LABOR IS A PARTNER
Catechetical Guild Educational Society: 1949 (32 pgs., paper-c)

nn-Anti-communism	18	36	54	105	165	250

Confidential Preview-(8-1/2x11", B&W, saddle stitched)-only one known copy; text varies from color version, advertises next book on secularism (If the Devil Would Talk)

	24	48	72	139	220	300

LADY AND THE TRAMP IN "BUTTER LATE THAN NEVER"
American Dairy Assoc. (Premium): 1955 (16 pgs., 5x7-1/4", soft-c) (Disney)

nn	10	20	30	54	72	90

LASSIE (TV)
Dell Publ. Co

The Adventures of... nn-(Red Heart Dog Food giveaway, 1949)-16 pgs, soft-c;

1st app. Lassie in comics	32	64	96	186	293	400

LEAVE IT TO CHANCE
Image Comics: 2003

Free Comic Book Day Edition - James Robinson-s/Paul Smith-a						2.50

LEGION OF SUPER-HEROES IN THE 31ST CENTURY
DC Comics: June, 2007 (Free Comic Book Day giveaway)

1-Reprints #1						2.50

LIFE OF THE BLESSED VIRGIN
Catechetical Guild (Giveaway): 1950 (68pgs.) (square binding)

nn-Contains "The Woman of the Promise" & "Mother of Us All" rebound

	6	12	18	31	38	45

LIGHTNING RACERS
DC Comics: 1989

1						4.50

LI'L ABNER (Al Capp's) (Also see Natural Disasters!)
Harvey Publ./Toby Press

...& the Creatures from Drop-Outer Space-nn (Job Corps giveaway; 36 pgs., in color) (entire book by Frank Frazetta)

	23	46	69	130	205	280
...Joins the Navy (1950) (Toby Press Premium)	11	22	33	62	86	110

Al Capp by Li'l Abner (Circa 1946, nd, giveaway) Al Capp bio and his life as an amputee

	11	22	33	62	86	110

LITTLE ALONZO
Macy's Dept. Store: 1938 (B&W, 5-1/2x8-1/2") (Christmas giveaway)

nn-By Ferdinand the Bull's Munro Leaf	9	18	27	50	65	80

LITTLE ARCHIE (See Archie Comics)

LITTLE DOT
Harvey Publications

Shoe store giveaway 2	4	8	12	26	41	55

LITTLE FIR TREE, THE
W. T. Grant Co.: nd (1942) (8-1/2x11") (12 pgs. with cover, color & B&W, heavy paper) (Christmas giveaway)

nn-Story by Hans Christian Anderson; 8 pg. Kelly-r/Santa Claus Funnies (not signed); X-Mas-c

	100	200	300	570	935	1300

LITTLE KLINKER
Little Klinker Ventures: Nov, 1960 (20 pgs.) (slick cover) (Montgomery Ward Giveaway)

nn	2	4	6	9	13	16

LITTLE MISS SUNBEAM COMICS
Magazine Enterprises/Quality Bakers of America

Bread Giveaway 1-4(Quality Bakers, 1949-50)-14 pgs. each						
	6	12	18	31	38	45
Bread Giveaway (1957,61; 16pgs, reg. size)	5	10	15	24	30	35

LITTLE ORPHAN ANNIE
David McKay Publ./Dell Publishing Co.

Junior Commandos (same-c as 4-Color #18, K.K. Publ.) (Big Shoe Store); same back cover as '47 Popped Wheat giveaway; 16 pgs; flag-c; r/strips 9/7/42-10/10/42

	28	56	84	162	256	350

Popped Wheat Giveaway ('47)-16 pgs. full color; reprints strips from 5/3/40 to 6/20/40

	4	8	12	18	22	25
Quaker Sparkies Giveaway (1940)	18	36	54	103	162	220

Quaker Sparkies Giveaway (1941, full color, 20 pgs.); "LOA and the Rescue";

Little Orphan Annie 1941 © UFS

Man of Steel Best Western #3 © DC

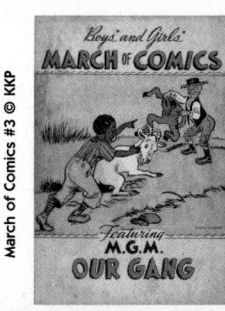

March of Comics #3 © KKP

	GD 2.0	VG 4.0	FN 6.0	VF 8.0	VF/NM 9.0	NM- 9.2
r/strips 4/13/39-6/21/39 & 7/6/39-7/17/39. "LOA and the Kidnappers"; r/strips 11/28/38-1/28/39	16	32	48	94	147	200
Quaker Sparkies Giveaway (1942, full color, 20 pgs.); "LOA and Mr. Gudge"; r/strips 2/13/38-3/21/38 & 4/18/37-5/30/37. "LOA and the Great Am"	15	30	45	88	137	185

LITTLE TREE THAT WASN'T WANTED, THE
W. T. Grant Co. (Giveaway): 1960, (Color, 28 pgs.)

	GD	VG	FN	VF	VF/NM	NM-
nn-Christmas story, puzzles and games	4	8	12	22	34	45

LOADED (Also see Re-Loaded)
DC Comics: 1995 (Interplay Productions)

1-Garth Ennis-s; promotes video game						4.00

LONE RANGER, THE
Dell Publishing Co.

	GD	VG	FN	VF	VF/NM	NM-
Cheerios Giveaways (1954, 16 pgs., 2-1/2x7", soft-c) #1- "The Lone Ranger, His Mask & How He Met Tonto". #2- "The Lone Ranger & the Story of Silver" each....	15	30	45	85	130	175
Doll Giveaways (Gabriel Ind.)(1973, 3-1/4x5")- "The Story of The Lone Ranger," "The Carson City Bank Robbery" & "The Apache Buffalo Hunt"	2	4	6	12	16	20
How the Lone Ranger Captured Silver Book(1936)-Silvercup Bread giveaway	59	118	177	369	610	850
...In Milk for Big Mike (1955, Dairy Association giveaway), soft-c; 5x7-1/4", 16 pgs.	14	28	42	80	115	150
Legend of The Lone Ranger (1969, 16 pgs., giveaway)-Origin The Lone Ranger	4	8	12	22	34	45
Merita Bread giveaway (1954, 16 pgs., 5x7-1/4")- "How to Be a Lone Ranger Health & Safety Scout"	18	36	54	103	162	220

LONE RANGER COMICS, THE
Lone Ranger, Inc.: Book 1, 1939(inside) (shows 1938 on-c) (52 pgs. in color; regular size) (Ice cream mail order)

	GD	VG	FN	VF	VF/NM	NM-
Book 1-(Scarce)-The first western comic devoted to a single character; not by Vallely	914	1828	2742	6400	-	-
2nd version w/large full color promo poster pasted over centerfold & a smaller poster pasted over back cover; includes new additional premiums not originally offered (Rare)	1000	2000	3000	7000	-	-

LOONEY TUNES
DC Comics: 1991, 1998

Claritin promotional issue (1998)						2.50
Colgate mini-comic (1998)						2.50
Tyson's 1-10 (1991)						4.00

LOVE FIGHTS
Oni Press: July, 2004 (Free Comic Book Day giveaway)

1-Flip book with r/Love Fights #1 and preview of Everest Facing the Goddess						2.50

LUCKY FIGHTS IT THROUGH (Also see The K. O. Punch)
Educational Comics: 1949 (Giveaway, 16 pgs. in color, paper-c)

	GD	VG	FN	VF	VF/NM	NM-
nn-(Very Rare)-1st Kurtzman work for E. C.; V.D. prevention	121	242	363	756	1253	1750
nn-Reprint in color (1977)						7.00

NOTE: Subtitled "The Story of That Ignorant, Ignorant Cowboy". Prepared for Communications Materials Center, Columbia University.

LUDWIG VON DRAKE (See Frito-Lay Giveaway)

MACO TOYS COMIC
Maco Toys/Charlton Comics: 1959 (Giveaway, 36 pgs.)

	GD	VG	FN	VF	VF/NM	NM-
1-All military stories featuring Maco Toys	2	4	6	11	16	20

MAD MAGAZINE
DC Comics: 1997, 1999

Special Edition (1997, Tang giveaway)						2.50
Stocking Stuffer (1999)						2.50

MAGAZINELAND
DC Comics: 1977

	GD	VG	FN	VF	VF/NM	NM-
nn-Kubert-c/a	3	6	9	14	19	24

MAGIC MORRO (Also see Super Comics #21, The Owl, & The Hurricane Kids)
K. K. Publications: 1941 (7-1/2 x 5-1/4", giveaway, soft-c)

	GD	VG	FN	VF	VF/NM	NM-
nn-Ken Ernst-a.	13	26	39	72	101	130

MAGIC OF CHRISTMAS AT NEWBERRYS, THE
E. S. London: 1967 (Giveaway) (B&W, slick-c, 20 pgs.)

	GD	VG	FN	VF	VF/NM	NM-
nn	1	3	4	6	8	10

MAJOR INAPAK THE SPACE ACE
Magazine Enterprises (Inapac Foods): 1951 (20 pgs.) (Giveaway)

	GD	VG	FN	VF	VF/NM	NM-
1-Bob Powell-c/a						6.00

NOTE: Many warehouse copies surfaced in 1973.

MAMMY YOKUM & THE GREAT DOGPATCH MYSTERY
Toby Press: 1951 (Giveaway)

	GD	VG	FN	VF	VF/NM	NM-
nn-Li'l Abner	15	30	45	88	137	185
nn-Reprint (1956)	5	10	15	22	26	30

MAN NAMED STEVENSON, A
Democratic National Committee: 1952 (20 pgs., 5 1/4 x 7")

	GD	VG	FN	VF	VF/NM	NM-
nn	9	18	27	47	61	75

MAN OF PEACE, POPE PIUS XII
Catechetical Guild: 1950 (See Pope Pius XII... & To V2#8)

	GD	VG	FN	VF	VF/NM	NM-
nn-All Powell-a	6	12	18	31	38	45

MAN OF STEEL BEST WESTERN
DC Comics: 1997 (Best Western hotels promo)

3-Reprints Superman's first post-Crisis meeting with Batman						4.00

MAN WHO WOULDN'T QUIT, THE
Harvey Publications Inc.: 1952 (16 pgs., paper cover)

	GD	VG	FN	VF	VF/NM	NM-
nn-The value of voting	4	8	12	18	22	25

MARCH OF COMICS (Boys' and Girls'...#3-353)
K. K. Publications/Western Publishing Co.: 1946 - No. 488, April, 1982 (#1-4 are not numbered) (K.K. Giveaway) (Founded by Sig Feuchtwanger)

Early issues were full size, 32 pages, and were printed with and without an extra cover of slick stock, just for the advertiser. The binding was stapled if the slick cover was added; otherwise, the pages were glued together at the spine. Most 1948 - 1951 issues were full size,24 pages, pulp covers. Starting in 1952 they were half-size (with a few exceptions) and 32 pages with slick covers.1959 and later issues had only 16 pages plus covers. 1952 -1959 issues read oblong; 1960 and later issues read upright. All have new stories except where noted.

	GD	VG	FN	VF	VF/NM	NM-
nn (#1, 1946)-Goldilocks; Kelly back-c (16 pgs., stapled)	43	86	129	262	431	600
nn (#2, 1946)-How Santa Got His Red Suit; Kelly-a (11 pgs., r/4-Color #61 from 1944) (16pgs., stapled)	30	60	90	174	275	375
nn (#3, 1947)-Our Gang (Walt Kelly)	40	80	120	235	368	500
nn (#4)-Donald Duck by Carl Barks, "Maharajah Donald", 28 pgs.; Kelly-c (Disney)	686	1372	2058	4800	8400	12,000
5-Andy Panda (Walter Lantz)	19	38	57	109	172	235
6-Popular Fairy Tales; Kelly-c; Noonan-a(2)	21	42	63	124	195	265
7-Oswald the Rabbit	19	38	57	112	176	240
8-Mickey Mouse, 32 pgs. (Disney)	46	92	138	281	466	650
9(nn)-The Story of the Gloomy Bunny	13	26	39	72	101	130
10-Out of Santa's Bag	12	24	36	67	94	120
11-Fun With Santa Claus	11	22	33	60	83	105
12-Santa's Toys	11	22	33	60	83	105
13-Santa's Surprise	11	22	33	60	83	105
14-Santa's Candy Kitchen	11	22	33	60	83	105
15-Hip-It-Ty Hop & the Big Bass Viol	11	22	33	60	83	95
16-Woody Woodpecker (1947)(Walter Lantz)	14	28	42	80	115	150
17-Roy Rogers (1948)	24	48	72	139	220	300
18-Popular Fairy Tales	12	24	36	69	97	125
19-Uncle Wiggily	11	22	33	62	86	110
20-Donald Duck by Carl Barks, "Darkest Africa", 22 pgs.; Kelly-c (Disney)	327	654	981	2125	3763	5400
21-Tom and Jerry	12	24	36	69	97	125
22-Andy Panda (Lantz)	11	22	33	62	86	110
23-Raggedy Ann & Andy; Kerr-a	14	28	42	80	115	150
24-Felix the Cat, 1932 daily strip reprints by Otto Messmer	21	42	63	122	191	260
25-Gene Autry	21	42	63	122	191	260
26-Our Gang; Walt Kelly	19	38	57	109	172	235
27-Mickey Mouse; r/in M. M. #240 (Disney)	36	72	108	208	329	450
28-Gene Autry	20	40	60	117	184	250
29-Easter Bonnet Shop	8	16	24	42	54	65
30-Here Comes Santa	8	16	24	40	50	60
31-Santa's Busy Corner	8	16	24	40	50	60
32-No book produced						
33-A Christmas Carol (12/48)	8	16	24	42	54	65
34-Woody Woodpecker	12	24	36	69	97	125
35-Roy Rogers (1948)	23	46	69	132	209	285
36-Felix the Cat(1949); by Messmer; '34 strip-r	17	34	51	100	158	215
37-Popeye	15	30	45	83	124	165
38-Oswald the Rabbit	10	20	30	54	72	90
39-Gene Autry	20	40	60	117	184	250
40-Andy and Woody	10	20	30	54	72	90
41-Donald Duck by Carl Barks, "Race to the South Seas", 22 pgs.; Kelly-c	315	630	945	2048	3624	5200
42-Porky Pig	10	20	30	56	76	95
43-Henry	9	18	27	52	69	85

	GD 2.0	VG 4.0	FN 6.0	VF 8.0	VF/NM 9.0	NM- 9.2		GD 2.0	VG 4.0	FN 6.0	VF 8.0	VF/NM 9.0	NM- 9.2
44-Bugs Bunny	11	22	33	60	83	105	117-Popeye	10	20	30	54	72	90
45-Mickey Mouse (Disney)	27	54	81	158	249	340	118-Flash Gordon; painted-c	12	24	36	67	94	120
46-Tom and Jerry	11	22	33	60	83	105	119-Tom and Jerry	5	10	15	22	26	30
47-Roy Rogers	19	38	57	112	176	240	120-Gene Autry	11	22	33	60	83	105
48-Greetings from Santa	6	12	18	31	38	45	121-Roy Rogers	11	22	33	60	83	105
49-Santa Is Here	6	12	18	31	38	45	122-Santa's Surprise (1954)	5	10	15	22	26	30
50-Santa Claus' Workshop (1949)	6	12	18	31	38	45	123-Santa's Christmas Book	5	10	15	22	26	30
51-Felix the Cat (1950) by Messmer	15	30	45	90	140	190	124-Woody Woodpecker (1955)	4	9	13	18	22	26
52-Popeye	13	26	39	74	105	135	125-Tarzan; Lex Barker photo-c	15	30	45	83	124	165
53-Oswald the Rabbit	9	18	27	52	69	85	126-Oswald the Rabbit	4	9	13	18	22	26
54-Gene Autry	17	34	51	100	158	215	127-Indian Chief	7	14	21	35	43	50
55-Andy and Woody	9	18	27	50	65	80	128-Tom and Jerry	4	9	13	18	22	26
56-Donald Duck; not by Barks; Barks art on back-c (Disney)							129-Henry	4	8	12	17	21	24
	30	60	90	174	275	375	130-Porky Pig	4	9	13	18	22	26
57-Porky Pig	9	18	27	52	69	85	131-Roy Rogers	11	22	33	60	83	105
58-Henry	8	16	24	42	54	65	132-Bugs Bunny	5	10	15	23	28	32
59-Bugs Bunny	10	20	30	56	76	95	133-Flash Gordon; painted-c	11	22	33	60	83	105
60-Mickey Mouse (Disney)	27	54	81	156	246	335	134-Popeye	8	16	24	42	54	65
61-Tom and Jerry	9	18	27	52	69	85	135-Gene Autry	10	20	30	56	76	95
62-Roy Rogers	19	38	57	109	172	235	136-Roy Rogers	10	20	30	56	76	95
63-Welcome Santa (1/2-size, oblong)	6	12	18	31	38	45	137-Gifts from Santa	4	7	10	14	17	20
64(nn)-Santa's Helpers (1/2-size, oblong)	6	12	18	31	38	45	138-Fun at Christmas (1955)	4	7	10	14	17	20
65(nn)-Jingle Bells (1950) (1/2-size, oblong)	6	12	18	31	38	45	139-Woody Woodpecker (1956)	4	9	13	18	22	26
66-Popeye (1951)	12	24	36	67	94	120	140-Indian Chief	7	14	21	35	43	50
67-Oswald the Rabbit	9	18	27	50	65	80	141-Oswald the Rabbit	4	9	13	18	22	26
68-Roy Rogers	18	36	54	105	165	225	142-Flash Gordon	11	22	33	60	83	105
69-Donald Duck; Barks-a on back-c (Disney)	26	52	78	152	239	325	143-Porky Pig	4	9	13	18	22	26
70-Tom and Jerry	9	18	27	47	61	75	144-Tarzan; Russ Manning-a; painted-c	14	28	42	80	115	150
71-Porky Pig	9	18	27	50	65	80	145-Tom and Jerry	4	9	13	18	22	26
72-Krazy Kat	10	20	30	56	76	95	146-Roy Rogers; photo-c	10	20	30	56	76	95
73-Roy Rogers	16	32	48	96	151	205	147-Henry	4	8	11	16	19	22
74-Mickey Mouse (1951)(Disney)	21	42	63	120	188	255	148-Popeye	8	16	24	42	54	65
75-Bugs Bunny	9	18	27	50	65	80	149-Bugs Bunny	5	10	15	22	26	30
76-Andy and Woody	9	18	27	47	61	75	150-Gene Autry	10	20	30	56	76	95
77-Roy Rogers	15	30	45	90	140	190	151-Roy Rogers	10	20	30	56	76	95
78-Gene Autry (1951); last regular size issue	15	30	45	86	133	180	152-The Night Before Christmas	4	8	11	16	19	22
Note: All pre #79 issues came with or without a slick protective wrap-around cover over the regular cover which advertised Poll Parrot Shoes, Sears, etc. This outer cover protects the inside pages making them in nicer condition.							153-Merry Christmas (1956)	4	9	13	18	22	26
							154-Tom and Jerry (1957)	4	9	13	18	22	26
							155-Tarzan; photo-c	14	28	42	78	112	145
Issues with the outer cover are worth 15-25% more							156-Oswald the Rabbit	4	9	13	18	22	26
79-Andy Panda (1952, 5x7" size)	7	14	21	35	43	50	157-Popeye	7	14	21	35	43	50
80-Popeye	10	20	30	58	79	100	158-Woody Woodpecker	4	9	13	18	22	26
81-Oswald the Rabbit	6	12	18	29	36	42	159-Indian Chief	7	14	21	35	43	50
82-Tarzan; Lex Barker photo-c	15	30	45	90	140	190	160-Bugs Bunny	5	10	15	22	26	30
83-Bugs Bunny	7	14	21	37	46	55	161-Roy Rogers	9	18	27	52	69	85
84-Henry	6	12	18	29	36	42	162-Henry	4	8	11	16	19	22
85-Woody Woodpecker	6	12	18	29	36	42	163-Rin Tin Tin (TV)	8	16	24	42	54	65
86-Roy Rogers	14	28	42	76	108	140	164-Porky Pig	4	9	13	18	22	26
87-Krazy Kat	8	16	24	44	57	70	165-The Lone Ranger	10	20	30	54	72	90
88-Tom and Jerry	6	12	18	31	38	45	166-Santa and His Reindeer	4	7	10	14	17	20
89-Porky Pig	6	12	18	29	36	42	167-Roy Rogers and Santa	9	18	27	52	69	85
90-Gene Autry	12	24	36	69	97	125	168-Santa Claus' Workshop (1957, full size)	4	8	11	16	19	22
91-Roy Rogers & Santa	13	26	39	74	105	135	169-Popeye (1958)	7	14	21	35	43	50
92-Christmas with Santa	5	10	15	24	30	35	170-Indian Chief	7	14	21	35	43	50
93-Woody Woodpecker (1953)	5	10	15	23	28	32	171-Oswald the Rabbit	4	8	12	17	21	24
94-Indian Chief	10	20	30	54	72	90	172-Tarzan	11	22	33	64	90	115
95-Oswald the Rabbit	5	10	15	23	28	32	173-Tom and Jerry	4	8	12	17	21	24
96-Popeye	10	20	30	54	72	90	174-The Lone Ranger	10	20	30	54	72	90
97-Bugs Bunny	7	14	21	35	43	50	175-Porky Pig	4	8	12	17	21	24
98-Tarzan; Lex Barker photo-c	15	30	45	86	133	180	176-Roy Rogers	9	18	27	47	61	75
99-Porky Pig	5	10	15	23	28	32	177-Woody Woodpecker	4	8	12	17	21	24
100-Roy Rogers	11	22	33	62	86	110	178-Henry	4	8	11	16	19	22
101-Henry	5	10	15	22	26	30	179-Bugs Bunny	4	8	12	17	21	24
102-Tom Corbett (TV)('53, early app.); painted-c	14	28	42	76	108	140	180-Rin Tin Tin (TV)	7	14	21	37	46	55
103-Tom and Jerry	5	10	15	23	28	32	181-Happy Holiday	4	7	9	14	16	18
104-Gene Autry	11	22	33	60	83	105	182-Happi Tim	4	8	11	16	19	22
105-Roy Rogers	11	22	33	60	83	105	183-Welcome Santa (1958, full size)	4	7	9	14	16	18
106-Santa's Helpers	5	10	15	24	30	35	184-Welcome Santa (1959)	4	8	11	16	19	22
107-Santa's Christmas Book - not published							185-Tarzan; photo-c	11	22	33	60	83	110
108-Fun with Santa (1953)	5	10	15	24	30	35	186-Oswald the Rabbit	4	8	11	16	19	22
109-Woody Woodpecker (1954)	5	10	15	24	30	35	187-Indian Chief	6	12	18	28	34	40
110-Indian Chief	6	12	18	31	38	45	188-Bugs Bunny	4	8	11	16	19	22
111-Oswald the Rabbit	5	10	15	22	26	30	189-Henry	4	7	10	14	17	20
112-Henry	4	9	13	18	22	26	190-Tom and Jerry	4	8	11	16	19	22
113-Porky Pig	5	10	15	22	26	30	191-Roy Rogers	8	16	24	44	57	70
114-Tarzan; Russ Manning-a	15	30	45	86	133	180	192-Porky Pig	4	8	11	16	19	22
115-Bugs Bunny	6	12	18	27	33	38	193-The Lone Ranger	9	18	27	52	69	85
116-Roy Rogers	11	22	33	60	83	105	194-Popeye	6	12	18	31	38	45

March of Comics #287 © WB
BUGS BUNNY
MAYCO CALIFORNIA

March of Comics #304 © KKP
The THREE STOOGES

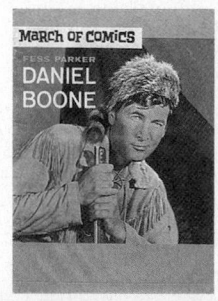

March of Comics #306 © DIS
FESS PARKER
DANIEL BOONE

	GD 2.0	VG 4.0	FN 6.0	VF 8.0	VF/NM 9.0	NM- 9.2
195-Rin Tin Tin (TV)	7	14	21	35	43	50
196-Sears Special - not published						
197-Santa Is Coming	4	7	10	14	17	20
198-Santa's Helpers (1959)	4	7	10	14	17	20
199-Huckleberry Hound (TV)(1960, early app.)	8	16	24	42	54	65
200-Fury (TV)	6	12	18	28	34	40
201-Bugs Bunny	4	8	11	16	19	22
202-Space Explorer	8	16	24	42	54	65
203-Woody Woodpecker	4	7	10	14	17	20
204-Tarzan	9	18	27	52	69	85
205-Mighty Mouse	6	12	18	33	41	48
206-Roy Rogers; photo-c	8	16	24	42	54	65
207-Tom and Jerry	4	7	10	14	17	20
208-The Lone Ranger; Clayton Moore photo-c	11	22	33	62	86	110
209-Porky Pig	4	7	10	14	17	20
210-Lassie (TV)	6	12	18	33	41	48
211-Sears Special - not published						
212-Christmas Eve	4	7	10	14	17	20
213-Here Comes Santa (1960)	4	7	10	14	17	20
214-Huckleberry Hound (TV)(1961)	7	14	21	35	43	50
215-Hi Yo Silver	8	16	24	40	50	60
216-Rocky & His Friends (TV)(1961); predates Rocky and His Fiendish Friends #1						
(see Four Color #1128)	10	20	30	58	79	100
217-Lassie (TV)	6	12	18	31	38	45
218-Porky Pig	4	7	10	14	17	20
219-Journey to the Sun	5	10	15	24	30	35
220-Bugs Bunny	4	8	11	16	19	22
221-Roy and Dale; photo-c	8	16	24	42	54	65
222-Woody Woodpecker	4	7	10	14	17	20
223-Tarzan	9	18	27	52	69	85
224-Tom and Jerry	4	7	10	14	17	20
225-The Lone Ranger	8	16	24	40	50	60
226-Christmas Treasury (1961)	4	7	10	14	17	20
227-Letters to Santa (1961)	4	7	10	14	17	20
228-Sears Special - not published?						
229-The Flintstones (TV)(1962); early app.; predates 1st Flintstones Gold Key issue (#7)						
	11	22	33	60	83	105
230-Lassie (TV)	6	12	18	27	33	38
231-Bugs Bunny	4	8	11	16	19	22
232-The Three Stooges	10	20	30	54	72	90
233-Bullwinkle (TV) (1962, very early app.)	10	20	30	58	79	100
234-Smokey the Bear	5	10	15	23	28	32
235-Huckleberry Hound (TV)	7	14	21	35	43	50
236-Roy and Dale	7	14	21	35	43	50
237-Mighty Mouse	6	12	18	27	33	38
238-The Lone Ranger	8	16	24	40	50	60
239-Woody Woodpecker	4	7	10	14	17	20
240-Tarzan	8	16	24	44	57	70
241-Santa Claus Around the World	4	7	9	14	16	18
242-Santa's Toyland (1962)	4	7	9	14	16	18
243-The Flintstones (TV)(1963)	8	16	24	44	57	70
244-Mister Ed (TV); early app.; photo-c	7	14	21	35	43	50
245-Bugs Bunny	4	8	11	16	19	22
246-Popeye	6	12	18	27	33	38
247-Mighty Mouse	6	12	18	27	33	38
248-The Three Stooges	10	20	30	54	72	90
249-Woody Woodpecker	4	7	10	14	17	20
250-Roy and Dale	7	14	21	35	43	50
251-Little Lulu & Witch Hazel	12	24	36	67	94	120
252-Tarzan; painted-c	8	16	24	42	54	65
253-Yogi Bear (TV)	8	16	24	40	50	60
254-Lassie (TV)	6	12	18	27	33	38
255-Santa's Christmas List	4	7	10	14	17	20
256-Christmas Party (1963)	4	7	10	14	17	20
257-Mighty Mouse	6	12	18	27	33	38
258-The Sword in the Stone (Disney)	8	16	24	42	54	65
259-Bugs Bunny	4	8	11	16	19	22
260-Mister Ed (TV)	6	12	18	31	38	45
261-Woody Woodpecker	4	7	10	14	17	20
262-Tarzan	8	16	24	40	50	60
263-Donald Duck; not by Barks (Disney)	9	18	27	52	69	85
264-Popeye	6	12	18	27	33	38
265-Yogi Bear (TV)	6	12	18	31	38	45
266-Lassie (TV)	5	10	15	23	28	32
267-Little Lulu; Irving Tripp-a	10	20	30	56	76	95
268-The Three Stooges	9	18	27	47	61	75
269-A Jolly Christmas	3	6	8	12	14	16
270-Santa's Little Helpers	3	6	8	12	14	16

	GD 2.0	VG 4.0	FN 6.0	VF 8.0	VF/NM 9.0	NM- 9.2
271-The Flintstones (TV)(1965)	8	16	24	44	57	70
272-Tarzan	8	16	24	40	50	60
273-Bugs Bunny	4	8	11	16	19	22
274-Popeye	6	12	18	27	33	38
275-Little Lulu; Irving Tripp-a	9	18	27	50	65	80
276-The Jetsons (TV)	14	28	42	76	108	140
277-Daffy Duck	4	8	11	16	19	22
278-Lassie (TV)	5	10	15	23	28	32
279-Yogi Bear (TV)	6	12	18	31	38	45
280-The Three Stooges; photo-c	9	18	27	47	61	75
281-Tom and Jerry	4	7	9	14	16	18
282-Mister Ed (TV)	6	12	18	31	38	45
283-Santa's Visit	4	7	9	14	16	18
284-Christmas Parade (1965)	4	7	9	14	16	18
285-Astro Boy (TV); 2nd app. Astro Boy	30	60	90	174	275	375
286-Tarzan	7	14	21	37	46	55
287-Bugs Bunny	4	8	11	16	19	22
288-Daffy Duck	4	7	10	14	17	20
289-The Flintstones (TV)	8	16	24	44	57	70
290-Mister Ed (TV); photo-c	5	10	15	24	30	35
291-Yogi Bear (TV)	6	12	18	27	33	38
292-The Three Stooges; photo-c	9	18	27	47	61	75
293-Little Lulu; Irving Tripp-a	8	16	24	42	54	65
294-Popeye	5	10	15	24	30	35
295-Tom and Jerry	4	7	9	14	16	18
296-Lassie (TV); photo-c	5	10	15	22	26	30
297-Christmas Bells	3	6	8	12	14	16
298-Santa's Sleigh (1966)	3	6	8	12	14	16
299-The Flintstones (TV)(1967)	8	16	24	44	57	70
300-Tarzan	7	14	21	37	46	55
301-Bugs Bunny	4	7	10	14	17	20
302-Laurel and Hardy (TV); photo-c	6	12	18	28	34	40
303-Daffy Duck	3	6	8	12	14	16
304-The Three Stooges; photo-c	8	16	24	44	57	70
305-Tom and Jerry	3	6	8	12	14	16
306-Daniel Boone (TV); Fess Parker photo-c	7	14	21	35	43	50
307-Little Lulu; Irving Tripp-a	7	14	21	37	46	55
308-Lassie (TV); photo-c	5	10	15	22	26	30
309-Yogi Bear (TV)	5	10	15	24	30	35
310-The Lone Ranger; Clayton Moore photo-c	11	22	33	62	86	110
311-Santa's Show	4	7	9	14	16	18
312-Christmas Album (1967)	4	7	9	14	16	18
313-Daffy Duck (1968)	3	6	8	12	14	16
314-Laurel and Hardy (TV)	6	12	18	27	33	38
315-Bugs Bunny	4	7	10	14	17	20
316-The Three Stooges	8	16	24	40	50	60
317-The Flintstones (TV)	8	16	24	42	54	65
318-Tarzan	7	14	21	35	43	50
319-Yogi Bear (TV)	5	10	15	24	30	35
320-Space Family Robinson (TV); Spiegle-a	12	24	36	69	97	125
321-Tom and Jerry	3	6	8	12	14	16
322-The Lone Ranger	7	14	21	37	46	55
323-Little Lulu; not by Stanley	5	10	15	24	30	35
324-Lassie (TV); photo-c	5	10	15	22	26	30
325-Fun with Santa	4	7	9	14	16	18
326-Christmas Story (1968)	4	7	9	14	16	18
327-The Flintstones (TV)(1969)	8	16	24	42	54	65
328-Space Family Robinson (TV); Spiegle-a	12	24	36	69	97	125
329-Bugs Bunny	4	7	10	14	17	20
330-The Jetsons (TV)	10	20	30	56	76	95
331-Daffy Duck	3	6	8	12	14	16
332-Tarzan	6	12	18	28	34	40
333-Tom and Jerry	3	6	8	12	14	16
334-Lassie (TV)	4	9	13	18	22	26
335-Little Lulu	5	10	15	24	30	35
336-The Three Stooges	8	16	24	40	50	60
337-Yogi Bear (TV)	5	10	15	24	30	35
338-The Lone Ranger	7	14	21	37	46	55
339-(Was not published)						
340-Here Comes Santa (1969)	3	6	8	12	14	16
341-The Flintstones (TV)	8	16	24	42	54	65
342-Tarzan	3	6	9	20	30	40
343-Bugs Bunny	2	4	6	10	14	18
344-Yogi Bear (TV)	3	6	9	16	23	30
345-Tom and Jerry	2	4	6	9	13	16
346-Lassie (TV)	3	6	9	15	21	26
347-Daffy Duck	2	4	6	9	13	16
348-The Jetsons (TV)	6	12	18	39	62	85

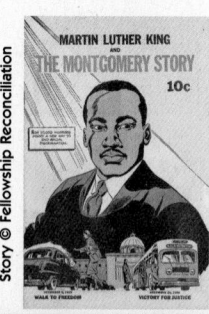
	GD 2.0	VG 4.0	FN 6.0	VF 8.0	VF/NM 9.0	NM- 9.2
349-Little Lulu; not by Stanley	3	6	9	16	23	30
350-The Lone Ranger	3	6	9	18	27	35
351-Beep-Beep, the Road Runner (TV)	2	4	6	11	16	20
352-Space Family Robinson (TV); Spiegle-a	8	16	24	54	90	125
353-Beep-Beep, the Road Runner (1971) (TV)	2	4	6	11	16	20
354-Tarzan (1971)	3	6	9	18	27	35
355-Little Lulu; not by Stanley	3	6	9	16	23	30
356-Scooby Doo, Where Are You? (TV)	6	12	18	43	69	95
357-Daffy Duck & Porky Pig	2	4	6	8	11	14
358-Lassie (TV)	3	6	9	14	19	24
359-Baby Snoots	2	4	6	10	14	18
360-H. R. Pufnstuf (TV); photo-c	6	12	18	43	69	95
361-Tom and Jerry	2	4	6	8	11	14
362-Smokey Bear (TV)	2	4	6	8	11	14
363-Bugs Bunny & Yosemite Sam	2	4	6	9	13	16
364-The Banana Splits (TV); photo-c	6	12	18	37	59	80
365-Tom and Jerry (1972)	2	4	6	8	11	14
366-Tarzan	3	6	9	18	27	35
367-Bugs Bunny & Porky Pig	2	4	6	9	13	16
368-Scooby Doo (TV)(4/72)	6	12	18	37	59	80
369-Little Lulu; not by Stanley	3	6	9	14	19	24
370-Lassie (TV); photo-c	3	6	9	14	19	24
371-Baby Snoots	2	4	6	9	13	16
372-Smokey the Bear (TV)	2	4	6	8	11	14
373-The Three Stooges	4	8	12	24	37	50
374-Wacky Witch	2	4	6	8	11	14
375-Beep-Beep & Daffy Duck (TV)	2	4	6	8	11	14
376-The Pink Panther (1972) (TV)	2	4	6	10	14	18
377-Baby Snoots (1973)	2	4	6	9	13	16
378-Turok, Son of Stone; new-a	8	16	24	56	93	130
379-Heckle & Jeckle New Terrytoons (TV)	2	4	6	8	11	14
380-Bugs Bunny & Yosemite Sam	2	4	6	8	11	14
381-Lassie (TV)	2	4	6	11	16	20
382-Scooby Doo, Where Are You? (TV)	5	10	15	32	51	70
383-Smokey the Bear (TV)	2	4	6	8	11	14
384-Pink Panther (TV)	2	4	6	8	11	14
385-Little Lulu	2	4	6	13	18	22
386-Wacky Witch	2	4	6	8	11	14
387-Beep-Beep & Daffy Duck (TV)	2	4	6	8	11	14
388-Tom and Jerry (1973)	2	4	6	8	11	14
389-Little Lulu; not by Stanley	2	4	6	13	18	22
390-Pink Panther (TV)	2	4	6	8	11	14
391-Scooby Doo (TV)	4	8	12	26	41	55
392-Bugs Bunny & Yosemite Sam	2	4	6	8	10	12
393-New Terrytoons (Heckle & Jeckle) (TV)	2	4	6	8	10	12
394-Lassie (TV)	2	4	6	9	13	16
395-Woodsy Owl	2	4	6	8	10	12
396-Baby Snoots	2	4	6	8	11	14
397-Beep-Beep & Daffy Duck (TV)	2	4	6	8	10	12
398-Wacky Witch	2	4	6	8	10	12
399-Turok, Son of Stone; new-a	7	14	21	50	83	115
400-Tom and Jerry	2	4	6	8	10	12
401-Baby Snoots (1975) (r/#371)	2	4	6	8	11	14
402-Daffy Duck (r/#313)	1	3	4	6	8	10
403-Bugs Bunny (r/#343)	2	4	6	8	10	12
404-Space Family Robinson (TV)(r/#328)	6	12	18	41	66	90
405-Cracky	1	3	4	6	8	10
406-Little Lulu (r/#355)	2	4	6	10	14	18
407-Smokey the Bear (TV)(r/#362)	2	4	6	8	10	12
408-Turok, Son of Stone; c-r/Turok #20 w/changes; new-a	6	12	18	39	62	85
409-Pink Panther (TV)	1	3	4	6	8	10
410-Wacky Witch	1	2	3	5	6	8
411-Lassie (TV)(r/#324)	2	4	6	9	13	16
412-New Terrytoons (1975) (TV)	1	2	3	5	6	8
413-Daffy Duck (1976) (r/#331)	1	2	3	5	6	8
414-Space Family Robinson (r/#328)	6	12	18	39	62	85
415-Bugs Bunny (r/#329)	1	2	3	5	6	8
416-Beep-Beep, the Road Runner (r/#353)(TV)	1	2	3	5	6	8
417-Little Lulu (r/#323)	2	4	6	10	14	18
418-Pink Panther (r/#384) (TV)	1	2	3	5	6	8
419-Baby Snoots (r/#377)	1	3	4	6	8	10
420-Woody Woodpecker	1	2	3	5	6	8
421-Tweety & Sylvester	1	2	3	5	6	8
422-Wacky Witch (r/#386)	1	2	3	5	6	8
423-Little Monsters	1	3	4	6	8	10
424-Cracky (12/76)	1	2	3	5	6	8
425-Daffy Duck	1	2	3	5	6	8

	GD 2.0	VG 4.0	FN 6.0	VF 8.0	VF/NM 9.0	NM- 9.2
426-Underdog (TV)	4	8	12	22	34	45
427-Little Lulu (r/#335)	2	4	6	8	11	14
428-Bugs Bunny	1	2	3	4	5	7
429-The Pink Panther (TV)	1	2	3	4	5	7
430-Beep-Beep, the Road Runner (TV)	1	2	3	4	5	7
431-Baby Snoots	1	2	3	5	6	8
432-Lassie (TV)	2	4	6	8	10	12
433-437: 433-Tweety & Sylvester. 434-Wacky Witch. 435-New Terrytoons (TV). 436-Wacky Advs. of Cracky. 437-Daffy Duck	1	2	3	4	5	7
438-Underdog (TV)	3	6	9	20	30	40
439-Little Lulu (r/#349)	2	4	6	8	11	14
440-442,444-446: 440-Bugs Bunny. 441-The Pink Panther (TV). 442-Beep-Beep, the Road Runner (TV). 444-Tom and Jerry. 445-Tweety and Sylvester. 446-Wacky Witch	1	2	3	5	6	8
443-Baby Snoots	1	2	3	5	6	8
447-Mighty Mouse	2	4	6	8	10	12
448-455,457,458: 448-Cracky. 449-Pink Panther (TV). 450-Baby Snoots. 451-Tom and Jerry. 452-Bugs Bunny. 453-Popeye. 454-Woody Woodpecker. 455-Beep-Beep, the Road Runner (TV). 457-Tweety & Sylvester. 458-Wacky Witch	1	2	3	5	6	8
456-Little Lulu (r/#369)	2	4	6	8	10	12
459-Mighty Mouse	2	4	6	8	10	12
460-466: 460-Daffy Duck. 461-The Pink Panther (TV). 462-Baby Snoots. 463-Tom and Jerry. 464-Bugs Bunny. 465-Popeye. 466-Woody Woodpecker	1	2	3	5	6	8
467-Underdog (TV)	3	6	9	18	27	35
468-Little Lulu (r/#385)	1	2	3	5	6	8
469-Tweety & Sylvester	1	2	3	5	6	8
470-Wacky Witch	1	2	3	5	6	8
471-Mighty Mouse	1	3	4	6	8	10
472-474,476-478: 472-Heckle & Jeckle(12/80). 473-Pink Panther(1/81)(TV). 474-Baby Snoots. 476-Bugs Bunny. 477-Popeye. 478-Woody Woodpecker	1	2	3	5	6	8
475-Little Lulu (r/#323)	1	3	4	6	8	10
479-Underdog (TV)	3	6	9	16	23	30
480-482: 480-Tom and Jerry. 481-Tweety and Sylvester. 482-Wacky Witch	1	2	3	4	5	8
483-Mighty Mouse	1	3	4	6	8	10
484-487: 484-Heckle & Jeckle. 485-Baby Snoots. 486-The Pink Panther (TV). 487-Bugs Bunny	1	2	3	4	5	8
488-Little Lulu (4/82) (r/#335) (Last issue)	2	4	6	10	14	18

MARGARET O'BRIEN (See The Adventures of...)

MARK STEEL
American Iron & Steel Institute: 1967, 1968, 1972 (Giveaway) (24 pgs.)

	GD 2.0	VG 4.0	FN 6.0	VF 8.0	VF/NM 9.0	NM- 9.2
1967,1968- "Journey of Discovery with..."; Neal Adams art	4	8	12	26	41	55
1972- "...Fights Pollution"; N. Adams-a	3	6	9	20	30	40

MARTIN LUTHER KING AND THE MONTGOMERY STORY
Fellowship Reconciliation: 1956 (Giveaway, 16 pgs.) (A Spanish edition also exists)
nn-In color with paper-c (a CGC 9.2 copy sold for $350 and a FN+ sold for $200 in 2004)

MARVEL ADVENTURES THREE-IN-ONE
Marvel Comics: 2007 (Free Comic Book Day giveaway)
1-Iron Man, Incredible Hulk and Franklin Richards app.   2.50

MARVEL AGE SPIDER-MAN
Marvel Comics: Aug, 2004 (Free Comic Book Day giveaway)
1-Spider-Man vs. The Vulture; Brooks-a   2.50

MARVEL AGE SPIDER-MAN TEAM-UP (Marvel Adventures on cover)
Marvel Comics: June, 2005 (Free Comic Book Day giveaway)
1-Spider-Man meets the Fantastic Four   2.50

MARVEL COLLECTOR'S EDITION: X-MEN
Marvel Comics: 1993 (3-3/4x6-1/2")
1-4-Pizza Hut giveaways   5.00

MARVEL COMICS PRESENTS
Marvel Comics: 1987, 1988 (4 1/4 x 6 1/4, 20 pgs.)
...Mini Comic Giveaway

	GD 2.0	VG 4.0	FN 6.0	VF 8.0	VF/NM 9.0	NM- 9.2
nn-(1988) Alf	1	2	3	5	6	8
nn-(1987) Captain America r/ #250	1	2	3	4	5	7
nn-(1987) Care Bears (Star Comics...)	1	2	3	4	5	7
nn-(1988) Flintstone Kids	1	2	3	5	6	8
nn-(1987) Heathcliffe (Star Comics...)	1	2	3	4	5	7
nn-(1988) Spider-Man-r/Spect. Spider-Man #21	1	2	3	4	5	7
nn-(1988) Spider-Man-r/Amazing Spider-Man #1	1	2	3	4	5	7
nn-(1988) X-Men-reprints X-Men #53; B. Smith-a	1	2	3	4	5	7

MARVEL GUIDE TO COLLECTING COMICS, THE

Marvel Collector's Edition: X-Men © MAR

The Matrix © WB

Mickey Mouse Magazine V1 #9 © DIS

	GD 2.0	VG 4.0	FN 6.0	VF 8.0	VF/NM 9.0	NM- 9.2

Marvel Comics: 1982 (16 pgs., newsprint pages and cover)
1-Simonson-c — 1 · 2 · 3 · 4 · 5 · 7

MARVEL HALLOWEEN ASHCAN 2006
Marvel Comics: 2006 (8-1/2"x 5-1/2", Halloween giveaway)
nn-r/Marvel Adventures The Avengers #1 — 2.00

MARVEL MINI-BOOKS
Marvel Comics Group: 1966 (50 pgs., B&W; 5/8x7/8") (6 different issues)
(Smallest comics ever published) (Marvel Mania Giveaways)
Captain America, Millie the Model, Sgt. Fury, Hulk, Thor
each... — 3 · 6 · 9 · 20 · 30 · 40
Spider-Man — 4 · 8 · 12 · 24 · 37 · 50
NOTE: *Each came in six different color covers, usually one color: Pink, yellow, green, etc.*

MARVEL SUPER-HERO ISLAND ADVENTURES
Marvel Comics: 1999 (Sold at the park polybagged with Captain America V3 #19, one other comic, 5 trading cards and a cloisonné pin)
1-Promotes Universal Studios Islands of Adventures theme park — 2.50

MARY'S GREATEST APOSTLE (St. Louis Grignion de Montfort)
Catechetical Guild (Topix) (Giveaway): No date (16 pgs.; paper cover)
nn — 5 · 10 · 15 · 22 · 26 · 30

MASK
DC Comics: 1985
1-3 — 5.00

MASKED PILOT, THE (See Popular Comics #43)
R.S. Callender: 1939 (7-1/2x5-1/4", 16 pgs., premium, non-slick-c)
nn-Bob Jenney-a — 10 · 20 · 30 · 56 · 76 · 95

MASTERS OF THE UNIVERSE (He-Man)
DC Comics: 1982 (giveaways with action figures, at least 35 different issues, unnumbered)
nn — 6.00

MATRIX, THE (1999 movie)
Warner Brothers: 1999 (Recalled by Warner Bros. over questionable content)
nn-Paul Chadwick-s/a (16 pgs.); Geof Darrow-c — 1 · 2 · 3 · 5 · 6 · 8

McCRORY'S CHRISTMAS BOOK
Western Printing Co: 1955 (36 pgs., slick-c) (McCrory Stores Corp. giveaway)
nn-Painted-c — 4 · 8 · 12 · 18 · 22 · 25

McCRORY'S TOYLAND BRINGS YOU SANTA'S PRIVATE EYES
Promotional Publ. Co.: 1956 (16 pgs.) (Giveaway)
nn-Has 9 pg. story plus 7 pgs. toy ads — 4 · 8 · 11 · 16 · 19 · 22

McCRORY'S WONDERFUL CHRISTMAS
Promotional Publ. Co.: 1954 (20 pgs., slick-c) (Giveaway)
nn — 4 · 8 · 12 · 18 · 22 · 25

McDONALDS COMMANDRONS
DC Comics: 1985
nn-Four editions — 5.00

MEET HIYA A FRIEND OF SANTA CLAUS
Julian J. Proskauer/Sundial Shoe Stores, etc.: 1949 (18 pgs.?, paper-c)(Giveaway)
nn — 6 · 12 · 18 · 31 · 38 · 45

MEET THE NEW POST-GAZETTE SUNDAY FUNNIES
Pittsburgh Post Gazette: 3/12/49 (7-1/4x10-1/4", 16 pgs., paper-c)
Commercial (insert in newspaper) (Rare)
Dick Tracy by Gould, Gasoline Alley, Terry & the Pirates, Brenda Starr, Buck Rogers by Yager, The Gumps, Peter Rabbit by Fago, Superman, Funnyman by Siegel & Shuster, The Saint, Archie, & others done especially for this book. A fine copy sold at auction in 1985 for $276.00.
— 400 · 800 · 1200 · 2600 · - · -

MEN OF COURAGE
Catechetical Guild: 1949
Bound Topix comics-V7#2,4,6,8,10,16,18,20 — 6 · 12 · 18 · 31 · 38 · 45

MEN WHO MOVE THE NATION
Publisher unknown: (Giveaway) (B&W)
nn-Neal Adams-a — 6 · 12 · 18 · 31 · 38 · 45

MERRY CHRISTMAS, A
K. K. Publications (Child Life Shoes): 1948 (Giveaway)
nn — 6 · 12 · 18 · 33 · 41 · 48

MERRY CHRISTMAS
K. K. Publications (Blue Bird Shoes Giveaway): 1956 (7-1/4x5-1/4")
nn — 4 · 8 · 12 · 18 · 22 · 25

MERRY CHRISTMAS FROM MICKEY MOUSE

K. K. Publications: 1939 (16 pgs.) (Color & B&W) (Shoe store giveaway)
nn-Donald Duck & Pluto app.; text with art (Rare); c-reprint/Mickey Mouse
Mag. V3#3 (12/37)(Rare) — 262 · 524 · 786 · 1638 · 2719 · 3800

MERRY CHRISTMAS FROM SEARS TOYLAND (See Santa's Christmas Comic)
Sears Roebuck Giveaway: 1939 (16 pgs.) (Color)
nn-Dick Tracy, Little Orphan Annie, The Gumps, Terry & the Pirates
— 110 · 220 · 330 · 688 · 1144 · 1600

MICKEY MOUSE (Also see Frito-Lay Giveaway)
Dell Publ. Co
...& Goofy Explore Business(1978) — 1 · 3 · 4 · 6 · 8 · 10
...& Goofy Explore Energy(1976-1978, 36 pgs.); Exxon giveaway in color;
regular size — 1 · 3 · 4 · 6 · 8 · 10
...& Goofy Explore Energy Conservation(1976-1978)-Exxon
— 1 · 3 · 4 · 6 · 8 · 10
...& Goofy Explore The Universe of Energy(1985, 20 pgs.); Exxon giveaway in
color; regular size — 2 · 3 · 4 · 5 · 7
The Perils of Mickey nn (1993, 5-1/4x7-1/4", 16 pgs.)-Nabisco giveaway w/
games, Nabisco coupons & 6 pgs. of stories; Phantom Blot app. — 5.00

MICKEY MOUSE MAGAZINE
Walt Disney Productions: V1#1, Jan, 1933 - V1#9, Sept, 1933 (5-1/4x7-1/4")
No. 1-3 published by Kamen-Blair (Kay Kamen, Inc.)
(Scarce)-Distributed by dairies and leading stores through their local theatres.
First few issues had 5¢ listed on cover, later ones had no price.
V1#1 — 540 · 1080 · 2160 · 6500 · - · -
2-4 — 225 · 450 · 900 · 1750 · - · -
5-9 — 175 · 350 · 700 · 1350 · - · -

MICKEY MOUSE MAGAZINE
Walt Disney Productions: V1#1, 11/33 - V2#12, 10/35 (Mills giveaways issued by different dairies)
V1#1 — 240 · 600 · 960 · 1350 · 2025 · 2700
2-12: 2-X-Mas issue — 80 · 200 · 320 · 475 · 688 · 900
V2#1-4,6-12: 2-X-Mas issue. 4-St. Valentine-c — 55 · 124 · 192 · 310 · 455 · 600
V2#5 (3/35) 1st app. Donald Duck in sailor outfit on-c — 96 · 192 · 288 · 600 · 975 · 1350

MICKEY MOUSE MAGAZINE
K.K. Publications: V4#1, Oct, 1938 (Giveaway)
V4#1 — 543 · 86 · 129 · 262 · 431 · 600

MIGHTY ATOM, THE
Whitman
Giveaway (1959, '63, Whitman)-Evans-a — 3 · 6 · 9 · 14 · 19 · 24
Giveaway ('64r, '65r, '66r, '67r, '68r)-Evans-r? — 2 · 4 · 6 · 8 · 11 · 14
Giveaway ('73r, '76r) — 1 · 3 · 4 · 6 · 8 · 10

MILES THE MONSTER (Initially sold only at the Dover Speedway track)
Dover International Speedway, Inc.: 2006 ($3.00)
1,2-Allan Gross-s/Mark Wheatley-a — 3.00

MILITARY COURTESY
Harvey Publications: (16 pgs.)
nn-Regulations and saluting instructions — 5 · 10 · 14 · 20 · 24 · 28

MINUTE MAN
Sovereign Service Station giveaway: No date (16 pgs., B&W, paper-c blue & red)
nn-American history — 3 · 6 · 8 · 12 · 14 · 16

MINUTE MAN ANSWERS THE CALL, THE
By M. C. Gaines: 1942,1943,1944,1945 (4 pgs.) (Giveaway inserted in Jr. JSA Membership Kit)
nn-Sheldon Moldoff-a — 21 · 42 · 63 · 122 · 191 · 260

MIRACLE ON BROADWAY
Broadway Comics: Dec, 1995 (Giveaway)
1-Ernie Colon-c/a; Jim Shooter & Co. story; 1st known digitally printed comic book;
1st app. Spire & Knights on Broadway (1150 print run) — 20.00
NOTE: *Miracle on Broadway was a limited edition comic given to 1100 VIPs in the entertainment industry for the 1995 Holiday Season.*

MISS SUNBEAM (See Little Miss Sunbeam Comics)

MR. BUG GOES TO TOWN (See Cinema Comics Herald)
K.K. Publications: 1941 (Giveaway, 52 pgs.)
nn-Cartoon movie (scarce) — 72 · 144 · 216 · 450 · 750 · 1050

MR. PEANUT, THE PERSONAL STORY OF
Planters Nut & Chocolate Co.: 1956
nn — 4 · 8 · 12 · 22 · 34 · 45

MOTHER OF US ALL
Catechetical Guild Giveaway: 1950? (32 pgs.)
nn — 5 · 10 · 15 · 23 · 28 · 32

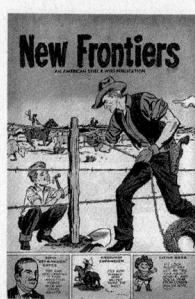

New Frontiers © U.S. Steel Corp.

Oxydol-Dreft #1 © TOBY

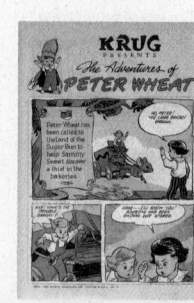

Peter Wheat #33 © Bakers Assoc.

	GD 2.0	VG 4.0	FN 6.0	VF 8.0	VF/NM 9.0	NM- 9.2

MOTION PICTURE FUNNIES WEEKLY (Amazing Man #5 on?)
First Funnies, Inc.: 1939 (Giveaway)(B&W, 36 pgs.) No month given; last panel in Sub-Mariner story dated 4/39 (Also see Colossus, Green Giant & Invaders No. 20)

1-Origin & 1st printed app. Sub-Mariner by Bill Everett (8 pgs.); Fred Schwab-c; reprinted in Marvel Mystery #1 with color added over the craft tint which was used to shade the black & white version; Spy Ring, American Ace (reprinted in Marvel Mystery #3) app.
(Rare)-only eight known copies, one near mint with white pages, the rest with brown pages.

		GD	VG	FN	VF	VF/NM
	4400	7700	11,000	17,800	29,000	-

Covers only to #2-4 (set) ... 1000
NOTE: Eight copies (plus one coverless) were discovered in 1974 in the estate of the deceased publisher. Covers only to issues No. 2-4 were also found which evidently were printed in advance along with #1. #1 was to be distributed only through motion picture movie houses. However, it is believed that only advanced copies were sent out and the motion picture houses not going for the idea. Possible distribution at local theaters in Boston suspected. The "pay" copy (graded at 9.0) was discovered after 1974, bringing the total known to nine. The last panel of Sub-Mariner contains a rectangular box with "Continued Next Week" printed in it. When reprinted in Marvel Mystery, the box was left in with lettering omitted.

MY DOG TIGE (Buster Brown's Dog)
Buster Brown Shoes: 1957 (Giveaway)

	GD	VG	FN	VF	VF/NM	NM-
nn	5	10	15	24	30	35

MY GREATEST THRILLS IN BASEBALL
Mission of California: Date? (16 pg. Giveaway)

	GD	VG	FN	VF	VF/NM	NM-
nn-By Mickey Mantle	55	110	165	344	572	800

MYSTERIOUS ADVENTURES OF SANTA CLAUS
Lansburgh's: 1948 (paper cover)

	GD	VG	FN	VF	VF/NM	NM-
nn	12	24	36	69	97	125

NATURAL DISASTERS!
Graphic Information Service/ Civil Defense: 1956 (16 pgs., soft-c)

nn-Al Capp Li'l Abner-c; Li'l Abner cameo (1 panel); narrated by Mr. Civil Defense

	GD	VG	FN	VF	VF/NM	NM-
	10	20	30	54	72	90

NAVY: HISTORY & TRADITION
Stokes Walesby Co./Dept. of Navy: 1958 - 1961 (nn) (Giveaway)
1772-1778, 1778-1782, 1782-1817, 1817-1865, 1865-1936, 1940-1945:

	GD	VG	FN	VF	VF/NM	NM-
1772-1778-16 pg. in color	5	10	15	22	26	30
1861: Naval Actions of the Civil War: 1865-36 pg. in color; flag-c						
	5	10	15	22	26	30

NEW ADVENTURES OF WALT DISNEY'S SNOW WHITE AND THE SEVEN DWARFS, A
(See Snow White Bendix Giveaway)

NEW ADVENTURES OF PETER PAN (Disney)
Western Publishing Co.: 1953 (5x7-1/4", 36 pgs.) (Admiral giveaway)

	GD	VG	FN	VF	VF/NM	NM-
nn	14	28	42	76	108	140

NEW AVENGERS...
Marvel Comics: 2005 (Giveaway for U.S Military personnel)

... Guest Starring the Fantastic Four (4/05) Bendis-s/Jurgens-a/c 3.00
...: Pot of Gold (AAFES 110th Anniversary Issue) (10/05) Jenkins-s/Nolan-a/c 3.00

NEW FRONTIERS
Harvey Information Press (United States Steel Corp.): 1958 (16 pgs., paper-c)

	GD	VG	FN	VF	VF/NM	NM-
nn-History of barbed wire	2	4	6	14	18	22

NEW TEEN TITANS, THE
DC Comics: Nov. 1983

nn(11/83-Keebler Co. Giveaway)-In cooperation with "The President's Drug Awareness Campaign"; came in Presidential envelope w/letter from White House (Nancy Reagan)

	GD	VG	FN	VF	VF/NM
	1	2	3	4	5 ... 7

nn-(re-issue of above on Mando paper for direct sales market); American Soft Drink Industry version; I.B.M. Corp. version 5.00

NOLAN RYAN IN THE WINNING PITCH (Kellogg's Tony's Sports Comics)
DC Comics: 1992 (Sports Illustrated)

nn 4.00

OLD GLORY COMICS
Chesapeake & Ohio Railway: 1944 (Giveaway)

	GD	VG	FN	VF	VF/NM	NM-
nn-Capt. Fearless reprint	8	16	24	40	50	60

ON THE AIR
NBC Network Comic: 1947 (Giveaway, paper-c)

	GD	VG	FN	VF	VF/NM	NM-
nn-(Rare)	24	48	72	139	220	300

OUT OF THE PAST A CLUE TO THE FUTURE
E. C. Comics (Public Affairs Comm.): 1946? (16 pgs.) (paper cover)

nn-Based on public affairs pamphlet "What Foreign Trade Means to You"

	GD	VG	FN	VF	VF/NM	NM-
	21	42	63	124	188	255

OUTSTANDING AMERICAN WAR HEROES
The Parents' Institute: 1944 (16 pgs., paper-c)

	GD	VG	FN	VF	VF/NM	NM-
nn-Reprints from True Comics	5	10	15	22	26	30

OVERSEAS COMICS (Also see G.I. Comics & Jeep Comics)
Giveaway (Distributed to U.S. Armed Forces): 1944 - No. 105?, 1946 (7-1/4x10-1/4"; 16 pgs. in color)

23-105-Bringing Up Father (by McManus), Popeye, Joe Palooka, Dick Tracy, Superman, Gasoline Alley, Buz Sawyer, Li'l Abner, Blondie, Terry & the Pirates, Out Our Way

	GD	VG	FN	VF	VF/NM	NM-
	7	14	21	35	43	50

OWL, THE (See Crackajack Funnies #25 & Popular Comics #72)(Also see The Hurricane Kids & Magic Morro)
Western Pub. Co./R.S. Callender: 1940 (Giveaway)(7-1/2x5-1/4")(Soft-c, color)

	GD	VG	FN	VF	VF/NM	NM-
nn-Frank Thomas-a	20	40	60	115	180	245

OXYDOL-DREFT
Toby Press:1950 (Set of 6 pocket-size giveaways; distributed through the mail as a set) (Scarce)

	GD	VG	FN	VF	VF/NM	NM-
1-3: 1-Li'l Abner. 2-Daisy Mae. 3-Shmoo	13	26	39	74	105	135
4-John Wayne; Williamson/Frazetta-c from John Wayne #3						
	15	30	45	88	137	185
5-Archie	15	30	45	85	130	175
6-Terrytoons Mighty Mouse	13	26	39	74	105	135
Mailing Envelope (has All Capp's Shmoo on front)	14	28	42	78	112	145

OZZIE SMITH IN THE KID WHO COULD (Kellogg's Tony's Sports Comics)
DC Comics: 1992 (Sports Illustrated)

nn-Ozzie Smith app. 5.00

PADRE OF THE POOR
Catechetical Guild: nd (Giveaway) (16 pgs., paper-c)

	GD	VG	FN	VF	VF/NM	NM-
nn	5	10	15	23	28	32

PAUL TERRY'S HOW TO DRAW FUNNY CARTOONS
Terrytoons, Inc. (Giveaway): 1940's (14 pgs.) (Black & White)

	GD	VG	FN	VF	VF/NM	NM-
nn-Heckle & Jeckle, Mighty Mouse, etc.	12	24	36	67	97	125

PETER PAN (See New Adventures of Peter Pan)

PETER PENNY AND HIS MAGIC DOLLAR
American Bankers Association, N.Y. (Giveaway): 1947 (16 pgs.; paper-c; regular size)

	GD	VG	FN	VF	VF/NM	NM-
nn-(Scarce)-Used in SOTI, pg. 310, 311	15	30	45	88	137	185
Diff. version (7-1/4x11")-redrawn, 16 pgs., paper-c	10	20	30	56	76	95

PETER WHEAT (The Adventures of...)
Bakers Associates Giveaway: 1948 - 1957? (16 pgs. in color) (paper covers)

	GD	VG	FN	VF	VF/NM	NM-
nn(No.1)-States on last page, end of 1st Adventure of...; Kelly-a	29	58	87	167	264	360
nn(4 issues)-Kelly-a	15	30	45	86	133	180
6-10-All Kelly-a	12	24	36	67	94	120
11-20-All Kelly-a	11	22	33	62	86	110
21-35-All Kelly-a	10	20	30	54	72	90
36-66	8	16	24	40	50	60
...Artist's Workbook ('54, digest size)	8	16	24	40	50	60
...Four-In-One Fun Pack (Vol. 2, '54), oblong, comics w/puzzles						
	8	16	24	44	57	70
...Fun Book ('52, 32 pgs., paper-c, B&W & color, 8-1/2x10-3/4")-Contains cut-outs, puzzles, games, magic & pages to color	10	20	30	58	79	100

NOTE: Al Hubbard art #36 on; written by Del Connell.

PETER WHEAT NEWS
Bakers Associates: 1948 - No. 30, 1950 (4 pgs. in color)

	GD	VG	FN	VF	VF/NM	NM-
Vol. 1-All have 2 pgs. Peter Wheat by Kelly	24	48	72	137	216	295
2-10	14	28	42	82	121	160
11-20	10	20	30	54	72	90
21-30	8	16	24	40	50	60

NOTE: Early issues have no date & Kelly art.

PINOCCHIO
Cocomalt/Montgomery Ward Co.: 1940 (10 pgs.; giveaway, linen-like paper)

	GD	VG	FN	VF	VF/NM	NM-
nn-Cocomalt edition	45	90	135	275	450	625
nn-store edition	38	76	114	219	347	475

PIUS XII MAN OF PEACE
Catechetical Guild: No date (12 pgs.; 5-1/2x8-1/2") (B&W)

	GD	VG	FN	VF	VF/NM	NM-
nn-Catechetical Guild Giveaway	6	12	18	31	38	45

PLOT TO STEAL THE WORLD, THE
Work & Unity Group: 1948, 16pgs., paper-c

	GD	VG	FN	VF	VF/NM	NM-
nn-Anti communism	17	34	51	98	154	210

POCAHONTAS
Pocahontas Fuel Company (Coal): 1941 - No. 2, 1942

nn(#1), 2-Feat. life story of Indian princess Pocahontas & facts about Pocahontas coal,

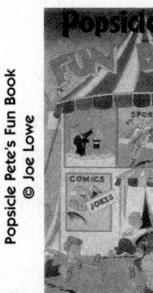

Popsicle Pete's Fun Book © Joe Lowe

Reddy Kilowatt #2 © EC

Robin Hood's Frontier Days © Robin Hood Shoes

	GD 2.0	VG 4.0	FN 6.0	VF 8.0	VF/NM 9.0	NM- 9.2
Pocahontas, VA.	15	30	45	85	130	175

POLL PARROT
Poll Parrot Shoe Store/International Shoe
K. K. Publications (Giveaway): 1950 - No. 4, 1951; No. 2, 1959 - No. 16, 1962

	GD 2.0	VG 4.0	FN 6.0	VF 8.0	VF/NM 9.0	NM- 9.2
1 ('50)-Howdy Doody; small size	18	36	54	107	169	230
2-4('51)-Howdy Doody	15	30	45	88	137	185

2('59)-16('62): 2-The Secret of Crumbley Castle. 5-Bandit Busters. 7-The Make-Believe Mummy. 8-Mixed Up Mission('60). 10-The Frightful Flight. 11-Showdown at Sunup. 12-Maniac at Mubu Island. 13-...and the Runaway Genie. 14-Bully for You. 15-Trapped In Tall Timber. 16-...& the Rajah's Ruby('62)

	GD 2.0	VG 4.0	FN 6.0	VF 8.0	VF/NM 9.0	NM- 9.2
	3	6	9	16	22	28

POPEYE
Whitman

	GD 2.0	VG 4.0	FN 6.0	VF 8.0	VF/NM 9.0	NM- 9.2
Bold Detergent giveaway (Same as regular issue #94)	2	4	6	8	11	14
Quaker Cereal premium (1989, 16pp, small size,4 diff.)(Popeye & the Time Machine, --On Safari, --& Big Foot, --vs. Bluto)	1	3	4	6	8	10

POPEYE
Charlton (King Features) (Giveaway): 1972 - 1974 (36 pgs. in color)

	GD 2.0	VG 4.0	FN 6.0	VF 8.0	VF/NM 9.0	NM- 9.2
E-1 to E-15 (Educational comics)	2	4	6	8	11	14
nn-Popeye Gettin' Better Grades-4 pgs. used as intro. to above giveaways (in color)	2	4	6	8	11	14

POPSICLE PETE FUN BOOK (See All-American Comics #6)
Joe Lowe Corp.: 1947, 1948

	GD 2.0	VG 4.0	FN 6.0	VF 8.0	VF/NM 9.0	NM- 9.2
nn-36 pgs. in color; Sammy 'n' Claras, The King Who Couldn't Sleep & Popsicle Pete stories, games, cut-outs	11	22	33	64	90	115
Adventure Book ('48)-Has Classics ad with checklist to HRN #343 (Great Expectations #43)	10	20	30	56	76	95

PORKY'S BOOK OF TRICKS
K. K. Publications (Giveaway): 1942 (8-1/2x5-1/2", 48 pgs.)

	GD 2.0	VG 4.0	FN 6.0	VF 8.0	VF/NM 9.0	NM- 9.2
nn-7 pg. comic story, text stories, plus games & puzzles	48	96	144	293	484	675

POST GAZETTE (See Meet the New...)

PUNISHER: COUNTDOWN (Movie)
Marvel Comics: 2004 (7 1/4" X 4 3/4" mini-comic packaged with Punisher DVD)

	GD 2.0	VG 4.0	FN 6.0	VF 8.0	VF/NM 9.0	NM- 9.2
nn-Prequel to 2004 movie; Ennis-s/Dillon-a/Bradstreet-c						2.50

PURE OIL COMICS (Also see Salerno Carnival of Comics, 24 Pages of Comics, & Vicks Comics)
Pure Oil Giveaway: Late 1930's (24 pgs., regular size, paper-c)

	GD 2.0	VG 4.0	FN 6.0	VF 8.0	VF/NM 9.0	NM- 9.2
nn-Contains 1-2 pg. strips; i.e., Hairbreadth Harry, Skyroads, Buck Rogers by Calkins & Yager, Olly of the Movies, Napoleon, S'Matter Pop, etc. Also a 16 pg. 1938 giveaway with Buck Rogers	37	74	111	213	337	460

QUAKER OATS (Also see Cap'n Crunch)
Quaker Oats Co.: 1965 (Giveaway) (2-1/2x5-1/2") (16 pgs.)

	GD 2.0	VG 4.0	FN 6.0	VF 8.0	VF/NM 9.0	NM- 9.2
"Plenty of Glutton", starring Quake & Quisp;	3	6	9	14	19	24
"Lava Come-Back", "Kite Tale"	1	3	4	6	8	10

RAILROADS DELIVER THE GOODS!
Assoc. of American Railroads: Dec, 1954; Sept, 1957 (16 pgs.)

	GD 2.0	VG 4.0	FN 6.0	VF 8.0	VF/NM 9.0	NM- 9.2
nn-The story of railway freight	6	12	18	28	34	40

RAILS ACROSS AMERICA!
Assoc. of American Railroads: nd (16 pgs.)

	GD 2.0	VG 4.0	FN 6.0	VF 8.0	VF/NM 9.0	NM- 9.2
nn	6	12	18	28	34	40

REAL FUN OF DRIVING!!, THE
Chrysler Corp.: 1965, 1966, 1967 (Regular size, 16 pgs.)

	GD 2.0	VG 4.0	FN 6.0	VF 8.0	VF/NM 9.0	NM- 9.2
nn-Schaffenberger-a (12 pgs.)	1	2	3	5	6	8

REAL HIT
Fox Features Publications: 1944 (Savings Bond premium)

	GD 2.0	VG 4.0	FN 6.0	VF 8.0	VF/NM 9.0	NM- 9.2
1-Blue Beetle-r	15	30	45	90	140	190

NOTE: Two versions exist, with and without covers. The coverless version has the title, No. 1 and price printed at top of splash page.

RED BALL COMIC BOOK
Parents' Magazine Institute: 1947 (Red Ball Shoes giveaway)

	GD 2.0	VG 4.0	FN 6.0	VF 8.0	VF/NM 9.0	NM- 9.2
nn-Reprints from True Comics	4	8	11	16	19	22

REDDY GOOSE
International Shoe Co. (Western Printing): No number, 1958?; No. 2, Jan, 1959 - No. 16, July, 1962 (Giveaway)

	GD 2.0	VG 4.0	FN 6.0	VF 8.0	VF/NM 9.0	NM- 9.2
nn (#1)	5	10	15	30	48	65
2-16	3	6	9	18	27	35

REDDY KILOWATT (5¢) (Also see Story of Edison)
Educational Comics (E. C.): 1946 - No. 2, 1947; 1956 - 1965 (no month) (16 pgs., paper-c)

	GD 2.0	VG 4.0	FN 6.0	VF 8.0	VF/NM 9.0	NM- 9.2
nn-A Visit With Reddy (1948-1954?)	9	18	27	50	65	80
nn-Reddy Made Magic (1946, 5¢)	13	26	39	72	101	130
nn-Reddy Made Magic (1958)	9	18	27	50	65	80
2-Edison, the Man Who Changed the World (3/4" smaller than #1) (1947, 5¢)	13	26	39	72	101	130
...Comic Book 2 (1954)- "Light's Diamond Jubilee"	9	18	27	54	72	90
...Comic Book 2 (1958, 16 pgs.)- "Wizard of Light"	9	18	27	50	65	78
...Comic Book 2 (1965, 16 pgs.)- "Wizard of Light"	4	8	12	28	44	60
...Comic Book 3 (1956, 8 pgs.)- "The Space Kite"; Orlando story; regular size	9	18	27	47	61	75
...Comic Book 3 (1960, 8 pgs.)- "The Space Kite"; Orlando story; regular size	4	8	12	28	44	60

NOTE: Several copies surfaced in 1979.

REDDY MADE MAGIC
Educational Comics (E. C.): 1956, 1958 (16 pgs., paper-c)

	GD 2.0	VG 4.0	FN 6.0	VF 8.0	VF/NM 9.0	NM- 9.2
1-Reddy Kilowatt-r (splash panel changed)	11	22	33	60	83	105
1 (1958 edition)	6	12	18	31	38	45

RED ICEBERG, THE
Impact Publ. (Catechetical Guild): 1960 (10¢, 16 pgs., Communist propaganda)

	GD 2.0	VG 4.0	FN 6.0	VF 8.0	VF/NM 9.0	NM- 9.2
nn-(Rare)- "We The People" back-c	30	60	90	225	413	600
2nd version- "Impact Press" back-c	26	52	78	195	348	500
3rd version- "Explains comic" back-c	26	52	78	195	348	500
4th version- "Impact Press w/World Wide Secret Heart Program ad"	26	52	78	195	348	500
5th version- "Chicago Inter-Student Catholic Action" back-c	26	52	78	195	348	500

NOTE: This book was the Guild's last anti-communist propaganda book and had very limited circulation. 3 - 4 copies surfaced in 1979 from the defunct publisher's files. Other copies do turn up.

RED RYDER COMICS
Dell Publ. Co.

	GD 2.0	VG 4.0	FN 6.0	VF 8.0	VF/NM 9.0	NM- 9.2
Buster Brown Shoes Giveaway (1941, color, soft-c, 32 pgs.)	24	48	72	139	220	300
Red Ryder Super Book of Comics (1944, paper-c, 32 pgs.; blank back-c) Magic Morro app.	26	52	78	154	242	330
Red Ryder Victory Patrol-nn(1942, 32 pgs.)(Langendorf bread; includes cut-out membership card and certificate, order blank and "Slide-Up" decoder, and a Super Book of Comics in color (same content as Super Book #4 w/diff. cover (Pan-Am)) (Rare)	300	600	900	1931	3366	4800
Red Ryder Victory Patrol-nn(1943, 32 pgs.)(Langendorf bread; includes cut-out "Rodeomatic" radio decoder, order coupon for "Magic V-Badge", cut-out membership card and certificate and a full color Super Book of comics comic book) (Rare)	300	600	900	1881	3141	4400
Red Ryder Victory Patrol-nn(1944, 32 pgs.)-r-/#43,44; comic has a paper-c & is stapled inside a triple cardboard fold-out-c; contains membership card, decoder, map of R.R. home range, etc. Herky app. (Langendorf Bread giveaway; sub-titled 'Super Book of Comics') (Rare)	300	600	900	1881	3141	4400
Wells Lamont Corp. giveaway (1950)-16 pgs. in color; regular size; paper-c; 1941-r	18	36	54	105	165	225

RELOADED (Also see Loaded)
DC Comics: 1996 (Interplay Productions, 16 pgs.)

	GD 2.0	VG 4.0	FN 6.0	VF 8.0	VF/NM 9.0	NM- 9.2
1-Promotes video game; Alan Grant-s/John Mueller-a						4.00

RICHIE RICH, CASPER & WENDY NATIONAL LEAGUE
Harvey Publications: June, 1976 (52 pgs.) (newsstand edition also exists)

	GD 2.0	VG 4.0	FN 6.0	VF 8.0	VF/NM 9.0	NM- 9.2
1 (Released-3/76 with 6/76 date)	3	6	9	14	19	24
1 (6/76)-2nd version w/San Francisco Giants & KTVU 2 logos; has "Compliments of Giants and Straw Hat Pizza" on-c	3	6	9	14	19	24
1-Variants for other 11 NL teams, similar to Giants version but with different ad on inside front-c	3	6	9	14	19	24

RIDE THE HIGH IRON!
Assoc. of American Railroads: Jan, 1957 (16 pgs.)

	GD 2.0	VG 4.0	FN 6.0	VF 8.0	VF/NM 9.0	NM- 9.2
nn-The Story of modern passenger trains	6	12	18	28	34	40

RIPLEY'S BELIEVE IT OR NOT!
Harvey Publications

	GD 2.0	VG 4.0	FN 6.0	VF 8.0	VF/NM 9.0	NM- 9.2
J. C. Penney giveaway (1948)	9	18	27	50	65	80

ROBIN HOOD (New Adventures of...)
Walt Disney Productions: 1952 (Flour giveaways, 5x7-1/4", 36 pgs.)

	GD 2.0	VG 4.0	FN 6.0	VF 8.0	VF/NM 9.0	NM- 9.2
"New Adventures of Robin Hood", "Ghosts of Waylea Castle", & "The Miller's Ransom" each....	5	10	15	24	30	35

ROBIN HOOD'S FRONTIER DAYS (...Western Tales, Adventures of... #1)
Shoe Store Giveaway (Robin Hood Stores): 1956 (20 pgs., slick-c)(7 issues?)

	GD 2.0	VG 4.0	FN 6.0	VF 8.0	VF/NM 9.0	NM- 9.2
nn	5	10	15	25	31	36
nn-Issues with Crandall-a	8	16	24	40	50	60

ROBOCOP (FRANK MILLER'S...)

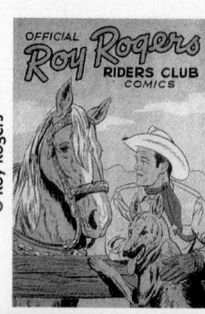

Roy Rogers Riders Club Comics © Roy Rogers

Santa's Secrets © Sam B. Anson

Sergeant Preston of the Yukon © FAW

	GD 2.0	VG 4.0	FN 6.0	VF 8.0	VF/NM 9.0	NM- 9.2

Avatar Press: Apr, 2003

Free Comic Book Day Edition - Previews Robocop & Stargate SG•1; Busch-c — 2.50

ROCKET COMICS: IGNITE
Dark Horse Comics: Apr, 2003 (Free Comic Book Day giveaway)

1-Previews Dark Horse series Syn, Lone, and Go Boy 7 — 2.50

ROCKETS AND RANGE RIDERS
Richfield Oil Corp.: May, 1957 (Giveaway, 16 pgs., soft-c)

| nn-Toth-a | 14 | 28 | 42 | 80 | 115 | 150 |

ROUND THE WORLD GIFT
National War Fund (Giveaway): No date (mid 1940's) (4 pgs.)

| nn | 11 | 22 | 33 | 64 | 90 | 115 |

ROY ROGERS COMICS
Dell Publishing Co.

...& the Man From Dodge City (Dodge giveaway, 16 pgs., 1954)-Frontier, Inc.

| (5x7-1/4") | 14 | 28 | 42 | 80 | 115 | 150 |

Official Roy Rogers Riders Club Comics (1952; 16 pgs., reg. size, paper-c)

| | 30 | 60 | 90 | 174 | 275 | 375 |

RUDOLPH, THE RED-NOSED REINDEER
Montgomery Ward: 1939 (2,400,000 copies printed); Dec, 1951 (Giveaway)

Paper cover-1st app. in print; written by Robert May; ill. by Denver Gillen

| | 14 | 28 | 42 | 82 | 121 | 160 |
| Hardcover version | 18 | 36 | 54 | 103 | 162 | 225 |

1951 Edition (Has 1939 date)-36 pgs., slick-c printed in red & brown; pulp interior printed in four mixed-ink colors: red, green, blue & brown

| | 11 | 22 | 33 | 60 | 83 | 105 |

1951 Edition with red-spiral promotional booklet printed on high quality stock, 8-1/2"x11", in red & brown, 25 pages composed of 4 fold outs, single sheets and the Rudolph comic book inserted (rare)

| | 46 | 92 | 138 | 281 | 466 | 650 |

SABRINA THE TEENAGE WITCH
Archie Comic Publications: (8 1/2"x 5 1/2", Diamond Comic Dist. Halloween giveaway)

... And The Archies (2004)-Tania Del Rio-s/a; manga-style; Josie and the Pussycats app. — 2.50

SAD CASE OF WAITING ROOM WILLIE, THE
American Visuals Corp. (For Baltimore Medical Society): (nd, 1950?)
(14 pgs. in color; paper covers; regular size)

| nn-By Will Eisner (Rare) | 45 | 90 | 135 | 275 | 450 | 625 |

SAD SACK COMICS
Harvey Publications: 1957-1962

Armed Forces Complimentary copies, HD #1-40 (1957-1962)

| | 3 | 6 | 9 | 14 | 19 | 24 |

SALERNO CARNIVAL OF COMICS (Also see Pure Oil Comics, 24 Pages of Comics, & Vicks Comics)
Salerno Cookie Co.: Late 1930s (Giveaway, 16 pgs, paper-c)

nn-Color reprints of Calkins' Buck Rogers & Skyroads, plus other strips from Famous Funnies

| | 43 | 86 | 129 | 262 | 431 | 600 |

SALUTE TO THE BOY SCOUTS
Association of American Railroads: 1960 (16 pgs.)

| nn-History of scouting and the railroad | 6 | 9 | 14 | 19 | 24 |

SANTA AND POLLYANNA PLAY THE GLAD GAME
Sales Promotion: Aug, 1960 (16 pgs.) (Disney giveaway)

| nn | 2 | 4 | 6 | 13 | 18 | 22 |

SANTA & THE BUCCANEERS
Promotional Publ. Co.: 1959 (Giveaway)

| nn-Reprints 1952 Santa & the Pirates | 2 | 4 | 6 | 11 | 16 | 20 |

SANTA & THE CHRISTMAS CHICKADEE
Murphy's: 1974 (Giveaway, 20 pgs.)

| nn | 2 | 4 | 6 | 8 | 10 | 12 |

SANTA & THE PIRATES
Promotional Publ. Co.: 1952 (Giveaway)

| nn-Marv Levy-c/a | 4 | 8 | 11 | 16 | 19 | 22 |

SANTA CLAUS FUNNIES (Also see The Little Fir Tree)
W. T. Grant Co./Whitman Publishing: nd; 1940 (Giveaway, 8x10"; 12 pgs., color & B&W, heavy paper)

| nn-(2 versions- no date and 1940) | 14 | 28 | 42 | 80 | 115 | 150 |

SANTA ON THE JOLLY ROGER
Promotional Publ. Co. (Giveaway): 1965

| nn-Marv Levy-c/a | 2 | 4 | 6 | 8 | 10 | 12 |

SANTA! SANTA!
R. Jackson: 1974 (20 pgs.) (Montgomery Ward giveaway)

| nn | 1 | 3 | 4 | 6 | 8 | 10 |

SANTA'S BUNDLE OF FUN
Gimbels: 1969 (Giveaway, B&W, 20 pgs.)

| nn-Coloring book & games | 2 | 4 | 6 | 8 | 10 | 12 |

SANTA'S CHRISTMAS COMIC VARIETY SHOW (See Merry Christmas From Sears Toyland)
Sears Roebuck & Co.: 1943 (24 pgs.)

Contains puzzles & new comics of Dick Tracy, Little Orphan Annie, Moon Mullins, Terry & the Pirates, etc.

| | 54 | 108 | 162 | 338 | 562 | 785 |

SANTA'S CHRISTMAS TIME STORIES
Premium Sales, Inc.: nd (Late 1940s) (16 pgs., paper-c) (Giveaway)

| nn | 6 | 12 | 18 | 31 | 38 | 45 |

SANTA'S CIRCUS
Promotional Publ. Co.: 1964 (Giveaway, half-size)

| nn-Marv Levy-c/a | 2 | 4 | 6 | 8 | 11 | 14 |

SANTA'S FUN BOOK
Promotional Publ. Co.: 1951, 1952 (Regular size, 16 pgs., paper-c) (Murphy's giveaway)

| nn | 5 | 10 | 15 | 23 | 28 | 32 |

SANTA'S GIFT BOOK
No Publisher: No date (16 pgs.)

| nn-Puzzles, games only | 4 | 8 | 11 | 16 | 19 | 22 |

SANTA'S NEW STORY BOOK
Wallace Hamilton Campbell: 1949 (16 pgs., paper-c) (Giveaway)

| nn | 6 | 12 | 18 | 31 | 38 | 45 |

SANTA'S REAL STORY BOOK
Wallace Hamilton Campbell/W. W. Orris: 1948, 1952 (Giveaway, 16 pgs.)

| nn | 6 | 12 | 18 | 31 | 38 | 45 |

SANTA'S RIDE
W. T. Grant Co.: 1959 (Giveaway)

| nn | 3 | 6 | 9 | 14 | 19 | 24 |

SANTA'S RODEO
Promotional Publ. Co.: 1964 (Giveaway, half-size)

| nn-Marv Levy-a | 2 | 4 | 6 | 8 | 11 | 14 |

SANTA'S SECRET CAVE
W.T. Grant Co.: 1960 (Giveaway, half-size)

| nn | 2 | 4 | 6 | 11 | 16 | 20 |

SANTA'S SECRETS
Sam B. Anson Christmas giveaway: 1951, 1952? (16 pgs., paper-c)

| nn-Has games, stories & pictures to color | 4 | 8 | 12 | 17 | 21 | 24 |

SANTA'S STORIES
K. K. Publications (Klines Dept. Store): 1953 (Regular size, paper-c)

| nn-Kelly-a | 15 | 30 | 45 | 88 | 137 | 185 |

| nn-Another version (1953, glossy-c, half-size, 7-1/4x5-1/4")-Kelly-a | 11 | 22 | 33 | 62 | 86 | 110 |

SANTA'S SURPRISE
K. K. Publications: 1947 (Giveaway, 36 pgs., slick-c)

| nn | 8 | 16 | 24 | 40 | 50 | 60 |

SANTA'S TOYTOWN FUN BOOK
Promotional Publ. Co.: 1953 (Giveaway)

| nn-Marv Levy-c | 4 | 8 | 11 | 16 | 19 | 22 |

SANTA TAKES A TRIP TO MARS
Bradshaw-Diehl Co., Huntington, W.VA.: 1950s (nd) (Giveaway, 16 pgs.)

| nn | 4 | 8 | 11 | 16 | 19 | 22 |

SCIENCE FAIR STORY OF ELECTRONICS
Radio Shack/Tandy Corp.: 1975 - 1987 (Giveaway)

11 different issues (approx. 1 per year) each.... — 3.00

SCOOBY-DOO!
DC Comics.: 2002 (Burger King/Cartoon Network giveaway)

1 — 2.50

SERGEANT PRESTON OF THE YUKON
Quaker Cereals: 1956 (4 comic booklets) (Soft-c, 16 pgs., 7x2-1/2" & 5x2-1/2")
Giveaways

"How He Found Yukon King", "The Case That Made Him A Sergeant", "How Yukon King Saved Him From The Wolves", "How He Became A Mountie"

| each... | 10 | 20 | 30 | 56 | 76 | 95 |

SHAZAM! (Visits Portland Oregon in 1943)

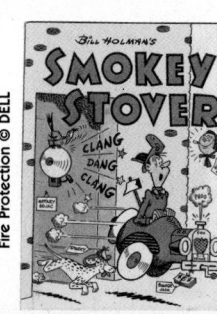

Smokey Stover National Fire Protection © DELL

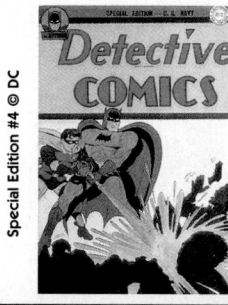

Special Edition #4 © DC

The Spirit 7/07/40 © Will Eisner

	GD 2.0	VG 4.0	FN 6.0	VF 8.0	VF/NM 9.0	NM- 9.2
DC Comics: 1989 (69¢ cover)						
nn-Promotes Super-Heroes exhibit at Oregon Museum of Science and Industry; reprints Golden Age Captain Marvel story	2	4	6	8	10	12
SHERIFF OF COCHISE, THE (TV) **Mobil:** 1957 (16 pgs.) Giveaway						
nn-Schaffenberger-a	4	8	12	17	21	24
SILLY PUTTY MAN DC Comics: 1978						
1	2	4	6	8	11	14
SKATING SKILLS Custom Comics, Inc./Chicago Roller Skates: 1957 (36 & 12 pgs.; 5x7", two versions) (10¢)						
nn-Resembles old ACG cover plus interior art	4	7	10	14	17	20
SKIPPY'S OWN BOOK OF COMICS (See Popular Comics) **No publisher listed:** 1934 (Giveaway, 52 pgs., strip reprints)						
nn-(Scarce)-By Percy Crosby	364	728	1092	2366	4183	6000
Published by Max C. Gaines for Phillip's Dental Magnesia to be advertised on the Skippy Radio Show and given away with the purchase of a tube of Phillip's Tooth Paste. This is the first four-color comic book of reprints about one character.						
SKY KING "RUNAWAY TRAIN" (TV) **National Biscuit Co.:** 1964 (Regular size, 16 pgs.)						
nn	6	12	18	41	66	90
SLAM BANG COMICS Post Cereal Giveaway: No. 9, No date						
9-Dynamic Man, Echo, Mr. E, Yankee Boy app.	9	18	27	50	65	80
SLAVE LABOR STORIES SLG Publishing: May, 2003 (Giveaway, B&W)						
1-Free Comic Book Day Edition; short stories by various; Dorkin Milk & Cheese-c						2.50
SMILIN' JACK Dell Publishing Co.						
Popped Wheat Giveaway (1947)-1938 strip reprints; 16 pgs. in full color	2	4	6	8	11	14
Shoe Store Giveaway-1938 strip reprints; 16 pgs.	5	10	15	24	30	35
Sparked Wheat Giveaway (1942)-16 pgs. in full color	5	10	15	24	30	35
SMOKEY BEAR (See Forest Fire for 1st app.) **Dell Publ. Co.:** 1959,1960						
True Story of..., The -U.S. Forest Service giveaway-Publ. by Western Printing Co.; reprints 1st 16 pgs. of Four Color #932. Inside front-c differs slightly in 1959 & 1960 editions	5	10	15	22	26	30
1964,1969 reprints	2	4	6	11	16	20
SMOKEY STOVER Dell Publishing Co.						
General Motors giveaway (1953)	8	16	24	40	50	60
National Fire Protection giveaway(1953 & 1954)-16 pgs., paper-c	8	16	24	40	50	60
SNOW FOR CHRISTMAS W. T. Grant Co.: 1957 (16 pgs.) (Giveaway)						
nn	4	8	12	18	22	25
SNOW WHITE AND THE SEVEN DWARFS Bendix Washing Machines: 1952 (32 pgs., 5x7-1/4", soft-c) (Disney)						
nn	11	22	33	62	86	110
SNOW WHITE AND THE SEVEN DWARFS Promotional Publ. Co.: 1957 (Small size)						
nn	6	12	18	28	34	40
SNOW WHITE AND THE SEVEN DWARFS Western Printing Co.: 1958 (16 pgs, 5x7-1/4", soft-c) (Disney premium)						
nn- "Mystery of the Missing Magic"	8	16	24	42	54	65
SNOW WHITE AND THE 7 DWARFS IN "MILKY WAY" American Dairy Assoc.: 1955 (16 pgs., soft-c, 5x7-1/4") (Disney premium)						
nn	10	20	30	58	79	100
SPACE GHOST COAST TO COAST Cartoon Network: Apr, 1994 (giveaway to Turner Broadcasting employees)						
1-(8 pgs.); origin of Space Ghost						6.00
SPACE PATROL (TV) **Ziff-Davis Publishing Co. (Approved Comics)**						
...'s Special Mission (8 pgs., B&W, Giveaway)	48	96	144	293	484	675
SPECIAL AGENT						

	GD 2.0	VG 4.0	FN 6.0	VF 8.0	VF/NM 9.0	NM- 9.2
Assoc. of American Railroads: Oct, 1959 (16 pgs.)						
nn-The Story of the railroad police	8	16	24	40	50	60
SPECIAL DELIVERY Post Hall Synd.: 1951 (32 pgs.; B&W) (Giveaway)						
nn-Origin of Pogo, Swamp, etc.; 2 pg. biog. on Walt Kelly (One copy sold in 1980 for $150.00)						
SPECIAL EDITION (U. S. Navy Giveaways) **National Periodical Publications:** 1944 - 1945 (Regular comic format with wording simplified, 52 pgs.)						
1-Action (1944)-Reprints Action #80	53	106	159	323	537	750
2-Action (1944)-Reprints Action #81	53	106	159	323	537	750
3-Superman (1944)-Reprints Superman #33	53	106	159	323	537	750
4-Detective (1944)-Reprints Detective #97	53	106	159	323	537	750
5-Superman (1945)-Reprints Superman #34	53	106	159	323	537	750
6-Action (1945)-Reprints Action #84	53	106	159	323	537	750
NOTE: *Wayne Boring* c-1, 2, 6. *Dick Sprang* c-4.						
SPIDER-MAN (See Amazing Spider-Man, The)						
SPIRIT, THE (Weekly Comic Book) **Will Eisner:** 6/2/40 - 10/5/52 (16 pgs.; 8 pgs.) (no cover) (in color) (Distributed through various newspapers and other sources)						
NOTE: *Eisner* script, pencils/inks for the most part from 6/2/40-4/26/42; a few stories assisted by Jack Cole, Fine, Powell and Kotsky.						
6/2/40(#1)-Origin/1st app. The Spirit; reprinted in Police #11; Lady Luck (Brenda Banks) (1st app.) by Chuck Mazoujian & Mr. Mystic (1st app.) by S. R. (Bob) Powell begin	69	138	207	431	716	1000
6/9/40(#2)	30	60	90	174	275	375
6/16/40(#3)-Black Queen app. in Spirit	20	40	60	117	184	250
6/23/40(#4)-Mr. Mystic receives magical necklace	15	30	45	88	137	185
6/30/40(#5)	15	30	45	88	137	185
7/7/40(#6)-1st app. Spirit carplane; Black Queen app. in Spirit	16	32	48	94	147	200
7/14/40(#7)-8/4/40(#10): 7/21/40-Spirit becomes fugitive wanted for murder	14	28	42	82	121	160
8/11/40-9/22/40	14	28	42	80	115	150
9/29/40-Ellen drops engagement with Homer Creep	14	28	42	76	108	140
10/6/40-11/3/40	14	28	42	76	108	140
11/10/40-The Black Queen app.	14	28	42	76	108	140
11/17/40, 11/24/40	14	28	42	76	108	140
12/1/40-Ellen spanking by Spirit on cover & inside; Eisner-1st 3 pgs., J. Cole rest	15	30	45	88	137	185
12/8/40-3/9/41	12	24	36	67	94	120
3/16/41-Intro. & 1st app. Silk Satin	14	28	42	82	121	160
3/23/41-6/1/41: 5/11/41-Last Lady Luck by Mazoujian; 5/18/41-Lady Luck by Nick Viscardi begins, ends 2/22/42	11	22	33	62	86	110
6/8/41-2nd app. Satin; Spirit learns Satin is also a British agent	13	26	39	72	101	130
6/15/41-1st app. Twilight	12	24	36	67	94	120
6/22/41-Hitler app. in Spirit	12	24	36	67	94	120
6/29/41-1/25/42,2/8/42	10	20	30	56	76	95
2/1/42-1st app. Duchess	12	24	36	67	94	120
2/15/42-4/26/42-Lady Luck by Klaus Nordling begins 3/1/42	11	22	33	60	83	105
5/3/42-8/16/42-Eisner/Fine/Quality staff assists on Spirit	9	18	27	50	65	80
8/23/42-Satin cover splash; Spirit by Eisner/Fine although signed by Fine	13	26	39	74	105	135
8/30/42,9/27/42-10/11/42,10/25/42-11/8/42-Eisner/Fine/Quality staff assists on Spirit	9	18	27	47	61	75
9/6/42-9/20/42,10/18/42-Fine/Belfi art on Spirit; scripts by Manly Wade Wellman	7	14	21	35	43	50
11/15/42-12/6/42,12/20/42,12/27/42,1/17/43-4/18/43,5/9/43-8/8/43-Wellman/ Woolfolk scripts, Fine pencils, Quality staff inks	7	14	21	35	43	50
12/13/42,1/3/43,1/10/43,4/25/43,5/2/43-Eisner scripts/layouts; Fine pencils, Quality staff inks	8	16	24	40	50	60
8/15/43-Eisner script/layout; pencils/inks by Quality staff; Jack Cole-a	6	12	18	31	38	45
8/22/43-12/12/43-Wellman/Woolfolk scripts, Fine pencils, Quality staff inks; Mr. Mystic by Guardineer-10/10/43-10/24/43	6	12	18	31	38	45
12/19/43-8/13/44-Wellman/Woolfolk/Jack Cole scripts; Cole, Fine & Robin King-a; Last Mr. Mystic-5/14/44	6	12	18	29	36	42
8/20/44-12/16/45-Wellman/Woolfolk scripts; Fine art with unknown staff assists	6	12	18	29	36	42
NOTE: *Scripts/layouts by Eisner, or Eisner/Nordling, Eisner/Mercer or Spranger/Eisner; inks by Eisner or Eisner/Spranger in issues 12/23/45-2/2/47.*						
12/23/45-1/6/46: 12/23/45-Christmas-c	7	14	21	37	46	55
1/13/46-Origin Spirit retold	10	20	30	54	72	90

The Spirit 12/31/44 © Will Eisner

The Spirit 8/03/52 © Will Eisner

Standard Oil Comics #5B © Standard Oil

	GD 2.0	VG 4.0	FN 6.0	VF 8.0	VF/NM 9.0	NM- 9.2
1/20/46-1st postwar Satin app.	9	18	27	47	61	75
1/27/46-3/10/46: 3/3/46-Last Lady Luck by Nordling	7	14	21	37	46	55
3/17/46-Intro. & 1st app. Nylon	9	18	27	47	61	75
3/24/46,3/31/46,4/14/46	7	14	21	37	46	55
4/7/46-2nd app. Nylon	8	16	24	42	54	65
4/21/46-Intro. & 1st app. Mr. Carrion & His Pet Buzzard Julia	9	18	27	52	69	85
4/28/46-5/12/46,5/26/46-6/30/46: Lady Luck by Fred Schwab in issues						
5/5/46-11/3/46	7	14	21	37	46	55
5/19/46-2nd app. Mr. Carrion	8	16	24	42	54	65
7/7/46-Intro. & 1st app. Dulcet Tone & Skinny	9	18	27	47	61	75
7/14/46-9/29/46	7	14	21	37	46	55
10/6/46-Intro. & 1st app. P'Gell	10	20	30	54	72	90
10/13/46-11/3/46,11/10/46-11/24/46	7	14	21	37	46	55
11/10/46-2nd app. P'Gell	8	16	24	44	57	70
12/1/46-3rd app. P'Gell	8	16	24	40	50	60
12/8/46-2/2/47	7	14	21	35	43	50
NOTE: Scripts, pencils/inks by Eisner except where noted in issues 2/9/47-12/19/48.						
2/9/47-7/6/47: 6/8/47-Eisner self satire	7	14	21	35	43	50
7/13/47-"Hansel & Gretel" fairy tales	9	18	27	47	61	75
7/20/47-Li'L Abner, Daddy Warbucks, Dick Tracy, Fearless Fosdick parody; A-Bomb blast-c						
	9	18	27	52	69	85
7/27/47-9/14/47	7	14	21	35	43	50
9/21/47-Pearl Harbor flashback	8	16	24	40	50	60
9/28/47-1st mention of Flying Saucers in comics-3 months after 1st sighting in Idaho						
on 6/25/47	14	28	42	76	108	140
10/5/47- "Cinderella" fairy tales	9	18	27	47	61	75
10/12/47-11/30/47	7	14	21	35	43	50
12/7/47-Intro. & 1st app. Powder Pouf	9	18	27	52	69	85
12/14/47-12/28/47	7	14	21	35	43	50
1/4/48-2nd app. Powder Pouf	8	16	24	40	50	60
1/11/48-1st app. Sparrow Fallon; Powder Pouf app.	8	16	24	40	50	60
1/18/48-He-Man ad cover; satire issue	8	16	24	40	50	60
1/25/48-Intro. & 1st app. Castanet	9	18	27	52	69	85
2/1/48-2nd app. Castanet	7	14	21	37	46	55
2/8/48-3/7/48	7	14	21	35	43	50
3/14/48-Only app. Kretchma	7	14	21	35	43	50
3/21/48,3/28/48,4/11/48-4/25/48	7	14	21	35	43	50
4/4/48-Only app. Wild Rice	7	14	21	35	43	50
5/2/48-2nd app. Sparrow	7	14	21	35	43	50
5/9/48-6/27/48,7/11/48,7/18/48: 6/13/48-TV issue	7	14	21	35	43	50
7/4/48-Spirit by Andre Le Blanc	6	12	18	29	36	42
7/25/48-Ambrose Bierce's "The Thing" adaptation classic by Eisner/Grandenetti						
	12	24	36	69	97	125
8/1/48-8/15/48,8/29/48-9/12/48	7	14	21	35	43	50
8/22/48-Poe's "Fall of the House of Usher" classic by Eisner/Grandenetti						
	12	24	36	69	97	125
9/19/48-Only app. Lorelei	8	16	24	40	50	60
9/26/48-10/31/48	7	14	21	35	43	50
11/7/48-Only app. Plaster of Paris	9	18	27	47	61	75
11/14/48-12/19/48	7	14	21	35	43	50
NOTE: Scripts by Eisner or Feiffer or Eisner/Feiffer or Nordling. Art by Eisner with backgrounds by Eisner, Grandenetti, Le Blanc, Stallman, Nordling, Dixon and/or others in issues 12/26/48-4/1/51 except where noted.						
12/26/48-Reprints some covers of 1948 with flashbacks						
	7	14	21	35	43	50
1/2/49-1/16/49	7	14	21	35	43	50
1/23/49,1/30/49-1st & 2nd app. Thorne	8	16	24	40	50	60
2/6/49-8/14/49	7	14	21	35	43	50
8/21/49,8/28/49-1st & 2nd app. Monica Veto	8	16	24	40	50	60
9/4/49,9/11/49	7	14	21	35	43	50
9/18/49-Love comic cover; has gag love comic ads on inside						
	8	16	24	40	50	60
9/25/49-Only app. Ice	7	14	21	37	46	55
10/2/49,10/9/49-Autumn News appears & dies in 10/9 issue						
	7	14	21	37	46	55
10/16/49-11/27/49,12/18/49,12/25/49	7	14	21	35	43	50
12/4/49,12/11/49-1st & 2nd app. Flaxen	7	14	21	37	46	55
1/1/50-Flashbacks to all of the Spirit girls-Thorne, Ellen, Satin, & Monica						
	10	20	30	56	76	95
1/8/50-Intro. & 1st app. Sand Saref	12	24	36	67	94	120
1/15/50-2nd app. Saref	9	18	27	52	69	85
1/22/50-2/5/50	7	14	21	35	43	50
2/12/50-Roller Derby issue	8	16	24	40	50	60
2/19/50-Half Dead Mr. Lox - Classic horror	9	18	27	47	61	75
2/26/50-4/23/50,5/14/50,5/28/50,7/23/50-9/3/50	7	14	21	35	43	50
4/30/50-Script/art by Le Blanc with Eisner framing	6	12	18	27	33	38
5/7/50,6/4/50-7/16/50-Abe Kanegson-a	6	12	18	27	33	38
5/21/50-Script by Feiffer/Eisner, art by Blaisdell, Eisner framing						

	GD 2.0	VG 4.0	FN 6.0	VF 8.0	VF/NM 9.0	NM- 9.2
9/10/50-P'Gell returns	6	12	18	27	33	38
9/17/50-1/7/51	8	16	24	40	50	60
	7	14	21	35	43	50
1/14/51-Life Magazine cover; brief biography of Comm. Dolan, Sand Saref, Silk Satin, P'Gell, Sammy & Willum, Darling O'Shea, & Mr. Carrion & His Pet Buzzard Julia, with pin-ups by Eisner	9	18	27	47	61	75
1/21/51,2/4/51-4/1/51	7	14	21	35	43	50
1/28/51- "The Meanest Man in the World" by Eisner	9	18	27	47	61	75
4/8/51-7/29/51,8/12/51-Last Eisner issue	7	14	21	35	43	50
8/5/51,8/19/51-7/20/52-Not Eisner	5	10	15	24	30	35
7/27/52-(Rare)-Denny Colt in Outer Space by Wally Wood; 7 pg. S/F story of E.C. vintage						
	27	54	81	158	249	340
8/3/52-(Rare)- "Mission...The Moon" by Wood	27	54	81	158	249	340
8/10/52-(Rare)- "A DP On The Moon" by Wood	27	54	81	158	249	340
8/17/52-(Rare)- "Heart" by Wood/Eisner	23	46	69	135	213	290
8/24/52-(Rare)- "Rescue" by Wood	27	54	81	158	249	340
8/31/52-(Rare)- "The Last Man" by Wood	27	54	81	158	249	340
9/7/52-(Rare)- "The Man in The Moon" by Wood	27	54	81	158	249	340
9/14/52-(Rare)-Eisner/Wenzel-a	12	24	36	69	97	125
9/21/52-(Rare)- "Denny Colt, Alias The Spirit/Space Report" by Eisner/Wenzel						
	14	28	42	76	108	140
9/28/52-(Rare)- "Return From The Moon" by Wood	26	52	78	154	242	330
10/5/52-(Rare)- "The Last Story" by Eisner	14	28	42	80	115	150

Large Tabloid pages from 1946 on (Eisner) - Price 200 percent over listed prices.
NOTE: Spirit sections came out in both large and small format. Some newspapers went to the 8-pg. format months before others. Some printed the pages so they cannot be folded in a small comic book section; these are worth less. (Also see Three Comics & Spiritman.)

SPY SMASHER
Fawcett Publications

	GD 2.0	VG 4.0	FN 6.0	VF 8.0	VF/NM 9.0	NM- 9.2
Well Known Comics (1944, 12 pgs., 8-1/2x10-1/2), paper-c, glued binding, printed in green;						
Bestmaid/Samuel Lowe giveaway	15	30	45	83	124	165

STANDARD OIL COMICS (Also see Gulf Funny Weekly)
Standard Oil Co.: 1932-1934 (Giveaway, tabloid size, 4 pgs. in color)

	GD 2.0	VG 4.0	FN 6.0	VF 8.0	VF/NM 9.0	NM- 9.2
nn (Dec. 1932)	55	110	165	344	572	800
1-Series has original art	48	96	144	293	484	675
2-5	21	42	63	124	195	265
6-14: 14-Fred Opper strip, 1 pg.	14	28	42	76	108	140
1A (Jan 1933)	50	100	150	305	503	700
2A-14A (1933)	32	64	96	186	293	400
1B (1934)	40	80	120	235	368	500
2B-?B (1934)	32	64	96	186	293	400

NOTE: Series A contains Frederick Opper's Si & Mirandi; Series B contains Goofus: He's From The Big City; McVittle by Walter O'Ehrle; interior strips include Pesty And His Pop & Smiling Slim by Sid Hicks.

STAR TEAM
Marvel Comics Group: 1977 (6-1/2x5", 20 pgs.) (Ideal Toy Giveaway)

	GD 2.0	VG 4.0	FN 6.0	VF 8.0	VF/NM 9.0	NM- 9.2
nn	2	4	6	11	16	20

STAR WARS
Dark Horse Comics: May, 2002; July, 2004 (Free Comic Book Day giveaways)

	Price
.... Clone Wars Adventures (7/04) based on Cartoon Network series; Fillbach Bros. -a	2.50
...: FCBD 2005 Special (5/05) Anakin & Obi-Wan during Clone Wars	2.50
...: FCBD 2006 Special (5/06) Clone Wars story; flip book with Conan FCBD Special	2.50
...: Tales - A Jedi's Weapon (5/02, 16 pgs.) Anakin Skywalker Episode 2 photo-c	2.50

STEVE CANYON COMICS
Harvey Publications

	GD 2.0	VG 4.0	FN 6.0	VF 8.0	VF/NM 9.0	NM- 9.2
Dept. Store giveaway #3(6/48, 36pp)	10	20	30	54	72	90
...'s Secret Mission (1951, 16 pgs., Armed Forces giveaway); Caniff-a	9	18	27	47	61	75
Strictly for the Smart Birds (1951, 16 pgs.)-Information Comics Div. (Harvey)						
Premium	8	16	24	40	50	60

STORIES OF CHRISTMAS
K. K. Publications: 1942 (Giveaway, 32 pgs., paper cover)

	GD 2.0	VG 4.0	FN 6.0	VF 8.0	VF/NM 9.0	NM- 9.2
nn-Adaptation of "A Christmas Carol"; Kelly story "The Fir Tree"; Infinity-c						
	31	62	93	180	285	390

STORY HOUR SERIES (Disney)
Whitman Publ. Co.: 1948, 1949; 1951-1953 (36 pgs., paper-c) (4-3/4x6-1/2")
Given away with subscription to Walt Disney's Comics & Stories

	GD 2.0	VG 4.0	FN 6.0	VF 8.0	VF/NM 9.0	NM- 9.2
nn(1948)-Mickey Mouse and the Boy Thursday	12	24	36	67	94	120
nn(1948)-Mickey Mouse the Miracle Master	12	24	36	67	94	120
nn(1948)-Minnie Mouse and Antique Chair	12	24	36	67	94	120
nn(1949)-The Three Orphan Kittens(B&W & color)	9	18	27	47	61	75
nn(1949)-Danny-The Little Black Lamb	9	18	27	47	61	75
800(1948)-Donald Duck in "Bringing Up the Boys"	15	30	45	88	137	185
1953 edition	11	22	33	64	90	115
801(1948)-Mickey Mouse's Summer Vacation	10	20	30	56	76	95

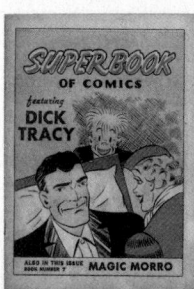

Super Book of Comics #7 © NYNS

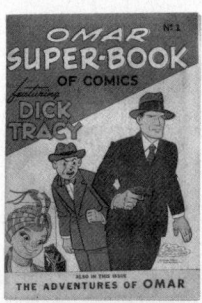

Super-Book of Comics #1 (Omar) © NYNS

Super Friends Special #1 © DC

	GD 2.0	VG 4.0	FN 6.0	VF 8.0	VF/NM 9.0	NM- 9.2
1951, 1952 editions	7	14	21	35	43	50
802(1948)-Bugs Bunny's Adventures	9	18	27	50	65	80
803(1948)-Bongo	8	16	24	40	50	60
804(1948)-Mickey and the Beanstalk	9	18	27	47	61	75
805-15(1949)-Andy Panda and His Friends	8	16	24	40	50	60
806-15(1949)-Tom and Jerry	8	16	24	44	57	70
808-15(1949)-Johnny Appleseed	8	16	24	40	50	60

1948, 1949 Hard Cover Edition of each....30% - 40% more.

STORY OF EDISON, THE
Educational Comics: 1956 (16 pgs.) (Reddy Kilowatt)

nn-Reprint of Reddy Kilowatt #2(1947)	7	14	21	35	43	50

STORY OF HARRY S. TRUMAN, THE
Democratic National Committee: 1948 (Giveaway, regular size, soft-c, 16 pg.)

nn-Gives biography on career of Truman; used in **SOTI**, pg. 311	14	28	42	76	108	140

STORY OF THE BALLET, THE
Selva and Sons, Inc.: 1954 (16 pgs., paper cover)

nn	4	8	11	16	19	22

STRANGE AS IT SEEMS
McNaught Syndicate: 1936 (B&W, 5" x 7", 24 pgs.)

nn-Ex-Lax giveaway	8	16	24	44	57	70

STRAY
Dark Horse Comics: 2004 (8 1/2"x 5 1/2", Diamond Comic Dist. Halloween giveaway)

nn-Reprint from The Dark Horse Book of Hauntings; Evan Dorkin-s/Jill Thompson-a						2.50

STRAY BULLETS
El Capitan Books: May, 2002 (48 pgs., B&W, flip book)

Free Comic Book Day giveaway-Reprints #2 with "Free Comic Book Day" banner on-c; flip book with The Matrix (printing of internet comic)						2.50

SUGAR BEAR
Post Cereal Giveaway: No date, circa 1975? (2 1/2" x 4 1/2", 16 pgs.)

"The Almost Take Over of the Post Office", "The Race Across the Atlantic", "The Zoo Goes Wild" each...	1	2	3	5	6	8

SUNDAY WORLD'S EASTER EGG FULL OF EASTER MEAT FOR LITTLE PEOPLE
Supplement to the New York World: 3/27/1898 (soft-c, 16pg, 4"x8" approx., opens at top, color & B&W)(Giveaway)(shaped like an Easter egg)

nn-By R.F. Outcault	18	36	54	103	162	220

SUPER BOOK OF COMICS
Western Publishing Co.: nd (1942-1943?) (Soft-c, 32 pgs.) (Pan-Am/Gilmore Oil/Kelloggs premiums)

nn-Dick Tracy (Gilmore)-Magic Morro app.	34	68	102	195	308	420
1-Dick Tracy & The Smuggling Ring; Stratosphere Jim app. (Rare) (Pan-Am)	34	68	102	195	308	420
1-Smilin' Jack, Magic Morro (Pan-Am)	13	26	39	74	105	135
2-Smilin' Jack, Stratosphere Jim (Pan-Am)	13	26	39	74	105	135
2-Smitty, Magic Morro (Pan-Am)	13	26	39	74	105	135
3-Captain Midnight, Magic Morro (Pan-Am)	24	48	72	139	220	300
3-Moon Mullins?	13	26	39	74	105	135
4-Red Ryder, Magic Morro (Pan-Am). Same content as Red Ryder Victory Patrol comic w/diff. cover	15	30	45	85	130	175
4-Smitty, Stratosphere Jim (Pan-Am)	13	26	39	74	105	135
5-Don Winslow, Magic Morro (Gilmore)	15	30	45	85	130	175
5-Don Winslow, Stratosphere Jim (Pan-Am)	15	30	45	85	130	175
5-Terry & the Pirates	17	34	51	98	154	210
6-Don Winslow, Stratosphere Jim (Pan-Am)-McWilliams-a	15	30	45	85	130	175
6-King of the Royal Mounted, Magic Morro (Pan-Am)	15	30	45	85	130	175
7-Dick Tracy, Magic Morro (Pan-Am)	20	40	60	115	180	245
7-Little Orphan Annie	11	22	33	64	90	115
8-Dick Tracy, Stratosphere Jim (Pan-Am)	17	34	51	98	154	210
8-Dan Dunn, Magic Morro (Pan-Am)	11	22	33	64	90	115
9-Terry & the Pirates, Magic Morro (Pan-Am)	17	34	51	98	154	210
10-Red Ryder, Magic Morro (Pan-Am)	15	30	45	85	130	175

SUPER BOOK OF COMICS
Western Publishing Co.: (Omar Bread & Hancock Oil Co. giveaways) 1944 - No. 30, 1947 (Omar); 1947 - 1948 (Hancock) (16 pgs.)

NOTE: The Hancock issues are all exact reprints of the earlier Omar issues. The issue numbers were removed in some of the reprints.

1-Dick Tracy (Omar, 1944)	16	32	48	94	147	200
1-Dick Tracy (Hancock, 1947)	14	28	42	78	112	145
2-Bugs Bunny (Omar, 1944)	8	16	24	40	50	60

	GD 2.0	VG 4.0	FN 6.0	VF 8.0	VF/NM 9.0	NM- 9.2
2-Bugs Bunny (Hancock, 1947)	6	12	18	32	39	46
3-Terry & the Pirates (Omar, 1944)	11	22	33	60	83	105
3-Terry & the Pirates (Hancock, 1947)	10	20	30	54	72	90
4-Andy Panda (Omar, 1944)	8	16	24	40	50	60
4-Andy Panda (Hancock, 1947)	6	12	18	32	39	46
5-Smokey Stover (Omar, 1945)	6	12	18	32	39	46
5-Smokey Stover (Hancock, 1947)	5	10	15	24	30	35
6-Porky Pig (Omar, 1945)	8	16	24	40	50	60
6-Porky Pig (Hancock, 1947)	6	12	18	32	39	46
7-Smilin' Jack (Omar, 1945)	8	16	24	40	50	60
7-Smilin' Jack (Hancock, 1947)	6	12	18	32	39	46
8-Oswald the Rabbit (Omar, 1945)	6	12	18	32	39	46
8-Oswald the Rabbit (Hancock, 1947)	5	10	15	24	30	35
9-Alley Oop (Omar, 1945)	11	22	33	64	90	115
9-Alley Oop (Hancock, 1947)	11	22	33	60	83	105
10-Elmer Fudd (Omar, 1945)	6	12	18	32	39	46
10-Elmer Fudd (Hancock, 1947)	5	10	15	24	30	35
11-Little Orphan Annie (Omar, 1945)	8	16	24	42	53	64
11-Little Orphan Annie (Hancock, 1947)	7	14	21	36	45	54
12-Woody Woodpecker (Omar, 1945)	6	12	18	32	39	46
12-Woody Woodpecker (Hancock, 1947)	5	10	15	24	30	35
13-Dick Tracy (Omar, 1945)	11	22	33	64	90	115
13-Dick Tracy (Hancock, 1947)	11	22	33	60	83	105
14-Bugs Bunny (Omar, 1945)	6	12	18	32	39	46
14-Bugs Bunny (Hancock, 1947)	5	10	15	24	30	35
15-Andy Panda (Omar, 1945)	6	12	18	28	34	40
15-Andy Panda (Hancock, 1947)	5	10	15	24	30	35
16-Terry & the Pirates (Omar, 1945)	11	22	33	60	83	105
16-Terry & the Pirates (Hancock, 1947)	9	18	27	47	61	75
17-Smokey Stover (Omar, 1946)	6	12	18	32	39	46
17-Smokey Stover (Hancock, 1948?)	5	10	15	24	30	35
18-Porky Pig (Omar, 1946)	6	12	18	28	34	40
18-Porky Pig (Hancock, 1948?)	5	10	15	24	30	35
19-Smilin' Jack (Omar, 1946)	6	12	18	32	39	46
nn-Smilin' Jack (Hancock, 1948)	5	10	15	24	30	35
20-Oswald the Rabbit (Omar, 1946)	6	12	18	28	34	40
nn-Oswald the Rabbit (Hancock, 1948)	5	10	15	24	30	35
21-Gasoline Alley (Omar, 1946)	8	16	24	42	53	64
nn-Gasoline Alley (Hancock, 1948)	7	14	21	36	45	54
22-Elmer Fudd (Omar, 1946)	6	12	18	28	34	40
nn-Elmer Fudd (Hancock, 1948)	5	10	15	24	30	35
23-Little Orphan Annie (Omar, 1946)	8	16	24	40	50	60
nn-Little Orphan Annie (Hancock, 1948)	6	12	18	32	39	46
24-Woody Woodpecker (Omar, 1946)	6	12	18	28	34	40
nn-Woody Woodpecker (Hancock, 1948)	5	10	15	24	30	35
25-Dick Tracy (Omar, 1946)	11	22	33	60	83	105
nn-Dick Tracy (Hancock, 1948)	9	18	27	50	65	80
26-Bugs Bunny (Omar, 1946))	6	12	18	28	34	40
nn-Bugs Bunny (Hancock, 1948)	5	10	15	24	30	35
27-Andy Panda (Omar, 1946)	6	12	18	28	34	40
27-Andy Panda (Hancock, 1948)	5	10	15	24	30	35
28-Terry & the Pirates (Omar, 1946)	11	22	33	60	83	105
28-Terry & the Pirates (Hancock, 1948)	9	18	27	47	61	75
29-Smokey Stover (Omar, 1947)	6	12	18	28	34	40
29-Smokey Stover (Hancock, 1948)	5	10	15	24	30	35
30-Porky Pig (Omar, 1947)	6	12	18	28	34	40
30-Porky Pig (Hancock, 1948)	5	10	15	24	30	35
nn-Bugs Bunny (Hancock, 1948)-Does not match any Omar book	6	12	18	28	34	40

SUPER CIRCUS (TV)
Cross Publishing Co.

1-(1951, Weather Bird Shoes giveaway)	8	16	24	40	50	60

SUPER FRIENDS
DC Comics: 1981 (Giveaway, no ads, no code or price)

...Special 1 -r/Super Friends #19 & 36	2	4	6	8	10	12

SUPERGEAR COMICS
Jacobs Corp.: 1976 (Giveaway, 4 pgs. in color, slick paper)

nn-(Rare)-Superman, Lois Lane; Steve Lombard app. (500 copies printed, over half destroyed)	19	38	57	142	254	365

SUPERGIRL
DC Comics: 1984, 1986 (Giveaway, Baxter paper)

nn-(American Honda/U.S. Dept. Transportation) Torres-c/a	2	4	6	8	10	12

SUPER HEROES PUZZLES AND GAMES
General Mills Giveaway (Marvel Comics Group): 1979 (32 pgs., regular size)

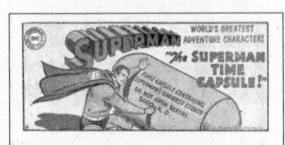

Superman (miniature) #1 © DC

Superman-Tim 3/48 © DC

Tastee-Freez Comics #3 © HARV

	GD 2.0	VG 4.0	FN 6.0	VF 8.0	VF/NM 9.0	NM- 9.2
nn-Four 2-pg. origin stories of Spider-Man, Captain America, The Hulk, & Spider-Woman						
	3	6	9	14	19	24

SUPERMAN
National Periodical Publ./DC Comics

	GD	VG	FN	VF	VF/NM	NM-
72-Giveaway(9-10/51)-(Rare)-Price blackened out; came with banner wrapped around book;						
without banner	72	144	216	450	750	1050
72-Giveaway with banner	103	206	309	644	1072	1500
Bradman birthday custom (1988)(extremely limited distribution) - no reported sales for 2006						
... For the Animals (2000, Doris Day Animal Foundation, 30 pgs.) polybagged with Gotham						
Adventures #22, Hourman #12, Impulse #58, Looney Tunes #62, Stars and S.T.R.I.P.E.						
#8 and Superman Adventures #41						2.50
Kelloggs Giveaway-(2/3 normal size, 1954)-r-two stories/Superman #55						
	30	60	90	174	275	375
Kenner: Man of Steel (Doomsday is Coming) (1995, 16 pgs.) packaged with set						
of Superman and Doomsday action figures						3.50
...Meets the Quik Bunny (1987, Nestles Quik premium, 36 pgs.)						
	1	2	3	5	6	8
Pizza Hut Premiums (12/77)-Exact reprints of 1950s comics except for paid ads						
(set of 6 exist?); Vol. 1-#97 (#113-r also known)	1	3	4	6	8	10
Radio Shack Giveaway-36 pgs. (7/80) "The Computers That Saved Metropolis", Starlin/						
Giordano-a; advertising insert in Action #509, New Advs. of Superboy #7, Legion of						
Super-Heroes #265, & House of Mystery #282. (All comics were 68 pgs.) Cover of inserts						
printed on newsprint. Giveaway contains 4 extra pgs. of Radio Shack advertising that						
inserts do not have	1	2	3	4	5	7
Radio Shack Giveaway-(7/81) "Victory by Computer"	1	2	3	4	5	7
Radio Shack Giveaway-(7/82) "Computer Masters of Metropolis"						
	1	2	3	4	5	7

SUPERMAN ADVENTURES, THE (TV)
DC Comics: 1996 (Based on animated series)

1-(1996) Preview issue distributed at Warner Bros. stores						4.00
Titus Game Edition (1998)						2.50

SUPERMAN AND THE GREAT CLEVELAND FIRE
National Periodical Publ.: 1948 (Giveaway, 4 pgs., no cover) (Hospital Fund)

nn-In full color	57	114	171	356	591	825

SUPERMAN/BATMAN
DC Comics: June, 2006 (Free Comic Book Day giveaway)

1-Reprints #1						2.50

SUPERMAN (Miniature)
National Periodical Publ.: 1942; 1955 - 1956 (3 issues, no #'s, 32 pgs.)
The pages are numbered in the 1st issue: 1-32; 2nd: 1A-32A, and 3rd: 1B-32B

No date-Py-Co-Pay Tooth Powder giveaway (8 pgs.; circa 1942)						
	53	106	159	323	537	750
1-The Superman Time Capsule (Kellogg's Sugar Smacks)(1955)						
	34	68	102	195	308	420
1A-Duel in Space (1955)	32	64	96	186	293	400
1B-The Super Show of Metropolis (also #1-32, no B)(1955)						
	32	64	96	186	293	400

NOTE: Numbering variations exist. Each title could have any combination-#1, 1A, or 1B.

SUPERMAN RECORD COMIC
National Periodical Publications: 1966 (Golden Records)

(With record)-Record reads origin of Superman from comic; came with iron-on patch, decoder,						
membership card & button; comic-r/Superman #125,146						
	14	28	42	102	181	260
Comic only	8	16	24	56	93	130

SUPERMAN'S BUDDY (Costume Comic)
National Periodical Publications: 1954 (4 pgs., slick paper-c; one-shot)
(Came in box w/costume)

1-With box & costume	131	262	393	819	1360	1900
Comic only	59	118	177	369	610	850
1-(1958 edition)-Printed in 2 colors	17	34	51	98	154	210

SUPERMAN'S CHRISTMAS ADVENTURE
National Periodical Publ.: 1940, 1944 (Giveaway, 16 pgs.)
Distributed by Nehi drinks, Bailey Store, Ivey-Keith Co., Kennedy's Boys Shop, Macy's Store, Boston Store

1(1940)-Burnley-a; F. Ray-c/r from Superman #6 (Scarce)-Superman saves Santa Claus.						
Santa makes real Superman Toys offered in 1940. 1st merchandising story						
	382	764	1146	2483	4392	6300
nn(1944) w/Santa Claus & X-mas tree-c	103	206	309	644	1072	1500
nn(1944) w/Candy cane & Superman-c	97	194	291	606	1003	1400

SUPERMAN-TIM (Becomes Tim)
Superman-Tim Stores/National Periodical Publ.: Aug, 1942 - May, 1950 (Half size)
(B&W Giveaway w/2 color covers) (Publ. monthly 2/43 on)

	GD 2.0	VG 4.0	FN 6.0	VF 8.0	VF/NM 9.0	NM- 9.2
8/42 (#1)-All have Superman illos.	121	242	363	756	1253	1750
1/43 (#2)	40	80	120	240	383	525
2/43 (#3)	40	80	120	235	368	500
3/43 (#4)	40	80	120	235	368	500
4/43, 5/43, 6/43, 7/43, 8/43	36	72	108	208	329	450
9/43, 10/43, 11/43, 12/43	30	60	90	174	275	375
1/44-12/44	26	52	78	150	235	320
1/45-5/45, 10-12/45, 1/46-8/46	23	46	69	135	213	290
6/45-Classic Superman-c	25	50	75	148	232	315
7/45-Classic Superman flag-c	25	50	75	148	232	315
9/45-1st stamp album issue	51	102	153	311	513	715
9/46-2nd stamp album issue	43	86	129	262	431	600
10/46-1st Superman story	31	62	93	178	282	385
11/46, 12/46, 1/47-8/47 issues-Superman story in each; 2/47-Infinity-c.						
All 36 pgs.	31	62	93	178	282	385
9/47-Stamp album issue & Superman story	41	82	123	256	416	575
10/47, 11/47, 12/47-Superman stories (24 pgs.)	31	62	93	178	282	385
1/48-7/48, 10/48, 11/48, 2/49, 4/49-11/49	25	50	75	148	232	315
8/48-Contains full page ad for Superman-Tim watch giveaway						
	25	50	75	148	232	315
9/48-Stamp album issue	34	68	102	195	308	420
420						
1/49-Full page Superman bank cut-out	25	50	75	148	232	315
3/49-Full page Superman boxing game cut-out	25	50	75	148	232	315
12/49-3/50, 5/50-Superman stories	27	54	81	158	249	340
4/50-Superman story, baseball stories; photo-c without Superman						
	31	62	93	178	282	385

NOTE: All issues have Superman illustrations throughout. The page count varies depending on whether a Superman-Tim comic story is inserted. If it is, the page count is either 36 or 24 pages. Otherwise all issues had 16 pages. Each issue has a special place for inserting a full color Superman stamp. The stamp album issues had spaces for the stamps given away the past year. The books were mailed as a subscription premium. The stamps were given away free (or when you made a purchase) only when you physically came into the store.

SUPER SEAMAN SLOPPY
Allied Pristine Union Council, Buffalo, NY: 1940s, 8pg., reg. size (Soft-c)

nn	4	8	12	17	21	24

SWAMP FOX, THE
Walt Disney Productions: 1960 (14 pgs, small size) (Canada Dry Premiums)
Titles: (A)-Tory Masquerade, (B)-Turnabout Tactics, (C)-Rindau Rampage;
each came in paper sleeve, books 1,2 & 3;

Set with sleeves	5	10	15	35	55	75
Comic only	2	4	6	13	18	22

SWORDQUEST
DC Comics/Atari Pub.: 1982, 52pg., 5"x7" (Giveaway with video games)

1,2-Roy Thomas & Gerry Conway-s; George Pérez & Dick Giordano-c/a in all						
	2	4	6	9	13	16
3-Low print	3	6	9	14	20	25

SYNDICATE FEATURES (Sci/fi)
Harry A. Chesler Syndicate: V1#3, 11/15/37 (Tabloid size, 3 colors, 4 pgs.) (Editors premium)
(Came folded)

V1#3-Dan Hastings daily strips-Guardineer-a	193	386	579	1206	2003	2800

TALES FROM RIVERDALE (See Archie Comics)

TASTEE-FREEZ COMICS (Also see Harvey Hits and Richie Rich)
Harvey Comics: 1957 (10¢, 36 pgs.)(6 different issues given away)

1-Little Dot on cover; Richie Rich "Ride 'Em Cowboy" story printed one year prior to being						
printed in Harvey Hits #9.	19	38	57	138	244	350
2,4,5: 2-Rags Rabbit. 4-Sad Sack. 5-Mazie	4	8	12	24	37	50
3-Casper	5	10	15	32	51	70
6-Dick Tracy	5	10	15	32	51	70

TAYLOR'S CHRISTMAS TABLOID
Dept. Store Giveaway: Mid 1930s, Cleveland, Ohio (Tabloid size; in color)

nn-(Very Rare)-Among the earliest pro work of Siegel & Shuster; one full color page called						
"The Battle in the Stratosphere", with a pre-Superman look; Shuster art throughout.						
(Only 1 known copy) Estimated value...						4000.00

TAZ'S 40TH BIRTHDAY BLOWOUT
DC Comics: 1994 (K-Mart giveaway, 16 pgs.)

nn-Six pg. story, games and puzzles						4.00

TEE AND VEE CROSLEY IN TELEVISION LAND COMICS (Also see Crosley's House of Fun)
Crosley Division, Avco Mfg. Corp. : 1951 (52 pgs.; 8x11"; paper cover; in color) (Giveaway)

Many stories, puzzles, cut-outs, games, etc.	7	14	21	35	43	50

TEEN TITANS GO!
DC Comics: Sept, 2004 (Free Comic Book Day giveaway)

1-Reprints Teen Titans Go! #1; 2 bound-in Wacky Packages stickers						2.50

Terry And The Pirates
Poll-Parrot Giveaway © DELL

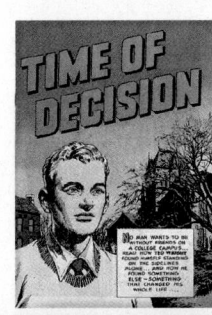

Time of Decision © HARV

Toy Land Funnies © Hecht's

	GD 2.0	VG 4.0	FN 6.0	VF 8.0	VF/NM 9.0	NM- 9.2

	GD 2.0	VG 4.0	FN 6.0	VF 8.0	VF/NM 9.0	NM- 9.2

TENNESSEE JED (Radio)
Fox Syndicate? (Wm. C. Popper & Co.): nd (1945) (16 pgs.; paper-c; reg. size; giveaway)

nn	20	40	60	115	180	245

TENNIS (...For Speed, Stamina, Strength, Skill)
Tennis Educational Foundation: 1956 (16 pgs.; soft cover; 10¢)
Book 1-Endorsed by Gene Tunney, Ralph Kiner, etc. showing how tennis has helped them

	6	12	18	28	34	40

TERRY AND THE PIRATES
Dell Publishing Co.: 1939 - 1953 (By Milton Caniff)
Buster Brown Shoes giveaway(1938)-32 pgs.; in color

	22	44	66	128	202	275

Canada Dry Premiums-Books #1-3(1953, 36 pgs., 2x5")-Harvey; #1-Hot Shot Charlie Flies Again; 2-In Forced Landing; 3-Dragon Lady in Distress)

	15	30	45	83	124	165
Gambles Giveaway (1938, 16 pgs.)	10	20	30	54	72	90
Gillmore Giveaway (1938, 24 pgs.)	10	20	30	56	76	95
Popped Wheat Giveaway(1938)-Strip reprints in full color; Caniff-a	2	4	6	8	10	12

Shoe Store giveaway (Weatherbird & Poll-Parrot)(1938, 16 pgs., soft-c)(2-diff.)

	10	20	30	56	76	95
Sparked Wheat Giveaway(1942, 16 pgs.)-In color	10	20	30	56	76	95

TERRY AND THE PIRATES
Libby's Radio Premium: 1941 (16 pgs.; reg. size)(shipped folded in the mail)
"Adventure of the Ruby of Genghis Khan" - Each pg. is a puzzle that must be completed to read the story

	400	800	1200	2600	-	-

THAT THE WORLD MAY BELIEVE
Catechetical Guild Giveaway: No date (16 pgs.) (Graymoor Friars distr.)

nn	4	8	12	18	22	25

30 DAYS OF NIGHT
IDW Publishing: July, 2004 (Free Comic Book Day edition)
Previews CSI: Bad Rap; The Shield: Spotlight; 24: One Shot; and 30 Days of Night 2.50

3-D COLOR CLASSICS (Wendy's Kid's Club)
Wendy's Int'l Inc.: 1995 (5 1/2" x 8", comes with 3-D glasses)
The Elephant's Child, Gulliver's Travels, Peter Pan, The Time Machine, 20,000 Leagues Under the Sea: Neal Adams-a in all   each.... ..... 3.50

350 YEARS OF AMERICAN DAIRY FOODS
American Dairy Assoc.: 1957 (5x7", 16 pgs.)

nn-History of milk	3	6	8	12	14	16

THUMPER (Disney)
Grosset & Dunlap: 1942 (50¢, 32pgs., hardcover book, 7"x8-1/2" w/dust jacket)
nn-Given away (along with a copy of Bambi) for a $2.00, 2-year subscription to WDC&S in 1942. (Xmas offer).   Book only

	15	30	45	90	140	190
Dust jacket only	10	20	30	56	76	95

TILLY AND TED-TINKERTOTLAND
W. T. Grant Co.: 1945 (Giveaway, 20 pgs.)

nn-Christmas comic	7	14	21	37	46	55

TIM (Formerly Superman-Tim; becomes Gene Autry-Tim)
Tim Stores: June, 1950 - Oct, 1950 (B&W, half-size)

4 issues: 6/50, 9/50, 10/50 known	17	34	51	98	154	210

TIM AND SALLY'S ADVENTURES AT MARINELAND
Marineland Restaurant & Bar, Marineland, CA: 1957 (5x7", 16 pgs., soft-c)

nn-copyright Oceanarium, Inc.	2	4	6	8	10	12

TIME MACHINE, THE
DC Comics: 2002 (10 pgs.)
nn-Promotes the 2002 DreamWorks movie 5.00

TIME OF DECISION
Harvey Publications Inc.: (16 pgs., paper cover)

nn-ROTC recruitment	4	7	10	14	17	20

TIM IN SPACE (Formerly Gene Autry Tim; becomes Tim Tomorrow)
Tim Stores: 1950 (1/2 size giveaway) (B&W)

nn	14	28	42	78	112	145

TIM TOMORROW (Formerly Tim In Space)
Tim Stores: 8/51, 9/51, 10/51, Christmas, 1951 (5x7-3/4")

nn-Prof. Fumble & Captain Kit Comet in all	14	28	42	78	112	145

TITANS BEAT (Teen Titans)
DC Comics: Aug, 1996 (16 pgs., paper-c)
1-Intro./preview new Teen Titans members; Pérez-a 4.00

TOMB RAIDER: THE SERIES (Also see Witchblade/Tomb Raider)
Image Comics (Top Cow Prod.): May, 2002
Free Comic Book Day giveaway-Reprints #1 with "Free Comic Book Day" banner on-c 2.50

TOM MIX (...Commandos Comics #10-12)
Ralston-Purina Co.: Sept, 1940 - No. 12, Nov, 1942 (36 pgs.); 1983 (one-shot)
Given away for two Ralston box-tops; 1983 came in cereal box

1-Origin (life) Tom Mix; Fred Meagher-a	276	552	828	1725	2863	4000
2	69	138	207	431	716	1000
3-9	50	100	150	305	503	700

10-12: 10-Origin Tom Mix Commando Unit; Speed O'Dare begins; Japanese sub-c.

12-Sci/fi-c	43	86	129	262	431	600

1983- "Taking of Grizzly Grebb", Toth-a; 16 pg. miniature

	2	4	6	9	12	15

TOM SAWYER COMICS
Giveaway: 1951? (Paper cover)
nn-Contains a coverless Hopalong Cassidy from 1951; other combinations known

	3	6	9	14	20	25

TOPPS COMICS PRESENTS
Topps Comics: No. 0, 1993 (Giveaway, B&W, 36 pgs.)
0-Dracula vs. Zorro, Teenagents, Silver Star, & Bill the Galactic Hero 2.50

TOWN THAT FORGOT SANTA, THE
W. T. Grant Co.: 1961 (Giveaway, 24 pgs.)

nn	3	6	9	16	23	30

TOY LAND FUNNIES (See Funnies On Parade)
Eastern Color Printing Co.: 1934 (32 pgs., Hecht Co. store giveaway)
nn-Reprints Buck Rogers Sunday pages #199-201 from Famous Funnies #5.
A rare variation of Funnies On Parade; same format, similar contents, same cover except for large Santa placed in center   (value will be based on sale)

TOY WORLD FUNNIES (See Funnies On Parade)
Eastern Color Printing Co.: 1933 (36 pgs., slick cover, Golden Eagle and Wanamaker giveaway)
nn-Contains contents from Funnies On Parade/Century Of Comics. A rare variation of Funnies On Parade; same format, similar contents, same cover except for large Santa placed in center   (value will be based on sale)

TRANSFORMERS
Dreamwave Productions/IDW Publishing: May, 2003; 2006
...Armada (Dreamwave Prods., 5/03) Free Comic Book Day Edition 3.00
.../Beast Wars Special (IDW, 2006) Free Comic Book Day Edition; flip book 3.00

TRAPPED
Harvey Publications (Columbia Univ. Press): 1951 (Giveaway, soft-c, 16 pgs)
nn-Drug education comic (30,000 printed?) distributed to schools.; mentioned in SOTI, pgs. 256,350

	2	4	6	8	10	12

NOTE: Many copies surfaced in 1979 causing a setback in price; beware of trimmed edges, because many copies have a brittle edge.

TRIPLE-A BASEBALL HEROES
Marvel Comics: 2007 (Minor league baseball stadium giveaway)
1-Special John Watson painted-c for Memphis, Durham and Buffalo; generic cover with team logos for each of the other 27 teams; Spider-Man, Iron Man, FF app. 3.00

TRIP TO OUTER SPACE WITH SANTA
Sales Promotions, Inc/Peoria Dry Goods: 1950s (paper-c)

nn-Comics, games & puzzles	5	10	15	22	26	30

TRIP WITH SANTA ON CHRISTMAS EVE, A
Rockford Dry Goods Co.: No date (Early 1950s) (Giveaway, 16 pgs., paper-c)

nn	5	10	15	22	26	30

TRUTH BEHIND THE TRIAL OF CARDINAL MINDSZENTY, THE (See Cardinal Mindszenty)

24 PAGES OF COMICS (No title) (Also see Pure Oil Comics, Salerno Carnival of Comics, & Vicks Comics)
Giveaway by various outlets including Sears: Late 1930s
nn-Contains strip reprints-Buck Rogers, Napoleon, Sky Roads, War on Crime

	34	68	102	195	308	420

TWISTED METAL (Video game)
DC Comics: 1996

nn						3.00

TWO FACES OF COMMUNISM (Also see Double Talk)
Christian Anti-Communism Crusade, Houston, Texas: 1961 (Giveaway, paper-c, 36 pgs.)

nn	15	30	45	85	130	175

2001, A SPACE ODYSSEY (Movie)
Marvel Comics Group
Howard Johnson giveaway (1968, 8pp); 6 pg. movie adaptation, 2 pg. games, puzzles;

Umbrella Academy FCBD Edition © DH

Walt Disney's Comics and Stories nn (1943) © DIS

Weather-Bird #1 © WEST

	GD 2.0	VG 4.0	FN 6.0	VF 8.0	VF/NM 9.0	NM- 9.2

	GD 2.0	VG 4.0	FN 6.0	VF 8.0	VF/NM 9.0	NM- 9.2

McWilliams-a | 2 | 4 | 6 | 9 | 12 | 15

ULTIMATE SPIDER-MAN
Marvel Comics: May, 2002

Free Comic Book Day giveaway - reprints #1 with "Free Comic Book Day" banner on-c   2.50
1-Kay Bee Toys variant edition | 2 | 4 | 6 | 9 | 12 | 15

ULTIMATE X-MEN
Marvel Comics: July, 2003

1-Free Comic Book Day Edition - reprints #1 with "Free Comic Book Day" banner on-c   2.50

UMBRELLA ACADEMY (Zero Killer & Pantheon City on back-c)
Dark Horse Comics: Apr, 2007

1-Free Comic Book Day Edition - previews of the upcoming series; James Jean-c   5.00

UNCLE SAM'S CHRISTMAS STORY
Promotional Publ. Co.: 1958 (Giveaway)

nn-Reprints 1956 Christmas USA | 2 | 4 | 6 | 10 | 13 | 16

UNKEPT PROMISE
Legion of Truth: 1949 (Giveaway, 24 pgs.)

nn-Anti-alcohol | 10 | 20 | 30 | 58 | 79 | 100

UNTOLD LEGEND OF THE BATMAN, THE
DC Comics: 1989 (28 pgs., 6X9", limited series of cereal premiums)

1-1st & 2nd printings known; Byrne-a | 1 | 2 | 3 | 5 | 7 | 9
2,3; 1st & 2nd printings known | 1 | 2 | 3 | 4 | 5 | 7

UNTOUCHABLES, THE (TV)
Leaf Brands, Inc.

Topps Bubblegum premiums produced by Leaf Brands, Inc.-2-1/2x4-1/2", 8 pgs. (3 diff. issues) "The Organization, Jamaica Ginger, The Otto Frick Story (drug), 3000 Suspects, The Antidote, Mexican Stakeout, Little Egypt, Purple Gang, Bugs Moran Story, & Lily Dallas Story" | 3 | 6 | 9 | 16 | 23 | 30

VICKS COMICS (See Pure Oil Comics, Salerno Carnival of Comics & 24 Pages of Comics)
Eastern Color Printing Co. (Vicks Chemical Co.): nd (circa 1938) (Giveaway, 68 pgs. in color)

nn-Famous Funnies-r (before #40); contains 5 pgs. Buck Rogers (4 pgs. from F.F. #15, & 1 pg. from #16) Joe Palooka, Napoleon, etc. app. | 58 | 116 | 174 | 363 | 602 | 840
nn-16 loose, untrimmed page giveaway; paper-c; r/Famous Funnies #14; Buck Rogers, Joe Palooka app. Has either "Vicks Comics" printed on cover or only a local store name as the logo. | 21 | 42 | 63 | 122 | 191 | 260

WALT DISNEY'S COMICS & STORIES
K.K. Publications: 1942-1963 known (7-1/3"x10-1/4", 4 pgs. color, slick paper) (folded horizontally once or twice as mailers) (Xmas subscription offer)

1942 mailer-r/Kelly cover to WDC&S 25; 2-year subscription + two Grosset & Dunlap hardcover books (32-pages each), of Bambi and of Thumper, offered for $2.00; came in an illustrated C&S envelope with an enclosed postage paid envelope
(Rare)   Mailer only | 23 | 46 | 69 | 132 | 209 | 285
                    with envelopes | 29 | 58 | 87 | 167 | 264 | 360
1947,1948 mailer | 17 | 34 | 51 | 98 | 154 | 210
1949 mailer-A rare Barks item: Same WDC&S cover as 1942 mailer, but with art changed so that nephew is handing teacher Donald a comic book rather than an apple, as originally drawn by Kelly. The tiny, 7/8"x1-1/4" cover shown was a rejected cover by Barks that was intended for C&S 110, but was redrawn by Kelly for C&S 111. The original art has been lost and this is its only app. (Rare) | 40 | 80 | 120 | 239 | 380 | 520
1950 mailer-P.1 r/Kelly cover to Dell Xmas Parade 1 (without title); p.2 r/Kelly cover to C&S 101 (w/o title), but with the art altered to show Donald reading C&S 122 (by Kelly); hardcover book, "Donald Duck in Bringing Up the Boys" given with a $1.00 one-year subscription; P.4 r/full Kelly Xmas cover to C&S 99 (Rare) | 17 | 34 | 51 | 98 | 154 | 210
1952 mailer-P1 r/cover WDC&S #88 | 14 | 28 | 42 | 80 | 115 | 150
1953 mailer-P.1 r/cover Dell Xmas Parade 4 (w/o title); insides offer "Donald Duck Full Speed Ahead," a 28-page, color, 5-5/8"x6-5/8" book, not of the Story Hour series; P.4 r/full Barks C&S 148 cover (Rare) | 14 | 28 | 42 | 80 | 115 | 150
1963 mailer-Pgs. 1,2 & 4 r/GK Xmas art; P.3 r/a 1963 C&S cover (Scarce) | 11 | 22 | 33 | 60 | 83 | 105

NOTE: It is assumed a different mailer was printed each Xmas for at least twenty years.

WALT DISNEY'S COMICS & STORIES
Walt Disney Productions: 1943 (36 pgs.) (Dept. store Xmas giveaway)

nn-X-Mas-c with Donald & the Boys; Donald Duck by Jack Hannah; Thumper by Ken Hultgren | 46 | 92 | 138 | 281 | 466 | 650

WALT DISNEY'S DONALD DUCK
Gemstone Publishing: 2006

... Free Comic Book Day (5/06) r/WDC&S #531; Rosa-s/a; P&S. Block-s/a; Van Horn-s/a   2.50
nn-(8-1/2"x 5-1/2") Halloween giveaway) r/"A Prank Above" -Barks-s/a; Rosa-s/a   2.50

WALT DISNEY'S DONALD DUCK ADVENTURES
Gemstone Publishing: May, 2003 (giveaway promoting 2003 return of Disney Comics)

...Free Comic Book Day Edition - cover logo on red background; reprints "Maharajah Donald" & "The Peaceful Hills" from March of Comics #4; Barks-s/a; Kelly original-c on back-c   2.50
...San Diego Comic-Con 2003 Edition - cover logo on gold background   2.50
...ANA World's Fair of Money Baltimore Edition - cover logo on green background   2.50
...WizardWorld Chicago 2003 Edition - cover logo on blue background   2.50

WALT DISNEY'S MICKEY MOUSE
Gemstone Publishing: May, 2007

... Free Comic Book Day (5/07) Floyd Gottfredson-s/a   2.50

WALT DISNEY'S MICKEY MOUSE AND UNCLE SCROOGE
Gemstone Publishing: June, 2004 (Free Comic Book Day giveaway)

nn-Flip book with r/Uncle Scrooge #15 and r/Mickey Mouse Four Color #79 (only Barks drawn Mickey Mouse story)   2.50

WALT DISNEY'S UNCLE SCROOGE
Gemstone Publishing: May, 2005 (Free Comic Book Day giveaway)

nn-Reprints Uncle Scrooge's debut in Four Color Comics #386; Barks-s/a   2.50

WATCH OUT FOR BIG TALK
Giveaway: 1950

nn-Dan Barry-a; about crooked politicians | 7 | 14 | 21 | 37 | 46 | 55

WEATHER-BIRD (See Comics From…, Dick Tracy, Free Comics to You…, Super Circus & Terry and the Pirates)
International Shoe Co./Western Printing Co.: 1958 - No. 16, July, 1962 (Shoe store giveaway)

1 | 4 | 8 | 12 | 24 | 37 | 50
2-16 | 2 | 4 | 6 | 13 | 18 | 22
NOTE: The numbers are located in the lower bottom panel, pg. 1. All feature a character called Weather-Bird.

WEATHER BIRD COMICS (See Comics From Weather Bird)
Weather Bird Shoes: 1957 (Giveaway)

nn-Contains a comic bound with new cover. Several combinations possible; contents determine price (40 - 60 percent of contents).

WEEKLY COMIC MAGAZINE
Fox Publications: May 12, 1940 (16 pgs.) (Others exist w/o super-heroes)

(1st Version)-8 pg. Blue Beetle story, 7 pg. Patty O'Day story; two copies known to exist. Estimated value…   625.00
(2nd Version)-7 two-pg. adventures of Blue Beetle, Patty O'Day, Yarko, Dr. Fung, Green Mask, Spark Stevens, & Rex Dexter; one copy known to exist. Estimated value…   525.00
(3rd version)-Captain Valor (only one known copy; it sold in 2005 for $480 in VG+)
Discovered with business papers, letters and exploitation material promoting **Weekly Comic Magazine** for use by newspapers in the same manner of **The Spirit** weeklies. Interesting note: these are dated three weeks before the first Spirit comic. Letters indicate that samples may have been sent to a few newspapers. These sections were actually 15-1/2x22" pages which would fold down to an approximate 8x10" comic booklet. Other various comic sections were found with the above, but were more like the Sunday comic sections in format.

WHAT DO YOU KNOW ABOUT THIS COMICS SEAL OF APPROVAL?
No publisher listed (DC Comics Giveaway): nd (1955) (4 pgs., slick paper-c)

nn-(Rare) | 72 | 144 | 216 | 450 | 750 | 1050

WHAT'S BEHIND THESE HEADLINES
William C. Popper Co.: 1948 (16 pgs.)

nn-Comic insert "The Plot to Steal the World" | 6 | 12 | 18 | 31 | 38 | 45

WHAT'S IN IT FOR YOU?
Harvey Publications Inc.: (16 pgs., paper cover)

nn-National Guard recruitment | 4 | 7 | 10 | 14 | 17 | 20

WHEATIES (Premiums)
Walt Disney Productions: 1950 & 1951 (32 titles, pocket-size, 32 pgs.)

Mailing Envelope (no art on front)(Designates sets A,B,C or D on front) | 9 | 18 | 27 | 47 | 61 | 75
(Set A-1 to A-8, 1950)
A-1-Mickey Mouse & the Disappearing Island, A-5-Mickey Mouse, Roving Reporter each… | 7 | 14 | 21 | 37 | 46 | 55
A-2-Grandma Duck, Homespun Detective, A-6-Li'l Bad Wolf, Forest Ranger, A-7-Goofy, Tightrope Acrobat, A-8-Pluto & the Bogus Money each… | 7 | 14 | 21 | 35 | 43 | 50
A-3-Donald Duck & the Haunted Jewels, A-4-Donald Duck & the Giant Ape each… | 9 | 18 | 27 | 52 | 69 | 85
(Set B-1 to B-8, 1950)
B-1-Mickey Mouse & the Pharoah's Curse, B-4-Mickey Mouse & the Mystery Sea Monster each… | 8 | 16 | 24 | 40 | 50 | 60
B-2-Pluto, Canine Cowpoke, B-5-Li'l Bad Wolf in the Hollow Tree Hideout, B-7-Goofy & the Gangsters each… | 7 | 14 | 21 | 35 | 43 | 50
B-3-Donald Duck & the Buccaneers, B-6-Donald Duck, Trail Blazer, B-8 Donald Duck, Klondike Kid each… | 9 | 18 | 27 | 52 | 69 | 85

Wisco/Klarer - Little Aspirin as the "Crook Catcher" © MAR

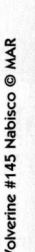

Wolverine #145 Nabisco © MAR

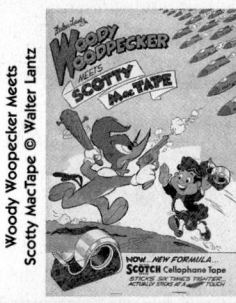

Woody Woopecker Meets Scotty MacTape © Walter Lantz

	GD 2.0	VG 4.0	FN 6.0	VF 8.0	VF/NM 9.0	NM- 9.2
(Set C-1 to C-8, 1951)						
C-1-Donald Duck & the Inca Idol, C-5-Donald Duck in the Lost Lakes,						
C-8-Donald Duck Deep-Sea Diver each...	9	18	27	52	69	85
C-2-Mickey Mouse & the Magic Mountain, C-6-Mickey Mouse & the Stagecoach Bandits						
each...	8	16	24	40	50	60
C-3-Li'l Bad Wolf, Fire Fighter, C-4-Gus & Jaq Save the Ship, C-7-Goofy, Big Game Hunter						
each...	7	14	21	35	43	50
(Set D-1 to D-8, 1951)						
D-1-Donald Duck in Indian Country, D-5-Donald Duck, Mighty Mystic						
each...	9	18	27	52	69	85
D-2-Mickey Mouse and the Abandoned Mine, D-6-Mickey Mouse & the Medicine Man						
each...	8	16	24	40	50	60
D-3-Pluto & the Mysterious Package, D-4-Bre'r Rabbit's Sunken Treasure,						
D-7-Li'l Bad Wolf and the Secret of the Woods, D-8-Minnie Mouse, Girl Explorer						
each...	7	14	21	35	43	50
NOTE: Some copies lack the Wheaties ad.						

WHIZ COMICS (Formerly Flash Comics & Thrill Comics #1)
Fawcett Publications

	GD 2.0	VG 4.0	FN 6.0	VF 8.0	VF/NM 9.0	NM- 9.2
Wheaties Giveaway(1946, Miniature, 6-1/2x8-1/4", 32 pgs.); all copies were taped at each						
corner to a box of Wheaties and are never found in very fine or mint condition;						
"Capt. Marvel & the Water Thieves", plus Golden Arrow, Ibis, Crime Smasher stories	150	375	600	—	—	—

WILD KINGDOM (TV) (Mutual of Omaha's...)
Western Printing Co.: 1965, 1966 (Giveaway, regular size, slick-c, 16 pgs.)

	GD 2.0	VG 4.0	FN 6.0	VF 8.0	VF/NM 9.0	NM- 9.2
nn-Front & back-c are different on 1966 edition	2	4	6	9	12	15

WISCO/KLARER COMIC BOOK (Miniature)
Marvel Comics/Vital Publ./Fawcett Publ.: 1948 - 1964 (3-1/2x6-3/4", 24 pgs.)

Given away by Wisco "99" Service Stations, Carnation Malted Milk, Klarer Health Wieners, Fleers Dubble Bubble Gum, Rodeo All-Meat Wieners, Perfect Potato Chips, & others; see ad in Tom Mix #21

	GD 2.0	VG 4.0	FN 6.0	VF 8.0	VF/NM 9.0	NM- 9.2
Blackstone & the Gold Medal Mystery (1948)	9	18	27	50	65	80
Blackstone "Solves the Sealed Vault Mystery" (1950)	9	18	27	50	65	80
Blaze Carson in "The Sheriff Shoots It Out" (1950)	9	18	27	50	65	80
Captain Marvel & Billy's Big Game (r/Capt. Marvel Adv. #76)						
	26	52	78	152	239	325
(Prices vary widely on this book)						
China Boy in "A Trip to the Zoo" #10 (1948)	6	12	18	31	38	45
Indoors-Outdoors Game Book	5	10	14	20	24	28
Jim Solar Space Sheriff in "Battle for Mars", "Between Two Worlds", "Conquers Outer Space",						
"The Creatures on the Comet", "Defeats the Moon Missile Men", "Encounter Creatures on						
Comet", "Meet the Jupiter Jumpers", "Meets the Man From Mars", "On Traffic Duty",						
"Outlaws of the Spaceways", "Pirates of the Planet X", "Protects Space Lanes", "Raiders						
From the Sun", "Ring Around Saturn", "Robots of Rhea", "The Sky Ruby", "Spacetts of						
the Sky", "Spidermen of Venus", "Trouble on Mercury"						
	8	16	24	44	57	70
Johnny Starboard & the Underseas Pirates (1948)	6	12	18	28	34	40
Kid Colt in "He Lived by His Guns" (1950)	10	20	30	54	72	90
Little Aspirin as the "Crook Catcher" #2 (1950)	5	10	15	22	26	30
Little Aspirin in "Naughty But Nice" #6 (1950)	5	10	15	22	26	30
Return of the Black Phantom (not M.E. character)(Roy Dare)(1948)						
	8	16	24	40	50	60
Secrets of Magic	5	10	15	23	28	32
Slim Morgan "Brings Justice to Mesa City" #3	5	10	15	23	28	32
Super Rabbit(1950)-Cuts Red Tape, Stops Crime Wave!						
	11	22	33	60	83	105
Tex Farnum, Frontiersman (1948)	6	12	18	28	34	40
Tex Taylor in "Draw or Die, Cowpoke!" (1950)	8	16	24	42	54	65
Tex Taylor in "An Exciting Adventure at the Gold Mine" (1950)						
	8	16	24	40	50	60
Wacky Quacky in "All-Aboard"	4	8	11	16	19	22
When School Is Out	4	8	11	16	19	22
Willie in a "Comic-Comic Book Fall" #1	4	9	13	18	22	26
Wonder Duck "An Adventure at the Rodeo of the Fearless Quacker!" (1950)						
	10	20	30	54	72	90
Rare uncut version of three; includes Capt. Marvel, Tex Farnum, Black Phantom						
Estimated value...						700.00
Rare uncut version of three; includes China Boy, Blackstone, Johnny Starboard						
& the Underseas Pirates Estimated value...						250.00

WOLVERINE
Marvel Comics

	GD 2.0	VG 4.0	FN 6.0	VF 8.0	VF/NM 9.0	NM- 9.2
145-(1999 Nabisco mail-in offer) Sienkiewicz-c	10	20	30	60	93	125
...Son of Canada (4/01, ed. of 65,000) Spider-Man & The Hulk app.; Lim-a						3.00

WOMAN OF THE PROMISE, THE
Catechetical Guild: 1950 (General Distr.) (Paper cover, 32 pgs.)

	GD 2.0	VG 4.0	FN 6.0	VF 8.0	VF/NM 9.0	NM- 9.2
nn	6	12	18	28	34	40

WONDERFUL WORLD OF DUCKS (See Golden Picture Story Book)
Colgate Palmolive Co.: 1975

	GD 2.0	VG 4.0	FN 6.0	VF 8.0	VF/NM 9.0	NM- 9.2
1-Mostly-r	1	3	4	6	8	10

WONDER WOMAN
DC Comics: 1977

	GD 2.0	VG 4.0	FN 6.0	VF 8.0	VF/NM 9.0	NM- 9.2
Pizza Hut Giveaways (12/77)-Reprints #60,62	2	4	6	10	12	15
... - The Minotaur (1981, General Foods giveaway, 8 pages, 3-1/2 x 6-3/4",						
oblong)	2	4	6	11	16	20

WONDER WORKER OF PERU
Catechetical Guild: No date (5x7", 16 pgs., B&W, giveaway)

	GD 2.0	VG 4.0	FN 6.0	VF 8.0	VF/NM 9.0	NM- 9.2
nn	5	10	15	27	33	38

WOODY WOODPECKER
Dell Publishing Co.

	GD 2.0	VG 4.0	FN 6.0	VF 8.0	VF/NM 9.0	NM- 9.2
Clover Stamp-Newspaper Boy Contest('56)-9 pg. story-(Giveaway)						
	7	14	21	37	46	55
In Chevrolet Wonderland(1954-Giveaway)(Western Publ.)-20 pgs., full story line;						
Chilly Willy app.	18	36	54	103	162	220
...Meets Scotty MacTape(1953-Scotch Tape giveaway)-16 pgs., full size						
	18	36	54	103	162	220

WOOLWORTH'S CHRISTMAS STORY BOOK
Promotional Publ. Co.(Western Printing Co.): 1952 - 1954 (16 pgs., paper-c) (See Jolly Christmas Book)

	GD 2.0	VG 4.0	FN 6.0	VF 8.0	VF/NM 9.0	NM- 9.2
nn: 1952 issue-Marv Levy c/a	6	12	18	33	41	48

WOOLWORTH'S HAPPY TIME CHRISTMAS BOOK
F. W. Woolworth Co. (Western Printing Co.): 1952 (Christmas giveaway)

	GD 2.0	VG 4.0	FN 6.0	VF 8.0	VF/NM 9.0	NM- 9.2
nn-36 pgs.	6	12	18	31	38	45

WORLD'S FINEST COMICS
National Periodical Publ./DC Comics

	GD 2.0	VG 4.0	FN 6.0	VF 8.0	VF/NM 9.0	NM- 9.2
Giveaway (c. 1944-45, 8 pgs., in color, paper-c)-Johnny Everyman-r/World's Finest						
	22	44	66	126	198	270
Giveaway (c. 1949, 8 pgs., in color, paper-c)- "Make Way For Youth" r/World's Finest;						
based on film of same name	18	36	54	107	169	230
#176, #179- Best Western reprint edition (1997)						3.00

WORLD'S GREATEST SUPER HEROES
DC Comics (Nutra Comics) (Child Vitamins, Inc.): 1977 (Giveaway, 3-3/4x3-3/4", 24 pgs.)

	GD 2.0	VG 4.0	FN 6.0	VF 8.0	VF/NM 9.0	NM- 9.2
nn-Batman & Robin app.; health tips	2	4	6	9	13	16

WORLDS OF ASPEN
Aspen MLT, Inc.: 2006; 2007 (Free Comic Book Day giveaway)

	GD 2.0	VG 4.0	FN 6.0	VF 8.0	VF/NM 9.0	NM- 9.2
...: FCBD 2006 Edition; Fathom, Soulfire, Shrugged short stories; Turner-c						2.50
...: FCBD 2007 Edition; Fathom, Soulfire, Shrugged short stories; Turner-c						2.50

XMAS FUNNIES
Kinney Shoes: No date (Giveaway, paper cover, 36 pgs.?)

	GD 2.0	VG 4.0	FN 6.0	VF 8.0	VF/NM 9.0	NM- 9.2
Contains 1933 color strip-r; Mutt & Jeff, etc.	31	62	93	180	285	390

X-MEN / RUNAWAYS
Marvel Comics: 2006 (Free Comic Book Day giveaway)

	GD 2.0	VG 4.0	FN 6.0	VF 8.0	VF/NM 9.0	NM- 9.2
...: FCBD 2006 Edition; new x-over story; Mighty Avengers preview; Jo Chen-c						2.50

X-MEN THE MOVIE
Marvel Comics/Toys R' Us: 2000

	GD 2.0	VG 4.0	FN 6.0	VF 8.0	VF/NM 9.0	NM- 9.2
Special Movie Prequel Edition						5.00

X2 PRESENTS THE ULTIMATE X-MEN #2
Marvel Comics/New York Post: July, 2003

	GD 2.0	VG 4.0	FN 6.0	VF 8.0	VF/NM 9.0	NM- 9.2
Reprint distributed inside issue of the New York Post						2.50

YALTA TO KOREA (Also see Korea My Home)
M. Phillip Corp. (Republican National Committee): 1952 (Giveaway, paper-c)

	GD 2.0	VG 4.0	FN 6.0	VF 8.0	VF/NM 9.0	NM- 9.2
nn-(8 pgs.)-Anti-communist propaganda book	18	36	54	103	162	220

YOGI BEAR (TV)
Dell Publishing Co.

	GD 2.0	VG 4.0	FN 6.0	VF 8.0	VF/NM 9.0	NM- 9.2
Giveaway ('84, '86)-City of Los Angeles, "Creative First Aid" & "Earthquake Preparedness						
for Children"	1	2	3	4	5	7

YOUR TRIP TO NEWSPAPERLAND
Philadelphia Evening Bulletin (Printed by Harvey Press): June, 1955 (14x11-1/2", 12 pgs.)

	GD 2.0	VG 4.0	FN 6.0	VF 8.0	VF/NM 9.0	NM- 9.2
nn-Joe Palooka takes kids on newspaper tour	5	10	15	24	30	35

YOUR VOTE IS VITAL!
Harvey Publications Inc.: 1952 (5" x 7", 16 pgs., paper cover)

	GD 2.0	VG 4.0	FN 6.0	VF 8.0	VF/NM 9.0	NM- 9.2
nn-The importance of voting	4	8	12	18	22	25

The American Comic Book: 1500s-1828
by Eric C. Caren ©2008

Want to avoid an argument in social discourse? Steer clear of politics and religion. In the latter category, the most controversial subject is human evolution. Collectors can become just as squeamish when you start messing with the evolution of a particular collectible. In most cases, the origin of a particular comic character will be universally agreed upon, but try tackling the origin of printed comics and you are asking for trouble. Perhaps I will make more friends than enemies amongst comic collectors if I first admit that in my own field of expertise, rare newspapers and other news forms – broadsides, tracts, newsletters, periodicals, etc. – 35 years of experience has left me somewhat at a loss to tell you what the first newspaper was. Actually, to be fair to myself, I could give you a list of at least a dozen good candidates and then it would be subjective as to which item on the list qualified as the godfather. It so happens that journalism and comics are not such distant cousins, and because a picture paints a thousand words, I have provided you with a number of pictorial exhibits to accompany this treatise. First printed comic? Ancestors of my Silver Age companions growing up in the 1960s? Yes, centuries before there was a Spider-Man, an Incredible Hulk, and the Fantastic Four, there were comics and cartoons!

My friend and fellow newspaper collector, Dr. Stephen A. Goldman, has always lived by the old maxim, "Knowledge is Power," and to that end he keeps an enormous personal library of books relating to journalism, history, and collectibles. Many years ago, I was perusing through the spines of a myriad of reference books in his print library (pre-Internet) and hit upon a title that really intrigued me – *The Early Comic Strip* by David Kunzle, published by The University of California Press in 1973. The subtitle of the tome is *Narrative Strips and Picture Stories in the European Broadsheet from c. 1450 to 1825*. Kunzle gets down to business in the flap copy. He states that "because the 'comic strip' has never been adequately defined, no one has known where to look for its ancestors…In this book the 'comic strip' is defined as a mass produced series of narrative images printed either on a single sheet, or else strung across several sheets…" The Kunzle book opened a whole new world for me, and I started adding many early items to my news archive. These would share space in the comics division of the archive with more familiar friends like the Yellow Kid, Little Nemo, and the Brownies.

In this article, I would like to share some of our mutual cousins with you in the hopes that you will be inspired to

Figure 1. German broadsheet, dated 1569.

look back at what I am calling "The Pioneer Age" of comics. There are many things out there from the 16th to the 19th centuries that would be interesting for comic connoisseurs to collect. While some items illustrated within this article are virtually unobtainable, others *can* be found, and many other similar items are out there just waiting for inspired collectors to seek them out. All of the items pictured are taken from originals in my personal collection, with the exception of the Franklin snake cartoon which is proudly owned by Dr. Goldman. As far as I know, his example is the only one in private hands.

Figure 2. The Murder of King Henry III (1589).

Before we begin, a bit of terminology is imperative. The terms 'broadsheet' and 'broadside' regarding works of the 16th and 17th centuries are fairly interchangeable and they essentially refer to the modern equivalent of a poster. Today, technically speaking, a broadside is a single sheet of paper printed only on the recto and a broadsheet is a piece of paper with printing on both sides. The earliest comic item illustrated in Kunzle is a ten-panel religious broadside probably printed in Strasburg (then Germany) circa 1460. Ten panels, biblical – hmm, what could it possibly depict? Guttenberg had invented moveable type only a few years earlier and used his printing press to print a now famous bible in Mainz, Germany, so it is no surprise that this early comic would be religious in nature. Non-secular matter would dominate the printing arts for well over a century to come. However, Kunzle does present us with a satirical and rather racy comic broadsheet done by one Casper of Regensburg, with a title that roughly translates to "My Heart doth Smart." This piece is replete with a picture of an alluring half-clothed maiden just out of her German bathing-house being admired by a kneeling young male observer. Kunzle dates this piece to circa 1485.

The earliest comic piece in my archive is a German broadside dated 1569 [Figure 1]. It is an illustrated attack on the Spanish Catholics led by the notoriously cruel Duke of Alva (center) who had recently occupied the Low Countries (Belgium and The Netherlands) and committed atrocities on the resident Protestant populace. It is half-allegorical, with the foreground consisting of the Devil and a nun blowing ill wind into the ear of the Duke of Alva who has in turn chained up the women of the Low Countries, and half-journalistic, with the upper half depicting the execution of Egmont and Horn in Antwerp.

The next two exhibits are particularly interesting to me. They are the work of the Hogenberg family of Cologne, Germany. Franz Hogenberg, and later his son Abraham, issued approximately 500 current event illustrated news

broadsides starting in the 1560s and ending around 1620. The father had already become famous for his extremely detailed and accurate city and town views that he had published with a partner named George Braun in atlas format. With correspondents all over Europe sending the Hogenberg family news and the city views already compiled, the Hogenbergs were able to have their news broadsides on the streets for sale within weeks of political and military events taking place in England and on the European Continent. In some cases, the news sheets were out of their print shop within days of the actual event, particularly when the event occurred in Germany. These sheets were of uniform size, approximately 10" x 13", sometimes numbered and interesting in that the graphics were always the dominant part of the broadside. Usually, text was relegated to a few lines of rhyming verse beneath the copperplate engravings. As literacy in this period was primarily confined to the nobility, this was a most pragmatic vehicle for dissemination of news – and often propaganda – to the populace at large. The picture told the story and the text could be read to groups of people who might remember it due to its catchy rhyming format.

A fair percentage of these news sheets were composed as strip narratives. One example of this is from 1589 [Figure 2] and shows the murder of King Henry III of France by the monk Jacques Clement near Paris. This four-panel broadside includes the stabbing of the king and concludes with Mr. Clement being drawn and quartered by four horses. The next work illustrated here is a 6-panel narrative strip with no text dating from 1617 [Figure 3]. The first panel depicts the shooting in Paris of the Italian Concini, who had ruled France while Louis XIII was still a young boy. The second panel shows the release of the birds from their cages to symbolize the new independence of the young King Louis, and the rest of the panels involve the common people attacking the corpse of Concini in various vicious ways.

The next piece is also the earliest English language piece in

Figure 3. The shooting of the Italian Concini (1617).

at a table sarcastically announces "I was to have took S. Sea [stock] at 2000 but chose rather to live here like a Knave than go to Jayl [sic] like a Fool."

The first successful American newspaper was the *Boston News-Letter* begun in 1704. From that point until the French and Indian War, there were precious few illustrations in any colonial newspaper. Some of the best information on early illustration in colonial newspapers can be found in the book *Journals and Journeymen* by Clarence Brigham, author of the most important bibliography of

my collection to employ word balloons. It is a trompe l'oeil, or collage, caricature satirizing the catastrophic South Sea Bubble, which ruined many investors in a manner similar to our own Tech Stock "New Economy" bubble of the 1990s. It is titled "The Bubblers Medley, or a Sketch of the Times/Being Europe's Memorial from the Year 1720" [Figure 4]. The most interesting scene to comic historians would have to be the one in the upper right corner depicting a number of men in a London coffeehouse – where merchants would regularly gather to read and discuss the latest news – speaking with word balloons. One of the gentlemen seated

colonial newspapers. In a chapter simply entitled "Illustration," Brigham points out that the first illustration in an American newspaper was a simple woodcut of a flag in an issue of the *Boston News-Letter* from January 26, 1708. Except for advertisements and title devices, Brigham could not find another illustration until 1733, when John Peter Zenger inserted a crude map of Louisburg into his *New York Weekly Journal*. Then, after perhaps one more map of Louisburg in 1745 came something in 1754 that was to have a lasting effect in the hearts and souls of the colonials right through the fight for independence.

Brigham tells us "Benjamin Franklin, in the *Pennsylvania Gazette* of May 9, 1754, published what may well be called the earliest American newspaper cartoon. That year, at a time when the prospect of a war with the French was imminent, a congress of the colonies was called at Albany to be held in June. Franklin, in a plea for united action, published an article on the situation on May 9. Accompanying the article was a cartoon woodcut engraving of a snake divided in eight parts [Figure 5]… Under the snake was the motto 'Join, Or Die…' The segmented snake device was of great importance in call-

Figure 4. "The Bubblers Medley" (1720).

Figure 5. "Join, or Die" from the
Pennsylvania Gazette, May 9, 1754.

Figure 6. The snake meets a dragon in the Massachusetts Spy (1774).

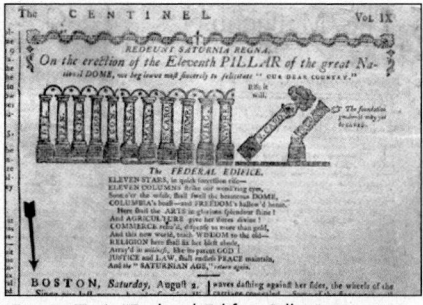

Figure 7. A "Federal Edifice Pillar" cartoon in the Massachusetts Centinel (1788).

ing the attention of the colonists to the necessity of union, and was revived at the time of the Stamp Act controversy in 1765 and again during the movement toward independence in 1774. That year, Isaiah Thomas used the snake cartoon device the full width of the first page in his *Massachusetts Spy*, and added a dragon, representing Great Britain, facing the snake…" [Figure 6]

The next time I find illustration in an American newspaper is at the time of our ratification process for the U.S. Constitution. *The Massachusetts Centinel* in 1787-1788 offered a series of what I call 'Federal Edifice Pillar' cartoons. Each time a state would ratify the Constitution, a new pillar would be added to the latest edifice cartoon. In Figure 7, we see the August 1788 cartoon with a headline reading "On the erection of the Eleventh Pillar of the great National Dome, we beg leave most sincerely to felicitate 'Our Dear Country.'" The cartoon thus shows that New York has ratified the Constitution. North Carolina's pillar is about to join New York according to the headline, which reads "Rise it Will," and lastly a fragmented Rhode Island Pillar is followed by a pointing hand which in turn is followed by the caption "The foundation Good – it may yet be SAVED." Under the cartoon can be found a dozen lines of verse called "The Federal Edifice." I have never seen any other illustrations in American newspapers dated before 1800. Therefore, it is safe to conclude that of the very few illustrations that were produced in American newspapers during the 18th century, the majority of them are cartoons!

Magazines of the 18th century offered more illustrations, perhaps because most of them were printed monthly, thereby giving the printer more time to produce an engraved plate or portrait to accompany the text of the periodical. Most of the illustrated magazines offered little in the way of cartoons; a notable exception was the *Royal American Magazine* printed in Boston. The famous silversmith and patriot, Paul Revere, produced the most famous cartoon of the era for this Boston magazine in June 1774 when he satirized the tea taxes and the closing down of Boston Harbor with a full page engraved cartoon entitled "The able Doctor or America Swallowing the Bitter Draught." This allegorical piece shows an Indian woman (representing colonials) having a pot of tea forced down her unwilling throat; a document labeled "Boston Port Bill" is thrown down at her simultaneously. The engraved cartoon was boldly signed in the lower right corner "P. Revere Sculp."

Much has been written about the icon "Bloody [Boston] Massacre…" by Paul Revere. It is claimed as an ancestor by

Figure 8. "Florizel granting Independency to Perdita" from The Ramblers Magazine (1783).

Figure 9. "Amusement for John Bull…" from The European Magazine (1783).

Figure 10. From The Anti-Jacobin Review and Magazine, January 1799.

young student). My friend Dr. Stephen A. Goldman says of Paul Revere's 1770 engraving of the Boston Massacre that it "has various elements common to early political cartoons. The piece has a distinct comic-like appearance, contains descriptive text (in verse), and is partly news, opinion, and propaganda. Revere in this work reveals himself to have much in common with later political cartoonists such as *Harper's Weekly*'s Thomas Nast (19th Century) and the *Washington Post*'s Herb Block (20th Century)" (for the image, see the color gallery later in this book).

collectors of newspapers, broadsides, printed Americana and, alas, comic/cartoon aficionados. I would add that nostalgia played a factor in my getting one for the collection many years ago (remembering it from history books as a

I have the first volume of a bawdy London monthly entitled *The Ramblers Magazine* that dates from the year that the American Revolution was officially ended by the Treaty of

Figure 11. "The Whiskers" in The New Wits Magazine (1805), annotated by the son of the illlustrator, George Cruikshank.

Figure 12. Cartoons satirizing Napoleon on the front page of the Connecticut Mirror, dated January 7, 1811.

Figure 13. Another Napoleon cartoon, this time dubbing him "The Corsican Munchausen, from the London Strand, December 4, 1813.

Paris (1783). The full title page contends that the magazine will be filled "With a Most Delicious Banquet of Amorous, Bacchanalian, Whimsical, Humorous, Theatrical and Polite [Not!] Entertainment." Almost every issue of this magazine contains a cartoon including word balloons. I have chosen one that is particularly delightful [Figure 8]. This is the first issue of the magazine, and it contains a plate entitled "Florizel granting Independency to Perdita." In it, a British aristocrat grabs the arm of a young maiden and his word balloon reads "Submit to my Royal Will." Seated on a sofa, the maiden responds "Declare me Independent and Then -----."

Another London periodical from April 1783, *The European Magazine*, contains a cartoon including a buffalo. It is believed that this is the first time that the buffalo was used to symbolize the young American nation. The plate is headed "Amusement for John Bull and his Cousin Paddy or, the Gambols of the American Buffalo, in St. James Street" [Figure 9]. An enormous 12" x 20" fold-out political cartoon was included in the January 1799 issue of *The Anti-Jacobin Review and Magazine* [Figure 10]. I am not familiar enough with the politics of the day to interpret the cartoon, but it is notable for its size and its extensive use of word balloons.

The earliest English language periodical identifying itself as a "Comic Work" which I have come across is *The New Wits Magazine* [Figure 11], printed in London. The printing on the very top of the outer wrapper reads "This Comic Work (which will be completed in Twenty-four Numbers, making three Volumes) may be had of every liberal bookseller in the United Kingdom – It is published regularly every fortnight

without any interruption whatever." The comic plate inside the issue is entitled "The Whiskers" and is dated December 1805. This is a remarkable issue in many ways; first of all, the pages are uncut, the original outer wrapper is present, and best of all, the plate is annotated in pencil and signed by the

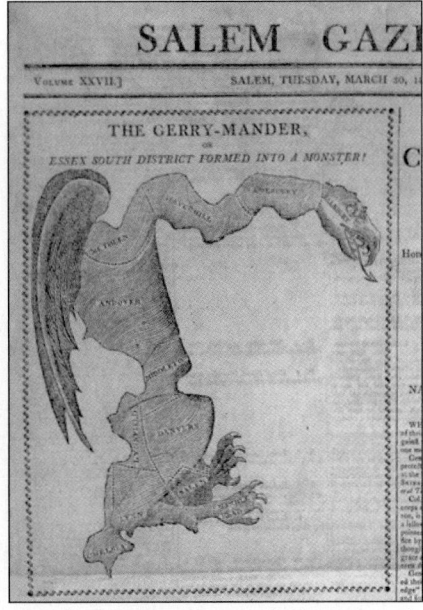

Figure 14. "The Gerry-Mander" as seen in the Salem Gazette, dated March 30, 1813.

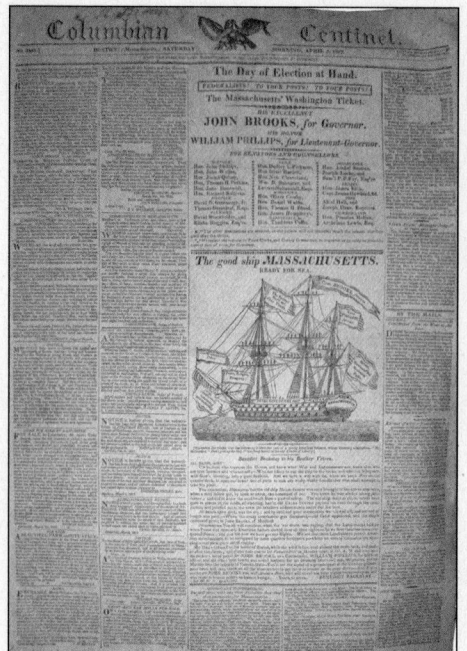

Figure 15. "The Good Ship Massachusetts Ready
for Sea" in the Columbian Centinel (1817).

Figure 16. The comic paper, "The Idiot," printed
in Boston in 1818.

most famous British illustrator of the 19th century – the illustrator for many of Charles Dickens' first editions, George Cruikshank. The blank space above the "Whisker" cartoon is filled with a pencil notation reading "engraved from a drawing by my father I. Cruikshank" and is signed in the same pencil with the initials "GCk." Isaac Cruikshank (c.1756-1811), father of George, was also a noted caricaturist. This then is George's own copy of a comic magazine illustrated by his father!

I have an issue of a Hartford, Connecticut newspaper entitled the *Connecticut Mirror* dated January 7, 1811. The front page contains what is known as a carrier's address. Newsboys would deliver a special issue either at Christmas or New Years, as in this case, with verse that would be specially prepared for that edition; to solicit tips, the newsboys used these carrier address issues. This particular title chose to grace the front page not only with verse but also three crude comic illustrations [Figure 12]. I am almost certain that the cartoons satirize Napoleon, as here is a sample of the accompanying comic verse: "...From deeds of bold and rash

Figure 17. "A Consultation at the Medical Board" from
The Pasquin or General Satirist (1821).

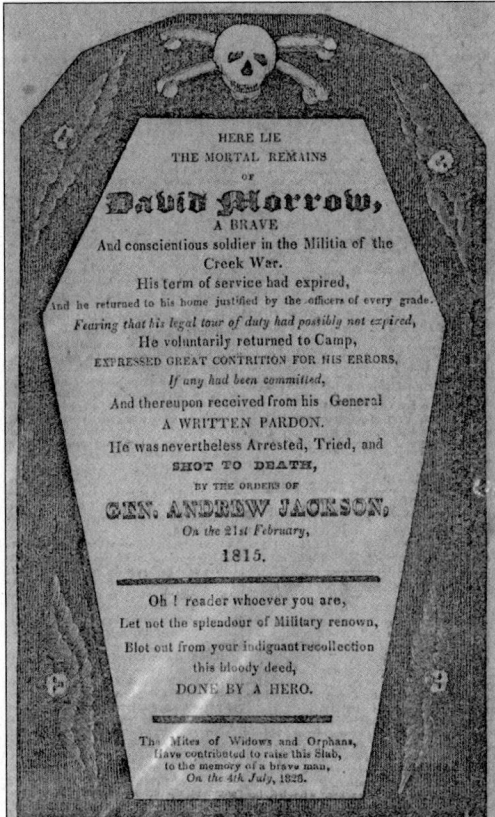

Figure 18. Above, the front page of The New Hampshire Journal, dated October 20, 1828, with multiple tombstone "panels." Immediately above is a detail of the bottom right tombstone.

emprize, to softer scenes we turn our eyes. Great Bonaparte's tender heart, Grows weary of his home-made queen, the mild, the beauteous Josephine…" It was not unusual to lampoon Napoleon, especially in Britain. "The Corsican Munchausen---Humming the Lads of Paris" [Figure 13] is a delightful hand-colored engraved cartoon "Published December 4, 1813" in the London *Strand*. Little Napoleon is spewing a multitude of word balloons ending with a particularly biting one that reads "Did I not burn Moscow – and leave 400,000 brave Soldiers to perish in the snow for the good of the French Nation?"

One of the most famous political cartoons in American history was first published in the *Salem Gazette* in Massachusetts on March 30, 1813. The front page contains "The Gerry-Mander, Essex South District Formed into a Monster!" [Figure 14] The expression gerrymandering has become famous when a geographical area is re-districted for the benefit of one political party over another. Elbridge Gerry, then Governor of Massachusetts, re-districted the state to get more Republican state senators than they otherwise would have netted. The cartoon puts the new district and the towns involved in a picture to resemble a winged dragon-like monster. Another Massachusetts newspaper called the *Columbian Centinel* issued a front-page endorsement in 1817 for John Brooks for Governor. Underneath this unabashed partisan endorsement is a cartoon of "The Good Ship Massachusetts Ready for Sea" [Figure 15] with all of the sails featuring either political slogans or the names of the candidates – Brooks, and his running mate for Lieutenant Governor, William Phillips.

Up until this point all of the American illustrations that I have discussed have been political cartoons of one sort or another. This would all change with the introduction of a comic paper called *The Idiot, or Invisible Rambler*, published under a pseudonym, "Samuel Simpleton." Printed in Boston in 1818, this publication was the earliest to present a recurring comic character that spoke with word balloons. This then is my choice for the 'Grandfather of all American Comics.' The comic is titled "Journal of Br. Jerry's Tour to the Ohio, (Continued)" [Figure 16]. The April 18, 1818 issue features the comic at the top of the first of the three columns on the front page of this four-page publication. It depicts two men on horses; one says to the other, "I am Going to Ohio." The other responds, "I have been." Ohio in 1818 was the Western frontier; it should be remembered that Lewis and Clark made their overland venture to the Pacific only about a dozen years earlier. Here, for the first time in American periodical publishing, do we encounter a secular and non-partisan comic of fictitious characters who speak with word balloons. Many of the elements that would later lead to familiar comic strip and comic book stylistic conventions are first found here.

Another really special publication in my holdings is an 1821 weekly British humor magazine in original green outer wrapper called *The Pasquin or General Satirist* [Figure 17]. I own issue #4, which has inserted into it a hand-colored word balloon cartoon relating to 'medical quackery.' One

Figure 19. Front and back views of
"The American Comic Almanac" (1833).

can only imagine the work that went into issuing a magazine with a hand-colored engraved cartoon. A poor patient stands before a doctor who is consulting with a mechanical robot made up of medical devices and tools. The consensus seems to be to "Bleed Him." The colored cartoon is titled "A Consultation at the Medical Board."

Did you know that the first full front-page illustration in an American newspaper was a cartoon? On Oct. 20, 1828, *The New Hampshire Journal* depicted a series of six coffins headed with skulls and bones. Each coffin has a biography describing various poor sods supposed to have been killed by General Andrew Jackson in duels, etc. Titled "Monumental Inscriptions" [Figure 18], who knows if it helped or hurt Jackson in his run for President. At any rate, he won the election and was re-elected President four years later.

Figure 20. The Gallery of 140 Comicalities, *a one-shot released by the newspaper*
Bell's Life in London *on June 24, 1831.*

Figure 21. One of the "Series of Comical Designs" regularly featured on the front page of The Boston Notion (1841).

Eric C. Caren was born (a collector) in 1959. By the age of 5 he had collected stamps, coins and baseball cards. He started collecting rare newspapers at the age of 11, after stumbling upon an abandoned house full of them in Rockland County, NY where he lived. In high school in the mid-1970s he apprenticed with a rare book dealer in Connecticut and actually set up as a dealer at a comic book convention in NYC sometime around 1975. He graduated from the University of Maryland with a Business degree in 1981. His first job was director of a gallery that dealt in rare newspapers in London in Covent Garden Market soon after it opened. He established The Caren Archive, a full-time business selling historical collectibles in 1983. He co-founded HCA Auctions with Dennis Holzman. He is a former Director of The Ephemera Society of America, a Member of The American Antiquarian Society, a Member of the Antiquarian Booksellers Association of America, and a Consultant to The Newseum, which will re-open in Washington DC on Pennsylvania Avenue in several years (his first newspaper collection will be the most substantial part of their permanent collection). He is a partner with Stephen A. Goldman in the business that bears his name as well as in OldNews, Inc. He has authored nine books using rare newspapers – The "Extra" series with Castle Books – and has recently co-authored his 10th book, "The Civil War" Smithsonian Institution Headliners Series with Dr. Stephen A. Goldman. Reprints of papers from his and Dr. Goldman's archive are sold at The Smithsonian Institution and The Holocaust Memorial Museum.

An interesting sidelight to the history of comics as they relate to newspapers and periodicals would be something that we might consider a distant cousin of everything in this *Guide*. I have the third issue of a series called "The American Comic Almanac" [Figure 19], dated 1833 and published in Philadelphia "With Whims, Scraps and Oddities," and of course lots of comics.

Bell's Life in London, a popular British newspaper in the first half of the 19th century, issued a one-shot on June 24, 1831 called *The Gallery of 140 Comicalities* [Figure 20]. It is subtitled "Which has appeared from time to time, in the most Popular Sporting Sunday Paper, 'Bell's Life in London'." The first British comic book? Let the Brits fight that one out!

The Boston Notion of 1841 not only had a comic nameplate, called a masthead by some, but some front pages of this title carried a column headed "Series of Comical Designs, Executed for The Boston Notion" [Figure 21]. Later in the 1840s, we start to see the advent of comic magazines in America styled after the successful British humor magazine *Punch*. The Victorian Age of comics dawned with titles such as *Yankee Doodle*, and *John Donkey*. Books composed of comics like Obadiah Oldbuck have previously been discussed in articles on the Victorian Age like the one featured in this edition of the *Guide*. One last note: It has previously been asserted, quite correctly, that *Harper's Monthly Magazine* started reprinting British comics in the back pages of its magazines in the early 1850s. But what about a regular comic feature in an American newspaper? Take a look at the May 31, 1856 issue of *Frank Leslie's Illustrated Newspaper* and you will find a page titled "Comic Department" [Figure 22]!

Figure 22. The "Comic Department" from the May 31, 1856 issue of Frank Leslie's Illustrated Newspaper.

Comic Strips and Books: 1646-1900
A Concise History & Price Index Of The Field As Of 2008

ORIGINS OF EARLY AMERICAN COMIC STRIPS BEFORE THE YELLOW KID

by Robert Lee Beerbohm, Richard Samuel West
& Richard D. Olson, PhD ©2008

(This article was originally created by Doug Wheeler, Robert Beerbohm and Richard D. Olson, PhD for CBPG #32 and continues to be revised annually by the current authors.) We welcome any and all corrections and additions. Special Thanks This Installment To Leonardo De Sa, Terrence Keegen, Gabriel Laderman and Joe Rainone.

Left: "The Burning of Mr. John Rogers," 1646 is the earliest-known North American cartoon printed on paper printed in the earliest children's primer in America.

"God's Revenge For Murder" By John Reynolds, unknown artist, 1656. Earliest-known sequential comic "panel" strip created in the English language.

OUR COMICS HISTORY IS BEING RE-WRITTEN RIGHT HERE, FOLKS!

Left: From his pamphlet Plain Truth 1747 containing Ben Franklin's earliest-known cartoon titled "Heaven Helps Only Those Who Help Themselves" depicting ancient "super hero" Hercules in the upper right corner.
Middle: "A Warm Place - Hell", one of two images definitely known to be drawn and engraved by Paul Revere, 1768. Word balloons had wide-spread usage in many cartoons in the 1700s. Right: The Tables Turned by James Gillray, 1797 commenting on an "invasion" of England by 1400 French convicts. The use of word balloons was wide spread in many parts of the world long before the Yellow Kid's parrot uttered a few words in 1896.

The Comic Almanac(k) debuted in America in 1831 with the earliest-known titles starting heavy with humor and sporting crude woodcut single panel cartoons. Ellm's American Comic Almanac was one of the first. By 1835 Davy Crockett, one of the nation's earliest national folk heroes, began issuing his own version. In the late 1840s

the Comic Almanac(k)s began to offer tall-tale sequential comic strips which became somewhat commonplace in the 1850s, fueled by the advent of the California Gold Rush. They were instrumental in the development of the American comic strip and we will be reporting more new finds next year after more research into American folklore.

We have a lot of new discoveries to share with you again this year as amply evident in the price index which follows this year's history lesson. A quantum leap has finally been achieved in the area of introducing the comic book collecting world to *American Comic Almanac(k)s* as well as a huge multitude of American humor periodicals, many of which contained sequential comic strips.

This Victorian Era section is devoted to comic strips and books published during the years the United States expanded across the North American continent, fought a Civil War, shifted from an agrarian to an industrial society, "welcomed" waves of immigrants, and struggled over race, class, religion, temperance, and suffrage - and all of it depicted and satirized by generations of mostly now long-forgotten cartoonists. The social attitudes, beliefs, and conventions of 19th century America, the good as well as the bad, are to be found in abundance. Perhaps the first question to pop into most readers' minds will be, "What, beyond the happenstance of publication date, are Victorian Era comics?"

There has been a long slow-motion evolution of the comic strip which was not invented in America, contrary to many previous history books on the subject. One must examine many aspects of concurrent popular culture. The main aspect that we believe most distinguishes Victorian Era comic strips from those of later eras was the extremely rare use of word balloons within sequential (multi-picture) comic stories. When word balloons were used, it was nearly always within single-panel cartoons. On the occasions when they appeared inside a strip, with very few exceptions, the ballooned dialogue was inconsequential. Nineteenth-century comics tended to place both narration and dialogue beneath comic panels rather than within the panel's borders as they were thought by many to interfere with the art. Many of these comics are to the word balloon-strewn post-Yellow Kid comics of the 20th Century as silent movies are to the later "talkies." Just as sound changed how stories were structured

on film, so too did comic strips change when the words were moved from beneath panels to inside them, and dialogue rather than narration drove the story in conjunction with the pictures.

The Victorian Era of actual comic strip books began on different dates in different nations, depending on when the first publication of a sequential comic book on their soil is known to have occurred. For the U.S. this happened when the American literary periodical *Brother Jonathan* printed the 40-page, 195-panel graphic novel *The Adventures of Mr. Obadiah Oldbuck* as a special extra dated September 14, 1842. Almost six decades later, America's Victorian comics came to their end, replaced by the onslaught of Platinum Age books reprinting newspaper strips from Bennett, Hearst, and Pulitzer Sunday comic sections, among many others.

There is considerable overlap between Victorian Era and Platinum Age comic books and strips. Those publications that continued from one century into the next, such as *Puck*, *Judge*, and *Life*, have their pre-1900 issues listed within the Victorian Age section, while their post-1899 issues can be found inside the Platinum Age. Some non-sequential (i.e., single-panel) American comic items existing prior to 1842 are also listed herein, going back to 1795. These belong to what could tentatively be called the Age of Caricature (1770s through 1830s). This was a fertile period for the art in England, when Gillray and Rowlandson, and, later, Cruikshank, Heath, and Seymour were that nation's top cartoonists. During the same period in the U.S., there were no artists who made their living as caricaturists, though William Charles, printer and engraver, did produce about two dozen spirited cartoon broadsides from 1805 to 1820, the most important ones concerning events of the War of 1812.

In addition, one can trace origins of American comic books to the humorous Comic Almanacs which began in earnest in the early 1830s.

The earliest known cartoon-like woodcut printed on paper

The Comus Offering, 1830 sample page of single panel cartoons using word balloons in every panel. Very Rare.

Outlines Illustrative of the Journal of F****** A*** K*****
Plate #6 By D.C. Johnston, 1835
Parodying a passage from the Journal of Fanny (Frances) A. Kemble,
a British woman who wrote a highly negative book about American
Culture after returning from the U.S. Word balloon use abounds.

in North America was in a Puritan children's book first published in 1646. Titled simply *The Burning of Mr. John Rogers*, it showed in flaming graphic detail what happens to those who stray from the flock and have to be burned at the stake. Dr. Wertham would have had a field day with that one!

Cartoon broadsides and other single panel images, often using word balloons, appeared from pre-Revolution days through the end of the 19th Century. The earliest known attributed cartoon, designed by the ubiquitous Benjamin Franklin, was "Heaven Helps Only Those Who Help Themselves," which first appeared in his pamphlet *Plain Truth* in 1747.

The most popularly remembered 18th-Century American cartoons are likely Franklin's *"Join or Die"* in 1754, representing the American Colonies as severed snake parts, and *"The Bloody Massacre Perpetrated in King Street"* -- Paul Revere's 1770 depiction of the Boston Massacre, which he pirated from the earlier Henry Pelham broadsheet cartoon *"The Fruits of Arbitrary Power."*

In September 1826, John Warner Barber, New Haven, Ct. (1798-1885) designed and self-published the broadside *The Drunkard's Progress, Or The Direct Road to Poverty, Wretchedness and Ruin* showing in four stages sequentially "The Morning Dram" which is "The Beginning of Sorrow, " "The Grog Shop" with its "Bad Company," "The

Adventures & Achievements of the Renowned Don Quixote & his Doughty Squire Sancho Panza by D.C. Johnston, 1837, America's earliest-known sequential comic broadside.

Confirmed Drunkard" in a state of "Beastly Intoxication," and the "Concluding Scene" with the family being driven off to the alms house. It is an interesting set of cuts, faintly reminiscent of Hogarth. Barber began his career in 1819, age 21, engraving on wood. He devoted most of his career to the multitude of art chores associated with book production. As late as 1870 he was issuing *Barber's Temperance Tracts*, which built upon his 1826 original plus four panels showing the positive effects of living without alcohol.

The first American whose fame was based primarily on his cartoons appears to be David Claypoole Johnston (1798-1865). Johnston provided illustrations for various almanacs, books, and periodicals, including the masthead for *Brother Jonathans*. Most notable of Johnston's comics work was his nine-issue series *Scraps*, which he self-published from 1828 to 1849. This series was highly influenced by George Cruikshank's series *Scraps and Sketches*, which first appeared in 1827. Because of the resemblance, Johnston became known in his day as "the American Cruikshank." Each issue of Johnston's *Scraps* consists of four large folio-sized pages, printed on one side, with nine to twelve single-panel cartoons per page, and each page often organized around a theme. Also popular was his comic album Outlines Illustrative of the Journal of F****** A*** K***** (1835), which parodied passages from the journal of recently published observations on America by British actress Fanny Kemble.

Johnston, himself a failed

Left: Cover to the subscriber version of the earliest-known sequential comic book published in America, The Adventures of Mr. Obadiah Oldbuck, Sept. 1842, Wilson & Co. New York, originally conceived in 1828 in Geneva Switzerland by creator Rodolphe Töpffer. Right: Pages 28 from this 40-page 1842 graphic novel which launched the comic book business in America....

actor, had an interest in the theater his entire career. In addition to producing a number of prints depicting American actors in famous roles, he collaborated with actor Henry J. Finn to produce the 1831 *(American) Comic Annual)*, with Finn as Editor and Johnston as artist, published by Richardson, Lord and Holbrook, Boston. It featured almost 30 full-page Johnston-designed copper engravings and woodcuts. Also that year, Finn solo produced *Finn's Comic Sketch Book*, a twelve-page album similar to Johnston's *Scraps* with upwards of half a dozen single-panel cartoons per page. It was published by Peabody and Co, of New York in business from 1831-1843. (Finn died tragically in a steamboat accident Jan. 13, 1840.)

Perhaps Johnston's most interesting contribution to the history of the comic strip in American came in 1837, when he produced the sequential comic broadside, *Illustrations of the Adventures & Achievements of the Renowned Don Quixote & his Doughty Squire Sancho Panza* (27.4 x 30.4 cm). This blank-reverse engraved print was an elaborate twelve-panel satire of the Andrew Jackson-Van Buren administration. It likely sold for 25 cents, seeing distribution in Boston, New York and Philadelphia. Much later, in 1863, Johnston drew another sequential comic broadside, *The House the Jeff Built* (27.5 x 36.7 cm), a bitter indictment of Jefferson Davis and the Southern slavocracy.

In July 1839, Wilson and Company, a newly formed New York printing firm, began publishing a mammoth newspaper by the name of *Brother Jonathan*. The publisher, J. Gregg Wilson had employed the newspaper format for *Brother Jonathan* to circumvent the higher postage rates imposed on magazines, but *Brother Jonathan* was a newspaper in format only -- it contained not a shred of news, instead specializing in serialized fiction, some of it written by Americans but most of it pirated from foreign sources. Despite the cost savings, the mammoth format had its limitations; when opened it measured a whopping three feet by four feet. So, once *Brother Jonathan* was an established success, Wilson and Day began in January 1841 the simultaneous publication of a magazine-sized quarto edition of *Brother Jonathan* that reprinted the contents of the mammoth edition.

Later that same year, to capitalize on the name recognition of their successful twin publications, Wilson and Company started issuing book-length *Brother Jonathan Extras* in the same format as the quarto magazine. These reprints are counted among the earliest paperback books in America. Most of the *Extra* numbers were pirated European novels. For example their eighth extra was the first American printing of a Charles Dickens novel. But for their ninth *Extra*, they did

EXPLOITS OF PETER PIPER.   21

But is fortunately rescued from immediate peril by the faithful elephant.

LIST of BOOKS for sale at the Brother Jonathan Office.

THE ADVENTURES OF OBADIAH OLDBUCK—A Book of Pictures, which set forth, in a laughable manner, the Curious, Comical, Cunning, Extraordinary, Extravagant, Funny, Farcical, Lively, Pathetic, Perplexing, Quizzical, and Wonderful Incidents which attended the Courtship and Marriage of that unfortunate and perplexed old gentleman—showing likewise how he attempted to commit suicide on five different occasions, and each time was saved by "invidious fate." The story of Mr. Oldbuck's Love, as set forth by these pictures, is one of the most admirable satires and caricatures of a love-sick old bachelor that can be imagined. It is full of genuine, original, sparkling wit—nothing old or borrowed. It will amuse the most refined person, and cannot fail to please everybody. This book comprises 80 pages of pictures, well printed on fine hot-pressed paper. It is one of the cheapest pictorial works ever published. We send it free of postage for 25 cents per copy.

A DAY'S SPORT—Or, Hunting Adventures of S. Winks Wattles, a shopkeeper, Thomas Titt, Esq., a "legal gent.," and Major Nicholas Noggin, a jolly good fellow generally. This story is told by Pictures, and is really a witty and amusing book—the drawings by Henry L. Stevens of Philadelphia. It will make you laugh out loud to look over this book. It is handsomely printed, and put up in an illustrated cover, suitable for the centre table. We send it free of postage for 12½ cents per copy.

THE SEA-WITCH—A Story of Life and Adventure on board an African Slaver, and on the Coast. One of the best novels we have issued in a long time. Sent free of postage for 25 cents.

Send cash for the above books to B. H. Day, 48 Beekman-st., New York.

B. H. Day's Brother Jonathan Cheap Book Establishment 1855 catalog with 32-panel comic strip "Peter Piper in Bengal'" by John Tenniel (later Alice of Wonderland fame) with two comic books for sale on the above page: Obadiah Oldbuck by Töpffer and A Day's Sport by Henry L. Stephens of Philadelphia, a scarce newly-rediscovered original American comic book.

something no American publisher had ever done before -- they pirated a graphic novel, Rodolphe Töpffer's *The Adventures of Mr. Obadiah Oldbuck*. By reformatting *Oldbuck* from its original small oblong strip design to fit *Brother Jonathan's* standard quarto format Wilson and Company inadvertently made this edition (alone) of *Obadiah Oldbuck* resemble a modern comic book. *Oldbuck's* arrival on the shores of the New World would directly inspire a wave of American imitators. [*This first Wilson printing of Oldbuck from 1842 was reprinted in same-size limited edition facsimile by the Naples Comicon in 2003. An English translation by Leonardo De Sá of Töpffer's original draft is at leonardo desa.interdinamica. net/comics/lds/*]

Even though in 1904 (in its September 3 edition), *The New York Times* accurately identified the *Brother Jonathan Extra* as the first American comic book as well as Wilson & Co. utilizing Tilt & Bougue's original printing plates as well as still being in print for sale in New York at such a late date, Töpffer has already been largely forgotten in the New World. It is high time Töpffer received credit long overdue as the inventor of the modern comic strip, laying previously long-held myths to rest.

Töpffer (1799-1846) was a playwright, novelist, artist, and teacher from Geneva, Switzerland, who in 1827 had begun producing what he called "picture novels," sharing them with his friends and students. His earliest editions were self-published via lithography on transfer paper as they use the word "autographie" in their imprints. The earliest printers were J. Freydig,

The Adventures of Obadiah Oldbuck, rare newly discovered 4th ediiton from mid 1850s. Says now "Published at Brother Jonathan Offices." Art & Story now accredited to the pseudonym "Timothy Crayon" - see Peter Piper ad previous page.

The Strange and Wonderful Adventures of Bachelor Butterfly by Rodolphe Töpffer (New York, 1846) was America's 3rd comic book; Wilson & Company's second comic book, this time out staying with the original European format.
Below: sample pages 15 & 16.

Frutiger (1830s) and Schmidt (1840s). These first sequential comic books, scripted in Töpffer's native French language, found their way to Paris and became an instant hit. According to Gombrich in *Art and Illusion* (1960), "Töpffer recognized that he could rely on the reader to supplement from their own lives what was omitted between the panels. This is crucial in the development of the sequential comic strip."

The demand for his comic books soon outstripped the supply, and pirated editions, redrawn by others, were created by Parisian publisher Aubert to capitalize on this. In a world where international copyright conventions did not exist, this was perfectly legal, if morally questionable. Thus, in 1841, London publisher Tilt and Bogue commissioned George Cruikshank to create an English version of Töpffer's *Les Amours de M. Vieux Bois* by pirating Aubert's pirated edition of the Geneva original.

This English translation, co-financed by George Cruikshank himself, sported a new cover page by George's brother Robert, based on a montage of Töpffer's scenes. Confirmation of this fact came when George Cruikshank's personal copy surfaced in auction recently with the inscription "Copied from a French book by my Brother Robert" above the title page with the same scene. This is the translation that was reprinted by America's Wilson and Company as *The Adventures of Mr. Obadiah Oldbuck* utilizing the original Tilt and Bogue printing plates.

Tilt and Bogue followed up their success by translating into English two additional stories of Töpffer's seven published graphic novels: *Beau Ogleby*, circa 1843 (originally Histoire de M. Jabot), and *Bachelor Butterfly* two years later (from *Histoire de M. Cryptogame*). David Bogue also published picture-story strip books by John Leighton using the pseudonym Luke Limner. He wrote and drew beautiful comic books titled *London Out of Town or The Adventures of the Browns At The Seaside; Comic Art-Manufactures; and The Ancient Story of the Old Dame and Her Pig* starting in 1847, but none of these seem to have ever been republished in America. They follow a definite Töpffer influence. This growing body of comic book production was made easier by the spreading understanding of transfer paper lithography, otherwise the panels would have had to have been drawn and lettered mirror reverse. Gombrich referred to Töpffer's comic books as "the innocent ancestors of today's manufactured dreams... everywhere in these countless episodes of almost surrealist inconsequence we find a mastery of physiognomic characterization which sets the standard for such influential humorous draftsmen in the 19th century as Wilhelm Busch in Germany."

A Register of The New York City Book Trades 1821-1842 by Sidney F. & Elizabeth Stege12, Huttner (The Bibliographical Society of America, NYC, 1993) mentions Benjamin H. Day bought into *Brother Jonathan*'s publisher, Wilson and Company, in this year, becoming at some point an equal partner with owner J. Gregg Wilson. The Register lists them both as publishers of *Brother Jonathan* at the same address of 162 Nassau Street. Other historical artifacts state Day eventually became sole-owner and publisher. Exactly when has not yet been determined, though we have figured out with certainly before 1850 .

This is the same Benjamin H. Day who started the first successful penny newspaper in 1833, *The (New York) Sun*, transforming it in four short years into the largest circulation daily in the world at that time. He sold out his ownership of the Sun to his brother-in-law during the financial "panic" of 1837, a mistake he regretted the rest of his life. He re-emerged heavily involved in *Brother Jonathan* definitely by 1840 and as a partner by 1841. *Brother Jonathan's* offices were right next door to Tamany Hall. (See the first 20 minutes of the 2002 movie *Gangs of New York* to visualize the period atmosphere and their customer base.) According to *The Brothers Harper* by Eugene Exmen (Harper & Row, 1965), on page 125, *"Brother Jonathan... offered in its weekly edition and also in special supplements very cheap reprints of English novels. In effect, it began a price-cutting war against the older established 'pirates' among the book publishers..."* Day, it appears, had found the perfect project on which to build a new empire.

Desirous of repeating the success they had with *Obadiah Oldbuck*, Wilson and Company published the first American edition of *Bachelor Butterfly* in 1846. Three years later, they reformatted *Obadiah Oldbuck* back into its original British shape using lithography, dropping a handful of comic panels

and altering the text to hide these deletions. Soon thereafter, they published other comic books for a steadily growing market that they had helped to stimulate. In recognition of their significant role in the dissemination of sequential comics, Wilson and Company deserve to be remembered as the first comic book publisher in America.

Back in Europe, perhaps inspired by his involvement with

Fisher's Comic Almanac, 1844, used a word balloon on its cover.

Töpffer's *Obadiah Oldbuck*, George Cruikshank soon created several sequential comic books of his own. These too found their way to America. *The Bachelor's Own Book*, published first in Britain in 1844, became the second known U.S. published sequential comic book when it was reprinted by Burgess, Stringer and Company the following year. Next was Cruikshank's masterpiece *The Bottle*, the Hogarthian-style tale of a man whose addiction to alcohol brings himself and his family to ruin. After debuting in London in 1847, it was reprinted the same year in a British-American co-publication between David Bogue and Americans Wiley and Putnam. Both printings were in huge folio form, available in either black and white or professionally hand-tinted versions. In 1848, the story saw American print again, this time in smaller form, placed at the front of the otherwise prose volume *Temperance Tales; Or, Six Nights with the Washing-tonians*. It continued to be reprinted by a variety of publishers into the early 20th Century. *The Bottle* was even reproduced onto painted glass slides and then projected by magic lantern onto a screen for the moral edification of temperance audiences. *The Drunkard's Children, Cruikshank's sequel to The Bottle*, was issued July 1, 1848 as a British-American-Australian co-publish-

The Bachelor's Own Book by George Cruikshank, published by Burgess, Stringer and Company, 1845, America's 2nd comic book, was also still a European reprint.

The Tooth-Ache by George Cruickshank 1849
© J. L. Smith, Philadelphia, PA. First American edition
opens up accordian-like into a single continuous
paper strip 7 feet, 3 inches long!

Thanks to Töpffer, Cruikshank, and a handful of enterprising American publishers, the 1840s should be remembered as the decade when America first fell in love with the comics. It had seen the U. S. publication of six sequential comic books, as well as the importation of other comics with foreign imprints. America's growing interest in graphic humor was further stimulated by the growth of two other fields: the cartoon broadside and the humor magazine.

ing venture, but was less successful, and had not nearly as many reprints.

The most clearly sequential, as well as f u n , of G e o r g e Cruickshank's comic books was *The Tooth-Ache*, first issued in London in 1849. It was reprinted in America later that same year by Philadelphia map maker J.L. Smith. An additional concurrent version was a l s o i s s u e d f r o m Boston.

When closed, this booklet appears an unassuming 5-1/4 inches tall by 3-1/4 inches wide. Its striking feature is that the book folds open accordion style, stretching the entire 43-panel story along one single strip of paper, which when fully extended is seven feet, three inches long! *The Tooth-Ache* was issued in both black and white and professionally hand-colored editions. Abridged editions of the story, printed in black and white and with a "normal" page-turning rather than foldout presentation, appeared inside promotional give-away comics issued by American companies in the 1880s.

As mentioned before, the cartoon broadside had been a part of the American scene since pre-Revolution days, but it did not flourish until stone lithography (introduced in 1818 and in wide use by the 1830s) made the reproduction of images relatively fast and cheap. From the early 1830s into the mid 1840s, the leading producer of cartoon broadsides in America was New York printer H. R. Robinson, who either drew his own cartoons or employed others, especially E. W. Clay, to do it. Clay is notable for having produced the first sequential comic broadside in America. Published in 1834 and entitled, "This Is the House that Jack Built" (50 x 32 cm), the nine-panel parody of the classic nursery rhyme was an attack on the Jackson Administration. The dominant theme of American cartoon broadsides was political, as befitted a nation where politics was the leading spectator sport. As the American electorate grew increasingly educated and prosperous, the demand for cartoon broadside also increased. During the 1840s, lithographers in New York, Boston, and Philadelphia, entered the field to satisfy that demand. The best known of these, Nathaniel Currier, later Currier and Ives, joined the fray in 1848. The firm employed

A few samples of the many humor magazines of the mid-1800s which ran cartoons. Wide-spread acceptance of the comic srtip slowly evolved over the decades. Right: Yankee Doodle #30, this title was the first American comic weekly which ran Oct 1846-Oct 1847; Second: Judy #1 ran Nov 28-Feb 20, 1847; Third: The John-Donkey #4 ran January-October 1848. Fourth: The Lantern #21, May 29, 1851 title ran Jan. 10, 1852-July 1853.

Davy Crockett's Alamnac #14, 1848, contains a 17 panel comic strip detailing tall tales of his life culminating with Crockett's death in The Alamo in 1836.

many artists, but its chief political cartoonist was Louis Maurer and its chief comic artist was Thomas Worth.

Except for the three previously cited sequential cartoon broadsides, nearly all of the cartoon broadsides published in America from 1832 to 1876, its dominant era, were single panels. From the 1860s onward, broadside series on a single comic theme became common, the most famous being Thomas Worth's *Darktown* series. These can be loosely categorized as sequential comics since they employed the same characters and formed a story of sorts when hung together on a wall, as was the publisher's expectation. Sequential art or not, the cartoon broadsides nearly always employed the speech balloons that later became one of the defining characteristic of the American comic strip.

During the same decade that sequential comics and cartoon broadsides were growing in popularity, the illustrated American humor magazine made its debut. The British comic weekly *Punch*, founded in 1841, was an immediate success, both in England and the United States. It was a handsomely printed quarto, initially twelve pages and later sixteen, with a repeating cover design, backed by a page of small advertisements, humorous text interspersed with comic spot art, and a single panel full-page cartoon. A significant subset of *Punch*'s subscriber base was located in the U.S., to which thousands of copies were exported on an ongoing trans-Atlantic basis. Inevitably, enterprising American publishers

Journey to the Gold Diggins By Jeremiah Saddlebags, June 1849, so far the earliest known sequential comic book by American creators, J.A. and D.F. Read. Below: a couple sample pages. Note similarity to Töpffer's comics especially Bachelor Butterfly

attempted to repulse this invader with a home-grown comic weekly. The first, *Yankee Doodle*, came to town (New York, that is) on October 10, 1846, for one year. *Judy* (November 28, 1846 to February 20, 1847), *The John-Donkey* (January 1 to October 21, 1848), and *The Elephant* (January 22 to February 19, 1848) soon followed. None of them was successful, but all of them continued to feed the growing American interest in comic art.

By the late 1840s, comic art was flourishing in America.

Illustrations of the Poets: From Passages in the Life of Little Billy Vidkins by Henry Stephens, S. Robinson, Phila, January, 1849, is an early American proto-comic book story told in poetry and reprinted several times. The Ohio State University Cartoon Research Library, Richard Samuel West Collection. RIGHT: In 1849 D.C. Johnston published his final issue of Scraps, nine years after the first series of eight issues. Mostly single panel cartoons all using word balloons.

Yankee Notions #1, January, 1852. This title began the first sequential comic strips in an American humor magazine, The Adventures of Jerimiah Old-Pot.

The conditions were right for the production of the earliest known American-created sequential comic book. Brothers James and Donald Read, who had worked for a time as cartoonists on *Yankee Doodle*, were the creators of *Journey to the Gold Diggins by Jeremiah Saddlebags*. This spirited send-up of the California gold rush craze was published in June 1849 by Stringer and Townsend, the late publishers of *Judy*, and, soon after, by U. P. James of Cincinnati. This Töpffer-influenced comic book chronicles the adventures of its hero *Jeremiah Saddlebags* in his get-rich-quick quest for gold in California. It is highly sought by collectors of Western Americana. Interestingly, the back cover of the Stringer and Townsend edition carries an advertisement for *Rose and Gertrude* - a Genevese Story, one of Rodolphe Töpffer's non-comics prose novels.

Stringer and Townsend was making something of a name for itself as a publisher of comic art. It will be remembered that it was one of the 1845 participants in the American publication of *The Bachelor's Own Book*. And, then, in 1846-47, it published *Judy*. Its decision to issue *Jeremiah Saddlebags* was all in due course.

The Gold Rush proved to be a gold mine for American comic artists. Aside from being a featured topic in the 1849 edition of David Claypool Johnston's *Scraps*, in comic almanacs, and in Currier cartoon prints, it was the subject of several other significant sequential series. The first, *The Adventures of Mr. Tom Plump* (a fat man who nearly starves to death in his failed attempt at California Gold riches), saw print in 1850. The second, *The Adventures of Jeremiah Old-Pot* (a twelve-part burlesque narrative of a New York businessman who attempts to get rich selling tin in price-inflated California), ran throughout 1852 in *Yankee Notions*. Though the narrative was distinctly American in its humor, the artwork was probably German in origin. *Yankee Notions'* Publisher, T. W. Strong, built his business on recycling old woodcuts with new captions attached. It should be noted that the *Old-Pot* series, borrowed or otherwise, was the first sequential art to appear in an American humor magazine. *Yankee Notions*, published from 1852 to 1875, also has the distinction of being the first comic monthly published in America.

"Moses Keyser the Bowery Bully's Trip to the California Gold Mines," was a 13-page comic story that appeared in *Elton's Californian Comic All-My-Nack* for 1850. It was reprinted at least twice in the circa 1850-51 booklet *The Clown, Or The Banquet of Wit* and later again in *Sam Slick's Comic Almanac* in 1857. *The Clown* is also notable as the earliest known anthology of sequential comics, with the bonus that each multi-panel story is by a different artist. Many of the artists are as yet unidentified, and how much of it is original American material versus that reprinted from Europe is presently unknown. But verified are cartoons by George Cruikshank, Elton (American), the Read brothers, Grandville (French), and Richard Doyle (British). The Doyle contribution reprints the comics story "Brown, Jones and Robinson and How They Went to a Ball," which originally saw print in the August 24, 1850 issue of *Punch*. This is the first known American appearance of these Doyle characters, and was almost certainly pirated.

Richard Doyle's *The Foreign Tour of Messrs. Brown, Jones, and Robinson* is basically a travelogue in illustrated form, told via humorous episodes, part sequential cartoon sequences, and part snapshots of moments jumping forward in time. This halfway sequential format was ideal for most 19th Century cartoonists, who, with rare exception, had not quite grasped how to maintain a single sequential story for much longer than two dozen successive panels. Doyle had simplified Töpffer's formula in a manner most artists could attempt to emulate. Episodes of *"Brown, Jones, and Robinson"* originally appeared in *Punch* in 1850, until a dispute between the Roman Catholic Doyle and Punch's editors over an anti-Papal joke ended with Doyle's resignation. Doyle redrew and expanded the story into a single album, first seeing print in 1854 from British publisher Bradbury and Evans.

New York Publisher D. Appleton brought the album to America, reprinting it in 1860, 1871, and 1877. Next, Dick and Fitzgerald of New York pirated Doyle's story sometime in

"Moses Keyser the Bowery Bully's Trip to the California Gold Mines" first appeared Elton's in 1850 ;was reprinted at least twice

the early 1870s. Doyle's format from *Foreign Tour* was
emulated again and again. Examples include: the 1857 *Mr.
Hardy Lee, His Yacht*, by Charles Stedman; the 1860s-
1870s G. W. Carleton-published *Our Artist In...* series, set
in various Latin American countries; the Augustus Hoppin
1870s sketch novels *On the Nile, Crossing the Atlantic*,
and *Ups and Downs on Land and Water*; and *Life*
founder John Ames Mitchell's 1881 (pre-*Life*) *The
Summer School of Philosophy at Mt. Desert*. D. Appleton,
the official, authorized American publisher of *Foreign Tour*,
even commissioned an American artist - Toby - to create a
sequel comic album involving Doyle's characters visiting the
U.S. and Canada, published in 1872 as *The American Tour
of Messrs Brown, Jones and Robinson*. In terms of influencing the development of mid-19th Century American comics,
Doyle's *Foreign Tour* ranks with the works of Töpffer,
Cruikshank, and Busch.

Doyle was also the author of an equally popular earlier
cartoon series for Punch, entitled, *In Manners and Customs
of Ye Englyshe, Mr. Pips Hys Diary*, which was reprinted in
1849. In this work, Doyle told his story using a deliberately
primitive almost stick-figure art style, combined with the
Hogarthian structure of large single panel cartoons leaping
forward in time with each picture.

Manners and Customs of Ye Harvard Studente, which
ran in the first year of the *Harvard Lampoon* (1876-cur-
rent), shows the clearest influence. The series by then student Francis Gilbert Attwood was collected in 1877 by
Houghton Mifflin. Attwood followed it up with *Manners and
Customs of Ye Bostonians*, again in the pages of the
Harvard Lampoon, but it is unknown whether that series
was ever reprinted in book form. Attwood later became one
of the regular artists in *Life*.

*The Extraordinary and Mirth-provoking Adventures by
Sea and Land of Oscar Shanghai*, inspired by Bachelor
Butterfly, was issued May 1855 by Garrett and Company,
Publishers, No. 18 Ann Street, New York. Oscar Shanghai has
many misadventures including being swallowed by a whale,
making a trip in a flying machine to Africa, where he is shot
out of a huge bow by a "Black Prince" for refusing to marry a
local princess of color. After more adventures, he makes it
back home.

Oscar Shanghai's first publisher was confirmed in 2002
with the discovery of a very rare 36-page catalog from 1856
of books, pamphlets and prints handled by B.H. Day (succes-
sor to Wilson and Company) who was by this time publishing
Brother Jonathan as a twice-a-year holiday pictorial only.

The catalog has a few crossover advertisement pages from an
associate publisher, Garrett and Company. This rediscovered
treasure, which sold for $750 in 2002, contains within a
sequential strip of one panel per page over 32 of those pages
titled *"Peter Piper in Bengal,"* by John Tenniel, reprinted
from four 1853 issues of *Punch*. In the narrative, Peter
Piper tries his hand hunting all different kinds of wild game
with many misadventures.

Amongst the many varied type of "Cheap Books" for sale in
this rare catalog are the comic books *The Adventures of
Obadiah Oldbuck, Bachelor Butterfly's Queer Love
Adventures and Misfortunes*, and *The Fortunes of
Ferdinand Flipper*, plus the aforementioned *Oscar
Shanghai*. All were priced at "25¢ per copy, postage free,
refunds paid out in stamps." There is also an advertisement
for a comic book entitled *A Day's Sport - Or, Hunting
Adventures of S. Winks Wattles, a Shopkeeper, Thomas
Titt, a "legal gent," and Major Nicholas Noggin, a Jolly
Good Fellow Generally* by Henry L. Stephens (1824-1882)
of Philadelphia.

Stephens, later the political cartoonist for *Vanity Fair* (New York, 1859-1863) and a leading children's book illustrator, produced his first work, *Illustrations of the Poets: From Passages in the Life of Little Billy Vidkins*, a small wrappered album of 32 comic woodcuts, in 1849. It was first published by S. Robinson, of Philadelphia, and reprinted with variant titles several times in the 1850s including *Yankee Notions*. It is likely that Little *Billy Vidkins* was printed before *Jeremiah Saddlebags*, though more research is needed before making this claim.

The New York Picayune v6 #46, Nov 10, 1855, later edited by Frank Bellew, regularly ran comic strips, this one right on the cover.

Garrett and Company was also responsible for the 1856 publication of *The Sad Tale of the Courtship of Chevalier Slyfox-Wikof, Showing His Heart-Rending Astounding and Most Wonderful Love Adventures with Fanny Elssler and Miss Gambol*. This book parodied the very public relationship between the then-famous wealthy American aristocrat Henry Wikoff, and the even more famous European actress/dancer Fanny Elssler. It is dated thusly because Wikoff's memoir is pictured in the comic book.

Apparently in late 1854 Garrett and Company formed a brief two-year partnership with Dick and Fitzgerald, officially becoming Garrett, Dick and Fitzgerald in November 1856, while continuing to operate out of the same 18 Ann Street address in New York. One month later they issued Richard Doyle's British published graphic novel *The Foreign Tour of Messrs. Brown, Jones, and Robinson,* reformatting it into the same oblong shape as Garrett's two prior comic books (which in turn were formatted in imitation of Töpffer's albums). This information came to light just this year. The interested

"The Flight of Abraham Lincoln," first appeared in Harper's Weekly, March 9, 1861.

scholar is encouraged to check out the new listings for Garrett's The Home Circle in the index.

In 1858, Garrett appears to have dropped out, leaving Dick and Fitzgerald alone with the former's book stock, his place of business, and most importantly, the printing plates for his comic books. For reasons unknown, Dick and Fitzgerald steered away from reprinting Garrett's comic books for more than a decade. But in the 1870s they resumed publication - not only of the three albums published by Garrett, but also of *Obadiah Oldbuck and Bachelor Butterfly* from Wilson and Company, and *Ferdinand Flipper* from *Brother Jonathan* - all of them also making use of the original printing plates. The inclusion of books from *Brother Jonathan*, Wilson and Company, and Garrett and Company all within the same promotional Peter Piper catalog from B.H. Day suggests that these early publishers of comic books had many over-lapping fields of interest,, and that Dick and Fitzgerald became the inheritor/acquirer of all of it. Dick and Fitzgerald also reprinted in the 1870s the earlier William T. Peter published *Ichabod Academicus* (how that title might have connected, if at all, with B.H. Day's business remains unclear). We can now say, though, that an evolving group of a handful of publishers was responsible, over a span of 46 years, beginning with the very first graphic novel published in America in 1842, for keeping in print in America a cluster of slightly over half a dozen graphic novels.

Tebbel's *History of Book Publishing* in the US (vol. 1, pages 351-2) states that Burgess and Stringer was dissolved in late 1840s and became two firms, Stringer and Townsend, and Burgess and Garrett. Burgess retired in 1850 and his nephew William Brisbane Dick stepped into the partnership, whereupon the new company was renamed Garrett, Dick and Fitzgerald. Garrett retired in 1851 and the firm became Dick and Fitzgerald. The firm persisted under that name until 1917.

Collections reprinting cartoons from Punch saw print in the U.S., such as *Merry Pictures by the Comic Hands*, imported for the 1859 Christmas Season, plus various John Leech, George Du Maurier, and Phil May books which appeared from the 1850s through 1910s. Finally, many American weekly newspapers and weekly and monthly magazines, humorous and non-humorous, reprinted cartoons from Punch. Such inclusions often became a prelude to switching to original material by American artists, if that publication find's cartoon section find American cartoonists of sufficient talent.

Harper's Monthly, the leading American monthly, was a prime example. Soon after it commenced publication in November 1850, it began to carry a few pages of single panel cartoons reprinted from *Punch* at the rear of each issue. This evolved into reprinting sequential comic pages from the British periodical *Town Talk*, and then, starting December 1853, original sequential comics by the great Frank Bellew.

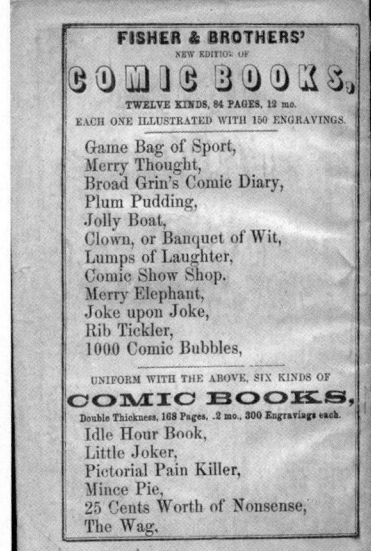

FISHER & BROTHERS'
NEW EDITION OF
COMIC BOOKS,
TWELVE KINDS, 84 PAGES, 12 mo.
EACH ONE ILLUSTRATED WITH 150 ENGRAVINGS.
Game Bag of Sport,
Merry Thought,
Broad Grin's Comic Diary,
Plum Pudding,
Jolly Boat,
Clown, or Banquet of Wit,
Lumps of Laughter,
Comic Show Shop.
Merry Elephant,
Joke upon Joke,
Rib Tickler,
1000 Comic Bubbles,

UNIFORM WITH THE ABOVE, SIX KINDS OF
COMIC BOOKS,
Double Thickness, 168 Pages, .2 mo., 300 Engravings each.
Idle Hour Book,
Little Joker,
Pictorial Pain Killer,
Mince Pie,
25 Cents Worth of Nonsense,
The Wag.

Earliest-known use of the description COMIC BOOKS dates from the early 1850s.

Bellew (1828-1888) should be regarded as the "Father of American Sequential Comics." Born in India, educated in France and England, he emigrated to America in 1850. His earliest work shows an influence from Doyle, but he rapidly developed his own unique art style. Bellew's comics, both sequential and single panel, graced nearly every American comic periodical published from the 1850s into the 1870s.

A month after the publication of the anonymous first installment of *Jeremiah Old-Pot* in *Yankee Notions*, Bellew began contributing his six-part, 18-panel comic series, *"Mr. Blobb in Search of a Physician"* to *The Lantern*, a New York comic weekly published from January 10, 1852 to July 2, 1853. The series ran in six of the nine issues published from January 31 through March 27, 1852. This was followed in April and May by the 16-panel, three-issue comic sequence *"Mr. Bulbear's Dream"*, which concluded with the main character awakened from his dream by falling out of bed, exactly like *Little Nemo* would do five decades later.

These two series were just the beginning for Bellew, who contributed a voluminous amount of work to the *New York Picayune* (1850-1860) (which he also edited for a time in 1857-58), *The Comic Monthly* (1859-1881), *Momus*, an 1860 comic daily, *The Phunniest of Awl* (1864-1867) (which he also edited), *Punchinello* (1870), and *Wild Oats* (1870-1881), to name the most prominent.

The Comic Monthly deserves special mention. Started in March 1859 and published by J. C. Haney and Company, of 119 Nassau Street, New York, *The Comic Monthly* was a profusely illustrated 16-page folio, the same size as *Harper's Weekly*. It focused its graphic satire on politics, the theater, and the comedy of everyday life. A preponderance of the

purely comic satire took the form of sequential art. Here are random samplings of highlights from issues from 1860:

• February: "A Day of Humiliation, Fasting, Supplica-tion, and Prayer (four panels, unsigned), "New Year Calls under the Influence of Hard Times" (twelve panels, unsigned), "Young Trouble-some; or, Master Jacky's Holidays" (nineteen panels covering three and half pages, unsigned);

• April: "Four Years After Marriage" (sixteen panels, unsigned), "Our Masked Ball" (twelve panel centerspread, Bellew), "Trials of a Witness" (eight panels, Bellew);

• May: "Precocities of Young Springles" (seven panels, unsigned), "The Fight for the Championship" (twenty-four panel centerspread, Bellew), "Steam Applied to Music" (three panels, unsigned), "The Course of True Love" (four panels, Bellew);

• June: "Further Particulars of the Fight" (nine panel cover, Bellew), "The Man Who Went to See the Fight" (twelve panels, unsigned);

• July: "Explaining American Politics to an Intelligent Foreigner" (twelve panels, unsigned), "The Meerschaum Mania" (two panels, Bellew), "The Art of Stump Speaking" (ten panels, unsigned), "Our Little Friend, Tom Noddy" (three panels, unsigned); "The Japanese in New York" (twelve panel centerspread, Bellew), "The Observant Child" (three panels, unsigned), "Mr. Dibbs Goes to Pike's Peak and Comes Back Again" (fourteen panel back cover, unsigned);

• September: "The Zouave Fever" (four panel cover, unsigned), "Mr. Lupell" (two panels, Bellew), "The Prince of Wales in America" (twenty-four panel centerspread, J. H. Howard), "D'ye Think It's True?" (three panels, Bellew);

• October: "The Duties of the Wide Awake" (four panels, Bellew), "Our Charley (two panels, unsigned), "The Three Young Friends" (eighteen panel back cover, unsigned);

• November: "The Hanlon's (sic) At Home" (nine panel back cover, unsigned);

• December: "The Target Excursion" (seventeen panel centerspread, signed with an unidentifiable monogram); "The Sporting Critic" two panels, Bellew).

The Comic Monthly also published many multi-panel cartoons grouped under a single heading, which were not strictly sequential in nature. Bellew was the monthly's chief artist, assisted by Thomas Nast, A. R Waud, and others. Some of the unsigned art was certainly by Bellew, some by journeymen artists, and some of it pirated from European journals.

The Comic Monthly was not the first folio-sized humor

magazine. Those laurels go to *The New York Picayune,* which began as a newspaper, switched to a folio in 1856, adopted *Punch's* format for thirty-five issues in 1857-58, and returned to a folio for the remainder of its run.

Frank Leslie's *Budget of Fun,* the greatest of the folio monthlies, began in January 1859 and was published until June 1878. Its star cartoonist during the sixties was William Newman (c. 1817-1870), one of the founding artists of Punch. As we have noted, *The Comic Monthly* began two months later.

Frank Leslie was born Henry Cart in Ipswich, England in 1821. He became a very skilled engraver before coming over to America in 1948. He first worked as manager for P.T. Barnum's *New York Illustrated News* for several years. in 1850 he legally had his name changed to Frank Leslie. He died in 1880 and his wife continued the numerous publications he was publishing. Many of Frank Leslie's periodicals had a lot of sequental comic art.

Quarto-sized monthlies to compete with the successful *Yankee Notions* were also proliferating. *Nick-Nax* was the first (May 1856 to December 1875), followed by *Phunny Phellow* (October 1859- 1876) and *Merryman's Comic Monthly* (January 1863 to December 1875), to name the most prominent.

Enterprising publishers continued to attempt an American comic weekly in the style of *Punch*. The most notable efforts, *Vanity Fair* (1859-1863), *Mrs. Grundy* (1865), and *Punchinello* (1870), were distinguished but unsuccessful.

Nearly all of them, weeklies and monthlies, to varying degrees, featured sequential comic art. By the time of the American Civil War, sequential comic art was a part of the American graphic landscape.

TOP: Frank Leslie's Budget of Fun #19 June 1860 sports a comic strip on its front cover.
BOTTOM: Likewise Comic Monthly v2#4 June 1860.

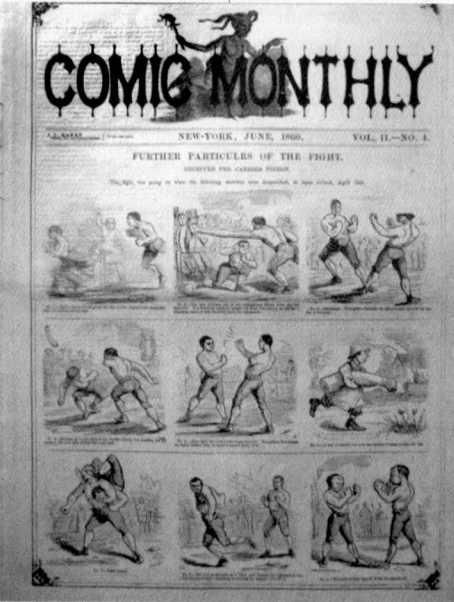

While Bellew stood out for his sequential comics, Thomas Nast (1840-1902) brought a new style to American political cartoons, of which he is regarded the father. Even though he created several sequential strips early in his career (especially for Nick-Nax in 1859), Nast made his name in the pages of the national news periodical, *Harper's Weekly,* for which he worked from 1862 until 1886. Nast was influenced more by the dark wood engravings of Franco-German illustrator Gustave Dore than by the cartoonists of *Punch*. His somber cartoons were a novelty in American cartooning. Nast in the pages of *Harper's Weekly* (and Newman in the pages of the *Budget of Fun*) popularized the extravagant double-page folio-sized cartoon, which had no precedent in European or American cartooning, save for the separately published cartoon broadsides. This format would come to full maturity after 1876 in the pages of *Puck* (1876-1918) and then *Judge* (1881-1947).

As Nast grew in prominence and success, American cartoonists increasingly emulated him. U.S. humor publications evolved towards an amalgamation of Nast and Punch, rather than sheer imitation of the latter. After the War, with Nast's style of cartoons more entrenched in American readers' minds, efforts to launch *Punch*-like American periodicals floundered quickly. *Mrs. Grundy,* ironically most famous for its cover design by Nast, died after a mere twelve issues (running July 8 to September 23, 1865). *Punchinello* (April 2 to December 24, 1870) struggled nine months before its backers gave up. *Punchinello* had been financed by Tammany Hall politicians Tweed and Sweeney, as counter-propaganda against Nast's ongoing assault upon their corruption. They attempted to buy and threaten Nast into silence, to no avail.

American comics continued their pull away from Anglo-

Franco imitation with the infusion of a third major European influence – the German humor magazine. The German-American community swelled significantly after the failed revolution of 1848. These émigrés brought with them a culture of humor, expressed most flamboyantly in their native humor magazines, the most famous being *Kladderadatsch, Fliegende Blätter*, and *Münchener Bilderbogen*. As high in quality, as were the graphic artists who contributed to them, one German comic artist in particular excelled beyond the rest, his stories breaking out and crossing over into English language translations, the demand for which resulted in numerous printings. This artist, of course, was Heinrich Christian Wilhelm Busch (1832-1908).

Sample panels from Frank Bellew Sr's The Flying Machine; And Professor High's Adventure therein in a Trip across the Ocean, Merryman's Monthly V3#5, May 1865.

Flag of Our Union, July 23, 1870, sample panels from Pt 1 of a 3 part comic strip depicting early baseball game.

Busch's work appeared in English in the 1860s in both British and American periodicals, often uncredited. For example, four of Busch's strips appeared in English in the pages of *Merryman's Monthly* in 1864, while in 1879 his graphic story "Fipps der Affe" was serialized across a 10-issue run of *Puck* as "Troddledums the Simian." The earliest known English language appearance of Busch in book form was *The Flying Dutchman, or The Wrath of Herr von Stoppelnoze*, in 1862, from New York publisher G. W. Carleton. Carleton not only pirated Busch's strip, but went so far as to credit the entire story to American poet John G. Saxe, with Busch's cartoons mere illustrations accompanying Saxe's prose!

The next known English language Busch book was **A** *Bushel of Merry Thoughts*, an 1868 London-published anthology collecting various Busch strips.

Some of these same stories later appeared in the U.S.-published *The Mischief Book* (1880), newly translated and with a few more Busch tales added. One of these additions was "Hans Huckebein," a tale of a mischievous pet raven who in the end gets drunk and accidentally hangs himself. It became, at least in the States, Busch's second most popular sequential comic story. The unrepentant bird was promoted to title character in two later collections: the rare *Hookeybeak the Raven and Other Tales* in 1878 and *Jack Huckaback, the Scapegrace Raven*, circa 1888. There were also at least three trade card series in the 1870s and 1880s that reprinted the ending sequence, as *Fritz Spindle-Shanks, The Raven Black*.

The most popular Busch tale, though, was easily Max und Moritz, which in the U.S. saw print as *Max and Maurice - A Juvenile History in Seven Tricks*. Published in Boston in 1871, this English language version saw at minimum of 60 reprintings by the century's end, plus countless more printings thereafter. A separate British translation debuted in 1874, under the title *Max and Moritz*. It is well known that the later Rudolph Dirks comic strip series, Katzenjammer Kids, beginning in late 1897, was based on *Max und Moritz*.

According to documents found by comics historian Alfredo Castelli, *Katzenjammer Kids* may not have been pirated as has been assumed but was licensed by William Randolph Hearst instead. Hearst's *New York Journal* was published in different language editions for New York City's immigrant communities. In the German edition, the strip was published under its original name, *Max und Moritz*. Numerous other translations of Busch were published in America - too many to name in this article.

Sample comics panels by Wilhelm Busch circa 1870.

Britain's famous Alley Sloper created by Marie Duvall made an early appearance in Day's Doings #168, August, 1871

Several can be found in the Victorian Age Price Index.

The most significant humor magazine of the 1870s, prior to the founding of the German-language *Puck* in 1876, was *Wild Oats* (1870-1881), which for part of its run also published a German-language edition, *Schnedereddeng*. In terms of the quality of its cartoons and comics, this New York City publication was in 1872 at an artistic level *Puck* would not achieve until 1880. Published by Winchell and Small (later Collin and Small) and distributed through the New York News Company, *Wild Oats* carried a cross-section of old and new generation comic artists, from the more established W. M. Avery, Frank Beard, Frank Bellew, E.S. Bisbee, Michael Angelo Woolf, and Thomas Worth, to up-and-comers such as Livingston Hopkins, Frederick Burr Opper, Palmer Cox, and James A. Wales.

Wild Oats began carrying sequential comic strips as early as #26, dated March 14, 1872, with the Livingston Hopkins strip pictured on the next page (we do not know anything yet about the first 25 issues). The very next issue has a Worth double-page spread titled "The Political Humpty Dumpty... Horace Greeley" told in eleven panels plus the sequential fictional "Graphic Account of the Assassination of Queen Victoria" and "Love As the Angels Love." "The Doings of the Japanese Embassy At Washington" related in twelve panels by W. M. Avery follows up in #28 April 11, 1872. An unknown hand drew "The Physiology of Moving" in six panels in #30. Hopkins returns with a beautiful intense 28-panel double-page spread in #31 May 23. Hopkins and Worth alternated for many issues with sequential comic strips on baseball, horse racing and other pertinent subjects of the day. In #45 December 5, 1872, E.S. Bisbee contributed his first sequential in seventeen panels and Worth showed up in "Humor and Pathos of a New England Thanksgiving" in eleven panels. Issue 47 expands the concept with a twelve-panel job by Bisbee, twenty-panel effort on one page by Hopkins and a three-panel effort by Worth. And on it goes through 1873 as well - comic strip after comic strip. Issue 58 June 5, 1873, includes a particularly humorous nineteen-panel double-pager drawn by someone still unknown titled "The Terrible Adventures of Messrs. Buster and Stumps, with the Indians" which begins with two white men heading out west in an effort to exterminate Indians - and their misadventures of not quite getting the job done. It reads across both pages in a unique evolution similar to Popeye #2052 (found in the Platinum listings). Issue 65 contains two nine-panel Thomas Worth strips "Only a Mad Dog Scare - Another Lesson For Nervous People" and "Only a Cholera Scare - Something For Nervous People to Read and Ponder Over." Issue 66 Sept 18, 1873, has the very funny Hopkins twelve-

Wild Oats #26, 14 March 1872 Livingston Hopkins sequential comic strip. Hopkins later moved to Australia and became its premiere political cartoonist.

Wild Oats #163, Feb 9, 1876 last six panels by Palmer Cox who began doing sequential comic strips some years before he created The Brownies.

panel strip as well as two more ten-panel Worth strips on the delights of Hunting and Fishing plus one by Hopkins titled "The Adventures of Mr Old Party with Jersey Mosquitoes" in twelve-panels. All told, four comic strips in this issue. They obviously liked what they were doing, judging from the exuberance of the work.

The next issue has Worth's nine-panel report on "The Adventures of Young Muttonhead among the Free Lovers" which was all about the "free sex" convention recently held in Chicago. Issue 68 has a nine-panel "An Adventure with a New Jersey Mosquito" which smacks of Winsor McCay in subject and even art style. Maybe McCay was inspired by this for his later animated cartoon as well as earlier Rarebit Fiend. We'll

Wild Oats #69, Oct 30, 1873 Frank Bellew early robot cover. The zine presented many 100s of sequential comic strips over its life time. Today loose issues remain rare to very rare.

never know for sure. On through 1875, *Wild Oats* presented sequential comic strips issue after issue. With #148, October 27, 1875, Frederick Opper contributes his very first Wild Oats cover, a political cartoon on inflation then rampant in the US. He does covers through at least #161 before a short break and then comes back with many more. In #158, January 5, 1876, Palmer Cox - some five years before inventing The Brownies - begins a wonderful series of 24-panel double page spread comic strips, with a couple sample titles being "The Adventures of Mr. and Mrs. Sprowl And Their Christmas Turkey-A Crashing Chasing Tearful Tragedy But Happily Ending Well" and "Bachelor Broke and Widow Snuggi: A Pictorial Account of Their Sleigh Ride and What Became of It."

Even though he had been contributing many covers and interior single panel jobs to *Wild Oats* for years, Frank Bellew does not show up with his first comic strip until #190, August 16, 1876, with a nine-panel effort he titled, "Rodger's Patent Mosquito Armour." By this time America's "Father of the sequential comic strip"

Wild Oats #190 August 16, 1876 by Frank Bellew Sr., Father of American Comic Strips. This one titled "Rodger's Patent Mosquito Armor."

had inspired many other cartoonists to try their hand telling stories with words and pictures.

Another highly desirable American graphic novel, sought especially by collectors of Western lore, is *Quiddities of an Alaskan Trip* by William H. Bell which debuted in 1873. Bell was Timothy O'Sullivan's assistant photographer on the 1871-74 expeditions of Lt. George Wheeler, surveying and mapping the western territories for the U.S. government. The story panels are laid out within ornate frames like those of stereograph cards, such as Bell was involved in creating on the expedition. It involves a parody of a trip from Washington, D.C., to survey the newly purchased territory of Alaska, which at the time was derisively referred to as "Seward's Folly." Bell published *Quiddities* in Portland, Oregon, in 1873, meaning that he drew it while he was on just such an expedition.

The seemingly disparate influences of Thomas Nast and German comics came together in the work of Austrian immigrant Joseph Keppler (1838-1894). Like many cartoonists in America, Keppler desired to rival Nast. Unlike most, he possessed the talent and drive to accomplish it. Keppler, trained as an artist but working as an actor, began contributing comic art to *Kikeriki* (1861-1923) in his native Vienna. He emigrated to St. Louis in 1868, where he took his first stab at starting a comic weekly, the German language *Die Vehme* (Aug 28, 1869 - Aug. 20, 1870). Seven months later, still in St. Louis, he tried again, launching another German language humor periodical, titled *Puck*. This German *Puck* began on March 18, 1871, joined by an English language version one year later, but both ended on Aug. 24, 1872.

Keppler moved to New York City and began working for Frank Leslie. His cartoons appeared in *Frank Leslie's Illustrated Newspaper*, Frank Leslie's *Budget of Fun*, and the Leslie-owned *Jolly Joker* and *Day's Doings*. (To capitalize on the 1876 Centennial Exposition in Philadelphia, Leslie published in that year a paperback collection of Centennial-related humor, *Centennial Fun*, most of which was

The Daily Graphic #1498, Jan 8, 1878, New York. Artist: Gray Parkxxx. This innovative paper carried all kinds of comic strips beginning more than 20 years before both Pulitzer and then Hearst got into the comic strip business. Largely overlooked by later historians, it is only recently being sought after once again.

Keppler's work.) Four years after the first *Puck* died, Keppler was ready to try again. He re-launched the German language edition of *Puck* in New York City on September 27, 1876.

This *Puck* was both familiar and exotic. Its format of an extravagant center-spread cartoon sandwiched between front and back cover cartoons had by this time become something of a comic periodical standard, certainly for the monthlies. But *Puck* was different from what had come before. The cartoons were lithographed, not engraved, which lent to them a softer, more pleasing quality, and they were in color, something virtually without precedent in American comic periodical literature.

Initially, the magazine's cartoons were tinted in just one color, but *Puck* appeared, ambitiously, every week, and the coloring set it apart from anything else on American stands. The parallel English language edition of *Puck* was launched six months after the German version, on March 14, 1877. This English edition of *Puck* was a money-loser for several years, kept afloat by the German edition's profits and the determination of the English edition's literary editor, H.C. Bunner, not to give up. By 1880, *Puck* was a huge success. It became the new model for American humor publications. In time, Keppler hired other artists, most notably Frederick Burr Opper, Eugene Zimmerman ("Zim") and F. M. Howarth, and added black and white sequential comics to the magazine's interior and then, with increasing frequency in the early 1890s to the magazine's back cover. *Funny Folks* by F. M. Howarth, 1899, collected many early sequential comics from *Puck;* one of the titles many consider bridges the Victorian

and Platinum Ages of comics. *Puck* was the model that inspired William Randolph Hearst to add a color comics section to his Sunday Journal in 1895.

With the first issue dated October 29, 1881, *Puck's* chief rival, *Judge*, was born. Founded by *Puck* artist James A. Wales, it also featured the work of Thomas Worth and Livingston Hopkins. *Judge* made several forays into *Puck's* talent pool over the years. Its best capture was Eugene Zimmerman ("Zim"), who became for Judge the star artist that Frederick Burr Opper was for Puck.

Judge struggled financially for several years, and likely would have ceased publication had it not been for Puck's powerful performance during the 1884 election. *Puck's* success galvanized Republican powerbrokers into recognizing the importance of the political cartoon weekly. They financed newspaperman W. J. Arkell's purchase of *Judge* in 1886 to turn it into a reliable Republican house organ.

Numerous other Puck imitators emerged in the 1880s but quickly died. Note should be made of two that did not: the *Puck*-like *San Francisco Wasp*, which debuted August 5, 1876 (too early for it to be considered a *Puck* knockoff), and the black and white *Texas Siftings*, which debuted on May 9, 1881. Though neither was as successful as *Puck* or *Judge*, both cut their own paths, managing to survive as cartoon humor magazines into the 1890s.

Also worthy of mention is the New York City newspaper *The Daily Graphic* (March 4, 1873 to Sept 23, 1889), which claims the distinction of being the first regularly illustrated daily newspaper in the world, published every day except Sundays and holidays. The majority of its illustrations were portraits or depictions of news events, but nearly every issue contained some comic drawing, many of them gracing the front cover.

With so many pages to fill on a daily basis, *The Daily Graphic* became a rotating door for many young American cartoonists in the early stages of their careers (making one suspect that it was not the best paying gig in town). Within its pages, like needles to be found in the haystack of its more than 4800 issues, is early work by Livingston Hopkins (who mysteriously appears, vanishes, reappears, etc., for months to whole years at a time, right up to his 1884 departure to Australia), pre-*Life* work by Kemble, pre-*Harper's* appearances by A.B. Frost and W.A. Rogers, pre-Puck and Judge Opper, C.J. Taylor, Hamilton, and Gillam. Old hats, too, appear at times, such as Michael Woolf and Frank Bellew, Sr.

Further, *The Daily Graphic* regularly plundered British periodicals for its back and sometimes center pages, not only

Leslie's Young America ran comic strips during its two year run 1881-82. Many are quite good. This example from #15 (10/15/81) reminds us of Zim.

A HAT OFF A PEG.

perpetrating the usual swipes of single-panel *Punch* cartoons, but also stealing sequential strips from Punch's two main rival publications, *Judy* and *Fun*. This included occasionally reprinting (albeit at random) episodes of continuing British strips "The British Workman" by James Sullivan, and "McNab of that Ilk" by James Brown, though, strangely enough, not Marie Duval's *Ally Sloper*, despite the fact that *The Daily Graphic* did reprint some of Duval's non-"Sloper" strips. ("Ally Sloper" was a continuing sequential strip character who debuted in 1867, lasting into the 1920s, and had very successful solo British book collections of his strip appearances published as early as 1873, more than two decades prior to *Yellow Kid in McFadden's Flats*).

Livingston Hopkins, whose art style changed like a chameleon from one year to the next, exhibited a definite Duval influence in his work within a year following the publication of the first *Ally Sloper* collection. Given that Hopkins worked for *The Daily Graphic* during the same period in which this newspaper was stealing cartoons from *Sloper*'s home publication, *Judy*, this can hardly be considered coincidental. Hopkins contributed a daily comic strip to *The Daily Graphic* in 1874-75, complete with word balloons. By the time Hopkins was preparing to emigrate to Australia to become lead cartoonist for the Sydney Bulletin, his art style was an imitation of Kemble's, who was also working at *The Daily Graphic*.

Life debuted on January 4, 1883, founded by J.A. Mitchell, and modeled after the Harvard Lampoon. It quickly rose to become the third main pillar of late 1800s American humor periodicals. Smaller in size, black and white, and priced the same as *Puck* and *Judge*, it nevertheless succeeded by appealing to a more genteel audience. Its earliest artists included Kemble and Palmer Cox, but its foremost artist was Charles Dana Gibson, becoming world renowned as the hand behind the graceful, aristocratic "Gibson Girls."

Unlike *Judge*, which had to become a low-brow imitation of *Life* to survive in the next century, and *Puck*, which attempted but failed to become an American version of the highbrow European humor magazines, Life transitioned into the 20th century virtually unaltered, and thrived. By the mid-1880s, with *Puck*, *Judge*, and *Life* all solidly in place, American comics and cartoon humor had come very much into their own, no longer

Sequence by A.B. Frost, from the MidSummer Puck 1887.

looking first at Europe to take their cues.

Almanacs began to appear in America starting in 1639. Humor was introduced as early as 1647 by Samuel Danforth. A very important one was *Leed Almanac* beginning in 1687. John Tulley produced the first humorous almanac in 1688. James Franklin, brother of Ben, began the *Rhode Island Almanac* in 1728 using the name "Poor Robin" and his younger brother began *Poor Richard's Almanac* in 1732. Farmer's Almanac began in 1792 and used some humor.

The first comic almanac totally devoted to humor was published by Charles Ellm in Boston in 1831 and featured the artwork of D.C. Johnston. Perhaps the most famous comic almanacs (certainly the most valuable) are the *Davy Crockett* series (1835-1856) which began in Nashville, Tennessee. The comic periodicals all ended up issuing comic almanacs beginning with *Yankee Notions* in 1856 and continuing into the 1890s with a one-shot comic almanac published by *Judge* for the year 1894.

Beginning in the 1850s, a new breed of almanacs appeared. Usually created by medicine and farm product companies, they were distributed for free to promote the company's product. Competition amongst companies, whose goal was to get customers to read the almanacs and the advertisements contained therein again and again, meant that attention-getting humorous cartoons soon found their way back into these giveaway pamphlets. Initially their cartoons were done cheap, either poorly drawn or pirated from elsewhere, such as those found in the Hostetter's and Wright's almanac series. More elaborate promotional almanacs eventually did evolve, though, and amongst the best of these was *Barker's Illustrated Almanac*, first produced for the year 1878, and annually into the 1930s. Each *Barker's Almanac* contained

THEY BEGIN IN A SMALL WAY, BUT "THEY GET THERE ALL THE SAME."

Texas Siftings v6#7 June 19, 1886 ran a whole slew of sequential comic strips for many years and is yet another sleeper for collectors to hunt.

ten to twelve full page cartoons, wonderful and bizarre in design, frequently racist, but also comically manic and crammed with details in a manner similar to Outcault's much later *Yellow Kid* pages. The cartoons in *Barker's Almanac* were so popular that in 1892, The Barker, Moore, and Mein Medicine Company published their first edition of *Barker's Komic Picture Souvenir*, reprinting nearly 150 pages of cartoons from their almanacs.

This first *Barker's Souvenir* features a wraparound color cover depicting people headed towards the Columbian World's Fair Exposition, which was to be held in Chicago the next year. It is the earliest confirmed "premium" comic book, sent to customers who mailed in a box label and outside wrapper from two different Barker's products. The *Souvenir* album was *Barker's* most in-demand premium. It was reprinted as a thick unnumbered booklet three more times in the 1890s, with the contents reorganized each time. Later, between 1901 and 1903, *Barker's* broke the album into three separate "Parts," each of which required still more box labels and wrappers to obtain. The 3-part series of reprint albums expanded to four parts circa 1906 or 1907. Both the 3 and 4-part album series had multiple printings.

Also very American in character were the country's promotional comics, which flourished throughout the latter half of the 19th century. They trace their beginnings to Comic Almanacs, which flourished in England and the United States since they first appeared in the 1830s. The first promotional comics which did not double as almanacs began to appear in the 1870s. They included the aforementioned reprints of Cruikshank and Busch strips, reprints of strips lifted from American sources (A.B. Frost's strip "The Bull Calf" was a particular favorite), and original material placing the product being promoted as the focus of the story. These original short cartoon dramas were in many ways similar in storyline to those found in modern television advertisements, except that the clothing is Victorian, and the claims, pre-F.D.A. and F.C.C., were unabashedly wild, over-the-top, and blunt. Chewing tobacco and snuff saved romances, calmed crying babies, and made the sick well. Stove polish that propelled you to wealth and power. Corsets that brought you a husband. The objective, of course, in an era before TV or radio, was to make each comic handout so entertaining that customers would want to keep and read the advertisement again and again.

The more wonderful graphics and outrageous claims tended to come from tobacco companies, who were using comic books and strips to sell their products more than a century before cries against "Joe Camel." The most elaborate of these were printed full color, and unfolded into a single long strip, just like Cruikshank's *The Tooth-Ache* from the 1840s, though usually limited to just the cover plus seven panels.

Examples are the Jackson Chewing Tobacco comics *How Adolphus Slim-Jim Used Jackson's Best* and *Ye Veracious Chronicle of Gruff and Pompey*, and Durham Smoking Tobacco's *Home Made Happy - A Romance for Married Men*. The artists of these comics are mostly unidentified, but their level of skill was equal to anything in *Puck* and *Judge*. *The Home Made Happy Comic*, in fact, was produced for Durham by The Graphic Company -- the publisher of *The Daily Graphic*, the aforementioned 1870s illustrated newspaper which included cartoons.

The earliest known anthology devoted to collecting the comic strips of a single American artist was A.B. Frost's *Stuff and Nonsense* in 1884. The next known American collection came in 1888, the very rare Frederick Burr Opper anthology, *Puck's Opper Book*. Both proved popular, so more Frost and Opper collections followed, to be joined within a few years by reprints collecting the cartoons and strips of Keppler, Kemble, Zim, Gibson, Mayer, Taylor, Frank Bellew's son "Chip," Howarth, Woolf, etc.

Puck, Judge, and *Texas Siftings* all began monthly Library series - 8-1/2" x 11" magazines, mostly black and white, which organized previously published material around one theme or one artist. For example, the first *Puck's Library* (July 1887) was titled "The National Game," and gathered

THE STORY OF A BLACK EYE.---In Six Pangs.

Young Men of America #527, Oct 13, 1887, by Frank Bellew towards the end of his illustrious career. By this time, he had the sequential comic art form down in most aspects, having published hundreds of them.

beneath one cover *Puck* material poking fun at the game of baseball. The third (March 1888) and ninth (November 1889) issues of *Judge's Serial (later named Judge's Library)* were devoted entirely to the work of Zim.

Life tended more towards hardcover collections, such as its annual ten-issue series *The Good Things of Life* (1884-1893), which included cartoons and strips by Palmer Cox, T.S. Sullivant, Hy Mayer, and others. *The Good Things of Life* was published initially by the firm of White, Stokes, and Allen, but which by the fourth book, had become simply Frederick A. Stokes. Stokes published a number of other cartoon books in the 1880s and 1890s, the majority of them reprint collections. The experience he gained at this time with these reprint albums placed Stokes in the perfect position to pick up the wealth of material about to be created for the comics supplements of William R. Hearst's newspapers, making Stokes the first major publisher of the coming Platinum Age.

In 1892, Charles Scribner's Sons published A. B. Frost's *Bull Calf and Other Tales*. It contains sequential comic strip art on quite a few pages as well as single panel cartoons. By 1898, Charles Scribner's Sons also issued Kemble's *The Billy Goat and Other Comicalities* as a 112-page hardcover, which also has sequential comic strips.

In the early 1890s, the slum children cartoons of artist Michael Woolf (many of which were reprinted in the 1896 collection *99 Woolfs from Truth* and in the posthumous 1899 collection *Sketches of Lowly Life in a Great City*) were popular. *Truth* magazine, which followed Puck's format of color front cover, back cover and centerspread cartoons, but in style was more akin to the aristocratic Life, was initially unable to secure Woolf's services, creating an opportunity for the young cartoonist Richard F. Outcault, who desired to break into one of the weekly comic periodicals.

It was in his Woolf-inspired slum children cartoons for *Truth* that Outcault's prototype of the *Yellow Kid* first emerged. The bald, sack-clothed youngster made four appearances in *Truth*, starting with #372 on June 2, 1894, prior to his newspaper debut.

During the rise of Yellow Kid's popularity, he appeared in American comic magazines in parodies drawn by others, with politicians, even Hearst and Pulitzer, dressed up as the *Yellow Kid*. Such cartoons are known to have appeared in *Judge, Life, The Bee,* and *Vim* plus various newspapers across the country. More about the *Yellow Kid's* importance can be found in the Platinum Age section of this book.

While comics definitely have their roots in Europe, and the earliest American comic books either reprinted or emulated those of Europe, the direction of influence was by no means one way. By at least the 1870s, American cartoons were being pub-

"A Family Discord" - One of many F.M. Howarth Puck back covers, this one later reprinted in Pickings From Puck #18 Dec 1895.

lished and seen in the Old World, as evidenced by the arrest in Spain of the on-the-lamb corrupt Tammany Hall politician Boss Tweed by Spanish police who recognized Tweed from a Nast cartoon.

European piracy of American cartoons was just as lucrative as the American piracy of Europeans. In the 1880s and '90s, the comics of Zim, Chip Bellew, and Charles Dana Gibson all saw reprint in Europe. In April 1899, *Pictorial Comedy*, a monthly magazine destined for a ten-year run, commenced publication in London. It was made up entirely of cartoons reprinted with permission from *Puck* and *Life*. F.M. Howarth's domestic comedies from *Puck* were favorites in France. American Hy Mayer was commissioned to create original comics work for *Black and White* (Britain), *Le Rire* (France), and *Fliegende Blätter*. Michael Woolf's slum children cartoons saw print in the British periodical *Pick-Me-Up*, during the same years that top British artist Phil May's first published work debuted in that publication. May later became famous for his Woolf-inspired street children cartoons as well as his influence on the development of comics in Australia.

As the 19th Century ended, American comics were coming to the fore worldwide, soon to explode into a position of dominance with the Platinum Age revolution brought about by the emergence of the color comic supplement in America's newspapers and the arrival of Richard F. Outcault's *Yellow Kid*.

END NOTE: Victorian Era comics were issued in many relatively obscure formats compared to what most of us are used to today.

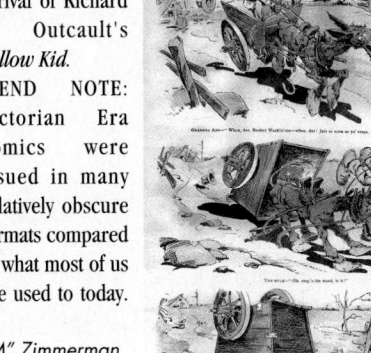

Judge 1896 Eugene "ZIM" Zimmerman "A Sagacious Animal" is but one of hundreds by mostly forgotten comics legend Zim who went on to run an early cartoonist training school.

ALONE.

Susy: "What's he cryin' for?"
Nelly (in a whisper): "That dead dog wuz his chum."

Michael Angelo Woolf cartoon from 99 Truths From Woolf. His many scenes from slum life in New York City was a major influence on Outcault's formulation of the Yellow Kid. Titled "Alone," The caption reads Susy: "What's he cryin' for?" Nelly (in a whisper): "That dog was his chum."

Time, One Minute by Hy Mayer, Truth, 1896
"Our artist-draws-a picture-before the kinetscope"
The last panel in this cinematic wonder says
"Thoz. A. Edizon," inventor of movies.
At the turn of the 19th Century, comic strips and movies
intersected on many levels.

The Victorian Era section can only grow as there are many more heretofore undiscovered comics from the 1800s which have fallen off the radar of history. Some may wonder why some of the earlier items listed contain as of yet no prices. The reason is simple. These books are part of a relatively "new" market which is still establishing itself.

High-grade copies are almost unheard of in almost all instances. Some books may truly have only a handful left in existence. We are sure there are some known to have been published which no (as of yet) known copies have survived the ravages of time and neglect.

Each year expect another quantum leap in our ever-expanding knowledge of the fascinating earliest origins of the comic strip as it relates to North America. Your input in helping this section of the Guide grow and mature is most welcome!

Robert Lee Beerbohm first sold comics through the legendary RBCC beginning in 1966, set up at his first comicon in 1967, helped found the northern California Comics & Comix chain of stores in August 1972, co-hosted Berkeleycon 1973, the first UG creator-owned comix con and operated comic book stores from 1972-1994. He now owns Robert Beerbohm Comic Art that specializes in buying and selling scarce comics and related material from the 1840s-1980s. He has been compiling a detailed history book of the business of the American comic book for some time now and hopes to complete it soon.

Contact Robert directly at www.BLBComics.com

Richard Olson is an Research Professor Emeritus at the University of New Orleans. He published the Richard Outcault Collector for years. Reach Richard directly at: rolsonredoak@bellsouth.net

Richard Samuel West is the author of Satire on Stone: The Political Cartoons of Joseph Keppler (University of Illinois, 1988) and The San Francisco Wasp: An Illustrate History (Periodyssey Press, 2004) and editor of several cartoon collections. He is the owner of Periodyssey, a business that specializes in buying and selling significant and unusual American magazines. Richard can be reached at:

www.oldmagazines.com

All three are life-long collectors and students of all forms of the comics who welcome corrections and additions to this concise compilation of our earliest American comics heritage dating back almost two centuries. Happy Hunting!

Judge #791, Dec 12, 1896,
depicting Tammany Hall politicians as
RFO's Yellow Kid & Cox's Brownies.
Art by Hamilton.

The American Comic Almanac #5
1835 © Charles Ellms, NYC

The Strange and Wonderful Adventures
of Bachelor Butterfly by Rodolphe Töpffer
1870s © Dick & Fitzgerald, NYC

Barker's "Komic" Picture Souvenir, 3rd Edition
1894 © Barker, Moore & Klein Medicine Co.

FR1.0   **GD**2.0   **FN**6.0   **FR**1.0   **GD**2.0   **FN**6.0

COLLECTOR'S NOTE: Some of books listed in this section were published well over a century before organized comics fandom began archiving and helping to preserve these fragile popular culture artifacts. Consequently, copies of most all of these comics almost never surface in Fine+ or better shape. Most are in the Poor to VG range. If you want to collect these only in high grade, your collection will be extremely small. This year the price blanks are filled in on most items. The past few years we had been more concerned with simply establishing what is known to exist. The prices given for Fair, Good and Fine categories are for strictly graded editions. If you need help grading your item, we refer you to the grading section in this book or contact the authors of this essay. Items marked Scarce, Rare or Very Rare we are trying to figure out how many copies might still be in existence. We welcome help from any interested parties at Robert@BLBcomics.com.

For ease ascertaining the contents of each item of this listing and the Platinum index list, we offer the following list of categories found immediately following most of the titles:
E - EUROPEAN ORIGINAL COMICS MATERIAL; Printed in Europe or reprinted in USA
G - GRAPHIC NOVEL (LONGER FORMAT COMIC TELLING A SINGLE STORY)
H - "HOW TO DRAW CARTOONS" BOOKS
I - ILLUSTRATED BOOKS NOTABLE FOR THE ARTIST, BUT NOT A COMIC.
M - MAGAZINE / PERIODICAL COMICS MATERIAL REPRINTS
N - NEWSPAPER COMICS MATERIAL REPRINTS
O - ORIGINAL COMIC MATERIAL NOT REPRINTED FROM ANOTHER SOURCE
P - PROMOTIONAL COMIC, EITHER GIVEN AWAY FOR FREE, OR A PREMIUM GIVEN IN CONJUNCTION WITH THE PURCHASE OF A PRODUCT.
S - SINGLE PANEL / NON-SEQUENTIAL CARTOONS

Measurements are in inches. The first dimension given is Height and the second is Width. Some original British editions are included in the section, so as to better explain and differentiate their American counterparts. This section created, revised, and expanded by Robert Beerbohm with acknowledgment to Bill Blackbeard, Chris Brown, Alfredo Castelli, Darrell Coons, Leonardo De Sá, Scott Deschaine, Joe Evans, Ron Friggle, Terrence Keegan, Tom Gordon III, Michel Kempeneers, Andy Konkykru, Don Kurtz, Richard Olson, Robert Quesinberry, Joseph Rainone, Steve Rowe, Randy Scott, John Snyder, Art Spiegelman, Steve Thompson, Richard Samuel West, Doug Wheeler and Richard Wright. Special Kudos to long-time collector and scholar Gabriel Laderman.

ACROBATIC ANIMALS
R.H. Russell: 1899 (9x11-7/8", 72 pgs, B&W, hard-c)
nn (Scarce)   40.00   80.00   160.00
NOTE: Animal strips by Gustave Verbeck, presented 1 panel per page.

ALMY'S SANTA CLAUS (P,E)
Edward C. Almy & Co., Providence, R.I.: nd (1880's) (5-3/4x4-5/8", 20 pgs, B&W, paper cover)
nn - (Rare)   12.50   40.00   80.00
NOTE: Department store Christmas giveaway containing an abbreviated 28-panel reprinting of George Cruikshank's The Tooth-ache. Santa Claus cover.

AMERICAN COMIC ALMANAC, THE (OLD AMERICAN COMIC ALMANAC 1839-1846)
Charles Ellms: 1831-1846 (5x8, 52 pgs, B&W)
1-16   100.00   200.00   400.00
NOTE:#1 from 1831 is the First American Comic Almanac

AMERICAN PUNCH
American Punch Publishing Co: Jan 1879-March 1881, J.A. Cummings Engraving Co (last 3 issues) (Quarto Monthly)
Most issues   25.00   50.00   150.00

THE AMERICAN WIT
Richardson & Collins, NY: 1867-68 (18-1/2x13. 8 pgs, B&W)
2/3 Frank Bellew single panels   50.00   100.00   200.00

AMERICAN WIT AND HUMOR
Harper & Bros, NY: 1859 (
nn - numerous McLenan sequential comic strips   100.00   200.00   400.00

ATTWOOD'S PICTURES - AN ARTIST'S HISTORY OF THE LAST TEN YEARS OF THE NINETEENTH CENTURY (M,S)
Life Publishing Company, New York: 1900 (11-1/4x9-1/8", 156 pgs, B&W, gilted blue hard-c)
nn - By Attwood   40.00   80.00   160.00
NOTE: Reprints monthly calendar cartoons which appeared in LIFE, for 1887 through 1899.

BACHELOR BUTTERFLY, THE VERITABLE HISTORY OF MR. (E,G)
D. Bogue, London: 1845 (5-1/2x10-1/4", 74 pgs, B&W, gilted hardcover)
nn - By Rodolphe Töpffer (Scarce)   500.00   1250.00 2500.00
nn - Hand colored edition (Very Rare)   (no known sales)
NOTE: This is the First Edition, translated from the re-engraved by Cham serialization found in L'Illustration - a periodical from Paris publisher Dubochet. Predates the first French collected edition. Third Töpffer comic book published in English. The first story page is numbered Page 3. Page 17 shows Bachelor Butterfly being swallowed by a whale.

BACHELOR BUTTERFLY, THE STRANGE ADVENTURES OF (E,G)
Wilson & Co., New York: 1846 (5-3/8x10-1/8", 68 pgs, B&W, soft-c)
nn - By Rodolphe Töpffer (Very Rare)   600.00   1500.00 3000.00
nn - At least one hand colored copy exists (Very Rare)   (no known sales)
NOTE: 2nd Töpffer comic book printed in the U.S., 3rd earliest known sequential comic book in the USA. Reprinted from the British D. Bogue 1845 edition, itself from the earlier French language Histoire de Mr.

Cryptogame. Released the same year as the French Dubochet edition. Two variations known, the earlier printing with Page number 17 placed on the inside (left) bottom corner in error, with slightly later printings corrected to place page number 17 on the outside (right) bottom corner of that page. Another first printing indicator is pages 17 and 20 are printed on the wrong side of the page. For both printings: the first story page is numbered 2. Page 17 shows Bachelor Butterfly already in the whale. In most panels with 3 lines of text, the third line is indented further than the second, which is in turn indented further than the first.

BACHELOR BUTTERFLY, THE STRANGE ADVENTURES
Brother Jonathan Press, NY: 1854 (5-1/2x10-5/8", 68 pgs, paper-c, B&W) (Very Rare)
nn - By Rodolphe Töpffer   250.00   500.00   1000.00

BACHELOR BUTTERFLY,THE STRANGE & WONDERFUL ADVENTURES OF
Dick & Fitzgerald, New York: 1870s-1888 (various printings 30 Cent cover price, 68 pgs, B&W, paper cover) (all versions Rare) (E,G)
nn - Black print on blue cover (5-1/2x10-1/2"); string bound   112.00   225.00   450.00
nn - Black print on green cover (5-1/2x10-1/2"); string bound 100.00   200.00   400.00
NOTE: Reprints the earlier Wilson & Co. edition. Page 2 is the first story page. Page 17 shows Bachelor Butterfly already in the whale. In most panels with 3 lines of text, the second and third lines are equally indented in from the first. Unknown which cover (blue or green) is earlier.

BACHELOR'S OWN BOOK. BEING THE PROGRESS OF MR. LAMBKIN, (GENT.) IN THE PURSUIT OF PLEASURE AND AMUSEMENT (E,O,G)
(See also PROGRESS OF MR. LAMBKIN)
D. Bogue, London: August 1, 1844 (5x8-1/4", 28 pgs printed one side only, cardboard cover & interior) (all versions Rare)
nn - First printing hand colored   (no known sales)
nn - First printing black & white   –   450.00   –
NOTE: First printing has misspellings in the title. "PURSUIT" is spelled "PERSUIT", and "AMUSEMENT" is spelled "AMUSEMEMT".
nn - Second printing hand colored   (no known sales)
nn - Second printing black & white   (no known sales)
NOTE: Second printing. The misspelling of "PURSUIT" has been corrected, but "AMUSEMEMT" error is still present.
nn - Third printing hand colored   No misspellings   (no known sales)
nn - Third printing black & white   (no known sales)
NOTE: By George Cruikshank. This is the British Edition. Issued both in black & white, and professionally hand-colored editions. Hand-colored editions have survived in higher quantities than uncolored. Originally made with thin paper sheets covering the plates.

BACHELOR'S OWN BOOK; OR, THE PROGRESS OF MR. LAMBKIN, (GENT.), IN THE PURSUIT OF PLEASURE AND AMUSEMENT, AND ALSO IN SEARCH OF HEALTH AND HAPPINESS, THE (E,O,G)
David Bryce & Son: Glasgow: 1884 (7-5/8 x5-7/8", 62 pgs printed one side only, illustrated hardcover, page edges guilt)
nn - Reprints the 1844 edition with altered title   (no known sales)

BACHELOR'S OWN BOOK. BEING TWENTY-FOUR PASSAGES IN THE LIFE OF MR. LAMBKIN, GENT. (E,G)
Burgess, Stringer & Co., New York on cover; Carey & Hart, Philadelphia on title page: 1845 (31-1/4 cents, 7-1/2x4-5/8", 52 pgs, B&W, paper cover)
nn - By George Cruikshank (Very Rare)   (no known sales)
NOTE: This is the second known sequential comic book story published in America. Reprints the earlier British edition. Pages printed on one side only. New cover art by an unknown artist.

BAD BOY'S FIRST READER (O,S)
G.W. Carleton & Co.: 1881 (5-3/4 x 4-1/8", 44 pgs, B&W, paper cover)
nn - By Frank Bellew (Senior)   50.00   100.00   200.00
NOTE: Parody of a children's ABC primer, one cartoon illustration plus text per page. Includes one panel of Boss Tweed. Frank Bellew is considered the "Father of the American Sequential Comics."

BALL OF YARN OR, QUEER, QUIANT & QUIZZICAL STORIES, UNRAVELED WITH NEARLY 200 COMIC ENGRAVINGS OF FREAKS, FOLLIES & FOIBLES OF QUEER FOLKS BY THAT PRINCE OF COMICS, ELTON, THE (M)
Philip. J. Cozans, 116 Nassau St, NY: early 1850s (7-1/4x3-1/2", 76 pgs, yellow-wraps)
nn - sequential comic strips plus singles   (no known sales)
NOTE: Mose Keyser-r, Jones, Smith & Robinson Goes To A Ball-r; The Adventures of Mr Goliah Starvemouse-r are all sequential comic strips printed in a number of sources

BARKER'S ILLUSTRATED ALMANAC (O,P,S)
Barker, Moore & Mein Medicine Co: 1878-1932+ (36 pgs, B&W, color paper-cr)
1878-1879 (Rare)   40.00   80.00   160.00
NOTE: Not known yet what the cover art is.
1880 Farmer Plowing Field-c   30.00   60.00   120.00
1881-1883 (Scarce,7-3/4x6-1/8") 4-mast ships & lighthouse-c 30.00   60.00   120.00
1884-1889 (8x6-1/4") Horse & Rider jumping picket fence-c   20.00   40.00   80.00
1890-1897 (8-1/8x6-1/4")   20.00   40.00   80.00
1898-1899 (7-3/8x5-7/8")   20.00   40.00   80.00
1900+: see the Platinum Age Comics section (7x5-7/8")
NOTE: Barker's Almanacs were actually issued in November of the year preceding the year which appears on the almanac. For example, the 1878 dated almanac was issued November 1877. They were given away to retailers of Barker's farm animal medicinal products, to in turn be given away to customers. Each Barker's Almanac contains 10 full page cartoons. These frequently included racist stereotypes of blacks. Each cartoon contained advertisements for Barker's products. It is unknown whether the cartoons appeared only in the almanacs, or if they also ran as newspaper ads or flyers. Originally issued with a metal hook attached in the upper left hand corner, which could be used to hang the almanac.

BARKER'S "KOMIC" PICTURE SOUVENIR (P,S)
Barker, Moore & Mein Medicine Co: nd (1892-94) (color cardboard cover, B&W interior)

The Comical Adventures of Beau Ogleby
1843 © Tilt & Bogue, London

The Bottle by George Cruickshank
1871 © Geo. Gebbie, Philadelphia

Brother Jonathan
Christmas New Years 1856 © Ben H Day Sr.

(all unnumbered editions Very Rare)

nn - (1892) (1st edition, 6-7/8x10-1/2, 150 pgs) wraparound cover showing
people headed towards Chicago for the 1893 World's Fair   150.00   300.00   650.00
nn - (1893) (2nd edition, ??? pgs) same cover as 1st edition 150.00   300.00   650.00
nn - (1894) (3rd edition, 180 pgs, 6-3/4x10-3/8")   150.00   300.00   650.00
NOTE: New cover art showing crowd of people laughing with a copy of Barker's Almanac. The crowd picture is flanked on both sides by picture of a tall thin person.
nn - (1894) (4th edition, 124 pgs, 6-3/8x9-3/8") same-c as 3rd edition
                                                  150.00   300.00   650.00
NOTE: Essentially same-c as 3rd edition, except flanking picture on left edge is now gone. The 2nd through 4th editions state their printing on the first interior page, in the paragraph beneath the picture of the Barker's Building. These have been confirmed as premium comic books, predating the Buster Brown premiums. They reprint advertising cartoons from Barker's Illustrated Almanac. For the 50 page booklets by this same name, numbered as "Part's, see the PLATINUM AGE SECTION. All "Editions in Parts", without exception, were published after 1900.

BEAU OGLEBY, THE COMICAL ADVENTURES OF (E,G)
Tilt & Bogue: nd (c1843) (5-7/8x9-1/8", 72 pgs, printed one side only, green gilted hard-c, B&W)

nn - By Rodolphe Töpffer (Rare)   300.00   600.00   1500.00
nn - Hand coloured edition (Very Rare)   (no known sales)
NOTE: British Edition; no known American Edition. 2nd Töpffer comic book illustrated in English. Translated from Paris publisher Aubert's unauthorized redrawn 1839 bootleg edition of Töpffer's Histoire de Mr. Jabot. The back most interior page is an advertisement for Obadiah Oldbuck, showing its comic book cover

BEE, THE
Bee Publishing Co: May 16 1898-Aug 2 1898 (Chromolithographic Weekly)

most issues   50.00   100.00   200.00
8 June Yellow Kid Hearst cover issue   150.00   300.00   650.00

BEFORE AND AFTER. A LOCOFOCO CHRISTMAS PRESENT. (O, C)
D.C. Johnston, Boston: 1837 (4-3/4x3", 1 page, hand colored cardboard)

nn - (Very Rare) by David Claypoole Johnston (sold at auction for $400 in GD)
NOTE: Pull-tab cartoon envelope, parodying the 1836 New York City mayoral election, picturing the candidate of the Locofoco Party smiling "Before the N.York election", then, when the tab is pulled, picturing him with an angry sneer "After the N.York election".

BILLY GOAT AND OTHER COMICALITIES, THE (M)
Charles Scribner's Sons: 1898 (6-3/4x8-1/2", 116 pgs., B&W, Hardcover)

nn - By E. W. Kemble   125.00   250.00   600.00

BLACKBERRIES, THE (N.S) (see Coontown's 400)
R. H. Russell: 1897 (9"x12", 76 pgs, hard-c, every other page in color, every other page in one color sepia tone)

nn - By E. W. Kemble   162.00   325.00   1300.00
NOTE: Tastefully done comics about Black Americana during the USA's Jim Crow days.

BOOK OF BUBBLES, YE (S)
Endicott & Co., New York: March 1864 (6-1/4 x 9-7/8",160 pgs, guilt-illus. hard-c, B&W

nn - By unknown   40.00   80.00   160.00
NOTE: Subtitle: A contribution to the New York Fair in aid of the Sanitary Commission; 68 single-sided pages of B&W cartoons, each with an accompanying limerick. A few are sequential.

BOOK OF DRAWINGS BY FRED RICHARDSON (N,S)
Lakeside Press, Chicago: 1899 (13-5/8x10-1/2", 116 pgs, B&W, hard-c)

nn - (Scarce)   80.00   160.00   320.00
NOTE: Reprinted from the Chicago Daily News. Mostly single panel. Includes one Yellow Kid parody, some Spanish-American War cartoons.

BOTTLE, THE (E,O) (see also THE DRUNKARD'S CHILDREN, and TEA GARDEN TO TEA POT, and TEMPERANCE TALES; OR, SIX NIGHTS WITH THE WASHINGTONIANS)
D. Bogue, London, with others in later editions: nd (1846) (16-1/2x11-1/2", 16 pgs, printed one side only, paper cover)

D. Bogue, London (nd; 1846): first edition:
nn - Black & white (Scarce)   200.00   400.00   900.00
nn - Hand colored (Rare)   (no known sales)
D. Bogue, London, and Wiley and Putnam, New York (nd; 1847) : second edition, misspells American publisher "Putnam" as "Putman":
nn - Black & white (Scarce)   150.00   300.00   600.00
nn - Hand colored (Rare)   (no known sales)
D. Bogue, London, and Wiley and Putnam, New York (nd; 1847) : third edition has "Putnam" spelled correctly.
nn - Black & white (Scarce)   150.00   300.00   600.00
nn - Hand colored (Rare)   (no known sales)
D. Bogue, London, Wiley and Putnam, New York, and J. Sands, Sydney, New South Wales: (nd; 1847) : fourth edition with no misspellings
nn - Black & white (Scarce)   150.00   300.00   600.00
nn - Hand colored (Rare)   (no known sales)
NOTE: By George Cruikshank. Temperance/anti-alcohol story. All editions are in precisely identical format. The only difference is to be found on the cover, where it lists who published it. Cover is text only - no cover art.

BOTTLE, THE HISTORY OF THE
J.C. Becket, 22 Great St James St, Montreal, Canada: 1851 (9-1/8x6", B&W)

nn - From Engravings by Cruikshank   150.00   300.00   650.00
NOTE: As published in The Canada Temperance Advocate.

BOTTLE, THE (E)
W. Tweedie, London: nd (1862) (11-1/2x17-1/3", 16 pgs, printed one side only, paper cover)

nn - Black & white; By George Cruikshank (Scarce) 100.00   200.00   400.00
nn - Hand colored (Scarce)   (no known sales)

BOTTLE, THE (E)
Geo. Gebbie, Philadelphia: nd (c.1871) (11-3/8x17-1/8", 42 pgs, tinted interior, hard-c)

nn - By George Cruikshank   100.00   200.00   400.00
NOTE: New cover art (cover not by Cruikshank).

BOTTLE, THE (E)
National Temperance, London: nd (1881) (11-1/2x16-1/2", 16 pgs, printed one side only, paper-c, color)

nn - By George Cruikshank   100.00   200.00   400.00
NOTE: See Platinum Age section for 1900s printings.

BROAD GRINS OF THE LAUGHING PHILOSOPHER
Dick & Fitzgerald,NY: 1870s

nn - (4) panel sequential strip   25.00   50.00   150.00

BROTHER JONATHAN
Wilson & Co/Benj H Day, 48 Beekman, NYC: 1839-??? (

July 4 1846 - ads for Obadiah & Butterfly   50.00   100.00   200.00
July 4 1856 catalog list - front cover comic strip 100.00   200.00   400.00
Xmas/New Years 1856   75.00   150.00   300.00
average large size issues   25.00   50.00   100.00
NOTE: has full page advert for Ferdinand Flipper comic book116
Various: nd (c1890's) (3-7/8x4-1/8", 16 pgs, B&W, paper-c)
nn - By A.B. Frost Creme Oatmeal Toilet Soap   25.00   50.00   150.00
nn - By A.B. Frost Thompson & Taylor Spice Co, Chicago 25.00   50.00   150.00
NOTE: Reprints the popular strip story by Frost, with the art modified to place a sign for Creme Oatmeal Soap within each panel. The back cover advertises the specific merchant who gave this booklet away - multiple variations exist.

BULL CALF AND OTHER TALES, THE (M)
Charles Scribner's Sons: 1892 (120 pgs., 6-3/4x8-7/8", B&W, illus. hard cover)

nn - By Arthur Burdett Frost   50.00   150.00   500.00
NOTE: Blue, grey, tan hard covers known to exist.

BULL CALF, THE STORY OF THE MAN OF HUMANITY AND THE (P,M)
C.H. Fargo & Co.: 1890 (5-1/4x6-1/4", 24 pgs, B&W, color paper-c)

nn - By A.B. Frost   42.50   85.00   185.00
NOTE: Fargo shoe company giveaway; pages alternate between shoe advertisements and the strip story.

BUSHEL OF MERRY THOUGHTS, A (see Mischief Book, The) (E)
Sampson Low Son & Marsten: 1868 (68 pgs, handcolored hardcover, B&W)

nn - (6-1/4 x 9-7/8", 138 pgs) red binding, publisher's name on title page only
                                                   200.00   400.00   800.00
nn - (6-1/2 x 10", 134 pgs) green binding, publisher's name on cover & title page
                                                   200.00   400.00   800.00
NOTE: Cover plus story title pages designed by Leighton Brothers, based on Busch art. Translated by Harry Rogers (who is credited instead of Busch). This is a British publication, notable as the earliest known English language anthology collection of Wilhelm Busch comic strips. Page 13 of second story missing from all editions (panel dropped). Unknown which of the two editions was published first. A modern reprint, by Dover in 1971.

BUTTON BURSTER, THE (M) (says on cover "ten cents hard cash")
M.J. Ivers & Co., 86 Nassau St., New York: 1873 (11x8-1/8", soft paper, B&W)

By various cartoonists (Very Rare)   125.00   250.00   500.00
NOTE: Reprints from various 1873 issues of Wild Oats; has (5) different sequential comic strips: (3) by Livingston Hopkins, (1) by Thomas Worth, other one creator presently unknown; Bellew, Sr. single panel cartoons.

BUZZ A BUZZ OR THE BEES (E)
Griffith & Farran, London: September 1872 (8-1/2x5-1/2", 168 pgs, printed one side only, orange, black & white hardcover, B&W interior)

nn - By Wilhelm Busch (Scarce)   112.00   225.00   450.00
NOTE: Reprint published by Phillipson & Golder, Chester; text written by English to accompany Busch art.

BUZZ A BUZZ OR THE BEES (E)
Henry Holt & Company, New York: 1873 (9x6", 96 pgs, gilted hardcover, hand colored)

nn - By Wilhelm Busch (Scarce)   100.00   200.00   450.00
NOTE: Completely different translation than the Griffith & Farran version. Also, contains 28 additional illustrations by Park Benjamin. The lower page count is because the Henry Holt version prints on both sides of each page, and the Griffith & Farran edition is printed one side only.

CALENDAR FOR THE MONTH; YE PICTORIAL LYSTE OF YE MATTERS OF INTEREST FOR SUMMER READING (P,M)
S.E. Bridgman & Company, Northampton, Mass: nd (c. late 1880's-1890's) (5-5/8x7-1/4", 64 pgs, paper-c, B&W)

nn - (Very Rare) T.S. Sullivant-c/a   100.00   200.00   400.00
NOTE: Book seller's catalog, with every other page reprinting cartoons and strips (from Life??). Art by: Chips Bellew, Gibson, Howarth, Kemble, Sullivant, Townsend, Woolf.

CARICATURE AND OTHER COMIC ART
Harper & Brothers, NY: 1877 (9-5/16x7-1/8", 360 pgs, B&W, green hard-c)

nn - By James Parton (over 200 illustrations)   50.00   110.00   200.00
NOTE: This is the earliest known serious history of comics & related genre from around the world produced by

The Carpet Bag #14
1851 © Snow & Wilder

Keppler Cover to Centennial Fun
July 1876 © Frank Leslie

Comic Monthly v2 #7
Sept. 1860 © J.C. Haney, NY

	FR1.0	GD2.0	FN6.0		FR1.0	GD2.0	FN6.0

an American. Parton was a cousin of Thomas Nast's wife Sarah. A large portion of this book was first serialized in **Harper's Monthly** in 1875.

CARICATURE HISTORY OF CANADIAN POLITICS (M,S)
Grip, Toronto: 1886; 1886 (12-3/4x10-3/8", 440 pgs, hard-c, B&W)

nn (Vol. 1) - (blue gilted-c) cartoon-r from 1849-1878   67.50   125.00à   250.00
NOTE: The pages of Volume 1 are heavily interlaced with advertising sheets for Toronto businesses (these are not part of the page count), including a smaller sized 96-pg machinery catalog, all bound into the volume.

Vol. 2 - (brown gilted-c) cartoon-r from 1879-1884   67.50   125.00   250.00
NOTE: Chronologically organized reprinting of single panel Canadian political cartoons, taken from a variety of Canadian publications. Each right-hand page is a full page cartoon, while each left-hand page is text describing the political situation which was being satirized.

CARPET BAG, THE
Snow & Wilder, later Wilder & Pickard, Boston: March 21 1851-March 26 1853

Each average issue   25.00   50.00   100.00
Samuel "Mark Twain" Clemmons issues (first app in print)   500.00   1000.00   2000.00
NOTE: Many issues contain cartoons by DC Johnston, Frank Bellew, others; literature includes Artemus Ward's Miss Partington who had a mischievous little Katzenjammer Kids-like brat. Carpet Bag was not considered derogatory pre-Civil War.

CARROT-POMADE (O,G)
James G. Gregory, Publisher, New York: 1864 (9x6-7/8", 36 pgs, B&W)

nn - By Augustus Hoppin   70.00   140.00   280.00
NOTE: The story of a quack remedy for baldness, sequentially told in the format parodying ABC primers. Has protective tissue pages (not part of page count).

CARTOONS BY HOMER C. DAVENPORT (M,N,S)
De Witt Publishing House: 1898 (16-1/8x12", 102 pgs, hard-c, B&W)

nn   70.00   140.00   280.00
NOTE: Reprinted from Harper's Weekly and the New York Journal. Includes cartoons about the Spanish-American War. Title page reads "Davenport's Cartoons".

CARTOONS BY WILL E. CHAPIN (P,N,S)
The Times-Mirror Printing and Binding House, Los Angeles: 1899 (15-1/4x12", 98 pgs, hard-c, B&W)

nn   75.00   150.00   300.00
NOTE: Premium item for subscribing to the Los-Angeles Times-Mirror newspaper, from which these cartoons were reprinted. Includes cartoons about the Spanish-American War.

CARTOONS OF OUR WAR WITH SPAIN (N,S)
Frederick A. Stokes Company: 1898 (11-1/2x10", 72 pgs, hardcover, B&W)

nn - By Charles Nelan (r-New York Herald)   40.00   100.00   200.00
nn - 2nd printing noted on copy right page   30.00   60.00   120.00

CARTOONS OF THE WAR OF 1898 (E,M,N,S)
Belford, Middlebrook & Co., Chicago: 1898 (7x10-3/8",190 pgs, B&W, hard-c)

nn   50.00   100.00   200.00
NOTE: Reprints single panel editorial cartoons on the Spanish-American War, from American, Spanish, Latino, and European newspapers and magazines, at rate of 2 to 6 cartoons per page. Art by Bart, Berryman, Bowman, Bradley, Chapin, Gillam, Nelan, Tenniel, others.

CENTENNIAL FUN (O,S) (Rare)
Frank Leslie, Philadelphia: (July) 1876 (25¢, 11x8", 32 pgs, paper cover, B&W)

nn - By Joseph Keppler-c/a;Thomas Worth-a   50.00   100.00   200.00
NOTE: Issued for the 1876 Centennial Exposition in Philadelphia. Exists with both black & white, and orange, black & white covers. One copy of the latter had an embossed newsstand label from Partland, Maine, implying that the orange cover version, at least, was distributed and sold outside of Philadelphia.

CHAMPAIGNE
Frank Leslie: June-Dec 1871

1-7   150.00   225.00   350.00

CHIC
Chic Publishing Co: 1880-81 (Chromolithographic Weekly)

1-38 Livingston Hopkins, Charles Kendrick, CW Weldon   50.00   100.00   200.00

CHILDREN'S CHRISTMAS BOOK, THE
The New York Sunday World: 1897 (10-1/4x8-3/4", 16 pgs, full color)

Dec 12, 1897 - By George Luks, G.H. Grant, Will Crawford, others) (Rare)
   50.00   100.00   280.00

CHIP'S DOGS (M)
R.H. Russell and Son Publishers: 1895 hardcover, B&W

nn - By Frank P. W. "Chip" Bellew   25.00   50.00   100.00
Early printing 80 pgs, 8-7/8x11-7/8"; dark green border of hardcover surrounds all four sides of pasted on cover image; pages arranged in error -- see NOTE below. (more scarce)
nn - By Frank P. W. "Chip" Bellew   12.50   25.00   50.00
Later printing 72 pgs, 8-7/8x11-3/4";green border only on the binding side (one side) of the cover image.
NOTE: Both are strip reprints from LIFE . The difference in page count is due to more blank pages in the first printing -- all printings have the same comics contents, but with the pages in the first printing arranged differently. This is noticeable particularly in the 2-page strip "Getting a Pointer", which appears on the 2nd & 3rd to last pages of the later printings, but in the early printing the first half of this strip is near the middle of the book, while the last half appears on the 2nd to last story page.

CHIP'S OLD WOOD CUTS (M,S)
R.H. Russell & Son: 1895 (8-7/8x11-3/4", 72 pgs, hardcover, B&W)

nn - By Frank P. W. ("Chip") Bellew   25.00   50.00   100.00
nn - 1897 reprint   15.00   30.00   60.00

CHIP'S UN-NATURAL HISTORY (O,S)
Frederick A. Stokes & Brother: 1888 (7x5-1/4", 64 pgs, hardcover, B&W)

nn - By Frank P. W. ("Chip") Bellew   12.50   25.00   50.00
NOTE: Title page lists publisher as "Successors to White, Stokes & Allen."

CLOWN, OR THE BANQUET OF WIT, THE (E,M,O)
Fisher & Brother, Philadelphia, Baltimore, New York, Boston: nd (c.1851) (7-3/8x4-1/2", 88 pgs, paper cover, B&W)

nn - (Very Rare; 3 known copies)   300.00   600.00   1200.00
NOTE: Earliest known multi-artist anthology of sequential comics; contains multiple sequential comics, plus numerous single panel cartoons. A mixture of reprinted and original material, involving both European and American artists. "Jones, Smith, and Robinson Goes to a Ball" by Richard Doyle (1st app. of Doyle's "Foreign Tour" in America, reprinted from PUNCH, August 24, 1850); "Moses Keyser The Bowery Bully's Trip to the Californian Gold Mines", by John H. Manning; "The Adventures of Mr. Gulp" (by the Read brothers?); more comics by artists unknown; cartoons by George Cruikshank, Grandville, Elton.

COLD CUTS AND PICKLED EELS' FEET; DONE BROWN BY JOHN BROWN
P.J. Cozans, New York: nd (c1855-60) (B&W)

nn (Very Rare)   100.00   200.00   300.00
NOTE: Mostly a children's book. But, pages 87 to 110, and 111 to 122, contain narrative sequential stories.

COLLEGE SCENES (O,G)
N. Hayward, Boston: 1850 (5x6-3/4", 72 pgs, printed one side only, B&W lithography)

nn - (Rare) by Nathan Hayward   200.00   400.00   600.00
NOTE: This is the 2nd such production for an American University; the first issued at Yale circa 1845, decent funny art of story about life of a Harvard student from his entrance thru graduation entirely in caricature. Has art on back cover as well.

COLLEGE CUTS Chosen From The Columbia Spectator 1880-81-82 (S)
White & Stokes, NY: 1882 (8x9-5/8", 92 pgs, B&W)

By F. Benedict Herzog, H. McVickar, W. Bard McVickar, others 20.00   40.00   80.00
nn - 2nd edition reprint (1888) (8-1/4x10-3/8)   10.00   20.00   40.00

COMICAL COONS (M)
R.H. Russell: 1898 (8-7/8 x 11-7/8", 68 pgs, hardcover, B&W)

nn - By E. W. Kemble   250.00   500.00   1000.00
NOTE: Black Americana collection of 2-panel stories.

COMIC ALMANAC, THE
John Berger. Baltimore: 1854-? (7-1/2x6-1/4, 36 pgs, B&W)

nn -   60.00   120.00   240.00

COMIC ANNUAL, AMERICAN (O,I)
Richardson, Lord, & Holbrook, Boston: 1831 (6-7/8x4-3/8", 268 pgs, B&W, hard-c)

nn - (Scarce)   150.00   300.00   600.00
NOTE: Mostly text; front & back cover illustrations, 13 full page, and scattered smaller illustrations by David Claypoole Johnston; edited by Henry J. Finn.

COMIC HISTORY OF THE UNITED STATES, (I)
Carleton & Co., NY: 1876 (6-7/8x5-1/8", 336 pgs, hardcover, B&W)

nn - By Livingston Hopkins.   12.50   25.00   50.00
2nd printing: Cassell, Petter, Galpin & Co.: 1880 (6-7/8x5-1/8", 336 pgs, hardcover, B&W)
nn - By Livingston Hopkins.   12.50   25.00   50.00
NOTE: Text with many B&W illustrations; some are multi-panel comics. Not to beconfused with Bill Nye's Comic History Of The U.S. which contains Frederick Opper illustrations.

COMIC MONTHLY, THE
J.C. Haney, N.Y.: March 1859-1880 (16 x 11-1/2", 30 pgs average, B&W)

	FR1.0	GD2.0	FN6.0
Certain average issues with sequential comics	50.00	100.00	200.00
11 (Jan 1860) Bellew-c	25.00	50.00	100.00
v2#2 (Apr 1860) Bellew-c	25.00	50.00	100.00
v2#3 (May 1860) Bellew-c	25.00	50.00	100.00
v2#4 (June 1860) Comic Strip Cover	50.00	100.00	200.00
v2#5 (July 1860) Bellew-c; (12) panel Explaining American Politics To An Intelligent Foreigner; (10) panel The Art of Stump Speaking; (15) panel Mr. Dibbs Goes to Pike's Peak and Comes Back Again	100.00	200.00	400.00
v2#7 (Sept 1860) Comic Strip Cover; (24) panel double page spread The Prince of Wales In America	50.00	100.00	200.00
v2#8 (18) panel The Three Young Friends Sillouette Strip	25.00	50.00	100.00
v2#9 (Nov 1860) (9) panel sequential	25.00	50.00	100.00
v2#10 11 not indexed	25.00	50.00	100.00
v2#12 (Jan 1861) (12) panel double page spread	25.00	50.00	100.00

COMIC TOKEN FOR 1836, A COMPANION TO THE COMIC ALMANAC, THE
Charles Ellms, Boston: 1836 (8x5', 48 pgs, B&W)

nn -   50.00   100.00   200.00

COMIC WEEKLY, THE
???, NYC: 1881-???

issues with comic strips (Chips, etc)   60.00   125.00   250.00

COMIC WORLD
???: 1876-1879 (Quarto Monthly)

issues with comic strips   37.50   75.00   150.00

COMICS FROM SCRIBNER'S MAGAZINE (M)
Scribner's: nd (1891) (10 cents, 9-1/2x6-5/8", 24 pgs, paper cover, side stapled, B&W)

The Comus Offering
1830-31 © B. Franklin Edmands

The Daily Graphic #158 Frank Bellew-c
Sept 4, 1873 © The Graphic Company, NY

Elton's Californian Comic All-My-Nack #17
1850 © Elton's, NY

	FR1.0	GD2.0	FN6.0

nn - (Rare) F.M.Howarth C&A — 100.00 / 200.00 / 400.00
NOTE: Advertised in SCRIBNER'S MAGAZINE in the June 1891 issue, page 793, as available by mail order for 10 cents. Collects together comics material which ran in the back pages of Scribner's Magazine. Art by Attwood, "Chip" Bellew, Dées, Frost, Gibson, Zim.

COMUS OFFERING CONTAINING HUMOROUS SCRAPS OF DIVERTING COMICALITIES, THE (O, S)
B. Franklin Edmands, 25 Court St, Boston: c1830-31 (8-7/8x10-3/4", 16 pgs, thin brown paper-c, blank on backs,

nn - (William F Straton, Engraver, 15 Water St, Boston) (no known sales)
NOTE: All hand-colored single panel cartoons format definitely inspired by D.C. Johnston's Scraps with every panel character using well-defined word balloons. Might become a seminal step in the evolution of the American comic book. More research is needed.

CONTRASTS AND CONCEITS FOR CONTEMPLATION BY LUKE LIMNER (O)
Ackerman & Co, 96 Strand, London: c1848 (9-3/4x6-1/4, 48 pgs, B&W)
nn - By John Leighton — 50.00 / 100.00 / 200.00

COONTOWN'S 400 (M) (see Blackberries) (M)
The Life (Magazine) Co.: 1899 (10-15/16x8-7/8, 68 pgs, cloth light-brown hard-c, B&W
nn - By E.W. Kemble (scarce) — 250.00 / 500.00 / 1500.00
NOTE: Tastefully drawn depictions of Black Americana over one hundred years ago during Jim Crow times.

CROSSING THE ATLANTIC (O,G)
James R. Osgood & Co., Boston: 1872 (10-7/8x16", 68 pgs, hardcover, B&W);
Houghton, Osgood & Co., Boston: 1880
1st printing - by Augustus Hoppin — 50.00 / 100.00 / 200.00
2nd printing (1880; 66 pgs; 8-1/8x11-1/8") — 32.50 / 65.00 / 150.00

C.R. PITT'S COMIC ALMANAC
C.R. Pitt: 1880 (7-1/2x4-5/8", 28 pgs)
nn - contains (8) panel sequential — 50.00 / 100.00 / 200.00

CRUIKSHANK'S OMNIBUS: A VEHICLE FOR FUN AND FROLIC (E,S)
E. Ferrett & Co., Philadelphia: 1845 (25 cents, 7-1/2" x 4-5/8", 96 pgs, B&W, paper-c)
nn - By George Cruikshank c/a (Very Rare) — 75.00 / 150.00 / 300.00
NOTE: Mostly prose, with 10 plates of cartoons printed on one-side (about half the plates with multiple cartoons), plus illustrated cover, all by George Cruikshank. First (perhaps only) American printing of Cruikshank's Omnibus, which was published first in Britain. It is only a partial reprinting.

CYCLISTS' DICTIONARY (S)
Morgan & Wright, Chicago: 1894 (5 x3-3/4, 80 pgs, soft-c, B&W
nn - By Unknown — 37.50 / 75.00 / 150.00

THE DAILY GRAPHIC
The Graphic Company, 39 Park Place, NY: 1873-Sept 23, 1889 (14x20-1/2, 8 pgs, B&W)
Average issues with comic strips — 7.50 / 15.00 / 30.00
Average issues without comic strips — 5.00 / 10.00 / 20.00
NOTE:

DAVY CROCKETT'S COMIC ALMANACK
???, Nashville, TN, then elsewhere: 1835-end (32 pages plus wraps)
1 — 500.00 / 1000.00 / 2000.00
2-13 15 end — 250.00 / 500.00 / 1000.00
14 contains (17) panel Crocket comic strip bio 1848 — 500.00 / 1000.00 / 2000.00

DAY'S DOINGS (was The Last Sensation) (Becomes New York Illustrated Times)
James Watts, NYC: 1-6 1868-early 1876 (11x16, 16 pgs, B&W)
average issue with comic strips — 10.00 / 15.00 / 25.00
Paul Pry & Alley Sloper character issues — 25.00 / 50.00 / 100.00
Aug 19 1871 - First Alley Sloper in America?? — 50.00 / 100.00 / 200.00
NOTE: James Watts was a shadow company for Frank Leslie; outright sold to Frank Leslie in 1873. There are a lot of issues with comic strips from 1868 up.

DAY'S SPORT - OR, HUNTING ADVENTURES OF S. WINKS WATTLES, A SHOPKEEPER, THOMAS TITT, A "LEGAL GENT," AND MAJOR NICHOLAS NOGGIN, A JOLLY GOOD FELLOW GENERALLY, A (O)
Brother Jonathan, NY: c1850s (5-7/8x8-1/4, 44 pgs)
nn - By Henry L. Stephens, Philadelphia (Very Rare) (no known sales)

DEVIL'S COMICAL OLDMANICK WITH COMIC ENGRAVINGS OF THE PRINCIPAL EVENTS OF TEXAS, THE
Turner & Fisher, NY & Philadelphia: 1837 (7-7/8x5", 24 pgs)
nn - many single panel cartoons — 100.00 / 200.00 / 400.00

DIE VEHME, ILLUSTRIRTES WOCHENBLATT FUR SCHERZ UND ERNEST (M,O)
Heinrich Binder, St. Louis: No.1 Aug 28, 1869 - No.?? Aug 20, 1870 (10 cents, 8 pgs, B&W, paper-c) (see also PUCK)
1-?? (Very Rare) by Joseph Keppler — 100.00 / 200.00 / 400.00
NOTE: Joseph Keppler's first attempt at a weekly American humor periodical. Entirely in German. The title translates into: "The Star Chamber: An Illustrated Weekly Paper in Fun and Ernest".

DOMESTIC MANNERS OF THE AMERICANS
The Imprint Society, Barre, Mass: 1969 (9-3/4 x 7-1/4", 390 pgs, hard-c in slipcase, B&W)
nn - — – / – / –
NOTE: Reprints the 1832 edition of this book by Mrs.Trollope with an added insert. The 28-page insert is what is of primary interest to us -- it reproduces SCRAPS No. 4 (1833) by D.C. Johnston.

DRUNKARD'S CHILDREN, THE (see also THE BOTTLE) (E,O)
David Bogue, London; John Wiley and G.P. Putnam, New York; J. Sands, Sydney, New South Wales: July 1, 1848 (16x11", 16 pgs, printed on one side only, paper-c)
nn - Black & white edition (Scarce) — 300.00 / 600.00 / 950.00
nn - Hand colored edition (Rare) (no known sales)
NOTE: Sequel story to THE BOTTLE, by George Cruikshank. Temperance/anti-alcohol story. British-American-Australian co-publication. Cover is text only - no cover art.

DRUNKARD'S PROGRESS, OR THE DIRECT ROAD TO POVERTY, WRETCHEDNESS & RUIN, THE
J. W. Barber, New Haven, Conn.: Sept 1826 (single sheet)
nn - By John Warner Barber (Very Rare) (no known sales)
NOTE: Broadside designed and printed by barber contains four large wood engravings showing "The Morning Dram" which is "The Beginning of Sorrow"; "The Grog Shop" with its "Bad Company"; "The Confirmed Drunkard" in a state of "Beastly Intoxication"; and the "Concluding Scene" with the family being drive off to the alms house. It is an interesting set of cuts, faintly reminiscent of Hogarth. Many modern reprints exist.

DUEL FOR LOVE, A (O,P)
E.C. DeWitt & Co., Chicago: nd (c1880's) (3-3/8" x 2-5/8", 12 pgs, B&W, paper-c)
nn - Art by F.M. Howarth (Rare) — 25.00 / 50.00 / 100.00
NOTE: Advertising giveaway for DeWitt's Little Early Risers, featuring an 8-panel strip story, spread out 1 panel per page.

DURHAM WHIFFS (O, P)
Blackwells Durham Tobacco Co: Jan 8 1878 (9x6.5", 8 pgs, color-c, B&W)
v1 #1 w/Trade Card Insert — 37.50 / 75.00 / 150.00

DYNALENE LAFLETS (P)
The Dynalene Company: nd (3 x 3-1/2", 16 pgs, B&W, paper cover)
nn - Dynalene Dyes promo (9) panel comic strip — 25.00 / 50.00 / 75.00

ELEPHANT, THE
William H Graham, Tribune Building, NYC: Jan 22 1848-Feb 19 1848 (11x8.5", B&W)
1-5 Rare - single panel cartoons — 150.00 / 300.00 / 600.00

ELTON'S COMIC ALL-MY-NACK (E,O,S)
Elton, Publisher, 18 Division & 98 Nassau St, NY: 1833-1852 (7-1/2x4-1/2", 36pgs, B&W
1-5 99% single panel cartoons — 60.00 / 120.00 / 240.00
6 (1839) — 60.00 / 120.00 / 240.00
NOTE: Two different covers & different interiors exist for this title and number
7-15 - 99% single panel cartoons — 60.00 / 120.00 / 240.00
16 - contains 6 panel "A Tales of A Tayl-or" 1848-49 — 200.00 / 400.00 / 600.00
17 - contains "Moses Keyser, The Bowery Bully's Trip to the California Gold Mines" 1850
By John H. Manning, early comics creator, told in 15 panels 200.00 / 400.00 / 600.00
18-19 presently unknown contents — 60.00 / 120.00 / 240.00
NOTE: Contains both original American, and pirated European, cartoons. All single panel material, except where noted. Almanacs are published near the end of the year prior to that for which they are printed -- like calendars today. Thus, the 1833 No. 1 issue was really published in the last months of 1832. #17 has Elton's Californian Comic-All-My-Nack on the cover.

ELTON'S COMIC ALMANAC (Publisher change)
GW Cottrell & Co, Publishers & C Cornhill, Boston, Mass: 1853 (7-7/8x4-5/8,36pgs,B&W
19
20 - (2) sequential comic strips (9) panel "Jones, Smith and Robinson Goes To A Ball; (21) panel "The Adventures of Mr. Gulp" — 200.00 / 400.00 / 600.00
NOTE: Both strips appear in The Clown, Or The Banquet of Wit

ELTON'S FUNNY ALMANACK (title change to Almanac)
Elton Publisher and Engraver, New York: 1846 (8x6-1/2", 36 pgs)
1 1846 — 50.00 / 100.00 / 200.00

ELTON'S FUNNY ALMANAC (#1 titled Almanack)
Elton & Co, New York: 1847-1853 (8x6-1/4, 36 pgs, B&W)
2 (1847) #3 (1848) — 50.00 / 100.00 / 200.00
nn 1853 (8-1/8x4-7/8"; (5) panel comic strip "The Adventures of Mr. Goliah Starvemouse"

ELTON'S RIPSNORTER COMIC ALMANAC
Elton, 90 Nassau St, NY: 1850 (8x5, 24 pgs, B&W, paper-c)

ENGLISH SOCIETY (S)
Harper & Brothers, Publishers, New York: 1897 (9-5/8x12-1/4", 206 pgs, B&W)
nn - by George Du Maurier — 25.00 / 50.00 / 75.00

ENGLISH SOCIETY AT HOME (S)
James R. Osgood and Company: 1881 (10-7/8x8-5/8, 182 pgss, protective sheets on some pages - not included in pages count, hard-c, B&W — 25.00 / 50.00 / 75.00
nn - by George Du Maurier

ENTER: THE COMICS (E,G)
University of Nebraska Press: 1965 (6-7/8x9-1/4", 120 pgs, hard-c)
nn - By Ellen Weisse — 25.00 / 50.00 / 100.00
NOTE: Contains overview of Töpffer's life and career plus only published English translation of Töpffer's Monsieur Crepin (1837); appears to have been re-drawn by Weisse in the days before xerox machines.

ESQUIRE BROWN AND HIS MULE, STORY OF
A.C. Meyer, Baltimore, Maryland: 1880s (5x3/7/8", 28 pgs, B&W)

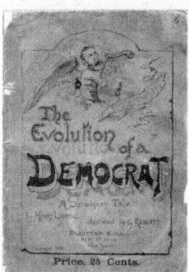

The Evolution Of A Democrat
1888 © Paquet & Co, NY

Frank Leslie's Boys & Girls Sample Comic Strip Page
1870s © Frank Leslie

Frank Leslie's Budget of Fun #79
Oct 1864 © Frank Leslie, NY

	FR1.0	GD2.0	FN6.0

Booklet (9 panel story plus cough remedies catalog) 25.00 50.00 100.00
Fold-Out of Booklet (9 panel version) 25.00 50.00 100.00

"EVENTS OF THE WEEK" REPRINTED FROM THE CHICAGO TRIBUNE
Henry O. Shepard Co, Chicago: 1894 (5-3/8x15-7/8", 110 pg, B&W, hard-c)

First Series, Second Series - By HR Heaton 37.50 75.00 150.00

EVERYBODY'S COMICK ALMANACK
Turner & Fisher, NY & Philadelphia: 1837 (7-7/8x5", 36 pgs, B&W)

nn 50.00 100.00 200.00

EVOLUTION OF A DEMOCRAT - A DARWINIAN TALE, THE (O,G)
Paquet & Co., New York: 1888 (25 cents, 7-7/8x5-1/2", 100 pgs, printed one side only, orange paper cover, B&W) (Very Rare)

nn - Written by Henry Liddell, art by G. Roberty 50.00 100.00 200.00
NOTE: Political parody about the rise of an Irishman through Tammany Hall. Grover Cleveland appears as linked with Tammany. Ireland becomes the next state in the USA.

FABLES FOR THE TIMES (S, I)
R.H. Russell & Son, New York: 1896 (9-1/8x12-1/8", 52 pgs, yellow hard-c)

nn - By H.W. Phillips and T.S. Sullivant 25.00 50.00 100.00

FERDINAND FLIPPER, ESQ., THE FORTUNES OF (O,G)
Brother Jonathan, Publisher, NY: nd (1851) (5-3/4 x 9-3/8", 84 pgs, B&W, printed both sides)

nn - By Various (Very Rare) 375.00 750.00 1500.00
NOTE: Extended title: "...Commencing With A Period of Four Months And Anterior To His Birth Going Thru The Various Stages of His Infancy, Childhood, Verdant Years, Manhood, Middle Life, and Green and Ripe Old Age, And Ending A Short Time Subsequent to His Sudden Decease With His Final Exit, Funeral And Burial." Extremely unique comic book, put together by gathering 145 independent single illustrations and cartoons, by various artists, and stringing them together into a sequential story. The majority of panels are by Grandville. Also included are at least 19 signed Charles Martin, reprinted from 1847 issues of Yankee Doodle, 5 panels from D.C. Johnston, plus other panels by F.O.C. Darley, T.H. Matheson, and others. The story also contains several panels of Gold Rush content . Printed by E.A. Alverds. The 1851 date is derived from an advertisement found in the Oct-Dec 1851 issue of the Brother Jonathan newspaper. It ispossible, however, that it actually came out even earlier.

FERDINAND FLIPPER, ESQ., THE FORTUNES OF (G)
Dick & Fitzgerald, New York: nd (1870's to 1888) (30 Cents, 84 pgs, B&W, paper cover)

nn - (Very Rare reprint - several editions possible) 150.00 300.00 500.00

FINN'S COMIC ALMANAC
Marsh, Capen, & Lyon; Boston: 1835-??? (4.5x7.5, 36 pgs, B&W)

nn 60.00 120.00 240.00

FINN'S COMIC SKETCHBOOK (S)
Peabody & Co., NY: 1831 (10-1/2x16", 12 pgs, B&W)

nn - By Henry J. Finn (Very Rare) (no known sales)
NOTE: Designs on copper plates; etched by J. Harris, NY; should have tissue paper in front of each plate.

50 GREAT CARTOONS (M,P,S)
Ram's Horn Press: 1899 (14x10-3/4, 112 pgs, hard-c)

nn - By Frank Beard 30.00 60.00 120.00
NOTE: Premium in return for a subscription to The Ram's Horn magazine.

FISHER'S COMIC ALMANAC
Ames Fisher and Brother, No 12 North Sixth St, Philadelphia , Charles Small in NYC, Also in Boston: 1841-1868 (4-1/2 x 7-1/4, 36 pgs, B&W)

1-7 (1841-1847) 60.00 120.00 240.00
12 reprints mermaid-c with word balloon (1868) 60.00 120.00 240.00

F*** A*** K*****, OUTLINES ILLUSTRATIVE OF THE JOURNAL OF** (O,S)
D.C. Johnston, Boston: 1835 (9-5/16 x 6", 12 pgs, printed one side only, blue paper cover, B&W interior) (also see SCRAPS)

nn - by David Claypoole Johnston (Scarce) 300.00 500.00 800.00
NOTE: This is a series of 8 plates lampooning passages from the Journal of Fanny (Frances) A. Kemble, a British woman who wrote a highly negative book about American Culture after returning from the U.S. Though remembered now for her campaign against slavery, she was prejudiced against most everything American culture, thus inspiring Johnston's satire. Contains 4 protective sheets (not part of page count.)

FLYING DUTCHMAN; OR, THE WRATH OF HERR VONSTOPPELNOZE, THE (E)
Carleton Publishing, New York: 1862 (7-5/8x5-1/4", 84 pgs, printed on one side only, gilted hardcover, B&W)

nn - By Wilhelm Busch (Scarce) 35.00 70.00 160.00
nn - 1975 Scarce 100 copy-r 74 pgs Visual Studies Workshop 5.00 10.00 20.00
NOTE: This is the earliest known English language book publication of a Wilhelm Busch work. The story is plagiarized by American poet John G. Saxe, who is credited with the text, while the uncredited Busch cartoons are described merely as accompanying illustrations.

FLYING LEAVES (E)
E.R. Herrick & Company, New York: nd (c1889/1890's) (8-1/4" x 11-1/2", 76 pgs, B&W interior, orange, b&w hard-c)

nn- (Scarce) 85.00 175.00 260.00
NOTE: Reprints strips and single panel cartoons from 1888 Fliegende Blatter issues, translated into English. Various artists, including Bechstein, Adolf Hengeler, Lothar Meggendorfer, Emil Reinicke.

FOOLS PARADISE WITH THE MANY ADVENTURES THERE AS SEEN IN THE STRANGE SURPRISING PEEP SHOW OF PROFESSOR WOLLEY COBBLE, THE (E)
(see also THE COMICAL PEEP SHOW)
John Camden Hotten, London: Nov 1871 (1 crown, 9-7/8x7-3/8", 172 pgs, printed one

	FR1.0	GD2.0	FN6.0

side only, gilted green hardcover, hand colored interior)

nn - By Wilhelm Busch (Rare) 400.00 800.00 1750.00
NOTE: Title on cover is: WALK IN! WALK IN!! JUST ABOUT TO BEGIN!!! the FOOLS PARADISE; below the above title page. Anthology of Wilhelm Busch comics, translated into English.

FOOLS PARADISE WITH THE MANY WONDERFUL SIGHTS AS SEEN IN THE STRANGE SURPRISING PEEP SHOW OF PROFESSOR WOLLEY COBBLE, FURTHER ADVENTURES IN (E)
Chatto & Windus, London: 1873 (10x7-3/8", 128 pgs, printed one side only, brown hardcover, hand colored interior)

nn - By Wilhelm Busch (Rare) 300.00 600.00 1320.00
NOTE: Sequel to the 1871 FOOLS PARADISE, containing a completely different set of Busch stories, translated into English.

FOOLS PARADISE MIRTH AND FUN FOR THE OLD & YOUNG (E)
Griffith & Farran, London: May 1883 (9-3/4x7-5/8", 78 pgs, color cover, color interior)

nn - By Wilhelm Busch (Rare) 100.00 200.00 420.00
NOTE: Collection of selected stories reprinted from both the 1871 & 1873 FOOLS PARADISE.

FOOLS PARADISE - MIRTH AND FUN FOR THE OLD & YOUNG (E)
E.P. Dutton and Co., NY: May 1883 (9-3/4x7-5/8", 78 pgs, color cover, color interior)

nn - By Wilhelm Busch (Rare) 100.00 200.00 420.00
NOTE: Collection of selected stories reprinted from both the 1871 & 1873 FOOLS PARADISE.

FOREIGN TOUR OFMESSRS. BROWN, JONES, AND ROBINSON, THE (see Messrs....,)

FRANK LESLIE'S BOYS AND GIRLS
Frank Leslie, NYC: Oct 13 1866-#905 Feb 9 1884

average issue with comic strip 10.00 20.00 40.00

FRANK LESLIE'S BUDGET OF FUN
Frank Leslie, Ross & Tousey, 121 Nassau St, NYC: Jan 1859-1878 (newspaper size)

1-5 no comic strips 50.00 100.00 200.00
6 June 1859 (9) panel "The Wonderful Hunting Tour of Mr Borridge After the Deer"
75.00 150.00 300.00
7-9 no comic strips 25.00 50.00 100.00
10 Sept 1859 sequential comic strip 50.00 100.00 200.00
11 (8) panel sequential "Apropos of the Great Eastern" 50.00 100.00 200.00
12-14 25.00 50.00 100.00
15 Feb 1860 (12) panel "The Ballet Girl" strip 50.00 100.00 200.00
16-18 25.00 50.00 100.00
19 June 1860 comic strip front cover 100.00 200.00 300.00
NOTE: Cover is (11) panel "The Very Latest Fashionable Amusement..."; Back cover comic strip "Mr Jogg's Reasons For Preferring to Board to Keeping House" (7) panels using word balloons. Plus centerfold double page (18) panel spread "The New York May, Moving in General, and Mrs. Grundy's In Particular."
20 24 25 no comic strips 25.00 50.00 100.00
21 (7/15/60) (8) panel Mr Septimus Verdilater Visits the Baltimore Convention"
50.00 100.00 200.00
22 (8/1/60) (3) panel 25.00 50.00 100.00
23 (8/15/60) (12) panel "Superb Scheme For Perfecting of Dramatic Entertainment"
50.00 100.00 200.00
25 (9/15/60 (9) panel sequential 50.00 100.00 200.00
27 AbrahamLincoln Word Balloon cover 50.00 100.00 200.00
28 Wilhelm Busch sequential strip-r begin 50.00 100.00 200.00
29, 31-51 to be indexed next year 25.00 50.00 100.00
30 (12/15/60) (3) panel sequential strip 25.00 50.00 100.00
31 (Jan 1861) (12) panel The Boarding School Miss 50.00 100.00 200.00
32 (Feb 1861) (10) panel Telegraphic Horrors; Or, Mr Buchanan
Undergoing A Series of Electric Shocks 50.00 100.00 200.00
35 (4/1/61) Abraham Lincoln Word Balloon cover 50.00 100.00 200.00
43 44 no sequential comic strips 25.00 50.00 100.00
45 (Nov 1861) (6) panel sequential; (11) panel The Budget Army and Infantry Tactics;
First Bellew here? - Many Bellew full pagers begin 50.00 100.00 200.00
48 (Feb 1862) Bellew-c; (2) panel Bellew strip plus singles 50.00 100.00 200.00
49 (Mar 1862) Bellew-c; (16) panel Wilhelm Busch "The Fly
Or The Disturbed Duchman A Story without Words" 50.00 100.00 200.00
50 (April 1862) Bellew-c "Succession Bath" plus singles 25.00 50.00 100.00
51 (May 1862) Bellew-c; (25) panel Busch The Toothache
(6) panel Definitions of the Day 50.00 100.00 200.00
52 (June 1862) Bellew-c; (9) panel A Cock & A Bull Expedition; (6) panel Bellew
The First Campaign of the Home Guard 50.00 100.00 200.00
NOTE: Johnny Bull & Louis Napolean with Brother Jonathan
53-67 To Be Indexed in the Future 25.00 50.00 100.00
68 (11/18///63) (6) panel Bellew strip "Cuts On Cowards" 25.00 50.00 100.00
NOTE: contains (1) panel William Newman 1817-1870, mentor to Thomas Nast
71 (Feb 1864) Wiord Balloon Jefferson Davis-c 25.00 50.00 100.00
72 (Mar 1864) Word Balloon-c 25.00 50.00 100.00
73 (April 1864) Word Balloon-c in (6) panels 25.00 50.00 100.00
74 (May 1864) Newman Word Balloon-c 25.00 50.00 100.00
75 77 78 no sequentials 25.00 50.00 100.00
76 (July 1864) Newman Word Balloon-c 25.00 50.00 100.00
79 (Oct 1864) Word Balloon-c 25.00 50.00 100.00
80 (Nov 1864) Robt E Lee & JeffDavis-c; no sequentials 25.00 50.00 100.00
81 (Dec 1864) Word Balloon "Abyss of War"-c 25.00 50.00 100.00

Frank Tousey's Illustrated New York Monthly #9
June 1882 © Frank Tousey

The Funnyest Of Awl And The Funniest Sort Of Phun v4#4
1865 © A.T. Bellew Word Balloon Cover

Funny Fellow's Own Book
1852 © Philip Cozans

	FR1.0	GD2.0	FN6.0
83 (2/18/65) Back-c (6) panel "Petroleum"	25.00	50.00	100.00
84 (Mar 1865) (6) panel sequential	25.00	50.00	100.00
85 (Apr 1865) Word Balloon-c	25.00	50.00	100.00
86 89 90 92 no sequentials	25.00	50.00	100.00
88 (7/6/65) (6) panel "Marriage"	25.00	50.00	100.00
91 (Oct 1865) (6) panel "Brief Confab At The Corner	25.00	50.00	100.00
93-98 yet to be indexed	25.00	50.00	100.00

99 (June 1866) (18) panel Mr Paul Peters Adventures
While Trout-Fishing In The Adirondacks — 50.00 100.00 200.00
100 (July 1866) (4) panel sequential comic strip — 25.00 50.00 100.00
102 (Sept 1866) (6) panel sequential comic strip — 25.00 50.00 100.00
103 (Oct 1866) (9) panel strip; (12) pane;l back cover
Adventures of McTiffin At Long Branch — 50.00 100.00 200.00
104 (Nov 1866) (4) panel; (23) panel "The Budget Rebuses; (2) panel
Glut On Treason Market;back-c; (6) sequential strip — 25.00 50.00 100.00
105 (12/18/66) Word Balloon-c; (20) panel sequential back-c — 37.50 65.00 130.00
NOTE: Artists include William Newman (1863-1868), William Henry Shelton, Joseph Keppler (1873-1876), James A. Wales (1876-1878), Frederick Burr Opper (1878)

FRANK LESLIE'S LADY'S MAGAZINE
Frank Leslie: Feb 1863-Dec 1882 (8.5x12", typically 152 pgs)
issues with comic strips — 10.00 20.00 40.00

FRANK LESLIE'S PICTORIAL WEEKLY
Frank Leslie, Ross & Tousey, 121 Nassau St, NYC:
average issue (Very Rare) — 50.00 100.00 200.00

FRANK TOUSEY'S NEW YORK COMIC MONTHLY
Frank Tousey, NYC: — (no known sales)

FREAKS
???, Philadelphia: Jan 8, 1881-April? 1881 (Chromolithographic Weekly)
(Very Rare) — 50.00 100.00 300.00

FREELANCE, THE
A.M. Soteldo Jr, Edito, 292 Broadway, NYC: 1874-75 (Folio Weekly)
(Rare) — 25.00 50.00 100.00

FREE MASONRY EXPOSED
Winchell & Small, 113 Fulton, NY: 1871 (7-5/8x10-1/2", 36pgs, blue paper-c, B&W)
nn- Thomas Worth — 25.00 50.00 100.00
NOTE: Scathing satirical look at Free Masons thru many cartoons, their power waning by the 1870s

FREETHINKERS' PICTORIAL TEXT-BOOK, THE (S,O)
The Truth Seeker Company, New York: 1890, 1896, 1898 (9x12, hard-c, B&W)
1 (1890 edition) - Scarce 382 pgs By Watson Heston — 100.00 200.00 450.00
1 (1896 edition) - Scarce 378 pgs By Watson Heston (1890-r) — 75.00 150.00 400.00
2 (1898 edition) - Scarce 408 pgs By Watson Heston — 125.00 250.00 450.00
NOTE: Sought after by collectors of Freethought/Atheism material. There is also 200 copy Modern Reprint.

FRITZ SPINDLE-SHANKS, THE RAVEN BLACK
Cosack & Co, Buffalo, NY: 1870/80s (4-3/8x2-3/4", color)
(10) card comic strip set by Wilhelm Busch — 25.00 50.00 100.00

FUN BY RALL
Unknown: circa 1865 (11x7-7/8", 68 pgs, soft-c, B&W)
nn - By presently unknown (Very Rare) — 100.00 200.00 350.00
NOTE: Wraparound soft cover like modern comic book; yellow paper cover with red & black ink.

FUN FOR THE FAMILY IN PICTURES
D. Lothrop and Company: 1886 (4 x 7", 48 pgs, Silver & Red stiff-c; interior pages have various single color inks)
nn - By unknown hand — 50.00 100.00 200.00
NOTE: Single panel cartoons and sequential stories.

FUN FROM LIFE
Frederick A Stokes & Brother, New York: 1889 (9 1/8 by 7 1/8, 72 pages, hard-c)
nn - Mostly by Frank "Chips" Bellew Jr — 62.50 125.00 250.00
NOTE: Contains both single panel and many sequential comics reprints from Life.

FUNNYEST OF AWL AND THE FUNNIEST SORT OF PHUN, THE
AT Bellew Or W. Jennings Demorest, 121 Nassau St, NY: 1865-67 (30 issues, 16x11 tabloid 16 pgs B&W Monthly, 1-8 © American News; 9-on © A.T. Bellews)
1 (April 1864) Bellew-c — 50.00 100.00 200.00
4 (1865) Bellew-c — 50.00 100.00 200.00
5 (1865) Busch (20) panel comic srtip The Toothache — 75.00 150.00 300.00
7 (1865) Bellew-c — 50.00 100.00 200.00
8 (1865) Special Petroleum oil issue - much cartoon art — 100.00 200.00 400.00
9 (July 1865) Bellew Bullfrog-c; centerfold double page spread hanging many Confederates; (6) panel strip hanging Jeff Davis — 100.00 200.00 400.00
10 (Aug 1865) Bellew-c (13) panel Busch strip with two ducks, a frog and a butcher who gets the ducks in the end — 100.00 200.00 400.00
11 (Sept 1865) Bellew Bull Frog Anti-French-c — 50.00 100.00 200.00
13 14 15 (12/65-1/66) Bellew-c no sequential comic strips — 50.00 100.00 200.00
16 (March 1866) address change to 39 Park Ave — 50.00 100.00 200.00
22 (Sept 1866) 133 Nassau St — 50.00 100.00 200.00

	FR1.0	GD2.0	FN6.0

34 (Oct 1867) 133 Nassau St (7) panel Baseball comic strip;
Last Known Issue - were there more? — 100.00 200.00 400.00
NOTE: Radical Republican politics distributed by Great American News Company; owned by Frank Bellew's wife as a front for her husband. When the Civil War ended, the brutal anti-Confederate comic strips and jokes switched to frogs and began attacking France. Funny thing, history says without France's help in the 1700s, there just might not have been a United States.

FUNNY ALMANAC
Elton & Co., NY: 1853 (8-1/8x4-7/8, 36 pgs)
nn - sequential comic strip — 50.00 100.00 200.00
NOTE: (5) panel strip "The Adventures of Mr. Goliah Starvemouse"

FUNNY FELLOWS OWN BOOK, A COMPANION FOR THE LOVERS OF FROLIC AND GLEE, THE (M,N)
Philip. J. Cozans, 116 Nassau ST, NY: 1852 (4-1/2x7-1/2", 196 pgs, burnt orange paper-c)
nn - contains many sequential comic strips (Very Rare) — (no known sales)
NOTE: Collected from many different Comic Alamac(k)s including Mose Keyser (Calif Gold Rush); Jones, Smith and Robinson Goes To A Ball; Adventures of Mr. Gulp, Or the Effects of A Dinner Party; The Bowery Bully's Trip To The California Gold Mines plus lots more. This one is a sleeper so far.

FUNNY FOLK (M)
E. P. Dutton: 1899 (12x16-1/2", 90 pgs,14 strips in color-rest in b&w, hard-c)
nn - By Franklin Morris Howarth — 162.50 325.00 1500.00
nn - London: J.M. Dent, 1899 embossed-c; same interior — 100.00 300.00 725.00
NOTE: Reprints many sequential strips & single panel cartoons from Puck. This is considered by many to be yet another "missing link" between Victorian & Platinum Age comic books. Most comic books 1900-1917 reprinting Sunday newspaper comic strips follow this size format, except using cardboard-c rather than hard-c.

GIBSON BOOK, THE (M,S)
Charles Scribner's Sons & R.H. Russell, New York: 1906 (11-3/8x17-5/8", gilted red hard-c, B&W)
Book I — 50.00 100.00 200.00
NOTE: Reprints in whole the books: Drawings, Pictures of People, London,Sketches and Cartoons, Education of Mr. Pipp, Americans. 414 pgs. 1907 2nd editions exist same value.
Book II — 50.00 100.00 200.00
NOTE: Reprints in whole the books: A Widow and Her Friends, The Weaker Sex, Everyday People, Our Neighbors. 314 pgs 1907 second edition for both also exists. Same value.

GIBSON'S PUBLISHED DRAWINGS, MR. (M,S) (see Plat index for later issues post 1900)
R.H. Russell, New York: No.1 1894 - No. 9 1904 (11x17-3/4", hard-c, B&W)
nn (No.1; 1894) Drawings 96 pgs — 30.00 60.00 120.00
nn (No.2; 1896) Pictures of People 92 pgs — 30.00 60.00 120.00
nn (No.3; 1898) Sketches and Cartoons 94 pgs — 30.00 60.00 120.00
nn (No.4; 1899) The Education of Mr. Pipp 88 pgs — 30.00 60.00 120.00
nn (No.5; 1900) Americans — 30.00 60.00 120.00
NOTE: By Charles Dana Gibson cartoons, reprinted from magazines, primarily LIFE. The Education of Mr. Pipp tells a story. Series continues how long after 1904? Each of these books originally came in a boxx and are worth more with the box.

GIRL WHO WOULDN'T MIND GETTING MARRIED, THE (O)
Frederick Warne & Co., London & New York: nd (c1870's) (9-1/2x11-1/2", 28 pgs, printed 1 side, paper-c, B&W)
nn - By Harry Parkes — 125.00 250.00
NOTE: Published simultaneously with its companion volume, The Man Who Would Like to Marry.

GOBLIN SNOB, THE (O)
DeWitt & Davenport, New York: nd (c1853-56) (24 x 17 cm, 96 pgs, B&W, color hard-c)
nn - (Rare) by H.L. Stephens — 250.00 500.00 1000.00

GOLDEN ARGOSY
Frank A. Munsey, 81 Warren St, NYC: 1880s (10-1/2x12, 16 pgs, B&W)
issues with full page comic strips by Chips and Bisbee — 12.50 25.00 50.00

GOLDEN DAYS, THE
James Elverson, Publisher, NYC: March 6 1880-May 11 1907 weekly, 16 pgs
issues with comic strips — 4.00 7.50 15.00
Horatio Alger issues — 10.00 20.00 40.00
v10 #49-v11#1 1889 first Stratemeyer story — 25.00 50.00 100.00

GOLDEN WEEKLY, THE
Frank Tousey, NYC: #1 Sept 25 1889-#145 Aug 18 1892 (10-3/4x14-1/2, 16 pgs, B&W)
average issue with comic striiips — 15.00 25.00 50.00

GREAT LOCOFOCO JUGGERNAUT, THE (S)
publisher unknown: Fall/Winter 1837 (7-5/8x3-1/4, handbill single page)
nn - By David Claypoole Johnston — (a VG copy sold for $2000 in 2005)
nn- Imprint Society: 1971 (reprint) — 6.00 12.00 25.00

HALF A CENTURY OF ENGLISH HISTORY (S. M)
G.P. Putnam's Sons - The Knickerbocker Press, New York and London: 1884 (7-3/4 x 5-3/4", 316 pgs., iiiustrated hard-c)
nn - By Various — 25.00 100.00 175.00
NOTE: Subtitle: Pictorially Presented in a Series of Cartoons from the Collection of Mr. Punch. Comprising 150 plates by Doyle, Leech, Tenniel, and others, in which are portrayed the political careers of Peel, Palmerston, Russell, Cobden, Bright, Beaconsfield, Derby, Salisbury, Gladstone and other English statesmen.

HAIL COLUMBIA! HISTORICAL, COMICAL, AND CENTENNIAL (O,S)
The Graphic Co., New York & Walter F. Brown, Providence, RI: 1876 (10x11-3/8",

The Story of Han's The Swapper Cover & First Two Panels
1865 © L. Pranc & Co, Boston

The Home Circle #20
August 1855 © Garrett & Co., NY

Imagerie d'Epinal
1888 © Mumoristic Publishing Co.

	FR1.0	GD2.0	FN6.0

60 pgs, red gilted hard-c, B&W)

nn - by Walter F. Brown (Scarce)	100.00	200.00	450.00

HANS HUCKEBEIN'S BATCH OF ODD STORIES ODDLY ILLUSTRATEDED
McLoughlin Bros., New York: 1880s (9-3/4x7-3/8, 36?? pg?

nn - By Wilhelm Busch (Rare)	37.50	75.00	150.00

HANS THE SWAPPER, THE STORY OF (O)
L. Pranc & Co., 159 Washington St, Boston: 1865 (33 inch long fold out in colors)

nn - unique fold out comic book on one long piece of paper	37.50	75.00	150.00

HARPER'S NEW MONTHLY MAGAZINE
Harper & Brothers, Franklin Square, NY: 1850-1870s (6-3/4x10, 140 pgs, paper-c, B&W)

1850s issues with comic strips in back advert section	10.00	20.00	40.00

HEALTH GUYED (I)
Frederick A. Stokes Company: 1890 (5-3/8 x 8-3/8, 56 pgs, hardcover, B&W)

nn - By Frank P.W. ("Chip") Bellew (Junior)	25.00	50.00	175.00

NOTE: Text & cartoon illustration parody of a health guide.

HITS AT POLITICS (M,S)
R.H. Russell, New York: 1899 (15" x 12", 156 pgs, B&W, hard-c)

nn - W.A. Rogers c/a	100.00	200.00	450.00

NOTE: Collection of W.A. Rogers cartoons, all reprinted from Harper's Weekly. Includes Spanish-American War cartoons.

THE HOME CIRCLE
Garrett & Co, NY: 1854-56 (26x19", 4 pgs, B&W)

1 (1/54) beautiful ad of Garrett Building	100.00	200.00	400.00
2/4 (4/66) Cover ad for Yale College Scraps	100.00	200.00	400.00
2/5 (5/55) First ad for Oscas Shanghai	75.00	150.00	300.00
2/6 (6/55) another ad forOscas Snanghai	75.00	150.00	300.00
2/8 (#20) (8/55) Oscar Shanghai comic book cover repro	200.00	400.00	800.00
3/1 (#25) (1/56)	200.00	400.00	800.00

NOTE: Garrett's 2nd comic book Courtship of Chavalier Slyfox-Wikoff

3/8 (#32) (8/56)	50.00	100.00	200.00
35 (11/56) first official Garrett, Dick & Fitzgerald issue	50.00	100.00	200.00
37 (1/57)	100.00	200.00	400.00

NOTE: Front page comic strip repro ad for Messrs. Brown, Jones, and Robinson's Foreign Tour; Back cover full of short sequentials, singles panel

HOME MADE HAPPY. A ROMANCE FOR MARRIED MEN IN SEVEN CHAPTERS (O,P)
Genuine Durham Smoking Tobacco & The Graphic Co.: nd (c1870's) (5-1/4 tall x 3-3/8" wide folded, 27" wide unfolded, color cardboard)

nn - With all 8 panels attached (Scarce)	30.00	60.00	200.00
nn - Individual panels/cards	5.00	10.00	25.00

NOTE: Consists of 8 attached cards, printed on one side, which unfold into a strip story of title card & 7 panels. Scrapbook hobbyists in the 19th Century tended to pull the panels apart to paste into their scrapbooks, making copies with all panels still attached scarce.

HOME PICTURE BOOK FOR LITTLE CHILDREN (E,P)
Home Insurance Company, New York: July 1887 (8 x 6-1/8", 36 pgs, b&w, color paper-c)

nn (Scarce)	40.00	80.00	160.00

NOTE: Contains an abbreviated 32-panel reprinting of "The Toothache" by George Cruikshank. Remainder of booklet does not contain comics. Some copies known to exist do not contain The Toothache - buyer beware!

HOOD'S COMICALITIES. COMICAL PICTURES FROM HIS WORKS (E,S)
Porter & Coates: 1880 (8-1/2x10-3/8", 104 pgs, printed one side, hard-c, B&W)

nn	20.00	40.00	80.00

NOTE: Reprints 4 cartoon illustrations per page from the British Hood's Comic Annuals, which were poetry books by Thomas Hood.

HOOKEYBEAK THE RAVEN, AND OTHER TALES (see also JACK HUCKABACK, THE SCAPEGRACE RAVEN) (E)
George Routledge and Sons, London & New York: nd (1878) (7-1/4x5-5/8", 104 pgs, hardcover, B&W)

nn - By Wilhelm Busch (Rare)	100.00	200.00	400.00

HOW ADOLPHUS SLIM-JIM USED JACKSON'S BEST, AND WAS HAPPY. A LENGTHY TALE IN 7 ACTS. (O,P)
Jackson's Best Chewing Tobacco & Donaldson Brothers: nd(c1870's) (5-1/8 tall x 3-3/8" wide folded, 27" wide unfolded, color cardboard)

nn - With all 8 panels attached (Scarce)	30.00	60.00	200.00
nn - Individual panels/cards	5.00	10.00	25.00

NOTE: Consists of 8 attached cards, printed on one side, which unfold into a strip story of title card & 7 panels. Scrapbook hobbyists in the 19th Century tended to pull the panels apart topaste into their scrapbooks, making copies with all panels still attached scarce.

HOW DAYS' DURHAM STANDARD OF THE WORLD SMOKING TOBACCO MADE TWO PAIRS OF TWINS HAPPY (O,P)
J.R. Day & Bro. Standard Durham Smoking Tobacco, Durham, NC: nd (c late 1870's/early 1880's) (3-5/8" x 5-1/2", folded, 21-3/4" tall unfolded, color cardboard)

nn- With all 6 panels attached (Scarce)	120.00	240.00	480.00
nn- Individual panels/cards	20.00	40.00	60.00

NOTE: Highly sought by both Black Americana and Tobacciana collectors. Recurring mid-19th Century story about two African-American twin brothers who romance and marry a pair of African-American twin sisters.

Although the text is racist at points, the art is not. Consists of 6 attached cards, printed on one side, which unfold downwards into a strip story of title card & 5 panels. Scrapbook hobbyists in the 19th Century tended to pull the panels apart and paste into their scrapbooks, making copies with all panels attached scarce. Note, there are numerous cartoon tellings of this same story, including several card series versions (with different art, and story variations, each time). But, the above is the only version which unfolds as a strip of attached cards. The cards from all the unattached versions are smaller sized, and thus distinguishable.

HUGGINIANA; OR, HUGGINS' FANTASY, BEING A COLLECTION OF THE MOST ESTEEMED MODERN LITERARY PRODUCTIONS (I,S,P)
H.C. Southwick, New York: 1808 (296 pgs, printed one side, B&W, hard-c)

nn - (Very Rare))		(no known sales)	

NOTE: The earliest known surviving collected promotional cartoons in America. This is a booklet collecting 7 folded plus 1 full page flyer advertisements for barber John Richard Desborus Huggins, who hired American artists Elkanah Tisdale and William S. Leney to modify previously published illustrations into cartoons referring to his barber shop.

HUMOROUS MASTERPIECES - PICTURES BY JOHN LEECH (E,M)
Frederick A. Stokes: nd (late 1900's - early 1910's) No.1-2 (5-5/8x3-7/8", 68 pgs, cardboard covers, B&W)

1- John Leech (single panel cartoon-r from **Punch**)	17.50	35.00	70.00
2- John Leech (single panel cartoon-r from **Punch**)	17.50	35.00	70.00

HUMOURIST, THE (E,I,S)
C.V. Nickerson and Lucas and Deaver, Baltimore: No.1 Jan 1829 - No.12 Dec 1829 (5-3/4x3-1/2", B&W text w/hand colored cartoon pg.)

Bound volume No.1-12 (Very Rare; copies in libraries 270 pgs)		(no known sales)	

NOTE: Earliest known American published periodical to contain a cartoon every issue. Surviving individual issues currently unknown -- all information comes from 1 surviving bound volume. Each issue is mostly text, with one full page hand-colored cartoon. Bound volume contains an additional hand-colored cartoons at front of each six month set (total of 14 cartoons in volume). Cartoons appear to be of British origin, possibly by George Cruikshank.

HUMPTY DUMPTY, ADVENTURES OF...(I,P)
1877 (Promotional 4x3-1/2", 12 page chapbook from Gantz, Jones & Co, 10¢-c.)

nn-Promotes Gantz Sea Foam Baking Powder; early app. of a costumed character, dressed as Humpty Dumpty	50.00	100.00	350.00

HUSBAND AND WIFE, OR THE STORY OF A HAIR. (O,P)
Garland Stoves and Ranges, Michigan Stove Co.: 1883 (4-3/16 tall x 2-11/16" wide folded, 16" wide unfolded, color cardboard)

nn - With all 6 panels attached (Scarce)	25.00	50.00	125.00
nn - Individual panels/cards	5.00	10.00	25.00

NOTE: Consists of 6 attached cards, printed on one side, which unfold into a strip story of title card & 5 panels. Scrapbook hobbyists in the 19th Century tended to pull the panels apart topaste into their scrapbooks, making copies with all panels still attached scarce.

ICHABOD ACADEMICUS, THE COLLEGE EXPERIENCES OF (O,G)
William T. Peters, New Haven, CT: 1850 (5-1/2x9-3/4",108 pgs, B&W)

nn - By William T. Peters (Rare)	350.00	775.00	1300.00

NOTE: Pages are not uniform in size. Also, a copy showed up on eBay with misspelled Academicus. Has "n" instead of "m" - not known yet which printing is earliest version.

ICHABOD ACADEMICUS, THE COLLEGE EXPERIENCES OF (O,G)
Dick & Fitzgerald, New York: nd (1870s-1888) (paper-c, B&W)

nn - By William T. Peters (Very Rare)	150.00	300.00	550.00

NOTE: Pages are uniform in size.

ILLUSTRATED SCRAP-BOOK OF HUMOR AND INTELLIGENCE (M)
John J. Dyer & Co.: nd (c1859-1860)

nn - Very Rare	200.00	400.00	–

NOTE: A "printed scrapbook" of images culled from some unidentified periodical. About half of it is illustrations that would have accompanied prose pieces. There are pages of single panel cartoons (multiple per page). And there are roughly 8 to 12 pages of sequential comics (all different stories, but appears to all be by the same presently unidentified artist).

THE ILLUSTRATED WEEKLY
Chars C Lucas & Co, 11 Dey St, NY: 1876 (15x18", 8pgs, 8¢ per issue)

2/8 (2/19/76) back-c all sequential comic strips	100.00	200.00	400.00
2/12 (3/18/76) full page of British-r sequentials	100.00	200.00	400.00
2/14 (4/1/76) April Fool Issue - (6) panel center; plus more	100.00	200.00	400.00
2/15 (4/8/76) (6) panel sequential	100.00	200.00	400.00
issues without comic strips	12.50	25.00	50.00

ILLUSTRATIONS OF THE POETS: FROM PASSAGES IN THE LIFE OF LITTLE BILLY VIDKINS (See A Day's Sport...)
S. Robinson, Philadelphia: May 1849 (14.7 cm x 11.3 cm, 32 pgs, B&W)

nn - by Henry Stephens (very rare)		(no known sales)	

NOTE: Newly listed, predates Journey to the Gold Diggins By Jeremiah Saddlebags by a few months and is an original American proto-comic strip book. More research needs to be done.

IMAGERIE d'EPINAL (untrimmed individual sheets) (E)
Pellerin for Humoristic Publishing Co, Kansas City, Mo.: nd (1888) No.1-60 (15-7/8x11-3/4",single sheets, hand colored) (All are Rare)

1-14, 15, 21, 22, 25-46, 49-60 - in the Album d'Images	17.50	35.00	70.00
15-20, 23,24, 47, 48 - not in the Album d'Images	30.00	60.00	120.00

NOTE: Printed and hand colored in France expressly for the Humoristic Publishing Company . Printed on one side only. These are single sheets, sold separately. Reprints and translates the sheets from their original French.

Journey To The Gold Diggings By Jeremiah Saddlebags
1849 © Various - First Original USA Comic Book

The Judge #1 Oct 29, 1881
1881 © Judge Publishing Co.

The Lantern Dec 18
1852 © Stringer & Townsend

	FR1.0	GD2.0	FN6.0

IMAGERIE d'EPINAL ALBUM d'IMAGES (E)
Pellerin for Humoristic Publishing Co., Kansas City. Mo: nd (1888)
(15-1/2x11-1/2",108 pgs plus full color hard-c, hand colored interior)

nn - Various French artists (Rare)	300.00	600.00	1800.00

NOTE: Printed and hand colored in France expressly for the Humoristic Publishing Company . Printed on one side only. This is supposedly a collection of sixty broadsheets, originally sold separately. All copies known only have fifty of the sixty known of these broadsheets (slightly bigger, before binding, trimming the margins in the process, down to 15-1/4x11-3/8"). Three slightly different covers known to exist, with or without the indication in French "Textes en Anglais" ("Texts in English"), with or without the general title "Contes de FEes" ("Fairy Tales"). A known copies were collected with sheets 15-20, 23,24, 47, and 48 missing.

IN LAUGHLAND (M)
R.H. Russell, New York: 1899 (14-9/16x12", 72 pgs, hard-c)

nn - By Henry "Hy" Mayer (scarce)	100.00	200.00	400.00

NOTE: Mostly strips plus single panel cartoon-r from various magazines. The majority are reprinted from Life, with the rest from: Truth, Dramatic Mirror, Black and White, Figaro Illustre, Le Rire, and Fliegende Blatter.

IN THE "400" AND OUT (M,S) (see also THE TAILOR-MADE GIRL)
Keppler & Schwarzmann, New York: 1888 (8-1/4x12", 64 pgs, hardc, B&W)

nn - By C.J. Taylor	42.50	85.00	170.00

NOTE: Cartoons reprinted from Puck. The "400" is a reference to New York City's aristocratic elite.

IN VANITY FAIR (M,S)
R.H.Russell & Son, New York: 1896 (11-7/8x17-7/8", 80 pgs, hard-c, B&W)

nn - By A.B.Wenzell, r-LIFE and HARPER'S	45.00	90.00	180.00

JACK HUCKABACK, THE SCAPEGRACE RAVEN (see also HOOKEYBEAK THE RAVEN) (E)
Stroefer & Kirchner, New York: nd (c1888) (9-3/8x6-3/8", 56 pgs, printed one side only, hand colored hardcover, B&W interior)

nn - By Wilhelm Busch (Rare)	55.00	110.00	350.00

NOTE: The 1888 date is derived from a gift signature on one known copy. The publication date might in truth be earlier. There are also professionally hand colored copies known to exist which would be worth more.

JEFF PETTICOATS
American News Company, NY: July 1865 (23 inches folded out; 6-1/4x8 folded,, B&W)

nn - Very Rare Frank Bellew (6) panel sequential foldout (10¢)		(no known sales)	

NOTE: printed also in FUNNYEST OF AWL AND THE FUNNIEST SORT OF PHUN #9 (July 1865) (6) panel strip hanging Jeff Davis; This sold hundreds of thousand of copies in its day

JINGO (M,O)
Art Newspaper Co., Boston & New York: Nov 1 Sept 10, 1884 - No.11 Nov 19, 1884 (10 cents, 13-7/8" x 10-1/4",16gs, color front/back-c and center, remainder B&W, paper-c)

1-11(Rare)	25.00	50.00	150.00

NOTE: Satirical Republican propaganda magazine, modeled after Puck and Judge, which was published during the last couple months of the 1884 Presidential Election campaign. The Republicans lost, Jingo ceased publication, and Republican backers soon after purchased Judge magazine.

JOHN-DONKEY, THE (O, S)
George Dexter, Burgess, Stringer & Co., NYC: 1848 (10x7.5",16 pgs,B&W, 6¢

1 Jan 1 1848	75.00	150.00	300.00
2-end (last issue Aug 12 1848)	50.00	100.00	200.00

JOLLY JOKER
Frank Leslie, NY: 1862-1878 (B&W, 10¢)

20/6 (July 1877) (Bellew Opper cover & single panels	150.00	300.00	600.00

JONATHAN'S WHITTLINGS OF THE WAR (O, S)
T.W. Strong, 98 Nassau St, NYC: April 1854-July 8 1854 (11.5x8.5", 16 pgs, B&W)

1 April 1854	100.00	200.00	400.00

NOTE: Begins Frank Bellew's sequential comic strip "Mr. Hookemcumsnivey, A Russian Gentleman, Hears That His Country Is In A State of War"

2-12 (July 8 1854) Many Bellew & Hopkins	100.00	200.00	400.00

JOURNEY TO THE GOLD DIGGINS BY JEREMIAH SADDLEBAGS (O,G)
Various publishers: 1849 (25 cents, 5-5/8 x 8-3/4", 68 pgs, green & black paper cover, B&W interior)

nn -- New York edition, Stringer & Townsend, Publishers (Very Rare) By J.A. and D.F. Read.	3500.00	6000.00	7800.00
nn -- Cincinnati, Ohio edition, published by U.P. James (Very Rare) By J.A. and D.F. Read.	3500.00	6000.00	7800.00
nn -- 1950 reprint, with introduction, published by William P. Wreden, Burlingame, California: 1950 (5-7/8 x 9", 92 pgs, hardcover, color interior) (390 copies printed) By J.A. and D.F. Read.	67.50	125.00	250.00

NOTE: Earliest known original sequential comic book by an American creator; directly inspired by Töpffer's Obadiah Oldbuck and Bachelor Butterfly. The New York and Cincinnati editions were both published in 1849, one soon after the other. Antiquarian Book sources have traditionally cited that the Cincinnati edition preceded the New York, but without referencing their evidence. Conflicting with this, the Cincinnati edition lists the New York publishers' 1849 copyright, while the New York edition makes no reference to the Cincinnati publishers. Such would indicate that the New York edition was first. Both are very rare, and until resolved both will be regarded as published simultaneously. A New York copy with missing back cover, detached front cover, and G/VG interior sold for $2000 in 2000. Two copies sold at auction in 2006 for $11,500 and 12,000. (Prices vary widely.)

JUDGE (M,O)
Judge Publishing, New York: No.1 Oct 29, 1881 - No. 950, Dec ??, 1899 (10 cents, color front/back c and centerspread, remainder B&W, paper-c)

1 (Scarce)		(no known sales)	

2-26 (Volume 1; Scarce)	20.00	40.00	80.00
27-790,792-950	12.50	25.00	50.00
791 (12/12/1896; Vol.31) - classic satirical-c depicting Tammany Hall politicians as the Yellow Kid & Cox's Brownies	50.00	150.00	350.00

Bound Volumes (six month, 26 issue run each):

Vol. 1 (Scarce)		(no known sales)	
Vol. 2-30,32-37	140.00	280.00	600.00
Vol. 31 - includes issue 791 YK/Brownies parody	165.00	230.00	725.00

NOTE: Rival publication to Puck. Purchased by Republican Party backers, following their loss in the 1884 Presidential Election, to become a Republican propaganda satire magazine.

JUDGE, GOOD THINGS FROM
Judge Publishing Co., NY: 1887 (13-3/4x10.5", 68 pgs, color paper-c)

1 first printing	50.00	100.00	200.00

NOTE: Zimmerman, Hamilton, Victor, Woolf, Beard, Ehrhart, De Meza, Howarth, Smith, Alfred Mitchell

JUDGE'S LIBRARY (M)
Judge Publishing, New York: No.1, April 1890 - No. 141, Dec 1899 (10 cents, 11x8-1/8", 36 pgs, color paper-c, B&W)

1	8.50	17.00	33.00
2-141	8.50	17.00	33.00
151-??? (post-1900 issues; see Platinum Age section)			

NOTE: Judge's Library was a monthly magazine reprinting cartoons & prose from Judge, with each issue's material organized around the same subject. The cover art was often original. All issues were kept in print for the duration of the series, so later issues are more scarce than earlier ones.

JUDGE'S QUARTERLY (M)
Judge Publishing Company/Arkell Publishing Company, New York: No.1 April 1892 - 31 Dec 1899 (25¢, 13-3/4x10-1/4", 64 pgs, color paper-c, B&W)

1-31	15.00	30.00	60.00

NOTE: Similar to Judge's Library, except larger in size, and issued quarterly. All reprint material, except for the cover art.

JUDGE'S SERIALS (M,S)
Judge Publishing, New York: March 1888 (10x7.5", 36 pgs)

#3 - Eugene Zimmerman	100.00	200.00	400.00

NOTE: A bit of sequential comic strips; mostly single panel cartoons.

JUDY
Burgess, Stringer & Co., 17 Ann St, NYC: Nov 28 1846-Feb 20 47 (11x8.5",12pgs,B&W)

1 Nov 28 1846	67.50	125.00	250.00
2-13	50.00	100.00	200.00

JUVENILE GEM, THE (see also THE ADVENTURES OF MR. TOM PLUMP, and OLD MOTHER MITTEN) (O,I)
Huestis & Cozans: nd (1850-1852) (6x3-7/8", 64 pgs, hand colored paper-c, B&W) (all versions Very Rare)

nn - First printing(s) publisher's address is 104 Nassau Street (1850-1851)			
		(1 copy sold for $800.00 in Fair)	
nn - 2nd printing(s) publisher's address is 116 Nassau Street (1851-1852) (no known sales)			
nn - 3rd printing(s) publisher's address is 107 Nassau Street (1852+)		(no known sales)	

NOTE: The JUVENILE GEM is a gathering of multiple booklets under a single, hand colored cover (none of the interior booklets have the covers which they were given when sold separately). The publisher appears to have gathered whichever printings of each booklet were available when copies of THE JUVENILE GEM was assembled, so that the booklets within, and the conglomerate cover, may be from a mixture of printings. Contains two sequential comic booklets: THE ADVENTURES OF MR. TOM PLUMP, and OLD MOTHER MITTEN and HER FUNNY KITTEN, along with five heavily illustrated children's booklets - The Pretty Primer, The Funny Book, The Picture Book, The Two Sisters, and Story Of The Little Drummer. Six of these -- including the two comic books -- were reprinted in the 1960's by Americana Review as a set of individual booklets, and included in a folder collectively titled "Six Children's Books of the 1850's".

LANTERN, THE
Stringer & Townsend:1852-1853 (11x8-3/8", 12 pgs, soft paper, 6 ¢)

1 Jan 10, 1852	37.50	75.00	150.00
2	25.00	50.00	100.00
3 First Frank Bellew cartoons onwards each issue	37.50	75.00	150.00
4 Bellew 's Mr Blobb begins 1/31/52	50.00	100.00	200.00

NOTE: Bellew serial sequential comic strip "Mr Blobb In Search Of A Physician" becomes 2nd earliest known recurring character in American comic strips plus full page single panel Bellew cartoon "The Modern Frankenstein" take-off on Shelly's story.

5 Hunsdale 2-panel "The Horrors of Slavery"; Mr Blobb	50.00	100.00	200.00
6 DF Read 15 panel "A Volley of Valentines"; Mr Blobb	50.00	100.00	200.00
7-8 10 Bellew's Mr Blobb continues	25.00	50.00	100.00
9 (4) panel "The Perils of Leap Year" MrBlobb	50.00	100.00	200.00
11 no Mr Blobb	20.00	40.00	80.00
12 Bellew's Mr Blobb continues 3/27/52	50.00	100.00	200.00
13 Bellew (10) panel sequential "Stump Speaking Studied"	50.00	100.00	200.00
14 no comic strips	20.00	40.00	80.00
15 Bellew's Mr Blobb ends (5) panel 4/17/52	50.00	100.00	200.00
16 Bellew begins new comic strip serial, "Mr. Bulbear, A Stockbroker, After having Supped at Delmonicos, Has A Dream", Part One, (6) panels	50.00	100.00	200.00
17 Bellew's Mr Bulbear continues	25.00	50.00	100.00
18 Bellew (8) panel "Trials of a Witness"	50.00	100.00	200.00
19 Bellew's Mr Bulbear's Dream continues	25.00	50.00	100.00
20-23 no comic strips	20.00	40.00	80.00

Leslie's Young America #1
1881 © Leslie & Company, NYC

Life Jan 3
1884 © J.A. Mitchell

Max and Maurice by Wilhelm Busch
1871 © Roberts Bros, Boston

	FR1.0	GD2.0	FN6.0

	FR1.0	GD2.0	FN6.0
24 Bellew "Trials of a Publisher" (6) panel	50.00	100.00	200.00
25 comic strip "Travels of Jonathan Verdant"recurring character	25.00	50.00	100.00
26-49 contents to be indexed soon			
50 (12/18/52) (2) panel Impertinent Smile	25.00	50.00	100.00
58 (2/12/53) (6) panel Trip to California	25.00	50.00	100.00
66 (4/9/53) (3) panel sequential strip	25.00	50.00	100.00

LAST SENSATION, THE (Becomes Day's Doings)
James Watts, NYC: Dec 27 1867-May 30 1868 (11x16 folio-size, 16 pgs, B&W)

issues with comic strips	50.00	100.00	200.00

LAUGH AND GROW FAT COMIC ALMANAC
Fisher & Brother, Philadelphia, New York & Boston: 1860-? (36 pgs)

nn	60.00	120.00	240.00

LEGEND OF SAM'L OF POSEN (O)
M.B. Curtis Company: 1884-85 (8x3-3/8", 44 pgs, Color-c, B&W interior)

nn - By M.B. Curtis	50.00	100.00	200.00

NOTE: Cover blurb says: From Early Days in Fatherland to affluence And Success in the Land of His Adoption, America

LESLIE'S YOUNG AMERICA (O. S)
Leslie & Co, 98 Chamber St, NY: 1881-82 (11-1/2x8", 5¢, B&W)

1 (7/9/81) back cover (6) panel strip	125.00	250.00	500.00
2 (7/16/81) back cover (9) panel strip	50.00	100.00	200.00
3 (7/23/81) back cover (16) panel Busch strip	67.50	125.00	250.00
9 (9/3/81) sequentials; Hopkins singles	50.00	100.00	200.00
15 (10/15/81) Zim or Frost? (6) panel strip	50.00	100.00	200.00
19 (11/12/81) (9) panel back-c strip	50.00	100.00	200.00
24 (4) panel strip 25 (2) panel back-c strip	50.00	100.00	200.00
26 27 (6) panel back-c strip	50.00	100.00	200.00
29 31 (12) panel strip	50.00	100.00	200.00
32 (2/11/82) (8) panel strip	50.00	100.00	200.00
issues without comic strips or Jules Verne	25.00	50.00	100.00

NOTE: Jules Verne stories begin with #1 and run thru at least #42

LIFE (M,O) (continues into Vol.35 No. 894+ in the Platinum Age section)
J.A.Mitchell: Vol.1 No.1 Jan. 4, 1883 - Vol.1 No.26 June 29, 1883 (10-1/4x8", 16 pgs, B&W, paper cover); J.A. Mitchell: Vol. 2 No. 27, July 5, 1883 - Vol. 6 No.148, Oct 29, 1885 (10-1/4x8-1/4", 16 pgs., B&W, paper cover); Mitchell & Miller: Vol No.149, Nov. 5, 1885 - Vol. 31, No. 796, March 17, 1898 (10-3/8x8-3/8", 16 pgs., B&W, paper cover); Life Publishing Company: Vol. 31 No. 797, March 24, 1898 - Vol. 34 No. 893, Dec 28, 1899 (10-3/8 x 8-1/2", 20 pgs., B&W, paper cover)

1-26 (Scarce)		(no known sales)	
27-799	5.00	10.00	20.00
800 (4/7/1898) parody Yellow Kid / Spanish-American War cover (not by Outcault)	67.50	125.00	250.00
801-893	5.00	10.00	20.00

NOTE: All covers for issues 1 - 26 are identical, apart from issue number & date.
Hard bound collected volumes:

V. 1 (No.1-26) (Scarce)	67.50	125.00	250.00
V. 2-34	45.00	90.00	180.00
V. 31 YK #800 parody-c not by RFO	70.00	140.00	280.00

NOTE: Because the covers of all issues in Volume 1 are identical, it was common practice to remove the covers before binding the issues together. This is not true of later volumes, though, in all volumes it was common to drop the advertising pages which appeared at the rear of each issue. Information on many more individual issues will expand next Guide.

LIFE AND ADVENTURES OF JEFF DAVIS (I)
J.C. Haney & Co., NY: 1865 (10 cents, 7-1/2" x 4", 36 pgs, B&W, paper-c)

nn - By McArone (Scarce)	150.00	300.00	650.00
nn - 1974 Reprint (350) copies 6-3/4x4-3/8	50.00	10.00	20.00
nn - 1997 Reprint (7th Fla. Sutler, Clearwater, 6-3/4x4-1/4")	−	−	2.00

NOTE: Humorous telling of the capture of Confederate President Jeff Davis in women's clothing, from the publisher of Merryman's Monthly. It contains an ad page for that publication; the material is perhaps reprinted from it. J.C. Haney licensed it to local printers, and so various publishers are found -- all printings currently regarded as simultaneous. (The Geo. H. Hees printing, Oswego, NY, contains an ad for the upcoming October 1865 issue of Merryman's Monthly, thus placing that printing in September 1865). Modern facsimile editions have been produced.

LIFE IN PHILADELPHIA
W. Simpson, 66 Chestnut, Philadelphia; Siltart, No. 65 South Third St, Philadelphia: 1830 (7-3/4x6-7/8", 15 loose plates, hand colored copies exist, maybe B&W also)

nn - By Edward Williams Clay (1799-1857) (Very Rare)		(no known sales)	

NOTE: First 13 plates etched, with many word balloons; scenes of exaggerated Black Americana in Philadelphia viewed one by one as broadsides. Had several publishers over the years. Was also eventually collected into a book of same name but only with the first 13 plates used; the last two not used in book. Collected book not yet viewed to share info.

LIFE'S BOOK OF ANIMALS (M,S)
Doubleday & McClure Co.: 1898 (7-1/4x10-1/8", 88 pgs, color hardcover, B&W)

nn	50.00	100.00	200.00

NOTE: Reprints funny animal single panel and strip cartoons reprinted from LIFE. Art by Blaisdell, Chip Bellew, Kemble, Hy Mayer, Sullivant, Woolf.

LIFE'S COMEDY (M,S)

Charles Scribner's Sons: Series 1 1897 - Series 3 1898 (12x9-3/8", hardcover, B&W)

1 (142 pgs). 2, 3 (138 pgs)	60.00	120.00	240.00

NOTE: Gibson a-1-3; c-3. Hy Mayer a-1-3. Rose O'Neill a-2-3. Stanlaws a-2-3. Sullivant a-1-2. Verbeek a-2. Wenzell a-1-3; c(painted)-2.

LIFE, THE GOOD THINGS OF (M,S)
White, Stokes, & Allen, NY: 1884 - No.3 1886 ; Frederick A. Stokes, NY: No.4 1887; Frederick Stokes & Brother, NY: No.5 1888 - No.6 1889; Frederick A. Stokes Company, NY: No. 7 1890 - No.10 1893 (8-3/8x10-1/2", 74 pgs, gilted hardcover, B&W)

nn - 1884 (most common issue)	32.50	65.00	130.00
2 - 1885	32.50	65.00	130.00
3 - 1886 (76 pgs)	32.50	65.00	130.00
4 - 1887 (76 pgs)	32.50	65.00	130.00
5 - 1888	32.50	65.00	130.00
6 - 1889	32.50	65.00	130.00
7 - 1890	32.50	65.00	130.00
8 - 1891 (scarce)	50.00	100.00	200.00
9 - 1892	32.50	65.00	130.00
10 - 1893	32.50	65.00	130.00

NOTE: Contains mostly single panel, and some sequential, comics reprinted from LIFE. Attwood a-1-4,10. Roswell Bacon a-5. Frank Bellew a-4,6. Palmer Cox a-1. H. E. Dey a-5. C. D. Gibson a-4-10. F.M. Howarth a-5-6. Kemble a-1-3. Klapp a-5. Walt McDougall a-1-2. H. McVickar a-5; J. A. Mitchell a-5. Peter Newell a-2-3. Gray Parker a-4-5,7. J. Smith a-5. Albert E. Steiner a-5; T. S. Sullivant a-7-9. Wenzell a-8-10. Wilder a-3. Woolf a-3-6.

LIFE, THE SPICE OF (E,M,)
White and Allen: NY & London: 1888 (8-3/8x10-1/2",76 pgs, hard-c, B&W)

nn	50.00	100.00	200.00

NOTE: Resembles THE GOOD THINGS OF LIFE in layout and format, and appears to be an attempt to compete with their former partner Frederick A. Stokes. However, the material is not from LIFE, but rather is reprinted and translated German sequential and single panel comics.

LIFE'S PICTURE GALLERY (becomes LIFE'S PRINTS) (M,S,P)
Life Publishing Company, New York: nd (1898-1899) (paper cover, B&W) (all are scarce)

nn - (nd; 1898, 100 pgs, 5-1/4x8-1/2") Gibson-c of a woman with closed umbrella; 1st interior page announcing that after January 1, 1899 Gibson will draw exclusively for LIFE; the word "SPECIMEN" is printed in red, diagonally, across every print; a-Gibson, Rose O'Neill, Sullivant	25.00	50.00	100.00
nn - (nd; 1899, 128 pgs, 4-7/8x7-3/8") Gibson-c of a woman golfer; 1st interior page announcing that Gibson & Hanna, Jr. draw exclusively for LIFE; the word "SPECIMEN" is printed in red, horizontally, across every print. Includes prints from Gibson's THE EDUCATION OF MR. PIPP: a-Gibson, Sullivant	25.00	50.00	100.00

NOTE: Catalog of prints reprinted from LIFE covers & centerspreads. The first catalog was given away free to anyone requesting it, but after many people got the catalog without ordering anything, subsequent catalogs were sold at 10 cents.

LONDON OUT OF TOWN, OR THE ADVENTURES OF THE BROWNS AT THE SEA SIDE BY LUKE LIMNER, ESQ. (O)
David Bogue, 86 Fleet St, London: c1847 (5-1/2x4-1/4, 32 pgs, yellow paper hard-c, B&W

nn - By John Leighton	100.00	200.00	400.00

NOTE: one long sequential comic strip multiple-panel story; each page crammed with panels inspired by the Töpffer comic books Bogue began several years earlier.

LORGNETTE, THE (S)
George J Coombes, New York: 1886 (6-1/2x8-3/4, 38 pgs, hard-c, B&W

nn - By J.K. Bangs	50.00	100.00	200.00

LOVING BALLAD OF LORD BATEMAN, THE (E,I)
G.W. Carleton & Co., Publishers, Madison Square, NY: 1871 (9x5-7/8",16 pgs, soft-c, 6¢)

nn - By George Cruikshank	50.00	100.00	200.00

MADISON'S EXPOSITION OF THE AWFUL & TERRIFYING CEREMONIES OF THE ODD FELLOWS
T.E. Peterson & Brothers, 306 Chestnut St, Phila: 1870s? (5-3/4x9-1/4, 68 pgs, B&W)

nn - single panel cartoons	50.00	100.00	200.00

MANNERS AND CUSTOMS OF YE HARVARD STUDENTE (M,S)
Houghton Mifflin & Co., Boston & Moses King, Cambridge: 1877 (7-7/8x11", 72 pgs, printed one side, hardc, B&W)

nn - by F.G. Attwood	75.00	150.00	300.00

NOTE: Collection of cartoons originally serialized in the Harvard Lampoon. Attwood later became a major cartoonist for Life.

MAN WHO WOULD LIKE TO MARRY, THE (O)
Frederick Warne & Co., London & New York: nd (c 1880's) (9-1/2x11-1/2", 28 pgs, printed 1 side, paper-c, B&W)

nn - By Harry Parkes	62.50	125.00	250.00

NOTE: Published simultaneously with its companion volume, The Girl Who Wouldn't Mind Getting Married.

MAX AND MAURICE: A JUVENILE HISTORY IN SEVEN TRICKS (E)
(see also Teasing Tom and Naughty Ned)
Roberts Brothers, Boston: 1871 first edition (8-1/8 x 5-1/2", 76 pgs, hard & soft-c B&W)

nn - By Wilhelm Busch (green or brown cloth hardbound)	275.00	550.00	1000.00
nn - exactly the same, but soft paper cover	162.00	325.00	650.00

NOTE: Page count includes 56 pgs of art, two blank endpapers at the front (one colored), 8 pgs of ads at the back, two blank endpapers at the end (one colored), and the covers. Green or brown illustrated hardcover. The

The Merry Thought, Or Laughter From Year To Year
early 1850s © Fisher & Brother, Phila, Baltimore

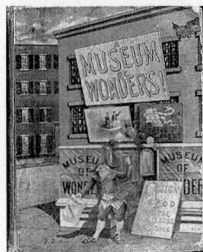

Museum of Wonders by F. Opper
1894 © Routledge & Sons

Nasby's Life Of Andy Jonson
1866 © Jesse Haney Company

name of the author is given on the title page as "William Busch." We assume this to be the 1st edition. Back side of title page states: Entered according to Act of Congress, in the year 1870, by Roberts Brothers, In the office of the Librarian of Congress at Washington.

nn - By Wilhelm Busch (1872 edition)	225.00	470.00	900.00
nn - 1875 reprint	100.00	200.00	450.00
nn - 1882 reprint (76 pgs, hand colored- c/a, 75¢)	100.00	200.00	400.00

NOTE: Each of the above contains 56 pages of art and text in a transitional format between a regular children's book and a comic book (the page count difference is ad pages in back). Seminal inspiration for William Randolph Hearst to acquire as a "new comic" (following the wild success of Outcault's Yellow Kid) to license M&M from Busch and hire Rudolph Dirks in late 1897 to create a New York American newspaper incarnation. In Hearst's English language newspapers it was called The Katzenjammer Kids and in his German language NYC newspaper it was titled Max & Moritz, Busch's original title. At least 50 other reprints versions are reputed to exist printed thru 1900. Translated from the 1865 German original. We are still sorting out the edition confusion.

MAX AND MAURICE: A JUVENILE HISTORY IN SEVEN TRICKS (E)
(see also Teasing Tom and Naughty Ned)
Little, Brown, and Company, Boston: 1898-1902 (8-1/8 x 5-3/4", 72 pgs, hardcover, black ink on orange paper) (various early reprints)

nn - 1898 , 1899 By Wilhelm Busch	50.00	100.00	200.00
nn - 1902 (64 pages, B&W)	10.00	30.00	90.00

MERRY MAPLE LEAVES Or A Summer In The Country (S)
E.P. Dutton And Company, New York: 1872 (9-3/8x7-3/8", 90 and 86 pgs pgs, hard-c)

nn - By Abner Perk	25.00	50.00	150.00

NOTE: Each drawing contained in a maple leaf motif by Livingston Hopkins and others.

MERRYMAN'S MONTHLY A COMIC MAGAZINE FOR THE FAMILY (M,O,E)
J.C. Haney & Co, NY: 1863-1875 (10-7/8x7-13/16", 30 pgs average, B&W)

Certain issues with sequential comics	100.00	200.00	400.00

NOTE: Sequential strips by Frank Bellew Sr, Wilhelm Busch found so far; others?

MERRYTHOUGHT, OR LAUGHTER FROM YEAR TO YEAR, THE
Fisher & Brother, Phila, Baltimore: early 1850s (4-1/2x7", B&W)

nn - many singles, some sequential (Very Rare)		(no known sales)

NOTE: See Vict article for back cover pic which is earliest known use of the term Comic Book

MESSRS. BROWN, JONES, AND ROBINSON, THE FOREIGN TOUR OF
(see also **THE CLOWN, OR THE BANQUET OF WIT**) (E,M,O,G)
Bradbury & Evans, London: 1854 (11-5/8x9-1/2", 196 pgs, gilted hard-c, B&W)

nn - By Richard Doyle	35.00	70.00	200.00
nn - Bradbury & Evans 1900 reprint	20.00	40.00	80.00

NOTE: Protective sheets between each page (not part of page count). Expanded and redrawn sequential comics story from the serialized episodes originally published in PUNCH. Also comes in a 174 pg 8-3/4x11" version.

MESSRS. BROWN, JONES, AND ROBINSON, THE LAUGHABLE ADVENTURES OF (E,M,G)
Garrett, Dick & Fitzgerald, NY: nd (1856 or 1857) (5-3/4x9-1/4", 100 pgs, printed one side only, paper-c, B&W)

nn - (Very Rare) by Richard Doyle c/a	300.00	500.00	1000.00

NOTE: 1st American reprinting of the "Foreign Tour"; reformatted into a small oblong format. Links the earlier Garrett & Co. to the later Dick & Fitzgerald. Back cover reprints full size the Garrett & Co. version cover for Oscar Shanghai. Interior front cover reprints full size the Garrett & Co. version cover for Slyfox-Wikof. Issued without a title page.

MESSRS. BROWN, JONES, AND ROBINSON, THE FOREIGN TOUR OF (E,M,G)
D. Appleton & Co., New York: 1860 & 1877 (11-5/8x9-1/2", 196 pgs, gilted hard-c, B&W)

nn - (1860 printing) by Richard Doyle	30.00	60.00	200.00
nn - (1871 printing) by Richard Doyle	30.00	60.00	150.00
nn - (1877 printing) by Richard Doyle	30.00	60.00	150.00

NOTE: Protective sheets between each page (not part of page count). Reprints the Bradbury & Evans edition.

MESSRS. BROWN JONES AND ROBINSON, THE AMERICAN TOUR OF (O,G)
D. Appleton & Co., New York: 1872 (11-5/8x9-1/2", 158 pgs, printed one side only, B&W, green gilted hard-c)

nn - By Toby	70.00	140.00	400.00

NOTE: Original American graphic novel sequel to Richard Doyle's Foreign Tour of Brown, Jones, and Robinson, with the same characters visiting New York, Canada, and Cuba. Protective sheets between each page (not part of page count).

MESSRS. BROWN, JONES, AND ROBINSON, THE LAUGHABLE ADVEN. OF (E,M,G)
Dick & Fitzgerald, NY: nd (late 1870's - 1888) (5-3/4x9-1/4", 100 pgs, printed one side only, green paper-c, B&W)

nn - (Scarce) by Richard Doyle	100.00	200.00	450.00

NOTE: Reprints the Garrett, Dick & Fitzgerald printing, with the following changes: Takes what had been page 12 in the Garrett, D&F printing (art by M.H. Henry), and makes it a title page, which is numbered page 1. The first story page, "Go to the Races", is numbered 2 (whereas it is numbered 1 in the Garrett, Dick & Fitzgerald version). Numbering stays ahead of the G,D&F edition by 1 page up through page 12, after which the page numbering becomes identical.

MINNEAPOLIS JOURNAL CARTOONS (N,S)
Minneapolis Journal: nn 1894 - No.2 1895 (7-3/4" x 10-7/8", 76 pgs, B&W, paper-c)

nn (1894) (Rare)	25.00	50.00	100.00
Second Series (1895) (Rare)	25.00	50.00	100.00
nn- "War Cartoons" Jan 1899 (9x8", 160 pgs, paperback, punched & string bound) (Scarce)	24.00	96.00	170.00

NOTE: Reprints single panel cartoons from the prior year, by Charles "Bart" L. Bartholomew.

MISCHIEF BOOK, THE (E)
R. Worthington, New York: 1880 (7-1/8 x 10-3/4", 176 pgs, hard-c, B&W)

nn - Green cloth binding; green on brown cover; cover art by R. Lewis based on Busch art by Wilhelm Busch	175.00	350.00	735.00
nn - Blue cloth binding; hand colored cover; completely different cover art based on Busch by Wilhelm Busch	175.00	350.00	735.00

NOTE: Translated by Abby Langdon Alger. American published anthology collection of Wilhelm Busch comic strips. Includes two of the strips found in the British "Bushel of Merry-Thoughts" collection, translated better, and with the dropped panel restored. Unknown which cover version was first.

MISSES BROWN, JONES AND ROBINSON, THE FOREIGN TOUR OF THE (E,O,G)
Bickers & Sons, London: nd (c1850's) (12-1/4" x 9-7/8", 108 pgs, printed on one side), B&W, hard-c)

nn- "by Miss Brown" (Rare)	35.00	70.00	180.00

NOTE: A female take on Doyle's Foreign Tour, by an unknown woman artist, using the pseudonym "Miss Brown."

MISS MILLY MILLEFLEUR'S CAREER (S)
Sheldon & Co., NY: 1869 (10-3/4x9-7/8", 74 pgs, purple hard-c)

nn - Artist unknown (Scarce)	25.00	50.00	150.00

MR PODGER AT COUP'S GREATEST SHOW ON EARTH HIS HAPS AND MISHAPS, THE ADVENTURES OF (O,S)
W.C. Coup, New York: 1884 (5-5/8x4-1/4", 20 pgs, color-c, B&W)

nn - Circus Themes; Similar to Barker's Comic Almanacs	20.00	40.00	80.00

MR. TOODLES' GREAT ELEPHANT HUNT (See Peter Piper in Bengal)
Brother Jonathan, NYC: 1850s (4-1/4x7-7/8", page count presently unknown)

nn - catalog contains comic strip (Very Rare)		(no known sales)

MR. TOODLES' TERRIFIC ELEPHANT HUNT
Dick & Fitzgerald, NYC: 1860s (5-3/4x9-1/4", 32 pgs, paper-c, B&W) (Very Rare)

nn - catalog reprint contains 28 panel comic strip	150.00	300.00	600.00

MRS GRUNDY
Mrs Grundy Publishing Co, NYC: July 8 1865-Sept 30 1865 (weekly)

1-13 Thomas Nast, Hoppin, Stephens,	50.00	100.00	200.00

MUSEUM OF WONDERS, A (O,I)
Routledge & Sons: 1894 (13x10", 64 pgs, color-c, color thru out)

nn - By Frederick Opper	100.00	200.00	450.00

MY FRIEND WRIGGLES, A (Laughter) Moving Panorama, of His Fortunes And Misfortunes, Illustrated With Over 200 Engravings, of Most Comic Catastrophes And Side-Splitting Merriment (O,G)
Stearn & Co, 202 Williams St, NY: 1850s (5-7/8x9-3/4", 100 pgs, B&W)

nn - By S. P. Avery (also the engraver) (Very Rare)	200.00	400.00	800.00

MY SKETCHBOOK (E,S)
Dana Estes & Charles E. Lauriat, Boston; J. Sabins & Sons, New York: circa 1880s (9-3/8x12", brown hard-c)

nn - By George Cruikshank	25.00	50.00	150.00

NOTE: Reprints British editions 1834-36; extensive usage of word balloons.

NASBY'S LIFE OF ANDY JONSON (O, M)
Jesse Haney Co., Publishers No. 119 Nassau St, NY: 1866 (4-1/2x7-1/2, 48 pgs, B&W)

nn - President Andrew Johnson satire	100.00	200.00	450.00

NOTE: Blurb further reads: With a True Pictorial History of His STumping Tour Out West By Petroleum V. Nasby, A Dimmicrat of Thirty Years Standing, And Who Allus Tuk His Licker Straight. Front of book has long sequential comic strip satire on President Andrew Johnson, misspelling his name on the cover on purpose.

NAST'S ILLUSTRATED ALMANAC
Harper & Brothers, Franklin Square, NYC: 1872-1874 (8x5.5", 80 pgs, B&W, 35¢)

nn	60.00	120.00	240.00

NAST'S WEEKLY (O,S)
???: 1892-93 (Quarto Weekly)

all issues scarce	50.00	100.00	200.00\

NATIONAL COMIC ALMANAC
An Association of Gentlemen, Boston: 1838-?? (8.25x4.75", 34 pgs, B&W)

nn	60.00	120.00	240.00

NEW AMERICAN COMIC ALL-IMAKE (ELTON'S BASKET OF COMICAL SCRAPS), THE
Elton, Publisher, New York: 1839 (7-1/2x4-5/8, 24 pgs)

1	100.00	200.00	400.00

NEW BOOK OF NONSENSE, THE: A Contribution To The Great Central Fair In Aid of the Sanitary Commission (O,S)
Ashmead & Evans, No. 724 Chestnut St, Philadelphia: June 1864 (red hard-c)

nn - Artists unknown (Scarce)	50.00	150.00	300.00

NEW YORK ILLUSTRATED NEWS
Frank Leslie, NYC: 10/14/76-June 1884

average issues with comic strips	10.00	20.00	40.00

NEW YORK PICAYUNE (see PHUN FOTOCRAPH)

Nonsense Or, A Treasure Box of Unconsidered Trifles
early 1850s © Fisher & Brother, Phila.

The Adventures of Obadiah Oldbuck 4th printing
mid-1850s © Brother Jonathan Offices, NY

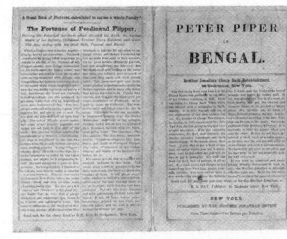

Peter Piper in Bengal Brother Jonathan Catalog
Front & Back Covers interior 32 page comic strip
1855 © B.H. Day, Brother Jonathan Offices

	FR1.0	GD2.0	FN6.0

Woodward & Hutchings: 1850-1855 newspaper-size weekly; 1856-1857 Folio Monthly 16x10.5; 1857-1858 Quarto Weekly; 1858-1860 Quarto Weekly

	FR1.0	GD2.0	FN6.0
Average Issue With Comic Strips	50.00	100.00	200.00
Issues with Full Front Page Comic Strip	100.00	200.00	400.00

NOTE: Many issues contain Frank Bellew sequential comic strips & single panel cartoons. Later issues published by Woodward, Levison & Robert Gun (1853-1857) ; Levison & Thompson (1857-1860)

99 "WOOLFS" FROM TRUTH (see Sketches of Lowly Life in a Great City, Truth)
Truth Company, NY: 1896 (9x5-1/2", 72 pgs, varnished paper-like cloth hard-c, 25 cents)

nn - By Michael Angelo Woolf (Rare)	100.00	200.00	400.00

NOTE: Woolf's cartoons are regarded as a primary influence on R.F. Outcault in the later development of The Yellow Kid newspaper strip. Copy sold in 2002 on eBay for $800.00.

NONSENSE OR, THE TREASURE BOX OF UNCONSIDERED TRIFLES
Fisher & Brother, 12 North Sixth St, Phila, PA, 64 Baltimore St, Baltimore, MD: early 1850s (4-1/2x7", 128 pgs, B&W)

nn - much Davy Crocket sequential story-telling comic strips	250.00	500.00	1000.00

OBADIAH OLDBUCK, THE ADVENTURES OF MR. (E,G)
Tilt & Bogue, London: nd (1840-41) (5-15/16x9-3/16", 176 pgs,B&W, gilted hard-c)

nn - By Rodolphe Töpffer	500.00	900.00	2500.00
nn - Hand coloured edition (Very Rare)			(no known sales)

NOTE: This is the British edition, translating the unauthorized redrawn 1839 edition from Parisian publisher Aubert, adapted from Töpffer's "Les Amours de Mr. Vieux Bois" (aka "Histoire de Mr. Vieux Bois"), originally published in French in Switzerland, in 1837 (2nd ed. 1839). Early 19th century books are often found rebound, with original cover and/or title page gone. To distinguish editions having no cover or title page: the British oblong editions (published by Tilt & Bogue) use Roman Numerals to number pages. American oblong shaped editions use Arabic Numerals. British are printed on one side only. This is the earliest known English language sequential comic book. Has a new title page with art by Robert Cruikshank.

OBADIAH OLDBUCK, THE ADVENTURES OF MR. (E,G)
Wilson and Company, New York: September 14, 1842 (11-3/4x9", 44 pgs, B&W, yellow paper-c on bookstand editions, hemp paper interior)

Brother Jonathan Extra No. IX - Rare bookstand edition	2200.00	4400.00	8800.00
Brother Jonathan Extra No. IX Very Rare subscriber/mailorder edition	2200.00	4400.00	8800.00

NOTE: By Rodolphe Töpffer. Earliest known sequential American comic book, reprinting the 1841 British edition. Pages are numbered with Roman numerals. States "BROTHER JONATHAN EXTRA - ADVENTURES OF MR. OBADIAH OLDBUCK." at the top of each page. Prints 2 to 3 tiers of panels on both sides of each page. Copies could be had for ten cents according to adverts in Brother Jonathan. By Rodolphe Töpffer with cover masthead design by David Claypool Johnston, and cover art beneath the masthead reprinting Robert Cruikshank's title page art taken from the Tilt & Bogue edition. A special, additional cover was added for copies sold on stands (it was not issued with mail order or subscriber copies). Only 1 known copy possesses (partially) this very thin outer yellow cover. A decent (subscriber) copy sold on eBay in October 2002 for over $3500.00. In 2005, a FR copy sold for $10,000; a G/VG for $20,000; and a VG for $20,000. A copy GVG sold in auction in 2007 for $9500. (Prices vary widely.)

OBADIAH OLDBUCK, THE ADVENTURES OF MR. (E,G)
Wilson & Co, New York: nd (1849) (5-11/16x8-3/8", 84 pgs, B&W,paper-c)

nn - by Rodolphe Töpffer; title page by Robert Cruikshank (Very Rare)			
	500.00	1200.00	4000.00

NOTE: 2nd Wilson & Co printing, reformatted into a small oblong format, with nine panels edited out, and text modified to smooth out this removal. Results in four less printed tiers/strips. Pages are numbered via Arabic numerals. Every panel on Pages 11, 14, 19, 21, 24, 34, 35 has one line of text. Reformatted to conform with British first edition.

OBADIAH OLDBUCK, THE ADVENTURES OF MR. (E,G)
Wilson & Co, 162 Nassau, NY: nd (early-1850s) (5-11/16x8-3/8", 84 pgs, B&W, yellow-c)

nn - 3rd Printing by Rodolphe Töpffer; title page by Robert Cruikshank (Very Rare)			
Says By Timothy Crayon, an obvious pseudonym	500.00	1200.00	4000.00

NOTE: Front cover banner the giant is holding says "Done With Drawings By Timothy Crayon, Gypsographer, 188 Comic Etchings On Antimony" Title page changes address to No. 15 Spruce-Street. (Late 162 Nassau Street.)

OBADIAH OLDBUCK, THE ADVENTURES OF MR..
Brother Jonathan Offices: ND (mid-1850s) (5-11/16x8-3/8", 84 pages, B&W, oblong)

nn - 4th printing; Originally by Rodolphe Töpffer (Very Rare)	500.00	1200.00	4000.00

NOTE: Cover States: "New York: Published at the Brother Jonathan Office". Front cover banner the giant is holding says "Done With Drawings By Timothy Crayon, Gypsographer, 188 Comic Designs On Antimony."

OBADIAH OLDBUCK, THE ADVENTURES OF MR. (E,G)
Dick & Fitzgerald, New York: nd (various printings; est. 1870s to 1888) (Thirty Cents, 84 pgs, B&W, paper-c) (all versions scarce)

nn - Black print on green cover (5-11/16x8-15/16"); string bound	200.00	400.00	800.00
nn - Black print on blue cover; same format as green-c	200.00	400.00	800.00
nn - Black print on white cover (5-13/16x9-3/16"); staple bound beneath cover)			
this is a later printing than the blue or green-c	200.00	400.00	800.00

NOTE: Reprints the abbreviated 1849 Wilson & Co. 2nd printing. Pages are numbered with Arabic numerals. Many of the panels on Pages 11, 14, 19, 21, 24, 34, 35 take two lines to print the same words found in the Wilson & Co version, which used only one text line for the same panels. Unknown whether the blue or green cover is earlier. White version has "thirty cents" line blackened out on the two copies known to exist. Robert Cruikshank's title page have been made the cover in the D&F editions.

OLD FOGY'S COMIC ALMANAC
Philip J. Cozans, NY: 1858 (4-7/8x7-1/4, 48 pgs)

nn - sequential comic strip told one panel per page	50.00	100.00	200.00

NOTE: Contains (12) called "Fourth of July in New York" sequential

OLD MOTHER MITTEN AND HER FUNNY KITTEN (see also The Juvenile Gem) (O)
Huestis & Cozans: nd(1850-1852) (6x3-7/8"12pgs, hand colored paper-c, B&W)

---

nn - first printing(s) publisher's address is 104 Nassau Street (1850-1851)			
(Very Rare)			(no known sales)

NOTE: A hand colored outer cover is highly rare, with only 1 recorded copy possessing it. Front cover image and text is repeated precisely on page 3 (albeit b&w), and only interior pages are numbered, together leading owners of coverless copies to believe they have the cover. The true back cover has ads for the publisher. Cover was issued only with copies which were sold separately - books which were bound together as part of THE JUVENILE GEM never had such covers.

OLD MOTHER MITTEN AND HER FUNNY KITTEN (see JUVENILE GEM) (O)
Philip J. Cozans: nd (1850-1852) (6x3-7/8",12 pgs, hand colored paper-c, B&W)

nn - Second printing(s) publisher's address is 116 Nassau Street (1851-1852)			
(Very Rare)			(no known sales)
nn - Third printing(s) publisher's address is 107 Nassau Street (1852+)			
(Very Rare)			(no known sales)

OLD MOTHER MITTEN AND HER FUNNY KITTEN
Americana Review, Scotia, NY: nd (1960's) (6-1/4x4-1/8", 8 pgs, side-stapled, cardboard, B&W)

nn - Modern reprint	2.50	5.00	10.00

NOTE: Issued within a folder titled SIX CHILDREN'S BOOKS OF THE 1850'S. States "Reprinted by American Review" at bottom of front cover. Reprints the 104 Nassau Street address.

ON THE NILE (O,G)
James R. Osgood & Co., Boston: 1874 ; **Houghton, Osgood & Co., Boston:** 1880 (112 pgs, gilted green hardcover, B&W)

1st printing (1874; 10-3/4x16") - by Augustus Hoppin	45.00	90.00	180.00
2nd printing (1880; smaller sized)	32.50	65.00	130.00

OSCAR SHANGHAI, THE EXTRAORDINARY AND MIRTH-PROVKING ADVENTURES BY SEA & LAND OF (O, G)
Garrett & Co., Publishers, No. 18 Ann Street, New York: May 1855 (5-3/4x9-1/4", 100 pgs, printed one side only, paper-c, 25¢, B&W)

nn - Samuel Avery-c; interior by ALC Very Rare)	450.00	900.00	1800.00

NOTE: Not much is known of this first edition as the data comes from a recently rediscovered Brother Jonathan catalog issued circa 1853-55. No original known yet to exist.

OSCAR SHANGHAI, THE WONDERFUL AND AMUSING DOINGS BY SEA AND LAND OF (G)
Dick & Fitzgerald, 10 Ann St, NY: nd (1870s-1888) (25 ¢, 5-3/4x9-1/4", 100 pgs, printed one side only, green paper-c, B&W)

nn - Cover by Samuel Avery; interior by ALC (Rare)	200.00	300.00	700.00

NOTE: Exact reprint of Garrett & Co original.

OUR ARTIST IN CUBA (O)
Carleton, New York: 1865 (6-5/8x4-3/8", 120 pgs, printed one side only, gilted hard-c, B&W)

nn - By Geo. W. Carleton	37.50	75.00	150.00

OUR ARTIST IN CUBA, PERU, SPAIN, AND ALGIERS (O)
Carleton: 1877 (6-1/2x5-1/8", 156 pgs, hard-c, B&W)

nn - By Geo. W. Carleton	50.00	100.00	200.00
nn - By Geo. W. Carleton (wraps paper cover) (Rare)	45.00	90.00	180.00

NOTE: Reprints OUR ARTIST IN CUBA and OUR ARTIST IN PERU, then adds new section on Spain and Algiers.

OUR ARTIST IN PERU (O)
Carleton, New York: 1866 (7-3/4x5-7/8", 68 pgs, gilted hardcover, B&W)

nn - By Geo. W. Carleton	37.50	75.00	150.00

NOTE: Contains advertisement for the upcoming books OUR ARTIST IN ITALY and OUR ARTIST IN FRANCE, but no such publications have been found to date.

PARSON SOURBALL'S EUROPEAN TOUR (O)
Duff and Ashmead: 1867 (6x7-1/2", 76 pgs, blue embossed title hard-c)

nn - By Horace Hope	45.00	60.00	180.00

PEN AND INK SKETCHES OF YALE NOTABLES (O,S)
Soule, Thomas and Winsor, St. Louis: 1872 (12-1/4x9-3/4", B&W)

By Squills	25.00	50.00	100.00

NOTE: Printed by Steamlith Press, The R.P. Studley Company, St Louis.

PETER PIPER IN BENGAL
Bengamin H Day.Publisher, Brother Jonathan Cheap Book Establishment, 48 Beekman, NY: 1953-55 (6-5/8x4-1/4, 36 pgs, yellow paper-c, B&W, 3 cents - two dollars per hundred) (Very Rare)

nn - By John Tenniel - 32 panel comic strip Punch-r	500.00	1000.00	2000.00

NOTE: Actually aka a catalogue of inexpensive books, prints, maps and half a dozen comic books for sale on separate pages from publishers Day and Garrett - see full story of this brand new find in the Victorian Era essay. A coverless copy with spine sold in November 2002 for $750.00. Published date most likely 1855.

THE PHILADELPHIA COMIC ALMANAC (S)
G. Strong, 44 Strawberry St, NYC: 1835 (8-1/2x5", 36 pgs)

nn -	100.00	200.00	600.00

NOTE: 77 engravings full of recurring cartoon characters but not sequential; early use of recurring characters.

PHIL MAY'S SKETCH BOOK (E,S,M)
R.H. Russell, New York: 1899 (14-5/8x10", 64 pgs, brown hard-c, B&W)

nn - By Phil May	32.50	65.00	130.00

NOTE: American reprint of the British edition.

PHUNNY PHELLOW, THE

Phun Fotocraft, Kewreus Konsweets Komically Illustrated By A Kweer Feller
1850s © The New York Picayune

Pictorial History of Senator Slim's Voyage To Europe
1860 © Dr. Herrick & Brother, Albany, NY

Puck #1
1877 © Keppler & Schwarzman, NY

	FR1.0	GD2.0	FN6.0

Oakie, Dayton & Jones: Oct 1859-1876; **Street & Smith** 1876: (Folio Monthly)

average issue with Thomas Nast	50.00	100.00	200.00

PHUN FOTOCRAFT, KEWREUS KONSEETS KOMICALLY ILLUSTRATED BY A KWEER FELLER (N) (see **NEW YORK PICAYUNE**)
The New York Picayune, NY: 1850s (104 pgs)

nn - Mostly Frank Bellew, some John Leach	250.00	500.00	1000.00

NOTE: Many sequential comic strips as well as single cartoons all collected from The New York Picayune. Ross & Tousey, Agents, 121 Nassau St, NY. The Picayune ran many sequential comic strips in this decade.

PICTORIAL HISTORY OF SENATOR SLIM'S VOYAGE TO EUROPE
Dr. Herrick & Brother, Chemists, Albany, NY: 1860 (3-1/4x4-3/4", 32 pgs, B&W)

nn - By John McLenan	50.00	100.00	200.00

PICTURES OF ENGLISH SOCIETY (Parchment-Paper Series, No.4) (M,S,E)
D. Appleton & Co., New York: 1884 (5-5/8x4-3/8", 108 pgs, paper-c, B&W)

4 - By George du Maurier; Punch-r	15.00	30.00	60.00

NOTE: Every other page is a full page cartoon, with the opposite page containing the cartoon's caption.

PICTURES OF LIFE AND CHARACTER (M,S,E)
Bradbury and Evans, London: No.1 1855 - No.5 c1864 (12-1/2x18", 100 pgs, illustrated hard-c, B&W)

nn (No.1) (1855)	32.50	65.00	130.00
2 (1858), 3 (1860)	32.50	65.00	130.00
4 (nd; c1862) 5 (nd; c1864)	32.50	65.00	130.00
nn (nd (late 1860's)	32.50	65.00	130.00

NOTE: 2-1/2x18-1/4", 494 pgs, green gilted-c) reprints 1-5 in one book

1-3 John Leech's... (nd; 12-3/8x10", ? pgs, red gilted-c).	25.00	50.00	100.00

NOTE: Reprints John Leech cartoons from Punch. note that the Volume Number is mentioned only on the last page of these versions.

PICTURES OF LIFE AND CHARACTER (E,M,S)
G.P. Putnam's Sons: 1880's (8-5/8x6-1/4", 218 pgs, hardcover, color-cr, B&W)

nn - John Leech (single panel Punch cartoon-r)	20.00	40.00	160.00

NOTE: Leech reprints which extend back to the 1850s.

PICTURES OF LIFE AND CHARACTER (Parchment-Paper Series) (E,M,S)
(see also Humerous Masterpieces)
D. Appleton & Co., NY: 1884 (30¢, 5-3/4 x 4-1/2", 104 pgs, paper-c, B&W)

nn - John Leech (single panel Punch cartoon-r)	20.00	40.00	160.00

NOTE: An advertisement in the back refers to a cloth-bound edition for 50 cents.

PIPPIN AMONG THE WIDE-AWAKES (O,S)
Werill & Chapin, 113 Nassau St, NYC, NY): 1860 (6x4-1/2", 36 pgs, 6 cents)

nn - Artist unknown (Very Rare)	100.00	200.00	400.00

PLISH AND PLUM (E,G)
Roberts Brothers, Boston: 1883 (8-1/8x5-3/4", 80 pgs, hardcover, B&W)

nn - By Wilhelm Busch	40.00	80.00	200.00
nn - Reprint (Roberts Brothers, 1895)	40.00	80.00	200.00
nn - Reprint (Little, Brown & Co., 1899)	40.00	80.00	200.00

NOTE: The adventures of two dogs.

POUNDS OF FUN
Frank Tousey, 34 North Moore St, NY: 1881 (6-1/2x9-1/2", 68pgs, B&W)

nn - Bellew, Worth, Woolf, Chips	40.00	80.00	200.00

PRESIDENTS MESSAGE, THE
G.P. Putnam's Sons, NY: 1887 (5-3/4x7-5/8, 44 pgs)

nn - (19) Thomas Nast single panel full page cartoons	40.00	80.00	200.00

PROGRESS OF MR. LAMBKIN, (GENT) (E,G) (see also Bachelor's Own Book)
David Bryce and Son, Glasgow: 1884 (1 shilling, 7-7/8x5-3/4", 60 pgs, printed one side only, cardboard cover, B&W)

nn	17.50	35.00	70.00

NOTE: Reprint of George Cruikshank's Bachelor's Own Book.

PUCK (German language edition, St. Louis) (M,O) (see also Die Vehme)
Publisher unknown, St. Louis: No.1, March 18, 1871 - No. ??, Aug. 24, 1872 (B&W, paper-c)

1-?? (Very Rare) by Joseph Keppler		(no known sales)	

NOTE: Joseph Keppler's second attempt at a weekly humor periodical, following **Die Vehme** one year earlier. This was his first attempt to launch using the title **Puck**. This German language version ran for a full year before being joined by an English language version.

PUCK (English language edition, St. Louis) (M,O)
Publisher unknown, St. Louis: No.1, March ?? 1872 - No. ??, Aug. 24, 1872 (B&W, paper c)

1-?? (Very Rare) by Joseph Keppler		(no known sales)	

NOTE: Same material as in the German language edition, but in English.

PUCK, ILLUSTRIRTES HUMORISTISCHES WOCHENBLATT (German language edition, NYC) (M,O)
Keppler & Schwarzmann, New York: No.1 Sept (27) 1876 - 1164 Dec ?? 1899 (10 cents, color front/back-c and centerspread, remainder B&W, paper-c)

1-26 (Volume 1; Rare) by Joseph Keppler - these issues precede the English language version, and contain cartoons not found in them. Includes cartoons on the controversial			

Tilden-Hayes 1876 Presidential Election debacle. (no known sales)

27-52 (Volume 2; Rare) by Joseph Keppler - contains some cartoon material not found in the English language editions. Particularly in the earlier issues.		(no known sales)	
53-1164	7.50	15.00	30.00

Bound Volumes (six month, 26 issue run each):

Vol. 1 (Rare)		(no known sales)	
Vol. 2-4 (Rare)		(no known sales)	
Vol. 5-47	62.50	125.00	250.00

NOTE: Joseph Keppler's second, and successful, attempt to launch **Puck**. In German. The first six months precede the launch of the English language edition. Soon after (but not immediately after) the launch of the English edition, both editions began sharing the same cartoons, but, their prose material always remained different. The German language edition ceased publication at the end of 1899, while the English language edition continued into the early 20th Century. First American periodical to feature printed color every issue.

PUCK (English language edition, NYC) (M,O)
Keppler & Schwarzmann, New York: No.1 March (14) 1877 - 1190 Dec ?? 1899 (10 cents, color front/back-c and centerspread, remainder B&W, paper-c)

1 (Rare) by Joseph Keppler		(no known sales)	
2-26 (Rare) by Joseph Keppler		(no known sales)	
27-1190	12.50	25.00	50.00

(see Platinum Age section for year 1900+ issues)
Bound volumes (six month, 26 issue run each):

Vol. 1 (Rare)		(one set sold on eBay for $2300.00)	
Vol. 2 (Scarce)		(one set sold on eBay for $1500.00)	
Vol. 3-6 (pre-1880 issues)	175.00	375.00	750.00
Vol. 7-46	140.00	300.00	600.00

NOTE: The English language editions began six months after the German editions, and so the English edition numbering is always one volume number, and 26 issue numbers, behind its parallel German language edition. Pre-1880 & post-1900 issues are more scarce than 1880's & 1890's.

PUCK (miniature) (M,P,I)
Keppler & Schwarzmann, New York: nd (c1895) (7x5-1/8", 12 pgs, color front & back paper-c, B&W interior)

nn - Scarce	25.00	50.00	110.00

NOTE: C.J.Taylor-a; F.M.Howarth-a; F.Opper-a; giveaway item promoting **Puck's** various publications. Mostly text, with art reprinted from **Puck.**

PUCK, CARTOONS FROM (M,S)
Keppler & Schwarzmann, New York: 1893 (14-1/4x11-1/2", 244 pgs, hard-c, mostly B&W)

nn - by Joseph Keppler (S/N)	25.00	50.00	100.00

NOTE: Reprints Keppler cartoons from 1877 to 1893, mostly in B&W, though a few in color, with a text opposite each cartoon explaining the situation then being satirized. Issued only in an edition of 300 numbered issues, signed by Keppler. Only 1/4 of the pages are cartoons.

PUCK'S LIBRARY (M)
Keppler & Schwarzmann, New York: No.1, July, 1887 - No. 174, Dec, 1899 (10 cents, 11-1/2x8-1/4", 36 pgs, color paper-c, B&W)

1- "The National Game" (Baseball)	50.00	100.00	200.00
2-149	7.50	15.00	30.00

NOTE: **Puck's Library** was a monthly magazine reprinting cartoons & prose from **Puck**, with each issue's material organized around the same subject. The cover art was often original. All issues were kept in print for the duration of the series, so later issues are more scarce than earlier ones.

PUCK, PICKINGS FROM (M)
Keppler & Schwarzmann, New York: No.1, Sept, 1891 - No. 34, Dec, 1899 (25 cents, 13-1/4x10-1/4", 68 pgs, color paper-c, B&W)

1-34	15.00	30.00	60.00

NOTE: Similar to **Puck's** Library, except larger in size, and issued quarterly. All reprint material, except for the cover art. There also exist variations with "RAILROAD EDITION 30 CENTS" printed on the cover in place of the standard 25 cent price.

PUCK'S OPPER BOOK (M)
Keppler & Schwarzmann, New York: 1888 (11-3/4x13-7/8", color paper-c, 68 pgs,interior B&W, 30¢)

nn - (Very Rare) by F. Opper	225.00	450.00	750.00

NOTE: **Puck's** first book collecting work by a single artist.; mostly sequential comic strips.

PUCK'S PRINTING BOOK FOR CHILDREN (S,O,I)
Keppler & Schwarzmann, Pubs, NY: 1891 (10-3/8x7-7/8", 52 pgs, color-c, B&W and color)

nn - Frederick B Opper (Very Rare)	-	-	-

NOTE: Left side printed in color; Right side B&W to be colored in.

PUCK PROOFS (M,P,S)
Keppler & Schwarzmann, New York: nd (1906-1909) (74 pgs, paper cover; B&W)
(all are Scarce)

nn - (c.1906, no price, 4-1/8x5-1/4") B&W painted -c of couple kissing over a chess board; 1905 & 1906-r	25.00	50.00	100.00
nn- (c.1909, 10 cents, 4-3/8x5-3/8") plain green paper-c; 76 pgs 1905-1909-r	25.00	50.00	100.00

NOTE: Catalog of prints available from **Puck,** reprinting mostly cover & centerspread art from **Puck.** There likely exist more as yet unreported **Puck** Proofs catalogs. Art by Rose O'Neill.

PUCK, THE TARIFF ?, CARTOONS AND COMMENTS FROM (M,S)
Keppler & Schwarzmann, New York: 1888 (10 cents, 6-7/8x10-3/8", 36 pgs, paper-c, B&W)

nn - (Scarce)	25.00	50.00	100.00

NOTE: Reprints both cartoons and commentary from **Puck,** concerning the issue of tariffs which were then being debated in Congress. Art by Gillam, Keppler, Opper, Taylor.

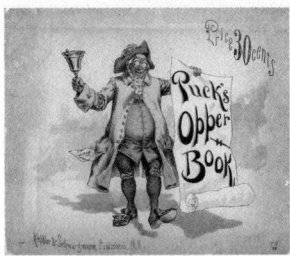

Puck's Opper Book
1888 © Keppler & Schwarzman

Sam Slick's Comic Almanac
1857 © Philip J Cozans, Publisher, NYC

Shakespeare Would Ride A Bicycle If Alive Today
1896 © Cleveland Bicycles, Toledo, OH.

	FR1.0	GD2.0	FN6.0

PUCK, WORLD'S FAIR
Keppler & Schwarzmann, PUCK BUILDING, World's Fair Grounds, Chicago: No.1 May 1, 1893 - No.26 Oct 30, 1893 (10 cents, 11-1/4x8-3/4, 14 pgs, paper-c, color front/back/center pages, rest B&W)(All issues Scarce to Rare)

	FR	GD	FN
1-26	30.00	60.00	130.00
1-26 bound volume:	500.00	1100.00	2200.00

NOTE: Art by Joseph Keppler, F. Opper, F.M. Howarth, C.J. Taylor, W.A. Rogers. This was a separate, parallel run of **Puck**, published during the 1893 Chicago World's Fair from within the fairgrounds, and containing all new and different material than the regular weekly **Puck**. Smaller sized and priced the same, this originally sold poorly, and had not as wide distribution as **Puck**, and so consequently issues are much more rare than regular **Puck** issues from the same period. Not to be confused with the larger sized regular **Puck** issues from 1893 which sometimes also contained World's Fair related material, and sometimes had the words "World's Fair" appear on the cover. Can also be distinguished by the fact that **Puck's** issue numbering was in the 800's in 1893, while these issue number 1 through 26.

PUNCHINELLO
Punchinello Publishing Co, NYC: April 2-Dec 24 1870 (weekly)

1-39 Henry L. Stephens, Frank Bellew, Bowlend	12.50	25.00	50.00

NOTE: Funded by the Tweed Ring, mild politics attacking Grant Admin & other NYC newspapers. Bound copies exist.

QUIDDITIES OF AN ALASKAN TRIP (O,G)
G.A. Steel & Co., Portland, OR: 1873 (6-3/4x10-1/2", 80 pgs, gilted hard-c, Red-c and Blue-c exist, B&W)

nn - By William H. Bell (Scarce)	350.00	750.00	1500.00

NOTE: Highly sought Western Americana collectors. Parody of a trip from Washington DC to Alaska, by a member of the team which went to survey Alaska, purchase commonly known than as "Seward's Folly".

"RAG TAGS" AND THEIR ADVENTURES, THE (N,S)
A. M. Robertson, San Francisco: 1899 (10-1/4x13-7/8, 84 pgs, color hard-c, B&W inside)

nn - By Arthur M. Lewis (SF Chronicle newspaper-r) (Scarce)	60.00	120.00	240.00

RAYS OF LIGHT (O,P)
Morse Bros., Canton, Mass.: No.1 1886 (7-1/8x5-1/8", 8 pgs, color paper-c, B&W)

1- (Rare)	50.00	100.00	200.00

NOTE: Giveaway pamphlet in guise of an educational publication, consisting entirely of a sequential story in which a teacher instructs her classroom of young girls in the use of Rising Sun Stove Polish. Color front & back covers.

RELIC OF THE ITALIAN REVOLUTION OF 1849, A
Gabici's Music Stores, New Orleans: 1849 (10-1/8x12-3/4", 144 pgs, hardcover)

nn - By G. Daelli (Scarce)	100.00	200.00	400.00

NOTE: From the title page: "Album of fifty line engravings, executed on copper, by the most eminent artists at Rome in 1849; secreted from the papal police after the 'Restoration of Order,' And just imported into America."

REMARKS ON THE JACOBINIAD (I,S)
E.W. Weld & W. Greenough, Boston: 1795-98 (8-1/4x5-1/8", 72 pgs, a number of B&W plates with text)

nn - Written by Rev. James Sylvester Gardner,artist unknown (Rare) (no known sales)			

NOTE: Early comics-type characters. Not sequential comics, but uses word balloons. Satire directed against "The Jacobin Club," supporters of the French Revolution and Radical Republicans. Gardner came to America from England in 1783, was minister of Trinity Church, Boston. There appears to be some reprints of this done as late as 1798.

REV. MR. SOURBALL'S EUROPEAN TOUR, THE RECREATION OF A CITY, THE
Duffield Ashmead, Philadelphia: 1867 (7-5/8x6-1/4", 72 pgs, turquoise blue soft wrappers)

By Horace Cope (Rare)	35.00	70.00	140.00
nn - Hard Cover version also exist	35.00	70.00	140.00

RHYMES OF NONSENSE TRUTH & FICTION (S)
G.W. Carleton & Co, Publishers, NY: 1874 (10x7-3/4", 44 pgs, hard-c, B&W) (Very Rare)

nn - By Chaucer Jones and Michael Angelo Raphael Smith	25.00	50.00	100.00

NOTE: Creator names obviously pseudonyms; looks like weak A.B. Frost.

ROMANCE OF A HAMMOCK, THE - AS RECITED BY MR. GUS WILLIAMS IN "ONE OF THE FINEST" (O,P)
Unknown: 1880s (5-1/2x3-5/8" folded, 7 attached cardboard cards which fold out into a strip, color)

nn - By presently unknown	25.00	50.00	100.00

NOTE: 12-panel story, which one begins reading on one side of the folded-out strip, then flip to the other side to continue -- unlike the vast majority of folded strips, which are printed on only one side. This was a promotional handout, for a play titled "One of the Finest". The story pictured comes from a poem read in the play by then famous New York stage actor Gus Williams, who is pictured on the "cover"/title card."

SAD TALE OF THE COURTSHIP OF CHEVALIER SLYFOX-WIKOF, SHOWING HIS HEART-RENDING ASTOUNDING & MOST RENDING LOVE ADVENTURES WITH FANNY ELSSLER AND MISS GAMBOL, THE (O,G)
Garrett & Co., NY: Jan 1856 (25 ¢, 5-3/4x9-1/4", 100 pages, paper-c, B&W)

nn - By T.C. Bond ?? (Very Rare)	200.00	400.00	800.00

NOTE: No surviving copies yet reported -- known via ads in Home Circle published by Garrett. Cover art by John McLenan and Samuel Avery. Graphic novel parodying the real-life romance between European actress/dancer Fanny Elssler and American aristocrat Henry Wikoff. The entire graphic novel is reprinted in the 1976 book "Fanny Elssler in America."

SAD TALE OF THE COURTSHIP OF CHEVALIER SLYFOX-WIKOF, SHOWING HIS HEART-RENDING ASTOUNDING & MOST RENDING LOVE ADVENTURES WITH FANNY ELSSLER AND MISS GUMBEL, THE (G) (25 cents printed on cover)
Dick And Fitzgerald, NY: 1870s-1888 (5-3/4x9-1/4", ??? pages, soft paper-c, B&W)

	FR1.0	GD2.0	FN6.0
nn - By T.C. Bond ?? (Very Rare)	100.00	200.00	500.00

NOTE: Reprint of Garrett original printing before G,D&F partnership begins.

SALT RIVER GUIDE FOR DISAPPOINTED POLITICIANS
Winchell, Small & Co., 113 Fulton St, NY: 1870s (16 pgs, 10¢)

nn - single panel cartoons from Wild Oats	50.00	100.00	200.00

SAM SLICK'S COMIC ALMANAC
Philip J. Cozans, NYC: 1857 (7.5x4.5, 48 pgs, B&W)

	100.00	200.00	400.00

NOTE: Contains reprint of "Moses Keyser the Bowery Bully's Trip to the California Gold Mines" from Elton's Comic Almanac #17 1850.

SCRAPS (O,S) (see also F****** A*** K*****)
D.C. Johnston, Boston: 1828 - No.8 1840; New Series No.1 1849 (12 pgs, printed one side only, paper-c, B&W)

1 - 1828 (9-1/4 x 11-3/4") (Very Rare)			(no known sales)
2 - 1830 (9-3/4 x 12-3/4") (Very Rare)			(no known sales)
3 - 1832 (10-7/8 x 13-1/8") (Very Rare)			(no known sales)
4 - 1833 (11 x 13-5/8") (Very Rare)			(no known sales)
5- 1834 (10-3/8 x 13-3/8") (Very Rare)			(no known sales)
6 - 1835 (10-3/8 x 13-1/4") red lettering in title SCRAPS (Very Rare)	250.00	500.00	1000.00
6 - 1835 (10-3/8 x 13-1/4") no red lettering in title (Scarce)	200.00	400.00	880.00
7 - 1837 (10-3/4 x 13-7/8") 1st Edition (Very Rare)	200.00	400.00	880.00
7 - 1837 (10-3/4 x 13-3/4") 2nd Edition (so stated)	100.00	175.00	375.00

NOTE: 20 pgs. of text (double-sided), 4 pgs. of art (single-sided), plus the covers. There are no protective sheets between the art pages.

8 - 1840 (10-1/2 x 13-7/8") (Rare)	200.00	400.00	880.00
New Series 1- 1849 (10-7/8 x 13-3/4")	125.00	250.00	475.00

NOTE: By David Claypoole Johnston. All issues consist of four one-sided sheets with 9 to 12 single panel cartoons per sheet. The other pages are blank or text. With #1-5 the size of the pages can vary up to an inch. Contains 4 protective sheets (not part of page count) Only 1 3 4 and the 1849 New Series Number 1 has cover art along with 4 art pgs. (single sided) with 4 protective sheets and no text pages.New Series Number 1, as well as #6 with to red lettering and the second printing of issue 7, have survived in higher numbers due to a 1940s warehouse discovery.

THE SETTLEMENT OF RHODE ISLAND (O)
The Graphic Co. Photo-Lith 39 & 41, Park Place, New York: 1874 (11-3/8x10, 40 pgs, gilted blue hard-c)

nn - Charles T. Miller & Walter F. Brown	50.00	100.00	250.00

NOTE: This is also the Same Walter F. Brown that did "Hail Columbia".

SHAKESPEARE WOULD RIDE THE BICYCLE IF ALIVE TODAY. "THE REASON WHY" (O,P,S)
Cleveland Bicycles H.A. Lozier & Co., Toledo, OH: 1896 (5-1/2x4",16 pgs, paper-c, color)

nn - By F. Opper (Rare)	70.00	140.00	300.00

NOTE: Original cartoons of Shakespearian characters riding bicycles; also popular amongst collectors of bicycle ephemera.

SHAKINGS - ETCHINGS FROM THE NAVAL ACADEMY BY A MEMBER OF THE CLASS OF '67 (O,S)
Lee & Shepard, Boston: 1867 (7-7/8x10", 132 pages, blue hard-c)

By: Park Benjamin	38.00	75.00	150.00

NOTE: Park Benjamin later became editor of Harper's Bazaar magazine.

SHOO FLY PICTORIAL (S)
John Stetson, Chestnut sT Theatre, Phila, PA: June 1870 (15-1/2x11-1/2", 8 pgs, B&W)

1	67.50	125.00	250.00

SHYS AT SHAKSPEARE
J.P. and T.C.P., Philadelphia: 1869 (9-1/4x6", 52 pgs)

nn - Artist unknown	35.00	70.00	140.00

SKETCHES OF LOWLY LIFE IN A GREAT CITY (M,S) (See 99 "Woolfs" From Truth)
G. P. Puntam's Sons: 1899 (8-5/8x11-1/4", 200 pgs, hard-c, B&W)
(reprints from Life and Judge of Woolf's cartoons of NYC slum children)

nn - By Michael Angelo Woolf	75.00	150.00	350.00

NOTE: Woolf's cartoons are regarded as a primary influence on R.F. Outcault in the later development of The Yellow Kid newspaper strip.

SLOVENLY PETER; or, Cheerful Stories and Funny Pictures, For Good Little People. (E,I)
Porter & Coates, Philadelphia: 1880 (4to, 100 pgs, handcolored hard-c)

nn - By Heinrich Hoffman	50.00	100.00	400.00

NOTE: The John C. Winston Co. did a number of reprints from at least 1901-1940 which range in price from $95 to $350 plus The Limited Editions Club, New York, published 1500 copies of a Samuel ("Mark Twain") Clemons translated version done in 1891 but in Berlin but not printed until 1935, ranges in price from $285 to $450.

SNAP (O,S)
Valentine & Townsend, Tribune Bldg, NYC: March 13,1885 (17x11, 8 pgs, B&W)

1-Contains a sequential comic strip	50.00	100.00	150.00

SOCIETY PICTURES (M,S,E)
Charles H. Sergel Company, Chicago: 1895 (5-1/4x7-3/4", 168 pgs, printed 1 side, paper-c, B&W)

nn - By George du Maurier; reprints from **Punch**.	12.50	25.00	50.00

Stumping It
1876 © Collin & Lee, NY

Texas Siftings v6 #2 May 15
1886 ©Texas Siftings Publishing Co.

The Adventures Of Mr. Tom Plump
1851 © Huestis & Cozans, NY

	FR1.0	GD2.0	FN6.0

SOLDIERS AND SAILORS HALF DIME TALES OF THE LATE REBELLION
Soldiers & Sailors Publishing Co: 1868 (5-1/4x7-7/8", 32 pgs)

	FR1.0	GD2.0	FN6.0
v1#1-#16 v2#1-#10	10.00	20.00	40.00
v2 #11 contains (5) page comic strip	20.00	40.00	80.00

NOTE: Changes to Soldiers & Sailors Half Dime Magazine with v2 #1.

SOUVENIR CONTAINING CARTOONS ISSUED BY THE PRESS BUREAU OF THE OHIO STATE REPUBLICAN EXECUTIVE COMMITTEE, A (S)
Ohio State Republican Executive Committee, Columbus, OH: 1899 (10-3/8x13-1/2, 248 pgs, Hard-c, B&W)

nn - By William L. Bloomer (Scarce)	50.00	100.00	200.00

SOUVENIR OF SOHMER CARTOONS FROM PUCK, JUDGE, AND FRANK LESLIE'S (M,S,P)
Sohmer Piano Co.: nd(c.1893) (6x4-3/4", 16 pgs, paper-c, B&W)

nn	20.00	40.00	80.00

NOTE: Reprints painted "cartoon" Sohmer Piano advertisements which appeared in the above publications. Artists include Keppler, Gillam, others.

SPORTING NEW YORKER, THE
Ornum & Co, Beekman ST, NYC: 1870s

issues with sequential comic strips (Rare)	50.00	100.00	200.00

STORY OF THE MAN OF HUMANITY AND THE BULL CALF, THE
(see Bull Calf, The Story of The Man Of Humanity And The)
NOTE: Reprints of two of A. B. Frost's mostfamous sequential comic strips.

STREET & SMITH'S LITERARY ALBUM
Street & Smith, NY: #1 Dec 23 1865-#225 Apr 9 1870 (11-3/4x16-3/4", 16 pgs, B&W)

1 (23 Dec 1865)	10.00	30.00	60.00
2-129 131-225 (issues with short sequential strips)	7.50	15.00	30.00
130 (Steam Man satire parody)	100.00	200.00	300.00

STUFF AND NONSENSE (Harper's Monthly strip-r) (M)
Charles Scribner's Sons: 1884 (10-1/4x7-3/4", 100 pgs, hardcover, B&W)

nn - By Arthur Burdett Frost	100.00	185.00	375.00
nn - By A.B. Frost (1888 reprint, 104 pgs)	40.00	80.00	180.00

NOTE: Earliest known anthology devoted to collecting the comic strips of a single American artist. 1888 2nd printing has a different cover and is layed out somewhat differently inside with a new title page, 3 added pages of cartoons, and a couple more illustrations. For more Frost, the 2nd is worth checki ng out also.

STUMPING IT (LAUGHING SERIES BRICKTOP STORIES #8) (O,S)
Collin & Small, NY: 1876 (6-5/8x9-1/4, 68 pgs, perfect bound, B&W)

nn - Thomas Worth art abounds (some sequentials)	75.00	150.00	300.00

NOTE: Mainly single panel cartoons w/text; however, some sequential comic strips inside worth picking up

SUMMER SCHOOL OF PHILOSOPHY AT MT. DESERT, THE
Henry Holt & Co.: 1881 (10-3/8x8-5/8", 60 pgs, illus. gilt hard-c, B&W)

nn - By J. A. Mitchell	60.00	120.00	240.00

NOTE: J.A.Mitchell went on to found LIFE two years later in 1883. Also, the long-running mascot for LIFE was Cupid - which you see multitudes of Cupids flying around in this story.

SURE WATER CURE, THE
Carey Grey & Hart, Phila, PA: c1841-43 (8-/2x5, 32 pgs, B&W)

nn - proto-comic-strip	75.00	150.00	300.00

TAILOR-MADE GIRL, HER FRIENDS, HER FASHIONS, AND HER FOLLIES, THE
(see also IN THE "400" AND OUT) (M)
Charles Scribner's Sons, New York: 1888 (8-3/8x10-1/2", 68 pgs, hard-c, B&W)

nn - Art by C.J. Taylor	17.50	35.00	70.00

NOTE: Format is a full page cartoon on every other page, with a script style vignette, written by Philip H. Welch, on every page opposite the art.

TALL STUDENT, THE
Roberts Brothers, Boston: 1873 (7x5", 48 pgs, printed one side only, gilted hard-c, B&W)

nn - By Wilhelm Busch (Scarce)	30.00	60.00	120.00

TARIFF ?, CARTOONS AND COMMENTS FROM PUCK, THE (see Puck, The Tariff...)

TEASING TOM AND NAUGHTY NED WITH A SPOOL OF CLARK'S COTTON, THE ADVENTURES OF (O,P)
Clark's O.N.T. Spool Cotton: 1879 (4-1/4x3", 12 pgs, B&W, paper-c)

nn	17.50	35.00	70.00

NOTE: Knock-off of the "First Trick" in Wilhelm Busch's Max and Maurice, modified to involve Clark's Spool Cotton in the story, with similar but new art by an artist identified as "HB". The back cover advertises the specific merchant who gave this booklet away -- multiple variations of back cover suspected.

TEMPERANCE TALES; OR, SIX NIGHTS WITH THE WASHINGTONIANS, VOL I & II
W.A. Leary, Philadelphia: 1848 (50¢, 6-1/8x4", 328 pgs, B&W, hard-c)

nn	100.00	200.00	400.00

NOTE: Mostly text. This edition gathers Volume I & II together. The first 8 pages reprints George Cruikshank's THE BOTTLE, re-drawn & re-engraved by Phil A. Pilliner. Later editions of this book do not include THE BOTTLE reprint and are therefore of little interest to comics collectors.

TEXAS SIFTINGS
Texas Siftings Publishing Co, Austin, Texas (1881-1887), NYC (1887-1897): 1881-1885 newspaper-size weekly; 1886-1897 folio weekly (15x10-3/4", 16 pgs, B&W 10¢

1881-1885 issues	25.00	50.00	100.00

	FR1.0	GD2.0	FN6.0
v6#1 (5/8/86) (8) panel strip Afterwhich He Emigrated;			
(16) panel The Tenor's Triumph Veni Vidi Vici	12.50	25.00	50.00
v6#2 (5/16/86) (5) panel sewuential	12.50	25.00	50.00
v6#3 no sequentials	12.50	25.00	50.00
v6#4 (5/29/86) Worth-c (4) panel Worth strip; (2) panel	12.50	25.00	50.00
v6#5 no sequentials	12.50	25.00	50.00
v6#6 (6/12/86) Comic Strip Cover (11) panels The Rise of a Great Artist			
(5) panel sequential	50.00	100.00	200.00
v6#7 (6/19/86) Worth-c (2) panel Wiorth;			
(10) panel Ha! Ha! The Honest Youth & the Lordly Villain	25.00	50.00	100.00
v6#8 (6/26/86) Worth-c; (15) panel The Kangaroo Hunter	25.00	50.00	100.00
v6#9 (7/3/86) Worth-c; Bellew (2) panel How Wives Get What They Want			
	12.50	25.00	50.00
v6#10 ((7/10/86) Baseball-c; (3) panel;			
(5) panel A Story Without Words from Fliegende Blätter	12.50	25.00	50.00
v6 #11 12 13 Worth-c no sequentials	12.50	25.00	50.00
v6#14 (8/7/86) Wiorth-c; (7) panel Mrs Cleveland Presents			
The President With A New Rocking Chair	12.50	25.00	50.00
v6#15 (8/14/86) Worth-c; (6) panel Worth strip	12.50	25.00	50.00
v6#16 (8/21/86) Worth-c Asleep At Post USA/Mexico Border			
(6) panel sequential	12.50	25.00	50.00
v6#17 no sequrntials	12.50	25.00	50.00
v6#18 (9/4/86) Worth-c; (3) panel from Fliegende	12.50	25.00	50.00
v6#19 (9/11/86) Worth Anarchist & Uncle Sam-c;			
(5) panel Duel of the Dudes	12.50	25.00	50.00
v6#20 (9/18/86) Worth-c (6) panel sequential	12.50	25.00	50.00
v6#21 (9/25/86) Worth-c; Verbeck single panel; (9) panel	12.50	25.00	50.00
v6#22 (10/2/86) Verbeck-c plus interiors	12.50	25.00	50.00
v6#23 (10/9/86) Worth-c Geronimo & Devil cover;			
Verbeck and Chips singles	25.00	50.00	100.00
v6#24 (10/16/86) Worth-c Verbeck strip "Evolution"	12.50	25.00	50.00
v6#25 no sequential strips	12.50	25.00	50.00
v6#26 (10/30/86) Worth-c; (6) panel Verbeck "A Warning To Smokers"			
	12.50	25.00	50.00

NOTE: Many Thomas Worth sequential comic strips. Frank Bellew and Dan McCarthy appear. Wilhelm Busch-r from German Fliegende Blaetter. Later issues in 1890s comics become sporadic

THAT COMIC PRIMER (S)
G.W. Carleton & Co., Publishers: 1877 (6-5/8x5", 52 pgs, paper soft-c, B&W)

nn - By Frank Bellew	35.00	70.00	140.00

NOTE: Premium for the United States Life Insurance Company, New York.

TIGER, THE LEFTENANT AND THE BOSUN, THE
Prudential Insurance Home Office, 878 & 880 Broad St, Newark, NJ: 1889 (4.5x3.25", 12 pgs) (Scarce)

nn - 8 panel sequential story in color	25.00	50.00	100.00

TOM PLUMP, THE ADVENTURES OF MR. (see also The Juvenile Gem) (O)
Huestis & Cozans, New York: nd (c1850-1851) (6x3-7/8", 12 pgs, hand colored paper-c, B&W)

nn- First printing(s) publisher's address is 104 Nassau Street (1850-1851)			
(Very Rare)	375.00	750.00	1500.00

NOTE: California Gold Rush story. The hand colored outer cover is highly rare, with only 1 recorded copy possessing it. The front cover image and text is repeated precisely on page 3 (albeit b&w), and only interior pages are numbered, together leading owners of coverless copies to believe they have the cover. The true back cover contains ads for the Juvenile Gem. The cover was issued only with copies which were sold separately - booklets which were bound together as part of THE JUVENILE GEM never had such covers.

TOM PLUMP, THE ADVENTURES OF MR. (see also The Juvenile Gem) (O)
Philip J. Cozans: nd (1851-1852) (6x3-7/8", 12 pgs,hand colored paper-c, B&W)

nn- Second printing(s) publisher's address is 116 Nassau Street (1851-1852)			
(Very Rare)	350.00	700.00	1300.00
nn- Third printing(s) publisher's address is 107 Nassau Street (1852+)			
(Very Rare)	350.00	700.00	1300.00

TOM PLUMP, THE ADVENTURES OF MR.
Americana Review, Scotia, NY: nd(1960's) (6-1/4x4-1/8", 8 pgs, side-stapled, cardboard-c, B&W)

nn - Modern reprint		12.00	24.00

NOTE: Issued within a folder titled SIX CHILDREN'S BOOKS OF THE 1850'S. States "Reprinted by American Review" at bottom of front cover. Reprints the 104 Nassau Street address.)

nn - Modern reprint (Scarce 1980s) (5-1/2x4-1/4", 8 pgs,side-stapled) -		5.00	10.00

NOTE: Photocopy reprint by a comix zine publisher, from an Americana Review copy, & available by mail order

TOOTH-ACHE, THE (E,O)
D. Bogue, London: 1849 (5-1/4x3-3/4)

nn - By Cruikshank, B&W (Very Rare)		(no known sales)	
nn - By Cruikshank, hand colored (Rare)		(no known sales)	

NOTE: Scripted by Horace Mayhew, art by George Cruikshank. This is the British edition. In British editions, the panels are not numbered. Publisher's name appears on cover. Booklet's "pages" unfold into a single, long, strip.

J.L. Smith, Philadelphia, PA: nd (1849) (5-1/8"x 3-3/4" folded, 86-7/8" wide unfolded, 26 pgs, cardboard-c, color, 15¢)

The Tramp Exposed #1 By Bellew Family
1878 © Dick & Fitzgerald

Uncle Josh's Trunk Full Of Fun
1870s © Dick & Fitzgerald

Wild Oats #115 March 10
1875 © Winchell & Small, NYC

	FR1.0	GD2.0	FN6.0

nn - By Cruikshank, hand colored (Very Rare)   (no known sales)
NOTE: Reprints the D. Bogue edition. In American editions, the panels are numbered (43 panels, not counting front & back cover). Publisher's name stamped on inside front cover, plus printed along left-hand side of first interior page. Page 1 is pasted to inside back cover, and unfolds from there. Front cover not attached to back cover by design. Booklet's "pages" unfold into a single, long, strip (made from four individual strips pasted together on the blank back side).

TOOTH-ACHE, THE (E)
Arts Council of Great Britain: nd (1974) (5-1/2x3-5/8", 28 pgs, B&W, cardboard-c, color interior)

nn - By Cruikshank, printed color   -   15.00   30.00
NOTE: Modern reprint of D. Bogue edition. 5000 copies printed, included in a catalogue issued with a show at the Victoria and Albert Museum, in London, 28 February-28 April 1974. Also included in the catalogue was a modern reprint of the Cruikshank booklet "A Comic Alphabet".

TRAMP, THE: His Tricks, Tallies, and Tell-Tales, with His Signs, Countersigns, Grips, Passwords and Villainies Exposed (0,S)
Dick & Fitzgerald, New York: 1878 (11-3/8x8, 36 pgs, paper-c, B&W, 25¢) (Rare)

1 Frank Bellew   150.00   300.00   600.00
NOTE: Edited by Frank Bellew, A Bee And A Chip (Bellew's daughter and son Frank).

TRUTH (See Platinum Age section for 1900-1906 issues)
Truth Company, NY: 1886-1906? (13-11/16x10-5/16", 16 pgs, process color-c & center-folds, rest B&W)

1886-1887 issues	20.00	40.00	100.00
1888-1893 issues	15.00	30.00	80.00
1894-1895 non Outcault issues	10.00	20.00	55.00
Mar 10 1894 - precursor Yellow Kid RFO	60.00	180.00	400.00
#372 June 2 1894 - first app Yellow Kid RFO	215.00	650.00	1300.00
June 23 1894 - precursor Yellow Kid R. F. Outcault	60.00	180.00	400.00
July 14 1894 -2nd app Yellow Kid RFO	110.00	330.00	700.00
Sept 15 1894 - (2) 3rd app YK RFO plus YK precursor	110.00	330.00	700.00
Feb 9 1895 - 4th app Yellow Kid RFO	110.00	330.00	700.00
1896-1899 issues	10.00	20.00	55.00

NOTE: This magazine contains the earliest known appearances of The Yellow Kid by Richard Felton Outcault. Feb 9 1895 issue's YK cartoon was reprinted one week later in the New York World Feb 17 1895 edition. We are still sorting out further Outcault appearances. Truth also contained full color sequential strips by Hy Mayer on the back plus Woolf, Verbeek, etc.

TRUTH, SELECTIONS FROM
Truth Company, NY: 1894-Spr 1897 (13-11/16x10-1/4, color-c, quarterly)

1-4	25.00	50.00	100.00
5-Outcault's early Yellow Kid	100.00	200.00	400.00
6-13	20.00	40.00	80.00

NOTE: #5 reprints all early Outcault Yellow Kid appearances

TURNER'S COMIC ALMANAC
Charles Strong, 298 Pearl St, NYC: ???-1843 (7.25x4.5", 36 pgs, B&W)

nn   60.00   120.00   240.00

TURNER'S COMICK ALMA-NACK
Turner & Fisher, NYC: 1844-?? (7.25x4.5", 36 pgs, B&W)

nn   60.00   120.00   240.00

TWO HUNDRED SKETCHES, HUMOROUS AND GROTESQUE, BY GUSTAVE DORE (E)
Frederick Warne & Co, London: 1867 (13-3/4x11-3/8, 94 pgs, hard-c, B&W)

nn - (1867) by Gustave Dore	100.00	200.00	500.00
nn - (Second Edition; 1871)- by Gustave Dore	50.00	100.00	240.00
nn - (Third Edition; 1870's)- by Gustave Dore	50.00	100.00	240.00
nn - (Fourth Edition; 1870's- by Gustave Dore	50.00	100.00	240.00

NOTE: Contains sequential comics stories, single panel cartoons, and sketches. Reprints and translates material which originally appeared in the French publications "Le Journal pour Rire", circa 1848-49. Although dated 1867, it was likely published & available for the 1866 Christmas Season, as has been confirmed for the American edition. Printed by Dalziel. The American & first British editions were printed simultaneously, the American edition is not a reprint of the British.

TWO HUNDRED SKETCHES, HUMOROUS AND GROTESQUE, BY GUSTAVE DORE (E)
Roberts Brothers, Boston: 1867 (13-3/4x11-3/8, 96 pgs, hard-c, B&W)

nn - By Gustave Dore   100.00   200.00   500.00
NOTE: Although dated 1867, it was published & available for the 1866 Christmas Season. Printed by Dalziel, in England, and imported to the USA expressly for a USA publisher.

UNCLE BANTAM'S FUNNY BOOKS, FOR THE AMUSEMENT OF HIS LITTLE NEPHEWS AND NIECES. WITH SEVENTY-FIVE ILLUSTRATIONS. (I)
Davis Porter & Co., Philadelphia : 1865 (Quarto, 54 pgs, col. ill. ; pictorial paper covered boards) (See also Slovenly Peter)

nn - By Heinrich Hoffman (Scarce)   250.00   500.00   1000.00
NOTE: Translation of "Der Struwwelpeter", first published in Germany in 1844. Hand-colored illustrations with lines of verse. This is a complete collection of six of the "Uncle Bantam's Funny Books" in one volume, each with 8 pgs.

UNCLE JOSH'S TRUNK-FUL OF FUN
Dick & Fitzgerald, 18 Ann St, NY: 1870s (5-3/4x9", 68 pgs, B&W & Red-c, B&W inside)

nn - Rare   75.00   125.00   200.00
NOTE: Many single panel cartoons; (2) pages of early boxing sequential strip

UNCLE SAM'S COMIC ALMANAC
M.J. Meyers, NY: 1879 (11x8", 32 pgs)

	FR1.0	GD2.0	FN6.0

nn -   50.00   100.00   200.00

UNDER THE GASLIGHT
Gaslight Publishing Co (Frank Tousey): Oct 13 1878-Apr 12 1879 (Folio, 16pgs)
1-27   75.00   125.00   200.00

UNITED STATES COMIC ALMANAC
King & Baird, Philadelphia: 1851-?? (7.5x4.5", 36 pgs, B&W)
nn   60.00   120.00   240.00

UNTIDY TOM & OTHER STORIES. (I)
Davis Porter & Co., Philadelphia: 1865 (8 pgs., color illustrations, 24 cm.)

nn - By Henrich Hoffman (Scarce)   (no known sales)
NOTE: Uncle Bantam's funny books for the amusement of his little nephews and nieces. Pub lisher's advertisement on back cover.(Contents: Untidy Tom -- Story of Johnny Look-in-the-Air -- Story of Augustus who would not have any soup -- Story of Little Suck-a-Thumb -- Story of Flying Robert.

UPS AND DOWNS ON LAND AND WATER (O,G)
James R. Osgood & Co., Boston: 1871 ; **Houghton, Osgood & Co., Boston:** 1880 (108 pgs, gilted hard-c, B&W)

1st printing (1871; 10-3/4x16") - By Augustus Hoppin   45.00   90.00   180.00
2nd printing (1880; smaller sized)   32.50   65.00   130.00
NOTE: Exists as blue or orange hard covers.

VANITY FAIR
William A. Stephens (for Thompson & Camac): Dec 29 1859-July 4 1863 Quarto Weekly

average issues with comic strips   12.50   25.00   50.00

VERDICT, THE
Verdict Publishing Co: Dec 19 1898-Nov 12 1900 (Chromolithographic Weekly)

Average Issues   50.00   100.00   200.00
NOTE: Artists included George B. Luks, Horace Taylor, MIRS. Striking anti-Republican weekly full o fsome of the most savage political cartoons of the era. The last brilliant burst of energy for the political cartoon weekly

VERY VERY FUNNY (M,S)
Dick & Fitzgerald, New York: nd(c1880's) (10¢, 7-1/2x5", 68 pgs, paper-c, B&W)

nn - (Rare)   22.50   45.00   90.00
NOTE: Unauthorized reprints of prose and cartoons extracted from Puck, Texas Siftings, and other publications. Includes art by Chips Bellew, Bisbee, Graetz, Opper, Wales, Zim.

VIM
H. Wimmel, NYC: June 22-Aug 24 1898 (Chromolithographic Weekly)

average issue   50.00   100.00   200.00
Yellow Kid by Leon Barritt issues   75.00   150.00   300.00

WAR IN THE MIDST OF AMERICA. FROM A NEW POINT OF VIEW. (E,O,G)
Ackermann & Co., London: 1864 (4-3/8" x 5-7/8", folded, 36 feet wide unfolded, 80 pgs, hard-c, B&W)

nn- by Charles Dryden (rare)   (no known sales)
NOTE: British graphic novel about the American Civil War, with a pro-Confederate bent. Adventures of a British artist who decides to visually summarize the American Civil War for his countrymen, from newspaper accounts. Reaching current events, he finds he can not finish the story until the War ends, and so he travels to America, to end it. Book unfolds into a single long strip (binding was issued split, to enable the unfolding).

WASP, THE ILLUSTRATED SAN FRANCISCO
F. Korbel & Bros and Numerous Others: August 5 1876-April 25 1941 (Chromolithographic Weekly)

average 1800s issues with comic strips   50.00   100.00   200.00

WHAT I KNOW OF FARMING: Founded On The Experience of Horace Greeley (S)
The American News Company, New York: 1871 (7-1/4x4-1/2", paper-c, B&W)

nn - By Joseph Hull (Scarce)   35.00   70.00   140.00
NOTE: Pay & Cox, Printers & Engravers, NY; political tract regarding Presidential elections.

WILD FIRE
Wild Fire Co, NYC: Nov 30 1877-at least#16 Mar 1878 (Folio, 16 pgs)
1-16   12.50   25.00   50.00

WILD OATS, An Illustrated Weekly Journal of Fun, Satire, Burlesque, and Nits at Persons and Events of the Day (O)
Winchell & Small, 113 Fulton St /48 Ann St, NYC: Feb 1870-1881 (16-1/4x11", generally 16 pages, B&W, began as monthly, then bi-weekly, then weekly) All loose issues Very Rare (See The Overstreet Price Guide #35 2005 for a detailed index of single issue contents)

1-25 Very Rare - contents to be indexed next year	50.00	100.00	200.00
26-28 30 32 35 36 39 40 41 43-46 1872 (sequential strips)	50.00	100.00	200.00
29 33 37 42 no sequential strips	40.00	80.00	160.00
31 34 38 47 Hopkins sequential comic strips	50.00	100.00	200.00
48 (1/16/73) Worth 13 panel sequential; first Woolf-c	50.00	100.00	200.00
49 51 53 54 60 62 61 64 65 66 67 69 1873 sequential strips	50.00	100.00	200.00
50 52 56 59 63 71 no sequential strips	40.00	80.00	160.00
51 (Worth 18 panel double page spread, Woolf 9 panel	50.00	100.00	200.00
55 Hopkins 22 panel double page spread; Bellew-c	50.00	150.00	300.00

57 intense unknown 6 panel "Two Relics of Barbarism, or A Few Contrasted Pictures, Showing the origin of the North American Indian   50.00   100.00   200.00
58 (6/5/73) unknown 19 panel double pager "The Terrible Adventures of Messrs Buster & Stumps, About Exterminating the Indians" reads across both pages like Popeye #2095 (1933); Woolf-c   100.00   200.00   400.00

Wild Oats #139 August 25
1875 © Winchell & Small, NY

Wreck-Elections Of Busy Life
Kellogg & Buckeley © 1864?

Yankee Notions #7 (v2#1)
July 1852 © T.W. Strong, NY

	FR1.0	GD2.0	FN6.0

68 (10/16/73) unknown 9 panel "Adv of New jersey Mosquito" looks like Winsor McCay
  type style: early inspiration for McCay's animated cartoon? 50.00 100.00 200.00
70 unknown 6 panel; Hopkins 6 panel "Hopkins novel: A Tale of True Love,
  with all the variations"; Bellew-c 50.00 100.00 200.00
72 (12/11/73) Worth 11 panel; Wales President Grant war-c 50.00 100.00 200.00
73 74 75 Hopkins sequential comic strip 75.00 150.00 300.00
76 77 sequential 50.00 100.00 200.00
78 Bellew 5 panel double pager 50.00 100.00 200.00
79-105 (March 1874-Dec 1874) contents presently unknown 50.00 100.00 200.00
106 107 111 no sequentials;Bellew-c #106 110;Wales-c #107 50.00 100.00 200.00
108 (1/20/75) Wales 12 panel double pg spread; Bellew-c 50.00 100.00 200.00
109 (1/27/75) unknown 6 panel; Wales-c 50.00 100.00 200.00
111 Busch 13 panel "The Conundrum of the Day - Is Lager Beer Intoxicating?"; Bellew-c
  50.00 100.00 200.00
112 116 sequential comic strips 50.00 100.00 200.00
113 114 115 no sequentials Worth-c #114 40.00 80.00 160.00
117 intense Wales 6 panel "One of the Oppresions of the Civil Rights Laws" Bellew-c
  75.00 150.00 300.00
118-137 (3/31/75-8/4/75) no sequential comic strips 40.00 80.00 160.00
138 (8/18/75) Bellew Sr & Bellew "Chips" Jr singles appear 50.00 100.00 200.00
139-143 145-147 154-157 159 no sequentials 40.00 80.00 160.00
144 (9/29/75) Hopkins 8 panel sequential; Wales-c 50.00 100.00 200.00
148 (10/27/75) Opper's first cover; many Opper singles 75.00 150.00 300.00
149 150 151 152 153 all Opper-c and much interior work 50.00 100.00 200.00
158 (1/5/76) Palmer Cox 1rst comic strip 24 panel double page spread "The Adv of Mr &
  Mrs Sprowl And Their Christmas Turkey - A Crashing Chasing Tearful Tragedy But
  Happily Ending Well"; Opper-c 100.00 200.00 400.00
159 160 162 165 167 169-173 no sequentials 40.00 80.00 160.00
161 163 164 166 168 179 182 Palmer Cox sequential strips 100.00 200.00 400.00
174 (4/26/76) Cox 24 panel double pager "The Tramp's Progress; A Story of the West
  And the Union Pacific Railroad" 100.00 200.00 400.00
175-178 183-189 no sequentials 40.00 80.00 160.00
180 (6/7/76) Beard & Opper jam; Woolf, Bellew singles 50.00 100.00 200.00
181 more Mann two panel jobs; Opper-c 50.00 100.00 200.00
190 Bellew 9 panel "Rodger's Patent Mosquito Armour" 75.00 150.00 300.00
191-end contents to be indexed in the near future 40.00 80.00 160.00
NOTE: There are very few known oose issues. All loose issues are Very Rare. Prices vary widely on this magazine. Issues with sequential comic strips would be in higher demand than issues with no comic strips. We present this index from the Library of Congress and New York Historical Society bound sets. We would love to hear from any one who turns up loose copies. This scarce humor bi-weekly contains easily a couple hundred original first-time published sequential comic strips found in most issues plus innumerable single panel cartoons in every issue

WYMAN'S COMIC ALMANAC FOR THE TIMES
T.W.Strong, NY: 1854 (8x5), 24 pgs)
nn - 50.00 100.00 200.00

WOMAN IN SEARCH OF HER RIGHTS, THE ADVENTURES OF (G)
Lee & Shepard, Boston And New York: early 1870s (8-3/8x13", 40 pgs, hard-c)
By Florence Claxton (Very Rare) 300.00 600.00 1000.00
NOTE: Earliest known original comic book sequential story by a woman; contains "nearly 100 original drawings by the author, which have been reproduced in fac-simile by the graphotype process of engraving". Tinted two color lithography; orange tint printed first, then printed 2nd time with black ink; early women's sufferage.

WORLD OVER, THE (I)
G. W. Dillingham Company, New York: 1897 (192 pgs, hard-c)
nn - By Joe Kerr; 80 illustrations by R.F. Outcault (Rare) 30.00 90.00 300.00
NOTE: soft cover editions also exist

WRECK-ELECTIONS OF BUSY LIFE (S)
Kellogg & Bulkeley: 1864? (9-1/4x11-3/4", ??? pages, soft-c)
nn - By J. Bowler (Rare) 45.00 90.00 200.00
NOTE: Says "Sold by American News Company, New York" on cover.

YANKEE DOODLE
W.H. Graham, Tribune Building, NYC: Oct 10 1846-Oct 2 1847 (Quarto weekly)
average issue 50.00 100.00 200.00

YANKEE NOTIONS, OR WHITTLINGS OF JONATHAN'S JACK-KNIFE
T.W. Strong, 98 Nassau St, NYC: Jan. 1852-1875 (11x8, 32 pgs, paper-c, 12.5¢, monthly)
1 Brother Jonathan character single panel cartoons 50.00 100.00 200.00
NOTE: Begins continuing character sequential comic strip, "The Adventures of Jeremiah Oldpot" in "A Bird in the Hand Is Worth Two in The Bush"
2-4 25.00 50.00 100.00
5 British X-Over 25.00 50.00 100.00
NOTE: Single panel of John Bull & Brother Jonathan exchanging civilities (issues of Punch & Yankee Notions)
6 end of Jeremiah Oldpot continued strip 25.00 50.00 100.00
v2#1 begin "Hoosier Bragg" sequential strip - six issue serial 25.00 50.00 100.00
v2#2 Feb 1853 two pg 12 panel sequential "Mr Vanity's Exploits, Arising Out Of A
  Valentine" 37.50 75.00 150.00
v2#3-v2#5 continues Hoosier Bragg 25.00 50.00 100.00
v2#6 Juen 1853 Lion Eats Hoosier Bragg, end of story 25.00 50.00 100.00
v3#1 begins referring to its cartoons as "Comic Art" 37.50 75.00 150.00
v4#1-V4#6 v5#1-v5#2 no sequential 20.00 40.00 80.00
v5#3 two sequential comic strips 37.50 75.00 150.00

NOTE: Mr Take-A-Drop And The Maine Law (5) panels and The First Segar (7) panels (about smoking tobacco)
v5#4 April 1856 begin Billy Vidkins 37.50 75.00 150.00
NOTE: Begins reprinting "From Passages in the Life of Little Billy Vidkins, first issued as a stand alone proto-comic book in 1849 Illustrations of the Poets
v5#5 The McBargem Guards (9) panel sequential; Vidkins 25.00 50.00 100.00
v5#6 v5 #9 no comics 20.00 40.00 80.00
v5#7 Billy Vidkins continues 25.00 50.00 100.00
v5#8 end of Vidkins By HL Stephens, Esq. 25.00 50.00 100.00
v5#10 (6) panel "How We Learn To Ride"; Timber is hero 25.00 50.00 100.00
v5#11 (7) panel "How Mr. Green Sparrowgrass Voted-A Warning For the Benefit of Quiet
  Citizens About To Excercize the Elective Franchise" plus Pt Two "How We Learn
  to Ride" 37.50 75.00 150.00
v5#12 (6) panel "How Mr Pipp Got Struck"; "The Eclipse" featuring Mr Phips;
  Pt 3 "How We Learn to Ride" 25.00 50.00 100.00
v6#1 (Jan 1857) (12) panel "A Tale of An Umbrella; (4) panel begins a serial
  "The Man Who Bought The Elephant; (8) panel How Our Young New Yorkers
  Celebrate New Years Day 25.00 50.00 100.00
v6#2 (Feb 1857) Pt 2 (4) panels The Man Who Bought the Elephant;
  (7) panel A Game of All Fours 25.00 50.00 100.00
v6#3 (Mar 1857) Pt 3 (4) panels The Man Who Bought the Elephant ending;
  (4) panel Ye Great Crinoline Monopoly 25.00 50.00 100.00
v6#4 no comic strips 25.00 50.00 100.00
v6#5 (May 1850) (3) panel A Short TRip to Mr Bumps, And How It Ended;
  (2) panel How mr Trembles Was Garrotted 25.00 50.00 100.00
v6#6 no comic strips 25.00 50.00 100.00
v6#7 (July 1857) (5) panel Alma Mater;
  (3) panel Three Tableaux In the Life of A Broadway Swell 25.00 50.00 100.00
v6 #8 9 no comic strips 25.00 50.00 100.00
v6#10 (Oct 1857) (3) panel Adv of Mr Near-Sight 25.00 50.00 100.00
v6#11 (Nov 1857) (11) panel Mrs Champignon's Dinner Party And the Way
  She Arranged Her Guests; (4) panel A Stroll in August 25.00 50.00 100.00
v6#12 (Dec 1857) (8) panel strip; (12) panel Young Fitz At A Blow Out in the Fifth Ave
  25.00 50.00 100.00
v10#1 (Jan 1860) comic strip Bibbs at Central Park Skating Pond using word balloons
  25.00 50.00 100.00

YE TRUE ACCOUNTE OF YE VISIT TO SPRINGFIELDE BY YE CONSTABEL HIS SPECIAL REPORTER
Frank Leslie: 1861 (5-1/8 x 5-1/4 or 93 inches when folded out, paper-c, B&W)
nn - Very Rare fold-out of 18 comic strip panels plus covers
NOTE: 8 panels contain word balloons (Very Rare - only one copy known to exist.) First printed in Frank Leslie's Budget of Fun Jan 1 1861 issue. Abraham Lincoln Biography.

YE VERACIOUS CHRONICLE OF GRUFF & POMPEY IN 7 TABLEAUX. (O,P)
Jackson's Best Chewing Tobacco & Donaldson Brothers: nd (c1870's) (5-1/8 tall x 3-3/8" wide folded, 27" unfolded, color cardboard)
nn - With all 8 panels attached (Scarce) 40.00 80.00 160.00
nn - Individual panels/cards 6.00 12.00 24.00
NOTE: Black Americana interest. Consists of 8 attached cards, printed on one side, which unfold into a strip story of title card & 7 panels. Scrapbook hobbyists in the 19th Century tended to pull the panels apart and paste into their scrapbooks, making copies with all panels attached scarce.

YOUNG AMERICA (continues as Yankee Doodle)
T.W. Strong, NYC: 1856 (
1-30 John McLennon 50.00 100.00 200.00
YOUNG AMERICA'S COMIC ALMANAC
T.W. Strong, NY: 1857 (7-1/2x5", 24 pgs)
nn 50.00 100.00 200.00

THE YOUNG MEN OF AMERICA (becomes Golden Weekly) (S)
Frank Tousey, NYC: 1887-88 (14x10-1/4", 16 pgs, B&W)
527 (10/13/87) Bellew strip "Story of A Black Eye" 25.00 50.00 100.00
530 (11/3/87) Thomas Worth (6) panel strip 125
531 (11/10/87) Thomas Worth(3) panel strip
537 (12/22/87) H.E. Patterson (3) panel strip
544 (2/9/88) Caran s'Ache (6) panel strip-r 37.50 75.00 100.00
555 (4/26/88) Thomas Worth (3) panel strip
556 (5/3/88) Thomas Worth (6) panel strip; Kit Carson-c 75.00 150.00 300.00
569 (8/21/88) Frank Bellew (2) panel strip
570 (8/9/88) Kemble (2) panel strip
571 (8/16/88) Kemble (2) panel strip; first Davy Crockett 75.00 150.00 300.00
Issues with just single panel cartoons 10.00 20.00 40.00

ZIM'S QUARTERLY (M)
(13-13/16x10-1/4", 60 pgs, color-c; most;y B&W, some interior color)
1 - Eugene Zimmerman 112.50 225.00 450.00
NOTE: Approx. half sequential comic strips, other half single panel cartoons.

For a free, lively e-mail discussion group of Victorian & Platinum Age comics collectors, fans, dealers, enthusiasts, and scholars you can join to look, listen, learn, and share at PlatinumAgeComics@Yahoogroups.com/subscribe.
Any additition or corrections to this section are always welcome, very much encouraged and can be sent to feedback@gemstonepub.com to be processed for next year's Guide.

The American Comic Book: 1883-1938
Further Concise History & Price Index Of The Field As Of 2008

NEWSPAPERS HARNESS COMICS POWER
MYRIAD FORMATS COMPETE

by Robert Lee Beerbohm and Richard D. Olson, PhD ©2008

(This article was originally created by Robert L. Beerbohm and Richard D. Olson
beginning in CBPG #27 1997 and is revised annually as new information comes to light.)

The story of the success of the modern comic strip as we know it today is tied closely to the companies who sponsored and bought licenses from the copyright holder for the purpose of advertising products. Platinum Age comic books have come back into their own after languishing mostly forgotten for a few decades. With this series of comics history research updates now marking its first decade, these historically important books are seem by many now as very collectible. Online sources such as eBay and bookfinder.com have demonstrate that many of these Platinum books are actually not scarce at all as previously thought, though they are in any type of higher-grade condition. Even so, most Platinum Age books are much rarer than so-called Golden Age comic books, yet despite this scarcity, *Mutt & Jeff, Bringing Up Father, The Katzenjammer Kids*, and many more were more popular than say Superman and Batman when they were introduced. Recent research has come up with some more amazing rediscoveries. There is much that can be learned and applied to today's comics market by a simple historical examination of the medium's evolution over more than 160 years.

It should be

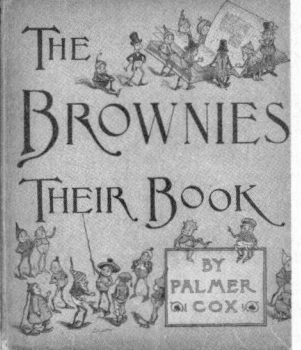

The Brownies' first book, 1877 by Palmer Cox, set a precedent for the Platinum Age, collecting and reprinting previously published material.

noted that "ages" are applied to historical periods in the history of comics for convenience. In fact, ages typically overlap and there is no discrete beginning or ending for any given "age." This is the case with the Platinum Age, which clearly began with Palmer Cox's creation of *The Brownies* in 1883 even though it overlaps with the Victorian Age which ran through the end of the 19th Century. Cox introduced a qualitative change to the field, not an incremental quantitative change. Specifically, he produced art and verse for children in children's magazines and then merchandised those characters. He published work for children not only in books but in magazines and newspapers, and he merchandised his creations to an extent that had never been done previously.

Palmer Cox was born in 1840 near Granby, Quebec. He journeyed to Oakland, California in 1863, and began publishing cartoon, prose and poems in the local press and media outlets such as *The San Francisco Examiner* wherein by 1867 it has been reported he also began creating sequential comic strips, though none have yet surfaced.

His first book, *Squibs of California*, was published in 1874. He subsequently moved to New York in 1875 and almost immediately began working for the magazine *Wild Oats*, of which more is written about in the preceding Victorian Age history introduction as well as a sample of his sequential work. He drew dozens of sequential comic strips for *Wild Oats*, a humor magazine so scarce only one issue has been offered on eBay in the past six years.

Soon thereafter he became a major contributor to the Scribner publications, including *The St. Nicholas*, an illustrated magazine for young folk. His first cartoon for them was "The Wasp And The Bee," published in the March 1879 cover-date issue. While it is now clear that Cox used elves and

The Brownies in the Philippines by Palmer Cox, Oct 1904 - scarce original art from the book. President Roosevelt is pictured within these multitudes of Brownie madness, a Cox "signature trademark." Cox's stories are comic strip-oriented in nature of time sequence as he boldly took his Brownies around the world.

brownie-like characters in his art for several different magazines as early as 1877 in *Harper's Young People* magazine as well as using Brownies-type characters beginning in the Feb 1881 issue of *Wide Awake*, the first true appearance of the Brownies in their own story using that title, a combination of art and verse was February, 1883, in *St. Nicholas*. Palmer Cox's *The Brownies* were the first North American comics-type characters to be internationally merchandised. Even though Cox was continuously doing sequential comic strips in magazines like *Wild Oats*, he left the popular medium of comics when he hit paydirt with *The Brownies*. For over a quarter of a century, Cox deftly combined the popular advertising motifs of animals and fairies into a wonderful, whimsical world of society at its best and worst.

The Brownies' first book was issued in 1887, titled *The Brownies: Their Book*; many more followed. Cox also added a run of his hugely popular characters in *Ladies Home Journal* from October 1891 through February 1895, as well as a special for December 1910. With the 1892-93 World's Fair, the merchandising exploded with a host of products, including pianos, paper dolls and other figurines, chairs, stoves, puzzles, cough drops, coffee, soap, boots, candy, and many more. *Brownies* material was being produced in Europe as well as the United States of America.

Cox tried out *The Brownies* as a newspaper strip in the *San Francisco Examiner* during 1898, where he had begun his newspaper career over 30 years before, and then in the *New York World* in 1900. It was then syndicated from 1903 through 1907. He seems to have retired from regularly drawing *The Brownies* with the January 1914 issue of *St. Nicholas* when he was 74. A wealthy man, he lived to the ripe old age of 84, spending his last decade in his home he affectionately called Brownie Castle, back in Granby, Quebec.

By the mid-1890s, while keeping careful track of steadily rising circulations of magazines with graphic humor such as *Harper's, Puck, St. Nicholas, Judge, Life* and *Truth*, New York based newspaper publishers began to recognize that illustrated humor would sell extra papers. This is what *The Yellow Kid* taught these publishers. Thus was born the Sunday "comic supplement." Most of the super star favorites were under contract with these magazines. However, there was an artist working for *Truth* who wasn't. Roy L McCardell, then a staffer at *Puck*, informed Morrill Goddard, Sunday

VOL. XXIII.,   SUNDAY MAY 27, 1894.   NO. 64.

THE TING-LINGS LISTEN TO THE PHONOGRAPH.

Chicago Inter Ocean Jr., May 27, 1894 Cover of **The Ting-Lings** by Charles W. Saalsburg, was inspired by Palmer Cox's **The Brownies** and later provided inspiration for Outcault's **Yellow Kid**.

Editor of *The New York World*, that he knew someone who could fit what was needed at the then-largest newspaper in America.

Richard F. Outcault (1863-1928) first introduced his street children strip in *Truth* #372, June 2, 1894, somewhat inspired by Michael Angelo Woolf's slum kids single panel cartoons in **Life** which had begun in the mid 1880s. The interested collector should seek out a copy of Woolf's *Sketches of Lowly Life In A Great City* (1899) listed in the *Guide* for comparison study. Edward Harrigan's play "O'Reilly and the Four Hundred," which had a song beginning with the words "Down in Hogan's Alley..." also likely provided direct inspiration.

It's also probable that Outcault's *Hogan's Alley* cast, including the *Yellow Kid*, was inspired by Charles W. Saalsburg's *The Ting Lings*, which began in the *Chicago Inter Ocean Jr* supplement post-dated May 1, 1894 in the April 29, 1894 edition of Chicago Inter Ocean. That first episode is titled: "The Brownies Welcome The Ting-Lings."

There is also a definite similarity in Mickey Dugan's appearance and clothing style to Saalsburg's creation which we will now examine in more detail thanks to welcome, ongoing research by long time comics historian Allan Holtz supplemented by living comics history legend Bill Blackbeard.

Charles Saalzburg was an artist who was also the genius behind color printing in newspapers. He seems to have pioneered the concept from whom all others learned their craft.

On June 23, 1892 the *Chicago Inter Ocean* introduced a section with mostly editorial cartoons titled the *Illustrated Supplement*, commemorating the Democratic National Convention held in that city. Early regulars included Thomas Nast and Art Young. Starting June 26, the *Inter Ocean* began steadily issuing this weekly four page supplement, typically featuring full page editorial cartoons on its front and back covers. In May 1893 the supplement began coming out twice a week, and even greater frequency to daily during the *World Columbian Exposition* held in Chicago later that same year as it was used as a wrapper to attract sales from fair goers. Art Young did some of the color cover art and comic strips for the early Fair supplements, printing them right at the Fair to goggle-eyed fair tourists. Thomas Nast did some art as well during a visit he made to the Fair.

. By September 10, 1893 the *Inter Ocean* introduced color, a multi-panel editorial comic strip by Charles Saalsburg. The supplement used yellow ink, a further nail in the coffin of various Yellow Kid myths which had clouded serious comics scholarship in earlier decades before being proven wrong.

On October 1, Tom E. Powers introduced their first sequential non-political comic strip in color, a humorous pantomime.

As the Exposition ended in November, the contents were soon aimed more at children, enhanced with color added to the center as well by December 24, 1893, then changing its title to *Inter Ocean Jr* in January 1894. This was accomplished easily by folding the single four page sheet into eight pages.

In the January 1894 Saalsburg began using Brownies-inspired characters in his color comic strips. The present theory is the *Ting-Ling* characters took over solo five months later in response to a presumed cease and desist letter which inevitably must have been issued from Palmer Cox to the *Inter Ocean*.

However, on July 8 1894, the *Inter Ocean Jr* stopped color and full page comics-type work in this supplement, devolving back to simple small spot art works. By mid-1894, color comics printing genius Saalburg had been lured to Pulitzer's New York World, becoming Art Director in charge of coloring for the new color printing press at the *New York World*. The color supplement was soon to be unleashed in the largest city in America.

By the November 18, 1894 issue of the *World*, Outcault was working for Goddard and Saalburg. Outcault produced a

successful Sunday newspaper sequential comic strip in color with "The Origin of a New Species" on the back page in the World's first colored Sunday supplement. Long time pro Walt McDougall, a famous cartoonist reputed to have turned the 1884 Presidential race with a single cartoon that ran in the *World*, handled the cartoon art on the front page. Earlier, *The World* began running full page color single panels on May 21, 1893. McDougall did various other page panels during 1893, but it was Jan. 28, 1894 when the first sequence of comic pictures in a New York World newspaper appeared in panels in the same format as our comic strips today. It was a full page cut up into nine panels. This historic sequence was drawn entirely in pantomime, with no words, by Mark Fenderson.

The second page to appear in panels was an eight panel strip from February 4, 1894, also lacking words except for the title. This page was a collaboration between Walt McDougall and Mark Fenderson titled "The Unfortunate Fate of a Well-Intentioned Dog." From then on, many full page color strips by McDougall and Fenderson appeared; they were the first cartoonists to draw for the Sunday newspaper comic section. It was Outcault, however, who soon became the most famous cartoonist featured. After first appearing in black and white in Pulitzer's *The New York World* on February 17, 1895 and again on March 10, 1895, *The Yellow Kid* was introduced to the public in color on May 5, 1895.

Some have erroneously reported in scholarly journals that perhaps it was Frank Ladendorf's "Uncle Reuben," first intro-

Left: Walt McDougall & Mark Fenderson, the 2nd sequential comic strip in New York World, February 4, 1894, predates Yellow Kid in The World by over a year. Mark Fenderson drew the first NY World newspaper comic strip and we are still hunting down an example to display here in future editions.
Right: New York World, Nov. 18, 1894 predates YK "Origin of A New Species," Richard F. Outcault.

"A Fair Champion" artwork by Richard F. Outcault, Truth, July 14, 1894 (2nd Yellow Kid app.). Many of RFO's comics were fully integrated down around the corner of Hogan's Alley and Ryan's Arcade.

"Fourth Ward Brownies," artwork by Richard F. Outcault, Feb. 17, 1895, the 4th Yellow Kid app. and 1st in Pulitzer's New York World. Note the Kid, second from left. This panel first saw print in Truth, Feb 9, 1895.

duced May 26, 1895, which became the first regularly recurring comics character in newspapers. This is wrong, as even Outcault's "Yellow Kid" began in Pulitzer's paper a good three months before *Uncle Reuben*. Until firm evidence to the contrary comes to light, that honor will forever be enshrined with Jimmy Swinnerton's *Little Bears* cartoon characters, found all over inside Hearst's *San Francisco Examiner* beginning October 14, 1893 with the first one called "Baby Monarch. Though never actually a comic strip, they nonetheless were the earliest presently-known recurring comics-type characters in American newspapers. In June 1895, a semi-regular "Little Bears" feature began. On January 26, 1896, children were introduced, the title eventually changed to "Little Bears and Tykes," forever confusing some scholars decades later. There never was a strip titled *Little Bears and Tigers,* as the *Tigers* were strictly for New York consumption when Hearst ordered Swinnerton to move to the Big Apple to compete better in the brewing comic strip wars.

The Yellow Kid's importance is widely recognized today as the first newspaper comic strip to demonstrate without a doubt that the general public was ready for full color comics. *The Yellow Kid* was the first in the USA to show

that comics could increase newspaper sales, and that comic characters could be merchandised. *The Yellow Kid* was the headlining spark of what was soon dubbed by Hearst as "eight pages of polychromatic effulgence that makes the rainbow look like a lead pipe."

Ongoing research suggests that Palmer Cox's fabulous success with *The Brownies* was a direct inspiration for Richard Outcault's future merchandising work. The ultimate proof lies in the fourth Yellow Kid cartoon, which appeared in the February 9, 1895 issue of *Truth*. It was reprinted in the *New York World* eight days later on February 17, 1895, becoming the first Yellow Kid cartoon in the newspapers. The caption read "FOURTH WARD BROWNIES. MICKEY, THE ARTIST (adding a finishing touch) Dere, Chimmy! If Palmer Cox wuz t' see yer, he'd git yer copyrighted in a minute." The Yellow Kid was widely licensed in the greater New York area for all kinds of products, including gum and cigarette cards, toys, pinbacks, cookies, postcards, tobacco products, and appliances. There was also a short-lived humor magazine from Street & Smith named *The Yellow Kid*, featuring exquisite Outcault covers, plus a 196-page comic book from Dillingham & Co. known as *The Yellow Kid in*

*Left: **The Yellow Kid** #1, March 20, 1897, Street & Smith as Howard Ainslee, NY cover by Richard F. Outcault; lasted six issues with RFO YK covers.*
*Right: **Yellow Kids On Parade** 1897 part of Gilmore & Leonard's Hogan's Alley Company; one of at least half a dozen Yellow Kid productions performed with collectiblesheet music generated.*

The Adventures of Foxy Grandpa, late 1900,
cover for the rare earliest known first edition of
Carl "Bunny" Schultze's famous creation.
He was one of the newspaper comics' first superstars.

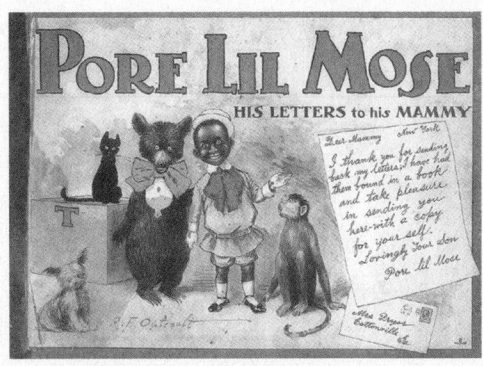

Pore Li'l Mose by Richard Outcault, 1901.
Bridges in between Yellow Kid and Buster Brown.
Becoming scarce because many copies have been cut up.

McFadden's Flats, dated to early 1897. Check out the covers in "The Platinum Age" three-page comic strip elsewhere in this Guide. In addition, there were several Yellow Kid plays produced, spawning other collectibles like show posters, programs and illustrated sheet music. (For those interested in more information regarding the Yellow Kid, it is available on the Internet at www.neponset.com/yellowkid.)

Mickey Dugan burned brightly for a few years as Outcault secured a copyright on the character with the United States Government by September 1896. By the time he completed the necessary paperwork, however, hundreds of business people nationwide had pirated the image of The Yellow Kid and plastered it all over every product imaginable; mothers were even dressing their newborns to look like Dugan. Outcault, however, kept regularly utilizing images of *The Yellow Kid* in his comics style advertising work confirmed as late as 1915. Outcault soon found himself in a maelstrom not of his choosing, which probably pushed him to eventually drop the character. Outcault's creation went back and forth between newspaper giants Pulitzer and Hearst until Bennett's New York Herald mercifully snatched the cartoonist away in 1900 to do what amounted to a few relatively short-run strips. Later, he did one particular strip for a year—a satire of rural Black America titled *Pore Li'l Mose His Letters to his Mammy,* and then his newer creation, *Buster Brown,* debuted May 4, 1902. *Mose* had a very rare comic book collection published in 1902 by Cupples & Leon, now highly sought after by today's savvy collectors. Outcault continued drawing him in the background of occasional *Buster Brown* strips for many years to come.

William Randolph Hearst loved the comic strip medium ever since he was a little boy growing up on *Max & Moritz* by Wilhelm Busch in American collected book editions translated from the original German (these collections were first published in book form in 1871, serving as the influence for *The Katzenjammer Kids*). One of the ways Hearst responded to losing Outcault in 1900 was by purchasing the highly successful 23-year-old humor magazine *Puck* from the heirs of founder

Joseph Keppler. With *Puck* and its exclusive cartoonist contracts, he commanded, among others, the very popular F. M. Howarth and Frederick Burr Opper's undivided attention. Opper first burst upon the comics scene in America back in 1880. Within a year Hearst had expanded this *National Lampoon* of its day into the colored Sunday comics section, *Puck-The Comic Weekly.* At first featuring Rudolph Dirk's *The Katzenjammer Kids* (1897), *Happy Hooligan* and other fine strips by the wildly popular Opper and a few others including Rudolph's brother Gus Dirks, the Hearst comic section steadily added more strips. For decades to come, there wasn't anything else that could compete with *Puck.* Hearst hired the best of the best and transformed *Puck* into the most popular comics section anywhere.

Outcault, meanwhile, followed in Palmer Cox's footprints a decade later by using the nexus of a World's Fair as a jumping off venue. *Buster Brown* was an instant sensation when he debuted as the new merchandising mascot of the Brown Shoe Company at the 1904 St. Louis World's Fair in a special Buster Brown Shoes pavilion. The character has the honor of being the first nationally licensed comic strip character in America with this time Outcault in almost full control. Many hundreds of different *Buster Brown* premiums have been issued. Comic books by Frederick A. Stokes Company featuring *Buster Brown & His Dog Tige* began as early as 1903 with *Buster Brown and His Resolutions,* simultaneously published in several different languages throughout the world.

After a few years, Buster and Outcault returned to Hearst in late 1905, joining what soon became the flagship of the comics world.

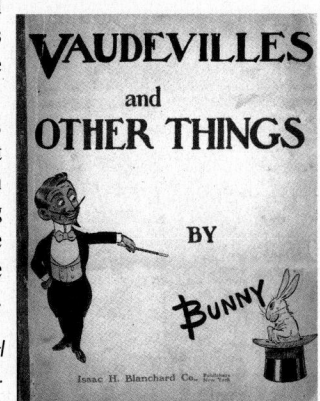

Vaudevilles And Other Things, 1900, first printing. Carl
Schultze later became famous for creating Foxy Grandpa.

The Chicago Tribune introduced a straight super hero with obvious super strength called "Hugo Hercules" by the unknown artist J. Koerner. This Sunday strip ran September 7, 1902 through January 11, 1903 and ran only in this one paper. It is entirely possible a very young Chicago-resident named Philip Wylie read "Hugo" since that was the same name he gave his super-heroic main character in his much-later book The Gladiator (1930). Other appearances have Hugo running with almost super speed.

Buster's popularity quickly spread all over the United States and then the world as he single-handedly spawned the first great comic strip licensing dynasty. For years, there were little people traveling from town to town performing as *Buster Brown* and selling shoes while accompanied by small dogs named Tige. Many other highly competitive licensed strips would soon follow. We suggest getting *Hake's Price Guide to Character Toys* for info on several hundred *Buster Brown* competitors, as well as several pages of the more fascinating *Buster Brown* material.

Soon there were many comic strip syndicates not only offering hundreds of various comic strips but also offering to license the characters for any company interested in paying the fee. The history of the comic strip with wide popularity since *The Yellow Kid* has been intertwined with giveaway premiums and character-based, store-bought merchandise of all kinds. Since its infancy as a profitable art form unto itself with *The Yellow Kid*, the comic strip world has profited from selling all sorts of "stuff" to the public featuring their favorite character or strip as its motif. American business gladly responded to the desire for comic character memorabilia with thousands of fun items to enjoy and collect. Most of the early comics were not aimed specifically at kids, though children understandably enjoyed them as well.

Comic books have generally been associated with almost all of the licensed merchandise in this century. In the Platinum Age section beginning right after this essay, you will find a great many comic books in varied formats and sizes published before the advent of the first successful monthly newsstand comic magazine, *Famous Funnies*. What drove each of

Katzenjammer Kids #1, 1902, by Rudolph Dirks was inspired by Wilhelm Busch.

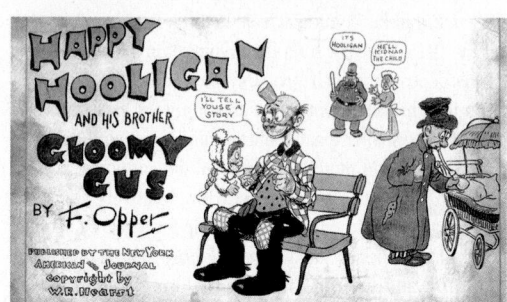

Happy Hooligan Book #1, 1902, by Frederick Opper, was wildly popular.

Katzenjammer Kids #2 by Rudolph Dirks. These Katz Kids have the longest running strip in America.

The second Happy Hooligan comic book, 1903, by Frederick Opper set a high standard.

Originally discovered listed for sale in a 1906 Lockwood Art School brochure, the existences of The Naughty Adventures of Vivacious Mr. Jack and Alphonse and Gaston New Edition 1903 were recently verified. Several copies of each are known to exist.

these evolutionary format changes was the need by their producers to make money so more books could be issued.

A very significant format was F. M. Howarth's *Funny Folks*, published in 1899 by E. P. Dutton and drawn from color as well as black and white pages of *Puck*. This rather large hardcover volume measured 16 1/2" wide by 12" tall. It contains numerous sequential comic strip pages as well as single gag illustrations. Howarth's art was a joy to behold and deserves wider recognition.

By Oct. 1900, Hearst had already caused Opper's *Folks In Funnyville* to be collected by publisher R. H. Russell, NY in a 12x9 hard cover format from his *New York Journal American Humorist* section. At the end of 1900, Carl Shultze had a first edition of *Vaudevilles and Other Things* published by Isaac H. Blanchard Co., NY. It measures 10 1/2" wide by 13" tall with 22 pages including covers. Each interior page is a 2 to 7 panel comic strip with lots of color.

There were also recently unearthed format variation second and third printings of *Vaudevilles* with the inscription "From the Originator of the 'Foxy Grandpa' Series" at the bottom of its front cover of the third printing. This note is lacking on the earlier first two editions, and it also switches format size to 11" tall by 13" wide. Discovered last year was a heretofore undocumented *The Adventures of Foxy Grandpa* - also issued in 1900 - new to the Platinum listings. The second number dated 1901 drops the words "The Adventures of..." from the title.

E. W. Kemble's *The Blackberries* had a color collection by 1901, also published by R. H. Russell, NY, as well as a few other comic-related volumes by Kemble still to be unearthed and properly identified. An earlier one was titled *Coontown's 400* (1899) newly listed this year. While the title is definitely not "PC" by today's standards, Kemble's drawings are excellent slices of African-American life in the USA with some humor injected. Kemble did a good job documenting aspects of life.

Confirmed is the exact format of Hearst's 1902 *The Katzenjammer Kids and Happy Hooligan And His Brother Gloomy Gus*. They both measure 15 5/16" wide by 10" tall and contain 88 pages including covers. Confirmed also is the fact that there are two separate editions with different covers for the pictured 1902 first edition and a 1903 Frederick Stokes edition of *Katzenjammer Kids* and *Happy Hooligan* with differing contents. They both are two different books entirely, and what confuses many collectors is that they have identical indicia title pages, but so does an entirely different *KK* from 1905.

Settling on a popular size of 17" wide by 11" tall, comic books were soon available that featured Charles "Bunny" Schultze's *Foxy Grandpa*, Rudolph Dirk's *The Katzenjammer Kids*, Winsor McCay's *Little Sammy Sneeze, Rarebit Fiend* and *Little Nemo*, and Fred Opper's *Happy Hooligan* and *Maud*, in addition to dozens of *Buster Brown* comic books. For well over a decade, these large-size, full-color volumes were the norm, retailing for 60¢. These collections offered

Little Sammy Sneeze, 1905, by Winsor McCay.

The Three FunMakers, 1908, the first anthology Platinum Age comic book.

Brainy Bowers and Drowsy Duggan by R.W. Taylor 1905 © Star Publishing Co - appears to be the first daily newspaper reprint comic book compilation ever. As such, this is a sleeper investment comic book.

The Three Fun Makers shown below.

With the ever-increasing popularity of Bud Fisher's new daily strip sensation, *Mutt & Jeff*, a new format was created for reprinting daily strips in black and white, a hardcover book about 15" wide by 5" tall, published by Ball starting in 1910 for five volumes. In 1912, Ball also branched out with at least the now-obscure *Doings of the Van Loons* by Fred I. Leipziger, a rare comic book in the

full-size Sunday comics with the back side blank per page.

Though not the first daily newspaper strip, the very rare *Brainy Bowers and Drowsy Dugan* by R. W. Taylor is now crowned the first collection of strip reprints from a daily newspaper published in America. There are now four different collections of Brainy Bower known to exist.

The Outbursts of Everett True by A. D. Condo and J. W. Raper was first published by Saalfield in 1907 in an 88-page hardcover collection. It qualifies as the second daily comic strip collection as it predates the first *Mutt & Jeff* collection from Ball by three years. Condo & Raper's creation began its regular run several times a week in 1905 daily newspapers and lasted until 1927, when Condo became too sick to continue. This same *Everett True* collection was later truncated a bit by Saalfield in 1921 to 56 strips in just 32 pages measuring the standard 10"x10" Cupples & Leon size.

By 1908 Stokes had a large backlist of full color comic books for sale at 60¢ each. Some of these titles date back to 1903 and were reprinted over and over as demand warranted. Note the number of titles in the advertisement pulled from the back of

same format as the *Mutt & Jeffs*.

Cartoons Magazine also began in 1912 and ran through 1921 before undergoing a radical format change. It is notable as a wonderful source for information on early comics and their creators. See also the Platinum index.

The next significant evolutionary change occurred in 1919, when Cupples & Leon began issuing their black and white daily strip reprint books in a new aforementioned format, about 10" wide by 10" tall, with four panels reprinted per page in a two by two matrix. These books were 52 pages for 25¢. The first ones featured *Bringing Up Father* and *Mutt & Jeff*; there were about 100 others.

By 1921, the last of the oblong (11"x15") color comic books were issued, with Cupples & Leon's *Jimmie Dugan* and *The Reg'lar Fellers* by Gene Byrne, and EmBee's *The Trouble Of Bringing Up Father* by self publisher George McManus. Of special historical interest, Embee issued the first 10¢ monthly comic book, *Comic Monthly*, with the first issue dated January 1922. A dozen 8-1/2"x9" issues were published, each featuring solo adventures of popular King

Left, The Outbursts of Everett True. 2nd daily strip collection, published 1907 Right: The earliest known comic book display ad, from in the back of 1908 Stokes comic books, 27 titles then in print. Cover prices are 60¢.

Features strips. The monthly 10¢ comic book concept had finally arrived, though it would be more than a decade before it became truly successful.

Skippy by Percy Crosby debuted in the long-running humor magazine *Life* in the March 22, 1923 issue. By 1924 the first hard cover collection, *Life Presents Skippy*, was published. The newspaper comic strip debuted June 23, 1925 with the McClure syndicate. Hearst soon picked up a Sunday page a year later in mid-1926, then added a daily strip in 1929. By the 1930s it was red hot - think *Calvin & Hobbes or Peanuts* in popularity. In its day, it was one of the most popular comic strips ever created. Read the Modern era essay for more on *Skippy's* immense popularity.

In 1926, Cupples & Leon added a new 7" wide by 9" tall format with *Little Orphan Annie, Smitty,* and others. These were issued in both softcover and hardcover editions with dust jackets, and became extremely popular at 60¢ per copy.

Dell began publishing all original material in *The Funnies* in late 1929 in a larger tabloid format. At least three dozen issues were published before Delacorte threw in the towel. Even the extremely popular *Big Little Book*, introduced in 1932, can be viewed as a smaller version of the existing formats. The competition amongst publishers now included Dell, McKay, Sonnet, Saalfield and Whitman. The 1930s saw a definite shift in merchandising comic strip material from adults to children. This was the decade when Kellogg's placed *Buck*

Above, Mutt & Jeff #5 by Bud Fisher, 1916, is fairly scarce as there was only one printing. Below, Reg'lar Fellers by Gene Byrne, 1921, one of the very last large oblong comics.

Rogers on the map, when Ovaltine issued tons of *Little Orphan Annie* material. Merchandising from such pioneers as Sam Gold and Kay Kamen spearheaded this next transformation of the comics biz beginning in the early 1930s.

Upwards of a thousand of these *Funnies On Parade* precursors, in all formats, were published through 1935 and were very popular. Towards the end of this era of once-popular comic book formats, beautiful collections of *Popeye, Mickey Mouse, Dick Tracy*, and many others were published which today command ever higher prices on the open market as they are rediscovered by the advanced collector who appreciates and enjoys truly great classic comics.

END NOTE: Each year we strive to add to the many 1930s variant formats. This Platinum Age section has grown as a result of advanced collectors who continue to report in with new finds. We encourage interested collectors and scholars to help with this section of the book, as each new data entry is very important for recovering our history. For corrections and additions to next year's next edition of *The Overstreet Guide* of some treasures you may have uncovered, please feel free to contact Gemstone Publishing at feedback@gemstonepub.com.

For further information on this era of American comic books, check out the previous evolving comics history essays in Guides #27,29-#37. Happy Hunting!

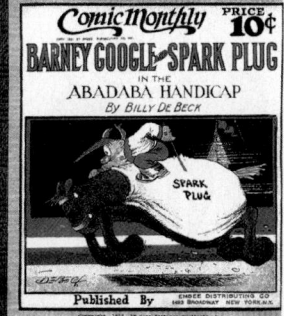

Comic Monthly #11 1922 (top), the first 10¢ monthly newsstand comic book title.

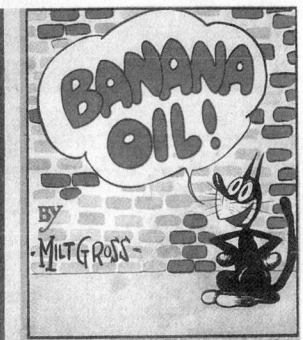

Banana Oil, a 1924 example of Cupples & Leon's then-revolutionary format from M.S. Publishers

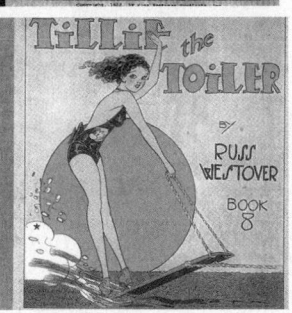

Tillie the Toiler #8 1933 from Cupples & Leon, another scarce number at the end of this once popular format.

David McKay published the last of the 10x10 comic books in 1935 as Famous Funnies grew in popularity.

The PLATINUM AGE
1883-1938

by J.C. Vaughn & Gene Gonzales

OKAY, I'VE GOT A QUESTION FOR YOU.

WHY WOULD ANYONE IGNORE FACTS IN FAVOR OF OPINION?

WHY IN THE FACE OF OVERWHELMING EMPIRICAL EVIDENCE WOULD SOMEONE SAY THAT THE COMIC BOOKS OF *THE VICTORIAN AGE* AND *THE PLATINUM AGE* AREN'T COMIC BOOKS?

GOSH, I FEEL LIKE THE RIDDLER.

THE FIRST COLLECTION OF PREVIOUSLY PUBLISHED STRIPS FEATURING *THE BROWNIES* WAS PRINTED IN 1887.

THE BROWNIES BECAME THE ROAD MAP FOR SUCCESSFUL LICENSED CHARACTERS . . .

THE PATH THAT WAS LATER FOLLOWED BY THE *YELLOW KID*, *MICKEY MOUSE*, AND *SUPERMAN*.

THE YELLOW KID IN MCFADDEN'S FLATS WAS COLLECTED R.F. OUTCAULT'S SUCCESSFUL CHARACTER IN BOOK FORM.

LIKE MANY OTHERS IN THAT TIME, IT WAS A HUGE SUCCESS.

BUT NO ONE WOULD CALL THIS COLLECTION A COMIC BOOK, WOULD THEY?

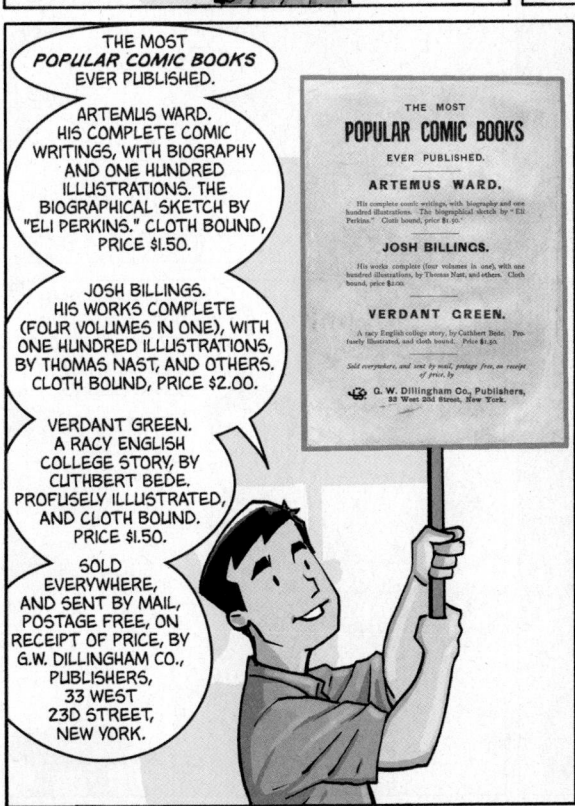

THE MOST *POPULAR COMIC BOOKS* EVER PUBLISHED.

ARTEMUS WARD. HIS COMPLETE COMIC WRITINGS, WITH BIOGRAPHY AND ONE HUNDRED ILLUSTRATIONS. THE BIOGRAPHICAL SKETCH BY "ELI PERKINS." CLOTH BOUND, PRICE $1.50.

JOSH BILLINGS. HIS WORKS COMPLETE (FOUR VOLUMES IN ONE), WITH ONE HUNDRED ILLUSTRATIONS, BY THOMAS NAST, AND OTHERS. CLOTH BOUND, PRICE $2.00.

VERDANT GREEN. A RACY ENGLISH COLLEGE STORY, BY CUTHBERT BEDE. PROFUSELY ILLUSTRATED, AND CLOTH BOUND. PRICE $1.50.

SOLD EVERYWHERE, AND SENT BY MAIL, POSTAGE FREE, ON RECEIPT OF PRICE, BY G.W. DILLINGHAM CO., PUBLISHERS, 33 WEST 23D STREET, NEW YORK.

SO, LET'S GET THIS STRAIGHT...

IN 1897 THESE GUYS KNEW IT WAS A COMIC BOOK, BUT THERE ARE STILL PEOPLE OUT THERE IN 2006 WHO DON'T?

The Adventures of Willie Green
© Frank M. Acton

Alphonse and Gaston by Opper
1902 © Hearst's NY American & Journal

Banana Oil by Milt Gross
1924 © M.S. Publishing Company

GD2.0   **FN**6.0   **VF**8.0   **GD**2.0   **FN**6.0   **VF**8.0

COLLECTOR'S NOTE: The books listed in this section were published many decades before organized comics fandom began archiving and helping to preserve these fragile popular culture artifacts. Consequently, copies of most all of these comics do not often surface in Fine+ or better shape. eBay is proving that many items once considered rare actually are not, though they are in higher grades. Most Platinum Age comic books are in the Fair to VG range. If you want to collect these only in high grade, your collection will be extremely small. The prices given for Good, Fine and Very Fine categories are for strictly graded editions. If you need help grading your item, we refer you to the grading section in the front of book or contact the authors of the Platinum essay. Items marked scarce we are trying to ascertain how many copies might still be in existence. Your input is always welcome.

For ease of ascertaining the contents of each item of this listing, there is a code letter or two following most titles. A helpful list of categories pertaining to these codes can be found at the beginning of the Victorian Age pricing sections. Most measurements are in inches. A few measurements are in centimeters. The first dimension given is Height and the second is Width. This section created, revised, and expanded by Robert Beerbohm with Richard Olson and able assistance from Ray Agricola, Jon Berk, Bill Blackbeard, Roy Bonario, Ray Bottorff Jr., Chris Brown, Alfredo Castelli, Darrell Coons, Sol Davidson, Leonardo De Sá, Scott Deschaine, Mitchell Duval, Joe Evans, Tom Gordon III, Bruce Hamilton, Andy Konkykru, Don Kurtz, Gabriel Laderman, Bruce Mason, Donald Puff, Robert Quesinberry, Steve Rowe, Randy Scott, John Snyder, Art Spiegelman, Steve Thompson, Joan Crosby Tibbets, Richard Samuel West, Doug Wheeler, Richard Wright and Craig Yoe.

ADVENTURES OF EVA, PORA AND TED (M)
Evaporated Milk Association: 1932 (5x15", 16 pgs, B&W)

nn - By Steve   10.00   30.00   70.00
NOTE: *Appears to have had green, blue or white paper cover versions.*

ADVENTURES OF HAWKSHAW (N) (See Hawkshaw The Detective)
The Saalfield Publishing Co.: 1917 (9-3/4x13-1/2", 48 pgs., color & two-tone)

nn - By Gus Mager*(only 24 pgs. of strips, reverse of each pg. is blank)
    30.00   150.00   260.00
nn - 1927 Reprints 1917 issue   30.00   150.00   260.00
NOTE: *Started Feb 23, 1913-Sept 4, 1922, then begins again Dec 13, 1931-Feb 11, 1952.*

ADVENTURES OF SLIM AND SPUD, THE (M)
Prairie Farmer Publ. Co.: 1924 (3-3/4x 9-3/4", 104 pgs., B&W strip reprints)

nn   21.00   84.00   150.00
NOTE: *Illustrated mailing envelope exists postmarked out of Chicago, add 50%.*

ADVENTURES OF WILLIE WINTERS, THE (O,P)
Kelloggs Toasted Corn Flake Co.: 1912 (6-7/8x9-1/2", 20 pgs, full color)

nn - By Byron Williams & Dearborn Melvill   54.00   189.00   350.00

ADVENTURES OF WILLIE GREEN, THE (N) (see The Willie Green Comics)
Frank M. Acton Co.: 1915 (50¢, 52 pgs, 8-1/2X16", B&W, soft-c)

Book 1 - By Harris Brown; strip-r   54.00   189.00   350.00

A. E. F. IN CARTOONS BY WALLY, THE (N)
Don Sowers & Co.: 1933 (12x10-1/8", 88 pgs, hardcover B&W)

nn - By Wally Wallgren (WW One Stars & Stripes-r)   25.00   90.00   150.00

AFTER THE TOWN GOES DRY (I)
The Howell Publishing Co, Chicago: 1919 (48 pgs, 6-1/2x4", hardbound two color-c)

nn - By Henry C. Taylor; illus by Frank King   20.00   70.00   140.00

AIN'T IT A GRAND & GLORIOUS FEELING? (N) (Also see Mr. & Mrs.)
Whitman Publishing Co.: 1922 (9x9-3/4", 52 pgs., stiff cardboard-c)

nn - 1921 daily strip-r; B&W, color-c; Briggs-a   36.00   143.00   250.00
nn -(9x9-1/2", 28pgs., stiff cardboard-c)-Sunday strip-r in color (inside front-c says "More of the Married Life of Mr. & Mrs".   36.00   143.00   250.00
NOTE: *Strip started in 1917; This is the 2nd Whitman comic book, after Brigg's MR. & MRS.*

ALL THE FUNNY FOLKS (I)
World Press Today, Inc.: 1926 (11-1/2x8-1/2", 112 pgs., color, hard-c)

nn-Barney Google, Spark Plug, Jiggs & Maggie, Tillie The Toiler, Happy Hooligan, Hans & Fritz, Toots & Casper, etc.   100.00   400.00   700.00
With Dust Jacket By Louis Biedermann   200.00   800.00   1600.00
NOTE: *Booklength race horse story masterfully enveloping all major King Features characters.*

ALPHONSE AND GASTON AND THEIR FRIEND LEON (N)
Hearst's New York American & Journal: 1902,1903 (10x15-1/4", Sunday strip reprints in color)

nn - (1902) - By Frederick Opper (scarce)   500.00   1800.00   –
nn - (1903) - By Frederick Opper (scarce) (72 pages)   500.00   1800.00   –
NOTE: *Strip ran Sept 22, 1901to at least July 17, 1904.*

ALWAYS BELITTLIN' (see Skippy; That Rookie From the 13th Squad; Between Shots)
Henry Holt & Co.: 1927 (6x8, hard-c with DJ,

nn -By Percy Crosby (text with cartoons)   43.00   172.00   300.00

ALWAYS BELITTLIN' (I) (see Skippy; That Rookie From the 13th Squad, Between Shots)
Percy Crosby, Publisher: 1933 (14 1/4 x 11", 72 pgs, hard-c, B&W)

nn - By Percy Crosby   43.00   172.00   300.00
NOTE: *Self-published; primarily political cartoons with text pages denouncing prohibition's gang warfare*

---

effects and cuts in the national defense budget as Crosby saw war looming in Europe and with Japan.

AMERICAN-JOURNAL-EXAMINER JOKE BOOK SPECIAL SUPPLEMENT (O)
New York American: 1911-12 (12 x 9 3/4", 16 pgs) (known issues) (Very Rare)

1 Tom Powers Joke Book(12/10/11)   80.00   280.00   –
2 Mutt & Jeff Joke Book (Bud Fisher 12/17/11)   100.00   350.00   –
3 TAD's Joke Book (Thomas Dorgan 12/24/11)   80.00   300.00   –
4 F. Opper's Joke Book (Frederick Burr Opper 12/31/11)
(contains Happy Hooligan)   100.00   350.00   –
5 not known to exist
6 Swinnerton's Joke Book (Jimmy Swinnerton 01/14/12)
(contains Mr. Jack)   100.00   350.00   –
7 The Monkey's Joke Book (Gus Mager 01/21/12)
(contains Sherlocko the Monk)   100.00   350.00   –
8 Joys And Glooms Joke Book (T. E. Powers 01/28/12)   80.00   280.00   –
9 The Dingbat Family's Joke Book (George Herriman 02/04/12)
(contains early Krazy Kat & Ignatz)   200.00   700.00   –
10 Valentine Joke Book, A (Opper, Howarth, Mager, T. E. Powers 02/11/12)
    80.00   280.00   –
11 Little Hatchet Joke Book (T. E. Powers 02/18/12)
    80.00   280.00   –
12 Jungle Joke Book (Dirks, McCay 02/25/12)   100.00   400.00   –
13 The Hayseeds Joke Book (03/03/12)   80.00   280.00   –
14 Married Life Joke Book (T.E. Powers 03/10/12)   80.00   280.00   –
NOTE: *These were insert newspaper supplements similar to Eisner's later Spirit sections. A Valentine Joke Book recently surfaced from Hearst's Boston Sunday American proving that other cities besides New York City had these special supplements. Each issue also contains work by other cartoonists besides the cover featured creator and those already listed above such as Sidney Smith, Winsor McCay, Hy Mayer, Grace Weiderseim (later Drayton), others.*

AMERICA'S BLACK & WHITE BOOK 100 Pictured Reasons Why We Are At War (N,S)
Cupples & Leon: 1917 (10 3/4 x 8", 216 pgs)

nn - W. A. Rogers (New York Herald-r)   32.00   114.00   195.00

AMONG THE FOLKS IN HISTORY
Rand McNally Print Guild: 1935 (192 pgs, 8-1/2x9-1/2", hard-c, B&W)

nn - By Gaar Williams   21.00   84.00   150.00

AMONG THE FOLKS IN HISTORY
The Book and Print Guild: 1935 (200 pgs, 8-1/2x9-1/2:,

nn - By Gaar Williams   21.00   84.00   150.00
NOTE: *Both the above are evidently different editions and contain largely full-page, single panel cartoons similar to Briggs' work of that sort. 8 or 10 pages are broken into panels, usually with a this is how it was in the old days, this is how it is today theme.*

ANGELIC ANGELINA (N)
Cupples & Leon Company: 1909 (11-1/2x17", 56 pgs., 2 colors)

nn - By Munson Paddock   67.00   233.00   400.00
NOTE: *Strip ran March 22, 1908-Feb 7, 1909.*

ANDY GUMP, HIS LIFE STORY (I)
The Reilly & Lee Co, Chicago: 1924 (192 pgs, hardbound)

nn - By Sidney Smith (over 100 illustrations)   20.00   80.00   150.00

ANIMAL CIRCUS, THE (from Puggery Wee)
Rand McNally + Company: 1908 (48 pgs, 11x8-1/2", color-c, 3-color insides)

nn - By unknown   20.00   80.00   150.00
NOTE: *Illustrated verse, many pages with multiple illustrations.*

ANIMAL SERIALS
T. Y. Crowell: 1906 (9x6-7/8, 214 pgs, hard-c, B&W)

nn - By E Warde Blaisdell   20.00   80.00   150.00
NOTE: *Multi-page comic strip stories. Reprints of Sunday strip "Bunny Bright He's All-Right".*

A NOBODY'S SCRAP BOOK
Frederik A. Stokes Co., New York: 1900 (11" x 8-5/8", hard-c, color)

nn- (Scarce)   67.00   233.00   400.00
NOTE: *Designed in England, printed in Holland, on English paper -- which likely explains the mispelling of Frederick Stokes' name. Highly fragile paper. Strips and cartoons, all by the same unidentified artist, "A Nobody", almost certainly reprinted from somewhere, as they are very professional.*

AT THE BOTTOM OF THE LADDER (M)
J.P. Lippincott Company: 1926 (11x8-1/4", 296 pgs, hardcover, B&W)

nn - By Camillus Kessler   45.00   157.50   300.00
NOTE: *Hilarious single panel cartoons showing first jobs of then important "captains of industry."*

AUTO FUN, PICTURES AND COMMENTS FROM "LIFE"
Thomas Y. Crowell & Co.: 1905 (152 pgs, 9x7", hard-c, B&W)

nn -By various   45.00   157.00   300.00
NOTE: *The cover just has "Auto Fun" but the title page also has the subheading listed here. This is similar to other reprint books of Life cartoons printed in the guide. Largely single panel cartoons but also several sequential. One or more cartoons by Kemble, Levering, Dirks, Flagg, Sullivant. Sequential cartoons by Kemble, Levering, Sullivant, and the highpoint, a 2 pg 6 panel piece by Winsor McCay.*

BANANA OIL (N)
MS Publ. Co.: 1924 (9-7/8x10", 52 pgs., B&W)

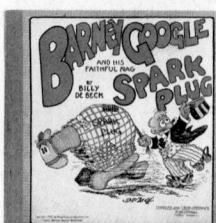

Barney Google and Spark Plug #1
© C&L

Bill the Boy Artist's Book by Ed Payne
1910 © C.M. Clark Publishing Co

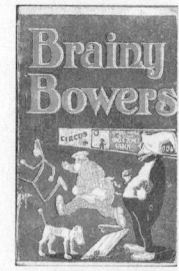

Brainy Bowers and Drowsy Duggan by R.W. Taylor
1905 © Star Publishing Co. - the first daily reprints

	GD2.0	FN6.0	VF8.0

nn - Milt Gross-a; not reprints 100.00 375.00 650.00

BARKER'S ILLUSTRATED ALMANAC (O,P,S) (See Barkers in Victorian Era section)
Barker, Moore & Mein Medicine Co: 1900-1932+ (36 pgs, B&W, color paper-c)

1900-1932+ (7x5-7/8") 20.00 70.00 125.00

BARKER'S "KOMIC" PICTURE SOUVENIR (P,S) (see Barker's in Victorian)
Barker, Moore & Mein Medicine Co: nd (Parts 1-3, 1901-1903; Parts 1-4, 1906+) (color cardboard-c, B&W interior, 50 pages)

Parts 1-3 (Rare, earliest printing, nd (1901)) 60.00 300.00 600.00
NOTE: Same cover as 4th edition in Victorian Age Section, except has "Part 1", "Part 2", or "Part 3" printed in the blank space beneath the crate on which central figure is sitting. States "Edition in 3 Parts" on the first interior or page, beneath the picture of the Barker's Building.
Parts 1-3 (nd, c1901-1903) 40.00 200.00 400.00
NOTE: New cover art on all Parts. States "Edition in 3 Parts" on the first interior page.
Parts 1-4 (nd, c1906+) 25.00 100.00 300.00
NOTE: States "Edition in 4 Parts" on the first interior page. Various printings known. These have been confirmed as premium comic books, predating the Buster Brown premiums. They reprint advertising cartoons from Barker's Illustrated Almanac. For the 50 page booklets by this same name, numbered as "Part"s, without exception, were published after 1900. Some editions are found to have 54 pages.

BARNEY GOOGLE AND SPARK PLUG (N) (See **Comic Monthly**)
Cupples & Leon Co.: 1923 - No.6, 1928 (9-7/8x9-3/4"; 52 pgs., B&W, daily-r)

1 (nn)-By Billy DeBeck 60.00 240.00 450.00
2-4 (#5 & #6 do not exist) 46.00 186.00 350.00
NOTE: Started June 17, 1919 as newspaper strip; Spark Plug introduced July 17, 1922; strip still running making it one of the oldest still in existence.

BART'S CARTOONS FOR 1902 FROM THE MINNEAPOLIS JOURNAL (N,S)
Minneapolis Journal: 1903 (11x9", 102 pgs, paperback, B&W)

nn - By Charles L. Bartholomew 28.00 99.00 170.00

BELIEVE IT OR NOT! by Ripley (N,S)
Simon & Schuster: 1929 (8x 5-1/4", 68 pgs, red, B&W cover, B&W interior)

nn - By Robert Ripley (strip-r text & art) 40.00 120.00 240.00
NOTE: 1929 was the first printing of many reprintings . Strip began Dec 19, 1918 and is still running.

BEN WEBSTER (N)
Standard Printing Company: 1928-1931 (13-3/4x4-7/16", 768 pgs, soft-c)

1 - "Bound to Win" 40.00 120.00 280.00
2 - "...in old Mexico 40.00 120.00 280.00
3 - "...At Wilderness Lake 40.00 120.00 280.00
4 - "...in the Oil Fields 40.00 120.00 280.00
NOTE: Self Published by Edwin Alger, also contains fan's letter pages.

BIG SMOKER
W.T. Blackwell & Co.: 1908 (16 pgs, 5-1/2x3-1/2", color-c & interior)

nn - By unknown 12.00 48.00 80.00
NOTE: Stated reprint of 1878 version. no known copies yet of original printing.

BILLY BOUNCE (I)
Donohue & Co.: 1906 (288 pgs, hardbound)

nn - By W.W. Denslow & Dudley Bragdon 150.00 525.00 900.00
NOTE: Billy Bounce was created in 1901 as a comic strip by W. W. Denslow (strip ran from 1901 NOV 11 to 1905 DEC 3), but the series is best remembered for the C. W. Kahles version (from 1902 SEP 28). Denslow resumed his character in the above illustrated book.

BILLY HON'S FAMOUS CARTOON BOOK (H)
Wasley Publishing Co.: 1927 (7-1/2x10", 68 pgs, softbound wraparound)

nn - By Billy Hon 12.00 48.00 80.00

BILLY THE BOY ARTIST'S BOOK OF FUNNY PICTURES (N)
C.M.Clark Publishing Co.: 1910 (9x12", hardcover-c, Boston Globe strip-r)

nn - By Ed Payne 125.00 400.00 750.00
NOTE: This long lived strip ran in **The Boston Globe** from Nov 5 1899-Jan 7 1955; one of the longer run strips.

BILLY THE BOY ARTIST'S PAINTING BOOK OF FUNNY PICTURES
(known to exist; more data required) — — —

BIRD CENTER CARTOONS: A Chronicle of Social Happenings (N,S)
A. C. McClurg & Co.: 1904 (12-3/8x9-1/2", 216 pgs, hardcover, B&W, single panels)

nn - By John McCutcheon 40.00 140.00 260.00
NOTE: Strip began in **The Chicago Tribune** in 1903. Satirical cartoons and text concerning a mythical town.

BLASTS FROM THE RAM'S HORN
The Rams Horn Company: 1902 (330 pgs, 7x9", B&W)

nn - By various 20.00 70.00 120.00
NOTE: Cartoons reprinted from what was, apparently, a religious newspaper. Many cartoons by Frank Beard. Mostly single panel but occasionally sequential. Allegorical cartoons similar to the Christian Cartoons book. This book mixes cartoons and text sort of like the Caricature books. One or more cartoons on every page.

BOBBY THATCHER & TREASURE CAVE (N)
Altemus Co.: 1932 (9x7", 86 pgs., B&W, hard-c)

nn - Reprints; Storm-a 54.00 189.00 400.00

BOBBY THATCHER'S ROMANCE (N)
The Bell Syndicate/Henry Altemus Co.: 1931 (8-3/4x7", color cover, B&W)

nn - By Storm 54.00 189.00 400.00

BOOK OF CARTOONS, A (M,S)
Edward T. Miller: 1903 (12-1/4x9-1/4", 120 pgs, hardcover, B&W)

nn - By Harry J. Westerman (Ohio State Journal-r) 20.00 70.00 120.00

BOOK OF DRAWINGS BY A.B. FROST, A (M,S)
P.F. Collier & Son: 1904 (15-3/8 x 11", 96 pgs, B&W)

nn - A.B. Frost 50.00 100.00 300.00
NOTE: Pages alternate verses by Wallace Irwin and full-page plated by A.B.Frost. 39 plates.

BOTTLE, THE (E) (see Victorian Age section for earlier printings)
Gowans & Gray, London & Glasgow: June 1905 (3-3/4x6", 72 pgs, printed one side only, paper cover, B&W)

nn - 1st printing (June 1905) 17.50 35.00 70.00
nn - 2nd printing (March 1906) 17.50 35.00 70.00
nn - 3rd printing (January 1911) 17.50 35.00 70.00
NOTE: By George Cruikshank. Reprints both THE BOTTLE and THE DRUNKARD'S CHILDREN. Cover is text only - no cover art.

BOTTLE, THE (E)
Frederick A. Stokes: nd (c1906) (3-3/4x6", 72 pgs, printed one side only, paper-c, B&W)

nn- by George Cruikshank 17.50 35.00 70.00
NOTE: Reprint of the Gowans & Gray edition. Reprints both THE BOTTLE and THE DRUNKARD'S CHILDREN. Cover is text only - no cover art.

BOYS AND FOLKS (N).
George H. Dornan Company: 1917 (10-1/4 x 8-1/4", 232 pgs. (single-sided), B&W strip-r.

nn - By Webster 21.00 64.00 150.00
NOTE: Four sections: Life's Darkest Moments, Mostly About Folks, The Thrill That Comes Once in a Lifetime, and Our Boyhood Ambitions. Most are single-panel cartoons, but there are some sequential comic strips.

BOY'S & GIRLS' BIG PAINTING BOOK OF INTERESTING COMIC PICTURES (N)
M. A. Donohue & Co.: 1914-16 (9x15, 70 pgs)

nn - By Carl "Bunny" Schultze (Foxy Grandpa-r) 81.00 284.00 –
#2 (1914) 81.00 284.00 –
#337 (1914) (sez "Big Painting & Drawing Book) 81.00 284.00 –
nn - (1916) (sez "Big Painting Book")(9-1/4x15") 81.00 284.00 –
NOTE: These are all Foxy Grandpa items.

BRAIN LEAKS: Dialogues of Mutt & Flea (N)
O. K. Printing Co. (Rochester Evening Times): 1911 (76 pgs, 6-5/8x4-5/8, hard-c, B&W)

nn - By Leo Edward O'Melia; newspaper strip-r 29.00 100.00 171.00

BRAINY BOWERS AND DROWSY DUGGAN (N)
Star Publishing: 1905 (7-1/4 x 4-9/16", 98 pgs., blue, brown & white color cover, B&W interior, 25¢) (daily strip-r 1902-04 Chicago Daily News)

#74 - By R. W. Taylor (Scarce) 400.00 1500.00 –
NOTE: Part of a series of Atlantic Library Heart Series. Strip begins in 1901 and runs thru 1915. Taylor also created Yen the Janitor for the **New York World**.

BRAIN BOWERS AND DROWSY DUGAN (N)
Max Stein Pub. House, Chicago: 1905 (6-3/16x4-3/8", 64 pgs, B&W)

nn - By R.W. Taylor (Scarce) 400.00 1500.00 –
NOTE: A coverless copy of this surfaced on eBay in 2002 selling for $700.00.;

BRAINY BOWERS AND DROWSY DUGGAN GETTING ON IN THE WORLD WITH NO VISIBLE MEANS OF SUPPORT (STORIES TOLD IN PICTURES TO MAKE THEIR TELLING SHORT) (N)
Max Stein/Star Publishing: 1905 (7-3/8x5 1/8", 164 pgs, slick black, red & tan color cover, interior newsprint) (daily strip-r 1902-04 Chicago Daily News)

nn - By R. W. Taylor (Scarce) 400.00 1500.00 –
nn - Possible hard cover edition also? – – –
NOTE: These Brainy Bowers editions are the earliest known daily newspaper strip reprint books.

BRINGING UP FATHER (N)
Star Co. (King Features): 1917 (5-1/2x16-1/2", 100 pgs., B&W, cardboard-c)

nn - (Scarcer)-Daily strip- by George McManus 158.00 553.00 950.00

BRINGING UP FATHER (N)
Cupples & Leon Co.: 1919 - No. 26, 1934 (10x10", 52 pgs., B&W, stiff cardboard-c) (No. 22 is 9-1/4x9-1/2")

1-Daily strip-r by George McManus in all 25.00 100.00 260.00
2-10 25.00 100.00 250.00
11-20 40.00 200.00 375.00
21-26 (Scarcer) 60.00 300.00 550.00
The Big Book 1 (1926)-Thick book (hardcover, 142 pgs.) 127.00 508.00 1000.00
w/dust jacket (rare) 183.00 732.00 1325.00
The Big Book 2 (1929) 96.00 384.00 700.00
w/dust jacket (rare) 183.00 732.00 1325.00
NOTE: The Big Books contain 3 regular issues rebound. Strip began Jan 2 1913-May 28 2000

BRINGING UP FATHER, THE TROUBLE OF (N)
Embee Publ. Co.: 1921 (9-3/4x15-3/4", 46 pgs, Sunday-r in color)

nn - (Rare) 100.00 350.00 600.00
NOTE: Ties with Mutt & Jeff (EmBee) and Jimmie Dugan And The Reg'lar Fellers (C&L) as the last of the oblong size era. This was self published by George McManus.

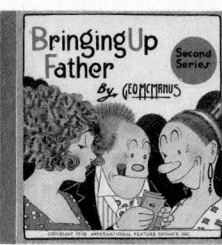

Bringing Up Father #2
© C&L

Brownie Clown of Brownie Town
© The Century Co.

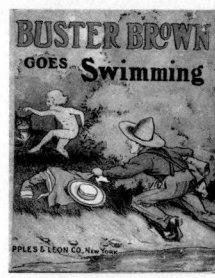

Buster Brown Nuggets - Goes Swimming
1907 © Cupples & Leon

	GD2.0	FN6.0	VF8.0		GD2.0	FN6.0	VF8.0

BRINGING UP FATHER (N) (see SAGARA'S ENGLISH CARTOONS
Publisher unknown (actually, unreadable), Tokyo: October 1924 (9-7/8" x 7-1/2", 90 pgs, color hard-c, B&W)

nn- (Scarce) by George McManus C&A		(no known sales)	

NOTE: *Published in Tokyo, Japan, with all strips in both English and Japanese, to facilitate learning English. Introduction by George McManus. Scarce in USA.*

BRONX BALLADS (I)
Simon & Schuster, NY: 1927 (9-1/2x7-1/4", hard-c, B&W)

nn - By Robert Simon and Harry Hershfield	36.00	143.00	250.00

BROWNIES, THE (not sequential comic strips)
The Century Co.: 1887 - 1914 (all came with dust jackets; add $100-150 to value if original dust jacket is included and intact)

Book 1 - The Brownies: Their Book (1887)	200.00	850.00	1320.00
Book 2 - Another Brownies Book (1890)	150.00	635.00	1000.00
Book 3 - The Brownies at Home (1893)	125.00	530.00	825.00
Book 4 - The Brownies Around the World (1894)	100.00	425.00	660.00
Book 5 - The Brownies Through the Union (1895)	100.00	425.00	660.00
Book 6 - The Brownies Abroad (1899)	100.00	425.00	660.00
Book 7 - The Brownies in the Philippines (1904)	100.00	425.00	660.00
Book 8 - The Brownies' Latest Adventures (1910)	100.00	425.00	660.00
Book 9 - The Brownies Many More Nights (1914)	100.00	425.00	660.00
...Raid on Kleinmaier Bros. (c. 1910, 16 pages) Kleinmaier Bros. Clothing, Marion, Ohio		(no known sales)	

BROWNIE CLOWN OF BROWNIE TOWN (N)
The Century Co.: 1908 (6-7/8 x 9-3/8", 112 pgs, color hardcover & interior)

nn - By Palmer Cox (rare; 1907 newspaper comic strip-r)	250.00	800.00	1400.00

NOTE: *The Brownies created 1883 in St Nicholas Magazine.*

BUDDY TUCKER & HIS FRIENDS (N) (also see **Buster Brown Nuggets**)
Cupples & Leon Co.: 1906 (11-5/8 x17", 58 pgs, color)

nn - 1905 Sunday strip-r by R. F. Outcault	300.00	950.00	1600.00

NOTE: *Strip began Apr 30, 1905 thru at least Oct 1905.*

BUFFALO BILL'S PICTURE STORIES
Street & Smith Publications: 1909 (Soft cardboard cover)

nn - Very rare	67.00	233.00	400.00

BUGHOUSE FABLES (N) (see also **Comic Monthly**)
Embee Distributing Co. (King Features): 1921 (10¢, 4x4-1/2", 48 pgs.)

1-By Barney Google (Billy DeBeck)	46.00	186.00	350.00

BUG MOVIES (O) (Also see Clancy The Cop & Deadwood Gulch)
Dell Publishing Co.: 1931 (9-13/16x9-7/8", 52 pgs., B&W)

nn - Original material; Stookie Allen-a	43.00	172.00	350.00

BULL
Bull Publishing Company, New York: No.1, March, 1916 - No.12, Feb, 1917 (10 cents, 10-3/4x8-3/4", 24 pgs, color paper-c, B&W)

1-12 (Very Rare)	–	–	–

NOTE: *Pro-German, Anti-British cartoon/humor monthly, whose goal was to keep the U.S. neutral and out of World War I. We know of no copies which have sold in the past few years.*

BUNNY'S BLUE BOOK (see also Foxy Grandpa)
Frederick A. Stokes Co.: 1911 (10x15, 60¢)

nn - By Carl "Bunny" Schultze strip-r	100.00	350.00	

BUNNY'S RED BOOK (see also Foxy Grandpa) (N)
Frederick A. Stokes Co.: 1912 (10-1/4x15-3/4", 64 pgs.)

nn - By Carl "Bunny" Schultze strip-r	100.00	350.00	

BUNNY'S GREEN BOOK (see also Foxy Grandpa) (N)
Frederick A. Stokes Co.: 1913 (10x15")

nn - By Carl "Bunny" Schultze	100.00	350.00	

BUSTER BROWN (C) (Also see Brown's Blue Ribbon Book of Jokes and Jingles & Buddy Tucker & His Friends)
Frederick A. Stokes Co.: 1903 - 1916 (Daily strip-r in color)

1903...& His Resolutions (11-1/4x16", 66 pgs.) by R. F. Outcault (Rare)-1st nationally distributed comic. Distr. through Sears & Roebuck	1600.00	5500.00	–
1904...His Dog Tige & Their Troubles (11-1/4x16-1/4", 66 pgs.)(Rare)	600.00	1875.00	–
1905...Pranks (11-1/4x16-3/8", 66 pgs.)	400.00	1450.00	–
1906...Antics (11x16-3/8", 66 pgs.)	400.00	1450.00	–
1906...And Company (11x16-1/2", 66 pgs.)	300.00	1050.00	–
1906...Mary Jane & Tige (11-1/4x16, 66 pgs.)	300.00	1050.00	–

NOTE: *Yellow Kid pictured on two pages.*

1908 Collection of Buster Brown Comics	250.00	835.00	
1909 Outcault's Real Buster and The Only Mary Jane (11x16, 66 pgs, Stokes)	250.00	835.00	
1910...Up to Date (10-1/8x15-3/4", 66 pgs.)	208.00	729.00	1315.00
1911...Fun And Nonsense (10-1/8x15-3/4", 66 pgs.)	183.00	642.00	1150.00

1912...The Fun Maker (10-1/8x15-3/4", 66 pgs.) -Yellow Kid (4 pgs.)	183.00	642.00	1150.00
1913...At Home (10-1/8x15-3/4", 56 pgs.)	167.00	583.00	1050.00
1914...And Tige Here Again (10x16, 62 pgs, Stokes)	153.00	535.00	1000.00
1915...And His Chum Tige (10x16, Stokes)	153.00	535.00	1000.00
1916...The Little Rogue (10-1/8x15-3/4", 62 pgs.)	162.00	567.00	1025.00
1917...And the Cat (5-1/2x 6-1/2, 26 pgs, Stokes)	115.00	402.00	750.00
1917...Disturbs the Family (5-1/2x 6 1/2, 26 pgs, Stokes)			
NOTE: *Story featuring statue of "the Chinese Yellow Kid"*	115.00	402.00	750.00
1917...The Real Buster Brown (5-1/2x 6 -/2, 26 pgs, Stokes	115.00	402.00	750.00

Frederick A. Stokes Co. Hard Cover Series (I)

...Abroad (1904, 10-1/4x8", 86 pgs., B&W, hard-c)-R. F. Outcault-a (Rare)	200.00	700.00	1260.00
...Abroad (1904, B&W, 67 pgs.)-R. F. Outcault-a	200.00	700.00	1260.00

NOTE: *Buster Brown Abroad is not an actual comic book, but prose with illustrations.*

..."Tige" His Story 1905 (10x8", 63 pgs., B&W) (63 illos.)			
nn-By RF Outcault	143.00	500.00	
...My Resolutions 1906 (10x8", B&W, 68 pgs.)-R.F. Outcault-a (Rare)	233.00	817.00	1475.00
...Autobiography 1907 (10x8", B&W, 71 pgs.) (16 color plates & 36 B&W illos)	67.00	233.00	440.00
...And Mary Jane's Painting Book 1907 (10x13-1/4", 60 pgs, both card & hardcover versions exist			
nn-RFO (first printing blank on top of cover)	67.00	233.00	440.00
First Series- this is a reprint if it says First Series	67.00	233.00	440.00
Volume Two - By RFO	67.00	233.00	440.00
... My Resolutions by Buster Brown (1907, 68 pgs, small size, cardboard covers) scarce	43.00	150.00	285.00

NOTE: *Not actual comic book per se, but a compilation of the Resolutions panels found at the end of Outcault's Buster Brown newspaper strips.*

BUSTER BROWN (N)
Cupples & Leon Co./N. Y. Herald Co.: 1906 - 1917 (11x17", color, strip-r)
NOTE: *Early issues by R. F. Outcault; most C&L editions are not by Outcault.*

1906...His Dog Tige And Their Jolly Times (11-3/8x16-5/8", 68 pgs.)	300.00	1100.00	1900.00
1906...His Dog Tige & Their Jolly Times (11x16, 46 pgs.)	163.00	600.00	1025.00
1907...Latest Frolics (11-3/8x16-5/8", 66 pgs., r/'05-06 strips)	163.00	600.00	1025.00
1908...Amusing Capers (58 pgs.)	129.00	475.00	815.00
1909...The Busy Body (11-3/8x16-5/8", 62 pgs.)	129.00	475.00	815.00
1910...On His Travels (11x16", 58 pgs.)	115.00	402.00	750.00
1911...Happy Days (11-3/8x16-5/8", 58 pgs.)	115.00	402.00	750.00
1912...In Foreign Lands (10x16", 58 pgs)	115.00	402.00	750.00
1913...And His Pets (11x16", 58 pgs.) STOKES????	115.00	402.00	750.00
1913...And His Pets (26 pg partial reprint)	–	–	–
1914...Funny Tricks (11-3/8x16-5/8", 58 pgs.)	115.00	402.00	750.00
1916...At Play (10x16, 58 pgs)	115.00	402.00	750.00

BUSTER BROWN NUGGETS (N)
Cupples & Leon Co./N.Y. Herald Co.: 1907 (1905, 7-1/2x6-1/2", 36 pgs., color, strip-r, hard-c)(By R. F. Outcault) (NOTE: Books are all unnumbered)

Buster Brown Goes Fishing, Goes Swimming, Plays Indian, Goes Shooting, Plays Cowboy, On Uncle Jack's Farm, Tige And the Bull, And Uncle Buster	39.00	137.00	275.00
Buddy Tucker Meets Alice in Wonderland	56.00	200.00	400.00
Buddy Tucker Visits The House That Jack Built	39.00	137.00	275.00

BUSTER BROWN MUSLIN SERIES (N)
Saalfield: 1907 (also contain copyright Cupples & Leon)

...Goes Fishing, Plays Indian, And the Donkey (1907, 6-7/8x6-1/8", 24 pgs., color)-r/1905 Sunday comics page by Outcault (Rare)	50.00	175.00	315.00
...Plays Cowboy (1907, 6-3/4x6", 10 pgs., color)-r/1905 Sunday comics page by Outcault (Rare)	50.00	175.00	315.00

NOTE: *These are muslin versions of the C&L BB Nugget series. Muslin books are all cloth books, made to be washable so as not easily stained/destroyed by very young children. The Muslin books contain one strip each (the title strip), to the more common NUGGET's three strips.*

BUSTER BROWN PREMIUMS (Advertising premium booklets)
Various Publishers: 1904 - 1912 (3x5" to 5x7"; sizes vary)

American Fruit Product Company, Rochester, NY

Buster Brown Duffy's 1842 Cider (1904, 7x5". 12 pgs, C.E. Sherin Co, NYC)			
nn - By R. F. Outcault (scarce)	100.00	350.00	600.00

The Brown Shoe Company, St. Louis, USA
Set of five books (5x7", 16 pgs., color)

Brown's Blue Ribbon Book of Jokes and Jingles Book 1 (nn, 1904)-By R. F. Outcault; Buster Brown & Tige, Little Tommy Tucker, Jack & Jill, Little Boy Blue, Dainty Jane; The Yellow Kid app. on back-c (1st BB comic book premium)	300.00	1050.00	1900.00
Buster Brown's Blue Ribbon Book of Jokes and Jingles Book 2 (1905)- Original color art by Outcault	200.00	600.00	1260.00

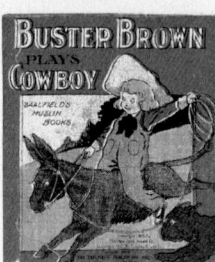

Buster Brown Nuggets -Buster Brown
Plays Cowboy © C&L

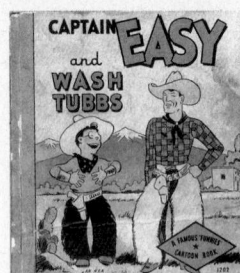

Captain Easy and Wash Tubbs by Roy Crane
1934 © Whitman Famous Comics Cartoon Book

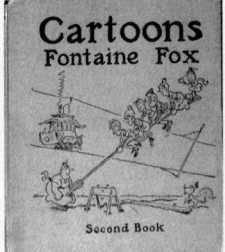

Cartoons Fontaine Fox Second Book
early 1920s © Harper & Bros, NY

Buster's Book of Jokes & Jingles Book 3 (1909)
not by R.F. Outcault 150.00 400.00 840.00
NOTE: Reprinted from the Blue Ribbon post cards with advert jingles added.
Buster's Book of Instructive Jokes and Jingles Book 4 (1910)-Original color art
not by R.F. Outcault 150.00 585.00 1050.00
...Book of Travels nn (1912, 3x5")-Original color art not signed by Outcault
117.00 408.00 735.00
NOTE: Estimated 5 or 6 known copies exist of books #1-4.
The Buster Brown Bread Company
"Buster Brown" Bread Book of Rhymes, The (1904, 4x6", 12 pgs., half color, half
B&W)- Original color art not signed by RFO 158.00 553.00 1000.00
Buster Brown's Hosiery Mills
"How Buster Brown Got The Pie" nn (nd, 7x5-1/4". 16 pgs, color paper cover and
color interior By R.F. Outcault 83.00 292.00 525.00
"The Autobiography of Buster Brown" nn (nd,9x6-1/8", 36 pgs, text story & art by
R.F. Outcault 83.00 292.00 525.00
NOTE: Similar to, but a distinctly different item than "Buster Brown's Autobiography."
The Buster Brown Stocking Company
Buster Brown Drawing Book, The nn (nd, 5x6", 20 pgs.)-B&W reproductions of 1903
R.F. Outcault art to trace 50.00 150.00 315.00
NOTE: Reprints a comic strip from Burr McIntosh Magazine, which includes Buster, Yellow Kid, and Pore Li'l
Mose (only known story involving all three.)
Buster Brown Stocking Magazine nn (Jan. 1906, 7-3/4x5-3/8", 36 pgs.) R.F. Outcault
50.00 100.00 200.00
NOTE: This was actually a store bought item selling for 5 cents per copy.
Collins Baking Company
Buster Brown Drawing Book nn (1904, 5x3", 12 pgs.)-Original B&W art to trace,
not signed by R.F. Outcault 50.00 150.00 315.00
C. H. Morton, St. Albans, VT
Merry Antics of Buster Brown, Buddy Tucker & Tige nn (nd, 3-1/2x5-1/2", 16 pgs.)
-Original B&W art by R.F. Outcault 83.00 292.00 525.00
Ivan Frank & Company
Buster Brown nn (1904, 3x5", 12 pgs.)-B&W repros of R. F. Outcault Sunday pages
(First premium to actually reproduce Sunday comic pages – may be first premium
comic strip-r book?) 125.00 438.00 785.00
Buster Brown's Pranks (1904, 3-1/2x5-1/8", 12 pgs.)-reprints intro of Buddy Tucker into
the BB newspaper strip before he was spun off into his own short lived newspaper strip
125.00 438.00 785.00
Kaufmann & Strauss
Buster Brown Drawing Book (1906, 28 pages, 5x3-1/2") Color Cover, B+W original story
signed by Outcault, tracing paper inserted as alternate pages. Back cover imprinted for
Nox' Em All Shoes 50.00 150.00 315.00
Pond's Extract
Buster Brown's Experiences With Pond's Extract nn (1904, 6-3/4x4-1/2", 28 pgs.)
Original color art by R.F. Outcault (may be the first BB premium comic book with
original art) 100.00 250.00 525.00
C. A. Cross & Co.
Red Cross Drawing Book nn (1906, 4-7/8x3-1/2", color paper -c, B&W interior, 12 pgs.)
50.00 150.00 315.00
NOTE: This is for Red Cross coffee; not the health organization.
Ringen Stove Company
Quick Meal Steel Ranges nn (nd, 5x3", 16 pgs.)-Original B&W art not signed
by R.F. Outcault 50.00 150.00 315.00
Steinwender Stoffregen Coffee Co.
"Buster Brown Coffee" (1905, 4-7/8x3", color paper cover, B&W interior, 12 printed pages,
plus 1 tracing paper page above each interior image (total of 8 sheets) (Very Rare)
83.00 292.00 525.00
NOTE: Part of a BB drawing contest. If instructions had been followed, most copies would have ended up
destroyed.
U. S. Playing Card Company
Buster Brown - My Own Playing Cards (1906, 2-1/2x1-3/4", full color)
nn - By R. F. Outcault 42.00 147.00 250.00
NOTE: Series of full color panels tell stories, average about 5 cards per story.
Publisher Unknown
The Drawing Book nn (1906, 3-9/16x5", 8 pgs.)-Original B&W art to trace
not by R.F. Outcault 50.00 150.00 300.00

BUTLER BOOK A Series of Clever Cartoons of Yale Undergraduate Life
Yale Record: June 16, 1913 (10-3/4 x 17", 34 pgs, paper cover B&W)
nn - By Alban Bernard Butler 21.00 73.00 130.00
NOTE: Cartoons and strips reprinted from The Yale Record student newspaper.

BUTTONS & FATTY IN THE FUNNIES
Whitman Publishing Co.: nd 1927 (10-1/4x15-1/2", 28pg.,color)
W936 - Signed "M.E.B.", probably M.E. Brady; strips in color copyright The Brooklyn
Daily Eagle; (very rare) 61.00 244.00 425.00
BY BRIGGS (M,N,P) (see also OLD GOLD THE SMOOTHER AND BETTER CIGARETTE)
Old Gold Cigarettes: nd (c1920's) (11" x 9-11/16", 44 pgs, cardboard-c, B&W)
nn- (Scarce) 20.00 70.00 130.00
NOTE: Collection reprinting strip cartoons by Clare Briggs, advertising Old Gold Cigarettes. These strips origi-

nally appeared in various magazines, play program booklets, newspapers, etc. Some of the strips involve regular Briggs strip series. Contains all of the strips in the smaller, color "OLD GOLD" giveaways, plus more.
CAMION CARTOONS
Marshall Jones Company: 1919 (7-1/2x5", 136 pgs, B&W)
nn - By Kirkland H. Day (W.W.One occupation) 20.00 70.00 120.00
CANYON COUNTRY KIDDIES (M)
Doubleday, Page & Co: 1923 (8x10-1/4", 88 pgs, hard-c, B&W)
nn - By James Swinnerton 39.00 137.00 260.00
CARLO (H)
Doubleday, Page & Co.: 1913 (8 x 9-5/8, 120 pgs, hardcover, B&W)
nn - By A.B. Frost 40.00 140.00 300.00
NOTE: Original sequential strips about a dog. Became short lived newspaper comic strip in 1914. Originally
published with a dust jacket which increases value 50%.
CARTOON BOOK, THE
Bureau of Publicity, War Loan Organization, Treasury Department, Washington, D.C.:
1918 (4-1/2x4-7/8", 48 pgs, paper cover, B&W)
nn - By various artists 31.00 108.00 185.00
NOTE: U.S. government issued booklet of WW I propaganda cartoons by 46 artists promoting the third sale of
Liberty Loan bonds. The artists include: Berryman, Clare Briggs, Cesare, J. N. "Ding" Darling, Rube Goldberg,
Kemble, McCutcheon, George McManus, F. Opper, T. E. Powers, Ripley, Satterfield, H. T. Webster, Gaar
Williams.
CARTOON CATALOGUE (S)
The Lockwood Art School, Kalamazoo, Mich.: 1919 (11-5/8x9, 52 pgs, B&W)
nn - Edited by Mr. Lockwood 20.00 60.00 140.00
NOTE: Jammed with 100s of single panel cartoons and some sequential comics; Mr Lockwood began the
very first cartoonist school back in 1892. Clare Briggs was one of his students.
CARTOON COMICS
Lasco Publications, Detroit, Mich: #1, April 1930 - #2, May 1930 (8-3/6x5-1/5")
1, 2 - By Lu Harris 20.00 60.00 100.00
NOTE: Contains recurring characters Hollywood Horace, Campus Charlie, Pair-A-Dice Alley and Jocko
Monkey. Not much is presently known about the creator(s) or publisher.
CARTOON HISTORY OF ROOSEVELT'S CAREER, A
The Review of Reviews Company: 1910 (276 pgs, 8-1/4x11",
nn - By various 43.00 129.00 325.00
NOTE: Reprints editorial cartoons about Teddy Roosevelt from U.S. and international newspapers and cartoons
from the humor magaines (Puck, Judge, etc.) A few cartoonists whose work is included are Dalrymple, Opper,
McDougall, McCutcheon, Remington, Rogers, Kemble. Mostly single panel but 10 or so are sequential strips.
CARTOON HUMOR
Collegian Press: 1938 (102 pgs, squarebound, B&W)
nn 20.00 70.00 120.00
NOTE: Contains cartoons & strips by Otto Soglow, Syd Hoff, Peter Arno, Abner Dean, others.
CARTOONIST'S PHILOSOPHY, A
Percy Crosby: 1931, HC, 252 pgs, 5-1/2x7-1/2", hard-c, celluloid dust wrapper
nn - By Percy Crosby (10 plates, 6 are of Skippy) 60.00 130.00
NOTE: Crosby's partial autobiography regarding his return to France in 1929, and portrayals of Normandy, the
"cliff dwellers" on Normandy cliffs (filmed in WWII), his visit to London, comments on art, philosophy, several poems, and political dialogue. His description of his Cockney driver, "Harold" is amusing. Also describes
his experience visiting Chicago to speak out against Capone, his concerns over the evils of Prohibition, and
the economy prior to the 1929 crash. This book reveals he was aware of the dangers of his outspoken views,
and is prophetic, re: his later years as political prisoner. Also reveals his religious beliefs.
CARTOONS BY BRADLEY: CARTOONIST OF THE CHICAGO DAILY NEWS
Rand McNally & Company: 1917 (11-1/4x8-3/4", 112 pgs, hardcover, B&W)
nn - By Luther D. Bradley (editorial) 20.00 70.00 120.00
CARTOONS BY FONTAINE FOX (Toonerville Trolley) (S)
Harper & Brothers Publishers: nd early '20s (9x7-7/8",102 pgs., hard-c, B&W)
Second Book- By Fontaine Fox (Toonerville-r) 56.00 200.00 400.00
CARTOONS BY HALLADAY (N,S)
Providence Journal Co., Rhode Island: Dec 1914 (116 pgs, 10-1/2x 7-3/4", hard-c, B&W)
nn- (Scarce) 50.00 125.00 250.00
NOTE: Cartoons on Rhode Island politics, plus some Teddy Roosevelt & WW I cartoons.
CARTOONS BY McCUTCHEON (S)
A. C. McClurg & Co.: 1903 (12-3/8x9-3/4", 212 pgs., hardcover, B&W)
nn - By John McCutcheon 20.00 70.00 120.00
CARTOONS BY W. A. IRELAND (S)
The Columbus-Evening Dispatch: 1907 (13-3/4 x 10-1/2", 66 pgs, hardcover)
nn - By W. A. Ireland (strip-r) 20.00 70.00 120.00
CARTOONS MAGAZINE (I,N,S)
H. H. Windsor, Chicago: Jan 1912-June 1921; July 1921-1923; 1923-1924; 1924-1927
(1912-July 1913 issues 12x9-1/4", 68-76 pgs; 1913-1921 issues 10x7", average 112 to 188
pgs, color covers)
1912-Jan-Dec 15.00 51.00 90.00
1913-1915 15.00 51.00 90.00
1916-1917 15.00 51.00 90.00

Cartoons Magazine v9 #5 by various creators
May 1916 © H. H. Windsor, Chicago

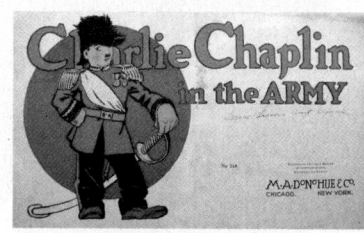

Charlie Chaplin in the Army by Segar
1917 © Essanay

Comic Monthly #2
© Embee Dist. Co.

	GD2.0	FN6.0	VF8.0
1917-(Apr) "How Comickers Regard Their Characters"	30.00	105.00	150.00
1917-(June) "A Genius of the Comic Page" - long article on George Herriman, Krazy Kat, etc with lots of Herriman art; "Cartoonists and Their Cars"	58.00	204.00	400.00
1918-1919	20.00	70.00	120.00
1920-June 1921	15.00	53.00	90.00
July 1921-1923 titled Wayside Tales & Cartoons Magazine	10.00	30.00	60.00
1923-1924 becomes Cartoons Magazine again	10.00	30.00	60.00
1924-1927 becomes Cartoons & Movie Magazine	10.00	30.00	60.00

NOTE: Many issues contain a wealth of historical background on then current cartoonists of the day with an international slant; each issue profusely illustrated with many cartoons. We are unsure if this magazine continued after 1927.

CARTOONS BY J. N. DARLING (S,N - some sequential strips)
The Register & Tribune Co., Des Moines, Iowa: 1909?-1920 (12x8-7/8",B&W)

Book 1	15.00	51.00	90.00
Book 2 Education of Alonzo Applegate (1910)	15.00	51.00	90.00
2nd printing	10.00	30.00	60.00
Book 3 Cartoons From The Files (1911)	15.00	51.00	90.00
Book 4	15.00	51.00	90.00
Book 5 In Peace And War (1916)	15.00	51.00	90.00
Book 6 Aces & Kings War Cartoons (Dec 1, 1918)	15.00	51.00	90.00
Book 7 The Jazz Era (Dec 1920)	15.00	51.00	90.00
Book 8 Our Own Outlines of History (1922)	15.00	51.00	90.00

NOTE: Some of the most inspired hard hitting cartoons ever printed. Are there more?

CARTOONS THAT MADE PRINCE HENRY FAMOUS, THE (N,S)
The Chicago Record-Herald: Feb/March 1902 (12-1/8" x 9", 32 pgs, paper-c, B&W)

nn- (Scarce) by McCutcheon	15.00	51.00	90.00

NOTE: Cartoons about the visit of the British Prince Henry to the U.S.

CAVALRY CARTOONS (O)
R. Montalboddi: nd (c1918) (14-1/4" x 11", 30 pgs, printed on one side, olive & black construction paper-c, B&W interior)

nn - By R.Montalboddi	15.00	51.00	90.00

NOTE: Comics about life in the U.S.Cavalry during World War I, by a soldier who was in the 1st Cavalry.

CHARLIE CHAPLIN (N)
Essanay/M. A. Donohue & Co.: 1917 (9x16", B&W, large size soft-c)
Series 1, #315-Comic Capers (9-3/4x15-3/4")-20 pgs. by Segar;

Series 1, #316-In the Movies	165.00	525.00	1200.00
#317-Up in the Air (20 pgs), #318-In the Army	165.00	525.00	1400.00
Funny Stunts-(12-1/2x16-3/8",16 color pgs)	165.00	525.00	1400.00

NOTE: All contain pre-Thimble Theatre Segar art. The thin paper used makes high grade copies very scarce.

CHASING THE BLUES (N)
Doubleday Page: 1912 (7-1/2x10", 108 pgs., B&W, hard-c)

nn - By Rube Goldberg	150.00	525.00	900.00

NOTE: Contains a dozen Foolish Questions, baseball, a few Goldberg poems and lots of sequential strips.

CHRISTIAN CARTOONS (N,S)
The Sunday School Times Company: 1922 (7-1/4 x 6-1/8,104 pgs, brown hard-c, B&W)

nn - E.J. Pace	15.00	51.00	90.00

NOTE: Religious cartoons reprinted from The Sunday School Times.

CLANCY THE COP (O))
Dell Publishing Co.: 1930 - No. 2, 1931 (10x10", 52 pgs., B&W, cardboard-c)
(Also see Bug Movies & Deadwood Gulch)

1, 2-By VEP Victor Pazimino (original material; not reprints)	50.00	200.00	400.00

CLIFFORD MCBRIDE'S IMMORTAL NAPOLEON & UNCLE ELBY (N)
The Castle Press: 1932 (12x17"; soft-c cartoon book)

nn - Intro. by Don Herod	36.00	144.00	250.00

COLLECTED DRAWINGS OF BRUCE BAIRNSFATHER, THE
W. Colston Leigh: 1931 (11-1/4x8-1/4 ", 168 pages, hardcover, B&W)

nn - By Bruce Bairnsfather	24.00	96.00	165.00

COMICAL PEEP SHOW
McLoughlin Bros: 1902 (36 pgs, B&W)

nn	24.00	96.00	165.00

NOTE: Comic stories of Wilhelm Busch redrawn; two versions with green or gold front cover logos; back covers different.

COMIC ANIMALS (I)
Charles E. Graham & Co.: 1903 (9-3/4x7-1/4", 90 pgs, color cover)

nn - By Walt McDougall (not comic strips)	43.0	150.00	260.00

COMIC CUTS (O)
H. L. Baker Co., Inc.: 5/19/34-7/28/34 (Tabloid size 10-1/2x15-1/2", 24 pgs., 5¢)
(full color, not reprints; published weekly; created for news stand sales)

V1#1 - V1#7(6/30/34), V1#8(7/14/34), V1#9(7/28/34)-Idle Jack strips	100.00	250.00	600.00

NOTE: According to a 1958 Lloyd Jacquet interview, this short-lived comics mag was the direct inspiration for Major Malcolm Wheeler-Nicholson's New Fun Comics, not Famous Funnies.

COMIC MONTHLY (N)

Embee Dist. Co.: Jan, 1922 - No. 12, Dec, 1922 (10¢, 8-1/2"x9", 28 pgs., 2-color covers)
(1st monthly newsstand comic publication) (Reprints 1921 B&W dailies)

1-Polly & Her Pals by Cliff Sterrett	375.00	1125.00	2225.00
2-Mike & Ike by Rube Goldberg	140.00	490.00	1000.00
3-S'Matter, Pop?	140.00	490.00	1000.00
4-Barney Google by Billy DeBeck	140.00	490.00	1000.00
5-Tillie the Toiler by Russ Westover	140.00	490.00	1000.00
6-Indoor Sports by Tad Dorgan	140.00	490.00	1000.00

NOTE: #6 contains more Judge Rummy than Indoor Sports.

7-Little Jimmy by James Swinnerton	140.00	490.00	1000.00
8-Toots and Casper b y Jimmy Murphy	140.00	490.00	1000.00
9-New Bughouse Fables by Barney Google	140.00	490.00	1000.00
10-Foolish Questions by Rube Goldberg	140.00	490.00	1000.00
11-Barney Google & Spark Plug by Billy DeBeck	140.00	490.00	1000.00
12-Polly & Her Pals by Cliff Sterrett	214.00	752.00	1500.00

NOTE: This series was published by George McManus (Bringing Up Father) as Em & Rudolph Block, Jr., son of Hearst's cartoon editor for many years, as "Bee." One would have thought this series should have done very well considering the tremendous amount of talent assembled. All issues are extremely hard to find these days and rarely show up in any type of higher grade.

COMIC PAINTING AND CRAYONING BOOK (H)
Saalfield Publ. Co.: 1917 (13-1/2x10", 32 pgs.) (No price on-c)

nn - Tidy Teddy by F. M. Follett, Clarence the Cop, Mr. & Mrs. Butt-In; regular comic stories to read or color	50.00	175.00	300.00

COMPLETE TRIBUNE PRIMER, THE (I)
Mutual Book Company: 1901 (7 1/4 x 5", 152 pgs, red hard-c)

nn - By Frederick Opper; has 75 Opper cartoons	25.00	88.00	150.00

COURTSHIP OF TAGS, THE (N)
McCormick Press: pre-1910 (9x4", 88 pgs, red & B&W-c, B&W interior)

nn - By O. E. Wertz (strip-r Wichita Daily Beacon)	25.00	88.00	150.00

DAFFYDILS (N)
Cupples & Leon Co.: 1911 (5-3/4x7-7/8", 52 pgs., B&W, hard-c)

nn - By "Tad" Dorgan	58.00	204.00	350.00

NOTE: Also exists in self-published TAD edition: The T.A. Dorgan Company; unknown which is first printing.

DAN DUNN SECRET OPERATIVE 48 (Also See Detective Dan) (N)
Whitman Publishing: 1937 ((5 1/2 x 7 1/4", 68pgs., color cardboard-c, B&W)

1010 And The Gangsters' Frame-Up	50.00	150.00	300.00

NOTE: There are two versions of the book the later printing has a 5 cent cover price. Dick Tracy look-alike character by Norman Marsh.

DANGERS OF DOLLY DIMPLE, THE (N)
Penn Tobacco Co.: nd (1930's) (9-3/8x7-7/8", 28 pgs, red cardboard-c, B&W)

nn - (Rare) by Walter Enright	25.00	88.00	150.00

NOTE: Reprints newspaper comic strip advertisements, in which in every episode, Dolly Dimple's life is saved by Penn's Smoking Tobacco. - how very un-P.C. by today's standards.

DEADWOOD GULCH (O) (See The Funnies 1929)(also see Bug Movies & Clancy The Cop)
Dell Publishing Co.: 1931 (10x10", 52 pgs., B&W, color covers, B&W interior)

nn - By Charles "Boody" Rogers (original material)	100.00	275.00	500.00

DESTINY A Novel In Pictures (O)
Farrar & Rinehart: 1930 (8x7", 424 pgs, B&W, hard-c, dust jacket?)

nn - By Otto Nuckel (original graphic novel)	25.00	100.00	175.00

DICK TRACY & DICK TRACY JR. CAUGHT THE RACKETEERS, HOW
Cupples & Leon Co.: 1933 (8-1/2x7", 88 pgs., hard-c) (See Treasure Box of Famous Comics) (N)

2-(Numbered on pg. 84)-Continuation of Stooge Viller book (daily strip reprints from 8/3/33 thru 11/8/33)(Rarer than #1)	94.00	376.00	750.00
With dust jacket.	118.00	472.00	900.00

DICK TRACY & DICK TRACY JR. AND HOW THEY CAPTURED "STOOGE" VILLER (N)
Cupples & Leon Co.: 1933 (8-1/2x7", 100 pgs., hard-c, one-shot)
Reprints 1932 & 1933 Dick Tracy daily strips

nn(No.1)-1st app. of "Stooge" Viller	94.00	376.00	750.00
With dust jacket.	118.00	472.00	900.00

DIMPLES By Grace Drayton (N) (See Dolly Dimples)
Hearst's International Library Co.: 1915 (6 1/4 x 5 1/4, 12 pgs) (5 known)

nn-Puppy and Pussy; nn-She Goes For a walk; nn-She Had A Sneeze; nn-She Has a Naughty Play Husband; nn-Wait Till Fido Comes Home	21.00	74.00	150.00

DOINGS OF THE DOO DADS, THE (N)
Detroit News (Universal Feat. & Specialty Co.): 1922 (50¢, 7-3/4x7-3/4", 34 pgs, B&W, red & white-c, square binding)

nn-Reprints 1921 newspaper strip "Text & Pictures" given away as prize in the Detroit News Doo Dads contest; by Arch Dale	43.00	173.00	360.00

DOING THE GRAND CANYON
Fred Harvey: 1922 (7 x 4-3/4", 24 pgs, B&W, paper cover)

nn - John McCutcheon	20.00	40.00	100.00

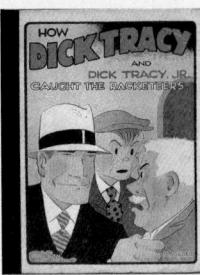

How Dick Tracy and Dick Tracy, Jr.
Caught the Racketeers by Chester Gould
1933 © Cupples & Leon

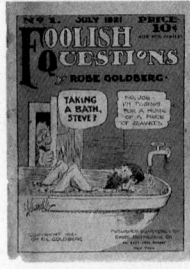

Foolish Questions by Rube Goldberg
1921 © EmBee Distributing Co., NY.

The Latest Adventures of Foxy Grandpa 1905
© Bunny Publ.

	GD2.0	FN6.0	VF8.0

NOTE: *Text & 8 cartoons about visiting the Grand Canyon.*

DOINGS OF THE VAN-LOONS (N) (from same company as Mutt & Jeff #1-#5)
Ball Publications: 1912 (5-3/4X15-1/2", 68pg., B&W, hard-c)

nn - By Fred I. Leipziger (scarce)	72.00	252.00	600.00

DOLLY DIMPLES & BOBBY BOUNCE (See Dimples)
Cupples & Leon Co.: 1933 (8-3/4x7", color hardcover, B&W)

nn - Grace Drayton-a	24.00	96.00	165.00

DOO DADS, THE (Sleepy Sam and Tiny the Elephant)
Universal Feature * Specialty Co: 1922 (5-1/4x14", 36 pgs.,B&W, R&W-c,square binding)

nn - By Arch Dale	35.00	125.00	250.00

DRAWINGS BY HOWARD CHANDLER CHRISTIE (S, M)
Moffat, Yard & Company, NY: 1905 (11-7/8x16-1/2", 68 pgs, hard-c, B&W)

nn - Howard C. Christie	30.00	60.00	120.00

NOTE: *Reprints1898-1905 from Haprer & Bros, Ch. Scribners Sons, Leslie's, MacMillians, McLurg, Russell.*

DREAMS OF THE RAREBIT FIEND (N)
Frederick A. Stokes Co.:1905 (10-1/4x7-1/2", 68 pgs, thin paper cover all B&W) newspaper reprints from the New York Evening Telegram printed on yellow paper

nn-By Winsor "Silas" McCay (Very Rare) (Five copies known to exist) Estimated value....	750.00	2500.00	–

NOTE: *A G/VG copy sold for $2,045 in May 2004.*

DRISCOLL'S BOOK OF PIRATES (O)
David McKay Publ.: 1934 (9x7", 124 pgs, B&W, hardcover)

nn - By Montford Amory ("Pieces of Eight strip-r)	21.00	64.00	150.00

DUCKY DADDLES
Frederick A. Stokes Co: July 1911 (15x10")

nn - By Grace Weiderseim (later Drayton) strip-r	50.00	175.00	300.00

DUMBUNNIES AND THEIR FRIENDS IN RABBITBORO, THE (O)
Albertine Randall Wheelan: 1931 (8-3/4x7-1/8", 82 pgs, color hardcover, B&W)

nn - By Albertine Randall Wheelan (self-pub)	34.00	103.00	240.00

EDISON - INSPIRATION TO YOUTH (N)(Also see Life of Thomas---)
Thomas A. Edison, Incorporated: 1939 (9-1/2 x 6-1/2, paper cover, B&W)

nn - Photo-c	46.00	138.00	275.00

NOTE: *Reprints strip material found in the 1928 Life of Thomas A. Edison in Word and Picture.*

'ERBIE AND 'IS PLAYMATES
Democratic National Committee: 1932 (8x9-1/2, 16 pgs, B&W)

nn - By Frederick Opper (Rare)	60.00	150.00	350.00

NOTE: *Anti-Hoover/Pro-Roosevelt political comics.*

EXPANSION BEING BART'S BEST CARTOONS FOR 1899
Minneapolis Journal: 1900 (10-1/4x8-1/4", 124 pgs, paperback, B&W)

v2#1 - By Charles L. Bartholomew	24.00	84.00	145.00

FAMOUS COMICS (N)
King Features Synd. (Whitman Pub. Co.): 1934 (100 pgs., daily newspaper-r) (3-1/2x8-1/2"; paper cover)(came in an illustrated box)

684 (#1) - Little Jimmy, Katzies & Barney Google	34.00	103.00	240.00
684 (#2) - Polly, Little Jimmy, Katzenjammer Kids	34.00	103.00	240.00
684 (#3) - Little Annie Rooney, Polly and Her Pals, Katzenjammer Kids	34.00	103.00	240.00
Box price...	34.00	102.00	275.00

FAMOUS COMICS CARTOON BOOKS (N)
Whitman Publishing Co.: 1934 (8x7-1/4", 72 pgs, B&W hard-c, daily strip-r)

1200-The Captain & the Kids; Dirks reprints credited to Bernard Dibble	29.00	86.00	200.00
1202-Captain Easy & Wash Tubbs by Roy Crane; 2 slightly different versions of cover exist	34.00	103.00	240.00
1203-Ella Cinders By Conselman & Plumb	28.00	84.00	195.00
1204-Freckles & His Friends	25.00	75.00	175.00

NOTE: *Called Famous Funnies Cartoon Books inside back area sales advertisement.*

FANTASIES IN HA-HA (M)
Meyer Bros & Co.: 1900 (14 x 11-7/8", 64 pgs, color cover hardcover, B&W)

nn - By Hy Mayer	40.00	140.00	280.00

FELIX (N)
Henry Altemus Company: 1931 (6-1/2"x8-1/4", 52 pgs., color, hard-c w/dust jacket)

1-3-Sunday strip reprints of Felix the Cat by Otto Messmer. Book No. 2 r/1931 Sunday panels mostly two to a page in a continuity format oddly arranged so each tier of panels reads across two pages, then drops to the next tier. (Books 1 & 3 have not been documented.)(Rare)

Each	104.00	416.00	750.00
With dust jacket	150.00	600.00	1050.00

FELIX THE CAT BOOK (N)
McLoughlin Bros.: 1927 (8"x15-3/4", 52 pgs, half in color-half in B&W)

nn - Reprints 23 Sunday strips by Otto Messmer from 1926 & 1927, every other one in color, two pages per strip. (Rare)	200.00	800.00	1550.00
260-Reissued (1931), reformatted to 9-1/2"x10-1/4" (same color plates, but one strip per every three pages), retitled ("Book" dropped from title) and abridged (only eight strips repeated from first issue, 28 pgs.).(Rare)	79.00	316.00	600.00

F. FOX'S FUNNY FOLK (see Toonerville Trolley; Cartoons by Fontaine Fox) (C)
George H. Doran Company: 1917 (10-1/4x8-1/4", 228 pgs, red, B&W cover, B&W interior, hardcover; dust jacket?)

nn - By Fontaine Fox (Toonerville Trolley strip-r)	125.00	300.00	600.00

52 CAREY CARTOONS (O,S)
Carey Cartoon Service, NY: 1915 (25 cents, 6-3/4" x 10-1/2", 118 pgs, printed on one side, color cardboard-c)

nn - (1915) War			

NOTE: *The Carey Cartoon Service supplied a weekly, hand-colored single panel cartoon broadsheet, on current news events, starting in 1906 or 1907, for window display in Carey Fountain Pen chain stores. These broadsheets were 22-1/2" x 33" in size. Starting circa 1915, Carey Fountain Pens began offering subscriptions for the broadsheets to other merchants, for window display in their stores as well. This collects, in B&W, the cartoons for 1915. An "Edition Deluxe" was also advertised, with all cartoons hand colored. It is currently unknown whether a reprint collection was only issued in 1915, or if other editions exist.*

52 LETTERS TO SALESMEN
Steven-Davis Company: 1927 (???)

nn - (Rare)	23.00	92.00	140.00

NOTE: *52 motivational letters to salesmen, with page of comics for each week, bound into embossed leather binder.*

FOLKS IN FUNNYVILLE (S)
R.H. Russell: 1900 (12"x9-1/4", 48 pgs.)(cardboard-c)

nn - By Frederick Opper	271.00	950.00	

NOTE: *Reprinted from Hearst's NY Journal American Humorist supplements.*

FOOLISH QUESTIONS (N)
Small, Maynard & Co.: 1909 (6-7/8 x 5-1/2", 174 pgs, hardcover, B&W)

nn - By Rube Goldberg (first Goldberg item)	100.00	300.00	500.00

NOTE: *Comic strip began Oct 23, 1908 running thru 1941. Also drawn by George Frink in 1909.*

FOOLISH QUESTIONS THAT ARE ASKED BY ALL
Levi Strauss & Co./Small, Maynard & Co.: 1909 (5-1/2x5-3/4", 24 pgs, paper-c, B&W)

nn- (Rare) by Rube Goldberg	46.00	160.00	300.00

FOOLISH QUESTIONS (Boxed card set) (S)
Wallie Dorr Co., N.Y.: 1919 (5-1/4x3-3/4")(box & card backs are red)

nn - Boxed set w/52 B&W comics on cards; each a single panel gag complete set w/box	75.00	263.00	450.00

NOTE: *There are two diff sets put out simultaneously with the first set, by the same company. One set continues/picks up the numbering of the cards from the other set.*

FOOLISH QUESTIONS (S)
EmBee Distributing Co.: 1921 (10¢, 4x5 1/2; 52 pgs, 3 color covers; B&W)

1-By Rube Goldberg	46.00	160.00	300.00

FOXY GRANDPA
Foxy Grandpa Company, 33 Wall St, NY: 1900 (9x15", 84 pgs, full color, cardboard-c)

nn - By Carl Schultze (By Permission of New York Herald)	271.00	1200.00	

NOTE: *This seminal comic strip began Jan 7, 1900 and was collected later that same year.*

FOXY GRANDPA (Also see The Funnies, 1st series) (N)
N. Y. Herald/Frederick A. Stokes Co./M. A. Donahue & Co./Bunny Publ.
(L. R. Hammersly Co.): 1901 - 1916 (Strip-r in color, hard-c)

1901- 9x15" in color-N. Y. Herald	313.00	1100.00	
1902- "Latest Larks of...", 32 pgs., 9-1/2x15-1/2"	164.00	575.00	
1902- "The Many Advs. of....", 9x12", 148 pgs., Hammersly Co.	179.00	625.00	
1903- "Latest Advs.", 9x15", 24 pgs., Hammersly Co.	164.00	575.00	
1903- "...'s New Advs.", 11x15", 66 pgs., Stokes	164.00	575.00	
1904- "Up to Date", 10x15", 66 pgs., Stokes	146.00	510.00	950.00
1904- "The Many Adventures of....", 9x15, 144pgs, Donahue	146.00	510.00	950.00
1905- "& Flip-Flaps", 9-1/2x15-1/2", 52 pgs.	146.00	510.00	950.00
1905- "The Latest Advs. of....", 9x15", 28, 52, & 68 pgs, M.A. Donahue Co.; re-issue of 1902 issue	104.00	365.00	700.00
1905- "Latest Larks of...", 9-1/2x15-1/2", 52 pgs., Donahue; re-issue of 1902 issue with more pages added	104.00	365.00	700.00
1905- "Latest Larks of...", 9-1/2x15-1/2", 24 pgs. edition, Donahue; re-issue of 1902 issue	104.00	365.00	700.00
1905- "Merry Pranks of...", 9-1/2x15-1/2", 28, 52 & 62 pgs., Donahue	104.00	365.00	700.00
1905-"...Surprises",10x15", color, 64 pg,Stokes, 60¢	104.00	365.00	700.00
1906- "Frolics", 10x15", 30 pgs., Stokes	104.00	365.00	700.00
1907?-"...& His Boys",10x15", 64 color pgs, Stokes	104.00	365.00	700.00
1907- "Triumphs", 10x15", 62 pgs, Stokes	104.00	365.00	700.00
1908-"...Mother Goose", Stokes	104.00	365.00	700.00
1909- "...& Little Brother", 10x15", 58 pgs, Stokes	104.00	365.00	700.00

Giggles
© Pratt Food Co.

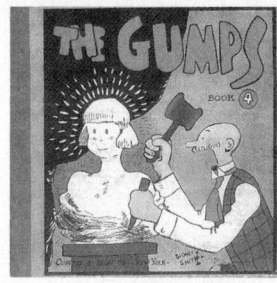

The Gumps by Sidney Smith
1927? © Cupples & Leon

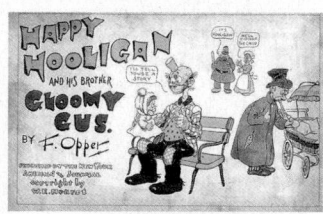

Happy Hooligan Book 1 1902
© Frederick A. Stokes

	GD2.0	FN6.0	VF8.0

1911- "Latest Tricks", r-1910,1911 Sundays-Stokes Co.

1914-(9-1/2x15-1/2", 24 pgs.)-6 color cartoons/page, Bunny Publ. Co.

1911- "Latest Tricks", r-1910,1911 Sundays-Stokes Co.	104.00	365.00	700.00
1914-(9-1/2x15-1/2", 24 pgs.)	88.00	306.00	575.00
1915 - ...Always Jolly (10x16, Stokes)	88.00	306.00	575.00
1916- "Merry Book", (10x15", 64 pgs, Stokes)	88.00	306.00	575.00
1917-"...Adventures (5 1/2 x 6 1/2, 26 pgs, Stokes)	57.00	200.00	400.00
1917-"...Frolics (5 1/2 x 6 1/2, 26 pgs, Stokes)	57.00	200.00	400.00
1917-"...Triumphs (5 1/2 x 6 1/2, 26 pgs, Stokes)	57.00	200.00	400.00

FOXY GRANDPA, FUNNY TRICKS OF (The Stump Books)
M.A. Donahue Co, Chicago: approx 1903 (1-7/8x6-3/8", 44 pgs, blue hardcover)

nn - By Carl Schultze	54.00	189.00	325.00

NOTE: One of a series of ten "stump" books; the only comics one.

FOXY GRANDPA'S MOTHER GOOSE (I)
Stokes: October 1903 (10-11/16x8-1/2", 86 pgs, hard-c)

nn - By Carl Schultze (not comics - illustrated book)	54.00	189.00	325.00

FOXY GRANDPA SPARKLETS SERIES (N)
M. A. Donahue & Co.: 1908 (7-3/4x6-1/2"; 24 pgs., color)

"… Rides the Goat", "…& His Boys", "…Playing Ball", "…Fun on the Farm", "…Fancy Shooting", "…Show His Boys Up-To-Date Sports", "…Plays Santa Claus"

each….	88.00	306.00	525.00
900- "Playing Ball"; Bunny illos; 8 pgs.; linen like pgs., no date	73.00	254.00	435.00

FOXY GRANDPA VISITS RICHMOND (O,P)
Dietz Printing Co., Richmond, VA / Hotel Rueger: nd (c1920's) (5-7/8" x 4-1/2", 16 pgs, paper-c, B&W)

nn - (Scarce) By Bunny	25.00	88.00	175.00

NOTE: Promotional comic given away to its guests by the Hotel Rueger, about Foxy Grandpa visiting and enjoying the Hotel. Originally came in an envelope, with the words "Foxy Grandpa Visits Richmond -- and Rueger's" printed on it.

FOXY GRANDPA VISITS WASHINGTON, D.C. (P)
Dietz Printing Co., Richmond, VA / Hamilton Hotel: nd (c1920's) (5-7/8" x 4-1/2", 16 pgs, paper-c, B&W)

nn - (Scarce) By Bunny	25.00	88.00	150.00

NOTE: Mostly reprints "… Visits Richmond", changing all references to Hotel Rueger, to Hamilton Hotel instead. Also, changes depictions of a waiter and a cook from black to white, plus incompletely erases the cover art on a book Foxy Grandpa falls asleep with (the latter is how we know that the Richmond version was first).

FRAGMENTS FROM FRANCE (S)
G. P. Putnam & Sons: 1917 (9x6-1/4", 168 pgs, hardcover, $1.75)

nn - By Bruce Bairnsfather	25.00	88.00	150.00

NOTE: WW1 trench warfare cartoons; color dust jacket.

FUNNIES, THE (H) (See Clancy the Cop, Deadwood Gulch, Bug Movies)
Dell Publishing Co.: 1929 - No. 36, 10/18/30 (10¢; 5¢ No. 22 on) (16 pgs.)
Full tabloid size in color; not reprints; published every Saturday

1-My Big Brudder, Jonathan, Jazzbo & Jim, Foxy Grandpa, Sniffy, Jimmy Jams & other strips begin; first four-color comic newsstand publication; also contains magic, puzzles & stories	200.00	700.00	1500.00
2-21 (1930, 10¢)	75.00	250.00	500.00
22(nn-7/12/30-5¢)	60.00	200.00	400.00
23(nn-7/19/30-5¢), 24(nn-7/26/30-5¢), 25(nn-8/2/30), 26(nn-8/9/30), 27(nn-8/16/30), 28(nn-8/23/30), 29(nn-8/30/30), 30(nn-9/6/30), 31(nn-9/13/30), 32(nn-9/20/30), 33(nn-9/27/30), 34(nn-10/4/30), 35(nn-10/11/30), 36(nn, no date-10/18/30)			
each….	60.00	200.00	400.00

GASOLINE ALLEY (Also see Popular Comics & Super Comics) (N)
Reilly & Lee Publishers: 1929 (8-3/4x7", B&W daily strip-r, hard-c)

nn - By King (96 pgs.)	75.00	260.00	600.00

Dust Wrapper - add 50% more

NOTE: Of all the Frank King reprint books, this is the only one to reprint actual complete newspaper strips - all others are illustrated prose text stories.

GIBSON'S PUBLISHED DRAWINGS, MR. (M,S) (See Victorian index for earlier issues)
R.H. Russell, New York: No.1 1894 - No. 9 1904 (11x17-3/4", hard-c, B&W)

nn (No.6; 1901) A Widow and her Friends (90 pgs.)	30.00	60.00	120.00
nn (No.7; 1902) The Social Ladder (88 pgs.)	30.00	60.00	120.00
8 - 1903 The Weaker Sex (88 pgs.)	30.00	60.00	120.00
9 - 1904 Everyday People (88 pgs.)	30.00	60.00	120.00

NOTE: By Charles Dana Gibson, reprinted from magazines, primarily LIFE. The Education of Mr. Pipp tells a story. Series continues how long after 1904?

GIGGLES
Pratt Food Co., Philadelphia, PA: 1908-09? (12x9", 8 pgs, color, 5 cents-c)

1-8: By Walt McDougall (#8 dated March 1909)	40.00	175.00	–

NOTE: Appears to be monthly; almost tabloid size; yearly subscriptions was 25 cents.

GOD'S MAN (H)
Jonathan Cape and Harrison Smith Inc.: 1929 (8-1/4x6", 298 pgs, B&W hardcover w/dust jacket) (original graphic novel in wood cuts)

nn - By Lynd Ward	43.00	171.00	300.00

GOLD DUST TWINS
N. K. Fairbank Co.: 1904 (4-5/8x6-3/4", 18 pgs, color and B&W)

nn - By E. W. Kemble (Rare)	30.00	60.00	130.00

NOTE: Promo comic for Gold DustWashing Powder; includes page of watercolor paints.

GOLF
Volland Co.: 1916 (9x12-3/4", 132 pgs, hard-c, B&W)

nn - By Clair Briggs	52.00	84.00	350.00

GUMPS, THE (N)
Landfield-Kupfer: No. 1, 1918 - No. 6, 1921; (B&W Daily strip-r)

Book No. 1(1918)(scarce)-cardboard-c, 5-1/4x13-1/3", 64 pgs., daily strip-r by Sidney Smith	75.00	250.00	500.00
Book No.2(1918)-(scarce)- 5-1/4x13-1/3"; paper cover; 36 pgs. daily strip reprints by Sidney Smith	75.00	250.00	500.00
Book No. 3	100.00	350.00	700.00
Book No. 4 (1918) 5-3/8x13-7/8", 20 pgs. Color card-c	100.00	350.00	700.00
Book No. 5 10-1/4x13-1/2", 20 pgs. Color paper-c	100.00	350.00	700.00
Book No. 6 (Rare, 20 pgs, 8x13-3/8, strip-r 1920-21)	121.00	423.00	725.00

GUMPS, ANDY AND MIN, THE (N)
Landfield-Kupfer Printing Co., Chicago/Morrison Hotel: nd (1920s) (Giveaway, 5-1/2"x14", 20 pgs., B&W, soft-c)

nn - Strip-r by Sidney Smith; art & logo embossed on cover w/hotel restaurant menu on back-c or a hotel promo ad; 4 different contents of issues known	50.00	175.00	300.00

GUMPS, THE (N)
Cupples & Leon: 1924-1930 (10x10, 52 pgs, B&W)

1 - By Sidney Smith	61.00	244.00	450.00
2-7	39.00	154.00	300.00

THE GUMPS (P)
Cupples & Leon Company: 1924 (9 x 7-1/2", 28 pgs, paper cover)

nn (1924)	50.00	175.00	300.00

NOTE: Promotional comic for Sunshine Andy Gump Biscuits. Daily strip-r from 1922-24.

GUMP'S CARTOON BOOK, THE (N)
The National Arts Company: 1931 (13-7/8x10", 36 pgs, color covers, B&W)

nn - By Sidney Smith	57.00	228.00	450.00

GUMPS PAINTING BOOK, THE (N)
The National Arts Company: 1931 (11 x 15 1/4", 20 pgs, half in full color)

nn - By Sidney Smith	57.00	228.00	450.00

HALT FRIENDS! (see also HELLO BUDDY)
???: 1918? (4-3/8x5-3/4", 36 pgs, color-c, B&W, no cover price listed)

nn - Unknown	10.00	30.00	70.00

NOTE: Says on front cover: "Comics of War Facts of Service Sold on its merits by Unemployed or Disabled Ex-Service Men. Credentials Shown On Request. Price - Pay What You Please." These are very common; exact contents vary widely.

HAMBONE'S MEDITATIONS
Jahl & Co.: no date 1920 (6-1/8 x 7-1/2, 108 pgs, paper cover, B&W)

nn - By J. P. Alley	33.00	132.00	250.00

NOTE: Reprint of racist single panel newspaper series, 2 cartoons per page.

HAN OLA OG PER (N)
Anundson Publishing Co, Decorah, Iowa: 1927 (10-3/8 x 15-3/4", 54 pgs, paper-c, B&W)

nn - American origin Norwegian language strips-r	33.00	131.00	230.00

NOTE: 1940s and modern reprints exist.

HANS UND FRITZ (N)
The Saalfield Publishing Co.: 1917, 1927-29 (10x13-1/2", 28 pgs., B&W)

nn - By R. Dirks (1917, r-1916 strips)	96.00	335.00	600.00
nn - By R. Dirks (1923 edition- reprint of 1917 edition)	58.00	204.00	350.00
nn - By R. Dirks (1926 edition- reprint of 1917 edition)	58.00	204.00	350.00
The Funny Larks Of... By R. Dirks (©1917 outside cover; ©1916 inside indicia)	96.00	335.00	600.00
The Funny Larks Of... (1927) reprints 1917 edition of 1916 strips Halloween-c	58.00	204.00	350.00
The Funny Larks Of... 2 (1929)	58.00	204.00	350.00
193 - By R. Dirks; contains 1916 Sunday strip reprints of Katzenjammer Kids & Hawkshaw the Detective - reprint of 1917 nn edition (1929) this edition is not rare	58.00	204.00	350.00

HAPPY DAYS (S)
Coward-McCann Inc.: 1929 (12-1/2x9-5/8", 110 pgs, hardcover B&W)

nn - By Alban Butler (WW 1 cartoons)	20.00	60.00	120.00

HAPPY HOOLIGAN (See Alphonse…) (N)
Hearst's New York American & Journal: 1902,1903

Book 1-(1902)-"And His Brother Gloomy Gus", By Fred Opper; has 1901-02-r; (yellow & black)(86 pgs.)(10x15-1/4")	450.00	1700.00	–
New Edition, 1903 -10x15" 82 pgs. in color	350.00	1400.00	–

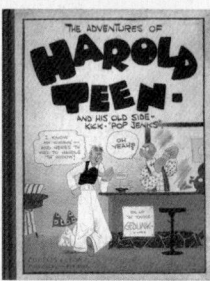

Harold Teen #2 by Carl Ed
1931 © Cupples & Leon

Jimmy and His Scrapes
© Frederick A. Stokes

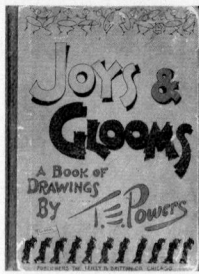

Joys & Glooms By T.E. Powers
1912 © Reilly & Britton Co.

GD2.0 FN6.0 VF8.0

NOTE: Strip ran March 26, 1900-Aug 14, 1932 and is widely recognized as setting the format standard for all newspaper comic strips which came after it. Opper (1857-1937) was going blind towards the end.

HAPPY HOOLIGAN (N) (By Fredrick Opper)
Frederick A. Stokes Co.: 1906-08 (10-1/4x15-3/4", cardboard color-c)

1906 - :Travels of...), 68 pgs,10-1/4x15-3/4", 1905-r	300.00	900.00	–
1907 - "--Home Again", 68 pgs., 10x15-3/4", 60¢; full color-c	300.00	900.00	–
1908 - "Handy--", 68 pgs, color	300.00	900.00	–

HAPPY HOOLIGAN, THE STORY OF (G)
McLoughlin Bros.: No. 281, 1932 (12x9-1/2", 20 pgs., soft-c)

281-Three-color text, pictures on heavy paper	57.00	228.00	400.00

NOTE: An homage to Opper's creation on its 30th Anniversary in 1932.

HAROLD HARDHIKE'S REJUVENATION
O'Sullivan Rubber: 1917 (6-1/4x3-1/2, 16 pgs, B&W)

nn	25.00	100.00	175.00

NOTE: Comic book to promote rubber shoe heels.

HAROLD TEEN (N)
Cupples & Leon Co.: 1929 (9-7/8x9-7/8", 52 pgs, cardboard covers)

1 - By Carl Ed	50.00	200.00	500.00
nn - (1931, 8-11/16x6-7/8", 96 pgs, hardcover w/dj)	41.00	164.00	290.00

NOTE: Title 2nd book: HAROLD TEEN AND HIS OLD SIDE-KICK-- POP JENKINS, (Adv. of...). Precursor for Archie Andrews & crew; strip began May 4, 1919 running into 1959.

HAROLD TEEN PAINT AND COLOR BOOK (N)
McLoughlin Bros Inc.: 1932 (13x9-3/4, 28 pgs, B&W and color)

#2054	25.00	100.00	175.00

HAWKSHAW THE DETECTIVE (See Advs. of..., Hans Und Fritz & Okay) (N)
The Saalfield Publishing Co.: 1917 (10-1/2x13-1/2", 24 pgs., B&W)

nn - By Gus Mager (Sunday strip-r)	54.00	190.00	350.00
nn - By Gus Mayer (1923 reprint of 1917 edition)	25.00	100.00	175.00
nn - By Gus Mayer (1926 reprint of 1917 edition)	25.00	100.00	175.00

NOTE: Runs Feb 23, 1913-Sept 4, 1922, starts again from Dec 13, 1931-Feb 11, 1952; Sherlock Holmes spoof.

HEALTH IN PICTURES
American Public Health Association, NYC: 1930 (6-1/2" x 5-3/16", 76 pgs, green & black paper-c, B&W interior)

nn - By various	15.00	51.00	90.00

NOTE: Collection of strips and cartoons put out by the Public Health Association, on topics ranging from boating and food safety, to small pox and typhoid prevention.

HE DONE HER WRONG (O)
Doubleday, Doran & Company: 1930 (8-1/4x 7-1/4", 276pgs, hard-c with dust jacket, B&W interiors)

nn - By Milt Gross	50.00	200.00	350.00

NOTE: A seminal original-material wordless graphic novel, not reprints. Several modern reprints.

HELLO BUDDY (see also HALT FRIENDS)
???: 1919? (4-3/8x5-3/4", 36 pgs, color-c, B&W, 15¢)

nn - Unknown	10.00	30.00	70.00

NOTE: Says on front cover: "Comics of War Facts of Service Sold on its merits by Unemployed or Disabled Ex-Service Men." These are very common; contents vary widely.

HENRY (N)
David McKay Co.: 1935 (25¢, soft-c)

Book 1 - By Carl Anderson	57.00	200.00	400.00

NOTE: Strip began March 19 1932; this book ties with Popeye (David McKay) and Little Annie Rooney (David McKay) as the last of the 10x10" Platinum Age comic books.

HENRY (M)
Greenberg Publishers Inc.: 1935 (11-1/4x 8-5/8", 72 pgs, red & blue color hard-c, dust jacket, B&W interiors) (strip-r from Saturday Evening Post)

nn - By Carl Anderson	57.00	200.00	400.00

HIGH KICKING KELLYS, THE (M)
Vaudeville News Corporation, NY: 1926 (5x11", B&W, two color soft-c)

nn - By Jack A. Ward (scarce)	40.00	160.00	280.00

HIGHLIGHTS OF HISTORY (N)
World Syndicate Publishing Co.: 1933-34 (4-1/2x4", 288 pgs)

nn - 5 different unnumbered issues; daily strip-r	10.00	40.00	70.00

NOTE: Titles include Buffalo Bill, Daniel Boone, Kit Carson, Pioneers of the Old West, Winning of the Old Northwest. There are line drawing color covers and embossed hardcover versions. It is unknown which came out first.

HOMER HOLCOMB AND MAY (N)
no publisher listed: 1920s (4 x 9-1/2", 40 pgs, paper cover, B&W)

nn - By Doc Bird Finch (strip-r)	10.00	40.00	70.00

HOME, SWEET HOME (N)
M.S. Publishing Co.: 1925 (10-1/4x10")

nn - By Tuthill	33.00	134.00	235.00

HOW THEY DRAW PROHIBITION (S)

GD2.0 FN6.0 VF8.0

Association Against Prohibition: 1930 (10x9", 100 pgs.)

nn - Single panel and multi-panel comics (rare)	71.00	285.00	500.00

NOTE: Contains art by J.N. "Ding" Darling, James Flagg, Rollin Kirby, Winsor McCay, T.E. Powers, H.T. Webster, others. Also comes with a loose sheet listing all the newspapers where the cartoons originally appeared.

HOW TO BE A CARTOONIST (H)
Saalfield Pub. Co.: 1936 (10-3/8x12-1/2", 16 pgs, color-c, B&W)

nn - By Chas. H. Kuhn	10.00	40.00	70.00

HOW TO DRAW: A PRACTICAL BOOK OF INSTRUCTION (H)
Harper & Brothers: 1904 (9-1/4x12-3/8", 128 pgs, hardcover, B&W)

nn - Edited By Leon Barritt	57.00	228.00	400.00

NOTE: Strips reprinted include: "Buster Brown" by Outcault, "Foxy Grandpa" by Bunny, "Happy Hooligan" by Opper, "Katzenjammer Kids" by Dirks, "Lady Bountiful" by Gene Carr, "Mr. Jack" by Swinnerton, "Panhandle Pete" by George McManus, "Mr E.Z. Mark" by F.M. Howarth others; non-character strips by Hy Mayer, Winsor McCay, T.E. Powers, others; single panel cartoons by Davenport, Frost, McDougall, Nast, W.A. Rogers, Sullivant, others.

HOW TO DRAW CARTOONS (H)
Garden City Publishing Co.: 1926, 1937 (10 1/4 x 7 1/2, 150 pgs)

1926 first edition By Clare Briggs	25.00	75.00	150.00
1937 2nd edition By Clare Briggs	20.00	60.00	120.00

NOTE: Seminal "how to" break into the comics syndicates with art by Briggs, Fisher, Goldberg, King, Webster, Opper, Tad, Hershfield, McCay, Ding, others. Came with Dust Jacket -add 50%.

HOW TO DRAW FUNNY PICTURES: A Complete Course in Cartooning (H)
Frederick J. Drake & Co., Chicago: 1936 (10-3/8x6-7/8", 168 pgs, hardcover, B&W)

nn - By E.C. Matthews (200 illus by Eugene Zimmerman)	20.00	60.00	120.00

HY MAYER (M)
Puck Publishing: 1915 (13-1/2 x 20-3/4", 52 pgs, hardcover cover, color & B&W interiors)

nn - By Hy Mayer(strip reprints from Puck)	40.00	140.00	300.00

HYSTERICAL HISTORY OF THE CIVILIAN CONSERVATION CORPS
Peerless Engraving: 1934 (10-3/4x7-1/2", 104 pgs, soft-c, B&W)

nn - By various	20.00	60.00	120.00

NOTE: Comics about CCC life, includes two color insert postcards in back.

INDOOR SPORTS (N,S)
National Specials Co., New York: nd circa 1912 (25 cents, 6 x 9", 68 pgs, B&W)

nn - Tad	35.00	125.00	225.00

NOTE: Cartoons reprinted from Hearst papers.

IT HAPPENS IN THE BEST FAMILIES (N)
Powers Photo Engraving Co.: 1920 (52 pgs.)(9-1/2x10-3/4")

nn - By Briggs; B&W Sunday strips-r	29.00	114.00	200.00
Special Railroad Edition (30¢)-r/strips from 1914-1920	26.00	103.00	180.00

JIMMIE DUGAN AND THE REG'LAR FELLERS (N)
Cupples & Leon: 1921, 46 pgs. (11"x16")

nn - By Gene Byrne	71.00	284.00	500.00

NOTE: Ties with EmBee's Mutt & Jeff and Trouble of Bringing Up Father as the last of this size.

JIMMY (N) (see Little Jimmy Picture & Story Book)
N. Y. American & Journal: 1905 (10x15", 84 pgs., color)

nn - By Jimmy Swinnerton (scarce)	250.00	800.00	1500.00

NOTE: James Swinnerton was one of the original first pioneers of the American newspaper comic strip.

JIMMY AND HIS SCRAPES (N)
Frederick A. Stokes: 1906, (10-1/4x15-1/4", 66 pgs, cardboard-c, color)

nn - By Jimmy Swinnerton (scarce)	150.00	450.00	750.00

JOE PALOOKA (N)
Cupples & Leon Co.: 1933 (9-13/16x10", 52 pgs., B&W daily strip-r)

nn - By Ham Fisher (scarce)	114.00	456.00	800.00

JOHN, JONATHAN AND MR. OPPER BY F. OPPER (S,I,N)
Grant, Richards, 48 Leicester Square, W.C.: 1903 (9-5/8x8-3/8", 108 pgs, hard-c B&W)

nn - Opper (Scarce)	50.00	200.00	380.00

NOTE: British precursor-type companion to WIllie And His Poppa reprints from Hearst's NY American & Journal Opper cartoons interfacing Uncle Sam precursor Brother Jonathan, John Bull. Uses name Happy Hooligan in one cartoon, has John Bull smoking opium in another.

JOLLY POLLY'S BOOK OF ENGLISH AND ETIQUETTE (S)
Jos. J. Frisch: 1931 (60 cents, 8 x 5-1/8, 88 pgs, paper-c, B&W)

nn - By Jos. J. Frisch	20.00	60.00	120.00

NOTE: Reprint of single panel newspaper series, 4 per page, of English and etiquette lessons taught by a flapper.

JOYS AND GLOOMS (N)
Reilly & Britton Co.: 1912 (11x8", 72 pgs, hard-c, B&W interior)

nn - By T. E. Powers (newspaper strip-r)	39.00	156.00	325.00

JUDGE - yet to be indexed

JUDGE'S LIBRARY - yet to be indexed

JUST KIDS COMICS FOR CRAYON COLORING

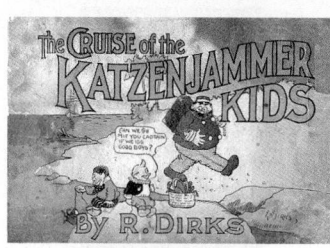

The Cruise of the Katzenjammer Kids
© NY American & Journal

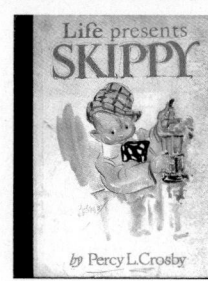

Life Presents Skippy by Percy L. Crosby
1924 © Life Publishing Company

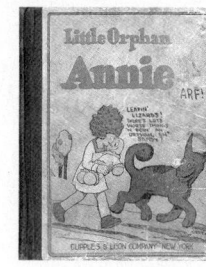

Little Orphan Annie 1926
© C&L

	GD2.0	FN6.0	VF8.0
King Features. NYC: 1928 (11x8-1/2, 16 pgs, soft-c)			
nn - By Ad Carter	33.00	100.00	200.00
NOTE: Porous better grade paper; top pics printed in color; lower in b&w to color.			
JUST KIDS, THE STORY OF (I)			
McLoughlin Bros.: 1932 (12x9-1/2, 20 pgs., paper-c)			
283-Three-color text, pictures on heavy paper	39.00	156.00	275.00
KAPTIN KIDDO AND PUPPO (N)			
Frederick A. Stokes Co.: 1910-1913 (11x16-1/2", 62 pgs)			
1910-By Grace Wiederseim (later Drayton)	40.00	140.00	240.00
1910-Turr-ble Tales of... By Grace Wiederseim (Edward Stern & Co., 11x16-1/2", 64 pgs.)			
	40.00	140.00	240.00
1913- ...'Speriences By Grace Drayton	40.00	140.00	240.00
NOTE: Strip ran approx. 1909-1912.			
KATZENJAMMER KIDS, THE (Also see Hans Und Fritz) (N)			
New York American & Journal: 1902,1903 (10x15-1/4, 86 pgs., color)			
(By Rudolph Dirks; strip first appeared in 1897) © W.R. Hearst			
NOTE: All KK books 1902-1905 all have the same exact title page with a 1902 copyright by W.R. Hearst; almost always look instead on the front cover.			
1902 (Rare) (red & black); has 1901-02 strips	650.00	2000.00	–
1903- **A New Edition** (Rare), 86 pgs	500.00	1800.00	–
1904- 10x15", 84 pgs	250.00	900.00	–
1905?-The Cruise of the, 10x15", 60¢, in color	250.00	900.00	–
1905-A Series of Comic Pictures, 10x15", 84 pgs. in color, possible reprint of 1904 edition	250.00	800.00	–
1905-Tricks of... (10x15", 66 pgs, Stokes)	250.00	800.00	–
1906-Stokes (10x16", 32 pgs. in color)	186.00	800.00	–
1907- The Cruise of the, 10x15", 62 pgs 1905-r?	186.00	800.00	–
1910-The Komical...(10x15)	150.00	450.00	800.00
1921-Embee Dist. Co., 10x16", 20 pgs. in color	150.00	450.00	800.00
KATZENJAMMER KIDS MAGIC DRAWING AND COLORING BOOK (N)			
Sam L Gabriel Sons And Company: 1931 (8 1/2 x 12", 36 pages, stiff-c			
838-By Knerr	50.00	200.00	350.00
KEEPING UP WITH THE JONESES (N)			
Cupples & Leon Co.: 1920 - No. 2, 1921 (9-1/4x9-1/4",52 pgs.,B&W daily strip-r)			
1,2-By Pop Momand	39.00	154.00	270.00
KID KARTOONS (N,S)			
The Century Co.: 1922 (232 pgs, printed 1 side, 9-3/4 x 7-3/4", hard-c, B&W)			
nn - By Gene Carr (Metropolitan Movies strip-r)	60.00	240.00	–
KING OF THE ROYAL MOUNTED (Also See Dan Dunn) (N)			
Whitman Publishing Co.: 1937 (5 1/2 x 7 1/4", 68 pgs., color cardboard-c, B&W)			
1010	36.00	144.00	250.00
LADY BOUNTIFUL (N)			
Saalfield Publ. Co./Press Publ. Co.: 1917 (13-3/8x10", 36 pgs, color cardboard-c, B&W interiors)			
nn - By Gene Carr; 2 panels per page	50.00	175.00	300.00
193S - 2nd printing (13-1/8x10",28 pgs color-c, B&W)	33.00	117.00	200.00
LAUGHS YOU MIGHT HAVE HAD From The Comic Pages of Six Week Day Issues of the Post-Dispatch (N)			
St. Louis Post-Dispatch: 1921 (9 x 10 1/2", 28 pgs, B&W, red ink cover)			
nn - Various comic strips	39.00	154.00	270.00
LIFE, DOGS FROM (M)			
Doubleday, Page & Company: nn 1920 - No.2 1926 (130 pgs, 11-1/4 x 9", color painted-c, hard-c, B&W)			
nn (No.1)	120.00	360.00	–
Second Litter	80.00	320.00	–
NOTE: Reprints strips & cartoons featuring dogs, from Life Magazine. Edited by Thomas L. Masson. Highly sought by collectors of dog ephemera. Art in both books is mostly by Robert L. Dickey. Other art: Carl Anderson-1,2; Barbes-1; Chip Bellew-1; Lang Campbell-1,2; Percy Crosby-1,2; Edwina-2; Frueh-2; R.B. Fuller-1; Gibson-1,2; Don Herold-2; Gus Mager-2; Orr-1; J.R. Shaver-1,2; T.S. Sullivant-2; Russ Westover-1,2; Crawford Young-1.			
LIFE OF DAVY CROCKETT IN PICTURE AND STORY, THE (N)			
Cupples & Leon: 1935 (8-3/4x7", 64 pgs, B&W hard-c, dust jacket?)			
nn - By C. Richard Schaare	29.00	116.00	200.00
LIFE OF THOMAS A. EDISON IN WORD AND PICTURE, THE (N)(Also see Edison...)			
Thomas A. Edison Industries: 1928 (10x8", 56 pgs, paper cover, B&W)			
nn - Photo-c	50.00	200.00	350.00
NOTE: Reprints newspaper strip which ran August to November 1927.			
LIFE'S LITTLE JOKES (S)			
M.S. Publ. Co.: No date (1924)(10-1/16x10", 52 pgs., B&W)			
nn - By Rube Goldberg	64.00	257.00	525.00
LIFE, MINIATURE (see also LIFE (miniature reprint of of issue No. 1)) (M,P,S)			
Life Publishing Co.: No. 1 - No. 4 1913, 1916, 1919 (5-3/4x4-5/8", 20 pgs, color paper-c			

	GD2.0	FN6.0	VF8.0
1- 3 (1913) 4 (1916) 5 (1919)	(no known sales)		
NOTE: Giveaway item from Life, to promote subscriptions. All reprint material. No.2: James Montgomery Flagg-c; a-Chip Bellew, Gus Dirks, Gibson, F.M.Howarth, Art Young.			
LIFE'S PRINTS (was LIFE'S PICTURE GALLERY - See Victorian Age section) (M,S,P)			
Life Publishing Company, New York: nd (c1907) (7x4-1/2", 132 pgs, paper cover, B&W)			
nn - (nd; c1907) unillustrated black construction paper cover; reprints art from 1895-1907; art by J.M.Flagg, A.B.Frost, Gibson (Scarce)	–	–	–
nn - (nd; c1908) b&w cardboard painted cover by Gibson, showing angel raising a champagne glass; reprints art from 1901-1908; art by J.M.Flagg, A.B.Frost, Gibson, Walt Kuhn, Art Young (Scarce)	–	–	–
NOTE: Catalog of prints reprinted from LIFE covers & centerspreads. There are likely more as yet unreported catalogs.			
LIFE, THE COMEDY OF LIFE			
Life Publishing Company: 1907 (130 pgs, 11-3/4x9-1/4",embossed printed cloth covered board-c, B+W			
nn - By various	20.00	80.00	120.00
NOTE: Single cartoons and some sequential cartoons. Artists include Charles Dana Gibson, Harrison Cady, E.W. Kemble, James Montgomery Flagg.			
LILY OF THE ALLEY IN THE FUNNIES			
Whitman Publishing Co.: No date (1927) (10-1/4x15-1/2", 28 pgs., color)			
W936 - By T. Burke (Rare)	57.00	228.00	400.00
LITTLE ANNIE ROONEY (N)			
David McKay Co.: 1935 (25¢, soft-c)			
Book 1	43.00	172.00	340.00
NOTE: Ties with Henry & Popeye (David McKay) as the last of the 10x10" size Plat comic books.			
LITTLE ANNIE ROONEY WISHING BOOK (G) (See Happy Hooligan, Story of #281)			
McLoughlin Bros.: 1932 (12x9-1/2", 16 pgs., soft-c, 3-color text, heavier paper)			
282 - By Darrell McClure	41.00	144.00	250.00
LITTLE BIRD TOLD ME, A (E)			
Life Publishing Co.: 1905? (96 pgs, hardbound)			
nn - By Walt Kuhn (Life-r)	41.00	144.00	250.00
LITTLE FOLKS PAINTING BOOK (N)			
The National Arts Company: 1931 (10-7/8 x 15-1/4", 20 pgs, half in full color)			
nn - By "Tack" Knight (strip-r)	41.00	144.00	250.00
LITTLE JIMMY PICTURE AND STORY BOOK (I) (see Jimmy)			
McLaughlin Bros., Inc.: 1932 (13-1/4 x 9-3/4", 20 pgs, cardstock color cover)			
284 Text by Marion Kincaird; illus by Swinnerton	57.00	228.00	400.00
LITTLE JOHNNY & THE TEDDY BEARS (Judge-r) (M) (see Teddy Bear Books)			
Reilly & Britton Co.: 1907 (10x14".; 68 pgs, green, red, black interior color)			
nn - By J. R. Bray-a/Robert D. Towne-s	67.00	233.00	400.00
LITTLE JOURNEY TO THE HOME OF BRIGGS THE SKY-ROCKET, THE			
Lockhart Art School: 1917 (10-3/4x7-7/8", 20 pgs, B&W) (I)			
nn - About Clare Briggs (bio & lots of early art)	41.00	144.00	250.00
LITTLE KING, THE (see New Yorker Cartoon Albums for 1st appearance) (M)			
Farrar & Reinhart, Inc: 1933 (10-1/4 x 8-3/4, 80 pgs, hardcover w/dust jacket			
nn - By Otto Soglow (strip-r The New Yorker)	75.00	200.00	400.00
NOTE: Copies with dust jacket are worth 50% more. Also exists in a 12x8-3/4 edition.			
LITTLE LULU BY MARGE (M)			
Rand McNally & Company, Chicago: 1936 (6-9/16x6", 68 pgs, yellow hard-c, B&W)			
nn - By Marjorie Henderson Buell	25.00	100.00	250.00
NOTE: Begins reprinting single panel Little Lulu cartoons which began with Saturday Evening Post Feb. 23, 1935. This book was reprinted several times as late as 1940.			
LITTLE NAPOLEON			
No publisher listed: 1924 , 50 pages, 10" by 10"; Color cardstock-c, B&W			
nn - By Bud Counihan (Cupples &Leon format)	25.00	100.00	240.00
LITTLE NEMO (...in Slumberland) (N) (see also Little Sammy Sneeze, Dreams...Rarebit F)			
Doffield & Co.(1906)/Cupples & Leon Co.(1909): 1906, 1909 (Sunday strip-r in color, cardboard covers)			
1906-11x16-1/2" by Winsor McCay; 30 pgs. (scarce)	1200.00	4500.00	–
1909-10x14" by Winsor McCay (scarce)	1000.00	3500.00	–
LITTLE ORPHAN ANNIE (See Treasure Box of Famous Comics) (N)			
Cupples & Leon Co.: 1926 - 1934 (8-3/4x7", 100 pgs., B&W daily strip-r, hard-c)			
1 (1926)-Little Orphan Annie (softback see Treasure Box)	50.00	200.00	375.00
2 (1927)-In the Circus (softback see Wonder Box...)	36.00	144.00	275.00
3 (1928)-The Haunted House (softback see Wonder Box...)	36.00	144.00	275.00
4 (1929)-Bucking the World	36.00	144.00	275.00
5 (1930)-Never Say Die	30.00	120.00	225.00
6 (1931)-Shipwrecked	30.00	120.00	225.00
7 (1932)-A Willing Helper	25.00	100.00	200.00
8 (1933)-In Cosmic City	25.00	100.00	200.00

The Trials of Lulu and Leander by Howarth
1906 © NY American & Journal

Maud the Mirthful Mule by Opper
1908 © Frederick A. Stokes

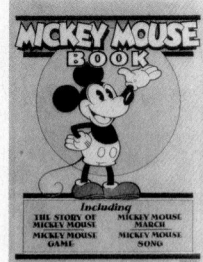

Mickey Mouse Book
1930 © Bibo & Lang

	GD2.0	FN6.0	VF8.0

9 (1934)-Uncle Dan (not rare) — 25.00 / 100.00 / 200.00
NOTE: Each book reprints dailies from the previous year. Each hardcover came with a dust jacket. Books with out dust jackets are worth 50% less. Many of copies of #9 Uncle Dan have been turning up on eBay recently.

LITTLE ORPHAN ANNIE RUMMY CARDS (N)
Whitman Publishing Co., Racine: 1935 (box: 5 x 6 1/2" Cards: 3 1/2 x 2 1/4")

nn-Harold Gray — 20.00 / 60.00 / 120.00
NOTE: 36 cards, including 1 instruction card, 5 character cards and 30 cards forming 5 sequential stories (6 cards each).

LITTLE SAMMY SNEEZE (N) (see also Little Nemo, Dreams of A Rarebit Fiend)
New York Herald Co.: Dec 1905 (11x16-1/2", 72 pgs., color)

nn - By Winsor McCay (Very Rare) — 1700.00 / 5000.00 / –
NOTE: Rarely found in fine to mint condition.

LIVE AND LET LIVE
Travelers Insurance Co.: 1936 (5-3/4x7/3/4", 16 pgs. color and B&W)

nn - Bill Holman, Carl Anderson, etc — 20.00 / 60.00 / 120.00

LULU AND LEANDER (N) (see also Funny Folk, 1899, in Victorian section)
New York American & Journal: 1904 (76 pgs); **William A Stokes & Co:** 1906

nn - By F.M. Howarth — 200.00 / 650.00 / 1200.00
nn - The Trials of...(1906, 10x16", 68 pgs. in color) — 200.00 / 650.00 / 1200.00
NOTE: F. M. Howarth helped pioneer the American comic strip in the pages of PUCK magazine in the early 1890s before the Yellow Kid.

MADMAN'S DRUM (O)
Jonathan Cape and Harrison Smith Inc.: 1930 (8-1/4x6", 274 pgs, B&W hardcover w/dust jacket) (original graphic novel in wood cuts)

nn - By Lynd Ward — 50.00 / 175.00 / 300.00

MAMA'S ANGEL CHILD IN TOYLAND (I)
Rand McNally, Chicago: 1915 (128 pgs, hardbound)

nn - By M.T. "Penny" Ross & Marie C, Sadler — 40.00 / 140.00 / 240.00
NOTE: Mama's Angel Child prefaced in a comic strip by the "Chicago Tribune" 1908 Mar 1 to 1920 Oct 17.This novel dedicated to Esther Starring Richartz, "the original Mama's Angel Kid."

MAUD (N) (see also Happy Hooligan)
Frederick A. Stokes Co.: 1906 - 1908? (10x15-1/2", cardboard-c)

1906-By Fred Opper (Scarce), 66 pgs. color — 257.00 / 1000.00 / –
1907-The Matchless, 10x15" 70 pgs in color — 200.00 / 800.00 / –
1908-The Mirthful Mule, 10x15", 64 pgs in color — 200.00 / 800.00 / –
NOTE: First run of strip began July 24, 1904 to at least Oct 6, 1907, spun out of Happy Hooligan.

MEMORIAL EDITION The Drawings of Clare Briggs (S)
Wm H. Wise & Company: 1930 (7-1/2x8-3/4", 284 pgs, pebbled false black leather, B&W) (posthumous boxed set of 7 books by Clare Briggs)

nn - The Days of Real Sport; nn-Golf; nn-Real Folks at Home; nn-Ain't it a Grand and Glorious Feeling?; nn-That Guiltiest Feeling; nn-Somebody's Always Taking the Joy Out of Life; nn-When a Feller Needs a Friend
Each book... — 30.00 / 120.00 / 210.00
NOTE: Also exists in a whitish cream colored paper back edition; first edition unknown presently.

MENACE CARTOONS (M, S)
Menace Publishing Company, Aurora, Missouri: 1914 (10-3/8x8", 80 pgs, cardboard-c, B&W)

nn - (Rare) — 50.00 / 150.00 / 450.00
NOTE: Reprints anti-Catholic cartoons from K.K.K. related publication The Menace.

MEN OF DARING (N)
Cupples & Leon Co.: 1933 (8-3/4x7", 100 pgs)

nn - By Stookie Allen, intro by Lowell Thomas — 30.00 / 90.00 / 200.00

MICKEY MOUSE BOOK
Bibo & Lang: 1930-1931 (12x9", stapled-c, 20 pgs., 4 printings)

nn - First Disney licensed publication (a magazine, not a book–see first book, Adventures of Mickey Mouse). Contains story of how Mickey met Walt and got his name; games, cartoons & song "Mickey Mouse (You Cute Little Feller)," written by Irving Bibo; Minnie, Clarabelle Cow, Horace Horsecollar & caricature of Walt shaking hands with Mickey. The changes made with the 2nd printing have been verified by billing affidavits in the Walt Disney Archives and include:Two Win Smith Mickey strips from 4/15/30 and 4/17/30 added to page 8 & back-c; "Printed in U.S.A." added to front cover; Bobette Bibo's age of 11 years added to title page; faulty type on the word "tail" corrected top of page 3; the word "start" added to bottom of page 7, removing the words "start 1 2 3 4" from the top of page 7; music and lyrics were rewritten on pages 12-14. A green ink border was added beginning with 2nd printing and some covers have inking variations. Art by Albert Barbelle, drawn in an Ub Iwerks style. Total circulation : 97,938 copies varying from 21,000 to 26,000 per printing.

1st printing. Contains the song lyrics **censored** in later printings, "When little Minnie's pursued by a big bad villain we feel so bad then we're glad when you up and kill him." Attached to the Nov. 15, 1930 issue of the Official Bulletin of the Mickey Mouse Club notes: "Attached to this Bulletin is a new Mickey Mouse Book that has just been published." This is thought to be the reason why a slightly disproportionate larger number of copies of the first printing still exist — 1200.00 / 6000.00 / 12,000.00
2nd printing with a theater/advertising. Christmas greeting added to inside front cover

(1 copy known with Dec. 27, 1930 date) — – / 12,000.00 / –
2nd-4th printings — 1050.00 / 5000.00 / 10,000.00
NOTE: Theater/advertising copies do not qualify as separate printings. Most copies are missing pages 9 & 10 which had a puzzle to be cut out. Puzzle (pages 9 and 10) cut out or missing, subtract 60% to 75%.

MICKEY MOUSE COLORING BOOK (S)
Saalfield Publishing Company:1931 (15-1/4x10-3/4", 32 pgs, color soft cover, half printed in full color interior, rest B&W)

871 - By Ub Iwerks & Floyd Gottfredson (rare) — 400.00 / 1200.00 / 2520.00
NOTE: Contains reprints of first MM daily strip ever, including the "missing" speck the chicken is after found only on the original daily strip art by Iwerks plus other very early MM art. There were several other Saalfield Mickey Mouse coloring books manufactured around the same time.

MICKEY MOUSE, THE ADVENTURES OF (I)
David McKay Co., Inc.: Book I, 1931 - Book II, 1932 (5-1/2"x8-1/2", 32 pgs.)

Book I-First Disney book, by strict definition (1st printing-50,000 copies)(see Mickey Mouse Book by Bibo & Lang). Illustrated text refers to Clarabelle Cow as "Carolyn" and Horace Horsecollar as "Henry". The name "Donald Duck" appears with a non-costumed generic duck on back cover & inside, not in the context of the character that later debuted in the Wise Little Hen.

Hardback w/characters on back-c — 75.00 / 300.00 / 650.00
Softcover w/characters on back-c — 38.00 / 151.00 / 350.00
Version without characters on back-c — 45.00 / 180.00 / 400.00
Book II-Less common than Book I. Character development brought into conformity with the Mickey Mouse cartoon shorts and syndicated strips. Captain Church Mouse, Tanglefoot, Peg-Leg Pete and Pluto appear with Mickey & Minnie — 46.00 / 186.00 / 400.00

MICKEY MOUSE COMIC (N)
David McKay Co.: 1931 - No. 4, 1934 (10"x9-3/4", 52 pgs., card board-c) (Later reprints exist)

1 (1931)-Reprints Floyd Gottfredson daily strips in black & white from 1930 & 1931, including the famous two week sequence in which Mickey tries to commit suicide — 229.00 / 914.00 / 1680.00
2 (1932)-1st app. of Pluto reprinted from 7/8/31 daily. All pgs. from 1931 — 164.00 / 656.00 / 1200.00
3 (1933)-Reprints 1932 & 1933 Sunday pages in color, one strip per page, including the "Lair of Wolf Barker" continuity pencilled by Gottfredson and inked by Al Taliaferro & Ted Thwaites. First app. Mickey's nephews, Morty & Ferdie, one identified by name of Mortimer Fieldmouse, not to be confused with Uncle Mortimer Mouse who is introduced in the Wolf Barker story — 214.00 / 856.00 / 1600.00
4 (1934)-1931 dailies, include the only known reprint of the infamous strip of 2/4/31 where the villainous Kat Nipp snips off the end of Mickey's tail with a pair of scissors — 140.00 / 560.00 / 1050.00

MICKEY MOUSE
Whitman Publishing Co.: 1933-34 (10x8-3/4", 34 pgs, cardboard-c)

948-1932 & 1933 Sunday strips in color, printed from the same plates as Mickey Mouse Book #3 by David McKay, but only pages 5-17 & 32-48 including all of the "Wolf Barker" continuity — 157.00 / 629.00 / 1100.00
NOTE: Some copies bound with back cover upside down. Variance doesn't affect value. Same art appears on front and back covers of all copies. Height of Whitman reissue trimmed 1/2 inch.

MILITARY WILLIE
J. I. Austen Co.: 1907 (7x9-1/2", 12 pgs., every other page in color, stapled)

nn - By F. R. Morgan — 70.00 / 245.00 / 400.00

MINNEAPOLIS TRIBUNE CARTOON BOOK (S)
Minneapolis Tribune: 1899-1903 (11-3/8x9-3/8", B&W, paper cover)

nn (#1) (1899) — 28.00 / 99.00 / 170.00
nn (#2) (1900) — 28.00 / 99.00 / 170.00
nn (#3) (1901) (published Jan 01, 1901) — 28.00 / 99.00 / 170.00
nn (#4) (1902) (114 pgs) — 28.00 / 99.00 / 170.00
nn (#5) (1903) (9x10-3/4",110 pgs, B&W; color-c) — 28.00 / 99.00 / 170.00
NOTE: All by Roland C. Bowman (editorial-r).

MINUTE BIOGRAPHIES: INTIMATE GLIMPSES INTO THE LIVES OF 150 FAMOUS MEN AND WOMEN
Grossett & Dunlap: 1931, 1933 (10-1/4x7-3/4", 168 pgs, hardcover, B&W)

nn - By Nisenson (art) & Parker(text) — 21.00 / 63.00 / 125.00
More.... (1933) — 21.00 / 63.00 / 125.00

MISCHIEVOUS MONKS OF CROCODILE ISLE, THE (N)
J. I. Austen Co., Chicago: 1908 (8-1/2x11-1/2", 12 pgs., 4 pgs. in color)

nn - By F. R. Morgan; reads longwise — 96.00 / 335.00 / 575.00

MR. & MRS. (Also see Ain't It A Grand and Glorious Feeling?) (N)
Whitman Publishing Co.: 1922 (9x9-1/2", 52 & 28 pgs., cardboard-c)

nn - By Briggs (B&W, 52 pgs.) — 37.00 / 149.00 / 260.00
nn - 28 pgs.-(9x9-1/2")-Sunday strips-r in color — 41.00 / 163.00 / 285.00
NOTE: The earliest presently-known Whitman comic books.

MR. BLOCK (N)
Industrial Workers of the World (IWW): 1913, 1919

nn - By Ernest Riebe (C) — 50.00 / 150.00 / –

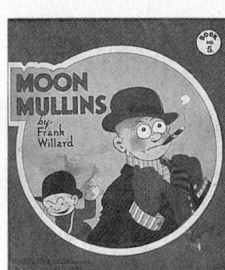

Moon Mullins #5 by Frank Willard
1931 @ Cupples & Leon

The Nebbs
© C&L

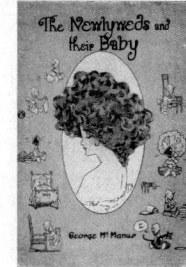

The Newlyweds by George McManus
1907 © Saalfield Publishing Co.

	GD2.0	FN6.0	VF8.0

...And The Profiteers (original material) (H)   50.00   150.00
NOTE: *Mr Block was a daily strip published from 1912 NOV 7 to 1913 SEP ? by the socialist newspaper "Industrial Worker"; Mr Block was a "square" guy (his head was in fact a block) who enthusiastically supported the same system that exploited him. The noted Joe Hill wrote a song about him (Mr Block,1913, on the air of "It loooks me like a big time tonight") for the "Industrial Worker Songbook".*

MR. TWEE-DEEDLE (N)
Cupples & Leon: 1913, 1917 (11-3/8 x 16-3/4" color strips-r from NY Herald)

nn - By John B. Gruelle (later of Raggedy Ann fame)	250.00	750.00	1600.00
nn - "Further Adventures of..." By Gruelle	200.00	700.00	1500.00

NOTE: *Strip ran Feb 5, 1911-March 10, 1918.*

MONKEY SHINES OF MARSELEEN AND SOME OF HIS ADVENTURES (C)
McLaughlin Bros. New York: 1906 (10 x 12-3/8", 36 pgs, full color hardcover)

nn - By Norman E. Jennett strip-r NY Evening Telegram	67.00	233.00	400.00

NOTE: *Strip ran in 1906 until at least March 13, 1910.*

MONKEY SHINES OF MARSELEEN (N)
Cupples & Leon Co.: 1909 (11-1/2 x 17", 58 pgs. in two colors)

nn - By Norman E. Jennett (strip-r New York Herald)	63.00	219.00	375.00

MOON MULLINS (N)
Cupples & Leon Co.: 1927 - 1933 (52 pgs., B&W daily strip-r)

Series 1 ('27)-By Willard	63.00	250.00	500.00
Series 2 ('28), Series 3 ('29), Series 4 ('30)	39.00	156.00	300.00
Series 5 ('31), 6 ('32), 7 ('33)	39.00	156.00	300.00
Big Book 1 ('30)-B&W (scarce)	100.00	400.00	750.00
w/dust jacket (rare)	183.00	732.00	1300.00

MOVING PICTURE FUNNIES
Saml Gabriel Sons & Company: 1918 (5-1/4 x 10-1/4", 52 pgs, B&W, illustrated hard-c)

nn	20.00	40.00	80.00

NOTE: *823 Comical illustrations that show a different scene when folded.*

MUTT & JEFF (...Cartoon, The) (N)
Ball Publications: 1911 - No. 5, 1916 (5-3/4 x 15-1/2", 72 pgs, B&W, hard-c)

1 (1910)(50¢) very common	71.00	286.00	500.00
2,3: 2 (1911)-Opium den panels; Jeff smokes opium (pipe dreams).			
3 (1912) both very common	71.00	286.00	500.00
2-(1913) Reprint of 1911 edition with black ink cover	50.00	175.00	300.00
4 (1915) (50¢) (Scarce)	150.00	350.00	650.00
5 (1916) (Rare) -Photos of Fisher, 1st pg. (68 pages)	200.00	480.00	900.00
5-Scarce 84 page reprint edition	150.00	450.00	800.00

NOTE: *Mutt & Jeff first appeared in newspapers in 1907. Cover variations exist showing Mutt & Jeff reading various newspapers; i.e., The Oregon Journal, The American, and The Detroit News. Reprinting of each issue began soon after publication. No. 4 and 5 may not have been reprinted. Values listed include the reprints. Mutt & Jeff was the first successful American daily newspaper comic strip and as such remains one of the seminal strips of all time.*

MUTT & JEFF (N)
Cupples & Leon Co.: No. 6, 1919 - No. 22, 1934? (9-1/2x9-1/2", 52 pgs, B&W dailies, stiff-c)

6, 7 - By Bud Fisher (very common)	32.00	128.00	225.00
8-10	46.00	186.00	325.00
11-18 (Somewhat Scarcer) (#19-#22 do not exist)	60.00	à240.00	420.00
nn (1920) (Advs. of...) 11x16"; 44 pgs.; full color reprints of 1919 Sunday strips	93.00	372.00	650.00
Big Book nn (1926, 144 pgs., hardcovers)	114.00	456.00	800.00
w/dust jacket	193.00	772.00	1350.00
Big Book 1 (1928) - Thick book (hardcovers)	114.00	456.00	800.00
w/dust jacket (rare)	182.00	729.00	1275.00
Big Book 2 (1929) - Thick book (hardcovers)	114.00	456.00	800.00
w/dust jacket (rare)	182.00	729.00	1275.00

NOTE: *The Big Books contain three previous issues rebound.*

MUTT & JEFF (N)
Embee Publ. Co.: 1921 (9x15", color cardboard-c & interior)

nn - Sunday strips in color (Rare)- BY Bud Fisher	143.00	572.00	1000.00

NOTE: *Ties in with The Trouble of Bringing Up Father (EmBee) and Jimmie Dugan & The Reg'lar Fellers (C&L) as the last of this size.*

MYSTERIOUS STRANGER AND OTHER CARTOONS, THE
McClure, Phillips & Co.: 1905 (12-3/8x9-3/4", 338 pgs, hardcover, B&W)

nn - By John McCutcheon	32.00	128.00	225.00

MY WAR - Szeged (Szuts)
Wm. Morrow Co.: 1932 (7x10-1/2", 210 pgs, hard-c, B&W)

nn - (All story panels, no words - powerful)	32.00	128.00	225.00

NAUGHTY ADVENTURES OF VIVACIOUS MR. JACK, THE
New York American & Journal: 1904 (15x10", color strips)

nn - By James Swinnerton; (Very Rare - 3 known copies)	600.00	1200.00	1800.00

NEBBS, THE (N)
Cupples & Leon Co.: 1928 (52 pgs., B&W daily strip-r)

nn - By Sol Hess; Carlson-a	40.00	160.00	280.00

	GD2.0	FN6.0	VF8.0

NERVY NAT'S ADVENTURES (E)
Leslie-Judge Co.: 1911 (90 pgs, 85¢, 1903 strip reprints from **Judge**)

nn - By James Montgomery Flagg	75.00	263.00	450.00

THE NEWLYWEDS AND THEIR BABY (N)
Saalfield Publ. Co.: 1907 (13x10", 52 pgs., hardcover)

...& Their Baby' by McManus; daily strips 50% color	250.00	900.00	–

NOTE: *Strip ran Apr 10, 1904 thru Jan 14, 1906 and then May 19, 1907-Dec 5, 1916; was a huge success with Baby Snookums long before McManus invented Bringing Up Father; Snookums brought back as a topper strip over BUF Nov 19, 1944-Dec 30, 1956.*

THE NEWLYWEDS AND THEIR BABY'S COMIC PICTURES FOR PAINTING AND CRAYONING (N)
Saalfield Publishing Company: 1916 (10-1/4x14-3/4", 52 pgs. Cardboard-c)

nn - 44 B&W pages, covers, and one color wrap glued to B&W title page.

Color wrap: color title pg. & 3 pgs of color strips	83.00	290.00	500.00
nn - (1917, 10x14", 20 pgs, oblong, cardboard-c) partial reprint of 1916 edition	31.00	124.00	275.00

THE NEWLYWEDS AND THEIR BABY (N)
Saalfield Publishing Company: 1917 (10-1/8x13-9/16 ", 52 pgs, full color cardstock-c, some pages full color, others two color (orange, blue))

nn	83.00	290.00	500.00

NEW YORKER CARTOON ALBUM, THE (M)
Doubleday, Doran & Company Inc.: (1928-1931); **Harper & Brothers.:** (1931-1933); **Random House** (1935-1937), 12x9", various pg counts, hardcovers w/dust jackets)

1928: nn-114 pgs Arno, Held, Soglow, Williams, etc	20.00	60.00	120.00
1928: SECOND-114 pgs Arno, Bairnsfather, Gross, Held, Soglow, Williams	10.00	30.00	60.00
1930: THIRD-172 pgs Arno, Bairnsfather, Held, Soglow, Art Young	10.00	30.00	60.00
1931: FOURTH-154 pgs Arno, Held, Soglow, Steig, Thurber, Williams, Art Young, "Little King" by Soglow begins	10.00	30.00	60.00
1932: FIFTH-156 pgs Arno, Bairnsfather, Held, Hoff, Soglow, Steig, Thurber, Williams	10.00	30.00	60.00
1933: SIXTH-156 pgs same as above	10.00	30.00	60.00
1935: SEVENTH-164 pgs	10.00	30.00	60.00
1937: 168 pgs; Charles Addams plus same as above but no Little King, two page "Gone With The Wind" parody strip	10.00	30.00	60.00

NOTE: *Some sequential strips but mostly single panel cartoons.*

NIPPY'S POP (N)
The Saalfield Publishing Co.: 1917 (10-1/2x13-1/2", 36 pgs., B&W, Sunday strip-r)

nn - Charles M Payne (better known as S'Matter Pop)	43.00	152.00	260.00

OH, MAN (A Bully Collection of Those Inimitable Humor Cartoons) (S)
P.F. Volland & Co.: 1919 (8-1/2x13"; 136 pgs.)

nn - By Briggs	43.00	152.00	260.00

NOTE: *Originally came in illustrated box with Briggs art (box is Rare - worth 50% more with box).*

OH SKIN-NAY! (S)
P.F. Volland & Co.: 1913 (8-1/2x13", 136 pgs.)

nn - The Days Of Real Sport by Briggs	43.00	152.00	260.00

NOTE: *Originally came in illustrated box with Briggs art (box is Rare - worth 50% more with box).*

OLD GOLD THE SMOOTHER AND BETTER CIGARETTE...NOT A COUGH IN A CARLOAD (M,N,P) (see also BY BRIGGS)
Old Gold Cigarettes: nd (c1920's) (16 pgs, paper-c, color) (both Scarce)
nn- (4-1/4" x 3-7/8") cover strip is "Oh, Man!"; also contains: "Real Folks at Home", "Ain't It a Grand and Glorious Feelin?", "It Happens in the Best Regulated Families", and "Mr. and Mrs."   (no known sales)
1440- (5-9/16" x 5-1/4") cover strip is "Frank and Ernest"; also contains: "That Guiltiest Feeling", "Real Folks at Home", "Oh, Man!", "When a Feller Needs a Friend".   (no known sales)

NOTE: *Collection reprinting sports cartoons by Clare Briggs, advertising Old Gold Cigarettes. These strips originally appeared in various magazines, play program booklets, newspapers, etc. Some of the strips involve regular Briggs strip series. The two booklets contain a completely different set of comics.*

ON AND OFF MOUNT ARARAT (also see Tigers) (N)
Hearst's New York American & Journal: 1902, 86pgs. 10x15-1/4"

nn - Rare Noah's Ark satire by Jimmy Swinnerton (rare)	340.00	1200.00	

ON THE LINKS (N)
Associated Feature Service: Dec, 1926 (9x10", 48 pgs.)

nn - Daily strip-r	25.00	100.00	175.00

ONE HUNDRED WAR CARTOONS (S)
Idaho Daily Statesman: 1918 (7-3/4x10", 102 pgs, paperback, B&W)

nn - By Villeneuve (WW I cartoons)	20.00	60.00	120.00

OUR ANTEDILUVIAN ANCESTORS (N,S)
New York Evening Journal, NY: 1903 (11-3/8x8-7/8", hardcover)

nn - By F Opper	25.00	100.00	250.00

NOTE: *There is a simultaneously published British edition, identical size and contents, from C. Arthur Pearson*

Oh Skin-nay! by Claire Briggs
1913 © P.F. Volland

The Adventures of Peck's Bad Boy With
the Teddy Bear Show by McDougall
1907 © Charles C. Thompson, Co.

Roger Bean, R.G. #4
© C&L

Ltd, London. A collection of single panel cartoons about cavemen. Similar to an earlier British cartoon book "Prehistoric Peeps from Punch", by E.T. Reed.

OUTBURSTS OF EVERETT TRUE, THE (N)
Saalfield Publ. Co.(Werner Co.): 1907 (92 pgs, 9-7/16x5-1/4")

1907 (2-4 panel strips-r)-By Condo & Raper	75.00	300.00	600.00
1921-Full color-c; reprints 56 of 88 cartoons from 1907 ed. (10x10", 32 pgs B&W)	37.00	148.00	260.00

OVER THERE COMEDY FROM FRANCE
Observer House Printing: nd (WW 1 era) (6x14", 60 pgs, paper cover)

nn - Artist(s) unknown	15.00	53.00	90.00

OWN YOUR OWN HOME (I)
Bobbs-Merrill Company, Indianapolis: 1919 (7-7/16x5-1/4")

nn - By Fontaine Fox	–	–	–

PECKS BAD BOY (N)
Charles C. Thompson Co, Chicago (by Walt McDougal): 1906-1908 (strip-r)

The Adventures of... (1906) 11-1/2x16-1/4", 68 pgs	100.00	400.00	800.00
...& His Country Cousin Cynthia (1907) 12x16-1/2," 34 pgs In color			
	100.00	400.00	800.00
Advs of...And His Country Cousins (1907) 5-1/2x10 1/2", 18 pgs In color			
	50.00	175.00	300.00
Advs of...And His Country Cousins (1907) 11-1/2x16-1/4", 36 pgs			
	50.00	175.00	300.00
...& Their Advs With The Teddy Bear (1907) 5-1/2x10-1/2", 18 pgs in color			
	50.00	175.00	300.00
...& Their Balloon Trip To the Country (1907) 5-1/2x 10-1/2, 18 pgs in color			
	50.00	175.00	300.00
...With the Teddy Bear Show (1907) 5-1/2x 10-1/2	50.00	175.00	300.00
...With The Billy Whiskers Goats (1907) 5-1/2 x 10-1/2, 18 pgs in color			
	50.00	175.00	300.00
...& His Chums (1908) - 11x16-3/8", 36 pgs. Stanton & Van Vliet Co			
	100.00	400.00	750.00
...& His Chums (1908)-Hardcover; full color;16 pgs.	100.00	350.00	600.00
Advs. of...in Pictures (1908) (11x17, 36 pgs)-In color; Stanton & V. Liet Co.			
	100.00	400.00	700.00

PERCY & FERDIE (N)
Cupples & Leon Co.: 1921 (10x10", 52 pgs., B&W dailies, cardboard-c)

nn - By H. A. MacGill (Rare)	61.00	244.00	450.00

PETER RABBIT (N)
John H. Eggers Co. The House of Little Books Publishers: 1922 - 1923
B1-B4-(Rare)-(Set of 4 books which came in a cardboard box)-Each book reprints half of a Sunday page per page and contains 8 B&W and 2 color pages; by Harrison Cady

(9-1/4x6-1/4", paper-c) each....	43.00	172.00	300.00
Box only	57.00	228.00	400.00

PHILATELIC CARTOONS (M)
Essex Publishing Company, Lynn, Mass.: 1916 (8-11/16" x 5-7/8", 40 pgs, light blue construction paper-c, B&W interior)

nn - By Leroy S. Bartlett	25.00	75.00	175.00

NOTE: Comics reprinted from The New England Philatelist.

PICTORIAL HISTORY OF THE DEPARTMENT OF COMMERCE UNDER HERBERT HOOVER (see Picture Life of a Great American) (O)
Hoover-Curtis Campaign Committee of New York State: no date, 1928 (3-1/4 x 5-1/4, 32 pgs, paper cover, B&W)

nn - By Satterfield (scarce)	40.00	120.00	240.00

NOTE: 1928 Presidential Campaign giveaway. Original material, contents completely different from Picture Life of a Great American.

PICTURE LIFE OF A GREAT AMERICAN (see Pictorial History of the Department of Commerce under Herbert Hoover) (O)
Hoover-Curtis Campaign Committee of New York State: no date, 1928 (paper cover, B&W)

nn - (8-3/4 x 7, 20 pgs) Text cover, 2 page text introduction, 18 pgs of comics (scarcer first print)	43.00	129.00	260.00
nn - (9 x 6-3/4,24 pgs) Illustrated cover,5 page text introduction, 18 pgs of comics (scarce)	43.00	129.00	260.00

NOTE: 1928 Presidential Campaign giveaway. Unknown which above version was published first. Both contain the same original comics material by Satterfield.

PINK LAFFIN (I)
Whitman Publishing Co.: 1922 (9x12")(Strip-r; some of these actually text joke books)
...the Lighter Side of Life, ...He Tells 'Em, ...and His Family, ...Knockouts;

Ray Gleason-a (All rare) each...	26.00	104.00	185.00

POLLY (AND HER PALS) - (N)
Newspaper Feature Service: 1916 (3x2-1/2", color)

Altogether: Three Rahs and a Tiger! by Cliff Sterrett	21.00	63.00	130.00
There Is A Limit To Pa's Patience by Cliff Sterrett	21.00	63.00	130.00
Pa's Lil Book Has Some Uncut Pages by Sterrett	21.00	63.00	130.00

NOTE: Single newsprint sheet printed in full color on both sides, unfolds to show 12 panel story.

POPEYE PAINT BOOK (N)
McLaughlin Bros, Inc., Springfield, Mass.: 1932 (9-7/8x13", 28 pgs, color-c)

2052 - By E. C. Segar	90.00	300.00	600.00

NOTE: Contains a full color panel above and the exact same art in below panel n B&W which one was to color in; strip-r panels.

POPEYE CARTOON BOOK (N)
The Saalfield Co.: 1934 (8-1/2x13", 40 pgs, cardboard-c)

2095-(scarce)-1933 strip reprints in color by Segar. Each page contains a vertical half of a Sunday strip, so the continuity reads row by row unevenly across each double page spread. If each page is read by itself, the continuity makes no sense. Each double page spread reprints one complete Sunday page from 1933	300.00	900.00	2700.00
12 Page Version	100.00	300.00	900.00

POPEYE (See **Thimble Theatre** for earlier Popeye-r from Sonnett) (N)
David McKay Publications: 1935 (25¢; 52 pgs, B&W) (By Segar)

1-Daily strip reprints- "The Gold Mine Thieves"	107.00	321.00	800.00
2-Daily strip-r (scarce)	100.00	300.00	750.00

NOTE: Ties with Henry & Little Annie Rooney (David McKay) as the last of the 10x10" size books.

PORE LI'L MOSE (N)
New York Herald Publ. by Grand Union Tea
Cupples & Leon Co.: 1902 (10-1/2x15", 78 pgs., color)

nn - By R. F. Outcault; Earliest known C&L comic book (scarce in high grade - very high demand)	1500.00	5500.00	–

NOTE: Black Americana one page newspaper strips; falls in between Yellow Kid & Buster Brown. Complete copies have become scarce. Some have cut this book apart thinking that reselling individual pages will bring them more money.

PRETTY PICTURES (M)
Farrar & Rinehart: 1931 (12 x 8-7/8", 104 pgs, color hardcover w/dust jacket, B&W; reprints from New Yorker, Judge, Life, Collier's Weekly)

nn - By Otto Soglow (contains "The Little King")	33.00	134.00	235.00

QUAINT OLD NEW ENGLAND (S)
Triton Syndicate: 1936 (5-1/4x6-1/4", 100 pgs, soft-c squarebound, B&W)

nn - By Jack Withycomb	36.00	144.00	250.00

NOTE: Comics about weird doings in Old New England.

RED CARTOONS (S)
Daily Worker Publishing Company: 1926 (12 x 9", 68 pgs,cardboard cover, B&W)

nn - By Various (scarce)	40.00	160.00	280.00

NOTE: Reprint of American Communist Party editorial cartoons, from The Daily Worker, The Workers Monthly, and the Liberator. Art by Fred Ellis, William Gropper, Clive Weed, Art Young.

REG'LAR FELLERS (See All-American Comics, Jimmie Dugan & The..., Popular Comics & Treasure Box of Famous Comics) (N)
Cupples & Leon Co./MS Publishing Co.: 1921-1929

1 (1921)-52 pgs. B&W dailies (Cupples & Leon, 10x10")	43.00	171.00	300.00
1925, 48 pgs. B&W dailies (MS Publ.)	39.00	157.00	275.00
Hardcover (1929, 8-3/4x7-1/2"; 96 pgs.)-B&W-r	54.00	214.00	375.00

REG'LAR FELLERS STORY PAINT BOOK
Whitman, Racine, Wisc.: 1932 (8-3/4x12-1/8", 132 pgs, red soft-c)

By Gene Byrnes	25.00	75.00	150.00

ROGER BEAN, R. G. (Regular Guy) (N)
The Indiana News Co. Distributers.: 1915 - No. 2, 1915 (5-3/8x17", 68 pgs., B&W, hardcovers); #3-#5 published by Chas. B. Jackson: 1916-1919
(No. 1 2 4 & 5 bound on side, No. 3 bound at top)

1-By Chas B. Jackson (68pgs.)(Scarce)	60.00	210.00	360.00
2- 5-5/8x17-1/8", 66 pgs (says 1913 inside - an obvious printing error) (red or green binding)	60.00	210.00	360.00
3-Along the Firing Line... (1916; 68 pgs, 6x17")	60.00	210.00	360.00
3-Along the Firing Line side-bound version	60.00	210.00	360.00
4-Into the Trenches and Out Again with... (1917, 68 pgs)	60.00	210.00	360.00
5 ...And The Reconstruction Period (1919, 5-3/8x15-1/2", 84 pgs) (Scarce) (has $1 printed on side)	60.00	210.00	360.00
Baby Grand Editions 1-5 (10x10", cardboard-c)	60.00	210.00	360.00

NOTE: 1 & 2 of the Baby Grands (nd) 8-1/4x10-7/8", 52 pgs. #3 & #4 9x10-7/8" Cardboard cover. B&W strip reprints. Cover also says "Politics Pickles People Police."

nn - 9x11, 68 pgs	60.00	210.00	360.00

NOTE: Has picture of Chic Jackson and a posthumous dedication from his three children. strip-r 1931-32

ROGER BEAN PHILOSOPHER
Schnull & Co: 1917 (5-1/2x17", 36 pgs., B&W, brown & black paper-c, square binding)

nn - By Chic Jackson	(no known sales)

ROOKIE FROM THE 13TH SQUAD, THAT (N) (also Between Shots; Always Belittlin';Skippy)
Harper & Brothers Publishers: Feb. 1918 (8x9-1/4", 72 pgs, hardcover, B&W)

nn - By Lieut. P(ercy) L. Crosby	58.00	204.00	375.00

NOTE: Strip began in 1917 at an Army base during basic training.

ROUND THE WORLD WITH THE DOO-DADS (see Doings of the Doo-Dads, Doo Dads)
Universal Feature And Specialty Co, Chicago: 1922 (12x10-1/2", 52 pgs, B&W, red &

Seaman Si
© Pierce Publ. Co.

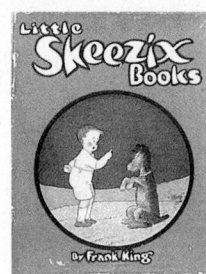

Little Skeezix Books by Frank King
1929 © Reilly & Lee

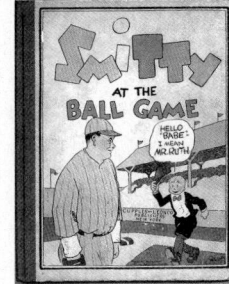

Smitty #2 By Walter Berndt
1929 © Cupples & Leon

	GD2.0	FN6.0	VF8.0

light blue-c, square binding)

nn - By Arch Dale newspaper strip-r   43.00   173.00   300.00
NOTE: Intermixed single panel and sequential comic strips with scenes from Scotland, Ireland, England, Holland, Italy, Spain, Egypt, Africa, and Lions & Elephants along the Nile River, China, Australia & back home.

RUBAIYKT OF THE EGG
The John C Winston Co, Philadelphia: 1905 (7x5/12", 64 pgs, purple-c, B&W)

nn - By Clare Victor Dwiggins   20.00   60.00   125.00
NOTE: Book is printed & cut into the shape of an egg.

RULING CLAWSS, THE (N,S)
The Daily Worker: 1935 (192 pgs, 10-1/4 x 7-3/8", hard-c, B&W)

nn - By Redfield   60.00   240.00   –
NOTE: Reprints cartoons from the American Communist Party newspaper The Daily Worker.

SAGARA'S ENGLISH CARTOONS AND CARTOON STORIES (N)
Bunkosha, Tokyo: nd (c1925) (6-5/8" x 4-1/4", 272 pgs, hard-c, B&W)

nn- (Scarce)   –   –   –
NOTE: Published in Tokyo, Japan, with all strips in both English and Japanese, to facilitate learning English. Majority of book is Bringing Up Father by George McManus. Also contains Japanese strip Father Takes it Easy, by T. Sagara, reprinted from the Kokusai News Agency.

SAM AND HIS LAUGH (N)
Frederick A. Stokes: 1906 (10x15", cardboard-c, Sunday strip-r in color)

nn - By Jimmy Swinnerton (Very Rare)   400.00   900.00   2000.00
NOTE: Strip ran July 24, 1904-Dec 26 1906; its ethnic humor might be considered racist by today's standards.

SCHOOL DAYS (N)
Harper & Bros.: 1919 (9x8", 104 pgs.)

nn - By Clare Victor Dwiggins   42.00   144.00   275.00

SEAMAN SI - A Book of Cartoons About the Funniest "Gob" in the Navy (N)
Pierce Publishing Co.: 1916 (4x8-1/2, 200 pgs, hardcover, B&W); 1918 (4-1/8x8-1/4, 104 pgs, hardcover, B&W)

nn - By Perce Pearce (1916)   50.00   150.00   300.00
nn - 1918 - (Reilly & Britton Co.)   30.00   125.00   200.00
NOTE: There exists two different covers for the 1918 reprints. The earlier edition was self published by the artist. The newspaper strip is sometimes also known as "The American Sailor."

SECRET AGENT X-9 (N)
David McKay Pbll.: 1934 (Book 1: 84 pgs; Book 2: 124 pgs.) (8x7-1/2")

Book 1-Contains reprints of the first 13 weeks of the strip by Dashiell Hammett & Alex Raymond, complete except for 2 dailies   100.00   300.00   750.00
Book 2-Contains reprints immediately following contents of Book 1, for 20 weeks by Dashiell Hammett & Alex Raymond; complete except for two dailies.
Last 5 strips misdated from 6/34, continuity correct   100.00   300.00   750.00

SILK HAT HARRY'S DIVORCE SUIT (N)
M. A. Donoghue & Co.: 1912 (5-3/4x15-1/2", oblong, B&W)

nn - Newspaper-r by Tad (Thomas A. Dorgan)   33.00   117.00   400.00

SINBAD A DOG'S LIFE (M)
Coward - McCann, Inc.: 1930 (11x 8-3/4", 104 pgs., single-sided, illustrated hard-c, B&W)

nn - By Edwina   11.00   33.00   100.00
Sinbad...Again (1932, 10-15/16x 8-9/16", 104 pgs.)   11.00   33.00   100.00
NOTE: Wordless comic strips from LIFE.

SIS HOPKINS OWN BOOK AND MAGAZINE OF FUN
Leslie-Judge Co.: 1899-July 1911 (36 pgs, color-c, B&W) (merged into Judge's Library, later titled Film Fun)

any issue - By various   11.00   33.00   100.00
NOTE: Zim, Flagg, Young, Newell, Adams, etc.

SKEEZIX (Also see Gasoline Alley & Little Skeezix Books listed below) (I)
Reilly & Lee Co.: 1925 - 1928 (Strip-r, soft covers) (pictures & text)

...and Uncle Walt (1924)-Origin   26.00   104.00   180.00
...and Pal (1925), ...at the Circus (1926)   21.00   84.00   160.00
...& Uncle Walt (1927) (does this actually exist? reprint?)   –   –   –
...Out West (1928)   21.00   84.00   180.00
Hardback Editions...   34.00   136.00   235.00

SKEEZIX BOOKS, LITTLE (Also see Skeezix, Gasoline Alley) (G)
Reilly & Lee Co.: No date (1928, 1929) (Boxed set of three Skeezix books)

nn - Box with 3 issues of Skeezix. Skeezix & Pal, Skeezix at the Circus, Skeezix & Uncle Walt known. 1928 Set...   60.00   180.00   360.00
nn - Box with set of three (3) above Skeezix plus "Out West"   80.00   330.00   550.00

SKEEZIX COLOR BOOK (N)
McLaughlin Bros. Inc, Springfield, Mass: 1929 (9-1/2x10-1/4", 28 pgs, one third in full color, rest in B&W)

2023 - By Frank King; strip-r to color   20.00   75.00   135.00

SKIPPY (see also Life Presents Skippy, Always Belittlin', That Rookie From 13th Squad)
No publisher listed: Circa 1920s (10x8", 16 pgs, color/B&W cartoons)

nn - By Percy Crosby   20.00   84.00   150.00

SKIPPY, LIFE PRESENTS (M)
Life Publishing Company & Henry Holt, NY: nd 1924 (134 pgs, 10-13/16x8-3/4", color hard-c, B&W)

nn   –   –   –
NOTE: Many sequential & single panel reprints from Skippy's earliest appearances in Life Magazine.

SKIPPY
Greenberg, Publisher, Inc, NY: 1925. (11-14x8-5/8, 72 pgs, hard-c, B&W and color

nn - By Percy L. Crosby   –   –   –
NOTE: Some but not all of these comics were also in Life Presents Skippy; issued with dust wrapper.

SKIPPY AND OTHER HUMOR
Greenberg: Publisher, NY: 1929 (11-1/4x8-1/2",72 pgs,tan hard-c, B&W and color)

nn - By Percy L. Crosby   50.00   175.00   300.00
NOTE: Came with a dust jacket.

SKIPPY (I)
Grossett & Dunlap: 1929 (7-3/8x6, 370 pgs, hardcover text with some art)

nn - By Percy Crosby (issued with a dust jacket)   23.00   92.00   160.00
NOTE: This is worth very little without the dust wrapper; very common without athe dust jacket.

SKIPPY
Greenberg Press: 1930 (soft cover, ca. 16 pp.,

nn - By Percy Crosby (scarce)   50.00   175.00   300.00
NOTE: Reprints from LIFE cartoons, color, b/w. Crosby told Greenberg to withdraw from the market as it cheapened the hard cover prior editions. Greenberg then stopped publishing per agreement, and sent Crosby all the copper & zinc bookplates, which were in Crosby estate until 1996.

SKIPPY CRAYON AND COLORING BOOK (N)
McLoughlin Bros, Inc., Springfield, MA: 1931 (13x9-3/4", 28 pgs, color-c, color & B&W)

2050 - By Percy Crosby   28.00   84.00   195.00
NOTE: This item says on the front cover: "Licensed by Percy Crosby" because he owned his creation. About half the pages have one panel pre-printed in full color with same one b&w below for person to copy the colors.

SKIPPY RAMBLES (I)
G.P. Putnam's Sons: 1932 (7 1/8 x 5 1/8, 202 pgs)

nn - By Percy Crosby   21.00   84.00   150.00
NOTE: Issued with a dustjacket. Has Skippy plates by Crosby every 4 or 5 pages.

SKUDDABUD STARRY STORY SERIES - FOLK FROM THE FUTURE (O,G)
no publisher listed: 1936 (9" x 11-7/8", 48 pgs, cardboard-c, B&W)

Book One (Rare) "Parachuting"   21.00   84.00   150.00
NOTE: By Columba Krebs. Top half of each page is a continuing strip story, while bottom half are different stories, in prose, about the same characters -- a race of aliens who have migrated to Earth, from their dying world.

S'MATTER POP? (N)
Saalfield Publ. Co.: 1917 (10x14", 44 pgs., B&W, cardboard-c,)

nn - By Charlie Payne; in full color; pages printed on one side   48.00   169.00   290.00

S'MATTER POP? (N) (25 ¢ cover price)
E.I. Company, New York: 1927 (8-15/16x7-1/8", 52 pgs, yellow soft-c perfect bound

nn - By C.M. Payne (scarce)   24.00   84.00   145.00
NOTE: First comic book published by Hugo Gernsback, noted for inventing Amazing Stories among other memorable science fiction pulps. The World Science Fiction Convention Award, The Hugo, is named for him.

SMITTY (See Treasure Box of Famous Comics) (N)
Cupples & Leon Co.: 1928 - 1933 (9x7", 96 pgs., B&W strip-r, hardcover)

1928-(96 pgs. 7x8-3/4") By Walter Berndt   43.00   172.00   300.00
1929-At the Ball Game (Babe Ruth on cover)   57.00   229.00   450.00
1930-The Flying Office Boy, 1931-The Jockey, 1932-In the North Woods
    each...   31.00   126.00   250.00
1933-At Military School   31.00   126.00   250.00
NOTE: Each hardbound was published with a dust jacket; worth 50% more with dust jacket. The 1923 edition is very popular with baseball collectors. Strip debuted Nov 27, 1922.

SMOKEY STOVER (See Dan Dunn & King of the Royal Mounted) (N)
Whitman Publishing: 1937 (5 1/2 x 7 1/4", 68pgs., color cardboard-c, B&W)

1010   36.00   144.00   250.00

SOCIAL COMEDY (M)
Life Publishing Company: 1902 (11-3/4 x 9-1/2", 128 pgs, B&W, illustrated hardcover)

nn - Artists include C.D. Gibson & Kemble.   20.00   70.00   120.00
NOTE: Reprints cartoons and a few sequential comics from LIFE. Came in unmarked slipcase.

SOCIAL HELL, THE (O)
Rich Hill: 1902

nn - By Ryan Walker   21.00   74.00   130.00
NOTE: "The conditions of workers and the corruption of a political system beholden to corporate interests have been a major focus of human rights concerns since the 19th century. This early graphic novel depicts the social evils of unreformed capitalism. Ryan Walker was a syndicate cartoonist for many mainstream newspapers as well as for the communist Daily Worker." This description comes from http://www.lib.ucomn.edu/DoddCenter/ascexh3.html, where you can find also a reproduction of the cover. I add that Ryan Walker was the editor of "The Saint Louis Republic" comic section since its inception in 1897; the supplement published "Alma and Oliver", George McManus's first series.

SPORT AND THE KID (see The Umbrella Man) (N)
Lowman & Hanford Co.: 1913 (6-1/4x6-5/8",114 pgs, hardcover, B&W&orange)

nn - By J.R. "Dok" Hager   20.00   70.00   120.00

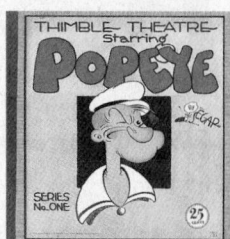

Thimble Theater #1 by E.C. Segar
1931 © Sonnet Publishing Co.

Tillie the Toiler #7 by Russ Westover
1932 © Cupples & Leon

Tim McCoy, Police Car 17
© Whitman Publ. Co.

	GD2.0	FN6.0	VF8.0

STORY OF CONNECTICUT (N)
The Hartford Times: Vol.1 1935 - Vol.3 1936 (10-1/2" x 7-3/8",304 pgs,color hard-c, B&W)

Vol.1 - 3	20.00	70.00	120.00

NOTE: Collects a newspaper strip on Connecticut State history, which ran in the Hartford Times. Strip is in a similar format to "Texas History Movies". Also published in a plain, blue hardcover.

STORY OF JAPAN IN CHINA, THE (N,S)
Trans-Pacific News Service, NYC: Vol. 3, No.1 March 10, 1938 (9" x 6", 36 pgs, construction paper-c, B&W)

Vol.3 No.1	21.00	64.00	150.00

NOTE: Part of the "China Reference-Series" of booklets, detailing the Japanese occupation and brutalization of China. Consists entirely of cartoons. The other booklets in the series have no cartoons. Art by: Ding, Fitzpatrick, Herblock, Herman, Rollin Kirby, Knox, Low, Manning, Orr, Shoemaker, Talburt.

STRANGE AS IT SEEMS (S)
Blue-Star Publishing Co.: 1932 (64 pgs., B&W, square binding)

1-Newspaper-r (Published with & without No. 1 and price on cover.)	32.00	128.00	225.00
Ex-Lax giveaway (1936, B&W, 24 pgs., 5x7") - McNaught Synd.	13.00	52.00	90.00

SULLIVANT'S ABC ZOO (I)
The Old Wine Press: 1946 (11-3/4x9-3/8", hardcover)

nn - By T.S. Sullivant	—	—	—

NOTE: Reprints Mitchell & Miller material 1895-1898 and Life Publishing 1898-1926.

TAILSPIN TOMMY STORY & PICTURE BOOK (I)
McLoughlin Bros.: No. 266, 1931? (nd) (10x10-1/2", color strip-r)

266 - By Forrest	43.00	172.00	300.00

TAILSPIN TOMMY (Also see Famous Feature Stories & The Funnies)(N)
Cupples & Leon Co.: 1932 (100 pgs., hard-c) (B&W 1930 strip reprints)

nn - (Scarce)- by Hal Forrest & Glenn Chaffin	50.00	150.00	375.00

TALES OF DEMON DICK AND BUNKER BILL (O)
Whitman Publishing Co.: 1934 (5-1/4x10-1/2", 80 pgs, color hardcover, B&W)

793 - By Spencer	33.00	100.00	300.00

TARZAN BOOK (The Illustrated...) (N)
Grosset & Dunlap: 1929 (9x7", 80 pgs.)
1(Rare)-Contains 1st B&W Tarzan newspaper comics from 1929. By Hal Foster
Cloth reinforced spine & dust jacket (50¢); Foster-c

With dust jacket...	86.00	344.00	630.00
Without dust jacket...	43.00	172.00	315.00

2nd Printing(1934, 25¢, 76 pgs.)-4 Foster pgs. dropped; paper spine, circle in lower right cover with 25¢ price. The 25¢ is barely visible on some copies

	34.00	136.00	250.00

1967-House of Greystoke reprint-7x10", using the complete 300 illustrations/text from the 1929 edition minus the original indicia, foreword, etc. Initial version bound in gold paper & sold for $5.00. Officially titled **Burroughs Bibliophile #2**. A very few additional copies were bound in heavier blue paper.

Gold binding...	2.25	6.75	20.00
Blue binding...	2.50	7.50	27.00

TARZAN OF THE APES TO COLOR (N)
Saalfield Publishing Co.: No. 988, 1933 (15-1/4x10-3/4", 24 pgs)
(Coloring book)
988-(Very Rare)-Contains 1929 daily reprints with some new art by Hal Foster. Two panels blown up large on each page with one at the top of opposing pages on every other double-page spread. Believed to be the only time these panels appeared in color. Most color panels are reproduced a second time in B&W to be colored

	271.00	1084.00	2000.00

TARZAN OF THE APES The Big Little Cartoon Book (N)
Whitman Publishing Company: 1933 (4-1/2x3 5/8", 320 pgs, color-c, B&W)

744 - By Hal Foster (comics on every page)	36.00	144.00	265.00

TECK HASKINS AT OHIO STATE (S)
Lea-Mar Press: 1908 (7-1/4x5-3/8", 84 pgs, B&W hardcover)

nn - By W.A. Ireland; football cartoons-r from Columbus Ohio Evening Dispatch	28.00	99.00	170.00

NOTE: Small blue & white patch of cover art pasted atop a color cloth quilt patter; pasted patch can easily peel off some copies.

TECK 1909 (S)
Lea-Mar Press: 1909 (8-5/8 x 8-1/8", 124 pgs., B&W hardcover, 25¢)

nn - By W.A. Ireland; Ohio State University baseball cartoons-r from Columbus Evening Dispatch	28.00	99.00	170.00

TEDDY BEAR BOOKS, THE (M) (see also LITTLE JOHNNY AND THE TEDDY BEARS)
Reilly & Britton Co., Chicago: 1907 (7-1/16" x 5-3/8", 24 pgs, hard-c, color

The Teddy Bears Come to Life, The Teddy Bears at the Circus, The Teddy Bears in a Smashup, The Teddy Bears on a Lark, The Teddy Bears on a Toboggan, The Teddy Bears at School, The Teddy Bears Go Fishing, The Teddy Bears in Hot Water

	21.00	84.00	130.00

NOTE: Books are all unnumbered. C & A by J.R. Bray; s-Robert D. Towne. Reprints "Little Johnny & the Teddy Bears" strips, from Judge Magazine. Similar in format to the Buster Brown Nuggets series. All eight

books debuted simultaneously.

TEDDY BEARS IN FUN AND FROLIC (M) (see LITTLE JOHNNY & THE TEDDY BEARS)
Reilly & Britton Co., Chicago: 1908 (8-3/4" x 8-3/4", 50 pgs, cardboard-c, color)

nn - (Rare) by J.R. Bray-a; Robert D. Towne-s	100.00	400.00	700.00

NOTE: Reprints "Little Johnny & the Teddy Bears" strips, from Judge Magazine. Unknown if there were any other "Teddy Bear" titles published in this format.

THE TEENIE WEENIES
Reilly & Britton, Chicago: 1916 (16-3/8x10-1/2", 52 pgs, cardboard-c, full color)

nn - By Wm. Donahey (Chicago Tribune-r)	100.00	400.00	700.00

TERROR OF THE TINY TADS (N)
Cupples & Leon: 1909 (11x17, 26 Sunday strips in Black & Red, Stiff cardboard-c)

nn - By Gustave Verbeek (Very Rare)	(no known sales)		

TEXAS HISTORY MOVIES (N)
Various editions, 1928 to 1986 (B&W)

Book I -1928 Southwest Press (7-1/4 x 5-3/8, 56 pgs, cardboard cover) for the Magnolia Petroleum Company	50.00	125.00	250.00
nn - 1928 Southwest Press (12-3/8 x 9-1/4, 232 pgs, HC)	75.00	200.00	400.00
nn - 1935 Magnolia Petroleum Company (6 x 9, 132 pgs, paper cover)	21.00	63.00	130.00

NOTE: Exists with either Wagon Train or Texas Flag & Lafitte/pirate covers.

nn - 1943 Magnolia Petroleum Company (132 pgs, paper cover)	16.00	48.00	100.00
nn - 1963 Graphic Ideas Inc (11 x 8-1/2, softcover)	12.00	37.00	75.00

NOTE: Reprints daily newspaper strips from the Dallas News, on Texas history. 1935 editions onward distributed within the Texas Public School System. Prior to that they appear to be giveaway comic books for the Magnolia Petroleum Company. There are many more editions than the ones pointed out above.

THAT SON-IN-LAW OF PA'S! (N)
Newspaper Feature Service: 1914 (2-1/2 by 3", color)

nn - Imprinted on back for THE LESTER SHOE STORE.	15.00	25.00	50.00

NOTE: Single sheet printed in full color on both sides, unfolds to show 12 panel story.

THIMBLE THEATRE STARRING POPEYE (See also Popeye) (N)
Sonnet Publishing Co.: 1931 - No. 2, 1932 (25¢, B&W, 52 pgs.)(Rare)

1-Daily strip serial-r in both by Segar	157.00	650.00	1300.00
2	136.00	544.00	1100.00

NOTE: The very first Popeye reprint book. The first Thimble Theatre Sunday page appeared Dec 19, 1919. Popeye first entered Thimble Theatre on Jan 17, 1929.

THREE FUN MAKERS, THE (N)
Stokes and Company: 1908 (10x15", 64 pgs., color) (1904-06 Sunday strip-r)

nn - Maud, Katzenjammer Kids, Happy Hooligan	600.00	1800.00	—

NOTE: This is the first comic book to compile more than one newspaper strip together.

TIGERS (Also see On and Off Mount Ararat) (N)
Hearst's New York American & Journal: 1902, 86 pgs. 10x15-1/4"

nn - Funny animal strip-r by Jimmy Swinnerton	600.00	1600.00	—

NOTE: The strip began as The Journal Tigers in The New York Journal Dec 12, 1897-Sept 28 1903

TILLIE THE TOILER (N)
Cupples & Leon Co.: 1925 - No. 8, 1933 (52 pgs., B&W, daily strip-r)

nn (#1) By Russ Westover	54.00	216.00	450.00
2-8	50.00	175.00	360.00

NOTE: First newspaper strip appearance was in January, 1921.

TILLIE THE TOILER MAGIC DRAWING AND COLORING BOOK
Sam L Gabriel Sons And Company: 1931 (8-1/2 x 12", 36 pages, stiff-c)

838-By Russ Westover	39.00	156.00	275.00

TIMID SOUL, THE (N)
Simon & Schuster: 1931 (12-1/4x9", 136 pgs, B&W hardcover, dust jacket?)

nn - By H. T. Webster (newspaper strip-r)	40.00	120.00	260.00

TIM McCOY, POLICE CAR 17 (O)
Whitman Publishing Co.: 1934 (14-3/4x11", 32 pgs, stiff color covers)

674-1933 original material	75.00	300.00	600.00

NOTE: Historically important as first movie adaptation in comic books.

TOAST BOOK
John C. Winston Co: 1905 (7-1/4 x 6,104 pgs, skull-shaped book, feltcover, B&W)

nn - By Clare Dwiggins	50.00	175.00	300.00

NOTE: Cartoon illustrations accompanying toasts/poems, most involving alcohol.

TOM SAWYER & HUCK FINN (N)
Stoll & Edwards Co.: 1925 (10x10-3/4", 52 pgs, stiff covers)

nn - "Dwig" Dwiggins; 1923, 1924-r color Sunday strip-r	39.00	156.00	325.00

NOTE: By Permission of the Estate of Samuel L. Clemons and the Mark Twain Company.

TOONERVILLE TROLLEY AND OTHER CARTOONS (N) (See Cartoons by Fontaine Fox)
Cupples & Leon Co.: 1921 (10 x10", 52 pgs., B&W, daily strip-r)

1 - By Fontaine Fox	60.00	300.00	550.00

TRAINING FOR THE TRENCHES (M)
Palmer Publishing Company: 1917 (5-3/8 x 7", 20 pgs., paper-c, 10¢)

When a Feller Needs a Friend
© P.F. Volland & Co.

Willie and His Papa & the Rest of the Family by Opper
1901 © Grossett & Dunlap

The Yellow Kid #4 cover by Outcault
1897 © Howard Ainslee & Co.

	GD2.0	FN6.0	VF8.0		GD2.0	FN6.0	VF8.0

nn - By Lieut. Alban B. Butler, Jr.   21.00   84.00   150.00
NOTE: Subtitle: "A book of humorous cartoons on a serious subject." Single-panels about military training.

TREASURE BOX OF FAMOUS COMICS (N) (see Wonder Chest of Famous Comics)
Cupples & Leon Co.: 1934 8-1/2x(6-7/8", 36 pgs, soft covers) (Boxed set of 5 books)

Little Orphan Annie (1926)	21.00	84.00	165.00
Reg'lar Fellers (1928)	19.00	76.00	145.00
Smitty (1928)	19.00	76.00	145.00
Harold Teen (1931)	19.00	76.00	145.00
How Dick Tracy & Dick Tracy Jr. Caught The Racketeers (1933)	26.00	104.00	205.00
Softcover set of five books in box	160.00	640.00	1250.00
Box only	57.00	228.00	450.00

NOTE: Dates shown are copyright dates; all books actually came out in 1934 or later. The softcovers are abbreviated versions of the hardcover editions listed under each character.

T.R. IN CARTOONS (N)
A.C. McClurg & Co., Chicago: June 13, 1910 (10-5/8" x 8", 104? pgs, paper-c, B&W)

nn - By McCutcheon about Teddy Roosevelt

TRUTH (See Victorian section for earlier issues including the first Yellow Kid appearances)
Truth Company, NY: 1886-1906? (13-11/16x10-5/16", 16 pgs, process color-c & center-folds, rest B&W)

1900-1906 issues	10.00	20.00	50.00

TRUTH SAVE IT FROM ABUSE & OVERWORK BEING THE EPISODE OF THE HIRED HAND & MRS. STIX PLASTER, CONCERTIST (N)
Radio Truth Society of WBAP: no date, 1924 (6-3/8 x 4-7/8, 40 pgs, paper cover, B&W)

nn - By V.T. Hamlin (Very Rare)   100.00   400.00   700.00
NOTE: Radio station WBAP giveaway reprints strips from the Ft. Worth Texas Star-Telegram set at local radio station. 1st collected work by V.T. Hamlin, pre-Alley Oop.

TWENTY FIVE YEARS AGO (see At The Bottom Of The Ladder) (M,S)
Coward-McCann: 1931 (5-3/4x4-1/4, 328 pgs, hardcover, B&W)

nn - By Camillus Kessler   32.00   128.00   225.00
NOTE: Multi-image panel cartoons showing historical events for dates during the year.

UMBRELLA MAN, THE (N) (See Sport And The Kid)
Lowman & Hanford Co.: 1911 (8-7/8x5-7/8", 112 pgs, hard-c, B&W & orange)

nn - By J.R. "Dok" Hager (Seattle Times-r)   20.00   70.00   120.00

UNCLE REMUS AND BRER RABBIT (N)
Frederick A. Stokes Co.: 1907 (64 pgs, hardbound, color)

nn - By Joel C Harris & J.M. Conde   50.00   175.00   300.00

UPSIDE DOWNS OF LITTLE LADY LOVEKINS AND OLD MAN MUFFAROO (N)
New York Herald: 1905 (?) (N)

nn - By Gustav Verbeck   100.00   350.00   650.00

VAUDEVILLES AND OTHER THINGS (N)
Isaac H. Blandiard Co.: 1900 (13x10-1/2", 22 pgs., color) plus two reprints

nn - By Bunny (Scarce)   271.00   950.00   –
nn - 2nd print "By the Creator of Foxy Grandpa" on-c but only has copyright info of 1900 (10-1/2x15 1/2, 28 pgs, color)   200.00   700.00   –
nn - 3rd print. "By the creator of Foxy Grandpa" on-c; has both 1900 and 1901 copyright info (11x13")   200.00   700.00   –

WALLY - HIS CARTOONS OF THE A.E.F. (N)
Stars & Stripes: 1917 (96 and 108 pgs, B&W)

nn - By Abian A "Wally" Wallgren (7x18; 96 pgs)   25.00   75.00   150.00
nn - another edition (108 pgs, 7x17-1/2)   25.00   75.00   150.00
NOTE: World War One cartoons reprints from Stars & Stripes; sold to U.S. servicemen with profits to go to French War Orphans Fund. Various editions from 1917-1920; there might be more than what we list here.

WAR CARTOONS (S)
Dallas News: 1918 (11x9", 112 pgs, hardcover, B&W)

nn - By John Knott (WWOne cartoons)   20.00   70.00   125.00

WAR CARTOONS FROM THE CHICAGO DAILY NEWS (N,S)
Chicago Daily News: 1914 (10 cents, 7-3/4x10-3/4", 68 pgs, paper-c, B&W)

nn - By L.D. Bradley   20.00   70.00   125.00

WEBER & FIELD'S FUNNYISMS (S,M,O)
Arkell Comoany, NY: 1904 (10-7/8x8", 112 pgs, color-c, B&W)

1 - By various (only issue?)   20.00   70.00   150.00
NOTE: Contains some sequential & many single panel strips by Outcault, George Luks, CA David, Houston, L Smith, Hy Mayer, Verbeck, Woolf, Sydney Adams, Frank "Chip" Bellew, Eugene "ZIM" Zimmerman, Phil May, FT Richards, Billy Marriner, Grosvenor and many others.

WE'RE NOT HEROES (O,S)
E.C. Wells and J.W. Moss: 1933 (8-11/16" x 5-7/8", 52 pgs, B&W interior)

nn - By Eddie Wells; red & black paper-c   10.00   30.00   60.00
NOTE: Amateurish cartoons about World War I vets in the Walter Reed Veteran's Hospital.

WHEN A FELLER NEEDS A FRIEND (S)
P. F. Volland & Co.: 1914 (11-11/16x8-7/8)

nn - By Clare Briggs   37.00   131.00   225.00
NOTE: Originally came in box with Briggs art (box is Rare); also numerous more modern reprints.

WILD PILGRIMAGE (O)
Harrison Smith & Robert Haas: 1932 (9-7/8x7", 210 pgs, B&W hardcover w/dust jacket) (original wordless graphic novel in woodcuts)

nn - By Lynd Ward   50.00   175.00   300.00

WILLIE AND HIS PAPA AND THE REST OF THE FAMILY (I)
Grossett & Dunlap: 1901 (9-1/2x8", 200 pgs, hardcover from N.Y. Evening Journal by Permission of W. R. Hearst) (pictures & text)

nn - By Frederick Opper   70.00   230.00   400.00
NOTE: Political satire series of single panel cartoons, involving whiny child Willie (President William McKinley), his rambunctious and uncontrollable cousin Teddy (Vice President Roosevelt), and Willie's Papa (trusts/monopolies) and their Maid (Senator) Hanna.

WILLIE GREEN COMICS, THE (N) (see Adventures of Willie Green)
Frank M. Acton Co./Harris Brown: 1915 (8x15, 36 pgs); 1921 (6x10-1/8", 52 pgs, color paper cover, B&W interior, 25¢)

Book No. 1 By Harris Brown	45.00	158.00	270.00
Book 2 (#2 sold via mail order directly from the artist)(very rare)	45.00	172.00	300.00

NOTE: Book No. 1 possible reprint of Adv. of Willie Green; definitely two different editions.

WILLIE WESTINGHOUSE EDISON SMITH THE BOY INVENTOR (N)
William A. Stokes Co.: 1906 (10x16", 36 pgs. in color)

nn - By Frank Crane (Scarce)   228.00   800.00   –
NOTE: Comic strip began May 27, 1900 and ran thru 1914. Parody of inventors Westinghouse and Edison.

WINNIE WINKLE (N) Strip began as a daily Sept 20, 1920.
Cupples & Leon Co.: 1930 - No. 4, 1933 (52 pgs., B&W daily strip-r)

1	43.00	172.00	400.00
2-4	29.00	116.00	300.00

WISDOM OF CHING CHOW, THE (see also The Gumps)
R. J. Jefferson Printing Co.: 1928 (4x3", 100 pgs, red & B&W cardboard cover) (newspaper strip-r The Chicago Tribune)

nn - By Sidney Smith (scarce)   30.00   90.00   150.00

WONDER CHEST OF FAMOUS COMICS (N) see Treasure Chest of Famous Comics
Cupples & Leon Co.: 1935? 8-1/2x(6-7/8", 36 pgs, soft covers) (Boxed set of 5 books)

Little Orphan Annie #2 (1927) (Haunted House)	21.00	84.00	130.00
Little Orphan Annie #3 (1928) (in the Circus)	19.00	76.00	130.00
Smitty #2 (1929) (Babe Ruth app.)	19.00	76.00	130.00
Dolly Dimples and Bobby Bounce (1933) by Grace Drayton	19.00	76.00	130.00
How Dick Tracy & Dick Tracy Jr. Caught The Racketeers (1933)	26.00	104.00	185.00
Softcover set of five books in box	160.00	640.00	1125.00
Box only	57.00	228.00	400.00

NOTE: Dates shown are original copyright dates of the first printings; all actually came out in 1934 or later. Extremely abbreviated versions of the hardcover editions listed under each character. It is suspected this came out the Christmas season following Teasure Chest of Famous Comics. which contains earlier editions.

WORLD OF TROUBLE, A (S)
Minneapolis Journal: 1901 (10x8-3/4, 100 pgs, 40 pgs full color)

v3#1 - By Charles L. Bartholomew (editorial-r)   28.00   99.00   170.00

WORLD OVER, THE (I)
G. W. Dillingham Company, New York: 1897 (192 pgs, hardbound)

nn - By Joe Kerr; 80 illus by R.F. Outcault   200.00   700.00   –

WRIGLEY'S "MOTHER GOOSE"
Wm. Wrigley Jr. Company, Chicago: 1915 (6" x 4", 28 pgs, full color)

nn - Promotional comics for Wrigley's gum. Intro Wrigley's "Spearmen   20.00   70.00   120.00
Book No. 2   20.00   70.00   120.00

YELLOW KID, THE (Magazine)(I) (becomes **The Yellow Book #10 on**)
Howard Ainslee & Co., N.Y.: Mar. 20, 1897 - #9, July 17, 1897 (5¢, B&W w/color covers, 52p., stapled) (not a comic book)

1-R.F. Outcault Yellow kid on-c only #1-6. The same Yellow Kid color ad app. on back-c #1-6 (advertising the New York Sunday Journal)	857.00	3500.00	–
2-6 (#2 4/3/97, #5 5/22/97, #6, 6/5/97)	743.00	2800.00	–
7-9 (Yellow Kid not on-c)	121.00	425.00	–

NOTE: Richard Outcault's Yellow Kid from the Hearst New York American represents the very first successful newspaper comic strip in America. Listed here due to historical importance.

YELLOW KID IN MCFADDEN'S FLATS, THE (I)
G. W. Dillingham Co., New York: 1897 (50¢, 7-1/2x5-1/2", 196 pgs., B&W, squarebound)

nn - The first "comic" book featuring The Yellow Kid; E. W. Townsend narrative w/R. F. Outcault Sunday comic page art-r & some original drawings   6000.00   13000.00   –
NOTE: A Fair condition copy sold for $2,901 in August 2004.; restored copy graded app VF sold for $10,500 in 2005. A copy in Fine+ (spine intact) and loose back cover sold for $17,000 in 2006.

YESTERDAYS (S)
The Reilly & Lee Co.: 1930 (8-3/4 x 7-1/2, 128 pgs, illustrated hard-c with dust jacket)

nn - Text and cartoons about Victorian times by Frank Wing   20.00   40.00   80.00

Any additions or corrections to this section are always welcome, very much encouraged and can be sent to **feedback@gemstonepub.com** to be processed for next year's Guide.

The American Comic Book: 1929-Present
A Concise History Of The Field As Of 2008
THE MODERN COMICS MAGAZINE
SUPPLANTS THE EARLIER FORMATS
by Robert Lee Beerbohm & Richard D. Olson, PhD ©2008

(This article was originally created by Robert Beerbohm and Richard Olson for CBPG #27 1997 and is revised annually.)

Although somewhat similar in appearance to comic books of the Golden Age of the superhero, the varied formats that comic publishing pioneers Stokes, Cupples & Leon and others popularized beginning in 1899 are quite different in appearance from today's comics. Even so, those many formats were consistently successful until the early 1930s, when they then had to compete against The Great Depression; the Depression eventually won. One major reason for a format change was that at a cost of 25¢ per book for the 10" x 10" cardboard style and 60¢ for the 7" x 8 1/2" dustjacketed hardcovers, the price became increasingly prohibitive for most consumers already stifled by the crushed economy. As a result, all Cupples & Leon style books published between 1929-1935 are much rarer than their earlier counterparts because most Americans had little money to spend after paying for necessities like food and shelter.

By the early 1930s, the era of the Prestige Format black & white reprint comic book was over. In 1932-33 a lot of format variations arose, collecting such newspaper strips as *Bobby Thatcher, Bringing Up Father, Buck Rogers, Dick Tracy, Happy Hooligan, Joe Palooka, The Little King, Little Orphan Annie, Mickey Mouse, Moon Mullins, Mutt & Jeff, Smitty, Tailspin Tommy, Tarzan, Thimble Theater starring Popeye, Tillie the Toiler, Winnie Winkle, and the Highlights of History.*

There had been Embee's *Comic Monthly's* dozen issues a decade earlier in 1922, and several dozen of Dell & Eastern's *The Funnies* tabloid in 1929-30. It contained only original material, went from a dime to a nickel and still it failed to catch a decent circulation.

A couple years ago it was discovered that Eastern Color and Dell were also co-partners in *The Funnies*. It is possible that Eastern came up with the idea and Delecorte agreed to publish it for general stand-alone distribution. Similar format Sunday sections of the same material have been discovered by comics historian Ken Barker to be published at the same time in the *Montreal Standard*,

a Canadian newspaper; it appears to have been an effort to get a new comics syndicate off the ground. The effort was not too successful as *The Standard* dropped the sections after just a few months. Allan Holtz went through the *E&P* yearbooks and found that this section (presumably a preprint) was advertised from 1930-34 by Eastern Color Printing out of New York City.

This is a re-discovery of important magnitude as it pushes back the time known for Eastern Color Printing Company and Dell Publishing Company to be partners by four years into late 1928. They had almost discovered the winning formula which has ruled the format of comic books in America for the last 70 years. Unfortunately, it would be another four years before they successfully figured it out.

With another format change including four colors, page counts beginning at 32 (soon hitting a whopping 68), and a hefty price reduction (starting for free as promotional premiums due to the nationwide numbing effects of worldwide deflation), the birthing pangs of the modern American comic book occurred in late 1932. Created out of desperation, to keep the printing presses rolling, the modern American comic book was born when a 45-year-old sales manager for Eastern Color Printing Company of New York reinvented the format from the failed tabloid *The Funnies*.

The Funnies #1, early 1929, Dell Publishing Company and Eastern Color. This was the very first original material newsstand comic book!

Harry I. Wildenberg's job was to come up with ideas that would sell color printing for Eastern, a company which also printed the comic sections for a score of newspapers along the eastern seaboard, including the *Boston Globe, the Brooklyn Times, the Providence Journal, and the Newark Ledger*. Down-time meant less take-home pay, so Wildenberg was always racking his brains to keep the color presses running. He was fascinated by the miles of funny sheets which rolled off Eastern's presses each week, and he constantly sought new ways to exploit their commercial possibilities. If the funny papers were this popular, he reasoned, they should prove a good advertising medium. He decided to pitch a comics tabloid to various oil company clients.

Brand new research conducted late in December 2005 has discovered the existence of a no number introduction issue of *Standard Oil Comics* dated to December 1932. Evidently it was Rockefeller's Standard Oil which decided before Gulf Oil to entice customers with a comics giveaway.

There are at least 14 issues each of at least a 1933 A and a 1934 B series of a four page tabloid-size full color comics giveaway titled *Standard Oil Comics*. The A issues all contain Fred Opper's *Si & Mirandi*, an older couple who interact with perennial favorites, *Happy Hooligan & Maud the Mule*, drawn by the grand old master himself, Frederick Opper, who had been a professional cartoonist for over 60 years by this time. This new "no number" 1932 precursor instructed readers to listen to the Si & Miandi radio show, come in regularly to Standard Oil stations and pick up *Standard Oil Comics*.

The 1934 B series front Goofus "He's From The Big City" McVittle by Walter O'Ehrle, set in humorous farming scenarios. Interior strips include *Pesty And His Pop & Smiling Slim* by Sid Hicks. Considering the concept of *Gulf Funny Weekly* has been well known for decades while *Standard Oil Comics* remains virtually unknown, what we now know is Gulf copied Standard in almost all respects.

Gulf Oil Company also liked the idea and hired a few artists to create an original comic called *Gulf Comic Weekly*. Their first issue was dated April 1933 and was 10 1/2" x 15". Gulf copied Standard Oil by advertising their giveaway nationally on the radio beginning April 30th. Its first artists were Stan Schendel doing *The Uncovered Wagon*, Victor doing *Curly and the Kids*, and Svess on a strip named *Smileage*. All were full page, full color comic strips. Wildenberg promptly had Eastern print this four page comic, making it probably the first tabloid newsprint comic published for American distribution outside of a newspaper in the 20th Century. Wildenberg and Gulf were astonished when the tabloids were grabbed up as fast as Gulf service stations could offer them. Distribution shot up to 3,000,000 copies a week after Gulf changed the

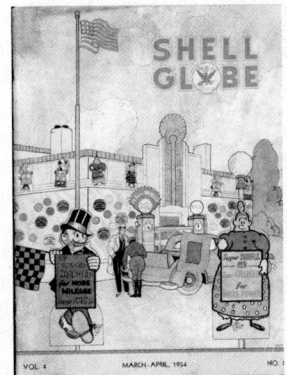

Top: Newly discovered Standard Oil Comics from Dec 1932. One copy presently known to exist. This rare giveaway ended in late in 1934. Standard Oil was the first to issue a regular giveaway using comics to bring in customers; Middle: Gulf Comic Weekly #1, April, 1933, copied what Standard Oil began. Gulf's weekly changed its name to Gulf Funny Weekly with #5; Bottom: Not to be outdone, by March 1934, Shell Oil began a huge comics promotion to compete with Standard and Gulf.

name to *Gulf Funny Weekly* with its 5th issue. It remained a tabloid until early 1939 & ran for 422 issues until May 23, 1941.

Recent research has also turned up "new" rediscovered comics material from other oil companies from this same time span of 1933-34. Perhaps spurred by the runaway success of first *Standard Oil Comics, then Gulf Funny Weekly*, these other oil companies found they had to compete with licensed comic strip material of their own in order to remain profitable.

Beginning with the March-April 1934 issue of *Shell Globe* (V4 #2), characters from Bud Fisher (*Mutt & Jeff*) and Fontaine Fox (*Toonerville Folks*) were licensed to sell gas & oil for this company. 52,000 eight foot standees were made for Fisher's *Mutt and Jeff* and Fox's *Powerful Katrinka* and *The Skipper* for placement around 13,000 Shell gas stations. Augmenting them was an army of 250,000 miniature figures of the same characters. In addition, more than 1,000,000 play masks were given away to children along with more than 285,000 window stickers. If that wasn't enough, hundreds of thousands of 3x5 foot posters featuring these characters were released in conjunction with twenty-four sheet outdoor billboards. Radio announcements of this promotion began running April 7th, 1934. It is presently unknown if Shell had a comics tabloid created to give away to customers.

In addition, new research has uncovered the Gilmore Oil Company issuing an eight page giveaway titled *The Gilmore Cub*. It appears to have carried "Starnge As It Seems" among other cartoon features by John Hix. At least one issue, v4 #2, May, 1938, is known to exist.

The authors of this essay are actively soliciting help in uncovering more information regarding these and potentially other oil comics giveaways.

With the 1933 newsstand appearance of Humor's *Detective Dan, Adventures of Detective Ace King, Bob Scully, Two Fisted Hick Detective*, and possibly the still unrediscovered, but definitely advertised, *Happy Mulligan*, these little understood original-material comic books from Humor were the direct inspiration for Jerry Siegel and Joe Shuster to transform their fanzine's evil character The Superman from *Science Fiction* #3 (January 1933) into a comic strip that would stand as a watershed heroic mark in American pop culture. The stage was set for a new frontier. The idea for creating an actual comic book as we know it today, however, did not occur to Wildenberg until later in 1933, when he said he was idly folding a newspaper in halves, then in quarters. As he looked at the twice-folded paper, it occurred to him that it was a convenient book size (actually it was late stage Dime Novel size, which companies like Street & Smith were pumping out). The format had its heyday from the 1880s through the 1910s, having been invented by the firm of Beadle and Adam in 1860 in more of a digest format. According to a 1942 article by Max Gaines (née Ginzberg), another contributing factor in the development of the format was an inspection of a promotional folder published by the Ledger Syndicate, in which four-color Sunday comic pages were printed in 7"x9".

According to a 1949 interview with Wildenberg, he thought "why not a comic book? It would have 32 or 64 pages and make a fine item for concerns which distribute premiums." All they did at Eastern Color that one fateful day is fold a tabloid newspaper format down to "dime novel" size running full color throughout on most of the comic strips, then staple it, and they hit upon their winning formula.

But they did not yet know this...as we will find out.

Working for Eastern Color at this same time were quite a few future legends of the comics business, such as Max Gaines, Lev Gleason and a fellow named Harold Moore (all sales staff directly underneath the supervision of Wilden-berg), Sol Harrison as a color separator, and George Dougherty Sr. as a printer.

Janosik, Wildenberg, Gaines, Gleason and crew obtained publishing rights to certain Associated, Bell, Fisher, McNaught and Public Ledger Syndicate comics, had an artist make up a few dummies by hand. The sales staff then walked them around to their biggest prospects. Wildenberg received a telegram from Proctor & Gamble for an order of a million copies for a 32-page color comic magazine called **Funnies on Parade**. The entire print

The Adventures of Detective Ace King, Bob Scully The Two Fisted Hick Detective & Detective Dan Secret Op. #48, early 1933, Humor Publishing Co. All issues Very Rare from the 2nd original newsstand comic book publisher; the direct inspiration for Jerry Siegel & Joe Shuster's 1933 conversion of The Superman into a comic book due to a promise of publication. This earliest Superman was never published.

run was given away in just a few weeks in the Spring of 1933. Most copies no longer exist and it is now hard to find. All of them worked on the *Funnies on Parade* project. Morris Margolis was brought in from Charlton in Derby, Connecticut to solve binding problems centered on getting the pages in proper numerical sequence on that last fold to "modern" comic book size. Most of them were infected with the comics bug for most of the rest of their lives.

The success of *Funnies on Parade* quickly led to Eastern publishing additional giveaway books in the same format by late 1933, including the 32-page *Famous Funnies A Carnival of Comics*, the 100-page *A Century of Comics* and the 52-page *Skippy's Own Book of Comics.*

The latter became the first "new" format comic book about a single character. Out of all the comic strips on the market in 1933, Eastern Color's growing comics market as devised by Harry Wildenberg, M.C. Gaines and Lev Gleason chose the Percy Crosby creation in *Skippy's Own Book of Comics* to be its first standalone title. This first solo effort in their new 52-page newsprint *Funnies On Parade* format had an initial print run of half a million, as did their 100-pager.

The idea that anyone would pay for them seemed fantastic to Wildenberg, so Max Gaines stickered ten cents on several dozen of the latest premium, *Famous Funnies A Carnival of Comics*, as a test, and talked a couple newsstands into participating in this experiment. The copies sold out over the weekend and newsies asked for more.

Eastern sales staffers then approached Woolworth's. The late Oscar Fitz-Alan Douglas, sales brains of Woolworth, showed some interest, but after several months of deliberation decided the book would not give enough value for ten cents. Kress, Kresge, McCrory, and several other dime stores turned them down even more abruptly. Wildenberg next went to George Hecht, editor of *Parents Magazine*, and tried to persuade him to run a comic supplement or publish a "higher level" comic magazine. Hecht also frowned on the idea.

In Wildenberg's 1949 interview, he noted that "even the comic syndicates couldn't see it. 'Who's going to read old comics?' they asked." With the failures of EmBee's *Comic Monthly* (1922) and Dell's *The Funnies* (1929) still fresh in some minds, no one could see why children would pay ten cents for a comic magazine when they could get all they wanted for free in a Sunday newspaper. But Wildenberg had become convinced that children as well as grown-ups were not getting all the comics they wanted in the Sunday papers; otherwise, *Standard Oil Comics, Gulf Comic Weekly* and the premium comics would not have met with such success. Wildenberg said, "I decided that if boys and girls were willing to work for premium coupons to obtain comic books, they might be willing to pay ten cents on the newsstands." This conviction was also strengthened by Max Gaines' ten cent sticker experiment.

George Janosik, the president of Eastern Color, then called on George Delacorte to form another 50-50 joint venture to publish and market a comic book "magazine" for retail sales as they did with *The Funnies* just a few years previously, but this time American News turned them down cold. The magazine monopoly remembered the abortive *The Funnies* from just a few years before. After much discussion on how to proceed, Delacorte finally agreed to publish it and a partnership was formed. Feeling cautious, they printed 40,000 copies for distribution to a few chain stores who agreed to try it out. Known today as *Famous Funnies Series One*, it clocks in at 68 pages, with half its pages coming from reprints of the reprints in *Funnies on Parade* and half from *Famous Funnies A Carnival of Comics*. It is the scarcest issue.

With 68 full-color pages at only ten cents a piece, it sold out in thirty days with not a single returned copy. Delacorte refused to print a second edition. "Advertisers won't use it," he complained. "They say it's not dignified enough." The profit, however, was approximately $2,000. This particular edition is the rarest of all these early Eastern comic book experiments.

In early 1934, while riding the train, another Eastern Color employee named Harold A. Moore read an account from a prominent New York newspaper that indicated they owed much of their circulation success to their comics section. Mr. Moore went back to Harry Gold, President of American News, with the article in hand. He succeeded in acquiring a print order for 250,000

Funnies on Parade, 1933 - what we recognize today as the first "modern" comic book with its slick cover.

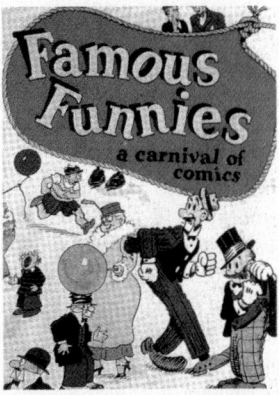

The fateful version Charlie Gaines stickered 10¢ a copy one weekend in late '33 which sold out over a weekend.

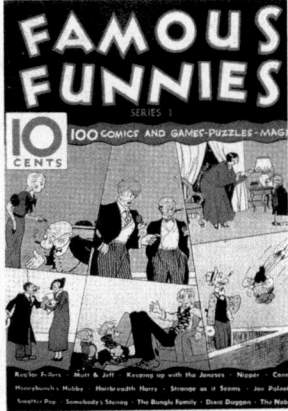

Famous Funnies Series One is the rare one, only 40,000 copies were printed.

copies for a proposed monthly comics magazine. In May 1934, *Famous Funnies* #1 (with a July cover date) hit the newsstands with Steven O. Douglass as its only editor (even though Harold Moore was listed as such in #1) until it ceased publication some twenty years later. It was a 64-page version of the 32-page giveaways, and more importantly, it still sold for a dime! The first issue lost $4,150.60. Ninety percent of the copies sold out and a second issue dated September debuted in July. From then on, the comic book was published monthly. *Famous Funnies* also began carrying original material, apparently as early as the second issue. With #3, Buck Rogers took center stage and stayed there for the next twenty years, with covers by Frank Frazetta towards the end of the run–some of his best comics work ever.

Delacorte got cold feet and sold back his interest to Eastern, even though the seventh issue cleared a profit of $2,664.25. Wildenberg emphasized that Eastern could make a manufacturer's profit by printing its own books as well as the publishing profits once it was distributed. Every issue showed greater sales than the preceding one, until within a year, close to a million 64-page books were being sold monthly at ten cents apiece; Eastern received the lion's share of the receipts, and soon found it was netting $30,000 per issue. The comic syndicates received $640 ($10 a page) for publishing rights. Original material could be obtained from budding professionals for just $5 a page. According to Will Eisner in R. C. Harvey's *The Art of the Comic Book*, the prices then paid for original material had a long range effect of keeping creator wages low for years.

Initially, Eastern's experiment was eyed with skepticism by the publishing world, but within a year or so after *Famous Funnies* was nonchalantly placed on sale alongside slicker magazines like *Atlantic Monthly* or *Harper's*, at least five other competitors tried this brand new format.

However, one other abortive periodical comics experiment was launched cover dated a full two months before the highly successful newsstand *Famous Funnies* format would have an important influence on a chain of events which led ultimately to *Superman* being published.

Comic Cuts #1, May 19, 1934, debuted published by H.L.

Famous Funnies #1, July 1934, was the first successful newsstand comic book, lasting until 1955.

Baker Co., Inc., 195 Main St, Buffalo, New York with editorial and execuitive offices at 381 Fourth St, NYC, same address as ULTEM (Centaur) would use just a couple years later - this address housed a number of publishers fighting to exist during the Great Depression. The indica says H. L. Baker was President & Treasurer and J. D. Geller was Vice President and Sec-retary. It lasted nine issues with the final one cover-dated July 28. It appears Jake Geller, Windsor, Ontario, Canada, acquired American rights to a number of comic strips from the publisher Amalgamated Press, publisher of *Comic Cuts* in England. He partnered in the publishing with H. L. Baker and they acquired the backing of S-M News Co., Inc. as their distributor. Most distributors back then functioned on many important levels. It was common practice for the distributor back then to front the funds to pay the paper company and the printer, collecting the revenue from the 900 I.D. distributors located around the country after months of on-sale time, then paying the publisher.

In late 1934, army officer/diplomat turned pulp writer turned publisher Major Wheeler-Nicholson (1890-1968) formed the under-funded National Allied Publishing which introduced *New Fun #1* (Feb 1935) at almost tabloid-size. *New Fun* was also distributed by S-M News. It is entirely possible Wheeler-Nicholson somehow convinced them he could

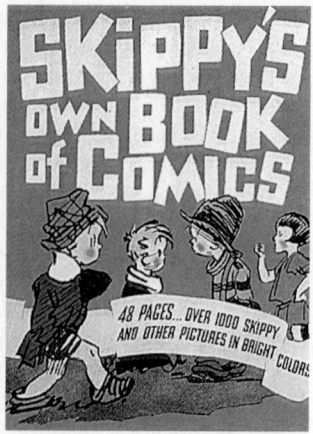

Skippy's Own Book of Comics, 1934, had half a million issues printed. It was the very first single character comic book in this "new" format.

grown. Coulton Waugh speculated in his 1947 history book *The Comics* on page 342: "...The Major had gone back to the 1929 idea of *The Funnies*, for the contents of *New Fun* were original material. (It should be recorded here that original art work had appeared in a one-color book called *Detective Dan*."

However, Lloyd Jacquet, a person definitely in a position to know better, wrote as Chapter One of a proposed "History of the Comic Book" in 1957, "When Major Malcolm Wheeler-Nicholson set up his card table and chair in an eleventh floor office of the Hatha-way Building in New York that Fall of 1934, these most modest beginnings sparked off what can rightly be called the 'comic book era.' When he came back to the U.S. after his last stay abroad, he looked over the American newsstand, and thought that the European juvenile weekly papers, with their picture-story continuities, their colorful illustrations, and their low price would appeal to the American boys and girls in the same way. He knew that those European publications were made up of new material, specially drawn and produced for each little magazine. He also knew that the American presentation of such material would have to be different, and merely importing, or translating European produced features for republication here was not the answer. This was about the time I joined with him in his project. It was still embryonic, but

beginning to take form under Nicholson's direction. We were in the depression then, & it was not too difficult to secure writers and artists - but it was a task to instruct them as to exactly what was wanted. We finally rounded up a small but gifted group of creative people, and we produced our first issue of a monthly magazine composed of original features

produce a superior "home-grown" package as the imported strips were not selling well. *New Fun* was basically the same as *Comic Cuts* while also containing all original USA material such as carried in *The Funnies* (1929-30) from Dell/Eastern. With *New Fun*, what S-M News offered was more familiar American home

Comic Cuts #8, July 14, 1934, issued weekly by H.L. Baker Co. Inc., Buffalo, New York; editorial offices at 381 Fourth Ave, NYC; co-owner Jake D. Geller was Canadian. Title provided inspiration for New Fun.

New Fun #1, Feb 1935. According to first-employee Lloyd Jacquet, the format Major Malcolm Wheeler-Nicholson used was directly inspired by Comic Cuts. Many of the non-comics features were the same.

and material, and which was called, simply, "*FUN*."

Around this same time in late 1934, M.C. Gaines left Eastern Color moving over to the McClure Newspaper Syndicate to become their manager of their Color Printing Department He immediately went to work convincing clients to issue promotional comics. Also, long-time comics publisher Whitman brought out the first original material movie adaptation, Tim McCoy Police Car 17, in the tabloid New Fun format with stiff card covers. A few years before, they had introduced the new comics formats known as the Big Little Book and the Big Big Book. The BLB and BBB formats would go toe-to-toe with Eastern's creation throughout the 1930s, but Eastern would win out with their new comics magazine format.

The very last 10" x 10" comic books pioneered by Cupples & Leon were published by the David McKay Publishing Company around mid-1935. Around this same time the Major published his 2nd comic book in which the editorial mentions amongst other exciting stories they were going to be showcasing the adventures of "hero supermen of the days to come."

By late 1935, Max Gaines (with his youthful assistant Sheldon Mayer) reached a business agreement with George Delacorte (who was re-entering the comic book business a third time) and McClure Syndicate (a growing newspaper comic strip enter-

prise) to be come editor of reprint newspaper comic strips in *Popular Comics.*

Also by late '35, Lev Gleason, another pioneer who participated in mercantiling *Funnies on Parade* and the early *Famous Funnies*, had become the first editor of United Feature's own *Tip Top Comics* with its first issue cover dated April 1936. In 1939 he would begin publishing his own titles starting with *Silver Streak*, created by the comics genius, Jack Cole, best known for Plastic Man. Gleason later created the crime comic book as a separate popular genre by 1942 with *Crime Does Not Pay* with a long run until 1955.

Wheeler-Nicholson introduced the concept of "the annual" into this new format with *Big Book of Fun Comics* #1 cover dated March 1936. It featured reprints from his earlier efforts in *New Fun* #1-5 as he struggled to make a go of it.

Industry giant King Features introduced *King Comics* #1 cover dated April 1936 through publisher David McKay, with Ruth Plumly Thompson as editor. McKay had already been issuing various format comic books with King Feature characters for a few years, including Mickey Mouse, Henry, Popeye and Secret Agent X-9, wherein Dashiell Hammett received cover billing and Alex Raymond was listed inside simply as "illustrator." McKay readily adapted to trying several formats. Soon many young comic book illustrators were copying Raymond.

The next month, William Cook & John Mahon, former dis-

Left, Charlie Gaines & Sheldon Mayer packaged Popular Comics #1, Feb. 1936, for George Delecorte in late 1935 after the former left Eastern Color. Middle, King Comics #1, April 1936, marked King Features Syndicate's entry into the new 64-page color comic market with their new heavyweights, Flash Gordon and Popeye. By this point, Hearst had been involved in publishing comic books for close to 40 years. Right, Lev Gleason left Eastern & Wildenberg about the same time as Gaines to edit Tip Top Comics #1, April 1936, for United Features.

Left, The Comics Magazine #2, June 1936, was the first title of what later became Centaur. Soon it had a name change and quickly made history. Middle, Wow What A Magazine is a rare title which ran four issues beginning in June 1936 with the first published work by youthful, eager Bernard Baily, Dick Briefer, Will Eisner & Bob Kane. Painted cover by Will Eisner. Western Picture Stories #1, Feb. 1937 has more art by Eisner, ties with Star Ranger Funnies #1 as first western comic book. Centaur also introduced the earliest crime comic book, Detective Picture Stories #1 dated December 1936.

gruntled employees of Major Wheeler-Nicholson, issued their first issue of *Comics Magazine* #1 in May 1936.

This was followed by Henle Publishing issuing *Wow What A Magazine*, which contained the earliest comic work of Will Eisner, Bob Kane, Dick Briefer & others. By the end of 1936, Cook and Mahon pioneered the first single theme comic books: *Funny Picture Stories* #1 in Nov. 1936 (adventure), *Detective Picture Stories* #1 in Feb. 1937 (crime), as well as *Western Picture Stories* #1 in Feb. 1937 (the Western). The company would eventually be known historically as Centaur Comics, and serve as the subject of endless debate among fan historians regarding their earliest origins as to who the owners were, where they came from and where they went.

Dell issued the second western genre comic book titled *Western Action Thrillers* #1 in April 1937. It was ten cents for one hundred pages as well as *100 Pages of Comics 101*, containing Big Little Book art reworked back into sequential comics.

Harry 'A' Chesler jumped ship from the Major, issuing his first comic books with **Star Comics** and **Star Ranger Funnies**, dated Feb 1937. Later that year, he sold these two titles to Ultem while remaining editor, and his newly set up art shop supplied contents. He then began **Feature Funnies** #1 in Oct. 1937, headlining Joe Palooka, at one time the #1 newspaper comic strip in America. Issue #2 sported a Rube Goldberg cover while #3 contains "Hawk of the Sea," Will Eisner's first work for what would soon become the Quality Comics Group when Everett "Busy" Arnold bought the company. **Feature Funnies** #3 also contains the first appearance of The Clock by George Brenner - the first costumed comic book hero.

Left, Feature Funnies #3, Dec. 1937, contains George Brenner's The Clock, the first comic book costumed hero plus Eisner's first work for Quality Comics, when still owned by Chesler. Circus the Comic Riot #1, June 1938, contains Basil Wolverton's earliest professional comic book work plus more Will Eisner and Bob Kane. Right, Action Comics #1, June 1938, began revolutionizing the industry when Superman by Jerome Siegel & Joseph Shuster debuted. The publishers did not understand what they had at first as Superman does not appear on a cover again until #7. Nobody knew at first, it seemed, except book-keeper Victor Fox counting copies sold, who quit and formed his own comic book company.

Left, Jumbo Comics #1, Sept. 1938, debuts pulp publisher Fiction House's entry into the growing comic book industry. Middle, Detective Comics #27 introduced Batman created by Bob Kane and Bill Finger - need we say more? Right, Wonder Comics #1, May 1939, became Victor Fox's first entry into the comics biz when he fast-talked a youthful Will Eisner into creating a near-exact clone of the creation of Siegel & Shuster's brainchild, Superman. There was a quick lawsuit and #2 featured Yarko The Great instead. Bob Kane was busy that May as he is also in Wonder #1.

Almost forty years after the first newspaper strip comic book compilations were issued at the dawn of international popularity for American comic strips, the race was on to get titles out of the starting block. In late 1937 the Major began stumbling when he couldn't pay his printing bill to Harry Donenfeld. In recent interviews, Harry's son, Irwin, who as a 12-year old read the original art to the first issue of *Action Comics* #1 and *Detective Comics* #27 said "in 1932 my father and Paul Sampliner started Independent News with Liebowitz as the accountant. The company was begun with Paul Sampliner's mother's money. If it hadn't been for her investments into building the distribution as well as purchasing color printing presses, there might never have been a DC Comics. My father took over Wheeler-Nicholson's company with the Major's books literally on the printing presses. Harry had to absorb debt that could not otherwise be paid." Irwin

told this writer "my dad did not originally willingly enter the comics business"

Soon after the Major lost control of his company, *Action Comics* #1 was published with a cover date of June 1938, and the first Golden Age of superhero comics had begun. Early in 1938 at McClure Syndicate, Max Gaines and Shelly Mayer showed editor Vin Sullivan a many times rejected sample strip. Sullivan then talked Donenfeld, Paul Sampliner and Jack Liebowitz into publishing Jerry Siegel & Joe Shuster's creation of "The Last Son of Krypton." This was followed in 1939 by a lucrative partnership for Gaines beginning with Harry Donenfeld as the All-American Comics Group.

While there's a great deal of controversy surrounding such labeling, the "Golden Age" is viewed by many these days as beginning with *Action Comics* #1 and continuing through the end of World War II. There was a time not that long ago that

Left, Marvel Comics #1, Oct. 1939, was the first Martin Goodman comic book, introducing Human Torch by Carl Burgos and Sub-Mariner by Bill Everett. Middle, Silver Streak #1, Dec. 1939, Lev Gleason's first published comic book, introduced Jack Cole's classic, The Claw, running until #24, when the title changed to Crime Does Not Pay. Right, Whiz Comics #2 (#1), Feb. 1940, ushered Fawcett onto the comic book scene with yet another Superman clone - Captain Marvel, who was successful from the get-go. At one time his main title was issued every three weeks.

Left, Crime Does Not Pay #43, Nov. 1945. Lev Gleason instigated a popular new genre which brought the industry unfairly under heavy fire from church and state. Middle, My Date #1, July 1947. Joe Simon and Jack Kirby created the romance genre when they developed the older female audience which lasted into the '70s. Right, Atomic War #1, Nov. 1952. Nuclear obliteration was heavy on the minds of most Americans. Due to the Korean War, there was a plethora of war titles and the genre survived well into the 1970s before being eventually marginalized by the super hero revival.

the newspaper reprint comic book was collected with more fervor than the heroic comics of the '40s. *Prince Valiant FB #26, Flash Gordon 4C #10* and *Tarzan SS #20* were some of the highest Holy Grails of collecting, but no more even though they contain fantastic art & story.

Today's marketplace dictates super heroes command the highest prices and are seemingly the most desirable. Maybe one day that pendulum will swing once again as there have been many years since they were introduced when super heroes almost disappeared completely from the racks.

The Atomic/Romance Age debuted with a bang by early 1946, revamping the industry once again as circulations soon hit their all-time highs with well over 1.3 billion periodical issues sold a year by the consignment honor system. By the

early 1950s one in three periodicals sold in the USA was a comic book. 90% of all children admitted they read and enjoyed comics. There were dozens of genres being published. There were comic books for every taste and style. Hundreds of titles were being issued every month.

For many readers, the pinnacle was reached with the "New Trend" Entertaining Comics (E.C.) began delivering to the newsstands in 1950. The company still has a large following even today - a testament to its emphasis on quality art & story.

Comic book publishers glutted the market place by 1952-53. The attacks on comics begun the late 1940s came back anew in 1954 brought on by over-zealous church people and district attorneys with an agenda.

This continued until the advent of the self-censoring,

Left, Crime Detective #9, July 1948. Some say the tied-up figure represents Dr. Fredric Wertham following his earliest attacks on the crime comic book. Hillman joined the first Code. Middle, Justice Traps the Guilty #56, Nov. 1953. The S&K studio placed themselves in the spotlight, with a pretty mother pointing out Joe Simon as the tall, dastardly ringleader. Jack Kirby is on the right end. Right, Thing #15, Apr. 1954. Ditko wreaks havoc on a world rising against comics as a giant worm eats Brooklyn in one of the most gruesome titles created. His early work is intense.

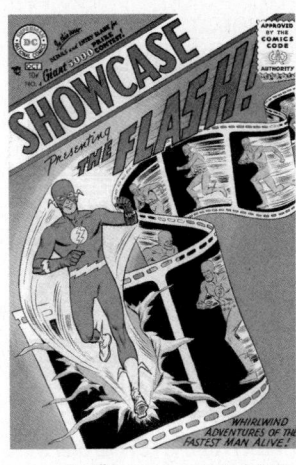

Left, By the early 1950s, Carl Barks increased the circulation of Walt Disney's C&S to over 4 million per issue & in 1952 his creation, Uncle Scrooge, got his own book, selling over a million an issue through the '50s while superheroes slumbered. Middle, Harvey Kurtzman created Mad Comics #1, 1952, as the comics industry went in an entirely "New" Direction and has directly inspired countless comics creators for years. Right, Showcase #4, Sept. 1956, the superhero revival starts a year after the Code, though it was three years before the Flash earned his own title once again.

industry-stifling Comics Code, created in response to a public outcry spearheaded by Dr. Frederic Wertham's tirade against the American comics industry, published as a book titled *Seduction of the Innocent*, which removed crime and horror comic books from the marketplace. Some of them were quite gruesome; however in his last book, *The World of Fanzines*, Wertham exhonerated comics fans for misinterpreting his data more than 20 years previous.

It took a year or two to recover from that moralistic assault, with many historians speculating the Silver Age of Superheroes began with the publication of *Showcase* #4 in 1956. Others point to the 1952 successful releases of Kurtzman's *MAD* #1 and Bark's *Uncle Scrooge Four Color* #386 as true Silver, since those titles soon broke the "million sold per issue" mark when the rest of the comic book industry was reeling from the effects of the public uproar fueled by Wertham. Within the Silver Era the term Bronze Age has been stated by some to begin when the Code approved newsstand comic book industry raised its standard cover price from 12 to 15 cents and Jack Kirby left Marvel for DC. As circulations plummeted after the Batman TV craze wore off by 1968 and the ensuing superhero glut withered on the stands, out in the Bay Area cartoonist Robert Crumb's creator-owned *Zap Comics* #1 appeared in Feb 1968, printed by Charles Plymell & Don Donahue on a small printing press. Soon after in Chicago, Jay Lynch and Skip Williamson brought out *Bijou Funnies*, Gilbert Shelton self-published *Feds 'N' Heads* while still in Austin, Texas, with Print Mint reprinting it almost immediately & Crumb let S. Clay Wilson, Victor Moscoso & Rick Griffin into Zap #2.

As originally published by the Print Mint beginning with #2

Left, Brave & Bold #28, Feb/Mar. 1960, gathered together the revived DC heroes, further expanding the resurging superhero market DC Comics ushered in. Middle, Fantastic Four #1, Nov. 1961, began the revitalization of Martin Goodman's moribund Marvel Comics Group, directly inspired by the success of the JLA's own regular series begun 2 years earlier in late 1960. Right, Amazing Fantasy #15, Aug. 1962, introduced the Amazing Spider-Man, created almost completely by Steve Ditko with some assists from Stan Lee and Jack Kirby, which revolutionized the way comic book stories could be told.

Left, Zap Comics #1, Plymell first printing, Feb. 1968, was the "direct" inspiration for the earliest successful origins of the Direct Market and has sold over a million copies. Most issues have been continuously in print for over 30 years. High grade first printings have sold for over $4500. Middle, soon afterwards Gilbert Shelton brought Feds 'N' Heads to Print Mint and later joined Zap. It has sold for $1000. Right, famed poster artist Rick Griffin edited his own comic book, Tales From the Tube in 1973, with most of the Zap crew joining him. It currently brings over $200 in NM high grade.

in 1968, *Zap Comics* almost single-handedly spawned an industry with tremendous growth in alternative comix running through the 1970s. During this decade the San Francisco Bay Area was an intense hotbed of comix being issued without a comics code "seal of approval" from companies such as Rip Off Press, Last Gasp, San Francisco Comic Book Company, Company & Sons, Weirdom Publications, Star*Reach, and Comics & Comix. Kitchen Sink prospered for many years in Wisconsin and many small press comix publishers scattered across the USA and Canada - all of whom created the Direct Sales Market. There were hundreds of people involved with an independent mind producing & distributing alternative underground comix, creating the direct market. Phil Seuling introduced DC, Marvel and Warren to this already developed for five years, San Francisco Bay Area-based, comix business system as a "new" way of selling comics in late 1973, acknowedged by Phil himself in his last interview in *Will Eisner's Quarterly* #3, Summer 1984.

After DC and Marvel joined the DM in a serious way in 1979, the last 20 years have generally been called the "Modern Age", although there are hints of a new age emerging since the mid-'90s. The jury is still out on naming it.

The comic book store as an industry came into its own in the 1980s. Thousands of fans & entrepreneurs opened stores, fulfilling a life's dream for many of them - fueled by a vibrant speculator's market which lasted until the early 1990s, its last hurrah being when DC "killed" Superman in 1992. The comic book marketplace has been rebuilding ever since. Much of that growth has been outside the super hero genre.

In each of the preceding eras, however, the secret for collectors has remained the same: buy what you enjoy. We did, and we are still collectors today! *Portions excerpted from* **Comics Archeology 101** *© 2006 Robert L. Beerbohm, a detailed, heavily researched book in progress covering the more than 160 year history of the American comic book business. You may contact him thru his web site at* www.BLBComics.com

Left, Conan #1, Oct. 1970, by Roy Thomas and Barry Windsor-Smith intro'd the sword & sorcery genre.
Middle, StarReach #1, April 1974, published by Mike Friedrich, was the first comic book directed specifically at comic book stores. Right, Giant-Size X-Men #1, Summer, 1975, introduced the new X-team, which later on revolutionized the comic book store system with its phenomenal sales once Chris Claremont and John Byrne teamed up on the title.

Golden Age & Beyond

The American Comic Book 1938–Present

by J.C. Vaughn & Gene Gonzales

EVERYTHING CHANGED IN JUNE 1938.

AT THE SAME TIME NOTHING CHANGED.

THE ERA OF THE SUPERHEROES ARRIVED, SO THE CONTENT OF COMICS DEFINITELY CHANGED . . .

. . . BUT NOTHING FUNDAMENTALLY CHANGED IN THE METHOD OF DELIVERING SEQUENTIAL STORYTELLING TO THE MASSES.

STILL, IT'S HARD TO IGNORE WHAT FOLLOWED.

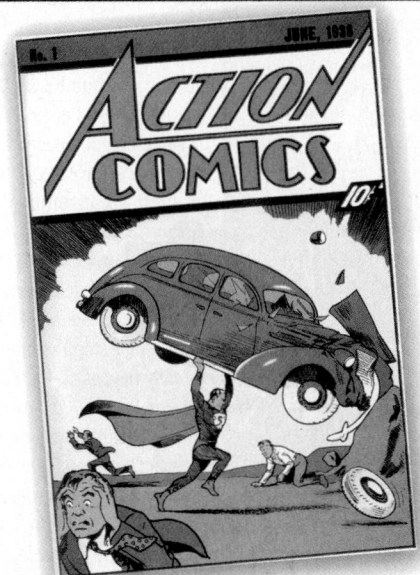

JUNE, 1938

No. 1

ACTION COMICS

10¢

AND IT'S HARD TO IGNORE THE VALUE ATTACHED TO SOME OF THE COMICS LISTED IN THIS SECTION.

FIRST, THOUGH, WE'LL TAKE A CLOSE-UP LOOK AT THE COMICS OF THE 1970S COURTESY OF *BACK ISSUE* EDITOR AND OVERSTREET ADVISOR MICHAEL EURY . . .

FOLLOWED BY OUR LARGEST PRICING SECTION.

TAKE IT AWAY, MICHAEL!

GOING FOR THE BRONZE: LIFE AFTER THE SILVER AGE

by Michael Eury

It was 1970, and the Silver Age was over.

The Silver Age's innovations, the Julie Schwartz-edited revamps of Golden Age favorites and the Lee/Kirby/et al.-constructed House of Ideas, had grown familiar, and in some cases, stale. The bottom had dropped out of the TV *Batman* superhero boom and the Big Two and its competitors, reeling from declining sales, scratched their heads and pondered, "What do we try next?"

Their answer: *Try everything!* The 1970s *was* the decade of excess, after all, when there was no such thing as "too much" and nothing we, as a culture, wouldn't try. Hair got longer, music got louder, lapels got wider, bras got burned, movies got bloodier, drugs got mainstreamed . . . and Mom wore pantsuits while Dad sprouted muttonchops. Marvel and DC also got "with it," trying new genres, new ideas, and new formats, all in a hungry pursuit of the one thing there could *never* be too much of: money.

Today, Mom's pantsuits may have elastic waistlines and Dad's muttonchops-and hair-may be a distant memory, but the decade we now call the Bronze Age-1970–1979-was, arguably, the most influential of all of comics' landmark eras. It could have been comics' last dance, but instead it became a decade of renaissance, when through trial and error inroads were made that paved the way for the innovations of the 1980s, the 1990s, and the comic book industry we know today.

In their quest to find the next big thing, the first place publishers looked was *outside* of comics. For a mere $200 licensing fee ($50 beyond tight-fisted publisher Martin Goodman's budgeted $150), Marvel Comics writer/editor Roy Thomas landed the publication rights to Robert E. Howard's famed swordsman Conan. And

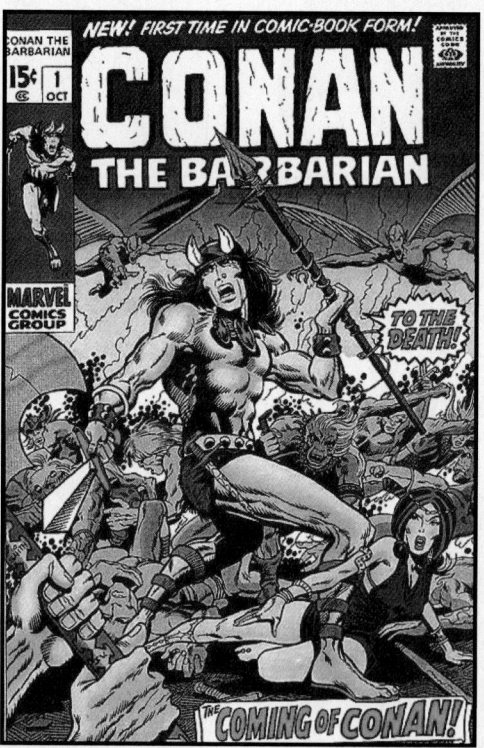

NEW! FIRST TIME IN COMIC-BOOK FORM!

CONAN THE BARBARIAN

15¢ 1 OCT

MARVEL COMICS GROUP

TO THE DEATH!

THE COMING OF CONAN!

while Marvel's *Conan the Barbarian* #1, written by Thomas, drawn by newcomer Barry (Windsor-) Smith, and cover-dated October 1970, didn't instantly ignite the comics world (*Conan* didn't look or read like the other material available, and early issues suffered from distribution challenges), before long the series developed a growing audience, and proved to publishers that they could sell material other than caped crusaders and lovesick all-American teens.

Sword-and-sorcery comics soon cut a swath through the stands, with licensed acquisitions Kull, Red Sonja, Thongor, and Solomon Kane joining Marvel's line, and DC countering with its acquisition of Fritz Leiber's Fafhrd and the Grey Mouser, in a 1973 series that made no attempt to hide the craze upon which it was capitalizing: *Sword and Sorcery* (original characters like the Warlord, Starfire, Stalker, Claw the Unconquered, IronJaw, and Wulf the Barbarian also premiered). Yet DC had already ventured into licensed terrain with its April 1972 cover–dated first issue of *Tarzan* (#207, continuing the numbering from previous publisher Gold Key). "[The estate of Tarzan creator Edgar Rice Burroughs] wanted their creative people on *Tarzan*," Carmine Infantino, at the time DC's Editorial Director, revealed, a request to which he responded, "No, I want my guys on the book"— actually his "guy," Joe Kubert, whose heralded stint as writer/artist/editor produced some of, perhaps *the*, finest illustrated Tarzan stories ever.

Tomb of Dracula (*TOD*), first seen in (cover date) April 1972, was not a licensed property but might have been had Bram Stoker's 1897 vampire novel not fallen into public domain. *TOD* and *Werewolf by Night*, which preceded it into print by two months in

Marvel Spotlight #2, were Marvel's response to the 1971 lifting of the Comics Code Authority's prohibition against the depiction of vampires, werewolves, and the undead (although Morbius the Living Vampire, who debuted in October 1971's *Amazing Spider-Man* #101, was first out the gruesome gate), and spawned one of the decade's most popular trends. Frankenstein, Swamp Thing, Man-Thing, Bog Beast, Brother Voodoo, the Demon, and the Living Mummy were among the macabre protagonists in 1970s comics ("I pray that you will discontinue this corruption of impressionable young minds. . ." penned one concerned mother in response to Marvel's hellspawned super-hero, the Son of Satan). Some of them have resurfaced in the 2000s and have achieved acclaim beyond the four-color pages, including Ghost Rider, the star of a 2006 motion picture starring Nicolas Cage—who was weaned on Bronze Age comics (and chose his stage name from Marvel's own Hero for Hire, Luke Cage, another prod-

uct of the 1970s).

Fu Manchu, the fictional "Yellow Peril" mastermind and subject of a series of novels by Sax Rohmer, brought his claw-fingered menace to comics in *Special Marvel Edition* #15 (December 1973), the first appearance of his created-for-comics son, Shang-Chi, better known as the Master of Kung Fu. Steve Englehart and Jim Starlin's response to the TV hit *Kung Fu* (1972–1975)—which itself was television's response to the trend of Hong Kong–born martial-arts movies and their patron saint, Bruce Lee—*Master of Kung Fu* became a long-running success for Marvel (most notably under Doug Moench and Paul Gulacy's tenure), and encouraged a gaggle of companions and imitators, including Sons of the Tiger, Iron Fist, Bronze Tiger, Lady Shiva, Karate Kid, and Richard Dragon, Kung Fu Fighter, as well as Seaboard/Atlas' 1975 copycat title *The Hands of the Dragon*.

Martial arts aside, Rohmer's Fu Manchu novels represented another 1970s' comics trend: pulp heroes. Doc Savage returned to spin racks in the form of a Marvel series in 1972. Dennis O'Neil and Michael Kaluta brought *The Shadow* to DC in 1973 (Jim Steranko, Alex Toth, and Bernie Wrightson were considered as the *Shadow* artist before then-newcomer Kaluta was signed). In 1975 DC also published four issues of *Justice, Inc.*, starring the chalk-skinned globe-trotter the Avenger, and Howard Chaykin's mid-1970s' Dominic Fortune (for Marvel) and the Scorpion (for Seaboard) mined this pulp vein.

Beyond the world of pop literature, Marvel found mass media a ripe market for exploitation. Rock stars KISS became super-heroes, even fighting Dr. Doom (premiering in a magazine-formatted comic featuring the audacious stunt of mixing the band's *blood* with the printer's ink!), and comics based upon popular sci-fi films *Logan's Run*, *Planet of the Apes*, *Godzilla*, and *2001: A Space Odyssey* invaded the

racks. DC was less ambitious in adapting cinematic properties, although its "DC TV Comic" line, including *Welcome Back, Kotter*, is noteworthy if for no other reason than the utter strangeness of it all.

No 1970s' screen property was more popular as a comic book than *Star Wars*, which premiered a few months before the May 25, 1977 release of the film, an anticipation-building maneuver brainstormed by Jedi master George Lucas. Roy Thomas was at the writing helm, and as he told *BACK ISSUE* in 2005, Lucas "had in mind the idea of Howard Chaykin as the artist." *Star Wars*' success title paved the way for other popular late-1970s' Marvel titles based upon sci-fi and toy properties, such as *Battlestar Galactica*, *The Micronauts*, and *Rom*.

Chaykin as Lucas' go-to artist illustrates another hallmark of 1970s' comics: the emergence of young talent. Comics publishing houses had been the exclusive domain of

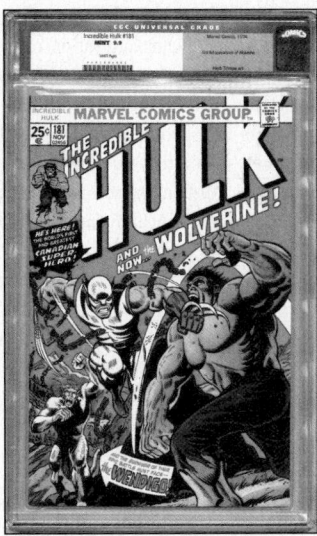

stuffed shirts in elbow-patched tweed jackets, but while looking outside of the field for new properties, the medium also looked *within* its fan base for the next talent wave. The transition, however, was not without its bumps in the road. As one of the "long-hairs" who broke the barrier, writer Denny O'Neil revealed, reflecting upon his visits to DC's headquarters, that "Steve Skeates and I were told by one of the functionaries not to walk past the Big Boss' office 'looking like that,' to take the long way around." "DC had been a closed shop," concurred Carmine Infantino, who "put aside a room for the freelance artists and writers, a place for them to go and discuss and enjoy each other's work." Another such site was Continuity Associates, the studio co-founded in 1971 by Neal Adams and Dick Giordano. Following the lead established in the late 1960s by visionaries Adams and his contemporary Steranko, who demonstrated that comics storytelling was not restricted to stodgy panel layouts or stereotypical dialogue, new artists and writers stormed the medium, daring to

do things differently, Frank Brunner, John Byrne, Chris Claremont, Gerry Conway, Dave Cockrum, José Luis Garcia-Lopez, Steve Gerber, Michael Golden, Mike Grell, George Pérez, Mike Ploog, Frank Miller, Marshall Rogers, Bill Sienkiewicz, Walter Simonson, Len Wein, and Marv Wolfman, among their number.

Not to rest on their laurels, established talent became energized by this exciting new climate: John Buscema, Nick Cardy, Gene Colan, Gil Kane, Jack Kirby, Joe Kubert, Stan Lee, and John Romita, Sr. produced some of their best work in the 1970s, as did Curt Swan and Murphy Anderson with their "Swanderson" pairing on *Superman*. Marvel and DC took chances with traditional characters and with new characters existing within their universes. The coming of Kirby's Fourth World, *Green Lantern/Green Arrow*, Swamp Thing, Jonah Hex, the Punisher and Wolverine, Howard the Duck, Warlock, ethnic characters, and the new X-Men, plus the Joker's return to his homicidal roots and the deaths of Gwen

Stacy and the Green Goblin, suggest that the most significant innovation of the 1970s might have been a willingness to explore new directions with icons.

With new properties, new talent, and new characters bombarding the reader at a dizzying pace, little stability was to be found in the *shapes* of the comic books themselves. Publishers experimented with a variety of formats, in a move initially inspired by that perennial enemy of the long-time comic-book reader: the price increase.

Two years after jumping from a 12- to a 15-cent cover price, the 25-cent comic originated in the summer of 1971, as DC's titles, with their August cover dates, were now 48 pages (52 counting covers), hyped as "bigger and better" with roughly 22–25 new story pages backed up by 6–12 pages of Golden and Silver Age reprints. Marvel sucker-punched DC, delaying their price hike by one month (while blurbing their covers "Still 15¢"), then matching DC's price the next month, but trumping their original page count with 34–35 new story pages—and *then* undercutting their competitor by reverting to the standard 32–page format the following month, but at the cover price of 20 cents. DC, however, offered its readers something that Marvel's streamlined package could not: history. Newer readers sampled adventures of long-retired characters like Starman and Sandman, or more recently cancelled heroes including Deadman, keeping them

alive in the fandom consciousness and inspiring budding writers and artists to, in later years, resuscitate them.

Is there any format that "says" the 1970s more than DC's 100-page Super Spectacular? In June and July 1971, DC published a trio of 100-pagers—*Weird Mystery Tales*, *Love Stories*, and *World's Greatest Super-Heroes*—each priced at 50 cents and reprinting material from the publisher's rich past. By 1973, 100-pagers returned as reprint specials, following in the footsteps of the Silver Age's beloved Annuals and 80-page giants. Before long several of DC's regular titles were converted to a bimonthly 100-page format, with new lead feature (or features) backed up by classics from yesteryear. (In December 1976 DC similarly converted some of its character-heavy titles like *Superman Family* into its new "Dollar Comic" format, featuring *all-new* stories in an 80-page [later a 64-page] package.)

Sharing the Super Spectacular's page count but at a much smaller size, the digest-sized comic (which began in the late 1960s at Gold Key) gained prominence in the 1970s in an attempt to broaden comics' availability. DC experimented with a 1972 *Tarzan* digest, announcing but never releasing a *Laurel and Hardy* digest (DC did, however, release a *Laurel and Hardy* one-shot comic). By decade's end, DC, Marvel, and Archie were publishing a host of reprint digests, aggressively fighting for rack space in supermarkets' highly visible checkouts. DC's and Marvel's digests were cancelled by the mid-1980s, but Archie's remain a durable fixture today, and the digest has morphed into a popular format for manga.

Comics reprints gained a bookstore presence throughout the 1970s, including Bonanza's trio of hardcovers, *Batman: From the 30's to the 70's*, *Superman: From the 30's to the 70's*, and *Shazam: From the 40's to the 70's*, the latter of which, not experiencing reprintings like the Batman and Superman editions, being quite scarce in today's collectibles market. Fireside's full-color trade paperback collections of Marvel and DC material were popular, particularly the Stan Lee–sanctioned line of super-hero trades beginning with *Origins of Marvel Comics* (1974). Near the end of the decade, Tempo Books' black-and-white paperback reprints of 1950s and 1960s DC material could be found in bookstores and K-Marts, as could Pocket Books' full-color line of reprints of early Marvels.

The *biggest* reprint format of the 1970s, bar none, was the tabloid, measuring approximately 10 1/4" x 13 1/4" and called "Treasury Editions" by Marvel and "Limited Collectors' Editions" by DC. Offering the added bonus of printing comics art close to full size (the standard dimensions of comics artboard of the day was 10" x 15"), these oversized comics soon housed all-new as well as classic material, and became the spotlight format for influential projects, including DC and Marvel's first super-hero team-up, *Superman vs. The Amazing Spider-Man* (1976).

Tabloids were envisioned as a doorway for comics to hop off the claustrophobic, kid-centric spin rack and be shelved alongside compatibly sized periodicals, but the black-and-white (B&W) comics magazine was most attrac-

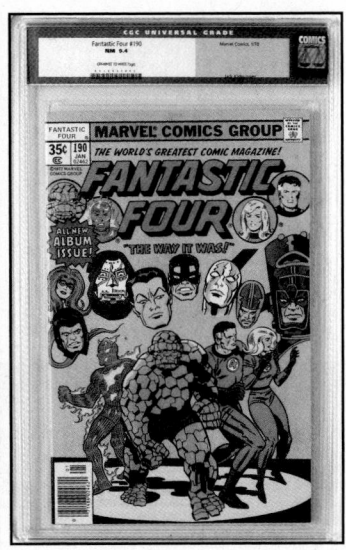

tive to publishers as a means of luring the older, more discerning reader to the comic-book art form. While the medium had previously dabbled in this arena, E.C.'s "Picto-Fiction" B&Ws of the 1950s being an early example, during the 1970s almost every comics house tried its hand at it, following the lead of publisher James Warren, the indisputable champ of black-and-whites since his 1964 launch of *Creepy*. Skywald's *Psycho*, Ross Andru and Mike Esposito's *Up Your Nose and Out Your Ear*, and Charlton's TV-licensed *The Six Million Dollar Man* were among 1970s' B&W comics magazine fare, but Marvel successfully milked this trend for several years, most notably with its long-running *Savage Sword of Conan*. A single issue each of Jack Kirby's ill-fated "Speak-Out" black-and-whites *In the Days of the Mob* and *Spirit World*, DC's 1971 attempt to stick an apprehensive toe in the B&W waters, was released under the banner of "Hampshire Distributor's Ltd." Always the trailblazer, Kirby had high hopes for finding a new audience with these magazines (he was developing two other titles, *True Divorce Cases* and *Soul Love*, but they were not produced), but spotty distribution of *Mob* and *Spirit* intimidated the publisher from releasing additional B&Ws.

The graphic novel was also born in the 1970s, thanks to Will Eisner's *A Contract with God* (1978). The biographical "comix" found in the undergrounds motivated Eisner to return to the fold after a hiatus, and at a time when he could have easily retired, Eisner essentially re-created the comics art form by producing this pioneering collection of intensely personal stories.

The final, but widest-reaching, breakthrough of the Bronze Age was merchandising. While popular comics stars had long been licensed for various products, comic-book characters became household names during the 1970s due to a ubiquitous barrage of Saturday-morning TV cartoons and primetime live-action dramas, action figures, records, coloring books, 7-11 Slurpee cups, lunchboxes, electric toothbrushes, Colorforms, clothing patches, View-Master reels, and Halloween costumes, culminating in *Superman: The Movie*'s elevation of the comic-book film to blockbuster status in 1978. While the innovations of 1970s publishing rebuilt the industry from within, the non-comics retailing of its characters cemented their statuses as cultural institutions.

Overstreet advisor Michael Eury is the Editor of TwoMorrows' *BACK ISSUE* magazine, the co-editor/co-author of *The Supervillain Book: The Ultimate Encyclopedia of Comic-Book and Hollywood Masterminds, Megalomaniacs, and Menaces* (Visible Ink Press, 2006), and the author of *The Justice League Companion* (2005), *Dick Giordano: Changing Comics, One Day at a Time* (2003), and *Captain Action: The Original Super-Hero Action Figure* (2002). A former editor for DC, Dark Horse, and Comico, Eury has written cartoons, comics, and copy for Nike, Toys R Us, Warner Bros., MSN, *Cracked*, and Bowen Designs. *Quotes for this article originally appeared in interviews in BACK ISSUE magazine and the book,* The Justice League Companion. *The author wishes to thank Dewey Cassell, Tom Field, Glenn Greenberg, Allan Harvey, Carmine Infantino, Dan Johnson, John Morrow, Dennis O'Neil, Diana Schutz, Tom Stewart, and Roy Thomas for their contributions.*

Abbott & Costello #2 © STJ

Ace Comics #55 © DMP

Acme Novelty Library #1 © Chris Ware

	GD 2.0	VG 4.0	FN 6.0	VF 8.0	VF/NM 9.0	NM- 9.2

The correct title listing for each comic book can be determined by consulting the indicia (publication data) on the beginning interior pages of the comic. The official title is determined by those words of the title in capital letters only, and not by what is on the cover. Titles are listed in this book as if they were one word, ignoring spaces, hyphens, and apostrophes, to make finding titles easier. Exceptions are made in rare cases. Comic books listed should be assumed to be in color unless noted "B&W".

Comic publishers are invited to send us sample copies for possible inclusion in future guides.

PRICING IN THIS GUIDE: Prices for **GD 2.0** (Good), **VG 4.0** (Very Good), **FN 6.0** (Fine), **VF 8.0** (Very Fine), **VF/NM 9.0** (Very Fine/Near Mint), and **NM– 9.2** (Near Mint–) are listed in whole U.S. dollars except for prices below $7 which show dollars and cents. **The minimum price listed is $2.25.** Many books listed at this price can be found in $1.00 boxes at conventions and dealers stores.

A-1 (See A-One)

ABADAZAD
CrossGen (Code 6): Mar, 2004 - No. 3, May, 2004 ($2.95)

1-3-Ploog-a/c; DeMatteis-s					3.00
1-2nd printing with new cover					3.00

ABBIE AN' SLATS (...With Becky No. 1-4) (See Comics On Parade, Fight for Love, Giant Comics Edition 2, Giant Comics Editions #1, Sparkler Comics, Tip Topper, Treasury of Comics, & United Comics)
United Features Syndicate: 1940; March, 1948 - No. 4, Aug, 1948 (Reprints)

	GD	VG	FN	VF	VF/NM	NM-
Single Series 25 ('40)	40	80	120	240	383	525
Single Series 28	34	68	102	197	311	425
1 (1948)	17	34	51	98	154	210
2-4: 3-r/Sparkler #68-72	10	20	30	58	79	100

ABBOTT AND COSTELLO (...Comics)(See Giant Comics Editions #1 & Treasury of Comics)
St. John Publishing Co.: Feb, 1948 - No. 40, Sept, 1956 (Mort Drucker-a in most issues)

1	59	118	177	369	615	860
2	34	68	102	199	315	430
3-9 (#8, 8/49; #9, 2/50)	22	44	66	126	198	270
10-Son of Sinbad story by Kubert (new)	26	52	78	150	235	320
11,13-20 (#11, 10/50; #13, 8/51; #15, 12/52)	16	32	48	94	147	200
12-Movie issue	17	34	51	98	154	210
21-30: 28-r/#8. 29,30-Painted-c	13	26	39	72	101	130
31-40: 33,38-Reprints	10	20	30	54	72	90
3-D #1 (11/53, 25¢)-Infinity-c	32	64	96	186	293	400

ABBOTT AND COSTELLO (TV)
Charlton Comics: Feb, 1968 - No. 22, Aug, 1971 (Hanna-Barbera)

1	8	16	24	54	90	125
2	4	8	12	28	44	60
3-10	4	8	12	22	34	45
11-22	3	6	9	18	27	35

ABC (See America's Best TV Comics)

ABC: A-Z (one-shots)
America's Best Comics: Nov, 2005 - Present ($3.99, one-shots)

... Greyshirt and Cobweb (1/06) character bios; Veitch-s/a; Gebbie-a; Dodson-c					4.00
... Terra Obscura and Splash Brannigan (3/06) character bios; Barta-a; Dodson-c					4.00
... Tom Strong and Jack B. Quick (11/05) character bios; Sprouse-a; Nowlan-a; Dodson-c					4.00
... Top Ten and Teams (7/06) character bios; Ha & Cannon-a; Veitch-a; Dodson-c					4.00

ABE SAPIEN: DRUMS OF THE DEAD
Dark Horse Comics: Mar, 1998 ($2.95, one-shot)

1-McDonald-s/Thompson-a. Hellboy back-up; Mignola-s/a/c					3.00

A. BIZARRO
DC Comics: Jul, 1999 - No. 4, Oct, 1999 (2.50, limited series)

1-4-Gerber-s/Bright-a					2.50

ABOMINATIONS (See Hulk)
Marvel Comics: Dec, 1996 - No. 3, Feb, 1997 (1.50, limited series)

1-3-Future Hulk storyline					2.50

ABRAHAM LINCOLN LIFE STORY (See Dell Giants)

ABRAHAM STONE
Marvel Comics (Epic): July, 1995 - No. 2, Aug, 1995 ($6.95, limited series)

1,2-Joe Kubert-s/a					7.00

ABSENT-MINDED PROFESSOR, THE

Dell Publishing Co.: Apr, 1961 (Disney)

	GD	VG	FN	VF	VF/NM	NM-
Four Color #1199-Movie, photo-c	8	16	24	56	93	130

ABSOLUTE VERTIGO
DC Comics (Vertigo): Winter, 1995 (99¢, mature)

nn-1st app. Preacher. Previews upcoming titles including Jonah Hex: Riders of the Worm, The Invisibles (King Mob), The Eaters, Ghostdancing & Preacher					
	1	2	3	5	7	9

ABYSS, THE (Movie)
Dark Horse Comics: June, 1989 - No. 2, July, 1989 ($2.25, limited series)

1,2-Adaptation of film; Kaluta & Moebius-a					3.00

ACCELERATE
DC Comics (Vertigo): Aug, 2000 - No. 4, Nov, 2000 ($2.95, limited series)

1-4-Pander Bros.-a/Kadrey-s					3.00

ACCLAIM ADVENTURE ZONE
Acclaim Books: 1997 ($4.50, digest size)

1-Short stories of Turok, Troublemakers, Ninjak and others					4.50

ACE COMICS
David McKay Publications: Apr, 1937 - No. 151, Oct-Nov, 1949 (All contain some newspaper strip reprints)

	GD	VG	FN	VF	VF/NM	NM-
1-Jungle Jim by Alex Raymond, Blondie, Ripley's Believe It Or Not, Krazy Kat begin (1st app. of each)	321	642	963	2087	3694	5300
2	95	190	285	594	985	1375
3-5	63	126	189	394	655	915
6-10	46	92	138	281	466	650
11-The Phantom begins (1st app., 2/38) (in brown costume)	81	162	243	506	841	1175
12-20	40	80	120	235	368	500
21-25,27-30	35	70	105	201	318	435
26-Origin & 1st app. Prince Valiant (5/39); begins series?	102	204	306	638	1057	1475
31-40: 37-Krazy Kat ends	25	50	75	145	228	310
41-60	18	36	54	107	169	230
61-64,66-76-(7/43; last 68 pgs.)	16	32	48	94	147	200
65-(8/42)-Flag-c	18	36	54	107	169	230
77-84 (3/44; all 60 pgs.)	14	28	42	80	115	150
85-99 (52 pgs.)	12	24	36	69	97	125
100 (7/45; last 52 pgs.)	14	28	42	80	115	150
101-134: 128-(11/47)-Brick Bradford begins. 134-Last Prince Valiant (all 36 pgs.)	10	20	30	56	76	95
135-151: 135-(6/48)-Lone Ranger begins	9	18	27	52	69	85

ACE KELLY (See Tops Comics & Tops In Humor)

ACE KING (See Adventures of Detective...)

ACES
Acme Press (Eclipse): Apr, 1988 - No. 5, Dec, 1988 ($2.95, B&W, magazine)

1-5					3.00

ACES HIGH
E.C. Comics: Mar-Apr, 1955 - No. 5, Nov-Dec, 1955

	GD	VG	FN	VF	VF/NM	NM-
1-Not approved by code	22	44	66	176	276	375
2	12	24	36	96	153	210
3-5	11	22	33	88	139	190

NOTE: *All have stories by* **Davis, Evans, Krigstein,** *and* **Wood.** *Evans c-1-5.*

ACES HIGH
Gemstone Publishing: Apr, 1999 - No. 5, Aug, 1999 ($2.50)

1-5-Reprints E.C. issues					2.50
Annual 1 ($13.50) r/#1-5					13.50

ACME NOVELTY LIBRARY, THE
Fantagraphics Books: Winter 1993-94 - Present (quarterly, various sizes)

	GD	VG	FN	VF	VF/NM	NM-
1-Introduces Jimmy Corrigan; Chris Ware-s/a in all	1	3	4	6	8	10
1-2nd and later printings						4.00
2,3: 2-Quimby						6.00
4-Sparky's Best Comics & Stories	1	2	3	4	5	7
5-12: Jimmy Corrigan in all						5.00
13,15-($10.95-c)						11.00
14-($12.95-c) Concludes Jimmy Corrigan saga						13.00
16-($15.95, hardcover) Rusty Brown						16.00
Jimmy Corrigan, The Smartest Kid on Earth (2000, Pantheon Books, Hardcover, $27.50, 380 pgs.) Collects Jimmy Corrigan stories; folded dust jacket						27.50

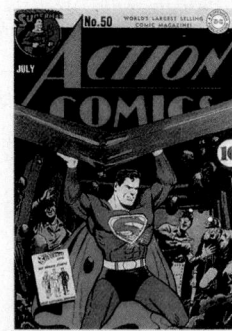

Action Comics #50 © DC

Action Comics #130 © DC

Action Comics #252 © DC

Jimmy Corrigan, The Smartest Kid on Earth (2003, Softcover, $17.95) ... 18.00
NOTE: *Multiple printings exist for most issues.*

ACROSS THE UNIVERSE: THE DC UNIVERSE STORIES OF ALAN MOORE (Also see DC Universe: The Stories of Alan Moore)
DC Comics: 2003 ($19.95, TPB)
nn-Reprints selected Moore stories from '85-'87; Superman, Batman, Swamp Thing app. 20.00

ACTION ADVENTURE (War) (Formerly Real Adventure)
Gillmor Magazines: V1#2, June, 1955 - No. 4, Oct, 1955

	GD 2.0	VG 4.0	FN 6.0	VF 8.0	VF/NM 9.0	NM- 9.2
V1#2-4	6	12	18	29	36	42

ACTION COMICS (...Weekly #601-642) (Also see The Comics Magazine #1, More Fun #14-17 & Special Edition) (Also see Promotional Comics section)
National Periodical Publ./Detective Comics/DC Comics: 6/38 - No. 583, 9/86; No. 584, 1/87 - Present

	GD 2.0	VG 4.0	FN 6.0	VF 8.0	VF/NM 9.0	NM- 9.2
1-Origin & 1st app. Superman by Siegel & Shuster, Marco Polo, Tex Thompson, Pep Morgan, Chuck Dawson & Scoop Scanlon; 1st app. Zatara & Lois Lane; Superman story missing 4 pgs. which were included when reprinted in Superman #1; Clark Kent works for Daily Star; story continued in #2	42,000	84,000	126,000	275,000	475,000	675,000

1-Reprint, Oversize 13-1/2x10". **WARNING:** This comic is an exact reprint of the original except for its size. DC published in 1974 with a second cover titling it as a Famous First Edition. There have been many reported cases of the outer cover being removed and the interior sold as the original edition. The reprint with the new outer cover removed is practically worthless. See Famous First Edition for value.

	GD 2.0	VG 4.0	FN 6.0	VF 8.0	VF/NM 9.0	NM- 9.2
2-O'Mealia non-Superman covers thru #6	4125	8250	12,375	29,906	47,953	66,000
3 (Scarce)-Superman apps. in costume in only one panel	2750	5500	8250	19,938	31,969	44,000
4-6: 6-1st Jimmy Olsen (called office boy)	1563	3126	4689	11,332	18,166	25,000
7-2nd Superman cover	3563	7126	10,689	25,832	41,416	57,000
8,9	1031	2062	3093	7475	11,988	16,500
10-3rd Superman cover by Siegel & Shuster; splash panel used as cover art for Superman #1	2250	4500	6750	16,313	26,157	36,000
11,14: 1st X-Ray Vision? 14-Clip Carson begins, ends #41; Zatara-c	514	1028	1542	3600	6300	9000
12-Has 1 panel Batman ad for Det. #27 (5/39); Zatara sci-fi cover	554	1108	1662	3878	6789	9700
13-Shuster Superman-c; last Scoop Scanlon	1000	2000	3000	7200	12,600	18,000
15-Guardineer Superman-c; has ad for Detective Comics #27	743	1486	2229	5200	9100	13,000
16	382	764	1146	2483	4392	6300
17-Superman cover; last Marco Polo	589	1178	1767	4123	7212	10,300
18-Origin 3 Aces	382	764	1146	2483	4392	6300
19-Superman covers begin; has a 1 panel ad for New York World's Fair 1939 at the end of the Superman story	554	1108	1662	3878	6789	9700
20-The 'S' left off Superman's chest; Clark Kent works at 'Daily Star'	531	1062	1593	3717	6509	9300
21-Has 2 ads for More Fun #52 (1st Spectre)	333	666	1000	2165	3833	5500
22,24,25: 24-Kent at Daily Planet. 25-Last app. Gargantua T. Potts, Tex Thompson's sidekick	327	654	981	2126	3763	5400
23-1st app. Luthor (w/red hair) & Black Pirate; Black Pirate by Moldoff; 1st mention of The Daily Planet (4/40)-Has 1 panel ad for Spectre in More Fun	771	1542	2313	5397	9449	13,500
26-28,30	317	634	951	1981	3291	4600
29-1st app. Lois Lane-c (10/40)	315	630	945	2048	3624	5200
31,32: 32-Intro/1st app. Krypto Ray Gun in Superman story by Burnley	197	394	591	1231	2041	2850
33-Origin Mr. America; Superman by Burnley; has half page ad for All Star Comics #3	203	406	609	1269	2110	2950
34,35,38,39	190	380	570	1188	1969	2750
36, 40: 36-Classic robot-c. 40-(9/41)-Intro/1st app. Star Spangled Kid & Stripesy; Jerry Siegel photo	198	396	594	1238	2057	2875
37-Origin Congo Bill	195	390	585	1219	2022	2825
41	172	344	516	1075	1788	2500
42-1st app./origin Vigilante; Bob Daley becomes Fat Man; origin Mr. America's magic flying carpet; The Queen Bee & Luthor app; Black Pirate app; not in #41	200	400	600	1250	2075	2900
43-46,48-50: 44-Fat Man's i.d. revealed to Mr. America. 45-1st app. Stuff (Vigilante's oriental sidekick)	162	324	486	1013	1682	2350
47-1st Luthor cover in comics (4/42)	238	476	714	1488	2469	3450
51-1st app. The Prankster	172	344	516	1075	1788	2500
52-Fat Man & Mr. America become the Ameri-commandos; origin Vigilante retold; classic Superman and back-ups-c	186	372	558	1163	1932	2700
53-56,59,60: 56-Last Fat Man. 59-Kubert Vigilante begins?, ends #70. 60-First app. Lois Lane as Super-woman	131	262	393	819	1360	1900
57-2nd Lois Lane-c in Action (3rd anywhere, 2/43)	148	296	444	925	1538	2150
58-"Slap a Jap-c"	148	296	444	925	1538	2150
61-Historic Atomic Radiation-c (6/43)	138	276	414	863	1432	2000
62,63-Japan war-c: 63-Last 3 Aces	131	262	393	819	1360	1900
64-Intro Toyman	138	276	414	863	1432	2000
65-70	112	224	336	700	1163	1625
71-79: 74-Last Mr. America	90	180	270	563	932	1300
80-2nd app. & 1st Mr. Mxyztplk-c (1/45)	121	242	363	756	1253	1750
81-88,90: 83-Intro Hocus & Pocus	83	166	249	519	860	1200
89-Classic rainbow cover	86	172	258	538	894	1250
91-99: 93-X-Mas-c. 99-1st small logo (8/46)	76	152	228	475	788	1100
100	112	224	336	700	1163	1625
101-Nuclear explosion-c (10/46)	145	290	435	906	1503	2100
102-107,109-120: 102-Mxyztplk-c. 105,117-X-Mas-c	69	138	207	431	716	1000
108-Classic molten metal-c	76	152	228	475	788	1100
121,122,124-126,128-140: 135,136,138-Zatara by Kubert	64	128	192	400	663	925
123-(8/48) 1st time Superman flies, not leaps	65	130	195	406	673	940
127-Vigilante by Kubert; Tommy Tomorrow begins (12/48, see Real Fact #6)	66	132	198	413	682	950
141-157,159-161: 151-Luthor/Mr. Mxyztplk/Prankster team-up. 156-Lois as Super Woman. 161-Last 52 pgs.	59	118	177	369	610	850
158-Origin Superman retold	124	248	372	775	1288	1800
162-180: 168,176-Used in POP, pg. 90. 173-Robot-c	55	110	165	344	572	800
181-201: 191-Intro. Janu in Congo Bill. 198-Last Vigilante. 201-Last pre-code issue	53	106	159	323	537	750
202-220,232: 212-(1/56)-Includes 1956 Superman calendar that is part of story. 232-1st Curt Swan-c in Action	46	92	138	281	466	650
221-231,233-240: 221-1st S.A. issue. 224-1st Golden Gorilla story. 228-(5/57)-Kongorilla in Congo Bill story (Congorilla try-out)	40	80	120	244	392	540
241,243-251: 241-Batman x-over. 248-Origin/1st app. Congorilla; Congo Bill renamed Congorilla. 251-Last Tommy Tomorrow	35	70	105	206	326	445
242-Origin & 1st app. Braniac (7/58); 1st mention of Shrunken City of Kandor	148	296	444	1258	2329	3400
252-Origin & 1st app. Supergirl (5/59); 1st app. Metallo	152	304	456	1315	2458	3600
253-2nd app. Supergirl	55	110	165	344	572	800
254-1st meeting of Bizarro & Superman-c/story	41	82	123	250	400	550
255-1st Bizarro Lois Lane-c/story & both Bizarros leave Earth to make Bizarro World; 3rd app. Supergirl	36	72	108	208	329	450
256-260: 259-Red Kryptonite used	24	48	72	139	220	300
261-1st X-Kryptonite which gave Streaky his powers; last Congorilla in Action; origin & 1st app. Streaky The Super Cat	26	52	78	154	242	330
262,264-266,268-270	21	42	63	122	191	260
263-Origin Bizarro World	27	54	81	156	246	335
267-(8/60)-3rd Legion app; 1st app. Chameleon Boy, Colossal Boy, & Invisible Kid; 1st app. of Supergirl as Superwoman.	50	100	150	305	503	700
271-275,277-282: 274-Lois Lane as Superwoman; 282-Last 10¢ issue	18	36	54	103	162	220
276-(5/61)-6th Legion app; 1st app. Braniac 5, Phantom Girl, Triplicate Girl, Bouncing Boy, Sun Boy, & Shrinking Violet; Supergirl joins Legion	32	64	96	186	293	400
283-(12/61)-Legion of Super-Villains app. 1st 12¢	12	24	36	87	156	225
284-(1/62)-Mon-el app.	12	24	36	87	156	225
285-(2/62)-12th Legion app; Braniac 5 cameo; Supergirl's existence revealed to world; JFK & Jackie cameos	16	32	48	118	209	300
286-287,289-292,294-299: 286-(3/62)-Legion of Super Villains app. 287-(4/62)-15th Legion app. (cameo). 289-(6/62)-16th Legion app. (Adult); Lightning Man & Saturn Woman's marriage 1st revealed. 290-(7/62)-Legion app. (cameo); Phantom Girl app. 1st Supergirl emergency squad. 291-1st meeting Supergirl & Mr. Mxyzptlk. 292-2nd app. Superhorse (see Adv.#293). 297-Mon-el app. 298-Legion cameo	10	20	30	71	126	180
288-Mon-el app; r-origin Supergirl	11	22	33	75	133	190
293-Origin Comet (Superhorse)	13	26	39	90	160	230
300-(5/63)	19	38	57	120	213	305
301-303,305,307,308,310-312,315-320: 307-Saturn Girl app. 317-Death of Nor-Kan of Kandor. 319-Shrinking Violet app.	8	16	24	54	90	125
304,306,313: 304-Origin/1st app. Black Flame (9/63). 306-Brainiac 5, Mon-el app. 313-Batman app.	8	16	24	56	93	130
309-(2/64)-Legion app; Batman & Robin-c & cameo; JFK app. (he died 11/22/63; on stands last week of Dec, 1963)	8	16	24	58	97	135
314-Retells origin Supergirl; J.L.A. x-over.	8	16	24	56	93	130
321-333,335-339: 336-Origin Akvar (Flamebird)	7	14	21	45	73	100
334-Giant G-20; origin Supergirl, Streaky, Superhorse & Legion (all-r)	11	22	33	75	133	190
340-Origin, 1st app. of the Parasite	7	14	21	49	80	110

341,344,350,358: 341-Batman app. in Supergirl back-up story. 344-Batman x-over.

Action Comics #376 © DC

Action Comics #738 © DC

Action Comics #847 © DC

	GD 2.0	VG 4.0	FN 6.0	VF 8.0	VF/NM 9.0	NM- 9.2

350-Batman, Green Arrow & Green Lantern app. in Supergirl back-up story. 358-Superboy meets Supergirl — 6 · 12 · 18 · 39 · 62 · 85

342,343,345,346,348,349,351-357,359: 342-UFO story. 345-Allen Funt/Candid Camera story. — 6 · 12 · 18 · 37 · 59 · 80

347,360-Giant Supergirl G-33,G-45; 347-Origin Comet-r plus Bizarro story. 360-Legion-r; r/origin Supergirl — 6 · 16 · 24 · 54 · 90 · 125

361-364,367-372,374-378: 361-2nd app. Parasite. 363-366-Leper/Death story. 370-New facts about Superman's origin. 376-Last Supergirl in Action. 377-Legion begins (thru #392).

378-Last 12¢ issue — 5 · 10 · 15 · 30 · 48 · 65

365,366: 365-JLA & Legion app. 366-JLA app. — 5 · 10 · 15 · 32 · 51 · 70

373-Giant Supergirl G-57; Legion-r — 7 · 14 · 21 · 50 · 83 · 115

379-399,401: 388-Sgt. Rock app. 392-Batman-c/app.; last Legion in Action; Saturn Girl gets new costume. 393-401-All Superman issues — 3 · 6 · 9 · 18 · 27 · 35

400 — 4 · 8 · 12 · 22 · 34 · 45

402-Last 15¢ issue; Superman vs. Supergirl duel — 3 · 6 · 9 · 19 · 29 · 38

403-413: All 52 pg. issues. 411-Origin Eclipso-(r). 413-Metamorpho begins, ends #418 — 3 · 6 · 9 · 19 · 29 · 38

414-424: 419-Intro. Human Target. 421-Intro Capt. Strong; Green Arrow begins.

422,423-Origin Human Target — 2 · 4 · 6 · 9 · 13 · 16

425-Neal Adams-a(p); The Atom begins — 3 · 6 · 9 · 14 · 19 · 24

426-431,433-436,438,439 — 2 · 4 · 6 · 8 · 10 · 12

432-1st Bronze Age Toyman app. (2/74) — 2 · 4 · 6 · 13 · 18 · 22

437,443-(100 pg. Giants) — 4 · 8 · 12 · 24 · 37 · 50

440-1st Grell-a on Green Arrow — 2 · 4 · 6 · 9 · 13 · 16

441,442,444-448: 441-Grell-a on Green Arrow continues — 1 · 3 · 4 · 6 · 8 · 10

449-(68 pgs.) — 1 · 3 · 4 · 6 · 9 · 13 · 16

450-465,467-483,486,489-499: 454-Last Atom. 456-Grell Jaws-c. 458-Last Green Arrow. — 1 · 2 · 3 · 4 · 5 · 7

466,485,487,488: 466-Batman, Flash app. 485-Adams-c. 487,488-(44 pgs.). 487-Origin & 1st app. Microwave Man; origin Atom retold — 1 · 2 · 3 · 5 · 7 · 9

481-483,492,495-499,501-505,507,508-Whitman variants (low print run; none show issue # on cover) — 1 · 3 · 4 · 6 · 8 · 10

484-Earth II Superman & Lois Lane wed; 40th anniversary issue(6/78) — 1 · 3 · 4 · 6 · 8 · 10

484-Variant includes 3-D Superman punchout doll in cello. pack; 4 different inserts; Canadian promo?) — 2 · 4 · 6 · 9 · 12 · 20

500-($1.00, 68 pgs.)-Infinity-c; Superman life story; shows Legion statues in museum — 1 · 3 · 4 · 6 · 8 · 10

501-543,545,547-551: 511-514-Airwave II solo stories. 513-The Atom begins. 517-Aquaman begins; ends #541. 521-1st app. The Vixen. 532,536-New Teen Titans cameo. 535,536-Omega Men app. 551-Starfire becomes Red-Star — — · — · — · — · — · 4.00

504,505,507,508-Whitman variants (no cover price) — 1 · 3 · 4 · 6 · 8 · 10

544-(6/83, Mando paper, 68 pgs.)-45th Anniversary issue; origins new Luthor & Brainiac; Omega Men cameo; Shuster-a (pin-up); article by Siegel — 1 · 2 · 3 · 4 · 5 · 7

546-J.L.A., New Teen Titans app. — 1 · 2 · 3 · 5 · 6 · 8

552,553-Animal Man-c & app. (2/84 & 3/84) — — · — · — · — · — · 5.00

554-582 — — · — · — · — · — · 3.00

583-Alan Moore scripts; last Earth 1 Superman story (cont'd from Superman #423) — 2 · 4 · 6 · 8 · 10 · 12

584-Byrne-a begins; New Teen Titans app. — — · — · — · — · — · 6.00

585-599: 586-Legends x-over. 596-Millennium x-over; Spectre app. 598-1st Checkmate — — · — · — · — · — · 3.00

600-($2.50, 84 pgs., 5/88) — — · — · — · — · — · 6.00

601-610,619-642: (#601-642 are weekly issues) ($1.50, 52 pgs.) 601-Re-intro The Secret Six; death of Katma Tui — — · — · — · — · — · 3.00

611-618: 611-614-Catwoman stories (new costume in #611). 613-618-Nightwing stories

643-Superman & monthly issues begin again; Perez-c/a scripts begin; swipes cover to Superman #1 — — · — · — · — · — · 4.00

644-649,651-661,663-673,675-683: 645-1st app. Maxima. 654-Part 3 of Batman storyline. 655-Free extra 8 pgs. 660-Death of Lex Luthor. 661-Begin $1.00-c. 667-($1.75, 52 pgs.). 675-Deathstroke cameo. 679-Last $1.00 issue. 683-Doomsday cameo — — · — · — · — · — · 2.50

650-($1.50, 52 pgs.)-Lobo cameo (last panel) — — · — · — · — · — · 3.00

662-Clark Kent reveals i.d. to Lois Lane; story cont'd in Superman #53 — — · — · — · — · — · 4.00

674-Nightwing logo & c/story (reintro) — — · — · — · — · — · 6.00

683-685-2nd & 3rd printings — — · — · — · — · — · 2.50

684-Doomsday battle issue — — · — · — · — · — · 3.00

685,686-Funeral for a Friend issues; Supergirl app. — — · — · — · — · — · 2.50

687-($1.95)-Collector's Ed.w/die-cut-c — — · — · — · — · — · 2.50

687-($1.50)-Newsstand Edition with mini-poster — — · — · — · — · — · 2.50

688-699,701-703-($1.50): 688-Guy Gardner-c/story. 697-Bizarro-c/story. 703-(9/94)-Zero Hour — — · — · — · — · — · 2.50

695-($2.50)-Collector's Edition w/embossed foil-c — — · — · — · — · — · 2.50

700-($2.95, 68 pgs.)-Fall of Metropolis Pt 1; Guice-a; Pete Ross marries Lana Lang and

Smallville flashbacks with Curt Swan art & Murphy Anderson inks — — · — · — · — · — · 3.00

700-Platinum — — · — · — · — · — · 15.00

700-Gold — — · — · — · — · — · 18.00

0(10/94), 704(11/94)-710-719,721-731: 710-Begin $1.95-c. 714-Joker app. 719-Batman-c/app. 721-Mr. Mxyzptlk app. 723-Dave Johnson-c. 727-Final Night x-over. — — · — · — · — · — · 2.50

720-Lois breaks off engagement w/Clark — — · — · — · — · — · 3.00

720-2nd print. — — · — · — · — · — · 2.50

732-749,751-767: 732-New powers. 733-New costume, Ray app. 738-Immonen-s/a(p) begins. 741-Legion app. 744-Millennium Giants x-over. 745-747-70's-style Superman vs. Prankster. 753-JLA-c/app. 757-Hawkman-c. 760-1st Encantadora. 761-Wonder Woman app. 765-Joker & Harley-c/app. 766-Batman-c/app. — — · — · — · — · — · 2.50

750-($2.95) — — · — · — · — · — · 3.00

768,769,771-774: 768-Begin $2.25-c; Marvel Family-c/app. 771-Nightwing-c/app. 772,773-Ra's al Ghul app. 774-Martian Manhunter-c/app. — — · — · — · — · — · 2.50

770-($3.50) Conclusion of Emperor Joker x-over — — · — · — · — · — · 3.50

775-($3.75) Bradstreet-c; intro. The Elite — — · — · — · — · — · 3.75

776-799: 776-Farewell to Krypton; Rivoche-c. 780-782-Our Worlds at War x-over. 781-Hippolyta and Major Lane killed. 782-War ends. 784-Joker: Last Laugh; Batman & Green Lantern app. 793-Return to Krypton. 795-The Elite app. 798-Van Fleet-c — — · — · — · — · — · 2.50

800-(4/03, $3.95) Struzan painted-c; guest artists include Ross, Jim Lee, Jurgens, Sale — — · — · — · — · — · 4.00

801-811: 801-Raney-a. 809-The Creeper app. 811-Mr. Majestic app. — — · — · — · — · — · 2.50

812-Godfall part 1; Turner-c; Caldwell-a(p) — — · — · — · — · — · 4.00

812-2nd printing; B&W sketch-c by Turner — — · — · — · — · — · 3.00

813-Godfall pt. 4; Turner-c; Caldwell-a(p) — — · — · — · — · — · 3.00

814-824, 826-828,830-836: 814-Reis-a/Art Adams-c; Darkseid app.; begin $2.50-c. 815,816-Teen Titans-c/app. 820-Doomsday app. 826-Capt. Marvel app. 827-Byrne-c/a begin. 831-Villains United tie-in. 835-Livewire app. 836-Infinite Crisis; revised origin — — · — · — · — · — · 2.50

825-($2.99, 40 pgs.) Doomsday app. — — · — · — · — · — · 5.00

829-Omac Project x-over Sacrifice pt. 2 — — · — · — · — · — · 2.50

829-(2nd printing) red tone cover — — · — · — · — · — · 2.50

837-843-One Year Later; powers return after Infinite Crisis; Johns & Busiek-s — — · — · — · — · — · 3.00

844-Donner & Johns-s/Adam Kubert-a/c begin; brown-toned cover — — · — · — · — · — · 4.00

844-Andy Kubert variant-c — — · — · — · — · — · 5.00

844-2nd printing with red-toned Adam Kubert cover — — · — · — · — · — · 3.00

845-849,851-855: 845-Bizarro-c/app.; re-intro. General Zod, Ursa & Non. 846-Jax-Ur app. 847-849-No Kubert-a. 851-Kubert-a/c. 855-Bizarro app.; Powell-a/c — — · — · — · — · — · 3.00

850-($3.99) Supergirl and LSH app.; origin re-told; Guedes-a/c — — · — · — · — · — · 2.50

#1,000,000 (11/98) Gene Ha-c; 853rd Century x-over — — · — · — · — · — · 2.50

Annual 1-6 ('87-'94, $2.95): 1-Art Adams-c/a(p); Batman app. 2-Perez-c/a(i). 3-Armageddon 2001. 4-Eclipso vs. Shazam. 5-Bloodlines; 1st app. Loose Cannon. 6-Elseworlds story — — · — · — · — · — · 4.00

Annual 7,9 ('95, '97, $3.95): 7-Year One story. 9-Pulp Heroes sty — — · — · — · — · — · 4.00

Annual 8 (1996, $2.95) Legends of the Dead Earth story — — · — · — · — · — · 3.00

Annual 10 ('07, $3.99) Short stories by Johns & Donner and various incl. A. Adams, J. Kubert, Wight, Morales; origin of Phantom Zone, Mon-El; Metallo app.; Adam & Joe Kubert-c — — · — · — · — · — · 4.00

NOTE:*Supergirl's* origin in 262, 280, 285, 291, 305, 309. N. Adams c-356, 358, 359, 361-364, 366, 367, 370-374, 377-379!, 398-400, 402, 404,405, 419p, 466, 468, 469, 473, 485. Aparo a-642. Austin c/a-682!. Baily a-29, 24, 25. Boring a-164, 194, 211, 223, 233, 241, 250, 261, 266-268, 346, 348, 352, 356, 357. Burnley a-28-33; c-487, 53-55, 58, 59?, 60-63, 65, 66p, 67p, 70p, 71p, 79p, 82p, 84-86p, 90-92p, 93p?, 94p, 107p, 108p. Byrne a-584-598p, 599!, 600p; c-584-591, 596-600. Ditko a-642. Giffen a-560, 563, 565, 577, 579; c-539, 560, 563, 565, 577, 579. Grell a-440-442, a144-448, 450-452, 456-458; c-456. Guardineer a-24, 25; c-8, 11, 12, 14-16, 18, 25. Guice a(p)-676-681, 683-698; a-700; c-683, 685, 686, 687(direct), 688-693; 694-696, 697!, 698-700. Infantino a-642. Kaluta c-613. Bob Kane's Clip Carson-14-41. Gil Kane a-443r, 493r, 539-541, 544-546, 551-554, 601-605, 642; c-535p, 540, 541, 544p, 545-549, 551-554, 580, 627. Kirby a-192-121(most). Mignola a-600. Moldoff a-23-25, 443r. Mooney a-667p. Mortimer c-153, 154, 159-172, 174, 178-181, 184, 186-189, 191-193, 196, 200, 206. Orlando a-617p; c-621. Perez a-600i, 643-653, 652p; Annual 2p; c-529p, 602, 643-651, Annual 2p. Quesada c-Annual 4p. Fred Ray c-34, 36-46, 50-52. Siegel & Shuster a-1-27. Paul Smith c-608. Starlin a-509; c-631. Leonard Starr a-597!(part), Staton a-525p, 526p, 531p, 535p, 536p. Swan/Moldoff c-281, 286, 287, 293, 298, 334. Thibert c-676, 677p, 678-681, 684. Toth a-406, 407, 413, 431; c-616. Tuska a-486p, 550. Williamson a-568!. Zeck c-Annual 5

ACTION COMICS

DC Comics: (no date)

1-Ashcan comic, not distributed to newsstands, only for in-house use. Cover art is the rejected art to Detective Comics #2 and interior from Detective Comics #1. A CGC certified 9.0 copy sold for $17,825 in 2002.

ACTION FORCE (Also see G.I. Joe European Missions)

Marvel Comics Ltd. (British): Mar, 1987 - No. 50, 1988 ($1.00, weekly, magazine)

1,3: British G.I. Joe series. 3-w/poster insert — 1 · 2 · 3 · 5 · 6 · 8

2,4 — — · — · — · — · — · 6.00

5-10 — — · — · — · — · — · 4.00

11-50 — — · — · — · — · — · 2.50

...Special 1 (7/87) Summer holiday special; Snake Eyes-c/app. — 1 · 2 · 3 · 5 · 6 · 8

...Special 2 (10/87) Winter special; — — · — · — · — · — · 5.00

ACTION FUNNIES

DC Comics: 1938

Adam-12 #10 © GK

Adventure Comics #48 © DC

Adventure Comics #116 © DC

	GD 2.0	VG 4.0	FN 6.0	VF 8.0	VF/NM 9.0	NM- 9.2

nn - Ashcan comic, not distributed to newsstands, only for in house use. Cover art is Action Comics #3 and interior from Detective Comics #10. The Mallette/Brown copy in VG+ condition sold for $15,000 in 2005.

ACTION GIRL
Slave Labor Graphics: Oct, 1994 - Present ($2.50/$2.75/$2.95, B&W)

1-19: 4-Begin $2.75-c. 19-Begin $2.95-c	3.00
1-6 ($2.75, 2nd printings): All read 2nd Print in indicia. 1-(2/96). 2-(10/95). 3-(2/96). 4-(7/96). 5-(2/97). 6-(9/97)	2.75
1-4 ($2.75, 3rd printings): All read 3rd Print in indicia.	2.75

ACTION PLANET COMICS
Action Planet: 1996 - No. 3, Sept, 1997 ($3.95, B&W, 44 pgs.)

1-3: 1-Intro Monster Man by Mike Manley & other stories	4.00
Giant Size Action Planet Halloween Special (1998, $5.95, oversized)	6.00

ACTUAL CONFESSIONS (Formerly Love Adventures)
Atlas Comics (MPI): No. 13, Oct, 1952 - No. 14, Dec, 1952

	GD 2.0	VG 4.0	FN 6.0	VF 8.0	VF/NM 9.0	NM- 9.2
13,14	8	16	24	44	57	70

ACTUAL ROMANCES (Becomes True Secrets #3 on?)
Marvel Comics (IPS): Oct, 1949 - No. 2, Jan, 1950 (52 pgs.)

	GD 2.0	VG 4.0	FN 6.0	VF 8.0	VF/NM 9.0	NM- 9.2
1	14	28	42	76	108	140
2-Photo-c	9	18	27	52	69	85

ADAM AND EVE
Spire Christian Comics (Fleming H. Revell Co.): 1975,1978 (35¢/39¢/49¢)

	GD 2.0	VG 4.0	FN 6.0	VF 8.0	VF/NM 9.0	NM- 9.2
nn-By Al Hartley	2	4	6	9	13	16

ADAM STRANGE (Also see Green Lantern #132, Mystery In Space #53 & Showcase #17)
DC Comics: 1990 - No. 3, 1990 ($3.95, 52 pgs, limited series, squarebound)

Book One - Three: Andy & Adam Kubert-c/a	4.00
...: The Man of Two Worlds (2003, $19.95, TPB) r/#1-3; sketch pages by Andy Kubert	20.00

ADAM STRANGE (Leads into the Rann/Thanagar War mini-series)
DC Comics: Nov, 2004 - No. 8, June, 2005 ($2.95, limited series)

1-8-Andy Diggle-s/Pascal Ferry-a/c. 1-Superman app.	3.00
...: Planet Heist TPB (2005, $19.99) r/series; sketch pages	20.00

ADAM-12 (TV)
Gold Key: Dec, 1973 - No. 10, Feb, 1976 (Photo-c)

	GD 2.0	VG 4.0	FN 6.0	VF 8.0	VF/NM 9.0	NM- 9.2
1	6	12	18	43	69	95
2-10	4	8	12	22	34	45

ADDAM OMEGA
Antarctic Press: Feb, 1997 - No. 4, Aug, 1997 ($2.95, B&W)

1-4	3.00

ADDAMS FAMILY (TV cartoon)
Gold Key: Oct, 1974 - No. 3, Apr, 1975 (Hanna-Barbera)

	GD 2.0	VG 4.0	FN 6.0	VF 8.0	VF/NM 9.0	NM- 9.2
1	9	18	27	61	103	145
2,3	6	12	18	41	66	90

ADLAI STEVENSON
Dell Publishing Co.: Dec, 1966

	GD 2.0	VG 4.0	FN 6.0	VF 8.0	VF/NM 9.0	NM- 9.2
12-007-612-Life story; photo-c	4	8	12	22	34	45

ADOLESCENT RADIOACTIVE BLACK BELT HAMSTERS (See Clint)
Comic Castle/Eclipse Comics: 1986 - No. 9, Jan, 1988 ($1.50, B&W)

1-9: 1st & 2nd printings exist	2.50
1-Limited Edition	6.00
1-In 3-D (7/86), 2-4 ($2.50)	2.50
Massacre The Japanese Invasion #1 (8/89, $2.00)	2.50

ADRENALYNN (See The Tenth)
Image Comics: Aug, 1999 - No. 4, Feb, 2000 ($2.50)

1-4-Tony Daniel-s/Marty Egeland-a; origin of Adrenalynn	2.50

ADULT TALES OF TERROR ILLUSTRATED (See Terror Illustrated)

ADVANCED DUNGEONS & DRAGONS (Also see TSR Worlds)
DC Comics: Dec, 1988 - No. 36, Dec, 1991 (Newsstand #1 is Holiday, 1988-89) ($1.25-$1.75)

1-Based on TSR role playing game	4.00
2-36: 25-$1.75-c begins	2.50
Annual 1 (1990, $3.95, 68 pgs.)	4.00

ADVENTURE BOUND
Dell Publishing Co.: Aug, 1949

	GD 2.0	VG 4.0	FN 6.0	VF 8.0	VF/NM 9.0	NM- 9.2
Four Color 239	6	12	18	39	62	85

ADVENTURE COMICS (Formerly New Adventure)(...Presents Dial H For Hero #479-490)
National Periodical Publications/DC Comics: No. 32, 11/38 - No. 490, 2/82; No. 491, 9/82 - No. 503, 9/83

	GD 2.0	VG 4.0	FN 6.0	VF 8.0	VF/NM 9.0	NM- 9.2
32-Anchors Aweigh (ends #52), Barry O'Neil (ends #60, not in #33), Captain Desmo (ends #47), Dale Daring (ends #47), Federal Men (ends #70), The Golden Dragon (ends #36), Rusty & His Pals (ends #52) by Bob Kane, Todd Hunter (ends #38) and Tom Brent (ends #39) begin	430	860	1290	2408	3354	4300
33-38: 37-Cover used on Double Action #2	210	420	630	1176	1638	2100
39(6/39)- Jack Wood begins, ends #42; 1st mention of Marijuana in comics	210	420	630	1176	1638	2100
40-(Rare, 7/39, on stands 6/10/39)-The Sandman begins by Bert Christman (who died in WWII); believed to be 1st conceived story (see N.Y. World's Fair for 1st published app.); Socko Strong, ends #54	500	10,000	15,000	37,500	66,250	95,000
41-O'Mealia shark-c	571	1142	1713	4000	7000	10,000
42,44-Sandman-c by Flessel. 44-Opium story	714	1428	2142	5000	8750	12,500
43,45	321	642	963	2087	3694	5300
46,47-Sandman covers by Flessel. 47-Steve Conrad Adventurer begins, ends #76	503	1006	1509	3521	6161	8800
48-Intro & 1st app. The Hourman by Bernard Baily; Baily-c (Hourman c-48,50,52-59)	2500	5000	7500	18,750	33,125	47,500
49,50: 50-Cotton Carver by Jack Lehti begins, ends #64	276	552	828	1725	2863	4000
51,60-Sandman-c: 51-Sandman-c by Flessel.	352	704	1056	2288	4044	5800
52-59: 53-1st app. Jimmy "Minuteman" Martin & the Minutemen of America in Hourman; ends #78. 58-Paul Kirk Manhunter begins (1st app.), ends #72	241	482	723	1506	2503	3500
61-1st app. Starman by Jack Burnley (4/41); Starman c-61-72; Starman by Burnley in #61-80	1160	2320	3480	8700	15,350	22,000
62-65,67,68,70: 67-Origin & 1st app. The Mist; classic Burnley-c. 70-Last Federal Men	200	400	600	1250	2075	2900
66-Origin/1st app. Shining Knight (9/41)	241	482	723	1506	2503	3500
69-1st app. Sandy the Golden Boy (Sandman's sidekick) by Paul Norris (in a Bob Kane style); Sandman dons new costume	210	420	630	1313	2182	3050
71-Jimmy Martin becomes costumed aide to the Hourman; 1st app. Hourman's Miracle Ray machine	193	386	579	1206	2003	2800
72-1st Simon & Kirby Sandman (3/42, 1st DC work)	1029	2058	3087	7718	13,359	19,000
73-Origin Manhunter by Simon & Kirby; begin new series; Manhunter-c (scarce)	1267	2534	3800	9500	16,750	24,000
74-78,80: 74-Thorndyke replaces Jimmy, Hourman's assistant; new Sandman-c begin by S&K. 75-Thor app. by Kirby (see Tales of the Unexpected #16). 77-Origin Genius Jones; Mist story. 80-Last S&K Manhunter & Burnley Starman	186	372	558	1163	1932	2700
79-Classic Manhunter-c	255	510	765	1594	2647	3700
81-90: 83-Last Hourman. 84-Mike Gibbs begins, ends #102	119	238	357	744	1235	1725
91-Last Simon & Kirby Sandman	110	220	330	688	1144	1600
92-99,101,102: 92-Last Manhunter. 101-Shining Knight origin retold. 102-Last Starman, Sandman, & Genius Jones; most-S&K-c (Genius Jones cont'd in More Fun #108)	97	194	291	606	1003	1400
100-S&K-c	131	262	393	819	1360	1900
103-Aquaman, Green Arrow, Johnny Quick & Superboy all move over from More Fun Comics #107; 8th app. Superboy; Superboy-c begin; 1st small logo (4/46)	317	634	951	1981	3291	4600
104	107	214	321	669	1110	1550
105-110	78	156	234	488	807	1125
111-120: 113-X-Mas-c	69	138	207	431	716	1000
121,122-126,128-130: 128-1st meeting Superboy & Lois Lane	61	122	183	381	633	885
127-Brief origin Shining Knight retold	62	124	186	388	644	900
131-141,143-149: 132-Shining Knight 1st return to King Arthur time; origin aide Sir Butch	53	106	159	323	529	735
142-Origin Shining Knight & Johnny Quick retold	55	110	165	344	560	775
150,151,153,155,157,159,161,163-All have 6 pg. Shining Knight stories by Frank Frazetta. 159-Origin Johnny Quick. 161-1st Lana Lang app. in this title	66	132	198	413	687	960
152,154,156,158,160,162,164-169: 166-Last Shining Knight. 168-Last 52 pg. issue	45	90	135	275	455	635
170-180	43	86	129	262	431	600
181-199: 189-B&W and color illo in POP	41	82	123	256	416	575
200 (5/54)	54	108	162	338	562	785
201-208: 207-Last Johnny Quick (not in 205)	40	80	120	237	376	515
209-Last pre-code issue; origin Speedy	40	80	120	242	389	535
210-1st app. Krypto (Superdog)-c/story (3/55)	275	550	825	2300	4150	6000
211-213,215-219	38	76	114	226	356	485

Adventure Comics #232 © DC · Adventure Comics #371 © DC · Adventure Comics #430 © DC

	GD 2.0	VG 4.0	FN 6.0	VF 8.0	VF/NM 9.0	NM- 9.2
214-2nd app. Krypto	60	120	180	375	625	875
220-Krypto-c/sty	41	82	123	250	400	550
221-246: 229-1st S.A. issue. 237-1st Intergalactic Vigilante Squadron (6/57). 239-Krypto-c	32	64	96	186	293	400
247(4/58)-1st Legion of Super Heroes app.; 1st app. Cosmic Boy, Saturn Girl & Lightning Boy (later Lightning Lad in #267) (origin)	400	800	1200	3600	6800	10,000
248-252,254,255-Green Arrow in all: 255-Intro. Red Kryptonite in Superboy (used in #252 but with no effect)	27	54	81	156	246	335
253-1st meeting of Superboy & Robin; Green Arrow by Kirby in #250-255 (also see World's Finest #96-99)	32	64	96	186	293	400
256-Origin Green Arrow by Kirby	66	132	198	413	682	950
257-259: 258-Green Arrow x-over in Superboy	23	46	69	130	205	280
260-1st Silver-Age origin Aquaman (5/59)	76	152	228	475	788	1100
261-265,268,270: 262-Origin Speedy in Green Arrow. 270-Congorilla begins, ends #281,283	18	36	54	107	169	230
266-(11/59)-Origin & 1st app. Aquagirl (tryout, not same as later character)	19	38	57	112	176	240
267(12/59)-2nd Legion of Super Heroes app.; Lightning Boy now called Lightning Lad; new costumes for Legion	95	190	285	594	985	1375
269-Intro. Aqualad (2/60); last Green Arrow (not in #206)	31	62	93	178	282	385
271-Origin Luthor retold	35	70	105	201	318	435
272-274,277-280: 279-Intro White Kryptonite in Superboy. 280-1st meeting Superboy & Lori Lemaris	17	34	51	98	154	210
275-Origin Superman-Batman team retold (see World's Finest #94)	24	48	72	139	220	300
276-(9/60) Robinson Crusoe-like story	18	36	54	103	162	220
281,284,287-289: 281-Last Congorilla. 284-Last Aquaman in Adv.; Mooney-a. 287,288-Intro Dev-Em, the Knave from Krypton. 287-1st Bizarro Perry White & Jimmy Olsen. 288-Bizarro-c. 289-Legion cameo (statues)	16	32	48	92	144	195
282(3/61)-5th Legion app; intro/origin Star Boy	30	60	90	174	275	375
283-Intro. The Phantom Zone	26	52	78	152	239	325
285-1st Tales of the Bizarro World-c/story (ends #299) in Adv. (see Action #255)	21	42	63	124	195	265
286-1st Bizarro Mxyzptlk; Bizarro-c	21	42	63	120	188	255
290(11/61)-9th Legion app; origin Sunboy in Legion (last 10¢ issue)	27	54	81	158	249	340
291,292,295-298: 291-1st 12¢ ish, (12/61). 292-1st Bizarro Lana Lang & Lucy Lane. 295-Bizarro-c; 1st Bizarro Titano	10	20	30	71	126	180
293(2/62)-13th Legion app; Mon-el & Legion of Super Pets (1st app./origin) app. (1st Superhorse). 1st Bizarro Luthor & Kandor	16	32	48	114	202	290
294-1st Bizarro Marilyn Monroe, Pres. Kennedy.	12	24	36	86	153	220
299-1st Gold Kryptonite (8/62)	16	30	70	73	129	185
300-Tales of the Legion of Super-Heroes series begins (9/62); Mon-el leaves Phantom Zone (temporarily), joins Legion	38	76	114	285	518	750
301-Origin Bouncing Boy	14	28	42	102	181	260
302-305: 303-1st app. Matter-Eater Lad. 304-Death of Lightning Lad in Legion	11	22	33	75	133	190
306-310: 306-Intro. Legion of Substitute Heroes. 307-1st app. Element Lad in Legion. 308-1st app. Lightning Lass in Legion	10	20	30	70	123	175
311-320: 312-Lightning Lad back in Legion. 315-Last new Superboy story; Colossal Boy app. 316-Origins & powers of Legion given. 317-Intro. Dream Girl in Legion; Lightning Lass becomes Light Lass; Hall of Fame series begins. 320-Dev-Em 2nd app.	9	18	27	60	100	140
321-Intro. Time Trapper	8	16	24	54	90	125
322-330: 325-Intro/1st app. Lone Wolf in Legion. 329-Intro The Bizarro Legionnaires; intro. Legion flight rings	7	14	21	49	80	110
331-340: 337-Chlorophyll Kid & Night Girl app. 340-Intro Computo in Legion	7	14	21	45	73	100
341-Triplicate Girl becomes Duo Damsel	6	12	18	41	66	90
342-345,347-351: 345-Last Hall of Fame; returns in 356,371. 348-Origin Sunboy; intro Dr. Regulus in Legion. 349-Intro Universo & Rond Vidar. 351-1st app. White Witch	6	12	18	39	62	85
346-1st app. Karate Kid, Princess Projectra, Ferro Lad & Nemesis Kid.	7	14	21	50	83	115
352,354-360: 354,355-Superman meets the Adult Legion. 355-Insect Queen joins Legion (4/67)	6	12	18	37	59	80
353-Death of Ferro Lad in Legion	7	14	21	47	76	105
361-364,366,368-370: 369-Mordru in Legion	5	10	15	32	51	70
365,367: 365-Intro Shadow Lass (memorial to Shadow Woman app. in #354's Adult Legion-s); lists origins & powers of L.S.H. 367-New Legion headquarters	5	10	15	35	55	75
371,372: 371-Intro. Chemical King (mentioned in #354's Adult Legion-s). 372-Timber Wolf & Chemical King join	5	10	15	35	55	75

	GD 2.0	VG 4.0	FN 6.0	VF 8.0	VF/NM 9.0	NM- 9.2
373,374,376-380: 373-Intro. Tornado Twins (Barry Allen Flash descendants). 374-Article on comics fandom. 380-Last Legion in Adventure; last 12¢-c	5	10	15	30	48	65
375-Intro Quantum Queen & The Wanderers	5	10	15	35	55	75
381-Supergirl begins; 1st full length Supergirl story & her 1st solo book (6/69)	10	20	30	71	126	180
382-389	4	8	12	26	41	55
390-Giant Supergirl G-69	6	12	18	43	69	95
391-396,398	3	6	9	21	32	42
397-1st app. new Supergirl	4	8	12	28	44	60
399-Unpubbed G.A. Black Canary story	4	8	12	23	36	48
400-New costume for Supergirl (12/70)	4	8	12	28	44	60
401,402,404-408-(15¢-c)	3	6	9	16	23	30
403-68 pg. Giant G-81; Legion-r/#304,305,308,312	6	12	18	41	66	90
409-411,413-415,417-420-(52 pgs.): 413-Hawkman by Kubert r/B&B #44; G.A. Robotman-r/Det. #178; Zatanna by Morrow. 414-r-2nd Animal Man/Str. Advs. #184. 415-Animal Man-r/Det. Adv.#190 (origin recap). 417-Morrow Vigilante; Frazetta Shining Knight-r/Adv. #161; origin The Enchantress; no Zatanna. 418-Prev. unpub. Dr. Mid-Nite story from 1948; no Zatanna. 420-Animal Man-r/Str. Adv. #195	3	6	9	18	27	35
412-(52 pgs.) Reprints origin & 1st app. of Animal Man from Strange Adventures #180	3	6	9	18	27	35
416-Also listed as DC 100 Pg. Super Spectacular #10; Golden Age-r; r/1st app. Black Canary from Flash #86; no Zatanna (see DC 100 Pg. Super Spectacular #10 for price)						
421-424: 424-Last Supergirl in Adventure	2	4	6	10	14	18
425-New look, content change to adventure; Kaluta-c; Toth-a, origin Capt. Fear	3	6	9	16	23	30
426,427: 426-1st Adventurers Club. 427-Last Vigilante	2	4	6	12	17	22
428-Origin/1st app. Black Orchid (c/story, 6-7/73)	6	12	18	37	59	80
429,430-Black Orchid-c/stories	3	6	9	21	32	42
431-Spectre by Aparo begins, ends #440.	6	12	18	41	66	90
432-439-Spectre app. 433-437-Cover title is Weird Adventure Comics. 436-Last 20¢ issue	4	8	12	22	34	45
440-New Spectre origin.	4	8	12	28	44	60
441-458: 441-452-Aquaman app. 443-Fisherman app. 445-447-The Creeper app. 446-Flag-c. 449-451-Martian Manhunter app. 450-Weather Wizard app. in Aquaman story. 453-458-Superboy app. 453-Intro. Mighty Girl. 457,458-Eclipso app.	1	2	3	5	7	9
459,460 (68 pgs.): 459-New Gods/Darkseid storyline concludes from New Gods #19 (#459 is dated 9-10/78) without missing a month. 459-Flash (ends #466), Deadman (ends #466), Wonder Woman (ends #464), Green Lantern (ends #460). 460-Aquaman (ends #478)	3	6	9	19	24	
461,462 ($1.00, 68 pgs.): 461-Justice Society begins; ends 466.	3	6	9	14	19	24
461,462-Death Earth II Batman	4	8	12	22	34	45
463-466 ($1.00 size, 68 pgs.)	2	4	6	9	13	16
467-Starman by Ditko & Plastic Man begins; 1st app. Prince Gavyn (Starman)	2	4	6	8	10	12
468-490: 470-Origin Starman. 479-Dial 'H' For Hero begins, ends #490. 478-Last Starman & Plastic Man. 480-490: Dial 'H' For Hero						5.00
491-503: 491-100pg. Digest size begins; r/Legion of Super Heroes/Adv. #247, 267; Spectre, Aquaman, Superboy, S&K Sandman, Black Canary-r & new Shazam by Newton begin. 492,495,496,499-S&K Sandman-r/Adventure in all. 493-Challengers of the Unknown begins by Tuska w/brief origin. 493-495,497-499-G.A. Captain Marvel-r. 494-499-Spectre-r/Adventure 1-3, 5-7. 496-Capt. Marvel Jr. new-s; Cockrum-a. 498-Mary Marvel new-s; Plastic Man-r begin; origin Bouncing Boy-r/ #301. 500-Legion-r (Digest size, 148 pgs.)	2	4	6	9	13	16
501-503: G.A.-r	2	4	6	9	13	16
... 80 Page Giant (10/98, $4.95) Wonder Woman, Shazam, Superboy, Supergirl, Green Arrow, Legion, Bizarro World stories						5.00

NOTE: Bizarro covers-285, 286, 288, 294, 295, 329. Vigilante app.-420, 426, 427. N. Adams a(r)-495i-498i; c-365-369, 371-373, 375-379, 381-383. Aparo a-431-433, 434i, 435, 436, 437i, 438i, 439-452, 503r; c-431-452. Austin a-449i 451i. Bernard Baily c-48, 50, 52-59. Buckler c-475. Burnley c-61-72, 116-120p. Chaykin a-438. Ditko a-467-478p; c-467p. Creig Flessel c-32, 33, 40, 42, 44, 46, 47, 51, 60. Giffen c-491p-494p, 500p. Grell c-435-437, 440. Guardineer c-34, 35, 45. Infantino a-416r. Kaluta c-425. Bob Kane a-38. G. Kane a-414r, 425; c-414r. Kirby a-250-256. Kubert a-413. Meskin a-81,127. Moldoff a-494i; c-49. Morrow a-413-415, 417, 422, 502r; 503r. Netzer/Nasser a-449-451. Newton a-493, 496, 498, 466, 491p, 492p. Paul Norris a-69. Orlando a-457p; 458p. Perez c-484-486, 490p. Simon/Kirby a-503r; c-73-97, 100-102. Starlin c-471. Staton a-445-447i, 456-458p, 459, 460, 461p-465p, 466,461p?; c-458, 461(back). Toth a-418, 419, 425, 431, 495p-497p. Tuska a-494p.

ADVENTURE COMICS (Also see All Star Comics 1999 crossover titles)
DC Comics: May, 1999 ($1.99, one-shot)

1-Golden Age Starman and the Atom; Snejbjerg-a						2.50

ADVENTURE INTO MYSTERY
Atlas Comics (BFP No. 1/OPI No. 2-8): May, 1956 - No. 8, July, 1957

	GD 2.0	VG 4.0	FN 6.0	VF 8.0	VF/NM 9.0	NM- 9.2
1-Powell s/f-a; Forte-a; Everett-c	40	80	120	235	368	500
2-Flying Saucer story	22	44	66	126	198	270

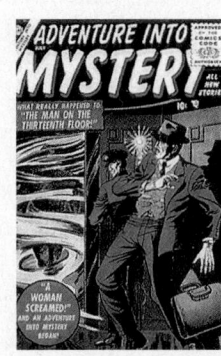

Adventure Into Mystery #2 © MAR

Adventures in the DC Universe #11 © DC

Adventures into the Unknown #13 © ACG

	GD 2.0	VG 4.0	FN 6.0	VF 8.0	VF/NM 9.0	NM- 9.2
3,6-Everett-c	19	38	57	109	172	235
4-7: 4-Williamson-a, 4 pgs; Powell-a. 5-Everett-c/a, Orlando-a. 7-Torres-a; Everett-c	21	42	63	120	188	255
8-Moreira, Sale, Torres, Woodbridge-a, Severin-c	19	38	57	109	172	235

ADVENTURE IS MY CAREER
U.S. Coast Guard Academy/Street & Smith: 1945 (44 pgs.)

nn-Simon, Milt Gross-a	21	42	63	120	188	255

ADVENTURERS, THE
Aircel Comics/Adventure Publ.: Aug, 1986 - No. 10, 1987? ($1.50, B&W)
V2#1, 1987 - V2#9, 1988; V3#1, Oct, 1989 - V3#6, 1990

1-Peter Hsu-a	1	2	3	5	6	8
1-Cover variant, limited ed.	2	4	6	9	12	15
1-2nd print (1986); 1st app. Elf Warrior						3.00
2,3, 0 (#4, 12/86)-Origin, 5-10, Book II, reg. & Limited Ed. #1						3.50
Book II, #2,3,0,4-9						2.50
Book III, #1 (10/89, $2.25)-Reg. & limited-c, Book II, #2-6						2.50

ADVENTURES (No. 2 Spectacular... on cover)
St. John Publishing Co.: Nov, 1949 - No. 2, Feb, 1950 (No. 1 ...in Romance on cover)
(Slightly larger size)

1(Scarce); Bolle, Starr-a(2)	26	52	78	154	242	330
2(Scarce)-Slave Girl; China Bombshell app.; Bolle, L. Starr-a	40	80	120	235	368	500

ADVENTURES FOR BOYS
Bailey Enterprises: Dec, 1954

nn-Comics, text, & photos	8	16	24	40	50	60

ADVENTURES IN PARADISE (TV)
Dell Publishing Co.: Feb-Apr, 1962

Four Color#1301	6	12	18	39	62	85

ADVENTURES IN ROMANCE (See Adventures)

ADVENTURES IN SCIENCE (See Classics Illustrated Special Issue)

ADVENTURES IN THE DC UNIVERSE
DC Comics: Apr, 1997 - No. 19, Oct, 1998 ($1.75/$1.95/$1.99)

1-Animated style in all: JLA-c/app						5.00
2-11,13-17,19: 2-Flash app. 3-Wonder Woman. 4-Green Lantern. 6-Aquaman. 7-Shazam Family. 8-Blue Beetle & Booster Gold. 9-Flash. 10-Legion. 11-Green Lantern & Wonder Woman. 13-Impulse & Martian Manhunter. 14-Superboy/Flash race						3.50
12,18-JLA-c/app						3.50
Annual 1(1997, $3.95)-Dr. Fate, Impulse, Rose & Thorn, Superboy, Mister Miracle app.						4.50

ADVENTURES IN THE RIFLE BRIGADE
DC Comics (Vertigo): Oct, 2000 - No. 3, Dec, 2000 ($2.50, limited series)

1-3-Ennis-s/Ezquerra-a/Bolland-c						2.50
TPB (2004, $14.95) r/series and Operation Bollock series						15.00

ADVENTURES IN THE RIFLE BRIGADE: OPERATION BOLLOCK
DC Comics (Vertigo): Oct, 2001 - No. 3, Jan, 2002 ($2.50, limited series)

1-3-Ennis-s/Ezquerra-a/Fabry-c						2.50

ADVENTURES IN 3-D (With glasses)
Harvey Publications: Nov, 1953 - No. 2, Jan, 1954 (25¢)

1-Nostrand, Powell-a, 2-Powell-a	17	34	51	98	154	210

ADVENTURES INTO DARKNESS (See Seduction of the Innocent 3-D)
Better-Standard Publications/Visual Editions: No. 5, Aug, 1952- No. 14, 1954

5-Katz-c/a; Toth-a(p)	41	82	123	256	416	575
6-Tuska, Katz-a	29	58	87	167	264	360
7-9: 7-Katz-c/a. 8,9-Toth-a(p)	29	58	87	167	264	360
10-12: 10,11-Jack Katz-a. 12-Toth-a; lingerie panel	26	52	78	152	239	325
13-Toth-a(p); Cannibalism story cited by T. E. Murphy articles	32	64	96	186	293	400
14	19	38	57	112	176	240

NOTE: *Fawcette* a-13. *Moreira* a-5. *Sekowsky* a-10, 11, 13(2).

ADVENTURES INTO TERROR (Formerly Joker Comics)
Marvel/Atlas Comics (CDS): No. 43, Nov, 1950 - No. 31, May, 1954

43(#1)	67	134	201	419	697	975
44(#2, 2/51)-Sol Brodsky-c	43	86	129	262	431	600
3(4/51), 4	31	62	93	178	282	385
5-Wolverton-c panel/Mystic #6; Rico-c panel also; Atom Bomb story	35	70	105	204	322	440
6,8: 8-Wolverton text illo r-/Marvel Tales #104	29	58	87	167	264	360

	GD 2.0	VG 4.0	FN 6.0	VF 8.0	VF/NM 9.0	NM- 9.2
7-Wolverton-a "Where Monsters Dwell", 6 pgs.; Tuska-c; Maneely-c panels	59	118	177	369	615	860
9,10,12-Krigstein-a. 9-Decapitation panels	25	50	75	148	232	315
11,13-20	22	44	66	128	202	275
21-24,26-31	20	40	60	117	184	250
25-Matt Fox-a	25	50	75	148	232	315

NOTE: *Ayers* a-21. *Colan* a-3, 5, 14, 21, 24, 25, 28, 29; c-27. *Colletta* a-30. *Everett* c-13, 21, 25. *Fass* a-28, 29. *Forte* a-28. *Heath* a-43, 44, 4-6, 22, 24, 26; c-43, 9, 11. *Lazarus* a-7. *Maneely* a-7(3 pg.), 10, 11, 21...22 c-15, 29. *Don Rico* a-4, 5(3 pg.). *Sekowsky* a-43, 3, 4. *Sinnott* a-8, 9, 11, 28. *Tuska* a-14; c-7.

ADVENTURES INTO THE UNKNOWN
American Comics Group: Fall, 1948 - No. 174, Aug, 1967 (No. 1-33: 52 pgs.)
(1st continuous series Supernatural comic; see Eerie #1)

1-Guardineer-a; adapt. of 'Castle of Otranto' by Horace Walpole	221	442	663	1381	2291	3200
2,3: 3-Feldstein-a (9 pgs)	78	156	234	488	807	1125
4,5: 5- 'Spirit Of Frankenstein' series begins, ends #12 (except #11)	41	82	123	256	416	575
6-10	35	70	105	204	322	440
11-16,18-20: 13-Starr-a	29	58	87	167	264	360
17-Story similar to movie 'The Thing'	34	68	102	195	308	420
21-26,28-30	25	50	75	148	232	315
27-Williamson/Krenkel-a (8 pgs)	31	62	93	180	285	390
31-50: 38-Atom bomb panels	20	40	60	117	184	250
51-(1/54)-(3-D effect-c/story)-Only white cover	38	76	225	355	420	485
52-58: (3-D effect-c/stories with black covers). 52-E.C. swipe/Haunt Of Fear #14	36	72	108	208	329	450
59-3-D effect story only; new logo	29	58	87	167	264	360
60-Woodesque-a by Landau	15	30	45	85	130	175
61-Last pre-code issue (1-2/55)	15	30	45	85	130	175
62-70	8	16	24	52	86	120
71-90	6	12	18	43	69	95
91,96(#95 on inside),107,116-All have Williamson-a	10	20	30	56	83	105
92-95,97-99,101-106,108-115,117-128: 109-113,118-Whitney painted-c. 128-Williamson/ Krenkel/Torres-a(r)/Forbidden Worlds #63; last 10¢ issue	5	10	15	32	51	70
100	6	12	18	39	62	85
129-153,157: 153,157-Magic Agent app.	4	8	12	24	37	50
154-Nemesis series begins (origin), ends #170	5	10	15	30	48	65
155,156,158-167,170-174	4	8	12	23	36	48
168-Ditko-a(p)	4	8	12	28	44	60
169-Nemesis battles Hitler	4	8	12	28	44	60

NOTE: *"Spirit of Frankenstein"* series in 5, 6, 8-10, 12, 16. *Buscema* a-100, 106, 108-110, 158; 165r. *Cameron* a-34. *Craig* a-152, 160. *Goode* a-45, 47, 60. *Landau* a-51, 59-63. *Lazarus* a-34, 48, 51, 52, 56, 58, 79, 87; c-31-56, 58. *Reinman* a-102, 111, 112, 115-118, 124, 130, 137, 141, 145, 164. *Whitney* c-12-30, 57, 59-on (most.) *Torres/Williamson* a-116.

ADVENTURES INTO WEIRD WORLDS
Marvel/Atlas Comics (ACI): Jan, 1952 - No. 30, June, 1954

1-Atom bomb panels	69	138	207	431	716	1000
2-Sci/fic stories (2); one by Maneely	40	80	120	235	368	500
3-10: 7-Tongue ripped out. 10-Krigstein, Everett-a	28	56	84	162	256	350
11-20	22	44	66	128	202	275
21-Hitler in Hell story	27	54	81	158	249	340
22-26: 24-Man holds hypo & splits in two	20	40	60	117	184	250
27-Matt Fox end of world story-a; severed head-c	40	80	120	235	368	500
28-Atom bomb story; decapitation panels	22	44	66	128	202	275
29,30	17	34	51	98	154	210

NOTE: *Ayers* a-18, 26. *Everett* a-5; c-6, 8, 10-13, 18, 19, 22, 24, 25. *Fass* a-7. *Forte* a-21, 24. *Al Hartley* a-2. *Heath* a-1, 4, 17, 22; c-7, 9, 20. *Maneely* a-2, 3, 11, 20, 22, 23, 25; c-1, 3, 22, 25-27, 29. *Reinman* a-24, 28. *Rico* a-13. *Robinson* a-13. *Sinnott* a-25, 30. *Tuska* a-1, 2, 12, 15. *Whitney* a-7. *Wildey* a-28. Bondage c-22.

ADVENTURES IN WONDERLAND
Lev Gleason Publications: April, 1955 - No. 5, Feb, 1956 (Jr. Readers Guild)

1-Maurer-a	11	22	33	62	86	110
2-4	7	14	21	37	46	55
5-Christmas issue	8	16	24	40	50	60

ADVENTURES OF ALAN LADD, THE
National Periodical Publ.: Oct-Nov, 1949 - No. 9, Feb-Mar, 1951 (All 52 pgs.)

1-Photo-c	81	162	243	506	841	1175
2-Photo-c	42	84	126	256	421	585
3-6: Last photo-c	34	68	102	195	308	420
7-9	27	54	81	158	249	340

NOTE: *Dan Barry* a-1. *Moreira* a-3-7.

ADVENTURES OF ALICE (Also see Alice in Wonderland & ...at Monkey Island)
Civil Service Publ./Pentagon Publishing Co.: 1945

Adventures of Bob Hope #5 © DC

Adventures of Jerry Lewis #60 © DC

Adventures of Mighty Mouse #5 © STJ

	GD 2.0	VG 4.0	FN 6.0	VF 8.0	VF/NM 9.0	NM- 9.2
1	15	30	45	83	124	165
2-Through the Magic Looking Glass	11	22	33	62	86	110

ADVENTURES OF BARON MUNCHAUSEN, THE
Now Comics: July, 1989 - No. 4, Oct, 1989 ($1.75, limited series)

1-4: Movie adaptation						2.50

ADVENTURES OF BARRY WEEN, BOY GENIUS, THE (Also see Free Comic Book Day Edition in the Promotional Comics section)
Image Comics: Mar, 1999 - No. 3, May, 1999 ($2.95, B&W, limited series)

1-3-Judd Winick-s/a						3.00
TPB (Oni Press, 11/99, $8.95)						9.00

ADVENTURES OF BARRY WEEN, BOY GENIUS 2.0, THE
Oni Press: Feb, 2000 - No. 3, Apr, 2000 ($2.95, B&W, limited series)

1-3-Judd Winick-s/a						3.00
TPB (2000, $8.95)						9.00

ADVENTURES OF BARRY WEEN, BOY GENIUS 3, THE : MONKEY TALES
Oni Press: Feb, 2001 - No. 6, Feb, 2002 ($2.95, B&W, limited series)

1-6-Judd Winick-s/a						3.00
TPB (2001, $8.95) r/#1-3; intro. by Peter David						9.00
...4 TPB (5/02, $8.95) r/#4-6						9.00

ADVENTURES OF BAYOU BILLY, THE (Based on video game)
Archie Comics: Sept, 1989 - No. 5, June, 1990 ($1.00)

1-5: Esposito-c/a(i). 5-Kelley Jones-c						3.00

ADVENTURES OF BOB HOPE, THE (Also see True Comics #59)
National Per. Publ.: Feb-Mar, 1950 - No. 109, Feb-Mar, 1968 (#1-10: 52pgs.)

	GD 2.0	VG 4.0	FN 6.0	VF 8.0	VF/NM 9.0	NM- 9.2
1-Photo-c	190	380	570	1188	1969	2750
2-Photo-c	83	166	249	519	860	1200
3,4-Photo-c	52	104	156	317	521	725
5-10	40	80	120	240	383	525
11-20	28	56	84	162	256	350
21-31 (2-3/55; last precode)	19	38	57	109	172	235
32-40	10	20	30	67	116	165
41-50	8	16	24	58	97	135
51-70	7	14	21	47	76	105
71-93	5	10	15	32	51	70
94-Aquaman cameo	5	10	15	32	51	70
95-1st app. Super-Hip & 1st monster issue (11/65)	7	14	21	47	76	105
96-105: Super-Hip and monster stories in all. 103-Batman, Robin, Ringo Starr cameos	5	10	15	32	51	70
106-109-All monster-c/stories by N. Adams-c/a	7	14	21	47	76	105

NOTE: Buzzy in #34. Kitty Karr of Hollywood in #15, 17-20, 23, 28. Liz in #26, 109. Miss Beverly Hills of Hollywood in #7, 8, 10, 13, 14. Miss Melody Lane of Broadway in #15. Rusty in #23, 25. Tommy in #24. No 2nd feature in #2-4, 6, 8, 11, 12, 28-108.

ADVENTURES OF CAPTAIN AMERICA
Marvel Comics: Sept, 1991 - No. 4, Jan, 1992 ($4.95, 52 pgs., squarebound, limited series)

1-4: 1-Origin in WW2; embossed-c; Nicieza scripts; Maguire-c/a(p) begins, ends #3. 2-4-Austin-c/a(i). 3,4-Red Skull app.						5.00

ADVENTURES OF CYCLOPS AND PHOENIX (Also See Askani'son & The Further Adventures of Cyclops And Phoenix)
Marvel Comics: May, 1994 - No. 4, Aug, 1994 ($2.95, limited series)

1-4-Characters from X-Men; origin of Cable						4.00
Trade paperback ($14.95)-reprints #1-4						15.00

ADVENTURES OF DEAN MARTIN AND JERRY LEWIS, THE
(The Adventures of Jerry Lewis #41 on) (See Movie Love #12)
National Periodical Publications: July-Aug, 1952 - No. 40, Oct, 1957

	GD 2.0	VG 4.0	FN 6.0	VF 8.0	VF/NM 9.0	NM- 9.2
1	107	214	321	669	1110	1550
2-3 pg origin on how they became a team	52	104	156	317	521	725
3-10: 3- I Love Lucy text featureine	31	62	93	178	282	385
11-19: Last precode (2/55)	20	40	60	115	180	245
20-30	15	30	45	85	130	175
31-40	13	26	39	74	105	135

ADVENTURES OF DETECTIVE ACE KING, THE (Also see Bob Scully-- & Detective Dan)
Humor Publ. Corp.: No date (1933) (36 pgs., 9-1/2x12") (10¢, B&W, one-shot) (paper-c)

Book 1-Along with Bob Scully & Detective Dan, the first comic w/original art & the first of a single theme.; Not reprints; Ace King by Martin Nadle (The American Sherlock Holmes).

	GD 2.0	VG 4.0	FN 6.0	VF 8.0	VF/NM 9.0	NM- 9.2
A Dick Tracy look-alike	375	750	1125	3000	-	-

ADVENTURES OF EVIL AND MALICE, THE
Image Comics: June, 1999 - No. 3, Nov, 1999 ($3.50/$3.95, limited series)

1,2-Jimmie Robinson-s/a						3.50
3-($3.95)						4.00

ADVENTURES OF FELIX THE CAT, THE
Harvey Comics: May, 1992 ($1.25)

1-Messmer-r						4.00

ADVENTURES OF FORD FAIRLANE, THE
DC Comics: May, 1990 - No. 4, Aug, 1990 ($1.50, limited series, mature)

1-4: Andrew Dice Clay movie tie-in; Don Heck inks						3.00

ADVENTURES OF HOMER COBB, THE
Say/Bart Prod. : Sept, 1947 (Oversized) (Published in the U.S., but printed in Canada)

	GD 2.0	VG 4.0	FN 6.0	VF 8.0	VF/NM 9.0	NM- 9.2
1-(Scarce)-Feldstein-c/a	32	64	96	186	293	400

ADVENTURES OF HOMER GHOST (See Homer The Happy Ghost)
Atlas Comics: June, 1957 - No. 2, Aug, 1957

	GD 2.0	VG 4.0	FN 6.0	VF 8.0	VF/NM 9.0	NM- 9.2
V1#1,2: 2-Robot-c	11	22	33	60	83	105

ADVENTURES OF JERRY LEWIS, THE (Adventures of Dean Martin & Jerry Lewis No. 1-40) (See Super DC Giant)
National Periodical Publ.: No. 41, Nov, 1957 - No. 124, May-June, 1971

	GD 2.0	VG 4.0	FN 6.0	VF 8.0	VF/NM 9.0	NM- 9.2
41	9	18	27	60	100	140
42-60	7	14	21	47	76	105
61-67,69-73,75-80	6	12	18	39	62	85
68,74-Photo-c (movie)	8	16	24	56	93	130
81,82,85-87,90,91,94,96,98,99	5	10	15	32	51	70
83,84,88: 83-1st Monsters-c/s. 84-Jerry as a Super-hero-c/s. 88-1st Witch, Miss Kraft	6	12	18	39	62	85
89-Bob Hope app.; Wizard of Oz & Alfred E. Neuman in MAD parody	6	12	18	43	69	95
92-Superman cameo	6	12	18	43	69	95
93-Beatles parody as babies	6	12	18	39	62	85
95-1st Uncle Hal Wack-A-Boy Camp-c/s	6	12	18	39	62	85
97-Batman/Robin/Joker-c/story; Riddler & Penguin app; Dick Sprang-c.	9	18	27	61	103	145
100	6	12	18	41	66	90
101,103,104-Neal Adams-c/a	7	14	21	47	76	105
102-Beatles app.; Neal Adams c/a	9	18	27	60	100	140
105-Superman x-over	6	12	18	43	69	95
106-111,113-116	4	8	12	26	41	55
112,117: 112-Flash x-over. 117-W. Woman x-over	6	12	18	43	69	95
118-124	4	8	12	24	37	50

NOTE: Monster-c/s-90,93,96,98,101. Wack-A-Buy Camp-c/s-96,99,102,107,108.

ADVENTURES OF JO-JOY, THE (See Jo-Joy)

ADVENTURES OF LASSIE, THE (See Lassie)

ADVENTURES OF LUTHER ARKWRIGHT, THE
Valkyrie Press/Dark Horse Comics: Oct, 1987 - No. 9, Jan, 1989 ($2.00, B&W) V2, #1, Mar, 1990 - V2#9, 1990 ($1.95, B&W)

1-9: 1-Alan Moore intro., V2#1-9 (Dark Horse): r-1st series; new-c						4.00
TPB (1997, $14.95) r/#1-9 w/Michael Moorcock intro.						15.00

ADVENTURES OF MIGHTY MOUSE (Mighty Mouse Adventures No. 1)
St. John Publishing Co.: No. 2, Jan, 1952 - No. 18, May, 1955

	GD 2.0	VG 4.0	FN 6.0	VF 8.0	VF/NM 9.0	NM- 9.2
2	25	50	75	145	228	310
3-5	14	28	42	81	118	155
6-18	11	22	33	60	83	105

ADVENTURES OF MIGHTY MOUSE (2nd Series) (Becomes Mighty Mouse No. 161 on)
No. 144's; formerly Paul Terry's Comics; No. 129-137 have nn's
St. John/Pines/Dell/Gold Key: No. 126, Aug, 1955 - No. 160, Oct, 1963

	GD 2.0	VG 4.0	FN 6.0	VF 8.0	VF/NM 9.0	NM- 9.2
126(8/55), 127(10/55), 128(11/55)-St. John	10	20	30	54	72	90
nn(129, 4/56)-144(8/59)-Pines	5	10	15	30	48	65
144(10-12/59)-155(7-9/62) Dell	4	8	12	28	44	60
156(10/62)-160(10/63) Gold Key	4	8	12	28	44	60

NOTE: Early issues titled "Paul Terry's Adventures of ...."

ADVENTURES OF MIGHTY MOUSE (Formerly Mighty Mouse)
Gold Key: No. 166, Mar, 1979 - No. 172, Jan, 1980

	GD 2.0	VG 4.0	FN 6.0	VF 8.0	VF/NM 9.0	NM- 9.2
166-172	1	2	3	5	6	8

ADVS. OF MR. FROG & MISS MOUSE (See Dell Junior Treasury No. 4)

ADVENTURES OF OZZIE & HARRIET, THE (See Ozzie & Harriet)

ADVENTURES OF PATORUZU
Green Publishing Co.: Aug, 1946 - Winter, 1946

Adventures of Rex the Wonder Dog #13 © DC

Adventures of Superman #625 © DC

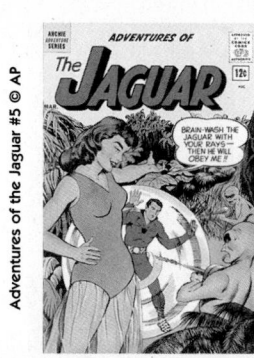

Adventures of the Jaguar #5 © AP

	GD 2.0	VG 4.0	FN 6.0	VF 8.0	VF/NM 9.0	NM- 9.2
nn's-Contains Animal Crackers reprints	6	12	18	28	34	40

ADVENTURES OF PINKY LEE, THE (TV)
Atlas Comics: July, 1955 - No. 5, Dec, 1955

	GD 2.0	VG 4.0	FN 6.0	VF 8.0	VF/NM 9.0	NM- 9.2
1	24	48	72	139	220	300
2-5	15	30	45	85	130	175

ADVENTURES OF PIPSQUEAK, THE (Formerly Pat the Brat)
Archie Publications (Radio Comics): No. 34, Sept, 1959 - No. 39, July, 1960

	GD 2.0	VG 4.0	FN 6.0	VF 8.0	VF/NM 9.0	NM- 9.2
34	3	6	9	21	32	42
35-39	3	6	9	17	25	32

ADVENTURES OF QUAKE & QUISP, THE (See Quaker Oats "Plenty of Glutton")

ADVENTURES OF REX THE WONDER DOG, THE (Rex...No. 1)
National Periodical Publ.: Jan-Feb, 1952 - No. 45, May-June, 1959; No. 46, Nov-Dec, 1959

	GD 2.0	VG 4.0	FN 6.0	VF 8.0	VF/NM 9.0	NM- 9.2
1-(Scarce)-Toth-c/a	129	258	387	806	1341	1875
2-(Scarce)-Toth-c/a	59	118	177	369	615	860
3-(Scarce)-Toth-a	46	92	138	281	466	650
4,5	40	80	120	235	368	500
6-10	31	62	93	178	282	385
11-Atom bomb-c/story; dinosaur-c/sty	37	74	111	213	337	460
12-19: 19-Last precode (1-2/55)	19	38	57	109	172	235
20-46	14	28	42	82	121	160

NOTE: *Infantino, Gil Kane* art in 5-19 (most)

ADVENTURES OF ROBIN HOOD, THE (Formerly Robin Hood)
Magazine Enterprises (Sussex Publ. Co.): No. 7, 9/57 - No. 8, 11/57
(Based on Richard Greene TV Show)

	GD 2.0	VG 4.0	FN 6.0	VF 8.0	VF/NM 9.0	NM- 9.2
7,8-Richard Greene photo-c. 7-Powell-a	15	30	45	83	124	165

ADVENTURES OF ROBIN HOOD, THE
Gold Key: Mar, 1974 - No. 7, Jan, 1975 (Disney cartoon) (36 pgs.)

	GD 2.0	VG 4.0	FN 6.0	VF 8.0	VF/NM 9.0	NM- 9.2
1(90291-403)-Part-r of $1.50 editions	2	4	6	11	16	20
2-7: 1-7 are part-r	2	4	6	8	10	12

ADVENTURES OF SNAKE PLISSKEN
Marvel Comics: Jan, 1997 ($2.50, one-shot)

1-Based on Escape From L.A. movie; Brereton-c	3.50

ADVENTURES OF SPAWN, THE
Image Comics (Todd McFarlane Prods.): Jan, 2007 ($5.99, one-shot)

1-Printed adaptation of the Spawn.com web comic; Khary Randolph-a	6.00

ADVENTURES OF SPIDER-MAN, THE (Based on animated TV series)
Marvel Comics: Apr, 1996 - No. 12, Mar, 1997 ($1.50)

1-12: 1-Punisher app. 2-Venom cameo. 3-X-Men. 6-Fantastic Four	3.00

ADVENTURES OF SUPERBOY, THE (See Superboy, 2nd Series)

ADVENTURES OF SUPERMAN (Formerly Superman)
DC Comics: No. 424, Jan, 1987 - No. 499, Feb, 1993; No. 500, Early June, 1993 - No. 649, Apr, 2006 (This title's numbering continues with Superman #650, May, 2006)

424-Ordway-c/a/Wolfman-s begin following Byrne's Superman revamp	3.00
425-435,437-462: 426-Legends x-over. 432-1st app. Jose Delgado who becomes Gangbuster in #434. 437-Millennium x-over. 438-New Brainiac app. 440-Batman app. 449-Invasion	3.00
436-Byrne scripts begin; Millennium x-over	3.50
463-Superman/Flash race; cover swipe/Superman #199	5.00
464-Lobo-c & app. (pre-dates Lobo #1)	4.00
465-495: 467-Part 2 of Batman story. 473-Hal Jordan, Guy Gardner x-over. 477-Legion app.	
491-Last $1.00-c. 480-($1.75, 52 pgs.). 495-Forever People-c/story; Darkseid app.	2.50
496,497: 496-Doomsday cameo. 497-Doomsday battle issue	3.00
496,497-2nd printings	2.50
498,499-Funeral for a Friend; Supergirl app.	2.50
498-2nd & 3rd printings	2.50
500-($2.95, 68 pgs.)-Collector's edition w/card	3.50
500-($2.50, 68 pgs.)-Regular edition w/different-c	2.50
500-Platinum edition	30.00
501-($1.95)-Collector's edition with die-cut-c	2.50
501-($1.50)-Regular edition w/mini-poster & diff.-c	2.50
502-516: 502-Supergirl-c/story. 508-Challengers of the Unknown app. 510-Bizarro-c/story.	
516-(9/94)-Zero Hour	2.50
505-($2.50)-Holo-grafx foil-c edition	2.50
0,517-523: 0-(10/94). 517-(11/94)	2.50
524-524g,551-580: 524-Begin $1.95-c. 527-Return of Alpha Centurion (Zero Hour). 533-Impulse-c/app. 535-Luthor-c/app. 536-Brainiac app. 537-Parasite app. 540-Final Night x-over. 541-Superboy-c/app.; Lois & Clark honeymoon. 545-New powers. 546-New costume. 555-Red & Blue Supermen battle. 557-Millennium Giants x-over. 558-560: Superman Silver Age-style story; Krypto app. 561-Begin $1.99-c. 565-JLA app.	2.50
550-($3.50)-Double sized	3.50
581-588: 581-Begin $2.25-c. 583-Emperor Joker. 588-Casey-s	2.50
589-595: 589-Return to Krypton; Rivoche-c. 591-Wolfman-s. 593-595-Our Worlds at War x-over. 593-New Suicide Squad formed. 594-Doomsday-c/app.	2.50
596-Aftermath of "War" x-over has panel showing damaged World Trade Center buildings; issue went on sale the day after the Sept. 11 attack	5.00
597-599,601-624: 597-Joker: Last Laugh. 604,605-Ultraman, Owlman, Superwoman app. 606-Return to Krypton. 612-616,619-623-Nowlan-s. 624-Mr. Majestic app.	2.50
600-($3.95) Wieringo-a; painted-c by Adel; pin-ups by various	4.00
625,626-Godfall parts 2,5; Turner-c; Caldwell-a(p)	3.00
627-641,643-648: 627-Begin $2.50-c, Rucka-s/Clark-a/Ha-c begin. 628-Wagner-c. 631-Bagged with Sky Captain CD; Lois shot. 634-Mxyzptlk visits DC offices. 639-Capt. Marvel & Eclipso app. 641-OMAC app. 643-Sacrifice aftermath; Batman & Wonder Woman app.	2.50
642-OMAC Project x-over Sacrifice pt. 3; JLA app.	5.00
642-(2nd printing) red tone cover	2.50
649-Last issue; Infinite Crisis x-over, Superman vs. Earth-2 Superman	3.00
#1,000,000 (11/98) Gene Ha-c; 853rd Century x-over	3.00
Annual 1 (1987, $1.25, 52 pgs.)-Starlin-c & scripts	4.00
Annual 2,3 (1990, 1991, $2.00, 68 pgs.): 2-Byrne-c/a(i); Legion '90 (Lobo) app.	
3-Armageddon 2001 x-over	3.00
Annual 4-6 ('92-'94, $2.50, 68 pgs.): 4-Guy Gardner/Lobo-c/story; Eclipso storyline; Quesada-c(p). 5-Bloodlines storyline. 6-Elseworlds sty.	3.00
Annual 7,9('95, '97, $3.95)-7-Year One story. 9-Pulp Heroes sty	4.00
Annual 8 (1996, $2.95)-Legends of the Dead Earth story	3.00

NOTE: *Erik Larsen* a-431.

ADVENTURES OF THE DOVER BOYS
Archie Comics (Close-up): September, 1950 - No. 2, 1950 (No month given)

	GD 2.0	VG 4.0	FN 6.0	VF 8.0	VF/NM 9.0	NM- 9.2
1,2	9	18	27	52	69	85

ADVENTURES OF THE FLY (The Fly #1-6; Fly Man No. 32-39; See The Double Life of Private Strong, The Fly, Laugh Comics & Mighty Crusaders)
Archie Publications/Radio Comics: Aug, 1959 - No. 30, Oct, 1964; No. 31, May, 1965

	GD 2.0	VG 4.0	FN 6.0	VF 8.0	VF/NM 9.0	NM- 9.2
1-Shield app.; origin The Fly; S&K-c/a	50	100	150	400	725	1050
2-Williamson, S&K-a	27	54	81	201	361	520
3-Origin retold; Davis, Powell-a	22	44	66	164	292	420
4-Neal Adams-a(p)(1 panel); S&K-c; Powell-a; 2 pg. Shield story	14	28	42	102	181	260
5,6,9,10: 9-Shield app. 9-1st app. Cat Girl. 10-Black Hood app.	10	20	30	68	119	170
7,8: 7-1st S.A. app. Black Hood (7/60). 8-1st S.A. app. Shield (9/60)	11	22	33	79	140	200
11-13,15-20: 13-1st app. Fly Girl w/o costume. 16-Last fly issue. 20-Origin Fly Girl retold	7	14	21	45	73	100
14-Origin & 1st app. Fly Girl in costume	8	16	24	52	86	120
21-30: 23-Jaguar cameo. 27-29-Black Hood 1 pg. strips. 30-Comet x-over (1st S.A. app.) in Fly Girl	5	10	15	35	55	75
31-Black Hood, Shield, Comet app.	6	12	18	37	59	80
Vol. 1 TPB ('04, $12.95) r/#1-4 & Double Life of Private Strong #1,2; foreward by Joe Simon						13.00

NOTE: *Simon* c-2-4. *Tuska* a-1. Cover title to #31 is Flyman; Advs. of the Fly inside.

ADVENTURES OF THE JAGUAR, THE (See Blue Ribbon Comics, Laugh Comics & Mighty Crusaders)
Archie Publications (Radio Comics): Sept, 1961 - No. 15, Nov, 1963

	GD 2.0	VG 4.0	FN 6.0	VF 8.0	VF/NM 9.0	NM- 9.2
1-Origin Jaguar (1st app?) by J. Rosenberger	20	40	60	146	261	375
2,3: 3-Last 10¢ issue	10	20	30	70	123	175
4-6-Catgirl app. (#4's-c is same as splash pg.)	8	16	24	54	90	125
7-10	7	14	21	45	73	100
11-15:13,14-Catgirl, Black Hood app. in both	6	12	18	39	62	85

ADVENTURES OF THE MASK (TV cartoon)
Dark Horse Comics: Jan, 1996 - No. 12, Dec, 1996 ($2.50)

1-12: Based on animated series	2.50

ADVENTURES OF THE NEW MEN (Formerly Newmen #1-21)
Maximum Press: No. 22, Nov, 1996; No. 23, March, 1997 ($2.50)

22,23-Sprouse-c/a	2.50

ADVENTURES OF THE OUTSIDERS, THE (Formerly Batman & The Outsiders; also see The Outsiders)
DC Comics: No. 33, May, 1986 - No. 46, June, 1987

33-46: 39-45-r/Outsiders #1-7 by Aparo	2.50

ADVENTURES OF THE SUPER MARIO BROTHERS (See Super Mario Bros.)
Valiant: 1990 - No. 9, Oct, 1991 ($1.50)

V2#1-9	5.00

ADVENTURES OF THE THING, THE (Also see The Thing)

After the Cape #1 © Howard Wong

Age of Bronze #3 © Eric Shanower

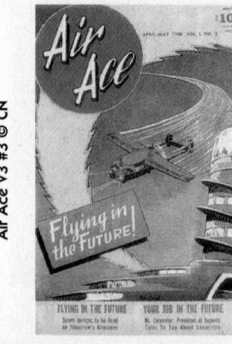

Air Ace V3 #3 © CN

	GD 2.0	VG 4.0	FN 6.0	VF 8.0	VF/NM 9.0	NM- 9.2		GD 2.0	VG 4.0	FN 6.0	VF 8.0	VF/NM 9.0	NM- 9.2

Marvel Comics: Apr, 1992 - No. 4, July, 1992, ($1.25, limited series)

1-4: 1-r/Marvel Two-In-One #50 by Byrne; Kieth-c. 2-4-r/Marvel Two-In-One #80,51 & 77; 2-Ghost Rider-c/story; Quesada-c. 3-Miller-r/Quesada-c; new Perez-a (4 pgs.)						2.50

ADVENTURES OF THE X-MEN, THE (Based on animated TV series)
Marvel Comics: Apr, 1996 - No. 12, Mar, 1997 (99¢)

1-12: 1-Wolverine/Hulk battle. 3-Spider-Man-c. 5,6-Magneto-c/app.						3.00

ADVENTURES OF TINKER BELL (See Tinker Bell, 4-Color No. 896 & 982)

ADVENTURES OF TOM SAWYER (See Dell Junior Treasury No. 10)

ADVENTURES OF YOUNG DR. MASTERS, THE
Archie Comics (Radio Comics): Aug, 1964 - No. 2, Nov, 1964

	GD	VG	FN	VF	VF/NM	NM-
1	3	6	9	18	27	35
2	3	6	9	14	19	24

ADVENTURES ON OTHER WORLDS (See Showcase #17 & 18)

ADVENTURES ON THE PLANET OF THE APES (Also see Planet of the Apes)
Marvel Comics Group: Oct, 1975 - No. 11, Dec, 1976

	GD	VG	FN	VF	VF/NM	NM-
1-Planet of the Apes magazine-r in color; Starlin-a; adapts movie thru #6	3	6	9	17	25	32
2-5: 5-(25¢-c edition)	2	4	6	10	14	18
5-7-(30¢-c variants, limited distribution)	4	8	12	24	37	50
6-10: 6,7-(25¢-c edition). 7-Adapts 2nd movie (thru #11)						
	2	4	6	11	16	20
11-Last issue; concludes 2nd movie adaptation	3	6	9	14	19	24

NOTE: **Alcala** a-6-11r. **Buckler** c-2p. **Nasser** c-7. **Ploog** a-1-9. **Starlin** c-6. **Tuska** a-1-5r.

AEON FLUX (Based on the 2005 movie which was based on the MTV animated series)
Dark Horse Comics: Oct, 2005 - No. 4, Jan, 2006 ($2.99, limited series)

1-4-Timothy Green II-a/Mike Kennedy-s						3.00
TPB (5/06, $12.95) r/series; cover gallery						13.00

AFRICA
Magazine Enterprises: 1955

	GD	VG	FN	VF	VF/NM	NM-
1(A-1 #137)-Cave Girl, Thun'da;Powell-c/a(4)	27	54	81	156	246	335

AFRICAN LION (Disney movie)
Dell Publishing Co.: Nov, 1955

	GD	VG	FN	VF	VF/NM	NM-
Four Color #665	6	12	18	37	59	80

AFTER DARK
Sterling Comics: No. 6, May, 1955 - No. 8, Sept, 1955

	GD	VG	FN	VF	VF/NM	NM-
6-8-Sekowsky-a in all	9	18	27	52	69	85

AFTER THE CAPE
Image Comics (Shadowline): Mar, 2007 - No. 3, May, 2007 ($2.99, B&W, limited series)

1-3-Jim Valentino-s/Marco Rudy-a						3.00
... Volume One TPB (9/07, $12.99) r/series; scripts, sketch pages, character profiles						13.00

AGAINST BLACKSHARD 3-D (Also see SoulQuest)
Sirius Comics: August, 1986 ($2.25)

1						3.50

AGENCY, THE
Image Comics (Top Cow): August, 2001 - No. 6, Mar, 2002 ($2.50/$2.95/$4.95)

1,2: 1-Jenkins-s/Hotz-a; three covers by Hotz, Turner, Silvestri						2.50
3-5 ($2.95)						3.00
6-($4.95) Flip-c preview of Jeremiah TV series						5.00
Preview (2001, 16 pgs.) B&W pages, cover previews, sketch pages						2.25

AGENT LIBERTY SPECIAL (See Superman, 2nd Series)
DC Comics: 1992 ($2.00, 52 pgs, one-shot)

1-1st solo adventure; Guice-c/a(i)						2.50

AGENTS, THE
Image Comics: Apr, 2003 - No. 6, Sept, 2003 ($2.95, B&W)

1-6-Ben Dunn-c/a						3.00

AGENTS OF ATLAS
Marvel Comics: Oct, 2006 - No. 6, Mar, 2007 ($2.99, limited series)

1-6: 1-Golden Age heroes Marvel Boy & Venus app.; Kirk-a						3.00
HC (2007, $24.99, dustjacket) r/#1-6, What If? #9, agents' debuts in '40s-'50s Atlas comics, creator interviews, character design art						25.00

AGENTS OF LAW (Also see Comic's Greatest World)
Dark Horse Comics: Mar, 1995 - No. 6, Sept, 1995 ($2.50)

1-6: 5-Predator app. 6-Predator app.; death of Law						2.50

AGENT X (Continued from Deadpool)
Marvel Comics: Sept. 2002 - No. 15, Dec, 2003 ($2.99/$2.25)

1-($2.99) Simone-s/Udon Studios-a; Taskmaster app.						3.00
2-9-($2.25) 2-Punisher app.						2.50
10-15-($2.99) 10,11-Evan Dorkin-s. 12-Hotz-a						3.00

AGE OF APOCALYPSE: THE CHOSEN
Marvel Comics: Apr, 1995 ($2.50, one-shot)

1-Wraparound-c						3.00

AGE OF BRONZE
Image Comics: Nov, 1998 - Present ($2.95/$3.50, B&W, limited series)

1-6-Eric Shanower-c/s/a						3.00
7-26-($3.50)						3.50
...Behind the Scenes (5/02, $3.50) background info and creative process						3.50
...Special (6/99, $2.95) Story of Agamemnon and Menelaus						3.00
A Thousand Ships (7/01, $19.95, TPB) r/#1-9						20.00
Sacrifice (9/04, $19.95, TPB) r/#10-19						20.00

AGE OF HEROES, THE
Halloween Comics/Image Comics #3 on: 1996 - No. 5, 1999 ($2.95, B&W)

1-5: James Hudnall scripts; John Ridgway-c/a						3.00
...Special ($4.95) r/#1,2						5.00
...Special 2 ($6.95) r/#3,4						7.00
...Wex 1 ('98, $2.95) Hudnall-s/Angel Fernandez-a						3.00

AGE OF INNOCENCE: THE REBIRTH OF IRON MAN
Marvel Comics: Feb, 1996 ($2.50, one-shot)

1-New origin of Tony Stark						3.00

AGE OF REPTILES
Dark Horse Comics: Nov, 1993 - No. 4, Feb, 1994 ($2.50, limited series)

1-4: Delgado-c/a;scripts in all						3.00

AGE OF REPTILES: THE HUNT
Dark Horse Comics: May, 1996 - No. 5, Sept, 1996 ($2.95, limited series)

1-5: Delgado-c/a;scripts in all; wraparound-c						3.00

AGGIE MACK
Four Star Comics Corp./Superior Comics Ltd.: Jan, 1948 - No. 8, Aug, 1949

	GD	VG	FN	VF	VF/NM	NM-
1-Feldstein-a, "Johnny Prep"	40	80	120	235	368	500
2,3-Kamen-c	20	40	60	117	184	250
4-Feldstein "Johnny Prep"; Kamen-c	27	54	81	156	246	335
5-8-Kamen-c/a	22	44	66	126	198	270

AGGIE MACK
Dell Publishing Co.: Apr - Jun, 1962

	GD	VG	FN	VF	VF/NM	NM-
Four Color #1335	4	8	12	26	41	55

AIR ACE (Formerly Bill Barnes No. 1-12)
Street & Smith Publications: V2#1, Jan, 1944 - V3#8(No. 20), Feb-Mar, 1947

	GD	VG	FN	VF	VF/NM	NM-
V2#1-Nazi concentration camp-c	41	82	123	256	416	575
V2#2-Classic-c	43	86	129	262	431	600
V2#3-12: 7-Powell-a	16	32	48	94	147	200
V3#1-6	14	28	42	80	115	150
V3#7-Powell bondage-c/a; all atomic issue	23	46	69	132	209	285
V3#8 (V5#8 on-c)-Powell-c/a	15	30	45	84	127	170

AIRBOY (Also see Airmaidens, Skywolf, Target: Airboy & Valkyrie)
Eclipse Comics: July, 1986 - No. 50, Oct, 1989 (#1-8, 50¢, 20 pgs., bi-weekly; #9-on, 36 pgs.; #34-on monthly)

1-4: 2-1st Marisa; Skywolf gets new costume. 3-The Heap begins						4.00
5-Valkyrie returns; Dave Stevens-c						6.00
6-49: 9-Begin $1.25-c; Skywolf begins. 11-Origin of G.A. Airboy & his plane Birdie. 28-Mr. Monster vs. The Heap. 33-Begin $1.75-c. 38-40-The Heap by Infantino. 41-r/1st app. Valkyrie from Air Fighters. 42-Begin $1.95-c. 46,47-part-r/Air Fighters. 48-Black Angel-r/A.F						3.00
50 ($4.95, 52 pgs.)-Kubert-c						5.00

NOTE: **Evans** c-21. **Gulacy** c-7, 20. **Spiegle** a-34, 35, 37. **Ken Steacy** painted c-17, 33.

AIRBOY COMICS (Air Fighters Comics No. 1-22)
Hillman Periodicals: V2#11, Dec, 1945 - V10#4, May, 1953 (No V3#3)

	GD	VG	FN	VF	VF/NM	NM-
V2#11	73	146	219	456	758	1060
12-Valkyrie-c/app.	51	102	153	311	516	720
V3#1,2(no #3)	40	80	120	240	383	525
4-The Heap app. in Skywolf	37	74	111	213	337	460
5,7,8,10,11	33	66	99	190	300	410
6-Valkyrie-c/app.	35	70	105	204	322	440

Air Fighters Comics V2 #6 © HILL

Akiko #16 © Mark Crilley

Alarming Tales #3 © HARV

	GD 2.0	VG 4.0	FN 6.0	VF 8.0	VF/NM 9.0	NM- 9.2
9-Origin The Heap	37	74	111	213	337	460
12-Skywolf & Airboy x-over; Valkyrie-c/app.	40	80	120	235	368	500
V4#1-Iron Lady app.	33	66	99	190	300	410
2,3,12: 2-Rackman begins	25	50	75	145	228	310
4-Simon & Kirby-c	29	58	87	167	264	360
5-9,11-All S&K-a	28	56	84	162	256	350
10-Valkyrie-c/app.	30	60	90	174	275	375
V5#1-4,6-11: 4-Infantino Heap. 10-Origin The Heap	19	38	57	112	176	235
5-Skull-c.	22	44	66	126	198	270
12-Krigstein-a(p)	20	40	60	115	180	245
V6#1-3,5-12: 6,8-Origin The Heap	18	36	54	103	162	220
4-Origin retold	22	44	66	126	198	270
V7#1-12: 7,8,10-Origin The Heap	18	36	54	103	162	220
V8#1-3,5-12	16	32	48	94	147	200
4-Krigstein-a	17	34	51	98	154	210
V9#1,3,4,6-12: 7-One pg. Frazetta ad	14	28	42	82	121	160
2-Valkyrie app.	15	30	45	85	130	175
5(#100)	15	30	45	85	130	175
V10#1-4	14	28	42	78	112	145

NOTE: *Barry* a-V2#3, 7. *Bolle* a-V4#12. *McWilliams* a-V3#7, 9. *Powell* a-V7#2, 3, V8#1, 6. *Starr* a-V5#1, 12. *Dick Wood* a-V4#12. Bondage-c V5#8.

AIRBOY MEETS THE PROWLER
Eclipse Comics: Nov, 1987 ($1.95, one-shot)

1-John Snyder, III-c/a						3.00

AIRBOY-MR. MONSTER SPECIAL
Eclipse Comics: Aug, 1987 ($1.75, one-shot)

1						3.00

AIRBOY VERSUS THE AIR MAIDENS
Eclipse Comics: July, 1988 ($1.95)

1						3.00

AIR FIGHTERS CLASSICS
Eclipse Comics: Nov, 1987 - No. 6, May, 1989 ($3.95, 68 pgs., B&W)

1-6: Reprints G.A. Air Fighters #2-7. 1-Origin Airboy						4.00

AIR FIGHTERS COMICS (Airboy Comics #23 (V2#11) on)
Hillman Periodicals: Nov, 1941; No. 2, Nov, 1942 - V2#10, Fall, 1945

	GD 2.0	VG 4.0	FN 6.0	VF 8.0	VF/NM 9.0	NM- 9.2
V1#1-(Produced by Funnies, Inc.); Black Commander only app.						
	276	552	828	1725	2863	4000
2(11/42)-(Produced by Quality artists & Biro for Hillman); Origin & 1st app. Airboy & Iron Ace; Black Angel (1st app.), Flying Dutchman & Skywolf (1st app.) begin; Fuje-a; Biro-c/a	412	824	1236	2678	4739	6800
3-Origin/1st app. The Heap; origin Skywolf; 2nd Airboy app./c	186	372	558	1163	1932	2700
4-Japan war-c	136	272	408	850	1413	1975
5-Japanese octopus War-c	116	232	348	725	1200	1675
6-Japanese soldiers as rats-c	152	304	456	950	1575	2200
7-Classic Nazi swastika-c	145	290	435	906	1503	2100
8-12: 8,10,11-War covers	83	166	249	519	860	1200
V2#1-Classic Nazi War-c	86	172	258	538	894	1250
2-Skywolf by Giunta; Flying Dutchman by Fuje; 1st meeting Valkyrie & Airboy (she worked for the Nazis in beginning); 1st app. Valkyrie (11/43); Valkyrie-c	114	228	342	713	1182	1650
3,4,6,8,9	62	124	186	388	644	900
5,7: 5-Flag-c; Fuje-a. 7-Valkyrie app.	66	132	198	413	687	960
10-Origin The Heap & Skywolf	71	142	213	444	735	1025

NOTE: *Fuje* a-V1#2, 5, 7, V2#2, 3, 5, 7-9. *Giunta* a-V2#2, 3, 7, 9.

AIRFIGHTERS MEET SGT. STRIKE SPECIAL, THE
Eclipse Comics: Jan, 1988 ($1.95, one-shot, stiff-c)

1-Airboy, Valkyrie, Skywolf app.						3.00

AIR FORCES (See American Air Forces)

AIRMAIDENS SPECIAL
Eclipse Comics: August, 1987 ($1.75, one-shot, Baxter paper)

1-Marisa becomes La Lupina (origin)						3.00

AIR RAIDERS
Marvel Comics (Star Comics)/Marvel #3 on: Nov, 1987- No. 5, Mar, 1988 ($1.00)

1,5: Kelley Jones-a in all						3.50
2-4: 2-Thunderhammer app.						2.50

AIRTIGHT GARAGE, THE (Also see Elsewhere Prince)
Marvel Comics (Epic Comics): July, 1993 - No. 4, Oct, 1993 ($2.50, lim. series, Baxter paper)

1-4: Moebius-c/a/scripts						4.00

AIR WAR STORIES
Dell Publishing Co.: Sept-Nov, 1964 - No. 8, Aug, 1966

	GD 2.0	VG 4.0	FN 6.0	VF 8.0	VF/NM 9.0	NM- 9.2
1-Painted-c; Glanzman-c/a begins	4	8	12	28	44	60
2-8: 2,3-Painted-c	3	6	9	18	27	35

A.K.A. GOLDFISH
Caliber Comics: 1994 - 1995 (B&W, $3.50/$3.95)

...:Ace; ...:Jack; ...:Queen; ...:Joker; ...:King -Brian Michael Bendis-s/a						4.00
TPB (1996, $17.95)						20.00
Goldfish: The Definitive Collection (Image, 2001, $19.95) r/series plus promo art and new prose story; intro. by Matt Wagner						20.00
10th Anniversary HC (Image, 2002, $49.95)						50.00

AKIKO
Sirius: Mar, 1996 - Present ($2.50/$2.95, B&W)

1-Crilley-c/a/scripts in all						5.00
2						4.00
3-39: 25-($2.95, 32 pgs.)-w/Asala back-up pages						3.00
40-49,51,52: 40-Begin $2.95-c						3.00
50-($3.50)						3.50
Flights of Fancy TPB (5/02, $12.95) r/various features, pin-ups and gags						13.00
TPB Volume 1,4 ('97, 2/00, $14.95) 1-r/#1-7. 4-r/#19-25						15.00
TPB Volume 2,3 ('98, '99, $11.95) 2-r/#8-13. 3- r/#14-18						12.00
TPB Volume 5 (12/01, $12.95) r/#26-31						13.00
TPB Volume 6,7 (6/03, 4/04, $14.95) 6-r/#32-38. 7-r/#40-47						15.00

AKIKO ON THE PLANET SMOO
Sirius: Dec, 1995 ($3.95, B&W)

V1#1-($3.95)-Crilley-c/a/scripts; gatefold-c						5.00
Ashcan ('95, mail offer)						3.00
Hardcover V1#1 (12/95, $19.95, B&W, 40 pgs.)						20.00
The Color Edition(2/00,$4.95)						5.00

AKIRA
Marvel Comics (Epic): Sept, 1988 - No. 38, Dec, 1995 ($3.50/$3.95/$6.95, deluxe, 68 pgs.)

	GD 2.0	VG 4.0	FN 6.0	VF 8.0	VF/NM 9.0	NM- 9.2
1-Manga by Katsuhiro Otomo	3	6	9	16	23	30
1,2-2nd printings (1989, $3.95)						5.00
2	2	4	6	9	12	15
3-5	2	4	6	8	10	12
6-16	1	2	3	5	7	9
17-33: 17-$3.95-c begins						6.00
34-37: 34-(1994)-$6.95-c begins. 35-37: 35-(1995). 37-Texeira back-up, Gibbons, Williams pin-ups	2	4	6	8	10	12
38-Moebius, Allred, Pratt, Toth, Romita, Van Fleet, O'Neill, Madureira pin-ups	2	4	6	8	11	14

ALADDIN & HIS WONDERFUL LAMP (See Dell Jr Treasury #2)

ALAN LADD (See The Adventures of...)

ALAN MOORE'S AWESOME UNIVERSE HANDBOOK (Also see Across the Universe:...)
Awesome Entertainment: Apr, 1999 ($2.95, B&W)

1-Alan Moore-text/ Alex Ross-sketch pages and 2 covers						5.00

ALAN MOORE...
DC Comics (WildStorm): TPB

...'s Complete WildC.A.T.S. (2007, $29.99) r/#21-34,50; ...Homecoming & ...Gang War						30.00
...: Wild Worlds (2007, $24.99) r/various WildStorm one-shots and limited series						25.00

ALARMING ADVENTURES
Harvey Publications: Oct, 1962 - No. 3, Feb, 1963

	GD 2.0	VG 4.0	FN 6.0	VF 8.0	VF/NM 9.0	NM- 9.2
1-Crandall/Williamson-a	8	16	24	54	90	125
2-Williamson/Crandall-a	5	10	15	35	55	75
3	5	10	15	30	48	65

NOTE: *Bailey* a-1. *Crandall* a-1p, 2i. *Powell* a-2(2). *Severin* c-1-3. *Torres* a-2? *Tuska* a-1. *Williamson* a-1i, 2p.

ALARMING TALES
Harvey Publications (Western Tales): Sept, 1957 - No. 6, Nov, 1958

	GD 2.0	VG 4.0	FN 6.0	VF 8.0	VF/NM 9.0	NM- 9.2
1-Kirby-c/a(4); Kamandi prototype story by Kirby	29	58	87	167	264	360
2-Kirby-a(4)	20	40	60	115	180	245
3,4-Kirby. 4-Powell, Wildey-a	15	30	45	86	133	180
5-Kirby/Williamson-a; Wildey-a; Severin-c	16	32	48	92	144	195
6-Williamson-a?; Severin-c	14	28	42	76	108	140

ALBEDO
Thoughts And Images: Apr, 1985 - No. 14, Spring, 1989 (B&W)
Antarctic Press: (Vol. 2) Jun, 1991 - No. 10 ($2.50)

Al Capp's Wolf Gal #1 © TOBY

Alias #20 © MAR

Alien Encounters #10 © ECL

	GD 2.0	VG 4.0	FN 6.0	VF 8.0	VF/NM 9.0	NM- 9.2
0-Yellow cover; 50 copies	14	28	42	99	175	250
0-White cover, 450 copies	7	14	21	47	76	105
0-Blue, 1st printing, 500 copies	6	12	18	41	66	90
0-Blue, 2nd printing, 1000 copies	4	8	12	22	34	45
0-3rd & 4th printing	2	4	6	11	16	20
1-Dark red - low print run	6	12	18	43	69	95
1-Bright red - low print run	5	10	15	30	48	65
2 -1st app. Usagi Yojimbo by Stan Sakai; 2000 copies - no 2nd printing	29	58	87	212	381	550
3	3	6	9	18	27	35
4-Usagi Yojimbo-c	3	6	9	20	30	40
5-14	1	2	3	5	6	8
(Vol. 2) 1-10, Color Special						4.00

ALBEDO ANTHROPOMORPHICS
Antarctic Press: (Vol. 3) Spring, 1994 - No. 4, Jan, 1996 ($2.95, color);
(Vol. 4) Dec, 1999 - No. 2, Jan, 1999 ($2.95/$2.99, B&W)

V3#1-4-Steve Gallacci-c/a. V4#1,2						3.00

ALBERTO (See The Crusaders)

ALBION (Inspired by 1960s IPC British comics characters)
DC Comics (WildStorm): Aug, 2005 - No. 6, Nov, 2006 ($2.99, limited series)

1-6-Alan Moore, Leah Moore & John Reppion-s/Shane Oakley-a; Dave Gibbons-c						3.00
TPB (2007, $19.99) r/series; intro by Neil Gaiman; reprints from 1960s British comics						20.00

ALBUM OF CRIME (See Fox Giants)

ALBUM OF LOVE (See Fox Giants)

AL CAPP'S DOGPATCH (Also see Mammy Yokum)
Toby Press: No. 71, June, 1949 - No. 4, Dec, 1949

71(#1)-Reprints from Tip Top #112-114	18	36	54	105	165	225
2-4: 4-Reprints from Li'l Abner #73	14	28	42	80	115	150

AL CAPP'S SHMOO (Also see Oxydol-Dreft & Washable Jones & Shmoo)
Toby Press: July, 1949 - No. 5, Apr, 1950 (None by Al Capp)

1-1st app. Super-Shmoo	34	68	102	195	308	420
2-5: 3-Sci-fi trip to moon. 4-X-Mas-c	23	46	69	130	205	280

AL CAPP'S WOLF GAL
Toby Press: 1951 - No. 2, 1952

1,2-Edited-r from Li'l Abner #63,64	27	54	81	158	249	340

ALEISTER ARCANE
IDW Publishing: Apr, 2004 - No. 3, June, 2004 ($3.99, limited series)

1-3-Steve Niles-s/Breehn Burns-a						4.00
TPB (10/04, $17.99) r/series; sketch pages						18.00

ALEXANDER THE GREAT (Movie)
Dell Publishing Co.: No. 688, May, 1956

Four Color 688-Buscema-a; photo-c	7	14	21	49	80	110

ALF (TV) (See Star Comics Digest)
Marvel Comics: Mar, 1988 - No. 50, Feb, 1992 ($1.00)

1-Photo-c						4.00
1-2nd printing						2.50
2-19: 6-Photo-c						2.50
20-22: 20-Conan parody. 21-Marx Brothers. 22-X-Men parody						3.00
23-30: 24-Rhonda-c/app. 29-3-D cover						2.50
31-43,46-49						3.00
44,45: 44-X-Men parody. 45-Wolverine, Punisher, Capt. America-c						4.00
50-($1.75, 52 pgs.)-Final issue; photo-c						4.00
Annual 1-3: 1-Rocky & Bullwinkle app. 2-Sienkiewicz-c. 3-TMNT parody						3.00
Comics Digest 1,2: 1-(1988)-Reprints Alf #1,2	1	3	4	6	8	10
Holiday Special 1,2 ('88, Wint. '89, 68 pgs.): 2-X-Men parody-c						3.00
Spring Special 1 (Spr/89, $1.75, 68 pgs.) Invisible Man parody						3.00
TPB (68 pgs.) r/#1-3; photo-c						5.00

ALFRED HARVEY'S BLACK CAT
Lorne-Harvey Productions: 1995 ($3.50, B&W/color)

1-Origin by Mark Evanier & Murphy Anderson; contains history of Alfred Harvey & Harvey Publications; 5 pg. B&W Sad Sack story; Hildebrandts-c						5.00

ALGIE (LITTLE...)
Timor Publ. Co.: Dec, 1953 - No. 3, 1954

1-Teenage	8	16	24	40	50	60
1-Misprint exists w/Secret Mysteries #19 inside	9	18	27	50	65	80

	GD 2.0	VG 4.0	FN 6.0	VF 8.0	VF/NM 9.0	NM- 9.2
2,3	5	10	15	24	30	35
Accepted Reprint #2(nd)	3	6	8	12	14	16
Super Reprint #15	2	4	6	8	11	14

ALIAS:
Now Comics: July, 1990 - No. 5, Nov, 1990 ($1.75)

1-5: 1-Sienkiewicz-c						2.50

ALIAS (Also see The Pulse)
Marvel Comics (MAX Comics): Nov, 2001 - No. 28, Jan, 2004 ($2.99)

1-Bendis-s/Gaydos-a/Mack-c; intro Jessica Jones; Luke Cage app.	1	2	3	5	6	8
2-4						5.00
5-28: 7,8-Sienkiewicz-a (2 pgs.) 16-21-Spider-Woman app. 22,23-Jessica's origin. 24-28-Purple; Avengers app.; flashback-a by Bagley						3.00
HC (2002, $29.99) r/#1-9; intro. by Jeph Loeb						30.00
Omnibus (2006, $69.99, hardcover with dustjacket) r/#1-28 and What If Jessica Jones Had Joined the Avengers?; original pitch, script and sketch pages						70.00
Vol. 1: TPB (2003, $19.99) r/#1-9						20.00
Vol. 2: Come Home TPB (2003, $13.99) r/#11-15						14.00
Vol. 3: The Underneath TPB (2003, $16.99) r/#10,16-21						17.00

ALICE (New Adventures in Wonderland)
Ziff-Davis Publ. Co.: No. 10, 7-8/51 - No. 11(#2), 11-12/51

10-Painted-c; Berg-a	26	52	78	150	235	320
11-(#2 on inside) Dave Berg-a	15	30	45	86	133	180

ALICE AT MONKEY ISLAND (See The Adventures of Alice)
Pentagon Publ. Co. (Civil Service): No. 3, 1946

3	10	20	30	54	72	90

ALICE IN WONDERLAND (Disney; see Advs. of Alice, Dell Jr. Treasury #1, The Dreamery, Movie Comics, Walt Disney Showcase #22, and World's Greatest Stories)
Dell Publishing Co.: No. 24, 1940; No. 331, 1951; No. 341, July, 1951

Single Series 24 (#1)(1940)	47	94	141	287	474	660
Four Color 331, 341-"Unbirthday Party w/..."	15	30	45	105	188	270
1-(Whitman, 3/84, pre-pack only) r/4-Color #331	2	4	6	10	14	18

ALIEN ENCOUNTERS (Replaces Alien Worlds)
Eclipse Comics: June, 1985 - No. 14, Aug, 1987 ($1.75, Baxter paper, mature)

1-10: Nudity, strong language in all. 9-Snyder-a						4.00
11-14-Low print run						5.00

ALIEN LEGION (See Epic & Marvel Graphic Novel #25)
Marvel Comics (Epic Comics): Apr, 1984 - No. 20, Sept, 1987

nn-With bound-in trading card; Austin-i						4.00
2-20: 2-$1.50-c. 7,8-Portacio-i						3.00

ALIEN LEGION (2nd Series)
Marvel Comics (Epic): Aug, 1987(indicia)(10/87 on-c) - No. 18, Aug, 1990

V2#1-18-Stroman-a in all. 7-18-Farmer-i						2.50
...: Force Nomad TPB (Checker Book Pub. Group, 2001, $24.95) r/#1-11						25.00
...: Piecemaker TPB (Checker Book Pub. Group, 2002, $19.95) r/#12-18						20.00

ALIEN LEGION: (Series of titles; all Marvel/Epic Comics)
--BINARY DEEP, 1993 ($3.50, one-shot, 52 pgs.), nn-With bound-in trading card

						3.50

--JUGGER GRIMROD, 8/92 ($5.95, one-shot, 52 pgs.) Book 1

						6.00

--ONE PLANET AT A TIME, 5/93 - Book 3, 7/93 ($4.95, squarebound, 52 pgs.)

Book 1-3: Hoang Nguyen-a						5.00

--ON THE EDGE (The... #2 & 3), 11/90 - No. 3, 1/91 ($4.50, 52 pgs.)

1-3-Stroman & Farmer-a						4.50

--TENANTS OF HELL, '91 - No. 2, '1 ($4.50, squarebound, 52 pgs.)

Book 1,2-Stroman-c/a(p)						4.50

ALIEN NATION (Movie)
DC Comics: Dec, 1988 ($2.50; 68 pgs.)

1-Adaptation of film; painted-c						4.00

ALIEN PIG FARM 3000
Image Comics (RAW Studios): Apr, 2007 - No. 4, July, 2007 ($2.99, limited series)

1-4-Steve Niles, Thomas Jane & Todd Farmer-s/Don Marquez-a						3.00

ALIEN RESURRECTION (Movie)
Dark Horse Comics: Oct, 1997 - No. 2, Nov, 1997 ($2.50; limited series)

1,2-Adaptation of film; Dave McKean-c						3.00

ALIENS, THE (Captain Johner and...)(Also see Magnus Robot Fighter...)
Gold Key: Sept-Dec, 1967; No. 2, May, 1982

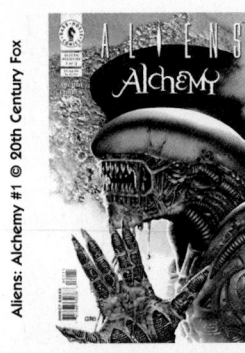

Aliens: Alchemy #1 © 20th Century Fox

Aliens: Hive #3 © 20th Century Fox

JERRY PROSSER • KELLEY JONES

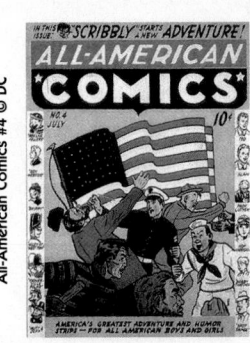

All-American Comics #4 © DC

	GD 2.0	VG 4.0	FN 6.0	VF 8.0	VF/NM 9.0	NM- 9.2

1-Reprints from Magnus #1,3,4,6-10; Russ Manning-a in all — 3 | 6 | 9 | 20 | 30 | 40
2-(Whitman) Same contents as #1 — 1 | 2 | 3 | 5 | 6 | 8

ALIENS (Movie) (See Alien: The Illustrated…, Dark Horse Comics & Dark Horse Presents #24)
Dark Horse Comics: May, 1988 - No. 6, July, 1989 ($1.95, B&W, limited series)

1-Based on movie sequel;1st app. Aliens in comics — 3 | 6 | 9 | 14 | 19 | 24
1-2nd - 6th printings; 4th w/new inside front-c — 3.00
2 — 1 | 3 | 4 | 6 | 8 | 10
2-2nd & 3rd printing, 3-6-2nd printings — 3.00
3 — 1 | 2 | 3 | 5 | 6 | 8
4-6 — 5.00
Mini Comic #1 (2/89, 4x6")-Was included with Aliens Portfolio — 4.00
Collection 1 ($10.95)-r/#1-6 plus Dark Horse Presents #24 plus new-a — 12.00
Collection 1-2nd printing (1991, $11.95)-On higher quality paper than 1st print; Dorman painted-c — 12.00
Hardcover ('90, $24.95, B&W)-r/1-6, DHP #24 — 30.00
... Omnibus Vol. 1 (7/07, $24.95, 9x6") r/1st & 2nd series and Aliens: Earth War — 25.00
... Outbreak (3rd printing, 8/96, $17.95)-Bolton-c — 18.00
Platinum Edition - (See Dark Horse Presents: Aliens Platinum Edition)

ALIENS
Dark Horse Comics: V2#1, Aug, 1989 - No. 4, 1990 ($2.25, limited series)
V2#1-Painted art by Denis Beauvais — 5.00
   1-2nd printing (1990), 2-4 — 3.00
...: Nightmare Asylum TPB (12/96, $16.95) r/series; Bolton-c — 17.00

ALIENS: (Series of titles, all Dark Horse)
--ALCHEMY, 10/97 - No. 3, 11/97 ($2.95),1-3-Corben-c/a, Arcudi-s — 3.00
--APOCALYPSE - THE DESTROYING ANGELS, 1/99 - No. 4, 4/99 ($2.95)
   1-4-Doug Wheatly-a/Schultz-s — 3.00
--BERSERKERS, 1/95 - No. 4, 4/95 ($2.50) 1-4 — 3.00
--COLONIAL MARINES, 1/93 - No. 10, 7/94 ($2.50) 1-10 — 3.00
--EARTH ANGEL. 8/94 ($2.95) 1-Byrne-a/story; wraparound-c — 3.00
--EARTH WAR, 6/90 - No. 4, 10/90 ($2.50) 1-All have Sam Kieth-a & Bolton painted-c — 5.00
   1-2nd printing, 3,4 — 3.00
   2 — 4.00
--GENOCIDE, 11/91 - No. 4, 2/92 ($2.50) 1-4-Suydam painted-c. 4-Wraparound-c, poster — 3.00
--GLASS CORRIDOR, 6/98 ($2.95) 1-David Lloyd-s/a — 3.00
--HARVEST (See Aliens: Hive)
--HAVOC, 6/97 - No. 2, 7/97 ($2.95) 1,2: Schultz-s, Kent Williams-c, 40 artists including Art Adams, Kelley Jones, Duncan Fegredo, Kevin Nowlan — 3.00
--HIVE, 2/92 - No. 4,5/92 ($2.50) 1-4: Kelley Jones-c/a in all — 3.00
...Harvest TPB ('98, $16.95) r/series; Bolton-c — 17.00
--KIDNAPPED, 12/97 - No. 3, 2/98 ($2.50) 1-3 — 3.00
--LABYRINTH, 9/93 - No. 4, 1/94 ($2.50)1-4: 1-Painted-c — 3.00
--LOVESICK, 12/96 ($2.95) 1 — 3.00
--MONDO HEAT, 2/96 ($2.50) nn-Sequel to Mondo Pest — 3.00
--MONDO PEST, 4/95 ($2.95, 44 pgs.)nn-r/Dark Horse Comics #22-24 — 3.00
--MUSIC OF THE SPEARS, 1/94 - No. 4, 4/94 ($2.50) 1-4 — 3.00
--NEWT'S TALE, 6/92 - No. 2, 7/92 ($4.95) 1,2-Bolton-c — 5.00
--PIG, 3/97 ($2.95)1 — 3.00
--PREDATOR: THE DEADLIEST OF THE SPECIES, 7/93 - No. 12,8/95 ($2.50)
   1-Bolton painted-c; Guice-a(p) — 5.00
   1-Embossed foil platinum edition — 10.00
   2-12: Bolton painted-c. 2,3-Guice-a(p) — 3.00
--PURGE, 8/97 ($2.95) nn-Hester-a — 3.00
--ROGUE, 4/993 - No. 4, 7/93 ($2.50)1-4: Painted-c — 3.00
--SACRIFICE, 5/93 ($4.95, 52 pgs.) nn-P. Milligan scripts; painted-c/a — 5.00
--SALVATION, 11/93 ($4.95, 52 pgs.) nn-Mignola-c/a(p); Gibbons script — 5.00
--SPECIAL, 6/97 ($2.50) 1 — 3.00
--STALKER, 6/98 ($2.50)1-David Wenzel-s/a — 3.00
--STRONGHOLD, 5/94 - No. 4, 9/94 ($2.50) 1-4 — 3.00
--SURVIVAL, 2/98 - No. 3, 4/98 ($2.95) 1-3-Tony Harris-c — 3.00
--TRIBES, 1992 ($24.95, hardcover graphic novel) Bissette text-s with Dorman painted-a — 25.00
   ...softcover ($9.95) — 10.00

ALIENS VS. PREDATOR (See Dark Horse Presents #36)
Dark Horse Comics: June, 1990 - No. 4, Dec, 1990 ($2.50, limited series)
1-Painted-c — 1 | 2 | 3 | 5 | 6 | 8
1-2nd printing — 3.00
0-(7/90, $1.95, B&W)-r/Dark Horse Pres. #34-36 — 1 | 2 | 3 | 5 | 7 | 9
2,3 — 5.00
4-Dave Dorman painted-c — 4.00
Annual (7/99, $4.95) Jae Lee-c — 5.00
... : Booty (1/96, $2.50) painted-c — 3.00
... Omnibus Vol. 1 (5/07, $24.95, 9x6") r/#1-4 & Annual; ...: War; ...: Eternal — 25.00
... Thrill of the Hunt (9/04, $6.95, digest-size TPB) Based on 2004 movie — 7.00
... Wraith 1 (7/98, $2.95) Jay Stephens-s — 3.00
--VS. PREDATOR: DUEL, 3/95 - No. 2, 4/95 ($2.50) 1,2 — 3.00
--VS. PREDATOR: ETERNAL, 6/98 - No. 4, 9/98 ($2.50)1-4: Edginton-s/Maleev-a; Fabry-c — 3.00
--VS. PREDATOR VS. THE TERMINATOR, 4/00 - No. 4, 7/00 ($2.95) 1-4: Ripley app. — 3.00
--VS. PREDATOR: WAR, No. 0, 5/95 - No. 4, 8/95 ($2.50) 0-4: Corben painted-c — 3.00
--VS. PREDATOR: XENOGENESIS, 12/99 - No. 4, 3/00 ($2.95) 1-4: Watson-s/Mel Rubi-a — 3.00
--XENOGENESIS, 8/99 - No. 4, 11/99 ($2.95) 1-4: T&M Bierbaum-s — 3.00

ALIEN TERROR (See 3-D Alien Terror)

ALIEN: THE ILLUSTRATED STORY (Also see Aliens)
Heavy Metal Books: 1980 ($3.95, soft-c, 8x11")
nn-Movie adaptation; Simonson-a — 3 | 6 | 9 | 14 | 19 | 24

ALIEN 3 (Movie)
Dark Horse Comics: June, 1992 - No. 3, July, 1992 ($2.50, limited series)
1-3: Adapts 3rd movie; Suydam painted-c — 3.00

ALIEN WORLDS (Also see Eclipse Graphic Album #22)
Pacific Comics/Eclipse: Dec, 1982 - No. 9, Jan, 1985
1,2,4: 2,4-Dave Stevens-c/a — 6.00
3,5-7 — 4.00
8,9 — 1 | 2 | 3 | 4 | 5 | 7
3-D No. 1-Art Adams 1st published art — 1 | 2 | 3 | 4 | 5 | 7

ALISON DARE, LITTLE MISS ADVENTURES (Also see Return of ...)
Oni Press: Sept, 2000 ($4.50, B&W, one-shot)
1-J. Torres-s/J.Bone-c/a — 4.50

ALISON DARE & THE HEART OF THE MAIDEN
Oni Press: Jan, 2002 - No. 2, Feb, 2002 ($2.95, B&W, limited series)
1,2-J. Torres-s/J.Bone-c/a — 3.00

ALISTER THE SLAYER
Midnight Press: Oct, 1995 ($2.50)
1-Boris-c — 2.50

ALL-AMERICAN COMICS (…Western #103-126, …Men of War #127 on; also see The Big All-American Comic Book)
All-American/National Periodical Publ.: April, 1939 - No. 102, Oct, 1948
1-Hop Harrigan (1st app.), Scribbly by Mayer (1st DC app.), Toonerville Folks, Ben Webster, Spot Savage, Mutt & Jeff, Red White & Blue (1st app.), Adventures in the Unknown, Tippie, Reg'lar Fellers, Skippy, Bobby Thatcher, Mystery Men of Mars, Daiseybelle, Wiley of West Point begin — 704 | 1408 | 2112 | 4224 | 6162 | 8100
2-Ripley's Believe It or Not begins, ends #24 — 204 | 408 | 612 | 1224 | 1787 | 2350
3-5: The American Way begins, ends #10 — 154 | 308 | 462 | 924 | 1350 | 1775
6,7-6: Last Spot Savage; Popsicle Pete begins, ends #26. 7-Last Bobby Thatcher — 115 | 230 | 345 | 719 | 1110 | 1500
8-The Ultra Man begins & 1st-c app. — 255 | 510 | 765 | 1594 | 2647 | 3700
9,10: 10-X-Mas-c — 95 | 190 | 285 | 594 | 985 | 1375
11,15: 11-Ultra Man-c. 15-Last Tippie & Reg'lar Fellars; Ultra Man-c — 110 | 220 | 330 | 688 | 1144 | 1600
12-14: 12-Last Toonerville Folks — 88 | 176 | 264 | 550 | 913 | 1275
16-(Rare)-Origin/1st app. Green Lantern by Sheldon Moldoff (c/a)(7/40) & begin series; appears in costume on-c & only one panel inside; created by Martin Nodell. Inspired in 1940 by a switchman's green lantern that would give trains the go ahead to proceed — 10,625 | 21,250 | 31,875 | 85,000 | 165,000 | 245,000
17-2nd Green Lantern — 1420 | 2840 | 4260 | 10,650 | 18,825 | 26,000
18-N.Y. World's Fair-c/story (scarce) — 1000 | 2000 | 3000 | 7400 | 12,950 | 18,500
19-Origin/1st app. The Atom (10/40); last Ultra Man — 1650 | 3300 | 4950 | 12,400 | 21,700 | 31,000
20-Atom dons costume; Ma Hunkle becomes Red Tornado, 11/40; 1st DC costumed heroine, forerunner for Wonder Woman, 11/40); Rescue on Mars begins, ends #25;
   1 pg. origin Green Lantern — 486 | 972 | 1458 | 3491 | 5950 | 8500

All-American Comics #21 © DC

All-American Men of War #2 © DC

All-American Western #103 © DC

	GD	VG	FN	VF	VF/NM	NM-		GD	VG	FN	VF	VF/NM	NM-
	2.0	4.0	6.0	8.0	9.0	9.2		2.0	4.0	6.0	8.0	9.0	9.2

	GD 2.0	VG 4.0	FN 6.0	VF 8.0	VF/NM 9.0	NM- 9.2
21-Last Wiley of West Point & Skippy; classic Moldoff-c	327	654	981	2126	3763	5400
22,23: 23-Last Daiseybelle; 3 idiots begin, end #82	317	634	951	1981	3291	4600
24-Sisty & Dinky become the Cyclone Kids; Ben Webster ends; origin Dr. Mid-Nite & Sargon, The Sorcerer in text with app.	315	630	945	2048	3624	5200
25-Origin & 1st story app. Dr. Mid-Nite by Stan Asch; Hop Harrigan becomes Guardian Angel; last Adventure in the Unknown (scarce)	971	1942	2913	6800	11,900	17,000
26-Origin/1st story app. Sargon, the Sorcerer	364	728	1092	2366	4183	6000
27: #27-32 are misnumbered in indicia with correct No. appearing on-c. Intro. Doiby Dickles, Green Lantern's sidekick	382	764	1146	2483	4392	6300
28-Hop Harrigan gives up costumed i.d.	190	380	570	1188	1969	2756
29,30	190	380	570	1188	1969	2756
31-40: 35-Doiby learns Green Lantern's i.d.	136	272	408	850	1413	1975
41-50: 50-Sargon ends	112	224	336	700	1163	1625
51-60: 59-Scribbly & the Red Tornado ends	97	194	291	606	1003	1400
61-Origin/1st app. Solomon Grundy (11/44)	571	1142	1713	4000	7000	10,000
62-70: 70-Kubert Sargon; intro Sargon's helper, Maximillian O'Leary	86	172	258	538	894	1250
71-88: 71-Last Red White & Blue. 72-Black Pirate begins (not in #74-82); last Atom. 73-Winky, Blinky & Noddy begins, ends #82. 79,83-Mutt & Jeff-c.	68	134	204	425	705	985
89-Origin & 1st app. Harlequin	116	232	348	725	1200	1675
90-99: 90-Origin/1st app. Icicle. 99-Last Hop Harrigan	112	224	336	700	1163	1625
100-1st app. Johnny Thunder by Alex Toth (8/48); western theme begins (Scarce)	197	394	591	1231	2041	2850
101-Last Mutt & Jeff (Scarce)	133	266	399	831	1378	1925
102-Last Green Lantern, Black Pirate & Dr. Mid-Nite (Scarce)	252	504	756	1575	2613	3650

NOTE: No Atom in 47, 62-69. Kinstler Black Pirate-89. Stan Aschmeier a (Dr. Mid-Nite) 25-84; c-7. Mayer c-1, 2(part), 6, 10. Moldoff c-16-23. Nodell c-31. Paul Reinman a (Green Lantern)-53-55p, 56-84, 87; (Black Pirate)-83-88, 90; c-52, 55-76, 78, 80, 81, 87. Toth a-88, 92, 96, 98-102; c(p)-92, 96-102. Scribbly by Mayer in #1-59. Ultra Man by Mayer in #8-19.

ALL AMERICAN COMICS
DC Comics: April 1939

nn - Ashcan comic, not distributed to newsstands, only for in house use. Cover art is Adventure Comics #33 and interior from Detective Comics #23   (no known sales)

ALL-AMERICAN COMICS (Also see All Star Comics 1999 crossover titles)
DC Comics: May, 1999 ($1.99, one-shot)

	GD 2.0	VG 4.0	FN 6.0	VF 8.0	VF/NM 9.0	NM- 9.2
1-Golden Age Green Lantern and Johnny Thunder; Barreto-a						2.50

ALL-AMERICAN MEN OF WAR (Previously All-American Western)
National Periodical Publ.: No. 127, Aug-Sept, 1952 - No. 117, Sept-Oct, 1966

	GD 2.0	VG 4.0	FN 6.0	VF 8.0	VF/NM 9.0	NM- 9.2
127 (#1, 1952)	87	174	261	740	1370	2000
128 (1952)	50	100	150	400	725	1050
2(12-1/52-53)-5	42	84	126	336	611	885
6-Devil Dog story; Ghost Squadron story	32	64	96	240	445	650
7-10: 8-Sgt. Storm Cloud-s	32	64	96	240	445	650
11-16,18: 18-Last precode; 1st Kubert-c (2/55)	29	58	87	216	388	560
17-1st Frogman-s in this title	31	62	93	222	404	585
19,20,22-27	21	42	63	156	278	400
21-Easy Co. prototype	25	50	75	184	330	475
28 (12/55)-1st Sgt. Rock prototype; Kubert-a	34	68	102	255	465	675
29,30,32-Wood-a	22	44	66	162	289	415
31,33-38,40: 34-Gunner prototype-s. 35-Greytone-c. 36-Little Sure Shot prototype-s.						
38-1st S.A. issue	18	36	54	132	234	335
39 (11/56)-2nd Sgt. Rock prototype; 1st Easy Co.?	29	58	87	212	381	550
41,43-47,49,50: 46-Tankbusters-c/s	15	30	45	107	191	275
42-Pre-Sgt. Rock Easy Co.-c/s	19	38	57	138	244	350
48-Easy Co.-c/s; Nick app.; Kubert-a	19	38	57	138	244	350
51-56,58-62,65,66: 61-Gunner-c/s	12	24	36	82	146	210
57(5/58),63,64 -Pre-Sgt. Rock Easy Co.-c/s	16	32	48	118	209	300
67-1st Gunner & Sarge by Andru & Esposito	32	64	96	240	445	650
68,69: 68-2nd app. Gunner & Sarge. 69-1st Tank Killer-c/s	14	28	42	102	181	260
70	11	22	33	79	140	200
71-80: 71,72,76-Tank Killer-c/s. 74-Minute Commandos-c/s	9	18	27	65	113	160
81,84-88: 88-Last 10¢ issue	8	16	24	54	90	125
82-Johnny Cloud begins(1st app.), ends #117	14	28	42	99	175	250
83-2nd Johnny Cloud						
89-100: 89-Battle Aces of 3 Wars begins, ends #98	6	12	18	39	62	85
101-111,113-116: 111,114,115-Johnny Cloud	5	10	15	30	48	65

	GD 2.0	VG 4.0	FN 6.0	VF 8.0	VF/NM 9.0	NM- 9.2
112-Balloon Buster series begins, ends #114,116	5	10	15	32	51	70
117-Johnny Cloud-c & 3-part story	5	10	15	32	51	70

NOTE: Frogman stories in 17, 38, 44, 45, 50, 51, 53, 55-58, 63, 65, 66, 72, 76, 77. Colan a-112. Drucker a-47, 58, 61, 63, 65, 69, 71, 74, 77. Grandenetti c(p)-127, 128, 2-17(most). Heath a-14, 27, 32, 38, 41, 45, 47, 50, 51, 55-58, 62, 64, 71, 75, 76, 78, 95, 111-117; c-85, 91, 94-96, 100, 101, 110-112, others? Infantino a-8. Kirby a-29. Krigstein a-128('52), 2, 3, 5. Kubert a-22, 24, 28, 29, 33, 34, 36, 38, 39, 41-43, 47-50, 52, 53, 55, 56, 59, 60, 63-65, 69, 71-73, 76, 102, 103, 105, 106, 108, 114; c-41, 44, 52, 54, 55, 58, 64, 69, 76, 77, 79, 102-106, 108, 113-117, others? Tank Killer in 69, 71, 76 by Kubert. P. Reinman c-55, 57, 61, 62, 71, 72, 74-76, 80. J. Severin a-58.

ALL AMERICAN MEN OF WAR
DC Comics: Aug/Sept. 1952

nn - Ashcan comic, not distributed to newsstands, only for in-house use. Cover art is All Star Western #58 and interior from Mr. District Attorney #21   (no known sales)

ALL-AMERICAN SPORTS
Charlton Comics: Oct, 1967

	GD 2.0	VG 4.0	FN 6.0	VF 8.0	VF/NM 9.0	NM- 9.2
1	3	6	9	19	29	38

ALL-AMERICAN WESTERN (Formerly All-American Comics; Becomes All-American Men of War)
National Periodical Publ.: No. 103, Nov, 1948 - No. 126, June-July, 1952

	GD 2.0	VG 4.0	FN 6.0	VF 8.0	VF/NM 9.0	NM- 9.2
103-Johnny Thunder & his horse Black Lightning continues by Toth, ends #126; Foley of The Fighting 5th, Minstrel Maverick, & Overland Coach begin; Captain Tootsie by Beck; mentioned in Love and Death	50	100	150	305	503	700
104-Kubert-a	37	74	111	213	337	460
105,107-Kubert-a	31	62	93	178	282	385
106,108-110,112: 112-Kurtzman's "Pot-Shot Pete" (1 pg.)	26	52	78	150	235	320
111,114-116-Kubert-a	27	54	81	156	246	335
113-Intro. Swift Deer, J. Thunder's new sidekick (4-5/50); classic Toth-c; Kubert-a	28	56	84	164	260	355
117-126: 121-Kubert-a; bondage-c	18	36	54	107	169	230

NOTE: G. Kane c(p)-112, 119, 120, 123. Kubert a-103-105, 107, 111, 112(1 pg.), 113-116, 121. Toth a-103-125; c(p)-103-111,113-116, 121, 122, 124-126. Some copies of #125 have #12 on-c.

ALL COMICS
Chicago Nite Life News: 1945

	GD 2.0	VG 4.0	FN 6.0	VF 8.0	VF/NM 9.0	NM- 9.2
1	15	30	45	83	124	165

ALLEGRA
Image Comics (WildStorm): Aug, 1996 - No. 4, Dec, 1996 ($2.50)

	GD 2.0	VG 4.0	FN 6.0	VF 8.0	VF/NM 9.0	NM- 9.2
1-4						2.50

ALLEY CAT (Alley Baggett)
Image Comics: July, 1999 - No. 6, Mar, 2000 ($2.50/$2.95)

	GD 2.0	VG 4.0	FN 6.0	VF 8.0	VF/NM 9.0	NM- 9.2
Preview Edition						6.00
Prelude						5.00
Prelude w/variant-c						6.00
1-Photo-c						2.50
1-Painted-c by Dorian						3.50
1-Another Universe Edition, 1-Wizard World Edition						7.00
2-4: 4-Twin towers on-c						2.50
5,6-($2.95)						3.00
Lingerie Edition (10/99, $4.95) Photos, pin-ups, cover gallery						5.00
...Vs. Lady Pendragon ('99, $3.00) Stinsman-c						3.00

ALLEY OOP (See The Comics, The Funnies, Red Ryder and Super Book #9)
Dell Publishing Co.: No. 3, 1942

	GD 2.0	VG 4.0	FN 6.0	VF 8.0	VF/NM 9.0	NM- 9.2
Four Color 3 (#1)	43	86	129	344	622	900

ALLEY OOP
Argo Publ.: Nov, 1955 - No. 3, Mar, 1956 (Newspaper reprints)

	GD 2.0	VG 4.0	FN 6.0	VF 8.0	VF/NM 9.0	NM- 9.2
1	16	32	48	92	144	195
2,3	12	24	36	67	94	120

ALLEY OOP
Dell Publishing Co.: 12-2/62-63 - No. 2, 9-11/63

	GD 2.0	VG 4.0	FN 6.0	VF 8.0	VF/NM 9.0	NM- 9.2
1	6	12	18	41	66	90
2	5	10	15	35	55	75

ALLEY OOP
Standard Comics: No. 10, Sept, 1947 - No. 18, Oct, 1949

	GD 2.0	VG 4.0	FN 6.0	VF 8.0	VF/NM 9.0	NM- 9.2
10	25	50	75	145	228	310
11-18: 17,18-Schomburg-c	20	40	60	115	180	245

ALLEY OOP ADVENTURES
Antarctic Press: Aug, 1998 - No. 3, Dec, 1998 ($2.95)

	GD 2.0	VG 4.0	FN 6.0	VF 8.0	VF/NM 9.0	NM- 9.2
1-3-Jack Bender-s/a						3.00

ALLEY OOP ADVENTURES (Alley Oop Quarterly in indicia)
Antarctic Press: Sept, 1999 - No. 3, Mar, 2000 ($2.50/$2.99, B&W)

All Flash #1 © DC

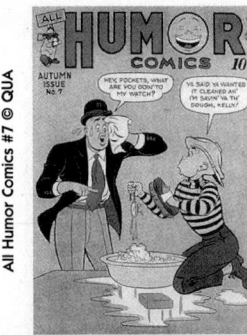

All Humor Comics #7 © QUA

All-New Comics #9 © HARV

	GD 2.0	VG 4.0	FN 6.0	VF 8.0	VF/NM 9.0	NM- 9.2

1-3-Jack Bender-s/a ... 3.00

ALL-FAMOUS CRIME (2nd series - Formerly Law Against Crime #1-3; becomes All-Famous Police Cases #6 on)
Star Publications: No. 8, 5/51 - No. 10, 11/51; No. 4, 2/52 - No. 5, 5/52;

8 (#1-1st series)	22	44	66	126	198	270
9 (#2)-Used in SOTI, illo- "The wish to hurt or kill couples in lovers' lanes is a not uncommon perversion;" L.B. Cole-c/a(r)/Law-Crime #3	36	72	108	208	329	450
10 (#3)	20	40	60	115	180	245
4 (#4-2nd series)-Formerly Law-Crime	18	36	54	107	169	230
5 (#5) Becomes All-Famous Police Cases #6	18	36	54	107	169	230

NOTE: All have L.B. Cole covers.

ALL FAMOUS CRIME STORIES (See Fox Giants)
ALL-FAMOUS POLICE CASES (Formerly All Famous Crime #5)
Star Publications: No. 6, Feb, 1952 - No. 16, Sept, 1954

6	19	38	57	112	176	240
7,8: 7-Baker story. 8-Marijuana story	18	36	54	105	165	225
9-16	16	32	48	94	147	200

NOTE: L. B. Cole c-all; a-15, 1pg. Hollingsworth a-15.

ALL-FLASH (...Quarterly No. 1-5)
National Per. Publ./All-American: Summer, 1941 - No. 32, Dec-Jan, 1947-48

1-Origin The Flash retold by E. E. Hibbard; Hibbard c-1-10,12-14,16,31/pg.	1417	2834	4251	10,628	18,314	26,500
2-Origin recap	352	704	1056	2288	4044	5800
3,4	176	352	528	1100	1825	2550
5-Winky, Blinky & Noddy begins (1st app.), ends #32	129	258	387	806	1341	1875
6-10	103	206	309	644	1072	1500
11-13: 12-Origin/1st The Thinker. 13-The King app.	89	178	267	556	921	1285
14-Green Lantern cameo	103	206	309	644	1072	1500
15-20: 18-Mutt & Jeff begins, ends #22	74	148	222	463	769	1075
21-31	64	128	192	400	663	925
32-Origin/1st app. The Fiddler; 1st Star Sapphire	116	252	348	725	1200	1675

NOTE: Book length stories in 2-13, 16. Bondage c-31, 32. Martin Nodell c-15, 17-28.

ALL FLASH (Leads into Flash [2nd series] #231)
DC Comics: Sept, 2007 ($2.99, one-shot)

1-Wally West hunts down Bart's killers; Waid-s; two covers by Middleton & Sienkiewicz ... 3.00

ALL FOR LOVE (Young Love V3#5-on)
Prize Publications: Apr-May, 1957 - V3#4, Dec-Jan, 1959-60

V1#1	7	14	21	49	80	110
2-6: 5-Orlando-c	4	8	12	28	44	60
V2#1-5 (1/59), 5(3/59)	4	8	12	22	34	45
V3#1(5/59), 1(7/59)-4: 2-Powell-a	3	6	9	18	27	35

ALL FUNNY COMICS
Tilsam Publ./National Periodical Publications (Detective): Winter, 1943-44 - No. 23, May-June, 1948

1-Genius Jones (1st app.), Buzzy (1st app., ends #4), Dover & Clover (see More Fun #93) begin; Bailey-a	47	94	141	287	474	660
2	23	46	69	132	209	285
3-10	15	30	45	83	124	165
11-13,15,18,19-Genius Jones app.	14	28	42	80	115	150
14,17,20-23	10	20	30	56	76	95
16-DC Super Heroes app.	32	64	96	186	293	400

ALL GOOD
St. John Publishing Co.: Oct, 1949 (50¢, 260 pgs.)

nn-(8 St. John comics bound together) ... 67 | 134 | 201 | 419 | 680 | 975
NOTE: Also see Li'l Audrey Yearbook & Treasury of Comics.

ALL GOOD COMICS (See Fox Giants)
Fox Features Syndicate: No.1, Spring, 1946 (36 pgs.)

1-Joy Family, Dick Transom, Rick Evans, One Round Hogan ... 27 | 54 | 81 | 156 | 246 | 335

ALL GREAT
William H. Wise & Co.: nd (1945?) (132 pgs.)

nn-Capt. Jack Terry, Joan Mason, Girl Reporter, Baron Doomsday; Torture scenes ... 41 | 82 | 123 | 252 | 406 | 560

ALL GREAT COMICS (See Fox Giants)
Fox Feature Syndicate: 1946 (36 pgs.)

1-Crazy House, Bertie Benson Boy Detective, Gussie the Gob ... 27 | 54 | 81 | 156 | 246 | 335

ALL GREAT COMICS (Formerly Phantom Lady #13? Dagar, Desert Hawk No. 14 on)
Fox Features Syndicate: No. 14, Oct, 1947 - No. 13, Dec, 1947 (Newspaper strip reprints)

14(#12)-Brenda Starr & Texas Slim-r (Scarce)	57	114	171	356	591	825
13-Origin Dagar, Desert Hawk; Brenda Starr (all-r); Kamen-c; Dagar covers begin	64	128	192	400	663	925

ALL-GREAT CONFESSIONS (See Fox Giants)
ALL GREAT CRIME STORIES (See Fox Giants)
ALL GREAT JUNGLE ADVENTURES (See Fox Giants)
ALL HALLOW'S EVE
Innovation Publishing: 1991 ($4.95, 52 pgs.)

1-Painted-c/a ... 1 | 2 | 3 | 4 | 5 | 7

ALL HERO COMICS
Fawcett Publications: Mar, 1943 (100 pgs.; cardboard-c)

1-Capt. Marvel Jr., Capt. Midnight, Golden Arrow, Ibis the Invincible, Spy Smasher, Lance O'Casey; 1st Banshee O'Brien; Raboy-c ... 172 | 344 | 516 | 1075 | 1788 | 2500

ALL HUMOR COMICS
Quality Comics Group: Spring, 1946 - No. 17, December, 1949

1	21	42	63	122	191	260
2-Atomic Tot story; Gustavson-a	13	26	39	72	101	130
3-9: 3-Intro Kelly Poole who is cover feature #3 on. 5-1st app. Hickory?						
8-Gustavson-a	8	16	24	44	57	70
10-17	8	16	24	40	50	60

ALLIANCE, THE
Image Comics (Shadowline Ink): Aug, 1995 - No. 3, Nov, 1995 ($2.50)

1-3: 2-(9/95) ... 2.50

ALL LOVE (...Romances No. 26)(Formerly Ernie Comics)
Ace Periodicals (Current Books): No. 26, May, 1949 - No. 32, May, 1950

26 (No. 1)-Ernie, Lily Belle app.	10	20	30	54	72	90
27-L.B. Cole-a	14	28	42	76	108	140
28-32	7	14	21	37	46	55

ALL-NEGRO COMICS
All-Negro Comics: June, 1947 (15¢)

1 (Rare) ... 1000 | 2000 | 3000 | 5500 | 7250 | 9000
NOTE: Seldom found in fine or mint condition; many copies have brown pages.

ALL-NEW ATOM, THE (See The Atom and DCU Brave New World)
DC Comics: Sept, 2006 - Present ($2.99)

1-15-Simone-s. 1-Intro Ryan Choi; Byrne-a thru #3. 4-11-Barrows-a. 12,13-Chronos app. 14,15-Countdown x-over						3.00
...: My Life in Miniature TPB (2007, $14.99) r/#1-6 and app. in DCU Brave New World #1						15.00

ALL-NEW COLLECTORS' EDITION (Formerly Limited Collectors' Edition: see for C-57, C-59)
DC Comics, Inc.: Jan, 1978 - Vol. 8, No. C-62, 1979 (No. 54-58: 76 pgs.)

C-53-Rudolph the Red-Nosed Reindeer	4	8	12	26	41	55
C-54-Superman Vs. Wonder Woman	4	8	12	23	36	48
C-55-Superboy & the Legion of Super-Heroes; Wedding of Lightning Lad & Saturn Girl; Grell-c/a	4	8	12	23	36	48
C-56-Superman Vs. Muhammad Ali: story & wraparound N. Adams-c/a	6	12	18	41	66	90
C-56-Superman Vs. Muhammad Ali (Whitman variant)-low print	7	14	21	47	76	105
C-57, C-59-(See Limited Collectors' Edition)						
C-58-Superman Vs. Shazam; Buckler-c/a	4	8	12	24	37	50
C-60-Rudolph's Summer Fun(8/78)	4	8	12	24	37	50
C-61-(See Famous First Edition-Superman #1)						
C-62-Superman the Movie (68 pgs.; 1979)-Photo-c from movie plus photos inside (also see DC Special Series #25)	3	6	9	14	20	25

ALL-NEW COMICS (...Short Story Comics No. 1-3)
Family Comics (Harvey Publications): Jan, 1943 - No. 14, Nov, 1946; No. 15, Mar-Apr, 1947 (10 x 13-1/2")

1-Steve Case, Crime Rover, Johnny Rebel, Kayo Kane, The Echo, Night Hawk, Ray O'Light, Detective Shane begin (all 1st app.?); Red Blazer on cover only; Sultan-a	300	600	900	1881	3141	4400
2-Origin Scarlet Phantom by Kubert	110	220	330	688	1144	1600
3-Nazi war-c	86	172	258	538	894	1250
4	71	142	213	444	735	1025
5-11: 5-Schomburg-a thru #11. 6-The Boy Heroes & Red Blazer (text story) begin, end #12; Black Cat app.; intro. Sparky in Red Blazer. 7-Kubert, Powell-a; Black Cat & Zebra begin. 8,9: 8-Shock Gibson app.; Kubert, Powell-a; Schomburg-c. 9-Black Cat app.; Kubert-a.						

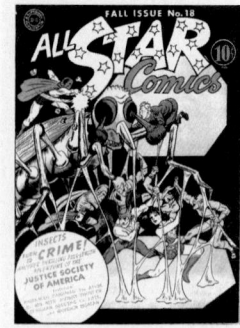

All-Select Comics #1 © MAR

All Star Batman & Robin, The Boy Wonder #6 © DC

All Star Comics #18 © DC

	GD	VG	FN	VF	VF/NM	NM-		GD	VG	FN	VF	VF/NM	NM-
	2.0	4.0	6.0	8.0	9.0	9.2		2.0	4.0	6.0	8.0	9.0	9.2

10-The Zebra app. (from Green Hornet Comics); Kubert-a(3). 11-Girl Commandos,
Man In Black app. 85 170 255 531 878 1225
12,13: 12-Kubert-a. 13-Stuntman by Simon & Kirby; Green Hornet, Joe Palooka, Flying Fool
app.; Green Hornet-c 59 118 177 369 615 860
14-The Green Hornet & The Man in Black Called Fate by Powell, Joe Flying Fool app.;
Flying Fool app.; J. Palooka-c by Ham Fisher 53 106 159 323 537 750
15-(Rare)-Small size (5-1/2x8-1/2"; B&W; 32 pgs.). Distributed to mail subscribers only.
Black Cat and Joe Palooka app. 110 220 330 688 1144 1600
NOTE: Also see Boy Explorers No. 2, Flash Gordon No. 5, and Stuntman No. 3. Powell a-11. Schomburg c-5-11. Captain Red Blazer & Spark on c-5-11 (w/Boy Heroes #12).

ALL-NEW OFFICIAL HANDBOOK OF THE MARVEL UNIVERSE A TO Z
Marvel Comics: 2006 - No. 12, 2006 ($3.99, limited series)
1-12-Profile pages of Marvel characters not covered in 2004-2005 Official Handbooks 4.00
...: Update 1-3 (2007, $3.99) Profile pages 4.00

ALL-OUT WAR
DC Comics: Sept-Oct, 1979 - No. 6, Aug, 1980 ($1.00, 68 pgs.)
1-The Viking Commando(origin), Force Three(origin), & Black Eagle Squadron begin
                                2 4 6 9 12 15
2-6 .... 1 2 3 5 7 9
NOTE: Ayers a(p)-1-6. Elias r-2. Evans a-1-6. Kubert c-16.

ALL PICTURE ADVENTURE MAGAZINE
St. John Publishing Co.: Oct., 1952 - No. 2, Nov, 1952 (100 pg. Giants, 25¢, squarebound)
1-War comics 32 64 96 186 293 400
2-Horror-crime comics 46 92 138 281 466 650
NOTE: Above books contain three St. John comics rebound; variations possible. Baker art known in both.

ALL PICTURE ALL TRUE LOVE STORY
St. John Publishing Co.: Oct., 1952 - No. 2, Nov, 1952 (100 pgs., 25¢)
1-Canteen Kate by Matt Baker .. 52 104 156 317 521 725
2-Baker-c/a 36 72 108 208 329 450

ALL-PICTURE COMEDY CARNIVAL
St. John Publishing Co.: October, 1952 (100 pgs., 25¢)(Contains 4 rebound comics)
1-Contents can vary; Baker-a .. 43 86 129 262 431 600

ALL REAL CONFESSION MAGAZINE (See Fox Giants)

ALL ROMANCES (Mr. Risk No. 7 on)
A. A. Wyn (Ace Periodicals): Aug, 1949 - No. 6, June, 1950
1 .... 11 22 33 64 90 115
2 .... 8 16 24 40 50 60
3-6 .... 7 14 21 35 43 50

ALL-SELECT COMICS (Blonde Phantom No. 12 on)
Timely Comics (Daring Comics): Fall, 1943 - No. 11, Fall, 1946
1-Capt. America (by Rico #1), Human Torch, Sub-Mariner begin; Black Widow
story (4 pgs.); Classic Schomburg-c 1266 2532 3800 9500 16,750 24,000
2-Red Skull app. 423 846 1269 2750 4875 7000
3-The Whizzer begins 290 580 870 1813 3007 4200
4,5-Sub-Mariner 214 428 642 1338 2219 3100
6-9: 6-The Destroyer app. 8-No Whizzer 172 344 516 1075 1788 2500
10-The Destroyer & Sub-Mariner app.; last Capt. America & Human Torch issue
                                172 344 516 1075 1788 2500
11-1st app. Blonde Phantom; Miss America app.; all Blonde Phantom-c by Shores
                                269 538 807 1681 2791 3900
NOTE: Schomburg c-1-10. Sekowsky a-7. #7 & 8 show 1944 in indicia, but should be 1945.

ALL SPORTS COMICS (Formerly Real Sports Comics; becomes All Time Sports Comics No. 4 on)
Hillman Periodicals: No. 2, Dec-Jan, 1948-49; No. 3, Feb-Mar, 1949
2-Krigstein-a(p), Powell, Starr-a 34 68 102 197 311 425
3-Mort Lawrence-a 23 46 69 130 205 280

ALL STAR BATMAN & ROBIN, THE BOY WONDER
DC Comics: Present (2005 - Present ($2.99)
1-Two covers; retelling of Robin's origin; Frank Miller-a/Jim Lee-a/c 3.00
1-Diamond Retailer Summit Edition (9/05) sketch-c 100.00
2-6-Two copies by Lee and Miller. 3-Black Canary app. 4-Six pg. Batcave gatefold 3.00
... Special Edition (2/06, $3.99) r/#1 with Lee pencil pages and Miller script; new Miller-c 4.00

ALL STAR COMICS
DC Comics: Spring 1940
1-Ashcan comic, not distributed to newsstands, only for in-house use. Cover art is Flash
Comics #1 and interior from Detective Comics #37. A CGC certified 7.0 copy sold for
$15,600 in 2002.

ALL STAR COMICS (All Star Western No. 58 on)

National Periodical Publ./All-American/DC Comics: Sum, '40 - No. 57, Feb-Mar, '51; No. 58,
Jan-Feb, '76 -No. 74, Sept-Oct, '78
1-The Flash (#1 by E.E. Hibbard), Hawkman (by Shelly), Hourman (by Bernard Baily),
The Sandman (by Creig Flessel), The Spectre (by Baily), Biff Bronson, Red White & Blue
(ends #2) begin; Ultra's only app. (#1-3 are quarterly; #4 begins bi-monthly issues)
                        1150 2300 3450 8600 15,300 22,000
2-Green Lantern (by Martin Nodell), Johnny Thunder begin; Green Lantern figure swipe from
the cover of All-American Comics #16; Flash figure swipe from cover of Flash Comics #8;
Moldoff/Baily-c (cut & paste-c.) 503 1006 1509 3521 6161 8800
3-Origin & 1st app. The Justice Society of America (Win/40); Dr. Fate & The Atom begin,
Red Tornado cameo 3950 7900 11,850 29,600 52,300 75,000
3-Reprint, Oversize 13-1/2x10". WARNING: This comic is an exact reprint of the original except for its
size. DC published it in 1974 with a second cover titling it as a Famous First Edition. There have been many
reported cases of the outer cover being removed and the interior sold as the original edition. The reprint with the
new outer cover removed is practically worthless. See Famous First Edition for value.
4-1st adventure for J.S.A. 529 1058 1587 3703 6477 9250
5-1st app. Shiera Sanders as Hawkgirl (1st costumed super-heroine, 6-7/41)
                                437 874 1311 3059 5355 7650
6-Johnny Thunder joins JSA ... 300 600 900 1894 3197 4500
7-Batman, Superman, Flash cameo; last Hourman; Doiby Dickles app.
                                327 654 981 2126 3763 5400
8-Origin & 1st app. Wonder Woman (12-1/41-42)(added as 9 pgs. making book 76 pgs.;
origin cont'd in Sensation #1; see W.W. #1 for more detailed info); Dr. Fate dons new
helmet; Hop Harrigan text stories & Starman begin; Shiera app.; Hop Harrigan JSA guest;
Starman & Dr. Mid-Nite become members 3150 6300 9450 23,600 41,800 60,000
9-11: 9-JSA's girlfriends cameo; Shiera app.; J. Edgar Hoover of FBI made associate member
of JSA. 10-Flash, Green Lantern cameo; Sandman new costume. 11-Wonder Woman
begins; Spectre cameo; Shiera app.; Moldoff Hawkman-c
                                300 600 900 1875 3113 4350
12-Wonder Woman becomes JSA Secretary 272 544 816 1700 2825 3950
13,15: Sandman w/Sandy in #14 & 15. 15-Origin & 1st app. Brain Wave; Shiera app.
                                248 496 744 1550 2575 3600
14-(12/42) Junior JSA Club begins; w/membership offer & premiums
                                255 510 765 1594 2647 3700
16-20: 19-Sandman w/Sandy. 20-Dr. Fate & Sandman cameo
                                193 386 579 1206 2003 2800
21-23: 21-Spectre & Atom cameo; Dr. Fate by Kubert; Dr. Fate, Sandman end.
22-Last Hop Harrigan; Flag-c. 23-Origin/1st app. Psycho Pirate; last Spectre
& Starman 162 324 486 1013 1682 2350
24-Flash & Green Lantern cameo; Mr. Terrific only app.; Wildcat, JSA guest; Kubert Hawkman
begins; Hitler-c 162 324 486 1013 1682 2350
25-27: 25-Flash & Green Lantern start again. 26-Robot-c. 27-Wildcat, JSA guest
(#24-26: only All-American imprint) 138 276 414 863 1432 2000
28-32 .... 121 242 363 756 1253 1750
33-Solomon Grundy & Doiby Dickles app.; classic Solomon Grundy cover & last G.A. app.
                                345 690 1035 2243 3972 5700
34,35-Johnny Thunder cameo in both 117 234 351 731 1216 1700
36-Batman & Superman JSA guests 276 552 828 1725 2863 4000
37-Johnny Thunder cameo; origin & 1st app. Injustice Society; last Kubert Hawkman
                                155 310 465 969 1610 2250
38-Black Canary begins; JSA Death issue 200 400 600 1250 2075 2900
39,40: 39-Last Johnny Thunder .. 114 228 342 713 1182 1650
41-Black Canary joins JSA; Injustice Society app. (2nd app.?)
                                114 228 342 713 1182 1650
42-Hawkman & the Hawkman don new costumes 114 228 342 713 1182 1650
43-49,51-56: 43-New logo; Robot-c. 55-Sci/Fi story. 56-Robot-c
                                114 228 342 713 1182 1650
50-Frazetta art, 3 pgs. 122 244 366 763 1269 1775
57-Kubert-a, 6 pgs. (Scarce); last app. G.A. Green Lantern, Flash & Dr. Mid-Nite
                                166 332 498 1038 1719 2400
V12 #58-(1976) JSA (Flash, Hawkman, Dr. Mid-Nite, Wildcat, Dr. Fate, Green Lantern, Robin
& Star Spangled Kid) app.; intro. Power Girl 5 10 15 32 51 70
V12 #59,60: 59-Estrada & Wood-a 3 6 9 15 21 26
V12 #61-68: 62-65-Superman app. 64,65-Wood-c/a; Vandal Savage app. 66-Injustice Society
app. 68-Psycho Pirate app. ... 3 6 9 15 21 26
V12 #69-1st app. Earth-2 Huntress (Helena Wayne) 4 8 12 22 34 45
V12 #70-73: 70-Full intro. of Huntress 3 6 9 15 21 26
V12 #74-(44 pgs.) Last issue, story continues in Adventure Comics #461 & 462 (death of
Earth-2 Batman; Staton-c/a ... 3 6 9 20 30 40
(See Justice Society Vol. 1 TPB for reprints of V12 revival)
NOTE: No Atom-27, 36; no Dr. Fate-13; no Flash-8, 9, 11-23; no Green Lantern-8, 9,11-23; Hawkman in 1-57 (only
one to app. in all 57 issues); no Johnny Thunder-5, 36; no Wonder Woman-9, 10, 23. Book length stories in 4-9, 11-
14, 18-22, 25, 26, 29, 30, 32-36, 40, 42, 43. Johnny Peril in #42-46, 48, 49, 51, 52,54-57. Baily a-1-10, 12, 13, 14i,
15-20. Burnley Starman-8-13; c-12, 13. Grell c-58. E.E. Hibbard c-3, 4, 6-10. Infantino c-40. Kubert Hawkman-24-
30, 33-37. Lampert/Baily/Flessel c-1, 2. Moldoff Hawkman-3-23; c-11. Mart Nodell c-25i, 26i, 27-32. Purcell c-5.

All-Star Squadron #18 © DC

All-Star Superman #2 © DC

All True Romance #3 © MAR

	GD 2.0	VG 4.0	FN 6.0	VF 8.0	VF/NM 9.0	NM- 9.2

Simon & Kirby *Sandman* 14-17, 19. **Staton** a-66-74p. c-74p. **Toth** a-37(2), 38(2), 40, 41; c-38, 41. **Wood** a-58i-63i, 64, 65; c-63i, 64, 65. Issues 1-7, 9-16 are 68 pgs.; #8 is 76 pgs.; #17-19 are 60 pgs.; #20-57 are 52 pgs.

ALL STAR COMICS (Also see crossover 1999 editions of Adventure, All-American, National, Sensation, Smash, Star Spangled and Thrilling Comics)
DC Comics: May, 1999 - No. 2, May, 1999 ($2.95, bookends for JSA x-over)

1,2-Justice Society in World War 2; Robinson-s/Johnson-c						3.00
1-RRP Edition (price will be based on future sales)						
...80-Page Giant (9/99, $4.95) Phantom Lady app.						5.00

ALL STAR INDEX, THE
Independent Comics Group (Eclipse): Feb, 1987 ($2.00, Baxter paper)

1		1	2	3	5	6	8

ALL-STAR SQUADRON (See Justice League of America #193)
DC Comics: Sept, 1981 - No. 67, Mar, 1987

1-Original Atom, Hawkman, Dr. Mid-Nite, Robotman (origin), Plastic Man, Johnny Quick, Liberty Belle, Shining Knight begin	1	2	3	4	5	7
2-10: 3-Solomon Grundy app. 4,7-Spectre app. 8-Re-intro Steel, the Indestructable Man						5.00
11-46,48,49: 12-Origin G.A. Hawkman retold. 23-Origin/1st app. The Amazing Man. 24-Batman app. 25-1st app. Infinity, Inc. (9/83), 26-Origin Infinity, Inc.(2nd app.) 27-Dr. Fate vs. The Spectre. 30-35-Spectre app. 33-Origin Freedom Fighters of Earth-X. 36,37-Superman vs. Capt. Marvel; Ordway-c. 41-Origin Starman						4.00
47-Origin Dr. Fate; McFarlane-a (1st full story)/part-c (7/85)						
	1	3	4	6	8	10
50-Double size; Crisis x-over						6.00
51-66: 51-56-Crisis x-over. 61-Origin Liberty Belle. 62-Origin The Shining Knight. 63-Origin Robotman. 65-Origin Johnny Quick. 66-Origin Tarantula						4.50
67-Last issue; retells first case of the Justice Society						6.00
Annual 1-3: 1(11/82)-Retells origin of G.A. Atom, Guardian & Wildcat; Jerry Ordway's 1st pencils for DC.(1st work was inking Carmine Infantino in Mystery in Space #94). 2(11/83)-Infinity, Inc. app. 3(9/84)						4.50

NOTE: *Buckler* a-1-5; c-1, 3-5, 51. *Kubert* c-2, 7-18. JLA app. in 14, 15. JSA app. in 4, 14, 15, 19, 27, 28.

ALL-STAR STORY OF THE DODGERS, THE
Stadium Communications: Apr, 1979 ($1.00)

1		2	4	6	9	13	16

ALL-STAR SUPERMAN
DC Comics: Jan, 2006 - Present ($2.99)

1-Grant Morrison-s/Frank Quitely-a/c						5.00
1-Variant-c by Neal Adams						20.00
2-8: 3-Lois gets super powers. 7,8-Bizarro app.						3.00
Vol. 1 HC (2007, $19.99, dustjacket) r/#1-6; Schreck intro.						20.00

ALL STAR WESTERN (Formerly All Star Comics No. 1-57)
National Periodical Publ.: No. 58, Mar/Apr, 1951 - No. 119, June-July, 1961

58-Trigger Twins (ends #116), Strong Bow, The Roving Ranger & Don Caballero begin	45	90	135	275	455	635
59,60: Last 52 pgs.	27	54	81	156	246	335
61-66: 61-64-Toth-a	22	44	66	128	202	275
67-Johnny Thunder begins; Gil Kane-a	28	56	84	162	256	350
68-81: Last precode (2-3/55)	14	28	42	82	121	160
82-98: 97-1st S.A. issue	13	26	39	72	101	130
99-Frazetta-r/Jimmy Wakely #4	13	26	39	74	105	135
100	13	26	39	74	105	135
101-107,109-116,118,119	11	22	33	62	86	110
108-Origin J. Thunder; J. Thunder logo begins	22	44	66	126	198	270
117-Origin Super Chief	14	28	42	80	115	150

NOTE: *Gil Kane* c(p)-58, 59, 61, 63, 64, 68, 69, 70-95(most), 97-199(most). *Infantino* art in most issues. Madame .44 app.- #117-119.

ALL-STAR WESTERN (Weird Western Tales No. 12 on)
National Periodical Publications: Aug-Sept, 1970 - No. 11, Apr-May, 1972

1-Pow-Wow Smith-r; Infantino-a/c	5	10	15	30	48	65
2-Outlaw begins; El Diablo by Morrow begins; has cameos by Williamson, Torres, Kane, Giordano & Phil Seuling	4	8	12	28	44	60
3-Origin El Diablo	4	8	12	26	41	55
4-6: 5-Last Outlaw issue. 6-Billy the Kid begins, ends #8						
	3	6	9	19	29	38
7-9-(52 pgs.) 9-Frazetta-a, 3pgs.(r)	4	8	12	22	34	45
10-(52 pgs.) Jonah Hex begins (1st app., 2-3/72)	35	70	105	263	482	700
11-(52 pgs.) 2nd app. Jonah Hex; 1st cover	15	30	45	105	188	270

NOTE: *Neal Adams* c-2-5; *Aparo* a-5. *G. Kane* a-3, 4, 6, 8. *Kubert* a-4r, 7-9r. *Morrow* a-2-4, 10, 11. No. 7-11 have 52 pgs...

ALL SURPRISE (Becomes Jeanie #13 on) (Funny animal)
Timely/Marvel (CPC): Fall, 1943 - No. 12, Winter, 1946-47

1-Super Rabbit, Gandy & Sourpuss begin	38	76	114	219	347	475
2	17	34	51	100	158	215
3-10,12	14	28	42	82	121	160
11-Kurtzman "Pigtales" art	15	30	45	84	127	170

ALL TEEN (Formerly All Winners; All Winners & Teen Comics No. 21 on)
Marvel Comics (WFP): No. 20, January, 1947

20-Georgie, Mitzi, Patsy Walker, Willie app.; Syd Shores-c	15	30	45	86	133	180

ALL-TIME SPORTS COMICS (Formerly All Sports Comics)
Hillman Per.: V2, No. 4, Apr-May, 1949 - V2, No. 7, Oct-Nov, 1949 (All 52 pgs.)

V2#4	23	46	69	132	209	285
5-7: 5-(V1#5 inside)-Powell-a; Ty Cobb sty. 7-Krigstein-p; Walter Johnson & Knute Rockne sty	17	34	51	100	158	215

ALL TOP
William H. Wise Co.: 1944 (132 pgs.)

nn-Capt. V, Merciless the Sorceress, Red Robbins, One Round Hogan, Mike the M.P., Snooky, Pussy Katnip app.	33	66	99	190	300	410

ALL TOP COMICS (My Experience No. 19 on)
Fox Features Synd./Green Publ./Norlen Mag.: 1945; No. 2, Sum, 1946 - No. 18, Mar, 1949; 1957 - 1959

1-Cosmo Cat & Flash Rabbit begin (1st app.)	24	48	72	139	220	300
2 (#1-7 are funny animal)	13	26	39	74	105	135
3-7-Two diff. issues (7/47 & 9/47)	10	20	30	54	72	90
8-Blue Beetle, Phantom Lady, & Rulah, Jungle Goddess begin (11/47); Kamen-c	269	538	807	1681	2791	3900
9-Kamen-c	140	280	420	875	1450	2025
10-Kamen bondage-c	145	290	435	906	1503	2100
11-13,15-17: 11,12-Rulah-c. 15-No Blue Beetle	116	232	348	725	1200	1675
14-No Blue Beetle; used in SOTI, illo- "Corpses of colored people strung up by their wrists"	155	310	465	969	1610	2250
18-Dagar, Jo-Jo app; no Phantom Lady or Blue Beetle	73	146	219	456	761	1065
6(1957-Green Publ.)-Patoruzu the Indian; Cosmo Cat on cover only. 6(1958-Literary Ent.)- Muggy Doo; Cosmo Cat on cover only. 6(1959-Norlen)-Atomic Mouse; Cosmo Cat on-c only. 6(1959)-Little Eva. 6(Cornell)-Supermouse on-c	5	10	15	24	30	35

NOTE: Jo-Jo by *Kamen*-12,18.

ALL TRUE ALL PICTURE POLICE CASES
St. John Publishing Co.: Oct, 1952 - No. 2, Nov, 1952 (100 pgs.)

1-Three rebound St. John crime comics	44	88	132	268	439	610
2-Three comics rebound	33	66	99	190	300	410

NOTE: Contents may vary.

ALL-TRUE CRIME (...Cases No. 26-35; formerly Official True Crime Cases)
Marvel/Atlas Comics: No. 26, Feb, 1948 - No. 52, Sept, 1952
(OFI #26,27/CFI #28,29/LCC #30-46/LMC #47-52)

26(#1)-Syd Shores-c	34	68	102	197	311	425
27(4/48)-Electric chair-c	27	54	81	156	246	335
28-41,43-48,50-52: 35-37-Photo-c	13	26	39	74	105	135
42,49-Krigstein-a. 49-Used in POP, Pg 79	14	28	42	78	112	145

NOTE: *Robinson* a-47, 50. *Shores* c-26. *Tuska* a-48(3).

ALL-TRUE DETECTIVE CASES (Kit Carson No. 5 on)
Avon Periodicals: #2, Apr-May, 1954 - No. 4, Aug-Sept, 1954

2(#1)-Wood-a	23	46	69	135	213	290
3-Kinstler-c	14	28	42	78	112	145
4-r/Gangsters And Gun Molls #2; Kamen-a	18	36	54	103	162	220
nn(100 pgs.)-7 pg. Kubert-a, Kinstler back-c	40	80	120	235	368	500

ALL TRUE ROMANCE (...Illustrated No. 3)
Artful Publ. #1-3/Harwell(Comic Media) #4-20?/Ajax-Farrell(Excellent Publ.) No. 22 on/Four Star Comic Corp.: 3/51 - No. 20, 12/54; No. 22, 3/55 - No. 30?, 7/57; No. 3(#31);No. 4(#32), 11/57; No. 33, 2/58 - No. 34, 6/58

1 (3/51)	17	34	51	98	154	210
2 (10/51; 11/51 on-c)	11	22	33	60	83	105
3(12/51) - #5 (5/52)	9	18	27	50	65	80
6-Wood-a, 9 pgs. (exceptional)	17	34	51	98	154	210
7-10 [two #7s: #7(11/52, 9/52 inside]; #7(11/52, 11/52 inside)]						
	8	16	24	44	57	70
11-13,16-19(9/54),20(12/54) (no #21)	7	14	21	35	43	50
14-Marijuana story	7	14	21	37	46	55
22: Last precode issue (1st Ajax, 3/55)	7	14	21	35	43	50
23-27,29,30(7/57): 29-Disbrow-a	6	12	18	28	34	40

All Winners Comics #3 © MAR

Alpha Flight #95 © MAR

Amazing Adult Fantasy #10 © MAR

	GD 2.0	VG 4.0	FN 6.0	VF 8.0	VF/NM 9.0	NM- 9.2

28 (9/56)-L. B. Cole, Disbrow-a — 11 / 22 / 33 / 60 / 83 / 105
3(#31, 9/57),4(#32, 11/57),33,34 (Farrell, '57-'58) — 5 / 10 / 15 / 24 / 30 / 35

ALL WESTERN WINNERS (Formerly All Winners; becomes Western Winners with No. 5; see Two-Gun Kid No. 5)
Marvel Comics(CDS): No. 2, Winter, 1948-49 - No. 4, April, 1949
2-Black Rider (origin/1st app.) & his horse Satan, Kid Colt & his horse Steel, & Two-Gun Kid & his horse Cyclone begin; Shores c-2-4 — 76 / 152 / 228 / 475 / 788 / 1100
3-Anti-Wertham editorial — 38 / 76 / 114 / 222 / 351 / 480
4-Black Rider i.d. revealed; Heath, Shores-a — 38 / 76 / 114 / 222 / 351 / 480

ALL WINNERS COMICS (All Teen #20) (Also see Timely Presents: ...)
USA No. 1-7/WFP No. 10-19/YAI No. 21: Summer, 1941 - No. 19, Fall, 1946; No. 21, Winter, 1946-47; (No #20) (No. 21 continued from Young Allies No. 20)
1-The Angel & Black Marvel only app.; Capt. America by Simon & Kirby, Human Torch & Sub-Mariner begin (#1 was advertised as All Aces); 1st app. All-Winners Squad in text story by Stan Lee — 2050 / 4100 / 6150 / 15,375 / 27,688 / 40,000
2-The Destroyer & The Whizzer begin; Simon & Kirby Captain America — 497 / 994 / 1491 / 3479 / 6090 / 8700
3 — 352 / 704 / 1056 / 2288 / 4044 / 5800
4-Classic War-c by Al Avison — 376 / 752 / 1128 / 2444 / 4322 / 6200
5 — 259 / 518 / 777 / 1619 / 2685 / 3750
6-The Black Avenger only app.; no Whizzer story; Hitler, Hirohito & Mussolini-c — 300 / 600 / 900 / 1894 / 3197 / 4500
7-10 — 224 / 448 / 672 / 1400 / 2325 / 3250
11,13-18: 11-1st Atlas globe on-c (Winter, 1943-44; also see Human Torch #14).
14-16-No Human Torch — 159 / 318 / 477 / 994 / 1647 / 2300
12-Red Skull story; last Destroyer; no Whizzer story — 203 / 406 / 609 / 1269 / 2110 / 2950
19-(Scarce)-1st story app. & origin All Winners Squad (Capt. America & Bucky, Human Torch & Toro, Sub-Mariner, Whizzer, & Miss America; r-in Fantasy Masterpieces #10 — 514 / 1028 / 1542 / 3600 / 6300 / 9000
21-(Scarce)-All Winners Squad; bondage-c — 429 / 858 / 1287 / 3000 / 5250 / 7500
NOTE: *Everett* Sub-Mariner-1, 3, 4; *Burgos* Torch-1, 3, 4. *Schomburg* c-1, 7-18. *Shores* c-19p, 21.
(2nd Series - August, 1948, Marvel Comics (CDS))
(Becomes All Western Winners with No. 2)
1-The Blonde Phantom, Capt. America, Human Torch, & Sub-Mariner app. — 297 / 594 / 891 / 1856 / 3078 / 4300

ALL YOUR COMICS (See Fox Giants)
Fox Feature Syndicate (R. W. Voight): Spring, 1946 (36 pgs.)
1-Red Robbins, Merciless the Sorceress app. — 22 / 44 / 66 / 126 / 198 / 270

ALMANAC OF CRIME (See Fox Giants)

AL OF FBI (See Little Al of the FBI)

ALONE IN THE DARK (Based on video game)
Image Comics: Feb, 2003 ($4.95)
1-Matt Haley-c/a; Jean-Marc & Randy Lofficier-s — 5.00

ALPHA AND OMEGA
Spire Christian Comics (Fleming H. Revell): 1978 (49¢)
nn — 2 / 4 / 6 / 8 / 11 / 14

ALPHA CENTURION (See Superman, 2nd Series & Zero Hour)
DC Comics: 1996 ($2.95, one-shot)
1 — 3.00

ALPHA FLIGHT (See X-Men #120,121 & X-Men/Alpha Flight)
Marvel Comics: Aug, 1983 - No. 130, Mar, 1994 (#52-on are direct sales only)
1-(52 pgs.) Byrne-a begins (thru #28) -Wolverine & Nightcrawler cameo — 4.00
2-28: 2-Vindicator becomes Guardian; origin Marrina & Alpha Flight. 3-Concludes origin Alpha Flight. 6-Origin Shaman. 7-Origin Snowbird. 10,11-Origin Sasquatch. 12-(52 pgs.)-Death of Guardian. 13-Wolverine app. 16,17-Wolverine cameo. 17-X-Men x-over (mostly r-/X-Men #109); 20-New headquarters. 25-Return of Guardian. 28-Last Byrne issue — 3.00
29-32,35-50: 39-47,49-Portacio-a(i). 50-Double size; Portacio-a — 2.50
33,34-1st & 2nd app. Lady Deathstrike; Wolverine app. 34-Origin Wolverine — 3.00
51-Jim Lee's 1st work at Marvel (10/87); Wolverine cameo; 1st Lee/Wolverine; Portacio-a(i) — 5.00
52,53-Wolverine app.; Lee-a on Wolverine; Portacio-a(i); 53-Lee/Portacio-a — 3.00
54-73,76-86,91-99,101-105: 54,63,64-No Jim Lee-a. 54-Portacio-a(i). 55-62-Jim Lee-a(p).
71-Intro The Sorcerer (villain). 91-Dr. Doom app. 94-F.F. x-over. 99-Galactus, Avengers app.
102-Intro Weapon Omega — 2.50
74,75,87-90,100: 74-Wolverine, Spider-Man & The Avengers app. 75-Double size ($1.95, 52 pgs.). 87-90-Wolverine. 4 part story w/Jim Lee-c. 89-Original Guardian returns. 100-($2.00, 52 pgs.)-Avengers & Galactus app. — 3.00
106-Northstar revelation issue — 2.50
106-2nd printing (direct sale only) — 2.25

107-109,112-119,121-129: 107-X-Factor x-over. 112-Infinity War x-overs — 2.25
110,111: Infinity War x-overs, Wolverine app. (brief). 111-Thanos cameo — 3.00
120-($2.25)-Polybagged w/Paranormal Registration Act poster — 2.50
130-($2.25, 52 pgs.) — 3.00
Annual 1,2 (9/86, 12/87) — 3.00
...Classics Vol. 1 TPB (2007, $24.99) r/#1-8; character profile pages; Byrne interview — 25.00
Special V2#1(6/92, $2.50, 52 pgs.)-Wolverine-c/story — 2.50
NOTE: *Austin* c-1i, 2i, 53i. *Byrne* c-81, 82. *Guice* c-85, 91-99. *Jim Lee* a(p)-51, 53, 55-62, 64; c-53, 87-90. *Mignola* a-29-31p. *Whilce Portacio* a(i)-39-47, 49-54.

ALPHA FLIGHT (2nd Series)
Marvel Comics: Aug, 1997 - No. 20, Mar, 1999 ($2.99/$1.99)
1-($2.99)-Wraparound cover — 6.00
2,3: 2-Variant-c — 4.00
4-11: 8,9-Wolverine-c/app. — 3.00
12-($2.99) Death of Sasquatch; wraparound-c — 4.00
13-20 — 3.00
.../Inhumans '98 Annual ($3.50) Raney-a — 3.50

ALPHA FLIGHT (3rd Series)
Marvel Comics: May, 2004 - No. 12, April, 2005 ($2.99)
1-12: 1-6-Lobdell-s/Henry-c/a — 3.00
... Vol. 1: You Gotta Be Kiddin' Me (2004, $14.99) r/#1-6 — 15.00

ALPHA FLIGHT: IN THE BEGINNING
Marvel Comics: July, 1997 ($1.95, one-shot)
(-1)-Flashback w/Wolverine — 2.50

ALPHA FLIGHT SPECIAL
Marvel Comics: July, 1991 - No. 4, Oct, 1991 ($1.50, limited series)
1-4: 1-3-r-a. Flight #97-99 w/covers. 4-r-a.Flight #100 — 2.50

ALPHA KORPS
Diversity Comics: Sept, 1996 ($2.50)
1-Origin/1st app. Alpha Korps — 2.50

ALTERED IMAGE
Image Comics: Apr, 1998 - No. 3, Sept, 1998 ($2.50, limited series)
1-3-Spawn, Witchblade, Savage Dragon; Valentino-s/a — 3.00

ALTER EGO
First Comics: May, 1986 - No. 4, Nov, 1986 (Mini-series)
1-4 — 2.50

ALTER NATION
Image Comics: Feb, 2004 - No. 4, Jun, 2004 ($2.95, limited series)
1-4: 1-Two covers by Art Adams and Barberi; Barberi-a — 3.00

ALVIN (TV) (See Four Color Comics No. 1042 or Three Chipmunks #1)
Dell Publishing Co.: Oct-Dec, 1962 - No. 28, Oct, 1973
12-021-212 (#1) — 9 / 18 / 27 / 60 / 100 / 140
2 — 5 / 10 / 15 / 35 / 55 / 75
3-10 — 5 / 10 / 15 / 30 / 48 / 65
11-"Chipmunks sing the Beatles' Hits" — 5 / 10 / 15 / 32 / 51 / 70
12-28 — 4 / 8 / 12 / 24 / 37 / 50
Alvin For President (10/64) — 4 / 8 / 12 / 28 / 44 / 60
...& His Pals in Merry Christmas with Clyde Crashcup & Leonardo 1 (02-120-402)-(12-2/64) — 7 / 14 / 21 / 50 / 83 / 115
Reprinted in 1966 (12-023-604) — 4 / 8 / 12 / 24 / 37 / 50

ALVIN & THE CHIPMUNKS
Harvey Comics: July, 1992 - No. 5, May, 1994
1-5: 1-Richie Rich app. — 4.00

AMALGAM AGE OF COMICS, THE: THE DC COMICS COLLECTION
DC Comics: 1996 ($12.95, trade paperback)
nn-r/Amazon, Assassins, Doctor Strangefate, JLX, Legends of the Dark Claw, & Super Soldier — 13.00

AMANDA AND GUNN
Image Comics: Apr, 1997 - No. 4, Oct, 1997 ($2.95, B&W, limited series)
1-4 — 3.00

AMAZING ADULT FANTASY (Formerly Amazing Adventures #1-6; becomes Amazing Fantasy #15) (See Amazing Fantasy for Omnibus HC reprint of #1-15)
Marvel Comics Group (AMI): No. 7, Dec, 1961 - No. 14, July, 1962
7-Ditko-c/a begins, ends #14 — 45 / 90 / 135 / 360 / 655 / 950
8-Last 10¢ issue — 36 / 72 / 108 / 270 / 498 / 725
9-13: 12-1st app. Mailbag. 13-Anti-communist sty — 35 / 70 / 105 / 263 / 482 / 700

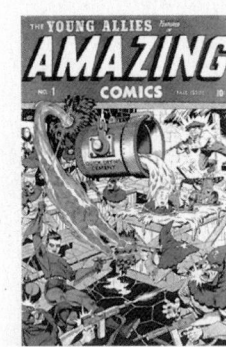

Amazing Comics #1 © MAR

Amazing Fantasy (2005) #8 © MAR

Amazing Man Comics #25 © CEN

	GD 2.0	VG 4.0	FN 6.0	VF 8.0	VF/NM 9.0	NM- 9.2		GD 2.0	VG 4.0	FN 6.0	VF 8.0	VF/NM 9.0	NM- 9.2
13-2nd printing (1994)	2	4	6	8	10	12	11,12: 11-(3/52)-Horror format begins. 12-Krigstein-a	36	72	108	208	329	450
14-Prototype issue (Professor X)	38	76	114	285	518	750	13-(Scarce)-Everett-a; electrocution-c/story	39	78	117	224	355	485
							14	31	62	93	180	285	390

AMAZING ADVENTURE FUNNIES (Fantoman No. 2 on)
Centaur Publications: June, 1940 - No. 2, Sept. 1940

NOTE: *Colan a-9. Maneely c-13. Sekowsky a-12. Sinnott a-13. Tuska a-10.*

1-The Fantom of the Fair by Gustavson (r/Amaz. Mystery Funnies V2#7,V2#8),													
The Arrow, Skyrocket Steele From the Year X by Everett (r/AMF #2);													
Burgos-a	172	344	516	1075	1788	2500							
2-Reprints; Published after Fantoman #2	110	220	330	688	1144	1600							

NOTE: *Burgos a-1(2). Everett a-1(3). Gustavson a-1(5), 2(3). Pinajian a-2.*

AMAZING FANTASY (Formerly Amazing Adult Fantasy #7-14)
Atlas Magazines/Marvel: #15, Aug, 1962 (Sept, 1962 shown in indicia); #16, Dec, 1995 - #18, Feb, 1996

AMAZING ADVENTURES (Also see Boy Cowboy & Science Comics)
Ziff-Davis Publ. Co.: 1950; No. 1, Nov, 1950 - No. 6, Fall, 1952 (Painted covers)

1950 (no month given) (8-1/2x11) (8 pgs.) Has the front & back cover plus Schomburg story used in Amazing Advs. #1 (Sent to subscribers of Z-D s/f magazines & ordered through mail for 10¢. Used to test market)	55	110	165	344	572	800							
1-Wood, Schomburg, Anderson, Whitney-a	79	158	237	494	822	1150							
2-5: 2-Schomburg-a. 2,4,5-Anderson-a. 3,5-Starr-a	40	80	120	240	383	525							
6-Krigstein-a	40	80	120	243	389	535							

15-Origin/1st app. of Spider-Man by Steve Ditko (11 pgs.); 1st app. Aunt May & Uncle Ben; Kirby/Ditko-c					1850 3700 5550	16,000	33,000	50,000					
16-18 ('95-'96, $3.95): Kurt Busiek scripts; painted-c/a by Paul Lee													4.00
Amazing Fantasy Omnibus HC ("Amazing Adult Fantasy" on-c) (2007, $75.00, dustjacket) r/Amazing Adventures #1-6, Amazing Adult Fantasy #7-14 and Amazing Fantasy #15 with letter pages; foreword by Bissette; cover gallery from '70s reprint titles													75.00

AMAZING ADVENTURES (Becomes Amazing Adult Fantasy #7 on) (See Amazing Fantasy for Omnibus HC reprint of #1-15)
Atlas Comics (AMI)/Marvel Comics No. 3 on: June, 1961 - No. 6, Nov, 1961

AMAZING FANTASY (Continues from #6 in Araña: The Heart of the Spider)
Marvel Comics: Aug, 2004 - No. 20, June, 2006 ($2.99)

1-Origin Dr. Droom (1st Marvel-Age Superhero) by Kirby; Kirby/Ditko-a (5 pgs.) Ditko & Kirby-a in all; Kirby monster c-1-6	109	218	327	927	1714	2500							
2	45	90	135	360	655	950							
3-6: 6-Last Dr. Droom	40	80	120	300	550	800							

1-Intro. Anya Corazon; Fiona Avery-s/Mark Brooks-c/a													4.00
2-14,16-20: 3,4-Roger Cruz-a. 7-Intro. new Scorpion; Kirk-a. 10-Intro. Vampire By Night 13,14-Back-up Captain Universe stories. 16-20-Death's Head													3.00
15-($3.99) Spider-Man app.; intro 6 new characters incl. Mastermind Excello seen in World War Hulk series; s/a by various													4.00
Death's Head 3.0: Unnatural Selection TPB (2006, $13.99) r/#16-20													14.00
Scorpion: Poison Tomorrow (2005, $7.99, digest) r/#7-13													8.00

AMAZING ADVENTURES
Marvel Comics Group: Aug, 1970 - No. 39, Nov, 1976

AMAZING GHOST STORIES (Formerly Nightmare)
St. John Publishing Co.: No. 14, Oct, 1954 - No. 16, Feb, 1955

1-Inhumans by Kirby(p) & Black Widow (1st app. in Tales of Suspense #52) double feature begins	6	12	18	39	62	85	14-Pit & the Pendulum story by Kinstler; Baker-c	34	68	102	195	308	420
2-4: 2-F.F. brief app. 4-Last Inhumans by Kirby	3	6	9	19	29	38	15-r/Weird Thrillers #5; Baker-c, Powell-a	25	50	75	145	228	310
5-8: Adams-a(p); 8-Last Black Widow; last 15¢-c	4	8	12	28	44	60	16-Kubert reprints of Weird Thrillers #4; Baker-c; Roussos, Tuska-a; Kinstler-a (1 pg.)	25	50	75	148	232	315
9,10: Magneto app. 10-Last Inhumans (origin-r by Kirby)	3	6	9	18	27	35							

AMAZING HIGH ADVENTURE
Marvel Comics: 8/84; No. 2, 10/85; No. 3, 10/86 - No. 5, 1986 ($2.00)

11-New Beast begins(1st app. in mutated form; origin in flashback); X-Men cameo in flashback (#11-17 are X-Men tie-ins)	14	28	42	99	175	250	1-5: Painted-c on all. 3,4-Baxter paper. 4-Bolton-c/a. 5-Bolton-a						3.50
12-17: 12-Beast battles Iron Man. 13-Brotherhood of Evil Mutants x-over from X-Men. 15-X-Men app. 16-Rutland Vermont - Bald Mountain Halloween x-over; Juggernaut app. 17-Last Beast (origin); X-Men app.	6	12	18	39	62	85							

NOTE: *Bissette a-4. Severin a-1, 3. Sienkiewicz a-1,2. Paul Smith a-2. Williamson a-2i.*

AMAZING JOY BUZZARDS
Image Comics: 2005 - No. 4, 2005 ($2.95, B&W with pink spot color in #1)

18-War of the Worlds begins (5/73); 1st app. Killraven; Neal Adams-a(p)	3	6	9	17	25	32	1-4-Mark Andrew Smith-s/Dan Hipp-a. 1-Mahfood back-c. 2-Morse back-c						3.00
							Vol. 1 TPB (2005, $11.95) r/#1-4; bonus art and character design sketches						12.00

AMAZING JOY BUZZARDS (Volume 2)
Image Comics: Oct, 2005 - No. 5, Aug, 2006 ($2.99, B&W)

19-35,38,39: 19-Chaykin-a. 25-Buckler-a. 35-Giffen's first published story (art), along with Deadly Hands of Kung-Fu #22 (3/76)	1	3	4	6	8	10	1-5: 1-Mark Andrew Smith-s/Dan Hipp-a. 4-Mahfood-a; Crosland-a. 5-Holgate-a						3.00
36,37-(Regular 25¢ edition)(7-8/76)	1	3	4	6	8	10	Vol. 2 TPB (2006, $12.99) r/#1-5; bonus art, pin-ups and character sketches						13.00
36,37-(30¢-c variants, limited distribution)	4	8	12	28	44	60							

NOTE: *N. Adams c-6-8. Buscema a-1p, 2p. Colan a-3-5p, 26p. Ditko a-24r. Everett a(i)3-5, 7-9. Giffen a-35i, 38p. G. Kane c-11, 25p, 29p. Ploog a-12i. Russell a-27-32, 34-37, 39; c-28, 30-32, 33i, 34, 35, 37, 39i. Starlling a-17. Starlin c-15p, 16, 17, 27. Sutton a-11-15p.*

AMAZING-MAN COMICS (Formerly Motion Picture Funnies Weekly?)
(Also see Stars And Stripes Comics)
Centaur Publications: No. 5, Sept, 1939 - No. 26, Jan, 1942

AMAZING ADVENTURES
Marvel Comics Group: Dec, 1979 - No. 14, Jan, 1981

V2#1-Reprints story/X-Men #1 & 38 (origins)	1	2	3	5	6	8	5(#1)-(Rare)-Origin/1st app. A-Man the Amazing Man by Bill Everett; The Cat-Man by Tarpe Mills (also #8), Mighty Man by Filchock, Minimidget & sidekick Ritty, & The Iron Skull by Burgos begins	1425	2850	4275	10,800	18,900	27,000
2-14: 2-6-Early X-Men-r. 7,8-Origin Iceman						6.00	6-Origin The Amazing Man retold; The Shark begins; Mighty Man by Tarpe Mills app.	333	666	1000	2165	3833	5500
							7-Magician From Mars begins; ends #11	241	482	723	1506	2503	3500

NOTE: *Byrne c-6p, 9p. Kirby a-1-14r; c-7, 9. Steranko a-12r. Tuska a-7-9.*

							8-Cat-Man dresses as woman	183	366	549	1144	1897	2650
							9-Magician From Mars battles the 'Elemental Monster', swiped into The Spectre in More Fun #54 & 55. Ties w/Marvel Mystery #4 for 1st Nazi War-c on a comic (2/40)	190	380	570	1188	1969	2750

AMAZING ADVENTURES
Marvel Comics: July, 1988 ($4.95, squarebound, one-shot, 80 pgs.)

1-Anthology; Austin, Golden-a						5.00	10,11: 11-Zardi, the Eternal Man begins; ends #16; Amazing Man dons costume; last Everett issue	134	268	402	838	1394	1950
							12,13	124	248	372	775	1288	1800

AMAZING ADVENTURES OF CAPTAIN CARVEL AND HIS CARVEL CRUSADERS, THE
(See Carvel Comics in the Promotional Comics section)

							14-Reef Kinkaid, Rocke Wayburn (ends #20) & Dr. Hypno (ends #21) begin; no Zardi or Chuck Hardy	98	196	294	613	1019	1425

AMAZING CHAN & THE CHAN CLAN, THE (TV)
Gold Key: May, 1973 - No. 4, Feb, 1974 (Hanna-Barbera)

1-Warren Tufts-a in all	4	8	12	22	34	45	15,17-20: 15-Zardi returns; no Rocke Wayburn. 17-Dr. Hypno returns; no Zardi	88	176	264	550	913	1275
2-4	3	6	9	16	23	30	16-Mighty Man's powers of super strength & ability to shrink & grow explained; Rocke Wayburn returns; no Dr. Hypno; Al Avison (a character) begins, ends #18 (a tribute to the famed artist)	91	182	273	569	947	1325

AMAZING COMICS (Complete Comics No. 2)
Timely Comics (EPC): Fall, 1944

1-The Destroyer, The Whizzer, The Young Allies (by Sekowsky), Sergeant Dix; Schomburg-c	248	496	744	1550	2575	3600	21-Origin Dash Dartwell (drug-use story); origin & only app. T.N.T.	199	291	606	1003	1400	

AMAZING DETECTIVE CASES (Formerly Suspense No. 2?)
Marvel/Atlas Comics (CCC): No. 3, Nov, 1950 - No. 14, Sept, 1952

							22-Dash Dartwell, the Human Meteor & The Voice app; last Iron Skull & The Shark; Silver Streak app. (classic-c)	166	332	498	1038	1719	2400
3	30	60	90	174	275	375	23-Two Amazing Man stories; intro/origin Tommy the Amazing Kid; The Marksman only app.	79	158	237	494	822	1150
4-6	17	34	51	98	154	210	24-King of Darkness, Nightshade, & Blue Lady begin; end #26; 1st app. Super-Ann						
7-10	15	30	45	88	137	185							

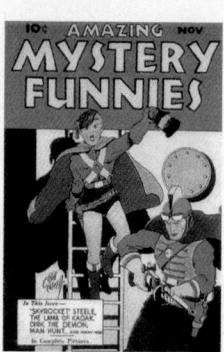

Amazing Mystery Funnies #3 © CEN

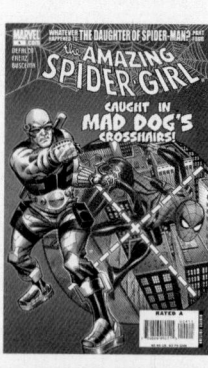

Amazing Spider-Girl #4 © MAR

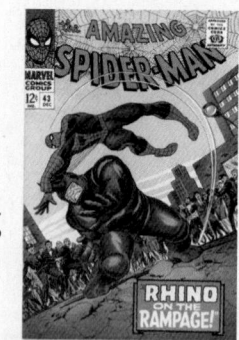

Amazing Spider-Man #43 © MAR

	GD 2.0	VG 4.0	FN 6.0	VF 8.0	VF/NM 9.0	NM- 9.2
25,26 (Scarce): Meteor Martin by Wolverton in both; 26-Electric Ray app.	79	158	237	494	822	1150
	124	248	372	775	1288	1800

NOTE: **Everett** a-5-11; c-5-11. **Gilman** a-14-20. **Giunta/Mirando** a-7-10. **Sam Glanzman** a-14-16, 18-21, 23. **Louis Glanzman** a-6, 9-11, 14-21; c-13-19, 21. **Robert Golden** a-9. **Gustavson** a-6; c-22, 23. **Lubbers** a-14-21. **Simon** a-10. **Frank Thomas** a-6, 9-11, 14, 15, 17-21.

AMAZING MYSTERIES (Formerly Sub-Mariner Comics No. 31)
Marvel Comics (CCC): No. 32, May, 1949 - No. 35, Jan, 1950 (1st Marvel Horror Comic)

	GD 2.0	VG 4.0	FN 6.0	VF 8.0	VF/NM 9.0	NM- 9.2
32-The Witness app.	84	168	252	525	875	1225
33-Horror format	40	80	120	240	383	525
34,35: Changes to Crime. 34,35-Photo-c	21	42	63	122	191	260

AMAZING MYSTERY FUNNIES
Centaur Publications: Aug, 1938 - No. 24, Sept, 1940 (All 52 pgs.)

	GD 2.0	VG 4.0	FN 6.0	VF 8.0	VF/NM 9.0	NM- 9.2
V1#1-Everett-c(1st); Dick Kent Adv. story; Skyrocket Steele in the Year X on cover only	364	728	1092	2366	4183	6000
2-Everett 1st-a (Skyrocket Steele)	186	372	558	1163	1932	2700
3	97	194	291	606	1003	1400
3(#4, 12/38)-nn on cover, #3 on inside; bondage-c	88	176	264	550	913	1275
V2#1-4,6: 2-Drug use story. 3-Air-Sub DX begins by Burgos. 4-Dan Hastings, Sand Hog begins (ends #5). 6-Last Skyrocket Steele	79	158	237	494	822	1150
5-Classic Everett-c	152	304	456	950	1575	2200
7 (Scarce)-Intro. The Fantom of the Fair & begins; Everett, Gustavson, Burgos-a	352	704	1056	2288	4044	5800
8-Origin & 1st app. Speed Centaur	145	290	435	906	1503	2100
9-11: 11-Self portrait and biog. of Everett; Jon Linton begins; early Robot cover (11/39)	79	158	237	494	822	1150
12 (Scarce)-1st app. Space Patrol; Wolverton-a (12/39); new costume Phantom of the Fair	193	386	579	1206	2003	2800
V3#1(#17, 1/40)-Intro. Bullet; Tippy Taylor serial begins, ends #24 (continued in The Arrow #2)	79	158	237	494	822	1150
18,20: 18-Fantom of the Fair by Gustavson	76	152	228	475	788	1100
19,21-24: Space Patrol by Wolverton in all	93	186	279	581	966	1350

NOTE: **Burgos** a-V2#3-9. **Eisner** a-V1#2, 3(2). **Everett** a-V1#2-4, V2#1, 3-6; c-V1#1-4, V2#3, 5, 18. **Filchock** a-V2#9. **Flessel** a-V2#6. **Guardineer** a-V1#4, V2#4-6; **Gustavson** a-V2#4, 5, 9-12, V3#1, 18, 19; c-V2#7, 9, 12, V3#1, 21, 22; **McWilliams** a-V2#9, 10. **TarpeMills** a-V2#2, 4-6, 9-12, V3#1. **Leo Morey**(Pulp artist) c-V2#10; text illo-V2#11. **FrankThomas** a-V2#11. **Webster** a-V2#4.

AMAZING SAINTS
Logos International: 1974 (39¢)

	GD 2.0	VG 4.0	FN 6.0	VF 8.0	VF/NM 9.0	NM- 9.2
nn-True story of Phil Saint	2	4	6	8	11	14

AMAZING SCARLET SPIDER
Marvel Comics: Nov, 1995 - No. 2, Dec, 1995 ($1.95, limited series)
1,2: Replaces "Amazing Spider-Man" for two issues. 1-Venom/Carnage cameos.
2-Green Goblin & Joystick-c/app. — 2.50

AMAZING SCREW-ON HEAD, THE
Dark Horse Comics (Maverick): May, 2002 ($2.99, one-shot)
1-Mike Mignola-s/a-c — 3.00

AMAZING SPIDER-GIRL
Marvel Comics: No. 0, 2006; No. 1, Dec, 2006 - Present ($2.99)
0-($1.99) Recap of the Spider-girl series and character profiles; A.F. #15 cover swipe — 2.50
1-12-($2.99) Frenz & Buscema-a. 9-Carnage returns — 3.00
... Vol. 1: What Ever Happened to the Daughter of Spider-Man? TPB (2007, $14.99) r/#0-6 — 15.00
... Vol. 2: Comes the Carnage! TPB (2007, $13.99) r/#7-12 — 14.00

AMAZING SPIDER-MAN, THE (See All Detergent Comics, Amazing Fantasy, America's Best TV Comics, Aurora, Deadly Foes of..., Fireside Book Series, Friendly Neighborhood..., Giant-Size..., Giant Size Super-Heroes Featuring..., Marvel Age..., Marvel Collectors Item Classics, Marvel Fanfare, Marvel Graphic Novel, Marvel Knoghts..., Marvel Spec. Ed., Marvel Tales, Marvel Team-Up, Marvel Treasury Ed., New Avengers, Nothing Can Stop the Juggernaut, Official Marvel Index To..., Peter Parker..., Power Record Comics, Spectacular..., Spider-Man, Spider-Man Digest, Spider-Man Saga, Spider-Man 2099, Spider-Man Vs. Wolverine, Spidey Super Stories, Strange Tales Annual #2, Superman Vs. ..., Try-Out Winner Book, Ultimate Marvel Team-Up, Ultimate Spider-Man, Web of Spider- Man & Within Our Reach)

AMAZING SPIDER-MAN, THE
Marvel Comics Group: March, 1963 - No. 441, Nov, 1998

	GD 2.0	VG 4.0	FN 6.0	VF 8.0	VF/NM 9.0	NM- 9.2
1-Retells origin by Steve Ditko; 1st Fantastic Four x-over (ties with F.F. #12 as first Marvel x-over); intro. John Jameson & The Chameleon; Spider-Man's 2nd app.; Kirby/Ditko-c; Ditko-c/a #1-38	1250	2500	3750	11,000	25,500	40,000
1-Reprint from the Golden Record Comic set	14	28	42	104	181	260
With record (1966)	22	44	66	155	258	360
2-1st app. the Vulture & the Terrible Tinkerer	340	680	1020	3060	5780	8500
3-1st app. Doc Octopus; 1st full-length story; Human Torch cameo; Spider-Man pin-up by Ditko	267	534	801	2336	4368	6400

4-Origin & 1st app. The Sandman (see Strange Tales #115 for 2nd app.); 1st monthly issue;

	GD 2.0	VG 4.0	FN 6.0	VF 8.0	VF/NM 9.0	NM- 9.2
intro. Betty Brant & Liz Allen	208	416	624	1820	3410	5000
5-Dr. Doom app.	171	342	513	1496	2798	4100
6-1st app. Lizard	156	312	468	1365	2558	3750
7-Vs. The Vulture	109	218	327	927	1714	2500
8-Fantastic Four app. in back-up story by Kirby & Ditko	98	196	294	833	1442	2050
9-Origin & 1st app. Electro (2/64)	117	234	351	995	1723	2450
10-1st app. Big Man & The Enforcers	100	200	300	850	1575	2300
11,12: 11-1st app. Bennett Brant. 12-Doc Octopus unmasks Spider-Man-c/story	72	144	216	612	1131	1650
13-1st app. Mysterio	100	200	300	850	1575	2300
14-(7/64)-1st app. The Green Goblin (c/story)(Norman Osborn); Hulk x-over	167	334	501	1461	2731	4000
15-1st app. Kraven the Hunter; 1st mention of Mary Jane Watson (not shown)	80	160	240	680	1265	1850
16-Spider-Man battles Daredevil (1st x-over 9/64); still in old yellow costume	63	126	189	536	993	1450
17-2nd app. Green Goblin (c/story); Human Torch x-over (also in #18 & #21)	72	144	216	612	1131	1650
18-1st app. Ned Leeds who later becomes Hobgoblin; Fantastic Four cameo; 3rd app. Sandman	50	100	150	400	725	1050
19-Sandman app.	40	80	120	300	550	800
20-Origin & 1st app. The Scorpion	57	114	171	485	893	1300
21-2nd app. The Beetle (see Strange Tales #123)	39	78	117	293	534	775
22-1st app. Princess Python	36	72	108	270	498	725
23-3rd app. The Green Goblin-c/story; Norman Osborn app.	46	92	138	368	672	975
24	30	60	90	225	413	600
25-(6/65)-1st brief app. Mary Jane Watson (face not shown); 1st app. Spencer Smythe; Norman Osborn app.	38	76	114	285	518	750
26-4th app. The Green Goblin-c/story; 1st app. Crime Master; dies in #27	40	80	120	311	568	825
27-5th app. The Green Goblin-c/story; Norman Osborn app.	38	76	114	285	518	750
28-Origin & 1st app. Molten Man (9/65, scarcer in high grade)	70	140	210	595	1098	1600
29,30	25	50	75	184	330	475
31-1st app. Harry Osborn who later becomes 2nd Green Goblin, Gwen Stacy & Prof. Warren.	31	62	93	233	429	625
32-38: 34-4th app. Kraven the Hunter. 36-1st app. Looter. 37-Intro. Norman Osborn. 38-(7/66)-2nd brief app. Mary Jane Watson (face not shown); last Ditko issue	22	44	66	165	295	425
39-The Green Goblin-c/story; Green Goblin's i.d. revealed as Norman Osborn; Romita-a begins (8/66; see Daredevil #16 for 1st Romita-a on Spider-Man)	32	64	96	240	445	650
40-1st told origin The Green Goblin	39	78	117	293	534	775
41-1st app. Rhino	30	60	90	225	413	600
42-(11/66)-3rd app. Mary Jane Watson (cameo in last 2 panels); 1st time face is shown	20	40	60	146	261	375
43-49: 44,45-2nd & 3rd app. The Lizard. 46-Intro. Shocker. 47-M. J. Watson & Peter Parker 1st date. 47-Green Goblin cameo; Harry & Norman Osborn app. 47,49-5th & 6th app. Kraven the Hunter	15	30	45	111	198	285
50-1st app. Kingpin (7/67)	72	144	216	459	855	1250
51-2nd app. Kingpin; Joe Robertson 1-panel cameo	21	42	63	156	278	400
52-58,60: 52-1st app. Joe Robertson & 3rd app. Kingpin. 56-1st app. Capt. George Stacy. 57,58-Ka-Zar app.	11	22	33	79	140	200
59-1st app. Brainwasher (alias Kingpin); 1st-c app. M. J. Watson	12	24	36	82	146	210
61-74: 61-1st Gwen Stacy cover app. 67-1st app. Randy Robertson. 69-Kingpin-c. 69,70-Kingpin app. 73-1st app. Silvermane. 74-Last 12¢ issue	9	18	27	63	107	150
75-83,87-89,91,92,95,99: 78,79-1st app. The Prowler. 83-1st app. Schemer & Vanessa (Kingpin's wife)	8	16	24	54	90	125
84-86,93: 84,85-Kingpin-c/story. 86-Re-intro & origin Black Widow in new costume. 93-1st app. Arthur Stacy	8	16	24	56	93	130
90-Death of Capt. Stacy	9	18	27	65	113	160
94-Origin retold	10	20	30	68	119	170
96-98-Green Goblin app. (97,98-Green Goblin-c); drug books not approved by CCA	10	20	30	70	123	175
100-Anniversary issue (9/71); Green Goblin cameo (2 pgs.)	15	30	45	107	191	275
101-1st app. Morbius the Living Vampire; Wizard cameo; last 15¢ issue (10/71)	16	32	48	114	202	290
101-Silver ink 2nd printing (9/92, $1.75)						2.50

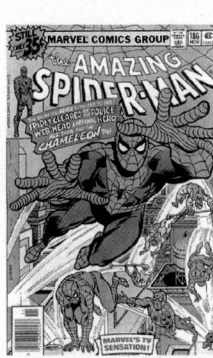

Amazing Spider-Man #186 © MAR

Amazing Spider-Man #246 © MAR

Amazing Spider-Man #352 © MAR

	GD 2.0	VG 4.0	FN 6.0	VF 8.0	VF/NM 9.0	NM- 9.2
102-Origin & 2nd app. Morbius (25¢, 52 pgs.)	10	20	30	73	129	185
103-118: 104,111-Kraven the Hunter-c/stories. 108-1st app. Sha-Shan. 109-Dr. Strange-c/story (6/72). 110-1st app. Gibbon. 113-1st app. Hammerhead. 116-118-reprints story from Spectacular Spider-Man Mag. in color with some changes	6	12	18	39	62	85
119,120-Spider-Man vs. Hulk (4 & 5/73)	8	16	24	54	90	125
121-Death of Gwen Stacy (6/73) (killed by Green Goblin) (reprinted in Marvel Tales #98 & 192)	19	38	57	138	244	350
122-Death of The Green Goblin-c/story (7/73) (reprinted in Marvel Tales #99 & 192)	19	38	57	141	251	360
123,126-128: 123-Cage app. 126-1st mention of Harry Osborn becoming Green Goblin	5	10	15	35	55	75
124-1st app. Man-Wolf (9/73)	6	12	18	41	66	90
125-Man-Wolf origin	6	12	18	37	59	80
129-1st app. The Punisher (2/74); 1st app. Jackal	35	70	105	263	482	700
130-133: 131-Last 20¢ issue	4	8	12	28	44	60
134-(7/74); 1st app. Tarantula; Harry Osborn discovers Spider-Man's ID; Punisher cameo	5	10	15	32	51	70
135-2nd full Punisher app. (8/74)	8	16	24	52	86	120
136-1st app. Harry Osborn Green Goblin in costume	7	14	21	49	80	110
137-Green Goblin-c/story (2nd Harry Osborn Goblin)	5	10	15	35	55	75
138-141: 139-1st Grizzly. 140-1st app. Glory Grant	3	6	9	21	32	42
142,143-Gwen Stacy clone cameos: 143-1st app. Cyclone	4	8	12	22	34	45
144-147: 144-Full app. of Gwen Stacy clone. 145,146-Gwen Stacy clone storyline continues. 147-Spider-Man learns Gwen Stacy is clone	4	8	12	22	34	45
148-Jackal revealed	4	8	12	22	37	50
149-Spider-Man clone story begins, clone dies (?); origin of Jackal	6	12	18	41	66	90
150-Spider-Man decides he is not the clone	4	8	12	23	36	48
151-Spider-Man disposes of clone body	4	8	12	23	36	48
152-160-(Regular 25¢ editions). 159-Last 25¢ issue(8/76)	3	6	9	17	25	32
155-159-(30¢-c variants, limited distribution)	6	12	18	37	59	80
161-Nightcrawler app. from X-Men; Punisher cameo; Wolverine & Colossus app.	3	6	9	20	30	40
162-Punisher, Nightcrawler app.; 1st Jigsaw	3	6	9	20	30	40
163-168,181-188: 167-1st app. Will O' The Wisp. 181-Origin retold; gives life history of Spidy; Punisher cameo in flashback (1 panel). 182-(7/78)-Peter's first proposal to Mary Jane, but she declines (in #183)	3	6	9	14	19	24
169-173-(Regular 30¢ edition). 169-Clone story recapped. 171-Nova app.	3	6	9	14	19	24
169-173-(35¢-c variants, limited dist.)(6-10/77)	14	28	42	99	175	250
174,175-Punisher app.	3	6	9	16	22	28
176-180-Green Goblin app.	3	6	9	16	23	30
189,190-Byrne-a	3	6	9	16	21	26
191-193,196-199: 193-Peter & Mary Jane break up. 196-Faked death of Aunt May	2	4	6	10	14	18

NOTE: Whitman 3-packs containing #192-194,196 exist.

	GD 2.0	VG 4.0	FN 6.0	VF 8.0	VF/NM 9.0	NM- 9.2
194-1st app. Black Cat	4	8	12	26	41	55
195-2nd app. Black Cat	3	6	9	14	19	24
200-Giant origin issue (1/80)	3	6	9	21	32	42
201,202-Punisher app.	2	4	6	11	16	20
203-205,207,208,210-219: 203-3rd app. Dazzler (4/80). 210-1st app. Madame Web. 212-1st app. Hydro Man; origin Sandman	2	4	6	8	10	12
206-Byrne-a	2	4	6	8	12	15
209-Origin & 1st app. Calypso (10/80)	2	4	6	11	16	20
220-237: 225-(2/82)-Foolkiller-c/story. 226,227-Black Cat returns. 234-Free 16 pg. insert "Marvel Guide to Collecting Comics". 235-Origin Will-'O-The-Wisp. 236-Tarantula dies	1	3	4	6	8	10
238-(3/83)-1st app. Hobgoblin (Ned Leeds); came with skin "Tattooz" decal.						

NOTE: The same decal appears in the more common Fantastic Four #252 which is being removed & placed in this issue as incentive to increase value

	GD 2.0	VG 4.0	FN 6.0	VF 8.0	VF/NM 9.0	NM- 9.2
(Value listed is with or without tattooz)	7	14	21	47	76	105
239-240 app. Hobgoblin & 1st battle w/Spidey	4	8	12	26	41	55
240-243,246-248: 241-Origin The Vulture. 242-Mary Jane Watson cameo (last panel). 243-Reintro Mary Jane after 4 year absence	1	2	3	5	7	9
244-3rd app. Hobgoblin (cameo)	2	4	6	8	12	15
245-(1/83)-4th app. Hobgoblin (cameo); Lefty Donovan gains powers of Hobgoblin & battles Spider-Man	1	2	3	6	9	12
249-251: 3 part Hobgoblin/Spider-Man battle. 249-Retells origin & death of 1st Green Goblin. 251-Last old costume	2	4	6	9	13	16

252-Spider-Man dons new black costume (5/84); ties with Marvel Team-Up #141 & Spectacular Spider-Man #90 for 1st new costume in regular title (See Marvel Super-Heroes

	GD 2.0	VG 4.0	FN 6.0	VF 8.0	VF/NM 9.0	NM- 9.2
Secret Wars #8 (12/84) for acquisition of costume)	4	8	12	24	37	50
253-1st app. The Rose	2	4	6	8	10	12
254-258: 256-1st app. Puma. 257-Hobgoblin cameo; 2nd app. Puma; M.J. Watson reveals she knows Spidey's i.d. 258-Hobgoblin app.	1	2	3	5	7	9
259-Full Hobgoblin app.; Spidey back to old costume; origin Mary Jane Watson	2	4	6	8	11	14
260-Hobgoblin app.	1	3	4	6	8	10
261-Hobgoblin-c/story; painted-c by Vess	2	4	6	8	10	12
262-Spider-Man unmasked; photo-c	1	2	3	5	7	9
263,264,266-274,277-280,282,283: 274-Zarathos (The Spirit of Vengeance) app. 277-Vess back-up art. 279-Jack O'Lantern-c/story. 282-X-Factor x-over	1	2	3	4	5	7
265-1st app. Silver Sable (6/85)	2	4	6	9	13	16
265-Silver ink 2nd printing ($1.25)						2.50
275-($1.25, 52 pgs.)-Hobgoblin-c/story; origin-r by Ditko	2	4	6	13	18	22
276-Hobgoblin app.	1	3	4	6	8	10
281-Hobgoblin battles Jack O'Lantern	1	3	4	6	8	10
284,285: 284-Punisher cameo; Gang War story begins; Hobgoblin-c/story. 285-Punisher app.; minor Hobgoblin app.	1	3	4	6	8	10
286-288: 286-Hobgoblin-c & app. (minor). 287-Hobgoblin app. (minor). 288-Full Hobgoblin app.; last Gang War	1	3	4	6	8	10
289-(6/87, $1.25, 52 pgs.)-Hobgoblin's i.d. revealed as Ned Leeds; death of Ned Leeds; Macendale (Jack O'Lantern) becomes new Hobgoblin (1st app.)	3	6	9	14	19	24
290-292,295-297: 290-Peter proposes to Mary Jane. 292-She accepts; leads into wedding in Amazing Spider-Man Annual #21	1	2	3	4	5	7
293,294-Part 2 & 5 of Kraven story from Web of Spider-Man. 294-Death of Kraven	1	3	4	6	8	10
298-Todd McFarlane-c/a begins (3/88); 1st brief app. Eddie Brock who becomes Venom; (last pg.)	5	10	12	28	44	60
299-1st brief app. Venom with costume	4	8	10	18	27	35
300-$1.50, 52 pgs.) 25th Anniversary)-1st full Venom app.; last black costume (5/88)	8	16	24	54	90	125
301-305: 301 ($1.00 issues begin). 304-1st bi-weekly issue	2	4	6	9	13	16
306-311,313,314: 306-Swipes-c from Action #1	2	4	6	8	11	14
312-Hobgoblin battles Green Goblin	2	4	6	11	16	20
315-317-Venom app.	2	4	6	13	18	22
318-323,325: 319-Bi-weekly begins again	1	2	3	5	7	9
324-Sabretooth app.; McFarlane cover only	1	2	3	5	7	9
326,327,329: 327-Cosmic Spidey continues from Spectacular Spider-Man (no McFarlane-c/a)						5.00
328-Hulk x-over; last McFarlane issue	1	3	4	6	8	10
330,331-Punisher app. 331-Minor Venom app.						4.00
332,333-Venom-c/story	1	2	3	5	7	9
334-336,338-343: 341-Tarantula app.						4.00
337-Hobgoblin app.						4.00
344-(2/91) 1st app. Cletus Kasady (Carnage)	2	4	6	8	11	14
345-1st full app. Cletus Kasady; Venom cameo on last pg.	2	4	6	8	11	14
346,347-Venom app.	1	2	3	5	7	9
348,349,351-359: 348-Avengers x-over. 351,352-New Warriors app. 353-Darkhawk app.; brief Punisher app. 354-Punisher cameo & Nova, Night Thrasher (New Warriors), Darkhawk & Moon Knight. 357,358-Punisher, Darkhawk, Moon Knight, Night Thrasher, Nova x-over. 358-3 part gatefold-c; last $1.00-c. 360-Carnage cameo						3.00
350-($1.50, 52pgs.)-Origin retold; Spidey vs. Dr. Doom; pin-ups; Uncle Ben app.						5.00
360-Carnage cameo						4.00
361-(4/92) Intro Carnage (the Spawn of Venom); begin 3 part story; recap of how Spidey's alien costume became Venom	2	4	6	9	12	15
361-($1.25)-2nd printing; silver-c						2.50
362,363-Carnage & Venom-c/story	1	2	3	5	7	9
362-2nd printing						2.50
364,366-374,376-387: 364-The Shocker app. (old villain). 366-Peter's parents-c/story. 369-Harry Osborn back-up (Gr. Goblin II). 373-Venom back-up. 374-Venom-c/story. 376-Cardiac app. 378-Maximum Carnage part 3. 381,382-Hulk app. 383-The Jury app. 384-Venom/carnage app. 387-New costume Vulture						3.00
365-($3.95, 84 pgs.)-30th anniversary issue w/silver hologram on-c; Spidey/Venom/Carnage pull-out back-up; contains 5 pg. preview of Spider-Man 2099 (1st app.); Spidey's origin retold; Lizard app.; reintro Peter's parents in Stan Lee 3 pg. text w/illo (story continues thru #370)						5.00
375-($3.95, 68 pgs.)-Holo-grafx foil-c; vs. Venom story; ties into Venom: Lethal Protector #1; Pat Olliffe-a.						5.00
388-($2.25, 68 pgs.)-Newsstand edition; Venom back-up & Cardiac & chance back-up						2.50

Amazing Spider-Man #411 © MAR

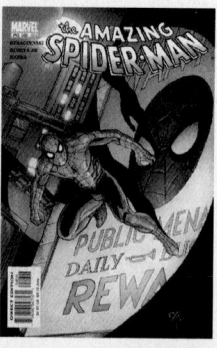

Amazing Spider-Man V2 #46 © MAR

Amazing Spider-Man #513 © MAR

	GD	VG	FN	VF	VF/NM	NM-		GD	VG	FN	VF	VF/NM	NM-
	2.0	4.0	6.0	8.0	9.0	9.2		2.0	4.0	6.0	8.0	9.0	9.2

388-($2.95, 68 pgs.)-Collector's edition w/foil-c 3.00
389-396,398,399,401-420: 389-$1.50-c begins; bound-in trading card sheet; Green Goblin app.
394-Power & Responsibility Pt. 2. 396-Daredevil-c & app. 403-Carnage app. 406-1st New Doc Octopus. 407-Human Torch, Silver Sable, Sandman app. 409-Kaine, Rhino app. 410-Carnage app. 414-The Rose app. 415-Onslaught story; Spidey vs. Sentinels. 416-Epilogue to Onslaught; Garney-a(p); Williamson-a(i) 2.50
390-($2.95)-Collector's edition polybagged w/16 pg. insert of new animated Spidey TV show plus animation cel 3.00
394-($2.95, 48 pgs.)-Deluxe edition; flip book w/Birth of a Spider-Man Pt. 2; silver foil both-c; Power & Responsibility Pt. 2 .... 3.00
397-($2.25)-Flip book w/Ultimate Spider-Man 2.50
400-($2.95)-Death of Aunt May 3.00
400-($2.95)-Death of Aunt May; embossed double-c 5.00
400-Collector's Edition; white-c 1 2 3 5 7 9
408-($2.95) Polybagged version with TV theme song cassette 8.00
421-424,426,428-433: 426-Begin $1.99-c. 432-Spiderhunt pt. 2 .... 2.50
425-($2.99)-48 pgs., wraparound-c 3.00
427-($2.25) Return of Dr. Octopus; double gatefold-c 2.50
434-440: 434-Double-c with "Amazing Ricochet #1". 438-Daredevil app. 439-Avengers-c/app.
440-Byrnes 2.50
441-Final issue; Byrne-s 4.00
#500-up (See Amazing Spider-Man Vol. 2; series resumed original numbering after Vol. 2 #58)
#(-1) Flashback issue (7/97, $1.95-c) 2.50
Annual 1 (1964, 72 pgs.)-Origin Spider-Man; 1st app. Sinister Six (Dr. Octopus, Electro, Kraven the Hunter, Mysterio, Sandman, Vulture) (new 41 pg. story); plus gallery of Spidey foes; early X-Men app. 85 170 255 723 1337 1950
Annual 2 (1965, 25¢, 72 pgs.)-Reprints from #1,2,5 plus New Doctor Strange story
from #11,12; Romita-a 34 68 102 255 465 675
Special 3 (11/66, 25¢, 72 pgs.)-New Avengers story & Hulk x-over; Doctor Octopus-r from #11,12; Romita-a 16 32 48 114 202 290
Special 4 (11/67, 25¢, 68 pgs.)-Spidey battles Human Torch (new 41 pg. story)
.... 13 26 39 95 168 240
Special 5 (11/68, 25¢, 68 pgs.)-New 40 pg. Red Skull story; 1st app. Peter Parker's parents; last appeared with new-a 12 24 36 82 146 210
Special 6 (11/69, 25¢, 68 pgs.)-Reprints 41 pg. Sinister Six story from annual #1 plus 2 Kirby/Ditko stories (r) 5 10 15 32 51 70
Special 7 (12/70, 25¢, 68 pgs.)-All-r(#1,2) new Vulture-c 5 10 15 32 51 70
Special 8 (12/71)-All-r 5 10 15 32 51 70
King Size 9 ('73)-Reprints Spectacular Spider-Man (mag.) #2; 40 pg. Green Goblin-c/story (re-edited from 58 pgs.) 5 10 15 32 51 70
Annual 10 (1976)-Origin Human Fly (vs. Spidey); new-a begins 3 6 9 14 20 25
Annual 11-13 ('77-'79):12-Spidey vs. Hulk-r/#119,120. 13-New Byrne/Austin-a; Dr. Octopus x-over w/Spectacular S-M Ann. #1 .... 2 4 6 9 13 16
Annual 14 (1980)-Miller-c/a(p); Dr. Strange app. 2 4 6 13 18 22
Annual 15 (1981)-Miller-c/a(p); Punisher app. 3 6 9 16 23 30
Annual 16-20:16 ('82)-Origin/1st app. new Capt. Marvel (female heroine). 17 ('83)-Kingpin app. 18 ('84)-Scorpion app.; JJJ weds. 19 ('85). 20 ('86)-Origin Iron Man of 2020
.... 1 2 3 4 5 7
Annual 21 (1987)-Special wedding issue; newsstand & direct sale versions exist & are worth same 2 4 6 8 10 12
Annual 22 (1988, $1.75, 68 pgs.)-1st app. Speedball; Evolutionary War x-over; Daredevil app. 6.00
Annual 23 (1989, $2.00, 68 pgs.)-Atlantis Attacks; origin Spider-Man retold; She-Hulk app.; Byrne-c; Liefeld-a(p), 23 pgs. 4.00
Annual 24 (1990, $2.00, 68 pgs.)-Ant-Man app. 3.00
Annual 25 (1991, $2.00, 68 pgs.)-3 pg. origin recap; Iron Man app.; 1st Venom solo story; Ditko-a (6 pgs.) 5.00
Annual 26 (1992, $2.25, 68 pgs.)-New Warriors-c/story; Venom solo story cont'd in Spectacular Spider-Man Annual #12 .... 4.00
Annual 27,28 ('93, '94, $2.95, 68 pgs.)-27-Bagged w/card; 1st app. Annex. 28-Carnage-c/story; Rhino & Cloak and Dagger back-ups 3.00
'96 Special-($2.95, 64 pgs.)-"Blast From The Past" 3.00
'97 Special-($2.99)-Wraparound-c,Sundown app. 3.00
Marvel Graphic Novel - Parallel Lives (3/89, $8.95) 2 4 6 8 10 12
Marvel Graphic Novel - Spirits of the Earth (1990, $18.95, HC)
.... 3 6 9 16 22 28
Super Special 1 (4/95, $3.95)-Flip Book 4.00
...: Skating on Thin Ice1(1990, $1.25, Canadian)-McFarlane-c; anti-drug issue; Electro app.
.... 1 2 3 5 7 9
...: Skating on Thin Ice 1 (2/93, $1.50, American) 4.00
...: Double Trouble 2 (1990, $1.25, Canadian) 6.00

...: Double Trouble 2 (2/93, $1.50, American) 3.00
...: Hit and Run 3 (1990, $1.25, Canadian)-Ghost Rider-c/story
.... 1 2 3 5 7 9
...: Hit and Run 3 (2/93, $1.50, American) 3.00
...: Carnage (6/93, $6.95)-r/ASM #344,345,359-363 1 2 3 4 5 7
...: Chaos in Calgary 4 (Canadian; part of 5 part series)-Turbine,Night Rider, Frightful app. 2 4 6 8 11 14
...: Chaos in Calgary 4 (2/93, $1.50, American) 3.00
...: Deadball 5 (1993, $1.60, Canadian)-Green Goblin-c/story; features Montreal Expos 2 4 6 10 14 18
Note: Prices listed above are for English Canadian editions. French editions are worth double.
...: Soul of the Hunter nn (8/92, $5.95, 52 pgs.)-Zeck-c/a(p) 6.00
Wizard #1 Ace Edition ($13.99) r/#1 w/ new Ramos acetate-c 14.00
Wizard #129 Ace Edition ($13.99) r/#129 w/ new Ramos acetate-c 14.00
NOTE: Austin a(i)-248, 335, 337, Annual 1; c(i)-188, 241, 242, 248, 331, 334, 343, Annual 25. J. Buscema a(p)-72, 73, 76-81, 84, 85. Byrne a-189p, 190p, 206p, Annual 3r, 6r, 7r, 13p; c-189p, 268, 296, Annual 12. Ditko a-1-38, Annual 1, Special 3(r), 2, 24(2); c-1i, 2-38. Guice c/a-Annual 18i. Gil Kane a(p)-89-105, 120-124, 150, Annual 10, 12i, 24p; c-90p, 96, 98, 99, 101-105p, 129p, 131p, 132p, 137-140p, 143p, 148p, 149p, 151p, 153p, 160p, 161p, Annual 10p, 24. Kirby a-8. Erik Larsen a-324, 327, 329-350; c-327, 329-350, 354i, Annual 25. McFarlane a-298p, 299p, 300-303, 304, 303-323p, 325p, 328. Miller c-218, 219. Mooney a-65i, 67-82i, 84-88i, 173i, 178i, 189i, 190i, 192i, 193i, 196-202i, 207i, 211-219i, 221i, 222i, 226i, 227i, 229-233i, Annual 11i, 17i. Nasser c-228p. Nebres a-Annual 24i. Russell c-357i. Simonson c-222, 337i. Starlin a-113i, 114i, 187p. Williamson a-365i.

AMAZING SPIDER-MAN (Volume 2) (Some issues reprinted in "Spider-Man, Best Of" hardcovers)
Marvel Comics: Jan, 1999 - Present ($2.99/$1.99/$2.25)
1-($2.99)-Byrne-a 6.00
1-($6.95) Dynamic Forces variant-c by the Romitas 1 3 4 6 8 10
2-($1.99) Two covers -by John Byrne and Andy Kubert 4.00
3-11: 4-Fantastic Four app. 5-Spider-Woman-c 2.50
12-($2.99) Sinister Six return (cont. in Peter Parker #12) 3.00
13-17: 13-Mary Jane's plane explodes 2.50
18,19,21-24,26-28: 18-Begin $2.25-c. 19-Venom-c. 24-Maximum Security 2.50
20-($2.99, 100 pg.) Spider-Slayer issue; new story and reprints 3.00
25-($2.99) Regular cover; Peter Parker becomes the Green Goblin 3.00
25-($3.99) Holo-foil enhanced cover 4.00
29-Peter is reunited with Mary Jane 2.50
30-Straczynski/Campbell-c begin; intro. Ezekiel 6.00
31-35: Battles Morlun 4.00
36-Black cover; aftermath of the Sept. 11 tragedy in New York 10.00
37-49: 39-'Nuff Said issue 42-Dr. Strange app. 43-45-Doctor Octopus app. 46-48-Cho-c 2.50
50-Peter and MJ reunite; Captain America & Dr. Doom app.; Campbell-c 3.00
51-58: 51,52-Campbell-c. 55,56-Avery scripts. 57,58-Avengers, FF, Cyclops app. 2.50
(After #58 [Nov, 2003] numbering reverted back to original Vol. 1 with #500, Dec, 2003)
500-($3.50) J. Scott Campbell-c; Romita Jr. & Sr.-a; Uncle Ben app. 3.50
501-524: 501-Harris-a. 503-504-Loki app. 506-508-Ezekiel app. 509-514-Sins Past; intro. Gabriel and Sarah Osborn; Deodato-a. 519-Moves into Avengers HQ. 521-Begin $2.50-c
524-Harris-c 2.50
525,526-Evolve or Die x-over. 525-David-s. 526-Hudlin-s; Spider-Man loses eye 4.00
525-526-2nd printings with variant-c. 525-Ben Reilly costume. 526-Six-Armed Spidey.
527-Spider-Man 2099. 528-Spider-Ham 5.00
527,528: Evolve or Die pt.9, 12 .... 2.50
529-Debut of red and gold costume; Garney-a 19.00
529-2nd printing 5.00
529-3rd printing with Wieringo-c 3.00
530,531-Titanium Man app.; Kirkham-a. 531-Begin $2.99-c 6.00
532-538-Civil War tie-in. 538-Aunt May shot 5.00
539-543-Back in Black. 539-Peter wears the black costume 5.00
544-($3.99) "One More Day" pt. 1; Quesada-a/Straczynski-a 4.00
1999, 2000 Annual (6/99, '00, $3.50) 1999-Buscema-a 3.50
2001 Annual ($2.99) Follows Peter Parker: S-M #29; last Mackie-s 3.00
Collected Edition #30-32 ($3.95) reprints #30-32 w/cover #30 .... 4.00
... 500 Covers HC (2004, $49.99) reprints covers for #1-500 & Annuals; yearly re-caps 50.00
... Omnibus HC (2007, $99.99, dustjacket) r/Amazing Fantasy #15, Amazing Spider-Man #1-38, Annual #1,2, Strange Tales Annual #2 & Fantastic Four Annual #1; letter pages, bonus art, intro. by Stan Lee; bios, essays, Marvel Tales cover gallery 100.00
...Vol. 1: Coming Home (2001, $15.95) r/#30-35; J. Scott Campbell-c 16.00
...Vol. 2: Revelations (2002, $8.99) r/#36-39; Kaare Andrews-c 9.00
...Vol. 3: Until the Stars Turn Cold (2002, $12.99) r/#40-45; Romita Jr.-c 13.00
...Vol. 4: The Life and Death of Spiders (2003, $11.99) r/#46-50; Campbell-c 12.00
...Vol. 5: Unintended Consequences (2003, $12.99) r/#51-56; Dodson-c 13.00
...Vol. 6: Happy Birthday (2003, $12.99) r/#57,58,500-502 .... 13.00
...Vol. 7: The Book of Ezekiel (2004, $12.99) r/#503-508; Romita Jr.-c 13.00
...Vol. 8: Sins Past (2005, $12.99) r/#509-514; cover sketch gallery 13.00
...Vol. 9: Skin Deep (2005, $9.99) r/#515-518 .... 10.00
...Vol. 10: New Avengers (2005, $14.99) r/#519-524 .... 15.00
Civil War: Amazing Spider-Man TPB (2007, $17.99) r/#532-538; variant covers 18.00

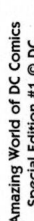

Amazing World of DC Comics
Special Edition #1 © DC

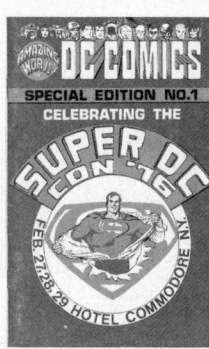

Amazons Attack #3 © DC

American Century #2
© Howard Chaykin & DC

	GD 2.0	VG 4.0	FN 6.0	VF 8.0	VF/NM 9.0	NM- 9.2		GD 2.0	VG 4.0	FN 6.0	VF 8.0	VF/NM 9.0	NM- 9.2

AMAZING WILLIE MAYS, THE
Famous Funnies Publ.: No date (Sept, 1954)

nn — 79 158 237 494 822 1150

AMAZING WORLD OF DC COMICS
DC Comics: Jul, 1974 - No. 17, 1978 ($1.50, B&W, mail-order DC Pro-zine)

1-Kubert interview; unpublished Kirby-a; Infantino-c 6 12 18 43 69 95
2-4: 3-Julie Schwartz profile. 4-Batman; Robinson-c 4 8 12 28 44 60
5-Sheldon Mayer 4 8 12 24 37 50
6,8,13: 6-Joe Orlando; EC-r; Wrightson pin-up. 8-Infantino; Batman-r from Pop Tart giveaway. 13-Humor; Aragonés-c; Wood/Ditko-a; photos from serials of Superman, Batman, Captain Marvel 3 6 9 19 29 38
7,10-12: 7-Superman; r/1955 Pep comic giveaway. 10-Behind the scenes at DC; Showcase article. 11-Super-Villains; unpubl. Secret Society of S.V. story.
12-Legion; Grell-c/interview; 3 6 9 20 30 40
9-Legion of Super-Heroes; lengthy bios and history; Cockrum-c 7 14 21 45 73 100
14-Justice League 3 6 9 21 32 42
15-Wonder Woman; Nasser-c 4 8 12 26 41 55
16-Golden Age heroes 4 8 12 24 37 50
17-Shazam; G.A., 70s, TV and Fawcett heroes 3 6 9 21 32 42
Special 1 (Digest size) 3 6 9 18 27 35

AMAZING WORLD OF SUPERMAN (See Superman)

AMAZING X-MEN
Marvel Comics: Mar, 1995 - No. 4, July, 1995 ($1.95, limited series)

1-Age of Apocalypse; Andy Kubert-c/a 3.50
2-4 2.50

AMAZON
Comico: Mar, 1989 - No. 3, May, 1989 ($1.95, limited series)

1-3: Ecological theme 2.25

AMAZON (Also see Marvel Versus DC #3 & DC Versus Marvel #4)
DC Comics (Amalgam): Apr, 1996 ($1.95, one-shot)

1-John Byrne-c/a/scripts 2.50

AMAZON ATTACK 3-D
The 3-D Zone: Sept, 1990 ($3.95, 28 pgs.)

1-Chaykin-a 6.00

AMAZONS ATTACK (See Wonder Woman #8 - 2006 series)
DC Comics: Jun, 2007 - No. 6, Late Oct, 2007 ($2.99, limited series)

1-6-Queen Hippolyta and Amazons attacks Wash., DC; Pfeifer-s/Woods-a 3.00

AMAZON WOMAN (1st Series)
FantaCo: Summer, 1994 - No. 2, Fall, 1994 ($2.95, B&W, limited series, mature)

1,2: Tom Simonton-c/a/scripts 3.00

AMAZON WOMAN (2nd Series)
FantaCo: Feb, 1996 - No. 4, May, 1996 ($2.95, B&W, limited series, mature)

1-4: Tom Simonton-a/scripts 3.00
...: Invaders of Terror ('96, $5.95) Simonton-a/s 6.00

AMBUSH (See Zane Grey, Four Color 314)

AMBUSH BUG (Also see Son of...)
DC Comics: June, 1985 - No. 4, Sept, 1985 (75¢, limited series)

1-4: Giffen-c/a in all 3.00
Nothing Special 1 (9/92, $2.50, 68pg.)-Giffen-c/a 3.00
Stocking Stuffer (2/86, $1.25)-Giffen-c/a 3.00

AMERICA AT WAR - THE BEST OF DC WAR COMICS (See Fireside Book Series)

AMERICA IN ACTION
Dell (Imp. Publ. Co.)/ Mayflower House Publ.: 1942; Winter, 1945 (36 pgs.)

1942-Dell-(68 pgs.) 17 34 51 98 154 210
1-(1945)-Has 3 adaptations from American history; Kiefer, Schrotter & Webb-a 14 28 42 76 108 140

AMERICAN, THE
Dark Horse Comics: July, 1987 - No. 8, 1989 ($1.50/$1.75, B&W)

1-8: ($1.50) 2.50
Collection ($5.95, B&W)-Reprints 6.00
Special 1 (1990, $2.25, B&W) 2.50

AMERICAN AIR FORCES, THE (See A-1 Comics)
William H. Wise(Flying Cadet Publ. Co./Hasan(No.1)/Life's Romances/ Magazine Ent. No. 5 on): Sept-Oct, 1944-No. 4, 1945; No. 5, 1951-No. 12, 1954

1-Article by Zack Mosley, creator of Smilin' Jack; German war-c 20 40 60 117 184 250
2-Classic-Japan war-c 32 64 96 186 293 400
3,4-Japan war-c 14 28 42 78 112 145
NOTE: *All part comic, part magazine. Art by **Whitney, Chas. Quinlan, H. C. Kiefer,** and **Tony Dipreta**.*
5(A-1 45)(Formerly Jet Powers), 6(A-1 54), 7(A-1 57), 8(A-1 65), 9(A-1 67), 10(A-1 74), 11(A-1 79), 12(A-1 91) 9 18 27 47 61 75
NOTE: *Powell c/a-5-12.*

AMERICAN CENTURY
DC Comics (Vertigo): May, 2001 - No. 27, Oct, 2003 ($2.50/$2.75)

1-Chaykin-s/painted-c; Tischman-a 4.00
2-27: 5-New story arc begins. 10-16,22-27-Orbik-c. 17-21-Silke-c. 18-$2.75-c begins 2.75
Hollywood Babylon (2002, $12.95, TPB) r/#5-9; w/sketch-to-art pages 13.00
Scars & Stripes (2001, $9.95, TPB) r/#1-4; Tischman intro. 9.00

AMERICAN FLAGG! (See First Comics Graphic Novel 3,9,12,21 & Howard Chaykin's..)
First Comics: Oct, 1983 - No. 50, Mar, 1988

1,21-27: 1-Chaykin-c/a begins. 21-27-Alan Moore scripts 4.00
2-20,28-49: 31-Origin Bob Violence 3.00
50-Last issue 4.00
Special 1 (11/86)-Introduces Chaykin's Time[2] 4.00

AMERICAN FREAK: A TALE OF THE UN-MEN
DC Comics (Vertigo): Feb, 1994 - No. 5, Jun, 1994 ($1.95, mini-series, mature)

1-5 2.50

AMERICAN GRAPHICS
Henry Stewart: No. 1, 1954; No. 2, 1957 (25¢)

1-The Maid of the Mist, The Last of the Eries (Indian Legends of Niagara) (sold at Niagara Falls) 11 22 33 60 83 105
2-Victory at Niagara & Laura Secord (Heroine of the War of 1812) 8 16 24 40 50 60

AMERICAN INDIAN, THE (See Picture Progress)

AMERICAN LIBRARY
David McKay Publ.: 1943 - No. 6, 1944 (15¢, 68 pgs., B&W, text & pictures)

nn (#1)-Thirty Seconds Over Tokyo (movie) 38 76 114 222 351 480
nn (#2)-Guadalcanal Diary; painted-c (only 10¢) 28 56 84 162 256 350
3-6: 3-Look to the Mountain. 4-Case of the Crooked Candle (Perry Mason)
5-Duel in the Sun. 6-Wingate's Raiders 15 30 45 85 130 175

AMERICAN: LOST IN AMERICA, THE
Dark Horse Comics: July, 1992 - No. 4, Oct, 1992 ($2.50, limited series)

1-4: 1-Dorman painted-c. 2-Phillips painted-c. 3-Mignola-c. 4-Jim Lee-c 2.50

AMERICAN SPLENDOR (Series of titles)
Dark Horse Comics: Aug, 1996 - Present (B&W, all one-shots)

--COMIC-CON COMICS (8/96) 1-H. Pekar script. --MUSIC COMICS (11/97) nn-H. Pekar-s/ Sacco-a; r/Village Voice jazz strips. --ODDS AND ENDS (12/97) 1-Pekar-s. --ON THE JOB (5/97) 1-Pekar-s. --A STEP OUT OF THE NEST (8/94) 1-Pekar-s. --TERMINAL (9/99) 1-Pekar-s. --TRANSATLANTIC (7/98) 1-"American Splendour" on cover; Pekar-s 3.00
--A PORTRAIT OF THE AUTHOR IN HIS DECLINING YEARS (4/01, $3.99) 1-Photo-c.
--BEDTIME STORIES (6/00, $3.95) 4.00

AMERICAN SPLENDOR
DC Comics: Nov, 2006 - No. 4, Feb, 2007 ($2.99, B&W)

1-4-Pekar-s/art by Haspiel and various. 1-Fabry-c 3.00
...: Another Day TPB (2007, $14.99) r/#1-4 15.00

AMERICAN SPLENDOR: UNSUNG HERO
Dark Horse Comics: Aug, 2002 - No. 3, Oct, 2002 ($3.99, B&W, limited series)

1-3-Pekar script/Collier-a; biography of Robert McNeill 4.00
TPB (8/03, $11.95) r/#1-3 12.00

AMERICAN SPLENDOR: WINDFALL
Dark Horse Comics: Sept, 1995 - No. 2, Oct,1995 ($3.95, B&W, limited series)

1,2-Pekar script 4.00

AMERICAN TAIL: FIEVEL GOES WEST, AN
Marvel Comics: Early Jan, 1992 - No. 3, Early Feb, 1992 ($1.00, limited series)

1-3-Adapts Universal animated movie; Wildman-a 3.00
1-($2.95-c, 69 pgs.) Deluxe squarebound edition 5.00

AMERICAN VIRGIN
DC Comics (Vertigo): May, 2006 - Present ($2.99)

1-18-Steven Seagle-s/Becky Cloonan-a. 1-3-Quitely-c. 4-14-Middleton-c 3.00
...: Head (2006, $9.99, TPB) r/#1-4; interviews with the creators and page development 10.00

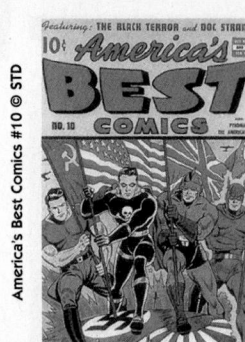

America's Best Comics #10 © STD

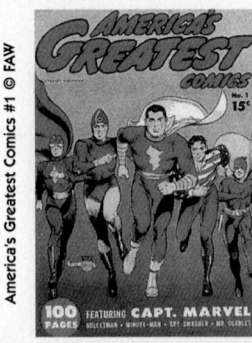

America's Greatest Comics #1 © FAW

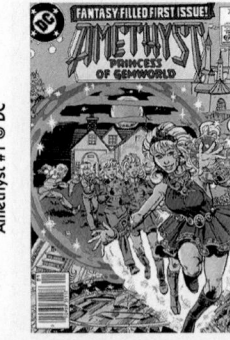

Amethyst #1 © DC

	GD 2.0	VG 4.0	FN 6.0	VF 8.0	VF/NM 9.0	NM- 9.2

...: Going Down (2007, $14.99, TPB) r/#5-9 — 15.00

AMERICAN WAY, THE
DC Comics (WildStorm): Apr, 2006 - No. 8, Nov, 2006 ($2.99, limited series)

1-8-John Ridley-s/Georges Jeanty-a/c — 3.00
TPB (2007, $19.99) r/series; covers; Jeanty sketch pages — 20.00

AMERICA'S BEST COMICS
Nedor/Better/Standard Publications: Feb, 1942; No. 2, Sept, 1942 - No. 31, July, 1949 (New logo with #9)

1-The Woman in Red, Black Terror, Captain Future, Doc Strange, The Liberator, & Don Davis, Secret Ace begin	300	600	900	1881	3141	4400
2-Origin The American Eagle; The Woman in Red ends	107	214	321	669	1110	1550
3-Pyroman begins (11/42, 1st app.; also see Startling Comics #18, 12/42)	83	166	249	519	860	1200
4-6: 5-Last Capt. Future (not in #4); Lone Eagle app. 6-American Crusader app.	62	124	186	388	644	900
7-Hitler, Mussolini & Hirohito-c	117	234	351	731	1216	1700
8-Last Liberator	60	120	180	375	625	875
9-The Fighting Yank begins; The Ghost app.	67	134	201	419	697	975
10-Flag-c	55	110	165	344	572	800
11-Hirohito & Tojo-c. (10/44)	74	148	222	463	769	1075
12-17,19-21: 14-American Eagle ends; Doc Strange vs. Hitler story. 21-Infinity-c	54	108	162	338	557	775
18-Classic-c	69	138	207	431	716	1000
22-Capt. Future app.	46	92	138	281	466	650
23-Miss Masque begins; last Doc Strange	54	108	162	338	557	775
24-Miss Masque bondage-c	53	106	159	323	537	750
25-Last Fighting Yank; Sea Eagle app.	40	80	120	244	392	540
26-31: 26-The Phantom Detective & The Silver Knight app.; Frazetta text illo & some panels in Miss Masque. 27,28-Commando Cubs. 27-Doc Strange. 28-Tuska Black Terror.						
29-Last Pyroman	40	80	120	240	383	525

NOTE: *American Eagle* not in 3, 8, 9, 13. *Fighting Yank* not in 10, 12. *Liberator* not in 2, 6, 7. *Pyroman* not in 9, 11, 14-16, 23, 25-27. *Schomburg* (Xela) c-5, 7-31. *Bondage* c-18, 24.

AMERICA'S BEST COMICS
America's Best Comics: 1999 - Present

Preview (1999, Wizard magazine supplement) - Previews Tom Strong, Top Ten, Promethea, Tomorrow Stories — 2.25
Sketchbook (2002, $5.95, square-bound)-Design sketches by Sprouse, Ross, Adams, Nowlan, Ha and others — 6.00
Special 1 (2/01, $6.95)-Short stories of Alan Moore's characters; art by various; Ross-c — 7.00
TPB (2004, $17.95) Reprints short stories and sketch pages from ABC titles — 18.00

AMERICA'S BEST TV COMICS (TV)
American Broadcasting Co. (Prod. by Marvel Comics): 1967 (25¢, 68 pgs.)

1-Spider-Man, Fantastic Four (by Kirby/Ayers), Casper, King Kong, George of the Jungle, Journey to the Center of the Earth stories (promotes new TV cartoon show)	13	26	39	97	171	245

AMERICA'S BIGGEST COMICS BOOK
William H. Wise: 1944 (196 pgs., one-shot)

1-The Grim Reaper, The Silver Knight, Zudo, the Jungle Boy, Commando Cubs, Thunderhoof app.	40	80	120	240	383	525

AMERICA'S FUNNIEST COMICS
William H. Wise: 1944 - No. 2, 1944 (15¢, 80 pgs.)

nn(#1), 2	30	60	90	174	275	375

AMERICA'S GREATEST COMICS
Fawcett Publications: May?, 1941 - No. 8, Summer, 1943 (15¢, 100 pgs., soft cardboard-c)

1-Bulletman, Spy Smasher, Capt. Marvel, Minute Man & Mr. Scarlet begin; Classic Mac Raboy-c. 1st time that Fawcett's major super-heroes appear together as a group on a cover. Fawcett's 1st squarebound comic	333	666	1000	2165	3833	5500
2	145	290	435	906	1503	2100
3	103	206	309	644	1072	1500
4,5: 4-Commando Yank begins; Golden Arrow, Ibis the Invincible & Spy Smasher cameo in Captain Marvel	76	152	228	475	788	1100
6,7: 7-Balbo the Boy Magician app.; Captain Marvel, Bulletman cameo in Mr. Scarlet	67	134	201	419	697	975
8-Capt. Marvel Jr. & Golden Arrow app.; Spy Smasher x-over in Capt. Midnight; no Minute Man or Commando Yank app.	67	134	201	419	697	975

AMERICA'S SWEETHEART SUNNY (See Sunny, ...)

AMERICA VS. THE JUSTICE SOCIETY
DC Comics: Jan, 1985 - No. 4, Apr, 1985 ($1.00, limited series)

1-Double size; Alcala-a(i) in all	1	2	3	5	7	9
2-4: 3,4-Spectre cameo	1	2	3	4	5	7

AMERICOMICS
Americomics: April, 1983 - No. 6, Mar, 1984 ($2.00, Baxter paper/slick paper)

1-Intro/origin The Shade; Intro. The Slayer, Captain Freedom and The Liberty Corps; Perez-c — 5.00
1,2-2nd printings ($2.00) — 2.25
2-6: 2-Messenger app. & 1st app. Tara on Jungle Island. 3-New & old Blue Beetle battle. 4-Origin Dragonfly & Shade. 5-Origin Commando D. 6-Origin the Scarlet Scorpion — 3.00
Special 1 (8/83, $2.00)-Sentinels of Justice (Blue Beetle, Captain Atom, Nightshade & The Question) — 4.50

AMETHYST
DC Comics: Jan, 1985 - No. 16, Aug, 1986 (75¢)

1-16: 8-Fire Jade's i.d. revealed — 2.50
Special 1 (10/86, $1.25), 1-4 (11/87 - 2/88)(Limited series) — 2.50

AMETHYST, PRINCESS OF GEMWORLD (See Legion of Super-Heroes #298)
DC Comics: May, 1983 - No. 12, Apr, 1984 (Maxi-series)

1-(60¢)						2.50
1,2-(75¢): tested in Austin & Kansas City	3	6	9	17	25	32
2-12, Annual 1(9/84): 5-11-Pérez-c(p)						2.50

AMORY WARS (Based on the Coheed and Cambria album The Second Stage Turbine Blade)
Image Comics: Jun, 2007 - No. 5 (2.99, limited series)

1-3: 1-Claudio Sanchez-s/Gus Vasquez-a — 3.00

AMY RACECAR COLOR SPECIAL (See Stray Bullets)
El Capitán Books: July, 1997; Oct, 1999 ($2.95/$3.50)

1,2-David Lapham-a/scripts. 2-($3.50) — 3.50

ANARCHO DICTATOR OF DEATH (See Comics Novel)

ANARKY (See Batman titles)
DC Comics: May, 1997 - No. 4, Aug, 1997 ($2.50, limited series)

1 — 3.50
2-4 — 2.50

ANARKY (See Batman titles)
DC Comics: May, 1999 - No. 8, Dec, 1999 ($2.50)

1-8: 1-JLA app. Grant-s/Breyfogle-a. 3-Green Lantern app. 7-Day of Judgment; Haunted Tank app. 8-Joker-c/app. — 2.50

ANCHORS ANDREWS (The Saltwater Daffy)
St. John Publishing Co.: Jan, 1953 - No. 4, July, 1953 (Anchors the Saltwater... No. 4)

1-Canteen Kate by Matt Baker (9 pgs.)	20	40	60	117	184	250
2-4	9	18	27	50	65	80

ANDY & WOODY (See March of Comics No. 40, 55, 76)

ANDY BURNETT (TV, Disney)
Dell Publishing Co.: Dec, 1957

Four Color 865-Photo-c	8	16	24	58	97	135

ANDY COMICS (Formerly Scream Comics; becomes Ernie Comics)
Current Publications (Ace Magazines): No. 20, June, 1948-No. 21, Aug, 1948

20,21: Archie-type comic	8	16	24	42	54	65

ANDY DEVINE WESTERN
Fawcett Publications: Dec, 1950 - No. 2, 1951

1	55	110	165	336	543	750
2	80	120	241	383	525	

ANDY GRIFFITH SHOW, THE (TV)(1st show aired 10/3/60)
Dell Publishing Co.: #1252, Jan-Mar, 1962; #1341, Apr-Jun, 1962

Four Color 1252(#1)	35	70	105	263	482	700
Four Color 1341-Photo-c	32	64	96	240	445	650

ANDY HARDY COMICS (See Movie Comics #3 by Fiction House)
Dell Publishing Co.: April, 1952 - No. 6, Sept-Nov, 1954

Four Color 389(#1)	5	10	15	35	55	75
Four Color 447,480,515, #5,#6	4	8	12	24	37	50

ANDY PANDA (Also see Crackajack Funnies #39, The Funnies, New Funnies & Walter Lantz...)
Dell Publishing Co.: 1943 - No. 56, Nov-Jan, 1961-62 (Walter Lantz)

Four Color 25(#1, 1943)	50	100	150	400	725	1050
Four Color 54(1944)	29	58	87	212	381	550
Four Color 85(1945)	16	32	48	118	209	300
Four Color 130(1946),154,198	11	22	33	79	140	200

A-Next #11 © MAR

Angel: The Curse #1 © 20th Century Fox

Animal Antics #19 © DC

	GD 2.0	VG 4.0	FN 6.0	VF 8.0	VF/NM 9.0	NM- 9.2
Four Color 216,240,258,280,297	8	16	24	56	93	130
Four Color 326,345,358	6	12	18	41	66	90
Four Color 383,409	5	10	15	32	51	70
16(11-1/52-53) - 30	4	8	12	24	37	50
31-56	3	6	9	18	27	35

(See March of Comics #5, 22, 79, & Super Book #4, 15, 27.)

A-NEXT (See Avengers)
Marvel Comics: Oct, 1998 - No. 12, Sept, 1999 ($1.99)

1-Next generation of Avengers; Frenz-a						3.00
2-12: 2-Two covers. 3-Defenders app.						2.50
Spider-Girl Presents Avengers Next Vol. 1: Second Coming (2006, $7.99, digest) r/#1-6						8.00

ANGEL
Dell Publishing Co.: Aug, 1954 - No. 16, Nov-Jan, 1958-59

	GD	VG	FN	VF	VF/NM	NM-
Four Color 576(#1, 8/54)	4	8	12	24	37	50
2(5-7/55) - 16	3	6	9	16	23	30

ANGEL (TV) (Also see Buffy the Vampire Slayer)
Dark Horse Comics: Nov, 1999 - No. 17, Apr, 2001 ($2.95/$2.99)

1-17: 1-3,5-7,10-14-Zanier-a. 1-4,7,10-Matsuda & photo-c. 16-Buffy-c/app.						3.00
...: Earthly Possessions TPB (4/01, $9.95) r/#5-7, photo-c						10.00
...: Surrogates TPB (12/00, $9.95) r/#1-3; photo-c						10.00

ANGEL (Buffy the Vampire Slayer)
Dark Horse Comics: Sept, 2001 - No. 4, May, 2002 ($2.99, limited series)

1-4-Joss Whedon & Matthews-s/Rubi-a; photo-c and Rubi-c on each						3.00

ANGEL (one-shots) (Buffy the Vampire Slayer)
IDW Publishing: ($3.99/$7.49)

...: Connor (8/06, $3.99) Jay Faerber-s/Bob Gill-a; 4 covers + 1 retailer cover						4.00
...: Doyle (7/06, $3.99) Jeff Mariotte-s/David Messina-a; 4 covers + 1 retailer cover						4.00
...: Gunn (5/06, $3.99) Dan Jolley-s/Mark Pennington-a; 4 covers + 2 retailer covers						4.00
...: Illyria (4/06, $3.99) Peter David-s/Nicola Scott-a; 4 covers + 2 retailer covers						4.00
...: Masks (10/06, $7.49) short stories of Angel, Illyria, Cordilia & Lindsay; puppet Angel app.						8.00
...: Wesley (6/06, $3.99) Scott Tipton-s/Mike Norton-a; 4 covers + 1 retailer cover						4.00
Spotlight TPB (12/06, $19.99) r/Connor, Doyle, Gunn, Illyria & Wesley one-shots						20.00

ANGELA
Image Comics (Todd McFarlane Prod.): Dec, 1994 - No. 3, Feb, 1995 ($2.95, lim. series)

	GD	VG	FN	VF	VF/NM	NM-
1-Gaiman scripts & Capullo-c/a in all; Spawn app.	1	2	3	5	6	8
2						6.00
3						5.00
Special Edition (1995)-Pirate Spawn-c	3	6	9	14	20	25
Special Edition (1995)-Angela-c	3	6	9	14	20	25
TPB ($9.95, 1995) reprints #1-3 & Special Ed. w/additional pin-ups						10.00

ANGELA/GLORY: RAGE OF ANGELS (See Glory/Angela: Rage of Angels)
Image Comics (Todd McFarlane Productions): Mar, 1996 ($2.50, one-shot)

1-Liefeld-c/Cruz-a(p); Darkchylde preview flip book						4.00
1-Variant-c						4.00

ANGEL AND THE APE (Meet Angel No. 7) (See Limited Collector's Edition C-34 & Showcase No. 77)
National Periodical Publications: Nov-Dec, 1968 - No. 6, Sept-Oct, 1969

	GD	VG	FN	VF	VF/NM	NM-
1-(11-12/68)-Not Wood-a	5	10	15	30	48	65
2-5-Wood inks in all. 4-Last 12¢ issue	3	6	9	20	30	40
6-Wood inks	4	8	12	22	34	45

ANGEL AND THE APE (2nd Series)
DC Comics: Mar, 1991 - No. 4, June, 1991 ($1.00, limited series)

1-4						3.00

ANGEL AND THE APE (3rd Series)
DC Comics (Vertigo): Oct, 2001 - No. 4, Jan 2002 ($2.95, limited series)

1-4-Chaykin & Tischman-s/Bond-a/Art Adams-c						3.00

ANGEL: AULD LANG SYNE (Buffy the Vampire Slayer)
IDW Publishing: Nov, 2006 - No. 5, Mar, 2007 ($3.99, limited series)

1-5: 1-Three covers plus photo-c; Tipton/s-Messina-a						4.00

ANGEL LOVE
DC Comics: Aug, 1986 - No. 8, Mar, 1987 (75¢, limited series)

1-8, Special 1 (1987, $1.25, 52 pgs.)						2.50

ANGEL OF LIGHT, THE (See The Crusaders)

ANGEL: OLD FRIENDS (Buffy the Vampire Slayer)
IDW Publishing: Nov, 2005 - No. 5, Mar, 2006 ($3.99, limited series)

1-5: Four covers plus photo-c on each; Mariotte-s/Messina-a; Gunn, Spike and Illyria app.						4.00
... Cover Gallery (6/06, $3.99) gallery of variant covers for the series						4.00
... Cover Gallery (12/06, $3.99) gallery of variant covers; preview of Angel: Auld Lang Syne						4.00
TPB (2006, $19.99) r/series; gallery of Messina covers						20.00

ANGEL: THE CURSE (Buffy the Vampire Slayer)
IDW Publishing: June, 2005 - No. 5, Oct, 2005 ($3.99, limited series)

1-5-Four covers on each; Mariotte-s/Messina-a						4.00
TPB (1/06, $19.99) r/#1-5; cover gallery of Messina covers						20.00

ANGELTOWN
DC Comics (Vertigo): Jan, 2005 - No. 5, May, 2005 ($2.95, limited series)

1-5-Gary Phillips-s/Shawn Martinbrough-a						3.00

ANGRY CHRIST COMIX (See Cry For Dawn)

ANIMA
DC Comics: Mar, 1994 - No. 15, July, 1995 ($1.75/$1.95/$2.25)

1-7,0,8-15: 7-(9/94)-Begin $1.95-c; Zero Hour x-over						2.50

ANIMAL ADVENTURES
Timor Publications/Accepted Publ. (reprints): Dec, 1953 - No. 3, May?, 1954

	GD	VG	FN	VF	VF/NM	NM-
1-Funny animal	8	16	24	40	50	60
2,3: 2-Featuring Soopermutt (2/54)	6	12	18	28	34	40
1-3 (reprints, nd)	3	6	8	11	13	15

ANIMAL ANTICS
DC Comics: Feb, 1946

nn - Ashcan comic, not distributed to newsstands, only for in-house use. Cover art is Star Spangled Comics #49 and interior from Boy Commandos #12 (no known sales)

ANIMAL ANTICS (Movietown... No. 24 on)
National Periodical Publ: Mar-Apr, 1946 - No. 23, Nov-Dec, 1949 (All 52 pgs.?)

	GD	VG	FN	VF	VF/NM	NM-
1-Raccoon Kids begins by Otto Feuer; many-c by Grossman; Seaman Sy Wheeler by Kelly in some issues; Grossman-a in most issues	45	90	135	275	450	625
2	25	50	75	145	228	310
3-10: 10-Post-c/a	16	32	48	92	144	195
11-23: 14,15,18,19-Post-a	12	24	36	67	94	120

ANIMAL COMICS
Dell Publishing Co.: Dec-Jan, 1941-42 - No. 30, Dec-Jan, 1947-48

	GD	VG	FN	VF	VF/NM	NM-
1-1st Pogo app. by Walt Kelly (Dan Noonan art in most issues)	97	194	291	606	1003	1400
2-Uncle Wiggily begins	50	100	150	305	503	700
3,5	28	56	84	227	384	540
4,6,7-No Pogo	16	32	48	118	209	300
8-10	19	38	57	141	251	360
11-15	13	26	39	93	164	235
16-20	9	18	27	63	107	150
21-30: 24-30- "Jigger" by John Stanley	8	16	24	52	86	120

NOTE: **Dan Noonan** a-18-30. **Gollub** art in most later issues; c-29, 30. **Kelly** c-7-26, part #27-30.

ANIMAL CRACKERS (Also see Adventures of Patoruzu)
Green Publ. Co./Norlen/Fox Feat.(Hero Books): 1946; No. 31, July, 1950; No. 9, 1959

	GD	VG	FN	VF	VF/NM	NM-
1-Super Cat begins (1st app.)	18	36	54	105	165	225
2	10	20	30	56	76	95
31(Fox)-Formerly My Love Secret	8	16	24	40	50	60
9(1959-Norlen)-Infinity-c	5	10	14	20	24	28
nn, nd ('50s), no publ.; infinity-c	5	10	14	20	24	28

ANIMAL FABLES
E. C. Comics (Fables Publ. Co.): July-Aug, 1946 - No. 7, Nov-Dec, 1947

	GD	VG	FN	VF	VF/NM	NM-
1-Freddy Firefly (clone of Human Torch), Korky Kangaroo, Petey Pig, Danny Demon begin	52	104	156	317	521	725
2-Aesop Fables begin	32	64	96	186	293	400
3-6	27	54	81	156	246	335
7-Origin Moon Girl	67	134	201	419	697	975

ANIMAL FAIR (Fawcett's...)
Fawcett Publications: Mar, 1946 - No. 11, Feb, 1947

	GD	VG	FN	VF	VF/NM	NM-
1	28	56	84	162	256	350
2	14	28	42	82	121	160
3-6	12	24	36	67	94	120
7-11	10	20	30	54	72	90

ANIMAL FUN
Premier Magazines: 1953 (25¢, came w/glasses)

	GD	VG	FN	VF	VF/NM	NM-
1-(3-D)-Ziggy Pig, Silly Seal, Billy & Buggy Bear	35	70	105	204	322	440

Animal Man #6 © DC

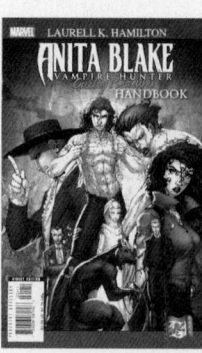

Anita Blake: Vampire Hunter Handbook © Laurell K. Hamilton

Annie Oakley #3 © MAR

	GD 2.0	VG 4.0	FN 6.0	VF 8.0	VF/NM 9.0	NM- 9.2

ANIMAL MAN (See Action Comics #552, 553, DC Comics Presents #77, 78, Secret Origins #39, Strange Adventures #180 & Wonder Woman #267, 268)
DC Comics (Vertigo imprint #57 on): Sept, 1988 - No. 89, Nov, 1995 ($1.25/$1.50/$1.75/$1.95/$2.25, mature)

	GD 2.0	VG 4.0	FN 6.0	VF 8.0	VF/NM 9.0	NM- 9.2
1-Grant Morrison scripts begin, ends #26	1	3	4	6	8	10
2-10: 2-Superman cameo. 6-Invasion tie-in. 9-Manhunter-c/story. 10-Psycho Pirate app.						6.00
11-49,51-55,57-89: 23,24-Psycho Pirate app. 24-Arkham Asylum story; Bizarro Superman app. 25-Inferior Five app. 26-Morrison apps. in story; part photo-c (of Morrison?)						3.00
50-($2.95, 52 pgs.)-Last issue w/Veitch scripts						5.00
56-($3.50, 68 pgs.)						5.00
Annual 1 (1993, $3.95, 68 pgs.)-Bolland-c; Children's Crusade Pt. 3						6.00
...: Deus Ex Machina TPB (2003, $19.95) r/#18-26; Morrison-a; new Bolland-c						20.00
...: Origin of the Species TPB (2002, $19.95) r/#10-17 & Secret Origins #39						20.00
NOTE: *Bolland* c-1-63. 71-**Sutton**-a(i).						

ANIMAL MYSTIC (See Dark One...)
Cry For Dawn/Sirius: 1993 - No. 4, 1995 ($2.95?/$3.50, B&W)

	GD 2.0	VG 4.0	FN 6.0	VF 8.0	VF/NM 9.0	NM- 9.2
1	3	6	9	14	19	24
1-Alternate	4	8	12	22	34	45
1-2nd printing						5.00
2	2	4	6	10	14	18
2,3-2nd prints (Sirius)						3.50
3 ,4: 4-Color poster insert, Linsner-s	1	2	3	5	7	9
TPB ($14.95) r/series						18.00

ANIMAL MYSTIC WATER WARS
Sirius: 1996 - No. 6 ($2.95, limited series)

1-6-Dark One-c/a/scripts						5.00

ANIMAL WORLD, THE (Movie)
Dell Publishing Co.: No. 713, Aug, 1956

	GD 2.0	VG 4.0	FN 6.0	VF 8.0	VF/NM 9.0	NM- 9.2
Four Color 713	4	8	12	26	41	55

ANIMANIACS (TV)
DC Comics: May, 1995 - No. 59, Apr, 2000 ($1.50/$1.75/$1.95/$1.99)

	GD 2.0	VG 4.0	FN 6.0	VF 8.0	VF/NM 9.0	NM- 9.2
1	1	2	3	4	5	7
2-20: 13-Manga issue. 19-X-Files parody; Miran Kim-c; Adlard-a (4 pgs.)						4.00
21-59: 26-E.C. parody-c. 34-Xena parody. 43-Pinky & the Brain take over						3.00
A Christmas Special (12/94, $1.50, "1" on-c)						3.00

ANIMATED COMICS
E. C. Comics: No date given (Summer, 1947?)

	GD 2.0	VG 4.0	FN 6.0	VF 8.0	VF/NM 9.0	NM- 9.2
1 (Rare)	79	158	237	494	822	1150

ANIMATED FUNNY COMIC TUNES (See Funny Tunes)

ANIMATED MOVIE-TUNES (Movie Tunes No. 3)
Margood Publishing Corp. (Timely): Fall, 1945 - No. 2, Sum, 1946

	GD 2.0	VG 4.0	FN 6.0	VF 8.0	VF/NM 9.0	NM- 9.2
1,2-Super Rabbit, Ziggy Pig & Silly Seal	30	60	90	174	275	375

ANIMAX
Marvel Comics (Star Comics): Dec, 1986 - No. 4, June, 1987

1-4: Based on toys; Simonson-a						3.00

ANITA BLAKE: VAMPIRE HUNTER GUILTY PLEASURES
Marvel Comics (Dabel Brothers): Dec, 2006 - Present ($2.99)

1-Laurell K. Hamilton-s/Brett Booth-a; blue cover						6.00
1-Variant-c by Greg Horn						20.00
1-Sketch cover						25.00
1-2nd printing with red cover						3.00
2-Two covers						5.00
3-6						3.00
...: Handbook (2007, $3.99) profile pages of characters; glossary						4.00
...: Volume One HC (6/07, $19.99, dust jacket) r/#1-6 plus new-a						

ANITA BLAKE: VAMPIRE HUNTER THE FIRST DEATH, (LAURELL K. HAMILTONs...)
Marvel Comics (Dabel Brothers): July, 2007 - No. 2 ($3.99)

1-Laurell K. Hamilton & Jonathon Green-s/Wellington Alves-a						4.00

ANNE RICE'S INTERVIEW WITH THE VAMPIRE
Innovation Books: 1991 - No. 12, Jan, 1994 ($2.50, limited series)

1-12: Adapts novel; Moeller-a						3.00

ANNE RICE'S THE MASTER OF RAMPLING GATE
Innovation Books: 1991 ($6.95, one-shot)

1-Bolton painted-c; Colleen Doran painted-a						7.00

ANNE RICE'S THE MUMMY OR RAMSES THE DAMNED
Millennium Publications: Oct, 1990 - No. 12, Feb, 1992 ($2.50, limited series)

1-12: Adapts novel; Mooney-p in all						3.00

ANNE RICE'S THE WITCHING HOUR
Millennium Publ./Comico: 1992 - No. 13, Jan, 1993 ($2.50, limited series)

1-13						3.00

ANNETTE (Disney, TV)
Dell Publishing Co.: No. 905, May, 1958; No. 1100, May, 1960 (Mickey Mouse Club)

	GD 2.0	VG 4.0	FN 6.0	VF 8.0	VF/NM 9.0	NM- 9.2
Four Color 905-Annette Funicello photo-c	27	54	81	202	361	520
Four Color 1100-...'s Life Story (Movie); A. Funicello photo-c	22	44	66	164	292	420

ANNEX (See Amazing Spider-Man Annual #27 for 1st app.)
Marvel Comics: Aug, 1994 - No. 4, Nov, 1994 ($1.75)

1-4: 1,4-Spider-Man app.						2.50

ANNIE
Marvel Comics Group: Oct, 1982 - No. 2, Nov, 1982 (60¢)

	GD 2.0	VG 4.0	FN 6.0	VF 8.0	VF/NM 9.0	NM- 9.2
1,2-Movie adaptation						4.00
Treasury Edition ($2.00, tabloid size)	3	6	9	17	25	32

ANNIE OAKLEY (See Tessie The Typist #19, Two-Gun Kid & Wild Western)
Marvel/Atlas Comics(MPI No. 1-4/CDS No. 5 on): Spring, 1948 - No. 4, 11/48; No. 5, 6/55 - No. 11, 6/56

	GD 2.0	VG 4.0	FN 6.0	VF 8.0	VF/NM 9.0	NM- 9.2
1 (1st Series, 1948)-Hedy Devine app.	45	90	135	275	455	635
2 (7/48, 52 pgs.)-Kurtzman-a, "Hey Look", 1 pg; Intro. Lana; Hedy Devine app; Captain Tootsie by Beck	26	52	78	154	242	330
3,4	23	46	69	130	205	280
5 (2nd Series, 1955)-Reinman-a ; Maneely-c	16	32	48	96	151	205
6-9: 6,8-Woodbridge-a. 9-Williamson-a (4 pgs)	14	28	42	80	115	150
10,11: 11-Severin-c	13	26	39	74	105	135

ANNIE OAKLEY AND TAGG (TV)
Dell Publishing Co./Gold Key: 1953 - No. 18, Jan-Mar, 1959; July, 1965 (Gail Davis photo-c #3 on)

	GD 2.0	VG 4.0	FN 6.0	VF 8.0	VF/NM 9.0	NM- 9.2
Four Color 438 (#1)	14	28	42	103	184	265
Four Color 481,575 (#2,3)	9	18	27	64	110	155
4(7-9/55)-10	8	16	24	56	93	130
11-18(1-3/59)	7	14	21	47	76	105
1(7/65-Gold Key)-Photo-c (c-r/#6)	5	10	15	30	48	65
NOTE: *Manning* a-13. Photo back c-4, 9, 11.						

ANNIHILATION
Marvel Comics: May, 2006 - No. 6, Mar, 2007 ($3.99/$2.99, limited x-over series)

Prologue (5/06, $3.99, one-shot) Nova, Thanos and Silver Surfer app.						4.00
1-6: 1-(10/06) Giffen-s/DiVito-a; Annihilus app.						3.00
...: Heralds of Galactus 1,2 (4/07-5/07, $3.99) 2-Silver Surfer app.						4.00
...: Nova 1-4 (6/06-9/06, $2.99) Abnett & Lanning-s/Walker-a/Dell'Otto-c. 2,3-Quasar app.						3.00
...: Ronan 1-4 (6/06-9/06, $2.99) Furman-s/Lucas-a/Dell'Otto-c						3.00
... Saga (2007, $1.99) re-cap of the series; DiVito-c						2.25
...: Silver Surfer 1-4 (6/06-9/06, $2.99) Giffen-s/Arlem-a/Dell'Otto-c						3.00
...: Super-Skrull 1-4 (6/06-9/06, $2.99) Grillo-Marxuach-s/Titus-a/Dell'Otto-c						3.00
...: The Nova Corps Files (2006, $3.99) profile pages of characters and alien races						4.00
Annihilation Book 1 HC (2007, $29.99, dustjacket) r/Drax the Destroyer #1-4, Annihilation Prologue and Annihilation: Nova #1-4; sketch and layout pages						30.00
Annihilation Book 1 SC (2007, $24.99) same content as HC						25.00
Annihilation Book 2 HC (2007, $29.99, dustjacket) r/Annihilation: Silver Surfer #1-4, ...: Super Skrull #1-4; sketch and layout pages						30.00
Annihilation Book 2 SC (2007, $24.99) same content as HC						25.00
Annihilation Book 3 HC (2007, $29.99, dustjacket) r/Annihilation/Annihilation #1-6, Annihilation: Heralds of Galactus 1,2 and Annihilation: Nova Corps Files; sketch pages						30.00
Annihilation Book 3 SC (2007, $24.99) same content as HC						25.00

ANNIHILATION: CONQUEST (Also see Nova 2007 series)
Marvel Comics: Sept, 2007 - No. 4 ($3.99/$2.99, limited x-over series)

Prologue (8/07, $3.99, one-shot) the new Quasar, Moondragon app.; Perkins-a						4.00
... - Quasar 1-3 (9/07-No. 4, $2.99) Gage-s/Lilly-a. 1-Super-Adaptoid app.						3.00
... - Starlord 1-3 (9/07-No. 4, $2.99) Giffen-s/Green-a						3.00
... - Wraith 1-3 (9/07-No. 4, $2.99) Hotz-a/Grillo-Marxuach-s						3.00

ANOTHER WORLD (See Strange Stories From...)

ANT
Image Comics: Aug, 2005 - Present ($2.99)

1-11: 1-Mario Gulley-s/a. 2-Savage Dragon & Spawn app. 3-Spawn-c/app.						3.00
Vol. 1: Reality Bites TPB (2006, $12.99) r/#1-4; sketch and concept art						13.00

ANTHRO (See Showcase #74)

Ant-Man's Big Christmas #1 © MAR

A-1 Comics #7 © ME

A-1 Comics #133 © ME

	GD 2.0	VG 4.0	FN 6.0	VF 8.0	VF/NM 9.0	NM- 9.2
National Periodical Publications: July-Aug, 1968 - No. 6, July-Aug, 1969						
1-(7-8/68)-Howie Post-a in all	6	12	18	37	59	80
2-5: 5-Last 12¢ issue	4	8	12	22	34	45
6-Wood-c/a (inks)	4	8	12	24	37	50

ANTI-HITLER COMICS
New England Comics Press: Summer, 1992 ($2.75, B&W, one-shot)

1-Reprints Hitler as Devil stories from wartime comics 5.00

ANT-MAN (See Irredeemable Ant-Man, The)

ANT-MAN'S BIG CHRISTMAS
Marvel Comics: Feb, 2000 ($5.95, square-bound, one-shot)

1-Bob Gale-s/Phil Winslade-a; Avengers app. 6.00

ANTONY AND CLEOPATRA (See Ideal, a Classical Comic)

ANYTHING GOES
Fantagraphics Books: Oct, 1986 - No. 6, 1987 ($2.00, #1-5 color & B&W/#6 B&W, lim. series)

1-6: 1-Flaming Carrot app. (1st in color?); G. Kane-a. 2-6: 2-Miller-c(p);
Kirby-a; early Sam Kieth-a (2 pgs.). 3-Capt. Jack, Cerebus app.; Cerebus-a by N. Adams.
4-Perez-c. 5-3rd color Teenage Mutant Ninja Turtles app. 3.50

A-1
Marvel Comics (Epic Comics): 1992 - No. 4, 1993 ($5.95, limited series, mature)

1-4: 1-Fabry-c/a, Russell-a. 3-Bisley-c; Kent Williams-a.						
4-McKean-a; Dorman-s/a	1	2	3	4	5	7

A-1 COMICS (A-1 appears on covers No. 1-17 only)(See individual title listings for #11-139)
(1st two issues not numbered.)
Life's Romances Publ.-No. 1/Compix/Magazine Ent.: 1944 - No. 139, Sept-Oct, 1955 (No #2)

nn-(1944) (See Kerry Drake Detective Cases)						
1-Dotty Dripple (1 pg.), Mr. Ex, Bush Berry, Rocky, Lew Loyal (20 pgs.)	14	28	42	82	121	160
3-8,10: Texas Slim & Dirty Dalton, The Corsair, Teddy Rich, Dotty Dripple, Inca Dinca, Tommy Tinker, Little Mexico & Tugboat Tim, The Masquerader & others. 7-Corsair-c/s. 8-Intro Rodeo Ryan	10	20	30	54	72	90
9-All Texas Slim	10	20	30	56	76	95

(See Individual Alphabetical listings for prices)

11-Teena; Ogden Whitney-c
13-Guns of Fact & Fiction (1948). Used in SOTI, pg. 19; Ingels & Johnny Craig-a
17-Tim Holt #2; photo-c; last issue to carry A-1 on cover (9-10/48)
19-Tim Holt #3; photo-c
22-Dick Powell (1949)-Photo-c
23-Cowboys of America #6; Doc Holiday-c/story
25-Fibber McGee & Molly (1949) (Radio)
26-Trail Colt #2-Ingels-c
28-Christmas (Koko & Kola #6) (“50)
30-Jet Powers #1-Powell-a
32-Jet Powers #2
33-Muggsy Mouse #1(‘51)
35-Jet Powers #3-Williamson/Evans-a
37-Ghost Rider #5-Frazetta-a (1951)
39-Muggsy Mouse #3
41-Cowboys ‘N’ Indians #7 (1951)
43-Dogface Dooley #2
45-American Air Forces #5-Powell-c/a
47-Thun’da, King of the Congo #1-Frazetta-c/a(‘52)
50-Danger Is Their Business #11 (‘52)-Powell-a
53-Dogface Dooley #4
55-U.S. Marines #5-Powell-a
56-Thun’da #2-Powell-c/a
58-American Air Forces #7-Powell-a
60-The U.S. Marines #6-Powell-a
62-Starr Flagg, Undercover Girl #5 (#1) reprinted from A-1 #24
65-American Air Forces #8-Powell-a
67-American Air Forces #9-Powell-a
69-Ghost Rider #9(10/52)
71-Ghost Rider #10(12/52)- Vs. Frankenstein

12,15-Teena
14-Tim Holt Western Adventures #1
16-Vacation Comics; The Pixies, Tom Tom, Flying Fredd, & Koko & Kola
18,20-Jimmy Durante; photo covers on both
21-Joan of Arc (1949)-Movie adaptation; Ingrid Bergman photo-covers & interior photos; Whitney-a
24-Trail Colt #1-Frazetta-r in-Manhunt #13; Ingels-c; L.B. Cole-a
27-Ghost Rider #1(1950)-Origin
29-Ghost Rider #2-Frazetta-c (1950)
31-Ghost Rider #3-Frazetta-c & origin (‘51)
34-Ghost Rider #4-Frazetta-c (1951)
36-Muggsy Mouse #2; Racist-c
38-Jet Powers #4-Williamson/Wood-a
40-Dogface Dooley #1(‘51)
42-Best of the West #1-Powell-a
44-Ghost Rider #6
46-Best of the West #2
48-Cowboys ‘N’ Indians #8
49-Dogface Dooley #3
51-Ghost Rider #7 (‘52)
52-Best of the West #3
54-American Air Forces #6(8/52)-Powell-a
57-Ghost Rider #8
59-Best of the West #4
61-Space Ace #5 (‘53)-Guardineer-a
63-Manhunt #13-Frazetta
64-Dogface Dooley #5
66-Best of the West #5
68-U.S. Marines #7-Powell-a
70-Best of the West #6
72-U.S. Marines #8-Powell-a(3)
73-Thun’da #3-Powell-c/a

74-American Air Forces #10-Powell-a
76-Best of the West #7
78-Thun’da #4-Powell-c/a
80-Ghost Rider #12(6/52)- One-eyed Devil-c
83-Thun’da #5-Powell-c/a
84-Ghost Rider #13(7-8/53)
86-Thun’da #6-Powell-c/a
88-Bobby Benson's B-Bar-B Riders #20
90-Red Hawk #11(1953)-Powell-c/a
91-American Air Forces #12-Powell-a
93-Great Western #8(‘54)-Origin The Ghost Rider; Powell-a
95-Muggsy Mouse #4
96-Cave Girl #12, with Thun’da; Powell-c/a
99-Muggsy Mouse #5
101-White Indian #12-Frazetta-a(r)
103-Dream Book of Romance #6 (4-6/54); Marlon Brando photo-c; Powell, Bolle, Guardineer-a
105-Great Western #9-Ghost Rider app.; Powell-a, 6 pgs.; Bolle-c
107-Hot Dog #1
108-Red Fox #15 (1954)-L.B. Cole-c; Powell-a
110-Dream Book of Romance #8 (10/54)-Movie photo-c
112-Ghost Rider #14 (‘54)
114-Dream Book of Love #2- Guardineer, Bolle-a; Piper Laurie, Victor Mature photo-c
118-Undercover Girl #7-Powell-c
120-Badmen of the West #2
121-Mysteries of Scotland Yard #1; reprinted from Manhunt (5 stories)
124-Dream Book of Romance #8 (10-11/54)
126-I'm a Cop #2-Powell-a
128-I'm a Cop #3-Powell-a
130-Strongman #1-Powell-a (2-3/55)
132-Strongman #2
134-Strongman #3
136-Hot Dog #4
138-The Avenger #4-Powell-c/a

75-Ghost Rider #11(3/52)
77-Manhunt #14
79-American Air Forces #11-Powell-a
81-Best of the West #8
82-Cave Girl #11(1953)-Powell-c/a; origin (#1)
85-Best of the West #9
87-Best of the West #10(9-10/53)
89-Home Run #3-Powell-a; Stan Musial photo-c
92-Dream Book of Romance #5- Photo-c; Guardineer
94-White Indian #11-Frazetta-a(r); Powell-c
97-Best of the West #11
98-Undercover Girl #6-Powell-c
100-Badmen of the West #1- Meskin-a(?)
103-Best of the West #12-Powell-a
104-White Indian #13-Frazetta-a(r) (‘54)
106-Dream Book of Love #1 (6-7/54) -Powell, Bolle-a; Montgomery Clift, Donna Reed photo-c
109-Dream Book of Romance #7 (7-8/54). Powell-a; movie photo-c
111-I'm a Cop #1 (‘54); drug mention story; Powell-a
113-Great Western #10; Powell-a
115-Hot Dog #3
116-Cave Girl #13-Powell-c/a
117-White Indian #14
119-Straight Arrow's Fury #1 (origin); Fred Meagher-c/a
122-Black Phantom #1 (11/54)
123-Dream Book of Love #3 (10-11/54)-movie photo-c
125-Cave Girl #14-Powell-c/a
127-Great Western #11(‘54)-Powell-a
129-The Avenger #1(‘55)-Powell-c
131-The Avenger #2(‘55)-Powell-c/a
133-The Avenger #3-Powell-c/a
135-White Indian #15
137-Africa #1-Powell-c/a(4)
139-Strongman #4-Powell-a

NOTE: *Bolle* a-110. Photo-c-17-22, 89, 92, 101, 106, 109, 110, 114, 123, 124.

APACHE
Fiction House Magazines: 1951

	GD 2.0	VG 4.0	FN 6.0	VF 8.0	VF/NM 9.0	NM- 9.2
1	23	46	69	130	205	280
I.W. Reprint No. 1-r/#1 above	3	6	9	18	27	35

APACHE KID (Formerly Reno Browne; Western Gunfighters #20 on)
(Also see Two-Gun Western & Wild Western)
Marvel/Atlas Comics(MPC No. 53-10/CPS No. 11 on): No. 53, 12/50 - No. 10, 1/52; No. 11, 12/54 - No. 19, 4/56

53(#1)-Apache Kid & his horse Nightwind (origin), Red Hawkins by Syd Shores begins						
	35	70	105	204	322	440
2(2/51)	17	34	51	98	154	210
3-5	13	26	39	72	101	130
6-10 (1951-52): 7-Russ Heath-a	11	22	33	60	83	105
11-19 (1954-56)	9	18	27	50	65	80

NOTE: *Heath* a-7, 13. *Maneely* a-53; c-53(#1), 12, 14-16. *Powell* a-14. *Severin* c-17.

APACHE MASSACRE (See Chief Victorio's...)

APACHE SKIES
Marvel Comics: Sept, 2002 - No. 4, Dec, 2002 ($2.99, limited series)

1-4-Apache Kid app.; Ostrander-s/Manco-c/a 3.00
TPB (2003, $12.99) r/#1-4 .... 13.00

APACHE TRAIL
Steinway/America's Best: Sept, 1957 - No. 4, June, 1958

	GD 2.0	VG 4.0	FN 6.0	VF 8.0	VF/NM 9.0	NM- 9.2
1	11	22	33	62	86	110
2-4: 2-Tuska-a	8	16	24	40	50	60

APE (Magazine)

Aphrodite IX #2 © TCOW

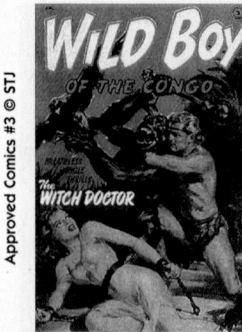

Approved Comics #3 © STJ

Aquaman (2003 series) #1 © DC

	GD 2.0	VG 4.0	FN 6.0	VF 8.0	VF/NM 9.0	NM- 9.2
Dell Publishing Co.: 1961 (52 pgs., B&W)						
1-Comics and humor	4	8	12	24	37	50
APHRODITE IX						
Image Comics (Top Cow): Sept, 2000 - No. 4, Mar, 2002 ($2.50)						
1-3: 1-Four covers by Finch, Turner, Silvestri, Benitez						4.00
1-Tower Record Ed.; Finch-c						3.00
1-DF Chrome ($14.99)						15.00
4-($4.95) Double-sized issue; Finch-c						5.00
Convention Preview						10.00
...: Time Out of Mind TPB (6/04, $14.99) r/#1-4, & #0; cover gallery						15.00
Wizard #0 (4/00), bagged w/Tomb Raider magazine) Preview & sketchbook						5.00
#0-(6/01, $2.95) r/Wizard #0 with cover gallery						3.00
APOCALYPSE NERD						
Dark Horse Comics: January, 2005 - No. 6 ($2.99, B&W)						
1-4-Peter Bagge-s/a						3.00
APPARITION						
Caliber Comics: 1995 ($3.95, 52 pgs., B&W)						
1 ($3.95)						4.00
V2#1-6 ($2.95)						3.00
Visitations						4.00
APPLESEED						
Eclipse Comics: Sept, 1988 - Book 4, Vol. 4, Aug, 1991 ($2.50/$2.75/$3.50, 52/68 pgs, B&W)						
Book One, Vol. 1-5: 5-(1/89), Book Two, Vol. 1(2/89) -5(7/89): Art Adams-c, Book Three,						
Vol. 1(8/89) -4 ($2.75), Book Three, Vol. 5 ($3.50), Book Four, Vol. 1 (1/91) - 4 (8/91)						
($3.50, 68 pgs.)						6.00
APPLESEED DATABOOK						
Dark Horse Comics: Apr, 1994 - No. 2, May, 1994 ($3.50, B&W, limited series)						
1,2: 1-Flip book format						3.50
APPROVED COMICS (Also see Blue Ribbon Comics)						
St. John Publishing Co. (Most have no c-price): March, 1954 - No. 12, Aug, 1954 (Painted-c on #1-5,7,8,10)						
1-The Hawk #5-r	10	20	30	56	76	95
2-Invisible Boy (3/54)-Origin; Saunders-c	16	32	48	92	144	195
3-Wild Boy of the Congo #11-r (4/54)	10	20	30	56	76	95
4,5: 4-Kid Cowboy-r. 5-Fly Boy-r	10	20	30	56	76	95
6-Daring Adv.-r (5/54); Krigstein-a(2); Baker-c	13	26	39	72	101	130
7-The Hawk #6-r	10	20	30	56	76	95
8-Crime on the Run (6/54); Powell-a; Saunders-c	10	20	30	56	76	95
9-Western Bandit Trails #3-r, with new-c; Baker-c/a	13	26	39	72	101	130
10-Dinky Duck (Terrytoons)	6	12	18	31	38	45
11-Fightin' Marines 3-r (8/54); Canteen Kate app; Baker-c/a	14	28	42	76	108	140
12-Northwest Mounties #4-r(8/54); new Baker-c	14	28	42	76	108	140
AQUAMAN (See Adventure Comics #260, Brave & the Bold, DC Comics Presents #5, DC Special #28, DC Special Series #1, DC Super Stars #7, Detective Comics, JLA, Justice League of America, More Fun #73, Showcase #30-33, Super DC Giant, Super Friends, and World's Finest Comics)						
AQUAMAN (1st Series)						
National Periodical Publications/DC Comics: Jan-Feb, 1962 - #56, Mar-Apr, 1971; #57, Aug-Sept,1977 - #63, Aug-Sept, 1978						
1-(1-2/62)-Intro. Quisp	78	156	234	663	1232	1800
2	31	62	93	233	429	625
3-5	19	38	57	138	244	350
6-10	12	24	36	87	156	225
11,18: 11-1st app. Mera. 18-Aquaman weds Mera; JLA cameo	10	20	30	68	119	170
12-17,19,20	9	18	27	65	113	160
21-32: 23-Birth of Aquababy. 26-Huntress app.(3-4/66). 29-1st app. Ocean Master, Aquaman's step-brother. 30-Batman & Superman-c & cameo	6	12	18	43	69	95
33-1st app. Aqua-Girl (see Adventure #266)	7	14	21	47	76	105
34-40: 35-1st app. Black Manta. 40-Jim Aparo's 1st DC work (8/68)	5	10	15	35	55	75
41-46,49: 45-Last 12¢-c	5	10	15	30	48	65
48-Origin reprinted	5	10	15	32	51	70
50-52-Deadman by Neal Adams	7	14	21	49	80	110
53-56('71): 56-1st app. Crusader; last 15¢-c	2	4	6	9	13	16
57('77)-63: 58-Origin retold	1	2	3	5	7	9
NOTE: *Aparo* c-1-40, 46p, 47-59; c-58-63. *Nick Cardy* c-1-40. *Newton* a-60-63.						
AQUAMAN (1st limited series)						
DC Comics: Feb, 1986 - No. 4, May, 1986 (75¢, limited series)						

	GD 2.0	VG 4.0	FN 6.0	VF 8.0	VF/NM 9.0	NM- 9.2
1-New costume; 1st app. Nuada of Thierna Na Oge.						5.50
2-4: 3-Retelling of Aquaman & Ocean Master's origins.						4.00
Special 1 (1988, $1.50, 52 pgs.)						3.75
NOTE: *Craig Hamilton* c/a-1-4p. *Russell* c-2-4i.						
AQUAMAN (2nd limited series)						
DC Comics: June, 1989 - No. 5, Oct, 1989 ($1.00, limited series)						
1-5: Giffen plots/breakdowns; Swan-a(p).						3.00
Special 1 (Legend of..., $2.00, 1989, 52 pgs.)-Giffen plots/breakdowns; Swan-a(p)						3.00
AQUAMAN (2nd Series)						
DC Comics: Dec, 1991 - No. 13, Dec, 1992 ($1.00/$1.25)						
1-5						2.50
6-13: 6-Begin $1.25-c. 9-Sea Devils app.						2.50
AQUAMAN (3rd Series)(Also see Atlantis Chronicles)						
DC Comics: Aug, 1994 - No. 75, Jan, 2001 ($1.50/$1.75/$1.95/$1.99/$2.50)						
1-(8/94)-Peter David scripts begin; reintro Dolphin						6.00
2-(9/94)-Aquaman loses hand						6.50
0-(10/94)-Aquaman replaces lost hand with hook.						6.50
3-8: 3-(11/94)-Superboy-c/app. 4-Lobo app. 6-Deep Six app.						3.50
9-69: 9-Begin $1.75-c. 10-Green Lantern app. 11-Reintro Mera. 15-Re-intro Kordax. 16-vs. JLA. 18-Reintro Ocean Master & Atlan (Aquaman's father). 19-Reintro Garth (Aqualad). 23-1st app. Deep Blue (Neptune Perkins & Tsunami's daughter). 23,24-Neptune Perkins, Nuada, Tsunami, Arion, Power Girl, & The Sea Devils app. 26-Final Night. 28-Martian Manhunter-c/app. 29-Black Manta-c/app. 32-Swamp Thing-c/app. 37-Genesis x-over. 41-Maxima-c/app. 43-Millennium Giants x-over; Superman-c/app. 44-G.A. Flash & Sentinel app. 50-Larsen-s begins. 53-Superman app. 60-Tempest marries Dolphin; Teen Titans app. 63-Kaluta covers begin. 66-JLA app.						2.50
70-75: 70-Begin $2.50-c. 71-73-Warlord-c/app. 75-Final issue						2.50
#1,000,000 (11/98) 853rd Century x-over						3.00
Annual 1 (1995, $3.50)-Year One story						3.50
Annual 2 (1996, $2.95)-Legends of the Dead Earth story						3.00
Annual 3 (1997, $3.95)-Pulp Heroes story						4.00
Annual 4,5 ('98, '99, $2.95)-4-Ghosts; Wrightson-c. 5-JLApe						3.00
...Secret Files 1 (12/98, $4.95) Origin-s and pin-ups						5.00
NOTE: *Art Adams*-c, Annual 5. *Mignola* c-6. *Simonson* c-15.						
AQUAMAN (4th Series)(Titled Aquaman: Sword of Atlantis #40-on) (Also see JLA #69-75)						
DC Comics: Feb, 2003 - Present ($2.50/$2.99)						
1-Veitch-s/Guichet-a/Maleev-c						3.00
2-14: 2-Martian Manhunter app. 8-11-Black Manta app.						2.50
15-39: 15-San Diego flooded; Pfeifer-s/Davis-c begin. 23,24-Sea Devils app. 33-Mera returns. 39-Black Manta app.						2.50
40-Sword of Atlantis; One Year Later begins ($2.99-c) Guice-a ; two covers						4.00
41-49,51-55: 41-Two covers. 42-Sea Devils app. 44-Ocean Master app.						3.00
50-($3.99) Tempest app.; McManus-a						4.00
...Secret Files 2003 (5/03, $4.95) background on Aquaman's new powers; pin-ups						5.00
...: Once and Future TPB (2006, $12.99) r/#40-45						13.00
...: The Waterbearer TPB (2003, $12.95) r/#1-4, stories from Aquaman Secret Files and JLA/JSA Secret Files #1; JG Jones-c						13.00
AQUAMAN: TIME & TIDE (3rd limited series) (Also see Atlantis Chronicles)						
DC Comics: Dec, 1993 - No. 4, Mar, 1994 ($1.50, limited series)						
1-4: Peter David scripts; origin retold.						3.00
Trade paperback ($9.95)						10.00
AQUANAUTS (TV)						
Dell Publishing Co.: May - July, 1961						
Four Color 1197-Photo-c	7	14	21	47	76	105
ARABIAN NIGHTS (See Cinema Comics Herald)						
ARACHNOPHOBIA (Movie)						
Hollywood Comics (Disney Comics): 1990 ($5.95, 68 pg. graphic novel)						
nn-Adaptation of film; Spiegle-a						6.00
Comic edition ($2.95, 68 pgs.)						3.00
ARAK/SON OF THUNDER (See Warlord #48)						
DC Comics: Sept, 1981 - No. 50, Nov, 1985						
1,24,50: 1-1st app. Angelica, Princess of White Cathay. 24,50-(52 pgs.)						3.00
2-23,25-49: 3-Intro Valda. 12-Origin Valda. 20-Origin Angelica						2.25
Annual 1(10/84)						3.00
ARAÑA THE HEART OF THE SPIDER (See Amazing Fantasy (2004) #1-6)						
Marvel Comics: March, 2005 - No. 12, Feb, 2006 ($2.99)						
1-12: 1-Avery-s/Cruz-a. 4-Spider-Man-c/app.						3.00
Vol. 1: Heart of the Spider (2005, $7.99, digest) r/Amazing Fantasy (2004) #1-6						8.00

Arcanum #7 © Brandon Peterson

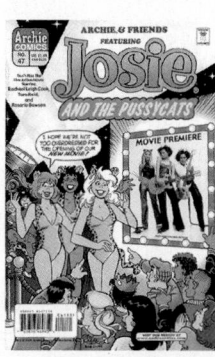

Archie and Friends #47 © AP

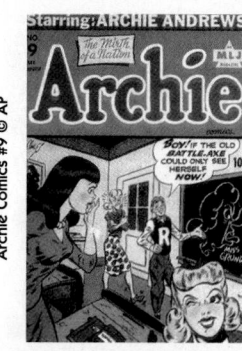

Archie Comics #9 © AP

	GD 2.0	VG 4.0	FN 6.0	VF 8.0	VF/NM 9.0	NM- 9.2

Vol. 2: In the Beginning (2005, $7.99, digest) r/#1-6	8.00
Vol. 3: Night of the Hunter (2006, $7.99, digest) r/#7-12	8.00

ARCANA (Also see Books of Magic limited & ongoing series and Mister E)
DC Comics (Vertigo): 1994 ($3.95, 68 pgs., annual)

1-Bolton painted-c; Children's Crusade/Tim Hunter story	4.00

ARCANUM
Image Comics (Top Cow Productions): Apr, 1997 - No. 8, Feb, 1998 ($2.50)

1/2 Gold Edition	12.00
1-Brandon Peterson-s/a(p), 1-Variant-c, 4-American Ent. Ed.	3.00
2-8	2.50
3-Variant-c	4.00
...: Millennium's End TPB (2005, $16.99) r/#1-8 & #1/2; cover gallery and sketch pages	17.00

ARCHANGEL (See Uncanny X-Men, X-Factor & X-Men)
Marvel Comics: Feb, 1996 ($2.50, B&W, one-shot)

1-Milligan story	2.50

ARCHARD'S AGENTS (See Ruse)
CrossGeneration Comics: Jan, 2003; Nov, 2003; Apr, 2004 ($2.95)

1-Dixon-s/Perkins-a	3.00
...: The Case of the Puzzled Pugilist (11/03) Dixon-s/Perkins-a	3.00
Vol. 3 - Deadly Dare (4/04) Dixon-s/McNiven-a; preview of Lady Death: The Wild Hunt	3.00

ARCHENEMIES
Dark Horse Comics: Apr, 2006 - No. 4, July, 2006 ($2.99, limited series)

1-4-Melbourne-s/Guichet-a	3.00

ARCHER & ARMSTRONG
Valiant: July (June inside), 1992 - No. 26, Oct, 1994 ($2.50)

	GD 2.0	VG 4.0	FN 6.0	VF 8.0	VF/NM 9.0	NM- 9.2
0-(7/92)-B. Smith-c/a; Reese-i assists						4.00
0-(Gold Logo)	2	4	6	8	10	12
1-7,9-26: 1-(8/92)-Origin & 1st app. Archer; Miller-c; B. Smith/Layton-a. 2-2nd app. Turok (c/story); Smith/Layton-a; Simonson-c. 3,4-Smith-c&a(p) & scripts. 10-2nd app. Ivar. 10,11-B. Smith-c. 21,22-Shadowman app. 22-w/bound-in trading card. 25-Eternal Warrior app. 26-Flip book w/Eternal Warrior #26						2.50
8-($4.50, 52 pgs.)-Combined with Eternal Warrior #8; B. Smith-c/a & scripts; 1st app. Ivar the Time Walker						4.50

ARCHIE (See Archie Comics) (Also see Christmas & Archie, Everything's..., Explorers of the Unknown, Jackpot, Little..., Oxydol-Dreft, Pep, Riverdale High, Teenage Mutant Ninja Turtles Adventures & To Riverdale and Back Again)

ARCHIE AMERICANA SERIES, BEST OF THE FORTIES
Archie Publications: 1991,2002 ($10.95, trade paperback)

Vol. 1,2-r/early strips from 1940's 1-Intro. by Steven King. 2-Intro. by Paul Castiglia	11.00

ARCHIE AMERICANA SERIES, BEST OF THE FIFTIES
Archie Publications: 1991 ($8.95, trade paperback)

V2-r/strips from 1950's;	9.00
2nd printing (1998, $9.95)	10.00
Book 2 (2003, $10.95)	11.00

ARCHIE AMERICANA SERIES, BEST OF THE SIXTIES
Archie Publications: 1995 ($9.95, trade paperback)

V3-r-strips from 1960's; intro. by Frankie Avalon.	10.00

ARCHIE AMERICANA SERIES, BEST OF THE SEVENTIES
Archie Publications: 1997 ($9.95, trade paperback)

V4-r/strips from 1970's	10.00

ARCHIE AMERICANA SERIES, BEST OF THE EIGHTIES
Archie Publications: 2001 ($10.95, trade paperback)

V5-r/strips from 1980's; foreword by Steve Geppi	11.00

ARCHIE AND BIG ETHEL
Spire Christian Comics (Fleming H. Revell Co.): 1982 (69¢)

	GD 2.0	VG 4.0	FN 6.0	VF 8.0	VF/NM 9.0	NM- 9.2
nn-(Low print run)	2	4	6	10	14	18

ARCHIE & FRIENDS
Archie Comics: Dec, 1992 - Present ($1.25/$1.50/$1.75/$1.79/$1.99/$2.19/$2.25, bi-monthly)

1	5.00
2,4,10-14,17,18,20-Sabrina app. 20-Archie's Band-c	4.00
3,5-9,16	2.50
15-Babewatch-s with Sabrina app.	6.00
19-Josie and the Pussycats app.; E.T. parody-c/s	5.00
21-46	2.50
47-All Josie and the Pussycats issue; movie and actress profiles/photos	3.00
48-115: 48-56,58,60,96-Josie and the Pussycats-c/s. 79-Cheryl Blossom returns.	

	GD 2.0	VG 4.0	FN 6.0	VF 8.0	VF/NM 9.0	NM- 9.2
100-The Veronicas-c/app. 101-Katy Keene begins						2.50

ARCHIE AND ME (See Archie Giant Series Mag. #578, 591, 603, 616, 626)
Archie Publications: Oct, 1964 - No. 161, Feb, 1987

	GD 2.0	VG 4.0	FN 6.0	VF 8.0	VF/NM 9.0	NM- 9.2
1	15	30	45	107	191	275
2	8	16	24	58	97	135
3-5	6	12	18	37	59	80
6-10	4	8	12	23	36	48
11-20	3	6	9	17	25	32
21(6/68)-26,28-30: 21-UFO story. 26-X-Mas-c	3	6	9	15	21	26
27-Groovyman & Knowman superhero-s; UFO-sty	3	6	9	17	25	32
31-42: 37-Japan Expo '70-c/s	2	4	6	10	14	18
43-48,50-63-(All Giants): 43-(8/71) Mummy-s. 44-Mermaid-s. 62-Elvis cameo-c.						
63-(2/74)	3	6	9	15	21	26
49-(Giant) Josie & the Pussycats-c/app.	3	6	9	18	27	35
64-66,68-99-(Regular size): 85-Bicentennial-s. 98-Collectors Comics						
	1	3	4	6	8	10
67-Sabrina app.(8/74)	2	4	6	9	13	16
100-(4/78)	2	4	6	8	10	12
101-120: 107-UFO-s						6.00
121(8/80)-159: 134-Riverdale 2001						5.00
160,161: 160-Origin Mr. Weatherbee. 161-Last issue						6.00

ARCHIE AND MR. WEATHERBEE
Spire Christian Comics (Fleming H. Revell Co.): 1980 (59¢)

	GD 2.0	VG 4.0	FN 6.0	VF 8.0	VF/NM 9.0	NM- 9.2
nn - (Low print run)	2	4	6	9	13	16

ARCHIE...ARCHIE ANDREWS, WHERE ARE YOU? (...Comics Digest #9, 10; ...Comics Digest Mag. No. 11 on)
Archie Publications: Feb, 1977 - No. 114, May, 1998 (Digest size, 160-128 pgs., quarterly)

	GD 2.0	VG 4.0	FN 6.0	VF 8.0	VF/NM 9.0	NM- 9.2
1	3	6	9	16	23	30
2,3,5,7-9-N. Adams-a; 8-r-/origin The Fly by S&K. 9-Steel Sterling-r						
	2	4	6	9	13	16
4,6,10 ($1.00/$1.50)	2	4	6	8	10	12
11-20: 17-Katy Keene story	1	2	3	5	7	9
21-50,100	1	2	3	4	5	7
51-70						4.00
71-114: 113-Begin $1.95-c						3.00

ARCHIE AS PUREHEART THE POWERFUL (Also see Archie Giant Series #142, Jughead as Captain Hero, Life With Archie & Little Archie)
Archie Publications (Radio Comics): Sept, 1966 - No. 6, Nov, 1967

	GD 2.0	VG 4.0	FN 6.0	VF 8.0	VF/NM 9.0	NM- 9.2
1-Super hero parody	10	20	30	67	116	165
2	6	12	18	39	62	85
3-6	5	10	15	34	52	70

NOTE: Evilheart cameos in all. Title: Archie As Pureheart the Powerful #1-3; ...As Capt. Pureheart-#4-6.

ARCHIE AT RIVERDALE HIGH (See Archie Giant Series Magazine #573, 586, 604 & Riverdale High)
Archie Publications: Aug, 1972 - No. 113, Feb, 1987

	GD 2.0	VG 4.0	FN 6.0	VF 8.0	VF/NM 9.0	NM- 9.2
1	6	12	18	39	62	85
2	3	6	9	20	30	40
3-5	3	6	9	16	23	30
6-10	2	4	6	11	16	20
11-30	2	4	6	8	10	12
31(12/75)-46,48-50(12/77)	1	2	3	5	7	9
47-Archie in drag-s; Betty mud wrestling-s	2	4	6	9	12	15
51-80,100 (12/84)						6.00
81(8/81)-88, 91,93-95,98: 96-Anti-smoking issue						5.00
89,90-Early Cheryl Blossom app. 90-Archies Band app.						
	2	4	6	9	13	16
92,96,97,99-Cheryl Blossom app.	2	4	6	8	10	12
101,102,104-109,111,112: 102-Ghost-c						4.00
103-Archie dates Cheryl Blossom-s	2	4	6	8	10	12
110,113: 110-Godzilla-s. 113-Last issue						6.00

ARCHIE COMICS (Archie #114 on; 1st Teen-age comic; Radio show aired 6/2/45 by NBC)
MLJ Magazines No. 1-19/Archie Publ. No. 20 on: Winter, 1942-43 - No. 19, 3-4/46; No. 20, 5-6/46 - Present

	GD 2.0	VG 4.0	FN 6.0	VF 8.0	VF/NM 9.0	NM- 9.2
1 (Scarce)-Jughead, Veronica app.; 1st app. Mrs. Andrews						
	1800	3600	5400	13,500	23,850	34,200
2	423	846	1269	2750	4875	7000
3 (60 pgs.)(scarce)	300	600	900	1931	3366	4800
4,5: 4-Article about Archie radio series	183	366	549	1144	1897	2650
6,8-10: 6-X-Mas-c. 9-1st Miss Grundy cover	128	256	384	800	1325	1850
7-1st definitive love triangle story	134	268	402	838	1394	1950

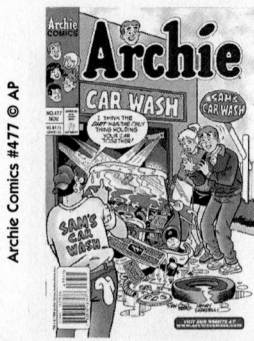

Archie Comics #33 © AP

Archie Comics #477 © AP

Archie Giant Series #13 © AP

	GD	VG	FN	VF	VF/NM	NM-
	2.0	4.0	6.0	8.0	9.0	9.2

11-20: 15,17,18-Dotty & Ditto by Woggon. 16,19-Woggon-a. 18-Halloween pumpkin-c.

	83	166	249	519	860	1200

21-30: 23-Betty & Veronica by Woggon. 25-Woggon-a. 30-Coach Piffle app., a Coach Kleets prototype. 34-Pre-Dilton try-out (named Dilbert)

	52	104	156	317	521	725
31-40	35	70	105	204	322	440
41-50	26	52	78	150	235	320
51-60	12	24	36	82	146	210
61-70 (1954): 65-70, Katy Keene app.	9	18	27	65	113	160
71-80: 72-74-Katy Keene app.	8	16	24	52	86	120
81-93,95-99	6	12	18	43	69	95
94-1st Coach Kleets	7	14	21	47	76	105
100	8	16	24	52	86	120
101-122,126,128-130 (1962)	5	10	15	30	48	65
123-125,127-Horror/SF covers. 123-UFO-c/s	6	12	18	37	59	80

131,132,134-157,159,160: 137-1st Caveman Archie gang story

	3	6	9	18	27	35
133 (12/62)-1st app. Cricket O'Dell	4	8	12	22	34	45
158-Archie in drag story	4	8	9	19	29	38

161(2/66)-184,186-188,190-195,197-199: 168-Superhero gag-c. 176,178-Twiggy-c 183-Caveman Archie gang story

	3	6	9	14	20	25
185-1st "The Archies" Band story	4	8	12	22	34	45

189 (3/69)-Archie's band meets Don Kirshner who developed the Monkees

	3	6	9	17	25	32
196 (12/69)-Early Cricket O'Dell app.	3	6	9	17	25	32
200 (6/70)	3	6	9	14	20	25

201-230(11/73): 213-Sabrina/Josie-c cameos. 229-Lost Child issue

	2	4	6	9	12	15
231-260(3/77): 253-Tarzan parody	1	3	4	6	8	10
261-282, 284-299	1	2	3	5	6	8

283(8/79)-Cover/story plugs "International Children's Appeal" which was a fraudulent charity, according to TV's 20/20 news program broadcast July 20, 1979

	1	2	3	5	7	9
300(1/81)-Anniversary issue	1	3	4	6	8	10
301-321,323-325,327-335,337-350: 323-Cheryl Blossom pin-up. 325-Cheryl Blossom app.						5.00
322-E.T. story						6.00
326-Early Cheryl Blossom story	2	4	6	9	13	16
336-Michael Jackson/Boy George parody						6.00
351-399: 356-Calgary Olympics Special. 393-Infinity-c; 1st comic book printed on recycled paper						4.00
400 (6/92)-Shows 1st meeting of Little Archie and Veronica						6.00
401-428						3.00
429-Love Showdown part 1						5.00
430-581: 467- "A Storm Over Uniforms" x-over parts 3,4. 538-Comic-Con issue						2.50
Annual 1 ('50)-116 pgs. (Scarce)	200	400	600	1250	2075	2900
Annual 2 ('51)	97	194	291	606	1003	1400
Annual 3 ('52)	55	110	165	344	572	800
Annual 4,5 (1953-54)	41	82	123	250	400	550
Annual 6-10 (1955-59): 8;9-(100 pgs.). 10-(84 pgs.) Elvis record on-c	15	30	45	107	191	275
Annual 11-15 (1960-65): 12,13-(84 pgs.). 14,15-(68 pgs.)	9	18	27	60	100	140
Annual 16-20 (1966-70)(all 68 pgs.): 20-Archie's band-c	5	10	15	35	55	75
Annual 21,22,24-26 (1971-75): 21,22-(68 pgs.). 22-Archie's band-s. 24-26-(52 pgs.). 25-Cavemen-s	3	6	9	18	27	35
Annual 23-Archie's band-c/s; Josie/Sabrina-c	4	8	12	24	37	50
Annual Digest 27 ('75)	3	6	9	20	30	40
...28-30	3	6	9	14	19	24
...31-34	2	4	6	9	13	16
...35-40 (...Magazine #35 on)	1	3	4	6	8	10
...41-65 ('94)						5.00
...66-69						3.00
...All-Star Specials (Winter '75, $1.25)-6 remaindered Archie comics rebound in each; titles: "The World of Giant Comics", "Giant Grab Bag of Comics", "Triple Giant Comics" & "Giant Spec. Comics	4	8	12	28	44	60
Special Edition-Christmas With Archie 1(1/75)-Treasury (rare)	6	12	18	41	66	90

NOTE: Archies Band-s-185, 188-192, 197, 198, 201, 204, 205, 208, 209, 215, 329, 330; Band-c-191, 330. Cavemen Archie Gang-s-183, 190, 218, 210, 220, 223, 282, 333, 335, 338, 340. Al Fagly c-17-35. Bob Montana c-38, 41-50, 58, Annual 1-4. Bill Woggon c-53, 54.

ARCHIE COMICS DIGEST (...Magazine No. 37-95)
Archie Publications: Aug, 1973 - Present (Small size, 160-128 pgs.)

1-1st Archie digest	9	18	27	63	107	150
2	5	10	15	32	51	70

3-5	4	8	12	24	37	50
6-10	3	6	9	16	23	30
11-33: 32,33-The Fly-r by S&K	2	4	6	10	14	18
34-60	1	3	4	6	8	10
61-80,100	1	2	3	5	6	8
81-99						5.00
101-140: 36-Katy Keene story						4.00
141-165						3.00

166-240: 194-Begin $2.39-c. 225-Begin $2.49-c. 236-65th Anniversary issue, r/1st app. in Pep #22 and entire Archie Comics #1 (1942)

						2.50

NOTE: Neal Adams a-1, 2, 4, 5, 19-21, 24, 25, 27, 29, 31, 33. X-mas c-88, 94, 100, 106.

ARCHIE COMICS PRESENTS: THE LOVE SHOWDOWN COLLECTION
Archie Publications: 1994 ($4.95, squarebound)

nn-r/Archie #429, Betty #19, Betty & Veronica #82, & Veronica #39

	1	2	3	4	5	7

ARCHIE GETS A JOB
Spire Christian Comics (Fleming H. Revell Co.): 1977

nn	2	4	6	10	14	18

ARCHIE GIANT SERIES MAGAZINE
Archie Publications: 1954 - No. 632, July, 1992 (No #36-135, no #252-451)
(#1 not code approved) (#1-233 are 68 pgs.; #12-184 are Giants; #185-194,197-233 are 52 pgs.; #195,196 are 84 pgs.; #234-up are 36 pgs.)

1-Archie's Christmas Stocking	138	276	414	863	1432	2000
2-Archie's Christmas Stocking('55)	74	148	222	463	769	1075
3-6-Archie's Christmas Stocking('56- '59)	52	104	156	317	521	725
7-10: 7-Katy Keene Holiday Fun(10/60); Bill Woggon-c. 8-Betty & Veronica Summer Fun (10/60); baseball story w/Babe Ruth & Lou Gehrig. 9-The World of Jughead (12/60); Neal Adams-a. 10-Archie's Christmas Stocking(1/61)	40	80	120	235	368	500
11,13,16,18: 11-Betty & Veronica Spectacular (10/61). 13-Betty & Veronica Summer Fun (10/61). 16-Betty & Veronica Spectacular (6/62). 18-Betty & Veronica Summer Fun (10/62)	25	50	75	148	232	315
12,14,15,17,19,20: 12-Katy Keene Holiday Fun (9/61). 14-The World of Jughead (12/61); Vampire-s. 15-Archie's Christmas Stocking (1/62). 17-Archie's Jokes (9/62); Katy Keene app. 19-The World of Jughead (12/62). 20-Archie's Christmas Stocking (1/63)	18	36	54	103	162	220
21,23,28: 21-Betty & Veronica Spectacular (6/63). 23-Betty & Veronica Summer Fun (10/63). 28-Betty & Veronica Summer Fun (9/64)	9	18	27	64	110	155
22,24,25,27,29,30: 22-Archie's Jokes (9/63). 24-The World of Jughead (12/63). 25-Archie's Christmas Stocking (1/64). 27-Archie's Jokes (8/64). 29-Around the World with Archie (10/64); Doris Day-s. 30-The World of Jughead (12/64)	8	16	24	56	93	130
26-Betty & Veronica Spectacular (6/64); all pin-ups; DeCarlo-c/a	8	16	24	65	113	160
31,33-35: 31-Archie's Christmas Stocking (1/65). 33-Archie's Jokes (8/65). 34-Betty & Veronica Summer Fun (9/65). 35-Around the World with Archie (10/65)	6	12	18	43	69	95
32-Betty & Veronica Spectacular (6/65); all pin-ups; DeCarlo-c/a	7	14	21	50	83	115

36-135-**Do not exist**

136-141: 136-The World of Jughead (12/65). 137-Archie's Christmas Stocking (1/66). 138-Betty & Veronica Spectacular (6/66). 139-Archie's Jokes (6/66). 140-Betty & Veronica Summer Fun (8/66). 141-Around the World with Archie (9/66)	6	12	18	43	69	95
142-Archie's Super-Hero Special (10/66)-Origin Capt. Pureheart, Capt. Hero, and Evilheart	7	14	21	49	80	110
143-The World of Jughead (12/66); Capt. Hero-c/s; Man From R.I.V.E.R.D.A.L.E., Pureheart, Superteen app.	6	12	18	39	62	85
144-160: 144-Archie's Christmas Stocking (1/67). 145-Betty & Veronica Spectacular (6/67). 146-Archie's Jokes (6/67). 147-Betty & Veronica Summer Fun (8/67) 148-World of Archie (9/67). 149-World of Jughead (10/67). 150-Archie's Christmas Stocking (1/68). 151-World of Archie (2/68). 152-World of Jughead (2/68). 153-Betty & Veronica Spectacular (6/68). 154-Archie Jokes (6/68). 155-Betty & Veronica Summer Fun (8/68). 156-World of Archie (10/68). 157-World of Jughead (12/68). 158-Archie's Christmas Stocking (1/69). 159-Betty & Veronica Christmas Spectacular (1/69). 160-World of Archie (2/69); Frankenstein-s each...	4	8	12	22	34	45
161-World of Jughead (2/69); Super-Jughead-s; 11 pg.early Cricket O'Dell-s	4	8	12	24	37	50
162-183: 162-Betty & Veronica Spectacular (6/69). 163-Archie's Jokes(8/69). 164-Betty & Veronica Summer Fun (9/69). 165-World of Archie (9/69). 166-World of Jughead (9/69). 167-Archie's Christmas Stocking (1/70). 168-Betty & Veronica Christmas Spect. (1/70). 169-Archie's Christmas Love-In (1/70). 170-Jughead's Eat-Out Comic Book Mag. (12/69). 171-World of Archie (2/70). 172-World of Jughead (2/70). 173-Betty & Veronica Spectacular (6/70). 174-Archie's Jokes (8/70). 175-Betty & Veronica Summer Fun (9/70). 176-Li'l Jinx Giant Laugh-Out (8/70). 177-World of Archie (9/70). 178-World of Jughead (9/70).						

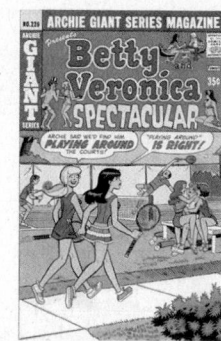

Archie Giant Series #226 © AP

Archie Giant Series #454 © AP

Archie Giant Series #610 © AP

	GD	VG	FN	VF	VF/NM	NM-		GD	VG	FN	VF	VF/NM	NM-
	2.0	4.0	6.0	8.0	9.0	9.2		2.0	4.0	6.0	8.0	9.0	9.2

179-Archie's Christmas Stocking(1/71). 180-Betty & Veronica Christmas Spect. (1/71). 181-Archie's Christmas Love-In (1/71). 182-World of Archie (2/71). 183-World of Jughead (2/71)-Last squarebound   each...   3   6   9   16   23   30

184-189,193,194,197-199 (52 pgs.): 184-Betty & Veronica Spectacular (6/71). 185-Li'l Jinx Giant Laugh-Out (6/71). 186-Archie's Jokes (8/71). 187-Betty & Veronica Summer Fun (9/71). 188-World of Archie (9/71). 189-World of Jughead (9/71). 193-World of Archie (3/72).194-World of Jughead (4/72). 197-Betty & Veronica Spectacular (6/72). 198-Archie's Jokes (8/72). 199-Betty & Veronica Summer Fun (9/72)   3   6   9   14   20   25

190-Archie's Christmas Stocking (12/71); Sabrina-c   4   8   12   24   37   50

191-Betty & Veronica Christmas Spect.(2/72); Sabrina app.   4   8   12   22   34   45

192-Archie's Christmas Love-In (1/72); Archie Band-c/s   3   6   9   19   29   38

195-(84 pgs.)-Li'l Jinx Christmas Bag (1/72).   3   6   9   21   32   42

196-(84 pgs.)-Sabrina's Christmas Magic (1/72)   5   10   15   35   55   75

200-(52 pgs.)-World of Archie (10/72)   3   6   9   19   29   38

201-206,208-219,221-230,232,233 (All 52 pgs.): 201-Betty & Veronica Spectacular (10/72). 202-World of Jughead (11/72). 203-Archie's Christmas Stocking (12/72). 204-Betty & Veronica Christmas Spectacular (2/73). 205-Archie's Christmas Love-In (1/73). 206-Li'l Jinx Christmas Bag (12/72). 208-World of Jughead (3/73). 209-World of Archie (4/73). 210-Betty & Veronica Spectacular (6/73). 211-Archie's Jokes (8/73). 212-Betty & Veronica Summer Fun (9/73). 213-World of Archie (10/73). 214-Betty & Veronica Spectacular (10/73). 215-World of Jughead (11/73). 216-Archie's Christmas Stocking (12/73). 217-Betty & Veronica Christmas Spectacular (2/74). 218-Archie's Christmas Love-In (1/74). 219-Li'l Jinx Christmas Bag (12/73). 221-Betty & Veronica Spectacular (Advertised as World of Archie) (6/74). 222-Archie's Jokes (advertised as World of Jughead) (8/74). 223-Li'l Jinx (8/74). 224-Betty & Veronica Summer Fun (9/74). 225-World of Archie (9/74). 226-Betty & Veronica Spectacular (10/74). 227-World of Jughead (10/74). 228-Archie's Christmas Stocking (12/74). 229-Betty & Veronica Christmas Spectacular (12/74). 230-Archie's Christmas Love-In (1/75). 232-World of Archie (3/75). 233-World of Jughead (4/75)   each...   2   4   6   9   13   16

207,220,231,243: Sabrina's Christmas Magic. 207-(12/72). 220-(12/73). 231-(1/75). 243-(1/76)   each...   3   6   9   16   23   30

234-242,244-251 (36 pgs.): 234-Betty & Veronica Spectacular (6/75). 235-Archie's Jokes (8/75). 236-Betty & Veronica Summer Fun (9/75). 237-World of Archie (9/75) 238-Betty & Veronica Spectacular (10/75). 239-World of Jughead (10/75). 240-Archie's Christmas Stocking (12/75). 241-Betty & Veronica Christmas Spectacular (12/75). 242-Archie's Christmas Love-In (1/76). 244-World of Archie (3/76). 245-World of Jughead (4/76). 246-Betty & Veronica Spectacular (6/76). 247-Archie's Jokes (8/76). 248-Betty & Veronica Summer Fun (9/76). 249-World of Archie (9/76). 250-Betty & Veronica Spectacular (10/76). 251-World of Jughead (10/76)   each....   2   4   6   8   11   14

252-451-Do not exist

452-454,456-466,468-478, 480-490,492-499: 452-Archie's Christmas Stocking (12/76). 453-Betty & Veronica Christmas Spectacular (12/76). 454-Archie's Christmas Love-In (1/77). 456-World of Archie (3/77). 457-World of Jughead (4/77). 458-Betty & Veronica Spectacular (6/77). 459-Archie's Jokes (8/77)-Shows 8/76 in error. 460-Betty & Veronica Summer Fun (9/77). 461-World of Archie (9/77). 462-Betty & Veronica Spectacular (10/77). 463-World of Jughead (10/77). 464-Archie's Christmas Stocking (12/77). 465-Betty & Veronica Christmas Spectacular (12/77). 466-Archie's Christmas Love-In (1/78). 468-World of Archie (2/78). 469-World of Jughead (2/78). 470-Betty & Veronica Spectacular(6/78). 471-Archie's Jokes (8/78). 472-Betty & Veronica Summer Fun (9/78). 473-World of Archie (9/78). 474-Betty & Veronica Spectacular (10/78). 475-World of Jughead (10/78). 476-Archie's Christmas Stocking (12/78). 477-Betty & Veronica Christmas Spectacular (12/78). 478-Archie's Christmas Love-In (1/79). 480-The World of Archie (3/79). 481-World of Jughead (4/79). 482-Betty & Veronica Spectacular (6/79). 483-Archie's Jokes (8/79). 484-Betty & Veronica Summer Fun(9/79). 485-The World of Archie (9/79). 486-Betty & Veronica Spectacular (10/79). 487-The World of Jughead (10/79). 488-Archie's Christmas Stocking (12/79). 489-Betty & Veronica Christmas Spectacular (1/80). 490-Archie's Christmas Love-in (1/80). 492-World of Archie (2/80). 493-The World of Jughead (4/80). 494-Betty & Veronica Spectacular (6/80). 495-Archie's Jokes (8/80). 496-Betty & Veronica Summer Fun (9/80). 497-The World of Archie (9/80). 498-Betty & Veronica Spectacular (10/80). 499-The World of Jughead (10/80)   each...   2   4   6   8   10   12

455,467,479,491,503-Sabrina's Christmas Magic: 455-(1/77). 467-(1/78). 479-(1/79) Dracula/ Werewolf-s. 491-(1/80). 503(1/81)   2   4   6   11   16   20

500-Archie's Christmas Stocking (12/80)   2   4   6   8   11   14

501-514,516-527,529-532,534-539,541-543,545-550: 501-Betty & Veronica Christmas Spectacular (12/80). 502-Archie's Christmas Love-in (1/81). 504-The World of Archie (3/81). 505-The World of Jughead (4/81). 506-Betty & Veronica Spectacular (6/81). 507-Archie's Jokes (8/81). 508-Betty & Veronica Summer Fun (9/81). 509-The World of Archie (9/81). 510-Betty & Vernonica Spectacular (9/81). 511-The World of Jughead (10/81). 512-Archie's Christmas Stocking (12/81). 513-Betty & Veronica Christmas Spectacular (12/81). 514-Archie's Christmas Love-In (1/82). 516-The World of Archie(3/82). 517-The World of Jughead (4/82). 518-Betty & Veronica Spectacular (6/82). 519-Archie's Jokes (8/82). 520-Betty & Veronica Summer Fun (9/82). 521-The World of Archie (9/82). 522-Betty & Veronica Spectacular (10/82). 523-The World of Jughead (10/82).524-Archie's Christmas Stocking (1/83). 525-Betty and Veronica Christmas Spectacular (1/83). 526-Betty and Veronica Spectacular (5/83). 527-Little Archie (8/83). 529-Betty and Veronica Summer Fun (8/83). 530-Betty and Veronica Spectacular (9/83). 531-The World of Jughead (9/83). 532-The World of Archie (10/83). 534-Little Archie (1/84). 535-Archie's Christmas Stocking (1/84). 536-Betty and Veronica Christmas Spectacular (1/84). 537-Betty and Veronica Spectacular (6/84). 538-Little Archie (8/84). 539-Betty and Veronica Summer Fun (8/84). 541-Betty and Veronica Spectacular (9/84). 542-The World of Jughead (9/84). 543-The World of Archie (10/84). 545-Little Archie (12/84). 546-Archie's Christmas Stocking (12/84). 547-Betty and Veronica Christmas Spectacular (12/84). 548-?. 549-Little Archie. 550-Betty and Veronica Summer Fun   each...   1   2   3   5   7   9

515,528,533,540,544: 515-Sabrina's Christmas Magic (1/82). 528-Josie and the Pussycats (8/83). 533-Sabrina; Space Pirates by Frank Bolling (10/83). 540-Josie and the Pussycats (8/84). 544-Sabrina the Teen-Age Witch (8/84)   each...   2   4   6   10   14   18

551,562,571,584,597-Josie and the Pussycats   2   4   6   8   10   12

552-561,563-570,572-583,585-596,598-600: 552-Betty & Veronica Spectacular. 553-The World of Jughead. 554-The World of Archie. 555-Betty's Diary. 556-Little Archie (1/86). 557-Archie's Christmas Stocking (1/86). 558-World of Archie Christmas Spectacular (1/86). 559-Betty & Veronica Spectacular. 560-Little Archie. 561-Betty & Veronica Summer Fun. 563-World of Jughead. 564-World of Archie. 565-World of Archie. 566-Little Archie. 567-Archie's Christmas Stocking. 568-Betty & Veronica Christmas Spectacular. 569-Betty & Veronica Spring Spectacular. 570-Little Archie. 571-Dracula-c/s. 572-Betty & Veronica Summer Fun. 573-Archie At Riverdale High. 574-World of Archie. 575-Betty & Veronica Spectacular. 576-Little Archie. 577-World of Jughead. 578-Archie And Me. 579-Archie's Christmas Stocking. 580-Betty and Veronica Christmas Spectacular. 581-Little Archie Christmas Special. 582-Betty & Veronica Spring Spectacular. 583-Little Archie. 585-Betty & Veronica Summer Fun. 586-Archie At Riverdale High. 587-The World of Archie (10/88); 1st app. Explorers of the Unknown. 588-Betty & Veronica Spectacular. 589-Pep (10/88). 590-The World of Jughead. 591-Archie & Me. 592-Archie's Christmas Stocking. 593-Betty & Veronica Christmas Spectacular. 594-Little Archie. 595-Betty & Veronica Spring Spectacular. 596-Little Archie. 598-Betty & Veronica Spectacular. 599-The World of Archie (10/89); 2nd app. Explorers of the Unknown. 600-Betty and Veronica Spectacular   each...   6.00

601,602,604-609,611-629: 601-Pep. 602-The World of Jughead. 604-Archie at Riverdale High. 605-Archie's Christmas Stocking. 606-Betty and Veronica Christmas Spectacular. 607-Little Archie. 608-Betty and Veronica Spectacular. 609-Little Archie. 611-Betty and Veronica Summer Fun. 612-The World of Archie. 613-Betty and Veronica Spectacular. 614-Pep (10/90). 615-Veronica's Summer Special. 616-Archie and Me. 617-Archie's Christmas Stocking. 618-Betty & Veronica Christmas Spectacular. 619-Little Archie. 620-Betty and Veronica Spectacular. 621-Betty and Veronica Summer Fun. 622-Josie & the Pussycats; not published. 623-Betty and Veronica Spectacular. 624-Pep Comics. 625-Veronica's Summer Special. 626-Archie and Me. 627-World of Archie. 628-Archie's Pals 'n' Gals Holiday Special. 629-Betty & Veronica Spectacular.   each...   4.00

603-Archie and Me; Titanic app.   5.00

610-Josie and the Pussycats   1   2   3   4   5   7

630-631: 630-Archie's Christmas Stocking. 631-Archie's Pals 'n' Gals   4.00

632-Last issue; Betty & Veronica Spectacular   1   2   3   4   5   7

NOTE: Archies Band-c-173,180,192; s-189,192. Archie Cavemen-165,225,232,244,249. Little Sabrina-527,534, 538,545,556,566. UFO-s-178,487,594.

ARCHIE MEETS THE PUNISHER (Same contents as The Punisher Meets Archie)
Marvel Comics & Archie Comics Publ.: Aug, 1994 ($2.95, 52 pgs., one-shot)

1-Batton Lash story, J. Buscema-a on Punisher, S. Goldberg-a on Archie   6.00

ARCHIE'S ACTIVITY COMICS DIGEST MAGAZINE
Archie Enterprises: 1985 - No. 4 (Annual, 128 pgs., digest size)

1 (Most copies are marked)   2   4   6   9   13   16
2-4   1   2   3   5   7   9

ARCHIE'S CAR
Spire Christian Comics (Fleming H. Revell co.): 1979 (49¢)

nn   2   4   6   8   11   14

ARCHIE'S CHRISTMAS LOVE-IN (See Archie Giant Series Mag. No. 169, 181,192, 205, 218, 230, 242, 454, 466, 478, 490, 502, 514)

ARCHIE'S CHRISTMAS STOCKING (See Archie Giant Series Mag. No. 1-6,10, 15, 20, 25, 31, 137, 144, 150, 158, 167, 179, 190, 203, 216, 228, 240, 452, 464, 476, 488, 500, 512, 524, 535, 546, 557, 567, 579, 592, 605, 617, 630)

ARCHIE'S CHRISTMAS STOCKING
Archie Comics: 1993 - No. 7, 1999 ($2.00-$2.29, 52 pgs.)(Bound-in calendar poster in all)

1-Dan DeCarlo-c/a   5.00
2-5   4.00
6,7: 6-(1998, $2.25). 7-(1999, $2.29)   3.00

Archie's Double Digest #72 © AP

Archie's Girls, Betty and Veronica #2 © AP

Archie's Joke Book #27 © AP

	GD	VG	FN	VF	VF/NM	NM-
	2.0	4.0	6.0	8.0	9.0	9.2

ARCHIE'S CLASSIC CHRISTMAS STORIES
Archie Comics: 2002 ($10.95, TPB)

	GD	VG	FN	VF	VF/NM	NM-
Volume 1 - Reprints stories from 1955-1964 Archie's Christmas Stocking issues						11.00

ARCHIE'S CLEAN SLATE
Spire Christian Comics (Fleming H. Revell Co.): 1973 (35/49¢)

	GD	VG	FN	VF	VF/NM	NM-
1-(35¢-c edition)(Some issues have nn)	2	4	6	10	14	18
1-(49¢-c edition)	2	4	6	9	12	15

ARCHIE'S DATE BOOK
Spire Christian comics (Fleming H. Revell Co.): 1981

	GD	VG	FN	VF	VF/NM	NM-
nn-(Low print)	2	4	6	10	14	18

ARCHIE'S DOUBLE DIGEST QUARTERLY MAGAZINE
Archie Comics: 1981 - Present ($1.95-$3.69, 256 pgs.) (Archie's Double Digest Magazine No. 10 on)

	GD	VG	FN	VF	VF/NM	NM-
1	3	6	9	16	23	30
2-10; 6-Katy Keene story.	2	4	6	10	14	18
11-30: 29-Pureheart story	2	4	6	8	10	12
31-50	1	2	3	4	5	7
51-70,100						5.00
71-99						4.00
101-184: 115-Begin $3.19-c. 123-Begin $3.29-c. 139-Begin $3.59-c. 170-Begin $3.69						3.75

ARCHIE'S FAMILY ALBUM
Spire Christian Comics (Fleming H. Revell Co.): 1978 (39¢/49¢, 36 pgs.)

	GD	VG	FN	VF	VF/NM	NM-
nn	2	4	6	9	12	15
nn (49¢-c edition)	1	3	4	6	8	10

ARCHIE'S FESTIVAL
Spire Christian Comics (Fleming H. Revell Co.): 1980 (49¢)

	GD	VG	FN	VF	VF/NM	NM-
nn	2	4	6	9	12	15

ARCHIE'S GIRLS, BETTY AND VERONICA (Becomes Betty & Veronica)(Also see Veronica)
Archie Publications (Close-Up): 1950 - No. 347, Apr, 1987

	GD	VG	FN	VF	VF/NM	NM-
1	235	470	705	1469	2435	3400
2	97	194	291	606	1003	1400
3-5: 3-Betty's 1st ponytail. 4-Dan DeCarlo's 1st Archie work	55	110	165	344	572	800
6-10: 10-Katy Keene app. (2 pgs.)	45	90	135	275	450	625
11-20: 11,13,14,17-19-Katy Keene app. 17-Last pre-code issue (3/55). 20-Debbie's Diary (2 pgs.)	35	70	105	204	322	440
21-30: 27,30-Katy Keene app. 29-Tarzan	24	48	72	139	220	300
31-43,45-50: 41-Marilyn Monroe and Brigitte Bardot mentioned. 45-Fabian 1 pg. photo & bio.	16	32	48	94	147	200
46-Bobby Darin 1 pg. photo & bio	18	36	54	107	169	230
51-55,57-74: 67-Jackie Kennedy homage. 73-Sci-fi-c	8	16	24	52	86	120
56-Elvis and Bobby Darin records parody	9	18	27	61	103	145
75-Betty & Veronica sell souls to Devil	14	28	42	102	181	260
76-99: 82-Bobby Rydell 1 pg. illustrated bio; Elvis mentioned on-c. 84-Connie Francis 1 pg. illustrated bio	5	10	15	35	55	75
100	6	12	18	41	66	90
101-104, 106-117,120 (12/65): 113-Monsters-s	4	8	12	26	41	55
105-Beatles wig parody (5 pg. story)(9/64)	4	8	12	28	44	60
118-(10/65) 1st app./origin Superteen (also see Betty & Me #3)	6	12	18	39	62	85
119-2nd app./last Superteen story	5	10	15	30	48	65
121,122,124-126,128-140 (8/67): 135,140-Mod-c. 136-Slave Girl-s	3	6	9	18	27	35
123-"Jingo"-Ringo parody-c	3	6	9	21	32	42
127-Beatles Fan Club-s	4	8	12	28	44	60
141-156,158-163,165-180 (12/70)	3	6	9	14	19	24
157,164-Archies Band	3	6	9	17	25	32
181-193,195-199	2	4	6	9	13	16
194-Sabrina-c/s	3	6	9	17	25	32
200-(8/72)	2	4	6	11	16	20
201-205,207,209,211-215,217-240	2	4	6	8	10	12
206,208,216-Sabrina c/app. 206-Josie-c. 210-Sabrina app.	3	6	9	14	19	24
241 (1/76)-270 (6/78)	1	3	4	6	8	10
271-299: 281-UFO-s	1	2	3	5	7	9
300 (12/80)-Anniversary issue	2	4	6	8	10	12
301-309	1	2	3	4	5	7
310-John Travolta parody story	1	3	4	6	8	10
311-319						6.00

320 (10/82)-Intro. of Cheryl Blossom on cover and inside story (she also appears, but not on the cover, in Jughead #325 with same 10/82 publication date)

	GD	VG	FN	VF	VF/NM	NM-
321,322-Cheryl Blossom app.	6	12	18	41	66	90
323,326,329,330,331,333-338: 333-Monsters-s	3	6	9	17	25	32
324,325-Crickett O'Dell app.	1	2	3	5	6	8
327,328-Cheryl Blossom app.	1	3	4	6	8	10
332,339: 332-Superhero costume party. 339-(12/85) Betty dressed as Madonna.	2	4	6	8	10	12
340-346 Low print	1	2	3	5	6	8
347 (4/87) Last issue; low print	1	2	3	5	7	9
Annual 1 (1953)	110	220	330	688	1144	1600
Annual 2 (1954)	45	90	135	275	450	625
Annual 3-5 (1955-1957)	37	74	111	213	337	460
Annual 6-8 (1958-1960)	26	52	78	150	235	320

ARCHIE'S HOLIDAY FUN DIGEST
Archie Comics: 1997 - Present ($1.75/$1.95/$1.99/$2.19/$2.39/$2.49, annual)

	GD	VG	FN	VF	VF/NM	NM-
1-12-Christmas stories						2.50

ARCHIE'S JOKEBOOK COMICS DIGEST ANNUAL (See Jokebook...)

ARCHIE'S JOKE BOOK MAGAZINE (See Joke Book ...)
Archie Publ.: 1953 - No. 3, Sum, 1954; No. 15, Fall, 1954 - No. 288, 11/82 (subtitled...Laugh-In #127-140; ...Laugh-Out #141-194)

	GD	VG	FN	VF	VF/NM	NM-
1953-One Shot (#1)	100	200	300	625	1038	1450
2	47	94	141	287	474	660
3 (no #4-14)	40	80	120	235	368	500
15-20: 15-Formerly Archie's Rival Reggie #14; last pre-code issue (Fall/54).	24	48	72	137	216	295
15-17-Katy Keene app.						
21-30	15	30	45	84	127	170
31-43: 42-Bio of Ed "Kookie" Byrnes. 43-story about guitarist Duane Eddy	11	22	33	64	90	115
44-1st professional comic work by Neal Adams, 4 pgs.	28	56	84	162	256	350
45-47-N. Adams-a in all, 2-6 pgs.	15	30	45	90	140	190
48-Four pgs. N. Adams-a	15	30	45	90	140	190
49,50	5	10	15	32	51	70
51-56,60 (1962)	4	8	12	24	37	50
57-Elvis mentioned; Marilyn Monroe cameo	5	10	15	32	51	70
58,59-Horror/Sci-Fi-c	4	8	12	28	44	60
61-80 (8/64): 66-(12¢ cover)	3	6	9	16	23	30
66-(15¢ cover variant)	3	6	9	18	27	35
81-89,91,92,94-99	2	4	6	13	18	22
90,93: 90-Beatles gag. 93-Beatles cameo	3	6	9	16	23	30
100 (5/66)	3	6	9	16	22	28
101,103-117,119-123,127,129,131-140 (9/69): 105-Superhero gag-c. 108-110-Archies Archers Band-s. 116-Beatles/Monkees/Bob Dylan cameos (posters)	2	4	6	10	14	18
102 (7/66) Archie Band prototype-c; Elvis parody panel, Rolling Stones mention	3	6	9	17	25	32
118,124,125,126,128,130: 118-Archie Band-c; Veronica & Groovers band-s. 124-Archies Band-c/app. 125-Beatles cameo (poster). 126,130-Monkees cameo. 128-Veronica/Archies Band app.	3	6	9		22	28
141-173,175-181,183-199	2	4	6	8	10	12
174-Sabrina-c. 182-Sabrina cameo	2	4	6	9	12	15
200 (9/74)	2	4	6	9	12	15
201-230 (3/77)	1	2	3	5	6	8
231-239,241-287						6.00
240-Elvis record-c	1	2	3	5	7	9
288-Last issue	1	2	3	4	5	7

NOTE: Archies Band-c-118,124,127,172; 1 pg.-s-127,128,138,140,143,147,167; 2 pg.-s-124,131, 155. Sabrina app.-247,248,252-259,261,262,264,266-270,274,277,284-286.

ARCHIE'S JOKES (See Archie Giant Series Mag. No. 17, 22, 27, 33, 139, 146, 154, 163, 174, 186, 198, 211, 222, 235, 247, 459, 471, 483, 495, 519)

ARCHIE'S LOVE SCENE
Spire Christian Comics (Fleming H. Revell Co.): 1973 (35¢/39¢/49¢/no price)

	GD	VG	FN	VF	VF/NM	NM-
1-(35¢ Edition)	2	4	6	10	14	18
1-(39¢/49¢ Edition/no price) (Some copies have nn)	2	4	6	8	10	12

ARCHIE'S LOVE SHOWDOWN SPECIAL
Archie Publications: 1994 ($2.00, one-shot)

	GD	VG	FN	VF	VF/NM	NM-
1-Concludes x-over from Archie #429, Betty #19, B&V #82, Veronica #39						4.00

ARCHIE'S MADHOUSE (Madhouse Ma-ad No. 67 on)
Archie Publications: Sept, 1959 - No. 66, Feb, 1969

	GD	VG	FN	VF	VF/NM	NM-
1-Archie begins	21	42	63	156	278	400

Archie's Pal, Jughead #166 © AP

Archie's Madhouse #4 © AP · Archie's Pals 'n' Gals #4 © AP

	GD 2.0	VG 4.0	FN 6.0	VF 8.0	VF/NM 9.0	NM- 9.2
2	11	22	33	79	140	200
3-5	8	16	24	56	93	130
6-10	6	12	18	39	62	85
11-17 (Last w/regular characters)	5	10	15	30	48	65
18-21,23,29: 18-New format begins. 23-No Sabrina	4	8	12	24	37	50
22-1st app. Sabrina, the Teen-age Witch (10/62)	23	46	69	171	306	440
24-2nd app.Sabrina a	10	20	30	67	116	165
25,26,28-Sabrina app. 25-1st app. Captain Sprocket (4/63)	7	14	21	49	80	110
27-Sabrina-c; no story	6	12	18	39	62	85
30,34,38-40: No Sabrina. 34-Bordered-c begin.	3	6	9	16	23	30
31,33,37-Sabrina app.	6	12	18	37	59	80
32-Sabrina app.?	3	6	9	16	23	30
35-Beatles cameo. No Sabrina	3	6	9	18	27	35
36-1st Salem the Cat w/Sabrina story	8	16	24	52	86	120
41-48,51-57,60-62,64-66; No Sabrina 43-Mighty Crusaders cameo. 44-Swipes Mad #4 (Super-Duperman) in "Bird Monsters From Outer Space"	3	6	9	14	19	24
49,50,58,59,63-Sabrina stories	4	8	12	28	44	60
Annual 1 (1962-63) no Sabrina	7	14	21	45	73	100
Annual 2 (1964) no Sabrina	4	8	12	28	44	60
Annual 3 (1965)-Origin Sabrina the Teen-Age Witch	9	18	27	63	107	150
Annual 4,5('66-68)(Becomes Madhouse Ma-ad Annual #7 on); no Sabrina	3	6	9	19	25	32
Annual 6 (1969)-Sabrina the Teen-Age Witch-sty	6	12	18	39	62	85

NOTE: Cover title to #61-65 is "Madhouse" and to #66 is "Madhouse Ma-ad Jokes". Sci-Fi/Horror covers 6, 8, 11, 13, 15-26, 29, 35, 36, 38, 42, 43, 48, 51, 58, 60.

ARCHIE'S MECHANICS
Archie Publications: Sept, 1954 - No. 3, 1955

	GD 2.0	VG 4.0	FN 6.0	VF 8.0	VF/NM 9.0	NM- 9.2
1-(15¢; 52 pgs.)	81	162	243	506	841	1175
2-(10¢)-Last pre-code issue	48	96	144	293	484	675
3-(10¢)	40	80	120	244	392	540

ARCHIE'S MYSTERIES (Continued from Archie's Weird Mysteries)
Archie Comics: No. 25, Feb, 2003 - No. 34, June, 2004 ($2.19)

25-34- Archie and gang as "Teen Scene Investigators" — 2.50

ARCHIE'S ONE WAY
Spire Christian Comics (Fleming H. Revell Co.): 1972 (35¢/39¢/49¢, 36 pgs.)

	GD 2.0	VG 4.0	FN 6.0	VF 8.0	VF/NM 9.0	NM- 9.2
nn-(35¢ Edition)	2	4	6	10	14	18
nn-(39¢, 49¢, no price editions)	2	4	6	8	10	12

ARCHIE'S PAL, JUGHEAD (Jughead No. 127 on)
Archie Publications: 1949 - No. 126, Nov, 1965

	GD 2.0	VG 4.0	FN 6.0	VF 8.0	VF/NM 9.0	NM- 9.2
1 (1949)-1st app. Moose (see Pep #33)	193	386	579	1206	2003	2800
2 (1950)	76	152	228	475	788	1100
3-5	45	90	135	275	450	625
6-10: 7-Suzie app.	32	64	96	186	293	400
11-20: 20-Jughead as Sherlock Holmes parody	21	42	63	122	191	260
21-30: 23-25,28-30-Katy Keene app. 23-Early Dilton-s. 28-Debbie's Diary app.	15	30	45	86	133	180
31-50: 49-Archies Rock 'N' Rollers band-c	7	14	21	45	73	100
51-57,59-70: 59- Bio of Will Hutchins of TV's Sugarfoot. 67-Betty becoming Jughead-c. 68-Early Archie Gang Cavemen-s	5	10	15	32	51	70
58-Neal Adams-a	6	12	18	37	59	80
71-76,83,84,89-99: 72-Jughead dates Betty & Veronica. 84-1st app. Big Ethel (5/62). 95-2nd app. Cricket O'Dell	3	6	9	20	30	40
77,78,80-82,85,86,88-Horror/Sci-Fi-c	5	10	15	30	48	65
79-Creature From the Black Lagoon-c	6	12	18	39	62	85
87-Early Big Ethel app.; UGAJ (United Girls Against Jughead)-s	4	8	12	26	41	55
100	4	8	12	24	37	50
101-Return of Big Ethyl	4	8	12	23	36	48
102-126	3	6	9	17	25	32
Annual 1 (1953, 25¢)	67	134	201	419	697	975
Annual 2 (1954, 25¢)-Last pre-code issue	40	80	120	243	389	535
Annual 3-5 (1955-57, 25¢)	29	58	87	167	264	360
Annual 6-8 (1958-60, 25¢)	18	36	54	105	165	225

ARCHIE'S PAL JUGHEAD COMICS (Formerly Jughead #1-45)
Archie Comic Publ.: No. 46, June, 1993 - Present ($1.25-$2.25)

46-60 — 3.00
61-186: 100-"A Storm Over Uniforms" x-over part 1,2. 166-Three Geeks cameo — 2.25

ARCHIE'S PALS 'N' GALS (Also see Archie Giant Series Magazine #628)
Archie Publ: 1952-53 - No. 6, 1957-58; No. 7, 1958 - No. 224, Sept, 1991

(...All News Stories on-c #49-59)

	GD 2.0	VG 4.0	FN 6.0	VF 8.0	VF/NM 9.0	NM- 9.2
1-(116 pgs., 25¢)	85	170	255	531	878	1225
2(Annual)('54, 25¢)	41	82	123	256	416	575
3-5(Annual, '55-57, 25¢): 3-Last pre-code issue	31	62	93	178	282	385
6-10('58-'60)	19	38	57	109	172	235
11,13,14,16,17,20-(84 pgs.): 17-B&V paper dolls	11	22	33	64	90	115
12,15-(84 pgs.) Neal Adams-a. 12-Harry Belafonte 2 pg. photos & bio.	13	26	39	72	101	130
18-(84 pgs.) Horror/Sci-Fi-c	12	24	36	69	97	125
19-Marilyn Monroe app.	15	30	45	90	140	190
21,22,24-28,30 (68 pgs.)	6	12	18	37	59	80
23-(Wint./62) 6 pg. Josie-s with Pepper and Melody (1st app.) by DeCarlo; Betty in towel pin-up	15	30	45	107	191	275
29-Beatles satire (68 pgs.)	8	16	24	56	93	130
31(Wint. 64/65)-39 -(68 pgs.)	5	10	15	32	51	70
40-Early Superteen-s; with Pureheart	6	12	18	41	66	90
41(8/67)-43,45-50(2/69) (68 pgs.)	4	8	12	22	34	45
44-Archies Band-s; WEB cameo	4	8	12	26	41	55
51(4/69),52,55-64(6/71): 62-Last squarebound	3	6	9	17	25	32
53-Archies Band-c/s	3	6	9	20	30	40
54-Satan meets Veronica-s	4	8	12	28	44	60
65(8/70),67-70,73-81,83(6/74) (52 pgs.)	2	4	6	13	18	22
66,82-Sabrina-c	3	6	9	19	29	38
71,72-Two part drug story (8/72,9/72)	3	6	9	18	27	35
75-Archies Band-s	3	6	9	16	23	30
84-99	1	3	4	6	8	10
100 (12/75)	2	4	6	9	12	15
101-130(3/79): 125,126-Riverdale 2001-s	1	2	3	5	6	8
131-160,162-170 (7/84)						6.00
161 (11/82) 3rd app./1st solo Cheryl Blossom-s and pin-up; 2nd Jason Blossom	3	6	9	19	29	38
171-173,175,177-197,199: 197-G. Colan-a						4.00
174,176,198: 174-New Archies Band-s. 176-Cyndi Lauper-c. 198-Archie gang on strike at Archie Ent. offices						6.00
200(9/88)-Illiteracy-s						6.00
201,203-223: Later issues $1.00 cover						3.00
202-Explains end of Archie's jalopy; Dezerland-c/s; James Dean cameo						6.00
224-Last issue						5.00

NOTE: Archies Band-c-45,47,49,53,56; s-44,53,75,174. UFO-s-50,63,209,220.

ARCHIE'S PALS 'N' GALS DOUBLE DIGEST MAGAZINE
Archie Comic Publications: Nov, 1992 - Present ($2.50-$3.69)

	GD 2.0	VG 4.0	FN 6.0	VF 8.0	VF/NM 9.0	NM- 9.2
1-Capt. Hero story; Pureheart app.	2	4	6	8	10	12
2-10: 2-Superduck story; Little Jinx in all. 4-Begin $2.75-c	1	2	3	4	5	7
11-29						4.00
30-117: 40-Begin $2.99-c. 48-Begin $3.19-c. 56-Begin $3.29-c. 72-Begin $3.59-c. 100-Story uses screen captures from classic animated series. 102-Begin $3.69-c						3.75

ARCHIE'S PARABLES
Spire Christian Comics (Fleming H. Revell Co.): 1973,1975 (39/49¢, 36 pgs.)

	GD 2.0	VG 4.0	FN 6.0	VF 8.0	VF/NM 9.0	NM- 9.2
nn-By Al Hartley; 39¢ Edition	2	4	6	10	14	18
49¢, no price editions	2	4	6	8	10	12

ARCHIE'S R/C RACERS (Radio controlled cars)
Archie Comics: Sept, 1989 - No. 10, Mar, 1991 (95¢/$1)

1 — 6.00
2,5-7,10: 5-Elvis parody. 7-Supervillain-c/s. 10-UFO-c/s — 4.00
3,4,8,9 — 3.00

ARCHIE'S RIVAL REGGIE (Reggie & Archie's Joke Book #15 on)
Archie Publications: 1949 - No. 14, Aug, 1954

	GD 2.0	VG 4.0	FN 6.0	VF 8.0	VF/NM 9.0	NM- 9.2
1-Reggie 1st app. in Jackpot Comics #5	85	170	255	531	878	1225
2	41	82	123	250	400	550
3-5	31	62	93	178	282	385
6-10	22	44	66	126	198	270
11-14: Katy Keene in No. 10-14, 1-2 pgs.	16	32	48	92	144	195

ARCHIE'S RIVERDALE HIGH (See Riverdale High)

ARCHIE'S ROLLER COASTER
Spire Christian Comics (Fleming H. Revell Co.): 1981 (69¢)

	GD 2.0	VG 4.0	FN 6.0	VF 8.0	VF/NM 9.0	NM- 9.2
nn-(Low print)	2	4	6	10	14	18

ARCHIE'S SOMETHING ELSE
Spire Christian Comics (Fleming H. Revell Co.): 1975 (39/49¢, 36 pgs.)

	GD 2.0	VG 4.0	FN 6.0	VF 8.0	VF/NM 9.0	NM- 9.2
nn-(39¢-c) Hell's Angels Biker on motorcycle-c	2	4	6	10	14	18

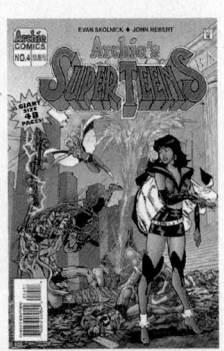
Archie's Super Teens #4 © AP

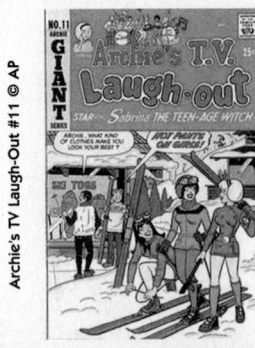
Archie's TV Laugh-Out #11 © AP

Aria Angela #1 © Avalon & TMP

	GD	VG	FN	VF	VF/NM	NM-
	2.0	4.0	6.0	8.0	9.0	9.2

nn-(49¢-c) — 2 4 6 8 10 12
Barbour Christian Comics Edition ('86, no price listed) — 1 2 3 5 7 9

ARCHIE'S SONSHINE
Spire Christian Comics (Fleming H. Revell Co.): 1973, 1974 (39/49¢, 36 pgs.)
39¢ Edition — 2 4 6 10 14 18
49¢, no price editions — 2 4 6 8 10 12

ARCHIE'S SPORTS SCENE
Spire Christian Comics (Fleming H. Revell Co.): 1983 (no cover price)
nn-(Low print) — 2 4 6 10 14 18

ARCHIE'S SPRING BREAK
Archie Comics: 1996 - Present ($2.00, 48 pgs., annual)
1-Dan DeCarlo-c — 4.00
2-4: 2-Dan DeCarlo-c — 3.00

ARCHIE'S STORY & GAME COMICS DIGEST MAGAZINE
Archie Enterprises: Nov, 1986 - No. 39, Jan, 1998 ($1.25-$1.95, 128 pgs., digest-size)
1: Marked-up copies are common — 2 4 6 10 14 18
2-10 — 1 3 4 6 8 10
11-20 — 6.00
21-38 — 3.00
39-($1.95) — 2.50

ARCHIE'S SUPER HERO SPECIAL (See Archie Giant Series Mag. No. 142)
ARCHIE'S SUPER HERO SPECIAL (...Comics Digest Mag. 2)
Archie Publications: Jan, 1979 - No. 2, Aug, 1979 (95¢, 148 pgs.)
1-Simon & Kirby r-/Double Life of Pvt. Strong #1,2; Black Hood, The Fly, Jaguar, The Web app. — 2 4 6 11 16 20
2-Contains contents to the never published Black Hood #1; origin Black Hood; N. Adams, Wood, McWilliams, Morrow, S&K-a(r); N. Adams-c. The Shield, The Fly, Jaguar, Hangman, Steel Sterling, The Web, The Fox-r — 2 4 6 11 16 20

ARCHIE'S SUPER TEENS
Archie Comic Publications, Inc.: 1994 - No. 4, 1996 ($2.00, 52 pgs.)
1-Staton/Esposito-c/a; pull-out poster — 4.00
2-4: 2-Fred Hembeck script; Bret Blevins/Terry Austin-a — 3.00

ARCHIE'S TV LAUGH-OUT ("...Starring Sabrina" on-c #1-50)
Archie Publications: Dec, 1969 - No. 105, Feb, 1986 (#1-7: 68 pgs.)
1-Sabrina begins, thru #106 — 10 20 30 71 126 160
2 (68 pgs.) — 6 12 18 37 59 80
3-6 (68 pgs.) — 4 8 12 28 44 60
7-Josie begins, thru #105; Archie's & Josie's Bands cover logos begin — 7 14 21 45 73 100
8-23 (52 pgs.): 10-1st Josie on-c. 12-1st Josie and Pussycats on-c. 14-Beatles cameo on poster — 4 8 12 24 37 50
24-40: 37,39,40-Bicenntennial-c — 3 6 9 14 20 25
41,47,56: 41-Alexandra rejoins J&P band. 47-Fonz cameo; voodoo-s. 56-Fonz parody: B&V with Farrah hair-c — 3 6 9 16 22 28
42-46,48-55,57-60 — 2 4 6 9 12 15
61-68,70-80: 63-UFO-s. 79-Mummy-s — 1 3 4 6 8 10
69-Sherlock Holmes parody — 1 3 4 6 8 10
81-90,94,95,97-99: 84 Voodoo-s — 1 2 3 5 6 8
91-Early Cheryl Blossom-s; Sabrina/Archies Band-c — 2 4 6 13 18 22
92-A-Team parody — 1 3 4 6 8 10
93-(2/84) Archie in drag-c; Hill Street Blues-s; Groucho Marx parody; cameo parody app. of Batman, Spider-Man, Wonder Woman and others — 2 4 6 9 12 15
96-MASH parody-s; Jughead in drag; Archies Band-c — 1 3 4 6 8 10
100-(4/85) Michael Jackson parody-c/s; J&P band and Archie band on-c — 2 4 6 9 12 15
101-104-Lower print run. 104-Miami Vice parody-c — 1 2 3 5 7 9
105-Wrestling/Hulk Hogan parody-c; J&P band-s — 2 4 6 9 12 15
106-Last issue; low print run — 2 4 6 8 10 12
NOTE: Dan DeCarlo-a 78-up(most), c-89-up(most). Archies Band-s 2,7,9-11,15,20,25,37,64,65,67,68,70,73, 76,78,79,83,84,86,90,96,100,101; Archies Band-c 2,17,20,91,94,96,99-103. Josie-s 12,21,26,35,52,78,80,90. Josie-c 10,91,94. Josie and the Pussycats (as a band in costume)-s 7,9,10,37,38,41,42,66,84,99-101,105. Josie w/Pussycats member Valerie &/or Melody-s 17,20,22,25,27-29,31,33,36,39,40,43-51,53-65,67-77,79,81-83,85-89,92-94,102-104. Josie w/Pussycats band-c 12,14,17,18,22,24. Sabrina-s 1-9,11-86,88-106. Sabrina-c 1-18,21,23,27,49,91,94.

ARCHIE'S VACATION SPECIAL
Archie Publications: Winter, 1994 - Present ($2.00/$2.25/$2.29/$2.49, annual)
1 — 4.00
2-8: 8-(2000, $2.49) — 3.00

ARCHIE'S WEIRD MYSTERIES (Continues as Archie's Mysteries)
Archie Comics: Feb, 2000 - No. 24, Dec, 2002 ($1.79/$1.99)
1 — 3.50
2-10: 3-Mighty Crusaders app. — 3.00
11-24: 14-Super Teens-c/app.; Mighty Crusaders app. — 2.50

ARCHIE'S WORLD
Spire Christian Comics (Fleming H. Revell Co.): 1973, 1976 (39/49¢)
39¢ Edition — 2 4 6 10 14 18
49¢ Edition, no price editions — 2 4 6 8 10 12

ARCHIE 3000
Archie Comics: May, 1989 - No. 16, July, 1991 (75¢/95¢/$1.00)
1,16: 16-Aliens-c/s — 4.00
2-15: 6-Begin $1.00-c; X-Mas-c — 3.00

ARCOMICS PREMIERE
Arcomics: July, 1993 ($2.95)
1-1st lenticular-c on a comic (flicker-c) — 3.00

AREA 52
Image Comics: Jan, 2001 - No. 4, June, 2001 ($2.95)
1-4-Haberlin-s/Henry-a — 3.00

ARES
Marvel Comics: Mar, 2006 - No. 5, July, 2006 ($2.99, limited series)
1-5-Oeming-s/Foreman-a — 3.00
....: God of War TPB (2006, $13.99) r/series — 14.00

ARGUS (See Flash, 2nd Series) (Also see Showcase '95 #1,2)
DC Comics: Apr, 1995 - No. 6, Oct, 1995 ($1.50, limited series)
1-6: 4-Begin $1.75-c — 2.50

ARIA
Image Comics (Avalon Studios): Jan, 1999 - Present ($2.50)
Preview (11/98, $2.95) — 5.00
1-Anacleto-c/a — 1 2 3 5 6 8
1-Variant-c by Michael Turner — 1 2 3 5 6 8
1-($10.00) Alternate-c by Turner — 6.00
1,2-(Blanc & Noir) Black and white printing of pencil art — 3.00
1-(Blanc & Noir) DF Edition — 5.00
2-4: 2,4-Anacleto-c/a. 3-Martinez-a — 3.00
4-($6.95) Glow in the Dark-c — 1 2 3 4 6 8
Aria Angela 1 (2/00, $2.95) Anacleto-a; 4 covers by Anacleto, JG Jones, Portacio and Quesada — 3.00
Aria Angela Blanc & Noir 1 (4/00, $2.95) Anacleto-c — 3.00
Aria Angela European Ashcan — 10.00
Aria Angela 2 (10/00, $2.95) Anacleto-a/c — 3.00
....: A Midwinter's Dream 1 (1/02, $4.95, 7"x7") text-s w/Anacleto panels — 5.00
....: The Enchanted Collection (5/04, $16.95) r/Summer's Spell & The Uses of Enchantment — 17.00

ARIA: SUMMER'S SPELL
Image Comics (Avalon Studios): Mar, 2002 - No. 2, Jun, 2002 ($2.95)
1,2-Anacleto-c/Holguin-s/Pajarillo & Medina-a — 3.00

ARIA: THE SOUL MARKET
Image Comics (Avalon Studios): Mar, 2001 - No. 6, Dec, 2001 ($2.95)
1-6-Anacleto-c/Holguin-s — 3.00
HC (2002, $26.95, 8.25" x 12.25") oversized r/#1-6 — 27.00
SC (2004, $16.95, 8.25" x 12.25") oversized r/#1-6 — 17.00

ARIA: THE USES OF ENCHANTMENT
Image Comics (Avalon Studios): Feb, 2003 - No. 4, Sept, 2003 ($2.95)
1-4-Anacleto-c/Holguin-s/Medina-a — 3.00

ARIANE AND BLUEBEARD (See Night Music #8)
ARIEL & SEBASTIAN (See Cartoon Tales & The Little Mermaid)
ARION, LORD OF ATLANTIS (Also see Warlord #55)
DC Comics: Nov, 1982 - No. 35, Sept, 1985
1-Story cont'd from Warlord #62 — 3.00
2-35, Special #1 (11/85) — 2.50

ARION THE IMMORTAL (Also see Showcase '95 #7)
DC Comics: July, 1992 - No. 6, Dec, 1992 ($1.50, limited series)
1 — 3.00
2-6: 4-Gustovich-a(i) — 2.50

ARISTOCATS (See Movie Comics & Walt Disney Showcase No. 16)

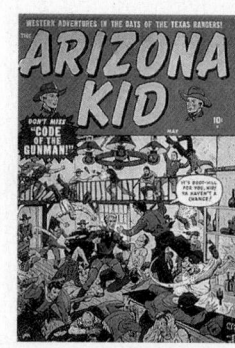

Arizone Kid #2 © MAR

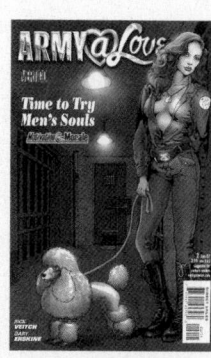

Army @ Love #2 © Rick Veitch

Army of Darkness: From the Ashes #1 © Orion Picts.

	GD 2.0	VG 4.0	FN 6.0	VF 8.0	VF/NM 9.0	NM- 9.2

ARISTOKITTENS, THE (…Meet Jiminy Cricket No. 1)(Disney)
Gold Key: Oct, 1971 - No. 9, Oct, 1975

1	3	6	9	20	30	40
2-5,7-9	3	6	9	14	19	24
6-(52 pgs.)	3	6	9	16	22	28

ARIZONA KID, THE (Also see The Comics & Wild Western)
Marvel/Atlas Comics(CSI): Mar, 1951 - No. 6, Jan, 1952

1	22	44	66	126	198	270
2-4: 2-Heath-a(3)	12	24	36	69	97	125
5,6	10	20	30	56	76	95

NOTE: *Heath* a-1-3; c-1-3. *Maneely* c-4-6. *Morisi* a-4-6. *Sinnott* a-6.

ARK, THE (See The Crusaders)

ARKAGA
Image Comics: Sept, 1997 ($2.95, one-shot)

1-Jorgensen-s/a		3.00

ARKANIUM
Dreamwave Productions: Sept, 2002 - No. 5 ($2.95)

1-5: 1-Gatefold wraparound-c		3.00

ARKHAM ASYLUM: LIVING HELL
DC Comics: July, 2003 - No. 6, Dec, 2003 ($2.50, limited series)

1-6-Ryan Sook-a; Batman app. 3-Batgirl-c/app.		2.50

ARMAGEDDON
Chaos! Comics: Oct, 1999 - No. 4, Jan, 2000 ($2.95, limited series)

Preview		5.00
1-4-Lady Death, Evil Ernie, Purgatori app.		3.00

ARMAGEDDON: ALIEN AGENDA
DC Comics: Nov, 1991 - No. 4, Feb, 1992 ($1.00, limited series)

1-4		2.50

ARMAGEDDON FACTOR, THE
AC Comics: 1987 - No. 2, 1987; No. 3, 1990 ($1.95)

1,2: Sentinels of Justice, Dragonfly, Femforce		2.50
3-($3.95, color)-Almost all AC characters app.		4.00

ARMAGEDDON: INFERNO
DC Comics: Apr, 1992 - No. 4, July, 1992 ($1.00, limited series)

1-4: Many DC heroes app. 3-A. Adams/Austin-a		2.50

ARMAGEDDON 2001
DC Comics: May, 1991 - No. 2, Oct, 1991 ($2.00, squarebound, 68 pgs.)

1-Features many DC heroes; intro Waverider		4.00
1-2nd & 3rd printings; 3rd has silver ink-c		2.50
2		3.00

ARMED & DANGEROUS
Acclaim Comics (Armada): Apr, 1996 - No.4, July, 1996 ($2.95, B&W)

1-4-Bob Hall-c/a & scripts		3.00
Special 1 (8/96, $2.95, B&W)-Hall-c/a & scripts.		3.00

ARMED & DANGEROUS HELL'S SLAUGHTERHOUSE
Acclaim Comics (Armada): Oct, 1996 - No. 4, Jan, 1997 ($2.95, B&W)

1-4: Hall-c/a/scripts.		3.00

ARMOR (AND THE SILVER STREAK) (Revengers Featuring… in indicia for #1-3)
Continuity Comics: Sept, 1985 - No.13, Apr, 1992 ($2.00)

1-13: 1-Intro/origin Armor & the Silver Streak; Neal Adams-c/a. 7-Origin Armor; Nebres-i		3.50

ARMOR (DEATHWATCH 2000)
Continuity Comics: Apr, 1993 - No. 6, Nov, 1993 ($2.50)

1-6: 1-3-Deathwatch 2000 x-over		3.00

ARMORINES (See X-O Manowar #25 for 16 pg. bound-in Armorines #0)
Valiant: June, 1994 - No. 12, June, 1995 ($2.25)

0-Stand-alone edition with cardstock-c		25.00
0-Gold		15.00
1-12: 7-Wraparound-c. 12-Byrne-c/swipe (X-Men, 1st Series #138)		2.50

ARMORINES (Volume 2)
Acclaim Comics: Oct, 1999 - No. 4 ($3.95/$2.50, limited series)

1-($3.95) Calafiore & P. Palmiotti-a		4.00
2,3-($2.50)		2.50

ARMOR X

Image Comics: March, 2005 - No. 4, June, 2005 ($2.95, limited series)

1-Keith Champagne-s/Andy Smith-a; flip covers on #2-4		3.00

ARMY AND NAVY COMICS (Supersnipe No. 6 on)
Street & Smith Publications: May, 1941 - No. 5, July, 1942

1-Cap Fury & Nick Carter	53	106	159	323	537	750
2-Cap Fury & Nick Carter	31	62	93	180	285	390
3,4: 4-Jack Farr-c/a	23	46	69	130	205	280
5-Supersnipe app.; see Shadow V2#3 for 1st app.; Story of Douglas MacArthur; George Marcoux-c/a	53	106	159	330	545	760

ARMY @ LOVE
DC Comics (Vertigo): May, 2007 - Present ($2.99)

1-6-Rick Veitch-s/a(p); Gary Erskine-a(i)		3.00

ARMY ATTACK
Charlton Comics: July, 1964 - No. 4, Feb, 1965; V2#38, July, 1965 - No. 47, Feb, 1967

V1#1	4	8	12	28	44	60
2-4(2/65)	3	6	9	18	27	35
V2#38(7/65)-47 (formerly U.S. Air Force #1-37)	3	6	9	15	21	26

NOTE: *Glanzman* a-1-3. *Montes/Bache* a-44.

ARMY AT WAR (Also see Our Army at War & Cancelled Comic Cavalcade)
DC Comics: Oct-Nov, 1978

1-Kubert-c; all new story and art	2	4	6	9	13	16

ARMY OF DARKNESS (Movie)
Dark Horse Comics: Nov, 1992 - No. 2, Dec, 1992 - No. 3, Oct, 1993 ($2.50, limited series)

1-3-Bolton painted-c/a	2	4	6	9	12	15
… Movie Adaptation TPB (2006, $14.99) r/#1-3; intro. by Busiek; Bruce Campbell interview						15.00

ARMY OF DARKNESS (Also see Marvel Zombies vs. Army of Darkness)
Dynamite Entertainment: 2005 - NO. 13, 2007 ($2.99)

1-4 (Vs. Re-Animator):1,2-Four covers; Greene-a/Kuhoric-s. 3,4-Three covers		3.00
5-13: 5-7-Kuhoric-s/Sharpe-a; four covers. 8-11-Ash Vs. Dracula. 12,13-Death of Ash		3.00

ARMY OF DARKNESS: ASHES 2 ASHES (Movie)
Devil's Due Publ.: July, 2004 - No. 4, 2004 ($2.99, limited series)

1-4-Four covers for each; Nick Bradshaw-a		3.00
1-Director's Cut (12/04, $4.99) r/#1, cover gallery, script and sketch pages		5.00
TPB (2005, $14.99) r/series; cover gallery; Bradshaw interview and sketch pages		15.00

ARMY OF DARKNESS: FROM THE ASHES
Dynamite Entertainment: 2007 - Present ($3.50)

1-Kuhoric-s/Blanco-a; covers by Blanco & Suydam		3.50

ARMY OF DARKNESS: SHOP TILL YOU DROP DEAD (Movie)
Devil's Due Publ.: Jan, 2005 - No. 4, July, 2005 ($2.99, limited series)

1-4:1-Five covers; Bradshaw-a/Kuhoric-s. 2-4: Two covers. 3-Greene-a		3.00

ARMY SURPLUS KOMIKZ FEATURING CUTEY BUNNY
Army Surplus Komikz/Eclipse Comics: 1982 - No. 5, 1985 ($1.50, B&W)

1-Cutey Bunny begins	2	4	6	8	10	12
2-5: 5-(Eclipse)-JLA/X-Men/Batman parody						4.50

ARMY WAR HEROES (Also see Iron Corporal)
Charlton Comics: Dec, 1963 - No. 38, June, 1970

1	5	10	15	30	48	65
2-10	3	6	9	18	27	35
11-21,23-30: 24-Intro. Archer & Corp. Jack series	3	6	9	14	20	25
22-Origin/1st app. Iron Corporal series by Glanzman	4	8	12	22	34	45
31-38	2	4	6	9	13	16
Modern Comics Reprint 36 ('78)						4.00

NOTE: *Montes/Bache* a-1, 16, 17, 21, 23-25, 27-30.

AROUND THE BLOCK WITH DUNC & LOO (See Dunc and Loo)

AROUND THE WORLD IN 80 DAYS (Movie) (See A Golden Picture Classic)
Dell Publishing Co.: Feb, 1957

Four Color 784-Photo-c	7	14	21	50	83	115

AROUND THE WORLD UNDER THE SEA (See Movie Classics)

AROUND THE WORLD WITH ARCHIE (See Archie Giant Series Mag. #29, 35, 141)

AROUND THE WORLD WITH HUCKLEBERRY & HIS FRIENDS (See Dell Giant No. 44)

ARRGH! (Satire)
Marvel Comics Group: Dec, 1974 - No. 5, Sept, 1975 (25¢)

1-Dracula story; Sekowsky-a(p)	3	6	9	16	23	30
2-5: 2-Frankenstein. 3-Mummy. 4-Nightstalker(TV); Dracula-c/app., Hunchback. 5-Invisible						

The Arrow #2 © CEN

Ascension #13 © TCOW

Ash: Fire and Crossfire #1 © Q&P

	GD	VG	FN	VF	VF/NM	NM-		GD	VG	FN	VF	VF/NM	NM-
	2.0	4.0	6.0	8.0	9.0	9.2		2.0	4.0	6.0	8.0	9.0	9.2

	GD 2.0	VG 4.0	FN 6.0	VF 8.0	VF/NM 9.0	NM- 9.2
Man, Dracula	2	4	6	12	16	20

NOTE: *Alcala a-2; c-3. Everett a-1r, 2r. Grandenetti a-4. Maneely a-4r. Sutton a-1-3.*

ARROW (See Protectors)
Malibu Comics: Oct, 1992 ($1.95, one-shot)

1-Moder-a(p)						2.50

ARROW, THE (See Funny Pages)
Centaur Publications: Oct, 1940 - No. 2, Nov, 1940; No. 3, Oct, 1941

	GD	VG	FN	VF	VF/NM	NM-
1-The Arrow begins(r/Funny Pages)	300	600	900	1945	3423	4900
2,3: 2-Tippy Taylor serial continues from Amazing Mystery Funnies #24. 3-Origin Dash Dartwell, the Human Meteor; origin The Rainbow-r; bondage-c	134	264	402	838	1394	1950

NOTE: *Gustavson a-1, 2; c-3.*

ARROWHEAD (See Black Rider and Wild Western)
Atlas Comics (CPS): April, 1954 - No. 4, Nov, 1954

	GD	VG	FN	VF	VF/NM	NM-
1-Arrowhead & his horse Eagle begin	15	30	45	88	137	185
2-4: 4-Forte-a	10	20	30	54	72	90

NOTE: *Heath c-3. Jack Katz a-3. Maneely c-2. Pakula a-2. Sinnott a-1-4; c-1.*

ARROWSMITH (Also see Astro City/Arrowsmith flip book)
DC Comics (Cliffhanger): Sept, 2003 - No. 6, May, 2004 ($2.95)

1-6-Pacheco-a/Busiek-s						3.00
...: So Smart in Their Fine Uniforms TPB (2004, $14.95) r/#1-6						15.00

ARSENAL (Teen Titans' Speedy)
DC Comics: Oct, 1998 - No. 4, Jan, 1999 ($2.50, limited series)

1-4: Grayson-s. 1-Black Canary app. 2-Green Arrow app.						2.50

ARSENAL SPECIAL (See New Titans, Showcase '94 #7 & Showcase '95 #8)
DC Comics: 1996 ($2.95, one-shot)

1						3.00

ARTBABE
Fantagraphics Books: May, 1996 - Apr, 1999 ($2.50/$2.95/$3.50, B&W)

V1 #5, V2 #1-3						3.00
#4-($3.50)						3.50

ARTEMIS: REQUIEM (Also see Wonder Woman, 2nd Series #90)
DC Comics: June, 1996 - No. 6, Nov, 1996 ($1.75, limited series)

1-6: Messner-Loebs scripts & Benes-c/a in all. 1,2-Wonder Woman app.						3.00

ARTESIA
Sirius Entertainment: Jan, 1999 - No. 6, June, 1999 ($2.95, limited series)

1-6-Mark Smylie-s/a						3.00
Annual 1 (1999, $3.50)						3.50
Annual 2 (2001, $3.95) Crilley back-c						4.00
Annual 3 (2004, $4.95) Timeline of the Known World						5.00

ARTESIA AFIELD
Sirius Entertainment: Jul, 2000 - No. 6, Feb, 2001 ($2.95, limited series)

1-6-Mark Smylie-s/a						3.00

ARTESIA AFIRE
Archaia Studios Press: June, 2003 - No. 6, Feb, 2004 ($3.95, limited series)

1-6-Mark Smylie-s/a						4.00

ARTESIA BESIEGED
Archaia Studios Press: June, 2006 - No. 6, ($3.95, limited series)

1-Mark Smylie-s/a						4.00

ART OF HOMAGE STUDIOS, THE
Image Comics: Dec, 1993 ($4.95, one-shot)

1-Short stories and pin-ups by Jim Lee, Silvestri, Williams, Portacio & Chiodo						5.00

ART OF ZEN INTERGALACTIC NINJA, THE
Entity Comics: 1994 - No. 2, 1994 ($2.95)

1,2						3.00

ARZACH (See Moebius...)
Dark Horse Comics: 1996 ($6.95, one-shot)

	GD	VG	FN	VF	VF/NM	NM-
nn-Moebius-c/a/scripts	1	2	3	4	5	7

ASCENSION
Image Comics (Top Cow Productions): Oct, 1997 - No. 22, Mar, 2000 ($2.50)

Preview						5.00
Preview Gold Edition						8.00
Preview San Diego Edition	2	4	6	8	10	12
0						4.00

1/2						6.00
1-David Finch-s/a(p)/Batt-s/a(i)						4.00
1-Variant-c w/Image logo at lower right						6.00
2-6						3.00
7-22						2.50
Fan Club Edition						5.00

...COLLECTED EDITION

1998 - No. 2 ($4.95, squarebound) 1,2: 1-r/#1,2. 2-r/#3,4						5.00

ASH
Event Comics: Nov, 1994 - No. 6, Dec, 1995; No. 0, May, 1996 ($2.50/$3.00)

0-Present & Future (Both 5/96, $3.00, foil logo-c)-w/pin-ups						3.00
0-Blue Foil logo-c (Present and Future) (1000 each)						4.00
0-Silver Prism logo-c (Present and Future) (500 each)						10.00
0-Red Prism logo-c (Present and Future) (250 each)						20.00
0-Gold Hologram logo-c (Present and Future) (1000 each)						8.00
1-Quesada-p/story; Palmiotti-i/story: Barry Windsor-Smith pin-up						

	GD	VG	FN	VF	VF/NM	NM-
	2	4	6	8	10	12
1	1	2	3	4	5	7

2-Mignola Hellboy pin-up						4.00
3,4: 3-Big Guy pin-up by Geoff Darrow. 4-Jim Lee pin-up						4.00
4-Fahrenheit Gold						7.00
4-6-Fahrenheit Red (5,6-1000)						8.00
4-6-Fahrenheit White						12.00
5, 6-Double-c w/Hildebrandt Bros.-a, Quesada & Palmiotti. 6-Texeira-c						3.00
5,6-Fahrenheit Gold (2000)						4.00
6-Fahrenheit White (500)-Texeira-c						12.00
Volume 1 (1996, $14.95, TPB)-r/#1-5, intro by James Robinson						15.00
Wizard Mini-Comic (1996, magazine supplement)						2.25
Wizard #1/2 (1997, mail order)						4.00

ASH: CINDER & SMOKE
Event Comics: May, 1997 - No. 6, Oct, 1997 ($2.95, limited series)

1-6: Ramos-a/Waid, Augustyn-s in all. 2-6-variant covers by Ramos and Quesada						3.00

ASH: FILES
Event Comics: Mar, 1997 ($2.95, one-shot)

1-Comics w/text						3.00

ASH: FIRE AND CROSSFIRE
Event Comics: Jan, 1999 - No. 5 ($2.95, limited series)

1,2-Robinson-s/Quesada & Palmiotti-c/a						3.00

ASH: FIRE WITHIN, THE
Event Comics: Sept, 1996 - No. 2, Jan, 1997 ($2.95, unfinished limited series)

1,2: Quesada & Palmiotti-c/s/a						3.00

ASH/ 22 BRIDES
Event Comics: Dec, 1996 - No. 2, Apr, 1997 ($2.95, limited series)

1,2: Nicieza-s/Ramos-c/a						3.00

ASKANI'SON (See Adventures of Cyclops & Phoenix limited series)
Marvel Comics: Jan, 1996 - No. 4, May, 1996 ($2.95, limited series)

1-4: Story cont'd from Advs. of Cyclops & Phoenix; Lobdell/Loeb story; Gene Ha-c/a(p)						3.00
TPB (1997, $12.99) r/#1-4; Gene Ha painted-c						13.00

ASPEN (MICHAEL TURNER PRESENTS:...) (Also see Fathom)
Aspen MLT, Inc.: July, 2003 - No. 3, Aug, 2003 ($2.99)

1-Fathom story; Turner-a/Johns-s; interviews w/Turner & Johns; two covers by Turner						3.00
2,3:2-Fathom story; Turner-a/Johns-s; two covers by Turner; pin-ups and interviews						3.00
... Seasons: Fall 2005 (12/05, $2.99) short stories by various; Turner-c						3.00
... Seasons: Spring 2005 (4/05, $2.99) short stories by various; Turner-c						3.00
... Seasons: Summer 2006 (10/06, $2.99) short stories by various; Turner-c						3.00
... Sketchbook 1 (2003, $2.99) sketch pages by Michael Turner and Talent Caldwell						3.00
... Splash: 2006 Swimsuit Spectacular 1 (3/06, $2.99) pin-up pages by various; Turner-c						3.00
... Splash: 2007 Swimsuit Spectacular 1 (8/07, $2.99) pin-up pages by various; Turner-c						3.00

ASSASSINETTE HARDCORE
Pocket Change Comics: 1995 - No. 2, 1995 ($2.50, B&W, limited series)

1,2						2.50

ASSASSINS
DC Comics (Amalgam): Apr, 1996 ($1.95)

1						2.50

ASTONISHING (Formerly Marvel Boy No. 1, 2)
Marvel/Atlas Comics(20CC): No. 3, Apr, 1951 - No. 63, Aug, 1957

	GD	VG	FN	VF	VF/NM	NM-
3-Marvel Boy continues; 3-5-Marvel Boy-c	93	186	279	581	966	1350
4-6-Last Marvel Boy; 4-Stan Lee app.	66	132	198	413	682	950

Astonishing #59 © MAR

Astonishing X-Men #3 © MAR

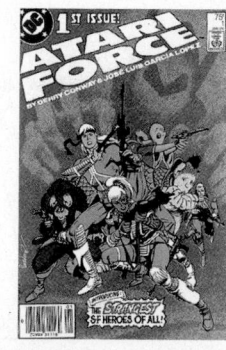

Atari Force #1 © Atari

	GD 2.0	VG 4.0	FN 6.0	VF 8.0	VF/NM 9.0	NM- 9.2
7-10: 7-Maneely s/f story. 10-Sinnott s/f story	34	68	102	199	315	430
11,12,15,17,20	30	60	90	174	275	375
13,14,16,18,19-Krigstein-a. 18-Jack The Ripper sty	31	62	93	178	282	385
21,22,24	26	52	78	150	235	320
23-E.C. swipe "The Hole In The Wall" from Vault Of Horror #16	26	52	78	154	242	330
25,29: 25-Crandall-a. 29-Decapitation-c	24	48	72	139	220	300
26-28	22	44	66	128	202	275
30-Tentacled eyeball-c/story; classic-c	43	86	129	262	431	600
31-37-Last pre-code issue	20	40	60	115	180	245
38-43,46,48-52,56,58,59,61	15	30	45	88	137	185
44,45,47,53-55,57,60: 44-Crandall swipe/Weird Fantasy #22. 45,47-Krigstein-a. 53-Ditko-a. 54-Torres-a, 55-Crandall, Torres-a. 57-Williamson/Krenkel-a (4 pgs.) 60-Williamson/Mayo-a (4 pgs)	16	32	48	94	147	200
62,63: 62-Torres, Powell-a. 63-Woodbridge-a	16	32	48	92	144	195

NOTE: Ayers a-16. Berg a-36, 53, 56. Cameron a-50. Gene Colan a-12, 20, 29, 56. Ditko a-53. Drucker a-41, 62. Everett a-3-6(3), 6, 10, 12, 37, 47, 48, 58. Heath a-c3-5, 13,15, 16, 18, 29, 47, 49, 51, 53-55, 57, 59-63. Fass a-11, 34. Forte a-53, 56, 60. Fuje a-11. Heath a-8, 29; c-8, 9, 19, 22, 25, 56. Kirby a-56. Lawrence a-28, 37, 38, 42. Maneely a-7(2); c-7, 31, 33, 34, 56. Moldoff a-33. Morisi a-10, 60. Morrow a-52, 61. Orlando a-47, 58, 61. Pakula a-10. Powell a-43, 44, 48. Ravielli a-28. Reinman a-32, 34, 38. Robinson a-29. Romita a-7, 18, 24, 43, 57,61. Roussos a-55. Sale a-28, 38, 59; c-32. Sekowsky a-13. Severin c-46. Shores a-16, 60. Sinnott a-11, 30. Whitney a-13. Ed Win a-20. Canadian reprints exist.

ASTONISHING TALES (See Ka-Zar)
Marvel Comics Group: Aug, 1970 - No. 36, July, 1976 (#1-7: 15¢; #8: 25¢)

	GD 2.0	VG 4.0	FN 6.0	VF 8.0	VF/NM 9.0	NM- 9.2
1-Ka-Zar (by Kirby(p) #1,2; by B. Smith #3-6) & Dr. Doom (by Wood #1-4; by Tuska #5,6; by Colan #7,8; 1st Marvel villain solo series) double feature begins; Kraven the Hunter-c/story; Nixon cameo	6	12	18	39	62	85
2-Kraven the Hunter-c/story; Kirby, Wood-a	3	6	9	20	30	40
3-6: B. Smith-p; Wood-a/3,4. 5,6-Red Skull 2-part story	4	8	12	22	34	45
7-Last 15¢ issue; Black Panther app.	3	6	9	15	21	26
8-(25¢, 52 pgs.)-Last Dr. Doom of series	3	6	9	20	30	40
9-All Ka-Zar issues begin; Lorna-r/Lorna #14	2	4	6	10	14	18
10-B. Smith/Sal Buscema-a.	3	6	9	14	19	24
11-Origin Ka-Zar & Zabu; death of Ka-Zar's father	2	4	6	11	16	20
12-2nd app.Man-Thing; by Neal Adams (see Savage Tales #1 for 1st app.)	4	8	12	22	34	45
13-3rd app.Man-Thing	3	6	9	17	25	32
14-20: 14-Jann of the Jungle-r (1950s); reprints censored Ka-Zar-s from Savage Tales #1. 17-S.H.I.E.L.D. begins. 19-Starlin-a(p). 20-Last Ka-Zar (continues into 1974 Ka-Zar series)	1	3	4	6	8	10
21-(12/73)-It! the Living Colossus begins, ends #24 (see Supernatural Thrillers #1)	3	6	9	19	29	38
22-24: 23,24-IT vs. Fin Fang Foom	3	6	9	16	22	28
25-1st app. Deathlok the Demolisher; full length stories begin, end #36; Perez's 1st work, 2 pgs. (8/74)	5	10	15	30	48	65
26-28,30	2	4	6	10	14	18
29-r/origin/1st app. Guardians of the Galaxy from Marvel Super-Heroes #18 plus-c w/4 pgs. omitted; no Deathlok story	1	3	4	6	8	10
31-34: 31-Watcher-r/Silver Surfer #3	2	4	6	8	11	14
35,36-(Regular 25¢ edition)(5,7/76)	2	4	6	8	11	14
35,36-(30¢-c, low distribution)	4	8	12	28	44	60

NOTE: Buckler a-13i, 16p, 25, 26p, 27p, 28, 29p-36p; c-13, 25p, 26-30, 32-35p, 36. John Buscema a-9, 12p-14p, 16p; c-4-6p, 12p. Colan a-7p, 8p. Ditko a-21r. Everett a-6i. G. Kane a-11p, 15p; c-9, 10p, 11p, 14, 15p, 21p. McWilliams a-30i. Starlin a-19p; c-16p. Sutton & Trimpe a-8. Tuska a-5p, 6p, 8p. Wood a-1-4. Wrightson c-31i.

ASTONISHING X-MEN
Marvel Comics: Mar, 1995 - No. 4, July, 1995 ($1.95, limited series)

1-Age of Apocalypse; Magneto-c	4.00
2-4	3.00

ASTONISHING X-MEN
Marvel Comics: Sept, 1999 - No.3, Nov, 1999 ($2.50, limited series)

1-3-New team, Cable & X-Man app.; Peterson-a	2.50
TPB (11/00, $15.95) r/#1-3, X-Men #92 & #95, Uncanny X-Men #375	16.00

ASTONISHING X-MEN
Marvel Comics: July, 2004 - Present ($2.99)

1-Whedon-s/Cassaday-c/a; team of Cyclops, Beast, Wolverine, Emma Frost & Kitty Pryde	3.00
1-Director's Cut (2004, $3.99) different Cassaday partial sketch-c; cover gallery, sketch pages and script excerpt	4.00
1-Variant-c by Cassaday	10.00
1-Variant-c by Dell'Otto	5.00
2,3,5,6-X-Men battle Ord	3.00
4-Colossus returns	4.00
4-Variant Colossus cover by Cassaday	5.00
7-22: 7-Fantastic Four app. 9,10-X-Men vs. the Danger Room	3.00
7,9,10-12,20-Second printing variant covers	3.00
... Saga (2006, $3.99) reprints highlights from #1-12; sketch pages and cover gallery	4.00
...Vol. 1 HC (2006, $29.99, dust jacket) r/#1-12; interviews, sketch pages and covers	30.00
...Vol. 1: Gifted (2004, $14.99) r/#1-6; variant cover gallery	15.00
...Vol. 2: Dangerous (2005, $14.99) r/#7-12; variant cover gallery	15.00
...Vol. 3: Torn (2007, $14.99) r/#13-18; variant & sketch cover gallery	15.00

ASTOUNDING SPACE THRILLS: THE COMIC BOOK
Image Comics: Apr, 2000 - No. 4, Dec, 2000 ($2.95, limited series)

1-4-Steve Conley-s/a. 2,3-Flip book w/Crater Kid	3.00
Galaxy-Sized Astounding Space Thrills 1 (10/01, $4.95)	5.00

ASTOUNDING WOLF-MAN
Image Comics: Jun, 2007 - Present ($2.99)

1-Free Comic Boy Day issue; Kirkman-s/Howard-a; origin story	3.00
2,3	3.00

ASTRA
CPM Manga: 2001 - No. 8 ($2.95, B&W, limited series)

1-8: Created by Jerry Robinson; Tanaka-a. 1-Balent variant-c	3.00
TPB (2002, $15.95) r/#1-8; JH Williams III-c from #3	16.00

ASTRO BOY (TV) (See March of Comics #285 & The Original...)
Gold Key: August, 1965 (12¢)

	GD 2.0	VG 4.0	FN 6.0	VF 8.0	VF/NM 9.0	NM- 9.2
1(10151-508)-Scarce;1st app. Astro Boy in comics	30	60	90	225	413	600

ASTRO CITY / ARROWSMITH (Flip book)
DC Comics (WildStorm Productions): Jun, 2004 ($2.95, one-shot flip book)

1-Intro. Black Badge; Ross-c; Arrowsmith a/c by Pacheco	3.00

ASTRO CITY (Also see Kurt Busiek's Astro City)
DC Comics (WildStorm Productions): Dec, 2004; Sept, 2006 (one-shots)

... A Visitor's Guide (12/04, $5.95) short story, city guide and pin-ups by various; Ross-c	6.00
...: Samaritan (9/06, $3.99) Busiek-s/Anderson-a/Ross-c; origin of Infidel	4.00

ASTRO CITY: DARK AGE
DC Comics (WildStorm Productions): Aug, 2005 - No. 4, Dec, 2005 ($2.95, limited series)

1-4-Busiek-s/Anderson-a/Ross-c; Silver Agent and The Blue Knight app.	3.00
Book Two #1-3 (1/07-6/07, $2.99) Busiek-s/Anderson-a/Ross-c	3.00

ASTRO CITY: LOCAL HEROES
DC Comics (WildStorm Productions): Apr, 2003 - No. 5, Feb, 2004 ($2.95, limited series)

1-5-Busiek-s/Anderson-a/Ross-c	3.00
HC (2005, $24.95) r/series; Kurt Busiek's Astro City V2 #21,22; stories from Astro City/ Arrowsmith #1; and 9-11, The World's Finest... Vol. 2; Alex Ross sketch pages	25.00
SC (2005, $17.99) same contents as HC	18.00

ASYLUM
Millennium Publications: 1993 ($2.50)

1-3: 1-Bolton-c/a; Russell 2-pg. illos	2.50

ASYLUM
Maximum Press: Dec, 1995 - No. 11, Jan, 1997 ($2.95/$2.99, anthology)
(#1-6 are flip books)

1-11: 1-Warchild by Art Adams, Beanworld, Avengelyne, Battlestar Galactica. 2-Intro Mike Deodato's Deathkiss. 4-1st app.Christian; painted Battlestar Galactica story begins. 6-Intro Bionix (Six Million Dollar Man & the Bionic Woman). 7-Begin $2.99-c. 8-B&W-a. 9- Foot Soldiers & Kid Supreme. 10-Lady Supreme by Terry Moore-c/app.	4.00

ATARI FORCE (Also see Promotional comics section)
DC Comics: Jan, 1984 - No. 20, Aug, 1985 (Mando paper)

1-(1/84)-Intro Tempest, Packrat, Babe, Morphea, & Dart	4.00
2-20	3.00
Special 1 (4/86)	3.00

NOTE: Byrne c-Special 1i. Giffen a-12p, 13i. Rogers a-18p, Special 1p.

A-TEAM, THE (TV) (Also see Marvel Graphic Novel)
Marvel Comics Group: Mar, 1984 - No. 3, May, 1984 (limited series)

	GD 2.0	VG 4.0	FN 6.0	VF 8.0	VF/NM 9.0	NM- 9.2
1-3						5.00
1,2-(Whitman bagged set) w/75¢-c	2	4	6	8	10	12
3-(Whitman, no bag) w/75¢-c	1	2	3	5	6	8

ATHENA INC. THE MANHUNTER PROJECT
Image Comics: Dec, 2001; Apr, 2002 - No. 6 ($2.95/$4.95/$5.95)

...The Beginning (12/01, $5.95) Anacleto-c/a; Haberlin-s	6.00
1-5: (4/02, $2.95) two covers by Anacleto	3.00
6-($4.95)	5.00

The Atom #1 © DC

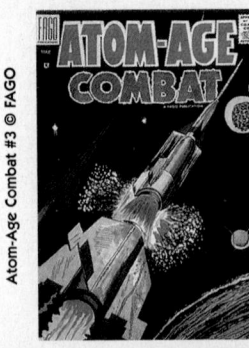

Atom-Age Combat #3 © FAGO

The Atomics #11 © Mike Allred

	GD 2.0	VG 4.0	FN 6.0	VF 8.0	VF/NM 9.0	NM- 9.2

...: Agents Roster #1 (11/02, $5.95, 8 1/2 x 11") bios and sketch pages by Anacleto ... 6.00
Vol. 1 TPB (4/03, $19.95) r/#1-6 & Agents Roster; cover gallery ... 20.00

ATLANTIS CHRONICLES, THE (Also see Aquaman, 3rd Series & Aquaman: Time & Tide)
DC Comics: Mar, 1990 - No. 7, Sept, 1990 ($2.95, limited series, 52 pgs.)
1-7: 1-Peter David scripts. 7-True origin of Aquaman; nudity panels ... 3.25

ATLANTIS, THE LOST CONTINENT
Dell Publishing Co.: May, 1961
Four Color #1188-Movie, photo-c   10   20   30   68   119   170

ATLAS (See 1st Issue Special)

ATLAS
Dark Horse Comics: Feb, 1994 - No. 4, 1994 ($2.50, limited series)
1-4 ... 2.50

ATMOSPHERICS
Avatar Press: June, 2002 ($5.95, B&W, one-shot graphic novel)
1-Warren Ellis-s/Ken Meyer Jr.-painted-a/c ... 6.00

ATOM, THE (See Action #425, All-American #19, Brave & the Bold, D.C. Special Series #1, Detective Comics, Flash Comics #80, Hawkman, Identity Crisis, JLA, Power Of The Atom, Showcase #34 -36, Super Friends, Sword of The Atom, Teen Titans & World's Finest)

ATOM, THE (....& the Hawkman No. 39 on)
National Periodical Publ.: June-July, 1962 - No. 38, Aug-Sept, 1968
1-(6-7/62)-Intro Plant-Master; 1st app. Maya   78   156   234   663   1232   1800
2   31   62   93   233   429   625
3-1st Time Pool story; 1st app. Chronos (origin)   21   42   63   156   278   400
4,5: 4-Snapper Carr x-over   16   32   48   118   209   300
6,9,10   12   24   36   84   150   215
7-Hawkman x-over (6-7/63); 1st Atom & Hawkman team-up!; 1st app. Hawkman since Brave & the Bold tryouts   28   56   84   227   381   535
8-Justice League, Dr. Light app.   12   24   36   87   156   225
11-15: 13-Chronos-c/story   9   18   27   65   113   160
16-20: 19-Zatanna x-over   7   14   21   50   83   115
21-28,30: 26-Two-page pin-up. 28-Chronos-c/story   7   14   21   45   73   100
29-1st solo Golden Age Atom x-over in S.A.   13   26   39   97   171   245
31-35,37,38: 31-Hawkman x-over. 37-Intro. Major Mynah; Hawkman cameo   6   12   18   37   59   80
36-G.A. Atom x-over   7   14   21   45   73   100
NOTE: *Anderson* a-1-11i, 13i; c-inks-1-25, 31-35, 37. *Sid Greene* a-8i-37i. *Gil Kane* a-1p-37p; c-1p-28p, 29, 33p, 34; c-26i. *George Roussos* a-38i. *Mike Sekowsky* a-38p. Time Pool stories also in 6, 9,12, 17, 21, 27, 35.

ATOM, THE (See All New Atom and Tangent Comics/ The Atom)

ATOM AGE (See Classics Illustrated Special Issue)

ATOM-AGE COMBAT
St. John Publishing Co.: June, 1952 - No. 5, Apr, 1953; Feb, 1958
1-Buck Vinson in all   47   94   141   287   474   660
2-Flying saucer story   30   60   90   172   271   370
3,5: 3-Mayo-a (6 pgs.). 5-Flying saucer-c/story   26   52   78   150   235   320
4 (Scarce)   30   60   90   172   271   370
1(2/58-St. John)   22   44   66   126   198   270

ATOM-AGE COMBAT
Fago Magazines: No. 2, Jan, 1959 - No. 3, Mar, 1959
2-A-Bomb explosion-c;   27   54   81   156   246   335
3   21   42   63   120   188   255

ATOMAN
Spark Publications: Feb, 1946 - No. 2, April, 1946
1-Origin & 1st app. Atoman; Robinson/Meskin-a; Kidcrusaders, Wild Bill Hickok, Marvin the Great app.   66   132   198   413   682   950
2-Robinson/Meskin-a; Robinson c-1,2   41   82   123   254   410   565

ATOM & HAWKMAN, THE (Formerly The Atom)
National Periodical Publ: No. 39, Oct-Nov, 1968 - No. 45, Oct-Nov, 1969
39-43: 40-41-Kubert/Anderson-a. 43-(7/69)-Last 12¢ issue; 1st app. Gentleman Ghost   5   10   15   35   55   75
44,45: 44-(9/69)-1st 15¢-c; origin Gentleman Ghost   5   10   15   35   55   75
NOTE: *M. Anderson* a-39, 40i, 41i, 43, 44. *Sid Greene* a-40i-45i. *Kubert* a-40p, 41p; c-39-45.

ATOM ANT (TV) (See Golden Comics Digest #2) (Hanna-Barbera)
Gold Key: January, 1966 (12¢)
1(10170-601)-1st app. Atom Ant, Precious Pup, and Hillbilly Bears   21   42   63   156   278   400

ATOM ANT & SECRET SQUIRREL (See Hanna-Barbera Presents)

	GD 2.0	VG 4.0	FN 6.0	VF 8.0	VF/NM 9.0	NM- 9.2

ATOMIC AGE
Marvel Comics (Epic Comics): Nov, 1990 - No. 4, Feb, 1991 ($4.50, limited series, square-bound, 52 pgs.)
1-4: Williamson-a(i); sci-fi story set in 1957 ... 4.50

ATOMIC ATTACK (True War Stories; formerly Attack, first series)
Youthful Magazines: No. 5, Jan, 1953 - No. 8, Oct, 1953 (1st story is sci/fi in all issues)
5-Atomic bomb-c; science fiction stories in all   40   80   120   235   368   500
6-8   25   50   75   148   232   315

ATOMIC BOMB
Jay Burtis Publications: 1945 (36 pgs.)
1-Airmale & Stampy (scarce)   69   138   207   431   716   1000

ATOMIC BUNNY (Formerly Atomic Rabbit)
Charlton Comics: No. 12, Aug, 1958 - No. 19, Dec, 1959
12   12   24   36   69   97   125
13-19   8   16   24   42   54   65

ATOMIC COMICS
Daniels Publications (Canadian): Jan, 1946 (Reprints, one-shot)
1-Rocketman, Yankee Boy, Master Key app.   40   80   120   235   368   500

ATOMIC COMICS
Green Publishing Co.: Jan, 1946 - No. 4, July-Aug, 1946 (#1-4 were printed w/o cover gloss)
1-Radio Squad by Siegel & Shuster; Barry O'Neal app.; Fang Gow cover-r/ Detective Comics (Classic-c)   117   234   351   731   1216   1700
2-Inspector Dayton; Kid Kane by Matt Baker; Lucky Wings, Congo King, Prop Powers (only app.) begin   59   118   177   369   610   850
3,4: 3-Zero Ghost Detective app.; Baker-a(2) each; 4-Baker-c   41   82   123   252   406   560

ATOMIC KNIGHTS (See Strange Adventures #117)

ATOMIC MOUSE (TV, Movies) (See Blue Bird, Funny Animals, Giant Comics Edition & Wotalife Comics)
Capitol Stories/Charlton Comics: 3/53 - No. 54, 6/63; No. 1, 12/84; V2#1, 19/85 - No. 12, 1/86
1-Origin & 1st app.; Al Fago-c/a in most   33   66   99   190   300   410
2   15   30   45   84   127   170
3-10: 5-Timmy The Timid Ghost app.; see Zoo Funnies   10   20   30   58   79   100
11-13,16-25   8   16   24   40   50   60
14,15-Hoppy The Marvel Bunny app.   9   18   27   50   65   80
26-(68 pgs.)   12   24   36   67   94   120
27-40: 36,37-Atom The Cat app.   6   12   18   29   36   42
41-54   5   10   15   22   26   30
1 (1984)-Low print run; rep/#7-c w/diff. stories   2   4   6   8   10   12
V2#10 (9/85) -12(1/86)-Low print run   1   3   4   6   8   10

ATOMIC RABBIT (Atomic Bunny #12 on; see Giant Comics #3 & Wotalife)
Charlton Comics: Aug, 1955 - No. 11, Mar, 1958
1-Origin & 1st app.; Al Fago-c/a in all?   30   60   90   174   275   375
2   14   28   42   80   115   150
3-10   10   20   30   56   76   90
11-(68 pgs.)   14   28   42   80   115   150

ATOMICS, THE
AAA Pop Comics: Jan, 2000 - No. 15, Nov, 2001 ($2.95)
1-11-Mike Allred-s/a; 1-Madman-c/app. ... 3.00
12-15-($3.50): 13-15-Savage Dragon-c/app. 15-Afterword by Alex Ross; colored reprint of 1st Frank Einstein story ... 3.50
...King-Size Giant Spectacular: Jigsaw (2000, $10.00) r/#1-4 ... 10.00
...King-Size Giant Spectacular: Lessons in Light, Lava, & Lasers (2000, $8.95) r/#5-8 ... 9.00
...King-Size Giant Spectacular: Running With the Dragon ('02, $8.95) r/#13-15 and r/1st Frank Einstein app. in color ... 9.00
...King-Size Giant Spectacular: Worlds Within Worlds ('01, $8.95) r/#9-12 ... 9.00
...: Spaced Out & Grounded in Snap City TPB (10/03, $12.95) r/one-shots - It Girl, Mr. Gum, Spaceman and Crash Metro & the Star Squad; sketch pages ... 13.00

ATOMIC SPY CASES
Avon Periodicals: Mar-Apr, 1950 (Painted-c)
1-No Wood-a; A-bomb blast panels; Fass-a   34   68   102   197   311   425

ATOMIC THUNDERBOLT, THE
Regor Company: Feb, 1946 (one-shot) (scarce)
1-Intro. Atomic Thunderbolt & Mr. Murdo   62   124   186   388   644   900

ATOMIC TOYBOX
Image Comics: Dec, 1999 ($2.95)

Attack #1 © YM

Authentic Police Cases #6 © STJ

The Authority #16 © WSP

	GD 2.0	VG 4.0	FN 6.0	VF 8.0	VF/NM 9.0	NM- 9.2
1- Aaron Lopresti-c/s/a						3.00

ATOMIC WAR!
Ace Periodicals (Junior Books): Nov, 1952 - No. 4, Apr, 1953

	GD 2.0	VG 4.0	FN 6.0	VF 8.0	VF/NM 9.0	NM- 9.2
1-Atomic bomb-c	97	194	291	606	1003	1400
2,3: 3-Atomic bomb-c	59	118	177	369	615	860
4-Used in POP, pg. 96 & illo.	59	118	177	369	615	860

ATOMIKA
Speakeasy Comics/Mercury Comics: Mar, 2005 - Present ($2.99)

1-6: 1-Alex Ross-c/Sal Abbinanti-a/Dabb-s. 3-Fabry-c. 4-Four covers; Romita back-c						3.00
... God is Red TPB (5/06, $19.99) r/#1-6; cover gallery; Dabb foreword						20.00

ATOMIK ANGELS
Crusade Comics: May, 1996 - No. 4, Nov. 1996 ($2.50)

1-4: 1-Freefall from Gen 13 app.						3.00
1-Variant-c						4.00
Intrep-Edition (2/96, B&W, giveaway at launch party)-Previews Atomik Angels #1; includes Billy Tucci interview.						4.00

ATOM SPECIAL (See Atom & Justice League of America)
DC Comics: 1993/1995 ($2.50/$2.95)(68pgs.)

1,2: 1-Dillon-c/a. 2-McDonnell-a/Bolland-c/Peyer-s						3.00

ATOM THE CAT (Formerly Tom Cat; see Giant Comics #3)
Charlton Comics: No. 9, Oct, 1957 - No. 17, Aug, 1959

	GD 2.0	VG 4.0	FN 6.0	VF 8.0	VF/NM 9.0	NM- 9.2
9	10	20	30	54	72	90
10,13-17	7	14	21	35	43	50
11,12: 11(64 pgs)-Atomic Mouse app. 12(100 pgs.)	11	22	33	62	86	110

ATTACK
Youthful Mag./Trojan No. 5 on: May, 1952 - No. 4, Nov, 1952; No. 5, Jan, 1953 - No. 5, Sept, 1953

	GD 2.0	VG 4.0	FN 6.0	VF 8.0	VF/NM 9.0	NM- 9.2
1-(1st series)-Extreme violence	32	64	96	186	293	400
2,3-Both Harrison-c/a; bondage, whipping	17	34	51	98	154	210
4-Krenkel-a (7 pgs.); Harrison-a (becomes Atomic Attack #5 on)	17	34	51	98	154	210
5-(#1, Trojan, 2nd series)	14	28	42	80	115	150
6-8 (#2-4), 5	10	20	30	58	79	100

ATTACK
Charlton Comics: No. 54, 1958 - No. 60, Nov, 1959

	GD 2.0	VG 4.0	FN 6.0	VF 8.0	VF/NM 9.0	NM- 9.2
54 (25¢, 100 pgs.)	12	24	36	67	94	120
55-60	6	12	18	31	38	45

ATTACK!
Charlton Comics: 1962 - No. 15, 3/75; No. 16, 8/79 - No. 48, 10/84

	GD 2.0	VG 4.0	FN 6.0	VF 8.0	VF/NM 9.0	NM- 9.2
nn(#1)-('62) Special Edition	5	10	15	31	48	65
2('63), 3(Fall, '64)	4	8	12	19	29	38
V4#3(10/66), 4(10/67)-(Formerly Special War Series #2; becomes Attack At Sea V4#5)	3	6	9	16	22	28
1(9/71)	3	6	9	16	22	28
2-5: 4-American Eagle app.	2	4	6	9	12	15
6-15(3/75):	1	3	4	6	8	10
16(8/79) - 40						5.00
41-47 Low print run						7.00
48(10/84)-Wood-r; S&K-c (low print)	1	3	4	6	8	10
Modern Comics 13('78)-r						4.00

NOTE: *Sutton a-9,10,13.*

ATTACK!
Spire Christian Comics (Fleming H. Revell Co.): 1975 (39¢/49¢, 36 pgs.)

	GD 2.0	VG 4.0	FN 6.0	VF 8.0	VF/NM 9.0	NM- 9.2
nn	2	4	6	8	11	14

ATTACK AT SEA (Formerly Attack!, 1967)
Charlton Comics: V4#5, Oct, 1968 (one-shot)

	GD 2.0	VG 4.0	FN 6.0	VF 8.0	VF/NM 9.0	NM- 9.2
V4#5	3	6	9	16	22	28

ATTACK ON PLANET MARS (See Strange Worlds #18)
Avon Periodicals: 1951

	GD 2.0	VG 4.0	FN 6.0	VF 8.0	VF/NM 9.0	NM- 9.2
nn-Infantino, Fawcette, Kubert & Wood-a; adaptation of Tarrano the Conqueror by Ray Cummings	79	158	237	494	822	1150

ATTITUDE LAD
Slave Labor Graphics: Apr, 1994 - No. 3, Nov, 1994 ($2.95, B&W)

1-3						3.00

AUDREY & MELVIN (Formerly Little...)(See Little Audrey & Melvin)
Harvey Publications: No. 62, Sept, 1974

	GD 2.0	VG 4.0	FN 6.0	VF 8.0	VF/NM 9.0	NM- 9.2
62	2	4	6	8	11	14

AUGIE DOGGIE (TV) (See Hanna-Barbera Band Wagon, Quick-Draw McGraw, Spotlight #2, Top Cat & Whitman Comic Books)
Gold Key: October, 1963 (12¢)

	GD 2.0	VG 4.0	FN 6.0	VF 8.0	VF/NM 9.0	NM- 9.2
1-Hanna-Barbera character	17	34	51	126	223	320

AUTHENTIC POLICE CASES
St. John Publishing Co.: 2/48 - No. 6, 11/48; No. 7, 5/50 - No. 38, 3/55

	GD 2.0	VG 4.0	FN 6.0	VF 8.0	VF/NM 9.0	NM- 9.2
1-Hale the Magician by Tuska begins	44	88	132	268	444	620
2-Lady Satan, Johnny Rebel app.	28	56	84	162	256	350
3-Veiled Avenger app.; blood drainage story plus 2 Lucky Coyne stories; used in SOTI, illo. from Red Seal #16	47	94	141	287	474	660
4,5: 4-Masked Black Jack app. 5-Late 1930s Jack Cole-a(r); transvestism story	28	56	84	162	256	350
6-Matt Baker-c; used in SOTI, illo- "An invitation to learning", r-in Fugitives From Justice #3; Jack Cole-a; also used by the N.Y. Legis. Comm.	49	98	147	299	492	685
7,8,10-14: 7-Jack Cole-a; Matt Baker-a begins #8, ends #?; Vic Flint in #10-14.	26	52	78	152	239	325
10-12-Baker-a(2 each)	26	52	78	152	239	325
9-No Vic Flint	21	42	63	122	191	260
15-Drug-c/story; Vic Flint app.; Baker-c	26	52	78	152	239	325
16,18,20,21,23: Baker-a(i)	16	32	48	94	147	200
17,19,22-Baker-c	19	38	57	112	176	240
24-28 (All 100 pgs.): 26-Transvestism	36	72	108	208	329	450
29,31,32-Baker-c	14	28	42	81	118	155
30	14	28	42	76	108	140
33-38: 33-Transvestism; Baker-c. 34-Baker-c; r/#9. 35-Baker-c/a(2); r/#10. 36-r/#11; Vic Flint strip-r; Baker-c/a(2) unsigned. 37-Baker-c; r/#17. 38- Baker-c/a; r/#18	15	30	45	88	137	185

NOTE: **Matt Baker** *c-6-16, 17, 19, 22, 27, 29, 31-38; a-13, 16. Bondage c-1, 3.*

AUTHORITY, THE (See Stormwatch and Jenny Sparks: The Secret History of...)
DC Comics (WildStorm): May, 1999 - No. 29, Jul, 2002 ($2.50)

	GD 2.0	VG 4.0	FN 6.0	VF 8.0	VF/NM 9.0	NM- 9.2
1-Wraparound-c; Warren Ellis-s/Bryan Hitch and Paul Neary-a	2	4	6	8	11	14
2-4	1	3	4	6	8	10
5-12: 12-Death of Jenny Sparks; last Ellis-s	1	2	3	5	6	8
13-Mark Millar-s/Frank Quitely-c/a begins	2	4	6	8	10	12
14-16-Authority vs. Marvel-esque villains	1	2	3	4	5	7
17-22: 17,18-Weston-a. 19,20,22-Quitely-a. 21-McCrea-a						5.00
23-29: 23-26-Peyer-s/Nguyen-a; new Authority. 24-Preview of "The Establishment." 25,26-Jenny Sparks app. 27,28-Millar-s/Adams-a/c						4.00
Annual 2000 ($3.50) Devil's Night x-over; Hamner-a/Bermejo-c	1	2	3	4	5	7
Absolute Authority Slipcased Hardcover (2002, $49.95) oversized r/#1-12 plus script pages by Ellis and sketch pages by Hitch						50.00
...: Earth Inferno and Other Stories TPB (2002, $14.95) r/#17-20, Annual 2000, and Wildstorm Summer Special; new Quitely-c						15.00
...: Human on the Inside HC (2004, $24.95, dust jacket) Ridley-s/Oliver-a/c						25.00
...: Human on the Inside SC (2004, $17.99) Ridley-s/Oliver-a/c						18.00
...: Kev (10/02, $4.95) Ennis-s/Fabry-c/a						5.00
...: Relentless TPB (2000, $17.95) r/#1-8						18.00
...: Scorched Earth (2/03, $4.95) Robbie Morrison-s/Frazer Irving-a/Ashley Wood-c						5.00
...: Transfer of Power TPB (2002, $17.95) r/#22-29						18.00
...: Under New Management TPB (2000, $17.95) r/#9-16; new Quitely-c						18.00

AUTHORITY, THE (See previews in Sleeper, Stormwatch: Team Achilles and Wildcats Version 3.0)
DC Comics (WildStorm): Jul, 2003 - No. 14, Oct, 2004 ($2.95)

1-14: 1-Robbie Morrison-s/Dwayne Turner-a. 5-Huat-a. 14-Portacio-a						3.00
#0 (10/03, $2.95) r/preview back-ups listed above; Turner sketch pages						3.00
...: Fractured Worlds TPB (2005, $17.95) r/#6-14; cover gallery						18.00
...: Harsh Realities TPB (2004, $14.95) r/#0-5; cover gallery						15.00
.../Lobo: Jingle Hell (2/04, $4.95) Bisley-c/a; Giffen & Grant-s						5.00
.../Lobo: Spring Break Massacre (8/05, $4.99) Bisley-c/a; Giffen & Grant-s						5.00

AUTHORITY, THE
DC Comics (WildStorm): Dec, 2006 - Present ($2.99)

1,2-Grant Morrison-s/Gene Ha-a/c						3.00
1-Variant cover by Art Adams						5.00

AUTHORITY, THE: MORE KEV
DC Comics (WildStorm): Jul, 2004 - No. 4, Dec, 2004 ($2.95, limited series)

1-4-Garth Ennis-s/Glenn Fabry-c/a						3.00
...: Kev TPB (2005, $14.99) r/Authority: Kev one-shot and Authority: More Kev series						15.00

AUTHORITY, THE: REVOLUTION
DC Comics (WildStorm): Dec, 2004 - No. 12, Dec, 2005 ($2.95/$2.99)

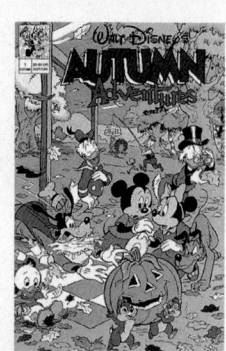

Autumn Adventures #1 © DIS

Avengers #2 © MAR

Avengers #11 © MAR

	GD 2.0	VG 4.0	FN 6.0	VF 8.0	VF/NM 9.0	NM- 9.2

1-12-Brubaker-s/Nguyen-a. 5-Henry Bendix returns. 7-Jenny Sparks app.   3.00
...: Book One TPB (2005, $14.99) r/#1-6; cover gallery and Nguyen sketch pages   15.00
...: Book Two TPB (2006, $14.99) r/#7-12; cover gallery and Nguyen sketch pages   15.00

AUTHORITY, THE: THE MAGNIFICENT KEV
DC Comics (WildStorm): Nov, 2005 - No. 5, Feb, 2006 ($2.99, limited series)
  1-5-Garth Ennis-s/Carlos Ezquerra-a/Glenn Fabry-c   3.00
TPB (2006, $14.99) r/#1-5   15.00

AUTOMATIC KAFKA
DC Comics (WildStorm): Sept, 2002 - No. 9, Jul, 2003 ($2.95)
  1-9-Ashley Wood-c/a; Joe Casey-s   3.00

AUTOMATON
Image Comics (Flypaper Press): Sept, 1998 - No. 3, 1998 ($2.95, lim. series)
  1-3-R.A. Jones-s/Peter Vale-a   3.00

AUTUMN
Caliber Comics: 1995 - No. 3, 1995 ($2.95, B&W)
  1-3   3.00

AUTUMN ADVENTURES (Walt Disney's...)
Disney Comics: Autumn, 1990; No. 2, Autumn, 1991 ($2.95, 68 pgs.)
  1-Donald Duck-r(2) by Barks, Pluto-r & new-a   4.00
  2-D. Duck-r by Barks; new Super Goof story   4.00

AVATAARS: COVENANT OF THE SHIELD
Marvel Comics: Sept, 2000 - No. 3, Nov, 2000 ($2.99, limited series)
  1-3-Kaminski-s/Oscar Jimenez-a   3.00

AVATAR
DC Comics: Feb, 1991 - No. 3, Apr, 1991 ($5.95, limited series, 100 pgs.)
  1-3: Based on TSR's Forgotten Realms   6.00

AVENGELYNE
Maximum Press: May, 1995 - No. 3, July, 1995 ($2.50/$3.50, limited series)

1/2	2	4	6	8	10	12
1/2 Platinum						15.00
1-Newsstand ($2.50)-Photo-c; poster insert						6.00
1-Direct Market ($3.50)-Chromium-c; poster	1	2	3	4	5	7
1-Glossy edition	2	4	6	12	16	20
1-Gold						12.00

2-3: 2-Polybagged w/card   3.00
3-Variant-c; Deodato pin-up   5.00
...Bible (10/96, $3.50)   4.00
.../Glory (9/95, $3.95) 2 covers   4.00
.../Glory Swimsuit Special (6/96, $2.95) photo and illos. covers   3.00
.../Glory: The Godyssey (9/96, $2.99) 2 covers (1 photo)   3.00
...Revelation One (Avatar, 1/01, $3.50) 3 covers by Haley, Rio, Shaw; Shaw-a   3.50
.../Shi (Avatar, 11/01, $3.50) Eight covers; Waller-a   3.50
...Swimsuit (8/95, $2.95)-Pin-ups/photos. 3-Variant-c exist (2 photo, 1 Liefeld-a)   4.00
...Swimsuit (1/96, $3.50, 2nd printing)-photo-c   4.00
Trade paperback (12/95, $9.95)   10.00
.../Warrior Nun Areala 1 (11/96, $2.99) also see Warrior Nun/Avengelyne   3.00

AVENGELYNE
Maximum Press: V2#1, Apr, 1996 - No. 14, Apr, 1997 ($2.95/$2.50)
V2#1-Four covers exist (2 photo-c).   4.00
V2#2-Three covers exist (1 photo-c); flip book w/Darkchylde   5.00
V2#0, 3-14: 0-(10/96).3-Flip book w/Priest preview. 5-Flip book w/Blindside   3.00

AVENGELYNE (Volume 3)
Awesome Comics: Mar, 1999 ($2.50)
  1-Fraga & Liefeld-a   3.00

AVENGELYNE: ARMAGEDDON
Maximum Press: Dec, 1996 - No. 3, Feb, 1997 ($2.99, limited series)
  1-3-Scott Clark-a(p)   3.00

AVENGELYNE: DEADLY SINS
Maximum Press: Feb, 1996 - No. 2, Mar, 1996 ($2.95, limited series)
  1,2: 1-Two-c exist (1 photo, 1 Liefeld-a). 2-Liefeld-c; Pop Mhan-a(p).   3.00

AVENGELYNE/POWER
Maximum Press: Nov, 1995 - No.3, Jan, 1996 ($2.95, limited series)
  1-3: 1,2-Liefeld-c/a. 3-Three variant-c. exist (1 photo-c)   3.00

AVENGELYNE • PROPHET
Maximum Press: May, 1996; No. 2, Feb. 1997 ($2.95, unfinished lim. series)

	GD 2.0	VG 4.0	FN 6.0	VF 8.0	VF/NM 9.0	NM- 9.2

1,2-Liefeld-c/a(p)   3.00

AVENGER, THE (See A-1 Comics)
Magazine Enterprises: Feb-Mar, 1955 - No. 4, Aug-Sept, 1955

1(A-1 #129)-Origin	40	80	120	238	379	520
2(A-1 #131), 3(A-1 #133) Robot-c, 4(A-1 #138)	27	54	81	158	249	340
IW Reprint #9('64)-Reprints #1 (new cover)	4	8	12	20	29	38

NOTE: *Powell a-2-4; c-1-4.*

AVENGERS, THE (TV)(Also see Steed and Mrs. Peel)
Gold Key: Nov, 1968 ("John Steed & Emma Peel" cover title) (15¢)

1-Photo-c	16	32	48	118	209	300
1-(Variant with photo back-c)	21	42	63	156	278	400

AVENGERS, THE (See Essential..., Giant-Size..., JLA/..., Kree/Skrull War Starring..., Marvel Graphic Novel #27, Marvel Super Action, Marvel Super Heroes('66), Marvel Treasury Ed., Marvel Triple Action, New Avengers, Solo Avengers, Tales Of Suspense #49, West Coast Avengers & X-Men Vs....)

AVENGERS, THE (The Mighty Avengers on cover only #63-69)
Marvel Comics Group: Sept, 1963 - No. 402, Sept, 1996

1-Origin & 1st app. The Avengers (Thor, Iron Man, Hulk, Ant-Man, Wasp); Loki app.	320	640	960	2880	5440	8000
2-Hulk leaves Avengers	70	140	210	595	1098	1600
3-2nd Sub-Mariner x-over outside the F.F. (see Strange Tales #107 for 1st); Sub-Mariner & Hulk team-up & battle Avengers; Spider-Man cameo (1/64)	50	100	150	400	725	1050
4-Revival of Captain America who joins the Avengers; 1st Silver Age app. of Captain America & Bucky (3/64)	128	256	384	1088	2019	2950
4-Reprint from the Golden Record Comic set	10	20	30	70	123	175
With Record (1966)	15	30	45	107	191	275
5-Hulk app.	34	68	102	255	465	675
6,8: 6-Intro/1st app. original Zemo & his Masters of Evil. 8-Intro Kang	25	50	75	184	330	475
7-Rick Jones app. in Bucky costume	30	60	90	220	398	575
9-Intro Wonder Man who dies in same story	31	62	93	233	429	625
10-Intro/1st app. Immortus; early Hercules app. (11/64)	22	44	66	165	295	425
11-Spider-Man-c & x-over (12/64)	27	54	81	203	364	525
12-15: 15-Death of original Zemo	15	30	45	111	198	285
16-New Avengers line-up-Hawkeye, Quicksilver, Scarlet Witch join; Thor, Iron Man, Giant-Man, Wasp leave)	19	38	57	141	251	360
17,18	11	22	33	79	140	200
19-1st app. Swordsman; origin Hawkeye (8/65)	12	24	36	87	156	225
20-22: Wood inks	8	16	24	58	97	135
23-30: 23-Romita Sr. inks (1st Silver Age Marvel work). 25-Dr. Doom-c/story. 28-Giant-Man becomes Goliath (5/66)	7	14	21	47	76	105
31-40	6	12	18	39	62	85
41-46,49-52,54-56: 43-1st app. Red Guardian (dies in #44). 46-Ant-Man returns (re-intro, 11/67). 52-Black Panther joins; 1st app. The Grim Reaper. 54-1st app. new Masters of Evil. 56-Zemo app; story explains how Capt. America became imprisoned in ice during WWII, only to be rescued in Avengers #4	5	10	15	35	55	75
47-Magneto-c/story	6	12	18	37	59	80
48-Origin/1st app. new Black Knight (1/68)	6	12	18	37	59	80
53-X-Men app.	7	14	21	50	83	115
57-1st app. S.A. Vision (10/68)	13	26	39	90	160	230
58-Origin The Vision	8	16	24	52	86	120
59-65: 59-Intro. Yellowjacket. 60-Wasp & Yellowjacket wed. 63-Goliath becomes Yellowjacket; Hawkeye becomes the new Goliath. 65-Last 12¢ issue	5	10	15	30	48	65
66,67-B. Smith-a	5	10	15	32	51	70
68-70: 69-Nighthawk cameo. 70-1st full app. Nighthawk	4	8	12	28	44	60
71-1st app. The Invaders (12/69); Black Knight joins	7	14	21	45	73	100
72-79,81,82,84-86,89-91: 82-Daredevil app	4	8	12	26	41	55
80-Intro. Red Wolf (9/70)	4	8	12	28	44	60
83-Intro. The Liberators (Wasp, Valkyrie, Scarlet Witch, Medusa & the Black Widow)	5	10	15	30	48	65
87-Origin The Black Panther	5	10	15	30	48	65
88-Written by Harlan Ellison	4	8	12	28	44	60
88-2nd printing (1994)	2	4	6	8	10	12
92-Last 15¢ issue; Neal Adams-c	5	10	15	32	51	70
93-(52 pgs.)-Neal Adams-c/a	12	24	36	82	146	210
94-96-Neal Adams-c/a	6	12	18	43	69	95
97-G.A. Capt. America, Sub-Mariner, Human Torch, Patriot, Vision, Blazing Skull, Fin, Angel, & new Capt. Marvel x-over	5	10	15	30	48	65
98,99: 98-Goliath becomes Hawkeye; Smith c/a(i). 99-Smith-c,						

Avengers #161 © MAR

Avengers #402 © MAR

Avengers V3 #2 © MAR

	GD 2.0	VG 4.0	FN 6.0	VF 8.0	VF/NM 9.0	NM- 9.2
Smith/Sutton-a	4	8	12	24	37	50
100-(6/72)-Smith-c/a; featuring everyone who was an Avenger	8	16	24	56	93	130
101-Harlan Ellison scripts	3	6	9	20	30	40
102-106,108,109	3	6	9	18	27	35
107-Starlin-a(p)	3	6	9	20	30	40
110,111-X-Men app.	4	8	12	28	44	60
112-1st app. Mantis	4	8	12	24	37	50
113-115,119-124,126-130: 123-Origin Mantis	3	6	9	16	22	28
116-118-Defenders/Silver Surfer app.	4	8	12	24	37	50
125-Thanos-c & brief app.	3	6	9	18	27	35
131-133,136-140: 136-Ploog-r/Amazing Advs. #12	2	4	6	10	14	18
134,135-Origin of the Vision revised (also see Avengers Forever mini-series)	3	6	9	16	22	28
141-143,145,152-163	1	3	4	6	8	11
144-Origin & 1st app. Hellcat	2	4	6	11	16	20
146-149-(Reg.25¢ editions)(4-7/76)	1	3	4	6	8	11
146-149-(30¢-c variants, limited distribution)	4	8	12	22	34	45
150-Kirby-a(r); new line-up: Capt. America, Scarlet Witch, Iron Man, Wasp, Yellowjacket, Vision & The Beast	2	4	6	8	11	14
150-(30¢-c variant, limited distribution)	3	6	9	18	27	35
151-Wonder Man returns w/new costume	2	4	6	8	10	12
160-164-(35¢-c variants, limited dist.)(6-10/77)	6	12	18	43	69	95
164-166: Byrne-a	2	4	6	8	10	12
167-180: 168-Guardians of the Galaxy app. 174-Thanos cameo. 176-Starhawk app.	1	2	3	4	5	7
181-191-Byrne-a: 181-New line-up: Capt. America, Scarlet Witch, Iron Man, Wasp, Vision, Beast & The Falcon. 183-Ms. Marvel joins. 185-Origin Quicksilver & Scarlet Witch	1	3	4	6	8	10
192-194,197-199						6.00
195,196: 195-1st Taskmaster cameo. 196-1st Taskmaster full app.	1	3	4	6	8	10
200-(10/80, 52 pgs.)-Ms. Marvel leaves.	1	3	4	6	8	10
201-213,217-238: 211-New line-up: Capt. America, Iron Man, Tigra, Thor, Wasp & Yellowjacket. 213-Yellowjacket leaves. 217-Yellowjacket & Wasp return. 221-Hawkeye & She-Hulk join. 227-Capt. Marvel (female) joins; origins of Ant-Man, Wasp, Giant-Man, Goliath, Yellowjacket, & Avengers. 230-Yellowjacket quits. 231-Iron Man leaves. 232-Starfox (Eros) joins.						
234-Origin Quicksilver, Scarlet Witch. 238-Origin Blackout						4.50
214-Ghost Rider-c/story						6.00
215,216,239,240,250: 215,216-Silver Surfer app. 216-Tigra leaves. 239-(1/84) Avengers app. on David Letterman show. 240-Spider-Woman revived. 250-($1.00, 52 pgs.)						4.00
241-244, 251-262						3.50
263-1st app. X-Factor (1/86)(story continues in Fant. Four #286)						2.50
264-297-Alpha Flight app. 291-$1.00 issues begin. 297-Black Knight, She-Hulk & Thor resign. 298-Inferno tie-in						3.00
300-(2/89, $1.75, 68 pgs.)-Thor joins; Simonson-a						4.00
301-304,306-313,319-325,327,329-343: 302-Re-intro Quasar. 320-324-Alpha Flight app. (320-cameo). 327-2nd app. Rage. 341,342-New Warriors app. 343-Last $1.00-c						3.00
305,314-318: 305-Byrne scripts begin. 314-318-Spider-Man x-over						3.50
326-1st app. Rage (11/90)						4.00
328,344-349,351-359,361,362,364,365,367: 328-Contains coupon for Hunt for Magneto contest. 365-Contains coupon						3.00
350-($2.50, 68 pgs.)-Double gatefold-c showing-c to #1; r/#53 w/cover in flip book format; vs. The Starjammers						3.50
360-($2.95, 52 pgs.)-Embossed all-foil-c; 30th ann.						4.00
363-($2.50, 52 pgs.)-All silver foil-c						4.00
366-($3.95, 68 pgs.)-Embossed all gold foil-c						4.00
368,370,374,376-399: 368-Bloodties part 1; Avengers/X-Men x-over. 374-bound-in trading card sheet. 380-Deodato-a. 390,391-"The Crossing." 395-Death of "old" Tony Stark; wraparound-c.						3.00
369-($2.95)-Foil embossed-c; Bloodties part 5						4.00
375-($2.00, 52 pgs.)-Regular ed.; Thunderstrike returns; leads into Malibu Comics' Black September.						3.00
375-($2.50)-Collector's ed. w/bound-in poster; leads into Malibu Comics' Black September.						3.50
400-402: Waid-s; 402-Deodato breakdowns; cont'd in X-Men #56 & Onslaught: Marvel Universe.						4.00
#500-503 (See Avengers Vol. 3; series resumed original numbering after Vol. 3 #84)						
Special 1 (9/67, 25¢, 68 pgs.)-New-a; original & new Avengers team-up	10	20	30	68	119	170
Special 2 (9/68, 25¢, 68 pgs.)-New-a; original vs. new Avengers	6	12	18	41	66	90
Special 3 (9/69, 25¢, 68 pgs.)-r/Avengers #4 plus 3 Capt. America stories by Kirby (art); origin Red Skull	4	8	12	24	37	50

	GD 2.0	VG 4.0	FN 6.0	VF 8.0	VF/NM 9.0	NM- 9.2
Special 4 (1/71, 25¢, 68 pgs.)-Kirby-r/Avengers #5,6	3	6	9	16	22	28
Special 5 (1/72, 52 pgs.)-Spider-Man x-over	3	6	9	16	22	28
Annual 6 (11/76) Peréz-a; Kirby-c	2	4	6	9	13	16
Annual 7 (11/77)-Starlin-c/a; Warlock dies; Thanos app.	4	8	12	28	44	60
Annual 8 (1978)-Dr. Strange, Ms. Marvel app.	1	3	4	6	8	10
Annual 9 (1979)-Newton-a(p)	1	2	3	5	6	8
Annual 10 (1981)-Golden-p; X-Men cameo; 1st app. Rogue & Madelyne Pryor	4	8	12	28	44	60
Annual 11-13: 11(1982)-Vs. The Defenders. 12('83), 13('84)						4.00
Annual 14-18: 14('85),15('86),16('87),17('88)-Evolutionary War x-over, 18('89)-Atlantis Attacks						4.00
Annual 19-23 (90-'94, 68 pgs.). 22-Bagged/card						3.00
...: Galactic Storm Vol. 1 ('06, $29.99, TPB) r/Kree-Shi'ar war from Avengers #345-346, Capt. America #398-399, Avengers West Coast #80-81, Quasar #32-33, Wonder Man #7-8, Iron Man #278 and Thor #445; new Epting-c						30.00
...: Galactic Storm Vol. 2 ('06, $29.99, TPB) r/Kree-Shi'ar war from Avengers #347, Capt. America #400-401, Avengers West Coast #82, Quasar #34-36, Wonder Man #9, Iron Man #279, Thor #446 and What If #55-56						30.00
...: Kang - Time and Time Again ('05, $19.99, TPB) r/Avengers #69-71 & 267-269, Thor #140 and Incredible Hulk #135						20.00
...Kree-Skrull War ('00, $24.95, TPB) new Neal Adams-c						25.00
...: Legends Vol. 3: George Perez ('03, $16.99) r/#161,162,194-196,201, Ann. #6 & 8						17.00
Marvel Double Feature...Avengers/Giant-Man #379 ($2.50, 52 pgs.)-Same as Avengers #379 w/Giant-Man flip book						2.50
Marvel Graphic Novel - Deathtrap: The Vault (1991, $9.95) Venom-c/app.	2	4	6	8	10	12
The Korvac Saga TPB (2003, $19.95)-r/#167,168,170-177; Perez-c						20.00
The Serpent Crown TPB (2005, $15.99)-r/#141-144,147-149; Hellcat app.						16.00
The Yesterday Quest ($6.95)-r/#181,182,185-187	1	2	3	4	5	7
Under Siege ('98, $16.95, TPB) r/#270,271,273-277						17.00
...: Vision and the Scarlet Witch TPB (2005, $15.99) r/wedding from Giant-Size Avengers #4 and "Vision and the Scarlet Witch" mini-series #1-4						16.00
...: Visionaries ('99, $16.95)-r/early George Perez art						17.00

NOTE: Austin c(i)-157, 167, 168, 170-177, 181, 183-188, 198-201, Annual 8. John Buscema a-41-44p, 46p, 47p, 49, 50, 51-62p, 74-77, 79-85, 87-91, 97, 105p, 121p, 124p,125p, 152, 153p, 255-279p, 281-302p; c-41-66, 68-71, 73-91, 97-99, 178, 256-259p, 261-279p, 281-302p. Byrne a-164-166p, 181-191p, 233p, Annual 13i, 14p; c-186-190p, 233p, 260, 305p; scripts-305-312. Colan a(p)-63-65, 111, 206-208, 210, 211; c(p)-65, 206-208, 210, 211. Ditko a-Annual 13. Guice a-Annual 12p. Don Heck a-9-15, 17-40, 157. Kane c-37p, 159p. Kane/Everett c-97. Kirby a-1-8p, Special 3r, 4r(p); c-1-30, 148, 151-158; layouts-14-16. Ron Lim a(p)-335-341. Miller c-193p. Mooney a-86i, 179p, 180p. Nebres a-178i; c-179i. Newton a-204p, Annual 9p. Perez a(p)-141, 143, 144, 148, 150, 154, 155, 160, 161, 162, 167,168, 170, 171, 194-196, 198-202, Annual 6, 8; c(p)-160-162, 164-169, 194-196, 201, 181,183-185, 191, 192, 194-201, 379-382, Annual 8. Starlin c-121, 135. Staton a-127-134i. Tuska a-47i,48i, 51i, 53i, 54i, 106p, 107p, 135p, 137-140p, 163p. Guardians of the Galaxy app. in #167, 168, 170, 173, 175, 181.

AVENGERS, THE (Volume Two)
Marvel Comics: V2#1, Nov, 1996 - No. 13, Nov, 1997 ($2.95/$1.95/$1.99) (Produced by Extreme Studios)

	GD 2.0	VG 4.0	FN 6.0	VF 8.0	VF/NM 9.0	NM- 9.2
1-($2.95)-Heroes Reborn begins; intro new team (Captain America, Swordsman, Scarlet Witch, Vision, Thor, Hellcat & Hawkeye); 1st app. Avengers Island; Loki & Enchantress app.; Rob Liefeld-a & plot; Chap Yaep-p; Jim Valentino art						5.00
1-($1.95)-Variant-c						6.00
2-13: Jeph Loeb scripts begin, Kang app. 4-Hulk-c/app. 5-Thor/Hulk battle; 2 covers. 10,11,13-"World War 3"-pt. 2, x-over w/Image characters. 12-($2.99) "Heroes Reunited"-pt. 2						4.00
Heroes Reborn: Avengers (2006, $29.99, TPB) r/#1-12; pin-up and cover gallery						30.00

AVENGERS, THE (Volume Three)(See New Avengers for next series)
Marvel Comics: Feb, 1998 - No. 84, Aug, 2004; No. 500, Sept, 2004 - No. 503, Dec, 2004 ($2.99/$1.99/$2.25)

	GD 2.0	VG 4.0	FN 6.0	VF 8.0	VF/NM 9.0	NM- 9.2
1-($2.99, 48 pgs.) Busiek-s/Perez-a/wraparound-c; Avengers reassemble after Heroes Return						5.00
1-Variant Heroes Return cover	1	2	3	4	5	7
1-Rough Cut-Features original script and pencil pages						3.00
2-($1.99)Perez-a, 2-Lago painted-c						4.00
3,4: 3-Wonder Man-c/app. 4-Final roster chosen; Perez poster						3.00
5-11: 5,6-Squadron Supreme-c/app. 8-Triathlon-c/app.						2.50
12-($2.99) Thunderbolts app.						3.00
12-Alternate-c of Avengers w/white background; no logo						15.00
13-24,26,28: 13-New Warriors app. 16-18-Ordway-s/a. 19-Ultron returns. 26-Immonen-a						2.50
16-Variant-c with purple background						5.00
25,27-($2.99) 25-vs. the Exemplars; Spider-Man app. 27-100 pgs.						3.00
29-33,35-47: 29-Begin $2.25-c. 35-Maximum Security x-over; Romita Jr.-a. 36-Epting-a; poster by Alan Davis. 38-Davis-a begins ($1.99-c)						2.50
34-($2.99) Last Pérez-a; Thunderbirds app.						3.00
48-($3.50, 100 pgs.) new story w/Dwyer-a & r/#98-100						3.50
49,51-59: 49-'Nuff Said story. 51-Anderson-a. 52-Reis-a. 57-Johns-s begin						2.50

	GD 2.0	VG 4.0	FN 6.0	VF 8.0	VF/NM 9.0	NM- 9.2

50,60-($3.50): 50 Dwyer-a; Quasar app.   3.50
61-84: 61,62-Frank-a; new line-up. 63-Davis-a. 64-Reis-a. 65-70-Coipel-a. 75-Hulk app.
  76-Jack of Hearts dies; Jae Lee-c. 77-(50¢-c) Coipel-a/Cassaday-c. 78,80,81Coipel-a.
  83,84-New Invaders app.   2.50
  (After #84 [Aug, 2004], numbering reverted back to original Vol. 1 with #500, Sept, 2004)
500-($3.50) "Avengers Disassembled" begins; Bendis-s/Finch-a; Ant-Man (Scott Lang) killed,
  Vision destroyed   3.50
500-Director's Cut ($4.99) Cassaday foil variant-c plus interviews and galleries   5.00
501, 502-($2.25): 502-Hawkeye killed   2.50
503-($3.50) "Avengers Disassembled" ends; reprint pages from Avengers V1#16   3.50
#11/2 (12/99, $2.50) Timm-c/a/Stern-s; 1963-style issue   2.50
.../ Squadron Supreme '98 Annual ($2.99)   3.00
1999, 2000 Annual (7/99, '00, $3.50) 1999-Manco-a. 2000-Breyfogle-a   3.50
2001 Annual ($2.99) Reis-a; back-up-s art by Churchill   3.00
...: Above and Beyond TPB ('05, $24.99) r/#36-40,56, Annual 2001, & Avengers: The Ultron
  Imperative; Alan Davis-c   25.00
... Assemble HC ('04, $29.95, oversized) r/#11-11 & '98 Annual; Busiek intro.; Pérez pencil art
  and Busiek script from Avengers #1   30.00
... Assemble Vol. 2 HC ('05, $29.95, oversized) r/#12-22, #0 & Ann. 1999; Ordway intro.   30.00
... Assemble Vol. 3 HC ('06, $34.99, oversized) r/#23-34, #11 1/2 & Thunderbolts #42-44   35.00
... Assemble Vol. 4 HC ('07, $34.99, oversized) r/#35-40, Avengers 2000, Avengers 2001,
  Avengers: The Ultron Imperative, Maximum Security #1-3 & ...Dangerous Planet   35.00
...: Clear and Present Dangers TPB ('01, $19.95) r/#8-15   20.00
...: Defenders War HC ('07, $19.99) r/#115-118 & Defenders #8-11; Englehart intro.   20.00
...: Disassembled HC ('06, $24.99) r/#500-503 & Avengers Finale; Director's Cut extras   25.00
...: Disassembled TPB ('05, $15.99) r/#500-503 & Avengers Finale; Director's Cut extras   16.00
...Finale 1 (1/05, $3.50) Epilogue to Avengers Disassembled; Neal Adams-c; art by various
  incl. Peréz, Maleev, Oeming, Powell, Mayhew, Mack, McNiven, Cheung, Frank   3.50
...: Living Legends TPB ('04, $19.99) r/#23-30; last Busiek/Pérez arc   20.00
...-Supreme Justice TPB (4/01, $17.95) r/Squadron Supreme appearances in Avengers #5-7,
  '98 Annual, Iron Man #7, Capt. America #8, Quicksilver #10; Pérez-c   18.00
The Kang Dynasty TPB ('02, $29.99) r/#41-55 & 2001 Annual   30.00
The Morgan Conquest TPB ('00, $14.95) r/#1-4   15.00
.../Thunderbolts Vol. 1: The Nefaria Protocols (2004, $19.99) r/#31-34, 42-44   20.00
Ultron Unleashed TPB (8/99, $3.50) reprints early app.   3.50
Ultron Unlimited TPB (4/01, $14.95) r/#19-22 & #0 prelude   15.00
Wizard #0-Ultron Unlimited prelude   2.50
Vol. 1: World Trust TPB ('03, $14.99) r/#57-62 & Marvel Double-Shot #2   15.00
Vol. 2: Red Zone TPB ('04, $14.99) r/#64-70   15.00
Vol. 3: The Search For She-Hulk TPB ('04, $12.99) r/#71-76   13.00
Vol. 4: The Lionheart of Avalon TPB ('04, $11.99) r/#77-81   12.00
Vol. 5: Once an Invader TPB ('04, $14.99) r/#82-84, V1 #71; Invaders #0 & Ann #1 ('77)   15.00

AVENGERS AND POWER PACK ASSEMBLE!
Marvel Comics: June, 2006 - No. 4 ($2.99, limited series)
1-4-GuriHiru-a/Sumerak-s. 1-Capt. America app. 2-Iron Man. 3-Spider-Man, Kang app.   3.00
TPB (2006, $6.99, digest-size) r/#1-4   7.00

AVENGERS: CELESTIAL QUEST
Marvel Comics: Nov, 2001 - No. 8, June, 2002 ($2.50/$3.50, limited series)
1-7-Englehart-s/Santamaría-a; Thanos app.   2.50
8-($3.50)   3.50

AVENGERS: CLASSIC
Marvel Comics: Aug, 2007 - Present ($3.99/$2.99)
1-($3.99)-Reprints Avengers #1 (1963) with new stories about that era; Art Adams-c   4.00
2-4-($2.99) R/#2-4 with back-up w/Oeming-a   3.00

AVENGERS COLLECTOR'S EDITION, THE
Marvel Comics: 1993 (Ordered through mail w/candy wrapper, 20 pgs.)
1-Contains 4 bound-in trading cards   5.00

AVENGERS: EARTH'S MIGHTIEST HEROES
Marvel Comics: Jan, 2005 - No. 8, Apr, 2005 ($3.50, limited series)
1-8-Retells origin; Casey-s/Kolins-a   3.50
HC (2005, $24.99, 7 1/2" x 11" with dustjacket) r/#1-8   25.00

AVENGERS: EARTH'S MIGHTIEST HEROES II
Marvel Comics: Jan, 2007 - No. 8, May, 2007 ($3.99, limited series)
1-8-Retells time when the Vision joined; Casey-s/Rosado-a. 6-Hank & Janet's wedding   4.00
HC (2007, $24.99, 7 1/2" x 11" with dustjacket) r/#1-8; cover sketches   25.00

AVENGERS FOREVER
Marvel Comics: Dec, 1998 - No. 12, Feb, 2000 ($2.99)
1-Busiek-s/Pacheco-a in all   4.00
2-12: 4-Four covers. 6-Two covers. 8-Vision origin revised. 12-Rick Jones becomes
  Capt. Marvel   3.00

TPB (1/01, $24.95) r/#1-12; Busiek intro.; new Pacheco-c   25.00

AVENGERS INFINITY
Marvel Comics: Sept, 2000 - No. 4, Dec, 2000 ($2.99, limited series)
1-4-Stern-s/Chen-a   3.00

AVENGERS/ JLA (See JLA/Avengers for #1 & #3)
DC Comics: No, 2, 2003; No. 4, 2003 ($5.95, limited series)
2-Busiek-s/Pérez-a; wraparound-c; Krona, Galactus app.   6.00
4-Busiek-s/Pérez-a; wraparound-c   6.00

AVENGERS LOG, THE
Marvel Comics: Feb, 1994 ($1.95)
1-Gives history of all members; Perez-c   2.50

AVENGERS NEXT (See A-Next and Spider-Girl)
Marvel Comics: Jan, 2007 - No. 5 ($2.99, limited series)
1-5-Lim-a/Wieringo-c; Spider-Girl app. 1-Avengers vs. zombies. 2-Thena app.   3.00
...: Rebirth TPB (2007, $13.99) r/#1-5   14.00

AVENGERS SPOTLIGHT (Formerly Solo Avengers #1-20)
Marvel Comics: No. 21, Aug, 1989 - No. 40, Jan, 1991 (75¢/$1.00)
21-Byrne-c/a   3.00
22-40: 26-Acts of Vengeance story. 31-34-U.S. Agent series. 36-Heck-i. 37-Mortimer-i.
  40-The Black Knight app.   2.50

AVENGERS STRIKEFILE
Marvel Comics: Jan, 1994 ($1.75, one-shot)
1   2.50

AVENGERS: THE CROSSING
Marvel Comics: July, 1995 ($4.95, one-shot)
1-Deodato-c/a; 1st app. Thor's new costume   5.00

AVENGERS: THE INITIATIVE (See Civil War and related titles)
Marvel Comics: Jun, 2007 - Present ($2.99)
1-6: 1-Caselli-a/Slott-s/Cheung-c; War Machine app. 4,5-World War Hulk. 6-Uy-a   3.00

AVENGERS: THE TERMINATRIX OBJECTIVE
Marvel Comics: Sept, 1993 - No. 4, Dec, 1993 ($1.25, limited series)
1 ($2.50)-Holo-grafx foil-c   3.00
2-4-Old vs. current Avengers   2.50

AVENGERS: THE ULTRON IMPERATIVE
Marvel Comics: Nov, 2001 ($5.99, one-shot)
1-Follow-up to the Ultron Unlimited ending in Avengers #42; BWS-c   6.00

AVENGERS/THUNDERBOLTS
Marvel Comics: May, 2004 - No. 6, Sept, 2004 ($2.99, limited series)
1-6: Busiek & Nicieza-s/Kitson-c. 1,2-Kitson-a. 3-6-Grummett-a   3.00
Vol. 2: Best Intentions (2004, $14.99) r/#1-6   15.00

AVENGERS: TIMESLIDE
Marvel Comics: Feb, 1996 ($4.95, one-shot)
1-Foil-c   5.00

AVENGERS TWO: WONDER MAN & BEAST
Marvel Comics: May, 2000 - No. 3, July, 2000 ($2.99, limited series)
1-3: Stern-s/Bagley-c/a   3.00

AVENGERS/ULTRAFORCE (See Ultraforce/Avengers)
Marvel Comics: Oct, 1995 ($3.95, one-shot)
1-Wraparound foil-c by Perez   4.00

AVENGERS UNITED THEY STAND
Marvel Comics: Nov, 1999 - No. 7, June, 2000 ($2.99/$1.99)
1-Based on the animated series   3.00
2-6-($1.99) 2-Avengers battle Hydra   2.50
7-($2.99) Devil Dinosaur-c/app.; reprints Avengers Action Figure Comic   3.00

AVENGERS UNIVERSE
Marvel Comics: Jun, 2000 - No. 3, Oct, 2000 ($3.99)
1-3-Reprints recent stories   4.00

AVENGERS UNPLUGGED
Marvel Comics: Oct, 1995 - No. 6, Aug, 1996 (99¢, bi-monthly)
1-6   2.50

AVENGERS WEST COAST (Formerly West Coast Avengers)
Marvel Comics: No. 48, Sept, 1989 - No. 102, Jan, 1994 ($1.00/$1.25)

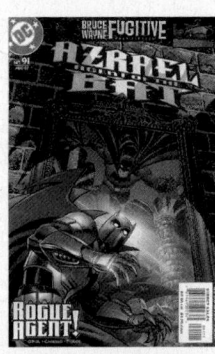

Azrael: Agent of the Bat #91 © DC

Babe #6 © PRIZE

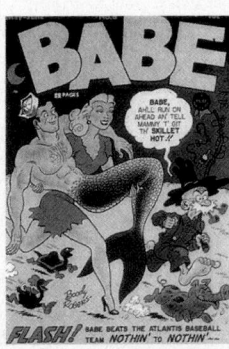

Baby Huey, The Baby Giant #2 © HARV

	GD 2.0	VG 4.0	FN 6.0	VF 8.0	VF/NM 9.0	NM- 9.2

48,49: 48-Byrne-c/a & scripts continue thru #57 — 3.00
50-Re-intro original Human Torch — 4.00
51-69,71-74,76-83,85,86,89-99: 54-Cover swipe/F.F. #1. 78-Last $1.00-c. 79-Dr. Strange x-over. 93-95-Darkhawk app. — 2.50
70,75,84,87,88: 70-Spider-Woman app. 75 (52 pgs.)-Fantastic Four x-over. 84-Origin Spider-Woman retold; Spider-Man app. (also in #85,86). 87,88-Wolverine-c/story — 3.00
100-($3.95, 68 pgs.)-Embossed all red foil-c — 4.00
101,102: 101-X-Men x-over — 4.00
Annual 5-8 ('90-'93, 68 pgs.)-5,6-West Coast Avengers in indicia. 7-Darkhawk app. 8-Polybagged w/card — 3.00
...: Vision Quest TPB (2005, $24.99) r/#42-50; Byrne-s/a — 25.00

AVIATION ADVENTURES AND MODEL BUILDING (True Aviation Advs. ...No. 15)
Parents' Magazine Institute: No. 16, Dec, 1946 - No. 17, Feb, 1947

| 16,17-Half comics and half pictures | 8 | 16 | 24 | 42 | 54 | 65 |

AVIATION CADETS
Street & Smith Publications: 1943

| nn | 19 | 37 | 57 | 109 | 172 | 235 |

A-V IN 3-D
Aardvark-Vanaheim: Dec, 1984 ($2.00, 28 pgs. w/glasses)

1-Cerebus, Flaming Carrot, Normalman & Ms. Tree — 4.00

AWAKENING, THE
Image Comics: Oct, 1997 - No. 4, Apr, 1998 ($2.95, B&W, limited series)

1-4-Stephen Blue-s/c-a — 3.00

AWESOME ADVENTURES
Awesome Entertainment: Aug, 1999 ($2.50)

1-Alan Moore-s/ Steve Skroce-a; Youngblood story — 3.00

AWESOME HOLIDAY SPECIAL
Awesome Entertainment: Dec, 1997 ($2.50, one-shot)

1-Flip book w/covers of Fighting American & Coven. Holiday stories also featuring Kaboom and Shaft by regular creators. — 3.00
1-Gold Edition — 5.00

AWFUL OSCAR (Formerly & becomes Oscar Comics with No. 13)
Marvel Comics: No. 11, June, 1949 - No. 12, Aug, 1949

| 11,12 | 14 | 28 | 42 | 76 | 108 | 140 |

AWKWARD UNIVERSE
Slave Labor Graphics: 12/95 ($9.95, graphic novel)

nn — 10.00

AXA
Eclipse Comics: Apr, 1987 - No. 2, Aug, 1987 ($1.75)

1,2 — 2.50

AXEL PRESSBUTTON (Pressbutton No. 5; see Laser Eraser &...)
Eclipse Comics: Nov, 1984 - No. 6, July, 1985 ($1.50/$1.75, Baxter paper)

1-6: Reprints Warrior (British mag.). 1-Bolland-c; origin Laser Eraser & Pressbutton — 3.00

AXIS ALPHA
Axis Comics: Feb, 1994 ($2.50, one-shot)

V1-Previews Axis titles including, Tribe, Dethgrip, B.E.A.S.T.I.E.S. & more; Pitt app. in Tribe story. — 3.00

AZRAEL (...Agent of the Bat #47 on)(Also see Batman: Sword of Azrael)
DC Comics: Feb, 1995 - No. 100, May, 2003 ($1.95/$2.25/$2.50/$2.95)

1-Dennis O'Neil scripts begin — 5.00
2,3 — 3.00
4-46,48-62: 5,6-Ras Al Ghul app. 13-Nightwing-c/app. 15-Contagion Pt. 5 (Pt. 4 on-c). 16-Contagion Pt. 10. 22-Batman-c/app. 23,27-Batman app. 27,28-Joker app. 35-Hitman app. 36-39-Batman, Bane app. 50-New costume. 53-Joker-c/app. 56,57,60-New Batgirl app. — 2.50
47-($3.95) Flip book with Batman: Shadow of the Bat #80 — 4.00
63-74,76-92: 63-Huntress-c/app.; Azrael returns to old costume. 67-Begin $2.50-c. 70-79-Harris-c. 83-Joker x-over. 91-Bruce Wayne: Fugitive pt. 15 — 2.50
75-($3.95) New costume; Harris-c — 4.00
93-100: 93-Begin $2.95-c. 95,96-Two-Face app. 100-Last issue; Zeck-c — 3.00
#1,000,000 (11/98) Giarrano-a — 2.50
Annual 1 (1995, $3.95)-Year One story — 4.00
Annual 2 (1996, $2.95)-Legends of the Dead Earth story — 3.00
Annual 3 (1997, $3.95)-Pulp Heroes story; Orbik-c — 4.00
Plus (12/96, $2.95)-Question-c/app. — 3.00

AZRAEL/ ASH

DC Comics: 1997 ($4.95, one-shot)

1-O'Neil-s/Quesada, Palmiotti-a — 5.00

AZTEC ACE
Eclipse Comics: Mar, 1984 - No. 15, Sept, 1985 ($2.25/$1.50/$1.75, Baxter paper)

1-$2.25-c (52 pgs.) — 3.00
2-15: 2-Begin 36 pgs. — 2.50
NOTE: *N. Redondo* a-1-8i, 10i. c-6-8i.

AZTEC: THE ULTIMATE MAN
DC Comics: Aug, 1996 - No. 10, May 1997 ($1.75)

1-1st app. Aztek & Synth; Grant Morrison & Mark Millar scripts in all — 6.00
2-9: 2-Green Lantern app. 3-1st app. Death-Doll. 4-Intro The Lizard King. 5-Origin. 6-Joker app.; Batman cameo. 7-Batman app. 8-Luthor app. 9-vs. Parasite-c/app. — 4.00
10-JLA-c/app.

| | | 1 | 2 | 4 | 6 | 8 | 10 |

NOTE: *Breyfogle* c-5p. *N. Steven Harris* a-1-5p. *Porter* c-1p. *Wieringo* c-2p.

BABE (...Darling of the Hills, later issues)(See Big Shot and Sparky Watts)
Prize/Headline/Feature: June-July, 1948 - No. 11, Apr-May, 1950

1-Boody Rogers-a	26	52	78	152	239	325
2-Boody Rogers-a	15	30	45	88	137	185
3-11-All by Boody Rogers	14	28	42	82	121	160

BABE
Dark Horse Comics (Legend): July, 1994 - No. 4, Jan, 1994 ($2.50, lim. series)

1-4: John Byrne-c/a/scripts; ProtoTykes back-up story — 2.50

BABE RUTH SPORTS COMICS (Becomes Rags Rabbit #11 on?)
Harvey Publications: April, 1949 - No. 11, Feb, 1951

1-Powell-a	41	82	123	250	400	550
2-Powell-a	28	56	84	162	256	350
3-11: Powell-a in most	23	46	69	132	209	285

NOTE: Baseball c-2-4, 9. Basketball c-1, 6. Football c-5. Yogi Berra c/story-8. Joe DiMaggio c/story-3. Bob Feller c/story-4. Stan Musial c-9.

BABES IN TOYLAND (Disney, Movie) (See Golden Pix Story Book ST-3)
Dell Publishing Co.: No. 1282, Feb-Apr, 1962

| Four Color 1282-Annette Funicello photo-c | 14 | 28 | 42 | 99 | 175 | 250 |

BABES OF BROADWAY
Broadway Comics: May, 1996 ($2.95, one-shot)

1-Pin-ups of Broadway Comics' female characters; Alan Davis, Michael Kaluta, J. G. Jones, Alan Weiss, Guy Davis & others-a; Giordano-c. — 3.00

BABE 2
Dark Horse Comics (Legend): Mar, 1995 - No. 2, May, 1995 ($2.50, lim. series)

1,2: John Byrne-c/a/scripts — 2.50

BABY HUEY
Harvey Comics: No. 1, Oct, 1991 - No. 9, June, 1994 ($1.00/$1.25/$1.50, quarterly)

1 ($1.00): 1-Cover says "Big Baby Huey" — 5.00
2-9 ($1.25-$1.50) — 3.00

BABY HUEY AND PAPA (See Paramount Animated...)
Harvey Publications: May, 1962 - No. 33, Jan, 1968 (Also see Casper The Friendly Ghost)

1	15	30	45	111	198	285
2	8	16	24	58	97	135
3-5	6	12	18	37	59	80
6-10	3	6	9	21	32	42
11-20	3	6	9	16	22	28
21-33	2	4	6	13	18	22

BABY HUEY DIGEST
Harvey Publications: June, 1992 (Digest-size, one-shot)

| 1-Reprints | 1 | 3 | 4 | 6 | 8 | 10 |

BABY HUEY DUCKLAND
Harvey Publications: Nov, 1962 - No. 15, Nov, 1966 (25¢ Giants, 68 pgs.)

1	12	24	36	82	146	210
2-5	6	12	18	39	62	85
6-15	4	8	12	22	34	45

BABY HUEY, THE BABY GIANT (Also see Big Baby Huey, Casper, Harvey Hits #22, Harvey Comics Hits #60, & Paramount Animated Comics)
Harvey Publ: 9/56 - #97, 10/71; #98, 10/72; #99, 10/80; #100, 10/90; #101, 11/90

1-Infinity-c	45	90	135	360	655	950
2	22	44	66	165	295	425
3-Baby Huey takes anti-pep pills	14	28	42	102	181	260
4,5	10	20	30	70	123	175

Babylon 5 #5 © WB

Backlash #9 © WSP

Badrock and Company #2 © Rob Liefeld

	GD 2.0	VG 4.0	FN 6.0	VF 8.0	VF/NM 9.0	NM- 9.2
6-10	7	14	21	45	73	100
11-20	5	10	15	35	55	75
21-40	4	8	12	24	37	50
41-60	3	6	9	16	23	30
61-79 (12/67)	2	4	6	13	18	22
80(12/68) - 95-All 68 pg. Giants	3	6	9	17	25	32
96,97-Both 52 pg. Giants	3	6	9	14	19	24
98-Regular size	2	4	6	9	12	15
99-Regular size	1	2	3	5	6	8
100,101 ($1.00)						4.00

BABYLON 5 (TV)
DC Comics: Jan, 1995 - No. 11, Dec, 1995 ($1.95/$2.50)

1	2	4	6	8	11	14
2-5	1	2	3	5	7	9
6-11: 7-Begin $2.50-c	1	2	3	4	5	7
... The Price of Peace (1998, $9.95, TPB) r/#1-4,11						10.00

BABYLON 5: IN VALEN'S NAME
DC Comics: Mar, 1998 - No. 3, May, 1998 ($2.50, limited series)

1-3						4.00

BABY SNOOTS (Also see March of Comics #359,371,396,401,419,431,443,450,462,474,485)
Gold Key: Aug, 1970 - No. 22, Nov, 1975

1	3	6	9	18	27	35
2-11	2	4	6	10	14	18
12-22: 22-Titled Snoots, the Forgetful Elefink	1	3	4	6	8	10

BACCHUS (Also see Eddie Campbell's ...)
Harrier Comics (New Wave): 1988 - No. 2, Aug, 1988 ($1.95, B&W)

1,2: Eddie Campbell-c/a/scripts.						2.50

BACHELOR FATHER (TV)
Dell Publishing Co.: No. 1332, 4-6/62 - No. 2, Sept.-Nov., 1962

Four Color 1332 (#1), 2-Written by Stanley	7	14	21	50	83	115

BACHELOR'S DIARY
Avon Periodicals: 1949 (15¢)

1(Scarce)-King Features panel cartoons & text-r; pin-up, girl wrestling photos; similar to Sideshow	55	110	165	344	572	800

BACKPACK MARVELS (B&W backpack-sized reprint collections)
Marvel Comics: Nov, 2000 ($6.95, B&W, digest-size)

Avengers 1 -r/Avengers #181-189; profile pages	7.00
Spider-Man 1-r/ASM #234-240	7.00
X-Men 1-r/Uncanny X-Men #167-173	7.00
X-Men 2-r/Uncanny X-Men #174-179; new painted-c by Greg Horn	7.00

BACK DOWN THE LINE
Eclipse Books: 1991 (Mature adults, 8-1/2 x 11", 52 pgs.)

nn (Soft-c, $8.95)-Bolton-c/a	9.00
nn (Limited Hard-c, $29.95)	30.00

BACKLASH (Also see The Kindred)
Image Comics (WildStorm Prod.): Nov,1994 - No. 32, May, 1997 ($1.95/$2.50)

1-Double-c; variant-double-c	3.00
2-7,9-32: 5-Intro Mindscape; 2 pinups. 19-Fire From Heaven Pt 2. 20-Fire From Heaven Pt 10. 31-WildC.A.T.S app.	2.50
8-($1.95, newsstand)-Wildstorm Rising Pt. 8	2.50
8-($2.50, direct market)-Wildstorm Rising Pt. 8	2.50
25-($3.95)-Double-size	4.00
...& Taboo's African Holiday (9/99, $5.95) Booth-s/a(p)	6.00

BACKLASH/SPIDER-MAN
Image Comics (WildStorm Productions): Aug, 1996 - No. 2, Sept, 1996 ($2.50, lim. series)

1,2: Pike (villain from WildC.A.T.S) & Venom app.	3.00

BACK TO THE FUTURE (Movie, TV cartoon)
Harvey Comics: Nov, 1991 - No. 4, June, 1992 ($1.25)

1-4: 1,2-Gil Kane-c; based on animated cartoon	3.00

BACK TO THE FUTURE: FORWARD TO THE FUTURE
Harvey Comics: Oct, 1992 - No. 3, Feb, 1993 ($1.50, limited series)

1-3	3.00

BAD BOY
Oni Press: Dec, 1997 ($4.95, one-shot)

1-Frank Miller-s/Simon Bisley-a/painted-c	5.00

BAD COMPANY
Quality Comics/Fleetway Quality #15 on: Aug, 1988 - No. 19?, 1990 ($1.50/$1.75, high quality paper)

1-19: 5,6-Guice-c	2.50

BADGE OF JUSTICE (Formerly Crime And Justice #21)
Charlton Comics: No. 22, 1/55 - No. 2, 4/55 - No. 4, 10/55

	GD 2.0	VG 4.0	FN 6.0	VF 8.0	VF/NM 9.0	NM- 9.2
22(#1)(1/55)	10	20	30	58	79	100
2-4	7	14	21	35	43	50

BADGER, THE
Capital Comics(#1-4)/First Comics: Dec, 1983 - No. 70, Apr, 1991; V2#1, Spring, 1991

1	5.00
2-70: 52-54-Tim Vigil-c/a	3.00
50-($3.95, 52 pgs.)	4.00
V2#1 (Spring, 1991, $4.95)	5.00

BADGER, THE
Image Comics: V3#78, May, 1997 - V3#88 ($2.95, B&W)

78-Cover lists #1, Baron-s	3.00
79/#2, 80/#3, 81(indicia lists #80)/#4,82-88/#5-11	3.00

BADGER GOES BERSERK
First Comics: Sept, 1989 - No. 4, Dec, 1989 ($1.95, lim. series, Baxter paper)

1-4: 2-Paul Chadwick-c/a(2pgs.)	3.00

BADGER: SHATTERED MIRROR
Dark Horse Comics: July, 1994 - No. Oct, 1994 ($2.50, limited series)

1-4	3.00

BADGER: ZEN POP FUNNY-ANIMAL VERSION
Dark Horse Comics: July, 1994 - No. 2, Aug, 1994 ($2.50, limited series)

1,2	3.00

BAD GIRLS
DC Comics: Oct, 2003 - No. 5, Feb, 2004 ($2.50, limited series)

1-5-Vance-s/Graves-a/Cook-c	2.50

BAD IDEAS
Image Comics: Apr, 2004 - No. 2, July, 2004 ($5.95, B&W, limited series)

1,2-Chinsang-s/Mahfood & Crosland-a	6.00
..., Vol. 1: Collected! (2005, $12.99) r/#1,2	13.00

BADLANDS
Vortex Comics: May, 1990 ($3.00, glossy stock, mature)

1-Chaykin-c	3.00

BADLANDS
Dark Horse Comics: July, 1991 - No. 6, Dec, 1991 ($2.25, B&W, limited series)

1-6: 1-John F. Kennedy-c; reprints Vortex Comics issue	2.50

BADMEN OF THE WEST
Avon Periodicals: 1951 (Giant) (132 pgs., painted-c)

	GD 2.0	VG 4.0	FN 6.0	VF 8.0	VF/NM 9.0	NM- 9.2
1-Contains rebound copies of Jesse James, King of the Bad Men of Deadwood, Badmen of Tombstone; other combinations possible. Issues with Kubert-a...	40	80	120	235	368	500

BADMEN OF THE WEST! (See A-1 Comics)
Magazine Enterprises: 1953 - No. 3, 1954

	GD 2.0	VG 4.0	FN 6.0	VF 8.0	VF/NM 9.0	NM- 9.2
1(A-1 100)-Meskin-a?	23	46	69	135	213	290
2(A-1 120), 3: 2-Larsen-a	15	30	45	85	130	175

BADMEN OF TOMBSTONE
Avon Periodicals: 1950

	GD 2.0	VG 4.0	FN 6.0	VF 8.0	VF/NM 9.0	NM- 9.2
nn	16	32	48	92	144	195

BAD PLANET
Image Comics (Raw Studios): Dec, 2005 - Present ($2.99)

1-3: 1-Thomas Jane & Steve Niles-s/Larosa & Bradstreet-a/c. 2-Wrightson-c. 3-3-D pages	3.00

BADROCK (Also see Youngblood)
Image Comics (Extreme Studios): Mar, 1995 - No. 2, Jan, 1996 ($1.75/$2.50)

1-Variant-c (3)	3.00
2-Liefeld-c/a & story; Savage Dragon app, flipbook w/Grifter/Badrock #2; variant-c exist	2.50
Annual 1(1995,$2.95)-Arthur Adams-c	
Annual 1 Commemorative ($9.95)-3,000 printed	10.00
.../Wolverine (6/96, $4.95, squarebound)-Sauron app; pin-ups; variant-c exists	5.00
.../Wolverine (6/96)-Special Comicon Edition	5.00

BADROCK AND COMPANY (Also see Youngblood)

Baffling Mysteries #5 © ACE

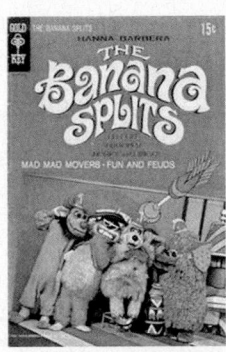

Banana Splits #1 © H-B

Barbie #45 © Mattel

	GD 2.0	VG 4.0	FN 6.0	VF 8.0	VF/NM 9.0	NM- 9.2

Image Comics (Extreme Studios): Sept, 1994 - No.6, Feb, 1995 ($2.50)

1-6 : 6-Indicia reads "October 1994"; story cont'd in Shadowhawk #17 ... 2.50

BAFFLING MYSTERIES (Formerly Indian Braves No. 1-4; Heroes of the Wild Frontier No. 26-on)
Periodical House (Ace Magazines): No. 5, Nov, 1951 - No. 26, Oct, 1955

	GD 2.0	VG 4.0	FN 6.0	VF 8.0	VF/NM 9.0	NM- 9.2
5	40	80	120	240	383	525
6-19,21-24: 8-Woodish-a by Cameron. 10-E.C. Crypt Keeper swipe on-c.						
24-Last pre-code issue	25	50	75	145	228	310
20-Classic-c	32	64	96	186	293	400
25-Reprints; surrealistic-c	19	38	57	109	172	235
26-Reprints	17	34	51	98	154	210

NOTE: *Cameron* a-8, 10, 16-18, 20-22. *Colan* a-5, 11, 25r/5. *Sekowsky* a-5, 6, 22. Bondage c-20, 23. Reprints in 18(1), 19(1), 24(3).

BALBO (See Master Comics #33 & Mighty Midget Comics)

BALDER THE BRAVE
Marvel Comics Group: Nov, 1985 - No. 4, 1986 (Limited series)

1-4: Simonson-c/a; character from Thor ... 3.00

BALLAD OF HALO JONES, THE
Quality Comics: Sept, 1987 - No. 12, Aug, 1988 ($1.25/$1.50)

1-12: Alan Moore scripts in all ... 2.50

BALL AND CHAIN
DC Comics (Homage): Nov, 1999 - No. 4, Feb, 2000 ($2.50, limited series)

1-4-Lobdell-s/Garza-a ... 2.50

BALLISTIC (Also See Cyberforce)
Image Comics (Top Cow Productions): Sept, 1995 - No. 3, Dec, 1995 ($2.50, limited series)

1-3: Wetworks app, Turner-c/a						3.00
... Action (5/96, $2.95) Pin-ups of Top Cow characters participating in outdoor sports						3.00
... Imagery (1/96, $2.50, anthology) Cyberforce app.						2.50
.../ Wolverine (2/97, $2.95) Devil's Reign pt. 4; Witchblade cameo (1 page)						4.00

BALOO & LITTLE BRITCHES (Disney)
Gold Key: Apr, 1968

	GD	VG	FN	VF	VF/NM	NM-
1-From the Jungle Book	4	8	12	23	34	45

BAMBI (Disney) (See Movie Classics, Movie Comics, and Walt Disney Showcase No. 31)
Dell Publishing Co.: No. 12, 1942; No. 30, 1943; No. 186, Apr, 1948; 1984

Four Color 12-Walt Disney's...	50	100	150	400	725	1050
Four Color 30-Bambi's Children (1943)	44	88	132	352	639	925
Four Color 186-Walt Disney's...; reprinted as Movie Classic Bambi #3 (1956)	16	32	48	118	209	300
1-(Whitman, 1984; 60¢)-r/Four Color #186 (3-pack)	2	4	6	9	13	16

BAMBI (Disney)
Grosset & Dunlap: 1942 (50¢, 7"x8-1/2", 32pg, hard-c w/dust jacket)

nn-Given away w/a copy of Thumper for a $2.00, 2-yr. subscription to WDC&S						
in 1942 (Xmas offer). Book only	22	44	66	126	198	270
w/dust jacket	40	80	120	235	368	500

BAMM BAMM & PEBBLES FLINTSTONE (TV)
Gold Key: Oct, 1964 (Hanna-Barbera)

1	9	18	27	60	100	140

BANANA SPLITS, THE (TV) (See Golden Comics Digest & March of Comics No. 364)
Gold Key: June, 1969 - No. 8, Oct, 1971 (Hanna-Barbera)

1-Photo-c on all	10	20	30	68	119	170
2-8	6	12	18	41	66	90

BANANA SUNDAY
Oni Press: July, 2005 - No. 4, Oct, 2005 ($2.99, B&W, limited series)

1-4-Root Nibot-s/Colleen Coover-a ... 3.00
TPB (3/06, $11.95) r/#1-4; sketch gallery ... 12.00

BAND WAGON (See Hanna-Barbera Band Wagon)

BANG-UP COMICS
Progressive Publishers: Dec, 1941 - No. 3, June, 1942

1-Cosmo Mann & Lady Fairplay begin; Buzz Balmer by Rick Yager in all (origin #1)						
	93	186	279	581	966	1350
2,3	45	90	135	275	450	625

BANISHED KNIGHTS (See Warlands)
Image Comics: Dec, 2001 - No. 4, June, 2002 ($2.95)

1-4-Two covers (Alvin Lee, Pat Lee) ... 3.00

BANNER COMICS (Becomes Captain Courageous No. 6)
Ace Magazines: No. 3, Sept, 1941 - No. 5, Jan, 1942

	GD 2.0	VG 4.0	FN 6.0	VF 8.0	VF/NM 9.0	NM- 9.2
3-Captain Courageous (1st app.) & Lone Warrior & Sidekick Dicky begin;						
Jim Mooney-c	107	214	321	669	1110	1550
4,5: 4-Flag-c	66	132	198	413	682	950

BARBARIANS, THE
Atlas Comics/Seaboard Periodicals: June, 1975

1-Origin, only app. Andrax; Iron Jaw app.; Marcos-a	2	4	6	8	10	12

BARBIE
Marvel Comics: Jan, 1991 - No. 63, Mar, 1996 ($1.00/$1.25/$1.50)

1-Polybagged w/doorknob hanger; Romita-c	2	4	6	9	12	15
2-49,51-62	1	2	3	5	7	9
50,63: 50-(Giant). 63-Last issue	2	4	6	8	10	12
... And Baby Sister Kelly (1995, 99¢-c, part of a Marvel 4-pack) scarce						
	2	4	6	11	16	20

BARBIE & KEN
Dell Publishing Co.: May-July, 1962 - No. 5, Nov-Jan, 1963-64

01-053-207(#1)-Based on Mattel toy dolls	36	72	108	270	498	725
2-4	29	58	87	216	388	560
5 (Rare)	30	60	90	223	407	590

BARBIE FASHION
Marvel Comics: Jan, 1991 - No. 53, May, 1995 ($1.00/$1.25/$1.50)

1-Polybagged w/Barbie Pink Card	2	4	6	9	12	15
2-49,51,52: 4-Contains preview to Sweet XVI. 14-Begin $1.25-c						
	1	2	3	5	7	9
50,53: 50-(Giant). 53-Last issue	2	4	6	8	10	12

BARBI TWINS, THE
Topps Comics: 1995 ($2.50/$5.00)

1-Razor app.						2.50
Swimsuit Art Calendar ($5.00)-art by Linsner, Bradstreet, Hughes; Julie Bell-c						5.00

BARB WIRE (See Comics' Greatest World)
Dark Horse Comics: Apr, 1994 - No. 9, Feb, 1995 ($2.00/$2.50)

1-9: 1-Foil logo						3.00
Trade paperback (1996, $8.95)-r/#2,3,5,6 w/Pamela Anderson bio						9.00

BARB WIRE: ACE OF SPADES
Dark Horse Comics: May, 1996 - No. 4, Sept, 1996 ($2.95, limited series)

1-4: Chris Warner-c/a(p)/scripts; Tim Bradstreet-c/a(i) in all ... 3.00

BARB WIRE COMICS MAGAZINE SPECIAL
Dark Horse Comics: May, 1996 ($3.50, B&W, magazine, one-shot)

nn-Adaptation of film; photo-c; poster insert. ... 3.50

BARB WIRE MOVIE SPECIAL
Dark Horse Comics: May, 1996 ($3.95, one-shot)

nn-Adaptation of film; photo-c; 1st app. new look ... 4.00

BARKER, THE (Also see National Comics #42)
Quality Comics Group/Comic Magazine: Autumn, 1946 - No. 15, Dec, 1949

1	23	46	69	130	205	280
2	14	28	42	76	108	140
3-10	10	20	30	58	79	100
11-14	9	18	27	47	61	75
15-Jack Cole-a(p)	9	18	27	50	65	80

NOTE: *Jack Cole* art in some issues.

BARNABY
Civil Service Publications Inc.: 1945 (25¢,102 pgs., digest size)

V1#1-r/Crocket Johnson strips from 1942	5	10	14	20	24	28

BARNEY AND BETTY RUBBLE (TV) (Flintstones' Neighbors)
Charlton Comics: Jan, 1973 - No. 23, Dec, 1976 (Hanna-Barbera)

1	4	8	12	24	37	50
2-11: 11(2/75)-1st Mike Zeck-a (illos)	3	6	9	14	20	25
12-23	2	4	6	10	14	18
Digest Annual (1972, B&W, 100 pgs.) (scarce)	3	6	9	20	30	40

BARNEY BAXTER (Also see Magic Comics)
David McKay/Dell Publishing Co./Argo: 1938 - No. 2, 1956

Feature Books 15(McKay-1938)	40	80	120	244	392	540
Four Color 20(1942)	25	50	75	186	333	480
1,2 (1956-Argo)	9	18	27	50	65	80

BARNEY BEAR ...
Spire Christian Comics (Fleming H. Revell Co.): 1977-1981

Barnyard Comics #8 © Nedor

Baseball Heroes © FAW

Batgirl #14 © DC

	GD 2.0	VG 4.0	FN 6.0	VF 8.0	VF/NM 9.0	NM- 9.2

...Home Plate nn-(1979, 49¢), ...Lost and Found nn-(1979, 49¢), Out of The Woods nn-(1980, 49¢), Sunday School Picnic nn-(1981, 69¢, The Swamp Gangl-(1977, 39¢)

	GD	VG	FN	VF	VF/NM	NM-
	1	3	4	6	8	11

BARNEY GOOGLE & SNUFFY SMITH
Dell Publishing Co./Gold Key: 1942 - 1943; April, 1964

Four Color 19(1942)	46	92	138	281	466	650
Four Color 40(1944)	21	42	63	156	278	400
Large Feature Comic 11(1943)	38	76	114	219	347	475
1(10113-404)-Gold Key (4/64)	4	8	12	26	41	55

BARNEY GOOGLE & SNUFFY SMITH
Toby Press: June, 1951 - No. 4, Feb, 1952 (Reprints)

1	14	28	42	76	108	140
2,3	8	16	24	44	57	70
4-Kurtzman-a "Pot Shot Pete", 5 pgs.; reprints John Wayne #5	12	24	36	69	97	125

BARNEY GOOGLE AND SNUFFY SMITH
Charlton Comics: Mar, 1970 - No. 6, Jan, 1971

1	3	6	9	16	23	30
2-6	2	4	6	10	14	18

BARNUM!
DC Comics (Vertigo): 2003; 2005 ($29.95, $19.95)

Hardcover (2003, $29.95, with dust jacket)-Chaykin & Tischman-s/Henrichon-a						30.00
Softcover (2005, $19.95)-Chaykin & Tischman-s/Henrichon-a						20.00

BARNYARD COMICS (Dizzy Duck No. 32 on)
Nedor/Polo Mag./Standard(Animated Cartoons): June, 1944 - No. 31, Sept, 1950; No. 10, 1957

1 (nn, 52 pgs.)-Funny animal	20	40	60	117	184	250
2 (52 pgs.)	12	24	36	69	97	125
3-5	9	18	27	52	69	85
6-12,16	8	16	24	44	57	70
13-15,17,21,23,26,27,29-All contain Frazetta text illos	10	20	30	54	72	90
18-20,22,24,25-All contain Frazetta-a & text illos	12	24	36	69	97	125
28,30,31	7	14	21	37	46	50
10 (1957)(Exist?)	4	7	10	14	17	20

BARRY M. GOLDWATER
Dell Publishing Co.: Mar, 1965 (Complete life story)

12-055-503-Photo-c	4	8	12	23	36	48

BARRY WINDSOR-SMITH: STORYTELLER
Dark Horse Comics: Oct, 1996 - No. 9, July, 1997 ($4.95, oversize)

1-9: 1-Intro Young Gods, Paradox Man & the Freebooters; Barry Smith-c/a/scripts						5.00
Preview						4.00

BAR SINISTER (Also see Shaman's Tears)
Acclaim Comics (Windjammer): Jun, 1995 - No. 4, Sept, 1995 ($2.50, lim. series)

1-4: Mike Grell-c/a/scripts						2.50

BARTMAN (Also see Simpson's Comics & Radioactive Man)
Bongo Comics: 1993 - No. 6, 1994 ($1.95/$2.25)

1-($2.95)-Foil-c; bound-in jumbo Bartman poster						6.00
2-6: 3-w/trading card						3.00

BART SIMPSON (See Simpsons Comics Presents Bart Simpson)

BASEBALL COMICS
Will Eisner Publications: Spring, 1949 (Reprinted later as a Spirit section)

1-Will Eisner-c/a	67	134	201	419	697	975

BASEBALL COMICS
Kitchen Sink Press: 1991 ($3.95, coated stock)

1-r/1949 ish. by Eisner; contains trading cards						6.00

BASEBALL HEROES
Fawcett Publications: 1952 (one-shot)

nn (Scarce)-Babe Ruth photo-c; baseball's Hall of Fame biographies	79	158	237	494	822	1150

BASEBALL'S GREATEST HEROES
Magnum Comics: Dec, 1991 - No. 2, May, 1992 ($1.75)

1-Mickey Mantle #1; photo-c; Sinnott-a(p)						5.00
2-Brooks Robinson #1; photo-c; Sinnott-a(i)						4.00

BASEBALL THRILLS

Ziff-Davis Publ. Co.: No. 10, Sum, 1951 - No. 3, Sum, 1952 (Saunders painted-c No.1,2)

10(#1)-Bob Feller, Musial, Newcombe & Boudreau stories						
	43	86	129	262	431	600
2-Powell-a(2)(Late Sum, '51); Feller, Berra & Mathewson stories						
	31	62	93	180	285	390
3-Kinstler-c/a; Joe DiMaggio story	31	62	93	180	285	390

BASEBALL THRILLS 3-D
The 3-D Zone: May, 1990 ($2.95, w/glasses)

1-New L.B. Cole-c; life stories of Ty Cobb & Ted Williams						6.00

BASICALLY STRANGE (Magazine)
John C. Comics (Archie Comics Group): Dec, 1982 ($1.95, B&W)

1-(21,000 printed; all but 1,000 destroyed; pgs. out of sequence)						
	3	6	9	16	23	30
1-Wood, Toth-a; Corben-c; reprints & new art	2	4	6	13	18	22

BASIC HISTORY OF AMERICA ILLUSTRATED
Pendulum Press: 1976 (B&W) (Soft-c $1.50; Hard-c $4.50)

07-1999-America Becomes a World Power 1890-1920. 07-2251-The Industrial Era 1865-1915. 07-226x-Before the Civil War 1830-1860. 07-2278-Americans Move Westward 1800-1850. 07-2286-The Civil War 1850-1876; Redondo-a. 07-2294-The Fight for Freedom 1750-1783. 07-2308-The New World 1500-1750. 07-2316-Problems of the New Nation 1800-1830. 07-2324-Roaring Twenties and the Great Depression 1920-1940. 07-2332-The United States Emerges 1783-1800. 07-2340-America Today 1945-1976. 07-2359-World War II 1940-1945

Softcover editions each	1	2	3	4	5	7
Hardcover editions each						14.00

BASIL (...the Royal Cat)
St. John Publishing Co.: Jan, 1953 - No. 4, Sept, 1953

1-Funny animal	7	14	21	37	46	55
2-4	5	10	15	22	26	30
I.W. Reprint 1	2	4	6	9	12	15

BASIL WOLVERTON'S FANTASTIC FABLES
Dark Horse Comics: Oct, 1993 - No. 2, Dec, 1993 ($2.50, B&W, limited series)

1,2-Wolverton-c/a(r)						6.00

BASIL WOLVERTON'S GATEWAY TO HORROR
Dark Horse Comics: June, 1988 ($1.75, B&W, one-shot)

1-Wolverton-r						6.00

BASIL WOLVERTON'S PLANET OF TERROR
Dark Horse Comics: Oct, 1987 ($1.75, B&W, one-shot)

1-Wolverton-r; Alan Moore-c						6.00

BASTARD SAMURAI
Image Comics: Apr, 2002 - No. 3, Aug, 2002 ($2.95)

1-3-Oeming & Gunter-s; Shannon-a/Oeming-i						3.00
TPB (2003, $12.95) r/#1-3; plus sketch pages and pin-ups						13.00

BATGIRL (See Batman: No Man's Land stories)
DC Comics: Apr, 2000 - No. 73, Apr, 2006 ($2.50)

1-Scott & Campanella-a						6.00
1-(2nd printing)						2.50
2-10: 8-Lady Shiva app.						4.50
11-24: 12-"Officer Down" x-over. 15-Joker-c/app. 24-Bruce Wayne: Murderer pt. 2.						4.00
25-($3.25) Batgirl vs Lady Shiva						3.50
26-29: 27- Bruce Wayne: Fugitive pt. 5; Noto-a. 29-B.W.:F. pt. 13						3.50
30-49,51-73: 30-32-Connor Hawke app. 39-Intro. Black Wind. 41-Superboy-c/app. 53-Robin (Spoiler) app. 54-Bagged with Sky Captain CD. 55-57-War Games. 63,64-Deathstroke app. 67-Birds of Prey app. 73-Lady Shiva origin; Sale-c						2.50
50-($3.25) Batgirl vs Batman						3.25
Annual 1 ('00, $3.50) Planet DC; intro. Aruna						3.50
...: A Knight Alone (2001, $12.95, TPB) r/#7-11,13,14						13.00
...: Death Wish (2003, $14.95, TPB) r/#17-20,22,23,25 & Secret Files and Origins #1						15.00
...: Destruction's Daughter (2006, $19.99, TPB) r/#65-73						20.00
...: Fists of Fury (2004, $14.95, TPB) r/#15,16,21,26-28						15.00
...: Kicking Assassins (2005, $14.99, TPB) r/#60-64						15.00
... Secret Files and Origins (8/02, $4.95) origin-s Noto-a; profile pages and pin-ups						5.00
...: Silent Running (2001, $12.95, TPB) r/#1-6						13.00

BATGIRL ADVENTURES (See Batman Adventures, The)
DC Comics: Feb, 1998 ($2.95, one-shot) (Based on animated series)

1-Harley Quinn and Poison Ivy app.; Timm-c						5.00

BATGIRL SPECIAL
DC Comics: 1988 ($1.50, one-shot, 52 pgs)

1-Kitson-a/Mignola-c	1	2	3	5	7	9

Batman #5 © DC

Batman #126 © DC

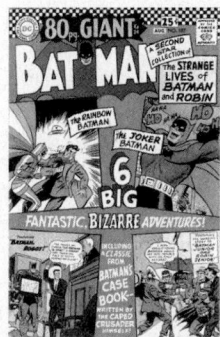

Batman #182 © DC

	GD 2.0	VG 4.0	FN 6.0	VF 8.0	VF/NM 9.0	NM- 9.2		GD 2.0	VG 4.0	FN 6.0	VF 8.0	VF/NM 9.0	NM- 9.2

BATGIRL: YEAR ONE
DC Comics: Feb, 2003 - No. 9, Oct, 2003 ($2.95, limited series)

1-9-Barbara Gordon becomes Batgirl; Killer Moth app.; Beatty & Dixon-s 3.00
TPB (2003, $17.95) r/#1-9 18.00

BAT LASH (See DC Special Series #16, Showcase #76, Weird Western Tales)
National Periodical Publications: Oct-Nov, 1968 - No. 7, Oct-Nov, 1969
(All 12¢ issues)

1-(10-11/68)-2nd app. Bat Lash 5 10 15 35 55 75
2-7 4 8 12 22 34 45

BATMAN (See All Star Batman & Robin, Anarky, Aurora [in Promo. Comics section], Azrael, The Best of DC #2, Blind Justice, The Brave & the Bold, Cosmic Odyssey, DC 100-Page Super Spec. #14,20, DC Special, DC Special Series, Detective, Dynamic Classics, 80-Page Giants, Gotham By Gaslight, Gotham Nights, Greatest Batman Stories Ever Told, Greatest Joker Stories Ever Told, Heroes Against Hunger, JLA,The Joker, Justice League of America, Justice League Int., Legends of the Dark Knight, Limited Coll. Ed., Man-Bat, Nightwing, Power Record Comics, Real Fact #5, Robin, Saga of Ra's Al Ghul, Shadow of the..., Star Spangled, Super Friends, 3-D Batman, Untold Legend of..., Wanted!... & World's Finest Comics)

BATMAN
National Per. Publ./Detective Comics/DC Comics: Spring, 1940 - Present
(#1-5 were quarterly)

1-Origin The Batman reprinted (2 pgs.) from Det. #33 w/splash from #34 by Bob Kane; see Detective #33 for 1st origin; 1st app. Joker (2 stories intended for 2 separate issues of Det. Comics which would have been 1st & 2nd app.); splash pg. to 2nd Joker story is similar to cover of Det. #40 (story intended for #40); 1st app. The Cat (Catwoman) (1st villainess in comics); has Batman story (w/Hugo Strange) without Robin originally planned for Det. #38; mentions location (Manhattan) where Batman lives (see Det. #31). This book was created entirely from the inventory of Det. Comics; 1st Batman/Robin pin-up on back-c; has text piece & photo of Bob Kane
  8200 16,400 24,600 57,400 121,200 185,000

1-Reprint, oversize 13-1/2x10". **WARNING:** This comic is an exact duplicate reprint of the original except for its size. DC published it in 1974 with a second cover titling it as a Famous First Edition. There have been many reported cases of the outer cover being removed and the interior sold as the original edition. The reprint with the outer cover removed is practically worthless. See Famous First Edition for value.

2-2nd app. The Joker; 2nd app. Catwoman (out of costume) in Joker story; 1st time called Catwoman (NOTE: A 15¢-c for Canadian distr. exists.)
  1385 2770 4155 10,400 18,700 27,000

3-3rd app Catwoman (1st in costume & 1st costumed villainess); 1st Puppet Master app.; classic Kane & Robinson-c 914 1828 2742 6400 11,200 16,000

4-3rd app. The Joker (see Det. #45 for 4th); 1st mention of Gotham City in a Batman comic (on newspaper)(Win/40) 714 1428 2142 5000 8750 12,500

5-1st app. the Batmobile with its bat-head front 520 1040 1560 3640 6370 9100

6,7: 7-Bullseye-c; Joker app. 446 892 1338 3122 5461 7800

8-Infinity-c by Fred Ray; Joker app. 376 752 1128 2444 4322 6200

9-10:9-1st Batman x-mas story; Burnley-c. 10-Catwoman story (gets new costume) 364 728 1092 2366 4183 6000

11-Classic Joker-c by Ray/Robinson (3rd Joker-c, 6-7/42); Joker & Penguin app. 743 1486 2229 5200 9100 13,000

12,15: 12-Joker app. 15-New costume Catwoman 300 600 900 1919 3310 4700

13-Jerry Siegel (Superman's co-creator) appears in a Batman story. 300 600 900 1931 3366 4800

14-2nd Penguin app.; Penguin app. (12-1/42-43) 300 600 900 1943 3422 4900

16-Intro/origin Alfred (4-5/43); cover is a reverse of #9 cover by Burnley; 1st small logo 520 1040 1560 3640 6370 9100

17,20: 17-Classic war-c; Penguin app. 20-1st Batmobile-c (12-1/43-44); Joker app. 255 510 765 1594 2647 3700

18-Hitler, Hirohito, Mussolini-c. 300 600 900 1931 3366 4800

19-Joker app. 204 408 612 1275 2113 2950

21,22,24,26,28,30: 21-1st skinny Alfred in Batman (2-3/44). 21,30-Penguin app. 22-1st Alfred solo-c/story (Alfred solo stories in 22-32,36); Catwoman & The Cavalier app. 28-Joker story 155 310 465 969 1610 2250

23-Joker-c/story; classic black-c 262 524 786 1638 2719 3800

25-Only Joker/Penguin team-up; 1st team-up between two major villains 241 482 723 1506 2503 3500

27-Classic Burnley Christmas-c; Penguin app. 207 414 621 1294 2147 3000

31,32,34,36,39: 32-Origin Robin retold; Joker app. 35-Catwoman story (in new costume w/o cat head mask). 36-Penguin app. 117 234 351 731 1216 1700

33-Christmas-c 134 268 402 838 1394 1950

37,40,44-Joker-c/stories 166 332 498 1038 1719 2400

38-Penguin-c/story 138 276 414 863 1432 2000

41,45,46: 41-1st Sci-fi cover/story in Batman; Penguin app.(6-7/47). 45-Christmas-c/story; Catwoman story. 46-Joker app. 86 172 258 538 894 1250

42-2nd Catwoman-c (1st in Batman)(8-9/47); Catwoman story also. 145 290 435 906 1503 2100

43-Penguin-c/story 121 242 363 756 1253 1750

47-1st detailed origin The Batman (6-7/48); 1st Bat-signal-c this title (see Detective #108); Batman tracks down his parent's killer and reveals i.d. to him 352 704 1056 2288 4044 5800

48-1000 Secrets of the Batcave; r-in #203; Penguin story 117 234 351 731 1216 1700

49-Joker-c/story; 1st app. Mad Hatter; 1st app. Vicki Vale 186 372 558 1163 1932 2700

50-Two-Face impostor app. 98 196 294 613 1019 1425

51,54,56,57,59,60: 57-Centerfold is a 1950 calendar; Joker app. 59-1st app. Deadshot; Batman in the future-c/story 83 166 249 519 860 1200

52,55-Joker-c/stories 117 234 351 731 1216 1700

53-Joker story 88 176 264 550 913 1275

58,61: 58-Penguin-c. 61-Origin Batman Plane II 93 186 279 581 966 1350

62-Origin Catwoman; Catwoman-c 134 268 402 838 1394 1950

63,80-Joker stories. 63-1st app. Killer Moth; flying saucer story(2-3/51) 79 158 237 494 822 1150

64,70-72,74-77,79: 70-Robot-c. 72-Last 52 pg. issue. 74-Used in **POP**, Pg. 90. 76-Penguin story. 79-Vicki Vale in "The Bride of Batman" 66 132 198 413 682 950

65,69-Catwoman-c/stories 93 186 279 581 966 1350

66,73-Joker-c/stories. 66-Pre-2nd Batman & Robin team try-out. 73-Vicki Vale story 97 194 291 606 1003 1400

67-Joker story 79 158 237 494 822 1150

68,81-Two-Face-c/stories 76 152 228 475 788 1100

78-(8-9/53)-Roh Kar, The Man Hunter from Mars story-the 1st lawman of Mars to come to Earth (green skinned) 81 162 243 506 841 1175

82,83,87-89: 89-Last pre-code issue 62 124 186 388 644 900

84-Catwoman-c/story; Two-Face app. 86 172 258 538 894 1250

85,86-Joker story. 86-Intro Batmarine (Batman's submarine) 64 128 192 400 663 925

90,91,93-96,98,99: 99-(4/56)-Last G.A. Penguin app. 53 106 159 329 545 760

92-1st app. Bat-Hound-c/story 83 166 249 519 860 1200

97-2nd app. Bat-Hound-c/story; Joker story 55 110 165 344 572 800

100-(6/56) 276 552 828 1725 2863 4000

101-(8/56)-Clark Kent x-over who protects Batman's i.d. (3rd story) 53 106 159 331 553 775

102-104,106-109: 103-1st S.A. issue; 3rd Bat-Hound-c/story 48 96 144 293 484 675

105-1st Batwoman in Batman (2nd anywhere) 66 132 198 413 682 950

110-Joker story 49 98 147 299 492 650

111-120: 112-1st app. Signalman (super villain). 113-1st app. Fatman; Batman meets his counterpart on Planet X w/a chest plate similar to S.A. Batman's design (yellow oval w/black design inside) 41 82 123 250 400 550

121- Origin/1st app. of Mr. Zero (Mr. Freeze) 53 106 159 331 553 775

122,124-126,128,130: 122,126-Batwoman-c/story. 124-2nd app. Signal Man. 128-Batwoman cameo. 130-Lex Luthor app. 32 64 96 186 293 400

123,127: 123-Joker story; Bat-Hound app. 127-(10/59)-Batman vs. Thor the Thunder God c/story; Joker story; Superman cameo 34 68 102 197 311 425

129-Origin Robin retold; bondage-c; Batwoman-c/story (reprinted in Batman Family #8) 28 56 114 219 347 475

131-135,137-139,141-143: 131-Intro 2nd Batman & Robin series (see #66; also in #135,145, 154,159,163). 133-1st Bat-Mite in Batman (3rd app. anywhere). 134-Origin The Dummy (not Vigilante's villain). 139-Intro 1st original Bat-Girl; only app. Signalman as the Blue Bowman. 141-2nd app. original Bat-Girl. 143-(10/61)-Last 10¢ issue 25 50 75 145 228 310

136-Joker-c/story 29 58 87 167 264 360

140-Batman story, Batwoman-c/s; Superman cameo 26 52 78 152 239 325

144-(12/61)-1st 12¢ issue; Joker story 17 34 51 126 223 320

145,148-Joker-c/stories 19 38 57 138 244 350

146,147,149,150 14 28 42 102 181 260

151-154,156-158,160-162,164-168,170: 152-Joker story. 156-Ant-Man/Robin team-up(6/63). 164-New Batmobile(6/64) new look & Mystery Analysts series begins 12 24 36 86 146 210

155-1st S.A. app. The Penguin (5/63) 30 60 90 220 398 575

159,163-Joker-c/stories. 159-Bat-Girl story 14 28 42 99 175 250

169-2nd SA Penguin app. 14 28 42 102 181 260

171-1st Riddler app.(5/65) since Dec. 1948 38 76 114 285 518 750

172-175,177,178,180,184 9 18 27 65 113 160

176-(80-Pg. Giant G-17); Joker-c/story; Penguin app. in strip-r; Catwoman reprint 11 22 33 79 140 200

179-2nd app. Silver Age Riddler 15 30 45 105 188 270

181-Batman & Robin poster insert; intro. Poison Ivy 18 36 54 134 237 340

182,187-(80 Pg. Giants G-24, G-30); Joker-c/stories 9 18 27 65 113 160

Batman #235 © DC

Batman #389 © DC

Batman #512 © DC

	GD 2.0	VG 4.0	FN 6.0	VF 8.0	VF/NM 9.0	NM- 9.2
183-2nd app. Poison Ivy	11	22	33	79	140	200
185-(80 Pg. Giant G-27)	9	18	27	64	110	155
186-Joker-c/story	9	18	27	64	110	155
188,191,192,194-196,199	7	14	21	47	76	105
189-1st S.A. app. Scarecrow; retells origin of G.A. Scarecrow from World's Finest #3(1st app.)	12	24	36	82	146	210
190-Penguin-c/app.	8	16	24	58	97	135
193-(80-Pg. Giant G-37)	9	18	27	60	100	140
197-4th S.A. Catwoman app. cont'd from Det. #369; 1st new Batgirl app. in Batman (5th anywhere)	9	18	27	65	113	160
198-(3/68) (80-Pg. Giant G-43); Joker-c/story-r/World's Finest #61; Catwoman-r/Det. #211; Penguin-r; origin-r/#47	9	18	27	63	107	150
200-(3/68)-Joker cameo; retells origin of Batman & Robin; 1st Neal Adams work this title (cover only)	11	22	33	79	140	200
201-Joker story	6	12	18	39	62	85
202,204-207,209-212: 210-Catwoman-c/app. 212-Last 12¢ issue	5	10	15	35	55	75
203-(80 Pg. Giant G-49); r/#48, 61, & Det. 185; Batcave Blueprints	7	14	21	47	76	105
208-(80 Pg. Giant G-55); New origin Batman by Gil Kane plus 3 G.A. Batman reprints w/Catwoman, Vicki Vale & Batwoman	7	14	21	47	76	105
213-(80-Pg. Giant G-61); 30th anniversary issue (7-8/69); origin Alfred (r/Batman #16), Joker(r/Det. #168), Clayface; new origin Robin with new facts	8	16	24	54	90	125
214-217: 214-Alfred given a new last name- "Pennyworth" (see Detective #96)	4	8	12	28	44	60
218-(80-Pg. Giant G-67)	6	12	18	41	66	90
219-Neal Adams-a	6	12	18	41	66	90
220,221,224-226,229-231	4	8	12	24	37	50
222-Beatles take-off; art lesson by Joe Kubert	5	10	15	35	55	75
223,228,233: 223,228-(80-Pg. Giants G-73,G-79). 233-G-85-(68 pgs., "64 pgs." on-c)	6	12	18	39	62	85
227-Neal Adams cover swipe of Detective #31	6	12	18	41	66	90
232-(6/71) N. Adams-a. Intro/1st app. Ra's al Ghul; origin Batman & Robin retold; last 15¢ issue (see Detective #411 (5/71) for Talia's debut)	14	28	42	99	175	250
234-(9/71)-1st modern app. of Harvey Dent/Two-Face; (see World's Finest #173 for Batman as Two-Face; only S.A. mention of character); N. Adams-a; 52 pg. issues begin; end #242	14	28	42	102	181	260
235,236,239-242: 239-XMas-c. 241-Reprint(#)	4	8	12	24	41	55
237-N. Adams-a. 1st Rutland Vermont - Bald Mountain Halloween x-over. G.A. Batman-r/Det. #37; 1st app. The Reaper; Wrightson/Ellison plots						
238-Also listed as DC 100 Page Super Spectacular #8; Batman, Legion, Aquaman-r; G.A. Atom, Sargon (r/Sensation #57), Plastic Man (r/Police #14) stories; Doom Patrol origin-r; N. Adams wraparound-c	10	20	30	70	123	175
(see DC 100 Pg. Super Spectacular #8 for price)						
243-245-Neal Adams-a	6	12	18	41	66	90
246-250,252,253: 246-Scarecrow app. 253-Shadow-c & app.	4	8	12	24	37	50
251-(9/73)-N. Adams-a; Joker-c/story	8	16	24	52	86	120
254,256-259,261-All 100 pg. editions; part-r: 254-(2/74)-Man-Bat-c & app. 256-Catwoman app. 257-Joker & Penguin app. 258-The Cavalier.-r. 259-Shadow-c/app.	6	12	18	37	59	80
255-(100 pgs.)-N. Adams-c/a; tells of Bruce Wayne's father who wore bat costume & fought crime (r/Det. #235); r/story Batman #22	7	14	21	45	73	100
260-Joker-c/story (100 pgs.)	7	14	21	45	73	100
262 (68pgs.)	4	8	12	24	37	50
263,264,266-285,287-290,292,293,295-299: 266-Catwoman back to old costume	2	4	6	10	14	18
265-Wrightson-a(i)	2	4	6	11	16	20
286,291,294: 294-Joker-c/stories	3	6	9	16	22	28
300-Double-size	3	6	9	16	23	30
301-(7/78)-310,312-315,317-320,325-331,333-352: 304-(44 pgs.). 306-3rd app. Black Spider. 308-Mr. Freeze app. 310-1st modern app. The Gentleman Ghost in Batman; Kubert-c. 312,314,346-Two-Face-c/stories. 313-2nd app. Calendar Man. 318-Intro Firebug. 319-2nd modern age app. The Gentleman Ghost; Kubert-c. 344-Poison Ivy app. 345-1st app. new Dr. Death. 345,346,351-Catwoman back-ups					9	12
306-308,311-320,323,324,326-(Whitman variants; low print run; none show issue # on cover)	4	8	12			18
311,316,322-324: 311-Batgirl-c/story; Batgirl reteams w/Batman. 316-Robin returns. 322-324-Catwoman (Selina Kyle) app. 322,323-Cat-Man cameos (1st in Batman, 1 panel each). 323-1st meeting Catwoman & Cat-Man. 324-1st full app. Cat-Man this title	3	6	9		12	15
321,353,359-Joker-c/stories	2	4	6	13	18	22

	GD 2.0	VG 4.0	FN 6.0	VF 8.0	VF/NM 9.0	NM- 9.2
332-Catwoman's 1st solo	2	4	6	10	14	18
354-356,358,360-365,369,370: 361-1st app Harvey Bullock	1	2	3	5	7	9
357-1st app. Jason Todd (3/83); see Det. #524; 1st brief app. Croc	2	4	6	9	13	16
366-Jason Todd 1st in Robin costume; Joker-c/story	2	4	6	11	16	20
367-Jason in red & green costume (not as Robin)	2	4	6	8	10	12
368-1st new Robin in costume (Jason Todd)	2	4	6	9	13	16
371-399,401-403: 371-Cat-Man-c/story; brief origin Cat-Man (cont'd in Det. #538). 386,387-Intro Black Mask (villain). 380-391-Catwoman app. 398-Catwoman & Two-Face app. 401-2nd app. Magpie (see Man of Steel #3 for 1st). 403-Joker cameo						6.00

NOTE: Issues 397-399, 401-403, 408-416, 421-425, 430-432 all have 2nd printings in 1989; some with up to 8 printings. Some are not identified as reprints but have newer ads copyrighted after cover dates. All reprints have different back-c ads. All reprints are scarcer than 1st prints and have same value to variant collectors.

	GD 2.0	VG 4.0	FN 6.0	VF 8.0	VF/NM 9.0	NM- 9.2
400 ($1.50, 68pgs.)-Dark Knight special; intro by Stephen King; Art Adams/Austin-a	3	6	9	16	23	30
404-Miller scripts begin (end 407); Year 1; 1st modern app. Catwoman (2/87)	3	6	9	15	21	26
405-407: 407-Year 1 ends (See Detective Comics #575-578 for Year 2)	2	4	6	11	16	20
408-410: New Origin Jason Todd (Robin)	2	4	6	11	16	20
411-416,421-425: 411-Two-face app. 412-Origin/1st app. Mime. 414-Starlin scripts begin, end #429. 416-Nightwing-c/story. 423-McFarlane-c						5.00
417-420: "Ten Nights of the Beast" storyline	2	4	6	8	10	12
426-($1.50, 52 pgs.)- "A Death In The Family" storyline begins, ends #429						
427- "A Death In The Family" part 2.	2	4	6	11	16	20
428-Death of Robin (Jason Todd)	2	4	6	9	12	15
429-Joker-c/story; Superman app.	2	4	6	11	16	20
430-432						3.00
433-435-Many Deaths of the Batman story by John Byrne-c/scripts						3.00
436-Year 3 begins (ends #439); origin original Robin retold by Nightwing (Dick Grayson); 1st app. Timothy Drake (8/89)						4.00
436-441: 436-2nd printing. 437-Origin Robin cont. 440,441: "A Lonely Place of Dying" Parts 1 & 3						3.00
442-1st app. Timothy Drake in Robin costume						4.00
443-456,458,459,462-464: 445-447-Batman goes to Russia. 448,449-The Penguin Affair Pts 1 & 3. 450-Origin Joker. 450,451-Joker-c/stories. 452-454-Dark Knight Dark City storyline; Riddler app. 455-Alan Grant scripts begin, ends #466, 470. 464-Last solo Batman story; free 16 pg. preview of Impact Comics line						3.00
457-Timothy Drake officially becomes Robin & dons new costume						5.00
457-Direct sale edition (has #000 in indicia)						5.00
460,461,465-487: 460,461-Two part Catwoman story. 465-Robin returns to action with Batman. 470-War of the Gods x-over. 475-1st app. Renee Montoya. 475,476-Return of Scarface.						3.00
488-Cont'd from Batman: Sword of Azrael #4; Azrael-c & app.	1	2	3	5	6	8
489-Newstand ed. w/app. Azrael in Bat-costume						5.00
490-Riddler-c/story; Azrael & Bane app.						6.00
491,492: 491-Knightfall lead-in; Joker-c/story; Azrael & Bane app.; Kelley Jones-c begin. 492-Knightfall part 1; Bane app.						4.00
492-Platinum edition (promo copy)						10.00
493-496,498: 493-Knightfall Pt. 3. 494-Knightfall Pt. 5; Joker-c & app. 495-Knightfall Pt. 7; brief Bane & Joker apps. 496-Knightfall Pt. 9, Joker-c/story; Bane cameo						3.00
497-(Late 7/93)-Knightfall Pt. 11; Bane breaks Batman's back; B&W outer-c; Aparo-a(p); Giordano-a(i)						5.00
497-499: 497-2nd printing. 497-Newsstand edition w/o outer cover. 498-Knightfall part 15; Bane & Catwoman-c & app. (see Showcase 93 #7 & 8) 499-Knightfall Pt. 17; Bane app.						3.00
500-($2.50, 68 pgs.)-Knightfall Pt. 19; Azrael in new Bat-costume; Bane-c/story						3.00
500-($3.95, 68 pgs.)-Collector's Edition w/die-cut double-c w/foil by Joe Quesada & 2 bound-in post cards						5.00
501-508,510,511: 501-Begin $1.50-c. 507-508 Knightquest. 503,504-Catwoman app. 507-Ballistic app.; Jim Balent-a(p). 510-KnightsEnd Pt. 7. 511-(9/94)-Zero Hour; Batgirl-c/story						2.50
509-($2.50, 52 pgs.)-KnightsEnd Pt. 1						3.00
512-514,516-518: 512-(11/94)-Dick Grayson assumes Batman role						2.50
515-Special Ed.($2.50)-Kelley Jones-a begins; all black embossed-c; Troika Pt. 1						3.00
515-Regular Edition						2.50
519-534,536-549: 519-Begin $1.95-c. 521-Return of Alfred. 522-Swamp Thing app. 525-Mr. Freeze app. 527,528-Two Face app. 529-Contagion Pt. 6. 530-532-Deadman app. 533-Legacy prelude. 534-Legacy Pt. 5. 536-Final Night x-over; Man-Bat/c/app. 540,541-Spectre-c-app. 544-546-Joker & The Demon. 548,549-Penguin-c/app.						2.50
530-532 ($2.50)-Enhanced edition; glow-in-the-dark-c.						3.00
535-(10/96, $2.95)-1st app. The Ogre						3.00

Batman #605 © DC

Batman #641 © DC

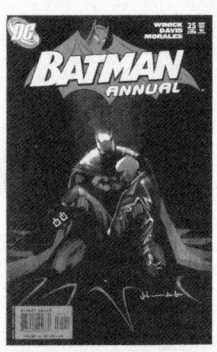

Batman Annual #25 © DC

	GD	VG	FN	VF	VF/NM	NM-		GD	VG	FN	VF	VF/NM	NM-
	2.0	4.0	6.0	8.0	9.0	9.2		2.0	4.0	6.0	8.0	9.0	9.2

535-(10/96, $3.95)-1st app. The Ogre; variant, cardboard, foldout-c ... 4.00
550-($3.50)-Collector's Ed.; includes 4 collector cards; intro. Chase, return of Clayface;
Kelley Jones-c 3.50
550-($2.95)-Standard Ed.; Williams & Gray-c 3.00
551,552,554-562: 551,552-Ragman c/app. 554-Cataclysm pt. 12. .... 2.50
553-Cataclysm pt.3 .... 4.00
563-No Man's Land; Joker-c by Campbell; Bob Gale-s 5.00
564-574: 569-New Batgirl-c/app. 572-Joker and Harley app. 2.50
575-579: 575-New look Batman begins; McDaniel-a 2.50
580-598: 580-Begin $2.25-c. 587-Gordon shot. 591,592-Deadshot-c/app. 2.50
599-Bruce Wayne: Murderer pt. 7 .... 2.50
600-($3.95) Bruce Wayne: Fugitive pt. 1; back-up homage stories in '50s, 60's, & 70s styles;
by Aragonés, Gaudiano, Shanower and others 5.00
600-(2nd printing) 4.00
601-604, 606,607: 601,603-Bruce Wayne: Fugitive pt.3,13. 606,607-Deadshot-c/app. ... 2.50
605-($2.95) Conclusion to Bruce Wayne: Fugitive x-over; Noto-c 3.00
608-(12/02) Jim Lee-a/c & Jeph Loeb-s begin; Poison Ivy & Catwoman app. 8.00
608-2nd printing; has different cover with Batman standing on gargoyle 12.00
608-Special Edition; has different cover; 200 printed; used for promotional purposes
(a CGC certified 9.2 copy sold for $700, and a CGC certified 9.8 copy sold for $2,100)
609-Huntress app. 9.00
610,611: 610-Killer Croc-c/app.; Batman & Catwoman kiss 8.00
612-Batman vs. Superman; 1st printing with full color cover 9.00
612-2nd printing with B&W sketch cover 15.00
613,614: 614-Joker-c/app. 7.00
615-617: 615-Reveals ID to Catwoman. 616-Ra's al Ghul app. 617-Scarecrow app. 5.00
618- Batman vs. "Jason Todd" 4.00
619-Newsstand cover; Hush story concludes; Riddler app. 5.00
619-Two variant tri-fold covers; one Heroes group, one Villains group 5.00
619-2nd printing with Riddler chess cover 5.00
620-Broken City pt. 1; Azzarello-s/Risso-a/c begin; Killer Croc app. 3.00
621-633: 621-625-Azzarello-s/Risso-a/c. 626-630-Winick-s/Nguyen-a/Wagner-c; Penguin &
Scarecrow app. 631-633-War Games. 633-Conclusion to War Games x-over 3.00
634-637-Winick-s/Nguyen-a/Wagner-c; Red Hood app. 637-Amazo app. 638-Red Hood
unmasked as Jason Todd 2.50
639-650: 640-Superman app. 641-Begin $2.50-c. 643,644-War Crimes; Joker app.
650-Infinite Crisis; Joker and Jason Todd app. 2.50
651-654-One Year Later; Bianchi-a. 3.00
655-Begin Grant Morrison-s/Andy Kubert-a; Kubert-c w/red background 5.00
655-Variant cover by Adam Kubert, brown-toned image 15.00
656-665: 656-Intro. Damien, son of Talia and Batman (see Batman: Son of the Demon).
657-Damien in Robin costume. 659-662-Mandrake-a. 663-Van Fleet-a. 664-Bane app. .. 3.00
666-668: 666-Future story of adult Damien; Kubert-a. 667,668-Williams III-a 3.00
#0 (10/94)-Zero Hour issue released between #511 & #512; Origin retold 2.50
#1,000,000 (11/98) 853rd Century x-over 2.50

Annual 1 (8-10/61)-Swan-c	55	110	165	468	872	1275
Annual 2	27	54	81	203	364	525
Annual 3 (Summer, '62)-Joker-c/story	28	56	84	227	381	535
Annual 4,5	14	28	42	99	175	250
Annual 6,7 (7/64, 25¢, 80 pgs.)	11	22	33	79	140	200
Annual V5#8 (1982)-Painted-c	1	2	3	5	6	8

Annual 9,10,12: 9(7/85). 10(1986). 12(1988, $1.50) 6.00

Annual 11 (1987, $1.25)-Penguin-c/story; Moore-s	1	2	3	5	6	8

Annual 13 (1989, $1.75, 68 pgs.)-Gives history of Bruce Wayne, Dick Grayson, Jason Todd,
Alfred, Comm. Gordon, Barbara Gordon (Batgirl) & Vicki Vale; Morrow-i 5.00
Annual 14-17 ('90-'93, 68 pgs.)-14-Origin Two-Face. 15-Armageddon 2001 x-over; Joker app.
15 (2nd printing). 16-Joker-c/s; Kieth'-c. 17 (1993, $2.50, 68 pgs.)-Azrael in Bat-costume;
intro Ballistic 3.00
Annual 18 (1994, $2.95) 3.00
Annual 19 (1995, $3.95)-Year One story; retells Scarecrow's origin 4.00
Annual 20 (1996, $2.95)-Legends of the Dead Earth story; Giarrano-a 3.00
Annual 21 (1997, $3.95)-Pulp Horror story 4.00
Annual 22,23 ('98, '99, $2.95)-22-Ghosts; Wrightson-c. 23-JLApe; Art Adams-c 3.00
Annual 24 ('00, $3.50)-Planet DC; intro. The Boggart; Aparo-a 3.50
Annual 25 ('06, $4.99) Infinite Crisis-revised story of Jason Todd; unused Aparo page .. 6.00
Annual 26 ('07, $3.99) Origin of Ra's al Ghul; Damien app. 3.00
NOTE: Art Adams a-400p. Neal Adams c-200, 203, 210, 217, 219-222, 224-227, 229, 230, 232, 234, 236-241, 243-
246, 251, 255, Annual 14. Aparo a-414-420, 426-435, 440-448, 450, 451, 480-483, 486-491, 494-500; c-414-416,
481, 482, 463i, 466, 467i. Bolland a-400; c-445-447. Burnley a-10, 12-18, 20, 22, 25, 27; c-9, 15, 16, 27, 28p, 40p,
42p. Byrne c-401, 433-435, 533-535, Annual 11. Travis Charest c-488-490p. Colan a-340p, 343-345p, 348-351p,
373p, 383p; c-343p, 345p, 350p. J. Cole a-239r. Cowan a-Annual 10p. Golden a-295p, 303p, 484, 485. Alan Grant
scripts-455-466, 470, 474-476, 479, 480, Annual 16(part). Grell a-287, 288p, 289p, 290; c-287-290.
Infantino/Anderson a-167, 173, 175, 181, 186, 191, 192, 194, 195, 198, 199. Infantino/Giella a-190. Kelley Jones
a-513-519, 521-525, 527; c-491-499, 500(newsstand), 501-510, 513. Kaluta c-242, 248, 253, Annual 12. G.
Kane/Anderson a-178-180. Bob Kane a-1, 2, 5; c-1-5, 7, 17. G. Kane a-(r)-254, 255, 259, 261, 353i. Kubert a-
238r, 400; c-310, 319p, 327, 328, 344. McFarlane c-423. Mignola c-426-429, 452-454, Annual 18. Moldoff c-101-

140. Moldoff/Giella a-164-175, 177-181, 183, 184, 186. Moldoff/Greene a-169, 172-174, 177-179, 181, 184.
Mooney a-255r. Morrow a-Annual 13i. Newton a-305, 306, 328p, 331p, 332p, 337p, 338p, 346p, 352-357p, 360-
372p, 374-378p; c-374p, 378p. Nino a-Annual 9. Irv Novick c-201, 202. Perez a-400; c-436-442. Fred Ray c-8, 10;
w/Robinson-11. Robinson/Roussos a-12-17, 20, 22, 24, 25, 27, 28, 31, 33, 37. Robinson a-12, 14, 18, 22-32,34,
36, 37, 255r, 260r, 261r; c-6, 10, 12-14, 18, 21, 24, 26, 30, 37, 39. Simonson a-300p, 312p, 321p; c-300p, 312p,
366, 413i. P. Smith a-Annual 9. Dick Sprang c-19, 20, 22, 23, 25, 29, 31-36, 38, 51, 55, 66, 73, 76. Starlin c/a-402.
Staton a-334. Sutton a-400. Wrightson a-265i, 400; c-320r. Bat-Hound app. in 92, 97, 103, 123, 125, 133, 156,
158. Bat-Mite app. in 133, 136, 144, 146, 158, 161. Batwoman app. in 105, 116, 122, 125, 128, 129, 131, 133, 139,
140, 141, 144, 145, 150, 151, 153, 154, 157, 159, 162, 163. Zeck c-417-420. Catwoman back-ups in 332, 345, 346,
348-351. Joker app. in 1, 2, 4, 5, 7-9, 11-13, 19, 20, 23, 25, 28, 32 & many more. Robin solo back-up stories in 337-
339, 341-343.

BATMAN (Hardcover books and trade paperbacks)
...: ABSOLUTION (2002, $24.95)-Hard-c.; DeMatteis-s/Ashmore painted-a 25.00
...: ABSOLUTION (2003, $17.95)-Soft-c.; DeMatteis-s/Ashmore painted-a 18.00
.... A LONELY PLACE OF DYING (1990, $3.95, 132 pgs.)-r/Batman #440-442 & New Titans
#60,61; Perez-c 4.00
...: ANARKY TPB (1999, $12.95) r/early appearances 13.00
...AND DRACULA: RED RAIN nn (1991, $24.95)-Hard-c.; Elseworlds storyline 32.00
...AND DRACULA: RED RAIN (1992, $9.95)-SC 12.00
ARKHAM ASYLUM Hard-c; Morrison-s/McKean-a (1989, $24.95) 30.00
ARKHAM ASYLUM Soft-c ($14.95) 15.00
ARKHAM ASYLUM 15TH ANNIVERSARY EDITION Hard-c (2004, $29.95) reprint with
Morrison's script and annotations, original page layouts; Karen Berger afterword ... 30.00
ARKHAM ASYLUM 15TH ANNIVERSARY EDITION Soft-c (2005, $17.99) 18.00
...: AS THE CROW FLIES-(2004, $12.95) r/#626-630; Nguyen sketch pages 13.00
BIRTH OF THE DEMON Hard-c (1992, $24.95)-Origin of Ra's al Ghul 25.00
BIRTH OF THE DEMON Soft-c (1993, $12.95) 13.00
BLIND JUSTICE nn (1992, $7.50)-r/Det. #598-600 .... 7.50
BLOODSTORM (1994, $24.95,HC) Kelley Jones-c/a 28.00
BRIDE OF THE DEMON Hard-c (1990, $19.95) 20.00
BRIDE OF THE DEMON Soft-c ($12.95) 13.00
....: BROKEN CITY HC-(2004, $24.95) r/#620-625; new Johnson-c; intro by Schreck ... 25.00
...: BROKEN CITY SC-(2004, $14.99) r/#620-625; new Johnson-c; intro by Schreck 15.00
...: BRUCE WAYNE: FUGITIVE Vol. 1 ('02, $12.95)-r/ story arc 13.00
...: BRUCE WAYNE: FUGITIVE Vol. 2 ('03, $12.95)-r/ story arc 13.00
...: BRUCE WAYNE: FUGITIVE Vol. 3 ('03, $12.95)-r/ story arc 13.00
...: BRUCE WAYNE-MURDERER? ('02, $19.95)-r/ story arc 20.00
...: CASTLE OF THE BAT ($5.95)-Elseworlds story 6.00
...: CATACLYSM ('99, $17.95)-r/ story arc 18.00
....: CHILD OF DREAMS (2003, $24.95, B&W, HC) Reprint of Japanese manga with Kia
Asamiya-s/a/c; English adaptation by Max Allan Collins; Asamiya interview 25.00
...: CHILD OF DREAMS (2003, $19.95, B&W, SC) 20.00
...CHRONICLES VOL. 1 (2005, $14.99)-r/apps. in Detective Comics #27-38; Batman #1 .. 15.00
...CHRONICLES VOL. 2 (2006, $14.99)-r/apps. in Detective Comics #39-45 and NY World's
Fair 1940; Batman #2,3 .... 15.00
...CHRONICLES VOL. 3 (2007, $14.99)-r/apps. in Detective Comics #46-50 and World's Best
Comics #1; Batman #4,5 .... 15.00
...: CITY OF CRIME (2006, $19.99) r/Detective Comics #800-808,811-814; Lapham-s .. 20.00
....: COLLECTED LEGENDS OF THE DARK KNIGHT nn (1994, $12.95)-r/Legends of the
Dark Knight #32-34,38,42,43 .... 13.00
...: CRIMSON MIST (1999, $24.95,HC)-Vampire Batman Elseworlds story
Doug Moench-s/Kelley Jones-c/a 25.00
...: CRIMSON MIST (2001, $14.95,SC) 15.00
...: DARK JOKER-THE WILD (1993, $24.95,HC)-Elseworlds story; Moench-s/Jones-c/a 25.00
...: DARK JOKER-THE WILD (1993, $9.95,SC) 10.00
...DARK KNIGHT DYNASTY nn (1997, $24.95)-Hard-c.; 3 Elseworlds stories; Barr-s/
S. Hampton painted-a, Gary Frank, McDaniel-a(p) 25.00
...DARK KNIGHT DYNASTY Softcover (2004, $14.95) Hampton-c 15.00
...DEADMAN: DEATH AND GLORY nn (1996, $24.95)-Hard-c.; Robinson-s/ Estes-c/a .. 25.00
...DEADMAN: DEATH AND GLORY (12.95)-SC 13.00
DEATH IN THE FAMILY (1988, $3.95, trade paperback)-r/Batman #426-429 by Aparo .. 5.00
DEATH IN THE FAMILY: (2nd - 5th printings) 4.00
...: DETECTIVE (2007, $14.99, SC)-r/Detective Comics #821-826 .... 15.00
....: DETECTIVE #27 HC (2003, $19.95)-Elseworlds; Uslan-s/Snejbjerg-a 20.00
...: DETECTIVE #27 SC (2004, $12.95)-Elseworlds; Uslan-s/Snejbjerg-a 13.00
DIGITAL JUSTICE nn (1990, $24.95, Hard-c.)-Computer generated art 25.00
...:EVOLUTION (2001, $12.95, SC)-r/Detective Comics #743-750 .... 13.00
...: FACES (1995, $9.95, TPB) 10.00
...: FACE THE FACE (2006, $14.99, TPB)-r/Batman #651-654 & Detective #817-820 .... 15.00
...: FORTUNATE SON HC (1999, $24.95) Gene Ha-a 25.00
...: FORTUNATE SON SC (2000, $14.95) Gene Ha-a 15.00
FOUR OF A KIND TPB (1998, $14.95)-r/1995 Year One Annuals featuring Poison Ivy, Riddler,
Scarecrow, & Man-Bat 15.00
...: GOTHAM BY GASLIGHT (2006, $12.99, TPB) r/Gotham By Gaslight & Master of the
Future one-shots; Elseworlds Batman vs. Jack the Ripper 13.00
...GOTHIC (1992, $12.95, TPB)-r/Legends of the Dark Knight #6-10 .... 13.00

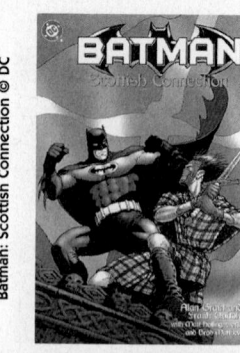

	GD 2.0	VG 4.0	FN 6.0	VF 8.0	VF/NM 9.0	NM- 9.2
...: HARVEST BREED-(2000, $24.95) George Pratt-s/painted-a						25.00
...: HARVEST BREED-(2003, $17.95) George Pratt-s/painted-a						18.00
...: HAUNTED KNIGHT-(1997, $12.95) r/ Halloween specials						13.00
...: HONG KONG HC (2003, $24.95, with dustjacket) Doug Moench-s/Tony Wong-a						25.00
...: HONG KONG SC (2004, $17.95) Doug Moench-s/Tony Wong-a						18.00
...: HUSH DOUBLE FEATURE-(2003, $3.95) r/#608,609(1st 2 Jim Lee-a issues)						4.00
...: HUSH VOLUME 1 HC-(2003, $19.95) r/#608-612; & new 2 pg. origin w/Lee-a						20.00
...: HUSH VOLUME 1 SC-(2004, $12.95) r/#608-612; includes CD of DC GN art						13.00
...: HUSH VOLUME 2 HC-(2003, $19.95) r/#613-619; Lee intro & sketchpages						20.00
...: HUSH VOLUME 2 SC-(2004, $12.95) r/#613-619; Lee intro & sketchpages						13.00
...: ILLUSTRATED BY NEAL ADAMS VOLUME 1 HC-(2003, $49.95) r/Batman, Brave and the Bold, and Detective Comics stories and covers						50.00
...: ILLUSTRATED BY NEAL ADAMS VOLUME 2 HC-(2004, $49.95) r/Adams' Batman art from 1969-71; intro. by Dick Giordano						50.00
... IN THE FORTIES TPB ($19.95) Intro. by Bill Schelly						20.00
... IN THE FIFTIES TPB ($19.95) Intro. by Michael Uslan						20.00
... IN THE SIXTIES TPB ($19.95) Intro. by Adam West						20.00
... IN THE SEVENTIES TPB ($19.95) Intro. by Dennis O'Neil						20.00
... IN THE EIGHTIES TPB ($19.95) Intro. by John Wells						20.00
...: JUDGE DREDD FILES (2004, $14.95) reprints cross-overs						15.00
... LEGACY-(1996,17.95) reprints Legacy						18.00
...: THE MANY DEATHS OF THE BATMAN (1992, $3.95, 84 pgs.)-r/Batman #433-435 w/new Byrne-c						4.00
...: THE MOVIES (1997, $19.95)-r/movie adaptations of Batman, Batman Returns, Batman Forever, Batman and Robin						20.00
...: NINE LIVES HC (2002, $24.95, sideways format) Motter-s/Lark-a						25.00
...: NINE LIVES SC (2003, $17.95, sideways format) Motter-s/Lark-a						18.00
...: OFFICER DOWN (2001, $12.95)-r/Commissioner shot x-over; Talon-c						13.00
...: PREY (1992, $12.95) Gulacy/Austin-a						13.00
...: PRODIGAL (1997, $14.95)-Gulacy/Austin-a						15.00
... SCARECROW TALES (2005, $19.99, TPB) r/Scarecrow stories & pin-ups from World's Finest #3 to present						20.00
SHAMAN (1993, $12.95)-r/Legends/D.K. #1-5						13.00
...: SNOW (2007, $14.99, TPB)-r/Legends of the Dark Knight #192-196; Fisher-a						15.00
... SON OF THE DEMON Hard-c (9/87, $14.95) (see Batman #655-658)						30.00
... SON OF THE DEMON limited signed & numbered Hard-c (1,700)						45.00
... SON OF THE DEMON Soft-c ($8.95)						10.00
...: SON OF THE DEMON Soft-c (1989, $9.95, 2nd printing - 5th printing)						10.00
...: STRANGE APPARITIONS ($12.95) r/'77-'78 Englehart/Rogers stories from Detective #469-479; also Simonson-a						13.00
...: TALES OF THE DEMON (1991, $17.95, 212 pgs.)-Intro by Sam Hamm; reprints by Neal Adams(3) & Golden; contains Saga of Ra's al Ghul #1						18.00
...: TEN NIGHTS OF THE BEAST (1994, $5.95)-r/Batman #417-420						6.00
...: TERROR (2003, $12.95, TPB)-r/Legends of the Dark Knight #137-141; Gulacy-c						13.00
...: THE CHALICE (HC, '99, $24.95) Van Fleet painted-a						25.00
...: THE CHALICE (SC, '00, $14.95) Van Fleet painted-a						15.00
...: THE GREATEST STORIES EVER TOLD (2005, $19.99, TPB) Les Daniels intro.						20.00
...: THE GREATEST STORIES EVER TOLD VOLUME TWO (2007, $19.99, TPB)						20.00
...: THE LAST ANGEL (1994, $12.95, TPB) Lustbader-s						13.00
...: THE RING, THE ARROW AND THE BAT (2003, $19.95, TPB) r/Legends of the DCU #7-9 & Batman: Legends of the Dark Knight #127-131; Green Lantern & Green Arrow app.						20.00
...: THRILLKILLER (1998, $12.95, TPB)-r/series & Thrillkiller '62						13.00
...: UNDER THE HOOD (2006, $9.99, TPB)-r/Batman #635-641						10.00
...: UNDER THE HOOD Vol. 2 (2006, $9.99, TPB)-r/Batman #645-650 & Annual #25						10.00
...: VENOM (1993, $4.95, TPB)-r/Legends of the Dark Knight #16-20; embossed-c						10.00
...: WAR CRIMES (2006, $12.99, TPB) r/x-over; James Jean-c						13.00
...: WAR DRUMS (2004, $17.95) r/Detective #790-796 & Robin #126-128						18.00
...: WAR GAMES ACT 1,2,3 (2005, $14.95/$14.99, TPB) r/x-over; James Jean-c; each..						15.00
... YEAR ONE Hard-c (1988, $12.95) r/Batman #404-407						18.00
YEAR ONE (1988, $9.95, TPB) r/Batman #404-407 by Miller; intro by Miller						10.00
YEAR ONE (TPB, 2nd & 3rd printings)						10.00
YEAR ONE Deluxe HC (2005, $19.99, die-cut d.j.) new intro. by Miller and developmental material from Mazzucchelli; script pages and sketches						20.00
YEAR ONE (Deluxe) SC (2007, $14.99) r/story plus bonus material from 2005 HC						15.00
YEAR TWO (TPB, 2nd & 3rd printings)-r/Det. 575-578 by McFarlane; wraparound-c						10.00
BATMAN (one-shots)						
... ABDUCTION (1998, $5.95)						6.00
... ALLIES SECRET FILES AND ORIGINS 2005 (8/05, $4.99) stories/pin-ups by various						5.00
... & ROBIN (1997, $5.95)-Movie adaptation						6.00
... ARKHAM ASYLUM - TALES OF MADNESS (5/98, $2.95) Cataclysm x-over pt. 16						3.00
... : BANE (1997, $4.95)-Dixon-s/Burchett-a; Stelfreeze-c; cover art interlocks w/Batman:(Batgirl, Mr. Freeze, Poison Ivy)						5.00
... : BATGIRL (1997, $4.95)-Puckett-s/Haley,Kesel-a; Stelfreeze-c; cover art interlocks w/Batman:(Bane, Mr. Freeze, Poison Ivy)						5.00
... : BATGIRL (6/98, $1.95)-Girlfrenzy; Balent-a						2.50
... : BLACKGATE (1/97, $3.95) Dixon-s						4.00
... : BLACKGATE - ISLE OF MEN (4/98, $2.95) Cataclysm x-over pt. 8; Moench-s/Aparo-a						3.00
... : BOOK OF SHADOWS, THE (1999, $5.95)						6.00
BROTHERHOOD OF THE BAT (1995, $5.95)-Elseworlds-s						6.00
... BULLOCK'S LAW (8/99, $4.95) Dixon-s						5.00
.../CAPTAIN AMERICA (1996, $5.95, DC/Marvel) Elseworlds story; Byrne-c/s/a						6.00
... : CATWOMAN DEFIANT nn (1992, $4.95, prestige format)-Milligan scripts; cover art interlocks w/Batman: Penguin Triumphant; special foil logo						5.00
... /DANGER GIRL (2/05, $4.95)-Leinil Yu-a/c; Joker, Harley Quinn & Catwoman app.						5.00
.../DAREDEVIL (2000, $5.95)-Barreto-a						6.00
... : DARK ALLEGIANCES (1996, $5.95)-Elseworlds story, Chaykin-c/a						6.00
... : DARK KNIGHT GALLERY (1/96, $3.50)-Pin-ups by Pratt, Balent, & others						3.50
...:DAY OF JUDGMENT (11/99, $3.95)						4.00
...:DEATH OF INNOCENTS (12/96, $3.95)-O'Neil-s/ Staton-a(p)						4.00
.../DEMON (1996, $4.95)-Alan Grant scripts						5.00
... /DEMON: A TRAGEDY (2000, $5.95)-Grant-s/Murray painted-a						6.00
... :D.O.A. (1999, $6.95)-Bob Hall-s/a						7.00
...:DREAMLAND (2000, $5.95)-Grant-s/Breyfogle-a						6.00
... : EGO (2000, $6.95)-Darwyn Cooke-s/a						7.00
... 80-PAGE GIANT (8/98, $4.95) Stelfreeze-c						6.00
... 80-PAGE GIANT 2 (10/99, $4.95) Luck of the Draw						5.00
... 80-PAGE GIANT 3 (7/00, $5.95) Calendar Man						6.00
... FOREVER (1995, $5.95, direct market)						6.00
... FOREVER (1995, $3.95, newsstand)						4.00
FULL CIRCLE nn (1991, $5.95, 68 pgs.)-Sequel to Batman: Year Two						6.00
...:GALLERY, The 1 (1992, $2.95)-Pin-ups by Miller, N. Adams & others						3.00
...:GOLDEN STREETS OF GOTHAM (2003, $6.95) Elseworlds in early 1900s						7.00
...:GOTHAM BY GASLIGHT (1989, $3.95) Elseworlds; Mignola-a/Augustyn-s						4.00
...:GOTHAM CITY SECRET FILES 1 (4/00, $4.95) Batgirl app.						5.00
...: GOTHAM NOIR (2001, $6.95)-Elseworlds; Brubaker-s/Phillips-c/a						7.00
.../GREEN ARROW: THE POISON TOMORROW nn (1992, $5.95, square-bound, 68 pgs.) Netzer-c/a						6.00
HOLY TERROR nn (1991, $4.95, 52 pgs.)-Elseworlds story						5.00
.../HOUDINI: THE DEVIL'S WORKSHOP (1993, $5.95)						6.00
... :HUNTRESS/SPOILER - BLUNT TRAUMA (5/98, $2.95) Cataclysm pt. 13; Dixon-s/Barreto & Sienkiewicz-a						3.00
... I, JOKER nn (1998, $4.95)-Elseworlds story; Bob Hall-s/a						5.00
... IN DARKEST KNIGHT nn (1994, $4.95, 52 pgs.)-Elseworlds story; Batman w/Green Lantern's ring.						5.00
...JOKER'S APPRENTICE (5/99, $3.95) Von Eeden-a						4.00
.../ JOKER: SWITCH (2003, $6.95)-Bolton-a/Grayson-s						7.00
.../JUDGE DREDD: JUDGEMENT ON GOTHAM nn (1991, $5.95, 68 pgs.) Simon Bisley-c/a; Grant/Wagner scripts						6.00
.../JUDGE DREDD: JUDGEMENT ON GOTHAM nn (2nd printing)						5.00
.../JUDGE DREDD: THE ULTIMATE RIDDLE (1995, $4.95)						5.00
.../JUDGE DREDD: VENDETTA IN GOTHAM (1993, $5.95)						6.00
... : KNIGHTGALLERY (1995, $3.50)-Elseworlds sketchbook.						3.50
.../ LOBO (2000, $5.95)-Elseworlds; Joker app.; Bisley-a						6.00
... : MASK OF THE PHANTASM (1994, $2.95)-Movie adapt.						3.00
... : MASK OF THE PHANTASM (1994, $4.95)-Movie adapt.						5.00
... : MASQUE (1997, $6.95)-Elseworlds; Grell-c/s/a						7.00
... : MASTER OF THE FUTURE nn (1991, $5.95, 68 pgs.)-Elseworlds; sequel to Gotham By Gaslight; Barreto-a; embossed-c						6.00
... : MITEFALL (1995, $4.95)-Alan Grant script, Kevin O'Neill-a						5.00
... : MR. FREEZE (1997, $4.95)-Dini-s/Buckingham-a; Stelfreeze-c; cover art interlocks w/Batman:(Bane, Batgirl, Poison Ivy)						5.00
.../NIGHTWING: BLOODBORNE (2002, $5.95) Cypress-a; McKeever-c						6.00
... : NOSFERATU (1999, $5.95) McKeever-a						6.00
... : OF ARKHAM (2000, $5.95)-Elseworlds; Grant-s/Alcatena-a						6.00
... : OUR WORLDS AT WAR (8/01, $2.95)-Jae Lee-c						3.00
... PENGUIN TRIUMPHANT nn (1992, $4.95)-Staton-a(p); foil logo						5.00
...•PHANTOM STRANGER nn (1997, $4.95)-nn-Grant-s/Russell						5.00
... : PLUS (2/97, $2.95) Arsenal-c/app.						3.00
... : POISON IVY (1997, $4.95)-J.F. Moore-s/Apthorp-a; Stelfreeze-c; cover art interlocks w/Batman:(Bane, Batgirl, Mr. Freeze)						5.00
.../POISON IVY: CAST SHADOWS (2004, $6.95) Van Fleet-c/a; Nocenti-s						7.00
...:REIGN OF TERROR ('99, $4.95) Elseworlds						5.00
...:RETURNS MOVIE SPECIAL (1992, $3.95)						4.00
...RETURNS MOVIE PRESTIGE (1992, $5.95, squarebound)-Dorman painted-c						6.00
...:RIDDLER-THE RIDDLE FACTORY (1995, $4.95)-Wagner script						5.00
... : ROOM FULL OF STRANGERS (2004, $5.95) Scott Morse-s/c/a						6.00
...: SCARECROW 3-D (12/98, $3.95) w/glasses						4.00

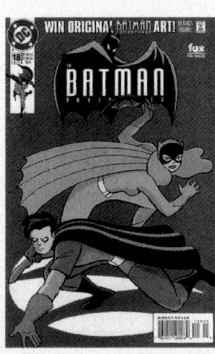

Batman Adventures #18 © DC

Batman and the Outsiders #10 © DC

Batman Beyond #1 © DC

	GD 2.0	VG 4.0	FN 6.0	VF 8.0	VF/NM 9.0	NM- 9.2		GD 2.0	VG 4.0	FN 6.0	VF 8.0	VF/NM 9.0	NM- 9.2

.../ SCARFACE: A PSYCHODRAMA (2001, $5.95)-Adlard-a/Sienkiewicz-c ... 6.00
.... SCAR OF THE BAT nn (1996, $4.95)-Elseworlds; Max Allan Collins script; Barreto-a ... 5.00
... :SCOTTISH CONNECTION (1998, $5.95) Quitely-a ... 6.00
... :SEDUCTION OF THE GUN nn (1992, $2.50, 68 pgs.) ... 3.00
.../SPAWN: WAR DEVIL nn (1994, $4.95, 52 pgs.) ... 5.00
... SPECIAL 1 (4/84)-Mike W. Barr story; Golden-c/a   1   2   3   6   8
.../SPIDER-MAN (1997, $4.95) Dematteis-s/Nolan & Kesel-a ... 5.00
... : THE ABDUCTION ('98, $5.95) ... 6.00
... : THE BLUE, THE GREY, & THE BAT (1992, $5.95)-Weiss/Lopez-a ... 6.00
... :THE HILL (5/00, $2.95)-Priest/s/Martinbrough-a ... 3.00
... :THE KILLING JOKE (1988, deluxe 52 pgs., mature readers)-Bolland-c/a; Alan Moore
   scripts; Joker cripples Barbara Gordon   2   4   6   10   14   18
... : THE KILLING JOKE (2nd thru 11th printings)   1   2   3   5   7   9
... :THE MAN WHO LAUGHS (2005, $6.95)-Retells 1st meeting with the Joker; Mahnke-a 7.00
... :THE OFFICIAL COMIC ADAPTATION OF THE WARNER BROS. MOTION PICTURE
  (1989, $2.50, regular format, 68 pgs.)-Ordway-c ... 3.00
... :THE OFFICIAL COMIC ADAPTATION OF THE WARNER BROS. MOTION PICTURE
  (1989, $4.95, prestige format, 68 pgs.)-same interiors but different-c ... 5.00
... :THE ORDER OF BEASTS (2004, $5.95)-Elseworlds; Eddie Campbell-a ... 5.00
... :THE SPIRIT (1/07, $4.99)-Loeb-s/Cooke-a; P'Gell & Commissioner Dolan app. ... 5.00
... :THE 10-CENT ADVENTURE (3/02, 10¢) intro. to the "Bruce Wayne: Murderer" x-over;
  Rucka-s/Burchett & Janson-a/Dave Johnson-c ... 2.00
NOTE: (Also see Promotional Comics section for alternate copies with special outer half-covers promoting local
comic shops)
... :THE 12-CENT ADVENTURE (10/04, 12¢) intro. to the "War Games" x-over;
  Grayson-s/Bachs-a; Catwoman & Spoiler app. ... 2.00
... : TWO-FACE-CRIME AND PUNISHMENT-(1995, $4.95)-McDaniel-a ... 5.00
... : TWO FACES (11/98, $4.95) Elseworlds ... 5.00
... :VENGEANCE OF BANE SPECIAL 1 (1992, $2.50, 68 pgs.)-Origin & 1st app. Bane
  (see Batman #491)   2   4   6   8   10   12
... :VENGEANCE OF BANE SPECIAL 1 (2nd printing) ... 3.00
..... :VENGEANCE OF BANE II nn (1995, $3.95)-sequel ... 4.00
... :Vs. THE INCREDIBLE HULK (1995, $3.95)-r/DC Special Series #27 ... 4.00
... :VILLAINS SECRET FILES (10/98, $4.95) Origin-s ... 5.00
... VILLAINS SECRET FILES AND ORIGINS 2005 (7/05, $4.99) Clayface origin w/ Mignola-a;
  Black Mask story, pin-up of villains by various; Barrionuevo-c ... 5.00

BATMAN ADVENTURES, THE (Based on animated series)
DC Comics: Oct, 1992 - No. 36, Oct, 1995 ($1.25/$1.50)
1-Penguin-c/story ... 4.00
1 ($1.95, Silver Edition)-2nd printing ... 2.50
2-6,8-19: 2,12-Catwoman-c/story. 3-Joker-c/story. 5-Scarecrow-c/story. 10-Riddler-c/story.
  11-Man-Bat-c/story. 12-Batgirl & Catwoman-c/story. 16-Joker-c/story; begin $1.50-c.
  18-Batgirl-c/story. 19-Scarecrow-c/story. ... 3.00
7-Special edition polybagged with Man-Bat trading card ... 5.00
20-24,26-32: 26-Batgirl app. ... 2.50
25-($2.50, 52 pgs.)-Superman app. ... 3.00
33-36: 33-Begin $1.75-c ... 2.50
Annual 1,2 ('94, '95): 2-Demon-c/story; Ra's al Ghul app. ... 3.50
...: Dangerous Dames & Demons (2003, $14.95, TPB) r/Annual 1,2, Mad Love & Adventures
  in the DC Universe #3; Bruce Timm painted-c ... 15.00
Holiday Special 1 (1995, $2.95) ... 4.00
The Collected Adventures Vol. 1,2 ('93, '95, $5.95) ... 6.00
TPB ('98, $7.95) r/#1-6; painted wraparound-c ... 8.00

BATMAN ADVENTURES (Based on animated series)
DC Comics: Jun, 2003 - No. 17, Oct, 2004 ($2.25)
1-Timm-c (2003 Free Comic Book Day edition is listed in Promotional Comics section) ... 2.25
2-17; 3,16-Joker-c/app. 4-Ra's al Ghul app. 6-8-Phantasm app. 14-Grey Ghost app. ... 2.50
Vol. 1: Rogues Gallery (2004, $6.95, digest size) r/#1-4 & Batman: Gotham Advs. #50 ... 7.00
Vol. 2: Shadows & Masks (2004, $6.95, digest size) r/#5-9 ... 7.00

BATMAN ADVENTURES, THE: MAD LOVE
DC Comics: Feb, 1994 ($3.95/$4.95)
1-Origin of Harley Quinn; Dini-s/Timm-c/a   2   4   6   8   10   12
1-($4.95, Prestige format) new Timm painted-c   1   2   3   5   8

BATMAN ADVENTURES, THE: THE LOST YEARS (TV)
DC Comics: Jan, 1998 - No. 5, May, 1998 ($1.95) (Based on animated series)
1-5-Leads into Fall '97's new animated episodes. 4-Tim Drake becomes Robin.
  5-Dick becomes Nightwing ... 2.50
TPB (1999, $9.95) r/series ... 10.00

BATMAN/ALIENS
DC Comics/Dark Horse: Mar, 1997 - No. 2, Apr, 1997 ($4.95, limited series)
1,2: Wrightson-c/a. ... 5.00

TPB-(1997, $14.95) w/prequel from DHP #101,102 ... 15.00

BATMAN/ALIENS II
DC Comics/Dark Horse: 2003 - No. 3, 2003 ($5.95, limited series)
1-3-Edginton-s/Staz Johnson-a ... 6.00
TPB-(2003, $14.95) r/#1-3 ... 15.00

BATMAN AND ROBIN ADVENTURES (TV)
DC Comics: Nov, 1995 - No. 25, Dec, 1997 ($1.75) (Based on animated series)
1-Dini-s. ... 3.00
2-24: 2-4-Dini script. 4-Penguin-c/story. 5-Joker-c/story; Poison Ivy, Harley Quinn/app.
  9-Batgirl & Talia-c/story. 10-Ra's al Ghul-c/story. 11-Man-Bat app. 12-Bane-c/app.
  13-Scarecrow-c/app. 15 Deadman-c/app. 16-Catwoman-c/app. 18-Joker-c/app.
  24-Poison Ivy app. ... 2.50
25-($2.95, 48 pgs.) ... 3.00
Annual 1,2 (11/96, 11/97): 1-Phantasm-c/app. 2-Zatara & Zatanna-c/app. ... 4.00
...: Sub-Zero(1998, $3.95) Adaptation of animated video ... 4.00

BATMAN AND SUPERMAN ADVENTURES: WORLD'S FINEST
DC Comics: 1997 ($6.95, square-bound, one-shot) (Based on animated series)
1-Adaptation of animated crossover episode; Dini-s/Timm-c. ... 7.00

BATMAN AND SUPERMAN: WORLD'S FINEST
DC Comics: Apr, 1999 - No. 10, Jan, 2000 ($4.95/$1.99, limited series)
1,10-($4.95, squarebound) Taylor-a ... 5.00
2-9-($1.99) 5-Batgirl app. 8-Catwoman-c/app. ... 2.50
TPB (2003, $19.95) r/#1-10 ... 20.00

BATMAN AND THE OUTSIDERS (The Adventures of the Outsiders #33 on)
(Also see Brave & The Bold #200 & The Outsiders) (Replaces The Brave and the Bold)
DC Comics: Aug, 1983 - No. 32, Apr, 1986 (Mando paper #5 on)
1-Batman, Halo, Geo-Force, Katana, Metamorpho & Black Lightning begin ... 4.00
2-32: 5-New Teen Titans x-over. 9-Halo begins. 11,12-Origin Katana. 18-More info on
  Metamorpho's origin. 28-31-Lookers origin. 32-Team disbands ... 2.50
Annual 1,2 (9/84, 9/85): 2-Metamorpho & Sapphire Stagg wed ... 3.00
NOTE: Aparo a-1-9, 11-13p, 16-20; c-1-4, 5i, 6-21, Annual 1, 2. B. Kane a-3r. Layton a-19i, 20i. Lopez a-3p. Miller
c-Annual 1. Perez c-5p. B. Willingham a-14p.

BATMAN: BANE OF THE DEMON
DC Comics: Mar, 1998 - No. 4, June, 1998 ($1.95, limited series)
1-4-Dixon-s/Nolan-a; prelude to Legacy x-over ... 2.50

BATMAN BEYOND (Based on animated series)(Mini-series)
DC Comics: Mar, 1999 - No. 6, Aug, 1999 ($1.99)
1-6: 1,2-Adaptation of pilot episode, Timm-c ... 2.50
TPB (1999, $9.95) r/#1-6 ... 10.00

BATMAN BEYOND (Based on animated series)(Continuing series)
DC Comics: Nov, 1999 - No. 24, Oct, 2001 ($1.99)
1-24: 1-Rousseau-a; Batman vs. Batman. 14-Demon-c/app. 21,22-Justice League
  Unlimited-c/app. ... 2.50
...: Return of the Joker (2/01, $2.95) adaptation of video release ... 3.00

BATMAN: BLACK & WHITE
DC Comics: June, 1996 - No. 4, Sept, 1996 ($2.95, B&W, limited series)
1-Stories by McKeever, Timm, Kubert, Chaykin, Goodwin; Jim Lee-c; Allred inside front-c;
  Moebius inside back-c ... 4.00
2-4: 2-Stories by Simonson, Corben, Bisley & Gaiman; Miller-c. 3-Stories by M. Wagner,
  Janson, Sienkiewicz, O'Neil & Kristiansen; B. Smith-c; Russell inside front-c; Silvestri inside
  back-c. 4-Stories by Bolland, Goodwin & Gianni, Strnad & Nowlan, O'Neil & Stelfreeze;
  Toth-c; pin-ups by Neal Adams & Alex Ross ... 3.00
Hardcover ('97, $39.95) r/series w/new art & cover plate ... 40.00
Softcover ('00, $19.95) r/series ... 20.00
Volume 2 HC ('02, $39.95, 7 3/4"x12") r/B&W back-ups from Batman: Gotham Knights #1-16;
  stories and art by various incl. Ross, Buscema, Byrne, Ellison, Sale; Mignola-c ... 40.00
Volume 2 SC ('03, $19.95, 7 3/4"x12") same contents as HC ... 20.00
Volume 3 HC ('07, $24.99, reg. size) r/B&W back-ups from Batman: Gotham Knights #17-49;
  stories and art by various incl. Davis, DeCarlo, Morse, Schwartz, Thompson; Miller-c ... 25.00

BATMAN: BOOK OF THE DEAD
DC Comics: Jun, 1999 - No. 2, July, 1999 ($4.95, limited series, prestige format)
1,2-Elseworlds; Kitson-a ... 5.00

BATMAN: CATWOMAN DEFIANT (See Batman one-shots)

BATMAN/ CATWOMAN: TRAIL OF THE GUN
DC Comics: 2004 - No. 2, 2004 ($5.95, limited series, prestige format)
1,2-Elseworlds; Van Sciver-a/Nocenti-s ... 6.00

BATMAN CHRONICLES, THE

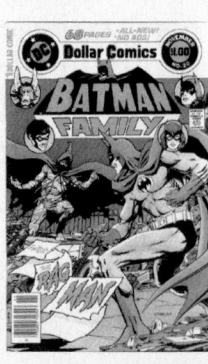

Batman Family #20 © DC

Batman: Gordon of Gotham #1 © DC

Batman: Gotham Knights #31 © DC

	GD 2.0	VG 4.0	FN 6.0	VF 8.0	VF/NM 9.0	NM- 9.2		GD 2.0	VG 4.0	FN 6.0	VF 8.0	VF/NM 9.0	NM- 9.2

DC Comics: Summer, 1995 - No. 23, Winter, 2001 ($2.95, quarterly)

1-3,5-19: 1-Dixon/Grant/Moench script. 3-Bolland-c. 5-Oracle Year One story, Richard Dragon
app.,Chaykin-c. 6-Kaluta-c; Ra's al Ghul story. 7-Superman-c/app.11-Paul Pope-s/a.
12-Cataclysm pt. 10. 18-No Man's Land 3.50
4-Hitman story by Ennis, Contagion tie-in; Balent-c   2   4   6   8   10   12
20-23: 20-Catwoman and Relative Heroes-c/app. 21-Pander Bros.-a 3.00
...Gallery (3/97, $3.50) Pin-ups 3.50
...Gauntlet, The (1997, $4.95, one-shot) 5.00

BATMAN: CITY OF LIGHT
DC Comics: Dec, 2003 - No. 8, July, 2004 ($2.95, limited series)

1-8-Pander Brothers-a/s; Paniccia-s 3.00

BATMAN CONFIDENTIAL
DC Comics: 2007 - Present ($2.99)

1-8: 1-6-Diggle-s/Portacio-a/c. 7,8-Cowan-a; Joker's origin 3.00

BATMAN: DARK DETECTIVE
DC Comics: Early July, 2005 - No. 6, Late September, 2005 ($2.99, limited series)

1-6-Englehart-s/Rogers & Austin-a; Silver St. Cloud and The Joker app. 3.00

BATMAN: DARK KNIGHT OF THE ROUND TABLE
DC Comics: 1999 - No. 2, 1999 ($4.95, limited series, prestige format)

1,2-Elseworlds; Giordano-a 5.00

BATMAN: DARK VICTORY
DC Comics: 1999 - No. 13, 2000 ($4.95/$2.95, limited series)

Wizard #0 Preview 2.25
1-($4.95) Loeb-s/Sale-c/a 5.00
2-12-($2.95) 3.00
13-($4.95) 5.00
Hardcover (2001, $29.95) with dust jacket; r/#0,1-13 .... 30.00
Softcover (2002, $19.95) r/#0,1-13 .... 20.00

BATMAN: DEATH AND THE MAIDENS
DC Comics: Oct, 2003 - No. 9, Aug, 2004 ($2.95, limited series)

1-Ra's al Ghul app.; Rucka-s/Janson-a 4.00
2-9: 9-Ra's al Ghul dies 3.00
TPB (2004, $19.95) r/#1-9 & Detective #783 .... 20.00

BATMAN/ DEATHBLOW: AFTER THE FIRE
DC Comics/WildStorm: 2002 - No. 3, 2002 ($5.95, limited series)

1-3-Azzarello-s/Bermejo & Bradstreet-a 6.00
TPB (2003, $12.95) r/#1-3; plus concept art 13.00

BATMAN FAMILY, THE
National Periodical Pub./DC Comics: Sept-Oct, 1975 - No. 20, Oct-Nov, 1978
(#1-4, 17-on: 68 pgs.) (Combined with Detective Comics with No. 481)

1-Origin/2nd app. Batgirl-Robin team-up (The Dynamite Duo); reprints plus one new story
begins; N. Adams-a(r); r/1st app. Man-Bat from Det. #400
                                              3   6   9   20   30   40
2-5: 2-r/Det. #369. 3-Batgirl & Robin learn each's i.d.; r/Batwoman app. from Batman #105.
4-r/1st Fatman app. from Batman #113. 5-r/1st Bat-Hound app. from Batman #92
                                              2   4   6   13   18   22
6,9-Joker's daughter on cover (1st app?) 3   6   9   15   21   26
7,8,14-16: 8-r/Batwoman app.14-Batwoman app. 15-3rd app. Killer Moth. 16-Bat-Girl cameo
(last app. in costume until New Teen Titans #47)   2   4   6   10   14   18
10-1st revival Batwoman; Cavalier app.; Killer Moth app.
                                              3   6   9   16   23   30
11-13,17-20: 11-13-Rogers-a(p): 11-New stories begin; Man-Bat begins. 13-Batwoman cameo.
17-($1.00 size)-Batman, Huntress begin; Batwoman & Catwoman 1st meet.
18-20: Huntress by Staton in all. 20-Origin Ragman retold
                                              3   6   9   16   22   28
NOTE: *Aparo* a-17; c-11-16. *Austin* a-12i. *Chaykin* a-14p. *Michael Golden* a-15-17,18-20p. *Grell* a-1; c-1. *Gil Kane*
a-2r. *Kaluta* c-17, 19. *Newton* a-13. *Robinson* a-1r, 3i(r), 9r. *Russell* a-18i, 19i. *Starlin* a-17; c-18, 20.

BATMAN: FAMILY
DC Comics: Dec, 2002 - No. 8, Feb, 2003 ($2.95/$2.25, weekly limited series)

1,8-($2.95). John Francis Moore-s/Hoberg & Gaudiano-a 3.00
2-7-($2.25). 3-Orpheus & Black Canary app. 2.50

BATMAN: GCPD
DC Comics: Aug, 1996 - No. 4, Nov, 1996 ($2.25, limited series)

1-4: Features Jim Gordon; Aparo/Sienkiewicz-a 2.50

BATMAN: GORDON OF GOTHAM
DC Comics: June, 1998 - No. 4, Sept, 1998 ($1.95, limited series)

1-4: Gordon's early days in Chicago 2.50

BATMAN: GORDON'S LAW
DC Comics: Dec, 1996 - No. 4, Mar, 1997 ($1.95, limited series)

1-4: Dixon-s/Janson-c/a 2.50

BATMAN: GOTHAM ADVENTURES (TV)
DC Comics: June, 1998 - No. 60, May, 2003 ($2.95/$1.95/$1.99/$2.25)

1-($2.95) Based on Kids WB Batman animated series 3.00
2-3-($1.95): 2-Two-Face-c/app. 2.50
4-22: 4-Begin $1.99-c. 6-Deadman-c. 13-MAD #1 cover swipe 2.50
23-60: 31,60-Joker-c/app. 50-Catwoman-c/app. 53-Begin $2.25-c. 58-Creeper-c/app. 2.50
TPB (2000, $9.95) r/#1-6 .... 10.00

BATMAN: GOTHAM COUNTY LINE
DC Comics: 2005 - No. 3, 2005 ($5.99, square-bound, limited series)

1-3-Steve Niles-s/Scott Hampton-a. 2,3-Deadman app. 6.00
TPB (2006, $17.99) r/#1-3 .... 18.00

BATMAN: GOTHAM KNIGHTS
DC Comics: Mar, 2000 - No. 74, Apr, 2006 ($2.50/$2.75)

1-Grayson-s; B&W back-up by Warren Ellis & Jim Lee 4.00
2-10-Grayson-s; B&W back-ups by various 2.75
11-($3.25) Bolland-c; Kyle Baker back-up story 3.25
12-24: 13-Officer Down x-over; Ellison back-up-s. 15-Colan back-up. 20-Superman-c/app. 2.75
25,26-Bruce Wayne: Murderer pt. 4,10 .... 3.00
27-31: 28,30,31-Bruce Wayne: Fugitive pt. 7,14,17 .... 2.75
32-49: 32-Begin $2.75-c; Kaluta-a back-up. 33,34-Bane-c/app. 35-Mahfood-a back-up.
38-Bolton-a back-up. 43-Jason Todd & Batgirl app. 44-Jason Todd flashback 2.75
50-54-Hush returns-Barrionuevo-a/Bermejo-a. 53,54-Green Arrow app. 3.00
55-($3.75) Batman vs. Hush; Joker & Riddler app. 4.00
56-74: 56-58-War Games; Jae Lee-c. 60-65-Hush app. 66-Villains United tie-in; Talia app. 2.50
Batman: Hush Returns TPB (2006, $12.99) r/#50-55,66; cover gallery 13.00

BATMAN: GOTHAM NIGHTS II (First series listed under Gotham Nights)
DC Comics: Mar, 1995 - No. 4, June, 1995 ($1.95, limited series)

1-4 .... 2.50

BATMAN/GRENDEL (1st limited series)
DC Comics: 1993 - No. 2, 1993 ($4.95, limited series, squarebound; 52 pgs.)

1,2: Batman vs. Hunter Rose. 1-Devil's Riddle; Matt Wagner-c/a/scripts. 2-Devil's Masque;
Matt Wagner-c/a/scripts 6.00

BATMAN/GRENDEL (2nd limited series)
DC Comics: June, 1996 - No. 2, July, 1996 ($4.95, limited series, squarebound)

1,2: Batman vs. Grendel Prime. 1-Devil's Bones. 2-Devil's Dance; Wagner-c/a/s ... 5.00

BATMAN: HARLEY & IVY
DC Comics: Jun, 2004 - No. 3, Aug, 2004 ($2.50, limited series)

1-3-Paul Dini-s/Bruce Timm-c/a 2.50
TPB (2007, $14.99) r/series; newly colored story from Batman: Gotham Knights #14 and
Harley and Ivy: Love on the Lam series 15.00

BATMAN: HARLEY QUINN
DC Comics: 1999 ($5.95, prestige format)

1-Intro. of Harley Quinn into regular DC continuity; Dini-s/Alex Ross-c 9.00
1-(2nd printing) 6.00

BATMAN: HAUNTED GOTHAM
DC Comics: 2000 - No. 4, 2000 ($4.95, limited series, squarebound)

1-4-Moench-s/Kelley Jones-c/a 5.00

BATMAN/ HELLBOY/STARMAN
DC Comics/Dark Horse: Jan, 1999 - No. 2, Feb, 1999 ($2.50, limited series)

1,2: Robinson-s/Mignola-a. 2-Harris-c 2.50

BATMAN: HOLLYWOOD KNIGHT
DC Comics: Apr, 2001 - No. 3, Jun, 2001 ($2.50, limited series)

1-3-Elseworlds Batman as a 1940's movie star; Giordano-a/Layton-s 2.50

BATMAN: HUNTRESS: CRY FOR BLOOD
DC Comics: Jun, 2000 - No. 6, Nov, 2000 ($2.50, limited series)

1-6: Rucka-s/Burchett-a; The Question app. 2.50
TPB (2002, $12.95) r/#1-6 .... 13.00

BATMAN: JEKYLL & HYDE
DC Comics: June, 2005 - No. 6, Nov, 2005 ($2.99, limited series)

1-6-Paul Jenkins-s; Two-Face app. 1-3-Jae Lee-a. 4-6-Sean Phillips-a 3.00

BATMAN: JOKER TIME (...: It's Joker Time! on cover)
DC Comics: 2000 - No. 3 ($4.95, limited series, squarebound)

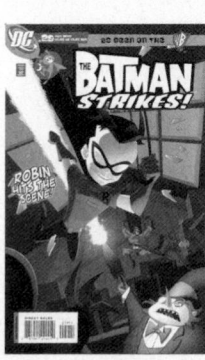

Batman: Legends of the Dark Knight #156 © DC

Batman: Shadow of the Bat #73 © DC

Batman Strikes! #29 © DC

	GD 2.0	VG 4.0	FN 6.0	VF 8.0	VF/NM 9.0	NM- 9.2

	GD 2.0	VG 4.0	FN 6.0	VF 8.0	VF/NM 9.0	NM- 9.2

1-3-Bob Hall-s/a 5.00

BATMAN: JOURNEY INTO KNGHT
DC Comics: Oct, 2005 - No. 12, Nov, 2006 ($2.50/$2.99, limited series)

1-9-Andrew Helfer-s/Tan Eng Huat-a/Pat Lee-c 2.50
10-12-($2.99) Joker app. 3.00

BATMAN/ JUDGE DREDD "DIE LAUGHING"
DC Comics: 1998 - No. 2, 1999 ($4.95, limited series, squarebound)

1,2: 1-Fabry-c/a. 2-Jim Murray-c/a 5.00

BATMAN: KNIGHTGALLERY (See Batman one-shots)

BATMAN: LEAGUE OF BATMEN
DC Comics: 2001 - No. 2, 2001 ($5.95, limited series, squarebound)

1,2-Elseworlds; Moench-s/Bright & Tanghal-a/Van Fleet-c 6.00

BATMAN: LEGENDS OF THE DARK KNIGHT (Legends of the Dark...#1-36)
DC Comics: Nov, 1989 - No. 214, Mar, 2007 ($1.50/$1.75/$1.95/$1.99/$2.25/$2.50/$2.99)

1- "Shaman" begins, ends #5; outer cover has four different color variations,
all worth same 4.00
2-10: 6-10- "Gothic" by Grant Morrison (scripts) 3.00
11-15: 11-15-Gulacy/Austin-a. 13-Catwoman app. 5.00
16-Intro drug Bane uses; begin Venom story 5.00
17-20 4.00
21-49,51-63: 38-Bat-Mite-c/story. 46-49-Catwoman app. w/Heath-c/a. 51-Ragman app.;
Joe Kubert-c. 59,60,61-Knightquest x-over. 62,63-KnightsEnd Pt. 4 & 10 3.00
50-($3.95, 68 pgs.)-Bolland embossed gold foil-c; Joker-c/story; pin-ups by Chaykin,
Simonson, Williamson, Kaluta, Russell, others 5.00
64-99: 64-(9/94)-Begin $1.95-c. 71-73-James Robinson-s/Watkiss-c/a. 74,75-McKeever-s/a.
76-78-Scott Hampton-c/a/s. 81-Card insert. 83,84-Ellis-s. 85-Robinson-s. 91-93-Ennis-s.
94-Michael T. Gilbert-s/a. 3.00
100-($3.95) Alex Ross painted-c; gallery by various 5.00
101-115: 101-Ezquerra-a. 102-104-Robinson-s 2.50
116-No Man's Land stories begin; Huntress-c 4.00
117-119,121-126: 122-Harris-c 2.50
120-ID of new Batgirl revealed 4.00
127-131: Return to Legends stories; Green Arrow app. 2.50
132-199, 201-204: 132-136 ($2.25-c) Archie Goodwin-s/Rogers-a. 137-141-Gulacy-a.
142-145-Joker and Ra's al Ghul app. 146-148-Kitson-a. 158-Begin $2.50-c
169-171-Tony Harris-c/a. 182-184-War Games. 182-Bagged with Sky Captain CD 2.50
200-($4.99) Joker-c/app. 5.00
205-214: 205-Begin $2.99-c. 207,208-Olivetti-a. 214-Deadshot app. 3.00
#0-(10/94)-Zero Hour; Quesada/Palmiotti-c; released between #64&65 3.00
Annual 1-7 ('91-'97, $3.50-$3.95, 68 pgs.): 1-Joker app. 2-Netzer-c/a. 3-New Batman (Azrael)
app. 4-Elseworlds story. 5-Year One; Man-Bat app. 6-Legend of the Dead Earth story.
7-Pulp Heroes story 4.00
Halloween Special 1 (12/93, $6.95, 84 pgs.)-Embossed & foil stamped-c

	1	2	3	4	5	7
Batman Madness-...Halloween Special (1994, $4.95)						5.00
Batman Ghosts-...Halloween Special (1995, $4.95)						5.00

NOTE: Aparo a-Annual 1. Chaykin scripts-24-26. Giffen a-Annual 1. Golden a-Annual 1. Alan Grant scripts-38,
52, 53. Gil Kane c/a-24-26. Mignola a-54; c-54, 62. Morrow a-Annual 3l. Quesada a-Annual 1. James Robinson
scripts- 71-73. Russell c/a-42, 43. Sears a-21, 23; c-21, 23. Zeck a-69, 70; c-69, 70.

BATMAN-LEGENDS OF THE DARK KNIGHT: JAZZ
DC Comics: Apr, 1995 - No. 3, June, 1995 ($2.50, limited series)

1-3 2.50

BATMAN: MANBAT
DC Comics: Oct, 1995 - No. 3, Dec, 1995 ($4.95, limited series)

1-3-Elseworlds-Delano-script; Bolton-a. 5.00
TPB-(1997, $14.95) r/#1-3 15.00

BATMAN: MITEFALL (See Batman one-shots)

BATMAN MINIATURE (See Batman Kellogg's)

BATMAN: NEVERMORE
DC Comics: June, 2003 - No. 5, Oct, 2003 ($2.50, limited series)

1-5-Elseworlds Batman & Edgar Allan Poe; Wrightson-c/Guy Davis-a/Len Wein-s 2.50

BATMAN: NO MAN'S LAND (Also see 1999 Batman titles)
DC Comics: (one-shots)

nn (3/99, $2.95) Alex Ross-c; Bob Gale-s; begins year-long story arc 3.00
Collector's Ed. (3/99, $3.95) Ross lenticular-c 5.00
#0 (: Ground Zero on cover) (12/99, $3.95) Orbik-c 5.00
...: Gallery (7/99, $3.95) Jim Lee-c 4.00
...: Secret Files (12/99, $4.95) Maleev-a 5.00
TPB ('99, $12.95) r/early No Man's Land stories; new Batgirl early app. 13.00

No Law and a New Order TPB(1999, $5.95) Ross-c 6.00
Volume 2 ('00, $12.95) r/later No Man's Land stories; Batgirl(Huntress) app.; Deodato-c 13.00
Volume 3-5 ('00,'01 $12.95) 3-Intro. new Batgirl. 4-('00). 5-('01) Land-c 13.00

BATMAN: ORPHEUS RISING
DC Comics: Oct, 2001 - No. 5, Feb, 2002 ($2.50, limited series)

1-5-Intro. Orpheus; Simmons-s/Turner & Miki-a 2.50

BATMAN: OUTLAWS
DC Comics: 2000 - No. 3, 2000 ($4.95, limited series)

1-3-Moench-s/Gulacy-a 5.00

BATMAN: PENGUIN TRIUMPHANT (See Batman one-shots)

BATMAN/PREDATOR III: BLOOD TIES
DC Comics/Dark Horse Comics: Nov, 1997 - No. 4, Feb, 1998 ($1.95, lim. series)

1-4: Dixon-s/Damaggio-c/a 2.50
TPB-(1998, $7.95) r/#1-4 8.00

BATMAN/RA'S AL GHUL (See Year One:...)

BATMAN RETURNS MOVIE SPECIAL (See Batman one-shots)

BATMAN: RIDDLER-THE RIDDLE FACTORY (See Batman one-shots)

BATMAN: RUN, RIDDLER, RUN
DC Comics: 1992 - Book 3, 1992 ($4.95, limited series)

Book 1-3: Mark Badger-a & plot 5.00

BATMAN SCARECROW (See Year One:...)

BATMAN: SECRET FILES
DC Comics: Oct, 1997 ($4.95)

1-New origin-s and profiles 5.00

BATMAN: SECRETS
DC Comics: May, 2006 - No. 5, Sept, 2006 ($2.99, limited series)

1-5-Sam Kieth-s/a/c; Joker app. 3.00
TPB (2007, $12.99) r/series 13.00

BATMAN: SHADOW OF THE BAT
DC Comics: June, 1992 - No. 94, Feb, 2000 ($1.50/$1.75/$1.95/$1.99)

1-The Last Arkham-c/story begins; Alan Grant scripts in all 4.00
1-($2.50)-Deluxe edition polybagged w/poster, pop-up & book mark 5.00
2-7: 4-The Last Arkham ends. 7-Last $1.50-c 3.00
8-28: 14,15-Staton-a(p). 16-18-Knightfall tie-ins. 19-28-Knightquest tie-ins w/Azrael as
Batman. 25-Silver ink-c; anniversary issue 2.50
29-($2.95, 52 pgs.)-KnightsEnd Pt. 2 3.00
30-72: 30-KnightsEnd Pt. 8. 31-(9/94)-Begin $1.95-c; Zero Hour. 32-(11/94). 33-Robin-c.
35-Troika-Pt.2. 43,44-Cat-Man & Catwoman-c. 48-Contagion Pt. 1; card insert.
49-Contagion Pt.7. 56,57,58-Poison Ivy-c/app. 62-Two-Face app. 69,70-Fate app. 2.50
35-($2.95)-Variant embossed-c 3.00
73,74,76-78: Cataclysm x-over pts. 1,9. 76-78-Orbik-c 2.50
75-($2.95) Mr. Freeze & Clayface app.; Orbik-c 3.00
79,81,82: 79-Begin $1.99-c 2.50
80-($3.95) Flip book with Azrael #47 4.00
83-No Man's Land; intro. new Batgirl (Huntress) 12.00
84,85-No Man's Land 4.00
86-94: 87-Deodato-a. 90-Harris-a. 92-Superman app. 93-Joker and Harley app.
94-No Man's Land ends 3.00
#0 (10/94) Zero Hour; released between #31&32 3.00
#1,000,000 (11/98) 853rd Century x-over; Orbik-c 2.50
Annual 1-5 ('93-'97 $2.95-$3.95, 68 pgs.): 3-Year One story; Poison Ivy app. 4-Legends of the
Dead Earth story; Starman cameo. 5-Pulp Heroes story; Poison Ivy app. 4.00

BATMAN: SON OF THE DEMON (Also see Batman #655-658 and Batman Hardcovers)
DC Comics: 2006 ($5.99, reprints the 1987 HC in comic book format)

nn-Talia has Batman's son; Mike W. Barr-s/Jerry Bingham-a; new Andy Kubert-c 6.00

BATMAN-SPAWN: WAR DEVIL (See Batman one-shots)

BATMAN SPECTACULAR (See DC Special Series No. 15)

BATMAN STRIKES!, THE (Based on the 2004 animated series) (2005 Free Comic Book Day
edition is listed in Promotional Comics section)
DC Comics: Nov, 2004 - Present ($2.25)

1,2,4-36: 1,11-Penguin app. 2-Man-Bat app. 4-Bane app. 9-Joker app. 18-Batgirl debut.
29-Robin debuts. 32,33-Cal Ripken 8-pg. insert 2.50
3-($2.95) Joker-c/app.; Catwoman & Wonder Woman-r from Advs. in the DCU 3.00
Jam Packed Action (2005, $7.99, digest) adaptations of two TV episodes 8.00
... Vol. 1: Crime Time (2005, $6.99, digest) r/#1-5 7.00
... Vol. 2: In Darkest Knight (2005, $6.99, digest) r/#6-10 7.00

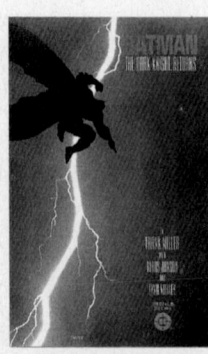

Batman: The Dark Knight Returns #1 © DC

Batman: The Mad Monk #1 © DC

Battle #9 © MAR

	GD 2.0	VG 4.0	FN 6.0	VF 8.0	VF/NM 9.0	NM- 9.2

BATMAN/ SUPERMAN/WONDER WOMAN: TRINITY
DC Comics: 2003 - No. 3, 2003 ($6.95, limited series, squarebound)

1-3-Matt Wagner-s/a/c. 1-Ra's al Ghul & Bizarro app.						7.00
HC (2004, $24.95, with dust-jacket) r/series; intro. by Brad Meltzer						30.00
SC (2004, $17.99) r/series; intro. by Brad Meltzer						18.00

BATMAN: SWORD OF AZRAEL (Also see Azrael & Batman #488,489)
DC Comics: Oct, 1992 - No. 4, Jan, 1993 ($1.75, limited series)

1-Wraparound gatefold-c; Quesada-c/a(p) in all; 1st app. Azrael						
		2	4	6	8	10	12
2-4- 4-Cont'd in Batman #488	1	2	3	5	6	8
Silver Edition 1-4 (1993, $1.95)-Reprints #1-4						2.25
Trade Paperback (1993, $9.95)-Reprints #1-4						10.00
Trade Paperback Gold Edition						15.00

BATMAN/ TARZAN: CLAWS OF THE CAT-WOMAN
Dark Horse Comics/DC Comics: Sept, 1999 - No. 4, Dec, 1999 ($2.95, limited series)

1-4- Marz-s/Kordey-a						3.00

BATMAN: TENSES
DC Comics: 2003 - No. 2, 2003 ($6.95, limited series)

1,2-Joe Casey-s/Cully Hamner-a; Bruce Wayne's first year back in Gotham						7.00

BATMAN: THE ANKH
DC Comics: 2002 - No. 2, 2002 ($5.95, limited series)

1,2-Dixon-s/Van Fleet-a						6.00

BATMAN: THE CULT
DC Comics: 1988 - No. 4, Nov, 1988 ($3.50, deluxe limited series)

1-Wrightson-a/painted-c in all						6.00
2-4						5.00
Trade Paperback ('91, $14.95)-New Wrightson-c						15.00

BATMAN: THE DARK KNIGHT RETURNS (Also see Dark Knight Strikes Again)
DC Comics: Mar, 1986 - No. 4, 1986 ($2.95, squarebound, limited series)

1-Miller story & c/a(p); set in the future	4	8	12	26	41	55
1,2-2nd & 3rd printings, 3-2nd printing						6.00
2-Carrie Kelly becomes 1st female Robin	3	6	9	14	20	25
3-Death of Joker; Superman app.	2	4	6	11	16	20
4-Death of Alfred; Superman app.	2	4	6	9	13	16
Hardcover, signed & numbered edition ($40.00)(4000 copies)						250.00
Hardcover, trade edition						50.00
Softcover, trade edition (1st printing only)	2	4	6	9	12	15
Softcover, trade edition (2nd thru 8th printings)	2	3	4	5	6	7
10th Anniv. Slipcase set ('96, $100.00): Signed & numbered hard-c edition (10,000 copies), sketchbook, copy of script for #1, 2 color prints						100.00
10th Anniv. Hardcover ('96, $45.00)						45.00
10th Anniv. Softcover ('97, $14.95)						15.00
Hardcover 2nd printing ('02, $24.95) with 3 1/4" tall partial dustjacket						25.00

NOTE: *The #2 second printings can be identified by matching the grey background colors on the inside front cover and facing page. The inside front cover of the second printing has a dark grey background which does not match the lighter grey of the facing page. On the true 1st printings, the backgrounds are both light grey. All other issues are clearly marked.*

BATMAN: THE DOOM THAT CAME TO GOTHAM
DC Comics: 2000 - No. 3, 2001 ($4.95, limited series)

1-3-Elseworlds; Mignola-c/s; Nixey-a; Etrigan app.						5.00

BATMAN: THE KILLING JOKE (See Batman one-shots)
BATMAN: THE LONG HALLOWEEN
DC Comics: Dec, 1996 - No. 13, Oct, 1997 ($2.95/$4.95, limited series)

1-($4.95)-Loeb-s/Sale-c/a in all	1	2	3	5	6	8
2-5($2.95)- 2-Solomon Grundy-c/app. 3-Joker-c/app., Catwoman, Poison Ivy app.						6.00
6-10- 6-Poison Ivy-c. 7-Riddler-c/app.						5.00
11,12						4.00
13-($4.95, 48 pgs.)-Killer revelations						5.00
Absolute Batman: The Long Halloween (2007, $75.00, oversized HC) r/series; interviews with the creators; Sale sketch pages; action figure line; unpubbed 4-page sequence						75.00
HC-($29.95) r/series						30.00
SC-($19.95)						20.00

BATMAN: THE MAD MONK ("Batman & the Mad Monk" on cover)
DC Comics: Oct, 2006 - No. 6, ($3.50, limited series)

1-5-Matt Wagner-s/a/c. 1-Catwoman app.						3.50
TPB (2007, $14.99) r/#1-6						

BATMAN: THE MONSTER MEN ("Batman & the Monster Men" on cover)
DC Comics: Jan, 2006 - No. 6, June, 2006 ($2.99, limited series)

1-6-Matt Wagner-s/a/c						3.00
TPB (2006, $14.99) r/#1-6						15.00

BATMAN: THE OFFICIAL COMIC ADAPTATION OF THE WARNER BROS. MOTION PICTURE
(See Batman one-shots)

BATMAN: THE ULTIMATE EVIL
DC Comics: 1995 ($5.95, limited series, prestige format)

1,2-Barrett, Jr. adaptation of Vachss novel.						6.00

BATMAN 3-D (Also see 3-D Batman)
DC Comics: 1990 ($9.95, w/glasses, 8-1/8x10-3/4")

nn-Byrne-a/scripts; Riddler, Joker, Penguin & Two-Face app. plus r/1953 3-D Batman; pin-ups by many artists	2	4	6	8	10	12

BATMAN: TOYMAN
DC Comics: Nov, 1998 - No. 4, Feb, 1999 ($2.25, limited series)

1-4-Hama-s						2.50

BATMAN: TURNING POINTS
DC Comics: Jan, 2001 - No. 5, Jan, 2001 ($2.50, weekly limited series)

1-5: 2-Giella-a. 3-Kubert-c/Giordano-a. 4-Chaykin-c/Brent Anderson-a. 5-Pope-c/a						2.50
TPB (2007, $14.99) r/#1-5						15.00

BATMAN: TWO-FACE-CRIME AND PUNISHMENT (See Batman one-shots)
BATMAN: TWO-FACE STRIKES TWICE
DC Comics: 1993 - No. 2, 1993 ($4.95, 52 pgs.)

1,2-Flip book format w/Staton-a (G.A. side)						5.00

BATMAN VERSUS PREDATOR
DC Comics/Dark Horse Comics: 1991 - No. 3, 1992 ($4.95/$1.95, limited series)
(1st DC/Dark Horse x-over)

1 (Prestige format, $4.95)-1 & 3 contain 8 Batman/Predator trading cards; Andy & Adam Kubert-a; Suydam painted-c						6.00
1-3 (Regular format, $1.95)-No trading cards						3.00
2,3-(Prestige)-2-Extra pin-ups inside; Suydam-c						5.00
TPB (1993, $5.95, 132 pgs.) r/#1-3 w/new introductions & forward plus new wraparound-c by Dave Gibbons						6.00

BATMAN VERSUS PREDATOR II: BLOODMATCH
DC Comics: Late 1994 - No. 4, 1995 ($2.50, limited series)

1-4-Huntress app.; Moench scripts; Gulacy-a						3.00
TPB (1995, $6.95)-r/#1-4						7.00

BATMAN VS. THE INCREDIBLE HULK (See DC Special Series No. 27)
BATMAN: WAR ON CRIME
DC Comics: Nov, 1999 ($9.95, treasury size, one-shot)

nn-Painted art by Alex Ross; story by Alex Ross and Paul Dini						10.00

BATMAN: WILDCAT
DC Comics: Apr, 1997 - No.3, June, 1997 ($2.25, mini-series)

1-3: Dixon/Smith-s: 1-Killer Croc app.						2.50

BATMAN: YEAR 100
DC Comics: 2006 - No. 4, 2006 ($5.99, squarebound, limited series)

1-4-Paul Pope-s/a/c						6.00
TPB (2007, $19.99) r/series						20.00

BAT MASTERSON (TV) (Also see Tim Holt #28)
Dell Publishing Co.: Aug-Oct, 1959; Feb-Apr, 1960 - No. 9, Nov-Jan, 1961-62

Four Color 1013 (#1) (8-10/59)	11	22	33	79	140	200
2-9: Gene Barry photo-c on all. 2-Two different back-c exist	7	14	21	45	73	100

BATS (See Tales Calculated to Drive You Bats)
BATS, CATS & CADILLACS
Now Comics: Oct, 1990 - No. 2, Nov, 1990 ($1.75)

1,2: 1-Gustovich-a(i); Snyder-c						2.50

BAT-THING
DC Comics (Amalgam): June, 1997 ($1.95, one-shot)

1-Hama-s/Damaggio & Sienkiewicz-a						2.50

BATTLE
Marvel/Atlas Comics(FPI #1-62/ Male #63 on): Mar, 1951 - No. 70, Jun, 1960

1	32	64	96	186	293	400
2	16	32	48	94	147	200

Battle Action #5 © ATLAS

Battle Chasers #2 © Joe Madureira

Battlefield #3 © MAR

	GD 2.0	VG 4.0	FN 6.0	VF 8.0	VF/NM 9.0	NM- 9.2
3-10: 4-1st Buck Pvt. O'Toole. 10-Pakula-a	14	28	42	76	108	140
11-20: 11-Check-a	11	22	33	60	83	105
21,23-Krigstein-a	11	22	33	64	90	115
22,24-36: 32-Tuska-a. 36-Everett-a	9	18	27	52	69	85
37-Kubert-a (Last precode, 2/55)	10	20	30	56	76	95
38-40,42-48	9	18	27	50	65	80
41,49: 41-Kubert/Moskowitz-a. 49-Davis-a	10	20	30	54	72	90
50-54,56-58	9	18	27	47	61	75
55-Williamson-a (5 pgs.)	10	20	30	54	72	90
59-Torres-a	9	18	27	50	65	80
60-62: 60,62-Combat Kelly app. 61-Combat Casey app.	9	18	27	47	61	75
63-Ditko-a	14	28	42	76	108	140
64-66-Kirby-a. 66-Davis-a; has story of Fidel Castro in pre-Communism days (an admiring profile)	15	30	45	84	127	170
67,68: 67-Williamson/Crandall-a (4 pgs.); Kirby, Davis-a. 68-Kirby/Williamson-a (4 pgs.); Kirby/Ditko-a	15	30	45	85	130	175
69,70: 69-Kirby-a. 70-Kirby/Ditko-a	15	30	45	84	127	170

NOTE: *Andru* a-37. *Berg* a-38, 14, 60-62. *Colan* a-33, 55. *Everett* a-36, 50, 70; c-56, 57. *Heath* a-6, 9, 13, 31, 69; c-6, 9, 12, 26, 35, 37. *Kirby* c-64-69. *Maneely* a-4, 6, 31, 61; c-4, 33, 59, 61. *Orlando* a-47. *Powell* a-53, 55. *Reinman* a-8, 9, 26, 32. *Robinson* a-9, 39. *Romita* a-26. *Severin* a-28, 32-34, 66-69; c-36, 55. *Sinnott* a-33, 37. *Woodbridge* a-52, 55.

BATTLE ACTION
Atlas Comics (NPI): Feb, 1952 - No. 12, 5/53; No. 13, 11/54 - No. 30, 8/57

	GD 2.0	VG 4.0	FN 6.0	VF 8.0	VF/NM 9.0	NM- 9.2
1-Pakula-a	26	52	78	154	242	330
2	15	30	45	83	124	165
3,4,6,7,9,10: 6-Robinson-c/a. 7-Partial nudity	10	20	30	56	76	95
5-Used in POP, pg. 93,94	10	20	30	58	79	100
8-Krigstein-a	11	22	33	60	83	105
11-15 (Last precode, 2/55)	10	20	30	54	72	90
16-30: 27,30-Torres-a	9	18	27	50	69	85

NOTE: Battle Brady app. 5-7, 10-12. *Berg* a-3. *Check* a-11. *Everett* a-7; c-13, 25. *Heath* a-9, 18; c-3,15, 18, 21. *Maneely* c-1; c-5. *Reinman* a-1. *Robinson* a-6, 7; c-6. *Shores* a-7(2), 12. *Sinnott* a-3, 27. *Woodbridge* a-28, 30.

BATTLE ATTACK
Stanmor Publications: Oct, 1952 - No. 8, Dec, 1955

	GD 2.0	VG 4.0	FN 6.0	VF 8.0	VF/NM 9.0	NM- 9.2
1	13	26	39	72	101	130
2	8	16	24	42	54	65
3-8: 3-Hollingsworth-a	7	14	21	37	46	55

BATTLEAXES
DC Comics (Vertigo): May, 2000 - No. 4, Aug, 2000 ($2.50, limited series)

1-4: Terry LaBan-s/Alex Horley-a						2.50

BATTLE BEASTS
Blackthorne Publishing: Feb, 1988 - No. 4, 1988 ($1.50/$1.75, B&W/color)

1-4: 1-3- (B&W)-Based on Hasbro toys. 4-Color						2.50

BATTLE BRADY (Formerly Men in Action No. 1-9; see 3-D Action)
Atlas Comics (IPC): No. 10, Jan, 1953 - No. 14, June, 1953

	GD 2.0	VG 4.0	FN 6.0	VF 8.0	VF/NM 9.0	NM- 9.2
10: 10-12-Syd Shores-c	16	32	48	92	144	195
11-Used in POP, pg. 95 plus B&W & color illos	10	20	30	58	79	100
12-14	9	18	27	52	69	85

BATTLE CHASERS
Image Comics (Cliffhanger): Apr, 1998 - No. 4, Dec, 1998;
DC Comics (Cliffhanger): No. 5, May, 1999 - No. 8, May, 2001 ($2.50)
Image Comics: No. 9, Sept, 2001 ($3.50)

	GD 2.0	VG 4.0	FN 6.0	VF 8.0	VF/NM 9.0	NM- 9.2
Prelude (2/98)	1	3	4	6	8	10
Prelude Gold Ed.	1	3	4	6	8	10
1-Madureira & Sharrieff-s/Madureira-a(p)/Charest-c	1	2	3	5	7	9
1-American Ent. Ed. w/"racy" cover	1	3	4	6	8	10
1-Gold Edition						9.00
1-Chromium cover						40.00
1-2nd printing						3.00
2						5.00
2-Dynamic Forces BattleChrome cover	2	4	6	8	10	12
3-Red Monika cover by Madureira						4.00
4-8: 4-Four covers. 6-Back-up by Warren-s/a. 7-3 covers (Madureira, Ramos, Campbell)						3.00
9-($3.50, Image) Flip cover/story by Adam Warren						3.50
...: A Gathering of Heroes HC ('99, $24.95) r/#1-5, Prelude, Frank Frazetta Fantasy Ill.; cover gallery						25.00
...: A Gathering of Heroes SC ('99, $14.95)						15.00
...Collected Edition 1,2 (11/98, $5.99, $5.95) 1-r/#1,2. 2-r/#3,4						6.00

BATTLE CLASSICS (See Cancelled Comic Cavalcade)
DC Comics: Sept-Oct, 1978 (44 pgs.)

	GD 2.0	VG 4.0	FN 6.0	VF 8.0	VF/NM 9.0	NM- 9.2
1-Kubert-r; new Kubert-c	1	3	4	6	8	10

BATTLE CRY
Stanmor Publications: 1952 (May) - No. 20, Sept, 1955

	GD 2.0	VG 4.0	FN 6.0	VF 8.0	VF/NM 9.0	NM- 9.2
1	15	30	45	85	130	175
2	9	18	27	52	69	85
3,5-10: 8-Pvt. Ike begins, ends #13,17	8	16	24	40	50	60
4-Classic E.C. swipe	9	18	27	47	61	75
11-20	7	14	21	35	43	50

NOTE: *Hollingsworth* a-9; c-20.

BATTLEFIELD (War Adventures on the...)
Atlas Comics (ACI): April, 1952 - No. 11, May, 1953

	GD 2.0	VG 4.0	FN 6.0	VF 8.0	VF/NM 9.0	NM- 9.2
1-Pakula, Reinman-a	22	44	66	126	198	270
2-5: 2-Heath, Maneely, Pakula, Reinman-a	13	26	39	74	105	135
6-11	10	20	30	56	76	95

NOTE: *Colan* a-11. *Everett* a-8. *Heath* a-1, 2, 5p; c-2, 8, 9, 11. *Ravielli* a-11.

BATTLEFIELD ACTION (Formerly Foreign Intrigues)
Charlton Comics: No. 16, Nov, 1957 - No. 62, 2-3/66; No. 63, 7/80 - No. 89, 11/84

	GD 2.0	VG 4.0	FN 6.0	VF 8.0	VF/NM 9.0	NM- 9.2
V2#16	8	16	24	40	50	60
17,20-30	5	10	15	23	28	32
18,19-Check-a (2 stories in #18)	3	6	9	19	29	38
31-62(1966)	3	6	9	14	19	24
63-80(1983-84)						5.00
81-83,85-89 (Low print run)	1	2	3	4	5	7
84-Kirby reprints; 3 stories	1	3	4	6	8	10

NOTE: *Montes/Bache* a-43, 55, 62. *Glanzman* a-87r.

BATTLE FIRE
Aragon Magazine/Stanmor Publications: Apr, 1955 - No. 7, 1955

	GD 2.0	VG 4.0	FN 6.0	VF 8.0	VF/NM 9.0	NM- 9.2
1	12	24	36	67	94	120
2	8	16	24	40	50	60
3-7	6	12	18	31	38	45

BATTLE FOR A THREE DIMENSIONAL WORLD
3D Cosmic Publications: May, 1983 (20 pgs., slick paper w/stiff-c, $3.00)

	GD 2.0	VG 4.0	FN 6.0	VF 8.0	VF/NM 9.0	NM- 9.2
nn-Kirby c/a in 3-D; shows history of 3-D	2	4	6	8	10	12

BATTLEFORCE
Blackthorne Publishing: Nov, 1987 - No. 2, 1988 ($1.75, color/B&W)

1,2: Based on game. 1-In color. 2-B&W						2.50

BATTLE FOR INDEPENDENTS, THE (Also See Cyblade/Shi & Shi/Cyblade: The Battle For Independents)
Image Comics (Top Cow Productions)/Crusade Comics: 1995 ($29.95)

	GD 2.0	VG 4.0	FN 6.0	VF 8.0	VF/NM 9.0	NM- 9.2
nn-boxed set of all editions of Shi/Cyblade & Cyblade/Shi plus new variant.	1	3	9	20	30	40

BATTLE FOR THE PLANET OF THE APES (See Power Record Comics)

BATTLEFRONT
Atlas Comics (PPI): June, 1952 - No. 48, Aug, 1957

	GD 2.0	VG 4.0	FN 6.0	VF 8.0	VF/NM 9.0	NM- 9.2
1-Heath-c	30	60	90	172	271	370
2-Robinson-a(4)	15	30	45	86	133	180
3-5	14	28	42	76	108	140
6-10: Combat Kelly in No. 6-10	13	26	42	62	86	110
11-22,24-28: 14,16-Battle Brady app. 22-Teddy Roosevelt & His Rough Riders story. 28-Last pre-code (2/55)	10	20	30	54	72	90
23,43-Everett-a	10	20	30	56	76	95
29-39,41,44-47	9	18	27	50	65	80
40,42-Williamson-a	10	20	30	54	72	90
48-Crandall-a	10	20	30	54	72	90

NOTE: *Ayers* a-19, 32. *Berg* a-44. *Colan* a-21, 22, 32, 33, 40. *Drucker* a-28, 29. *Everett* a-44. *Heath* c-23, 26, 27, 29, 32. *Maneely* a2, 23; c-2, 7, 13, 22, 34, 35. *Morisi* a-42. *Morrow* a-41. *Orlando* a-47. *Powell* a-19, 21, 25, 29, 32, 40, 47. *Robinson* a-1-4, 5(4); c-4, 5. *Robert Sale* a-19. *Severin* a-32; c-40, 45. *Woodbridge* a-45, 46.

BATTLEFRONT
Standard Comics: No. 5, June, 1952

	GD 2.0	VG 4.0	FN 6.0	VF 8.0	VF/NM 9.0	NM- 9.2
5-Toth-a	15	30	45	83	124	165

BATTLE GODS: WARRIORS OF THE CHAAK
Dark Horse Comics: Apr, 2000 - No. 4, July, 2000 ($2.95)

1-4-Francisco Ruiz Velasco-s/a						3.00

BATTLE GROUND
Atlas Comics (OMC): Sept, 1954 - No. 20, Aug, 1957

	GD 2.0	VG 4.0	FN 6.0	VF 8.0	VF/NM 9.0	NM- 9.2
1	22	44	66	126	198	270
2-Jack Katz-a	13	26	39	74	105	135
3,4-Last precode (3/55)	10	20	30	58	79	100

Battle of the Planets: Manga #1 © SFFII

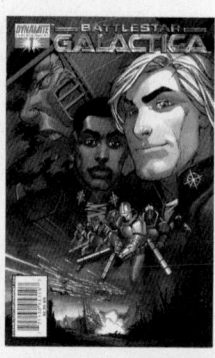

Battlestar Galactica (Classic...) #1 © USA Cable

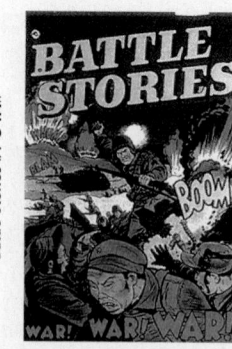

Battle Stories #1 © FAW

	GD 2.0	VG 4.0	FN 6.0	VF 8.0	VF/NM 9.0	NM- 9.2
5-8,10	10	20	30	54	72	90

9,11,13,18: 9-Krigstein-a. 11,13,18-Williamson-a in each

	GD 2.0	VG 4.0	FN 6.0	VF 8.0	VF/NM 9.0	NM- 9.2
		11	22	33	62	86	110
12,15-17,19,20	9	18	27	52	69	85
14-Kirby-a	12	24	36	69	97	125

NOTE: **Ayers** a-4, 13, 16. **Colan** a-11, 13. **Drucker** a-7, 12, 13, 20. **Heath** c-2, 5, 13. **Maneely** a-14, 19; c-1, 18, 19. **Orlando** a-17.**Pakula** a-11. **Severin** a-4, 5, 12, 19. c-20. **Tuska** a-11.

BATTLE HEROES
Stanley Publications: Sept, 1966 - No. 2, Nov, 1966 (25¢, squarebound giants)

	GD 2.0	VG 4.0	FN 6.0	VF 8.0	VF/NM 9.0	NM- 9.2
1	3	6	9	21	32	42
2	3	6	9	16	22	28

BATTLE HYMN
Image Comics: Jan, 2005 - No. 5, Oct, 2005 ($2.95/$2.99, limited series)
1-5-WW2 super team; B. Clay Moore-s/Jeremy Haun-a; flip cover on #1-4   3.00

BATTLE OF THE BULGE (See Movie Classics)

BATTLE OF THE PLANETS (Based on syndicated cartoon by Sandy Frank)
Gold Key/Whitman No. 6 on: 6/79 - No. 10, 12/80

	GD 2.0	VG 4.0	FN 6.0	VF 8.0	VF/NM 9.0	NM- 9.2
1: Mortimer a-1-4,7-10	4	8	12	22	34	45
2-6,10	3	6	9	16	22	28
7-Low print run	4	8	12	28	44	60
8,9-Low print run: 8(11/80). 9-(3-pack only?)	4	8	12	24	37	50

BATTLE OF THE PLANETS (Also see Thundercats/...)
Image Comics (Top Cow): Aug, 2002 - No. 12, Sept, 2003 ($2.95/$2.99)
1-($2.95) Alex Ross-c & art director; Tortosa-a(p); re-intro. G-Force   3.00
1-($5.95) Holofoil-c by Ross   6.00
2-11-($2.99) Ross-c on all   3.00
12-($4.99)   5.00
#1/2 (7/03, $2.99) Benitez-c; Alex Ross sketch pages   3.00
... Battle Book 1 (5/03, $4.99) background info on characters, equipment, stories   5.00
... : Jason 1 (7/03, $4.99) Ross-c; Erwin David-a; preview of Tomb Raider: Epiphany   5.00
... : Mark 1 (5/03, $4.99) Ross-c; Erwin David-a; preview of BotP: Jason   5.00
.../Thundercats 1 (Image/WildStorm, 5/03, $4.99) 2 covers by Ross & Campbell   5.00
.../Witchblade 1 (2/03, $5.95) Ross-c; Christina and Jo Chen-a   6.00
Vol. 1: Trial By Fire (2003, $7.99) r/#1-3   8.00
Vol. 2: Blood Red Sky (9/03, $16.95) r/#4-9   17.00
Vol. 3: Destroy All Monsters (11/03, $19.95) r/#10-12, ...: Jason, .../Witchblade   20.00
Vol. 1: Digest (1/04, $9.99, 7-3/8x5", B&W) r/#1-9 & ...: Mark   10.00
Vol. 2: Digest (8/04, $9.99, B&W) r/#10-12, ...: Jason, ...: Manga 1-3, .../Witchblade   10.00

BATTLE OF THE PLANETS: MANGA
Image Comics (Top Cow): Nov, 2003 - No. 3, Jan, 2004 ($2.99, B&W)
1-3-Edwin David-a/David Wohl-s; previews for Wanted & Tomb Raider #35   3.00

BATTLE OF THE PLANETS: PRINCESS
Image Comics (Top Cow): Nov, 2004 - No. 6, May, 2005 ($2.99, B&W, limited series)
1-6-Tortosa-a/Wohl-s. 1-Ross-c. 2-Tortosa-c   3.00

BATTLE POPE
Image Comics: June, 2005 - No. 14, Apr, 2007 ($2.99/$3.50, reprints 2000 B&W series in color)
1-5-Kirkman-s/Moore-a   3.00
6-10,12-14-($3.50) 14-Wedding   3.50
11-($4.99) Christmas issue   5.00
... Vol. 1: Genesis TPB (2006, $12.95) r/#1-4; sketch pages   13.00
... Vol. 2: Mayhem TPB (2006, $12.99) r/#5-8; sketch pages   13.00
... Vol. 3: Pillow Talk TPB (2007, $12.99) r/#9-11; sketch pages   13.00

BATTLER BRITTON (British comics character who debuted in 1956)
DC Comics (WildStorm): Sept, 2006 - No. 5, Jan, 2007 ($2.99, limited series)
1-5-WWII fighter pilots; Garth Ennis-s/Colin Wilson-a   3.00
TPB (2007, $19.99) r/#1-5; background of the character's British origins in the 1950s   20.00

BATTLE REPORT
Ajax/Farrell Publications: Aug, 1952 - No. 6, June, 1953

	GD 2.0	VG 4.0	FN 6.0	VF 8.0	VF/NM 9.0	NM- 9.2
1	10	20	30	58	79	100
2-6	7	14	21	35	43	50

BATTLE SQUADRON
Stanmor Publications: April, 1955 - No. 5, Dec, 1955

	GD 2.0	VG 4.0	FN 6.0	VF 8.0	VF/NM 9.0	NM- 9.2
1	10	20	30	54	72	90
2-5: 3-Iwo Jima & flag-c	6	12	18	31	38	45

BATTLESTAR GALACTICA (TV) (Also see Marvel Comics Super Special #8)
Marvel Comics Group: Mar, 1979 - No. 23, Jan, 1981

	GD 2.0	VG 4.0	FN 6.0	VF 8.0	VF/NM 9.0	NM- 9.2
1: 1-5 adapt TV episodes	2	4	6	8	10	12
2-23: 1-3-Partial-r	1	2	3	5	6	8

NOTE: **Austin** c-9i, 10i. **Golden** c-18. **Simonson** a(p)-4, 5, 11-13, 15-20, 22, 23; c(p)-4, 5,11-17, 19, 20, 22, 23.

BATTLESTAR GALACTICA (TV) (Also see Asylum)
Maximum Press: July, 1995 - No. 4, Nov, 1995 ($2.50, limited series)
1-4: Continuation of 1978 TV series   4.00
Trade paperback (12/95, $12.95)-reprints series   13.00

BATTLESTAR GALACTICA (1978 TV series)
Realm Press: Dec, 1997 - No. 5, July, 1998 ($2.99)
1-5-Chris Scalf-s/painted-a/c   3.00
...Search For Sanctuary (9/98, $2.99) Scalf & Kuhoric-s   3.00
...Search For Sanctuary Special (4/00, $3.99) Kuhoric-s/Scalf & Scott-a   4.00

BATTLESTAR GALACTICA (2003-Present TV series)
Dynamite Entertainment: No. 0, 2006 - No. 12, 2007 (25¢/$2.99)
0-(25¢-c) Two covers; Pak-s/Raynor-a   2.25
1-($2.99) Covers by Turner, Tan, Raynor & photo-c; Pak-s/Raynor-a   3.00
2-12-Four covers on each   3.00
... Volume 1 TPB (2007, $14.99) r/#0-4; cover gallery; Raynor sketch pages; commentary 15.00

BATTLESTAR GALACTICA, (Classic...) (1978 TV series characters)
Dynamite Entertainment: 2006 - Present ($2.99)
1-5: 1-Two covers by Dorman & Caldwell; Rafael-a. 2-Two covers   3.00

BATTLESTAR GALACTICA: APOLLO'S JOURNEY (1978 TV series)
Maximum Press: Apr, 1996 - No. 3, June, 1996 ($2.95, limited series)
1-3 Richard Hatch scripts   4.00

BATTLESTAR GALACTICA: CYLON APOCALYPSE (1978 TV series characters)
Dynamite Entertainment: 2007 - No. 4, 2007 ($2.99, limited series)
1-4-Carlos Rafael-a; 4 covers on each   3.00

BATTLESTAR GALACTICA: JOURNEY'S END (1978 TV series)
Maximum Press: Aug, 1996 - No. 4, Nov, 1996 ($2.99, limited series)
1-4-Continuation of the T.V. series   4.00

BATTLESTAR GALACTICA: SEASON III
Realm Press: June/July, 1999 - No. 3, Sept, 1999 ($2.99)
1-3: 1-Kuhoric-s/Scalf & Scott-a; two covers by Scalf & Jae Lee. 2,3-Two covers   3.00
Gallery (4/00, $3.99) short story and pin-ups   4.00
1999 Tour Book (5/99, $2.99)   3.00
1999 Tour Book Convention Edition (5/99)   7.00
...Special: Centurion Prime (12/99, $3.99) Kuhoric-s   4.00

BATTLESTAR GALACTICA: SEASON ZERO (2003-Present TV series)
Dynamite Entertainment: 2007 - Present ($2.99)
1-Set 2 years before the Cylon attack; multiple covers   3.00

BATTLESTAR GALACTICA: SPECIAL EDITION (TV) (one-shot)
Maximum Press: Jan, 1997 ($2.99, one-shot)
1-Fully painted; Scalf-c/s/a; r/Asylum   3.00

BATTLESTAR GALACTICA: STARBUCK (TV)
Maximum Press: Dec, 1995 - No. 3, Mar, 1996 ($2.50, limited series)
1-3   4.00

BATTLESTAR GALACTICA: THE COMPENDIUM (TV)
Maximum Press: Feb, 1997 ($2.99, one-shot)
1   4.00

BATTLESTAR GALACTICA: THE ENEMY WITHIN (TV)
Maximum Press: Nov, 1995 - No. 3, Feb, 1996 ($2.50, limited series)
1-3: 3-Indicia reads Feb, 1995 in error.   4.00

BATTLESTAR GALACTICA ZAREK (2003 series)
Dynamite Entertainment: 2007 - No. 4, 2007 ($3.50, limited series)
1-4-Origin story of political activist Tom Zarek; 2 covers on each   3.50

BATTLE STORIES (See XMas Comics)
Fawcett Publications: Jan, 1952 - No. 11, Sept, 1953

	GD 2.0	VG 4.0	FN 6.0	VF 8.0	VF/NM 9.0	NM- 9.2
1-Evans-a	16	32	48	92	144	195
2	10	20	30	56	76	95
3-11	9	18	27	47	61	75

BATTLE STORIES
Super Comics: 1963 - 1964

	GD 2.0	VG 4.0	FN 6.0	VF 8.0	VF/NM 9.0	NM- 9.2
Reprints #10-13,15-18: 10-r/U.S Tank Commandos #? 11-r/? 11, 12,17-r/Monty Hall #?; 13-Kintsler-a (1pg).15-r/American Air Forces #7 by Powell; Bolle-r. 18-U.S. Fighting Air Force #?	2	4	6	9	13	16

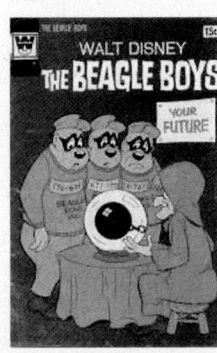

Beagle Boys #16 © DIS

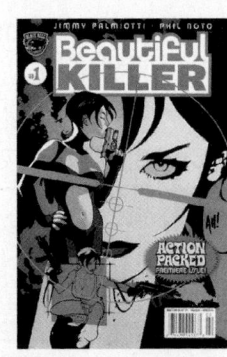

Beautiful Killer #1 © Black Bull

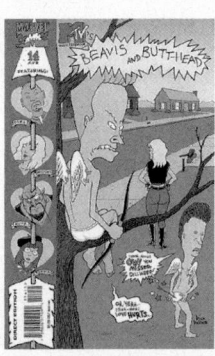

Beavis and Butthead #14 © MTV

	GD	VG	FN	VF	VF/NM	NM-
	2.0	4.0	6.0	8.0	9.0	9.2

	GD	VG	FN	VF	VF/NM	NM-
	2.0	4.0	6.0	8.0	9.0	9.2

BATTLETECH (See Blackthorne 3-D Series #41 for 3-D issue)
Blackthorne Publishing: Oct, 1987 - No. 6, 1988 ($1.75/$2.00)

1-6: Based on game. 1-Color. 2-Begin B&W						3.00
Annual 1 ($4.50, B&W)						5.00

BATTLETECH
Malibu Comics: Feb, 1995 ($2.95)

0						3.00

BATTLETECH FALLOUT
Malibu Comics: Dec, 1994 - No. 4, Mar, 1995 ($2.95)

1-4-Two edi. exist #1; normal logo						3.00
1-Gold version w/foil logo stamped "Gold Limited Edition						8.00
1-Full-c holographic limited edition						6.00

BATTLETIDE (Death's Head II & Killpower…)
Marvel Comics UK, Ltd.: Dec, 1992 - No. 4, Mar, 1993 ($1.75, mini-series)

1-4: Wolverine, Psylocke, Dark Angel app.						2.50

BATTLETIDE II (Death's Head II & Killpower…)
Marvel Comics UK, Ltd.: Aug, 1993 - No. 4, Nov, 1993 ($1.75, mini-series)

1-($2.95)-Foil embossed logo						3.00
2-4: 2-Hulk-c/story						2.50

BAY CITY JIVE
DC Comics (WildStorm): Jul, 2001 - No. 3, Sept, 2001 ($2.95, limited series)

1-3: Intro Sugah Rollins in 1970s San Francisco; Layman-s/Johnson-a						3.00

BAYWATCH COMIC STORIES (TV) (Magazine)
Acclaim Comics (Armada): May, 1996 - No. 4, 1997 ($4.95) (Photo-c on all)

1-4: Photo comics based on TV show						5.00

BEACH BLANKET BINGO (See Movie Classics)

BEAGLE BOYS, THE (Walt Disney)(See The Phantom Blot)
Gold Key: 11/64; No. 2, 11/65; No. 3, 8/66 - No. 47, 2/79 (See WDC&S #134)

1	5	10	15	30	48	65
2-5	3	6	9	17	25	32
6-10	3	6	9	15	21	26
11-20: 11,14,19-r	2	4	6	11	16	20
21-30: 27-r	2	4	6	8	11	14
31-47	1	3	4	6	8	10

BEAGLE BOYS VERSUS UNCLE SCROOGE
Gold Key: Mar, 1979 - No. 12, Feb, 1980

1	2	4	6	9	13	16
2-12: 9-r	1	2	3	5	6	8

BEANBAGS
Ziff-Davis Publ. Co. (Approved Comics): Winter, 1951 - No. 2, Spring, 1952

1,2	12	24	36	69	97	125

BEANIE THE MEANIE
Fago Publications: No. 3, May, 1959

3	5	10	15	24	30	35

BEANY AND CECIL (TV) (Bob Clampett's…)
Dell Publishing Co.: Jan, 1952 - 1955; July-Sept, 1962 - No. 5, July-Sept, 1963

Four Color 368	24	48	72	179	320	460
Four Color 414,448,477,530,570,635(1/55)	15	30	45	105	188	270
01-057-209 (#1)	14	28	42	100	178	255
2-5	10	20	30	68	119	170

BEAR COUNTRY (Disney)
Dell Publishing Co.: No. 758, Dec, 1956

Four Color 758-Movie	5	10	15	35	55	75

BEAST (See X-Men)
Marvel Comics: May, 1997 - No. 3, 1997 ($2.50, mini-series)

1-3-Giffen-s/Nocon-a						3.00

BEAST BOY (See Titans)
DC Comics: Jan, 2000 - No. 4, Apr, 2000 ($2.95, mini-series)

1-4-Justiano-c/a; Raab & Johns-s						3.00

B.E.A.S.T.I.E.S. (Also see Axis Alpha)
Axis Comics: Apr, 1994 ($1.95)

1-Javier Saltares-c/a/scripts						2.50

BEATLES, THE (See Girls' Romances #109, Go-Go, Heart Throbs #101, Herbie #5, Howard the Duck

Mag. #4, Laugh #166, Marvel Comics Super Special #4, My Little Margie #54, Not Brand Echh, Strange Tales #130, Summer Love, Superman's Pal Jimmy Olsen #79, Teen Confessions #37, Tippy's Friends & Tippy Teen)

BEATLES, THE (Life Story)
Dell Publishing Co.: Sept-Nov, 1964 (35¢)

1-(Scarce)-Stories with color photo pin-ups; Paul S. Newman-s	40	80	120	300	550	800

BEATLES EXPERIENCE, THE
Revolutionary Comics: Mar, 1991 - No. 8, 1991 ($2.50, B&W, limited series)

1-8: 1-Gold logo						5.00

BEATLES YELLOW SUBMARINE (See Movie Comics under Yellow…)

BEAUTIFUL KILLER
Black Bull Comics: Sept., 2002 - No. 3, Jan, 2003 ($2.99, limited series)

…Limited Preview Edition (5/02, $5.00) preview pgs. & creator interviews						5.00
1-Noto-a/Palmiotti-s; Hughes-c; intro Brigit Cole						3.00
2,3: 2-Jusko-c. 3-Noto-c						3.00
TPB (5/03, $9.99) r/#1-3; cover gallery and Adam Hughes sketch pages						10.00

BEAUTIFUL PEOPLE
Slave Labor Graphics: Apr, 1994 ($4.95, 8-1/2x11", one-shot)

nn						5.00

BEAUTIFUL STORIES FOR UGLY CHILDREN
DC Comics (Piranha Press): 1989 - No. 30, 1991 ($2.00/$2.50, B&W, mature)

Vol. 1-20: 12-$2.50-c begins						3.50
21-25						4.50
26-30-(Lower print run)						6.00
A Cotton Candy Autopsy ($12.95, B&W)-Reprints 1st two volumes						13.00

BEAUTY AND THE BEAST, THE
Marvel Comics Group: Jan, 1985 - No. 4, Apr, 1985 (limited series)

1-4: Dazzler & the Beast from X-Men; Sienkiewicz-c on all						3.00

BEAUTY AND THE BEAST (Graphic novel)(Also see Cartoon Tales & Disney's New Adventures of…)
Disney Comics: 1992

nn-($4.95, prestige edition)-Adapts animated film						7.00
nn-($2.50, newsstand edition)						3.00

BEAUTY AND THE BEAST
Disney Comics: Sept., 1992 - No. 2, 1992 ($1.50, limited series)

1,2						3.00

BEAUTY AND THE BEAST: PORTRAIT OF LOVE (TV)
First Comics: May, 1989 - No. 2, Mar, 1990 ($5.95, 60 pgs., squarebound)

1,2: 1-Based on TV show, Wendy Pini-a/scripts. 2-…: Night of Beauty; by Wendy Pini						6.00

BEAVER VALLEY (Movie)(Disney)
Dell Publishing Co.: No. 625, Apr, 1955

Four Color 625	6	12	18	41	66	90

BEAVIS AND BUTTHEAD (MTV's…)(TV cartoon)
Marvel Comics: Mar, 1994 - No. 28, June, 1996 ($1.95)

1-Silver ink-c. 1, 2-Punisher & Devil Dinosaur app.						4.00
1-2nd printing						2.50
2,3: 2-Wolverine app. 3-Man-Thing, Spider-Man, Venom, Carnage, Mary Jane & Stan Lee cameos; John Romita, Sr. art (2 pgs.)						2.50
4-28: 5-War Machine, Thor, Loki, Hulk, Captain America & Rhino cameos. 6-Psylocke, Polaris, Daredevil & Bullseye app. 7-Ghost Rider & Sub-Mariner app. 8-Quasar & Eon app. 9-Prowler & Nightwatch app. 11-Black Widow app. 12-Thunderstrike & Bloodaxe app. 13-Night Thrasher app. 14-Spider-Man 2099 app. 15-Warlock app. 16-X-Factor app. 25-Juggernaut app.						2.50

BECK & CAUL INVESTIGATIONS
Gauntlet Comics (Caliber): Jan, 1994 - No. 5, 1995? ($2.95, B&W)

1-5						3.00
Special 1 ($4.95)						5.00

BEDKNOBS AND BROOMSTICKS (See Walt Disney Showcase No. 6 & 50)

BEDLAM!
Eclipse Comics: Sept, 1985 - No. 2, Sept, 1985 (B&W-r in color)

1,2: Bissette-a						3.00

BEDTIME STORY (See Cinema Comics Herald)

BEELZEVIS
Slave Labor Graphics: Feb, 1994 ($2.95, B&W, one-shot)

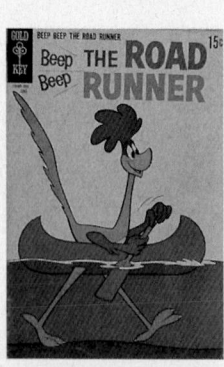

Beep Beep, The Road Runner #12 © WB

Behind Prison Bars #1 © AVON

Ben Casey #5 © Bing Crosby Prods.

	GD 2.0	VG 4.0	FN 6.0	VF 8.0	VF/NM 9.0	NM- 9.2
1						3.00

BEEP BEEP, THE ROAD RUNNER (TV) (See Dell Giant Comics Bugs Bunny Vacation Funnies #8 for 1st app.) (Also see Daffy & Kite Fun Book)
Dell Publishing Co./Gold Key No. 1-88/Whitman No. 89 on: July, 1958 - No. 14, Aug-Oct, 1962; Oct, 1966 - No. 105, 1984

	GD	VG	FN	VF	VF/NM	NM-
Four Color 918 (#1, 7/58)	10	20	30	71	126	180
Four Color 1008,1046 (11-1/59-60)	6	12	18	41	66	90
4(2-4/60)-14(Dell)	6	12	18	37	59	80
1(10/66, Gold Key)	6	12	18	37	59	80
2-5	4	8	12	23	36	48
6-14	3	6	9	17	25	32
15-18,20-40	3	6	9	14	19	24
19-With pull-out poster	3	6	9	21	32	42
41-50	2	4	6	10	14	18
51-70	2	4	6	8	10	12
71-88	1	2	3	5	6	8
89,90,94-101: 100(3/82), 101(4/82)	1	2	3	5	7	9
91(8/80), 92(9/80), 93 (3-pack?) (low printing)	3	6	9	20	30	40
102-105 (All #90189 on-c; nd or date code; pre-pack) 102(6/83), 103(7/83),						
104(5/84), 105(6/84)	3	6	9	14	19	24
#63-2970 (Now Age Books/Pendulum Pub. Comic Digest, 1971, 75¢, 100 pages, B&W)						
collection of one-page gags	4	8	12	24	37	50

NOTE: See March of Comics #351, 353, 375, 387, 397, 416, 430, 442, 455. #5, 8-10, 35, 53, 59-62, 68-r; 96-102, 104 are 1/3-r.

BEETLE BAILEY (See Giant Comic Album, Sarge Snorkel; also Comics Reading Libraries in the Promotional Comics section)
Dell Publishing Co./Gold Key #39-53/King #54-66/Charlton #67-119/Gold Key #120-131/ Whitman #132: #459, 5/53 - #38, 5-7/62; #39, 11/62 - #53, 5/66; #54, 8/66 - #65, 12/67;#67, 2/69 - #119, 11/76; #120, 4/78 - #132, 4/80

	GD	VG	FN	VF	VF/NM	NM-
Four Color 469 (#1)-By Mort Walker	10	20	30	71	126	180
Four Color 521,552,622	6	12	18	41	66	90
5(2-4/56)-10(5-7/57)	5	10	15	35	55	75
11-20(4-5/59)	4	8	12	24	37	50
21-38(5-7/62)	3	6	9	18	27	35
39-53(5/66)	3	6	9	16	22	28
54-65 (No. 66 publ. overseas only?)	2	4	6	13	18	22
67-69: 69-Last 12¢ issue	2	4	6	11	16	20
70-99	2	4	6	9	12	15
100	2	4	6	11	16	20
101-111,114-119	1	3	4	6	8	10
112,113-Byrne illos. (4 each)	2	4	6	9	12	15
120-132						6.00

BEETLE BAILEY
Harvey Comics: V2#1, Sept, 1992 - V2#9, Aug, 1994 ($1.25/$1.50)

V2#1						4.00
2-9-($1.50)						3.00
Big Book 1(11/92),2(5/93)(Both $1.95, 52 pgs.)						3.50
Giant Size V2#1(10/92),2(3/93)(Both $2.25,68 pgs.)						3.50

BEETLEJUICE (TV)
Harvey Comics: Oct, 1991 ($1.25)

1						3.00

BEETLEJUICE CRIMEBUSTERS ON THE HAUNT
Harvey Comics: Sept, 1992 - No. 3, Jan, 1993 ($1.50, limited series)

1-3						3.00

BEE 29, THE BOMBARDIER
Neal Publications: Feb, 1945

	GD	VG	FN	VF	VF/NM	NM-
1-(Funny animal)	31	62	93	178	282	385

BEFORE THE FANTASTIC FOUR: BEN GRIMM AND LOGAN
Marvel Comics: July, 2000 - No. 3, Sept, 2000 ($2.99, limited series)

1-3-The Thing and Wolverine app.; Hama-s						3.00

BEFORE THE FANTASTIC FOUR: REED RICHARDS
Marvel Comics: Sept, 2000 - No. 3, Dec, 2000 ($2.99, limited series)

1-3-Peter David-s/Duncan Fegredo-c/a						3.00

BEFORE THE FANTASTIC FOUR: THE STORMS
Marvel Comics: Dec, 2000 - No. 3, Feb, 2001 ($2.99, limited series)

1-3-Adlard-a						3.00

BEHIND PRISON BARS
Realistic Comics (Avon): 1952

	GD	VG	FN	VF	VF/NM	NM-
1-Kinstler-c	32	64	96	186	293	400

BEHOLD THE HANDMAID
George Pflaum: 1954 (Religious) (25¢ with a 20¢ sticker price)

	GD	VG	FN	VF	VF/NM	NM-
nn	6	12	18	28	34	40

BELIEVE IT OR NOT (See Ripley's...)

BELLE STARR: QUEEN OF BANDITS
Moonstone: 2005 - Present ($2.95, B&W)

1,2-Ricketts-s/Buccallato-a/Beck-c						3.00

BEN AND ME (Disney)
Dell Publishing Co.: No. 539, Mar, 1954

	GD	VG	FN	VF	VF/NM	NM-
Four Color 539	4	8	12	26	41	55

BEN BOWIE AND HIS MOUNTAIN MEN
Dell Publishing Co.: 1952 - No. 17, Nov-Jan, 1958-59

	GD	VG	FN	VF	VF/NM	NM-
Four Color 443 (#1)	8	16	24	56	93	130
Four Color 513,557,599,626,657	5	10	15	30	48	65
7(5-7/56)-11: 11-Intro/origin Yellow Hair	4	8	12	24	37	50
12-17	4	8	12	22	34	45

BEN CASEY (TV)
Dell Publishing Co.: June-July, 1962 - No. 10, June-Aug, 1965 (Photo-c)

	GD	VG	FN	VF	VF/NM	NM-
12-063-207 (#1)	6	12	18	41	66	90
2(10/62),3,5-10	4	8	12	24	37	50
4-Marijuana & heroin use story	4	8	12	28	44	60

BEN CASEY FILM STORY (TV)
Gold Key: Nov, 1962 (25¢) (Photo-c)

	GD	VG	FN	VF	VF/NM	NM-
30009-211-All photos	8	16	24	52	86	120

BENEATH THE PLANET OF THE APES (See Movie Comics & Power Record Comics)

BEN FRANKLIN (See Kite Fun Book)

BEN HUR
Dell Publishing Co.: No. 1052, Nov, 1959

	GD	VG	FN	VF	VF/NM	NM-
Four Color 1052-Movie, Manning-a	10	20	30	67	116	165

BEN ISRAEL
Logos International: 1974 (39¢)

	GD	VG	FN	VF	VF/NM	NM-
nn-Christian religious	2	4	6	9	13	16

BEOWULF (Also see First Comics Graphic Novel #1)
National Periodical Publications: Apr-May, 1975 - No. 6, Feb-Mar, 1976

	GD	VG	FN	VF	VF/NM	NM-
1	2	4	6	8	11	14
2,3,5,6: 5-Flying saucer-c/story	1	2	3	5	6	8
4-Dracula-c/s	1	2	3	5	7	9

BERNI WRIGHTSON, MASTER OF THE MACABRE
Pacific Comics/Eclipse Comics No. 5: July, 1983 - No. 5, Nov, 1984 ($1.50, Baxter paper)

1-5: Wrightson-c/a(r). 4-Jeff Jones-r (11 pgs.)						5.00

BERRYS, THE (Also see Funny World)
Argo Publ.: May, 1956

	GD	VG	FN	VF	VF/NM	NM-
1-Reprints daily & Sunday strips & daily Animal Antics by Ed Nofziger	6	12	18	29	36	42

BERZERKERS (See Youngblood V1#2)
Image Comics (Extreme Studios): Aug, 1995 - No. 3, Oct, 1995 ($2.50, limited series)

1-3: Beau Smith scripts, Fraga-a						2.50

BEST COMICS
Better Publications: Nov, 1939 - No. 4, Feb, 1940(10-11/16" wide x 8" tall, reads sideways)

	GD	VG	FN	VF	VF/NM	NM-
1-(Scarce)-Red Mask begins(1st app.) & c/s-all	86	172	258	538	894	1250
2-4: 4-Cannibalism story	48	96	114	293	484	675

BEST FROM BOY'S LIFE, THE
Gilberton Company: Oct, 1957 - No. 5, Oct, 1958 (35¢)

	GD	VG	FN	VF	VF/NM	NM-
1-Space Conquerors & Kam of the Ancient Ones begin, end #5; Bob Cousy photo/story						
	13	26	39	72	101	130
2,3,5	8	16	24	42	54	65
4-L.B. Cole-a	8	16	24	44	57	70

BEST LOVE (Formerly Sub-Mariner Comics No. 32)
Marvel Comics (MPI): No. 33, Aug, 1949 - No. 36, April, 1950 (Photo-c 33-36)

	GD	VG	FN	VF	VF/NM	NM-
33-Kubert-a	14	28	42	78	112	145
34	9	18	27	50	65	80
35,36-Everett-a	10	20	30	56	76	95

The Best of DC #45 © DC

Best Romance #5 © STD

Betty #57 © AP

	GD 2.0	VG 4.0	FN 6.0	VF 8.0	VF/NM 9.0	NM- 9.2

BEST OF BUGS BUNNY, THE
Gold Key: Oct, 1966 - No. 2, Oct, 1968

	GD 2.0	VG 4.0	FN 6.0	VF 8.0	VF/NM 9.0	NM- 9.2
1,2-Giants	4	8	12	28	44	60

BEST OF DC, THE (Blue Ribbon Digest) (See Limited Coll. Ed. C-52)
DC Comics: Sept-Oct, 1979 - No. 71, Apr, 1986 (100-148 pgs; mostly reprints)

1-Superman, w/"Death of Superman"-r	2	4	6	11	16	20
2,5-9: 2-Batman 40th Ann. Special. 5-Best of 1979. 6,8-Superman. 7-Superboy. 9-Batman, Creeper app.	2	4	6	8	10	12
3-Superfriends	2	4	6	9	12	15
4-Rudolph the Red Nosed Reindeer	2	4	6	9	13	16
10-Secret Origins of Super Villains; 1st ever Penguin origin-s	3	6	9	16	22	28

11-16,18-20: 11-The Year's Best Stories. 12-Superman Time and Space Stories.13-Best of DC Comics Presents. 14-New origin stories of Batman villains. 15-Superboy. 16-Superman Anniv. 18-Teen Titans new-s., Adams, Kane-a. 19-Superman. 20-World's Finest

	1	2	3	5	7	9
17-Supergirl	2	4	6	8	10	12

21,22: 21-Justice Society. 22-Christmas; unpublished Sandman story w/Kirby-a

	2	4	6	10	14	18

23-27: 23-(148 pgs.)-Best of 1981. 24 Legion, new story and 16 pgs. new costumes. 25-Superman. 26-Brave & Bold. 27-Superman vs. Luthor

	2	4	6	9	12	15

28,29: 28-Binky, Sugar & Spike app. 29-Sugar & Spike, 3 new stories; new Stanley & his Monster story

	2	4	6	9	13	16

30,32-36,38,40: 30-Detective Comics. 32-Superman. 33-Secret origins of Legion Heroes and Villains. 34-Metal Men; has #497 on-c from Adv. Comics. 35-The Year's Best Comics Stories (148 pgs.). 36-Superman vs. Kryptonite. 38-Superman. 40-World of Krypton

	2	4	6	9	12	15
31-JLA	2	4	6	10	14	18
37,39: 37-"Funny Stuff", Mayer-a. 39-Binky	2	4	6	10	14	18

41,43,45,47,49,53,55,58,60,63,65,68,70: 41-Sugar & Spike new stories with Mayer-a. 43,49,55-Funny Stuff. 45,53,70-Binky. 47,58,65,68-Sugar & Spike. 60-Plop!; Wood-c(r) & Aragonés-r (5/85). 63-Plop!; Wrightson-a(r)

	3	6	9	14	19	24

42,44,46,48,50-52,54,56,57,59,61,62,64,66,67,69,71: 42,56-Superman vs. Aliens. 44,57,67-Superboy & LSH. 46-Jimmy Olsen. 48-Superman Team-ups. 50-Year's best Superman. 51-Batman Family. 52 Best of 1984. 54,56,59-Superman. 61-(148 pgs.)Year's best. 62-Best of Batman 1985. 69-Year's best Team stories. 71-Year's best

	2	4	6	10	14	18

NOTE: **N. Adams** a-2r, 14r, 18r, 26, 51. **Aparo** a-9, 14, 26, 30; c-9, 14, 26. **Austin** a-51i. **Buckler** a-40p; c-16, 22. **Giffen** a-50, 52; c-33p. **Grell** a-33p. **Grossman** a-37. **Heath** a-26. **Infantino** a-10r, 18. **Kaluta** a-14. **G. Kane** a-10r, 18r; c-40, 44. **Kubert** a-10r, 21, 26. **Layton** a-21. **S. Mayer** c-29, 37, 41, 43, 47; a-28, 29, 37, 41, 43, 47, 58, 65, 68. **Moldoff** c-64p. **Morrow** a-40; c-40. **W. Mortimer** a-39p. **Newton** a-5, 51. **Perez** a-24, 50p; c-18, 21, 23. **Rogers** a-14, 51p. **Simonson** a-11r. **Spiegle** a-52. **Starlin** a-51. **Staton** a-5, 21. **Tuska** a-24. **Wolverton** a-60. **Wood** a-60, 63; c-60, 63. **Wrightson** a-60. New art in #14, 18, 24.

BEST OF DENNIS THE MENACE, THE
Hallden/Fawcett Publications: Summer, 1959 - No. 5, Spring, 1961 (100 pgs.)

1-All reprints; Wiseman-a	7	14	21	45	73	100
2-5	4	8	12	28	44	60

BEST OF DONALD DUCK, THE
Gold Key: Nov, 1965 (12¢, 36 pgs.)(Lists 2nd printing in indicia)

1-Reprints Four Color #223 by Barks	8	16	24	54	90	125

BEST OF DONALD DUCK & UNCLE SCROOGE, THE
Gold Key: Nov, 1964 - No. 2, Sept, 1967 (25¢ Giants)

1(30022-411)('64)-Reprints 4-Color #189 & 408 by Carl Barks; cover of F.C. #189 redrawn by Barks	9	18	27	60	100	140
2(30022-709)('67)-Reprints 4-Color #256 & "Seven Cities of Cibola" & U.S. #8 by Barks	7	14	21	50	83	115

BEST OF HORROR AND SCIENCE FICTION COMICS
Bruce Webster: 1987 ($2.00)

1-Wolverton, Frazetta, Powell, Ditko-r						5.00

BEST OF JOSIE AND THE PUSSYCATS
Archie Comics: 2001 ($10.95, TPB)

1-Reprints 1st app. and noteworthy stories						11.00

BEST OF MARMADUKE, THE
Charlton Comics: 1960

1-Brad Anderson's strip reprints	3	6	9	19	29	38

BEST OF MS. TREE, THE
Pyramid Comics: 1987 - No. 4, 1988 ($2.00, B&W, limited series)

1-4						2.50

BEST OF RAY BRADBURY, THE
ibooks: 2003 ($18.95, TPB)

The Graphic Novel - Reprints from Ray Bradbury Comics; adaptations by various						19.00

BEST OF THE BRAVE AND THE BOLD, THE (See Super DC Giant)
DC Comics: Oct, 1988 - No. 6, Jan, 1989 ($2.50, limited series)

1-6: Neal Adams-r, Kubert-r & Heath-r in all						4.00

BEST OF THE SPIRIT, THE
DC Comics: 2005 ($14.99, TPB)

nn-Reprints 1st app. and noteworthy stories; intro by Neil Gaiman; Eisner bio.						15.00

BEST OF THE WEST (See A-1 Comics)
Magazine Enterprises: 1951 - No. 12, April-June, 1954

1(A-1 42)-Ghost Rider, Durango Kid, Straight Arrow, Bobby Benson begin	41	82	123	250	400	550
2(A-1 46)	22	44	66	128	202	275
3(A-1 52), 4(A-1 59), 5(A-1 66)	18	36	54	105	165	225
6(A-1 70), 7(A-1 76), 8(A-1 81), 9(A-1 85), 10(A-1 87), 11(A-1 97), 12(A-1 103)	15	30	45	84	127	170

NOTE: **Bolle** a-9. **Borth** a-12. **Guardineer** a-5, 12. **Powell** a-1, 12.

BEST OF UNCLE SCROOGE & DONALD DUCK, THE
Gold Key: Nov, 1966 (25¢)

1(30030-611)-Reprints part 4-Color #159 & 456 & Uncle Scrooge #6,7 by Carl Barks	8	16	24	52	86	120

BEST OF WALT DISNEY COMICS, THE
Western Publishing Co.: 1974 ($1.50, 52 pgs.) (Walt Disney)
(8-1/2x11" cardboard covers; 32,000 printed of each)

96170-Reprints 1st two stories less 1 pg. each from 4-Color #62	5	10	15	35	55	75
96171-Reprints Mickey Mouse and the Bat Bandit of Inferno Gulch from 1934 (strips) by Gottfredson	5	10	15	35	55	75
96172-r/Uncle Scrooge #386 & two other stories	5	10	15	35	55	75
96173-Reprints "Ghost of the Grotto" (from 4-Color #159) & "Christmas on Bear Mountain" (from 4-Color #178)	5	10	15	35	55	75

BEST ROMANCE
Standard Comics (Visual Editions): No. 5, Feb-Mar, 1952 - No. 7, Aug, 1952

5-Toth-a; photo-c	14	28	42	76	108	140
6,7-Photo-c	8	16	24	42	54	65

BEST SELLER COMICS (See Tailspin Tommy)

BEST WESTERN (Formerly Terry Toons? or Miss America Magazine
Marvel Comics (IPC): V7#24(#57)?; Western Outlaws & Sheriffs No. 60 on)
No. 58, June, 1949 - No. 59, Aug, 1949

58,59-Black Rider, Kid Colt, Two-Gun Kid app.; both have Syd Shores-c	21	42	63	120	188	255

BETTIE PAGE COMICS
Dark Horse Comics: Mar, 1996 ($3.95)

1-Dave Stevens-c; Blevins & Heath-a; Jaime Hernandez pin-up	1	2	3	4	5	7

BETTIE PAGE COMICS: QUEEN OF THE NILE
Dark Horse Comics: Dec, 1999 - No. 3, Apr, 2000 ($2.95, limited series)

1-3-Silke-s/a; Stevens-c						3.00

BETTIE PAGE COMICS: SPICY ADVENTURE
Dark Horse Comics: Jan, 1997 ($2.95, one-shot, mature)

nn-Silke-c/s/a						4.00

BETTY (See Pep Comics #22 for 1st app.)
Archie Comics: Sept, 1992 - Present ($1.25/$1.50/$1.75/$1.79/$1.99/$2.19/$2.25)

1						5.00
2-18,20-24: 20-1st Super Sleuther-s						3.00
19-Love Showdown part 2						5.00
25-Pin-up page of Betty as Marilyn Monroe, Madonna, Lady Di						5.00
26-50						3.00
51-170: 57- "A Storm Over Uniforms" x-over part 5,6						2.50

BETTY AND HER STEADY (Going Steady with Betty No. 1)
Avon Periodicals: No. 2, Mar-Apr, 1950

2	10	20	30	54	72	90

BETTY AND ME
Archie Publications: Aug, 1965 - No. 200, Aug, 1992

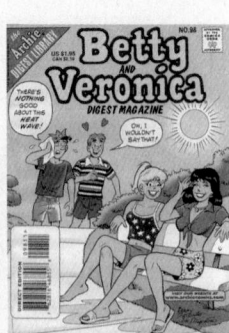

Betty and Veronica Digest #98 © AP

Betty and Veronica Spectacular #64 © AP

Beware #6 © TM

	GD 2.0	VG 4.0	FN 6.0	VF 8.0	VF/NM 9.0	NM- 9.2
1	9	18	27	63	107	150
2,3: 3-Origin Superteen	5	10	15	35	55	75
4-8: Superteen in new costume #4-7; dons new helmet in #5, ends #8.	4	8	12	24	37	50
9,10: Girl from R.I.V.E.R.D.A.L.E. 9-UFO-s	3	6	9	19	29	38
11-15,17-20(4/69)	3	6	9	16	23	30
16-Classic cover; w/risqué cover dialogue	4	8	12	24	37	50
21,24-35: 33-Paper doll page	2	4	6	13	18	22
22-Archies Band-s	3	6	9	14	20	25
23-I Dream of Jeannie parody	3	6	9	16	23	30
36(8/71),37,41-55 (52 pgs.): 42-Betty as vamp-s	3	6	9	14	19	24
38-Sabrina app.	3	6	9	21	32	42
39-Josie and Sabrina cover cameos	3	6	9	17	25	32
40-Archie & Betty share a cabin	3	6	9	14	20	25
56(4/71)-80(12/76): 79 Betty Cooper mysteries thru #86. 79-81-Drago the Vampire-s	2	4	6	8	11	14
81-99: 83-Harem-s. 84-Jekyll & Hyde-c/s	1	3	4	6	8	10
100(3/79)	2	4	6	8	11	14
101,118: 101-Elvis mentioned. 118-Tarzan mentioned	1	2	3	5	6	8
102-117,119-130(9/82): 103,104-Space-s. 124-DeCarlo-a begins						6.00
131-138,140,142-147,149-154,156-158: 135,136-Jason Blossom app. 136-Cheryl Blossom cameo. 137-Space-s. 138-Tarzan parody						4.00
139,141,148: 139-Katy Keene collecting-s; Archie in drag-s. 141-Tarzan parody-s. 148-Cyndi Lauper parody-s						5.00
155,159,160(8/87): 155-Archie in drag-s. 159-Superhero gag-c. 160-Wheel of Fortune parody						5.00
161-169,171-199						3.00
170,200: 170-New Archie Superhero-s						5.00

BETTY AND VERONICA (Also see Archie's Girls...)
Archie Enterprises: June, 1987 - Present (75¢ /$1.25/$1.50/$1.75/$1.79/$1.99/$2.19/$2.25)

1	1	2	3	5	7	9
2-10						5.50
11-30						4.00
31-50						3.00
51-81						2.50
82-Love Showdown part 3						5.00
83-158						2.50
159-232						2.25
Summer Fun 1 (1994, $2.00, 52 pgs. plus poster)						3.00

NOTE: 2005 Free Comic Book Day edition is listed in Promotional Comics section.

BETTY & VERONICA ANNUAL DIGEST (...Digest Magazine #1-4, 44 on; ...Comics Digest Mag. #5-43)
Archie Publications: Nov, 1980 - Present ($1.00/-$2.49, digest size)

1	3	6	9	16	22	28
2-10: 2(11/81-Katy Keene story), 3(8/82)	2	4	6	9	13	16
11-30	1	3	4	6	8	10
31-50	1	2	3	4	5	7
51-70						4.00
71-180: 110-Begin $2.19-c. 135-Begin $2.39-c. 165-Begin $2.49						2.50

BETTY & VERONICA ANNUAL DIGEST MAGAZINE
Archie Comics: Sept, 1989 - No. 16, Aug, 1997 ($1.50/$1.75/$1.79, 128 pgs.)

1	1	2	3	5	7	9
2-10: 9-Neon ink logo						5.00
11-16: 16-Begin $1.79-c						3.00

BETTY & VERONICA CHRISTMAS SPECTACULAR (See Archie Giant Series Magazine #159, 168, 180, 191, 204, 217, 229, 241, 453, 465, 477, 489, 501, 513, 525, 536, 547, 558, 568, 580, 593, 606, 618)

BETTY & VERONICA DOUBLE DIGEST MAGAZINE
Archie Enterprises: 1987 - Present ($2.25-$3.69, digest size, 256 pgs.)(...Digest #12 on)

1	2	4	6	8	10	12
2-10	1	2	3	4	5	7
11-25: 5,17-Xmas-c. 16-Capt. Hero story						5.00
26-50						4.00
51-150: 87-Begin $3.19-c. 95-Begin $3.29-c. 114-Begin $3.59-c. 142-Begin $3.69-c						3.75
151-157: 151-(7/07)-Realistic style Betty & Veronica debuts						4.00
Betty & Veronica: in Bad Boy Trouble Vol.1 TPB (2007, $7.49) r/new style from #151-154						8.00

BETTY & VERONICA SPECTACULAR (See Archie Giant Series Magazine #11, 16, 21, 26, 32, 138, 145, 153, 162, 173, 184, 197, 201, 210, 214, 221, 226, 234, 238, 246, 250, 458, 462, 470, 482, 486, 494, 498, 506, 510, 518, 522, 526, 530, 537, 552, 559, 563, 569, 575, 582, 588, 600, 608, 613, 620, 623, and Betty & Veronica)

BETTY AND VERONICA SPECTACULAR
Archie Comics: Oct, 1992 - Present ($1.25/$1.50/$1.75/$1.99/$2.19/$2.25)

1-Dan DeCarlo-c/a						5.00

	GD 2.0	VG 4.0	FN 6.0	VF 8.0	VF/NM 9.0	NM- 9.2
2-20						3.00
21-80: 48-Cheryl Blossom leaves Riverdale. 64-Cheryl Blossom returns						2.25

BETTY & VERONICA SPRING SPECTACULAR (See Archie Giant Series Magazine #569, 582, 595)

BETTY & VERONICA SUMMER FUN (See Archie Giant Series Mag. #8, 13, 18, 23, 28, 34, 140, 147, 155, 164, 175, 187, 199, 212, 224, 236, 248, 460, 484, 496, 508, 520, 529, 539, 550, 561, 572, 585, 598, 611, 621)
Archie Comics: 1994 - Present ($2.00/$2.25/$2.29)

1-6: 5-($2.25-c). 6-($2.29-c)						2.50
Vol. 1 (2003, $10.95) reprints stories from Archie Giant Series editions						11.00

BETTY BOOP'S BIG BREAK
First Publishing: 1990 ($5.95, 52 pgs.)

nn-By Joshua Quagmire; 60th anniversary ish.						6.00

BETTY PAGE 3-D COMICS
The 3-D Zone: 1991 ($3.95, "7-1/2x10-1/4", 28 pgs., no glasses)

1-Photo inside covers; back-c nudity	1	2	3	5	6	8

BETTY'S DIARY (See Archie Giant Series Magazine No. 555)
Archie Enterprises: April, 1986 - No. 40, Apr, 1991 (#1:65¢; 75¢/95¢)

1						6.00
2-10						4.00
11-40						2.50

BETTY'S DIGEST
Archie Enterprises: Nov, 1996 - No. 2 ($1.75/$1.79)

1,2						3.00

BEVERLY HILLBILLIES (TV)
Dell Publishing Co.: 4-6/63 - No. 18, 8/67; No. 19, 10/69; No. 20, 10/70; No. 21, Oct, 1971

1-Photo-c	15	30	45	109	195	280
2-Photo-c	9	18	27	60	100	140
3-9: All have photo covers	7	14	21	47	76	105
10: No photo cover	5	10	15	32	51	70
11-21: All have photo covers. 18-Last 12¢ issue. 19-21-Reprint #1-3 (covers and insides)	6	12	18	37	59	80

NOTE: #1-9, 11-21 are photo covers.

BEWARE (Formerly Fantastic; Chilling Tales No. 13 on)
Youthful Magazines: No. 10, June, 1952 - No. 12, Oct, 1952

10-E.A. Poe's Pit & the Pendulum adaptation by Wildey; Harrison/Bache-a; atom bomb and shrunken head-c	57	114	171	356	591	825
11-Harrison-a; Ambrose Bierce adapt.	38	76	114	219	347	475
12-Used in SOTI, pg. 388; Harrison-a	38	76	114	219	347	475

BEWARE
Trojan Magazines/Merit Publ. No. ?: No. 13, 1/53 - No. 16, 7/53; No. 5, 9/53 - No. 15, 5/55

13(#1)-Harrison-a	56	112	168	350	580	810
14(#2, 3/53)-Krenkel/Harrison-c; dismemberment, severed head panels	38	76	114	219	347	475
15,16(#3, 5/53; #4, 7/53)-Harrison-a	33	66	99	190	300	410
5,9,12,13	32	64	96	186	293	400
6-Ill. in SOTI- "Children are first shocked and then desensitized by all this brutality." Corpse on cover swipe/V.O.H. #26; girl on cover swipe/Advs. Into Darkness #10	60	120	180	375	625	875
7,8-Check-a	33	66	99	190	300	410
10-Frazetta/Check-c; Disbrow, Check-a	68	136	204	425	705	985
11-Disbrow-a; heart torn out, blood drainage	38	76	114	219	347	475
14,15: 14-Myron Fass-c. 15-Harrison-a	27	54	81	158	249	340

NOTE: Fass a-5, 6, 8; c-6, 11, 14. Forte a-8. Hollingsworth a-15(#3), 16(#4); 9; c-16(#4), 8, 9. Kiefer a-16(#4), 5, 6, 10.

BEWARE (Becomes Tomb of Darkness No. 9 on)
Marvel Comics Group: Mar, 1973 - No. 8, May, 1974 (All reprints)

1-Everett-c; Kirby & Sinnott-a ('54)	3	6	9	14	20	25
2-8: 2-Forte, Colan-r. 6-Tuska-a. 7-Torres-r/Mystical Tales #7	2	4	6	9	13	16

NOTE: Infantino a-4r. Gil Kane c-4. Wildey a-7r.

BEWARE TERROR TALES
Fawcett Publications: May, 1952 - No. 8, July, 1953

1-E.C. art swipe/Haunt of Fear #5 & Vault of Horror #26	46	92	138	281	466	650
2	31	62	93	180	285	390
3-5,7	26	52	78	150	235	320
6-Classic skeleton-c	27	54	81	158	249	340
8-Tothish-a; people being cooked-c	30	60	90	176	278	380

NOTE: Andru a-2. Bernard Bailey a-1; c-1-5. Powell a-1, 2, 8. Sekowsky a-2.

Beware the Creeper #1 © DC

The Beyond #9 © ACE

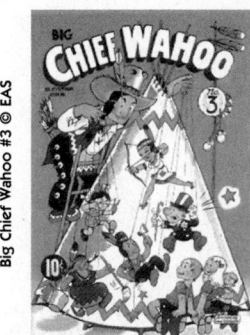

Big Chief Wahoo #3 © EAS

	GD 2.0	VG 4.0	FN 6.0	VF 8.0	VF/NM 9.0	NM- 9.2

	GD 2.0	VG 4.0	FN 6.0	VF 8.0	VF/NM 9.0	NM- 9.2

BEWARE THE CREEPER (See Adventure, Best of the Brave & the Bold, Brave & the Bold, 1st Issue Special, Flash #318-323, Showcase #73, World's Finest Comics #249)
National Periodical Publications: May-June, 1968 - No. 6, Mar-Apr, 1969 (All 12¢ issues)

1-(5-6/68)-Classic Ditko-c; Ditko-a in all	9	18	27	63	107	150
2-6: 2-5-Ditko-c. 2-Intro. Proteus. 6-Gil Kane-c	5	10	15	35	55	75

BEWARE THE CREEPER
DC Comics (Vertigo): June, 2003 - No. 5, Oct, 2003 ($2.95, limited series)

1-5-Female vigilante in 1920s Paris; Jason Hall-s/Cliff Chiang-a						3.00

BEWITCHED (TV)
Dell Publishing Co.: 4-6/65 - No. 11, 10/67; No. 12, 10/68 - No. 13, 1/69; No. 14, 10/69

1-Photo-c	15	30	45	105	188	270
2-No photo-c	8	16	24	54	90	125
3-13-All have photo-c. 12-Rep. #1. 13-Last 12¢-c	7	14	21	47	76	105
14-No photo-c; reprints #2	5	10	15	35	55	75

BEYOND!
Marvel Comics: Sept, 2006 - No. 6, Feb, 2007 ($2.99, limited series)

1-6-McDuffie-s/Kolins-a; Spider-Man, Venom, Gravity, Wasp app. 6-Gravity dies						3.00
HC (2007, $19.99, dustjacket) r/series; cover sketches and sketch design pages						20.00

BEYOND, THE
Ace Magazines: Nov, 1950 - No. 30, Jan, 1955

1-Bakerish-a(p)	43	86	129	262	431	600
2-Bakerish-a(p)	28	56	84	162	256	350
3-10: 10-Woodish-a by Cameron	20	40	60	115	180	245
11-20: 18-Used in **POP**, pgs. 81,82	15	30	45	90	140	190
21-26,28-30	15	30	45	88	137	185
27-Used in **SOTI**, pg. 111	15	30	45	90	140	190

NOTE: *Cameron* a-10, 11p, 12p, 15, 16, 21-27, 30; c-20. *Colan* a-6, 13, 17. *Sekowsky* a-2, 3, 5, 7, 11, 14, 27r. No. 1 was to appear as Challenge of the Unknown No. 7.

BEYOND THE GRAVE
Charlton Comics: July, 1975 - No. 6, June, 1976; No. 7, Jan, 1983 - No. 17, Oct, 1984

1-Ditko-a (6 pgs.); Sutton painted-c	3	6	9	17	25	32
2-6: 2-5-Ditko-a; Ditko c-2,3,6	2	4	6	9	13	16
7-17: ('83-'84) Reprints. 13-Aparo-c(r). 15-Sutton-c (low print run)						6.00
Modern Comics Reprint 2('78)						4.00

NOTE: *Howard* a-4. *Kim* a-13. *Larson* a-4, 6.

BIBLE, THE: EDEN
IDW Publishing: 2003 ($21.99, hardcover graphic novel)

HC-Scott Hampton painted-a; adaptation of Genesis by Dave Elliot and Keith Giffen						22.00

BIBLE TALES FOR YOUNG FOLK (...Young People No. 3-5)
Atlas Comics (OMC): Aug, 1953 - No. 5, Mar, 1954

1	26	52	78	152	239	325
2-Everett, Krigstein-a	18	36	54	105	165	225
3-5: 4,5-Robinson-c	15	30	45	88	137	185

BIG (Movie)
Hit Comics (Dark Horse Comics): Mar, 1989 ($2.00)

1-Adaptation of film; Paul Chadwick-c						2.50

BIG ALL-AMERICAN COMIC BOOK, THE (See All-American Comics)
All-American/National Per. Publ.: 1944 (132 pgs., one-shot) (Early DC Annual)

1-Wonder Woman, Green Lantern, Flash, The Atom, Wildcat, Scribbly, The Whip, Ghost Patrol, Hawkman by Kubert (1st on Hawkman), Hop Harrigan, Johnny Thunder, Little Boy Blue, Mr. Terrific, Mutt & Jeff app.; Sargon on cover only; cover by Kubert/Hibbard/Mayer and others	800	1600	2400	5600	9,800	14,000

BIG BABY HUEY (See Baby Huey)

BIG BANG COMICS (Becomes Big Bang #4)
Caliber Press: Spring, 1994 - No. 4, Feb, 1995; No. 0, May, 1995 ($1.95, lim. series)

1-4-($1.95-c)						2.50
0-(5/95, $2.95) Alex Ross-c; color and B&W pages						3.00
Your Big Book of Big Bang Comics TPB ('98, $11.00) r/#0-2						11.00

BIG BANG COMICS (Volume 2)
Image Comics (Highbrow Ent.): V2#1, May, 1996 - No. 35, Jan, 2001 ($1.95-$3.95)

1-23,26: 1-Mighty Man app. 2-4-S.A. Shadowhawk app. 5-Begin B&W. 7-Curt Swan/Murphy Anderson-a. 7-Begin B&W. 12-Savage Dragon-c/app. 16,17,21-Shadow Lady 24,25,27-35-($3.95): 24,27-History of Big Bang Comics Vol. 1,2. 35-Big Bang vs. Alan Moore's "1963" characters						3.00
...Presents the Ultiman Family (2/05, $3.50)						4.00
...Round Table of America (2/04, $3.95) Don Thomas-a						3.50
...Summer Special (8/03, $4.95) World's Nastiest Nazis app.						4.00
						5.00

BIG BANG PRESENTS (Volume 3)
Big Bang Comics: July, 2006 - Present ($2.95/$3.95, B&W)

1,2: 1-Protoplasman (Plastic Man homage)						3.00
3-5-($3.95) 3-Origin of Protoplasman. 4-Flip book						4.00

BIG BLACK KISS
Vortex Comics: Sep, 1989 - No, 3, Nov, 1989 ($3.75, B&W, lim. series, mature)

1-3-Chaykin-s/a						4.00

BIG BLOWN BABY (Also see Dark Horse Presents)
Dark Horse Comics: Aug, 1996 - No. 4, Nov, 1996 ($2.95, lim. series, mature)

1-4: Bill Wray-c/a/scripts						3.00

BIG BOOK OF ..., THE
DC Comics (Paradox Press): 1994 - Present (B&W)($12.95 - $14.95)

nn-...BAD,1998 ($14.95),...CONSPIRACIES, 1995 ($12.95), ...DEATH,1994 ($12.95), ...FREAKS, 1996 ($14.95), ...GRIMM, 1999 ($14.95), ...HOAXES, 1996 ($14.95), ...LITTLE CRIMINALS, 1996 ($14.95), ...LOSERS,1997 ($14.95), MARTYRS, 1997 ($14.95), ...SCANDAL,1997 ($14.95), ...THE WEIRD WILD WEST,1998 ($14.95), ...THUGS, 1997 ($14.95), ...UNEXPLAINED, 1997 ($14.95), ...URBAN LEGENDS, 1994 ($12.95), ...VICE, 1999 ($14.95),...WEIRDOS, 1995 ($12.95)				cover price		

BIG BOOK OF FUN COMICS (See New Book of Comics)
National Periodical Publications: Spring, 1936 (Large size, 52 pgs.)
(1st comic book annual & DC annual)

1 (Very rare)-r/New Fun #1-5	2250	4500	6750	14,700	-	-

BIG BOOK ROMANCES
Fawcett Publications: Feb, 1950 (no date given) (148 pgs.)

1-Contains remaindered Fawcett romance comics - several combinations possible	41	82	123	250	400	550

BIG BRUISERS
Image Comics (WildStorm Productions): July, 1996 ($3.50, one-shot)

1-Features Maul from WildC.A.T.S, Impact from Cyberforce & Badrock from Youngblood						3.50

BIG CHIEF WAHOO
Eastern Color Printing/George Dougherty (distr. by Fawcett): July, 1942 - No. 7, Wint., 1943/44?(no year given)(Quarterly)

1-Newspaper-r (on sale 6/15/42)	41	82	123	256	416	575
2-Steve Roper app.	23	46	69	132	209	285
3-5: 4-Chief is holding a Katy Keene comic	18	36	54	103	162	220
6-7	14	28	42	82	121	160

NOTE: *Kerry Drake* in some issues.

BIG CIRCUS, THE (Movie)
Dell Publishing Co.: No. 1036, Sept-Nov, 1959

Four Color 1036-Photo-c	6	12	18	43	69	95

BIG COUNTRY, THE (Movie)
Dell Publishing Co.: No. 946, Oct, 1958

Four Color 946-Photo-c	7	14	21	47	76	105

BIG DADDY DANGER
DC Comics: Oct, 2002 - No. 9, June, 2003 ($2.95, limited series)

1-9-Adam Pollina-a/c						3.00

BIG DADDY ROTH (Magazine)
Millar Publications: Oct-Nov, 1964 - No. 4, Apr-May, 1965 (35¢)

1-Toth-a	17	34	51	126	223	320
2-4-Toth-a	11	22	33	79	140	200

BIGFOOT
IDW Publishing: Feb, 2005 - No. 4, May, 2005 ($3.99, limited series)

1-4-Steve Niles & Rob Zombie-s/Richard Corben-a/c						4.00

BIGG TIME
DC Comics (Vertigo): 2002 ($14.95, B&W, graphic novel)

nn-Ty Templeton-s/c-a						15.00

BIG GUY AND RUSTY THE BOY ROBOT, THE (Also See Madman Comics #6,7 & Martha Washington Stranded In Space)
Dark Horse (Legend): July, 1995 - No. 2, Aug, 1995 ($4.95, oversize, limited series)

1,2-Frank Miller scripts & Geoff Darrow-c/a	1	2	3	4	5	7
Trade paperback (10/96, $14.95)-r/1,2 w/cover gallery						15.00

BIG HERO ADVENTURES (See Jigsaw)

BIG HAIR PRODUCTIONS
Image Comics: Feb, 2000 - No. 2, Mar, 2000 ($3.50, B&W)

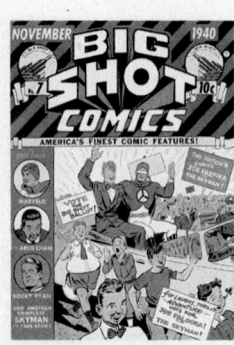

Big Shot Comics #7 © CCG

Big-3 #3 © FOX

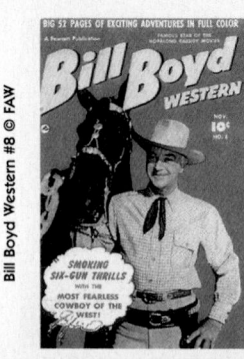

Bill Boyd Western #8 © FAW

	GD 2.0	VG 4.0	FN 6.0	VF 8.0	VF/NM 9.0	NM- 9.2
1,2						3.50

BIG JON & SPARKIE (Radio)(Formerly Sparkie, Radio Pixie)
Ziff-Davis Publ. Co.: No. 4, Sept-Oct, 1952 (Painted-c)

	GD 2.0	VG 4.0	FN 6.0	VF 8.0	VF/NM 9.0	NM- 9.2
4-Based on children's radio program	18	36	54	107	169	230

BIG LAND, THE (Movie)
Dell Publishing Co.: No. 812, July, 1957

Four Color 812-Alan Ladd photo-c	9	18	27	60	100	140

BIG RED (See Movie Comics)

BIG SHOT COMICS
Columbia Comics Group: May, 1940 - No. 104, Aug, 1949

1-Intro. Skyman; The Face (1st app.; Tony Trent), The Cloak (Spy Master), Marvelo, Monarch of Magicians, Joe Palooka, Charlie Chan, Tom Kerry, Dixie Dugan, Rocky Ryan begin; Charlie Chan moves over from Feature Comics #31 (4/40)	252	504	756	1575	2613	3650
2	88	176	264	550	913	1275
3-The Cloak called Spy Chief; Skyman-c	78	156	234	488	807	1125
4,5	57	114	171	356	591	825
6-10: 8-Christmas-c	45	90	135	275	455	635
11-13	41	82	123	256	416	575
14-Origin & 1st app. Sparky Watts (6/41)	45	90	135	275	450	625
15-Origin The Cloak	45	90	135	278	457	635
16-20	35	70	105	204	322	440
21-23,26,27,29,30: 29-Intro. Capt. Yank; Bo (a dog) newspaper strip-r by Frank Beck begin, ends #104. 30-X-Mas-c	30	60	90	172	271	370
24-Classic Tojo-c	47	94	141	287	474	660
25-Hitler-c	40	80	120	239	380	520
28-Hitler, Tojo & Mussolini-c	52	104	156	317	521	725
31,33-40	22	44	66	128	202	275
32-Vic Jordan newspaper strip reprints begin, ends #52; Hitler, Tojo & Mussolini-c	41	82	123	252	406	560
41,42,44,45,47-50: 42-No Skyman. 50-Origin The Face retold	19	38	57	109	172	235
43-Hitler-c	37	74	111	213	337	460
46-Hitler, Tojo-c (6/44)	35	70	105	201	318	435
51-56,58-60	16	32	48	92	144	195
57-Hitler, Tojo Halloween mask-c	26	52	78	152	239	325
61-70: 63 on-Tony Trent, the Face	14	28	42	80	115	150
71-80: 73-The Face cameo. 74-(2/47)-Mickey Finn begins. 74,80-The Face app. in Tony Trent. 78-Last Charlie Chan strip-r	14	28	42	76	108	140
81-90: 85-Tony Trent marries Babs Walsh. 86-Valentines-c	11	22	33	62	86	110
91-99,101-104: 69-94-Skyman in Outer Space. 96-Xmas-c	10	20	30	56	76	95
100	11	22	33	64	90	115

NOTE: *Mart Bailey* art on "The Face" No. 1-104. *Guardineer* a-5. Sparky Watts by *Boody Rogers* No. 14-42, 77-104, (by others No. 43-76). Others than Tony Trent wear "The Face" mask in No. 46-63, 93. Skyman by *Ogden Whitney*-No. 1, 2, 4, 12-37, 49, 70-101. Skyman covers-No. 1, 3, 7-12, 14, 16, 20, 27, 89, 95, 100.

BIG SMASH BARGAIN COMICS
No publisher listed: Early 1950s (25¢, 160pgs., Canadian reprints)

1-4: Contains 4 comics from various companies bundled with new cover (scarce)	28	56	84	162	256	350

BIG TEX
Toby Press: June, 1953

1-Contains (3) John Wayne stories-r with name changed to Big Tex	10	20	30	58	79	100

BIG-3
Fox Features Syndicate: Fall, 1940 - No. 7, Jan, 1942

1-Blue Beetle, The Flame, & Samson begin	221	442	663	1381	2291	3200
2	83	166	249	519	860	1200
3-5	59	118	177	369	610	850
6,7: 6-Last Samson. 7-V-Man app.	45	90	135	275	450	625

BIG TOP COMICS, THE (TV's Great Circus Show)
Toby Press: 1951 - No. 2, 1951 (No month)

1	11	22	33	62	86	100
2	9	18	27	47	61	75

BIG TOWN (Radio/TV) (Also see Movie Comics, 1946)
National Periodical Publ: Jan, 1951 - No. 50, Mar-Apr, 1958 (No. 1-9: 52pgs.)

1-Dan Barry-a begins	66	132	198	413	682	950
2	35	70	105	201	318	435

	GD 2.0	VG 4.0	FN 6.0	VF 8.0	VF/NM 9.0	NM- 9.2
3-10	21	42	63	120	188	255
11-20	15	30	45	88	137	185
21-31: Last pre-code (1-2/55)	12	24	36	69	97	125
32-50: 46-Grey tone cover	10	20	30	54	72	90

BIG VALLEY, THE (TV)
Dell Publishing Co.: June, 1966 - No. 5, Oct, 1967; No. 6, Oct, 1969

1: Photo-c #1-5	5	10	15	35	55	75
2-6: 6-Reprints #1	4	8	12	22	34	45

BIKER MICE FROM MARS (TV)
Marvel Comics: Nov, 1993 - No. 3, Jan, 1994 ($1.50, limited series)

1-3: 1-Intro Vinnie, Modo & Throttle. 2-Origin						3.50

BILL & TED'S BOGUS JOURNEY
Marvel Comics: Sept, 1991 ($2.95, squarebound, 84 pgs.)

1-Adapts movie sequel						3.00

BILL & TED'S EXCELLENT COMIC BOOK (Movie)
Marvel Comics: Dec, 1991 - No. 12, 1992 ($1.00/$1.25)

1-12: 3-Begin $1.25-c						2.50

BILL BARNES COMICS (...America's Air Ace Comics No. 2 on) (Becomes Air Ace V2#1 on; also see Shadow Comics)
Street & Smith Publications: Oct, 1940(No. month given) - No. 12, Oct, 1943

1-23 pgs.-comics; Rocket Rooney begins	86	172	258	538	894	1250
2-Barnes as The Phantom Flyer app.; Tuska-a	43	86	129	262	431	600
3-5	40	80	120	235	368	500
6-12	34	68	102	195	308	420

BILL BATTLE, THE ONE MAN ARMY (Also see Master Comics No. 133)
Fawcett Publications: Oct, 1952 - No. 4, Apr, 1953 (All photo-c)

1	14	28	42	76	108	140
2	8	16	24	44	57	70
3,4	8	16	24	40	50	60

BILL BLACK'S FUN COMICS
Paragon #1-3/Americomics #4: Dec, 1982 - No. 4, Mar, 1983 ($1.75/$2.00, Baxter paper) (1st AC comic)

1-(B&W fanzine; 7x8-1/2"; low print) Intro. Capt. Paragon, Phantom Lady & Commando D	2	4	6	13	18	22
2-4: 2,3-(B&W fanzines; 8-1/2x11"). 3-Kirby-c. 4-($2.00, color)-Origin Nightfall (formerly Phantom Lady); Nightveil app.; Kirby-a	1	3	4	6	8	10

BILL BOYD WESTERN (Movie star; see Hopalong Cassidy & Western Hero)
Fawcett Publ: Feb, 1950 - No. 23, June, 1952 (1-3,7,11,14-on: 36 pgs.)

1-Bill Boyd & his horse Midnite begin; photo front/back-c	43	86	129	262	421	580
2-Painted-c	24	48	72	138	214	290
3-Photo-c begin, end #23; last photo back-c	19	38	57	108	167	225
4-6(52 pgs.)	16	32	48	89	137	185
7,11(36 pgs.)	14	28	42	76	108	140
8-10,12,13(52 pgs.)	14	28	42	78	112	145
14-22	13	26	39	72	101	130
23-Last issue	14	28	42	76	108	140

BILL BUMLIN (See Treasury of Comics No. 3)

BILL ELLIOTT (See Wild Bill Elliott)

BILLI 99
Dark Horse Comics: Sept, 1991 - No. 4, 1991 ($3.50, B&W, lim. series, 52 pgs.)

1-4: Tim Sale-c/a						3.50

BILL STERN'S SPORTS BOOK
Ziff-Davis Publ. Co.(Approved Comics): Spring-Sum, 1951 - V2#2, Win, 1952

V1#10-(1951)	21	42	63	122	191	260
2-(Sum/52; reg. size)	16	32	48	92	144	195
V2#2-(1952, 96 pgs.)-Krigstein, Kinstler-a	22	44	66	126	198	270

BILL THE BULL: ONE SHOT, ONE BOURBON, ONE BEER
Boneyard Press: Dec, 1994 ($2.95, B&W, mature)

1						3.00

BILLY AND BUGGY BEAR (See Animal Fun)
I.W. Enterprises/Super: 1958; 1964

I.W. Reprint #1, #7('58)-All Surprise Comics #?(Same issue-r for both)

	2	4	6	10	14	18
Super Reprint #10(1964)	2	4	6	8	11	14

Billy the Kid #7 © TOBY

Bionic Woman #3 © CC

Birds of Prey #56 © DC

	GD 2.0	VG 4.0	FN 6.0	VF 8.0	VF/NM 9.0	NM- 9.2

BILLY BUCKSKIN WESTERN (2-Gun Western No. 4)
Atlas Comics (IMC No. 1/MgPC No. 2,3): Nov, 1955 - No. 3, Mar, 1956

1-Mort Drucker-a; Maneely-c/a	16	32	48	88	137	185
2-Mort Drucker-a	10	20	30	56	76	95
3-Williamson, Drucker-a	12	24	36	67	94	120

BILLY BUNNY (Black Cobra No. 6 on)
Excellent Publications: Feb-Mar, 1954 - No. 5, Oct-Nov, 1954

1	9	18	27	47	61	75
2	6	12	18	27	33	38
3-5	5	10	15	23	28	32

BILLY BUNNY'S CHRISTMAS FROLICS
Farrell Publications: 1952 (25¢ Giant, 100 pgs.)

1	20	40	60	117	184	250

BILLY COLE
Cult Press: May, 1994 - No. 4, Aug, 1994 ($2.75, B&W, limited series)

1-4						2.75

BILLY MAKE BELIEVE
United Features Syndicate: No. 14, 1939

Single Series 14	31	62	93	178	282	385

BILLY NGUYEN, PRIVATE EYE
Caliber Press: V2#1, 1990 ($2.50)

V2#1						2.50

BILLY THE KID (Formerly The Masked Raider; also see Doc Savage Comics
& Return of the Outlaw)
Charlton Publ. Co.: No. 9, Nov, 1957 - No. 121, Dec, 1976; No. 122, Sept, 1977 - No. 123,
Oct, 1977; No. 124, Feb, 1978 - No. 153, Mar, 1983

9	10	20	30	56	76	95
10,12,14,17-19: 12-2 pg Check-sty	7	14	21	37	46	55
11-(68 pgs.)-Origin & 1st app. The Ghost Train.	9	18	27	47	61	75
13-Williamson/Torres-a	8	16	24	42	54	65
15-Origin; Williamson-a	8	16	24	42	54	65
16-Williamson-a, 2 pgs.	8	16	24	40	50	60
20-26-Severin-a(3-4 each)	8	16	24	42	54	65
27-30: 30-Masked Rider app.	3	6	9	18	27	35
31-40	3	6	9	14	20	25
41-60	2	4	6	11	16	20
61-65	2	4	6	9	12	15
66-Bounty Hunter series begins.	2	4	6	10	14	18
67-80: Bounty Hunter series; not in #79,82,84-86	2	4	6	8	11	14
81-84,86-90: 87-Last Bounty Hunter	1	2	3	5	7	9
85-Early Kaluta-a (4 pgs.)	2	4	6	8	10	12
91-123: 110-Dr. Young of Boothill app. 111-Origin The Ghost Train. 117-Gunsmith & Co., The Cheyenne Kid app.						6.00
124(2/78)-153						4.00
Modern Comics 109 (1977 reprint)						4.00

NOTE: *Boyette* a-91-110. *Kim* a-73. *Morisi* a-12,14. *Sattler* a-118-123. *Severin* a(r)-121-129, 134; c-23, 25. *Sutton* a-111.

BILLY THE KID ADVENTURE MAGAZINE
Toby Press: Oct, 1950 - No. 29, 1955

1-Williamson/Frazetta-a (2 pgs) r/from John Wayne Adventure Comics #2; photo-c	31	62	93	178	282	385
2-Photo-c	12	24	36	67	94	120
3-Williamson/Frazetta "The Claws of Death", 4 pgs. plus Williamson art	34	68	102	197	311	425
4,5,7,8,10: 4,7-Photo-c	9	18	27	50	65	80
6-Frazetta assist on "Nightmare"; photo-c	15	30	45	83	124	165
9-Kurtzman Pot-Shot Pete; photo-c	11	22	33	64	90	115
11,12,15-20: 11-Photo-c	8	16	24	42	54	65
13-Kurtzman-r/John Wayne #12 (Genius)	9	18	27	47	61	75
14-Williamson/Frazetta; r-of #1 (2 pgs.)	10	20	30	56	76	95
21,23-29	7	14	21	37	46	55
22-Williamson/Frazetta-r(1pg.)/#1; photo-c	8	16	24	42	54	65

BILLY THE KID AND OSCAR (Also see Fawcett's Funny Animals)
Fawcett Publications: Winter, 1945 - No. 3, Summer, 1946 (Funny animal)

1	15	30	45	84	127	170
2,3	10	20	30	56	76	95

BILLY THE KID'S OLD TIMEY ODDITIES
Dark Horse Comics: Apr, 2005 - No. 4, July, 2005 ($2.99, limited series)

	GD 2.0	VG 4.0	FN 6.0	VF 8.0	VF/NM 9.0	NM- 9.2
1-4-Eric Powell-s/c; Kyle Hotz-a						3.00
TPB (2005, $13.95) r/series						14.00

BILLY WEST (Bill West No. 9,10)
Standard Comics (Visual Editions): 1949-No. 9, Feb, 1951; No. 10, Feb, 1952

1	14	28	42	82	121	160
2	9	18	27	50	65	80
3-6,9,10	8	16	24	42	54	65
7,8-Schomburg-c	9	18	27	47	61	75

NOTE: *Celardo* a-1-6, 9; c-1-3. *Moreira* a-3. *Roussos* a-2.

BING CROSBY (See Feature Films)

BINGO (...Comics) (H. C. Blackerby)
Howard Publ.: 1945 (Reprints National material)

1-L. B. Cole opium-c; blank back-c	36	72	108	208	329	450

BINGO, THE MONKEY DOODLE BOY
St. John Publishing Co.: Aug, 1951; Oct, 1953

1(8/51)-By Eric Peters	8	16	24	40	50	60
1(10/53)	6	12	18	28	34	40

BINKY (Formerly Leave It to...)
National Periodical Publ./DC Comics: No. 72, 4-5/70 - No. 81, 10-11/71; No. 82, Summer/77

72-76	3	6	9	19	29	38
77-79: (68 pgs.). 77-Bobby Sherman 1pg. story w/photo. 78-1 pg. sty on Barry Williams of Brady Bunch. 79-Osmonds 1pg. story.	5	10	15	32	51	70
80,81 (52 pgs.)-Sweat Pain story	4	8	12	26	41	55
82 (1977, one-shot)	3	6	9	20	30	40

BINKY'S BUDDIES
National Periodical Publications: Jan-Feb, 1969 - No. 12, Nov-Dec, 1970

1	6	12	18	39	62	85
2-12: 3-Last 12¢ issue	3	6	9	21	32	42

BIONIC WOMAN, THE (TV)
Charlton Publications: Oct, 1977 - No. 5, June, 1978

1	3	6	9	16	23	30
2-5	2	4	6	10	14	18

BIRDS OF PREY (Also see Black Canary/Oracle: Birds of Prey)
DC Comics: Jan, 1999 - Present ($1.99/$2.50)

1-Dixon-s/Land-c/a	1	3	4	6	8	10
2-4						6.00
5-7,9-15: 15-Guice-a begins.						4.00
8-Nightwing-c/app.; Barbara & Dick's circus date	2	4	6	9	12	15
16-38: 23-Grodd-c/app. 26-Bane app. 32-Noto-c begin						2.50
39,40-Bruce Wayne: Murderer pt. 5,12						3.00
41-Bruce Wayne: Fugitive pt. 2						4.00
42-46: 42-Fabry-a. 45-Deathstroke-c/app.						2.50
47-74,76-91: 47-49-Terry Moore-s/Conner & Palmiotti-a; Noto-c. 50-Gilbert Hernandez-s begin. 52,54-Metamorpho app. 56-Simone-s/Benes-a begin. 65,67,68,70-Land-c. 76-Debut of Black Alice (from Day of Vengeance). 86-Timm-a (7 pgs.)						2.50
75-($2.95) Pearson-c; back-up story of Lady Blackhawk						3.00
92-99,101-109: 92-One Year Later. 94-Begin $2.99-c; Prometheus app. 96,97-Black Alice app. 98,99-New Batgirl app. 99-Black Canary leaves the team. 104-107-Secret Six app.						3.00
100-($3.99) new team recruited; Black Canary origin re-told						4.00
TPB (1999, $17.95) r/ previous stories and one-shots						18.00
...: Batgirl 1 (2/98, $2.95) Dixon-s/Frank-c						5.00
...: Batgirl/Catwoman 1 ('03, $5.95) Robertson-a; cont'd in BOP: Catwoman/Oracle 1						6.00
...: Between Dark & Dawn TPB (2006, $14.99) r/#69-75						15.00
...: Blood and Circuits TPB (2007, $17.99) r/#96-103						18.00
...: Catwoman/Oracle 1 ('03, $5.95) Cont'd from BOP: Batgirl/Catwoman 1; David Ross-a						6.00
...: Of Like Minds TPB (2004, $14.95) r/#55-61						15.00
...: Old Friends, New Enemies TPB (2003, $17.95) r/#1-6, ...: Batgirl, ...: Wolves						18.00
...: Perfect Pitch TPB (2007, $17.99) r/#86-90,92-95						18.00
...: Revolution 1 (1997, $2.95) Frank-c/Dixon-s						5.00
...: Secret Files 2003 (8/03, $4.95) Short stories, pin-ups and profile pages; Noto-c						5.00
...: Sensei and Student TPB (2005, $17.95) r/#62-68						18.00
...: The Battle Within TPB (2006, $17.99) r/#76-85						18.00
...: The Ravens 1 (6/98, $1.95)-Dixon-s; Girlfrenzy issue						4.00
...: Wolves 1 (10/97, $2.95) Dixon-s/Giordano & Faucher-a						5.00

BIRDS OF PREY: MANHUNT
DC Comics: Sept, 1996 - No. 4, Dec, 1996 ($1.95, limited series)

1-Features Black Canary, Oracle, Huntress, & Catwoman; Chuck Dixon scripts; Gary Frank-c on all. 1-Catwoman cameo only	1	2	3	5	6	8
2-4						6.00

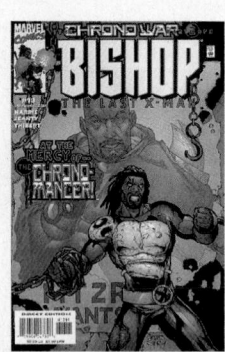

Bishop The Last X-Man #13 © MAR

Black Canary #1 © DC

Black Cat Comics #11 © HARV

	GD 2.0	VG 4.0	FN 6.0	VF 8.0	VF/NM 9.0	NM- 9.2

	GD 2.0	VG 4.0	FN 6.0	VF 8.0	VF/NM 9.0	NM- 9.2

NOTE: *Gary Frank c-1-4. Matt Haley a-1-4p. Wade Von Grawbadger a-1i.*

BIRTH CAUL, THE
Eddie Campbell Comics: 1999 ($5.95, B&W, one-shot)
1-Alan Moore-s/Eddie Campbell-a ... 6.00

BIRTH OF THE DEFIANT UNIVERSE, THE
Defiant Comics: May, 1993
nn-Contains promotional artwork & text; limited print run of 1000 copies.
	2	4	6	8	10	12

BISHOP (See Uncanny X-Men & X-Men)
Marvel Comics: Dec, 1994 - No.4, Mar, 1995 ($2.95, limited series)
1-4: Foil-c; Shard & Mountjoy in all. 1-Storm app. ... 3.00

BISHOP THE LAST X-MAN
Marvel Comics: Oct, 1999 - No. 16, Jan, 2001 ($2.99/$1.99/$2.25)
1-($2.99)-Jeanty-a ... 3.50
2-8-($1.99): 2-Two covers ... 2.50
9-11,13-16: 9-Begin $2.25-c. 15-Maximum Security x-over; Xavier app. ... 2.50
12-($2.99) ... 3.00

BISHOP: XAVIER SECURITY ENFORCER
Marvel Comics: Jan, 1998 - No.3, Mar, 1998 ($2.50, limited series)
1-3: Ostrander-s ... 3.00

BITE CLUB
DC Comics (Vertigo): Jun, 2004 - No. 6, Nov, 2004 ($2.95, limited series)
1-6-Chaykin-s/Tischman-a/Quitely-c ... 3.00
TPB Digest (2005, $9.99) r/#1-6; cover gallery ... 10.00

BITE CLUB: VAMPIRE CRIME UNIT
DC Comics (Vertigo): Jun, 2006 - No. 5 ($2.99, limited series)
1-5:1-Chaykin & Tischman-s/Hahn-a/Quitely-c. 4-Chaykin-c ... 3.00

BIZARRE ADVENTURES (Formerly Marvel Preview)
Marvel Comics Group: No. 25, 3/81 - No. 34, 2/83 (#25-33: Magazine-$1.50)
25,26: 25-Lethal Ladies. 26-King Kull; Bolton-c/a
	1	3	4	6	8	10
27,28: 27-Phoenix, Iceman & Nightcrawler app. 28-The Unlikely Heroes; Elektra by Miller;
Neal Adams-a
	2	4	6	9	13	16
29,30,32,33: 29-Stephen King's Lawnmower Man. 30-Tomorrow; 1st app. Silhouette. 32-Gods;
Thor-c/s. 33-Horror; Dracula app.; photo-c
	1	2	3	5	7	9
31-After The Violence Stops; new Hangman story; Miller-a
	1	3	4	6	8	10
34 ($2.00, Baxter paper, comic size)-Son of Santa; Christmas special; Howard
the Duck by Paul Smith
	1	2	3	5	6	8
NOTE: *Alcala a-27i. Austin a-25i, 28i. Bolton a-26, 32. J. Buscema a-27p, 29, 30p; c-26. Byrne a-31 (2 pg.). Golden a-25p, 28p. Perez a-27p. Rogers a-25p. Simonson a-29; c-29. Paul Smith a-34.*

BIZARRO COMICS!
DC Comics: 2001 ($29.95, hardcover, one-shot)
HC-Short stories of DC heroes by various alternative cartoonists including Dorkin, Pope, Haspiel, Kidd, Kochalka, Millionaire, Stephens, Wray; includes "Superman's Babysitter" by Kyle Baker from Elseworlds 80-Page Giant recalled by DC; Groening-c ... 30.00
Softcover (2003, $19.95) ... 20.00

BIZARRO WORLD
DC Comics: 2005 ($29.95, hardcover, one-shot)
HC-Short stories by various alternative cartoonists including Bagge, Baker, Dorkin, Dunn, Kupperman, Morse, Oswalt, Pekar, Simpson, Stewart; Jaime Hernandez-c ... 30.00
Softcover (2006, $19.99) ... 20.00

BLACK ADAM (See 52 and Countdown)
DC Comics: Oct, 2007 - No. 6 ($2.99, limited series)
1-Mahnke-a/c; Isis returns ... 3.00

BLACK AND WHITE (See Large Feature Comic, Series I)

BLACK & WHITE (Also see Codename: Black & White)
Image Comics (Extreme): Oct,1994 - No. 3, Jan,1995 ($1.95, limited series)
1-3: Thibert-c/story ... 2.50

BLACK & WHITE MAGIC
Innovation Publishing: 1991 ($2.95, 98 pgs., B&W w/30 pgs. color, squarebound)
1-Contains rebound comics w/covers removed; contents may vary ... 3.00

BLACK AXE
Marvel Comics (UK): Apr, 1993 - No. 7, Oct, 1993 ($1.75)
1-4: 1-Romita Jr.-c. 2-Sunfire-c/s ... 3.00
5-7: 5-Janson-c; Black Panther app. 6,7-Black Panther-c/s ... 3.00

BLACKBALL COMICS
Blackball Comics: Mar, 1994 ($3.00)
1-Trencher-c/story by Giffen; John Pain by O'Neill ... 3.00

BLACKBEARD'S GHOST (See Movie Comics)

BLACK BEAUTY (See Son of Black Beauty)
Dell Publishing Co.: No. 440, Dec, 1952
Four Color 440	5	10	15	30	48	65

BLACKBURNE COVENANT, THE
Dark Horse Comics: Apr, 2003 - No. 4, July, 2003 ($2.99, limited series)
1-4-Nicieza-s/Raffaele-a ... 3.00
TPB (2003, $12.95) r/#1-4 ... 13.00

BLACK CANARY (See All Star Comics #38, Flash Comics #86, Justice League of America #75 & World's Finest #244)
DC Comics: Nov, 1991 - No. 4, Feb, 1992 ($1.75, limited series)
1-4 ... 2.50

BLACK CANARY
DC Comics: Jan, 1993 - No. 12, Dec, 1993 ($1.75)
1-7 ... 2.50
8-12: 8-The Ray-c/story. 9,10-Huntress-c/story ... 3.00

BLACK CANARY (Follows Oliver Queen's marriage proposal in Green Arrow #75)
DC Comics: Early Sept, 2007 - No. 4, Late Oct, 2007 ($2.99, bi-weekly limited series)
1-4-Bedard-s/Siqueira-a ... 3.00
... Wedding Planner 1 (11/07, $2.99) Roux-c/Ferguson & Norrie-a ... 3.00

BLACK CANARY/ORACLE: BIRDS OF PREY (Also see Showcase '96 #3)
DC Comics: 1996 ($3.95, one-shot)
1-Chuck Dixon scripts & Gary Frank-c/a.
	1	2	3	5	7	9

BLACK CAT COMICS (...Western #16-19; ...Mystery #30 on)
(See All-New #7,9, The Original Black Cat, Pocket & Speed Comics)
Harvey Publications (Home Comics): June-July, 1946 - No. 29, June, 1951
1-Kubert-a; Joe Simon c-1,2	72	144	216	450	750	1050
2-Kubert-a	40	80	120	235	368	500
3,4: 4-The Red Demons begin (The Demon #4 & 5)
| | 32 | 64 | 96 | 186 | 293 | 400 |
5,6,7: 5,6-The Scarlet Arrow app. in ea. by Powell; S&K-a in both. 6-Origin Red Demon.
7-Vagabond Prince by S&K plus 1 more story | 40 | 80 | 120 | 235 | 368 | 500 |
8-S&K-a; Kerry Drake begins, ends #13 | 35 | 70 | 105 | 201 | 318 | 435 |
9-Origin Stuntman (r/Stuntman #1) | 38 | 76 | 114 | 222 | 351 | 480 |
10-20: 14,15,17-Mary Worth app. plus Invisible Scarlet O'Neil-#15,20,24
| | 26 | 52 | 78 | 152 | 239 | 325 |
21-26 | 21 | 42 | 63 | 124 | 195 | 265 |
27,28: 27-Used in SOTI, pg. 193; X-Mas-c; 2 pg. John Wayne story. 28-Intro.
Kit, Black Cat's new sidekick | 23 | 46 | 69 | 130 | 205 | 280 |
29-Black Cat bondage-c; Black Cat stories | 22 | 44 | 66 | 128 | 202 | 275 |

BLACK CAT MYSTERY (Formerly Black Cat; ...Western Mystery #54; ...Western #55,56; ...Mystery #57; ...Mystic #58-62; Black Cat #63-65)
Harvey Publications: No. 30, Aug, 1951 - No. 65, Apr, 1963
30-Black Cat on cover and splash page only	31	62	93	178	282	385
31,32,34,37,38,40	25	50	75	145	228	310
33-Used in POP, pg. 89; electrocution-c	27	54	81	156	246	335
35-Atomic disaster cover/story	30	60	90	174	275	375
36,39-Used in SOTI: #36-Pgs. 270,271; #39-Pgs. 386-388
| | 29 | 58 | 87 | 167 | 264 | 360 |
41-43 | 24 | 48 | 72 | 139 | 220 | 300 |
44-Eyes, ears, tongue cut out; Nostrand-a | 26 | 52 | 78 | 152 | 239 | 325 |
45-Classic "Colorama" by Powell; Nostrand-a | 41 | 82 | 123 | 253 | 407 | 560 |
46-49,51-Nostrand-a in all | 30 | 60 | 90 | 174 | 275 | 375 |
50-Check-a; classic Warren Kremer-c showing a man's face & hands burning away
| | 86 | 172 | 258 | 538 | 894 | 1250 |
52,53 (r/#34 & 35) | 16 | 32 | 48 | 92 | 144 | 195 |
54-Two Black Cat stories (2/55, last pre-code) | 18 | 36 | 54 | 107 | 169 | 230 |
55,56-Black Cat stories | 16 | 32 | 48 | 92 | 144 | 195 |
57(7/56)-Kirby-c | 16 | 32 | 48 | 94 | 147 | 200 |
58-60-Kirby-a(4). 58,59-Kirby-c. 60,61-Simon-c | 21 | 42 | 63 | 122 | 191 | 260 |
61-Nostrand-a; "Colorama" r/#45 | 18 | 36 | 54 | 107 | 169 | 230 |
62 (3/58)-E.C. story swipe | 15 | 30 | 45 | 88 | 137 | 185 |
63-65: Giants(10/62,1/63, 4/63); Reprints; Black Cat app. 63-origin Black Kitten.
65-1 pg. Powell-a | 18 | 36 | 54 | 107 | 169 | 230 |
NOTE: *Kremer a-37, 39, 43; c-36, 37, 47. Meskin a-51. Palais a-30, 31(2), 32(2), 33-35, 37-40. Powell a-32-35,*

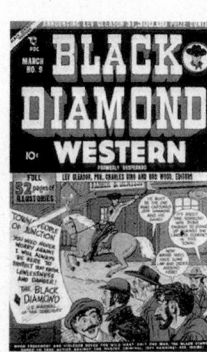

Black Diamond Western #9 © LEV

Blackhawk #19 © QUA

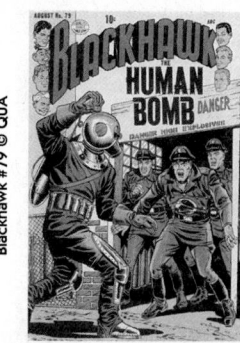

Blackhawk #79 © QUA

	GD 2.0	VG 4.0	FN 6.0	VF 8.0	VF/NM 9.0	NM- 9.2

36(2), 40, 41, 43-53, 57. Simon c-63-65. Sparling a-44. Bondage c-32, 34, 43.

BLACK COBRA (Bride's Diary No. 4 on) (See Captain Flight #8)
Ajax/Farrell Publications(Excellent Publ.): No. 1, 10-11/54; No. 6(No. 2), 12-1/54-55; No. 3, 2-3/55

1-Re-intro Black Cobra & The Cobra Kid (costumed heroes)						
	35	70	105	201	318	435
6(#2)-Formerly Billy Bunny	18	36	54	107	169	230
3-(Pre-code)-Torpedoman app.	17	34	51	100	158	215

BLACK CONDOR (Also see Crack Comics, Freedom Fighters & Showcase '94 #10,11)
DC Comics: June, 1992 - No. 12, May, 1993 ($1.25)

1-8-Heath-c	2.50
9-12: 9,10,12-Heath-c. 9,10-The Ray app. 12-Batman-c/app.	3.00

BLACK CROSS SPECIAL (See Dark Horse Presents)
Dark Horse Comics: Jan, 1988 ($1.75, B&W, one-shot)(Reprints & new-a)

1-1st printing	3.00
1-(2nd printing) has 2 pgs. new-a	2.50

BLACK CROSS: DIRTY WORK (See Dark Horse Presents)
Dark Horse Comics: Apr, 1997 ($2.95, one-shot)

1-Chris Warner-c/s/a	3.00

BLACK DIAMOND
Americomics: May, 1983 - No. 5, 1984 (no month)($2.00-$1.75, Baxter paper)

1-3-Movie adapt.; 1-Colt back-up begins	4.00
4,5	3.00

NOTE: *Bill Black a-1; c-1. Gulacy c-2-5. Sybil Danning photo back-c-1.*

BLACK DIAMOND WESTERN (Formerly Desperado No. 1-8)
Lev Gleason Publ.: No. 9, Mar, 1949 - No. 60, Feb, 1956 (No. 9-28: 52 pgs.)

9-Black Diamond & his horse Reliapon begin; origin & 1st app. Black Diamond						
	21	42	63	122	191	260
10	12	24	36	69	97	125
11-15	10	20	30	54	72	90
16-28(11/49-11/51)-Wolverton's Bingbang Buster	14	28	42	76	108	140
29-40: 31-One pg. Frazetta anti-drug ad	9	18	27	47	61	75
41-50,53-59	8	16	24	40	50	60
51-3-D effect-c/story	15	30	45	85	130	175
52-3-D effect story	14	28	42	81	118	155
60-Last issue	8	16	24	44	57	70

NOTE: *Biro c-9-35?. Fass a-58, c-54-56, 58. Guardineer a-9, 15, 18. Kida a-9. Maurer a-10. Ed Moore a-16. Morisi a-55. Tuska a-10, 48.*

BLACK DRAGON, THE
Marvel Comics (Epic Comics): 5/85 - No. 6, 10/85 (Baxter paper, mature)

1-6: 1-Chris Claremont story & John Bolton painted-c/a in all	3.00

BLACK DRAGON, THE
Dark Horse Comics: Apr, 1996 ($17.95, B&W, trade paperback)

nn-Reprints Epic Comics limited series; intro by Anne McCaffrey	18.00

BLACK FLAG (See Asylum #5)
Maximum Press: Jan, 1995 - No.4, 1995; No. 0, July, 1995 ($2.50, B&W) (No. 0 in color)

Preview Edition (6/94, $1.95, B&W)-Fraga/McFarlane-c.	3.00
0-4: 0-(7/95)-Liefeld/Fraga-c. 1-(1/95).	3.00
1-Variant cover	5.00
2,4-Variant covers	3.00

NOTE: *Fraga a-0-4, Preview Edition; c-1-4. Liefeld/Fraga c-0. McFarlane/Fraga c-Preview Edition.*

BLACK FOREST, THE
Image Comics: Mar, 2004; 2005 ($9.95/$6.99, B&W, graphic novels)

nn-Livingston & Tinnell-s/Vokes-a/Oeming-c	10.00
... 2:Castle of Shadows (2005, $6.99) Livingston & Tinnell-s/Vokes-a/c	7.00

BLACK FURY (Becomes Wild West No. 58) (See Blue Bird)
Charlton Comics Group: May, 1955 - No. 57, Mar-Apr, 1966 (Horse stories)

1	9	18	27	50	65	80
2	6	12	18	28	34	40
3-10	5	10	15	22	26	30
11-15,19,20	4	7	9	14	16	18
16-18-Ditko-a	9	18	27	50	65	80
21-30	3	6	8	12	14	16
31-57	2	4	6	8	10	12

BLACK GOLIATH (See Avengers #32-35,41,54 and Civil War #4)
Marvel Comics Group: Feb, 1976 - No. 5, Nov, 1976

1-Tuska-a(p) thru #3	2	4	6	9	13	16

2-5: 2-4-(Regular 25¢ editions). 4-Kirby-c/Buckler-a	1	3	4	6	8	10
2-4-(30¢-c variants, limited distribution)(4,6,8/76)	3	6	9	20	30	40

BLACKHAWK (Formerly Uncle Sam #1-8; see Military & Modern Comics)
Comic Magazines(Quality)No. 9-107(12/56); National Periodical Publications No. 108 (1/57) -250; DC Comics No. 251 on: No. 9, Winter, 1944 - No. 243, 10-11/68; No. 244, 1-2/76 - No. 250, 1-2/77; No. 251, 10/82 - No. 273, 11/84

9 (1944)	352	704	1056	2288	4044	5800
10 (1946)	119	238	357	744	1235	1725
11-15: 14-Ward-a; 13,14-Fear app.	83	166	249	519	860	1200
16-20: 20-Ward Blackhawk	68	136	204	425	705	985
21-30 (1950)	45	90	135	275	455	635
31-40: 31-Chop Chop by Jack Cole	38	76	114	219	347	475
41-49,51-60: 42-Robot-c	31	62	93	178	282	385
50-1st Killer Shark; origin in text	34	68	102	197	311	425
61,62: 61-Used in POP, pg. 91. 62-Used in POP, pg. 92 & color illo						
	27	54	81	158	249	340
63-70,72-80: 65-H-Bomb explosion panel. 66-B&W & color illos POP. 67-Hitler-s. 70-Return						
of Killer Shark; atomic explosion panel. 75-Intro. Blackie the Hawk						
	26	52	78	150	235	320
71-Origin retold; flying saucer-c; A-Bomb panels	29	58	87	170	268	365
81-86: Last precode (3/55)	23	46	69	130	205	280
87-92,94-99,101-107: 91-Robot-c. 105-1st S.A.	18	36	54	105	165	225
93-Origin in text	18	36	54	107	169	230
100	23	46	69	130	205	280
108-1st DC issue (1/57); re-intro. Blackie, the Hawk, their mascot; not in #115						
	38	76	114	285	518	750
109-117: 117-(10/57)-Mr. Freeze app.	14	28	42	103	184	265
118-(11/57)-Frazetta-r/Jimmy Wakely #4 (3 pgs.)	15	30	45	109	195	280
119-130 (11/58): 120-Robot-c	11	22	33	75	133	190
131-140 (9/59): 133-Intro. Lady Blackhawk	9	18	27	64	110	155
141-150,152-163,165,166: 141-Cat-Man returns-c/s. 143-Kurtzman-r/Jimmy Wakely #4.						
150-(7/60)-King Condor returns. 166-Last 10¢ issue						
	7	14	21	49	80	110
151-Lady Blackhawk receives & loses super powers	8	16	24	52	86	120
164-Origin retold	8	16	24	52	86	120
167-180	5	10	15	35	55	75
181-190	4	8	12	28	44	60
191-196,199,201,202,204-210: 196-Combat Diary series begins.						
	4	8	12	22	34	45
197,198,200: 197-New look for Blackhawks. 198-Origin retold						
	4	8	12	24	37	50
203-Origin Chop Chop (12/64)	4	8	12	26	41	55
211-227,229-243(1968): 230-Blackhawks become superheroes; JLA cameo						
242-Return to old costumes	3	6	9	18	27	35
228-Batman, Green Lantern, Superman, The Flash cameos.						
	3	6	9	20	30	40
244 ('76) -250: 250-Chuck dies	1	2	3	4	5	7
251-273: 251-Origin retold; Black Knights return. 252-Intro Domino. 253-Part origin						
Hendrickson. 258-Blackhawk's Island destroyed. 259-Part origin Chop-Chop.						
265-273 (75¢ cover price)						3.00

NOTE: *Chaykin a-260; c-257-260, 262. Crandall a-10, 11, 13, 16?, 18-20, 22-26, 30-33, 35p, 36(2), 37, 38?, 39-44, 46-50, 52-58, 60, 63, 64, 66, 67; c-14-20, 22-63(most except #28-33, 36, 37, 39). Evans a-244, 245,246, 248-250i. G. Kane c-263, 264. Kubert a-244, 245. Newton a-266p. Severin a-257. Spiegle a-261-267, 269-273; c-265-272. Toth a-260p. Ward a-16-27(Chop Chop, 8pgs. ea.); pencilled stories No. 17-63(approx.). Wildey a-268. Chop Chop solo stories in #10-95?*

BLACKHAWK
DC Comics: Mar, 1988 - No. 3, May, 1988 ($2.95, limited series, mature)

1-3: Chaykin painted-c/a/scripts	4.00

BLACKHAWK (Also see Action Comics #601)
DC Comics: Mar, 1989 - No. 16, Aug, 1990 ($1.50, mature)

1	3.50
2-6,8-16: 16-Crandall-c swipe	2.50
7-($2.50, 52 pgs.)-Story-r/Military #1	3.00
Annual 1 (1989, $2.95, 68 pgs.)-Recaps origin of Blackhawk, Lady Blackhawk, and others	3.50
Special 1 (1992, $3.50, 68 pgs.)-Mature readers	3.50

BLACKHAWK INDIAN TOMAHAWK WAR, THE
Avon Periodicals: 1951 (Also see Fighting Indians of the Wild West)

nn-Kinstler-c; Kit West story	20	40	60	115	180	245

BLACK HEART ASSASSIN
Iguana Comics: Jan, 1994 ($2.95)

1	3.00

Black Knight #1 © MAR

Black Lightning #11 © DC

Black Orchid #19 © DC

	GD	VG	FN	VF	VF/NM	NM-		GD	VG	FN	VF	VF/NM	NM-
	2.0	4.0	6.0	8.0	9.0	9.2		2.0	4.0	6.0	8.0	9.0	9.2

BLACK HOLE (See Walt Disney Showcase #54) (Disney, movie)
Whitman Publishing Co.: Mar, 1980 - No. 4, Sept, 1980

11295(#1) (1979, Golden, $1.50-c, 52 pgs., graphic novel; 8 1/2x11") Photo-c; Spiegle-a.	2	4	6	11	16	20
1-3: 1,2-Movie adaptation. 3-Spiegle-a; photo-c.						
3-New stories	1	3	4	6	8	10
4-Sold only in pre-packs; new story; Spiegle-a	4	8	12	28	44	60

BLACK HOOD, THE (See Blue Ribbon, Flyman & Mighty Comics)
Red Circle Comics (Archie): June, 1983 - No. 3, Oct, 1983 (Mandell paper)

1-Morrow, McWilliams, Wildey-a; Toth-c		6.00
2,3: The Fox by Toth-c/a; Boyette-a. 3-Morrow-a; Toth wraparound-c		4.00

(Also see Archie's Super-Hero Special Digest #2)

BLACK HOOD
DC Comics (Impact Comics): Dec, 1991 - No. 12, Dec, 1992 ($1.00)

1		3.50
2-12: 11-Intro The Fox. 12-Origin Black Hood		2.50
Annual 1 (1992, $2.50, 68 pgs.)-w/Trading card		3.00

BLACK HOOD COMICS (Formerly Hangman #2-8; Laugh Comics #20 on; also see
Black Swan, Jackpot, Roly Poly & Top-Notch #9)
MLJ Magazines: No. 9, Wint., 1943-44 - No. 19, Sum., 1946 (on radio in 1943)

9-The Hangman & The Boy Buddies cont'd	109	218	327	681	1128	1575
10-Hangman & Dusty, the Boy Detective app.	62	124	186	388	644	900
11-Dusty app.; no Hangman	48	96	144	293	484	675
12-18: 14-Kinstler blood-c. 17-Hal Foster swipe from Prince Valiant; 1st issue with "An Archie Magazine" on-c	42	84	126	256	423	590
19-I.D. exposed; last issue	52	104	156	317	521	725

NOTE: *Hangman by Fuje in 9, 10. Kinstler a-15, c-14-16.*

BLACK JACK (Rocky Lane's...; formerly Jim Bowie)
Charlton Comics: No. 20, Nov, 1957 - No. 30, Nov, 1959

20	9	18	27	52	69	85
21,27,29,30	6	12	18	31	* 38	45
22,23: 22-(68 pgs.). 23-Williamson/Torres-a	8	16	24	42	54	65
24-26,28-Ditko-a	10	20	30	56	76	95

BLACK KNIGHT, THE
Toby Press: May, 1953; 1963

1-Bondage-c	27	54	81	158	249	340
Super Reprint No. 11 (1963)-Reprints 1953 issue	3	6	9	19	25	32

BLACK KNIGHT, THE
Atlas Comics (MgPC): May, 1955 - No. 5, April, 1956

1-Origin Black Knight; Maneely-c/a	86	172	258	538	894	1250
2-Maneely-c/a(4)	60	120	180	375	623	870
3-5: 4-Maneely-c/a. 5-Maneely-c, Shores-a	46	92	138	281	461	640

BLACK KNIGHT (See The Avengers #48, Marvel Super Heroes & Tales To Astonish #52)
Marvel Comics: June, 1990 - No. 4, Sept, 1990 ($1.50, limited series)

1-4: 1-Original Black Knight returns. 3,4-Dr. Strange app.		2.50

NOTE: *Buckler c-1-4p.*

BLACK KNIGHT: EXODUS
Marvel Comics: Dec, 1996 ($2.50, one-shot)

1-Raab-c; Apocalypse-c/app.		2.50

BLACK LAMB, THE
DC Comics (Helix): Nov, 1996 - No, 6, Apr, 1997 ($2.50, limited series)

1-6: Tim Truman-c/a/scripts		2.50

BLACKLIGHT (From ShadowHawk)
Image Comics: June, 2005 - Present ($2.99)

1,2-Toledo & Deering-a/Wherle-s		3.00

BLACK LIGHTNING (See The Brave & The Bold, Cancelled Comic Cavalcade, DC Comics Presents #16, Detective #490 and World's Finest #257)
National Periodical Publ./DC Comics: Apr, 1977 - No. 11, Sept-Oct, 1978

1-Origin Black Lightning	2	4	6	8	10	12
2,3,6-10						6.00
4,5-Superman-c/s. 4-Intro Cyclotronic Man	1	2	3	4	5	7
11-The Ray new solo story	1	2	3	5	7	9

NOTE: *Buckler c-1-3p, 6-11p. #11 is 44 pgs.*

BLACK LIGHTNING (2nd Series)
DC Comics: Feb, 1995 - No. 13, Feb, 1996 ($1.95/$2.25)

1-5-Tony Isabella scripts begin, ends #8		3.00
6-13: 6-Begin $2.25-c. 13-Batman-c/app.		3.00

BLACK MAGIC (...Magazine) (Becomes Cool Cat V8#6 on)
Crestwood Publ. V1#1-4,V6#1-V7#5/Headline V1#5-V5#3, V7#6-V8#5: 10-11/50 - V4#1,
6-7/53: V4#2, 9-10/53 - V5#3, 11-12/54; V6#1, 9-10/57 - V7#2, 11-12/58: V7#3, 7-8/60 - V8#5,
11-12/61 (V1#1-5, 52pgs.; V1#6-V3#3, 44pgs.)

V1#1-S&K-a, 10 pgs.; Meskin-a(2)	138	276	414	863	1432	2000
2-S&K-a, 17 pgs.; Meskin-a	61	122	183	381	633	885
3-6(8-9/51)-S&K-a, Roussos, Meskin-a	53	106	159	329	545	760
V2#1(10-11/51),4,5,7(#13),9(#15),12(#18)-S&K-a	38	76	114	219	347	475
2,3,6,8,10,11,(#17)	29	58	87	167	264	360
V3#1(#19, 12/52) - 6(#24, 5/53)-S&K-a	30	60	90	174	275	375
V4#1(#25, 6-7/53), 2(#26, 9-10/53)-S&K-a(3-4)	31	62	93	178	282	385
3(#27, 11-12/53)-S&K-a; Ditko-a (2nd published-a); also see Captain 3-D, Daring Love #1, Strange Fantasy #9, & Fantastic Fears #5 (Fant. Fears was 1st drawn, but not 1st publ.)	48	96	144	293	484	675
4(#28)-Eyes ripped out/story-S&K, Ditko-a	40	80	120	243	389	535
5(#29, 3-4/54)-S&K, Ditko-a	32	64	96	186	293	400
6(#30, 5-6/54)-S&K, Powell?-a	25	50	75	148	232	315
V5#1(#31, 7-8/54 - 3(#33, 11-12/54)-S&K-a	18	36	54	107	169	230
V6#1(#34, 9-10/57), 2(#35, 11-12/57)	11	22	33	64	90	115
3(1-2/58) - 6(7-8/58)	11	22	33	64	90	115
V7#1(9-10/58) - 3(7-8/60)	10	20	30	56	76	95
4(9-10/60)	11	22	33	60	83	105
5(11-12/60)-Hitler-c; Torres-a	14	28	42	80	115	150
6(1-2/61)-Powell-a(2)	11	22	33	60	76	95
V8#1(3-4/61)-Powell-c/a	10	20	30	56	76	95
2(5-6/61)-E.C. story swipe/W.F. #22; Ditko, Powell-a						
	11	22	33	60	83	105
3(7-8/61)-E.C. story swipe/W.F. #22; Powell-a(2)	11	22	33	60	83	105
4(9-10/61)-Powell-a(5)	10	20	30	56	76	95
5-E.C. story swipe/W.S.F. #28; Powell-a(3)	11	22	33	60	83	105

NOTE: *Bernard Baily a-V4#6?, V5#3(2). Grandenetti a-V2#3, 11. Kirby c-V1#1-6, V2#1-12, V3#1-6, V4#1, 2, 4-6, V5#1-3. McWilliams a-V3#2i. Meskin a-V1#1(2), 2, 3, 5(2), 6, V2/1, 2, 3(2), 4(3), 5, 6(2), 7-9, 11, 12i, V3#1(2), 5, 6, V5#1(2), 2. Orlando a-V6#1, 4, V7#2; c-V6/1-6. Powell a-V5#1?. Roussos a-V1#3-5, 6(2), V2#3(2), 4, 5(2), 6, 8, 10-12, V3#1(2); 5, 6, V5#2. Simon a-V1#1, 2(2), 3-6, V2#1, 4, 5, 7, 9, 12, V3#1-6, V4#1(3), 2(4), 3(2), 4(2), 5, 6, V5#1-3; c-V2#1. Leonard Starr a-V1#1. Tuska a-V6#3, 4. Woodbridge a-V7#4.*

BLACK MAGIC
National Periodical Publications: Oct-Nov, 1973 - No. 9, Apr-May, 1975

1-S&K reprints	3	6	9	18	23	30
2-8-S&K reprints	2	4	6	9	13	16
9-S&K reprints	2	4	6	10	14	18

BLACKMAIL TERROR (See Harvey Comics Library)

BLACK MASK
DC Comics: 1993 - No. 3, 1994 ($4.95, limited series, 52 pgs.)

1-3		5.00

BLACK OPS
Image Comics (WildStorm): Jan, 1996 - No. 5, May, 1996 ($2.50, lim. series)

1-5		2.50

BLACK ORCHID (See Adventure Comics #428 & Phantom Stranger)
DC Comics: Holiday, 1988-89 - No. 3, 1989 ($3.50, lim. series, prestige format)

Book 1,3: Gaiman scripts & McKean painted-a in all						6.00
Book 2-Arkham Asylum story; Batman app.	1	2	3	5	6	8
TPB (1991, $19.95) r/#1-3; new McKean-c						20.00

BLACK ORCHID
DC Comics: Sept, 1993 - No. 22, June, 1995 ($1.95/$2.25)

1-22: Dave McKean-c all issues		2.50
1-Platinum Edition		12.00
Annual 1 (1993, $3.95, 68 pgs.)-Children's Crusade		4.00

BLACKOUTS (See Broadway Hollywood...)

BLACK PANTHER, THE (Also see Avengers #52, Fantastic Four #52, Jungle Action & Marvel Premiere #51-53)
Marvel Comics Group: Jan, 1977 - No. 15, May, 1979

1-Jack Kirby-s/a thru #12	3	6	9	17	25	32
2-13: 4,5-(Regular 30c editions). 8-Origin	2	4	6	8	10	12
4,5-(35c-c variants, limited dist.)(7,9/77)	5	10	15	35	55	75
14,15-Avengers x-over. 14-Origin	2	4	6	10	14	18
...By Jack Kirby Vol. 1 TPB (2005, $19.99) r/#1-7; unused covers and sketch pages						20.00
...By Jack Kirby Vol. 2 TPB (2006, $19.99) r/#8-12 by Kirby and #13 non-Kirby						20.00

NOTE: *J. Buscema c-15p. Layton c-13i.*

BLACK PANTHER

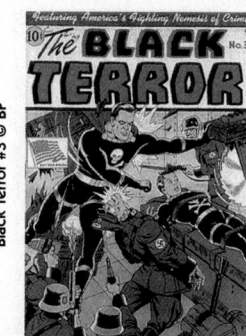

Black Panther #17 © MAR

Blackstone, Master Magician #1 © Vital

Black Terror #3 © BP

	GD 2.0	VG 4.0	FN 6.0	VF 8.0	VF/NM 9.0	NM- 9.2

	GD 2.0	VG 4.0	FN 6.0	VF 8.0	VF/NM 9.0	NM- 9.2

Marvel Comics Group: July, 1988 - No. 4, Oct, 1988 ($1.25)

1-4-Gillis-s/Cowan & Delarosa-a — 2.50

BLACK PANTHER (Marvel Knights)
Marvel Comics: Nov, 1998 - No. 62, Sept, 2003 ($2.50)

1-Texeira-a/c; Priest-s — 6.00
1-($6.95) DF edition w/Quesada & Palmiotti-c — 1 — 2 — 3 — 5 — 6 — 8
2-4: Two covers by Texeira and Timm. 3-Fantastic Four app. — 3.50
5-35,37-40: 5-Evans-a. 6-8-Jusko-a. 8-Avengers-c/app. 15-Hulk app. 22-Moon Knight app. 23-Avengers app. 25-Maximum Security x-over. 26-Storm-c/app. 28-Magneto & Sub-Mariner-c/app. 29-WWII flashback meeting w/Captain America. 35-Defenders-c/app. 37-Luke Cage and Falcon-c/app. — 2.50
36-($3.50, 100 pgs.) 35th Anniversary issue incl. r/1st app. in FF #52 — 3.50
41-56: 41-44-Wolverine app. 47-Thor app. 48,49-Magneto app. — 2.50
57-62: 57-Begin $2.99-c. 59-Falcon app. — 3.00
...: The Client (6/01, $14.95, TPB) r/#1-5 — 15.00
... 2099 #1 (11/04, $2.99) Kirkman-s/Hotz-a/Pat Lee-c — 3.00

BLACK PANTHER (Marvel Knights)
Marvel Comics: Apr, 2005 - Present ($2.99)

1-Reginald Hudlin-s/John Romita Jr. & Klaus Janson-a; covers by Romita & Ribic — 5.00
1-2nd printing; variant-c by Ribic — 3.00
2-7,9,15,17-20: 7-House of M; Hairsine-a. 10-14-Blade app. 17-Linsner-c. 19-Doctor Doom app. — 3.00
8-Cho-c; X-Men app. — 4.00
8-2nd printing variant-c — 3.00
16-($3.99) Wedding of T'Challa and Storm; wraparound Cho-c; Hudlin-s/Eaton-a — 4.00
21-Civil War x-over; Namor app. — 8.00
21-2nd printing with new cover and Civil War logo — 3.00
22-25-Civil War: 23-25-Turner-c — 4.00
26-30-T'Challa and Storm join the Fantastic Four. 27-30-Marvel Zombies app. 28-30-Suydam-c — 3.00
...: Bad Mutha TPB (2006, $10.99) r/#10-13 — 11.00
...: Civil War TPB (2007, $17.99) r/#19-25 — 18.00
...: The Bride TPB (2006, $14.99) r/#14-18; interview with the dress designer — 15.00
...: Who Is The Black Panther HC (2005, $21.99) r/#1-6; Hudlin afterword; cover gallery — 22.00
...: Who Is The Black Panther SC (2006, $14.99) r/#1-6; Hudlin afterword; cover gallery — 15.00

BLACK PANTHER: PANTHER'S PREY
Marvel Comics: May, 1991 - No. 4, Oct, 1991 ($4.95, squarebound, lim. series, 52 pgs.)

1-4-McGregor-s/Turner-a — 5.00

BLACK PEARL, THE
Dark Horse Comics: Sept, 1996 - No. 5, Jan, 1997 ($2.95, limited series)

1-5-Mark Hamill scripts — 3.00

BLACK PHANTOM (See Tim Holt #25, 38)
Magazine Enterprises: Nov, 1954 (one-shot) (Female outlaw)

1 (A-1 #122)-The Ghost Rider story plus 3 Black Phantom stories; Headlight-c/a — 36 — 72 — 108 — 208 — 329 — 450

BLACK PHANTOM
AC Comics: 1989 - No. 3, 1990 ($2.50, B&W; #2 color)(Reprints & new-a)

1-3: 1-Ayers-r, Bolle-r/B.P. #1-3-Redmask-r — 2.75

BLACK PHANTOM, RETURN OF THE (See Wisco)

BLACK RIDER (Western Winners #1-7; Western Tales of Black Rider #28-31; Gunsmoke Western #32 on)(See All Western Winners, Best Western, Kid Colt, Outlaw Kid, Rex Hart, Two-Gun Kid, Two-Gun Western, Western Gunfighters, Western Winners, & Wild Western)
Marvel/Atlas Comics(CDS No. 8-17/CPS No. 19 on): No. 8, 3/50 - No. 18, 1/52; No. 19, 11/53 - No. 27, 3/55

8 (#1)-Black Rider & his horse Satan begin; 36 pgs; Stan Lee photo-c as Black Rider — 42 — 84 — 126 — 256 — 421 — 585
9-52 pgs. begin, end #14 — 23 — 46 — 69 — 130 — 205 — 280
10-Origin Black Rider — 27 — 54 — 81 — 158 — 249 — 340
11-14: 14-Last 52pgs. — 17 — 34 — 51 — 98 — 154 — 210
15-19: 19-Two-Gun Kid app. — 15 — 30 — 45 — 85 — 130 — 175
20-Classic-c; Two-Gun Kid app. — 16 — 32 — 48 — 92 — 144 — 195
21-27: 21-23-Two-Gun Kid app. 24,25-Arrowhead app. 26-Kid Colt app. 27-Last issue; last precode. Kid Colt app. The Spider (a villain) burns to death — 14 — 28 — 42 — 81 — 118 — 155
NOTE: *Ayers* c-22. *Jack Keller* a-15, 26, 27. *Maneely* a-14; c-16, 17, 25, 27. *Syd Shores* a-19, 21, 22, 23(3), 24(3), 25-27; c-19, 21, 23. *Sinnott* a-24, 25. *Tuska* a-12, 19-21.

BLACK RIDER RIDES AGAIN!, THE
Atlas Comics (CPS): Sept, 1957

1-Kirby-a(3); Powell-a; Severin-c — 25 — 50 — 75 — 145 — 228 — 310

BLACK SEPTEMBER (Also see Avengers/Ultraforce, Ultraforce (1st series) #10 & Ultraforce/Avengers)
Malibu Comics (Ultraverse): 1995 ($1.50, one-shot)

Infinity-Intro to the newUltraverse; variant-c exists. — 2.50

BLACKSTONE (See Super Magician Comics & Wisco Giveaways)

BLACKSTONE, MASTER MAGICIAN COMICS
Vital Publ./Street & Smith Publ.: Mar-Apr, 1946 - No. 3, July-Aug, 1946

1 — 32 — 64 — 96 — 186 — 293 — 400
2,3 — 19 — 38 — 57 — 112 — 176 — 240

BLACKSTONE, THE MAGICIAN (...Detective on cover only #3 & 4)
Marvel Comics (CnPC): No. 2, May, 1948 - No. 4, Sept, 1948 (No #1) (Cont'd from E.C. #1?)

2-The Blonde Phantom begins, ends #4 — 64 — 128 — 192 — 400 — 663 — 925
3,4: 3-Blonde Phantom by Sekowsky — 40 — 80 — 120 — 239 — 380 — 520

BLACKSTONE, THE MAGICIAN DETECTIVE FIGHTS CRIME
E. C. Comics: Fall, 1947

1-1st app. Happy Houlihans — 50 — 100 — 150 — 305 — 503 — 700

BLACK SUN (X-Men Black Sun on cover)
Marvel Comics: Nov, 2000 - No. 5, Nov, 2000 ($2.99, weekly limited series)

1-(...: X-Men), 2-(...: Storm), 3-(...: Banshee and Sunfire), 4-(...: Colossus and Nightcrawler), 5-(...: Wolverine and Thunderbird); Claremont-s in all; Evans interlocking painted covers; Magik returns — 3.00

BLACK SUN
DC Comics (WildStorm): Nov, 2002 - No. 6, Jun, 2003 ($2.95, limited series)

1-6-Andreyko-s/Scott-a — 3.00

BLACK SWAN COMICS
MLJ Magazines (Pershing Square Publ. Co.): 1945

1-The Black Hood reprints from Black Hood No. 14; Bill Woggon-a; Suzie app. — 21 — 42 — 63 — 122 — 191 — 260

BLACK TARANTULA (See Feature Presentations No. 5)

BLACK TERROR (See America's Best Comics & Exciting Comics)
Better Publications/Standard: Winter, 1942-43 - No. 27, June, 1949

1-Black Terror, Crime Crusader begin — 300 — 600 — 900 — 1931 — 3366 — 4800
2 — 117 — 234 — 351 — 731 — 1216 — 1700
3 — 81 — 162 — 243 — 506 — 841 — 1175
4,5 — 68 — 136 — 204 — 425 — 705 — 985
6-10: 7-The Ghost app. — 57 — 114 — 171 — 356 — 596 — 835
11-20: 20-The Scarab app. — 50 — 100 — 150 — 305 — 503 — 700
21-Miss Masque app. — 53 — 106 — 159 — 323 — 537 — 750
22-Part Frazetta-a on one Black Terror story — 50 — 100 — 150 — 305 — 503 — 700
23,25-27 — 45 — 90 — 135 — 275 — 450 — 625
24-Frazetta-a (1/4 pg.) — 45 — 90 — 135 — 277 — 456 — 635
NOTE: *Schomburg (Xela)* c-2-27; bondage c-2, 17, 24. *Meskin* a-27. *Moreira* a-27. *Robinson/Meskin* a-23, 24(3), 25, 26. *Roussos/Mayo* a-24. *Tuska* a-26, 27.

BLACK TERROR, THE (Also see Total Eclipse)
Eclipse Comics: Oct, 1989 - No. 3, June, 1990 ($4.95, 52 pgs., limited series)

1-3: Beau Smith & Chuck Dixon scripts; Dan Brereton painted-c/a — 5.00

BLACKTHORNE 3-D SERIES
Blackthorne Publishing Co.: May, 1985 - No. 80, 1989 ($2.25/$2.50)

1-Sheena in 3-D #1. D. Stevens-c/retouched-a — 1 — 2 — 3 — 5 — 6 — 8
2-10: 2-MerlinRealm in 3-D #1. 3-3-D Heroes #1. Goldyn in 3-D #1. 5-Bizarre 3-D Zone #1. 6-Salimba in 3-D #1. 7-Twisted Tales in 3-D #1. 8-Dick Tracy in 3-D #1. 9-Salimba in 3-D #2. 10-Gumby in 3-D #1 — 6.00
11-19: 11-Betty Boop in 3-D #1. 12-Hamster Vice in 3-D #1. 13-Little Nemo in 3-D #1. 14-Gumby in 3-D #2. 15-Hamster Vice #6 in 3-D. 16-Laffin' Gas #6 in 3-D. 17-Gumby in 3-D #3. 18-Bullwinkle and Rocky in 3-D #1. 19-The Flintstones in 3-D #1 — 6.00
20(#1),26(#2),35(#3),39(#4),52(#5),62,71(#6)-G.I. Joe in 3-D. 62-G.I. Joe Annual — 2 — 4 — 6 — 8 — 11 — 14
21-24,27-28: 21-Gumby in 3-D #4. 22-The Flintstones in 3-D #2. 23-Laurel & Hardy in 3-D #1. 24-Bozo the Clown in 3-D #1. 27-Bravestarr in 3-D #1. 28- Gumby in 3-D #5 — 6.00
25,29,37-The Transformers in 3-D — 2 — 4 — 6 — 10 — 14 — 18
30-Star Wars in 3-D #1 — 3 — 6 — 9 — 14 — 19 — 24
31-34,36,38,40: 31-The California Raisins in 3-D #1. 32-Richie Rich & Casper in 3-D #1. 33-Gumby in 3-D #6. 34-Laurel & Hardy in 3-D #2. 36-The Flintstones in 3-D #3. 38-Gumby in 3-D #7. 40-Bravestarr in 3-D #2 — 6.00
41-46,49,50: 41-Battletech in 3-D #1. 42-The Flintstones in 3-D #4. 43-Underdog in 3-D #1. 44-The California Raisins in 3-D #2. 45-Red Heat in 3-D #1 (movie adapt.). 46-The California Raisins in 3-D #3. 49-Rambo in 3-D #1. 49-Sad Sack in 3-D #1. 50-Bullwinkle For President in 3-D #1 — 6.00

	GD	VG	FN	VF	VF/NM	NM-
	2.0	4.0	6.0	8.0	9.0	9.2

47,48-Star Wars in 3-D #2,3
51,53-60: 51-Kull in 3-D #1. 53-Red Sonja in 3-D #1. 54-Bozo in 3-D #2. 55-Waxwork in 3-D #1 (movie adapt.). 57-Casper in 3-D #1. 58-Baby Huey in 3-D #1. 59-Little Dot in 3-D #1. 60-Solomon Kane in 3-D #1

| | | 2 | 4 | 6 | 9 | 13 | 16 |

60-Solomon Kane in 3-D #1 ... 6.00
61,63-70,72-80: 61-Werewolf in 3-D #1. 63-The California Raisins in 3-D #4. 64-To Die For in 3-D #1. 65-Capt. Holo in 3-D #1. 66-Playful Little Audrey in 3-D #1. 67-Kull in 3-D #2. 69-The California Raisins in 3-D #5. 70-Wendy in 3-D #1. 72-Sports Hall of Shame #1. 74-The Noid in 3-D #1. 75-Moonwalker in 3-D #1 (Michael Jackson movie adapt.). 76-79.
80-The Noid in 3-D #2 ... 1 2 3 4 5 7

BLACK WIDOW (Marvel Knights) (Also see Marvel Graphic Novel)
Marvel Comics: May, 1999 - No. 3, Aug, 1999 ($2.99, limited series)
1-(June on-c) Devin Grayson-s/J.G. Jones-c/a; Daredevil app. ... 5.00
1-Variant-c by J.G. Jones ... 6.00
2,3 ... 4.00
...Web of Intrigue (6/99, $3.50) r/origin & early appearances ... 3.50
TPB (7/01, $15.95) r/Vol. 1 & 2; Jones-c ... 16.00

BLACK WIDOW (Marvel Knights) (Volume 2)
Marvel Comics: Jan, 2001 - No. 3, May, 2001 ($2.99, limited series)
1-3-Grayson & Rucka-s/Scott Hampton-c/a; Daredevil app. ... 3.00

BLACK WIDOW (Marvel Knights)
Marvel Comics: Nov, 2004 - No. 6, Apr, 2005 ($2.99, limited series)
1-6-Sienkiewicz-a/Land-c ... 3.00

BLACK WIDOW: PALE LITTLE SPIDER (Marvel Knights) (Volume 3)
Marvel Comics: Jun, 2002 - No. 3, Aug, 2002 ($2.99, limited series)
1-3-Rucka-s/Kordey-a/Horn-c ... 3.00

BLACK WIDOW 2 (THE THINGS THEY SAY ABOUT HER) (Marvel Knights)
Marvel Comics: Nov, 2005 - No. 6, Apr, 2006 ($2.99, limited series)
1-6-Phillips & Sienkiewicz-a/Morgan-a; Daredevil app. ... 3.00
TPB (2006, $15.99) r/#1-6 ... 16.00

BLACKWULF
Marvel Comics: June, 1994 - No. 10, Mar, 1995 ($1.50)
1-($2.50)-Embossed-c; Angel Medina-a ... 3.00
2-10 ... 2.50

BLADE (The Vampire Hunter)
Marvel Comics
1-(3/98, $3.50) Colan-a(p)/Christopher Golden-s ... 3.50
... Black & White TPB (2004, $15.99, B&W) reprints from magazines Vampire Tales #8,9;
    Marvel Preview #3,6; Crescent City Blues #1 and Marvel Shadow and Light #1 ... 16.00
San Diego Con Promo (6/97) Wesley Snipes photo-c ... 3.00
...Sins of the Father (10/98, $5.99) Sears-a; movie adaption ... 6.00
Blade 2: Movie Adaptation (5/02, $5.95) Ponticelli-a/Bradstreet-c ... 6.00

BLADE (The Vampire Hunter)
Marvel Comics: Nov, 1998 - No. 3, Jan, 1999 ($3.50/$2.99)
1-($3.50) Contains Movie insider pages; McKean-a ... 3.50
2,3-($2.99): 2-Two covers ... 3.00

BLADE (Volume 2)
Marvel Comics (MAX): May, 2002 -No. 6, Oct, 2002 ($2.99)
1-6-Bradstreet-c/Hinz-a. 1-5-Pugh-a. 6-Homs-a ... 3.00

BLADE
Marvel Comics: Nov, 2006 - No. 12, Oct, 2007 ($2.99)
1-12: 1-Chaykin-a/Guggenheim-s; origin retold; Spider-Man app. 2-Dr. Doom-c/app.
    5-Civil War tie-in; Wolverine app. 6-Blade loses a hand. 10-Spider-Man app. ... 3.00
...: Undead Again TPB (2007, $14.99) r/#1-6; letters pages from #1&2 ... 15.00

BLADE OF THE IMMORTAL (Manga)
Dark Horse Comics: June, 1996 - Present ($2.95/$2.99/$3.95, B&W)
1-Hiroaki Samura-s/a in all ... 1 3 4 6 8 10
2-5: 2-#1 on cover in error ... 6.00
6-10 ... 5.00
11,19,20,34-($3.95, 48 pgs.): 34-Food one-shot ... 4.00
12-18,21-33,35-41,43-105,107-128: 12-20-Dreamsong. 21-28-On Silent Wings. 29-33-Dark
    Shadow. 35-42-Heart of Darkness. 43-57-The Gathering ... 3.00
42-($3.50) Ends Heart of Darkness ... 3.50
106-($3.99) ... 4.00

BLADE RUNNER (Movie)
Marvel Comics Group: Oct, 1982 - No. 2, Nov, 1982
1,2-r/Marvel Super Special #22; 1-Williamson-c/a. 2-Williamson-a ... 3.50

BLADE: THE VAMPIRE-HUNTER
Marvel Comics: July, 1994 - No. 10, Apr, 1995 ($1.95)
1-($2.95)-Foil-c; Dracula returns; Wheatley-c/a ... 3.50
2-10: 2,3,10-Dracula-c/app. 8-Morbius app. ... 2.50

BLADE: VAMPIRE-HUNTER
Marvel Comics: Dec, 1999 - No. 6, May, 2000 ($3.50/$2.50)
1-($3.50)-Bart Sears-s; Sears and Smith-a ... 3.50
2-6-($2.50): 2-Regular & Wesley Snipes photo-c ... 2.50

BLAIR WITCH CHRONICLES, THE
Oni Press: Mar, 2000 - No. 4, July, 2000 ($2.95, B&W, limited series)
1-4-Van Meter-s.1-Guy Davis-a. 2-Mireault-a ... 3.00
1-DF Alternate-c by John Estes ... 7.00
TPB (9/00, $15.95) r/#1-4 & Blair Witch Project one-shot ... 16.00

BLAIR WITCH: DARK TESTAMENTS
Image Comics: Oct, 2000 ($2.95, one-shot)
1-Edington-s/Adlard-a; story of murderer Rustin Parr ... 3.00

BLAIR WITCH PROJECT, THE (Movie companion, not adaption)
Oni Press: July, 1999 ($2.95, B&W, one-shot)
1-(1st printing) History of the Blair Witch, art by Edwards, Mireault, and Davis; Van Meter-s;
    only the stick figure is red on the cover ... 12.00
1-(2nd printing) Stick figure and title lettering are red on cover ... 4.00
1-(3rd printing) Stick figure, title, and creator credits are red on cover ... 3.00
DF Glow in the Dark variant-c ($10.00) ... 10.00

BLAST (Satire Magazine)
G & D Publications: Feb, 1971 - No. 2, May, 1971
1-Wrightson & Kaluta-a/Everette-c ... 7 14 21 47 76 105
2-Kaluta-c/a ... 5 10 15 35 55 75

BLAST CORPS
Dark Horse Comics: Oct, 1998 ($2.50, one-shot, based on Nintendo game)
1-Reprints from Nintendo Power magazine; Mahn-a ... 2.50

BLASTERS SPECIAL
DC Comics: 1989 ($2.00, one-shot)
1-Peter David scripts; Invasion spin-off ... 2.50

BLAST-OFF (Three Rocketeers)
Harvey Publications (Fun Day Funnies): Oct, 1965 (12¢)
1-Kirby/Williamson-a(2); Williamson/Crandall-a; Williamson/Torres/Krenkel-a; Kirby/Simon-c
... 6 12 18 41 66 90

BLAZE
Marvel Comics: Aug, 1994 - No. 12, July, 1995 ($1.95)
1-($2.95)-Foil embossed-c ... 3.50
2-12: 2-Man-Thing-c/story. 11,12-Punisher app. ... 2.50

BLAZE CARSON (Rex Hart #6 on)(See Kid Colt, Tex Taylor, Wild Western, Wisco)
Marvel Comics (USA): Sept, 1948 - No. 5, June, 1949
1: 1,2-Shores-c ... 27 54 81 156 246 335
2,4,5: 4-Two-Gun Kid app. 5-Tex Taylor app. ... 18 36 54 105 165 225
3-Used by N.Y. State Legis. Comm. (injury to eye splash); Tex Morgan app. ... 19 38 57 112 176 240

BLAZE: LEGACY OF BLOOD (See Ghost Rider & Ghost Rider/Blaze)
Marvel Comics (Midnight Sons imprint): Dec, 1993 - No. 4, Mar, 1994 ($1.75, limited series)
1-4 ... 2.50

BLAZE OF GLORY
Marvel Comics: Feb, 2000 - No. 4, Mar, 2000 ($2.99, limited series)
1-4-Ostrander-s/Manco-a; Two-Gun Kid, Rawhide Kid, Red Wolf and Ghost Rider app. ... 3.00
TPB (7/02, $9.99) r/#1-4 ... 10.00

BLAZE THE WONDER COLLIE (Formerly Molly Manton's Romances #1?)
Marvel Comics(SePI): No. 2, Oct, 1949 - No. 3, Feb, 1950 (Both have photo-c)
2(#1), 3-(Scarce) ... 23 46 69 132 209 285

BLAZING BATTLE TALES
Seaboard Periodicals (Atlas): July, 1975
1-Intro. Sgt. Hawk & the Sky Demon; Severin, McWilliams, Sparling-a; Nazi-c by Thorne
... 2 4 6 8 11 14

BLAZING COMBAT (Magazine)
Warren Publishing Co.: Oct, 1965 - No. 4, July, 1966 (35¢, B&W)
1-Frazetta painted-c on all ... 22 44 66 165 295 425

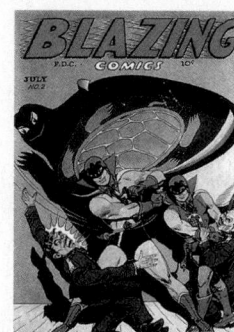

Blazing Comics #2 © Enwil

Blazing West #7 © ACG

Blonde Phantom #22 © MAR

	GD	VG	FN	VF	VF/NM	NM-
	2.0	4.0	6.0	8.0	9.0	9.2

	GD 2.0	VG 4.0	FN 6.0	VF 8.0	VF/NM 9.0	NM- 9.2
2	7	14	21	49	80	110
3,4: 4-Frazetta half pg. ad	6	12	18	43	69	95
nn-Anthology (reprints from No. 1-4) (low print)	7	14	21	47	76	105

NOTE: **Adkins** a-4. **Colan** a-3,4,nn. **Crandall** a-all. **Evans** a-1,4. **Heath** a-4,nn. **Morrow** a-1-3,nn. **Orlando** a-1-3,nn. **J. Severin** a-all. **Torres** a-1-4. **Toth** a-all. **Williamson** a-2. and **Wood** a-3,4,nn.

BLAZING COMBAT: WORLD WAR I AND WORLD WAR II
Apple Press: Mar, 1994 ($3.75, B&W)

	GD 2.0	VG 4.0	FN 6.0	VF 8.0	VF/NM 9.0	NM- 9.2
1,2: 1-r/Colan, Toth, Goodwin, Severin, Wood-a. 2-r/Crandall, Evans, Severin, Torres, Williamson-a						4.00

BLAZING COMICS (Also see Blue Circle Comics and Red Circle Comics)
Enwil Associates/Rural Home: 6/44 - #3, 9/44; #4, 2/45; #5, 3/45; #5(V2#2), 3/55 - #6(V2#3), 1955?

	GD 2.0	VG 4.0	FN 6.0	VF 8.0	VF/NM 9.0	NM- 9.2
1-The Green Turtle, Red Hawk, Black Buccaneer begin; origin Jun-Gal	50	100	150	305	503	700
2-5: 3-Briefer-a. 5-(V2#2 inside)	34	68	102	197	311	425
5(3/55, V2#2-inside)-Black Buccaneer-c, 6(V2#3-inside, 1955)-Indian/Japanese-c; cover is from Apr. 1945	17	34	51	100	158	215

NOTE: No. 5 & 6 contain remaindered comics rebound and the contents can vary. Cloak & Dagger, Will Rogers, Superman 64, Star Spangled 130, Kaanga known. Value would be half of contents.

BLAZING SIXGUNS
Avon Periodicals: Dec, 1952

	GD 2.0	VG 4.0	FN 6.0	VF 8.0	VF/NM 9.0	NM- 9.2
1-Kinstler-c/a; Larsen/Alascia-a(2), Tuska?-a; Jesse James, Kit Carson, Wild Bill Hickok app.	17	34	51	98	154	210

BLAZING SIXGUNS
I.W./Super Comics: 1964

	GD 2.0	VG 4.0	FN 6.0	VF 8.0	VF/NM 9.0	NM- 9.2
I.W. Reprint #1,8,9: 1-r/Wild Bill Hickok #26, Western True Crime #? & Blazing Sixguns #1 by Avon; Kinstler-c. 8-r/Blazing Western #?; Kinstler-c. 9-r/Blazing Western #1; Ditko-c; Kintsler-c reprinted from Dalton Boys #1	2	4	6	10	14	18
Super Reprint #10,11,15-17: 10,11-r/The Rider #2,1. 15-r/Silver Kid Western #?. 16-r/Buffalo Bill #?; Wildey-r; Severin-c. 17(1964)-r/Western True Crime #?	2	4	6	10	14	18
12-Reprints Bullseye #3; S&K-a	4	8	12	19	29	38
18-r/Straight Arrow #? by Powell; Severin-c	2	4	6	10	14	18

BLAZING SIX-GUNS (Also see Sundance Kid)
Skywald Comics: Feb, 1971 - No. 2, Apr, 1971 (52 pgs.)

	GD 2.0	VG 4.0	FN 6.0	VF 8.0	VF/NM 9.0	NM- 9.2
1-The Red Mask (3-D effect, not true 3-D), Sundance Kid begin (new-s), Avon's Geronimo reprint by Kinstler; Wyatt Earp app.	3	6	9	14	20	25
2-Wild Bill Hickok, Jesse James, Kit Carson-r plus M.E. Red Mask-r (3-D effect)	2	4	6	10	14	18

BLAZING WEST (The Hooded Horseman #21 on)
American Comics Group (B&I Publ./Michel Publ.): Fall, 1948 - No. 20, Nov-Dec, 1951

	GD 2.0	VG 4.0	FN 6.0	VF 8.0	VF/NM 9.0	NM- 9.2
1-Origin & 1st app. Injun Jones, Tenderfoot & Buffalo Belle; Texas Tim & Ranger begins, ends #13	20	40	60	117	184	250
2,3 (1-2/49)	11	22	33	62	86	110
4-Origin & 1st app. Little Lobo; Starr-a (3-4/49)	10	20	30	56	76	95
5-10: 5-Starr-a	9	18	27	50	65	80
11-13	8	16	24	42	54	65
14(11-12/50)-Origin/1st app. The Hooded Horseman	13	26	39	74	105	135
15-20: 15,16,18,19-Starr-a	9	18	27	50	65	80

BLAZING WESTERN
Timor Publications: Jan, 1954 - No. 5, Sept, 1954

	GD 2.0	VG 4.0	FN 6.0	VF 8.0	VF/NM 9.0	NM- 9.2
1-Ditko-a (1st Western-a?); text story by Bruce Hamilton	16	32	48	94	147	200
2-4	9	18	27	50	65	80
5-Disbrow-a	9	18	27	52	69	85

BLINDSIDE
Image Comics (Extreme Studios): Aug, 1996 ($2.50)

	GD 2.0	VG 4.0	FN 6.0	VF 8.0	VF/NM 9.0	NM- 9.2
1-Variant-c exists						2.50

BLINK (See X-Men Age of Apocalypse storyline)
Marvel Comics: March, 2001 - No. 4, June, 2001 ($2.99, limited series)

	GD 2.0	VG 4.0	FN 6.0	VF 8.0	VF/NM 9.0	NM- 9.2
1-4-Adam Kubert-c/Lobdell-s/Winick-script; leads into Exiles #1						3.00

BLIP
Marvel Comics Group: 2/1983 - 1983 (Video game mag. in comic format)

	GD 2.0	VG 4.0	FN 6.0	VF 8.0	VF/NM 9.0	NM- 9.2
1-1st app. Donkey Kong & Mario Bros. in comics, 6pgs. comics; photo-c	1	2	3	5	6	8
2-Spider-Man photo-c; 6pgs. Spider-Man comics w/Green Goblin	1	3	4	6	8	10
3,4,6						5.00

	GD 2.0	VG 4.0	FN 6.0	VF 8.0	VF/NM 9.0	NM- 9.2
5-E.T., Indiana Jones; Rocky-c						6.00
7-6pgs. Hulk comics; Pac-Man & Donkey Kong Jr. Hints	1	2	3	4	5	7

BLISS ALLEY
Image Comics: July, 1997 - No. 2, Sept, 1997 ($2.95, B&W)

	GD 2.0	VG 4.0	FN 6.0	VF 8.0	VF/NM 9.0	NM- 9.2
1,2-Messner-Loebs-s/a						3.00

BLITZKRIEG
National Periodical Publications: Jan-Feb, 1976 - No. 5, Sept-Oct, 1976

	GD 2.0	VG 4.0	FN 6.0	VF 8.0	VF/NM 9.0	NM- 9.2
1-Kubert-c on all	4	8	12	22	34	45
2-5	3	6	9	14	20	25

BLONDE PHANTOM (Formerly All-Select #1-11; Lovers #23 on)(Also see Blackstone, Marvel Mystery, Millie The Model #2, Sub-Mariner Comics #25 & Sun Girl)
Marvel Comics (MPC): No. 12, Winter, 1946-47 - No. 22, Mar, 1949

	GD 2.0	VG 4.0	FN 6.0	VF 8.0	VF/NM 9.0	NM- 9.2
12-Miss America begins, ends #14	169	338	507	1056	1753	2450
13-Sub-Mariner begins (not in #16)	100	200	300	625	1038	1450
14,15: 15-Kurtzman's "Hey Look"	93	186	279	581	966	1350
16-Captain America with Bucky story by Rico(p), 6 pgs.; Kurtzman's "Hey Look" (1 pg.)	124	248	372	775	1288	1800
17-22: 22-Anti Wertham editorial	78	156	234	488	807	1125

NOTE: **Shores** c-12-18.

BLONDIE (See Ace Comics, Comics Reading Libraries (Promotional Comics section), Dagwood, Daisy & Her Pups, Eat Right to Work…, King & Magic Comics)
David McKay Publications: 1942 - 1946

	GD 2.0	VG 4.0	FN 6.0	VF 8.0	VF/NM 9.0	NM- 9.2
Feature Books 12 (Rare)	81	162	243	506	841	1175
Feature Books 27-29,31,34(1940)	21	42	63	124	195	265
Feature Books 36,38,40,42,43,45,47	20	40	60	117	184	250
…1944 (Hard-c, 1938, B&W, 128 pgs.)-1944 daily strip-r	16	32	48	94	147	200

BLONDIE & DAGWOOD FAMILY
Harvey Publ. (King Features Synd.): Oct, 1963 - No. 4, Dec, 1965 (68 pgs.)

	GD 2.0	VG 4.0	FN 6.0	VF 8.0	VF/NM 9.0	NM- 9.2
1	5	10	15	32	51	70
2-4	3	6	9	20	30	40

BLONDIE COMICS (…Monthly No. 16-141)
David McKay #1-15/Harvey #16-163/King #164-175/Charlton #177 on:
Spring, 1947 - No. 163, Nov, 1965; No. 164, Aug, 1966 - No. 175, Dec, 1967; No. 177, Feb, 1969 - No. 222, Nov, 1976

	GD 2.0	VG 4.0	FN 6.0	VF 8.0	VF/NM 9.0	NM- 9.2
1	30	60	90	176	278	380
2	15	30	45	90	140	190
3-5	14	28	42	76	108	140
6-10	11	22	33	62	86	110
11-15	9	18	27	47	61	75
16-(3/50; 1st Harvey issue)	10	20	30	56	76	95
17-20: 20-(3/51)-Becomes Daisy & Her Pups #21 & Chamber of Chills #21	5	10	15	32	51	70
21-30	4	8	12	28	44	60
31-50	4	8	12	22	34	45
51-80	3	6	9	20	30	40
81-99	3	6	9	18	27	35
100	4	8	12	22	34	45
101-124,126-130	3	6	9	16	22	28
125 (80 pgs.)	4	8	12	24	37	50
131-136,138,139	3	6	9	14	20	25
137,140-(80 pgs.)	4	8	12	23	36	48
141-147,149-154,156,160,164-167	3	6	9	14	20	25
148,155,157-159,161-163 are 68 pgs.	3	6	9	19	29	38
168-175	2	4	6	10	14	18
177-199 (no #176)	2	4	6	8	11	14
200	2	4	6	9	13	16
201-210,213-222	1	3	4	6	8	10
211,212-1st & 2nd app. Super Dagwood	2	4	6	8	11	14
Blondie, Dagwood & Daisy by Chic Young #1(Harvey, 1953, 100 pg. squarebound giant) new stories; Popeye (1 pg.) app.	26	52	78	152	239	325

BLOOD
Marvel Comics (Epic Comics): Feb, 1988 - No. 4, Apr, 1988 ($3.25, mature)

	GD 2.0	VG 4.0	FN 6.0	VF 8.0	VF/NM 9.0	NM- 9.2
1-4: DeMatteis scripts & Kent Williams-c/a						3.50

BLOOD AND GLORY (Punisher & Captain America)
Marvel Comics: Oct, 1992 - No. 3, Dec, 1992 ($5.95, limited series)

	GD 2.0	VG 4.0	FN 6.0	VF 8.0	VF/NM 9.0	NM- 9.2
1-3: 1-Embossed wraparound-c by Janson; Chichester & Clarke-s						6.00

BLOOD & ROSES: FUTURE PAST TENSE (Bob Hickey's…)
Sky Comics: Dec, 1993 ($2.25)

Blood: A Tale #2
© DeMatteis & Williams

Blood Pack #1 © DC

Blood Syndicate #18 © Milestone

	GD 2.0	VG 4.0	FN 6.0	VF 8.0	VF/NM 9.0	NM- 9.2

1-Silver ink logo 2.50

BLOOD & ROSES: SEARCH FOR THE TIME-STONE (Bob Hickey's…)
Sky Comics: Apr, 1994 ($2.50)

1 2.50

BLOOD AND SHADOWS
DC Comics (Vertigo): 1996 - Book 4, 1996 ($5.95, squarebound, mature)

Books 1-4: Joe R. Lansdale scripts; Mark A. Nelson-c/a. 6.00

BLOOD AND WATER
DC Comics (Vertigo): May, 2003 - No. 5, Sept, 2003 ($2.95, limited series)

1-5-Judd Winick-s/Tomm Coker-a/Brian Bolland-c 3.00

BLOOD: A TALE
DC Comics (Vertigo): Nov, 1996 - No. 4, Feb, 1997 ($2.95, limited series)

1-4: Reprints Epic series w/new-c; DeMatteis scripts; Kent Williams-c/a 3.00
TPB (2004, $19.95) r/#1-4 20.00

BLOODBATH
DC Comics: Early Dec, 1993 - No. 2, Late Dec, 1993 ($3.50, 68 pgs.)

| 1-Neon ink-c; Superman app.; new Batman-c /app. | | | | | | 3.50 |
| 2-Hitman 2nd app. | 1 | 2 | 3 | 4 | 5 | 7 |

BLOODHOUND
DC Comics: Sept, 2004 - No. 10, June, 2005 ($2.95)

1-10: 1-Jolley-s/Kirk-a/Johnson-c. 5-Firestorm app. (cont. from Firestorm #7) 3.00

BLOOD LEGACY
Image Comics (Top Cow): May, 2000 - No. 4, Nov, 2000; Apr, 2003 ($2.50/$4.99)

…: The Story of Ryan 1-4-Kerri Hawkins-s. 1-Andy Park-a(p); 3 covers 2.50
…: The Young Ones 1 (4/03, $4.99, one-shot) Basaldua-c/a 5.00
Preview Special ('00, $4.95) B&W flip-book w/The Magdalena Preview 5.00

BLOODLINES: A TALE FROM THE HEART OF AFRICA (See Tales From the Heart of Africa)
Marvel Comics (Epic Comics): 1992 ($5.95, 52 pgs.)

1-Story cont'd from Tales From… 6.00

BLOOD OF DRACULA
Apple Comics: Nov, 1987 - No. 20?, 1990 ($1.75/$1.95, B&W)($2.25 #14,16 on)

1-3,5-14,20: 1-10-Chadwick-c 4.00
4,16-19-Lost Frankenstein pgs. by Wrightson 6.00
15-Contains stereo flexidisc ($3.75) 5.00

BLOOD OF THE DEMON (Etrigan the Demon)
DC Comics: May, 2005 - No. 17, Sept, 2006 ($2.50/$2.99)

1-14-Byrne-a(p) & plot/Pfeifer-script. 3,4-Batman app. 13-One Year Later 2.50
15-17-($2.99) 3.00

BLOOD OF THE INNOCENT (See Warp Graphics Annual)
WaRP Graphics: 1/7/86 - No. 4, 1/28/86 (Weekly mini-series, mature)

1-4 2.50

BLOODPACK
DC Comics: Mar, 1995 - No. 4, June,1995 ($1.50, limited series)

1-4 2.50

BLOODPOOL
Image Comics (Extreme): Aug, 1995 - No. 4, Nov, 1995 ($2.50, limited series)

1-4: Jo Duffy scripts in all 2.50
Special (3/96, $2.50)-Jo Duffy scripts 2.50
Trade Paperback (1996, $12.95)-r/#1-4 13.00

BLOODSCENT
Comico: Oct, 1988 ($2.00, one-shot, Baxter paper)

1-Colan-p 2.50

BLOODSEED
Marvel Comics (Frontier Comics): Oct, 1993 - No. 2, Nov, 1993 ($1.95)

1,2: Sharp/Cam Smith-a 3.00

BLOODSHOT (See Eternal Warrior #4 & Rai #0)
Valiant/Acclaim Comics (Valiant): Feb, 1993 - No. 51, Aug, 1996 ($2.25/$2.50)

0-(3/94, $3.50)-Wraparound chromium-c by Quesada(p); origin 4.00
0-Gold variant; no cover price 10.00
Note: There is a "Platinum variant" ; press run error of Gold ed. (25 copies exist)
(A CGC certified 9.8 copy sold for $2,067 in 2004)
1-($3.50)-Chromium embossed-c by B. Smith w/poster 4.00
2-5,8-14: 3-$2.25-c begins; cont'd in Hard Corps #5. 4-Eternal Warrior-c/story. 5-Rai &
Eternal Warrior app. 14-(3/94)-Reese-c(i) 2.50

6,7: 6-1st app. Ninjak (out of costume). 7-In costume 2.50
15(4/94)-51: 16-w/bound-in trading card. 51-Bloodshot dies? 2.50
Yearbook 1 (1994, $3.95) 4.00
Special 1 (3/94, $5.95)-Zeck-c/a(p); Last Stand 6.00

BLOODSHOT (Volume Two)
Acclaim Comics (Valiant): July, 1997 - No. 16, Oct, 1998 ($2.50)

1-16: 1-Two covers. 5-Copycat-c. X-O Manowar-c/app 2.50

BLOODSTONE
Marvel Comics: Dec, 2001 - No. 4, Mar, 2002 ($2.99)

1-4-Intro. Elsa Bloodstone; Abnett & Lanning-s/Lopez-a 3.00

BLOODSTREAM
Image Comics: Jan, 2004 - No. 4, Dec, 2004 ($2.95)

1-4-Adam Shaw painted-a 3.00

BLOODSTRIKE (See Supreme V2#3)
Image Comics (Extreme Studios): 1993 - No. 22, May, 1995; No. 25, May, 1994 ($1.95/$2.50)

1-22, 25: Liefeld layouts in early issues. 1-Blood Brothers prelude. 2-1st app. Lethal.
5-1st app. Noble. 9-Black and White part 6 by Art Thibert; Liefeld pin-up. 9,10-Have coupon
#3 & 7 for Extreme Prejudice for Extreme Prejudice #0. 10-(4/94). 11-(7/94). 16-Platt-c; Prophet app.
17-19-polybagged w/card . 25-(5/94)-Liefeld/Fraga-c 3.00
NOTE: Giffen story/layouts-4-6. Jae Lee c-7, 8. Rob Liefeld layouts-1-3. Art Thibert c-6i.

BLOODSTRIKE ASSASSIN
Image Comics (Extreme Studios): June, 1995 - No. 3, Aug, 1995; No. 0, Oct, 1995 ($2.50, limited series)

0-3: 8-(8/95)-Quesada-c. 0-(10/95)-Battlestone app. 3.00

BLOOD SWORD, THE
Jademan Comics: Aug, 1988 - No. 53, Dec, 1992 ($1.50/$1.95, 68 pgs.)

1-53-Kung Fu stories in all 3.00

BLOOD SWORD DYNASTY
Jademan Comics: 1989 -No. 41, Jan, 1993 ($1.25, 36 pgs.)

1-Ties into Blood Sword 2.50
2-41: Ties into Blood Sword 2.50

BLOOD SYNDICATE
DC Comics (Milestone): Apr, 1993 - No. 35, Feb, 1996 ($1.50/-$3.50)

1-($2.95)-Collector's Edition; polybagged with poster, trading card, & acid-free backing board
(direct sale only) 3.50
1-9,11-24,26,27,29,33-34: 8-Intro Kwai. 15-Byrne-c. 16-Worlds Collide Pt. 6; Superman-c/app.
17-Worlds Collide Pt. 13. 29-(99¢; Long Hot Summer x-over 2.50
10,28,30-32: 10-Simonson-c. 30-Long Hot Summer x-over 2.50
25-($2.95, 52 pgs.) 3.00
35-Kwai disappears; last issue 3.50

BLOODWULF
Image Comics (Extreme): Feb, 1995 - No. 4, May, 1995 ($2.50, limited series)

1-4: 1-Liefeld-c w/4 diferent captions & alternate-c. 2.50
Summer Special (1995, $2.50)-Jeff Johnson-c/a; Supreme app; story takes place
between Legend of Supreme #3 & Supreme #23. 2.50

BLOODY MARY
DC Comics (Helix): Oct, 1996 - No. 4, Jan, 1997 ($2.25, limited series)

1-4: Garth Ennis scripts; Ezquerra-c/a in all 3.50
TPB (2005, $19.99) r/#1-4 and Bloody Mary: Lady Liberty #1-4 20.00

BLOODY MARY: LADY LIBERTY
DC Comics (Helix): Sept, 1997 - No. 4, Dec, 1997 ($2.50, limited series)

1-4: Garth Ennis scripts; Ezquerra-c/a in all 3.00

BLUE
Image Comics (Action Toys): Aug, 1999 - No. 2, Apr, 2000 ($2.50)

1,2-Aronowitz-s/Struzan-c 2.50

BLUEBEARD
Slave Labor Graphics: Nov, 1993 - No. 3, Mar, 1994 ($2.95, B&W, lim. series)

1-3: James Robinson scripts. 2-(12/93) 3.00
Trade paperback (6/94, $9.95) 13.00
Trade paperback (2nd printing, 7/96, $12.95)-New-c 13.00

BLUE BEETLE, THE (Also see All Top, Big-3, Mystery Men & Weekly Comic Magazine)
Fox Publ. No. 1-11, 31-60; Holyoke No. 12-30: Winter, 1939-40 - No. 57, 7/48; No. 58, 4/50 -
No. 60, 8/50

1-Reprints from Mystery Men #1-5; Blue Beetle origin; Yarko the Great-r/from Wonder Comics
/Wonderworld #2-5 all by Eisner; Master Magician app.; (Blue Beetle

Blue Beetle #8 © FOX

Blue Beetle #15 © DC

Blue Bolt V2 #11 © NOVP

	GD 2.0	VG 4.0	FN 6.0	VF 8.0	VF/NM 9.0	NM- 9.2
in 4 different costumes)	457	914	1371	3200	5600	8000
2-K-51-r by Powell/Wonderworld #8,9	159	318	477	994	1647	2300
3-Simon-c	116	232	348	725	1200	1675
4-Marijuana drug mention story	78	156	234	488	807	1125
5-Zanzibar The Magician by Tuska	68	136	204	425	705	985
6-Dynamite Thor begins (1st); origin Blue Beetle	64	128	192	400	663	925
7,8-Dynamo app. in both. 8-Last Thor	58	116	174	363	599	835
9-12: 9,10-The Blackbird & The Gorilla app. in both. 10-Bondage/hypo-c. 11(2/42)-The Gladiator app. 12(6/42)-The Black Fury app.	53	106	159	320	528	735
13-V-Man begins (1st app.), ends #18; Kubert-a; centerfold spread	60	120	180	375	625	875
14,15-Kubert-a in both. 14-Intro. side-kick (c/text only), Sparky (called Spunky #17-19)	53	106	159	323	527	750
16-18: 17-Brodsky-c	43	86	129	262	431	600
19-Kubert-a	45	90	135	275	450	625
20-Origin/1st app. Tiger Squadron; Arabian Nights begin	47	94	141	287	474	660
21-26: 24-Intro. & only app. The Halo. 26-General Patton story & photo	37	74	111	213	337	460
27-Tamaa, Jungle Prince app.	34	68	102	197	311	425
28-30(2/44)	30	60	90	174	275	375
31(6/44), 33,34,36-40: 34-38-"The Threat from Saturn" serial.	28	56	84	162	256	350
32-Hitler-c	50	100	150	305	503	700
35-Extreme violence	34	68	102	197	311	425
41-45 (#43 exist?)	26	52	78	152	239	325
46-The Puppeteer app.	29	58	87	170	268	365
47-Kamen & Baker-a begin	131	262	393	819	1360	1900
48-50	100	200	300	625	1038	1450
51,53	86	172	258	538	889	1240
52-Kamen bondage-c; true crime stories begin	126	252	378	788	1307	1825
54-Used in SOTI. Illo, "Children call these 'headlights' comics"	172	344	516	1075	1788	2500
55-57: 56-Used in SOTI, pgs. 145. 57(7/48)-Last Kamen issue; becomes Western Killers)	83	166	249	519	860	1200
58(4/49)-60-No Kamen-a	45	90	135	275	450	625

NOTE: **Kamen** a-47-51, 53, 55-57; c-47, 49-52. **Powell** a-4(2). Bondage-c 9-12, 46, 52.

BLUE BEETLE (Formerly The Thing; becomes Mr. Muscles No. 22 on)
(See Charlton Bullseye & Space Adventures)
Charlton Comics: No. 18, Feb, 1955 - No. 21, Aug, 1955

	GD 2.0	VG 4.0	FN 6.0	VF 8.0	VF/NM 9.0	NM- 9.2
18,19-(Pre-1944-r). 18-Last pre-code issue. 19-Bouncer, Rocket Kelly-r	21	42	63	122	191	260
20-Joan Mason by Kamen	26	52	78	150	235	320
21-New material	20	40	60	117	184	250

BLUE BEETLE (Unusual Tales #1-49; Ghostly Tales #55 on)(See Captain Atom #83 & Charlton Bullseye)
Charlton Comics: V2#1, June, 1964 - V2#5, Mar-Apr, 1965; V3#50, July, 1965 - V3#54, Feb-Mar, 1966; #1, June, 1967 - #5, Nov, 1968

	GD 2.0	VG 4.0	FN 6.0	VF 8.0	VF/NM 9.0	NM- 9.2
V2#1-Origin/1st S.A. app. Dan Garrett-Blue Beetle	8	16	24	56	93	130
2-5: 5-Weiss illo; 1st published-a	5	10	15	35	55	75
V3#50-54-Formerly Unusual Tales	5	10	15	32	51	70
1(1967)-Question series begins by Ditko	10	20	30	68	119	170
2-Origin Ted Kord-Blue Beetle (see Capt. Atom #83 for 1st Ted Kord Blue Beetle); Dan Garrett x-over	6	12	18	37	59	80
3-5 (All Ditko-c/a in #1-5)	5	10	15	32	51	70
1,3(Modern Comics-1977)-Reprints	1	2	3	5	6	8

NOTE: #6 only appeared in the fanzine 'The Charlton Portfolio.'

BLUE BEETLE (Also see Americomics, Crisis On Infinite Earths, Justice League & Showcase '94 #2-4)
DC Comics: June, 1986 - No. 24, May, 1988

1-Origin retold; intro. Firefist						4.00
2-10,15-19,21-24: 2-Origin Firefist. 5-7-The Question app. 21-Millennium tie-in						2.50
11-14-New Teen Titans x-over						3.00
20-Justice League app.; Millennium tie-in						3.00

BLUE BEETLE (See Infinite Crisis)
DC Comics: May, 2006 - Present ($2.99)

1-Hamner-a/Giffen & Rogers-s; Guy Gardner app.						4.00
2-nd & 3rd printings						3.00
2-18: 2-2nd printing exists. 2-4-Oracle app. 5-Phantom Stranger app. 14-Guy Gardner. 16-Eclipso app. 18-Teen Titans app.						3.00
...: Road Trip TPB (2007, $12.99) r/#7-12						13.00
...: Shellshocked TPB (2006, $12.99) r/#1-6						13.00

BLUEBERRY (See Lt. Blueberry & Marshal Blueberry)
Marvel Comics (Epic Comics): 1989 - No. 5, 1990 ($12.95/$14.95, graphic novel)

	GD 2.0	VG 4.0	FN 6.0	VF 8.0	VF/NM 9.0	NM- 9.2
1,3,4,5-($12.95)-Moebius-a in all	2	4	6	11	16	20
2-($14.95)	2	4	6	13	18	22

BLUE BOLT
Funnies, Inc. No. 1/Novelty Press/Premium Group of Comics: June, 1940 - No. 101 (V10#2), Sept-Oct, 1949

	GD 2.0	VG 4.0	FN 6.0	VF 8.0	VF/NM 9.0	NM- 9.2
V1#1-Origin Blue Bolt by Joe Simon, Sub-Zero Man, White Rider & Super Horse, Dick Cole, Wonder Boy & Sgt. Spook (1st app. of each)	315	630	945	2048	3624	5200
2-Simon & Kirby's 1st art & 1st super-hero (Blue Bolt)	179	358	537	1119	1860	2600
3-1 pg. Space Hawk by Wolverton; 2nd S&K-a on Blue Bolt (same cover date as Red Raven #1); 1st time S&K names app. in a comic; Simon-c	155	310	465	969	1610	2250
4-S&K-a; classic Everett shark-c	152	304	456	950	1575	2200
5-S&K-a; Everett-a begins on Sub-Zero	133	266	399	831	1378	1925
6,8-10-S&K-a	121	242	363	756	1253	1750
7-S&K-c/a	141	282	423	881	1466	2050
11,12: 11-Robot-c	114	228	342	713	1182	1650
V2#1-Origin Dick Cole & The Twister; Twister x-over in Dick Cole, Sub-Zero, & Blue Bolt; origin Simba Karno who battles Dick Cole thru V2#5 & becomes main supporting character V2#6 on; battle-c	40	80	120	244	392	540
2-Origin The Twister retold in text	34	68	102	195	308	420
3-5: 5-Intro. Freezum	30	60	90	174	275	375
6-Origin Sgt. Spook retold	26	52	78	150	235	320
7-12-Lois Blake becomes Blue Bolt's costume aide; last Twister. 12-Text-sty by Mickey Spillane	22	44	66	126	198	270
V3#1-3	18	36	54	103	162	220
4-12: 4-Blue Bolt abandons costume	15	30	45	84	127	170
V4#1-Hitler, Tojo, Mussolini-c	39	78	117	225	355	485
V4#2-12: 2-Shows V4#3 on-c, V4#4 inside (9-10/43). 5-Infinity-c. 8-Last Sub-Zero	12	24	36	69	97	125
V5#1-8, V6#1-3,5-10, V7#1-12	11	22	33	62	86	110
V6#4-Racist cover	18	36	54	103	162	220
V8#1-6,8-12, V9#1-4,7,8, V10#1(#100),V10#2(#101)-Last Dick Cole, Blue Bolt	10	20	30	56	76	95
V8#7,V9#6,9-L. B. Cole-c	22	44	66	128	202	275
V9#5-Classic fish in the face-c	21	42	63	122	199	250

NOTE: **Everett** c-V1#4, 11, V2#1, 2. **Gustavson** a-V1#1-2, V2#1-7. **Kiefer** c-V3#1. **Rico** a-V6#10, V7#4. Blue Bolt not in V9#8.

BLUE BOLT (Becomes Ghostly Weird Stories #120 on; continuation of Novelty Blue Bolt)
(...Weird Tales of Terror #111,112,...Weird Tales #113-119)
Star Publications: No. 102, Nov-Dec, 1949 - No. 119, May-June, 1953

	GD 2.0	VG 4.0	FN 6.0	VF 8.0	VF/NM 9.0	NM- 9.2
102-The Chameleon, & Target app.	39	78	117	229	360	490
103,104-The Chameleon app. 104-Last Target	38	76	114	216	343	470
105-Origin Blue Bolt (from #1) retold by Simon; Chameleon & Target app.; opium den story	55	110	165	344	572	800
106-Blue Bolt by S&K begins; Spacehawk reprints from Target by Wolverton begin, ends #110; Sub-Zero begins; ends #109	53	106	159	323	537	750
107-110: 108-Last S&K Blue Bolt reprint. 109-Wolverton-c(r)/inside Spacehawk splash. 110-Target app.	52	104	156	317	521	725
111,112: 111-Red Rocket & The Mask-r; last Blue Bolt; 1pg. L. B. Cole-a. 112-Last Torpedo Man app.	47	94	141	287	474	660
113-Wolverton's Spacehawk-r/Target V3#7	49	98	147	299	492	685
114,116: 116-Jungle Jo-r	47	94	141	287	474	660
115-Sgt. Spook app.	49	98	147	299	492	685
117-Jo-Jo & Blue Bolt-r	48	96	144	293	484	675
118-"White Spirit" by Wood	49	98	147	299	492	685
119-Disbrow/Cole; Jungle Jo-r	48	96	144	293	484	675
Accepted Reprint #103(1957?, nd)	14	28	42	78	112	145

NOTE: **L. B. Cole** c-102-108, 110 on. **Disbrow** a-112(2), 113(3), 114(2), 115(2), 116-118. **Hollingsworth** a-117. **Palais** a-112r. Sci/Fi c-105-110. Horror c-111.

BLUE BULLETEER, THE (Also see Femforce Special)
AC Comics: 1989 ($2.25, B&W, one-shot)

1-Origin by Bill Black; Bill Ward-a						4.00

BLUE BULLETEER (Also see Femforce Special)
AC Comics: 1996 ($5.95, B&W, one-shot)

1-Photo-c						6.00

BLUE CIRCLE COMICS (Also see Red Circle Comics, Blazing Comics & Roly Poly Comic Book)
Enwil Associates/Rural Home: June, 1944 - No. 6, Apr, 1945

Blue Circle Comics #6 © Enwil

Blue Ribbon Comics #19 © AP

Bob Colt #4 © FAW

	GD	VG	FN	VF	VF/NM	NM-
	2.0	4.0	6.0	8.0	9.0	9.2

1-The Blue Circle begins (1st app.); origin & 1st app. Steel Fist
| | 32 | 64 | 96 | 186 | 293 | 400 |

2
| | 20 | 40 | 60 | 117 | 184 | 250 |

3-Hitler parody-c
| | 29 | 58 | 87 | 167 | 264 | 360 |

4-6: 5-Last Steel Fist.
| | 17 | 34 | 51 | 98 | 154 | 210 |

6-(Dated 4/45, Vol. #2#3 inside)-Leftover covers to #6 were later restapled over early 1950's coverless comics; variations of the coverless comics exist.
Colossal Features known.
| | 16 | 32 | 48 | 94 | 147 | 200 |

BLUE DEVIL (See Fury of Firestorm #24, Underworld Unleashed, Starman (2nd) #38, Infinite Crisis and Shadowpact)
DC Comics: June, 1984 - No. 31, Dec, 1986 (75¢/$1.25)

1					4.00
2-16,19-31: 4-Origin Nebiros. 7-Gil Kane-a. 8-Giffen-a					2.50
17,18-Crisis x-over					3.00
Annual 1 (11/85)-Team-ups w/Black Orchid, Creeper, Demon, Madame Xanadu, Man-Bat & Phantom Stranger					3.00

BLUE MONDAY: ... (one-shots)
Oni Press: Feb, 2002 - Present (B&W, Chynna Clugston-Major-s/a/c in all)

Dead Man's Party (10/02, $2.95) Dan Brereton painted back-c	3.00
Inbetween Days (9/03, $9.95, 8" x 5-1/2") r/Dead Man's Party, Lovecats, & Nobody's Fool	10.00
Lovecats (2/02, $2.95) Valentine's Day themed	3.00
Nobody's Fool (2/03, $2.95) April Fool's Day themed	3.00

BLUE MONDAY: ABSOLUTE BEGINNERS
Oni Press: Feb, 2001 - No. 4, Sept, 2001 ($2.95, B&W, limited series)

1-4-Chynna Clugston-Major-s/a/c	3.00
TPB (12/01, $11.95, 8" x 6") r/series	12.00

BLUE MONDAY: PAINTED MOON
Oni Press: Feb, 2004 - No. 4, Mar, 2005 ($2.99, B&W, limited series)

1-4-Chynna Clugston-Major-s/a/c	3.00
TPB (4/05, $11.95, digest-sized) r/series; sketch pages	12.00

BLUE MONDAY: THE KIDS ARE ALRIGHT
Oni Press: Feb, 2000 - No. 3, May, 2000 ($2.95, B&W, limited series)

1-3-Chynna Clugston-Major-s/a/c. 1-Variant-c by Warren. 2-Dorkin-c	3.00
3-Variant cover by J. Scott Campbell	4.00
TPB (12/00, $10.95, digest-sized) r/#1-3 & earlier short stories	11.00

BLUE PHANTOM, THE
Dell Publishing Co.: June-Aug, 1962

1(01-066-208)-by Fred Fredericks
| | 3 | 6 | 9 | 21 | 32 | 42 |

BLUE RIBBON COMICS (...Mystery Comics No. 9-18)
MLJ Magazines: Nov, 1939 - No. 22, Mar, 1942 (1st MLJ series)

1-Dan Hastings, Richy the Amazing Boy, Rang-A-Tang the Wonder Dog begin
(1st app. of each); Little Nemo app. (not by W. McCay); Jack Cole-a(3)
(1st MLJ comic)
| | 321 | 642 | 963 | 2087 | 3694 | 5300 |

2-Bob Phantom, Silver Fox (both in #3), Rang-A-Tang Club & Cpl. Collins begin
(1st app. of each); Jack Cole-a
| | 117 | 234 | 351 | 731 | 1216 | 1700 |

3-J. Cole-a
| | 78 | 156 | 234 | 488 | 807 | 1125 |

4-Doc Strong, The Green Falcon, & Hercules begin (1st app. each); origin & 1st app.
The Fox & Ty-Gor, Son of the Tiger
| | 86 | 172 | 258 | 538 | 894 | 1250 |

5-8: 8-Last Hercules; 6,7-Biro, Meskin-a. 7-Fox app. on-c
| | 63 | 126 | 189 | 394 | 652 | 910 |

9-(Scarce)-Origin & 1st app. Mr. Justice (2/41)
| | 300 | 600 | 900 | 1902 | 3251 | 4600 |

10-13: 12-Last Doc Strong. 13-Inferno, the Flame Breather begins. Devil-c
| | 103 | 206 | 309 | 644 | 1072 | 1500 |

14,15,17,18: 15-Last Green Falcon
| | 87 | 174 | 261 | 544 | 902 | 1260 |

16-Origin & 1st app. Captain Flag (9/41)
| | 162 | 324 | 486 | 1013 | 1682 | 2350 |

19-22: 20-Last Ty-Gor. 22-Origin Mr. Justice retold
| | 87 | 174 | 261 | 544 | 902 | 1260 |

NOTE: *Biro* c-3-5; a-2 (Cpl. Collins & Scoop Cody). **S. Cooper** c-9-17. 20-22 contain "Tales From the Witch's Cauldron" (same strip as "Stories of the Black Witch" in Zip Comics). Mr. Justice c-9-18. Captain Flag c-16(w/Mr. Justice), 19-22.

BLUE RIBBON COMICS (Becomes Teen-Age Diary Secrets #4)
(Also see Approved Comics, Blue Ribbon Comics and Heckle &Jeckle)
Blue Ribbon (St. John): Feb, 1949 - No. 6, Aug, 1949

1-Heckle & Jeckle (Terrytoons)
| | 14 | 28 | 42 | 76 | 108 | 140 |

2(4/49)-Diary Secrets; Baker-c
| | 27 | 54 | 81 | 158 | 249 | 340 |

3-Heckle & Jeckle (Terrytoons)
| | 10 | 20 | 30 | 58 | 79 | 100 |

4(6/49)-Teen-Age Diary Secrets; Baker c/a(2)
| | 27 | 54 | 81 | 158 | 249 | 340 |

5(8/49)-Teen-Age Diary Secrets; Oversize; photo-c; Baker-a(2)- Continues
as Teen-Age Diary Secrets
| | 32 | 64 | 96 | 186 | 293 | 400 |

6-Dinky Duck(8/49)(Terrytoons)
| | 8 | 16 | 24 | 42 | 54 | 65 |

BLUE RIBBON COMICS
Red Circle Prod./Archie Ent. No. 5 on: Nov, 1983 - No. 14, Dec, 1984

1-S&K-r/Advs. of the Fly #1,2; Williamson/Torres-r/Fly #2; Ditko-c	6.00
2-7,9,10: 3-Origin Steel Sterling. 5-S&K Shield-r; new Kirby-c. 6,7-The Fox app.	5.00
8-Toth centerspread; Black Hood app.; Neal Adams-a(r)	6.00
11,13,14: 11-Black Hood. 13-Thunder Bunny. 14-Web & Jaguar	5.00
12-Thunder Agents; Noman new Ditko-a.	6.00

NOTE: **N. Adams** a(r)-8. **Buckler** a-4i. **Nino** a-2i. **McWilliams** a-8. **Morrow** a-8.

BLUE STREAK (See Holyoke One-Shot No. 8)

BLUNTMAN AND CHRONIC TPB(Also see Jay and Silent Bob, Clerks, and Oni Double Feature)
Image Comics: Dec, 2001 ($14.95, TPB)

nn-Tie-in for "Jay & Silent Bob Strike Back" movie; new Kevin Smith-s/Michael Oeming-a;
r/app. from Oni Double Feature #12 in color; Ben Affleck & Jason Lee afterwords   15.00

BLYTHE (Marge's)
Dell Publishing Co.: No. 1072, Jan-Mar, 1960

Four Color 1072
| | 5 | 10 | 15 | 35 | 55 | 75 |

B-MAN (See Double-Dare Adventures)

BO (Tom Cat #4 on) (also see Big Shot #29 & Dixie Dugan)
Charlton Comics Group: June, 1955 - No. 3, Oct, 1955 (A dog)

1-3: Newspaper reprints by Frank Beck
| | 8 | 16 | 24 | 40 | 50 | 60 |

BOATNIKS, THE (See Walt Disney Showcase No. 1)

BOB BURDEN'S ORIGINAL MYSTERYMEN PRESENTS
Dark Horse Comics: 1999 - No. 4 ($2.95/$3.50)

1-3-Bob Burden-s/Sadowski-a(p)	3.50
4-($3.50) All Villain issue	3.50

BOBBY BENSON'S B-BAR-B RIDERS (Radio) (See Best of The West, The Lemonade Kid & Model Fun)
Magazine Enterprises/AC Comics: May-June, 1950 - No. 20, May-June, 1953

1-The Lemonade Kid begins; Powell-a (Scarce)
| | 41 | 82 | 123 | 256 | 416 | 575 |

2
| | 17 | 34 | 51 | 98 | 154 | 210 |

3-5: 4,5-Lemonade Kid-c (#4-Spider-c)
| | 14 | 28 | 42 | 76 | 108 | 140 |

6-8,10
| | 13 | 26 | 39 | 72 | 101 | 130 |

9,11,13-Frazetta-c; Ghost Rider in #13-15 by Ayers-a. 13-Ghost Rider-c
| | 36 | 72 | 108 | 208 | 329 | 450 |

12,17-20: 20-(A-1 #88)
| | 11 | 22 | 33 | 64 | 90 | 115 |

14-Decapitation/Bondage-c & story; classic horror-c
| | 28 | 56 | 84 | 162 | 256 | 350 |

15-Ghost Rider-c
| | 22 | 44 | 66 | 128 | 202 | 275 |

16-Photo-c
| | 14 | 28 | 42 | 80 | 115 | 150 |

1 (1990, $2.75, B&W)-Reprints; photo-c & inside covers   3.00

NOTE: *Ayers* a-13-15, 20. **Powell** a-1-12(4 ea.), 13(3), 14-16(Red Hawk only); c-1-8,1 0, 12. Lemonade Kid in most 1-13.

BOBBY COMICS
Universal Phoenix Features: May, 1946

1-By S. M. Iger
| | 9 | 18 | 27 | 47 | 61 | 75 |

BOBBY SHERMAN (TV)
Charlton Comics: Feb, 1972 - No. 7, Oct, 1972

1-Based on TV show "Getting Together"
| | 5 | 10 | 15 | 35 | 55 | 75 |

2-7: 2,4-Photo-c
| | 4 | 8 | 12 | 22 | 34 | 45 |

BOB COLT (Movie star)(See XMas Comics)
Fawcett Publications: Nov, 1950 - No. 10, May, 1952

1-Bob Colt, his horse Buckskin & sidekick Pablo begin; photo front/back-c
begin
| | 39 | 78 | 117 | 224 | 350 | 475 |

2
| | 20 | 40 | 60 | 115 | 178 | 240 |

3-5
| | 16 | 32 | 48 | 92 | 141 | 190 |

6-Flying Saucer story
| | 14 | 28 | 42 | 82 | 121 | 160 |

7-10: 9-Last photo back-c
| | 14 | 28 | 42 | 78 | 112 | 145 |

BOB HOPE (See Adventures of... & Calling All Boys #12)

BOB MARLEY, TALE OF THE TUFF GONG (Music star)
Marvel Comics: Aug, 1994 - No, 3, Nov, 1994 ($5.95, limited series)

1-3   6.00

BOB POWELL'S TIMELESS TALES
Eclipse Comics: March, 1989 ($2.00, B&W)

1-Powell-r/Black Cat #5 (Scarlet Arrow), 9 & Race for the Moon #1   3.00

BOB SCULLY, THE TWO-FISTED HICK DETECTIVE (Also see Advs. of Detective Ace King and Detective Dan)
Humor Publ. Co.: No date (1933) (36 pgs., 9-1/2x11", B&W, paper-c; 10¢-c)

Body Doubles #1 © DC

Bomb Queen III #2 © Jimmie Robinson

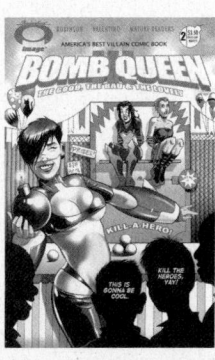

Bone #33 © Jeff Smith

	GD 2.0	VG 4.0	FN 6.0	VF 8.0	VF/NM 9.0	NM- 9.2		GD 2.0	VG 4.0	FN 6.0	VF 8.0	VF/NM 9.0	NM- 9.2

nn-By Howard Dell; not reprints; along with Advs. of Det. Ace King and Detective Dan, the first comic w/original art & the first of a single theme; has a blue 2-tone cover — 375 750 1125 3000 — —

BOB SON OF BATTLE
Dell Publishing Co.: No. 729, Nov, 1956
Four Color 729 — 4 8 12 24 37 50

BOB STEELE WESTERN (Movie star)
Fawcett Publications/AC Comics: Dec, 1950 - No. 10, June, 1952; 1990
1-Bob Steele & his horse Bullet begin; photo front/back-c begin — 48 96 114 293 472 650
2 — 25 50 75 144 222 300
3-5: 4-Last photo back-c — 18 36 54 104 160 215
6-10: 10-Last photo-c — 15 30 45 83 124 165
1 (1990, $2.75, B&W)-Bob Steele & Rocky Lane reprints; photo-c & inside covers — 3.00

BOB SWIFT (Boy Sportsman)
Fawcett Publications: May, 1951 - No. 5, Jan, 1952
1 — 10 20 30 58 79 100
2-5: Saunders painted-c #1-5 — 7 14 21 35 43 50

BOB, THE GALACTIC BUM
DC Comics: Feb, 1995 - No. 4, June, 1995 ($1.95, limited series)
1-4: 1-Lobo app. — 2.50

BODY BAGS
Dark Horse Comics (Blanc Noir): Sept, 1996 - No. 4, Jan, 1997 ($2.95, mini-series, mature) (1st Blanc Noir series)
1-Jason Pearson-c/a/scripts in all. 1-Intro Clownface & Panda. — 1 2 3 5 6 8
2 — 1 3 4 6 8 10
3,4 — 6.00
Body Bags 1 (Image Comics, 7/05, $5.99) r/#1&2 — 6.00
Body Bags 2 (Image Comics, 8/05, $5.99) r/#3&4 — 6.00
: 3 The Hard Way (Image, 2/06, $5.99) new story & r/Dark Horse Presents Annual 1997 and Dark Horse Maverick 2000; Pearson-c — 6.00

BODYCOUNT (Also see Casey Jones & Raphael)
Image Comics (Highbrow Entertainment): Mar, 1996 - No. 4, July, 1996 ($2.50, lim. series)
1-4: Kevin Eastman-a(p)/scripts; Simon Bisley-c/a(i); Turtles app. — 2.50

BODY DOUBLES (See Resurrection Man)
DC Comics: Oct, 1999 - No. 4, Jan, 2000 ($2.50, limited series)
1-4-Lanning & Abnett-s. 2-Black Canary app. 4-Wonder Woman app. — 2.50
...(Villains) (2/98, $1.95, one-shot) 1-Pearson-c; Deadshot app. — 2.50

BOFFO LAFFS
Paragraphics: 1986 - No. 5 ($2.50/$1.95)
1-($2.50) First comic cover with hologram — 3.00
2-5 — 2.50

BOLD ADVENTURES
Pacific Comics: Oct, 1983 - No. 3, June, 1984 ($1.50)
1-Time Force, Anaconda, & The Weirdling begin — 3.00
2,3: 2-Soldiers of Fortune begins. 3-Spitfire — 3.00
NOTE: Kaluta c-3. Nebres a-1-3. Nino a-2, 3. Severin a-3.

BOLD STORIES (Also see Candid Tales & It Rhymes With Lust)
Kirby Publishing Co.: Mar, 1950 - July, 1950 (Digest size, 144 pgs.)
March issue (Very Rare) - Contains "The Ogre of Paris" by Wood — 138 276 414 863 1432 2000
May issue (Very Rare) - Contains "The Cobra's Kiss" by Graham Ingels (21 pgs.) — 122 244 366 763 1269 1775
July issue (Very Rare) - Contains "The Ogre of Paris" by Wood — 110 220 330 688 1144 1600

BOLT AND STAR FORCE SIX
Americomics: 1984 ($1.75)
1-Origin Bolt & Star Force Six — 3.00
Special 1 (1984, $2.00, 52pgs., B&W) — 3.00

BOMBARDIER (See Bee 29, the Bombardier & Cinema Comics Herald)

BOMBAST
Topps Comics: 1993 ($2.95, one-shot) (Created by Jack Kirby)
1-Polybagged w/Kirbychrome trading card; Savage Dragon app.; Kirby-c; has coupon for Amberchrome Secret City Saga #0 — 3.00

BOMBA THE JUNGLE BOY (TV)

National Periodical Publ.: Sept-Oct, 1967 - No. 7, Sept-Oct, 1968 (12¢)
1-Intro. Bomba; Infantino/Anderson-c — 4 8 12 24 37 50
2-7 — 3 6 9 16 23 30

BOMBER COMICS
Elliot Publ. Co./Melverne Herald/Farrell/Sunrise Times: Mar, 1944 - No. 4, Winter, 1944-45
1-Wonder Boy, & Kismet, Man of Fate begin — 80 160 240 500 830 1160
2-Hitler-c — 69 138 207 431 716 1000
3: 2-4-Have Classics Comics ad to HRN 20 — 45 90 135 275 450 625
4-Hitler, Tojo & Mussolini-c; Sensation Comics #13-c/swipe; has Classics Comics ad to HRN 20. — 69 138 207 431 716 1000

BOMB QUEEN
Image Comics (Shadowline): Feb, 2006 - No. 4, May, 2006 ($3.50, mature)
1-4-Jimmie Robinson-s/a — 3.50
... Vs. Blacklight One Shot #1 (8/06, $3.50) Robinson-a; Shadowhawk app. — 3.50
..., Vol. 1: WMD: Woman of Mass Destruction TPB (7/06, $12.99) r/#1-4; bonus art — 13.00

BOMB QUEEN II
Image Comics (Shadowline): Oct, 2006 - No. 3, Dec, 2006 ($3.50, mature)
1-3-Jimmie Robinson-s/a; intro. The Four Queens — 3.50
..., Vol. 2: Dirty Bomb - Queen of Hearts TPB (7/07, $14.99) r/#1-3 & Blacklight One Shot; bonus art; Robinson interview — 15.00

BOMB QUEEN III THE GOOD, THE BAD & THE LOVELY
Image Comics (Shadowline): Mar, 2007 - No. 4, Jun, 2007 ($3.50, mature)
1-4-Jimmie Robinson-a/Jim Valentino-s; Blacklight & Rebound app. 1-Linsner-c — 3.50

BOMB QUEEN IV SUICIDE BOMBER
Image Comics (Shadowline): Aug, 2007 - No. 4 ($3.50, mature)
1-Jim Robinson-s/a — 3.50

BONANZA (TV)
Dell/Gold Key: June-Aug, 1960 - No. 37, Aug, 1970 (All Photo-c)
Four Color 1110 (6-8/60) — 31 62 93 233 429 625
Four Color 1221,1283, & #01070-207, 01070-210 — 17 34 51 124 220 315
1(12/62-Gold Key) — 18 36 54 130 230 330
2 — 10 20 30 67 116 165
3-10 — 8 16 24 52 86 120
11-20 — 6 12 18 39 62 85
21-37: 29-Reprints — 5 10 15 32 51 70

BONE
Cartoon Books #1-20, 28 on/Image Comics #21-27: Jul, 1991 - No. 55, Jun, 2004 ($2.95, B&W)
1-Jeff Smith-c/a in all — 7 14 21 45 73 100
1-2nd printing — 2 4 6 8 10 12
1-3rd thru 5th printings — 4.00
2-1st printing — 4 8 12 24 37 50
2-2nd & 3rd printings — 4.00
3-1st printing — 3 6 9 19 29 38
3-2nd thru 4th printings — 4.00
4,5 — 2 4 6 11 16 20
6-10 — 1 3 4 6 8 10
11-37: 21-1st Image issue — 4.00
13 1/2 (1/95, Wizard) — 1 3 4 6 8 10
13 1/2 (Gold) — 2 4 6 8 10 12
38-($4.95) Three covers by Miller, Ross, Smith — 5.00
39-55-($2.95) — 3.00
1-27-($2.95): 1-Image reprints begin w/new-c. 2-Allred pin-up. — 3.00
... Holiday Special (1993, giveaway) — 3.00
... Reader -($9.95) Behind the scenes info — 10.00
... Sourcebook-San Diego Edition — 3.00
...10th Anniversary Edition (8/01, $5.95) r/#1 in color; came with figure — 6.00
Complete Bone Adventures Vol 1,2 ('93, '94, $12.95, r/#1-6 & #7-12) — 13.00
...: One Volume Edition (2004, $39.95, 1300 pgs.) r/#1-54; extra material — 40.00
Volume 1-($19.95, hard-c)-"Out From Boneville" — 20.00
Volume 1-($12.95, soft-c) — 13.00
Volume 2,5-($22.95, hard-c)-"The Great Cow Race" & "Rock Jaw" — 23.00
Volume 2,5-($14.95, soft-c) — 15.00
Volume 3,4-($24.95, hard-c)-"Eyes of the Storm" & "The Dragonslayer" — 25.00
Volume 3,4,7-($16.95, soft-c) — 17.00
Volume 6-($15.95, soft-c)-"Old Man's Cave" — 16.00
Volume 8-($24.95, hard-c)-"Ghost Circles" — 25.00
Volume 8-($23.95, hard-c)-"Treasure Hunters" — 24.00
NOTE: Printings not listed sell for cover price.

BONGO (See Story Hour Series)

Book of the Dead #2 © MAR

Books of Faerie #3 © DC

Books of Magic: Life During Wartime #1 © DC

	GD	VG	FN	VF	VF/NM	NM-
	2.0	4.0	6.0	8.0	9.0	9.2

BONGO & LUMPJAW (Disney, see Walt Disney Showcase #3)
Dell Publishing Co.: No. 706, June, 1956; No. 886, Mar, 1958

Four Color 706 (#1)	6	12	18	37	59	80
Four Color 886	5	10	15	30	48	65

BONGO COMICS PRESENTS RADIOACTIVE MAN (See Radioactive Man)

BON VOYAGE (See Movie Classics)

BOOF
Image Comics (Todd McFarlane Prod.): July, 1994 - No. 6, Dec, 1994 ($1.95)

1-6						2.50

BOOF AND THE BRUISE CREW
Image Comics (Todd McFarlane Prod.): July, 1994 - No. 6, Dec, 1994 ($1.95)

1-6						2.50

BOOK AND RECORD SET (See Power Record Comics)

BOOK OF ALL COMICS
William H. Wise: 1945 (196 pgs.)(Inside f/c has Green Publ. blacked out)

nn-Green Mask, Puppeteer & The Bouncer	43	86	129	262	431	600

BOOK OF ANTS, THE
Artisan Entertainment: 1998 ($2.95, B&W)

1-Based on the movie Pi; Aronofsky-s						3.00

BOOK OF BALLADS AND SAGAS, THE
Green Man Press: Oct, 1995 - No. 4 ($2.95/$3.50/$3.25, B&W)

1-4: 1-Vess-c/a; Gaiman story.						3.50

BOOK OF COMICS, THE
William H. Wise: No date (1944) (25¢, 132 pgs.)

nn-Captain V app.	40	80	120	244	392	540

BOOK OF FATE, THE (See Fate)
DC Comics: Feb, 1997 - No. 12, Jan, 1998 ($2.25/$2.50)

1-12: 4-Two-Face-c/app. 6-Convergence. 11-Sentinel app.						3.00

BOOK OF LOST SOULS, THE
Marvel Comics (Icon): Dec, 2005 - No. 6, June, 2006 ($2.99)

1-6-Colleen Doran-a/c; J. Michael Straczynski-s						3.00
... Vol. 1: Introductions All Around TPB (2006, $16.99) r/series						17.00

BOOK OF LOVE (See Fox Giants)

BOOK OF NIGHT, THE
Dark Horse Comics: July, 1987 - No. 3, 1987 ($1.75, B&W)

1-3: Reprints from Epic Illustrated; Vess-a						2.50
TPB-r/#1-3						15.00
Hardcover-Black-c with red crest						100.00
Hardcover w/slipcase (1991) signed and numbered						50.00

BOOK OF THE DEAD
Marvel Comics: Dec, 1993 - No. 4, Mar, 1994 ($1.75, limited series, 52 pgs.)

1-4: 1-Ploog Frankenstein & Morrow Man-Thing-r begin; Wrightson-r/Chamber of Darkness
#7. 2-Morrow new painted-c; Chaykin/Morrow Man-Thing; Krigstein-r/Uncanny Tales #54;
r/Fear #10. 3-r/Astonishing Tales #10 & Starlin Man-Thing. 3,4-Painted-c

	1	2	3	4	5	7

BOOKS OF DOOM (Dr. Doom from Fantastic Four)
Marvel Comics: Jan, 2006 - No. 6, June, 2006 ($2.99, limited series)

1-6-Life story/origin of Dr. Doom; Brubaker-s/Raimondi-a/Rivera-c						3.00
Fantastic Four: Books of Doom HC (2006, $19.99) r/#1-6						20.00
Fantastic Four: Books of Doom SC (2007, $14.99) r/#1-6						15.00

BOOKS OF FAERIE, THE
DC Comics (Vertigo): Mar, 1997 - No. 3, May, 1997 ($2.50, limited series)

1-3-Gross-a						3.00
TPB (1998, $14.95) r/#1-3 & Arcana Annual #1						15.00

BOOKS OF FAERIE, THE : AUBERON'S TALE
DC Comics (Vertigo): Aug, 1998 - No. 3, Oct, 1998 ($2.50, limited series)

1-3-Gross-a						3.00

BOOKS OF FAERIE, THE : MOLLY'S STORY
DC Comics (Vertigo): Sept, 1999 - No. 4, Dec, 1999 ($2.50, limited series)

1-4-Ney Rieber-s/Mejia-a						3.00

BOOKS OF MAGIC
DC Comics: 1990 - No. 4, 1991 ($3.95, 52 pgs., limited series, mature)

1-Bolton painted-c/a; Phantom Stranger app.; Gaiman scripts in all						
	1	3	4	6	8	10
2,3: 2-John Constantine, Dr. Fate, Spectre, Deadman app. 3-Dr. Occult app.;						
minor Sandman app.	1	2	3	4	5	7
4-Early Death-c/app. (early 1991)	1	2	3	5	6	8
Trade paperback-($7.95)-Reprints limited series						20.00

BOOKS OF MAGIC (Also see Hunter: The Age of Magic and Names of Magic)
DC Comics (Vertigo): May, 1994 - No. 75, Aug, 2000 ($1.95/$2.50, mature)

1-Charles Vess-c	2	4	6	8	10	12
1-Platinum	2	4	6	13	18	22
2-4: 4-Death app.	1	2	3	4	5	7
5-14: Charles Vess-c						4.00
15-50: 15-$2.50-c begins. 22-Kaluta-c. 25-Death-c/app; Bachalo-c						3.00
51-75: 51-Peter Gross-s/a begins. 55-Medley-a						2.50
Annual 1-3 (2/97, 2/98, '99, $3.95)						4.00
Bindings (1995, $12.95, TPB)-r/#1-4						13.00
Death After Death (2001, $19.95, TPB)-r/#42-50						20.00
Girl in the Box (1999, $14.95, TPB)-r/#26-32						15.00
Reckonings (1997, $12.95, TPB)-r/#14-20						13.00
Summonings (1996, $17.50, TPB)-r/#5-13, Vertigo Rave #1						17.50
The Burning Girl (2000, $17.95, TPB)-r/#33-41						18.00
Transformations (1998, $12.95, TPB)-r/#21-25						13.00

BOOKS OF MAGICK, THE : LIFE DURING WARTIME (See Books of Magic)
DC Comics (Vertigo): Sept, 2004 - No. 15, Dec, 2005 ($2.50/$2.75)

1-15: 1-Spencer-s/Ormston-a/Quitely-c; Constantine app. 2-Bagged with Sky Captain CD						
6-Fegredo-a. 7-Constantine & Zatanna-c						2.75
... Book One TPB (2005, $9.95) r/#1-5						10.00

BOOSTER GOLD (See Justice League #4)
DC Comics: Feb, 1986 - No. 25, Feb, 1988 (75¢)

1-Dan Jurgens-s/a(p)						3.00
2-25: 4-Rose & Thorn app. 6-Origin. 6,7,23-Superman app. 8,9-LSH app. 22-JLI app.						
24,25-Millennium tie-ins						2.50
NOTE: *Austin* c-22i. *Byrne* c-23i.						

BOOSTER GOLD (See DC's weekly series 52)
DC Comics: Oct, 2007 - Present ($3.50)

1-Geoff Johns-s/Dan Jurgens-a(p); covers by Jurgens and Art Adams; Rip Hunter app.						3.50

BOOTS AND HER BUDDIES
Standard Comics/Visual Editions/Argo (NEA Service):
No. 5, 9/48 - No. 9, 9/49; 12/55 - No. 3, 1956

5-Strip-r	16	32	48	94	147	200
6,8	11	22	33	64	90	115
7-(Scarce)	14	28	42	80	115	150
9-(Scarce)-Frazetta-a (2 pgs.)	26	52	78	150	235	320
1-3(Argo-1955-56)-Reprints	6	12	18	31	38	45

BOOTS & SADDLES (TV)
Dell Publ. Co.: No. 919, July, 1958; No. 1029, Sept, 1959; No. 1116, Aug, 1960

Four Color 919 (#1)-Photo-c	7	14	21	50	83	115
Four Color 1029, 1116-Photo-c	5	10	15	35	55	75

BORDERLINE
Friction Press: June, 1992 ($2.25, B&W)

0-Ashcan edition; 1st app. of Cliff Broadway						2.25
1-Painted-c						3.00
1-Special Edition (bagged w/ photo, S&N)						4.00

BORDER PATROL
P. L. Publishing Co.: May-June, 1951 - No. 3, Sept-Oct, 1951

1	14	28	42	80	115	150
2,3	10	20	30	54	72	90

BORDER WORLDS (Also see Megaton Man)
Kitchen Sink Press: 7/86 - No. 7, 1987; V2#1, 1990 - No. 4, 1990 ($1.95-$2.00, B&W, mature)

1-7, V2#1-4: Donald Simpson-c/a/scripts						3.00

BORIS KARLOFF TALES OF MYSTERY (TV) (...Thriller No. 1,2)
Gold Key: No. 3, April. 1963 - No. 97, Feb, 1980

3-5-(Two #5's, 10/63,11/63): 5-(10/63)-11 pgs. Toth-a.						
	4	8	12	28	44	60
6-8,10: 10-Orlando-a	3	6	9	21	32	42
9-Wood-a	4	8	12	22	34	45
11-Williamson-a, 8 pgs.; Orlando-a, 5 pgs.	4	8	12	22	34	45
12-Torres, McWilliams-a; Orlando-a(2)	3	6	9	18	27	35

Bouncer #11 © FOX

Boy Comics #6 © LEV

Boy Commandos #8 © DC

	GD 2.0	VG 4.0	FN 6.0	VF 8.0	VF/NM 9.0	NM- 9.2
13,14,16-20	3	6	9	16	23	30
15-Crandall	3	6	9	17	25	32
21-Jeff Jones-a(3 pgs.) "The Screaming Skull"	3	6	9	17	25	32
22-Last 12¢ issue	3	6	9	14	19	24
23-30: 23-Reprint; photo-c	2	4	6	13	18	22
31-50: 36-Weiss-a	2	4	6	10	14	18
51-74: 74-Origin & 1st app. Taurus	2	4	6	8	11	14
75-79,87-97: 90-r/Torres, McWilliams-a/#12; Morrow-c	1	3	4	6	8	10
80-86-(52 pgs.)	2	4	6	8	11	14
Story Digest 1(7/70-Gold Key)-All text/illos.; 148 pp.	5	10	15	32	51	70

(See Mystery Comics Digest No. 2, 5, 8, 11, 14, 17, 20, 23, 26)
NOTE: **Bolle** a-51-54, 56, 58, 59. **McWilliams** a-12, 14, 18, 19, 72, 80, 81, 93. **Orlando** a-11-15, 21. Reprints: 78, 81-86, 89, 90, 92, 95, 97.

BORIS KARLOFF THRILLER (TV) (Becomes Boris Karloff Tales…)
Gold Key: Oct, 1962 - No. 2, Jan, 1963 (84 pgs.)

	GD 2.0	VG 4.0	FN 6.0	VF 8.0	VF/NM 9.0	NM- 9.2
1-Photo-c	9	18	27	64	110	155
2	6	12	18	41	66	90

BORIS THE BEAR
Dark Horse Comics/Nicotat Comics #13 on: Aug, 1986 - No. 34, 1990 ($1.50/$1.75/$1.95, B&W)

1, Annual 1 (1988, $2.50)						3.00
1 (2nd printing),2,3,4A,4B,5-12, 14-34: 8-(44 pgs.)						2.50
13-1st Nicotat Comics issue						3.00

BORIS THE BEAR INSTANT COLOR CLASSICS
Dark Horse Comics: July, 1987 - No. 3, 1987 ($1.75/$1.95)

1-3						2.50

BORN
Marvel Comics: 2003 - No. 4, 2003 ($3.50, limited series)

1-4-Frank Castle (the Punisher) in 1971 Vietnam; Ennis-s/Robertson-a						3.50
HC (2004, $17.99) oversized reprint of series; proposal, layout pages						18.00
Punisher: Born SC (2004, $13.99) r/series; proposal, layout pages						14.00

BORN AGAIN
Spire Christian Comics (Fleming H. Revell Co.): 1978 (39¢)

	GD 2.0	VG 4.0	FN 6.0	VF 8.0	VF/NM 9.0	NM- 9.2
nn-Watergate, Nixon, etc.	2	4	6	8	11	14

BOUNCER, THE (Formerly Green Mask #9)
Fox Features Syndicate: 1944 - No. 14, Jan, 1945

	GD 2.0	VG 4.0	FN 6.0	VF 8.0	VF/NM 9.0	NM- 9.2
nn(1944, #10?)	31	62	93	178	282	385
11 (9/44)-Origin; Rocket Kelly, One Round Hogan app.	23	46	69	135	213	290
12-14: 14-Reprints no # issue	18	36	54	107	169	230

BOUNTY GUNS (See Luke Short's…, Four Color 739)

BOX OFFICE POISON
Antarctic Press: 1996 - No. 21, Sept, 2000 ($2.95, B&W)

	GD 2.0	VG 4.0	FN 6.0	VF 8.0	VF/NM 9.0	NM- 9.2
1-Alex Robinson-s/a in all	1	2	3	4	5	7
2-5						4.00
6-21, ...Kolor Karnival 1 (5/99, $2.99)						3.00
...Super Special 0 (5/97, $4.95)						5.00
Sherman's March: Collected BOP Vol. 1 (9/98, $14.95) r/#0-4						15.00
TPB (2002, $29.95, 608 pgs.) r/entire series						30.00

BOY AND HIS 'BOT, A
Now Comics: Jan, 1987 ($1.95)

1-A Holiday Special						3.00

BOY AND THE PIRATES, THE (Movie)
Dell Publishing Co.: No. 1117, Aug, 1960

	GD 2.0	VG 4.0	FN 6.0	VF 8.0	VF/NM 9.0	NM- 9.2
Four Color 1117-Photo-c	6	12	18	43	69	95

BOY COMICS (Captain Battle No. 1 & 2; Boy Illustories No. 43-108) (Stories by Charles Biro) (Also see Squeeks)
Lev Gleason Publ. (Comic House): No. 3, Apr, 1942 - No. 119, Mar, 1956

	GD 2.0	VG 4.0	FN 6.0	VF 8.0	VF/NM 9.0	NM- 9.2
3(No.1)-1st app. & origin Crimebuster, Bombshell & Young Robin Hood; Yankee Longago, Case 1001-1008, Swoop Storm & Boy Movies begin; 1st app. Iron Jaw; Crimebuster's pet monkey Squeeks begins	306	612	918	1989	3445	4900
4-Hitler, Tojo, Mussolini-c	131	262	393	819	1360	1900
5	90	180	270	563	932	1300
6-Origin Iron Jaw; origin & death of Iron Jaw's son; Little Dynamite begins, ends #39; 1st Iron Jaw-c	300	600	900	1931	3366	4800
7-Flag & Hitler, Tojo, Mussolini-c	98	196	294	613	1019	1425
8-Death of Iron Jaw; Iron Jaw-c	97	194	291	606	1003	1400
9-Iron Jaw-c	86	172	258	538	894	1250

	GD 2.0	VG 4.0	FN 6.0	VF 8.0	VF/NM 9.0	NM- 9.2
10-Return of Iron Jaw; classic Biro-c; Iron Jaw-c	128	256	384	800	1325	1850
11-Classic Iron Jaw-c	90	180	270	563	932	1300
12,13: 12-Torture-c	55	110	165	344	572	800
14-Iron Jaw-c	65	130	195	406	671	935
15-Death of Iron Jaw	74	148	222	463	769	1075
16,18-20	40	80	120	242	389	535
17-Flag-c	41	82	123	250	400	550
21-29,31,32-(All 68 pgs.). 28-Yankee Longago ends. 32-Swoop Storm & Young Robin Hood end	27	54	81	158	249	340
30-(68 pgs.)-Origin Crimebuster retold	37	74	111	213	337	460
33-40: 34-Crimebuster story(2); suicide-c/story	21	42	63	122	191	260
41-50	17	34	51	98	154	210
51-59: 57-Dilly Duncan begins, ends #71	15	30	45	85	133	180
60-Iron Jaw returns	16	32	48	92	144	195
61-Origin Crimebuster & Iron Jaw retold	18	36	54	103	162	220
62-Death of Iron Jaw explained	17	34	51	98	154	210
63-73: 63-McWilliams-a. 73-Frazetta 1-pg. ad	13	26	39	72	101	130
74-88: 80-1st app. Rocky X of the Rocketeers; becomes "Rocky X" #101; Iron Jaw, Sniffer & the Deadly Dozen in 80-118	10	20	30	58	79	100
89-92-The Claw serial app. in all	11	22	33	60	83	105
93-Claw cameo; Rocky X by Sid Check	10	20	30	58	79	100
94-97,99	10	20	30	56	76	95
98,100: 98-Rocky X by Sid Check	10	20	30	58	79	100
101-107,109,111,119: 101-Rocky X becomes spy strip. 106-Robin Hood app. 119-Last Crimebuster. 111-Crimebuster becomes Chuck Chandler.	9	18	27	52	69	85
108,110,112-118-Kubert-a; 108-Ditko-a	10	20	30	56	76	95

(See Giant Boy Book of Comics)
NOTE: *Boy Movies* in 3-5,40,41. *Iron Jaw* app.-3, 4, 6, 8, 10, 11, 13-15; returns-60-62, 68, 69, 72-79, 81-118. **Biro** c-all. **Briefer** a-5, 13, 14, 16-20 among others. **Fuje** a-55, 18 pgs. **Palais** a-14, 16, 17, 19, 20 among others.

BOY COMMANDOS (See Detective #64 & World's Finest Comics #8)
National Periodical Publications: Winter, 1942-43 - No. 36, Nov-Dec, 1949

	GD 2.0	VG 4.0	FN 6.0	VF 8.0	VF/NM 9.0	NM- 9.2
1-Origin Liberty Belle; The Sandman & The Newsboy Legion x-over in Boy Commandos; S&K-a, 48 pgs.; S&K cameo? (classic WWII-c)	503	1006	1509	3521	6161	8800
2-Last Liberty Belle; Hitler-c; S&K-a, 46 pgs.; WWII-c	221	442	663	1381	2291	3200
3-S&K-a, 45 pgs.; WWII-c	131	262	393	819	1360	1900
4-6: All WWII-c. 6-S&K-a	83	166	249	519	860	1200
7-10: All WWII-c	53	106	159	323	537	750
11-13: All WWII-c. 11-Infinity-c	40	80	120	235	368	500
14,16,18-19-All have S&K-a. 18-2nd Crazy Quilt-c	31	62	93	178	282	385
15-1st app. Crazy Quilt, their arch nemesis	40	80	120	240	383	525
17,20-Sci/fi-c/stories	38	76	114	219	347	475
21,22,25: 22-3rd Crazy Quilt-c; Judy Canova x-over	25	50	75	145	228	310
23-S&K c/a(all)	34	68	102	195	308	420
24-1st costumed superhero satire-c (11-12/47).	30	60	90	172	271	370
26-Flying Saucer story (3-4/48)-4th of this theme; see The Spirit 9/28/47(1st), Shadow Comics V7#10 (2nd, 1/48) & Captain Midnight #60 (3rd, 2/48)	30	60	90	174	275	375
27,28,30: 30-Cleveland Indians story	24	48	72	139	220	300
29-S&K story (1)	26	52	78	150	235	320
31-35: 32-Dale Evans app. on-c & in story. 33-Last Crazy Quilt-c. 34-Intro. Wolf, their mascot	22	44	66	126	198	270
36-Intro The Atomobile c/sci-fi story (Scarce)	40	80	120	240	383	525

NOTE: Most issues signed by **Simon & Kirby** are not by them. **S&K** c-1-9, 13, 14, 17, 21, 23, 24, 30-32. **Feller** c-30.

BOY COMMANDOS
National Per. Publ.: Sept-Oct, 1973 - No. 2, Nov-Dec, 1973 (G.A. S&K reprints)

	GD 2.0	VG 4.0	FN 6.0	VF 8.0	VF/NM 9.0	NM- 9.2
1,2: 1-Reprints story from Boy Commandos #1 plus-c & Detective #66 by S&K. 2-Infantino/Orlando-c	2	4	6	9	13	16

BOY COMMANDOS COMICS
DC Comics: Sept/Oct. 1942

1-Ashcan comic, not distributed to newsstands, only for in-house use. Cover art is the splash page from the Boy Commandos story in Detective Comics #68 interior is from an unidentified interior of Detective Comics	(no known sales)
nn - (9-10/42) Ashcan comic, not distributed to newsstands, only for in-house use. Cover art is the splash page from the Boy Commandos story in Detective Comics #68 interior is from Detective Comics #68	(no known sales)

BOY COWBOY (Also see Amazing Adventures & Science Comics)
Ziff-Davis Publ. Co.: 1950 (8 pgs. in color)

	GD 2.0	VG 4.0	FN 6.0	VF 8.0	VF/NM 9.0	NM- 9.2
nn-Sent to subscribers of Ziff-Davis mags. & ordered through mail for 10¢; used to test market for Kid Cowboy	27	54	81	158	249	340

BOY DETECTIVE

The Boys #10
© Spitfire & Darick Robertson

Boys' Ranch #2 © HARV

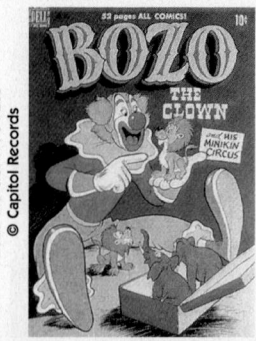

Bozo the Clown FC #285
© Capitol Records

	GD	VG	FN	VF	VF/NM	NM-		GD	VG	FN	VF	VF/NM	NM-
	2.0	4.0	6.0	8.0	9.0	9.2		2.0	4.0	6.0	8.0	9.0	9.2

Avon Periodicals: May-June, 1951 - No. 4, May, 1952

1	20	40	60	115	180	245
2-4: 3,4-Kinstler-c	14	28	42	78	112	145

BOY EXPLORERS COMICS (Terry and The Pirates No. 3 on)
Family Comics (Harvey Publ.): May-June, 1946 - No. 2, Sept-Oct, 1946

1-Intro The Explorers, Duke of Broadway, Calamity Jane & Danny Dixon...Cadet; S&K-c/a, 24 pgs.	65	130	195	406	673	940
2-(Scarce)-Small size (5-1/2x8-1/2"; B&W; 32 pgs.) Distributed to mail subscribers only; S&K-a	114	228	342	713	1182	1650

(Also see All New No. 15, Flash Gordon No. 5, and Stuntman No. 3)

BOY ILLUSTORIES (See Boy Comics)

BOY LOVES GIRL (Boy Meets Girl No. 1-24)
Lev Gleason Publications: No. 25, July, 1952 - No. 57, June, 1956

25(#1)	10	20	30	54	72	90
26,27,29-33: 30-33-Serial, 'Loves of My Life	7	14	21	37	46	55
34-42: 39-Lingerie panels	7	14	21	35	43	50
28-Drug propaganda story	7	14	21	37	46	55
43-Toth-a	8	16	24	40	50	60
44-50: 47-Toth-a? 50-Last pre-code (2/55)	6	12	18	31	38	45
51-57: 57-Ann Brewster-a	6	12	18	27	33	38

BOY MEETS GIRL (Boy Loves Girl No. 25 on)
Lev Gleason Publications: Feb, 1950 - No. 24, June, 1952 (No. 1-17: 52 pgs.)

1-Guardineer-a	14	28	42	82	121	160
2	9	18	27	50	65	80
3-10	8	16	24	44	57	70
11-24	8	16	24	42	54	65

NOTE: Briefer a-24. Fuje c-3,7. Painted-c 1-17. Photo-c 19-21, 23.

BOYS, THE
DC Comics (WildStorm)/Dynamite Ent. #7 on: Oct, 2006 - Present ($2.99, mature)

1-Garth Ennis-s/Darick Robertson-a	6.00
2-6	4.00
7-10-(Dynamite Ent.,)	3.00
... Volume 1: The Name of the Game TPB (2007, $14.99) r/#1-6; intro. by Simon Pegg	15.00

BOYS' AND GIRLS' MARCH OF COMICS (See March of Comics)

BOYS' RANCH (Also see Western Tales & Witches' Western Tales)
Harvey Publ.: Oct, 1950 - No. 6, Aug, 1951 (No.1-3, 52 pgs.; No. 4-6, 36 pgs.)

1-S&K-c/a(3)	60	120	180	375	625	875
2-S&K-c/a(3)	41	82	123	252	406	560
3-S&K-c/a(2); Meskin-a	40	80	120	235	368	500
4-S&K-c/a, 5 pgs.	35	70	105	201	318	435
5,6-S&K-c, splashes & centerspread only; Meskin-a	20	40	60	117	184	250

BOZO (Larry Harmon's Bozo, the World's Most Famous Clown)
Innovation Publishing: 1992 ($6.95, 68 pgs.)

1-Reprints Four Color #285(#1)	1	2	3	4	5	7

BOZO THE CLOWN (TV) (Bozo No. 7 on)
Dell Publishing Co.: July, 1950 - No. 4, Oct-Dec, 1963

Four Color 285(#1)	18	36	54	134	237	340
2(7-9/51)-7(10-12/52)	10	20	30	73	129	185
Four Color 464,508,551,594(10/54)	9	18	27	64	110	155
1(nn, 5-7/62)	7	14	21	49	80	110
2 - 4(1963)	6	12	18	37	59	80

BOZZ CHRONICLES, THE
Marvel Comics (Epic Comics): Dec, 1985 - No. 6, 1986 (Lim. series, mature)

1-6-Logan/Wolverine look alike in 19th century. 1,3,5- Blevins-a	3.00

B.P.R.D.: GARDEN OF SOULS
Dark Horse Comics: Mar, 2007 - No. 5, July, 2007 ($2.99, limited series)

1-5-Mignola & Arcudi-s/Guy Davis-a/Mignola-c	3.00

B.P.R.D.: HOLLOW EARTH (Mike Mignola's...)
Dark Horse Comics: Jan, 2002 - No. 3, June, 2002 ($2.99, limited series)

1-3-Mignola, Golden & Sniegoski-s/Sook-a/Mignola-c; Hellboy and Abe Sapien app.	3.00
... and Other Stories TPB (1/03; 7/04, $17.95) r/#1-3, Hellboy; Box Full of Evil, Abe Sapien: Drums of the Dead, and Dark Horse Extra; plus sketch pages	18.00
B.P.R.D Dark Waters (7/03, $2.99) Guy Davis-c/a; Augustyn-s	3.00
B.P.R.D Night Train (9/03, $2.99) Johns & Kolins-s; Kolins & Stewart-a	3.00
B.P.R.D There's Something Under My Bed (11/03, $2.99) Pollina-a/c	3.00
B.P.R.D The Soul of Venice (5/03, $2.99) Oeming-a/c; Gunter & Oeming-s	3.00

B.P.R.D The Soul of Venice and Other Stories TPB (8/04, $17.95) r/one-shots & new story by Mignola and Cam Stewart; sketch pages by various	18.00

B.P.R.D.: KILLING GROUND
Dark Horse Comics: Aug, 2007 - No. 5, ($2.99, limited series)

1-Mignola & Arcudi-s/Guy Davis-a/c	3.00

B.P.R.D.: PLAGUE OF FROGS
Dark Horse Comics: Mar, 2004 - No. 5, July, 2004 ($2.99, limited series)

1-5-Mignola-s/Guy Davis-a/c	3.00
TPB (1/05, $17.95) r/series; sketchbook pages & afterword by Davis & Mignola	18.00

B.P.R.D.: THE BLACK FLAME
Dark Horse Comics: Sept, 2005 - No. 6, Jan, 2006 ($2.99, limited series)

1-6-Mignola & Arcudi-s/Guy Davis-a/ Mignola-c	3.00
TPB (7/06, $17.95) r/series; sketchbook pages & afterword by Davis & Mignola	18.00

B.P.R.D.: THE DEAD
Dark Horse Comics: Nov, 2004 - No. 5, Mar, 2005 ($2.99, limited series)

1-5-Mignola-s/Guy Davis-c/a	3.00

B.P.R.D.: THE UNIVERSAL MACHINE
Dark Horse Comics: Apr, 2006 - No. 5, Aug, 2006 ($2.99, limited series)

1-5-Mignola & Arcudi-s/Guy Davis-a/Mignola-c. 5-Mignola-a (5 pgs.)	3.00
TPB (1/07, $17.95) r/series; sketchbook pages by Davis; Mignola afterword	18.00

BRADLEYS, THE (Also see Hate)
Fantagraphics Books: Apr, 1999 - No. 6, Jan, 2000 ($2.95, B&W, limited series)

1-6-Reprints Peter Bagge's-s/a	3.00

BRADY BUNCH, THE (TV)(See Kite Fun Book and Binky #78)
Dell Publishing Co.: Feb, 1970 - No. 2, May, 1970

1	11	22	33	75	133	190
2	8	16	24	54	90	125

BRAIN, THE
Sussex Publ. Co./Magazine Enterprises: Sept, 1956 - No. 7, 1958

1-Dan DeCarlo-a in all including reprints	12	24	36	67	94	120
2,3	8	16	24	40	50	60
4-7	8	12	24	37	50	
I.W. Reprints #1-4,8-10('63),14: 2-Reprints Sussex #2 with new cover added	2	4	6	9	13	16
Super Reprint #17,18(nd)	2	4	6	9	13	16

BRAINBANX
DC Comics (Helix): Mar, 1997 - No. 6, Aug, 1997 ($2.50, limited series)

1-6: Elaine Lee-s/Temujin-a	2.50

BRAIN BOY
Dell Publishing Co.: Apr-June, 1962 - No. 6, Sept-Nov, 1963 (Painted c#1-6)

Four Color 1330(#1)-Gil Kane-a; origin	11	22	33	79	140	200
2(7-9/62),3-6: 4-Origin retold	7	14	21	49	80	110

BRAM STOKER'S BURIAL OF THE RATS (Movie)
Roger Corman's Cosmic Comics: Apr, 1995 - No.3, June, 1995 ($2.50)

1-3: Adaptation of film; Jerry Prosser scripts	2.50

BRAM STOKER'S DRACULA (Movie)(Also see Dracula: Vlad the Impaler)
Topps Comics: Oct, 1992 - No. 4, Jan, 1993 ($2.95, limited series, polybagged)

1-(1st & 2nd printing)-Adaptation of film begins; Mignola-c/a in all; 4 trading cards & poster; photo scenes of movie	3.00
1-Crimson foil edition (limited to 500)	8.00
2-4: 2-Bound-in poster & cards. 4 trading cards in both. 3-Contains coupon to win 1 of 500 crimson foil-c edition of #1. 4-Contains coupon to win 1 of 500 uncut sheets of all 16 trading cards	3.00

BRAND ECHH (See Not Brand Echh)

BRAND OF EMPIRE (See Luke Short's...Four Color 771)

BRASS
Image Comics (WildStorm Productions): Aug, 1996 - No. 3, May, 1997 ($2.50, lim. series)

1-($4.50) Folio Ed.; oversized	4.50
1-3: Wiesenfeld-s/Bennett-a. 3-Grunge & Roxy(Gen 13) cameo	2.50

BRASS
DC Comics (WildStorm): Aug, 2000 - No. 6, Jan, 2001 ($2.50, limited series)

1-6-Arcudi-s	2.50

BRATH
CrossGeneration Comics: Feb, 2003 - No. 14, June, 2004 ($2.95)

Brave and the Bold #21 © DC

Brave and the Bold #55 © DC

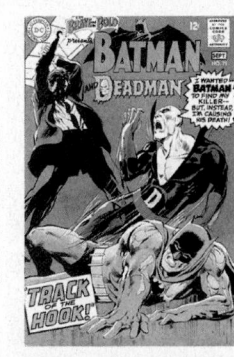

Brave and the Bold #79 © DC

	GD 2.0	VG 4.0	FN 6.0	VF 8.0	VF/NM 9.0	NM- 9.2

Prequel-Dixon-s/Di Vito-a — 3.00
1-14: 1-(3/03)-Dixon-s/Di Vito-a — 3.00
Vol. 1: Hammer of Vengeance (2003, $9.95) Digest-sized reprint of Prequel & #1-6 — 10.00

BRATPACK/MAXIMORTAL SUPER SPECIAL
King Hell Press: 1996 ($2.95, B&W, limited series)
1,2: Veitch-s/a — 3.00

BRATS BIZARRE
Marvel Comics (Epic/Heavy Hitters): 1994 - No. 4, 1994 ($2.50, limited series)
1-4: All w/bound-in trading cards — 2.50

BRAVADOS, THE (See Wild Western Action)
Skywald Publ. Corp.: Aug, 1971 (52 pgs., one-shot)
1-Red Mask, The Durango Kid, Billy Nevada-r; Bolle-a; 3-D effect story — 3 6 9 14 19 24

BRAVE AND THE BOLD, THE (See Best Of… & Super DC Giant) (Replaced by Batman & The Outsiders)
National Periodical Publ./DC Comics: Aug-Sept, 1955 - No. 200, July, 1983
1-Viking Prince by Kubert, Silent Knight, Golden Gladiator begin; part Kubert-c — 263 526 789 2300 4300 6300
2 — 109 218 327 927 1714 2500
3,4 — 59 118 177 502 926 1350
5-Robin Hood begins (4-5/56, 1st DC app.), ends #15; see Robin Hood Tales #7 — 61 122 183 519 960 1400
6-10: 6-Robin Hood by Kubert; last Golden Gladiator app.; Silent Knight; no Viking Prince. 8-1st S.A. issue — 44 88 132 352 639 925
11-22,24: 12,14-Robin Hood-c. 18,21-23-Grey tone-c. 22-Last Silent Knight. 24-Last Viking Prince by Kubert (2nd solo book) — 35 70 135 263 482 700
23-Viking Prince by Kubert; 1st B&B single theme issue & 1st Viking Prince solo book — 44 88 132 352 639 925
25-1st app. Suicide Squad (8-9/59) — 41 82 123 328 594 860
26,27-Suicide Squad — 29 58 87 212 381 550
28-(2-3/60)-Justice League intro./1st app.; origin/1st app. Snapper Carr — 460 920 1380 4209 7855 11,500
29-Justice League (4-5/60)-2nd app. battle the Weapons Master; robot-c — 175 350 525 1531 2866 4200
30-Justice League (6-7/60)-3rd app.; vs. Amazo — 143 286 429 1216 2258 3300
31-1st app. Cave Carson (8-9/60); scarce in high grade; 1st try-out series — 38 76 114 285 518 750
32,33-Cave Carson — 22 44 66 165 295 425
34-Origin/1st app. Silver-Age Hawkman, Hawkgirl & Byth (2-3/61); Gardner Fox story, Kubert-c/a ; 1st S.A. Hawkman tryout series; 2nd in #42-44; both series predate Hawkman #1 (4-5/64) — 175 350 525 1531 2866 4200
35-Hawkman by Kubert (4-5/61)-2nd app. — 43 86 129 344 622 900
36-Hawkman by Kubert; origin & 1st app. Shadow Thief (6-7/61)-3rd app. — 39 78 117 293 534 775
37-Suicide Squad (2nd tryout series) — 21 42 63 152 271 390
38,39-Suicide Squad. 38-Last 10¢ issue — 18 36 54 132 234 335
40,41-Cave Carson Inside Earth (2nd try-out series). 40-Kubert-a. 41-Meskin-a — 14 28 42 102 181 260
42-Hawkman by Kubert (2nd tryout series); Hawkman earns helmet wings; Byth app. — 27 54 81 202 361 520
43-Hawkman by Kubert; more detailed origin — 32 64 96 236 436 635
44-Hawkman by Kubert; grey-tone-c — 26 52 78 187 336 485
45-49-Strange Sports Stories by Infantino — 9 18 27 64 110 155
50-The Green Arrow & Manhunter From Mars (10-11/63); 1st Hawkman x-over outside of Detective Comics (pre-dates House of Mystery #143); team-ups begin — 18 36 54 130 230 330
51-Aquaman & Hawkman (12-1/63-64); pre-dates Hawkman #1 — 21 42 63 156 278 400
52-(2-3/64)-3 Battle Stars; Sgt. Rock, Haunted Tank, Johnny Cloud, & Mlle. Marie team-up for 1st time by Kubert (c/a) — 20 40 60 146 261 375
53-Atom & The Flash by Toth — 17 34 51 63 107 150
54-Kid Flash, Robin & Aqualad; 1st app./origin Teen Titans (6-7/64) — 30 60 90 220 398 575
55-Metal Men & The Atom — 8 16 24 54 90 125
56-The Flash & Manhunter From Mars — 8 16 24 54 90 125
57-Origin & 1st app. Metamorpho (12-1/64-65) — 17 34 51 122 216 310
58-2nd app. Metamorpho by Fradon — 9 18 27 64 110 155
59-Batman & Green Lantern; 1st Batman team-up in Brave and the Bold — 11 22 33 77 136 195
60-Teen Titans (2nd app.)-1st app. new Wonder Girl (Donna Troy), who joins Titans (6-7/65) — 12 24 36 87 156 225
61-Origin Starman & Black Canary by Anderson — 12 24 36 86 153 220

62-Origin Starman & Black Canary cont'd. 62-1st S.A. app. Wildcat (10-11/65); 1st S.A. app. of G.A. Huntress (W.W. villain) — 11 22 33 75 133 190
63-Supergirl & Wonder Woman — 8 16 24 52 86 120
64-Batman Versus Eclipso (see H.O.S. #61) — 8 16 24 54 90 125
65-Flash & Doom Patrol (4-5/66) — 6 12 18 37 59 80
66-Metamorpho & Metal Men (6-7/66) — 6 12 18 37 59 80
67-Batman & The Flash by Infantino; Batman team-ups begin, end #200 (8-9/66) — 7 14 21 45 73 100
68-Batman/Metamorpho/Joker/Riddler/Penguin-c/story; Batman as Bat-Hulk (Hulk parody) — 8 16 24 58 97 135
69-Batman & Green Lantern — 6 12 18 39 62 85
70-Batman & Hawkman; Craig-a(p) — 6 12 18 39 62 85
71-Batman & Green Arrow — 6 12 18 39 62 85
72-Spectre & Flash (6-7/67); 4th app. The Spectre; predates Spectre #1 — 6 12 18 41 66 90
73-Aquaman & The Atom — 6 12 18 37 59 80
74-Batman & Metal Men — 6 12 18 37 59 80
75-Batman & The Spectre (12-1/67-68); 6th app. Spectre; came out between Spectre #1 & #2 — 6 12 18 39 62 85
76-Batman & Plastic Man (2-3/68); came out between Plastic Man #8 & #9 — 6 12 18 37 59 80
77-Batman & The Atom — 6 12 18 37 59 80
78-Batman, Wonder Woman & Batgirl — 6 12 18 37 59 80
79-Batman & Deadman by Neal Adams (8-9/68); early Deadman app. — 8 16 24 56 93 130
80-Batman & Creeper (10-11/68); N. Adams-a; early app. The Creeper; came out between Creeper #3 & #4 — 7 14 21 47 76 105
81-Batman & Flash; N. Adams-a — 7 14 21 47 76 105
82-Batman & Aquaman; N. Adams-a; origin Ocean Master retold (2-3/69) — 7 14 21 47 76 105
83-Batman & Teen Titans; N. Adams-a (4-5/69) — 7 14 21 47 76 105
84-Batman (G.A., 1st S.A. app.) & Sgt. Rock; last 12¢ issue (6-7/69) — 7 14 21 47 76 105
85-Batman & Green Arrow; 1st new costume for Green Arrow by Neal Adams (8-9/69) — 9 18 27 49 80 110
86-Batman & Deadman (10-11/69); N. Adams-a; story concludes from Strange Adventures #216 (1-2/69) — 7 14 21 47 76 105
87-Batman & Wonder Woman — 4 8 12 24 37 50
88-Batman & Wildcat — 4 8 12 24 37 50
89-Batman & Phantom Stranger (4-5/70); early Phantom Stranger app. (came out between Phantom Stranger #6 & 7 — 4 8 12 22 34 45
90-Batman & Adam Strange — 4 8 12 22 34 45
91-Batman & Black Canary (8-9/70) — 4 8 12 22 34 45
92-Batman; intro the Bat Squad — 4 8 12 24 37 50
93-Batman-House of Mystery; N. Adams-a — 6 12 18 39 62 85
94-Batman-Teen Titans — 3 6 9 20 30 40
95-Batman & Plastic Man — 3 6 9 19 29 38
96-Batman & Sgt. Rock; last 15¢ issue — 3 6 9 20 30 40
97-Batman & Wildcat; 52 pg. issues begin, end #102; reprints origin & 1st app. Deadman from Strange Advs. #205 — 3 6 9 20 30 40
98-Batman & Phantom Stranger; 1st Jim Aparo Batman-a? — 3 6 9 20 30 40
99-Batman & Flash — 3 6 9 20 30 40
100-(2-3/72, 25¢, 52 pgs.)-Batman-Green Lantern-Green Arrow-Black Canary-Robin; Deadman-r by Adams/Str. Advs. #210 — 6 12 18 37 59 80
101-Batman & Metamorpho; Kubert Viking Prince — 3 6 9 19 29 38
102-Batman-Teen Titans; N. Adams-a(p) — 4 8 12 28 44 60
103-107,109,110: Batman team-ups: 103-Metal Men. 104-Deadman. 105-Wonder Woman. 106-Green Arrow. 107-Black Canary. 109-Demon. 110-Wildcat — 2 4 6 13 18 22
108-Sgt. Rock — 3 6 9 14 19 24
111-Batman/Joker-c/story — 3 6 9 15 25 32
112-117: All 100 pgs.; Batman team-ups: 112-Mr. Miracle. 113-Metal Men; reprints origin/1st Hawkman from Brave and the Bold #34; r/origin Multi-Man/Challengers #14. 114-Aquaman. 115-Atom; r/origin Viking Prince from #23; r/Dr. Fate/Hourman/Solomon Grundy/Green Lantern from Showcase #55. 116-Spectre. 117-Sgt. Rock; last 100 pg. issue — 4 8 12 28 44 60
118-Batman/Wildcat/Joker-c/story — 3 6 9 16 23 30
119,121-123,125-128,132-140: Batman team-ups: 119-Man-Bat. 121-Metal Men. 122-Swamp Thing. 123-Plastic Man/Metamorpho. 125-Flash. 126-Aquaman. 127-Wildcat. 128-Mr. Miracle. 132-Kung-Fu Fighter. 133-Deadman. 134-Green Lantern. 135-Metal Men. 136-Metal Men/Green Arrow. 137-Demon. 138-Mr. Miracle. 139-Hawkman. 140-Wonder Woman — 2 4 6 8 10 12
120-Kamandi (68 pgs.) — 3 6 9 14 19 24

Brave and the Bold #141 © DC

Brave and the Bold #5 © DC

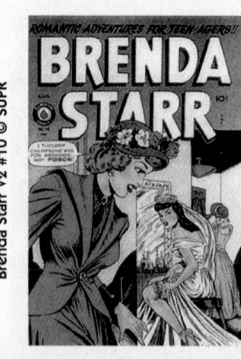

Brenda Starr V2 #10 © SUPR

	GD	VG	FN	VF	VF/NM	NM-
	2.0	4.0	6.0	8.0	9.0	9.2

124-Sgt. Rock` — 2 4 6 9 12 15
129,130-Batman/Green Arrow/Atom parts 1 & 2; Joker & Two Face-c/stories — 2 4 6 13 18 22
131-Batman & Wonder Woman vs. Catwoman-c/sty — 2 4 6 10 14 18
141-Batman/Black Canary vs. Joker-c/story — 2 4 6 13 18 22
142-160: Batman team-ups: 142-Aquaman. 143-Creeper; origin Human Target (44 pgs.). 144-Green Arrow; origin Human Target part 2 (44 pgs.). 145-Phantom Stranger. 146-G.A. Batman/Unknown Soldier. 147-Supergirl. 148-Plastic Man; X-Mas-c. 149-Teen Titans. 150-Anniversary issue; Superman. 151-Flash. 152-Atom. 153-Red Tornado. 154-Metamorpho. 155-Green Lantern. 156-Dr. Fate. 157-Batman vs. Kamandi (ties into Kamandi #59). 158-Wonder Woman. 159-Ra's Al Ghul. 160-Supergirl. — 1 3 4 6 8 10
145(11/79)-147,150-159,165(8/80)-(Whitman variants; low print run; none show issue # on cover) — 2 4 6 9 13 16
161-181,183-190,192-195,198,199: Batman team-ups: 161-Adam Strange. 162-G.A. Batman/Sgt. Rock. 163-Black Lightning. 164-Hawkman. 165-Man-Bat. 166-Black Canary; Nemesis (intro) back-up story begins, ends #192; Penguin-c/story. 167-G.A. Batman/Blackhawk; origin Nemesis. 168-Green Arrow. 169-Zatanna. 170-Nemesis. 171-Scalphunter. 172-Firestorm. 173-Guardians of the Universe. 174-Green Lantern. 175-Lois Lane. 176-Swamp Thing. 177-Elongated Man. 178-Creeper. 179-Legion. 180-Spectre. 181-Hawk & Dove. 183-Riddler. 184-Huntress. 185-Green Arrow. 186-Hawkman. 187-Metal Men. 188,189-Rose & the Thorn. 190-Adam Strange. 192-Superboy vs. Mr. I.Q. 193-Nemesis. 194-Flash. 195-I...Vampire. 198-Karate Kid. 199-Batman vs. The Spectre — 6.00
182-G.A. Robin; G.A. Starman app.; 1st modern app. G.A. Batwoman — 2 4 6 8 10 12
191-Batman/Joker-c/story; Nemesis app. — 2 4 6 8 11 14
196-Ragman; origin Ragman retold. — 1 2 3 5 6 8
197-Catwoman; Earth II Batman & Catwoman marry; 2nd modern app. of G.A. Batwoman — 2 4 6 9 12 15
200-Double-sized (64 pgs.); printed on Mando paper; Earth One & Earth Two Batman app. in separate stories; intro/1st app. Batman & The Outsiders — 1 3 4 6 8 10

NOTE: **Neal Adams** a-79-86, 93, 100r, 102; c-75, 76, 79-86, 88-90, 93, 95, 99, 100r. **M. Anderson** a-115r; c-72i, 96i. **Aparo** a-98, 100-102, 104-125, 126i, 127-136, 138-145, 147, 148i, 149-152, 154, 155, 157-162, 168-170, 173-178, 180-182, 184, 186i-189i, 191i-193i, 195, 196, 200; c-105-109, 111-136, 137i, 138-175, 177, 180-184, 186-200. **Austin** a-166i. **Bernard Baily** c-32, 33, 58. **Buckler** a-185, 186p; c-137, 178p, 185p, 186p. **Giordano** a-143, 144. **Infantino** a-67p, 72p, 97r, 98r, 115r, 172p, 183p, 190p, 194p; c-45-49, 67p, 69p, 72p, 72p, 96p, 98r. **Kaluta** c-176. **Kane** a-175; c-59, 64. **Kubert &/or Heath** a-1-24; reprints-101, 113, 115, 117. **Kubert** a-99r; c-22-24, 34-36, 40, 42-44, 52. **Mooney** a-114r. **Mortimer** a-64, 69. **Newton** a-153p, 156p, 165p. **Irv Novick** c-1(part), 2-21. **Fred Ray** a-78r. **Roussos** a-50, 76i, 114r. **Staton** 148p. 52 pgs.-97, 100; 68 pgs.-120; 100 pgs.-112-117.

BRAVE AND THE BOLD, THE
DC Comics: Dec, 1991 - No. 6, June, 1992 ($1.75, limited series)
1-6: Green Arrow, The Butcher, The Question in all; Grell scripts in all — 2.50
NOTE: Grell c-3, 4-6.

BRAVE AND THE BOLD, THE
DC Comics: Apr, 2007 - Present ($2.99)
1-Batman & Green Lantern team-up; Roulette app.; Waid-c/Peréz-c/a; 2 covers — 4.00
2-6: 2-GL & Supergirl. 3-Batman & Blue Beetle vs. Fatal Five; Lobo app. 4-6-LSH app. — 3.00

BRAVE AND THE BOLD ANNUAL NO. 1 1969 ISSUE, THE
DC Comics: 2001 ($5.95, one-shot)
1-Reprints silver age team-ups in 1960s-style 80 pg. Giant format — 6.00

BRAVE AND THE BOLD SPECIAL, THE (See DC Special Series No. 8)

BRAVE EAGLE (TV)
Dell Publishing Co.: No. 705, June, 1956 - No. 929, July, 1958
Four Color 705 (#1)-Photo-c — 6 12 18 43 69 95
Four Color 770, 816, 879 (2/58), 929-All photo-c — 4 8 12 26 41 55

BRAVE NEW WORLD (See DCU Brave New World)

BRAVE OLD WORLD (V2K)
DC Comics (Vertigo): Feb, 2000 - No. 4, May, 2000 ($2.50, mini-series)
1-4-Messner-Loeb-s/Guy Davis & Phil Hester-a — 2.50

BRAVE ONE, THE (Movie)
Dell Publishing Co.: No. 773, Mar, 1957
Four Color 773-Photo-c — 5 10 15 35 55 75

BRAVURA
Malibu Comics (Bravura): 1995 (mail-in offer)
0-wraparound holographic-c; short stories and promo pin-ups of Chaykin's Power & Glory, Gil Kane's & Steven Grant's Edge, Starlin's Breed, & Simonson's Star Slammers — 5.00
1 1/2 — 7.00

BREACH
DC Comics: Mar, 2005 - No. 11, Jan, 2006 ($2.95/$2.50)
1-11: 1-Marcos Martin-a/Bob Harras-s; origin. 4-JLA-c/app. — 3.00

BREAKDOWN
Devil's Due Publ.: Oct, 2004 - No. 6, Apr, 2005 ($2.95)
1-6: 1-Two covers by Dave Ross and Leinil Yu; Dixon-s/Ross-a — 3.00

BREAKFAST AFTER NOON
Oni Press: May, 2000 - No. 6, Jan, 2001($2.95, B&W, limited series)
1-6-Andi Watson-s/a — 3.00
TPB (2001, $19.95) r/series — 20.00

BREAKNECK BLVD.
MotioN Comics/Slave Labor Graphics Vol. 2: No. 0, Feb, 1994 - No. 2, Nov, 1994; Vol. 2#1, Jul, 1995 - #6, Dec., 1996 ($2.50/$2.95, B&W)
0-2, V2#1-6: 0-Perez/Giordano-c — 3.00

BREAK-THRU (Also see Exiles V1#4)
Malibu Comics (Ultraverse): Dec, 1993 - No. 2, Jan, 1994 ($2.50, 44 pgs.)
1,2-Perez-c/a(p); has x-overs in Ultraverse titles — 2.50

BREATHTAKER
DC Comics: 1990 - No. 4, 1990 ($4.95, 52 pgs., prestige format, mature)
Book 1-4: Mark Wheatley-painted-c/a & scripts; Marc Hempel-a — 5.00
TPB (1994, $14.95) r/#1-4; intro by Neil Gaiman — 15.00

'BREED
Malibu Comics (Bravura): Jan, 1994 - No. 6, 1994 ($2.50, limited series)
1-6: 1-(48 pgs.)-Origin/1st app. of 'Breed by Starlin; contains Bravura stamps; spot varnish-c. — 3.00
2-5-contains Bravura stamps. 6-Death of Rachel — 3.00
....Book of Genesis (1994, $12.95)-reprints #1-6 — 13.00

'BREED II
Malibu Comics (Bravura): Nov, 1994 - No. 6, Apr, 1995 ($2.95, limited series)
1-6: Starlin-c/a/scripts in all. 1-Gold edition — 3.00

BREEZE LAWSON, SKY SHERIFF (See Sky Sheriff)

BRENDA LEE'S LIFE STORY
Dell Publishing Co.: July-Sept., 1962
01-078-209 — 8 16 24 52 86 120

BRENDA STARR (Also see All Great)
Four Star Comics Corp./Superior Comics Ltd.: No. 13, 9/47; No. 14, 3/48; V2#3, 6/48 - V2#12, 12/49
V1#13-By Dale Messick — 83 166 249 519 860 1200
  14-Classic Kamen bondage-c — 121 242 363 756 1253 1750
V2#3-Baker-a? — 67 134 201 419 697 975
  4-Used in SOTI, pg. 21; Kamen-c — 81 162 243 506 841 1175
  5-10 — 66 132 198 413 682 950
  11,12 (Scarce) — 67 134 201 419 697 975
NOTE: Newspaper reprints plus original material through #6. All original #7 on.

BRENDA STARR (...Reporter)(Young Lovers No. 16 on?)
Charlton Comics: No. 13, June, 1955 - No. 15, Oct, 1955
13-15-Newspaper-r — 32 64 96 186 293 400

BRENDA STARR REPORTER
Dell Publishing Co.: Oct, 1963
1 — 13 26 39 90 160 230

BRER RABBIT (See Kite Fun Book, Walt Disney Showcase #28 and Wheaties)
Dell Publishing Co.: No. 129, 1946; No. 208, Jan, 1949; No. 693, 1956 (Disney)
Four Color 129 (#1)-Adapted from Disney movie "Song of the South" — 26 52 78 195 348 500
Four Color 208 (1/49) — 11 22 33 75 133 200
Four Color 693-Part-r #129 — 8 16 24 56 93 130

BRIAN BOLLAND'S BLACK BOOK
Eclipse Comics: July, 1985 (one-shot)
1-British B&W-r in color — 3.00

BRIAN PULIDO'S LADY DEATH... (See Lady Death)

BRICK BRADFORD (Also see Ace Comics & King Comics)
King Features Syndicate/Standard: No. 5, July, 1948 - No. 8, July, 1949 (Ritt & Grey reprints)
5 — 19 38 57 109 172 235
6-Robot-c (by Schomburg?). — 34 68 102 197 311 425
7-Schomburg-c. 8-Says #7 inside, #8 on-c — 16 32 48 92 144 195

BRIDE'S DIARY (Formerly Black Cobra No. 3)

Brides Romances #6 © QUA

Broncho Bill #11 © STD

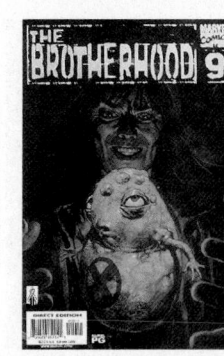

Brotherhood #9 © MAR

	GD 2.0	VG 4.0	FN 6.0	VF 8.0	VF/NM 9.0	NM- 9.2

Ajax/Farrell Publ.: No. 4, May, 1955 - No. 10, Aug, 1956

	GD 2.0	VG 4.0	FN 6.0	VF 8.0	VF/NM 9.0	NM- 9.2
4 (#1)	9	18	27	47	61	75
5-8	6	12	18	29	36	42
9,10-Disbrow-a	8	16	24	40	50	60

BRIDES IN LOVE (Hollywood Romances & Summer Love No. 46 on)
Charlton Comics: Aug, 1956 - No. 45, Feb, 1965

1	10	20	30	58	79	100
2	7	14	21	35	43	50
3-6,8-10	3	6	9	19	29	38
7-(68 pgs.)	4	8	12	24	37	50
11-20	3	6	9	14	20	25
21-45	2	4	6	9	13	16

BRIDES ROMANCES
Quality Comics Group: Nov, 1953 - No. 23, Dec, 1956

1	14	28	42	82	121	160
2	8	16	24	44	57	70
3-10: Last precode (3/55)	8	16	24	42	54	65
11-17,19-22: 15-Baker-a(p)?; Colan-a	8	16	24	40	50	60
18-Baker-a	8	16	24	44	57	70
23-Baker-c/a	11	22	33	62	86	110

BRIDE'S SECRETS
Ajax/Farrell(Excellent Publ.)/Four-Star: Apr-May, 1954 - No. 19, May, 1958

1	11	22	33	64	90	115
2	7	14	21	37	46	55
3-6: Last precode (3/55)	6	12	18	29	36	42
7-11,13-19: 18-Hollingsworth-a	6	12	18	27	33	38
12-Disbrow-a	6	12	18	31	38	45

BRIDE-TO-BE ROMANCES (See True...)

BRIGADE
Image Comics (Extreme Studios): Aug, 1992 - No. 4, 1993 ($1.95, lim. series)

1-Liefeld part plots/scripts in all, Liefeld-c(p); contains 2 Brigade trading cards						3.00
1-Gold foil stamped logo edition						8.00
2-Contains coupon for Image Comics #0 & 2 trading cards						3.00
2-With coupon missing						2.25
3,4: 3-Contains 2 trading cards; 1st Birds of Prey. 4-Flip book featuring Youngblood #5						2.50

BRIGADE
Image Comics (Extreme): V2#1, May, 1993 - V2#22, July, 1995, V2#25, May, 1996 ($1.95/$2.50)

V2#1-22,25: 1-Gatefold-c; Liefeld co-plots; Blood Brothers part 1; Bloodstrike app. 2-(6/93, V2#1 on inside)-Foil merricote-c (newsstand ed. w/out foil-c exists). 3-Perez-c(i); Liefeld scripts. 8,9-Coupons #2 & 6 for Extreme Prejudice #0 bound-in. 11-(8/94, $2.50) WildC.A.T.S app. 16-Polybagged w/ trading card. 22-"Supreme Apocalypse" Pt. 4; w/ trading card 2.50
0-(9/93)-Liefeld scripts; 1st app. Warcry; Youngblood & Wildcats app.;						2.50
20-Variant-c by Quesada & Palmiotti						2.50
Sourcebook 1 (8/94, $2.95)						3.00

BRIGADE
Awesome Entertainment: July, 2000 ($2.99)

1-Flip book w/Century preview						3.00

BRIGAND, THE (See Fawcett Movie Comics No. 18)

BRINGING UP FATHER
Dell Publishing Co.: No. 9, 1942 - No. 37, 1944

Large Feature Comic 9	30	60	90	174	275	375
Four Color 37	19	38	57	138	244	350

BRING BACK THE BAD GUYS (Also see Fireside Book Series)
Marvel Comics: 1998 ($24.95, TPB)

1-Reprints stories of Marvel villains' secrets						25.00

BRING ON THE BAD GUYS (See Fireside Book Series)

BROADWAY HOLLYWOOD BLACKOUTS
Stanhall: Mar-Apr, 1954 - No. 3, July-Aug, 1954

1	13	26	39	74	105	135
2,3	9	18	27	50	65	80

BROADWAY ROMANCES
Quality Comics Group: January, 1950 - No. 5, Sept, 1950

1-Ward-c/a (9 pgs.); Gustavson-a	38	76	114	219	347	475
2-Ward-a (9 pgs.); photo-c	26	52	78	152	239	325
3-5: All-Photo-c	14	28	42	82	121	160

BROKEN ARROW (TV)
Dell Publishing Co.: No. 855, Oct, 1957 - No. 947, Nov, 1958

Four Color 855 (#1)-Photo-c	6	12	18	37	59	80
Four Color 947-Photo-c	5	10	15	32	51	70

BROKEN CROSS, THE (See The Crusaders)

BRONCHO BILL (See Comics On Parade, Sparkler & Tip Top Comics)
United Features Syndicate/Standard(Visual Editions) No. 5-on: 1939 - 1940; No. 5, 1?/48 - No. 16, 8?/50

Single Series 2 ('39)	52	104	156	317	521	725
Single Series 19 ('40)(#2 on cvr)	42	84	126	256	421	585
5	15	30	45	83	124	165
6(4/48)-10(4/49)	9	18	27	52	69	85
11(6/49)-16	8	16	24	44	57	70

NOTE: *Schomburg c-6, 7, 9-13, 16.*

BROOKLYN DREAMS
DC Comics (Paradox Press): 1994 ($4.95, B&W, limited series, mature)

1-4						5.00

BROOKS ROBINSON (See Baseball's Greatest Heroes #2)

BROTHER BILLY THE PAIN FROM PLAINS
Marvel Comics Group: 1979 (68pgs.)

1-B&W comics, satire, Jimmy Carter-c & x-over w/Brother Billy peanut jokes. Joey Adams-a (scarce)	3	6	9	20	30	40

BROTHERHOOD, THE (Also see X-Men titles)
Marvel Comics: July, 2001 - No. 9, Mar, 2002 ($2.25)

1-Intro. Orwell & the Brotherhood; Ribic-a/X-s/Sienkiewicz-c						2.50
2-9: Two covers (JG Jones & Sienkiewicz). 4-6-Fabry-c. 7-9-Phillips-c/a						2.50

BROTHER POWER, THE GEEK (See Saga of Swamp Thing Annual & Vertigo Visions)
National Periodical Publications: Sept-Oct, 1968 - No. 2, Nov-Dec, 1968

1-Origin; Simon-c(i)	5	10	15	35	55	75
2	3	6	9	20	30	40

BROTHERS, HANG IN THERE, THE
Spire Christian Comics (Fleming H. Revell Co.): 1979 (49¢)

nn	2	4	6	8	11	14

BROTHERS OF THE SPEAR (Also see Tarzan)
Gold Key/Whitman No. 18: June, 1972 - No. 17, Feb, 1976; No. 18, May, 1982

1	4	8	12	28	44	60
2-Painted-c begin, end #17	3	6	9	16	23	30
3-10	2	4	6	13	18	22
11-18: 12-Line drawn-c. 13-17-Spiegle-a. 18(5/82)-r/#2; Leopard Girl-r	2	4	6	9	12	15

BROTHERS, THE CULT ESCAPE, THE
Spire Christian Comics (Fleming H. Revell Co.): 1980 (49¢)

nn	2	4	6	8	10	12

BROWNIES (See New Funnies)
Dell Publishing Co.: No. 192, July, 1948 - No. 605, Dec, 1954

Four Color 192(#1)-Kelly-a	14	28	42	99	175	250
Four Color 244(9/49), 293 (9/50)-Last Kelly c/a	10	20	30	68	119	170
Four Color 337(7-8/51), 365(12-1/51-52), 398(5/52)	6	12	18	37	59	80
Four Color 436(11/52), 482(7/53), 522(12/53), 605	5	10	15	35	55	75

BRUCE GENTRY
Better/Standard/Four Star Publ./Superior No. 3: Jan, 1948 - No. 8, Jul, 1949

1-Ray Bailey strip reprints begin, end #3; E. C. emblem appears as a monogram on stationery in story; negligee panels	55	110	165	344	572	800
2,3	37	74	111	213	337	460
4-8	25	50	75	148	232	315

NOTE: *Kamen ish a-2-7; c-1-8.*

BRUCE LEE (Also see Deadly Hands of Kung Fu)
Malibu Comics: July, 1994 - No. 6, Dec, 1994 ($2.95, 36 pgs.)

1-6: 1-(44 pgs.)-Mortal Kombat prev., 1st app. in comics. 2,6-(36 pgs.)						5.00

BRUCE JONES' OUTER EDGE
Innovation: 1993 ($2.50, B&W, one-shot)

1-Bruce Jones-c/a/script						2.50

BRUCE WAYNE: AGENT OF S.H.I.E.L.D. (Also see Marvel Vs. DC #3 & DC Vs. Marvel #4)
Marvel Comics (Amalgam): Apr, 1996 ($1.95, one-shot)

1-Chuck Dixon scripts & Cary Nord-c/a.						2.50

Brute Force #1 © MAR

Buccaneers #24 © QUA

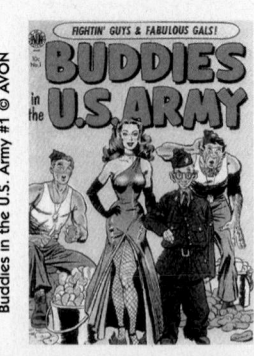

Buddies in the U.S. Army #1 © AVON

	GD 2.0	VG 4.0	FN 6.0	VF 8.0	VF/NM 9.0	NM- 9.2

BRUISER
Anthem Publications: Feb, 1994 ($2.45)

1						2.50

BRUTE, THE
Seaboard Publ. (Atlas): Feb, 1975 - No. 3, July, 1975

1-Origin & 1st app; Sekowsky-a(p)	2	4	6	8	10	12
2-Sekowsky-a(p); Fleisher-s	1	2	3	5	6	8
3-Brunner/Starlin/Weiss-a(p)	1	2	3	5	7	9

BRUTE & BABE
Ominous Press: July, 1994 - No. 2, Aug, 1994

1-($3.95, 8 tablets plus-c)-"…It Begins…"; tablet format						4.00
2-($2.50, 36 pgs.)-"Mael's Rage", 2-(40 pgs.)-Stiff additional variant-c						2.50

BRUTE FORCE
Marvel Comics: Aug, 1990 - No. 4, Nov, 1990 ($1.00, limited series)

1-4: Animal super-heroes; Delbo & DeCarlo-a						2.50

B-SIDES (The Craptacular…)
Marvel Comics: Nov, 2002 - No. 3, Jan, 2003 ($2.99, limited series)

1-3-Kieth/Weldele-a. 2-Dorkin-a (1 pg.) 2-FF cameo. 3-FF app.						3.00

BUBBLEGUM CRISIS: GRAND MAL
Dark Horse Comics: Mar, 1994 - No. 4, June, 1994 ($2.50, limited series)

1-4-Japanese manga						2.50

BUCCANEER
I. W. Enterprises: No date (1963)

I.W. Reprint #1(r-/Quality #20), #8(r-/#23): Crandall-a in each		3	6	9	16	23	30

BUCCANEERS (Formerly Kid Eternity)
Quality Comics: No. 19, Jan, 1950 - No. 27, May, 1951 (No. 24-27: 52 pgs.)

19-Captain Daring, Black Roger, Eric Falcon & Spanish Main begin; Crandall-a	48	96	144	293	484	675
20,23-Crandall-a	36	72	108	208	329	450
21-Crandall-c/a	40	80	120	235	368	500
22-Bondage-c	28	56	84	162	256	350
24-26: 24-Adam Peril, U.S.N. begins. 25-Origin & 1st app. Corsair Queen.						
26-last Spanish Main	24	48	72	139	220	300
27-Crandall-a	35	70	105	204	322	440
Super Reprint #12 (1964)-Crandall-r/#21	3	6	9	16	23	30

BUCCANEERS, THE (TV)
Dell Publishing Co.: No. 800, 1957

Four Color 800-Photo-c	7	14	21	47	76	105

BUCKAROO BANZAI (Movie)
Marvel Comics Group: Dec, 1984 - No. 2, Feb, 1985

1,2-Movie adaptation; r/Marvel Super Special #33; Texiera-c/a						3.00

BUCKAROO BANZAI: RETURN OF THE SCREW
Moonstone: 2006 - No. 3, 2006 ($3.50, limited series)

1-3: 1-Three covers by Haley, Stribling, Beck; Thompson-a						3.50
Preview (2006, 50¢) B&W preview; history of movie and spin-off projects						2.25

BUCK DUCK
Atlas Comics (ANC): June, 1953 - No. 4, Dec, 1953

1-Funny animal stories in all	15	30	45	84	127	170
2-4: 2-Ed Win-a(5)	9	18	27	52	69	85

BUCK JONES (Also see Crackajack Funnies, Famous Feature Stories, Master Comics #7 & Wow Comics #1, 1936)
Dell Publishing Co.: No. 299, Oct, 1950 - No. 850, Oct, 1957 (All Painted-c)

Four Color 299(#1)-Buck Jones & his horse Silver-B begin; painted back-c begins, ends #5						
	13	26	39	93	164	235
2(4-6/51)	7	14	21	50	83	115
3-8(10-12/52)	6	12	18	43	69	95
Four Color 460,500,546,589	6	12	18	41	66	90
Four Color 652,733,850	5	10	15	32	51	70

BUCK ROGERS (Also see Famous Funnies, Pure Oil Comics, Salerno Carnival of Comics, 24 Pages of Comics, & Vicks Comics)
Famous Funnies: Winter, 1940-41 - No. 6, Sept, 1943
NOTE: Buck Rogers first appeared in the pulp magazine Amazing Stories Vol. 3 #5 in Aug, 1928.

1-Sunday strip reprints by Rick Yager; begins with strip #190; Calkins-c						
	300	600	900	1970	3485	5000

	GD 2.0	VG 4.0	FN 6.0	VF 8.0	VF/NM 9.0	NM- 9.2

2 (7/41)-Calkins-c	129	258	387	806	1341	1875
3 (12/41), 4 (7/42)	112	224	336	700	1163	1625
5,6: 5-Story continues with Famous Funnies No. 80; Buck Rogers, Sky Roads. 6-Reprints of 1939 dailies; contains B.R. story "Crater of Doom" (2 pgs.) by Calkins not-r from Famous Funnies						
	95	190	285	594	985	1375

BUCK ROGERS
Toby Press: No. 100, Jan, 1951 - No. 9, May-June, 1951

100(#7)-All strip-r begin	30	60	90	174	275	375
101(#8), 9-All Anderson-a(1947-49-r/dailies)	23	46	69	132	209	285

BUCK ROGERS (…in the 25th Century No. 5 on) (TV)
Gold Key/Whitman No. 7 on: Oct, 1964; No. 2, July, 1979 - No. 16, May, 1982 (No #10; story was written but never released. #17 exists only as a press proof without covers and was never published)

1(10128-410, 12¢)-1st S.A. app. Buck Rogers & 1st new B. R. in comics since 1933 giveaway; painted-c; back-c pin-up	10	20	30	67	116	165
2(7/79)-6: 3,4,6-Movie adaptation; painted-c	2	4	6	9	12	15
7,11 (Whitman)	2	4	6	11	16	20
8,9 (prepack)(scarce)	3	6	9	18	27	35
12-16: 14(2/82), 15(3/82), 16(5/82)	2	4	6	8	10	12
Giant Movie Edition 11296(64pp, Whitman, $1.50), reprints GK #2-4 minus cover; tabloid size; photo-c (See Marvel Treasury)	3	6	9	19	26	34
Giant Movie Edition 02489(Western/Marvel, $1.50), reprints GK #2-4 minus cover	3	6	9	17	25	32

NOTE: Bolle a-2p,3p, Movie Ed.(p). McWilliams a-2i,3i, 5-11, Movie Ed.(i). Painted c-1-9,11-13.

BUCK ROGERS (Comics Module)
TSR, Inc.: 1990 - No. 10, 1991 ($2.95, 44 pgs.)

1-10 (1990): 1-Begin origin in 3 parts. 2-Indicia says #1. 2,3-Black Barney back-up story. 4-All Black Barney issue; B. B.-c. 5-Indicia says #6; Black Barney-c & lead story; Buck Rogers back-up story. 10-Flip book (72pgs.)						3.00

BUCKSKIN (TV)
Dell Publishing Co.: No. 1011, July, 1959 - No. 1107, June-Aug, 1960

Four Color 1011 (#1)-Photo-c	7	14	21	47	76	105
Four Color 1107-Photo-c	6	12	18	43	69	95

BUCKY O'HARE (Funny Animal)
Continuity Comics: 1988 ($5.95, graphic novel)

1-Golden-c/a(r); r/serial-Echo of Futurepast #1-6	1	2	3	4	5	7
Deluxe Hardcover ($40.00, 52 pg., 8 x 11")						40.00

BUCKY O'HARE
Continuity Comics: Jan, 1991 - No. 5, 1991 ($2.00)

1-6: 1-Michael Golden-c/a						2.50

BUDDIES IN THE U.S. ARMY
Avon Periodicals: Nov, 1952 - No. 2, 1953

1-Lawrence-c	14	28	42	80	115	150
2-Mort Lawrence-c/a	10	20	30	54	72	90

BUFFALO BEE
Dell Publishing Co.: No. 957, Nov, 1958 - No. 1061, Dec-Feb, 1959-60

Four Color 957 (#1)	8	16	24	58	97	135
Four Color 1002 (8-10/59), 1061	7	14	21	45	73	100

BUFFALO BILL (See Frontier Fighters, Super Western Comics & Western Action Thrillers)
Youthful Magazines: No. 2, Oct, 1950 - No. 9, Dec, 1951

2-Annie Oakley story	14	28	42	78	112	145
3-9: 2-4-Walter Johnson-c/a. 9-Wildey-a	10	20	30	54	72	90

BUFFALO BILL CODY (See Cody of the Pony Express)

BUFFALO BILL, JR. (TV) (See Western Roundup)
Dell/Gold Key: Jan, 1956 - No. 13, Aug-Oct, 1959; 1965 (All photo-c)

Four Color 673 (#1)	9	18	27	60	100	140
Four Color 742,766,798,828,856(11/57)	6	12	18	39	62	85
7(2-4/58)-13	5	10	15	35	55	75
1(6/65, Gold Key)-Photo-c(r/F.C. #798); photo-b/c	4	8	12	24	37	50

BUFFALO BILL PICTURE STORIES
Street & Smith Publications: June-July, 1949 - No. 2, Aug-Sept, 1949

1,2-Wildey, Powell-a in each	14	28	42	78	112	145

BUFFY THE VAMPIRE SLAYER (Based on the TV series)(Also see Tales of the Vampires)
Dark Horse Comics: 1998 - No. 63, Nov, 2003 ($2.95/$2.99)

1-Bennett-a/Watson-s; Art Adams-c	1	2	3	5	7	9
1-Variant photo-c	1	2	3	5	7	9

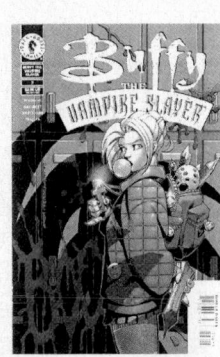

Buffy the Vampire Slayer #2
© 20th Century Fox

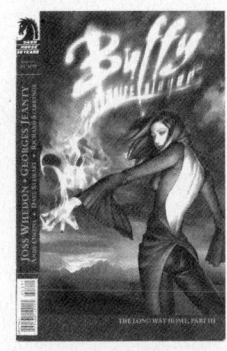

Buffy the Vampire Slayer #3
© 20th Century Fox

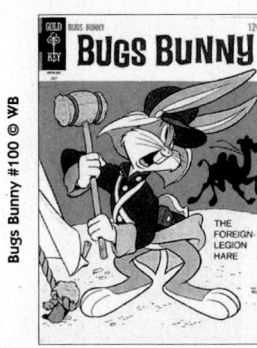

Bugs Bunny #100 © WB

	GD	VG	FN	VF	VF/NM	NM-		GD	VG	FN	VF	VF/NM	NM-
	2.0	4.0	6.0	8.0	9.0	9.2		2.0	4.0	6.0	8.0	9.0	9.2

1-Gold foil logo Art Adams-c		15.00
1-Gold foil logo photo-c		20.00
2-15-Regular and photo-c. 4-7-Gomez-a. 5,8-Green-c		5.00
16-48: 29,30-Angel x-over. 43-45-Death of Buffy. 47-Lobdell-s begin. 48-Pike returns		3.00
50-($3.50) Scooby gang battles Adam; back-up story by Watson		3.50
51-63: 51-54-Viva Las Buffy; pre-Sunnydale Buffy & Pike in Vegas		3.00

Annual '99 ($4.95)-Two stories and pin-ups ...... 1 ...... 2 ...... 3 ...... 4 ...... 5 7

...: A Stake to the Heart TPB (3/04, $12.95) r/#60-63	13.00
...: Chaos Bleeds (6/03, $2.99) Based on the video game; photo & Campbell-a	3.00
...: Creatures of Habit (3/02, $17.95) text with Horton & Paul Lee-a	18.00
...: Jonathan 1 (1/01, $2.99) two covers; Richards-a	3.00
...: Lost and Found 1 (3/02, $2.99) aftermath of Buffy's death; Richards-a	3.00
...: Lovers Walk (2/01, $2.99) short stories by various; Richards & photo-c	3.00
...: Note From the Underground (3/03, $12.95) r/#47-50	13.00
...: Omnibus Vol. 1 (7/07, $24.95, 9x6") r/Spike & Dru #3, Origin #1-3 and Buffy #51-59	25.00
...: Omnibus Vol. 2 (9/07, $24.95, 9x6") r/Buffy #60-63 and various one-shots & specials	25.00
...: Reunion (6/02, $3.50) Buffy & Angel's; Espenson-s; art by various	3.50
...: Slayer Interrupted TPB (2003, $14.95) r/#56-59	15.00
...: Tales of the Slayers (10/02, $3.50) art by Matsuda and Colan; art & photo-c	3.50
...: The Death of Buffy TPB (8/02, $15.95) r/#43-46	16.00
...: Viva Las Buffy TPB (7/03, $12.95) r/#51-54	13.00

Wizard #1/2 ...... 1 ...... 2 ...... 3 ...... 6 ...... 8 9

BUFFY THE VAMPIRE SLAYER ("Season Eight" of the TV series)
Dark Horse Comics: Mar, 2007 - Present ($2.99)

1-Joss Whedon-s/Georges Jeanty-a/Jo Chen-c	8.00
1-Variant cover by Jeanty	10.00
1-RRP with B&W Jeanty cover (edition of 1000)	70.00
1-2nd & 3rd printings with Chen-c with different credit graphics	4.00
2-6-Chen-c. 6-Faith app.; Vaughan-s	4.00
2-6-Variant-c by Jeanty	6.00

BUFFY THE VAMPIRE SLAYER: ANGEL
Dark Horse Comics: May, 1999 - No. 3, July, 1999 ($2.95, limited series)

1-3-Gomez-a; Matsuda-c & photo-c for each	3.00

BUFFY THE VAMPIRE SLAYER: GILES
Dark Horse Comics: Oct, 2000 ($2.95, one-shot)

1-Eric Powell-a; Powell & photo-c	3.00

BUFFY THE VAMPIRE SLAYER: HAUNTED
Dark Horse Comics: Dec, 2001 - No. 4, Mar, 2002 ($2.99, limited series)

1-4-Faith and the Mayor app.; Espenson-s/Richards-a	3.00
TPB (9/02, $12.95) r/series; photo-c	13.00

BUFFY THE VAMPIRE SLAYER: OZ
Dark Horse Comics: July, 2001 - No. 3, Sept, 2001 ($2.99, limited series)

1-3-Totleben & photo-c; Golden-s	3.00

BUFFY THE VAMPIRE SLAYER: SPIKE AND DRU
Dark Horse Comics: Apr, 1999; No. 2, Oct, 1999; No. 3, Dec, 2000 ($2.95)

1-3: 1,2-Photo-c. 3-Two covers (photo & Sook)	3.00

BUFFY THE VAMPIRE SLAYER: THE ORIGIN (Adapts movie screenplay)
Dark Horse Comics: Jan, 1999 - No. 3, Mar, 1999 ($2.95, limited series)

1-3-Brereton-s/Bennett-a; reg & photo-c for each	3.00

BUFFY THE VAMPIRE SLAYER: WILLOW & TARA
Dark Horse Comics: Apr, 2001 ($2.99, one-shot)

1-Terry Moore-a/Chris Golden & Amber Benson-s; Moore-c & photo-c	3.00
TPB (4/03, $9.95) r/#1 & W&T - Wilderness; photo-c	10.00

BUFFY THE VAMPIRE SLAYER: WILLOW & TARA - WILDERNESS
Dark Horse Comics: Jul, 2002 - No. 2, Sept, 2002 ($2.99, one-shot)

1,2-Chris Golden & Amber Benson-s; Jothikaumar-c & photo-c	3.00

BUG
Marvel Comics: Mar, 1997 ($2.99, one-shot)

1-Micronauts character	3.00

BUGALOOS (TV)
Charlton Comics: Sept, 1971 - No. 4, Feb, 1972

1		5	10	15	30	48	65
2-4		3	6	9	19	29	38

NOTE: No. 3(1/72) went on sale late in 1972 (after No. 4) with the 1/73 issues.

BUGBOY
Image Comics: June, 1998 ($3.95, B&W, one-shot)

1-Mark Lewis-s/a	4.00

BUGHOUSE (Satire)
Ajax/Farrell (Excellent Publ.): Mar-Apr, 1954 - No. 4, Sept-Oct, 1954

V1#1	21	42	63	120	188	255
2-4	14	28	42	76	108	140

BUGS BUNNY (See The Best of..., Camp Comics, Comic Album #2, 6, 10, 14, Dell Giant #28, 32, 46, Dynabrite, Golden Comics Digest #1, 3, 5, 6, 8, 10, 14, 15, 17, 21, 26, 30, 34, 39, 42, 47, Kite Fun Book, Large Feature Comic #8, Looney Tunes and Merry Melodies, March of Comics #44, 59, 75, 83, 97, 115, 132, 149, 160, 179, 188, 201, 220, 231, 245, 259, 273, 287, 301, 315, 329, 343, 363, 367, 380, 392, 403, 415, 428, 440, 452, 464, 476, 487, Porky Pig, Puffed Wheat, Story Hour Series #802, Super Book #14, 26 and Whitman Comic Books)

BUGS BUNNY (See Dell Giants for annuals)
Dell Publishing Co./Gold Key No. 86-218/Whitman No. 219 on: 1942 - No. 245, April, 1984

Large Feature Comic 8(1942)-(Rarely found in fine-mint condition)

	GD	VG	FN	VF	VF/NM	NM-
	186	372	558	1163	1932	2700
Four Color 33 ('43)	96	192	288	816	1508	2200
Four Color 51	32	64	96	240	445	650
Four Color 88	22	44	66	164	292	420
Four Color 123('46),142,164	15	30	45	111	198	285
Four Color 187,200,217,233	11	22	33	80	143	205
Four Color 250-Used in SOTI, pg. 309	12	24	36	84	150	215
Four Color 266,274,281,289,298('50)	9	18	27	64	110	155
Four Color 307,317(#1),327(#2),338,347,355,366,376,393						
	8	16	24	58	97	135
Four Color 407,420,432(10/52)	7	14	21	49	80	110
Four Color 498(9/53),585(9/54), 647(9/55)	6	12	18	37	59	80
Four Color 724(9/56),838(9/57),1064(12/59)	5	10	15	32	51	70
28(12-1/52-53)-30	6	12	18	37	59	80
31-50	4	8	12	28	44	60
51-85(7-9/62)	4	8	12	22	34	45
86(10/62)-88-Bugs Bunny's Showtime-(25¢, 80pgs.)	6	12	18	41	66	90
89-99	3	6	9	16	23	30
100	3	6	9	17	25	32
101-118: 108-1st Honey Bunny. 118-Last 12¢ issue	2	4	6	13	18	22
119-140	2	4	6	10	14	18
141-170	2	4	6	8	11	14
171-218	1	3	4	6	8	10
219,220,225-237(5/82): 229-Swipe of Barks story/WDC&S #223. 233(2/82)						
	1	3	6	8	11
221(9/80),222(11/80)-Pre-pack? (Scarce)	3	6	9	18	27	35
223 (1/81, 50¢-c), 224 (3/81)-Low distr.	2	4	6	10	14	18
223 (1/81, 40¢-c) Cover price error variant	3	6	9	18	28	22
238-245 (#90070 on-c, nd, nd code; pre-pack): 238(5/83), 239(6/83), 240(7/83), 241(7/83),						
242(8/83), 243(8/83), 244(3/84), 245(4/84)	2	4	6	11	16	20

NOTE: Reprints-100,102-104,110,115,123,143,144,147,167,173,175-177,179-185,187,190.

nn (Xerox Pub. Comic Digest, 1971, 100 pages, B&W) collection of one-page gags	3	6	9	20	30	40
...Comic-Go-Round 11196-(224 pgs.)($1.95)(Golden Press, 1979)						
	4	8	12	22	34	45
...Winter Fun 1(12/67-Gold Key)-Giant	5	10	15	30	48	65

BUGS BUNNY
DC Comics: June, 1990 - No. 3, Aug, 1990 ($1.00, limited series)

1-3: Daffy Duck, Elmer Fudd, others app.	4.00

BUGS BUNNY (...Monthly on-c)
DC Comics: 1993 - No. 3, 1994? ($1.95)

1-3-Bugs, Porky Pig, Daffy, Road Runner	3.50

BUGS BUNNY (Digest-size reprints from Looney Tunes)
DC Comics: 2005 - Present ($6.99, digest)

Vol. 1: What's Up Doc? - Reprints from Looney Tunes #37,41,43-45,48,52,55,57-59,63	7.00

BUGS BUNNY & PORKY PIG
Gold Key: Sept, 1965 (Paper-c, giant, 100 pgs.)

1(30025-509)		7	14	21	49	80	110

BUGS BUNNY'S ALBUM (See Bugs Bunny, Four Color 498,585,647,724)

BUGS BUNNY LIFE STORY ALBUM (See Bugs Bunny, Four Color No. 838)

BUGS BUNNY MERRY CHRISTMAS (See Bugs Bunny, Four Color No. 1064)

BUILDING, THE
Kitchen Sink Press: 1987; 2000 (8 1/2" x 11" sepia toned graphic novel)

nn-Will Eisner-s/c/a	10.00
nn-(DC Comics, 9/00, $9.95) reprints 1987 edition	10.00

Bulletman #1 © FAW

Bullet Points #4 © MAR

Buster Crabbe #12 © FF

	GD 2.0	VG 4.0	FN 6.0	VF 8.0	VF/NM 9.0	NM- 9.2

BULLET CROW, FOWL OF FORTUNE
Eclipse Comics: Mar, 1987 - No. 2, Apr, 1987 ($2.00, B&W, limited series)

	GD 2.0	VG 4.0	FN 6.0	VF 8.0	VF/NM 9.0	NM- 9.2
1,2-The Comic Reader-r & new-a						2.50

BULLETMAN (See Fawcett Miniatures, Master Comics, Mighty Midget Comics, Nickel Comics & XMas Comics)
Fawcett Publications: Sum, 1941 - #12, 2/12/43; #14, Spr, 1946 - #16, Fall, 1946 (No #13)

	GD 2.0	VG 4.0	FN 6.0	VF 8.0	VF/NM 9.0	NM- 9.2
1-Silver metallic-c	376	752	1128	2444	4322	6200
2-Raboy-c	162	324	486	1013	1682	2350
3,5-Raboy-c each	119	238	357	744	1235	1725
4	97	194	291	606	1003	1400
6-10: 7-Ghost Stories told by night watchman of cemetery begins; Eisnerish-a; hidden message "Chic Stone is a jerk". 10-Intro. Bulletdog	79	158	237	494	822	1150
11,12,14-16 (nn 13): 12-Robot-c	60	120	180	375	625	875

NOTE: *Mac Raboy* c-1-3, 5, 6, 10. "Bulletman the Flying Detective" on cover #8 on.

BULLET POINTS
Marvel Comics: Jan, 2007 - No. 5 ($2.99, limited series)

	GD 2.0	VG 4.0	FN 6.0	VF 8.0	VF/NM 9.0	NM- 9.2
1-5: 1-Steve Rogers becomes Iron Man; Straczynski-s/Edwards-a. 4,5-Galactus app.						3.00
TPB (2007, $13.99) r/#1-5; layout pages by Edwards						14.00

BULLETPROOF MONK (Inspired the 2003 film)
Image Comics (Flypaper Press): 1998 - No. 3, 1999 ($2.95, limited series)

	GD 2.0	VG 4.0	FN 6.0	VF 8.0	VF/NM 9.0	NM- 9.2
1-3-Oeming-a						3.00
...:-Tales of the BPM (3/03, $2.95) Flip book; 2 covers by Sale; art by Sale, Oeming, Dave Johnson; Seann William Scott afterword						3.00
TPB (2002, $9.95) r/#1-3; foreword by John Woo						10.00

BULLETS AND BRACELETS (Also see Marvel Versus DC #3 & DC Versus Marvel #4)
Marvel Comics (Amalgam): Apr, 1996 ($1.95)

	GD 2.0	VG 4.0	FN 6.0	VF 8.0	VF/NM 9.0	NM- 9.2
1-John Ostrander script & Gary Frank-c/a						2.50

BULLSEYE: GREATEST HITS (Daredevil villain)
Marvel Comics: Nov, 2004 - No. 5, Mar, 2005 ($2.99, limted series)

	GD 2.0	VG 4.0	FN 6.0	VF 8.0	VF/NM 9.0	NM- 9.2
1-5-Origin of Bullseye; Steve Dillon-a/Deodato-c. 3-Punisher app.						3.00
TPB (2005, $13.99) r/#1-5						14.00

BULLS-EYE (Cody of The Pony Express No. 8 on)
Mainline No. 1-5/Charlton No. 6,7: 7-8/54-No. 5, 3-4/55; No. 6, 6/55; No. 7, 8/55

	GD 2.0	VG 4.0	FN 6.0	VF 8.0	VF/NM 9.0	NM- 9.2
1-S&K-c, 2 pgs.-a	55	110	165	344	572	800
2-S&K-c/a	46	92	138	281	466	650
3-5-S&K-c/a(2 each). 4-Last pre-code issue (1-2/55). 5-Censored issue with tomahawks removed in battle scene	40	80	120	240	383	525
6-S&K-c/a	35	70	105	201	318	435
7-S&K-c/a(3)	40	80	120	240	383	525

BULLS-EYE COMICS (Formerly Komik Pages #10; becomes Kayo #12)
Harry 'A' Chesler: No. 11, 1944

	GD 2.0	VG 4.0	FN 6.0	VF 8.0	VF/NM 9.0	NM- 9.2
11-Origin K-9, Green Knight's sidekick, Lance; The Green Knight, Lady Satan, Yankee Doodle Jones app.	43	86	129	262	431	600

BULLWHIP GRIFFIN (See Movie Comics)

BULLWINKLE (...and Rocky No. 22 on; See March of Comics #233 and Rocky & Bullwinkle) (TV) (Jay Ward)
Dell/Gold Key: 3-5/62 - #11, 4/74; #12, 6/76 - #19, 3/78; #20, 4/79 - #25, 2/80

	GD 2.0	VG 4.0	FN 6.0	VF 8.0	VF/NM 9.0	NM- 9.2
Four Color 1270 (3-5/62)	18	36	54	132	234	335
01-090-209 (Dell, 7-9/62)	14	28	42	103	184	265
1(11/62, Gold Key)	13	26	39	93	164	235
2(2/63)	8	16	24	58	97	135
3(4/72)-11(4/74-Gold Key)	5	10	15	32	51	70
12-14: 12(6/76)-Reprints. 13(9/76), 14-New stories	3	6	9	16	23	30
15-25	2	4	6	10	14	18
Mother Moose Nursery Pomes 01-530-207 (5-7/62, Dell)	17	34	51	124	220	315

NOTE: *Reprints: 6, 7, 20-24.*

BULLWINKLE (...& Rocky No. 2 on)(TV)
Charlton Comics: July, 1970 - No. 7, July, 1971

	GD 2.0	VG 4.0	FN 6.0	VF 8.0	VF/NM 9.0	NM- 9.2
1	6	12	18	41	66	90
2-7	4	8	12	28	44	60

BULLWINKLE AND ROCKY
Star Comics/Marvel Comics No. 3 on: Nov, 1987 - No. 9, Mar, 1989

	GD 2.0	VG 4.0	FN 6.0	VF 8.0	VF/NM 9.0	NM- 9.2
1-9: Boris & Natasha in all. 3,5,8-Dudley Do-Right app. 4-Reagan-c						4.00
Marvel Moosterworks (1/92, $4.95)	1	3	4	6	8	10

BUMMER
Fantagraphics Books: June, 1995 ($3.50, B&W, mature)

	GD 2.0	VG 4.0	FN 6.0	VF 8.0	VF/NM 9.0	NM- 9.2
1						3.50

BUNNY (Also see Harvey Pop Comics)
Harvey Publications: Dec, 1966 - No. 20, Dec, 1971; No. 21, Nov, 1976

	GD 2.0	VG 4.0	FN 6.0	VF 8.0	VF/NM 9.0	NM- 9.2
1-68 pg. Giants begin	8	16	24	52	86	120
2-10	4	8	12	28	44	60
11-18: 18-Last 68 pg. Giant	4	8	12	26	41	55
19-21-52 pg. Giants: 21-Fruitman app.	4	8	12	24	37	50

BURKE'S LAW (TV)
Dell Publ.: 1-3/64; No. 2, 5-7/64; No. 3, 3-5/65 (All have Gene Barry photo-c)

	GD 2.0	VG 4.0	FN 6.0	VF 8.0	VF/NM 9.0	NM- 9.2
1-Photo-c	5	10	15	35	55	75
2,3-Photo-c	4	8	12	24	37	50

BURNING ROMANCES (See Fox Giants)

BUSTER BEAR
Quality Comics Group (Arnold Publ.): Dec, 1953 - No. 10, June, 1955

	GD 2.0	VG 4.0	FN 6.0	VF 8.0	VF/NM 9.0	NM- 9.2
1-Funny animal	11	22	33	60	83	105
2	7	14	21	35	43	50
3-10	6	12	18	28	34	40
I.W. Reprint #9,10 (Super on inside)	2	4	6	9	13	16

BUSTER BROWN COMICS (See Promotional Comics section)

BUSTER BUNNY
Standard Comics(Animated Cartoons)/Pines: Nov, 1949 - No. 16, Oct, 1953

	GD 2.0	VG 4.0	FN 6.0	VF 8.0	VF/NM 9.0	NM- 9.2
1-Frazetta 1 pg. text illo.	11	22	33	60	83	105
2	7	14	21	35	43	50
3-14,16	6	12	18	28	34	40
15-Racist-c	8	16	24	40	50	60

BUSTER CRABBE (TV)
Famous Funnies Publ.: Nov, 1951 - No. 12, 1953

	GD 2.0	VG 4.0	FN 6.0	VF 8.0	VF/NM 9.0	NM- 9.2
1-1st app.(?) Frazetta anti-drug ad; text story about Buster Crabbe & Billy the Kid	40	80	120	235	368	500
2-Williamson/Evans-c; text story about Wild Bill Hickok & Pecos Bill	38	76	114	216	343	470
3-Williamson/Evans-c/a	40	80	120	235	368	500
4-Frazetta-c/a, 1pg.; bondage-c	48	96	144	293	484	675
5-Frazetta-c; Williamson/Krenkel/Orlando-a, 11pgs. (per Mr. Williamson)	122	244	366	763	1269	1775
6,8	19	38	57	109	172	235
7-Frazetta one pg. ad	19	38	57	112	176	240
9-One pg. Frazetta Boy Scouts ad (1st?)	16	32	48	92	144	195
10-12	12	24	36	69	97	125

NOTE: Eastern Color sold 3 dozen each NM file copies of #s 9-12 a few years ago.

BUSTER CRABBE (The Amazing Adventures of...)(Movie star)
Lev Gleason Publications: Dec, 1953 - No. 4, June, 1954

	GD 2.0	VG 4.0	FN 6.0	VF 8.0	VF/NM 9.0	NM- 9.2
1,4: 1-Photo-c. 4-Flash Gordon-c	21	42	63	122	191	260
2,3-Toth-a	19	38	57	109	172	235

BUTCH CASSIDY
Skywald Publications: June, 1971 - No. 3, Oct, 1971 (52 pgs.)

	GD 2.0	VG 4.0	FN 6.0	VF 8.0	VF/NM 9.0	NM- 9.2
1-Pre-code reprints and new material; Red Mask reprint, retitled Maverick; Bolle-a; Sutton-a	3	6	9	14	19	24
2,3: 2-Whip Wilson-r. 3-Dead Canyon Days reprint/Crack Western No. 63; Sundance Kid app.; Crandall-a	2	4	6	9	13	16

BUTCH CASSIDY (...& the Wild Bunch)
Avon Periodicals: 1951

	GD 2.0	VG 4.0	FN 6.0	VF 8.0	VF/NM 9.0	NM- 9.2
1-Kinstler-c/a	19	38	57	109	172	235

NOTE: *Reinman story; Issue number on inside spine.*

BUTCH CASSIDY (See Fun-In No. 11 & Western Adventure Comics)

BUTCHER, THE (Also see Brave and the Bold, 2nd Series)
DC Comics: May, 1990 - No. 5, Sept, 1990 ($1.50, mature)

	GD 2.0	VG 4.0	FN 6.0	VF 8.0	VF/NM 9.0	NM- 9.2
1-5: 1-No indicia inside						2.50

BUTCHER KNIGHT
Image Comics (Top Cow): Jan, 2001 - No. 4, June, 2001 ($2.95, limited series)

	GD 2.0	VG 4.0	FN 6.0	VF 8.0	VF/NM 9.0	NM- 9.2
Preview (B&W, 16 pgs.) Dwayne Turner-c/a						2.25
1-4-Dwayne Turner-c/a						3.00

BUZ SAWYER (Sweeney No. 4 on)
Standard Comics: June, 1948 - No. 3, 1949

	GD 2.0	VG 4.0	FN 6.0	VF 8.0	VF/NM 9.0	NM- 9.2
1-Roy Crane-a	24	48	72	139	220	300
2-Intro his pal Sweeney	15	30	45	85	130	175

Buzzy #2 © DC

Cable #2 © MAR

Cage V3 #1 © MAR

	GD 2.0	VG 4.0	FN 6.0	VF 8.0	VF/NM 9.0	NM- 9.2
3	12	24	36	67	94	120

BUZ SAWYER'S PAL, ROSCOE SWEENEY (See Sweeney)

BUZZ, THE (Also see Spider-Girl)
Marvel Comics: July, 2000 - No. 3, Sept, 2000 ($2.99, limited series)

1-3-Buscema-a/DeFalco & Frenz-s						3.00

BUZZ BUZZ COMICS MAGAZINE
Horse Press: May, 1996 ($4.95, B&W, over-sized magazine)

1-Paul Pope-c/a/scripts; Moebius-a						5.00

BUZZY (See All Funny Comics)
National Periodical Publications/Detective Comics: Winter, 1944-45 - No. 75, 1-2/57; No. 76, 10/57; No. 77, 10/58

	GD	VG	FN	VF	VF/NM	NM-
1 (52 pgs. begin); "America's favorite teenster"	31	62	93	178	282	385
2 (Spr, 1945)	15	30	45	90	140	190
3-5	12	24	36	69	97	125
6-10	10	20	30	56	76	95
11-20	9	18	27	50	65	80
21-30	8	16	24	42	54	65
31,35-38	8	16	24	40	50	60
32-34,39-Last 52 pgs. Scribbly story by Mayer in each (these four stories were done for Scribbly #14 which was delayed for a year)	8	16	24	44	57	70
40-77: 62-Last precode (2/55)	7	14	21	37	46	55

BUZZY THE CROW (See Harvey Comics Hits #60 & 62, Harvey Hits #18 & Paramount Animated Comics #1)

BY BIZARRE HANDS
Dark Horse Comics: Apr, 1994 - No. 3, June, 1994 ($2.50, B&W, mature)

1-3: Lansdale stories						2.50

CABBOT: BLOODHUNTER (Also see Bloodstrike & Bloodstrike: Assassin)
Maximum Press: Jan, 1997 ($2.50, one-shot)

1-Rick Veitch-a/script; Platt-c; Thor, Chapel & Prophet cameos						2.50

CABLE (See Ghost Rider &..., & New Mutants #87) (Title becomes Soldier X)
Marvel Comics: May, 1993 - No. 107, Sept, 2002 ($3.50/$1.95/$1.50-$2.25)

1-($3.50, 52 pgs.)-Gold foil & embossed-c; Thibert a-1-4p; c-1-3						5.00
2-15: 3-Extra 16 pg. X-Men/Avengers ann. preview. 4-Liefeld-a assist; last Thibert-a(p). 6-8-Reveals that Baby Nathan is Cable; gives background on Stryfe. 9-Omega Red-c/story. 11-Bound-in trading card sheet						3.50
16-Newsstand edition						2.50
16-Enhanced edition						5.00
17-20-($1.95)-Deluxe edition, 20-w/bound in '95 Fleer Ultra cards						3.00
17-20-($1.50)-Standard edition						2.50
21-24, 26-44, -1(7/97): 21-Begin $1.95-c; return from Age of Apocalypse. 24-Grizzly dies. 28-vs. Sugarman; Mr. Sinister app. 30-X-Man-c/app.; Exodus app. 31-vs. X-Man. 32-Post app. 33-Post-c/app; Mandarin app (flashback); includes "Onslaught Update". 34-Onslaught x-over; Hulk-c/app; Apocalypse app. (cont'd in Hulk #444). 35-Onslaught x-over; Apocalypse vs. Cable. 36-w/card insert. 38-Weapon X-c/app; Psycho Man & Micronauts app. 40-Scott Clark-a(p). 41-Bishop-c/app.						3.00
25 ($3.50)-Foil gatefold-c						4.00
45-49,51-74: 45-Operation Zero Tolerance. 51-1st Casey-s. 54-Black Panther. 55-Domino-c/app. 62-Nick Fury-c/app.63-Stryfe-c/app. 67,68-Avengers-c/app. 71,73-Liefeld-a						2.50
50-($2.99) Double sized w/wraparound-c						3.00
75 -($2.99) Liefeld-c/a; Apocalypse: The Twelve x-over						3.00
76-79: 76-Apocalypse: The Twelve x-over						2.50
80-96: 80-Begin $2.25-c. 87-Mystique-c/app.						2.50
97-99,101-107: 97-Tischman-s/Kordey-a/c begin						2.50
100-($3.99) Dialogue-free 'Nuff Said back-up story						4.00
.../Machine Man '98 Annual ($2.99) Wraparound-c						3.00
.../X-Force '96 Annual ($2.95) Wraparound-c						3.00
...'99 Annual ($3.50) vs. Sinister; computer photo-c						3.50
...Second Genesis 1 (9/99, $3.99) r/new Mutants #99, 100 and X-Force #1; Liefeld-c						4.00
...: The End (2002, $14.99, TPB) r/#101-107						15.00

CABLE - BLOOD AND METAL (Also see New Mutants #87 & X-Force #8)
Marvel Comics: Oct, 1992 - No. 2, Nov, 1992 ($2.50, limited series, 52 pgs.)

1-Fabian Nicieza scripts; John Romita, Jr.-c/a in both; Cable vs. Stryfe; 2nd app. of The Wild Pack (becomes The Six Pack); wraparound-c						4.00
2-Prelude to X-Cutioner's Song						3.00

CABLE/DEADPOOL ("Cable & Deadpool" on cover)
Marvel Comics: May, 2004 - Present ($2.99)

1-45: 1-Nicieza-s/Liefeld-c. 7-9-X-Men app. 17-House of M. 21-Heroes For Hire app. 30,31-Civil War. 30-Great Lakes Avengers app. 33-Liefeld-a. 43,44-Wolverine app.						3.00
... Vol. 1: If Looks Could Kill TPB (2004, $14.99) r/#1-6						15.00

	GD 2.0	VG 4.0	FN 6.0	VF 8.0	VF/NM 9.0	NM- 9.2
... Vol. 2: The Burnt Offering TPB (2005, $14.99) r/#7-12						15.00
... Vol. 3: The Human Race TPB (2005, $14.99) r/#13-18						15.00
... Vol. 4: Bosom Buddies TPB (2006, $14.99) r/#19-24						15.00
... Vol. 5: Living Legends TPB (2006, $13.99) r/#25-29						14.00
... Vol. 6: Paved With Good Intentions TPB (2007, $14.99) r/#30-35						15.00
... Vol. 7: Separation Anxiety TPB (2007, $17.99) r/#36-42; sketch pages						18.00

CADET GRAY OF WEST POINT (See Dell Giants)

CADILLACS & DINOSAURS (TV)
Marvel Comics (Epic Comics): Nov, 1990 - No. 6, Apr, 1991 ($2.50, limited series)

1-6: r/Xenozoic Tales in color w/new-c						3.00
...In 3-D #1 (7/92, $3.95, Kitchen Sink)-With glasses						6.00

CADILLACS AND DINOSAURS (TV)
Topps Comics: V2#1, Feb, 1994 - V2#9, 1995 ($2.50, limited series)

V2#1-($2.95)-Collector's edition w/Stout-c & bound-in poster; Buckler-a; foil stamped logo; Giordano-a in all						6.00
V2#1-9: 1-Newsstand edition w/Giordano-c. 2,3-Collector's editions w/Stout-c & posters. 2,3-Newsstand ed. w/Giordano-c; w/o posters. 4-6-Collectors & Newsstand editions; Kieth-c. 7-9-Linsner-c						3.00

CAGE (Also see Hero for Hire, Power Man & Punisher)
Marvel Comics: Apr, 1992 - No. 20, Nov, 1993 ($1.25)

1,3,10,12: 3-Punisher-c & minor app. 10-Rhino & Hulk-c/app. 12-(52 pgs.)-Iron Fist app.						3.00
2,4-9,11,13-20: 9-Rhino-c/story; Hulk cameo						2.50

CAGE (Volume 3)
Marvel Comics (MAX): Mar, 2002 - No. 5, Sept, 2002 ($2.99, mature)

1-5-Corben-c/a; Azzarello-s						3.00
HC (2002, $19.99, with dustjacket) r/#1-5; intro. by Darius James; sketch pages						20.00
SC (2003, $13.99) r/#1-5; intro. by Darius James						14.00

CAGED HEAT 3000 (Movie)
Roger Corman's Cosmic Comics: Nov, 1995 - No. 3, Jan, 1996 ($2.50)

1-3: Adaptation of film						2.50

CAGES
Tundra Publ.: 1991 - No. 10, May, 1996 ($3.50/$3.95/$4.95, limited series)

	GD	VG	FN	VF	VF/NM	NM-
1-Dave McKean-c/a in all	2	4	6	8	10	12
2-Misprint exists	1	2	3	5	6	8
3-9: 5-$3.95-c begins						4.00
10-($4.95)						5.00

CAIN'S HUNDRED (TV)
Dell Publishing Co.: May-July, 1962 - No. 2, Sept-Nov, 1962

	GD	VG	FN	VF	VF/NM	NM-
nn(01-094-207)	3	6	9	20	30	40
2	3	6	9	16	22	28

CAIN/VAMPIRELLA FLIP BOOK
Harris Comics: Oct, 1994 ($6.95, one-shot, squarebound)

nn-contains Cain #3 & #4; flip book is r/Vampirella story from 1993 Creepy Fearbook	1	2	3	5	7	9

CALIBER PRESENTS
Caliber Press: Jan, 1989 - No. 24, 1991 ($1.95/$2.50, B&W, 52 pgs.)

	GD	VG	FN	VF	VF/NM	NM-
1-Anthology; 1st issue by Vigil; Tim Vigil-c/a	6	12	18	37	59	80
2-Deadworld story; Tim Vigil-a	2	4	6	9	13	16
3-24: 15-24 ($3.50, 68 pgs.)						3.50

CALIBER PRESENTS: CINDERELLA ON FIRE
Caliber Press: 1994 ($2.95, B&W, mature)

1						3.00

CALIBER SPOTLIGHT
Caliber Press: May, 1995 ($2.95, B&W)

1-Kabuki app						3.50

CALIBRATIONS
Caliber: 1996 - No. 5 (99¢, anthology)

1-5: 1-Jill Thompson-c/a. 1,2-Atmospherics by Warren Ellis						2.50

CALIFORNIA GIRLS
Eclipse Comics: June, 1987 - No. 8, May, 1988 ($2.00, 40 pgs, B&W)

1-8: All contain color paper dolls						3.00

CALL, THE
Marvel Comics: June, 2003 - No. 4, Sept, 2003 ($2.25)

1-4-Austen-s/Olliffe-a						2.50

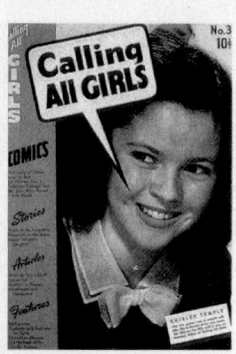

Calling All Girls #3 © PMI

Camera Comics #2 © USCPC

Candy Comics #3 © WHW

	GD 2.0	VG 4.0	FN 6.0	VF 8.0	VF/NM 9.0	NM- 9.2

CALLING ALL BOYS (Tex Granger No. 18 on)
Parents' Magazine Institute: Jan, 1946 - No. 17, May, 1948 (Photo c-1-5,7,8)

	GD 2.0	VG 4.0	FN 6.0	VF 8.0	VF/NM 9.0	NM- 9.2
1	14	28	42	80	115	150
2-Contains Roy Rogers article	8	16	24	44	57	70
3-7,9,11,14-17: 6-Painted-c. 11-Rin Tin Tin photo on-c; Tex Granger begins. 14-J. Edgar Hoover photo on-c. 15-Tex Granger-c begin	7	14	21	35	43	50
8-Milton Caniff story	9	18	27	50	65	80
10-Gary Cooper photo on-c	9	18	27	47	61	75
12-Bob Hope photo on-c	13	26	39	74	105	135
13-Bing Crosby photo on-c	11	22	33	64	90	115

CALLING ALL GIRLS
Parents' Magazine Institute: Sept, 1941 - No. 89, Sept, 1949 (Part magazine, part comic)

1	17	34	51	98	154	210
2-Photo-c	10	20	30	56	76	95
3-Shirley Temple photo-c	14	28	42	76	108	140
4-10: 4,5,7,9-Photo-c. 9-Flag-c	9	18	27	47	61	75
11-Tina Thayer photo-c; Mickey Rooney photo-b/c; B&W photo inside of Gary Cooper as Lou Gehrig in "Pride of Yankees"	10	20	30	56	76	95
12-20	8	16	24	40	50	60
21-39,41-43(10/11/45)-Last issue with comics	7	14	21	37	46	55
40-Liz Taylor photo-c	19	38	57	112	176	240
44-51(7/46)-Last comic book size issue	6	12	18	29	36	42
52-89	5	10	15	23	28	32

NOTE: *Jack Sparling* art in many issues; becomes a girls' magazine "Senior Prom" with #90.

CALLING ALL KIDS (Also see True Comics)
Parents' Magazine Institute: Dec-Jan, 1945-46 - No. 26, Aug, 1949

1-Funny animal	14	28	42	80	115	150
2	8	16	24	44	57	70
3-10	7	14	21	35	43	50
11-26	6	12	18	31	38	45

CALL OF DUTY, THE : THE BROTHERHOOD
Marvel Comics: Aug, 2002 - No. 6, Jan, 2003 ($2.25)

1-Exploits of NYC Fire Dept.; Finch-c/a; Austen & Bruce Jones-s		4.00
2-6-Austen-s		2.50
...Vol 1: The Brotherhood & The Wagon TPB (2002, $14.99) r/#1-6 & ...The Wagon #1-4		15.00

CALL OF DUTY, THE : THE PRECINCT
Marvel Comics: Sept, 2002 - No. 5, Jan, 2003 ($2.25, limited series)

1-Exploits of NYC Police Dept.; Finch-c; Bruce Jones-s/Mandrake-a		3.00
2-4		2.50
...Vol 2: The Precinct TPB (2003, $9.99) r/#1-4		10.00

CALL OF DUTY, THE : THE WAGON
Marvel Comics: Oct, 2002 - No. 4, Jan, 2003 ($2.25, limited series)

1-4-Exploits of NYC EMS Dept.; Finch-c; Austen-s/Zelzej-a		2.50

CALVIN (See Li'l Kids)

CALVIN & THE COLONEL (TV)
Dell Publishing Co.: No. 1354, Apr-June, 1962 - No. 2, July-Sept, 1962

Four Color 1354(#1)	8	16	24	56	93	130
2	6	12	18	39	62	85

CAMELOT 3000
DC Comics: Dec, 1982 - No. 11, July, 1984; No. 12, Apr, 1985 (Direct sales, maxi series, Mando paper)

1-12: 1-Mike Barr scripts & Brian Bolland-c/a begin. 5-Intro Knights of New Camelot		3.00
TPB (1988, $12.95) r/#1-12		13.00

NOTE: *Austin* a-7i-12i. *Bolland* a-1-12p; c-1-12.

CAMERA COMICS
U.S. Camera Publishing Corp./ME: July, 1944 - No. 9, Summer, 1946

nn (7/44)	25	50	75	145	228	310
nn (9/44)	18	36	54	107	169	230
1(10/44)-The Grey Comet (slightly smaller page size than subsequent issues)	18	36	54	107	169	230
2-16 pgs. of photos with 32 pgs. of comics	14	28	42	82	121	160
3-Nazi WW II-c; photos	14	28	42	82	121	160
4-9: All 1/3 photos	13	26	39	74	105	135

CAMP CANDY (TV)
Marvel Comics: May, 1990 - No. 6, Oct, 1990 ($1.00, limited series)

1-6: Post-c/a(p); featuring John Candy		4.00

CAMP COMICS
Dell Publishing Co.: Feb, 1942 - No. 3, April, 1942 (All have photo-c)

	GD 2.0	VG 4.0	FN 6.0	VF 8.0	VF/NM 9.0	NM- 9.2
1- "Seaman Sy Wheeler" by Kelly, 7 pgs.; Bugs Bunny app.; Mark Twain adaptation (scarce)	81	162	243	506	841	1175
2-Kelly-a, 12 pgs.; Bugs Bunny app.; classic-c	81	162	243	506	841	1175
3-(Scarce)-Dave Berg & Walt Kelly-a	62	124	186	388	644	900

CAMP RUNAMUCK (TV)
Dell Publishing Co.: Apr, 1966

1-Photo-c	4	8	12	21	32	42

CAMPUS LOVES
Quality Comics Group (Comic Magazines): Dec, 1949 - No. 5, Aug, 1950

1-Ward-c/a (9 pgs.)	35	70	105	204	322	440
2-Ward-c/a	26	52	78	152	239	325
3-5	14	28	42	81	118	155

NOTE: *Gustavson* a-1-5. Photo c-3-5.

CAMPUS ROMANCE (...Romances on cover)
Avon Periodicals/Realistic: Sept-Oct, 1949 - No. 3, Feb-Mar, 1950

1-Walter Johnson-a; c/Avon paperback #348	26	52	78	150	235	320
2-Grandenetti-a; c/Avon paperback #151	18	36	54	105	165	225
3-c/Avon paperback #201	18	36	54	105	165	225
Realistic reprint	9	18	27	52	69	85

CANADA DRY PREMIUMS (See Swamp Fox, The, & Terry & The Pirates in the Promotional Comics section)

CANCELLED COMIC CAVALCADE (See the Promotional Comics section)

CANDID TALES (Also see Bold Stories & It Rhymes With Lust)
Kirby Publ. Co.: April, 1950; June, 1950 (Digest size) (144 pgs.) (Full color)

nn-(Scarce) Contains Wood female pirate story, 15 pgs., and 14 pgs. in June issue; Powell-a	100	200	300	625	1038	1450

NOTE: Another version exists with Dr. Kilmore by Wood; no female pirate story.

CANDY
William H. Wise & Co.: Fall, 1944 - No. 3, Spring, 1945

1-Two Scoop Scuttle stories by Wolverton	40	80	120	235	368	500
2,3-Scoop Scuttle by Wolverton, 2-4 pgs.	26	52	78	152	239	325

CANDY (Teen-age)(Also see Police Comics #37)
Quality Comics Group (Comic Magazines): Autumn, 1947 - No. 64, Jul, 1956

1-Gustavson-a	23	46	69	135	213	290
2-Gustavson-a	14	28	42	76	108	140
3-10	10	20	30	54	72	90
11-30	8	16	24	40	50	60
31-64: 64-Ward-c(p)?	7	14	21	35	43	50
Super Reprint No. 2,10,12,16,17,18('63- '64):17-Candy #12						
	2	4	6	10	14	18

NOTE: *Jack Cole* 1-2 pg. art in many issues.

CANNON (See Heroes, Inc. Presents Cannon)

CANNON: DAWN OF WAR (Michael Turner's...)
Aspen MLT, Inc.: Nov, 2004 ($2.99)

1-Turnbull-a; two covers by Turnbull and Turner		3.00

CANNONBALL COMICS
Rural Home Publishing Co.: Feb, 1945 - No. 2, Mar, 1945

1-The Crash Kid, Thunderbrand, The Captive Prince & Crime Crusader begin; skull-c	90	180	270	563	932	1300
2-Devil-c	67	134	201	419	697	975

CANTEEN KATE (See All Picture All True Love Story & Fightin' Marines)
St. John Publishing Co.: June, 1952 - No. 3, Nov, 1952

1-Matt Baker-c/a	66	132	198	413	682	950
2-Matt Baker-c/a	44	88	132	268	439	610
3-(Rare)-Used in POP, pg. 75; Baker-c/a	51	102	153	311	511	710

CAPER
DC Comics: Dec, 2003 - No. 12, Nov, 2004 ($2.95, limited series)

1-12: 1-4-Judd Winick-s/Farel Dalrymple-a. 5-8-John Severin-a. 9-12-Fowler-a		3.00

CAPES
Image Comics: Sept, 2003 - No. 3, Nov, 2003 ($3.50)

1-3-Robert Kirkman-s/Mark Englert-a/c		3.50

CAP'N QUICK & A FOOZLE (Also see Eclipse Mag. & Monthly)
Eclipse Comics: July, 1984 - No. 3, Nov, 1985 ($1.50, color, Baxter paper)

1-3-Rogers-c/a		3.00

CAPTAIN ACTION (Toy)
National Periodical Publications: Oct-Nov, 1968 - No. 5, June-July, 1969 (Based on Ideal toy)

Captain Aero Comics V2 #2 © HOKE

Captain America #115 © MAR

Captain America #431 © MAR

	GD 2.0	VG 4.0	FN 6.0	VF 8.0	VF/NM 9.0	NM- 9.2
1-Origin; Wood-a; Superman-c app.	7	14	21	49	80	110
2,3,5-Kane/Wood-a	6	12	18	39	62	85
4	5	10	15	32	51	70

CAPTAIN AERO COMICS (Samson No. 1-6; also see Veri Best Sure Fire & Veri Best Sure Shot Comics)
Holyoke Publishing Co.: V1#7(#1), Dec, 1941 - V2#4(#10), Jan, 1943; V3#9(#11), Sept, 1943 -V4#3(#17), Oct, 1944; #21, Dec, 1944 - #26, Aug, 1946 (No #18-20)

V1#7(#1)-Flag-Man & Solar, Master of Magic, Captain Aero, Cap Stone, Adventurer begin; Nazi WWII-c	176	352	528	1100	1325	2550
8,10: 8(#2)-Pals of Freedom app. 10(#4)-Origin The Gargoyle; Kubert-a	90	180	270	563	932	1300
9(#3)-Hitler-sty; Catman back-c; Alias X begins; Pals of Freedom app.	100	200	300	625	1038	1450
11,12(#5,6)-Kubert-a; Miss Victory in #6	72	144	216	450	750	1050
V2#1,2(#7,8): 8-Origin The Red Cross; Miss Victory app.; Brodsky-c(i)	43	86	129	262	431	600
3(#9)-Miss Victory app.	40	80	120	244	392	540
4(#10)-Miss Victory app.; Japanese WWII-c	34	68	102	199	315	430
V3#9 - V3#12(#11-14): 9-Quinlan Japanese WWII-c; Miss Victory app.	28	56	84	162	256	350
V3#13(#15),V4#2(#16): Schomburg Japanese WWII-c. 13-Miss Victory app.	30	60	90	174	275	375
V4#3(#17), 21-24-L. B. Cole Japanese WWII covers. 22-Intro/origin Mighty Mite.	50	100	150	305	503	700
25-L B. Cole SciFi-c	50	100	150	305	503	700
26-L B. Cole SciFi-c; Palais-a(2) (scarce)	103	206	309	644	1072	1500

NOTE: *L.B. Cole* c-17. *Hollingsworth* a-23. *Infantino* a-23, 26. *Schomburg* c-15, 16.

CAPTAIN AMERICA (See Adventures of…, All-Select, All Winners, Aurora, Avengers #4, Blood and Glory, Captain Britain 16-20, Giant-Size…, The Invaders, Marvel Double Feature, Marvel Fanfare, Marvel Mystery, Marvel Super-Action, Marvel Super Heroes V2#3, Marvel Team-Up, Marvel Treasury Special, Power Record Comics, Ultimates, USA Comics, Young Allies & Young Men)

CAPTAIN AMERICA (Formerly Tales of Suspense #1-99) (Captain America and the Falcon #134-223 & Steve Rogers: Captain America #444-454 appears on cover only)
Marvel Comics Group: No. 100, Apr, 1968 - No. 454, Aug, 1996

100-Flashback on Cap's revival with Avengers & Sub-Mariner; story continued from Tales of Suspense #99; Kirby-c/a begins	24	48	72	175	313	450
101-The Sleeper-c/story; Red Skull app.	7	14	21	50	83	115
102-104: 102-Sleeper-c/s. 103,104-Red Skull-c/sty	6	12	18	39	62	85
105-108	5	10	15	32	51	70
109-Origin Capt. America retold	7	14	21	49	80	110
109-2nd printing (1994)	2	4	6	8	10	12
110-Rick becomes Cap's partner; Hulk x-over	9	18	27	63	107	150
111,113-Classic Steranko-c/a: 111-Death of Steve Rogers. 113-Cap's funeral	8	16	24	54	90	125
112-S.A. recovery retold; last Kirby-c/a	4	8	12	28	44	60
114-116,118-120: 115-Last 12¢ issue	3	6	9	20	30	40
117-1st app. The Falcon (9/69)	8	16	24	54	90	125
121-136,139,140: 121-Retells origin. 133-The Falcon becomes Cap's partner; origin Modok						
140-Origin Grey Gargoyle retold	3	6	9	16	22	28
137,138-Spider-Man x-over	3	6	9	18	27	35
141,142: 142-Last 15¢ issue	2	4	6	13	18	22
143-(52 pgs.)	3	6	9	16	23	30
144-153: 144-New costume Falcon. 153-1st brief app. Jack Monroe	2	4	6	10	14	18
154-1st full app. Jack Monroe (Nomad)(10/72)	2	4	6	11	16	20
155-Origin re-told; origin Jack Monroe	2	4	6	11	16	20
156-171,176-179: 155-1st app Cap's strength increased. 160-1st app. Solarr. 164-1st app. Nightshade. 176-End of Capt. America.	2	4	6	8	10	12
172-175: X-Men x-over	2	4	6	11	16	20
180-Intro/origin of Nomad (Steve Rogers)	2	4	6	13	18	22
181-Intro/origin new Cap.	2	4	6	10	14	18
182,184-192: 186-True origin The Falcon	1	2	3	5	7	9
183-Death of new Cap; Nomad becomes Cap	2	4	6	8	11	14
193-Kirby-c/a begins	2	4	6	13	18	22
194-199-(Regular 25¢ edition (4-7/76)	2	4	6	10	14	18
196-199-30¢-c variants, limited distribution	5	10	15	32	51	70
200-(Regular 25¢ edition)(8/76)	2	4	6	11	16	20
200-(30¢-c variant, limited distribution)	6	12	18	37	59	80
201-214-Kirby-c/a	2	4	6	8	11	14
210-214-35¢-c variants, limited dist.)(6-10/77)	7	14	21	45	73	100
215,216,218-229,231-234,236-240,242-246: 215-Retells Cap's origin. 216-r/story from Strange Tales #114. 229-Marvel Man app. 233-Death of Sharon Carter. 234-Daredevil x-over.						
244,245-Miller-c						5.00
217,230,235: 217-1st app. Marvel Man (later Quasar). 230-Battles Hulk-c/story cont'd in Hulk #232. 235-(7/79) Daredevil x-over; Miller-a(p)	1	2	3	4	5	7
241-Punisher app.; Miller-c.	3	6	9	16	23	30
241-2nd print						3.00
247-255-Byrne-a. 255-Origin; Miller-c.	1	2	3	5	7	9
256-281,284,285,289-322,324-326,328-331: 264-Old X-Men cameo in flashback. 265,266-Nick Fury & Spider-Man app. 267-1st app. Everyman. 269-1st Team America. 279-(3/83)-Contains Tattooz skin decals. 281-1950s Bucky returns. 284-Patriot (Jack Mace) app. 285-Death of Patriot. 298-Origin Red Skull. 328-Origin & 1st app. D-Man						3.00
282-Bucky becomes new Nomad (Jack Monroe)						5.00
282-Silver ink 2nd print ($1.75) w/original date (6/83)						2.50
283,327,333-340: 283-2nd app. Nomad. 327-Capt. Amer. battles Super Patriot. 333-Intro & origin new Captain (Super Patriot). 339-Fall of the Mutants tie-in						4.00
286-288-Deathlok app.						4.00
323-1st app. new Super Patriot (see Nick Fury)						4.00
332-Old Cap resigns	1	2	3	4	6	8
341-343,345-349						3.00
344-($1.50, 52 pgs.)-Ronald Reagan cameo						4.00
350-($1.75, 68 pgs.)-Return of Steve Rogers (original Cap) to original costume						4.00
351-382,384-396: 351-Nick Fury app. 354-1st app. U.S. Agent (6/89, see Avengers West Coast). 360-1st app. Crossbones. 375-Daredevil app. 386-U.S. Agent app. 387-389-Red Skull back-up stories. 396-Last $1.00-c. 396,397-1st app. all new Jack O'Lantern						2.50
383-($2.00, 68 pgs.)-New Jack O'Lantern app. in back-up story. 406-Cable & Shatterstar cameo. 407-Capwolf vs. Cable-c/story. 408-Infinity War x-over; Falcon solo back-up.						4.00
397-399,401-424,425: 402-Begin 6 part Man-Wolf story w/Wolverine in #403-407. 405-410-New Jack O'Lantern app. in back-up story.						2.50
423-Vs. Namor-c/story						2.50
400-($2.25, 84 pgs.)-Flip book format w/double gatefold-c; r/Avengers #4 plus-c; contains cover pin-ups						3.00
425-($2.95, 52 pgs.)-Embossed Foil-c ed.n; Fighting Chance Pt. 1						3.00
426-443,446,447,449-453: 427-Begin $1.50-c; bound-in trading card sheet. 449-Thor app. 450-"Man Without A Country" storyline begins, ends #453; Bill Clinton app; variant-c exists. 451-1st app.Cap's new costume. 453-Cap gets old costume back; Bill Clinton app.						2.50
444-Mark Waid scripts & Ron Garney-c/a(p) begins, ends #454; Avengers app.						5.00
445,454: 445-Sharon Carter & Red Skull return.						3.00
448-($2.95, double-sized issue)-Waid script & Garney-c/a; Red Skull "dies"						4.00
Special 1(1/71)-Origin retold	5	10	15	30	48	65
Special 2(1/72, 52 pgs.)-Colan-a/Not Brand Echh; all-r	3	6	9	18	27	35
Annual 3(76, 52 pgs.)-Kirby-c/a(new)	3	6	9	14	19	24
Annual 4('77, 34 pgs.)-Magneto-c/story	3	6	9	14	19	24
Annual 5-7: (52 pgs.)('81-'83)						5.00
Annual 8(9/86)-Wolverine-c/story	3	6	9	19	29	38
Annual 9-13('90-'94, 68 pgs.)-9-Nomad back-up. 10-Origin retold (2 pgs.). 11-Falcon solo story. 12-Bagged w/card. 13-Red Skull-c/story						3.00
…Ashcan Edition ('95, 75¢)						3.00
… and the Falcon: Madbomb TPB (2004, $16.99) r/#193-200; Kirby-s/a						17.00
… and the Falcon: Nomad TPB (2006, $24.99) r/#177-186; Cap becomes Nomad						25.00
… and the Falcon: Secret Empire TPB (2005, $19.99) r/#169-176						20.00
… and the Falcon: The Swine TPB (2006, $29.99) r/#206-214 & Annual #3,4						30.00
… By Jack Kirby: Bicentennial Battles TPB (2005, $19.99) r/#201-205 & Marvel Treasury Special Featuring Captain America's Bicentennial Battles; Kirby-s/a						20.00
…: Deathlok Lives! nn(10/93, $4.95)-r/#286-288						5.00
…Drug War 1-(1994, $2.00, 52 pgs.)-New Warriors app.						3.00
…Man Without a Country(1998, $12.99, TPB)-r/#450-453						13.00
…Medusa Effect 1 (1994, $4.95, 68 pgs.)-Origin Baron Zemo						3.00
…Operation Rebirth (1996, $9.95)-r/#445-448						10.00
…65th Anniversary Special (5/06, $3.99) WWII flashback with Bucky; Brubaker-s						4.00
…Streets of Poison ($15.95)-r/#372-378						16.00
…. The Movie Special nn (5/92, $3.50, 52 pgs.)-Adapts movie; printed on coated stock; The Red Skull app.						3.50

NOTE: *Austin* c-225, 239i, 246i. *Buscema* a-115p, 217p; c-136p, 217, 297. *Byrne* c-223(part), 238, 239, 247p-254p, 290, 291, 313p; a-247-254p, 255, 313p, 350. *Colan* a(p)-116-137, 256, Annual 2(layouts), Annual 3, 4; c(p)-116-123, 126, 129. *Everett* a-136i, 137i; c-126i. *Garney* a(p)-444-454. *Gil Kane* a-145p; c-147p, 149p, 150p, 170p, 172-174, 180, 181p, 183-190p, 215, 216, 220, 221. *Kirby* a(p)-100-109, 112, 126p, 193-214. *Ron Lim* a(p)-366, 368-378, 380-386; c-366p, 368-378p, 379, 380-393p. *Miller* c-241p, 244p, 245p, 255p, Annual 5. *Mooney* a-149i. *Morrow* a-144i. *Perez* a-243p, 246p. *Robbins* c(p)-183-187, 189-192, 225. *Roussos* a-140i, 168i. *Starlin/Sinnott* c-162. *Sutton* a-244i. *Tuska* a-112i, 215p, Special 2. *Waid* scripts-444-454. *Williamson* a-313i. *Wood* a-127i. *Zeck* a-263-289; c-300.

CAPTAIN AMERICA (Volume Two)
Marvel Comics: V2#1, Nov, 1996 - No. 13, Nov, 1997($2.95/$1.95/$1.99) (Produced by Extreme Studios)

1-($2.95)-Heroes Reborn begins; Liefeld-c/a; Loeb scripts; reintro Nick Fury						6.00
1-($3.95)-(Variant-c)-Liefeld-c/a						6.00
1-(7/96, $2.95)-(Exclusive Comicon Ed.)-Liefeld-c/a. 1	2	3	5	6	8
2-11,13: 5-Two-c. 6-Cable-c/app. 13-"World War 3"-pt. 4, x-over w/Image						3.00

Captain America #25 © MAR

Captain America and the Falcon #5 © MAR

Captain America Comics #7 © MAR

	GD 2.0	VG 4.0	FN 6.0	VF 8.0	VF/NM 9.0	NM- 9.2

	GD 2.0	VG 4.0	FN 6.0	VF 8.0	VF/NM 9.0	NM- 9.2

12-($2.99) "Heroes Reunited"-pt. 4 — 4.00
Heroes Reborn: Captain America (2006, $29.99, TPB) r/#1-12 & Heroes Reborn #1/2 — 30.00

CAPTAIN AMERICA (Vol. Three) (Also see Capt. America: Sentinel of Liberty)
Marvel Comics: Jan, 1998 - No. 50, Feb, 2002 ($2.99/$1.99/$2.25)

1-($2.99) Mark Waid-s/Ron Garney-a — 4.00
1-Variant cover — 6.00
2-($1.99): 2-Two covers — 3.00
3-11: 3-Returns to old shield. 4-Hawkeye app. 5-Thor-c/app. 7-Andy Kubert-c/a begin.
9-New shield — 2.50
12-($2.99) Battles Nightmare; Red Skull back-up story — 3.50
13-17,19-Red Skull returns — 2.50
18-($2.99) Cap vs. Korvac in the Future — 3.00
20-24,26-29: 20,21-Sgt. Fury back-up story painted by Evans — 2.50
25-($2.99) Cap & Falcon vs. Hatemonger — 3.00
30-49: 30-Begin $2.25-c. 32-Ordway-a. 33-Jurgens-s/a begins; U.S. Agent app. 36-Maximum
Security x-over. 41,46-Red Skull app. — 2.50
.../Citizen V '98 Annual ($3.50) Busiek & Kesel-s — 3.50
50-($5.95) Stories by various incl. Jurgens, Quitely, Immonen; Ha-c — 6.00
1999 Annual ($3.50) Flag Smasher app. — 3.50
2000 Annual ($3.50) Continued from #35 vs. Protocide; Jurgens-s — 3.50
2001 Annual ($2.99) Golden Age flashback; Invaders app. — 3.00
...: To Serve and Protect TPB (2/02, $17.95) r/Vol. 3 #1-7 — 18.00

CAPTAIN AMERICA (Volume 4)
Marvel Comics: Jun, 2002 - No. 32, Dec, 2004 ($3.99/$2.99)

1-Ney Rieber-s/Cassaday-c/a — 4.00
2-9-($2.99) 3-Cap reveals Steve Rogers ID. 7-9-Hairsine-a — 3.00
10-32: 10-16-Jae Lee-a. 17-20-Gibbons-s/Weeks-a. 21-26-Bachalo-a. 26-Bucky flashback.
27,28-Eddie Campbell-a. 29-32-Red Skull app. — 3.00
...Vol. 1: The New Deal HC (2003, $22.99) r/#1-6; foreward by Max Allan Collins — 23.00
...Vol. 2: The Extremists TPB (2003, $13.99) r/#7-11; Cassaday-c — 14.00
...Vol. 3: Ice TPB (2003, $12.99) r/#12-16; Jae Lee-a; Cassaday-c — 13.00
...Vol. 4: Cap Lives TPB (2004, $12.99) r/#17-22 & Tales of Suspense #66 — 13.00
Avengers Disassembled: Captain America TPB (2004, $17.99) r/#29-32 and
Captain America and the Falcon #5-7 — 18.00

CAPTAIN AMERICA
Marvel Comics: Jan, 2005 - Present ($2.99)

1-Brubaker-s/Epting-c/a; Red Skull app. — 4.00
2-24: 10-House of M. 11-Origin of the Winter Soldier. 13-Iron Man app. 24-Civil War — 3.00
6,8-Retailer variant covers — 6.00
25-($3.99) Captain America shot dead; handcuffed red glove cover by Epting — 8.00
25-($3.99) Variant edition with running Cap cover by McGuinness — 12.00
25-($3.99) 2nd printing with "The Death of The Dream" cover by Epting — 4.00
25 Director's Cut-($4.99) w/script with Brubaker commentary; pencil pages, variant and
un-used covers gallery; article on media hype — 5.00
26-30-Falcon & Winter Soldier app. — 3.00
... By Ed Brubaker Omnibus Vol. 1 HC (2007, $74.99, dustjacket) r/#1-25; Capt. America 65th
Anniv. Spec. and Winter Soldier: Winter Kills; Brubaker intro.; bonus material — 75.00
Civil War: Captain America TPB (2007, $11.99) r/#22-24 & Winter Soldier: Winter Kills — 12.00
...: Red Menace Vol. 1 SC (2006, $11.99) r/#15-17 and 65th Anniversary Special — 12.00
...: Red Menace Vol. 2 SC (2006, $10.99) r/#18-21; Brubaker interview — 11.00
...Vol. 1: Winter Soldier HC (2005, $21.99) r/#1-7; concept sketches — 22.00
...Vol. 1: Winter Soldier SC (2006, $16.99) r/#1-7; concept sketches — 17.00
...: Winter Soldier Vol. 2 HC (2006, $19.99) r/#8,9,11-14 — 20.00
...: Winter Soldier Vol. 2 SC (2006, $14.99) r/#8,9,11-14 — 15.00

CAPTAIN AMERICA AND THE FALCON
Marvel Comics: May, 2004 - No. 14, June, 2005 ($2.99, limited series)

1-4-Priest-s/Sears-a — 3.00
5-14: 5-8-Avengers Disassembled x-over. 6,7-Scarlet Witch app. 8-12-Modok app. — 3.00
... Vol. 1: Two Americas (2005, $9.99) r/#1-4 — 10.00
... Vol. 2: Brothers and Keepers (2005, $17.99) r/#8-14 — 18.00

CAPTAIN AMERICA COMICS
Timely/Marvel Comics (TCI 1-20/CmPS 21-68/MjMC 69-75/Atlas Comics (PrPI 76-78): Mar,
1941 - No. 75, Feb, 1950; No. 76, 5/54 - No. 78, 9/54
(No. 74 & 75 titled Capt. America's Weird Tales)

1-Origin & 1st app. Captain America & Bucky by S&K; Hurricane, Tuk the Caveboy begin by
S&K; 1st app. Red Skull; Hitler-c (by Simon?); intro of the "Capt. America Sentinels of
Liberty Club" (advertised on inside front-c.); indicia reads Vol. 2, Number 1

	GD 2.0	VG 4.0	FN 6.0	VF 8.0	VF/NM 9.0	NM- 9.2
	7700	15,400	23,100	55,000	115,000	175,000

2-S&K Hurricane; Tuk by Avison (Kirby splash); classic Hitler-c

	GD 2.0	VG 4.0	FN 6.0	VF 8.0	VF/NM 9.0	NM- 9.2
	1400	2800	4200	10,500	18,750	27,000

3-Classic Red Skull-c & app; Stan Lee's 1st text (1st work for Marvel)

	GD 2.0	VG 4.0	FN 6.0	VF 8.0	VF/NM 9.0	NM- 9.2
	1125	2250	3375	8400	15,200	22,000
4-Early use of full pg. panel in comic	771	1542	2313	5397	9449	13,500
5	714	1428	2142	5000	8750	12,500
6-Origin Father Time; Tuk the Caveboy ends	611	1222	1833	4277	7489	10,700
7-Red Skull app.; classic-c	686	1372	2058	4800	8400	12,000
8-10-Last S&K issue, (S&K centerfold #6-10)	497	994	1491	3479	6090	8700
11-Last Hurricane, Headline Hunter; Al Avison Captain America begins, ends #20;						
Avison-c(p)	423	846	1269	2750	4875	7000
12-The Imp begins, ends #16; last Father Time	400	800	1200	2600	4600	6600
13-Origin The Secret Stamp; classic-c	429	858	1287	3000	5250	7500
14,15	400	800	1200	2600	4600	6600
16-Red Skull unmasks Cap; Red Skull-c	486	972	1458	3400	5950	8500
17-The Fighting Fool only app.	345	690	1035	2243	3972	5700
18-Classic-c	345	690	1035	2243	3972	5700
19-Human Torch begins #19	328	656	984	2050	3400	4750
20-Sub-Mariner app.; no H. Torch	300	600	900	1919	3310	4700
21-25: 25-Cap drinks liquid opium	300	600	900	1881	3141	4400
26-30: 27-Last Secret Stamp; last 68 pg. issue. 28-60 pg. issues begin.						
	290	580	870	1813	3007	4200
31-35,38-40: 34-Centerfold poster of Cap	252	504	756	1575	2613	3650
36-Classic Hitler-c	315	630	945	2048	3624	5200
37-Red Skull app.	300	600	900	1894	3197	4500
41-45,47: 41-Last Jap War-c. 47-Last German War-c						
	214	428	642	1338	2219	3100
46-German Holocaust-c; classic	290	580	870	1813	3007	4200
48-58,60	155	310	465	969	1610	2250
59-Origin retold	300	600	900	1970	3485	5000
61-Red Skull-c/story	317	634	951	1981	3291	4600
62,64,65: 65-Kurtzman's "Hey Look"	200	400	600	1250	2075	2900
63-Intro/origin Asbestos Lady	203	406	609	1269	2110	2950
66-Bucky is shot; Golden Girl teams up with Captain America & learns his i.d;						
origin Golden Girl	241	482	723	1506	2503	3500
67-73: 67-Captain America/Golden Girl team-up; Mxyztplk swipe; last Toro in Human Torch.						
68,70-Sub-Mariner/Namora, and Captain America/Golden Girl team-up in each. 69-Human						
Torch/Sun Girl team-up. 70-Science fiction-c/story. 71-Anti Wertham editorial; The Witness,						
Bucky app.	235	470	705	1469	2435	3400
74-(Scarce)(10/49)-Titled "Captain America's Weird Tales"; Red Skull-c & app.;						
classic-c	657	1314	1971	4600	8050	11,500
75(2/50)-Titled "C.A.'s Weird Tales"; no C.A. app.; horror cover/stories						
	235	470	705	1469	2435	3400
76-78(1954): Human Torch/Toro stories; all have communist-c/stories						
	134	268	402	838	1394	1950
132-Pg. Issue (B&W-1942)(Canadian)-Very rare. Has blank inside-c and back-c; contains						
Marvel Mystery #33 & Captain America #18 w/cover from Captain America #22;						
same contents as one version of the Marvel Mystery annuals						
	4667	9334	14,000	28,000	—	—

NOTE: *Crandall* a-2i, 3i, 9i, 10i. *Kirby* c-1, 2, 5-8p. *Rico* c-69-71. *Romita* c-77, 78. *Schomburg* c-3, 4, 26-29, 31, 33, 37-39, 41, 42, 45-54, 58. *Sekowsky* c-55, 56. *Shores* c-1i, 2i, 5-7i, 11i, 20-25, 30, 32, 34, 35, 40, 57, 59-67. *S&K* c-9, 10. Bondage c-3, 7, 15, 16, 34, 38.

CAPTAIN AMERICA: DEAD MEN RUNNING
Marvel Comics: Mar, 2002 - No. 3, May, 2002 ($2.99, limited series)

1-3-Macan-s/Zezelj-a — 3.00

CAPTAIN AMERICA/NICK FURY: BLOOD TRUCE
Marvel Comics: Feb, 1995 ($5.95, one-shot, squarebound)

nn-Chaykin story — 6.00

CAPTAIN AMERICA/NICK FURY: THE OTHERWORLD WAR
Marvel Comics: Oct, 2001 ($6.95, one-shot, squarebound)

nn-Manco-a; Bucky and Red Skull app. — 7.00

CAPTAIN AMERICA: RED, WHITE & BLUE
Marvel Comics: Sept, 2002 ($29.99, one-shot, hardcover with dustjacket)

nn-Reprints from Lee & Kirby, Steranko, Miller and others; and new short stories and pin-ups
by various incl. Ross, Dini, Timm, Waid, Dorkin, Sienkiewicz, Miller, Bruce Jones, Collins,
Piers-Rayner, Pope, Deodato, Quitely, Nino; Stelfreeze-c — 30.00
TPB (2007, $19.99) — 20.00

CAPTAIN AMERICA, SENTINEL OF LIBERTY (See Fireside Book Series)

CAPTAIN AMERICA, SENTINEL OF LIBERTY
Marvel Comics: Sept, 1998 - No. 12, Aug, 1999 ($1.99)

1-Waid-s/Garney-a — 3.00
1-Rough Cut ($2.99) Features original script and pencil pages — 3.00
2-5: 2-Two-c; Invaders WW2 story — 2.50
6-($2.99) Iron Man-c/app. — 3.00

Captain America: Sentinel of Liberty #5 © MAR

Captain Battle, Jr. #1 © LEV

Captain Carrot and His Amazing Zoo Crew #13 © DC

	GD 2.0	VG 4.0	FN 6.0	VF 8.0	VF/NM 9.0	NM- 9.2

7-11: 8-Falcon-c/app. 9-Falcon poses as Cap — 2.50
12-($2.99) Final issue; Bucky-c/app. — 3.00

CAPTAIN AMERICA SPECIAL EDITION
Marvel Comics Group: Feb, 1984 - No. 2, Mar, 1984 ($2.00, Baxter paper)

1-Steranko-c/a(r) in both; r/ Captain America #110,111 — 6.00
2-Reprints the scarce Our Love Story #5, and C.A. #113

	1	2	3	5	6	8

CAPTAIN AMERICA: THE CHOSEN
Marvel Comics: Nov, 2007 - No. 6 ($3.99, limited series)

1,2-Breitweiser-a/Morrell-s — 4.00

CAPTAIN AMERICA: THE CLASSIC YEARS
Marvel Comics: Jun, 1998 -No. 2 (trade paperbacks)

1-($19.95) Reprints Captain America Comics #1-5 — 25.00
2-($24.95) Reprints Captain America Comics #6-10 — 25.00

CAPTAIN AMERICA: THE LEGEND
Marvel Comics: Sept, 1996 ($3.95, one-shot)

1-Tribute issue; wraparound-c — 4.00

CAPTAIN AMERICA: WHAT PRICE GLORY
Marvel Comics: May, 2003 - No. 4, May, 2003 ($2.99, weekly limited series)

1-4-Bruce Jones-s/Steve Rude & Mike Royer-a — 3.00

CAPTAIN AND THE KIDS, THE (See Famous Comics Cartoon Books)

CAPTAIN AND THE KIDS, THE (See Comics on Parade, Katzenjammer Kids, Okay Comics & Sparkler Comics)
United Features Syndicate/Dell Publ. Co.: 1938 -12/39; Sum, 1947 - No. 32, 1955; Four Color No. 881, Feb, 1958

	GD 2.0	VG 4.0	FN 6.0	VF 8.0	VF/NM 9.0	NM- 9.2
Single Series 1(1938)	97	194	291	606	1003	1400
Single Series 1(Reprint)(12/39- "Reprint" on-c)	48	96	144	293	484	675
1(Summer, 1947-UFS)-Katzenjammer Kids	16	32	48	94	147	200
2	10	20	30	58	79	100
3-10	9	18	27	50	65	80
11-20	8	16	24	40	50	60
21-32 (1955)	7	14	21	37	46	55

50th Anniversary issue-(1948)-Contains a 2 pg. history of the strip, including an account of the famous Supreme Court decision allowing both Pulitzer & Hearst to run the same strip

under different names	15	30	45	88	137	185
Special Issue, Fall issue (1948)	10	20	30	58	79	100
Four Color 881 (Dell)	4	8	12	28	44	60

CAPTAIN ATOM
Nationwide Publishers: 1950 - No. 7, 1951 (5¢, 5x7-1/4", 52 pgs.)

1-Science fiction	41	82	123	250	400	550
2-7	20	44	66	128	202	275

CAPTAIN ATOM (Formerly Strange Suspense Stories #77)(Also see Space Adventures)
Charlton Comics: V2#78, Dec, 1965 - V2#89, Dec, 1967

V2#78-Origin retold; Bache-a (3 pgs	8	16	24	54	90	125
79-82: 79-1st app. Dr. Spectro; 3 pg. Ditko cut & paste /Space Adventures #24.						
82-Intro. Nightshade (9/66)	5	10	15	35	55	75
83-86: Ted Kord Blue Beetle in all. 83-(11/66)-1st app. Ted Kord. 84-1st app. new Captain						
Atom	5	10	15	32	51	70
87-89: Nightshade by Aparo in all	5	10	15	32	51	70
83-85-(Modern Comics-1977)-reprints	1	2	3	4	5	7

NOTE: Aparo a-87-89. Ditko c/a(p) 78-89. #90 only published in fanzine 'The Charlton Bullseye' #1, 2.

CAPTAIN ATOM (Also see Americomics & Crisis On Infinite Earths)
DC Comics: Mar, 1987 - No. 57, Sept, 1991 (Direct sales only #35 on)

1-(44 pgs.)-Origin/1st app. with new costume — 4.00
2-49: 5-Firestorm x-over. 6-Intro. new Dr. Spectro. 11-Millennium tie-in. 14-Nightshade app. 16-Justice League app. 17-$1.00-c begins; Swamp Thing app. 20-Blue Beetle x-over.
24,25-Invasion tie-in — 2.50
51-57: 50-($2.00, 52 pgs.). 57-War of the Gods x-over — 2.50
Annual 1,2 ('88, '89)-1-Intro Major Force — 3.00

CAPTAIN ATOM: ARMAGEDDON (Restarts the WildStorm Universe)
DC Comics (WildStorm): Dec, 2005 - No. 9, Aug, 2006 ($2.99, limited series)

1-9-Captain Atom appears in WildStorm Universe; Pfeifer-s/Camuncoli-a. 1-Lee-c — 3.00
TPB (2007, $19.99) r/series — 20.00

CAPTAIN BATTLE (Boy Comics #3 on) (See Silver Streak Comics)
New Friday Publ./Comic House: Summer, 1941 - No. 2, Fall, 1941

1-Origin Blackout by Rico; Captain Battle begins (1st appeared in Silver Streak #10, 5/41)

	145	290	435	906	1503	2100

2	79	158	237	494	822	1150

CAPTAIN BATTLE (2nd Series)
Magazine Press/Picture Scoop No. 5: No. 3, Wint, 1942-43; No. 5, Sum, 1943 (No #4)

3-Origin Silver Streak-r/SS#3; origin Lance Hale-r/Silver Streak; Simon-a(r) (52 pgs., nd)

	71	142	213	444	735	1025
5-Origin Blackout retold (68 pgs.)	50	100	150	305	503	700

CAPTAIN BATTLE, JR.
Comic House (Lev Gleason): Fall, 1943 - No. 2, Winter, 1943-44

1-The Claw vs. The Ghost | 134 | 268 | 402 | 838 | 1394 | 1950
2-Wolverton's Scoop Scuttle; Don Rico-c/a; The Green Claw story is reprinted from Silver Streak #6; bondage/torture-c | 79 | 158 | 237 | 494 | 822 | 1150

CAPTAIN BEN DIX (See Promotional Comics section)

CAPTAIN BRITAIN (Also see Marvel Team-Up No. 65, 66)
Marvel Comics International: Oct. 13, 1976 - No. 39, July 6, 1977 (Weekly)

1-Origin; with Capt. Britain's face mask inside	2	4	6	9	13	16
2-Origin, part II; Capt. Britain's Boomerang inside	1	3	4	6	8	10
3-11: 3,8-Vs. Bank Robbers. 4-7-Vs. Hurricane. 9-11: Vs. Dr. Synne						5.00
12-23,25-27: (scarce)-12,13-Vs. Dr. Synne. 14,15-Vs. Mastermind. 16-23,25,26-With Captain America. 17 misprinted & color section reprinted in #18. 27-Origin retold						
			6	8	10	12
24-With C.B.'s Jet Plane inside	2	4	6	9	13	16
28-32,36-39: 28-32-Vs. Lord Hawk. 37-39-Vs. Highwayman & Manipulator						3.50
33-35-More on origin						4.00
Annual (1978, Hardback, 64 pgs.)-Reprints #1-7 with pin-ups of Marvel characters						
	2	4	6	8	11	14
Summer Special (1980, 52 pgs.)-Reprints						5.00

NOTE: No. 1, 2, & 24 are rarer in mint due to inserts. Distributed in Great Britain only. Nick Fury-r by Steranko in 1-20, 24-31, 35-37. Fantastic Four-r by J. Buscema-a in 24-30. Story from No. 39 continues in Super Spider-Man (British weekly) No. 231-247. Following cancellation of his series, new Captain Britain stories appeared in "Super Spider-Man" (British weekly) No. 231-247. Captain Britain stories which appear in Super-Spider-Man No. 248-253 are reprints of Marvel Team-Up No. 65&66. Capt. Britain strips also appeared in Hulk Comic (weekly) 1, 3-30, 42-55, 57-60, in Marvel Superheroes (monthly) 377-388, in Daredevils (monthly) 1-11, Mighty World of Marvel (monthly) 7-16 & Captain Britain (monthly) 1-14. Issues 1-23 have B&W & color, paper-c, & are 32 pgs. Issues 24 on are all B&W w/glossy-c & are 36 pgs.

CAPTAIN CANUCK
Comely Comix (Canada) (All distr. in U. S.): 7/75 - No. 4, 7/77; No. 4, 7-8/79 - No. 14, 3-4/81

1-1st app. Bluefox						5.00
2,3(5-7/76)-2-1st app. Dr. Walker, Redcoat & Kebec. 3-1st app. Heather						4.00
4(1st printing-2/77)-10x14-1/2"; (5.00); B&W; 300 copies serially numbered and signed with one certificate of authenticity	7	14	21	49	80	110
4(2nd printing-7/77)-11x17", B&W; only 15 copies printed; signed by creator Richard Comely, serially #d and two certificates of authenticity inserted; orange cardboard covers (Very Rare)	9	18	27	65	113	160
4-14: 4(7-8/79)-1st app. Tom Evans & Mr. Gold; origin The Catman. 5-Origin Capt. Canuck's powers; 1st app. Earth Patrol & Chaos Corps. 8-Jonn 'The Final Chapter'. 9-1st World Beyond. 11-'Chariots of Fire' story						4.00
15-(8/04, $15.00) Limited edition of unpublished issue from 1981; serially #d edition of 150; signed by creator Richard Comely	3	6	9	16	23	30
... Legacy 1 (9-10/06) Comely-s/a						3.00
... Legacy Special Edition (52 pgs., limited ed. of 1000) Comely-s/a						6.00
Special Collectors Pack (polybagged)	1	3	4	6	8	10
Summer Special 1(7-9/80, 95¢, 64 pgs.)						4.00

NOTE: 30,000 copies of No. 2 were destroyed in Winnipeg.

CAPTAIN CANUCK: UNHOLY WAR
Comely Comix: Oct, 2004 - No. 3 ($2.50, limited series)

1-Riel Langlois-s/Drue Langlois-a — 2.50

CAPTAIN CARROT AND HIS AMAZING ZOO CREW (Also see New Teen Titans & Oz-Wonderland War)
DC Comics: Mar, 1982 - No. 20, Nov, 1983

1-20: 1-Superman app. 3-Re-intro Dodo & The Frog. 9-Re-intro Three Mouseketeers, the Terrific Whatzit. 10,11- Pig Iron reverts back to Peter Porkchops. 20-Changeling app. — 3.00

CAPTAIN CARVEL AND HIS CARVEL CRUSADERS (See Carvel Comics)

CAPTAIN CONFEDERACY
Marvel Comics (Epic Comics): Nov, 1991 - No. 4, Feb, 1992 ($1.95)

1-4-All new stories — 2.25

CAPTAIN COURAGEOUS COMICS (Banner #3-5; see Four Favorites #5)
Periodical House (Ace Magazines): No. 6, March, 1942

6-Origin & 1st app. The Sword; Lone Warrior, Capt. Courageous app.; Capt. moves to Four Favorites #5 in May | 76 | 152 | 228 | 475 | 788 | 1100

Captain Easy #16 © NEA

Captain Flight Comics #11 © Four Star

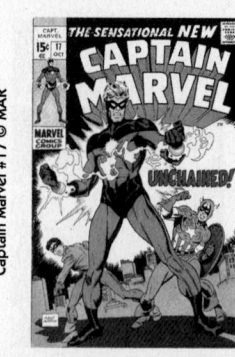

Captain Marvel #17 © MAR

	GD 2.0	VG 4.0	FN 6.0	VF 8.0	VF/NM 9.0	NM- 9.2
CAPT'N CRUNCH COMICS (See Cap'n...)						
CAPTAIN DAVY JONES						
Dell Publishing Co.: No. 598, Nov, 1954						
Four Color 598	5	10	15	30	48	65
CAPTAIN EASY (See The Funnies & Red Ryder #3-32)						
Hawley/Dell Publ./Standard(Visual Editions)/Argo: 1939 - No. 17, Sept, 1949; April, 1956						
nn-Hawley(1939)-Contains reprints from The Funnies & 1938 Sunday strips by Roy Crane	88	176	264	550	913	1275
Four Color 24 (1943)	50	100	150	305	503	700
Four Color 111(6/46)	14	28	42	99	175	250
10(Standard-10/47)	13	26	39	72	101	130
11,12,14,15,17: 11-17 all contain 1930s & '40s strip-r	10	20	30	54	72	90
13,16: Schomburg-c	11	22	33	62	86	110
Argo 1(4/56)-Reprints	7	14	21	37	46	55
CAPTAIN EASY & WASH TUBBS (See Famous Comics Cartoon Books)						
CAPTAIN ELECTRON						
Brick Computer Science Institute: Aug, 1986 ($2.25)						
1-Disbrow-a						2.50
CAPTAIN EO 3-D (Disney)						
Eclipse Comics: July, 1987 (Eclipse 3-D Special #18, $3.50, Baxter)						
1-Adapts 3-D movie						4.00
1-2-D limited edition	1	2	3	4	5	7
1-Large size (11x17", 8/87)-Sold only at Disney Theme parks ($6.95)	2	4	6	10	14	18
CAPTAIN FEARLESS COMICS (Also see Holyoke One-Shot #6, Old Glory Comics & Silver Streak #1)						
Helnit Publishing Co. (Holyoke Publ. Co.): Aug, 1941 - No. 2, Sept, 1941						
1-Origin Mr. Miracle, Alias X, Captain Fearless, Citizen Smith Son of the Unknown Soldier; Miss Victory (1st app.) begins (1st patriotic heroine? before Wonder Woman)	83	166	249	519	860	1200
2-Grit Grady, Captain Stone app.	50	100	150	305	503	700
CAPTAIN FLAG (See Blue Ribbon Comics #16)						
CAPTAIN FLASH						
Sterling Comics: Nov, 1954 - No. 4, July, 1955						
1-Origin; Sekowsky-a; Tomboy (female super hero) begins; only pre-code issue; atomic rocket-c	40	80	120	238	379	520
2-4: 4-Flying saucer invasion-c	22	44	66	128	202	275
CAPTAIN FLEET (Action Packed Tales of the Sea)						
Ziff-Davis Publishing Co.: Fall, 1952						
1-Painted-c	15	30	45	88	137	185
CAPTAIN FLIGHT COMICS						
Four Star Publications: Mar, 1944 - No. 10, Dec, 1945; No. 11, Feb-Mar, 1947						
nn	43	86	129	262	431	600
2-4: 4-Rock Raymond begins, ends #7	25	50	75	145	228	310
5-Bondage, classic torture-c; Red Rocket begins; the Grenade app. (scarce)	110	220	330	688	1144	1600
6	46	92	138	301	513	590
7-10: 7-L. B. Cole covers begin, end #11. 8-Yankee Girl begins; intro. Black Cobra & Cobra Kid app. 9-Torpedoman app.; last Yankee Girl; Kinstler-a. 10-Deep Sea Dawson, Zoom of the Jungle, Rock Raymond, Red Rocket, & Black Cobra app; bondage-c	52	104	156	317	521	725
11-Torpedoman, Blue Flame (Human Torch clone) app.; last Black Cobra, Red Rocket; classic L. B. Cole robot-c (scarce)	138	276	414	863	1432	2000
CAPTAIN GALLANT (...of the Foreign Legion) (TV) (Texas Rangers in Action No. 5 on?)						
Charlton Comics: 1955; No. 2, Jan, 1956 - No. 4, Sept, 1956						
Non-Heinz version (#1)-Buster Crabbe photo on-c; full page Buster Crabbe photo inside front-c	9	18	27	47	61	75
(Heinz version is listed in the Promotional Comics section)						
2-4: Buster Crabbe in all	8	16	24	42	54	65
CAPTAIN GLORY						
Topps Comics: Apr, 1993 ($2.95) (Created by Jack Kirby)						
1-Polybagged w/Kirbychrome trading card; Ditko-a & Kirby-c; has coupon for Amberchrome Secret City Saga #0						3.00
CAPTAIN HERO (See Jughead as...)						
CAPTAIN HERO COMICS DIGEST MAGAZINE						
Archie Publications: Sept, 1981						
1-Reprints of Jughead as Super-Guy	2	4	6	10	14	18
CAPTAIN HOBBY COMICS						
Export Publication Ent. Ltd. (Dist. in U.S. by Kable News Co.): Feb, 1948 (Canadian)						
1	8	16	24	40	50	60
CAPT. HOLO IN 3-D (See Blackthorne 3-D Series #65)						
CAPTAIN HOOK & PETER PAN (Movie)(Disney)						
Dell Publishing Co.: No. 446, Jan, 1953						
Four Color 446	9	18	27	60	100	140
CAPTAIN JET (Fantastic Fears No. 7 on)						
Four Star Publ./Farrell/Comic Media: May, 1952 - No. 5, Jan, 1953						
1-Bakerish-a	23	46	69	130	205	280
2	14	28	42	76	108	140
3-5,6(?)	11	22	33	64	90	115
CAPTAIN JOHNER & THE ALIENS						
Valiant: May, 1995 - No. 2, May, 1995 ($2.95, shipped in same month)						
1,2: Reprints Magnus Robot Fighter 4000 A.D. back-up stories; new Paul Smith-c						3.00
CAPTAIN JUSTICE (TV)						
Marvel Comics: Mar, 1988 - No. 2, Apr, 1988 (limited series)						
1,2-Based on the 1987 "Once a Hero" television series						2.50
CAPTAIN KANGAROO (TV)						
Dell Publishing Co.: No. 721, Aug, 1956 - No. 872, Jan, 1958						
Four Color 721 (#1)-Photo-c	16	32	48	116	206	290
Four Color 780, 872-Photo-c	13	26	39	93	167	235
CAPTAIN KIDD (Formerly Dagar; My Secret Story #26 on)(Also see Comic Comics & Fantastic Comics)						
Fox Feature Syndicate: No. 24, June, 1949 - No. 25, Aug, 1949						
24,25: 24-Features Blackbeard the Pirate	15	30	45	83	124	165
CAPTAIN MARVEL (See All Hero, All-New Collectors' Ed., America's Greatest, Fawcett Miniature, Gift, JSA, Kingdom Come, Legends, Limited Collectors' Ed., Marvel Family, Master No. 21, Mighty Midget Comics, Power of Shazam!, Shazam, Special Edition Comics, Whiz, Wisco (in Promotional Comics section), World's Finest #253 and XMas Comics)						
CAPTAIN MARVEL (Becomes ...Presents the Terrible 5 No. 5)						
M. F. Enterprises: April, 1966 - No. 4, Nov, 1966 (25¢ Giants)						
nn-(#1 on pg. 5)-Origin; created by Carl Burgos	4	8	12	26	41	55
2-4: 3-(#3 on pg. 4)-Fights the Bat	3	6	9	17	25	32
CAPTAIN MARVEL (Marvel's Space-Born Super-Hero! Captain Marvel #1-6; see Giant-Size..., Life Of..., Marvel Graphic Novel #1, Marvel Spotlight V2#1 & Marvel Super-Heroes #12)						
Marvel Comics Group: May, 1968 - No. 19, Dec, 1969; No. 20, June, 1970 - No. 21, Aug, 1970; No. 22, Sept, 1972 - No. 62, May, 1979						
1	12	24	36	82	146	210
2-Super Skrull-c/story	5	10	15	35	55	75
3-5: 4-Captain Marvel battles Sub-Mariner	4	8	12	26	41	55
6-11: 11-Capt. Marvel given great power by Zo the Ruler; Smith/Trimpe-c; Death of Una	3	6	9	18	27	35
12,13,15-20: 16,17-New costume	3	6	9	18	27	35
14,21: 14-Capt. Marvel vs. Iron Man; last 12¢ issue. 21-Capt. Marvel battles Hulk; last 12¢ issue	3	6	9	18	27	35
22-24	2	4	6	10	14	18
25,26: 25-Starlin-c/a begins; Starlin's 1st Thanos saga begins (3/73), ends #34; Thanos cameo (5 panels). 26-Minor Thanos app. (see Iron Man #55); 1st Thanos-c	3	6	9	22	34	45
27,28-1st & 2nd full app. Thanos. 28-Thanos-c/s	3	6	9	20	30	40
29,30-Thanos cameos. 29-C.M. gains more powers	3	6	9	14	20	25
31,32: Thanos app. 31-Last 20¢ issue. 32-Thanos-c	3	6	9	16	22	28
33-Thanos-c & app.; Capt. Marvel battles Thanos; 1st origin Thanos	3	6	9	20	30	40
34-1st app. Nitro; C.M. contracts cancer which eventually kills him; last Starlin-c/a	3	6	9	14	20	25
35,37-40,42,46-48,50,53-56,58-62: 39-Origin Watcher. 58-Thanos cameo	1	2	3	5	7	9
36,41,43,49: 36-R-origin/1st app. Capt. Marvel from Marvel Super-Heroes #12. 41,43-Wrightson part inks; #43-c(i). 49-Starlin & Weiss-p assists	1	2	3	5	7	9
44,45-(Regular 25¢ editions)(5,7/76)	1	3	4	6	8	10
44,45-(30¢-c variants, limited distribution)	4	8	12	24	37	50
51,52-(Regular 30¢ editions)(7,9/77)	1	2	3	5	7	9
51,52-(35¢-c variants, limited distribution)	4	8	12	28	44	60
57-Thanos appears in flashback	2	4	6	8	10	12

Captain Marvel #1 © MAR

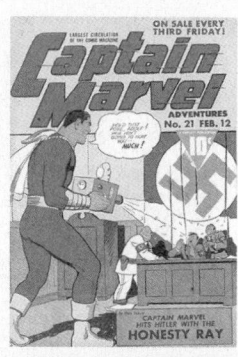

Captain Marvel Adventures #21 © FAW

Captain Marvel, Jr. #8 © FAW

	GD	VG	FN	VF	VF/NM	NM-
	2.0	4.0	6.0	8.0	9.0	9.2

NOTE: Alcala a-35. Austin a-46i, 49-53i; c-52i. Buscema a-18p-21p. Colan a(p)-1-4; c(p)-1-4, 8, 9. Heck a-5-10p, 16p. Gil Kane a-17-21p; c-17-24p, 37p, 53. Starlin a-36. McWilliams a-40i. #25-34 were reprinted in The Life of Captain Marvel.

CAPTAIN MARVEL
Marvel Comics: Nov, 1989 ($1.50, one-shot, 52 pgs.)

1-Super-hero from Avengers; new powers						3.00

CAPTAIN MARVEL
Marvel Comics: Feb, 1994 ($1.75, 52 pgs.)

1-(Indicia reads Vol 2 #2)-Minor Captain America app.						2.50

CAPTAIN MARVEL
Marvel Comics: Dec, 1995 - No. 6, May, 1996 ($2.95/$1.95)

1 ($2.95)-Advs. of Mar-Vell's son begins; Fabian Nicieza scripts; foil-c						3.50
2-6: 2-Begin $1.95-c						2.50

CAPTAIN MARVEL (Vol. 3) (See Avengers Forever)
Marvel Comics: Jan, 2000 - No. 35, Oct, 2002 ($2.50)

1-Peter David-s in all; two covers						4.00
2-10: 2-Two covers; Hulk app. 9-Silver Surfer app.						3.00
11-35: 12-Maximum Security x-over. 17,18-Starlin-a. 27-30-Spider-Man 2099 app.						2.50
Wizard #0-Preview and history of Rick Jones						4.00
....: First Contact (8/01, $16.95, TPB) r/#0,1-6						17.00

CAPTAIN MARVEL (Vol. 4) (See Avengers Forever)
Marvel Comics: Nov, 2002 - No. 25, Sept, 2004 ($2.25/$2.99)

1-Peter David-s/Chriscross-a ; 3 covers by Ross, Jusko & Chriscross						3.00
2-7: 2,3-Punisher app. 5-New costume debuts. 4-Noto-c. 7-Thor app.						2.50
3-Sketchbook Edition-($3.50) includes Ross' concept design pages for new costume						3.00
8-25: 8-Begin $2.99-c; Thor app.; Manco-c. 10-Spider-Man-c/app. 15-Neal Adams-c						3.00
Vol. 1: Nothing To Lose (2003, $14.99, TPB) r/#1-6						15.00
Vol. 2: Coven (2003, $14.99, TPB) r/#7-12						15.00
Vol. 3: Crazy Like a Fox (2004, $14.99, TPB) r/#13-18						15.00
Vol. 4: Odyssey (2004, $16.99, TPB) r/#19-25						17.00

CAPTAIN MARVEL ADVENTURES (See Special Edition Comics for pre #1)
Fawcett Publications: 1941 (March) - No. 150, Nov, 1953 (#1 on stands 1/16/41)

	GD	VG	FN	VF	VF/NM	NM-
nn(#1)-Captain Marvel & Sivana by Jack Kirby. The cover was printed on unstable paper stock and is rarely found in Fine or Mint condition; blank back inside-c	2750	5500	8250	21,000	35,500	50,000
2-(Advertised as #3, which was counting Special Edition Comics as the real #1); Tuska-a	423	846	1269	2855	5028	7200
3-Metallic silver-c	300	600	900	1881	3141	4400
4-Three Lt. Marvels app.	207	414	621	1294	2147	3000
5	159	318	477	994	1647	2300
6-10: 9-1st Otto Binder scripts on Capt. Marvel	121	242	363	756	1253	1750
11-15: 12-Capt. Marvel joins the Army. 13-Two pg. Capt. Marvel pin-up. 15-Comic cards on back-c begin, end #26	93	186	279	581	966	1350
16,17: 17-Painted-c	88	176	264	550	913	1275
18-Origin & 1st app. Mary Marvel & Marvel Family (12/11/42); painted-c; Mary Marvel by Marcus Swayze	241	482	723	1506	2503	3500
19-Mary Marvel x-over; Christmas-c	75	150	225	469	777	1085
20,21,23-Attached to the cover, each has a miniature comic just like the Mighty Midget Comics #11, except that each has a full color promo ad on the back cover. Most copies were circulated without the miniature comic. These issues with miniatures attached are very rare, and should not be confused for copies with the similar Mighty Midget glued in its place. The Mighty Midgets had blank back covers except for a small victory stamp seal. Only the Capt. Marvel, Captain Marvel Jr. and Golden Arrow No. 11 miniatures have been positively documented as having been affixed to these covers. Each miniature was only partially glued by its back cover to the Captain Marvel comic making it easy to see if it's the genuine miniature rather than a Mighty Midget.						
with comic attached....	355	710	1065	2308	4079	5850
20,23-Without miniature	68	136	204	425	705	985
21-Without miniature; Hitler-c	110	220	330	688	1144	1600
22-Mr. Mind serial begins; 1st app. Mr. Mind	95	190	285	594	985	1375
24,25	66	132	198	413	687	960
26-28,30: 26-Flag-c. 27-1st Mr. Mind app. (his voice was heard over the radio before now) (9/43)	55	110	165	344	572	800
29-1st Mr. Mind-c (11/43)	58	116	174	363	602	840
31-35: 35-Origin Radar (5/44, see Master #50)	49	98	147	299	492	685
36-40: 37-Mary Marvel x-over	45	90	135	275	455	635
41-46: 42-Christmas-c. 43-Capt. Marvel 1st meets Uncle Marvel; Mary Batson cameo. 46-Mr. Mind serial ends	40	80	120	235	368	500
47-50	38	76	114	216	343	470
51-53,55-60: 51-63-Bi-weekly issues. 52-Origin & 1st app. Sivana Jr.; Capt. Marvel Jr. x-over	32	64	96	186	293	400
54-Special oversize 68 pg. issue	33	66	99	190	300	410
61-The Cult of the Curse serial begins	35	70	105	204	322	440
62-65-Serial cont.; Mary Marvel x-over in #65	32	64	96	186	293	400

	GD	VG	FN	VF	VF/NM	NM-
	2.0	4.0	6.0	8.0	9.0	9.2
66-Serial ends; Atomic War-c	36	72	108	208	329	450
67-77,79: 69-Billy Batson's Christmas; Uncle Marvel, Mary Marvel, Capt. Marvel Jr. x-over. 71-Three Lt. Marvels app. 79-Origin Mr. Tawny	29	58	87	167	264	360
78-Origin Mr. Atom	33	66	99	190	300	410
80-Origin Capt. Marvel retold	64	128	192	400	663	925
81-84,86-90: 81,90-Mr. Atom app. 82-Infinity-c. 82,86,88,90-Mr. Tawny app.	27	54	81	158	249	340
85-Freedom Train issue	32	64	96	186	293	400
91-99: 92-Mr. Tawny app. 96-Gets 1st name "Tawky"	26	52	78	154	242	330
100-Origin retold; silver metallic-c	46	92	138	281	466	650
101-115,117-120	26	52	78	150	235	320
116-Flying Saucer issue (1/51)	29	58	87	170	268	365
121-Origin retold	34	68	102	195	308	420
122-137,139,140	25	50	75	145	228	310
138-Flying Saucer issue (11/52)	29	58	87	170	268	365
141-Pre-code horror story "The Hideous Head-Hunter"	26	52	78	154	242	330
142-149: 142-used in POP, pgs. 92,96	26	52	78	150	235	320
150-(Low distribution)	46	92	138	281	466	650

NOTE: Swayze a-12, 14, 15, 18, 19, 40; c-12, 15, 19.

CAPTAIN MARVEL AND THE GOOD HUMOR MAN (Movie)
Fawcett Publications: 1950

nn-Partial photo-c w/Jack Carson & the Captain Marvel Club Boys	46	92	138	281	466	650

CAPTAIN MARVEL COMIC STORY PAINT BOOK (See Comic Story...)

CAPTAIN MARVEL, JR. (See Fawcett Miniatures, Marvel Family, Master Comics, Mighty Midget Comics, Shazam & Whiz Comics)

CAPTAIN MARVEL, JR.
Fawcett Publications: Nov, 1942 - No. 119, June, 1953 (No #34)

	GD	VG	FN	VF	VF/NM	NM-
1-Origin Capt. Marvel Jr. retold (Whiz #25); Capt. Nazi app. Classic Raboy-c	543	1086	1629	3800	6650	9500
2-Vs. Capt. Nazi; origin Capt. Nippon	200	400	600	1250	2075	2900
3	111	222	333	694	1152	1610
4-Classic Raboy-c	117	234	351	731	1216	1700
5-Vs. Capt. Nazi	95	190	285	594	985	1375
6-8: 8-Vs. Capt. Nazi	78	156	234	488	807	1125
9-Classic flag-c	84	168	252	525	875	1225
10-Hitler-c	110	220	330	688	1144	1600
11,12,15-Capt. Nazi app.	67	134	201	419	697	975
13-Classic Hitler, Tojo and Mussolini football-c	110	220	330	688	1144	1600
14,16-20: 14-X-Mas-c. 16-Capt. Marvel & Sivana x-over. 19-Capt. Nazi & Capt. Nippon app.	55	110	165	344	572	800
21-30: 25-Flag-c	45	90	135	275	455	635
31-33,36-40: 37-Infinity-c	32	64	96	186	293	400
35-#34 on inside; cover shows origin of Sivana Jr. which is not on inside. Evidently the cover to #35 was printed out of sequence and bound with contents to #34	32	64	96	186	293	400
41-70: 42-Robot-c. 53-Atomic Bomb-c/story	26	52	78	152	239	325
71-99,101-104: 87-Robot-c. 104-Used in POP, pg. 89	20	40	60	117	184	250
100	24	48	72	139	220	300
105-114,116-118: 116-Vampira, Queen of Terror app.	19	38	57	109	172	235
115-Injury to eye-c; Eyeball story w/injury-to-eye panels	45	90	135	275	450	625
119-Electric chair-c (scarce)	50	100	150	305	503	700

NOTE: Mac Raboy c-1-28, 30-32, 57, 59 among others.

CAPTAIN MARVEL PRESENTS THE TERRIBLE FIVE
M. F. Enterprises: Aug, 1966; V2#5, Sept, 1967 (No #2-4) (25¢)

	GD	VG	FN	VF	VF/NM	NM-
1	4	8	12	26	41	55
V2#5-(Formerly Captain Marvel)	3	6	9	17	25	32

CAPTAIN MARVEL'S FUN BOOK
Samuel Lowe Co.: 1944 (1/2" thick) (cardboard covers)(25¢)

nn-Puzzles, games, magic, etc.; infinity-c	36	72	108	208	329	450

CAPTAIN MARVEL SPECIAL EDITION (See Special Edition)

CAPTAIN MARVEL STORY BOOK
Fawcett Publications: Summer, 1946 - No. 4, Summer?, 1948

	GD	VG	FN	VF	VF/NM	NM-
1-Half text	52	104	156	317	521	725
2-4	37	74	111	213	337	460

CAPTAIN MARVEL THRILL BOOK (Large-Size)

Captain Midnight #21 © FAW

Captain Steve Savage #6 © AVON

Captain Science #7 © YM

	GD 2.0	VG 4.0	FN 6.0	VF 8.0	VF/NM 9.0	NM- 9.2

Fawcett Publications: 1941 (B&W w/color-c)

1-Reprints from Whiz #8,10, & Special Edition #1 (Rare) — 300 600 900 3000 – –

NOTE: *Rarely found in Fine or Mint condition.*

CAPTAIN MIDNIGHT (TV, radio, films) (See The Funnies, Popular Comics & Super Book of Comics)(Becomes Sweethearts No. 68 on)
Fawcett Publications: Sept, 1942 - No. 67, Fall, 1948 (#1-14: 68 pgs.)

1-Origin Captain Midnight, star of radio and movies; Captain Marvel cameo on cover — 300 600 900 1970 3485 5000
2-Smashes the Jap Juggarnaut — 138 276 414 863 1432 2000
3-Classic Nazi war-c — 124 248 372 775 1288 1800
4,5: 4-Grapples the Gremlins — 109 218 327 681 1128 1575
6-8 — 67 134 201 419 697 975
9-Raboy-c — 69 138 207 431 716 1000
10-Raboy Flag-c — 71 142 213 444 735 1025
11-20: 11,17,18-Raboy-c. 16 (1/44) — 50 100 150 305 503 700
21-Classic-c — 43 86 129 262 431 600
22,23,25-30: 22-War savings stamp-c — 41 82 123 250 400 550
24-Japan flag sunburst-c — 48 96 144 293 484 675
31-40 — 32 64 96 186 293 400
41-59,61-67: 50-Sci/fi theme begins? — 24 48 72 139 220 300
60-Flying Saucer issue (2/48)-3rd of this theme; see The Spirit 9/28/47(1st), Shadow Comics V7#10 (2nd, 1/48) & Boy Commandos #26 (4th, 3-4/48) — 35 70 105 201 318 435

CAPTAIN NICE (TV)
Gold Key: Nov, 1967 (one-shot)

1(10211-711)-Photo-c — 7 14 21 47 76 105

CAPTAIN N: THE GAME MASTER (TV)
Valiant Comics: 1990 - No. 6? ($1.95, thick stock, coated-c)

1-6: 4-6-Layton-c — 3.00

CAPTAIN PARAGON (See Bill Black's Fun Comics)
Americomics: Dec, 1983 - No. 4, 1985

1-Intro/1st app. Ms. Victory — 4.00
2-4 — 3.00

CAPTAIN PARAGON AND THE SENTINELS OF JUSTICE
AC Comics: April, 1985 - No. 6, 1986 ($1.75)

1-6: 1-Capt. Paragon, Commando D., Nightveil, Scarlet Scorpion, Stardust & Atoman — 3.00

CAPTAIN PLANET AND THE PLANETEERS (TV cartoon)
Marvel Comics: Oct, 1991 - No. 12, Oct, 1992 ($1.00/$1.25)

1-N. Adams painted-c — 4.00
2-12: 3-Romita-c — 3.00

CAPTAIN POWER AND THE SOLDIERS OF THE FUTURE (TV)
Continuity Comics: Aug, 1988 - No. 2, 1988 ($2.00)

1,2: 1-Neal Adams-c/layouts/inks; variant-c exists. — 3.00

CAPTAIN PUREHEART (See Archie as...)

CAPTAIN ROCKET
P. L. Publ. (Canada): Nov, 1951

1 — 43 86 129 262 431 600

CAPT. SAVAGE AND HIS LEATHERNECK RAIDERS (...And His Battlefield Raiders #9 on)
Marvel Comics Group (Animated Timely Features): Jan, 1968 - No. 19, Mar, 1970
(See Sgt. Fury No. 10)

1-Sgt. Fury & Howlers cameo — 4 8 12 28 44 60
2,7,11: 2,4-Origin Hydra. 7-Pre-"Thing" Ben Grimm story. 11-Sgt. Fury app. — 3 6 9 16 23 30
3-6,8-10,12-14: 14-Last 12¢ issue — 3 6 9 14 20 25
15-19 — 2 4 6 13 18 22

NOTE: *Ayres/Shores a-1-8,11. Ayres/Severin a-9,10,17-19. Heck/Shores a-12-15.*

CAPTAIN SCIENCE (Fantastic No. 8 on)
Youthful Magazines: Nov, 1950 - No. 7, Dec, 1951

1-Wood-a; origin; 2 pg. text w/ photos of George Pal's "Destination Moon." — 88 176 264 550 913 1275
2 — 45 90 135 275 455 635
3,6,7: 3,6-Bondage c-swipes/Wings #94,91 — 41 82 123 256 416 575
4,5-Wood/Orlando-c/a(2) each — 81 162 243 506 841 1175

NOTE: *Fass a-4. Bondage c-3, 6, 7.*

CAPTAIN SILVER'S LOG OF SEA HOUND (See Sea Hound)

CAPTAIN SINBAD (Movie Adaptation) (See Fantastic Voyages of... & Movie Comics)

CAPTAIN STERNN: RUNNING OUT OF TIME
Kitchen Sink Press: Sept, 1993 - No. 5, 1994 ($4.95, limited series, coated stock, 52 pgs.)

1-5: Berni Wrightson-c/a/scripts — 6.00
1-Gold ink variant — 10.00

CAPTAIN STEVE SAVAGE (...& His Jet Fighters, No. 2-13)
Avon Periodicals: 1950 - No. 8, 1/53; No. 5, 9-10/54 - No. 13, 5-6/56

nn(1st series)-Wood art, 22 pgs. (titled "...Over Korea") — 40 80 120 235 368 500
1(4/51)-Reprints nn issue (Canadian) — 16 32 48 96 151 205
2-Kamen-a — 13 26 39 74 105 135
3-11 (#6, 9-10/54, last precode) — 10 20 30 54 72 90
12-Wood-a (6 pgs.) — 14 28 42 76 108 140
13-Check, Lawrence-a — 10 20 30 56 76 95

NOTE: *Kinstler c-2-5, 7-9, 11. Lawrence a-8. Ravielli a-5, 9.*

5(9-10/54-2nd series)(Formerly Sensational Police Cases) — 9 18 27 52 69 80
6-Reprints nn issue; Wood-a — 10 20 30 56 76 95
7-13: 9,10-Kinstler-c. 10-r/cover #2 (1st series). 13-r/cover #8 (1st series) — 8 16 24 42 54 65

CAPTAIN STONE (See Holyoke One-Shot No. 10)

CAPT. STORM (Also see G. I. Combat #138)
National Periodical Publications: May-June, 1964 - No. 18, Mar-Apr, 1967

1-Origin — 7 14 21 50 83 115
2-7,9-18: 3,6,13-Kubert-a. 4-Colan-a. 12-Kubert-c — 5 10 15 30 48 65
8-Grey-tone-c — 6 12 18 37 59 80

CAPTAIN 3-D (Super hero)
Harvey Publications: December, 1953 (25¢, came with 2 pairs of glasses)

1-Kirby/Ditko-a (Ditko's 3rd published work tied with Strange Fantasy #9, see also Daring Love #1 & Black Magic V4 #3); shows cover in 3-D on inside; Kirby/Meskin-a — 12 24 36 69 97 125

NOTE: *Half price without glasses*

CAPTAIN THUNDER AND BLUE BOLT
Hero Comics: Sept, 1987 - No. 10, 1988 ($1.95)

1-10: 1-Origin Blue Bolt. 3-Origin Capt. Thunder. 6-1st app. Wicket. 8-Champions x-over — 2.50

CAPTAIN TOOTSIE & THE SECRET LEGION (Advs. of...)(Also see Monte Hale #30,39 & Real Western Hero)
Toby Press: Oct, 1950 - No. 2, Dec, 1950

1-Not Beck-a; both have sci-fi covers — 32 64 96 186 293 400
2-The Rocketeer Patrol app.; not Beck-a — 20 40 60 117 184 250

CAPTAIN TRIUMPH (See Crack Comics #27)

CAPTAIN UNIVERSE... (5-part x-over)
Marvel Comics: 2005; Jan, 2006

.../ Daredevil 1 (1/06, $2.99) Part 2; Faerber-s/Santacruz-a — 3.00
.../ Hulk 1 (1/06, $2.99) Part 1; Faerber-s/Magno-a — 3.00
.../ Invisible Woman 1 (1/06, $2.99) Part 4; Faerber-s/Raiza-a; Gladiator app. — 3.00
.../ Silver Surfer 1 (1/06, $2.99) Part 5; Faerber-s/Magno-a — 3.00
.../ X-23 1 (1/06, $2.99) Part 3; Faerber-s/Portella-a; Scorpion app. — 3.00
...: Power Unimaginable TPB (2005, $19.99)-Reprints from Marvel Spotlight #9-11, Incredible Hulk Ann. #10, Marvel Fanfare #25, Web of Spider-Man Ann. #5&6, Marvel Comics Presents #148, Cosmic Power Unlimited #5 — 20.00
...: Universal Heroes TPB (2005, $13.99) reprints .../Hulk, .../Daredevil, ...X-23 and back-up stories from Amazing Fantasy (2005) #13,14 — 14.00

CAPTAIN VENTURE & THE LAND BENEATH THE SEA (See Space Family Robinson)
Gold Key: Oct, 1968 - No. 2, Oct, 1969

1-r/Space Family Robinson serial; Spiegle-a — 4 8 12 28 44 60
2-Spiegle-a — 4 8 12 24 37 50

CAPTAIN VICTORY AND THE GALACTIC RANGERS
Pacific Comics: Nov, 1981 - No. 13, Jan, 1984 ($1.00, direct sales, 36-48 pgs.) (Created by Jack Kirby)

1-1st app. Mr. Mind — 4.00
2-13: 3-N. Adams-a — 3.00
Special 1-(10/83)-Kirby c/a(p) — 4.00

NOTE: *Conrad a-10, 11. Ditko a-6. Kirby a-1-3p; c-1-13.*

CAPTAIN VICTORY AND THE GALACTIC RANGERS
Jack Kirby Comics: July, 2000 - No. 2, Sept, 2000 ($2.95, B&W)

1,2-New Jeremy Kirby-s with reprinted Jack Kirby-a; Liefeld pin-up art — 3.00

CAPTAIN VIDEO (TV) (See XMas Comics)

Car 54, Where Are You? #3 © DELL

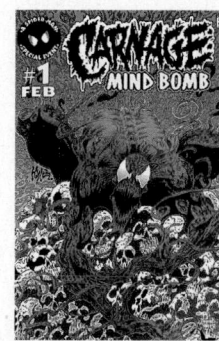

Carnage: Mind Bomb #1 © MAR

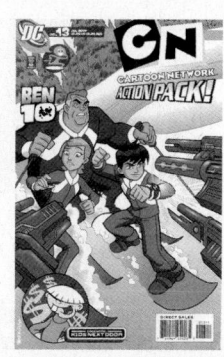

Cartoon Network Action Pack #13 © Cartoon Network

	GD 2.0	VG 4.0	FN 6.0	VF 8.0	VF/NM 9.0	NM- 9.2

Fawcett Publications: Feb, 1951 - No. 6, Dec, 1951 (No. 1,5,6-36pgs.; 2-4, 52pgs.) (All photo-c)

	GD 2.0	VG 4.0	FN 6.0	VF 8.0	VF/NM 9.0	NM- 9.2
1-George Evans-a(2); 1st TV hero comic	107	214	321	669	1085	1500
2-Used in **SOTI**, pg. 382	70	140	210	438	707	975
3-6-All Evans-a except #5 mostly Evans	57	114	171	356	578	800

NOTE: Minor Williamson assists on most issues. Photo c-1, 5, 6; painted c-2-4.

CAPTAIN WILLIE SCHULTZ (Also see Fightin' Army)
Charlton Comics: No. 76, Oct, 1985 - No. 77, Jan, 1986

76,77-Low print run	1	2	3	4	5	7

CAPTAIN WIZARD COMICS (See Meteor, Red Band & Three Ring Comics)
Rural Home: 1946

1-Capt. Wizard dons new costume; Impossible Man, Race Wilkins app.						
	34	68	102	195	308	420

CARE BEARS (TV, Movie)(See Star Comics Magazine)
Star Comics/Marvel Comics No. 15 on: Nov, 1985 - No. 20, Jan, 1989

1-20: Post-a begins. 11-$1.00-c begins. 13-Madballs app.						4.00

CAREER GIRL ROMANCES (Formerly Three Nurses)
Charlton Comics: June, 1964 - No. 78, Dec, 1973

V4#24-31	3	6	9	14	20	25
32-Elvis Presley, Herman's Hermits, Johnny Rivers line drawn-c						
	10	20	30	68	119	170
33-38,40-50	2	4	6	13	18	22
39-(4/67) 1st app. Tiffany Sinn, C.I.A. Sweetheart, Undercover Agent (also see Secret Agent #10; Dominguel-a	3	6	9	16	23	30
51-78	2	4	6	9	13	16

CAR 54, WHERE ARE YOU? (TV)
Dell Publishing Co.: Mar-May, 1962 - No. 7, Sept-Nov, 1963; 1964 - 1965 (All photo-c)

Four Color 1257(#1, 3-5/62)	8	16	24	56	93	130
2(6-8/62)-7	5	10	15	32	51	70
2,3(10-12/64), 4(1-3/65)-Reprints #2,3,&4 of 1st series						
	3	6	9	20	30	40

CARL BARKS LIBRARY OF WALT DISNEY'S GYRO GEARLOOSE COMICS AND FILLERS IN COLOR, THE
Gladstone: 1993 ($7.95, 8-1/2x11", limited series, 52 pgs.)

1-6: Carl Barks reprints	1	3	4	6	8	10

CARL BARKS LIBRARY OF WALT DISNEY'S COMICS AND STORIES IN COLOR, THE
Gladstone: Jan, 1992 - No. 51, Mar, 1996 ($8.95, 8-1/2x11", 60 pgs.)

1,2,6,8-51: 1-Barks Donald Duck-r/WDC&S #31-35; 2-r/#36,38-41; 6-r/#57-61; 8-r/#67-71; 9-r/#72-76; 10-r/#77-81; 11-r/#82-86; 12-r/#87-91; 13-r/#92-96; 14-r/#97-101; 15-r/#102-106; 16-r/#107-111; 17-r/#112,114,117,124,125; 18-r/#126-130; 19-r/#131,132(2),133,134; 20-r/#135-139; 21-r/#140-144; 22-r/#145-149; 23-r/#150-154; 24-r/#155-159; 25-r/#160-164; 26-r/#165-169; 27-r/#170-174;28-r/#175-179; 29-r/#180-184; 30-r/#185-189; 31-r/#190-194; 32-r/#195-199;33-r/#200-204; 34-r/#205-209; 35-r/#210-214; 36-r/#215-219; 37-r/#220-224; 38-r/#225-229; 39-r/#230-234; 40-r/#235-239; 41-r/#240-244; 42r/#245-249; 43-r/#250-254; 44-50; All contain one Heroes & Villains trading card each						
	1	3	4	6	8	10
3,4,7: 3-r/#42-46. 4-r/#47-51. 7-r/#62-66.	2	4	6	9	12	15
5-r/#52-56	2	4	6	11	16	20

CARL BARKS LIBRARY OF WALT DISNEY'S DONALD DUCK ADVENTURES IN COLOR, THE
Gladstone: Jan, 1994 - No. 25, Jan, 1996 ($7.95-$9.95, 44-68 pgs., 8-1/2"x11")
(all contain one Donald Duck trading card each)

1-5,7,25-Carl Barks-r: 1-r/FC #9; 2-r/FC #29; 3-r/FC #62; 4-r/FC #108; 5-r/FC #147 & #79(Mickey Mouse); 7-r/FC #159. 8-r/FC #178 & 189. 9-r/FC #199 & 203; 10-r/FC 223 & 238; 11-r/Christmas Parade #1 & 2; 12-r/FC #296; 13-r/FC #263; 14-r/MOC #20 & 41; 15-r/FC 275 & 282; 16-r/FC #291&300; 17-r/FC #308 & 318; 18-r/Vac. Parade #1 & Summer Fun #2; 19-r/FC #328 & 367	3	6	9	8	10	12
6-r/MOC #4, Cheerios "Atom Bomb", D.D. Tells About Kites						
	2	4	6	11	16	20

CARL BARKS LIBRARY OF WALT DISNEY'S DONALD DUCK CHRISTMAS STORIES IN COLOR, THE
Gladstone: 1992 ($7.95, 44pgs., one-shot)

nn-Reprints Firestone giveaways 1945-1949	2	4	6	9	12	15

CARL BARKS LIBRARY OF WALT DISNEY'S UNCLE SCROOGE COMICS ONE PAGERS IN COLOR, THE
Gladstone: 1992 - No. 2, 1993 ($8.95, limited series, 60 pgs., 8-1/2x11")

1-Carl Barks one pg. reprints	3	6	9	14	20	25
2-Carl Barks one pg. reprints	2	4	6	9	12	15

CARNAGE: IT'S A WONDERFUL LIFE

Marvel Comics: Oct, 1996 ($1.95, one-shot)

1-David Quinn scripts						3.00

CARNAGE: MIND BOMB
Marvel Comics: Feb, 1996 ($2.95, one-shot)

1-Warren Ellis script; Kyle Hotz-a						3.00

CARNATION MALTED MILK GIVEAWAYS (See Wisco)

CARNEYS, THE
Archie Comics: Summer, 1994 ($2.00, 52 pgs)

1-Bound-in pull-out poster						2.50

CARNIVAL COMICS (Formerly Kayo #12; becomes Red Seal Comics #14)
Harry 'A' Chesler/Pershing Square Publ. Co.: 1945

nn (#13)-Guardineer-a	18	36	54	103	162	220

CAROLINE KENNEDY
Charlton Comics: 1961 (one-shot)

nn-Interior photo covers of Kennedy family	9	18	27	60	100	140

CAROUSEL COMICS
F. E. Howard, Toronto: V1#8, April, 1948

V1#8	8	16	24	42	54	65

CARTOON CARTOONS (Anthology)
DC Comics: Mar, 2001 - No. 33, Oct, 2004 ($1.99/$2.25)

1-33-Short stories of Cartoon Network characters. 3,6,10,13,15-Space Ghost. 13-Begin $2.25-c. 17-Dexter's Laboratory begins						2.50

CARTOON KIDS
Atlas Comics (CPS): 1957 (no month)

1-Maneely-c/a; Dexter The Demon, Willie The Wise-Guy, Little Zelda app.						
	11	22	33	62	86	110

CARTOON NETWORK ACTION PACK (Anthology)
DC Comics: July, 2006 - Present ($2.25)

1-16-Short stories of Cartoon Network characters. 1,4,6-Rowdyruff Boys app.						2.50

CARTOON NETWORK BLOCK PARTY (Anthology)
DC Comics: Nov, 2004 - Present ($2.25)

1,2,4,4-36-Short stories of Cartoon Network characters						2.50
3-($2.95) Bonus pages						3.00
... Vol. 1: Get Down! (2005, $6.99, digest) reprints from Dexter's Lab and Cartoon Cartoons						7.00
... Vol. 2: Read All About It! (2005, $6.99, digest) reprints						7.00
... Vol. 3: Can You Dig It?; ... Vol. 4: Blast Off! (2006, $6.99, digest) reprints						7.00

CARTOON NETWORK PRESENTS
DC Comics: Aug, 1997 - No. 24, Aug, 1999 ($1.75-$1.99, anthology)

1-Dexter's Lab						5.00
1-Platinum Edition	1	2	3	5	7	9
2-10: 2-Space Ghost						3.50
11-24: 12-Bizarro World						2.50

CARTOON NETWORK PRESENTS SPACE GHOST
Archie Comics: Mar, 1997 ($1.50)

1-Scott Rosema-p						6.00

CARTOON NETWORK STARRING... (Anthology)
DC Comics: Sept, 1999 - No. 18, Feb, 2001 ($1.99)

1-Powerpuff Girls						5.00
2-18: 2,8,11,14,17-Johnny Bravo. 12,15,18-Space Ghost						3.00

CARTOON TALES (Disney's...)
W.D. Publications (Disney): nd, nn (1992) ($2.95, 6-5/8x9-1/2", 52 pgs.)

nn-Ariel & Sebastian-Serpent Teen; Beauty and the Beast; A Tale of Enchantment; Darkwing Duck - Just Us Justice Ducks; 101 Dalmatians - Canine Classics; Tale Spin - Surprise in the Skies; Uncle Scrooge - Blast to the Past						4.00

CARVERS
Image Comics (Flypaper Press): 1998 - No. 3, 1999 ($2.95)

1-3-Pander Bros.-a/Fleming-s						3.00

CAR WARRIORS
Marvel Comics (Epic): June, 1991 - No. 4, Sept, 1991 ($2.25, lim. series)

1-4: 1-Says April in indicia						2.50

CASANOVA
Image Comics: June, 2006 - Present ($1.99, B&W& olive green or blue)

1-9: 1-7-Matt Fraction-s/Gabriel Bá-a/c. 8,9-Fabio Moon-a						2.25

Case Files: Sam & Twitch #22 © TMP

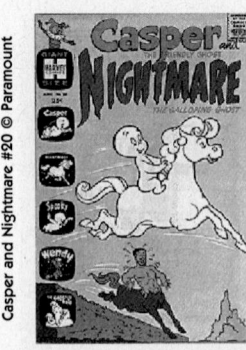

Casper and Nightmare #20 © Paramount

Casper Giant Size #1 © HARV

	GD 2.0	VG 4.0	FN 6.0	VF 8.0	VF/NM 9.0	NM- 9.2

CASE FILES: SAM & TWITCH (Also see the Spawn titles)
Image Comics: May, 2003 - No. 25, July, 2006 ($2.50/$2.95, color #1-6/B&W #7-on)

1-25: 1-5-Scott Morse-a/Marc Andreyko-s. 7-13-Paul Lee-a. 13-Niles-s						3.00

CASE OF THE SHOPLIFTER'S SHOE (See Perry Mason, Feature Book No.50)

CASE OF THE WINKING BUDDHA, THE
St. John Publ. Co.: 1950 (132 pgs.; 25¢; B&W; 5-1/2x7-5-1/2x8")

nn-Charles Raab-a; reprinted in Authentic Police Cases No. 25	29	58	87	167	264	360

CASEY-CRIME PHOTOGRAPHER (Two-Gun Western No. 5 on)(Radio)
Marvel Comics (BFP): Aug, 1949 - No. 4, Feb, 1950

1-Photo-c; 52 pgs.	25	50	75	145	228	310
2-4: Photo-c	17	34	51	98	154	210

CASEY JONES (TV)
Dell Publishing Co.: No. 915, July, 1958

Four Color 915-Alan Hale photo-c	5	10	15	35	55	75

CASEY JONES & RAPHAEL (See Bodycount)
Mirage Studios: Oct, 1994 ($2.75, unfinished limited series)

1-Bisley-c; Eastman story & pencils						2.75

CASEY JONES: NORTH BY DOWNEAST
Mirage Studios: May, 1994 - No. 2, July, 1994 ($2.75, limited series)

1,2-Rick Veitch script & pencils; Kevin Eastman story & inks						2.75

CASPER ADVENTURE DIGEST
Harvey Comics: V2#1, Oct, 1992 - V2#8, Apr, 1994 ($1.75/$1.95, digest-size)

V2#1: Casper, Richie Rich, Spooky, Wendy						5.00
2-8						3.50

CASPER AND...
Harvey Comics: Nov, 1987 - No. 12, June, 1990 (.75/$1.00, all reprints)

1-Ghostly Trio						5.00
2-12: 2-Spooky; begin $1.00-c. 3-Wendy. 4-Nightmare. 5-Ghostly Trio. 6-Spooky. 7-Wendy. 8-Hot Stuff. 9-Baby Huey. 10-Wendy.11-Ghostly Trio. 12-Spooky						3.00

CASPER AND FRIENDS
Harvey Comics: Oct, 1991 - No. 5, July, 1992 ($1.00/$1.25)

1-Nightmare, Ghostly Trio, Wendy, Spooky						4.00
2-5						3.00

CASPER AND FRIENDS MAGAZINE: Mar, 1997 - No. 3, July, 1997 ($3.99)

1-3						4.00

CASPER AND NIGHTMARE (See Harvey Hits# 37, 45, 52, 56, 59, 62, 65, 68,71, 75)

CASPER AND NIGHTMARE (Nightmare & Casper No. 1-5)
Harvey Publications: No. 6, 11/64 - No. 44, 10/73; No. 45, 6/74 - No. 46, 8/74 (25¢)

6: 68 pg. Giants begin, ends #32	5	10	15	30	48	65
7-10	3	6	9	21	32	42
11-20	3	6	9	17	25	32
21-37: 33-37-(52 pg. Giants)	3	6	9	14	19	24
38-46	2	4	6	9	12	15

NOTE: Many issues contain reprints.

CASPER AND SPOOKY (See Harvey Hits No. 20)
Harvey Publications: Oct, 1972 - No. 7, Oct, 1973

1	3	6	9	17	25	32
2-7	2	4	6	9	13	16

CASPER AND THE GHOSTLY TRIO
Harvey Pub.: Nov, 1972 - No. 7, Nov, 1973; No. 8, Aug, 1990 - No. 10, Dec, 1990

1	3	6	9	17	25	32
2-7	2	4	6	9	13	16
8-10						5.00

CASPER AND WENDY
Harvey Publications: Sept, 1972 - No. 8, Nov, 1973

1: 52 pg. Giant	3	6	9	17	25	32
2-8	2	4	6	9	13	16

CASPER BIG BOOK
Harvey Comics: V2#1, Aug, 1992 - No. 3, May, 1993 ($1.95, 52 pgs.)

V2#1-Spooky app.						4.00
2,3						3.00

CASPER CAT (See Dopey Duck)
I. W. Enterprises/Super: 1958; 1963

1,7:1-Wacky Duck #?.7-Reprint, Super No. 14('63)	2	4	6	9	13	16

CASPER DIGEST (...Magazine #?; ...Halloween Digest #8, 10)
Harvey Publications: Oct, 1986 - No. 18, Jan, 1991 ($1.25/$1.75, digest-size)

1	1	3	4	6	8	10
2-18: 11-Valentine-c. 18-Halloween-c						6.00

CASPER DIGEST (...Magazine #? on)
Harvey Comics: V2#1, Sept, 1991 - V2#14, Nov, 1994 ($1.75/$1.95, digest-size)

V2#1						5.00
2-14						3.50

CASPER DIGEST STORIES
Harvey Publications: Feb, 1980 - No. 4, Nov, 1980 (95¢, 132 pgs., digest size)

1	2	4	6	9	13	16
2-4	1	2	3	5	7	9

CASPER DIGEST WINNERS
Harvey Publications: Apr, 1980 - No. 3, Sept, 1980 (95¢, 132 pgs., digest-size)

1	2	4	6	9	13	16
2,3	1	2	3	5	7	9

CASPER ENCHANTED TALES DIGEST
Harvey Comics: May, 1992 - No. 10, Oct, 1994 ($1.75, digest-size, 98 pgs.)

1-Casper, Spooky, Wendy stories						5.00
2-10						3.50

CASPER GHOSTLAND
Harvey Comics: May, 1992 ($1.25)

1						3.00

CASPER GIANT SIZE
Harvey Comics: Oct, 1992 - No. 4, Nov, 1993 ($2.25, 68 pgs.)

V2#1-Casper, Wendy, Spooky stories						5.00
2-4						4.00

CASPER HALLOWEEN TRICK OR TREAT
Harvey Publications: Jan, 1976 (52 pgs.)

1	3	6	9	17	25	32

CASPER IN SPACE (Formerly Casper Spaceship)
Harvey Publications: No. 6, June, 1973 - No. 8, Oct, 1973

6-8	2	4	6	9	13	16

CASPER'S GHOSTLAND
Harvey Publications: Winter, 1958-59 - No. 97, 12/77; No. 98, 12/79 (25¢)

1-84 pgs. begin, ends #10	18	36	54	134	237	340
2	9	18	27	65	113	160
3-10	7	14	21	49	80	110
11-20: 11-68 pgs. begin, ends #61. 13-X-mas-c	6	12	18	39	62	85
21-40	4	8	12	28	44	60
41-61	3	6	9	17	25	32
62-77: 62-52 pgs. begin	2	4	6	9	13	16
78-98: 94-X-Mas-c	2	4	6	8	10	12

NOTE: Most issues contain reprints w/new stories.

CASPER SPACESHIP (Casper in Space No. 6 on)
Harvey Publications: Aug, 1972 - No. 5, April, 1973

1: 52 pg. Giant	3	6	9	18	27	35
2-5	2	4	6	10	14	18

CASPER STRANGE GHOST STORIES
Harvey Publications: October, 1974 - No. 14, Jan, 1977 (All 52 pgs.)

1	3	6	9	18	27	35
2-14	2	4	6	10	14	18

CASPER, THE FRIENDLY GHOST (See America's Best TV Comics, Famous TV Funday Funnies, The Friendly Ghost..., Nightmare &..., Richie Rich and..., Tastee-Freez, Treasury of Comics, Wendy the Good Little Witch & Wendy Witch World)

CASPER, THE FRIENDLY GHOST (Becomes Harvey Comics Hits No. 61 (No. 6), and then continued with Harvey issue No. 7)(1st Series)
St. John Publishing Co.: Sept. 1949 - No. 5, Aug, 1951

1(1949)-Origin & 1st app. Baby Huey & Herman the Mouse (1st comic app. of Casper and the 1st time the name Casper app. in any media, even films)	241	482	723	1506	2503	3500
2,3 (2/50 & 8/50)	90	180	270	563	932	1300
4,5 (3/51 & 8/51)	69	138	207	431	716	1000

CASPER, THE FRIENDLY GHOST (Paramount Picture Star...)(2nd Series)

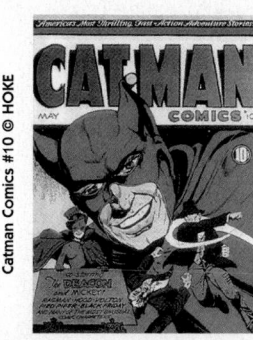

Casual Heroes #1 © Motown Animation

Catman Comics #10 © HOKE

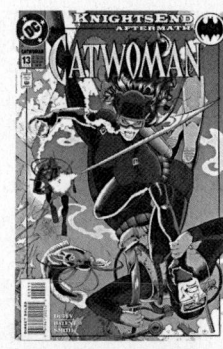

Catwoman #13 © DC

	GD 2.0	VG 4.0	FN 6.0	VF 8.0	VF/NM 9.0	NM- 9.2
Harvey Publications (Family Comics): No. 7, Dec, 1952 - No. 70, July, 1958						
Note: No. 6 is Harvey Comics Hits No. 61 (10/52)						
7-Baby Huey begins, ends #9	32	64	96	240	445	650
8,9	20	40	60	146	261	375
10-Spooky begins (1st app., 6/53), ends #70?	24	48	72	175	313	450
11,12: 2nd & 3rd app. Spooky	14	28	42	99	175	250
13-18: Alfred Harvey app. in story	12	24	36	87	156	225
19-1st app. Nightmare (4/54)	20	40	60	146	261	375
20-Wendy the Witch begins (1st app., 5/54)	24	48	72	179	320	460
21-30: 24-Infinity-c	9	18	27	65	113	160
31-40: 38-Early Wendy app. 39-1st app. Samson Honeybun. 40-1st app. Dr. Brainstorm						
	8	16	24	52	86	120
41-1st Wendy app. on-c	8	16	24	54	90	125
42-50: 43-2nd Wendy-c. 46-1st app. Spooky's girl Pearl.						
	6	12	18	41	66	90
51-70 (Continues as Friendly Ghost... 8/58) 58-Early app. Bat Balfrey. 63-2nd app. Something						
the Baby Ghost. 66-1st app. Wildcat Witch	5	10	15	32	51	70
Harvey Comics Classics Vol. 1 TPB (Dark Horse Books, 6/07, $19.95) Reprints Casper's						
earliest appearances in this title, Little Audrey, and The Friendly Ghost Casper, mostly B&W						
with some color stories; history, early concept drawings and animation art						20.00
NOTE: Baby Huey app. 7-9, 11, 121, 14, 16, 20. Nightmare app. 19, 27, 36, 37, 42, 46, 51,						
53, 56, 70. Spooky app. 10-70. Wendy app. 20, 29-31, 35, 37, 38, 41-49, 51, 52, 54-58, 61, 64, 68.						
CASPER THE FRIENDLY GHOST (Formerly The Friendly Ghost...)(3rd Series)						
Harvey Comics: No. 254, July, 1990 - No. 260, Jan, 1991 ($1.00)						
254-260						3.00
CASPER THE FRIENDLY GHOST (4th Series)						
Harvey Comics: Mar, 1991 - No. 28, Nov, 1994 ($1.00/$1.25/$1.50)						
1-Casper becomes Mighty Ghost; Spooky & Wendy app.						5.00
2-10: 7,8-Post-a						3.00
11-28-($1.50)						2.50
CASPER T.V. SHOWTIME						
Harvey Comics: Jan, 1980 - No. 5, Oct, 1980						
1	2	4	6	9	12	15
2-5	1	2	3	5	6	8
CASSETTE BOOKS (Classics Illustrated)						
Cassette Book Co./I.P.S. Publ.: 1984 (48 pgs, b&w comic with cassette tape)						
NOTE: This series was illegal. The artwork was illegally obtained, and the Classics Illustrated copyright owner,						
Twin Circle Publ. sued to get an injunction to prevent the continued sale of this series. Many C.I. collectors						
obtained copies before the 1987 injunction, but now they are already scarce. Here again the market is just devel-						
oping, but sealed mint copies of com ic and tape should be worth at least $25.						
1001 (CI#1-A2)New-PC 1002(CI#3-A2)CI-PC 1003(CI#13-A2)CI-PC						
1004(CI#25)CI-LDC 1005(CI#10-A2)New-PC 1006(CI#64)CI-LDC						
CASTILIAN (See Movie Classics)						
CASTLEVANIA: THE BELMONT LEGACY						
IDW Publishing: March 2005 - No. 5, July, 2005 ($3.99, limited series)						
1-5-Marc Andreyko-s/E.J. Su-a						4.00
CASTLE WAITING						
Olio: 1997 - No. 7, 1999 ($2.95, B&W)						
Cartoon Books: Vol. 2, Aug, 2000 - No. 16 ($2.95/$3.95, B&W)						
Fantagraphics Books: Vol. 3, 2006 - Present ($5.95/$3.95, B&W)						
1-Linda Medley-s/a in all	1	2	3	5	6	8
2						4.00
3-7						3.00
The Lucky Road TPB r/#1-7						17.00
Hiatus Issue (1999) Crilley-c; short stories and previews						3.00
Vol. 2 #1-6,14-16 (#5&6 also have #12&13 on cover, for series numbering)						3.00
Vol. 3 #1 ($5.95) r/#15,16 and new story						6.00
Vol. 3 #2-8 ($3.95)						4.00
CASUAL HEROES						
Image Comics (Motown Machineworks): Apr, 1996 ($2.25, unfinished lim. series)						
1-Steve Rude-c						2.50
CAT, T.H.E. (TV) (See T.H.E. Cat)						
CAT, THE (See Movie Classics)						
CAT, THE (Female hero)						
Marvel Comics Group: Nov, 1972 - No. 4, June, 1973						
1-Origin & 1st app. The Cat (who later becomes Tigra); Mooney-a(i); Wood-c(i)/a(i)						
	4	8	12	23	36	48
2,3: 2-Marie Severin/Mooney-a. 3-Everett inks	3	6	9	14	19	24
4-Starlin/Weiss-a(p)	3	6	9	15	21	26

	GD 2.0	VG 4.0	FN 6.0	VF 8.0	VF/NM 9.0	NM- 9.2
CATALYST: AGENTS OF CHANGE (Also see Comics' Greatest World)						
Dark Horse Comics: Feb, 1994 - No.7, Nov, 1994 ($2.00, limited series)						
1-7: 1-Foil stamped logo						2.50
CAT & MOUSE						
EF Graphics (Silverline): Dec, 1988 ($1.75, color w/part B&W)						
1-1st printing (12/88, 32 pgs.), 1-2nd printing (5/89, 36 pgs.)						2.50
CAT FROM OUTER SPACE (See Walt Disney Showcase #46)						
CATHOLIC COMICS (See Heroes All Catholic...)						
Catholic Publications: June, 1946 - V3#10, July, 1949						
1	30	60	90	176	278	380
2	15	30	45	90	140	190
3-13(7/47)	14	28	42	81	118	155
V2#1-10	11	22	33	60	83	105
V3#1-10: Reprints 10-part Treasure Island serial from Target V2#2-11 (see Key Comics #5)						
	11	22	33	62	86	110
CATHOLIC PICTORIAL						
Catholic Guild: 1947						
1-Toth-a(2) (Rare)	40	80	120	240	383	525
CATMAN COMICS (Formerly Crash Comics No. 1-5)						
Holyoke Publishing Co./Continental Magazines V2#12, 7/44 on:						
5/41 - No. 17, 1/43; No. 18, 7/43 - No. 22, 12/43; No. 23, 3/44 - No. 26,						
11/44; No. 27, 4/45 - No. 30, 12/45; No. 31, 6/46 - No. 32, 8/46						
1(V1#6)-Origin The Deacon & Sidekick Mickey, Dr. Diamond & Rag-Man; The Black Widow						
app.; The Catman by Chas. Quinlan & Blaze Baylor begin						
	394	788	1182	2561	4531	6500
2(V1#7)	159	318	477	994	1647	2300
3(V1#8)-The Pied Piper begins; classic Hitler, Stalin & Mussolini-c						
	141	282	423	881	1466	2050
4(V1#9)	107	214	321	669	1110	1550
5(V2#10)-1st app. Kitten; The Hood begins (c-redated), 6,7(V2#11,12)						
	88	176	264	550	913	1275
8(V2#13,3/42)-Origin Little Leaders; Volton by Kubert begins (his 1st comic book work)						
	110	220	330	688	1144	1600
9,10(V2#14,15): 10-Origin Blackout; Phantom Falcon begins						
	72	144	216	450	750	1050
11 (V3#1)-Kubert-a	72	144	216	450	750	1050
12 (V3#2), 14, 15, 17. 12-Volton by Brodsky, not Kubert. 14-Brodsky-a						
	59	118	177	369	610	850
13-(scarce)	100	200	300	625	1038	1450
16 (V3#5)-Hitler, Tojo, Mussolini, Goehring-c	93	186	279	581	966	1350
18(V3#6), 19-20.	67	134	201	419	697	975
19,20: 19 (V2#6)-Hitler, Tojo, Mussolini-c. 20 (V2#7): Classic Hitler-c						
	98	196	294	613	1019	1425
21-23 (V2#10, 3/44)	57	114	171	356	591	825
nn(V3#13, 5/44)-Rico-a; Schomburg bondage-c	55	110	165	344	572	800
nn(V2#12, 7/44, nn(V3#1, 9/44)-Origin The Golden Archer; Leatherface app.						
	52	104	156	317	521	725
nn(V3#2, 11/44)-L. B. Cole-c	90	180	270	563	932	1300
27-Origins Catman & Kitten retold; L. B. Cole Flag-c; Infantino-a						
	107	214	321	669	1110	1550
28-Dr. Macabre app.; L. B. Cole-c/a	117	234	351	731	1216	1700
29-32-L. B. Cole-c; bondage-#30	103	206	309	644	1072	1500
NOTE: Fuje a-11, 27, 28(2), 29(3), 30. Palais a-11, 16, 27, 28, 29(2), 30(2), 32; c-25(7/44). Rico a-11(2), 23, 27,						
28.						
CAT TALES (3-D)						
Eternity Comics: Apr, 1989 ($2.95)						
1-Felix the Cat-r in 3-D						5.00
CATWOMAN (Also see Action Comics Weekly #611, Batman #404-407, Detective Comics,						
& Superman's Girlfriend Lois Lane #70, 71)						
DC Comics: Feb, 1989 - No. 4, May, 1989 ($1.50, limited series, mature)						
1	1	3	4	6	8	10
2-4: 3-Batman cameo. 4-Batman app.	1	2	3	5	7	9
Her Sister's Keeper (1991, $9.95, trade paperback)-r/#1-4						10.00
CATWOMAN (Also see Showcase '93, Showcase '95 #4, & Batman #404-407)						
DC Comics: Aug, 1993 - No. 94, Jul, 2001 ($1.50-$2.25)						
0-(10/94)-Zero Hour; origin retold. Released between #14&15						3.00
1-($1.95)-Embossed-c; Bane app.; Balent c-1-10; a-1-10p						4.00
2-20: 3-Bane flashback cameo. 4-Brief Bane app. 6,7-Knightquest tie-ins; Batman (Azrael)						
app. 8-1st app. Zephyr. 12-KnightsEnd pt. 6. 13-new Knights End Aftermath						

Catwoman #66 © DC

Cave Kids #5 © H-B

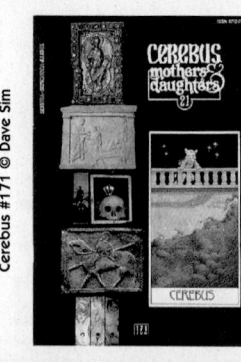

Cerebus #171 © Dave Sim

	GD	VG	FN	VF	VF/NM	NM-
	2.0	4.0	6.0	8.0	9.0	9.2

14-(9/94)-Zero Hour						3.00
21-24, 26-30, 33-49: 21-$1.95-c begins. 28,29-Penguin cameo app. 36-Legacy pt. 2.						
38-40-Year Two; Batman, Joker, Penguin & Two-Face app. 46-Two-Face app.						2.50
25,31,32: 25-($2.95)-Robin app. 31,32-Contagion pt. 4 (Reads pt. 5 on-c) & pt. 9.						3.00
50-($2.95, 48 pgs.)-New armored costume						3.00
50-($2.95, 48 pgs.)-Collector's Ed.w/metallic ink-c						3.00
51-77: 51-Huntress-c/app. 54-Grayson-s begins. 56-Cataclysm pt.6. 57-Poison Ivy-c/app.						
63-65-Joker-c/app. 72-No Man's Land; Ostrander-s begins						2.50
78-82: 80-Catwoman goes to jail						2.50
83-94: 83-Begin $2.25-c. 83,84,89-Harley Quinn-c/app.						2.50
#1,000,000 (11/98) 853rd Century x-over						2.50
Annual 1 (1994, $2.95, 68 pgs.)-Elseworlds story; Batman app.; no Balent-a						3.00
Annual 2,4 ('95, '97, $3.95) 2-Year One story. 4-Pulp Heroes						4.00
Annual 3 (1996, $2.95)-Legends of the Dead Earth story						3.00
...Plus 1 (11/97, $2.95) Screamqueen (Scare Tactics) app.						3.00
TPB ($9.95) r/#15-19, Balent-c						10.00
CATWOMAN (Also see Detective Comics #759-762)						
DC Comics: Jan, 2002 - Present ($2.50/$2.99)						
1-Darwyn Cooke & Mike Allred-a; Ed Brubaker-s						6.00
2-4						3.00
5-54: 5-9-Rader-a/Paul Pope-c. 10-Morse-c. 16-JG Jones-c. 22-Batman-c/app.						
34-36-War Games. 43-Killer Croc app. 44-Hughes-c begin. 50-Zatanna app.						
52-Catwoman kills Black Mask. 53-One Year Later; Helena born						2.50
55-70: 55-Begin $2.99-c. 56-58-Wildcat app.						3.00
...: Crooked Little Town TPB (2003, $14.95) r/#5-10 & Secret Files; Oeming-c						15.00
...: Relentless TPB (2005, $19.95) r/#12-19 & Secret Files						20.00
... Secret Files and Origins (10/02, $4.95) origin-s Oeming-a; profiles and pin-ups						5.00
...Selina's Big Score HC (2002, $24.95) Cooke-s/a by various						25.00
...Selina's Big Score SC (2003, $17.95) Cooke-s/a; pin-ups by various						18.00
...: The Dark End of the Street TPB (2002, $12.95) r/#1-4 & Slam Bradley back-up stories from Detective Comics #759-762						13.00
...: The Replacements TPB (2007, $14.99) r/#53-58						
...: Wild Ride TPB (2005, $14.99) r/#20-24 & Secret Files #1						15.00
CATWOMAN/ GUARDIAN OF GOTHAM						
DC Comics: 1999 - No. 2, 1999 ($5.95, limited series)						
1,2-Elseworlds; Moench-s/Balent-a						6.00
CATWOMAN: NINE LIVES OF A FELINE FATALE						
DC Comics: 2004 ($14.95, TPB)						
nn-Reprints notable stories from Batman #1 to the present; pin-ups by various; Bolland-c						15.00
CATWOMAN: THE MOVIE (2004 Halle Berry movie)						
DC Comics: 2004 ($4.95/$9.95)						
1-($4.95) Movie adaptation; Jim Lee-c and sketch pages; Derenick-a						5.00
... & Other Cat Tales TPB (2004, $9.95)-r/Movie adaptation; Jim Lee sketch pages, r/Catwoman #0, Catwoman (2nd series) #11 & 25; photo-c						10.00
CATWOMAN/VAMPIRELLA: THE FURIES						
DC Comics/Harris Publ.: Feb, 1997 ($4.95, squarebound, 46 pgs.) (1st DC/Harris x-over)						
nn-Reintro Pantha; Chuck Dixon scripts; Jim Balent-c/a						5.00
CATWOMAN: WHEN IN ROME						
DC Comics: Nov, 2004 - No. 6, Aug, 2005 ($3.50, limited series)						
1-6-Jeph Loeb-s/Tim Sale-a/c; Riddler app.						3.50
HC (2005, $19.95, dustjacket); intro by Mark Chiarello; sketch pages						20.00
SC (2007, $12.99) r/series; intro by Mark Chiarello; sketch pages						13.00
CATWOMAN/WILDCAT						
DC Comics: Aug, 1998 - No. 4, Nov, 1998 ($2.50, limited series)						
1-4-Chuck Dixon & Beau Smith-s; Stelfreeze-c						3.00
CAUGHT						
Atlas Comics (VPI): Aug, 1956 - No. 5, Apr, 1957						
1	23	46	69	130	205	280
2-4: 3-Maneely, Pakula, Torres-a. 4-Maneely-a	13	26	39	74	105	135
5-Crandall, Krigstein-a	14	28	42	78	112	145
NOTE: *Drucker* a-2. *Heck* a-4. *Severin* c-1, 2, 4, 5. *Shores* a-4.						
CAVALIER COMICS						
A. W. Nugent Publ. Co.: 1945; 1952 (Early DC reprints)						
2(1945)-Speed Saunders, Fang Gow	21	42	63	120	188	255
2(1952)	11	22	33	64	90	115
CAVE GIRL (Also see Africa)						
Magazine Enterprises: No. 11, 1953 - No. 14, 1954						
11(A-1 82)-Origin; all Cave Girl stories	46	92	138	281	466	650

12(A-1 96), 13(A-1 116), 14(A-1 125)-Thunda by Powell in each						
	36	72	108	208	329	450
NOTE: *Powell* c/a in all.						
CAVE GIRL						
AC Comics: 1988 ($2.95, 44 pgs.) (16 pgs. of color, rest B&W)						
1-Powell-r/Cave Girl #11; Nyoka photo back-c from movie; Powell/Bill Black-c; Special Limited Edition on-c						4.00
CAVE KIDS (TV) (See Comic Album #16)						
Gold Key: Feb, 1963 - No. 16, Mar, 1967 (Hanna-Barbera)						
1	7	14	21	45	73	100
2-5	4	8	12	24	37	50
6-16: 7,12-Pebbles & Bamm Bamm app. 16-1st Space Kidettes						
	3	6	9	20	30	40
CAVEWOMAN						
Basement Comics: Jan, 1994 - No. 6, 1995 ($2.95)						
1	3	6	9	16	23	30
2	2	4	6	9	12	15
3-6	1	2	3	5	6	8
...: Meets Explorers ('97, $2.95)						3.00
...: One-Shot Special (7/00, $2.95) Massey-s/a						3.00
CELESTINE (See Violator Vs. Badrock #1)						
Image Comics (Extreme): May, 1996 - No. 2, June, 1996 ($2.50, limited series)						
1,2: Warren Ellis scripts						2.50
CENTURION OF ANCIENT ROME, THE						
Zondervan Publishing House: 1958 (no month listed) (B&W, 36 pgs.)						
(Rare) All by Jay Disbrow	55	110	165	344	572	800
CENTURIONS (TV)						
DC Comics: June, 1987 - No. 4, Sept, 1987 (75¢, limited series)						
1-4						2.50
CENTURY: DISTANT SONS						
Marvel Comics: Feb, 1996 ($2.95, one-shot)						
1-Wraparound-c						3.00
CENTURY OF COMICS (See Promotional Comics section)						
CEREBUS BI-WEEKLY						
Aardvark-Vanaheim: Dec. 2, 1988 - No. 26, Nov. 11, 1989 ($1.25, B&W)						
Reprints Cerebus The Aardvark#1-26						
1-16, 18, 19, 21-26:						3.00
17-Hepcats app.	2	4	6	8	10	12
20-Milk & Cheese app.	2	4	6	10	12	15
CEREBUS: CHURCH & STATE						
Aardvark-Vanaheim: Feb, 1991 - No. 30, Apr, 1992 ($2.00, B&W, bi-weekly)						
1-30: r/Cerebus #51-80						3.00
CEREBUS: HIGH SOCIETY						
Aardvark-Vanaheim: Feb, 1990 - No. 25, 1991 ($1.70, B&W)						
1-25: r/Cerebus #26-50						3.00
CEREBUS JAM						
Aardvark-Vanaheim: Apr, 1985						
1-Eisner, Austin, Dave Sim-a (Cerebus vs. Spirit)						6.00
CEREBUS THE AARDVARK (See A-V in 3-D, Nucleus, Power Comics)						
Aardvark-Vanaheim: Dec, 1977 - No. 300, March, 2004 ($1.70/$2.00/$2.25, B&W)						
0						3.00
0-Gold						20.00
1-1st app. Cerebus; 2000 print run; most copies poorly printed						
	43	86	129	344	622	900
Note: There is a counterfeit version known to exist. It can be distinguished from the original in the following ways: inside cover is glossy instead of flat, black background on the front cover is blotted or spotty. Reports show that a counterfeit #2 also exists.						
2-Dave Sim art in all	12	24	36	82	146	210
3-Origin Red Sophia	10	20	30	67	116	165
4-Origin Elrod the Albino	8	16	24	52	86	120
5,6	6	12	18	43	69	95
7-10	5	10	15	35	55	75
11,12: 11-Origin The Cockroach	4	8	12	26	41	55
13-15: 14-Origin Lord Julius	4	8	12	22	34	45
16-20	3	6	9	16	22	28
21-B. Smith letter in letter column	5	10	15	32	51	70
22-Low distribution; no cover price	3	6	9	19	29	38

Chain Gang War #6 © DC

Challengers of the Unknown #79 © DC

Chamber of Chills #23 © HARV

	GD 2.0	VG 4.0	FN 6.0	VF 8.0	VF/NM 9.0	NM- 9.2

23-30: 23-Preview of Wandering Star by Teri S. Wood. 26-High Society begins, ends #50

	2	4	6	11	16	20

31-Origin Moonroach

	2	4	6	13	18	22

32-40, 53-Intro. Wolveroach (brief app.)

	1	3	4	6	8	10

41-50,52: 52-Church & State begins, ends #111; Cutey Bunny app.

	1	2	3	5	6	8

51,54: 51-Cutey Bunny app. 54-1st full Wolveroach story

	2	4	6	8	10	12

55,56-Wolveroach app.; Normalman back-ups by Valentino

	1	2	3	5	7	9

57-100: 61,62: Flaming Carrot app. 65-Gerhard begins 4.00
101-160: 104-Flaming Carrot app. 112/113-Double issue. 114-Jaka's Story begins, ends #136.
139-Melmoth begins, ends #150. 151-Mothers & Daughters begins, ends #200 3.00

161-Bone app.

	1	3	4	6	8	10

162-231: 175-($2.25, 44 pgs). 186-Strangers in Paradise cameo. 201-Guys storyline begins; Eddie Campbell's Bacchus app. 220-231-Rick's Story 2.50
232-265-Going Home 2.50
266-288,291-299-Latter Days: 267-Five-Bar Gate. 276-Spore (Spawn spoof) 2.50
289&290 ($4.50) Two issues combined 5.00
300-Final issue 2.50
Free Cerebus (Giveaway, 1991-92?, 36 pgs.)-All-r 4.00

CHAIN GANG WAR
DC Comics: July, 1993 - No. 12, June, 1994 ($1.75)

1-($2.50)-Embossed silver foil-c, Dave Johnson-c/a 3.00
2-4,6-12: 3-Deathstroke app. 4-Brief Deathstroke app. 6-New Batman (Azrael) cameo.
11-New Batman-c/story. 12-New Batman app. 2.50
5-($2.50)-Foil-c; Deathstroke app; new Batman cameo (1 panel) 3.00

CHAINS OF CHAOS
Harris Comics: Nov, 1994 - No. 3, Jan, 1995 ($2.95, limited series)

1-3-Re-Intro of The Rook w/ Vampirella 3.00

CHALLENGE OF THE UNKNOWN (Formerly Love Experiences)
Ace Magazines: No. 6, Sept, 1950 (See Web Of Mystery No. 19)

6- "Villa of the Vampire" used in N.Y. Joint Legislative Comm. Publ; Sekowsky-a

	35	70	105	201	318	435

CHALLENGER, THE
Interfaith Publications/T.C. Comics: 1945 - No. 4, Oct-Dec, 1946

nn; nd; 32 pgs.; Origin the Challenger Club; Anti-Fascist with funny animal filler

	48	96	144	293	484	675

2-4: Kubert-a; 4-Fuje-a

	38	76	114	219	347	475

CHALLENGERS OF THE FANTASTIC
Marvel Comics (Amalgam): June 1997 ($1.95, one-shot)

1-Karl Kesel-s/Tom Grummett-a 2.50

CHALLENGERS OF THE UNKNOWN (See Showcase #6, 7, 11, 12, Super DC Giant, and Super Team Family) (See Showcase Presents for B&W reprints)
National Per. Publ./DC Comics: 4-5/58 - No. 77, 12-1/70-71; No. 78, 2/73 - No. 80, 6-7/73; No. 81, 6-7/77 - No. 87, 6-7/78

1-Kirby/Stein-a(2); Kirby-c

	196	392	588	1715	3208	4700

2-Kirby/Stein-a(2)

	64	128	192	544	1010	1475

3-Kirby/Stein-a(2)

	55	110	165	468	872	1275

4-8-Kirby/Wood-a plus cover to #8

	43	86	129	344	622	900

9,10

	26	52	78	194	340	485

11-Grey tone-c

	20	40	60	146	261	375

12-15: 14-Origin/1st app. Multi-Man (villain)

	17	34	51	128	227	325

16-22: 18-Intro. Cosmo, the Challengers Spacepet. 22-Last 10¢ issue

	12	24	36	87	156	225

23-30

	8	16	24	54	90	125

31-Retells origin of the Challengers

	8	16	24	56	93	130

32-40

	6	12	18	39	62	85

41-47,49,50,52-60: 43-New look begins. 49-Intro. Challenger Corps. 55-Death of Red Ryan.
60-Red Ryan returns

	4	8	12	26	41	55

48,51: 48-Doom Patrol app. 51-Sea Devils app.

	4	8	12	28	44	60

61-68: 64,65-Kirby origin-r, parts 1 & 2. 66-New logo. 68-Last 12¢ issue.

	3	6	9	18	27	35

69-73,75-80: 69-1st app. Corinna. 77-Last 15¢ issue

	2	4	6	10	14	18

74-Deadman by Tuska/Adams; 1 pg. Wrightson-a

	5	10	15	30	48	65

81,83-87: 81-(6-7/77). 83-87-Swamp Thing app. 84-87-Deadman app.

	1	3	4	6	8	10

82-Swamp Thing app. (thru #87, c/s

	1	3	6	9	11	14

NOTE: *N. Adams* c-67, 68, 70, 72, 74l, 81l. *Buckler* c-83-86p. *Giffen* a-83-87p. *Kirby* a-75-80r; c-75, 77, 78. *Kubert* c-64, 66, 69, 76, 79. *Nasser* a-81p, 82p. *Tuska* a-73. *Wood* r-76.

CHALLENGERS OF THE UNKNOWN
DC Comics: Mar, 1991 - No. 8, Oct, 1991 ($1.75, limited series)

1-Jeph Loeb scripts & Tim Sale-a in all (1st work together); Bolland-c 3.00
2-8: 2-Superman app. 3-Dr. Fate app. 6-G. Kane-c(p). 7-Steranko-c/swipe by Art Adams 2.50
... Must Die! (2004, $19.95, TPB) r/series; intro by Bendis; Sale sketch pages 20.00
NOTE: *Art Adams* c-7. *Hempel* c-5. *Gil Kane* c-6p. *Sale* a-1-8; c-3, 8. *Wagner* c-4.

CHALLENGERS OF THE UNKNOWN
DC Comics: Feb, 1997 - No. 18, July, 1998 ($2.25)

1-18: 1-Intro new team; Leon-c/a(p) begins. 4-Origin of new team. 11,12-Batman app.
15-Millennium Giants x-over; Superman-c/app. 2.50

CHALLENGERS OF THE UNKNOWN
DC Comics: Aug, 2004 - No. 6, Jan, 2005 ($2.95, limited series)

1-6-Intro. new team; Howard Chaykin-s/a 3.00

CHALLENGE TO THE WORLD
Catechetical Guild: 1951 (10¢, 36 pgs.)

nn

	6	12	18	27	33	38

CHAMBER (See Generation X and Uncanny X-Men)
Marvel Comics: Oct, 2002 - No. 4, Jan, 2003 ($2.99, limited series)

1-4-Bachalo-c/Vaughan-s/Ferguson-a. 1-Cyclops app. 3.00

CHAMBER OF CHILLS (Formerly Blondie Comics #20; ...of Clues No. 27 on)
Harvey Publications/Witches Tales: No. 21, June, 1951 - No. 26, Dec, 1954

21 (#1)

	48	96	144	293	484	675

22,24 (#2,4)

	34	68	102	195	308	420

23 (#3)-Excessive violence; eyes torn out

	36	72	108	208	329	450

5(2/52)-Decapitation, acid in face scene

	36	72	108	208	329	450

6-Woman melted alive

	35	70	105	201	318	435

7-Used in **SOTI**, pg. 389; decapitation/severed head panels

	33	66	99	190	300	410

8-10: 8-Decapitation panels

	27	54	81	156	246	335

11,12,14

	22	44	66	126	198	270

13,15-24-Nostrand-a in all. 13,21-Decapitation panels. 18-Atom bomb panels. 20-Nostrand-c

	27	54	81	156	246	335

25,26

	17	34	51	98	154	210

NOTE: *About half the issues contain bondage, torture, sadism, perversion, gore, cannabalism, eyes ripped out, acid in face, etc. Elias* c-4-11, 14-19, 21-26. *Kremer* a-12, 17. *Palais* a-21(1), 23. *Nostrand/Powell* a-13, 15, 16. *Powell* a-21, 23, 24('51), 5-8, 11, 13, 18-21, 23-25. *Bondage*-c-21, 24('51), 7. 25-r/#5; 26-r/#9.

CHAMBER OF CHILLS
Marvel Comics Group: Nov, 1972 - No. 25, Nov, 1976

1-Harlan Ellison adaptation

	3	6	9	18	27	35

2-5: 2-1st app. John Jakes' Brak the Barbarian

	2	4	6	9	13	16

6-25: 22,23-(Regular 25¢ editions)

	2	4	6	8	10	12

22,23-(30¢-c variants, limited distribution)(5,7/76)

	3	6	9	20	30	40

NOTE: *Adkins* a-1i, 2i. *Brunner* a-2-4; c-4. *Chaykin* a-4. *Ditko* r-14, 16, 19, 23, 24. *Everett* a-3i, 11i,21r. *Heath* a-1r. *Gil Kane* c-2p. *Kirby* r-11, 18, 19, 22. *Powell* a-13r. *Russell* a-1p, 2p. *Shores* a-5. *Williamson/Mayo* a-13r. *Robert E. Howard* horror story adaptation-2, 3.

CHAMBER OF CLUES (Formerly Chamber of Chills)
Harvey Publications: No. 27, Feb, 1955 - No. 28, April, 1955

27-Kerry Drake-r/#19; Powell-a; last pre-code

	7	14	21	35	43	50

28-Kerry Drake

	6	12	18	28	34	40

CHAMBER OF DARKNESS (Monsters on the Prowl #9 on)
Marvel Comics Group: Oct, 1969 - No. 8, Dec, 1970

1-Buscema-a(p)

	6	12	18	41	66	90

2,3: 2-Neal Adams scripts. 3-Smith, Buscema-a

	4	8	12	22	34	45

4-A Conan-esque tryout by Smith (4/70); reprinted in Conan #16; Marie Severin/Everett-c

	7	14	21	50	83	115

5,8: 5-H.P. Lovecraft adaptation. 8-Wrightson-c

	3	6	9	19	29	38

6

	3	6	9	17	25	32

7-Wrightson-c/a, 7pgs. (his 1st work at Marvel); Wrightson draws himself in 1st & last panels; Kirby/Ditko-r; last 15¢-c

	4	8	12	28	44	60

1-(1/72; 25¢ Special, 52 pgs.)

	4	8	12	22	34	45

NOTE: *Adkins/Everett* a-8. *Buscema* a-Special 1r. *Craig* a-5. *Ditko* a-6-9r. *Heck* a-1, 2, 8, Special 1r. *Kirby* a(p)-4, 5, 7r. *Kirby/Everett* c-5. *Severin/Everett* c-6. *Shores* a-2, 3i, Special 1r. *Sutton* a-1, 2i, 4, 7, Special 1r. *Wrightson* c-7, 8.

CHAMP COMICS (Formerly Champion No. 1-10)
Worth Publ. Co./Champ Publ./Family Comics(Harvey Publ.): No. 11, Oct, 1940 - No. 24, Dec, 1942; No. 25, April, 1943

11-Human Meteor cont'd. from Champion

	91	182	273	569	947	1325

12-17,20: 14,15-Crandall-c. 20-The Green Ghost app.

	71	142	213	444	735	1025

18,19-Simon-c. 19-The Wasp app.

	88	176	264	550	913	1275

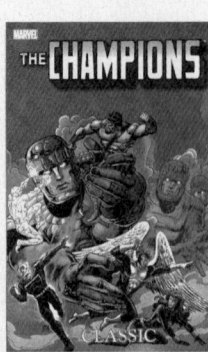

Champions Classic V2 TPB © MAR

Charlie Chan #8 © PRIZE

Charlton Bullseye #8 © CC

	GD 2.0	VG 4.0	FN 6.0	VF 8.0	VF/NM 9.0	NM- 9.2
21-23,25: 22-The White Mask app. 23-Flag-c	52	104	156	317	521	725
24-Hitler, Tojo & Mussolini-c	63	126	189	394	652	910

CHAMPION (See Gene Autry's...)

CHAMPION COMICS
Worth Publ. Co.: Oct, 1939 (ashcan)

nn-Ashcan comic, not distributed to newsstands, only for in house use				(no known sales)		

CHAMPION COMICS (Formerly Speed Comics #1?; Champ Comics No. 11 on)
Worth Publ. Co.(Harvey Publications): No. 2, Dec, 1939 - No. 10, Aug, 1940 (no No.1)

	GD 2.0	VG 4.0	FN 6.0	VF 8.0	VF/NM 9.0	NM- 9.2
2-The Champ, The Blazing Scarab, Neptina, Liberty Lads, Jungleman, Bill Handy, Swingtime Sweetie begin	172	344	516	1075	1788	2500
3-7: 7-The Human Meteor begins?	79	158	237	494	822	1150
8-10: 8-Simon-a. 9-1st S&K-c (1st collaboration together). 10-Bondage-c by Kirby	162	324	486	1013	1682	2350

CHAMPIONS, THE
Marvel Comics Group: Oct, 1975 - No. 17, Jan, 1978

	GD 2.0	VG 4.0	FN 6.0	VF 8.0	VF/NM 9.0	NM- 9.2
1-Origin & 1st app. The Champions (The Angel, Black Widow, Ghost Rider, Hercules, Iceman); Venus x-over	4	8	12	22	34	45
2-4,8-10,16: 2,3-Venus x-over	2	4	6	10	14	18
5-7-(Regular 25¢ edition)(4-8/76) 6-Kirby-c	2	4	6	10	14	18
5-7-(30¢-c variants, limited distribution)	4	8	12	24	37	50
11-14,17-Byrne-a. 14-(Regular 30¢ edition)	2	4	6	10	14	18
14,15-(35¢-c variant, limited distribution)	5	10	15	32	51	70
15-(Regular 30¢ edition)(9/77)-Byrne-a	2	4	6	10	14	18
... Classic Vol. 1 TPB (2006, $19.99) r/#1-11; unused cover to #7						20.00
... Classic Vol. 2 TPB (2007, $19.99) r/#12-17, Iron Man Ann.#4, Avengers #163, Super-Villain Team-Up #14 and Peter Parker, The Spectacular Spider-Man #17-18						20.00

NOTE: *Buckler/Adkins c-3. Byrne a-11-15, 17. Kane/Adkins c-1. Kane/Layton c-11. Tuska a-3p, 4p, 6p, 7p. Ghost Rider c-1-4, 7, 8, 10, 14, 16, 17 (4, 10, 14 are more prominent).*

CHAMPIONS (Game)
Eclipse Comics: June, 1986 - No. 6, Feb, 1987 (limited series)

1-6: 1-Intro Flare; based on game. 5-Origin Flare						2.50

CHAMPIONS (Also see The League of Champions)
Hero Comics: Sept, 1987 - No. 12, 1989 ($1.95)

1-12: 1-Intro The Marksman & The Rose. 14-Origin Malice						2.50
Annual 1(1988, $2.75, 52pgs.)-Origin of Giant						2.75

CHAMPION SPORTS
National Periodical Publications: Oct-Nov, 1973 - No. 3, Feb-Mar, 1974

	GD 2.0	VG 4.0	FN 6.0	VF 8.0	VF/NM 9.0	NM- 9.2
1	3	6	9	16	23	30
2,3	2	4	6	9	12	15

CHANNEL ZERO
Image Comics: Feb, 1998 - No. 5 ($2.95, B&W, limited series)

1-5, ...Dupe (1/99) -Brian Wood-s/a						3.00

CHAOS (See The Crusaders)

CHAOS! BIBLE
Chaos! Comics: Nov, 1995 ($3.30, one-shot)

1-Profiles of characters & creators						3.50

CHAOS! CHRONICLES
Chaos! Comics: Feb, 2000 ($3.50, one-shot)

1-Profiles of characters, checklist of Chaos! comics and products						3.50

CHAOS EFFECT, THE
Valiant: 1994

Alpha (Giveaway w/trading card checklist)						2.25
Alpha-Gold variant, Alpha-Red variant, Omega-Gold variant						5.00
Omega (11/94, $2.25); Epilogue Pt. 1, 2 (12/94, 1/95; $2.95)						3.00

CHAOS! GALLERY
Chaos! Comics: Aug, 1997 ($2.95, one-shot)

1-Pin-ups of characters						3.00

CHAOS! QUARTERLY
Chaos! Comics: Oct, 1995 -No. 3, May, 1996 ($4.95, quarterly)

1-3: 1-anthology; Lady Death-c by Julie Bell. 2-Boris "Lady Demon"-c						5.00
1-Premium Edition (7,500)						25.00

CHAPEL (Also see Youngblood & Youngblood Strikefile #1-3)
Image Comics (Extreme Studios): No. 1 Feb, 1995 - No. 2, Mar, 1995 ($2.50, limited series)

1,2						2.50

CHAPEL (Also see Youngblood & Youngblood Strikefile #1-3)

Image Comics (Extreme Studios): V2 #1, Aug, 1995 - No. 7, Apr, 1996 ($2.50)

V2#1-7: 4-Babewatch x-over. 5-vs. Spawn. 7-Shadowhawk-c/app; Shadowhunt x-over						2.50
#1-Quesada & Palmiotti variant-c						2.50

CHAPEL (Also see Youngblood & Youngblood Strikefile #1-3)
Awesome Entertainment: Sept, 1997 ($2.99, one-shot)

1 (Reg. & alternate covers)						3.00

CHARLEMAGNE (Also see War Dancer)
Defiant Comics: Mar, 1994 - No. 5, July, 1994 ($2.50)

1/2 (Hero Illustrated giveaway)-Adam Pollina-c/a.						
1-(3/94, $3.50, 52 pgs.)-Adam Pollina-c/a.						3.50
2,3,5: Adam Pollina-c/a. 2-War Dancer app. 5-Pre-Schism issue.						2.50
4-($3.25, 52 pgs.)						3.25

CHARLIE CHAN (See Big Shot Comics, Columbia Comics, Feature Comics & The New Advs. of...)

CHARLIE CHAN (The Adventures of...) (Zaza The Mystic No. 10 on) (TV)
Crestwood(Prize) No. 1-5; Charlton No. 6(6/55) on: 6-7/48 - No. 5, 2-3/49; No.6, 6/55 - No. 9, 3/56

	GD 2.0	VG 4.0	FN 6.0	VF 8.0	VF/NM 9.0	NM- 9.2
1-S&K-c, 2 pgs.; Infantino-a	81	162	243	506	841	1175
2-5-S&K-c; 3-S&K c/a	49	98	147	299	492	685
6 (6/55-Charlton)-S&K-c	37	74	111	213	337	460
7-9	20	40	60	115	180	245

CHARLIE CHAN
Dell Publishing Co.: Oct-Dec, 1965 - No. 2, Mar, 1966

	GD 2.0	VG 4.0	FN 6.0	VF 8.0	VF/NM 9.0	NM- 9.2
1-Springer-a	5	10	15	35	55	75
2	4	8	12	22	34	45

CHARLIE McCARTHY (See Edgar Bergen Presents...)
Dell Publishing Co.: No. 171, Nov, 1947 - No. 571, July, 1954 (See True Comics #14)

	GD 2.0	VG 4.0	FN 6.0	VF 8.0	VF/NM 9.0	NM- 9.2
Four Color 171	24	48	72	175	313	450
Four Color 196-Part photo-c; photo back-c	16	32	48	114	202	290
1(3-5/49)-Part photo-c; photo back-c	14	28	42	102	181	260
2-9(7/52); #5,6-52 pgs.	8	16	24	56	93	130
Four Color 445,478,527,571	6	12	18	39	62	85

CHARLTON BULLSEYE
CPL/Gang Publications: 1975 - No. 5, 1976 ($1.50, B&W, bi-monthly, magazine format)

	GD 2.0	VG 4.0	FN 6.0	VF 8.0	VF/NM 9.0	NM- 9.2
1: 1 & 2 are last Capt. Atom by Ditko/Byrne intended for the never published Capt. Atom #90; Nightshade app.; Jeff Jones-a	5	10	15	30	48	65
2-Part 2 Capt. Atom story by Ditko/Byrne	3	6	9	21	32	42
3-Wrong Country by Sanho Kim	2	4	6	13	18	22
4-Doomsday + 1 by John Byrne	3	6	9	17	25	32
5-Doomsday + 1 by Byrne, The Question by Toth; Neal Adams back-c; Toth-c	4	8	12	24	37	50

CHARLTON BULLSEYE
Charlton Publications: June, 1981 - No. 10, Dec, 1982; Nov, 1986

	GD 2.0	VG 4.0	FN 6.0	VF 8.0	VF/NM 9.0	NM- 9.2
1-Blue Beetle, The Question app.; 1st app. Rocket Rabbit	1	2	3	5	7	9
2-5: 2-1st app. Neil The Horse; Rocket Rabbit app. 4-Vanguards						6.00
6-10: Low print run. 6-Origin & 1st app. Thunderbunny	1	2	3	5	7	9

NOTE: *Material intended for issue #11-up was published in Scary Tales #37-up.*

CHARLTON CLASSICS
Charlton Comics: Apr, 1980 - No. 9, Aug, 1981

1-Hercules-r by Glanzman in all						6.00
2-9						5.00

CHARLTON CLASSICS LIBRARY (1776)
Charlton Comics: V10 No.1, Mar, 1973 (one-shot)

	GD 2.0	VG 4.0	FN 6.0	VF 8.0	VF/NM 9.0	NM- 9.2
1776 (title) - Adaptation of the film musical "1776"; given away at movie theatres; also a newsstand version	3	6	9	14	19	24

CHARLTON PREMIERE (Formerly Marine War Heroes)
Charlton Comics: V1#19, July, 1967; V2#1, Sept, 1967 - No. 4, May, 1968

	GD 2.0	VG 4.0	FN 6.0	VF 8.0	VF/NM 9.0	NM- 9.2
V1#19, V2#1,2,4: V1#19-Marine War Heroes. V2#1-Trio; intro. Shape. Tyro Team & Spookman. 2-Children of Doom; Boyette classic-a. 4-Unlikely Tales; Aparo, Ditko-a	3	6	9	16	22	28
V2#3-Sinistro Boy Fiend; Blue Beetle & Peacemaker x-over	3	6	9	18	27	35

CHARLTON SPORT LIBRARY - PROFESSIONAL FOOTBALL
Charlton Comics: Winter, 1969-70 (Jan. on cover) (68 pgs.)

	GD 2.0	VG 4.0	FN 6.0	VF 8.0	VF/NM 9.0	NM- 9.2
1	3	6	9	20	30	40

Chassis #3 © Hurricane

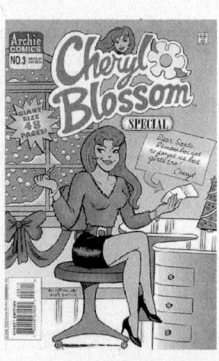

Cheryl Blossom Special #3 © AP

Cheval Noir #22 © DH

	GD 2.0	VG 4.0	FN 6.0	VF 8.0	VF/NM 9.0	NM- 9.2

CHASE (See Batman #550 for 1st app.)
DC Comics: Feb, 1998 - No. 9, Oct, 1998; #1,000,000 Nov, 1998 ($2.50)

1-9: Williams III & Gray-a. 1-Includes 4 Chase cards. 4-Teen Titans app. 7,8-Batman app. 9-GL Hal Jordan-c/app.					2.50
#1,000,000 (11/98) Final issue; 853rd Century x-over					2.50

CHASING DOGMA (See Jay and Silent Bob)

CHASSIS
Millenium Publications: 1996 - No. 3 ($2.95)

1-3: 1-Adam Hughes-c. 2-Conner var-c.					3.00

CHASSIS
Hurricane Entertainment: 1998 - No. 3 ($2.95)

0,1-3: 1-Adam Hughes-c. 0-Green var-c.					3.00

CHASSIS (Vol. 3)
Image Comics: Nov, 1999 - No. 4 ($2.95, limited series)

1-4: 1-Two covers by O'Neil and Green. 2-Busch var-c.					3.00
1-($6.95) DF Edition alternate-c by Wieringo					7.00

CHASTITY
Chaos! Comics: (one-shots)

#1/2 (1/01, $2.95) Batista-a					3.00
Heartbreaker (3/02, $2.99) Adrian-a/Molenaar-c					3.00
Love Bites (3/01, $2.99) Vale-a/Romano-c					3.00
Reign of Terror 1 (10/00, $2.95) Grant-s/Ross-a/Rio-c					3.00
Re-Imagined 1 (7/02, $2.99) Conner-c; Toledo-a					3.00

CHASTITY: CRAZYTOWN
Chaos! Comics: Apr, 2002 - No. 3, June, 2002 ($2.99, limited series)

1-3-Nicieza-s/Batista-c/a					3.00

CHASTITY: LUST FOR LIFE
Chaos! Comics: May, 1999 - No. 3, July, 1999 ($2.95, limited series)

1-3-Nutman-s/Benes-c/a					3.00

CHASTITY: ROCKED
Chaos! Comics: Nov, 1998 - No. 4, Feb, 1999 ($2.95, limited series)

1-4-Nutman-s/Justiniano-c/a					3.00

CHASTITY: SHATTERED
Chaos! Comics: Jun, 2001 - No. 3, Sept, 2001 ($2.99, limited series)

1-3-Kaminski & Pulido-s/Batista-c/a					3.00

CHASTITY: THEATER OF PAIN
Chaos! Comics: Feb, 1997 - No. 3, June, 1997 ($2.95, limited series)

1-3-Pulido-s/Justiniano-c/a					3.00
TPB (1997, $9.95) r/#1-3					10.00

CHECKMATE (TV)
Gold Key: Oct, 1962 - No. 2, Dec, 1962

	GD	VG	FN	VF	VF/NM	NM-
1-Photo-c on both	6	12	18	37	59	80
2	5	10	15	32	51	70

CHECKMATE! (See Action Comics #598 and The OMAC Project)
DC Comics: Apr, 1988 - No. 33, Jan, 1991 ($1.25)

1-33: 13: New format begins					2.50

NOTE: *Gil Kane c-2, 4, 7, 8, 10, 11, 15-19.*

CHECKMATE (See Infinite Crisis and The OMAC Project)
DC Comics: Jun, 2006 - Present ($2.99)

1-Rucka-s/Saiz-a/Bermejo-c; Alan Scott, Mr. Terrific, Sasha Bordeaux app.					4.00
1-2nd printing with B&W cover					3.00
2-17: 2,3-Kobra, King Faraday, Amanda Waller, Fire app. 13-15-Outsiders app.					3.00
...: A King's GameTPB (2007, $14.99) r/#1-7					15.00

CHERYL BLOSSOM (See Archie's Girls, Betty and Veronica #320 for 1st app.)
Archie Publications: Sept, 1995 - No. 3, Nov, 1995 ($1.50 series)

1-3					6.00
Special 1-4 ('95, '96, $2.00)					6.00

CHERYL BLOSSOM (Cheryl's Summer Job)
Archie Publications: July, 1996 - No. 3, Sept, 1996 ($1.50 series)

1-3					4.50

CHERYL BLOSSOM (...Goes Hollywood)
Archie Publications: Dec, 1996 - No. 3, Feb, 1997 ($1.50 series)

1-3					4.00

CHERYL BLOSSOM
Archie Publications: Apr, 1997 - No. 37, Mar, 2001 ($1.50/$1.75/$1.99/$1.99)

	GD	VG	FN	VF	VF/NM	NM-
1-Dan DeCarlo-c/a	1	2	3	4	5	7
2-10: 2-7-Dan DeCarlo-c/a						4.00
11-37: 32-Begin $1.99-c. 34-Sabrina app.						2.50

CHESTY SANCHEZ
Antarctic Press: Nov, 1995 - No. 2, Mar, 1996 ($2.95, B&W)

1,2					3.00
...Super Special (2/99, $5.99)					6.00

CHEVAL NOIR
Dark Horse Comics: 1989 - No. 48, Nov, 1993 ($3.50, B&W, 68 pgs.)

1-8,10 ($3.50): 6-Moebius poster insert					3.50
9,11,13,15,17,20,22 ($4.50, 84 pgs.)					4.50
12,18,19,21,23,25,26 ($3.95): 12-Geary-a; Mignola-c. 26-Moebius-a begins					4.00
14 ($4.95, 76 pgs.)(7 pgs. color)					5.00
16,24 ($3.75): 16-19-Contain trading cards					3.75
27-48 ($2.95): 33-Snyder III-c					3.00

NOTE: *Bolland* a-2, 6, 7, 13, 14. *Bolton* a-2, 4, 45; c-4, 20. *Chadwick* c-13. *Dorman* painted c-16. *Geary* a-13, 14. *Kelley Jones* c-27. *Kaluta* a-6; c-6, 18. *Moebius* c-5, 9, 26. *Dave Stevens* c-1, 7. *Sutton* painted c-36.

CHEYENNE (TV)
Dell Publishing Co.: No. 734, Oct, 1956 - No. 25, Dec-Jan, 1961-62

	GD	VG	FN	VF	VF/NM	NM-
Four Color 734(#1)-Clint Walker photo-c	15	30	45	111	198	285
Four Color 772,803: Clint Walker photo-c	9	18	27	60	100	140
4(8-10/57) - 20: 4-9,13-20-Clint Walker photo-c. 10-12-Ty Hardin photo-c	6	12	18	43	69	95
21-25-Clint Walker photo-c on all	7	14	21	45	73	100

CHEYENNE AUTUMN (See Movie Classics)

CHEYENNE KID (Formerly Wild Frontier No. 1-7)
Charlton Comics: No. 8, July, 1957 - No. 99, Nov, 1973

	GD	VG	FN	VF	VF/NM	NM-
8 (#1)	8	16	24	40	50	65
9,15-19	6	12	18	29	36	42
10-Williamson/Torres-a(3); Ditko-c	11	22	33	60	83	105
11-(68 pgs.)-Cheyenne Kid meets Geronimo	10	20	30	58	79	100
12-Williamson/Torres-a(2)	10	20	30	58	79	100
13-Williamson/Torres-a (5 pgs.)	8	16	24	44	57	70
14-Williamson-a (5 pgs.?)	8	16	24	42	54	65
20-22,24,25-Severin c/a(3) each	3	6	9	21	32	42
23,27-29	3	6	9	14	20	25
26,30-Severin-a	3	6	9	17	25	32
31-59	2	4	6	9	13	16
60-65,67-80	2	4	6	8	10	12
66-Wander by Aparo begins, ends #87	2	4	6	9	13	16
81-99: Apache Red begins #88, origin in #89	2	4	6	8	10	12
Modern Comics Reprint 87,89(1978)						4.00

CHIAROSCURO (THE PRIVATE LIVES OF LEONARDO DA VINCI)
DC Comics (Vertigo): July, 1995 - No. 10, Apr, 1996 ($2.50/$2.95, limited series, mature)

1-9: McGreal and Rawson-s/Truog & Kayanan-a					2.50
10-($2.95)					3.00
TPB (2005, $24.99) r/series; intro. by Alisa Kwitney, afterword by Pat McGreal					25.00

CHICAGO MAIL ORDER (See C-M-O Comics)

CHIEF, THE (Indian Chief No. 3 on)
Dell Publishing Co.: No. 290, Aug, 1950 - No. 2, Apr-June, 1951

	GD	VG	FN	VF	VF/NM	NM-
Four Color 290(#1)	7	14	21	47	76	105
2	6	12	18	37	59	80

CHIEF CRAZY HORSE (See Wild Bill Hickok #21)
Avon Periodicals: 1950 (Also see Fighting Indians of the Wild West!)

	GD	VG	FN	VF	VF/NM	NM-
nn-Fawcette-c	21	42	63	120	188	255

CHIEF VICTORIO'S APACHE MASSACRE (See Fight Indians of/Wild West!)
Avon Periodicals: 1951

	GD	VG	FN	VF	VF/NM	NM-
nn-Williamson/Frazetta-a (7 pgs.); Larsen-a; Kinstler-c	45	90	135	275	450	625

CHILDREN OF FIRE
Fantagor Press: Nov, 1987 - No. 3, 1988 ($2.00, limited series)

1-3:by Richard Corben					4.00

CHILDREN OF THE VOYAGER (See Marvel Frontier Comics Unlimited)
Marvel Frontier Comics: Sept, 1993 - No. 4, Dec, 1993 ($1.95, limited series)

1-($2.95)-Embossed glow-in-the-dark-c; Paul Johnson-c/a					3.00

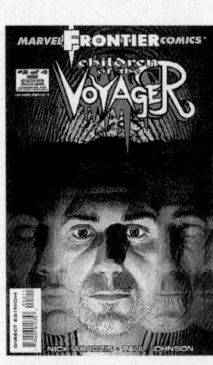

Children of the Voyager #3 © MAR

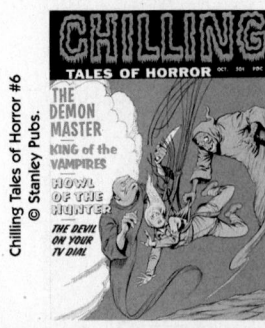

Chilling Tales of Horror #6 © Stanley Pubs.

Chip 'n' Dale #71 © DIS

	GD 2.0	VG 4.0	FN 6.0	VF 8.0	VF/NM 9.0	NM- 9.2
2-4						2.50

CHILDREN'S BIG BOOK
Dorene Publ. Co.: 1945 (25¢, stiff-c, 68 pgs.)

	GD 2.0	VG 4.0	FN 6.0	VF 8.0	VF/NM 9.0	NM- 9.2
nn-Comics & fairy tales; David Icove-a	14	28	42	76	108	140

CHILDREN'S CRUSADE, THE
DC Comics (Vertigo): Dec, 1993 - No. 2, Jan, 1994 ($3.95, limited series)

1,2-Neil Gaiman scripts & Chris Bachalo-a; framing issues for Children's Crusade x-over						4.00

CHILD'S PLAY: THE SERIES (Movie)
Innovation Publishing: May, 1991 - #3, 1991 ($2.50, 28pgs.)

1-3						2.50

CHILD'S PLAY 2 THE OFFICIAL MOVIE ADAPTATION (Movie)
Innovation Publishing: 1990 - No. 3, 1990 ($2.50, bi-weekly limited series)

1-3: Adapts movie sequel						2.50

CHILI (Millie's Rival)
Marvel Comics Group: 5/69 - No. 17, 9/70; No. 18, 8/72 - No. 26, 12/73

	GD 2.0	VG 4.0	FN 6.0	VF 8.0	VF/NM 9.0	NM- 9.2
1	8	16	24	52	86	120
2,4,5	4	8	12	28	44	60
3-Millie & Chili visit Marvel and meet Stan Lee & Stan Goldberg (6 pgs.)	5	10	15	30	48	65
6-17	4	8	12	22	34	45
18-26	3	6	9	18	27	35
Special 1(12/71, 52 pgs.)	5	10	15	30	48	65

CHILLER
Marvel Comics (Epic): Nov, 1993 - No. 2, Dec, 1993 ($7.95, lim. series)

	GD 2.0	VG 4.0	FN 6.0	VF 8.0	VF/NM 9.0	NM- 9.2
1,2-(68 pgs.)	1	2	3	5	6	8

CHILLING ADVENTURES IN SORCERY (...as Told by Sabrina #1, 2)
(Red Circle Sorcery No. 6 on)
Archie Publications: 9/72 - No. 2, 10/72; No. 3, 10/73 - No. 5, 2/74

	GD 2.0	VG 4.0	FN 6.0	VF 8.0	VF/NM 9.0	NM- 9.2
1-Sabrina cameo as narrator	4	8	12	28	44	60
2-Sabrina cameo as narrator	3	6	9	16	23	30
3-5: Morrow-c/a, all. 4,5-Alcazar-a	2	4	6	9	13	16

CHILLING TALES (Formerly Beware)
Youthful Magazines: No. 13, Dec, 1952 - No. 17, Oct, 1953

	GD 2.0	VG 4.0	FN 6.0	VF 8.0	VF/NM 9.0	NM- 9.2
13(No.1)-Harrison-a; Matt Fox-c/a	66	132	198	413	682	950
14-Harrison-a	43	86	129	262	431	600
15-Has #14 on-c; Matt Fox-c; Harrison-a	52	104	156	317	521	725
16-Poe adapt.-'Metzengerstein'; Rudyard Kipling adapt.- 'Mark of the Beast,' by Kiefer; bondage-c	40	80	120	235	368	500
17-Matt Fox-c; Sir Walter Scott & Poe adapt.	43	86	129	262	431	600

CHILLING TALES OF HORROR (Magazine)
Stanley Publications: V1#1, 6/69 - V1#7, 12/70; V2#2, 2/71 - V2#6, 10/71(50¢, B&W, 52 pgs.)

	GD 2.0	VG 4.0	FN 6.0	VF 8.0	VF/NM 9.0	NM- 9.2
V1#1	7	14	21	45	73	100
2-4,(no #5),6,7: 7-Cameron-a	4	8	12	28	44	60
V2#2-6: 2-Two different #2 issues exist (2/71 & 4/71). 2-(2/71) Spirit of Frankenstein -r/Adventures into the Unknown #16. 4-(8/71) different from other V2#4(6/71)	4	8	12	26	41	55
V2#4-(6/71) r/9 pg. Feldstein-a from Adventures into the Unknown #3	4	8	12	28	44	60

NOTE: *Two issues of V2#2 exist, Feb, 1971 and April, 1971. Two issues of V2#4 exist, Jun, 1971 and Aug, 1971.*

CHILLY WILLY (Also see New Funnies #211)
Dell Publ. Co.: No. 740, Oct, 1956 - No. 1281, Apr-June, 1962 (Walter Lantz)

	GD 2.0	VG 4.0	FN 6.0	VF 8.0	VF/NM 9.0	NM- 9.2
Four Color 740 (#1)	7	14	21	45	73	100
Four Color 852 (2/58),967 (2/59),1017 (9/59),1074 (2-4/60),1122 (8/60), 1177 (4-6/61), 1212 (7-9/61), 1281	5	10	15	30	48	65

CHIMERA
CrossGeneration Comics: Mar, 2003 - No. 4, July, 2003 ($2.95, limited series)

1-4-Marz-s/Peterson-c/a						3.00
Vol. 1 TPB (2003, $15.95) r/#1-4 plus sketch pages, 3-D models, how-to guides						16.00

CHINA BOY (See Wisco in the Promotional Comics section)

CHIP 'N' DALE (Walt Disney)(See Walt Disney's C&S #204)
Dell Publishing Co./Gold Key/Whitman No. 65 on: Nov, 1953 - No. 30, June-Aug, 1962; Sept, 1967 - No. 83, July, 1984

	GD 2.0	VG 4.0	FN 6.0	VF 8.0	VF/NM 9.0	NM- 9.2
Four Color 517(#1)	10	20	30	70	123	175
Four Color 581,636	6	12	18	41	66	90
4(12/55-2/56)-10	5	10	15	35	55	75
11-30	4	8	12	28	44	60
1(Gold Key, 1967)-Reprints	3	6	9	18	27	35
2-10	2	4	6	10	14	18
11-20	2	4	6	8	10	12
21-40	1	2	3	5	7	9
41-64,70-77: 75(2/82), 76(2-3/82), 77(3/82)	1	2	3	4	5	7
65,66 (Whitman)	1	3	4	6	8	10
67-69 (3-pack? 1980): 67(8/80), 68(10/80) (scarce)	3	6	9	20	30	40
78-83 (All #90214; 3-pack, nd, nd code): 78(4/83), 79(5/83), 80(7/83), 81(8/83), 82(5/84), 83(7/84)	3	6	9	14	19	24

NOTE: *All Gold Key/Whitman issues have reprints except No. 32-35, 38-41, 45-47. No. 23-28, 30-42, 45-47, 49 have new covers.*

CHIP 'N DALE RESCUE RANGERS
Disney Comics: June, 1990 - No. 19, Dec, 1991 ($1.50)

1-New stories; origin begins						3.00
2-19: 2-Origin continued						2.50

CHITTY CHITTY BANG BANG (See Movie Comics)

C.H.I.X.
Image Comics (Studiosaurus): Jan, 1998 ($2.50)

1-Dodson, Haley, Lopresti, Randall, and Warren-s/c/a						3.00
1-($5.00) "X-Ray Variant" cover						5.00
C.H.I.X. That Time Forgot 1 (8/98, $2.95)						3.00

CHOICE COMICS
Great Publications: Dec, 1941 - No. 3, Feb, 1942

	GD 2.0	VG 4.0	FN 6.0	VF 8.0	VF/NM 9.0	NM- 9.2
1-Origin Secret Circle; Atlas the Mighty app.; Zomba, Jungle Fight, Kangaroo Man, & Fire Eater begin	152	304	456	950	1575	2200
2	76	152	228	475	788	1100
3-Double feature; Features movie "The Lost City" (classic cover); continued from Great Comics #3	131	262	393	819	1360	1900

CHOLLY AND FLYTRAP (Arthur Suydam's...)
Image Comics: Nov, 2004 - No. 4, June, 2005 ($4.95/$5.95, limited series)

1-($4.95) Arthur Suydam-s/a/c						5.00
2-4-($5.95)						6.00

CHOO CHOO CHARLIE
Gold Key: Dec, 1969

	GD 2.0	VG 4.0	FN 6.0	VF 8.0	VF/NM 9.0	NM- 9.2
1-John Stanley-a	9	18	27	63	107	150

CHOSEN
Dark Horse Comics: Jan, 2004 - No. 3, Aug, 2004 ($2.99, limited series)

1-3-Story of the second coming; Mark Millar-s/Peter Gross-a						3.00

CHRISTIAN (See Asylum)
Maximum Press: Jan, 1996 ($2.99, one-shot)

1-Pop Mhan-a						3.00

CHRISTIAN HEROES OF TODAY
David C. Cook: 1964 (36 pgs.)

	GD 2.0	VG 4.0	FN 6.0	VF 8.0	VF/NM 9.0	NM- 9.2
nn	3	6	9	16	22	28

CHRISTMAS (Also see A-1 Comics)
Magazine Enterprises: No. 28, 1950

	GD 2.0	VG 4.0	FN 6.0	VF 8.0	VF/NM 9.0	NM- 9.2
A-1 28	7	14	21	37	46	55

CHRISTMAS ADVENTURE, A (See Classics Comics Giveaways, 12/69)

CHRISTMAS ALBUM (See March of Comics No. 312)

CHRISTMAS ANNUAL
Golden Special: 1975 ($1.95, 100 pgs., stiff-c)

	GD 2.0	VG 4.0	FN 6.0	VF 8.0	VF/NM 9.0	NM- 9.2
nn-Reprints Mother Goose stories with Walt Kelly-a	3	6	9	21	32	42

CHRISTMAS & ARCHIE
Archie Comics: Jan, 1975 ($1.00, 68 pgs., 10-1/4x13-1/4" treasury-sized)

	GD 2.0	VG 4.0	FN 6.0	VF 8.0	VF/NM 9.0	NM- 9.2
1-(scarce)	6	12	18	37	59	80

CHRISTMAS BELLS (See March of Comics No. 297)

CHRISTMAS CARNIVAL
Ziff-Davis Publ. Co./St. John Publ. Co. No. 2: 1952 (25¢, one-shot, 100 pgs.)

	GD 2.0	VG 4.0	FN 6.0	VF 8.0	VF/NM 9.0	NM- 9.2
nn	35	70	105	201	318	435
2-Reprints Ziff-Davis issue plus-c	17	34	51	98	154	210

CHRISTMAS CAROL, A (See March of Comics No. 33)

CHRISTMAS EVE, A (See March of Comics No. 212)

CHRISTMAS IN DISNEYLAND (See Dell Giants)

Christmas With Mother Goose FC #126 © DELL

Cinderella Love #11 © Z-D

Circus of Fun Comics #2 © A.W. Nugent

	GD 2.0	VG 4.0	FN 6.0	VF 8.0	VF/NM 9.0	NM- 9.2

CHRISTMAS PARADE (See Dell Giant No. 26, Dell Giants, March of Comics No. 284, Walt Disney Christmas Parade & Walt Disney's...)

CHRISTMAS PARADE (Walt Disney's)
Gold Key: 1962 (no month listed) - No. 9, Jan, 1972 (#1,5: 80 pgs.; #2-4,7-9: 36 pgs.)

	GD	VG	FN	VF	VF/NM	NM-
1 (30018-301)-Giant	9	18	27	63	107	150
2-6: 2-r/F.C. #367 by Barks. 3-r/F.C. #178 by Barks. 4-r/F.C. #203 by Barks. 5-r/Christmas Parade #1 (Dell) by Barks; giant. 6-r/Christmas Parade #2 (Dell) by Barks; giant	7	14	21	45	73	100
7-Pull-out poster (half price w/o poster)	5	10	15	35	55	75
8-r/F.C. #367 by Barks; pull-out poster	7	14	21	45	73	100
9	4	8	12	28	44	60

CHRISTMAS PARTY (See March of Comics No. 256)

CHRISTMAS STORIES (See Little People No. 959, 1062)

CHRISTMAS STORY (See March of Comics No. 326 in the Promotional Comics section)

CHRISTMAS STORY BOOK (See Woolworth's Christmas Story Book)

CHRISTMAS TREASURY, A (See Dell Giants & March of Comics No. 227)

CHRISTMAS WITH ARCHIE
Spire Christian Comics (Fleming H. Revell Co.): 1973, 1974 (49¢, 52 pgs.)

	GD	VG	FN	VF	VF/NM	NM-
nn-Low print run	2	4	6	11	16	20

CHRISTMAS WITH MOTHER GOOSE
Dell Publishing Co.: No. 90, Nov, 1945 - No. 253, Nov, 1949

	GD	VG	FN	VF	VF/NM	NM-
Four Color 90 (#1)-Kelly-a	17	34	51	126	223	320
Four Color 126 ('46), 172 (11/47)-By Walt Kelly	13	26	39	93	164	235
Four Color 201 (10/48), 253-By Walt Kelly	11	22	33	79	140	200

CHRISTMAS WITH SANTA (See March of Comics No. 92)

CHRISTMAS WITH THE SUPER-HEROES (See Limited Collectors' Edition)
DC Comics: 1988; No. 2, 1989 ($2.95)

	GD	VG	FN	VF	VF/NM	NM-
1,2: 1-(100 pgs.)-All reprints; N. Adams-r, Byrne-c; Batman, Superman, JLA, LSH Christmas stories; r-Miller's 1st Batman/DC Special Series #21. 2-(68 pgs.)-Superman by Chadwick; Batman, Wonder Woman, Deadman, Green Lantern, Flash app.; Morrow-a; Enemy Ace by Byrne; all new-a						5.00

CHROMA-TICK, THE (...Special Edition, #1,2) (Also see The Tick)
New England Comics Press: Feb, 1992 - No. 8, Nov, 1993 ($3.95/$3.50, 44 pgs.)

	GD	VG	FN	VF	VF/NM	NM-
1,2-Includes serially numbered trading card set						5.00
3-8 ($3.50, 36 pgs.): 6-Bound-in card						4.00

CHROME
Hot Comics: 1986 - No. 3, 1986 ($1.50, limited series)

	GD	VG	FN	VF	VF/NM	NM-
1-3						2.50

CHROMIUM MAN, THE
Triumphant Comics: Aug, 1993 - No.10, May, 1994 ($2.50)

	GD	VG	FN	VF	VF/NM	NM-
1-1st app. Mr. Death; all serially numbered						2.50
2-10: 2-1st app. Prince Vandal. 3-1st app. Candi, Breaker & Coil. 4,5-Triumphant Unleashed x-over. 8,9-(3/94). 10-(5/94)						2.50
0-(4/94)-Four color-c, 0-All pink-c & all blue-c; no cover price						2.50

CHROMIUM MAN: VIOLENT PAST, THE
Triumphant Comics: Jan, 1994 - No. 2, Jan, 1994 ($2.50, limited series)

	GD	VG	FN	VF	VF/NM	NM-
1,2-Serially numbered to 22,000 each						2.50

CHRONICLES OF CONAN, THE (See Conan the Barbarian)

CHRONICLES OF CORUM, THE (Also see Corum)
First Comics: Jan, 1987 - No. 12, Nov, 1988 ($1.75/$1.95, deluxe series)

	GD	VG	FN	VF	VF/NM	NM-
1-12: Adapts Michael Moorcock's novel						2.50

CHRONOS
DC Comics: Mar, 1998 - No. 11, Feb. 1999 ($2.50)

	GD	VG	FN	VF	VF/NM	NM-
1-11-J.F. Moore-s/Guinan-a						2.50
#1,000,000 (11/98) 853rd Century x-over						2.50

CHUCKLE, THE GIGGLY BOOK OF COMIC ANIMALS
R. B. Leffingwell Co.: 1945 (132 pgs., one-shot)

	GD	VG	FN	VF	VF/NM	NM-
1-Funny animal	22	44	66	126	198	270

CHUCK NORRIS (TV)
Marvel Comics (Star Comics): Jan, 1987 - No. 4, July, 1987

	GD	VG	FN	VF	VF/NM	NM-
1-3: Ditko-a						3.50
4-No Ditko-a (low print run)						5.00

CHUCK WAGON (See Sheriff Bob Dixon's...)

CHUCKY (Based on the 1988 killer doll movie Child's Play)
Devil's Due Publishing: Apr, 2007 - Present ($3.50)

	GD	VG	FN	VF	VF/NM	NM-
1-3-Pulido-s/Medors-a; art & photo covers						3.50

CHYNA (WWF Wrestling)
Chaos! Comics: Sept, 2000; July, 2001 ($2.95/$2.99, one-shots)

	GD	VG	FN	VF	VF/NM	NM-
1-Grant-s/Barrows-a; photo-c						3.00
1-($9.95) Premium Edition; Cleavenger-c						10.00
II -(7/01, $2.99) Deodato-a; photo-c						3.00

CICERO'S CAT
Dell Publishing Co.: July-Aug, 1959 - No. 2, Sept-Oct, 1959

	GD	VG	FN	VF	VF/NM	NM-
1-Cat from Mutt & Jeff	5	10	15	30	48	65
2	4	8	12	26	41	55

CIMARRON STRIP (TV)
Dell Publishing Co.: Jan, 1968

	GD	VG	FN	VF	VF/NM	NM-
1-Stuart Whitman photo-c	4	8	12	24	37	50

CINDER AND ASHE
DC Comics: May, 1988 - No. 4, Aug, 1988 ($1.75, limited series)

	GD	VG	FN	VF	VF/NM	NM-
1-4: Mature readers						2.50

CINDERELLA (Disney) (See Movie Comics)
Dell Publishing Co.: No. 272, Apr, 1950 - No. 786, Apr, 1957

	GD	VG	FN	VF	VF/NM	NM-
Four Color 272	12	24	36	86	153	220
Four Color 786-Partial-r #272	7	14	21	45	73	100

CINDERELLA
Whitman Publishing Co.: Apr, 1982

	GD	VG	FN	VF	VF/NM	NM-
nn-Reprints 4-Color #272	1	2	3	4	5	7

CINDERELLA LOVE
Ziff-Davis/St. John Publ. Co. No. 12 on: No. 10, 1950; No. 11, 4-5/51; No. 12, 9/51; No. 4, 10-11/51 - No. 11, Fall, 1952; No. 12, 10/53 - No. 15, 8/54; No. 25, 12/54 - No. 29, 10/55 (No #16-24)

	GD	VG	FN	VF	VF/NM	NM-
10(#1)(1st Series, 1950)-Painted-c	15	30	45	86	133	180
11(#2, 4-5/51)-Crandall-a; Saunders painted-c	11	22	33	60	83	105
12(#3, 9/51)-Photo-c	9	18	27	52	69	85
4-8: 4,6,7-Photo-c	9	18	27	47	61	75
9-Kinstler-a; photo-c	10	20	30	54	72	90
10,11(Fall/52), 14: 10,11-Photo-c. 14-Baker-a	9	18	27	52	69	85
12(St. John-10/53)-#13:13-Painted-c.	8	16	24	44	57	70
15(8/54)-Matt Baker-c	10	20	30	56	76	95
25(2nd Series)(Formerly Romantic Marriage) Baker-c	8	16	24	44	57	70
26-Baker-c; last precode (2/55)	10	20	30	56	76	95
27,29: Both Matt Baker-c	10	20	30	56	76	95
28	8	16	24	40	48	60

CINDY COMICS (...Smith No. 39, 40; Crime Can't Win No. 41 on)(Formerly Krazy Komics) (See Junior Miss & Teen Comics)
Timely Comics: No. 27, Fall, 1947 - No. 40, July, 1950

	GD	VG	FN	VF	VF/NM	NM-
27-Kurtzman-a, 3 pgs.: Margie, Oscar begin	22	44	66	128	202	275
28-31-Kurtzman-a	14	28	42	81	118	155
32-40: 33-Georgie story; anti-Wertham editorial	11	22	33	60	83	105

NOTE: Kurtzman's "Hey Look"-#27(3), 29(2), 30(2), 31; 'Giggles 'n' Grins'-28.

CINNAMON: EL CICLO
DC Comics: Oct, 2003 - No. 5, Feb, 2004 ($2.50, limited series)

	GD	VG	FN	VF	VF/NM	NM-
1-5-Van Meter-s/Chaykin-c/Paronzini-a						2.50

CIRCUS (...the Comic Riot)
Globe Syndicate: June, 1938 - No. 3, Aug, 1938

	GD	VG	FN	VF	VF/NM	NM-
1-(Scarce)-Spacehawks (2 pgs.), & Disk Eyes by Wolverton (2 pgs.), Pewee Throttle by Cole (2nd comic book work; see Star Comics V1#11), Beau Gus, Ken Craig & The Lords of Crillon, Jack Hinton by Eisner, Van Bragger by Kane	514	1028	1542	3600	6300	9000
2,3-(Scarce)-Eisner, Cole, Wolverton, Bob Kane-a in each	300	600	900	1881	3141	4400

CIRCUS BOY (TV) (See Movie Classics)
Dell Publishing Co.: No. 759, Dec, 1956 - No. 813, June, 1957

	GD	VG	FN	VF	VF/NM	NM-
Four Color 759 (#1)-The Monkees' Mickey Dolenz photo-c	12	24	36	86	153	220
Four Color 785 (4/57), 813-Mickey Dolenz photo-c	10	20	30	70	123	175

CIRCUS COMICS
Farm Women's Pub. Co./D. S. Publ.: 1945 - No. 2, Jun, 1945; Wint., 1948-49

	GD	VG	FN	VF	VF/NM	NM-
1-Funny animal	14	28	42	78	112	145

Cisco Kid #3 © DELL

Civil War #3 © MAR

Civil War: Young Avengers and Runaways #1 © MAR

	GD 2.0	VG 4.0	FN 6.0	VF 8.0	VF/NM 9.0	NM- 9.2
2	9	18	27	50	65	80
1(1948)-D.S. Publ.; 2 pgs. Frazetta	24	48	72	139	220	300

CIRCUS OF FUN COMICS
A. W. Nugent Publ. Co.: 1945 - No. 3, Dec, 1947 (A book of games & puzzles)

	GD 2.0	VG 4.0	FN 6.0	VF 8.0	VF/NM 9.0	NM- 9.2
1	15	30	45	83	124	165
2,3	10	20	30	54	72	90

CISCO KID, THE (TV)
Dell Publishing Co.: July, 1950 - No. 41, Oct-Dec, 1958

Four Color 292(#1)-Cisco Kid, his horse Diablo, & sidekick Pancho & his horse Loco begin;

	GD 2.0	VG 4.0	FN 6.0	VF 8.0	VF/NM 9.0	NM- 9.2
painted-c begin	22	44	66	164	292	420
2(1/51)	11	22	33	79	140	200
3-5	10	20	30	70	123	175
6-10	9	18	27	60	100	140
11-20	8	16	24	52	86	120
21-36-Last painted-c	6	12	18	43	69	95
37-41: All photo-c	8	16	24	58	97	135

NOTE: **Buscema** a-40. **Ernest Nordli** painted c-5-16, 20, 35.

CISCO KID COMICS
Bernard Bailey/Swappers Quarterly: Winter, 1944 (one-shot)

	GD 2.0	VG 4.0	FN 6.0	VF 8.0	VF/NM 9.0	NM- 9.2
1-Illustrated Stories of the Operas: Faust; Funnyman by Giunta; Cisco Kid (1st app.) & Superbaby begin; Giunta-c	43	86	129	262	431	600

CITIZEN SMITH (See Holyoke One-Shot No. 9)

CITIZEN V AND THE V-BATTALION (See Thunderbolts)
Marvel Comics: June, 2001 - No. 3, Aug, 2001 ($2.99, limited series)

1-3-Nicieza-a; Michael Ryan-c/a		3.00
.... The Everlasting 1-4 (3/02 - No. 4, 7/02) Nicieza-s/LaRosa-a(p)		3.00

CITY OF HEROES (Online game)
Dark Horse Comics/Blue King Studios: Sept, 2002; May, 2004 - No. 7 ($2.95)

1-(no cover price) Dakan-s/Zombo-a		2.50
1-7-($2.95)		3.00

CITY OF HEROES (Online game)
Image Comics: June, 2005 - No. 20, Aug, 2007 ($2.99)

1-20: 1-Waid-s; Pérez-c. 6-Flp-c with City of Villains. 7,9-Jurgens-s		3.00

CITY OF OTHERS
Dark Horse Comics: Apr, 2007 - No. 4, Aug, 2007 ($2.99, limited series)

1-4-Bernie Wrightson-a/c; Steve Niles & Wrightson-s		3.00

CITY OF SILENCE
Image Comics: May, 2000 - No. 3, July, 2000 ($2.50)

1-3-Ellis-s/Erskine-a		2.50
TPB (6/04, $9.95) r/#1-3; pin-up gallery		10.00

CITY OF THE LIVING DEAD (See Fantastic Tales No. 1)
Avon Periodicals: 1952

	GD 2.0	VG 4.0	FN 6.0	VF 8.0	VF/NM 9.0	NM- 9.2
nn-Hollingsworth-c/a	47	94	141	287	474	660

CITY OF TOMORROW
DC Comics (WildStorm): June, 2005 - No. 6, Nov, 2005 ($2.99, limited series)

1-6-Howard Chaykin-s/a		3.00
TPB (2006, $19.99) r/#1-6		20.00

CITY PEOPLE NOTEBOOK
Kitchen Sink Press: 1989 ($9.95, B&W, magazine sized)

nn-Will Eisner-s/a		10.00
nn-(DC Comics, 2000) Reprint		10.00

CITY SURGEON (Blake Harper…)
Gold Key: August, 1963

	GD 2.0	VG 4.0	FN 6.0	VF 8.0	VF/NM 9.0	NM- 9.2
1(10075-308)-Painted-c	4	8	12	23	36	48

CIVIL WAR (Also see Amazing Spider-Man for TPB)
Marvel Comics: July, 2006 - No. 7, Jan, 2007 ($3.99/$2.99, limited series)

	GD 2.0	VG 4.0	FN 6.0	VF 8.0	VF/NM 9.0	NM- 9.2
1-($3.99) Millar-s/McNiven-a & wraparound-c	1	2	3	5	6	8
1-Variant cover by Michael Turner	2	4	6	9	12	15
1-Aspen Comics Variant cover by Turner	2	4	6	9	12	15
1-Director's Cut (2006, $4.99) r/#1 plus promo art, variant covers, sketches and script						5.00
2-($2.99) Spider-Man unmasks	1	2	3	4	5	7
2-Turner variant cover						5.00
2-B&W sketch variant cover						20.00
2-2nd printing						4.00
3-7: 3-Thor returns. 4-Goliath killed						4.00

3-7-Turner variant covers		5.00
3-7-B&W sketch variant covers		15.00
TPB (2007, $24.99) r/#1-7; gallery of variant covers		25.00
...: Battle Damage Report (2007, $3.99) Post-Civil War character profiles; McGuiness-c		4.00
...: Choosing Sides (2/07, $3.99) Colan-c; Howard the Duck app.; 2 covers by Yu & Colan		4.00
... Companion TPB (2007, $13.99) r/Civil War Files, ...:Battle Damage Report, Marvel Spotlight: Millar/McNiven; Civil War Aftermath and Daily Bugle CW		14.00
Daily Bugle Civil War Newspaper Special #1 (9/06, 50¢, newsprint) Daily Bugle "newspaper" overview of the crossover; Mayhew-a		2.50
...Files (2006, $3.99) profile pages of major Civil War characters; McNiven-c		4.00
...: Marvel Universe TPB (2007, $11.99) r/Civil War: Choosing Sides, CW: The Return, She-Hulk #8, CW: The Initiative; She-Hulk sketch page; variant cover gallery		12.00
...: The Initiative (4/07, $4.99) Silvestri-c/a; previews of post-Civil War series		5.00
...: The Return (3/07, $2.99) Captain Marvel returns; The Sentry app.; Raney-a		3.00
...: The Road to Civil War TPB (2007, $14.99) r/New Avengers: Illuminati, Fantastic Four #536 & 537, Amazing Spider-Man #529-531; Spider-Man costume sketches by Bachalo		15.00
... War Crimes (2/07, $3.99) Kingpin in prison; Tieri-s/Staz Johnson-a		4.00
... War Crimes TPB (2007, $17.99) r/Civil War: War Crimes one-shot and Underworld #1-5		18.00
... X-Men Universe TPB (2007, $14.99) r/Cable & Deadpool #30-32; X-Factor #8,9		14.00

CIVIL WAR CHRONICLES (Reprints of Civil War and related Marvel issues)
Marvel Comics: Oct, 2007 - Present ($4.99, limited series)

1-3:1-Reprints Civil War #1 and Civil War: Frontline #1. 2-R/Civil War #2 & AS-M #532,533 3-R/Civil War: Frontline #2-4		5.00

CIVIL WAR: FRONTLINE (Tie-in to Civil War and related Marvel issues)
Marvel Comics: Aug, 2006 - No. 11, Apr, 2007 ($2.99, limited series)

1-Jenkins-s/Bachs-a/Watson-c; back-up stories by various		5.00
2-11: 9-Green Goblin app. 11-Aftermath of Civil War #7		3.00
... Book 1 TPB (2007, $14.99) r/#1-6		15.00
... Book 2 TPB (2007, $14.99) r/#7-11		15.00

CIVIL WAR MUSKET, THE (Kadets of America Handbook)
Custom Comics, Inc.: 1960 (25¢, half-size, 36 pgs.)

	GD 2.0	VG 4.0	FN 6.0	VF 8.0	VF/NM 9.0	NM- 9.2
nn	3	6	9	16	22	28

CIVIL WAR: X-MEN (Tie-in to Civil War)
Marvel Comics: Sept, 2006 - No. 4, Dec, 2006 ($2.99, limited series)

1-4-Paquette-a/Hine-s; Bishop app.		3.00
1-Variant cover by Michael Turner		10.00
TPB (2007, $11.99) r/#1-4, profile pages of minor characters		12.00

CIVIL WAR: YOUNG AVENGERS & RUNAWAYS (Tie-in to Civil War)
Marvel Comics: Sept, 2006 - No. 4, Dec, 2006 ($2.99, limited series)

1-4-Caselli-a/Wells-s/Cheung-c		3.00
TPB (2007, $11.99) r/#1-4, profile pages of characters		12.00

CLAIRE VOYANT (Also see Keen Teens)
Leader Publ./Standard/Pentagon Publ.: 1946 - No. 4, 1947 (Sparling strip reprints)

	GD 2.0	VG 4.0	FN 6.0	VF 8.0	VF/NM 9.0	NM- 9.2
nn	66	132	198	413	682	950
2,4: 2-Kamen-c. 4-Kamen bondage-c	49	98	147	299	492	685
3-Kamen bridal-c; contents mentioned in Love and Death, a book by Gershom Legman(1949) referenced by Dr. Wertham in SOTI	57	114	171	356	578	800

CLANDESTINE (Also see Marvel Comics Presents & X-Men: ClanDestine)
Marvel Comics: Oct, 1994 - No.12, Sept, 1995 $2.95/$2.50)

1-($2.95)-Alan Davis-s/a(p)/scripts & Mark Farmer-c/a(i) begin, ends #8; Modok app.; Silver Surfer cameo; gold foil-c		3.00
2-12: 2-Wraparound-c. 2,3-Silver Surfer app. 5-Origin of ClanDestine. 6-Capt. America, Hulk, Spider-Man, Thing & Thor-c; Spider-Man cameo. 7-Spider-Man-c/app; Punisher cameo. 8-Invaders & Dr. Strange app. 10-Captain Britain-c/app. 11-Sub-Mariner app.		2.50
Preview (10/94, $1.50)		2.50

CLASH
DC Comics: 1991 - No. 3, 1991 ($4.95, limited series, 52 pgs.)

Book One - Three: Adam Kubert-c/a		5.00

CLASSIC BATTLESTAR GALACTICA (See Battlestar Galactica, Classic...)

CLASSIC COMICS/ILLUSTRATED - INTRODUCTION
by Dan Malan

Since the first publication of this special introduction to the **Classics** section, a number of revisions have been made to further clarify the listings. **Classics** reprint editions prior to 1963 had either incorrect dates or no dates listed. Those reprint editions should be identified only by the highest number on the reorder list (HRN). Past *Guides* listed what were calculated to be approximately correct dates, but many people found it confusing for the *Guide* to list a date not

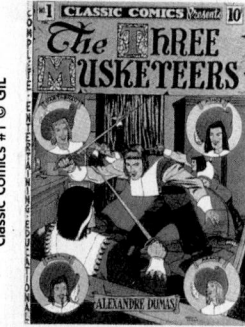

Classic Comics #1 © GIL

Classic Comics #2 © GIL

Classic Comics #3 © GIL

	GD	VG	FN	VF	VF/NM	NM-		GD	VG	FN	VF	VF/NM	NM-
	2.0	4.0	6.0	8.0	9.0	9.2		2.0	4.0	6.0	8.0	9.0	9.2

listed in the comic itself.

We have also attempted to clear up confusion about edition variations, such as color, printer, etc. Such variations are identified by letters. Editions are determined by three categories. Original edition variations are designated as Edition 1A, 1B, etc. All reprint editions prior to 1963 are identified by HRN only. All reprint editions from 9/63 on are identified by the correct date listed in the comic.

Information is also included on four reprintings of **Classics**. From 1968-1976, Twin Circle, the Catholic newspaper, serialized over 100 **Classics** titles. That list can be found under non-series items at the end of this section. In 1972, twelve **Classics** were reissued as **Now Age Books Illustrated**. They are listed under **Pendulum Illustrated Classics**. In 1982, 20 **Classics** were reissued, adapted for teaching English as a second language. They are listed under **Regents Illustrated Classics**. Then in 1984, six **Classics** were reissued with cassette tapes. See the listing under **Cassette Books**.

UNDERSTANDING CLASSICS ILLUSTRATED
by Dan Malan

Since **Classics Illustrated** is the most complicated comic book series, with all its reprint editions and variations, changes in covers and artwork, a variety of means of identifying editions, and the most extensive worldwide distribution of any comic-book series, this introductory section is provided to assist you in gaining expertise about this series.

THE HISTORY OF CLASSICS

The **Classics** series was the brain child of Albert L. Kanter, who saw in the new comic-book medium a means of introducing children to the great classics of literature. In October of 1941 his Gilberton Co. began the **Classic Comics** series with **The Three Musketeers**, with 64 pages of storyline. In those early years, the struggling series saw irregular schedules and numerous printers, not to mention variable art quality and liberal story adaptations. With No.13 the page total was reduced to 56 (except for No. 33, originally scheduled to be No. 9), and with No. 15 the coming-next ad on the outside back cover moved inside. In 1945 the Jerry Iger Shop began producing all new CC titles, beginning with No. 23. In 1947 the search for a classier logo resulted in **Classics Illustrated**, beginning with No. 35, **Last Days of Pompeii**. With No. 45 the page total dropped again to 48, which was to become the standard.

Two new developments in 1951 had a profound effect upon the success of the series. One was the introduction of painted covers, instead of the old line drawn covers, beginning with No. 81, **The Odyssey**. The second was the switch to the major national distributor Curtis. They raised the cover price from 10 to 15 cents, making it the highest priced comic-book, but it did not slow the growth of the series, because they were marketed as books, not comics. Because of this higher quality image, **Classics** flourished during the fifties while other comic series were reeling from outside attacks. They diversified with their new **Juniors**, **Specials**, and **World Around Us** series.

Classics artwork can be divided into three distinct periods. The pre-Iger era (1941-44) was mentioned above for its variable art quality. The Iger era (1945-53) was a major improvement in art quality and adaptations. It came to be dominated by artists Henry Kiefer and Alex Blum, together accounting for some 50 titles. Their styles gave the finest real personality to the series. The EC era (1954-62) resulted from the demise of the EC horror series, when many of their artists made the major switch to classical art.

But several factors brought the production of new CI titles to a complete halt in 1962. Gilberton lost its 2nd class mailing permit. External factors like television, cheap paperback books, and Cliff Notes were all eating away at their market. Production halted with No.167, **Faust**, even though many more titles were already in the works. Many of those found their way into foreign series, and are very desirable to collectors. In 1967, **Classics Illustrated** was sold to Patrick Frawley and his Catholic publication, Twin Circle. They issued two new titles in 1969 as part of an attempted revival, but succumbed to major distribution problems in 1971. In 1988, First Publishing acquired the rights to use the old CI series art, logo, and name from the Frawley Group, and released a short-lived series featuring contributions of modern creators. Acclaim Books and Twin Circles issued a series of **Classics** reprints from 1997-1998.

One of the unique aspects of the **Classics Illustrated** (CI) series was the proliferation of reprint editions. Some titles had as many as 25 editions. Reprinting began in 1943. Some **Classic Comics** (CC) reprints (r) had the logo format revised to a banner logo, and added a motto under the banner. In 1947 CC titles changed to the CI logo, but kept their line drawn covers (LDC). In 1948, Nos. 13, 18, 29 and 41 received second covers (LDC2), replacing covers considered too violent, and reprints of Nos. 13-44 had pages reduced to 48, except for No. 26, which had 48 pages to begin with.

Starting in the mid-1950s, 70 of the 80 LDC titles were reissued with new painted covers (PC). Thirty of them also received new interior artwork (A2). The new artwork was generally higher quality with larger art panels and more faithful but abbreviated storylines. Later on, there were 29 second painted covers (PC2), mostly by Twin Circle. Altogether there were 199 interior art variations (169 (O)s and 30 A2 editions) and 272 different covers (169 (O)s, four LDC2s, 70 new PCs of LDC (O)s, and 29 PC2s). It is mildly astounding to realize that there are nearly 1400 different editions in the U.S. CI series.

FOREIGN CLASSICS ILLUSTRATED

If U.S. Classics variations are mildly astounding, the veritable plethora of foreign CI variations will boggle your imagination. While we still anticipate additional discoveries, we presently know

about series in 25 languages and 27 countries. There were 250 new CI titles in foreign series, and nearly 400 new foreign covers of U.S. titles. The 1400 U.S. CI editions pale in comparison to the 4000 plus foreign editions. The very nature of CI lent itself to flourishing as an international series. Worldwide, they published over one billion copies! The first foreign CI series consisted of six Canadian Classic Comic reprints in 1946.

The following chart shows when CI series first began in each country:

1946: Canada. 1947: Australia. 1948: Brazil/The Netherlands. 1950: Italy. 1951: Greece/Japan/Hong Kong(?)/England/Argentina/Mexico. 1952: West Germany. 1954: Norway. 1955: New Zealand/South Africa. 1956: Denmark/Sweden/Iceland. 1957: Finland/France. 1962: Singapore(?). 1964: India (8 languages). 1971: Ireland (Gaelic). 1973: Belgium(?) /Philippines(?) & Malaysia(?).

Significant among the early series were Brazil and Greece. In 1950, Brazil was the first country to begin doing its own new titles. They issued nearly 80 new CI titles by Brazilian authors. In Greece in 1951 they actually had debates in parliament about the effects of Classics Illustrated on Greek culture, leading to the inclusion of 88 new Greek History & Mythology titles in the CI series.

But by far the most important foreign CI development was the joint European series which began in 1956 in 10 countries simultaneously. By 1960, CI had the largest European distribution of any American publication, not just comics! So when all the problems came up with U.S. distribution, they literally moved the CI operation to Europe in 1962, and continued producing new titles in all four CI series. Many of them were adapted and drawn in the U.S., the most famous of which was the British CI #158A. Dr. No, drawn by Norman Nodel. Unfortunately, the British CI series ended in late 1963, which limited the European CI titles available in English to 15. Altogether there were 82 new CI art titles in the joint European series, which ran until 1976.

IDENTIFYING CLASSICS EDITIONS

HRN: This is the highest number on the reorder list. It should be listed in ( ) after the title number. It is crucial to understanding various CI editions.

ORIGINALS (O): This is the all-important First Edition. To determine (O)s, there is one primary rule and two secondary rules (with exceptions):

Rule No. 1: All (O)s and only (O)s have coming-next ads for the next number. **Exceptions:** No. 14(15) (reprint) has an ad on the last inside text page only. No. 14(0) also has a full-page outside back cover ad (also rule 2). Nos.55(75) and 57(75) have coming-next ads. (Rules 2 and 3 apply here). Nos. 168(O) and 169(O) do not have coming-next ads. No.168 was never reprinted; No. 169(O) has HRN (166). No. 169(169) is the only reprint.

Rule No. 2: On nos.1-80, all (O)s and only (O)s list 10c on the front cover. **Exceptions:** Reprint variations of Nos. 37(62), 39(71), and 46(62) list 10c on the front cover. (Rules 1 and 3 apply here.)

Rule No. 3: All (O)s have HRN close to that title No. **Exceptions:** Some reprints also have HRNs close to that title number: a few CC(r)s, 58(62), 60(62), 149(149), 152(149) 153(149), and title nos. in the 160's. (Rules 1 and 2 apply here.)

DATES: Many reprint editions list either an incorrect date or no date. Since Gilberton apparently kept track of CI editions by HRN, they often left the (O) date on reprints. Often, someone with a CI collection for sale will swear that all their copies are originals. That is why we are so detailed in pointing out how to identify original editions. Except for original editions, which should have a coming-next ad, etc., all CI dates prior to 1963 are incorrect! So you want to go by HRN only if it is (165) or below, and go by listed date if it is 1963 or later. There are a few (167) editions with incorrect dates. They could be listed either as (167) or (62/3), which is meant to indicate that there were issued sometime between late 1962 and early 1963.

COVERS: A change from CC to LDC indicates a logo change, not a cover change; while a change from LDC to LDC2, LDC to PC, or from PC to PC2 does indicate a new cover. New PCs can be identified by HRN, and PC2s can be identified by HRN and date. Several covers had color changes, particularly from purple to blue.

Notes: If you see 15 cents in Canada on a front cover, it does not necessarily indicate a Canadian edition. Editions with an HRN between 44 and 75, with 15 cents on the cover are Canadian. Check the publishers address. An HRN listing two numbers with a / between them indicates that there are two different reorder lists in the front and back covers. Official Twin Circle editions have a full-page back cover ad for their TC magazine, with no CI reorder list. Any CI with just a Twin Circle sticker on the front is not an official TC edition.

TIPS ON LISTING CLASSICS FOR SALE

It may be easy to just list Edition 17, but Classics collectors keep track of CI editions in terms of HRN and/or date, (O) or (r), CC or LDC, PC or PC2, A1 or A2, soft or stiff cover, etc. Try to help them out. For originals, just list (0), some have variations such as color (Nos. 10 and 61), printer (Nos. 18-22), HRN (Nos. 95, 108, 160), etc. For reprints, just list HRN if it's (165) or below. Above that, list HRN and date. Also, please list type of logo/cover/art for the convenience of buyers. They will appreciate it.

CLASSIC COMICS (Also see Best from Boys Life, Cassette Books, Famous Stories, Fast Fiction, Golden Picture Classics, King Classics, Marvel Classics Comics, Pendulum Illustrated Classics, Picture Parade, Picture Progress, Regents Ill. Classics, Spitfire, Stories by Famous Authors, Superior Stories, and World Around Us.)

CLASSIC COMICS (Classics Illustrated No. 35 on)
Elliot Publishing #1-3 (1941-1942)/**Gilberton Publications #4-167** (1942-1967) /**Twin Circle Pub. (Frawley) #168-169** (1968-1971):

Classic Comics #4 © GIL

Classic Comics #5 © GIL

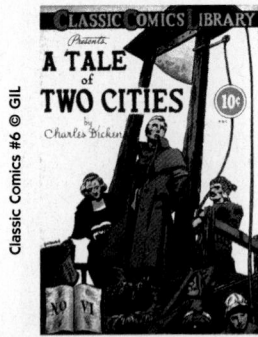

Classic Comics #6 © GIL

	GD	VG	FN	VF	VF/NM	NM-
	2.0	4.0	6.0	8.0	9.0	9.2

10/41 - No. 34, 2/47; No. 35, 3/47 - No. 169, Spring 1969
(Reprint Editions of almost all titles 5/43 - Spring 1971)
(Painted Covers (0)s No. 81 on, and (r)s of most Nos. 1-80)

Abbreviations:
A–Art; C or c–Cover; CC–Classic Comics; CI–Classics Ill.; Ed–Edition; LDC–Line Drawn Cover;
PC–Painted Cover; r–Reprint

1. The Three Musketeers

Ed	HRN	Date	Details	A	C	GD 2.0	VG 4.0	FN 6.0	VF 8.0	VF/NM 9.0	NM- 9.2
1	–	10/41	Date listed-1941; Elliot Pub; 68 pgs.	1	1	440	880	1320	3080	5390	7700
2	10	–	10¢ price removed on all (r)s; Elliot Pub; CC-r	1	1	34	68	102	195	308	420
3	15	–	Long Isl. Ind. Ed.; CC-r	1	1	24	48	72	139	220	300
4	18/20	–	Sunrise Times Ed.; CC-r	1	1	17	34	51	98	154	210
5	21	–	Richmond Courier Ed.; CC-r	1	1	15	30	45	88	137	185
6	28	1946	CC-r	1	1	14	28	42	76	108	140
7	36	–	LDC-r	1	1	8	16	24	42	54	65
8	60	–	LDC-r	1	1	6	12	18	27	33	38
9	64	–	LDC-r	1	1	5	10	15	22	26	30
10	78	–	C-price 15¢;LDC-r	1	1	4	9	13	18	22	26
11	93	–	LDC-r	1	1	4	9	13	18	22	26
12	114	–	Last LDC-r	1	1	4	8	11	16	19	22
13	134	–	New-c; old-a; 64 pg. PC-r	1	2	3	6	9	17	25	32
14	143	–	Old-a; PC-r; 64 pg.	1	2	2	4	6	11	16	20
15	150	–	New-a; PC-r; Evans/Crandall-a	2	2	3	6	9	16	22	28
16	149	–	PC-r	2	2	2	4	6	8	10	12
17	167	–	PC-r	2	2	2	4	6	8	10	12
18	167	4/64	PC-r	2	2	2	4	6	8	10	12
19	167	1/65	PC-r	2	2	2	4	6	8	10	12
20	167	3/66	PC-r	2	2	2	4	6	8	10	12
21	166	11/67	PC-r	2	2	2	4	6	8	10	12
22	166	Spr/69	C-price 25¢ ; stiff-c; PC-r	2	2	2	4	6	8	10	12
23	169	Spr/71	PC-r; stiff-c	2	2	2	4	6	8	10	12

2. Ivanhoe

Ed	HRN	Date	Details	A	C	GD 2.0	VG 4.0	FN 6.0	VF 8.0	VF/NM 9.0	NM- 9.2
1	(O)	12/41?	Date listed-1941; Elliot Pub; 68 pgs.	1	1	228	456	684	1425	2363	3300
2	10	–	Price & 'Presents' removed; Elliot Pub; CC-r	1	1	31	62	93	178	282	385
3	15	–	Long Isl. Ind. ed.; CC-r	1	1	19	38	57	112	176	240
4	18/20	–	Sunrise Times ed.; CC-r	1	1	17	34	51	98	154	210
5	21	–	Richmond Courier ed.; CC-r	1	1	15	30	45	88	137	185
6	28	1946	Last 'Comics'-r	1	1	14	28	42	76	108	140
7	36	–	1st LDC-r	1	1	9	18	27	47	61	75
8	60	–	LDC-r	1	1	6	12	18	27	33	38
9	64	–	LDC-r	1	1	5	10	15	22	26	30
10	78	–	C-price 15¢; LDC-r	1	1	4	9	13	18	22	26
11	89	–	LDC-r	1	1	4	8	12	17	21	24
12	106	–	LDC-r	1	1	4	7	10	14	17	20
13	121	–	Last LDC-r	1	1	4	7	10	14	17	20
14	136	–	New-c&a; PC-r	2	2	5	10	15	23	28	32
15	142	–	PC-r	2	2	2	4	6	8	11	14
16	153	–	PC-r	2	2	2	4	6	8	11	14
17	149	–	PC-r	2	2	2	4	6	8	11	14
18	167	–	PC-r	2	2	2	4	6	8	10	12
19	167	5/64	PC-r	2	2	2	4	6	8	10	12
20	167	1/65	PC-r	2	2	2	4	6	8	10	12
21	167	3/66	PC-r	2	2	2	4	6	8	10	12
22A	166	9/67	PC-r	2	2	2	4	6	8	10	12
22B	166	–	Center ad for	2	2	7	14	21	47	76	105

Children's Digest & Young Miss; rare; PC-r

Ed	HRN	Date	Details	A	C	GD 2.0	VG 4.0	FN 6.0	VF 8.0	VF/NM 9.0	NM- 9.2
23	166	R/68	C-Price 25¢; PC-r	2	2	2	4	6	8	10	12
24	169	Win/69	Stiff-c	2	2	2	4	6	8	10	12
25	169	Win/71	PC-r; stiff-c	2	2	2	4	6	8	10	12

3. The Count of Monte Cristo

Ed	HRN	Date	Details	A	C	GD 2.0	VG 4.0	FN 6.0	VF 8.0	VF/NM 9.0	NM- 9.2
1	(O)	3/42	Elliot Pub; 68 pgs.	1	1	145	290	435	906	1503	2100
2	10	–	Conray Prods; CC-r1	1		26	52	78	150	235	320
3	15	–	Long Isl. Ind. ed.; CC-r	1	1	20	40	60	115	180	245
4	18/20	–	Sunrise Times ed.; CC-r	1	1	18	36	54	103	162	220
5	20	–	Sunrise Times ed.; CC-r	1	1	16	32	48	92	144	195
6	21	–	Richmond Courier ed.; CC-r	1	1	15	30	45	88	137	185
7	28	1946	CC-r; new Banner logo	1	1	14	28	42	76	108	140
8	36	–	1st LDC-r	1	1	9	18	27	47	61	75
9	60	–	LDC-r	1	1	6	12	18	27	33	38
10	62	–	LDC-r	1	1	6	12	18	29	36	42
11	71	–	LDC-r	1	1	5	10	14	20	24	28
12	87	–	C-price 15¢; LDC-r	1	1	4	9	13	18	22	26
13	113	–	LDC-r	1	1	4	7	10	14	17	20
14	135	–	New-c&a; PC-r; Cameron-a	2	2	3	6	9	16	23	30
15	143	–	PC-r	2	2	2	4	6	8	11	14
16	153	–	PC-r	2	2	2	4	6	8	11	14
17	161	–	PC-r	2	2	2	4	6	8	11	14
18	167	–	PC-r	2	2	2	4	6	8	10	12
19	167	7/64	PC-r	2	2	2	4	6	8	10	12
20	167	7/65	PC-r	2	2	2	4	6	8	10	12
21	167	7/66	PC-r	2	2	2	4	6	8	10	12
22	166	R/68	C-price 25¢; PC-r	2	2	2	4	6	8	10	12
23	169	–	Win/69 Stiff-c; PC-r	2	2	2	4	6	8	10	12

4. The Last of the Mohicans

Ed	HRN	Date	Details	A	C	GD 2.0	VG 4.0	FN 6.0	VF 8.0	VF/NM 9.0	NM- 9.2
1	(O)	8/42	Date listed-1942; Gilberton #4(0) on; 68 pgs.	1	1	124	248	372	775	1288	1800
2	12	–	Elliot Pub; CC-r	1	1	26	52	78	150	235	320
3	15	–	Long Isl. Ind. ed.; CC-r	1	1	20	40	60	115	180	245
4	20	–	Long Isl. Ind. ed.; CC-r; banner logo	1	1	17	34	51	98	154	210
5	21	–	Queens Home News ed.; CC-r	1	1	15	30	45	88	137	185
6	28	1946	Last CC-r; new	1	1	14	28	42	76	108	140
7	36	–	1st LDC-r	1	1	9	18	27	47	61	75
8	60	–	LDC-r	1	1	6	12	18	27	33	38
9	64	–	LDC-r	1	1	5	10	14	20	24	28
10	78	–	C-price 15¢; LDC-r	1	1	4	9	13	18	22	26
11	89	–	LDC-r	1	1	4	8	12	17	21	24
12	117	–	Last LDC-r	1	1	4	7	10	14	17	20
13	135	–	New-c; PC-r	1	2	5	10	15	22	26	30
14	141	–	PC-r	1	2	3	6	8	12	14	16
15	150	–	New-a; PC-r; Severin, L.B. Cole-a	2	2	5	10	15	23	28	32
16	161	–	PC-r	2	2	2	4	6	8	10	12
17	167	–	PC-r	2	2	2	4	6	8	10	12
18	167	6/64	PC-r	2	2	2	4	6	8	10	12
19	167	8/65	PC-r	2	2	2	4	6	8	10	12
20	167	8/66	PC-r	2	2	2	4	6	8	10	12
21	166	R/67	C-price 25¢; PC-r	2	2	2	4	6	8	10	12
22	169	Spr/69	Stiff-c; PC-r	2	2	2	4	6	8	10	12

5. Moby Dick

Ed	HRN	Date	Details	A	C	GD 2.0	VG 4.0	FN 6.0	VF 8.0	VF/NM 9.0	NM- 9.2
1A	(O)	9/42	Date listed-1942; Gilberton; 68 pgs.	1	1	152	304	456	950	1575	2200
1B			inside-c, rare free promo			228	456	684	1425	2363	3300

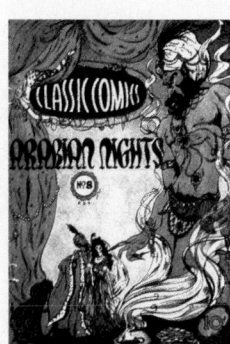

Classic Comics #8 © GIL

Classic Comics #9 © GIL

CLASSIC COMICS ROBINSON CRUSOE BY DANIEL DEFOE

Classic Comics #10 © GIL

					GD 2.0	VG 4.0	FN 6.0	VF 8.0	VF/NM 9.0	NM- 9.2
2	10	–	Conray Prods; Pg. 64 changed from 105 title list to letter from Editor; CC-r	1 1	27	54	81	158	249	340
3	15	–	Long Isl. Ind. ed.; Pg. 64 changed from Letter to the Editor to Ill. poem-Concord Hymn; CC-r	1 1	23	46	69	130	205	280
4	18/20	–	Sunrise Times ed.; CC-r	1 1	18	36	54	103	162	220
5	20	–	Sunrise Times ed.; CC-r	1 1	17	34	51	98	154	210
6	21	–	Sunrise Times ed.; CC-r	1 1	15	30	45	88	137	185
7	28	1946	CC-r; new banner logo	1 1	14	28	42	80	115	150
8	36	–	1st LDC-r	1 1	9	18	27	47	61	75
9	60	–	LDC-r	1 1	6	12	18	27	33	38
10	62	–	LDC-r	1 1	6	12	18	29	36	42
11	71	–	LDC-r	1 1	5	10	15	22	26	30
12	87	–	C-price 15¢; LDC-r	1 1	5	10	14	20	24	28
13	118	–	LDC-r	1 1	4	8	12	17	21	24
14	131	–	New c&a; PC-r	2 2	5	10	15	23	28	32
15	138	–	PC-r	2 2	2	4	6	8	11	14
16	148	–	PC-r	2 2	2	4	6	8	11	14
17	158	–	PC-r	2 2	2	4	6	8	11	14
18	167	–	PC-r	2 2	2	4	6	8	10	12
19	167	6/64	PC-r	2 2	2	4	6	8	10	12
20	167	7/65	PC-r	2 2	2	4	6	8	10	12
21	167	3/66	PC-r	2 2	2	4	6	8	10	12
22	166	9/67	PC-r	2 2	2	4	6	8	10	12
23	166	New/69	New-c & c-price 25¢; Stiff-c; PC-r	2 3	3	6	9	14	19	24
24	169	Win/71	PC-r	2 3	2	4	6	13	18	22

6. A Tale of Two Cities

Ed	HRN	Date	Details	A C	GD 2.0	VG 4.0	FN 6.0	VF 8.0	VF/NM 9.0	NM- 9.2
1	(O)	10/42	Date listed-1942; 68 pgs. Zeckerberg c/a	1 1	124	248	372	775	1288	1800
2	14	–	Elliot Pub; CC-r	1 1	24	48	72	139	220	300
3	18	–	Long Isl. Ind. ed.; CC-r	1 1	19	38	57	109	172	235
4	20	–	Sunrise Times ed.; CC-r	1 1	17	34	51	98	154	210
5	28	1946	Last CC-r; new banner logo	1 1	14	28	42	76	108	140
6	51	–	1st LDC-r	1 1	8	16	24	42	54	65
7	64	–	LDC-r	1 1	5	10	15	23	28	32
8	78	–	C-price 15¢; LDC-r	1 1	5	10	14	20	24	28
9	89	–	LDC-r	1 1	4	7	10	14	17	20
10	117	–	LDC-r	1 1	4	7	10	14	17	20
11	132	–	New-c&a; PC-r; Joe Orlando-a	2 2	5	10	15	23	28	32
12	140	–	PC-r	2 2	2	4	6	8	10	12
13	147	–	PC-r	2 2	2	4	6	8	10	12
14	152	–	PC-r; very rare	2 2	16	32	48	94	147	200
15	153	–	PC-r	2 2	2	4	6	8	11	14
16	149	–	PC-r	2 2	2	4	6	8	11	14
17	167	–	PC-r	2 2	2	4	6	8	10	12
18	167	6/64	PC-r	2 2	2	4	6	8	10	12
19	167	8/65	PC-r	2 2	2	4	6	8	10	12
20	166	5/67	PC-r	2 2	2	4	6	8	10	12
21	166	Fall/68	New-c & 25¢; PC-r	2 3	3	6	9	16	22	28
22	169	Sum/70	Stiff-c; PC-r	2 3	2	4	6	11	16	20

7. Robin Hood

Ed	HRN	Date	Details	A C	GD 2.0	VG 4.0	FN 6.0	VF 8.0	VF/NM 9.0	NM- 9.2
1	(O)	12/42	Date listed-1942; first Gift Box ad-bc; 68 pgs.	1 1	93	186	279	581	966	1350
2	12	–	Elliot Pub; CC-r	1 1	23	46	69	135	213	290
3	18	–	Long Isl. Ind. ed.; CC-r	1 1	18	36	54	105	165	225
4	20	–	Nassau Bulletin	1 1	17	34	51	98	154	210

					GD 2.0	VG 4.0	FN 6.0	VF 8.0	VF/NM 9.0	NM- 9.2
5	22	–	Queens Cty. Times ed.; CC-r	1 1	15	30	45	88	137	185
6	28	–	CC-r	1 1	14	28	42	80	115	150
7	51	–	LDC-r	1 1	8	16	24	42	54	65
8	64	–	LDC-r	1 1	5	10	15	24	30	35
9	78	–	LDC-r	1 1	4	9	13	18	22	26
10	97	–	LDC-r	1 1	4	8	12	17	21	24
11	106	–	LDC-r	1 1	4	7	10	14	17	20
12	121	–	LDC-r	1 1	4	7	10	14	17	20
13	129	–	New-c; PC-r	1 2	5	10	15	23	28	32
14	136	–	New-a; PC-r	2 2	5	10	15	22	26	30
15	143	–	PC-r	2 2	2	4	6	8	11	14
16	153	–	PC-r	2 2	2	4	6	8	11	14
17	164	–	PC-r	2 2	2	4	6	8	10	12
18	167	–	PC-r	2 2	2	4	6	8	10	12
19	167	6/64	PC-r	2 2	2	4	6	8	10	12
20	167	5/65	PC-r	2 2	2	4	6	8	10	12
21	167	7/66	PC-r	2 2	2	4	6	8	10	12
22	166	12/67	PC-r	2 2	2	4	6	8	10	12
23	169	Sum/69	Stiff-c; c-price 25¢; PC-r	2 2	2	4	6	8	10	12

8. Arabian Nights

Ed	HRN	Date	Details	A C	GD 2.0	VG 4.0	FN 6.0	VF 8.0	VF/NM 9.0	NM- 9.2
1	(O)	2/43	Original; 68 pgs. Lilian Chestney-c/a	1 1	148	296	444	925	1538	2150
2	17	–	Long Isl. ed.; pg. 64 changed from Gift Box ad to Letter from British Medical Worker; CC-r	1 1	52	104	156	317	521	725
3	20	–	Nassau Bulletin; Pg. 64 changed from letter to article-Three Men Named Smith; CC-r	1 1	42	84	126	256	421	585
4A	28	1946	CC-r; new banner logo, slick-c	1 1	31	62	93	178	282	385
4B	28	1946	Same, but w/stiff-c	1 1	31	62	93	178	282	385
5	51	–	LDC-r	1 1	22	44	66	126	198	270
6	64	–	LDC-r	1 1	18	36	54	105	165	225
7	78	–	LDC-r	1 1	17	34	51	98	154	210
8	164	–	New-c&a; PC-r	2 2	15	30	45	85	130	175

9. Les Miserables

Ed	HRN	Date	Details	A C	GD 2.0	VG 4.0	FN 6.0	VF 8.0	VF/NM 9.0	NM- 9.2
1A	(O)	3/43	Original; slick paper cover; 68 pgs.	1 1	93	186	279	581	966	1350
1B	(O)	3/43	Original; rough, pulp type-c; 68 pgs.	1 1	110	220	330	688	1144	1600
2	14	–	Elliot Pub; CC-r	1 1	26	52	78	150	235	320
3	18	3/44	Nassau Bul. Pg. 64 changed from Gift Box ad to Bill of Rights article; CC-r	1 1	22	44	66	126	198	270
4	20	–	Richmond Courier ed.; CC-r	1 1	18	36	54	103	162	220
5	28	1946	Gilberton; pgs. 60-64 rearranged/ illos added; CC-r	1 1	14	28	42	80	115	150
6	51	–	LDC-r	1 1	9	18	27	47	61	75
7	71	–	LDC-r	1 1	6	12	18	29	36	42
8	87	–	C-price 15¢; LDC-r	1 1	6	12	18	27	33	38
9	161	–	New-c&a; PC-r	2 2	7	14	21	35	43	50
10	167	9/63	PC-r	2 2	2	4	6	11	16	20
11	167	12/65	PC-r	2 2	2	4	6	11	16	20
12	166	R/1968	New-c & price 25¢; PC-r	2 3	3	6	9	16	23	30

10. Robinson Crusoe (Used in SOTI, pg. 142)

Ed	HRN	Date	Details	A C	GD 2.0	VG 4.0	FN 6.0	VF 8.0	VF/NM 9.0	NM- 9.2
1A	(O)	4/43	Original; Violet-c; 68 pgs; Zuckerberg c/a	1 1	83	166	249	519	860	1200
1B	(O)	4/43	Original; blue-grey-c, 68 pgs.	1 1	91	182	273	569	947	1325

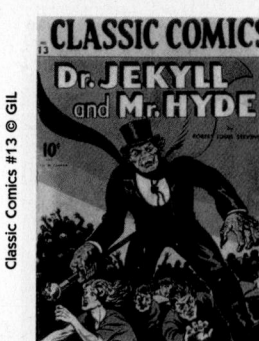

Classic Comics #12 © GIL

Classic Comics #13 © GIL

Classic Comics #15 © GIL

Ed	HRN	Date	Details	A	C	GD 2.0	VG 4.0	FN 6.0	VF 8.0	VF/NM 9.0	NM- 9.2
2A	14	–	Elliot Pub; violet-c; 68 pgs; CC-r	1	1	28	56	84	162	256	350
2B	14	–	Elliot Pub; blue-grey-c; CC-r	1	1	25	50	75	145	228	310
3	18	–	Nassau Bul. Pg. 64 changed from Gift Box ad to Bill of Rights article; CC-r	1	1	18	36	54	105	165	225
4	20	–	Queens Home News ed.; CC-r	1	1	15	30	45	88	137	185
5	28	1946	Gilberton; pg. 64 changes from Bill of Rights to WWII article-One Leg Shot Away; last CC-r	1	1	14	28	42	76	108	140
6	51	–	LDC-r	1	1	8	16	24	42	54	65
7	64	–	LDC-r	1	1	6	12	18	27	33	38
8	78	–	C-price 15¢; LDC-r	1	1	5	10	14	20	24	28
9	97	–	LDC-r	1	1	4	9	13	18	22	26
10	114	–	LDC-r	1	1	4	7	10	14	17	20
11	130	–	New-c; PC-r	1	2	5	10	15	23	28	32
12	140	–	New-a; PC-r	2	2	5	10	15	22	26	30
13	153	–	PC-r	2	2	2	4	6	8	10	12
14	164	–	PC-r	2	2	2	4	6	8	10	12
15	167	–	PC-r	2	2	2	4	6	8	10	12
16	167	7/64	PC-r	2	2	2	4	6	10	13	16
17	167	5/65	PC-r	2	2	2	4	6	10	13	16
18	167	6/66	PC-r	2	2	2	4	6	8	10	12
19	166	Fall/68	C-price 25¢; PC-r	2	2	2	4	6	8	10	12
20	166	R/68	(No Twin Circle ad)	2	2	2	4	6	8	11	14
21	169	Sm/70	Stiff-c; PC-r	2	2	2	4	6	8	11	14

11. Don Quixote

Ed	HRN	Date	Details	A	C	GD 2.0	VG 4.0	FN 6.0	VF 8.0	VF/NM 9.0	NM- 9.2
1	10	5/43	First (O) with HRN list; 68 pgs.	1	1	86	172	258	538	894	1250
2	18	–	Nassau Bulletin ed.; CC-r	1	1	23	46	69	130	205	280
3	21	–	Queens Home News ed.; CC-r	1	1	18	36	54	105	165	225
4	28	–	CC-r	1	1	14	28	42	80	115	150
5	110	–	New-PC; PC-r	1	2	6	12	18	31	38	45
6	156	–	Pgs. reduced 68 to 52; PC-r	1	2	4	7	10	14	17	20
7	165	–	PC-r	1	2	2	4	6	9	11	14
8	167	1/64	PC-r	1	2	2	4	6	9	11	14
9	167	11/65	PC-r	1	2	2	4	6	9	11	14
10	166	R/1968	New-c & price 25¢; PC-r	1	3	3	6	9	17	25	32

12. Rip Van Winkle and the Headless Horseman

Ed	HRN	Date	Details	A	C	GD 2.0	VG 4.0	FN 6.0	VF 8.0	VF/NM 9.0	NM- 9.2
1	11	6/43	Original; 68 pgs.	1	1	86	172	258	538	894	1250
2	15	–	Long Isl. Ind. ed.; CC-r	1	1	23	46	69	130	205	280
3	20	–	Long Isl. Ind. ed.; CC-r	1	1	18	36	54	105	165	225
4	22	–	Queens Cty. Times ed.; CC-r	1	1	15	30	45	88	137	185
5	28	–	CC-r	1	1	14	28	42	76	108	140
6	60	–	1st LDC-r	1	1	8	16	24	40	50	60
7	62	–	LDC-r	1	1	5	10	15	23	28	32
8	71	–	LDC-r	1	1	4	9	13	18	22	26
9	89	–	C-price 15¢; LDC-r	1	1	4	8	12	17	21	24
10	118	–	LDC-r	1	1	4	7	10	14	17	20
11	132	–	New-c; PC-r	1	2	5	10	15	22	26	32
12	150	–	New-a; PC-r	2	2	5	10	15	23	28	30
13	158	–	PC-r	2	2	2	4	6	8	11	14
14	167	–	PC-r	2	2	2	4	6	8	11	14
15	167	12/63	PC-r	2	2	2	4	6	8	10	12
16	167	4/65	PC-r	2	2	2	4	6	8	10	12
17	167	4/66	PC-r	2	2	2	4	6	8	10	12
18	166	R/1968	New-c&price 25¢; PC-r; stiff-c	2	3	3	6	9	14	19	24
19	169	Sm/70	PC-r; stiff-c	2	2	2	4	6	8	13	16

13. Dr. Jekyll and Mr. Hyde (Used in SOTI, pg. 143)(1st horror comic?)

Ed	HRN	Date	Details	A	C	GD 2.0	VG 4.0	FN 6.0	VF 8.0	VF/NM 9.0	NM- 9.2
1	12	8/43	Original 60 pgs.	1	1	128	256	384	800	1325	1850
2	15	–	Long Isl. Ind. ed.; CC-r	1	1	33	66	99	190	300	410
3	20	–	Long Isl. Ind. ed.; CC-r	1	1	23	46	69	130	205	280
4	28	–	No c-price; CC-r	1	1	17	34	51	98	154	210
5	60	–	New-c; Pgs. reduced from 60 to 52; H.C. Kiefer-c; LDC-r	1	2	8	16	24	44	57	70
6	62	–	LDC-r	1	2	6	12	18	28	34	40
7	71	–	LDC-r	1	2	5	10	15	23	28	32
8	87	–	Date returns (erroneous); CC-r	1	2	5	10	15	22	26	30
9	112	–	New-c&a; PC-r; Cameron-a	2	3	6	12	18	31	38	45
10	153	–	PC-r	2	3	2	4	6	9	12	15
11	161	–	PC-r	2	3	2	4	6	9	12	15
12	167	–	PC-r	2	3	2	4	6	8	10	12
13	167	8/64	PC-r	2	3	2	4	6	8	10	12
14	167	11/65	PC-r	2	3	2	4	6	8	10	12
15	166	R/68	C-price 25¢; PC-r	2	3	2	4	6	8	10	12
16	169	Wn/69	PC-r; stiff-c	2	3	2	4	6	8	10	12

14. Westward Ho!

Ed	HRN	Date	Details	A	C	GD 2.0	VG 4.0	FN 6.0	VF 8.0	VF/NM 9.0	NM- 9.2
1	13	9/43	Original; last outside bc coming-next ad; 60 pgs.	1	1	193	386	579	1206	2003	2800
2	15	–	Long Isl. Ind. ed.; CC-r	1	1	55	110	165	344	572	800
3	21	–	Queens Home News; Pg. 56 changed from coming-next ad to Three Men Named Smith; CC-r	1	1	45	90	135	275	450	625
4	28	1946	Gilberton; Pg. 56 changed again to WWII article-Speaking for America; last CC-r	1	1	40	80	120	235	368	500
5	53	–	Pgs. reduced from 60 to 52; LDC-r	1	1	35	70	105	204	322	440

15. Uncle Tom's Cabin (Used in SOTI, pgs. 102, 103)

Ed	HRN	Date	Details	A	C	GD 2.0	VG 4.0	FN 6.0	VF 8.0	VF/NM 9.0	NM- 9.2
1	14	11/43	Original; Outside-bc ad: 2 Gift Boxes; 60 pgs.; color var. on-c; green trunk,root on left & brown trunk, root on left	1	1	72	144	216	450	750	1050
2	15	–	Long Isl. Ind. listed- bottom inside-fc; also Gilberton listed bottom-pg. 1; CC-r; green root vs. brown root var. occurs again	1	1	25	50	75	145	228	310
3	21	–	Nassau Bulletin ed.; CC-r	1	1	19	38	57	109	172	235
4	28	–	No c-price; CC-r	1	1	14	28	42	80	115	150
5	53	–	Pgs. reduced 60 to 52; LDC-r	1	1	8	16	24	42	54	65
6	71	–	LDC-r	1	1	6	12	18	27	33	38
7	89	–	C-price 15¢; LDC-r	1	1	5	10	15	24	30	35
8	117	–	New-c/lettering changes; PC-r	1	2	5	10	15	23	28	32
9	128	–	'Picture Progress' promo; PC-r	1	2	2	4	6	9	13	16
10	137	–	PC-r	1	2	2	4	6	8	11	14
11	146	–	PC-r	1	2	2	4	6	8	11	14
12	154	–	PC-r	1	2	2	4	6	8	11	14
13	161	–	PC-r	1	2	2	4	6	8	10	12
14	167	–	PC-r	1	2	2	4	6	8	10	12
15	167	6/64	PC-r	1	2	2	4	6	8	10	12
16	167	5/65	PC-r	1	2	2	4	6	8	10	12

Classic Comics #17 © GIL

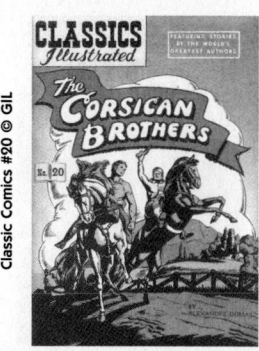

Classic Comics #20 © GIL

Classic Comics #21 © GIL

Ed	HRN	Date	Details	A	C	GD 2.0	VG 4.0	FN 6.0	VF 8.0	VF/NM 9.0	NM- 9.2
17	166	5/67	PC-r	1	2	2	4	6	8	10	12
18	166	Wn/69	New-stiff-c; PC-r	1	3	3	6	9	14	19	24
19	169	Sm/70	PC-r; stiff-c	1	3	2	4	6	10	13	16

16. Gullivers Travels

Ed	HRN	Date	Details	A	C	GD 2.0	VG 4.0	FN 6.0	VF 8.0	VF/NM 9.0	NM- 9.2
1	15	12/43	Original-Lilian Chestney c/a; 60 pgs.	1	1	74	148	222	463	769	1075
2	18/20	–	Price deleted; Queens Home News ed; CC-r	1	1	22	44	66	126	198	270
3	22	–	Queens Cty. Times ed.; CC-r	1	1	17	34	51	98	154	210
4	28	–	CC-r	1	1	14	28	42	76	108	140
5	60	–	Pgs. reduced to 48; LDC-r	1	1	6	12	18	31	38	45
6	62	–	LDC-r	1	1	5	10	15	23	28	32
7	78	–	C-price 15¢; LDC-r	1	1	5	10	14	20	24	28
8	89	–	LDC-r	1	1	4	8	12	17	21	24
9	155	–	New-c	1	2	5	10	15	23	28	32
10	165	–	PC-r	1	2	2	4	6	8	10	12
11	167	5/64	PC-r	1	2	2	4	6	8	10	12
12	167	11/65	PC-r	1	2	2	4	6	8	10	12
13	166	R/1968	C-price 25¢; PC-r	1	2	2	4	6	8	10	12
14	169	Wn/69	PC-r; stiff-c	1	2	2	4	6	8	10	12

17. The Deerslayer

Ed	HRN	Date	Details	A	C	GD 2.0	VG 4.0	FN 6.0	VF 8.0	VF/NM 9.0	NM- 9.2
1	16	1/44	Original; Outside-bc ad: 3 Gift Boxes; 60 pgs.	1	1	64	128	192	400	663	925
2A	18	–	Queens Cty Times (inside-fc); CC-r	1	1	23	46	69	132	209	285
2B	18	–	Gilberton (bottom-pg. 1); CC-r; Scarce	1	1	33	66	99	190	300	410
3	22	–	Queens Cty. Times ed.; CC-r	1	1	18	36	54	105	165	225
4	28	–	CC-r	1	1	14	28	42	80	115	150
5	60	–	Pgs.reduced to 52; LDC-r	1	1	7	14	21	37	46	55
6	64	–	LDC-r	1	1	5	10	15	22	26	30
7	85	–	C-price 15¢; LDC-r	1	1	4	8	12	17	21	24
8	118	–	LDC-r	1	1	4	7	10	14	17	20
9	132	–	LDC-r	1	1	4	7	10	14	17	20
10	167	11/66	Last LDC-r	1	1	2	4	6	11	16	20
11	166	R/1968	New-c & price 25¢; PC-r	1	2	3	6	9	16	23	30
12	169	Spr/71	Stiff-c; letters from parents & educators; PC-r	1	2	2	4	6	10	14	18

18. The Hunchback of Notre Dame

Ed	HRN	Date	Details	A	C	GD 2.0	VG 4.0	FN 6.0	VF 8.0	VF/NM 9.0	NM- 9.2
1A	17	3/44	Orig.; Gilberton ed; 60 pgs.	1	1	86	172	258	538	894	1250
1B	17	3/44	Orig.; Island Pub. Ed.; 60 pgs.	1	1	76	152	228	475	788	1100
2	18/20	–	Queens Home News ed.; CC-r	1	1	24	48	72	139	220	300
3	22	–	Queens Cty. Times ed.; CC-r	1	1	18	36	54	105	165	225
4	28	–	CC-r	1	1	15	30	45	88	137	185
5	60	–	New-c; 8pgs. deleted; Kiefer-c; LDC-r	1	2	8	16	24	44	57	70
6	62	–	LDC-r	1	2	5	10	15	22	26	30
7	78	–	C-price 15¢; LDC-r	1	2	5	10	14	20	24	28
8A	89	–	H.C.Kiefer on bottom right-fc; LDC-r	1	2	4	9	13	18	22	26
8B	89	–	Name omitted; LDC-r	1	2	5	10	15	24	30	35
9	118	–	LDC-r	1	2	4	8	12	17	21	24
10	140	–	New-c; PC-r	1	3	6	12	18	31	38	45
11	146	–	PC-r	1	3	4	9	13	18	22	26
12	158	–	New-c&a; PC-r; Evans/Crandall-a	2	4	5	10	15	23	28	32
13	165	–	PC-r	2	4	2	4	6	8	11	14
14	167	9/63	PC-r	2	4	2	4	6	8	11	14
15	167	10/64	PC-r	2	4	2	4	6	8	11	14
16	167	4/66	PC-r	2	4	2	4	6	8	10	12
17	166	R/1968	New price 25¢; PC-r	2	4	2	4	6	8	10	12
18	169	Sp/70	Stiff-c; PC-r	2	4	2	4	6	8	10	12

19. Huckleberry Finn

Ed	HRN	Date	Details	A	C	GD 2.0	VG 4.0	FN 6.0	VF 8.0	VF/NM 9.0	NM- 9.2
1A	18	4/44	Orig.; Gilberton ed.; 60 pgs.	1	1	53	106	159	323	537	750
1B	18	4/44	Orig.; Island Pub.; 60 pgs.	1	1	55	110	165	344	572	800
2	18	–	Nassau Bulletin ed.; fc-price 15¢-Canada; no coming-next ad; CC-r	1	1	23	46	69	130	205	280
3	22	–	Queens City Times ed.; CC-r	1	1	18	36	54	105	165	225
4	28	–	CC-r	1	1	14	28	42	76	108	140
5	60	–	Pgs. reduced to 48; LDC-r	1	1	6	12	18	31	38	45
6	62	–	LDC-r	1	1	5	10	15	23	28	32
7	78	–	LDC-r	1	1	4	9	13	18	22	26
8	89	–	LDC-r	1	1	4	8	12	17	21	24
9	117	–	LDC-r	1	1	4	7	10	14	17	20
10	131	–	New-c&a; PC-r	2	2	5	10	15	22	26	30
11	140	–	PC-r	2	2	2	4	6	8	11	14
12	150	–	PC-r	2	2	2	4	6	8	11	14
13	158	–	PC-r	2	2	2	4	6	8	11	14
14	165	–	PC-r (scarce)	2	2	3	6	9	14	19	24
15	167	–	PC-r	2	2	2	4	6	8	10	12
16	167	6/64	PC-r	2	2	2	4	6	8	10	12
17	167	6/65	PC-r	2	2	2	4	6	8	10	12
18	167	10/65	PC-r	2	2	2	4	6	8	10	12
19	166	9/67	PC-r	2	2	2	4	6	8	10	12
20	166	Win/69	C-price 25¢; PC-r; stiff-c	2	2	2	4	6	8	10	12
21	169	Sm/70	PC-r; stiff-c	2	2	2	4	6	9	11	12

20. The Corsican Brothers

Ed	HRN	Date	Details	A	C	GD 2.0	VG 4.0	FN 6.0	VF 8.0	VF/NM 9.0	NM- 9.2
1A	20	6/44	Orig.; Gilberton ed.;1 bc-ad: 4 Gift Boxes; 60 pgs.	1	1	46	92	138	281	486	650
1B	20	6/44	Orig.; Courier ed.; 60 pgs.	1	1	40	80	120	240	383	525
1C	20	6/44	Orig.; Long Island Ind. ed.; 60 pgs.	1	1	40	80	120	240	383	525
2	22	–	Queens Cty. Times ed.; white logo banner; CC-r	1	1	19	38	57	109	172	235
3	28	–	CC-r	1	1	18	36	54	105	165	225
4	60	–	CI logo; no price; 48 pgs.; LDC-r	1	1	15	30	45	88	137	185
5A	62	–	LDC-r; Classics Ill. logo at top of pgs.	1	1	14	28	42	82	121	160
5B	62	–	w/o logo at top of pg. (scarcer)	1	1	15	30	45	85	130	175
6	78	–	C-price 15¢; LDC-r	1	1	14	28	42	80	115	150
7	97	–	LDC-r	1	1	14	28	42	76	108	140

21. 3 Famous Mysteries ("The Sign of the 4", "The Murders in the Rue Morgue", "The Flayed Hand")

Ed	HRN	Date	Details	A	C	GD 2.0	VG 4.0	FN 6.0	VF 8.0	VF/NM 9.0	NM- 9.2
1A	21	7/44	Orig.; Gilberton ed.; 60 pgs.	1	1	93	186	279	581	966	1350
1B	21	7/44	Orig. Island Pub. Co.; 60 pgs.	1	1	97	194	291	606	1003	1400
1C	21	7/44	Original; Courier Ed.; 60 pgs.	1	1	83	166	249	519	860	1200
2	22	–	Nassau Bulletin ed.; CC-r	1	1	38	76	114	219	347	475
3	30	–	CC-r	1	1	27	54	81	158	249	340
4	62	–	LDC-r; 8 pgs. deleted; LDC-r	1	1	22	44	66	126	198	270

Classic Comics #24 © GIL · Classic Comics #26 © GIL · Classic Comics #28 © GIL

Ed	HRN	Date	Details	A	C	GD 2.0	VG 4.0	FN 6.0	VF 8.0	VF/NM 9.0	NM- 9.2
5	70	–	LDC-r	1	1	19	38	57	112	176	240
6	85	–	C-price 15¢; LDC-r	1	1	17	34	51	98	154	210
7	114	–	New-c; PC-r	1	2	17	34	51	98	154	210

22. The Pathfinder

Ed	HRN	Date	Details	A	C	GD 2.0	VG 4.0	FN 6.0	VF 8.0	VF/NM 9.0	NM- 9.2
1A	22	10/44	Orig.; No printer listed; ownership statement inside fc lists Gilberton & date; 60 pgs.	1	1	45	90	135	275	450	625
1B	22	10/44	Orig.; Island Pub. ed.; 60 pgs.	1	1	40	80	120	240	383	525
1C	22	10/44	Orig.; Queens Cty Times ed. 60 pgs.	1	1	40	80	120	240	383	525
2	30	–	C-price removed; CC-r	1	1	14	28	42	82	121	160
3	60	–	Pgs. reduced to 52; LDC-r	1	1	6	12	18	27	33	38
4	70	–	LDC-r	1	1	5	10	15	22	26	30
5	85	–	C-price 15¢; LDC-r	1	1	4	9	13	18	22	26
6	118	–	LDC-r	1	1	4	8	12	17	21	24
7	132	–	LDC-r	1	1	4	7	10	14	17	20
8	146	–	LDC-r	1	1	4	7	10	14	17	20
9	167	11/63	New-c; PC-r	1	2	4	8	12	22	34	45
10	167	12/65	PC-r	1	2	2	4	6	11	16	20
11	166	8/67	PC-r	1	2	2	4	6	11	16	20

23. Oliver Twist (1st Classic produced by the Iger Shop)

Ed	HRN	Date	Details	A	C	GD 2.0	VG 4.0	FN 6.0	VF 8.0	VF/NM 9.0	NM- 9.2
1	23	7/45	Original; 60 pgs.	1	1	45	90	135	275	450	625
2A	30	–	Printers Union logo on bottom left-fc same as 23(Orig.) (very rare); CC-r	1	1	30	60	90	174	275	375
2B	30	–	Union logo omitted; CC-r	1	1	14	28	42	80	115	150
3	60	–	Pgs. reduced to 48; LDC-r	1	1	6	12	18	29	36	42
4	62	–	LDC-r	1	1	5	10	15	23	28	32
5	71	–	LDC-r	1	1	5	10	14	20	24	28
6	85	–	C-price 15¢; LDC-r	1	1	4	9	13	18	22	26
7	94	–	LDC-r	1	1	4	7	10	14	17	20
8	118	–	LDC-r	1	1	4	7	10	14	17	20
9	136	–	New-PC, old-a; PC-r	1	2	5	10	15	22	26	30
10	150	–	Old-a; PC-r	1	2	4	7	10	14	17	20
11	164	–	Old-a; PC-r	1	2	4	8	11	16	19	22
12	164	–	New-a; Evans/Crandall-a PC-r	2	2	4	8	12	22	34	45
13	167	–	PC-r	2	2	2	4	6	11	16	20
14	167	8/64	PC-r	2	2	2	4	6	8	10	12
15	167	12/65	PC-r	2	2	2	4	6	8	10	12
16	166	R/1968	New 25¢; PC-r	2	2	2	4	6	8	10	12
17	169	Win/69	Stiff-c; PC-r	2	2	2	4	6	8	10	12

24. A Connecticut Yankee in King Arthur's Court

Ed	HRN	Date	Details	A	C	GD 2.0	VG 4.0	FN 6.0	VF 8.0	VF/NM 9.0	NM- 9.2
1	–	9/45	Original	1	1	40	80	120	240	383	525
2	30	–	No price circle; CC-r	1	1	14	28	42	80	115	150
3	60	–	8 pgs. deleted; LDC-r	1	1	6	12	18	27	33	38
4	62	–	LDC-r	1	1	5	10	15	23	28	32
5	71	–	LDC-r	1	1	5	10	15	22	26	30
6	87	–	C-price 15¢; LDC-r	1	1	4	9	13	18	22	26
7	121	–	LDC-r	1	1	4	8	12	17	21	24
8	140	–	New-c&a; PC-r	2	2	5	10	15	23	28	32
9	153	–	PC-r	2	2	2	4	6	8	11	14
10	164	–	PC-r	2	2	2	4	6	8	10	12
11	167	–	PC-r	2	2	2	4	6	8	10	12
12	167	7/64	PC-r	2	2	2	4	6	8	10	12
13	167	6/66	PC-r	2	2	2	4	6	8	10	12
14	166	R/1968	C-price 25¢; PC-r	2	2	2	4	6	8	10	12
15	169	Spr/71	PC-r; stiff-c	2	2	2	4	6	8	10	12

25. Two Years Before the Mast

Ed	HRN	Date	Details	A	C	GD 2.0	VG 4.0	FN 6.0	VF 8.0	VF/NM 9.0	NM- 9.2
1	–	10/45	Original; Webb/Heames-a&c	1	1	40	80	120	240	383	525
2	30	–	Price circle blank; CC-r	1	1	14	28	42	80	115	150
3	60	–	8 pgs. deleted; LDC-r	1	1	6	12	18	27	33	38
4	62	–	LDC-r	1	1	5	10	15	23	28	32
5	71	–	LDC-r	1	1	4	9	13	18	22	26
6	85	–	C-price 15¢; LDC-r	1	1	4	8	12	17	21	24
7	114	–	LDC-r	1	1	4	7	10	14	17	20
8	156	–	3 pgs. replaced by fillers; new-c; PC-r	1	2	5	10	15	23	28	32
9	167	12/63	PC-r	1	2	2	4	6	8	10	12
10	167	12/65	PC-r	1	2	2	4	6	8	10	12
11	166	9/67	PC-r	1	2	2	4	6	8	10	12
12	169	Win/69	C-price 25¢; stiff-c PC-r	1	2	2	4	6	8	10	12

26. Frankenstein (2nd horror comic?)

Ed	HRN	Date	Details	A	C	GD 2.0	VG 4.0	FN 6.0	VF 8.0	VF/NM 9.0	NM- 9.2
1	26	12/45	Orig.; Webb/Brewster a&c; 52 pgs.	1	1	100	200	300	625	1038	1450
2A	30	–	Price circle blank; no indicia; CC-r	1	1	29	58	87	167	264	360
2B	30	–	With indicia; scarce; CC-r	1	1	34	68	102	195	308	420
3	60	–	LDC-r	1	1	15	30	45	88	137	185
4	62	–	LDC-r	1	1	14	28	42	82	121	160
5	71	–	LDC-r	1	1	7	14	21	37	46	55
6A	82	–	C-price 15¢; soft-c LDC-r	1	1	6	12	18	31	38	45
6B	82	–	Stiff-c; LDC-r	1	1	7	14	21	37	46	55
7	117	–	LDC-r	1	1	4	8	12	18	22	25
8	146	–	New Saunders-c; PC-r	1	2	6	12	18	27	33	38
9	152	–	Scarce; PC-r	1	2	7	14	21	37	46	55
10	153	–	PC-r	1	2	2	4	6	8	11	14
11	160	–	PC-r	1	2	2	4	6	8	11	14
12	165	–	PC-r	1	2	2	4	6	8	10	12
13	167	–	PC-r	1	2	2	4	6	8	10	12
14	167	6/64	PC-r	1	2	2	4	6	8	10	12
15	167	6/65	PC-r	1	2	2	4	6	8	10	12
16	167	10/65	PC-r	1	2	2	4	6	8	10	12
17	166	9/67	PC-r	1	2	2	4	6	8	10	12
18	169	Fall/69	C-price 25¢; stiff-c PC-r	1	2	2	4	6	8	10	12
19	169	Spr/71	PC-r; stiff-c	1	2	2	4	6	8	10	12

27. The Adventures of Marco Polo

Ed	HRN	Date	Details	A	C	GD 2.0	VG 4.0	FN 6.0	VF 8.0	VF/NM 9.0	NM- 9.2
1	–	4/46	Original	1	1	40	80	120	240	383	525
2	30	–	Last 'Comics' reprint; CC-r	1	1	14	28	42	80	115	150
3	70	–	8 pgs. deleted; no c-price; LDC-r	1	1	5	10	15	24	30	35
4	87	–	C-price 15¢; LDC-r	1	1	4	9	13	18	22	26
5	117	–	LDC-r	1	1	4	7	10	14	17	20
6	154	–	New-c; PC-r	1	2	5	10	15	22	26	30
7	165	–	PC-r	1	2	2	4	6	8	10	12
8	167	4/64	PC-r	1	2	2	4	6	8	10	12
9	167	6/66	PC-r	1	2	2	4	6	8	10	12
10	169	Spr/69	New price 25¢; stiff-c; PC-r	1	2	2	4	6	8	10	12

28. Michael Strogoff

Ed	HRN	Date	Details	A	C	GD 2.0	VG 4.0	FN 6.0	VF 8.0	VF/NM 9.0	NM- 9.2
1	–	6/46	Original	1	1	40	80	120	240	383	525
2	51	–	8 pgs. cut; LDC-r	1	1	14	28	42	80	115	150
3	115	–	New-c; PC-r	1	2	6	12	18	28	34	40
4	155	–	PC-r	1	2	4	7	10	14	17	20
5	167	11/63	PC-r	1	2	2	4	6	9	13	16
6	167	7/66	PC-r	1	2	2	4	6	9	13	16
7	169	Sm/69	C-price 25¢; stiff-c PC-r	1	2	3	6	9	15	21	26

29. The Prince and the Pauper

Classic Comics #30 © GIL

Classic Comics #32 © GIL

Classics Illustrated #37 © GIL

Ed	HRN	Date	Details	A	C	GD 2.0	VG 4.0	FN 6.0	VF 8.0	VF/NM 9.0	NM- 9.2
1	–	7/46	Orig.; "Horror"-c	1	1	57	114	171	356	591	825
2	60	–	8 pgs. cut; new-c by Kiefer; LDC-r	1	2	9	18	27	47	61	75
3	62	–	LDC-r	1	2	5	10	15	24	30	35
4	71	–	LDC-r	1	2	4	9	13	18	22	26
5	93	–	LDC-r	1	2	4	8	12	17	21	24
6	114	–	LDC-r	1	2	4	7	10	14	17	20
7	128	–	New-c; PC-r	1	3	5	10	15	22	26	30
8	138	–	PC-r	1	3	2	4	6	8	11	14
9	150	–	PC-r	1	3	2	4	6	8	11	14
10	164	–	PC-r	1	3	2	4	6	8	10	12
11	167	–	PC-r	1	3	2	4	6	8	10	12
12	167	7/64	PC-r	1	3	2	4	6	8	10	12
13	167	11/65	PC-r	1	3	2	4	6	8	10	12
14	166	R/68	C-price 25¢; PC-r	1	3	2	4	6	8	10	12
15	169	Sm/70	PC-r; stiff-c	1	3	2	4	6	8	10	12

30. The Moonstone

Ed	HRN	Date	Details	A	C	GD 2.0	VG 4.0	FN 6.0	VF 8.0	VF/NM 9.0	NM- 9.2
1	–	9/46	Original; Rico-c/a	1	1	40	80	120	240	383	525
2	60	–	LDC-r; 8pgs. cut	1	1	8	16	24	44	57	70
3	70	–	LDC-r	1	1	8	16	24	40	50	60
4	155	–	New L.B. Cole-c; PC-r	1	2	4	8	12	26	41	55
5	165	–	PC-r; L.B. Cole-c	1	2	3	6	9	16	23	30
6	167	1/64	PC-r; L.B. Cole-c	1	2	2	4	6	10	14	18
7	167	9/65	PC-r; L.B. Cole-c	1	2	2	4	6	9	13	16
8	166	R/1968	C-price 25¢; PC-r	1	2	2	4	6	8	11	14

31. The Black Arrow

Ed	HRN	Date	Details	A	C	GD 2.0	VG 4.0	FN 6.0	VF 8.0	VF/NM 9.0	NM- 9.2
1	30	10/46	Original	1	1	38	76	114	219	347	475
2	51	–	CI logo; LDC-r 8pgs. deleted	1	1	6	12	18	31	38	45
3	64	–	LDC-r	1	1	4	9	13	18	22	26
4	87	–	C-price 15¢; LDC-r	1	1	4	8	12	17	21	24
5	108	–	LDC-r	1	1	4	7	10	14	17	20
6	125	–	LDC-r	1	1	4	7	10	14	17	20
7	131	–	New-c; PC-r	1	2	5	10	15	22	26	30
8	140	–	PC-r	1	2	2	4	6	8	11	14
9	148	–	PC-r	1	2	2	4	6	8	11	14
10	161	–	PC-r	1	2	2	4	6	8	10	12
11	167	–	PC-r	1	2	2	4	6	8	10	12
12	167	7/64	PC-r	1	2	2	4	6	8	10	12
13	167	11/65	PC-r	1	2	2	4	6	8	10	12
14	166	R/1968	C-price 25¢; PC-r	1	2	2	4	6	8	10	12

32. Lorna Doone

Ed	HRN	Date	Details	A	C	GD 2.0	VG 4.0	FN 6.0	VF 8.0	VF/NM 9.0	NM- 9.2
1	–	12/46	Original; Matt Baker c&a	1	1	40	80	120	240	383	525
2	53/64	–	8 pgs. deleted; LDC-r	1	1	8	16	24	44	57	70
3	85	1951	C-price 15¢; LDC-r; Baker c&a	1	1	7	14	21	35	43	50
4	118	–	LDC-r	1	1	4	9	13	18	22	26
5	138	–	New-c; old-c becomes new title pg.; PC-r	1	2	5	10	15	24	30	35
6	150	–	PC-r	1	2	2	4	6	8	10	12
7	165	–	PC-r	1	2	2	4	6	8	10	12
8	167	1/64	PC-r	1	2	2	4	6	8	11	14
9	167	11/65	PC-r	1	2	2	4	6	8	11	14
10	166	R/1968	New-c; PC-r	1	3	3	6	9	17	25	32

33. The Adventures of Sherlock Holmes

Ed	HRN	Date	Details	A	C	GD 2.0	VG 4.0	FN 6.0	VF 8.0	VF/NM 9.0	NM- 9.2
1	33	1/47	Original; Kiefer-c; contains Study in Scarlet & Hound of the Baskervilles; 68 pgs.	1	1	121	242	363	756	1253	1750
2	53	–	"A Study in Scarlet" (17 pgs.) deleted; LDC-r	1	1	45	90	135	275	450	625
3	71	–	LDC-r	1	1	36	72	108	208	329	450
4A	89	–	C-price 15¢; LDC-r	1	1	29	58	87	167	264	360
4B	89	–	Kiefer's name omitted from-c	1	1	30	60	90	174	275	375

34. Mysterious Island (Last "Classic Comic")

Ed	HRN	Date	Details	A	C	GD 2.0	VG 4.0	FN 6.0	VF 8.0	VF/NM 9.0	NM- 9.2
1	35	2/47	Original; Webb/Heames-c/a	1	1	40	80	120	240	383	525
2	60	–	8 pgs. deleted; LDC-r	1	1	7	14	21	35	43	50
3	62	–	LDC-r	1	1	5	10	15	23	28	32
4	71	–	LDC-r	1	1	6	12	18	31	38	45
5	78	–	C-price 15¢ in circle; LDC-r	1	1	5	10	14	20	24	28
6	92	–	LDC-r	1	1	4	9	13	18	22	26
7	117	–	LDC-r	1	1	4	7	10	14	17	20
8	140	–	New-c; PC-r	1	2	5	10	15	22	26	30
9	156	–	PC-r	1	2	2	4	6	8	11	14
10	167	10/63	PC-r	1	2	2	4	6	8	10	12
11	167	5/64	PC-r	1	2	2	4	6	8	10	12
12	167	6/66	PC-r	1	2	2	4	6	8	10	12
13	166	R/1968	C-price 25¢; PC-r	1	2	2	4	6	8	10	12

35. Last Days of Pompeii (First "Classics Illustrated")

Ed	HRN	Date	Details	A	C	GD 2.0	VG 4.0	FN 6.0	VF 8.0	VF/NM 9.0	NM- 9.2
1	35	3/47	Original; LDC; Kiefer-c/a	1	1	40	80	120	240	383	525
2	161	–	New c&a; 15¢; PC-r; Kirby/Ayers-a	2	2	4	8	12	28	44	60
3	167	1/64	PC-r	2	2	3	6	9	15	21	26
4	167	7/66	PC-r	2	2	3	6	9	15	21	26
5	169	Spr/70	New price 25¢; stiff-c; PC-r	2	2	3	6	9	15	21	26

36. Typee

Ed	HRN	Date	Details	A	C	GD 2.0	VG 4.0	FN 6.0	VF 8.0	VF/NM 9.0	NM- 9.2
1	36	4/47	Original	1	1	26	52	78	152	239	325
2	64	–	No c-price; 8 pg. ed.; LDC-r	1	1	7	14	21	35	43	50
3	155	–	New-c; PC-r	1	2	5	10	15	22	26	30
4	167	9/63	PC-r	1	2	2	4	6	9	12	15
5	167	7/65	PC-r	1	2	2	4	6	9	12	15
6	169	Sm/69	C-price 25¢; stiff-c PC-r	1	2	2	4	6	9	12	15

37. The Pioneers

Ed	HRN	Date	Details	A	C	GD 2.0	VG 4.0	FN 6.0	VF 8.0	VF/NM 9.0	NM- 9.2
1	37	5/47	Original; Palais-c/a	1	1	24	48	72	139	220	300
2A	62	–	8 pgs. cut; LDC-r; price circle blank	1	1	6	12	18	28	34	40
2B	62	–	10¢; LDC-r	1	1	26	52	78	152	239	325
3	70	–	LDC-r	1	1	4	8	12	17	21	24
4	92	–	15¢; LDC-r	1	1	4	8	11	16	19	22
5	118	–	LDC-r	1	1	4	7	10	14	17	20
6	131	–	LDC-r	1	1	4	7	10	14	17	20
7	132	–	LDC-r	1	1	4	7	10	14	17	20
8	153	–	LDC-r	1	1	4	7	10	14	17	20
9	167	5/64	LDC-r	1	1	2	4	6	8	11	14
10	167	6/66	LDC-r	1	1	2	4	6	8	11	14
11	166	R/1968	New-c; 25¢; PC-r	1	2	3	6	9	17	25	32

38. Adventures of Cellini

Ed	HRN	Date	Details	A	C	GD 2.0	VG 4.0	FN 6.0	VF 8.0	VF/NM 9.0	NM- 9.2
1	–	6/47	Original; Froehlich c/a	1	1	32	64	96	186	293	400
2	164	–	New-c&a; PC-r	2	2	3	6	9	17	25	32
3	167	1/64	PC-r	2	2	2	4	6	10	14	18
4	167	7/66	PC-r	2	2	2	4	6	10	14	18
5	169	Spr/70	Stiff-c; new price 25¢; PC-r	2	2	2	4	6	11	16	20

39. Jane Eyre

Ed	HRN	Date	Details	A	C	GD 2.0	VG 4.0	FN 6.0	VF 8.0	VF/NM 9.0	NM- 9.2
1	–	7/47	Original	1	1	31	62	93	178	282	385
2	60	–	No c-price; 8 pgs. cut; LDC-r	1	1	6	12	18	31	38	45
3	62	–	LDC-r	1	1	5	10	15	24	30	35
4	71	–	LDC-r; c-price 10¢	1	1	5	10	15	22	26	30

Classics Illustrated #44 © GIL

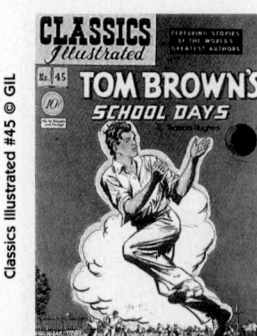
Classics Illustrated #45 © GIL

Classics Illustrated #47 © GIL

#	HRN	Date	Details	A	C	GD 2.0	VG 4.0	FN 6.0	VF 8.0	VF/NM 9.0	NM- 9.2
5	92	–	C-price 15¢; LDC-r	1	1	4	9	13	18	22	26
6	118	–	LDC-r	1	1	4	8	12	17	21	24
7	142	–	New-c; old-a; PC-r	1	2	5	10	15	24	30	35
8	154	–	Old-a; PC-r	1	2	4	8	12	17	21	24
9	165	–	New-a; PC-r	2	2	3	6	9	16	23	30
10	167	12/63	PC-r	2	2	3	6	9	14	19	24
11	167	4/65	PC-r	2	2	2	4	6	13	18	22
12	167	8/66	New-c; PC-r	2	2	2	4	6	13	18	22
13	166	R/1968	New-c; PC-r	2	3	5	10	15	32	51	70

40. Mysteries ("The Pit and the Pendulum", "The Advs. of Hans Pfall" & "The Fall of the House of Usher")

Ed	HRN	Date	Details	A	C	GD 2.0	VG 4.0	FN 6.0	VF 8.0	VF/NM 9.0	NM- 9.2
1	40	8/47	Original; Kiefer-c/a, Froehlich, Griffiths-a	1	1	59	118	177	369	615	860
2	62	–	LDC-r; 8pgs. cut	1	1	23	46	69	130	205	280
3	75	–	LDC-r	1	1	19	38	57	109	172	235
4	92	–	C-price 15¢; LDC-r	1	1	16	32	48	94	147	200

41. Twenty Years After

Ed	HRN	Date	Details	A	C	GD 2.0	VG 4.0	FN 6.0	VF 8.0	VF/NM 9.0	NM- 9.2
1	–	9/47	Original; 'horror'-c	1	1	39	78	117	224	355	485
2	62	–	New-c; no c-price 8 pgs. cut; LDC-r; Kiefer-c	1	2	7	14	21	35	43	50
3	78	–	C-price 15¢; LDC-r	1	2	5	10	15	23	28	32
4	156	–	New-c; PC-r	1	3	5	10	15	22	26	30
5	167	12/63	PC-r	1	3	2	4	6	8	10	12
6	167	11/66	PC-r	1	3	2	4	6	8	10	12
7	169	Spr/70	New price 25¢; stiff-c; PC-r	1	3	2	4	6	8	10	12

42. Swiss Family Robinson

Ed	HRN	Date	Details	A	C	GD 2.0	VG 4.0	FN 6.0	VF 8.0	VF/NM 9.0	NM- 9.2
1	42	10/47	Orig.; Kiefer-c&a	1	1	23	46	69	132	209	285
2A	62	–	8 pgs. cut; outside bc: Gift Box ad; LDC-r	1	1	6	12	18	31	38	45
2B	62	–	8 pgs. cut; outside-bc: Reorder list; scarce; LDC-r	1	1	10	20	30	56	76	95
3	75	–	LDC-r	1	1	5	10	14	20	24	28
4	93	–	LDC-r	1	1	5	10	14	20	24	28
5	117	–	LDC-r	1	1	3	6	9	14	19	24
6	131	–	New-c; old-a; PC-r	1	2	3	6	9	15	21	26
7	137	–	Old-a; PC-r	1	2	2	4	6	10	14	18
8	141	–	Old-a; PC-r	1	2	2	4	6	10	14	18
9	152	–	New-a; PC-r	2	2	3	6	9	16	22	28
10	158	–	PC-r	2	2	2	4	6	8	10	12
11	165	–	PC-r	2	2	2	4	6	8	10	12
12	167	12/63	PC-r	2	2	2	4	6	8	11	14
13	167	4/65	PC-r	2	2	2	4	6	8	10	12
14	167	5/66	PC-r	2	2	2	4	6	8	10	12
15	166	11/67	PC-r	2	2	2	4	6	8	10	12
16	169	Spr/69	PC-r; stiff-c	2	2	2	4	6	8	10	12

43. Great Expectations (Used in SOTI, pg. 311)

Ed	HRN	Date	Details	A	C	GD 2.0	VG 4.0	FN 6.0	VF 8.0	VF/NM 9.0	NM- 9.2
1	43	11/47	Original; Kiefer-a/c	1	1	88	176	264	550	913	1275
2	62	–	No c-price; 8 pgs. cut; LDC-r	1	1	57	114	171	356	596	835

44. Mysteries of Paris (Used in SOTI, pg. 323)

Ed	HRN	Date	Details	A	C	GD 2.0	VG 4.0	FN 6.0	VF 8.0	VF/NM 9.0	NM- 9.2
1A	44	12/47	Original; 56 pgs.; Kiefer-c/a	1	1	64	128	192	400	663	925
1B	44	12/47	Orig.; printed on white/heavier paper; (rare)	1	1	74	148	222	463	769	1075
2A	62	–	8 pgs. cut; outside-bc: Gift Box ad; LDC-r	1	1	29	58	87	167	264	360
2B	62	–	8 pgs. cut; outside-bc: reorder list; LDC-r	1	1	29	58	87	167	264	360
3	78	–	C-price 15¢; LDC-r	1	1	24	48	72	139	220	300

45. Tom Brown's School Days

Ed	HRN	Date	Details	A	C	GD 2.0	VG 4.0	FN 6.0	VF 8.0	VF/NM 9.0	NM- 9.2
1	44	1/48	Original; 1st 48pg. issue	1	1	17	34	51	98	154	210
2	64	–	No c-price; LDC-r	1	1	7	14	21	35	43	50
3	161	–	New-c&a; PC-r	2	2	3	6	9	16	22	28
4	167	2/64	PC-r	2	2	2	4	6	8	11	14
5	167	8/66	PC-r	2	2	2	4	6	8	11	14
6	166	R/1968	C-price 25¢; PC-r	2	2	2	4	6	8	11	14

46. Kidnapped

Ed	HRN	Date	Details	A	C	GD 2.0	VG 4.0	FN 6.0	VF 8.0	VF/NM 9.0	NM- 9.2
1	47	4/48	Original; Webb-c/a	1	1	17	34	51	98	154	210
2A	62	–	Price circle blank; LDC-r	1	1	6	12	18	31	38	45
2B	62	–	C-price 10¢; rare; LDC-r	1	1	30	60	90	174	275	375
3	78	–	C-price 15¢; LDC-r	1	1	5	10	14	20	24	28
4	87	–	LDC-r	1	1	4	9	13	18	22	26
5	118	–	LDC-r	1	1	4	7	10	14	17	20
6	131	–	New-c; PC-r	1	2	5	10	14	20	24	28
7	140	–	PC-r	1	2	2	4	6	8	11	14
8	150	–	PC-r	1	2	2	4	6	8	11	14
9	164	–	Reduced pg.width; PC-r	1	2	2	4	6	8	10	12
10	167	–	PC-r	1	2	2	4	6	8	10	12
11	167	3/64	PC-r	1	2	2	4	6	8	10	12
12	167	6/65	PC-r	1	2	2	4	6	8	10	12
13	167	12/65	PC-r	1	2	2	4	6	8	10	12
14	166	9/67	PC-r	1	2	2	4	6	8	10	12
15	166	Win/69	New price 25¢; PC-r; stiff-c	1	2	2	4	6	8	10	12
16	169	Sm/70	PC-r; stiff-c	1	2	2	4	6	8	10	12

47. Twenty Thousand Leagues Under the Sea

Ed	HRN	Date	Details	A	C	GD 2.0	VG 4.0	FN 6.0	VF 8.0	VF/NM 9.0	NM- 9.2
1	47	5/48	Orig.; Kiefer-a&c	1	1	18	36	54	105	165	225
2	64	–	No c-price; LDC-r	1	1	6	12	18	27	33	38
3	78	–	C-price 15¢; LDC-r	1	1	4	9	13	18	22	26
4	94	–	LDC-r	1	1	4	8	12	17	21	24
5	118	–	LDC-r	1	1	4	7	10	14	17	20
6	128	–	New-c; PC-r	1	2	5	10	15	22	26	30
7	133	–	PC-r	1	2	2	4	6	9	13	16
8	140	–	PC-r	1	2	2	4	6	8	11	14
9	148	–	PC-r	1	2	2	4	6	8	11	14
10	156	–	PC-r	1	2	2	4	6	8	11	14
11	165	–	PC-r	1	2	2	4	6	8	11	14
12	167	–	PC-r	1	2	2	4	6	8	11	14
13	167	3/64	PC-r	1	2	2	4	6	8	11	14
14	167	8/65	PC-r	1	2	2	4	6	8	11	14
15	167	10/66	PC-r	1	2	2	4	6	8	11	14
16	166	R/1968	C-price 25¢; new-c PC-r	1	2		4	6	11	16	20
17	169	Spr/70	Stiff-c; PC-r	1	3		4	6	11	16	20

48. David Copperfield

Ed	HRN	Date	Details	A	C	GD 2.0	VG 4.0	FN 6.0	VF 8.0	VF/NM 9.0	NM- 9.2
1	47	6/48	Original; Kiefer-c/a	1	1	17	34	51	98	154	210
2	64	–	Price circle replaced by motif of boy reading; LDC-r	1	1	6	12	18	27	33	38
3	87	–	C-price 15¢; LDC-r	1	1	4	8	12	17	21	24
4	121	–	New-c; PC-r	1	2	4	9	13	18	22	26
5	130	–	PC-r	1	2	2	4	6	8	11	14
6	140	–	PC-r	1	2	2	4	6	8	11	14
7	148	–	PC-r	1	2	2	4	6	8	11	14
8	156	–	PC-r	1	2	2	4	6	8	11	14
9	167	–	PC-r	1	2	2	4	6	8	10	12
10	167	4/64	PC-r	1	2	2	4	6	8	10	12
11	167	6/65	PC-r	1	2	2	4	6	8	10	12
12	166	5/67	PC-r	1	2	2	4	6	8	10	12
13	166	R/67	PC-r; C-price 25¢	1	2	2	4	6	9	13	16
14	166	Spr/69	C-price 25¢; stiff-c	1	2	2	4	6	8	10	12
15	169	Win/69	Stiff-c; PC-r	1	2	2	4	6	8	10	12

49. Alice in Wonderland

Classics Illustrated #53 © GIL

Classics Illustrated #56 © GIL

Classics Illustrated #58 © GIL

Ed	HRN	Date	Details	A	C	GD 2.0	VG 4.0	FN 6.0	VF 8.0	VF/NM 9.0	NM- 9.2
1	47	7/48	Original; 1st Blum a & c	1	1	21	42	63	122	191	260
2	64	–	No c-price; LDC-r	1	1	7	14	21	37	46	55
3A	85	–	C-price 15¢; soft-c LDC-r	1	1	6	12	18	31	38	45
3B	85	–	Stiff-c; LDC-r	1	1	7	14	21	35	43	50
4	155	–	New PC, similar to orig.; PC-r	1	2	4	8	12	22	34	45
5	165	–	PC-r	1	2	3	6	9	16	23	30
6	167	3/64	PC-r	1	2	3	6	9	15	21	26
7	167	6/66	PC-r	1	2	3	6	9	15	21	26
8A	166	Fall/68	New-c; soft-c; 25¢ c-price; PC-r	1	3	4	8	12	22	34	45
8B	166	Fall/68	New-c; stiff-c; 25¢ c-price; PC-r	1	3	6	12	18	43	69	95

50. Adventures of Tom Sawyer (Used in SOTI, pg. 37)

Ed	HRN	Date	Details	A	C	GD 2.0	VG 4.0	FN 6.0	VF 8.0	VF/NM 9.0	NM- 9.2
1A	51	8/48	Orig.; Aldo Rubano a&c	1	1	17	34	51	98	154	210
1B	51	9/48	Orig.; Rubano c&a	1	1	17	34	51	98	154	210
1C	51	9/48	Orig.; outside-bc: blue & yellow only; rare	1	1	23	46	69	130	205	280
2	64	–	No c-price; LDC-r	1	1	5	10	15	23	28	32
3	78	–	C-price 15¢; LDC-r	1	1	4	8	12	17	21	24
4	94	–	LDC-r	1	1	4	7	10	14	17	20
5	117	–	LDC-r	1	1	2	4	6	10	14	18
6	132	–	LDC-r	1	1	2	4	6	10	14	18
7	140	–	New-c; PC-r	1	2	3	6	9	16	23	30
8	150	–	PC-r	1	2	2	4	6	8	11	14
9	164	–	New-a; PC-r	2	2	3	6	9	16	23	30
10	167	–	PC-r	2	2	2	4	6	8	11	14
11	167	1/65	PC-r	2	2	2	4	6	8	10	12
12	167	5/66	PC-r	2	2	2	4	6	8	10	12
13	166	12/67	PC-r	2	2	2	4	6	8	10	12
14	169	Fall/69	C-price 25¢; stiff-c; PC-r	2	2	2	4	6	8	10	12
15	169	Win/71	PC-r	2	2	2	4	6	8	10	12

51. The Spy

Ed	HRN	Date	Details	A	C	GD 2.0	VG 4.0	FN 6.0	VF 8.0	VF/NM 9.0	NM- 9.2
1A	51	9/48	Original; inside-bc illo: Christmas Carol	1	1	16	32	48	94	147	200
1B	51	9/48	Original; inside-bc illo: Man in Iron Mask	1	1	16	32	48	94	147	200
1C	51	8/48	Original; outside-bc: full color	1	1	16	32	48	94	147	200
1D	51	8/48	Original; outside-bc: blue & yellow only; scarce	1	1	18	36	54	103	162	220
2	89	–	C-price 15¢; LDC-r	1	1	5	10	14	20	24	28
3	121	–	LDC-r	1	1	4	8	12	17	21	24
4	139	–	New-c; PC-r	1	2	3	6	9	16	23	30
5	156	–	PC-r	1	2	2	4	6	8	11	14
6	167	11/63	PC-r	1	2	2	4	6	8	10	12
7	167	7/66	PC-r	1	2	2	4	6	8	10	12
8A	166	Win/69	C-price 25¢; soft-c; scarce; PC-r	1	2	3	6	9	15	21	26
8B	166	Win/69	C-price 25¢; stiff-c; PC-r	1	2	2	4	6	8	10	12

52. The House of the Seven Gables

Ed	HRN	Date	Details	A	C	GD 2.0	VG 4.0	FN 6.0	VF 8.0	VF/NM 9.0	NM- 9.2
1	53	10/48	Orig.; Griffiths a&c	1	1	16	32	48	94	147	200
2	89	–	C-price 15¢; LDC-r	1	1	5	10	14	20	24	28
3	121	–	LDC-r	1	1	4	8	12	17	21	24
4	142	–	New-c&a; PC-r; Woodbridge-a	2	2	5	10	15	23	28	32
5	156	–	PC-r	2	2	2	4	6	8	11	14
6	165	–	PC-r	2	2	2	4	6	8	10	12
7	167	5/64	PC-r	2	2	2	4	6	8	11	14
8	167	3/66	PC-r	2	2	2	4	6	8	10	12
9	166	R/1968	C-price 25¢; PC-r	2	2	2	4	6	8	10	12
10	169	Spr/70	Stiff-c; PC-r	2	2	2	4	6	8	10	12

53. A Christmas Carol

Ed	HRN	Date	Details	A	C	GD 2.0	VG 4.0	FN 6.0	VF 8.0	VF/NM 9.0	NM- 9.2
1	53	11/48	Original & only ed; Kiefer-c/a	1	1	22	44	66	128	202	275

54. Man in the Iron Mask

Ed	HRN	Date	Details	A	C	GD 2.0	VG 4.0	FN 6.0	VF 8.0	VF/NM 9.0	NM- 9.2
1	55	12/48	Original; Froehlich-a, Kiefer-c	1	1	16	32	48	94	147	200
2	93	–	C-price 15¢; LDC-r	1	1	5	10	15	23	28	32
3A	111	–	(O) logo lettering; scarce; LDC-r	1	1	6	12	18	31	38	45
3B	111	–	New logo as PC; LDC-r	1	1	5	10	15	23	28	32
4	142	–	New-c&a; PC-r	2	2	5	10	15	22	26	30
5	154	–	PC-r	2	2	2	4	6	8	11	14
6	165	–	PC-r	2	2	2	4	6	8	10	12
7	167	5/64	PC-r	2	2	2	4	6	8	10	12
8	167	4/66	PC-r	2	2	2	4	6	8	10	12
9A	166	Win/69	C-price 25¢; soft-c PC-r	2	2	3	6	9	15	21	26
9B	166	Win/69	Stiff-c	2	2	2	4	6	8	10	12

55. Silas Marner (Used in SOTI, pgs. 311, 312)

Ed	HRN	Date	Details	A	C	GD 2.0	VG 4.0	FN 6.0	VF 8.0	VF/NM 9.0	NM- 9.2
1	55	1/49	Original-Kiefer-c	1	1	16	32	48	94	147	200
2	75	–	Price circle blank; 'Coming Next' ad; LDC-r	1	1	5	10	15	24	30	35
3	97	–	LDC-r	1	1	3	6	9	14	19	24
4	121	–	New-c; PC-r	1	2	3	6	9	16	23	30
5	130	–	PC-r	1	2	2	4	6	8	11	14
6	140	–	PC-r	1	2	2	4	6	8	11	14
7	154	–	PC-r	1	2	2	4	6	8	11	14
8	165	–	PC-r	1	2	2	4	6	8	10	12
9	167	2/64	PC-r	1	2	2	4	6	8	10	12
10	167	6/65	PC-r	1	2	2	4	6	8	10	12
11	166	5/67	PC-r	1	2	2	4	6	8	10	12
12A	166	Win/69	C-price 25¢; soft-c PC-r	1	2	3	6	9	15	21	26
12B	166	Win/69	C-price 25¢; stiff-c PC-r	1	2	2	4	6	8	10	12

56. The Toilers of the Sea

Ed	HRN	Date	Details	A	C	GD 2.0	VG 4.0	FN 6.0	VF 8.0	VF/NM 9.0	NM- 9.2
1	55	2/49	Original; A.M. Froehlich-a	1	1	24	48	72	139	220	300
2	165	–	New-c&a; PC-r; Angelo Torres-a	2	2	7	14	21	35	43	50
3	167	3/64	PC-r	2	2	3	6	9	16	22	28
4	167	10/66	PC-r	2	2	3	6	9	16	22	28

57. The Song of Hiawatha

Ed	HRN	Date	Details	A	C	GD 2.0	VG 4.0	FN 6.0	VF 8.0	VF/NM 9.0	NM- 9.2
1	55	3/49	Original; Alex Blum-c/a	1	1	15	30	45	88	137	185
2	75	–	No c-price w/15¢ sticker; 'Coming Next' ad; LDC-r	1	1	5	10	15	24	30	35
3	94	–	C-price 15¢; LDC-r	1	1	5	10	14	20	24	28
4	118	–	LDC-r	1	1	3	6	9	14	19	24
5	134	–	New-c; PC-r	1	2	3	6	9	16	23	30
6	139	–	PC-r	1	2	2	4	6	8	11	14
7	167	–	Has orig.date; PC-r	1	2	2	4	6	8	10	12
8	167	9/64	PC-r	1	2	2	4	6	8	10	12
9	167	9/64	PC-r	1	2	2	4	6	8	10	12
10	167	10/65	PC-r	1	2	2	4	6	8	10	12
11	166	F/1968	C-price 25¢; PC-r	1	2	2	4	6	8	10	12

58. The Prairie

Ed	HRN	Date	Details	A	C	GD 2.0	VG 4.0	FN 6.0	VF 8.0	VF/NM 9.0	NM- 9.2
1	60	4/49	Original; Palais c/a	1	1	15	30	45	88	137	185
2A	62	–	No c-price; no coming-next ad; LDC-r	1	1	9	18	27	47	61	75
2B	62	–	10¢ (rare)	1	1	17	34	51	100	158	215

					GD	VG	FN	VF	VF/NM	NM-
					2.0	4.0	6.0	8.0	9.0	9.2

#	HRN	Date	Details	A	C	2.0	4.0	6.0	8.0	9.0	9.2
3	78	–	C-price 15¢ in dbl. circle; LDC-r	1	1	5	10	15	22	26	30
4	114	–	LDC-r	1	1	4	8	12	17	21	24
5	131	–	LDC-r	1	1	4	7	10	14	17	20
6	132	–	LDC-r	1	1	4	7	10	14	17	20
7	146	–	New-c; PC-r	1	2	5	10	14	20	24	28
8	155	–	PC-r	1	2	2	4	6	8	11	14
9	167	5/64	PC-r	1	2	2	4	6	8	10	12
10	167	4/66	PC-r	1	2	2	4	6	8	10	12
11	169	Sm/69	New price 25¢; stiff-c; PC-r	1	2	2	4	6	8	10	12

59. Wuthering Heights

Ed	HRN	Date	Details	A	C	2.0	4.0	6.0	8.0	9.0	9.2
1	60	5/49	Original; Kiefer-c/a	1	1	16	32	48	94	147	200
2	85	–	C-price 15¢; LDC-r	1	1	6	12	18	28	34	40
3	156	–	New-c; PC-r	1	2	5	10	15	23	28	32
4	167	1/64	PC-r	1	2	2	4	6	8	11	14
5	167	10/66	PC-r	1	2	2	4	6	8	11	14
6	169	Sm/69	C-price 25¢; stiff-c; PC-r	1	2	2	4	6	8	11	14

60. Black Beauty

Ed	HRN	Date	Details	A	C	2.0	4.0	6.0	8.0	9.0	9.2
1	62	6/49	Original; Froehlich-c/a	1	1	15	30	45	88	137	185
2	62	–	No c-price; no coming-next ad; LDC-r (rare)	1	1	17	34	51	100	158	215
3	85	–	C-price 15¢; LDC-r	1	1	5	10	15	23	28	32
4	158	–	New L.B. Cole-c/a; PC-r	2	2	6	12	18	31	38	45
5	167	2/64	PC-r	2	2	2	4	6	11	16	20
6	167	3/66	PC-r	2	2	2	4	6	11	16	20
7	166	R/1968	New-c&price, 25¢; PC-r	2	3	5	10	15	30	48	65

61. The Woman in White

Ed	HRN	Date	Details	A	C	2.0	4.0	6.0	8.0	9.0	9.2
1A	62	7/49	Original; Blum-c/a fc-purple; bc: top illos light blue	1	1	16	32	48	94	147	200
1B	62	7/49	Original; Blum-c/a fc-pink; bc: top illos light violet	1	1	16	32	48	94	147	200
2	156	–	New-c; PC-r	1	2	5	10	15	24	30	35
3	167	1/64	PC-r	1	2	2	4	6	11	16	20
4	166	R/1968	C-price 25¢; PC-r	1	2	2	4	6	11	16	20

62. Western Stories ("The Luck of Roaring Camp" and "The Outcasts of Poker Flat")

Ed	HRN	Date	Details	A	C	2.0	4.0	6.0	8.0	9.0	9.2
1	62	8/49	Original; Kiefer-c/a	1	1	15	30	45	85	130	175
2	89	–	C-price 15¢; LDC-r	1	1	5	10	15	23	28	32
3	121	–	LDC-r	1	1	3	6	9	15	21	26
4	137	–	New-c; PC-r	1	2	3	6	9	16	23	30
5	152	–	PC-r	1	2	2	4	6	8	10	12
6	167	10/63	PC-r	1	2	2	4	6	8	10	12
7	167	6/64	PC-r	1	2	2	4	6	8	10	12
8	167	11/66	PC-r	1	2	2	4	6	8	10	12
9	166	R/1968	New-c&price 25¢; PC-r	1	3	3	6	9	16	22	28

63. The Man Without a Country

Ed	HRN	Date	Details	A	C	2.0	4.0	6.0	8.0	9.0	9.2
1	62	9/49	Original; Kiefer-c/a	1	1	15	30	45	88	137	185
2	78	–	C-price 15¢ in double circle; LDC-r	1	1	5	10	15	23	28	32
3	156	–	New-c, old-a; PC-r	1	2	5	10	15	24	30	35
4	165	–	New-a & text pgs.; PC-r; A. Torres-a	2	2	5	10	14	20	24	28
5	167	3/64	PC-r	2	2	2	4	6	8	10	12
6	167	8/66	PC-r	2	2	2	4	6	8	10	12
7	169	Sm/69	New price 25¢; stiff-c; PC-r	2	2	2	4	6	8	10	12

64. Treasure Island

Ed	HRN	Date	Details	A	C						

					GD	VG	FN	VF	VF/NM	NM-
					2.0	4.0	6.0	8.0	9.0	9.2

Ed	HRN	Date	Details	A	C	2.0	4.0	6.0	8.0	9.0	9.2
1	62	10/49	Original; Blum-c/a	1	1	16	32	48	94	147	200
2A	82	–	C-price 15¢; soft-c	1	1	5	10	15	22	26	30
2B	82	–	Stiff-c; LDC-r	1	1	5	10	15	23	28	32
3	117	–	LDC-r	1	1	3	6	9	15	21	26
4	131	–	New-c; PC-r	1	2	3	6	9	16	23	30
5	138	–	PC-r	1	2	2	4	6	8	11	14
6	146	–	PC-r	1	2	2	4	6	8	11	14
7	158	–	PC-r	1	2	2	4	6	8	11	14
8	165	–	PC-r	1	2	2	4	6	8	10	12
9	167	–	PC-r	1	2	2	4	6	8	10	12
10	167	6/64	PC-r	1	2	2	4	6	8	10	12
11	167	12/65	PC-r	1	2	2	4	6	8	10	12
12A	166	10/67	PC-r	1	2	2	4	6	8	10	12
12B	166	10/67	w/Grit ad stapled in book	1	2	9	18	27	63	107	150
13	169	Spr/69	New price 25¢; stiff-c; PC-r	1	2	2	4	6	8	11	14
14	–	1989	Long John Silver's Seafood Shoppes; $1.95, First/Berkley Publ.; Blum-r	1	2						5.00

65. Benjamin Franklin

Ed	HRN	Date	Details	A	C	2.0	4.0	6.0	8.0	9.0	9.2
1	64	11/49	Original; Kiefer-c; Iger Shop-a	1	1	15	30	45	88	137	185
2	131	–	New-c; PC-r	1	2	5	10	15	23	28	32
3	154	–	PC-r	1	2	2	4	6	9	12	15
4	167	2/64	PC-r	1	2	2	4	6	8	11	14
5	167	4/66	PC-r	1	2	2	4	6	8	11	14
6	169	Fall/69	New price 25¢; stiff-c; PC-r	1	2	2	4	6	8	11	14

66. The Cloister and the Hearth

Ed	HRN	Date	Details	A	C	2.0	4.0	6.0	8.0	9.0	9.2
1	67	12/49	Original & only ed; Kiefer-a & c	1	1	30	60	90	174	275	375

67. The Scottish Chiefs

Ed	HRN	Date	Details	A	C	2.0	4.0	6.0	8.0	9.0	9.2
1	67	1/50	Original; Blum-a&c	1	1	14	28	42	82	121	160
2	85	–	C-price 15¢; LDC-r	1	1	5	10	15	23	28	32
3	118	–	LDC-r	1	1	3	6	9	15	21	26
4	136	–	New-c; PC-r	1	2	3	6	9	17	25	32
5	154	–	PC-r	1	2	2	4	6	8	11	14
6	167	11/63	PC-r	1	2	2	4	6	9	13	16
7	167	8/65	PC-r	1	2	2	4	6	8	11	14

68. Julius Caesar (Used in **SOTI**, pgs. 36, 37)

Ed	HRN	Date	Details	A	C	2.0	4.0	6.0	8.0	9.0	9.2
1	70	2/50	Original; Kiefer-c/a	1	1	14	28	42	82	121	160
2	85	–	C-price 15¢; LDC-r	1	1	5	10	15	22	26	30
3	108	–	LDC-r	1	1	4	9	13	18	22	26
4	156	–	New L.B. Cole-c; PC-r	1	2	5	10	15	24	30	35
5	165	–	New-a by Evans, Crandall; PC-r	2	2	5	10	15	22	26	30
6	167	2/64	PC-r	2	2	2	4	6	8	10	12
7	167	10/65	Tarzan books inside cover; PC-r	2	2	2	4	6	8	10	12
8	166	R/1967	PC-r	2	2	2	4	6	8	10	12
9	169	Win/69	PC-r; stiff-c	2	2	2	4	6	8	10	12

69. Around the World in 80 Days

Ed	HRN	Date	Details	A	C	2.0	4.0	6.0	8.0	9.0	9.2
1	70	3/50	Original; Kiefer-c/a	1	1	14	28	42	82	121	160
2	87	–	C-price 15¢; LDC-r	1	1	5	10	15	22	26	30
3	125	–	LDC-r	1	1	4	9	13	18	22	26
4	136	–	New-c; PC-r	1	1	5	10	15	23	28	32
5	146	–	PC-r	1	2	2	4	6	8	11	14
6	152	–	PC-r	1	2	2	4	6	8	11	14
7	164	–	PC-r	1	2	2	4	6	8	10	12
8	167	–	PC-r	1	2	2	4	6	8	10	12
9	167	7/64	PC-r	1	2	2	4	6	8	10	12
10	167	11/65	PC-r	1	2	2	4	6	8	10	12
11	166	7/67	PC-r	1	2	2	4	6	8	10	12
12	169	Spr/69	C-price 25¢; stiff-c;	1	2	2	4	6	8	10	12

Classics Illustrated #71 © GIL

Classics Illustrated #75 © GIL

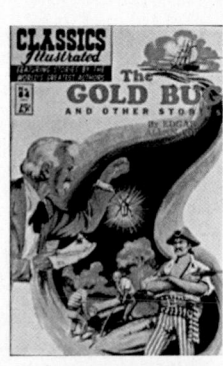

Classics Illustrated #84 © GIL

				GD 2.0	VG 4.0	FN 6.0	VF 8.0	VF/NM 9.0	NM- 9.2
			PC-r						
70. The Pilot									
Ed	HRN	Date	Details	A	C				
1	71	4/50	Original; Blum-c/a	1	1	12	24	36	69	97	125
2	92	–	C-price 15¢; LDC-r	1	1	5	10	15	23	28	32
3	125	–	LDC-r	1	1	4	9	13	18	22	26
4	156	–	New-c; PC-r	1	2	5	10	15	24	30	35
5	167	2/64	PC-r	1	2	2	4	6	11	16	20
6	167	5/66	PC-r	1	2	2	4	6	9	13	16
71. The Man Who Laughs									
Ed	HRN	Date	Details	A	C				
1	71	5/50	Original; Blum-c/a	1	1	17	34	51	98	154	210
2	165	–	New-c&a; PC-r	2	2	14	28	42	76	108	140
3	167	4/64	PC-r	2	2	11	22	33	60	83	105
72. The Oregon Trail									
Ed	HRN	Date	Details	A	C				
1	73	6/50	Original; Kiefer-c/a	1	1	12	24	36	69	97	125
2	89	–	C-price 15¢; LDC-r	1	1	5	10	15	23	28	32
3	121	–	LDC-r	1	1	4	9	13	18	22	26
4	131	–	New-c; PC-r	1	2	5	10	15	23	28	32
5	140	–	PC-r	1	2	2	4	6	8	11	14
6	150	–	PC-r	1	2	2	4	6	8	11	14
7	164	–	PC-r	1	2	2	4	6	8	10	12
8	167	–	PC-r	1	2	2	4	6	8	10	12
9	167	8/64	PC-r	1	2	2	4	6	8	10	12
10	167	10/65	PC-r	1	2	2	4	6	8	10	12
11	166	R/1968	C-price 25¢; PC-r	1	2	2	4	6	8	10	12
73. The Black Tulip									
Ed	HRN	Date	Details	A	C				
1	75	7/50	1st & only ed.; Alex Blum-c/a	1	1	35	70	105	201	318	435
74. Mr. Midshipman Easy									
Ed	HRN	Date	Details	A	C				
1	75	8/50	1st & only edition	1	1	35	70	105	201	318	435
75. The Lady of the Lake									
Ed	HRN	Date	Details	A	C				
1	75	9/50	Original; Kiefer-c/a	1	1	12	24	36	69	97	125
2	85	–	C-price 15¢; LDC-r	1	1	5	10	15	24	30	35
3	118	–	LDC-r	1	1	5	10	14	20	24	28
4	139	–	New-c; PC-r	1	2	5	10	15	23	28	32
5	154	–	PC-r	1	2	2	4	6	8	11	14
6	165	–	PC-r	1	2	2	4	6	8	10	12
7	167	4/64	PC-r	1	2	2	4	6	8	10	12
8	167	5/66	PC-r	1	2	2	4	6	8	10	12
9	169	Spr/69	New price 25¢; stiff-c; PC-r	1	2	2	4	6	8	10	12
76. The Prisoner of Zenda									
Ed	HRN	Date	Details	A	C				
1	75	10/50	Original; Kiefer-c/a	1	1	12	24	36	67	97	125
2	85	–	C-price 15¢; LDC-r	1	1	5	10	15	23	28	32
3	111	–	LDC-r	1	1	3	6	9	16	21	26
4	128	–	New-c; PC-r	1	2	3	6	9	16	23	30
5	152	–	PC-r	1	2	2	4	6	8	11	14
6	165	–	PC-r	1	2	2	4	6	8	10	12
7	167	4/64	PC-r	1	2	2	4	6	8	10	12
8	167	9/66	PC-r	1	2	2	4	6	8	10	12
9	169	Fall/69	New price 25¢; stiff-c; PC-r	1	2	2	4	6	8	10	12
77. The Iliad									
Ed	HRN	Date	Details	A	C				
1	78	11/50	Original; Blum-c/a	1	1	12	24	36	69	97	125
2	87	–	C-price 15¢; LDC-r	1	1	5	10	15	24	30	35
3	121	–	LDC-r	1	1	3	6	9	15	21	26
4	139	–	New-c; PC-r	1	2	3	6	9	16	22	28
5	150	–	PC-r	1	2	2	4	6	8	11	14
6	165	–	PC-r	1	2	2	4	6	8	10	12
7	167	10/63	PC-r	1	2	2	4	6	8	10	12
8	167	7/64	PC-r	1	2	2	4	6	8	10	12
9	167	5/66	PC-r	1	2	2	4	6	8	10	12
10	166	R/1968	C-price 25¢; PC-r	1	2	2	4	6	8	10	12
78. Joan of Arc									
Ed	HRN	Date	Details	A	C				
1	78	12/50	Original; Kiefer-c/a	1	1	12	24	36	69	97	125
2	87	–	C-price 15¢; LDC-r	1	1	5	10	15	23	28	32
3	113	–	LDC-r	1	1	3	6	9	15	21	26
4	128	–	New-c; PC-r	1	2	3	6	9	16	23	30
5	140	–	PC-r	1	2	2	4	6	8	11	14
6	150	–	PC-r	1	2	2	4	6	8	11	14
7	159	–	PC-r	1	2	2	4	6	8	11	14
8	167	–	PC-r	1	2	2	4	6	8	10	12
9	167	12/63	PC-r	1	2	2	4	6	8	10	12
10	167	6/65	PC-r	1	2	2	4	6	8	10	12
11	166	6/67	PC-r	1	2	2	4	6	8	10	12
12	166	Win/69	New-c&price, 25¢; PC-r; stiff-c	1	3	3	6	9	16	23	30
79. Cyrano de Bergerac									
Ed	HRN	Date	Details	A	C				
1	78	1/51	Orig.; movie promo inside front-c; Blum-c/a	1	1	12	24	36	69	97	125
2	85	–	C-price 15¢; LDC-r	1	1	5	10	15	23	28	32
3	118	–	LDC-r	1	1	3	6	9	17	23	28
4	133	–	New-c; PC-r	1	2	3	6	9	16	22	28
5	156	–	PC-r	1	2	2	4	6	11	16	20
6	167	8/64	PC-r	1	2	2	4	6	11	16	20
80. White Fang (Last line drawn cover)									
Ed	HRN	Date	Details	A	C				
1	79	2/51	Orig.; Blum-c/a	1	1	12	24	36	69	97	125
2	87	–	C-price 15¢; LDC-r	1	1	5	10	15	24	30	35
3	125	–	LDC-r	1	1	3	6	9	15	21	26
4	132	–	New-c; PC-r	1	2	3	6	9	16	22	28
5	140	–	PC-r	1	2	2	4	6	8	11	14
6	153	–	PC-r	1	2	2	4	6	8	11	14
7	167	–	PC-r	1	2	2	4	6	8	10	12
8	167	9/64	PC-r	1	2	2	4	6	8	10	12
9	167	7/65	PC-r	1	2	2	4	6	8	10	12
10	166	6/67	PC-r	1	2	2	4	6	8	10	12
11	169	Fall/69	New price 25¢; PC-r; stiff-c	1	2	2	4	6	8	10	12
81. The Odyssey (1st painted cover)									
Ed	HRN	Date	Details	A	C				
1	82	3/51	First 15¢ Original; Blum-c	1	1	12	24	36	69	97	125
2	167	8/64	PC-r	1	1	2	4	6	11	16	20
3	167	10/66	PC-r	1	1	2	4	6	11	16	20
4	169	Spr/69	New, stiff-c; PC-r	1	2	3	6	9	17	25	32
82. The Master of Ballantrae									
Ed	HRN	Date	Details	A	C				
1	82	4/51	Original; Blum-c	1	1	10	20	30	58	79	100
2	167	8/64	PC-r	1	1	3	6	9	14	19	24
3	166	Fall/68	New, stiff-c; PC-r	1	2	3	6	9	17	25	32
83. The Jungle Book									
Ed	HRN	Date	Details	A	C				
1	85	5/51	Original; Blum-c; Bossert/Blum-a	1	1	10	20	30	58	79	100
2	110	–	PC-r	1	1	2	4	6	9	13	16
3	125	–	PC-r	1	1	2	4	6	8	11	14
4	134	–	PC-r	1	1	2	4	6	8	11	14
5	142	–	PC-r	1	1	2	4	6	8	11	14
6	150	–	PC-r	1	1	2	4	6	8	11	14
7	159	–	PC-r	1	1	2	4	6	8	11	14
8	167	–	PC-r	1	1	2	4	6	8	10	12
9	167	3/65	PC-r	1	1	2	4	6	8	10	12
10	167	11/65	PC-r	1	1	2	4	6	8	10	12
11	167	5/66	PC-r	1	1	2	4	6	8	10	12
12	166	R/1968	New c&a; stiff-c; PC-r	2	2	3	6	9	17	25	32
84. The Gold Bug and Other Stories ("The Gold Bug", "The Tell-Tale Heart", "The Cask of Amontillado")									
Ed	HRN	Date	Details	A	C				
1	85	6/51	Original; Blum-c/a; Palais, Laverly-a	1	1	14	28	42	80	115	150
2	167	7/64	PC-r	1	1	10	20	30	58	79	100

85. The Sea Wolf

Ed	HRN	Date	Details	A	C	GD 2.0	VG 4.0	FN 6.0	VF 8.0	VF/NM 9.0	NM- 9.2
1	85	7/51	Original; Blum-c/a	1	1	10	20	30	54	72	90
2	121	–	PC-r	1	1	2	4	6	8	11	14
3	132	–	PC-r	1	1	2	4	6	8	11	14
4	141	–	PC-r	1	1	2	4	6	8	11	14
5	161	–	PC-r	1	1	2	4	6	8	10	12
6	167	2/64	PC-r	1	1	2	4	6	8	10	12
7	167	11/65	PC-r	1	1	2	4	6	8	10	12
8	169	Fall/69	New price 25¢; stiff-c; PC-r	1	1	2	4	6	8	10	12

86. Under Two Flags

Ed	HRN	Date	Details	A	C	GD 2.0	VG 4.0	FN 6.0	VF 8.0	VF/NM 9.0	NM- 9.2
1	87	8/51	Original; first delBourgo-a	1	1	10	20	30	54	72	90
2	117	–	PC-r	1	1	2	4	6	9	13	16
3	139	–	PC-r	1	1	2	4	6	8	11	14
4	158	–	PC-r	1	1	2	4	6	8	11	14
5	167	2/64	PC-r	1	1	2	4	6	8	10	12
6	167	8/66	PC-r	1	1	2	4	6	8	10	12
7	169	Sm/69	New price 25¢; stiff-c; PC-r	1	1	2	4	6	8	10	12

87. A Midsummer Nights Dream

Ed	HRN	Date	Details	A	C	GD 2.0	VG 4.0	FN 6.0	VF 8.0	VF/NM 9.0	NM- 9.2
1	87	9/51	Original; Blum c/a	1	1	10	20	30	54	72	90
2	161	–	PC-r	1	1	2	4	6	8	11	14
3	167	4/64	PC-r	1	1	2	4	6	8	10	12
4	167	5/66	PC-r	1	1	2	4	6	8	10	12
5	169	Sm/69	New price 25¢; stiff-c; PC-r	1	1	2	4	6	8	10	12

88. Men of Iron

Ed	HRN	Date	Details	A	C	GD 2.0	VG 4.0	FN 6.0	VF 8.0	VF/NM 9.0	NM- 9.2
1	89	10/51	Original	1	1	10	20	30	54	72	90
2	154	–	PC-r	1	1	2	4	6	8	11	14
3	167	1/64	PC-r	1	1	2	4	6	8	10	12
4	166	R/1968	C-price 25¢; PC-r	1	1	2	4	6	8	10	12

89. Crime and Punishment (Cover illo. in POP)

Ed	HRN	Date	Details	A	C	GD 2.0	VG 4.0	FN 6.0	VF 8.0	VF/NM 9.0	NM- 9.2
1	89	11/51	Original; Palais-a	1	1	10	20	30	54	72	90
2	152	–	PC-r	1	1	2	4	6	8	11	14
3	167	4/64	PC-r	1	1	2	4	6	8	10	12
4	167	5/66	PC-r	1	1	2	4	6	8	10	12
5	169	Fall/69	New price 25¢; stiff-c; PC-r	1	1	2	4	6	8	10	12

90. Green Mansions

Ed	HRN	Date	Details	A	C	GD 2.0	VG 4.0	FN 6.0	VF 8.0	VF/NM 9.0	NM- 9.2
1	89	12/51	Original; Blum-c/a	1	1	10	20	30	54	72	90
2	148	–	New L.B. Cole-c	1	2	4	9	13	18	22	26
3	165	–	PC-r	1	2	2	4	6	8	10	12
4	167	4/64	PC-r	1	2	2	4	6	8	10	12
5	167	9/66	PC-r	1	2	2	4	6	8	10	12
6	169	Sm/69	New price 25¢; stiff-c; PC-r	1	2	2	4	6	8	10	12

91. The Call of the Wild

Ed	HRN	Date	Details	A	C	GD 2.0	VG 4.0	FN 6.0	VF 8.0	VF/NM 9.0	NM- 9.2
1	92	1/52	Orig.; delBourgo-a	1	1	10	20	30	54	72	90
2	112	–	PC-r	1	1	2	4	6	8	11	14
3	125	–	'Picture Progress' on back-c; PC-r	1	1	2	4	6	8	11	14
4	134	–	PC-r	1	1	2	4	6	8	11	14
5	143	–	PC-r	1	1	2	4	6	8	11	14
6	165	–	PC-r	1	1	2	4	6	8	11	14
7	167	–	PC-r	1	1	2	4	6	8	10	12
8	167	4/65	PC-r	1	1	2	4	6	8	10	12
9	167	3/66	PC-r	1	1	2	4	6	8	10	12
10	166	11/67	PC-r	1	1	2	4	6	8	10	12
11	169	Spr/70	New price 25¢; stiff-c; PC-r	1	1	2	4	6	8	10	12

92. The Courtship of Miles Standish

Ed	HRN	Date	Details	A	C	GD 2.0	VG 4.0	FN 6.0	VF 8.0	VF/NM 9.0	NM- 9.2
1	92	2/52	Original; Blum-c/a	1	1	10	20	30	54	72	90
2	165	–	PC-r	1	1	2	4	6	8	11	14
3	167	3/64	PC-r	1	1	2	4	6	8	11	14
4	166	5/67	PC-r	1	1	2	4	6	8	11	14
5	169	Win/69	New price 25¢; stiff-c; PC-r	1	1	2	4	6	8	11	14

93. Pudd'nhead Wilson

Ed	HRN	Date	Details	A	C	GD 2.0	VG 4.0	FN 6.0	VF 8.0	VF/NM 9.0	NM- 9.2
1	94	3/52	Orig.; Kiefer-c/a;	1	1	10	20	30	54	72	90
2	165	–	New-c; PC-r	1	2	2	4	6	11	16	20
3	167	3/64	PC-r	1	2	2	4	6	8	11	14
4	166	R/1968	New price 25¢; soft-c; PC-r	1	2	2	4	6	9	12	15

94. David Balfour

Ed	HRN	Date	Details	A	C	GD 2.0	VG 4.0	FN 6.0	VF 8.0	VF/NM 9.0	NM- 9.2
1	94	4/52	Original; Palais-a	1	1	10	20	30	54	72	90
2	167	5/64	PC-r	1	1	2	4	6	11	16	20
3	166	R/1968	C-price 25¢; PC-r	1	1	2	4	6	13	18	22

95. All Quiet on the Western Front

Ed	HRN	Date	Details	A	C	GD 2.0	VG 4.0	FN 6.0	VF 8.0	VF/NM 9.0	NM- 9.2
1A	96	5/52	Orig.; del Bourgo-a	1	1	13	26	39	74	105	135
1B	99	5/52	Orig.; del Bourgo-a	1	1	11	22	33	62	86	110
2	167	10/64	PC-r	1	1	3	6	9	15	21	26
3	167	11/66	PC-r	1	1	3	6	9	15	21	26

96. Daniel Boone

Ed	HRN	Date	Details	A	C	GD 2.0	VG 4.0	FN 6.0	VF 8.0	VF/NM 9.0	NM- 9.2
1	97	6/52	Original; Blum-a	1	1	9	18	27	52	69	85
2	117	–	PC-r	1	1	2	4	6	8	11	14
3	128	–	PC-r	1	1	2	4	6	8	11	14
4	132	–	PC-r	1	1	2	4	6	8	11	14
5	134	–	"Story of Jesus" on back-c; PC-r	1	1	2	4	6	8	11	14
6	158	–	PC-r	1	1	2	4	6	8	11	14
7	167	1/64	PC-r	1	1	2	4	6	8	10	12
8	167	5/65	PC-r	1	1	2	4	6	8	10	12
9	167	11/66	PC-r	1	1	2	4	6	8	10	12
10	166	Win/69	New-c; price 25¢; PC-r; stiff-c	1	2	3	6	9	14	19	24

97. King Solomon's Mines

Ed	HRN	Date	Details	A	C	GD 2.0	VG 4.0	FN 6.0	VF 8.0	VF/NM 9.0	NM- 9.2
1	96	7/52	Orig.; Kiefer-a	1	1	9	18	27	52	69	85
2	118	–	PC-r	1	1	2	4	6	8	11	14
3	131	–	PC-r	1	1	2	4	6	8	11	14
4	141	–	PC-r	1	1	2	4	6	8	11	14
5	158	–	PC-r	1	1	2	4	6	8	11	14
6	167	2/64	PC-r	1	1	2	4	6	8	10	12
7	167	9/65	PC-r	1	1	2	4	6	8	10	12
8	169	Sm/69	New price 25¢; stiff-c; PC-r	1	1	2	4	6	8	10	12

98. The Red Badge of Courage

Ed	HRN	Date	Details	A	C	GD 2.0	VG 4.0	FN 6.0	VF 8.0	VF/NM 9.0	NM- 9.2
1	98	8/52	Original	1	1	9	18	27	52	69	85
2	118	–	PC-r	1	1	2	4	6	8	11	14
3	132	–	PC-r	1	1	2	4	6	8	11	14
4	142	–	PC-r	1	1	2	4	6	8	11	14
5	152	–	PC-r	1	1	2	4	6	8	11	14
6	161	–	PC-r	1	1	2	4	6	8	11	14
7	167	–	Has orig.date; PC-r	1	1	2	4	6	8	11	14
8	167	9/64	PC-r	1	1	2	4	6	8	11	14
9	167	10/65	PC-r	1	1	2	4	6	8	11	14
10	166	R/1968	New-c&price 25¢; stiff-c	1	2	3	6	9	15	21	26

99. Hamlet (Used in POP, pg. 102)

Ed	HRN	Date	Details	A	C	GD 2.0	VG 4.0	FN 6.0	VF 8.0	VF/NM 9.0	NM- 9.2
1	98	9/52	Original; Blum-a	1	1	10	20	30	54	72	90
2	121	–	PC-r	1	1	2	4	6	8	11	14
3	141	–	PC-r	1	1	2	4	6	8	11	14
4	158	–	PC-r	1	1	2	4	6	8	11	14
5	167	–	Has orig.date; PC-r	1	1	2	4	6	8	10	12
6	167	7/65	PC-r	1	1	2	4	6	8	10	12
7	166	4/67	PC-r	1	1	2	4	6	8	10	12
8	169	Spr/69	New-c&price 25¢; PC-r; stiff-c	1	2	3	6	9	15	21	26

Classics Illustrated #104 © GIL

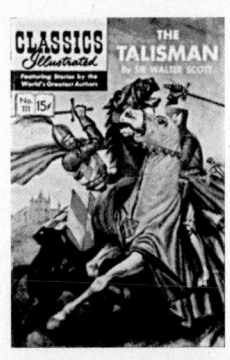

Classics Illustrated #111 © GIL

Classics Illustrated #115 © GIL

100. Mutiny on the Bounty

Ed	HRN	Date	Details	A	C	GD 2.0	VG 4.0	FN 6.0	VF 8.0	VF/NM 9.0	NM- 9.2
1	100	10/52	Original	1	1	9	18	27	52	69	85
2	117	–	PC-r	1	1	2	4	6	8	11	14
3	132	–	PC-r	1	1	2	4	6	8	11	14
4	142	–	PC-r	1	1	2	4	6	8	11	14
5	155	–	PC-r	1	1	2	4	6	8	11	14
6	167	–	Has orig. date;PC-r	1	1	2	4	6	8	10	12
7	167	5/64	PC-r	1	1	2	4	6	8	10	12
8	167	3/66	PC-r	1	1	2	4	6	8	10	12
9	169	Spr/70	PC-r; stiff-c	1	1	2	4	6	8	10	12

101. William Tell

Ed	HRN	Date	Details	A	C	GD 2.0	VG 4.0	FN 6.0	VF 8.0	VF/NM 9.0	NM- 9.2
1	101	11/52	Original; Kiefer-c delBourgo-a	1	1	9	18	27	52	69	85
2	118	–	PC-r	1	1	2	4	6	8	11	14
3	141	–	PC-r	1	1	2	4	6	8	11	14
4	158	–	PC-r	1	1	2	4	6	8	11	14
5	167	–	Has orig. date; PC-r	1	1	2	4	6	8	10	12
6	167	11/64	PC-r	1	1	2	4	6	8	10	12
7	166	4/67	PC-r	1	1	2	4	6	8	10	12
8	169	Win/69	New price 25¢; stiff-c; PC-r	1	1	2	4	6	8	10	12

102. The White Company

Ed	HRN	Date	Details	A	C	GD 2.0	VG 4.0	FN 6.0	VF 8.0	VF/NM 9.0	NM- 9.2
1	101	12/52	Original; Blum-a	1	1	12	24	36	67	94	120
2	165	–	PC-r	1	1	3	6	9	16	22	28
3	167	4/64	PC-r	1	1	3	6	9	16	22	28

103. Men Against the Sea

Ed	HRN	Date	Details	A	C	GD 2.0	VG 4.0	FN 6.0	VF 8.0	VF/NM 9.0	NM- 9.2
1	104	1/53	Original; Kiefer-c; Palais-a	1	1	10	20	30	54	72	90
2	114	–	PC-r	1	1	4	8	11	16	19	22
3	131	–	New-c; PC-r	1	2	5	10	15	22	26	30
4	158	–	PC-r	1	2	4	7	10	14	17	20
5	149	–	White reorder list; came after HRN-158; PC-r	1	2	5	10	15	22	26	30
6	167	3/64	PC-r	1	2	2	4	6	8	11	14

104. Bring 'Em Back Alive

Ed	HRN	Date	Details	A	C	GD 2.0	VG 4.0	FN 6.0	VF 8.0	VF/NM 9.0	NM- 9.2
1	105	2/53	Original; Kiefer-c/a	1	1	9	18	27	52	69	85
2	118	–	PC-r	1	1	2	4	6	8	11	14
3	133	–	PC-r	1	1	2	4	6	8	11	14
4	150	–	PC-r	1	1	2	4	6	8	11	14
5	158	–	PC-r	1	1	2	4	6	8	11	14
6	167	10/63	PC-r	1	1	2	4	6	8	10	12
7	167	9/65	PC-r	1	1	2	4	6	8	10	12
8	169	Win/69	New price 25¢; stiff-c; PC-r	1	1	2	4	6	8	10	12

105. From the Earth to the Moon

Ed	HRN	Date	Details	A	C	GD 2.0	VG 4.0	FN 6.0	VF 8.0	VF/NM 9.0	NM- 9.2
1	106	3/53	Original; Blum-a	1	1	9	18	27	52	69	85
2	118	–	PC-r	1	1	2	4	6	8	11	14
3	132	–	PC-r	1	1	2	4	6	8	11	14
4	141	–	PC-r	1	1	2	4	6	8	11	14
5	146	–	PC-r	1	1	2	4	6	8	11	14
6	156	–	PC-r	1	1	2	4	6	8	11	14
7	167	–	Has orig. date; PC-r	1	1	2	4	6	8	10	12
8	167	5/64	PC-r	1	1	2	4	6	8	10	12
9	167	5/65	PC-r	1	1	2	4	6	8	10	12
10A	166	10/67	PC-r	1	1	2	4	6	8	10	12
10B	166	10/67	w/Grit ad stapled in book	1	1	7	14	21	50	83	115
11	169	Sm/69	New price 25¢; stiff-c; PC-r	1	1	2	4	6	8	10	12
12	169	Spr/71	PC-r	1	1	2	4	6	8	10	12

106. Buffalo Bill

Ed	HRN	Date	Details	A	C	GD 2.0	VG 4.0	FN 6.0	VF 8.0	VF/NM 9.0	NM- 9.2
1	107	4/53	Orig.; delBourgo-a	1	1	9	18	27	50	65	80
2	118	–	PC-r	1	1	2	4	6	8	11	14
3	132	–	PC-r	1	1	2	4	6	8	11	14
4	142	–	PC-r	1	1	2	4	6	8	11	14
5	161	–	PC-r	1	1	2	4	6	8	10	12
6	167	3/64	PC-r	1	1	2	4	6	8	10	12
7	166	7/67	PC-r	1	1	2	4	6	8	10	12
8	169	Fall/69	PC-r; stiff-c	1	1	2	4	6	8	10	12

107. King of the Khyber Rifles

Ed	HRN	Date	Details	A	C	GD 2.0	VG 4.0	FN 6.0	VF 8.0	VF/NM 9.0	NM- 9.2
1	108	5/53	Original	1	1	9	18	27	50	65	80
2	118	–	PC-r	1	1	2	4	6	8	11	14
3	146	–	PC-r	1	1	2	4	6	8	11	14
4	158	–	PC-r	1	1	2	4	6	8	11	14
5	167	–	Has orig.date; PC-r	1	1	2	4	6	8	10	12
6	167	–	PC-r	1	1	2	4	6	8	10	12
7	167	10/66	PC-r	1	1	2	4	6	8	10	12

108. Knights of the Round Table

Ed	HRN	Date	Details	A	C	GD 2.0	VG 4.0	FN 6.0	VF 8.0	VF/NM 9.0	NM- 9.2
1A	108	6/53	Original; Blum-a	1	1	10	20	30	54	72	90
1B	109	6/53	Original; scarce	1	1	9	18	27	56	75	95
2	117	–	PC-r	1	1	2	4	6	8	11	14
3	165	–	PC-r	1	1	2	4	.6	8	11	14
4	167	4/64	PC-r	1	1	2	4	6	8	10	12
5	166	4/67	PC-r	1	1	2	4	6	8	10	12
6	169	Sm/69	New price 25¢; stiff-c; PC-r	1	1	2	4	6	8	10	12

109. Pitcairn's Island

Ed	HRN	Date	Details	A	C	GD 2.0	VG 4.0	FN 6.0	VF 8.0	VF/NM 9.0	NM- 9.2
1	110	7/53	Original; Palais-a	1	1	10	20	30	54	72	90
2	165	–	PC-r	1	1	2	4	6	8	11	14
3	167	3/64	PC-r	1	1	2	4	6	8	11	14
4	166	6/67	PC-r	1	1	2	4	6	8	11	14

110. A Study in Scarlet

Ed	HRN	Date	Details	A	C	GD 2.0	VG 4.0	FN 6.0	VF 8.0	VF/NM 9.0	NM- 9.2
1	111	8/53	Original	1	1	14	28	42	80	115	150
2	165	–	PC-r	1	1	10	20	30	58	79	100

111. The Talisman

Ed	HRN	Date	Details	A	C	GD 2.0	VG 4.0	FN 6.0	VF 8.0	VF/NM 9.0	NM- 9.2
1	112	9/53	Original; last H.C. Kiefer-a	1	1	10	20	30	54	72	90
2	165	–	PC-r	1	1	2	4	6	8	11	14
3	167	5/64	PC-r	1	1	2	4	6	8	11	14
4	166	Fall/68	C-price 25¢; PC-r	1	1	2	4	6	8	11	14

112. Adventures of Kit Carson

Ed	HRN	Date	Details	A	C	GD 2.0	VG 4.0	FN 6.0	VF 8.0	VF/NM 9.0	NM- 9.2
1	113	10/53	Original; Palais-a	1	1	9	18	27	52	69	85
2	129	–	PC-r	1	1	2	4	6	8	11	14
3	141	–	PC-r	1	1	2	4	6	8	11	14
4	152	–	PC-r	1	1	2	4	6	8	11	14
5	161	–	PC-r	1	1	2	4	6	8	10	12
6	167	–	PC-r	1	1	2	4	6	8	10	12
7	167	2/65	PC-r	1	1	2	4	6	8	10	12
8	167	5/66	PC-r	1	1	2	4	6	8	10	12
9	166	Win/69	New-c&price 25¢; PC-r; stiff-c	1	2	2	4	6	11	16	20

113. The Forty-Five Guardsmen

Ed	HRN	Date	Details	A	C	GD 2.0	VG 4.0	FN 6.0	VF 8.0	VF/NM 9.0	NM- 9.2
1	114	11/53	Orig.; delBourgo-a	1	1	11	22	33	62	86	110
2	166	7/67	PC-r	1	1	3	6	9	18	27	35

114. The Red Rover

Ed	HRN	Date	Details	A	C	GD 2.0	VG 4.0	FN 6.0	VF 8.0	VF/NM 9.0	NM- 9.2
1	115	12/53	Original	1	1	11	22	33	62	86	110
2	167	1/67	PC-r	1	1	3	6	9	18	27	35

115. How I Found Livingstone

Ed	HRN	Date	Details	A	C	GD 2.0	VG 4.0	FN 6.0	VF 8.0	VF/NM 9.0	NM- 9.2
1	116	1/54	Original	1	1	12	24	36	67	94	120
2	167	1/67	PC-r	1	1	4	8	12	23	36	48

116. The Bottle Imp

Ed	HRN	Date	Details	A	C	GD 2.0	VG 4.0	FN 6.0	VF 8.0	VF/NM 9.0	NM- 9.2
1	117	2/54	Orig.; Cameron-a	1	1	12	24	36	67	94	120
2	167	1/67	PC-r	1	1	4	8	12	23	36	48

Classics Illustrated #122 © GIL

Classics Illustrated #127 © GIL

Classics Illustrated #132 © GIL

117. Captains Courageous

Ed	HRN	Date	Details	A	C	GD 2.0	VG 4.0	FN 6.0	VF 8.0	VF/NM 9.0	NM- 9.2
1	118	3/54	Orig.; Costanza-a	1	1	11	22	33	62	86	110
2	167	2/67	PC-r	1	1	3	6	9	14	19	24
3	169	Fall/69	New price 25¢; stiff-c; PC-r	1	1	3	6	9	14	19	24

118. Rob Roy

Ed	HRN	Date	Details	A	C	GD 2.0	VG 4.0	FN 6.0	VF 8.0	VF/NM 9.0	NM- 9.2
1	119	4/54	Original; Rudy & Walter Palais-a	1	1	12	24	36	67	94	120
2	167	2/67	PC-r	1	1	4	8	12	23	36	48

119. Soldiers of Fortune

Ed	HRN	Date	Details	A	C	GD 2.0	VG 4.0	FN 6.0	VF 8.0	VF/NM 9.0	NM- 9.2
1	120	5/54	Schaffenberger-a	1	1	10	20	30	58	79	100
2	166	3/67	PC-r	1	1	3	6	9	14	19	24
3	169	Spr/70	New price 25¢; stiff-c; PC-r	1	1	3	6	9	14	19	24

120. The Hurricane

Ed	HRN	Date	Details	A	C	GD 2.0	VG 4.0	FN 6.0	VF 8.0	VF/NM 9.0	NM- 9.2
1	121	6/54	Orig.; Cameron-a	1	1	10	20	30	58	79	100
2	166	3/67	PC-r	1	1	3	6	9	18	27	35

121. Wild Bill Hickok

Ed	HRN	Date	Details	A	C	GD 2.0	VG 4.0	FN 6.0	VF 8.0	VF/NM 9.0	NM- 9.2
1	122	7/54	Original	1	1	9	18	27	50	65	80
2	132	–	PC-r	1	1	2	4	6	8	11	14
3	141	–	PC-r	1	1	2	4	6	8	11	14
4	154	–	PC-r	1	1	2	4	6	8	11	14
5	167	–	PC-r	1	1	2	4	6	8	10	12
6	167	8/64	PC-r	1	1	2	4	6	8	10	12
7	166	4/67	PC-r	1	1	2	4	6	8	10	12
8	169	Win/69	PC-r; stiff-c	1	1	2	4	6	8	10	12

122. The Mutineers

Ed	HRN	Date	Details	A	C	GD 2.0	VG 4.0	FN 6.0	VF 8.0	VF/NM 9.0	NM- 9.2
1	123	9/54	Original	1	1	10	20	30	54	72	90
2	136	–	PC-r	1	1	2	4	6	8	11	14
3	146	–	PC-r	1	1	2	4	6	8	11	14
4	158	–	PC-r	1	1	2	4	6	8	11	14
5	167	11/63	PC-r	1	1	2	4	6	8	10	12
6	167	3/65	PC-r	1	1	2	4	6	8	10	12
7	166	8/67	PC-r	1	1	2	4	6	8	10	12

123. Fang and Claw

Ed	HRN	Date	Details	A	C	GD 2.0	VG 4.0	FN 6.0	VF 8.0	VF/NM 9.0	NM- 9.2
1	124	11/54	Original	1	1	10	20	30	54	72	90
2	133	–	PC-r	1	1	2	4	6	8	11	14
3	143	–	PC-r	1	1	2	4	6	8	11	14
4	154	–	PC-r	1	1	2	4	6	8	11	14
5	167	–	Has orig.date; PC-r	1	1	2	4	6	8	10	12
6	167	9/65	PC-r	1	1	2	4	6	8	10	12

124. The War of the Worlds

Ed	HRN	Date	Details	A	C	GD 2.0	VG 4.0	FN 6.0	VF 8.0	VF/NM 9.0	NM- 9.2
1	125	1/55	Original; Cameron-c/a	1	1	12	24	36	67	94	120
2	131	–	PC-r	1	1	2	4	6	9	13	16
3	141	–	PC-r	1	1	2	4	6	9	13	16
4	148	–	PC-r	1	1	2	4	6	9	13	16
5	156	–	PC-r	1	1	2	4	6	9	13	16
6	165	–	PC-r	1	1	2	4	6	11	16	20
7	167	–	PC-r	1	1	2	4	6	8	11	14
8	167	11/64	PC-r	1	1	2	4	6	9	13	16
9	167	11/65	PC-r	1	1	2	4	6	8	11	14
10	166	R/1968	C-price 25¢; PC-r	1	1	2	4	6	8	11	14
11	169	Sm/70	PC-r; stiff-c	1	1	2	4	6	8	11	14

125. The Ox Bow Incident

Ed	HRN	Date	Details	A	C	GD 2.0	VG 4.0	FN 6.0	VF 8.0	VF/NM 9.0	NM- 9.2
1	–	3/55	Original; Picture Progress replaces reorder list	1	1	9	18	27	50	65	80
2	143	–	PC-r	1	1	2	4	6	8	11	14
3	152	–	PC-r	1	1	2	4	6	8	11	14
4	149	–	PC-r	1	1	2	4	6	8	11	14
5	167	–	PC-r	1	1	2	4	6	8	10	12
6	167	11/64	PC-r	1	1	2	4	6	8	10	12
7	166	4/67	PC-r	1	1	2	4	6	8	10	12
8	169	Win/69	New price 25¢; stiff-c; PC-r	1	1	2	4	6	8	10	12

126. The Downfall

Ed	HRN	Date	Details	A	C	GD 2.0	VG 4.0	FN 6.0	VF 8.0	VF/NM 9.0	NM- 9.2
1		5/55	Orig.; 'Picture Progress' replaces reorder list; Cameron-c/a	1	1	10	20	30	54	72	90
2	167	8/64	PC-r	1	1	2	4	6	11	16	20
3	166	R/1968	C-price 25¢; PC-r	1	1	2	4	6	11	16	20

127. The King of the Mountains

Ed	HRN	Date	Details	A	C	GD 2.0	VG 4.0	FN 6.0	VF 8.0	VF/NM 9.0	NM- 9.2
1	128	7/55	Original	1	1	10	20	30	54	72	90
2	167	6/64	PC-r	1	1	2	4	6	9	13	16
3	166	F/1968	C-price 25¢; PC-r	1	1	2	4	6	9	13	16

128. Macbeth (Used in POP, pg. 102)

Ed	HRN	Date	Details	A	C	GD 2.0	VG 4.0	FN 6.0	VF 8.0	VF/NM 9.0	NM- 9.2
1	128	9/55	Orig.; last Blum-a	1	1	10	20	30	54	72	90
2	143	–	PC-r	1	1	2	4	6	8	11	14
3	158	–	PC-r	1	1	2	4	6	8	11	14
4	167	–	PC-r	1	1	2	4	6	8	10	12
5	167	6/64	PC-r	1	1	2	4	6	8	10	12
6	167	4/67	PC-r	1	1	2	4	6	8	10	12
7	166	R/1968	C-Price 25¢; PC-r	1	1	2	4	6	8	10	12
8	169	Spr/70	Stiff-c; PC-r	1	1	2	4	6	8	10	12

129. Davy Crockett

Ed	HRN	Date	Details	A	C	GD 2.0	VG 4.0	FN 6.0	VF 8.0	VF/NM 9.0	NM- 9.2
1	129	11/55	Orig.; Cameron-a	1	1	14	28	42	76	108	140
2	167	9/66	PC-r	1	1	10	20	30	56	76	95

130. Caesar's Conquests

Ed	HRN	Date	Details	A	C	GD 2.0	VG 4.0	FN 6.0	VF 8.0	VF/NM 9.0	NM- 9.2
1	130	1/56	Original; Orlando-a	1	1	10	20	30	54	72	90
2	142	–	PC-r	1	1	2	4	6	8	11	14
3	152	–	PC-r	1	1	2	4	6	8	11	14
4	149	–	PC-r	1	1	2	4	6	8	11	14
5	167	–	PC-r	1	1	2	4	6	8	10	12
6	167	10/64	PC-r	1	1	2	4	6	8	10	12
7	167	4/66	PC-r	1	1	2	4	6	8	10	12

131. The Covered Wagon

Ed	HRN	Date	Details	A	C	GD 2.0	VG 4.0	FN 6.0	VF 8.0	VF/NM 9.0	NM- 9.2
1	131	3/56	Original	1	1	6	12	18	37	59	80
2	143	–	PC-r	1	1	2	4	6	8	11	14
3	152	–	PC-r	1	1	2	4	6	8	11	14
4	158	–	PC-r	1	1	2	4	6	8	11	14
5	167	–	PC-r	1	1	2	4	6	8	10	12
6	167	11/64	PC-r	1	1	2	4	6	8	10	12
7	167	4/66	PC-r	1	1	2	4	6	8	10	12
8	169	Win/69	New price 25¢; stiff-c; PC-r	1	1	2	4	6	8	10	12

132. The Dark Frigate

Ed	HRN	Date	Details	A	C	GD 2.0	VG 4.0	FN 6.0	VF 8.0	VF/NM 9.0	NM- 9.2
1	132	5/56	Original	1	1	10	20	30	54	72	90
2	150	–	PC-r	1	1	2	4	6	9	12	15
3	167	1/64	PC-r	1	1	2	4	6	8	11	14
4	166	5/67	PC-r	1	1	2	4	6	8	11	14

133. The Time Machine

Ed	HRN	Date	Details	A	C	GD 2.0	VG 4.0	FN 6.0	VF 8.0	VF/NM 9.0	NM- 9.2
1	132	7/56	Orig.; Cameron-a	1	1	7	14	21	45	73	100
2	142	–	PC-r	1	1	2	4	6	9	13	16
3	152	–	PC-r	1	1	2	4	6	9	13	16
4	158	–	PC-r	1	1	2	4	6	8	11	14
5	167	–	PC-r	1	1	2	4	6	8	11	14
6	167	6/64	PC-r	1	1	2	4	6	8	11	13
7	167	3/66	PC-r	1	1	2	4	6	8	11	14
8	166	12/67	PC-r	1	1	2	4	6	8	11	14
9	169	Win/71	New price 25¢; stiff-c; PC-r	1	1	2	4	6	8	11	14

134. Romeo and Juliet

Ed	HRN	Date	Details	A	C	GD 2.0	VG 4.0	FN 6.0	VF 8.0	VF/NM 9.0	NM- 9.2
1	134	9/56	Original; Evans-a	1	1	6	12	18	41	66	90

Ed	HRN	Date	Details	A	C	GD 2.0	VG 4.0	FN 6.0	VF 8.0	VF/NM 9.0	NM- 9.2
2	161	–	PC-r	1	1	2	4	6	8	11	14
3	167	9/63	PC-r	1	1	2	4	6	8	10	12
4	167	5/65	PC-r	1	1	2	4	6	8	10	12
5	166	6/67	PC-r	1	1	2	4	6	8	10	12
6	166	Win/69	New c&price 25¢; stiff-c; PC-r	1	2	3	6	9	16	22	28

135. Waterloo

Ed	HRN	Date	Details	A	C	GD 2.0	VG 4.0	FN 6.0	VF 8.0	VF/NM 9.0	NM- 9.2
1	135	11/56	Orig.; G. Ingels-a	1	1	6	12	18	41	66	90
2	153	–	PC-r	1	1	2	4	6	8	11	14
3	167	–	PC-r	1	1	2	4	6	8	10	12
4	167	9/64	PC-r	1	1	2	4	6	8	10	12
5	166	R/1968	C-price 25¢; PC-r	1	1	2	4	6	8	10	12

136. Lord Jim

Ed	HRN	Date	Details	A	C	GD 2.0	VG 4.0	FN 6.0	VF 8.0	VF/NM 9.0	NM- 9.2
1	136	1/57	Original; Evans-a	1	1	6	12	18	41	66	90
2	165	–	PC-r	1	1	2	4	6	8	10	12
3	167	3/64	PC-r	1	1	2	4	6	8	10	12
4	167	9/66	PC-r	1	1	2	4	6	8	10	12
5	169	Sm/69	New price 25 ¢; stiff-c; PC-r	1	1	2	4	6	8	10	12

137. The Little Savage

Ed	HRN	Date	Details	A	C	GD 2.0	VG 4.0	FN 6.0	VF 8.0	VF/NM 9.0	NM- 9.2
1	136	3/57	Original; Evans-a	1	1	6	12	18	41	66	90
2	148	–	PC-r	1	1	2	4	6	8	11	14
3	156	–	PC-r	1	1	2	4	6	8	11	14
4	167	–	PC-r	1	1	2	4	6	8	10	12
5	167	10/64	PC-r	1	1	2	4	6	8	10	12
6	166	8/67	PC-r	1	1	2	4	6	8	10	12
7	169	Spr/70	New price 25¢; stiff-c; PC-r	1	1	2	4	6	8	10	12

138. A Journey to the Center of the Earth

Ed	HRN	Date	Details	A	C	GD 2.0	VG 4.0	FN 6.0	VF 8.0	VF/NM 9.0	NM- 9.2
1	136	5/57	Original	1	1	7	14	21	50	83	115
2	146	–	PC-r	1	1	2	4	6	10	14	18
3	156	–	PC-r	1	1	2	4	6	10	14	18
4	158	–	PC-r	1	1	2	4	6	10	14	18
5	167	–	PC-r	1	1	2	4	6	8	11	14
6	167	6/64	PC-r	1	1	2	4	6	11	16	20
7	167	4/66	PC-r	1	1	2	4	6	11	16	20
8	166	R/68	C-price 25¢; PC-r	1	1	2	4	6	9	13	16

139. In the Reign of Terror

Ed	HRN	Date	Details	A	C	GD 2.0	VG 4.0	FN 6.0	VF 8.0	VF/NM 9.0	NM- 9.2
1	139	7/57	Original; Evans-a	1	1	6	12	18	37	59	80
2	154	–	PC-r	1	1	2	4	6	8	11	14
3	167	–	Has orig.date; PC-r	1	1	2	4	6	8	10	12
4	167	7/64	PC-r	1	1	2	4	6	8	10	12
5	166	R/1968	C-price 25¢; PC-r	1	1	2	4	6	8	10	12

140. On Jungle Trails

Ed	HRN	Date	Details	A	C	GD 2.0	VG 4.0	FN 6.0	VF 8.0	VF/NM 9.0	NM- 9.2
1	140	9/57	Original	1	1	6	12	18	37	59	80
2	150	–	PC-r	1	1	2	4	6	8	11	14
3	160	–	PC-r	1	1	2	4	6	8	11	14
4	167	9/63	PC-r	1	1	2	4	6	8	10	12
5	167	9/65	PC-r	1	1	2	4	6	8	10	12

141. Castle Dangerous

Ed	HRN	Date	Details	A	C	GD 2.0	VG 4.0	FN 6.0	VF 8.0	VF/NM 9.0	NM- 9.2
1	141	11/57	Original	1	1	6	12	18	43	69	95
2	152	–	PC-r	1	1	2	4	6	8	11	14
3	167	–	PC-r	1	1	2	4	6	8	11	14
4	166	7/67	PC-r	1	1	2	4	6	8	11	14

142. Abraham Lincoln

Ed	HRN	Date	Details	A	C	GD 2.0	VG 4.0	FN 6.0	VF 8.0	VF/NM 9.0	NM- 9.2
1	142	1/58	Original	1	1	6	12	18	41	66	90
2	154	–	PC-r	1	1	2	4	6	8	11	14
3	158	–	PC-r	1	1	2	4	6	8	11	14
4	167	10/63	PC-r	1	1	2	4	6	8	10	12
5	167	7/65	PC-r	1	1	2	4	6	8	10	12
6	166	11/67	PC-r	1	1	2	4	6	8	10	12
7	169	Fall/69	New price 25¢; stiff-c; PC-r	1	1	2	4	6	8	10	12

143. Kim

Ed	HRN	Date	Details	A	C	GD 2.0	VG 4.0	FN 6.0	VF 8.0	VF/NM 9.0	NM- 9.2
1	143	3/58	Original; Orlando-a	1	1	6	12	18	37	59	80
2	165	–	PC-r	1	1	2	4	6	8	10	12
3	167	11/63	PC-r	1	1	2	4	6	8	10	12
4	167	8/65	PC-r	1	1	2	4	6	8	10	12
5	169	Win/69	New price 25¢; stiff-c; PC-r	1	1	2	4	6	8	10	12

144. The First Men in the Moon

Ed	HRN	Date	Details	A	C	GD 2.0	VG 4.0	FN 6.0	VF 8.0	VF/NM 9.0	NM- 9.2
1	143	5/58	Original; Woodbridge/Williamson/Torres-a	1	1	7	14	21	45	73	100
2	152	–	(Rare)-PC-r	1	1	7	14	21	50	83	115
3	153	–	PC-r	1	1	2	4	6	8	11	14
4	161	–	PC-r	1	1	2	4	6	8	10	12
5	167	–	PC-r	1	1	2	4	6	8	10	12
6	167	12/65	PC-r	1	1	2	4	6	8	10	12
7	166	Fall/68	New-c&price 25¢; PC-r; stiff-c	1	2	3	6	9	14	19	24
8	169	Win/69	Stiff-c; PC-r	1	2	2	4	6	10	14	18

145. The Crisis

Ed	HRN	Date	Details	A	C	GD 2.0	VG 4.0	FN 6.0	VF 8.0	VF/NM 9.0	NM- 9.2
1	143	7/58	Original; Evans-a	1	1	6	12	18	41	66	90
2	156	–	PC-r	1	1	2	4	6	8	11	14
3	167	10/63	PC-r	1	1	2	4	6	8	10	12
4	167	3/65	PC-r	1	1	2	4	6	8	10	12
5	166	R/68	C-price 25¢; PC-r	1	1	2	4	6	8	10	12

146. With Fire and Sword

Ed	HRN	Date	Details	A	C	GD 2.0	VG 4.0	FN 6.0	VF 8.0	VF/NM 9.0	NM- 9.2
1	143	9/58	Original; Woodbridge-a	1	1	6	12	18	41	66	90
2	156	–	PC-r	1	1	2	4	6	9	13	16
3	167	11/63	PC-r	1	1	2	4	6	8	11	14
4	167	3/65	PC-r	1	1	2	4	6	8	11	14

147. Ben-Hur

Ed	HRN	Date	Details	A	C	GD 2.0	VG 4.0	FN 6.0	VF 8.0	VF/NM 9.0	NM- 9.2
1	147	11/58	Original; Orlando-a	1	1	6	12	18	39	62	85
2	152	–	Scarce; PC-r	1	1	6	12	18	37	59	90
3	153	–	PC-r	1	1	2	4	6	8	11	14
4	158	–	PC-r	1	1	2	4	6	8	11	14
5	167	–	Orig.date; but PC-r	1	1	2	4	6	8	10	12
6	167	2/65	PC-r	1	1	2	4	6	8	10	12
7	167	9/66	PC-r	1	1	2	4	6	8	10	12
8A	166	Fall/68	New-c&price 25¢; PC-r; soft-c	1	2	3	6	9	16	22	28
8B	166	Fall/68	New-c&price 25¢; PC-r; stiff-c; scarce	1	2	4	8	12	22	34	45

148. The Buccaneer

Ed	HRN	Date	Details	A	C	GD 2.0	VG 4.0	FN 6.0	VF 8.0	VF/NM 9.0	NM- 9.2
1	148	1/59	Orig.; Evans/Jenny-a; Saunders-c	1	1	6	12	18	37	59	80
2	568	–	Juniors list only PC-r	1	1	2	4	6	8	11	14
3	167	–	PC-r	1	1	2	4	6	8	10	12
4	167	9/65	PC-r	1	1	2	4	6	8	10	12
5	169	Sm/69	New price 25¢; PC-r; stiff-c	1	1	2	4	6	8	10	12

149. Off on a Comet

Ed	HRN	Date	Details	A	C	GD 2.0	VG 4.0	FN 6.0	VF 8.0	VF/NM 9.0	NM- 9.2
1	149	3/59	Orig.;G.McCann-a; blue reorder list	1	1	6	12	18	41	66	90
2	155	–	PC-r	1	1	2	4	6	8	11	14
3	149	–	PC-r; white reorder list; no coming-next ad	1	1	2	4	6	8	11	14
4	167	12/63	PC-r	1	1	2	4	6	8	10	12
5	167	2/65	PC-r	1	1	2	4	6	8	10	12
6	167	10/66	PC-r	1	1	2	4	6	8	10	12
7	166	Fall/68	New-c & price 25¢; PC-r	1	2	3	6	9	15	21	26

150. The Virginian

Classics Illustrated #151 © GIL

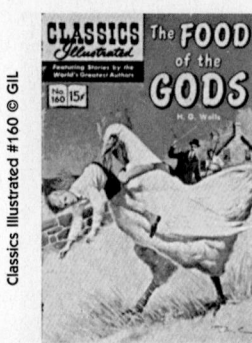

Classics Illustrated #160 © GIL

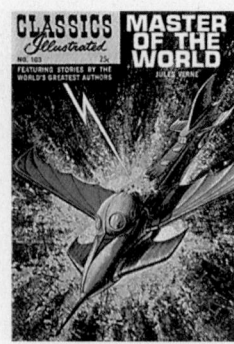

Classics Illustrated #163 © GIL

Ed	HRN	Date	Details	A	C	GD 2.0	VG 4.0	FN 6.0	VF 8.0	VF/NM 9.0	NM- 9.2
1	150	5/59	Original	1	1	6	12	18	43	69	95
2	164	–	PC-r	1	1	2	4	6	11	16	20
3	167	10/63	PC-r	1	1	3	6	9	15	21	26
4	167	12/65	PC-r	1	1	2	4	6	11	16	20

151. Won By the Sword

Ed	HRN	Date	Details	A	C	GD 2.0	VG 4.0	FN 6.0	VF 8.0	VF/NM 9.0	NM- 9.2
1	150	7/59	Original	1	1	6	12	18	41	66	90
2	164	–	PC-r	1	1	2	4	6	9	13	16
3	167	10/63	PC-r	1	1	2	4	6	9	13	16
4	166	7/67	PC-r	1	1	2	4	6	9	13	16

152. Wild Animals I Have Known

Ed	HRN	Date	Details	A	C	GD 2.0	VG 4.0	FN 6.0	VF 8.0	VF/NM 9.0	NM- 9.2
1	152	9/59	Orig.; L.B. Cole c/a	1	1	7	14	21	45	73	100
2A	149	–	PC-r; white reorder list; no coming-next ad; IBC; Jr. list #572	1	1	2	4	6	8	11	14
2B	149	–	PC-r; inside-bc: Jr. list to #555			2	4	6	12	15	
2C	149	–	PC-r; inside-bc: has World Around Us ad; scarce	1	1	3	6	9	15	21	26
3	167	9/63	PC-r	1	1	2	4	6	8	10	12
4	167	8/65	PC-r	1	1	2	4	6	8	10	12
5	169	Fall/69	New price 25¢; stiff-c; PC-r	1	1	2	4	6	8	10	12

153. The Invisible Man

Ed	HRN	Date	Details	A	C	GD 2.0	VG 4.0	FN 6.0	VF 8.0	VF/NM 9.0	NM- 9.2
1	153	11/59	Original	1	1	7	14	21	49	80	110
2A	149	–	PC-r; white reorder list; no coming-next ad; inside-bc: Jr. list to #572	1	1	2	4	6	10	14	18
2B	149	–	PC-r; inside-bc: Jr. list to #555			2	4	6	11	16	20
3	167	–	PC-r	1	1	2	4	6	9	12	15
4	167	2/65	PC-r	1	1	2	4	6	9	12	15
5	167	9/66	PC-r	1	1	2	4	6	9	12	15
6	166	Win/69	New price 25¢; PC-r; stiff-c	1	1	2	4	6	9	12	15
7	169	Spr/71	Stiff-c; letters spelling 'Invisible Man' are 'solid' not 'invisible'; PC-r	1	1	2	4	6	9	12	15

154. The Conspiracy of Pontiac

Ed	HRN	Date	Details	A	C	GD 2.0	VG 4.0	FN 6.0	VF 8.0	VF/NM 9.0	NM- 9.2
1	154	1/60	Original	1	1	6	12	18	43	69	95
2	167	11/63	PC-r	1	1	2	4	6	11	16	20
3	167	7/64	PC-r	1	1	2	4	6	11	16	20
4	166	12/67	PC-r	1	1	2	4	6	11	16	20

155. The Lion of the North

Ed	HRN	Date	Details	A	C	GD 2.0	VG 4.0	FN 6.0	VF 8.0	VF/NM 9.0	NM- 9.2
1	154	3/60	Original	1	1	6	12	18	41	66	90
2	167	1/64	PC-r	1	1	2	4	6	10	14	18
3	166	R/1967	C-price 25¢; PC-r	1	1	2	4	6	9	12	15

156. The Conquest of Mexico

Ed	HRN	Date	Details	A	C	GD 2.0	VG 4.0	FN 6.0	VF 8.0	VF/NM 9.0	NM- 9.2
1	156	5/60	Orig.; Bruno Premiani-c/a	1	1	6	12	18	41	66	90
2	167	1/64	PC-r	1	1	2	4	6	9	12	15
3	166	8/67	PC-r	1	1	2	4	6	9	12	15
4	169	Spr/70	New price 25¢; stiff-c; PC-r	1	1	2	4	6	8	10	12

157. Lives of the Hunted

Ed	HRN	Date	Details	A	C	GD 2.0	VG 4.0	FN 6.0	VF 8.0	VF/NM 9.0	NM- 9.2
1	156	7/60	Orig.; L.B. Cole-c	1	1	6	12	18	43	69	95
2	167	2/64	PC-r	1	1	2	4	6	11	16	20
3	166	10/67	PC-r	1	1	2	4	6	11	16	20

158. The Conspirators

Ed	HRN	Date	Details	A	C	GD 2.0	VG 4.0	FN 6.0	VF 8.0	VF/NM 9.0	NM- 9.2
1	156	9/60	Original	1	1	6	12	18	43	69	95
2	167	7/64	PC-r	1	1	2	4	6	11	16	20
3	166	10/67	PC-r	1	1	2	4	6	11	16	20

159. The Octopus

Ed	HRN	Date	Details	A	C	GD 2.0	VG 4.0	FN 6.0	VF 8.0	VF/NM 9.0	NM- 9.2
1	159	11/60	Orig.; Gray Morrow-a; L.B. Cole-c	1	1	6	12	18	43	69	95
2	167	2/64	PC-r	1	1	2	4	6	11	16	20
3	166	R/1967	C-price 25¢; PC-r	1	1	2	4	6	11	16	20

160. The Food of the Gods

Ed	HRN	Date	Details	A	C	GD 2.0	VG 4.0	FN 6.0	VF 8.0	VF/NM 9.0	NM- 9.2
1A	159	1/61	Original	1	1	7	14	21	45	73	100
1B	160	1/61	Original; same, except for HRN	1	1	6	12	18	43	69	95
3	166	6/67	PC-r	1	1	2	4	6	11	16	20

161. Cleopatra

Ed	HRN	Date	Details	A	C	GD 2.0	VG 4.0	FN 6.0	VF 8.0	VF/NM 9.0	NM- 9.2
1	161	3/61	Original	1	1	6	12	18	43	69	95
2	167	1/64	PC-r	1	1	2	4	6	13	18	22
3	166	8/67	PC-r	1	1	2	4	6	13	18	22

162. Robur the Conqueror

Ed	HRN	Date	Details	A	C	GD 2.0	VG 4.0	FN 6.0	VF 8.0	VF/NM 9.0	NM- 9.2
1	162	5/61	Original	1	1	6	12	18	43	69	95
2	167	7/64	PC-r	1	1	2	4	6	13	18	22
3	166	8/67	PC-r	1	1	2	4	6	13	18	22

163. Master of the World

Ed	HRN	Date	Details	A	C	GD 2.0	VG 4.0	FN 6.0	VF 8.0	VF/NM 9.0	NM- 9.2
1	163	7/61	Original; Gray Morrow-a	1	1	6	12	18	43	69	95
2	167	1/65	PC-r	1	1	2	4	6	12	16	20
3	166	R/1968	C-price 25¢; PC-r	1	1	2	4	6	12	16	20

164. The Cossack Chief

Ed	HRN	Date	Details	A	C	GD 2.0	VG 4.0	FN 6.0	VF 8.0	VF/NM 9.0	NM- 9.2
1	164	(1961)	Orig.; nd(10/61?)	1	1	7	14	21	40	60	80
2	167	4/65	PC-r	1	1	2	4	6	11	16	20
3	166	Fall/68	C-price 25¢; PC-r	1	1	2	4	6	11	16	20

165. The Queen's Necklace

Ed	HRN	Date	Details	A	C	GD 2.0	VG 4.0	FN 6.0	VF 8.0	VF/NM 9.0	NM- 9.2
1	164	1/62	Original; Morrow-a	1	1	6	12	18	43	69	95
2	167	4/65	PC-r	1	1	2	4	6	11	16	20
3	166	Fall/68	C-price 25¢; PC-r	1	1	2	4	6	11	16	20

166. Tigers and Traitors

Ed	HRN	Date	Details	A	C	GD 2.0	VG 4.0	FN 6.0	VF 8.0	VF/NM 9.0	NM- 9.2
1	165	5/62	Original	1	1	8	16	24	56	93	130
2	167	2/64	PC-r	1	1	3	6	9	19	29	38
3	166	11/66	PC-r	1	1	3	6	9	19	29	38

167. Faust

Ed	HRN	Date	Details	A	C	GD 2.0	VG 4.0	FN 6.0	VF 8.0	VF/NM 9.0	NM- 9.2
1	165	8/62	Original	1	1	12	24	36	82	146	210
2	167	2/64	PC-r	1	1	5	10	15	35	55	75
3	166	6/67	PC-r	1	1	5	10	15	35	55	75

168. In Freedom's Cause

Ed	HRN	Date	Details	A	C	GD 2.0	VG 4.0	FN 6.0	VF 8.0	VF/NM 9.0	NM- 9.2
1	169	Win/69	Original; Evans/Crandall-a; stiff-c; 25¢; no coming-next ad;	1	1	13	26	39	95	168	240

169. Negro Americans The Early Years

Ed	HRN	Date	Details	A	C	GD 2.0	VG 4.0	FN 6.0	VF 8.0	VF/NM 9.0	NM- 9.2
1	166	Spr/69	Orig. & last issue; 25¢; Stiff-c; no coming-next ad; other sources indicate publication date of 5/69	1	1	12	24	36	84	150	215
2	169	Spr/69	Stiff-c	1	1	7	14	21	45	73	100

NOTE: Many other titles were prepared or planned but were only issued in British/European series.

CLASSIC PUNISHER (Also see Punisher)
Marvel Comics: Dec, 1989 ($4.95, B&W, deluxe format, 68 pgs.)

1-Reprints Marvel Super Action #1 & Marvel Preview #2 plus new story 5.00

Classics Illustrated Junior #503 © GIL

Classics Illustrated Special #141A © GIL

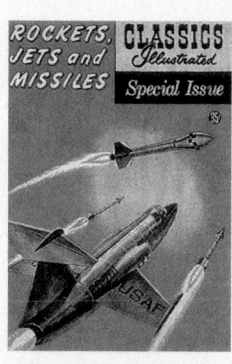

Classics Illustrated Special #159A © GIL

	GD 2.0	VG 4.0	FN 6.0	VF 8.0	VF/NM 9.0	NM- 9.2

CLASSICS ILLUSTRATED

First Publishing/Berkley Publishing: Feb, 1990 - No. 27, July, 1991 ($3.75/$3.95, 52 pgs.)

1-27: 1-Gahan Wilson-c/a. 4-Sienkiewicz painted-c/a. 6-Russell scripts/layouts. 7-Spiegle-a. 9-Ploog-c/a. 16-Staton-a. 18-Gahan Wilson-c/a; 20-Geary-a. 26-Aesop's Fables (6/91). 26,27-Direct sale only 5.00

CLASSICS ILLUSTRATED

Acclaim Books/Twin Circle PublishingCo.: Feb, 1997 - Present ($4.99, digest-size) (Each book contains study notes)

A Christmas Carol-(12/97), A Connecticut Yankee in King Arthur's Court-(5/97), All Quiet on the Western Front-(1/98), A Tale of Two Cities-(2/97)Joe Orlando-r, Captains Courageous-(11/97), Crime and Punishment-(3/97), Dr. Jekyll and Mr. Hyde-(10/97), Don Quixote-(12/97), Frankenstein-(10/97), Great Expectations-(4/97), Hamlet-(3/97), Huckleberry Finn-(3/97), Jane Eyre-(2/97), Kidnapped-(1/98), Les Miserables-(5/97), Lord Jim-(9/97),Macbeth-(9/97), Moby Dick-(4/97), Oliver Twist-(5/97), Robinson Crusoe-(9/97), Romeo & Juliet-(2/97), Silas Marner-(11/97), The Call of the Wild-(9/97), The Count of Monte Cristo-(1/98), The House of the Seven Gables-(9/97), The Iliad-(12/97), The Invisible Man-(10/97), The Last of the Mohicans-(12/97), The Master of Ballantrae-(11/97), The Odyssey-(3/97), The Prince and the Pauper-(4/97), The Red Badge Of Courage-(9/97), Tom Sawyer-(2/97) Wuthering Heights-(11/97) 5.00

NOTE: *Stories reprinted from the original Gilberton Classic Comics and Classics Illustrated.*

CLASSICS ILLUSTRATED GIANTS

Gilberton Publications: Oct, 1949 (One-Shots - "OS")

These Giant Editions, all with new front and back covers, were advertised from 10/49 to 2/52. They were 50¢ on the newsstand and 60¢ by mail. They are actually four Classics in one volume. All the stories are reprints of the Classics Illustrated Series.

NOTE: There were also British hardback Adventure & Indian Giants in 1952, with the same covers but different contents: Adventure - 2, 7, 10; Indian - 17, 22, 37, 58. They are also rare.

	GD 2.0	VG 4.0	FN 6.0	VF 8.0	VF/NM 9.0	NM- 9.2
"An Illustrated Library of Great Adventure Stories" - reprints of No. 6,7,8,10 (Rare); Kiefer-c	145	290	435	906	1503	2100
"An Illustrated Library of Exciting Mystery Stories" - reprints of No. 30,21,40, 13 (Rare); Blum-c	157	314	471	981	1628	2275
"An Illustrated Library of Great Indian Stories" - reprints of No. 4,17,22,37 (Rare); Blum-c	145	290	435	906	1503	2100

INTRODUCTION TO CLASSICS ILLUSTRATED JUNIOR

Collectors of Juniors can be put into one of two categories: those who want any copy of each title, and those who want all the originals. Those seeking every original and reprint edition are a limited group, primarily because Juniors have no changes in art or covers to spark interest, and because reprints are so low in value it is difficult to get dealers to look for specific reprint editions.

In recent years it has become apparent that most serious Classics collectors seek Junior originals. Those seeking reprints seek them for low cost. This has made the previous note about the comparative market value of reprints inadequate. Three particular reprint editions are worth even more. For the 535-Twin Circle edition, see Giveaways. There are also reprint editions of 501 and 503 which have a full-page bc ad for the very rare Junior record. Those may sell as high as $10-$15 in mint. Original editions of 557 and 558 also have that ad.

There are no reprint editions of 577. The only edition, from 1969, is a 25 cent stiff-cover edition with no ad for the next issue. All other original editions have coming-next ad. But 577, like C.I. #168, was prepared in 1962 but not issued. Copies of 577 can be found in 1963 British/European series, which then continued with dozens of additional new Junior titles.

PRICES LISTED BELOW ARE FOR ORIGINAL EDITIONS, WHICH HAVE AN AD FOR THE NEXT ISSUE.

NOTE: *Non HRN 576 copies- many are written on or colored . Reprints with 576 HRN are worth about 1/3 original prices. All other HRN #'s are 1/2 original price*

CLASSICS ILLUSTRATED JUNIOR

Famous Authors Ltd. (Gilberton Publications): Oct, 1953 - Spring, 1971

	GD 2.0	VG 4.0	FN 6.0	VF 8.0	VF/NM 9.0	NM- 9.2
501-Snow White & the Seven Dwarfs; Alex Blum-a	12	24	36	67	94	120
502-The Ugly Duckling	9	18	27	47	61	75
503-Cinderella	7	14	21	37	46	55
504-512: 504-The Pied Piper. 505-The Sleeping Beauty. 506-The Three Little Pigs. 507-Jack & the Beanstalk. 508-Goldilocks & the Three Bears. 509-Beauty and the Beast. 510-Little Red Riding Hood. 511-Puss-N Boots. 512-Rumpelstiltskin	6	12	18	27	33	38
513-Pinocchio	7	14	21	37	46	55
514-The Steadfast Tin Soldier	8	16	24	44	57	70
515-Johnny Appleseed	6	12	18	27	33	38
516-Aladdin and His Lamp	6	12	18	29	36	42
517-519: 517-The Emperor's New Clothes. 518-The Golden Goose. 519-Paul Bunyan	6	12	18	27	33	38
520-Thumbelina	6	12	18	29	36	42
521-King of the Golden River	6	12	18	27	33	38
522,523,530: 522-The Nightingale. 523-The Gallant Tailor. 530-The Golden Bird	5	10	15	24	30	35

	GD 2.0	VG 4.0	FN 6.0	VF 8.0	VF/NM 9.0	NM- 9.2
524-The Wild Swans	6	12	18	29	36	42
525,526: 525-The Little Mermaid. 526-The Frog Prince	6	12	18	29	36	42
527-The Golden-Haired Giant	6	12	18	27	33	38
528-The Penny Prince	6	12	18	27	33	38
529-The Magic Servants	6	12	18	27	33	38
531-Rapunzel	6	12	18	31	38	45
532-534: 532-The Dancing Princesses. 533-The Magic Fountain. 534-The Golden Touch	5	10	15	23	28	32
535-The Wizard of Oz	8	16	24	44	57	70
536-The Chimney Sweep	6	12	18	27	33	38
537-The Three Fairies	6	12	18	28	34	40
538-Silly Hans	5	10	15	23	28	32
539-The Enchanted Fish	6	12	18	31	38	45
540-The Tinder-Box	6	12	18	31	38	45
541-Snow White & Rose Red	5	10	15	24	30	35
542-The Donkey's Tale	5	10	15	24	30	35
543-The House in the Woods	6	12	18	27	33	38
544-The Golden Fleece	6	12	18	31	38	45
545-The Glass Mountain	5	10	15	24	30	35
546-The Elves & the Shoemaker	5	10	15	24	30	35
547-The Wishing Table	6	12	18	27	33	38
548-551: 548-The Magic Pitcher. 549-Simple Kate. 550-The Singing Donkey. 551-The Queen Bee	5	10	15	23	28	32
552-The Three Little Dwarfs	6	12	18	27	33	38
553,556: 553-King Thrushbeard. 556-The Elf Mound	5	10	15	23	28	32
554-The Enchanted Deer	6	12	18	29	36	42
555-The Three Golden Apples	5	10	15	24	30	35
557-Silly Willy	6	12	18	28	34	40
558-The Magic Dish; L.B. Cole-c; soft and stiff-c exist on original	7	14	21	35	43	50
559-The Japanese Lantern; 1 pg. Ingels-a; L.B. Cole-c	7	14	21	35	43	50
560-The Doll Princess; L.B. Cole-c	7	14	21	35	43	50
561-Hans Humdrum; L.B. Cole-c	6	12	18	29	36	42
562-The Enchanted Pony; L.B. Cole-c	7	14	21	35	43	50
563,565-568,570: 563-The Wishing Well; L.B. Cole-c. 565-The Silly Princess; L.B. Cole-c. 566-Clumsy Hans; L.B. Cole-c. 567-The Bearskin Soldier; L.B. Cole-c. 570-The Pearl Princess; L.B. Cole-c	6	12	18	27	33	38
564-The Salt Mountain; L.B.Cole-c. 568-The Happy Hedgehog; L.B. Cole-c.	6	12	18	28	34	40
569,573: 569-The Three Giants.573-The Crystal Ball	5	10	15	23	28	32
571,572: 571-How Fire Came to the Indians. 572-The Drummer Boy	6	12	18	29	36	42
574-Brightboots	5	10	15	24	30	35
575-The Fearless Prince	6	12	18	28	34	40
576-The Princess Who Saw Everything	7	14	21	35	43	50
577-The Runaway Dumpling	8	16	24	44	57	70

NOTE: *Prices are for original editions. Last reprint - Spring, 1971.* **Costanza & Schaffenberger** *art in many issues.*

CLASSICS ILLUSTRATED SPECIAL ISSUE

Gilberton Co.: (Came out semi-annually) Dec, 1955 - Jul, 1962 (35¢, 100 pgs.)

	GD 2.0	VG 4.0	FN 6.0	VF 8.0	VF/NM 9.0	NM- 9.2
129-The Story of Jesus (titled ...Special Edition) "Jesus on Mountain" cover	13	26	39	72	101	130
"Three Camels" cover (12/58)	14	28	42	80	115	150
"Mountain" cover (no date)-Has checklist on inside b/c to HRN #161 & different testimonial on back-c	11	22	33	60	83	105
"Mountain" cover (1968 re-issue; has white 50¢ circle)	8	16	24	44	57	70
132A-The Story of America (6/56); Cameron-a	10	20	30	56	76	95
135A-The Ten Commandments(12/56)	9	18	27	52	69	85
138A-Adventures in Science(6/57); HRN to 137	9	18	27	50	65	80
138A-(6/57)-2nd version w/HRN to 149	7	14	21	35	43	50
138A-(12/61)-3rd version w/HRN to 149	7	14	21	35	43	50
141A-The Rough Rider (Teddy Roosevelt)(12/57); Evans-a	9	18	27	52	69	85
144A-Blazing the Trails West(6/58)- 73 pgs. of Crandall/Evans plus Severin-a	10	20	30	54	72	90
147A-Crossing the Rockies(12/58)-Crandall/Evans-a	9	18	27	52	69	85
150A-Royal Canadian Police (6/59)-Ingels, Sid Check-a	9	18	27	52	69	85
153A-Men, Guns & Cattle(12/59)-Evans-a (26 pgs.); Kinstler-a	9	18	27	52	69	85
156A-The Atomic Age(6/60)-Crandall/Evans, Torres-a	9	18	27	52	69	85
159A-Rockets, Jets and Missiles(12/60)-Evans, Morrow-a	9	18	27	52	69	85

Classic Star Wars #4 © LucasFilm

Claws #3 © MAR

Clerks Holiday Special © View Askew

	GD	VG	FN	VF	VF/NM	NM-
	2.0	4.0	6.0	8.0	9.0	9.2

162A-War Between the States(6/61)-Kirby & Crandall/Evans-a; Ingels-a

	15	30	45	85	130	175

165A-To the Stars(12/61)-Torres, Crandall/Evans, Kirby-a

	10	20	30	58	79	100

166A-World War II('62)-Torres, Crandall/Evans, Kirby-a

	12	24	36	69	97	125

167A-Prehistoric World(7/62)-Torres & Crandall/Evans-a; two versions exist
(HRN to 165 & HRN to 167)

	12	24	36	69	97	115

nn Special Issue-The United Nations"(1964; 50¢; scarce); this is actually part of the European
Special Series, which cont'd on after the U.S. series stopped issuing new titles in 1962.
This English edition was prepared specifically for sale at the U.N. It was printed in Norway

	38	76	114	219	347	475

NOTE: There was another U.S. Special Issue prepared in 1962 with artwork by Torres entitled World War I.
Unfortunately, it was never issued in any English-language edition. It was issued in 1964 in West Germany, The
Netherlands, and some Scandanavian countries, with another edition in 1974 with a new cover.

CLASSICS LIBRARY (See King Classics)

CLASSIC STAR WARS (Also see Star Wars)
Dark Horse Comics: Aug, 1992 - No. 20, June, 1994 ($2.50)

1-Begin Star Wars strip-r by Williamson; Williamson redrew portions of the panels to fit
comic book format ... 6.00
2-10: 8-Polybagged w/Star Wars Galaxy trading card. 8-M. Schultz-c ... 4.00
11-19: 13-Yeates-c. 17-M. Schultz-c. 19-Evans-c ... 3.00
20-($3.50, 52 pgs.)-Polybagged w/trading card ... 3.50
Escape To Hoth TPB ($16.95) r/#15-20 ... 17.00
The Rebel Storm TPB - r/#8-14 ... 17.00
Trade paperback ($29.95, slip-cased)-Reprints all movie adaptations ... 30.00
NOTE: Williamson c-1-5,7,9,10,14,15,20.

CLASSIC STAR WARS: (Title series). **Dark Horse Comics**

--A NEW HOPE, 6/94 - No. 2, 7/94 ($3.95)
1,2: 1-r/Star Wars #1-3, 7-9 publ; 2-r/Star Wars #4-6, 10-12 publ. by Marvel Comics4.00
--DEVILWORLDS, 8/96 - No.2, 9/96 ($2.50s)1,2: r/Alan Moore-s ... 2.50
--HAN SOLO AT STARS' END, 3/97 - No. 3, 5/97 ($2.95)
1-3: r/strips by Alfredo Alcala ... 3.00
--RETURN OF THE JEDI, 10/94 - No.2, 11/94 ($3.50)
1,2: 1-r/1983-84 Marvel series; polybagged with w/trading card ... 3.50
--THE EARLY ADVENTURES, 8/94 - No. 9, 4/95 ($2.50)1-9 ... 2.50
--THE EMPIRE STRIKES BACK, 8/94 - No. 2, 9/94 ($3.95)
1-r/Star Wars #39-44 published by Marvel Comics ... 4.00

CLASSIC X-MEN (Becomes X-Men Classic #46 on)
Marvel Comics Group: Sept, 1986 - No. 45, Mar, 1990

1-Begins-r of New X-Men ... 5.00
2-10: 10-Sabretooth app. ... 4.00
11-45: 11-1st origin of Magneto in back-up story. 17-Wolverine-c. 27-r/X-Men #121.
26-r/X-Men #120; Wolverine-c/app. 35-r/X-Men #129. 39-New Jim Lee back-up story
(2nd-a on X-Men). 43-Byrne-c/a(r); $1.75, double-size ... 3.00
NOTE: Art Adams c(p)-1-10, 12-16, 18-23. Austin c-10,15-21,24-28i. Bolton back up stories in 1-28,30-35.
Williamson c-12-14i.

CLAW (See Capt. Battle, Jr., Daredevil Comics & Silver Streak Comics)

CLAWS
Marvel Comics: Oct, 2006 - No. 3, Dec, 2006 ($3.99, limited series)

1-3-Wolverine and Black Cat team-up; Linsner-a/c ... 4.00
Wolverine & Black Cat: Claws HC (2007, $17.99, dustjacket) r/#1-3 & bonus Linsner art 18.00

CLAW THE UNCONQUERED (See Cancelled Comic Cavalcade)
National Periodical Publications/DC Comics: 5-6/75 - No. 9, 9-10/76; No. 10, 4-5/78 - No.
12, 8-9/78

1-1st app. Claw

	1	3	4	6	8	10

2-12: 3-Nudity panel. 9-Origin ... 6.00
NOTE: Giffen a-8-12p. Kubert c-10-12. Layton a-9i, 12i.

CLAW THE UNCONQUERED (See Red Sonja/Claw: The Devil's Hands)
DC Comics: Aug, 2006 - No. 6, Jan, 2007 ($2.99)

1-6: 1,2-Chuck Dixon-s/Andy Smith; two covers by Smith & Van Sciver ... 3.00
TPB (2007, $17.99) r/#1-6; cover gallery ... 18.00

CLAY CODY, GUNSLINGER
Pines Comics: Fall, 1957

1-Painted-c

	6	12	18	31	38	45

CLEAN FUN, STARRING "SHOOGAFOOTS JONES"
Specialty Book Co.: 1944 (10¢, B&W, oversized covers, 24 pgs.)

nn-Humorous situations involving Negroes in the Deep South

White cover issue...

	15	30	45	84	127	170

Dark grey cover issue...

	15	30	45	86	133	180

CLEMENTINA THE FLYING PIG (See Dell Jr. Treasury)

CLEOPATRA (See Ideal, a Classical Comic No. 1)

CLERKS: THE COMIC BOOK (Also see Tales From the Clerks and Oni Double Feature #1)
Oni Press: Feb, 1998 ($2.95, B&W, one-shot)

1-Kevin Smith-s

	2	4	6	8	10	12

1-Second printing ... 4.00
...Holiday Special (12/98, $2.95) Smith-s ... 5.00
...The Lost Scene (12/99, $2.95) Smith-s/Hester-a ... 5.00

CLIFFHANGER (See Battle Chasers, Crimson, and Danger Girl)
WildStorm Prod./Wizard Press: 1997 (Wizard supplement)

0-Sketchbook preview of Cliffhanger titles ... 6.00

CLIMAX! (Mystery)
Gillmor Magazines: July, 1955 - No. 2, Sept, 1955

1

	16	32	48	94	147	200

2

	14	28	42	76	108	140

CLINT (Also see Adolescent Radioactive Black Belt Hamsters)
Eclipse Comics: Sept, 1986 - No. 2, Jan, 1987 ($1.50, B&W)

1,2 ... 2.50

CLINT & MAC (TV, Disney)
Dell Publishing Co.: No. 889, Mar, 1958

Four Color 889-Alex Toth-a, photo-c

	11	22	33	79	140	200

CLIVE BARKER'S BOOK OF THE DAMNED: A HELLRAISER COMPANION
Marvel Comics (Epic): Oct, 1991 - No. 3, Nov, 1992 ($4.95, semi-annual)

Volume 1-3-(52 pgs.): 1-Simon Bisley-c. 2-(4/92). 3-(11/92)-McKean-a (1 pg.) ... 5.00

CLIVE BARKER'S HELLRAISER (Also see Epic, Hellraiser Nightbreed –Jihad, Revelations,
Son of Celluloid, Tapping the Vein & Weaveworld)
Marvel Comics (Epic Comics): 1989 - No. 20, 1993 ($4.50-6.95, mature, quarterly, 68 pgs.)

Book 1-4,10-16,18,19: Based on Hellraiser & Hellbound movies; Bolton-c/a;
Spiegle & Wrightson-a (graphic album). 10-Foil-c. 12-Sam Kieth-a ... 6.00
Book 5-9 ($5.95): 7-Bolton-a. 8-Morrow-a ... 6.00
Book 17-Alex Ross-a, 34 pgs.

	2	4	6	8	10	12

Book 20-By Gaiman/McKean

	1	2	3	5	6	8

...Collected Best (Checker Books, '02, $21.95)-r/by various incl. Ross, Gaiman, Mignola 22.00
...Collected Best II ('03, $19.95)-r/by various incl. Bolton, L. Wachowski, Dorman ... 20.00
...Collected Best III ('04, $26.95)-r/by various incl. Bolton, L. Wachowski, Wrightson ... 27.00
...Dark Holiday Special ('92, $4.95)-Conrad-a ... 6.00
...Spring Slaughter 1 ('94, $6.95, 52 pgs.)-Painted-c ... 7.00
...Summer Special 1 ('92, $5.95, 68 pgs.) ... 6.00

CLIVE BARKER'S NIGHTBREED (Also see Epic)
Marvel Comics (Epic Comics): Apr, 1990 - No. 25, Mar, 1993 ($1.95/$2.25/$2.50, mature
readers)

1-25: 1-4-Adapt horror movie. 5-New stories; Guice-a(p) ... 2.50

CLIVE BARKER'S THE HARROWERS
Marvel Comics (Epic Comics): Dec, 1993 - No. 6, May, 1994 ($2.50)

1-($2.95)-Glow-in-the-dark-c; Colan-c/a in all ... 3.00
2-6 ... 2.50
NOTE: Colan a(p)-1-6; c-1-3, 4p, 5p. Williamson a(i)-2, 4, 5(part).

CLOAK AND DAGGER
Ziff-Davis Publishing Co.: Fall, 1952

1-Saunders painted-c

	28	56	84	160	253	345

CLOAK AND DAGGER (Also see Marvel Fanfare)
Marvel Comics Group: Oct, 1983 - No. 4, Jan, 1984 (Mini-series)
(See Spectacular Spider-Man #64)

1-4-Austin-c/a(i) in all. 4-Origin ... 3.00

CLOAK AND DAGGER (2nd Series)(Also see Marvel Graphic Novel #34 & Strange Tales)
Marvel Comics Group: July, 1985 - No. 11, Jan, 1987

1-11: 9-Art Adams-p ... 2.50
...And Power Pack (1990, $7.95, 68 pgs.) ... 8.00
NOTE: Mignola c-7, 8.

CLOAK AND DAGGER (3rd Series listed as Mutant Misadventures Of...)

CLOBBERIN' TIME
Marvel Comics: Sept, 1995 ($1.95) (Based on card game)

nn-Overpower game guide; Ben Grimm story ... 2.25

Clue Comics #4 © HILL

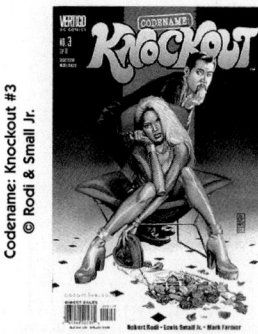

Codename: Knockout #3 © Rodi & Small Jr.

Code of Honor #2 © MAR

	GD 2.0	VG 4.0	FN 6.0	VF 8.0	VF/NM 9.0	NM- 9.2
CLOCK MAKER, THE						
Image Comics: Jan, 2003 - No. 4, May, 2003 ($2.50, comic unfolds to 10"x13" pages)						
1-4-Krueger-s						2.50
... Act Two (4/04, $4.95, standard format) Krueger-s/Matt Smith-c						5.00
CLONEZONE SPECIAL						
Dark Horse Comics/First Comics: 1989 ($2.00, B&W)						
1-Back-up series from Badger & Nexus						2.50
CLOSE ENCOUNTERS (See Marvel Comics Super Special & Marvel Special Edition)						
CLOSER						
Oni Press: May, 2004 ($14.95, B&W, digest size, graphic novel)						
nn-Antony Johnston-s/Mike Norton-a						15.00
CLOSE SHAVES OF PAULINE PERIL, THE (TV cartoon)						
Gold Key: June, 1970 - No. 4, March, 1971						
1	3	6	9	21	32	42
2-4	3	6	9	16	22	28
CLOWN COMICS (No. 1 titled Clown Comic Book)						
Clown Comics/Home Comics/Harvey Publ.: 1945 - No. 3, Win, 1946						
nn (#1)	13	26	39	74	105	135
2,3	9	18	27	47	61	75
CLOUDBURST						
Image Comics: June, 2004 ($7.95, squarebound)						
1-Gray & Palmiotti-s/Shy & Gouveia-a						8.00
CLOUDFALL						
Image Comics: Nov, 2003 ($4.95, B&W, squarebound)						
1-Kirkman-s/Su-a/c						5.00
CLOWNS, THE (I Pagliacci)						
Dark Horse Comics: 1998 ($2.95, B&W, one-shot)						
1-Adaption of the opera; P. Craig Russell-script						3.00
CLUBHOUSE RASCALS (#1 titled ...Presents?) (Also see Three Rascals)						
Sussex Publ. Co. (Magazine Enterprises): June, 1956 - No. 2, Oct, 1956						
1-The Brain app. in both; DeCarlo-a	8	16	24	44	57	70
2	7	14	21	35	43	50
CLUB "16"						
Famous Funnies: June, 1948 - No. 4, Dec, 1948						
1-Teen-age humor	14	28	42	76	108	140
2-4	8	16	24	44	57	70
CLUE COMICS (Real Clue Crime V2#4 on)						
Hillman Periodicals: Jan, 1943 - No. 15(V2#3), May, 1947						
1-Origin The Boy King, Nightmare, Micro-Face, Twilight, & Zippo						
	155	310	465	969	1610	2250
2 (scarce)	79	158	237	494	822	1150
3-5 (9/43)	43	86	129	262	431	600
6,8,9: 8-Palais-c/a(2)	33	66	99	190	300	410
7-Classic concentration camp torture-c (3/44)	59	118	177	369	610	850
10-Origin/1st app. The Gun Master & begin series; content changes to crime (10/46)	34	68	102	197	311	425
11(12/46)	24	48	72	139	220	300
12-Origin Rackman; McWilliams-a, Guardineer-a(2)	30	60	90	174	275	375
V2#1-Nightmare new origin; Iron Lady app.; Simon & Kirby-a (3/47)						
	53	106	159	323	529	735
V2#2-S&K-a(2)-Bondage/torture-c; man attacks & kills people with electric iron. Infantino-a	68	136	204	425	705	985
V2#3-S&K-a(3)	53	106	159	329	545	760
CLUELESS SPRING SPECIAL (TV)						
Marvel Comics: May, 1997 ($3.99, magazine sized, one-shot)						
1-Photo-c from TV show						4.00
CLUTCHING HAND, THE						
American Comics Group: July-Aug, 1954						
1	40	80	120	235	368	500
CLYDE BEATTY COMICS (Also see Crackajack Funnies)						
Commodore Productions & Artists, Inc.: October, 1953 (84 pgs.)						
1-Photo front/back-c; movie scenes and comics	25	50	75	145	228	310
CLYDE CRASHCUP (TV)						
Dell Publishing Co.: Aug-Oct, 1963 - No. 5, Sept-Nov, 1964						

	GD 2.0	VG 4.0	FN 6.0	VF 8.0	VF/NM 9.0	NM- 9.2
1-All written by John Stanley	10	20	30	70	123	175
2-5	9	18	27	60	100	140
COBALT BLUE (Also see Power Comics)						
Innovation Publishing: Sept, 1989 - No. 2, Oct, 1989 ($1.95, 28 pgs.)						
1,2-Gustovich-c/a/scripts						2.50
The Graphic Novel ($6.95, color, 52 pgs.)-r/1,2						7.00
COBB						
IDW Publishing: May, 2006 - No. 3, July, 2007 ($3.99, B&W)						
1-3-Beau Smith-s/Eduardo Barreto-a/c; regular and retailer incentive covers						4.00
CODE NAME: ASSASSIN (See 1st Issue Special)						
CODENAME: DANGER						
Lodestone Publishing: Aug, 1985 - No. 4, May, 1986 ($1.50)						
1-4						2.50
CODENAME: FIREARM (Also see Firearm)						
Malibu Comics (Ultraverse): June, 1995 - No. 5, Sept, 1995 ($2.95, bimonthly limited series)						
0-5: 0-2-Alec Swan back-up story by James Robinson						3.00
NOTE: Perez c-0.						
CODENAME: GENETIX						
Marvel Comics UK: Jan, 1993 - No. 4, May, 1993 ($1.75, limited series)						
1-4: Wolverine in all						3.00
CODENAME: KNOCKOUT						
DC Comics (Vertigo): No. 0, Jun, 2001 - No. 23, June, 2003 ($2.50/$2.75)						
0-15: Rodi-s in all. 0-6-Small Jr. -a. 1-Two covers by Chiodo & Cho. 7,8,10,11,12-Paquette-a. 9,13,14-Conner-a						2.50
16-23: 16-Begin $2.75-c. 23-Last issue; JG Jones-c						2.75
CODENAME SPITFIRE (Formerly Spitfire And The Troubleshooters)						
Marvel Comics Group: No. 10, July, 1987 - No. 13, Oct, 1987						
10-13: 10-Rogers-c/a (low printing)						3.50
CODENAME: STRYKE FORCE (Also See Cyberforce V1#4 & Cyberforce/Stryke Force: Opposing Forces)						
Image Comics (Top Cow Productions): Jan, 1994 - No. 14, Sept, 1995 ($1.95-$2.25)						
0,1-14: 1-2-Silvestri stories, Peterson-a. 4-Stormwatch app. 14-Story continues in Cyberforce/Stryke Force: Opposing Forces; Turner-a						2.50
1-Gold, 1-Blue						4.00
CODE NAME: TOMAHAWK						
Fantasy General Comics: Sept, 1986 ($1.75, high quality paper)						
1-Sci/fi						2.50
CODE OF HONOR						
Marvel Comics: Feb, 1997 - No. 4, May, 1997 ($5.95, limited series)						
1-4-Fully painted by various; Dixon-s						6.00
CODY OF THE PONY EXPRESS (See Colossal Features Magazine)						
Fox Features Syndicate: Sept, 1950 (See Women Outlaws)(One shot)						
1-Painted-c	14	28	42	81	118	155
CODY OF THE PONY EXPRESS (Buffalo Bill...) (Outlaws of the West #11 on; Formerly Bullseye)						
Charlton Comics: No. 8, Oct, 1955; No. 9, Jan, 1956; No. 10, June, 1956						
8-Bullseye on splash pg; not S&K-a	8	16	24	44	57	70
9,10: Buffalo Bill app. in all	6	12	18	29	36	42
CODY STARBUCK (1st app. in Star Reach #1)						
Star Reach Productions: July, 1978						
nn-Howard Chaykin-c/a	2	4	6	12	16	20
2nd printing	1	2	3	5	6	8
NOTE: Both printings say First Printing. True first printing is on lower-grade paper, somewhat off-register, and snow in snow sequence has green tint.						
CO-ED ROMANCES						
P. L. Publishing Co.: November, 1951						
1	9	18	27	47	61	75
COFFEE WORLD						
World Comics: Oct, 1995 ($1.50, B&W, anthology)						
1-Shannon Wheeler's Too Much Coffee Man story						3.00
COFFIN, THE						
Oni Press: Sept, 2000 - No. 4, May, 2001 ($2.95, B&W, limited series)						
1-4-Hester-s/Huddleston-a						3.00
TPB (8/01, $11.95, TPB) r/#1-4						12.00

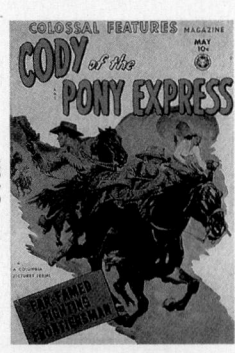

Colossal Features Magazine #33 © FOX

Combat Kelly #1 © MAR

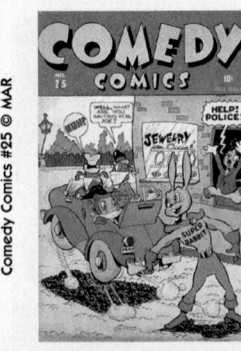

Comedy Comics #25 © MAR

	GD 2.0	VG 4.0	FN 6.0	VF 8.0	VF/NM 9.0	NM- 9.2

COLLECTORS DRACULA, THE
Millennium Publications: 1994 - No. 2, 1994 ($3.95, color/B&W, 52 pgs., limited series)

1,2-Bolton-a (7 pgs.) ... 4.00

COLLECTORS ITEM CLASSICS (See Marvel Collectors Item Classics)

COLORS IN BLACK
Dark Horse Comics: Mar, 1995 - No. 4, June, 1995 ($2.95, limited series)

1-4 ... 3.00

COLOSSAL FEATURES MAGAZINE (Formerly I Loved) (See Cody of the Pony Express)
Fox Features Syndicate: No. 33, 5/50 - No. 34, 7/50; No. 3, 9/50 (Based on Columbia serial)

33,34: Cody of the Pony Express begins. 33-Painted-c. 34-Photo-c

	14	28	42	80	115	150
3-Authentic criminal cases	14	28	42	80	115	150

COLOSSAL SHOW, THE (TV)
Gold Key: Oct, 1969

| 1 | 5 | 10 | 15 | 32 | 51 | 70 |

COLOSSUS (See X-Men)
Marvel Comics: Oct, 1997 ($2.99, 48 pgs., one-shot)

1-Raab-s/Hitch & Neary-a, wraparound-c ... 3.00

COLOSSUS COMICS (See Green Giant & Motion Picture Funnies Weekly)
Sun Publications (Funnies, Inc.?): March, 1940

1-(Scarce)-Tulpa of Tsang(hero); Colossus app. 629 1258 1887 4400 7700 11,000
NOTE: Cover by artist that drew Colossus in Green Giant Comics.

COLOUR OF MAGIC, THE (Terry Pratchett's…)
Innovation Publishing: 1991 - No. 4, 1991 ($2.50, limited series)

1-4: Adapts 1st novel of the Discworld series ... 3.00

COLT .45 (TV)
Dell Publishing Co.: No. 924, 8/58 - No. 1058, 11-1/59-60; No. 4, 2-4/60 - No. 9, 5-7/61

Four Color 924(#1)-Wayde Preston photo-c on all	10	20	30	70	123	175
Four Color 1004,1058, #4,5,7-9: 1004-Photo-b/c	8	16	24	56	93	130
6-Toth-a	9	18	27	60	100	140

COLUMBIA COMICS
William H. Wise Co.: 1943

1-Joe Palooka, Charlie Chan, Capt. Yank, Sparky Watts, Dixie Dugan app.
| | 27 | 54 | 81 | 158 | 249 | 340 |

COLUMBUS
Dark Horse Comics: Sept, 1992 ($2.50, B&W, one-shot)

1-Yeates painted-c ... 2.50

COMANCHE
Dell Publishing Co.: No. 1350, Apr-Jun, 1962

Four Color 1350-Disney movie; reprints FC #966 with title change from "Tonka" to "Comanche"; Sal Mineo photo-c
| | 5 | 10 | 15 | 35 | 55 | 75 |

COMANCHEROS, THE
Dell Publishing Co.: No. 1300, Mar-May, 1962

Four Color 1300-Movie, John Wayne photo-c
| | 15 | 30 | 45 | 105 | 188 | 270 |

COMBAT
Atlas Comics (ANC): June, 1952 - No. 11, April, 1953

1	26	52	78	150	235	320
2-Heath-c/a	14	28	42	82	121	160
3,5-9,11: 9-Robert Q. Sale-a	11	22	33	62	86	110
4-Krigstein-a	11	22	33	64	90	115
10-B&W and color illos. in POP	11	22	33	62	86	110
NOTE: Combat Casey in 7-11. Heath c-1, 2, 9. Maneely a-1; c-3. Pakula a-1. Reinman a-1.

COMBAT
Dell Publishing Co.: Oct-Nov, 1961 - No. 40, Oct, 1973 (No #9)

1	6	12	18	41	66	90
2,3,5:	4	8	12	24	37	50
4-John F. Kennedy c/story (P.T. 109)	5	10	15	32	51	70
6,7,8(4-6/63), 8(7-9/63)	4	8	12	22	34	45
10-26: 26-Last 12¢ issue	3	6	9	18	27	35
27-40(reprints #1-14). 30-r/#4	3	6	9	14	19	24

COMBAT CASEY (Formerly War Combat)
Atlas Comics (SAI): No. 6, Jan, 1953 - No. 34, July, 1957

| 6 (Indicia shows 1/52 in error) | 16 | 32 | 48 | 94 | 147 | 200 |
| 7 | 10 | 20 | 30 | 58 | 79 | 100 |

8-Used in POP, pg. 94	10	20	30	54	72	90
9	9	18	27	50	65	80
10,13-19-Violent art by R. Q. Sale; Battle Brady x-over #10						
	13	26	39	72	101	130
11,12,20-Last Precode (2/55)	9	18	27	50	65	80
21-34	9	18	27	47	61	75
NOTE: Everett a-6. Heath c-10, 17, 19, 23, 30. Maneely c-6, 8. Powell a-29(5), 30(5), 34. Severin c-26, 33.

COMBAT KELLY
Atlas Comics (SPI): Nov, 1951 - No. 44, Aug, 1957

1-1st app. Combat Kelly; Heath-a	31	62	93	178	282	385
2	15	30	45	86	133	180
3-10	12	24	36	69	97	125
11-Used in POP, pgs. 94,95 plus color illo.	10	20	30	56	76	95
12-Color illo. in POP	10	20	30	56	76	95
13-16	9	18	27	52	69	85
17-Violent art by R. Q. Sale; Combat Casey app.	13	26	39	72	101	130
18-20,22-44: 18-Battle Brady app. 28-Last precode (1/55). 38-Green Berets story (8/56)						
	9	18	27	50	65	80
21-Transvestism-c	9	18	27	52	69	85
NOTE: Berg a-8, 12-14, 16, 17, 19-23, 25, 26, 28, 31-36, 42-44; c-2. Colan a-42. Heath a-4; c-31. Lawrence a-23. Maneely a-4(2), 6, 7(3), 8; c-4, 5, 7, 8, 10, 25. R.Q. Sale a-17, 25. Severin c-41, 42. Whitney a-5.

COMBAT KELLY (…and the Deadly Dozen)
Marvel Comics Group: June, 1972 - No. 9, Oct, 1973

1-Intro & origin new Combat Kelly; Ayers/Mooney-a; Severin-c (20¢)						
	3	6	9	16	23	30
2,5-8	2	4	6	9	12	15
3,4: 3-Origin. 4-Sgt. Fury-c/s	2	4	6	11	16	20
9-Death of the Deadly Dozen	2	4	6	13	18	22

COMBAT ZONE: TRUE TALES OF GIS IN IRAQ
Marvel Comics: 2005 ($19.99, squarebound)

Vol. 1-Karl Zinsmeister scripts adapted from his non-fiction books; Dan Jurgens-a ... 20.00

COMBINED OPERATIONS (See The Story of the Commandos)

COMEBACK (See Zane Grey 4-Color 357)

COMEDY CARNIVAL
St. John Publishing Co.: no date (1950's) (100 pgs.)

nn-Contains rebound St. John comics
| | 35 | 70 | 105 | 201 | 318 | 435 |

COMEDY COMICS (1st Series) (Daring Mystery #1-8) (Becomes Margie Comics #35 on)
Timely Comics (TCI 9,10): No. 9, April, 1942 - No. 34, Fall, 1946

9-(Scarce)-The Fin by Everett, Capt. Dash, Citizen V, & The Silver Scorpion app.; Wolverton-a; 1st app. Comedy Kid; satire on Hitler & Stalin; The Fin, Citizen V & Silver Scorpion cont. from Daring Mystery
| | 300 | 600 | 900 | 1894 | 3197 | 4500 |
10-(Scarce)-Origin The Fourth Musketeer, Victory Boys; Monstro, the Mighty app.
	228	456	684	1425	2363	3300
11-Vagabond, Stuporman app.	53	106	159	323	537	750
12,13	16	32	48	94	147	200
14-Origin/1st app. Super Rabbit (3/43) plus-c	53	106	159	323	537	750
15-20	15	30	45	88	137	185
21-32	13	26	39	74	105	135
33-Kurtzman-a (5 pgs.)	15	30	45	83	124	165
34-Intro Margie; Wolverton-a (5 pgs.)	22	44	66	128	202	275

COMEDY COMICS (2nd Series)
Marvel Comics (ACI): May, 1948 - No. 10, Jan, 1950

1-Hedy, Tessie, Millie begin; Kurtzman's "Hey Look" (he draws himself)
	36	72	108	208	329	450
2	15	30	45	90	140	190
3,4-Kurtzman's "Hey Look" (?&3)	16	32	48	94	147	200
5-10	11	22	33	60	83	105

COMET, THE (See The Mighty Crusaders & Pep Comics #1)
Red Circle Comics (Archie): Oct, 1983 - No. 2, Dec, 1983

1-Re-intro & origin The Comet; The American Shield begins. Nino & Infantino art in both. Hangman in both ... 5.00
2-Origin continues. ... 4.00

COMET, THE
DC Comics (Impact Comics): July, 1991 - No. 18, Dec, 1992 ($1.00/$1.25)

1 ... 3.00
2-18: 4-Black Hood app. 6-Re-intro Hangman. 8-Web x-over. 10-Contains Crusaders trading card. 4-Origin. Netzer(Nasser) c(p)-11,14-17 ... 2.50
Annual 1 (1992, $2.50, 68 pgs.)-Contains Impact trading card; Shield back-up story ... 2.50

Comic Album #12 © DELL

Comic Cavalcade #11 © DC

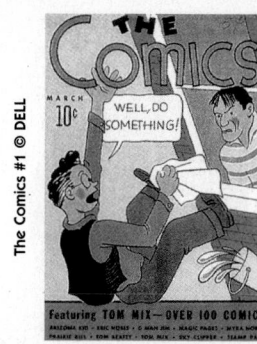

The Comics #1 © DELL

	GD 2.0	VG 4.0	FN 6.0	VF 8.0	VF/NM 9.0	NM- 9.2

COMET MAN, THE (Movie)
Marvel Comics Group: Feb, 1987 - No. 6, July, 1987 (limited series)

1-6: 3-Hulk app. 4-She-Hulk shower scene-c/s. Fantastic 4 app. 5-Fantastic 4 app.   2.50
NOTE: *Kelley Jones a-1-6p.*

COMIC ALBUM (Also see Disney Comic Album)
Dell Publishing Co.: Mar-May, 1958 - No. 18, June-Aug, 1962

	GD	VG	FN	VF	VF/NM	NM-
1-Donald Duck	9	18	27	60	100	140
2-Bugs Bunny	5	10	15	32	51	70
3-Donald Duck	7	14	21	47	76	105
4-6,8-10: 4-Tom & Jerry. 5-Woody Woodpecker. 6,10-Bugs Bunny. 8-Tom & Jerry. 9-Woody Woodpecker	4	8	12	28	44	60
7,11,15: Popeye. 11-(9-11/60)	6	12	18	33	49	65
12-14: 12-Tom & Jerry. 13-Woody Woodpecker. 14-Bugs Bunny	5	10	15	30	48	60
16-Flintstones (12-2/61-62)-3rd app. Early Cave Kids app.	8	16	24	54	90	125
17-Space Mouse (3rd app.)	5	10	15	32	51	70
18-Three Stooges; photo-c	8	16	24	54	90	125

COMIC BOOK
Marvel Comics-#1/Dark Horse Comics-#2: 1995 ($5.95, oversize)

	GD	VG	FN	VF	VF/NM	NM-
1-Spumco characters by John K.	1	2	3	4	5	7
2-(Dark Horse)						6.00

COMIC CAPERS
Red Circle Mag./Marvel Comics: Fall, 1944 - No. 6, Summer, 1946

	GD	VG	FN	VF	VF/NM	NM-
1-Super Rabbit, The Creeper, Silly Seal, Ziggy Pig, Sharpy Fox	30	60	90	174	275	375
2	15	30	45	90	140	190
3-6	14	28	42	80	115	150

COMIC CAVALCADE
All-American/National Periodical Publications: Winter, 1942-43 - No. 63, June-July, 1954
(Contents change with No. 30, Dec-Jan, 1948-49 on)

	GD	VG	FN	VF	VF/NM	NM-
1-The Flash, Green Lantern, Wonder Woman, Wildcat, The Black Pirate by Moldoff (also #2), Ghost Patrol, and Red White & Blue begin; Scribbly app.; Minute Movie	857	1714	2571	6000	10,500	15,000
2-Mutt & Jeff begin; last Ghost Patrol & Black Pirate; Minute Movies	241	482	723	1506	2503	3500
3-Hop Harrigan & Sargon, the Sorcerer begin; The King app.	159	318	477	994	1647	2300
4,5: 4-The Gay Ghost, The King, Scribbly, & Red Tornado app. 5-Christmas-c. 5-Prints ad for Jr. JSA membership kit that includes "The Minute Man Answers The Call"	145	290	435	906	1503	2100
6-10: 7-Red Tornado & Black Pirate app.; last Scribbly. 9-Fat & Slat app.; X-Mas-c	116	232	348	725	1200	1675
11,12,14: 12-Last Red White & Blue	97	194	291	606	1003	1400
13-Solomon Grundy app.; X-Mas-c	160	320	480	1000	1663	2325
15-Just a Story begins	98	196	294	606	1016	1425
16-20: 19-Christmas-c	89	178	267	556	921	1285
21-23: 22-Johnny Peril begins. 23-Harry Lampert-c (Toth swipes)	85	170	255	531	878	1225
24-Solomon Grundy x-over in Green Lantern	113	226	339	706	1173	1640
25-28: 25-Black Canary app.; X-Mas-c. 26-28-Johnny Peril app. 28-Last Mutt & Jeff	116	232	348	725	1200	1675
29-(10-11/48)-Last Flash, Wonder Woman, Green Lantern & Johnny Peril; Wonder Woman invents "Thinking Machine"; 2nd computer in comics (after Flash Comics #52); Leave It to Binky story (early app.)	86	172	258	538	894	1250
30-(12-1/48-49)-The Fox & the Crow, Dodo & the Frog & Nutsy Squirrel begin	41	82	123	250	400	550
31-35	24	48	72	139	220	300
36-49: 41-Last squarebound issue	17	34	51	98	154	210
50-62(Scarce)	21	42	63	124	195	265
63(Rare)	34	68	102	195	308	420

NOTE: *Grossman a-30-63. E.E. Hibbard c-(Flash only)-1-4, 7-14, 16-19, 21. Sheldon Mayer a(2-3)-40-63. Moulson c(G.L.)-7, 15. Nodell c(G.L.)-9. H.G. Peter c(W. Woman only)-1, 3-21, 24. Post a-31, 36. Purcell c(G.L.)-2-5, 10. Reinman a(Green Lantern)-4-6, 8, 9, 13, 15-21; c(Gr. Lantern)-6, 8, 19. Toth a(Green Lantern)-26-28; c-27. Atom app.-22, 23.*

COMIC COMICS
Fawcett Publications: Apr, 1946 - No. 10, Feb, 1947

	GD	VG	FN	VF	VF/NM	NM-
1-Captain Kid; Nutty Comics #1 in indicia	15	30	45	124	124	165
2-10-Wolverton-a, 4 pgs. each. 5-Captain Kidd app. Mystic Moot by Wolverton in #2-10?	15	30	45	84	127	170

COMIC LAND

Fact and Fiction Publ.: March, 1946

	GD	VG	FN	VF	VF/NM	NM-
1-Sandusky & the Senator, Sam Stupor, Sleuth, Marvin the Great, Sir Passer, Phineas Gruff app.; Irv Tirman & Perry Williams art	15	30	45	84	127	170

COMICO CHRISTMAS SPECIAL
Comico: Dec, 1988 ($2.50, 44pgs.)

1-Rude/Williamson-a; Dave Stevens-c   4.00

COMICO COLLECTION (Also see Grendel)
Comico: 1987 ($9.95, slipcased collection)

nn-Contains exclusive Grendel: Devil's Vagary, 9 random Comico comics, a poster & newsletter in black slipcase w/silver ink   25.00

COMICO PRIMER (See Primer)

COMIC PAGES (Formerly Funny Picture Stories)
Centaur Publications: V3#4, July, 1939 - V3#6, Dec, 1939

	GD	VG	FN	VF	VF/NM	NM-
V3#4-Wood-a	53	106	159	323	537	750
5,6: 6-Schwab-a	43	86	129	262	431	600

COMICS AND STORIES (See Walt Disney's Comics and Stories)

COMICS & STORIES (Also see Wolf & Red)
Dark Horse Comics: Apr, 1996 - No. 4, July, 1996 ($2.95, lim. series) (Created by Tex Avery)

1-4: Wolf & Red reads Comics and Stories on-c. 1-Terry Moore-a. 2-Reed Waller-a 3.00

COMICS CALENDAR, THE (The 1946…)
True Comics Press (ordered through the mail): 1946 (25¢, 116 pgs.) (Stapled at top)

	GD	VG	FN	VF	VF/NM	NM-
nn-(Rare) Has a "strip" story for every day of the year in color	40	80	120	235	368	500

COMICS DIGEST (Pocket size)
Parents' Magazine Institute: Winter, 1942-43 (B&W, 100 pgs)

	GD	VG	FN	VF	VF/NM	NM-
1-Reprints from True Comics (non-fiction World War II stories)	10	20	30	54	72	90

COMICS EXPRESS
Eclipse Comics: Nov, 1989 - No. 2, Jan, 1990 ($2.95, B&W, 68pgs.)

1,2: Collection of strip-r; 2(12/89-c, 1/90 inside)   3.00

COMICS FOR KIDS
London Publ. Co./Timely: 1945 (no month); No. 2, Sum, 1945 (Funny animal)

	GD	VG	FN	VF	VF/NM	NM-
1,2-Puffy Pig, Sharpy Fox	16	32	48	94	147	200

COMICS' GREATEST WORLD
Dark Horse Comics: Jun, 1993 - V4#4, Sept, 1993 ($1.00, weekly, lim. series)

	GD	VG	FN	VF	VF/NM	NM-
Arcadia (Wk 1): V1#1,2,4: 1-X: Frank Miller-c. 2-Pit Bulls. 4-Monster.						2.50
1-B&W Press Proof Edition (1500 copies)	1	3	4	6	8	10
1-Silver-c; distr. retailer bonus w/print & cards	1	2	3	5	6	8
3-Ghost, Dorman-c; Hughes-a						4.00
Retailer's Prem. Emb. Silver Foil Logo-r/V1#1-4	1	3	4	6	8	10
Golden City (Wk 2): V2#1-4: 1-Rebel; Ordway-c. 2-Mecha; Dave Johnson-c.						
3-Titan; Walt Simonson-c. 4-Catalyst; Perez-c.						2.50
1-Gold-c; distr. retailer bonus w/print & cards.						6.00
Retailer's Prem. Embos. Gold Foil Logo-r/V2#1-4	1	2	3	5	6	8
Steel Harbor (Week 3): V3#1-Barb Wire; Dorman-c; Gulacy-a(p)						4.00
2-4: 2-The Machine. 3-Wolfgang. 4-Motorhead						2.50
1-Silver-c; distr. retailer bonus w/print & cards.	1	3	4	6	8	10
Retailer's Prem. Emb. Red Foil Logo-r/V3#1-4.	1	3	4	6	8	10
Vortex (Week 4): V4#1-4: 1-Division 13; Dorman-c. 2-Hero Zero; Art Adams-c.						2.50
3-King Tiger; Chadwick-a(p); Darrow-c. 4-Vortex; Miller-c.						2.50
1-Gold-c; distr. retailer bonus w/print & cards.						6.00
Retailer's Prem. Emb. Blue Foil Logo-r/V4#1-4.	1	2	3	5	6	8

COMICS' GREATEST WORLD: OUT OF THE VORTEX (See Out of The Vortex)

COMICS HITS (See Harvey Comics Hits)

COMICS MAGAZINE, THE (…Funny Pages #3)(Funny Pages #6 on)
Comics Magazine Co. (1st Comics Mag./Centaur Publ.): May, 1936 - No. 5, Sept, 1936 (Paper covers)

1-1st app. Dr. Mystic (a.k.a. Dr. Occult) by Siegel & Shuster (the 1st app. of a Superman

---

COMICS, THE
Dell Publ. Co.: Mar, 1937 - No. 11, Nov, 1938 (Newspaper strip-r; bi-monthly)

	GD	VG	FN	VF	VF/NM	NM-
1-1st app. Tom Mix in comics; Wash Tubbs, Tom Beatty, Myra North, Arizona Kid, Erik Noble & International Spy w/Doctor Doom begin	186	372	558	1163	1932	2700
2	82	164	246	513	849	1185
3-11: 3-Alley Oop begins	66	132	198	413	682	950

Comics on Parade #21 © UFS

Commando Adventures #1 © MAR

Complete Love Magazine V26 #3 © ACE

	GD 2.0	VG 4.0	FN 6.0	VF 8.0	VF/NM 9.0	NM- 9.2

prototype in comics). Dr. Mystic is not in costume but later appears in costume as a more pronounced prototype in More Fun #14-17. (1st episode of "The Koth and the Seven"; continues in More Fun #14; originally scheduled for publication at DC). 1 pg. Kelly-a; Sheldon Mayer-a .... 2500 5000 7500 16,500 – –
2-Federal Agent (a.k.a. Federal Men) by Siegel & Shuster; 1 pg. Kelly-a
| | 330 | 660 | 990 | 1980 | 2640 | 3300 |
| 3-5 | 280 | 560 | 840 | 1680 | 2240 | 2800 |

COMICS NOVEL (Anarcho, Dictator of Death)
Fawcett Publications: 1947

| 1-All Radar; 51 pg anti-fascism story | 32 | 64 | 96 | 186 | 293 | 400 |

COMICS ON PARADE (No. 30 on are a continuation of Single Series)
United Features Syndicate: Apr, 1938 - No. 104, Feb, 1955

1-Tarzan by Foster; Captain & the Kids, Little Mary Mixup, Abbie & Slats, Ella Cinders, Broncho Bill, Li'l Abner begin
	358	716	1074	2327	4114	5900
2 (Tarzan & others app. on-c of #1-3,17)	126	252	378	788	1307	1825
3	97	194	291	606	1003	1400
4,5	76	152	228	475	788	1100
6-10	53	106	159	323	537	750
11-16,18-20	42	84	126	256	421	585
17-Tarzan-c	49	98	147	299	492	685
21-29: 22-Son of Tarzan begins. 22,24,28-Tailspin Tommy-c. 29-Last Tarzan issue
	36	72	108	208	329	450
30-Li'l Abner	20	40	60	117	184	250
31-The Captain & the Kids	15	30	45	85	130	175
32-Nancy & Fritzi Ritz	14	28	42	78	112	145
33,36,39,42-Li'l Abner	16	32	48	94	147	200
34,37,40-The Captain & the Kids (10/41,6/42,3/43)	15	30	45	83	124	165
35,38-Nancy & Fritzi Ritz. 38-Infinity-c	14	28	42	76	108	140
41-Nancy & Fritzi Ritz	11	22	33	60	83	105
43-The Captain & the Kids	15	30	45	83	124	165
44 (3/44),47,50: Nancy & Fritzi Ritz	11	22	33	60	83	105
45-Li'l Abner	15	30	45	84	127	170
46,49-The Captain & the Kids	13	26	39	74	105	135
48-Li'l Abner (3/45)	15	30	45	84	127	170
51,54-Li'l Abner	14	28	42	76	108	140
52-The Captain & the Kids (3/46)	10	20	30	56	76	95
53,55,57-Nancy & Fritzi Ritz	10	20	30	56	76	95
56-The Captain & the Kids (r/Sparkler)	10	20	30	56	76	95
58-Li'l Abner; continues as Li'l Abner #61?	14	28	42	76	108	140
59-The Captain & the Kids	9	18	27	47	61	75
60-70-Nancy & Fritzi Ritz	8	16	24	44	57	70
71-99,101-104-Nancy & Sluggo: 71-76-Nancy only	8	16	24	42	54	65
100-Nancy & Sluggo	8	16	24	42	57	70
Special Issue, 7/46; Summer, 1948 - The Captain & the Kids app.
	10	20	30	58	79	100
NOTE: Bound Volume (Very Rare) includes No. 1-12; bound by publisher in pictorial comic boards & distributed at the 1939 World's Fair and through mail order from ads in comic books also (see Tip Top)
	276	552	828	1725	2863	4000
NOTE: Li'l Abner reprinted from Tip Top.

COMICS READING LIBRARIES (See the Promotional Comics section)

COMICS REVUE
St. John Publ. Co. (United Features Synd.): June, 1947 - No. 5, Jan, 1948

1-Ella Cinders & Blackie	11	22	33	64	90	115
2,4: 2-Hap Hopper (7/47). 4-Ella Cinders (9/47)	9	18	27	47	61	75
3,5: 3-Iron Vic (8/47). 5-Gordo No. 1 (1/48)	8	16	24	44	57	70

COMIC STORY PAINT BOOK
Samuel Lowe Co.: 1943 (Large size, 68 pgs.)

1055-Captain Marvel & a Captain Marvel Jr. story to read & color; 3 panels in color per pg. (reprints)
| | 75 | 150 | 225 | 469 | 777 | 1085 |

COMIX BOOK
Marvel Comics Group/Krupp Comics Works No. 4,5: 1974 - No. 5, 1976 ($1.00, B&W, magazine) (#1-3 newsstand; #4,5 were direct distribution only)

1-Underground comic artists; 2 pgs. Wolverton-a	3	6	9	16	22	28
2,3: 2-Wolverton-a (1 pg.)	3	6	9	14	19	24
4(2/76), 4(5/76), 5 (Low distribution)	3	6	9	15	21	26
NOTE: Print run No. 1-3: 200-250M; No. 4&5: 10M each.

COMIX INTERNATIONAL
Warren Magazines: Jul, 1974 - No. 5, Spring, 1977 (Full color, stiff-c, mail only)

1-Low distribution; all Corben story remainders from Warren; Corben-c on all
| | 8 | 16 | 24 | 58 | 97 | 135 |
2,4: 2-Two Dracula stories; Wood, Wrightson-r; Crandall-a; Maroto-a.

| 4-Printing w/ 3 Corben sty | 5 | 10 | 15 | 30 | 48 | 65 |
3-5: 3-Dax story. 4-(printing without Corben story). 4-Crandall-a, 4,5-Vampirella stories.
| 5-Spirit story; Eisner-a | 4 | 8 | 12 | 24 | 37 | 50 |
NOTE: No. 4 had two printings with extra Corben story in one. No. 3 may also have a variation. No. 3 has two Jeff Jones reprints from Vampirella.

COMMANDER BATTLE AND THE ATOMIC SUB
Amer. Comics Group (Titan Publ. Co.): Jul-Aug, 1954 - No. 7, Aug-Sep, 1955

| 1 (3-D effect)-Moldoff flying saucer-c | 47 | 94 | 141 | 287 | 474 | 660 |
2,4-7: 2-Moldoff-c. 4-(1-2/55)-Last pre-code; Landau-a. 5-3-D effect story
(2 pgs.). 6,7-Landau-a. 7-Flying saucer-c
| | 31 | 62 | 93 | 178 | 282 | 385 |
3-H-Bomb-c; Atomic Sub becomes Atomic Spaceship
| | 32 | 64 | 96 | 186 | 293 | 400 |

COMMANDO ADVENTURES
Atlas Comics (MMC): June, 1957 - No. 2, Aug, 1957

| 1-Severin-c | 13 | 26 | 39 | 74 | 105 | 135 |
| 2-Severin-c; Drucker-a? | 10 | 20 | 30 | 54 | 72 | 90 |

COMMANDOS
DC Comics: Oct. 1942

1-Ashcan comic, not distributed to newsstands, only for in-house use. Cover art is Boy Commandos #1 with interior being a Boy Commandos story from an unidentified issue of Detective Comics (no known sales)

COMMANDO YANK (See The Mighty Midget Comics & Wow Comics)

COMMON GROUNDS
Image Comics (Top Cow): Feb, 2004 - No. 6, July, 2004 ($2.99)

| 1-6: 1-Two covers; art by Jurgens and Oeming. 3-Bachalo, Jurgens-a. 4-Peréz-a | | | | | | 3.00 |
| ...: Baker's Dozen TPB (12/04, $14.99) r/#1-6; cover gallery; Holey Crullers pages | | | | | | 15.00 |

COMPLETE BOOK OF COMICS AND FUNNIES
William H. Wise & Co.: 1944 (25¢, one-shot, 196 pgs.)

1-Origin Brad Spencer, Wonderman; The Magnet, The Silver Knight by Kinstler, & Zudo the Jungle Boy app.
| | 43 | 86 | 129 | 262 | 431 | 600 |

COMPLETE BOOK OF TRUE CRIME COMICS
William H. Wise & Co.: No date (Mid 1940's) (25¢, 132 pgs.)

nn-Contains Crime Does Not Pay rebound (includes #22)
| | 121 | 242 | 363 | 756 | 1253 | 1750 |

COMPLETE COMICS (Formerly Amazing Comics No. 1)
Timely Comics (EPC): No. 2, Winter, 1944-45

2-The Destroyer, The Whizzer, The Young Allies & Sergeant Dix; Schomburg-c
| | 162 | 324 | 486 | 1013 | 1682 | 2350 |

COMPLETE FRANK MILLER BATMAN, THE
Longmeadow Press: 1989 ($29.95, hardcover, silver gilded pages)

| HC-Reprints Batman: Year One, Wanted: Santa Claus--Dead or Alive, and The Dark Knight Returns | | | | | | 30.00 |

COMPLETE GUIDE TO THE DEADLY ARTS OF KUNG FU AND KARATE
Marvel Comics: 1974 (68 pgs., B&W magazine)

| V1#1-Bruce Lee-c and 5 pg. story (scarce) | 6 | 12 | 18 | 39 | 62 | 75 |

COMPLETE LOVE MAGAZINE (Formerly a pulp with same title)
Ace Periodicals (Periodical House): V26#2, May-June, 1951 - V32#4(#191), Sept, 1956

V26#2-Painted-c (52 pgs.)	10	20	30	54	72	90
V26#3-6(2/52), V27#1(4/52)-6(1/53)	8	16	24	42	54	65
V28#1(3/53), V28#2(5/53), V29#3(7/53)-6(12/53)	8	16	24	40	50	60
V30#1(2/54), V30#1(#176, 4/54),2,4-6(#181, 1/55)	8	16	24	40	50	60
V30#3(#178)-Rock Hudson photo-c	8	16	24	42	54	65
V31#1(#182, 3/55)-Last precode	7	14	21	37	46	55
V31#2(5/55)-6(#187, 1/56)	7	14	21	35	43	50
V32#1(#188, 3/56)-4(#191, 9/56)	7	14	21	35	43	50
NOTE: (34 total issues). Photo-c V27#5-on. Painted-c V26#3.

COMPLETE MYSTERY (True Complete Mystery No. 5 on)
Marvel Comics (PrPI): Aug, 1948 - No. 4, Feb, 1949 (Full length stories)

| 1-Seven Dead Men | 45 | 90 | 135 | 275 | 450 | 625 |
2-4: 2-Jigsaw of Doom! 3-Fear in the Night; Burgos-c/a (28 pgs.). 4-A Squealer Dies Fast
| | 39 | 78 | 117 | 225 | 355 | 485 |

COMPLETE ROMANCE
Avon Periodicals: 1949

| 1-(Scarce)-Reprinted as Women to Love | 40 | 80 | 120 | 243 | 389 | 535 |

CONAN (See Chamber of Darkness #4, Giant-Size..., Handbook of..., King Conan, Marvel Graphic Novel #19, 28, Marvel Treasury Ed., Power Record Comics, Robert E. Howard's.., Savage Sword of Conan, and Savage

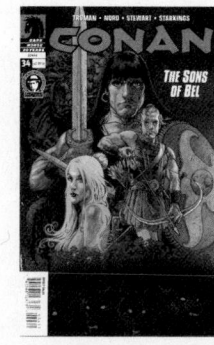

Conan #34 © Conan Props.

Conan Saga #57 © Conan Props.

Conan the Barbarian #150 © Conan Props.

	GD	VG	FN	VF	VF/NM	NM-		GD	VG	FN	VF	VF/NM	NM-
	2.0	4.0	6.0	8.0	9.0	9.2		2.0	4.0	6.0	8.0	9.0	9.2

Tales)

CONAN
Dark Horse Comics: Feb, 2004 - Present ($2.99)

0-(11/03, 25¢-c) Busiek-s/Nord-a						2.25
1-($2.99) Linsner-c/Busiek-s/Nord-a						5.00
1-(2nd printing) J. Scott Campell-c						3.00
1-(3rd printing) Nord-c						3.00
2-43: 18-Severin & Timm-a. 22-Kaluta-a (6 pgs.) 23-Ruth-a. 24-Harris-c. 29-31-Mignola-s						3.00
24-Variant-c with nude woman (also see Conan and the Demons of Khitai #3 for ad)						20.00
... and the Daughters of Midora (10/04, $4.99) Texiera-a/c						5.00
HC Vol. 1: The Frost Giant's Daughter and Other Stories (2005, $24.95) r/#1-6, partial 7; signed by Busiek; Nord sketch pages						25.00
Vol. 1: The Frost Giant's Daughter and Other Stories (2005, $15.95) r/#1-6, partial 7						16.00
Vol. 2: The God in the Bowl and Other Stories HC (2005, $24.95) r/#9-14						25.00
Vol. 2: The God in the Bowl and Other Stories SC (2006, $15.95) r/#9-14						16.00
Vol. 3: The Tower of the Elephant and Other Stories HC (5/06, $24.95) r/#0,16,17,19-22						25.00
Vol. 3: The Tower of the Elephant and Other Stories SC (6/06, $15.95) r/#0,16,17,19-22						16.00
Vol. 4: The Hall of the Dead and Other Stories HC (5/07, $24.95) r/#0,24,25,29-31,33,34						25.00
Vol. 4: The Hall of the Dead and Other Stories SC (6/07, $17.95) r/#0,24,25,29-31,33,34						18.00

CONAN AND THE DEMONS OF KHITAI
Dark Horse Comics: Oct, 2005 - No. 4, Jan, 2006 ($2.99, limited series)

1,2,4-Paul Lee-a/Akira Yoshida-s/Pat Lee-c						3.00
3-1st printing with red cover logo; letters page has image of Conan #24 nude variant-c						5.00
3-2nd printing with black cover logo; letters page has image of Conan #24 regular-c						3.00
TPB (7/06, $12.95) r/series						13.00

CONAN AND THE JEWELS OF GWAHLUR
Dark Horse Comics: Apr, 2005 - No. 3, June, 2005 ($2.99, limited series)

1-3-P. Craig Russell-s/a/c						3.00
HC (12/05, $13.95) r/series; P. Craig Russell interview and sketch pages						14.00

CONAN AND THE MIDNIGHT GOD
Dark Horse Comics: Dec, 2006 - No. 5, May, 2007 ($2.99, limited series)

1-5-Dysart-s/Conrad-a/Alexander-c						3.00

CONAN AND THE SONGS OF THE DEAD
Dark Horse Comics: July, 2006 - No. 5, Nov, 2006 ($2.99, limited series)

1-5-Timothy Truman-a/c; Joe Lansdale-s						3.00
TPB (4/07, $14.95) r/series; Truman sketch pages						15.00

CONAN: (Title Series): Marvel Comics

CONAN, 8/95 - No. 11, 6/96 ($2.95), 1-11: 4-Malibu Comic's Rune app.						3.00
...CLASSIC, 6/94 - No. 11, 4/95 ($1.50), 1-11: 1-r/Conan #1 by B. Smith, r/covers w/changes. 2-11-r/Conan #2-11 by Smith. 2-Bound w/cover to Conan The Adventurer #2 by mistake						2.50
...DEATH COVERED IN GOLD, 9/99 - No. 3, 11/99 ($2.99), 1-3-Roy Thomas-s/ John Buscema-a						3.00
...FLAME AND THE FIEND, 8/00 - No. 3, 10/00 ($2.99), 1-3-Thomas-s						3.00
...RETURN OF STYRM, 9/98 - No. 3, 11/98 ($2.99), 1-3-Parente & Soresina-a; painted-c						3.00
...RIVER OF BLOOD, 6/98 - No. 3, 8/98 ($2.50), 1-3						2.50
...SCARLET SWORD, 12/98 - No. 3, 2/99 ($2.99), 1-3-Thomas-s/Raffaele-a						3.00

CONAN SAGA, THE
Marvel Comics: June, 1987 - No. 97, Apr, 1995 ($2.00/$2.25, B&W, magazine)

1-Barry Smith-r; new Smith-c	1	2	3	4	5	7
2-27: 2-9,11-new Barry Smith-c. 13,15-Boris-c. 17-Adams-r.18,25-Chaykin-r. 22-r/Giant-Size Conan 1,2						4.00
28-90: 28-Begin $2.25-c. 31-Red Sonja-r by N. Adams/SSOC #1; 1 pg. Jeff Jones-r. 32-Newspaper strip-r begin by Buscema. 33-Smith/Conrad-a. 39-r/Kull #1('71) by Andru & Wood. 44-Swipes-c/Savage Tales #1. 57-Brunner-r/SSOC #30. 66-r/Conan Annual #2 by Buscema. 79-r/Conan #43-45 w/Red Sonja. 85-Based on Conan #57-63						3.00
91-96						4.00
97-Last issue						5.00

NOTE: **J. Buscema** r-32-on; c-86. **Chaykin** r-34. **Chiodo** painted c-63, 65, 66, 82. **G. Colan** a-47p. **Jusko** painted c-64, 83. **Kaluta** c-84. **Nino** a-37. **Ploog** a-50. **N. Redondo** painted c-48, 50, 51, 53, 57, 62. **Simonson** r-50-54, 56. **B. Smith** r-51. **Starlin** c-34. **Williamson** r-50i.

CONAN THE ADVENTURER
Marvel Comics: June, 1994 - No. 14, July, 1995 ($1.50)

1-($2.50)-Embossed foil-c; Kayaran-a						3.00
2-14						2.50
2-Contents are Conan Classics #2 by mistake						2.50

CONAN THE BARBARIAN
Marvel Comics: Oct, 1970 - No. 275, Dec, 1993

	GD	VG	FN	VF	VF/NM	NM-
1-Origin/1st app. Conan (in comics) by Barry Smith; 1st brief app. Kull; #1-9 are 15¢ issues	20	40	60	146	261	375
2	8	16	24	56	93	130
3-(Low distribution in some areas)	13	26	39	90	160	230
4,5	7	14	21	47	76	105
6-9: 8-Hidden panel message, pg. 14. 9-Last 15¢-c	6	12	18	37	59	80
10,11 (25¢ 52 pg. giants): 10-Black Knight-r; Kull story by Severin						
	7	14	21	45	73	100
12,13: 12-Wrightson-c(i)	5	10	15	32	51	70
14,15-Elric app.	6	12	18	39	62	85
16,19,20: 16-Conan-r/Savage Tales #1	5	10	15	30	48	65
17,18-No Barry Smith-a	4	8	12	22	34	45
21,22: 22-Has reprint from #1	4	8	12	24	37	50
23-1st app. Red Sonja (2/73)	5	10	15	35	55	75
24-1st full Red Sonja story; last Smith-a	5	10	15	32	51	70
25-John Buscema-c/a begins	3	6	9	15	21	26
26-30	2	4	6	10	14	18
31-36,38-40	2	4	6	8	10	12
37-Neal Adams-c/a; last 20¢ issue; contains pull-out subscription form						
	3	6	9	16	22	28
41-43,46-50: 48-Origin retold	1	2	3	5	7	9
44,45-N. Adams-i(Crusty Bunkers). 45-Adams-c	2	4	6	8	10	12
51-57,59,60: 59-Origin Belit						6.00
58-2nd Belit app. (see Giant-Size Conan #1)	1	3	4	6	8	10
61-65-(Regular 25¢ editions)(4-8/76)						5.00
61-65-(30¢-c variants, limited distribution)	4	8	12	24	37	50
66-99: 68-Red Sonja story cont'd from Marvel Feature #7. 75-79-(Reg. 30¢-c). 84-Intro. Zula. 85-Origin Zula. 87-r/Savage Sword of Conan #3 in color						4.00
75-79-(35¢-c variants, limited distribution)	3	6	9	20	30	40
100-(52 pg. Giant)-Death of Belit						6.00
101-114						2.50
115-Double size						3.00
116-199,201-231,233-249: 116-r/Power Record Comic PR31. 244-Zula returns						2.50
200,232: 200-(52 pgs.). 232-Young Conan storyline begins; Conan is born						4.00
250-(60 pgs.)						3.50
251-270: 262-Adapted from R.E. Howard story						3.00
271-274						5.00
275-($2.50, 68 pgs.)-Final issue; painted-c (low print)	2	4	6	8	10	12
King Size 1(1973, 35¢)-Smith-r/#2,4; Smith-c	3	6	9	16	23	30
Annual 2(1976, 50¢)-New full length story	2	4	6	8	10	12
Annual 3,4: 3('78)-Chaykin/N. Adams-r/SSOC #2. 4('78)-New full length story						
	1	2	3	5	6	8
Annual 5,6: 5(1979)-New full length Buscema story & part-c. 6(1981)-Kane-c/a						5.00
Annual 7-12: 7('82)-Based on novel "Conan of the Isles" (new-a). 8(1984). 9(1984). 10(1986). 11(1986). 12(1987)						4.00
Special Edition 1 (Red Nails)						4.00
The Chronicles of Conan Vol. 1: Tower of the Elephant and Other Stories (Dark Horse, 2003, $15.95) r/#1-8; afterword by Roy Thomas						16.00
The Chronicles of Conan Vol. 2: Rogues in the House and Other Stories (Dark Horse, 2003, $15.95) r/#9-13,16; afterword by Roy Thomas						16.00
The Chronicles of Conan Vol. 3: The Monster of the Monoliths and Other Stories (Dark Horse, 2003, $15.95) r/#14,15,17-21; afterword by Roy Thomas						16.00
The Chronicles of Conan Vol. 4: The Song of Red Sonja and Other Stories (Dark Horse, 2004, $15.95) r/#23-26 & "Red Nails" from Savage Tales; afterword by Roy Thomas						16.00
The Chronicles of Conan Vol. 5: The Shadow in the Tomb and Other Stories (Dark Horse, 2004, $15.95) r/#27-34; afterword by Roy Thomas						16.00
The Chronicles of Conan Vol. 6: The Curse of the Skull and Other Stories (Dark Horse, 2004, $15.95) r/#35-42; afterword by Roy Thomas						16.00
The Chronicles of Conan Vol. 7: The Dweller in the Pool and Other Stories (Dark Horse, 2005, $15.95) r/#43-51; afterword by Roy Thomas						16.00
The Chronicles of Conan Vol. 8: Brothers of the Blade and Other Stories (Dark Horse, 2005, $16.95) r/#52-59; afterword by Roy Thomas						17.00
The Chronicles of Conan Vol. 9: Riders of the River-Dragons and Other Stories (Dark Horse, 11/05, $16.95) r/#60-63,65,69-71; afterword by Roy Thomas						17.00
The Chronicles of Conan Vol. 10: When Giants Walk the Earth and Other Stories (Dark Horse, 3/06, $16.95) r/#72-77,79-82; afterword by Roy Thomas						17.00
The Chronicles of Conan Vol. 11: The Dance of the Skull and Other Stories (Dark Horse, 2/07, $16.95) r/#82-86,88-90; afterword by Roy Thomas						17.00
The Chronicles of Conan Vol. 12: The King Beast of Abombi and Other Stories (Dark Horse, 7/07, $16.95) r/#91,93-100; afterword by Roy Thomas						17.00
The Chronicles of Conan Vol. 13: Whispering Shadows and Other Stories (Dark Horse, 12/07, $16.95) r/#92,100-107; afterword by Roy Thomas						17.00

Conan: River of Blood #1 © Conan Props.

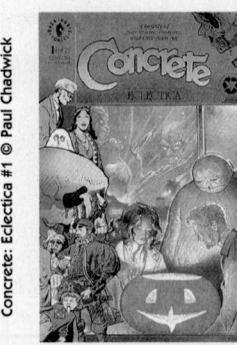

Concrete: Eclectica #1 © Paul Chadwick

Congo Bill #5 © DC

	GD 2.0	VG 4.0	FN 6.0	VF 8.0	VF/NM 9.0	NM- 9.2

CONAN THE BARBARIAN (Volume 2)
Marvel Comics: July, 1997 - No. 3, Oct, 1997 ($2.50, limited series)

1-3-Castellini-a ... 2.50

CONAN THE BARBARIAN MOVIE SPECIAL (Movie)
Marvel Comics Group: Oct, 1982 - No. 2, Nov, 1982

1,2-Movie adaptation; Buscema-a ... 3.00

CONAN THE BARBARIAN: THE USURPER
Marvel Comics: Dec, 1997 - No. 3, Feb, 1998 ($2.50, limited series)

1-3-Dixon-s ... 2.50

CONAN: THE BOOK OF THOTH
Dark Horse Comics: Mar, 2006 - No. 4, June, 2006 ($4.99, limited series)

1-4-Origin of Thoth-amon; Len Wein & Kurt Busiek-s/Kelley Jones-a/c ... 5.00
TPB (12/06, $17.95) r/#1-4 ... 18.00

CONAN THE DESTROYER (Movie)
Marvel Comics Group: Jan, 1985 - No. 2, Mar, 1985

1,2-r/Marvel Super Special ... 2.50

CONAN THE KING (Formerly King Conan)
Marvel Comics Group: No. 20, Jan, 1984 - No. 55, Nov, 1989

20-49 ... 3.00
50-54 ... 4.00
55-Last issue ... 6.00
NOTE: **Kaluta** c-20-23, 24i, 26, 27, 30, 50, 52. **Williamson** a-37i; c-37i, 38i.

CONAN: THE LEGEND (See Conan 2004 series)

CONAN: THE LORD OF THE SPIDERS
Marvel Comics: Mar, 1998 - No. 3, May, 1998 ($2.50, limited series)

1-3-Roy Thomas-s/Raffaele-a ... 2.50

CONAN THE SAVAGE
Marvel Comics: Aug, 1995 - No. 10, May, 1996 ($2.95, B&W, Magazine)

1-10: 1-Bisley-c. 4-vs. Malibu Comics' Rune. 5,10-Brereton-c ... 3.00

CONAN VS. RUNE (Also See Conan #4)
Marvel Comics: Nov, 1995 ($2.95, one-shot)

1-Barry Smith-c/a/scripts ... 3.00

CONCRETE (Also see Dark Horse Presents & Within Our Reach)
Dark Horse Comics: March, 1987 - No. 10, Nov, 1988 ($1.50, B&W)

1-Paul Chadwick-c/a in all	1	3	4	6	8	10

1-2nd print ... 3.00
2 ... 6.00
3-Origin ... 5.00
4-10 ... 4.00
A New Life 1 (1989, $2.95, B&W)-r/#3,4 plus new-a (11 pgs.) ... 3.00
Celebrates Earth Day 1990 ($3.50, 52 pgs.) ... 6.00
Color Special 1 (2/89, $2.95, 44 pgs.)-r/1st two Concrete apps. from Dark Horse Presents #1,2 plus new-a ... 6.00
Depths TPB (7/05, $12.95)-r/#1-5, stories from DHP #1,8,10,150; other short stories ... 13.00
Land And Sea 1 (2/89, $2.95, B&W)-r/#1,2 ... 6.00
Odd Jobs 1 (7/90, $3.50)-r/5,6 plus new-a ... 3.50
...Vol. 1: Depths ('05, $12.95, 9"x6") r/#1-5 & short stories ... 13.00
...Vol. 2: Heights ('05, $12.95, 9"x6") r/#6-10 & short stories ... 13.00
...Vol. 3: Fragile Creatures (1/06, $12.95, 9"x6") r/mini-series & short stories from DHP ... 13.00
...Vol. 4: Killer Smile (3/06, $12.95, 9"x6") r/mini-series & short stories from various ... 13.00
...Vol. 5: Think Like a Mountain (5/06, $12.95, 9"x6") r/mini-series & short stories ... 13.00
...Vol. 6: Strange Armor (7/06, $12.95, 9"x6") r/mini-series & short stories ... 13.00
...Vol. 7: The Human Dilemma (4/06, $12.95, 9"x6") r/mini-series ... 13.00

CONCRETE: (Title series), **Dark Horse Comics**

--**ECLECTICA**, 4/93 - No. 2, 5/93 ($2.95) 1,2 ... 3.00
--**FRAGILE CREATURE**, 6/91 - No. 4, 2/92 ($2.50) 1-4 ... 3.00
--**KILLER SMILE**, (Legend), 7/94 - No. 4, 10/94 ($2.9) 1-4 ... 3.00

--**STRANGE ARMOR**, 12/97 - No. 5, 5/98 ($2.95, color) 1-5-Chadwick-s/c/a; retells origin ... 3.00
--**THE HUMAN DILEMMA**, 12/04 - No. 6, 5/05 ($3.50)
1-6: Chadwick-a/c & scripts; Concrete has a child ... 3.50
--**THINK LIKE A MOUNTAIN**, (Legend), 3/96 - No. 6, 8/96 ($2.95)
1-6: Chadwick-a/scripts & Darrow-c in all ... 3.00

CONDORMAN (Walt Disney)
Whitman Publishing: Oct, 1981 - No. 3, Jan, 1982

1-3: 1,2-Movie adaptation; photo-c	1	3	4	6	8	10

CONEHEADS
Marvel Comics: June, 1994 - No. 4, 1994 ($1.75, limited series)

1-4 ... 2.50

CONFESSIONS ILLUSTRATED (Magazine)
E. C. Comics: Jan-Feb, 1956 - No. 2, Spring, 1956

1-Craig, Kamen, Wood, Orlando-a	28	56	84	162	256	350
2-Craig, Crandall, Kamen, Orlando-a	20	40	60	117	184	250

CONFESSIONS OF LOVE
Artful Publ.: Apr, 1950 - No. 2, July, 1950 (25¢, 7-1/4x5-1/4", 132 pgs.)

1-Bakerish-a	28	56	84	162	256	350
2-Art & text; Bakerish-a	16	32	48	94	147	200

CONFESSIONS OF LOVE (Formerly Startling Terror Tales #10; becomes Confessions of Romance No. 7 on)
Star Publications: No. 11, 7/52 - No. 14, 1/53; No. 4, 3/53- No. 6, 8/53

11-13; 12,13-Disbrow-a	15	30	45	90	140	190
14,5,6	14	28	42	78	112	145
4-Disbrow-a	14	28	42	81	118	155

NOTE: All have **L. B. Cole** covers.

CONFESSIONS OF ROMANCE (Formerly Confessions of Love)
Star Publications: No. 7, Nov, 1953 - No. 11, Nov, 1954

7	15	30	45	90	140	190
8	14	28	42	78	112	145
9-Wood-a	15	30	45	84	127	170
10,11-Disbrow-a	14	28	42	81	118	155

NOTE: All have **L. B. Cole** covers.

CONFESSIONS OF THE LOVELORN (Formerly Lovelorn)
American Comics Group (Regis Publ./Best Synd. Features): No. 52, Aug, 1954 - No. 114, June-July, 1960

52 (3-D effect)	29	58	87	167	264	360
53,55	10	20	30	58	79	100
54 (3-D effect)	29	58	87	167	264	360
56-Anti-communist propaganda story, 10 pgs; last pre-code (2/55)						
	14	28	42	76	108	140
57-90,100	8	16	24	42	54	65
91-Williamson-a	10	20	30	54	72	90
92-99,101-114	7	14	21	37	46	55

NOTE: **Whitney** a-most issues; c-52, 53. Painted c-106, 107.

CONFIDENTIAL DIARY (Formerly High School Confidential Diary; Three Nurses #18 on)
Charlton Comics: No. 12, May, 1962 - No. 17, Mar, 1963

12-17	3	6	9	15	21	26

CONGO BILL (See Action Comics & More Fun Comics #56)
National Periodical Publication: Aug-Sept, 1954 - No. 7, Aug-Sept, 1955

1 (Scarce)	181	362	543	1450	–	–
2,7 (Scarce)	121	242	363	965	–	–
3-6 (Scarce). 4-Last pre-code issue	95	190	285	760	–	–

NOTE: (Rarely found in fine to mint condition.) **Nick Cardy** c-1-7.

CONGO BILL
DC Comics (Vertigo): Oct, 1999 - No. 4, Jan, 2000 ($2.95, limited series)

1-4-Corben-c ... 3.00

CONGORILLA (Also see Actions Comics #224)
DC Comics: Nov, 1992 - No. 4, Feb, 1993 ($1.75, limited series)

1-4: 1,2-Brian Bolland-c ... 3.00

CONJURORS
DC Comics: Apr, 1999 - No. 3, Jun, 1999 ($2.95, limited series)

1-3-Elseworlds; Phantom Stranger app.; Barreto-c/a ... 3.00

CONNECTICUT YANKEE, A (See King Classics)

CONNOR HAWKE: DRAGON'S BLOOD (Also see Green Arrow titles)

Consumed #1 © Platinum Studios

CooCoo Comics #40 © STD

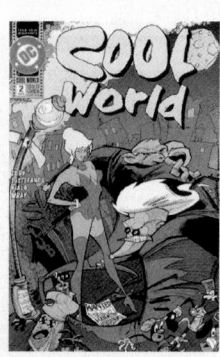

Cool World #2 © Paramount Picts.

	GD 2.0	VG 4.0	FN 6.0	VF 8.0	VF/NM 9.0	NM- 9.2

DC Comics: Jan, 2007 - No. 6, Jun, 2007 ($2.99, limited series)
1-6-Chuck Dixon-s/Derec Donovan-a/c 3.00

CONQUEROR, THE
Dell Publishing Co.: No., 690, Mar, 1956

Four Color 690-Movie, John Wayne photo-c	16	32	48	114	202	290

CONQUEROR COMICS
Albrecht Publishing Co.: Winter, 1945

nn	21	42	63	122	191	260

CONQUEROR OF THE BARREN EARTH (See The Warlord #63)
DC Comics: Feb, 1985 - No. 4, May, 1985 (Limited series)
1-4: Back-up series from Warlord 2.50

CONQUEST
Store Comics: 1953 (6¢)

1-Richard the Lion Hearted, Beowulf, Swamp Fox	7	14	21	35	43	50

CONQUEST
Famous Funnies: Spring, 1955

1-Crandall-a, 1 pg.; contains contents of 1953 ish.	5	10	15	22	26	30

CONSPIRACY
Marvel Comics: Feb, 1998 - No. 2, Mar, 1998 ($2.99, limited series)
1,2-Painted art by Korday/Abnett-s 3.00

CONSTANTINE (Also see Hellblazer)
DC Comics (Vertigo): 2005 (Based on the 2005 Keanu Reeves movie)
...: The Hellblazer Collection (2005, $14.95) Movie adaptation and r/#1, 27, 41; photo-c 15.00
...: The Official Movie Adaptation (2005, $6.95) Seagle-s/Randall-a/photo-c 7.00

CONSTRUCT
Caliber (New Worlds): 1996 - No. 6, 1997 ($2.95, B&W, limited series)
1-6: Paul Jenkins scripts 3.00

CONSUMED
Platinum Studios: July, 2007 - No. 4 ($2.99, limited series)
1,2-Linsner-c/Budd-a/Shumskas-Tait-s 3.00

CONTACT COMICS
Aviation Press: July, 1944 - No. 12, May, 1946

nn-Black Venus, Flamingo, Golden Eagle, Tommy Tomahawk begin						
	53	106	159	325	543	760
2-5: 3-Last Flamingo. 3,4-Black Venus by L. B. Cole. 5-The Phantom Flyer app.						
	40	80	120	237	379	520
6,11-Kurtzman's Black Venus; 11-Last Golden Eagle, last Tommy Tomahawk; Feldstein-a	46	92	138	281	466	650
7-10	40	80	120	235	368	500
12-Sky Rangers, Air Kids, Ace Diamond app.; L.B. Cole sci-fi cover						
	103	206	309	644	1072	1500

NOTE: *L. B. Cole a-3, 9; c-1-12. Giunta a-3. Hollingsworth a-5, 7, 10. Palais a-11, 12.*

CONTEMPORARY MOTIVATORS
Pendelum Press: 1977 - 1978 ($1.45, 5-3/8x8", 31 pgs., B&W)
14-3002 The Caine Mutiny; 14-3010 Banner in the Sky; 14-3029 God Is My Co-Pilot; 14-3037 Guadalcanal Diary; 14-3045 Hiroshima; 14-3053 Hot Rod; 14-3061 Just Dial a Number; 14-3088 The Diary of Anne Frank; 14-3096 Lost Horizon

		1	3	4	6	8	10

NOTE: *Also see Pendulum Illustrated Classics. Above may have been distributed the same.*

CONTEST OF CHAMPIONS (See Marvel Super-Hero...)
CONTEST OF CHAMPIONS II
Marvel Comics: Sept, 1999 - No. 5 ($2.50, limited series)
1-5-Claremont-s/Jimenez-a 2.50

CONTRACTORS
Eclipse Comics: June, 1987 ($2.00, B&W, one-shot)
1-Funny animal 2.25

CONTRACT WITH GOD, A
Baronet Publishing Co./Kitchen Sink Press: 1978 ($4.95/$7.95, B&W, graphic novel)

nn-Will Eisner-s/a		2	4	6	13	18	22
Reprint (DC Comics, 2000, $12.95)						13.00

CONVOCATIONS: A MAGIC THE GATHERING GALLERY
Acclaim Comics (Armada): Jan, 1996 ($2.50, one-shot)
1-pin-ups by various artists including Kaluta, Vess, and Dringenberg 2.50

COO COO COMICS (...the Bird Brain No. 57 on)

Nedor Publ. Co./Standard (Animated Cartoons): Oct, 1942 - No. 62, Apr, 1952

1-Origin/1st app. Super Mouse & begin series (cloned from Superman); the first funny animal super hero series (see Looney Tunes #5 for 1st funny animal super hero)						
	31	62	93	180	285	390
2	15	30	45	85	130	175
3-10: 10-(3/44)	11	22	33	60	83	105
11-33: 33-1 pg. Ingels-a	9	18	27	50	65	80
34-40,43-46,48-Text illos by Frazetta in all. 36-Super Mouse covers begin						
	11	22	33	64	90	115
41-Frazetta-a (6-pg. story & 3 text illos)	21	42	63	120	188	255
42,47-Frazetta-a & text illos.	15	30	45	86	133	180
49-(1/50)-3-D effect story; Frazetta text illo	14	28	42	76	108	140
50,51-3-D effect c only. 50-Frazetta text illo	13	26	39	72	101	130
52-62: 56-Last Supermouse?	8	16	24	42	54	65

"COOKIE" (Also see Topsy-Turvy)
Michel Publ./American Comics Group(Regis Publ.): Apr, 1946 - No. 55, Aug-Sept, 1955

1-Teen-age humor	22	44	66	126	198	270
2	13	26	39	74	105	135
3-10	10	20	30	58	79	100
11-20	9	18	27	50	65	80
21-23,26,28-30	8	16	24	40	50	60
24,25,27-Starlett O'Hara stories	8	16	24	42	54	65
31-34,37-48,50,52-55	7	14	21	35	43	50
35,36-Starlett O'Hara stories	8	16	24	40	50	60
49,51: 49-(6-7/54)-3-D effect-c/s. 51-(10-11/54) 8pg. TrueVision 3-D effect story						
	11	22	33	64	90	115

COOL CAT (Formerly Black Magic)
Prize Publications: V8#6, Mar-Apr, 1962 - V9#2, July-Aug, 1962

V8#6, nn(V9#1, 5-6/62), V9#2	3	6	9	16	23	30

COOL WORLD (Movie by Ralph Bakshi)
DC Comics: Apr, 1992 - No. 4, Sept, 1992 ($1.75, limited series)
1-4: Prequel to animated/live action movie. 1-Bakshi-c. Bill Wray inks in all 2.50
Movie Adaptation nn ('92, $3.50, 68pg.)-Bakshi-c 3.50

COPPER CANYON (See Fawcett Movie Comics)

COPS (TV)
DC Comics: Aug, 1988 - No. 15, Aug, 1989 ($1.00)
1 ($1.50, 52 pgs.)-Based on Hasbro Toys 3.00
2-15: 14-Orlando-c(p) 2.50

COPS: THE JOB
Marvel Comics: June, 1992 - No. 4, Sept, 1992 ($1.25, limited series)
1-4: All have Jusko scripts & Golden-c 2.50

CORBEN SPECIAL, A
Pacific Comics: May, 1984 (one-shot)
1-Corben-c/a; E.A. Poe adaptation 5.00

CORKY & WHITE SHADOW (Disney, TV)
Dell Publishing Co.: No. 707, May, 1956 (Mickey Mouse Club)

Four Color 707-Photo-c	7	14	21	47	76	105

CORLISS ARCHER (See Meet Corliss Archer)

CORMAC MAC ART (Robert E. Howard's...)
Dark Horse Comics: June - No. 4, 1990 ($1.95, B&W, mini-series)
1-4: All have Bolton painted-c; Howard adapts. 3.00

CORNY'S FETISH
Dark Horse Comics: Apr, 1998 ($4.95, B&W, one-shot)
1-Renée French-s/a; Bolland-c 5.00

CORPORAL RUSTY DUGAN (See Holyoke One-Shot #2)

CORPSES OF DR. SACOTTI, THE (See Ideal a Classical Comic)

CORSAIR, THE (See A-1 Comics No. 5, 7, 10 under Texas Slim)

CORTEZ AND THE FALL OF THE AZTECS
Tome Press: 1993 ($2.95, B&W, limited series)
1 .... 3.00

CORUM: THE BULL AND THE SPEAR (See Chronicles Of Corum)
First Comics: Jan, 1989 - No. 4, July, 1989 ($1.95)
1-4: Adapts Michael Moorcock's novel 2.50

COSMIC BOOK, THE
Ace Comics: Dec, 1986 - No. 1, 1987 ($1.95)

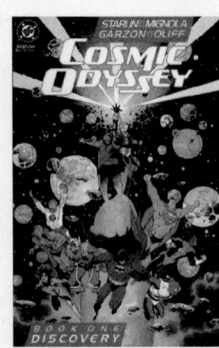

Cosmic Odyssey #1 © DC

Countdown #39 © DC

Coven #6 © Awesome Ent.

	GD 2.0	VG 4.0	FN 6.0	VF 8.0	VF/NM 9.0	NM- 9.2		GD 2.0	VG 4.0	FN 6.0	VF 8.0	VF/NM 9.0	NM- 9.2

1,2: 1-(44pgs.)-Wood, Toth-a. 2-(B&W)   2.25

COSMIC BOY (Also see The Legion of Super-Heroes)
DC Comics: Dec, 1986 - No. 4, Mar, 1987 (limited series)
1-4: Legends tie-ins all issues   2.50

COSMIC GUARD
Devil's Due Publ.: Aug, 2004 - No. 6, Dec, 2005 ($2.99)
1-6-Jim Starlin-s/a   3.00

COSMIC HEROES
Eternity/Malibu Graphics: Oct, 1988 - No. 11, Dec, 1989 ($1.95, B&W)
1-11: Reprints 1934-1936's Buck Rogers newspaper strips #1-728   2.25

COSMIC ODYSSEY
DC Comics: 1988 - No. 4, 1988 ($3.50, limited series, squarebound)
1-4: Reintro. New Gods into DC continuity; Superman, Batman, Green Lantern (John Stewart) app.; Starlin scripts, Mignola-c/a in all. 2-Darkseid merges Demon & Jason Blood (separated in Demon limited series #4)   5.00
Trade paperback-r/#1-4.   20.00

COSMIC POWERS
Marvel Comics: Mar, 1994 - No. 6, Aug, 1994 ($2.50, limited series)
1-6: 1-Ron Lim-c/a(p). 1,2-Thanos app. 2-Terrax. 3-Ganymede & Jack of Hearts app.   2.50

COSMIC POWERS UNLIMITED
Marvel Comics: May, 1995 - No. 5, May, 1996 ($3.95, quarterly)
1-5   4.00

COSMIC RAY
Image Comics: June, 1999 - No. 2 ($2.95, B&W)
1,2-Steven Blue-s/a   3.00

COSMIC SLAM
Ultimate Sports Entertainment: 1999 ($3.95, one-shot)
1-McGwire, Sosa, Bagwell, Justice battle aliens; Sienkiewicz-c   4.00

COSMO CAT (Becomes Sunny #10 on; also see All Top & Wotalife Comics)
Fox Publications/Green Publ. Co./Norlen Mag.: July-Aug, 1946 - No. 10, Oct, 1947; 1957; 1959

	GD	VG	FN	VF	VF/NM	NM-
1	27	54	81	158	249	340
2	15	30	45	84	127	170
3-Origin (11-12/46)	18	36	54	107	169	230
4-Robot-c	14	28	42	76	108	140
5-10	11	22	33	60	83	105
2-4(1957-Green Publ. Co.)	6	12	18	27	33	38
2-4(1959-Norlen Mag.)	5	10	15	23	28	32
I.W. Reprint #1	2	4	6	11	16	20

COSMO THE MERRY MARTIAN (Radio Comics)
Archie Publications: Sept, 1958 - No. 6, Oct, 1959

	GD	VG	FN	VF	VF/NM	NM-
1-Bob White-a in all	15	30	45	84	127	170
2-6	11	22	33	60	83	105

COTTON WOODS
Dell Publishing Co.: No. 837, Sept, 1957

	GD	VG	FN	VF	VF/NM	NM-
Four Color 837	4	8	12	24	37	50

COUGAR, THE (Cougar No. 2)
Seaboard Periodicals (Atlas): April, 1975 - No. 2, July, 1975

	GD	VG	FN	VF	VF/NM	NM-
1,2: 1-Vampire; Adkins-a(p). 2-Cougar origin; werewolf-s; Buckler-c(p)	1	2	3	5	7	9

COUNTDOWN (See Movie Classics)

COUNTDOWN
DC Comics (WildStorm): June, 2000 - No. 8, Jan, 2001 ($2.95)
1-8-Mariotte-s/Lopresti-a   3.00

COUNTDOWN (Continued from 52 weekly series)
DC Comics: No. 51, July, 2007 - No. 0 ($2.99, weekly, limited series) (issue #s go in reverse)
51-Gatefold wraparound-c by Andy Kubert; Duela Dent killed; the Monitors app.   3.00
50-39: 50-Joker-c. 48-Lightray dies. 47-Mary Marvel gains Black Adam's powers. 46-Intro. Forerunner. 43-Funeral for Bart Allen. 39-Karate Kid-c   3.00

COUNTDOWN TO ADVENTURE
DC Comics: Oct, 2007 - No. 8 ($3.99, limited series)
1-Adam Strange, Animal Man and Starfire app.; origin of Forerunner   4.00

COUNTDOWN TO INFINITE CRISIS (See DC Countdown)

COUNT DUCKULA (TV)
Marvel Comics: Nov, 1988 - No. 15, Jan, 1991 ($1.00)
1,8: 1-Dangermouse back-up. 8-Geraldo Rivera photo-c/& app.; Sienkiewicz-a(i)   5.00
2-7,9-15: Dangermouse back-ups in all   4.00

COUNT OF MONTE CRISTO, THE
Dell Publishing Co.: No. 794, May, 1957

	GD	VG	FN	VF	VF/NM	NM-
Four Color 794-Movie, Buscema-a	8	16	24	56	93	130

COUP D'ETAT (Oneshots)
DC Comics (WildStorm): April, 2004 ($2.95, weekly limited series)
...: Sleeper 1 (part 1 of 4) Jim Lee-a; 2 covers by Lee and Bermejo   3.00
...: Stormwatch 1 (part 2 of 4) D'Anda-a; 2 covers by D'Anda and Bermejo   3.00
...: Wildcats Version 3.0 1 (part 3 of 4) Garza-a; 2 covers by Garza and Bermejo   3.00
...: The Authority 1 (part 4 of 4) Portacio-a; 2 covers by Portacio and Bermejo   3.00
...: Afterword 1 (5/04) Profile pages and prelude stories for Sleeper & Wetworks   3.00
TPB (2004, $12.95) r/series and profile pages from Afterword   13.00

COURAGE COMICS
J. Edward Slavin: 1945

	GD	VG	FN	VF	VF/NM	NM-
1,2,77	14	28	42	80	115	150

COURTNEY CRUMRIN & THE COVEN OF MYSTICS
Oni Press: Dec, 2002 - No. 4, March, 2003 ($2.95, B&W, limited series)
1-4-Ted Naifeh-s/a   3.00
TPB (9/03, $11.95, 8" x 5-1/2") r/#1-4   12.00

COURTNEY CRUMRIN & THE NIGHT THINGS (Also see Promotional Section for FCBD Ed.)
Oni Press: Mar, 2002 - No. 4, June, 2002 ($2.95, B&W, limited series)
1-4-Ted Naifeh-s/a   3.00
TPB (12/02, $11.95) r/#1-4   12.00

COURTNEY CRUMRIN IN THE TWILIGHT KINGDOM
Oni Press: Dec, 2003 - No. 4, May, 2004 ($2.99, B&W, limited series)
1-4-Ted Naifeh-s/a   3.00
TPB (9/04, $11.95, digest-size) r/#1-4   12.00

COURTNEY CRUMRIN TALES
Oni Press: July, 2005 ($5.95, B&W, series of one-shots)
... Portrait of the Warlock as a Young Man (7/05) origin Uncle Aloysius; Ted Naifeh-s/a   6.00

COURTSHIP OF EDDIE'S FATHER (TV)
Dell Publishing Co.: Jan, 1970 - No. 2, May, 1970

	GD	VG	FN	VF	VF/NM	NM-
1-Bill Bixby photo-c on both	6	12	18	37	59	80
2	4	8	12	24	37	50

COVEN
Awesome Entertainment: Aug, 1997 - No. 5, Mar, 1998 ($2.50)

	GD	VG	FN	VF	VF/NM	NM-
Preview	1	2	3	5	6	8
1-Loeb-s/Churchill-a; three covers by Churchill, Liefeld, Pollina	1	2	3	5	6	8
1-Fan Appreciation Ed.(3/98); new Churchill-c						3.00
1+ :Includes B&W art from Kaboom	1	3	4	6	8	10
2-Regular-c w/leaping Fantom						6.00
2-Variant-c w/circle of candles	1	2	3	5	6	8
3-6-Contains flip book preview of ReGex						3.00
3-White variant-c	1	2	3	4	5	7
3,4: 3-Halloween wraparound-c. 4-Purple variant-c						3.00
...Black & White (9/98) Short stories						3.00
...Fantom Special (2/98) w/sketch pages						5.00

COVEN
Awesome Entertainment: Jan, 1999 - No. 3, June, 1999 ($2.50)
1-3: 1-Loeb-s/Churchill-a; 6 covers by various. 2-Supreme-c/app. 3-Flip book w/Kaboom preview   2.50
... Dark Origins (7/99, 2.50) w/Lionheart gallery   2.50

COVENANT, THE
Image Comics (Top Cow): 2005 ($9.99, squarebound, one-shot)
nn-Tone Rodriguez/Aron Coleite-s   10.00

COVERED WAGONS, HO (Disney, TV)
Dell Publishing Co.: No. 814, June, 1957 (Donald Duck)

	GD	VG	FN	VF	VF/NM	NM-
Four Color 814-Mickey Mouse app.	5	10	15	35	55	75

COWBOY ACTION (Formerly Western Thrillers No. 1-4; Becomes Quick-Trigger Western No. 12 on)
Atlas Comics (ACI): No. 5, March, 1955 - No. 11, March, 1956

Cowgirl Romances #9 © FH

Cow Puncher #5 © AVON

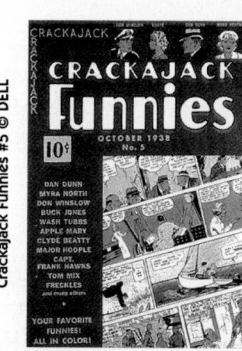

Crackajack Funnies #5 © DELL

	GD 2.0	VG 4.0	FN 6.0	VF 8.0	VF/NM 9.0	NM- 9.2
5	14	28	42	76	108	140
6-10: 6-8-Heath-c	10	20	30	54	72	90
11-Williamson-a (4 pgs.); Baker-a	11	22	33	60	83	105

NOTE: Ayers a-8. Drucker a-6. Maneely c/a-5, 6. Severin c-10. Shores a-7.

COWBOY COMICS (Star Ranger #12, Stories #14)(Star Ranger Funnies #15)
Centaur Publishing Co.: No. 13, July, 1938 - No. 14, Aug, 1938

	GD 2.0	VG 4.0	FN 6.0	VF 8.0	VF/NM 9.0	NM- 9.2
13-(Rare)-Ace and Deuce, Lyin Lou, Air Patrol, Aces High, Lee Trent, Trouble Hunters begin	126	252	378	788	1307	1825
14-Filchock-c	86	172	258	538	894	1250

NOTE: Guardineer a-13, 14. Gustavson a-13, 14.

COWBOY IN AFRICA (TV)
Gold Key: Mar, 1968

	GD 2.0	VG 4.0	FN 6.0	VF 8.0	VF/NM 9.0	NM- 9.2
1(10219-803)-Chuck Connors photo-c	4	8	12	26	41	55

COWBOY LOVE (Becomes Range Busters?)
Fawcett Publications/Charlton Comics No. 28 on: 7/49 - V2#10, 6/50; No. 11, 1951; No. 28, 2/55 - No. 31, 8/55

	GD 2.0	VG 4.0	FN 6.0	VF 8.0	VF/NM 9.0	NM- 9.2
V1#1-Rocky Lane photo back-c	16	32	48	89	137	185
2	8	16	24	44	57	70
V1#3,4,6 (12/49)	8	16	24	40	50	60
5-Bill Boyd photo back-c (11/49)	9	18	27	47	61	75
V2#7-Williamson/Evans-a	10	20	30	54	72	90
V2#8-11	7	14	21	35	43	50
V1#28 (Charlton)-Last precode (2/55) (Formerly Romantic Story?)	6	12	18	31	38	45
V1#29-31 (Charlton; becomes Sweetheart Diary #32 on)	6	12	18	28	34	40

NOTE: Powell a-10. Marcus Swayze a-2, 3. Photo c-1-11. No. 1-3, 5-7, 9, 10 are 52 pgs.

COWBOY ROMANCES (Young Men No. 4 on)
Marvel Comics (IPC): Oct, 1949 - No. 3, Mar, 1950 (All photo-c & 52 pgs.)

	GD 2.0	VG 4.0	FN 6.0	VF 8.0	VF/NM 9.0	NM- 9.2
1-Photo-c	23	46	69	132	209	285
2-William Holden, Mona Freeman "Streets of Laredo" photo-c	16	32	48	94	147	200
3-Photo-c	15	30	45	84	127	170

COWBOYS 'N' INJUNS (...and Indians on No. 6 on)
Compix No. 1-5/Magazine Enterprises No. 6 on: 1946 - No. 5, 1947; No. 6, 1949 - No. 8, 1952

	GD 2.0	VG 4.0	FN 6.0	VF 8.0	VF/NM 9.0	NM- 9.2
1-Funny animal western	14	28	42	82	121	160
2-5-All funny animal western	10	20	30	54	72	90
6(A-1 23)-Half violent, half funny; Ayers-a	13	26	39	74	105	135
7(A-1 41, 1950), 8(A-1 48)-All funny	9	18	27	47	61	75
I.W. Reprint No. 1,7 (Reprinted in Canada by Superior, No. 7)	2	4	6	11	16	20
Super Reprint #10 (1963)	2	4	6	11	16	20

COWBOY WESTERN COMICS (TV)(Formerly Jack In The Box; Becomes Space Western No. 40-45 & Wild Bill Hickok & Jingles No. 68 on; title:Cowboy Western Heroes No. 47 & 48; Cowboy Western No. 49 on)
Charlton (Capitol Stories): No. 17, 7/48 - No. 39, 8/52; No. 46, 10/53; No. 47, 12/53; No. 48, Spr, '54; No. 5-6/54 - No. 67, 3/58 (nn 40-45)

	GD 2.0	VG 4.0	FN 6.0	VF 8.0	VF/NM 9.0	NM- 9.2
17-Jesse James, Annie Oakley, Wild Bill Hickok begin; Texas Rangers app.	17	34	51	98	154	210
18,19-Orlando-c/a. 18-Paul Bunyan begins. 19-Wyatt Earp story	11	22	33	62	86	110
20-25: 21-Buffalo Bill story. 22-Texas Rangers-c/story. 24-Joel McCrea photo-c & adaptation from movie "Three Faces West". 25-James Craig photo-c & adaptation from movie "Northwest Stampede".	10	20	30	54	72	90
26-George Montgomery photo-c and adaptation from movie "Indian Scout"; 1 pg. bio on Will Rogers	11	22	33	62	86	110
27-Sunset Carson photo-c & adapts movie "Sunset Carson Rides Again" plus 1 other Sunset Carson story	43	86	129	262	431	600
28-Sunset Carson line drawn-c; adapts movies "Battling Marshal" & "Fighting Mustangs" starring Sunset Carson	23	46	69	132	209	285
29-Sunset Carson photo-c; adapts movies "Rio Grande" with Sunset Carson & "Winchester '73" w/James Stewart plus 5 pg. life history of Sunset Carson featuring Tom Mix	23	46	69	132	209	285
30-Sunset Carson photo-c; adapts movie "Deadline" starring Sunset Carson plus 1 other Sunset Carson story	43	86	129	262	431	600
31-34,38,39,47-50 (no #40-45): 50-Golden Arrow, Rocky Lane & Blackjack (r?) stories	9	18	27	47	61	75
35,36-Sunset Carson-c/stories (2 in each). 35-Inside front-c photo of Sunset Carson plus photo on-c	23	46	69	132	209	285
37-Sunset Carson stories (2)	17	34	51	98	154	210

	GD 2.0	VG 4.0	FN 6.0	VF 8.0	VF/NM 9.0	NM- 9.2
46-(Formerly Space Western)-Space western story	17	34	51	98	154	210
51-57,59-66: 51-Golden Arrow(r?) & Monte Hale-r renamed Rusty Hall. 53,54-Tom Mix-r. 55-Monte Hale story(r?). 66-Young Eagle story. 67-Wild Bill Hickok and Jingles-c/story	7	14	21	37	46	55
58-(1/56, 15¢, 68 pgs.)-Wild Bill Hickok, Annie Oakley & Jesse James stories; Forgione-a	9	18	27	47	61	75
67-(15¢, 68 pgs.)-Williamson/Torres-a, 5 pgs.	9	18	27	52	69	85

NOTE: Many issues trimmed 1" shorter. Maneely a-67(5). Inside front/back photo c-29.

COWGIRL ROMANCES
Marvel Comics (CCC): No. 28, Jan, 1950 (52 pgs.)

	GD 2.0	VG 4.0	FN 6.0	VF 8.0	VF/NM 9.0	NM- 9.2
28(#1)-Photo-c	21	42	63	122	191	260

COWGIRL ROMANCES
Fiction House Magazines: 1950 - No. 12, Winter, 1952-53 (No. 1-3: 52 pgs.)

	GD 2.0	VG 4.0	FN 6.0	VF 8.0	VF/NM 9.0	NM- 9.2
1-Kamen-a	40	80	120	240	383	525
2	20	40	60	117	184	250
3-5: 5-12-Whitman-c (most)	17	34	51	98	154	210
6-9,11,12	16	32	48	94	147	200
10-Frazetta?/Williamson?-a; Kamen?/Baker-a; r/Mitzi story from Movie Comics #4 w/all new dialogue	31	62	93	178	282	385

COW PUNCHER (...Comics)
Avon Periodicals: Jan, 1947; No. 2, Sept, 1947 - No. 7, 1949

	GD 2.0	VG 4.0	FN 6.0	VF 8.0	VF/NM 9.0	NM- 9.2
1-Clint Cortland, Texas Ranger, Kit West, Pioneer Queen begin; Kubert-a; Alabam stories begin	43	86	129	262	431	600
2-Kubert, Kamen/Feldstein-a; Kamen-c	38	76	114	216	343	470
3-5,7- 3-Kiefer story	27	54	81	156	246	335
6-Opium drug mention story; bondage, headlight-c; Reinman-a	35	70	105	201	318	435

COWPUNCHER
Realistic Publications: 1953 (nn) (Reprints Avon's No. 2)

	GD 2.0	VG 4.0	FN 6.0	VF 8.0	VF/NM 9.0	NM- 9.2
nn-Kubert-a	11	22	33	64	90	115

COWSILLS, THE (See Harvey Pop Comics)

COW SPECIAL, THE
Image Comics (Top Cow): Spring-Summer 2000; 2001 ($2.95)

1-Previews upcoming Top Cow projects; Yancy Butler photo-c		3.00
Vol. 2 #1-Witchblade-c; previews and interviews		3.00

COYOTE
Marvel Comics (Epic Comics): June, 1983 - No. 16, Mar, 1986

1-10,15: 7-10-Ditko-a		2.50
11-1st McFarlane-a.		6.00
12-14,16: 12-14-McFarlane-a. 14-Badger x-over. 16-Reagan c/app.		3.00
Coyote Collection Vol. 1 (2005, $14.99) reprints from Coyote #1-7 & Scorpio Rose #1,2 plus Rogers layout pages for unpublished #3; Englehart intro.		15.00
Coyote Collection Vol. 2 (2005, $12.99) reprints from Coyote #1-4		13.00
Coyote Collection Vol. 3 (2006, $12.99) reprints from Coyote #5-8		13.00
Coyote Collection Vol. 4 (2007, $14.99) reprints from Coyote #9-12		15.00
Coyote Collection Vol. 5 (2007, $12.99) reprints from Coyote #13-16		13.00

CRACKAJACK FUNNIES (Also see The Owl)
Dell Publishing Co.: June, 1938 - No. 43, Jan, 1942

	GD 2.0	VG 4.0	FN 6.0	VF 8.0	VF/NM 9.0	NM- 9.2
1-Dan Dunn, Freckles, Myra North, Wash Tubbs, Apple Mary, The Nebbs, Don Winslow, Tom Mix, Buck Jones, Major Hoople, Clyde Beatty, Boots begin	235	470	705	1469	2435	3400
2	90	180	270	563	932	1300
3	66	132	198	413	682	950
4	50	100	150	305	503	700
5-Nude woman on cover	52	104	156	317	521	725
6-8,10: 8-Speed Bolton begins (1st app.)	41	82	123	256	416	575
9-(3/39)-Red Ryder strip-r begin by Harman; 1st app. in comics & 1st cover app.	186	372	558	1163	1932	2700
11-14	80	160	240	235	368	500
15-Tarzan text feature begins by Burroughs (9/39); not in #26,35	41	82	123	252	406	560
16-24: 18-Stratosphere Jim begins (1st app., 12/39). 23-Ellery Queen begins plus-c (1st comic book app., 5/40)	32	64	96	186	293	400
25-The Owl begins (1st app., 7/40); in new costume #26 by Frank Thomas (also see Popular Comics #72)	79	158	237	494	822	1150
26-30: 28-Part Owl-c	53	106	159	323	529	735
31-Owl covers begin, end #42	53	106	159	326	543	760
32-Origin Owl Girl	58	116	174	363	599	835
33-38: 36-Last Tarzan issue. 37-Cyclone & Midge begin (1st app.)						

Crack Comics #13 © QUA

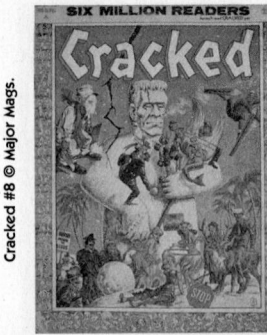

Cracked #8 © Major Mags.

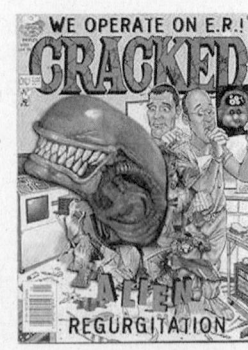

Cracked #323 © Major Mags.

	GD 2.0	VG 4.0	FN 6.0	VF 8.0	VF/NM 9.0	NM- 9.2
	52	104	156	317	521	735
39-Andy Panda begins (intro/1st app., 9/41)	61	122	183	381	633	885
40-42: 42-Last Owl-c.	40	80	120	235	368	500
43-Terry & the Pirates-r	30	60	90	174	275	375

NOTE: *McWilliams* art in most issues.

CRACK COMICS (Crack Western No. 63 on)
Quality Comics Group: May, 1940 - No. 62, Sept, 1949

1-Origin & 1st app. The Black Condor by Lou Fine, Madame Fatal, Red Torpedo, Rock Bradden & The Space Legion; The Clock, Alias the Spider (by Gustavson), Wizard Wells, & Ned Brant begin; Powell-a; Note: Madame Fatal is a man dressed as a woman						
	463	926	1389	3241	5671	8100
2	221	442	663	1381	2291	3200
3	152	304	456	950	1575	2200
4	121	242	363	756	1253	1750
5-10: 5-Molly The Model begins. 10-Tor, the Magic Master begins						
	91	182	273	569	947	1325
11-20: 13-1 pg. J. Cole-a. 15-1st app. Spitfire	81	162	243	506	841	1175
21-24: 23-Pen Miller begins; continued from National Comics #22. 24-Last Fine Black Condor						
	64	128	192	400	663	925
25,26: 26-Flag-c	48	96	144	293	484	675
27-(1/43)-Intro & origin Captain Triumph by Alfred Andriola (Kerry Drake artist) & begin series						
	90	180	270	563	932	1300
28-30	41	82	123	250	400	550
31-39: 31-Last Black Condor	24	48	72	139	220	300
40-46	17	34	51	98	154	210
47-57,59,60-Capt. Triumph by Crandall	18	36	54	105	165	225
58,61,62-Last Captain Triumph	15	30	45	84	127	170

NOTE: *Black Condor* by *Fine*: No. 1, 2, 5, 6, 8, 10-24; by *Sultan*: No. 3, 7; by *Fugitani*: No. 9. *Cole* a-34. *Crandall* a-61(unsigned); c-48, 49, 51-61. *Guardineer* a-17. *Gustavson* a-1, 2, 4, 7, 13, 17, 23. *McWilliams* a-15-27. *Black Condor* c-2, 4, 6, 8, 10, 12, 14, 16, 18, 20-26. *Capt. Triumph* c-27-62. *The Clock* c-1, 3, 5, 7, 9, 11, 13, 15, 17, 19.

CRACK COMICS
Quality Comics: May 1940

1-Ashcan comic, not distributed to newsstands, only for in-house use. Cover art is the same as published version of Crack Comics #1with exception of text panel on bottom left of cover. A CGC certified 4.0 copy sold for $1,495 in 2005.						

CRACKED (Magazine) (Satire) (Also see The 3-D Zone #19)
Major Magazines(#1-212)/Globe Communications(#213-346/American Media #347 on):
Feb-Mar, 1958 - Present

1-One pg. Williamson-a; Everett-c; Gunsmoke-s	17	34	51	126	223	320
2-1st Shut-Ups & Bonus Cut-Outs; Superman parody-c by Severin (his 1st cover on the title)						
Frankenstein-s	9	18	27	63	107	150
3-5	7	14	21	47	76	105
6-10: 7-Reprints 1st 6 covers on-c. 8-Frankenstein-c. 10-Wolverton-c						
	6	12	18	37	59	80
11-12, 13(nn,3/60),	5	10	15	32	51	70
14-Kirby-a	6	12	18	37	59	80
15-17, 18(nn,2/61), 19,20	5	10	15	30	48	65
21-27(11/62), 27(No.28, 2/63; mis-#d), 29(5/63)	4	8	12	26	41	55
30-40(11/64): 37-Beatles and Superman cameos	4	8	12	22	34	45
41-45,47-56,59,60: 47,49,52-Munsters. 51-Beatles inside-c. 59-Laurel and Hardy photos						
	3	6	9	18	27	35
46,57,58: 46,58-Man From U.N.C.L.E. 46-Beatles. 57-Rolling Stones						
	3	6	9	19	29	38
61-80: 62-Beatles cameo. 69-Batman, Superman app. 70-(8/68) Elvis cameo.						
71-Garrison's Gorillas; W.C. Fields photos	3	6	9	15	21	26
81-99: 99-Alfred E. Neuman c/s	2	4	6	13	18	22
100	3	6	9	17	25	32
101-119: 104-Godfather-c/s. 108-Archie Bunker-s. 112,119-Kung Fu (TV). 113-Tarzan-s. 115-MASH. 117-Cannon. 118-The Sting-c/s	2	4	6	9	13	16
120(12/74) Six Million Dollar Man-c/s; Ward-a	2	4	6	11	16	20
121,122,124-126,128-133,136-140: 121-American Graffiti. 122-Korak-c/s. 124,131-Godfather-c/s. 128-Capone-c. 129,131-Jaws. 132-Baretta-c/s. 133-Space 1999. 136-Laverne and Shirley/Fonz-c. 137-Travolta/Kotter-c/s. 138-Travolta/Laverne and Shirley/ Fonz-c. 139-Barney Miller-c/s. 140-King Kong-c/s; Fonz-s						
	2	4	6	9	13	16
123-Planet of the Apes-c/s; Six Million Dollar Man	2	4	6	11	16	20
127,134,135: 127-Star Trek-c/s; Ward-a. 134-Fonz-c/s. 135-Starsky and Hutch. 135-Bionic Woman-c/s; Ward-a	2	4	6	10	14	18
141,151-Charlie's Angels-c/s. 151-Frankenstein	2	4	6	11	16	22
142,143,150,152-155,157: 142-MASH-c/s. 143-Rocky-c/s; King Kong-s. 150-(5/78) Close Encounters-c/s. 152-Close Enc./Star Wars-c/s. 153-Close Enc./Fonz-c/s. 154-Jaws II-c/s; Star Wars. 155-Star Wars/Fonz-c						
	2	4	6	9	14	18
144,149,156,158-160: 144-Fonz/Happy Days-c. 149-Star Wars/Six Mil.$ Man-c/s.						

	GD 2.0	VG 4.0	FN 6.0	VF 8.0	VF/NM 9.0	NM- 9.2
156-Grease/Travolta-c. 158-Mork & Mindy. 159-Battlestar Galactica-c/s; MASH-s.						
160-Superman-c/s	2	4	6	10	14	18
145,147-Both have insert postcards: 145-Fonz/Rocky/L&S-c/s. 147-Star Wars-s; Farrah photo page (missing postcards-1/2 price)	3	6	9	14	19	24
146,148: 46-Star Wars-c/s with stickers insert (missing stickers-1/2 price). 148-Star Wars-c/s with inside-c color poster	3	6	9	16	22	28
161,170-Ward-a: 161-Mork & Mindy-c/s. 170-Dukes of Hazzard-c/s						
	2	4	6	8	10	12
162,165-168,171,172,175-178,180-Ward-a: 162-Sherlock Holmes-s. 165-Dracula-c/s. 167-Mork-c/s. 168,175-MASH-s. 168-Mork-s. 172-Dukes of Hazzard/CHiPs-c/s. 176-Barney Miller-c/s				6	8	10
163,179:163-Postcard insert; Mork & Mindy-c/s. 179-Insult cards insert; Popeye, Dukes of Hazzard-c/s	3	6	9	13	18	22
164,169,173,174: 164-Alien movie-c/s; Mork & Mindy-c. 169-Star Trek. 173,174-Star Wars- Empire Strikes Back. 173-SW poster	2	4	6	9	12	15
181,182,185-191,193,194,196-198-most Ward-a: 182-MASH-c/s. 185-Dukes of Hazzard-c/s; Jefferson. 187-Love Boat. 188-Fall Guy-c. 189-Fonz/Happy Days-c. 190,194-MASH-s. 191-Magnum P.I./Rocky-c; Magnum-s. 193-Knight Rider-s. 196-Dukes of Hazzard/Knight Rider-c/s. 198-Jaws III-c/s; Fall Guy-s	1	2	3	5	7	9
183,184,192,195,199,200-Ward-a in all: 183-Superman-c/s. 184-Star Trek-c/s. 192-E.T.-c/s. 195-Rocky-c. 195-E.T.-c/s. 199-Jabba-c/s; Star Wars-s. 200-(12/83)						
	1	3	6	8	10	
201,203,210-A-Team-s						6.00
202,204-206,211-224,226,227,230-233: 202-Knight Rider-s. 204-Magnum P.I.; A-Team-s. 206-Michael Jackson/Mr. T-c/s. 212-Prince-s; Cosby-s. 213-Monsters issue-c/s. 215-Hulk Hogan/Mr. T-c/s. 216-Miami Vice-s; James Bond-s. 217-Rambo-c; Cosby-s; A-Team-s. 218-Rocky-c/s. 219-Arnold/Commando-c/s; Rocky-s; Godzilla. 220-Rocky-c/s. 221-Stephen King app. 223-Miami Vice-s. 224-Cosby-s. 226-29th Anniv.; Tarzan-s; Aliens-s; Family Ties-s. 227-Cosby, Family Ties. 230-Monkees-s; Elvis on-c; 232-Alf, Cheers, Street Hawk-s. 233-Superman/James Bond-c/s; Robocop, Predator-s						5.00
207-209,225,234: 207-Michael Jackson-s. 208-Indiana Jones-c/s. 209-MichaelJackson/ Gremlins-c/s; Star Trek III-s. 225-Schwarzenegger/Stallone/G.I. Joe-c/s. 234-Don Martin-a begins; Batman/Robocop/Clint Eastwood-c/s						6.00
228,229: 228-Star Trek-c/s; Alf, Pee Wee Herman-s. 229-Monsters issue-c/s; centerfold with many superheroes						6.00
235,239,243,249: 235-1st Martin-c; Star Trek:TNG-s; Alf-s. 239-Beetlejuice-c/s; Mike Tyson-s. 243-X-Men and other heroes app. 249-Batman/Indiana Jones/Ghostbusters-c/s						6.00
236,244,245,248: 236-Madonna/Stallone-c/s; Twilight Zone-s. 244-Elvis-c/s; Martin-c. 245-Roger Rabbit-c/s. 248-Batman issue						6.00
237,238,240-242,246,247,250: 237-Robocop-s. 238-Rambo-c/s; Star Trek-s. 242-Dirty Harry-s, Ward-a. 246-Alf-s; Star Trek-s. 247-Star Trek-s. 250-Batman/Ghostbusters-c						4.00
251-253,255,256,259,261-265,275-278,281,284,286-297,299: 252-Star Trek-s. 253-Back to the Future-c/s. 255-TMNT-c/s. 256-TMNT-c/s. 259-Die Hard II, Robocop-s. 261-TMNT, Twin Peaks-s. 262-Rocky-c/s; Rocky Horror-s. 265-TMNT-s. 276-Aliens III, Batman-s. 277-Clinton-c. 284-Bart Simpson-c; 90210-s. 297-Van Damme-s/photo-c. 299-Dumb & Dumber-c/s						4.00
254,257,266,267,272,280,282,285,298,300: 254-Back to the Future, Punisher-s; Wolverton-a, Batman-s, Ward-a. 257-Batman, Simpsons-s; Spider-Man and other heroes app. 266-Terminator-s. 267-Toons-c/s. 272-Star Trek VI-s. 280-Swimsuit issue. 282-Cheers-c/s. 285-Jurassic Park-c/s. 298-Swimsuit issue; Martin-c. 300-(8/95) Brady Bunch-c/s						5.00
258,260,264,279,283: 258-Simpsons-c/s. 260-Back to the Future-s. 260-Spider-Man-c/s; Simpsons-s. 274-Batman-c/s. 279-Madonna-c/s. 283-Jurassic Park-c/s; Wolverine app. inside back-c						5.00
301-305,307-348						2.50
306-Toy Story-c/s						4.00
Biggest... (Winter, 1977)	2	4	6	11	16	20
Biggest, Greatest... nn('65)	4	8	12	28	44	60
Biggest, Greatest... 2('66/67) - #5('69/70)	3	6	9	18	27	35
Biggest, Greatest... 6('70) - #12(Wint. '77)	2	4	6	13	18	22
Biggest, Greatest...13(Fall '78) - #21(Fall/Wint. '86)	2	4	6	8	10	12
...Blockbuster 1(Sum '87), 2('88), 3(Sum. '89)	1	2	3	5	7	9
...Blockbuster 4 - 6(Sum. '92)						6.00
...Collectors' Edition 4 ('73; formerly ...Special)	2	4	6	11	16	20
5-9,10(10/75)	2	4	6	10	14	18
11-19,20(11/17)	2	4	6	8	10	12
21,22,23(5/78): 23-Ward-a	2	4	6	8	10	12
(#24-62,64 not numbered)						
1978 (nn; July, Sept, Nov, Dec) (#24-27)	2	4	6	8	10	12
1979 (nn; May, July, Sept, Nov, Dec) (#28-33)	2	4	6	8	10	12
1980 (nn; Feb, May, July, Sept, Nov, Dec) (#34-39)	1	2	3	5	7	9
1981 (nn; Feb, May, July, Sept, Nov, Dec) (#40-45)	1	2	3	5	7	9
1982 (nn; Feb, May, July, Sept, Nov, Dec) (#46-51)	1	2	3	5	7	9
1983 (nn; Feb, May, Sept, Nov, Dec) (#52-56)	1	2	3	5	7	9
1984 (nn; Feb, May, July, Nov) (#57-60)						6.00

Crack Western #71 © QUA

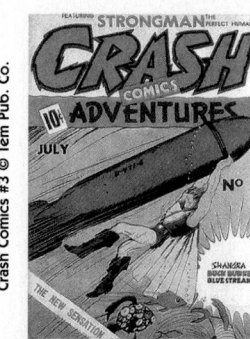

Crash Comics #3 © Tem Pub. Co.

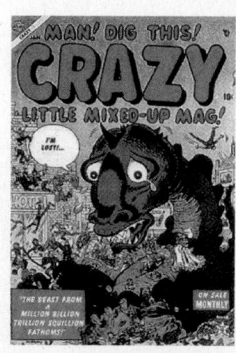

Crazy #2 © MAR

	GD 2.0	VG 4.0	FN 6.0	VF 8.0	VF/NM 9.0	NM- 9.2
1985 (nn; Feb) (#61)						6.00
62(9/85), nn(#63, 11/85), 64(12/85), 65-69, 70(4/87)						6.00
71,72,73(100 pgs.), 1/88), 74-79, 80(9/89)						4.00
81-96, 97(two diff. issues), 98-115: 83-Elvis, Batman parodies						4.00
116('98)-Last issue?						5.00
...Digest 1(Fall, '86, 148 pgs.), 2(1/87)	1	2	3	5	7	9
...Digest 3-5	1	2	3	4	5	7
...Party Pack 1,2('88) - 4('90)						4.00
...Shut-Ups 1(2/72)	3	6	9	17	25	32
...Shut-Ups 2('72) becomes Cracked Spec. #3	2	4	6	13	18	22
...Special 3('73; formerly Cracked Shut-Ups; ...Collectors' Edition#4 on)	2	4	6	11	16	20
... Summer Special 1(Sum. '91), 2(Sum. '92)-Don Martin-a						4.00
... Summer Special 3(Sum. '93) - 8(Sum. '98)						3.00
... Super (Vol. 2, formerly Super Cracked) 5(Wint. '91/92) - 14(Wint.'97/98)						3.00
Extra Special... 1(Spr. '76)	2	4	6	10	14	18
Extra Special... 2(Spr./Sum. '77)	2	4	6	9	12	15
Extra Special... 3(Wint. '79) - 9(Wint. '86)						6.00
Giant... nn('65)	5	10	15	32	51	70
Giant... 2('66) - 5('69)	3	6	9	20	30	40
Giant...6('70) - 12('76)	3	6	9	16	23	30
Giant...nn(9/77, #13), nn(1/78, #14), nn(3/78, #15), nn(5/78, #16), nn(7/78, #17), nn(11/78, #18), nn(3/79, #19), nn(7/79, #20), nn(10/79, #21), nn(12/79, #22), nn(3/80, #23), nn(7/80, #24)	2	4	6	10	14	18
Giant...nn(10/80, #25), nn(12/80, #26), nn(3/81, #27), nn(7/81, #28), nn(10/81, #29), nn(3/79, #30), nn(7/82, #31), nn(12/82, #32), nn(7/83, #34), nn(12/81, #30), nn(7/82, #31), nn(12/82, #32), nn(7/83, #34),	2	4	6	8	10	12
Giant...nn(10/83, #35), nn(12/83, #36), nn(3/84, #37), nn(7/84, #38), nn(10/84, #39), nn(3/85, #40), nn(7/85, #41), nn(10/85, #42)	1	2	3		5	8
Giant...43(3/86) - 46(1/87), 47(Wint. '88), 48(Wint. '89)						6.00
King Sized... 1('67)	4	8	12	24	37	50
King Sized... 2('68) - 5('71)	3	6	9	17	25	32
King Sized... 6('72) - 11('77)	3	6	9	14	19	24
King Sized... 12(Fall '78) - 17(Sum. '83)	2	4	6	8	10	12
King Sized... 18-20 (Sum/'86) (#21,22 exist?)	1	2	3	5	7	9
Spaced Out... 1-4 ('93 - '94)						5.00
Super... 1('68)	4	8	12	24	37	50
Super... 2('69) - 6('73)	3	6	9	14	20	25
Super... 7('74), 8(Spr. '75) - 10(Spr. '77)	3	6	9	14	20	25
Super... 11(Sum. '78) - 16(Fall '81)	2	4	6	10	14	18
Super... 17(Spr. '82) - 22(Fall '83)	2	4	6	8	10	12
Super... 23(Sum. '84, mis-numbered as #24)	2	4	6	8	10	12
Super... 24(Fall '84, correctly numbered)	2	4	6	8	10	12
Super... 25('Wint. '85) - 32(Fall '86)	1	3	4	6	8	10
Super... (Vol. 2) 1('87, 100 pgs.)-Severin & Elder-a	2	3		5	7	9
Super... (Vol. 2) becomes Cracked Super)						5.00

NOTE: *Burgos* a-1-10. *Colan* a-257. *Davis* a-5, 11-17, 24, 40, 80; c-12-14, 16. *Elder* a-5, 6, 10-13; c-10. *Everett* a-1-10, 23-85, in all issues. *Heath* a-1-3, 6, 13, 14, 17, 110; c-6. *Jaffee* a-5, 6. *Don Martin* c-235, 244, 247, 259, 261, 264. *Morrow* a-8-10. *Reinman* a-1-4. *Severin* c/a in most all issues. *Shores* a-3-7. *Torres* a-7-10. *Ward* a-22-24, 27, 35, 40, 120-193, 195-197, 199-205, 242, 244, 246, 247, 250, 252-257. *Williamson* a-1 (1 pg.). *Wolverton* a-1-2 pgs.), *Giant* nn('65). *Wood* a-27, 35, 40. Alfred E. Neuman c-177, 200, 202. Batman c-234, 248, 249, 256, 274. Captain America c-256. Christmas c-234, 243. Spider-Man c-260. Star Trek c-127, 169, 207, 228. Star Wars c-145, 146, 148, 149, 152, 155, 173, 174, 199. Superman c-183, 233. #144, 146 have free full-color pre-glued stickers. #145, 147, 155, 163 have free full-color postcards. #123, 137, 154, 157 have free iron-ons.

CRACKED MONSTER PARTY
Globe Communications: July, 1988 - No. 27, Wint. 1999/2000

	GD 2.0	VG 4.0	FN 6.0	VF 8.0	VF/NM 9.0	NM- 9.2
1	2	4	6	9	12	15
2-10	1	3	4	6	8	10
11-26						6.00
27-Interview with a Vampire-c/s	1	3	4	6	8	10

CRACKED'S FOR MONSTERS ONLY
Major Magazines: Sept, 1969 - No. 9, Sept, 1969; June, 1972

	GD 2.0	VG 4.0	FN 6.0	VF 8.0	VF/NM 9.0	NM- 9.2
1	4	8	12	28	44	60
2-9, nn(6/72)	3	6	9	18	27	35

CRACK WESTERN (Formerly Crack Comics; Jonesy No. 85 on)
Quality Comics Group: No. 63, Nov, 1949 - No. 84, May, 1953 (36 pgs., 63-68,74-on)

	GD 2.0	VG 4.0	FN 6.0	VF 8.0	VF/NM 9.0	NM- 9.2
63(#1)-Ward-c; Two-Gun Lil (origin & 1st app.)(ends #84), Arizona Ames, his horse Thunder (with sidekick Spurs & his horse Calico), Frontier Marshal (ends #70), & Dead Canyon Days (ends #69) begin; Crandall-a	19	38	57	112	176	240
64,65: 64-Ward-c. Crandall-a in both.	15	30	45	85	130	175
66,68-Photo-c. 66-Arizona Ames becomes A. Raines (ends #84)	14	28	42	76	108	140
67-Randolph Scott photo-c; Crandall-a	15	30	45	83	124	165
69(52pgs.)-Crandall-a	14	28	42	76	108	140
70(52pgs.)-The Whip (origin & 1st app.) & his horse Diablo begin (ends #84); Crandall-a	14	28	42	76	108	140
71(52pgs.)-Frontier Marshal becomes Bob Allen F. Marshal (ends #84); Crandall-c/a	15	30	45	83	124	165
72(52pgs.)-Tim Holt photo-c	13	26	39	72	101	130
73(52pgs.)-Photo-c	11	22	33	60	83	105
74-76,78,79,81,83-Crandall-c. 83-Crandall-a(p)	12	24	36	67	94	120
77,80,82	9	18	27	47	61	75
84-Crandall-c/a	13	26	39	72	101	130

NOTE: *Crandall* c-71p, 74-81, 83p(w/Cuidera-i).

CRASH COMICS (Catman Comics No. 6 on)
Tem Publishing Co.: May, 1940 - No. 5, Nov, 1940

	GD 2.0	VG 4.0	FN 6.0	VF 8.0	VF/NM 9.0	NM- 9.2
1-The Blue Streak, Strongman (origin), The Perfect Human, Shangra begin (1st app. of each); Kirby-a	315	630	945	2048	3624	5200
2-Simon & Kirby-a	159	318	477	994	1647	2300
3,5-Simon & Kirby-a	134	268	402	838	1394	1950
4-Origin & 1st app. The Catman; S&K-a	315	630	945	2048	3624	5200

NOTE: *Solar Legion by Kirby* No. 1-5 (5 pgs. each). Strongman c-1-4. Catman c-5.

CRASH DIVE (See Cinema Comics Herald)

CRASH METRO AND THE STAR SQUAD
Oni Press: May, 1999 ($2.95, B&W, one-shot)

	GD 2.0	VG 4.0	FN 6.0	VF 8.0	VF/NM 9.0	NM- 9.2
1-Allred-s/Ontiveros-a						3.00

CRASH RYAN (Also see Dark Horse Presents #44)
Marvel Comics (Epic): Oct, 1984 - No. 4, Jan, 1985 (Baxter paper, lim. series)

	GD 2.0	VG 4.0	FN 6.0	VF 8.0	VF/NM 9.0	NM- 9.2
1-4						2.50

CRAZY (Also see This Magazine is Crazy)
Atlas Comics (CSI): Dec, 1953 - No. 7, July, 1954

	GD 2.0	VG 4.0	FN 6.0	VF 8.0	VF/NM 9.0	NM- 9.2
1-Everett-c/a	30	60	90	174	275	375
2	19	38	57	109	172	250
3-7: 4-I Love Lucy satire. 5-Satire on censorship	16	32	48	94	147	200

NOTE: *Ayers* a-5. *Berg* a-1, 2. *Burgos* c-5, 6. *Drucker* a-6. *Everett* a-1-4. *Al Hartley* a-4. *Heath* a-3, 7; c-7. *Maneely* a-1-7, c-3, 4. *Post* a-3-6. Funny monster c-1-4.

CRAZY (Satire)
Marvel Comics Group: Feb, 1973 - No. 3, June, 1973

	GD 2.0	VG 4.0	FN 6.0	VF 8.0	VF/NM 9.0	NM- 9.2
1-Not Brand Echh-r; Beatles cameo (r)	3	6	9	14	20	25
2,3-Not Brand Echh-r; Kirby-a	2	4	6	9	13	16

CRAZY MAGAZINE (Satire)
Oct, 1973 - No. 94, Apr, 1983 (40-90¢, B&W magazine)
Marvel Comics (#1, 44 pgs; #2-90, reg. issues, 52 pgs; #92-95, 68 pgs)'

	GD 2.0	VG 4.0	FN 6.0	VF 8.0	VF/NM 9.0	NM- 9.2
1-Wolverton(1 pg.), Bode-a; 3 pg. photo story of Neal Adams & Dick Giordano; Harlan Ellison story; TV Kung Fu sty.	4	8	12	28	44	60
2-"Live & Let Die" c/s; 8pgs; Adams/Buscema-a; McCloud w5 pgs. Adams-a; Kurtzman's "Hey Look" 2 pg.-r	3	6	9	19	29	38
3-5: 3-"High Plains Drifter" w/Clint Eastwood c/s; Waltons app; Drucker, Reese-a. 4-Shaft-c/s; Ploog-a; Nixon 3 pg. app; Freas-a. 5-Michael Crichton's "Westworld" c/s; Nixon app.	3	6	9	16	23	30
6,7,18: 6-Exorcist c/s; Nixon app. 7-TV's Kung Fu c/s; Nixon app; Ploog & Freas-a. 18-Six Million Dollar Man/Bionic Woman c/s; Welcome Back Kotter story	3	6	9	15	21	26
8-10: 8-Serpico c/s; Casper parody; TV's Police Story. 9-Joker cameo; Chinatown story; Eisner s/a begins; Has 1st 8 covers on-c. 10-Playboy Bunny-c; M. Severin-a; Lee Marrs-a begins; "Deathwish" story	3	6	9	14	19	24
11-17,19: 11-Towering Inferno. 12-Rhoda. 13-"Tommy" the Who Rock Opera. 14-Mandingo. 15-Jaws story. 16-Santa/Xmas-c; "Good Times" TV story; Jaws. 17-Bicentennial issue; Baretta; Woody Allen. 19-King Kong-c; Reagan, J. Carter, Howard the Duck cameos, "Laverne & Shirley"	2	4	6	13	18	22
20,24,27: 20-Bicentennial-c; Space 1999 sty; Superheroes song sheet, 4pgs. 24-Charlie's Angels. 27-Charlie's Angels/Travolta/Fonz-c; Bionic Woman sty	2	4	6	13	18	22
21-23,25,26,28-30: 21-Starsky & Hutch. 22-Mount Rushmore/J. Carter-c; TV's Barney Miller; Superheroes spoof. 23-Santa/Xmas-c; "Happy Days" sty; "Omen" sty. 25-J. Carter-c/s; Grandenetti-a begins; TV's Alice; Logan's Run. 26-TV Stars-c/s; Mary Hartman, King Kong. 28-Donny & Marie Osmond-c/s; Marathon Man. 29-Travolta/Kotter-c; "One Day at a Time", Gong Show. 30-1977, 84 pgs. w/bonus; Jaws, Baretta, King Kong, Happy Days	1	3	4	8	11	14
31,33-35,38,40: 31- "Rocky"-c/s; TV game shows. 33-Peter Benchley's "Deep". 34-J. Carter-c; TV's "Fish". 35-Xmas-c with Fonz/Six Million Dollar Man/Wonder Woman/Darth Vader/Travolta, TV's "Mash" & "Family Matters". 38-Close Encounters of the Third Kind-c/s. 40- "Three's Company-c/s	1	3	4	6	8	10
32-Star Wars/Darth Vader-c/s; "Black Sunday"	2	4	6	13	18	22
36,42,47,49: 36-Farrah Fawcett/Six Million Dollar Man-c/s; TV's Nancy Drew & Hardy Boys;						

Crazy #53 © MAR

Creature Commandos #3 © DC

Creed: Cranial Disorder #3 © Trent Kaniuga

	GD 2.0	VG 4.0	FN 6.0	VF 8.0	VF/NM 9.0	NM- 9.2		GD 2.0	VG 4.0	FN 6.0	VF 8.0	VF/NM 9.0	NM- 9.2

1st app. Howard The Duck in Crazy, 2 pgs. 42-84 pgs. w/bonus: TV Hulk/Spider-Man-c; Mash, Gong Show, One Day at a Time, Disco, Alice. 47-Battlestar Galactica xmas-c; movie "Foul Play". 49-1979, 84 pgs. w/bonus; Mork & Mindy-c; Jaws, Saturday Night Fever, Three's Company

| | 2 | 4 | 6 | 8 | 11 | 14 |

37-1978, 84 pgs. w/bonus. Darth Vader-c; Barney Miller, Laverne & Shirley, Good Times, Rocky, Donny & Marie Osmond, Bionic Woman

| | 2 | 4 | 6 | 11 | 16 | 20 |

39,44: 39-Saturday Night Fever-c/s. 44-"Grease"-c w/Travolta/O. Newton-John

| | 2 | 4 | 6 | 10 | 14 | 18 |

41-Kiss-c & 1pg. photos; Disaster movies, TV's "Family", Annie Hall

| | 4 | 8 | 12 | 26 | 41 | 55 |

43,45,46,48,51: 43-Jaws-c; Saturday Night Fever. 43-E.C. swipe from Mad #131. 45-Travolta/O. Newton-John/J. Carter-c; Eight is Enough. 46-TV Hulk-c/s; Punk Rock. 48-"Wiz"-c, Battlestar Galactica-s. 51-Grease/Mork & Mindy/D&M Osmond-c, Mork & Mindy-sty. "Boys from Brazil"

| | 1 | 3 | 4 | 6 | 8 | 10 |

50,58: 50-Superman movie-c/sty, Playboy Mag., TV Hulk, Fonz; Howard the Duck, 1 pg. 58-1980, 84 pgs. w/32 pg. color comic bonus insert-Full reprint of Crazy Comic #1, Battlestar Galactica, Charlie's Angels, Starsky & Hutch

| | 2 | 4 | 6 | 10 | 14 | 18 |

52,59,60,64: 52-1979, 84 pgs. w/bonus. Marlon Brando-c; TV Hulk, Grease. Kiss, 1 pg. photos. 59-Santa Ptd-c by Larkin; "Alien", "Moonraker", Rocky-2, Howard the Duck, 1 pg. 60-Star Trek w/Muppets-c; Star Trek sty; 1st app/origin Teen Hulk; Severin-a. 64-84 pgs. w/bonus Monopoly game satire. "Empire Strikes Back", 8 pgs., One Day at a Time

| | 2 | 4 | 6 | 10 | 14 | 18 |

53,54,65,67-70: 53-"Animal House"-c/sty; TV's "Vegas", Howard the Duck, 1 pg. 54-Love at First Bite-c/sty, Fantasy Island sty, Howard the Duck 1 pg. 65-(Has #66 on-c, Aug/'80). "Black Hole" w/Janson-a; Kirby,Wood/Severin-a(r), 5 pgs. Howard the Duck, 3 pgs.; Broderick-a; Buck Rogers, Mr. Rogers. 67-84 pgs. w/bonus; TV's Kung Fu, Exorcist; Ploog-a(r). 68-American Gigolo, Dukes of Hazzard, Teen Hulk; Howard the Duck, 3 pgs. Broderick-a; Monster sty/5 pg. Ditko-a(r). 69-Obnoxio the Clown-c/sty; Stephen King's "Shining", Teen Hulk, Richie Rich, Howard the Duck, 3pgs; Broderick-a. 70-84 pgs. Towering Inferno, Daytime TV; Trina Robbins-a

| | 1 | 2 | 3 | 5 | 7 | 9 |

55-57,61,63: 55-84 pgs. w/bonus; Love Boat, Mork & Mindy, Fonz, TV Hulk. 56-Mork/Rocky/ J. Carter-c; China Syndrome. 57-TV Hulk with Miss Piggy-c; Dracula, Sting, Muppets. 61-1980, 84 pgs. Adams-a(r), McCloud, Pro wrestling, Casper, TV's Police Story. 63-Apocalypse Now-Coppola's cult movie; 3rd app. Teen Hulk, Howard the Duck, 3 pgs.

| | 2 | 4 | 6 | 8 | 10 | 12 |

62-Kiss-c & 2 pg. app; Quincy, 2nd app. Teen Hulk

| | 8 | 14 | 22 | 34 | 45 |

66-Sept/'80, Empire Strikes Back-c/sty; Teen Hulk by Severin, Howard the Duck, 3pgs. by Broderick

| | 2 | 4 | 6 | 10 | 13 | 16 |

71,72,75-77,79: 71-Blues Brothers parody, Teen Hulk, Superheroes parody, WKRP in Cincinnati, Howard the Duck, 3pgs. by Broderick. 72-Jackie Gleason/Smokey & the Bandit II-c/sty; Teen Hulk. Howard the Duck, 3pgs. by Broderick. 75-Flash Gordon movie c/sty; Teen Hulk, Cat in the Hat, Howard the Duck 3pgs. by Broderick. 76-84 pgs. w/bonus; Monster-sty w/ Crandall-a(r), Monster-stys(2) w/Kirby-a(r), 5pgs. ea; Mash, TV Hulk, Chinatown. 77-Popeye movie/R. Williams-c/sty; Teen Hulk, Love Boat, Howard the Duck 3 pgs. 79-84 pgs. w/bonus color stickers; has new material; "9 to 5" w/Dolly Parton, Teen Hulk, Magnum P.I., Monster-sty w/5pgs, Ditko-a(r), "Rat" w/Sutton-a(r), Everett-a, 4 pgs.(r)

| | 1 | 2 | 3 | 5 | 7 | 9 |

73,74,78,80: 73-84 pgs. w/bonus Hulk/Spiderman Finger Puppets-c & bonus; "Live & Let Die, Jaws, Fantasy Island. 74-Dallas/"Who Shot J.R."-c/sty; Elephant Man, Howard the Duck 3pgs. by Broderick. 78-Clint Eastwood-c/sty; Teen Hulk, Superheroes parody, Lou Grant. 80-Star Wars, 2 pg. app; "Howling", TV's "Greatest American Hero"

| | 2 | 4 | 6 | 8 | 10 | 12 |

81,84,86,87,89: 81-.Superman Movie II-c/sty; Wolverine cameo, Mash, Teen Hulk. 84-American Werewolf in London, Johnny Carson app; Teen Hulk. 86-Time Bandits-c/sty; Private Benjamin. 87-Rubix Cube-c; Hill Street Blues, "Ragtime", Origin Obnoxio the Clown; Teen Hulk. 89-Burt Reynolds "Sharkey's Machine", Teen Hulk

| | 1 | 2 | 3 | 5 | 7 | 9 |

82-X-Men-c w/new Byrne-a, 84 pgs. w/new material; Fantasy Island, Teen Hulk, "For Your Eyes Only", Spiderman/Human Torch-r by Kirby/Ditko; Sutton-a(r); Rogers-a; Hunchback of Notre Dame, 5 pgs.

| | 2 | 4 | 6 | 10 | 14 | 18 |

83-Raiders of the Lost Ark-c/sty; Hart to Hart; Reese-a; Teen Hulk

| | 2 | 4 | 6 | 8 | 11 | 14 |

85,88: 85-84 pgs; Escape from New York, Teen Hulk; Kirby-a(r), 5 pgs, Posiedon Adventure, Flintstones, Sesame Street. 88-84 pgs. w/bonus Dr. Strange Game, some new material; Jeffersons, X-Men/Wolverine, 10 pgs.; Byrne-a; Apocalypse Now, Teen Hulk

| | 1 | 3 | 4 | 6 | 8 | 10 |

90-94: 90-Conan-c/sty; M. Severin-a; Teen Hulk. 91-84 pgs, some new material; Bladerunner-c/sty, "Deathwish-II, Teen Hulk, Black Knight, 10 pgs.-'50s-r w/Maneely-a. 92-Wrath of Khan Star Trek-c/sty; Joanie & Chachi, Teen Hulk. 93-"E.T."-c/sty, Teen Hulk, Archie Bunkers Place, Dr. Doom Game. 94-Poltergeist, Smurfs, Teen Hulk, Casper, Avengers parody-8pgs. Adams-a

| | 2 | 4 | 6 | 8 | 13 | 16 |

Crazy Summer Special #1 (Sum, '75, 100 pgs.)-Nixon, TV Kung Fu, Babe Ruth, Joe Namath, Waltons, McCloud, Chariots of the Gods

| | 2 | 4 | 6 | 13 | 18 | 22 |

NOTE: **N. Adams** a-2, 61r, 94p. **Austin** a-82i. **Buscema** a-2, 82. **Byrne** c-82p. **Nick Cardy** c-7, 8, 10, 12-16, Super Special 1. **Crandall** a-76r. **Ditko** a-68r, 79r, 82r. **Drucker** a-3. **Eisner** a-9-16. **Kelly Freas** c-1-6, 9, 11; a-7. **Kirby/Wood** a-66r. **Ploog** a-1, 4, 7, 67r, 73r. **Rogers** a-82. **Sparling** a-92. **Wood** a-65r. Howard the Duck in 36, 50, 51, 53, 54, 59, 63, 65, 66, 68, 69, 71, 72, 74, 75, 77. Hulk in 46, c-42, 46, 57, 73. Star Wars in 32, 66; c-37.

CRAZYMAN
Continuity Comics: Apr, 1992 - No. 3, 1992 ($2.50, high quality paper)

1-($3.95, 52 pgs.)-Embossed-c; N. Adams part-i 4.00
2,3 ($2.50): 2-N. Adams/Bolland-c 2.50

CRAZYMAN
Continuity Comics: V2#1, 5/93 - No. 4, 1/94 ($2.50, high quality paper)

V2#1-4: 1-Entire book is die-cut. 2-(12/93)-Adams-c(p) & part scripts. 3-(12/93). 4-Indicia says #3, Jan. 1993 .... 2.50

CRAZY, MAN, CRAZY (Magazine) (Becomes This Magazine is...?) (Formerly From Here to Insanity)
Humor Magazines (Charlton): V2#1, Dec, 1955 - V2#2, June, 1956

V2#1,V2#2-Satire; Wolverton-a, 3 pgs. | 15 | 30 | 45 | 84 | 127 | 170 |

CREATURE, THE (See Movie Classics)

CREATURE COMMANDOS (See Weird War Tales #93 for 1st app.)
DC Comics: May, 2000 - No. 8, Dec, 2000 ($2.50, limited series)

1-8: Truman-s/Eaton-a 2.50

CREATURES OF THE ID
Caliber Press: 1990 ($2.95, B&W)

1-Frank Einstein (Madman) app.; Allred-a | 3 | 6 | 9 | 16 | 23 | 30 |

CREATURES OF THE NIGHT
Dark Horse Books: Nov, 2004 ($12.95, hardcover graphic novel)

HC-Neil Gaiman-s/Michael Zulli-a/c 13.00

CREATURES ON THE LOOSE (Formerly Tower of Shadows No. 1-9)(See Kull)
Marvel Comics: No. 10, March, 1971 - No. 37, Sept, 1975 (New-a & reprints)

10-(15¢)-1st full app. King Kull; see Kull the Conqueror; Wrightson-a

| | 6 | 12 | 18 | 43 | 69 | 95 |

11-15: 15-Last 15¢ issue | 3 | 6 | 9 | 15 | 21 | 26 |
16-Origin Warrior of Mars (begins, ends #21) | 2 | 4 | 6 | 13 | 18 | 22 |
17-20 | 2 | 4 | 6 | 8 | 11 | 14 |
21-Steranko-c | 2 | 4 | 6 | 13 | 18 | 22 |
22-Steranko-c; Thongor stories begin | 3 | 6 | 9 | 14 | 19 | 24 |
23-29-Thongor-c/stories | 1 | 2 | 3 | 5 | 7 | 9 |
30-Manwolf begins | 3 | 6 | 9 | 16 | 22 | 28 |
31-33 | 2 | 4 | 6 | 8 | 11 | 14 |
34-37 | 2 | 4 | 6 | 8 | 10 | 12 |

NOTE: **Crandall** a-13. **Ditko** r-15, 17, 18, 20, 22, 24, 27, 28. **Everett** a-16i(new). **Matt Fox** r-21i. **Howard** a-26i. **Gil Kane** a-16p, 17p, 19i; c-16, 17, 19, 20, 25, 29, 33p, 35p, 36p. **Kirby** a-10-15i; 16(2)i, 17r, 19r. **Morrow** a-20, 21. **Perez** a-33-37; c-34p. **Shores** a-11. **innott** r-21. **Sutton** c-10. **Tuska** a-31p, 32p.

CREECH, THE
Image Comics: Oct, 1997 - No. 3, Dec, 1997 ($1.95/$2.50, limited series)

1-3: 1-Capullo-s/c/a(p) 2.50
TPB (1999, $9.95) r/#1-3, McFarlane intro. 10.00
Out for Blood 1-3 (7/01 - No. 3, 11/01; $4.95) Capullo-s/c/a 5.00

CREED
Hall of Heroes Comics: Dec, 1994 - No. 2, Jan, 1995 ($2.50, B&W)

1 | | 2 | 4 | 6 | 9 | 12 | 15 |
2 | | 2 | 4 | 6 | 8 | 10 | 12 |

CREED
Lightning Comics: June, 1995 - No. 3 ($2.75/$3.00, B&W/color)

1-($2.75) 4.00
1-($3.00, color) 5.00
1-($9.95)-Commemorative Edition 10.00
1-TwinVariant (1250? print run) 10.00
1-Special Edition; polybagged w/certificate 4.00
1 Gold Collectors Edition; polybagged w/certificate 3.00
2,3-($3.00, color)-Butt Naked Edition & regular-c 3.00
3-($9.95)-Commemorative Edition; polybagged w/certificate & card 10.00

CREED: CRANIAL DISORDER
Lightning Comics: Oct, 1996 ($3.00, limited series)

1-3-Two covers 3.00
1-($5.95)-Platinum Edition 6.00
2,3-($9.95)Ltd.l Edition 10.00

CREED/TEENAGE MUTANT NINJA TURTLES

The Creeper #5 © DC

Creepy #25 © WP

Crime and Justice #15 © CC

	GD 2.0	VG 4.0	FN 6.0	VF 8.0	VF/NM 9.0	NM- 9.2

Lightning Comics: May, 1996 ($3.00, one-shot)
- 1-Kaniuga(p)/scripts; Laird-c; variant-c exists ... 3.00
- 1-($9.95)-Platinum Edition ... 10.00
- 1-Special Edition; polybagged w/certificate ... 5.00

CREEPER, THE (See Beware… , Showcase #73 & 1st Issue Special #7)
DC Comics: Dec, 1997 - No. 11; #1,000,000 Nov, 1998 ($2.50)
- 1-11-Kaminski-s/Martinbrough-a(p). 7,8-Joker-c/app. ... 3.00
- #1,000,000 (11/98) 853rd Century x-over ... 3.00

CREEPER, THE (See DCU Brave New World)
DC Comics: Oct, 2006 - No. 6, Mar, 2007 ($2.99, limited series)
- 1-6-Niles-s/Justiniano-a/c; Jack Ryder becomes the Creeper. 2-6-Batman app. ... 3.00

CREEPS
Image Comics: Oct, 2001 - No. 4, May, 2002 ($2.95)
- 1-4-Mandrake-a/Mishkin-s ... 3.00

CREEPSHOW
Plume/New American Library Pub.: July, 1982 (softcover graphic novel)

	GD 2.0	VG 4.0	FN 6.0	VF 8.0	VF/NM 9.0	NM- 9.2
1st edition-nn-(68 pgs.) Kamen-c/Wrightson-a; screenplay by Stephen King for the George Romero movie	3	6	9	19	29	38
2nd-7th printings	3	6	9	14	19	24

CREEPSVILLE
Laughing Reindeer Press: V2#1, Winter, 1995 ($4.95)
- V2#1-Comics w/text ... 5.00

CREEPY (See Warren Presents)
Warren Publishing Co./Harris Publ. #146: 1964 - No. 145, Feb, 1983; No. 146, 1985 (B&W, magazine)

	GD 2.0	VG 4.0	FN 6.0	VF 8.0	VF/NM 9.0	NM- 9.2
1-Frazetta-a (his last story in comics?); Jack Davis-c; 1st Warren all comics magazine; 1st app. Uncle Creepy	11	22	33	79	140	200
2-Frazetta-c & 1 pg. strip	7	14	21	47	76	105
3-8,11-13,15-17: 3-7,9-11,15-17-Frazetta-a. 7-Frazetta 1 pg. strip. 15,16-Adams-a. 16-Jeff Jones-a	4	8	12	28	44	60
9-Creepy fan club sketch by Wrightson (1st published-a); has 1/2 pg. anti-smoking strip by Frazetta; Frazetta-a; 1st Wood and Ditko art on this title; Toth-a (low print)	7	14	21	45	73	100
10-Brunner fan club sketch (1st published work)	5	10	15	30	48	65
14-Neal Adams 1st Warren work	5	10	15	30	48	65
18-28,30,31: 27-Frazetta-c	3	6	9	21	32	42
29,34: 29-Jones-a	4	8	12	22	34	45
32-(scarce) Frazetta-c; Harlan Ellison sty	5	10	15	37	59	80
33,35,37,39,40,42-47,49: 35-Hitler/Nazi-a. 39-1st Uncle Creepy solo-s, Cousin Eerie app.; early Brunner-a. 42-1st San Julian-a. 44-1st Ploog-a. 46-Corben-a	3	6	9	19	29	38
36-(11/70)1st Corben art at Warren	4	8	12	23	36	48
38,41-(scarce): 38-1st Kelly-c. 41-Corben-a	4	8	12	26	41	55
48,55,65-(1972, 1973, 1974 Annuals) #55 & 65 contain an 8 pg. slick comic insert. 48-(84 pgs.). 55-Color poster bonus (1/2 price if missing). 65-(100 pgs.) Summer Giant	4	8	12	23	36	48
50-Vampirella/Eerie/Creepy-c	4	8	12	26	41	55
51,54,56-61,64: All contain an 8 pg. slick comic insert in middle. 59-Xmas horror. 54,64-Chaykin-a	3	6	9	21	32	42
52,53,66,71,72,75,76,78-80: 71-All Bermejo-a; Space & Time issue. 72-Gual-a. 78-Fantasy issue. 79,80-Monsters issue	3	6	9	16	22	28
62,63-1st & 2nd full Wrightson story art; Corben-a; 8 pg. color comic insert	3	6	9	21	32	42
67,68,73	3	6	9	17	25	32
69,70-Edgar Allan Poe issues; Corben-a	3	6	9	16	23	30
74,77: 74-All Crandall-a. 77-Xmas Horror issue; Corben-a,Wrightson-a	3	6	9	19	29	38
81,84,85,88-90,92-94,96-99,102,104-112,114-118,120,122-130: 84,93-Sports issue. 85,97,102-Monster issue. 89-All war issue; Nino-a. 94-Weird Children issue. 96,109-Aliens issue. 99-Disasters. 103-Corben-a. 104-Robots issue. 106-Sword & Sorcery.107-Sci-fi. 116-End of Man. 125-Xmas Horror	2	4	6	9	12	15
82,100,101: 82-All Maroto issue. 100-(8/78) Anniversary. 101-Corben-a	2	4	6	13	18	22
83,95-Wrightson-a. 83-Corben-a. 95-Gorilla/Apes.	2	4	6	10	14	18
86,87,91,103-Wrightson-a. 86-Xmas Horror	2	4	6	10	14	18
113-All Wrightson-r issue	3	6	9	16	22	28
119,121: 119-All Nino issue.121-All Severin-r issue	2	4	6	10	14	18
131,133-136,138,140: 135-Xmas issue	2	4	6	10	14	18
132,137,139: 132-Corben. 137-All Williamson-r issue. 139-All Toth-r issue	2	4	6	13	18	22
141,143,144 (low dist.): 144-Giant, $2.25; Frazetta-c	3	6	9	15	21	26
142,145 (low dist.): 142-(10/82, 100 pgs.) All Torres issue. 145-(2/83) last Warren issue	3	6	9	15	21	26
146 ($2.95)-1st from Harris; resurrection issue	6	12	18	43	69	95
Year Book '68-'70: '70-Neal Adams, Ditko-a(r)	5	10	15	30	48	65
Annual 1971,1972	4	8	12	28	44	60
1993 Fearbook ($3.95)-Harris Publ.; Brereton-c; Vampirella by Busiek-s/Art Adams-a; David-s; Paquette-a	4	8	12	24	37	50
…:The Classic Years TPB (Harris/Dark Horse, '91, $12.95) Kaluta-c; art by Frazetta,Torres, Crandall, Ditko, Morrow, Williamson, Wrightson						25.00

NOTE: All issues contain many good artists works: *Neal Adams, Brunner, Corben, Craig (Taycee), Crandall, Ditko, Evans, Frazetta, Heath, Jeff Jones, Krenkel, McWilliams, Morrow, Nino, Orlando, Ploog, Severin, Torres, Toth, Williamson, Wood, & Wrightson; covers by Crandall, Davis, Frazetta, Morrow, San Julian, Todd/Bode; Otto Binder's "Adam Link" stories in No. 2, 4, 6, 8, 9, 12, 13, 15 with Orlando art. Frazetta c-2-7, 9-11, 15-17, 27, 32, 83r, 89r, 91r. E.A. Poe adaptations in 66, 69, 70.*

CREEPY (Mini-series)
Harris Comics/Dark Horse: 1992 - Book 4, 1992 (48 pgs, B&W, squarebound)

	GD 2.0	VG 4.0	FN 6.0	VF 8.0	VF/NM 9.0	NM- 9.2
Book 1-4: Brereton painted-c on all. Stories and art by various incl. David (all), Busiek(2), Infantino(2), Guice(3), Colan(1)	2	4	6	8	10	12

CREEPY THINGS
Charlton Comics: July, 1975 - No. 6, June, 1976

	GD 2.0	VG 4.0	FN 6.0	VF 8.0	VF/NM 9.0	NM- 9.2
1-Sutton-c/a	2	4	6	12	16	20
2-6: Ditko-a in 3,5. Sutton-c-3,4. 6-Zeck-c	1	3	4	6	8	10
Modern Comics Reprint 2-6(1977)						4.00

NOTE: *Larson a-2,6. Sutton a-1,2,4,6. Zeck a-2.*

CREW, THE
Marvel Comics: July, 2003 - No. 7, Jan, 2004 ($2.50)
- 1-7-Priest-s/Bennett-a; James Rhodes (War Machine) app. ... 2.50

CRIME AND JUSTICE (Badge Of Justice #22 on; Rookie Cop? No. 27 on)
Capitol Stories/Charlton Comics: March, 1951 - No. 21; No. 23 - No. 26, Sept, 1955 (No #22)

	GD 2.0	VG 4.0	FN 6.0	VF 8.0	VF/NM 9.0	NM- 9.2
1	34	68	102	195	308	420
2	14	28	42	82		160
3-8,10-13: 6-Negligee panels	13	26	39	72	101	130
9-Classic story "Comics Vs. Crime"	24	48	72	139	220	300
14-Color illos in POP; gory story of man who beheads women	20	40	60	117	184	250
15-17,19-21,23,24: 15-Negligee panels. 23-Rookie Cop (1st app.)	10	20	30	54	72	90
18-Ditko-a	25	50	75	145	228	310
25,26: (scarce)	14	28	42	82	121	160

NOTE: *Alascia c-20. Ayers a-17. Shuster a-19-21; c-19. Bondage c-11, 12.*

CRIME AND PUNISHMENT (Title inspired by 1935 film)
Lev Gleason Publications: April, 1948 - No. 74, Aug, 1955

	GD 2.0	VG 4.0	FN 6.0	VF 8.0	VF/NM 9.0	NM- 9.2
1-Mr. Crime app. on-c	36	72	108	208	329	450
2	18	36	54	103	162	220
3-Used in SOTI, pg. 112; injury-to-eye panel; Fuje-a	20	40	60	117	184	250
4,5	14	28	42	82	121	160
6-10	13	26	39	72	101	130
11-20	11	22	33	62	86	110
21-30	10	20	30	54	72	90
31-38,40-44,46: 46-One pg. Frazetta-a	9	18	27	47	61	75
39-Drug mention story "The 5 Dopes"	13	26	39	72	101	130
45- "Hophead Killer" drug story	13	26	39	72	101	130
47-57,60-65,70-74:	8	16	24	44	57	70
58-Used in POP, pg. 79	9	18	27	47	61	75
59-Used in SOTI, illo "What comic-book America stands for"	30	60	90	176	278	380
66-Toth-c/a(4); 3-D effect issue (3/54); 1st "Deep Dimension" process	40	80	120	235	368	500
67- "Monkey on His Back" heroin story; 3-D effect issue	36	72	108	208	329	450
68-3-D effect issue; Toth-c (7/54)	30	60	90	174	275	375
69- "The Hot Rod Gang" dope crazy kids	13	26	39	72	101	130

NOTE: *Biro c-most. Everett a-31. Fuje a-2-4, 12, 13, 17, 18, 20, 26, 27. Guardineer a-2-4, 10, 14, 17, 18, 20, 26-28, 32, 38-44,54. Kinstler c-69. McWilliams a-41, 48, 49. Tuska a-28, 30, 51, 64, 70.*

CRIME AND PUNISHMENT: MARSHALL LAW TAKES MANHATTAN
Marvel Comics (Epic Comics): 1989 ($4.95, 52 pgs., direct sales only, mature)
- nn-Graphic album featuring Marshall Law ... 5.00

CRIME CAN'T WIN (Formerly Cindy Smith)
Marvel/Atlas Comics (TCI 41/CCC 42,43,4-12): No. 41, 9/50 - No. 43, 2/51;

Crime Cases #9 © MAR

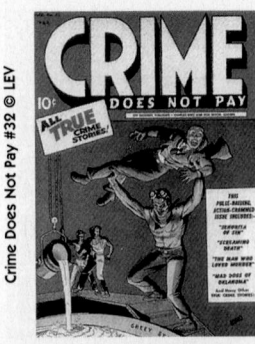

Crime Does Not Pay #32 © LEV

Crime Illustrated #2 © WMG

	GD	VG	FN	VF	VF/NM	NM-
	2.0	4.0	6.0	8.0	9.0	9.2

No. 4, 4/51 - No. 12, 9/53

	GD	VG	FN	VF	VF/NM	NM-
41(#1)	26	52	78	150	235	320
42(#2)	15	30	45	85	130	175
43(#3)-Horror story	18	36	54	103	162	220
4(4/51),5-12: 10-Possible use in SOTI, pg. 161	14	28	42	76	108	140

NOTE: *Robinson a-9-11. Tuska a-43.*

CRIME CASES COMICS (Formerly Willie Comics)
Marvel/Atlas Comics(CnPC No.24-8/MJMC No.9-12): No. 24, 8/50 - No. 27, 3/51; No. 5, 5/51 - No. 12, 7/52

24 (#1, 52 pgs.)-True police cases	18	36	54	103	162	220
25-27(#2-4): 27-Morisi-a	14	28	42	76	108	140
5-12: 11-Robinson-a. 12-Tuska-a	12	24	36	67	94	120

CRIME CLINIC
Ziff-Davis Publishing Co.: No. 10, July-Aug, 1951 - No. 5, Summer, 1952

10(#1)-Painted-c; origin Dr. Tom Rogers	28	56	84	162	256	350
11(#2),4,5: 4,5-Painted-c	18	36	54	107	169	230
3-Used in SOTI, pg. 18	19	38	57	112	176	240

NOTE: *All have painted covers by Saunders. Starr a-10.*

CRIME CLINIC
Slave Labor Graphics: May, 1995 - No. 2, Oct, 1995 ($2.95, B&W, limited series)

1,2						3.00

CRIME DETECTIVE COMICS
Hillman Periodicals: Mar-Apr, 1948 - V3#8, May-June, 1953

V1#1-The Invisible 6, costumed villains app; Fuje-c/a, 15 pgs.	30	60	90	174	275	375
2,5: 5-Krigstein-a	14	28	42	82	121	160
3,4,6,7,10-12: 6-McWilliams-a	12	24	36	69	97	125
8-Kirbyish-a by McCann	12	24	36	69	97	125
9-Used in SOTI, pg. 16 & "Caricature of the author in a position comic book publishers wish he were in permanently" illo.	37	74	111	213	337	460
V2#1,4,7-Krigstein-a: 1-Tuska-a	11	22	33	64	90	115
2,3,5,6,8-12 (1-2/52)	10	20	30	54	72	90
V3#1-Drug use-c	10	20	30	56	76	95
2-8	9	18	27	47	61	75

NOTE: *Briefer a-11, V3#1. Kinstlerish-a by McCann-V2#7, V3#2. Powell a-11, 11. Starr a-10.*

CRIME DETECTOR
Timor Publications: Jan, 1954 - No. 5, Sept, 1954

1	21	42	63	120	188	255
2	12	24	36	69	97	125
3,4	10	20	30	58	79	100
5-Disbrow-a (classic)	22	44	66	126	198	270

CRIME DOES NOT PAY (Formerly Silver Streak Comics No. 1-21)
Comic House/Lev Gleason/Golfing: No. 22, June, 1942 - No. 147, July, 1955
(1st crime comic)(Title inspired by)

22 (23 on cover, 22 on indicia)-Origin The War Eagle & only app.; Chip Gardner begins; #22 was rebound in Complete Book of True Crime (Scarce)	300	600	900	1894	3197	4500
23 (Scarce)	166	332	498	1038	1719	2400
24-Intro. & 1st app. Mr. Crime (Scarce).	138	276	414	863	1432	2000
25,26,28-30: 30-Wood and Biro app.	62	124	186	388	644	900
27-Classic Biro-c	71	142	213	444	735	1025
31,32,34-40	40	80	120	240	383	525
33-Classic Biro Hanging & hatchet-c	55	110	165	344	572	800
41-Origin & 1st app. Officer Common Sense	31	62	93	178	282	385
42-Electrocution-c	40	80	120	235	368	500
43-46,48-50: 44,45,46,50 are 68 pg. issues; 44-"legs" diamond story	20	40	60	117	184	250
47-Electric chair-c	35	70	105	204	322	440
51-70: 63,64-Possible use in SOTI, pg. 306. 63-Contains Biro & Gleason's self censorship code of 12 listed restrictions (5/48)	16	32	48	94	147	200
71-99: 87-Chip Gardner begins, ends #100	15	30	45	83	124	165
100	15	30	45	88	137	185
101-104,107-110: 102-Chip Gardner app	12	24	36	69	97	125
105-Used in POP, pg. 84	13	26	39	74	105	135
106,114-Frazetta-a, 1 pg.	12	24	36	69	97	125
111-Used in POP, pgs. 80 & 81; injury-to-eye sty illo 13	13	26	39	74	105	135
112,113,115-130	10	20	30	54	72	90
131-140	9	18	27	47	61	75
141,142-Last pre-code issue; Kubert-a(1)	10	20	30	56	76	95
143-Kubert-a in one story	10	20	30	56	76	95
144-146	9	18	27	47	61	75
147-Last issue (scarce); Kubert-a	15	30	45	83	124	165
1(Golfing-1945)	8	16	24	42	54	65

The Best of...(1944, 128 pgs.)-Series contains 4 rebound issues

	83	166	249	519	860	1200
...1945 issue	61	122	183	381	633	885
...1946-48 issues	45	90	135	275	435	635
...1949-50 issues	41	82	123	250	400	550
...1951-53 issues	36	72	108	208	329	450

NOTE: *Many issues contain violent covers and stories. Who Dunnit by Guardineer-39-42, 44-105, 108-110; Chip Gardner by Bob Fujitani (Fuje)-88-103. Alderman a-29, 41-44, 49. Dan Barry a-67, 75. Biro c-1-76, 122, 142. Briefer a-29(2), 30, 31, 33, 37, 39. G. Colan a-105. Fuje c-88, 89, 91-94, 96, 98, 99, 102, 103. Guardineer a-51, 57, 67, 68, 71, 74. Kubert c-143. Landau a-118. Maurer a-29, 39, 41, 42. McWilliams a-91, 93, 95, 100-103. Palais a-30, 33, 37, 39, 41-43, 44(2), 46, 49. Powell a-146, 147. Tuska a-48, 50(2), 51, 52, 56, 57(2), 60-64, 66, 67, 68, 71, 74. Painted c-87-102. Bondage c-43, 62, 98.*

CRIME EXPOSED
Marvel Comics (PPI)/Marvel Atlas Comics (PrPI): June, 1948; Dec, 1950 - No. 14, June, 1952

1(6/48)	34	68	102	197	311	425
1(12/50)	20	40	60	117	184	250
2	14	28	42	80	115	150
3-9,11,14	12	24	36	67	94	120
10-Used in POP, pg. 81	13	26	39	72	101	130
12-Krigstein & Robinson-a	13	26	39	72	101	130
13-Used in POP, pg. 81; Krigstein-a	13	26	39	74	105	135

NOTE: *Maneely c-8. Robinson a-11, 12. Tuska a-3, 4.*

CRIMEFIGHTERS
Marvel Comics (CmPS 1-3/CCC 4-10): Apr, 1948 - No. 10, Nov, 1949

1-Some copies are undated & could be reprints	25	50	75	145	228	310
2,3: 3-Morphine addict story	14	28	42	81	118	155
4-10: 4-Early John Buscema-a. 6-Anti-Wertham editorial. 9,10-Photo-c	14	28	42	81	118	155
	13	26	39	72	101	130

CRIME FIGHTERS (...Always Win)
Atlas Comics (CnPC): No. 11, Sept, 1954 - No. 13, Jan, 1955

11-13: 11-Maneely-a,13-Pakula, Reinman, Severin-a	12	24	36	69	97	125

CRIME-FIGHTING DETECTIVE (Shock Detective Cases No. 20 on; formerly Criminals on the Run)
Star Publications: No. 11, Apr-May, 1950 - No. 19, June, 1952 (Based on true crime cases)

11-L. B. Cole-c/a (2 pgs.); L. B. Cole-c on all	18	36	54	107	169	230
12,13,15-19: 17-Young King Cole & Dr. Doom app.	15	30	45	83	124	165
14-L. B. Cole-c; r/Law-Crime #2	15	30	45	140	140	190

CRIME FILES
Standard Comics: No. 5, Sept, 1952 - No. 6, Nov, 1952

5-1pg. Alex Toth-a; used in SOTI, pg. 4 (text)	23	46	69	130	205	280
6-Sekowsky-a	14	28	42	76	108	140

CRIME ILLUSTRATED (Magazine)
E. C. Comics: Nov-Dec, 1955 - No. 2, Spring, 1956 (25¢, Adult Suspense Stories on-c)

1-Ingels & Crandall-a	17	34	51	98	154	210
2-Ingels & Crandall-a	14	28	42	81	118	155

NOTE: *Craig a-2. Crandall a-1, 2; c-2. Evans a-1. Davis a-2. Ingels a-1, 2. Krigstein/Crandall a-1. Orlando a-1, 2; c-1.*

CRIME INCORPORATED (Formerly Crimes Incorporated)
Fox Features Syndicate: No. 2, Aug, 1950; No. 3, Aug, 1951

2	26	52	78	150	235	320
3(1951)-Hollingsworth-a	18	36	54	105	165	225

CRIME MACHINE (Magazine reprints pre-code crime and gangster comics)
Skywald Publications: Feb, 1971 - No. 2, May, 1971 (B&W, 68 pgs., roundbound)

1-Kubert-a(2)(r)(Avon); bikini girl in cake-c	6	12	18	37	59	80
2-Torres, Wildey-a; violent-c/a	4	8	12	24	37	50

CRIME MUST LOSE! (Formerly Sports Action?)
Sports Action (Atlas Comics): No. 4, Oct, 1950 - No. 12, April, 1952

4-Ann Brewster-a in all; c-used in N.Y. Legis. Comm. documents	18	36	54	105	165	225
5-12: 9-Robinson-a. 11-Used in POP, pg. 89	14	28	42	78	112	145

CRIME MUST PAY THE PENALTY (Formerly Four Favorites; Penalty #47, 48)
Ace Magazines (Current Books): No. 33, Feb, 1948; No. 2, Jun, 1948 - No. 48, Jan, 1956

33(#1, 2/48)-Becomes Four Teeners #34?	36	72	108	208	329	450
2(6/48)-Extreme violence; Palais-a?	22	44	66	126	198	270

Crime Reporter #2 © STJ

Crime SuspenStories #19 © WMG

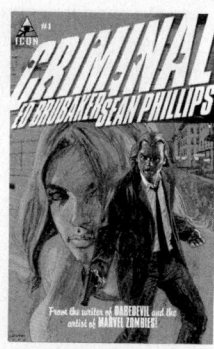

Criminal #1 © Brubaker & Phillips

	GD 2.0	VG 4.0	FN 6.0	VF 8.0	VF/NM 9.0	NM- 9.2
3,4,8: 3- "Frisco Mary" story used in Senate Investigation report, pg. 7. 4,8-Transvestism stories	16	32	48	94	147	200
5-7,9,10	13	26	39	72	101	130
11-19	12	24	36	67	94	120
20-Drug story "Dealers in White Death"	15	30	45	85	130	175
21-32,34-40,42-48: 44-Last pre-code	9	18	27	52	69	85
33(7/53)- "Dell Fabry-Junk King" drug story; mentioned in Love and Death	13	26	39	74	105	135
41-reprints "Dealers in White Death"	10	20	30	54	72	90

NOTE: Cameron a-29-31, 34, 35, 39-41. Colan a-20, 31. Kremer a-3, 37r. Larsen a-32. Palais a-5?,37.

CRIME MUST STOP
Hillman Periodicals: October, 1952 (52 pgs.)

	GD	VG	FN	VF	VF/NM	NM-
V1#1(Scarce)-Similar to Monster Crime; Mort Lawrence, Krigstein-a	72	144	216	450	750	1050

CRIME MYSTERIES (Secret Mysteries #16 on; combined with Crime Smashers #7 on)
Ribage Publ. Corp. (Trojan Magazines): May, 1952 - No. 15, Sept, 1954

	GD	VG	FN	VF	VF/NM	NM-
1-Transvestism story; crime & terror stories begin	57	114	171	356	591	825
2-Marijuana story (7/52)	40	80	120	240	383	525
3-One pg. Frazetta-a	37	74	111	213	337	460
4-Cover shows girl in bondage having her blood drained; 1 pg. Frazetta-a	57	114	171	356	591	825
5-10	31	62	93	178	282	385
11,12,14	29	58	87	167	264	360
13-(5/54)-Angelo Torres 1st comic work (inks over Check's pencils); Check-a	35	70	105	201	318	435
15-Acid in face-c	41	82	123	250	400	550

NOTE: Fass a-13; c-4, 10. Hollingsworth a-10-13, 15; c-2, 12, 13, 15. Kiefer a-4. Woodbridge a-13? Bondage-c-1, 8, 12.

CRIME ON THE RUN (See Approved Comics #8)

CRIME ON THE WATERFRONT (Formerly Famous Gangsters)
Realistic Publications: No. 4, May, 1952 (Painted cover)

	GD	VG	FN	VF	VF/NM	NM-
4	28	56	84	162	256	350

CRIME PATROL (Formerly International #1-5; International Crime Patrol #6; becomes Crypt of Terror #17 on)
E. C. Comics: No. 7, Summer, 1948 - No. 16, Feb-Mar, 1950

	GD	VG	FN	VF	VF/NM	NM-
7-Intro. Captain Crime	71	142	213	444	735	1025
8-14: 12-Ingels-a	61	122	183	381	633	885
15-Intro. of Crypt Keeper (inspired by Witches Tales radio show) & Crypt of Terror (see Tales From the Crypt #33 for origin); used by N.Y. Legis. Comm.; last pg. Feldstein-a	259	518	777	2072	3236	4400
16-2nd Crypt Keeper app.; Roussos-a	169	338	507	1352	2114	2875

NOTE: Craig c/a in most issues. Feldstein a-9-16. Kiefer a-8, 10, 11. Moldoff a-7.

CRIME PATROL
Gemstone Publishing: Apr, 2000 - No. 10, Jan, 2001 ($2.50)

1-10: E.C. reprints		2.50
Volume 1,2 (2000, $13.50) 1-r/#1-5. 2-r/#6-10		14.00

CRIME PHOTOGRAPHER (See Casey...)

CRIME REPORTER
St. John Publ. Co.: Aug, 1948 - No. 3, Dec, 1948 (Indicia shows Oct.)

	GD	VG	FN	VF	VF/NM	NM-
1-Drug club story	53	106	159	323	529	735
2-Used in SOTI: illo- "Children told me what the man was going to do with the red-hot poker;" r/Dynamic #17 with editing; Baker-c; Tuska-a	72	144	216	450	750	1050
3-Baker-c; Tuska-a	40	80	120	243	389	535

CRIMES BY WOMEN
Fox Features Syndicate: June, 1948 - No. 15, Aug, 1951; 1954 (True crime cases)

	GD	VG	FN	VF	VF/NM	NM-
1-True love story of Bonnie Parker	121	242	363	756	1253	1750
2,3: 3-Used in SOTI, pg. 234	63	126	189	394	652	910
4,5,7-9,11-15: 8-Used in POP, pg. 14-Bondage-c	57	114	171	356	596	835
6-Classic girl fight-c; acid-in-face panel	66	132	198	413	682	950
10-Used in SOTI, pg. 72; girl fight-c	59	118	177	369	610	850
54(M.S. Publ.-'54)-Reprint; (formerly My Love Secret)	24	48	72	139	220	300

CRIMES INCORPORATED (Formerly My Past)
Fox Features Syndicate: No. 12, June, 1950 (Crime Incorporated No. 2 on)

	GD	VG	FN	VF	VF/NM	NM-
12	21	42	63	122	191	260

CRIMES INCORPORATED (See Fox Giants)

CRIME SMASHER (See Whiz #76)
Fawcett Publications: Summer, 1948 (one-shot)

	GD 2.0	VG 4.0	FN 6.0	VF 8.0	VF/NM 9.0	NM- 9.2
1-Formerly Spy Smasher	42	84	126	256	421	585

CRIME SMASHERS (Becomes Secret Mysteries No. 16 on)
Ribage Publishing Corp.(Trojan Magazines): Oct, 1950 - No. 15, Mar, 1953

	GD	VG	FN	VF	VF/NM	NM-
1-Used in SOTI, pg. 19,20, & illo "A girl raped and murdered;" Sally the Sleuth begins	88	176	264	550	913	1275
2-Kubert-c	46	92	138	281	466	650
3,4	38	76	114	219	347	475
5-Wood-a	45	90	135	275	450	625
6,8-11: 8-Lingerie panel	29	58	87	170	268	365
7-Female heroin junkie story	33	66	99	190	300	410
12-Injury to eye panel; 1 pg. Frazetta-a	32	64	96	186	293	400
13-Used in POP, pgs. 79,80; 1 pg. Frazetta-a	32	64	96	186	293	400
14,15	24	48	72	139	220	300

NOTE: Hollingsworth a-14. Kiefer a-15. Bondage c-7, 9.

CRIME SUSPENSTORIES (Formerly Vault of Horror No. 12-14)
E. C. Comics: No. 15, Oct-Nov, 1950 - No. 27, Feb-Mar, 1955

15-Identical to #1 in content; #1 printed on outside front cover. #15 (formerly "The Vault of Horror") printed and blackened out on inside front cover with Vol. 1, No. 1 printed over it. Evidently, several of No. 15 were printed before a decision was made not to drop the Vault of Horror and Haunt of Fear series. The print run was stopped on No. 15 and continued on No. 1. All of the No. 15 issues were changed as described above.

	GD	VG	FN	VF	VF/NM	NM-
	147	294	441	1176	1838	2500
1	112	224	336	896	1398	1900
2	59	118	177	472	736	1000
3-5: 3-Poe adaptation. 3-Old Witch stories begin	41	82	123	328	514	700
6-10: 9-Craig bio.	35	70	105	280	440	600
11,12,14,15: 15-The Old Witch guest stars	27	54	81	216	341	465
13,16-Williamson-a	29	58	87	232	366	500
17-Williamson/Frazetta-a (6 pgs.) Williamson bio.	35	70	105	280	440	600
18,19: 19-Used in SOTI, pg. 235	35	70	105	280	440	600
20-Cover used in SOTI, illo "Cover of a children's comic book"		58	87	232	366	500
21,24-26: 24- "Food For Thought" similar to "Cave In" in Amazing Detective Cases #13 (1952)	17	34	51	136	213	290
22-Used in Senate investigation on juvenile delinquency; Ax decapitation-c	32	64	96	256	403	550
23-Used in Senate investigation on juvenile delinquency	24	48	72	192	296	400
27-Last issue (Low distribution)	21	42	63	168	264	360

NOTE: Craig a-1-21; c-1-18, 20-22. Crandall a-18-26. Davis a-4, 5, 7, 9-12, 20. Elder a-17,18. Evans a-15, 19, 21, 23, 25, 27; c-23, 24. Feldstein c-19. Ingels a-1-12, 14, 15, 27. Kamen a-2, 4, 18, 20-27; c-25-27. Krigstein a-22, 24, 25, 27. Kurtzman a-1, 3. Orlando a-16, 22, 24, 26. Wood a-1. Issues No. 1-3 were printed in Canada as "Weird Suspenstories". Issues No. 11-15 have E. C. "quickie" stories. No. 25 contains the famous "Are You a Red Dupe?" editorial. Ray Bradbury adaptations-15, 17.

CRIME SUSPENSTORIES
Russ Cochran/Gemstone Publ.: Nov, 1992 - No. 27, May, 1999 ($1.50/$2.00/$2.50)

1-27: Reprints Crime SuspenStories series		3.00

CRIMINAL
Marvel Comics (Icon): Oct, 2006 - Present ($2.99)

1-9-Ed Brubaker-s/Sean Phillips-a/c		3.00
... Vol. 1: Coward TPB (2007, $14.99) r/#1-5; intro. by Tom Fontana		15.00

CRIMINAL MACABRE: A CAL MCDONALD MYSTERY (Also see Last Train to Deadsville)
Dark Horse Comics: May, 2003 - No. 5, Sept, 2003 ($2.99)

1-5-Niles-s/Templesmith-a		3.00
... :Feat of Clay (6/06, $2.99) Niles-s/Hotz-a/c		3.00

CRIMINAL MACABRE: TWO RED EYES
Dark Horse Comics: Dec, 2006 - No. 4, Mar, 2007 ($2.99)

1-4-Niles-s/Hotz-a/Bradstreet-c		3.00

CRIMINALS ON THE RUN (Formerly Young King Cole) (Crime Fighting Detective No. 11 on)
Premium Group (Novelty Press): V4#1, Aug-Sep, 1948-#10, Dec-Jan, 1949-50

	GD	VG	FN	VF	VF/NM	NM-
V4#1-Young King Cole continues	29	58	87	170	268	365
2-6: 6-Dr. Doom app.	25	50	75	148	232	315
7-Classic "Fish in the Face" c by L. B. Cole	53	106	159	323	537	750
V5#1,2 (#8,9),10: 9,10-L. B. Cole-c	23	46	69	130	205	280

NOTE: Most issues have L. B. Cole covers. McWilliams a-V4#6, 7, V5#2; c-V4#5.

CRIMSON (Also see Cliffhanger #0)
Image Comics (Cliffhanger Productions): May, 1998 - No. 7, Dec, 1998;
DC Comics (Cliffhanger Prod.): No. 8, Mar, 1999 - No. 24, Apr, 2001 ($2.50)

1-Humberto Ramos-a/Augustyn-s		5.00
1-Variant-c by Warren		8.00
1-Chromium-c		20.00
2-Ramos-c with street crowd, 2-Variant-c by Art Adams		3.00

Crimson #24 © Humberto Ramos

Crisis on Infinite Earths #12 © DC

Crossgen Chronicles #2 © CRO

	GD 2.0	VG 4.0	FN 6.0	VF 8.0	VF/NM 9.0	NM- 9.2

	GD 2.0	VG 4.0	FN 6.0	VF 8.0	VF/NM 9.0	NM- 9.2

2-Dynamic Forces CrimsonChrome cover ... 15.00
3-7: 3-Ramos Moon background-c. 7-3 covers by Ramos, Madureira, & Campbell ... 3.50
8-23: 8-First DC issue ... 2.50
24-($3.50) Final issue; wraparound-c ... 3.50
DF Premiere Ed. 1998 ($6.95) covers by Ramos and Jae Lee ... 7.00
Crimson: Scarlet X Blood on the Moon (10/99, $3.95) ... 4.00
Crimson Sourcebook (11/99, $2.95) Pin-ups and info ... 3.00
Earth Angel TPB (2001, $14.95) r/#13-18 ... 15.00
Heaven and Earth TPB (1/00, $14.95) r/#7-12 ... 15.00
Loyalty and Loss TPB ('99, $12.95) r/#1-6 ... 13.00
Redemption TPB ('01, $14.95) r/#19-24 ... 15.00

CRIMSON AVENGER, THE (See Detective Comics #20 for 1st app.)(Also see Leading Comics #1 & World's Best/Finest Comics)
DC Comics: June, 1988 - No. 4, Sept, 1988 ($1.00, limited series)
1-4 ... 2.50

CRIMSON DYNAMO
Marvel Comics (Epic): Oct, 2003 - No. 6, Apr, 2004 ($2.50/$2.99)
1-4,6: 1-John Jackson Miller-s/Steve Ellis-a/c ... 2.50
5-($2.99) Iron Man-c/app. ... 3.00

CRIMSON PLAGUE
Event Comics: June, 1997 ($2.95, unfinished mini-series)
1-George Perez-a ... 3.00

CRIMSON PLAGUE (George Pérez's...)
Image Comics (Gorilla): June, 2000 - No. 2, Aug, 2000 ($2.95, mini-series)
1-George Perez-a; reprints 6/97 issue with 16 new pages ... 3.00
2-($2.50) ... 2.50

CRISIS AFTERMATH: THE BATTLE FOR BLUDHAVEN (Also see Infinite Crisis)
DC Comics: Jun, 2006 - No. 6, Sept, 2006 ($2.99, limited series)
1-Atomic Knights return; Teen Titans app.; Jurgens-a/Acuna-c ... 4.00
1-2nd printing with pencil cover ... 3.00
2-6: 2-Intro S.H.A.D.E. (new Freedom Fighters) ... 3.00
TPB (2007, $14.99) r/#1-6 ... 13.00

CRISIS AFTERMATH: THE SPECTRE (Also see Infinite Crisis, Gotham Central and Tales of the Unexpected)
DC Comics: Jul, 2006 - No. 3, Sept, 2006 ($2.99, limited series)
1-3-Crispus Allen becomes the Spectre; Pfeifer-s/Chiang-a/c ... 3.00
TPB (2007, $12.99) r/#1-3 and Tales of the Unexpected #1-3 ... 13.00

CRISIS ON INFINITE EARTHS (Also see Official... Index and Legends of the DC Universe)
DC Comics: Apr, 1985 - No. 12, Mar, 1986 (maxi-series)
1-1st DC app. Blue Beetle & Detective Karp from Charlton; Pérez-c on all ... 2 4 6 9 13 16
2-6: 6-Intro Charlton's Capt. Atom, Nightshade, Question, Judomaster, Peacemaker & Thunderbolt into DC Universe ... 1 3 4 6 8 10
7-Double size; death of Supergirl ... 2 4 6 13 16 22
8-Death of the Flash (Barry Allen) ... 2 4 6 11 16 20
9-11: 9-Intro. Charlton's Ghost into DC Universe. 10-Intro Charlton's Banshee, Dr. Spectro, Image, Punch & Jewellee into DC Universe; Starman (Prince Gavyn) dies ... 1 3 4 6 8 10
12-(52 pgs.)-Deaths of Dove, Kole, Lori Lemaris, Sunburst, G.A. Robin &Huntress; Kid Flash becomes new Flash; 3rd & final DC app. of the 3 Lt. Marvels; Green Fury gets new look (becomes Green Flame in Infinity, Inc. #32) ... 2 4 6 8 11 14
Slipcased Hardcover (1998, $99.95) Wraparound dust-jacket cover by Pérez and Alex Ross; sketch pages by Pérez; intro by Wolfman ... 125.00
TPB (2000, $29.95) Wraparound-c by Pérez and Ross ... 30.00
NOTE: Crossover issues: All Star Squadron 50-56,60; Amethyst 13; Blue Devil 17,18; DC Comics Presents 78,86-88,95; Detective Comics 558; Fury of Firestorm 41,42; G.I. Combat 274; Green Lantern 194-196,198; Infinity, Inc. 18-25 & Annual 1, Justice League of America 244,245 & Annual 3; Legion of Super-Heroes 16,18; Losers Special 1; New Teen Titans 13,14; Omega Men 31,33; Superman 413-415; Swamp Thing 44,46; Wonder Woman 327-329.

CRISIS ON MULTIPLE EARTHS
DC Comics: 2002, 2003, 2004 ($14.95, trade paperbacks)
TPB-(2003) Reprints 1st 4 Silver Age JLA/JSA crossovers from J.L.ofA. #21,22; 29,30; 37,38; 46,47; new painted-c by Alex Ross; intro. by Mark Waid ... 15.00
Volume 2 (2003, $14.95) r/J.L.ofA. #55,56; 64,65; 73,74; 82,83; new Ordway-c ... 15.00
Volume 3 (2004, $14.95) r/J.L.ofA. #91,92; 100-102; 107,108; 113; Wein intro.. Ross-c ... 15.00
Volume 4 (2006, $14.99) r/J.L.ofA. #123-124 (Earth-Prime),135-137 (Fawcett's Shazam characters), 147-148 (Legion of Super-Heroes); Ross-c ... 15.00
... The Team-Ups Volume 1 (2005, $14.99) r/Flash #123,129,137,151; Showcase #55,56; Green Lantern #40, Brave and the Bold #61 and Spectre #7; new Ordway-c ... 15.00

CRITICAL MASS (See A Shadowline Saga: Critical Mass)

CRITTERS (Also see Usagi Yojimbo Summer Special)
Fantagraphics Books: 1986 - No. 50, 1990 ($1.70/$2.00, B&W)
1-Cutey Bunny, Usagi Yojimbo app. ... 1 3 4 6 8 10
2,4,5,8,9 ... 6.00
3,6,7,10-Usagi Yojimbo app. ... 1 2 3 4 5 7
11-22,24-37,39,40: 11,14-Usagi Yojimbo app. 11-Christmas Special (68 pgs.); Usagi Yojimbo. ... 2.50
22-Watchmen parody; two diff. covers exist ... 5.00
23-With Alan Moore Flexi-disc ($3.95) ... 3.00
38-($2.75-c) Usagi Yojimbo app. ... 4.00
41-49 ...
50 ($4.95, 84 pgs.)-Neil the Horse, Capt. Jack, Sam & Max & Usagi Yojimbo app.; Quagmire, Shaw-a ... 1 2 3 4 5 7
Special 1 (1/88, $2.00) ... 3.00

CROSS
Dark Horse Comics: No. 0, Oct, 1995 - No. 6, Apr, 1995 ($2.95, limited series, mature)
0-6: Darrow-c & Vachss scripts in all ... 3.00

CROSS AND THE SWITCHBLADE, THE
Spire Christian Comics (Fleming H. Revell Co.): 1972 (35-49¢)
1-Some issues have nn ... 2 4 6 9 13 16

CROSS BRONX, THE
Image Comics: Sept, 2006 - No. 4, Dec, 2006 ($2.99, limited series)
1-4: 1-Oeming-a/c; Oeming & Brandon-s; Ribic var-c. 2-Johnson var-c. 4-Mack var-c ... 3.00

CROSSFIRE
Spire Christian Comics (Fleming H. Revell Co.): 1973 (39/49¢)
nn ... 2 4 6 9 12 15

CROSSFIRE (Also see DNAgents)
Eclipse Comics: 5/84 - No. 17, 3/86; No. 18, 1/87 - No. 26, 2/88 ($1.50, Baxter paper) (#18-26 are B&W)
1-11,14-26: 1-DNAgents x-over; Spiegle-c/a begins ... 2.50
12,13-Death of Marilyn Monroe. 12-Dave Stevens-c ... 4.00

CROSSFIRE AND RAINBOW (Also see DNAgents)
Eclipse Comics: June, 1986 - No. 4, Sept, 1986 ($1.25, deluxe format)
1-3: Spiegle-a. 4-Dave Stevens-c ... 2.50

CROSSGEN...
CrossGeneration Comics
CrossGenesis (1/00) Previews CrossGen universe; cover gallery ... 3.00
...Primer (1/00) Wizard supplement; intro. to the CrossGen universe ... 2.50
...Sampler (2/00) Retailer preview book ... 3.00

CROSSGEN CHRONICLES
CrossGeneration Comics: June, 2000 - No. 8 ($3.95)
1-Intro. to CrossGen characters & company ... 4.00
1-(no cover price) same contents, customer preview ... 4.00
2-8: 2-(3/01) George Pérez-c/a. 3-5-Pérez-a/Waid-s. 6,7-Nebres-c/a ... 4.00

CROSSING MIDNIGHT
DC Comics (Vertigo): Jan, 2007 - Present ($2.99)
1-10: 1-Carey-s/Fern-a/Williams III-c. 10-Nguyen-a ... 3.00
...: Cut Here TPB ($9.99) r/#1-5 ... 10.00

CROSSING THE ROCKIES (See Classics Illustrated Special Issue)

CROSSOVERS, THE
CrossGeneration Comics: Feb, 2003 - No. 12 ($2.95)
1-12-Robert Rodi-s. 1-6-Mauricet & Ernie Colon-a. 7-Staton-a begins ... 3.00
Vol. 1: Cross Currents (2003, $9.95) digest-sized reprints #1-6 ... 10.00

CROW, THE (Also see Caliber Presents)
Caliber Press: Feb, 1989 - No. 4, 1989 ($1.95, B&W, limited series)
1-James O'Barr-c/a/scripts ... 5 10 15 30 48 65
1-3-2nd printing ... 6.00
2-4 ... 3 6 9 18 27 35
2-3rd printing ... 4.00

CROW, THE
Tundra Publishing, Ltd.: Jan, 1992 - No. 3, 1992 ($4.95, B&W, 68 pgs.)
1-3: 1-r/#1,2 of Caliber series. 2-r/#3 of Caliber series w/new material. 3-All new material ... 1 2 3 5 6 8

CROW, THE
Kitchen Sink Press: 1/96 - No. 3, 3/96 ($2.95, B&W)
1-3: James O'Barr-c/scripts ... 5.00

Crown Comics #2 © Golfing

The Crusades #12 © Seagle & Jones

Crypt of Dawn #3 © JM Linsner

	GD 2.0	VG 4.0	FN 6.0	VF 8.0	VF/NM 9.0	NM- 9.2

#0-A Cycle of Shattered Lives (12/98, $3.50) new story by O'Barr ... 4.00

CROW, THE
Image Comics (Todd McFarlane Prod.): Feb, 1999 - No. 10, Nov, 1999 ($2.50)

1-10: 1-Two covers by McFarlane and Kent Williams; Muth-s in all. 2-6,10-Paul Lee-a ... 3.00
Book 1 - Vengeance (2000, $10.95, TPB) r/#1-3,5,6 ... 11.00
Book 2 - Evil Beyond Reach (2000, $10.95, TPB) r/#4,7-10 ... 11.00
Todd McFarlane Presents The Crow Magazine 1 (3/00, $4.95) ... 5.00

CROW, THE: CITY OF ANGELS (Movie)
Kitchen Sink Press: July, 1996 - No. 3, Sept, 1996 ($2.95, limited series)

1-3: Adaptation of film; two-c (photo & illos.). 1-Vincent Perez interview ... 3.00

CROW, THE: FLESH AND BLOOD
Kitchen Sink Press: May, 1996 - No. 3, July, 1996 ($2.95, limited series)

1-3: O'Barr-c ... 3.00

CROW, THE: RAZOR - KILL THE PAIN
London Night Studios: Apr, 1998 - No. 3, July, 1998 ($2.95, B&W, lim. series)

1-3-Hartsoe-s/O'Barr-painted-c ... 3.00
0(10/98) Dorien painted-c, Finale (2/99) ... 3.00
The Lost Chapter (2/99, $4.95), Tour Book-(12/97) pin-ups; 4 diff.-c ... 5.00

CROW, THE: WAKING NIGHTMARES
Kitchen Sink Press: Jan, 1997 - No. 4, 1998 ($2.95, B&W, limited series)

1-4-Miran Kim-c ... 5.00

CROW, THE: WILD JUSTICE
Kitchen Sink Press: Oct, 1996 - No. 3, Dec, 1996 ($2.95, B&W, limited series)

1-3-Prosser-s/Adlard-a ... 3.00

CROWN COMICS
Golfing/McCombs Publ.: Wint, 1944-45; No. 2, Sum, 1945 - No. 19, July, 1949

	GD 2.0	VG 4.0	FN 6.0	VF 8.0	VF/NM 9.0	NM- 9.2
1- "The Oblong Box" E.A. Poe adaptation	40	80	120	244	392	540
2,3-Baker-a; 3-Voodah by Baker	28	56	84	162	256	350
4-6-Baker-c/a; Voodah app.#4,5	29	58	87	170	268	365
7-Feldstein, Baker, Kamen-a; Baker-c	30	60	90	172	271	370
8-Baker-a; Voodah app.	24	48	72	139	220	300
9-11,13-19; Voodah in #10-19. 13-New logo	16	32	48	94	147	200
12-Master Marvin by Feldstein, Starr-a; Voodah-c	17	34	51	98	154	210

NOTE: Bolle a-11, 13-16, 18, 19; c-11p, 15. Powell a-19. Starr a-11-13; c-11i.

CRUCIBLE
DC Comics (Impact): Feb, 1993 - No. 6, July, 1993 ($1.25, limited series)

1-6: 1-(99¢)-Neon ink-c. 1,2-Quesada-c(p). 1-4-Quesada layouts ... 2.50

CRUEL AND UNUSUAL
DC Comics (Vertigo): June, 1999 - No. 4, Sept, 1999 ($2.95, limited series)

1-4-Delano & Peyer-s/McCrea-c/a ... 3.00

CRUSADER FROM MARS (See Tops in Adventure)
Ziff-Davis Publ. Co.: Jan-Mar, 1952 - No. 2, Fall, 1952 (Painted-c)

	GD 2.0	VG 4.0	FN 6.0	VF 8.0	VF/NM 9.0	NM- 9.2
1-Cover is dated Spring	75	150	225	469	777	1085
2-Bondage-c	53	106	159	323	537	750

CRUSADER RABBIT (TV)
Dell Publishing Co.: No. 735, Oct, 1956 - No. 805, May, 1957

	GD 2.0	VG 4.0	FN 6.0	VF 8.0	VF/NM 9.0	NM- 9.2
Four Color 735 (#1)	26	52	78	195	348	500
Four Color 805	20	40	60	148	264	380

CRUSADERS, THE (Religious)
Chick Publications: 1974 - Vol. 17, 1988 (39/69¢, 36 pgs.)

	GD 2.0	VG 4.0	FN 6.0	VF 8.0	VF/NM 9.0	NM- 9.2
Vol.1-Operation Bucharest ('74). Vol.2-The Broken Cross ('74). Vol.3-Scarface ('74). Vol.4-Exorcists ('75). Vol.5-Chaos ('75)	2	4	6	9	13	16
Vol.6-Primal Man? ('76)-(Disputes evolution theory). Vol.7-The Ark-(claims proof of existence, destroyed by Bolsheviks). Vol.8-The Gift-(Life story of Christ). Vol.9-Angel of Light-(Story of the Devil). Vol.10-Spellbound?-(Tells how rock music is Satanic & produced by witches). 11-Sabotage?. 12-Alberto. 13-Double Cross. 14-The Godfathers. (No. 6-14 low in distribution; loaded with religious propaganda.). 15-The Force. 16-The Four Horsemen	2	4	6	9	13	16
Vol. 17-The Prophet (low print run)	2	4	6	10	14	18

CRUSADERS (Southern Knights No. 2 on)
Guild Publications: 1982 (B&W, magazine size)

	GD 2.0	VG 4.0	FN 6.0	VF 8.0	VF/NM 9.0	NM- 9.2
1-1st app. Southern Knights	1	3	4	6	8	10

CRUSADERS, THE (Also see Black Hood, The Jaguar, The Comet, The Fly, Legend of the Shield, The Mighty... & The Web)
DC Comics (Impact): May, 1992 - No. 8, Dec, 1992 ($1.00/$1.25)

1-8-Contains 3 Impact trading cards ... 2.50

CRUSADES, THE
DC Comics (Vertigo): 2001 - No. 20, Dec, 2002 ($3.95/$2.50)

...: Urban Decree ('01, $3.95) Intro. the Knight; Seagle-s/Kelley Jones-c/a ... 4.00
1-(5/01, $2.50) Sienkiewicz-c ... 3.00
2-20: 2-Moeller-c. 18-Begin $2.95-c ... 3.00

CRUSH
Dark Horse Comics: Oct, 2003 - No. 4, Jan, 2004 ($2.99, limited series)

1-4-Jason Hall-s/Sean Murphy-a ... 3.00

CRUSH, THE
Image Comics (Motown Machineworks): Jan, 1996 - No. 5, July, 1996 ($2.25, limited series)

1-5: Baron scripts ... 3.00

CRUX
CrossGeneration Comics: May, 2001 - No. 33, Feb, 2004 ($2.95)

1-33: 1-Waid-s/Epting & Magyar-a/c. 6-Pelletier-a. 13-Dixon-s begin. 25-Cover has fake creases and other aging ... 3.00
Atlantis Rising Vol. 1 TPB (2002, $15.95) r/#1-6 ... 16.00
Test of Time Vol. 2 TPB (12/02, $15.95) r/#7-12 ... 16.00
Vol. 3: Strangers in Atlantis (2003, $15.95) r/#13-18 ... 16.00
Vol. 4: Chaos Reborn (2003, $15.95) r/#19-24 ... 16.00

CRY FOR DAWN
Cry For Dawn Pub.: 1989 - No. 9 ($2.25, B&W, mature)

	GD 2.0	VG 4.0	FN 6.0	VF 8.0	VF/NM 9.0	NM- 9.2
1	7	14	21	45	73	100
1-2nd printing	3	6	9	18	27	35
1-3rd printing	3	6	9	14	20	25
2	4	8	12	28	44	60
2-2nd printing	2	4	6	11	16	20
3	3	6	9	20	30	40
3a-HorrorCon Edition (1990, less than 400 printed, signed inside-c)						200.00
4-6	2	4	6	11	16	20
5-2nd printing	1	2	3	5	6	8
7-9	2	4	6	8	11	14
4-9-Signed & numbered editions	3	6	9	14	20	25

Angry Christ Comix HC (4/03, $29.99) reprints various stories; and 30 pgs. new material ... 30.00
...Calendar (1993) ... 35.00

CRYIN' LION COMICS
William H. Wise Co.: Fall, 1944 - No. 3, Spring, 1945

	GD 2.0	VG 4.0	FN 6.0	VF 8.0	VF/NM 9.0	NM- 9.2
1-Funny animal	15	30	45	83	124	165
2-Hitler app.	13	26	39	74	105	135
3	10	20	30	56	76	95

CRYPT
Image Comics (Extreme): Aug, 1995 - No.2, Oct. 1995 ($2.50, limited series)

1,2-Prophet app. ... 2.50

CRYPTIC WRITINGS OF MEGADETH
Chaos! Comics: Sept, 1997 - No. 4, Jun, 1998 ($2.95, quarterly)

1-4-Stories based on song lyrics by Dave Mustaine ... 3.00

CRYPT OF DAWN (see Dawn)
Sirius: 1996 ($2.95, B&W, limited series)

1-Linsner-c/s; anthology. ... 5.00
2, 3 (2/98) ... 4.00
4,5: 4- (6/98), 5-(11/98) ... 3.00
Ltd. Edition ... 20.00

CRYPT OF SHADOWS
Marvel Comics Group: Jan, 1973 - No. 21, Nov, 1975 (#1-9 are 20¢)

	GD 2.0	VG 4.0	FN 6.0	VF 8.0	VF/NM 9.0	NM- 9.2
1-Wolverton-r/Advs. Into Terror #7	3	6	9	14	20	25
2-10: 2-Starlin/Everett-c	2	4	6	9	13	16
11-21: 18,20-Kirby-a	2	4	6	8	11	14

NOTE: Briefer a-2r. Ditko a-13r, 18-20r. Everett a-6, 14r; c-2i. Heath a-1r. Gil Kane c-1, 6. Mort Lawrence a-1r, 8r. Maneely a-2r. Moldoff a-8. Powell a-12r, 14r. Tuska a-2r.

CRYPT OF TERROR (Formerly Crime Patrol; Tales From the Crypt No. 20 on)
(Also see EC Archives • Tales From the Crypt)
E. C. Comics: No. 17, Apr-May, 1950 - No. 19, Aug-Sept, 1950

	GD 2.0	VG 4.0	FN 6.0	VF 8.0	VF/NM 9.0	NM- 9.2
17-1st New Trend to hit stands	282	564	846	2256	3528	4800
18,19	162	324	486	1296	2023	2750

NOTE: Craig a-17-19. Feldstein a-17-19. Ingels a-19. Kurtzman a-18. Wood a-18. Canadian reprints known; see Table of Contents.

CSI: CRIME SCENE INVESTIGATION (Based on TV series)

CSI: Thicker Than Blood © CBS

Curse of the Spawn #23 © TMP

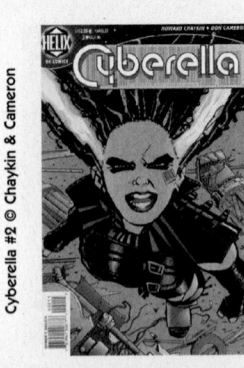

Cyberella #2 © Chaykin & Cameron

	GD 2.0	VG 4.0	FN 6.0	VF 8.0	VF/NM 9.0	NM- 9.2

IDW Publishing: Jan, 2003 - No. 5, May, 2003 ($3.99, limited series)

1-Two covers (photo & Ashley Wood); Max Allan Collins-s						4.00
2-5						4.00
...: Case Files Vol. 1 TPB (8/06, $19.99) B&W rep/Serial TPB, CSI - Bad Rap and CSI - Demon House limited series						20.00
...: Serial TPB (2003, $19.99) r/#1-5; bonus short story by Collins/Wood						20.00
...: Thicker Than Blood (7/03, $6.99) Mariotte-s/Rodriguez-a						7.00

CSI: CRIME SCENE INVESTIGATION - BAD RAP
IDW Publishing: Aug, 2003 - No. 5, Dec, 2003 ($3.99, limited series)

1-5-Two photo covers; Max Allan Collins-s/Rodriguez-a						4.00
TPB (3/04, $19.99) r/#1-5						20.00

CSI: CRIME SCENE INVESTIGATION - DEMON HOUSE
IDW Publishing: Feb, 2004 - No. 5, Jun, 2004 ($3.99, limited series)

1-5-Photo covers on all; Max Allan Collins-s/Rodriguez-a						4.00
TPB (10/04, $19.99) r/#1-5						20.00

CSI: CRIME SCENE INVESTIGATION - DOMINOS
IDW Publishing: Aug, 2004 - No. 5, Dec, 2004 ($3.99, limited series)

1-5-Photo covers on all; Oprisko-s/Rodriguez-a						4.00

CSI: CRIME SCENE INVESTIGATION - DYING IN THE GUTTERS
IDW Publishing: Aug, 2006 - No. 5, Dec, 2006 ($3.99, limited series)

1-5-"Rich Johnston" murdered; comic creators (Quesada, Rucka, David, Brubaker, Silvestri and others) appear as suspects; Stephen Mooney-a; photo-c						4.00

CSI: CRIME SCENE INVESTIGATION - SECRET IDENTITY
IDW Publishing: Feb, 2005 - No. 5, Jun, 2005 ($3.99, limited series)

1-5-Photo covers on all; Steven Grant-s/Gabriel Rodriguez-a						4.00

CSI: MIAMI
IDW Publishing: Oct, 2003; Apr, 2004 ($6.99, one-shots)

... - Blood Money (9/04) Oprisko-s/Guedes & Perkins-a						7.00
... - Smoking Gun (10/03) Mariotte-s/Avilés & Wood-a						7.00
... - Thou Shalt Not... (4/04) Oprisko-s/Guedes & Wood-a						7.00
TPB (2/05, $19.99) reprints one-shots						20.00

CSI: NY - BLOODY MURDER
IDW Publishing: July, 2005 - No. 5, Nov, 2005 ($3.99, limited series)

1-5-Photo covers on all; Collins-s/Woodward-a						4.00

C-23 (Jim Lee's...) (Based on Wizards of the Coast card game)
Image Comics: Apr, 1998 - No. 8, Nov, 1998 ($2.50)

1-8: 1,2-Choi & Mariotte-s/ Charest-c by Jim Lee. 4-Ryan Benjamin-c. 5,8-Corben var-c. 6-Flip book with Planetary preview; Corben-c						3.00

CUD
Fantagraphics Books: 8/92 - No. 8, 12/94 ($2.25-$2.75, B&W, mature)

1-8: Terry LaBan scripts & art in all. 6-1st Eno & Plum						3.00

CUD COMICS
Dark Horse Comics: Jan, 1995 - No. 8, Sept, 1997 ($2.95, B&W)

1-8: Terry LaBan-c/a/scripts. 5-Nudity; marijuana story						3.00
Eno and Plum TPB (1997, $12.95) r/#1-4, DHP #93-95						13.00

CUPID
Marvel Comics (U.S.A.): Dec, 1949 - No. 2, Mar, 1950

	GD	VG	FN	VF	VF/NM	NM-
1-Photo-c	15	30	45	88	137	185
2-Bettie Page ('50s pin-up queen) photo-c; Powell-a (see My Love #4)	40	80	120	235	368	500

CURIO
Harry 'A' Chesler: 1930's(?) (Tabloid size, 16-20 pgs.)

	GD	VG	FN	VF	VF/NM	NM-
nn	18	36	54	107	169	230

CURLY KAYOE COMICS (Boxing)
United Features Syndicate/Dell Publ. Co.: 1946 - No. 8, 1950; Jan, 1958

	GD	VG	FN	VF	VF/NM	NM-
1 (1946)-Strip-r (Fritzi Ritz); biography of Sam Leff, Kayoe's artist	18	36	54	103	162	220
2	11	22	33	62	86	110
3-8	10	20	30	54	72	90
United Presents...(Fall, 1948)	10	20	30	54	72	90
Four Color 871 (Dell, 1/58)	4	8	12	24	37	50

CURSED
Image Comics (Top Cow): Oct, 2003 - No. 4, Feb, 2004 ($2.99)

1-4-Avery & Blevins-s/Molenaar-a						3.00

	GD 2.0	VG 4.0	FN 6.0	VF 8.0	VF/NM 9.0	NM- 9.2

CURSE OF DRACULA, THE
Dark Horse Comics: July, 1998 - No. 3, Sept, 1998 ($2.95, limited series)

1-3-Marv Wolfman-s/Gene Colan-a						3.00
TPB (2005, $9.95) r/series; intro. by Marv Wolfman						10.00

CURSE OF DREADWOLF
Lightning Comics: Sept, 1994 ($2.75, B&W)

1						2.75

CURSE OF RUNE (Becomes Rune, 2nd Series)
Malibu Comics (Ultraverse): May, 1995 - No. 4, Aug, 1995 ($2.50, lim. series)

1-4: 1-Two covers form one image						2.50

CURSE OF THE SPAWN
Image Comics (Todd McFarlane Prod.): Sept, 1996 - No. 29, Mar, 1999 ($1.95)

	GD	VG	FN	VF	VF/NM	NM-
1-Dwayne Turner-a(p)						6.00
1-B&W Edition	2	4	6	9	13	16
2-3						4.00
4-29: 12-Movie photo-c of Melinda Clarke (Priest)						2.50
Blood and Sutures ('99, $9.95, TPB) r/#5-8						10.00
Lost Values ('00, $10.95, TPB) r/#12-14,22; Ashley Wood-c						11.00
Sacrifice of the Soul ('99, $9.95, TPB) r/#1-4						10.00
Shades of Gray ('00, $9.95, TPB) r/#9-11,29						10.00
The Best of the Curse of the Spawn (6/06, $16.99, TPB) B&W r/#1-8,12-16,20-29						17.00

CURSE OF THE WEIRD
Marvel Comics: Dec, 1993 - No. 4, Mar, 1994 ($1.25, limited series)
(Pre-code horror-r)

	GD	VG	FN	VF	VF/NM	NM-
1-4: 1,3,4-Wolverton-r(1-Eye of Doom; 3-Where Monsters Dwell; 4-The End of the World).						
2-Orlando-r. 4-Zombie-r by Everett; painted-c	1	2	3	4	5	7

NOTE: *Briefer* r-2. *Davis* a-4r. *Ditko* a-1r, 2r, 4r; c-1r. *Everett* r-1. *Heath* r-1-3. *Kubert* r-3. *Wolverton* a-1r, 3r, 4r.

CUSTER'S LAST FIGHT
Avon Periodicals: 1950

	GD	VG	FN	VF	VF/NM	NM-
nn-Partial reprint of Cowpuncher #1	15	30	45	88	137	185

CUTEY BUNNY (See Army Surplus Komikz Featuring...)

CUTIE PIE
Junior Reader's Guild (Lev Gleason): May, 1955 - No. 3, Dec, 1955; No. 4, Feb, 1956; No. 5, Aug, 1956

	GD	VG	FN	VF	VF/NM	NM-
1	8	16	24	42	54	65
2-5: 4-Misdated 2/55	6	12	18	28	34	40

CUTTING EDGE
Marvel Comics: Dec, 1995 ($2.95)

1-Hulk-c/story; Messner-Loebs scripts						3.00

CVO: COVERT VAMPIRIC OPERATIONS
IDW Publishing: June, 2003 ($5.99, one-shot)

1-Alex Garner-s/Mindy Lee-a(p)						6.00
... - Human Touch 1 (8/04, $3.99, one-shot) Hernandez & Garner-a						4.00
TPB (9/04, $19.99) r/#1 and ... - Artifact #1-3; intro. by Garner						20.00

CVO: COVERT VAMPIRIC OPERATIONS - AFRICAN BLOOD
IDW Publishing: Sept, 2006 - No. 4, May, 2007 ($3.99, limited series)

1-4-El Torres-s/Luis Czerniawski-a						4.00

CVO: COVERT VAMPIRIC OPERATIONS - ARTIFACT
IDW Publishing: Oct, 2003 - No. 3, Dec, 2003 ($3.99, limited series)

1-3-Jeff Mariotte-s/Gabriel Hernandez-a/Alex Garner-c						4.00

CVO: COVERT VAMPIRIC OPERATIONS - ROGUE STATE
IDW Publishing: Nov, 2004 - No. 5, Mar, 2005 ($3.99, limited series)

1-5-Jeff Mariotte-s/Vazquez-a						4.00
TPB (7/05, $19.99) r/#1-5; cover gallery						20.00

CYBERELLA
DC Comics (Helix): Sept, 1996 - No. 12, Aug, 1997 ($2.25/$2.50)(1st Helix series)

1-12: 1-5-Chaykin & Cameron-a. 1,2-Chaykin-c. 3-5-Cameron-c						2.50

CYBERFORCE
Image Comics (Top Cow Productions): Oct, 1992 - No. 4, 1993; No. 0, Sept, 1993 ($1.95, limited series)

1-Silvestri-c/a in all; coupon for Image Comics #0; 1st Top Cow Productions title						6.00
1-With coupon missing						2.50
2-4: 0: 2-(3/93). 3-Pitt-c/story. 4-Codename: Stryke Force back-up (1st app.); foil-c.						
0-(9/93)-Walt Simonson-c/a/scripts						3.00

CYBERFORCE

Cyberforce #6 © TCOW

Cyclone Comics #1 © Bilbara

Cyclops #1 © MAR

	GD	VG	FN	VF	VF/NM	NM-
	2.0	4.0	6.0	8.0	9.0	9.2

Image Comics (Top Cow Productions)/Top Cow Comics No. 28 on:
V2#1, Nov, 1993 - No. 35, Sept. 1997 ($1.95)

V2#1-24: 1-7-Marc Silvestri/Keith Williams-c/a. 8-McFarlane-c/a. 10-Painted variant-c exists.
18-Variant-c exists. 23-Velocity-c. 2.50
1-3: 1-Gold Logo-c. 2-Silver embossed-c. 3-Gold embossed-c 10.00
1-(99¢, 3/96, 2nd printing) 2.50
25-($3.95)-Wraparound, foil-c 4.00
26-35: 28-(11/96)-1st Top Cow Comics iss. Quesada & Palmiotti's Gabriel app.
27-Quesada & Palmiotti's Ash app. 2.50
Annual 1,2 (3/95, 8/96, $2.50, $2.95) 3.00
NOTE: Annuals read Volume One in the indica.

CYBERFORCE (Volume 2)
Image Comics (Top Cow): Apr, 2006 - No. 6, Nov, 2006 ($2.99)

1-6: 1-Pat Lee/Ron Marz-s; three covers by Pat Lee, Marc Silvestri and Dave Finch 3.00
#0-(6/06, $2.99) reprints origin story from Image Comics Hardcover Vol. 1 ..... 3.00
...X-Men 1 (1/07, $3.99) Pat Lee-a/Ron Marz-s; 2 covers by Lee and Silvestri 4.00
Vol. 1 TPB (12/06, $14.99) r/#1-6, #0 & story from The Cow Quarterly; cover gallery 15.00

CYBERFORCE ORIGINS
Image Comics (Top Cow Productions): Jan, 1995 - No. 3, Nov, 1995 ($2.50)

1-Cyblade (1/95) 5.00
1-Cyblade (3/96, 99¢, 2nd printing) 2.25
1A-Exclusive Ed.; Tucci-c 4.00
2,3: 2-Stryker (2/95)-1st Mike Turner-a. 3-Impact 2.50
(#4) Misery (12/95, $2.95) 3.00

CYBERFORCE/STRYKEFORCE: OPPOSING FORCES (See Codename: Stryke Force #15)
Image Comics (Top Cow Productions): Sept, 1995 - No.2, Oct, 1995 ($2.50, limited series)

1,2: 2-Stryker disbands Strykeforce. 2.50

CYBERFORCE UNIVERSE SOURCEBOOK
Image Comics (Top Cow Productions): Aug, 1994/Feb, 1995 ($2.50)

1,2-Silvestri-c 2.50

CYBERFROG
Hall of Heroes: June, 1994 - No. 2, Dec, 1994 ($2.50, B&W, limited series)

1,2 ..... 3.00

CYBERFROG
Harris Comics: Feb, 1996 - No. 3, Apr, 1996 ($2.95)

0-3: Van Sciver-c/a/scripts. 2-Variant-c exists 5.00

CYBERFROG: (Title series), **Harris Comics**
--RESERVOIR FROG, 9/96 - No. 2, 10/96 ($2.95) 1,2: Van Sciver-c/a/scripts;
wraparound-c 3.00
--3RD ANNIVERSARY SPECIAL, 1/97 - #2, ($2.50, B&W) 1,2 ..... 3.00
--VS. CREED, 7/97 ($2.95, B&W)1 ..... 3.00

CYBERNARY (See Deathblow #1)
Image Comics (WildStorm Productions): Nov, 1995 - No.5, Mar, 1996 ($2.50)

1-5 ..... 2.50

CYBERNARY 2.0
DC Comics (WildStorm): Sept, 2001 - No. 6, Apr, 2002 ($2.95, limited series)

1-6: Joe Harris-s/Eric Canete-a. 6-The Authority app. 3.00

CYBERPUNK
Innovation Publishing: Sept, 1989 - No. 2, Oct, 1989 ($1.95, 28 pgs.) Book 2, #1, May, 1990 - No. 2, 1990 ($2.25, 28 pgs.)

1,2, Book 2 #1,2:1,2-Ken Steacy painted-covers (Adults) 2.50

CYBERPUNK: THE SERAPHIM FILES
Innovation Publishing: Nov, 1990 - No. 2, Dec, 1990 ($2.50, 28 pgs., mature)

1,2: 1-Painted-c; story cont'd from Seraphim 2.50

CYBERPUNX
Image Comics (Extreme Studios): Mar, 1996 ($2.50)

1 ..... 3.00

CYBERRAD
Continuity Comics: 1991 - No. 7, 1992 ($2.00)(Direct sale & newsstand-c variations)
V2#1, 1993 ($2.50)

1-7: 5-Glow-in-the-dark-c by N. Adams (direct sale only). 6-Contains 4 pg. fold-out poster;
N. Adams layouts 2.50
V2#1-($2.95, direct sale ed.)-Die-cut-c w/B&W hologram on-c; Neal Adams sketches 3.00
V2#1-($2.50, newsstand ed.)-Without sketches 2.50

CYBERRAD DEATHWATCH 2000 (Becomes CyberRad w/#2, 7/93)
Continuity Comics: Apr, 1993 - No. 2, 1993 ($2.50)

1,2: 1-Bagged w/2 cards; Adams-c & layouts & plots. 2-Bagged w/card; Adams scripts 2.50

CYBER 7
Eclipse Comics: Mar, 1989 - #7, Sept, 1989; V2#1, Oct, 1989 - #10, 1990 ($2.00, B&W)

1-7, Book 2 #1-10: Stories translated from Japanese 2.50

CYBLADE
Image Comics (Top Cow Productions): (one-shots)

.../ Ghost Rider 1 (Marvel/Top Cow, 1/97, $2.95) Devil's Reign pt. 2 ..... 4.00
...: Pilot Season 1 (9/07, $2.99) Rick Mays-a 3.00

CYBLADE/SHI (Also see Battle For The Independents & Shi/Cyblade: The Battle For The Independents)
Image Comics (Top Cow Productions): 1995 ($2.95, one-shot)

San Diego Preview	3	6	9	16	20	25
1-($2.95)-1st app. Witchblade	2	4	6	12	16	20
1-($2.95)-variant-c; Tucci-a	2	4	6	10	12	15

CYBRID
Maximum Press: July, 1995; No. 0, Jan, 1997 ($2.95/$3.50)

1-(7/95) 3.50
0-(1/97)-Liefeld-a/script; story cont'd in Avengelyne #4 ..... 3.50

CYCLONE COMICS (Also see Whirlwind Comics)
Bilbara Publishing Co.: June, 1940 - No. 5, Nov, 1940

1-Origin Tornado Tom; Volton (the human generator), Tornado Tom, Kingdom of the Moon, Mister Q begin (1st app. of each)	138	276	414	863	1432	2000
2	69	138	207	431	716	1000
3-Classic-c (scarce)	103	206	309	644	1072	1500
4	65	130	195	406	673	940
5-(Scarce)	81	162	243	506	841	1175

Ashcan - Not distributed to newsstands, only for in house use. Cover produced on green stock paper. A CGC certified FN (6.0) copy sold for $2,000 in 2006.

CYCLOPS (X-Men)
Marvel Comics: Oct, 2001 - No. 4, Jan, 2002 ($2.50, limited series)

1-4-Texeira-c/a. 1,2-Black Tom and Juggernaut app. 2.50

CYCLOPS: RETRIBUTION
Marvel Comics: 1994 ($5.95, trade paperback)

nn-r/Marvel Comics Presents #17-24 ..... 6.00

CY-GOR (See Spawn #38 for 1st app.)
Image Comics (Todd McFarlane Prod.): July, 1999 - No. 6, Dec, 1999 ($2.50)

1-6-Veitch-s 2.50

CYNTHIA DOYLE, NURSE IN LOVE (Formerly Sweetheart Diary)
Charlton Publications: No. 66, Oct, 1962 - No. 74, Feb, 1964

66-74	3	6	9	14	19	24

DAFFY (Daffy Duck No. 18 on)(See Looney Tunes)
Dell Publishing Co./Gold Key No. 31-127/Whitman No. 128 on: #457, 3/53 - #30, 7-9/62;
#31, 10-12/62 - #145, 6/84 (No #132,133)

Four Color 457(#1)-Elmer Fudd x-overs begin	10	20	30	68	119	170
Four Color 536,615('55)	6	12	18	39	62	85
4(1-3/56)-11('57)	5	10	15	30	48	65
12-19(1958-59)	4	8	12	22	34	45
20-40(1960-64)	3	6	9	16	23	30
41-60(1964-68)	2	4	6	13	18	22
61-90(1969-74)-Road Runner in most. 76-82-"Daffy Duck and the Road Runner" on-c	2	4	6	9	13	16
91-110	1	3	4	6	8	10
111-127	1	2	3	5	6	8
128,134-141: 139(2/82), 140(2-3/82), 141(4/82)	1	3	4	6	8	10
129(8/80),130,131 (pre-pack?) (scarce). 129-Sherlock Holmes parody-s						
142-145(#90029 on-c; nd, nd code, pre-pack): 142(6/83), 143(8/83), 144(3/84), 145(6/84)	3	6	9	19	29	38
Mini-Comic 1 (1976); 3-1/4x6-1/2")	1	2	3	6	9	24

NOTE: Reprint issues-No.41-46, 48, 50, 53-55, 58, 59, 65, 67, 69, 73, 81, 96, 103-108; 136-142, 144, 145(1/3-2/3-r). (See March of Comics No. 277, 288, 303, 313, 331, 347, 357,375, 387, 397, 402, 413, 425, 437, 460).

DAFFY DUCK (Digest-size reprints from Looney Tunes)
DC Comics: 2005 - Present (digest)

Vol. 1: You're Despicable! - Reprints from Looney Tunes #38,43,45,47,51,53,54,58,61,62,66,70 ..... 7.00

DAFFY TUNES COMICS

Dagar, Desert Hawk #22 © FOX

Dagwood #1 © KFS

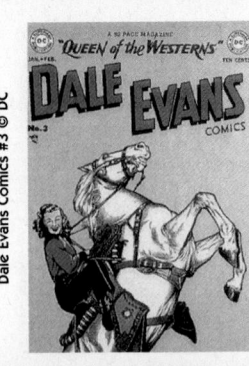

Dale Evans Comics #3 © DC

	GD	VG	FN	VF	VF/NM	NM-			GD	VG	FN	VF	VF/NM	NM-
	2.0	4.0	6.0	8.0	9.0	9.2			2.0	4.0	6.0	8.0	9.0	9.2

Four-Star Publications: June, 1947; No. 12, Aug, 1947

nn	9	18	27	50	65	80
12-Al Fago-c/a; funny animal	8	16	24	44	57	70

DAGAR, DESERT HAWK (Captain Kidd No. 24 on; formerly All Great)
Fox Features Syndicate: No. 14, Feb, 1948 - No. 23, Apr, 1949 (No #17,18)

14-Tangi & Safari Cary begin; Good bondage-c/a	78	156	234	488	807	1125
15,16-E. Good-a; 15-Bondage-c	46	92	138	281	466	650
19,20,22: 19-Used in SOTI, pg. 180 (Tangi)	41	82	123	256	416	575
21,23: 21-Bondage-c; "Bombs & Bums Away" panel in "Flood of Death" story used in SOTI.						
23-Bondage-c	45	90	135	275	450	625

NOTE: *Tangi by Kamen-14-16, 19, 20; c-20, 21.*

DAGAR THE INVINCIBLE (Tales of Sword & Sorcery…) (Also see Dan Curtis Giveaways &
Gold Key Spotlight)
Gold Key: Oct, 1972 - No. 18, Dec, 1976; No. 19, Apr, 1982

1-Intro; intro. Villains Olstellon & Scor	3	6	9	20	30	40
2-5: 3-Intro. Graylin, Dagar's woman; Jarn x-over	2	4	6	11	16	20
6-1st Dark Gods story	2	4	6	9	12	15
7-10: 9-Intro. Torgus. 10-1st Three Witches story	2	4	6	9	12	15
11-18: 13-Durak & Torgus x-over; story continues in Dr. Spektor #15.						
14-Dagar's origin retold. 18-Origin retold	1	3	4	6	8	10
19(4/82)-Origin-r/#18						6.00

NOTE: *Durak app. in 7, 12, 13. Tragg app. in 5, 11.*

DAGWOOD (Chic Young's) (Also see Blondie Comics)
Harvey Publications: Sept, 1950 - No. 140, Nov, 1965

1	15	30	45	105	188	270
2	8	16	24	56	93	130
3-10	7	14	21	45	73	100
11-20	6	12	18	37	59	80
21-30	5	10	15	30	48	65
31-50	4	8	12	26	41	55
51-70	3	6	9	19	29	38
71-100	3	6	9	16	22	28
101-121,123-128,130,135	3	6	9	14	19	24
122,129,131-134,136-140-All are 68-pg. issues	3	6	9	19	29	38

NOTE: *Popeye and other one page strips appeared in early issues.*

DAI KAMIKAZE!
Now Comics: June, 1987 - No. 12, Aug, 1988 ($1.75)

1-1st app. Speed Racer; 2nd print exists	4.00
2-12	2.50

DAILY BUGLE (See Spider-Man)
Marvel Comics: Dec, 1996 - No. 3, Feb, 1997 ($2.50, B&W, limited series)

1-3-Paul Grist-s	2.50

DAISY AND DONALD (See Walt Disney Showcase No. 8)
Gold Key/Whitman No. 42 on: May, 1973 - No. 59, July, 1984 (no No. 48)

1-Barks-r/WDC&S #280,308	3	6	9	20	30	40
2-5: 4-Barks-r/WDC&S #224	2	4	6	11	16	20
6-10	2	4	6	9	12	15
11-20	1	3	4	6	8	10
21-41: 32-r/WDC&S #308	1	2	3	5	6	8
42-44 (Whitman)	2	4	6	8	11	14
45 (8/80),46-(pre-pack?)(scarce)	4	8	12	22	34	45
47-(12/80)-Only distr. in Whitman 3-pack (scarce)	5	10	15	35	55	75
48(3/81)-50(8/81): 50-r/#3	2	4	6	10	14	18
51-54: 51-Barks-r/4-Color #1150. 52-r/#2. 53(2/82), 54(4/82)						
	2	4	6	9	13	16
55-59-(all #90284 on-c, nd, nd code, pre-pack): 55(5/83), 56(7/83), 57(8/83),						
58(8/83), 59(7/84)	3	6	9	14	19	24

DAISY & HER PUPS (Dagwood & Blondie's Dogs)(Formerly Blondie Comics #20)
Harvey Publications: No. 21, 7/51 - No. 27, 7/52; No. 8, 9/52 - No. 18, 5/54

21 (#1)-Blondie's dog Daisy and her 5 pups led by Elmer begin. Rags Rabbit app.						
	6	12	18	39	62	85
22-27 (#2-7): 26 has No. 6 on cover but No. 26 on inside. 23,25-The Little King app.						
24-Bringing Up Father by McManus app. 25-27-Rags Rabbit app.						
	4	8	12	26	41	55
8-18: 8,9-Rags Rabbit app. 8,17-The Little King app. 11-The Flop Family Swan begins.						
22-Cookie app. 11-Felix The Cat app. by 17,18-Popeye app.						
	4	8	12	24	37	50

DAISY DUCK & UNCLE SCROOGE PICNIC TIME (See Dell Giant #33)

DAISY DUCK & UNCLE SCROOGE SHOW BOAT (See Dell Giant #55)

DAISY DUCK'S DIARY (See Dynabrite Comics, & Walt Disney's C&S #298)
Dell Publishing Co.: No. 600, Nov, 1954 - No. 1247, Dec-Fef, 1961-62 (Disney)

Four Color 600 (#1)	7	14	21	47	76	105
Four Color 659, 743 (11/56)	6	12	18	37	59	80
Four Color 858 (11/57), 948 (11/58), 1247 (12-2/61-62)						
	5	10	15	32	51	70
Four Color 1055 (11-1/59-60), 1150 (12-1/60-61)-By Carl Barks						
	9	18	27	60	100	140

DAISY HANDBOOK
Daisy Manufacturing Co.: 1946; No. 2, 1948 (10¢, pocket-size, 132 pgs.)

1-Buck Rogers, Red Ryder; Wolverton-a (2 pgs.)	35	70	105	204	322	375
2-Captain Marvel & Ibis the Invincible, Red Ryder, Boy Commandos & Robotman; Wolverton-a (2 pgs.); contains 8 pg. color catalog	35	70	105	204	322	375

DAISY MAE (See Oxydol-Dreft)

DAISY'S RED RYDER GUN BOOK
Daisy Manufacturing Co.: 1955 (25¢, pocket-size, 132 pgs.)

nn-Boy Commandos, Red Ryder, 1pg. Wolverton-a	21	42	63	122	191	260

DAKKON BLACKBLADE ON THE WORLD OF MAGIC: THE GATHERING
Acclaim Comics (Armada): June, 1996 ($5.95, one-shot)

1-Jerry Prosser scripts; Rags Morales-a.	6.00

DAKOTA LIL (See Fawcett Movie Comics)

DAKTARI (Ivan Tors) (TV)
Dell Publishing Co.: July, 1967 - No. 3, Oct, 1968; No. 4, Oct, 1969

1-Marshall Thompson photo-c on all	4	8	12	24	37	50
2-4	3	6	9	18	27	35

DALE EVANS COMICS (Also see Queen of the West…)(See Boy Commandos #32)
National Periodical Publications: Sept-Oct, 1948 - No. 24, Jul-Aug, 1952 (No. 1-19: 52 pgs.)

1-Dale Evans & her horse Buttermilk begin; Sierra Smith begins by Alex Toth						
	76	152	228	475	788	1100
2-Alex Toth-a	40	80	120	235	368	500
3-11-Alex Toth-a	24	48	72	139	220	300
12-20: 12-Target-c	15	30	45	83	124	165
21-24	15	30	45	85	130	175

NOTE: *Photo-c 1, 2, 4-14.*

DALGODA
Fantagraphics Books: Aug, 1984 - No. 8, Feb, 1986 (High quality paper)

1,8: 1- Fujitake-c/a in all. 8-Alan Moore story	4.00
2-7: 2,3-Debut Grimwood's Daughter.	2.50

DALTON BOYS, THE
Avon Periodicals: 1951

1-(Number on spine)-Kinstler-c	17	34	51	98	154	210

DAMAGE
DC Comics: Apr, 1994 - No. 20, Jan, 1996 ($1.75/$1.95/$2.25)

1-20: 6-(9/94)-Zero Hour. 0-(10/94). 7-(11/94). 14-Ray app.	3.00

DAMAGE CONTROL (See Marvel Comics Presents)
Marvel Comics: 5/89 - No. 4, 8/89; V2#1, 12/89 - No. 4, 2/90 ($1.00)
V3#1, 6/91 - No. 4, 9/91 ($1.25, all are limited series)

V1#1-4, V2#1-4, V3#1-4: V1#4-Wolverine app. V2#2,4-Punisher app. 1-Spider-Man app.	
2-New Warriors app. 3,4-Silver Surfer app. 4-Infinity Gauntlet parody	2.50

DAMNED
Image Comics (Homage Comics): June, 1997 - No. 4, Sept, 1997 ($2.50, limited series)

1-4-Steven Grant-s/Mike Zeck-c/a in all	2.50

DAMN NATION
Dark Horse Comics: Feb, 2005 - No. 3, Apr, 2005 ($2.99, limited series)

1-3-J. Alexander-a/Andrew Cosby-s	3.00

DANCES WITH DEMONS (See Marvel Frontier Comics Unlimited)
Marvel Frontier Comics: Sept, 1993 - No. 4, Dec, 1993 ($1.95, limited series)

1-($2.95)-Foil embossed-c; Charlie Adlard & Rod Ramos-a	3.00
2-4	2.50

DANDEE: Four Star Publications: 1947 (Advertised, not published)

DAN DUNN (See Crackajack Funnies, Detective Dan, Famous Feature Stories & Red Ryder)

DANDY COMICS (Also see Happy Jack Howard)
E. C. Comics: Spring, 1947 - No. 7, Spring, 1948

1-Funny animal; Vince Fago-a in all; Dandy in all	40	80	120	235	368	500

Danger Girl #5 © J. Scott Campbell

Danger Trail #5 © DC

Danny Blaze #1 © CC

	GD 2.0	VG 4.0	FN 6.0	VF 8.0	VF/NM 9.0	NM- 9.2
2	27	54	81	156	246	335
3-7: 3-Intro Handy Andy who is c-feature #3 on	21	42	63	122	191	260

DANGER
Comic Media/Allen Hardy Assoc.: Jan, 1953 - No. 11, Aug, 1954

	GD 2.0	VG 4.0	FN 6.0	VF 8.0	VF/NM 9.0	NM- 9.2
1-Heck-c/a	25	50	75	145	228	310
2,3,5,7,9-11:	14	28	42	81	118	155
4-Marijuana cover/story	16	32	48	94	147	200
6- "Narcotics" story; begin spy theme	15	30	45	85	130	175
8-Bondage/torture/headlights panels	17	34	51	98	154	210

NOTE: Morisi a-2, 5, 6(3), 10; c-2. Contains some reprints from Danger & Dynamite.

DANGER (Formerly Comic Media title)
Charlton Comics Group: No. 12, June, 1955 - No. 14, Oct, 1955

	GD 2.0	VG 4.0	FN 6.0	VF 8.0	VF/NM 9.0	NM- 9.2
12(#1)	12	24	36	67	94	120
13,14: 14-r/#12	10	20	30	54	72	90

DANGER
Super Comics: 1964

Super Reprint #10-12 (Black Dwarf; #10-r/Great Comics #1 by Novack. #11-r/Johnny Danger #1. #12-r/Red Seal #14), #15-r/Spy Cases #26. #16-Unpublished Chesler material (Yankee Girl), #17-r/Scoop #8 (Capt. Courage & Enchanted Dagger), #18(nd)-r/Guns Against Gangsters #5 (Gun-Master, Annie Oakley, The Chameleon), L.B. Cole-r)

	GD 2.0	VG 4.0	FN 6.0	VF 8.0	VF/NM 9.0	NM- 9.2
	2	4	6	11	16	20

DANGER AND ADVENTURE (Formerly This Magazine Is Haunted; Robin Hood and His Merry Men No. 28 on)
Charlton Comics: No. 22, Feb, 1955 - No. 27, Feb, 1956

	GD 2.0	VG 4.0	FN 6.0	VF 8.0	VF/NM 9.0	NM- 9.2
22-Ibis the Invincible-c/story; Nyoka app.; last pre-code issue	11	22	33	62	86	110
23-Lance O'Casey-c/sty; Nyoka app.; Ditko-a thru #27	13	26	39	72	101	130
24-27: 24-Mike Danger & Johnny Adventure begin	9	18	27	50	65	80

DANGER GIRL (Also see Cliffhanger #0)
Image Comics (Cliffhanger Productions): Mar, 1998 - No. 4, Dec, 1998;
DC Comics (Cliffhanger Prod.): No. 5, July, 1999 - No. 7, Feb, 2001

	GD 2.0	VG 4.0	FN 6.0	VF 8.0	VF/NM 9.0	NM- 9.2
Preview-Bagged in DV8 #14 Voyager Pack						4.00
Preview Gold Edition						8.00
1-($2.95) Hartnell & Campbell-s/Campbell/Garner-a	1	2	3	5	6	8
1-($4.95) Chromium cover						45.00
1-American Entertainment Ed.						8.00
1-American Entertainment Gold Ed., 1-Tourbook edition						10.00
1-"Danger-sized" ed.; over-sized format	3	6	9	16	23	30
2-($2.50)						4.00
2-Smoking Gun variant cover, 2-Platinum Ed., 2-Dynamic Forces Omnichrome variant-c	2	4	6	9	13	16
2-Gold foil cover						9.00
2-Ruby red foil cover						90.00
3,4: 3-c by Campbell, Charest and Adam Hughes. 4-Big knife variant-c						3.00
3,5: 3-Gold foil cover. 5-DF Bikini variant-c						3.00
4-6						3.00
7-($5.95) Wraparound gatefold-c; Last issue						6.00
...: Hawaiian Punch (5/03, $4.95) Campbell-c; Phil Noto-a						5.00
...: Odd Jobs TPB (2004, $14.95) r/one-shots Hawaiian Punch, Viva Las Danger & Special; Campbell-c						15.00
San Diego Preview (8/98, B&W) flip book w/Wildcats preview						5.00
Sketchbook (2001, $6.95) Campbell-a; sketches for comics, toys, games						7.00
...Special (2/00, $3.50) art by Campbell, Chiodo, and Art Adams						3.50
... 3-D #1 (4/03, $4.95) bagged with 3-D glasses) r/ Preview & #1 in 3-D						5.00
.... Viva Las Danger (1/04, $4.95) Noto-a/Campbell-c						5.00
...:The Dangerous Collection nn(8/98; r-#1)						6.00
...:The Dangerous Collection 2,3: 2-(11/98, $5.95) r/#2,3. 3-('99) r/#4,5						6.00
...:The Dangerous Collection nn, 2-($10.00) Gold foil logo						10.00
...:The Ultimate Collection HC ($29.95) r/#1-7; intro by Bruce Campbell						30.00
...:The Ultimate Collection SC ($19.95) r/#1-7; intro by Bruce Campbell						20.00

DANGER GIRL: BACK IN BLACK
DC Comics (Cliffhanger): Jan, 2006 - No. 4, Apr, 2006 ($2.99, limited series)

	GD 2.0	VG 4.0	FN 6.0	VF 8.0	VF/NM 9.0	NM- 9.2
1-4-Hartnell-s/Bradshaw-a. 1-Campbell-c						3.00
TPB (2007, $12.99) r/series & covers						13.00

DANGER GIRL: BODY SHOTS
DC Comics (WildStorm): Jun, 2007 - No. 4, Sept, 2007 ($2.99, limited series)

	GD 2.0	VG 4.0	FN 6.0	VF 8.0	VF/NM 9.0	NM- 9.2
1-4-Hartnell-s/Bradshaw-a						3.00

DANGER GIRL KAMIKAZE

DC Comics (Cliffhanger): Nov, 2001 - No. 2, Dec., 2001 ($2.95, lim. series)

	GD 2.0	VG 4.0	FN 6.0	VF 8.0	VF/NM 9.0	NM- 9.2
1,2-Tommy Yune-s/a						3.00

DANGER IS OUR BUSINESS!
Toby Press: 1953(Dec.) - No. 10, June, 1955

	GD 2.0	VG 4.0	FN 6.0	VF 8.0	VF/NM 9.0	NM- 9.2
1-Captain Comet by Williamson/Frazetta-a, 6 pgs. (science fiction)	44	88	132	268	444	620
2	14	28	42	80	115	150
3-10	12	24	36	67	94	120
I.W. Reprint #9('64)-Williamson/Frazetta-r/#1; Kinstler-c	8	16	24	52	86	120

DANGER IS THEIR BUSINESS (Also see A-1 Comic)
Magazine Enterprises: No. 50, 1952

	GD 2.0	VG 4.0	FN 6.0	VF 8.0	VF/NM 9.0	NM- 9.2
A-1 50-Powell-a	14	28	42	78	112	145

DANGER MAN (TV)
Dell Publishing Co.: No. 1231, Sept-Nov, 1961

	GD 2.0	VG 4.0	FN 6.0	VF 8.0	VF/NM 9.0	NM- 9.2
Four Color 1231-Patrick McGoohan photo-c	10	20	30	71	126	180

DANGER TRAIL (Also see Showcase #50, 51)
National Periodical Publ.: July-Aug, 1950 - No. 5, Mar-Apr, 1951 (52 pgs.)

	GD 2.0	VG 4.0	FN 6.0	VF 8.0	VF/NM 9.0	NM- 9.2
1-King Faraday begins, ends #4; Toth-a in all	124	248	372	775	1288	1800
2	86	172	258	538	894	1250
3-(Rare) one of the rarest early '50s DCs	124	248	372	775	1288	1800
4,5: 5-Johnny Peril-c/story (moves to Sensation Comics #107); new logo (also see Comic Cavalcade #15-29)	67	134	201	419	697	975

DANGER TRAIL
DC Comics: Apr, 1993 - No. 4, July, 1993 ($1.50, limited series)

	GD 2.0	VG 4.0	FN 6.0	VF 8.0	VF/NM 9.0	NM- 9.2
1-4: Gulacy-c on all						2.50

DANGER UNLIMITED (See San Diego Comic Con Comics #2 & Torch of Liberty Special)
Dark Horse (Legend): Feb, 1994 - No. 4, May, 1994 ($2.00, limited series)

	GD 2.0	VG 4.0	FN 6.0	VF 8.0	VF/NM 9.0	NM- 9.2
1-4: Byrne-c/a/scripts in all; origin stories of both original team (Doc Danger, Thermal, Miss Mirage, & Hunk) & future team (Thermal, Belebet, & Caucus). 1-Intro Torch of Liberty & Golgotha (cameo) in back-up story. 4-Hellboy & Torch of Liberty cameo in lead story						2.50
TPB (1995, $14.95) r/#1-4; includes last pg. originally cut from #4						15.00

DAN HASTINGS (See Syndicate Features)

DANIEL BOONE (See The Exploits of..., Fighting... Frontier Scout...,The Legends of... & March of Comics No. 306)
Dell Publishing Co.: No. 1163, Mar-May, 1961

	GD 2.0	VG 4.0	FN 6.0	VF 8.0	VF/NM 9.0	NM- 9.2
Four Color 1163-Marsh-a	5	10	15	35	55	75

DANIEL BOONE (TV) (See March of Comics No. 306)
Gold Key: Jan, 1965 - No. 15, Apr, 1969 (All have Fess Parker photo-c)

	GD 2.0	VG 4.0	FN 6.0	VF 8.0	VF/NM 9.0	NM- 9.2
1-Back-c and last eight pages fold in half to form "Official Handbook Fess Parker as Daniel Boone Trail Blazers Club"	8	16	24	56	93	130
2-Back-c pin-up	5	10	15	32	51	70
3-5-Back-c pin-ups	4	8	12	26	41	55
6-15: 7,8-Back-c pin-up	3	6	9	20	30	40

DAN'L BOONE
Sussex Publ. Co.: Sept, 1955 - No. 8, Sept, 1957

	GD 2.0	VG 4.0	FN 6.0	VF 8.0	VF/NM 9.0	NM- 9.2
1	14	28	42	80	115	150
2	10	20	30	54	72	90
3-8	8	16	24	40	50	60

DANNY BLAZE (...Firefighter) (Nature Boy No. 3 on)
Charlton Comics: Aug, 1955 - No. 2, Oct, 1955

	GD 2.0	VG 4.0	FN 6.0	VF 8.0	VF/NM 9.0	NM- 9.2
1	13	26	39	72	101	130
2	9	18	27	50	65	80

DANNY DINGLE (See Sparkler Comics)
United Features Syndicate: No. 17, 1940

	GD 2.0	VG 4.0	FN 6.0	VF 8.0	VF/NM 9.0	NM- 9.2
Single Series 17	26	52	78	152	239	325

DANNY THOMAS SHOW, THE (TV)
Dell Publishing Co.: No. 1180, Apr-June, 1961 - No. 1249, Dec-Feb, 1961-62

	GD 2.0	VG 4.0	FN 6.0	VF 8.0	VF/NM 9.0	NM- 9.2
Four Color 1180-Toth-a, photo-c	15	30	45	111	198	285
Four Color 1249-Manning-a, photo-c	14	28	42	103	184	265

DARBY O'GILL & THE LITTLE PEOPLE (Movie)(See Movie Comics)
Dell Publishing Co.: 1959 (Disney)

	GD 2.0	VG 4.0	FN 6.0	VF 8.0	VF/NM 9.0	NM- 9.2
Four Color 1024-Toth-a; photo-c.	9	18	27	65	113	160

DAREDEVIL (...& the Black Widow #92-107 on-c only; see Giant-Size..., Marvel Advs., Marvel

Daredevil #2 © MAR

Daredevil #100 © MAR

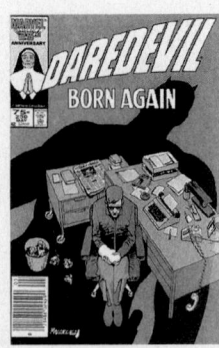

Daredevil #230 © MAR

	GD 2.0	VG 4.0	FN 6.0	VF 8.0	VF/NM 9.0	NM- 9.2		GD 2.0	VG 4.0	FN 6.0	VF 8.0	VF/NM 9.0	NM- 9.2

Graphic Novel #24, Marvel Super Heroes, '66 & Spider-Man &...)
Marvel Comics Group: Apr, 1964 - No. 380, Oct, 1998

1-Origin/1st app. Daredevil; intro Foggy Nelson & Karen Page; death of Battling Murdock;
Bill Everett-c/a; reprinted in Marvel Super Heroes #1 (1966)
250 500 750 2188 4094 6000
2-Fantastic Four cameo; 2nd app. Electro (Spidey villain); Thing guest star
63 126 189 536 993 1450
3-Origin & 1st app. The Owl (villain) 41 82 123 328 589 850
4-Origin & 1st app. The Purple Man 34 68 102 255 470 685
5-Minor costume change; Wood-a begins 26 52 78 187 336 485
6-Mr. Fear app. 17 34 51 128 227 325
7-Daredevil battles Sub-Mariner & dons red costume for 1st time (4/65)
61 122 183 519 960 1400
8-10: 8-Origin/1st app. Stilt-Man 14 28 42 103 184 265
11-15: 12-1st app. Plunderer; Ka-Zar app. 13-Facts about Ka-Zar's origin; Kirby-a
10 20 30 68 119 170
16,17-Spider-Man x-over. 16-1st Romita-a on Spider-Man (5/66)
15 30 45 111 198 285
18-Origin & 1st app. Gladiator 9 18 27 63 107 150
19,20 7 14 21 50 83 115
21-26,28-30: 24-Ka-Zar app. 7 12 18 39 62 85
27-Spider-Man x-over 7 14 21 45 73 100
31-40: 38-Fantastic Four x-over; cont'd in F.F. #73. 39-1st Exterminator (later becomes
Death-Stalker). 10 15 32 51 70
41,42,44-49: 41-Death Mike Murdock. 42-1st app. Jester. 45-Statue of Liberty
photo-c 4 8 12 28 44 60
43-Daredevil battles Captain America; origin partially retold
6 12 18 39 62 85
50-53: 50-52-B. Smith-a. 53-Origin retold; last 12¢ issue
5 10 15 30 48 65
54-56,58-60: 54-Spider-Man cameo. 56-1st app. Death's Head (9/69); story cont'd in #57
(not same as new Death's Head) 3 6 9 19 29 38
57-Reveals i.d. to Karen Page; Death's Head app. 4 8 12 22 34 45
61-76,78-80: 79-Stan Lee cameo. 80-Last 15¢ issue 3 6 9 17 25 32
77-Spider-Man x-over 4 8 12 22 34 45
81-(52 pgs.) Black Widow begins (11/71) 4 8 12 24 37 50
82,84-99: 87-Electro-c/story 3 6 9 14 19 24
83-B. Smith layouts/Weiss-p 3 6 9 16 22 28
100-Origin retold 3 6 9 20 30 40
101-104,106-120: 107-Starlin-c; Thanos cameo. 113-1st brief app. Deathstalker.
114-1st full app. Deathstalker 2 4 6 11 16 20
105-Origin Moondragon by Starlin (12/73); Thanos cameo in flashback (early app.)
3 6 9 14 19 24
121-130,137: 124-1st app. Copperhead; Black Widow leaves. 126-1st new Torpedo
2 4 6 9 13 16
131-Origin/1st app. new Bullseye (see Nick Fury #15) 7 14 21 47 76 105
132-2nd app. new Bullseye (Regular 25¢ edition) 4 8 12 28 44 60
132-(30¢-c variant, limited distribution)(4/76) 7 14 21 49 80 110
133-136-(Regular 25¢ editions) 2 4 6 9 12 15
133-136-(30¢-c variants, limited distribution)(5-8/76) 3 6 9 16 23 30
138-Ghost Rider-c/story; Death's Head is reincarnated; Byrne-a
3 6 9 14 19 24
139,140,142-145,147-157: 142-Nova cameo. 147,148-(Reg. 30¢-c). 150-1st app. Paladin.
151-Reveals i.d. to Heather Glenn. 155-Black Widow returns. 156-The '60s Daredevil app.
2 4 6 9 12 15
141,146-Bullseye app. 3 6 9 17 25 32
146-(35¢-c variant, limited distribution) 6 12 18 39 62 85
147,148-(35¢-c variants, limited distribution) 4 8 12 28 44 60
158-Frank Miller art begins (5/79); origin/death of Deathstalker (see Captain America #235
& Spectacular Spider-Man #27 7 14 21 50 83 115
159 4 8 12 26 41 55
160,161-Bullseye app. 3 6 9 21 32 42
162-Ditko-a; no Miller-a 2 4 6 8 11 14
163,164: 163-Hulk cameo. 164-Origin retold 3 6 9 16 22 28
165-167,170 3 6 9 14 19 24
168-Origin/1st app. Elektra; 1st Miller scripts 9 18 27 63 107 150
169-2nd Elektra app. 4 8 12 26 41 55
171-173 2 4 6 13 18 22
174,175-Elektra app. 3 6 9 15 21 26
176-180-Elektra app. 178-Cage app. 179-Anti-smoking issue mentioned in the Congressional
Record 3 6 9 14 19 24
181-(52 pgs.)-Death of Elektra; Punisher cameo out of costume
3 6 9 21 32 42
182-184-Punisher app. by Miller (drug issues) 2 4 6 10 14 18

185-191: 187-New Black Widow. 189-Death of Stick. 190-($1.00, 52 pgs.)-Elektra returns,
part origin. 191-Last Miller Daredevil 1 3 4 6 8 10
192-195,198,199,201-207,209-218,220-226,234-237: 226-Frank Miller plots begin 3.50
196-Wolverine-c/app. 2 4 6 8 11 14
197-Bullseye-c/app.; 1st app. Yuriko Oyama (who becomes Lady Deathstrike) 5.00
200,238: 200-Bullseye app. 238-Mutant Massacre; Sabretooth app. 6.00
208,219,228-233: 208-Harlan Ellison scripts borrowed from Avengers TV episode "House that
Jack Built". 219-Miller-c/script. 228-233-Last Miller scripts 4.00
227-Miller scripts begin 5.00
239,240,242-247 3.00
241-Todd McFarlane-a(p) 5.00
248,249-Wolverine app. 6.00
250,251,253,258: 250-1st app. Bullet. 258-Intro The Bengal (a villain) 3.00
252,260 (52 pgs.): 252-Fall of the Mutants. 260-Typhoid Mary app. 5.00
254-Origin & 1st app. Typhoid Mary (5/88) 1 2 3 4 5 8
255,256,258: 255,256-2nd/3rd app. Typhoid Mary. 259-Typhoid Mary app. 5.00
257-Punisher app. (x-over w/Punisher #10) 1 3 4 6 8 10
261-281,283-294,296-299,301-304,307-318: 270-1st app. Black Heart. 272-Intro Shotgun
(villain). 281-Silver Surfer cameo. 283-Capt. America app. 297-Typhoid Mary app.; Kingpin
storyline begins. 292-D.G. Chichester scripts begin. 303-Re-intro the
Owl. 304-Garney-c/a. 309-Punisher-c.; Terror app. 310-Calypso-c 2.50
282,295,300,305,306: 282-Silver Surfer app. 295-Ghost Rider app. 300-($2.00, 52 pgs.)-
Kingpin story ends. 305,306-Spider-Man-c 3.00
319-Prologue to Fall From Grace; Elektra returns 6.00
319-2nd printing w/black-c 2.50
320-Fall From Grace Pt 1 5.00
321-Fall From Grace regular ed.; Pt 2; new costume; Venom app. 5.00
321-($2.00)-Wraparound Glow-in-the-dark-c ed. 5.00
322-Fall From Grace Pt 3; Eddie Brock app. 4.00
323,324-Fall From Grace Pt 4 & 5: 323-Vs. Venom-c/story. 324-Morbius-c/story 4.00
325-($2.50, 52 pgs.)-Fall From Grace ends; contains bound-in poster 4.00
326-349,351-353: 326-New logo. 328-Bound-in trading card sheet. 330-Gambit app. 348-1st
Cary Nord art in DD (1/96);"Dec" on-c. 353-Karl Kesel scripts; Nord-c/a begins;
Mr. Hyde-c/app. 2.50
350-($2.95)-Double-sized 3.00
350-($3.50)-Double-sized; gold ink-c 3.50
354-374,376-379: Kesel scripts, Nord-c/a in all. 354-$1.50-c begins. 355-Larry Hama layouts;
Pyro app. 358-Mysterio-c/app. 359-Absorbing Man cameo. 360-Absorbing Man-c/app.
361-Black Widow-c/app. 363,366-370-Gene Colan-a(p). 368-Omega Red-c/app.
372-Ghost Rider-c/app. 376-379-"Flying Blind", DD goes undercover for S.H.I.E.L.D. 2.50
375-($2.99) Wraparound-c; Mr. Fear-c/app. 3.00
380-($2.99) Final issue; flashback story 4.00
Special 1(9/67, 25¢, 68 pgs.)-New art/story 6 12 18 39 62 85
Special 2,3: 2(2/71, 25¢, 52 pgs.)-Entire book has Powell/Wood-r; Wood-a
3(1/72, 52 pgs.)-Reprints 3 6 9 16 22 28
Annual 4(10/76) 4
Annual 4(#5)-10: ('89-94 68 pgs.)-5-Atlantis Attacks. 6-Sutton-a. 7-Guice-a (7 pgs.).
8-Deathlok-c/story. 9-Polybagged w/card
...:Born Again TPB ($17.95)-r/#227-233; Miller-s/Mazzucchelli-a & new-c 20.00
... By Frank Miller and Klaus Janson Omnibus HC (2007, $99.99, dustjacket) r/#158-161,
163-191 and What If...? #28; intros by Miller and Janson; interviews, bonus art 100.00
.../Deadpool- (Annual '97, $2.99)-Wraparound-c 3.00
...:Fall From Grace TPB ($19.95)-r/#319-325 20.00
...:Gang War TPB ($15.95)-r/#169-172,180; Miller-s/a(p) 16.00
...:Legends: (Vol. 4) Typhoid Mary TPB (2003, $19.95) r/#254-257,259-263 16.00
...:Love's Labors Lost TPB ($19.99)-r/#215-217,219-222,225,226; Mazzucchelli-c 20.00
.../Punisher TPB (1988, $4.95)-r/D.D. #182-184 (all printings) 5.00
...Visionaries: Frank Miller Vol. 1 TPB ($17.95) r/#158-161,163-167 18.00
...Visionaries: Frank Miller Vol. 2 TPB ($24.95) r/#168-182; new Miller-c 25.00
...Visionaries: Frank Miller Vol. 3 TPB ($24.95)-r/#183-191, What If? #28,35 &
Bizarre Adventures #28; new Miller-c 25.00
... Vs. Bullseye Vol. 1 TPB ($15.99)-r/#131-132,146,169,181,191 14.00
Wizard Ace Edition: Daredevil (Vol. 1) #1 (4/03, $13.99) Acetate Campbell-c 14.00

NOTE: **Art Adams** c-238p, 239. **Austin** a-191i; c-151i, 200i. **John Buscema** a-136, 137p, 234p, 235p; c-86p, 136i, 137p, 142, 219. **Byrne** a-200p, 201, 203, 223. **Capullo** a-286p. **Colan** a(p)-20-49, 53-82, 84-98, 100, 110, 112, 124, 153, 154, 156, 157, 163, 366-370, Spec. 1; c(p)-20-42, 44-49, 70p, 71, 92, 98, 138, 153, 154, 156, 157, 366-370. **Craig** a-50i, 52i. **Ditko** a-162, 234p, 235p, 264p; c-162. **Everett** c/a-1; inks-21, 83. **Garney** c/a-304. **Gil Kane** a-141p, 144-148p, 151p; c(p)-85, 90, 91, 93, 94, 115, 116, 119, 120, 125-128, 133, 139, 147, 152. **Kirby** c-2-4, 9p, 12p, 13, 43, 136p. **Layton** c-202. **Miller** scripts-168-182, 183(part), 184-191, 219, 227-233; a-158-161p, 163-184p, 191p; c-158-161p, 163-184p, 185-189, 190p, 191. **Orlando** a-2-4p. **Powell** a-9p, 11p, Special 1r, 2r. **Simonson** c-199, 236p. **B. Smith** a-236p; c-51p, 52p, 217. **Starlin** a-105p. **Steranko** c-44i. **Tuska** a-39i, 145p. **Williamson** a(i)-237, 239, 240, 243, 248-257, 259-282, 293-300; c(i)-237, 243, 244, 248-257, 259-263, 265-278, 280-289, Annual 8. **Wood** a-5-8, 9i, 10, 11i, Spec. 2i; c-5i, 6-11, 164i.

DAREDEVIL (Volume 2) (Marvel Knights)
Marvel Comics: Nov, 1998 - Present ($2.50/$2.99)

DA

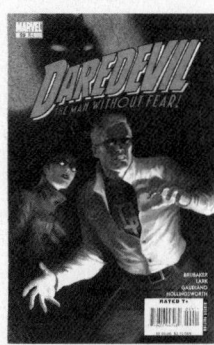

Daredevil V2 #99 © MAR

Daredevil: Yellow #1 © MAR

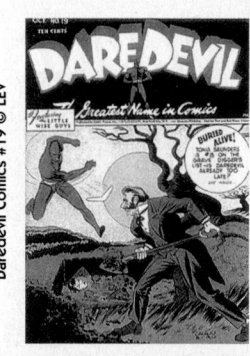

Daredevil Comics #19 © LEV

	GD	VG	FN	VF	VF/NM	NM-
	2.0	4.0	6.0	8.0	9.0	9.2

1-Kevin Smith-s/Quesada & Palmiotti-a 12.00
1-($6.95) DF Edition w/Quesada & Palmiotti var.-c 15.00
1-($6.00) DF Sketch Ed. w/B&W-c 10.00
2-Two covers by Campbell and Quesada/Palmiotti 9.00
3-8: 4,5-Bullseye app. 5-Variant-c exists. 8-Spider-Man-c/app.; last Smith-s 3.00
9-15: 9-11-David Mack-s; intro Echo. 12-Begin $2.99-c; Haynes-a. 13,14-Quesada-a 3.00
16-19-Direct editions; Bendis-s/Mack-c/painted-a 3.00
18,19,21,22-Newsstand editions with variant cover logo "Marvel Unlimited Featuring... ..... 3.00
20-($3.50) Gale-s/Winslade-a; back-up by Stan Lee-s/Colan-a; Mack-c 3.50
21-40: 21-25-Gale-s. 26-38-Bendis-s/Maleev-a. 32-Daredevil's ID revealed.
　　35-Spider-Man-c/app. 38-Iron Fist & Luke Cage app. 40-Dodson-a 3.00
41-(25¢-c) Begins "Lowlife" arc; Maleev-a; intro Milla Donovan 2.50
41-(Newsstand edition with 2.99¢-c) 4.00
42-45-"Lowlife" arc; Maleev-a 2.50
46-50-($2.99). 46-Typhoid Mary returns. 49-Bullseye app. 50-Art panels by various incl.
　　Romita, Colan, Mack, Janson, Oeming, Quesada 3.00
51-64,66-74,76-81: 51-55-Mack-s/a; Echo app. 54-Wolverine-c/app. 61-64-Black Widow app.
　　71-Decalogue begins. 76-81-The Murdock Papers. 81-Last Bendis-s/Maleev-a 3.00
65-($3.99) 40th Anniversary issue; Land-c; art by Maleev, Horn, Bachalo and others 4.00
75-($3.99) Decalogue ends; Jester app. 4.00
82-99: 82-Brubaker-s/Lark-a begin; Foggy "killed". 84-86-Punisher app. 87-Other Daredevil ID
　　revealed. 94-Romita-c 3.00
82-Variant-c by McNiven 4.00
100-($3.99) Three covers (Djurdjevic, Bermejo and Turner); art by Romita Sr., Colan, Lark,
　　Sienkiewicz, Maleev, Bermejo & Djurdjevic; sketch art gallery; r/Daredevil #90 (1972) 4.00
2099 #1 (11/04, $2.99) Kirkman-s/Moline-a 3.00
TPB ($9.95) r/#1-3 ..... 10.00
...Vol. 1 HC (2001, $29.99, with dustjacket) r/#1-11,13-15 ..... 30.00
...Vol. 1 HC (2003, $29.99, with dustjacket) r/#1-11,13-15; larger page size 30.00
...Vol. 2 HC (2002, $29.99, with dustjacket) r/#26-37; afterword by Bendis 30.00
...Vol. 3 HC (2004, $29.99, with dustjacket) r/#38-50; Maleev sketch pages 30.00
...Vol. 4 HC (2005, $29.99, with dustjacket) r/#56-65; Vol. 1 #81 (1971) Black Widow 30.00
...Vol. 5 HC (2006, $29.99, with dustjacket) r/#66-75 ..... 30.00
...Vol. 6 HC (2006, $34.99, with dustjacket) r/#76-81 & What If Karen Page Had Lived? 35.00
(Vol. 1) Visionaries TPB ($19.95) r/#1-8; Ben Affleck intro. 20.00
(Vol. 2) Parts of a Hole TPB (1/02, $17.95) r/#9-15; David Mack intro. 18.00
(Vol. 3) Wake Up TPB (7/02, $9.99) r/#16-19 ..... 10.00
...Vol. 4: Underboss TPB (8/02, $14.99) r/#26-31 ..... 15.00
...Vol. 5: Out TPB (2003, $19.99) r/#32-40 ..... 20.00
...Vol. 6: Lowlife TPB (2003, $13.99) r/#41-45 ..... 14.00
...Vol. 7: Hardcore TPB (2003, $13.99) r/#46-50 ..... 14.00
...Vol. 8: Echo - Vision Quest TPB (2004, $13.99) r/#51-55; David Mack-s/a 14.00
...Vol. 9: King of Hell's Kitchen TPB (2004, $13.99) r/#56-60 ..... 14.00
...Vol. 10: The Widow TPB (2004, $16.99) r/#61-65 & Vol. 1 #81 ..... 17.00
...Vol. 11: Golden Age TPB (2005, $13.99) r/#66-70 ..... 14.00
...Vol. 12: Decalogue TPB (2005, $14.99) r/#71-75 ..... 15.00
...Vol. 13: The Murdock Papers TPB (2006, $14.99) r/#76-81 ..... 15.00
...: The Devil Inside and Out Vol. 1 (2006, $14.99) r/#82-87; Brubaker & Lark interview 15.00
...: The Devil Inside and Out Vol. 2 (2007, $14.99) r/#88-93; Bermejo cover sketches 15.00
...: Hell To Pay Vol. 1 (2007, $14.99) r/#94-99; Djurdjevic cover sketches 15.00

DAREDEVIL/ BATMAN (Also see Batman/Daredevil)
Marvel Comics/ DC Comics: 1997 ($5.99, one-shot)
nn-McDaniel-c/a 6.00

DAREDEVIL/ BATTLIN' JACK MURDOCK
Marvel Comics: Aug, 2007 - No. 4, Nov, 2007 ($3.99, limited series)
1-4-Wells-s/DiGiandomenico-a; flashback to the fixed fight 4.00

DAREDEVIL/ ELEKTRA: LOVE AND WAR
Marvel Comics: 2003 ($29.99, hardcover with dust jacket)
HC-Larger-size reprints of Daredevil: Love and War (Marvel Graphic Novel #24) &
　　Elektra: Assassin; Frank Miller-s; Bill Sienkiewicz-a 30.00

DAREDEVIL/ FATHER
Marvel Comics: June, 2004 - No. 6, Feb, 2007 ($3.50/$2.99, limited series)
1-Quesada-s/a; Isanove-painted color 3.50
1-Director's Cut ($2.99) cover and page development art; partial sketch-c 3.00
2-6: 2-($2.99,10/05). 3-Santerians app. 3.00
HC (2006, $24.99) r/series; Lindelof intro.; sketch pages, cover pencils and bonus art 25.00

DAREDEVIL/ NINJA
Marvel Comics: Dec, 2000 - No. 3, Feb, 2001 ($2.99, limited series)
1-3: Bendis-s/Haynes-a 3.00
1-Dynamic Forces foil-c 10.00
TPB (7/01, $12.95) r/#1-3 with cover and sketch gallery 13.00

DAREDEVIL: REDEMPTION
Marvel Comics: Apr, 2005 - No. 6, Aug, 2005 ($2.99, limited series)
1-6-Hine-s/Gaydos-a/Sienkiewicz-c 3.00
TPB (2005, $14.99) r/#1-6 ..... 15.00

DAREDEVIL/ SHI (See Shi/ Daredevil)
Marvel Comics/ Crusade Comics: Feb,1997 ($2.95, limited series)
1 ..... 3.00

DAREDEVIL/ SPIDER-MAN
Marvel Comics: Jan, 2001 - No. 4, Apr, 2001 ($2.99, limited series)
1-4-Jenkins-s/Winslade-a/Alex Ross-c; Stilt Man app. 3.00
TPB (2001, $12.95) r/#1-4; Ross-c 13.00

DAREDEVIL THE MAN WITHOUT FEAR
Marvel Comics: Oct, 1993 - No. 5, Feb, 1994 ($2.95, limited series) (foil embossed covers)
1-Miller scripts; Romita, Jr./Williamson-c/a 6.00
2-5 ..... 5.00
Hardcover 100.00
Trade paperback 20.00

DAREDEVIL: THE MOVIE (2003 movie adaptation)
Marvel Comics: March, 2003 ($3.50/$12.95, one-shot)
1-Photo-c of Ben Affleck; Bruce Jones-s/Manuel Garcia-a 3.50
TPB ($12.95) r/movie adaptation; Daredevil #32; Ultimate Daredevil & Elektra #1 and
　　Spider-Man's Tangled Web #4; photo-c of Ben Affleck 13.00

DAREDEVIL: THE TARGET (Daredevil Bullseye on cover)
Marvel Comics: Jan, 2003 ($3.50, unfinished limited series)
1-Kevin Smith-s/Glenn Fabry-c/a 3.50

DAREDEVIL VS. PUNISHER
Marvel Comics: Sept, 2005 - No. 6, Jan, 2006 ($2.99, limited series)
1-5-David Lapham-s/a 3.00
TPB (2005, $15.99) r/#1-6 ..... 16.00

DAREDEVIL: YELLOW
Marvel Comics: Aug, 2001 - No. 6, Jan, 2002 ($3.50, limited series)
1-6-Jeph Loeb-s/Tim Sale-a/c; origin & yellow costume days retold 3.50
HC (5/02, $29.95) r/#1-6 with dustjacket; intro by Stan Lee; sketch pages 30.00
Daredevil Legends Vol. 1: Daredevil Yellow (2002, $14.99, TPB) r/#1-6 ..... 15.00

DAREDEVIL COMICS (See Silver Streak Comics)
Lev Gleason Publications (Funnies, Inc. No. 1): July, 1941 - No. 134, Sept, 1956
(Charles Biro stories)

	GD	VG	FN	VF	VF/NM	NM-

1-No. 1 titled "Daredevil Battles Hitler"; The Silver Streak, Lance Hale, Cloud Curtis, Dickey
　　Dean, Pirate Prince team up w/Daredevil and battle Hitler; Daredevil battles the Claw;
　　Origin of Hitler feature story. Hitler photo app. on-c
　　| 1216 | 2432 | 3648 | 9120 | 15,810 | 22,500 |
2-London, Pat Patriot (by Reed Crandall), Nightro, Real American No. 1 (by Briefer #2-11),
　　Dickie Dean, Pirate Prince, & Times Square begin; intro. & only app. The Pioneer,
　　Champion of America | 315 | 630 | 945 | 2048 | 3624 | 5200 |
3-Origin of 13 | 235 | 470 | 705 | 1469 | 2435 | 3400 |
4 | 183 | 366 | 549 | 1144 | 1897 | 2650 |
5-Intro. Sniffer & Jinx; Ghost vs. Claw begins by Bob Wood, ends #20
　　| 134 | 268 | 402 | 838 | 1394 | 1950 |
6 | 112 | 224 | 336 | 700 | 1163 | 1625 |
7-10: 7-(Shows #6 on cover). 8-Nightro ends | 91 | 182 | 273 | 569 | 947 | 1325 |
11-London, Pat Patriot end; classic bondage/torture-c
　　| 166 | 332 | 498 | 1038 | 1719 | 2400 |
12-Origin of The Claw; Scoop Scuttle by Wolverton begins (2-4 pgs.), ends #22,
　　not in #21 | 131 | 262 | 393 | 819 | 1360 | 1900 |
13-Intro. of Little Wise Guys (10/42) | 107 | 214 | 321 | 669 | 1110 | 1550 |
14 | 64 | 128 | 192 | 400 | 663 | 925 |
15-Death of Meatball | 91 | 182 | 273 | 569 | 947 | 1325 |
16,17 | 59 | 118 | 177 | 369 | 610 | 850 |
18-New origin of Daredevil (not same as Silver Streak #6). Hitler, Mussolini Tojo and
　　Mickey Mouse app. on-c | 117 | 234 | 351 | 731 | 1216 | 1700 |
19,20 | 53 | 106 | 159 | 323 | 537 | 750 |
21-Reprints cover of Silver Streak #6 (on inside) plus intro. of The Claw from
　　Silver Streak #1 | 83 | 166 | 249 | 519 | 860 | 1200 |
22-26,28-30 | 41 | 82 | 123 | 250 | 400 | 550 |
27-Bondage/torture-c | 41 | 82 | 123 | 256 | 416 | 575 |
31-Death of The Claw | 76 | 152 | 228 | 475 | 788 | 1100 |
32-37,39-41: 35-Two Daredevil stories begin, end #68 (35-41 are 64 pgs.)
　　| 31 | 62 | 93 | 178 | 282 | 385 |
38-Origin Daredevil retold from #18 | 45 | 90 | 135 | 275 | 450 | 625 |

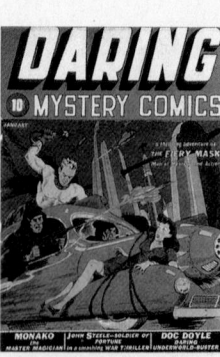

Daring Mystery Comics #1 © MAR

Daring New Adventures of Supergirl #1 © DC

Dark Angel #8 © MAR

	GD 2.0	VG 4.0	FN 6.0	VF 8.0	VF/NM 9.0	NM- 9.2
42-50: 42-Intro. Kilroy in Daredevil	26	52	78	150	235	320
51-69-Last Daredevil issue (12/50)	18	36	54	103	162	220
70-Little Wise Guys take over book; McWilliams-a; Hot Rock Flanagan begins, ends #80	12	24	36	69	97	125
71-78,81	10	20	30	54	72	90
79,80: 79-Daredevil returns. 80-Daredevil x-over	10	20	30	56	76	95
82,90,100: 82,90-One pg. Frazetta ad in both	10	20	30	54	72	90
83-89,91-99,101-134	9	18	27	50	65	80

NOTE: *Biro* c/a-all? *Bolle* a-125. *Maurer* a-75. *McWilliams* a-73, 75, 79, 80.

DARIA JONTAK
JMJ Media Group: Jan, 2001 ($4.99)

1-Matt Busch-s/a						5.00

DARING ADVENTURES (Also see Approved Comics)
St. John Publishing Co.: Nov, 1953 (25¢, 3-D, came w/glasses)

1 (3-D)-Reprints lead story from Son of Sinbad #1 by Kubert	28	56	84	162	256	350

DARING ADVENTURES
I.W. Enterprises/Super Comics: 1963 - 1964

I.W. Reprint #8-r/Fight Comics #53; Matt Baker-a	5	10	15	30	48	65
I.W. Reprint #9-r/Blue Bolt #115; Disbrow-a(3)	5	10	15	32	51	70
Super Reprint #10,11('63)-r/Dynamic #24,16; 11-Marijuana story; Yankee Boy app.; Mac Raboy-a	4	8	12	22	34	45
Super Reprint #12('64)-Phantom Lady from Fox (r/#14 only? w/splash pg. omitted); Matt Baker-a	10	20	30	67	116	165
Super Reprint #15('64)-r/Hooded Menace #1	6	12	18	43	69	95
Super Reprint #16('64)-r/Dynamic #12	3	6	9	20	30	40
Super Reprint #17('64)-r/Green Lama #3 by Raboy	4	8	12	26	41	55
Super Reprint #18-Origin Atlas from unpublished Atlas Comics #1	4	8	12	24	37	50

DARING COMICS (Formerly Daring Mystery) (Jeanie Comics No. 13 on)
Timely Comics (HPC): No. 9, Fall, 1944 - No. 12, Fall, 1945

9-Human Torch, Toro & Sub-Mariner begin	134	268	402	838	1394	1950
10-12: 10-The Angel only app. 11,12-The Destroyer app.	109	218	327	681	1128	1575

NOTE: *Schomburg* c-9-11. *Sekowsky* c-12? Human Torch, Toro & Sub-Mariner c-9-12.

DARING CONFESSIONS (Formerly Youthful Hearts)
Youthful Magazines: No. 4, 11/52 - No. 7, 5/53; No. 8, 10/53

4-Doug Wildey-a; Tony Curtis story	16	32	48	92	144	195
5-8: 5-Ray Anthony photo on-c. 6,8-Wildey-a	13	26	39	72	101	130

DARING ESCAPES
Image Comics: Sept, 1998 - No. 4, Mar, 1999 ($2.95/$2.50, mini-series)

1-Houdini; following app. in Spawn #19,20						3.00
2-4-($2.50)						2.50

DARING LOVE (Radiant Love No. 2 on)
Gilmor Magazines: Sept-Oct, 1953

1–Steve Ditko's 1st published work (1st drawn was Fantastic Fears #5)(Also see Black Magic #27)(scarce)	69	138	207	431	716	1000

DARING LOVE (Formerly Youthful Romances)
Ribage/Pix: No. 15, 12/52; No. 16, 2/53-c, 4/53-Indicia; No. 17-4/53-c & indicia

15	12	24	36	67	94	120
16,17: 17-Photo-c	10	20	30	58	79	100

NOTE: *Colletta* a-15. *Wildey* a-17.

DARING LOVE STORIES (See Fox Giants)

DARING MYSTERY COMICS (Comedy Comics No. 9 on; title changed to Daring Comics with No. 9)
Timely Comics (TPI 1-6/TCI 7,8): 1/40 - No. 5, 6/40; No. 6, 9/40; No. 7, 4/41 - No. 8, 1/42

1-Origin The Fiery Mask (1st app.) by Joe Simon; Monako, Prince of Magic (1st app.), John Steele, Soldier of Fortune (1st app.), Doc Denton (1st app.) begin; Flash Foster & Barney Mullen, Sea Rover only app; bondage-c	1900	3800	5700	14,250	25,125	36,000
2-(Rare)-Origin The Phantom Bullet (1st & only app.); The Laughing Mask & Mr. E only app.; Trojak the Tiger Man begins, ends #6; Zephyr Jones & K-4 & His Sky Devils app., also #4	1050	2100	3150	7400	12,700	18,000
3-The Phantom Reporter, Dale of FBI, Captain Strong only app.; Breeze Barton, Marvex the Super-Robot, The Purple Mask begin	503	1006	1509	3521	6161	8800
4,5: 4-Last Purple Mask; Whirlwind Carter begins; Dan Gorman, G-Man app. 5-The Falcon begins (1st app.); The Fiery Mask, Little Hercules app. by Sagendorf in the Segar style; bondage-c	339	678	1017	2204	3902	5600

6-Origin & only app. Marvel Boy by S&K; Flying Flame, Dynaman, & Stuporman only app.; The Fiery Mask by S&K; S&K-c	423	846	1269	2855	5028	7200
7-Origin and 1st app. The Blue Diamond, Captain Daring by S&K, The Fin by Everett, The Challenger, The Silver Scorpion & The Thunderer by Burgos; Mr. Millions app	352	704	1056	2288	4044	5800
8-Origin Citizen V; Last Fin, Silver Scorpion, Capt. Daring by Borth, Blue Diamond & The Thunderer; Kirby & part solo Simon-c; Rudy the Robot only app.; Citizen V, Fin & Silver Scorpion continue in Comedy #9	317	634	951	1981	3291	4600

NOTE: *Schomburg* c-1-4, 7. *Simon* a-2, 3, 5. Cover features: 1-Fiery Mask; 2-Phantom Bullet; 3-Purple Mask; 4-G-Man; 5-The Falcon; 6-Marvel Boy; 7, 8-Multiple characters.

DARING NEW ADVENTURES OF SUPERGIRL, THE
DC Comics: Nov, 1982 - No. 13, Nov, 1983 (Supergirl No. 14 on)

1-Origin retold; Lois Lane back-ups in #2-12	1	2	3	5	6	8
2-13: 8,9-Doom Patrol app. 13-New costume; flag-c						4.00

NOTE: *Buckler* c-1p, 2p. *Giffen* c-3p, 4p. *Gil Kane* c-6,8, 9, 11-13.

DARK, THE
Continuum Comics: Nov, 1990 - No. 4, Feb, 1993; V2#1, May, 1993 - V2#7, Apr?, 1994 ($1.95)

1-4: 1-Bright-p; Panosian, Hanna-i; Stroman-c. 2-(1/92)-Stroman-c/a(p).						3.00
4-Perez-c & part-i						3.00
V2#1,V2#2-6: V2#1-Red foil Bart Sears-c. V2#1-Red non-foil variant-c. V2#1-2nd printing w/blue foil Bart Sears-c. V2#2-Stroman/Bryant-a. 3-Perez-c(i). 3-6-Foil-c. 4-Perez-c & part-i; bound-in trading cards. 5,6-(2/3/94)-Perez-c(i). 7-(B&W)-Perez-c(i)						2.50
Convention Book 1 ,2(Fall/94, 10/94)-Perez-c						2.50

DARK ANGEL (Formerly Hell's Angel)
Marvel Comics UK, Ltd.: No. 6, Dec, 1992 - No. 16, Dec, 1993 ($1.75)

6-8,13-16: 6-Excalibur-c/story. 8-Psylocke app.						2.50
9-12-Wolverine/X-Men app.						2.50

DARK ANGEL: PHOENIX RESURRECTION (Kia Asamiya's...)
Image Comics: May, 2000 - No. 4, Oct, 2001 ($2.95)

1-4-Kia Asamiya-s/a. 2-Van Fleet variant-c						3.00

DARKCHYLDE (Also see Dreams of the Darkchylde)
Maximum Press #1-3/ Image Comics #4 on: June, 1996 - No. 5, Sept, 1997 ($2.95/ $2.50)

1-Randy Queen-c/a/scripts; "Roses" cover						6.00
1-American Entertainment Edition-wraparound-c						6.00
1-"Fashion magazine"-style" variant-c	1	2	3	4	5	7
1-Special Comicon Edition (contents of #1) Winged devil variant-c						5.00
1-($2.50)-Remastered Ed.-wraparound-c						4.00
2(Reg-c),2-Spiderweb and Moon variant-c						6.00
3(Reg-c),3-"Kalvin Clein" variant-c by Drew						3.00
4,5(Reg-c), 4-Variant-c						4.00
5-B&W Edition, 5-Dynamic Forces Gold Ed.						8.00
0-(3/98, $2.50)						2.50
0-Remastered (1/01, $2.95) includes Darkchylde: Redemption preview						3.00
1/2-Wizard offer						4.00
1/2 Variant-c						6.00
... The Descent TPB ('98, $19.95) r/#1-5; bagged with Darkchylde The Legacy Preview Special 1998; listed price is for TPB only						20.00

DARKCHYLDE LAST ISSUE SPECIAL
Darkchylde Entertainment: June, 2002 ($3.95)

1-Wraparound-c; cover gallery						4.00

DARKCHYLDE REDEMPTION
Darkchylde Entertainment: Feb, 2001 - No. 2, Dec, 2001 ($2.95)

1,2: 1-Wraparound-c						3.00
1-Dynamic Forces alternate-c						6.00
1-Dynamic Forces chrome-c						16.00

DARKCHYLDE SKETCH BOOK
Image Comics (Dynamic Forces): 1998

1-Regular-c						8.00
1-DarkChrome cover						16.00

DARKCHYLDE SUMMER SWIMSUIT SPECTACULAR
DC Comics (WildStorm): Aug, 1999 ($3.95, one-shot)

1-Pin-up art by various						4.00

DARKCHYLDE SWIMSUIT ILLUSTRATED
Image Comics: 1998 ($2.50, one-shot)

1-Pin-up art by various						2.50
1-(6.95) Variant cover						7.00
1-Chromium cover						15.00

DARKCHYLDE THE DIARY

Darkdevil #2 © MAR

Darkhawk #6 © MAR

Dark Horse Comics #6 © DH

	GD 2.0	VG 4.0	FN 6.0	VF 8.0	VF/NM 9.0	NM- 9.2		GD 2.0	VG 4.0	FN 6.0	VF 8.0	VF/NM 9.0	NM- 9.2

Image Comics: June, 1997 ($2.50, one-shot)

1-Queen-c/s/ art by various						2.50
1-Variant-c						5.00
1-Holochrome variant-c						8.00

DARKCHYLDE THE LEGACY
Image Comics/DC (WildStorm) #3 on: Aug, 1998 - No. 3, June, 1999 ($2.50)

1-3: 1-Queen-c. 2-Two covers by Queen and Art Adams						2.50

DARK CLAW ADVENTURES
DC Comics (Amalgam): June, 1997 ($1.95, one-shot)

1-Templeton-c/s/a & Burchett-a						2.50

DARK CROSSINGS: DARK CLOUDS RISING
Image Comics (Top Cow): June, 2000; Oct, 2000 ($5.95, limited series)

1-Witchblade, Darkness, Tomb Raider crossover; Dwayne Turner-a						6.00
1-(Dark Clouds Overhead)						6.00

DARK CRYSTAL, THE (Movie)
Marvel Comics Group: April, 1983 - No. 2, May, 1983

1,2-Adaptation of film						3.00

DARK DAYS (See 30 Days of Night)
IDW Publishing: June, 2003 - No. 6, Dec, 2003 ($3.99, limited series)

1-6-Sequel to 30 Days of Night; Niles-s/Templesmith-a						4.00
1-Retailer variant (Diamond/Alliance Fort Wayne 5/03 summit)						15.00
TPB (2004, $19.99) r/#1-6; cover gallery; intro. by Eric Red						20.00

DARKDEVIL (See Spider-Girl)
Marvel Comics: Nov, 2000 - No. 3, Jan, 2001 ($2.99, limited series)

1-3: 1-Origin of Darkdevil; Kingpin-c/app.						3.00

DARK DOMINION
Defiant: Oct, 1993 - No. 10, July, 1994 ($2.50)

1-10-Len Wein scripts begin. 4-Free extra 16 pgs. 7-9-J.G. Jones-c/a. 10-Pre-Schism issue; Shooter/Wein script; John Ridgway-a						2.50

DARKER IMAGE (Also see Deathblow, The Maxx, & Bloodwulf)
Image Comics: Mar, 1993 ($1.95, one-shot)

1-The Maxx by Sam Kieth begins; Bloodwulf by Rob Liefeld & Deathblow by Jim Lee begin (both 1st app.); polybagged w/1 of 3 cards by Kieth, Lee or Liefeld						2.50
1-B&W interior pgs. w/silver foil logo						6.00

DARKEWOOD
Aircel Publishing: 1987 - No. 5, 1988 ($2.00, 28pgs, limited series)

1-5						2.50

DARK FANTASIES
Dark Fantasy: 1994 - No. 8, 1995 ($2.95)

1-Test print Run (3,000)-Linsner-c	1	2	3	5	6	8
1-Linsner-c						5.00
2-8: 2-4 (Deluxe), 2-4 (Regular), 5-8 (Deluxe; $3.95)						4.00
5-8 (Regular; $3.50)						3.50

DARK GUARD
Marvel Comics UK: Oct, 1993 - No. 4, Jan, 1994 ($1.75)

1-($2.95)-Foil stamped-c						3.00
2-4						2.50

DARKHAWK
Marvel Comics: Mar, 1991 - No. 50, Apr, 1995 ($1.00/$1.25/$1.50)

1-Origin/1st app. Darkhawk; Hobgoblin cameo						4.00
2,3,13,14: 2-Spider-Man & Hobgoblin app. 3-Spider-Man & Hobgoblin app. 13,14-Venom-c/story						3.00
4-12,15-24,26-49: 6-Capt. America & Daredevil x-over. 9-Punisher app. 11,12-Tombstone app. 19-Spider-Man & Brotherhood of Evil Mutants-c/story. 20-Spider-Man app. 22-Ghost Rider-c/story. 23-Origin begins, ends #25. 27-New Warriors-c/story. 35-Begin 3 part Venom story. 39-Bound-in trading card sheet						2.50
25,50: (52 pgs.)-Red holo-grafx foil-c w/double gatefold poster; origin of Darkhawk armor						3.00
Annual 1-3 ('92-'94,68 pgs.)-1-Vs. Iron Man. 2 -Polybagged w/card						3.00

DARKHOLD: PAGES FROM THE BOOK OF SINS (See Midnight Sons Unlimited)
Marvel Comics (Midnight Sons imprint #15 on): Oct, 1992 - No. 16, Jan, 1994

1-($2.75, 52 pgs.)-Polybagged w/poster by Andy & Adam Kubert; part 4 of Rise of the Midnight Sons storyline						3.00
2-10,12-16: 3-Reintro Modred the Mystic (see Marvel Chillers #1). 4-Sabertooth-c/sty. 5-Punisher & Ghost Rider app. 15-Spot varnish-c. 15,16-Siege of Darkness pt. 4&12						2.50
11-($2.25)-Outer-c is a Darkhold envelope made of black parchment w/gold ink						2.50

DARK HORSE BOOK OF... , THE
Dark Horse Comics: Aug, 2003 - Nov, 2006 ($14.95/$15.95, HC, 9 1/4" x 6 1/4")

... Hauntings (8/03, $14.95)-Short stories by various incl. Mignola (Hellboy), Thompson, Dorkin, Russell; Gianni-c						15.00
... Monsters (11/06, $15.95)-Short-s by Mignola, Thompson, Dorkin, Giffen, Busiek; Gianni-c						16.00
... The Dead (6/05, $14.95)-Short-s by Mignola, Thompson, Dorkin, Powell; Gianni-c						15.00
... Witchcraft (6/04, $14.95)-Short-s by Mignola, Thompson, Dorkin, Millionaire; Gianni-c						15.00

DARK HORSE CLASSICS (Title series), **Dark Horse Comics**

1992 ($3.95, B&W, 52 pgs. nn's): The Last of the Mohicans. 20,000 Leagues Under the Sea						4.00

DARK HORSE CLASSICS, 5/96 ($2.95) 1-r/Predator: Jungle Tales | | | | | | 3.00

--ALIENS VERSUS PREDATOR, 2/97 - No. 6, 7/97 ($2.95), 1-6: r/Aliens Versus Predator | | | | | | 3.00

--GODZILLA: KING OF THE MONSTERS, 4/98 ($2.95) 1-6: 1-r/Godzilla: Color Special; Art Adams-a | | | | | | 3.00

--STAR WARS: DARK EMPIRE, 3/97 - No. 6, 8/97 ($2.95) 1-6: r/Star Wars: Dark Empire | | | | | | 3.00

--TERROR OF GODZILLA, 8/98 - No. 6, 1/99 ($2.95) 1-6-r/manga Godzilla in color; Art Adams-c | | | | | | 3.00

DARK HORSE COMICS
Dark Horse Comics: Aug, 1992 - No. 25, Sept, 1994 ($2.50)

1-Dorman double gategold painted-c; Predator, Robocop, Timecop (3-part) & Renegade stories begin						3.00
2-6,11-25: 2-Mignola-c. 3-Begin 3-part Aliens story; Aliens-c. 4-Predator-c. 6-Begin 4 part Robocop story. 12-Begin 2-part Aliens & 3-part Predator stories. 13-Thing From Another World begins w/Nino-a(i). 15-Begin 2-part Aliens: Cargo story. 16-Begin 3-part Predator story. 17-Begin 3-part StarWars: Droids story & 3-part Aliens: Alien story; Droids-c. 19-Begin 2-part X story; X cover						2.50
7-Begin Star Wars: Tales of the Jedi 3-part story	1	2	3	4	5	7
8-1st app. X and begins; begin 4-part James Bond						6.00
9,10-Star Wars ends. 10-X ends; Begin 3-part Predator & Godzilla stories						4.00

NOTE: *Art Adams c-11.*

DARK HORSE DOWN UNDER
Dark Horse Comics: June, 1994 - No. 3, Oct, 1994 ($2.50, B&W, limited series)

1-3						2.50

DARK HORSE MAVERICK
Dark Horse Comics: July, 2000; July, 2001; Sept, 2002 (B&W, annual)

2000-($3.95) Short stories by Miller, Chadwick, Sakai, Pearson						4.00
2001-($4.99) Short stories by Sakai, Wagner and others; Miller-c						5.00
...: Happy Endings (9/02, $9.95) Short stories by Bendis, Oeming, Mahfood, Mignola, Miller, Kieth and others; Miller-c						10.00

DARK HORSE MONSTERS
Dark Horse Comics: Feb, 1997 ($2.95, one-shot)

1-reprints						3.00

DARK HORSE PRESENTS
Dark Horse Comics: July, 1986 - No. 157, Sept, 2000 ($1.50-$2.95, B&W)

1-1st app. Concrete by Paul Chadwick		2	4	6	8	11	14
1-2nd printing (1988, $1.50)						2.50
1-Silver ink 3rd printing (1992, $2.25)-Says 2nd printing inside						2.50
2-9: 2-6,9-Concrete app.						6.00
10-1st app. The Mask; Concrete app.		2	4	6	9	12	15
11-19,21-23: 11-19,21-Mask stories. 12,14,16,18,22-Concrete app. 15(2/88). 17-All Roachmill issue						6.00
20-(68 pgs.)-Concrete, Flaming Carrot, Mask	1	3	4	6	8	10
24-Origin Aliens-c/story (11/88); Mr. Monster app.	2	4	6	10	14	18
25-31,33,37-41,44,45,47-49: 28-(52 pgs.)-Concrete app.; Mr. Monster story (homage to Graham Ingels). 33-(44 pgs.). 38-Concrete. 40-(52 pgs.)-1st Argosy story. 44-Crash Ryan. 48,49-Contain 2 trading cards						4.00
32,34,35: 32-(68 pgs.)-Annual; Concrete, American. 34-Aliens-c/story. 35-Predator/c-app.						4.00
36-1st Aliens Vs. Predator story; painted-c, 36-Variant line drawn-c						5.00
42,43,46: 42,43-Aliens-c/stories. 46-Prequel to new Predator II mini-series						3.00
50-S/F story by Perez; contains 2 trading cards						4.00
51-53-Sin City by Frank Miller, parts 2-4; 51,53-Miller-c (see D.H.P. Fifth Anniversary Special for pt. 1)	1	2	3	4	6	8
54-61: 54-(9/91) The Next Men begins (1st app.) by Byrne; Miller-a/Morrow-c. Homicide by Morrow (also in #55). 55-2nd app. The Next Men; parts 5 & 6 of Sin City by Miller; Miller-c. 56-(68 pg. annual)-part 7 of Sin City by Miller; part prologue to Aliens: Genocide; Next Men by Byrne. 57-(52 pgs.)-Part 8 of Sin City by Miller; Next Men by Byrne; Byrne-c; Alien Fire story; swipes cover to Daredevil #1. 58,59-Alien Fire stories. 58-61- Part 9-12 Sin City by Miller						5.00
62-Last Sin City (entire book by Miller, c/a; 52 pgs.)	1	3	4	6	8	10

	GD 2.0	VG 4.0	FN 6.0	VF 8.0	VF/NM 9.0	NM- 9.2

63-66,68-79,81-84-($2.25): 64-Dr. Giggles begins (1st app.), ends #66; Boris the Bear story. 66-New Concrete-c/story by Chadwick. 71-Begin 3 part Dominque story by Jim Balent; Balent-c. 72-(3/93)-Begin 3-part Eudaemon (1st app.) story by Nelson 3.00

67-($3.95, 68 pgs.)-Begin 3-part prelude to Predator: Race War mini-series; Oscar Wilde adapt. by Russell 4.00

80-Art Adams-c/a (Monkeyman & O'Brien) 4.00

85-87,92-99: 85-Begin $2.50-c. 92, 93, 95-Too Much Coffee Man 3.00

88-91-Hellboy by Mignola. 6.00

NOTE: *There are 5 different Dark Horse Presents #100 issues*

100-1-Intro Lance Blastoff by Miller; Milk & Cheese by Evan Dorkin 4.00

100-2-Hellboy-c by Wrightson; Hellboy story by Mignola; includes Roberta Gregory & Paul Pope stories 6.00

100-3-100-5: 100-3-Darrow-c, Concrete by Chadwick; Pekar story. 100-4-Gibbons-c: Miller story, Geary story/a. 100-5-Allred-c, Adams, Dorkin, Pope 3.00

101-125: 101-Aliens c/a by Wrightson, story by Pope. 103-Kirby gatefold-c. 106-Big Blown Baby by Bill Wray. 107-Mignola-c/a. 109-Begin $2.95-c; Paul Pope-c. 110-Ed Brubaker-a/s. 114-Flip books begin; Lance Blastoff by Miller; Star Slammers by Simonson. 115-Miller-c. 117-Aliens-c/app. 118-Evan Dorkin-c/a. 119-Monkeyman & O'Brien. 124-Predator. 125-Nocturnals 3.00

126-($3.95, 48 pgs.)-Flip book: Nocturnals, Starship Troopers 4.00

127-134,136-140: 127-Nocturnals. 129-The Hammer. 132-134-Warren-a 3.00

135-($3.50) The Mark 3.50

141-All Buffy the Vampire Slayer issue 4.00

142-149: 142-Mignola-c. 143-Tarzan. 146,147-Aliens vs. Predator. 148-Xena 3.00

150-($4.50) Buffy-c by Green; Buffy, Concrete, Fish Police app. 4.50

151-157: 151-Hellboy-c/app. 153-155-Angel flic-c. 156,157-Witch's Son 3.00

Annual 1997 ($4.95, 64 pgs.)-Flip book; Body Bags, Aliens. Pearson-c; stories by Allred & Stephens, Pope, Smith & Morrow 1 2 3 5 6 8

Annual 1998 ($4.95, 64 pgs.) 1st Buffy the Vampire Slayer comic app.; Hellboy story and cover by Mignola 1 2 3 4 5 7

Annual 1999 (7/99, $4.95) Stories of Xena, Hellboy, Ghost, Luke Skywalker, Groo, Concrete, the Mask and Usagi Yojimbo in their youth. 5.00

Annual 2000 ($4.95) Girl sidekicks; Chiodo-c and flip photo Buffy-c 5.00

...Aliens Platinum Edition (1992)-r/DHP #24,43,43,56 & Special 11.00

...Fifth Anniversary Special nn (4/91, $9.95)-Part 1 of Sin City by Frank Miller (c/a); Aliens, Aliens vs. Predator, Concrete, Roachmill, Give Me Liberty & The American stories 25.00

The One Trick Rip-off (1997, $12.95, TPB)-r/stories from #101-112 13.00

NOTE: *Geary a-59, 60. Miller a-Special, 51-53, 55-62; c-59-62, 100-1; c-51, 53, 55, 59-62, 100-1. Moebius a-63; c-63, 70. Vess a-78; c-75, 78.*

DARK HORSE TWENTY YEARS
Dark Horse Comics: 2006 (25¢, one-shot)

nn-Pin-ups by a host of other artists' Dark Horse characters; Mignola-c 2.50

DARK KNIGHT (See Batman: The Dark Knight Returns & Legends of the...)

DARK KNIGHT STRIKES AGAIN, THE (Also see Batman: The Dark Knight Returns)
DC Comics: 2001 - No. 3, 2002 ($7.95, prestige format, limited series)

1-Frank Miller-s/a/c; sequel 3 years after Dark Knight Returns; 2 covers 8.00

2,3 8.00

HC (2002, $29.95) intro. by Miller; sketch pages and exclusive artwork; cover has 3 1/4" tall partial dustjacket 30.00

SC (2002, $19.95) intro. by Miller; sketch pages 20.00

DARKLON THE MYSTIC (Also see Eerie Magazine #79,80)
Pacific Comics: Oct, 1983 (one-shot)

1-Starlin-c/a(r) 4.00

DARKMAN (Movie)
Marvel Comics: Sept, 1990; Oct, 1990 - No. 3, Dec, 1990 ($1.50)

1 (9/90, $2.25, B&W mag., 68 pgs.)-Adaptation of film 3.00

1-3: Reprints B&W magazine 2.50

DARKMAN
Marvel Comics: V2#1, Apr, 1993 -No. 6, Sept, 1993 ($2.95, limited series)

V2#1 ($3.95, 52 pgs.) 4.00

2-6 3.00

DARKMAN VS. THE ARMY OF DARKNESS (Movie crossover)
Dynamite Entertainment: 2006 - No. 4, 2007 ($3.50)

1-4: 1-Busiek & Stern-a; photo-c and Perez and Bradshaw covers 3.50

DARK MANSION OF FORBIDDEN LOVE, THE (Becomes Forbidden Tales of Dark Mansion No. 5 on)
National Periodical Publ.: Sept-Oct, 1971 - No. 4, Mar-Apr, 1972 (52 pgs.)

1 17 34 51 126 223 320

2-4: 2-Adams-c. 3-Jeff Jones-c 8 16 24 58 97 135

DARKMINDS
Image Comics (Dreamwave Prod.): July, 1998 - No. 8, Apr, 1999 ($2.50)

1-Manga; Pat Lee-s/a; 2 covers 1 3 4 6 8 10

1-2nd printing 2.50

2, 0-(1/99, $5.00) Story and sketch pages 5.00

3-8, 1/2-(5/99, $2.50) Story and sketch pages 2.50

... Collected 1,2 (1/99,3/99; $7.95) 1-r/#1-3. 2-r/#4-6 8.00

... Collected 3 (5/99; $5.95) r/#7,8 6.00

DARKMINDS (Volume 2)
Image Comics (Dreamwave Prod.): Feb, 2000 - No. 10, Apr, 2001 ($2.50)

1-10-Pat Lee-c 2.50

0-(7/00) Origin of Mai Murasaki; sketchbook 2.50

DARKMINDS: MACROPOLIS
Image Comics (Dreamwave Prod.): Jan, 2002 - No. 4, Dec, 2002 ($2.95)

Preview (8/01) Flip book w/Banished Knights preview 2.50

1-4-Jo Chen-a 3.00

DARKMINDS: MACROPOLIS (Volume 2)
Dreamwave Prod.: Sept, 2003 - No. 4, Jul, 2004 ($2.95)

1-4-Chris Sarracini-s/Kwang Mook Lim-a 3.00

DARKMINDS / WITCHBLADE (Also see Witchblade/Dark Minds)
Image Comics (Top Cow/Dreamwave Prod.): Aug, 2000 ($5.95, one-shot)

1-Wohl-s/Pat Lee-a; two covers by Silvestri and Lee 6.00

DARK MYSTERIES (Thrilling Tales of Horror & Suspense)
"Master" - "Merit" Publications: June-July, 1951 - No. 24, July, 1955

1-Wood-c/a (8 pgs.) 119 238 357 744 1235 1725

2-Wood/Harrison-c/a (8 pgs.) 81 162 243 506 841 1175

3-9: 7-Dismemberment, hypo blood drainage stys 45 90 135 275 450 625

10-Cannibalism story; witch burning-c 48 96 144 293 484 675

11-13,15-18: 11-Severed head panels. 13-Dismemberment-c/story. 17-The Old Gravedigger host 40 80 120 240 383 525

14-Several E.C. Craig swipes 40 80 120 243 389 535

19-Injury-to-eye panel; E.C. swipe; torture-c 48 96 144 293 484 675

20-Female bondage, blood drainage story 43 86 129 262 431 600

21,22: 21-Devil-c. 22-Last pre-code issue, misdated 3/54 instead of 3/55 29 58 87 167 264 360

23,24 21 42 63 122 191 260

NOTE: *Cameron a-1, 2. Myron Fass c/a-21. Harrison a-3, 7; c-3. Hollingsworth a-7-17, 20, 21, 23. Wildey a-5. Woodish art by Fleishman-9; c-10, 14-17. Bondage c-10, 18, 19.*

DARK NEMESIS (VILLAINS) (See Teen Titans)
DC Comics: Feb, 1998 ($1.95, one-shot)

1-Jurgens-s/Pearson-c 2.50

DARKNESS, THE (See Witchblade #10)
Image Comics (Top Cow Productions): Dec, 1996 - No. 40, Aug, 2001 ($2.50)

Special Preview Edition-(7/96, B&W)-Ennis script; Silvestri-a(p) 2 4 6 9 13 16

0 2 4 6 8 10 12

0-Gold Edition 16.00

1/2 1 3 4 6 8 10

1/2-Christmas-c 3 6 9 14 19 24

1/2-(3/01, $2.95) r/#1/2 w/new 6 pg. story & Silvestri-c 3.00

1-Ennis-s/Silvestri-a, 1-Black variant-c 2 4 6 9 12 15

1-Platinum variant-c 20.00

1-DF Green variant-c 12.00

1,2: 1-Fan Club Ed. 1 3 4 6 8 10

3-5 6.00

6-10: 9,10-Witchblade "Family Ties" x-over pt. 2,3 4.00

7-Variant-c w/concubine 2 3 5 7 9

8-American Entertainment 6.00

8-10-American Entertainment Gold Ed. 7.00

11-Regular Ed.; Ennis-s/Silverstri & D-Tron-c 3.00

11-Nine (non-chromium) variant-c (Benitez, Cabrera, the Hildebrandts, Finch, Keown, Peterson, Portacio, Tan, Turner 4.50

11-Chromium-c by Silvestri & Batt 20.00

12-19: 13-Begin Benitez-a(p) 3.00

20-24,26-40: 34-Ripclaw app. 2.50

25-($3.99) Two covers (Benitez, Silvestri) 4.00

25-Chromium-c variant by Silvestri 8.00

.../ Batman (8/99, $5.95) Silvestri, Finch, Lansing-a(p) 6.00

...Collected Editions #1-4 ($4.95,TPB) 1-r/#1,2. 2-r/#3,4. 3- r/#5,6. 4- r/#7,8 6.00

Dark Shadows #8 © Dan Curtis Prods.

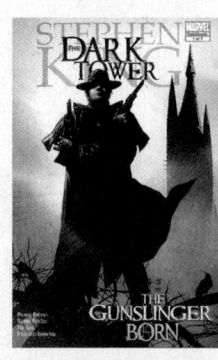

Dark Tower: The Gunslinger Born #1 © Stephen King

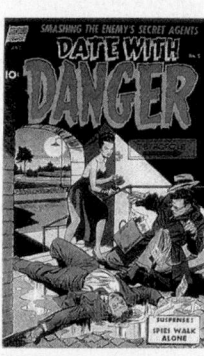

Date With Danger #5 © STD

	GD	VG	FN	VF	VF/NM	NM-		GD	VG	FN	VF	VF/NM	NM-
	2.0	4.0	6.0	8.0	9.0	9.2		2.0	4.0	6.0	8.0	9.0	9.2

...Collected Editions #5,6 ($5.95, TPB)5- r/#11,12. 6-r/#13,14 — 6.00
Deluxe Collected Editions #1 (12/98, $14.95, TPB) r/#1-6 & Preview — 15.00
...: Heart of Darkness (2001, $14.95, TPB) r/ #7,8, 11-14 — 15.00
Holiday Pin-up-American Entertainment — 5.00
Holiday Pin-up Gold Ed.-American Entertainment — 7.00
Infinity #1 (8/99, $3.50) Lobdell-s — 3.50
Prelude-American Entertainment — 4.00
Prelude Gold Ed.-American Entertainment — 9.00
Volume 1 Compendium (2006, $59.99) r/#1-40, V2 #1, Tales of the Darkness #1-4; #1/2,
   Darkness/Witchblade #1/2, Darkness: Wanted Dead; cover and sketch gallery — 60.00
...: Wanted Dead 1 (8/03, $2.99) Texiera-a/Tieri-s — 3.00
Wizard ACE Ed.- Reprints #1 — 2 4 6 8 10 12

DARKNESS (Volume 2)
Image Comics (Top Cow Productions): Dec, 2002 - No. 24, Oct, 2004 ($2.99)
1-24: 1-6-Jenkins-s/Keown-a. 17-20-Lapham-s. 23,24-Magdalena app. — 3.00
... Black Sails (3/05, $2.99) Marz-s/Cha-a; Hunter-Killer preview — 3.00
... and Tomb Raider (4/05, $2.99) r/Darkness Prelude & Tomb Raider/Darkness Special — 3.00
...: Resurrection TPB (2/04, $16.99) r/#1-6 & Vol. 1 #40 — 17.00
.../ The Incredible Hulk (7/04, $2.99) Keown-a/Jenkins-s — 3.00
.../ Vampirella (7/05, $2.99) Terry Moore-s; two covers by Basaldua and Moore — 3.00
... Vol. 5 TPB (2006, $19.99) r/#7-16 & The Darkness: Wanted Dead #1; cover gallery — 20.00
... vs Mr Hyde Monster War 2005 (9/05, $2.99) x-over w/Witchblade, Tomb Raider and
   Magdalena; two covers — 3.00
.../ Wolverine (2006, $2.99) Kirkham-a/Tieri-s — 3.00

DARKNESS: LEVEL...
Image Comics (Top Cow): No. 0, Dec, 2006 - No. 5, Aug, 2007 ($2.99, limited series)
0-5: 0-Origin of The Darkness in WW1; Jenkins-s. 1-Jackie's origin retold; Sejic-a — 3.00

DARKNESS/ PITT
Image Comics (Top Cow): Dec, 2006 - Present ($2.99)
...: First Look (12/06) Jenkins script pages with Keown B&W and color art — 3.00

DARKNESS/ SUPERMAN
Image Comics (Top Cow Productions): Jan, 2005 - No. 2, Feb, 2005 ($2.99, limited series)
1,2-Marz-s/Kirkham & Banning-a/Silvestri-c — 3.00

DARKSEID (VILLAINS) (See Jack Kirby's New Gods and New Gods)
DC Comics: Feb, 1998 ($1.95, one-shot)
1-Byrne-s/Pearson-c — 2.50

DARKSEID VS. GALACTUS: THE HUNGER
DC Comics: 1995 ($4.95, one-shot) (1st DC/Marvel x-over by John Byrne)
nn-John Byrne-c/a/script — 5.00

DARK SHADOWS
Steinway Comic Publ. (Ajax)(America's Best): Oct, 1957 - No. 3, May, 1958

	GD	VG	FN	VF	VF/NM	NM-
1	27	54	81	156	246	335
2,3	19	38	57	109	172	235

DARK SHADOWS (TV) (See Dan Curtis Giveaways)
Gold Key: Mar, 1969 - No. 35, Feb, 1976 (Photo-c: 1-7)

	GD	VG	FN	VF	VF/NM	NM-
1(30039-903)-With pull-out poster (25¢)	22	44	66	165	295	425
1-With poster missing	8	16	24	56	93	130
2	7	14	21	49	80	110
3-With pull-out poster	11	22	33	75	133	170
3-With poster missing	6	12	18	41	66	90
4-7: 7-Last photo-c	6	12	18	43	69	95
8-10	5	10	15	32	51	70
11-20	4	8	12	28	44	60
21-35: 30-Last painted-c	4	8	12	24	37	50
Story Digest 1 (6/70, 148pp.)-Photo-c (low print)	8	16	24	54	90	125

DARK SHADOWS (TV) (See Nightmare on Elm Street)
Innovation Publishing: June, 1992 - No. 4, Spring, 1993 ($2.50, limited series, coated stock)
1-Based on 1991 NBC TV mini-series; painted-c — 5.00
2-4 — 4.00

DARK SHADOWS: BOOK TWO
Innovation Publishing: 1993 - No. 4, July, 1993 ($2.50, limited series)
1-4-Painted-c. 4-Maggie Thompson scripts — 4.00

DARK SHADOWS: BOOK THREE
Innovation Publishing: Nov, 1993 ($2.50)
1-(Whole #9) — 4.00

DARKSTARS, THE
DC Comics: Oct, 1992 - No. 38, Jan, 1996 ($1.75/$1.95)

1-1st app. The Darkstars — 3.00
2-24,0,25-38: 5-Hawkman & Hawkwoman app. 18-20-Flash app. 24-(9/94)-Zero Hour. 0-(10/94).
   25-(11/94). 30-Green Lantern app. 31-...vs. Darkseid. 32-Green Lantern app. — 2.50
NOTE: *Travis Charest* a(p)-4-7; c(p)-2-5; c-6-11. *Stroman* a-1-3; c-1.

DARK TOWER: THE GUNSLINGER BORN (Based on Stephen King's Dark Tower series)
Marvel Comics: Apr, 2007 - No. 7, Oct, 2007 ($3.99, limited series)
1-Peter David & Robin Furth-s/Jae Lee & Richard Isanove-a; boyhood of Roland Deschain;
   afterword by Ralph Macchio; map of New Canaan — 6.00
1-Variant cover by Quesada — 8.00
1-Second printing with variant-c by Quesada — 5.00
1-Sketch cover variant by Jae Lee — 40.00
2-6-Jae Lee-c — 4.00
2-Second printing with variant-c by Immonen — 4.00
2-7-Variant covers. 2-Finch-c. 3-Yu-c. 4-McNiven-c. 5-Land-c. 6-Campbell. 7-Coipel — 6.00
2-7-B&W sketch-c by Jae Lee — 20.00
... Sketchbook (2006, no cover price) pencil art and designs by Lee; coloring process — 5.00
Datk Tower: Gunslinger's Guidebook (2007, $3.99) profile pages with Jae Lee-a — 4.00

DARKWING DUCK (TV cartoon) (Also see Cartoon Tales)
Disney Comics: Nov, 1991 - No. 4, Feb, 1992 ($1.50, limited series)
1-4: Adapts hour-long premiere TV episode — 3.00

DARLING LOVE
Close Up/Archie Publ. (A Darling Magazine): Oct-Nov, 1949 - No. 11, 1952 (no month)
(52 pgs.)(Most photo-c)

	GD	VG	FN	VF	VF/NM	NM-
1-Photo-c	18	36	54	103	162	220
2-Photo-c	11	22	33	64	90	115
3-8,10,11: 3-6-photo-c	10	20	30	54	72	90
9-Krigstein-a	10	20	30	58	79	100

DARLING ROMANCE
Close Up (MLJ Publications): Sept-Oct, 1949 - No. 7, 1951 (All photo-c)

	GD	VG	FN	VF	VF/NM	NM-
1-(52 pgs.)-Photo-c	23	46	69	132	209	285
2	12	24	36	69	97	125
3-7	10	20	30	56	76	95

DARQUE PASSAGES (See Master Darque)
Acclaim (Valiant): April, 1998 ($2.50)
1-Christina Z.-s/Manco-c/a — 2.50

DART (Also see Freak Force & Savage Dragon)
Image Comics (Highbrow Entertainment): Feb, 1996 - No. 3, May, 1996 ($2.50, lim. series)
1-3 — 3.00

DASTARDLY & MUTTLEY (See Fun-In No. 1-4, 6 and Kite Fun Book)

DATE WITH DANGER
Standard Comics: No. 5, Dec, 1952 - No. 6, Feb, 1953

	GD	VG	FN	VF	VF/NM	NM-
5,6-Secret agent stories: 6-Atom bomb story	9	18	27	52	69	85

DATE WITH DEBBI (Also see Debbi's Dates)
National Periodical Publ.: Jan-Feb, 1969 - No. 17, Sept-Oct, 1971; No. 18, Oct-Nov, 1972

	GD	VG	FN	VF	VF/NM	NM-
1-Teenage	6	12	18	37	59	80
2-5,17-(52 pgs) James Taylor sty.	3	6	9	20	30	40
6-12,18-Last issue	3	6	9	19	29	38
13-16-(68 pgs.): 14-1 pg. story on Jack Wild. 15-Marlo Thomas/"That Girl" story	4	8	12	22	34	45

DATE WITH JUDY, A (Radio/TV, and 1948 movie)
National Periodical Publications: Oct-Nov, 1947 - No. 79, Oct-Nov, 1960 (No. 1-25: 52 pgs.)

	GD	VG	FN	VF	VF/NM	NM-
1-Teenage	29	58	87	167	264	360
2	14	28	42	82	121	160
3-10	12	24	36	67	94	120
11-20	9	18	27	50	65	80
21-40	8	16	24	44	57	70
41-45: 45-Last pre-code (2-3/55)	8	16	24	40	50	60
46-79: 79-Drucker-c/a	7	14	21	37	46	55

DATE WITH MILLIE, A (Life With Millie No. 8 on)(Teenage)
Atlas/Marvel Comics (MPC): Oct, 1956 - No. 7, Aug, 1957; Oct, 1959 - No. 7, Oct, 1960

	GD	VG	FN	VF	VF/NM	NM-
1(10/56)-(1st Series)-Dan DeCarlo-a in #1-7	26	52	78	154	242	330
2	15	30	45	83	124	165
3-7	11	22	33	64	90	115
1(10/59)-(2nd Series)	15	30	45	83	124	165
2-7	10	20	30	56	76	95

DATE WITH PATSY, A (Also see Patsy Walker)
Atlas Comics: Sept, 1957 (One-shot)

Davy Crockett, Frontier Fighter #2 © CC

Day of Judgment #5 © DC

Dazzler #35 © MAR

	GD 2.0	VG 4.0	FN 6.0	VF 8.0	VF/NM 9.0	NM- 9.2
1-Starring Patsy Walker	12	24	36	69	97	125

DAUGHTERS OF THE DRAGON (See Heroes For Hire)
Marvel Comics: 2005; Mar, 2006 - No. 6, Aug, 2006 ($2.99, limited series)

1-6-Palmiotti & Gray-s/Evans-a. 1-Rhino app. 5,6-Iron Fist app.						3.00
...: Deadly Hands Special (2005, $3.99) reprints app. from Deadly Hands of Kung Fu #32,33 & Bizarre Adventures #25; Claremont-s/Rogers-a; new Rogers-c & interview						4.00
...: Samurai Bullets TPB (2006, $15.99) r/#1-6						16.00

DAVID AND GOLIATH (Movie)
Dell Publishing Co.: No. 1205, July, 1961

Four Color 1205-Photo-c	6	12	18	43	69	95

DAVID BORING (See Eightball)
Pantheon Books: 2000 ($24.95, hardcover w/dust jacket)

Hardcover - reprints David Boring stories from Eightball; Clowes-s/a						25.00

DAVID CASSIDY (See Partridge Family, Swing With Scooter #33 & Time For Love #30)
Charlton Comics: Feb, 1972 - No. 14, Sept, 1973

1-Most have photo covers	6	12	18	41	66	90
2-5	4	8	12	24	37	50
6-14	4	8	12	22	34	45

DAVID LADD'S LIFE STORY (See Movie Classics)

DAVY CROCKETT (See Dell Giants, Fightin..., Frontier Fighters, It's Game Time, Power Record Comics, Western Tales & Wild Frontier)

DAVY CROCKETT (Frontier Fighter...)
Avon Periodicals: 1951

nn-Tuska?, Reinman-a; Fawcette-c	18	36	54	105	165	225

DAVY CROCKETT (...King of the Wild Frontier No. 1,2)(TV)
Dell Publishing Co./Gold Key: 5/55 - No. 671, 12/55; No. 1; No. 2, 11/69 (Walt Disney)

Four Color 631(#1)-Fess Parker photo-c	17	34	51	126	223	320
Four Color 639-Photo-c	14	28	42	102	181	260
Four Color 664,671(Marsh-a)-Photo-c	13	26	39	97	171	245
1(12/63-Gold Key)-Fess Parker photo-c; reprints	12	24	36	87	156	225
2(11/69)-Fess Parker photo-c	4	8	12	28	44	60

DAVY CROCKETT (...Frontier Fighter #1,2; Kid Montana #9 on)
Charlton Comics: Aug, 1955 - No. 8, Jan, 1957

1	10	20	30	56	76	95
2	7	14	21	35	43	50
3-8	5	10	15	24	30	35

DAWN
Sirius Entertainment/Image Comics: June, 1995 - No. 6, 1996 ($2.95)

1/2-w/certificate	1	2	3	5	6	8
1/2-Variant-c	2	4	6	10	14	18
1-Linsner-c/a	1	2	3	5	6	8
1-Black Light Edition	2	4	6	9	13	16
1-White Trash Edition	3	6	9	16	23	30
1-Look Sharp Edition	3	6	9	19	29	38
2-4: Linsner-c/a						4.50
2-Variant-c, 3-Limited Edition	2	4	6	13	18	22
4-6-Vibrato-c						3.50
4, 5-Limited Edition	2	4	6	8	10	12
6-Limited Edition	2	4	6	8	10	12
...Convention Sketchbook (Image Comics, 2002, $2.95) pin-ups						3.00
...2003 Convention Sketchbook (Image Comics, 3/03, $2.95) pin-ups						3.00
...2004 Convention Sketchbook (Image Comics, 4/04, $2.95) pin-ups						3.00
...2005 Convention Sketchbook (Image Comics, 5/05, $2.95) pin-ups						3.00
Genesis Special ('99, Wizard supplement) previews Return of the Goddess						2.50
Lucifer's Halo TPB (11/97, $19.95) r/Drama, Dawn #1-6 plus 12 pages of new artwork						20.00
...: Tenth Anniversary Special (9/99, $2.95) Interviews						3.00
The Portable Dawn ($9.95, 5"x4", 64 pgs.) Pocket-sized cover gallery						10.00

DAWN OF THE DEAD (George A. Romaro's...)
IDW Publishing: Apr, 2004 - No. 3, Jun, 2004 ($3.99, limited series)

1-3-Adaptation of the 2004 movie; Niles-s						4.00
TPB (9/04, $17.99) r/#1-3; intro. by George A. Romero						18.00

DAWN: THE RETURN OF THE GODDESS
Sirius Entertainment: Apr, 1999 - No. 4, July, 2000 ($2.95, limited series)

1-4-Linsner-s/a						3.00
TPB (4/02, $12.95) r/#1-4; intro. by Linsner						13.00

DAWN: THREE TIERS

Image Comics: Jun, 2003 - No. 6, Aug, 2005 ($2.95, limited series)

1-6-Linsner-s/a. 2-Preview of Vampire's Christmas						3.00

DAYDREAMERS (See Generation X)
Marvel Comics: Aug, 1997 - No. 3, Oct, 1997 ($2.50, limited series)

1-3-Franklin Richards, Howard the Duck, Man-Thing app.						2.50

DAY OF JUDGMENT
DC Comics: Nov, 1999 - No. 5, Nov, 1999 ($2.95/$2.50, limited series)

1-($2.95) Spectre possessed; Matt Smith-a						3.00
2-5: Parallax returns. 5-Hal Jordan becomes the Spectre						3.00
...Secret Files 1 (11/99, $4.95) Harris-c						5.00

DAY OF VENGEANCE (Prelude to Infinite Crisis)(Also see Birds of Prey #76 for 1st app. of Black Alice)
DC Comics: June, 2005 - No. 6, Nov, 2005 ($2.50, limited series)

1-6: 1-Jean Loring becomes Eclipso; Spectre, Ragman, Enchantress, Detective Chimp, Shazam app.; Justiniano-a. 2,3-Capt. Marvel app. 4-6-Black Alice app.						2.50
...: Infinite Crisis Special 1 (3/06, $4.99) Justiniano-a/Simonson-c						5.00
TPB (2005, $12.99) r/series & Action #826, Advs. of Superman #639, Superman #216						13.00

DAYS OF THE DEFENDERS (See Defenders, The)
Marvel Comics: Mar, 2001 ($3.50, one-shot)

1-Reprints early team-ups of members, incl. Marvel Feature #1; Larsen-c						3.50

DAYS OF THE MOB (See In the Days of the Mob)

DAZEY'S DIARY
Dell Publishing Co.: June-Aug, 1962

01-174-208: Bill Woggon-c/a	4	8	12	28	44	60

DAZZLER, THE (Also see Marvel Graphic Novel & X-Men #130)
Marvel Comics Group: Mar, 1981 - No. 42, Mar, 1986

1,22,24,27,28,38,42: 1-X-Men app. 22 (12/82)-vs. Rogue Battle-c/story. 24-Full app. Rogue w/Powerman (Iron Fist). 27-Rogue app. 28-Rogue app. Rogue; Mystique app. 38-Wolverine-c/app.; X-Men app. 42-Beast-c/app.						4.00
2-21,23,25,26,29-37,39-41: 2-X-Men app. 10,11-Galactus app. 21-Double size; photo-c. 23-Rogue/Mystique 1 pg. app. 26-Jusko-c. 33-Michael Jackson thriller swipe-c/story. 40-Secret Wars II						3.00

NOTE: No. 1 distributed only through comic shops. Alcala a-1i, 2i. Chadwick a-38-42p; c(p)-39, 41, 42. Guice a-38i, 42i; c-8, 40.

DC CHALLENGE (Most DC superheroes appear)
DC Comics: Nov, 1985 - No. 12, Oct, 1986 ($1.25/$2.00, maxi-series)

1-11: 1-Colan-a. 2,8-Batman-c/app. 4-Gil Kane-c/a						2.50
12-($2.00-c) Giant; low print						3.00

NOTE: Batman app. in 1-4, 6-12. Joker app. in 7. Infantino a-3. Ordway c-12. Swan/Austin c-10.

DC COMICS PRESENTS
DC Comics: July-Aug, 1978 - No. 97, Sept, 1986 (Superman team-ups in all)

1-4th Superman/Flash race	3	6	9	16	23	30
1-(Whitman variant)	3	6	9	18	27	35
2-Part 2 of Superman/Flash race	2	4	6	10	14	18
2-4,9-12,14-16,19,21,22-(Whitman variants, low print run, none have issue # on cover)	2	4	6	10	14	18
3-10: 4-Metal Men. 6-Green Lantern. 8-Swamp Thing. 9-Wonder Woman	1	2	3	5	7	9
11-25,27-40: 13-Legion of Super-Heroes. 19-Batgirl. 31-Robin. 35-Man-Bat						6.00
26-(10/80)-Green Lantern; intro Cyborg, Starfire, Raven (1st app. New Teen Titans in 16 pg. preview); Starlin-c/a; Sargon the Sorcerer back-up	4	8	12	22	34	45
41,72,77,78,97: 41-Superman/Joker-c/story. 72-Joker/Phantom Stranger-c/story. 77,78-Animal Man app. 97-Phantom Zone						5.00
42-46,48-50,52-71,73-76,79-83: 42-Sandman. 43,80-Legion of Super-Heroes. 52-Doom Patrol. 58-Robin. 82-Adam Strange. 83-Batman & Outsiders						4.00
47-He-Man-c/s (1st app. in comics)	2	4	6	10	14	18
51-Preview insert (16 pgs.) of He-Man (2nd app.)	1	2	3	5	6	8
84-Challengers of the Unknown; Kirby-c/s.						6.00
85-Swamp Thing; Alan Moore scripts						6.00
86,88-96: 86-88-Crisis x-over. 88-Creeper						4.00
87-Origin/1st app. Superboy of Earth Prime	1	3	4	6	8	10
Annual 1,4: 1(9/82)-G.A. Superman; 1pt. app. Alexander Luther. 4(10/85)-Superwoman						4.00
Annual 2,3: 2(7/83)-Intro/origin Superwoman. 3(9/84)-Shazam						4.00

NOTE: Adkins a-2, 54; c-2. Buckler a-33, 34; c-30, 33, 34. Giffen a-39; c-59. Gil Kane a-28, 35, Annual 3; c-48p, 56, 58, 60, 62, 64, 68, Annual 2, 3. Kirby a-84. Kubert a/c-66. Morrow c/a-65. Newton c/a-54p. Orlando c-53i. Perez a-26p, 61p; c-38, 61, 94. Starlin a-26-29p, 36p, 37p; c-26-29, 36, 37, 93. Toth a-84. Williamson i-79, 85, 87.

DC COMICS PRESENTS: ...(Julie Schwartz tribute series of one-shots based on classic covers)
DC Comics: Sept, 2004 - Oct, 2004 ($2.50)

The Atom -(Based on cover of Atom #10) Gibbons-s/Oliffe-a; Waid-s/Jurgens-a; Bolland-c						2.50

DC Comics Presents: Green Lantern © DC

DC One Million #4 © DC

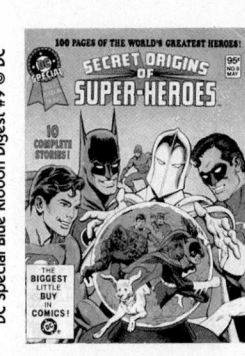

DC Special Blue Ribbon Digest #9 © DC

	GD 2.0	VG 4.0	FN 6.0	VF 8.0	VF/NM 9.0	NM- 9.2

Batman -(Batman #183) Johns-s/Infantino-a; Wein-s/Kuhn-a; Hughes-c ... 2.50
The Flash -(Flash #163) Loeb-s/McGuinness-a; O'Neil-s/Mahnke-a; Ross-c ... 2.50
Green Lantern -(Green Lantern #31) Azzarello-s/Breyfogle-a; Pasko-s/McDaniel-a; Bolland-c ... 2.50
Hawkman -(Hawkman #6) Bates-s/Byrne-a; Busiek-s/Simonson-a; Garcia-Lopez-c ... 2.50
Justice League of America -(J.L. of A. #53) Ellison & David-s/Giella-a; Wolfman-s/Nguyen-a; Garcia-Lopez-c ... 2.50
Mystery in Space -(M.I.S. #82) Maggin-s/Williams-a; Morrison-s/Ordway-a; Ross-c ... 2.50
Superman -(Superman #264) Stan Lee-s/Cooke-a; Levitz-s/Giffen-a; Hughes-c ... 2.50

DC COUNTDOWN (To Infinite Crisis)
DC Comics: May, 2005 ($1.00, 80 pages, one-shot)
1-Death of Blue Beetle; prelude to OMAC Project, Day of Vengeance, Rann/Thanagar War and Villains United mini-series; s/a by various; Jim Lee/Alex Ross-c ... 3.00

DC FIRST: ...(series of one-shots)
DC Comics: July, 2002 ($3.50)
Batgirl/Joker 1-Sienkiewicz & Terry Moore-a; Nowlan-c ... 3.50
Green Lantern/Green Lantern 1-Alan Scott & Hal Jordan vs. Krona ... 3.50
Flash/Superman 1-Superman races Jay Garrick; Abra Kadabra app. ... 3.50
Superman/Lobo 1-Giffen-s; Nowlan-c ... 3.50

DC GRAPHIC NOVEL (Also see DC Science Fiction...)
DC Comics: Nov, 1983 - No. 7, 1986 ($5.95, 68 pgs.)
1-3,5,7: 1-Star Raiders. 2-Warlords; not from regular Warlord series. 3-The Medusa Chain; Ernie Colon story/a. 5-Me and Joe Priest; Chaykin-c. 7-Space Clusters; Nino-c/a
   2   4   6   9   12   15
4-The Hunger Dogs by Kirby; Darkseid kills Himon from Mister Miracle & destroys New Genesis
   5   10   15   30   48   65
6-Metalzoic; Sienkiewicz-c ($6.95)
   2   4   6   9   12   15

DC/MARVEL: ALL ACCESS (Also see DC Versus Marvel & Marvel Versus DC)
DC Comics: 1996 - No. 4, 1997 (limited series)
1-4: 1-Superman & Spider-Man app. 2-Robin & Jubilee app. 3-Dr. Strange & Batman-c/app., X-Men, JLA app. 4-X-Men vs. JLA-c/app. rebirth of Amalgam ... 3.00

DC/MARVEL: CROSSOVER CLASSICS
DC Comics: 1998; 2003 ($14.95, TPB)
Vol. II-Reprints Batman/Punisher: Lake of Fire, Punisher/Batman: Deadly Knights, Silver Surfer/Superman, Batman & Capt. America ... 15.00
Vol. 4 (2003, $14.95) Reprints Green Lantern/Silver Surfer: Unholy Alliances, Darkseid/Galactus: The Hunger, Batman & Spider-Man, and Superman/Fantastic Four ... 15.00

DC 100 PAGE SUPER SPECTACULAR
(Title is 100 Page... No. 14 on)(Square bound) (Reprints, 50¢)
National Periodical Publications: No. 4, Summer, 1971 - No. 13, 6/72; No. 14, 2/73 - No. 22, 11/73 (No #1-3)
4-Weird Mystery Tales; Johnny Peril & Phantom Stranger; cover & splashes by Wrightson; origin Jungle Boy of Jupiter
   17   34   51   128   227   325
5-Love Stories; Wood inks (7 pgs.)(scarcer)
   44   88   132   352   639   925
6-"World's Greatest Super-Heroes"; JLA, JSA, Spectre, Johnny Quick, Vigilante & Hawkman; contains unpublished Wildcat story; N. Adams wrap-around-c; r/JLA #21,22
   17   34   51   128   227   325
6-Replica Edition (2004, $6.95) complete reprint w/wraparound-c ... 7.00
7-(Also listed as Superman #245) Air Wave, Kid Eternity, Hawkman-r; Atom-r/Atom #3
   9   18   27   60   100   140
8-(Also listed as Batman #238) Batman, Legion, Aquaman-r; G.A. Atom, Sargon (r/Sensation #57), Plastic Man (r/Police #14) stories; Doom Patrol origin-r; Neal Adams wraparound-c
   10   20   30   71   126   180
9-(Also listed as Our Army at War #242) Kubert-a   9   18   27   60   100   140
10-(Also listed as Adventure Comics #416) Golden Age-reprints; r/1st app. Black Canary from Flash #86; no Zatanna
   10   20   30   70   123   175
11-(Also listed as Flash #214) origin Metal Men-r/Showcase #37; never before published G.A. Flash story.
   8   16   24   52   86   120
12,14: 12-Legion-c/story; Teen Titans, Kid Eternity (r/Hit #46), Star Spangled Kid-r(S.S. #55). 14-Batman-r/Detective #31,32,156; Atom-r/Showcase #34
   7   14   21   45   73   100
13-(Also listed as Superman #252) Ray(r/Smash #17), Black Condor, (r/Crack #18), Hawkman(r/Flash #24); Starman-r/Adv. #67; Dr. Fate & Spectre-r/More Fun #57; Neal Adams-c
   5   10   15   35   55   75
15,16,18,19,21,22: 15-r/2nd Boy Commandos/Det. #64. 21-Superboy-r/Brave & Bold #54. 22-r/All-Flash #13.
17,20: 17-JSA-r/All Star #37 (10-11/47, 38 pgs.), Sandman-r/Adv. #65 (8/41), JLA #23 (11/63) & JLA #43 (3/66). 20-Batman-r/Det. #66,68, Spectre; origin Two-Face
   5   10   15   35   55   75
... : Love Stories Replica Edition (2000, $6.95) reprints #5 ... 7.00
NOTE: Anderson r-11, 14, 18i, 22. B. Bailey r-18. Burnley r-18. Crandall r-14p, 20. Drucker r-4. Grandenetti a-22(2)r. Heath a-22r. Infantino r-17, 20, 22. G. Kane r-18. Kirby r-15. Kubert r-6, 7, 16, 17; c-16, 19. Manning a-19r. Meskin r-4, 22. Mooney r-15, 21. Toth r-17, 20.

DC ONE MILLION (Also see crossover #1,000,000 issues and JLA One Million TPB)
DC Comics: Nov, 1998 - No. 4, Nov, 1998 ($2.95/$1.99, weekly lim. series)
1-($2.95) JLA travels to the 853rd century; Morrison-s ... 3.00
2-4-($1.99) ... 2.50
...Eighty-Page Giant (8/99, $4.95) ... 5.00
TPB ('99, $14.95) r/#1-4 and several x-over stories ... 15.00

DC SCIENCE FICTION GRAPHIC NOVEL
DC Comics: 1985 - No. 7, 1987 ($5.95)
SF1-SF7: SF1-Hell on Earth by Robert Bloch; Giffen-p. SF2-Nightwings by Robert Silverberg; G. Colan-p. SF3-Frost & Fire by Bradbury. SF4-Merchants of Venus. SF5-Demon With A Glass Hand by Ellison; M. Rogers-a. SF6-The Magic Goes Away by Niven. SF7-Sandkings by George R.R. Martin
   2   4   6   8   11   14

DC SILVER AGE CLASSICS
DC Comics: 1992 ($1.00, all reprints)
...Action Comics #252-r/1st Supergirl. Adventure Comics #247-r/1st Legion of Super-Heroes. The Brave and the Bold #28-r/1st JLA. Detective Comics #225-r/1st Martian Manhunter. Detective Comics #327-r/1st new look Batman. Green Lantern #76-r/1st Green Lantern/Green Arrow. House of Secrets #92-r/1st Swamp Thing. Showcase #4-r/1st S.A. Flash. Showcase #22-r/1st S.A. Green Lantern ... 2.50
...Sugar and Spike #99; includes 2 unpublished stories ... 4.00

DC SPECIAL (Also see Super DC Giant)
National Per. Publ.: 10-12/68 - No. 15, 11-12/71; No. 16, Spr/75 - No. 29, 8-9/77
1-All Infantino issue; Flash, Batman, Adam Strange-r; begin 68 pg. issues, end #21
   8   16   24   52   86   120
2-Teen humor; Binky, Buzzy, Harvey app.
   9   18   27   65   113   160
3-All-Girl issue; unpubl. GA Wonder Woman story
   8   16   24   58   97   135
4,11: 4-Horror (1st Abel, brief). 11-Monsters
   8   16   24   48   65
5-10,12-15: 5-All Kubert issue; Viking Prince, Sgt. Rock-r. 6-Western. 7,9,13-Strangest Sports. 12-Viking Prince; Kubert-c/a (r/B&B almost entirely). 15-G.A. Plastic Man origin-r/Police #14; origin Woozy by Cole; 14,15-(52 pgs.)
   4   8   12   24   37   50
16-27: 16-Super Heroes Battle Super Gorillas; r/Capt. Storm #1, 1st Johnny Cloud/All-Amer. Men of War #82. 17-Early S.A. Green Lantern-r. 22-Origin Robin Hood. 26-Enemy Ace. 27-Captain Comet story
   3   6   9   14   20   25
28-Earth Shattering Disaster Stories; Legion of Super-Heroes story
   3   6   9   14   20   25
29-New "The Untold Origin of the Justice Society"; Staton-a/Neal Adams-c; Hitler app. in story and on cover
   3   6   9   20   30   40
NOTE: N. Adams c-3, 4, 6, 11, 29. Grell a-20; c-17, 20. Heath a-12r. G. Kane a-6p, 13r, 17r, 19-21r. Kirby a-4,11. Kubert a-6r, 12r, 22r. Meskin a-10. Moreira a-10. Staton a-29p. Toth a-13, 20r. #1-15: 25c; 16-27: 50c; 28, 29: 60c. #1-13, 16-21: 68 pgs.; 14, 15: 52 pgs.; 25-27: oversized.

DC SPECIAL BLUE RIBBON DIGEST
DC Comics: Mar-Apr, 1980 - No. 24, Aug, 1982
1,2,4,5: 1-Legion reprints. 2-Flash. 4-Green Lantern. 5-Secret Origins; new Zatara and Zatanna
   2   4   6   8   10   12
3-Justice Society
   2   4   6   8   10   12
6,8-10: 6-Ghosts. 8-Legion. 9-Secret Origins. 10-Warlord-"The Deimos Saga"-Grell-s/c/a
   2   4   6   8   10   12
7-Sgt. Rock's Prize Battle Tales
   2   4   6   11   16   20
11,16: 11-Justice League. 16-Green Lantern/Green Arrow-r; all Adams-a
   4   6   10   14   16
12-Haunted Tank; reprints 1st app.
   2   4   6   11   16   20
13-15,17-19: 13-Strange Sports Stories. 14-UFO Invaders; Adam Strange app. 15-Secret Origins of Super Villains; JLA app. 17-Ghosts. 18-Sgt. Rock; Kubert front & back-c. 19-Doom Patrol; new Perez-c
   2   4   6   11   16   20
20-Dark Mansion of Forbidden Love (scarce)
   4   8   12   28   44   60
21-Our Army at War
   2   4   6   9   14   20
22-24: 22-Secret Origins. 23-Green Arrow, w/new 7 pg. story. 24-House of Mystery; new Kubert wraparound-c
   2   4   6   11   16   20
NOTE: N. Adams a-16(i)r, 17r, 23r; c-16. Aparo a-6r, 24r; c-23. Grell a-8, 10; c-10. Heath a-14. Infantino a-15r. Kaluta a-17r. Gil Kane a-15r, 22r. Kirby a-5, 9, 23r. Kubert a-3, 18r, 21r; c-7, 12, 14, 17, 18, 21, 24. Morrow a-24r. Orlando a-17, 21; c-1, 20. Toth a-21r, 24r. Wood a-3, 17r, 24r. Wrightson a-16r, 17r, 20r.

DC SPECIAL SERIES
National Periodical Publications/DC Comics: 9/77 - No. 16, Fall, 1978; No. 17, 8/79 - No. 27, Fall, 1981 (No. 18, 19, 23, 24 - digest size, 100 pgs.; No. 25-27 - Treasury sized)
1-"5-Star Super-Hero Spectacular 1977"; Batman, Atom, Flash, Green Lantern, Aquaman, (in)to stories, Neal Adams-c
   3   6   9   17   28   40
2(#1)-"The Original Swamp Thing Saga 1977"-r/Swamp Thing #1&2 by Wrightson; new Wrightson wraparound-c.
   2   4   6   8   11   14
3,4,6-8: 3-Sgt. Rock. 4-Unexpected. 6-Secret Society of Super Villains, Jones-a. 7-Ghosts

DC Super-Stars #7 © DC

DC Holiday Bash III © DC

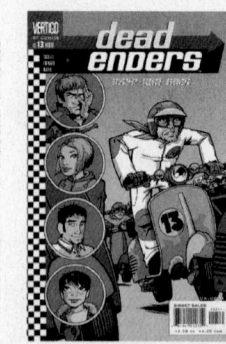

Dead Enders #13 © Brubaker & Pleece

	GD	VG	FN	VF	VF/NM	NM-		GD	VG	FN	VF	VF/NM	NM-
	2.0	4.0	6.0	8.0	9.0	9.2		2.0	4.0	6.0	8.0	9.0	9.2

Special. 8-Brave and Bold w/ new Batman, Deadman & Sgt Rock team-up
| | | 2 | 4 | 6 | 9 | 13 | 16 |
5-"Superman Spectacular 1977"-(84 pg, $1.00)-Superman vs. Brainiac & Lex Luthor,
new 63 pg. story | 2 | 4 | 6 | 13 | 18 | 22
9-Wonder Woman; Ditko-a (11 pgs.) | 2 | 4 | 6 | 13 | 18 | 22
10-"Secret Origins of Superheroes Special 1978"-(52 pgs.)-Dr. Fate, Lightray & Black Canary
on-c/new origin stories; Staton, Newton-a | 2 | 4 | 6 | 11 | 16 | 20
11-"Flash Spectacular 1978"-(84 pgs.) Flash, Kid Flash, GA Flash & Johnny Quick vs. Grodd;
Wood-i on Kid Flash chapter | 2 | 4 | 6 | 9 | 13 | 16
12-"Secrets of Haunted House Special Spring 1978" 2 | 4 | 6 | 9 | 13 | 16
13-"Sgt. Rock Special Spring 1978", 50 pg new story 2 | 4 | 6 | 10 | 14 | 18
14,17,20-"Original Swamp Thing Saga", Wrightson-a: 14-Sum '78, r/#3,4. 17-Sum '79 r/#5-7.
20-Jan/Feb '80, r/#8-10 | 1 | 3 | 4 | 6 | 9 | 12
15-"Batman Spectacular Summer 1978", Ra's Al Ghul-app.; Golden-a. Rogers-a/front & back-c
| | | 3 | 6 | 9 | 16 | 23 | 30
16-"Jonah Hex Spectacular Fall 1978"; death of Jonah Hex, Heath-a; Bat Lash and
Scalphunter stories | 6 | 12 | 18 | 37 | 59 | 80
18,19-Digest size: 18-"Sgt. Rock's Prize Battle Tales Fall 1979". 19-"Secret Origins of
Super-Heroes Fall 1979"; origins Wonder Woman (new-a), r/Robin, Batman-Superman
team, Aquaman, Hawkman and others | 2 | 4 | 6 | 9 | 13 | 16
21-"Super-Star Holiday Special Spring 1980", Frank Miller-a in "Batman--Wanted Dead or Alive"
(1st Batman story); Jonah Hex, Sgt. Rock, Superboy & LSH and House of Mystery/
Witching Hour-c/stories | 3 | 6 | 9 | 20 | 30 | 40
22-"G.I. Combat Sept. 1980", Kubert-c. Haunted Tank-s 2 | 4 | 6 | 10 | 14 | 18
23,24-Digest size: 23-World's Finest-r. 24-Flash | 2 | 4 | 6 | 9 | 13 | 16
V5#25-($2.95).-"Superman II, the Adventure Continues Summer 1981"; photos from movie &
photo-c (see All-New Coll. Ed. C-62) | 2 | 4 | 6 | 13 | 18 | 22
26-($2.50)-"Superman and His Incredible Fortress of Solitude Summer 1981"
| | | 2 | 4 | 6 | 13 | 18 | 22
27-($2.50)-"Batman vs. The Incredible Hulk Fall 1981" 4 | 8 | 12 | 22 | 34 | 45
NOTE: *Aparo* c-8. *Heath* a-12i, 16. *Infantino* a-19r. *Kirby* a-23, 19r. *Kubert* c-13, 19r. *Nasser/Netzer* a-1, 10i, 15. *Newton* a-10. *Nino* a-4, 7. *Starlin* c-12. *Staton* a-1. *Tuska* a-19r. #25 & 26. were advertised as All-New Collectors'
Edition C-63, C-64. #26 was originally planned as All-New Collectors' Ed. C-30?; has C-630 & A.N.C.E. on cover.

DC SPECIAL: THE RETURN OF DONNA TROY
DC Comics: Aug, 2005 - No. 4, Late Oct, 2005 ($2.99, limited series)
1-4-Jimenez-s/Garcia-Lopez-a(p)/Pérez-i | | | | | | 3.00

DC SUPER-STARS
National Periodical Publications/DC Comics: March, 1976 - No. 18, Winter, 1978 (No.3-18:
52 pgs.)
1-(68 pgs.)-Re-intro Teen Titans (predates T. T. #44 (11/76); tryout iss.) plus r/Teen Titans;
W.W. as girl was original Wonder Girl | 3 | 6 | 9 | 16 | 23 | 30
2-7,9,11,12,16: 2,4,6,8-Adam Strange; 2-(68 pgs.)-r/1st Adam Strange/Hawkman team-up
from Mystery in Space #90 plus Atomic Knights origin-r. 3-Legion issue.
4-r/Tales/Unexpected #45 | 1 | 3 | 4 | 6 | 8 | 10
8-r/1st Space Ranger from Showcase #15, Adam Strange-r/Mystery in Space #89 &
Star Rovers-r/M.I.S. #80 | 2 | 4 | 6 | 8 | 10 | 12
10-Strange Sports Stories; Batman/Joker-c/story 2 | 4 | 6 | 8 | 11 | 14
13-Sergio Aragonés Special | 2 | 4 | 6 | 13 | 18 | 22
14,15,18: 15-Sgt. Rock | 2 | 4 | 6 | 8 | 10 | 12
17-Secret Origins of Super-Heroes (origin of The Huntress); origin Green Arrow by Grell;
Legion app.; Earth II Batman & Catwoman marry (1st revealed; also see B&B #197 &
Superman Family #211) | 4 | 8 | 12 | 28 | 44 | 60
NOTE: *M. Anderson* r-2, 4, 6. *Aparo* c-7, 14, 18. *Austin* a-11i. *Buckler* a-14p; c-10. *Grell* a-17. *G. Kane* a-17r, 10r.
Kubert c-15. *Layton* c/a-16i, 17i. *Mooney* a-4r, 6r. *Morrow* c/a-11r. *Nasser* a-1, 10. *Newton* c/a-16p. *Staton* a-17; c-
17. No. 10, 12-18 contain all new material; the rest are reprints. #1 contains new and reprint material.

DC: THE NEW FRONTIER
DC Comics: Mar, 2004 - No. 6, Nov, 2004 ($6.95, limited series)
1-6-DCU in the 1940s-60s; Darwyn Cooke-c/s/a in all. 1-Hal Jordan and The Losers app.
2-Origin Martian Manhunter; Barry Allen app. 3-Challengers of the Unknown
| | | | | | | 7.00
...Volume One (2004, $19.95, TPB) r/#1-3; cover gallery & intro. by Paul Levitz | 20.00
...Volume Two (2005, $19.99, TPB) r/#4-6; cover gallery & afterword by Cooke | 20.00

DC 2000
DC Comics: 2000 - No. 2, 2000 ($6.95, limited series)
1,2-JLA visit 1940s JSA; Semeiks-a | | | | | | 7.00

DCU BRAVE NEW WORLD (See Infinite Crisis and tie-ins)
DC Comics: Aug, 2006 ($1.00, 80 pgs., one-shot)
1-Previews 2006 series Martian Manhunter, OMAC, The Creeper, The All-New Atom, The
Trials of Shazam, and Uncle Sam and the Freedom Fighters; the Monitor app. | 3.00

DCU HEROES SECRET FILES
DC Comics: Feb, 1999 ($4.95, one-shot)
1-Origin-s and pin-ups; new Star Spangled Kid app. | | | | | 5.00

DCU INFINITE HOLIDAY SPECIAL
DC Comics: Feb, 2007 ($4.99, one-shot)
1-Christmas anthology by various; Batwoman app.; Porter-c | | | 5.00

DC UNIVERSE CHRISTMAS, A
DC Comics: 2000 ($19.95)
TPB-Reprints DC Christmas stories by various | | | | 20.00

DC UNIVERSE HOLIDAY BASH
DC Comics: 1997- 1999 ($3.95)
I,II-(X-mas '96,'97) Christmas stories by various | | | 5.00
III (1999, for Christmas '98, $4.95) | | | | 5.00

DC UNIVERSE: THE STORIES OF ALAN MOORE (Also see Across the Universe:...)
DC Comics: 2006 ($19.99)
TPB-Reprints Batman: The Killing Joke, "Whatever Happened to the Man of Tomorrow", "For
The Man Who Has Everything, and other classic Moore DC stories; Bolland-c | 20.00

DC UNIVERSE: TRINITY
DC Comics: Aug, 1993 - No. 2, Sept, 1993 ($2.95, 52 pgs, limited series)
1,2-Foil-c; Green Lantern, Darkstars, Legion app. | | | | 3.50

DCU VILLAINS SECRET FILES
DC Comics: Apr, 1999 ($4.95, one-shot)
1-Origin-s and profile pages | | | | | 5.00

DC VERSUS MARVEL (See Marvel Versus DC) (Also see Amazon, Assassins, Bruce Wayne:
Agent of S.H.I.E. L.D., Bullets & Bracelets, Doctor Strangefate, JLX, Legend of the Dark Claw,
Magneto & The Magnetic Men, Speed Demon, Spider-Boy, Super Soldier, X-Patrol)
DC Comics: No. 1, 1996, No. 4, 1996 ($3.95, limited series)
1,4: 1-Marz script, Jurgens-a(p); 1st app. of Access. | | | 4.00
.../Marvel Versus DC ($12.95, trade paperback) r/1-4 | | 13.00

D-DAY (Also see Special War Series)
Charlton Comics (no No. 3): Sum/63; No. 2, Fall/64; No. 4, 9/66; No. 5, 10/67; No. 6, 11/68
1,2: 1(1963)-Montes/Bache-a. 2(Fall '64)-Wood-a(4) 4 | 8 | 12 | 22 | 34 | 45
4-6('66-'68)-Montes/Bache-a #5 | 3 | 6 | 9 | 14 | 20 | 25

DEAD AIR
Slave Labor Graphics: July, 1989 ($5.95, graphic novel)
nn-Mike Allred's 1st published work | | | | | 6.00

DEAD CORPSe
DC Comics (Helix): Sept, 1998 - No. 4, Dec, 1998 ($2.50, limited series)
1-4-Pugh-a/Hinz-s | | | | | 2.50

DEAD END CRIME STORIES
Kirby Publishing Co.: April, 1949 (52 pgs.)
nn-(Scarce)-Powell, Roussos-a; painted-c | 50 | 100 | 150 | 305 | 503 | 700

DEAD ENDERS
DC Comics (Vertigo): Mar, 2000 - No. 16, June, 2001 ($2.50)
1-16-Brubaker-s/Pleece's | | | | | 2.50
Stealing the Sun (2000, $9.95, TPB) r/#1-4, Vertigo Winter's Edge #3 | 10.00

DEAD-EYE WESTERN COMICS
Hillman Periodicals: Nov-Dec, 1948 - V3#1, Apr-May, 1953
V1#1-(52 pgs.)-Krigstein, Roussos-a | 19 | 38 | 57 | 112 | 176 | 240
V1#2,3-(52 pgs.) | 12 | 24 | 36 | 67 | 94 | 120
V1#4-12-(52 pgs.) | 9 | 18 | 27 | 47 | 61 | 75
V2#1,2,5-8,10-12: 1-7-(52 pgs.) | 8 | 16 | 24 | 40 | 50 | 60
3,4-Krigstein-a | 8 | 16 | 24 | 44 | 57 | 70
9-One pg. Frazetta ad | 8 | 16 | 24 | 40 | 50 | 60
V3#1 | 8 | 16 | 24 | 40 | 50 | 60
NOTE: *Briefer* a-V1#6. Kinstleresque stories by *McCann*-12, V2#1, 2, V3#1. *McWilliams* a-V1#5. *Ed Moore* a-
V1#4.

DEADFACE: DOING THE ISLANDS WITH BACCHUS
Dark Horse Comics: July, 1991 - No. 3, Sept, 1991 ($2.95, B&W, lim. series)
1-3: By Eddie Campbell | | | | | 3.00

DEADFACE: EARTH, WATER, AIR, AND FIRE
Dark Horse Comics: July, 1992 - No. 4, Oct, 1992 ($2.50, B&W, limited series; British-r)
1-4: By Eddie Campbell | | | | | 3.00

DEAD IN THE WEST
Dark Horse Comics: Oct, 1993 - No. 2, Mar, 1994 ($3.95, B&W, 52 pgs.)
1,2-Timothy Truman-c | | | | | 4.00

DEAD KING (See Evil Ernie)

Deadly Hands of Kung Fu #3 © MAR

Dead Of Night #8 © MAR

Deadman #8 © DC

	GD	VG	FN	VF	VF/NM	NM-		GD	VG	FN	VF	VF/NM	NM-
	2.0	4.0	6.0	8.0	9.0	9.2		2.0	4.0	6.0	8.0	9.0	9.2

Chaos! Comics: May, 1998 - No. 4, Aug, 1998, ($2.95, limited series)

1-4-Fisher-s ... 3.00

DEADLIEST HEROES OF KUNG FU (Magazine)
Marvel Comics Group: Summer, 1975 (B&W)(76 pgs.)

1-Bruce Lee vs. Carradine painted-c; TV Kung Fu, 4pgs. photos/article; Enter the Dragon, 24 pgs. photos/article w/ Bruce Lee; Bruce Lee photo pinup ... 4 8 12 22 34 45

DEADLINE
Marvel Comics: June, 2002 - No. 4, Sept, 2002 ($2.99, limited series)

1-4: 1-Intro. Kat Farrell; Bill Rosemann-s/Guy Davis-a; Horn painted-c ... 3.00
TPB (2002, $9.99) r/#1-4 ... 10.00

DEADLY DUO, THE
Image Comics (Highbrow Entertainment): Nov, 1994 - No. 3, Jan, 1995 ($2.50, lim. series)

1-3: 1-1st app. of Kill Cat ... 2.50

DEADLY DUO, THE
Image Comics (Highbrow Entertainment): June, 1995 - No. 4, Oct, 1995 ($2.50, lim. series)

1-4: 1-Spawn app. 2-Savage Dragon app. 3-Gen 13 app. ... 2.50

DEADLY FOES OF SPIDER-MAN (See Lethal Foes of...)
Marvel Comics: May, 1991 - No. 4, Aug, 1991 ($1.00, limited series)

1-4: 1-Punisher, Kingpin, Rhino app. ... 2.50

DEADLY HANDS OF KUNG FU, THE (See Master of Kung Fu)
Marvel Comics Group: April, 1974 - No. 33, Feb, 1977 (75¢) (B&W, magazine)

1(V1#4 listed in error)-Origin Sons of the Tiger; Shang-Chi, Master of Kung Fu begins (ties w/Master of Kung Fu #17 as 3rd app. Shang-Chi); Bruce Lee painted-c by Neal Adams; 2pg. memorial photo pinup w/8 pgs. photos/articles; TV Kung Fu, 9 pgs. photos/articles; 15 pgs. Starlin-a ... 5 10 15 32 51 70
2-Adams painted-c; 1st time origin of Shang-Chi, 34 pgs. by Starlin. TV Kung Fu, 15 pgs. photos & article w/2 pg. pinup. Bruce Lee, 11 pgs. ph/a ... 4 8 12 24 37 50
3,4,7,10: 3-Adams painted-c; Gulacy-a. Enter the Dragon, photos/articles, 8 pgs. 4-TV Kung Fu painted-c by Neal Adams; TV Kung Fu 7 pg. article/art; Fu Manchu; Enter the Dragon, 10 pg. photos/article w/Bruce Lee. 7-Bruce Lee painted-c & 9 pgs. photos/articles-Return of Dragon plus 1 pg. photo pinup. 10-(3/75)-Iron Fist painted-c & 34 pg. sty-Early app. ... 3 6 9 18 27 35
5,6: 5-1st app. Manchurian, 6 pgs. Gulacy-a. TV Kung Fu, 4 pg. article; reprints books w/Barry Smith-a. Capt. America-sty, 10 pgs. Kirby-a(r). 6-Bruce Lee photos/article, 6 pgs.; 15 pgs. early Perez-a ... 3 6 9 17 25 32
8,9,11: 9-Iron Fist, 2 pg. Preview pinup; Nebres-a. 11-Billy Jack painted-c by Adams; 17 pgs. photos/article ... 3 6 9 16 23 30
12,13: 12-James Bond painted-c by Adams; 14 pg. photos/article. 13-16 pgs. early Perez-a; Piers Anthony, 7 pgs. photos/article ... 3 6 9 16 22 28
14-Classic Bruce Lee painted-c by Adams. Lee pinup by Chaykin. Lee 16 pg. photos/article w/2 pgs. Green Hornet TV ... 6 12 18 39 62 85
15,19: 15-Sum, '75 Giant Annual #1. 20pgs. Starlin-a. Bruce Lee photo pinup & 3 pg. photos/article re book; Man-Thing app. Iron Fist-c/sty; Gulacy-a 18pgs. 19-Iron Fist painted-c & series begins; 1st White Tiger ... 3 6 9 18 23 30
16,18,20: 16-1st app. Corpse Rider, a samurai w/Sanho Kim-a. 20-Chuck Norris painted-c & 16 pgs. interview w/photos/article; Bruce Lee vs. C. Norris pinup by Ken Barr. Origin The White Tiger, Perez-a ... 3 6 9 15 21 26
17-Bruce Lee painted-c by Adams; interview w/R. Clouse, director Enter Dragon 7 pgs. w/B. Lee app. 1st Giffen-a (1pg. 11/75) ... 4 8 12 24 37 50
21-Bruce Lee 1pg. photos/article ... 3 6 9 11 16 21 26
22,30-32: 22-1st brief app. Jack of Hearts. 1st Giffen sty-a (along w/Amazing Adv. #35, 3/76). 30-Swordquest-c/sty & conclusion; Jack of Hearts app. 31-Jack of Hearts app; Staton-a. 32-1st Daughters of the Dragon-c/sty, 21 pgs. M. Rogers-a/Claremont-sty; Iron Fist pinup ... 3 6 9 12 17 19 24
23-26,29: 23-1st full app. Jack of Hearts. 24-Iron Fist-c & centerfold pinup. early Zeck-a; Shang Chi pinup; 6 pgs. Piers Anthony text sty w/Perez/Austin-a; Jack of Hearts app. early Giffen-a. 25-1st app. Shimuru, "Samurai", 20 pgs. Mantlo-s/Broderick-a; "Swordquest"-c & begins 17 pg. sty by Sanho Kim; 11 pgs. photos/article; partly Bruce Lee. 26-Bruce Lee painted-c & pinup; 16 pgs. interviews w/Kwon & Clouse; talk about Bruce Lee.re-filming of Lee legend. 29-Ironfist vs. Shang Chi battle-c/sty; Jack of Hearts app. ... 3 6 9 16 23 30
27 ... 2 4 6 13 18 22
28-All Bruce Lee Special Issue; (1st time in comics). Bruce Lee painted-c by Ken Barr & pinup. 36 pgs. comics chronicling Bruce Lee's life; 15 pgs. B. Lee photos/article (Rare in high grade) ... 7 14 21 47 76 105
33-Shang Chi-c/sty; Classic Daughters of the Dragon, 21 pgs. M. Rogers-a/Claremont-story with nudity; Bob Wall interview, photos/article, 14 pgs. ... 3 6 9 18 27 35

...Special Album Edition 1(Summer, '74)-Iron Fist-c/story (early app., 3rd?); 10 pgs. Adams-i; Shang Chi/Fu Manchu, 10 pgs.; Sons of Tiger, 11 pgs.; TV Kung Fu, 6 pgs. photos/article ... 3 6 9 20 30 40
NOTE: *Bruce Lee:* 1-7, 14, 15, 17, 25, 26, 28. *Kung Fu (TV):* 1, 2, 4. *Jack of Hearts:* 22, 23, 29-33. *Shang Chi Master of Kung Fu:* 1-9, 11-18, 29, 31, 33. *Sons of Tiger:* 1, 3, 4, 6-14, 16-19. *Swordquest:* 25-27, 29-33. *White Tiger:* 19-24, 26, 27, 29-33. *N. Adams* a-1i(part), 27i; c-1, 2-4i, 11, 12, 14, 17. *Giffen* a-22p, 24p. *G. Kane* a-23p. *Kirby* a-5r. *Nasser* a-27p, 28. *Perez* a(p)-6-14, 16, 17, 19, 21. *Rogers* a-26, 32, 33. *Starlin* a-1, 2r, 15r. *Staton* a-28p, 31, 32.

DEADMAN (See The Brave and the Bold & Phantom Stranger #39)
DC Comics: May, 1985 - No. 7, Nov, 1985 ($1.75, Baxter paper)

1-7: 1-Deadman-r by Infantino, N. Adams in all. 5-Batman-c/story-r/Strange Adventures. 7-Batman-r ... 3.00

DEADMAN
DC Comics: Mar, 1986 - No. 4, June, 1986 (75¢, limited series)

1-4: Lopez-c/a. 4-Byrne-c(p) ... 3.00

DEADMAN
DC Comics: Feb, 2002 - No. 9, Oct, 2002 ($2.50)

1-9: 1-4-Vance-s/Beroy-a. 3,4-Mignola-c. 5,6-Garcia-Lopez-a ... 2.50

DEADMAN
DC Comics (Vertigo): Oct, 2006 - Present ($2.99)

1-12: 1-Bruce Jones-s/John Watkiss-a/c; intro Brandon Cayce ... 3.00
....: Deadman Walking TPB (2007, $9.99) r/#1-5 ... 10.00

DEADMAN: DEAD AGAIN (Leads into 2002 series)
DC Comics: Oct, 2001 - No. 5, Oct, 2001 ($2.50, weekly limited series)

1-5: Deadman at the deaths of the Flash, Robin, Superman, Hal Jordan ... 2.50

DEADMAN: EXORCISM
DC Comics: 1992 - No. 2, 1992 ($4.95, limited series, 52 pgs.)

1,2: Kelley Jones-c/a in both ... 5.00

DEADMAN: LOVE AFTER DEATH
DC Comics: 1989 - No. 2, 1990 ($3.95, 52 pgs., limited series, mature)

Book One, Two: Kelley Jones-c/a in both. 1-contains nudity ... 4.00

DEAD OF NIGHT
Marvel Comics Group: Dec, 1973 - No. 11, Aug, 1975

1-Horror reprints ... 3 6 9 16 23 30
2-10: 10-Kirby-a. 6-Jack the Ripper-c/s ... 2 4 6 10 14 18
11-Intro Scarecrow; Kane/Wrightson-a ... 3 6 9 20 30 40
NOTE: *Ditko* r-7, 10. *Everett* c-2. *Sinnott* r-1.

DEAD OR ALIVE - A CYBERPUNK WESTERN
Image Comics (Shok Studio): Apr, 1998 - No. 4, July, 1998 ($2.50, lim. series)

1-4 ... 3.00

DEADPOOL (See New Mutants #98)
Marvel Comics: Aug, 1994 - No. 4, Nov, 1994 ($2.50, limited series)

1-4: Mark Waid's 1st Marvel work; Ian Churchill-c/a ... 4.00

DEADPOOL (... : Agent of Weapon X on cover #57-60) (title becomes Agent X)
Marvel Comics: Jan, 1997 - No. 69, Sept, 2002 ($2.95/$1.95/$1.99)

1-($2.95)-Wraparound-c ... 1 2 3 4 5 7
2-Begin-$1.95-c ... 5.00
3-10,12-22,24: 4-Hulk-c/app. 12-Variant-c. 14-Begin McDaniel-a. 22-Cable app. ... 5.00
11-($3.99)-Deadpool replaces Spider-Man from Amazing Spider-Man #47; Kraven, Gwen Stacy app. ... 6.00
23,25-($2.99): 23-Dead Reckoning pt. 1; wraparound-c ... 4.00
26-40: 27-Wolverine-c/app. 37-Thor app. ... 3.00
41-53,56-60: 41-Begin $2.25-c. 44-Black Panther-c/app. 46-49-Chadwick-a 51-Cover swipe of Detective #38. 57-60-BWS-c ... 3.00
54,55-Punisher-c/app. 54-Dillon-c. 55-Bradstreet-c ... 3.00
61-69: 61-64-Funeral For a Freak on cover. 65-69-Udon Studios-a. 67-Dazzler-c/app. ... 2.50
#(-1) Flashback (7/97) Lopresti-a; Wade Wilson's early days ... 3.00
...Death '98 Annual ($2.99) Kelly-s, ... Team-Up (12/98, $2.99) Widdle Wade-c/app., Baby's First Deadpool Book (12/98, $2.99), Encyclopædia Deadpoolica (12/98, $2.99) Synopses ... 3.00
.../GLI - Summer Fun Spectacular #1 (9/07, $3.99) short stories; Pelletier-c ... 4.00
Mission Improbable TPB (9/98, $14.95) r/#1-5 ... 15.00
Wizard #0 ('98, bagged with Wizard #87) ... 2.50

DEADPOOL: THE CIRCLE CHASE (See New Mutants #98)
Marvel Comics: Aug, 1993 - No. 4, Nov, 1993 ($2.00, limited series)

1-($2.50)-Embossed-c ... 4.00
2-4 ... 3.00

Dear Beatrice Fairfax #6 © STD

Death Dealer #1 © Frank Frazetta

Deathlok #7 © MAR

	GD 2.0	VG 4.0	FN 6.0	VF 8.0	VF/NM 9.0	NM- 9.2

DEADSHOT (See Batman #59, Detective Comics #474, & Showcase '93 #8)
DC Comics: Nov, 1988 - No. 4, Feb, 1989 ($1.00, limited series)

	GD 2.0	VG 4.0	FN 6.0	VF 8.0	VF/NM 9.0	NM- 9.2
1-4						2.50

DEADSHOT
DC Comics: Feb, 2005 - No. 5, June 2005 ($2.95, limited series)

1-5-Zeck-c/Gage-s/Cummings-a. 3-Green Arrow app.						3.00

DEAD WHO WALK, THE (See Strange Mysteries, Super Reprint #15, 16)
Realistic Comics: 1952 (one-shot)

nn	53	106	159	323	537	750

DEADWORLD (Also see The Realm)
Arrow Comics/Caliber Comics: Dec, 1986 - No. 26 ($1.50/$1.95/#15-28: $2.50, B&W)

1-4						4.00
5-26-Graphic cover version						4.00
5-26-Tame cover version						3.00
...Archives 1-3 (1992, $2.50)						3.00

DEAN MARTIN & JERRY LEWIS (See Adventures of...)

DEAR BEATRICE FAIRFAX
Best/Standard Comics (King Features): No. 5, Nov, 1950 - No. 9, Sept, 1951
(Vern Greene art)

5-All have Schomburg air brush-c	12	24	36	67	94	120
6-9	8	16	24	44	57	70

DEAR HEART (Formerly Lonely Heart)
Ajax: No. 15, July, 1956 - No. 16, Sept, 1956

15,16	7	14	21	35	43	50

DEAR LONELY HEART (...Illustrated No. 1-6)
Artful Publications: Mar, 1951; No. 2, Oct, 1951 - No. 8, Oct, 1952

1	17	34	51	98	154	210
2	10	20	30	54	72	90
3-Matt Baker Jungle Girl story	20	40	60	117	184	250
4-8	9	18	27	50	65	80

DEAR LONELY HEARTS (Lonely Heart #9 on)
Harwell Publ./Mystery Publ. Co. (Comic Media): Aug, 1953 -No. 8, Oct, 1954

1	12	24	36	67	94	120
2-8	8	16	24	44	57	70

DEARLY BELOVED
Ziff-Davis Publishing Co.: Fall, 1952

1-Photo-c	17	34	51	98	154	210

DEAR NANCY PARKER
Gold Key: June, 1963 - No. 2, Sept, 1963

1-Painted-c on both	4	8	12	23	36	48
2	3	6	9	17	25	32

DEATH: AT DEATH'S DOOR (See Sandman: The Season of Mists)
DC Comics: 2003 ($9.95, graphic novel one-shot, B&W, 7-1/2" x 5")

1-Jill Thompson-s/a/c; manga-style; Morpheus and the Endless app.						10.00

DEATHBLOW (Also see Batman/Deathblow and Darker Image)
Image Comics (WildStorm Productions): May (Apr. inside), 1993 - No. 29, Aug, 1996
($1.75/$1.95/$2.50)

0-(8/96, $2.95, 32 pgs.)-r/Darker Image w/new story & art; Jim Lee & Trevor Scott-a; new Jim Lee-c						3.00
1-($2.50)-Red foil stamped logo on black varnish-c; Jim Lee-c/a; flip-book side has Cybernary -c/story (#2 also)						3.00
1-($1.95)-Newsstand version w/no foil-c & varnish						2.50
2-29: 2-(8/93)-Lee-a; with bound-in poster. 2-($1.75)-Newsstand version w/o poster. 4-Jim Lee-c/Tim Sale-a begin. 13-W/pinup poster by Tim Sale & Jim Lee. 16-($1.95 Newsstand & $2.50 Direct Market editions)-Wildstorm Rising Pt. 6. 17-Variant "Chicago Comicon" edition exists. 20,21-Gen 13 app. 23-Backlash-c/app. 24,25-Grifter-c/app; Gen 13 & Dane from Wetworks app. 28-Deathblow dies. 29-Memorial issue						2.50
5-Alternate Portacio-c (Forms larger picture when combined with alternate-c for Gen 13 #5, Kindred #3, Stormwatch #10, Team 7 #1, Union #0, Wetworks #2 & WildC.A.T.S #11)						6.00
....Sinners and Saints TPB ('99, $19.95) r/#1-12; Sale-c						20.00

DEATHBLOW (Volume 2)
DC Comics (WildStorm): Dec, 2006 - Present ($2.99)

1-6: 1-Azzarello-s/D'Anda-a; two covers by D'Anda & Platt						3.00

DEATHBLOW BY BLOWS

DC Comics (WildStorm): Nov, 1999 - No. 3, Jan, 2000 ($2.95, limited series)

1-3-Alan Moore-s/Jim Baikie-a						3.00

DEATHBLOW/WOLVERINE
Image Comics (WildStorm Productions)/ Marvel Comics: Sept, 1996 - No. 2, Feb, 1997
($2.50, limited series)

1,2: Wiesenfeld-s/Bennett-a						2.50
TPB (1997, $8.95) r/#1,2						9.00

DEATHDEALER (Also see Frank Frazetta's...)
Verotik: July, 1995 - No. 4, July, 1997 ($5.95)

1-Frazetta-c; Bisley-a	1	2	3	5	6	8
1-2nd print, 2-4-($6.95)-Frazetta-c; embossed logo	1	2	3	4	5	7

DEATH, JR.
Image Comics: Apr, 2005 - No. 3, Aug, 2005 ($4.99, squarebound, limited series)

1-3-Gary Whitta-s/Ted Naifeh-a						5.00
Vol. 1 TPB (2005, $14.99) r/series; concept and promotional art						15.00

DEATH, JR. (Volume 2)
Image Comics: Jul, 2006 - No. 3, May, 2007 ($4.99, squarebound, limited series)

1-3-Gary Whitta-s/Ted Naifeh-a. 1-Dan Brereton-c						5.00
Vol. 2 TPB (2007, $14.99) r/series; Halloween story w/Guy Davis-a; promotional art						15.00

DEATHLOK (Also see Astonishing Tales #25)
Marvel Comics: July, 1990 - No. 4, Oct, 1990 ($3.95, limited series, 52 pgs.)

1-4: 1,2-Guice-a(p). 3,4-Denys Cowan-a, c-4						4.00

DEATHLOK
Marvel Comics: July, 1991 - No. 34, Apr, 1994 ($1.75)

1-Silver ink cover; Denys Cowan-c/a(p) begins						3.00
2-18,20-24,26-34: 2-Forge (X-Men) app. 3-Vs. Dr. Doom. 5-X-Men & F.F. x-over. 6,7-Punisher x-over. 9,10-Ghost Rider-c/story. 16-Infinity War x-over. 17-Jae Lee-c. 22-Black Panther app. 27-Siege app.						2.50
19-($2.25)-Foil-c						3.00
25-($2.95, 52 pgs.)-Holo-grafx foil-c						3.00
Annual 1 (1992, $2.25, 68 pgs.)-Guice-p; Quesada-c(p)						3.00
Annual 2 (1993, $2.95, 68 pgs.)-Bagged w/card; intro Tracer						3.00
NOTE: *Denys Cowan a(p)-9-13, 15, Annual 1; c-9-12, 13p, 14. Guice/Cowan c-8.*						

DEATHLOK
Marvel Comics: Sept, 1999 - No. 11, June, 2000 ($1.99)

1-11: 1-Casey-s/Manco-a. 2-Two covers. 4-Canete-a						2.50

DEATHLOK SPECIAL
Marvel Comics: May, 1991 - No. 4, June, 1991 ($2.00, bi-weekly lim. series)

1-4: r/1-4(1990) w/new Guice-c #1,2; Cowan c-3,4						2.50
1-2nd printing w/white-c						2.50

DEATHMASK
Future Comics: Mar, 2003 - No. 3, June, 2003 ($2.99)

1-3-Giordano-a(p)/Michelinie & Layton-s						3.00

DEATHMATE
Valiant (Prologue/Yellow/Blue)/Image Comics (Black/Red/Epilogue):
Sept, 1993 - Epilogue (#6), Feb, 1994 ($2.95/$4.95, limited series)

Preview-(7/93, 8 pgs.)						2.25
Prologue (#1)–Silver foil; Jim Lee/Layton-c; B. Smith/Lee-a; Liefeld-a(p)						3.00
Prologue–Special gold foil ed. of silver ed.						4.00
Black (#2)-(9/93, $4.95, 52 pgs.)-Silvestri/Jim Lee-c; pencils by Peterson/Silvestri/Capullo/ Jim Lee/Portacio; 1st story app. Gen 13 telling their rebellion against the Troika (see WildC.A.T.S. Trilogy)						6.00
Black-Special gold foil edition						7.00
Yellow (#3)-(10/93, $4.95, 52 pgs)-Yellow foil-c; Indicia says Prologue Sept 1993 by mistake; 3rd app. Ninjak; Thibert-c(i)						5.00
Yellow-Special gold foil edition						6.00
Blue (#4)-(10/93, $4.95, 52 pgs.)-Thibert blue foil-c(i); Reese-a(i)						5.00
Blue-Special gold foil edition						6.00
Red (#5), Epilogue (#6)-(2/94, $2.95)-Silver foil Quesada/Silvestri-c; Silvestri-a(p)						3.00

DEATH METAL
Marvel Comics UK: Jan, 1994 - No. 4, Apr, 1994 ($1.95, limited series)

1-4: 1-Silver ink-c. Alpha Flight app.						2.50

DEATH METAL VS. GENETIX
Marvel Comics UK: Dec, 1993 - No. 2, Jan, 1994 (Limited series)

1-($2.95)-Polybagged w/2 trading cards						3.00
2-($2.50)-Polybagged w/2 trading cards						2.50

Death's Head II #9 © MAR

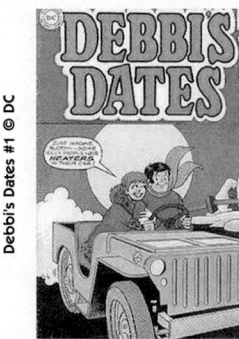

Debbi's Dates #1 © DC

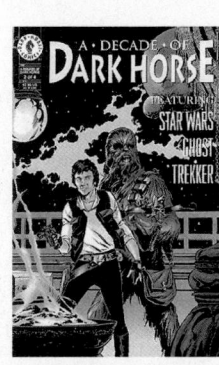

Decade of Dark Horse #2 © DH

	GD 2.0	VG 4.0	FN 6.0	VF 8.0	VF/NM 9.0	NM- 9.2

DEATH OF CAPTAIN MARVEL (See Marvel Graphic Novel #1)

DEATH OF MR. MONSTER, THE (See Mr. Monster #8)

DEATH OF SUPERMAN (See Superman, 2nd Series)

DEATH RACE 2020
Roger Corman's Cosmic Comics: Apr, 1995 - No. 8, Nov, 1995 ($2.50)

	GD	VG	FN	VF	VF/NM	NM-
1-8: Sequel to the Movie						2.50

DEATH RATTLE (Formerly an Underground)
Kitchen Sink Press: V2#1, 10/85 - No. 18, 1988, 1994 ($1.95, Baxter paper, mature); V3#1, 11/95 - No. 5, 6/96 ($2.95, B&W)

V2#1-7,9-18: 1-Corben-c. 2-Unpubbed Spirit story by Eisner. 5-Robot Woman-r by Wolverton. 6-B&W issues begin. 10-Savage World-r by by Williamson/Torres/ Krenkel/Frazetta from Witzend #1. 16-Wolverton Spacehawk-r 4.00
8-(12/86)-1st app. Mark Schultz's Xenozoic Tales/Cadillacs & Dinosaurs

	GD	VG	FN	VF	VF/NM	NM-
8	1	3	4	6	8	10
8-(1994)-r plus interview w/Mark Schultz						3.00
V3#1-5 ($2.95-c)						3.00

DEATH'S HEAD (See Daredevil #56, Dragon's Claws #5 & Incomplete...)(See Amazing Fantasy (2004) for Death's Head 3.0)
Marvel Comics: Dec, 1988 - No. 10, Sept, 1989 ($1.75)

	GD	VG	FN	VF	VF/NM	NM-
1-Dragon's Claws spin-off						3.00
2-Fantastic Four app.; Dragon's Claws x-over						3.00
3-10: 8-Dr. Who app. 9-F. F. x-over; Simonson-c(p)						2.50

DEATH'S HEAD II (Also see Battletide)
Marvel Comics UK, Ltd.: Mar, 1992 - No. 4, June (May inside), 1992 ($1.75, color, lim. series)

	GD	VG	FN	VF	VF/NM	NM-
1-4: 2-Fantastic Four app. 4-Punisher, Spider-Man, Daredevil, Dr. Strange, Capt. America & Wolverine in the year 2020						2.50
1,2-Silver ink 2nd printiings						2.50

DEATH'S HEAD II (Also see Battletide)
Marvel Comics UK, Ltd.: Dec, 1992 - No. 16, Mar, 1994 ($1.75/$1.95)

	GD	VG	FN	VF	VF/NM	NM-
V2#1-13,15,16: 1-Gatefold-c. 1-4-X-Men app.15-Capt. America & Wolverine app.						2.50
14-($2.95)-Foil flip-c w/Death's Head II Gold #0						3.00
...Gold 1 (1/94, $3.95, 68 pgs.)-Gold foil-c						4.00

DEATH'S HEAD II & THE ORIGIN OF DIE CUT
Marvel Comics UK, Ltd.: Aug, 1993 - No. 2, Sept, 1993 (limited series)

	GD	VG	FN	VF	VF/NM	NM-
1-($2.95)-Embossed-c						3.00
2 ($1.75)						2.50

DEATHSTROKE: THE TERMINATOR (Deathstroke: The Hunted #0-47; Deathstroke #48-60)
(Also see Marvel & DC Present, New Teen Titans #2, New Titans, Showcase '93 #7,9 & Tales of the Teen Titans #42-44)
DC Comics: Aug, 1991 - No. 60, June, 1996 ($1.75-$2.25)

	GD	VG	FN	VF	VF/NM	NM-
1-New Titans spin-off; Mike Zeck c-1-28						4.00
1-Gold ink 2nd printing ($1.75)						2.50
2						3.00
3-40,(10/94),41(11/94)-49,51-60: 6,8-Batman cameo. 7,9-Batman-c/story. 9-1st brief app. new Vigilante (female). 10-1st full app. new Vigilante; Perez-i. 13-Vs. Justice League; Team Titans cameo on pg. 14-Total Chaos, part 1; TeamTitans-c/story cont'd in New Titans #90. 40-(9/94). 0-(10/94)-Begin Deathstroke, The Hunted, ends #47.						2.50
50 ($3.50)						3.50
Annual 1-4 ('92-'95, 68 pgs.): 1-Nightwing & Vigilante app.; minor Eclipso app. 2-Bloodlines Deathstorm; 1st app. Gunfire. 3-Elseworlds story. 4-Year One story						4.00

NOTE: *Golden* a-12. *Perez* a-11i. *Zeck* c-Annual 1, 2.

DEATH: THE HIGH COST OF LIVING (See Sandman #8) (Also see the Books of Magic limited & ongoing series)
DC Comics (Vertigo): Mar, 1993 - No. 3, May, 1993 ($1.95, limited series)

	GD	VG	FN	VF	VF/NM	NM-
1-Bachalo/Buckingham-a; Dave McKean-c; Neil Gaiman scripts in all						6.00
1-Platinum edition						40.00
2						3.50
3-Pgs. 19 & 20 had wrong placement						3.00
3-Corrected version w/pgs. 19 & 20 facing each other; has no-c & ads for Sebastion O & The Geek added						4.00
Death Talks About Life-giveaway about AIDS prevention						5.00
Hardcover (1994, $19.95)-r/#1-3 & Death Talks About Life; intro. by Tori Amos						20.00
Trade paperback (6/94, $12.95, Titan Books)-r/#1-3 & Death Talks About Life; prism-c						13.00

DEATH: THE TIME OF YOUR LIFE (See Sandman #8)
DC Comics (Vertigo): Apr, 1996 - No. 3, July, 1996 ($2.95, limited series)

	GD	VG	FN	VF	VF/NM	NM-
1-3: Neil Gaiman story & Bachalo/Buckingham-a; Dave McKean-c. 2-(5/96)						3.00
Hardcover (1997, $19.95)-r/#1-3 w/3 new pages & gallery art by various						20.00
TPB (1997, $12.95)-r/#1-3 & Visions of Death gallery; Intro. by Claire Danes						13.00

DEATH 3
Marvel Comics UK: Sept, 1993 - No. 4, Dec, 1993 ($1.75, limited series)

	GD	VG	FN	VF	VF/NM	NM-
1-($2.95)-Embossed-c						3.00
2-4						2.50

DEATH VALLEY (Cowboys and Indians)
Comic Media: Oct, 1953 - No. 6, Aug, 1954

	GD	VG	FN	VF	VF/NM	NM-
1-Billy the Kid; Morisi-a; Andru/Esposito-c/a	15	30	45	90	140	190
2-Don Heck-c	10	20	30	58	79	100
3-6: 3,5-Morisi-a. 5-Discount-a	10	20	30	56	76	95

DEATH VALLEY (Becomes Frontier Scout, Daniel Boone No.10-13)
Charlton Comics: No. 7, 6/55 - No. 9, 10/55 (Cont'd from Comic Media series)

	GD	VG	FN	VF	VF/NM	NM-
7-9: 8-Wolverton-a (half pg.)	9	18	27	50	65	80

DEATHWISH
DC Comics (Milestone Media): Dec, 1994 - No. 4, Mar, 1995 (2.50, lim. series)

	GD	VG	FN	VF	VF/NM	NM-
1-4						2.50

DEATH WRECK
Marvel Comics UK: Jan, 1994 - No. 4, Apr, 1994 ($1.95, limited series)

	GD	VG	FN	VF	VF/NM	NM-
1-4: 1-Metallic ink logo; Death's Head II app.						2.50

DEBBIE DEAN, CAREER GIRL
Civil Service Publ.: April, 1945 - No. 2, July, 1945

	GD	VG	FN	VF	VF/NM	NM-
1,2-Newspaper reprints by Bert Whitman	14	28	42	76	108	140

DEBBI'S DATES (Also see Date With Debbi)
National Periodical Publications: Apr-May, 1969 - No. 11, Dec-Jan, 1970-71

	GD	VG	FN	VF	VF/NM	NM-
1	6	12	18	37	59	80
2,3,5,7-11: 2-Last 12¢ issue	3	6	9	19	29	38
4-Neal Adams text illo	4	8	12	23	36	48
6-Superman cameo	5	10	15	35	55	75

DECADE OF DARK HORSE, A
Dark Horse Comics: Jul, 1996 - No. 4, Oct, 1996 ($2.95, B&W/color, lim. series)

	GD	VG	FN	VF	VF/NM	NM-
1-4: 1-Sin City-c/story by Miller; Grendel by Wagner; Predator. 2-Star Wars wraparound-c. 3-Aliens-c/story; Nexus, Mask stories						3.00

DECAPITATOR (Randy Bowen's...)
Dark Horse Comics: Jun, 1998 - No. 4, ($2.95)

	GD	VG	FN	VF	VF/NM	NM-
1-4-Bowen-s/art by various. 1-Mahnke-c. 3-Jones-c						4.00

DECEPTION, THE
Image Comics (Flypaper Press): 1999 - No. 3, 1999 ($2.95, B&W, mini-series)

	GD	VG	FN	VF	VF/NM	NM-
1-3-Horley painted-c						3.00

DECIMATION: THE HOUSE OF M
Marvel Comics: Jan, 2006 ($3.99)

	GD	VG	FN	VF	VF/NM	NM-
... - The Day After (one-shot) Claremont-s/Green-a						4.00

DEEP, THE (Movie)
Marvel Comics Group: Nov, 1977 (Giant)

	GD	VG	FN	VF	VF/NM	NM-
1-Infantino-c/a	1	3	4	6	8	10

DEEP SLEEPER
Oni Press/Image Comics: Feb, 2004 - No. 4, Sept, 2004 ($3.50/$2.95, B&W, limited series)

	GD	VG	FN	VF	VF/NM	NM-
1,2-(Oni Press, $3.50)-Hester-s/Huddleston-a						3.50
3,4-(Image Comics, $2.95)						3.00
... Omnibus (Image, 8/04, $5.95) r/#1,2						6.00
... Vol. 1 TPB (2005, $12.95) r/#1-4; cover gallery						13.00

DEFCON 4
Image Comics (WildStorm Productions): Feb, 1996 - No. 4, Sept, 1996 ($2.50, lim. series)

	GD	VG	FN	VF	VF/NM	NM-
1/2	1	2	3	5	7	9
1/2 Gold-(1000 printed)						14.00
1-Main Cover by Mat Broome & Edwin Rosell						3.00
1-Hordes of Cymulants variant-c by Michael Golden						5.00
1-Backs to the Wall variant-c by Humberto Ramos & Alex Garner						5.00
1-Defcon 4-Way variant-c by Jim Lee	1	2	3	4	5	7
2-4						2.50

DEFENDERS, THE (TV)
Dell Publishing Co.: Sept-Nov, 1962 - No. 2, Feb-Apr, 1963

	GD	VG	FN	VF	VF/NM	NM-
12-176-211(#1)	4	8	12	26	41	55
12-176-304(#2)	3	6	9	21	32	42

DEFENDERS, THE (Also see Giant-Size..., Marvel Feature, Marvel Treasury Edition, Secret Defenders & Sub-Mariner #34, 35; The New...#140-on)

Defenders #101 © MAR

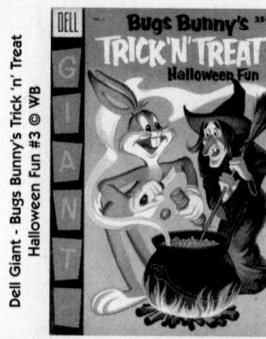

Dell Giant - Bugs Bunny's Trick 'n' Treat Halloween Fun #3 © WB

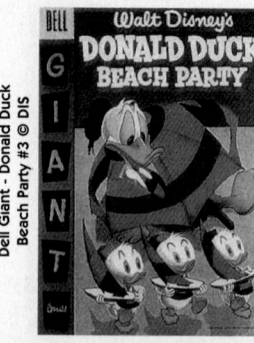

Dell Giant - Donald Duck Beach Party #3 © DIS

	GD 2.0	VG 4.0	FN 6.0	VF 8.0	VF/NM 9.0	NM- 9.2

Marvel Comics Group: Aug, 1972 - No. 152, Feb, 1986

	GD 2.0	VG 4.0	FN 6.0	VF 8.0	VF/NM 9.0	NM- 9.2
1-The Hulk, Doctor Strange, Sub-Mariner begin	10	20	30	73	129	185
2-Silver Surfer x-over	6	12	18	37	59	80
3-5: 3-Silver Surfer x-over. 4-Valkyrie joins	4	8	12	24	37	50
6,7: 6-Silver Surfer x-over	3	6	9	17	25	32
8,9,11: 8-11-Defenders vs. the Avengers (Crossover with Avengers #115-118)						
8,11-Silver Surfer x-over	3	6	9	21	32	42
10-Hulk vs. Thor battle	7	14	21	47	76	105
12-14: 12-Last 20¢ issue	2	4	6	10	14	18
15,16-Magneto & Brotherhood of Evil Mutants app. from X-Men						
	2	4	6	11	16	20
17-20: 17-Power Man x-over (11/74)	1	3	4	6	8	10
21-25: 24,25-Son of Satan app.	1	2	3	4	5	7
26-29-Guardians of the Galaxy app. (#26 is 8/75; pre-dates Marvel Presents #3): 28-1st full app. Starhawk (1st brief app. #27). 29-Starhawk joins Guardians						
	1	2	3	5	7	9
30-33,39-50: 31,32-Origin Nighthawk. 44-Hellcat joins. 45-Dr. Strange leaves.						
47-49-Early Moon Knight app. (5/77). 48-50-(Reg. 30¢-c)						5.00
34-38-(Regular 25¢ editions): 35-Intro New Red Guardian						5.00
34-38-(30¢-c variants, limited distribution)(4-8/76)	3	6	9	18	24	30
48-52-(30¢-c variants, limited distribution)(6-10/77)	4	8	12	24	37	50
51-60: 51,52-(Reg. 30¢-c). 53-1st brief app. Lunatik (Lobo lookalike). 55-Origin Red Guardian; Lunatik cameo. 56-1st full Lunatik story						4.00
61-75: 61-Lunatik & Spider-Man app. 70-73-Lunatik (origin #71). 73-75-Foolkiller II app. (Greg Salinger). 74-Nighthawk resigns						3.00
76-93,95,97-99,102-119,123,124,126-149,151: 77-Origin Omega. 78-Original Defenders return thru #101. 104-The Beast joins. 105-Son of Satan joins. 106-Death of Nighthawk.						
129-New Mutants cameo (3/84, early x-over)						2.50
94,101,120-122: 94-1st Gargoyle. 101-Silver Surfer-c & app. 120,121-Son of Satan-c/stories.						
122-Final app. Son of Satan (2 pgs.)						4.00
96-Ghost Rider app.						4.00
100-(52 pgs.)-Hellcat (Patsy Walker) revealed as Satan's daughter						5.00
125,150: 125-(52 pgs.)-Intro new Defenders. 150-(52 pgs.)-Origin Cloud						4.00
152-(52 pgs.)-Ties in with X-Factor & Secret Wars II						4.00
Annual 1 (1976, 52 pgs.)-New book-length story	3	6	9	16	23	30

NOTE: *Art Adams* c-142p. *Austin* a-53i; c-65i, 119i, 145i. *Frank Bolle* a-7i, 10i, 11i. *Buckler* c(p)-34, 38, 76, 77, 79-86, 90, 91. *J. Buscema* c-66. *Giffen* a-42-49p, 50, 51-54p. *Golden* a-53p, 54p; c-94, 96. *Guice* c-129. *G. Kane* c(p)-13, 16, 18, 19, 21-26, 31-33, 35-37, 40, 41, 52, 55. *Kirby* c-42-45. *Mooney* a-3i, 31-34i, 62i, 63i, 85i. *Nasser* c-88p. *Perez* c(p)-51, 53, 54. *Rogers* c-98. *Starlin* c-110. *Tuska* a-57p. Silver Surfer in No. 2, 3, 6, 8-11, 92, 98-101, 107, 112-115, 122-125.

DEFENDERS, THE (Volume 2) (Continues in The Order)
Marvel Comics: Mar, 2001 - No. 12, Feb, 2002 ($2.99/$2.25)

1-Busiek & Larsen-s/Larsen & Janson-a/c						3.00
2-11: 2-Two covers by Larsen & Art Adams. Valkyrie app. 4-Frenz-a						2.50
12-($3.50) 'Nuff Said issue; back-up-s Reis-a						3.50

DEFENDERS, THE
Marvel Comics: Sept, 2005 - No. 5, Jan, 2006 ($2.99, limited series)

1-5-Giffen & DeMatteis-s/Maguire-a. 2-Dormammu app.						3.00
...: Indefensible HC (2006, $19.99, dust jacket) r/#1-5; Giffen & Maguire sketch page						20.00
...: Indefensible SC (2007, $13.99) r/#1-5; Giffen & Maguire sketch page						14.00

DEFENDERS OF DYNATRON CITY
Marvel Comics: Feb, 1992 - No. 6, July, 1992 ($1.25, limited series)

1-6-Lucasarts characters. 2-Origin						3.00

DEFENDERS OF THE EARTH (TV)
Marvel Comics (Star Comics): Jan, 1987 - No. 4, July, 1987

1-4: The Phantom, Mandrake The Magician, Flash Gordon begin. 3-Origin Phantom. 4-Origin Mandrake						4.00

DEFEX
Devil's Due Publ.: Oct, 2004 - No. 6, Apr, 2005 ($2.95)

1-6: 1-Wolfman-s/Caselli-a. 6-Pérez-c						3.00

DEFIANCE
Image Comics: Feb, 2002 - No. 8, Jun, 2003 ($2.95)

Preview Edition (12/01)						2.50
1-8-Barré-s/Kang & Suh-a						3.00

DEFINITIVE DIRECTORY OF THE DC UNIVERSE, THE (See Who's Who...)

DELECTA OF THE PLANETS (See Don Fortune & Fawcett Miniatures)

DELICATE CREATURES
Image Comics (Top Cow): 2001 ($16.95, hardcover with dust jacket)

nn-Fairy tale storybook; J. Michael Straczynski-s; Michael Zulli-a						17.00

DELLA VISION (...The Television Queen) (Patty Powers #4 on)
Atlas Comics: April, 1955 - No. 3, Aug, 1955

	GD 2.0	VG 4.0	FN 6.0	VF 8.0	VF/NM 9.0	NM- 9.2
1-Al Hartley-c	15	30	45	90	140	190
2,3	11	22	33	62	86	110

DELL GIANT COMICS

Dell Publishing began to release square bound comics in 1949 with a 132-page issue called Christmas Parade #1. The covers were of a heavier stock to accommodate the increased number of pages. The books proved profitable at 25 cents, but the average number of pages was quickly reduced to 100. Ten years later they were converted to a numbering system similar to the Four Color Comics, for greater ease in distribution and the page counts cut back to mostly 84 pages. The label "Dell Giant" began to appear on the covers in 1954. Because of the size of the books and the heavier, less pliant cover stock, they are rarely found in high grade condition, and with the exception of a small quantity of copies released from Western Publishing's warehouse–are almost never found in near mint.

	GD 2.0	VG 4.0	FN 6.0	VF 8.0	VF/NM 9.0	NM- 9.2
Abraham Lincoln Life Story 1(3/58)	8	16	24	64	107	150
Bugs Bunny Christmas Funnies 1(11/50, 116pp)	19	38	57	152	261	370
...Christmas Funnies 2(11/51, 116pp)	11	22	33	88	157	225
...Christmas Funnies 3-5(11/52-11/54,)-Becomes Christmas Party #6						
	10	20	30	80	138	195
...Christmas Funnies 7-9(12/56-12/58)	9	18	27	72	124	175
...Christmas Party 6(11/55)-Formerly Bugs Bunny Christmas Funnies						
	9	18	27	72	124	175
...County Fair 1(9/57)	10	20	30	80	140	200
...Halloween Parade 1(10/53)	11	22	33	88	157	225
...Halloween Parade 2(10/54)-Trick 'N' Treat Halloween Fun #3 on						
	9	18	27	72	129	185
...Trick 'N' Treat Halloween Fun 3,4(10/55-10/56)-Formerly Halloween Parade #2						
	9	18	27	72	129	185
...Vacation Funnies 1(7/51, 112pp)	18	36	54	144	252	360
...Vacation Funnies 2('52)	13	26	39	104	180	255
...Vacation Funnies 3-5('53-'55)	10	20	30	80	138	195
...Vacation Funnies 6,7,9('56-'59)	9	18	27	72	124	175
...Vacation Funnies 8('58) 1st app. Beep Beep the Road Runner, Wile E. Coyote (1st meeting), Mathilda (Mrs. Beep Beep) and their 3 children who hatch from eggs; one month before Four Color #918						
	10	20	30	80	140	200
Cadet Gray Of West Point 1(4/58)-Williamson-a, 10pgs.; Buscema-a; photo-c						
	8	16	24	64	107	150
Christmas In Disneyland 1(12/57)-Barks-a, 18 pgs.	25	50	75	200	350	500
Christmas Parade 1(11/49)(132 pgs.)(1st Dell Giant)-Donald Duck (25pgs. by Barks, r-in G.K. Christmas Parade #5); Mickey Mouse & other film oriented stories; Cinderella (prior to movie), 7 Dwarfs, Bambi & Thumper, So Dear To My Heart, Flying Mouse, Dumbo, Cookieland & others	60	120	180	480	840	1200
Christmas Parade 2('50)-Donald Duck (132 pgs.)(25 pgs. by Barks, r-in Gold Key's Christmas Parade #6). Mickey, Pluto, Chip & Dale, etc. Contents shift to a holiday expansion of W.D. C&S type format	42	84	126	336	588	840
Christmas Parade 3-7('51-'55, #3-116pgs)(#4-7, 100 pgs.)						
	14	28	42	112	196	280
Christmas Parade 8(12/56)-Barks-a, 8 pgs.	22	44	66	176	306	435
Christmas Parade 9(12/58)-Barks-a, 20 pgs.	25	50	75	200	350	500
Christmas Treasury, A 1(11/54)	9	18	27	72	126	180
Davy Crockett, King Of The Wild Frontier 1(9/55)-Fess Parker photo-c; Marsh-a						
	19	38	57	152	269	385
Disneyland Birthday Party 1(10/58)-Barks-a, 16 pgs. r-by Gladstone						
	25	50	75	200	350	500
Donald and Mickey In Disneyland 1(5/58)	11	22	33	88	157	225
Donald Duck Beach Party 1(7/54)-Has an Uncle Scrooge story (not by Barks) that prefigures the later rivalry with Flintheart Glomgold and tells of Scrooge's wild rivalry with another millionaire	16	32	48	128	224	320
...Beach Party 2(1955)-Lady & Tramp	11	22	33	88	157	225
...Beach Party 3-5(1956-58)	11	22	33	88	152	215
...Beach Party 6(8/59, 84pp)-Stapled	8	16	24	64	115	165
Donald Duck Fun Book 1,2(1953 & 10/54)-Games, puzzles, comics & cut-outs (very rare in unused condition)(most copies commonly have defaced interior pgs.)	60	120	180	480	840	1200
Donald Duck In Disneyland 1(9/55)-1st Disneyland Dell Giant						
	15	30	45	120	210	300
Golden West Rodeo Treasury 1(10/57)	10	20	30	80	135	190
Huey, Dewey and Louie Back To School 1(9/58)	9	18	27	72	126	180
Lady and The Tramp 1(6/55)	17	34	51	136	233	330
Life Stories of American Presidents 1(11/57)-Buscema-a						
	8	16	24	64	107	150
Lone Ranger Golden West 3(8/55)-Formerly Lone Ranger Western Treasury						
	18	36	54	144	255	365

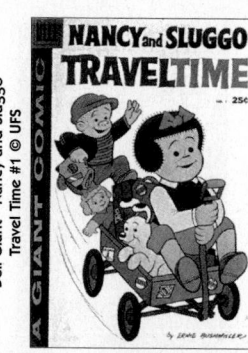
Dell Giant - Nancy and Sluggo Travel Time #1 © UFS

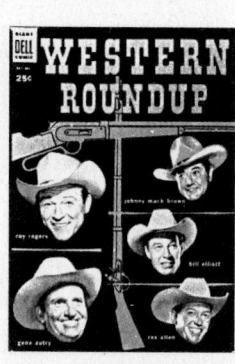
Dell Giant - Western Roundup #8 © DELL

Dell Giant #26 © DIS

DE

	GD	VG	FN	VF	VF/NM	NM-		GD	VG	FN	VF	VF/NM	NM-
	2.0	4.0	6.0	8.0	9.0	9.2		2.0	4.0	6.0	8.0	9.0	9.2

Lone Ranger Movie Story nn(3/56)-Origin Lone Ranger in text; Clayton Moore photo-c
36 72 108 288 507 725

...Western Treasury 1(9/53)-Origin Lone Ranger, Silver, & Tonto; painted cover
23 46 69 184 325 465

...Western Treasury 2(8/54)-Becomes Lone Ranger Golden West #3
18 36 54 144 255 365

Marge's Little Lulu & Alvin Story Telling Time 1(3/59)-r/#2,5,3,11,30,10,21,17,8, 14,16; Stanley-a
14 28 42 112 196 280

...& Her Friends 4(3/56)-Tripp-a
14 28 42 112 191 270

...& Her Special Friends 3(3/55)-Tripp-a
15 30 45 120 210 300

...& Tubby At Summer Camp 5,2: 5(10/57)-Tripp-a. 2(10/58)-Tripp-a
13 26 39 104 182 260

...& Tubby Halloween Fun 6,2: 6(10/57)-Tripp-a. 2(10/58)-Tripp-a
13 26 39 104 182 260

...& Tubby In Alaska 1(7/59)-Tripp-a
13 26 39 104 177 250

...On Vacation 1(7/54)-r/4C-110,14,4C-146,5,4C-97,4,4C-158,3,1;Stanley-a
25 50 75 200 350 500

...& Tubby Annual 1(3/53)-r/4C-165,4C-74,4C-146,4C-97,4C-158, 4C-139, 4C-131; Stanley-a (1st Lulu Dell Giant)
30 60 90 240 420 600

...& Tubby Annual 2('54)-r/4C-139,6,4C-115,4C-74,5,4C-97,3,4C-146,18; Stanley-a
25 50 75 200 350 500

Marge's Tubby & His Clubhouse Pals 1(10/56)-1st app. Gran'pa Feeb;1st app. Janie; written by Stanley; Tripp-a
15 30 45 120 210 300

Mickey Mouse Almanac 1(12/57)-Barks-a, 8pgs.
27 54 81 216 378 540

...Birthday Party 1(9/53)-r/entire 48pgs. of Gottfredson's "Mickey Mouse in Love Trouble" from WDC&S 36-39. Quality equal to original. Also reprints one story each from Four Color 27, 79, & 181 plus 6 panels of highlights in the career of Mickey Mouse
31 62 93 248 434 620

...Club Parade 1(12/55)-r/4-Color 16 with some death trap scenes redrawn by Paul Murry & recolored with night turned into day; quality less than original
22 44 66 176 308 440

...In Fantasy Land 1(5/57)
13 26 39 104 180 255

...In Frontier Land 1(5/56)-Mickey Mouse Club iss.
13 26 39 104 180 255

...Summer Fun 1(8/58)-Mobile cut-outs on back-c; becomes Summer Fun with #2
13 26 39 104 180 255

Moses & The Ten Commandments 1(8/57)-Not based on movie; Dell's adaptation; Sekowsky-a
7 14 21 56 98 140

Nancy & Sluggo Travel Time 1(9/58)
8 16 24 64 115 165

Peter Pan Treasure Chest 1(1/53, 212pp)-Disney; contains 54-page movie adaptation & other Peter Pan stories; plus Donald & Mickey stories w/P. Pan; a 32-page retelling of "D. Duck Finds Pirate Gold" with yellow beak, called "Capt. Hook & the Buried Treasure"
113 226 339 904 1577 2250

Picnic Party 6,7(7/55-6/56)(Formerly Vacation Parade)-Uncle Scrooge, Mickey & Donald
12 24 36 96 166 235

Picnic Party 8(7/57)-Barks-a, 6pgs
21 42 63 168 289 410

Pogo Parade 1(9/53)-Kelly-a(r-/Pogo from Animal Comics in this order: #11,13,21,14,27,16,23,9,18,15,17)
25 50 75 200 350 500

Raggedy Ann & Andy 1(2/55)
16 32 48 128 224 320

Santa Claus Funnies 1(11/52)-Dan Noonan -A Christmas Carol adaptation
9 18 27 72 126 180

Silly Symphonies 1(9/52)-Redrawing of Gotfredson's Mickey Mouse strip of "The Brave Little Tailor;" 2 Good Housekeeping pages (from 1943); Lady and the Two Siamese Cats, three years before "Lady & the Tramp;" a retelling of Donald Duck's first app. in "The Wise Little Hen" & other stories based on 1930's Silly Symphony cartoons
29 58 87 232 409 585

Silly Symphonies 2(9/53)-M. Mouse in "The Sorcerer's Apprentice", 2 Good Housekeeping pages (from 1944); The Pelican & the Snipe, Elmer Elephant, Peculiar Penguins, Little Hiawatha, & others
24 48 72 192 336 480

Silly Symphonies 3(2/54)-r/Mickey & The Beanstalk (4-Color #157, 39pgs.), Little Minnehaha, Pablo, The Flying Gauchito, Pluto, & Bongo, & 2 Good Housekeeping pages (1944)
20 40 60 160 275 390

Silly Symphonies 4(8/54)-r/Dumbo (4-Color 234), Morris The Midget Moose, The Country Cousin, Bongo, & Clara Cluck
20 40 60 160 275 390

Silly Symphonies 5-8: 5(2/55)-r/Cinderella (4-Color 272), Bucky Bug, Pluto, Little Hiawatha, The 7 Dwarfs & Dumbo. 6(8/55)-r/Pinocchio (WDC&S 63), The 7 Dwarfs & Thumper (WDC&S 45), M. Mouse "Adventures With Robin Hood" (40 pgs.), Johnny Appleseed, Pluto & Peter Pan, & Bucky Bug; Cut-out on back-c. 7(2/56)-r/Reluctant Dragon, Ugly Duckling, M. Mouse & Peter Pan, Jiminy Cricket, Peter & The Wolf, Brer Rabbit, Bucky Bug; Cut-out on back-c. 8(2/58)-r/Thumper Meets The 7 Dwarfs (4-Color #19), Jiminy Cricket, Niok, Brer Rabbit; Cut-out on back-c
16 32 48 128 224 320

Silly Symphonies 9(2/59)-r/Paul Bunyan, Humphrey Bear, Jiminy Cricket, The Social Lion, Goliath II; cut-out on back-c
15 30 45 120 210 300

Sleeping Beauty 1(4/59)
25 50 75 200 350 500

Summer Fun 2(8/59, 84pp, stapled binding)(Formerly Mickey Mouse...)-Barks-a(2), 24 pgs.
24 48 72 192 336 480

Tarzan's Jungle Annual 1(8/52)-Lex Barker photo on-c of #1,2
15 30 45 120 210 300

...Annual 2(8/53)
11 22 33 88 152 215

...Annual 3-7('54-9/58)(two No. 5s)-Manning-a-No. 3,5-7; Marsh-a in No. 1-7 plus painted-c 1-7
9 18 27 72 124 175

Tom And Jerry Back To School 1(9/56)
12 24 36 96 168 240

...Picnic Time 1(7/58)
10 20 30 80 135 190

...Summer Fun 1(7/54)-Droopy written by Barks
15 30 45 120 205 290

...Summer Fun 2-4(7/55-7/57)
8 16 24 64 107 150

...Toy Fair 1(6/58)
9 18 27 72 126 180

...Winter Carnival 1(12/52)-Droopy written by Barks
20 40 60 160 280 400

...Winter Carnival 2(12/53)-Droopy written by Barks
16 32 48 128 224 320

...Winter Fun 3(12/54)
8 16 24 64 115 165

...Winter Fun 4-7(12/55-11/58)
7 14 21 56 101 145

Treasury of Dogs, A 1(10/56)
7 14 21 56 101 145

Treasury of Horses, A (9/55)
7 14 21 56 101 145

Uncle Scrooge Goes To Disneyland 1(8/57p)-Barks-a, 20pgs.r-by Gladstone
26 52 78 208 359 510

Vacation In Disneyland 1(8/58)
11 22 33 88 157 225

Vacation Parade 1(7/50, 132pp)-Donald Duck & Mickey Mouse; Barks-a, 55 pgs.
89 178 267 712 1244 1775

Vacation Parade 2(7/51,116pp)
25 50 75 200 350 500

Vacation Parade 3-5(7/52-7/54)-Becomes Picnic Party No. 6 on #4-Robin Hood Advs.
14 28 42 112 194 275

Western Roundup 1(6/52)-Photo-c; Gene Autry, Roy Rogers, Johnny Mack Brown, Rex Allen, & Bill Elliott begin; photo back-c begin, end No. 14,16,18
25 50 75 200 350 500

Western Roundup 2(2/53)-Photo-c
14 28 42 112 196 280

Western Roundup 3-5(7-9/53 - 1-3/54)-Photo-c
11 22 33 88 157 225

Western Roundup 6-10(4-6/54 - 4-6/55)-Photo-c
11 22 33 88 149 210

Western Roundup 11-17,25: 11-17-Photo-c; 11-13,16,17-Manning-a. 11-Flying A's Range Rider, Dale Evans begin
9 18 27 72 129 185

Western Roundup 18-Toth-a; last photo-c; Gene Autry ends
11 22 33 88 149 210

Western Roundup 19-24-Manning-a. 19-Buffalo Bill Jr. begins (7-9/57; early app.). 19,20,22-Toth-a. 21-Rex Allen, Johnny Mack Brown end. 22-Jace Pearson's Texas Rangers, Rin Tin Tin, Tales of Wells Fargo (2nd app., 4-6/58) & Wagon Train (2nd app.) begin
9 18 27 72 129 185

Woody Woodpecker Back To School 1(10/52)
10 20 30 80 140 200

...Back To School 2-4,6('53-10/57)-County Fair No. 5
8 16 24 64 112 160

...County Fair 5(9/56)-Formerly Back To School
8 16 24 64 112 160

...County Fair 2(11/58)
7 14 21 56 101 145

DELL GIANTS (Consecutive numbering)
Dell Publishing Co.: No. 21, Sept. 1959 - No. 55, Sept. 1961 (Most 84 pgs., 25¢)
21-(#1)-M.G.M.'s Tom & Jerry Picnic Time (84pp, stapled binding)-Painted-c
11 22 33 88 157 225

22-Huey, Dewey & Louie Back to School (Disney; 10/59, 84pp, square binding begins)
9 18 27 72 129 185

23-Marge's Little Lulu & Tubby Halloween Fun (10/59)-Tripp-a
12 24 36 96 168 240

24-Woody Woodpecker's Family Fun (11/59)(Walter Lantz)
8 16 24 64 112 160

25-Tarzan's Jungle World(11/59)-Marsh-a; painted-c
11 22 33 88 152 215

26-Christmas Parade(Disney; 12/59)-Barks-a, 16pgs.; Barks draws himself on wanted poster on pg. 13
21 42 63 168 289 410

27-Walt Disney's Man in Space (10/59) r-/4-Color 716,866, & 954 (100 pgs., 35¢)(TV)
9 18 27 72 129 185

28-Bugs Bunny's Winter Fun (2/60)
9 18 27 72 126 180

29-Marge's Little Lulu & Tubby in Hawaii (4/60)-Tripp-a
12 24 36 96 166 235

30-Disneyland USA(Disney; 6/60)
12 24 36 96 124 175

31-Huckleberry Hound Summer Fun (7/60)(TV)(HannaBarbera)-Yogi Bear & Pixie & Dixie app.
12 24 36 96 173 250

32-Bugs Bunny Beach Party
7 14 21 56 101 145

33-Daisy Duck & Uncle Scrooge Picnic Time (Disney; 9/60)
9 18 27 72 124 175

34-Nancy & Sluggo Summer Camp (8/60)
7 14 21 56 101 145

35-Huey, Dewey & Louie Back to School (Disney; 10/60)-1st app. Daisy Duck's Nieces, April, May & June
12 24 36 96 163 230

36-Marge's Little Lulu & Witch Hazel Halloween Fun (10/60)-Tripp-a
11 22 33 88 157 225

37-Tarzan, King of the Jungle (11/60)-Marsh-a; painted-c

Dell Giant #48 © H-B

The Demon #1 © DC

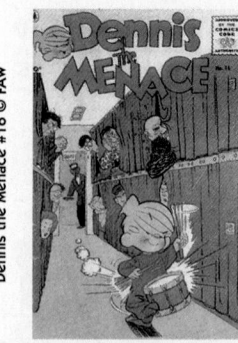
Dennis the Menace #16 © FAW

	GD 2.0	VG 4.0	FN 6.0	VF 8.0	VF/NM 9.0	NM- 9.2

	9	18	27	72	129	185
38-Uncle Donald & His Nephews Family Fun (Disney; 11/60)-Cover painting based on a pencil sketch by Barks	12	24	36	96	173	250
39-Walt Disney's Merry Christmas (Disney; 12/60)-Cover painting based on a pencil sketch by Barks	12	24	36	96	173	250
40-Woody Woodpecker Christmas Parade (12/60)(Walter Lantz)	6	12	18	48	87	125
41-Yogi Bear's Winter Sports (12/60)(TV)(Hanna-Barbera)-Huckleberry Hound, Pixie & Dixie, Augie Doggie app.	12	24	36	96	173	250
42-Marge's Little Lulu & Tubby in Australia (4/61)	11	22	33	88	157	225
43-Mighty Mouse in Outer Space (5/61)	18	36	54	144	252	360
44-Around the World with Huckleberry and His Friends (7/61)(TV)(Hanna-Barbera)-Yogi Bear, Pixie & Dixie, Quick Draw McGraw, Augie Doggie app.; 1st app. Yakky Doodle	13	26	39	104	182	260
45-Nancy & Sluggo Summer Camp (8/61)	7	14	21	56	96	135
46-Bugs Bunny Beach Party (8/61)	7	14	21	56	96	135
47-Mickey & Donald in Vacationland (Disney; 8/61)	8	16	24	64	115	165
48-The Flintstones (No. 1)(Bedrock Bedlam)(7/61)(TV)(Hanna-Barbera) 1st app. in comics	19	38	57	152	269	385
49-Huey, Dewey & Louie Back to School (Disney; 9/61)	9	18	27	72	124	175
50-Marge's Little Lulu & Witch Hazel Trick 'N' Treat (10/61)	11	22	33	88	157	225
51-Tarzan, King of the Jungle by Jesse Marsh (11/61)-Painted-c	8	16	24	64	110	155
52-Uncle Donald & His Nephews Dude Ranch (Disney; 11/61)	8	16	24	64	115	165
53-Donald Duck Merry Christmas (Disney; 12/61)	8	16	24	64	112	160
54-Woody Woodpecker's Christmas Party (12/61)-Issued after No. 55	7	14	21	56	98	140
55-Daisy Duck & Uncle Scrooge Showboat (Disney; 9/61)	8	16	24	64	117	170

NOTE: All issues printed with & without ad on back cover.

DELL JUNIOR TREASURY
Dell Publishing Co.: June, 1955 - No. 10, Oct, 1957 (15¢) (All painted-c)

1-Alice in Wonderland; r/4-Color #331 (52 pgs.)	9	18	27	63	107	150
2-Aladdin & the Wonderful Lamp	7	14	21	49	80	110
3-Gulliver's Travels (1/56)	6	12	18	43	69	95
4-Adventures of Mr. Frog & Miss Mouse	7	14	21	45	73	100
5-The Wizard of Oz (7/56)	7	14	21	49	80	110
6-10: 6-Heidi (10/56). 7-Santa and the Angel. 8-Raggedy Ann and the Came with the Wrinkled Knees. 9-Clementina the Flying Pig. 10-Adventures of Tom Sawyer	6	12	18	43	69	95

DEMOLITION MAN
DC Comics: Nov, 1993 - No. 4, Feb, 1994 ($1.75, color, limited series)

1-4-Movie adaptation						2.50

DEMON, THE (See Detective Comics No. 482-485)
National Periodical Publications: Aug-Sept, 1972 - V3#16, Jan, 1974

1-Origin; Kirby-c/a in all	6	12	18	37	59	80
2-5	3	6	9	20	30	40
6-16	3	6	9	15	21	26

DEMON, THE (1st limited series)(Also see Cosmic Odyssey #2)
DC Comics: Nov, 1986 - No. 4, Feb, 1987 (75¢, limited series)(#2 has #4 of 4 on-c)

1-4: Matt Wagner-a(p) & scripts in all. 4-Demon & Jason Blood become separate entities.						3.00

DEMON, THE (2nd Series)
DC Comics: July, 1990 - No. 58, May, 1995 ($1.50/$1.75/$1.95)

1-Grant scripts begin, ends #39: 1-4-Painted-c						4.00
2-18,20-27,29-39,41,42: 3,8-Batman app. (cameo #4). 12-Bisley painted-c. 12-15,21-Lobo app. (1 pg. cameo #11). 23-Robin app. 29-Superman app. 31,33-39-Lobo app.						2.50
19,28,40: 19-($2.50, 44 pgs.)-Lobo poster stapled inside. 28-Superman-c/story; begin $1.75-c. 40-Garth Ennis scripts begin						4.00
43-45-Hitman app.	1	2	3	5	7	9
46-48 Return of The Haunted Tank-c/s. 48-Begin $1.95-c.						5.00
49,51,0-(10/94),55-58: 51-(9/94)						2.50
50 ($2.95, 52 pgs.)						3.00
52-54-Hitman-s						5.00
Annual 1 (1992, $3.00, 68 pgs.)-Eclipso-c/story						3.00
Annual 2 (1993, $3.50, 68 pgs.)-1st app. of Hitman	2	4	6	9	13	16

NOTE: *Alan Grant* scripts in #1-16, 20, 21, 23-25, 30-39, Annual 1. *Wagner* a/scripts-22.

DEMON DREAMS

Pacific Comics: Feb, 1984 - No. 2, May, 1984

1,2-Mostly r-/Heavy Metal						2.50

DEMON: DRIVEN OUT
DC Comics: Nov, 2003 - No. 6, Apr, 2004 ($2.50, limited series)

1-6-Dysart-s/Mhan-a						2.50

DEMON-HUNTER
Seaboard Periodicals (Atlas): Sept, 1975

1-Origin/1st app. Demon-Hunter; Buckler-c/a	1	2	3	5	6	9

DEMON KNIGHT: A GRIMJACK GRAPHIC NOVEL
First Publishing: 1990 ($8.95, 52 pgs.)

nn-Flint Henry-a						9.00

DEMONWARS (R.A. Salvatore's...) ("The Demon Awakens" on cover)
Devil's Due Publishing: Jan, 2007 - No. 3 ($4.99/$5.50, limited series)

1-Daab-s/Seeley-a						5.00
2,3-($5.50)						5.50

DEMONWARS: EYE FOR AN EYE (R.A. Salvatore's...)
CrossGeneration Comics (Code 6 Comics): Jun, 2003 - No. 5, Nov, 2003 ($2.95, lim. series)

1-5-Ciencin-s/Tocchini-a						3.00

DEMONWARS: TRIAL BY FIRE (R.A. Salvatore's...)
CrossGeneration Comics (Code 6 Comics): Jan, 2003 - No. 5, May, 2003 ($2.95, lim. series)

1-5-Ciencin-s/Wagner-a						3.00
TPB (2003, $9.95) r/#1-5; new short story by Salvatore						10.00

DENNIS THE MENACE (TV with 1959 issues) (Becomes ...Fun Fest Series; See The Best of... & The Very Best of...)(...Fun Fest on-c only to #156-166)
Standard Comics/Pines/Hallden (Fawcett) No.32 on: 8/53 - #14, 1/56; #15, 3/56 - #31, 11/58; #32, 1/59 - #166, 11/79

1-1st app. Dennis, Mr. & Mrs. Wilson, Ruff & Dennis' mom & dad; Wiseman-a, written by Fred Toole-most issues	72	144	216	450	750	1050
2	31	62	93	178	282	385
3-10: 8-Last pre-code issue	16	32	48	94	147	200
11-20	13	26	39	72	101	130
21,23-30	10	20	30	56	76	95
22-1st app. Margaret w/blonde hair	12	24	36	69	97	125
31-1st app. Joey	12	24	36	69	97	125
32-38,40(1/60): 37-A-bomb blast panel	8	16	24	40	50	60
39-1st app. Gina (11/59)	8	16	24	44	57	70
41-60(7/62)	4	8	12	21	30	40
61-80(9/65),100(1/69)	3	6	9	14	19	24
81-99	2	4	6	11	16	20
101-117: 102-Last 12¢ issue	2	4	6	9	12	15
118(1/72)-131 (All 52 pages)	2	4	6	10	14	18
132(1/74)-142,144-160	1	2	3	5	7	9
143(3/76) Olympic-c/s; low print	2	4	6	10	14	18
161-166	1	3	4	6	8	10

NOTE: *Wiseman* c/a-1-46, 53, 68, 69.

DENNIS THE MENACE (Giants) (No. 1 titled Giant Vacation Special; becomes Dennis the Menace Bonus Magazine No. 76 on)
(#1-8,18,23,25,30,38: 100 pgs.; rest to #41: 84 pgs.; #42-75: 68 pgs.)
Standard/Pines/Hallden(Fawcett): Summer, 1955 - No. 75, Dec, 1969

nn-Giant Vacation Special (Summ/55-Standard)	16	32	48	94	147	200
nn-Christmas issue (Winter '55)	15	30	45	85	130	175
2-Giant Vacation Special (Summer '56-Pines)	14	28	42	76	108	140
3-Giant Christmas issue (Winter '56-Pines)	13	26	39	72	101	130
4-Giant Vacation Special (Summer '57-Pines)	12	24	36	67	94	120
5-Giant Christmas issue (Winter '57-Pines)	12	24	36	67	94	120
6-In Hawaii (Giant Vacation Special)(Summer '58-Pines)	11	22	33	62	86	110
6-In Hawaii (Summer '59-Hallden)-2nd printing; says 3rd large printing on-c						
6-In Hawaii (Summer '60)-3rd printing; says 4th large printing on-c						
6-In Hawaii (Summer '62)-4th printing; says 5th large printing on-c each....	8	16	24	42	54	65
6-Giant Christmas issue (Winter '58)	11	22	33	62	86	110
7-In Hollywood (Winter '59-Hallden)	5	10	15	32	51	70
7-In Hollywood (Summer '61)-2nd printing	3	6	9	21	32	42
8-In Mexico (Winter '60, 100 pgs.-Hallden/Fawcett)	5	10	15	32	51	70
8-In Mexico (Summer '62, 2nd printing)	3	6	9	21	32	42
9-Goes to Camp (Summer '61, 84 pgs.)-1st CCA approved issue	5	10	15	32	51	70
9-Goes to Camp (Summer '62)-2nd printing	3	6	9	21	32	42

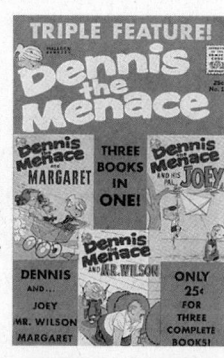

Dennis the Menace Triple Feature #1 © FAW

Desperado #2 © LEV

Desperadoes: Quiet of the Grave #3 © WSP

	GD	VG	FN	VF	VF/NM	NM-
	2.0	4.0	6.0	8.0	9.0	9.2

10-12: 10-X-Mas issue (Winter '61), 11-Giant Christmas issue (Winter '62),
12-Triple Feature (Winter '62)

		5	10	15	35	55	75

13-17: 13-Best of Dennis the Menace (Spring '63)-Reprints, 14-And His Dog Ruff
(Summer '63), 15-In Washington, D.C. (Summer '63), 16-Goes to Camp (Summer '63)-
Reprints No. 9, 17-& His Pal Joey (Winter '63)

	4	8	12	22	34	45
18-In Hawaii (Reprints No. 6)	3	6	9	18	27	35
19-Giant Christmas issue (Winter '63)	4	8	12	22	34	45
20-Spring Special (Spring '64)	4	8	12	22	34	45
21-40 (Summer '66): 30-r/#6. #35-Xmas spec.Wint,'65	3	6	9	17	25	32
41-60 (Fall '68)	2	4	6	13	18	22
61-75 (12/69): 68-Partial-r/#6	2	4	6	10	14	18

NOTE: Wiseman c/a-1-8, 12, 14, 15, 17, 20, 22, 27, 28, 31, 35, 36, 41, 49.

DENNIS THE MENACE
Marvel Comics Group: Nov, 1981 - No. 13, Nov, 1982

1-New-a	2	4	6	8	10	12
2-13: 2-New art. 3-Part-r. 4,5-r. 5-X-Mas-c & issue, 7-Spider Kid-c/sty	1	2	3	4	5	7

NOTE: Hank Ketcham c-most; a-3, 12. Wiseman a-4, 5.

DENNIS THE MENACE AND HIS DOG RUFF
Hallden/Fawcett: Summer, 1961

1-Wiseman-c/a	5	10	15	32	51	70

DENNIS THE MENACE AND HIS FRIENDS
Fawcett Publ.: 1969; No. 5, Jan, 1970 - No. 46, April, 1980 (All reprints)

Dennis the Menace & Joey No. 2 (7/69)	2	4	6	13	18	22
Dennis the Menace & Ruff No. 2 (9/69)	2	4	6	13	18	22
Dennis the Menace & Mr. Wilson No. 1 (10/69)	3	6	9	16	22	28
Dennis & Margaret No. 1 (Winter '69)	3	6	9	16	22	28
5-12: 5-Dennis the Menace & Margaret. 6-...& Joey. 7-...& Ruff. 8-...& Mr. Wilson	2	4	6	8	11	14
13-21-(52 pg Giants): 13-(1/72). 21-(1/74)	2	4	6	10	14	18
22-37	1	3	4	6	8	10
38-46 (Digest size, 148 pgs.), 4/78, 95¢)	2	4	6	8	11	14

NOTE: Titles rotate every four issues, beginning with No. 5. Joey issues: #2(7/69),6,10,14,18,22,26,30,34. Ruff issues: #2(9/69), 7,11,15,19,23,27,31,35. Mr. Wilson issues: #1(10/69),8,12,16,20,24,28,32,36. Margaret issues: #1(Wint'69),5,9,13,17,21,25,29,33,37.

DENNIS THE MENACE AND HIS PAL JOEY
Fawcett Publ.: Summer, 1961 (10¢) (See Dennis the Menace Giants No. 45)

1-Wiseman-c/a	5	10	15	32	51	70

DENNIS THE MENACE AND THE BIBLE KIDS
Word Books: 1977 (36 pgs.)

1-6: 1-Jesus. 2-Joseph. 3-David. 4-The Bible Girls. 5-Moses. 6-More About Jesus

	2	4	6	8	10	12

7-9-Low print run: 7-The Lord's Prayer. 8-Stories Jesus told. 9-Paul, God's Traveller

	2	4	6	11	16	20
10-Low print run; In the Beginning	3	6	9	16	23	30

NOTE: Ketcham c/a in all.

DENNIS THE MENACE BIG BONUS SERIES
Fawcett Publications: No. 10, Feb, 1980 - No. 11, Apr, 1980

10,11	1	2	3	5	6	8

DENNIS THE MENACE BONUS MAGAZINE (Formerly Dennis the Menace Giants Nos. 1-75)
(...Big Bonus Series on-c for #174-194)
Fawcett Publications: No. 76, 1/70 - No. 95, 7/71; No. 95, 7/71; No. 97, '71; No. 194, 10/79;
(No. 76-124: 68 pgs.; No. 125-163: 52 pgs.; No. 164 on: 36 pgs.)

76-90(3/71)	2	4	6	10	14	18
91-95, 97-110(10/72): Two #95's with same date(7/71) A-Summer Games, and						
B-That's Our Boy. No #96	2	4	6	9	13	16
111-124	2	4	6	8	10	12
125-163-(52 pgs.)	2	4	6	8	10	12
164-190: 166-Indicia printed backwards	1	2	3	4	5	7

DENNIS THE MENACE COMICS DIGEST
Marvel Comics Group: April, 1982 - No. 3, Aug, 1982 ($1.25, digest-size)

1-3-Reprints	1	3	4	6	8	10
1-Mistakenly printed with DC emblem on cover	2	4	6	10	12	15

NOTE: Ketcham c-all. Wiseman a-all. A few thousand #1's were published with a DC emblem on cover.

DENNIS THE MENACE FUN BOOK
Fawcett Publications/Standard Comics: 1960 (100 pgs.)

1-Part Wiseman-a	6	12	18	39	62	85

DENNIS THE MENACE FUN FEST SERIES (Formerly Dennis the Menace #166)

Hallden (Fawcett): No. 16, Jan, 1980 - No. 17, Mar, 1980 (40¢)

16,17-By Hank Ketcham	1	2	3	4	5	7

DENNIS THE MENACE POCKET FULL OF FUN!
Fawcett Publications (Hallden): Spring, 1969 - No. 50, March, 1980 (196 pgs.) (Digest size)

1-Reprints in all issues	5	10	15	32	51	70
2-10	4	8	12	22	34	45
11-20	3	6	9	14	20	25
21-28	2	4	6	10	14	18
29-50: 35,40,46-Sunday strip-r	2	4	6	8	10	12

NOTE: No. 1-28 are 196 pgs.; No. 29-36: 164 pgs.; No. 37: 148 pgs.; No. 38 on: 132 pgs. No. 8, 11, 15, 21, 25, 29 all contain strip reprints.

DENNIS THE MENACE TELEVISION SPECIAL
Fawcett Publ. (Hallden Div.): Summer, 1961 - No. 2, Spring, 1962 (Giant)

1	6	12	18	37	59	80
2	3	6	9	21	32	42

DENNIS THE MENACE TRIPLE FEATURE
Fawcett Publications: Winter, 1961 (Giant)

1-Wiseman-c/a	6	12	18	37	59	80

DEPUTY, THE (TV)
Dell Publishing Co.: No. 1077, Feb-Apr, 1960 - No. 1225, Oct-Dec, 1961
(all-Henry Fonda photo-c)

Four Color 1077 (#1)-Buscema-a	11	22	33	79	140	200
Four Color 1130 (9-11/60)-Buscema-a,1225	9	18	27	63	107	150

DEPUTY DAWG (TV) (Also see New Terrytoons)
Dell Publishing Co./Gold Key: Oct-Dec, 1961 - No. 1299, 1962; No. 1, Aug, 1965

Four Color 1238,1299	10	20	30	73	129	185
1(10164-508)(8/65)-Gold Key	10	20	30	73	129	185

DEPUTY DAWG PRESENTS DINKY DUCK AND HASHIMOTO-SAN (TV)
Gold Key: August, 1965

1(10159-508)	10	20	30	67	116	165

DESERT GOLD (See Zane Grey 4-Color 467)

DESIGN FOR SURVIVAL (Gen. Thomas S. Power's...)
American Security Council Press: 1968 (36 pgs. in color) (25¢)

nn-Propaganda against the Threat of Communism-Aircraft cover; H-Bomb panel

	3	6	9	17	25	32
Twin Circle Edition-Cover shows panels from inside	2	4	6	11	16	20

DESOLATION JONES
DC Comics (WildStorm): July, 2005 - Present ($2.95/$2.99)

1-8: 1-6-Warren Ellis-s/J.H. Williams-a. 7,8-Zezelj-a						3.00
...: Made in England TPB (2006, $14.99) r/series; cover gallery						15.00

DESPERADO (Becomes Black Diamond Western No. 9 on)
Lev Gleason Publications: June, 1948 - No. 8, Feb, 1949 (All 52 pgs.)

1-Biro-c on all; contains inside photo-c of Charles Biro, Lev Gleason & Bob Wood						
	15	30	45	86	133	180
2	10	20	30	54	72	90
3-Story with over 20 killings	10	20	30	56	76	95
4-8	8	16	24	42	54	65

NOTE: Barry a-2. Fuje a-4, 8. Guardineer a-5-7. Kida a-3-7. Ed Moore a-4, 6.

DESPERADO PRIMER
Image Comics (Desperado): Apr, 2005 ($1.99, one-shot)

1-Previews of Roundeye, World Traveler, A Mirror To The Soul; Bolland-c						2.50

DESPERADOES
Image Comics (Homage): Sept, 1997 - No. 5, June, 1998 ($2.50/$2.95)

1-5-Mariotte-s/Cassaday-c/a: 1-($2.50-c). 2-5-($2.95)						3.00
...: A Moment's Sunlight TPB ('98, $16.95) r/#1-5						17.00
...: Epidemic! (11/99, $5.95) Mariotte-s						6.00

DESPERADOES: BANNERS OF GOLD
IDW Publishing: Dec, 2004 - No. 5, Apr, 2005 ($3.99, limited series)

1-5: Mariotte-s/Haun-a. 1-Cassaday-c						4.00

DESPERADOES: BUFFALO DREAMS
IDW Publishing: Jan, 2007 - No. 4, Apr, 2007 ($3.99, limited series)

1-4: Mariotte-s/Dose-a/c						4.00

DESPERADOES: QUIET OF THE GRAVE
DC Comics (Homage): Jul, 2001 - No. 5, Nov, 2001 ($2.95)

1-5-Jeff Mariotte-s/John Severin-c/a						3.00

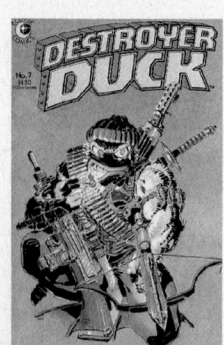
Destroyer Duck #7 © Gerber & Kirby

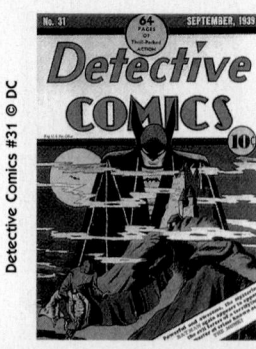
Detective Comics #31 © DC

Detective Comics #73 © DC

	GD 2.0	VG 4.0	FN 6.0	VF 8.0	VF/NM 9.0	NM- 9.2

TPB (2002, $14.95) r/#1-5; intro. by Brian Keene   15.00

DESPERATE TIMES (See Savage Dragon)
Image Comics: Jun, 1998 - No. 4, Dec, 1998; Nov, 2000 - No. 4, July, 2001 ($2.95, B&W)
1-4-Chris Eliopoulos-s/a   3.00
(Vol. 2) 1-4   3.00
(Vol. 3) 0-(1/04, $3.50) Pages read sideways   3.50
(Vol. 3) 1-Pages read sideways   3.00

DESTINATION MOON (See Fawcett Movie Comics, Space Adventures #20, 23, & Strange Adventures #1)

DESTINY: A CHRONICLE OF DEATHS FORETOLD (See Sandman)
DC Comics (Vertigo): 1997 - No.3, 1998 ($5.95, limited series)
1-3-Alisa Kwitney-s in all: 1-Kent Williams & Michael Zulli-a, Williams painted-c. 2-Williams &
Scott Hampton-painted-c/a. 3-Williams & Guay-a   6.00
TPB (2000, $14.95) r/series   15.00

DESTROY!!
Eclipse Comics: 1986 ($4.95, B&W, magazine-size, one-shot)
1   5.00
3-D Special 1-r-/#1 ($2.50)   5.00

DESTROYER, THE
Marvel Comics: Nov, 1989 - No. 9, Jun, 1990 ($2.25, B&W, magazine, 52 pgs.)
1-Based on Remo Williams movie, paperbacks   6.00
2-9: 2-Williamson part inks. 4-Ditko-a   4.00

DESTROYER, THE
Marvel Comics: V2#1, March, 1991 ($1.95, 52 pgs.)
V3#1, Dec, 1991 - No. 4, Mar, 1992 ($1.95, mini-series)
V2#1,V3#1-4: Based on Remo Williams paperbacks. V3#1-4-Simonson-c. 3-Morrow-a   2.50

DESTROYER,THE (Also see Solar, Man of the Atom)
Valiant: Apr, 1995 ($2.95, color, one-shot)
0-Indicia indicates #1   3.00

DESTROYER DUCK
Eclipse Comics: Feb, 1982 - No. 7, May, 1984 (#2-7: Baxter paper) ($1.50)

	GD 2.0	VG 4.0	FN 6.0	VF 8.0	VF/NM 9.0	NM- 9.2
1-Origin Destroyer Duck; 1st app. Groo; Kirby-c/a(p) 1	3	4	6	8		10
2-5: 2-Starling back-up begins; Kirby-c/a(p) thru #5						5.00
6,7						4.00

NOTE: *Neal Adams* c-1i. *Kirby* c/a-1-5p. *Miller* c-7.

DESTRUCTOR, THE
Atlas/Seaboard: February, 1975 - No. 4, Aug, 1975

	GD 2.0	VG 4.0	FN 6.0	VF 8.0	VF/NM 9.0	NM- 9.2
1-Origin/1st app.; Ditko/Wood-a; Wood-c(i)	1	3	4	6	8	10
2-4: 2-Ditko/Wood-a. 3,4-Ditko-a(p)	1	2	3	5	6	8

DETECTIVE COMICS (Also see other Batman titles)
National Periodical Publications/DC Comics: Mar, 1937 - Present

1-(Scarce)-Slam Bradley & Spy by Siegel & Shuster, Speed Saunders by Guardineer, Flat
Foot Flannigan by Gustavson, Cosmo, the Phantom of Disguise, Buck Marshall, Bruce
Nelson begin; Chin Lung in 'Claws of the Red Dragon' serial begins; Vincent Sullivan-c
   9,700 19,400 29,100 68,000 – –
2 (Rare)-Creig Flessel-a begin; new logo 2700 5400 8100 19,000 – –
3 (Rare) 2000 4000 6000 14,000 – –
4,5: 5-Larry Steele begins 1053 2106 3159 5528 7764 10,000
6,7,9,10 758 1516 2274 3980 5590 7200
8-Mister Chang-c; classic-c 1137 2274 3411 5969 8385 10,800
11-17,19: 16-Has interior ad for Action Comics #1. 17-1st app. Fu Manchu in Detective
  590 1180 1770 3098 4349 5600
18-Fu Manchu-s; last Flessel-c 947 1894 2841 4972 6986 9000
20-The Crimson Avenger begins (1st app.) 884 1768 2652 4641 6521 8400
21,23-25 463 926 1389 2431 3416 4400
22-1st Crimson Avenger-c by Chambers (12/38) 632 1264 1896 3318 4659 6000
26 432 864 1296 2268 3184 4100
27-The Bat-Man & Commissioner Gordon begin (1st app.), created by Bill Finger & Bob Kane
(5/39); Batman-c (1st)(by Kane). Bat-Man's secret identity revealed as Bruce Wayne in 6pg.
sty. Signed Rob't Kane (also see Det. Picture Stories #5 & Funny Pages V3#1)
  35,000 70,000 105,000 225,000 375,000 525,000
27-Reprint, Oversize 13-1/2x10". WARNING: This comic is an exact duplicate reprint of the original
except for its size. DC published it in 1974 with a second cover titling it as Famous First Edition. There have been
many reported cases of the outer cover being removed and the interior sold as the original edition. The reprint
with the new outer cover removed is practically worthless; see Famous First Edition for value.
28-2nd app. The Batman (6 pg. story); non-Bat-Man-c; signed Rob't Kane
  2050 4100 6150 15,400 27,700 40,000
29-1st app. Doctor Death-c/story, Batman's 1st name villain. 1st 2 part story (10 pgs.).
2nd Batman-c by Kane 3385 6770 10,155 25,400 45,700 66,000

	GD 2.0	VG 4.0	FN 6.0	VF 8.0	VF/NM 9.0	NM- 9.2

30-Dr. Death app. Story concludes from issue #29. Classic Batman splash panel by Kane.
  829 1658 2487 5803 10,152 14,500
31-Classic Batman over castle cover; 1st app. The Monk & 1st Julie Madison (Bruce Wayne's
1st love interest); 1st Batplane (Bat-Gyro) and Batarang; 2nd 2-part Batman adventure.
Gardner Fox takes over script from Bill Finger. 1st mention of locale (New York City) where
Batman lives 3700 7400 11,100 27,750 48,875 70,000
32-Batman story concludes from issue #31. 1st app. Dala (Monk's assistant). Batman uses
gun for 1st time to slay The Monk and Dala. This was the 1st time a costumed hero used a
gun in comic books. 1st Batman head logo on cover
  714 1428 2142 5000 8750 12,500
33-Origin The Batman (2 pgs.)(1st told origin); Batman gun holster-c; Batman w/smoking gun
panel at end of story. Batman story now 12 pgs. Classic Batman-c
  4125 8250 12,375 31,000 55,500 80,000
34-2nd Crimson Avenger-c by Creig Flessel and last non Batman-c. Story from issue #32
x-over as Bruce Wayne sees Julie Madison off to America from Paris. Classic Batman
splash panel used later in Batman #1 for origin story. Steve Malone begins
  543 1086 1629 3800 6650 9500
35-Classic Batman hypodermic needle-c that reflects story in issue #34. Classic
Batman with smoking .45 automatic splash panel. Batman-c begin
  1266 2532 3800 9500 16,750 24,000
36-Batman-c that reflects adventure in issue #35. Origin/1st app. of Dr. Hugo
Strange (1st major villain, 2/40). 1st finned-gloves worn by Batman
  914 1828 2742 6400 11,200 16,000
37-Last solo Golden-Age Batman adventure in Detective Comics. Panel at end of story
reflects solo Batman adventure in Batman #1 that was originally planned for
Detective #38. Cliff Crosby begins 800 1600 2400 5600 9800 14,000
38-Origin/1st app. Robin the Boy Wonder (4/40); Batman and Robin-c; cover by Kane
& Robinson taken from splash page 3850 7700 11,550 29,000 52,000 75,000
39-Opium story; Clayface app. in 1 panel ad at the end of the Batman story
  629 1258 1887 4400 7700 11,000
40-Origin & 1st app. Clay Face (Basil Karlo); 1st Joker cover app. (6/40); Joker story intended
for this issue was used in Batman #1 instead; cover is similar to splash page in
2nd Joker story in Batman #1 743 1486 2229 5200 9100 13,000
41-Robin's 1st solo 376 752 1128 2444 4322 6200
42-44: 44-Crimson Avenger-new costume 290 580 870 1813 3007 4200
45-1st Joker story in Det. (3rd book app. & 4th story app. over all, 11/40)
  376 752 1128 2444 4322 6200
46-50: 46-Death of Hugo Strange. 48-1st time car called Batmobile (2/41); Gotham City 1st
mention in Detective (1st mentioned in Wow #1; also see Batman #4).
  269 538 807 1681 2791 3900
49-Last Clay Face 269 538 807 1681 2791 3900
51-57 179 358 537 1119 1860 2600
58-1st Penguin app. (12/41); last Speed Saunders; Fred Ray-c
  440 880 1320 3080 5390 7700
59,60: 59-Last Steve Malone; 2nd Penguin; Wing becomes Crimson Avenger's aide.
60-Intro. Air Wave; Joker app. (2nd in Det.) 186 372 558 1163 1932 2700
61,63-Last Cliff Crosby; 1st app. Mr. Baffle 166 332 498 1038 1719 2400
62-Joker-c/story (2nd Joker-c, 4/42) 297 594 891 1856 3078 4300
64-Origin & 1st app. Boy Commandos by Simon & Kirby (6/42); Joker app.
  382 764 1146 2483 4392 6300
65-1st Boy Commandos-c (S&K-a on Boy Commandos & Ray/Robinson-a on
Batman & Robin on-c; 4 artists on one-c) 300 600 900 1881 3141 4400
66-Origin & 1st app. Two-Face 423 846 1269 2750 4875 7000
67-1st Penguin-c (9/42) 276 552 828 1725 2863 4000
68-Two-Face-c/story; 1st Two-Face-c 190 380 570 1188 1969 2750
69-Joker-c/story 190 380 570 1188 1969 2750
70 138 276 414 863 1432 2000
71-Joker-c/story 179 358 537 1119 1860 2600
72,74,75: 74-1st app Tweedledum & Tweedledee plus-c; S&K-a
  117 234 351 731 1216 1700
73-Scarecrow-c/story (1st Scarecrow-c) 152 304 456 950 1575 2200
76-Newsboy Legion & The Sandman x-over in Boy Commandos; S&K-a;
Joker-c/story 179 358 537 1119 1860 2600
77-79: All S&K-a 121 242 363 756 1253 1750
80-Two-Face app.; S&K-a 134 268 402 838 1394 1950
81,82,84,86-90: 81-1st Cavalier-c & app. 89-Last Crimson Avenger; 2nd Cavalier-c & app.
  95 190 285 594 985 1375
83-1st "skinny" Alfred (1/44)(see Batman #21); last S&K Boy Commandos (also #92,128);
most issues #84 on signed S&K are not by them
  103 206 309 644 1072 1500
85-Joker-c/story; last Spy; Kirby/Klech Boy Commandos
  131 262 393 819 1360 1900
91,102-Joker-c/story 124 248 373 775 1288 1800
92-98: 96-Alfred's last name 'Beagle' revealed, later changed to 'Pennyworth' in #214
  79 158 237 494 822 1150

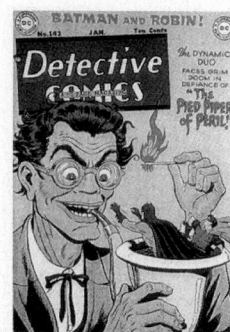

Detective Comics #143 © DC

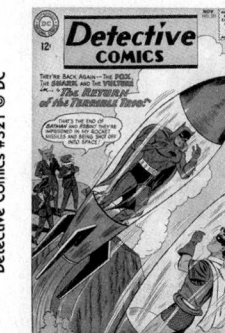

Detective Comics #321 © DC

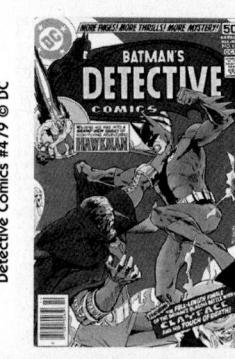

Detective Comics #479 © DC

	GD 2.0	VG 4.0	FN 6.0	VF 8.0	VF/NM 9.0	NM- 9.2
99-Penguin-c/story	121	242	363	756	1253	1750
100 (6/45)	121	242	363	756	1253	1750
101,103-108,110-113,115-117,119: 108-1st Bat-signal-c (2/46). 114-1st small logo (8/46)	72	144	216	450	750	1050
109,114,118-Joker-c/stories	109	218	327	681	1128	1575
120-Penguin-c/story (white-c, rare above fine)	172	344	516	1075	1788	2500
121,123,125,127,129,130	69	138	207	431	716	1000
122-1st Catwoman-c (4/47)	152	304	456	950	1575	2200
124,128-Joker-c/stories	100	200	300	625	1038	1450
126-Penguin-c	100	200	300	625	1038	1450
131-134,136,139: 134-Penguin-c/story	64	128	192	400	663	925
135-Frankenstein-c/story	81	162	243	506	841	1175
137-Joker-c/story; last Air Wave	85	170	255	531	878	1225
138-Origin Robotman (see Star Spangled #7 for 1st app.); series ends #202	110	220	330	688	1144	1600
140-The Riddler-c/story (1st app., 10/48)	457	914	1371	3200	5600	8000
141,143-148,150: 150-Last Boy Commandos	64	128	192	400	663	925
142-2nd Riddler-c/story	124	248	372	775	1288	1800
149-Joker-c/story	85	170	255	531	878	1225
151-Origin & 1st app. Pow Wow Smith, Indian lawman (9/49) & begins series	74	148	222	463	769	1075
152,154,155,157-160: 152-Last Slam Bradley	64	128	192	400	663	925
153-1st app. Roy Raymond TV Detective (11/49) ; origin The Human Fly	68	136	204	425	705	985
156(2/50)-The new classic Batmobile	90	180	270	563	932	1300
161-167,169,170,172-176: Last 52 pg. issue	59	118	177	369	610	850
168-Origin the Joker	352	704	1056	2288	4044	5800
171-Penguin-c	90	180	270	563	932	1300
177-179,181-186,188,189,191,192,194-199,201,202,204,206-210,212,214-216: 184-1st app. Fire Fly. 185-Secret of Batman's utility belt. 187-Two-Face app. 202-Last Robotman & Pow Wow Smith. 215-1st app. of Batmen of all Nations. 216-Last precode (2/55)	54	108	162	338	557	775
180,193-Joker-c/story	64	128	192	400	663	925
187-Two-Face-c/story	59	118	177	369	610	850
190-Origin Batman retold	78	156	234	488	807	1125
200(10/53), 205: 205-Origin Batcave	71	142	213	444	740	1035
203,211-Catwoman-c/stories	66	132	198	413	682	950
213-Origin & 1st app. Mirror Man	66	132	198	413	682	950
217-224: 218-Batman Jr. & Robin Sr. app.	47	94	141	287	474	660
225-(11/55)-1st app. Martian Manhunter (J'onn J'onzz); origin begins; also see Batman #78	372	744	1116	3348	6324	9300
226-Origin Martian Manhunter cont'd (2nd app.)	138	276	414	863	1432	2000
227-229: Martian Manhunter stories in all	54	108	162	338	557	775
230-1st app. Mad Hatter; brief recap origin of Martian Manhunter	57	114	171	356	591	825
231-Brief origin recap Martian Manhunter	43	86	129	262	431	600
232,234,237-240: 239-Early DC grey tone-c	41	82	123	252	406	560
233-Origin & 1st app. Batwoman (7/56)	152	304	456	950	1575	2200
235-Origin Batman & his costume; tells how Bruce Wayne's father (Thomas Wayne) wore Bat costume & fought crime (reprinted in Batman #255)	66	132	198	413	682	950
236-1st S.A. issue; J'onn J'onzz talks to parents and Mars-1st since being stranded on Earth; 1st app. Bat-Tank?	45	90	135	275	450	625
241-260: 246-Intro. Diane Meade, John Jones' girl. 249-Batwoman-c/app. 253-Intro. & 1st app. The Terrible Trio. 254-Bat-Hound-c/story. 257-Intro. & 1st app. Whirly Bats. 259-1st app. The Calendar Man	36	72	108	208	329	450
261-264,266,268-271: 261-J. Jones tie-in to sci/fi movie "Incredible Shrinking Man"; 1st app. Dr. Double X. 262-Origin Jackal. 268,271-Manhunter origin recap	28	56	84	162	256	350
265-Batman's origin retold with new facts	40	80	120	240	383	525
267-Origin & 1st app. Bat-Mite (5/59)	41	82	123	252	406	560
272,274,275,277-280	23	46	69	130	205	280
273-J'onn J'onzz i.d. revealed for 1st time	23	46	69	135	213	290
276-2nd app. Bat-Mite	27	54	81	156	246	335
281-292, 294-297: 286,292-Batwoman-c/app. 287-Origin J'onn J'onzz retold. 289-Bat-Mite-c/story. 292-Last Roy Raymond. 297-Last 10¢ issue (11/61)	18	36	54	103	162	220
293-(7/61)-Aquaman begins (pre #1); ends #300	18	36	54	107	169	230
298-(12/61)-1st modern Clayface (Matt Hagen)	23	46	69	171	306	440
299, 300-(2/62)-Aquaman ends	11	22	33	79	140	200
301-(3/62)-J'onn J'onzz returns to Mars (1st time since stranded on Earth six years before)	9	18	27	65	113	160
302-317,319-321,323,324,326,329,330: 302,307-Batwoman-c/app. 311-Intro. Zook in John Jones; 1st app. Cat-Man. 321-2nd Terrible Trio. 326-Last J'onn J'onzz, story cont'd in House of Mystery #143; intro. Idol-Head of Diabolu	8	16	24	58	97	135
318,322,325: 318,325-Cat-Man-c/story (2nd & 3rd app.); also 1st & 2nd app. Batwoman as the Cat-Woman. 322-Bat-Girl's 1st/only app. in Det. (6th in all); Batman cameo in J'onn J'onzz (only hero to app. in series)	9	18	27	60	100	140
327-(5/64)-Elongated Man begins, ends #383; 1st new look Batman with new costume; Infantino/Giella new look-a begins; Batman with gun	12	24	36	82	146	210
328-Death of Alfred; Bob Kane biog, 2 pgs.	11	22	33	75	133	190
331,333-340: 334-1st app. The Outsider	7	14	21	47	76	105
342-358,360,361,366-368: 345-Intro Block Buster. 347-"What If" theme story (1/66). 351-Elongated Man new costume. 355-Zatanna x-over in Elongated Man. 356-Alfred brought back in Batman, early SA app.	6	12	18	41	66	90
332,341,365-Joker-c/stories	8	16	24	58	97	135
359-Intro/origin Batgirl (Barbara Gordon)-c/story (1/67); 1st Silver Age app. Killer Moth	15	30	45	105	188	270
362-364: 362,364-S.A. Riddler app. (early). 363-2nd app. new Batgirl	7	14	21	49	80	110
369(11/67)-N. Adams-a (Elongated Man); 3rd app. S.A. Catwoman (cameo; leads into Batman #197); 4th app. new Batgirl	9	18	27	63	107	150
370-1st Neal Adams-a on Batman (cover only, 12/67)	7	14	21	47	76	105
371-(1/68) 1st new Batmobile from TV show; classic Batgirl-c	8	16	24	54	90	125
372-376,378-386,389,390: 375-New Batmobile-c	5	10	15	35	55	75
377-S.A. Riddler-c/sty	6	12	18	39	62	85
387-r/1st Batman story from #27 (30th anniversary, 5/69); Joker-c; last 12¢ issue	7	14	21	50	83	115
388-Joker-c/story	7	14	21	47	76	105
391-394,396,398,399,401,403,405,406,409: 392-1st app. Jason Bard. 401-2nd Batgirl/Robin team-up. 405-Debut League of Assassins	4	8	12	28	44	60
395,397,402,404,407,408,410-Neal Adams-a. 404-Tribute to Enemy Ace	6	12	18	43	69	95
400-(6/70)-Origin & 1st app. Man-Bat; 1st Batgirl/Robin team-up (cont'd in #401); Neal Adams-a	15	30	45	107	191	275
411-(5/71) Intro. Talia, daughter of Ra's al Ghul (Ra's mentioned, but doesn't appear until Batman #232 (6/71); Bob Brown-a	4	8	12	28	44	60
412-413: 413-Last 15¢ issue	4	8	12	22	34	45
414-424: All-25¢, 52 pgs. 418-Creeper x-over. 424-Last Batgirl	4	8	12	24	37	50
425-436: 426,430,436-Elongated Man app. 428,434-Hawkman begins, ends #467	3	6	9	16	23	30
437-New Manhunter begins (10-11/73, 1st app.) by Simonson, ends #443	4	8	12	28	44	60
438-445 (All 100 Page Super Spectaculars): 438-Kubert Hawkman-r. 439-Origin Manhunter. 440-G.A. Manhunter(Adv. #79) by S&K, Hawkman, Dollman, Green Lantern, Toth-a. 441-G.A. Plastic Man, Batman, Ibis-r. 442-G.A. Newsboy Legion, Black Canary, Elongated Man, Dr. Fate-r. 443-Origin The Creeper-r; death of Manhunter; G.A. Green Lantern, Spectre-r; Batman-r/Batman #18. 444-G.A. Kid Eternity-r. 445-G.A. Dr. Midnite-r	6	12	18	37	59	80
446-460: 457-Origin retold & updated	2	4	6	13	18	22
461-465,470,480: 480-(44 pgs.). 463-1st app. Black Spider. 464-2nd app. Black Spider	3	6	9	10	14	18
466-468,471-474,478,479-Rogers-a in all: 466-1st app. Signalman since Batman #139. 470,471-1st modern app. Hugo Strange. 474-1st app. new Deadshot. 478-1st app. 3rd Clayface (Preston Payne). 479-(44 pgs.)	3	6	9	20	30	40
469-Intro/origin Dr. Phosphorous; Simonson-a	3	6	9	18	27	35
475,476-Joker-c/stories; Rogers-a	6	12	18	39	62	85
477-Neal Adams-a(r); Rogers-a (3 pgs.)	3	6	9	18	27	35
481-(Combined with Batman Family, 12-1/78-79, begin $1.00, 68 pg. issues, ends #495); 481-495-Batgirl, Robin solo stories	2	4	6	13	18	22
482-Starlin/Russell, Golden-a; The Demon begins (origin-r), ends #485 (by Ditko #483-485)	2	4	6	9	13	16
483-40th Anniversary issue; origin retold; Newton Batman begins	2	4	6	11	16	20
484-495 (68 pgs): 484-Origin Robin. 485-Death of Batwoman. 487-The Odd Man by Ditko. 489-Robin/Batgirl team-up. 490-Black Lightning begins. 491-(#492 on inside)	2	4	6	8	12	18
496-499	1	2	3	5	7	9
500-($1.50, 52 pgs.)-Batman/Deadman team-up; new Hawkman story by Joe Kubert; incorrectly says 500th anniv. of Det.	2	4	6	10	14	18
501-503,505-523: 512-2nd app. new Dr. Death. 519-Last Batgirl. 521-Green Arrow series begins. 523-Solomon Grundy app.						6.00
504-Joker-c/story	2	4	6	8	11	14
524-2nd app. Jason Todd (cameo)(3/83)	1	2	3	5	7	9

Detective Comics #546 © DC

Detective Comics #831 © DC

Devi #8 © Virgin Comics

	GD	VG	FN	VF	VF/NM	NM-			GD	VG	FN	VF	VF/NM	NM-
	2.0	4.0	6.0	8.0	9.0	9.2			2.0	4.0	6.0	8.0	9.0	9.2

525-3rd app. Jason Todd (See Batman #357)   1   2   3   5   7   9

526-Batman's 500th app. in Detective Comics ($1.50, 68 pgs.); Death of Jason Todd's parents, Joker-c/story (55 pgs.); Bob Kane pin-up   2   4   6   13   18   22

527-531,533,534,536-568,571,573: 538-Cat-Man-c/story cont'd from Batman #371.

542-Jason Todd quits as Robin (becomes Robin again #547). 549,550-Alan Moore scripts (Green Arrow). 554-1st new Black Canary (9/85). 566-Batman villains profiled.

567-Harlan Ellison scripts.   5.00

532,569,570-Joker-c/stories   2   4   6   8   10   12

535-Intro new Robin (JasonTodd)-1st appeared in Batman   1   2   3   5   6   8

572-(3/87, $1.25, 60 pgs.)-50th Anniv. of Det. Comics   6.00

574-Origin Batman & Jason Todd retold   1   2   3   5   6   8

575-Year 2 begins, ends #578   2   4   6   13   18   22

576-578: McFarlane-c/a. 578-Clay Face app.   2   4   6   13   18   22

579-597,599,601-610: 579-New bat wing logo. 583-1st app. villains Scarface & Ventriloquist.

589-595-(52 pgs.)-Each contain free 16 pg. Batman stories. 604-607-Mudpack storyline. 604,607-Contain Batman mini-posters. 610-Faked death of Penguin; artists names app. on tombstone on-c   3.00

598-($2.95, 84 pgs.)- "Blind Justice" storyline begins by Batman movie writer Sam Hamm, ends #600   4.00

600-(5/89, $2.95, 84 pgs.)-50th Anniv. of Batman in Det.; 1 pg. Neal Adams pin-up, among other artists   4.00

611-626,628-658: 612-1st new look Cat-Man; Catwoman app. 615- "The Penguin Affair" part 2 (See Batman #448,449). 617-Joker-c/story. 624-1st new Catwoman (w/death) & 1st new Batwoman. 626-Batman's 600th app. 642-Return of Scarface, part 2.

644-Last $1.00-c. 652,653-Huntress-c/story w/new costume plus Charest-c on both   3.00

627-($2.95, 84 pgs.)-Batman's 601st app. in Det.; reprints 1st story/#27 plus 3 versions (2 new) of same story   4.00

659-664: 659-Knightfall part 2; Kelley Jones-c. 660-Knightfall part 4; Bane-c by Sam Kieth. 661-Knightfall part 6; brief Joker & Riddler app. 662-Knightfall part 8; Riddler app.; Sam Kieth-c. 663-Knightfall part 10; Kelley Jones-c. 664-Knightfall part 12; Bane-c/story; Joker app.; continued in Showcase 93 #7 & 8; Jones-c   3.00

665-675: 665,666-Knightfall parts 16 & 18; 666-Bane-c/story. 667-Knightquest: The Crusade & new Batman begins (1st app. in Batman #500). 669-Begin $1.50-c; Knightquest, cont'd in Robin 1. 671,673-Joker app.   2.75

675-($2.95)-Collectors edition w/foil-c   3.50

676-($2.50, 52 pgs.)-KnightsEnd pt. 3   3.00

677,678: 677-KnightsEnd pt. 9. 678-(9/94)-Zero Hour tie-in.   2.75

679-685: 679-(11/94). 682-Troika pt. 3   2.75

682-($2.50) Embossed-c Troika pt. 3   3.00

686-699,701-719: 686-Begin $1.95-c. 693,694-Poison Ivy-c/app. 695-Contagion pt. 2; Catwoman, Penguin app. 698-Two-Face-c/app. 701-Legacy pt. 6; Batman vs. Bane-c/app. 702-Legacy Epilogue. 703-Final Night x-over. 705-707-Riddler-app. 714,715-Martian Manhunter-app.   2.75

700-($4.95, Collectors Edition)-Legacy pt. 1; Ra's Al Ghul-c/app; Talia & Bane app; book displayed at shops in envelope   5.00

700-($2.95, Regular Edition)-Different-c   3.00

720-740: 720,721-Cataclysm pts. 5,14. 723-Green Arrow app. 730-740-No Man's Land stories   2.75

741-($2.50) Endgame; Joker-c/app.   3.00

742-749,751-765: 742-New look Batman begins; 1st app. Crispus Allen (who later becomes the Spectre). 751,752-Poison Ivy app. 756-Superman-c/app. 759-762-Catwoman back-up   2.75

750-($4.95, 64 pgs.) Ra's al Ghul-c   5.00

766-772: 766,767-Bruce Wayne: Murderer pt. 1,8. 769-772-Bruce Wayne: Fugitive pts. 4,8,12,16   3.00

773,774,776-799: 773-Begin $2.75-c; Sienkiewicz-c. 777-784-Sale-c. 784-786-Alan Scott app. 787-Mad Hatter app. 793-Begin $2.95-c. 797-799-War Games   3.00

775-($3.50) Sienkiewicz-c   3.50

800-($3.50) Jock-c; aftermath of War Games; back-up by Lapham   3.50

801-816: 801-814-Lapham-s. 804-Mr. Freeze app. 809-War Crimes   3.00

817-836: 817-820: One Year Later 8-part x-over with Batman #651-654; Robinson-s/Bianchi-c. 819-Begin $2.99-c. 820-Dini-s/Williams III-a. 825-Doctor Phosperous app. 827-Debut of new Scarface. 831-Harley app.; Dini-s. 833,834-Zatanna & Joker app.   3.00

817,818-2nd printings. 817-Combo-c of #817&#819 cover images. 818-Combo-c of #818 and Batman #653 cover images   3.00

#0-(10/94) Zero Hour tie-in.   2.75

#1,000,000 (11/98) 853rd Century x-over   2.75

Annual 1 (1988, $1.50)   5.00

Annual 2-7,9 ('89-'94, '96, 68 pgs.)-4-Painted-c. 5-Joker-c/story (54 pgs.) continued in Robin Annual 1; Sam Kieth-c; Eclipso app. 6-Azrael as Batman in new costume; intro Geist the Twilight Man; Bloodlines storyline. 7-Elseworlds story. 9-Legends of the Dead Earth story   3.00

Annual 8 (1995, $3.95, 68 pgs.)-Year One story   4.00

Annual 10 (1997, $3.95)-Pulp Heroes story   4.00

NOTE: *Neal Adams* c-370, 372, 385, 389, 391, 392, 394-422, 439. *Aparo* a-437, 438, 444-446, 500, 625-632p, 638-643p; c-430, 437, 440-446, 448, 468-470, 480, 484(back), 492-502,508, 509, 515, 518-522, 641, 716, 719, 722, 724. *Austin* a(i)-450, 451, 463-468, 471-476; c(i)-474-476, 478. *Baily* a-443r. *Buckler* a-434, 446p, 479p; c(p)-467, 482, 505-507, 511, 513-516, 518. *Burnley* a(Batman)-65, 75, 78, 83, 100, 103, 125; c(-p)-63i, 64, 73i, 78, 83p, 96p, 103p, 105p, 106, 108, 121p, 123p, 125p. *Chaykin* a-441. *Colan* a(p)-510, 512, 517, 523, 528-538, 540-546, 555-567; c(p)-510, 512, 528, 530-535, 537, 538, 540, 541, 543-545, 556-558, 560-564. *J. Craig* a-488. *Ditko* a-443r, 483-485, 487. *Golden* a-482p; c-625, 626, 628-631, 633, 644-646. *Alan Grant* scripts-584-597, 601-621, 641, 642, Annual 5. *Grell* a-445, 455, 463p, 464p; c-455. *Guardineer* c-23, 24, 26, 28, 30, 32. *Gustavson* a-441r. *Infantino* a-354, 442(2)r, 500, 572. *Infantino/Anderson* c-333, 337-340, 343, 344, 347, 351, 352, 359, 361-368, 371. *Kelley Jones* c-651, 657i, 658i, 659, 661, 663-675. *Kaluta* c-423, 424, 426-428, 431, 434, 438, 484, 486, 572. *Bob Kane* a-Most early issues #27 on. 297i, 356r, 438-440r, 442r. *Kane/Robinson* c-33. *Gil Kane* c(a/p)-368, 370-374, 384, 385, 388-407, 438r, 439r, 520. *Kane/Anderson* c-369. *Sam Kieth* c-654-656 (657, 658 w/Kelley Jones), 660, 662, Annual #5. *Kubert* a-438r, 439r, 500; c-348, 350. *McFarlane* c(a/p)-576-578, 583. *Meskin* a-420r. *Mignola* c-583. *Moldoff* c-233-354, 259, 266, 267, 275, 287, 289, 290, 297, 300. *Moldoff/Giella* a-328, 330, 332, 334, 336, 338, 340, 342, 344, 346, 348, 350, 352, 354, 356. *Mooney* a-447. *Moreira* a-153-300, 419r, 444r, 445r. *Nasser/Netzer* a-654, 655, 657, 658. *Newton* a(p)-480, 481, 483-499, 501-509, 511, 513-516, 518-520, 524, 526, 539; c-526p. *Irv Novick* c-375-377, 383. *Robbins* a-426p, 429p. *Robinson* a-part: 66, 68, 71-73; all: 74-76, 79, 80; c-62, 64, 66, 68-74, 76, 79, 82, 86, 88, 442r, 443r. *Rogers* a-466-468, 471-479p, 481p; c-471p, 472p, 473, 474-479p. *Roussos* Ainwave-76-105(most); c(i)-71, 72, 74-76, 79, 107. *Russell* a-481i, 482i. *Simon/Kirby* a-440r, 442r. *Simonson* a-437-443, 450, 469, 470, 500. *Dick Sprang* c-77, 82, 84, 85, 87, 89-93, 95-100, 102, 103i, 104i, 106, 108, 114, 117, 118, 122, 123, 128, 129, 131, 133, 135, 141, 148, 149, 448p. *Starlin* a-481p, 482p; c-503, 504, 567p. *Starr* a-444r. *Toth* a-442; r-414, 416, 418, 424, 440-441, 443, 444. *Tuska* a-486, 490p. *Matt Wagner* c-647-649. *Wrightson* c-425.

DETECTIVE DAN, SECRET OP. 48 (Also see Adventures of Detective Ace King and Bob Scully, The Two-Fisted Hick Detective)

Humor Publ. Co. (Norman Marsh): 1933 (10¢, 10x13", 36 pgs., B&W, one-shot) (3 color, cardboard-c)

nn-By Norman Marsh, 1st comic w/ original-a; 1st newsstand-c; Dick Tracy look-alike; forerunner of Dan Dunn. (Title and Wu Fang character inspired Detective Comics #1 four years later.) (1st comic of a single theme)   1600   3200   4800   9600   –   –

DETECTIVE EYE (See Keen Detective Funnies)

Centaur Publications: Nov, 1940 - No. 2, Dec, 1940

1-Air Man (see Keen Detective) & The Eye Sees begins; The Masked Marvel & Dean Denton app.   228   456   684   1425   2363   3300

2-Origin Don Rance and the Mysticape; Binder-a; Frank Thomas-c   121   242   363   756   1253   1750

DETECTIVE PICTURE STORIES (Keen Detective Funnies No. 8 on?)

Comics Magazine Company: Dec, 1936 - No. 5, Apr, 1937 (1st comic of a single theme)

1 (all issues are very scarce)   550   1100   1650   2915   4208   5500

2-The Clock app. (1/37, early app.)   235   470   705   1246   1798   2350

3,4: 4-Eisner-a   155   310   465   822   1186   1550

5-The Clock-c/story (4/37); 1st detective/adventure art by Bob Kane; Bruce Wayne prototype app.(see Funny Pages V3/1)   180   360   540   954   1377   1800

DETECTIVES, THE (TV)

Dell Publishing Co.: No. 1168, Mar-May, 1961 - No. 1240, Oct-Dec, 1961

Four Color 1168 (#1)-Robert Taylor photo-c   9   18   27   65   113   160

Four Color 1219-Robert Taylor, Adam West photo-c   8   16   24   56   93   130

Four Color 1240-Tufts-a; Robert Taylor photo-c   8   16   24   56   93   130

DETECTIVES, INC. (See Eclipse Graphic Album Series)

Eclipse Comics: Apr, 1985 - No. 2, Apr, 1985 ($1.75, both w/April dates)

1,2: 2-Nudity   2.50

DETECTIVES, INC.: A TERROR OF DYING DREAMS

Eclipse Comics: Jun, 1987 - No. 3, Dec, 1987 ($1.75, B&W& sepia)

1-3: Colan-a   2.50

TPB ('99, $19.95) r/series   20.00

DETENTION COMICS

DC Comics: Oct, 1996 ($3.50, 56 pgs., one-shot)

1-Robin story by Dennis O'Neil & Norm Breyfogle; Superboy story by Ron Marz & Ron Lim; Warrior story by Ruben Diaz & Joe Phillips; Phillips-c   5.00

DETONATOR (Mike Baron's...)

Image Comics: Nov, 2004 - No. 4 ($2.50/$2.95)

1-4-Mike Baron-s/Mel Rubi-a   3.00

DEVASTATOR

Image Comics/Halloween: 1998 - No. 3 ($2.95, B&W, limited series)

1,2-Hudnall-s/Horn-c/a   3.00

DEVI (Shekhar Kapur's...)

Virgin Comics: July, 2006 - Present ($2.99)

1-13: 1-Mukesh Singh-a/Siddharth Kotian-s. 2-Greg Horn-c   3.00

... Vol. 1 TPB (5/07, $14.99) r/#1-5 and Story from Virgin Comics Preview #0   15.00

DEVIL CHEF

Devil Dinosaur #4 © MAR

Diary of Horror #1 © AVON

Dick Cole #6 © STAR

	GD	VG	FN	VF	VF/NM	NM-
	2.0	4.0	6.0	8.0	9.0	9.2

Dark Horse Comics: July, 1994 ($2.50, B&W, one-shot)

	GD	VG	FN	VF	VF/NM	NM-
nn						2.50

DEVIL DINOSAUR
Marvel Comics Group: Apr, 1978 - No. 9, Dec, 1978

1-Kirby/Royer-a in all; all have Kirby-c	2	4	6	11	16	20
2-9: 4-7-UFO/sci. fic. 8-Dinoriders-c/sty	1	3	4	6	8	10
... By Jack Kirby Omnibus HC (2007, $29.99, dustjacket) r/#1-9; intro. by Brevoort						30.00

DEVIL DINOSAUR SPRING FLING
Marvel Comics: June, 1997 ($2.99. one-shot)

1-(48pgs.) Moon-Boy-c/app.						3.00

DEVIL-DOG DUGAN (Tales of the Marines No. 4 on)
Atlas Comics (OPI): July, 1956 - No. 3, Nov, 1956

1-Severin-c	13	26	39	74	105	135
2-Iron Mike McGraw x-over; Severin-c	8	16	24	44	57	70
3	8	16	24	40	50	60

DEVIL DOGS
Street & Smith Publishers: 1942

1-Boy Rangers, U.S. Marines	28	56	84	162	256	350

DEVILINA (Magazine)
Atlas/Seaboard: Feb, 1975 - No. 2, May, 1975 (B&W)

1-Art by Reese, Marcos; "The Tempest" adapt.	3	6	9	16	23	30
2 (Low printing)	3	6	9	18	27	35

DEVIL KIDS STARRING HOT STUFF
Harvey Publications (Illustrated Humor): July, 1962 - No. 107, Oct, 1981 (Giant-Size #41-55)

1 (12¢ cover price #1-#41-9/69)	21	42	63	152	271	390
2	10	20	30	71	126	180
3-10 (1/64)	8	16	24	52	86	120
11-20	5	10	15	35	55	75
21-30	4	8	12	24	37	50
31-40: 40-(6/69)	3	6	9	18	27	35
41-50: All 68 pg. Giants	3	6	9	20	30	40
51-55: All 52 pg. Giants	3	6	9	18	27	35
56-70	2	4	6	10	14	18
71-90	2	4	6	8	10	12
91-107	1	2	3	4	5	7

DEVIL'S FOOTPRINTS, THE
Dark Horse Comics: March, 2003 - No. 4, June, 2003 ($2.99, limited series)

1-4-Paul Lee-c/a; Scott Allie-s						3.00

DEXTER COMICS
Dearfield Publ.: Summer, 1948 - No. 5, July, 1949

1-Teen-age humor	11	22	33	60	83	105
2-Junie Prom app.	8	16	24	42	54	65
3-5	7	14	21	35	43	50

DEXTER'S LABORATORY (Cartoon Network)
DC Comics: Sept, 1999 - No. 34, Apr, 2003 ($1.99/$2.25)

1						4.00
2-10: 2-McCracken-s						3.00
11-24, 26-34: 31-Begin $2.25-c. 32-34-Wray-c						2.50
25-(50¢-c) Tartakovsky-s/a; Action Hank-c/app.						2.50

DEXTER THE DEMON (Formerly Melvin The Monster)(See Cartoon Kids & Peter the Little Pest)
Atlas Comics (HPC): No. 7, Sept, 1957

7	8	16	24	42	54	65

DHAMPIRE: STILLBORN
DC Comics (Vertigo): 1996 ($5.95, one-shot, mature)

1-Nancy Collins script; Paul Lee-c/a						6.00

DIARY CONFESSIONS (Formerly Ideal Romance)
Stanmor/Key Publ.(Medal Comics): No. 9, May, 1955 - No. 14, Apr, 1955

9	8	16	24	44	57	70
10-14	6	12	18	31	38	45

DIARY LOVES (Formerly Love Diary #1; G. I. Sweethearts #32 on)
Quality Comics Group: No. 2, Nov, 1949 - No. 31, April, 1953

2-Ward-c/a, 9 pgs.	17	34	51	98	154	210
3 (1/50)-Photo-c begin, end #27?	9	18	27	52	69	85
4-Crandall-a	10	20	30	58	79	100
5-7,10	8	16	24	44	57	70

8,9-Ward-a 6,8 pgs. 8-Gustavson-a; Esther Williams photo-c	13	26	39	74	105	135
11,13,14,17-20	8	16	24	42	54	65
12,15,16-Ward-a 9,7,8 pgs.	12	24	36	67	94	120
21-Ward-a, 7 pgs.	11	22	33	60	83	105
22-31: 31-Whitney-a	8	16	24	40	50	60

NOTE: *Photo c-3-10, 12-27.*

DIARY OF HORROR
Avon Periodicals: December, 1952

1-Hollingsworth-c/a; bondage-c	43	86	129	262	431	600

DIARY SECRETS (Formerly Teen-Age Diary Secrets)(See Giant Comics Ed.)
St. John Publishing Co.: No. 10, Feb, 1952 - No. 30, Sept, 1955

10-Baker-c/a most issues	23	46	69	132	209	285
11-16,18,19	15	30	45	90	140	190
17,20: Kubert-r/Hollywood Confessions #1. 17-r/Teen Age Romances #9	15	30	45	90	140	190
21-30: 22,27-Signed stories by Estrada. 28-Last precode (3/55)	12	24	36	69	97	125
nn-(25¢ giant, nd (1950)?-Baker-c & rebound St. John comics	57	114	171	356	591	825

DICK COLE (Sport Thrills No. 11 on)(See Blue Bolt & Four Most #1)
Curtis Publ./Star Publications: Dec-Jan, 1948-49 - No. 10, June-July, 1950

1-Sgt. Spook; L. B. Cole-c; McWilliams-a; Curt Swan's 1st work	34	68	102	195	308	420
2,5	15	30	45	88	137	185
3,4,6-10: All-L.B. Cole-c. 10-Joe Louis story	23	46	69	130	205	280
Accepted Reprint #7(V1#6 on-c)(1950's)-Reprints #7; L.B. Cole-c	8	16	24	44	57	70
Accepted Reprint #9(nd)-(Reprints #9 & #8-c)	8	16	24	44	57	70

NOTE: *L. B. Cole c-1, 3, 4, 6-10. Al McWilliams a-6. Dick Cole in 1-9. Baseball c-10. Basketball c-9. Football c-8.*

DICKIE DARE
Eastern Color Printing Co.: 1941 - No. 4, 1942 (#3 on sale 6/15/42)

1-Caniff-a, bondage-c by Everett	60	120	180	375	625	875
2	28	56	84	162	256	350
3,4-Half Scorchy Smith by Noel Sickles who was very influential in Milton Caniff's development	30	60	90	174	275	375

DICK POWELL (Also see A-1 Comics)
Magazine Enterprises: No. 22, 1949 (one shot)

A-1 22-Photo-c	23	46	69	135	213	

DICK QUICK, ACE REPORTER (See Picture News #10)

DICKS
Caliber Comics: 1997 - No. 4, 1998 ($2.95, B&W)

1-4-Ennis-s/McCrea-c/a; r/Fleetway						3.00
TPB ('98, $12.95) r/series						13.00

DICK'S ADVENTURES
Dell Publishing Co.: No. 245, Sept, 1949

Four Color 245	6	12	18	41	66	90

DICK TRACY (See Famous Feature Stories, Harvey Comics Library, Limited Collectors' Ed., Mammoth Comics, Merry Christmas, The Original..., Popular Comics, Super Book No. 1, 7, 13, 25, Super Comics & Tastee-Freez)
David McKay Publications: May, 1937 - Jan, 1938

Feature Books nn - 100 pgs., partially reprinted as 4-Color No. 1 (appeared before Large Feature Comics, 1st Dick Tracy comic book) (Very Rare-five known copies; two incomplete)	914	1828	2742	6400	11,200	16,000
Feature Books 4 - Reprints nn issue w/new-c	129	258	387	806	1341	1875
Feature Books 6,9	94	188	282	588	974	1360

DICK TRACY (...Monthly #1-24)
Dell Publishing Co.: 1939 - No. 24, Dec, 1949

Large Feature Comic 1 (1939) -Dick Tracy Meets The Blank	179	358	537	1119	1860	2600
Large Feature Comic 4,8	93	186	279	581	966	1350
Large Feature Comic 11,13,15	82	164	246	513	849	1185
Four Color 1(1939)('35-r)	857	1714	2571	6000	10,500	15,000
Four Color 6(1940)('37-r)-(Scarce)	207	414	621	1294	2147	3000
Four Color 8(1940)('38-'39-r)	103	206	309	644	1072	1500
Four Color Comic 3(1941, Series II)	81	162	243	506	841	1175
Four Color 21('41)('38-r)	78	156	234	488	807	1125
Four Color 34('43)('39-'40-r)	40	80	120	300	550	800

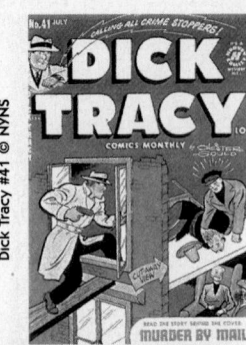

Dick Tracy #41 © NYNS

Digitek #1 © MAR

Dilly #1 © LEV

	GD 2.0	VG 4.0	FN 6.0	VF 8.0	VF/NM 9.0	NM- 9.2

	GD 2.0	VG 4.0	FN 6.0	VF 8.0	VF/NM 9.0	NM- 9.2
Four Color 56('44)('40-r)	35	70	105	263	482	700
Four Color 96('46)('40-r)	24	48	72	175	313	450
Four Color 133('47)('40-'41-r)	19	38	57	142	254	365
Four Color 163('47)('41-r)	17	34	51	122	216	310
Four Color 215('48)-Titled "Sparkle Plenty", Dick Tracy-r						
	11	22	33	79	140	200
1(1/48)('34-r)	37	74	111	278	507	735
2,3	20	40	60	150	268	385
4-10	17	34	51	128	227	325
11-18: 13-Bondage-c	14	28	42	99	175	250
19-1st app. Sparkle Plenty, B.O. Plenty & Gravel Gertie in a 3-pg. strip not						
by Gould	14	28	42	103	184	265
20-1st app. Sam Catchem; c/a not by Gould	13	26	39	95	168	240
21-24-Only 2 pg. Gould-a in each	13	26	39	90	160	230

NOTE: No. 19-24 have a 2 pg. biography of a famous villain illustrated by Gould: 19-Little Face; 20-Flattop; 21-Breathless Mahoney; 22-Measles; 23-Itchy; 24-The Brow.

DICK TRACY (Continued from Dell series)(...Comics Monthly #25-140)
Harvey Publications: No. 25, Mar, 1950 - No. 145, April, 1961

	GD 2.0	VG 4.0	FN 6.0	VF 8.0	VF/NM 9.0	NM- 9.2
25-Flat Top-c/story (also #26,27)	14	28	42	103	184	265
26-28,30: 28-Bondage-c. 28,29-The Brow-c/stories	11	22	33	79	140	200
29-1st app. Gravel Gertie in a Gould-r	13	26	39	97	171	245
31,32,34,35,37-40: 40-Intro/origin 2-way wrist radio (6/51)						
	9	18	27	65	113	160
33- "Measles the Teen-Age Dope Pusher"	11	22	33	79	140	200
36-1st app. B.O. Plenty in a Gould-r	11	22	33	79	140	200
41-50	9	18	27	60	100	140
51-56,58-80: 51-2pgs Powell-a	8	16	24	52	86	120
57-1st app. Sam Catchem in a Gould-r	9	18	27	60	100	140
81-99,101-140: 99-109-Painted-c	7	14	21	49	80	110
100, 141-145 (25¢) Titled "Dick Tracy"	8	16	24	52	86	120

NOTE: Powell a(1-2pgs.)-43, 44, 104, 108, 109, 145. No. 110-120, 141-145 are all reprints from earlier issues.

DICK TRACY
Blackthorne Publishing: 12/84 - No. 24, 6/89 (1-12: $5.95; 13-24: $6.95, B&W, 76 pgs.)

1-8-1st printings; hard-c ed. ($14.95)						15.00
1-3-2nd printings, 1986; hard-c ed.						15.00
1-12-1st & 2nd printings; squarebound. thick-c						7.00
13-24 ($6.95): 21,22-Regular-c & stapled						7.00

NOTE: Gould daily & Sunday strip-r in all. 1-12 r-12/31/45-4/5/49; 13-24 r-7/13/41-2/20/44.

DICK TRACY (Disney)
WD Publications: 1990 - No. 3, 1990 (color) (Book 3 adapts 1990 movie)

Book One ($3.95, 52pgs.)-Kyle Baker-c/a						6.00
Book Two, Three ($5.95, 68pgs.)-Direct sale						6.00
Book Two, Three ($2.95, 68pgs.)-Newsstand						3.00

DICK TRACY ADVENTURES
Gladstone Publishing: May, 1991 ($4.95, 76 pgs.)

1-Reprints strips 2/1/42-4/18/42						5.00

DICK TRACY, EXPLOITS OF
Rosdon Books, Inc.: 1946 ($1.00, hard-c strip reprints)

	GD 2.0	VG 4.0	FN 6.0	VF 8.0	VF/NM 9.0	NM- 9.2
1-Reprints the near complete case of "The Brow" from 6/12/44 to 9/24/44 (story starts a few weeks late)	25	50	75	148	232	315
with dust jacket...	40	80	120	240	383	525

DICK TRACY MONTHLY/WEEKLY
Blackthorne Publishing: May, 1986 - No. 99, 1989 ($2.00, B&W)
(Becomes Weekly #26 on)

	GD 2.0	VG 4.0	FN 6.0	VF 8.0	VF/NM 9.0	NM- 9.2
1-60: Gould-r. 30,31-Mr. Crime app.						3.00
61-90						4.00
91-95						6.00
96-99-Low print	1	2	3	5	7	9

NOTE: #1-10 reprint strips 3/10/40-7/13/41; #10(pg.8)-51 reprint strips 4/6/49-12/31/55; #52-99 reprint strips 12/26/56-4/26/64.

DICK TRACY SPECIAL
Blackthorne Publ.: Jan, 1988 - No. 3, Aug. (no month), 1989 ($2.95, B&W)

1-3: 1-Origin D. Tracy; 4/strips 10/12/31-3/30/32						3.00

DICK TRACY: THE EARLY YEARS
Blackthorne Publishing: Aug, 1987 - No. 4, Aug (no month) 1989 ($6.95, B&W, 76 pgs.)

	GD 2.0	VG 4.0	FN 6.0	VF 8.0	VF/NM 9.0	NM- 9.2
1-3: 1-4-r/strips 10/12/31(1st daily)-8/31/32 & Sunday strips 6/12/32-8/28/32; Big Boy apps. in #1-3	1	2	3	4	5	7
4 ($2.95, 52pgs.)						3.00

DICK TRACY UNPRINTED STORIES

	GD 2.0	VG 4.0	FN 6.0	VF 8.0	VF/NM 9.0	NM- 9.2

Blackthorne Publishing: Sept, 1987 - No. 4, June, 1988 ($2.95, B&W)

1-4: Reprints strips 1/1/56-12/25/56						3.00

DICK TURPIN (See Legend of Young...)

DIE-CUT
Marvel Comics UK, Ltd: Nov, 1993 - No. 4, Feb, 1994 ($1.75, limited series)

1-4: 1-Die-cut-c; The Beast app.						2.50

DIE-CUT VS. G-FORCE
Marvel Comics UK, Ltd: Nov, 1993 - No. 2, Dec, 1993 ($2.75, limited series)

1,2-($2.75)-Gold foil-c on both						2.75

DIE, MONSTER, DIE (See Movie Classics)

DIGIMON DIGITAL MONSTERS (TV)
Dark Horse Comics: May, 2000 - No. 12, Nov, 2000 ($2.95/$2.99)

1-12						3.00

DIGITEK
Marvel UK, Ltd: Dec, 1992 - No. 4, Mar, 1993 ($1.95/$2.25, mini-series)

1-4: 3-Deathlock-c/story						2.50

DILLY (Dilly Duncan from Daredevil Comics; see Boy Comics #57)
Lev Gleason Publications: May, 1953 - No. 3, Sept, 1953

	GD 2.0	VG 4.0	FN 6.0	VF 8.0	VF/NM 9.0	NM- 9.2
1-Teenage; Biro-c	7	14	21	37	46	55
2,3-Biro-c	5	10	15	23	28	32

DILTON'S STRANGE SCIENCE (See Pep Comics #78)
Archie Comics: May, 1989 - No. 5, May, 1990 (75¢/$1.00)

1-5						3.00

DIME COMICS
Newsbook Publ. Corp.: 1945; 1951

	GD 2.0	VG 4.0	FN 6.0	VF 8.0	VF/NM 9.0	NM- 9.2
1-Silver Streak-c/story; L. B. Cole-c	83	166	249	519	860	1200
1(1951)	11	22	33	60	83	105

DINGBATS (See 1st Issue Special)

DING DONG
Compix/Magazine Enterprises: Summer?, 1946 - No. 5, 1947 (52 pgs.)

	GD 2.0	VG 4.0	FN 6.0	VF 8.0	VF/NM 9.0	NM- 9.2
1-Funny animal	27	54	81	156	246	335
2 (9/46)	14	28	42	78	112	145
3 (Wint '46-'47) - 5	11	22	33	62	86	110

DINKY DUCK (Paul Terry's...) (See Approved Comics, Blue Ribbon, Giant Comics Edition #5A & New Terrytoons)
St. John Publishing Co./Pines No. 16 on: Nov, 1951 - No. 16, Sept, 1955; No. 16, Fall, 1956; No. 17, May, 1957 - No. 19, Summer, 1958

	GD 2.0	VG 4.0	FN 6.0	VF 8.0	VF/NM 9.0	NM- 9.2
1-Funny animal	13	26	39	72	101	130
2	8	16	24	42	54	65
3-10	6	12	18	29	36	42
11-16(9/55)	6	12	18	27	33	38
16(Fall, '56) - 19	5	10	15	22	26	30

DINKY DUCK & HASHIMOTO-SAN (See Deputy Dawg Presents...)

DINO (TV)(The Flintstones)
Charlton Publications: Aug, 1973 - No. 20, Jan, 1977 (Hanna-Barbera)

	GD 2.0	VG 4.0	FN 6.0	VF 8.0	VF/NM 9.0	NM- 9.2
1	3	6	9	18	27	35
2-10	2	4	6	10	14	18
11-20	2	4	6	8	10	12
Digest nn (w/Xerox Pub., 1974) (low print run)	2	4	6	11	16	20

DINO ISLAND
Mirage Studios: Feb, 1994 - No. 2, Mar, 1994 ($2.75, limited series)

1,2-By Jim Lawson						2.75

DINO RIDERS
Marvel Comics: Feb, 1989 - No. 3, 1989 ($1.00)

1-3: Based on toys						3.00

DINOSAUR REX
Upshot Graphics (Fantagraphics): 1986 - No. 3, 1986 ($2.00, limited series)

1-3						2.50

DINOSAURS, A CELEBRATION
Marvel Comics (Epic): Oct, 1992 - No. 4, Oct, 1992 ($4.95, lim. series, 52 pgs.)

1-4: 2-Bolton painted-c						5.00

DINOSAURS ATTACK! THE GRAPHIC NOVEL
Eclipse Comics: 1991 ($3.95, coated stock, stiff-c)

Dinosaurs For Hire #7 © Tom Mason

Disney's Aladdin #10 © DIS

Disney's Beauty and the Beast #4 © DIS

	GD 2.0	VG 4.0	FN 6.0	VF 8.0	VF/NM 9.0	NM- 9.2

Book One- Based on Topps trading cards — 4.00

DINOSAURS FOR HIRE
Malibu Comics: Feb, 1993 - No. 12, Feb, 1994 ($1.95/$2.50)

1-12: 1,10-Flip bk. 8-Bagged w/Skycap; Staton-c. 10-Flip book — 2.50

DINOSAURS GRAPHIC NOVEL (TV)
Disney Comics: 1992 - No. 2, 1993 ($2.95, 52 pgs.)

1,2-Staton-a; based on Dinosaurs TV show — 3.00

DINOSAURUS
Dell Publishing Co.: No. 1120, Aug, 1960

Four Color 1120-Movie, painted-c — 8 16 24 56 93 130

DIPPY DUCK
Atlas Comics (OPI): October, 1957

1-Maneely-a; code approved — 10 20 30 54 72 90

DIRECTORY TO A NONEXISTENT UNIVERSE
Eclipse Comics: Dec, 1987 ($2.00, B&W)

1 — 2.50

DIRTY DOZEN (See Movie Classics)

DIRTY PAIR (Manga)
Eclipse Comics: Dec, 1988 - No. 4, Apr, 1989 ($2.00, B&W, limited series)

1-4: Japanese manga with original stories — 3.00
...: Start the Violence (Dark Horse, 9/99, $2.95) r/B&W stories in color from Dark Horse Presents #132-134; covers by Warren & Pearson — 3.00

DIRTY PAIR: FATAL BUT NOT SERIOUS (Manga)
Dark Horse Comics: July, 1995 - No. 5, Nov, 1995 ($2.95, limited series)

1-5 — 3.00

DIRTY PAIR: RUN FROM THE FUTURE (Manga)
Dark Horse Comics: Jan, 2000 - No. 4, Mar, 2000 ($2.95, limited series)

1-4-Warren-s/c/a. Var.-c by Hughes(1), Stelfreeze(2), Timm(3), Ramos(4) — 3.00

DIRTY PAIR: SIM HELL (Manga)
Dark Horse Comics: May, 1993 - No. 4, Aug, 1993 ($2.50, B&W, limited series)

1-4 — 3.00
...Remastered #1-4 (5/01 - 8/01) reprints in color, with pin-up gallery — 3.00

DIRTY PAIR II (Manga)
Eclipse Comics: June, 1989 - No. 5, Mar, 1990 ($2.00, B&W, limited series)

1-5: 3-Cover is misnumbered as #1 — 3.00

DIRTY PAIR III, THE (A Plague of Angels) (Manga)
Eclipse Comics: Aug, 1990 - No. 5, July, 1991 ($2.00/$2.25, B&W, lim. series)

1-5 — 3.00

DISHMAN
Eclipse Comics: Sept, 1988 ($2.50, B&W, 52 pgs.)

1 — 2.50

DISNEY AFTERNOON, THE (TV)
Marvel Comics: Nov, 1994 - No.10?, Aug, 1995 ($1.50)

1-10: 3-w/bound-in Power Ranger Barcode Card — 3.00

DISNEY COMIC ALBUM
Disney Comics: 1990(no month, year) - No. 8, 1991 ($6.95/$7.95)

1,2 ($6.95): 1-Donald Duck and Gyro Gearloose by Barks(r). 2-Uncle Scrooge by Barks(r); Jr. Woodchucks app. — 9.00
3-8: 3-Donald Duck-r/F.C. 308 by Barks; begin $7.95-c. 4-Mickey Mouse Meets the Phantom Blot; r/M.M Club Parade (censored 1956 version of story). 5-Chip 'n' Dale Rescue Rangers; new-a. 6-Uncle Scrooge. 7-Donald Duck in Too Many Pets; Barks-r(4) including F.C. #29. 8-Super Goof; r/S.G. #1, D.D. #102 — 9.00

DISNEY COMIC HITS
Marvel Comics: Oct, 1995 - No. 16, Jan, 1997 ($1.50/$2.50)

1-16: 4-Toy Story. 6-Aladdin. 7-Pocahontas. 10-The Hunchback of Notre Dame (Same story in Disney's The Hunchback of Notre Dame). 13-Aladdin and the Forty Thieves — 4.00

DISNEY COMICS
Disney Comics: June, 1990

Boxed set of #1 issues includes Donald Duck Advs., Ducktales, Chip 'n Dale Rescue Rangers, Roger Rabbit, Mickey Mouse Advs. & Goofy Advs.; limited to 10,000 sets — 2 4 6 9 12 15

DISNEYLAND BIRTHDAY PARTY (Also see Dell Giants)
Gladstone Publishing Co.: Aug, 1985 ($2.50)

1-Reprints Dell Giant with new-photo-c — 2 4 6 8 10 12
...Comics Digest #1-(Digest) — 2 4 6 8 11 14

DISNEYLAND MAGAZINE
Fawcett Publications: Feb. 15, 1972 - ? (10-1/4"x12-5/8", 20 pgs, weekly)

1-One or two page painted art features on Dumbo, Snow White, Lady & the Tramp, the Aristocats, Brer Rabbit, Peter Pan, Cinderella, Jungle Book, Alice & Pinocchio. Most standard characters app. — 3 6 9 16 23 30

DISNEYLAND, USA (See Dell Giant No. 30)

DISNEY MOVIE BOOK
Walt Disney Productions (Gladstone): 1990 ($7.95, 8-1/2"x11", 52 pgs.) (w/pull-out poster)

1-Roger Rabbit in Tummy Trouble; from the cartoon film strips adapted to the comic format. Ron Dias-c — 2 4 6 8 10 12

DISNEY'S ACTION CLUB
Acclaim Books: 1997 - No. 4 ($4.50, digest size)

1-4: 1-Hercules. 4-Mighty Ducks — 4.50

DISNEY'S ALADDIN (Movie)
Marvel Comics: Oct, 1994 - No. 11, 1995 ($1.50)

1-11 — 3.00

DISNEY'S BEAUTY AND THE BEAST (Movie)
Marvel Comics: Sept, 1994 - No. 13, 1995 ($1.50)

1-13 — 3.00

DISNEY'S BEAUTY AND THE BEAST HOLIDAY SPECIAL
Acclaim Books: 1997 ($4.50, digest size, one-shot)

1-Based on The Enchanted Christmas video — 4.50

DISNEY'S COLOSSAL COMICS COLLECTION
Disney Comics: 1991 - No. 10, 1993 ($1.95, digest-size, 96/132 pgs.)

1-10: Ducktales, Talespin, Chip 'n Dale's Rescue Rangers. 4-r/Darkwing Duck #1-4. 6-Goofy begins. 8-Little Mermaid — 5.00

DISNEY'S COMICS IN 3-D
Disney Comics: 1992 ($2.95, w/glasses, polybagged)

1-Infinity-c; Barks, Rosa, Gottfredson-r — 5.00

DISNEY'S ENCHANTING STORIES
Acclaim Books: 1997 - No. 5 ($4.50, digest size)

1-5: 1-Hercules. 2-Pocahontas — 4.50

DISNEY'S NEW ADVENTURES OF BEAUTY AND THE BEAST (Also see Beauty and the Beast & Disney's Beauty and the Beast)
Disney Comics: 1992 - No. 2, 1992 ($1.50, limited series)

1,2-New stories based on movie — 3.00

DISNEY'S POCAHONTAS (Movie)
Marvel Comics: 1995 ($4.95, one-shot)

1-Movie adaptation — 1 2 3 4 5 7

DISNEY'S TALESPIN LIMITED SERIES: "TAKE OFF" (TV) (See Talespin)
W. D. Publications (Disney Comics): Jan, 1991 - No. 4, Apr, 1991 ($1.50, lim. series, 52 pgs.)

1-4: Based on animated series; 4 part origin — 2.50

DISNEY'S TARZAN (Movie)
Dark Horse Comics: June, 1999 - No. 2, July, 1999 ($2.95, limited series)

1,2: Movie adaptation — 3.00

DISNEY'S THE LION KING (Movie)
Marvel Comics: July, 1994 - No. 2, July, 1994 ($1.50, limited series)

1,2: 2-part movie adaptation — 3.00
1-($2.50, 52 pgs.)-Complete story — 5.00

DISNEY'S THE LITTLE MERMAID (Movie)
Marvel Comics: Sept, 1994 - No. 12, 1995 ($1.50)

1-12 — 4.00

DISNEY'S THE LITTLE MERMAID LIMITED SERIES (Movie)
Disney Comics: Feb, 1992 - No. 4, May, 1992 ($1.50, limited series)

1-4: Peter David scripts — 3.00

DISNEY'S THE LITTLE MERMAID: UNDERWATER ENGAGEMENTS
Acclaim Books: 1997 ($4.50, digest size)

1-Flip book — 4.50

DISNEY'S THE HUNCHBACK OF NOTRE DAME (Movie)(See Disney's Comic Hits #10)
Marvel Comics: July, 1996 ($4.95, squarebound, one-shot)

A Distant Soil #24 © Colleen Doran

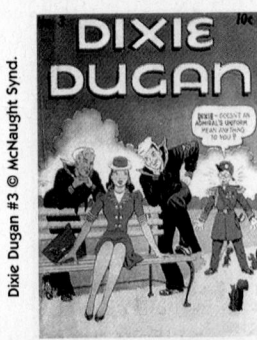

Dixie Dugan #3 © McNaught Synd.

Doc Samson #1 © MAR

	GD 2.0	VG 4.0	FN 6.0	VF 8.0	VF/NM 9.0	NM- 9.2
1-Movie adaptation.	1	2	3	4	5	7

NOTE: A different edition of this series was sold at Wal-Mart stores with new covers depicting scenes from the 1989 feature film. Inside contents and price were identical.

DISNEY'S THE THREE MUSKETEERS (Movie)
Marvel Comics: Jan, 1994 - No. 2, Feb, 1994 ($1.50, limited series)

1,2-Morrow-c; Spiegle-a; Movie adaptation						2.50

DISNEY'S TOY STORY (Movie)
Marvel Comics: Dec, 1995 ($4.95, one-shot)

	GD	VG	FN	VF	VF/NM	NM-
nn-Adaptation of film	1	2	3	4	5	7

DISTANT SOIL, A (1st Series)
WaRP Graphics: Dec, 1983 - No. 9, Mar 1986 ($1.50, B&W)

1-Magazine size						4.00
2-9: 2-4 are magazine size						3.00

NOTE: Second printings exist of #1, 2, 3 & 6.

DISTANT SOIL, A
Donning (Star Blaze): Mar, 1989 ($12.95, trade paperback)

nn-new material						13.00

DISTANT SOIL, A (2nd Series)
Aria Press/Image Comics (Highbrow Entertainment) #15 on:
June, 1991 - Present ($1.75/$2.50/$2.95/$3.95, B&W)

1-27: 13-$2.95-c begins. 14-Sketchbook. 15-(8/96)-1st Image issue						3.00
29-33,35,37-($3.95)						4.00
34-($4.95, 64 pages) includes sketchbook pages						5.00
36,38-($4.50) 36-Back-up story by Darnall & Doran. 38-Includes sketch pages						4.50
The Aria ('01, $16.95,TPB) r/#26-31						17.00
The Ascendant ('98, $18.95,TPB) r/#13-25						19.00
The Gathering ('97, $18.95,TPB) r/#1-13; intro. Neil Gaiman						19.00
Vol. 4: Coda (2005, $17.99, TPB) r/#32-38						18.00

NOTE: Four separate printings exist for #1 and are clearly marked. Second printings exist of #2-4 and are also clearly marked.

DISTANT SOIL, A: IMMIGRANT SONG
Donning (Star Blaze): Aug, 1987 ($6.95, trade paperback)

nn-new material						7.00

DISTRICT X (Also see X-Men titles) (Also see Mutopia X)
Marvel Comics: July, 2004 - No. 14, Aug, 2005 ($2.99)

1-14: 1-3-Bishop app.; Yardin-a/Hine-s						3.00
...Vol. 1: Mr. M (2005, $14.99) r/#1-6; sketch page by Yardin						15.00
...Vol. 2: Underground (2005, $19.99) r/#7-14; prologue from X-Men Unlimited #2						20.00

DIVER DAN (TV)
Dell Publishing Co.: Feb-Apr, 1962 - No. 2, June-Aug, 1962

	GD	VG	FN	VF	VF/NM	NM-
Four Color 1254(#1), 2	5	10	15	35	55	75

DIVINE RIGHT
Image Comics (WildStorm Prod.): Sept, 1997 - No. 12, Nov, 1999 ($2.50)

Preview						5.00
1,2: 1-Jim Lee-s/a(p)/c, 1-Variant-c by Charest						4.00
1-($3.50)-Voyager Pack w/Stormwatch preview						3.50
1-American Entertainment Ed.						6.00
2-Variant-c of Exotica & Blaze						5.00
3-Chromium-c by Jim Lee						5.00
3-12: 3-5-Fairchild & Lynch app. 4-American Entertainment Ed. 8-Two covers. 9-1st DC issue. 11,12-Divine Intervention pt. 1,4						3.00
5-Pacific Comicon Ed.						6.00
6-Glow in the dark variant-c, European Tour Edition						20.00
...Book One TPB (2002, $17.95) r/#1-7						18.00
...Book Two TPB (2002, $17.95) r/#8-12 & Divine Intervention Gen13, ...Wildcats						18.00
...Collected Edition #1-3 ($5.95, TPB) 1-r/#1,2. 2-r/#3,4. 3-r/#5,6						6.00
Divine Intervention/Gen 13 (11/99, $2.50) Part 3; D'Anda-a						2.50
Divine Intervention/Wildcats (11/99, $2.50) Part 2; D'Anda-a						2.50

DIVISION 13 (See Comic's Greatest World)
Dark Horse Comics: Sept, 1994 - Jan, 1995 ($2.50, color)

1-4: Giffen story in all. 1-Art Adams-c						2.50

DIXIE DUGAN (See Big Shot, Columbia Comics & Feature Funnies)
McNaught Syndicate/Columbia/Publication Ent.: July, 1942 - No. 13, 1949
(Strip reprints in all)

	GD	VG	FN	VF	VF/NM	NM-
1-Joe Palooka x-over by Ham Fisher	27	54	81	158	249	340
2	15	30	45	85	130	175
3	12	24	36	69	97	125
4,5(1945-46)-Bo strip-r	10	20	30	54	72	90

	GD 2.0	VG 4.0	FN 6.0	VF 8.0	VF/NM 9.0	NM- 9.2
6-13(1/47-49): 6-Paperdoll cut-outs	9	18	27	47	61	75

DIXIE DUGAN
Prize Publications (Headline): V3#1, Nov, 1951 - V4#4, Feb, 1954

	GD	VG	FN	VF	VF/NM	NM-
V3#1	9	18	27	52	69	85
2-4	7	14	21	35	43	50
V4#1-4(#5-8)	6	12	18	28	34	40

DIZZY DAMES
American Comics Group (B&M Distr. Co.): Sept-Oct, 1952 - No. 6, Jul-Aug, 1953

	GD	VG	FN	VF	VF/NM	NM-
1-Whitney-c	15	30	45	86	133	180
2	10	20	30	54	72	90
3-6	8	16	24	44	57	70

DIZZY DON COMICS
F. E. Howard Publications/Dizzy Don Ent. Ltd (Canada): 1942 - No. 22, Oct, 1946; No. 3, Apr, 1947 (Most B&W)

	GD	VG	FN	VF	VF/NM	NM-
1 (B&W)	21	42	63	122	191	260
2 (B&W)	13	26	39	72	101	130
4-21 (B&W)	10	20	30	58	79	100
22-Full color, 52 pgs.	21	42	63	122	191	260
3 (4/47)-Full color, 52 pgs.	21	46	63	122	191	260

DIZZY DUCK (Formerly Barnyard Comics)
Standard Comics: No. 32, Nov, 1950 - No. 39, Mar, 1952

	GD	VG	FN	VF	VF/NM	NM-
32-Funny animal	10	20	30	54	72	90
33-39	6	12	18	31	38	45

DMZ
DC Comics (Vertigo): Jan, 2006 - Present ($2.99)

1-22: 1-10-Brian Wood-s/Riccardo Burchielli-a. 11-Donaldson-a. 12-Wood-s/a						3.00
...: Body of a Journalist TPB (2007, $12.99) r/#6-12; intro. by D. Randall Blythe						13.00
...: On the Ground TPB (2006, $9.99) r/#1-5; intro. by Brian Azzarello						10.00

DNAGENTS (The New DNAgents V2/1 on)(Also see Surge)
Eclipse Comics: March, 1983 - No. 24, July, 1985 ($1.50, Baxter paper)

1,24: 1-Origin. 4-Amber app. 24-Dave Stevens-c						3.00
2-23: 8-Infinity-c						2.50

DOBERMAN (See Sgt. Bilko's Private...)

DOBIE GILLIS (See The Many Loves of...)

DOC CHAOS: THE STRANGE ATTRACTOR
Vortex Comics: Apr, 1990 - No. 3, 1990 ($3.00, 32 pgs.)

1-3: The Lust For Order						3.00

DOC FRANKENSTEIN
Burlyman Entertainment: Nov, 2004 - Present ($3.50)

1-5-Wachowski brothers-s/Skroce-a						3.50

DOC SAMSON (Also see Incredible Hulk)
Marvel Comics: Jan, 1996 - No. 4, Apr, 1996 ($1.95, limited series)

1-4: 1-Hulk c/app. 2-She-Hulk-c/app. 3-Punisher-c/app. 4-Polaris-c/app.						2.50

DOC SAMSON (Incredible Hulk)
Marvel Comics: Mar, 2006 - No. 5, July, 2006 ($2.99, limited series)

1-5: 1-DiFilippo-s/Fiorentino-a. 3-Conner-c						3.00

DOC SAVAGE
Gold Key: Nov, 1966

	GD	VG	FN	VF	VF/NM	NM-
1-Adaptation of the Thousand-Headed Man; James Bama c-r/1964 Doc Savage paperback	10	20	30	71	126	180

DOC SAVAGE (Also see Giant-Size...)
Marvel Comics Group: Oct, 1972 - No. 8, Jan, 1974

	GD	VG	FN	VF	VF/NM	NM-
1	3	6	9	17	25	32
2,3-Steranko-c	2	4	6	10	14	18
4-8	2	4	6	8	10	12

NOTE: *Gil Kane* c-5, 6. *Mooney* a-1i. No. 1, 2 adapts pulp story "The Man of Bronze"; No. 3, 4 adapts "Death in Silver"; No. 5, 6 adapts "The Monsters"; No. 7, 8 adapts "The Brand of The Werewolf".

DOC SAVAGE (Magazine)
Marvel Comics Group: Aug, 1975 - No. 8, Spring, 1977 ($1.00, B&W)

	GD	VG	FN	VF	VF/NM	NM-
1-Cover from movie poster; Ron Ely photo-c	2	4	6	13	18	22
2-5: 3-Buscema-a. 5-Adams-a(1 pg.), Rogers-a(1 pg)	2	4	6	8	10	12
6-8	2	4	6	8	11	14

DOC SAVAGE
DC Comics: Nov, 1987 - No. 4, Feb, 1988 ($1.75, limited series)

1-4						3.00

Doc Savage Comics V2 #3 © CN

Doctor Mid-Nite #2 © DC

Doctor Solar, Man of the Atom #7 © GK

	GD	VG	FN	VF	VF/NM	NM-		GD	VG	FN	VF	VF/NM	NM-
	2.0	4.0	6.0	8.0	9.0	9.2		2.0	4.0	6.0	8.0	9.0	9.2

DOC SAVAGE
DC Comics: Nov, 1988 - No. 24, Oct, 1990 ($1.75/$2.00: #13-24)

1-16,19-24						3.00
17,18-Shadow x-over						4.00
Annual 1 (1989, $3.50, 68 pgs.)						4.00

DOC SAVAGE COMICS (Also see Shadow Comics)
Street & Smith Publ.: May, 1940 - No. 20, Oct, 1943 (1st app. in Doc Savage pulp, 3/33)

1-Doc Savage, Cap Fury, Danny Garrett, Mark Mallory, The Whisperer, Captain Death,
Billy the Kid, Sheriff Pete & Treasure Island begin; Norgil, the Magician app.

	GD	VG	FN	VF	VF/NM	NM-
1	486	972	1458	3400	5950	8500
2-Origin & 1st app. Ajax, the Sun Man; Danny Garrett, The Whisperer end; classic sci-fi cover	204	408	612	1275	2113	2950
3	128	256	384	800	1325	1850
4-Treasure Island ends; Tuska-a	103	206	309	644	1072	1500
5-Origin & 1st app. Astron, the Crocodile Queen, not in #9 & 11; Norgi the Magician app.; classic-c	93	186	279	581	966	1350
6-10: 6-Cap Fury ends; origin & only app. Red Falcon in Astron story. 8-Mark Mallory ends; Charlie McCarthy app. on-c plus true life story. 9-Supersnipe app. 10-Origin & only app. The Thunderbolt	61	122	183	381	633	885
11,12	52	104	156	317	521	725

V2#1-8(#13-20): 15-Origin of Ajax the Sun Man; Jack Benny on-c; Hitler app. 16-The Pulp
Hero, The Avenger app.; Fanny Brice story. 17-Sun Man ends; Nick Carter begins; Duffy's
Tavern part photo-c & story. 18-Huckleberry Finn part-c/story. 19-Henny Youngman part
photo-c & life story. 20-Only all funny-c w/Huckleberry Finn

	46	92	138	281	466	650

DOC SAVAGE: CURSE OF THE FIRE GOD
Dark Horse Comics: Sept, 1995 - No, 4, Dec, 1995 ($2.95, limited series)

1-4						3.00

DOC SAVAGE: THE MAN OF BRONZE
Skylark Pub: Mar, 1979, 68pgs. (B&W comic digest, 5-1/4x7-5/8")(low print)

	GD	VG	FN	VF	VF/NM	NM-
15406-0: Whitman-a, 60 pgs., new comics	3	6	9	20	30	40

DOC SAVAGE: THE MAN OF BRONZE
Millennium Publications: 1991 - No. 4, 1991 ($2.50, limited series)

1-4: 1-Bronze logo						3.00
...: The Manual of Bronze 1 ($2.50, B&W, color, one-shot)-Unpublished proposed Doc Savage strip in color, with Doc Savage strip-r						3.00

DOC SAVAGE: THE MAN OF BRONZE, DOOM DYNASTY
Millennium Publ.: 1992 (Says 1991) - No. 2, 1992 ($2.50, limited series)

1,2						3.00

DOC SAVAGE: THE MAN OF BRONZE - REPEL
Innovation Publishing: 1992 ($2.50)

1-Dave Dorman painted-c						3.00

DOC SAVAGE: THE MAN OF BRONZE THE DEVIL'S THOUGHTS
Millennium Publ.: 1992 (Says 1991) - No. 3, 1992 ($2.50, limited series)

1-3						3.00

DOC STEARN...MR. MONSTER (See Mr. Monster)

DR. ANTHONY KING, HOLLYWOOD LOVE DOCTOR
Minoan Publishing Corp./Harvey Publications No. 4: 1952(Jan) - No. 3, May, 1953; No. 4, May, 1954

	GD	VG	FN	VF	VF/NM	NM-
1	14	28	42	80	115	150
2-4: 4-Powell-a	9	18	27	50	65	80

DR. ANTHONY'S LOVE CLINIC (See Mr. Anthony's...)

DR. BOBBS
Dell Publishing Co.: No. 212, Jan, 1949

	GD	VG	FN	VF	VF/NM	NM-
Four Color 212	6	12	18	37	59	80

DOCTOR CYBORG
Attention! Publishing: 1996 - No. 5 ($2.95, B&W)

1-5						3.00
The Clone Conspiracy TPB (1998, $14.95) r/#1-5						15.00

DR. DOOM'S REVENGE
Marvel Comics: 1989 (Came w/computer game from Paragon Software)

V1#1-Spider-Man & Captain America fight Dr. Doom						3.00

DR. FATE (See 1st Issue Special, The Immortal..., Justice League, More Fun #55, & Showcase)

DOCTOR FATE
DC Comics: July, 1987 - No. 4, Oct, 1987 ($1.50, limited series, Baxter paper)

1-4: Giffen-c/a in all						3.00

DOCTOR FATE
DC Comics: Winter, 1988-`89 - No. 41, June, 1992 ($1.25/$1.50 #5 on)

1,15: 15-Justice League app.						3.50
2-14						3.00
16-41: 25-1st new Dr. Fate. 36-Original Dr. Fate returns						2.50
Annual 1(1989, $2.95, 68 pgs.)-Sutton-a						3.50

DOCTOR FATE
DC Comics: Oct, 2003 - No. 5, Feb, 2004 ($2.50, limited series)

1-5-Golden-s/Kramer-a						2.50

DR. FU MANCHU (See The Mask of...)
I.W. Enterprises: 1964

	GD	VG	FN	VF	VF/NM	NM-
1-r/Avon's "Mask of Dr. Fu Manchu"; Wood-a	7	14	21	49	80	110

DR. GIGGLES (See Dark Horse Presents #64-66)
Dark Horse Comics: Oct, 1992 - No. 2, Oct, 1992 ($2.50, limited series)

1,2-Based on movie						2.50

DOCTOR GRAVES (Formerly The Many Ghosts of...)
Charlton Comics: No. 73, Sept, 1985 - No. 75, Jan, 1986

	GD	VG	FN	VF	VF/NM	NM-
73-75-Low print run	1	2	3	4	5	7

DR. JEKYLL AND MR. HYDE (See A Star Presentation & Supernatural Thrillers #4)

DR. KILDARE (TV)
Dell Publishing Co.: No. 1337, 4-6/62 - No. 9, 4-6/65 (All Richard Chamberlain photo-c)

	GD	VG	FN	VF	VF/NM	NM-
Four Color 1337(#1, 1962)	8	16	24	58	97	135
2-9	6	12	18	43	69	95

DR. MASTERS (See The Adventures of Young...)

DOCTOR MID-NITE (Also see All-American #25)
DC Comics: 1999 - No. 3, 1999 ($5.95, square-bound, limited series)

1-3-Matt Wagner-s/John K. Snyder III-painted art						6.00
TPB (2000, $19.95) r/series						20.00

DOCTOR OCTOPUS: NEGATIVE EXPOSURE
Marvel Comics: Dec, 2003 - No. 5, Apr, 2004 ($2.99, limited series)

1-5-Vaughan-s/Staz Johnson-a; Spider-Man app.						3.00
Spider-Man/Doctor Octopus: Negative Exposure TPB (2004, $13.99) r/series						14.00

DR. ROBOT SPECIAL
Dark Horse Comics: Apr, 2000 ($2.95, one-shot)

1-Bernie Mireault-s/a; some reprints from Madman Comics #12-15						3.00

DOCTOR SOLAR, MAN OF THE ATOM (See The Occult Files of Dr. Spektor #14 & Solar)
Gold Key/Whitman No. 28 on: 10/62 - No. 27, 4/69; No. 28, 4/81 - No. 31, 3/82 (1-27 have painted-c)

	GD	VG	FN	VF	VF/NM	NM-
1-(#10000-210)-Origin/1st app. Dr. Solar (1st original Gold Key character)	18	36	54	134	237	340
2-Prof. Harbinger begins	9	18	27	60	100	140
3,4	6	12	18	41	66	90
5-Intro. Man of the Atom in costume	6	12	18	43	69	95
6-10	5	10	15	32	51	70
11-14,16-20	4	8	12	24	37	50
15-Origin retold	4	8	12	26	41	55
21-23: 23-Last 12¢ issue	3	6	9	20	30	40
24-27	3	6	9	19	29	38
28-31: 29-Magnus Robot Fighter begins. 31-(3/82)The Sentinel app.	2	4	6	11	16	20
Hardcover Volume One (Dark Horse Books, 2004, $49.95) r/#1-7; creator bios						50.00
Hardcover Volume Two (Dark Horse Books, 6/05, $49.95) r/#8-14; Jim Shooter foreword						50.00
Hardcover Volume Three (Dark Horse Books, 9/05, $49.95) r/#15-22; Mike Baron foreword						50.00

NOTE: *Frank Bolle* a-6-19, 29-31; c-29l. *Bob Fugitani* a-1-5. *Spiegle* a-29-31. *Al McWilliams* a-20-31.

DOCTOR SOLAR, MAN OF THE ATOM
Valiant Comics: 1990 - No. 2, 1991 ($7.95, card stock-c, high quality, 96 pgs.)

	GD	VG	FN	VF	VF/NM	NM-
1,2: Reprints Gold Key series	1	2	3	4	5	7

DOCTOR SPECTRUM (See Supreme Power)
Marvel Comics: Oct, 2004 - No. 6, Mar, 2005 ($2.99, limited series)

1-6-Origin; Sara Barnes-s/Travel Foreman-a						3.00
TPB (2005, $16.99) r/#1-6						17.00

DOCTOR SPEKTOR (See The Occult Files of..., & Spine-Tingling Tales)

DOCTOR STRANGE (Formerly Strange Tales #1-168) (Also see The Defenders, Giant-Size...,
Marvel Fanfare, Marvel Graphic Novel, Marvel Premiere, Marvel Treasury Edition, Strange &

Doctor Strange #75 © MAR

Doctor Strange, Sorcerer Supreme #69 © MAR

Doctor Zero #1 © MAR

	GD 2.0	VG 4.0	FN 6.0	VF 8.0	VF/NM 9.0	NM- 9.2

Strange Tales, 2nd Series)
Marvel Comics Group: No. 169, 6/68 - No. 183, 11/69; 6/74 - No. 81, 2/87

169(#1)-Origin retold; panel swipe/M.D. #1-c	12	24	36	86	153	220
170-177: 177-New costume	4	8	12	24	37	50
178-183: 178-Black Knight app. 179-Spider-Man story-r. 180-Photo montage-c.						
181-Brunner-c(part-i), last 12¢ issue	4	8	12	22	34	45
1(6/74, 2nd series)-Brunner-c/a	6	12	18	41	66	90
2	3	6	9	20	30	40
3-5	3	6	9	14	19	24
6-10	2	4	6	8	10	12
11-13,15,20: 13,15-17-(Regular 25¢ editions)	1	2	3	4	5	7
13,15-17-(25¢-c variants, limited distribution)	3	6	9	18	27	35
14-(5/76) Dracula app.; (regular 25¢ edition)	2	4	6	8	10	12
14-(30¢-c variant, limited distribution)	4	8	12	28	44	60
21-40: 21-Origin-r/Doctor Strange #169. 23-25-(Regular 30¢ editions). 31-Sub-Mariner-c/story						4.00
23-25-(35¢-c variants, limited distribution)(6,8,10/77)	1	2	3	5	6	8
41-57,63-77,79-81: 56-Origin retold						3.50
58-62: 58-Re-intro Hannibal King (cameo). 59-Hannibal King full app. 59-62-Dracula app. (Darkhold storyline). 61,62-Doctor Strange, Blade, Hannibal King & Frank Drake team-up to battle. Dracula. 62-Death of Dracula & Lilith						5.00
78-New costume						3.00
Annual 1(1976, 52 pgs.)-New Russell-a (35 pgs.)	2	4	6	10	14	18
.../Silver Dagger Special Edition 1 (3/83, $2.50)-r/#1,2,4,5; Wrightson-c						3.00
... Vs. Dracula TPB (2006, $19.99) r/#14,58-62 and Tomb of Dracula #44						20.00
...What Is It That Disturbs You, Stephen? #1 (10/97, $5.99, 48 pgs.) Russell-a/Andreyko & Russell-s, retelling of Annual #1 story						6.00

NOTE: *Adkins* a-169, 170, 171i; c-169-171, 172i, 173. *Adams* a-4i. *Austin* a(i)-48-60, 66, 68, 70, 73; c(i)-38, 47-53, 55, 58-60, 70. *Brunner* a-1-5p; c-1-6, 22, 28-30, 33. *Colan* a(p)-172-178, 180-183, 6-18, 36-45, 47; c(p)-172, 174-183, 11-21, 23, 27, 35, 36, 47. *Ditko* a-179r, 3r. *Everett* c-183i. *Golden* a-46p, 55p; c-42-44, 46, 55p. *G. Kane* c(p)-8-10. *Miller* c-46p. *Nebres* a-20, 22, 23, 24i, 26i, 32i; c-32i, 34. *Rogers* a-48-53p; c-47p-53p. *Russell* a-34i, 46i, Annual 1. *B. Smith* c-179. *Paul Smith* a-54p, 56p, 65, 66p, 68p, 69, 71-73; c-56, 65, 66, 68, 71. *Starlin* a-23p, 26; c-25, 26. *Sutton* a-27-29p, 31i, 33i, 34p. Painted c-62, 63.

DOCTOR STRANGE (Volume 2)
Marvel Comics: Feb, 1999 - No. 4, May, 1999 ($2.99, limited series)
1-4: 1,2-Tony Harris-a/painted cover. 3,4-Chadwick-a 3.00

DOCTOR STRANGE CLASSICS
Marvel Comics Group: Mar, 1984 - No. 4, June, 1984 ($1.50, Baxter paper)
1-4: Ditko-r; Byrne-a. 4-New Golden pin-up 3.00
NOTE: *Byrne* c-1i, 2-4.

DOCTOR STRANGEFATE (See Marvel Versus DC #3 & DC Versus Marvel #4)
DC Comics (Amalgam): Apr, 1996 ($1.95)
1-Ron Marz script w/Jose Garcia-Lopez-(p) & Kevin Nowlan-(i). Access &
Charles Xavier app. 2.50

DOCTOR STRANGE MASTER OF THE MYSTIC ARTS (See Fireside Book Series)

DOCTOR STRANGE, SORCERER SUPREME
Marvel Comics (Midnight Sons imprint #60 on): Nov, 1988 - No. 90, June, 1996
($1.25/$1.50/$1.75/$1.95, direct sales only, Mando paper)
1 ($1.25) 4.00
2-9,12-14,16-25,27,29-40,42-49,51-64: 3-New Defenders app. 5-Guice-c/a begins.
  14-18-Morbius story line. 31-36-Infinity Gauntlet x-overs. 31-Silver Surfer app.
  33-Thanos-c & cameo. 36-Warlock app. 37-Silver Surfer app. 40-Daredevil x-over.
  41-Wolverine-c/story. 42-47-Infinity War x-overs. 47-Gamora app. 52,53-Morbius-c/stories.
  60,61-Siege of Darkness pt. 7 & 15. 60-Spot varch-c. 61-New Doctor Strange begins
  (cameo, 1st app.). 62-Dr. Doom & Morbius app. 2.50
10,11,26,28,41: 10-Re-intro Morbius w/new costume (11/89). 11-Hobgoblin app. 3.00
26-Werewolf by Night app. 28-Ghost Rider-s cont'd from G.R. #12; published at same time
  as Doctor Strange/Ghost Rider Special #1(4/91) 4.00
15-Unauthorized Amy Grant photo-c 4.00
50-($2.95, 52 pgs.)-Holo-grafx foil-c; Hulk, Ghost Rider & Silver Surfer app.; leads into new
  Secret Defenders series 3.00
65-74, 76-90: 65-Begin $1.95-c; bound-in card sheet. 72-Silver ink-c. 80-82- Ellis-s.
  84-DeMatteis story begins. 87-Death of Baron Mordo 2.50
75 ($2.50) 3.00
75 ($3.50)-Foil-c 4.00
Annual 2-4 ('92-'94, 68 pgs.)-2-Defenders app. 3-Polybagged w/card 3.00
Ashcan (1995, 75¢) 2.25
.../Ghost Rider Special 1 (4/91, $1.50)-Same book as D.S.S.S. #28 2.50
...Vs. Dracula 1 (3/94, $1.75, 52 pgs.)-r/Tomb of Dracula #44 & Dr. Strange #14 2.50
NOTE: *Colan* c/a-19. *Golden* c-28. *Guice* a-5-16, 18, 20-24; c-5-12, 20-24. See 1st series for Annual #1.

DOCTOR STRANGE: THE OATH
Marvel Comics: Dec, 2006 - No. 5, Apr, 2007 ($2.99, limited series)

1-5-Vaughan-s/Martin-a; Night Nurse app.						3.00
TPB (2007, $13.99) r/#1-5; sketch pages and promotional art						14.00

DR. TOM BRENT, YOUNG INTERN
Charlton Publications: Feb, 1963 - No. 5, Oct, 1963

1	3	6	9	16	22	28
2-5	2	4	6	10	14	18

DR. TOMORROW
Acclaim Comics (Valiant): Sept, 1997 - No. 12 ($2.50)
1-12: 1-Mignola-c 2.50

DR. VOLTZ (See Mighty Midget Comics)

DR. WEIRD
Big Bang Comics: Oct, 1994 - No. 2, May, 1995 ($2.95, B&W)
1,2: 1-Frank Brunner-c 4.00

DR. WEIRD SPECIAL
Big Bang Comics: Feb, 1994 ($3.95, B&W, 68 pgs.)
1-Origin-r by Starlin; Starlin-c. 4.00

DOCTOR WHO (Also see Marvel Premiere #57-60)
Marvel Comics Group: Oct, 1984 - No. 23, Aug, 1986 ($1.50, direct sales, Baxter paper)
1-15-British-r 4.00
16-23 5.00
Graphic Novel Voyager (1985, $8.95) color reprints of B&W comic pages from
  Doctor Who Magazine #88-99; Colin Baker afterword 12.00

DR. WHO & THE DALEKS (See Movie Classics)

DR. WONDER
Old Town Publishing: June, 1996 - No. 5 ($2.95, B&W)
1-5: 1-Intro & origin of Dr. Wonder; Dick Ayers-c/a; Irwin Hasen-a 3.00

DOCTOR ZERO
Marvel Comics (Epic Comics): Apr, 1988 - No. 8, Aug, 1989 ($1.25/$1.50)
1-8: 1-Sienkiewicz-c. 6,7-Spiegle-a 2.50
NOTE: *Sienkiewicz* a-3i, 4i; c-1. *Spiegle* a-6, 7.

DO-DO (Funny Animal Circus Stories)
Nation-Wide Publishers: 1950 - No. 7, 1951 (5¢, 5x7-1/4" Miniature)

1 (52 pgs.)	26	52	78	150	235	320
2-7	14	28	42	82	121	160

DODO & THE FROG, THE (Formerly Funny Stuff)
National Periodical Publications: No. 80, 9-10/54 - No. 88, 1-2/56; No. 89, 8-9/56; No. 90, 10-11/56; No. 91, 9/57; No. 92, 11/57 (See Comic Cavalcade)

80-1st app. Doodles Duck by Sheldon Mayer	20	40	60	117	184	250
81-91: Doodles Duck by Mayer in #81,83-90	14	28	42	76	108	140
92-(Scarce)-Doodles Duck by S. Mayer	18	36	54	105	165	225

DOGFACE DOOLEY
Magazine Enterprises: 1951 - No. 5, 1953

1(A-1 40)	8	16	24	40	50	60
2(A-1 43), 3(A-1 49), 4(A-1 53), 5(A-1 54)	6	12	18	28	34	40
I.W. Reprint #1('64), Super Reprint #17	2	4	6	9	13	16

DOG MOON
DC Comics (Vertigo): 1996 ($6.95, one-shot)
1-Robert Hunter-scripts; Tim Truman-c/a. 7.00

DOG OF FLANDERS, A
Dell Publishing Co.: No. 1088, Mar, 1960

Four Color 1088-Movie, photo-c	5	10	15	30	48	65

DOGPATCH (See Al Capp's... & Mammy Yokum)

DOGS OF WAR (Also see Warriors of Plasm)
Defiant: Apr, 1994 - No. 5, Aug, 1994 ($2.50)
1-5 2.50

DOGS-O-WAR
Crusade Comics: June, 1996 - No. 3, Jan, 1997 ($2.95, B&W, limited series)
1-3: 1,2-Photo-c 3.00

DOLLFACE & HER GANG (Betty Betz'...)
Dell Publishing Co.: No. 309, Jan, 1951

Four Color 309	5	10	15	35	55	75

DOLLMAN (Movie)
Eternity Comics: Sept, 1991 - No. 4, Dec, 1991 ($2.50, limited series)

Doll Man Quarterly #6 © QUA

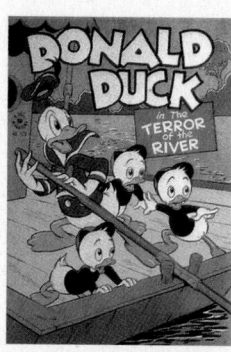

Donad Duck FC #108 © DIS

Donad Duck #29 © DIS

	GD 2.0	VG 4.0	FN 6.0	VF 8.0	VF/NM 9.0	NM- 9.2

1-4: Adaptation of film — — — — — 2.50

DOLL MAN QUARTERLY, THE (Doll Man #17 on; also see Feature Comics #27 & Freedom Fighters)
Quality Comics: Fall, 1941 - No. 7, Fall, '43; No. 8, Spr, '46 - No. 47, Oct, 1953

	GD 2.0	VG 4.0	FN 6.0	VF 8.0	VF/NM 9.0	NM- 9.2
1-Dollman (by Cassone), Justin Wright begin	327	654	981	2126	3763	5400
2-The Dragon begins; Crandall-a(5)	138	276	414	863	1432	2000
3,4	88	176	264	550	913	1275
5-Crandall-a	81	162	243	506	841	1175
6,7(1943)	53	106	159	333	549	765
8(1946)-1st app. Torchy by Bill Ward	162	324	486	1013	1682	2350
9	53	106	159	323	537	750
10-20	41	82	123	250	400	550
21-30: 28-Vs. The Flame	35	70	105	204	322	440
31-36,38,40: 31-(12/50)-Intro Elmo, the wonder dog (Dollman's faithful dog).
32-34-Jeb Rivers app.; 34 by Crandall(p)	32	64	96	186	293	400
37-Origin & 1st app. Dollgirl; Dollgirl bondage-c	46	92	138	281	466	650
39- "Narcotics…the Death Drug" c-/story	36	72	108	208	329	450
41-47	23	46	69	132	209	285
Super Reprint #11('64, r/#20),15(r/#23),17(r/#28): 15,17-Torchy app.; Andru/Esposito-c	3	6	9	20	30	40

NOTE: *Ward* Torchy in 8, 9, 11, 12, 14-24, 27; by Fox-#26, 30, 35-47. *Crandall* a-2, 5, 10, 13 & Super #11, 17, 18. *Crandall/Cuidera* c-40-42. *Guardineer* a-3. Bondage c-27, 37, 38, 39.

DOLLS
Sirius: June, 1996 ($2.95, B&W, one-shot)

1	—	—	—	—	—	3.00

DOLLY
Ziff-Davis Publ. Co.: No. 10, July-Aug, 1951 (Funny animal)

	GD	VG	FN	VF	VF/NM	NM-
10-Painted-c	8	16	24	44	57	70

DOLLY DILL
Marvel Comics/Newsstand Publ.: 1945

	GD	VG	FN	VF	VF/NM	NM-
1	18	36	54	105	165	225

DOLLZ, THE
Image Comics: Apr, 2001 - No. 2, June, 2001 ($2.95)

1,2: 1-Four covers; Sniegoski & Green-s/Green-a — — — — — 3.00

DOMINATION FACTOR
Marvel Comics: Nov, 1999 - 4.8, Feb, 2000 ($2.50, interconnected mini- series)

1.1, 2.3, 3.5, 4.7-Fantastic Four; Jurgens-s/a — — — — — 2.50
1.2, 2.4, 3.6, 4.8-Avengers; Ordway-s/a — — — — — 2.50

DOMINION
Image Comics: Jan, 2003 - No. 2 ($2.95)

1,2-Keith Giffen-s/a — — — — — 3.00

DOMINION (Manga)
Eclipse Comics: Dec, 1990 - No. 6., July, 1990 ($2.00, B&W, limited series)

1-6 — — — — — 3.00

DOMINION: CONFLICT 1 (Manga)
Dark Horse Comics: Mar, 1996 - No. 6, Aug, 1996 ($2.95, B&W, limited series)

1-6: Shirow-c/a/scripts — — — — — 3.00

DOMINIQUE: KILLZONE
Caliber Comics: May, 1995 ($2.95, B&W)

1 — — — — — 3.00

DOMINO (See X-Force)
Marvel Comics: Jan, 1997 - No. 3, Mar, 1997 ($1.95, limited series)

1-3: 2-Deathstrike-c/app. — — — — — 2.50

DOMINO (See X-Force)
Marvel Comics: June, 2003 - No. 4, Aug, 2003 ($2.50, limited series)

1-4-Stelfreeze c/a; Pruett-s. — — — — — 2.50

DOMINO CHANCE
Chance Enterprises: May-June, 1982 - No. 9, May, 1985 (B&W)

1-9: 7-1st app. Gizmo, 2 pgs. 8-1st full Gizmo story. 1-Reprint, May, 1985 — — — — — 2.50

DONALD AND MICKEY IN DISNEYLAND (See Dell Giants)

DONALD AND SCROOGE
Disney Comics: 1992 ($8.95, squarebound, 100 pgs.)

	GD	VG	FN	VF	VF/NM	NM-
nn-Don Rosa reprint special; r/U.S., D.D. Advs.	1	3	4	6	8	10
1-3 (1992, $1.50)-r/D.D. Advs. (Disney) #1,22,24 & U.S. #261-263,269	—	—	—	—	—	3.00

DONALD AND THE WHEEL (Disney)

Dell Publishing Co.: No. 1190, Nov, 1961

	GD	VG	FN	VF	VF/NM	NM-
Four Color 1190-Movie, Barks-c	8	16	24	54	90	125

DONALD DUCK (See Adventures of Mickey Mouse, Cheerios, Donald & Mickey, Ducktales, Dynabrite Comics, Gladstone Comic Album, Mickey & Donald, Mickey Mouse Mag., Story Hour Series, Uncle Scrooge, Walt Disney's Comics & Stories, W. D.'s Donald Duck, Wheaties & Whitman Comic Books, Wise Little Hen, The)

DONALD DUCK
Whitman Publishing Co./Grosset & Dunlap/K.K.: 1935, 1936 (All pages on heavy linen-like finish cover stock in color;1st book ever devoted to Donald Duck; see Advs. of Mickey Mouse for 1st app.) (9-1/2x13")

	GD	VG	FN	VF	VF/NM	NM-
978(1935)-16 pgs.; Illustrated text story book	300	600	900	1600	2800	4000
nn(1936)-36 pgs.plus hard cover & dust jacket. Story completely rewritten with B&W illos added. Mickey appears and his nephews are named Morty & Monty
Book only	285	570	855	1540	2670	3800
Dust jacket only….	65	130	195	350	575	800

DONALD DUCK (Walt Disney's) (10¢)
Whitman/K.K. Publications: 1938 (8-1/2x11-1/2", B&W, cardboard-c)
(Has D. Duck with bubble pipe on-c.)

	GD	VG	FN	VF	VF/NM	NM-
nn-The first Donald Duck & Walt Disney comic book; 1936 & 1937 Sunday strip-r(in B&W); same format as the Feature Books; 1st strips with Huey, Dewey & Louie from 10/17/37	380	760	1140	2090	3295	4500

DONALD DUCK (Walt Disney's…#262 on; see 4-Color listings for titles & Four Color No. 1109 for origin story)
Dell Publ. Co./Gold Key #85-216/Whitman #217-245/Gladstone #246 on: 1940 - No. 84, Sept-Nov, 1962; No. 85, Dec, 1962 - No. 245, July, 1984; No. 246, Oct, 1986 - No. 279, May, 1990; No. 280, Sept, 1993 - No. 307, Mar,1998

	GD	VG	FN	VF	VF/NM	NM-
Four Color 4(1940)-Daily 1939 strip-r by Al Taliaferro	1100	2200	3300	8250	14,875	21,500
Large Feature Comic 16(1/41?)-1940 Sunday strips-r in B&W	543	1086	1629	3800	6650	9500
Large Feature Comic 20('41)-Comic Paint Book, r-single panels from Large Feature #16 at top of each pg. to color; daily strip-r across bottom of each pg.	571	1142	1713	3997	7000	10,000
Four Color 9('42)- "Finds Pirate Gold"; 64 pgs. by Carl Barks & Jack Hannah (pgs. 1,2,5,12-40 are by Barks, his 1st Donald Duck comic book art work; © 8/17/42)	971	1942	2913	6800	11,900	17,000
Four Color 29(9/43)- "Mummy's Ring" by Barks; reprinted in Uncle Scrooge & Donald Duck #1('65), W. D. Comics Digest #44('73) & Donald Duck Advs. #14	686	1372	2058	4800	8400	12,000
Four Color 62(1/45)- "Frozen Gold"; 52 pgs. by Barks, reprinted in The Best of W.D. Comics & Donald Duck Advs. #4	196	392	588	1715	3208	4700
Four Color 108(1946)- "Terror of the River"; 52 pgs. by Carl Barks; reprinted in Gladstone Comic Album #2	143	286	429	1216	2258	3300
Four Color 147(5/47)-in "Volcano Valley" by Barks	96	192	288	816	1508	2200
Four Color 159(8/47)-in "The Ghost of the Grotto";52 pgs. by Carl Barks; reprinted in Best of Uncle Scrooge & Donald Duck #1 ('66) & The Best of W.D. Comics & D.D. Advs. #9; two Barks stories	85	170	255	723	1337	1950
Four Color 178(12/47)-1st app. Uncle Scrooge by Carl Barks; reprinted in Gold Key Christmas Parade #3 & The Best of Walt Disney Comics	115	230	345	978	1814	2650
Four Color 189(6/48)-by Carl Barks; reprinted in Best of Donald Duck & Uncle Scrooge #1('64) & D.D. Advs. #19	72	144	216	612	1131	1650
Four Color 199(10/48)-by Carl Barks; mentioned in Love and Death; r/in Gladstone Comic Album #5	78	156	234	663	1232	1800
Four Color 203(12/48)-by Barks; reprinted as Gold Key Christmas Parade #4	54	108	162	459	855	1250
Four Color 223(4/49)-by Barks; reprinted as Best of Donald Duck #1 & Donald Duck Advs. #3	72	144	216	612	1131	1650
Four Color 238(8/49)-in "Voodoo Hoodoo" by Barks	54	108	162	459	855	1250
Four Color 256(12/49)-by Barks; reprinted in Best of Donald Duck & Uncle Scrooge #2('67, Gladstone Comic Album #16 & W.D. Comics Digest #44('73)	46	92	138	368	672	975
Four Color 263(2/50)-Two Barks stories; r-in D.D. #278	45	90	135	360	655	950
Four Color 275(5/50), 282(7/50), 291(9/50), 300(11/50)-All by Carl Barks; 275, 282 reprinted in W.D. Comics Digest #44('73). #275 r/in Gladstone Comic Album #10. #291 r/in D. Duck Advs. #16	44	88	132	352	639	925
Four Color 308(1/51), 318(3/51)-by Barks; #318-reprinted in W.D. Comics Digest #34 & D.D. Advs. #2,19	41	82	123	334	600	865
Four Color 328(5/51)-by Carl Barks	41	82	123	328	589	850
Four Color 339(7-8/51), 379-2nd Uncle Scrooge-c; art not by Barks.	11	22	33	79	140	200
Four Color 348(9-10/51), 356,394-Barks-c only	19	38	57	141	251	360
Four Color 367(1-2/52)-by Barks; reprinted as Gold Key Christmas Parade #2 & #8						

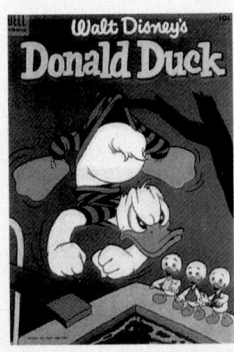

Donald Duck #31 © DIS

Donald Duck #268 © DIS

Don Fortune Magazine #4 © Don Fortune Pub.

	GD 2.0	VG 4.0	FN 6.0	VF 8.0	VF/NM 9.0	NM- 9.2
	32	64	96	240	445	650
Four Color 408(7-8/52), 422(9-10/52)-All by Carl Barks. #408-r-in Best of Donald Duck & Uncle Scrooge #1('64) & Gladstone Comic Album #13	32	64	96	240	445	650
26(11-12/52)-In "Trick or Treat" (Barks-a, 36pgs.) 1st story r-in Walt Disney Digest #16 & Gladstone C.A. #23	32	64	96	240	445	650
27-30-Barks-c only	12	24	36	82	146	210
31-44,47-50	7	14	21	45	73	100
45-Barks-a (6 pgs.)	14	28	42	99	175	250
46- "Secret of Hondorica" by Barks, 24 pgs.; reprinted in Donald Duck #98 & 154	19	38	57	138	244	350
51-Barks-a,1/2 pg.	7	14	21	45	73	100
52- "Lost Peg-Leg Mine" by Barks, 10 pgs.	14	28	42	99	175	250
53,55-59	6	12	18	39	62	85
54- "Forbidden Valley" by Barks, 26 pgs. (10¢ & 15¢ versions exist)	16	32	48	114	202	290
60- "Donald Duck & the Titanic Ants" by Barks, 20 pgs. plus 6 more pgs.	16	32	48	114	202	290
61-67,69,70	5	10	15	32	51	70
68-Barks-a, 5 pgs.	10	20	30	68	119	170
71-Barks-r, 1/2 pg.	5	10	15	32	51	70
72-78,80,82-97,99,100: 96-Donald Duck Album	5	10	15	30	48	65
79,81-Barks-a, 1pg.	5	10	15	32	51	70
98-Reprints #46 (Barks)	5	10	15	32	51	70
101,103-111,113-135: 120-Last 12¢ issue. 134-Barks-r/#52 & WDC&S 194. 135-Barks-r/WDC&S 198, 19 pgs.	3	6	9	20	30	40
102-Super Goof. 112-1st Moby Duck	3	6	9	21	32	42
136-153,155,156,158: 149-20¢-c begin	3	6	9	14	19	24
154-Barks-r(#46)	3	6	9	16	23	30
157,159,160,164: 157-Barks-r(#45); 25¢-c begin. 159-Reprints/WDC&S #192 (10 pgs.). 160-Barks-r(#26). 164-Barks-r/#79)	3	6	9	14	19	24
161-163,165-173,175-187,189-191: 175-30¢-c begin. 187-Barks r/#68.	2	4	6	11	16	20
174,188: 174-r/4-Color #394.	2	4	6	13	18	22
192-Barks-r(40 pgs.) from Donald Duck #60 & WDC&S #226,234 (52 pgs.)	3	6	9	15	21	26
193-200,202-207,209-211,213-216	2	4	6	9	13	16
201,208,212: 201-Barks-r/Christmas Parade #26, 16pgs. 208-Barks-r/#60 (6 pgs.). 212-Barks-r/WDC&S #130	2	4	6	9	13	16
217-219: 217 has 216 on-c. 219-Barks-r/WDC&S #106,107, 10 pgs. ea.	2	4	6	10	14	18
220,225-228: 228-Barks-r/F.C. #275	2	4	6	13	18	22
221,223,224: Scarce; only sold in pre-packs. 221(8/80), 223(11/80), 224(12/80)	5	10	15	32	51	70
222-(9-10/80)-(Very low distribution)	16	32	48	116	206	295
229-240: 229-Barks-r/FC #282. 230-Barks-r/ #52 & WDC&S #194. 236(2/82), 237(2-3/82), 238(3/82), 239(4/82), 240(5/82)	2	4	6	9	13	16
241-245: 241(4/83), 242(5/83), 243(3/84), 244(4/84), 245(7/84)(low print)	3	6	9	14	19	24
246-(1st Gladstone issue)-Barks-r/FC #422	3	6	9	15	21	26
247-249,251: 248,249-Barks-r/DD #54 & 26. 251-Barks-r/1945 Firestone	2	4	6	9	13	16
250-($1.50, 68 pgs.)-Barks-r/4-Color #9	2	4	6	10	14	18
252-277,280: 254-Barks-r/FC #328. 256-Barks-r/FC #147. 257-($1.50, 52 pgs.)-Barks-r/ Vacation Parade #1. 261-Barks-r/FC #300. 275-Kelly-r/FC #92. 280 (#1, 2nd Series)	1	2	3	5	6	8
278,279,286: 278,279 ($1.95, 68 pgs.); 278-Rosa-r/ Barks-r/FC #263. 279-Rosa-c; Barks-r/MOC #4. 286-Rosa-a	1	2	3	4	5	7
281,282,284	1	2	3	5	6	8
283-Don Rosa-a, part-c & scripts						5.00
285,287-307						6.00
286 ($2.95, 68 pgs.)-Happy Birthday, Donald						6.00
Mini-Comic #1(1976)-(3-1/4x6-1/2"); r/D.D. #150	2	4	6	8	11	14

NOTE: *Carl Barks* wrote all issues he illustrated, but #117, 126, 138 contain his script only. Issues 4-Color #189, 199, 203, 223, 238, 256, 263, 275, 282, 308, 348, 356, 367, 394, 408, 422, 26-30, 35, 44, 46, 52, 55, 57, 60, 65, 70-73, 77, 80,82, 83, 101, 103, 105, 106, 111, 126, 246r, 266r, 271r, 275r, 278r(F.C. 263) all have *Barks* covers. *Barks* r-263-267, 269-278-282, 284, 285. #96 titled "Comic Album", #99-"Christmas Album". New art issues (not reprints)-106-46, 148-63, 167, 169, 170, 172, 173, 175, 178, 179, 196, 209, 223, 225, 236. *Taliaferro* daily news-paper strips #258-260, 264, 284, 285; Sunday strips #247, 280-283.

DONALD DUCK ADVENTURES (See Walt Disney's Donald Duck Adventures)

DONALD DUCK ALBUM (See Comic Album No. 1,3 & Duck Album)
Dell Publishing Co./Gold Key: 5-7/59 - F.C. No. 1239, 10-12/61; 1962; 8/63 - No. 2, Oct, 1963

	GD 2.0	VG 4.0	FN 6.0	VF 8.0	VF/NM 9.0	NM- 9.2
Four Color 995 (#1)	6	12	18	43	69	95

	GD 2.0	VG 4.0	FN 6.0	VF 8.0	VF/NM 9.0	NM- 9.2
Four Color 1099,1140,1239-Barks-c	7	14	21	45	73	100
Four Color 1182, 01204-207 (1962-Dell)	5	10	15	32	51	70
1(8/63-Gold Key)-Barks-c	6	12	18	39	62	85
2(10/63)	5	10	15	30	48	65

DONALD DUCK AND THE BOYS (Also see Story Hour Series)
Whitman Publishing Co.: 1948 (5-1/4x5-1/2", 100pgs., hard-c; art & text)

	GD 2.0	VG 4.0	FN 6.0	VF 8.0	VF/NM 9.0	NM- 9.2
845-(49) new illos by Barks based on his Donald Duck 10-pager in WDC&S #74, Expanded text not written by Barks; Cover not by Barks	50	100	150	350	600	850

(Prices vary widely on this book)

DONALD DUCK AND THE CHRISTMAS CAROL
Whitman Publishing Co.: 1960 (A Little Golden Book, 6-3/8"x7-5/8", 28 pgs.)

	GD 2.0	VG 4.0	FN 6.0	VF 8.0	VF/NM 9.0	NM- 9.2
nn-Story book pencilled by Carl Barks with the intended title "Uncle Scrooge's Christmas Carol." Finished art adapted by Norman McGary. (Rare)-Reprinted in Uncle Scrooge in Color.	30	60	90	150	210	270

DONALD DUCK BEACH PARTY (Also see Dell Giants)
Gold Key: Sept, 1965 (12¢)

	GD 2.0	VG 4.0	FN 6.0	VF 8.0	VF/NM 9.0	NM- 9.2
1(#10158-509)-Barks-r/WDC&S #45; painted-c	6	12	18	43	69	95

DONALD DUCK BOOK (See Story Hour Series)

DONALD DUCK COMICS DIGEST
Gladstone Publishing: Nov, 1986 - No. 5, July, 1987 ($1.25/$1.50, 96 pgs.)

	GD 2.0	VG 4.0	FN 6.0	VF 8.0	VF/NM 9.0	NM- 9.2
1,3: 1-Barks-c/a-r	1	3	4	6	8	10
2,4,5: 4,5-$1.50-c						6.00

DONALD DUCK FUN BOOK (See Dell Giants)

DONALD DUCK IN DISNEYLAND (See Dell Giants)

DONALD DUCK MARCH OF COMICS (See March of Comics #4,20,41,56,69,263)

DONALD DUCK MERRY CHRISTMAS (See Dell Giant No. 53)

DONALD DUCK PICNIC PARTY (See Picnic Party listed under Dell Giants)

DONALD DUCK TELLS ABOUT KITES (See Kite Fun Book)

DONALD DUCK, THIS IS YOUR LIFE (Disney, TV)
Dell Publishing Co.: No. 1109, Aug-Oct, 1960

	GD 2.0	VG 4.0	FN 6.0	VF 8.0	VF/NM 9.0	NM- 9.2
Four Color 1109-Gyro flashback to WDC&S #141; origin Donald Duck (1st told)	14	28	42	102	181	260

DONALD DUCK XMAS ALBUM (See regular Donald Duck No. 99)

DONALD IN MATHMAGIC LAND (Disney)
Dell Publishing Co.: No. 1051, Oct-Dec, 1959 - No. 1198, May-July, 1961

	GD 2.0	VG 4.0	FN 6.0	VF 8.0	VF/NM 9.0	NM- 9.2
Four Color 1051 (#1)-Movie	9	18	27	63	107	150
Four Color 1198-Reprint of above	6	12	18	43	69	95

DONATELLO, TEENAGE MUTANT NINJA TURTLE
Mirage Studios: Aug, 1986 ($1.50, B&W, one-shot, 44 pgs.)

	GD 2.0	VG 4.0	FN 6.0	VF 8.0	VF/NM 9.0	NM- 9.2
1	1	2	3	5	7	9

DONDI
Dell Publishing Co.: No. 1176, Mar-May, 1961 - No. 1276, Dec, 1961

	GD 2.0	VG 4.0	FN 6.0	VF 8.0	VF/NM 9.0	NM- 9.2
Four Color 1176 (#1)-Movie; origin, photo-c	5	10	15	35	55	75
Four Color 1276	4	8	12	22	34	45

DON FORTUNE MAGAZINE
Don Fortune Publishing Co.: Aug, 1946 - No. 6, Feb, 1947

	GD 2.0	VG 4.0	FN 6.0	VF 8.0	VF/NM 9.0	NM- 9.2
1-Delecta of the Planets by C. C. Beck in all	26	52	78	150	235	320
2	14	28	42	82	121	160
3-6: 3-Bondage-c	13	26	39	74	105	135

DONKEY KONG (See Blip #1)

DONNA MATRIX
Reactor, Inc.: Aug, 1993 ($2.95, 52 pgs.)

	GD 2.0	VG 4.0	FN 6.0	VF 8.0	VF/NM 9.0	NM- 9.2
1-Computer generated-c/a by Mike Saenz; 3-D effects						3.00

DON NEWCOMBE
Fawcett Publications: 1950 (Baseball)

	GD 2.0	VG 4.0	FN 6.0	VF 8.0	VF/NM 9.0	NM- 9.2
nn-Photo-c	43	86	129	262	431	600

DON ROSA'S COMICS AND STORIES
Fantagraphics Books (CX Comics): 1983 ($2.95)

	GD 2.0	VG 4.0	FN 6.0	VF 8.0	VF/NM 9.0	NM- 9.2
1,2: 1-(68 pgs.) Reprints Rosa's The Pertwillaby Papers episodes #128-133. 2-(60 pgs.) Reprints episodes #134-138	2	4	6	11	16	20

DON SIMPSON'S BIZARRE HEROES (Also see Megaton Man)
Fiasco Comics: May, 1990 - No. 17, Sept, 1996 ($2.50/$2.95, B&W)

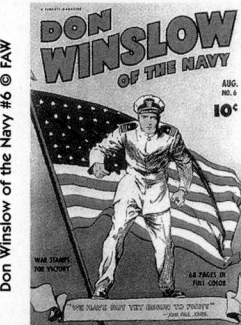

Don Winslow of the Navy #6 © FAW

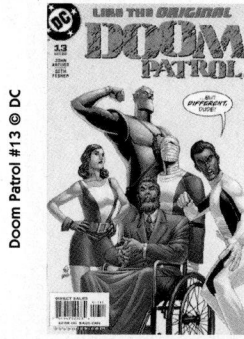

Doom Patrol #13 © DC

Doom 2099 #19 © MAR

	GD 2.0	VG 4.0	FN 6.0	VF 8.0	VF/NM 9.0	NM- 9.2

1-10,0,11-17: 0-Begin $2.95-c; r/Bizarre Heroes #1. 17-(9/96)-Indicia also reads Megaton
Man #0; intro Megaton Man and the Fiascoverse to new readers 3.00

DON'T GIVE UP THE SHIP
Dell Publishing Co.: No. 1049, Aug, 1959

Four Color 1049-Movie, Jerry Lewis photo-c	9	18	27	61	103	145

DON WINSLOW OF THE NAVY
Merwil Publishing Co.: Apr, 1937 - No. 2, May, 1937 (96 pgs.)(A pulp/comic book cross;
stapled spine)

V1#1-Has 16 pgs. comics in color. Captain Colorful & Jupiter Jones by Sheldon Mayer; complete Don Winslow novel	653	1306	1959	4900	–	–
2-Sheldon Mayer-a	177	354	531	1325	–	–

DON WINSLOW OF THE NAVY (See Crackajack Funnies, Famous Feature Stories, Popular Comics & Super Book #5,6)
Dell Publishing Co.: No. 2, Nov, 1939 - No. 22, 1941

Four Color 2 (#1)-Rare	186	372	558	1163	1932	2700
Four Color 22	45	90	135	275	450	625

DON WINSLOW OF THE NAVY (See TV Teens/ Movie, Radio, TV) (Fightin' Navy No. 74 on)
Fawcett Publications/Charlton No. 70 on: 2/43 - #64, 12/48; #65, 1/51 - #69, 9/51; #70, 3/55 - #73, 9/55

1-(68 pgs.)-Captain Marvel on cover	120	240	360	750	1213	1675
2	46	92	138	281	453	625
3	38	76	114	216	333	450
4-6: 6-Flag-c	29	58	87	167	259	350
7-10: 8-Last 68 pg. issue?	21	42	63	121	186	250
11-20	16	32	48	92	141	190
21-40	14	28	42	76	108	140
41-43,45-64: 51,60-Singapore Sal (villain) app. 64-(12/48)						
	11	22	33	64	90	115
44-Classic spider-c	24	48	72	139	220	300
65(1/51)-Flying Saucer attack; photo-c	18	36	54	105	165	225
66 - 69(9/51): All photo-c. 66-sci-fi story	14	28	42	80	115	150
70(3/55)-73: 70-73 r-/#26,58 & 59	9	18	27	47	61	75

DOOM
Marvel Comics: Oct, 2000 - No. 3, Dec, 2000 ($2.99, limited series)

1-3-Dr. Doom; Dixon-s/Manco-a 3.00

DOOM FORCE SPECIAL
DC Comics: July, 1992 ($2.95, 68 pgs., one-shot, mature) (X-Force parody)

1-Morrison scripts; Simonson, Steacy, & others-a; Giffen/Mignola-c 3.00

DOOM PATROL, THE (Formerly My Greatest Adventure No. 1-85; see Brave and the Bold,
DC Special Blue Ribbon Digest 19, Official... Index & Showcase No. 94-96)
National Periodical Publ.: No. 86, 3/64 - No. 121, 9-10/68; No. 122, 2/73 - No. 124, 6-7/73

86-1 pg. origin (#86-121 are 12¢ issues)	10	20	30	70	123	175
87-98: 88-Origin The Chief. 91-Intro. Mento	7	14	21	50	83	115
99-Intro. Beast Boy (later becomes the Changeling in New Teen Titans)						
	9	18	27	60	100	140
100-Origin Beast Boy; Robot-Maniac series begins (12/65)						
	9	18	27	60	100	140
101-110: 102-Challengers of the Unknown app. 105-Robot-Maniac series ends.						
106-Negative Man begins (origin)	6	12	18	37	59	80
111-120	5	10	15	30	48	65
121-Death of Doom Patrol; Orlando-c.	9	18	27	65	113	160
122-124: All reprints	2	4	6	8	10	12

DOOM PATROL
DC Comics (Vertigo imprint #64 on): Oct, 1987 - No, 87, Feb, 1995 (75¢-$1.95, new format)

1-Wraparound-c; Lightle-a 5.00
2-18: 3-1st app. Lodestone. 4-1st app. Karma. 8,15,16-Art Adams-c(i). 18-Invasion tie-in 3.00
19-(2/89)-Grant Morrison scripts begin, ends #63; 1st app Crazy Jane; $1.50-c
& new format begins. | 1 | 2 | 3 | 5 | 6 | 8 |
20-30: 29-Superman app. 30-Night Breed fold-out 5.00
31-34,37-41,45-49,51-56,58-60: 39-World Without End preview 2.50
35-1st brief app. of Flex Mentallo 5.00
36-1st full app. of Flex Mentallo 6.00
42-44-Origin of Flex Mentallo 4.00
50,57 ($2.50, 52 pgs.) 2.50
61-87: 61,70-Photo-c. 73-Death cameo (2 panels) 3.00
...And Suicide Squad 1 (3/88, $1.50, 52 pgs.)-Wraparound-c 2.50
Annual 1 (1988, $1.50, 52 pgs.) 2.50
Annual 2 (1994, $3.95, 68 pgs.)-Children's Crusade tie-in. 4.00
...: Crawling From the Wreckage TPB (2004, $19.95) r/#19-25; Morrison-s 20.00

...: Down Paradise Way TPB (2005, $19.99) r/#35-41; Morrison-s 20.00
...: Magic Bus TPB (2007, $19.99) r/#51-57; Morrison-s; new Bolland-c 20.00
...: Musclebound TPB (2006, $19.99) r/#42-50; Morrison-s; new Bolland-c 20.00
...: The Painting That Ate Paris TPB (2004, $19.95) r/#26-34; Morrison-s 20.00
NOTE: *Bisley* painted c-26-48, 55-58. *Bolland* c-64, 75. *Dringenberg* a-42(p). *Steacy* a-53.

DOOM PATROL
DC Comics: Dec, 2001 - No. 22, Sept, 2003 ($2.50)

1-Intro. new team with Robotman; Tan Eng Huat-c/a; John Arcudi-s 3.00
2-22: 4,5-Metamorpho & Elongated Man app. 13,14-Fisher-a. 20-Geary-a 2.50

DOOM PATROL (see JLA #94-99)
DC Comics: Aug, 2004 - No. 18, Jan, 2006 ($2.50)

1-18-John Byrne-s/a. 1-Green Lantern, Batman app. 2.50

DOOM PATROL (See Tangent Comics/ Doom Patrol)

DOOMSDAY
DC Comics: 1995 ($3.95, one-shot)

1-Year One story by Jurgens, L. Simonson, Ordway, and Gil Kane; Superman app. 4.00

DOOMSDAY + 1 (Also see Charlton Bullseye)
Charlton Comics: July, 1975 - No. 6, June, 1976; No. 7, June, 1978 - No. 12, May, 1979

1: #1-5 are 25¢ issues	3	6	9	15	20	25
2-6: 4-Intro Lor. 5-Ditko-a(1 pg.) 6-Begin 30¢-c	2	4	6	10	13	16
V3#7-12 (reprints #1-6)						6.00
5 (Modern Comics reprint, 1977)						4.00
NOTE: *Byrne* c/a-1-12; Painted covers-2-7.

DOOMSDAY SQUAD, THE
Fantagraphics Books: Aug, 1986 - No. 7, 1987 ($2.00)

1-7: Byrne-a in all. 1-3-New Byrne-c. 3-Usagi Yojimbo app. (1st in color). 4-Neal Adams-c.
5-7-Gil Kane-c 3.00

DOOM'S IV
Image Comics (Extreme): July, 1994 - No.4, Oct, 1994 ($2.50, limited series)

1-4-Liefeld story 2.50
1,2-Two alternate Liefeld-c each, 4 covers form 1 picture 5.00

DOOM: THE EMPEROR RETURNS
Marvel Comics: Jan, 2002 - No. 3, Mar, 2002 ($2.50, limited series)

1-3-Dixon-s/Manco-a; Franklin Richards app. 2.50

DOOM 2099 (See Marvel Comics Presents #118 & 2099: World of Tomorrow)
Marvel Comics: Jan, 1993 - No. 44, Aug, 1996 ($1.25/$1.50/$1.95)

1-24,26-44: 1-Metallic foil stamped-c. 4-Ron Lim-c(p). 17-bound-in trading card sheet.
40-Namor & Doctor Strange app. 41-Daredevil app., Namor-c/app. 44-Intro The Emissary;
story contin'd in 2099: World of Tomorrow 2.50
1-2nd printing 2.50
18-Variant polybagged with Sega Sub-Terrania poster 4.00
25 ($2.25, 52 pgs.) 2.50
25 ($2.95, 52pgs.) Foil embossed cover 3.00
29 ($2.50)-acetate-c. 3.50

DOORWAY TO NIGHTMARE (See Cancelled Comic Cavalcade)
DC Comics: Jan-Feb, 1978 - No. 5, Sept-Oct, 1978

1-Madame Xanadu in all	2	4	6	9	13	16
2-5: 4-Craig-a	1	3	4	6	8	10
NOTE: *Kaluta* covers on all. Merged into The Unexpected with No. 190.

DOPEY DUCK COMICS (Wacky Duck No. 3) (See Super Funnies)
Timely Comics (NPP): Fall, 1945 - No. 2, Apr, 1946

1,2-Casper Cat, Krazy Krow	23	46	69	130	205	280

DORK
Slave Labor: June, 1993 - Present ($2.50-$3.50, B&W, mature)

1-7,9-11: Evan Dorkin-c/a/scripts in all. 1(8/95),2(1/96)-(2nd printings). 1(3/97) (3rd printing).
1-Milk & Cheese app. 3-Eltingville Club starts. 6-Reprints 1st Eltingville Club app. from
Instant Piano #1 .... 3.00
8-($3.00) 3.50
Who's Laughing Now? TPB (2001, $11.95) reprints most of #1-5 .... 12.00
The Collected Dork, Vol. 2: Circling the Drain (6/03, $13.95) r/most of #7-10 & other-s 14.00

DOROTHY LAMOUR (Formerly Jungle Lil)(Stage, screen, radio)
Fox Features Syndicate: No. 2, June, 1950 - No. 3, Aug, 1950

2,3-Wood-a(3) each, photo-c	27	54	81	156	246	335

DOT DOTLAND (Formerly Little Dot Dotland)
Harvey Publications: No. 62, Sept, 1974 - No. 63, Nov, 1974

62,63		2	4	6	9	12	15

Double Comics 1941 © EP

Down With Crime #1 © FAW

Dracula Lives! Annual #1 © MAR

	GD 2.0	VG 4.0	FN 6.0	VF 8.0	VF/NM 9.0	NM- 9.2

DOTTY (...& Her Boy Friends)(Formerly Four Teeners; Glamorous Romances No. 41 on)
Ace Magazines (A. A. Wyn): No. 35, June, 1948 - No. 40, May, 1949

35-Teen-age	9	18	27	47	61	75
36-40: 37-Transvestism story	6	12	18	31	38	45

DOTTY DRIPPLE (Horace & Dotty Dripple No. 25 on)
Magazine Ent.(Life's Romances)/Harvey No. 3 on: 1946 - No. 24, June, 1952 (Also see A-1 No. 1, 3-8, 10)

1 (nd) (10¢)	11	22	33	62	86	110
2	7	14	21	37	46	55
3-10: 3,4-Powell-a	6	12	18	31	38	45
11-24	5	10	15	24	30	35

DOTTY DRIPPLE AND TAFFY
Dell Publishing Co.: No. 646, Sept, 1955 - No. 903, May, 1958

Four Color 646 (#1)	5	10	15	32	51	70
Four Color 691,718,746,801,903	4	8	12	22	34	45

DOUBLE ACTION COMICS
National Periodical Publications: No. 2, Jan, 1940 (68 pgs.), B&W

2-Contains original stories(?); pre-hero DC contents; same cover as Adventure No. 37. (seven known copies, five in high grade) (not an ashcan)

		1500	3000	4500	9200	13,850	18,500

NOTE: The cover to this book was probably reprinted from Adventure #37. #1 exists as an ash can copy with B&W cover; contains a coverless comic on inside with 1st & last page missing. Two copies exist in fair & fine condition proving at least limited newsstand distribution. #2 cover proof only sold in 2005 for $4,000.

DOUBLE COMICS
Elliot Publications: 1940 - 1944 (132 pgs.)

1940 issues; Masked Marvel-c & The Mad Mong vs. The White Flash covers known

		245	490	735	1531	2541	3550

1941 issues; Tornado Tim-c, Nordac-c, & Green Light covers known

		162	324	486	1013	1682	2350
1942 issues	117	234	351	731	1216	1700
1943,1944 issues	97	194	291	606	1003	1400

NOTE: Double Comics consisted of an almost endless combination of pairs of remaindered, unsold issues of comics representing most publishers and usually mixed publishers in the same book; e.g., a Captain America with a Silver Streak, or a Feature with a Detective, etc., could appear inside the same cover. The actual contents would have to determine its price. Prices listed are for average contents. Any containing rare origin or first issues are worth much more. Covers also vary in same year. Value would be approximately 50% contents of contents.

DOUBLE-CROSS (See The Crusaders)

DOUBLE-DARE ADVENTURES
Harvey Publications: Dec, 1966 - No. 2, Mar, 1967 (35¢/25¢, 68 pgs.)

1-Origin Bee-Man, Glowing Gladiator, & Magic-Master; Simon/Kirby-a (last S&K art as a team?)

	6	12	18	41	66	90
2-Williamson/Crandall-a; r/Alarming Adv. #3('63)	4	8	12	28	44	60

NOTE: Powell a-1. Simon/Sparling c-1, 2.

DOUBLE DRAGON
Marvel Comics: July, 1991 - No. 6, Dec, 1991 ($1.00, limited series)

1-6: Based on video game. 2-Art Adams-c ... 2.50

DOUBLE EDGE
Marvel Comics: Alpha, 1995; Omega, 1995 ($4.95, limited series)

Alpha ($4.95)- Punisher story, Nick Fury app. ... 5.00
Omega ($4.95)-Punisher, Daredevil, Ghost Rider app. Death of Nick Fury ... 5.00

DOUBLE IMAGE
Image Comics: Feb, 2001 - No. 5, July, 2001 ($2.95)

1-5: 1-Flip covers of Codeflesh (Casey-s/Adlard-a) and The Bod (Young-s). 2-Two covers. 5-"Trust in Me" begins; Chaudhary-a ... 3.00

DOUBLE LIFE OF PRIVATE STRONG, THE
Archie Publications/Radio Comics: June, 1959 - No. 2, Aug, 1959

1-Origin & re-intro The Shield; Simon & Kirby-c/a, their re-entry into the super-hero genre; intro./1st app. The Fly; 1st S.A. super-hero for Archie Publ.

	47	94	141	376	681	985
2-S&K-c/a; Tuska-a; The Fly app. (2nd or 3rd?)	29	58	87	216	388	560

DOUBLE TROUBLE
St. John Publishing Co.: Nov, 1957 - No. 2, Jan-Feb, 1958

1,2: Tuffy & Snuffy by Frank Johnson; dubbed "World's Funniest Kids"

	6	12	18	31	38	45

DOUBLE TROUBLE WITH GOOBER
Dell Publishing Co.: No. 417, Aug, 1952 - No. 556, May, 1954

Four Color 417	4	8	12	28	44	60
Four Color 471,516,556	3	6	9	20	30	40

DOUBLE UP
Elliott Publications: 1941 (Pocket size, 200 pgs.)

1-Contains rebound copies of digest sized issues of Pocket Comics, Speed Comics, & Spitfire Comics

	79	158	237	494	822	1150

DOVER & CLOVER (See All Funny & More Fun Comics #93)

DOVER BOYS (See Adventures of the...)

DOVER THE BIRD
Famous Funnies Publishing Co.: Spring, 1955

1-Funny animal; code approved

	7	14	21	35	43	50

DOWN
Image Comics (Top Cow): Dec, 2005 - No. 4, Mar, 2006 ($2.99)

1-4-Warren Ellis-s. 1-Tony Harris-a/c. 2-4-Cully Hamner-a. ... 3.00
Down & Top Cow's Best of Warren Ellis TPB (6/06, $15.99) r/#1-4 & Tales of the Witchblade #3,4; Ellis-s; script for Down #1 with Harris sketch pages ... 16.00

DOWN WITH CRIME
Fawcett Publications: Nov, 1952 - No. 7, Nov, 1953

1	36	72	108	208	329	450
2,4,5: 2,4-Powell-a in each. 5-Bondage-c	18	36	54	103	162	220
3-Used in POP, pg. 106; "H is for Heroin" drug story						
	20	40	60	117	184	250
6,7: 6-Used in POP, pg. 80	15	30	45	85	130	175

DO YOU BELIEVE IN NIGHTMARES?
St. John Publishing Co.: Nov, 1957 - No. 2, Jan, 1958

1-Mostly Ditko-c/a	50	100	150	305	503	700
2-Ayers-a	28	56	84	162	256	350

D.P. 7
Marvel Comics Group (New Universe): Nov, 1986 - No. 32, June, 1989

1-20, Annual #1 (11/87)-Intro. The Witness ... 2.50
21-32-Low print ... 4.00
... Classic Vol. 1 TPB (2007, $24.99) r/#1-9; Mark Gruenwald-s/Paul Ryan-a in all ... 25.00
NOTE: Williamson a-9i, 11i; c-9i.

DRACULA (See Bram Stoker's Dracula, Giant-Size..., Little Dracula, Marvel Graphic Novel, Requiem for Dracula, Spider-Man Vs...., Stoker's..., Tomb of... & Wedding of...; also see Movie Classics under Universal Presents as well as Dracula)

DRACULA (See Movie Classics for #1)(Also see Frankenstein & Werewolf)
Dell Publ. Co.: No. 2, 11/66 - No. 4, 3/67; No. 6, 7/72 - No. 8, 7/73 (No #5)

2-Origin & 1st app. Dracula (11/66) (super hero)	4	8	12	28	44	60
3,4: 4-Intro. Fleeta ('67)	3	6	9	19	29	38
6-('72)-r/#2 w/origin	3	6	9	15	21	26
7,8,-r/#3, #4	2	4	6	11	16	20

DRACULA (Magazine)
Warren Publishing Co.: 1979 (120 pgs., full color)

Book 1-Maroto art; Spanish material translated into English (mail order only)

	6	12	18	39	62	85

DRACULA CHRONICLES
Topps Comics: Apr, 1995 - No. 3, June, 1995 ($2.50, limited series)

1-3-Linsner-c ... 3.00

DRACULA LIVES! (Magazine)(Also see Tomb of Dracula) (Reprinted in Stoker's Dracula)
Marvel Comics Group: 1973(no month) - No. 13, July, 1975 (75¢, B&W) (76 pgs.)

1-Boris painted-c	6	12	18	43	69	95
2 (7/73)-1st time origin Dracula; Adams, Starlin-a	4	8	12	28	44	60
3-1st app. Robert E. Howard's Soloman Kane; Adams-c/a						
	4	8	12	28	44	60
4,5: 4-Ploog-a. 5(V2#1)-Bram Stoker's Classic Dracula adapt. begins						
	3	6	9	20	30	40
6-9: 6-8-Bram Stoker adapt. 9-Bondage-c	3	6	9	20	30	40
10 (1/75)-16 pg. Lilith solo (1st?)	4	8	12	24	37	50
11-13: 11-21 pg. Lilith solo sty. 12-31 pg. Dracula sty	3	6	9	20	30	40
Annual 1(Summer, 1975, $1.25, 92 pgs.)-Morrow painted-c; 6 Dracula stys.						
25 pgs. Adams-a(?)	4	8	12	22	34	45

NOTE: N. Adams a-2, 3, 10i, Annual 1r(2, 3i). Alcala a-9. Buscema a-3p, 6p, Annual 1p. Colan a(p)-1, 2, 5, 6, 8. Evans a-7. Gulacy a-9. Heath a-1r, 13. Pakula a-6r. Sutton a-13. Weiss r-Annual 1p. 4 Dracula stories each in 1, 609; 3 Dracula stories each in 2, 4, 5,, 13.

DRACULA: LORD OF THE UNDEAD
Marvel Comics: Dec, 1998 - No. 3, Dec, 1998 ($2.99, limited series)

1-3-Olliffe & Palmer-a ... 3.00

DRACULA: RETURN OF THE IMPALER

Dracula: Vlad the Impaler #1 © Topps

Dragon Ball pt. 4 #1 © Bird Studios

Dragon Lines #2 © MAR

	GD	VG	FN	VF	VF/NM	NM-			GD	VG	FN	VF	VF/NM	NM-
	2.0	4.0	6.0	8.0	9.0	9.2			2.0	4.0	6.0	8.0	9.0	9.2

Slave Labor Graphics: July, 1993 - No. 4, Oct, 1994 ($2.95, limited series)

1-4 .... 3.00

DRACULA'S REVENGE
IDW Publishing: Apr, 2004 - No. 3 ($3.99, limited series)

1,2-Forbeck-s/Kudranski-a 4.00

DRACULA VERSUS ZORRO
Topps Comics: Oct, 1993 - No. 2, Nov, 1993 ($2.95, limited series)

1,2: 1-Spot varnish & red foil-c. 2-Polybagged w/16 pg. Zorro #0 ..... 3.00

DRACULA VERSUS ZORRO
Dark Horse Comics: Sept, 1998 - No. 2, Oct, 1998 ($2.95, limited series)

1,2 .... 3.00

DRACULA: VLAD THE IMPALER (Also see Bram Stoker's Dracula)
Topps Comics: Feb, 1993 - No. 3, Apr, 1993 ($2.95, limited series)

1-3-Polybagged with 3 trading cards each; Maroto-c/a 3.00

DRAFT, THE
Marvel Comics: 1988 ($3.50, one-shot, squarebound)

1-Sequel to "The Pitt" 3.50

DRAG 'N' WHEELS (Formerly Top Eliminator)
Charlton Comics: No. 30, Sept, 1968 - No. 59, May, 1973

30		4	8	12	28	44	60
31-40-Scot Jackson begins		3	6	9	19	29	38
41-50		3	6	9	17	25	32
51-59: Scot Jackson		2	4	6	13	18	22
Modern Comics Reprint 58('78)							5.00

DRAGON, THE (Also see The Savage Dragon)
Image Comics (Highbrow Ent.): Mar, 1996 - No. 5, July, 1996 (99¢, lim. series)

1-5: Reprints Savage Dragon limited series w/new story & art. 5-Youngblood app; includes 5 pg. Savage Dragon story from 1984 ..... 2.50

DRAGON ARCHIVES, THE (Also see The Savage Dragon)
Image Comics: Jun, 1998 - No. 4, Jan, 1999 ($2.95, B&W)

1-4: Reprints early Savage Dragon app. 3.00

DRAGON, THE: BLOOD & GUTS (Also see The Savage Dragon)
Image Comics (Highbrow Entertainment): Mar, 1995 - No. 3, May, 1995 ($2.50, lim. series)

1-3: Jason Pearson-c/a/scripts 2.50

DRAGON BALL
Viz Comics: 1998 - Present ($2.95, B&W, Manga reprints read right to left)

Part 1: 1-Akira Toriyama-s/a		1	2	3	5	6	8
2-12							5.00
1-12 (2nd & 3rd printings)							3.00
Part 2: 1-15: 15-($3.50-c)							4.00
Part 3: 1-14							3.00
Part 4: 1-10							3.00
Part 5: 1-7							3.00
Part 6: 1,2							3.50

DRAGON BALL Z
Viz Comics: 1998 - Present ($2.95, B&W, Manga reprints read right to left)

Part 1: 1-Akira Toriyama-s/a		2	4	6	8	10	12
2-9							5.00
1-9 (2nd & 3rd printings)							3.00
Part 2: 1-14							4.00
Part 3: 1-10							3.00
Part 4: 1-15							3.00
Part 5: 1-10							3.00

DRAGON CHIANG
Eclipse Books: 1991 ($3.95, B&W, squarebound, 52 pgs.)

nn-Timothy Truman-c/a(p) 4.00

DRAGONFLIGHT
Eclipse Books: Feb, 1991 - No. 3, 1991 ($4.95, 52 pgs.)

Book One - Three: Adapts 1968 novel 5.00

DRAGONFLY (See Americomics #4)
Americomics: Sum, 1985 - No. 8, 1986 ($1.75/$1.95)

1 .... 3.50
2-8 .... 2.50

DRAGONFORCE

Aircel Publishing: 1988 - No. 13, 1989 ($2.00)

1-Dale Keown-c/a/scripts in #1-12 .... 3.00
2-13: 13-No Keown-a 2.50
...Chronicles Book 1-5 ($2.95, B&W, 60 pgs.): Dale Keown-r/Dragonring & Dragonforce 3.00

DRAGONHEART (Movie)
Topps Comics: May, 1996 - No. 2, June, 1996 ($2.95/$4.95, limited series)

1-($2.95, 24 pgs.)-Adaptation of the film; Hildebrandt Bros-c; Lim-a 3.00
2-($4.95, 64 pgs.) 5.00

DRAGONLANCE (Also see TSR Worlds)
DC Comics: Dec, 1988 - No. 34, Sept, 1991 ($1.25/$1.50, Mando paper)

1-Based on TSR game 4.00
2-34: Based on TSR game. 30-32-Kaluta-c 3.00

DRAGONLANCE: CHRONICLES
Devil's Due Publ.: Aug, 2005 - No. 8, Mar, 2006 ($2.95)

1-8-Dabb-s/Kurth-a 3.00
...: Dragons of Autumn Twilight TPB (2006, $17.95) r/#1-8 ...... 18.00

DRAGONLANCE: CHRONICLES (Volume 2)
Devil's Due Publ.: July, 2006 - No. 4, Jan, 2007 ($4.95/$4.99, 48 pgs.)

1-4-Dragons of Winter Night; Dabb-s/Kurth-a 5.00
...: Dragons of Winter Night TPB (3/07, $18.99) r/#1-4; cover gallery 19.00

DRAGONLANCE: CHRONICLES (Volume 3)
Devil's Due Publ.: Mar, 2007 - No. 12, 3/2008 ($3.50)

1-3-Dragons of Spring Dawning; Dabb-s/Cope-a 3.50

DRAGONLANCE: THE LEGEND OF HUMA
Devil's Due Publ.: Jan, 2004 - No. 6, Oct, 2005 ($2.95)

1-6-Mike Miller & Rael-a 3.00

DRAGON LINES
Marvel Comics (Epic Comics/Heavy Hitters): May, 1993 - No. 4, Aug, 1993 ($1.95, limited series)

1-($2.50)-Embossed-c; Ron Lim-c/a in all 3.00
2-4 .... 2.50

DRAGON LINES: WAY OF THE WARRIOR
Marvel Comics (Epic Comics/ Heavy Hitters): Nov, 1993 - No. 2, Jan, 1994 ($2.25, limited series)

1,2-Ron Lim-c/a(p) 2.50

DRAGONQUEST
Silverwolf Comics: Dec, 1986 - No. 2, 1987 ($1.50, B&W, 28 pgs.)

1,2-Tim Vigil-c/a in all 5.00

DRAGONRING
Aircel Publishing: 1986 - V2#15, 1988 ($1.70/$2.00, B&W/color)

1-6: 6-Last B&W issue, V2#1-15($2.00, color) 2.50

DRAGON'S CLAWS
Marvel UK, Ltd.: July, 1988 - No. 10, Apr, 1989 ($1.25/$1.50/$1.75, British)

1-10: 3-Death's Head (1st app.). 4-Silhouette of Death's Head on last pg. 5-1st full app. new Death's Head 2.50

DRAGON'S LAIR: SINGE'S REVENGE (Based on the Don Bluth video game)
CrossGen Comics: Sept, 2003 - No. 3 ($2.95, limited series)

1-3-Mangels-s/Laguna-a 3.00

DRAGONSLAYER (Movie)
Marvel Comics Group: October, 1981 - No. 2, Nov, 1981

1,2-Paramount Disney movie adaptation 2.50

DRAGON'S STAR 2
Caliber Press: 1994 ($2.95, B&W)

1 .... 3.00

DRAGON STRIKE
Marvel Comics: Feb, 1994 ($1.25)

1-Based on TSR role playing game 2.50

DRAGOON WELLS MASSACRE
Dell Publishing Co.: No. 815, June, 1957

Four Color 815-Movie, photo-c		7	14	21	50	83	115

DRAGSTRIP HOTRODDERS (World of Wheels No. 17 on)
Charlton Comics: Sum, 1963; No. 2, Jan, 1965 - No. 16, Aug, 1967

1		7	14	21	49	80	110

	GD 2.0	VG 4.0	FN 6.0	VF 8.0	VF/NM 9.0	NM- 9.2
2-5	4	8	12	26	41	55
6-16	4	8	12	22	34	45

DRAIN
Image Comics: Nov, 2006 - Present ($2.99)

1-4: 1-Cebulski-s/Takeda-a; two covers by Takeda and Finch						3.00

DRAKUUN
Dark Horse Comics: Feb, 1997 - No. 25, Mar, 1999 ($2.95, B&W, manga)

1-25; 1-6- Johji Manabe-s/a in all. Rise of the Dragon Princess series. 7-12-Revenge of Gustav. 13-18-Shadow of the Warlock. 19-25-The Hidden War						3.00

DRAMA
Sirius: June, 1994 ($2.95, mature)

1-1st full color Dawn app. in comics	2	4	6	11	16	20
1-Limited edition (1400 copies); signed & numbered; fingerprint authenticity	4	8	12	24	37	50

NOTE: Dawn's 1st full color app. was a pin-up in Amazing Heroes' Swimsuit Special #5.

DRAMA OF AMERICA, THE
Action Text: 1973 ($1.95, 224 pgs.)

1- "Students' Supplement to History"						5.00

DRAWING ON YOUR NIGHTMARES
Dark Horse Comics: Oct, 2003 ($2.99, one-shot)

1-Short stories; The Goon, Criminal Macabre, Tales of the Vampires; Templesmith-c						3.00

DRAX THE DESTROYER
Marvel Comics: Nov, 2005 - No. 4, Feb, 2006 ($2.99, limited series)

1-4-Giffen-s/Breitweiser-a						3.00
...: Earthfall TPB (2006, $10.99) r/#1-4; character design page						11.00

DREADLANDS (Also see Epic)
Marvel Comics (Epic Comics): 1992 - No. 4, 1992 ($3.95, lim. series, 52 pgs.)

1-4: Stiff-c						4.00

DREADSTAR
Marvel Comics (Epic Comics)/First Comics No. 27 on: Nov, 1982 - No. 64, Mar, 1991

1						4.00
2-5,8-49						3.00
6,7,51-64: 6,7-1st app. Interstellar Toybox; 8pgs. ea.; Wrightson-a. 51-64-Lower print run						4.00
50						5.00
Annual 1 (12/83)-r/The Price						4.00

DREADSTAR
Malibu Comics (Bravura): Apr, 1994 - No. 6, Jan, 1995 ($2.50, limited series)

1-6-Peter David scripts: 1,2-Starlin-c						2.50

NOTE: Issues 1-6 contain Bravura stamps.

DREADSTAR AND COMPANY
Marvel Comics (Epic Comics): July, 1985 - No. 6, Dec, 1985

1-6: 1,3,6-New Starlin-c: 2-New Wrightson-c; reprints of Dreadstar series						2.50

DREAM BOOK OF LOVE (Also see A-1 Comics)
Magazine Enterprises: No. 106, June-July, 1954 - No. 123, Oct-Nov, 1954

A-1 106 (#1)-Powell, Bolle-a; Montgomery Clift, Donna Reed photo-c	14	28	42	80	115	150
A-1-114 (#2)-Guardineer, Bolle-a; Piper Laurie, Victor Mature photo-c	10	20	30	58	79	100
A-1 123 (#3)-Movie photo-c	10	20	30	54	72	90

DREAM BOOK OF ROMANCE (Also see A-1 Comics)
Magazine Enterprises: No. 92, 1954 - No. 124, Oct-Nov, 1954

A-1 92 (#5)-Guardineer-a; photo-c	14	28	42	76	108	140
A-1 101 (#6)(4-6/54)-Marlon Brando photo-c; Powell, Bolle, Guardineer-a	21	42	63	122	191	260
A-1 109,110,124: 109 (#7)(7-8/54)-Powell-a; movie photo-c. 110 (#8)(1/54)- Movie photo-c. 124 (#8)(10-11/54)	11	22	33	60	83	105

DREAMER, THE
Kitchen Sink Press: 1986 ($6.95, B&W, graphic novel)

nn-Will Eisner-s/a						12.00
DC Comics Reprint ($7.95, 6/00)						8.00

DREAMERY, THE
Eclipse Comics: Dec, 1986 - No. 14, Feb, 1989 ($2.00, B&W, Baxter paper)

1-14: 2-7-Alice In Wonderland adapt.						2.50

DREAMING, THE (See Sandman, 2nd Series)
DC Comics (Vertigo): June, 1996 - No. 60, May, 2001 ($2.50)

	GD 2.0	VG 4.0	FN 6.0	VF 8.0	VF/NM 9.0	NM- 9.2
1-McKean-c on all.; LaBan scripts & Snejbjerg-a						4.00
2-30,32-60: 2,3-LaBan scripts & Snejbjerg-a. 4-7-Hogan scripts; Parkhouse-a. 8-Zulli-a. 9-11-Talbot-s/Taylor-a(p). 41-Previews Sandman: The Dream Hunters. 50-Hempel, Fegredo, McManus, Totleben-a						2.50
31-($3.95) Art by various						4.00
...Beyond The Shores of Night TPB ('97, $19.95) r/#1-8						20.00
...Special (7/98, $5.95, one-shot) Trial of Cain						6.00
...Through The Gates of Horn and Ivory TPB ('99, $19.95) r/#15-19,22-25						20.00

DREAM OF LOVE
I. W. Enterprises: 1958 (Reprints)

1,2,8: 1-r/Dream Book of Love #1; Bob Powell-a. 2-r/Great Lover's Romances #10. 8-Great Lover's Romances #1; also contains 2 Jon Juan stories by Siegel & Schomburg; Kinstler-c.	2	4	6	10	14	18
9-Kinstler-c; 1pg. John Wayne interview & Frazetta illo from John Wayne Adv. Comics #2	2	4	6	10	14	18

DREAM POLICE
Marvel Comics (Icon): Aug, 2005 ($3.99)

1-Straczynski-s/Deodato-a/c						4.00

DREAMS OF THE DARKCHYLDE
Darkchylde Entertainment: Oct, 2000 - No. 6, Sept, 2001 ($2.95)

1-6-Randy Queen-s in all. 1-Brandon Peterson-c/a						3.00

DREAM TEAM (See Battlezones: Dream Team 2)
Malibu Comics (Ultraverse): July, 1995 ($4.95, one-shot)

1-Pin-ups teaming up Marvel & Ultraverse characters by various artists including Allred, Romita, Darrow, Balent, Quesada & Palmiotti						5.00

DREAMWAVE PRODUCTIONS PREVIEW
Dreamwave Productions: May, 2002 ($1.00, one-shot)

nn-Previews Arkanium, Transformers: The War Within and other series						2.50

DRIFT FENCE (See Zane Grey 4-Color 270)

DRIFT MARLO
Dell Publishing Co.: May-July, 1962 - No. 2, Oct-Dec, 1962

01-232-207 (#1)	5	10	15	32	51	70
2 (12-232-212)	4	8	12	28	44	60

DRISCOLL'S BOOK OF PIRATES
David McKay Publ. (Not reprints): 1934 (B&W, hardcover; 124 pgs, 7x9")

nn-By Montford Amory	25	50	75	144	222	300

DROIDS (Based on Saturday morning cartoon) (Also see Dark Horse Comics)
Marvel Comics (Star Comics): April, 1986 - No. 8, June, 1987

1-R2D2 & C-3PO from Star Wars app. in all	2	4	6	11	16	20
2-8: 2,5,7,8-Williamson-a(i)	2	4	6	8	10	12

NOTE: Romita a-3p. Sinnott a-3i.

DROOPY (see Tom & Jerry #60)

DROOPY (Tex Avery's)
Dark Horse Comics: Oct, 1995 - No. 3, Dec, 1995 ($2.50, limited series)

1-3: Characters created by Tex Avery; painted-c						2.50

DROPSIE AVENUE: THE NEIGHBORHOOD
Kitchen Sink Press: June, 1995 ($15.95/$24.95, B&W)

nn-Will Eisner (softcover)						16.00
nn-Will Eisner (hardcover)						25.00

DROWNED GIRL, THE
DC Comics (Piranha Press): 1990 ($5.95, 52 pgs, mature)

nn						6.00

DRUG WARS
Pioneer Comics: 1989 ($1.95)

1-Grell-c						2.50

DRUID
Marvel Comics: May, 1995 - No. 4, Aug, 1995 ($2.50, limited series)

1-4: Warren Ellis scripts.						3.00

DRUM BEAT
Dell Publishing Co.: No. 610, Jan, 1955

Four Color 610-Movie, Alan Ladd photo-c	8	16	24	56	93	130

DRUMS OF DOOM
United Features Syndicate: 1937 (25¢)(Indian)(Text w/color illos.)

nn-By Lt. F.A. Methot; Golden Thunder app.; Tip Top Comics ad in comic; nice-c						

Duckman #2 © Paramount

Durango Kid #4 © ME

DV8 #11 © WSP

	GD 2.0	VG 4.0	FN 6.0	VF 8.0	VF/NM 9.0	NM- 9.2

DRUNKEN FIST
Jademan Comics: Aug, 1988 - No. 54, Jan, 1993 ($1.50/$1.95, 68 pgs.)

	35	70	105	201	318	435

1	4.00
2-50	3.00
51-54	2.50

DUCK ALBUM (See Donald Duck Album)
Dell Publishing Co.: No. 353, Oct, 1951 - No. 840, Sept, 1957
Four Color 353 (#1)-Barks-c; 1st Uncle Scrooge-c (also appears on back-c).

	GD	VG	FN	VF	VF/NM	NM-
	10	20	30	70	123	175
Four Color 450-Barks-c	7	14	21	49	80	110
Four Color 492,531,560,586,611,649,686,	6	12	18	41	66	90
Four Color 726,782,840	5	10	15	35	55	75

DUCKMAN
Dark Horse Comics: Sept, 1990 ($1.95, B&W, one-shot)
1-Story and art by Everett Peck 4.00

DUCKMAN
Topps Comics: Nov, 1994 - No. 5, May, 1995; No. 0, Feb, 1996 ($2.50)
0 (2/96, $2.95, B&W)-r/Duckman #1 from Dark Horse Comics 4.00
1-5: 1-w/ coupon #A for Duckman trading card. 2-w/Duckman 1st season episode guide 3.00

DUCKMAN: THE MOB FROG SAGA
Topps Comics: Nov, 1994 - No. 3, Dec, 1995 ($2.50, limited series)
1-3: 1-w/coupon #B for Duckman trading card, S. Shaw!-c 2.50

DUCKTALES
Gladstone Publ.: Oct, 1988 - No. 13, May, 1990 (1,2,9-11: $1.50; 3-8: 95¢)
1-Barks-r 6.00
2-11: 2-7,9-11-Barks-r 4.00
12,13 ($1.95, 68 pgs.)-Barks-r; 12-r/F.C. #495 .... 5.00
Disney Presents Carl Barks' Greatest DuckTales Stories Vol. 1 (Gemstone Publ., 2006, $10.95)
 r/stories adapted from the animated TV series including "Back to the Klondike" 11.00
Disney Presents Carl Barks' Greatest DuckTales Stories Vol. 2 (Gemstone Publ., 2006, $10.95)
 r/stories adapted for the animated TV series; "Robot Robbers" app. 11.00

DUCKTALES (TV)
Disney Comics: June, 1990 - No. 18, Nov, 1991 ($1.50)
1-All new stories 3.00
2-18 .... 2.50
The Movie nn (1990, $7.95, 68 pgs.)-Graphic novel adapting animated movie 9.00

DUDLEY (Teen-age)
Feature/Prize Publications: Nov-Dec, 1949 - No. 3, Mar-Apr, 1950

	GD	VG	FN	VF	VF/NM	NM-
1-By Boody Rogers	15	30	45	83	124	165
2,3	10	20	30	54	72	90

DUDLEY DO-RIGHT (TV)
Charlton Comics: Aug, 1970 - No. 7, Aug, 1971 (Jay Ward)

	GD	VG	FN	VF	VF/NM	NM-
1	8	16	24	58	97	135
2-7	6	12	18	41	66	90

DUEL MASTERS (Based on a trading card game) (Also see Free Comic Book Day Edition in the Promotional Comics section)
Dreamwave Productions: Nov, 2003 - Present ($2.95)
1-8: 1-Bagged with card; Augustyn-s 3.00

DUKE OF THE K-9 PATROL
Gold Key: Apr, 1963

	GD	VG	FN	VF	VF/NM	NM-
1 (10052-304)	4	8	12	24	37	50

DUMBO (Disney; see Movie Comics, & Walt Disney Showcase #12)
Dell Publishing Co.: No. 17, 1941 - No. 668, Jan, 1958
Four Color 17 (#1)-Mickey Mouse, Donald Duck, Pluto app.

	GD	VG	FN	VF	VF/NM	NM-
	255	510	765	1594	2647	3700
Large Feature Comic 19 ('41)-Part-r 4-Color 17	290	580	870	1813	3007	4200
Four Color 234 ('49)	13	26	39	95	168	240

Four Color 668 (12/55)-1st of two printings. Dumbo on-c with starry sky. Same-c as #234

	GD	VG	FN	VF	VF/NM	NM-
	10	20	30	70	123	175

Four Color 668 (1/58)-2nd printing. Same cover altered with Timothy Mouse added. Same

	GD	VG	FN	VF	VF/NM	NM-
contents	7	14	21	45	73	100

DUMBO COMIC PAINT BOOK (See Dumbo, Large Feature Comic No. 19)

DUNC AND LOO (#1-3 titled "Around the Block with Dunc and Loo")
Dell Publishing Co.: Oct-Dec, 1961 - No. 8, Oct-Dec, 1963

	GD 2.0	VG 4.0	FN 6.0	VF 8.0	VF/NM 9.0	NM- 9.2
1	9	18	27	60	100	140
2	6	12	18	43	69	95
3-8	5	10	15	35	55	75

NOTE: Written by John Stanley; Bill Williams art.

DUNE (Movie)
Marvel Comics: Apr, 1985 - No. 3, June, 1985
1-3-r/Marvel Super Special; movie adaptation 3.00

DURANGO KID, THE (Also see Best of the West, Great Western & White Indian)
(Charles Starrett starred in Columbia's Durango Kid movies)
Magazine Enterprises: Oct-Nov, 1949 - No. 41, Oct-Nov, 1955 (All 36 pgs.)

	GD	VG	FN	VF	VF/NM	NM-
1-Charles Starrett photo-c; Durango Kid & his horse Raider begin; Dan Brand & Tipi (origin) begin by Frazetta & continue through #16	72	144	216	450	750	1050
2-Starrett photo-c.	37	74	111	213	327	440
3-5-All have Starrett photo-c.	32	64	96	184	285	385
6-10: 7-Atomic weapon-c/story	17	34	51	96	148	200
11-16-Last Frazetta issue	14	28	42	80	115	150
17-Origin Durango Kid	17	34	51	96	148	200
18-30: 18-Fred Meagher-a on Dan Brand begins. 19-Guardineer-c/a(3) begins, end #41. 23-Intro. The Red Scorpion	10	20	30	58	79	100
31-Red Scorpion returns	10	20	30	54	72	90

32-41-Bolle/Frazetta!sh-a (Dan Brand; true in later issues?)

	GD	VG	FN	VF	VF/NM	NM-
	9	18	27	52	69	85

NOTE: #6, 8, 14, 15 contain Frazetta art not reprinted in White Indian. Ayers c-18. Guardineer a(3)-19-41; c-19-41. Fred Meagher a-18-29 at least.

DURANGO KID, THE
AC Comics: 1990 - #2, 1990 ($2.50,$2.75, half-color)
1,2: 1-Starrett photo front/back-c; Guardineer-r. 2-B&W)-Starrett photo-c; White Indian-r by Frazetta; Guardineer-r (50th anniversary of films) 3.00

DUSTCOVERS: THE COLLECTED SANDMAN COVERS 1989-1997
DC Comics (Vertigo): 1997 ($39.95, Hardcover)
Reprints Dave McKean's Sandman covers with Gaiman text 40.00
Softcover (1998, $24.95) 25.00

DUSTY STAR
Image Comics (Desperado Studios): No. 0, Apr, 1997 - No. 1 ($2.95, B&W)
0,1-Pruett-s/Robinson-a 3.00

DUSTY STAR
Image Comics (Desperado Publishing): June, 2006 - Present ($3.50)
1-Pruett-s/Robinson-s/a 3.50

DV8 (See Gen 13)
Image Comics (WildStorm Productions): Aug, 1996 - No. 25, Dec, 1998;
DC Comics (WildStorm Prod.): No. 0, Apr, 1999 - No. 32, Nov, 1999 ($2.50)
1/2 .... 6.00
1-Warren Ellis scripts & Humberto Ramos-c/a(p) 4.00
1-(7-variant covers, w/1 by Jim Lee) ...each 4.00
2-4: 3-No Ramos-a 3.00
5-32: 14-Regular-c, 14-Variant-c by Charest. 26-(5/99)-McGuinness-c 2.50
14-($3.50) Voyager Pack w/Danger Girl preview 5.00
0-(4/99, $2.95) Two covers (Rio and McGuinness) 3.00
Annual 1 (1/98, $2.95) 3.00
Annual 1999 ($3.50) Slipstream x-over with Gen13 .... 3.50
Rave-(7/96, $1.75)-Ramos-c; pinups & interviews 3.00
...: Neighborhood Threat TPB (2002, $14.95) r/#1-6 & #1/2; Ellis intro.; Ramos-c 15.00

DV8 VS. BLACK OPS
Image Comics (WildStorm): Oct, 1997 - No. 3, Dec, 1997 ($2.50, lim. series)
1-3-Bury-s/Norton-a 3.00

DWIGHT D. EISENHOWER
Dell Publishing Co.: December, 1969

	GD	VG	FN	VF	VF/NM	NM-
01-237-912 - Life story	5	10	15	30	48	65

DYNABRITE COMICS
Whitman Publishing Co.: 1978 - 1979 (69¢, 10x7-1/8", 48 pgs., cardboard-c)
(Blank inside covers)
11350 - Walt Disney's Mickey Mouse & the Beanstalk (4-C 157). 11350-1 - Mickey Mouse Album (4-C 1057, 1151,1246). 11351 - Mickey Mouse & His Sky Adventure (4-C 214, 343). 11354 - Goofy: A Gaggle of Giggles. 11354-1 - Super Goof Meets Super Thief. 11356 - (?). 11359 - Bugs Bunny-r. 11360 - Winnie the Pooh Fun and Fantasy (Disney-r).

	GD	VG	FN	VF	VF/NM	NM-
each....	2	4	6	8	10	12

11352 - Donald Duck (4-C 408, Donald Duck 45,52)-Barks-a. 11352-1 - Donald Duck (4-C 318, 10 pg. Barks/WDC&S 125,128)-Barks-c(r). 11353 - Daisy Duck's Diary (4-C 1055,1150) Barks-a. 11355 - Uncle Scrooge (Barks-a/U.S. 12,33). 11355-1 - Uncle Scrooge (Barks-a/U.S. 13,16) Barks-a. 11357 - Star Trek (r/-Star Trek 33,41). 11358 - Star Trek (r/-Star Trek 34,36). 11361 - Gyro Gearloose and the Disney Ducks (r/4-C 1047,1184)-

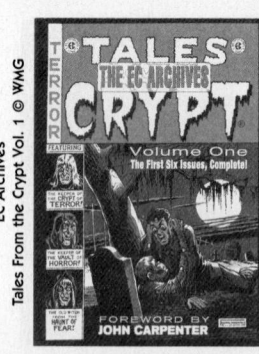

	GD	VG	FN	VF	VF/NM	NM-
	2.0	4.0	6.0	8.0	9.0	9.2

Barks-c(r)
each....   2   4   6   8   11   14

DYNAMIC ADVENTURES
I. W. Enterprises: No. 8, 1964 - No. 9, 1964

	GD	VG	FN	VF	VF/NM	NM-
8-Kayo Kirby-r by Baker?/Fight Comics 53.	3	6	9	14	20	25
9-Reprints Avon's "Escape From Devil's Island"; Kinstler-c	3	6	9	16	23	30
nn (no date)-Reprints Risks Unlimited with Rip Carson, Senorita Rio; r/Fight #53	3	6	9	16	22	28

DYNAMIC CLASSICS (See Cancelled Comic Cavalcade)
DC Comics: Sept-Oct, 1978 (44 pgs.)

	GD	VG	FN	VF	VF/NM	NM-
1-Neal Adams Batman, Simonson Manhunter-r	2	4	6	8	10	12

DYNAMIC COMICS (No #4-7)
Harry 'A' Chesler: Oct, 1941 - No. 3, Feb, 1942; No. 8, Mar, 1944 - No. 25, May, 1948

	GD	VG	FN	VF	VF/NM	NM-
1-Origin Major Victory by Charles Sultan (reprinted in Major Victory #1), Dynamic Man & Hale the Magician; The Black Cobra only app.; Major Victory & Dynamic Man begin	90	180	270	563	932	1300
2-Origin Dynamic Boy & Lady Satan; intro. The Green Knight & sidekick Lance Cooper	200	400	600	1250	2075	2900
3-1st small logo, resumes with #10	88	176	264	550	913	1275
8-Classic-c; Dan Hastings, The Echo, The Master Key, Yankee Boy begin; Yankee Doodle Jones app.; hypo story	100	200	300	625	1038	1450
9-Mr. E begins; Mac Raboy-c	74	148	222	463	769	1075
10-Small logo begins	57	114	171	356	591	825
11-16: 15-The Sky Chief app. 16-Marijuana story	50	100	150	305	503	700
17(1/46)-Illustrated in SOTI, "The children told me what the man was going to do with the hot poker," but Wertham saw this in Crime Reporter #2	60	120	180	375	625	875
18,19,21,22,25: 21-Dinosaur-c; new logo	41	82	123	250	400	550
20-Bare-breasted woman-c	76	152	228	475	788	1100
23,24-(68 pgs.): 23-Yankee Girl app.	40	80	120	237	379	520
I.W. Reprint #1,8('64): 1-r/#23. 8-Exist?	3	7	10	18	27	35

NOTE: Kinstler c-IW #1. Tuska art in many issues, #3, 9, 11, 12, 16, 19. Bondage c-16.

DYNAMITE (Becomes Johnny Dynamite No. 10 on)
Comic Media/Allen Hardy Publ.: May, 1953 - No. 9, Sept, 1954

	GD	VG	FN	VF	VF/NM	NM-
1-Pete Morisi-a; Don Heck-c; r-as Danger #6	31	62	93	178	282	385
2	15	30	45	90	140	190
3-Marijuana story; Johnny Dynamite (1st app.) begins by Pete Morisi(c/a); Heck text-a; man shot in face at close range	20	40	60	117	184	250
4-Injury-to-eye, prostitution; Morisi-c/a	19	38	57	112	176	240
5-9-Morisi-c/a in all. 7-Prostitute story & reprints	15	30	45	85	130	175

DYNAMO (Also see Tales of Thunder & T.H.U.N.D.E.R. Agents)
Tower Comics: Aug, 1966 - No. 4, June, 1967 (25¢)

	GD	VG	FN	VF	VF/NM	NM-
1-Crandall/Wood, Ditko/Wood-a; Weed series begins; NoMan & Lightning cameos; Wood-c/a	9	18	27	60	100	140
2-4: Wood-c/a in all	5	10	15	35	55	75

NOTE: Adkins/Wood a-2. Ditko a-4?. Tuska a-2, 3.

DYNAMO 5 (See Noble Causes: Extended Family #2 for debut of Captain Dynamo)
Image Comics: Jan, 2007 - Present ($3.50)

1-Intro. the offspring of Captain Dynamo; Faerber-s/Asrar-a						8.00
2						5.00
3-7; 5-Intro. Synergy						3.50

DYNAMO JOE (Also see First Adventures & Mars)
First Comics: May, 1986 - No. 15, Jan, 1988 (#12-15: $1.75)

1-15: 4-Cargonauts begin, Special 1(1/87)-Mostly-r/Mars						2.25

DYNOMUTT (TV)(See Scooby-Doo (3rd series))
Marvel Comics Group: Nov, 1977 - No. 6, Sept, 1978 (Hanna-Barbera)

	GD	VG	FN	VF	VF/NM	NM-
1-The Blue Falcon, Scooby Doo in all	4	8	12	22	34	45
2-6-All newsstand only	3	6	9	16	23	30

EAGLE, THE (1st Series) (See Science Comics & Weird Comics #8)
Fox Features Syndicate: July, 1941 - No. 4, Jan, 1942

	GD	VG	FN	VF	VF/NM	NM-
1-The Eagle begins; Rex Dexter of Mars app. by Briefer; all issues feature German war covers	179	358	537	1119	1860	2600
2-The Spider Queen begins (origin)	85	170	255	531	878	1225
3,4: 3-Joe Spook begins (origin)	67	134	201	419	697	975

EAGLE (2nd Series)
Rural Home Publ.: Feb-Mar, 1945 - No. 2, Apr-May, 1945

	GD	VG	FN	VF	VF/NM	NM-
1-Aviation stories	48	96	144	293	484	675
2-Lucky Aces	26	52	78	152	239	325

NOTE: *L. B. Cole* c/a in each.

EAGLE
Crystal Comics/Apple Comics #17 on: Sept, 1986 - No. 23, 1989 ($1.50/1.75/1.95, B&W)

1-23: 12-Double size origin issue ($2.50)						2.50
1-Signed and limited						4.00

EARTH 4 (Also see Urth 4)
Continuity Comics: Dec, 1993 - No. 4, Jan, 1994 ($2.50)

1-4: 1-3 all listed as Dec, 1993 in indicia						2.50

EARTH 4 DEATHWATCH 2000
Continuity Comics: Apr, 1993 - No. 3, Aug, 1993 ($2.50)

1-3						2.50

EARTH MAN ON VENUS (An...) (Also see Strange Planets)
Avon Periodicals: 1951

	GD	VG	FN	VF	VF/NM	NM-
nn-Wood-a (26 pgs.); Fawcette-c	133	266	399	831	1378	1925

EARTHWORM JIM (TV, cartoon)
Marvel Comics: Dec, 1995 - No. 3, Feb, 1996 ($2.25)

1-3: Based on video game and toys						3.00

EARTH X
Marvel Comics: No. 0, Mar, 1999 - No. 12, Apr, 2000 ($3.99/$2.99, lim. series)

	GD	VG	FN	VF	VF/NM	NM-
nn- (Wizard supplement) Alex Ross sketchbook; painted-c	1	3	4	6	8	10
Sketchbook (2/99) New sketches and previews						6.00
0-(3/99)-Prelude; Leon-a(p)/Ross-c	1	2	3	4	5	7
1-(4/99)-Leon-a(p)/Ross-c	1	2	3	4	5	7
1-2nd printing						3.00
2-12						3.50
#X (6/00, $3.99)						4.00
HC (2005, $49.99) r/#0,1-12, #/2, X; forward by Joss Whedon; Ross sketch pages						50.00
TPB (12/00, $24.95) r/#0,1-12, X; forward by Joss Whedon						25.00

EASTER BONNET SHOP (See March of Comics No. 29)

EASTER WITH MOTHER GOOSE
Dell Publishing Co.: No. 103, 1946 - No. 220, Mar, 1949

	GD	VG	FN	VF	VF/NM	NM-
Four Color 103 (#1)-Walt Kelly-a	17	34	51	128	227	325
Four Color 140 ('47)-Kelly-a	14	28	42	102	181	260
Four Color 185 ('48),220-Kelly-a	13	26	39	93	164	235

EAST MEETS WEST
Innovation Publishing: Apr, 1990 - No. 2, 1990 ($2.50, limited series, mature)

1,2: 1-Stevens part-i; Redondo-c(i). 2-Stevens-c(i); 1st app. Cheech & Chong in comics						2.50

EC ARCHIVES
Gemstone Publishing: 2006 - Present ($49.95, hardcover with dustjacket)

Shock SuspenStories Vol. 1 - Recolored reprints of #1-6; forward by Steven Spielberg						50.00
Shock SuspenStories Vol. 2 - Recolored reprints of #7-12; forward by Dean Kamen						50.00
Tales From the Crypt Vol. 1 - Recolored reprints of Crypt of Terror #17-19 and Tales From the Crypt #20-22; forward by John Carpenter; Al Feldstein behind-the-scenes info						50.00
Tales From the Crypt Vol. 2 - Recolored reprints of #23-28; forward by Joe Dante						50.00
Two-Fisted Tales Vol. 1 - Recolored reprints of #18-23; forward by Stephen Geppi						50.00
Two-Fisted Tales Vol. 2 - Recolored reprints of #24-29; forward by Rocco Versaci, Ph.D.						50.00
Weird Science Vol. 1 - Recolored reprints of #1-6; forward by George Lucas						50.00
Weird Science Vol. 2 - Recolored reprints of #7-12; forward by Paul Levitz						50.00

E. C. CLASSIC REPRINTS
East Coast Comix Co.: May, 1973 - No. 12, 1976 (E. C. Comics reprinted in color minus ads)

	GD	VG	FN	VF	VF/NM	NM-
1-The Crypt of Terror #1 (Tales from the Crypt #46)	2	4	6	10	14	18
2-12: 1-Weird Science #15('52). 3-Shock SuspenStories #12. 4-Haunt of Fear #12. 5-Weird Fantasy #13('52). 6-Crime SuspenStories #25. 7-Vault of Horror #26. 8-Shock SuspenStories #6. 9-Two-Fisted Tales #34. 10-Haunt of Fear #23. 11-Weird Science 12(#1). 12-Shock SuspenStories #2	2	4	6	8	10	12

EC CLASSICS
Russ Cochran: Aug, 1985 - No. 12, 1986? (High quality paper; each-r 8 stories in color) (#2-12 were resolicited in 1990)($4.95, 56 pgs., 8x11")

	GD	VG	FN	VF	VF/NM	NM-
1-12: 1-Tales From the Crypt. 2-Weird Science. 3-Two-Fisted Tales. 4-Frontline Combat (r/9). 4-Shock SuspenStories. 5-Weird Fantasy. 6-Vault of Horror. 7-Weird Science-Fantasy (r/23,24). 8-Crime SuspenStories (r/17,18). 9-Haunt of Fear (r/14,15). 10-Panic (r/1,2). 11-Tales From the Crypt (r/23,24). 12-Weird Science (r/20,22)	1	2	3	4	5	7

Eclipse Graphic Album #35 © ECL

Eclipso #10 © DC

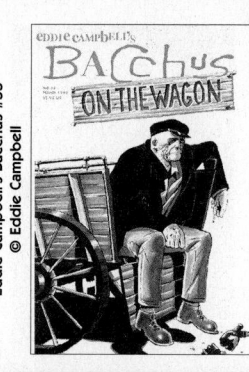

Eddie Campbell's Bacchus #33 © Eddie Campbell

	GD 2.0	VG 4.0	FN 6.0	VF 8.0	VF/NM 9.0	NM- 9.2

ECHO
Image Comics (Dreamwave Prod.): Mar, 2000 - No. 5, Sept, 2000 ($2.50)

1-5: 1-3-Pat Lee-c — 2.50
0-(7/00) — 2.50

ECHO OF FUTUREPAST
Pacific Comics/Continuity Com.: May, 1984 - No. 9, Jan, 1986 ($2.95, 52 pgs.)

1-9: Neal Adams-c/a in all? — 6.00
NOTE: **N. Adams** a-1-6,7i,9i; c-1-3, 5p,7i,8,9i. **Golden** a-1-6 (Bucky O'Hare). c-6. **Toth** a-6,7.

ECLIPSE GRAPHIC ALBUM SERIES
Eclipse Comics: Oct, 1978 - 1989 (8-1/2x11") (B&W #1-5)

1-Sabre (10/78, B&W, 1st print.); Gulacy-a; 1st direct sale graphic novel — 16.00
1-Sabre (2nd printing, 1/79) — 8.00
1-Sabre (3rd printing, $5.95) — 6.00
3,4: 3-Detectives, Inc. (5/80, B&W, $6.95)-Rogers-a. 4-Stewart The Rat (1980, B&W)
-G. Colan-a — 10.00
5-The Price (10/81, B&W)-Starlin-a — 16.00
2,6,7,13: 2-Night Music (11/79, B&W)-Russell-a. 6-I Am Coyote (11/84, color)-Rogers-c/a.
7-The Rocketeer (2nd print, $7.95). 7-The Rocketeer (3rd print, 1991, $8.95).
13-The Sisterhood of Steel ('87, $8.95, color) — 10.00
7-The Rocketeer (9/85, color)-Dave Stevens-a (r/chapters 1-5)(see Pacific Presents &
Starslayer); has 7 pgs. new-a — 14.00
7-The Rocketeer, signed & limited HC — 60.00
7-The Rocketeer, hardcover (1986, $19.95) — 20.00
7-The Rocketeer, unsigned HC (3rd, $32.95) — 33.00
8-Zorro In Old California ('86, color) — 14.00
8,12-Hardcover — 18.00
9,10: 9-Sacred And The Profane ('86)-Steacy-a. 10-Somerset Holmes ('86, $15.95)-Adults,
soft-c — 16.00
9,10,12-Hardcover ($24.95). 12-signed & #'d — 25.00
11-Floyd Farland, Citizen of the Future ('87, $2.95, B&W) Chris Ware-s/a — 7.00
12,28,31,35: 12-Silverheels ('87, $7.95, color). 28-Miracleman Book I ($5.95). 31-Pigeons
From Hell by R. E. Howard (11/88). 35-Rael: Into The Shadow of the Sun ('88, $7.95) 10.00
14,16,18,20,23,24: 14-Samurai, Son of Death ('87, $4.95, B&W). 16,18,20,23-See Airfighters
Classics #1-4. 24-Heartbreak ($4.95, B&W) — 7.00
14 (2nd pr.),17,21: 14-Samurai, Son of Death ($3.95, 2nd printing). 17-Valkyrie, Prisoner of
the Past SC ('88, $3.95, color). 21-XYR-Multiple ending comic ('88, $3.95, B&W) — 6.00
15,22,27: 15-Twisted Tales (11/87, color)-Dave Stevens-c. 22-Alien Worlds #1
(5/88, $3.95, 52 pgs.)-Nudity. 27-Fast Fiction (She) ($5.95, B&W) — 8.00
17-Valkyrie, Prisoner of the Past S&N Hardcover ('88, $19.95) — 20.00
19-Scout: The Four Monsters ('88, $14.95, color)-r/Scout #1-7; soft-c — 15.00
25,30,32-34: 25-Alex Toth's Zorro Vol. 1 ,2($10.95, B&W). 30-Brought To Light; Alan Moore
scripts ('89). 32-Teenaged Dope Slaves and Reform School Girls. 33-Bogie.
34-Air Fighters Classics #5 — 12.00
29-Real Love: Best of Simon & Kirby Romance Comics(10/88, $12.95) — 15.00
30,31: Limited hardcover ed. ($29.95). 31-signed — 30.00
36-Dr. Watchstop: Adventures in Time and Space ('89, $8.95) — 10.00

ECLIPSE MAGAZINE (Becomes Eclipse Monthly)
Eclipse Publishing: May, 1981 - No. 8, Jan, 1983 ($2.95, B&W, magazine)

1-8: 1-1st app. Cap'n Quick and a Foozle by Rogers, Ms. Tree by Beatty, and Dope by Trina
Robbins. 2-1st app. I Am Coyote by Rogers. 7-1st app. Masked Man by Boyer — 3.00
NOTE: **Colan** a-3, 5, 8. **Golden** c/a-2. **Gulacy** a-6, c-1. 6. **Kaluta** c/a-5. **Mayerik** a-2, 3. **Rogers** a-1-8.
Starlin a-1. **Sutton** a-6.

ECLIPSE MONTHLY
Eclipse Comics: Aug, 1983 - No. 10, Jul, 1984 (Baxter paper, $2.00/$1.50/$1.75)

1-10: ($2.00, 52 pgs.)-Cap'n Quick and a Foozle by Rogers, Static by Ditko, Dope by Trina
Robbins, Rio by Wildey, The Masked Man by Boyer begin. 3-Ragamuffins begins — 2.50
NOTE: **Boyer** c-6. **Ditko** a-1-3. **Rogers** a-1-4; c-2, 4, 7. **Wildey** a-1, 2, 5, 9, 10; c-5, 10.

ECLIPSO (See Brave and the Bold #64, House of Secrets #61 & Phantom Stranger, 1987)
DC Comics: Nov, 1992 - No. 18, Apr, 1994 ($1.25)

1-18: 1-Giffen plots/breakdowns begin. 10-Darkseid app. Creeper in #3-6,9,11-13.
18-Spectre-c/s — 2.50
Annual 1 (1993, $2.50, 68 pgs.)-Intro Prism — 2.50

ECLIPSO: THE DARKNESS WITHIN
DC Comics: July, 1992 - No. 2, Oct, 1992 ($2.50, 68 pgs.)

1,2: 1-With purple gem attached to-c; 1-Without gem; Superman, Creeper app.,
2-Concludes Eclipso storyline from annuals — 2.50

E. C. 3-D CLASSICS (See Three Dimensional...)

ECTOKID (See Razorline)
Marvel Comics: Sept, 1993 - No. 9, May, 1994 ($1.75/$1.95)

1-($2.50)-Foil embossed-c; created by C. Barker — 3.00
2-9: 2-Origin. 5-Saint Sinner x-over — 2.50
...: Unleashed! 1 (10/94, $2.95, 52 pgs.) — 3.00

ED "BIG DADDY" ROTH'S RATFINK COMIX (Also see Ratfink)
World of Fandom/ Ed Roth: 1991 - No. 3, 1991 ($2.50)

1-3: Regular Ed., 1-Limited double cover	1	3	4	6	8	10

EDDIE CAMPBELL'S BACCHUS
Eddie Campbell Comics: May, 1995 - Present ($2.95, B&W)

1-Cerebus app.	1	2	3	5	6	8

1-2nd printing (5/97) — 3.00
2-10: 9-Alex Ross back-c — 5.00
11-60 — 3.00
Doing The Islands With Bacchus ('97, $17.95) — 18.00
Earth, Water, Air & Fire ('98, $9.95) — 10.00
King Bacchus ('99, $12.95) — 13.00
The Eyeball Kid ('98, $8.50) — 8.50

EDDIE STANKY (Baseball Hero)
Fawcett Publications: 1951 (New York Giants)

nn-Photo-c	34	68	102	197	311	425

EDEN'S TRAIL
Marvel Comics: Jan, 2003 - No. 6 ($2.99, limited series, Marvelscope-printed sideways)

1-5-Chuck Austen-s/Steve Uy-a — 3.00

EDGAR ALLAN POE'S - THE FALL OF THE HOUSE OF USHER AND OTHER TALES OF HORROR
Catlan Communications Pub.: Sept. 1985 (hardcover graphic novel)

nn-Reprints of Poe story issues from Warren comic mags; all Richard Corben-a;
numbered edition of 350 signed by Corben — 110.00

EDGAR BERGEN PRESENTS CHARLIE McCARTHY
Whitman Publishing Co. (Charlie McCarthy Co.): No. 764, 1938 (36 pgs.; 15x10-1/2"; color)

764	74	148	222	463	769	1075

EDGAR RICE BURROUGHS' TARZAN: A TALE OF MUGAMBI
Dark Horse Comics: 1995 ($2.95, one-shot)

1 — 3.00

**EDGAR RICE BURROUGHS' TARZAN: IN THE LAND THAT TIME FORGOT
AND THE POOL OF TIME**
Dark Horse Comics: 1996 ($12.95, trade paperback)

nn-r/Russ Manning-a — 13.00

EDGAR RICE BURROUGHS' TARZAN OF THE APES
Dark Horse Comics: May, 1999 ($12.95, trade paperback)

nn-reprints — 13.00

EDGAR RICE BURROUGHS' TARZAN: THE LOST ADVENTURE
Dark Horse Comics: Jan, 1995 - No. 4, Apr, 1995 ($2.95, B&W, limited series)

1-4: ERB's last Tarzan story, adapted by Joe Lansdale — 3.00
Hardcover (12/95, $19.95) — 20.00
Limited Edition Hardcover ($99.95)-signed & numbered — 100.00

EDGAR RICE BURROUGHS' TARZAN: THE RETURN OF TARZAN
Dark Horse Comics: May, 1997 - No. 3, July, 1997 ($2.95, limited series)

1-3 — 3.00

EDGAR RICE BURROUGHS' TARZAN: THE RIVERS OF BLOOD
Dark Horse Comics: Nov, 1999 - No. 4, Feb, 2000 ($2.95, limited series)

1-4-Kordey-c/a — 3.00

EDGE
Malibu Comics (Bravura): July, 1994 - No. 3, Apr, 1995 ($2.50/$2.95, unfinished lim.series)

1,2-S. Grant-story & Gil Kane-c/a; w/Bravura stamp — 2.50
3-($2.95-c) — 3.00

EDGE (Re-titled as Vector starting with #13)
CrossGeneration Comics: May, 2002 - No. 12, Apr, 2003 ($9.95/$11.95/$7.95, TPB)

1-3: Reprints from various CrossGen titles — 10.00
4-8-($11.95) — 12.00
9-12-$7.95, 8-1/4" x 5-1/2") digest-sized reprints — 8.00

EDGE OF CHAOS
Pacific Comics: July, 1983 - No. 3, Jan, 1984 (Limited series)

1-3-Morrow c/a; all contain nudity — 2.50

ED WHEELAN'S JOKE BOOK STARRING FAT & SLAT (See Fat & Slat)

Eerie #4 © AVON

Eerie #15 © WP

Egbert #7 © QUA

	GD 2.0	VG 4.0	FN 6.0	VF 8.0	VF/NM 9.0	NM- 9.2

EERIE (Strange Worlds No. 18 on)
Avon Per.: No. 1, Jan, 1947; No. 1, May-June, 1951 - No. 17, Aug-Sept, 1954

1(1947)-1st supernatural comic; Kubert, Fugitani-a; bondage-c	423	846	1269	2908	5104	7300
1(1951)-Reprints story from 1947 #1	71	142	213	444	735	1025
2-Wood-c/a; bondage-c	72	144	216	450	750	1050
3-Wood-c; Kubert, Wood/Orlando-a	72	144	216	450	750	1050
4,5-Wood-c/a	59	118	177	369	610	850
6,8,13,14: 8-Kinstler-a; bondage-c; Phantom Witch Doctor story	34	68	102	197	311	425
7-Wood/Orlando-c; Kubert-a	45	90	135	275	455	635
9-Kubert-a; Check-c	38	76	114	219	347	475
10,11: 10-Kinstler-a. 11-Kinstlerish-a by McCann	34	68	102	197	311	425
12-Dracula story from novel, 25 pgs.	40	80	120	235	368	500
15-Reprints No. 1('51) minus-c(bondage)	24	48	72	139	220	300
16-Wood-a r-/No. 2	24	48	72	139	220	300
17-Wood/Orlando & Kubert-a; reprints #3 minus inside & outside Wood-c	24	48	72	139	220	300

NOTE: *Hollingsworth a-9-11; c-10, 11.*

EERIE
I. W. Enterprises: 1964

I.W. Reprint #1('64)-Wood-c(r); r-story/Spook #1	4	8	12	22	34	45
I.W. Reprint #2,6,8: 8-Dr. Drew by Grandenetti from Ghost #9	3	6	9	20	30	40
I.W. Reprint #9-r/Tales of Terror #1(Toby); Wood-c	4	8	12	24	37	50

EERIE (Magazine)(See Warren Presents)
Warren Publ. Co.: No. 1, Sept, 1965; No. 2, Mar, 1966 - No. 139, Feb, 1983

1-24 pgs., black & white, small size (5-1/4x7-1/4"), low distribution; cover from inside back cover of Creepy No. 2; stories reprinted from Creepy No. 7, 8. At least three different versions exist.

First Printing - B&W, 5-1/4" wide x 7-1/4" high, evenly trimmed. On page 18, panel 5, in the upper left-hand corner, the large rear view of a bald headed man blends into solid black and is unrecognizable. Overall printing quality is poor.

	43	86	129	344	622	900

Second Printing - B&W, 5-1/4x7-1/4", with uneven, untrimmed edges (if one of these were trimmed evenly, the size would be less than as indicated). The figure of the bald headed man on page 18, panel 5 is clear and discernible. The staples have a 1/4" blue stripe.

	15	30	45	111	198	285

Other subsequent reproductions for comparison's sake would be practically worthless. One known version was probably shot off a first printing copy with some loss of detail; the finer lines tend to disappear in this version which can be determined by looking at the lower right-hand corner of page one, first story. The roof of the house is shaded with straight lines. These lines are sharp and distinct on original, but broken on this version.

NOTE: **The Overstreet Comic Book Price Guide** recommends that, before buying a 1st issue, you consult an expert.

2-Frazetta-c; Toth-a; 1st app. host Cousin Eerie	10	20	30	67	116	165
3-Frazetta-c & half pg. ad (rerun in #4); Toth, Williamson, Ditko-a	8	16	24	52	86	120
4-7: 4-Frazetta-a (1/2 pg. ad). 5,7-Frazetta-c. Ditko-a in all.	5	10	15	32	51	70
8-Frazetta-c; Ditko-a	6	12	18	37	59	80
9-11,25: 9,10-Neal Adams-a, Ditko-a. 11-Karloff Mummy adapt.-Wood-s/a. 25-Steranko-c	5	10	15	35	55	75
12-16,18-22,24,32-35,40,45: 12,13,20-Poe-s. 12-Bloch-s. 12,15-Jones-a. 13-Lovecraft-s. 14,16-Toth-a. 16,19,24-Stoker-s. 16,32,33,43-Corben-a. 34-Early Boris-c. 35-Early Brunner-a. 35,40-Early Ploog-a. 40-Frankenstein; Ploog-a (6/72, 6 months before Marvel's series)	4	8	12	24	37	50
17-(low distribution)	11	22	33	79	140	200
23-Frazetta-c; Adams-a(reprint)	6	12	18	37	59	80
26-31,36-38,43,44	3	6	9	20	30	40
39,41: 39-1st Dax the Warrior; Maroto-a. 41-(low distribution)	4	8	12	26	41	55
42,51: 42-('73 Annual, 84 pgs.) Spooktacular; Williamson-a. 51-('74 Annual, 76 pgs.) Color poster insert; Toth-a	4	8	12	24	37	50
46,48: 46-Dracula series by Sutton begins; 2pgs. Vampirella. 48-Begin "Mummy Walks" and "Curse of the Werewolf" series (both continue in #49,50,52,53)	3	6	9	21	32	42
47,49,50,52,53: 47-Lilith. 49-Marvin the Dead Thing. 50-Satanna, Daughter of Satan. 52-Hunter by Neary begins. 53-Adams-a	3	6	9	20	30	40
54,55-Color insert Spirit story by Eisner, reprints sections 12/21/47 & 6/16/46 54-Dr. Archaeus series begins	3	6	9	18	27	35
56,57,59,63,69,77,78: All have 8 pg. slick color insert. 56,57,77-Corben-a. 59-(100 pgs.) Summer Special, all Dax issue. 69-Summer Special, all Hunter issue, Neary-a. 78-All Mummy issue	3	6	9	18	27	35
58,60,62,68,72,: 8 pg. slick color insert & Wrightson-a in all. 58,60,62-Corben-a. 60-Summer Giant (9/74, $1.25) 1st Exterminator One; Wood-a. 62-Mummies Walk. 68-Summer Special (84 pgs.)	3	6	9	20	30	40

61,64-67,71: 61-Mummies Walk-s, Wood-a. 64-Corben-a. 64,65,67-Toth-a. 65,66-El Cid. 67-Hunter II. 71-Goblin-c/1st app.	3	6	9	16	23	30
70,73-75	2	4	6	13	18	22
76-1st app. Darklon the Mystic by Starlin-s/a	3	6	9	19	29	38
79,80-Origin Darklon the Mystic by Starlin	3	6	9	18	24	30
81,86,97: 81-Frazetta-c, King Kong; Corben-a. 86-(92 pgs.) All Corben issue. 97-Time Travel/ Dinosaur issue, Corben,Adams-a	3	6	9	16	23	26
82-Origin/1st app. The Rook	3	6	9	17	25	32
83,85,88,89,91-93,98,99: 98-Rook (31 pgs.). 99-1st Horizon Seekers.	2	4	6	9	13	16
84,87,90,96,100: 84,100-Starlin-a. 87-Hunter 3; Nino-a. 87,90-Corben-a. 96-Summer Special (92 pgs.). 100-(92 pgs.) Anniverary issue; Rook (30 pgs.)	2	4	6	11	16	20
94,95-The Rook & Vampirella team-up. 95-Vampirella-c; 1st MacTavish	3	6	9	16	23	30
101,106,112,115,118,120,121,128: 101-Return of Hunter II, Starlin-a. 106-Hard John Nuclear Hit Parade Special, Corben-a. 112-All Maroto issue, Luana-s. 115-All José Ortiz issues. 118-1st Haggarth. 120-1st Zud Kamish. 121-Hunter/Darklon. 128-Starlin-a, Hsu-a	2	4	6	9	13	16
102-105,107-111,113,114,116,117,119,122-124,126,127,129: 104-Beast World. 103-105,109-111-Gulacy-a	2	4	6	8	11	14
125-(10/81, 84 pgs.) all Neal Adams issue	2	4	6	13	18	22
130-(76 pgs.) Vampirella-c/sty (54 pgs.); Pantha, Van Helsing, Huntress, Dax, Schreck, Hunter, Exterminator One, Rook app.	3	6	9	16	22	28
131-(Lower distr.); all Wood issue	3	6	9	14	19	24
132-134,136: 132-Rook returns. 133-All Ramon Torrents-a issue. 134,136-Color comic insert	2	4	6	9	13	16
135-(Lower distr. 10/82, 100 pgs.) All Ditko issue	3	6	9	14	19	24
137-139 (lower distr.):137-All Super-Hero issue. 138-Sherlock Holmes. 138,139-Color comic insert	4	8	12	26	41	55
Yearbook '70-Frazetta-c	6	12	18	37	59	80
Annual '71, '72-Reprints in both	4	8	12	26	41	55

NOTE: The above books contain art by many good artists: **N. Adams, Brunner, Corben, Craig (Taycee), Crandall, Ditko, Eisner, Evans, Jeff Jones, Krenkel, McWilliams, Morrow, Orlando, Ploog, Severin, Starlin, Torres, Toth, Williamson, Wood, and Wrightson; covers by Bode', Corben, Davis, Frazetta, Morrow, and Orlando.** Frazetta-2, 3, 7, 8, 23. Annuals from 1973-on are included in regular numbering. 1970-74 Annuals are complete reprints. Annuals from 1975-on are in the format of the regular issues.

EERIE ADVENTURES (Also see Weird Adventures)
Ziff-Davis Publ. Co.: Winter, 1951 (Painted-c)

1-Powell-a(2), McCann-a; used in **SOTI**; bondage-c; Krigstein back-c	43	86	129	262	431	600

NOTE: Title dropped due to similarity to Avon's Eerie & legal action.

EERIE TALES (Magazine)
Hastings Associates: 1959 (Black & White)

1-Williamson, Torres, Tuska-a, Powell(2), & Morrow(2)-a	15	30	45	83	124	165

EERIE TALES
Super Comics: 1963-1964

Super Reprint No. 10,11,12,18: 10('63)-r/Spook #27. Purple Claw in #11,12 ('63); #12-r/Avon's Eerie (#51)-Kida-r	3	6	9	17	25	32
15-Wolverton-a, Spacehawk-r/Blue Bolt Weird Tales #113; Disbrow-a	5	10	15	30	48	65

EGBERT
Arnold Publications/Quality Comics Group: Spring, 1946 - No. 20, 1950

1-Funny animal; intro Egbert & The Count	20	40	60	115	180	245
2	11	22	33	62	86	110
3-10	9	18	27	47	61	75
11-20	7	14	21	37	46	55

EGON
Dark Horse Comics: Jan, 1998 - No.2, Feb, 1998 ($2.95, limited series)

1,2-Horley-painted-c						3.00

EGYPT
DC Comics (Vertigo): Aug, 1995 - No.7, Feb, 1996 ($2.50, lim. series, mature)

1-7: Milligan scripts in all.						3.00

EH! (...Dig This Crazy Comic) (From Here to Insanity No. 8 on)
Charlton Comics: Dec, 1953 - No. 7, Nov-Dec, 1954 (Satire)

1-Davis-ish-c/a by Ayers, Wood-ish-a by Giordano; Atomic Mouse app.	36	72	108	208	329	450
2-Ayers-c/a	21	42	63	120	188	255
3,5,7	18	36	54	107	169	230

Eightball #22 © Dan Clowes

Elektra V2 #2 © MAR

Elektra: Glimpse & Echo #1 © MAR

	GD 2.0	VG 4.0	FN 6.0	VF 8.0	VF/NM 9.0	NM- 9.2
4,6: Sexual innuendo-c. 6-Ayers-a	20	40	60	115	180	245

EIGHTBALL (Also see David Boring)
Fantagraphics Books: Oct, 1989 - Present ($2.75/$2.95/$3.95, semi-annually, mature)

	GD 2.0	VG 4.0	FN 6.0	VF 8.0	VF/NM 9.0	NM- 9.2
1 (1st printing) Daniel Clowes-s/a in all	2	4	6	8	10	12
2,3	1	2	3	5	6	8
4-8						6.00
9-19: 17-(8/96)						4.00
20-($4.50)						4.50
21-($4.95) Concludes David Boring 3-parter						5.00
22-($5.95) 29 short stories						6.00
23-($7.00, 9" x 12") The Death Ray						7.00
Twentieth Century Eightball (2002, $19.00) r/Clowes strips						19.00

EIGHTH WONDER, THE
Dark Horse Comics: Nov, 1997 ($2.95, one-shot)

nn-Reprints stories from Dark Horse Presents #85-87						3.00

EIGHT IS ENOUGH KITE FUN BOOK (See Kite Fun Book 1979 in the Promotional Comics section)

EIGHT LEGGED FREAKS
DC Comics (WildStorm): 2002 ($6.95, one-shot, squarebound)

nn-Adaptation of 2002 mutant spider movie; Joe Phillips-a; intro by Dean Devlin						7.00

80 PAGE GIANT (...Magazine No. 2-15)
National Periodical Publications: 8/64 - No. 15, 10/65; No. 16, 11/65 - No. 89, 7/71 (25¢)
(All reprints (#1-56: 84 pgs.; #57-89: 68 pgs.)

	GD 2.0	VG 4.0	FN 6.0	VF 8.0	VF/NM 9.0	NM- 9.2
1-Superman Annual; originally planned as Superman Annual #9 (8/64)	38	76	114	285	518	750
2-Jimmy Olsen	21	42	63	156	278	400
3,4: 3-Lois Lane. 4-Flash-G.A.-r; Infantino-a	17	34	51	122	216	310
5-Batman; has Sunday newspaper strip; Catwoman-r; Batman's Life Story-r (25th anniversary special)	17	34	51	122	216	310
6-Superman	15	30	45	105	188	270
7-Sgt. Rock's Prize Battle Tales; Kubert-c/a	20	40	60	150	268	385
8-More Secret Origins-origins of JLA, Aquaman, Robin, Atom, & Superman; Infantino-a	30	60	90	222	404	585
9-15: 9-Flash (r/Flash #106,117,123 & Showcase #14); Infantino-a. 10-Superboy. 11-Superman(all Luthor issue. 12-Batman; has Sunday newspaper strip. 13-Jimmy Olsen. 14-Lois Lane. 15-Superman and Batman; Joker-c/story	14	28	42	102	181	260

Continued as part of regular series under each title in which that particular book came out, a Giant being published instead of the regular size. Issues No. 16 to No. 89 are listed for your information. See individual titles for prices.
16-JLA #39 (11/65), 17-Batman #176, 18-Superman #183, 19-Our Army at War #164, 20-Action #334, 21-Flash #160, 22-Superboy #129, 23-Superman #187, 24-Batman #182, 25-Jimmy Olsen #95, 26-Lois Lane #68, 27-Batman #185, 28-World's Finest #161, 29-JLA #48, 30-Batman #187, 31-Superman #193, 32-Our Army at War #177, 33-Action #347, 34-Flash #169, 35-Superboy #138, 36-Superman #197, 37-Batman #193, 38-Jimmy Olsen #104, 39-Lois Lane #77, 40-World's Finest #170, 41-JLA #58, 42-Superman #202, 43-Batman #198, 44-Our Army at War #190, 45-Action #360, 46-Flash #178, 47-Superboy #147, 48-Superman #207, 49-Batman #203, 50-Jimmy Olsen #113, 51-Lois Lane #86, 52-World's Finest #179, 53-JLA #67, 54-Superman #212, 55-Batman #208, 56-Our Army at War #203, 57-Action #373, 58-Flash #187, 59-Superboy #156, 60-Superman #217, 61-Batman #213, 62-Jimmy Olsen #122, 63-Lois Lane #95, 64-World's Finest #188, 65-JLA #76, 66-Superman #222, 67-Batman #218, 68-Our Army at War #216, 69-Adventure #390, 70-Flash #196, 71-Superboy #165, 72-Superman #227, 73-Batman #223, 74-Jimmy Olsen #131, 75-Lois Lane #104, 76-World's Finest #197, 77-JLA #85, 78-Superman #232, 79-Batman #228, 80-Our Army at War #229, 81-Adventure #403, 82-Flash #205, 83-Superboy #174, 84-Superman #239, 85-Batman #233, 86-Jimmy Olsen #140, 87-Lois Lane #113, 88-World's Finest #206, 89-JLA #93.

87TH PRECINCT (TV) (Based on the Ed McBain novels)
Dell Publishing Co.: Apr-June, 1962 - No. 2, July-Sept, 1962

	GD 2.0	VG 4.0	FN 6.0	VF 8.0	VF/NM 9.0	NM- 9.2
Four Color 1309(#1)-Krigstein-a	9	18	27	65	113	160
2	8	16	24	56	93	130

EL BOMBO COMICS
Standard Comics/Frances M. McQueeny: 1946

	GD 2.0	VG 4.0	FN 6.0	VF 8.0	VF/NM 9.0	NM- 9.2
nn(1946), 1(no date)	12	24	36	69	97	125

EL CAZADOR
CrossGen Comics: Oct, 2003 - No. 6, Jun, 2004 ($2.95)

1-Dixon-s/Epting-a						5.00
2-6: 5-Lady Death preview						3.00
Collected Edition (2003, $5.95) r/#1-3						6.00
...: The Bloody Ballad of Blackjack Tom 1 (4/04, $2.95, one-shot) Cariello-a						3.00

EL CID
Dell Publishing Co.: No. 1259, 1961

	GD 2.0	VG 4.0	FN 6.0	VF 8.0	VF/NM 9.0	NM- 9.2
Four Color 1259-Movie, photo-c	7	14	21	47	76	105

EL DIABLO (See All-Star Western #2 & Weird Western Tales #12)
DC Comics: Aug, 1989 - No. 16, Jan, 1991 ($1.50/$1.75, color)

1 ($2.50, 52pgs.)-Masked hero						3.00

	NM- 9.2
2-16	2.50

EL DIABLO
DC Comics (Vertigo): Mar, 2001 - No. 4, Jun, 2001 ($2.50, limited series)

	NM- 9.2
1-4-Azzarello-s/Zezelj-a/Sale-c	2.50

EL DORADO (See Movie Classics)

ELECTRIC UNDERTOW (See Strikeforce Morituri: Electric Undertow)

ELECTRIC WARRIOR
DC Comics: May, 1986 - No. 18, Oct, 1987 ($1.50, Baxter paper)

	NM- 9.2
1-18	2.50

ELECTROPOLIS
Image Comics: May, 2001 - No. 4, Jan, 2003 ($2.95/$5.95)

	NM- 9.2
1-3-Dean Motter-a/a. 3-(12/01)	3.00
4-(1/03, $5.95, 72 pages) The Infernal Machine pts. 4-6	6.00

ELEKTRA (Also see Daredevil #319-325)
Marvel Comics: Mar, 1995 - No. 4, June, 1995 ($2.95, limited series)

	NM- 9.2
1-4-Embossed-c; Scott McDaniel-a	3.00

ELEKTRA (Also see Daredevil)
Marvel Comics: Nov, 1996 - No. 19, Jun, 1998 ($1.95)

	NM- 9.2
1-Peter Milligan scripts; Deodato-c/a	3.00
1-Variant-c	5.00
2-19: Dr. Strange-c/app. 10-Logan-c/app.	2.50
#(-1) Flashback (7/97) Matt Murdock-c/app.; Deodato-c/a	2.50
.../Cyblade (Image, 3/97,$2.95) Devil's Reign pt. 7	3.00

ELEKTRA (Vol. 2) (Marvel Knights)
Marvel Comics: Sept, 2001 - No. 35, Jun, 2004 ($3.50/$2.99)

	NM- 9.2
1-Bendis-s/Austen-a/Horn-c	4.00
2-6: 2-Two covers	3.00
3-Initial printing with panel of nudity; most copies pulped	18.00
7-35: 7-Rucka-s begin. 9,10,17-Bennett-a. 19-Meglia-a. 23-25-Chen-a; Sienkiewicz-a	3.00
...Vol. 1: Introspect TPB (2002, $16.99) r/#10-15; Marvel Knights: Double Shot #3	17.00
...Vol. 2: Everything Old is New Again TPB (2003, $16.99) r/#16-22	17.00
...Vol. 3: Relentless TPB (2004, $14.99) r/#23-28	15.00
...Vol. 4: Frenzy TPB (2004, $17.99) r/#29-35	18.00

ELEKTRA & WOLVERINE: THE REDEEMER
Marvel Comics: Jan, 2002 - No. 3, Mar, 2002 ($5.95, square-bound, lim. series)

	NM- 9.2
1-3-Greg Rucka-s/Yoshitaka Amano-a/c	6.00
HC (5/02, $29.95, with dustjacket) r/#1-3, interview with Greg Rucka	30.00

ELEKTRA: ASSASSIN (Also see Daredevil)
Marvel Comics (Epic Comics): Aug, 1986 - No. 8, June, 1987 (Limited series, mature)

	NM- 9.2
1,8-Miller scripts in all; Sienkiewicz-c/a.	6.00
2-7	5.00
Signed & numbered hardcover (Graphitti Designs, $39.95, 2000 print run)- reprints 1-8	50.00
TPB (2000, $24.95)	25.00

ELEKTRA: GLIMPSE & ECHO
Marvel Comics: Sept, 2002 - No. 4, Dec, 2002 ($2.99, limited series)

	NM- 9.2
1-4-Scott Morse-s/painted-a	3.00

ELEKTRA LIVES AGAIN (Also see Daredevil)
Marvel Comics (Epic Comics): 1990 ($24.95, oversize, hardcover, 76 pgs.)
(Produced by Graphitti Designs)

	NM- 9.2
nn-Frank Miller-c/a/scripts; Lynn Varley painted-a; Matt Murdock & Bullseye app.	35.00
2nd printing (9/02, $24.99)	25.00

ELEKTRA MAGAZINE
Marvel Comics: Nov, 1996 - No. 2, Dec, 1996 ($3.95, 96 pgs., reprints, limited series)

	NM- 9.2
1,2: Reprints Frank Miller's Elektra stories in Daredevil	4.00

ELEKTRA SAGA, THE
Marvel Comics Group: Feb, 1984 - No. 4, June, 1984 ($2.00, limited series, Baxter paper)

	NM- 9.2
1-4-r/Daredevil 168-190; Miller-c/a	4.00

ELEKTRA: THE HAND
Marvel Comics: Nov, 2004 - No. 5, Feb, 2005 ($2.99, limited series)

	NM- 9.2
1-5-Gossett-a/Sienkiewicz-c/Yoshida-s; origin of the Hand in the 16th century	3.00
TPB (2005, $13.99) r/#1-5	14.00

ELEKTRA: THE MOVIE
Marvel Comics: Feb, 2005 ($5.99)

	NM- 9.2
1-Movie adaptation; McKeever-s/Perkins-a; photo-c	6.00

Elementals #19 © Bill Willingham

Elflord Cuts Loose #1 © Warp

Elfquest New Blood #18 © Warp

	GD	VG	FN	VF	VF/NM	NM-
	2.0	4.0	6.0	8.0	9.0	9.2

TPB (2005, $12.95) r/movie adaptation, Daredevil #168, 181 & Elektra #(-1) — 13.00

ELEMENTALS, THE (See The Justice Machine & Morningstar Spec.)
Comico The Comic Co. : June, 1984 - No. 29, Sept, 1988; V2#1, Mar, 1989 - No. 28, 1994? ($1.50/$2.50, Baxter paper); V3#1, Dec, 1995 - No. 3 ($2.95)

1-Willingham-c/a, 1-8 — 5.00
2-29, V2#1-28: 9-Bissette-a(p). 10-Photo-c. V2#6-1st app. Strike Force America. 18-Prelude to Avalon mini-series. 27-Prequel to Strike Force America series — 3.00
V3#1-3: 1-Daniel-a(p), bagged w/gaming card — 3.00
Lingerie (5/96, $2.95) — 3.00
Special 1,2 (3/86, 1/89)-1-Willingham-a(p) — 3.00

ELEMENTALS: (Title series), Comico
--GHOST OF A CHANCE, 12/95 ($5.95)-graphic novel, nn-Ross-c. — 6.00
--HOW THE WAR WAS WON, 6/96 - No. 2, 8/96 ($2.95) 1,2-Tony Daniel-a, & 1-Variant-c; no logo — 3.00
--SEX SPECIAL, 1991 - No. 4, Feb, 1993 ($2.95, color) 2 covers for each — 3.00
--SEX SPECIAL, 5/97 - No. 2, 6/97 ($2.95, B&W) 1-Tony Daniel, Jeff Moy-a, 2-Robb Phipps, Adam McDaniel-a — 3.00
--SWIMSUIT SPECTACULAR 1996, 6/96 ($2.95), 1-pin-ups, 1-Variant-c; no logo — 3.00
--THE VAMPIRE'S REVENGE, 6/96 - No. 2 8/96 ($2.95), 1,2-Willingham-s, 1-Variant-c; no logo — 3.00

ELEPHANTMEN
Image Comics: July, 2006 - Present ($2.99) (Flip covers on most)
1-10: 1-Starkings-s/Moritat-a/Ladronn-c. 6-Campbell flip-c — 3.00
...: The Pilot (5/07, $2.99) short stories and pin-ups by various incl. Sale, Jim Lee, Jae Lee — 3.00

1111 (ELEVEN ELEVEN)
Crusade Entertainment: Oct, 1996 ($2.95, B&W, one-shot)
1-Wrightson-c/a — 4.00

ELEVEN OR ONE
Sirius: Apr, 1995 ($2.95)

1-Linsner-c/a	1	3	4	6	8	10
1-(6/96) 2nd printing						3.50

ELFLORD
Nightwind Productions: Jun, 1980 - Vol. 2 #1, 1982 (B&W, magazine-size)

1-1st Barry Blair-s/c/a in comics; B&W-c; limited print run for all	11	22	33	79	140	200
2-5-B&W-c	5	10	15	35	55	75
6-14: 9-14-Color-c	4	8	12	28	44	60
Vol. 2 #1 (1982)	4	8	12	24	37	50

ELFLORD
Aircel Publ.: 1986 - No. 6, Oct, 1989 ($1.70, B&W); V2#1- V2#31, 1995 ($2.00)

1 — 3.00
2-4,V2#1-20,22-30: 4-6: Last B&W issue. V2#1-Color-a begin. 22-New cast. 25-Begin B&W — 2.50
1,2-2nd printings — 2.50
21-Double size ($4.95) — 5.00

ELFLORD
Warp Graphics: Jan, 1997-No.4, Apr, 1997 ($2.95, B&W, mini-series)
1-4 — 3.00

ELFLORD (CUTS LOOSE) (Vol. 2)
Warp Graphics: Sept, 1997 - No. 7, Apr, 1998 ($2.95, B&W, mini-series)
1-7 — 3.00

ELFLORD: DRAGON'S EYE
Night Wynd Enterprises: 1993 ($2.50, B&W)
1 — 2.50

ELFLORD: THE RETURN
Mad Monkey Press: 1996 ($6.95, magazine size)
1 — 7.00

ELFQUEST (Also see Fantasy Quarterly & Warp Graphics Annual)
Warp Graphics, Inc.: No. 2, Aug, 1978 - No. 21, Feb, 1985 (All magazine size)
No. 1, Apr, 1979
NOTE: *Elfquest* was originally published as one of the stories in Fantasy Quarterly #1. When the publisher went out of business, the creative team, Wendy and Richard Pini, formed WaRP Graphics and continued the series, beginning with *Elfquest #2*. *Elfquest #1,* which reprinted the story from *Fantasy Quarterly*, was published about the same time *Elfquest #4* was released. Thereafter, most issues were reprinted as demand warranted, until Marvel announced it would reprint the entire series under its Epic imprint (Aug., 1985).

1(4/79)-Reprints Elfquest story from Fantasy Quarterly No. 1

	GD	VG	FN	VF	VF/NM	NM-
1st printing ($1.00-c)	4	8	12	22	34	45
2nd printing ($1.25-c)	1	3	4	6	8	10
3rd printing ($1.50-c)						3.00
4th printing; different-c ($1.50-c)						3.00
2(8/78)-5: 1st printings ($1.00-c)	2	4	6	13	18	22
2nd printings ($1.25-c)						4.00
3rd & 4th printings ($1.50-c)(all 4th prints 1989)						3.00
6-9: 1st printings ($1.25-c)	2	4	6	8	10	12
2nd printings ($1.50-c)						3.50
3rd printings ($1.50-c)						3.00
10-21: ($1.50-c); 16-8pg. preview of A Distant Soil	1	2	3	4	6	8
10-14: 2nd printings ($1.50)						3.00

ELFQUEST
Marvel Comics (Epic Comics): Aug, 1985 - No. 32, Mar, 1988
1-Reprints in color the Elfquest epic by Warp Graphics — 3.00
2-32 — 2.50

ELFQUEST
DC Comics: 2003 - Present
Archives Vol. 1 (2003, $49.95, HC) r/#1-5 — 50.00
Archives Vol. 2 (2005, $49.95, HC) r/#6-10 & Epic Illustrated #1 — 50.00
25th Anniversary Special (2003, $2.95) r/Elfquest #1 (Apr, 1979); interview w/Pinis — 3.00

ELFQUEST (Title series), Warp Graphics
'89 - No. 4, '89 ($1.50, B&W) 1-4: R-original Elfquest series — 2.50

ELFQUEST (Volume 2),Warp Graphics: V2#1, 5/96 - No. 33, 2/99 ($4.95/$2.95, B&W)
V2#1-31: 1,3,5,8,10,12,13,18,21,23,25-Wendy Pini-c — 5.00
32,33-($2.95-c) — 3.00

--BLOOD OF TEN CHIEFS, 7/93 - No. 20, 9/95 ($2.00/$2.50) 1-20-By Richard & Wendy Pini — 3.00
--HIDDEN YEARS, 5/92 - No. 29, 3/96 ($2.00/$2.25)1-9,9 1/2, 10-29 — 3.00
--JINK, 11/94 - No. 12, 2/6 ($2.25/$2.50) 1-12-W. Pini/John Byrne-back-c — 3.00
--KAHVI, 10/95 - No. 6,3/96 ($2.25, B&W) 1-6 — 3.00
--KINGS CROSS, 11/97 - No. 2, 12/97 ($2.95, B&W) 1,2 — 3.00
--KINGS OF THE BROKEN WHEEL, 6/90 - No. 9, 2/92 ($2.00, B&W) (3rd Elfquest saga) 1-9: By R. & W. Pini; 1-Color insert — 3.00
1-2nd printing — 2.50
--METAMORPHOSIS, 4/96 ($2.95, B&W) 1 — 3.00
--NEW BLOOD (...Summer Special on-c #1 only), 8/92 - No. 35, 1/96 ($2.00-$2.50, color/ B&W) 1-($3.95, 68 pgs.....Summer Special on-c)-Byrne-a/scripts (16 pgs.) — 4.00
2-35: Barry Blair-a in all — 3.00
1993 Summer Special ($3.95) Byrne-a/scripts — 4.00
--SHARDS, 8/94 - No. 16, 3/96 ($2.25/$2.50) 1-16 — 3.00
--SIEGE AT BLUE MOUNTAIN, WaRP Graphics/Apple 3/87 - No. 8, 12/88 ($1.75/ $1.95, B&W) 1-Staton-a(i) in all; 2nd Elfquest saga — 4.00
1-3-2nd printing, 3-8 — 2.50
2 — 3.00
--THE REBELS, 11/94 - No. 12, 3/96 ($2.25/$2.50, B&W/color) 1-12 — 3.00
--TWO-SPEAR, 10/95 - No. 5, 2/96 ($2.25, B&W) 1-5 — 3.00
--WAVE DANCERS, 12/93 - No. 6, 3/96, 1-6: 1-Foil-c & poster — 3.00
Special 1 ($2.95) — 3.00
--WORLDPOOL, 7/97 ($2.95, B&W) 1-Richard Pini-s/Barry Blair-a — 3.00

ELFQUEST: THE DISCOVERY
DC Comics: March,2006 - No. 4, Sept, 2006 ($3.99, limited series)
1-4-Wendy Pini-a/Wendy & Richard Pini-s — 4.00
TPB (2006, $14.99) r/#1-4 — 15.00

ELFQUEST: THE GRAND QUEST
DC Comics: 2004 - Present ($9.95/$9.99, B&W, digest-size)
Vol. 1-6 ('04)1-r/Elfquest #1-5; new W. Pini-c. 2-r/#5-8. 3-r/#8-11. 4-r/#11-15. 5-r/#15-18 6-r/#18-20 — 10.00
Vol. 7-9 ('05) 7-r/Siege At Blue Mountain #1-3. 8-r/SABM #3-5. 9-r/SABM #6-8 — 10.00
Vol. 10-14 ('05) 10-r/Kings of the Broken Wheel #1-3. 11-KotBW #5-7 & Frazetta Fant. Ill. 12-r/Kings of the Broken Wheel V2 #4-18. 14-r/Hidden Years #4-9 1/2 — 10.00

ELFQUEST: THE SEARCHER AND THE SWORD
DC Comics: 2004 ($24.95/$14.99, graphic novel)
HC (2004, $24.95, with dust jacket)-Wendy and Richard Pini-s/a/c — 25.00
SC (2004, $14.99) — 15.00

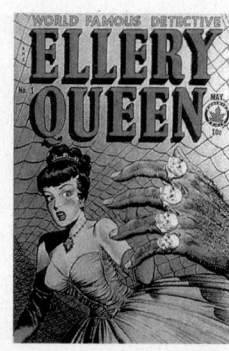

Ellery Queen #1 © SUPR

Elseworlds 80-Page Giant #1 © DC

Elvira, Mistress of the Dark #166 © Queen B Prods.

	GD 2.0	VG 4.0	FN 6.0	VF 8.0	VF/NM 9.0	NM- 9.2		GD 2.0	VG 4.0	FN 6.0	VF 8.0	VF/NM 9.0	NM- 9.2

ELFQUEST: WOLFRIDER
DC Comics: 2003 - Present ($9.95, digest-size)

Volume 1 ('03, $9.95, digest-size) r/Elfquest V2#19,21,23,25,27,29,31; Blood of Ten Chiefs #2; Hidden Years #5; New Blood Special #1; New Blood 1993 Special #1; new W. Pini-c ... 10.00
Volume 2 ('03, $9.95, digest-size) r/Elfquest V2#33; Blood of Ten Chiefs #10,11,19; Warp Graphics Annual #1 ... 10.00

ELF-THING
Eclipse Comics: March, 1987 ($1.50, B&W, one-shot)
1 ... 2.25

ELIMINATOR (Also see The Solution #16 & The Night Man #16)
Malibu Comics (Ultraverse): Apr, 1995 - No. 3, Jul, 1995 ($2.95/$2.50, lim. series)
0-Mike Zeck-a in all ... 3.00
1-3-($2.50): 1-1st app. Siren ... 2.50
1-($3.95)-Black cover edition ... 4.00

ELIMINATOR FULL COLOR SPECIAL
Eternity Comics: Oct, 1991 ($2.95, one-shot)
1-Dave Dorman painted-c ... 3.00

ELLA CINDERS (See Comics On Parade, Comics Revue #1,4, Famous Comics Cartoon Book, Giant Comics Editions, Sparkler Comics, Tip Top & Treasury of Comics)

ELLA CINDERS
United Features Syndicate: 1938 - 1940

	GD 2.0	VG 4.0	FN 6.0	VF 8.0	VF/NM 9.0	NM- 9.2
Single Series 3(1938)	40	80	120	244	392	540
Single Series 21(#2 on-c, #21 on inside), 28('40)	35	70	105	204	322	440

ELLA CINDERS
United Features Syndicate: Mar, 1948 - No. 5, Mar, 1949

	GD 2.0	VG 4.0	FN 6.0	VF 8.0	VF/NM 9.0	NM- 9.2
1-(#2 on cover)	14	28	42	80	115	150
2	10	20	30	54	72	90
3-5	8	16	24	40	50	60

ELLERY QUEEN
Superior Comics Ltd.: May, 1949 - No. 4, Nov, 1949

	GD 2.0	VG 4.0	FN 6.0	VF 8.0	VF/NM 9.0	NM- 9.2
1-Kamen-c; L.B. Cole-a; r-in Haunted Thrills	52	104	156	317	521	725
2-4: 3-Drug use stories(2)	40	80	120	235	368	500

NOTE: Iger shop art in all issues.

ELLERY QUEEN (TV)
Ziff-Davis Publishing Co.: 1-3/52 (Spring on-c) - No. 2, Summer/52 (Saunders painted-c)

	GD 2.0	VG 4.0	FN 6.0	VF 8.0	VF/NM 9.0	NM- 9.2
1-Saunders-c	46	92	138	281	461	640
2-Saunders bondage, torture-c	39	78	117	225	355	485

ELLERY QUEEN (Also see Crackajack Funnies No. 23)
Dell Publishing Co.: No. 1165, Mar-May, 1961 - No.1289, Apr, 1962

	GD 2.0	VG 4.0	FN 6.0	VF 8.0	VF/NM 9.0	NM- 9.2
Four Color 1165 (#1)	10	20	30	70	123	175
Four Color 1243 (11-1/61-61), 1289	8	16	24	56	93	130

ELMER FUDD (Also see Camp Comics, Daffy, Looney Tunes #1 & Super Book #10, 22)
Dell Publishing Co.: No. 470, May, 1953 - No. 1293, Mar-May, 1962

	GD 2.0	VG 4.0	FN 6.0	VF 8.0	VF/NM 9.0	NM- 9.2
Four Color 470 (#1)	8	16	24	52	86	120
Four Color 558,628,689('56)	5	10	15	30	48	65
Four Color 725,783,841,888,938,977,1032,1081,1131,1171,1222,1293('62)	4	8	12	26	41	55

ELMO COMICS
St. John Publishing Co.: Jan, 1948 (Daily strip-r)

	GD 2.0	VG 4.0	FN 6.0	VF 8.0	VF/NM 9.0	NM- 9.2
1-By Cecil Jensen	10	20	30	54	72	90

ELONGATED MAN (See Flash #112 & Justice League of America #105)
DC Comics: Jan, 1992 - No. 4, Apr, 1992 ($1.00, limited series)
1-4: 3-The Flash app. ... 2.50

ELRIC (Of Melnibone)(See First Comics Graphic Novel #6 & Marvel Graphic Novel #2)
Pacific Comics: Apr, 1983 - No. 6, Apr, 1984 ($1.50, Baxter paper)
1-6: Russell-c/a(i) in all ... 3.00

ELRIC
Topps Comics: 1996 ($2.95, one-shot)
0—One Life: Russell-c/a; adapts Neil Gaiman's short story "One Life--Furnished in Early Moorcock." ... 3.00

ELRIC, SAILOR ON THE SEAS OF FATE
First Comics: June, 1985 - No. 7, June, 1986 ($1.75, limited series)
1-7: Adapts Michael Moorcock's novel ... 3.00

ELRIC, STORMBRINGER
Dark Horse Comics/Topps Comics: 1997 - No. 7, 1997($2.95, limited series)
1-7: Russell-c/s/a; adapts Michael Moorcock's novel ... 3.00

ELRIC: THE BANE OF THE BLACK SWORD
First Comics: Aug, 1988 - No. 6, June, 1989 ($1.75/$1.95, limited series)
1-6: Adapts Michael Moorcock's novel ... 3.00

ELRIC: THE VANISHING TOWER
First Comics: Aug, 1987 - No. 6, June, 1988 ($1.75, limited series)
1-6: Adapts Michael Moorcock's novel ... 3.00

ELRIC: WEIRD OF THE WHITE WOLF
First Comics: Oct, 1986 - No. 5, June, 1987 ($1.75, limited series)
1-5: Adapts Michael Moorcock's novel ... 3.00

EL SALVADOR - A HOUSE DIVIDED
Eclipse Comics: March, 1989 ($2.50, B&W, Baxter paper, stiff-c, 52 pgs.)
1-Gives history of El Salvador ... 2.50

ELSEWHERE PRINCE, THE (Moebius' Airtight Garage)
Marvel Comics (Epic): May, 1990 - No. 6, Oct, 1990 ($1.95, limited series)
1-6: Moebius scripts & back-up-a in all ... 3.00

ELSEWORLDS 80-PAGE GIANT
DC Comics: Aug, 1999 ($5.95, one-shot)

	GD 2.0	VG 4.0	FN 6.0	VF 8.0	VF/NM 9.0	NM- 9.2
1-Most copies destroyed by DC over content of the "Superman's Babysitter" story; some UK shipments sold before recall	10	20	30	70	123	175

ELSEWORLD'S FINEST
DC Comics: 1997 - No. 2, 1997 ($4.95, limited series)
1,2: Elseworlds story-Superman & Batman in the 1920's ... 5.00

ELSEWORLD'S FINEST: SUPERGIRL & BATGIRL
DC Comics: 1998 ($5.95, one-shot)
1-Haley-a ... 6.00

ELSIE THE COW
D. S. Publishing Co.: Oct-Nov, 1949 - No. 3, July-Aug, 1950

	GD 2.0	VG 4.0	FN 6.0	VF 8.0	VF/NM 9.0	NM- 9.2
1-(36 pgs.)	25	50	75	145	228	310
2,3	18	36	54	105	165	225

ELSINORE
Alias Entertainment: Apr, 2005 - Present (75¢/$2.99/$3.25)
1-5: 1-(75¢-c) Brian Denham-a/Kenneth Lillie-Paetz-s. 2-($2.99-c). 4-($3.25-c) 5-Sparacio-a ... 3.25

ELSON'S PRESENTS
DC Comics: 1981 (100 pgs., no cover price)

	GD 2.0	VG 4.0	FN 6.0	VF 8.0	VF/NM 9.0	NM- 9.2
Series 1-6: Repackaged 1981 DC comics; 1-DC Comics Presents #29, Flash #303, Batman #331. 2-Superman #335, Ghosts #96, Justice League of America #186. 3-New Teen Titans #3, Secrets of Haunted House #32, Wonder Woman #275. 4-Secrets of the LSH #1, Brave & the Bold #170, New Adv. of Superboy #13. 5-LSH #271, Green Lantern #136, Super Friends #40. 6-Action #515, Mystery in Space #115, Detective #498	2	4	6	10	14	18

ELVEN (Also see Prime)
Malibu Comics (Ultraverse): Oct, 1994 - No. 4, Feb, 1995 ($2.50, lim. series)
0 ($2.95)-Prime app. ... 3.00
1-4: 2,4-Prime app. 3-Primevil app. ... 2.50
1-Limited Foil Edition- no price on cover ... 3.00

ELVIRA MISTRESS OF THE DARK
Marvel Comics: Oct, 1988 ($2.00, B&W, magazine size)
1-Movie adaptation ... 5.00

ELVIRA MISTRESS OF THE DARK
Claypool Comics (Eclipse): May, 1993 - No. 166, Feb, 2007 ($2.50, B&W)
1-Austin-a(i). Spiegle-a ... 6.00
2-6: Spiegle-a ... 4.00
7-99,101-166-Photo-c ... 2.50
100-(8/01) Kurt Busiek back-up-s; art by DeCarlo and others ... 2.50
TPB ($12.95) ... 13.00

ELVIRA'S HOUSE OF MYSTERY
DC Comics: Jan, 1986 - No. 11, Jan, 1987
1,11: 11-Dave Stevens-c ... 6.00
2-10: 9-Photo-c, Special 1 (3/87, $1.25) ... 4.00

ELVIS MANDIBLE, THE
DC Comics (Piranha Press): 1990 ($3.50, 52 pgs., B&W, mature)

E-Man #3 © CC

Empire #1 © Waid & Kitson

Enchanting Love #3 © Kirby Publ.

	GD 2.0	VG 4.0	FN 6.0	VF 8.0	VF/NM 9.0	NM- 9.2

nn   3.50

ELVIS PRESLEY (See Career Girl Romances #32, Go-Go, Howard Chaykin's American Flagg #10, Humbug #8, I Love You #60 & Young Lovers #18)

EL ZOMBO FANTASMA
Dark Horse Comics (Rocket Comics): Apr, 2004 - No. 3, June, 2004 ($2.99)

1-3-Wilkins-s&a/Munroe-s   3.00

E-MAN
Charlton Comics: Oct, 1973 - No. 10, Sept, 1975 (Painted-c No. 7-10)

1-Origin & 1st app. E-Man; Staton c/a in all	3	6	9	16	22	28
2-4: 2,4-Ditko-a. 3-Howard-a	2	4	6	8	11	14
5-Miss Liberty Belle app. by Ditko	2	4	6	8	10	12
6-10: 6,7,9,10-Early Byrne-a (#6 is 1/75). 6-Disney parody. 8-Full-length story; Nova begins as E-Man's partner	2	4	6	10	14	18
1-4,9,10 (Modern Comics reprints, '77)						4.00

NOTE: *Killjoy* app.-No. 2, 4. *Liberty Belle* app.-No. 5. *Rog 2000* app.-No. 6, 7, 9, 10. *Travis* app.-No. 3. *Sutton* a-1.

E-MAN
Comico: Sept, 1989 ($2.75, one-shot, no ads, high quality paper)

1-Staton-c/a; Michael Mauser story   2.75

E-MAN
Comico: V4#1, Jan, 1990 - No. 3, Mar, 1990 ($2.50, limited series)

1-3: Staton-c/a   2.50

E-MAN
Alpha Productions: Oct, 1993 ($2.75)

V5#1-Staton-c/a; 20th anniversary issue   2.75

E-MAN COMICS (Also see Michael Mauser & The Original E-Man)
First Comics: Apr, 1983 - No. 25, Aug, 1985 ($1.00/$1.25, direct sales only)

1-25: 2-X-Men satire. 3-X-Men/Phoenix satire. 6-Origin retold. 8-Cutey Bunny app. 10-Origin Nova Kane. 24-Origin Michael Mauser   2.50
NOTE: *Staton* a-1-5, 6-25; c-1-25.

E-MAN RETURNS
Alpha Productions: 1994 ($2.75, B&W)

1-Joe Staton-c/a(p)   2.75

EMERALD DAWN
DC Comics: 1991 ($4.95, trade paperback)

nn-Reprints Green Lantern: Emerald Dawn #1-6   5.00

EMERALD DAWN II (See Green Lantern...)

EMERGENCY (Magazine)
Charlton Comics: June, 1976 - No. 4, Jan, 1977 (B&W)

1-Neal Adams-c/a; Heath, Austin-a	4	8	12	22	34	45
2,3: 2-N. Adams-c. 3-N. Adams-a.	3	6	9	19	29	38
4-Alcala-a	3	6	9	14	20	25

EMERGENCY (TV)
Charlton Comics: June, 1976 - No. 4, Dec, 1976

1-Staton-c; early Byrne-a (22 pages)	3	6	9	19	29	38
2-4: 2-Staton-c. 2,3-Byrne text illos.	3	6	9	14	20	25

EMERGENCY DOCTOR
Charlton Comics: Summer, 1963 (one-shot)

1	3	6	9	19	29	38

EMIL & THE DETECTIVES (See Movie Comics)

EMISSARY (Jim Valentino's...)
Image Comics (Shadowline): May, 2006 - Present ($3.50)

1-6: 1-Rand-s/Ferreyra-a. 4-6-Long-s   3.50

EMMA FROST
Marvel Comics: Aug, 2003 - No. 18, Feb, 2005 ($2.50/$2.99)

1-7-Emma in high school; Bollers-s/Green-a/Horn-c   2.50
8-18-($2.99)   3.00
... Vol. 1: Higher Learning TPB (2004, $7.99, digest size) r/#1-6   8.00
... Vol. 2: Mind Games TPB (2005, $7.99, digest size) r/#7-12   8.00
... Vol. 3: Bloom TPB (2005, $7.99, digest size) r/#13-18   8.00

EMMA PEEL & JOHN STEED (See The Avengers)

EMPEROR'S NEW CLOTHES, THE
Dell Publishing Co.: 1950 (10¢, 68 pgs., 1/2 size, oblong)

nn - (Surprise Books series)	6	12	18	28	34	40

EMPIRE

Image Comics (Gorilla): May, 2000 - No. 2, Sept, 2000 ($2.50)
DC Comics: No. 0, Aug, 2003; Sept, 2003 - No. 6, Feb, 2004 ($4.95/$2.50, limited series)

1,2: 1 (5/00)-Waid-s/Kitson-s; w/Crimson Plague prologue   2.50
0-(8/03) reprints #1,2   5.00
1-6: 1-(9/03) new Waid-s/Kitson-a/c   2.50
TPB (DC, 2004, $14.95) r/series; Kitson sketch pages; Waid intro.   15.00

EMPIRE STRIKES BACK, THE (See Marvel Comics Super Special #16 & Marvel Special Edition)

EMPTY LOVE STORIES
Slave Labor #1 & 2/Funny Valentine Press: Nov, 1994 - Present ($2.95, B&W)

1,2: Steve Darnall scripts in all. 1-Alex Ross-c. 2-(8/96)-Mike Allred-c   4.00
1,2-2nd printing (Funny Valentine Press)   3.00
... 1999-Jeff Smith-c; Doran-a   3.00
..."Special" (2.95) Ty Templeton-c   3.00

ENCHANTED
Sirius Entertainment: 1997 - No. 3 ($2.50, B&W, limited series)

1-3-Robert Chang-s/a   2.50

ENCHANTED (Volume 2)
Sirius Entertainment: 1998 - No. 3 ($2.95, limited series)

1-Robert Chang-s/a   3.00

ENCHANTED APPLES OF OZ, THE (See First Comics Graphic Novel #5)

ENCHANTER
Eclipse Comics: Apr, 1987 - No. 3, Aug. 1987 ($2.00, B&W, limited series)

1-3   2.50

ENCHANTING LOVE
Kirby Publishing Co.: Oct, 1949 - No. 6, July, 1950 (All 52 pgs.)

1-Photo-c	15	30	45	86	133	180
2-Photo-c; Powell-a	10	20	30	54	72	90
3,4,6: 3-Jimmy Stewart photo-c	9	18	27	52	69	85
5-Ingels-a, 9 pgs.; photo-c	15	30	45	88	137	185

ENCHANTMENT VISUALETTES (Magazine)
World Editions: Dec, 1949 - No. 5, Apr, 1950 (Painted-c-1)

1-Contains two romance comic strips each	15	30	45	85	130	175
2	11	22	33	64	90	115
3-5	10	20	30	56	76	90

ENEMY
Dark Horse Comics: May, 1994 - No. 5, Sept, 1994 ($2.50, limited series)

1-5   2.50

ENEMY ACE SPECIAL (Also see Our Army at War #151, Showcase #57, 58 & Star Spangled War Stories #138)
DC Comics: 1990 ($1.00, one-shot)

1-Kubert-r/Our Army #151,153; c-r/Showcase 57   5.00

ENEMY ACE: WAR IDYLL
DC Comics: 1990 (Graphic novel)

Hardcover-George Pratt-s/painted-a   30.00
Softcover (1991, $14.95)   15.00

ENEMY ACE: WAR IN HEAVEN
DC Comics: 2001 - No. 2, 2001 ($5.95, squarebound, limited series)

1,2-Ennis-s; Von Hammer in WW2. 1-Weston & Alamy-a. 2-Heath-a   6.00
TPB (2003, $14.95) r/#1,2 & Star Spangled War Stories #139; Jim Dietz-painted-c   15.00

ENGINEHEAD
DC Comics: June, 2004 - No. 6, Nov, 2004 ($2.50, limited series)

1-6-Joe Kelly-s/Ted McKeever-a/c. 6-Metal Men app.   2.50

ENIGMA
DC Comics (Vertigo): Mar, 1993 - No. 8, Oct, 1993 ($2.50, limited series)

1-8: Milligan scripts   2.50
Trade paperback ($19.95)-reprints   20.00

ENO AND PLUM (Also see Cud Comics)
Oni Press: Mar, 1998 ($2.95, B&W)

1-Terry LaBan-s/c/a   3.00

ENSIGN O'TOOLE (TV)
Dell Publishing Co.: Aug-Oct, 1963 - No. 2, 1964

1	3	6	9	20	30	40
2	3	6	9	16	23	30

ENSIGN PULVER (See Movie Classics)

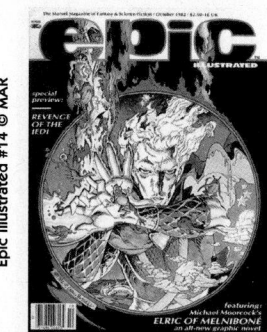

Epic Illustrated #14 © MAR

ESPers #5 © James Hudnall

Essential Hulk Vol. 1 © MAR

	GD	VG	FN	VF	VF/NM	NM-
	2.0	4.0	6.0	8.0	9.0	9.2

EPIC
Marvel Comics (Epic Comics): 1992 - Book 4, 1992 ($4.95, lim. series, 52 pgs.)

Book One-Four: 2-Dorman painted-c 5.00
NOTE: *Alien Legion in #3. Cholly & Flytrap by* **Burden***(scripts) &* **Suydam***(art) in 3, 4. Dinosaurs in #4. Dreadlands in #1. Hellraiser in #2. Nightbreed in #2. Sleeze Brothers in #1-4. Stalkers in #1-4. Wild Cards in #1-4.*

EPIC ANTHOLOGY
Marvel Comics (Epic Comics): Apr, 2004 ($5.99)

1-Short stories by various 6.00

EPIC ILLUSTRATED (Magazine)
Marvel Comics Group: Spring, 1980 - No. 34, Feb, 1986 ($2.00/$2.50, B&W/color, mature)

1-Frazetta-c; Silver Surfer/Galactus-sty; Wendy Pini-s/a; Suydam-s/a; Metamorphosis Odyssey begins (thru #9) Starlin-a	2	4	6	8	10	12
2-10: 2-Bissette/Veitch-a; Goodwin-s. 3-Goodwin-s. 4-Ellison 15 pg. story w/art by Steacy; Hempel-s/a; Veitch-s/a. 5-Hildebrandts-c/interview; Jusko-a; Vess-s/a. 6-Ellison-s (26 pgs.). 7-Adams-s/a(16 pgs.); BWS interview. 8-Suydam-s/a; Vess-s/a. 9-Conrad-c. 10-Marada the She-Wolf-c/sty(21 pgs.) by Claremont/Bolton	1	2	3	4	5	7
11-20: 11-Wood-a; Jusko-a. 12-Wolverton Spacehawk-r edited & recolored w/article on him; Muth-a. 13-Blade Runner preview by Williamson. 14-Elric of Melnibone by Russell; Revenge of the Jedi preview. 15-Vallejo-c & interview; 1st Dreadstar story (cont'd in Dreadstar #1. 16-B. Smith-c/a(2); Sim-s/a. 17-Starslammers preview. 18-Go Nagai; Williams-a. 19-Jabberwocky w/Hampton-a; Cheech Wizard-s. 20-The Sacred & the Profane begins by Ken Steacy; Elric by Gould; Williams-a	1	2	3	5	6	8
21-30: 21-Vess-a. 22-Frankenstein w/Wrightson-a. 26-Galactus series begins (thru #34). Cerebus the Aardvark story by Dave Sim. 27-Groo. 28-Cerebus. 29-1st Sheeva. 30-Cerebus; History of Dreadstar, Starlin-s/a; Williams-a; Vess-a	1	3	4	6	8	10
31-33: 31-Bolton-c/a. 32-Cerebus portfolio	2	4	6	8	10	12
34-R.E.Howard tribute by Thomas-s/Plunkett-a; Moore-s/Veitch-a; Cerebus; Cholly & Flytrap w/Suydam-a; BWS-a	2	4	6	10	14	18

NOTE: *N. Adams a-7; c-6. Austin a-15-20i. Bode a-19, 23, 27r. Bolton a-7, 10-12, 15, 18, 22-25; c-10, 18, 22-23. Boris c/a-15. Brunner c-1; c/a. Buscema a-1p, 9p, 11-13p. Byrne/Austin a-26-34. Chaykin a-2; c-8. Conrad a-2-5, 7-9, 25-34; c-17. Corben a-15; c-2. Frazetta c-1. Golden a-3r. Gulacy c/a-3. Jeff Jones c-25. Kaluta a-17r, 21, 24r, 26; c-4, 28. Nebres a-1. Reese a-22. Russell a-14, 9, 14, 33; c-14. Simonson a-17. B. Smith c/a-7, 16. Starlin a-1-9, 14, 15, 34. Steranko c-19. Williamson a-13, 27, 34. Wrightson a-13p, 22, 25, 27, 34; c-30.*

EPIC LITE
Marvel Comics (Epic Comics): Sept, 1991 ($3.95, 52 pgs., one-shot)

1-Bob the Alien, Normalman by Valentino 4.00

EPICURUS THE SAGE
DC Comics (Piranha Press): Vol. 1, 1991 - Vol. 2, 1991 ($9.95, 8-1/8x10-7/8")

Volume 1,2-Sam Kieth-c/a; Messner-Loebs-s 10.00
TPB (2003, $19.95) r/ #1,2, Fast Forward Rising the Sun; new story 20.00

EPSILON WAVE
Independent Comics/Elite Comics No. 5 on: Oct, 1985 - V2#2, 1987 ($1.50/$1.25/$1.75)

1-8,V2#1,2: 1-3,6-Seadragon app. V2 (B&W) 2.50

ERADICATOR
DC Comics: Aug, 1996 - No. 3, Oct, 1996 ($1.75, limited series)

1-3: Superman app. 3.00

ERNIE COMICS (Formerly Andy Comics #21; All Love Romances #26 on)
Current Books/Ace Periodicals: No. 22, Sept, 1948 - No. 25, Mar, 1949

nn (9/48,11/48); #22,23)-Teenage humor	8	16	24	40	50	60
24,25	6	12	18	28	34	40

ESCAPADE IN FLORENCE (See Movie Comics)

ESCAPE FROM DEVIL'S ISLAND
Avon Periodicals: 1952

1-Kinstler-c; r/as Dynamic Adventures #9	40	80	120	235	368	500

ESCAPE FROM THE PLANET OF THE APES (See Power Record Comics)

ESCAPE TO WITCH MOUNTAIN (See Walt Disney Showcase No. 29)

ESCAPISTS, THE (See Michael Chabon Presents The Amazing Adventures of the Escapist)
Dark Horse Comics: July, 2006 - No. 6, Dec, 2006 ($1.00/$2.99, limited series)

1-($1.00) Frank Miller-c; r/Vaughan story from Michael Chabon... #8 2.50
2-6($2.99) Vaughan-s/Rolston & Alexander-a. 2-James Jean-c. 3-Cassaday-c 3.00

ESPERS (Also see Interface)
Eclipse Comics: July, 1986 - No. 5, Apr, 1987 ($1.25/$1.75, Mando paper)

1-5-James Hudnall story & David Lloyd-a. 3.00

ESPERS
Halloween Comics: V2#1, 1996 - No. 6, 1997 ($2.95, B&W)
(1st Halloween Comics series)

V2#1-6: James D. Hudnall scripts 3.00
Undertow TPB ('98, $14.95) r/#1-6 15.00

ESPERS
Image Comics: V3#1, 1997 - Present ($2.95, B&W, limited series)

V3#1-7: James D. Hudnall scripts 3.00
Black Magic TPB ('98, $14.95) r/#1-4 15.00

ESPIONAGE (TV)
Dell Publishing Co.: May-July, 1964 - No. 2, Aug-Oct, 1964

1,2	3	6	9	20	30	40

ESSENTIAL (Title series), Marvel Comics

--ANT-MAN, '02 (B&W- r) V1-Reprints app. from Tales To Astonish #27, #35-69; Kirby-c	15.00
--AVENGERS, '98 (B&W- r) V1-R-Avengers #1-24; new Immonen-c	15.00
V2(6/00)-Reprints Avengers #25-46, King-Size Special #1; Immonen-c	15.00
V3(3/01)-Reprints Avengers #47-68, Annual #2; Immonen-c	15.00
V4('04)-Reprints Avengers #69-97, Incredible Hulk #140; Neal Adams-c	17.00
V5('06)-Reprints Avengers #98-119, Daredevil #99, Defenders #8-11	17.00
--CAPTAIN AMERICA, '00 (B&W-r) V1-Reprints stories from Tales of Suspense #59-99, Captain America #100-102; new Romita & Milgrom-c	15.00
V2(1/02)-Reprints #103-126; Steranko-c	15.00
V3('06)-Reprints #127-153	17.00
--CLASSIC X-MEN, '06 - Present (B&W- r) (See Essential Uncanny X-Men for V1)	
V2-($16.99) R-X-Men #25-53 & Avengers #53; Gil Kane-c	17.00
--CONAN, '00 (B&W- r) V1-R-Conan the Barbarian#1-25; new Buscema-c	15.00
--DAREDEVIL, '02 - Present (B&W-r)	
V1-R-Daredevil #1-25	15.00
V2-($16.99) R-Daredevil #26-48, Special #1, Fantastic Four #73	17.00
V3-($16.99) R-Daredevil #49-74, Iron Man #35-38	17.00
V4-($16.99) R-Daredevil #75-101, Avengers #111	17.00
--DAZZLER, '07 (B&W- r) V1-R/#1-21, X-Men #130-131, Amaz. Spider-Man #203	17.00
--DEFENDERS, '05 (B&W-r) V1-Reprints Doctor Strange #183, Sub-Mariner #22,34,35, Incredible Hulk #126, Marvel Feature #1-3, Defenders #1-14, Avengers #115-118	17.00
V2-($16.99) R- Defenders #15-30, Giant-Size Defenders #1-4, Marvel Two-In-One #6,7, Marvel Team-Up #33-35 and Marvel Treasury Edition #12	17.00
V3-($16.99) R- Defenders #31-60 and Annual #1	17.00
--DOCTOR STRANGE, '04 - Present (B&W-r)	
V1-($15.95) Reprints Strange Tales #110,111,114-168	16.00
V1 (2nd printing) -(2006, $16.99) Reprints Strange Tales #110,111,114-168	17.00
V2-($16.99) R-Doctor Strange #169-178,180-183; Avengers #61, Sub-Mariner #22 Marvel Feature #1, Incredible Hulk #126 and Marvel Premiere #3-14	17.00
--FANTASTIC FOUR, '98 - Present (B&W-r)	
V1-Reprints FF #1-20, Annual #1; new Alan Davis-c; multiple printings exist	17.00
V2-Reprints FF #21-40, Annual #1; Davis and Farmer-c	15.00
V3-Reprints FF #41-63, Annual #3,4; Davis-c	15.00
V4-Reprints FF #64-83, Annual #5,6	17.00
V5-Reprints FF #84-110	17.00
V6-Reprints FF #111-137	17.00
--GHOST RIDER, '05 (B&W-r) V1-Reprints Marvel Spotlight #5-12, Ghost Rider #1-20 and Daredevil #138	17.00
V2-Reprints Ghost Rider #21-50	17.00
--GODZILLA, '06 (B&W-r) V1-Godzilla #1-24	20.00
--HOWARD THE DUCK, '02 (B&W- r) V1-Reprints #1-27, Annual #1; plus stories from Marvel Treasury Ed. #12, Man-Thing #4,5, Fear #19; Bolland-c	15.00
--HULK, '99 (B&W-r) V1-R-Incred. Hulk #1-6, Tales To Astonish stories; new Timm-c	15.00
V2-Reprints Tales To Astonish #102-117, Annual #1	15.00
V3-Reprints Incredible Hulk #118-142, Capt. Marvel #20&21, Avengers #88	17.00
V4-Reprints Incredible Hulk #143-170	17.00
--HUMAN TORCH, '03 (B&W-r) V1-Strange Tales #101-134 & Ann. 2; Kirby-c	15.00
--IRON MAN, '00 - Present (B&W-r)	
V1-Tales Of Suspense #39-72; new Timm-c and back-c	15.00
V2-Reprints Tales of Suspense #73-99, Tales To Astonish #82 & Iron Man #1-11	17.00
--KILLRAVEN, '05 (B&W-r) V1-Reprints Amazing Adventures V2 #18-39, Marvel Team-Up #45, Marvel Graphic Novel #7, Killraven #1 (2001)	17.00
--LUKE CAGE, POWER MAN, '05 (B&W-r) V1-Hero For Hire #1-16 & Power Man #17-27	17.00
V2-Reprints Power Man #28-49 & Annual #1	17.00
--MAN-THING, '06 (B&W-r) V1-Reprints Savage Tales #1, Astonishing Tales #12-13, Adventure Into Fear #10-19, Man-Thing #1-14, Giant-Size Man-Thing #1-2 & Monsters	

Essential Spider-Man Vol. 5 © MAR

The Establishment #1 © DC

Eternals #1 © MAR

	GD 2.0	VG 4.0	FN 6.0	VF 8.0	VF/NM 9.0	NM- 9.2

Unleashed #5,8,9 · · · · · 17.00

--MARVEL HORROR, '06 (B&W-r) V1-R/#Ghost Rider #1-2, Marvel Spotlight #12-24, Son of
Satan #1-8, Marvel Two-In-One #14, Marvel Team-Up #32,80,81, Vampire Tales #2-3,
Haunt of Horror #2,4,5, Marvel Premiere #27, & Marvel Preview #7 · · · 17.00

--MARVEL TEAM-UP, '02 - Present (B&W-r) V1('02, '06)-R/#1-24 · · · 17.00
V2-R/#25-51 and Marvel Two-In-One #17 · · · 17.00

--MARVEL TWO-IN-ONE, '05 - Present (B&W-r)
V1-Reprints Marvel Feature #11&12, Marvel Two-In-One #1-20,22-25 & Annual #1,
Marvel Team-Up #47 and Fantastic Four Ann. #11 · · · 17.00
V2-R/#26-52 & Annual #2,3 · · · 17.00

--MONSTER OF FRANKENSTEIN, '04 (B&W-r) V1-Reprints Monster of Frankenstein #1-5,
Frankenstein Monster #6-18, Giant-Size Werewolf #2, Monsters Unleashed #2,4-10 &
Legion of Monsters #1 · · · 17.00

--MOON KNIGHT, '06 (B&W-r) V1-Reprints Moon Knight #1-10 and early apps. · · · 17.00

--MS. MARVEL, '07 (B&W-r) V1-Reprints Ms. Marvel #1-23, Marvel Super-Heroes
Magazine #10,11, and Avengers Annual #10 · · · 17.00

--NOVA, '06 (B&W-r) V1-Reprints Nova #1-25, AS-M #175, Marvel Two-In-One Ann. #3 · 17.00

--OFFICIAL HANDBOOK OF THE MARVEL UNIVERSE, '06 (B&W-r) V1-Reprints #1-15
profiling Abomination through Zzzax; dead and inactive characters; weapons & hardware;
wraparound-c by Byrne · · · 17.00

--OFFICIAL HANDBOOK OF THE MARVEL UNIVERSE - DELUXE EDITION, '06 (B&W-r)
V1-Reprints #1-7 profiling Abomination through Magneto; wraparound-c by Byrne · 17.00
V2-Reprints #8-14 profiling Magus through Wolverine; wraparound-c by Byrne · 17.00
V3-Reprints #15-20 profiling Wonder Man through Zzzax & Book of the Dead · 17.00

--OFFICIAL HANDBOOK OF THE MARVEL UNIVERSE - UPDATE '89, '06 (B&W-r)
V1-Reprints #1-8; wraparound-c by Frenz · · · 17.00

--PETER PARKER, THE SPECTACULAR SPIDER-MAN, '05 (B&W-r) V1-Reprints #1-31 17.00
V2-Reprints #32-53 & Annual #1,2; Amazing Spider-Man Annual #13 · 17.00
V3-Reprints #54-74 & Annual #3; Frank Miller-c · · · 17.00

--PUNISHER, '04, '06 - Present (B&W-r) V1-Reprints early app. in Amazing Spider-Man,
Captain America, Daredevil, Marvel Preview and Punisher #1-5 (2 printings) · 17.00
V2-Punisher #1-20, Annual #1 and Daredevil #257 · · · 17.00

--SAVAGE SHE-HULK, '06 (B&W-r) V1-R/#1-25 · · · 17.00

--SILVER SURFER, '98 - Present (B&W-r)
V1-R-material from SS#1-18 and Fantastic Four Ann. #5 · · · 15.00
V2-R-SS#1(1982), SS#1-18 & Ann#1(1987), Epic Illustrated #1, Marvel Fanfare #51 17.00

--SPIDER-MAN, '96 - Present (B&W-r)
V1-R-AF #15, Amaz. S-M #1-20, Ann. #1 (2 printings) · · · 15.00
V2-R-Amaz. Spider-Man #21-43, Annual #2,3 · · · 15.00
V3-R-Amaz. Spider-Man #44-68 · · · 15.00
V4-R-Amaz. Spider-Man #69-89; Annual #4,5; new Timm-f&b-c · · · 15.00
V5-R-Amaz. Spider-Man #90-113; new Romita-c · · · 15.00
V6-R-Amaz. Spider-Man #114-137, Giant-Size Super-Heroes #1 G-S S-M #1,2 · 17.00
V7-R-Amaz. Spider-Man #138-160, Annual #10; Giant-Size Spider-Man #3-5 · 17.00
V8-R-Amaz. Spider-Man #161-185, Annual #11; G-S Spider-Man #6; Nova #12 · 17.00

--SPIDER-WOMAN, '05 (B&W-r) V1-Reprints Marvel Spotlight #32, Marvel Two-In-One #29-33,
Spider-Woman #1-25 · · · 17.00
V2-R-Spider-Woman #26-50, Marvel Team-Up #97 & Uncanny X-Men #148 · 17.00

--SUPER-VILLAIN TEAM-UP, '04 (B&W-r) V1-r/S-V T-U #1-14 & 16-17, Giant-Size S-V T-U #1,2;
Avengers #154-156; Champions #16, & Astonishing Tales #1-8 · · · 17.00

--TALES OF THE ZOMBIE, '06 (B&W-r) V1-($16.99) r/#1-10 & Dracula Lives #1,2 · 17.00

--THOR, '01 (B&W-r) V1-R-Journey Into Mystery #83-112 · · · 15.00
V2-($16.99) R-Thor #113-136 & Annual #1,2 · · · 17.00
V3-($16.99) R-Thor #137-166 · · · 17.00

--TOMB OF DRACULA, '03 - Present (B&W-r) V1-R-Tomb of Dracula #1-25,
Werewolf By Night #15, Giant-Size Chillers #1 · · · 15.00
V2-($16.99) R-Tomb of Dracula #26-49, Giant-Size Dracula #2-5, Dr. Strange #14 · 17.00
V3-($16.99) R-Tomb of Dracula #50-70, Tomb of Dracula Magazine #1-4 · 17.00
V4-($16.99) R/Stories from Tomb of Dracula Magazine #2-6, Dracula Lives! #1-13, and
Frankenstein Monster #7-9 · · · 17.00

--UNCANNY X-MEN, '99 - Present (B&W reprints) (See Essential Classic X-Men for V2)
V1-Reprints X-Men (1st series) #1-24; Timm-c · · · 15.00

ESSENTIAL VERTIGO: THE SANDMAN
DC Comics (Vertigo): Aug, 1996 - No. 32, Mar, 1999 ($1.95/$2.25, reprints)
1-13,15-31: Reprints Sandman, 2nd series · · · 3.00
14-($2.95) · · · 3.50
32-($4.50) Reprints Sandman Special #1 · · · 4.50

ESSENTIAL VERTIGO: SWAMP THING
DC Comics: Nov, 1996 - No. 24, Oct, 1998 ($1.95/$2.25,B&W, reprints)
1-11,13-24: 1-9-Reprints Alan Moore's Swamp Thing stories · · · 3.00
12-($3.50) r/Annual #2 · · · 3.50

ESSENTIAL WEREWOLF BY NIGHT
Marvel Comics: 2005 - Present (B&W reprints)
V1-($16.99) r/Marvel Spotlight #2-4, Werewolf By Night 1-23, Marvel Team-Up #12, Tomb of
Dracula #18, Giant-Size Creatures #1 · · · 17.00

ESSENTIAL WOLVERINE
Marvel Comics: 1999 - Present (B&W reprints)
V1-r/#1-23, V2-r/#24-47, V3-R/#48-69, V4-R/#70-90 · · · 17.00

ESSENTIAL X-FACTOR
Marvel Comics: 2005 - Present (B&W reprints)
V1-($16.99) r/X-Factor #1-16 & Annual #1, Avengers #262, Fantastic Four #286,
Thor #373&374 and Power Pack #27 · · · 17.00
V2-Reprints X-Factor #17-35 & Annual #2, Thor #378 · · · 17.00

ESSENTIAL X-MEN
Marvel Comics: 1996 - Present (B&W reprints)
V1-V4: V1-R/Giant Size X-Men #1, X-Men #94-119. V2-R-X-Men #120-144. V3-R-Uncanny
X-Men #145-161, Ann. #3-5. V4-Uncanny X-Men #162-179, Ann. #6 · · · 15.00
V5-($16.99) R/Uncanny X-Men #180-198, Ann. #7-8 · · · 17.00
V6-($16.99) R/Uncanny X-Men #199-213, Ann. #9, New Mutants Special Edition #1,
X-Factor #9-11, New Mutants #46, Thor #373-374 and Power Pack #27 · 17.00
V7-($16.99) R/Uncanny X-Men #214-228, Ann. #10,11, and F.F. vs. The X-Men #1-4 · 17.00

ESTABLISHMENT, THE (Also see The Authority and The Monarchy)
DC Comics (WildStorm): Nov, 2001 - No. 13, Nov, 2002 ($2.50)
1-13-Edginton-s/Adlard-a · · · 2.50

ETERNAL, THE
Marvel Comics (MAX): Aug, 2003 - No. 6, Jan, 2004 ($2.99, mature)
1-6-Austen-s/Walker-a · · · 3.00

ETERNAL BIBLE, THE
Authentic Publications: 1946 (Large size) (16 pgs. in color)

	GD 2.0	VG 4.0	FN 6.0	VF 8.0	VF/NM 9.0	NM- 9.2
1	15	30	45	84	127	170

ETERNALS, THE
Marvel Comics Group: July, 1976 - No. 19, Jan, 1978

	GD 2.0	VG 4.0	FN 6.0	VF 8.0	VF/NM 9.0	NM- 9.2
1-(Regular 25¢ edition)-Origin & 1st app. Eternals	3	6	9	14	19	24
1-(30¢-c variant, limited distribution)	3	6	9	18	27	36
2-(Reg. 25¢ edition)-1st app. Ajak & The Celestials	2	4	6	8	10	12
2-(30¢-c variant, limited distribution)	2	4	6	10	14	18
3-19: 14,15-Cosmic powered Hulk-c/story	1	3	4	6	8	10
12-16-(35¢-c variants, limited distribution)	2	4	6	9	12	15
Annual 1(10/77)	1	3	4	6	8	10

Eternals by Jack Kirby HC (2006, $75.00, dust jacket) r/#1-19 & Annual #1; intro by Royer;
letter pages from #1,2,Annual #1; afterwords by Robert Greenberger · · · 75.00
NOTE: Kirby c/a(p) in all.

ETERNALS, THE
Marvel Comics: Oct, 1985 - No. 12, Sept, 1986 (Maxi-series, mando paper)
1,12 (52 pgs.): 12-Williamson-a(i) · · · 3.00
2-11 · · · 2.50

ETERNALS
Marvel Comics: Aug, 2006 - No. 7, Mar, 2007 ($3.99, limited series)
1-7-Neil Gaiman-s/John Romita Jr.-a/Rick Berry-c · · · 4.00
1-7-Variant covers by Romita Jr. · · · 4.00
1-Variant cover by Coipel · · · 4.00
... Sketchbook (2006, $1.99, B&W) character sketches and sketch pages from #1 · 2.25
HC (2007, $29.99, dustjacket) r/#1-7; gallery of variant covers; sketches, Gaiman interview,
Gaiman's original proposal; background essay on Kirby's Eternals · · · 30.00

ETERNALS: THE HEROD FACTOR
Marvel Comics: Nov, 1991 ($2.50, 68 pgs.)
1 · · · 2.50

ETERNAL WARRIOR (See Solar #10 & 11)
Valiant/Acclaim Comics (Valiant): Aug, 1992 - No. 50, Mar, 1996 ($2.25/$2.50)
1-Unity x-over; Miller-c; origin Eternal Warrior & Aram (Armstrong) · · · 4.00
1-($2.25-c) Gold logo · · · 5.00
1-Gold foil logo on embossed cover; no cover price · · · 6.00
2-8: 2-Unity x-over; Simonson-c. 3-Archer & Armstrong x-over. 4-1st brief app. Bloodshot

Etta Kett #11 © KING

Eva: Daughter of the Dragon #1 © DE

Everything's Archie #157 © AP

	GD	VG	FN	VF	VF/NM	NM-
	2.0	4.0	6.0	8.0	9.0	9.2

(last pg.); see Rai #0 for 1st full app.; Cowan-c. 5-2nd full app. Bloodshot (12/92;						
see Rai #0). 6,7: 6-2nd full app. Master Darque. 8-Flip book w/Archer & Armstrong #8						3.00
9-25,27-34: 9-1st Book of Geomancer. 14-16-Bloodshot app. 18-Doctor Mirage cameo.						
19-Doctor Mirage app. 22-W/bound-in trading card. 25-Archer & Armstrong app.;						
cont'd from A&A #25						2.50
26-($2.75, 44 pgs.)-Flip book w/Archer & Armstrong						2.75
35-50: 35-Double-c; $2.50-c begins. 50-Geomancer app.						2.50
Special 1 (2/96, $2.50)-Wings of Justice; Art Holcomb script						2.50
Yearbook 1 (1993, $3.95), 2(1994, $3.95)						4.00

ETERNAL WARRIORS: BLACKWORKS
Acclaim Comics (Valiant Heroes): Mar, 1998 ($3.50, one-shot)

1						3.50

ETERNAL WARRIORS: DIGITAL ALCHEMY
Acclaim Comics (Valiant Heroes): Vol. 2, Sep, 1997 ($3.95, one-shot, 64 pgs.)

Vol. 2-Holcomb-s/Eaglesham-a(p)						4.00

ETERNAL WARRIORS: FIST AND STEEL
Acclaim Comics (Valiant): May, 1996 - No. 2, June, 1996 ($2.50, lim. series)

1,2: Geomancer app. in both. 1-Indicia reads "June." 2-Bo Hampton-a						2.50

ETERNAL WARRIORS: TIME AND TREACHERY
Acclaim Comics (Valiant Heroes): Vol. 1, Jun, 1997 ($3.95, one-shot, 48 pgs.)

Vol. 1-Reintro Aram, Archer, Ivar the Timewalker, & Gilad the Warmaster; 1st app. Shalla						
Redburn; Art Holcomb script						4.00

ETERNITY SMITH
Renegade Press: Sept, 1986 - No. 5, May, 1987 ($1.25/$1.50, 36 pgs.)

1-5: 1st app. Eternity Smith. 5-Death of Jasmine						2.50

ETERNITY SMITH
Hero Comics: Sept, 1987 - No. 9, 1988 ($1.95)

V2#1-9: 8-Indigo begins						2.50

ETTA KETT
King Features Syndicate/Standard: No. 11, Dec, 1948 - No. 14, Sept, 1949

	GD	VG	FN	VF	VF/NM	NM-
11-Teenage	11	22	33	60	83	105
12-14	8	16	24	42	54	65

EVA: DAUGHTER OF THE DRAGON
Dynamite Entertainment: 2007 ($4.99, one-shot)

1-Two covers by Jo Chen and Edgar Salazar; Jerwa-s/Salazar-a						5.00

EVANGELINE (Also see Primer)
Comico/First Comics V2#1 on/Lodestone Publ.: 1984 - #2, 6/84; V2#1, 5/87 - V2#12, 1989 (Baxter paper)

1,2, V2#1 (5/87) - 12, Special #1 (1986, $2.00)-Lodestone Publ.						2.50

EVA THE IMP
Red Top Comic/Decker: 1957 - No. 2, Nov, 1957

	GD	VG	FN	VF	VF/NM	NM-
1,2	5	10	14	20	24	28

EVEN MORE FUND COMICS (Benefit book for the Comic Book Legal Defense Fund)
(Also see More Fund Comics)
Sky Dog Press: Sept, 2004 ($10.00, B&W, trade paperback)

nn-Anthology of short stories and pin-ups by various; Spider-Man-c by Cho						10.00

E.V.E. PROTOMECHA
Image Comics (Top Cow): Mar, 2000 - No. 6, Sept, 2000 ($2.50)

	GD	VG	FN	VF	VF/NM	NM-
Preview ($5.95) Flip book w/Soul Saga preview	2	4	6	8	10	12
1-6: 1-Covers by Finch, Madureira, Garza. 2-Turner var-c						3.00
1-Another Universe variant-c						5.00
TPB (5/01, $17.95) r/#1-6 plus cover galley and sketch pages						18.00

EVERQUEST: ... (Based on online role-playing game)
DC Comics (WildStorm): 2002 ($5.95, one-shots)

The Ruins of Kunark - Jim Lee & Dan Norton-a; McQuaid & Lee-s; Lee-c						6.00
Transformations - Philip Tan-a; Devin Grayson-s; Portacio-c						6.00

EVERYBODY'S COMICS (See Fox Giants)

EVERYMAN, THE
Marvel Comics (Epic Comics): Nov, 1991 ($4.50, one-shot, 52 pgs.)

	GD	VG	FN	VF	VF/NM	NM-
1-Mike Allred-a	1	2	3	4	5	7

EVERYTHING HAPPENS TO HARVEY
National Periodical Publications: Sept-Oct, 1953 - No. 7, Sept-Oct, 1954

	GD	VG	FN	VF	VF/NM	NM-
1	28	56	84	162	256	350
2	15	30	45	88	137	185

	GD	VG	FN	VF	VF/NM	NM-
	2.0	4.0	6.0	8.0	9.0	9.2
3-7	14	28	42	80	115	150

EVERYTHING'S ARCHIE
Archie Publications: May, 1969 - No. 157, Sept, 1991 (Giant issues No. 1-20)

	GD	VG	FN	VF	VF/NM	NM-
1-(68 pages)	8	16	24	52	86	120
2-(68 pages)	5	10	15	30	48	65
3-5-(68 pages)	4	8	12	24	37	50
6-13-(68 pages)	3	6	9	17	25	32
14-31-(52 pages)	2	4	6	11	16	20
32 (7/74)-50 (8/76)	1	3	4	6	8	10
51-80 (12/79),100 (4/82)	1	2	3	5	6	8
81-99						6.00
101-120						5.00
121-156: 142,148-Gene Colan-a						4.00
157-Last issue						5.00

EVERYTHING'S DUCKY (Movie)
Dell Publishing Co.: No. 1251, 1961

	GD	VG	FN	VF	VF/NM	NM-
Four Color 1251	5	10	15	30	48	65

EVIL ERNIE
Eternity Comics: Dec, 1991 - No. 5, 1992 ($2.50, B&W, limited series)

	GD	VG	FN	VF	VF/NM	NM-
1-1st app. Lady Death by Steven Hughes (12,000 print run); Lady Death app. in all issues						
	4	8	12	24	37	50
2,3: 2-1st Lady Death-c. 2,3-(7,000 print run)	3	6	9	14	20	25
4-(8,000 print run)	2	4	6	11	16	20
5	2	4	6	9	13	16
Special Edition 1	3	6	9	14	20	25
Youth Gone Wild! ($9.95, trade paperback)-r/#1-5	1	3	4	6	8	10
Youth Gone Wild! Director's Cut ($4.95)-Limited to 15,000, shows the making of the comic						5.00

EVIL ERNIE (Monthly series)
Chaos! Comics: July, 1998 - No. 10, Apr, 1999 ($2.95)

1-10-Pulido & Nutman-s/Brewer-a						3.00
1-($10.00) Premium Ed.						10.00

EVIL ERNIE: BADDEST BATTLES
Chaos! Comics: Jan, 1997 ($1.50, one-shot)

1-Pin-ups, 1-Variant-c						3.00

EVIL ERNIE: DEPRAVED
Chaos! Comics: Jul, 1999 - No. 3, Sept, 1999 ($2.95, limited series)

1-3-Pulido-s/Brewer-a						3.00

EVIL ERNIE: DESTROYER
Chaos! Comics: Oct, 1997 - No. 9, Jun, 1998 ($2.95, limited series)

Preview ($2.50), 1-9-Flip cover						3.00

EVIL ERNIE: IN SANTA FE
Devil's Due Publ.: Sept, 2005 - Mar, 2006 ($2.95, limited series)

1-4-Alan Grant-s/Tommy Castillo-a/Alex Horley-c						3.00

EVIL ERNIE: PIECES OF ME
Chaos! Comics: Nov, 2000 ($2.95, B&W, one-shot)

1-Flashback story; Pulido-s/Beck-a						3.00

EVIL ERNIE: RELENTLESS
Chaos! Comics (Black Label Graphics): May, 2002 ($4.99, B&W, one-shot)

1-Pulido-s/Beck, Bonk, & Brewer-a						5.00

EVIL ERNIE: RETURNS
Chaos! Comics (Black Label Graphics): Oct, 2001 ($3.99, B&W, one-shot)

1-Pulido-s/Beck-a						4.00

EVIL ERNIE: REVENGE
Chaos! Comics: June, 1994 - No.4, Feb, 1995 ($2.95, limited series)

	GD	VG	FN	VF	VF/NM	NM-
1-Glow-in-the-dark-c; Lady Death app. 1-3-flip book w. Kilzone Preview (series of 3)						5.00
1-Commemorative-(4000 print run)	1	3	4	6	8	10
2-4						4.00
Trade paperback (10/95, $12.95)						13.00

EVIL ERNIE: STRAIGHT TO HELL
Chaos! Comics: Oct, 1995 - No. 5, May, 1996 ($2.95, limited series)

1-5: 1-fold-out-c						3.00
1,3:1-($19.95) Chromium Ed. 3-Chastity Chase-c-(4000 printed)						20.00
Special Edition (10,000)						20.00

EVIL ERNIE: THE RESURRECTION
Chaos! Comics: 1993 - No. 4, 1994 (Limited series)

Ewoks #2 © LucasFilm

Excalibur #116 © MAR

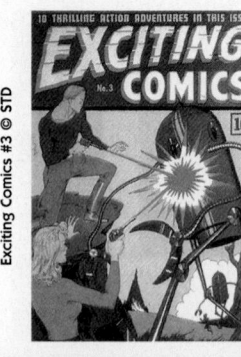

Exciting Comics #3 © STD

	GD 2.0	VG 4.0	FN 6.0	VF 8.0	VF/NM 9.0	NM- 9.2
0						5.00
1	2	4	6	8	10	12
1A-Gold	3	6	9	16	23	30
2-4	1	2	3	5	6	8

EVIL ERNIE VS. THE MOVIE MONSTERS
Chaos! Comics: Mar, 1997 ($2.95, one-shot)

1						3.00
1-Variant-"Chaos•Scope•Terror Vision" card stock-c						5.00

EVIL ERNIE VS. THE SUPER HEROES
Chaos! Comics: Aug, 1995; Sept, 1998 ($2.95)

1-Lady Death poster						3.00
1-Foil-c variant (limited to 10,000)	2	4	6	11	16	20
1-Limited Edition (1000)	2	4	6	11	16	20
2-(9/98) Ernie vs. JLA and Marvel parodies						3.00

EVIL ERNIE: WAR OF THE DEAD
Chaos! Comics: Nov, 1999 - No. 3, Jan, 2000 ($2.95, limited series)

1-3-Pulido & Kaminski-s/Brewer-a. 3-End of Evil Ernie						3.00

EVIL EYE
Fantagraphics Books: June, 1998 - Present ($2.95/$3.50/$3.95, B&W)

1-7-Richard Sala-s/c						3.00
8-10-($3.50)						3.50
11,12-($3.95)						4.00

EVO (Crossover from Tomb Raider #25 & Witchblade #60)
Image Comics (Top Cow): Feb, 2003 ($2.99, one-shot)

1-Silvestri-s/a(p); Endgame x-over pt. 3; Sara Pezzini & Lara Croft app.						3.00

EWOKS (Star Wars) (TV) (See Star Comics Magazine)
Marvel Comics (Star Comics): June, 1985 - No. 14, Jul, 1987 (75¢/$1.00)

1,10: 10-Williamson-a (From Star Wars)	2	4	6	9	12	15
2-9	2	4	6	8	10	12
11-14: 14-($1.00-c)	2	4	6	8	11	14

EXCALIBUR (Also see Marvel Comics Presents #31)
Marvel Comics: Apr, 1988; Oct, 1988 - No. 125, Oct, 1998 ($1.50/$1.75/$1.99)

Special Edition nn (The Sword is Drawn)(4/88, $3.25)-1st Excalibur comic						6.00
Special Edition nn (4/88)-no price on-c	1	3	4	6	8	10
Special Edition nn (2nd & print, 10/88, 12/89)						3.00
...The Sword is Drawn (Apr, 1992, $4.95)						3.00
1($1.50, 10/88)-X-Men spin-off; Nightcrawler, Shadowcat(Kitty Pryde), Capt. Britain, Phoenix & Meggan begin						5.00
2-4						4.00
5-10						3.00
11-49,51-70,72-74,76: 10,11-Rogers/Austin-a. 21-Intro Crusader X. 22-Iron Man x-over. 24-John Byrne app. in story. 26-Ron Lim-c/a. 27-B. Smith-a(p). 37-Dr. Doom & Iron Man app. 41-X-Men (Wolverine) app.; Cable cameo. 49-Neal Adams c-swipe. 52,57-X-Men (Cyclops, Wolverine) app. 53-Spider-Man-c/story. 58-X-Men (Wolverine, Gambit, Cyclops, etc.)-c/story. 61-Phoenix returns. 68-Starjammers-c/story						2.50
50-($2.75, 56 pgs.)-New logo						3.00
71-($3.95, 52 pgs.)-Hologram on-c; 30th anniversary						5.00
75-($3.50, 52 pgs.)-Holo-grafx foil-c						4.00
75-($2.25, 52 pgs.)-Regular edition						2.50
77-81,83-86: 77-Begin $1.95-c; bound-in trading card sheet. 83-86-Deluxe Editions and Standard Editions. 86-1st app. Pete Wisdom						2.50
82-($2.50)-Newsstand edition						3.00
82-($3.50)-Enhanced edition						4.00
87-89,91-99,101-110: 87-Return from Age of Apocalypse. 92-Colossus-c/app. 94-Days of Future Tense 95-X-Man-c/app. 96-Sebastian Shaw & the Hellfire Club app. 99-Onslaught app. 101-Onslaught tie-in. 102-w/card insert. 103-Last Warren Ellis scripts; Belasco app. 104,105-Hitch & Neary-c/a. 109-Spiral-c/app.						2.50
90,100-($2.95)-double-sized. 100-Onslaught tie-in; wraparound-c						4.00
111-124: 111-Begin $1.99-c, wraparound-c. 119-Calafiore-a						2.50
125-($2.99) Wedding of Capt. Britain and Meggan						4.00
Annual 1,2 ('93, '94, 68 pgs.)-1st app. Khaos. 2-X-Men & Psylocke app.						3.00
#(-1) Flashback (7/97)						2.50
...Air Apparent nn (12/91, $4.95)-Simonson-c						5.00
...Mojo Mayhem nn (12/89, $4.50)-Art Adams/Austin-c/a						5.00
...: The Possession nn (7/91, $2.95, 52 pgs.)						3.00
...: XX Crossing (7/92, 5/92-inside, $2.50)-vs. the X-Men						3.00
...Vol. 1: The Sword is Drawn TPB (2005, $19.99) r/#1-5 & Special Edition nn (The Sword is Drawn)						20.00
...Vol. 2: Two-Edged Sword TPB (2006, $24.99) r/#6-11						25.00
...Vol. 3: Cross-Time Caper Book 1 TPB (2007, $24.99) r/#12-20						25.00

EXCALIBUR
Marvel Comics: Feb, 2001 - No. 4, May, 2001 ($2.99)

1-4-Return of Captain Britain; Raimondi-a						3.00

EXCALIBUR (X-Men Reloaded title) (Leads into House of M series, then New Excalibur)
Marvel Comics: July, 2004 - No. 14, July, 2005 ($2.99)

1-14: 1-Claremont-s/Lopresti-a/Park-c; Magneto returns. 6-11-Beast app. 13,14-Prelude to House of M; Dr. Strange app.						3.00
House of M Prelude: Excalibur TPB (2005, $11.99) r/#11-14						12.00
...Vol. 1: Forging the Sword (2004, $9.99) r/#1-4						10.00
...Vol. 2: Saturday Night Fever (2005, $14.99) r/#5-10						15.00

EXCITING COMICS
Nedor/Better Publications/Standard Comics: Apr, 1940 - No. 69, Sept, 1949

	GD 2.0	VG 4.0	FN 6.0	VF 8.0	VF/NM 9.0	NM- 9.2
1-Origin & 1st app. The Mask, Jim Hatfield, Sgt. Bill King, Dan Williams begin; early Robot-c (see Smash #1)	406	812	1218	2639	4670	6700
2-The Sphinx begins; The Masked Rider app.; Son of the Gods begins, ends #8	169	338	507	1056	1753	2450
3-Robot-c	121	242	363	756	1253	1750
4-6	78	156	234	488	807	1125
7,8	62	124	186	388	644	900
9-Origin/1st app. of The Black Terror & sidekick Tim, begin series (5/41) (Black Terror c-9-21,23-52,54,55)	943	1886	2829	6600	11,550	16,500
10-2nd app. Black Terror	300	600	900	1881	3141	4400
11	152	304	456	950	1575	2200
12,13	100	200	300	625	1038	1450
14-Last Sphinx, Dan Williams	72	144	216	450	750	1050
15-The Liberator begins (origin)	100	200	300	625	1038	1450
16-20: 20-The Mask ends	57	114	171	356	591	825
21,23-25: 25-Robot-c	48	96	144	293	484	675
22-Origin The Eaglet; The American Eagle begins	57	114	171	356	591	825
26-Schomburg-c	72	144	216	450	750	1050
27,29,30	66	132	198	413	682	950
28-(Scarce) Crime Crusader begins, ends #58	110	220	330	688	1144	1600
31-38: 35-Liberator ends, not in 31-33	58	116	174	363	602	840
39-Nazis giving poison candy to kids on cover; origin Kara, Jungle Princess	86	172	258	538	894	1250
40-50: 42-The Scarab begins. 45-Schomburg Robot-c. 49-Last Kara, Jungle Princess.						
50-Last American Eagle	59	118	177	369	615	860
51-Miss Masque begins (1st app.)	63	126	189	394	652	910
52-54: Miss Masque ends. 53-Miss Masque-c	54	108	162	329	552	775
55-58: 55-Judy of the Jungle begins (origin), ends #69; 1 pg. Ingels-a; Judy of the Jungle c-56-66. 57,58-Airbrush-c	54	108	162	329	552	775
59-Frazetta art in Caniff style; signed Frank Frazeta (one 1), 9 pgs.	54	108	162	338	562	785
60-66: 60-Rick Howard, the Mystery Rider begins. 66-Robinson/Meskin-a	50	100	150	305	503	700
67-69-All western covers	21	42	63	122	191	260

NOTE: **Schomburg (Xela)** c-26-68; airbrush c-57-66. Black Terror by **R. Moreira**-#65. **Roussos** a-62. Bondage-c 9, 12, 13, 20, 23, 25, 30, 59.

EXCITING ROMANCES
Fawcett Publications: 1949 (nd); No. 2, Spring, 1950 - No. 5, 10/50; No. 6 (1951, nd); No. 7, 9/51 -No. 12, 1/53

	GD 2.0	VG 4.0	FN 6.0	VF 8.0	VF/NM 9.0	NM- 9.2
1,3: 1(1949). 3-Wood-a	14	28	42	80	115	150
2,4,5-(1950)	10	20	30	54	72	90
6-12	9	18	27	47	61	75

NOTE: **Powell** a-8-10. **Marcus Swayze** a-5, 6, 9. Photo c-1-7, 10-12.

EXCITING ROMANCE STORIES (See Fox Giants)

EXCITING WAR (Korean War)
Standard Comics (Better Publ.): No. 5, Sept, 1952 - No. 8, May, 1953; No. 9, Nov, 1953

	GD 2.0	VG 4.0	FN 6.0	VF 8.0	VF/NM 9.0	NM- 9.2
5	10	20	30	54	72	90
6,7,9	7	14	21	35	43	50
8-Toth-a	8	16	24	44	57	70

EXCITING X-PATROL
Marvel Comics (Amalgam): June, 1997 ($1.95, one-shot)

1-Barbara Kesel-s/ Bryan Hitch-a						2.50

EXILES (Also see Break-Thru)
Malibu Comics (Ultraverse): Aug, 1993 - No. 4, Nov, 1993 ($1.95)

	GD 2.0	VG 4.0	FN 6.0	VF 8.0	VF/NM 9.0	NM- 9.2
1,2,4: 1,2-Bagged copies of each exist. 4-Team dies; story cont'd in Break-Thru #1						2.50
3-($2.50, 40 pgs.)-Rune flip-c/story by B. Smith (3 pgs.)						2.50
1-Holographic-c edition	1	2	3	5	6	8

EXILES (All New, The) (2nd Series) (Also see Black September)

Exiles #78 © MAR

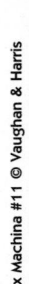

Ex Machina #11 © Vaughan & Harris

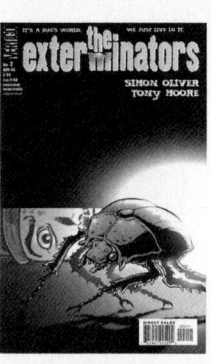

Exterminators #2 © Oliver & Moore

	GD	VG	FN	VF	VF/NM	NM-		GD	VG	FN	VF	VF/NM	NM-
	2.0	4.0	6.0	8.0	9.0	9.2		2.0	4.0	6.0	8.0	9.0	9.2

Malibu Comics (Ultraverse): Sept, 1995 - V2#11, Aug, 1996 ($1.50)

Infinity (9/95, $1.50)-Intro new team including Marvel's Juggernaut & Reaper						2.50	
Infinity (2000 signed), V2#1 (2000 signed)	1	3	4	6	8	10	
V2#1-4,6-11: 1-(10/95, 64 pgs.)-Reprint of Ultraforce V2#1 follows lead story. 2-1st app.							
Hellblade. 8-Intro Maxis. 11-Vs. Maxis; Ripfire app.; cont'd in Ultraforce #12						2.50	
V2#5-($2.50) Juggernaut returns to the Marvel Universe.						2.50	

EXILES (Also see X-Men titles)
Marvel Comics: Aug, 2001 - Present ($2.99/$2.25)

1-($2.99) Blink and parallel world X-Men; Winick-s/McKone & McKenna-a	1	2	3	4	5	7	
2-10-($2.25) 2-Two covers (McKone & JH Williams III). 5-Alpha Flight app.						3.00	
11-24: 22-Blink leaves; Magik joins. 23,24-Walker-a; alternate Weapon-X app.						2.50	
25-98: 25-Begin $2.99-c; Inhumans app.; Walker-a. 26-30-Austen-s. 33-Wolverine app.							
35-37-Fantastic Four app. 37-Sunfire dies, Blink returns. 38-40-Hyperion app.							
69-71-House of M. 77,78-Squadron Supreme app. 85,86-Multiple Wolverines.							
90-Claremont-s begin; Psylocke app.						3.00	
Annual 1 (2/07, $3.99) Bedard-s/Raney-a/c						4.00	
TPB (3/02, $12.95) r/#1-4						13.00	
...: A World Apart TPB (7/02, $14.99) r/#5-11						15.00	
...: Vol. 3: Out of Time TPB (2003, $17.99) r/#12-19						18.00	
...: Vol. 4: Legacy TPB (2003, $12.99) r/#20-25						13.00	
...: Vol. 5: Unnatural Instinct TPB (2003, $14.99) r/#26-30						15.00	
...: Vol. 6: Fantastic Voyage TPB (2004, $17.99) r/#31-37						18.00	
...: Vol. 7: A Blink in Time TPB (2004, $19.99) r/#38-45						20.00	
...: Vol. 8: Earn Your Wings TPB (2004, $14.99) r/#46-51						15.00	
...: Vol. 9: Bump in the Night TPB (2005, $17.99) r/#52-58						18.00	
...: Vol. 10: Age of Apocalypse TPB ('05, $12.99) r/#59-61 & Official Handbook:AoA 2005						13.00	
...: Vol. 11: Time Breakers TPB (2006, $17.99) r/#62-68						18.00	
...: Vol. 12: World Tour Book 1 TPB (2006, $16.99) r/#69-74						17.00	
...: Vol. 13: World Tour Book 2 TPB (2006, $23.99) r/#75-83						24.00	
...: Vol. 14: The New Exiles TPB (2007, $14.99) r/#84-89 and Annual #1						15.00	
...: Vol. 15: Enemy of the Stars TPB (2007, $13.99) r/#90-94						14.00	

EXILES VS. THE X-MEN
Malibu Comics (Ultraverse): Oct, 1995 (one-shot)

0-Limited Super Premium Edition; signed w/certificate; gold foil logo,							
0-Limited Premium Edition	1	3	4	6	8	10	

EX MACHINA
DC Comics: Aug, 2004 - Present ($2.95/$2.99)

1-Intro. Mitchell Hundred; Vaughan-s/Harris-a/c						4.00	
2-29: 12-Intro. Automaton						3.00	
...: Inside the Machine (4/07, $2.99) script pages and Harris art and cover process						3.00	
...: Masquerade Special (10/07, $3.50) John Paul Leon-a; Harris-c						3.50	
... Special 1,2 (6/06 - No. 2, 8/06, $2.99) Sprouse-a; flashback to the Great Machine						3.00	
... March To War (2006, $12.99) r/#17-20 and Special #1,2						13.00	
...: Smoke Smoke (2007, $12.99) r/#21-25						13.00	
...: The First Hundred Days (2005, $9.95) r/#1-5; photo reference and sketch pages						10.00	
... Tag (2005, $12.99) r/#6-10; Harris sketch pages						13.00	

EX-MUTANTS
Malibu Comics: Nov, 1992 - No. 18, Apr, 1994 ($1.95/$2.25/$2.50)

1-18: 1-Polybagged w/Skycap; prismatic cover						2.50	

EXORCISTS (See The Crusaders)

EXOSQUAD (TV)
Topps Comics: No. 0, Jan, 1994 ($1.25)

0-($1.00, 20 pgs.)-1st app.; Staton-a(p); wraparound-c						2.25	

EXOTIC ROMANCES (Formerly True War Romances)
Quality Comics Group (Comic Magazines): No. 22, Oct, 1955-No. 31, Nov, 1956

22		11	22	33	64	90	115
23-26,29		8	16	24	40	50	60
27,31-Baker-c/a		14	28	42	80	115	150
28,30-Baker-a		12	24	36	67	94	120

EXPATRIOT
Image Comics: Feb, 2005 - Present ($2.95)

1-4-B. Clay Moore-s/Jason Latour-a. 1,4-Flip-c						3.00	

EXPLOITS OF DANIEL BOONE
Quality Comics Group: Nov, 1955 - No. 6, Oct, 1956

1-All have Cuidera-c(i)		22	44	66	126	198	270
2		15	30	45	86	133	180
3-6		14	28	42	80	115	150

EXPLOITS OF DICK TRACY (See Dick Tracy)

EXPLORER JOE
Ziff-Davis Comic Group (Approved Comics): Win, 1951 - No. 2, Oct-Nov, 1952

1-2: Saunders painted covers; 2-Krigstein-a		14	28	42	76	108	140

EXPLORERS OF THE UNKNOWN (See Archie Giant Series #587, 599)
Archie Comics: June, 1990 - No. 6, Apr, 1991 ($1.00)

1-6: Featuring Archie and the gang						3.00	

EXPOSED (...True Crime Cases; ...Cases in the Crusade Against Crime #5-9)
D. S. Publishing Co.: Mar-Apr, 1948 - No. 9, July-Aug, 1949

1		24	48	72	139	220	300
2-Giggling killer story with excessive blood; two injury-to-eye panels;							
electrocution panel		30	60	90	172	271	370
3,8,9		14	28	42	76	108	140
4-Orlando-a		14	28	42	80	115	150
5-Breeze Lawson, Sky Sheriff by E. Good		14	28	42	80	115	150
6,7: 6-Ingels-a; used in SOTI, illo. "How to prepare an alibi" 7-Illo. in SOTI, "Diagram for							
housebreakers;" used by N.Y. Legis. Committee	34	68	102	195	308	420	

EXTERMINATORS, THE
DC Comics (Vertigo): Mar, 2006 - Present ($2.99)

1-21: 1-7,9,10,13,14-Simon Oliver-s/Tony Moore-a. 11,12-Hawthorne-a						3.00	
...: Bug Brothers TPB (2006, $9.99) r/#1-5; intro. by screenwriter Josh Olson						10.00	
...: Insurgency TPB (2007, $12.99) r/#6-10						13.00	

EXTINCT!
New England Comics Press: Wint, 1991-92 - No. 2, Fall, 1992 ($3.50, B&W)

1,2-Reprints and background info of "perfectly awful" Golden Age stories						3.50	

EXTINCTION EVENT
DC Comics (WildStorm): Sept, 2003 - No. 5, Jan, 2004 ($2.50, limited series)

1-5-Booth-a/Weinberg-s						2.50	

EXTRA!
E. C. Comics: Mar-Apr, 1955 - No. 5, Nov-Dec, 1955

1-Not code approved		19	38	57	152	241	330
2-5		12	24	36	96	153	210
NOTE: *Craig, Crandall, Severin* art in all.

EXTRA!
Gemstone Publishing: Jan, 2000 - No. 5, May, 2000 ($2.50)

1-5-Reprints E.C. series						2.50	

EXTRA COMICS
Magazine Enterprises: 1948 (25¢, 3 comics in one)

1-Giant; consisting of rebound ME comics. Two versions known; (1)-Funnyman by Siegel &							
Shuster, Space Ace, Undercover Girl, Red Fox by L.B. Cole, Trail Colt & (2)-All Funnyman							
by L.B. Cole		54	108	162	338	557	775

EXTREME
Image Comics (Extreme Studios): Aug, 1993 (Giveaway)

0						3.00	

EXTREME DESTROYER
Image Comics (Extreme Studios): Jan, 1996 ($2.50)

Prologue 1-Polybagged w/card; Liefeld-c, Epilogue 1-Liefeld-c						2.50	

EXTREME JUSTICE
DC Comics: No. 0, Jan, 1995 - No. 18, July, 1996 ($1.50/$1.75)

0-18						3.00	

EXTREMELY YOUNGBLOOD
Image Comics (Extreme Studios): Sept, 1996 ($3.50, one-shot)

1						3.50	

EXTREME SACRIFICE
Image Comics (Extreme Studios): Jan, 1995 ($2.50, limited series)

Prelude (#1)-Liefeld wraparound-c; polybagged w/ trading card						2.50	
Epilogue (#2)-Liefeld wraparound-c; polybagged w/trading card						2.50	
Trade paperback (6/95, $16.95)-Platt-a						17.00	

EXTREME SUPER CHRISTMAS SPECIAL
Image Comics (Extreme Studios): Dec, 1994 ($2.95, one-shot)

1						3.00	

EXTREMIST, THE
DC Comics (Vertigo): Sept, 1993 - No. 4, Dec, 1993 ($1.95, limited series)

1-4-Peter Milligan scripts; McKeever-c/a						2.50	

Fables #49 © Bill Willingham & DC

Fairy Tale Parade #4 © WEST

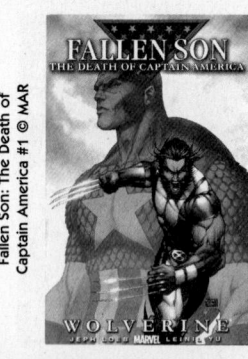

Fallen Son: The Death of Captain America #1 © MAR

	GD 2.0	VG 4.0	FN 6.0	VF 8.0	VF/NM 9.0	NM- 9.2

	GD 2.0	VG 4.0	FN 6.0	VF 8.0	VF/NM 9.0	NM- 9.2

1-Platinum Edition — 5.00

EYE OF THE STORM
Rival Productions: Dec, 1994 - No. 7, June, 1995? ($2.95)

1-7: Computer generated comic — 3.00

EYE OF THE STORM
DC Comics (WildStorm): Sept, 2003 ($4.95)

Annual 1-Short stories by various incl. Portacio, Johns, Coker, Pearson, Arcudi — 5.00

FABLES
DC Comics (Vertigo): July, 2002 - Present ($2.50/$2.75/$2.99)

1-Willingham-s/Medina-a; two covers by Maleev & Jean — 8.00
#1: Special Edition (12/06, 25¢) r/#1 with preview of 1001 Nights of Snowfall — 2.50
2-Medina-a — 5.00
3-5 — 4.00
6-37: 6-10-Buckingham-a. 11-Talbot-a. 18-Medley-a. 26-Preview of The Witching — 3.00
6-RRP Edition wraparound variant-c; promotional giveaway for retailers (200 printed) — 50.00
38-49,51-64: 38-Begin $2.75-c. 49-Begin $2.99-c. 57,58-Allred-a — 3.00
50-($3.99) Wedding of Snow White and Bigby Wolf; preview of Jack of Fables series — 4.00
Animal Farm (2003, $12.95, TPB) r/#6-10; sketch pages by Buckingham & Jean — 13.00
...: Arabian Nights (And Days) (2006, $14.99, TPB) r/#42-47 — 15.00
...: Homelands (2005, $14.99, TPB) r/#34-41 — 15.00
Legends in Exile (2002, $9.95, TPB) r/#1-5; new short story Willingham-s/a — 10.00
...: March of the Wooden Soldiers (2004, $17.95, TPB) r/#19-21 & ...: The Last Castle — 18.00
...: Sons of Empire (2007, $17.99, TPB) r/#52-59 — 18.00
...: Storybook Love (2004, $14.95, TPB) r/#11-18 — 15.00
...: The Last Castle (2003, $5.95) Hamilton-a/Willingham-s; prequel to title — 6.00
...: The Mean Seasons (2005, $14.99, TPB) r/#22,28-33 — 15.00
...: Wolves (2006, $17.99, TPB) r/#48-51; script to #50 — 18.00

FACE
DC Comics (Vertigo): Jan, 1995 ($4.95, one-shot)

1 — 5.00

FACE, THE (Tony Trent, the Face No. 3 on) (See Big Shot Comics)
Columbia Comics Group: 1941 - No. 2, 1943

1-The Face; Mart Bailey-c	86	172	258	538	894	1250
2-Bailey-c	50	100	150	305	503	700

FACTOR X
Marvel Comics: Mar, 1995 - No. 4, July, 1995 ($1.95, limited series)

1-Age of Apocalypse — 3.00
2-4 — 2.50

FACULTY FUNNIES
Archie Comics: June, 1989 - No. 5, May, 1990 (75¢/95¢ #2 on)

1-5: 1,2-The Awesome Four app. — 3.00

FADE FROM GRACE
Beckett Comics: Aug, 2004 - No. 5, Mar, 2005 (99¢/$1.99)

1-(99¢) Jeff Amano-a/c; Gabriel Benson-s; origin of Fade — 2.50
2-5-($1.99) — 2.50
TPB (2005, $14.99) r/#1-5; cover gallery, afterword by David Mack — 15.00

FAFHRD AND THE GREY MOUSER (Also see Sword of Sorcery & Wonder Woman #202)
Marvel Comics: Oct, 1990 - No. 4, 1991 ($4.50, 52 pgs., squarebound)

1-4: Mignola/Williamson-a; Chaykin scripts — 4.50

FAGIN THE JAW
Doubleday: Oct, 2003 ($15.95, softcover graphic novel)

nn-Will Eisner-s/a; story of Fagin from Dickens' Oliver Twist — 16.00

FAIRY TALE PARADE (See Famous Fairy Tales)
Dell Publishing Co.: June-July, 1942 - No. 121, Oct, 1946 (Most by Walt Kelly)

1-Kelly-a begins	96	192	288	816	1508	2200
2(8-9/42)	43	86	129	344	622	900
3-5 (10-11/42 - 2-4/43)	31	62	93	233	429	625
6-9 (5-7/43 - 11-1/43-44)	25	50	75	184	330	475
Four Color 50('44),69('45), 87('45)	24	48	72	175	313	450
Four Color 104,114('46)-Last Kelly issue	19	38	57	138	244	350
Four Color 121('46)-Not by Kelly	12	24	36	82	146	210

NOTE: #1-9, 4-Color #50, 69 have **Kelly** c/a; 4-Color #87, 104, 114-**Kelly** art only. #9 has a redrawn version of The Reluctant Dragon. This series contains all the classic fairy tales from Jack In The Beanstalk to Cinderella.

FAIRY TALES
Ziff-Davis Publ. Co. (Approved Comics): No. 10, Apr-May, 1951 - No. 11, June-July, 1951

10,11-Painted-c	20	40	60	117	184	250

FAITH
DC Comics (Vertigo): Nov, 1999 - No. 5, Mar, 2000 ($2.50, limited series)

1-5-Ted McKeever-s/c/a — 2.50

FAITHFUL
Marvel Comics/Lovers' Magazine: Nov, 1949 - No. 2, Feb, 1950 (52 pgs.)

1,2-Photo-c	11	22	33	60	83	105

FAKER
DC Comics (Vertigo): Sept, 2007 - No. 6 ($2.99, limited series)

1-3-Mike Carey-s/Jock-a/c — 3.00

FALCON (See Marvel Premiere #49, Avengers #181 & Captain America #117 & 133)
Marvel Comics Group: Nov, 1983 - No. 4, Feb, 1984 (Mini-series)

1-4: 1-Paul Smith-c/a(p). 2-Paul Smith-c/Mark Bright-a. 3-Kupperberg-c — 3.00

FALLEN ANGEL
DC Comics: Sept, 2003 - No. 20, July, 2005 ($2.50/$2.95)

1-9-Peter David-s/David Lopez-a/Stelfreeze-c; intro. Lee — 2.50
10-20: 10-Begin $2.95-c. 13,17-Kaluta-a. 20-Last issue; Pérez-a — 3.00
TPB (2004, $12.95) r/#1-9; intro. by Harlan Ellison — 13.00
Down to Earth TPB (2007, $14.99) r/#7-12 — 15.00

FALLEN ANGEL
IDW Publ.: Dec, 2005 - Present ($3.99)

1-17: 1-14-Peter David-s/J.K Woodward. Retailer variant-c for each. 15-Donaldson-a.
17-Flip cover with Shi story; Tucci-a — 4.00
...: To Serve in Heaven TPB (8/06, $19.99) r/#1-5; gallery of reg & variant covers — 20.00

FALLEN ANGEL ON THE WORLD OF MAGIC: THE GATHERING
Acclaim (Armada): May, 1996 ($5.95, one-shot)

1-Nancy Collins story — 6.00

FALLEN ANGELS
Marvel Comics Group: April, 1987 - No. 8, Nov, 1987 (Limited series)

1-8 — 2.50

FALLEN SON: THE DEATH OF CAPTAIN AMERICA
Marvel Comics: June, 2007 - No. 5, Aug, 2007 ($2.99, limited series)

1-5: Loeb-s in all. 1-Wolverine; Yu-a/c. 2-Avengers; McGuinness-a/c. 3-Captain America;
Romita Jr.-a/c; Hawkeye app. 4-Spider-Man; Finch-c/a. 5-Cassaday-a/c — 3.00
1-5-Variant covers by Turner — 3.00

FALLING IN LOVE
Arleigh Pub. Co./National Per. Pub.: Sept-Oct, 1955 - No. 143, Oct-Nov, 1973

1	40	80	120	235	368	500
2	20	40	60	117	184	250
3-10	13	26	39	74	105	135
11-20	11	22	33	62	86	110
21-40	9	18	27	50	65	80
41-47: 47-Last 10¢ issue?	8	16	24	42	54	65
48-70	4	8	12	22	34	45
71-99,108: 108-Wood-a (4 pgs., 7/69)	3	6	9	16	23	30
100	4	8	12	22	34	45
101-107,109-124	2	4	6	13	18	22
134-143	2	4	6	10	14	18
125-133: 52 pgs.	3	6	9	19	29	38

NOTE: **Colan** c/a-75, 81. 52 pgs.-#125-133.

FALLING MAN, THE
Image Comics: Feb, 1998 ($2.95)

1-McCorkindale-s/Hester-a — 3.00

FALL OF THE HOUSE OF USHER, THE (See A Corben Special & Spirit section 8/22/48)

FALL OF THE ROMAN EMPIRE (See Movie Comics)

FAMILY AFFAIR (TV)
Gold Key: Feb, 1970 - No. 4, Oct, 1970 (25¢)

1-With pull-out poster; photo-c	6	12	18	39	62	85
1-With poster missing	3	6	9	18	27	35
2-4-Photo-c	3	6	9	21	32	42

FAMILY FUNNIES
Parents' Magazine Institute: No. 9, Aug-Sept, 1946

9	5	10	15	24	30	35

FAMILY FUNNIES (Tiny Tot Funnies No. 9)
Harvey Publications: Sept, 1950 - No. 8, Apr, 1951

1-Mandrake (has over 30 King Feature strips)	10	20	30	58	79	100

Famous Crimes #14 © FOX

Famous First Edition C-26 © DC

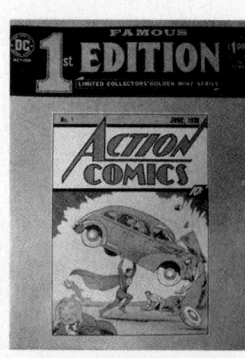

Famous Funnies #4 © EAS

	GD 2.0	VG 4.0	FN 6.0	VF 8.0	VF/NM 9.0	NM- 9.2
2-Flash Gordon, 1 pg.	8	16	24	40	50	60
3-8: 4,5,7-Flash Gordon, 1 pg.	6	12	18	31	38	45

FAMILY GUY (TV)
Devil's Due Publ.: 2006 - Present ($6.95)

nn-101 Ways to Kill Lois; 2-Peter Griffin's Guide to Parenting; 3-Books Don't Taste Very Good						7.00
... A Big Book o' Crap TPB (10/06, $16.95) r/nn,2,3						17.00

FAMILY MATTER
Kitchen Sink Press: 1998 ($24.95/$15.95, graphic novel)

Hardcover ($24.95) Will Eisner-s/a						25.00
Softcover ($15.95)						16.00

FAMOUS AUTHORS ILLUSTRATED (See Stories by…)

FAMOUS CRIMES
Fox Features Syndicate/M.S. Dist. No. 51,52: June, 1948 - No. 19, Sept, 1950; No. 20, Aug, 1951; No. 51, 52, 1953

	GD 2.0	VG 4.0	FN 6.0	VF 8.0	VF/NM 9.0	NM- 9.2
1-Blue Beetle app. & crime story-r/Phantom Lady #16	50	100	150	305	503	700
2-Has woman dissolved in acid; lingerie-c/panels	40	80	120	235	368	500
3-Injury-to-eye story used in SOTI, pg. 112; has two electrocution stories	48	96	144	293	484	675
4-6	23	46	69	135	213	290
7- "Tarzan, the Wyoming Killer" (SOTI, pg. 44)	40	80	120	235	368	500
8-20: 17-Morisi-a. 20-Same cover as #15	17	34	51	98	154	210
51 (nd, 1953)	15	30	45	88	137	185
52 (Exist?)	12	24	36	67	94	120

FAMOUS FEATURE STORIES
Dell Publishing Co.: 1938 (7-1/2x11", 68 pgs.)

	GD 2.0	VG 4.0	FN 6.0	VF 8.0	VF/NM 9.0	NM- 9.2
1-Tarzan, Terry & the Pirates, King of the Royal Mtd., Buck Jones, Dick Tracy, Smilin' Jack, Dan Dunn, Don Winslow, G-Man, Tailspin Tommy, Mutt & Jeff, Little Orphan Annie reprints - all illustrated text	75	140	210	455	710	965

FAMOUS FIRST EDITION (See Limited Collectors' Edition)
National Periodical Publications/DC Comics: ($1.00, 10x13-1/2", 72 pgs.) (No.6-8, 68 pgs.) 1974 - No. 8, Aug-Sept, 1975; C-61, 1979
(Hardbound editions available from Lyle Stuart, Inc.)

	GD 2.0	VG 4.0	FN 6.0	VF 8.0	VF/NM 9.0	NM- 9.2
C-26-Action Comics #1; gold ink outer-c	4	8	12	28	44	60
C-26-Hardbound edition w/dust jacket	15	30	45	107	191	275
C-28-Detective #27; silver ink outer-c	6	12	18	39	62	85
C-28-Hardbound edition w/dust jacket	21	42	63	148	242	335
C-30-Sensation #1(1974); bronze ink outer-c	4	8	12	28	44	60
C-30-Hardbound edition w/dust jacket	15	30	45	107	191	275
F-4-Whiz Comics #2(#1)(10-11/74)-Cover not identical to original (dropped "Gangway for Captain Marvel" from cover); gold ink on outer-c	4	8	12	28	44	60
F-4-Hardbound edition w/dust jacket	15	30	45	107	191	275
F-5-Batman #1(F-6 inside); silver ink on outer-c	5	10	15	32	51	70
F-5-Hardbound edition w/dust jacket	15	30	45	107	191	275
V2#F-6-Wonder Woman #1	4	8	12	28	44	60
F-6-Wonder Woman #1 Hardbound w/dust jacket	15	30	45	107	191	275
F-7-All-Star Comics #3	4	8	12	28	44	60
F-8-Flash Comics #1(8-9/75)	4	8	12	28	44	60
V8#C-61-Superman #1(1979, $2.00)	4	8	12	17	34	45
V8#C-61-(Whitman variant)	4	8	12	24	37	50
V8#C-61-(HC in slipcase, edition of 250 copies) Each signed by Jerry Siegel and Joe Shuster						500.00

Warning: The above books are almost exact reprints of the originals that they represent except for the Giant-Size format. None of the originals are Giant-Size. The first five issues and C-61 were printed with two covers. Reprint information can be found on the outside cover, but not on the inside cover which was reprinted exactly like the original (inside and out).

FAMOUS FUNNIES
Eastern Color: 1934; July, 1934 - No. 218, July, 1955

A Carnival of Comics (See Promotional Comics section)
Series 1-(Very rare)(nd-early 1934)(68 pgs.) No publisher given (Eastern Color Printing Co.); sold in chain stores for 10c. 35,000 print run. Contains Sunday strip reprints of Mutt & Jeff, Reg'lar Fellers, Nipper, Hairbreadth Harry, Strange As It Seems, Joe Palooka, Dixie Dugan, The Nebbs, Keeping Up With the Jones, and others. Inside front and back covers and pages 1-16 reprinted from Famous Funnies Series 1, #s 49-64 reprinted from Famous Funnies, A Carnival of Comics, and most of pages 17-48 reprinted from Funnies on Parade.

	GD 2.0	VG 4.0	FN 6.0	VF 8.0	VF/NM 9.0	NM- 9.2
	4058	8116	12,174	29,000	–	–

No. 1 (Rare)(7/34-on stands 5/34) - Eastern Color First monthly newsstand comic book. Contains Sunday strip reprints of Toonerville Folks, Mutt & Jeff, Hairbreadth Harry, S'Matter Pop, Nipper, Dixie Dugan, The Bungle Family, Connie, Ben Webster, Tailspin Tommy, The Nebbs, Joe Palooka, & others.

	GD 2.0	VG 4.0	FN 6.0	VF 8.0	VF/NM 9.0	NM- 9.2
	3043	6086	9129	22,000	–	–
2 (Rare, 9/34)	613	1226	1839	4600	–	–

	GD 2.0	VG 4.0	FN 6.0	VF 8.0	VF/NM 9.0	NM- 9.2
3-Buck Rogers Sunday strip-r by Rick Yager begins, ends #218; not in #191-208; 1st comic book app. of Buck Rogers; the number of the 1st strip reprinted is pg. 190, Series No. 1	800	1600	2400	6000	–	–
4	253	506	759	1900	–	–
5-1st Christmas-c on a newsstand comic	240	480	720	1800	–	–
6-10	170	340	510	1275	–	–
11,12,18-Four pgs. of Buck Rogers in each issue, completes stories in Buck Rogers #1 which lacks these pages. 18-Two pgs. of Buck Rogers reprinted in Daisy Comics #1	102	204	306	612	944	1275
13-17,19,20: 14-Has two Buck Rogers panels missing. 17-2nd Christmas-c on a newsstand comic (12/35)	79	158	237	474	730	985
21,23-30: 27-(10/36)-War on Crime begins (4 pgs.); 1st true crime in comics (reprints); part photo-c. 29-X-Mas-c (12/36)	60	120	180	360	560	760
22-Four pgs. of Buck Rogers needed to complete stories in Buck Rogers #1	63	126	189	378	582	785
31,33,34,36,37,39,40: 33-Careers of Baby Face Nelson & John Dillinger traced	42	84	126	252	389	525
32-(3/37) 1st app. the Phantom Magician (costume hero) in Advs. of Patsy	46	92	138	276	426	575
35-Two pgs. Buck Rogers omitted in Buck Rogers #2	46	92	138	276	426	575
38-Full color portrait of Buck Rogers	44	88	132	264	407	550
40-41: 41,53-X-Mas-c. 55-Last bottom panel, pg. 4 in Buck Rogers redrawn in Buck Rogers #3	30	60	90	174	275	375
61,63,64,66,67,69,70	23	46	69	135	213	290
62,65,68,73-78-Two pgs. Kirby-a "Lightnin' & the Lone Rider". 65,77-X-Mas-c	25	50	75	148	232	315
71,79,80: 80-(3/41)-Buck Rogers story continues from Buck Rogers #5	17	34	51	100	158	215
72-Speed Spaulding begins by Marvin Bradley (artist), ends #88. This series was written by Edwin Balmer & Philip Wylie (later appeared as film & book "When Worlds Collide")	20	40	60	117	184	250
81-Origin & 1st app. Invisible Scarlet O'Neil (4/41); strip begins #82, ends #167; 1st non-funny-c (Scarlet O'Neil)	21	42	63	120	188	255
82-Buck Rogers-c	21	42	63	122	191	260
83-87,90: 86-Connie vs. Monsters on the Moon-c (sci/fi). 87 has last Buck Rogers full page-r. 90-Bondage-c	15	30	45	90	140	190
88,89: 88-Buck Rogers in "Moon's End" by Calkins, 2 pgs.(not reprints). Beginning with #88, all Buck Rogers pgs. have rearranged panels. 89-Origin & 1st app. Fearless Flint, the Flint Man	16	32	48	94	147	200
91-93,95,96,98-99,101,103-110: 105-Series 2 begins (Strip Page #1)	14	28	42	82	121	160
94-Buck Rogers in "Solar Holocaust" by Calkins, 3 pgs.(not reprints)	15	30	45	86	133	180
97-War Bond promotion, Buck Rogers by Calkins, 2 pgs.(not reprints)	15	30	45	86	133	180
100-1st comic to reach #100; 100th Anniversary cover features 11 major Famous Funnies characters, including Buck Rogers	18	36	54	105	165	225
102-Chief Wahoo vs. Hitler,Tojo & Mussolini-c (1/43)	55	110	165	344	572	800
111-130 (5/45): 113-X-Mas-c	11	22	33	64	90	115
131-150 (1/47): 137-Strip page No. 110 omitted. 144-(7/46) 12th Anniversary cover	10	20	30	58	79	100
151-162,164-168	10	20	30	54	72	90
163-St. Valentine's Day-c	10	20	30	56	76	95
169,170-Two text illos. by Williamson, his 1st comic book work	12	24	36	69	97	125
171-190: 171-Strip pgs. 227,229,230, Series 2 omitted. 172-Strip Pg. 232 omitted. 190-Buck Rogers ends with start of strip pg. 302, Series 2; Oaky Doaks-c/story	9	18	27	50	65	80
191-197,199,201,203,206-208: No Buck Rogers. 191-Barney Carr, Space detective begins, ends #192	9	18	27	47	61	75
198,200,202,205-One pg. Frazetta ads; no B. Rogers	9	18	27	50	65	80
204-Used in POP, pg. 79,99; war-c begin, end #208	9	18	27	52	69	85
209-216: Frazetta-c. 209-Buck Rogers begins (12/53) w/strip pg. 480, Series 2; 211-Buck Rogers ads by Anderson begins, ends #217. #215-Contains B. Rogers reprint pg. 515-518, series 2 followed by pgs.179-181, Series 3	117	234	351	731	1216	1700
217,218-B. Rogers ends with pg. 199, Series 3. 218-Wee Three-c/story	9	18	27	52	69	85

NOTE: *Rick Yager* did the Buck Rogers Sunday strips reprinted in Famous Funnies. The Sundays were formerly done by Russ Keaton and Lt. Dick Calkins did the dailies, but would sometimes assist Yager on a panel or two from time to time. Strip No. 169 is Yager's first full Buck Rogers page. Yager did the strip until 1958 when *Murphy Anderson* took over. Tuska art from 4/26/59 - 1965. Virtually every panel was rewritten for Famous Funnies. Not identical to the original Sunday page. The Buck Rogers reprints run continuously through Famous Funnies issue No. 190 (Strip No. 302) with no break in story line. The story line has no continuity after No. 190. The Buck Rogers news-paper strips came out in four series: Series 1, 3/30/30 - 9/21/41 (No. 1 - 600); Series 2, 9/28/41 -10/21/51 (No. 1 - 525)(Strip No. 110-1/2 (1/2 pg.) published in only a few newspapers); Series 3, 10/28/51 -2/9/58 (No. 100-428)(No

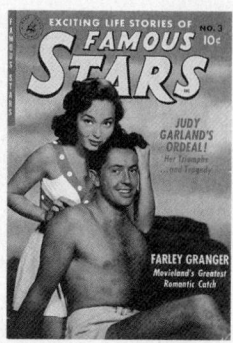

Famous Stars #3 © Z-D

Fantastic Fears #5 © AJAX

Fantastic Four #4 © MAR

	GD	VG	FN	VF	VF/NM	NM-
	2.0	4.0	6.0	8.0	9.0	9.2

No.1-99); Series 4, 2/16/58 - 6/13/65 (No numbers, dates only). **Everett** c-85, 86. **Moulton** a-100. Chief Wahoo c-93, 97, 102, 116, 136, 139, 151. Dickie Dare c-83, 88. Fearless Flint c-89. Invisible Scarlet O'Neil c-81, 87, 95, 121(part), 132. Scorchy Smith c-84, 90.

FAMOUS FUNNIES
Super Comics: 1964

Super Reprint Nos. 15-18:17-r/Double Trouble #1. 18-Space Comics #?

| | | | 2 | 4 | 6 | 9 | 12 | 15 |

FAMOUS GANGSTERS (Crime on the Waterfront No. 4)
Avon Periodicals/Realistic No. 3: Apr, 1951 - No. 3, Feb, 1952

1-3: 1-Capone, Dillinger; c-/Avon paperback #329. 2-Dillinger Machine Gun Killer; Wood-c/a (1 pg.); r/Saint #7 & retitled "Mike Strong". 3-Lucky Luciano & Murder, Inc; c-/Avon paperback #66 ... 37 74 111 213 337 460

FAMOUS INDIAN TRIBES
Dell Publishing Co.: July-Sept, 1962; No. 2, July, 1972

12-264-209(#1) (The Sioux) ... 3 6 9 15 21 26
2(7/72)-Reprints above ... 1 3 4 6 8 10

FAMOUS STARS
Ziff-Davis Publ. Co.: Nov-Dec, 1950 - No. 6, Spring, 1952 (All have photo-c)

1-Shelley Winters, Susan Peters, Ava Gardner, Shirley Temple; Jimmy Stewart & Shelley Winters photo-c; Whitney-a ... 37 74 111 213 337 460
2-Betty Hutton, Bing Crosby, Colleen Townsend, Gloria Swanson; Betty Hutton photo-c; Everett-a(2) ... 23 46 69 135 213 290
3-Farley Granger, Judy Garland's ordeal (life story; she died 6/22/69 at the age of 47), Alan Ladd; Farley Granger photo-c; Whitney-a ... 28 56 84 162 256 350
4-Al Jolson, Bob Mitchum, Ella Raines, Richard Conte, Vic Damone; Bob Mitchum photo-c; Crandall-a, 6pgs. ... 20 40 60 117 184 250
5-Liz Taylor, Betty Grable, Esther Williams, George Brent, Mario Lanza; Liz Taylor photo-c; Krigstein-a ... 43 86 129 294 431 600
6-Gene Kelly, Hedy Lamarr, June Allyson, William Boyd, Janet Leigh, Gary Cooper; Gene Kelly photo-c ... 18 36 54 103 162 220

FAMOUS STORIES (...Book No. 2)
Dell Publishing Co.: 1942 - No. 2, 1942

1,2: 1-Treasure Island. 2-Tom Sawyer ... 30 60 90 174 275 375

FAMOUS TV FUNDAY FUNNIES
Harvey Publications: Sept, 1961 (25¢ Giant)

1-Casper the Ghost, Baby Huey, Little Audrey ... 6 12 18 37 59 80

FAMOUS WESTERN BADMEN (Formerly Redskin)
Youthful Magazines: No. 13, Dec, 1952 - No. 15, Apr, 1953

13-Redskin story ... 14 28 42 76 108 140
14,15: 15-The Dalton Boys story ... 10 20 30 56 76 95

FAN BOY
DC Comics: Mar, 1999 - No. 6, Aug, 1999 ($2.50, limited series)

1-6: 1-Art by Aragonés and various in all. 2-Green Lantern-c/a by Gil Kane. 3-JLA. 4-Sgt. Rock art by Heath, Marie Severin. 5-Batman art by Sprang, Adams, Miller, Timm. 6-Wonder Woman; art by Rude, Grell ... 2.50
TPB (2001, $12.95) r/#1-6 ... 13.00

FANTASTIC (Formerly Captain Science; Beware No. 10 on)
Youthful Magazines: No. 8, Feb, 1952 - No. 9, Apr, 1952

8-Capt. Science by Harrison ... 41 82 123 256 416 575
9-Harrison-a; decapitation, shrunken head panels ... 34 68 102 197 311 425

FANTASTIC ADVENTURES
Super Comics: 1963 - 1964 (Reprints)

9,10,12,15,16,18: 9-r/? 10-r/He-Man #2(Toby). 11-Disbrow-a. 12-Unpublished Chesler material? 15-r/Spook #23. 16-r/Dark Shadows #2(Steinway). Briefer-a.18-r/Superior Stories #1 ... 3 6 9 18 27 35
11-Wood-a; r/Blue Bolt #118 ... 4 8 12 24 37 50
17-Baker-a(2) r/Seven Seas #6 ... 4 8 12 24 37 50

FANTASTIC COMICS
Fox Features Syndicate: Dec, 1939 - No. 23, Nov, 1941

1-Intro/origin Samson; Stardust, The Super Wizard, Sub Saunders (by Kiefer), Space Smith, Capt. Kidd begin ... 480 960 1440 3360 5880 8400
2-Powell text illos ... 248 496 744 1550 2575 3600
3-Classic Lou Fine Robot-c; Powell text illos ... 1200 2400 3600 6000 8400 12,000
4,5: Last Lou Fine-c ... 193 386 579 1206 2003 2800
6,7-Simon-c ... 141 282 423 881 1466 2050
8-10: 10-Intro/origin David, Samson's aide ... 97 194 291 606 1003 1400
11-17,19,20: 16-Stardust ends ... 78 156 234 488 807 1125

	GD	VG	FN	VF	VF/NM	NM-
	2.0	4.0	6.0	8.0	9.0	9.2

18,23: 18-1st app. Black Fury & sidekick Chuck; ends #23. 23-Origin The Gladiator ... 79 158 237 494 822 1150
21-The Banshee begins(origin); ends #23; Hitler-c ... 85 170 255 531 878 1225
22-Hitler-c (likeness of Hitler as furnace on cover) ... 93 186 279 581 966 1350
NOTE: **Lou Fine** c-1-5. **Tuska** a-3-5, 8. Bondage c-6, 8, 9. Issue #11 has indicia in Mystery Men Comics #15. All issues feature Samson covers.

FANTASTIC COMICS (Fantastic Fears #1-9; Becomes Samson #12)
Ajax/Farrell Publ.: No. 10, Nov-Dec, 1954 - No. 11, Jan-Feb, 1955

10 (#1) ... 21 42 63 122 191 260
11-Robot-c ... 26 52 78 150 235 320

FANTASTIC FABLES
Silverwolf Comics: Feb, 1987 - No. 2, 1987 ($1.50, 28 pgs., B&W)

1,2: 1-Tim Vigil-a (6 pgs.). 2-Tim Vigil-a (7 pgs.) ... 4.00

FANTASTIC FEARS (Formerly Captain Jet) (Fantastic Comics #10 on)
Ajax/Farrell Publ.: No. 7, May, 1953 - No. 9, Sept-Oct, 1954

7(#1, 5/53)-Tales of Stalking Terror ... 49 98 147 299 492 685
8(#2, 7/53) ... 36 72 108 208 329 450
3,4 ... 28 56 84 162 256 350
5-(1-2/54)-Ditko story (1st drawn) is written by Bruce Hamilton; r-in Weird V2#8 (1st pro work for Ditko but Daring Love #1 was published 1st) ... 88 176 264 550 913 1275
6-Decapitation-girl's head w/paper cutter (classic) ... 55 110 165 344 572 800
7(5-6/54), 9(9-10/54) ... 28 56 84 162 256 350
8(7-8/54)-Contains story intended for Jo-Jo; name changed to Kaza; decapitation story ... 23 46 69 132 209 285

FANTASTIC FIVE
Marvel Comics: Oct, 1999 - No. 5, Feb, 2000 ($1.99)

1-5: 1-M2 Universe; recaps origin; Ryan-a. 2-Two covers ... 2.50
Spider-Girl Presents Fantastic Five: In Search of Doom (2006, $7.99, digest) r/#1-5 ... 8.00

FANTASTIC FIVE
Marvel Comics: Sept, 2007 - No. 5, Nov, 2007 ($2.99, limited series)

1-5-DeFalco-s/Lim-a; Dr. Doom returns vs. the future Fantastic Five ... 3.00

FANTASTIC FORCE
Marvel Comics: Nov, 1994 - No. 18, Apr, 1996 ($1.75)

1-($2.50)-Foil wraparound-c; intro Fantastic Force w/Huntara, Delvor, Psi-Lord & Vibraxas ... 3.00
2-18: 13-She-Hulk app. ... 2.50

FANTASTIC FOUR (See America's Best TV..., Fireside Book Series, Giant-Size..., Giant Size Super-Stars, Marvel Age..., Marvel Collectors Item Classics, Marvel Knights 4, Marvel Milestone Edition, Marvel's Greatest, Marvel Treasury Edition, Marvel Triple Action, Official Marvel Index to..., Power Record Comics & Ultimate...)

FANTASTIC FOUR
Marvel Comics Group: Nov, 1961 - No. 416, Sept, 1996 (Created by Stan Lee & Jack Kirby)

1-Origin & 1st app. The Fantastic Four: Mr. Fantastic, Johnny Storm: The Human Torch, Sue Storm: The Invisible Girl, & Ben Grimm: The Thing–Marvel's 1st superhero group since the G.A.; 1st app. S.A. Human Torch); origin/1st app. The Mole Man ... 1250 2500 3750 12,500 26,750 41,000
1-Golden Record Comic Set Reprint (1966)-cover not identical to original ... 17 34 51 126 223 320
with Golden Record ... 25 50 75 186 333 480
2-Vs. The Skrulls (last 10¢ issue) ... 360 720 1080 3240 6120 9000
3-Fantastic Four don costumes & establish Headquarters; brief 1pg. origin; intro. The Fantasti-Car; Human Torch drawn w/two left hands on-c ... 258 516 744 2258 4229 6200
4-1st S. A. Sub-Mariner app. (5/62) ... 292 584 876 2555 4778 7000
5-Origin & 1st app. Doctor Doom ... 368 736 1104 3312 6256 9200
6-Sub-Mariner, Dr. Doom team up; 1st Marvel villain team-up (2nd S.A. Sub-Mariner app. ... 152 304 456 1315 2458 3600
7-10: 7-1st app. Kurrgo. 8-1st app. Puppet-Master & Alicia Masters. 9-3rd Sub-Mariner app. ... 104 208 312 884 1642 2400
10-Stan Lee & Jack Kirby app. in story ... 104 208 312 884 1642 2400
11-Origin/1st app. The Impossible Man (2/63) ... 91 182 273 774 1437 2100
12-Fantastic Four vs. The Hulk (1st meeting); 1st Hulk x-over & ties w/Amazing Spider-Man #1 as 1st Marvel x-over.; (3/63) ... 225 450 675 1969 3685 5400
13-Intro. The Watcher; 1st app. The Red Ghost ... 54 108 162 459 855 1250
14-19: 14-Sub-Mariner x-over. 15-1st app. Mad Thinker. 16-1st Ant-Man x-over (7/63); Wasp cameo. 18-Origin/1st app. The Super Skrull. 19-Intro. Rama-Tut; Stan Lee & Jack Kirby cameo ... 43 86 129 344 622 900
20-Origin/1st app. The Molecule Man ... 43 86 129 346 628 910
21-Intro. The Hate Monger; 1st Sgt. Fury x-over (12/63) ... 40 80 120 311 568 825
22-24: 22-Sue Storm gains more powers ... 27 54 81 203 364 525
25,26-The Hulk vs. The Thing (their 1st battle). 25-3rd Avengers x-over (1st time w/Captain

Fantastic Four #27 © MAR

Fantastic Four #244 © MAR

Fantastic Four #391 © MAR

	GD 2.0	VG 4.0	FN 6.0	VF 8.0	VF/NM 9.0	NM- 9.2

America)(cameo, 4/64); 2nd S.A. app. Cap (takes place between Avengers #4 & 5.)

26-4th Avengers x-over — 51 / 102 / 153 / 434 / 805 / 1175

27-1st Doctor Strange x-over (6/64) — 32 / 64 / 96 / 240 / 445 / 650

28-Early X-Men x-over (7/64); same date as X-Men #6 — 45 / 90 / 135 / 360 / 655 / 950

29,30: 30-Intro. Diablo — 22 / 44 / 66 / 165 / 295 / 425

31-40: 31-Early Avengers x-over (10/64). 33-1st app. Attuma; part photo-c. 35-Intro/1st app. Dragon Man. 36-Intro/1st app. Madam Medusa & the Frightful Four (Sandman, Wizard, Paste Pot Pete). 39-Wood inks on Daredevil (early x-over) — 18 / 36 / 54 / 134 / 237 / 340

41-44,47: 41-43-Frightful Four app. 44-Intro. Gorgon — 18 / 22 / 33 / 79 / 140 / 200

45-Intro/1st app. The Inhumans (c/story, 12/65); also see Incredible Hulk Special #1 & Thor #146, & 147 — 18 / 36 / 54 / 134 / 237 / 340

46-1st Black Bolt-c (Kirby) & 1st full app. — 12 / 24 / 36 / 86 / 153 / 220

48-Partial origin/1st app. The Silver Surfer & Galactus (3/66) by Lee & Kirby; Galactus brief app. in last panel; 1st of 3 part story — 51 / 102 / 153 / 434 / 805 / 1175

49-2nd app./1st cover Silver Surfer & Galactus — 36 / 72 / 108 / 270 / 498 / 725

50-Silver Surfer battles Galactus; full S.S.-c — 40 / 80 / 120 / 311 / 568 / 825

51-Classic "This Man...This Monster" story — 16 / 32 / 48 / 118 / 209 / 300

52-1st app. The Black Panther (7/66) — 26 / 52 / 78 / 195 / 348 / 500

53-Origin & 2nd app. The Black Panther — 14 / 28 / 42 / 102 / 181 / 260

54-Inhumans cameo — 9 / 18 / 27 / 65 / 113 / 160

55-Thing battles Silver Surfer; 4th app. Silver Surfer — 16 / 32 / 48 / 118 / 209 / 300

56-Silver Surfer cameo — 9 / 18 / 27 / 65 / 113 / 160

57-60: Dr. Doom steals Silver Surfer's powers (also see Silver Surfer: Loftier Than Mortals).

59,60-Inhumans cameo — 8 / 16 / 24 / 58 / 97 / 135

61-65,68-71: 61-Silver Surfer cameo; Sandman-c/s — 7 / 14 / 21 / 45 / 73 / 100

66-Begin 2 part origin of Him (Warlock); does not app. (9/67) — 11 / 22 / 33 / 75 / 133 / 190

66,67-2nd printings (1994) — 4 / 6 / 8 / 10 / 12

67-Origin/1st brief app. Him (Warlock); 1 page; see Thor #165,166 for 1st full app. — 11 / 22 / 33 / 75 / 133 / 190

72-Silver Surfer-c/story (pre-dates Silver Surfer #1) — 11 / 22 / 33 / 71 / 113 / 175

73-Spider-Man, D.D., Thor x-over; cont'd from Daredevil #38 — 10 / 20 / 30 / 70 / 123 / 160

74-77: Silver Surfer app.(#77 is same date/S.S. #1) — 8 / 16 / 24 / 54 / 90 / 125

78-80 — 6 / 12 / 18 / 37 / 59 / 80

81-88: 81-Crystal joins & dons costume. 82,83-Inhumans app. 84-87-Dr. Doom app.

88-Last 12¢ issue — 5 / 10 / 15 / 32 / 51 / 70

89-99,101: 94-Intro. Agatha Harkness. — 4 / 8 / 12 / 28 / 44 / 60

100 (7/70): F.F. vs Thinker and Puppet-Master — 9 / 18 / 27 / 64 / 110 / 155

102-104: F.F. vs. Sub-Mariner. 104-Magneto-c/story — 5 / 10 / 15 / 30 / 48 / 65

105-109,111: 108-Last Kirby issue (not in #103-107) — 4 / 8 / 12 / 28 / 44 / 60

110-Initial version w/green Thing and blue faces and pink uniforms on-c — 5 / 10 / 15 / 32 / 51 / 70

110-Corrected-c w/accurately colored faces and uniforms and orange Thing — 5 / 10 / 15 / 30 / 48 / 65

112-Hulk Vs. Thing (7/71) — 12 / 24 / 36 / 82 / 146 / 210

113-115: 115-Last 15¢ issue — 4 / 8 / 12 / 22 / 34 / 45

116 (52 pgs.) — 5 / 10 / 15 / 32 / 51 / 70

117-120 — 3 / 6 / 9 / 20 / 30 / 40

121-123-Silver Surfer-c/stories. 122,123-Galactus — 4 / 8 / 12 / 24 / 37 / 50

124,125,127,129-149: 129-Intro. Thundra. 130-Sue leaves F.F. 131-Quicksilver app. 132-Medusa joins. 133-Thundra Vs. Thing. 142-Kirbyish-a by Buckler app.

143-Dr. Doom-c/story. 1st full app. — 3 / 6 / 9 / 16 / 23 / 30

126-Origin F.F. retold; cover swipe of F.F. #1 — 3 / 6 / 9 / 18 / 27 / 35

128-Four pg. insert of F.F. Friends & Foes — 3 / 6 / 9 / 18 / 27 / 35

150-Crystal & Quicksilver's wedding — 3 / 6 / 9 / 19 / 29 / 38

151-154,158-160: 151-Origin Thundra. 159-Medusa leaves; Sue rejoins — 2 / 4 / 6 / 10 / 14 / 18

155-157: Silver Surfer in all — 3 / 6 / 9 / 15 / 21 / 26

161-165,168,174-180: 164-The Crusader (old Marvel Boy) revived (origin #165); Lois app. Frankie Raye. 168-170-Cage app. 176-Re-intro Impossible Man; Marvel artists app. 180-r/#101 by Kirby — 1 / 3 / 4 / 6 / 8 / 10

166,167-vs. Hulk — 2 / 4 / 6 / 14 / 18 / 24

169-173-(Regular 25¢ edition)(4-8/75) — 1 / 3 / 4 / 6 / 8 / 10

169-173-(30¢-c, limited distribution) — 1 / 3 / 4 / 14 / 19 / 30

181-199: 189-G.A. Human Torch app. & origin retold. 190,191-Fantastic Four break up — 1 / 2 / 3 / 5 / 6 / 8

183-187-(35¢-c variants, limited dist.)(6-10/77) — 4 / 8 / 12 / 24 / 37 / 50

200-(11/78, 52 pgs.)-F.F. re-united vs. Dr. Doom — 4 / 6 / 9 / 12 / 15

201-208,219,222-231: 207-Human Torch vs. Spider-Man-c/story. 211-1st app. Terrax. 224-Contains unused alternate-c for FF #3 and pin-ups — 5.00

209-216,218,220,221-Byrne-a. 209-1st Herbie the Robot. 220-Brief origin — 6.00

217-Early app. Dazzler (4/80); by Byrne — 6.00

232-Byrne-a begins — 6.00

233-235,237-249,251-260: All Byrne-a. 238-Origin Frankie Raye. 244-Frankie Raye becomes Nova, Herald of Galactus. 252-Reads sideways; Annihilus app.; contains skin "Tattooz" decals — 5.00

236-20th Anniversary issue(11/81, 68 pgs., $1.00)-Brief origin F.F.; Byrne-c/a(p); new Kirby-a(p) — 6.00

250-(52 pgs)-Spider-Man x-over; Byrne-a; Skrulls impersonate New X-Men — 6.00

261-285: 261-Silver Surfer. 262-Origin Galactus; Byrne writes & draws himself into story. 264-Swipes-c of F.F. #1. 274-Spider-Man's alien costume app. (4th app., 1/85, 2 pgs.) — 4.00

286-2nd app. X-Factor continued from Avengers #263; story continues in X-Factor #1 — 5.00

287-295: 291-Action Comics #1 cover swipe. 292-Nick Fury app. 293-Last Byrne-a 296-($1.50)-Barry Smith-c/a; Thing rejoins — 4.00

297-318,321-330: 300-Johnny Storm & Alicia Masters wed. 306-New team begins (9/87). 311-Re-intro The Black Panther. 327-Mr. Fantastic & Invisible Girl return — 3.00

319,320: 319-Double size. 320-Thing vs. Hulk — 4.00

331-346,351-357,359,360: 334-Simonson-c/scripts begin. 337-Simonson-a begins. 342-Spider-Man cameo. 356-F.F. vs. The New Warriors; Paul Ryan-c/a begins. 360-Last $1.00-c — 3.00

347-Ghost Rider, Wolverine, Spider-Man, Hulk-c/stories thru #349; Arthur Adams-c/a(p) in each — 4.00

347,348-Gold 2nd printing — 2.50

348-350: 350-($1.50, 52 pgs.)-Dr. Doom app. — 4.00

358-(11/91, $2.25, 88 pgs.)-30th anniversary issue; gives history of F.F.; die cut-c; Art Adams back-up story-a — 3.00

361-368,370,372-374,376-380,382-386: 362-Spider-Man app. 367-Wolverine app. (brief). 370-Infinity War x-over; Thanos & Magus app. 374-Secret Defenders (Ghost Rider, Hulk, Wolverine) x-over — 2.50

369-Infinity War x-over; Thanos app. — 2.50

371-All white embossed ($2.00) — 4.00

371-All red 2nd printing ($2.00) — 2.50

375-($2.95, 52 pgs.)-Holo-grafx foil-c; ann. issue — 4.00

376-($2.95)-Variant polybagged w/Dirt Magazine #4 and music tape — 5.00

381-Death of Reed Richards (Mister Fantastic) & Dr. Doom — 4.00

387-Newsstand ed. ($1.25) — 2.25

387-($2.95)-Collector's Ed. w/die-cut foil-c — 3.00

388-393,395-397: 388-bound-in trading card sheet. 394-($1.50-c) — 3.00

394,398,399: 394 ($2.95)-Collector's Edition-polybagged w/16 pg. Marvel Action Hour book and acetate print; pink logo. 398,399-Rainbow Foil-C — 3.00

400-Rainbow-Foil-c — 4.00

401-415: 401,402-Atlantis Rising. 407,408-Return of Reed Richards. 411-Inhumans app. 414-Galactus vs. Hyperstorm. 415-Onslaught tie-in; X-Men app. — 2.50

416-($2.50)-Onslaught tie-in; Dr. Doom app.; wraparound-c — 3.00

#500-up (See Fantastic Four Vol. 3; series resumed original numbering after Vol. 3 #70)

Annual 1('63)-Origin F.F.; Ditko-i; early Spidey app. — 70 / 140 / 210 / 595 / 1098 / 1600

Annual 2('64)-Dr. Doom origin & c/story — 38 / 76 / 114 / 285 / 518 / 750

Annual 3('65)-Reed & Sue wed; r/#6,11 — 17 / 34 / 51 / 128 / 227 / 325

Special 4('66)-G.A. Torch x-over (1st S.A. app.) & origin retold; r/#25,26 (Hulk vs. Thing); Torch vs. Torch battle — 11 / 22 / 33 / 79 / 140 / 200

Special 5(11/67)-New art; Intro. Psycho-Man; early Black Panther, Inhumans & Silver Surfer (1st solo story) — 12 / 24 / 36 / 82 / 146 / 210

Special 6(11/68)-Intro. Annihilus; birth of Franklin Richards; new 48 pg. movie length epic; last non-reprint annual — 8 / 16 / 24 / 54 / 90 / 125

Special 7(11/69)-r/F.F. #1,2; Marvel staff photos — 4 / 8 / 12 / 26 / 41 / 55

Special 8-10: All reprints. 8(12/70)-F.F. vs. Sub-Mariner plus gallery of F.F. foes. 9(12/71). 10('73) — 3 / 6 / 9 / 12 / 18 / 30

Annual 11-14: 11(1976)-New art begins again. 12(1978). 13(1978). 14(1979) — 2 / 4 / 6 / 10 / 14 / 18

Annual 15-17: 15('80, 68 pgs.). 17(1983)-Byrne-c/a — 5.00

Annual 18-27: 21(1988)-Evolutionary War x-over. 22-Atlantis Attacks x-over; Sub-Mariner & The Avengers app.; Buckler-a. 23-Byrne-c; Guice-p. 24-2 pg. origin recap of Fantastic Four; Guardians of the Galaxy x-over. 25-Moondragon app. 26-Bagged w/card — 3.00

Best of the Fantastic Four Vol. 1 HC (2005, $29.99) oversized reprints of classic stories from FF#1,39,40,51,100,116,176,236,267, Ann.2, V3#56,60 and more; Brevoort intro. — 30.00

Maximum Fantastic Four HC (2005, $49.99, dust jacket) r/Fantastic Four #1 with super-sized art; historical background from Walter Mosley and Mark Evanier; dust jacket unfolds to poster: giant FF#1 cover on one side, gallery of interior pages on other — 50.00

...: Monsters Unleashed nn (1992, $5.95)-r/F.F. #347-349 w/new Arthur Adams-c — 6.00

...Nobody Gets Out Alive (1994, $15.95) TPB r/#387-392 — 16.00

...Omnibus Vol. 1 HC (2005, $99.99) r/#1-30 & Annual 1 plus letter pages; 3 intros. and a 1974 essay by Stan Lee; original plot synopsis for FF #1; essays and Kirby art — 100.00

...Omnibus Vol. 2 HC (2007, $99.99) r/#31-60, Annual 2-4 and Not Brand Echh #1 plus letter pages and essays by Stan Lee, Reginald Hudlin, RoyThomas and others — 100.00

Special Edition 1(5/84)-r/Annual #1; Byrne-c/a — 3.00

Fantastic Four V2 #6 © MAR

Fantastic Four #543 © MAR

Fantastic Four: The End #6 © MAR

	GD	VG	FN	VF	VF/NM	NM-
	2.0	4.0	6.0	8.0	9.0	9.2

... Visionaries: George Pérez Vol. 1 (2005, $19.99) r/#164-167,170,176-178,184-186 — 20.00
... Visionaries: George Pérez Vol. 2 (2006, $19.99) r/#187-188,191-192, Annual #14-15, Marvel Two-In-One #60 and back-up story from Adventures of the Thing #3 — 20.00
... Visionaries (11/01, $19.95) r/#232-240 by John Byrne — 20.00
... Visionaries Vol. 2 (2004, $24.99) r/#241-250 by John Byrne — 25.00
... Visionaries John Byrne Vol. 3 (2004, $24.99) r/#251-257; Annual #17; Avengers #233 and Thing #2 — 25.00
... Visionaries John Byrne Vol. 4 (2005, $24.99) r/#258-267; Alpha Flight #4 & Thing #10 — 25.00
... Visionaries John Byrne Vol. 5 (2005, $24.99) r/#268-275; Annual #18 & Thing #19 — 25.00
... Visionaries John Byrne Vol. 6 ('06, $24.99) r/#276-284; Secret Wars II #2 & Thing #23 — 25.00
... Visionaries John Byrne Vol. 7 ('07, $24.99) r/#285,286, Ann. #19, Avengers #263 & Ann. #14, and X-Factor #1 — 25.00
... Visionaries: Walter Simonson Vol. 1 (2007, $19.99) r/#334-341 — 20.00
NOTE: **Arthur Adams** c/a-347-349p. **Austin** c(i)-232-236, 238, 240-242, 250i, 286i. **Buckler** c-151, 168. **John Buscema** a(p)-107, 108(w/**Kirby, Sinnott & Romita**),109-130, 132, 134-141, 160, 173-175, 202, 296-309p, Annual 11, 13; c(p)-107-122, 124-129, 133-139, 202, Annual 12p, Special 10. **Byrne** a-209-218p, 220p, 221p, 232-265, 266i, 267-273, 274-293p, Annual 17, 19; c-211-214p, 220p, 232-236p, 237, 238p, 239, 240-242p, 243-249, 250p, 251-267, 269-277, 278-281p, 283p, 284, 285, 286p, 288-293, Annual 17, 18. **Ditko** a-13i, 14i(w/**Kirby**-p), Annual 16. **G. Kane** c-145p, 146p, 150p, 160p. **Kirby** a-1-102p, 108p, 180i, 189i, 236p, Special 1-10; c-1-101, 164, 167, 171-177, 180, 181, 190, 200, Annual 1-1, Special 1-7, 9. **Marcos** a-Annual 14i. **Mooney** a-118i, 152i. **Perez** a(p)-164-167, 170-172, 176-178, 184-188, 191p, 192p. Annual 14p, 15p; c(p)-183-188, 191, 192, 194-197. **Simonson** a-337-341, 343, 344p, 345p, 346, 350p, 352-354; c-212, 334-341, 342p, 343-346, 350, 353, 354. **Steranko** c-130-132p. **Williamson** c-357i.

FANTASTIC FOUR (Volume Two)
Marvel Comics: V2#1, Nov, 1996 - No. 13, Nov, 1997 ($2.95/$1.95/$1.99) (Produced by WildStorm Productions)

1-($2.95)-Reintro Fantastic Four; Jim Lee-c/a; Brandon Choi scripts; Mole Man app.						5.00
1-($2.95)-Variant-c		1	2	3	4	7
2-9: 2-Namor-c/app. 3-Avengers-c/app. 4-Two covers; Dr. Doom cameo						3.00
10,11,13: All $1.99-c. 13-"World War 3"-pt. 1, x-over w/Image						3.00
12-($2.99) "Heroes Reunited"-pt. 1						4.00
...: Heroes Reborn (7/00, $17.95, TPB) r/#1-6						18.00
Heroes Reborn: Fantastic Four (2006, $29.99, TPB) r/#1-12; Jim Lee intro.; pin-ups						30.00

FANTASTIC FOUR (Volume Three)
Marvel Comics: V3#1, Jan, 1998 - Present ($2.99/$1.99/$2.25)

1-($2.99)-Heroes Return; Lobdell-s/Davis & Farmer-a						6.00
1-Alternate Heroes Return-c		1	2	3	5	8
2-4,12: 2-2-covers. 4-Claremont-s/Larroca-a begin; Silver Surfer c/app.						
12-($2.99) Wraparound-c by Larroca						4.00
5-11: 6-Heroes For Hire app. 9-Spider-Man-c/app.						3.50
13-24: 13,14-Ronan-c/app.						3.00
25-($2.99) Dr. Doom returns						3.50
26-49: 27-Dr. Doom marries Sue. 30-Begin $2.25-c. 32,42-Namor-c/app. 35-Regular cover; Pacheco-s/a begins. 37-Super-Skrull-c/app. 38-New Baxter Building						3.00
35-($3.25) Variant foil enhanced-c; Pacheco-s/a begins						3.50
50-($3.99, 64 pgs.) BWS-c; Grummett, Pacheco, Rude, Udon-a						4.00
51-53,55-59: 51-53-Bagley-a(p)/Wieringo-c; Inhumans app. 55,56-Immonen-a						
57-59-Warren-s/Grant-a						3.00
54-($3.50, 100 pgs.) Birth of Valeria; r/Annual #6 birth of Franklin						4.00
60-(9¢-c) Waid-s/Wieringo-a begin						3.00
60-($2.25 newsstand edition)(also see Promotional Comics section)						3.00
61-70: 62-64-FF vs. Modulus. 65,66-Buckingham-a. 68-70-Dr. Doom app.						3.00

(After #70 [Aug, 2003] numbering reverted back to original Vol. 1 with #500, Sept, 2003)

500-($3.50) Regular edition; concludes Dr. Doom app.; Dr. Strange app.; Rivera painted-c						3.00
500-($4.99) Director's Cut Edition; chromium-c by Wieringo; sketch and script pages						8.00
501-516: 501,502-Casey Jones-a. 503-508-Porter-a. 509-Wieringo-c/a resumes.						
512,513-Spider-Man app. 514-516-Ha-c/Medina-a						3.00
517-537: 517-Begin $2.99-c. 519-523-Galactus app. 527-Straczynski-s begins. 537-Dr. Doom.						3.00
527-Variant Edition with different McKone-c						3.00
527-Wizard World Philadelphia Edition with B&W McKone sketch-c						3.00
536-Variant cover by Bryan Hitch						5.00
537-B&W variant cover						5.00
538-542-Civil War. 538-Don Blake reclaims Thor's hammer						4.00
543-45th Anniversary; Black Panther and Storm replace Reed and Sue; Granov-c						4.00
544-549: 544-546-Silver Surfer app.; Turner-c						3.00
...'98 Annual ($3.50) Immonen-a						3.50
...'99 Annual ($3.50) Ladronn-a						3.50
...'00 Annual ($3.50) Larocca-a; Marvel Girl back-up story						3.50
...'01 Annual ($2.99) Maguire-a; Thing back-up w/Yu-a						3.00
... : A Death in the Family (7/06, $3.99, one-shot) Weeks-a/c; and r/F.F. #245						4.00
... By J. Michael Straczynski Vol. 1 (2005, $19.99, HC) r/#527-532						20.00
Civil War: Fantastic Four TPB (2007, $17.99) r/#538-543; 45th Anniversary Toasts						18.00
Fantastic 4th Voyage of Sinbad (9/01, $5.95) Claremont-s/Ferry-a						6.00

Flesh and Stone (8/01, $12.95, TPB) r/#35-39 — 13.00
.../Inhumans TPB (2007, $19.99) r/#51-54 and Inhumans ('00) #1-4 — 20.00
... Presents: Franklin Richards 1 (11/05, $2.99) r/back-up stories from Power Pack #1-4 plus new 5 pg. story; Sumerak-s/Eliopoulos-a (Also see Franklin Richards) — 3.00
...Special (2/06, $2.99) McDuffie-s/Casey Jones-a; dinner with Dr. Doom — 3.00
...Tales Vol. 1 (2005, $7.99, digest) r/Marvel Age: FF Tales #1, Tales of the Thing #1-3, and Spider-Man Team-Up Special — 8.00
... : The Wedding Special 1 (1/06, $5.00) 40th Anniversary new story & r/FF Annual #3 — 5.00
... Vol. 1 HC (2004, $29.99, dust jacket) oversized reprint r/#60-70, 500-502; Mark Waid intro and series proposal; cover gallery — 30.00
... Vol. 2 HC (2005, $29.99, d.j.) oversized r/#503-513; Waid intro.; deleted scenes — 30.00
... Vol. 3 HC (2005, $29.99, d.j.) oversized r/#514-524; Waid commentaries; cover sketches — 30.00
... Vol. 1: Imaginauts (2003, $17.99, TPB) r/#56,60-66; Mark Waid's series proposal — 18.00
... Vol. 2: Unthinkable (2003, $17.99, TPB) r/#67-70,500-502; #500 Director's Cut extras — 18.00
... Vol. 3: Authoritative Action (2004, $12.99, TPB) r/#503-508 — 13.00
... Vol. 4: Hereafter (2004, $11.99, TPB) r/#509-513 — 12.00
... Vol. 5: Disassembled (2004, $14.99, TPB) r/#514-519 — 15.00
... Vol. 6: Rising Storm (2005, $13.99, TPB) r/#520-524 — 14.00
...: The Life Fantastic TPB (2006, $16.99) r/#533-535; The Wedding Special, Special (2/06) and A Death in the Family one-shots — 17.00
Wizard #1/2 -Lim-a — 10.00

FANTASTIC FOUR AND POWER PACK
Marvel Comics: Sept, 2007 - No. 4 ($2.99, limited series)
1-3-Gurihiru/Van Lente-s; the Wizard app. — 3.00

FANTASTIC FOUR: ATLANTIS RISING
Marvel Comics: June, 1995 - No. 2, July, 1995 ($3.95, limited series)
1,2: Acetate-c — 5.00
Collector's Preview (5/95, $2.25, 52 pgs.) — 2.50

FANTASTIC FOUR: BIG TOWN
Marvel Comics: Jan, 2001 - No. 4, Apr, 2001 ($2.99, limited series)
1-4-"What If?" story; McKone-a/Englehart-s — 3.00

FANTASTIC FOUR: FIREWORKS
Marvel Comics: Jan, 1999 - No. 3, Mar, 1999 ($2.99, limited series)
1-3-Remix; Jeff Johnson-a — 3.00

FANTASTIC FOUR: FIRST FAMILY
Marvel Comics: May, 2006 - No. 6, Oct, 2006 ($2.99, limited series)
1-6-Casey-s/Weston-a; flashback to the days after the accident — 3.00
TPB (2006, $15.99) r/#1-6 — 16.00

FANTASTIC FOUR: FOES
Marvel Comics: Mar, 2005 - No. 6, Aug, 2005 ($2.99, limited series)
1-6-Kirkman-s/Rathburn-a. 1-Puppet Master app. 3-Super-Skrull app. 4-Mole Man app. — 3.00
TPB (2005, $16.99) r/#1-6 — 17.00

FANTASTIC FOUR: HOUSE OF M (Reprinted in House of M: Fantastic Four/ Iron Man TPB)
Marvel Comics: Sept, 2005 - No. 3, Nov, 2005 ($2.99, limited series)
1-3: Fearsome Four by Doom; Scot Eaton-a — 3.00

FANTASTIC FOUR INDEX (See Official...)

FANTASTIC FOUR/ IRON MAN: BIG IN JAPAN
Marvel Comics: Dec, 2005 - No. 4, Mar, 2006 ($3.50, limited series)
1-4-Seth Fisher-a/c; Zeb Wells-s; wraparound-c on each — 3.50
TPB (2006, $12.99) r/#1-4 and Seth Fisher illustrated story from Spider-Man Unlimited #8 — 13.00

FANTASTIC FOUR: 1 2 3 4
Marvel Comics: Oct, 2001 - No. 4, Jan, 2002 ($2.99, limited series)
1-4-Morrison-s/Jae Lee-a. 2-4-Namor-c/app. — 3.00
TPB (2002, $9.99) r/#1-4 — 10.00

FANTASTIC FOUR ROAST
Marvel Comics Group: May, 1982 (75¢, one-shot, direct sales)
1-Celebrates 20th anniversary of F.F.#1; X-Men, Ghost Rider & many others cameo; Golden, Miller, Buscema, Rogers, Byrne, Anderson art; Hembeck/Austin-c — 4.00

FANTASTIC FOUR: THE END
Marvel Comics: Jan, 2007 - No. 6, May, 2007 ($2.99, limited series)
1-6-Alan Davis-s/a; last adventure of the future FF. 1-Dr. Doom-c/app. — 3.00
Roughcut #1 ($3.99) B&W pencil art for full story and text script; B&W sketch cover — 4.00
HC (2007, $19.99, dustjacket) r/#1-6 — 20.00

FANTASTIC FOUR: THE LEGEND
Marvel Comics: Oct, 1996 ($3.95, one-shot)
1-Tribute issue — 4.00

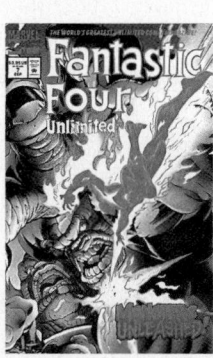

Fantastic Four Unlimited #7 © MAR

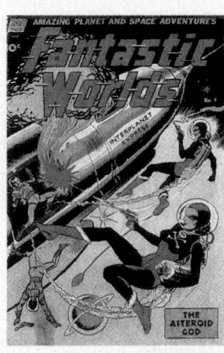

Fantastic Worlds #7 © STD

Fast Fiction #1 © Seaboard

	GD 2.0	VG 4.0	FN 6.0	VF 8.0	VF/NM 9.0	NM- 9.2

FANTASTIC FOUR: THE MOVIE
Marvel Comics: Aug, 2005 ($4.99/$12.99, one-shot)

1-($4.99) Movie adaptation; Jurgens-a; behind the scenes feature; Doom origin; photo-c						5.00
TPB-($12.99) Movie adaptation, r/Fantastic Four #5 & 190, and FF Vol. 3 #60, photo-c						13.00

FANTASTIC FOUR 2099
Marvel Comics: Jan, 1996 - No. 8, Aug, 1996 ($3.95/$1.95)

1-($3.95)-Chromium-c; X-Nation preview						4.00
2-8: 4-Spider-Man 2099-c/app. 5-Doctor Strange app. 7-Thibert-c						2.50

NOTE: *Williamson* a-1i; c-1i.

FANTASTIC FOUR UNLIMITED
Marvel Comics: Mar, 1993 - No. 12, Dec, 1995 ($3.95, 68 pgs.)

1-12: 1-Black Panther app. 4-Thing vs. Hulk. 5-Vs. The Frightful Four. 6-Vs. Namor. 7, 9-12-Wraparound-c						4.00

FANTASTIC FOUR UNPLUGGED
Marvel Comics: Sept, 1995 - No. 6, Aug 1996 (99¢, bi-monthly)

1-6						2.50

FANTASTIC FOUR - UNSTABLE MOLECULES
(Indicia for #1 reads STARTLING STORIES: ... ; #2 reads UNSTABLE MOLECULES)
Marvel Comics: Mar, 2003 - No. 4, June, 2003 ($2.99, limited series)

1-4-Guy Davis-a						3.00
Fantastic Four Legends Vol. 1 TPB (2003, $13.99) r/#1-4, origin from FF #1 (1963)						14.00
TPB (2005, $13.99) r/#1-4						14.00

FANTASTIC FOUR VS. X-MEN
Marvel Comics: Feb, 1987 - No. 4, June, 1987 (Limited series)

1-4: 4-Austin-a(i)						4.00

FANTASTIC FOUR: WORLD'S GREATEST COMICS MAGAZINE
Marvel Comics: Feb, 2001 - No. 12 (Limited series)

1-12: Homage to Lee & Kirby era of F.F.; s/a by Larsen & various. 5-Hulk-c/app. 10-Thor app.						3.00

FANTASTIC GIANTS (Formerly Konga #1-23)
Charlton Comics: V2#24, Sept, 1966 (25¢, 68 pgs.)

	GD	VG	FN	VF	VF/NM	NM-
V2#24-Special Ditko issue; origin Konga & Gorgo reprinted plus two new Ditko stories	6	12	18	43	69	95

FANTASTIC TALES
I. W. Enterprises: 1958 (no date) (Reprint, one-shot)

	GD	VG	FN	VF	VF/NM	NM-
1-Reprints Avon's "City of the Living Dead"	3	6	9	20	30	40

FANTASTIC VOYAGE (See Movie Comics)
Gold Key: Aug, 1969 - No. 2, Dec, 1969

	GD	VG	FN	VF	VF/NM	NM-
1 (TV)	4	8	12	28	44	60
2	3	6	9	20	30	40

FANTASTIC VOYAGES OF SINDBAD, THE
Gold Key: Oct, 1965 - No. 2, June, 1967

	GD	VG	FN	VF	VF/NM	NM-
1-Painted-c on both	6	12	18	43	69	95
2	5	10	15	32	51	70

FANTASTIC WORLDS
Standard Comics: No. 5, Sept, 1952 - No. 7, Jan, 1953

	GD	VG	FN	VF	VF/NM	NM-
5-Toth, Anderson-a	36	72	108	208	329	450
6-Toth-c/a	30	60	90	174	275	375
7	20	40	60	115	180	245

FANTASY FEATURES
Americomics: 1987 - No. 2, 1987 ($1.75)

1,2						3.00

FANTASY ILLUSTRATED
New Media Publ.: Spring 1982 ($2.95, B&W magazine)

			GD	VG	FN	VF	VF/NM	NM-
1-P. Craig Russell-c/a; art by Ditko, Sekowsky, Sutton; Englehart-s		1	2	3	4	5	7

FANTASY MASTERPIECES (Marvel Super Heroes No. 12 on)
Marvel Comics Group: Feb, 1966 - No. 11, Oct, 1967; V2#1, Dec, 1979 - No. 14, Jan, 1981

	GD	VG	FN	VF	VF/NM	NM-
1-Photo of Stan Lee (12¢-c #1,2)	7	14	21	45	73	100
2-r/1st Fin Fang Foom from Strange Tales #89	4	8	12	28	44	60
3-8: 3-G.A. Capt. America-r begin, end #11; 1st 25¢ Giant; Colan-r. 3-6-Kirby-c(p). 4-Kirby-c(p)(i). 7-Begin G.A. Sub-Mariner, Torch-r/M. Mystery. 8-Torch battles the Sub-Mariner-r/Marvel Mystery #9	5	10	15	30	48	65
9-Origin Human Torch-r/Marvel Comics #1	5	10	15	32	51	70
10,11: 10-r/origin & 1st app. All Winners Squad from All Winners #19. 11-r/origin of Toro						

(H.T. #1) & Black Knight #1

	GD	VG	FN	VF	VF/NM	NM-
	4	8	12	28	44	60

V2#1(12/79, 75¢, 52 pgs.)-r/origin Silver Surfer from Silver Surfer #1 with editing plus reprints cover; J. Buscema-a						6.00
2-14-Reprints Silver Surfer #2-14 w/covers						4.00

NOTE: *Buscema* c-V2#7-9(in part). *Ditko* r-1-3, 7, 9. *Everett* r-1,7-9. *Matt Fox* r-9i. *Kirby* r-1-11; c(p)-3, 4i, 5, 6. *Starlin* r-8-13. Some direct sale V2#14's had a 50¢ cover price. #3-11 contain Capt. America-r/Capt. America #3-10. #7-11 contain G.A.Human Torch & Sub-Mariner-r.

FANTASY QUARTERLY (Also see Elfquest)
Independent Publishers Syndicate: Spring, 1978 (B&W)

	GD	VG	FN	VF	VF/NM	NM-
1-1st app. Elfquest; Dave Sim-a (6 pgs.)	6	12	18	41	66	90

FANTOMAN (Formerly Amazing Adventure Funnies)
Centaur Publications: No. 2, Aug, 1940 - No. 4, Dec, 1940

	GD	VG	FN	VF	VF/NM	NM-
2-The Fantom of the Fair, The Arrow, Little Dynamite-r begin; origin The Ermine by Filchock; Fantoman app. in 2-4; Burgos, J. Cole, Ernst, Gustavson-a	110	220	330	688	1144	1600
3,4: Gustavson-r. 4-Red Blaze story	86	172	258	538	894	1250

FAREWELL MOONSHADOW (See Moonshadow)
DC Comics (Vertigo): Jan, 1997 ($7.95, one-shot)

nn-DeMatteis-s/Muth-c/a						8.00

FARGO KID (Formerly Justice Traps the Guilty)(See Feature Comics #47)
Prize Publications: No. 3(#1), June-July, 1958 - V11#5, Oct-Nov, 1958

	GD	VG	FN	VF	VF/NM	NM-
V11#3(#1)-Origin Fargo Kid; Severin-c/a; Williamson-a(2); Heath-a	18	36	54	103	162	220
V11#4,5-Severin-c/a	13	26	39	74	105	135

FARMER'S DAUGHTER, THE
Stanhall Publ./Trojan Magazines: Feb-Mar, 1954 - No. 3, June-July, 1954; No. 4, Oct, 1954

	GD	VG	FN	VF	VF/NM	NM-
1-Lingerie, nudity panel	32	64	69	186	293	400
2-4(Stanhall)	18	36	54	105	165	225

FARSCAPE: WAR TORN (Based on TV series)
DC Comics (WildStorm): Apr, 2002 - No. 2, May, 2002 ($4.95, limited series)

1,2-Teranishi-a/Wolfman-s; photo-c						5.00

FASHION IN ACTION
Eclipse Comics: Aug, 1986 - Feb, 1987 (Baxter paper)

Summer Special 1 , Winter Special 1, each Snyder III-c/a						2.50

FASTBALL EXPRESS (Major League Baseball)
Ultimate Sports Force: 2000 ($3.95, one-shot)

1-Polybagged with poster; Johnson, Maddux, Park, Nomo, Clemens app.						4.00

FASTEST GUN ALIVE, THE (Movie)
Dell Publishing Co.: No. 741, Sept, 1956 (one-shot)

	GD	VG	FN	VF	VF/NM	NM-
Four Color 741-Photo-c	8	16	24	51	78	105

FAST FICTION (...Action) (Stories by Famous Authors Illustrated #6 on)
Seaboard Publ./Famous Authors Ill.: Oct, 1949 - No. 5, Mar, 1950
(All have Kiefer-c)(48 pgs.)

	GD	VG	FN	VF	VF/NM	NM-
1-Scarlet Pimpernel; Jim Lavery-c/a	32	64	96	180	278	375
2-Captain Blood; H. C. Kiefer-a	27	54	81	155	240	325
3-She, by Rider Haggard; Vincent Napoli-a	34	68	102	192	296	400
4-(1/50, 52 pgs.)-The 39 Steps; Lavery-c/a	20	40	60	115	178	240
5-Beau Geste; Kiefer-c/a	20	40	60	115	178	240

NOTE: *Kiefer* a-2, 5; c-2, 3,5. *Lavery* c/a-1, 4. *Napoli* a-3.

FAST FORWARD
DC Comics (Piranha Press): 1992 - No. 3, 1993 ($4.95, 68 pgs.)

1-3: 1-Morrison scripts; McKean-c/a. 3-Sam Kieth-a						5.00

FAST WILLIE JACKSON
Fitzgerald Periodicals, Inc.: Oct, 1976 - No. 7, 1977

	GD	VG	FN	VF	VF/NM	NM-
1	2	4	6	13	18	22
2-7	2	4	6	11	14

FAT ALBERT (...& the Cosby Kids) (TV)
Gold Key: Mar, 1974 - No. 29, Feb, 1979

	GD	VG	FN	VF	VF/NM	NM-
1	4	8	12	22	34	45
2-10	3	6	9	14	19	24
11-29	2	4	6	10	14	18

FATALE (Also see Powers That Be #1 & Shadow State #1,2)
Broadway Comics: Jan, 1996 - No. 6, Aug, 1996 ($2.50)

1-6: J.G. Jones-c/a in all, Preview Edition 1 (11/95, B&W)						2.50

FAT AND SLAT (Ed Wheelan) (Becomes Gunfighter No. 5 on)

Fathom #2 © Michael Turner

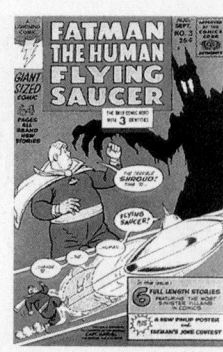

Fatman, The Human Flying Saucer #3 © Milson Publ.

Fawcett Movie Comic #17 © FAW

	GD 2.0	VG 4.0	FN 6.0	VF 8.0	VF/NM 9.0	NM- 9.2

E. C. Comics: Summer, 1947 - No. 4, Spring, 1948

	GD	VG	FN	VF	VF/NM	NM-
1-Intro/origin Voltage, Man of Lightning; "Comics" McCormick, the World's No. 1 Comic Book Fan begins, ends #4	37	74	111	213	337	460
2-4: 4-Comics McCormick-c feature	24	48	72	139	220	300

FAT AND SLAT JOKE BOOK
All-American Comics (William H. Wise): Summer, 1944 (52 pgs., one-shot)

nn-by Ed Wheelan	28	56	84	162	256	350

FATE (See Hand of Fate & Thrill-O-Rama)

FATE
DC Comics: Oct, 1994 - No. 22, Sept, 1996 ($1.95/$2.25)

0,1-22: 8-Begin $2.25-c. 11-14-Alan Scott (Sentinel) app. 10,14-Zatanna app. 21-Phantom Stranger app. 22-Spectre app. ... 2.50

FATHOM
Comico: May, 1987 - No. 3, July, 1987 ($1.50, limited series)

1-3 ... 2.50

FATHOM
Image Comics (Top Cow Prod.): Aug, 1998 - No. 14, May, 2002 ($2.50)

Preview	12.00
0-Wizard supplement	7.00
0-($6.95) DF Alternate	7.00
1/2 (Wizard) origin of Cannon; Turner-a	6.00
1/2 (3/03, $2.99) origin of Cannon	3.00
1-Turner-s/a; three covers; alternate story pages	6.00
1-Wizard World Ed.	9.00
2-14: 12-14-Witchblade app. 13,14-Tomb Raider app.	3.00
9-Green foil-c edition	15.00
9,12-Holofoil editions	18.00
12,13-DFE alternate-c	6.00
13,14-DFE Gold edition	8.00
14-DFE Blue	15.00
... Collected Edition 1 (3/99, $5.95) r/Preview & all three #1's	6.00
... Collected Edition 2-4 (3-12/99, $5.95) 2-r/#2,3. 3-r/#4,5. 4-r/#6,7	6.00
... Collected Edition 5 (4/00, $5.95) 5-r/#8,9	6.00
... Swimsuit Special (5/99, $2.95) Pin-ups by various	3.00
... Swimsuit Special 2000 (12/00, $2.95) Pin-ups by various; Turner-c	3.00
Michael Turner's Fathom HC ('01, $39.95) r/#1-9, black-c w/silver foil	40.00
Michael Turner's Fathom SC ('01, $24.95) r/#1-9, new Turner-c	25.00

FATHOM (MICHAEL TURNER'S...) (Volume 2)
Aspen MLT, Inc.: No. 0, Apr, 2005 - Present ($2.50/$2.99)

0-($2.50) Turnbull-a/Turner-c	2.50
1-11-($2.99) 1-Five covers. 2-Two covers. 4-Six covers	3.00
... Beginnings (2005, $1.99) Two covers; Turnbull-a	2.50
...: Killian's Vessel 1 (7/07, $2.99) 3 covers; Odagawa-a	3.00
... Prelude (6/05, $2.99) Seven covers; Garza-a	3.00

FATHOM: CANNON HAWKE (MICHAEL TURNER'S...)
Aspen MLT, Inc.: Nov, 2005 - No. 5, Feb, 2006 ($2.99)

1-5-To-a/Turner-c	3.00
... Prelude (11/05, $2.50) Turner-c	2.50

FATHOM: DAWN OF WAR (MICHAEL TURNER'S...)
Aspen MLT, Inc.: Oct, 2004 - No. 3, Dec, 2004 ($2.99, limited series)

0-Caldwell-a	2.50
1-3-Caldwell-a	3.00
...: Cannon Hawke #0 ('04, $2.50) Turner-c	2.50
... The Complete Saga Vol. 1 (2005, $9.99) r/series with cover gallery	10.00

FATHOM: KIANI (MICHAEL TURNER'S...)
Aspen MLT, Inc.: No. 0, Feb, 2007 - No. 4, ($2.99, limited series)

0-3-Marcus To-a. 1-Six covers ... 3.00

FATHOM: KILLIAN'S TIDE
Image Comics (Top Cow Prod.): Apr, 2001 - No. 4, Nov, 2001 ($2.95)

1-4-Caldwell-a(p); two covers by Caldwell and Turner. 2-Flip-book preview of Universe	3.00
1-DFE Blue, 1-Holographic logo	12.00
4-Foil-c	12.00

FATIMA...CHALLENGE TO THE WORLD
Catechetical Guild: 1951, 36 pgs. (15¢)

nn same as 'Challenge to the World'	5	10	15	23	28	32

FATMAN, THE HUMAN FLYING SAUCER
Lightning Comics(Milson Publ. Co.): April, 1967 - No. 3, Aug-Sept, 1967 (68 pgs.)

(Written by Otto Binder)

	GD	VG	FN	VF	VF/NM	NM-
1-Origin/1st app. Fatman & Tinman by Beck	6	12	18	39	62	85
2-C. C. Beck-a	4	8	12	24	37	50
3-(Scarce)-Beck-a	6	12	18	41	66	90

FAULTLINES
DC Comics (Vertigo): May, 1997 - No. 6, Oct, 1997 ($2.50, limited series)

1-6-Lee Marrs-s/Bill Koeb-a in all ... 2.50

FAUNTLEROY COMICS (Super Duck Presents...)
Close-Up/Archie Publications: 1950; No. 2, 1951; No. 3, 1952

1-Super Duck-c/stories by Al Fagaly in all	9	18	27	50	65	80
2,3	6	12	18	31	38	45

FAUST
Northstar Publishing/Rebel Studios #7 on: 1989 - No 11, 1997 ($2.00/$2.25, B&W, mature themes)

1-Decapitation-c; Tim Vigil-c/a in all	3	6	9	14	19	24
1-2nd - 4th printings						3.00
2	2	4	6	8	10	12
2-2nd & 3rd printings, 3,5-2nd printing						3.00
3	1	3	4	6	8	10
4-10: 7-Begin Rebel Studios series						5.00
11-($2.25)						3.00

FAWCETT MOTION PICTURE COMICS (See Motion Picture Comics)

FAWCETT MOVIE COMIC
Fawcett Publications: 1949 - No. 20, Dec, 1952 (All photo-c)

	GD	VG	FN	VF	VF/NM	NM-
nn- "Dakota Lil"; George Montgomery & Rod Cameron (1949)						
	28	56	84	161	248	335
nn- "Copper Canyon"; Ray Milland & Hedy Lamarr (1950)						
	20	40	60	115	178	240
nn- "Destination Moon" (1950)	75	150	225	469	760	1050
nn- "Montana"; Errol Flynn & Alexis Smith (1950)	20	40	60	115	178	240
nn- "Pioneer Marshal"; Monte Hale (1950)	20	40	60	115	178	240
nn- "Powder River Rustlers"; Rocky Lane (1950)	29	58	87	167	259	350
nn- "Singing Guns"; Vaughn Monroe, Ella Raines & Walter Brennan (1950)						
	18	36	54	101	156	210
7- "Gunmen of Abilene"; Rocky Lane; Bob Powell-a (1950)						
	22	44	66	125	193	260
8- "King of the Bullwhip"; Lash LaRue; Bob Powell-a (1950)						
	32	64	96	184	285	385
9- "The Old Frontier"; Monte Hale; Bob Powell-a (2/51; mis-dated 2/50)						
	21	42	63	121	186	250
10- "The Missourians"; Monte Hale (4/51)	21	42	63	121	186	250
11- "The Thundering Trail"; Lash LaRue (6/51)	27	54	81	154	237	320
12- "Rustlers on Horseback"; Rocky Lane (8/51)	21	42	63	121	186	250
13- "Warpath"; Edmond O'Brien & Forrest Tucker (10/51)						
	16	32	48	89	137	185
14- "Last Outpost"; Ronald Reagan (12/51)	36	72	108	204	315	425
15-(Scarce)- "The Man From Planet X"; Robert Clark; Schaffenberger-a (2/52)						
	241	482	723	1506	2503	3500
16- "10 Tall Men"; Burt Lancaster	14	28	42	78	112	145
17- "Rose of Cimarron"; Jack Buetel & Mala Powers	11	22	33	62	86	110
18- "The Brigand"; Anthony Dexter & Anthony Quinn; Schaffenberger-a						
	11	22	33	62	86	110
19- "Carbine Williams"; James Stewart; Costanza-a; James Stewart photo-c						
	12	24	36	69	97	125
20- "Ivanhoe"; Robert Taylor & Liz Taylor photo-c	19	38	57	108	167	225

FAWCETT'S FUNNY ANIMALS (No. 1-26, 80-on titled "Funny Animals"; becomes Li'l Tomboy No. 92 on?)
Fawcett Publications/Charlton Comics No. 84 on: 12/42 - #79, 4/53; #80, 6/53 - #83, 12?/53; #84, 4/54 - #91, 2/56

1-Capt. Marvel on cover; intro. Hoppy The Captain Marvel Bunny, cloned from Capt. Marvel; Billy the Kid & Willie the Worm begin	58	116	174	363	602	840
2-Xmas-c	35	70	105	201	318	435
3-5: 3(2/43)-Spirit of '43-c	25	50	75	145	228	310
6,7,9,10	15	30	45	85	130	175
8-Flag-c	15	30	45	88	137	185
11-20: 14-Cover is a 1944 calendar	12	24	36	67	94	120
21-40: 25-Xmas-c. 26-St. Valentine's Day-c	9	18	27	52	69	85
41-86,90,91	8	16	24	44	57	70
87-89(10-54-2/55)-Merry Mailman ish (TV/Radio)-part photo-c						
	9	18	27	52	69	85

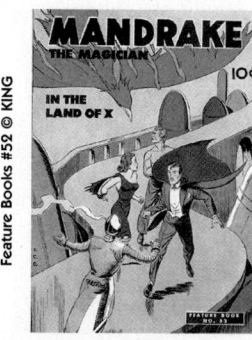

Fear #20 © MAR

Feature Books #52 © KING

Feature Comics #80 © QUA

	GD	VG	FN	VF	VF/NM	NM-		GD	VG	FN	VF	VF/NM	NM-
	2.0	4.0	6.0	8.0	9.0	9.2		2.0	4.0	6.0	8.0	9.0	9.2

NOTE: *Marvel Bunny in all issues to at least No. 68 (not in 49-54).*

FAZE ONE FAZERS
AC Comics: 1986 - No. 4, Sept, 1986 (Limited series)

1-4						2.50

F.B.I., THE
Dell Publishing Co.: Apr-June, 1965

1-Sinnott-a	3	6	9	18	27	35

F.B.I. STORY, THE (Movie)
Dell Publishing Co.: No. 1069, Jan-Mar, 1960

Four Color 1069-Toth-a; James Stewart photo-c	9	18	27	63	107	150

FEAR (Adventure into…)
Marvel Comics Group: Nov, 1970 - No. 31, Dec, 1975

1-Fantasy & Sci-Fi-r in early issues; 68 pg. Giant size; Kirby-a(r)	5	10	15	30	48	65
2-6: 2-4-(68 pgs.). 5,6-(52 pgs.) Kirby-a(r)	3	6	9	18	27	35
7-9-Kirby-a(r)	2	4	6	11	16	20
10-Man-Thing begins (10/72, 4th app.), ends #19; see Savage Tales #1 for 1st app.; 1st solo series; Chaykin/Morrow-c/a;	4	8	12	26	41	55
11,12: 11-N. Adams-c. 12-Starlin/Buckler-a	2	4	6	13	18	22
13,14,16-18: 17-Origin/1st app. Wundarr	2	4	6	10	14	18
15-1st full-length Man-Thing story (8/73)	3	6	9	14	19	24
19-Intro. Howard the Duck (12/73)	4	8	12	26	41	55
20-Morbius, the Living Vampire begins, ends #31; has history recap of Morbius with X-Men & Spider-Man	4	8	12	26	41	55
21-23,25	2	4	6	10	14	18
24-Blade-c/sty	3	6	9	18	27	35
26-31	2	4	6	8	11	14

NOTE: *Bolle a-13i. Brunner c-15-17. Buckler a-11p, 12i. Chaykin a-10i. Colan a-23r. Craig a-10p. Ditko a-5i. Evans a-30. Everett a-9, 10i, 21r. Gulacy a-20p. Heath a-12r. Heck a-8r, 13r. Gil Kane a-21p; c(p)-20, 21, 23-28, 31. Kirby a-1-9r. Maneely a-24r. Mooney a-11i, 26r. Morrow a-11i. Paul Reinman a-14r. Robbins a(p)-25-27, 31. Russell a-23p, 24p. Severin c-8. Starlin c-12p.*

FEAR AGENT
Image Comics: Oct, 2005 - Present ($2.99)

1-11: 1-Remender-s/Moore-a. 5-Opeña a begins. 11-Francavilla-a						3.00
... The Last Goodbye 1,2 (6/07 - Present)						3.00
... Vol 1.: Re-Ignition TPB (2006, $9.99) r/#1-4						10.00
... Vol 2.: My War TPB (Dark Horse Books, 2007, $14.95) r/#5-10; Opeña sketch pages						15.00

FEAR AGENT: THE LAST GOODBYE
Dark Horse Comics: June, 2007 - No. 4 ($2.99)

1-Remender-s/Moore-a						3.00

FEARBOOK
Eclipse Comics: April, 1986 ($1.75, one-shot, mature)

1-Scholastic Mag- r; Bissette-a						2.50

FEAR EFFECT (Based on the video game)
Image Comics (Top Cow): May, 2000; March, 2001 ($2.95)

Retro Helix 1 (3/01), Special 1 (5/00)						3.00

FEAR IN THE NIGHT (See Complete Mystery No. 3)

FEARLESS FAGAN
Dell Publishing Co.: No. 441, Dec, 1952 (one-shot)

Four Color 441	4	8	12	24	37	50

FEATURE BOOK (Dell) (See Large Feature Comic)

FEATURE BOOKS (Newspaper-r, early issues)
David McKay Publications: May, 1937 - No. 57, 1948 (B&W)
(Full color, 68 pgs. begin #26 on)

Note: See individual alphabetical listings for prices

nn-Popeye & the Jeep (#1, 100 pgs.); reprinted as Feature Book #3(Very Rare; only 3 known copies, 1-VF, 2-in low grade)

nn-Dick Tracy (#1)-Reprinted as Feature Book #4 (100 pgs.) & in part as 4-Color #1 (Rare, less than 10 known copies)

NOTE: *Above books were advertised together with different covers from Feat. Books #3 & #4.*

1-King of the Royal Mtd. (#1)
2-Popeye (6/37) by Segar
3-Popeye (7/37) by Segar; same as nn issue but a new cover added
4-Dick Tracy (8/37)-Same as nn issue but a new cover added
5-Popeye (9/37) by Segar
6-Dick Tracy (10/37)
7-Little Orphan Annie (#1, 11/37) (Rare)-Reprints strips from 12/31/34 to 7/17/35
8-Secret Agent X-9 (12/37) -Not by Raymond
9-Dick Tracy (1/38)
10-Popeye (2/38)

11-Little Annie Rooney (#1, 3/38)
13-Inspector Wade (5/38)
15-Barney Baxter (#1) (7/38)
17-Gangbusters (#1, 9/38) (1st app.)
20-Phantom (#1, 12/38)
22-Phantom
24-Lone Ranger (1941)
26-Prince Valiant (1941)-Hal Foster
 -c/a; newspaper strips reprinted, pgs. 1-28,30-63; color & 68 pg. issues begin; Foster cover is only original comic book artwork by him
36('43),38,40('44),42,43, 45,47-Blondie
39-Phantom
46-Mandrake in the Fire World-(58 pgs.)
48-Maltese Falcon by Dashiell Hammett('46)
51,54-Rip Kirby; Raymond-c/s; origin-#51
53,56,57-Phantom

NOTE: *All Feature Books through #25 are over-sized 8-1/2x11-3/8" comics with color covers and black and white interiors. The covers are rough, heavy stock. The page counts, including covers, are as follows: nn, #3, 4-100 pgs.; #1, 2-52 pgs.; #5-25 are all 76 pgs. #33 was found in bound set from publisher.*

12-Blondie (#1) (4/38) (Rare)
14-Popeye (6/38) by Segar
16-Red Eagle (8/38)
18,19-Mandrake
21-Lone Ranger
23-Mandrake
25-Flash Gordon (#1)-Reprints not by Raymond
27-29,31,34-Blondie
30-Katzenjammer Kids (#1, 1942)
32,35,41,44-Katzenjammer Kids
33(nn)-Romance of Flying; World War II photos
37-Katzenjammer Kids; has photo & biog. of Harold H. Knerr (1883-1949) who took over strip from Rudolph Dirks in 1914
49,50-Perry Mason; based on Gardner novels
52,55-Mandrake

FEATURE COMICS (Formerly Feature Funnies)
Quality Comics Group: No. 21, June, 1939 - No. 144, May, 1950

21-The Clock, Jane Arden & Mickey Finn continue from Feature Funnies	66	132	198	363	544	725
22-26: 23-Charlie Chan begins (8/39, 1st app.)	46	92	138	253	377	500
26-(nn, nd)-Cover in one color, (10c, 36 pgs.; issue No. blanked out. Two variations exist, each contain half of the regular #26)	46	92	138	253	377	500
27-(Rare)-Origin/1st app. Doll Man by Eisner (scripts) & Lou Fine (art); Doll Man begins, ends #139	486	972	1458	3400	5950	8500
28-2nd app. Doll Man by Lou Fine	193	386	579	1206	2003	2800
29	103	206	309	644	1072	1500
30-1st Doll Man-c	152	304	456	950	1575	2200
31-Last Clock & Charlie Chan issue (4/40); Charlie Chan moves to Big Shot #1 following month (5/40)	71	142	213	444	735	1025
32,34,36: 32-Rusty Ryan & Samar begin. 34-Captain Fortune app.	65	130	195	406	671	935
33,35,37: 37-Last Fine Doll Man	46	92	138	281	466	650

Note: *A 15¢ Canadian version of Feature Comics #37, made in the US, exists.*

38,40-Dollman covers. 38-Origin the Ace of Space. 40-Bruce Blackburn in costume	52	104	156	317	521	725
39,41: 39-Origin The Destroying Demon, ends #40; X-Mas-c.	40	80	120	235	368	500
42,46,48,50-Dollman covers. 42-USA, the Spirit of Old Glory begins. 46-Intro. Boyville Brigadiers in Rusty Ryan. 48-USA ends	42	84	126	248	384	520
43,45,47,49: 47-Doll Man by Crandall begins, ends #63; Crandall-a(2)	29	58	87	170	268	365
44-Doll Man by Crandall begins, ends #63; Crandall-a(2)	52	104	156	317	521	725
51,53,55,57,59: 57-Spider Widow begins	44	88	132	258	409	550
52,54,56,58,60-Dollman covers. 56-Marijuana story in Swing Sisson strip.	44	66	128	202	275	
60-Raven begins, ends #71	31	62	93	178	282	385
61,63,65,67	20	40	60	117	184	250
62,64,66,68-Dollman covers. 68-(5/43)	27	54	81	158	249	340
69,71-Phantom Lady x-over in Spider Widow	22	44	66	128	202	275
70-Dollman-c; Phantom Lady x-over	30	60	90	172	271	370
72,74,77-80,100-Dollman covers. 72-Spider Widow ends	22	44	66	126	198	270
73,75,76	16	32	48	94	147	200
81-99-All Dollman covers	15	30	45	88	137	185
101-144: 139-Last Doll Man & last Doll Man cover. 140-Stuntman Stetson begins (Stuntman Stetson c-140-144)	14	28	42	80	115	150

NOTE: *Celardo a-37-43. Crandall a-44-60, 62, 63-on(most). Gustavson a-(Rusty Ryan)- 32-134. Powell a-34, 64-73. The Clock c-25, 28, 29. Doll Man c-30, 32, 34, 36, 38, 40, 42, 44, 46, 48, 50, 52, 54, 56, 58, 60, 62, 64, 66, 68, 70, 72, 74, 77-139. Joe Palooka c-21, 24, 27.*

FEATURE FILMS
National Periodical Publ.: Mar-Apr, 1950 - No. 4, Sept-Oct, 1950 (All photo-c)

1- "Captain China" with John Payne, Gail Russell, Lon Chaney & Edgar Bergen	66	132	198	413	682	950
2- "Riding High" with Bing Crosby	69	138	207	431	716	1000
3- "The Eagle & the Hawk" with John Payne, Rhonda Fleming & D. O'Keefe	66	132	198	413	682	950

Feature Funnies #9 © QUA

Felix the Cat #19 © KING

Femforce #92 © AC

	GD 2.0	VG 4.0	FN 6.0	VF 8.0	VF/NM 9.0	NM- 9.2
4- "Fancy Pants"; Bob Hope & Lucille Ball	72	144	216	450	750	1050

FEATURE FUNNIES (Feature Comics No. 21 on)
Harry 'A' Chesler: Oct, 1937 - No. 20, May, 1939

1(V9#1-indicia)-Joe Palooka, Mickey Finn (1st app.), The Bungles, Jane Arden, Dixie Dugan (1st app.), Big Top, Ned Brant, Strange As It Seems, & Off the Record strip reprints begin						
	322	644	966	1770	2635	3500
2-The Hawk app. (11/37); Goldberg-c	150	300	450	825	1213	1600
3-Hawks of Seas begins by Eisner, ends #12; The Clock begins; Christmas-c						
	117	234	351	644	947	1250
4,5	86	172	258	473	699	925
6-12: 11-Archie O'Toole by Bud Thomas begins, ends #22						
	67	134	201	369	542	715
13-Espionage, Starring Black X begins by Eisner, ends #20						
	71	142	213	391	578	765
14-20	50	100	150	275	408	540

NOTE: Joe Palooka covers 1, 6, 9, 12, 15, 18.

FEATURE PRESENTATION, A (Feature Presentations Magazine #6)
(Formerly Women in Love) (Also see Startling Terror Tales #11)
Fox Features Syndicate: No. 5, April, 1950

5(#1)-Black Tarantula	40	80	120	244	392	540

FEATURE PRESENTATIONS MAGAZINE (Formerly A Feature Presentation #5; becomes Feature Stories Magazine #3 on)
Fox Features Syndicate: No. 6, July, 1950

6(#2)-Moby Dick; Wood-c	32	64	96	186	293	400

FEATURE STORIES MAGAZINE (Formerly Feature Presentations Mag. #6)
Fox Features Syndicate: No. 3, Aug, 1950

3-Jungle Lil, Zegra stories; bondage-c	35	70	105	201	318	435

FEDERAL MEN COMICS
DC Comics: 1936

nn-Ashcan comic, not distributed to newsstands, only for in house use (no known sales)

FEDERAL MEN COMICS (See Adventure Comics #32, The Comics Magazine, New Adventure Comics, New Book of Comics, New Comics & Star Spangled Comics #91)
Gerard Publ. Co.: No. 2, 1945 (DC reprints from 1930's)

2-Siegel/Shuster-a; cover redrawn from Det. #9	39	78	117	224	355	485

FELICIA HARDY: THE BLACK CAT
Marvel Comics: July, 1994 - No. 4, Oct, 1994 ($1.50, limited series)

1-4: 1,4-Spider-Man app.						2.50

FELIX'S NEPHEWS INKY & DINKY
Harvey Publications: Sept, 1957 - No. 7, Oct, 1958

1-Cover shows Inky's left eye with 2 pupils	10	20	30	54	72	90
2-7	6	12	18	31	38	45

NOTE: Messmer art in 1-6. Oriolo a-1-7.

FELIX THE CAT (See Cat Tales 3-D, The Funnies, March of Comics #24,36,51, New Funnies & Popular Comics)
Dell Publ. No. 1-19/Toby No. 20-61/Harvey No. 62-118/Dell No. 1-12:
1943 - No. 118, Nov, 1961; Sept-Nov, 1962 - No. 12, July-Sept, 1965

Four Color 15	72	144	216	612	1131	1650
Four Color 46('44)	40	80	120	300	550	800
Four Color 77('45)	38	76	114	285	518	750
Four Color 119('46)-All new stories begin	32	64	96	240	445	650
Four Color 135('46)	23	42	69	171	306	440
Four Color 162(9/47)	17	34	51	128	227	325
1(2-3/48)(Dell)	26	52	78	211	348	485
2	14	28	42	99	175	250
3-5	10	20	30	73	129	185
6-19(2-3/51-Dell)	8	16	24	58	97	135
20-30,32,33,36,38-61(6/55)-All Messmer issues.(Toby): 28-(2/52)-Some copies have #29 on cover, #28 on inside (Rare in high grade)	16	32	48	118	209	300
31,34,35-No Messmer-a; Messmer-c only 31,34	8	16	24	58	97	135
37-(100 pgs., 25 ¢, 1/15/53, X-Mas-c, Toby; daily & Sunday-r (rare)						
	38	76	114	285	518	750
62(8/55)-80.100 (Harvey)	4	8	12	28	44	60
81-99	4	8	12	24	37	50
101-118(11/61): 101-117-Reprints. 118-All new-a	3	6	9	18	27	35
12-269-211(#1, 9-11/62)(Dell)-No Messmer	5	10	15	30	44	65
2-12(7-9/65)(Dell, TV)-No Messmer	4	8	12	24	37	50
3-D Comic Book 1(1953-One Shot, 25¢)-w/glasses	22	44	66	165	295	425
Summer Annual nn ('53, 25¢, 100 pgs., Toby)-Daily & Sunday-r						

	31	62	93	233	429	625
Winter Annual 2 ('54, 25¢, 100 pgs., Toby)-Daily & Sunday-r						
	31	62	93	222	404	585

(Special note: Despite the covers on Toby 37 and the Summer Annual above proclaiming "all new stories," they were actually reformatted newspaper strips)

NOTE: *Otto Messmer* went to work for Universal Film as an animator in 1915 and then worked for the Pat Sullivan animation studio in 1916. He created a black cat in the cartoon short, *Feline Follies* in 1919 that became known as Felix in the early 1920s. The Felix Sunday strip began Aug. 14, 1923 and continued until Sept. 19, 1943 when *Messmer* took the character to Dell (Western Publishing) and began doing Felix comic books, first adapting strips to the comic format. The first all new Felix comic was Four Color #119 in 1946 (#4 in the Dell run). The daily Felix was begun on May 9, 1927 by another artist, but by the following year, *Messmer* did it too. King Features took the daily away from *Messmer* in 1954 and he began to do some of his most dynamic art for Toby Press. The daily was continued by *Joe Oriolo* who drew it until it was discontinued Jan. 9, 1967. *Oriolo* was *Messmer's* assistant for many years and inked some of *Messmer's* pencils through the Toby run, as well as doing some of the Sunday strips by himself. Though *Messmer* continued to work for Harvey, his contirubitons were limited, and no all *Messmer* stories appeared after the Toby run until some early Felix reprints were published in the 1990s Harvey revival of the title. 4-Color No. 15, 46, 77 and the Toby Annuals are all daily or Sunday newspaper reprints from the 1930's-1940's drawn by *Otto Messmer*. #101-r/#64; 102-r/#65; 103-r/#67; 104-117-r/#68-81. *Messmer*-a in all Dell/Toby/Harvey issues except #31, 34, 35, 97, 98, 100, 118. *Oriolo* a-20; 31-on.

FELIX THE CAT (Also see The Nine Lives of...)
Harvey Comics/Gladstone: Sept, 1991 - No. 7, Jan, 1993 ($1.25/$1.50, bi-monthly)

1: 1950s-r/Toby issues by Messmer begins. 1-Inky and Dinky back-up story (produced by Gladstone)						4.00
2-7, Big Book, V2#1 (9/92), $1.95, 52 pgs.						3.00

FELIX THE CAT AND FRIENDS
Felix Comics: 1992 - No. 5, 1993 ($1.95)

1-5: 1-Contains Felix trading cards						3.00

FELIX THE CAT & HIS FRIENDS (Pat Sullivan's...)
Toby Press: Dec, 1953 - No. 3, 1954 (Indicia title for #2&3 as listed)

1 (Indicia title, "Felix and His Friends," #1 only)	30	60	90	174	275	375
2-3	18	36	54	105	165	225

FELIX THE CAT DIGEST MAGAZINE
Harvey Comics: July, 1992 ($1.75, digest-size, 98 pgs.)

1-Felix, Richie Rich stories						6.00

FELIX THE CAT KEEPS ON WALKIN'
Hamilton Comics: 1991 ($15.95, 8-1/2"x11", 132 pgs.)

nn-Reprints 15 Toby Press Felix the Cat and Felix and His Friends stories in new color 16.00

FELL
Image Comics: Sept, 2005 - Present ($1.99)

1-8-Warren Ellis-s/Ben Templesmith-a						2.50
..., Vol. 1: Feral City TPB (2007, $14.99) r/#1-8						15.00

FELON
Image Comics (Minotaur Press): Nov, 2001 - No. 4, Apr, 2002 ($2.95, B&W)

1-4-Rucka-s/Clark-a/c						3.00

FEM FANTASTIQUE
AC Comics: Aug, 1988 ($1.95, B&W)

V2#1-By Bill Black; Betty Page pin-up						4.00

FEMFORCE (Also see Untold Origin of the Femforce)
Americomics: Apr, 1985 - No. 109 (1.75-/2.95, B&W #16-56)

1-Black-a in most; Nightveil, Ms. Victory begin	1	3	4	6	8	10
2-10						4.00
11-43: 25-Origin/1st app. new Ms. Victory. 28-Colt leaves. 29,30-Camilla-r by Mayo from Jungle Comics. 36-(2.95, 52 pgs.)						4.00
44,64: 44-W/mini-comic, Catman & Kitten #0. 64-Re-intro Black Phantom						5.00
45-63,65-99: 50 (2.95, 52 pgs.)-Contains flexi-disc; origin retold; most AC characters app. 51-Photo-c from movie. 57-Begin color issues. 95-Photo-c						3.00
100-($3.95)						5.00
100-($6.90)-Polybagged	1	2	3	5	6	8
101-109-($4.95)						5.00
Special 1 (Fall, '84)(B&W, 52pgs.)-1st app. Ms. Victory, She-Cat, Blue Bulleteer, Rio Rita & Lady Luger						4.00
Bad Girl Backlash-(12/95, $5.00)						5.00
Frightbook 1 ('92, $2.95, B&W)-Halloween special, In the House of Horror 1 (`89, 2.50, B&W), Night of the Demon 1 ('90, 2.75, B&W), Out of the Asylum Special 1 ('87, B&W, $1.95), Pin-Up Portfolio						3.50
Pin-Up Portfolio (5 issues)						4.00

FEMFORCE UP CLOSE
AC Comics: Apr, 1992 - No. 11, 1995 ($2.75, quarterly)

1-11: 1-Stars Nightveil; inside f/c photo from Femforce movie. 2-Stars Stardust. 3-Stars Dragonfly. 4-Stars She-Cat						3.50

The Ferret #9 © MAL

52 #46 © DC

Fight Comics #13 © FH

	GD 2.0	VG 4.0	FN 6.0	VF 8.0	VF/NM 9.0	NM- 9.2

FERDINAND THE BULL (See Mickey Mouse Magazine V4#3)
Dell Publishing Co.: 1938 (10¢, large size, some color w/rest B&W)

| nn | 19 | 38 | 57 | 112 | 176 | 240 |

FERRET
Malibu Comics: Sept, 1992; May, 1993 - No. 10, Feb, 1994 ($1.95)

1-(1992, one-shot)						3.00
1-10: 1-Die-cut-c. 2-4-Collector's Ed. w/poster. 5-Polybagged w/Skycap						2.50
2-4-($1.95)-Newsstand Edition w/different-c						2.50

F5
Image Comics/Dark Horse: Jan, 2000 - No. 4, Oct, 2000 ($2.50/$2.95)

Preview (1/00, $2.50) Character bios and b&w pages; Daniel-s/a						2.50
1-($2.95, 48 pages) Tony Daniel-s/a						3.00
1-($20.00) Variant bikini-c						20.00
2-4-($2.50)						2.50
F5 Origin (Dark Horse Comics, 11/01, $2.99) w/cove gallery & sketches						3.00

FIBBER McGEE & MOLLY (Radio)(Also see A-1 Comics)
Magazine Enterprises: No. 25, 1949 (one-shot)

| A-1 25 | 11 | 22 | 33 | 64 | 90 | 115 |

55 DAYS AT PEKING (See Movie Comics)

FICTION ILLUSTRATED
Byron Preiss Visual Publ./Pyramid: No. 1, Jan, 1975 - No. 4, Jan, 1977 ($1.00, #1,#2 are digest size, $3.4 are graphic novels for mail order and specialty bookstores only)

1,2: 1-Schlomo Raven; Sutton-a. 2-Starfawn; Stephen Fabian-a.						
	2	4	6	12	16	20
3-($1.00-c, 4 3/4 x 6 1/2" digest size) Chandler; new Steranko-a						
	3	6	9	14	19	24
3-($4.95-c, 8 1/2 x 11" graphic novel; low print) same contents and indicia, but "Chandler" is the cover feature title	5	10	15	32	51	70
4-($4.95-c, 8 1/2 x 11" graphic novel; low print) Son of Sherlock Holmes; Reese-a						
	4	8	12	26	41	55

FIERCE
Dark Horse Comics (Rocket Comics): July, 2004 - No. 4, Dec, 2004 ($2.99, limited series)

| 1-4-Jeremy Love-s/Robert Love-a | | | | | | 3.00 |

52 (Leads into Countdown series)
DC Comics: Week One, July, 2006 - Week Fifty-Two, Jul, 2007 ($2.50, weekly series)

1-Chronicles the year after Infinite Crisis; Johns, Morrison, Rucka & Waid-s; JG Jones-c						4.00
2-10: 2-History of the DC Universe back-up thru #11. 7-Intro. Kate Kane. 10-Supernova						3.00
11-Batwoman debut (single panel cameo in #9)						4.00
12-52: 12-Isis gains powers; back-up 2 pg. origins begin. 15-Booster Gold killed. 17-Lobo returns. 30-Batman-c/Robin & Nightwing app. 37-Booster Gold returns. 38-The Question dies. 42-Ralph Dibny dies. 44-Isis dies. 48-Renee becomes the Question. 50-World War III. 51-Mister Mind evolves. 52-The Multiverse is re-formed; wraparound-c						2.50
....: Volume One TPB (2007, $19.99) r/#1-13; sample of page development; cover gallery						20.00
....: Volume Two TPB (2007, $19.99) r/#14-26; creator notes and sketches; cover gallery						20.00

52 AFTERMATH: THE FOUR HORSEMEN (Takes place during 52 Week Fifty)
DC Comics: Oct, 2007 - No. 6 ($2.99, limited series)

| 1-Giffen-s/Olliffe-a; Superman & Wonder Woman app. | | | | | | 3.00 |

52/WWIII (Takes place during 52 Week Fifty)
DC Comics: Part One, Jun, 2007 - Part Four, Jun, 2007 ($2.50, 4 issues came out same day)

| Part One - Part Four: Van Sciver-c; heroes vs. Black Adam. 3-Terra dies | | | | | | 2.50 |

FIGHT AGAINST CRIME (Fight Against the Guilty #22, 23)
Story Comics: May, 1951 - No. 21, Sept, 1954

1-True crime stories #1-4	40	80	120	240	383	525
2	21	42	63	122	191	260
3,5: 5-Frazetta-a, 1 pg.; content change to horror & suspense						
	18	36	54	103	162	220
4-Drug story "Hopped Up Killers"	19	38	57	109	172	235
6,7: 6-Used in POP, pgs. 83,84	16	32	48	92	144	195
8-Last crime format issue	15	30	45	86	133	180
NOTE: No. 9-21 contain violent, gruesome stories with blood, dismemberment, decapitation, E.C. style plot twists and several E.C. swipes. Bondage c-4, 6, 18, 19.						
9-11,13	38	76	114	219	347	475
12-Morphine drug story "The Big Dope"	40	80	120	240	383	525
14-Tothish art by Ross Andru; electrocution-c	40	80	120	235	368	500
15-B&W & color illos in POP	38	76	114	219	347	475
16-E.C. story swipe/Haunt of Fear #19; Tothish-a by Ross Andru; bondage-c	40	80	120	240	383	525
17-Wildey E.C. swipe/Shock SuspenStories #9; knife through neck-c (1/54)						

	GD 2.0	VG 4.0	FN 6.0	VF 8.0	VF/NM 9.0	NM- 9.2
	40	80	120	240	383	525
18,19: 19-Bondage/torture-c	37	74	111	213	337	460
20-Decapitation cover; contains hanging, ax murder, blood & violence						
	64	128	192	400	663	925
21-E.C. swipe	31	62	93	178	282	385
NOTE: Cameron a-4, 5, 8. Hollingsworth a-3-7, 9, 10, 13. Wildey a-6, 15, 16.						

FIGHT AGAINST THE GUILTY (Formerly Fight Against Crime)
Story Comics: No. 22, Dec, 1954 - No. 23, Mar, 1955

22-Tothish-a by Ross Andru; Ditko-a; E.C. story swipe; electrocution-c (Last pre-code)						
	31	62	93	178	282	385
23-Hollingsworth-a	21	42	63	122	191	260

FIGHT COMICS
Fiction House Magazines: Jan, 1940 - No. 83, 11/52; No. 84, Wint, 1952-53; No. 85, Spring, 1953; No. 86, Summer, 1954

1-Origin Spy Fighter, Starring Saber; Jack Dempsey life story; Shark Brodie & Chip Collins begin; Fine-c; Eisner-a	333	666	1000	2165	3833	5500
2-Joe Louis life story; Fine/Eisner-c	121	242	363	756	1253	1750
3-Rip Regan, the Power Man begins (3/40)	103	206	309	644	1072	1500
4,5: 4-Fine-c	66	132	198	413	687	960
6-10: 6,7-Powell-c	49	98	147	299	492	685
11-14: Rip Regan ends	45	90	135	275	455	635
15-1st app. Super American plus-c (10/41)	59	118	177	369	610	850
16-Captain Fight begins (12/41); Spy Fighter ends	59	118	177	369	610	850
17,18: Super American ends	45	90	135	275	455	635
19-Captain Fight ends; Senorita Rio begins (6/42, origin & 1st app.); Rip Carson, Chute Trooper begins	48	96	144	293	484	675
20	41	82	123	250	400	550
21-30	38	76	114	219	347	475
31-Classic decapitation-c	66	132	198	413	682	950
32-Tiger Girl begins (6/44, 1st app.?)	40	80	120	235	368	500
33-50: 44-Capt. Fight returns. 48-Used in Love and Death by Legman. 49-Jungle-c begin, end #81	31	62	93	178	282	385
51-Origin Tiger Girl; Patsy Pin-Up app.	38	76	114	216	343	470
52-60,62-64-Last Baker issue	22	44	66	128	202	275
61-Origin Tiger Girl retold	23	46	69	135	213	290
65-78: 78-Used in POP, pg. 99	18	36	54	107	169	230
79-The Space Rangers app.	19	38	57	112	176	240
80-85: 81-Last jungle-c. 82-85-War-c/stories	15	30	45	90	140	190
86-Two Tigerman stories by Evans-r/Rangers Comics #40,41; Moreira-r/Rangers Comics #45	15	30	45	90	140	190
NOTE: Bondage covers, Lingerie, headlights panels are common. Captain Fight by Kamen-51-66. Kayo Kirby by Baker-#43-64, 67(not by Baker). Senorita Rio by Kamen-#57-64; by Grandenetti-#65. Tiger Girl by Baker-#36-60, 62-64; Eisner c-1-3, 5, 10, 11. Kamen a-54?, 57? Tuska a-1, 5, 8, 10, 21, 29, 34. Whitman c-73-84. Zolnerwich c-16, 17, 22. Power Man c-5, 6, 9. Super American c-15-17. Tiger Girl c-49-81.						

FIGHT FOR LOVE
United Features Syndicate: 1952 (no month)

| nn-Abbie & Slats newspaper-r | 9 | 18 | 27 | 47 | 61 | 75 |

FIGHT FOR TOMORROW
DC Comics (Vertigo): Nov, 2002 - No. 6, Apr, 2003 ($2.50, limited series)

| 1-6-Denys Cowan-a/Brian Wood-s. 1-Jim Lee-c | | | | | | 2.50 |

FIGHTING AIR FORCE (See United States Fighting Air Force)

FIGHTIN' AIR FORCE (Formerly Sherlock Holmes?; Never Again? War and Attack #54 on)
Charlton Comics: No. 3, Feb, 1956 - No. 53, Feb-Mar, 1966

V1#3	9	18	27	47	61	75
4-10	6	12	18	31	38	45
11(3/58, 68 pgs.)	8	16	24	42	54	65
12 (100 pgs.)-U.S. Nukes Russia	11	22	33	64	90	115
13-30: 13,24-Glanzman-a. 24-Glanzman-c	3	6	9	18	27	35
31-50: 50-American Eagle begins	3	6	9	14	19	24
51-53	2	4	6	11	16	20

FIGHTING AMERICAN
Headline Publ./Prize (Crestwood): Apr-May, 1954 - No. 7, Apr-May, 1955

1-Origin & 1st app. Fighting American & Speedboy (Capt. America & Bucky clones); S&K-c/a(3); 1st super hero satire series	172	344	516	1075	1788	2500
2-S&K-a(3)	80	160	240	500	830	1160
3-5: 3,4-S&K-a(3). 5-S&K-a(2); Kirby/?-a	62	124	186	388	644	900
6-Origin-r (4 pgs.) plus 2 pgs. by S&K	59	118	177	369	615	860
7-Kirby-a	53	106	159	323	537	750
NOTE: Simon & Kirby covers on all. 6 is last pre-code issue.						

FIGHTING AMERICAN
Harvey Publications: Oct, 1966 (25¢)

Fightin' Army #17 © CC

Fighting Leathernecks #1 © TOBY

Fightin' Marines #5 © STJ

Column headers: **GD 2.0 · VG 4.0 · FN 6.0 · VF 8.0 · VF/NM 9.0 · NM- 9.2**

1-Origin Fighting American & Speedboy by S&K-r; S&K-c/a(3); 1 pg. Neal Adams ad   5 10 15 35 55 75

FIGHTING AMERICAN
DC Comics: Feb, 1994 - No. 6, 1994 ($1.50, limited series)
1-6   2.50

FIGHTING AMERICAN (Vol. 3)
Awesome Entertainment: Aug, 1997 - No. 2, Oct, 1997 ($2.50)
Preview-Agent America (pre-lawsuit)   1 2 3 5 6 7
1-Four covers by Liefeld, Churchill, Platt, McGuinness   2.50
1-Platinum Edition, 1-Gold foil Edition   10.00
1-Comic Cavalcade Edition, 2-American Ent. Spice Ed.   4.00
2-Platt-c, 2-Liefeld variant-c   2.50

FIGHTING AMERICAN: DOGS OF WAR
Awesome-Hyperwerks: Sept, 1998 - No. 3, May, 1999 ($2.50)
Limited Convention Special (7/98, B&W) Platt-a   2.50
1-3-Starlin-s/Platt-a/c   2.50

FIGHTING AMERICAN: RULES OF THE GAME
Awesome Entertainment: Nov, 1997 - No. 3, Mar, 1998 ($2.50, lim. series)
1-3: 1-Loeb-s/McGuinness-a/c. 2-Flip book with Swat! preview   2.50
1-Liefeld SPICE variant-c, 1-Dynamic Forces Ed.; McGuinness-c   2.50
1-Liefeld Fighting American & cast variant-c   2.50

FIGHTIN' ARMY (Formerly Soldier and Marine Comics) (See Captain Willy Schultz)
Charlton Comics: No. 16, 1/56 - No. 127, 12/76; No. 128, 9/77 - No. 172, 11/84
16   9 18 27 47 61 75
17-19,21-23,25-30   6 12 18 31 38 45
20-Ditko-a   9 18 27 47 61 75
24 (3/58, 68 pgs.)   8 16 24 40 50 60
31-45   3 6 9 17 25 32
46-60   3 6 9 15 21 26
61-74   2 4 6 11 16 20
75-1st The Lonely War of Willy Schultz   3 6 9 16 23 30
76-80: 76-92-The Lonely War of Willy Schultz. 79-Devil Brigade   2 4 6 11 16 20
81-88,91,93-99: 82,83-Devil Brigade   2 4 6 9 12 15
89,90,92-Ditko-a   2 4 6 13 18 22
100   2 4 6 10 14 18
101-127   2 4 6 8 10 12
128-140   1 2 3 5 6 8
141-165   6.00
166-172-Low print run   1 2 3 5 6 8
108(Modern Comics-1977)-Reprint   4.00
NOTE: Aparo c-154. Glanzman a-77-88. Montes/Bache a-48, 49, 51, 69, 75, 76, 170r.

FIGHTING CARAVANS (See Zane Grey 4-Color 632)

FIGHTING DANIEL BOONE
Avon Periodicals: 1953
nn-Kinstler-c/a, 22 pgs.   18 36 54 105 165 225
I.W. Reprint #1-Reprints #1 above; Kinstler-c/a; Lawrence/Alascia-a   3 6 9 14 19 24

FIGHTING DAVY CROCKETT (Formerly Kit Carson)
Avon Periodicals: No. 9, Oct-Nov, 1955
9-Kinstler-c   10 20 30 54 72 90

FIGHTIN' FIVE, THE (Formerly Space War) (Also see The Peacemaker)
Charlton Comics: July, 1964 - No. 41, Jan, 1967; No. 42, Oct, 1981 - No. 49, Dec, 1982
V2#28-Origin/1st app. Fightin' Five; Montes/Bache-a   6 12 18 39 62 85
29-39,41-Montes/Bache-a in all   3 6 9 21 32 42
40-Peacemaker begins (1st app.)   6 12 18 41 66 90
41-Peacemaker (2nd app.)   4 8 12 28 44 60
42-49: Reprints   5.00

FIGHTING FRONTS!
Harvey Publications: Aug, 1952 - No. 5, Jan, 1953
1   10 20 30 54 72 90
2-Extreme violence; Nostrand/Powell-a   11 22 33 60 83 105
3-5: 3-Powell-a   7 14 21 37 46 55

FIGHTING INDIAN STORIES (See Midget Comics)

FIGHTING INDIANS OF THE WILD WEST!
Avon Periodicals: Mar, 1952 - No. 2, Nov, 1952
1-Geronimo, Chief Crazy Horse, Chief Victorio, Black Hawk begin; Larsen-a; McCann-a(2)   17 34 51 98 154 210
2-Kinstler-c & inside-c only; Larsen, McCann-a   12 24 36 69 97 125
100 Pg. Annual (1952, 25¢)-Contains three comics rebound; Geronimo, Chief Crazy Horse, Chief Victorio; Kinstler-c   34 68 102 195 308 420

FIGHTING LEATHERNECKS
Toby Press: Feb, 1952 - No. 6, Dec, 1952
1- "Duke's Diary"; full pg. pin-ups by Sparling   14 28 42 80 115 150
2-5: 2- "Duke's Diary". 3-5- "Gil's Gals"; full pg. pin-ups   10 20 30 54 72 90
6-(Same as No. 3-5?)   10 20 30 54 72 90

FIGHTING MAN, THE (War)
Ajax/Farrell Publications(Excellent Publ.): May, 1952 - No. 8, July, 1953
1   14 28 42 80 115 150
2   9 18 27 47 61 75
3-8   8 16 24 40 50 60
Annual 1 (1952, 25¢, 100 pgs.)   24 48 72 139 220 300

FIGHTIN' MARINES (Formerly The Texan; also see Approved Comics)
St. John(Approved Comics)/Charlton Comics No. 14 on:
No. 15, 8/51 - No. 12, 3/53; No. 14, 5/55 - No. 132, 11/76; No. 133, 10/77 - No. 176, 9/84 (No #13?) (Korean War #1-3)
15(#1)-Matt Baker c/a "Leatherneck Jack"; slightly large size; Fightin' Texan No. 16 & 17?   41 82 123 256 416 575
2-1st Canteen Kate by Baker; slightly large size; partial Baker-c   48 96 144 293 484 675
3-9,11-Canteen Kate by Baker; Baker c-#2,3,5-11; 4-Partial Baker-c   27 54 81 158 249 340
10-Matt Baker-c   13 26 39 72 101 130
12-No Baker-a; Last St. John issue?   8 16 24 40 50 60
14 (5/55; 1st Charlton issue; formerly?)-Canteen Kate by Baker; all stories reprinted from #2   18 36 54 105 165 225
15-Baker-c   10 20 30 58 79 100
16,18-20-Not Baker-c   6 12 18 33 41 48
17-Canteen Kate by Baker   14 28 42 82 121 160
21-24   6 12 18 29 36 42
25-(68 pgs.)(3/58)-Check-a?   10 20 30 54 72 90
26-(100 pgs.)(8/58)-Check-a(5)   14 28 42 80 115 150
27-50   3 6 9 17 25 32
51-81: 78-Shotgun Harker & the Chicken series begin   3 6 9 14 19 24
82-(100 pgs.)   4 8 12 28 44 60
83-85: 85-Last 12¢ issue   2 4 6 14 13 22
86-94: 94-Last 15¢ issue   2 4 6 9 12 16
95-100,122: 122-(1975) Pilot issue for "War" title (Fightin' Marines Presents War)   2 4 6 8 11 14
101-121   1 3 4 6 8 10
123-140   1 2 3 5 6 8
141-170   6.00
171-176-Low print run   1 2 3 5 6 8
120(Modern Comics reprint, 1977)   4.00
NOTE: No. 14 & (CC) reprint St. John issues; No. 16 reprints St. John insignia on cover. Colan a-3, 7. Glanzman c/a-92, 94. Montes/Bache a-48, 53, 55, 64, 65, 72-74, 77-83, 176r.

FIGHTING MARSHAL OF THE WILD WEST (See The Hawk)

FIGHTIN' NAVY (Formerly Don Winslow)
Charlton Comics: No. 74, 1/56 - No. 125, 4-5/66; No. 126, 8/83 - No. 133, 10/84
74   5 10 15 35 55 75
75-81   3 6 9 21 32 42
82-Sam Glanzman-a (68 pg. Giant)   4 8 12 28 44 60
83-(100 pgs.)   6 12 18 39 62 85
84-99,101: 101-UFO story   3 6 9 16 23 30
100   3 6 9 17 25 32
102-105,106-125('66)   2 4 6 13 18 22
126-133 (1984)-Low print run   1 2 3 5 6 8
NOTE: Montes/Bache a-109. Glanzman a-82, 92, 96, 98, 100, 131r.

FIGHTING PRINCE OF DONEGAL, THE (See Movie Comics)

FIGHTIN' TEXAN (Formerly The Texan & Fightin' Marines?)
St. John Publishing Co.: No. 16, Sept, 1952 - No. 17, Dec, 1952
16,17: Tuska-a each. 17-Cameron-c/a   16 32 48 94 157 220

FIGHTING UNDERSEA COMMANDOS (See Undersea Fighting…)
Avon Periodicals: May, 1952 - No. 5, April, 1953 (U.S. Navy frogmen)
1-Cover title is Undersea Fighting… #1 only   15 30 45 84 127 170

Fighting Yank #8 © Nedor

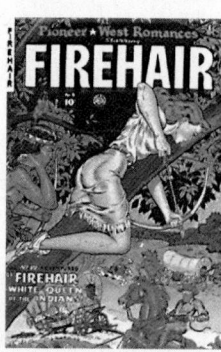

Firehair Comics #6 © FH

Fireside Books - The Superhero Women © MAR

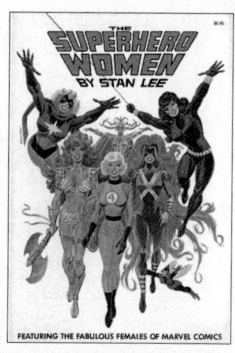

	GD 2.0	VG 4.0	FN 6.0	VF 8.0	VF/NM 9.0	NM- 9.2
2	10	20	30	56	76	95
3-5: 1,3-Ravielli-c. 4-Kinstler-c	9	18	27	50	65	80

FIGHTING WAR STORIES
Men's Publications/Story Comics: Aug, 1952 - No. 5, 1953

1	10	20	30	54	72	90
2-5	6	12	18	31	38	45

FIGHTING YANK (See America's Best Comics & Startling Comics)
Nedor/Better Publ./Standard: Sept, 1942 - No. 29, Aug, 1949

1-The Fighting Yank begins; Mystico, the Wonder Man app; bondage-c	276	552	828	1725	2863	4000
2	114	228	342	713	1182	1650
3,4: 4-Schomburg-c begin	83	166	249	519	860	1200
5,6,8-10: 8,10-Bondage/torture-c	65	130	195	406	671	935
7-Hitler special bomb-c; Grim Reaper app.	69	138	207	431	716	1000
11,13-20: 11-The Oracle app. 15-Bondage/torture-c. 18-The American Eagle app.	53	106	159	323	537	750
12-Hirohito bondage-c	71	142	213	444	735	1025
21,24: 21-Kara, Jungle Princess app.; lingerie-c. 24-Miss Masque app.	47	94	141	287	474	660
22-Miss Masque-c/story	53	106	159	323	537	750
23-Classic Schomburg hooded vigilante-c	69	138	207	431	716	1000
25-Robinson/Meskin-a; strangulation, lingerie panel; The Cavalier app.	52	104	156	317	521	725
26-29: All-Robinson/Meskin-a. 28-One pg. Williamson-a	43	86	129	262	431	600

NOTE: *Schomburg (Xela)* c-4-29; airbrush-c 28, 29. Bondage-c 1, 4, 8, 10, 11, 12, 15, 17.

FIGHTMAN
Marvel Comics: June, 1993 ($2.00, one-shot, 52 pgs.)

1						2.50

FIGHT THE ENEMY
Tower Comics: Aug, 1966 - No. 3, Mar, 1967 (25¢, 68 pgs.)

1-Lucky 7 & Mike Manly begin	4	8	12	26	41	55
2-1st Boris Vallejo comic art; McWilliams-a	3	6	9	20	30	40
3-Wood-a (1/2 pg.); McWilliams, Bolle-a	3	6	9	20	30	40

FILM FUNNIES
Marvel Comics (CPC): Nov, 1949 - No. 2, Feb, 1950 (52 pgs.)

1-Krazy Krow, Wacky Duck	19	38	57	112	176	240
2-Wacky Duck	14	28	42	82	121	160

FILM STARS ROMANCES
Star Publications: Jan-Feb, 1950 - No. 3, May-June, 1950 (True life stories of movie stars)

1-Rudy Valentino & Gregory Peck stories; L. B. Cole-c; lingerie panels	43	86	129	262	431	600
2-Liz Taylor/Robert Taylor photo-c & true life story	54	108	162	338	557	775
3-Douglas Fairbanks story; photo-c	26	52	78	152	239	325

FILTH, THE
DC Comics (Vertigo): Aug, 2002 - No. 13, Oct, 2003 ($2.95, limited series)

1-13-Morrison-s/Weston & Erskine-a						3.00
TPB (2004, $19.95) r/#1-13						20.00

FINAL CYCLE, THE
Dragon's Teeth Productions: July, 1987 - No. 4, 1988 (Limited series)

1-4						2.50

FINAL NIGHT, THE (See DC related titles and Parallax: Emerald Night)
DC Comics: Nov, 1996 - No. 4, Nov, 1996 ($1.95, weekly limited series)

1-4: Kesel-s/Immonen-a(p) in all. 4-Parallax's final acts						3.50
Preview						2.50
TPB (1998, $12.95) r/#1-4, Parallax: Emerald Night #1, and preview						13.00

FINALS
DC Comics (Vertigo): Sept, 1999 - No. 4, Dec, 1999 ($2.95, limited series)

1-4-Will Pfeifer-s/Jill Thompson-a						3.00

FIRE
Caliber Press: 1993 - No. 2, 1993 ($2.95, B&W, limited series, 52 pgs.)

1,2-Brian Michael Bendis-s/a						3.00
TPB (1999, 2001, $9.95) Restored reprints of series						10.00

FIREARM (Also see Codename: Firearm, Freex #15, Night Man #4 & Prime #10)
Malibu Comics (Ultraverse): Sept, 1993 - No. 18, Mar, 1995 ($1.95/$2.50)

0 ($14.95)-Came w/ video containing 1st half of story (comic contains 2nd half);						

	GD 2.0	VG 4.0	FN 6.0	VF 8.0	VF/NM 9.0	NM- 9.2
1st app. Duet						15.00
1,3-6: 1-James Robinson scripts begin; Cully Hamner-a; Chaykin-c; 1st app. Alec Swan. 3-Intro The Sportsmen; Chaykin-c. 4-Break-Thru x-over; Chaykin-c. 5-1st app. Ellen (Swan's girlfriend);2 pg. origin of Prime. 6-Prime app. (story cont'd in Prime #10); Brereton-c						2.50
1-($2.50)-Newsstand edition polybagged w/card						3.00
1-Ultra Limited silver foil-c						5.00
2 ($2.50, 44 pgs.)-Hardcase app.;Chaykin-c; Rune flip-c/story by B. Smith (3 pgs.)						3.00
7-10,12-17: 12-The Rafferty Saga begins, ends #18; 1st app. Rafferty. 15-Night Man & Freex app. 17-Swan marries Ellen						2.50
11-($3.50, 68 pgs.)-Flip book w/Ultraverse Premiere #5						3.50
18-Death of Rafferty; Chaykin-c						3.00

NOTE: *Brereton* c-6. *Chaykin* c-1-4, 14, 16, 18. *Hamner* a-1-4. *Herrera* a-12. *James Robinson* scripts-0-18.

FIRE BALL XL5 (See Steve Zodiac & The ...)

FIREBIRDS (See Noble Causes)
Image Comics: Nov, 2004 ($5.95)

1-Faerber-s/Ponce-a/c; intro. Firebird						6.00

FIREBRAND (Also see Showcase '96 #4)
DC Comics: Feb, 1996 - No. 9, Oct, 1996 ($1.75)

1-9: Brian Augustyn scripts; Velluto-c/a in all. 9-Daredevil #319-c/swipe						2.50

FIREBREATHER
Image Comics: Jan, 2003 - No. 4, Apr, 2003 ($2.95)

1-4-Hester-s/Kuhn-a						3.00
...: The Iron Saint (12/04, $6.95, squarebound) Hester-s/Kuhn-a						7.00
TPB (7/04, $13.95) r/#1-4; foreword by Brad Meltzer; gallery and sketch pages						14.00

FIRE FROM HEAVEN
Image Comics (WildStorm Productions): Mar, 1996 ($2.50)

1,2-Moore-s						2.50

FIREHAIR COMICS (Formerly Pioneer West Romances #3-6; also see Rangers Comics)
Fiction House Magazines (Flying Stories): Winter/48-49; No. 2, Wint/49-50; No. 7, Spr/51 - No. 11, Spr/52

1-Origin Firehair	43	86	129	262	431	600
2-Continues as Pioneer West Romances for #3-6	22	44	66	128	202	275
7-11	16	32	48	92	144	195
I.W. Reprint 8-(nd)-Kinstler-c; reprints Rangers #57; Dr. Drew story by Grandenetti	3	6	9	18	24	30

FIRESIDE BOOK SERIES (Hard and soft cover editions)
Simon and Schuster: 1974 - 1980 (130-260 pgs.), Square bound, color

		GD 2.0	VG 4.0	FN 6.0	VF 8.0	VF/NM 9.0	NM- 9.2
Amazing Spider-Man, The, 1979, 130 pgs., $3.95, Bob Larkin-c	HC	8	16	24	56	93	130
	SC	6	12	18	37	59	80
America At War–The Best of DC War Comics, 1979, $6.95, 260 pgs, Kubert-c	HC	11	22	33	79	140	200
	SC	7	14	21	50	83	115
Best of Spidey Super Stories (Electric Company) 1978, $3.95,	SC	6	12	18	43	69	95
Bring On The Bad Guys (Origins of the Marvel Comics Villains) 1976, $6.95, 260 pgs.; Romita-c	HC	8	16	24	54	90	125
	SC	5	10	15	35	55	75
Captain America, Sentinel of Liberty,1979, 130 pgs., $12.95, Cockrum-c	HC	8	16	24	56	93	130
	SC	6	12	18	37	59	80
Doctor Strange Master of the Mystic Arts, 1980, 130 pgs.	HC	8	16	24	56	93	130
	SC	6	12	18	37	59	80
Fantastic Four, The, 1979, 130 pgs.	HC	8	16	24	54	90	125
	SC	5	10	15	35	55	75
Heart Throbs–The Best of DC Romance Comics, 1979, 260 pgs., $6.,95	HC	16	32	48	114	202	290
	SC	9	18	27	65	113	160
Incredible Hulk, The, 1978, 260 pgs. (8 1/4" x 11")	HC	8	16	24	54	90	125
	SC	5	10	15	35	55	75
Marvel's Greatest Superhero Battles, 1978, 260 pgs., $6.95, Romita-c	HC	10	20	30	67	116	165
	SC	6	12	18	43	69	95
Mysteries in Space, 1980, $7,95, Anderson-c, r-DC sci/fi stories	HC	9	18	27	61	103	145
	SC	6	12	18	39	62	85
Origins of Marvel Comics, 1974, 260 pgs., $5.95. r-covers & origins of Fantastic Four, Hulk, Spider-Man, Thor, & Doctor Strange	HC	8	16	24	54	90	125
	SC	5	10	15	35	55	75
Silver Surfer, The, 1978, 130 pgs., $4.95, Norem-c	HC	8	16	24	56	93	130
	SC	6	12	18	39	62	85

Firestorm, The Nuclear Man #85 © DC

1st Issue Special #3 © DC

First Love Illustrated #11 © HARV

	GD 2.0	VG 4.0	FN 6.0	VF 8.0	VF/NM 9.0	NM- 9.2
	GD 2.0	VG 4.0	FN 6.0	VF 8.0	VF/NM 9.0	NM- 9.2

Son of Origins of Marvel Comics, 1975, 260 pgs., $6.95, Romita-c. Reprints
covers & origins of X-Men, Iron Man, HC 8 16 24 54 90 125
Avengers, Daredevil, Silver Surfer SC 5 10 15 35 55 75
Superhero Women, The–Featuring the HC 10 20 30 67 116 165
Fabulous Females of Marvel Comics, SC 6 12 18 43 69 95
1977, 260 pgs., $6.95, Romita-c
Note: Prices listed are for 1st printings. Later printings have lesser value.

FIRESTAR
Marvel Comics Group: Mar, 1986 - No. 4, June, 1986 (75¢)(From Spider-Man TV series)
1,2: 1-X-Men & New Mutants app. 2-Wolverine-c (not real Wolverine?); Art Adams-a(p) 5.00
3,4: 3-Art Adams/Sienkiewicz-c. 4-B. Smith-c 3.00
X-Men: Firestar Digest (2006, $7.99, digest-size) r/#1-4; profile pages 8.00

FIRESTONE (See Donald And Mickey Merry Christmas)

FIRESTORM (See Cancelled Comic Cavalcade, DC Comics Presents, Flash #289,
The Fury of... & Justice League of America #179)
DC Comics: March, 1978 - No. 5, Oct-Nov, 1978
1,5: 1-Origin & 1st app. 1 3 4 6 8 10
2-4: 2-Origin Multiplex. 3-Origin & 1st app. Killer Frost. 4-1st app. Hyena 6.00

FIRESTORM
DC Comics: July, 2004 - Present ($2.50/$2.99)
1-24: 1-Intro. Jason Rusch; Jolley-s/ChrisCross-a. 6-Identity Crisis tie-in. 7-Bloodhound x-over
8-Killer Frost returns. 9-Ronnie Raymond returns. 17-Villains United tie-in. 21-Infinite Crisis.
24-One Year Later; Killer Frost app. 2.50
25-35: 25-Begin $2.99-c; Mr. Freeze app. 33-35-Mister Miracle & Orion app. 3.00
...: Reborn TPB (2007, $14.99) r/#23-27 15.00

FIRESTORM, THE NUCLEAR MAN (Formerly Fury of Firestorm)
DC Comics: No. 65, Nov, 1987 - No. 100, Aug, 1990
65-99: 66-1st app. Zuggernaut; Firestorm vs. Green Lantern. 71-Death of Capt. X.
67,68-Millennium tie-ins. 83-1st new look 2.50
100-($2.95, 68 pgs.) 4.00
Annual 5 (10/87)-1st app. new Firestorm 3.00

FIRST, THE
CrossGeneration Comics: Jan, 2001 - No. 37, Jan, 2004 ($2.95)
1-3: 1-Barbara Kesel-s/Bart Sears & Andy Smith-a 5.00
4-10 4.00
11-37 3.00
Preview (11/00, free) 8 pg. intro 2.25
Two Houses Divided Vol. 1 TPB (11/01, $19.95) r/#1-7; new Moeller-c 20.00
Magnificent Tension Vol. 2 TPB (2002, $19.95) r/#8-13 20.00
Sinister Motives Vol. 3 TPB (2003, $15.95) r/#14-19 16.00
Vol. 4 Futile Endeavors (2003, $15.95) r/#20-25 16.00
Vol. 5 Liquid Alliances (2003, $15.95) r/#26-31 16.00
Vol. 6 Ragnarok (2004, $15.95) r/#32-37 16.00

FIRST ADVENTURES
First Comics: Dec, 1985 - No. 5, Apr, 1986 ($1.25)
1-5: Blaze Barlow, Whisper & Dynamo Joe in all 2.50

FIRST AMERICANS, THE
Dell Publishing Co.: No. 843, Sept, 1957
Four Color 843-Marsh-a 8 16 24 56 93 130

FIRST BORN (See Witchblade and Darkness titles)
Image Comics (Top Cow): Aug, 2007 - No. 3 ($2.99, limited series)
... First Look (6/07, 99¢) Preview; The Darkness app.; Sejic-a; 2 covers (color & B&W) 2.25
1-($2.99) Two covers; Marz-s/Sejic-a 3.00
1-B&W variant Sejic cover 5.00

FIRST CHRISTMAS, THE (3-D)
Fiction House Magazines (Real Adv. Publ. Co.): 1953 (25¢, 8-1/4x10-1/4", oversize)(Came
w/glasses)
nn-(Scarce)-Kelly Freas painted-c; Biblical theme, birth of Christ; Nativity-c
31 62 93 180 285 390

FIRST COMICS GRAPHIC NOVEL
First Comics: Jan, 1984 - No. 21? (52 pgs./176 pgs., high quality paper)
1,2: 1-Beowulf ($5.95)(both printings). 2-Time Beavers 9.00
3($11.95, 100 pgs.)-American Flagg! Hard Times (2nd printing exists) 15.00
4-Nexus ($6.95)-r/B&W 1-3 12.00
5,7: 5-The Enchanted Apples of Oz ($7.95, 52 pgs.)-Intro by Harlan Ellison (1986).
7-The Secret Island Of Oz ($7.95) 10.00
6-Elric of Melnibone ($14.95, 176 pgs.)-Reprints with new color 18.00

8,10,14,18: Teenage Mutant Ninja Turtles Book I -IV ($9.95, 132 pgs.)-8-r/TMNT #1-3 in color
w/12 pgs. new-a; origin. 10-r/TMNT #4-6 in color. 14-r/TMNT #7,8 in color plus new 12 pg.
story. 18-r/TMNT #10,11 plus 3 pg. fold-out 11.00
9-Time 2: The Epiphany by Chaykin (11/86, $7.95, 52pgs. - indicia says #8) 10.00
11-Sailor On The Sea of Fate ($14.95) 16.00
nn-Time 2: The Satisfaction of Black Mariah (9/87) 10.00
12-American Flagg! Southern Comfort (10/87, $11.95) 14.00
13,16,17,21: 13-The Ice King Of Oz. 16-The Forgotten Forest of Oz ($8.95). 17-Mazinger
(68 pgs., $8.95). 21-Elric, The Weird of the White Wolf; r/#1-5 10.00
15,19: 15-Hex Breaker: Badger ($7.95). 19-The Original Nexus Graphic Novel
($7.95, 104 pgs.)-Reprints First Comics Graphic Novel #4 12.00
20-American Flagg!: State of the Union ($11.95, 96 pgs.); r/A.F. #7-9 15.00
NOTE: Most or all issues have been reprinted.

1ST FOLIO (The Joe Kubert School Presents...)
Pacific Comics: Mar, 1984 ($1.50, one-shot)
1-Joe Kubert-c/a(2 pgs.); Adam & Andy Kubert-a 3.00

1ST ISSUE SPECIAL
National Periodical Publications: Apr, 1975 - No. 13, Apr, 1976 (Tryout series)
1,6: 1-Intro. Atlas; Kirby-c/a/script. 6-Dingbats 2 4 6 9 12 15
2,12: 2-Green Team (see Cancelled Comic Cavalcade). 12-Origin/1st app. "Blue" Starman
(2nd app. in Starman, 2nd Series #3); Kubert-c 1 3 4 6 8 10
3-Metamorpho by Ramona Fradon 1 3 4 6 8 10
4,10,11: 4-Lady Cop. 10-The Outsiders. 11-Code Name: Assassin; Grell-c
1 2 3 5 7 9
5-Manhunter; Kirby-c/a/script 2 4 6 11 16 20
7,9: 7-The Creeper by Ditko (c/a). 9-Dr. Fate; Kubert-c/Simonson-a
2 4 6 9 13 16
8-Origin/1st app. The Warlord; Grell-c/a (11/75) 3 6 9 18 27 35
13-Return of the New Gods; Darkseid app.; 1st new costume Orion; predates New Gods #12
by more than a year 3 6 9 16 22 28

FIRST KISS
Charlton Comics: Dec, 1957 - No. 40, Jan, 1965
V1#1 4 8 12 28 44 60
V1#2-10 3 6 9 18 27 35
11-40 2 4 6 13 18 22

FIRST LOVE ILLUSTRATED
Harvey Publications(Home Comics)(True Love): 2/49 - No. 9, 6/50; No. 10, 1/51 - No. 86,
3/58; No. 87, 9/58 - No. 88, 11/58; No. 89, 11/62, No. 90, 2/63
1-Powell-a(2) 18 36 54 107 169 230
2-Powell-a 11 22 33 64 90 115
3-"Was I Too Fat To Be Loved" story 12 24 36 69 97 125
4-10 9 18 27 47 61 75
11-30: 13-"I Joined a Teen-age Sex Club" story. 30-Lingerie panel
7 14 21 37 46 55
31-34,37,39-49: 49-Last pre-code (2/55) 7 14 21 35 43 50
35-Used in **SOTI**, illo "The title of this comic book is First Love"
19 38 57 112 176 240
36-Communism story, "Love Slaves" 10 20 30 58 79 100
38-Nostrand-a 8 16 24 44 57 70
50-66,71-90 7 14 21 35 43 50
67-70-Kirby-a 7 14 21 37 46 55
NOTE: *Disbrow a-13. Orlando c-87. Powell a-1, 3-5, 7, 10, 11, 13-17, 19-24, 26-29, 33,35-41, 43, 45, 46, 50, 54, 55, 57, 58, 61-63, 65, 71-73, 76, 79r, 82, 84, 88.*

FIRST MEN IN THE MOON (See Movie Comics)

FIRST ROMANCE MAGAZINE
Home Comics(Harvey Publ.)/True Love: 8/49 - #6, 6/50; #7, 6/51 - #50, 2/58; #51, 9/58 -
#52, 11/58
1 16 32 48 94 147 200
2 10 20 30 58 79 100
3-5 9 18 27 47 61 75
6-10,28: 28-Nostrand-a(Powell swipe) 8 16 24 40 50 60
11-20 7 14 21 35 43 50
21-27,29-32: 32-Last pre-code issue (2/55) 6 12 18 31 38 45
33-40,44-52 6 12 18 28 34 40
41-43-Kirby-c 7 14 21 37 46 55
NOTE: *Powell a-1-5, 8-10, 14, 18, 20-22, 24, 25, 28, 36, 46, 48, 51.*

FIRST TRIP TO THE MOON (See Space Adventures No. 20)

FIRST WAVE (Based on Sci-Fi Channel TV series)
Andromeda Entertainment: Dec, 2000 - No. 4, Jun, 2001 ($2.99)
1-4-Kuhoric-s/Parsons-a/Busch-c 3.00

The Flame #1 © FOX

Flaming Carrot Comics (2004 series) #1 © Bob Burden

The Flash #169 © DC

	GD 2.0	VG 4.0	FN 6.0	VF 8.0	VF/NM 9.0	NM- 9.2

FISH POLICE (Inspector Gill of the...#2, 3)
Fishwrap Productions/Comico V2#5-17/Apple Comics #18 on:
Dec, 1985 - No. 11, Nov, 1987 ($1.50, B&W); V2#5, April, 1988 - V2#17, May, 1989 ($1.75, color) No. 18, Aug, 1989 - No. 26, Dec, 1990 ($2.25, B&W)

1-11, 1(5/86),2-nd print, V2#5-17-(Color): V2#5-11. 12-17, new-a, 18-26 ($2.25-c, B&W). 18-Origin Inspector Gill						2.50
Special 1($2.50, 7/87, Comico)						2.50
Graphic Novel: Hairballs (1987, $9.95, TPB) r/#1-4 in color						10.00

FISH POLICE
Marvel Comics: V2#1, Oct, 1992 - No. 6, Mar, 1993 ($1.25)

V2#1-6: 1-Hairballs Saga begins; r/#1 (1985)						2.50

5 CENT COMICS (Also see Whiz Comics)
Fawcett Publ.: Feb, 1940 (8 pgs., reg. size, B&W)

nn - 1st app. Dan Dare. Ashcan comic, not distributed to newsstands, only for in-house use. A CGC certified 9.6 copy sold for $10,800 in 2003.						

5-STAR SUPER-HERO SPECTACULAR (See DC Special Series No. 1)

FLAK RIOT
Image Comics: June, 2005 - Present ($2.95)

1-Michael O'Hare-a/Robert Place Napton-s						3.00

FLAME, THE (See Big 3 & Wonderworld Comics)
Fox Features Synd.: Sum, 1940 - No. 8, Jan, 1942 (#1,2: 68 pgs; #3-8: 44 pgs.)

1-Flame stories reprinted from Wonderworld #5-9; origin The Flame; Lou Fine-a (36 pgs.),	300	600	900	1931	3366	4800
2-Fine-a(2); Wing Turner by Tuska; r/Wonderworld #3,10	121	242	363	756	1253	1750
3-8: 3-Powell-a	79	158	237	494	822	1150

FLAME, THE (Formerly Lone Eagle)
Ajax/Farrell Publications (Excellent Publ.): No. 5, Dec-Jan, 1954-55 - No. 3, April-May, 1955

5(#1)-1st app. new Flame	45	90	135	275	450	625
2,3	29	58	87	170	268	365

FLAMING CARROT COMICS (Also see Junior Carrot Patrol)
Killian Barracks Press: Summer-Fall, 1981 ($1.95, one shot) (Lg size, 8-1/2x11")

1-Bob Burden-c/a/scripts; serially #'ed to 6500	5	10	15	32	51	70

FLAMING CARROT COMICS (See Anything Goes, Cerebus, Teenage Mutant Ninja Turtles/Flaming Carrot Crossover & Visions)
Aardvark-Vanaheim/Renegade Press #6-17/Dark Horse #18-31:
May, 1984 - No. 5, Jan, 1985; No. 6, Mar, 1985 - No. 31, Oct, 1994 ($1.70/$2.00, B&W)

1-Bob Burden story/art	4	8	12	26	41	55
2	3	6	9	16	22	28
3	2	4	6	10	14	18
4-6	2	4	6	8	11	14
7-9	1	3	4	6	8	10
10-12						6.50
13-15						4.00
15-Variant without cover price						6.00
16-(6/87) 1st app. Mystery Men	1	2	3	5	6	8
17-20: 18-1st Dark Horse issue						4.00
21-23,25: 25-Contains trading cards; TMNT app.						3.00
24-(2.50, 52 pgs.)-10th anniversary issue						3.00
26-28: 26-Begin $2.25-c. 26,27-Teenage Mutant Ninja Turtles x-over. 27-McFarlane-c						3.00
29-31-(2.50)						3.00
Annual 1(1/97, $5.00)						5.00
... & Reid Fleming, World's Toughest Milkman (12/02, $3.99) listed as #32 in indicia						4.00
...:Fortune Favors the Bold (1998, $16.95, TPB) r/#19-24						17.00
...:Men of Mystery (7/97, $12.95, TPB) r/#1-3, + new material						13.00
...'s Greatest Hits (4/98, $17.95, TPB) r/#12-18, + new material						18.00
...:The Wild Shall Wild Remain (1997, $17.95, TPB) r/#4-11, + new s/a						18.00

FLAMING CARROT COMICS
Image Comics (Desperado): Dec, 2004 - Present ($2.95/$3.50, B&W)

1-3-Bob Burden story/art						3.00
4-($3.50-c)						3.50
... Special #1 (3/06, $3.50) All Photo comic						3.50
... Vol. 6 (2006, $14.99) r/1-4 & Special #1; intro. by Brian Bolland						15.00

FLAMING LOVE
Quality Comics Group (Comic Magazines): Dec, 1949 - No. 6, Oct, 1950 (Photo covers #2-6) (52 pgs.)

1-Ward-c/a (9 pgs.)	40	80	120	235	368	500
2	18	36	54	103	162	220

3-Ward-a (9 pgs.); Crandall-a	26	52	78	152	239	325
4-6: 4-Gustavson-a	15	30	45	86	133	180

FLAMING WESTERN ROMANCES (Formerly Target Western Romances)
Star Publications: No. 3, Mar-Apr, 1950

3-Robert Taylor, Arlene Dahl photo on-c with biographies inside; L. B. Cole-c	38	76	114	222	351	480

FLARE (Also see Champions for 1st app. & League of Champions)
Hero Comics/Hero Graphics Vol. 2 on: Nov, 1988 - No. 3, Jan, 1989 ($2.75, color, 52 pgs); V2#1, Nov, 1990 - No. 7, Oct, 1991 ($2.95/$3.50, color, mature, 52 pgs.);V2#8, Oct, 1992 - No. 16, Feb, 1994 ($3.50/$3.95, B&W, 36 pgs.)

V1#1-3, V2#1-16: 5-Eternity Smith returns. 6-Intro The Tigress						4.00
Annual 1(1992, $4.50, B&W, 52 pgs.)-Champions-r						4.50

FLARE ADVENTURES
Hero Graphics: Feb, 1992 - No. 12, 1993? ($3.50/$3.95)

1 (90¢, color, 20 pgs.)						2.50
2-12-Flip books w/Champions Classics						4.00

FLASH, THE (See Adventure Comics, The Brave and the Bold, Crisis On Infinite Earths, DC Comics Presents, DC Special, DC Special Series, DC Super-Stars, The Greatest Flash Stories Ever Told, Green Lantern, Impulse, JLA, Justice League of America, Showcase, Super Team Family, Titans & World's Finest)

FLASH, THE (1st Series)(Formerly Flash Comics)(See Showcase #4,8,13,14)
National Periodical Publ./DC: No. 105, Feb-Mar, 1959 - No. 350, Oct, 1985

105-(2-3/59)-Origin Flash(retold), & Mirror Master (1st app.)	446	892	1338	4014	8257	12,500
106-Origin Grodd & Pied Piper; Flash's 1st visit to Gorilla City; begin Grodd the Super Gorilla trilogy (Scarce)	167	334	501	1461	2731	4000
107-Grodd trilogy, part 2	96	192	288	816	1508	2200
108-Grodd trilogy ends	78	156	234	663	1232	1800
109-2nd app. Mirror Master	61	122	183	519	960	1400
110-Intro/origin Kid Flash who later becomes Flash in Crisis On Infinite Earths #12; begin Kid Flash trilogy, ends #112 (also in #114,116,118); 1st app. & origin of The Weather Wizard	143	286	429	1216	2258	3300
111-2nd Kid Flash tryout; Cloud Creatures	46	92	138	368	672	975
112-Origin & 1st app. Elongated Man (4-5/60); also apps. in #115,119,130	50	100	150	413	757	1100
113-Origin & 1st app. Trickster	45	90	135	360	655	950
114-Captain Cold app. (see Showcase #8)	38	76	114	285	518	750
115,116,118-120: 119-Elongated Man marries Sue Dearborn. 120-Flash & Kid Flash team-up for 1st time	30	60	90	220	398	575
117-Origin & 1st app. Capt. Boomerang; 1st & only S.A. app. Winky Blinky & Noddy	34	68	102	255	465	675
121,122: 122-Origin & 1st app. The Top	24	48	72	175	313	450
123-(9/61)-Re-intro. Golden Age Flash; origins of both Flashes; 1st mention of an Earth II where DC G. A. heroes live	130	260	390	1105	2053	3000
124-Last 10¢ issue	19	38	57	138	244	350
125-128,130: 127-Return of Grodd-c/story. 128-Origin & 1st app. Abra Kadabra. 130-(7/62)-1st Gauntlet of Super-Villains (Mirror Master, Capt. Cold, The Top, Capt. Boomerang & Trickster)	17	34	51	128	227	325
129-2nd G.A. Flash x-over; J.S.A. cameo in flashback (1st S.A. app. G.A. Green Lantern, Hawkman, Atom, Black Canary & Dr. Mid-Nite. Wonder Woman (1st S.A. app.?) appears)	29	58	87	212	381	550
131-136,138,140: 131-Early Green Lantern x-over (9/62). 135-1st app. of Kid Flash's yellow costume (3/63). 136-1st Dexter Miles. 140-Origin & 1st app. Heat Wave	14	28	42	99	175	250
137-G.A. Flash x-over; J.S.A. cameo (1st S.A. app.)(1st real app. since 2-3/51); 1st S.A. app. Vandal Savage & Johnny Thunder; JSA team decides to re-form	38	76	114	285	518	750
139-Origin & 1st app. Prof. Zoom	15	30	45	107	191	275
141-150: 142-Trickster app.	11	22	33	75	133	190
151-Engagement of Barry Allen & Iris West; G.A. Flash vs. The Shade.	12	24	36	86	153	220
152-159: 159-Dr. Mid-Nite cameo	9	18	27	65	113	160
160-(80-Pg. Giant G-21); G.A. Flash & Johnny Quick-r	12	24	36	84	150	215
161-164,166,167: 167-New facts about Flash's origin	8	16	24	54	90	125
165-Barry Allen weds Iris West	8	16	24	58	97	135
168,170: 168-Green Lantern-c/app. 170-Dr. Mid-Nite, Dr. Fate, G.A. Flash x-over	8	16	24	54	90	125
169-(80-pg. Giant G-34)-New facts about origin	9	18	27	61	103	145
171,172,174,176,177,179,180: 171-JLA, Green Lantern, Atom flashbacks. 174-Barry Allen reveals I.D. to wife. 179-(5/68)-Flash travels to Earth-Prime and meets DC editor Julie Schwartz; 1st unnamed app. Earth-Prime (See Justice League of America #123 for 1st named app. & 3rd app. overall)	7	14	21	49	80	110

The Flash #173 © DC

The Flash (2nd series) #149 © DC

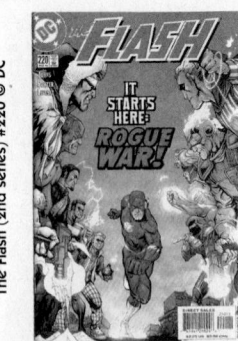

The Flash (2nd series) #220 © DC

	GD 2.0	VG 4.0	FN 6.0	VF 8.0	VF/NM 9.0	NM- 9.2
173-G.A. Flash x-over	8	16	24	54	90	125
175-2nd Superman/Flash race (12/67) (See Superman #199 & World's Finest #198,199); JLA cameo; gold kryptonite used (on J'onn J'onzz impersonating Superman)	16	32	48	114	202	290
178-(80-Pg. Giant G-46)	8	16	24	56	93	130
181-186,188,189: 186-Re-intro. Sargon. 189-Last 12¢-c	6	12	18	37	59	80
187,196: (68-Pg. Giants G-58, G-70)	6	12	18	41	66	90
190-195,197-199	4	8	12	26	41	55
200	5	10	15	30	48	65
201-204,206,207: 201-New G.A. Flash story. 206-Elongated Man app. 207-Last 15¢ issue	3	6	9	20	30	40
205-(68-Pg. Giant G-82)	5	10	15	35	55	75
208-213-(52 pg.): 211-G.A. Flash origin-r/#104. 213-Reprints #137	4	8	12	22	34	45
214-DC 100 Page Super Spectacular DC-11; origin Metal Men-r/Showcase #37; never before published G.A. Flash story. (see DC 100 pg. Super Spec. #11 for price)						
215 (52 pgs.)-Flash-r/Showcase #4; G.A. Flash x-over, continued in #216	4	8	12	24	37	50
216,220: 220-1st app. Turtle since Showcase #4			9	16	23	30
217-219: Neal Adams-a in all. 217-Green Lantern/Green Arrow series begins (9/72); 2nd G.L. & G.A. team-up series (see Green Lantern #76). 219-Last Green Arrow	4	8	12	24	37	50
221-225,227,228,230,231,233: 222-G. Lantern x-over. 228-(7-8/74)-Flash writer Cary Bates travels to Earth-One & meets Flash, Iris Allen & Trickster; 2nd unnamed app. Earth-Prime (See Justice League of America #123 for 1st named app. & 3rd app. overall)	2	4	6	11	16	20
226-Neal Adams-p	3	6	9	16	22	28
229,232-(100 pg. issues)-G.A. Flash-r & new-a	4	8	12	26	41	55
234-250: 235-Green Lantern x-over. 243-Death of The Top. 245-Origin The Floronic Man in Green Lantern back-up, ends #246. 246-Last Green Lantern. 247-Jay Garrick app. 250-Intro Golden Glider	2	4	6	9	12	15
251-274: 256-Death of The Top retold. 265-267-(44 pgs.). 267-Origin of Flash's uniform. 270-Intro The Clown	1	3	4	6	8	10
268,273-276,278,283,286-(Whitman variants; low print run; no issue #s shown on covers)	2	4	6	8	10	12
275,276-Iris Allen dies	2	4	6	8	10	12
277-288,290: 286-Intro/origin Rainbow Raider	1	2	3	4	5	7
289-1st Perez DC art (Firestorm); new Firestorm back-up series begins (9/80), ends #304	1	2	3	5	7	9
291-299,301-305: 291-1st app. Saber-Tooth (villain). 295-Gorilla Grodd-c/story. 298-Intro & origin new Shade. 301-Atomic bomb-c. 303-The Top returns. 304-Intro/origin Colonel Computron; 305-G.A. Flash x-over						5.00
300-(52 pgs.)-Origin Flash retold; 25th ann. issue	1	2	3	4	5	7
306-313-Dr. Fate by Giffen. 309-Origin Flash retold						5.00
314-340: 318-323-Creeper back-ups. 323,324-Two part Flash vs. Flash story. 324-Death of Reverse Flash (Professor Zoom). 328-Iris West Allen's death retold. 329-JLA app. 340-Trial of the Flash begins						4.00
341-349: 344-Origin Kid Flash						5.00
350-Double size ($1.25) Final issue						6.00
Annual 1 (10-12/63, 84 pgs.)-Origin Elongated Man & Kid Flash-r; origin Grodd; G.A. Flash-r	36	72	108	270	498	725
Annual 1 Replica Edition (2001, $6.95)-Reprints the entire 1963 Annual						7.00

The Flash Spectacular (See DC Special Series No. 11)
The Life Story of the Flash (1997, $19.95, Hardcover) "Iris Allen's" chronicle of Barry Allen's life; comic panels w/additional text; Waid & Augustyn-s/ Kane & Staton-a/Orbik painted-c ... 20.00
The Life Story of the Flash (1998, $12.95, Softcover) New Orbik-c ... 13.00
NOTE: N. Adams c-194, 195, 203, 204, 206-208, 211, 213, 215, 226p, 246. M. Anderson c-165, a(i)-195, 200-204, 206-208. Austin a-233i, 234i, 246i. Buckler a-271p, 272p; c(p)-247-250, 252, 253p, 255, 256p, 258, 262, 265-267, 269-271. Giffen a-306-313p; c-310p, 315. Giordano a-226i. Sid Greene a-167-174i, 229i(r). Grell a-237p, 238p, 240-243p; c-236. Heck a-198p. Infantino/Anderson a-135. c-135, 170-174, 192, 200, 201, 328-330. Infantino/Giella c-105-112, 163, 164, 166-168. G. Kane a-195p, 197-199p, 229r, 232r; c-197-199, 312p. Kubert a-108p, 215i(r); c-189-191. Lopez c-272. Meskin a-229r, 232r. Perez a-289-293p; c-293. Starlin a-294-296p. Staton c-263p, 264p. Swan c-cover-version-131, 143, 168, 171, 191.

FLASH (2nd Series)(See Crisis on Infinite Earths #12 and All Flash #1)
DC Comics: June, 1987 - No. 230, Mar, 2006; No. 231, Oct. 2007 - Present (75¢-$2.50)

	GD 2.0	VG 4.0	FN 6.0	VF 8.0	VF/NM 9.0	NM- 9.2
1-Guice-c/a begins; New Teen Titans app.			3	6	8	10
2-10: 3-Intro. Kilgore. 5-Intro. Speed McGee. 7-1st app. Blue Trinity. 8,9-Millennium tie-ins. 9-1st app. The Chunk						4.00
11-61: 12-Free extra 16 pg. Dr. Light story. 19-Free extra 16 pg. Flash story. 28-Capt. Cold app. 29-New Phantom Lady app. 40-Dr. Alchemy app. 50-($1.75, 52 pgs.)						3.00

62-78,80: 62-Flash: Year One begins, ends #65. 65-Last $1.00-c. 66-Aquaman app. 69,70-Green Lantern app. 70-Gorilla Grodd story ends. 73-Re-intro Barry Allen & begin saga ("Barry Allen's" true ID revealed in #78). 76-Re-intro of Max Mercury (Quality Comics' Quicksilver), not in uniform until #77. 80-($1.25-c) Regular Edition ... 4.00
79,80 ($2.50): 79-(68 pgs.) Barry Allen saga ends. 80-Foil-c ... 5.00
81-91,93,94,0,95-99,101: 81,82-Nightwing & Starfire app. 84-Razer app. 94-Zero Hour. 0-(10/94). 95-"Terminal Velocity" begins, ends #100. 96,98,99-Kobra app. 97-Origin Max Mercury; Chillblaine app. ... 4.00

	GD 2.0	VG 4.0	FN 6.0	VF 8.0	VF/NM 9.0	NM- 9.2
92-1st Impulse	1	3	4	6	8	10

100 ($2.50)-Newsstand edition; Kobra & JLA app. ... 4.00
100 ($3.50)-Foil-c edition; Kobra & JLA app. ... 5.00
102-131: 102-Mongul app.; begin-$1.75-c. 105-Mirror Master app. 107-Shazam app. 108-"Dead Heat" begins; 1st app. Savitar. 109-"Dead Heat" Pt. 2 (cont'd in Impulse #10). 110-"Dead Heat" Pt. 4 (cont'd in Impulse #11). 111-"Dead Heat" finale; Savitar disappears into the Speed Force; John Fox cameo (2nd app.). 112-"Race Against Time" begins, ends #118; re-intro John Fox. 113-Tornado Twins app. 119-Final Night x-over. 127-129-Rogue's Gallery & Neron. 128,129-JLA-app.130-Morrison & Millar-s begin ... 3.50
132-150: 135-GL & GA app. 142-Wally almost marries Linda; Waid-s return. 144-Cobalt Blue origin. 145-Chain Lightning begins.147-Professor Zoom app. 149-Barry Allen app. 150-($2.95) Final showdown with Cobalt Blue ... 3.00
151-162: 151-Casey-s. 152-New Flash-c. 154-New Flash ID revealed. 159-Wally marries Linda. 162-Last Waid-s. ... 3.00
163-187,189-196,198,199,201-206: 163-Begin $2.25-c. 164-186-Bolland-c. 183-New Trickster. 196-Winslade-a. 201-Dose-a begins. 205-Batman-c/app. ... 2.50
188-($2.95) Mirror Master, Weather Wizard, Trickster app. ... 3.00
197-Origin of Zoom (6/03) ... 6.00
200-($3.50) Flash vs. Zoom; Barry Allen & Hal Jordan app.; wraparound-c ... 3.50
207-230: 207-211-Turner-c/Porter-a. 209-JLA app. 210-Nightwing app. 212-Origin Mirror Master. 214-216-Identity Crisis x-over. 219-Wonder Woman app. 220-Rogue War 224-Zoom & Prof. Zoom app. 225-Twins born; Barry Allen app.; last Johns-s ... 2.50
231-(10/07) Waid-s/Acuña-a ... 3.00
#1,000,000 (11/98) 853rd Century x-over ... 2.50
Annual 1-7,9: 2-('87-'94,'96, 68 pgs), 3-Gives history of G.A.,S.A., & Modern Age Flash in text. 4-Armaggeddon 2001. 5-Eclipso-c/story. 7-Elseworlds story. 9-Legends of the Dead Earth story; J.H. Williams-a(p); Mick Gray-a(i) ... 3.00
Annual 8 (1995, $3.50)-Year One story ... 3.50
Annual 10 (1997, $3.95)-Pulp Heroes stories ... 4.00
Annual 11,12 ('98, '99)-11-Ghosts; Wrightson-c. 12-JLApe; Art Adams-c ... 3.00
Annual 13 ('00, $3.50) Planet DC; Alcatena-c/a ... 3.50
...: Blitz (2004, $19.95, TPB)-r/#192-200; Kolins-c ... 20.00
...: Blood Will Run (2002, $17.95, TPB)-r/#170-176, Secret Files #3 ... 18.00
...: Crossfire (2004, $17.95, TPB)-r/#183-191 & parts of Flash Secret Files #3 ... 18.00
Dead Heat (2000, $14.95, TPB)-r/#108-111, Impulse #10,11 ... 15.00
...80-Page Giant (8/98, $4.95) Flash family stories by Waid, Millar and others; Mhan-c ... 5.00
...80-Page Giant 2 (4/99, $4.95) Stories of Flash family, future Kid Flash, original Teen Titans and XS ... 5.00
...: Ignition (2005, $14.95, TPB)-r/#201-206 ... 15.00
...: Iron Heights (2001, $5.95)-Van Sciver-c/a; intro. Murmur ... 6.00
...: Our Worlds at War I (10/01, $2.95)-Jae Lee-c; Black Racer app. ... 3.00
...Plus 1 (1/1997, $2.95)-Nightwing-c/app. ... 3.00
Race Against Time (2001, $14.95, TPB)-r/#112-118 ... 15.00
...: Rogues (2003, $14.95, TPB)-r/#177-182 ... 15.00
...: Rogue War (2006, $17.99, TPB)-r/#2,212,218,220-225; cover gallery ... 18.00
...Secret Files 1 (11/97, $4.95) Origin-s & pin-ups ... 5.00
...Secret Files 2 (11/99, $4.95) Origin of Reverse Flash ... 5.00
...Secret Files 3 (11/01) Intro. Hunter Zolomon (who later becomes Zoom) ... 5.00
Special 1 (1990, $2.95, 84 pgs.)-50th anniversary issue; Kubert-c; 1st Flash story by Mark Waid; 1st app. John Fox (27th Century Flash) ... 3.00
Terminal Velocity (1996, $12.95, TPB)-r/#95-100. ... 13.00
The Return of Barry Allen (1996, $12.95, TPB)-r/#74-79 ... 13.00
The Secret of Barry Allen (2005, $19.99, TPB)-r/#207-211,213-217; Turner sketch page ... 20.00
...: Time Flies (2002, $5.95)-Seth Fisher-c/a; Rozum-s ... 6.00
TV Special 1 (1991, $3.95, 76 pgs.)-Photo-c plus behind the scenes photos of TV show; Saltares-a, Byrne scripts ... 6.00
Wizard #1/2 (2005) prelude to Rogue Wars; Justiano-a ... 10.00
NOTE: Guice a-1-9p, 11p, Annual 1p; c-1-9p, Annual 1p. Perez c-15-17, Annual 2i. Charest c/a-Annual 5p.

FLASH: THE FASTEST MAN ALIVE (3rd Series)(See Infinite Crisis)
DC Comics: Aug, 2006 - No. 13, Aug, 2007 ($2.99)
1-Bart Allen becomes the Flash; Lashley-a/Bilson & Demeo-s ... 3.00
1-Variant-c by Joe and Andy Kubert ... 5.00
2-12: 5-Cyborg app. 7-Inertia returns. 10-Zoom app. ... 3.00
13-Bart Allen dies; 2 covers ... 3.00
13-DC Nation Edition from the 2007 San Diego Comic-Con ... 8.00
...: Lightning in a Bottle TPB (2007, $12.99) r/#1-6 ... 13.00
FLASH, THE (See Tangent Comics/ The Flash)

Flash: The Fastest Man Alive #9 © DC

Flash Comics #10 © DC

Flash Gordon #1 © KING

	GD 2.0	VG 4.0	FN 6.0	VF 8.0	VF/NM 9.0	NM- 9.2

FLASH AND GREEN LANTERN: THE BRAVE AND THE BOLD
DC Comics: Oct, 1999 - No. 6, Mar, 2000 ($2.50, limited series)

	GD 2.0	VG 4.0	FN 6.0	VF 8.0	VF/NM 9.0	NM- 9.2
1-6-Waid & Peyer-s/Kitson-a. 4-Green Arrow app.; Grindberg-a(p)						2.50
TPB (2001, $12.95) r/#1-6						13.00

FLASH COMICS
DC Comics:. Dec. 1939

1-Ashcan comic, not distributed to newsstands, only for in-house use. Cover art is Adventure Comics #41 and interior from All-American Comics #8. A CGC certified 9.6 sold for $12,000 in 2003.

FLASH COMICS (Whiz Comics No. 2 on)
Fawcett Publications: Jan, 1940 (12 pgs., B&W, regular size)
(Not distributed to newsstands; printed for in-house use)

NOTE: *Whiz Comics* #2 was preceded by two books, *Flash Comics* and *Thrill Comics*, both dated Jan, 1940, (12 pgs, B&W, regular size) and were not distributed. These two books are identical except for the title, and were sent out to major distributors as ad copies to promote sales. It is believed that the complete 68 page issue of Fawcett's *Flash* and *Thrill Comics* #1 was finished and ready for publication with the January date. Since DC Comics was also about to publish a book with the same date and title, Fawcett hurriedly printed up the black and white version of *Flash Comics* to secure copyright before DC. The inside covers are blank, with the covers and inside pages printed on a high quality uncoated paper stock. The eight page origin story of Captain Thunder is composed of pages 1-7 and 13 of the Captain Marvel story essentially as they appeared in the first issue of *Whiz Comics*. The balloon dialogue on page thirteen was relettered to tie the story into the end of page seven in *Flash* and *Thrill Comics* to produce a shorter version of the origin story for copyright purposes. Obviously, DC acquired the copyright and Fawcett dropped *Flash* as well as *Thrill* and came out with *Whiz Comics* a month later. Fawcett never used the cover to *Flash* and *Thrill* #1, designing a new cover for *Whiz Comics*. Fawcett also must have discovered that Captain Thunder had already been used by another publisher (Captain Terry Thunder by Fiction House). All references to Captain Thunder were relettered to Captain Marvel before appearing in *Whiz*.

1 (nn on-c, #1 on inside)-Origin & 1st app. Captain Thunder. Cover by C.C. Beck. Eight copies of Flash and three copies of Thrill exist. All 3 copies of Thrill sold in 1986 for between $4,000-$10,000 each. A NM copy of Thrill sold in 1987 for $12,000. A VG copy of Thrill sold in 1987 for $9000 cash. A VF(8.0) copy of Thrill sold in 2003 for $11,400. A CGC certified 9.0 copy of the Flash Comics version sold for $10,117.50 in 2006. A CGC certified 9.0 copy of the Thrill Comics version sold for $8,000 in 2006.

FLASH COMICS (The Flash No. 105 on) (Also see All-Flash)
National Periodical Publ./All-American: Jan, 1940 - No. 104, Feb, 1949

	GD 2.0	VG 4.0	FN 6.0	VF 8.0	VF/NM 9.0	NM- 9.2
1-The Flash (origin/1st app.) by Harry Lampert, Hawkman (origin/1st app.) by Gardner Fox, The Whip, & Johnny Thunder (origin/1st app.) by Stan Asch; Cliff Cornwall by Moldoff, Flash Picture Novelettes (last Minute Movies w/#12) begin; Moldoff (Shelly) cover; 1st app. Shiera Sanders who later becomes Hawkgirl; #24; reprinted in Famous First Edition on sale 11/10/39; The Flash-c	6850	13,700	20,550	51,500	90,750	130,000
1-Reprint, Oversize 13-1/2x10". WARNING: This comic is an exact reprint of the original except for its size. DC published it in 1974 with a second cover titling it as a Famous First Edition. There have been many reported cases of the outer cover being removed and the interior sold as the original edition. The reprint with the new outer cover removed is practically worthless. See Famous First Edition for value.						
2-Rod Rian begins, ends #11; Hawkman-c	771	1542	2313	5397	9449	13,500
3-King Standish begins (1st app.), ends #41 (called The King #16-37,39-41); E.E. Hibbard-a begins on Flash	531	1062	1593	3717	6509	9300
4-Moldoff (Shelly) Hawkman begins; The Whip-c	423	846	1269	2750	4875	7000
5-The King-c	352	704	1056	2288	4044	5800
6-2nd Flash-c (alternates w/Hawkman #6 on)	497	994	1491	3479	6090	8700
7-2nd Hawkman-c; 1st Moldoff Hawkman-c	480	960	1440	3360	5880	8400
8-New logo begins; classic Moldoff Flash-c	300	600	900	1970	3485	5000
9,10: 9-Moldoff Hawkman-c. 10-Classic Moldoff Flash-c	327	654	981	2126	3763	5400
11-13,15-20: 12-Les Watts begins; "Sparks" #16 on. 17-Last Cliff Cornwall	217	434	651	1356	2253	3150
14-World War II cover	255	510	765	1594	2647	3700
21-Classic Hawkman-c	207	414	621	1294	2147	3000
22,23	190	380	570	1188	1969	2750
24-Shiera becomes Hawkgirl (12/41); see All-Star Comics #5 for 1st app.	228	456	684	1425	2363	3300
25-28,30: 28-Last Les Sparks.	122	244	366	763	1269	1775
29-Ghost Patrol begins (origin/1st app.), ends #104	128	256	384	800	1325	1850
31,33-Classic Hawkman-c. 33-Origin Shade	124	248	372	775	1288	1800
32,34-40: 36-1st app. Rag Doll	110	220	330	688	1144	1600
41-50	97	194	291	606	1003	1400
51-61: 52-1st computer in comics, c/s (4/44). 59-Last Minute Movies. 61-Last Moldoff Hawkman	88	176	264	550	913	1275
62-Hawkman by Kubert begins	112	224	336	700	1163	1625
63-85: 66-68-Hop Harrigan in all. 70-Mutt & Jeff app. 80-Atom begins, ends #104	78	156	234	488	807	1125
86-Intro. The Black Canary in Johnny Thunder (8/47); see All-Star #38.	297	594	891	1856	3078	4300
87,88,90: 87-Intro. The Foil. 88-Origin Ghost.	124	248	372	775	1288	1800
89-Intro villain The Thorn	179	358	537	1119	1860	2600
91,93-99: 98-Atom & Hawkman don new costumes	131	262	393	819	1360	1900
92-1st solo Black Canary plus-c; rare in Mint due to black ink smearing on white-c	345	690	1035	2243	3972	5700
100 (10/48),103(Scarce)-52 pgs. each	293	586	879	1831	3041	4250
101,102(Scarce)	252	504	756	1575	2613	3650
104-Origin The Flash retold (Scarce)	657	1314	1971	4599	8050	11,500

NOTE: *Irwin Hasen* a-Wheaties Giveaway. c-97, Wheaties Giveaway. *E.E. Hibbard* c-6, 12, 20, 24, 26, 28, 30, 44, 46, 48, 50, 62, 66, 68, 69, 72, 74, 76, 78, 80, 82. *Infantino* a-86p; 90, 93-95, 99-104; c-90, 92, 93, 97, 99, 101, 103. *Kinstler* a-87, 89(Hawkman); c-87. *Chet Kozlak* c-77, 79, 81. *Krigstein* a-94. *Kubert* a-62-76, 83, 85, 86, 88-104; c-63, 65, 67, 70, 71, 73, 75, 83, 85, 86, 88, 89, 91, 94, 96, 98, 100, 104. *Moldoff* a-3; c-3, 7-11, 13-17, plus odd #'s 19-61. *Martin Naydell* c-52, 54, 56, 58, 60, 64, 84.

FLASH DIGEST, THE (See DC Special Series #24)

FLASH GORDON (See Defenders Of The Earth, Eat Right to Work..., Giant Comic Album, King Classics, King Comics, March of Comics #118, 133, 142, The Phantom #18, Street Comix & Wow Comics, 1st series)

FLASH GORDON
Dell Publishing Co.: No. 25, 1941; No. 10, 1943 - No. 512, Nov, 1953

	GD 2.0	VG 4.0	FN 6.0	VF 8.0	VF/NM 9.0	NM- 9.2
Feature Books 25 (#1)(1941)(1)-r-not by Raymond	121	242	363	756	1253	1750
Four Color 10(1942)-by Alex Raymond; reprints "The Ice Kingdom"	79	158	237	672	1249	1825
Four Color 84(1945)-by Alex Raymond; reprints "The Fiery Desert"	41	82	123	328	589	850
Four Color 173	19	38	57	138	544	350
Four Color 190-Bondage-c; "The Adventures of the Flying Saucers"; 5th Flying Saucer story (6/48)- see The Spirit 9/28/47(1st), Shadow Comics V7#10 (2nd, 1/48), Captain Midnight #60 (3rd, 2/48) & Boy Commandos #26 (4th, 3-4/48)	20	40	60	150	268	385
Four Color 204,247	15	30	45	107	191	275
Four Color 424-Painted-c	11	22	33	77	136	195
2(5-7/53-Dell)-Painted-c; Evans-a?	8	16	24	58	97	135
Four Color 512-Painted-c	8	16	24	58	97	135

FLASH GORDON (See Tiny Tot Funnies)
Harvey Publications: Oct, 1950 - No. 4, April, 1951

	GD 2.0	VG 4.0	FN 6.0	VF 8.0	VF/NM 9.0	NM- 9.2
1-Alex Raymond-a; bondage-c; reprints strips from 7/14/40 to 12/8/40	36	72	108	208	329	450
2-Alex Raymond-a; r/strips 12/15/40-4/27/41	23	46	69	132	209	285
3,4-Alex Raymond-a; 3-bondage-c; r/strips 5/4/41-9/21/41. 4-r/strips 10/24/37-3/27/38	21	42	63	122	191	260
5-(Rare)-Small size-5-1/2x8-1/2"; B&W; 32 pgs.; Distributed to some mail subscribers only	59	118	177	369	610	850
(Also see All-New No. 15, Boy Explorers No. 2, and Stuntman No. 3)						

FLASH GORDON
Gold Key: Jan, 1965

	GD 2.0	VG 4.0	FN 6.0	VF 8.0	VF/NM 9.0	NM- 9.2
1 (1947 reprint)-Painted-c	6	12	18	39	62	85

FLASH GORDON (Also see Comics Reading Libraries in the Promotional Comics section)
King #1-11/Charlton #12-18/Gold Key #19-23/Whitman #28 on:
9/66 - #11, 12/67; #12, 2/69 - #18, 1/70; #19, 9/78 - #37, 3/82 (Painted covers Nos. 19-30, 34)

	GD 2.0	VG 4.0	FN 6.0	VF 8.0	VF/NM 9.0	NM- 9.2
1-1st S.A. app Flash Gordon; Williamson c/a(2); E.C. swipe/Incredible S.F. #32; Mandrake story	7	14	21	47	76	105
1-Army giveaway(1968)("Complimentary" on cover)(Same as regular #1 minus Mandrake story & back-c)	4	8	12	26	41	55
2-8: 2-Bolle, Gil Kane-c; Mandrake story. 3-Williamson-a. 4-Secret Agent X-9 begins, Williamson-c/a(3). 5-Williamson-c/a(2). 6,8-Crandall-a. 7-Raboy-a (last in comics?).	4	8	12	22	34	45
8-Secret Agent X-9-r	4	8	12	24	37	50
9-13: 9,10-Raymond-r. 10-Buckler's 1st pro work (11/67). 11-Crandall-a. 12-Crandall-c/a.	4	8	12	22	34	45
13-Jeff Jones-a (15 pgs.)	4	8	12	20	30	40
14,15: 15-Last 12¢ issue	3	6	9	17	25	32
16,17: 17-Brick Bradford story	3	6	9	15	21	26
18-Kaluta-a (3rd pro work?)(see Teen Confessions #18)	3	6	9	18	27	35
19(9/78, G.K.), 20-26	1	3	4	6	8	10
27-29,34-37: 34-37-Movie adaptation	2	4	6	8	10	12
30 (10/80)-(scarce)	3	6	9	16	23	30
30 (7/81; re-issue), 31-33-single issues	2	4	6	8	10	12
31-33 (Bagged 3-pack): Movie adaptation; Williamson-a.						36.00

NOTE: *Aparo* a-8. *Bolle* a-21, 22. *Boyette* a-14-18. *Briggs* c-10. *Buckler* a-10. *Crandall* c-6. *Estrada* a-3. *Gene Fawcette* a-29, 30, 34, 37. *McWilliams* a-31-33, 36.

FLASH GORDON
DC Comics: June, 1988 - No. 9, Holiday, 1988-'89 ($1.25, mini-series)

	GD 2.0	VG 4.0	FN 6.0	VF 8.0	VF/NM 9.0	NM- 9.2
1-9: 1,5-Painted-c						3.00

FLASH GORDON
Marvel Comics: June, 1995 - No. 2, July, 1995 ($2.95, limited series)

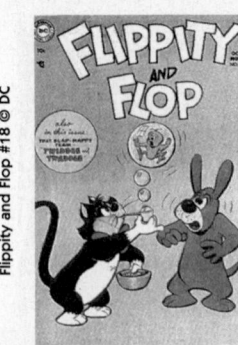

	GD 2.0	VG 4.0	FN 6.0	VF 8.0	VF/NM 9.0	NM- 9.2
1,2: Schultz scripts; Williamson-a						3.00

FLASH GORDON THE MOVIE
Western Publishing Co.: 1980 (8-1/4 x 11", $1.95, 68 pgs.)

	GD 2.0	VG 4.0	FN 6.0	VF 8.0	VF/NM 9.0	NM- 9.2
11294-Williamson-c/a; adapts movie	2	4	6	10	14	18
13743-Hardback edition	3	6	9	15	21	26

FLASH/ GREEN LANTERN: FASTER FRIENDS (See Green Lantern/Flash...)
DC Comics: No. 2, 1997 ($4.95, continuation of Green Lantern/Flash: Faster Friends #1)

2-Waid/Augustyn-s						5.00

FLASHPOINT (Elseworlds Flash)
DC Comics: Dec, 1999 - No. 3, Feb, 2000 ($2.95, limited series)

1-3-Paralyzed Barry Allen; Breyfogle-a/McGreal-s						3.00

FLAT-TOP
Mazie Comics/Harvey Publ.(Magazine Publ.) No. 4 on: 11/53 - No. 3, 5/54; No. 4, 3/55 - No. 7, 9/55

	GD 2.0	VG 4.0	FN 6.0	VF 8.0	VF/NM 9.0	NM- 9.2
1-Teenage; Flat-Top, Mazie, Mortie & Stevie begin	8	16	24	44	57	70
2,3	5	10	15	24	30	35
4-7	5	10	15	22	26	30

FLESH & BLOOD
Brainstorm Comics: Dec, 1995 ($2.95, B&W, mature)

1-Balent-c; foil-c.						3.00

FLESH AND BONES
Upshot Graphics (Fantagraphics Books): June, 1986 - No. 4, Dec, 1986 (Limited series)

1-4: Alan Moore scripts (r) & Dalgoda by Fujitake						3.00

FLESH CRAWLERS
Kitchen Sink Press: Aug, 1993 - No. 3, 1995 ($2.50, B&W, limited series, mature)

1-3						2.50

FLEX MENTALLO (Man of Muscle Mystery) (See Doom Patrol, 2nd Series)
DC Comics (Vertigo): Jun, 1996 - No. 4, Sept, 1996 ($2.50, lim. series, mature)

	GD 2.0	VG 4.0	FN 6.0	VF 8.0	VF/NM 9.0	NM- 9.2
1-4: Grant Morrison scripts & Frank Quitely-c/a in all; banned from reprints due to Charles Atlas legal action	2	4	6	8	11	14

FLINCH (Horror anthology)
DC Comics (Vertigo): Jun, 1999 - No. 16, Jan, 2001 ($2.50)

1-16: 1-Art by Jim Lee, Quitely, and Corben. 5-Sale-c. 11-Timm-a						2.50

FLINTSTONE KIDS, THE (TV) (See Star Comics Digest)
Star Comics/Marvel Comics #5 on: Aug, 1987 - No. 11, Apr, 1989

1-11						4.50

FLINTSTONES, THE (TV)(See Dell Giant #48 for No. 1)
Dell Publ. Co./Gold Key No. 7 (10/62) on: No. 2, Nov-Dec, 1961 - No. 60, Sept, 1970 (Hanna-Barbera)

	GD 2.0	VG 4.0	FN 6.0	VF 8.0	VF/NM 9.0	NM- 9.2
2-2nd app. (TV show debuted on 9/30/60); 1st app. of Cave Kids; 15¢ thru #5	10	20	30	70	123	175
3-6(7-8/62): 3-Perry Gunnite begins. 6-1st 12¢-c	7	14	21	45	73	100
7 (10/62; 1st GK)	7	14	21	45	73	100
8-10	6	12	18	37	59	80
11-1st app. Pebbles (6/63)	8	16	24	58	97	135
12-15,17-20	5	10	15	30	48	65
16-1st app. Bamm-Bamm (1/64)	8	16	24	54	90	125
21-23,25-30,33: 26,27-2nd & 3rd app. The Grusomes. 30-1st app. Martian Mopheads (10/65). 33-Meet Frankenstein & Dracula	4	8	12	28	44	60
24-1st app. The Grusomes	6	12	18	39	62	85
31,32,35-40: 31-Xmas-c. 36-Adaptation of "the Man Called Flintstone" movie. 39-Reprints	4	8	12	24	37	50
34-1st app. The Great Gazoo	6	12	18	39	62	85
41-60: 45-Last 12¢ issue	3	6	9	21	32	42
At N. Y. World's Fair ('64)-J.W. Books (25¢)-1st printing; no date on-c (29¢ version exists, 2nd print?) Most H-B characters app.; including Yogi Bear, Top Cat, Snagglepuss and the Jetsons	5	10	15	35	55	75
At N. Y. World's Fair (1965 on-c; re-issue; Warren Pub.)						
NOTE: Warehouse find in 1984	2	4	6	10	14	18
Bigger & Boulder 1(#30013-211) (Gold Key Giant, 11/62, 25¢, 84 pgs.)	8	16	24	54	90	125
Bigger & Boulder 2-(1966, 25¢)-Reprints B&B No. 1	5	10	15	32	51	70
...On the Rocks (9/61, $1.00, 6-1/4x9", cardboard-c, high quality paper,116 pgs.) B&W new material	9	18	27	63	107	150
...With Pebbles & Bamm Bamm (100 pgs., G.K.)-30028-511 (paper-c, 25¢) (11/65)	8	16	24	54	90	125

NOTE: (See Comic Album #16, Bamm-Bamm & Pebbles Flintstone, Dell Giant 48, Golden Comics Digest, March of

Comics #229, 243, 271, 289, 299, 317, 327, 341, Pebbles Flintstone, Top Comics #2-4, and Whitman Comic Book.)

FLINTSTONES, THE (TV)(...& Pebbles)
Charlton Comics: Nov, 1970 - No. 50, Feb, 1977 (Hanna-Barbera)

	GD 2.0	VG 4.0	FN 6.0	VF 8.0	VF/NM 9.0	NM- 9.2
1	8	16	24	52	86	120
2	4	8	12	28	44	60
3-7,9,10	3	6	9	20	30	40
8- "Flintstones Summer Vacation" (Summer, 1971, 52 pgs.)	5	10	15	35	55	75
11-20,36: 36-Mike Zeck illos (early work)	3	6	9	16	23	30
21-35,38-41,43-45	3	6	9	14	19	24
37-Byrne text illos (early work; see Nightmare #20)	3	6	9	16	23	30
42-Byrne-a (2 pgs.)	3	6	9	16	23	30
46-50	2	4	6	13	18	22
Digest nn (1972, B&W, 100 pgs.) (low print run)	3	6	9	20	30	40

(Also see Barney & Betty Rubble, Dino, The Great Gazoo, & Pebbles & Bamm-Bamm)

FLINTSTONES, THE (TV)(See Yogi Bear, 3rd series) (Newsstand sales only)
Marvel Comics Group: October, 1977 - No. 9, Feb, 1979 (Hanna-Barbera)

	GD 2.0	VG 4.0	FN 6.0	VF 8.0	VF/NM 9.0	NM- 9.2
1,7-9: 1-(30¢-c). 7-9-Yogi Bear app.	3	6	9	20	30	40
1-(35¢-c variant, limited distribution)	9	18	27	60	100	140
2,3,5,6: Yogi Bear app.	3	6	9	16	22	28
4-The Jetsons app.	3	6	9	17	25	32

FLINTSTONES, THE (TV)
Harvey Comics: Sept, 1992 - No. 13, Jun, 1994 ($1.25/$1.50) (Hanna-Barbera)

V2#1-13						3.00
...Big Book 1,2 (11/92, 3/93; both $1.95, 52 pgs.)						3.50
...Giant Size 1-3 (10/92, 4/93, 11/93; $2.25, 68 pgs.)						3.50

FLINTSTONES, THE (TV)
Archie Publications: Sept, 1995 - No. 22, June, 1997 ($1.50)

1-22						3.00

FLINTSTONES AND THE JETSONS, THE (TV)
DC Comics: Aug, 1997 - No. 21, May, 1999 ($1.75/$1.95/$1.99)

1						6.00
2-21: 19-Bizarro Elroy-c						3.00

FLINTSTONES CHRISTMAS PARTY, THE (See The Funtastic World of Hanna-Barbera No. 1)

FLIP
Harvey Publications: April, 1954 - No. 2, June, 1954 (Satire)

	GD 2.0	VG 4.0	FN 6.0	VF 8.0	VF/NM 9.0	NM- 9.2
1,2-Nostrand-a each. 2-Powell-a	22	44	66	128	202	275

FLIPPER (TV)
Gold Key: Apr, 1966 - No. 3, Nov, 1967 (All have photo-c)

	GD 2.0	VG 4.0	FN 6.0	VF 8.0	VF/NM 9.0	NM- 9.2
1	7	14	21	45	73	100
2,3	5	10	15	30	48	65

FLIPPITY & FLOP
National Per. Publ. (Signal Publ. Co.): 12-1/51-52 - No. 46, 8-10/59; No. 47, 9-11/60

	GD 2.0	VG 4.0	FN 6.0	VF 8.0	VF/NM 9.0	NM- 9.2
1-Sam dog & his pets Flippity The Bird and Flop The Cat begin; Twiddle and Twaddle begin	27	54	81	158	249	340
2	15	30	45	84	127	170
3-5	14	28	42	76	108	140
6-10	11	22	33	62	86	110
11-20: 20-Last precode (3/55)	10	20	30	56	76	95
21-47	9	18	27	50	65	80

FLOATERS
Dark Horse Comics: Sept, 1993 - No. 5, Jan, 1994 ($2.50, B&W, lim. series)

1-5						2.50

FLOYD FARLAND (See Eclipse Graphic Album Series #11)

FLY, THE (Also see Adventures of..., Blue Ribbon Comics & Flyman)
Archie Enterprises, Inc.: May, 1983 - No. 9, Oct, 1984

1,2: 1-Mr. Justice app; origin Shield; Kirby-a; Steranko-c. 2-Ditko-a; Flygirl app.						5.00
3-5: Ditko-a in all. 4,5-Ditko-c(p)						4.00
6-9: Ditko-a in all. 6-8-Ditko-c(p)						5.00

NOTE: Ayers c-3. Buckler a-1, 2. Kirby a-1. Nebres c-3, 4, 5i, 6, 7i. Steranko c-1, 2.

FLY, THE
Impact Comics (DC): Aug, 1991 - No. 17, Dec, 1992 ($1.00)

1						3.00
2-17: 4-Vs. The Black Hood. 9-Trading card inside						2.50
Annual 1 ('92, $2.50, 68 pgs.)-Impact trading card						3.00

FLYBOY (Flying Cadets)(Also see Approved Comics #5)

Flying A's Range Rider #18 © DELL

Fly Man #37 © AP

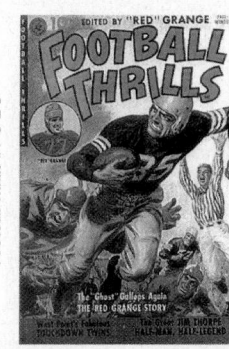

Football Thrills #1 © Z-D

	GD 2.0	VG 4.0	FN 6.0	VF 8.0	VF/NM 9.0	NM- 9.2
Ziff-Davis Publ. Co. (Approved): Spring, 1952 - No. 2, Oct-Nov, 1952						
1-Saunders painted-c	19	38	57	112	176	240
2-(10-11/52)-Saunders painted-c	14	28	42	80	115	150
FLYING ACES (Aviation stories)						
Key Publications: July, 1955 - No. 5, Mar, 1956						
1	8	16	24	40	50	60
2-5: 2-Trapani-a	5	10	15	22	26	30
FLYING A'S RANGE RIDER, THE (TV)(See Western Roundup under Dell Giants)						
Dell Publishing Co.: #404, 6-7/52; #2, June-Aug, 1953 - #24, Aug, 1959 (All photo-c)						
Four Color 404(#1)-Titled "The Range Rider"	10	20	30	71	126	180
2	7	14	21	47	76	105
3-10	6	12	18	39	62	85
11-16,18-24	5	10	15	35	55	75
17-Toth-a	6	12	18	41	66	90
FLYING CADET (WW II Plane Photos)						
Flying Cadet Publ. Co.: Jan, 1943 - V2#8, 1944 (Half photos, half comics)						
V1#1-Painted-c	15	30	45	83	124	165
2	9	18	27	50	65	80
3-9 (Two #6's, Sept. & Oct.): 5,6a,6b-Photo-c	8	16	24	44	57	70
V2#1-7(#10-16)	8	16	24	40	50	60
7(#17 on cover)-Bare-breasted woman-c	18	36	54	103	162	220
FLYING COLORS 10th ANNIVERSARY SPECIAL						
Flying Colors Comics: Fall 1998 ($2.95, one-shot)						
1-Dan Brereton-c; pin-ups by Jim Lee and Jeff Johnson						3.00
FLYIN' JENNY						
Pentagon Publ. Co./Leader Enterprises #2: 1946 - No. 2, 1947 (1945 strip-r)						
nn-Marcus Swayze strip-r (entire insides)	15	30	45	83	124	165
2-Baker-c; Swayze strip reprints	16	32	48	94	147	200
FLYING MODELS						
H-K Publ. (Health-Knowledge Publs.): V61#3, May, 1976 (5¢, 16 pgs.)						
V61#3 (Rare)	9	18	27	50	65	80
FLYING NUN (TV)						
Dell Publishing Co.: Feb, 1968 - No. 4, Nov, 1968						
1-Sally Field photo-c	6	12	18	39	62	85
2-4: 2-Sally Field photo-c	4	8	12	24	37	50
FLYING NURSES (See Sue & Sally Smith…)						
FLYING SAUCERS (See The Spirit 9/28/47(1st app.), Shadow Comics V7#10 (2nd, 1/48), Captain Midnight #60 (3rd, 2/48), Boy Commandos #26 (4th, 3-4/48) & Flash Gordon Four Color 190 (5th, 6/48))						
FLYING SAUCERS						
Avon Periodicals/Realistic: 1950; 1952; 1953						
1(1950)-Wood-a, 21 pgs.; Fawcette-c	80	160	240	500	830	1160
nn(1952)-Cover altered plus 2 pgs. of Wood-a not in original	46	92	138	281	461	640
nn(1953)-Reprints above	35	70	105	204	322	440
FLYING SAUCERS (Comics)						
Dell Publishing Co.: April, 1967 - No. 4, Nov, 1967; No. 5, Oct, 1969						
1	4	8	12	24	37	50
2-5	3	6	9	18	27	35
FLY MAN (Formerly Adventures of The Fly; Mighty Comics #40 on)						
Mighty Comics Group (Radio Comics) (Archie): No. 32, July, 1965 - No. 39, Sept, 1966 (Also see Mighty Crusaders)						
32,33-Comet, Shield, Black Hood, The Fly & Flygirl x-over. 33-Re-intro Wizard, Hangman (1st S.A. appearances)	5	10	15	35	55	75
34-39: 34-Shield begins. 35-Origin Black Hood. 36-Hangman x-over in Shield; re-intro. & origin of Web (1st S.A. app.). 37-Hangman, Wizard x-over in Flyman; last Shield issue. 38-Web story. 39-Steel Sterling (1st S.A. app.)	4	8	12	24	37	50
FOLLOW THE SUN (TV)						
Dell Publishing Co.: May-July, 1962 - No. 2, Sept-Nov, 1962 (Photo-c)						
01-280-207(No.1)	5	10	15	30	48	65
12-280-211(No.2)	5	10	15	30	48	65
FOODANG						
Continuum Comics: July, 1994 ($1.95, B&W, bi-monthly)						
1						2.50
FOODINI (TV)(The Great…; see Jingle Dingle & Pinhead &…)						
Continental Publ. (Holyoke): March, 1950 - No. 4, Aug, 1950 (All have 52 pgs.)						

	GD 2.0	VG 4.0	FN 6.0	VF 8.0	VF/NM 9.0	NM- 9.2
1-Based on TV puppet show (very early TV comic)	22	44	66	126	198	270
2-Jingle Dingle begins	13	26	39	74	105	135
3,4	10	20	30	56	76	95
FOOEY (Magazine) (Satire)						
Scoff Publishing Co.: Feb, 1961 - No. 4, May, 1961						
1	5	10	15	30	48	65
2-4	3	6	9	20	30	40
FOOFUR (TV)						
Marvel Comics (Star Comics)/Marvel No. 5 on: Aug, 1987 - No. 6, Jun, 1988						
1-6						3.00
FOOLKILLER (Also see The Amazing Spider-Man #225, The Defenders #73, Man-Thing #3 & Omega the Unknown #8)						
Marvel Comics: Oct, 1990 - No. 10, Oct, 1991 ($1.75, limited series)						
1-10: 1-Origin 3rd Foolkiller; Greg Salinger app; DeZuniga-a(i) in 1-4. 8-Spider-Man x-over						2.50
FOOM (Friends Of Ol' Marvel)						
Marvel Comics: 1973 - No. 22, 1979 (Marvel fan magazine)						
1	7	14	21	45	73	100
2-Hulk-c by Steranko	5	10	15	30	48	65
3,4	4	8	12	28	44	60
5-11: 11-Kirby-a and interview	4	8	12	24	37	50
12-15: 12-Vision-c. 13-Daredevil-c. 14-Conan. 15-Howard the Duck	4	8	12	24	37	50
16-20: 16-Marvel bullpen. 17-Stan Lee issue. 19-Defenders	3	6	9	20	30	40
21-Star Wars	4	8	12	22	34	45
22-Spider-Man-c; low print run final issue	5	10	15	35	55	75
FOOTBALL THRILLS (See Tops In Adventure)						
Ziff-Davis Publ. Co.: Fall-Winter, 1951-52 - No. 2, Fall, 1952 (Edited by "Red" Grange)						
1-Powell a(2); Saunders painted-c; Red Grange, Jim Thorpe stories	27	54	81	158	249	340
2-Saunders painted-c	18	36	54	105	165	225
FOOT SOLDIERS, THE						
Dark Horse Comics: Jan, 1996 - No. 4, Apr, 1996 ($2.95, limited series)						
1-4: Krueger story & Avon Oeming-a. in all. 1-Alex Ross-c. 4-John K. Snyder, III-c						3.00
FOOT SOLDIERS, THE (Volume Two)						
Image Comics: Sept, 1997 - No. 5, May, 1998 ($2.95, limited series)						
1-5: 1-Yeowell-a. 2-McDaniel, Hester, Sienkiewicz, Giffen-a						3.00
FOR A NIGHT OF LOVE						
Avon Periodicals						
nn-Two stories adapted from the works of Emile Zola; Astarita, Ravielli-a; Kinstler-c	31	62	93	178	282	385
FORBIDDEN KNOWLEDGE: ADVENTURE BEYOND THE DOORWAY TO SOULS WITH RADICAL DREAMER (Also see Radical Dreamer)						
Mark's Giant Economy Size Comics: 1996 ($3.50, B&W, one-shot, 48 pgs.)						
nn-Max Wrighter app.; Wheatley-c/a/script; painted infinity-c						3.50
FORBIDDEN LOVE						
Quality Comics Group: Mar, 1950 - No. 4, Sept, 1950 (52 pgs.)						
1-(Scarce)-Classic photo-c; Crandall-a	76	152	228	475	788	1100
2-(Scarce)-Classic photo-c	63	126	189	394	652	910
3-(Scarce)-Classic photo-c	40	80	120	240	383	525
4-(Scarce)-Ward/Cuidera-a; photo-c	40	80	120	244	392	540
FORBIDDEN LOVE (See Dark Mansion of...)						
FORBIDDEN PLANET						
Innovation Publishing: May, 1992 - No. 4, 1992 ($2.50, limited series)						
1-4: Adapts movie; painted-c						2.50
FORBIDDEN TALES OF DARK MANSION (Formerly Dark Mansion of Forbidden Love #1-4)						
National Periodical Publ.: No. 5, May-June, 1972 - No. 15, Feb-Mar, 1974						
5-(52 pgs.)	5	10	15	32	51	70
6-15: 13-Kane/Howard-a	3	6	9	16	22	28
NOTE: **N. Adams** c-9. **Alcala** a-9-11, 13. **Chaykin** a-7,15. **Evans** a-14. **Heck** a-5. **Kaluta** a-7i, 8-12; c-7, 8, 13. **G. Kane** a-13. **Kirby** a-6. **Nino** a-8, 12, 15. **Redondo** a-14.						
FORBIDDEN WORLDS						
American Comics Group: 7-8/51 - No. 34, 10-11/54; No. 35, 8/55 - No. 145, 8/67 (No. 1-5: 52 pgs.; No. 6-8: 44 pgs.)						
1-Williamson/Frazetta-a (10 pgs.)	155	310	465	969	1610	2250
2	66	132	198	413	682	950

Forbidden Worlds #136 © ACG

Force Works #11 © MAR

Forever People #4 © DC

	GD 2.0	VG 4.0	FN 6.0	VF 8.0	VF/NM 9.0	NM- 9.2

3-Williamson/Orlando-a (7 pgs.); Wood (2 panels); Frazetta (1 panel)

	67	134	201	419	697	975
4	43	86	129	262	431	600
5-Krenkel/Williamson-a (8 pgs.)	53	106	159	330	548	765
6-Harrison/Williamson-a (8 pgs.)	47	94	141	287	474	660
7,8,10: 7-1st monthly issue	32	64	96	186	293	400
9-A-Bomb explosion story	35	70	105	201	318	435
11-20	21	42	63	124	195	265
21-33: 24-E.C. swipe by Landau	16	32	48	94	147	200
34(10-11/54)(Scarce)(becomes Young Heroes #35 on)-Last pre-code issue;						
A-Bomb explosion story	18	36	54	107	169	230
35(8/55)-Scarce	18	36	54	103	162	220
36-62	13	26	39	72	101	130
63,69,76,78-Williamson-a in all; w/Krenkel #69	13	26	39	74	105	135
64,66-68,70-72,74,75,77,79-85,87-90	10	20	30	56	76	95
65- "There's a New Moon Tonight" listed in #114 as holding 1st record fan mail response						
	13	26	39	74	105	135
73-1st app. Herbie by Ogden Whitney	42	84	126	248	384	520
86-Flying saucer-c by Schaffenberger	11	22	33	62	86	110
91-93,95-100	5	10	15	35	55	75
94-Herbie (2nd app.)	9	18	27	63	107	150
101-109,111-113,115,117-120	4	8	12	28	44	60
110,116-Herbie app. 116-Herbie goes to Hell	6	12	18	43	69	95
114-1st Herbie-c; contains list of editor's top 20 ACG stories						
	8	16	24	54	90	125
121-123	4	8	12	22	34	45
124,126-130: 124-Magic Agent app. 126-Herbie	4	8	12	24	37	50
125-Magic Agent app.; intro. & origin Magicman series, ends #141; Herbie app.						
	5	10	15	35	55	75
131-139: 133-Origin/1st app. Dragonia in Magicman (1-2/66); returns in #138.						
136-Nemesis x-over in Magicman	4	8	12	22	34	45
140-Mark Midnight app. by Ditko	4	8	12	24	37	50
141-145	3	6	9	20	30	40

NOTE: *Buscema* a-75, 79, 81, 82, 140r. *Cameron* a-5. *Disbrow* a-10. *Ditko* a-137p, 138, 140. *Landau* a-24, 27-29, 31-34, 48, 86r, 96, 143-45. *Lazarus* a-18, 23, 24, 57. *Moldoff* a-27, 31, 139r. *Reinman* a-93. *Whitney* a-115, 116, 137; c-40, 46, 57, 60, 68, 78, 79, 90, 93, 94, 100, 102, 103, 106-108, 114, 129.

FORCE, THE (See The Crusaders)

FORCE MAJEURE: PRAIRIE BAY (Also see Wild Stars)
Little Rocket Publications: May, 2002 ($2.95, B&W)

1-Tierney-s/Gil-c/a						3.00

FORCE OF BUDDHA'S PALM THE
Jademan Comics: Aug, 1988 - No. 55, Feb, 1993 ($1.50/$1.95, 68 pgs.)

1,55-Kung Fu stories in all						3.00
2-54						2.50

FORCE WORKS
Marvel Comics: July, 1994 - No. 22, Apr, 1996 ($1.50)

1-($3.95)-Fold-out pop-up-c; Iron Man, Wonder Man, Spider-Woman, U.S. Agent & Scarlet Witch (new costume)						4.00
2-11, 13-22: 13-Spider-Man app.						2.50
5-Blue logo & pink versions. 9-Intro Dreamguard. 13-Avengers app.						
5-Pink logo ($2.95)-polybagged w/ 16pg. Marvel Action Hour Preview & acetate print						3.00
12 ($2.50)-Flip book w/War Machine.						2.50

FORD ROTUNDA CHRISTMAS BOOK (See Christmas at the Rotunda)

FOREIGN INTRIGUES (Formerly Johnny Dynamite; becomes Battlefield Action #16 on)
Charlton Comics: No. 14, 1956 - No. 15, Aug, 1956

14,15-Johnny Dynamite continues	8	16	24	42	54	65

FOREMOST BOYS (See 4Most)

FOREVER AMBER
Image Comics: July, 1999 - Oct, 1999 ($2.95, B&W)

1-4-Don Hudson-s/a						3.00

FOREVER DARLING (Movie)
Dell Publishing Co.: No. 681, Feb, 1956

Four Color 681-w/Lucille Ball & Desi Arnaz; photo-c	11	22	33	79	140	200

FOREVER MAELSTROM
DC Comics: Jan, 2003 - No. 6, Jun, 2003 ($2.95, limited series)

1-6-Chaykin & Tischman-s/Lucas & Barreto-a						3.00

FOREVER PEOPLE, THE
National Periodical Publications: Feb-Mar, 1971 - No. 11, Oct-Nov, 1972 (Fourth World)
(#1-3, 10-11 are 36 pgs.; #4-9 are 52 pgs.)

1-1st app. Forever People; Superman x-over; Kirby-c/a begins; 1st full app. Darkseid (3rd anywhere, 3 weeks before New Gods #1); Darkseid storyline begins, ends #8

(app. in 1-4,6,8; cameos in 5,11)	7	14	21	49	80	110
2-9: 4-G.A. reprints thru #9. 9,10-Deadman app.	4	8	12	26	41	55
10,11	3	6	9	20	30	40
Jack Kirby's Forever People TPB ('99, $14.95, B&W&Grey) r/#1-11 plus cover gallery						15.00

NOTE: *Kirby* c/a(p)-1-11; #4-9 contain Sandman reprints from Adventure #85, 84, 75, 80, 77, 74 in that order.

FOREVER PEOPLE
DC Comics: Feb, 1988 - No. 6, July, 1988 ($1.25, limited series)

1-6						3.00

FORGE
CrossGeneration Comics: Feb, 2002 - No. 13, May, 2003 ($9.95/$11.95/$7.95, TPB)

1-3: Reprints from various CrossGen titles						10.00
4-8-($11.95)						12.00
9-13-($7.95, 8-1/4" x 5-1/2") digest-sized reprints						8.00

FOR GIRLS ONLY
Bernard Baily Enterprises: 11/53 - No. 2, 6/54 (100 pgs., digest size, 25¢)

1-25% comic book, 75% articles, illos, games	15	30	45	83	124	165
2-Eddie Fisher photo & story.	10	20	30	58	79	100

FORGOTTEN FOREST OF OZ, THE (See First Comics Graphic Novel #16)

FORGOTTEN REALMS (Also see Avatar & TSR Worlds)
DC Comics: Sept, 1989 - No. 25, Sept, 1991 ($1.50/$1.75)

1, Annual 1 (1990, $2.95, 68 pgs.)						3.00
2-25: Based on TSR role-playing game. 18-Avatar story						2.50

FORGOTTEN REALMS (Based on Wizards of the Coast game)
Devil's Due Publ.: June, 2005 - No. 3, Aug, 2005 ($4.95)

1-3-Salvatore-s/Seeley-a						5.00
...Exile (11/05 - No. 3, 1/06, $4.95) 1-3-Daab-s/Seeley-a. 1-Flip cover						5.00
The Legend of Drizzt Book II: Exile (2006, $14.95, TPB) r/#1-3						15.00
...Sojourn (3/06 - No. 3, 6/06, $4.95) 1-3-Daab-s/Seeley-a						5.00
...: Streams of Silver (12/06 - No. 3, $5.50) 1-3-Daab-s/Semeiks-a						5.50
...The Crystal Shard (8/06 - No. 3, 12/06, $4.95) 1-3-Daab-s/Semeiks-a						5.00
...The Halfling's Gem (8/07 - No. 3, $5.50) 1-Daab-s/Seeley-a; two covers						5.50

FORLORN RIVER (See Zane Grey Four Color 395)

FOR LOVERS ONLY (Formerly Hollywood Romances)
Charlton Comics: No. 60, Aug, 1971 - No. 87, Nov, 1976

60	3	6	9	20	30	40
61-87: 81-Psychedelic cover	2	4	6	11	16	20

FORMERLY KNOWN AS THE JUSTICE LEAGUE
DC Comics: Sept, 2003 - No. 6, Feb, 2004 ($2.50, limited series)

1-Giffen & DeMatteis-s/Maguire-a; Booster Gold, Blue Beetle, Captain Atom, Mary Marvel, Fire, and Elongated Man app.						3.00
2-6: 3,4-Roulette app. 6-JLA app.						2.50
TPB (2004, $12.95) r/#1-6						13.00

FORT: PROPHET OF THE UNEXPLAINED
Dark Horse Comics: June, 2002 - No. 4, Sept, 2002 ($2.99, B&W, limited series)

1-4-Peter Lenkov-s/Frazer Irving-c/a						3.00
TPB (2003, $9.95) r/#1-4						10.00

FORTUNE AND GLORY
Oni Press: Dec, 1999 - No. 3, Apr, 2000 ($4.95, B&W, limited series)

1-3-Brian Michael Bendis in Hollywood						5.00
TPB ($14.95)						15.00

40 BIG PAGES OF MICKEY MOUSE
Whitman Publ. Co.: No. 945, Jan, 1936 (10-1/4x12-1/2", 44 pgs., cardboard-c)

945-Reprints Mickey Mouse Magazine #1, but with a different cover; ads were eliminated and some illustrated stories had expanded text. The book is 3/4" shorter than Mickey Mouse Mag. #1, but the reprints are same size (Rare)	164	328	492	1025	1663	2300

40 oz. COLLECTED
Image Comics: Nov, 2003 ($9.95, digest-size, B&W)

Vol. 1-Reprints Jim Mahfood's mini-comics plus 20 pgs. new material; Grrl Scouts app.						10.00

FOR YOUR EYES ONLY (See James Bond)

FOUNTAIN, THE (Companion graphic novel to the Darren Aronofsky film)
DC Comics (Vertigo): 2005 ($39.99, hardcover with dust jacket)

1-Darren Aronofsky-s/Kent Williams-a						40.00

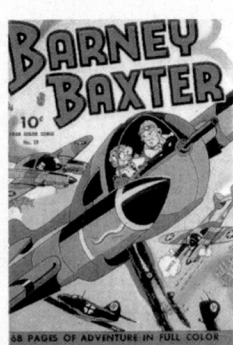
Four Color Comics #20 © KING

Four Color Comics #49 © DIS

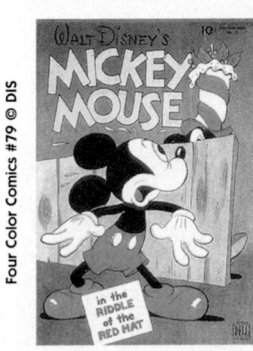
Four Color Comics #79 © DIS

	GD 2.0	VG 4.0	FN 6.0	VF 8.0	VF/NM 9.0	NM- 9.2

FOUR (Fantastic Four; See Marvel Knights 4 #28-30)

FOUR COLOR

Dell Publishing Co.: Sept?, 1939 - No. 1354, Apr-June, 1962
(Series I are all 68 pgs.)

NOTE: Four Color only appears on issues #19-25, 1-99,101. Dell Publishing Co. filed these as Series I, #1-25, and Series II, #1-1354. Issues beginning with #710? were printed with and without ads on back cover. Issues without ads are worth more.

SERIES I:

	GD 2.0	VG 4.0	FN 6.0	VF 8.0	VF/NM 9.0	NM- 9.2
1(nn)-Dick Tracy	857	1714	2571	6000	10,500	15,000
2(nn)-Don Winslow of the Navy (#1) (Rare) (11/39)						
	186	372	558	1163	1932	2700
3(nn)-Myra North (1/40)	95	190	285	594	985	1375
4-Donald Duck by Al Taliaferro (1940)(Disney)(3/40?)						
	1100	2200	3300	8250	14,875	21,500
(Prices vary widely on this book)						
5-Smilin' Jack (#1) (5/40?)	71	142	213	444	735	1025
6-Dick Tracy (Scarce)	207	414	621	1294	2147	3000
7-Gang Busters	48	96	144	293	484	675
8-Dick Tracy	103	206	309	644	1072	1500
9-Terry and the Pirates-r/Super #9-29	67	134	201	419	692	965
10-Smilin' Jack	61	122	183	381	633	885
11-Smitty (#1)	45	90	135	275	450	625
12-Little Orphan Annie; reprints strips from 12/19/37 to 6/4/38						
	57	114	171	356	591	825
13-Walt Disney's Reluctant Dragon('41)-Contains 2 pgs. of photos from film; 2 pg. foreword to Fantasia by Leopold Stokowski; Donald Duck, Goofy, Baby Weems & Mickey Mouse (as the Sorcerer's Apprentice) app. (Disney)	214	428	642	1338	2219	3100
14-Moon Mullins (#1)	45	90	135	275	450	625
15-Tillie the Toiler (#1)	45	90	135	275	455	635
16-Mickey Mouse (#1) (Disney) by Gottfredson	1250	2500	3750	14,500		
17-Walt Disney's Dumbo, the Flying Elephant (#1)(1941)-Mickey Mouse, Donald Duck, & Pluto app. (Disney)	255	510	765	1594	2647	3700
18-Jiggs and Maggie (#1)(1936-38-r)	48	96	144	293	484	675
19-Barney Google and Snuffy Smith (#1)-(1st issue with Four Color on the cover)						
	46	92	138	281	466	650
20-Tiny Tim	37	74	114	213	339	465
21-Dick Tracy	78	156	234	488	807	1125
22-Don Winslow	45	90	135	275	450	625
23-Gang Busters	40	80	120	235	368	500
24-Captain Easy	50	100	150	305	503	700
25-Popeye (1942)	83	166	249	519	860	1200
SERIES II:						
1-Little Joe (1942)	50	100	150	400	725	1050
2-Harold Teen	29	58	87	212	381	550
3-Alley Oop (#1)	43	86	129	344	622	900
4-Smilin' Jack	38	76	114	285	518	750
5-Raggedy Ann and Andy (#1)	45	90	135	360	655	950
6-Smitty	21	42	63	156	278	400
7-Smokey Stover (#1)	28	56	84	227	384	540
8-Tillie the Toiler	23	46	69	169	302	435
9-Donald Duck Finds Pirate Gold, by Carl Barks & Jack Hannah (Disney) (© 8/17/42)	971	1942	2913	6800	11,900	17,000
10-Flash Gordon by Alex Raymond; reprinted from "The Ice Kingdom"						
	79	158	237	672	1249	1825
11-Wash Tubbs	28	56	84	227	384	540
12-Walt Disney's Bambi (#1)	50	100	150	400	725	1050
13-Mr. District Attorney (#1)-See The Funnies #35 for 1st app.						
	27	54	81	203	364	525
14-Smilin' Jack	30	60	90	225	413	600
15-Felix the Cat (#1)	72	144	216	612	1131	1650
16-Porky Pig (#1)(1942)- "Secret of the Haunted House"						
	80	160	240	680	1265	1850
17-Popeye	42	84	126	336	606	875
18-Little Orphan Annie's Junior Commandos; Flag-c; reprints strips from 6/14/42 to 11/21/42						
19-Walt Disney's Thumper Meets the Seven Dwarfs (Disney); reprinted in Silly Symphonies						
	46	92	138	368	672	975
20-Barney Baxter	25	50	75	186	333	480
21-Oswald the Rabbit (#1)(1943)	42	84	126	336	606	875
22-Tillie the Toiler	17	34	51	126	223	320
23-Raggedy Ann and Andy	34	68	102	255	465	675
24-Gang Busters	26	52	78	211	348	485

	GD 2.0	VG 4.0	FN 6.0	VF 8.0	VF/NM 9.0	NM- 9.2
25-Andy Panda (#1) (Walter Lantz)	50	100	150	400	725	1050
26-Popeye	42	84	126	336	606	875
27-Walt Disney's Mickey Mouse and the Seven Colored Terror						
	76	152	228	646	1198	1750
28-Wash Tubbs	19	38	57	141	251	360
29-Donald Duck and the Mummy's Ring, by Carl Barks (Disney) (9/43)						
	686	1372	2058	4800	8400	12,000
30-Bambi's Children (1943)-Disney	44	88	132	352	639	925
31-Moon Mullins	17	34	51	128	227	325
32-Smitty	15	30	45	111	198	285
33-Bugs Bunny "Public Nuisance #1"	96	192	288	816	1508	2200
34-Dick Tracy	40	80	120	300	550	800
35-Smokey Stover	16	32	48	118	209	300
36-Smilin' Jack	22	44	66	160	285	410
37-Bringing Up Father	19	38	57	138	244	350
38-Roy Rogers (#1, © 4/44)-1st western comic with photo-c (see Movie Comics #3)	167	334	501	1461	2731	4000
39-Oswald the Rabbit (1944)	29	58	87	212	381	550
40-Barney Google and Snuffy Smith	21	42	63	156	278	400
41-Mother Goose and Nursery Rhyme Comics (#1)-All by Walt Kelly						
	22	44	66	165	295	425
42-Tiny Tim (1934-r)	16	32	48	118	209	300
43-Popeye (1938-'42-r)	31	62	93	222	404	585
44-Terry and the Pirates (1938-r)	34	68	102	255	465	675
45-Raggedy Ann	29	58	87	216	388	560
46-Felix the Cat and the Haunted Castle	40	80	120	300	550	800
47-Gene Autry (copyright 6/16/44)	41	82	123	326	551	775
48-Porky Pig of the Mounties by Carl Barks (7/44)	87	174	261	740	1370	2000
49-Snow White and the Seven Dwarfs (Disney)	50	100	150	402	731	1060
50-Fairy Tale Parade-Walt Kelly art (1944)	24	48	72	175	313	450
51-Bugs Bunny Finds the Lost Treasure	32	64	96	240	445	650
52-Little Orphan Annie; reprints strips from 6/18/38 to 11/19/38						
	26	52	78	211	348	485
53-Wash Tubbs	14	28	42	102	181	260
54-Andy Panda	29	58	87	212	381	550
55-Tillie the Toiler	13	26	39	97	171	245
56-Dick Tracy	35	70	105	263	482	700
57-Gene Autry	39	78	117	293	497	700
58-Smilin' Jack	22	44	66	160	285	410
59-Mother Goose and Nursery Rhyme Comics-Kelly c/a						
	18	36	54	134	237	340
60-Tiny Folks Funnies	15	30	45	111	198	285
61-Santa Claus Funnies(11/44)-Kelly art	22	44	66	165	295	425
62-Donald Duck in Frozen Gold, by Carl Barks (Disney) (1/45)						
	196	392	588	1715	3208	4700
63-Roy Rogers; color photo-all 4 covers	41	82	123	328	589	850
64-Smokey Stover	13	26	39	93	164	235
65-Smitty	13	26	39	90	160	230
66-Gene Autry	39	78	117	293	497	700
67-Oswald the Rabbit	17	34	51	126	223	320
68-Mother Goose and Nursery Rhyme Comics, by Walt Kelly						
	18	36	54	134	237	340
69-Fairy Tale Parade, by Walt Kelly	24	48	72	175	313	450
70-Popeye and Wimpy	22	44	66	165	295	425
71-Walt Disney's Three Caballeros, by Walt Kelly (© 4/45)-(Disney)						
	62	124	186	310	868	1425
72-Raggedy Ann	24	48	72	179	320	460
73-The Gumps (#1)	12	24	36	82	146	210
74-Marge's Little Lulu (#1)	115	230	345	961	1781	2600
75-Gene Autry and the Wildcat	31	62	93	225	383	540
76-Little Orphan Annie; reprints strips from 2/28/40 to 6/24/40						
	21	42	63	156	278	400
77-Felix the Cat	38	76	114	285	518	750
78-Porky Pig and the Bandit Twins	26	52	78	195	348	500
79-Walt Disney's Mickey Mouse in The Riddle of the Red Hat by Carl Barks (8/45)						
	91	182	273	774	1437	2100
80-Smilin' Jack	14	28	42	103	184	265
81-Moon Mullins	10	20	30	73	129	185
82-Lone Ranger	38	76	114	285	518	750
83-Gene Autry in Outlaw Trail	31	62	93	225	383	540
84-Flash Gordon by Alex Raymond-Reprints from "The Fiery Desert"						
	41	82	123	328	589	850
85-Andy Panda and the Mad Dog Mystery	16	32	48	118	209	300
86-Roy Rogers; photo-c	31	62	93	222	404	585

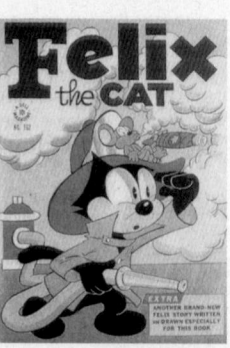

Four Color Comics #125 © Lone Ranger Inc.

Four Color Comics #162 © KING

Four Color Comics #212 © KING

	GD 2.0	VG 4.0	FN 6.0	VF 8.0	VF/NM 9.0	NM- 9.2
87-Fairy Tale Parade by Walt Kelly; Dan Noonan-c	24	48	72	175	313	450
88-Bugs Bunny's Great Adventure (Sci/fi)	22	44	66	164	292	420
89-Tillie the Toiler	13	26	39	97	171	245
90-Christmas with Mother Goose by Walt Kelly (11/45)						
	17	34	51	126	223	320
91-Santa Claus Funnies by Walt Kelly (11/45)	17	34	51	128	227	325
92-Walt Disney's The Wonderful Adventures Of Pinocchio (1945); Donald Duck by Kelly, 16 pgs. (Disney)	50	100	150	406	741	1075
93-Gene Autry In The Bandit of Black Rock	29	58	87	211	348	485
94-Winnie Winkle (1945)	12	24	36	87	156	225
95-Roy Rogers Comics; photo-c	31	62	93	222	404	585
96-Dick Tracy	24	48	72	175	313	450
97-Marge's Little Lulu (1946)	51	102	153	408	742	1075
98-Lone Ranger, The	29	58	87	212	381	550
99-Smitty	10	20	30	73	129	185
100-Gene Autry Comics; 1st Gene Autry photo-c	31	62	93	224	380	535
101-Terry and the Pirates	22	44	66	165	295	425

NOTE: No. 101 is last issue to carry "Four Color" logo on cover; all issues beginning with No. 100 are marked "...O.S." (One Shot) which can be found in the bottom left-hand panel on the first page; the numbers following "O.S." relate to the year/month issued.

	GD 2.0	VG 4.0	FN 6.0	VF 8.0	VF/NM 9.0	NM- 9.2
102-Oswald the Rabbit-Walt Kelly art, 1 pg.	14	28	42	102	181	260
103-Easter with Mother Goose by Walt Kelly	17	34	51	128	227	325
104-Fairy Tale Parade by Walt Kelly	19	38	57	138	244	350
105-Albert the Alligator and Pogo Possum (#1) by Kelly (4/46)	51	102	153	434	805	1175
106-Tillie the Toiler (5/46)	10	20	30	68	119	170
107-Little Orphan Annie; reprints strips from 11/16/42 to 3/24/43	18	36	54	134	237	340
108-Donald Duck in The Terror of the River, by Carl Barks (Disney) (© 4/16/46)	143	286	429	1216	2258	3300
109-Roy Rogers Comics; photo-c	23	46	69	171	306	440
110-Marge's Little Lulu	36	72	108	270	498	725
111-Captain Easy	14	28	42	99	175	250
112-Porky Pig's Adventure in Gopher Gulch	16	32	48	118	209	300
113-Popeye; all new Popeye stories begin	14	28	42	102	181	260
114-Fairy Tale Parade by Walt Kelly	19	38	57	138	244	350
115-Marge's Little Lulu	35	70	105	263	482	700
116-Mickey Mouse and the House of Many Mysteries (Disney)	26	52	78	211	348	485
117-Roy Rogers Comics; photo-c	19	38	57	138	244	350
118-Lone Ranger, The	29	58	87	212	381	550
119-Felix the Cat; all new Felix stories begin	32	64	96	240	445	650
120-Marge's Little Lulu	30	60	90	225	413	600
121-Fairy Tale Parade-(not Kelly)	12	24	36	82	146	210
122-Henry (#1) (10/46)	14	28	42	99	175	250
123-Bugs Bunny's Dangerous Venture	15	30	45	111	198	285
124-Roy Rogers Comics; photo-c	19	38	57	138	244	350
125-Lone Ranger, The	20	40	60	150	268	385
126-Christmas with Mother Goose by Walt Kelly (1946)	13	26	39	93	164	235
127-Popeye	14	28	42	102	181	260
128-Santa Claus Funnies- "Santa & the Angel" by Gollub; "A Mouse in the House" by Kelly	14	28	42	102	181	260
129-Walt Disney's Uncle Remus and His Tales of Brer Rabbit (#1) (1946)-Adapted from Disney movie "Song of the South"	26	52	78	195	348	500
130-Andy Panda (Walter Lantz)	11	22	33	79	140	200
131-Marge's Little Lulu	30	60	90	225	413	600
132-Tillie the Toiler (1947)	10	20	30	68	119	170
133-Dick Tracy	19	38	57	142	254	365
134-Tarzan and the Devil Ogre; Marsh-c/a	52	104	156	442	821	1200
135-Felix the Cat	23	42	69	171	306	440
136-Lone Ranger, The	20	40	60	150	268	385
137-Roy Rogers Comics; photo-c	19	38	57	138	244	350
138-Smitty	9	18	27	64	110	155
139-Marge's Little Lulu (1947)	30	60	90	220	398	575
140-Easter with Mother Goose by Walt Kelly	14	28	42	102	181	260
141-Mickey Mouse and the Submarine Pirates (Disney)	21	42	63	156	278	400
142-Bugs Bunny and the Haunted Mountain	15	30	45	111	198	285
143-Oswald the Rabbit & the Prehistoric Egg	9	18	27	63	107	150
144-Roy Rogers Comics (1947)-Photo-c	19	38	57	138	244	350
145-Popeye	14	28	42	102	181	260
146-Marge's Little Lulu	30	60	90	220	398	575
147-Donald Duck in Volcano Valley, by Carl Barks (Disney) (5/47)	96	192	288	816	1508	2200

	GD 2.0	VG 4.0	FN 6.0	VF 8.0	VF/NM 9.0	NM- 9.2
148-Albert the Alligator and Pogo Possum by Walt Kelly (5/47)	43	86	129	344	622	900
149-Smilin' Jack	10	20	30	68	119	170
150-Tillie the Toiler (6/47)	9	18	27	63	107	150
151-Lone Ranger, The	17	34	51	128	227	325
152-Little Orphan Annie; reprints strips from 1/2/44 to 5/6/44	12	24	36	87	156	225
153-Roy Rogers Comics; photo-c	17	34	51	124	220	315
154-Walter Lantz Andy Panda	11	22	33	79	140	200
155-Henry (7/47)	9	18	27	65	113	160
156-Porky Pig and the Phantom	12	24	36	82	146	210
157-Mickey Mouse & the Beanstalk (Disney)	21	42	63	156	278	400
158-Marge's Little Lulu	30	60	90	220	398	575
159-Donald Duck in the Ghost of the Grotto, by Carl Barks (Disney) (8/47)	85	170	255	723	1337	1950
160-Roy Rogers Comics; photo-c	17	34	51	124	220	315
161-Tarzan and the Fires Of Tohr; Marsh-c/a	48	96	144	384	692	1000
162-Felix the Cat (9/47)	17	34	51	128	227	325
163-Dick Tracy	17	34	51	122	216	310
164-Bugs Bunny Finds the Frozen Kingdom	15	30	45	111	198	285
165-Marge's Little Lulu	30	60	90	220	398	575
166-Roy Rogers Comics (52 pgs.)-Photo-c	17	34	51	124	220	315
167-Lone Ranger, The	17	34	51	128	227	325
168-Popeye (10/47)	14	28	42	102	181	260
169-Woody Woodpecker (#1)- "Manhunter in the North"; drug use story	17	34	51	126	223	320
170-Mickey Mouse on Spook's Island (11/47)(Disney)-reprinted in Mickey Mouse #103	18	36	54	134	237	340
171-Charlie McCarthy (#1) and the Twenty Thieves	24	48	72	175	313	450
172-Christmas with Mother Goose by Walt Kelly (11/47)	13	26	39	93	164	235
173-Flash Gordon	19	38	57	138	244	350
174-Winnie Winkle	8	16	24	58	97	135
175-Santa Claus Funnies by Walt Kelly (1947)	14	28	42	102	181	260
176-Tillie the Toiler (12/47)	9	18	27	63	107	150
177-Roy Rogers Comics (36 pgs.); Photo-c	16	32	48	118	209	300
178-Donald Duck "Christmas on Bear Mountain" by Carl Barks; 1st app. Uncle Scrooge (Disney)(12/47)	115	230	345	978	1814	2650
179-Uncle Wiggily (#1)-Walt Kelly-c	15	30	45	111	198	285
180-Ozark Ike (#1)	10	20	30	67	116	165
181-Walt Disney's Mickey Mouse in Jungle Magic	18	36	54	134	237	340
182-Porky Pig in Ever-Never Land (2/48)	12	24	36	82	146	210
183-Oswald the Rabbit (Lantz)	9	18	27	63	107	150
184-Tillie the Toiler	9	18	27	63	107	150
185-Easter with Mother Goose by Walt Kelly (1948)	13	26	39	93	164	235
186-Walt Disney's Bambi (4/48)-Reprinted as Movie Classic Bambi #3 (1956)	16	32	48	118	209	300
187-Bugs Bunny and the Dreadful Dragon	11	22	33	80	143	205
188-Woody Woodpecker (Lantz, 5/48)	11	22	33	79	140	200
189-Donald Duck in The Old Castle's Secret, by Carl Barks (Disney) (6/48)	72	144	216	612	1131	1650
190-Flash Gordon (6/48); bondage-c; "The Adventures of the Flying Saucers" story- see The Spirit 9/28/47(1st), Shadow Comics V7#10 (2nd, 1/48), Captain Midnight #60 (3rd, 2/48) & Boy Commandos #26 (4th, 3-4/48)	20	40	60	150	268	385
191-Porky Pig to the Rescue	12	24	36	82	146	210
192-The Brownies (#1)-by Walt Kelly (7/48)	14	28	42	99	175	250
193-M.G.M. Presents Tom and Jerry (#1)(1948)	22	44	66	165	295	425
194-Mickey Mouse in The World Under the Sea (Disney)-Reprinted in Mickey Mouse #101	18	36	54	134	237	340
195-Tillie the Toiler	7	14	21	50	83	115
196-Charlie McCarthy in The Haunted Hide-Out; part photo-c	16	32	48	114	202	290
197-Spirit of the Border (#1) (Zane Grey) (1948)	11	22	33	79	140	200
198-Andy Panda	11	22	33	79	140	200
199-Donald Duck in Sheriff of Bullet Valley, by Carl Barks; Barks draws himself on wanted poster, last page; used in Love & Death (Disney) (10/48)	78	156	234	663	1232	1800
200-Bugs Bunny, Super Sleuth (10/48)	11	22	33	80	143	205
201-Christmas with Mother Goose by W. Kelly	11	22	33	79	140	200
202-Woody Woodpecker	8	16	24	58	97	135
203-Donald Duck in the Golden Christmas Tree, by Carl Barks (Disney) (12/48)	54	108	162	459	855	1250

Four Color Comics #260 © WB

Four Color Comics #283 © KING

Four Color Comics #319 © Gene Autry

	GD 2.0	VG 4.0	FN 6.0	VF 8.0	VF/NM 9.0	NM- 9.2
204-Flash Gordon (12/48)	15	30	45	107	191	275
205-Santa Claus Funnies by Walt Kelly	13	26	39	93	164	235
206-Little Orphan Annie; reprints strips from 11/10/40 to 1/11/41	8	16	24	54	90	125
207-King of the Royal Mounted (#1) (12/48)	14	28	42	97	175	250
208-Brer Rabbit Does It Again (Disney) (1/49)	11	22	33	75	133	200
209-Harold Teen	6	12	18	39	62	85
210-Tippie and Cap Stubbs	5	10	15	32	51	70
211-Little Beaver (#1)	8	16	24	56	93	130
212-Dr. Bobbs	6	12	18	37	59	80
213-Tillie the Toiler	7	14	21	50	83	115
214-Mickey Mouse and His Sky Adventure (2/49)(Disney)-Reprinted in Mickey Mouse #105	14	28	42	99	175	250
215-Sparkle Plenty (Dick Tracy-r by Gould)	11	22	33	79	140	200
216-Andy Panda and the Police Pup (Lantz)	8	16	24	56	93	130
217-Bugs Bunny in Court Jester	11	22	33	80	143	205
218-Three Little Pigs and the Wonderful Magic Lamp (Disney) (3/49)(#1)	10	20	30	71	126	180
219-Swee'pe	8	16	24	56	93	130
220-Easter with Mother Goose by Walt Kelly	13	26	39	93	164	235
221-Uncle Wiggily-Walt Kelly cover in part	9	18	27	63	107	150
222-West of the Pecos (Zane Grey)	7	14	21	47	76	105
223-Donald Duck "Lost in the Andes" by Carl Barks (Disney-4/49) (square egg story)	72	144	216	612	1131	1650
224-Little Iodine (#1), by Hatlo (4/49)	11	22	33	79	140	200
225-Oswald the Rabbit (Lantz)	7	14	21	45	73	100
226-Porky Pig and Spoofy, the Spook	10	20	30	67	116	165
227-Seven Dwarfs (Disney)	9	18	27	65	113	160
228-Mark of Zorro, The (#1) (1949)	20	40	60	146	261	375
229-Smokey Stover	6	12	18	41	66	90
230-Sunset Pass (Zane Grey)	7	14	21	47	76	105
231-Mickey Mouse and the Rajah's Treasure (Disney)	14	28	42	99	175	250
232-Woody Woodpecker (Lantz, 6/49)	8	16	24	58	97	135
233-Bugs Bunny, Sleepwalking Sleuth	11	22	33	80	143	205
234-Dumbo in Sky Voyage (Disney)	13	26	39	95	168	240
235-Tiny Tim	6	12	18	37	59	80
236-Heritage of the Desert (Zane Grey) (1949)	7	14	21	47	76	105
237-Tillie the Toiler	7	14	21	50	83	115
238-Donald Duck in Voodoo Hoodoo, by Carl Barks (Disney) (8/49)	54	108	162	459	855	1250
239-Adventure Bound (8/49)	6	12	18	39	62	85
240-Andy Panda (Lantz)	8	16	24	56	93	130
241-Porky Pig, Mighty Hunter	10	20	30	67	116	165
242-Tippie and Cap Stubbs	4	8	12	26	41	55
243-Thumper Follows His Nose (Disney)	11	22	33	79	140	200
244-The Brownies by Walt Kelly	10	20	30	68	119	170
245-Dick's Adventures (9/49)	6	12	18	41	66	90
246-Thunder Mountain (Zane Grey)	5	10	15	32	51	70
247-Flash Gordon	15	30	45	107	191	275
248-Mickey Mouse and the Black Sorcerer (Disney)	14	28	42	99	175	250
249-Woody Woodpecker in the "Globetrotter" (10/49)	8	16	24	58	97	135
250-Bugs Bunny in Diamond Daze; used in SOTI, pg. 309	12	24	36	84	150	215
251-Hubert at Camp Moonbeam	6	12	18	39	62	85
252-Pinocchio (Disney)-not by Kelly; origin	10	20	30	73	129	185
253-Christmas with Mother Goose by W. Kelly	11	22	33	79	140	200
254-Santa Claus Funnies by Walt Kelly; Pogo & Albert story by Kelly (11/49)	13	26	39	93	164	235
255-The Ranger (Zane Grey) (1949)	5	10	15	32	51	70
256-Donald Duck in "Luck of the North" by Carl Barks (Disney) (12/49)-Shows #257 on inside	46	92	138	368	672	975
257-Little Iodine	8	16	24	56	93	130
258-Andy Panda and the Balloon Race (Lantz)	8	16	24	56	93	130
259-Santa and the Angel (Gollub art-condensed from #128) & Santa at the Zoo (12/49) -two books in one	5	10	15	35	55	75
260-Porky Pig, Hero of the Wild West (12/49)	10	20	30	67	116	165
261-Mickey Mouse and the Missing Key (Disney)	14	28	42	99	175	250
262-Raggedy Ann and Andy	10	20	30	67	116	165
263-Donald Duck in "Land of the Totem Poles" by Carl Barks (Disney) (2/50)-Has two Barks stories	45	90	135	360	655	950
264-Woody Woodpecker in the Magic Lantern (Lantz)	8	16	24	58	97	135
265-King of the Royal Mounted (Zane Grey)	8	16	24	58	97	135

	GD 2.0	VG 4.0	FN 6.0	VF 8.0	VF/NM 9.0	NM- 9.2
266-Bugs Bunny on the "Isle of Hercules" (2/50)-Reprinted in Best of Bugs Bunny #1	9	18	27	64	110	155
267-Little Beaver; Harmon-c/a	5	10	15	35	55	75
268-Mickey Mouse's Surprise Visitor (1950)(Disney)	13	26	39	95	168	240
269-Johnny Mack Brown (#1)-Photo-c	22	44	66	160	285	410
270-Drift Fence (Zane Grey) (3/50)	5	10	15	32	51	70
271-Porky Pig in Phantom of the Plains	10	20	30	67	116	165
272-Cinderella (Disney) (4/50)	12	24	36	86	153	220
273-Oswald the Rabbit (Lantz)	7	14	21	45	73	100
274-Bugs Bunny, Hare-brained Reporter	9	18	27	64	110	155
275-Donald Duck in "Ancient Persia" by Carl Barks (Disney) (5/50)	44	88	132	352	639	925
276-Uncle Wiggily	8	16	24	52	86	120
277-Porky Pig in Desert Adventure (5/50)	10	20	30	67	116	165
278-(Wild) Bill Elliott Comics (#1)-Photo-c	13	26	39	90	160	230
279-Mickey Mouse and Pluto Battle the Giant Ants (Disney); reprinted in Mickey Mouse #102 & 245	10	20	30	70	123	175
280-Andy Panda in The Isle Of Mechanical Men (Lantz)	8	16	24	56	93	130
281-Bugs Bunny in The Great Circus Mystery	9	18	27	64	110	155
282-Donald Duck and the Pixilated Parrot by Carl Barks (Disney) (© 5/23/50)	44	88	132	352	639	925
283-King of the Royal Mounted (7/50)	8	16	24	58	97	135
284-Porky Pig in The Kingdom of Nowhere	10	20	30	67	116	165
285-Bozo the Clown & His Minikin Circus (#1) (TV)	18	36	54	134	237	340
286-Mickey Mouse in The Uninvited Guest (Disney)	10	20	30	70	123	175
287-Gene Autry's Champion in The Ghost Of Black Mountain; photo-c	12	24	36	82	146	210
288-Woody Woodpecker in Klondike Gold (Lantz)	8	16	24	58	97	135
289-Bugs Bunny in "Indian Trouble"	9	18	27	64	110	155
290-The Chief (#1) (8/50)	7	14	21	47	76	105
291-Donald Duck in "The Magic Hourglass" by Carl Barks (Disney) (9/50)	44	88	132	352	639	925
292-The Cisco Kid Comics (#1)	22	44	66	164	292	420
293-The Brownies-Kelly-c/a	10	20	30	68	119	170
294-Little Beaver	5	10	15	35	55	75
295-Porky Pig in President Porky (9/50)	10	20	30	67	116	165
296-Mickey Mouse in Private Eye for Hire (Disney)	10	20	30	70	123	175
297-Andy Panda in The Haunted Inn (Lantz, 10/50)	8	16	24	56	93	130
298-Bugs Bunny in Sheik for a Day	9	18	27	64	110	155
299-Buck Jones & the Iron Horse Trail (#1)	13	26	39	93	164	235
300-Donald Duck in "Big-Top Bedlam" by Carl Barks (Disney) (11/50)	44	88	132	352	639	925
301-The Mysterious Rider (Zane Grey)	5	10	15	32	51	70
302-Santa Claus Funnies (11/50)	7	14	21	45	73	100
303-Porky Pig in The Land of the Monstrous Flies	7	14	21	50	83	115
304-Mickey Mouse in Tom-Tom Island (Disney) (12/50)	9	18	27	63	107	150
305-Woody Woodpecker (Lantz)	6	12	18	41	66	90
306-Raggedy Ann	7	14	21	50	83	115
307-Bugs Bunny in Lumber Jack Rabbit	8	16	24	58	97	135
308-Donald Duck in "Dangerous Disguise" by Carl Barks (Disney) (1/51)	41	82	123	334	600	865
309-Betty Betz' Dollface and Her Gang (1951)	5	10	15	35	55	75
310-King of the Royal Mounted (1/51)	6	12	18	43	69	95
311-Porky Pig in Midget Horses of Hidden Valley	7	14	21	50	83	115
312-Tonto (#1)	11	22	33	75	133	190
313-Mickey Mouse in The Mystery of the Double-Cross Ranch (#1) (Disney) (2/51)	9	18	27	63	107	150

Note: Beginning with the above comic in 1951 Dell/Western began adding #1 in small print on the covers of several long running titles with the evident intention of switching these titles to their own monthly numbers, but when the conversions were made, there was no connection. It is thought that the post office may have stepped in and decreed the sequences should commence as though the first four colors printed had each begun with number one, or the first issues sold by subscription. Since the regular series' numbers don't correctly match to the numbers of earlier issues published, it's not known whether or not the numbering was in error.

	GD 2.0	VG 4.0	FN 6.0	VF 8.0	VF/NM 9.0	NM- 9.2
314-Ambush (Zane Grey)	5	10	15	32	51	70
315-Oswald the Rabbit (Lantz)	6	12	18	39	62	85
316-Rex Allen (#1)-Photo-c; Marsh-a	14	28	42	102	181	260
317-Bugs Bunny in Hair Today Gone Tomorrow (#1)	8	16	24	58	97	135
318-Donald Duck in "No Such Varmint" by Carl Barks (#1)-Indicia shows #317 (Disney, © 1/23/51)	41	82	123	334	600	865
319-Gene Autry's Champion; painted-c	7	14	21	45	73	100
320-Uncle Wiggily (#1)	8	16	24	52	86	120

Four Color Comics #335 © David Stern   Four Color Comics #361 © W.E. Grant   Four Color Comics #406 © WB

	GD 2.0	VG 4.0	FN 6.0	VF 8.0	VF/NM 9.0	NM- 9.2
321-Little Scouts (#1) (3/51)	4	8	12	28	44	60
322-Porky Pig in Roaring Rockets (#1 on-c)	7	14	21	50	83	115
323-Susie Q. Smith (#1) (3/51)	5	10	15	32	51	70
324-I Met a Handsome Cowboy (3/51)	8	16	24	56	93	130
325-Mickey Mouse in The Haunted Castle (#2) (Disney) (4/51)	9	18	27	63	107	150
326-Andy Panda (#1) (Lantz)	6	12	18	41	66	90
327-Bugs Bunny and the Rajah's Treasure (#2)	8	16	24	58	97	135
328-Donald Duck in Old California (#2) by Carl Barks-Peyote drug use issue (Disney) (5/51)	41	82	123	328	589	850
329-Roy Roger's Trigger (#1)(5/51)-Painted-c	14	28	42	103	184	265
330-Porky Pig Meets the Bristled Bruiser (#2)	7	14	21	50	83	115
331-Alice in Wonderland (Disney) (1951)	15	30	45	105	188	270
332-Little Beaver	5	10	15	35	55	75
333-Wilderness Trek (Zane Grey) (5/51)	5	10	15	32	51	70
334-Mickey Mouse and Yukon Gold (Disney) (6/51)	9	18	27	63	107	150
335-Francis the Famous Talking Mule (#1, 6/51)-1st Dell non animated movie comic (all issues based on movie)	10	20	30	71	126	180
336-Woody Woodpecker (Lantz)	6	12	18	41	66	90
337-The Brownies-not by Walt Kelly	6	12	18	37	59	80
338-Bugs Bunny and the Rocking Horse Thieves	8	16	24	58	97	135
339-Donald Duck and the Magic Fountain-not by Carl Barks (Disney) (7-8/51)	11	22	33	79	140	200
340-King of the Royal Mounted (7/51)	6	12	18	43	69	95
341-Unbirthday Party with Alice in Wonderland (Disney) (7/51)	15	30	45	105	188	270
342-Porky Pig the Lucky Peppermint Mine; r/in Porky Pig #3	6	12	18	39	62	85
343-Mickey Mouse in The Ruby Eye of Homar-Guy-Am (Disney)-Reprinted in Mickey Mouse #104	8	16	24	54	90	125
344-Sergeant Preston from Challenge of The Yukon (#1) (TV)	12	24	36	82	146	210
345-Andy Panda in Scotland Yard (8-10/51) (Lantz)	6	12	18	41	66	90
346-Hideout (Zane Grey)	5	10	15	32	51	70
347-Bugs Bunny the Frigid Hare (8-9/51)	8	16	24	58	97	135
348-Donald Duck "The Crocodile Collector"; Barks-c only (Disney) (9-10/51)	19	38	57	141	251	360
349-Uncle Wiggily	6	12	18	43	69	95
350-Woody Woodpecker (Lantz)	6	12	18	41	66	90
351-Porky Pig & the Grand Canyon Giant (9-10/51)	6	12	18	39	62	85
352-Mickey Mouse in The Mystery of Painted Valley (Disney)	8	16	24	54	90	125
353-Duck Album (#1)-Barks-c (Disney)	10	20	30	70	123	175
354-Raggedy Ann & Andy	7	14	21	50	83	115
355-Bugs Bunny Hot-Rod Hare	8	16	24	58	97	135
356-Donald Duck in "Rags to Riches"; Barks-c only	19	38	57	141	251	360
357-Comeback (Zane Grey)	4	8	12	28	44	60
358-Andy Panda (Lantz) (11-1/52)	6	12	18	41	66	90
359-Frosty the Snowman (#1)	9	18	27	63	107	150
360-Porky Pig in Tree of Fortune (11-12/51)	6	12	18	39	62	85
361-Santa Claus Funnies	7	14	21	45	73	100
362-Mickey Mouse and the Smuggled Diamonds (Disney)	8	16	24	54	90	125
363-King of the Royal Mounted	6	12	18	39	62	85
364-Woody Woodpecker (Lantz)	5	10	15	35	55	75
365-The Brownies-not by Kelly	6	12	18	37	59	80
366-Bugs Bunny Uncle Buckskin Comes to Town (12-1/52)	8	16	24	58	97	135
367-Donald Duck in "A Christmas for Shacktown" by Carl Barks (Disney) (1-2/52)	32	64	96	240	445	650
368-Bob Clampett's Beany and Cecil (#1)	24	48	72	179	320	460
369-The Lone Ranger's Famous Horse Hi-Yo Silver (#1); Silver's origin	10	20	30	71	126	180
370-Porky Pig in Trouble in the Big Trees	6	12	18	39	62	85
371-Mickey Mouse in The Inca Idol Case (1952) (Disney)	8	16	24	54	90	125
372-Riders of the Purple Sage (Zane Grey)	4	8	12	28	44	60
373-Sergeant Preston (TV)	8	16	24	52	86	120
374-Woody Woodpecker (Lantz)	5	10	15	35	55	75
375-John Carter of Mars (E. R. Burroughs)-Jesse Marsh-a; origin	25	50	75	186	333	480
376-Bugs Bunny, "The Magic Sneeze"	8	16	24	58	97	135
377-Susie Q. Smith	4	8	12	26	41	55
378-Tom Corbett, Space Cadet (#1) (TV)-McWilliams-a						
379-Donald Duck in "Southern Hospitality"; Not by Barks (Disney)	16	32	48	118	209	300
380-Raggedy Ann & Andy	11	22	33	79	140	200
381-Marge's Tubby (#1)	7	14	21	50	83	115
382-Snow White and the Seven Dwarfs (Disney)-origin; partial reprint of Four Color #49 (Movie)	20	40	60	146	261	375
383-Andy Panda (Lantz)	9	18	27	65	113	160
384-King of the Royal Mounted (3/52)(Zane Grey)	5	10	15	32	51	70
385-Porky Pig in The Isle of Missing Ships (3-4/52)	6	12	18	39	62	85
386-Uncle Scrooge (#1)-by Carl Barks (Disney) in "Only a Poor Old Man" (3/52)	152	304	456	1292	2396	3500
387-Mickey Mouse in High Tibet (Disney) (4-5/52)	8	16	24	54	90	125
388-Oswald the Rabbit (Lantz)	6	12	18	39	62	85
389-Andy Hardy Comics (#1)	5	10	15	35	55	75
390-Woody Woodpecker (Lantz)	5	10	15	35	55	75
391-Uncle Wiggily	6	12	18	43	69	95
392-Hi-Yo Silver	6	12	18	41	66	90
393-Bugs Bunny	8	16	24	58	97	135
394-Donald Duck in Malayalaya-Barks-c only (Disney)	19	38	57	141	251	360
395-Forlorn River(Zane Grey)-First Nevada (5/52)	4	8	12	28	44	60
396-Tales of the Texas Rangers(#1)(TV)-Photo-c	10	20	30	73	129	185
397-Sergeant Preston of the Yukon (TV) (5/52)	8	16	24	52	86	120
398-The Brownies-not by Kelly	6	12	18	37	59	80
399-Porky Pig in The Lost Gold Mine	6	12	18	39	62	85
400-Tom Corbett, Space Cadet (TV)-McWilliams-c/a	10	20	30	68	119	170
401-Mickey Mouse and Goofy's Mechanical Wizard (Disney) (6-7/52)	6	12	18	43	69	95
402-Mary Jane and Sniffles	7	14	21	50	83	115
403-Li'l Bad Wolf (Disney) (6/52)(#1)	7	14	21	47	76	105
404-The Range Rider (#1) (Flying A's...)(TV)-Photo-c	10	20	30	71	126	180
405-Woody Woodpecker (Lantz) (6-7/52)	5	10	15	35	55	75
406-Tweety and Sylvester (#1)	10	20	30	71	126	180
407-Bugs Bunny, Foreign-Legion Hare	7	14	21	49	80	110
408-Donald Duck and the Golden Helmet by Carl Barks (Disney) (7-8/52)	32	64	96	240	445	650
409-Andy Panda (7-9/52)	5	10	15	32	51	70
410-Porky Pig in the Water Wizard (7/52)	6	12	18	39	62	85
411-Mickey Mouse and the Old Sea Dog (Disney) (8-9/52)	6	12	18	43	69	95
412-Nevada (Zane Grey)	4	8	12	28	44	60
413-Robin Hood (Disney-Movie) (8/52)-Photo-c (1st Disney movie Four Color book)	9	18	27	65	113	160
414-Bob Clampett's Beany and Cecil (TV)	15	30	45	105	188	270
415-Rootie Kazootie (#1) (TV)	9	18	27	65	113	160
416-Woody Woodpecker (Lantz)	5	10	15	35	55	75
417-Double Trouble with Goober (#1) (8/52)	4	8	12	28	44	60
418-Rusty Riley, a Boy, a Horse, and a Dog (#1)-Frank Godwin-a (strip reprints) (8/52)	5	10	15	32	51	70
419-Sergeant Preston (TV)	8	16	24	52	86	120
420-Bugs Bunny in The Mysterious Buckaroo (8-9/52)	7	14	21	49	80	110
421-Tom Corbett, Space Cadet (TV)-McWilliams-a	10	20	30	71	119	170
422-Donald Duck and the Gilded Man, by Carl Barks (Disney) (9-10/52) (#423 on inside)	32	64	96	240	445	650
423-Rhubarb, Owner of the Brooklyn Ball Club (The Millionaire Cat) (#1)-Painted cover	6	12	18	39	62	85
424-Flash Gordon-Test Flight in Space (9/52)	11	22	33	77	136	195
425-Zorro, the Return of	12	24	36	82	146	210
426-Porky Pig in The Scalawag Leprechaun	6	12	18	39	62	85
427-Mickey Mouse and the Wonderful Whizzix (Disney) (10-11/52)-Reprinted in Mickey Mouse #100	6	12	18	43	69	95
428-Uncle Wiggily	5	10	15	35	55	75
429-Pluto in "Why Dogs Leave Home" (Disney) (10/52)(#1)	9	18	27	64	110	155
430-Marge's Tubby, the Shadow of a Man-Eater	12	24	36	82	146	210
431-Woody Woodpecker (10/52) (Lantz)	5	10	15	35	55	75
432-Bugs Bunny and the Rabbit Olympics	7	14	21	49	80	110
433-Wildfire (Zane Grey) (11-1/52-53)	4	8	12	28	44	60
434-Rin Tin Tin "In Dark Danger" (#1) (TV) (11/52)-Photo-c	14	28	42	102	181	260
435-Frosty the Snowman (11/52)	6	12	18	37	59	80
436-The Brownies-not by Kelly (11/52)	5	10	15	35	55	75
437-John Carter of Mars (E.R. Burroughs)-Marsh-a	15	30	45	111	198	285

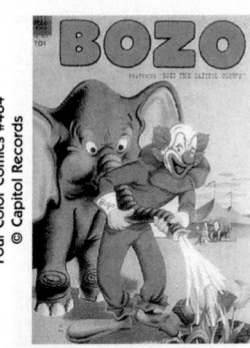

Four Color Comics #464 © Capitol Records

Four Color Comics #517 © DIS

Four Color Comics #534 © DELL

	GD 2.0	VG 4.0	FN 6.0	VF 8.0	VF/NM 9.0	NM- 9.2
438-Annie Oakley (#1) (TV)	14	28	42	103	184	265
439-Little Hiawatha (Disney) (12/52))(#1)	6	12	18	39	62	85
440-Black Beauty (12/52)	5	10	15	30	48	65
441-Fearless Fagan	4	8	12	24	37	50
442-Peter Pan (Disney) (Movie)	10	20	30	70	123	175
443-Ben Bowie and His Mountain Men (#1)	8	16	24	56	93	130
444-Marge's Tubby	12	24	36	82	146	210
445-Charlie McCarthy	6	12	18	39	62	85
446-Captain Hook and Peter Pan (Disney)(Movie)(1/53)	9	18	27	60	100	140
447-Andy Hardy Comics	4	8	12	24	37	50
448-Bob Clampett's Beany and Cecil (TV)	15	30	45	105	188	270
449-Tappan's Burro (Zane Grey) (2-4/53)	4	8	12	28	44	60
450-Duck Album; Barks-c (Disney)	7	14	21	49	80	110
451-Rusty Riley-Frank Godwin-a (strip-r) (2/53)	4	8	12	26	41	50
452-Raggedy Ann & Andy (1953)	7	14	21	50	83	115
453-Susie Q. Smith (2/53)	4	8	12	26	41	55
454-Krazy Kat Comics; not by Herriman	5	10	15	32	51	70
455-Johnny Mack Brown Comics(3/53)-Photo-c	7	14	21	47	76	105
456-Uncle Scrooge Back to the Klondike (#2) by Barks (3/53) (Disney)	78	156	234	663	1232	1800
457-Daffy (#1)	10	20	30	68	119	170
458-Oswald the Rabbit (Lantz)	5	10	15	32	51	70
459-Rootie Kazootie (TV)	7	14	21	47	76	105
460-Buck Jones (4/53)	6	12	18	41	66	90
461-Marge's Tubby	10	20	30	71	126	180
462-Little Scouts	4	8	12	22	34	45
463-Petunia (4/53)	4	8	12	26	41	55
464-Bozo (4/53)	9	18	27	64	110	155
465-Francis the Famous Talking Mule	6	12	18	41	66	90
466-Rhubarb, the Millionaire Cat; painted-c	5	10	15	35	55	75
467-Desert Gold (Zane Grey) (5-7/53)	4	8	12	28	44	60
468-Goofy (#1) (Disney)	12	24	36	82	146	210
469-Beetle Bailey (#1) (5/53)	10	20	30	71	126	180
470-Elmer Fudd	8	16	24	52	86	120
471-Double Trouble with Goober	3	6	9	20	30	40
472-Wild Bill Elliott (6/53)-Photo-c	5	10	15	35	55	75
473-Li'l Bad Wolf (Disney) (6/53)(#2)	5	10	15	32	51	70
474-Mary Jane and Sniffles	7	14	21	47	76	105
475-M.G.M.'s The Two Mouseketeers (#1)	8	16	24	52	86	120
476-Rin Tin Tin (TV)-Photo-c	8	16	24	56	93	130
477-Bob Clampett's Beany and Cecil (TV)	15	30	45	105	188	270
478-Charlie McCarthy	6	12	18	39	62	85
479-Queen of the West Dale Evans (#1)-Photo-c	19	38	57	141	251	360
480-Andy Hardy Comics	4	8	12	24	37	50
481-Annie Oakley And Tagg (TV)	9	18	27	64	110	155
482-Brownies-not by Kelly	5	10	15	35	55	75
483-Little Beaver (7/53)	5	10	15	30	48	65
484-River Feud (Zane Grey) (8-10/53)	4	8	12	28	44	60
485-The Little People-Walt Scott (#1)	8	16	24	52	86	120
486-Rusty Riley-Frank Godwin strip-r	4	8	12	26	41	50
487-Mowgli, the Jungle Book (Rudyard Kipling's)	6	12	18	37	59	80
488-John Carter of Mars (Burroughs)-Marsh-a; painted-c	15	30	45	111	198	285
489-Tweety and Sylvester	6	12	18	41	66	90
490-Jungle Jim (#1)	7	14	21	49	80	110
491-Silvertip (#1) (Max Brand)-Kinstler-a (8/53)	8	16	24	52	86	120
492-Duck Album (Disney)	6	12	18	41	66	90
493-Johnny Mack Brown; photo-c	7	14	21	47	76	105
494-The Little King (#1)	9	18	27	60	100	140
495-Uncle Scrooge (#3) (Disney)-by Carl Barks (9/53)	52	104	156	442	821	1200
496-The Green Hornet; painted-c	23	46	69	171	306	440
497-Zorro (Sword of...)-Kinstler-a	12	24	36	87	156	225
498-Bugs Bunny's Album (9/53)	6	12	18	37	59	80
499-M.G.M.'s Spike and Tyke (#1) (9/53)	6	12	18	41	66	90
500-Buck Jones	6	12	18	41	66	90
501-Francis the Famous Talking Mule	5	10	15	32	51	70
502-Rootie Kazootie (10/53)	7	14	21	47	76	105
503-Uncle Wiggily (10/53)	5	10	15	35	55	75
504-Krazy Kat; not by Herriman	5	10	15	32	51	70
505-The Sword and the Rose (Disney) (10/53)(Movie)-Photo-c	8	16	24	56	93	130
506-The Little Scouts	4	8	12	22	34	45

	GD 2.0	VG 4.0	FN 6.0	VF 8.0	VF/NM 9.0	NM- 9.2
507-Oswald the Rabbit (Lantz)	5	10	15	32	51	70
508-Bozo (10/53)	9	18	27	64	110	155
509-Pluto (Disney) (10/53)	6	12	18	41	66	90
510-Son of Black Beauty	4	8	12	26	41	55
511-Outlaw Trail (Zane Grey)-Kinstler-a	5	10	15	32	51	70
512-Flash Gordon (11/53)	8	16	24	58	97	135
513-Ben Bowie and His Mountain Men	5	10	15	30	48	65
514-Frosty the Snowman (11/53)	6	12	18	37	59	80
515-Andy Hardy	4	8	12	24	37	50
516-Double Trouble With Goober	3	6	9	20	30	40
517-Chip 'N' Dale (#1) (Disney)	10	20	30	70	123	175
518-Rivets (11/53)	4	8	12	24	37	50
519-Steve Canyon (#1)-Not by Milton Caniff	8	16	24	56	93	130
520-Wild Bill Elliott-Photo-c	5	10	15	35	55	75
521-Beetle Bailey (12/53)	6	12	18	41	66	90
522-The Brownies	5	10	15	35	55	75
523-Rin Tin Tin (TV)-Photo-c (12/53)	8	16	24	56	93	130
524-Tweety and Sylvester	6	12	18	41	66	90
525-Santa Claus Funnies	7	14	21	45	73	100
526-Napoleon	4	8	12	24	37	50
527-Charlie McCarthy	6	12	18	39	62	85
528-Queen of the West Dale Evans; photo-c	10	20	30	70	123	175
529-Little Beaver	5	10	15	30	48	65
530-Bob Clampett's Beany and Cecil (TV) (1/54)	15	30	45	105	188	270
531-Duck Album (Disney)	6	12	18	41	66	90
532-The Rustlers (Zane Grey) (2-4/54)	4	8	12	28	44	60
533-Raggedy Ann and Andy	7	14	21	50	83	115
534-Western Marshal(Ernest Haycox's)-Kinstler-a	6	12	18	39	62	85
535-I Love Lucy (#1) (TV) (2/54)-Photo-c	45	90	135	360	655	950
536-Daffy (3/54)	6	12	18	39	62	85
537-Stormy, the Thoroughbred... (Disney-Movie) on top 2/3 of each page; Pluto story on bottom 1/3 of each page (2/54)	5	10	15	30	48	65
538-The Mask of Zorro; Kinstler-a	12	24	36	87	156	225
539-Ben and Me (Disney)	4	8	12	26	41	55
540-Knights of the Round Table (3/54) (Movie)-Photo-c	7	14	21	47	76	105
541-Johnny Mack Brown; photo-c	7	14	21	47	76	105
542-Super Circus Featuring Mary Hartline (TV) (3/54)	7	14	21	47	76	105
543-Uncle Wiggily (3/54)	5	10	15	35	55	75
544-Rob Roy (Disney-Movie)-Manning-a; photo-c	7	14	21	50	83	115
545-The Wonderful Adventures of Pinocchio-Partial reprint of Four Color #92 (Disney-Movie)	7	14	21	47	76	105
546-Buck Jones	6	12	18	41	66	90
547-Francis the Famous Talking Mule	5	10	15	32	51	70
548-Krazy Kat; not by Herriman (4/54)	5	10	15	30	48	65
549-Oswald the Rabbit (Lantz)	5	10	15	32	51	70
550-The Little Scouts	4	8	12	22	34	45
551-Bozo (4/54)	9	18	27	64	110	155
552-Beetle Bailey	6	12	18	41	66	90
553-Susie Q. Smith	4	8	12	26	41	55
554-Rusty Riley (Frank Godwin strip-r)	4	8	12	26	41	50
555-Range War (Zane Grey)	4	8	12	28	44	60
556-Double Trouble With Goober (5/54)	3	6	9	20	30	40
557-Ben Bowie and His Mountain Men	5	10	15	30	48	65
558-Elmer Fudd (5/54)	5	10	15	30	48	65
559-I Love Lucy (#2) (TV)-Photo-c	30	60	90	217	391	565
560-Duck Album (Disney) (5/54)	6	12	18	41	66	90
561-Mr. Magoo (5/54)	10	20	30	68	119	170
562-Goofy (#2)	7	14	21	47	76	105
563-Rhubarb, the Millionaire Cat (6/54)	5	10	15	35	55	75
564-Li'l Bad Wolf (Disney)(#3)	5	10	15	32	51	70
565-Jungle Jim	5	10	15	30	48	65
566-Son of Black Beauty	4	8	12	26	41	55
567-Prince Valiant (#1)-By Bob Fuje (Movie)-Photo-c	10	20	30	73	129	185
568-Gypsy Colt (Movie) (6/54)	5	10	15	32	51	70
569-Priscilla's Pop	4	8	12	26	41	55
570-Bob Clampett's Beany and Cecil (TV)	15	30	45	105	188	270
571-Charlie McCarthy	6	12	18	39	62	85
572-Silvertip (Max Brand) (7/54); Kinstler-a	5	10	15	30	48	65
573-The Little People by Walt Scott	5	10	15	32	51	70
574-The Hand of Zorro; Kinstler-a	12	24	36	87	156	225
575-Annie Oakley and Tagg (TV)-Photo-c	9	18	27	64	110	155

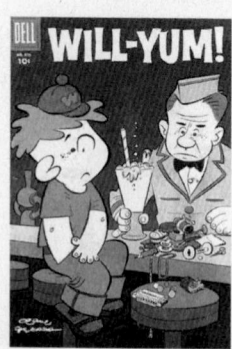

Four Color Comics #639 © DIS

Four Color Comics #641 © Field Ents.

Four Color Comics #676 © DELL

	GD 2.0	VG 4.0	FN 6.0	VF 8.0	VF/NM 9.0	NM- 9.2
576-Angel (#1) (8/54)	4	8	12	24	37	50
577-M.G.M.'s Spike and Tyke	4	8	12	26	41	55
578-Steve Canyon (8/54)	5	10	15	35	55	75
579-Francis the Famous Talking Mule	5	10	15	32	51	70
580-Six Gun Ranch (Luke Short-8/54)	4	8	12	28	44	60
581-Chip 'N' Dale (#2) (Disney)	6	12	18	41	66	90
582-Mowgli Jungle Book (Kipling) (8/54)	5	10	15	30	48	65
583-The Lost Wagon Train (Zane Grey)	4	8	12	28	44	60
584-Johnny Mack Brown-Photo-c	7	14	21	47	76	105
585-Bugs Bunny's Album	6	12	18	37	59	80
586-Duck Album (Disney)	6	12	18	41	66	90
587-The Little Scouts	4	8	12	22	34	45
588-King Richard and the Crusades (Movie) (10/54) Matt Baker-a; photo-c	9	18	27	63	107	150
589-Buck Jones	6	12	18	41	66	90
590-Hansel and Gretel; partial photo-c	6	12	18	43	69	95
591-Western Marshal(Ernest Haycox's)-Kinstler-a	5	10	15	35	55	75
592-Super Circus (TV)	6	12	18	43	69	95
593-Oswald the Rabbit (Lantz)	5	10	15	32	51	70
594-Bozo (10/54)	9	18	27	64	110	155
595-Pluto (Disney)	5	10	15	32	51	70
596-Turok, Son of Stone (#1)	50	100	150	413	757	1100
597-The Little King	5	10	15	35	55	75
598-Captain Davy Jones	5	10	15	30	48	65
599-Ben Bowie and His Mountain Men	5	10	15	30	48	65
600-Daisy Duck's Diary (#1) (Disney) (11/54)	7	14	21	47	76	105
601-Frosty the Snowman	6	12	18	37	59	80
602-Mr. Magoo and Gerald McBoing-Boing	10	20	30	68	119	170
603-M.G.M.'s The Two Mouseketeers	6	12	18	37	59	80
604-Shadow on the Trail (Zane Grey)	4	8	12	28	44	60
605-The Brownies-not by Kelly (12/54)	5	10	15	35	55	75
606-Sir Lancelot (not TV)	7	14	21	49	80	110
607-Santa Claus Funnies	7	14	21	45	73	100
608-Silvertip- "Valley of Vanishing Men" (Max Brand)-Kinstler-a	5	10	15	30	48	65
609-The Littlest Outlaw (Disney-Movie) (1/55)-Photo-c	6	12	18	43	69	95
610-Drum Beat (Movie); Alan Ladd photo-c	8	16	24	56	93	130
611-Duck Album (Disney)	6	12	18	41	66	90
612-Little Beaver (1/55)	5	10	15	30	48	65
613-Western Marshal (Ernest Haycox's) (2/55)-Kinstler-a	5	10	15	35	55	75
614-20,000 Leagues Under the Sea (Disney) (Movie) (2/55)-Painted-c	8	16	24	58	97	135
615-Daffy	6	12	18	39	62	85
616-To the Last Man (Zane Grey)	4	8	12	28	44	60
617-The Quest of Zorro	12	24	36	82	146	210
618-Johnny Mack Brown; photo-c	7	14	21	47	76	105
619-Krazy Kat; not by Herriman	5	10	15	30	48	65
620-Mowgli Jungle Book (Kipling)	5	10	15	30	48	65
621-Francis the Famous Talking Mule (4/55)	4	8	12	28	44	60
622-Beetle Bailey	6	12	18	41	66	90
623-Oswald the Rabbit (Lantz)	4	8	12	28	44	60
624-Treasure Island(Disney-Movie)(4/55)-Photo-c	8	16	24	54	90	125
625-Beaver Valley (Disney-Movie)	6	12	18	41	66	90
626-Ben Bowie and His Mountain Men	5	10	15	30	48	65
627-Goofy (Disney) (5/55)	7	14	21	47	76	105
628-Elmer Fudd	5	10	15	30	48	65
629-Lady and the Tramp with Jock (Disney)	7	14	21	47	76	105
630-Priscilla's Pop	4	8	12	26	41	55
631-Davy Crockett, Indian Fighter (#1) (Disney) (5/55) (TV)-Fess Parker photo-c	17	34	51	126	223	320
632-Fighting Caravans (Zane Grey)	4	8	12	28	44	60
633-The Little People by Walt Scott (6/55)	5	10	15	32	51	70
634-Lady and the Tramp Album (Disney) (6/55)	5	10	15	32	51	70
635-Bob Clampett's Beany and Cecil (TV)	15	30	45	105	188	270
636-Chip 'N' Dale (Disney)	6	12	18	41	66	90
637-Silvertip (Max Brand) Kinstler-a	5	10	15	30	48	65
638-M.G.M.'s Spike and Tyke (8/55)	4	8	12	26	41	55
639-Davy Crockett at the Alamo (Disney) (7/55) (TV)-Fess Parker photo-c	14	28	42	102	181	260
640-Western Marshal(Ernest Haycox's)-Kinstler-a	5	10	15	35	55	75
641-Steve Canyon (1955)-by Caniff	5	10	15	35	55	75
642-M.G.M.'s The Two Mouseketeers	6	12	18	37	59	80

	GD 2.0	VG 4.0	FN 6.0	VF 8.0	VF/NM 9.0	NM- 9.2
643-Wild Bill Elliott; photo-c	5	10	15	30	48	65
644-Sir Walter Raleigh (5/55)-Based on movie "The Virgin Queen"; photo-c	7	14	21	45	73	100
645-Johnny Mack Brown; photo-c	7	14	21	47	76	105
646-Dotty Dripple and Taffy (#1)	5	10	15	32	51	70
647-Bugs Bunny's Album (9/55)	6	12	18	37	59	80
648-Jace Pearson of the Texas Rangers (TV)-Photo-c	6	12	18	41	66	90
649-Duck Album (Disney)	6	12	18	41	66	90
650-Prince Valiant; by Bob Fuje	7	14	21	50	83	115
651-King Colt (Luke Short) (9/55)-Kinstler-a	4	8	12	28	44	60
652-Buck Jones	5	10	15	32	51	70
653-Smokey the Bear (#1) (10/55)	10	20	30	71	126	180
654-Pluto (Disney)	5	10	15	32	51	70
655-Francis the Famous Talking Mule	4	8	12	28	44	60
656-Turok, Son of Stone (#2) (10/55)	30	60	90	225	413	600
657-Ben Bowie and His Mountain Men	5	10	15	30	48	65
658-Goofy (Disney)	7	14	21	47	76	105
659-Daisy Duck's Diary (Disney)(#2)	6	12	18	37	59	80
660-Little Beaver	5	10	15	30	48	65
661-Frosty the Snowman	6	12	18	37	59	80
662-Zoo Parade (TV)-Marlin Perkins (11/55)	5	10	15	32	51	70
663-Winky Dink (TV)	8	16	24	52	86	120
664-Davy Crockett in the Great Keelboat Race (TV) (Disney) (11/55)-Fess Parker photo-c	13	26	39	97	171	245
665-The African Lion (Disney-Movie) (11/55)	6	12	18	37	59	80
666-Santa Claus Funnies	7	14	21	45	73	100
667-Silvertip and the Stolen Stallion (Max Brand) (12/55)-Kinstler-a	5	10	15	30	48	65
668-Dumbo (Disney) (12/55)-First of two printings. Dumbo on cover with starry sky. Reprints 4-Color #234?; same-c as #234	10	20	30	70	123	175
668-Dumbo (Disney) (1/58)-Second printing. Same cover altered, with Timothy Mouse added. Same contents as above	7	14	21	45	73	100
669-Robin Hood (Disney-Movie) (12/55)-Reprints #413 plus-c; photo-c	6	12	18	37	59	80
670-M.G.M.'s Mouse Musketeers (#1) (1/56)-Formerly the Two Mouseketeers	5	10	15	35	55	75
671-Davy Crockett and the River Pirates (TV) (Disney) (12/55)-Jesse Marsh-a; Fess Parker photo-c	13	26	39	97	171	245
672-Quentin Durward (1/56) (Movie)-Photo-c	7	14	21	45	73	100
673-Buffalo Bill, Jr. (#1) (TV)-James Arness photo-c	9	18	27	60	100	140
674-The Little Rascals (#1) (TV)	9	18	27	60	100	140
675-Steve Donovan, Western Marshal (#1) (TV)-Kinstler-a; photo-c	8	16	24	52	86	120
676-Will-Yum!	4	8	12	26	41	55
677-Little King	5	10	15	35	55	75
678-The Last Hunt (Movie)-Photo-c	7	14	21	50	83	115
679-Gunsmoke (#1) (TV)-Photo-c	16	32	48	118	209	300
680-Out Our Way with the Worry Wart (2/56)	4	8	12	24	37	50
681-Forever Darling (Movie) with Lucille Ball & Desi Arnaz (2/56)-; photo-c	11	22	33	79	140	200
682-The Sword & the Rose (Disney-Movie)-Reprint of #505; Renamed When Knighthood Was in Flower for the novel; photo-c	7	14	21	47	76	105
683-Hi and Lois (3/56)	5	10	15	30	48	65
684-Helen of Troy (Movie)-Buscema-a; photo-c	9	18	27	65	113	160
685-Johnny Mack Brown	7	14	21	47	76	105
686-Duck Album (Disney)	6	12	18	41	66	90
687-The Indian Fighter (Movie)-Kirk Douglas photo-c	7	14	21	50	83	115
688-Alexander the Great (Movie) (5/56)-Buscema-a; photo-c	7	14	21	47	80	110
689-Elmer Fudd (3/56)	5	10	15	30	48	65
690-The Conqueror (Movie) - John Wayne photo-c	16	32	48	114	202	290
691-Dotty Dripple and Taffy	4	8	12	28	44	60
692-The Little People-Walt Scott	5	10	15	32	51	70
693-Song of the South (Disney) (1956)-Partial reprint of #129	8	16	24	56	93	130
694-Super Circus (TV)-Photo-c	6	12	18	43	69	95
695-Little Beaver	5	10	15	30	48	65
696-Krazy Kat; not by Herriman (4/56)	5	10	15	30	48	65
697-Oswald the Rabbit (Lantz)	4	8	12	28	44	60
698-Francis the Famous Talking Mule (4/56)	4	8	12	28	44	60
699-Prince Valiant-by Bob Fuje	7	14	21	50	83	115
700-Water Birds and the Olympic Elk (Disney-Movie) (4/56)	5	10	15	35	55	75

Four Color Comics #760 © DIS

Four Color Comics #769 © CBS

Four Color Comics #812 © WB

	GD 2.0	VG 4.0	FN 6.0	VF 8.0	VF/NM 9.0	NM- 9.2
701-Jiminy Cricket (#1) (Disney) (5/56)	8	16	24	56	93	130
702-The Goofy Success Story (Disney)	7	14	21	47	76	105
703-Scamp (#1) (Disney)	8	16	24	58	97	135
704-Priscilla's Pop (5/56)	4	8	12	26	41	55
705-Brave Eagle (#1) (TV)-Photo-c	6	12	18	43	69	95
706-Bongo and Lumpjaw (Disney) (6/56)	6	12	18	37	59	80
707-Corky and White Shadow (5/56)-Mickey Mouse Club (TV); photo-c	7	14	21	47	76	105
708-Smokey the Bear	6	12	18	41	66	90
709-The Searchers (Movie) - John Wayne photo-c	23	46	69	171	306	440
710-Francis the Famous Talking Mule	4	8	12	28	44	60
711-M.G.M's Mouse Musketeers	4	8	12	26	41	55
712-The Great Locomotive Chase (Disney-Movie) (9/56)-Photo-c	7	14	21	47	76	105
713-The Animal World (Movie) (8/56)	4	8	12	26	41	55
714-Spin and Marty (#1) (TV) (Disney)-Mickey Mouse Club (6/56); photo-c	12	24	36	87	156	225
715-Timmy (8/56)	5	10	15	30	48	65
716-Man in Space (Disney)(A science feature from Tomorrowland)	8	16	24	56	93	130
717-Moby Dick (Movie)-Gregory Peck photo-c	8	16	24	56	93	130
718-Dotty Dripple and Taffy	4	8	12	22	34	45
719-Prince Valiant; by Bob Fuje (8/56)	7	14	21	50	83	115
720-Gunsmoke (TV)-James Arness photo-c	9	18	27	61	103	145
721-Captain Kangaroo (TV)-Photo-c	16	32	48	116	206	290
722-Johnny Mack Brown-Photo-c	7	14	21	47	76	105
723-Santiago (Movie)-Kinstler-a (9/56); Alan Ladd photo-c	9	18	27	63	107	150
724-Bugs Bunny's Album	5	10	15	32	51	70
725-Elmer Fudd (9/56)	4	8	12	26	41	55
726-Duck Album (Disney) (9/56)	5	10	15	35	55	75
727-The Nature of Things (TV) (Disney)-Jesse Marsh-a	5	10	15	35	55	75
728-M.G.M's Mouse Musketeers	4	8	12	26	41	55
729-Bob Son of Battle (11/56)	4	8	12	24	37	50
730-Smokey Stover	5	10	15	32	51	70
731-Silvertip and The Fighting Four (Max Brand)-Kinstler-a	5	10	15	30	48	65
732-Zorro, the Challenge of (10/56)	12	24	36	82	146	210
733-Buck Jones	5	10	15	32	51	70
734-Cheyenne (#1) (TV) (10/56)-Clint Walker photo-c	15	30	45	111	198	285
735-Crusader Rabbit (#1) (TV)	26	52	78	195	348	500
736-Pluto (Disney)	5	10	15	32	51	70
737-Steve Canyon-Caniff-a	5	10	15	35	55	75
738-Westward Ho, the Wagons (Disney-Movie)-Fess Parker photo-c	9	18	27	63	107	150
739-Bounty Guns (Luke Short)-Drucker-a	4	8	12	26	41	55
740-Chilly Willy (#1) (Walter Lantz)	7	14	21	45	73	100
741-The Fastest Gun Alive (Movie)(9/56)-Photo-c	8	16	24	51	78	105
742-Buffalo Bill, Jr. (TV)	6	12	18	39	62	85
743-Daisy Duck's Diary (Disney) (11/56)	6	12	18	37	59	80
744-Little Beaver	5	10	15	30	48	65
745-Francis the Famous Talking Mule	4	8	12	28	44	60
746-Dotty Dripple and Taffy	4	8	12	22	34	45
747-Goofy (Disney)	7	14	21	47	76	105
748-Frosty the Snowman (11/56)	5	10	15	32	51	70
749-Secrets of Life (Disney-Movie)-Photo-c	5	10	15	32	51	70
750-The Great Cat Family (Disney-TV/Movie)-Pinocchio & Alice app.	6	12	18	43	69	95
751-Our Miss Brooks (TV)-Photo-c	7	14	21	50	83	115
752-Mandrake, the Magician	10	20	30	70	123	175
753-Walt Scott's Little People (11/56)	5	10	15	32	51	70
754-Smokey the Bear	6	12	18	41	66	90
755-The Littlest Snowman (12/56)	5	10	15	32	51	70
756-Santa Claus Funnies	7	14	21	45	73	100
757-The True Story of Jesse James (Movie)-Photo-c	8	16	24	58	97	135
758-Bear Country (Disney-Movie)	5	10	15	35	55	75
759-Circus Boy (TV)-The Monkees' Mickey Dolenz photo-c (12/56)	12	24	36	86	153	220
760-The Hardy Boys (#1) (TV) (Disney)-Mickey Mouse Club; photo-c	10	20	30	70	123	175
761-Howdy Doody (TV) (1/57)	10	20	30	71	126	180
762-The Sharkfighters (Movie) (1/57); Buscema-a; photo-c	7	14	21	50	83	115
763-Grandma Duck's Farm Friends (#1) (Disney)	8	16	24	52	86	120
764-M.G.M's Mouse Musketeers	4	8	12	26	41	55
765-Will-Yum!	4	8	12	26	41	55
766-Buffalo Bill, Jr. (TV)-Photo-c	6	12	18	39	62	85
767-Spin and Marty (TV) (Disney)-Mickey Mouse Club (2/57)	9	18	27	63	107	150
768-Steve Donovan, Western Marshal (TV)-Kinstler-a; photo-c	6	12	18	43	69	95
769-Gunsmoke (TV)-James Arness photo-c	9	18	27	61	103	145
770-Brave Eagle (TV)-Photo-c	4	8	12	26	41	55
771-Brand of Empire (Luke Short)(3/57)-Drucker-a	4	8	12	26	41	55
772-Cheyenne (TV)-Clint Walker photo-c	9	18	27	60	100	140
773-The Brave One (Movie)-Photo-c	5	10	15	35	55	75
774-Hi and Lois (3/57)	4	8	12	24	37	50
775-Sir Lancelot and Brian (TV)-Buscema-a; photo-c	9	18	27	65	113	160
776-Johnny Mack Brown; photo-c	7	14	21	47	76	105
777-Scamp (Disney) (3/57)	6	12	18	43	69	95
778-The Little Rascals (TV)	6	12	18	39	62	85
779-Lee Hunter, Indian Fighter (3/57)	5	10	15	33	55	75
780-Captain Kangaroo (TV)-Photo-c	13	26	39	93	167	235
781-Fury (#1) (TV) (3/57)-Photo-c	8	16	24	52	86	120
782-Duck Album (Disney)	5	10	15	35	55	75
783-Elmer Fudd	4	8	12	26	41	55
784-Around the World in 80 Days (Movie) (2/57)-Photo-c	7	14	21	50	83	115
785-Circus Boy (TV) (4/57)-The Monkees' Mickey Dolenz photo-c	10	20	30	70	123	175
786-Cinderella (Disney) (3/57)-Partial-r of #272	7	14	21	45	73	100
787-Little Hiawatha (Disney) (4/57)(#2)	5	10	15	30	48	65
788-Prince Valiant; by Bob Fuje	7	14	21	47	76	105
789-Silvertip-Valley Thieves (Max Brand) (4/57)-Kinstler-a	5	10	15	30	48	65
790-The Wings of Eagles (Movie) (John Wayne)-Toth-a; John Wayne photo-c; 10¢ & 15¢ editions exist	14	28	42	100	178	255
791-The 77th Bengal Lancers (TV)-Photo-c	7	14	21	47	76	105
792-Oswald the Rabbit (Lantz)	4	8	12	28	44	60
793-Morty Meekle	4	8	12	22	34	45
794-The Count of Monte Cristo (5/57) (Movie)-Buscema-a	8	16	24	56	93	130
795-Jiminy Cricket (Disney)(#2)	6	12	18	43	69	95
796-Ludwig Bemelman's Madeleine and Genevieve	4	8	12	24	37	50
797-Gunsmoke (TV)-Photo-c	9	18	27	61	103	145
798-Buffalo Bill, Jr. (TV)-Photo-c	6	12	18	39	62	85
799-Priscilla's Pop	4	8	12	26	41	55
800-The Buccaneers (TV)-Photo-c	7	14	21	47	76	105
801-Dotty Dripple and Taffy	4	8	12	22	34	45
802-Goofy (Disney) (5/57)	7	14	21	47	76	105
803-Cheyenne (TV)-Clint Walker photo-c	9	18	27	60	100	140
804-Steve Canyon-Caniff-a (1957)	5	10	15	35	55	75
805-Crusader Rabbit (TV)	20	40	60	148	264	380
806-Scamp (Disney) (6/57)	6	12	18	43	69	95
807-Savage Range (Luke Short)-Drucker-a	4	8	12	26	41	55
808-Spin and Marty (TV)(Disney)-Mickey Mouse Club; photo-c	9	18	27	63	107	150
809-The Little People (Walt Scott)	5	10	15	32	51	70
810-Francis the Famous Talking Mule	4	8	12	26	41	55
811-Howdy Doody (TV) (7/57)	10	20	30	71	126	180
812-The Big Land (Movie); Alan Ladd photo-c	9	18	27	60	100	140
813-Circus Boy (TV)-The Monkees' Mickey Dolenz photo-c	10	20	30	70	123	175
814-Covered Wagons, Ho! (Disney)-Donald Duck (6/57); Mickey Mouse app.	5	10	15	35	55	75
815-Dragoon Wells Massacre (Movie)-photo-c	7	14	21	50	83	115
816-Brave Eagle (TV)-photo-c	4	8	12	26	41	55
817-Little Beaver	5	10	15	30	48	65
818-Smokey the Bear (6/57)	6	12	18	41	66	90
819-Mickey Mouse in Magicland (Disney) (7/57)	6	12	18	37	59	80
820-The Oklahoman (Movie)-Photo-c	8	16	24	58	97	135
821-Wringle Wrangle (Disney)-Based on movie "Westward Ho, the Wagons"; Marsh-a; Fess Parker photo-c	8	16	24	52	86	120
822-Paul Revere's Ride with Johnny Tremain (TV) (Disney)-Toth-a	8	16	24	58	97	135

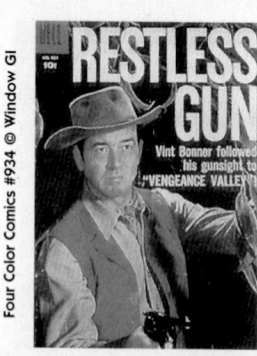
	GD 2.0	VG 4.0	FN 6.0	VF 8.0	VF/NM 9.0	NM- 9.2
823-Timmy	4	8	12	26	41	55
824-The Pride and the Passion (Movie) (8/57)-Frank Sinatra & Cary Grant photo-c	9	18	27	63	107	150
825-The Little Rascals (TV)	6	12	18	39	62	85
826-Spin and Marty and Annette (TV) (Disney)-Mickey Mouse Club; Annette Funicello photo-c	22	44	66	160	285	410
827-Smokey Stover (8/57)	5	10	15	32	51	70
828-Buffalo Bill, Jr. (TV)-Photo-c	6	12	18	39	62	85
829-Tales of the Pony Express (TV) (8/57)-Painted-c	5	10	15	30	48	65
830-The Hardy Boys (TV) (Disney)-Mickey Mouse Club (8/57); photo-c	9	18	27	60	100	140
831-No Sleep 'Til Dawn (Movie)-Karl Malden photo-c	6	12	18	43	69	95
832-Lolly and Pepper (#1)	5	10	15	30	48	65
833-Scamp (Disney) (9/57)	6	12	18	43	69	95
834-Johnny Mack Brown; photo-c	7	14	21	47	76	105
835-Silvertip-The False Rider (Max Brand)	5	10	15	30	48	65
836-Man in Flight (Disney) (TV) (9/57)	7	14	21	47	76	105
837-All-American Athlete Cotton Woods	4	8	12	24	37	50
838-Bugs Bunny's Life Story Album (9/57)	5	10	15	32	51	70
839-The Vigilantes (Movie)	7	14	21	47	76	105
840-Duck Album (Disney) (9/57)	5	10	15	35	55	75
841-Elmer Fudd	4	8	12	26	41	55
842-The Nature of Things (Disney-Movie) ('57)-Jesse Marsh-a (TV series)	5	10	15	35	55	75
843-The First Americans (Disney) (TV)-Marsh-a	8	16	24	56	93	130
844-Gunsmoke (TV)-Photo-c	9	18	27	61	103	145
845-The Land Unknown (Movie)-Alex Toth-a	11	22	33	79	140	200
846-Gun Glory (Movie)-by Alex Toth; photo-c	8	16	24	58	97	135
847-Perri (squirrels) (Disney-Movie)-Two different covers published	5	10	15	35	55	75
848-Marauder's Moon (Luke Short)	4	8	12	26	41	55
849-Prince Valiant; by Bob Fuje	7	14	21	47	76	105
850-Buck Jones	5	10	15	32	51	70
851-The Story of Mankind (Movie) (1/58)-Hedy Lamarr & Vincent Price photo-c	7	14	21	47	76	105
852-Chilly Willy (2/58) (Lantz)	5	10	15	30	48	65
853-Pluto (Disney) (10/57)	5	10	15	32	51	70
854-The Hunchback of Notre Dame (Movie)-Photo-c	12	24	36	87	156	225
855-Broken Arrow (TV)-Photo-c	6	12	18	37	59	80
856-Buffalo Bill, Jr. (TV)-Photo-c	6	12	18	39	62	85
857-The Goofy Adventure Story (Disney) (11/57)	7	14	21	47	76	105
858-Daisy Duck's Diary (Disney) (11/57)	5	10	15	32	51	70
859-Topper and Neil (TV) (11/57)	5	10	15	30	48	65
860-Wyatt Earp (#1) (TV)-Manning-a; photo-c	9	18	27	65	113	160
861-Frosty the Snowman	5	10	15	32	51	70
862-The Truth About Mother Goose (Disney-Movie) (11/57)	7	14	21	49	80	110
863-Francis the Famous Talking Mule	4	8	12	26	41	55
864-The Littlest Snowman	5	10	15	32	51	70
865-Andy Burnett (TV) (Disney) (12/57)-Photo-c	8	16	24	58	97	135
866-Mars and Beyond (Disney-TV)(A science feature from Tomorrowland)	8	16	24	56	93	130
867-Santa Claus Funnies	7	14	21	45	73	100
868-The Little People (12/57)	5	10	15	32	51	70
869-Old Yeller (Disney-Movie)-Photo-c	5	10	15	35	55	75
870-Little Beaver (1/58)	5	10	15	30	48	65
871-Curly Kayoe	4	8	12	24	37	50
872-Captain Kangaroo (TV)-Photo-c	13	26	39	93	167	235
873-Grandma Duck's Farm Friends (Disney)	6	12	18	37	59	80
874-Old Ironsides (Disney-Movie with Johnny Tremain) (1/58)	6	12	18	43	69	95
875-Trumpets West (Luke Short) (2/58)	4	8	12	26	41	55
876-Tales of Wells Fargo (#1)(TV)(2/58)-Photo-c	9	18	27	60	100	140
877-Frontier Doctor with Rex Allen (TV)-Alex Toth-a; Rex Allen photo-c	9	18	27	63	107	150
878-Peanuts (#1)-Schulz-c only (2/58)	19	38	57	138	244	350
879-Brave Eagle (2/58) Photo-c	4	8	12	26	41	55
880-Steve Donovan. Western Marshal-Drucker-a (TV)-Photo-c	5	10	15	30	48	65
881-The Captain and the Kids (2/58)	4	8	12	28	44	60
882-Zorro (Disney)-1st Disney issue; by Alex Toth (2/58); photo-c	15	30	45	107	191	275
883-The Little Rascals (TV)	6	12	18	37	59	80
884-Hawkeye and the Last of the Mohicans (TV) (3/58); photo-c	7	14	21	47	76	105
885-Fury (TV) (3/58)-Photo-c	6	12	18	41	66	90
886-Bongo and Lumpjaw (Disney) (3/58)	5	10	15	30	48	65
887-The Hardy Boys (TV) (Disney)-Mickey Mouse Club (1/58)-Photo-c	9	18	27	60	100	140
888-Elmer Fudd (3/58)	4	8	12	26	41	55
889-Clint and Mac (Disney) (TV) (3/58)-Alex Toth-a; photo-c	11	22	33	79	140	200
890-Wyatt Earp (TV)-by Russ Manning; photo-c	7	14	21	49	80	110
891-Light in the Forest (Disney-Movie) (3/58)-Fess Parker photo-c	7	14	21	50	83	115
892-Maverick (#1) (TV) (4/58)-James Garner photo-c	22	44	66	165	295	425
893-Jim Bowie (TV)-Photo-c	6	12	18	39	62	85
894-Oswald the Rabbit (Lantz)	4	8	12	28	44	60
895-Wagon Train (#1) (TV) (3/58)-Photo-c	10	20	30	71	126	180
896-The Adventures of Tinker Bell (Disney)	8	16	24	56	93	130
897-Jiminy Cricket (Disney)	6	12	18	43	69	95
898-Silvertip (Max Brand)-Kinstler-a (4/58)	5	10	15	30	48	65
899-Goofy (Disney) (5/58)	5	10	15	32	51	70
900-Prince Valiant; by Bob Fuje	7	14	21	47	76	105
901-Little Hiawatha (Disney)	5	10	15	30	48	65
902-Will-Yum!	4	8	12	26	41	55
903-Dotty Dripple and Taffy	4	8	12	22	34	45
904-Lee Hunter, Indian Fighter	4	8	12	26	41	55
905-Annette (Disney) (TV) (5/58)-Mickey Mouse Club; Annette Funicello photo-c	27	54	81	202	361	520
906-Francis the Famous Talking Mule	4	8	12	26	41	55
907-Sugarfoot (#1) (TV)Toth-a; photo-c	12	24	36	84	150	215
908-The Little People and the Giant-Walt Scott (5/58)	5	10	15	32	51	70
909-Smitty	4	8	12	24	37	50
910-The Vikings (Movie)-Buscema-a; Kirk Douglas photo-c	8	16	24	54	90	125
911-The Gray Ghost (TV)-Photo-c	8	16	24	56	93	130
912-Leave It to Beaver (#1) (TV)-Photo-c	16	32	48	114	202	290
913-The Left-Handed Gun (Movie) (7/58); Paul Newman photo-c	9	18	27	63	107	150
914-No Time for Sergeants (Movie)-Andy Griffith photo-c; Toth-a	9	18	27	65	113	160
915-Casey Jones (TV)-Alan Hale photo-c	5	10	15	35	55	75
916-Red Ryder Ranch Comics (7/58)	5	10	15	35	55	75
917-The Life of Riley (TV)-Photo-c	10	20	30	70	123	175
918-Beep Beep, the Roadrunner (#1) (7/58)-Published with two different back covers	10	20	30	71	126	180
919-Boots and Saddles (#1) (TV)-Photo-c	7	14	21	50	83	115
920-Zorro (Disney) (6/58)Toth-a; photo-c	11	22	33	80	143	205
921-Wyatt Earp (TV)-Manning-a; photo-c	7	14	21	49	80	110
922-Johnny Mack Brown by Russ Manning; photo-c	7	14	21	45	73	100
923-Timmy	4	8	12	26	41	55
924-Colt .45 (#1) (TV) (8/58)-W. Preston photo-c	10	20	30	70	123	175
925-Last of the Fast Guns (Movie) (8/58)-Photo-c	7	14	21	47	76	105
926-Peter Pan (Disney)-Reprint of #442	4	8	12	28	44	60
927-Top Gun (Luke Short) Buscema-a	4	8	12	26	41	55
928-Sea Hunt (#1) (9/58) (TV)-Lloyd Bridges photo-c	11	22	33	79	140	200
929-Brave Eagle (TV)-Photo-c	4	8	12	26	41	55
930-Maverick (TV) (7/58)-James Garner photo-c	11	22	33	75	133	190
931-Have Gun, Will Travel (#1) (TV)-Photo-c	13	26	39	95	168	240
932-Smokey the Bear (His Life Story)	6	12	18	41	66	90
933-Zorro (Disney, 9/58) (TV)-Alex Toth-a; photo-c	11	22	33	80	143	205
934-Restless Gun (#1) (TV)-Photo-c	10	20	30	71	126	180
935-King of the Royal Mounted	4	8	12	28	44	60
936-The Little Rascals (TV)	6	12	18	37	59	80
937-Ruff and Reddy (#1) (9/58) (TV) (1st Hanna-Barbera comic book)	12	24	36	84	150	215
938-Elmer Fudd (9/58)	4	8	12	26	41	55
939-Steve Canyon - not by Caniff	5	10	15	35	55	75
940-Lolly and Pepper (10/58)	4	8	12	22	34	45
941-Pluto (10/58)	4	8	12	28	44	60
942-Pony Express (Tales of the ...) (TV)	5	10	15	30	48	65
943-White Wilderness (Disney-Movie) (10/58)	6	12	18	43	69	95
944-The 7th Voyage of Sinbad (Movie) (9/58)-Buscema-a; photo-c	12	24	36	87	156	225
945-Maverick (TV)-James Garner/Jack Kelly photo-c	11	22	33	75	133	190

Four Color Comics #976 © DIS

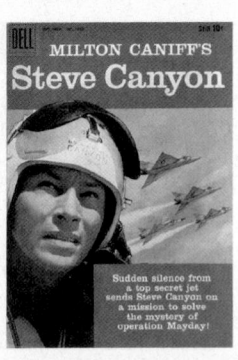

Four Color Comics #1033 © Field Ents.

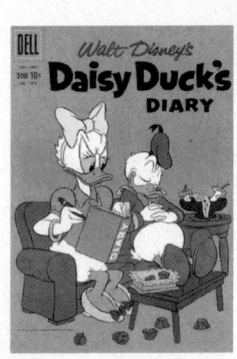

Four Color Comics #1055 © DIS

	GD 2.0	VG 4.0	FN 6.0	VF 8.0	VF/NM 9.0	NM- 9.2
946-The Big Country (Movie)-Photo-c	7	14	21	47	76	105
947-Broken Arrow (TV)-Photo-c (11/58)	5	10	15	32	51	70
948-Daisy Duck's Diary (Disney) (11/58)	5	10	15	32	51	70
949-High Adventure(Lowell Thomas')(TV)-Photo-c	6	12	18	37	59	80
950-Frosty the Snowman	5	10	15	32	51	70
951-The Lennon Sisters Life Story (TV)-Toth-a, 32 pgs.; photo-c						
	13	26	39	95	168	240
952-Goofy (Disney) (11/58)	5	10	15	32	51	70
953-Francis the Famous Talking Mule	4	8	12	26	41	55
954-Man in Space-Satellites (TV)	7	14	21	47	76	105
955-Hi and Lois (11/58)	4	8	12	24	37	50
956-Ricky Nelson #1 (TV)-Photo-c	17	34	51	126	223	320
957-Buffalo Bee (#1) (TV)	8	16	24	58	97	135
958-Santa Claus Funnies	6	12	18	41	66	90
959-Christmas Stories-(Walt Scott's Little People) (1951-56 strip reprints)						
	5	10	15	32	51	70
960-Zorro (Disney) (TV) (12/58)-Toth art; photo-c	11	22	33	80	143	205
961-Jace Pearson's Tales of the Texas Rangers (TV)-Spiegle-a; photo-c						
	6	12	18	37	59	80
962-Maverick (1) (1/59)-James Garner/Jack Kelly photo-c						
	11	22	33	75	133	190
963-Johnny Mack Brown; photo-c	7	14	21	47	76	105
964-The Hardy Boys (TV) (Disney) (1/59)-Mickey Mouse Club; photo-c						
	9	18	27	60	100	140
965-Grandma Duck's Farm Friends (Disney)(1/59)	5	10	15	32	51	70
966-Tonka (starring Sal Mineo; Disney-Movie)-Photo-c						
	8	16	24	58	97	135
967-Chilly Willy (2/59) (Lantz)	5	10	15	30	48	65
968-Tales of Wells Fargo (TV)-Photo-c	8	16	24	56	93	130
969-Peanuts (2/59)	12	24	36	82	146	210
970-Lawman (#1) (TV)-Photo-c	12	24	36	87	156	225
971-Wagon Train (TV)-Photo-c	7	14	21	45	73	100
972-Tom Thumb (Movie)-George Pal (1/59)	8	16	24	58	97	135
973-Sleeping Beauty and the Prince(Disney)(5/59)	10	20	30	71	126	180
974-The Little Rascals (3/59)	6	12	18	37	59	80
975-Fury (TV)-Photo-c	6	12	18	41	66	90
976-Zorro (Disney) (TV)-Toth-a; photo-c	11	22	33	80	143	205
977-Elmer Fudd (3/59)	4	8	12	26	41	55
978-Lolly and Pepper	4	8	12	22	34	45
979-Oswald the Rabbit (Lantz)	4	8	12	28	44	60
980-Maverick (TV) (4-6/59)-James Garner/Jack Kelly photo-c						
	11	22	33	75	133	190
981-Ruff and Reddy (TV) (Hanna-Barbera)	8	16	24	52	86	120
982-The New Adventures of Tinker Bell (TV) (Disney)						
	8	16	24	52	86	120
983-Have Gun, Will Travel (TV) (4-6/59)-Photo-c	9	18	27	60	100	140
984-Sleeping Beauty's Fairy Godmothers (Disney)	8	16	24	58	97	135
985-Shaggy Dog (Disney-Movie)-Photo-all four covers; Annette on back-c(5/59)						
	7	14	21	50	83	115
986-Restless Gun (TV)-Photo-c	8	16	24	52	86	120
987-Goofy (Disney) (7/59)	5	10	15	32	51	70
988-Little Hiawatha (Disney)	6	12	18	30	48	65
989-Jiminy Cricket (Disney) (5-7/59)	6	12	18	43	69	95
990-Huckleberry Hound (#1)(TV)(Hanna-Barbera); 1st app. Huck, Yogi Bear, & Pixie & Dixie & Mr. Jinks	12	24	36	86	153	220
991-Francis the Famous Talking Mule	4	8	12	26	41	55
992-Sugarfoot (TV)-Toth-a; photo-c	11	22	33	77	136	195
993-Jim Bowie (TV)-Photo-c	5	10	15	35	55	75
994-Sea Hunt (TV)-Lloyd Bridges photo-c	8	16	24	54	90	125
995-Donald Duck Album (Disney) (5-7/59)(#1)	6	12	18	43	69	95
996-Nevada (Zane Grey)	4	8	12	28	44	60
997-Walt Disney Presents-Tales of Texas John Slaughter (#1) (TV) (Disney)-Photo-c; photo of W. Disney inside-c	7	14	21	49	80	110
998-Ricky Nelson (TV)	17	34	51	126	223	320
999-Leave It to Beaver (TV)-Photo-c	13	26	39	95	168	240
1000-The Gray Ghost (TV) (6-8/59)-Photo-c	8	16	24	56	93	130
1001-Lowell Thomas' High Adventure (TV) (8-10/59)-Photo-c						
	5	10	15	35	55	75
1002-Buffalo Bee (TV)	7	14	21	45	73	100
1003-Zorro (TV) (Disney)-Toth-a; photo-c	11	22	33	80	143	205
1004-Colt .45 (TV) (6-8/59)-Photo-c	8	16	24	56	93	130
1005-Maverick (TV)-James Garner/Jack Kelly photo-c						
	11	22	33	75	133	190
1006-Hercules (Movie)-Buscema-a; photo-c	9	18	27	60	100	140

	GD 2.0	VG 4.0	FN 6.0	VF 8.0	VF/NM 9.0	NM- 9.2
1007-John Paul Jones (Movie)-Robert Stack photo-c	5	10	15	35	55	75
1008-Beep Beep, the Road Runner (7-9/59)	6	12	18	41	66	90
1009-The Rifleman (#1) (TV)-Photo-c	21	42	63	156	278	400
1010-Grandma Duck's Farm Friends (Disney)-by Carl Barks						
	12	24	36	87	156	225
1011-Buckskin (#1) (TV)-Photo-c	7	14	21	47	76	105
1012-Last Train from Gun Hill (Movie) (7/59)-Photo-c	8	16	24	56	93	130
1013-Bat Masterson (#1) (TV) (8/59)-Gene Barry photo-c						
	11	22	33	79	140	200
1014-The Lennon Sisters (TV)-Toth-a; photo-c	12	24	36	87	156	225
1015-Peanuts-Schulz-c	12	24	36	82	146	210
1016-Smokey the Bear Nature Stories	4	8	12	28	44	60
1017-Chilly Willy (Lantz)	5	10	15	30	48	65
1018-Rio Bravo (Movie)(6/59)-John Wayne; Toth-a; John Wayne, Dean Martin & Ricky Nelson photo-c	22	44	66	160	285	410
1019-Wagon Train (TV)-Photo-c	7	14	21	45	73	100
1020-Jungle Jim-McWilliams-a	4	8	12	26	41	55
1021-Jace Pearson's Tales of the Texas Rangers (TV)-Photo-c						
	6	12	18	37	59	80
1022-Timmy	4	8	12	26	41	55
1023-Tales of Wells Fargo (TV)-Photo-c	8	16	24	56	93	130
1024-Darby O'Gill and the Little People (Disney-Movie)-Toth-a; photo-c						
	9	18	27	65	113	160
1025-Vacation in Disneyland (8-10/59)-Carl Barks-a(24pgs.) (Disney)						
	16	32	48	114	202	290
1026-Spin and Marty (TV) (Disney) (9-11/59)-Mickey Mouse Club; photo-c						
	8	16	24	52	86	120
1027-The Texan (#1)(TV)-Photo-c	8	16	24	56	93	130
1028-Rawhide (#1) (TV) (9-11/59)-Clint Eastwood photo-c; Tufts-a						
	22	44	66	160	285	410
1029-Boots and Saddles (TV) (9/59)-Photo-c	5	10	15	35	55	75
1030-Spanky and Alfalfa, the Little Rascals (TV)	6	12	18	37	59	80
1031-Fury (TV)-Photo-c	6	12	18	41	66	90
1032-Elmer Fudd	4	8	12	26	41	55
1033-Steve Canyon-not by Caniff; photo-c	5	10	15	35	55	75
1034-Nancy and Sluggo Summer Camp (9-11/59)	5	10	15	32	51	70
1035-Lawman (TV)-Photo-c	8	16	24	54	90	125
1036-The Big Circus (Movie)-Photo-c	6	12	18	43	69	95
1037-Zorro (Disney) (TV)-Tufts-a; Annette Funicello photo-c						
	14	28	42	100	178	255
1038-Ruff and Reddy (TV)(Hanna-Barbera)(1959)	8	16	24	52	86	120
1039-Pluto (Disney) (11-1/60)	4	8	12	28	44	60
1040-Quick Draw McGraw (#1) (TV) (Hanna-Barbera) (12-2/60)						
	13	26	39	95	168	240
1041-Sea Hunt (TV) (10-12/59)-Toth-a; Lloyd Bridges photo-c						
	8	16	24	54	90	125
1042-The Three Chipmunks (Alvin, Simon & Theodore) (#1) (TV) (10-12/59)						
	7	14	21	47	76	105
1043-The Three Stooges (#1)-Photo-c	25	50	75	184	330	475
1044-Have Gun, Will Travel (TV)-Photo-c	9	18	27	60	100	140
1045-Restless Gun (TV)-Photo-c	8	16	24	52	86	120
1046-Beep Beep, the Road Runner (11-1/60)	6	12	18	41	66	90
1047-Gyro Gearloose (#1) (Disney)-All Barks-c/a	17	34	51	128	227	325
1048-The Horse Soldiers (Movie) (John Wayne)-Sekowsky-a; painted cover featuring John Wayne	13	26	39	95	168	240
1049-Don't Give Up the Ship (Movie) (8/59)-Jerry Lewis photo-c						
	9	18	27	61	103	145
1050-Huckleberry Hound (TV) (Hanna-Barbera) (10-12/59)						
	8	16	24	56	93	130
1051-Donald in Mathmagic Land (Disney-Movie)	9	18	27	63	107	150
1052-Ben-Hur (Movie) (11/59)-Manning-a	10	20	30	67	116	165
1053-Goofy (Disney) (11-1/60)	5	10	15	32	51	70
1054-Huckleberry Hound Winter Fun (TV) (Hanna-Barbera) (12/59)						
	8	16	24	56	93	130
1055-Daisy Duck's Diary (Disney)-by Carl Barks (11-1/60)						
	9	18	27	60	100	140
1056-Yellowstone Kelly (Movie)-Clint Walker photo-c	6	12	18	37	59	80
1057-Mickey Mouse Album (Disney)	5	10	15	32	51	70
1058-Colt .45 (Movie)-Photo-c	8	16	24	56	93	130
1059-Sugarfoot (TV)-Photo-c	8	16	24	58	97	135
1060-Journey to the Center of the Earth (Movie)-Pat Boone & James Mason photo-c						
	10	20	30	73	129	185
1061-Buffalo Bee (TV)	7	14	21	45	73	100
1062-Christmas Stories (Walt Scott's Little People strip-r)						

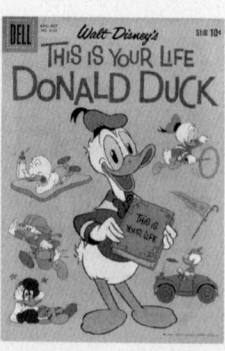

Four Color Comics #1109 © DIS

Four Color Comics #1115 © Ozzie Nelson

Four Color Comics #1170 © DELL

	GD 2.0	VG 4.0	FN 6.0	VF 8.0	VF/NM 9.0	NM- 9.2
1063-Santa Claus Funnies	5	10	15	32	51	70
1064-Bugs Bunny's Merry Christmas (12/59)	6	12	18	41	66	90
1065-Frosty the Snowman	5	10	15	32	51	70
1066-77 Sunset Strip (#1) (TV)-Toth-a (1-3/60)-Efrem Zimbalist, Jr. & Edd "Kookie" Byrnes photo-c	10	20	30	71	126	180
1067-Yogi Bear (#1) (TV) (Hanna-Barbera)	10	20	30	71	126	180
1068-Francis the Famous Talking Mule	4	8	12	26	41	55
1069-The FBI Story (Movie)-Toth-a; James Stewart photo on-c	9	18	27	63	107	150
1070-Solomon and Sheba (Movie)-Sekowsky-a	8	16	24	58	97	135
1071-The Real McCoys (#1) (TV) (1-3/60)-Toth-a; Walter Brennan photo-c	9	18	27	60	100	140
1072-Blythe (Marge's)	5	10	15	35	55	75
1073-Grandma Duck's Farm Friends-Barks-c/a (Disney)	12	24	36	87	156	225
1074-Chilly Willy (Lantz)	5	10	15	30	48	65
1075-Tales of Wells Fargo (TV)-Photo-c	8	16	24	56	93	130
1076-The Rebel (#1) (TV)-Sekowsky-a; photo-c	9	18	27	65	113	160
1077-The Deputy (#1) (TV)-Buscema-a; Henry Fonda photo-c	11	22	33	79	140	200
1078-The Three Stooges (2-4/60)-Photo-c	13	26	39	95	168	240
1079-The Little Rascals (TV) (Spanky & Alfalfa)	6	12	18	37	59	80
1080-Fury (TV) (2-4/60)-Photo-c	6	12	18	41	66	90
1081-Elmer Fudd	4	8	12	26	41	55
1082-Spin and Marty (Disney) (TV)-Photo-c	8	16	24	52	86	120
1083-Men into Space (TV)-Anderson-a; photo-c	5	10	15	35	55	75
1084-Speedy Gonzales	5	10	15	35	55	75
1085-The Time Machine (H.G. Wells) (Movie) (3/60)-Alex Toth-a; Rod Taylor photo-c	14	28	42	100	178	255
1086-Lolly and Pepper	4	8	12	22	34	45
1087-Peter Gunn (TV)-Photo-c	8	16	24	58	97	135
1088-A Dog of Flanders (Movie)-Photo-c	5	10	15	30	48	65
1089-Restless Gun (TV)-Photo-c	8	16	24	52	86	120
1090-Francis the Famous Talking Mule	4	8	12	26	41	55
1091-Jacky's Diary (4-6/60)	5	10	15	30	48	65
1092-Toby Tyler (Disney-Movie)-Photo-c	6	12	18	43	69	95
1093-MacKenzie's Raiders (Movie/TV)-Richard Carlson photo-c from TV show	6	12	18	43	69	95
1094-Goofy (Disney)	5	10	15	32	51	70
1095-Gyro Gearloose (Disney)-All Barks-c/a	9	18	27	65	113	160
1096-The Texan (TV)-Rory Calhoun photo-c	8	16	24	52	86	120
1097-Rawhide (TV)-Manning-a; Clint Eastwood photo-c	14	28	42	102	181	260
1098-Sugarfoot (TV)-Photo-c	8	16	24	58	97	135
1099-Donald Duck Album (Disney) (5-7/60)-Barks-c	7	14	21	45	73	100
1100-Annette's Life Story (Disney-Movie) (5/60)-Annette Funicello photo-c	22	44	66	164	292	420
1101-Robert Louis Stevenson's Kidnapped (Disney-Movie) (5/60); photo-c	6	12	18	43	69	95
1102-Wanted: Dead or Alive (#1) (TV) (5-7/60); Steve McQueen photo-c	12	24	36	87	156	225
1103-Leave It to Beaver (TV)-Photo-c	13	26	39	95	168	240
1104-Yogi Bear Goes to College (TV) (Hanna-Barbera) (6-8/60)	7	14	21	49	80	110
1105-Gale Storm (Oh! Susanna) (TV)-Toth-a; photo-c	11	22	33	77	136	195
1106-77 Sunset Strip(TV)(6-8/60)-Toth-a; photo-c	8	16	24	58	97	135
1107-Buckskin (TV)	6	12	18	43	69	95
1108-The Troubleshooters (TV)-Keenan Wynn photo-c	5	10	15	35	55	75
1109-This Is Your Life, Donald Duck (Disney) (TV) (8-10/60)-Gyro flashback to WDC&S #141; origin Donald Duck (1st told)	14	28	42	102	181	260
1110-Bonanza (#1) (TV) (6-8/60)-Photo-c	31	62	93	233	429	625
1111-Shotgun Slade (TV)-Photo-c	6	12	18	41	66	90
1112-Pixie and Dixie and Mr. Jinks (#1) (TV) (Hanna-Barbera) (7-9/60)	7	14	21	50	83	115
1113-Tales of Wells Fargo (TV)-Photo-c	8	16	24	56	93	130
1114-Huckleberry Finn (Movie) (7/60)-Photo-c	5	10	15	35	55	75
1115-Ricky Nelson (TV)-Manning-a; photo-c	14	28	42	100	178	255
1116-Boots and Saddles (TV) (8/60)-Photo-c	5	10	15	35	55	75
1117-Boy and the Pirates (Movie)-Photo-c	6	12	18	43	69	95
1118-The Sword and the Dragon (Movie) (6/60)-Photo-c						
1119-Smokey the Bear Nature Stories	7	14	21	50	83	115
1120-Dinosaurus (Movie)-Painted-c	4	8	12	28	44	60
1121-Hercules Unchained (Movie) (8/60)-Crandall/Evans-a	8	16	24	56	93	130
1122-Chilly Willy (Lantz)	9	18	27	60	100	140
1123-Tombstone Territory (TV)-Photo-c	5	10	15	30	48	65
1124-Whirlybirds (#1) (TV)-Photo-c	8	16	24	56	93	130
1125-Laramie (#1) (TV)-Photo-c; G. Kane/Heath-a	8	16	24	58	97	135
1126-Hotel Deparee - Sundance (TV) (8-10/60)-Earl Holliman photo-c	6	12	18	43	69	95
1127-The Three Stooges-Photo-c (8-10/60)	13	26	39	95	168	240
1128-Rocky and His Friends (#1) (TV) (Jay Ward) (8-10/60)	29	58	87	212	381	550
1129-Pollyanna (Disney-Movie)-Hayley Mills photo-c	7	14	21	50	83	115
1130-The Deputy (TV)-Buscema-a; Henry Fonda photo-c	9	18	27	63	107	150
1131-Elmer Fudd (9-11/60)	4	8	12	26	41	55
1132-Space Mouse (Lantz) (8-10/60)	4	8	12	28	44	60
1133-Fury (TV)-Photo-c	6	12	18	41	66	90
1134-Real McCoys (TV)-Toth-a; photo-c	9	18	27	60	100	140
1135-M.G.M.'s Mouse Musketeers (9-11/60)	4	8	12	24	37	50
1136-Jungle Cat (Disney-Movie)-Photo-c	6	12	18	43	69	95
1137-The Little Rascals (TV)	6	12	18	37	59	80
1138-The Rebel (TV)-Photo-c	8	16	24	56	93	130
1139-Spartacus (Movie) (11/60)-Buscema-a; Kirk Douglas photo-c	12	24	36	87	156	225
1140-Donald Duck Album (Disney)-Barks-c	7	14	21	45	73	100
1141-Huckleberry Hound for President (TV) (Hanna-Barbera) (10/60)	8	16	24	52	86	120
1142-Johnny Ringo (TV)-Photo-c	7	14	21	47	76	105
1143-Pluto (TV) (11-1/61)	4	8	12	28	44	60
1144-The Story of Ruth (Movie)-Photo-c	8	16	24	58	97	135
1145-The Lost World (Movie)-Gil Kane-a; photo-c; 1 pg. Conan Doyle biography by Torres	9	18	27	64	110	155
1146-Restless Gun (TV)-Photo-c; Wildey-a	8	16	24	52	86	120
1147-Sugarfoot (TV)-Photo-c	8	16	24	58	97	135
1148-I Aim at the Stars-the Wernher Von Braun Story (Movie) (11-1/61)-Photo-c	7	14	21	47	76	105
1149-Goofy (Disney) (11-1/61)	5	10	15	32	51	70
1150-Daisy Duck's Diary (Disney) (12-1/61) by Carl Barks	9	18	27	60	100	140
1151-Mickey Mouse Album (Disney) (11-1/61)	5	10	15	32	51	70
1152-Rocky and His Friends (TV) (Jay Ward) (12-2/61)	19	38	57	138	244	350
1153-Frosty the Snowman	5	10	15	32	51	70
1154-Santa Claus Funnies	6	12	18	41	66	90
1155-North to Alaska (Movie)-John Wayne photo-c (12/60)	16	32	48	114	202	290
1156-Walt Disney Swiss Family Robinson (Movie) (12/60)-Photo-c	7	14	21	49	80	110
1157-Master of the World (Movie) (7/61)	6	12	18	41	66	90
1158-Three Worlds of Gulliver (2 issues exist with different covers) (Movie)-Photo-c	7	14	21	45	73	100
1159- 77 Sunset Strip (TV)-Toth-a; photo-c	8	16	24	58	97	135
1160-Rawhide (TV)-Clint Eastwood photo-c	14	28	42	102	181	260
1161-Grandma Duck's Farm Friends (Disney) by Carl Barks (2-4/61)	12	24	36	87	156	225
1162-Yogi Bear Joins the Marines (TV) (Hanna-Barbera) (5-7/61)	7	14	21	49	80	110
1163-Daniel Boone (3-5/61); Marsh-a	5	10	15	35	55	75
1164-Wanted: Dead or Alive (TV)-Steve McQueen photo-c	9	18	27	63	107	150
1165-Ellery Queen (#1) (3-5/61)	10	20	30	70	123	175
1166-Rocky and His Friends (TV) (Jay Ward)	19	38	57	138	244	350
1167-Tales of Wells Fargo (TV)-Photo-c	8	16	24	52	86	120
1168-The Detectives (TV)-Robert Taylor photo-c	9	18	27	65	113	160
1169-New Adventures of Sherlock Holmes	14	28	42	102	181	260
1170-The Three Stooges (3-5/61)-Photo-c	13	26	39	95	168	240
1171-Elmer Fudd	4	8	12	26	41	55
1172-Fury (TV)-Photo-c	6	12	18	41	66	90
1173-The Twilight Zone (#1) (TV) (5/61)-Crandall/Evans-c/a; Crandall tribute to Ingles	21	42	63	156	278	400
1174-The Little Rascals (TV)	5	10	15	30	48	65
1175-M.G.M.'s Mouse Musketeers (3-5/61)	4	8	12	24	37	50

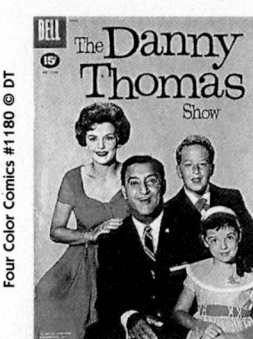

Four Color Comics #1180 © DT

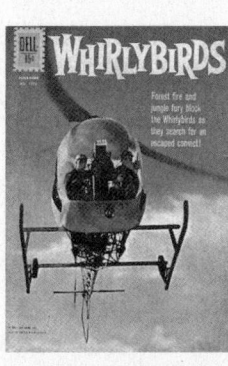

Four Color Comics #1216 © DELL

Four Color Comics #1289 © DELL

	GD 2.0	VG 4.0	FN 6.0	VF 8.0	VF/NM 9.0	NM- 9.2
1176-Dondi (Movie)-Origin; photo-c	5	10	15	35	55	75
1177-Chilly Willy (Lantz) (4-6/61)	5	10	15	30	48	65
1178-Ten Who Dared (Disney-Movie) (12/60)-Painted-c; cast member photo on back-c	7	14	21	49	80	110
1179-The Swamp Fox (TV) (Disney)-Leslie Nielsen photo-c	8	16	24	56	93	130
1180-The Danny Thomas Show (TV)-Toth-a; photo-c	15	30	45	111	198	285
1181-Texas John Slaughter (TV) (Walt Disney Presents...) (4-6/61)-Photo-c	7	14	21	47	76	105
1182-Donald Duck Album (Disney) (5-7/61)	5	10	15	32	51	70
1183-101 Dalmatians (Disney-Movie) (3/61)	9	18	27	65	113	160
1184-Gyro Gearloose; All Barks-c/a (Disney) (5-7/61) Two variations exist	9	18	27	65	113	160
1185-Sweetie Pie	5	10	15	30	48	65
1186-Yak Yak (#1) by Jack Davis (2 versions - one minus 3-pg. Davis-c/a)	8	16	24	58	97	135
1187-The Three Stooges (6-8/61)-Photo-c	13	26	39	95	168	240
1188-Atlantis, the Lost Continent (Movie) (5/61)-Photo-c	10	20	30	68	119	170
1189-Greyfriars Bobby (Disney-Movie) (11/61)-Photo-c (scarce)	7	14	21	47	76	105
1190-Donald and the Wheel (Disney-Movie) (11/61); Barks-a	8	16	24	54	90	125
1191-Leave It to Beaver (TV)-Photo-c	13	26	39	95	168	240
1192-Ricky Nelson (TV)-Manning-a; photo-c	14	28	42	100	178	255
1193-The Real McCoys (TV) (6-8/61)-Photo-c	8	16	24	56	93	130
1194-Pepe (Movie) (4/61)-Photo-c	4	8	12	22	34	45
1195-National Velvet (#1) (TV)-Photo-c	7	14	21	49	80	110
1196-Pixie and Dixie and Mr. Jinks (TV) (Hanna-Barbera) (7-9/61)	6	12	18	37	59	80
1197-The Aquanauts (TV) (5-7/61)-Photo-c	7	14	21	47	76	105
1198-Donald in Mathmagic Land (Disney-Movie)-Reprint of #1051	6	12	18	43	69	95
1199-The Absent-Minded Professor (Disney-Movie) (4/61)-Photo-c	8	16	24	56	93	130
1200-Hennessey (TV) (8-10/61)-Gil Kane-a; photo-c	7	14	21	47	76	105
1201-Goofy (Disney) (8-10/61)	5	10	15	32	51	70
1202-Rawhide (TV)-Clint Eastwood photo-c	14	28	42	102	181	260
1203-Pinocchio (Disney) (3/62)	5	10	15	35	55	75
1204-Scamp (Disney)	4	8	12	28	44	60
1205-David and Goliath (Movie) (7/61)-Photo-c	6	12	18	43	69	95
1206-Lolly and Pepper (9-11/61)	4	8	12	22	34	45
1207-The Rebel (TV)-Sekowsky-a; photo-c	8	16	24	56	93	130
1208-Rocky and His Friends (Jay Ward) (TV)	19	38	57	138	244	350
1209-Sugarfoot (TV)-Photo-c (10-12/61)	8	16	24	58	97	135
1210-The Parent Trap (Disney-Movie) (8/61)-Hayley Mills photo-c	9	18	27	60	100	140
1211-77 Sunset Strip (TV)-Manning-a; photo-c	8	16	24	54	90	125
1212-Chilly Willy (Lantz) (7-9/61)	5	10	15	30	48	65
1213-Mysterious Island (Movie)-Photo-c	8	16	24	56	93	130
1214-Smokey the Bear	4	8	12	28	44	60
1215-Tales of Wells Fargo (TV) (10-12/61)-Photo-c	8	16	24	52	86	120
1216-Whirlybirds (TV)-Photo-c	8	16	24	52	86	120
1218-Fury (TV)-Photo-c	6	12	18	41	66	90
1219-The Detectives (TV)-Robert Taylor & Adam West photo-c	8	16	24	56	93	130
1220-Gunslinger (TV)-Photo-c	8	16	24	56	93	130
1221-Bonanza (TV) (9-11/61)-Photo-c	17	34	51	124	220	315
1222-Elmer Fudd (9-11/61)	4	8	12	26	41	55
1223-Laramie (TV)-Gil Kane-a; photo-c	6	12	18	43	69	95
1224-The Little Rascals (TV) (10-12/61)	5	10	15	30	48	65
1225-The Deputy (TV)-Henry Fonda photo-c	9	18	27	63	107	150
1226-Nikki, Wild Dog of the North (Disney-Movie) (9/61)-Photo-c	5	10	15	35	55	75
1227-Morgan the Pirate (Movie)-Photo-c	7	14	21	50	83	115
1229-Thief of Baghdad (Movie)-Crandall/Evans-a; photo-c	7	14	21	45	73	100
1230-Voyage to the Bottom of the Sea (#1) (Movie)-Photo insert on-c	10	20	30	70	123	175
1231-Danger Man (TV) (9-11/61)-Patrick McGoohan photo-c	10	20	30	71	126	180
1232-On the Double (Movie)	5	10	15	30	48	65
1233-Tammy Tell Me True (Movie) (1961)	6	12	18	43	69	95

	GD 2.0	VG 4.0	FN 6.0	VF 8.0	VF/NM 9.0	NM- 9.2
1234-The Phantom Planet (Movie) (1961)	7	14	21	47	76	105
1235-Mister Magoo (#1) (12-2/62)	8	16	24	56	93	130
1235-Mister Magoo (3-5/65) 2nd printing; reprint of 12-2/62 issue	6	12	18	41	66	90
1236-King of Kings (Movie)-Photo-c	7	14	21	50	83	115
1237-The Untouchables (#1) (TV)-Not by Toth; photo-c	20	40	60	146	261	375
1238-Deputy Dawg (TV)	10	20	30	73	129	185
1239-Donald Duck Album (Disney) (10-12/61)-Barks-c	7	14	21	45	73	100
1240-The Detectives (TV)-Tufts-a; Robert Taylor photo-c	8	16	24	56	93	130
1241-Sweetie Pie	4	8	12	24	37	50
1242-King Leonardo and His Short Subjects (#1) (TV) (11-1/62)	12	24	36	84	150	215
1243-Ellery Queen	8	16	24	56	93	130
1244-Space Mouse (Lantz) (11-1/62)	4	8	12	28	44	60
1245-New Adventures of Sherlock Holmes	13	26	39	90	160	230
1246-Mickey Mouse Album (Disney)	5	10	15	32	51	70
1247-Daisy Duck's Diary (Disney) (12-2/62)	5	10	15	32	51	70
1248-Pluto (Disney)	4	8	12	28	44	60
1249-The Danny Thomas Show (TV)-Manning-a; photo-c	14	28	42	103	184	265
1250-The Four Horsemen of the Apocalypse (Movie)-Photo-c	6	12	18	43	69	95
1251-Everything's Ducky (Movie) (1961)	5	10	15	30	48	65
1252-The Andy Griffith Show (TV)-Photo-c; 1st show aired 10/3/60	35	70	105	263	482	700
1253-Space Man (#1) (1-3/62)	7	14	21	49	80	110
1254-"Diver Dan" (#1) (TV) (2-4/62)-Photo-c	5	10	15	35	55	75
1255-The Wonders of Aladdin (Movie) (1961)	6	12	18	43	69	95
1256-Kona, Monarch of Monster Isle (#1) (2-4/62)-Glanzman-a	9	18	27	60	100	140
1257-Car 54, Where Are You? (#1) (TV) (3-5/62)-Photo-c	8	16	24	56	93	130
1258-The Frogmen (#1)-Evans-a	8	16	24	52	86	120
1259-El Cid (Movie) (1961)-Photo-c	7	14	21	47	76	105
1260-The Horsemasters (TV, Movie) (Disney) (12-2/62)-Annette Funicello photo-c	12	24	36	87	156	225
1261-Rawhide (TV)-Clint Eastwood photo-c	14	28	42	102	181	260
1262-The Rebel (TV)-Photo-c	8	16	24	56	93	130
1263-77 Sunset Strip (TV) (12-2/62)-Manning-a; photo-c	8	16	24	54	90	125
1264-Pixie and Dixie and Mr. Jinks (TV) (Hanna-Barbera)	6	12	18	37	59	80
1265-The Real McCoys (TV)-Photo-c	8	16	24	56	93	130
1266-M.G.M.'s Spike and Tyke (12-2/62)	4	8	12	22	34	45
1267-Gyro Gearloose; Barks-c/a, 4 pgs. (Disney) (12-2/62)	8	16	24	54	90	125
1268-Oswald the Rabbit (Lantz)	4	8	12	28	44	60
1269-Rawhide (TV)-Clint Eastwood photo-c	14	28	42	102	181	260
1270-Bullwinkle and Rocky (#1) (TV) (Jay Ward) (3-5/62)	18	36	54	132	234	335
1271-Yogi Bear Birthday Party (TV) (Hanna-Barbera) (11/61) (Given away for 1 box top from Kellogg's Corn Flakes)	6	12	18	37	59	80
1272-Frosty the Snowman	5	10	15	32	51	70
1273-Hans Brinker (Disney-Movie)-Photo-c (2/62)	6	12	18	43	69	95
1274-Santa Claus Funnies (12/61)	6	12	18	41	66	90
1275-Rocky and His Friends (TV) (Jay Ward)	19	38	57	138	244	350
1276-Dondi	4	8	12	22	34	45
1278-King Leonardo and His Short Subjects (TV)	12	24	36	84	150	215
1279-Grandma Duck's Farm Friends (Disney)	5	10	15	32	51	70
1280-Hennesey (TV)-Photo-c	6	12	18	43	69	95
1281-Chilly Willy (Lantz) (4-6/62)	5	10	15	30	48	65
1282-Babes in Toyland (Disney-Movie) (1/62); Annette Funicello photo-c	14	28	42	99	175	250
1283-Bonanza (TV) (2-4/62)-Photo-c	17	34	51	124	220	315
1284-Laramie (TV)-Heath-a; photo-c	6	12	18	43	69	95
1285-Leave It to Beaver (TV)-Photo-c	13	26	39	95	168	240
1286-The Untouchables (TV)-Photo-c	14	28	42	102	181	260
1287-Man from Wells Fargo (TV)-Photo-c	6	12	18	37	59	80
1288-Twilight Zone (TV) (4/62)-Crandall/Evans-c/a	12	24	36	87	156	225
1289-Ellery Queen	8	16	24	56	93	130
1290-M.G.M.'s Mouse Musketeers	4	8	12	24	37	50

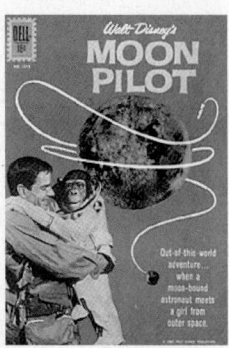
Four Color Comics #1313 © DIS

Four Favorites #3 © ACE

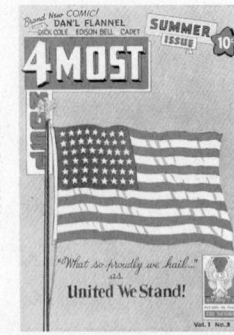
4Most #3 © NOVP

	GD 2.0	VG 4.0	FN 6.0	VF 8.0	VF/NM 9.0	NM- 9.2
1291-77 Sunset Strip (TV)-Manning-a; photo-c	8	16	24	54	90	125
1293-Elmer Fudd (3-5/62)	4	8	12	26	41	55
1294-Ripcord (TV)	7	14	21	47	76	105
1295-Mister Ed, the Talking Horse (#1) (TV) (3-5/62)-Photo-c						
	12	24	36	87	156	225
1296-Fury (TV) (3-5/62)-Photo-c	6	12	18	41	66	90
1297-Spanky, Alfalfa and the Little Rascals (TV)	5	10	15	30	48	65
1298-The Hathaways (TV)-Photo-c	5	10	15	30	48	65
1299-Deputy Dawg (TV)	10	20	30	73	129	185
1300-The Comancheros (Movie) (1961)-John Wayne photo-c						
	15	30	45	105	188	270
1301-Adventures in Paradise (TV) (2-4/62)	6	12	18	39	62	85
1302-Johnny Jason, Teen Reporter (2-4/62)	4	8	12	24	37	50
1303-Lad: A Dog (Movie)-Photo-c	4	8	12	28	44	60
1304-Nellie the Nurse (3-5/62)-Stanley-a	7	14	21	47	76	105
1305-Mister Magoo (3-5/62)	8	16	24	56	93	130
1306-Target: The Corruptors (#1) (TV) (3-5/62)-Photo-c						
	6	12	18	37	59	80
1307-Margie (TV) (3-5/62)	6	12	18	37	59	80
1308-Tales of the Wizard of Oz (TV) (3-5/62)	11	22	33	79	140	200
1309-87th Precinct (#1) (TV) (4-6/62)-Krigstein-a; photo-c						
	9	18	27	65	113	160
1310-Huck and Yogi Winter Sports (TV) (Hanna-Barbera) (3/62)						
	8	16	24	56	93	130
1311-Rocky and His Friends (TV) (Jay Ward)	19	38	57	138	244	350
1312-National Velvet (TV)-Photo-c	4	8	12	28	44	60
1313-Moon Pilot (Disney-Movie)-Photo-c	7	14	21	47	76	105
1328-The Underwater City (Movie) (1961)-Evans-a; photo-c						
	7	14	21	47	76	105
1329-See Gyro Gearloose #01329-207						
1330-Brain Boy (#1)-Gil Kane-a	11	22	33	79	140	200
1332-Bachelor Father (TV)	7	14	21	50	83	115
1333-Short Ribs (4-6/62)	5	10	15	35	55	75
1335-Aggie Mack (4-6/62)	4	8	12	26	41	55
1336-On Stage; not by Leonard Starr	5	10	15	30	48	65
1337-Dr. Kildare (#1) (TV) (4-6/62)-Photo-c	8	16	24	58	97	135
1341-The Andy Griffith Show (TV) (4-6/62)-Photo-c	32	64	96	240	445	650
1348-Yak Yak (#2)-Jack Davis-c/a	8	16	24	52	86	120
1349-Yogi Bear Visits the U.N. (TV) (Hanna-Barbera) (1/62)-Photo-c						
	8	16	24	58	97	135
1350-Comanche (Disney-Movie)(1962)-Reprints 4-Color #966 (title change from "Tonka" to "Comanche") (4-6/62)-Sal Mineo photo-c						
	5	10	15	35	55	75
1354-Calvin & the Colonel (#1) (TV) (4-6/62)	8	16	24	56	93	130
NOTE: *Missing numbers probably do not exist.*

4-D MONKEY, THE (Adventures of... #? on)
Leung's Publications: 1988 - No. 11, 1990 ($1.80/$2.00, 52 pgs.)

1-11: 1-Karate Pig, Ninja Flounder & 4-D Monkey (48 pgs., centerfold is a Christmas card).						
2-4 (52 pgs.)						2.50

FOUR FAVORITES (Crime Must Pay the Penalty No. 33 on)
Ace Magazines: Sept, 1941 - No. 32, Dec, 1947

	GD	VG	FN	VF	VF/NM	NM-
1-Vulcan, Lash Lightning (formerly Flash Lightning in Sure-Fire), Magno the Magnetic Man & The Raven begin; flag/Hitler-c	176	352	528	1100	1825	2550
2-The Black Ace only app.	62	124	186	388	644	900
3-Last Vulcan	52	104	156	317	521	725
4,5: 4-The Raven & Vulcan end; Unknown Soldier begins (see Our Flag), ends #28.						
5-Captain Courageous begins (5/42), ends #28 (moves over from Captain Courageous #6); not in #6	45	90	135	275	450	625
6-8: 6-The Flag app.; Mr. Risk begins (7/42)	41	82	123	256	416	575
9-Kurtzman-a (Lash Lightning); robot-c	45	90	135	275	455	635
10-Classic Kurtzman-c/a (Magno & Davey)	53	106	159	320	529	735
11-Kurtzman-a; Hitler, Mussolini, Hirohito-c; L.B. Cole-a; Unknown Soldier by Kurtzman	72	144	216	450	750	1050
12-L.B. Cole-a	39	78	117	224	355	485
13-20: 18,20-Palais-c/a	34	68	102	195	308	420
21-No Unknown Soldier; The Unknown app.	23	46	69	135	213	290
22-26: 22-Captain Courageous drops costume. 23-Unknown Soldier drops costume.						
25-29-Hap Hazard app. 26-Last Magno	23	46	69	135	213	290
27-29: Hap Hazard app. in all	19	38	57	112	176	240
30-32: 30-Funny-c begin (teen humor), end #32	14	28	42	82	121	160
NOTE: *Dave Berg c-5. Jim Mooney a-6; c-1-3. Palais a-18-20; c-18-25. Torture chamber c-5.*

FOUR HORSEMEN, THE (See The Crusaders)
FOUR HORSEMEN

DC Comics (Vertigo): Feb, 2000 - No. 4, May, 2000 ($2.50, limited series)

	GD 2.0	VG 4.0	FN 6.0	VF 8.0	VF/NM 9.0	NM- 9.2
1-4-Essad Ribic-c/a; Robert Rodi-s						2.50

FOUR HORSEMEN OF THE APOCALYPSE, THE (Movie)
Dell Publishing Co.: No. 1250, Jan-Mar, 1962 (one-shot)

Four Color 1250-Photo-c	6	12	18	43	69	95

4MOST (Foremost Boys No. 32-40; becomes Thrilling Crime Cases #41 on)
Novelty Publications/Star Publications No. 37-on:
Winter, 1941-42 - V8#5(#36), 9-10/49; #37, 11-12/49 - #40, 4-5/50

	GD	VG	FN	VF	VF/NM	NM-
V1#1-The Target by Sid Greene, The Cadet & Dick Cole begin with origins retold; produced by Funnies Inc.; quarterly issues begin, end V6#3						
	152	304	456	950	1575	2200
2-Last Target (Spr/42); WWII cover	62	124	186	388	644	900
3-Dan'l Flannel begins; flag-c	46	92	138	281	466	650
4-1pg. Dr. Seuss (signed) (Aut/42); fish in the face-c						
	49	98	147	299	492	685
V2#1-3	19	38	57	109	172	235
4-Hitler, Tojo & Mussolini app. as pumpkins in all	39	78	117	224	355	485
V3#1-4	15	30	45	86	133	180
V4#1-4: 2-Walter Johnson-c	13	26	39	74	105	135
V5#1-4: 1-The Target & Targeteers app.	11	22	33	64	90	115
V6#1-4	10	20	30	56	76	95
5-L. B. Cole-c	20	40	60	115	180	245
V7#1,3,5, V8#1, 37	10	20	30	56	76	95
2,4,6-L. B. Cole-c. 6-Last Dick Cole	20	40	60	115	180	245
V8#2,3,5-L. B. Cole-c/a	23	46	69	132	209	285
4-L. B. Cole-a	15	30	45	83	124	165
38-40: 38-Johnny Weismuller (Tarzan) life story & Jim Braddock (boxer) life story.						
38-40-L.B. Cole-c. 40-Last White Rider	17	34	51	98	154	210
Accepted Reprint 38-40 (nd): 40-r/Johnny Weismuller life story; all have L.B. Cole-c						
	10	20	30	56	76	95

411
Marvel Comics: June, 2003 - No. 3 ($3.50, limited series)

1,2-Tributes to peacemakers; s/a by various. 1-Millar, Quitely, Mack, Winslade & others-s/a						
2-Harris, Phillips, Manco, Bruce Jones.						3.50

FOUR-STAR BATTLE TALES
National Periodical Publications: Feb-Mar, 1973 - No. 5, Nov-Dec, 1973

1-Reprints begin	3	6	9	16	23	30
2-5	2	4	6	10	14	18
NOTE: *Drucker r-1, 3-5. Heath r-2, 5; c-1. Krigstein r-5. Kubert r-4; c-2.*

FOUR STAR SPECTACULAR
National Periodical Publications: Mar-Apr, 1976 - No. 6, Jan-Feb, 1977

1	2	4	6	10	14	18
2-6: Reprints in all. 2-Infinity cover	3	4	6	8	10	
NOTE: *All contain DC Superhero reprints. #1 has 68 pgs.; #2-6, 52 pgs. #1, 4-Hawkman app.; #2-Kid Flash app.; #3-Green Lantern app; #2, 4, 5-Wonder Woman, Superboy app; #5-Green Arrow, Vigilante app; #6-Blackhawk G.A.-r.*

FOUR TEENERS (Formerly Crime Must Pay The Penalty; Dotty No. 35 on)
A. A. Wyn: No. 34, April, 1948 (52 pgs.)

34-Teen-age comic; Dotty app.; Curly & Jerry continue from Four Favorites						
	8	16	24	42	54	65

FOURTH WORLD GALLERY, THE (Jack Kirby's...)
DC Comics: 1996 (9/96) ($3.50, one-shot)

nn-Pin-ups of Jack Kirby's Fourth World characters (New Gods, Forever People & Mister Miracle) by John Byrne, Rick Burchett, Dan Jurgens, Walt Simonson & others						3.50

FOUR WOMEN
DC Comics (Homage): Dec, 2001 - No. 5, Apr, 2002 ($2.95, limited series)

1-5-Sam Kieth-s/a						3.00
TPB (2002, $17.95) r/series; foreward by Kieth						18.00

FOX AND THE CROW (Stanley & His Monster No. 109 on) (See Comic Cavalcade & Real Screen Comics)
National Periodical Publications: Dec-Jan, 1951-52 - No. 108, Feb-Mar, 1968

	GD	VG	FN	VF	VF/NM	NM-
1	117	234	351	731	1216	1700
2(Scarce)	53	106	159	331	553	775
3-5	37	74	111	213	337	460
6-10	26	52	78	152	239	325
11-20	19	38	57	112	176	240
21-30: 22-Last precode issue (2/55)	14	28	42	82	121	160
31-40	12	24	36	69	97	125
41-60	6	12	18	43	69	95

Fox and the Crow #89 © DC

Fox Giant - Book of Love nn © FOX

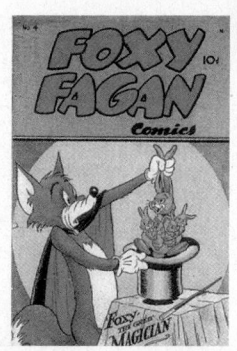

Foxy Fagan Comics #4 © Dearfield

	GD	VG	FN	VF	VF/NM	NM-
	2.0	4.0	6.0	8.0	9.0	9.2

	GD 2.0	VG 4.0	FN 6.0	VF 8.0	VF/NM 9.0	NM- 9.2
61-80	5	10	15	35	55	75
81-94: 94-(11/65)-The Brat Finks begin	4	8	12	26	41	55
95-Stanley & His Monster begins (origin & 1st app)	5	10	15	35	55	75
96-99,101-108	3	6	9	20	30	40
100 (10-11/66)	4	8	12	22	34	45

NOTE: Many later covers by Mort Drucker.

FOX AND THE HOUND, THE (Disney)(Movie)
Whitman Publishing Co.: Aug, 1981 - No. 3, Oct, 1981

11292- Golden Press Graphic Novel	2	4	6	8	10	12
1-3-Based on animated movie	1	2	3	5	7	9

FOXFIRE (See The Phoenix Resurrection)
Malibu Comics (Ultraverse): Feb, 1996 - No. 4, May, 1996 ($1.50)

1-4: Sludge, Ultraforce app. 4-Punisher app.						2.50

FOX GIANTS (Also see Giant Comics Edition)
Fox Features Syndicate: 1944 - 1950 (25¢, 132 - 196 pgs.)

	GD 2.0	VG 4.0	FN 6.0	VF 8.0	VF/NM 9.0	NM- 9.2
Album of Crime nn(1949, 132p)	50	100	150	305	503	700
Album of Love nn(1949, 132p)	46	92	138	281	466	650
All Famous Crime Stories nn('49, 132p)	50	100	150	305	503	700
All Good Comics 1(1944, 132p)(R.W. Voigt)-The Bouncer, Purple Tigress,Rick Evans, Puppeteer, Green Mask; Infinity-c	40	80	120	240	383	525
All Great nn(1944, 132p)-Capt. Jack Terry, Rick Evans, Jaguar Man	40	80	120	240	383	525
All Great nn(Chicago Nite Life News)(1945, 132p)-Green Mask, Bouncer, Puppeteer, Rick Evans, Rocket Kelly	40	80	120	240	383	525
All-Great Confessions nn(1949, 132p)	45	90	135	275	450	625
All Great Crime Stories nn('49, 132p)	50	100	150	305	503	700
All Great Jungle Adventures nn('49, 132p)	54	108	162	338	557	775
All Real Confession Magazine 3 (3/49, 132p)	45	90	135	275	450	625
All Real Confession Magazine 4 (4/49, 132p)	45	90	135	275	450	625
All Your Comics 1(1944, 132p)-The Puppeteer, Red Robbins & Merciless the Sorcerer	40	80	120	240	383	525
Almanac Of Crime nn(1948, 148p)-Phantom Lady	55	110	165	344	572	800
Almanac Of Crime 1(1950, 132p)	49	98	147	299	495	690
Book Of Love nn(1950, 132p)	43	86	129	262	431	600
Burning Romances 1(1949, 132p)	52	104	156	317	521	725
Crimes Incorporated nn(1950, 132p)	45	90	135	275	450	625
Daring Love Stories nn(1950, 132p)	43	86	129	262	431	600
Everybody's Comics 1(1944, 50¢, 196p)-The Green Mask, The Puppeteer, The Bouncer, Rocket Kelly, Rick Evans	45	90	135	275	450	625
Everybody's Comics 1(1946, 196p)-Green Lama, The Puppeteer	40	80	120	235	368	500
Everybody's Comics 1(1946, 196p)-Same as 1945 Ribtickler	31	62	93	180	285	390
Everybody's Comics nn(1947, 132p)-Jo-Jo, Purple Tigress, Cosmo Cat, Bronze Man	41	82	123	237	374	510
Exciting Romance Stories nn(1949, 132p)	46	92	138	281	466	650
Famous Love nn(1950, 132p)	43	86	129	262	431	600
Intimate Confessions nn(1950, 132p)	43	86	129	262	431	600
Journal Of Crime nn(1949, 132p)	50	100	150	305	503	700
Love Problems nn(1949, 132p)	45	90	135	275	450	625
Love Thrills nn(1950, 132p)	44	88	132	268	442	615
March of Crime nn('48, 132p)-Female w/rifle-c	48	96	144	293	484	675
March of Crime nn('49, 132p)-Cop w/pistol-c	46	92	138	281	466	650
March of Crime nn(1949, 132p)-Coffin & man w/machine-gun-c	46	92	138	281	466	650
Revealing Love Stories nn(1950, 132p)	43	86	129	262	431	600
Ribtickler nn(1945, 50¢, 196p)-Chicago Nite Life News; Marvel Mutt, Cosmo Cat, Flash Rabbit, The Nebbs app.	40	80	120	235	368	500
Romantic Thrills nn(1950, 132p)	43	86	129	262	431	600
Secret Love Stories nn(1949, 132p)	46	92	138	281	466	650
Strange Love nn(1950, 132p)-Photo-c	50	100	150	305	503	700
Sweetheart Scandals nn(1950, 132p)	43	86	129	262	431	600
Teen-Age Love nn(1950, 132p)	43	86	129	262	431	600
Throbbing Love nn(1950, 132p)-Photo-c; used in POP, pg. 107	50	100	150	305	503	700
Truth About Crime nn(1949, 132p)	50	100	150	305	503	700
Variety Comics 1(1946, 132p)-Blue Beetle, Jungle Jo	41	82	123	250	400	550
Variety Comics nn(1950, 132p)-Jungle Jo, My Secret Affair(w/Harrison/Wood-a), Crimes by Women & My Story	40	80	120	240	383	525
Western Roundup nn('50, 132p)-Hoot Gibson; Cody of the Pony Express app.	40	80	120	235	368	500

NOTE: Each of the above usually contain four remaindered Fox books minus covers. Since these missing covers

---

often had the first page of the first story, most Giants therefore are incomplete. Approximate values are listed. Books with appearances of Phantom Lady, Rulah, Jo-Jo, etc. could bring more.

FOXHOLE (Becomes Never Again #8?)
Mainline/Charlton No. 5 on: 9-10/54 - No. 4, 3-4/55; No. 5, 7/55 - No. 7, 3/56

	GD 2.0	VG 4.0	FN 6.0	VF 8.0	VF/NM 9.0	NM- 9.2
1-Classic Kirby-c	46	92	138	281	466	650
2-Kirby-c/a(2); Kirby scripts based on his war time experiences	34	68	102	195	308	420
3-5-Kirby-c only	20	40	60	117	184	250
6-Kirby-c/a(2)	29	58	87	167	264	360
7	11	22	33	62	86	110
Super Reprints #10,15-17: 10-r/? 15,16-r/United States Marines #5,8.						
17-r/Monty Hall a?	2	4	6	11	16	20
11,12,18-r/Foxhole #1,2,3; Kirby-c	3	6	9	17	25	32

NOTE: Kirby a(r)-Super #11, 12. Powell a(r)-Super #15, 16. Stories by actual veterans.

FOXY FAGAN COMICS (Funny Animal)
Dearfield Publishing Co.: Dec, 1946 - No. 7, Summer, 1948

1-Foxy Fagan & Little Buck begin	13	26	39	72	101	130
2	8	16	24	42	54	65
3-7: 6-Rocket ship-c	7	14	21	37	46	55

FRACTION
DC Comics (Focus): June, 2004 - No. 6, Nov, 2004 ($2.50, limited series)

1-6-David Tischman-s/Timothy Green II-a						2.50

FRACTURED FAIRY TALES (TV)
Gold Key: Oct, 1962 (Jay Ward)

1 (10022-210)-From Bullwinkle TV show	10	20	30	71	126	180

FRAGGLE ROCK (TV)
Marvel Comics (Star Comics)/Marvel V2#1 on: Apr, 1985 - No. 8, Sept, 1986; V2#1, Apr, 1988 - No. 6, Sept, 1988

1-6 (75¢-c)						5.00
7,8						6.00
V2#1-6-($1.00): Reprints 1st series						2.50

FRANCIS, BROTHER OF THE UNIVERSE
Marvel Comics Group: 1980 (75¢, 52 pgs., one-shot)

nn-John Buscema/Marie Severin-a; story of Francis Bernadone celebrating his 800th birthday in 1982						4.00

FRANCIS THE FAMOUS TALKING MULE (All based on movie)
Dell Publishing Co.: No. 335 (#1), June, 1951 - No. 1090, March, 1960

Four Color 335 (#1)	10	20	30	71	126	180
Four Color 465	6	12	18	41	66	90
Four Color 501,547,579	5	10	15	32	51	70
Four Color 621,655,698,710,745	4	8	12	28	44	60
Four Color 810,863,906,953,991,1068,1090	4	8	12	26	41	55

FRANK
Nemesis Comics (Harvey): Apr (Mar inside), 1994 - No. 4, 1994 ($1.75/$2.50, limited series)

1-4-($2.50, direct sale): 1-Foil-c Edition						3.00
1-4-($1.75)-Newsstand Editions; Cowan-a in all						2.50

FRANK
Fantagraphics Books: Sept, 1996 ($2.95, B&W)

1-Woodring-c/a/scripts						3.00

FRANK BUCK (Formerly My True Love)
Fox Features Syndicate: No. 70, May, 1950 - No. 3, Sept, 1950

70-Wood a(p)(3 stories)-Photo-c	32	64	96	186	293	400
71-Wood a (9 pgs.); photo/painted-c	17	3	51	98	154	210
3: 3-Photo/painted-c	14	28	42	80	115	150

NOTE: Based on "Bring 'Em Back Alive" TV show.

FRANKENSTEIN (See Dracula, Movie Classics & Werewolf)
Dell Publishing Co.: Aug-Oct, 1964 - No. 2, Sept, 1966 - No. 4, Mar, 1967

1(12-283-410)(1964)(2nd printing; see Movie Classics for 1st printing)	5	10	15	35	55	75
2-Intro. & origin super-hero character (9/66)	4	8	12	26	41	55
3,4	3	6	9	18	27	35

FRANKENSTEIN (The Monster of…; also see Monsters Unleashed #2, Power Record Comics, Psycho & Silver Surfer #7)
Marvel Comics Group: Jan, 1973 - No. 18, Sept, 1975

1-Ploog-c/a begins, ends #6	6	12	18	41	66	90
2	4	8	12	22	34	45
3-5	3	6	9	17	25	32

Frankenstein #25 © PRIZE

Fray #1 © Joss Whedon

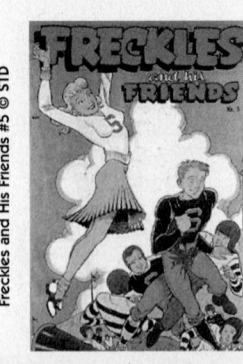

Freckles and His Friends #5 © STD

	GD 2.0	VG 4.0	FN 6.0	VF 8.0	VF/NM 9.0	NM- 9.2		GD 2.0	VG 4.0	FN 6.0	VF 8.0	VF/NM 9.0	NM- 9.2

6,7,10: 7-Dracula cameo — 3, 6, 9, 15, 21, 26
8,9-Dracula c/sty. 9-Death of Dracula — 4, 8, 12, 24, 37, 50
11-17 — 2, 4, 6, 11, 16, 20
18-Wrightson-c(i) — 3, 6, 9, 14, 19, 24
NOTE: *Adkins c-17l. Buscema a-7-10p. Ditko a-12r. G. Kane c-15p. Orlando a-8r. Ploog a-1-3, 4p, 5p, 6; c-1-6l. Wrightson c-18l.*

FRANKENSTEIN (Mary Wollstonecraft Shelley's...; A Marvel Illustrated Novel)
Marvel Pub.: 1983 ($8.95, B&W, 196 pgs., 8x11" TPB)
nn-Wrightson-a; 4 pg. intro. by Stephen King — 4, 8, 12, 22, 34, 45
Limited HC Edition — 150.00

FRANKENSTEIN COMICS (Also See Prize Comics)
Prize Publ. (Crestwood/Feature): Sum, 1945 - V5#5(#33), Oct-Nov, 1954
1-Frankenstein begins by Dick Briefer (origin); Frank Sinatra parody — 117, 234, 351, 731, 1216, 1700
2 — 54, 108, 162, 338, 557, 775
3-5 — 41, 82, 123, 256, 416, 575
6-10: 7-S&K a(r)/Headline Comics. 8(7-8/47)-Superman satire — 38, 76, 114, 219, 347, 475
11-17(1-2/49)-11-Boris Karloff parody-c/story. 17-Last humor issue — 33, 66, 99, 190, 300, 410
18(3/52)-New origin, horror series begins — 42, 84, 126, 256, 421, 585
19,20(V3#4, 8-9/52) — 28, 56, 84, 162, 256, 350
21(V3#5), 22(V3#6), 23(V4#1) - #28(V4#6) — 26, 52, 78, 152, 239, 325
29(V5#1) - #33(V5#5) — 25, 50, 75, 148, 232, 315
NOTE: *Briefer c/a-all. Meskin a-21, 29.*

FRANKENSTEIN/DRACULA WAR, THE
Topps Comics: Feb, 1995 - No. 3, May, 1995 ($2.50, limited series)
1-3 — 3.00

FRANKENSTEIN, JR. (...& the Impossibles) (TV)
Gold Key: Jan, 1966 (Hanna-Barbera)
1-Super hero (scarce) — 10, 20, 30, 73, 129, 185

FRANKENSTEIN MOBSTER
Image Comics: No. 0, Oct, 2003 - No. 7, Dec, 2004 ($2.95)
0-7: 0-Two covers by Wheatley and Hughes; Wheatley-s/a. 1-Variant-c by Wieringo — 3.00

FRANKENSTEIN: OR THE MODERN PROMETHEUS
Caliber Press: 1994 ($2.95, one-shot)
1 — 3.00

FRANK FRAZETTA FANTASY ILLUSTRATED (Magazine)
Quantum Cat Entertainment: Spring 1998 - No. 8 ($5.95, quarterly)
1-Anthology; art by Corben, Horley, Jusko — 1, 2, 3, 4, 5, 7
1-Linsner variant-c — 10.00
2-Battle Chasers by Madureira; Harris-a — 8.00
2-Madureira Battle Chasers variant-c — 12.00
3-8-Frazetta-c — 6.00
3-Tony Daniel variant-c — 15.00
5,6-Portacio variant-c, 7,8-Alex Nino variant-c — 10.00
8-Alex Ross Chicago Comicon variant-c — 10.00

FRANK FRAZETTA'S DEATH DEALER
Image Comics: Mar, 2007 - No. 6 ($3.99)
1-4-Nat Jones-a; 3 covers (Frazetta, Jones, Jones sketch) — 4.00

FRANK FRAZETTA'S THUN'DA TALES
Fantagraphics Books: 1987 ($2.00, one-shot)
1-Frazetta-r — 6.00

FRANK FRAZETTA'S UNTAMED LOVE (Also see Untamed Love)
Fantagraphics Books: Nov, 1987 ($2.00, one-shot)
1-Frazetta-r from 1950's romance comics — 6.00

FRANKIE COMICS (...& Lana No. 13-15) (Formerly Movie Tunes; becomes Frankie Fuddle No. 16 on)
Marvel Comics (MgPC): No. 4, Wint, 1946-47 - No. 15, June, 1949
4-Mitzi, Margie, Daisy app. — 15, 30, 45, 83, 124, 165
5-9 — 10, 20, 30, 54, 72, 90
10-15: 13-Anti-Wertham editorial — 9, 18, 27, 50, 65, 80

FRANKIE DOODLE (See Sparkler, both series)
United Features Syndicate: No. 7, 1939
Single Series 7 — 33, 66, 99, 190, 300, 410

FRANKIE FUDDLE (Formerly Frankie & Lana)
Marvel Comics: No. 16, Aug, 1949 - No. 17, Nov, 1949

16,17 — 9, 18, 27, 50, 65, 80

FRANKLIN RICHARDS (Fantastic Four)
Marvel Comics: April, 2006 - Present ($2.99, one-shots)
... One Shot (4/06, $2.99) short stories by Eliopoulos-a/Sumerak-s — 3.00
...: Happy Franksgiving (1/07, $2.99) Thanksgiving stories by Eliopoulos-a/Sumerak-s — 3.00
...: Lab Brat (2007, $7.99, digest) reprints one-shots and Masked Marvel back-ups — 8.00
...: March Madness (5/07, $2.99) More science gone wrong by Eliopoulos-a/Sumerak-s — 3.00
...: Monster Mash (11/07, $2.99) Science mishaps by Eliopoulos-a/Sumerak-s — 3.00
...: Super Summer Spectacular (9/06, $2.99) short stories by Eliopoulos-a/Sumerak-s — 3.00
...: World Be Warned (8/07, $2.99) short stories by Eliopoulos-a/Sumerak-s; Hulk app. — 3.00

FRANK LUTHER'S SILLY PILLY COMICS (See Jingle Dingle...)
Children's Comics (Maltex Cereal): 1950 (10¢)
1-Characters from radio, records, & TV — 8, 16, 24, 44, 57, 70

FRANK MERRIWELL AT YALE (Speed Demons No. 5 on?)
Charlton Comics: June, 1955 - No. 4, Jan, 1956 (Also see Shadow Comics)
1 — 7, 14, 21, 37, 46, 55
2-4 — 5, 10, 15, 24, 30, 35

FRANTIC (Magazine) (See Ratfink & Zany)
Pierce Publishing Co.: Oct, 1958 - V2#2, Apr, 1959 (Satire)
V1#1 — 12, 24, 36, 69, 97, 125
2 — 9, 18, 27, 52, 69, 85
V2#1,2: 1-Burgos-a, Severin-c/a; Powell-a? — 8, 16, 24, 42, 54, 65

FRAY
Dark Horse Comics: June, 2001 - No. 8, July, 2003 ($2.99, limited series)
1-Joss Whedon-s/Moline & Owens-a — 1, 2, 3, 5, 6, 8
1-DF Gold edition — 2, 4, 6, 9, 12, 15
2-8: 6-(3/02). 7-(4/03) — 4.00
TPB (11/03, $19.95) r/#1-8; intros by Whedon & Loeb; Moline sketch pages — 20.00

FREAK FORCE (Also see Savage Dragon)
Image Comics (Highbrow Ent.): Dec, 1993 - No. 18, July, 1995 ($1.95/$2.50)
1-18-Superpatriot & Mighty Man in all; Erik Larsen scripts in all. 4-Vanguard app. 8-Begin $2.50-c. 9-Cyberforce-c & app. 13-Variant-c — 3.00

FREAK FORCE (Also see Savage Dragon)
Image Comics: Apr, 1997 - No. 3, July, 1997 ($2.95)
1-3-Larsen-s — 3.00

FREAK SHOW
Image Comics (Desperado): 2006 ($5.99, B&W, one-shot)
nn-Bruce Jones-s/Bernie Wrightson-c/a — 6.00

FREAKS OF THE HEARTLAND
Dark Horse Comics: Jan, 2004 - No. 6, Nov, 2004 ($2.99)
1-6-Steve Niles-s/Greg Ruth-a — 3.00

FRECKLES AND HIS FRIENDS (See Crackajack Funnies, Famous Comics Cartoon Book, Honeybee Birdwhistle... & Red Ryder)

FRECKLES AND HIS FRIENDS
Standard Comics/Argo: No. 5, 11/47 - No. 12, 8/49; 11/55 - No. 4, 6/56
5-Reprints — 9, 18, 27, 50, 65, 80
6-12-Reprints. 7-9-Airbrush-c (by Schomburg?). 11-Lingerie panels — 7, 14, 21, 35, 43, 50
NOTE: *Some copies of No. 8 & 9 contain a printing oddity. The negatives were elongated in the engraving process, probably to conform to page dimensions on the filler pages. Those pages only look normal when viewed at a 45 degree angle.*
1(Argo,'55)-Reprints (NEA Service) — 6, 12, 18, 28, 34, 40
2-4 — 4, 8, 12, 18, 22, 25

FREDDY (Formerly My Little Margie's Boy Friends) (Also see Blue Bird)
Charlton Comics: V2#12, June, 1958 - No. 47, Feb, 1965
V2#12 — 3, 6, 9, 20, 30, 40
13-15 — 3, 6, 9, 14, 20, 25
16-47 — 2, 4, 6, 10, 14, 18

FREDDY
Dell Publishing Co.: May-July, 1963 - No. 3, Oct-Dec, 1964
1 — 3, 6, 9, 18, 27, 35
2,3 — 3, 6, 9, 14, 19, 24

FREDDY KRUEGER'S A NIGHTMARE ON ELM STREET
Marvel Comics: Oct, 1989 - No. 2, Dec, 1989 ($2.25, B&W, movie adaptation, magazine)
1,2: Origin Freddy Krueger; Buckler/Alcala-a — 6.00

FREDDY'S DEAD: THE FINAL NIGHTMARE

Freedom Fighters #3 © DC

Friendly Neighborhood Spider-Man #17 © MAR

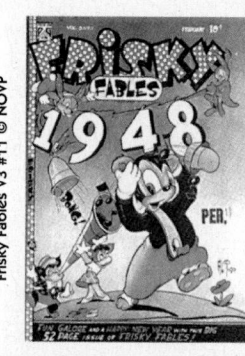

Frisky Fables V3 #11 © NOVP

	GD 2.0	VG 4.0	FN 6.0	VF 8.0	VF/NM 9.0	NM- 9.2

Innovation Publishing: Oct, 1991 - No. 3, Dec 1991 ($2.50, color mini-series, adapts movie)
1-3: Dismukes (film poster artist) painted-c ... 3.00

FRED HEMBECK DESTROYS THE MARVEL UNIVERSE
Marvel Comics: July, 1989 ($1.50, one-shot)
1-Punisher app.; Staton-i (5 pgs.) ... 3.00

FRED HEMBECK SELLS THE MARVEL UNIVERSE
Marvel Comics: Oct, 1990 ($1.25, one-shot)
1-Punisher, Wolverine parodies; Hembeck/Austin-c ... 3.00

FREEDOM AGENT (Also see John Steele)
Gold Key: Apr, 1963 (12¢)
1 (10054-304)-Painted-c ... 4 8 12 26 41 55

FREEDOM FIGHTERS (See Justice League of America #107,108)
National Periodical Publ./DC Comics: Mar-Apr, 1976 - No. 15, July-Aug, 1978
1-Uncle Sam, The Ray, Black Condor, Doll Man, Human Bomb, & Phantom Lady begin
(all former Quality characters) ... 4 8 12 16 20
2-9: 4,5-Wonder Woman x-over. 7-1st app. Crusaders 2 4 8 10 12
10-15:-Origin Doll Man; Cat-Man-c/story (4th app; 1st revival since Detective #325).
11-Origin The Ray. 12-Origin Firebrand. 13-Origin Black Condor. 14-Batgirl & Batwoman
app. 15-Batgirl & Batwoman app.; origin Phantom Lady
... 2 4 6 8 11 14
NOTE: *Buckler c-5-11p, 13p, 14p.*

FREEDOM FORCE
Image Comics: Jan, 2005 - No. 6, June, 2005 ($2.95)
1-6-Eric Dieter-s/Tom Scioli-a ... 3.00

FREEMIND
Future Comics: No. 0, Aug, 2002; Nov, 2002 - No. 7, June, 2003 ($3.50)
0-($2.25) Giordano-a ... 2.50
0-($2.25) Variant-c by Layton ... 2.50
1-7 ($3.50) 1-Two covers by Giordano & Layton; Giordano-a thru #3. 4,5-Leeke-a ... 3.50

FREEX
Malibu Comics (Ultraverse): July, 1993 - No. 18, Mar, 1995 ($1.95)
1-3,5-14,16-18: 1-Polybagged w/trading card. 2-Some were polybagged w/card.
6-Nightman-c/story. 7-2 pg. origin Hardcase by Zeck. 17-Rune app. ... 2.50
1-Holographic-c edition ... 6.00
1-Ultra 5,000 limited silver ink-c ... 3.00
4-($2.50, 48 pgs.)-Rune flip-c/story by B. Smith (3 pgs.); 3 pg. Night Man preview ... 2.50
15 ($3.50)-w/Ultraverse Premiere #9 flip book; Alec Swan & Rafferty app. ... 3.50
Giant Size 1 (1994, $2.50)-Prime app. ... 2.50
NOTE: *Simonson c-1.*

FRENZY (Magazine) (Satire)
Picture Magazine: Apr, 1958 - No. 6, Mar, 1959
1 ... 12 24 36 69 97 125
2-6 ... 8 16 24 44 57 70

FRESHMEN
Image Comics: Jul, 2005 - No. 6, Mar, 2006 ($2.99)
1-Sterbakov-s/Kirk-a; co-created by Seth Green; covers by Pérez, Migliari, Linsner ... 3.00
2-6-Migliari-c ... 3.00
... Yearbook (1/06, $2.99) profile pages of characters; art by various incl. Chaykin, Kirk ... 3.00
... Vol. 1 (3/06, $16.99, TPB) r/#1-6 & Yearbook; cover gallery with concept art ... 17.00

FRESHMEN (Volume 2)
Image Comics: Nov, 2006 - No. 6, Aug, 2007 ($2.99)
1-6: 1-Sterbakov-s/Conrad-a; 4 covers ... 3.00
... Vol. 2 Fundamentals of Fear (6/07, $16.99, TPB) r/#1-6; cover gallery, journals ... 17.00

FRIDAY FOSTER
Dell Publishing Co.: October, 1972
1 ... 3 6 9 20 30 40

FRIDAY THE 13TH (Based on the horror movie franchise)
DC Comics (WildStorm): Feb, 2007 - No. 6, July, 2007 ($2.99, mature)
1-6: 1-Two covers by Sook and Bradstreet; Gray & Palmiotti-s ... 3.00
...: Pamela's Tale 1,2 (9/07 - No. 2, 10/07, $2.99) Andreyko-s/Moll-a/Nguyen-c ... 3.00

FRIENDLY GHOST, CASPER, THE (Becomes Casper... #254 on)
Harvey Publications: Aug, 1958 - No. 224, Oct, 1982; Oct, 1986 - No. 253, June, 1990
1-Infinity-c ... 32 64 96 240 445 650
2 ... 15 30 45 109 195 280
3-10: 6-X-Mas-c ... 9 18 27 61 103 145

11-20: 18-X-Mas-c ... 7 14 21 45 73 100
21-30 ... 5 10 15 30 48 65
31-50 ... 4 8 12 22 34 45
51-70,100: 54-X-Mas-c ... 3 6 9 18 27 35
71-99 ... 3 6 9 16 22 28
101-131: 131-Last 12¢ issue ... 3 6 9 14 19 24
132-159 ... 2 4 6 10 14 18
160-163: All 52 pg. Giants ... 3 6 9 14 19 24
164-199: 173,179,185-Cub Scout Specials ... 1 3 4 6 8 10
200 ... 2 4 6 8 10 12
201-224 ... 1 2 3 5 6 8
225-237: 230-X-mas-c. 232-Valentine's-c ... 5.00
238-253: 238-Begin $1.00-c. 238,244-Halloween-c. 243-Last new material ... 4.00

FRIENDLY NEIGHBORHOOD SPIDER-MAN
Marvel Comics: Dec, 2005 - Present ($2.99)
1-Evolve or Die pt. 1; Peter David-s/Mike Wieringo-a; Morlun app. ... 4.00
1-Variant Wieringo-c with regular costume ... 3.00
2-4: 2-New Avengers app. 3-Spider-Man dies ... 3.00
2-4-var-c: 2-Bag-Head Fantastic Four costume. 3-Captain Universe. 4-Wrestler ... 5.00
5-23: 6-Red & gold costume. 8-10-Uncle Ben app. 17-Black costume; Sandman app. ... 3.00
Annual 1 (7/07, $3.99) Origin of The Sandman; back-up w/Doran-a ... 4.00
... Vol. 1: Derailed (2006, $14.99) r/#5-10; Wieringo sketch pages ... 15.00
... Vol. 2: Mystery Date (2007, $13.99) r/#11-16 ... 14.00

FRIENDS OF MAXX (Also see Maxx)
Image Comics (I Before E): Apr, 1996 - No. 3, Mar, 1997 ($2.95)
1-3: Sam Kieth-c/a/scripts. 1-Featuring Dude Japan ... 3.00

FRIGHT
Atlas/Seaboard Periodicals: June, 1975 (Aug on inside)
1-Origin/1st app. The Son of Dracula; Frank Thorne-c/a ... 1 3 4 6 8 10

FRIGHT NIGHT
Now Comics: Oct, 1988 - No. 22, 1990 ($1.75)
1-22: 1,2 Adapts movie. 8, 9-Evil Ed horror photo-c from movie ... 2.50

FRIGHT NIGHT II
Now Comics: 1989 ($3.95, 52 pgs.)
1-Adapts movie sequel ... 4.00

FRISKY ANIMALS (Formerly Frisky Fables; Super Cat #56 on)
Star Publications: No. 44, Jan, 1951 - No. 55, Sept, 1953
44-Super Cat; L.B. Cole ... 23 46 69 130 205 280
45-Classic L. B. Cole-c ... 32 64 96 186 293 400
46-51,53-55: Super Cat. 54-Super Cat-c begin ... 21 42 63 122 191 260
52-L. B. Cole-c/a, 3 1/2 pgs.; X-Mas-c ... 23 46 69 130 205 280
NOTE: *All have L. B. Cole-c. No. 47-No Super Cat. Disbrow a-49, 52. Fago a-51.*

FRISKY ANIMALS ON PARADE (Formerly Parade Comics; becomes Superspook)
Ajax-Farrell Publ. (Four Star Comic Corp.): Sept, 1957 - No. 3, Dec-Jan, 1957-1958
1-L. B. Cole-c ... 19 38 57 109 172 235
2-No L. B. Cole-c ... 10 20 30 56 76 95
3-L. B. Cole-c ... 6 32 48 92 144 195

FRISKY FABLES (Frisky Animals No. 44 on)
Premium Group/Novelty Publ./Star Publ. V5#4 on: Spring, 1945 - No. 43, Oct, 1950
V1#1-Funny animal; Al Fago-c/a #1-38 ... 22 44 66 126 198 270
2,3(Fall & Winter, 1945) ... 12 24 36 69 97 125
V2#1(#4, 4/46), 9,11,12(#15, 3/47): 4-Flag-c ... 10 20 30 54 72 90
10-Christmas-c. 12-Valentine's-c ... 10 20 30 56 76 95
V3#1(#16, 4/47) - 12(#27, 3/48): 4-Flag-c. 7,9-Infinity-c. 10-X-Mas-c. 12-Washington
crossing the Delaware parody-c ... 9 18 27 47 61 75
V4#1(#28, 4/48) - 7(#34, 2-3/49) ... 8 16 24 44 57 70
V5#1(#35, 4-5/49) - 4(#38, 10-11/49) ... 8 16 24 44 57 70
39-43-L. B. Cole-c. 40-Xmas-c ... 23 46 69 130 205 280
Accepted Reprint No. 43 (nd); L.B. Cole-c ... 10 20 30 54 72 90

FRITZI RITZ (See Comics On Parade, Single Series #5, 1(reprint), Tip Top & United Comics)
FRITZI RITZ (United Comics No. 8-26) (Also see Tip Topper for early Peanuts by Schulz)
United Features Synd./St. John No. 37-55/Dell No. 56 on:
1939; Fall, 1948; No. 3, 1949 - No. 7, 1949; No. 37, 3-4/53 - No. 36, 9-10/54; No. 37 - No. 55,
9-11/57; No. 56, 12-2/57-58 - No. 59, 9-11/58
Single Series #5 (1939) ... 32 64 96 186 293 400
nn(1948)-Special Fall issue; by Ernie Bushmiller ... 17 34 51 98 154 210
3(#1) ... 12 24 36 67 94 120

Frogman Comics #11 © HILL

Frontline Combat #2 © WMG

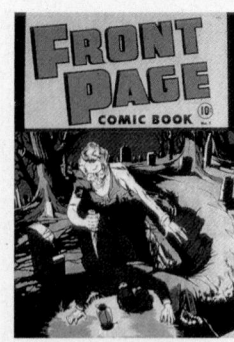
Front Page Comic Book #1 © HARV

	GD 2.0	VG 4.0	FN 6.0	VF 8.0	VF/NM 9.0	NM- 9.2
4-7(1949): 6-Abbie & Slats app.	9	18	27	50	65	80
27(1953)-33,37-50,57-59-Early Peanuts (1-4 pgs.) by Schulz. 29-Five pg. Abbie & Slats; 1 pg. Mamie by Russell Patterson. 38(9/55)-41(4/56)-Low print run	9	18	27	47	61	75
34-36,51-56: 36-1 pg. Mamie by Patterson	8	16	24	40	50	60

NOTE: Abbie & Slats in #6,7, 27-31. Li'l Abner in #32-36.

FROGMAN COMICS
Hillman Periodicals: Jan-Feb, 1952 - No. 11, May, 1953

	GD 2.0	VG 4.0	FN 6.0	VF 8.0	VF/NM 9.0	NM- 9.2
1	15	30	45	84	127	170
2	9	18	27	52	69	85
3,4,6-11: 4-Meskin-a	8	16	24	40	50	60
5-Krigstein-a	8	16	24	44	57	70

FROGMEN, THE
Dell Publishing Co.: No. 1258, Feb-Apr, 1962 - No. 11, Nov-Jan, 1964-65 (Painted-c)

	GD 2.0	VG 4.0	FN 6.0	VF 8.0	VF/NM 9.0	NM- 9.2
Four Color 1258(#1)-Evans-a	8	16	24	52	86	120
2,3-Evans-a; part Frazetta inks in #2,3	6	12	18	37	59	80
4,6-11	4	8	12	24	37	50
5-Toth-a	4	8	12	28	44	60

FROM BEYOND THE UNKNOWN
National Periodical Publications: 10-11/69 - No. 25, 11-12/73

	GD 2.0	VG 4.0	FN 6.0	VF 8.0	VF/NM 9.0	NM- 9.2
1	5	10	15	32	51	70
2-6	3	6	9	18	27	35
7-11: (64 pgs.) 7-Intro Col. Glenn Merrit	3	6	9	20	30	40
12-17: (52 pgs.) 13-Wood-a(i)(r). 17-Pres. Nixon-c	3	6	9	16	23	30
18-25: Star Rovers-r begin #18,19. Space Museum in #23-25	2	4	6	10	14	18

NOTE: N. Adams c-3, 6, 8, 9. Anderson c-2, 4, 5, 10, 11i, 15-17, 22; reprints-3, 4, 6-8, 10, 11, 13-16, 24, 25. Infantino r-1-5, 7-19, 23-25; c-11p. Kaluta c-18, 19. Gil Kane a-9r. Kubert c-1, 7, 12-14. Toth a-2r. Wood a-13i. Photo c-22.

FROM DUSK TILL DAWN (Movie)
Big Entertainment: 1996 ($4.95, one-shot)

nn-Adaptation of the film; Brereton-c	5.00
nn-($9.95)Deluxe Ed. w/ new material	10.00

FROM HELL
Mad Love/Tundra Publishing/Kitchen Sink: 1991 - No. 11, Sept, 1998 (B&W)

	GD 2.0	VG 4.0	FN 6.0	VF 8.0	VF/NM 9.0	NM- 9.2
1-Alan Moore and Eddie Campbell's Jack The Ripper story collected from the Taboo anthology series	2	4	6	11	16	20
1-(2nd printing)	2	4	6	8	10	12
1-(3rd printing)	1	2	3	4	5	7
2	1	2	3	5	6	8
2-(2nd printing)						6.00
2-(3rd printing)						4.00
3-1st Kitchen Sink Press issue	1	2	3	5	6	8
3-(2nd printing)						5.00
4-10: 10-(8/96)	1	2	3	4	5	7
11-Dance of the Gull Catchers (9/98, $4.95) Epilogue	2	4	6	9	12	15
Tundra Publishing reprintings 1-5 ('92)	1	2	3	4	5	7
HC						125.00
HC Ltd. Edition of 1,000 (signed and numbered)						225.00
TPB-1st printing (11/99)						60.00
TPB-2nd printing (3/00)						50.00
TPB-3rd printing (11/00)						40.00
TPB-4th printing (7/01) Regular and movie covers						35.00
TPB-5th printing - Regular and movie covers						35.00

FROM HERE TO INSANITY (Satire) (Formerly Eh! #1-7) (See Frantic & Frenzy)
Charlton Comics: No. 8, Feb, 1955 - V3#1, 1956

	GD 2.0	VG 4.0	FN 6.0	VF 8.0	VF/NM 9.0	NM- 9.2
8	17	34	51	98	154	210
9	15	30	45	88	137	185
10-Ditko-c/a (3 pgs.)	23	46	69	135	213	290
11,12-All Kirby except 4 pgs.	33	66	99	190	300	410
V3#1(1956)-Ward-c/a(2) (signed McCartney); 5 pgs. Wolverton-a; 3 pgs. Ditko-a; magazine format (cover says "Crazy, Man, Crazy" and becomes Crazy, Man, Crazy with V2#2)	42	84	126	238	379	520

FROM THE PIT
Fantagor Press: 1994 ($4.95, one-shot, mature)

	GD 2.0	VG 4.0	FN 6.0	VF 8.0	VF/NM 9.0	NM- 9.2
1-R. Corben-a; HP Lovecraft back-up story	1	2	3	5	6	8

FRONTIER DOCTOR (TV)
Dell Publishing Co.: No. 877, Feb, 1958 (one-shot)

	GD 2.0	VG 4.0	FN 6.0	VF 8.0	VF/NM 9.0	NM- 9.2
Four Color 877-Toth-a, Rex Allen photo-c	9	18	27	63	107	150

FRONTIER FIGHTERS
National Periodical Publications: Sept-Oct, 1955 - No. 8, Nov-Dec, 1956

	GD 2.0	VG 4.0	FN 6.0	VF 8.0	VF/NM 9.0	NM- 9.2
1-Davy Crockett, Buffalo Bill (by Kubert), Kit Carson begin (Scarce)	55	110	165	344	572	800
2	37	74	111	214	340	465
3-8	34	68	102	197	311	425

NOTE: Buffalo Bill by Kubert in all.

FRONTIER ROMANCES
Avon Periodicals/I. W.: Nov-Dec, 1949 - No. 2, Feb-Mar, 1950 (Painted-c)

	GD 2.0	VG 4.0	FN 6.0	VF 8.0	VF/NM 9.0	NM- 9.2
1-Used in SOTI, pg. 180 (General reference) & illo. "Erotic spanking in a western comic book"	48	96	144	293	484	675
2 (Scarce)-Woodish-a by Stallman	37	74	111	213	337	460
I.W. Reprint #1-Reprints Avon's #1	4	8	12	22	34	45
I.W. Reprint #9-Reprints ?	3	6	9	16	22	28

FRONTIER SCOUT: DAN'L BOONE (Formerly Death Valley; The Masked Raider No. 14 on)
Charlton Comics: No. 10, Jan, 1956 - No. 13, Aug, 1956; V2#14, Mar, 1965

	GD 2.0	VG 4.0	FN 6.0	VF 8.0	VF/NM 9.0	NM- 9.2
10	10	20	30	54	72	90
11-13(1956)	6	12	18	31	38	45
V2#14(3/65)	5	10	14	20	24	28

FRONTIER TRAIL (The Rider No. 1-5)
Ajax/Farrell Publ.: No. 6, May, 1958

	GD 2.0	VG 4.0	FN 6.0	VF 8.0	VF/NM 9.0	NM- 9.2
6	6	12	18	28	34	40

FRONTIER WESTERN
Atlas Comics (PrPI): Feb, 1956 - No. 10, Aug, 1957

	GD 2.0	VG 4.0	FN 6.0	VF 8.0	VF/NM 9.0	NM- 9.2
1	19	38	57	109	172	235
2,3,6-Williamson-a, 4 pgs. each	14	28	42	80	115	150
4,7,9,10: 10-Check-a	10	20	30	56	76	95
5-Crandall, Baker, Davis-a; Williamson text illos	14	28	42	76	108	140
8-Crandall, Morrow, & Wildey-a	10	20	30	58	79	100

NOTE: Baker a-9. Colan a-2, 6. Drucker a-3, 4. Heath c-5. Maneely c/a-2, 7, 9. Maurera a-2. Romita a-7. Severin c-6, 8, 10. Tuska a-2. Wildey a-5, 8. Ringo Kid in No. 4.

FRONTLINE COMBAT
E. C. Comics: July-Aug, 1951 - No. 15, Jan, 1954

	GD 2.0	VG 4.0	FN 6.0	VF 8.0	VF/NM 9.0	NM- 9.2
1-Severin/Kurtzman-a	66	132	198	528	827	1125
2	36	72	108	288	449	610
3	28	56	84	224	350	475
4-Used in SOTI, pg. 257; contains "Airburst" by Kurtzman which is his personal all-time favorite story	26	52	78	208	324	440
5-John Severin and Bill Elder bios.	22	44	66	176	276	375
6-10: 6-Kurtzman bio.	19	38	57	152	239	325
11-15	14	28	42	112	179	245

NOTE: Davis a-in all; c-11, 12. Evans a-10-15. Heath a-1. Kubert a-14. Kurtzman a-1-5; c-1-9. Severin a-5-7, 9, 13, 15. Severin/Elder a-2-11; c-10. Toth a-8, 12. Wood a-1-4, 6-10, 12-15; c-13-15. Special issues: No. 7 (Iwo Jima), No. 9 (Civil War), No. 12 (Air Force).
(Canadian reprints known; see Table of Contents.)

FRONTLINE COMBAT
Russ Cochran/Gemstone Publishing: Aug, 1995 - No. 14 ($2.00/$2.50)

1-14-E.C. reprints in all	3.00

FRONT PAGE COMIC BOOK
Front Page Comics (Harvey): 1945

	GD 2.0	VG 4.0	FN 6.0	VF 8.0	VF/NM 9.0	NM- 9.2
1-Kubert-a; intro. & 1st app. Man in Black by Powell; Fuje-c	40	80	120	239	380	520

FROST AND FIRE (See DC Science Fiction Graphic Novel)

FROSTY THE SNOWMAN
Dell Publishing Co.: No. 359, Nov, 1951 - No. 1272, Dec-Feb?/1961-62

	GD 2.0	VG 4.0	FN 6.0	VF 8.0	VF/NM 9.0	NM- 9.2
Four Color 359 (#1)	9	18	27	63	107	150
Four Color 435,514,601,661	6	12	18	37	59	80
Four Color 748,861,950,1065,1153,1272	5	10	15	32	51	70

FRUITMAN SPECIAL
Harvey Publications: Dec, 1969 (68 pgs.)

	GD 2.0	VG 4.0	FN 6.0	VF 8.0	VF/NM 9.0	NM- 9.2
1-Funny super hero	3	6	9	20	30	40

F-TROOP (TV)
Dell Publishing Co.: Aug, 1966 - No. 7, Aug, 1967 (All have photo-c)

	GD 2.0	VG 4.0	FN 6.0	VF 8.0	VF/NM 9.0	NM- 9.2
1	9	18	27	63	107	150
2-7	6	12	18	37	59	80

FUGITIVES FROM JUSTICE
St. John Publishing Co.: Feb, 1952 - No. 5, Oct, 1952

Fun Comics #9 © STAR

The Funnies #61 © DELL

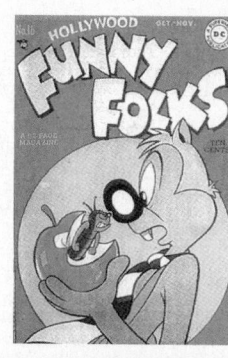

Funny Folks #16 © DC

	GD 2.0	VG 4.0	FN 6.0	VF 8.0	VF/NM 9.0	NM- 9.2
1	22	44	66	126	198	270
2-Matt Baker-r/Northwest Mounties #2; Vic Flint strip reprints begin	22	44	66	126	198	270
3-Reprints panel from Authentic Police Cases that was used in SOTI with changes; Tuska-a	21	42	63	122	191	260
4	12	24	36	67	94	120
5-Last Vic Flint-r; bondage-c	14	28	42	76	108	140

FUGITOID
Mirage Studios: 1985 (B&W, magazine size, one-shot)

	GD 2.0	VG 4.0	FN 6.0	VF 8.0	VF/NM 9.0	NM- 9.2
1-Ties into Teenage Mutant Ninja Turtles #5	1	2	3	4	5	7

FULL OF FUN
Red Top (Decker Publ.)(Farrell)/I. W. Enterprises: Aug, 1957 - No. 2, Nov, 1957; 1964

	GD 2.0	VG 4.0	FN 6.0	VF 8.0	VF/NM 9.0	NM- 9.2
1(1957)-Funny animal; Dave Berg-a	7	14	21	37	46	55
2-Reprints Bingo, the Monkey Doodle Boy	5	10	15	22	26	30
8-I.W. Reprint('64)	2	4	6	9	12	15

FUN AT CHRISTMAS (See March of Comics No. 138)

FUN CLUB COMICS (See Interstate Theatres...)

FUN COMICS (Formerly Holiday Comics #1-8; Mighty Bear #13 on)
Star Publications: No. 9, Jan, 1953 - No. 12, Oct, 1953

	GD 2.0	VG 4.0	FN 6.0	VF 8.0	VF/NM 9.0	NM- 9.2
9-(25¢ Giant)-L. B. Cole X-Mas-c; X-Mas issue	23	46	69	132	209	285
10-12-L. B. Cole-c. 12-Mighty Bear-c/story	18	36	54	105	165	225

FUNDAY FUNNIES (See Famous TV..., and Harvey Hits No. 35,40)

FUN-IN (TV)(Hanna-Barbera)
Gold Key: Feb, 1970 - No. 10, Jan, 1972; No. 11, 4/74 - No. 15, 12/74

	GD 2.0	VG 4.0	FN 6.0	VF 8.0	VF/NM 9.0	NM- 9.2
1-Dastardly & Muttley in Their Flying Machines; Perils of Penelope Pitstop in #1-4; It's the Wolf in all	6	12	18	41	66	90
2-4,6-Cattanooga Cats in 2-4	3	6	9	21	32	42
5,7-Motormouse & Autocat, Dastardly & Muttley in both; It's the Wolf in #7	4	8	12	23	36	48
8,10-The Harlem Globetrotters, Dastardly & Muttley in #10	4	8	12	23	36	48
9-Where's Huddles?, Dastardly & Muttley, Motormouse & Autocat app.	4	8	12	23	36	48
11-Butch Cassidy	3	6	9	19	29	38
12-15: 12,15-Speed Buggy. 13-Hair Bear Bunch. 14-Inch High Private Eye	3	6	9	19	29	38

FUNKY PHANTOM, THE (TV)
Gold Key: Mar, 1972 - No. 13, Mar, 1975 (Hanna-Barbera)

	GD 2.0	VG 4.0	FN 6.0	VF 8.0	VF/NM 9.0	NM- 9.2
1	5	10	15	32	51	70
2-5	3	6	9	18	27	35
6-13	3	6	9	15	21	26

FUNLAND
Ziff-Davis (Approved Comics): No date (1940s) (25¢)

	GD 2.0	VG 4.0	FN 6.0	VF 8.0	VF/NM 9.0	NM- 9.2
nn-Contains games, puzzles, cut-outs, etc.	18	36	54	105	165	225

FUNLAND COMICS
Croyden Publishers: 1945

	GD 2.0	VG 4.0	FN 6.0	VF 8.0	VF/NM 9.0	NM- 9.2
1-Funny animal	15	30	45	85	130	175

FUNNIES, THE (New Funnies No. 65 on)
Dell Publishing Co.: Oct, 1936 - No. 64, May, 1942

	GD 2.0	VG 4.0	FN 6.0	VF 8.0	VF/NM 9.0	NM- 9.2
1-Tailspin Tommy, Mutt & Jeff, Alley Oop (1st app?), Capt. Easy (1st app.), Don Dixon begin	400	800	1200	2300	3450	4600
2 (11/36)-Scribbly by Mayer begins (see Popular Comics #6 for 1st app.)	178	356	534	1024	1537	2050
3	122	244	366	702	1051	1400
4,5: 4(1/37)-Christmas-c	91	182	273	523	787	1050
6-10	70	140	210	403	602	800
11-20: 16-Christmas-c	65	130	195	374	562	750
21-29: 25-Crime Busters by McWilliams(4pgs.)	52	104	156	299	450	600
30-John Carter of Mars (origin/1st app.) begins by Edgar Rice Burroughs; Warner Bros.' Bosko-c (4/39)	145	290	435	906	1503	2100
31-34,36-44: 33-John Coleman Burroughs art begins on John Carter. 34-Last funny-c.	78	156	234	488	807	1125
35-(9/39)-Mr. District Attorney begins; based on radio show; 1st cover app. John Carter of Mars	83	166	249	519	860	1200
45-Origin/1st app. Phantasmo, the Master of the World (Dell's 1st super-hero, 7/40) & his sidekick Whizzer McGee	91	182	273	569	947	1325
46-50: 46-The Black Knight begins, ends #62	55	110	165	344	572	800
51-56-Last ERB John Carter of Mars	46	92	138	281	466	650

	GD 2.0	VG 4.0	FN 6.0	VF 8.0	VF/NM 9.0	NM- 9.2
57-Intro. & origin Captain Midnight (7/41)	345	690	1035	2243	3972	5700
58-60: 58-Captain Midnight-c begin, end #63	86	172	258	538	894	1250
61-Andy Panda begins by Walter Lantz	93	186	279	581	966	1350
62,63: 63-Last Captain Midnight-c; bondage-c	67	134	201	419	697	975
64-Format change; Oswald the Rabbit, Felix the Cat, Li'l Eight Ball app.; origin & 1st app. Woody Woodpecker in Oswald; last Capt. Midnight; Oswald, Andy Panda, Li'l Eight Ball-c	134	268	402	838	1394	1950

NOTE: *Mayer* c-26, 48. *McWilliams* art in many issues on "Rex King of the Deep". *Alley Oop* c-17, 20. *Captain Midnight* c-57(i/2), 58-63. *John Carter* c-35-37, 40. *Phantasmo* c-45-56, 57(1/2), 58-61(part). *Rex King* c-38, 39, 42. *Tailspin Tommy* c-41.

FUNNIES ANNUAL, THE
Avon Periodicals: 1959 ($1.00, approx. 7x10", B&W; tabloid-size)

	GD 2.0	VG 4.0	FN 6.0	VF 8.0	VF/NM 9.0	NM- 9.2
1-(Rare)-Features the best newspaper comic strips of the year: Archie, Snuffy Smith, Beetle Bailey, Henry, Blondie, Steve Canyon, Buz Sawyer, The Little King, Hi & Lois, Popeye, & others. Also has a chronological history of the comics from 2000 B.C. to 1959.	43	86	129	262	431	600

FUNNIES ON PARADE (See Promotional Comics section)

FUNNY ANIMALS (See Fawcett's Funny Animals)
Charlton Comics: Sept, 1984 - No. 2, Nov, 1984

	GD 2.0	VG 4.0	FN 6.0	VF 8.0	VF/NM 9.0	NM- 9.2
1,2-Atomic Mouse-r; low print						6.00

FUNNYBONE (... The Laugh-Book of Comical Comics)
La Salle Publishing Co.: 1944 (25¢, 132 pgs.)

	GD 2.0	VG 4.0	FN 6.0	VF 8.0	VF/NM 9.0	NM- 9.2
nn	29	58	87	167	264	360

FUNNY BOOK (...Magazine for Young Folks) (Hocus Pocus No. 9)
Parents' Magazine Press (Funny Book Publishing Corp.):
Dec, 1942 - No. 7, Aug-Sept, 1946 (Comics, stories, puzzles, games)

	GD 2.0	VG 4.0	FN 6.0	VF 8.0	VF/NM 9.0	NM- 9.2
1-Funny animal; Alice In Wonderland app.	15	30	45	84	127	170
2-Gulliver in Giant-Land	10	20	30	54	72	90
3-9: 4-Advs. of Robin Hood. 9-Hocus-Pocus strip	8	16	24	44	57	70

FUNNY COMICS
Modern Store Publ.: 1955 (7¢, 5x7", 36 pgs.)

	GD 2.0	VG 4.0	FN 6.0	VF 8.0	VF/NM 9.0	NM- 9.2
1-Funny animal	4	8	12	22	34	45

FUNNY COMIC TUNES (See Funny Tunes)

FUNNY FABLES
Decker Publications (Red Top Comics): Aug, 1957 - V2#2, Nov, 1957

	GD 2.0	VG 4.0	FN 6.0	VF 8.0	VF/NM 9.0	NM- 9.2
V1#1	6	12	18	31	38	45
V1#2,V2#1,2: V1#2 (11/57)-Reissue of V1#1	5	10	14	20	24	28

FUNNY FILMS (Features funny animal characters from films)
American Comics Group(Michel Publ./Titan Publ.): Sept-Oct, 1949 - No. 29, May-June, 1954 (No. 1-4: 52 pgs.)

	GD 2.0	VG 4.0	FN 6.0	VF 8.0	VF/NM 9.0	NM- 9.2
1-Puss N' Boots, Blunderbunny begin	18	36	54	105	165	225
2	11	22	33	62	86	110
3-10: 3-X-Mas-c	9	18	27	47	61	75
11-20	7	14	21	35	43	50
21-29	6	12	18	28	34	40

FUNNY FOLKS
DC Comics: Feb, 1946

nn-Ashcan comic, not distributed to newsstands, only for in house use					(no known sales)	

FUNNY FOLKS (Hollywood... on cover only No. 16-26; becomes Hollywood Funny Folks No. 27 on)
National Periodical Publ.: April-May, 1946 - No. 26, June-July, 1950 (52 pgs., #15 on)

	GD 2.0	VG 4.0	FN 6.0	VF 8.0	VF/NM 9.0	NM- 9.2
1-Nutsy Squirrel begins (1st app.) by Rube Grossman; Grossman-a in most issues	40	80	120	240	383	525
2	20	40	60	115	180	245
3-5: 4-1st Nutsy Squirrel-c	15	30	45	84	127	170
6-10: 6,9-Nutsy Squirrel-c begin	11	22	33	62	86	110
11-26: 15-Begin 52 pg. issue (8-9/48)	10	20	30	54	72	90

NOTE: *Sheldon Mayer* a-in some issues. *Post* a-18. Christmas c-12.

FUNNY FROLICS
Timely/Marvel Comics (SPI): Summer, 1945 - No. 5, Dec, 1946

	GD 2.0	VG 4.0	FN 6.0	VF 8.0	VF/NM 9.0	NM- 9.2
1-Sharpy Fox, Puffy Pig, Krazy Krow	25	50	75	145	228	310
2	14	28	42	81	118	155
3,4	11	22	33	64	90	115
5-Kurtzman-a	13	26	39	72	101	130

FUNNY FUNNIES
Nedor Publishing Co.: April, 1943 (68 pgs.)

	GD 2.0	VG 4.0	FN 6.0	VF 8.0	VF/NM 9.0	NM- 9.2
1-Funny animals; Peter Porker app.	19	38	57	109	172	235

Funny Pages V3 #9 © CEN

Funny Tunes #3 © AVON

Fury of Firestorm #4 © DC

	GD	VG	FN	VF	VF/NM	NM-		GD	VG	FN	VF	VF/NM	NM-
	2.0	4.0	6.0	8.0	9.0	9.2		2.0	4.0	6.0	8.0	9.0	9.2

FUNNYMAN (Also see Cisco Kid Comics & Extra Comics)
Magazine Enterprises: Dec, 1947; No. 1, Jan, 1948 - No. 6, Aug, 1948

nn(12/47)-Prepublication B&W undistributed copy by Siegel & Shuster-(5-3/4x8"), 16 pgs.;
    Sold at auction in 1997 for $575.00
1-Siegel & Shuster-a in all; Dick Ayers 1st pro work (as assistant) on 1st few issues

	45	90	135	275	450	625
2	27	54	81	158	249	340
3-6	23	46	69	130	205	280

FUNNY MOVIES (See 3-D Funny Movies)

FUNNY PAGES (Formerly The Comics Magazine)
Comics Magazine Co./Ultem Publ.(Chesler)/Centaur Publications:
No. 6, Nov, 1936 - No. 42, Oct, 1940

V1#6 (nn, nd)-The Clock begins (2 pgs., 1st app.), ends #11; The Clock is the 1st masked						
comic book hero	255	510	765	1594	2647	3700
7-11	97	194	291	606	1003	1400
V2#1-V2#3: V2#1 (9/37)(V2#2 on-c; V2#1 in indicia). V2#2 (10/37)(V2#3 on-c; V2#2 in indicia).						
V2#3(11/37)-5	68	136	204	425	705	985
6(1st Centaur, 3/38)	91	182	273	569	947	1325
7-9	68	136	204	425	705	985
10(Scarce, 9/38)-1st app. of The Arrow by Gustavson (Blue costume)						
	339	678	1017	2204	3902	5600
11,12	121	242	363	756	1253	1750
V3#1-Bruce Wayne prototype in "Case of the Missing Heir," by Bob Kane, 3 months before						
app. Batman (See Det. Pic. Stories #5)	128	256	384	800	1325	1850
2-6,8-10-Last funny covers	110	220	330	688	1144	1600
7-1st Arrow-c (9/39)	290	580	870	1813	3007	4200
9-Tarpe Mills jungle-c	121	242	363	756	1253	1750
10-2nd Arrow-c	235	470	705	1469	2435	3400

V4#1(1/40, Arrow-c)-(Rare)-The Owl & The Phantom Rider app.; origin Mantoka, Maker of
    Magic by Jack Cole. Mad Ming begins, ends #42; Tarpe Mills-a

	276	552	828	1725	2863	4000
35-Classic Arrow-c	276	552	828	1725	2863	4000
36-38-Mad Ming-c	117	234	351	731	1216	1700
39-41-Arrow-c	200	400	600	1250	2075	2900
42 (Scarce,10/40)-Last Arrow; Arrow-c	207	414	621	1294	2147	3000

NOTE: *Biro* c-V2#9. *Burgos* c-V3#10. *Jack Cole* a-V2#3, 7, 8, 10, 11, V3#2, 6, 9, 10. *Jack Cole* a-V2#3, 7, 8, 10, 11, V3#2, 6, 9.
Eisner a-V1#7, 8?, 10. *Ken Ernst* a-V1#7, 8. *Everett* a-V2#11 (illos). *Filchock* c-V2#10, V3#6. *Gill Fox* a-V2#11.
Sid Greene a-39. *Guardineer* a-V2#2, 3, 5. *Gustavson* a-V2#5, 11, 12, V3#1-10, 35, 38-42; c-V3#7, 35, 39-42.
Bob Kane a-V3#1. *McWilliams* a-V2#12, V3#1, 3-6. *Tarpe Mills* a-V3#8-10, V4#1; c-V3#9. *Ed Moore Jr.* a-
V2#12. *Schwab* c-V3#1. *Bob Wood* a-V2#2, 3, 5.

FUNNY PICTURE STORIES (Comic Pages V3#4 on)
Comics Magazine Co./Centaur Publications: Nov, 1936 - V3#3, May, 1939

V1#1-The Clock begins (c-feature)(see Funny Pages for 1st app.)						
	345	690	1035	2243	3972	5700
2	124	248	372	775	1288	1800
3-7(6/37): 4-Eisner-a; X-Mas-c. 7-Racial humor-c	83	166	249	519	860	1200
V2#1 (9/37)-V1#10 on-c; V2#1 in indicia)-Jack Strand begins						
	54	108	162	338	557	775
2 (10/37), V1#11 on-c; V2#2 in indicia	54	108	162	338	557	775
3-5,7-11(11/38)-4-Xmas-c	48	96	144	293	484	675
6(1st Centaur, 3/38)	79	158	237	494	822	1150
V3#1(1/39)-3	46	92	138	281	466	650

NOTE: *Biro* c-V2#1, 8, 9, 11. *Guardineer* a-V1#11; c-V2#6, V3#5. *Bob Wood* c/a-V1#11, V2#2; c-V2#3, 5.

FUNNY STUFF (Becomes The Dodo & the Frog No. 80)
All-American/National Periodical Publications No. 7 on: Summer, 1944 - No. 79, July-Aug,
1954 (#1-7 are quarterly)

1-The Three Mouseketeers (ends #28) & The "Terrific Whatzit" begin;						
Sheldon Mayer-a; Grossman-a in most issues	88	176	264	550	913	1275
2-Sheldon Mayer-a	42	84	126	256	421	585
3-5: 3-Flash parody. 5-All Mayer-a/scripts issue	30	60	90	174	275	375
6-10 10-(6/46)	20	40	60	117	184	250
11-17,19	15	30	45	90	140	190
18-The Dodo and the Frog (2/47, 1st app?) begin?; X-Mas-c						
	27	54	81	158	249	340
19-1st Dodo & the Frog-c (3/47)	18	36	54	105	165	225
20-2nd Dodo & the Frog-c (4/47)	14	28	42	80	115	150
21,23-30: 24-Infinity-c. 30-Christmas-c	11	22	33	62	86	110
22-Superman cameo	38	76	114	222	351	480
31-79: 70-1st Bo Bunny by Mayer & begins	10	20	30	56	76	95

NOTE: *Mayer* a-1-8, 55, .57, 58, 61, 62, 64, 65, 68, 70, 72, 74-79; c-2, 5, 6, 8.

FUNNY STUFF STOCKING STUFFER
DC Comics: Mar, 1985 ($1.25, 52 pgs.)

| 1-Almost every DC funny animal featured | | | | | | 4.00 |

FUNNY 3-D
Harvey Publications: December, 1953 (25¢, came with 2 pair of glasses)

| 1-Shows cover in 3-D on inside | 11 | 22 | 33 | 62 | 86 | 110 |

FUNNY TUNES (Animated Funny Comic Tunes No. 16-22; Funny Comic Tunes No. 23,
on covers only; Oscar No. 24 on)
U.S.A. Comics Magazine Corp. (Timely): No. 16, Summer, 1944 - No. 23, Fall, 1946

16-Silly Seal, Ziggy Pig, Krazy Krow begin	15	30	45	88	137	185
17 (Fall/44)-Becomes Gay Comics #18 on?	13	26	39	74	105	135
18-22: 21-Super Rabbit app.	11	22	33	62	86	110
23-Kurtzman-a	12	24	36	69	97	125

FUNNY TUNES (Becomes Space Comics #4 on)
Avon Periodicals: July, 1953 - No. 3, Dec-Jan, 1953-54

1-Space Mouse, Peter Rabbit, Merry Mouse, Spotty the Pup, Cicero the Cat begin;						
all continue in Space Comics	11	22	33	60	83	105
2,3	8	16	24	44	57	70

FUNNY WORLD
Marbak Press: 1947 - No. 3, 1948

| 1-The Berrys, The Toodles & other strip-r begin | 9 | 18 | 27 | 47 | 61 | 75 |
| 2,3 | 6 | 12 | 18 | 31 | 38 | 45 |

FUNTASTIC WORLD OF HANNA-BARBERA, THE (TV)
Marvel Comics Group: Dec, 1977 - No. 3, June, 1978 ($1.25, oversized)

| 1-3: 1-The Flintstones Christmas Party(12/77). 2-Yogi Bear's Easter Parade(3/78). | | | | | | |
| 3-Laff-a-lympics(6/78) | 4 | 8 | 12 | 24 | 37 | 50 |

FUN TIME
Ace Periodicals: Spring, 1953; No. 2, Sum, 1953; No. 3(nn), Fall, 1953; No. 4, Wint, 1953-54

| 1-(25¢, 100 pgs.)-Funny animal | 18 | 36 | 54 | 105 | 165 | 225 |
| 2-4 (All 25¢, 100 pgs.) | 15 | 30 | 45 | 85 | 130 | 175 |

FUN WITH SANTA CLAUS (See March of Comics No. 11, 108, 325)

FURTHER ADVENTURES OF CYCLOPS AND PHOENIX (Also see Adventures of Cyclops
and Phoenix, Uncanny X-Men & X-Men)
Marvel Comics: June, 1996 - No. 4, Sept, 1996 ($1.95, limited series)

| 1-4: Origin of Mr. Sinister; Milligan scripts; John Paul Leon-c/a(p). 2-4-Apocalypse app. | | | | | | 3.00 |
| Trade Paperback (1997, $14.99) r/1-4 | | | | | | 15.00 |

FURTHER ADVENTURES OF INDIANA JONES, THE (Movie) (Also see
Indiana Jones and the Last Crusade & Indiana Jones and the Temple of Doom)
Marvel Comics Group: Jan, 1983 - No. 34, Mar, 1986

| 1-Byrne/Austin-a; Austin-c | | | | | | 4.00 |
| 2-34: 2-Byrne/Austin-c/a | | | | | | 2.50 |

NOTE: *Austin* a-1i, 2i, 6i, 9i; c-1, 2i, 6i, 9i. *Byrne* a-1p, 2p; c-2p. *Chaykin* a-6p; c-6p, 8p-10p. *Ditko* a-21p, 25-28,
34. *Golden* c-24, 25. *Simonson* c-9. Painted c-14.

FURTHER ADVENTURES OF NYOKA, THE JUNGLE GIRL, THE (See Nyoka)
AC Comics: 1988 - No. 5, 1989 ($1.95, color; $2.25/$2.50, B&W)

| 1-5 : 1,2-Bill Black-a plus reprints. 3-Photo-c. 5-(B&W)-Reprints plus movie photos | | | | | | 2.50 |

FURY (Straight Arrow's Horse...) (See A-1 No. 119)

FURY (TV) (See March of Comics No. 178)

FURY (of Nukla No. #200)
Dell Publishing Co./Gold Key: No. 781, Mar, 1957 - Nov, 1962 (All photo-c)

Four Color 781	8	16	24	52	86	120
Four Color 885,975,1031,1080,1133,1172,1218,1296	6	12	18	41	66	90
01292-208(#1-'62), 10020-211(11/62-G.K.)	6	12	18	37	59	80

FURY
Marvel Comics: May, 1994 ($2.95, one-shot)

| 1-Iron Man, Red Skull, FF, Hatemonger, Logan app.; Origin Nick Fury | | | | | | 3.00 |

FURY (Volume 3)
Marvel Comics (MAX): Nov, 2001 - No. 6, Apr, 2002 ($2.99, mature content)

| 1-6-Ennis-s/Robertson-a | | | | | | 3.00 |

FURY/ AGENT 13
Marvel Comics: June, 1998 - No. 2, July, 1998 ($2.99, limited series)

| 1,2-Nick Fury returns | | | | | | 3.00 |

FURY OF FIRESTORM, THE (Becomes Firestorm The Nuclear Man on cover with #50,
in indicia with #65) (Also see Firestorm)
DC Comics: June, 1982 - No. 64, Oct, 1987 (75¢ on)

| 1-Intro The Black Bison; brief origin | | | | | | 6.00 |
| 2-40,43-64: 4-JLA x-over. 17-1st app. Firehawk. 21-Death of Killer Frost. 22-Origin. 23-Intro. | | | | | | |

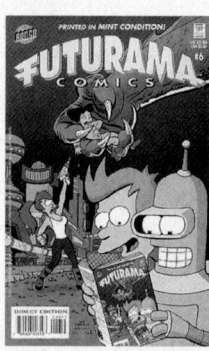

Futurama Comics #6 © Bongo

Future Comics #1 © DMP

Galactus the Devourer #1 © MAR

	GD	VG	FN	VF	VF/NM	NM-		GD	VG	FN	VF	VF/NM	NM-
	2.0	4.0	6.0	8.0	9.0	9.2		2.0	4.0	6.0	8.0	9.0	9.2

Byte. 24-(6/84)-1st app. Blue Devil & Bug (origin); origin Byte. 34-1st app./origin Killer Frost II. 39-Weasel's ID revealed. 48-Intro. Moonbow. 53-Origin/1st app. Silver Shade.
55,56-Legends x-over. 58-1st app./origin new Parasite ... 2.50
41,42-Crisis x-over ... 3.00
61-Test cover variant; Superman logo ... 4 8 12 22 34 45
Annual 1-4: 1(1983), 2(1984), 3(1985), 4(1986) ... 3.00
NOTE: *Colan* a-19p, Annual 4p. *Giffen* a-Annual 4p. *Gil Kane* c-30. *Nino* a-37. *Tuska* a-(p)-17, 18, 32, 45.

FURY OF SHIELD
Marvel Comics: Apr, 1995 - No. 4, July, 1995 ($2.50/$1.95, limited series)
1 ($2.50)-Foil-c ... 3.00
2-4: 4-Bagged w/ decoder ... 2.50

FURY: PEACEMAKER
Marvel Comics: Apr, 2006 - No. 6, Sept, 2006 ($3.50, limited series)
1-6-Flashback to WW2; Ennis-s/Robertson-a. 1-Deodato-c. 2-Texeira-c. 5-Dillon-c ... 3.50
TPB (2006, $17.99) r/#1-6 ... 18.00

FUSED
Image Comics: Mar, 2002 - No. 4, Jan, 2003 ($2.95)
1-4-Steve Niles-s. 1,2-Paul Lee-a. 3-Brad Rader-a. 4-Templesmith-a ... 3.00
Canned Heat TPB (Dark Horse, 6/04, $12.95) r/series; Dan Wickline intro. ... 13.00

FUSED
Dark Horse Comics: Dec, 2003 - No. 4, Mar, 2004 ($2.95)
1-4-Steve Niles-s/Josh Medors-a. 1-Powell-c ... 3.00

FUSION
Eclipse Comics: Jan, 1987 - No. 17, Oct, 1989 ($2.00, B&W, Baxter paper)
1-17: 11-The Weasel Patrol begins (1st app.?) ... 2.50

FUTURAMA (TV)
Bongo Comics: 2000 - Present ($2.50/$2.99, bi-monthly)
1-Based on the FOX-TV animated series; Groening/Morrison-c ... 3.50
1-San Diego Comic-Con Premiere Edition ... 5.00
2-32: 8-CGC cover spoof; X-Men parody ... 3.00
Futurama Adventures TPB (2004, $14.95) r/#5-9 ... 15.00
Futurama Conquers the Universe TPB (2007, $14.95) r/#10-13 ... 15.00
Futurama-O-Rama TPB (2002, $12.95) r/#1-4; sketch pages of Fry's development ... 13.00
...: The Time Bender Trilogy TPB (2006, $14.95) r/#16-19; cover gallery ... 15.00

FUTURAMA/SIMPSONS INFINITELY SECRET CROSSOVER CRISIS (TV) (See Simpsons/Futurama Crossover Crisis II for sequel)
Bongo Comics: 2002 - No. 2, 2002 ($2.50, limited series)
1,2-Evil Brain Spawns put Futurama crew into the Simpsons' Springfield ... 2.50

FUTURE COMICS
David McKay Publications: June, 1940 - No. 4, Sept, 1940
1-(6/40, 64 pgs.)-Origin The Phantom (1st in comics) (4 pgs.); The Lone Ranger (8 pgs.) & Saturn Against the Earth (4 pgs.) begin ... 283 566 849 1769 2935 4100
2 ... 121 242 363 756 1253 1750
3,4 ... 86 172 258 538 894 1250

FUTURE COP L.A.P.D. (Electronic Arts video game) (Also see Promotional Comics section)
DC Comics (WildStorm): Jan, 1999 ($4.95, magazine sized)
1-Stories & art by various ... 5.00

FUTURE WORLD COMICS
George W. Dougherty: Summer, 1946 - No. 2, Fall, 1946
1,2: H. C. Kiefer-c; preview of the World of Tomorrow ... 31 62 93 178 282 385

FUTURE WORLD COMIX (Warren Presents...)
Warren Publications: Sept, 1978 (B&W magazine, 84 pgs.)
1-Corben, Maroto, Morrow, Nino, Sutton-a; Todd-c/a; contains nudity panels ... 2 4 6 8 10 12

FUTURIANS, THE (See Marvel Graphic Novel #9)
Lodestone Publishing/Eternity Comics: Sept, 1985 - No. 3, 1985 ($1.50)
1-3: Indicia title "Dave Cockrum's..." ... 2.25
Graphic Novel 1 ($9.95, Eternity)-r/#1-3, plus never published #4 issue ... 10.00

G-8 (Listed as G-Eight)

GABBY (Formerly Ken Shannon) (Teen humor)
Quality Comics Group: No. 11, Jul, 1953; No. 2, Sep, 1953 - No. 9, Sep, 1954
11(#1)(7/53) ... 8 16 24 44 57 70
2 ... 6 12 18 28 34 40
3-9 ... 5 10 15 23 28 32

GABBY GOB (See Harvey Hits No. 85, 90, 94, 97, 100, 103, 106, 109)

GABBY HAYES ADVENTURE COMICS
Toby Press: Dec, 1953
1-Photo-c ... 15 30 45 88 137 185

GABBY HAYES WESTERN (Movie star)(See Monte Hale, Real Western Hero & Western Hero)
Fawcett Publications/Charlton Comics No. 51 on: Nov, 1948 - No. 50, Jan, 1953; No. 51, Dec, 1954 - No. 59, Jan, 1957
1-Gabby & his horse Corker begin; photo front/back-c begin ... 43 86 129 262 419 575
2 ... 22 44 66 127 196 265
3-5 ... 16 32 48 89 137 185
6-10: 9-Young Falcon begins ... 14 28 42 78 112 145
11-20: 19-Last photo back-c ... 11 22 33 64 90 115
21-49: 20,22,24,26,28,29-(52 pgs.) ... 9 18 27 52 69 85
50-(1/53)-Last Fawcett issue; last photo-c? ... 10 20 30 58 79 100
51-(12/54)-1st Charlton issue; photo-c ... 11 22 33 60 83 105
52-59(1955-57): 53,55-Photo-c. 58-Swayze-a ... 8 16 24 42 54 65

GAGS
United Features Synd./Triangle Publ. No. 9 on: Jul, 1937 - V3#10, Oct, 1944 (13-3/4x10-3/4")
1(7/37)-52 pgs.; 20 pgs. Grin & Bear It, Fellow Citizen ... 10 20 30 54 72 90
V1#9 (36 pgs.) (7/42) ... 6 12 18 28 34 40
V3#10 ... 5 10 15 24 30 35

GALACTICA: THE NEW MILLENNIUM
Realm Press: Sept, 1999 ($2.99)
1-Stories by Shooter, Braden, Kuhoric ... 3.00

GALACTIC GUARDIANS
Marvel Comics: July, 1994 - No. 4, Oct, 1994 ($1.50, limited series)
1-4 ... 2.50

GALACTIC WARS COMIX (Warren Presents... on cover)
Warren Publications: Dec, 1978 (B&W magazine, 84 pgs.)
nn-Wood, Williamson-r; Battlestar Galactica/Flash Gordon photo/text stories ... 2 4 6 8 10 12

GALACTUS THE DEVOURER
Marvel Comics: Sept, 1999 - No. 6, Mar, 2000 ($3.50/$2.50, limited series)
1-($3.50) L. Simonson-s/Muth & Sienkiewicz-a ... 3.50
2-5-($2.50) Buscema & Sienkiewicz-a ... 2.50
6-($3.50) Death of Galactus; Buscema & Sienkiewicz-a ... 3.50

GALAXIA (Magazine)
Astral Publ.: 1981 ($2.50, B&W, 52 pgs.)
1-Buckler/Giordano-c; Texeira/Guice-a; 1st app. Astron, Sojourner, Bloodwing, Warlords; Buckler-s/a ... 2 4 6 8 10 12

GALLANT MEN, THE (TV)
Gold Key: Oct, 1963 (Photo-c)
1(1008-310)-Manning-a ... 3 6 9 20 30 40

GALLEGHER, BOY REPORTER (Disney, TV)
Gold Key: May, 1965
1(10149-505)-Photo-c ... 3 6 9 17 25 32

GAMBIT (See X-Men #266 & X-Men Annual #14)
Marvel Comics: Dec, 1993 - No. 4, Mar, 1994 ($2.00, limited series)
1-($2.50)-Lee Weeks-c/a in all; gold foil stamped-c ... 5.00
1 (Gold) ... 2 4 6 9 12 15
2-4 ... 3.00

GAMBIT
Marvel Comics: Sept, 1997 - No. 4, Dec, 1997 ($2.50, limited series)
1-4-Janson-a/Mackie & Kavanagh-s ... 3.00

GAMBIT
Marvel Comics: Feb, 1999 - No. 25, Feb, 2001 ($2.99/$1.99)
1-($2.99) Five covers; Nicieza-a/Skroce-a ... 4.00
2-11,13-16-($1.99): 2-Two covers (Skroce & Adam Kubert) ... 2.50
12-($2.99) ... 3.50
17-24: 17-Begin $2.25-c. 21-Mystique-c/app. ... 2.50
25-($2.99) Leads into "Gambit & Bishop" ... 3.00
...1999 Annual ($3.50) Nicieza-s/McDaniel-a ... 3.50
...2000 Annual ($3.50) Nicieza-s/Derenick & Smith-a ... 3.50

Gambit #11 © MAR

Gamekeeper #2 © Virgin Comics

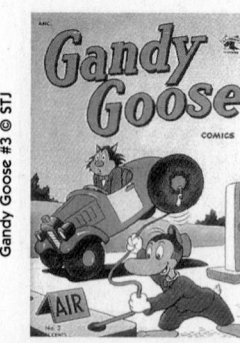

Gandy Goose #3 © STJ

	GD 2.0	VG 4.0	FN 6.0	VF 8.0	VF/NM 9.0	NM- 9.2

GAMBIT
Marvel Comics: Nov, 2004 - No. 12, Aug, 2005 ($2.99)

	GD 2.0	VG 4.0	FN 6.0	VF 8.0	VF/NM 9.0	NM- 9.2
1-12: 1-Jeanty-a/Land-c/Layman-s. 5-Wolverine-c/app. 9-Brother Voodoo-c/app.						3.00
...: Hath No Fury TPB (2005, $14.99) r/#7-12						15.00
...: House of Cards TPB (2005, $14.99) r/#1-6; Land cover sketches; unused covers						15.00

GAMBIT & BISHOP (... : Sons of the Atom on cover)
Marvel Comics: Feb, 2001 - No. 6, May, 2001 ($2.25, bi-weekly limited series)

Alpha (2/01) Prelude to series; Nord-a						2.50
1-6-Jeanty-a/Williams-c						2.50
Genesis (3/01, $3.50) reprints their first apps. and first meeting						3.50

GAMBIT AND THE X-TERNALS
Marvel Comics: Mar, 1995 - No. 4, July, 1995 ($1.95, limited series)

1-4-Age of Apocalypse						2.50

GAMEBOY (Super Mario covers on all)
Valiant: 1990 - No. 5 ($1.95, coated-c)

1-5: 3,4-Layton-c. 4-Morrow-a. 5-Layton-c(i)						4.00

GAMEKEEPER (Guy Ritchie's...)
Virgin Comics: Mar, 2007 - Present ($2.99)

1-4-Andy Diggle-s/Mukesh Singh-a; 2 covers on each						3.00
1-Extended Edition (6/07, $2.99) r/#1 with script excerpt and sketch art						3.00

GAMERA
Dark Horse Comics: Aug, 1996 - No. 4, Nov, 1996 ($2.95, limited series)

1-4						3.00

GAMMARAUDERS
DC Comics: Jan, 1989 - No. 10, Dec, 1989 ($1.25/$1.50/$2.00)

1-10-Based on TSR game						2.50

GAMORRA SWIMSUIT SPECIAL
Image Comics (WildStorm Productions): June, 1996 ($2.50, one-shot)

1-Campbell wraparound-c; pinups						2.50

GANDY GOOSE (Movies/TV)(See All Surprise, Giant Comics Edition #5A &10,
Paul Terry's Comics & Terry-Toons)
St. John Publ. Co./Pines No. 5,6: Mar, 1953 - No. 5, Nov, 1953; No. 5, Fall, 1956 - No. 6,
Sum/58

	GD 2.0	VG 4.0	FN 6.0	VF 8.0	VF/NM 9.0	NM- 9.2
1-All St. John issues are pre-code	10	20	30	56	76	95
2	6	12	18	33	41	48
3-5(1953)(St. John)	6	12	18	29	36	42
5,6(1956-58)(Pines)-CBS Television Presents...	5	10	15	23	28	32

GANG BUSTERS (See Popular Comics #38)
David McKay/Dell Publishing Co.: 1938 - 1943

	GD 2.0	VG 4.0	FN 6.0	VF 8.0	VF/NM 9.0	NM- 9.2
Feature Books 17(McKay)('38)-1st app.	65	130	195	406	671	935
Large Feature Comic 10('39)-Scarce)	65	130	195	406	671	935
Large Feature Comic 17('41)	45	90	135	275	450	625
Four Color 7(1940)	48	96	144	293	484	675
Four Color 23('42)	40	80	120	235	368	500
Four Color 24('43)	26	52	78	211	348	485

GANG BUSTERS (Radio/TV)(Gangbusters #14 on)
National Periodical Publ.: Dec-Jan, 1947-48 - No. 67, Dec-Jan, 1958-59 (No. 1-23: 52 pgs.)

	GD 2.0	VG 4.0	FN 6.0	VF 8.0	VF/NM 9.0	NM- 9.2
1	83	166	249	519	860	1200
2	40	80	120	235	368	500
3-5	28	56	84	162	256	350
6-10: 9-Dan Barry-a. 9,10-Photo-c	21	42	63	122	191	260
11-13-Photo-c	17	34	51	98	154	210
14,17-Frazetta-a, 8 pgs. each. 14-Photo-c	36	72	108	208	329	450
15,16,18-20,26: 26-Kirby-a	15	30	45	84	127	170
21-25,27-30	14	28	42	76	108	140
31-44: 44-Last Pre-code (2-3/55)	12	24	36	67	94	120
45-67	10	20	30	54	72	90

NOTE: **Barry** a-6, 8, 10. **Drucker** a-51. **Moreira** a-48, 50, 59. **Roussos** a-8.

GANGLAND
DC Comics (Vertigo): Jun, 1998 - No. 4, Sept, 1998 ($2.95, limited series)

1-4:Crime anthology by various. 2-Corben-a						3.00
TPB-(2000, $12.95) r/#1-4; Bradstreet-c						13.00

GANGSTERS AND GUN MOLLS
Avon Per./Realistic Comics: Sept, 1951 - No. 4, June, 1952 (Painted c-1-3)

	GD 2.0	VG 4.0	FN 6.0	VF 8.0	VF/NM 9.0	NM- 9.2
1-Wood-a, 1 pg; c-/Avon paperback #292	49	98	147	299	492	685
2-Check-a, 8 pgs.; Kamen-a; Bonnie Parker story	40	80	120	235	368	500

	GD 2.0	VG 4.0	FN 6.0	VF 8.0	VF/NM 9.0	NM- 9.2
3-Marijuana mentioned; used in **POP**, pg. 84,85	38	76	114	219	347	475
4-Syd Shores-c	29	58	87	167	264	360

GANGSTERS CAN'T WIN
D. S. Publishing Co.: Feb-Mar, 1948 - No. 9, June-July, 1949 (All 52 pgs?)

	GD 2.0	VG 4.0	FN 6.0	VF 8.0	VF/NM 9.0	NM- 9.2
1-True crime stories	36	72	108	208	329	450
2	18	36	54	105	165	225
3,5,6	16	32	48	94	147	200
4-Acid in face story	21	42	63	122	191	260
7-9	14	28	42	80	115	150

NOTE: **Ingles** a-5, 6. **McWilliams** a-5, 7, 8. **Reinman** c-6.

GANG WORLD
Standard Comics: No. 5, Nov, 1952 - No. 6, Jan, 1953

	GD 2.0	VG 4.0	FN 6.0	VF 8.0	VF/NM 9.0	NM- 9.2
5-Bondage-c	19	38	57	109	172	235
6	15	30	45	83	124	165

GARGOYLE (See The Defenders #94)
Marvel Comics Group: June, 1985 - No. 4, Sept, 1985 (75¢, limited series)

1-Wrightson-c; character from Defenders						3.50
2-4						2.50

GARGOYLES (TV cartoon)
Marvel Comics: Feb, 1995 - No. 17, June, 1996 ($2.50)

1-17: Based on animated series						3.00

GARRISON'S GORILLAS (TV)
Dell Publishing Co.: Jan, 1968 - No. 4, Oct, 1968; No. 5, Oct, 1969 (Photo-c)

	GD 2.0	VG 4.0	FN 6.0	VF 8.0	VF/NM 9.0	NM- 9.2
1	5	10	15	30	48	65
2-5: 5-Reprints #1	3	6	9	20	30	40

GARY GIANNI'S THE MONSTERMEN
Dark Horse Comics: Aug, 1999 ($2.95, one-shot)

1-Gianni-s/c/a; back-up Hellboy story by Mignola						3.00

GASM
Stories, Layouts & Press, Inc.: Nov, 1977 - nn(No. 4), Jun, 1978 (B&W/color)

	GD 2.0	VG 4.0	FN 6.0	VF 8.0	VF/NM 9.0	NM- 9.2
1-Mark Wheatley-s/a; Gene Day-s/a; Workman-a	2	4	6	11	16	20
nn(#2, 2/78) Day-s/a; Wheatley-a; Workman-a	2	4	6	8	11	14
nn(#3, 4/78) Day-s/a; Wheatley-a; Corben-a	2	4	6	13	18	22
nn(#4, 6/78) Hempel-a; Howarth-a; Corben-a	3	6	9	14	19	24

GASOLINE ALLEY (Top Love Stories No. 3 on?)
Star Publications: Sept-Oct, 1950 - No. 2, Dec, 1950 (Newspaper-r)

	GD 2.0	VG 4.0	FN 6.0	VF 8.0	VF/NM 9.0	NM- 9.2
1-Contains 1 pg. intro. history of the strip (The Life of Skeezix); reprints 15 scenes of highlights from 1921-1935, plus an adventure from 1935 and 1936 strips; a 2-pg. filler is included on the life of the creator Frank King, with photo of the cartoonist.						
	21	42	63	120	188	255
2-(1936-37 reprints)-L. B. Cole-c	23	46	69	135	213	290

(See Super Book No. 21)

GASP!
American Comics Group: Mar, 1967 - No. 4, Aug, 1967 (12¢)

	GD 2.0	VG 4.0	FN 6.0	VF 8.0	VF/NM 9.0	NM- 9.2
1	4	8	12	28	44	60
2-4	3	6	9	18	27	35

GATECRASHER
Black Bull Entertainment: Mar, 2000 - No. 4, Jun, 2000 ($2.50, limited series)

1,2-Waid-s/Conner & Palmiotti-c/a; 1,2-variant-c by J.G. Jones						2.50
3,4: 3-Jusko var-c. 4-Linsner-c						2.50
... Ring of Fire TPB (11/00, $12.95) r/#1-4; Hughes-c; Ennis intro.						13.00

GATECRASHER (Regular series)
Black Bull Entertainment: Aug, 2000 - No. 6, Jan, 2001 ($2.50, limited series)

1-6-Waid-s/Conner & Palmiotti-c/a; 1-3-Variant-c by Fabry. 4-Hildebrandts variant-c. 5-Art Adams var-c. 6-Texeira var-c						2.50

GAY COMICS (Honeymoon No. 41)
Timely Comics/USA Comic Mag. Co. No. 18-24: Mar, 1944 (no month);
No. 18, Fall, 1944 - No. 40, Oct, 1949

	GD 2.0	VG 4.0	FN 6.0	VF 8.0	VF/NM 9.0	NM- 9.2
1-Wolverton's Powerhouse Pepper; Tessie the Typist begins; 1st app. Willie (one shot)	54	108	162	338	557	775
18-(Formerly Funny Tunes #17?)-Wolverton-a	36	72	108	208	329	450
19-29: Wolverton-a in all. 21,24-6 pg., 7 pg. Powerhouse Pepper; additional 2 pg. story in 24. 23-7 pg Wolverton story & 2 two pg stories(total of 11pgs.).						
24,29-Kurtzman-a (24-"Hey Look"(2))	32	64	96	186	293	400
30,33,36,37-Kurtzman's "Hey Look"	14	28	42	76	108	140
31-Kurtzman's "Hey Look" (1), Giggles 'N' Grins (1-1/2)						
	14	28	42	76	108	140

Gay Comics #24 © MAR

Gene Autry Comics #73 © DELL

Generation X #40 © MAR

	GD 2.0	VG 4.0	FN 6.0	VF 8.0	VF/NM 9.0	NM- 9.2
32,35,38-40: 35-Nellie The Nurse begins?	12	24	36	69	97	125
34-Three Kurtzman's "Hey Look"	14	28	42	80	115	150

GAY COMICS (Also see Smile, Tickle, & Whee Comics)
Modern Store Publ.: 1955 (7¢, 5x7-1/4", 52 pgs.)

1	4	8	12	22	34	45

GAY PURR-EE (See Movie Comics)

GAZILLION
Image Comics: Nov, 1998 ($2.50, one-shot)

1-Howard Shum-s/ Keron Grant-a						2.50

GEAR STATION, THE
Image Comics: Mar, 2000 - No. 5, Nov, 2000 ($2.50)

1-Four covers by Ross, Turner, Pat Lee, Fraga						2.50
1-($6.95) DF Cover						7.00
2-5: 2-Two covers by Fraga and Art Adams						2.50

GEEK, THE (See Brother Power... & Vertigo Visions)

GEEKSVILLE (Also see 3 Geeks, The)
3 Finger Prints/ Image: Aug, 1999 - No. 6 Mar, 2001 ($2.75/$2.95, B&W)

1,2,4-6-The 3 Geeks by Koslowski; Innocent Bystander by Sassaman						3.00
3-Includes "Babes & Blades" mini-comic						5.00
0-(3/00) First Image issue						3.00
(Vol. 2) 1-4-($2.95) 3-Mini-comic insert by the Geeks. 4-Steve Borock app.						3.00

G-8 AND HIS BATTLE ACES (Based on pulps)
Gold Key: Oct, 1966

1 (10184-610)-Painted-c	4	8	12	25	38	50

G-8 AND HIS BATTLE ACES
Blazing Comics: 1991 ($1.50, one-shot)

1-Glanzman-a; Truman-c						2.50

NOTE: Flip book format with "The Spider's Web" #1 on other side w/**Glanzman**-a, **Truman**-c.

GEISHA (Also see Oni Press Summer Vacation Supercolor Fun Special)
Oni Press: Sept, 1998 - No. 4, Dec, 1998 ($2.95, limited series)

1-4-Andi Watson-s/a. 2-Adam Warren-c						3.00
...One Shot (5/00, $4.50)						4.50
The Complete Geisha TPB (5/03, $15.95, digest size) r/#1-4, One Shot & story from Oni Press Summer Vacation Supercolor Fun Special						16.00

GEM COMICS
Spotlight Publishers: Apr, 1945 (52 pgs)

1-Little Mohee, Steve Strong app.; Jungle bondage-c	48	96	144	293	484	675

GEMINAR
Image Comics: July, 2000 ($4.95, B&W)

1-(72-Page Special) Terry Collins-s/Al Bigley-a						5.00

GEMINI BLOOD
DC Comics (Helix): Sept, 1996 - No. 9, May, 1997 ($2.25, limited series)

1-9: 5-Simonson-c						2.50

GEN ACTIVE
DC Comics (WildStorm): May, 2000 - No. 6, Aug, 2001 ($3.95)

1-6: 1-Covers by Campbell and Madureira; Gen 13 & DV8 app. 5-Mahfood-a; Quitely and Stelfreeze-c. 6-Portacio-a/c						4.00

GENE AUTRY (See March of Comics No. 25, 28, 39, 54, 78, 90, 104, 120, 135, 150 in the Promotional Comics section & Western Roundup under Dell Giants)

GENE AUTRY COMICS (Movie, Radio star; singing cowboy)
Fawcett Publications: 1941 (On sale 12/31/41) - No. 10, 1943 (68 pgs.)
(Dell takes over with No. 11)

1 (Rare)-Gene Autry & his horse Champion begin	706	1412	2118	4942	8471	12,000
2-(1942)	150	300	450	938	1519	2100
3-5: 3-(11/1/42)	91	182	273	569	922	1275
6-10	71	142	213	444	722	1000

GENE AUTRY COMICS (...& Champion No. 102 on)
Dell Publishing Co.: No. 11, 1943 - No. 121, Jan-Mar, 1959 (TV - later issues)

11 (1943, 60 pgs.)-Continuation of Fawcett series; photo back-c; first Dell issue	46	92	138	368	622	875
12 (2/44, 60 pgs.)	41	82	123	326	551	775
Four Color 47 (1944, 60 pgs.)	41	82	123	326	551	775
Four Color 57 (11/44),66('45)(52 pgs. each)	39	78	117	293	497	700

	GD 2.0	VG 4.0	FN 6.0	VF 8.0	VF/NM 9.0	NM- 9.2
Four Color 75,83 ('45, 36 pgs. each)	31	62	93	225	383	540
Four Color 93 ('45, 36 pgs.)	29	58	87	211	348	485
Four Color 100 ('46, 36 pgs.) First Gene Autry photo-c	31	62	93	224	380	535
1 (5-6/46, 52 pgs.)	41	82	123	326	551	775
2 (7-8/46)-Photo-c begin, end #111	23	46	69	163	269	375
3-5: 4-Intro Flapjack Hobbs	17	34	51	118	197	275
6-10	15	30	45	106	173	240
11-20: 20-Panhandle Pete begins	13	26	39	87	144	200
21-29 (36 pgs.)	11	22	33	73	119	165
30-40 (52 pgs.)	10	20	30	65	103	140
41-56 (52 pgs.)	9	18	27	55	85	115
57-66 (36 pgs.): 58-X-mas-c	8	16	24	47	71	95
67-80 (52 pgs.): 70-X-mas-c	8	16	24	47	71	95
81-90 (52 pgs.): 82-X-mas-c. 87-Blank inside-c	7	14	21	43	64	85
91-99 (36 pgs. No. 91-on). 94-X-mas-c	6	12	18	38	57	75
100	7	14	21	40	60	80
101-111-Last Gene Autry photo-c	6	12	18	35	53	70
112-121-All Champion painted-c, most by Savitt	6	12	18	33	49	65

NOTE: Photo back covers 4-18, 20-45, 48-65. **Manning** a-118. **Jesse Marsh** art: 4-Color No. 66, 75, 93, 100, No. 1-25, 27-37, 39, 40.

GENE AUTRY'S CHAMPION (TV)
Dell Publ. Co.: No. 287, 8/50; No. 319, 2/51; No. 3, 8-10/51 - No. 19, 8-10/55

Four Color 287(#1)('50, 52pgs.)-Photo-c	12	24	36	82	146	210
Four Color 319(#2, '51), 3: 2-Painted-c begin, most by Sam Savitt	7	14	21	45	73	100
4-19: 19-Last painted-c	5	10	15	33	55	75

GENE DOGS
Marvel Comics UK: Oct, 1993 - No. 4, Jan, 1994 ($1.75, limited series)

1-($2.75)-Polybagged w/4 trading cards						3.00
2-4: 2-Vs. Genetix						2.50

GENE POOL
IDW Publishing: Oct, 2003 ($6.99, squarebound)

nn-Wein & Wolfman-s/Cummings-a						7.00

GENERAL DOUGLAS MACARTHUR
Fox Features Syndicate: 1951

nn-True life story	20	40	60	117	184	250

GENERIC COMIC, THE
Marvel Comics Group: Apr, 1984 (one-shot)

1						3.00

GENERATION HEX
DC Comics (Amalgam): June, 1997 ($1.95, one-shot)

1-Milligan-s/ Pollina & Morales-a						2.50

GENERATION M (Follows House of M x-over)
Marvel Comics: Jan, 2006 - No. 5, May, 2006 ($2.99, limited series)

1-5-Jenkins-s/Bachs-a. 1-Chamber app. 2-Jubilee app. 3-Blob-c. 4-Angel-c						3.00
Decimation: Generation M TPB (2006, $13.99) r/#1-5						14.00

GENERATION NEXT
Marvel Comics: Mar, 1995 - No. 4, June, 1995 ($1.95, limited series)

1-4-Age of Apocalypse; Scott Lobdell scripts & Chris Bachalo-c/a						2.50

GENERATION X (See Gen [13]/ Generation X)
Marvel Comics: Oct, 1994 - No. 75, June, 2001 ($1.50/$1.95/$1.99/$2.25)

Collectors Preview ($1.75), "Ashcan" Edition						2.25
-1(7/97) Flashback story						3.00
1/2 (San Diego giveaway)	2	4	6	8	10	12
1-($3.95)-Wraparound chromium-c; Scott Lobdell scripts & Chris Bachalo-a begins						6.00
2-($1.95)-Deluxe edition, Bachalo-a						4.00
3,4-($1.95)-Deluxe Edition; Bachalo-a						3.00
2-10: 2-4 Standard Edition. 5-Returns from "Age of Apocalypse," begin $1.95-c. 6-Bachalo-a(p) ends, returns #17. 7-Roger Cruz-a(p). 10-Omega Red-c/app.						3.00
11-24, 26-28: 13,14-Bishop-app. 17-Stan Lee app. (Stan Lee scripts own dialogue); Bachalo/Buckingham-a; Onslaught update. 18-Toad cameo. 20-Franklin Richards app; Howard the Duck cameo. 21-Howard the Duck app. 22-Nightmare app.						2.50
25-($2.99)-Wraparound-c. Black Tom, Howard the Duck app.						3.50
29-37: 29-Begin $1.99-c, "Operation Zero Tolerance". 33-Hama-s						2.50
38-49: 38-Dodson-a begins. 40-Penance ID revealed. 49-Maggott app.						2.50
50,57-($2.99): 50-Crossover w/X-Man #50						3.50
51-56, 58-62: 59-Avengers & Spider-Man app.						2.50
63-74: 63-Ellis-s begin. 64-Begin $2.25-c. 69-71-Art Adams-c						2.50

Gen 12 #1 © WSP

Gen 13 #25 © WSP

Gen 13 (2007 series) #7 © WSP

	GD	VG	FN	VF	VF/NM	NM-		GD	VG	FN	VF	VF/NM	NM-
	2.0	4.0	6.0	8.0	9.0	9.2		2.0	4.0	6.0	8.0	9.0	9.2

75-($2.99) Final issue; Chamber joins the X-Men; Lim-a ... 3.00
'95 Special-($3.95) ... 4.00
'96 Special-($2.95)-Wraparound-c; Jeff Johnson-c/a ... 3.50
'97 Special-($2.99)-Wraparound-c; ... 3.50
'98 Annual-($3.50)-vs. Dracula ... 3.50
'99 Annual-($3.50)-Monet leaves ... 3.50
75¢ Ashcan Edition ... 3.00
...Holiday Special 1 (2/99, $3.50) Pollina-a ... 3.50
...Underground Special 1 (5/98, $2.50, B&W) Mahfood-a ... 2.50

GENERATION X/ GEN 13 (Also see Gen 13/ Generation X)
Marvel Comics: 1997 ($3.99, one-shot)

1-Robinson-s/Larroca-a(p) ... 4.00

GENE RODDENBERRY'S LOST UNIVERSE
Tekno Comix: Apr, 1995 - No. 7, Oct, 1995 ($1.95)

1-7: 1-3-w/ bound-in game piece & trading card. 4-w/bound-in trading card ... 2.50

GENE RODDENBERRY'S XANDER IN LOST UNIVERSE
Tekno Comix: No. 0, Nov, 1995; No. 1, Dec, 1995 - No. 8, July, 1996 ($2.25)

0,1-8: 1-5-Jae Lee-c. 4-Polybagged. 8-Pt. 5 of The Big Bang x-over ... 2.50

GENESIS (See DC related titles)
DC Comics: Oct, 1997 - No. 4, Oct, 1997 ($1.95, weekly limited series)

1-4: Byrne-s/Wagner-a(p) in all. ... 3.00

GENESIS: THE #1 COLLECTION (WildStorm Archives)
WildStorm Productions: 1998 ($9.99, TPB, B&W)

nn-Reprints #1 issues of WildStorm titles and pin-ups ... 10.00

GENETIX
Marvel Comics UK: Oct, 1993 - No. 6, Mar, 1994 ($1.75, limited series)

1-($2.75)-Polybagged w/4 cards; Dark Guard app. ... 3.00
2-6: 2-Intro Tektos. 4-Vs. Gene Dogs ... 2.50

GEN 12 (Also see Gen 13 and Team 7)
Image Comics (WildStorm Productions): Feb, 1998 - No. 5, June, 1998 ($2.50, lim. series)

1-5: 1-Team 7 & Gen13 app.; wraparound-c ... 3.00

GEN 13 (Also see Wild C.A.T.S. #1 & Deathmate Black #2)
Image Comics (WildStorm Productions): Feb, 1994 - No. 5, July 1994 ($1.95, limited series)

0 (8/95, $2.50)-Ch. 1 w/Jim Lee-p; Ch.4 w/Charest-p ... 3.00

	1	2	3	4	5	7
1/2	1	2	3	4	5	7
1-($2.50)-Created by Jim Lee	1	3	4	6	8	10

1-2nd printing ... 2.50
1-"3-D" Edition (9/97, $4.95)-w/glasses ... 5.00

| 2-($2.50) | 1 | 2 | 3 | 4 | 5 | 7 |

3-Pitt-c & story ... 4.00
4-Pitt-c & story; wraparound-c ... 3.00
5 ... 4.00
5-Alternate Portacio-c; see Deathblow #5 ... 6.00
...Collected Edition ('94, $12.95)-r/#1-5 ... 13.00
...Rave ($1.50, 3/95)-wraparound-c ... 3.00
...: Who They Are And How They Came To Be... (2006, $14.99) r/#1-5; sketch gallery ... 15.00
NOTE: Issues 1-4 contain coupons redeemable for the ashcan edition of Gen 13 #0. Price listed is for a complete book.

GEN 13
Image Comics (WildStorm Productions): Mar, 1995 - No. 36, Dec, 1998;
DC Comics (WildStorm): No. 37, Mar, 1999 - No. 77, Jul, 2002 ($2.95/$2.50)

1-A (Charge)-Campbell/Garner-c ... 4.50
1-B (Thumbs Up)-Campbell/Garner-c ... 4.50
1-C-1-F,1-I-1-M: 1-C (Lil' GEN 13)-Campbell-c. 1-D (Barbari-GEN)-Simon Bisley-c. 1-E (Your Friendly Neighborhood Grunge)-Cleary-c. 1-F (GEN 13 Goes Madison Ave.)-Golden-c.
1-I (That's the way we became GEN 13)-Campbell/Gibson-c. 1-J (All Dolled Up)-Campbell/McWeeney-c. 1-K (Verti-GEN)-Dunn-c. 1-L (Picto-Fiction). 1-M (Do it Yourself Cover)

	1	2	3	4	5	7
1-G (Lin-GEN-re)-Michael Lopez-c	2	4	6	8	10	12
1-H (GEN-et Jackson)-Jason Pearson-c	2	4	6	8	10	12
1-Chromium-c by Campbell	4	8	12	28	44	60
1-Chromium-c by Jim Lee	6	12	18	37	59	80

1-"3-D" Edition (2/98, $4.95)-w/glasses ... 5.00
2 ($1.95, Newsstand)-WildStorm Rising Pt. 4; bound-in card ... 2.50
2-12: 2-($2.50, Direct Market)-WildStorm Rising Pt. 4, bound-in card. 6,7-Jim Lee-c/a(p).
9-Ramos-a. 10,11-Fire From Heaven Pt. 3, & Pt.9 ... 3.00
11-($4.95)-Special European Tour Edition; chromium-c

| | 2 | 4 | 6 | 10 | 14 | 18 |

13A,13B,13C-($1.30, 13 pgs.): 13A-Archie & Friends app. 13B-Bone-c/app.;

Teenage Mutant Ninja Turtles, Madman, Spawn & Jim Lee app. ... 3.00
14-24: 20-Last Campbell-a ... 2.50
25-($3.50)-Two covers by Campbell and Charest ... 3.50
25-($3.50)-Voyager Pack w/Danger Girl preview ... 4.50
25-Foil-c ... 10.00
26-32,34: 26-Arcudi-s/Frank-a begins. 34-Back-up story by Art Adams ... 2.50
33-Flip book w/Planetary preview ... 4.00
35-49: 36,38,40-Two covers. 37-First DC issue. 41-Last Frank-a ... 2.50
50-($3.95) Two covers by Lee and Benes; art by various ... 4.00
51-76: 51-Moy-a; Fairchild loses her powers. 60-Warren-s/a. 66-Art by various incl. Campbell (3 pgs.). 70,75,76-Mays-a. 76-Original team dies ... 2.50
77-($3.50) Mays, Andrews, Warren-a ... 3.50
Annual 1 (1997, $2.95) Ellis-s/ Dillon-c/a. ... 3.50
Annual 1999 ($3.50, DC) Slipstream x-over w/ DV8 ... 3.50
Annual 2000 ($3.50) Devil's Night x-over w/WildStorm titles; Bermejo-c ... 3.50
...: A Christmas Caper (1/00, $5.95, one-shot) McWeeney-s/a ... 6.00
... Archives (4/98, $12.99) B&W reprints of mini-series, #0,1/2,1-13ABC; includes cover gallery and sourcebook ... 13.00
...: Carny Folk (2/00, $3.50) Collect back-up stories ... 3.50
... European Vacation TPB ($6.95) r/#6,7 ... 7.00
.../ Fantastic Four (2001, $5.95) Maguire-s/c/a(p) ... 6.00
... Going West (6/99, $2.50, one-shot) Pruett-s ... 2.50
... Grunge Saves the World (5/99, $5.95, one-shot) Altieri-c/a ... 6.00
... I Love New York TPB ($9.95) r/part #25, 26-29; Frank-c ... 10.00
... London, New York, Hell TPB ($6.95) r/Annual #1 & Bootleg Ann. #1 ... 7.00
... Lost in Paradise TPB ($6.95) r/#3-5 ... 7.00
.../ Maxx (12/95, $3.50, one-shot) Messner-Loebs-a, 1st Coker-c/a. ... 3.50
... Meanwhile (2003, $17.95) r/#43,44,66-70; all Warren-s; art by various ... 18.00
... Medicine Song (2001, $5.95) Brent Anderson-c/a(p)/Raab-s ... 6.00
... Science Friction (2001, $5.95) Haley & Lopresti-a ... 6.00
... Starting Over TPB ($14.95) r/#1-7 ... 15.00
... Superhuman Like You TPB ($12.95) r/#60-65; Warren-a ... 13.00
... #13 A,B&C Collected Edition ($6.95, TPB) r/#13A,B&C ... 7.00
... 3-D Special (1997, $4.95, one-shot)-w/glasses ... 5.00
... The Unreal World (7/96, $2.95, one-shot) Humberto Ramos-a ... 3.00
... We'll Take Manhattan TPB ($14.95) r/#45-50; new Benes-c ... 15.00
... Wired (4/99, $2.50, one-shot) Richard Bennett-c/a ... 2.50
... Yearbook 1997 (6/97, $2.50) College-themed stories and pin-ups by various ... 2.50
...'Zine (12/96, $1.95, B&W, digest size) Campbell/Garner-a ... 2.50
Variant Collection-Four editions all 13 variants w/Chromium variant-limited, signed) ... 100.00

GEN 13
DC Comics (WildStorm): No. 0, Sept, 2002 - No. 16, Feb, 2004 ($2.95)

0-(13¢-c) Intro. new team; includes previews of 21 Down & The Resistance ... 2.50
1-Claremont-s/Garza-c/a; Fairchild app. ... 3.00
2-16: 8-13-Bachs-a. 16-Original team returns ... 3.00
...: September Song TPB (2003, $19.95) r/#0-6; Garza sketch pages ... 20.00

GEN 13 (Volume 4)
DC Comics (WildStorm): Dec, 2006 - Present ($2.99)

1-11: 1-Simone-s/Caldwell-a; re-intro the original team; Caldwell-c. 8-The Authority app. ... 3.00
1-Variant-c by J. Scott Campbell ... 5.00
...: Best of a Bad Lot TPB (2007, $14.99) r/#1-6 ... 15.00

GEN 13 BOOTLEG
Image Comics (WildStorm): Nov, 1996 - No. 20, Jul, 1998 ($2.50)

1-Alan Davis-a; alternate costumes-c ... 2.50
1-Team falling variant-c ... 3.00
2-7: 2-Alan Davis-a. 5,6-Terry Moore-s. 7-Robinson-s/Scott Hampton-a ... 2.50
8-10-Adam Warren-s/a ... 4.00
11-20: 11,12-Lopresti-a/s & Simonson-s. 13-Wieringo-s/a. 14-Marriotte-s/Phillips-a. 15,16-Strnad-s/Shaw-a. 18-Altieri-s/a(p)/c, 18-Variant-c by Bruce Timm ... 2.50
Annual 1 (2/98, $2.95) Ellis-s/Dillon-c/a ... 3.00
... Grunge: The Movie (12/97, $9.95) r/#8-10, Warren-c ... 10.00
...Vol. 1 TPB (10/98, $11.95) r/#1-4 ... 12.00

GEN 13/ GENERATION X (Also see Generation X / Gen 13)
Image Comics (WildStorm Publications): July, 1997 ($2.95, one-shot)

1-Choi-s/ Art Adams-p/Garner-i. Variant covers by Adams/Garner and Campbell/McWeeney ... 3.00
1-($4.95) 3-D Edition w/glasses; Campbell-c ... 5.00

GEN 13 INTERACTIVE
Image Comics (WildStorm): Oct, 1997 - No. 3, Dec, 1997 ($2.50, lim. series)

1-3-Internet voting used to determine storyline ... 2.50
... Plus! (7/98, $11.95) r/series & 3-D Special (in 2-D) ... 12.00

Georgie Comics #11 © MAR

Get Smart #5 © DELL

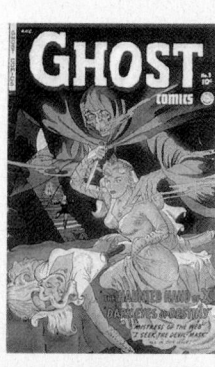

Ghost #3 © FH

	GD 2.0	VG 4.0	FN 6.0	VF 8.0	VF/NM 9.0	NM- 9.2

GEN 13 : MAGICAL DRAMA QUEEN ROXY
Image Comics (WildStorm): Oct, 1998 - No. 3, Dec, 1998 ($3.50, lim. series)
1-3-Adam Warren-s/c/a; manga style, 2-Variant-c by Hiroyuki Utatane — 3.50
1-($6.95) Dynamic Forces Ed. w/Variant Warren-c — 7.00

GEN 13/MONKEYMAN & O'BRIEN
Image Comics (WildStorm): Jun, 1998 - No. 2, July, 1998 ($2.50, lim. series)
1,2-Art Adams-s/a(p); 1-Two covers — 2.50
1-($4.95) Chromium-c — 5.00
1-($6.95) Dynamic Forces Ed. — 7.00

GEN 13: ORDINARY HEROES
Image Comics (WildStorm Publications): Feb, 1996 - No. 2, July, 1996 ($2.50, limited series)
1,2-Adam Hughes-c/a/scripts — 3.00
TPB (2004, $14.95) r/series, Gen13 Bootleg #1&2 and Wildstorm Thunderbook; new Hughes-c and art pages — 15.00

GENTLE BEN (TV)
Dell Publishing Co.: Feb, 1968 - No. 5, Oct, 1969 (All photo-c)

	GD	VG	FN	VF	VF/NM	NM-
1	4	8	12	26	41	55
2-5: 5-Reprints #1	3	6	9	16	23	30

GEOMANCER (Also see Eternal Warrior: Fist & Steel)
Valiant: Nov, 1994 - No. 8, June, 1995 ($3.75/$2.25)
1 ($3.75)-Chromium wraparound-c; Eternal Warrior app. — 3.75
2-8 — 2.50

GEORGE OF THE JUNGLE (TV)(See America's Best TV Comics)
Gold Key: Feb, 1969 - No. 2, Oct, 1969 (Jay Ward)

	GD	VG	FN	VF	VF/NM	NM-
1	9	18	27	65	113	160
2	6	12	18	41	66	90

GEORGE PAL'S PUPPETOONS (Funny animal puppets)
Fawcett Publications: Dec, 1945 - No. 18, Dec, 1947; No. 19, 1950

	GD	VG	FN	VF	VF/NM	NM-
1-Captain Marvel-c	42	84	126	256	421	585
2	23	46	69	132	209	285
3-10	15	30	45	86	133	180
11-19	13	26	39	74	105	135

GEORGIE COMICS (...& Judy Comics #20-35?; see All Teen & Teen Comics)
Timely Comics/GPI No. 1-34: Spr, 1945 - No. 39, Oct, 1952 (#1-3 are quarterly)

	GD	VG	FN	VF	VF/NM	NM-
1-Dave Berg-a	29	58	87	167	264	360
2	15	30	45	86	133	180
3-5,7,8	14	28	42	80	115	150
6-Georgie visits Timely Comics	15	30	45	86	133	180
9,10-Kurtzman's "Hey Look" (1 & ?); Millie the Model & Margie app.	14	28	42	80	115	150
11,12: 11-Margie, Millie app.	11	22	33	62	86	110
13-Kurtzman's "Hey Look", 3 pgs.	12	24	36	67	94	120
14-Wolverton-a(1 pg.); Kurtzman's "Hey Look"	13	26	39	72	101	130
15,16,18-20	10	20	30	58	79	100
17,29-Kurtzman's "Hey Look", 1 pg.	11	22	33	62	86	110
21-24,27,28,30-39: 21-Anti-Wertham editorial. 33-38-Hy Rosen-c	10	20	30	54	72	90
25-Painted-c by classic pin-up artist Peter Driben	13	26	39	72	101	130
26-Logo design swipe from Archie Comics	10	20	30	56	76	95

GERALD McBOING-BOING AND THE NEARSIGHTED MR. MAGOO (TV)
(Mr. Magoo No. 6 on)
Dell Publishing Co.: Aug-Oct, 1952 - No. 5, Aug-Oct, 1953

	GD	VG	FN	VF	VF/NM	NM-
1	11	22	33	75	133	190
2-5	9	18	27	63	107	150

GERONIMO (See Fighting Indians of the Wild West!)
Avon Periodicals: 1950 - No. 4, Feb, 1952

	GD	VG	FN	VF	VF/NM	NM-
1-Indian Fighter; Maneely-a; Texas Rangers-r/Cowpuncher #1; Fawcette-c	19	38	57	109	172	235
2-On the Warpath; Kit West app.; Kinstler-c/a	13	26	39	74	105	135
3-And His Apache Murderers; Kinstler-c/a(2); Kit West-r/Cowpuncher #6	13	26	39	74	105	135
4-Savage Raids of; Kinstler-c & inside front-c; Kinstlerish-a by McCann(3)	12	24	36	69	97	125

GERONIMO JONES
Charlton Comics: Sept, 1971 - No. 9, Jan, 1973

	GD	VG	FN	VF	VF/NM	NM-
1	2	4	6	11	16	20
2-9	1	3	4	6	8	10

Modern Comics Reprint #7('78) — 4.00

GETALONG GANG, THE (TV)
Marvel Comics (Star Comics): May, 1985 - No. 6, Mar, 1986
1-6: Saturday morning TV stars — 3.00

GET LOST
Mikeross Publications/New Comics: Feb-Mar, 1954 - No. 3, June-July, 1954 (Satire)

	GD	VG	FN	VF	VF/NM	NM-
1-Andru/Esposito-a in all?	31	62	93	178	282	385
2-Andru/Esposito-c; has 4 pg. E.C. parody featuring "The Sewer Keeper"	21	42	63	120	188	255
3-John Wayne 'Hondo' parody	17	34	51	98	154	210
1,2 (10,12/87-New Comics)-B&W r-original						2.50

GET SMART (TV)
Dell Publ. Co.: June, 1966 - No. 8, Sept, 1967 (All have Don Adams photo-c)

	GD	VG	FN	VF	VF/NM	NM-
1	10	20	30	67	116	165
2,3-Ditko-a	7	14	21	47	76	105
4-8: 8-Reprints #1 (cover and insides)	6	12	18	37	59	80

GHOST (...Comics #9)
Fiction House Magazines: 1951(Winter) - No. 11, Summer, 1954

	GD	VG	FN	VF	VF/NM	NM-
1-Most covers by Whitman	76	152	228	475	788	1100
2-Ghost Gallery & Werewolf Hunter stories	40	80	120	240	383	525
3-9: 3,6,7,9-Bondage-c. 9-Abel, Discount-c	34	68	102	197	311	425
10,11-Dr. Drew by Grandenetti in each, reprinted from Rangers; 11-Evans-r/Rangers #39; Grandenetti-r/Rangers #49	29	58	87	167	264	360

GHOST (See Comic's Greatest World)
Dark Horse Comics: Apr, 1995 - No. 36, Apr, 1998 ($2.50/$2.95)

	GD	VG	FN	VF	VF/NM	NM-
1-Adam Hughes-a	1	2	3	5	6	8
2,3-Hughes-a						4.00
4-24: 4-Barb Wire app. 5,6-Hughes-c. 12-Ghost/Hellboy preview. 15,21-X app. 18,19-Barb Wire app.						3.00
25-($3.50)-48 pgs. special						3.50
26-36: 26-Begin $2.95-c. 29-Flip book w/Timecop. 33-36-Jade Cathedral; Harris painted-c						3.00
Special 1 (7/94, $3.95, 48 pgs.)	1	2	3	4	5	7
Special 2 (6/98, $3.95) Barb Wire app.						4.00
...Black October (1/99, $14.95, trade paperback)-r/#6-9,26,27						15.00
...Nocturnes (1996, $9.95, trade paperback)-r/#1-3 & 5						10.00
...Stories (1995, $9.95, trade paperback)-r/Early Ghost app.						10.00

GHOST (Volume 2)
Dark Horse Comics: Sept, 1998 - No. 22, Aug, 2000 ($2.95)
1-22: 1-4-Ryan Benjamin-c/Zanier-a — 3.00
Handbook (8/99, $2.95) guide to issues and characters — 3.00
Special 3 (12/98, $3.95) — 4.00

GHOST AND THE SHADOW
Dark Horse Comics: Dec, 1995 ($2.95, one-shot)
1-Moench scripts — 3.00

GHOST/BATGIRL
Dark Horse Comics: Aug, 2000 - No. 4, Dec, 2000 ($2.95, limited series)
1-4-New Batgirl; Oracle & Bruce Wayne app.; Benjamin-c/a — 3.00

GHOST/HELLBOY
Dark Horse Comics: May, 1996 - No. 2, June, 1996 ($2.50, limited series)
1,2: Mike Mignola-c/scripts & breakdowns; Scott Benefiel finished-a — 3.00

GHOST BREAKERS (Also see Racket Squad in Action, Red Dragon & (CC) Sherlock Holmes Comics)
Street & Smith Publications: Sept, 1948 - No. 2, Dec, 1948 (52 pgs.)

	GD	VG	FN	VF	VF/NM	NM-
1-Powell-c/a(3); Dr. Neff (magician) app.	41	82	123	256	416	575
2-Powell-c/a(2); Maneely-a	34	68	102	195	308	420

GHOSTBUSTERS (TV) (Also, see Real...and Slimer)
First Comics: Feb, 1987 - No. 6, Aug, 1987 ($1.25)
1-6: Based on new animated TV series — 3.00

GHOSTBUSTERS: LEGION (Movie)
88 MPH Studios: Feb, 2004 - No. 4, May, 2004 ($2.95/$3.50)
1-4-Steve Kurth-a/Andrew Dabb-s — 3.00
1-3-($3.50) Brereton variant-c — 3.50

GHOSTBUSTERS II
Now Comics: Oct, 1989 - No. 3, Dec, 1989 ($1.95, mini-series)
1-3: Movie Adaptation — 3.00

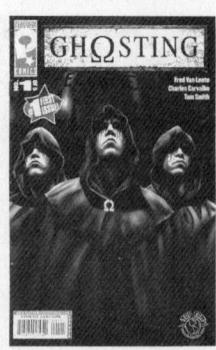

Ghosting #1 © Platinum Studios

Ghostly Haunts #20 © CC

Ghost Manor #15 © CC

	GD	VG	FN	VF	VF/NM	NM-
	2.0	4.0	6.0	8.0	9.0	9.2

GHOST CASTLE (See Tales of...)

GHOSTING
Platinum Studios: 2007 - No. 5 ($2.99, limited series)

	GD	VG	FN	VF	VF/NM	NM-
1-Van Lente-s/Carvalho-a/Wolfe-c						3.00

GHOST IN THE SHELL (Manga)
Dark Horse: Mar, 1995 - No. 8, Oct, 1995 ($3.95, B&W/color, lim. series)

	GD	VG	FN	VF	VF/NM	NM-
1,2	2	4	6	13	18	22
3	2	4	6	8	10	12
4-8	1	2	3	5	6	8

GHOST IN THE SHELL 2: MAN-MADE INTERFACE (Manga)
Dark Horse Comics: Jan, 2003 - No. 11, Dec, 2003 ($3.50, color/B&W, lim. series)

	GD	VG	FN	VF	VF/NM	NM-
1-11-Masamune Shirow-s/a. 5-B&W						3.50

GHOSTLY HAUNTS (Formerly Ghost Manor)
Charlton Comics: #20, 9/71 - #53, 12/76; #54, 9/77 - #55, 10/77; #56, 1/78 - #58, 4/78

	GD	VG	FN	VF	VF/NM	NM-
20	3	6	9	16	23	30
21	2	4	6	9	13	16
22-25,27,31-34,36,37-Ditko-c/a. 27-Dr. Graves x-over. 32-New logo. 33-Back to old logo	2	4	6	13	18	22
26,29,30,35-Ditko-c	2	4	6	9	13	16
28,38-40-Ditko-a. 39-Origin & 1st app. Destiny Fox	2	4	6	9	13	16
41,42: 41-Sutton-c; Ditko-a. 42-Newton-c/a	2	4	6	10	14	18
43-46,48,50,52-Ditko-a	2	4	6	9	12	15
47,54,56-Ditko-c/a. 56-Ditko-a(r).	2	4	6	10	14	18
49,51,53,55,57	1	3	4	6	8	10
58 (4/78) Last issue	2	4	6	10	14	18
40,41(Modern Comics-r, 1977, 1978)						4.00

NOTE: *Ditko* a-22-25, 27, 28, 31-34, 36-41, 43-48, 50, 52, 54, 56r; c-22-27, 29, 30, 33-37, 47, 54, 56. *Glanzman* a-20. *Howard* a-27, 30, 35, 40-43, 48, 54, 57. *Kim* a-38, 41, 57. *Larson* a-48, 50. *Newton* c/a-42. *Staton* a-32, 35; c-28, 46. *Sutton* c-33, 37, 39, 41.

GHOSTLY TALES (Formerly Blue Beetle No. 50-54)
Charlton Comics: No. 55, 4-5/66 - No. 124, 12/76; No. 125, 9/77 - No. 169, 10/84

	GD	VG	FN	VF	VF/NM	NM-
55-Intro. & origin Dr. Graves; Ditko-a	6	12	18	41	66	90
56-58,60,61,70,71-Ditko-a. 70-Dr. Graves ends. 71-Last 12¢ issue	3	6	9	20	30	40
59,62-66,68	3	6	9	16	22	28
67,69-Ditko-c/a	4	8	12	23	36	48
72,75,76,79-82,85-Ditko-a	2	4	6	13	18	22
73,77,78,83,84,86-90,92-95,97,99-Ditko-c/a	3	6	9	16	22	28
74,91,98,119,123,124,127-130: 127,130-Sutton-a	2	4	6	8	11	14
96-Ditko-c	2	4	6	11	16	20
100-Ditko-c; Sutton-a	2	4	6	11	16	20
101,103-105-Ditko-a	2	4	6	13	18	22
102,109-Ditko-a	2	4	6	13	18	22
110,113-Sutton-c; Ditko-a	2	4	6	10	14	18
106-Ditko & Sutton-a; Sutton-c	2	4	6	10	14	18
107-Ditko, Wood, Sutton-a	2	4	6	11	16	20
108,116,117,126-Ditko-a	2	4	6	10	14	18
111,118,120-122,125-Ditko-c/a	2	4	6	13	18	22
112,114,115: 112,114-Ditko, Sutton-a. 114-Newton-a. 115-Newton, Ditko-a.	2	4	6	10	14	18
131-134,151,157,163-Ditko-c/a	2	4	6	9	13	16
135,142,145-150,153,154,156,158-160	1	2	3	5	6	8
136-141,143,144,152,155-Ditko-a	1	3	4	6	8	10
161,162,164-168-Lower print run. 162-Nudity panel	2	4	6	8	11	14
169 (10/84) Last issue; lower print run	2	4	6	10	14	18

NOTE: *Aparo* a-65, 66, 68, 72, 137, 141r, 142r; c-71, 72, 74-76, 81, 146r, 149. *Ditko* a-55-58, 60, 61, 67, 69-73, 75-90, 92-95, 97, 99-118, 120-122, 125-133, 147, 148, 151, 157-160, 163. *Glanzman* a-167. *Howard* a-55, 98, 99, 108, 117, 129, 131; c-98, 107, 120, 121, 141. *Larson* a-117, 119, 136, 159; c-136. *Morisi* a-83, 84, 86. *Newton* a-114; c-115(painted). *Palais* a-161; *Staton* a-161; c-117. *Sutton* a-106, 107, 111-114, 127, 130, 162; c-100, 106, 110, 113(painted). *Wood* a-107.

GHOSTLY WEIRD STORIES (Formerly Blue Bolt Weird)
Star Publications: No. 120, Sept, 1953 - No. 124, Sept, 1954

	GD	VG	FN	VF	VF/NM	NM-
120-Jo-Jo-r	40	80	120	240	383	525
121-124: 121-Jo-Jo-r. 122-The Mask-r/Capt. Flight #5; Rulah-r; has 1pg. story 'Death and the Devil Pills'-r/Western Outlaws #17. 123-Jo-Jo; Disbrow-a(2). 124-Torpedo Man	37	74	111	210	337	460

NOTE: *Disbrow* a-120-124. *L. B. Cole* covers-all issues #122 is a sci-fi cover).

GHOST MANOR (Ghostly Haunts No. 20 on)
Charlton Comics: July, 1968 - No. 19, July, 1971

	GD	VG	FN	VF	VF/NM	NM-
1	5	10	15	32	51	70
2-6: 6-Last 12¢ issue	3	6	9	18	27	35
7-12,17: 17-Morisi-a	3	6	9	16	22	28
13,14,16-Ditko-a	3	6	9	18	27	35
15,18,19-Ditko-c/a	3	6	9	21	32	42

GHOST MANOR (2nd Series)
Charlton Comics: Oct, 1971-No. 32, Dec, 1976; No. 33, Sept, 1977-No. 77, 11/84

	GD	VG	FN	VF	VF/NM	NM-
1	4	8	12	26	41	55
2,3,5-7,9-Ditko-c	3	6	9	15	21	26
4,10-Ditko-c/a	3	6	9	17	25	32
8-Wood, Ditko-a; Sutton-c	3	6	9	17	25	32
11,14-Ditko-c/a	3	6	9	15	21	26
12,17,27,30	2	4	6	8	11	14
13,15,16,23-26,29: 13-Ditko-a. 15,16-Ditko-c. 23-Sutton-a. 24-26,29-Ditko-a.	2	4	6	10	14	18
18-(3/74) Newton 1st pro art; Ditko-a; Sutton-c	3	6	9	14	20	25
19-21: 19-Newton, Sutton-a; nudity panels. 20-Ditko-a. 21-E-Man, Blue Beetle, Capt. Atom cameos; Ditko-a.	2	4	6	10	14	18
22-Newton-c/a; Ditko-a	2	4	6	11	16	20
25,28,31,37,38-Ditko-a; c- 28-Nudity panels	2	4	6	11	16	20
32-36,39,41,45,48-50,53: 34-Black Cat by Kim	1	2	3	5	7	9
40-Ditko-a; torture & drug use	2	4	6	10	14	18
42,43,46,47,51,52,60,62,69-Ditko-c/a	2	4	6	9	13	16
44,54,71-Ditko-a	2	4	6	8	10	12
55,56,58,59,61,63,65-68,70	1	2	3	4	5	7
57-Wood, Ditko, Howard-a	2	4	6	8	11	14
64-Ditko & Newton-a	2	4	6	8	10	12
71-76 (low print)	1	2	3	5	6	8
77-(11/84) Last issue Aparo-r/Space Adventures V3#60 (Paul Mann)	2	4	6	9	13	16
19 (Modern Comics reprint, 1977)						4.00

NOTE: *Ditko* a-4, 8, 10, 11(2), 13, 14, 18, 20-22, 24-26, 28, 29, 31, 37r, 38r, 40r, 42-44r, 46r, 47, 51r, 52r, 54r, 57, 60, 62(4r), 64r, 69, 71; c-2-7, 9-11, 14-16, 28, 31, 37, 38, 42, 43, 46, 47, 51, 52, 60, 62, 64. *Howard* a-4, 8, 12, 17, 57; c-11, 41, 45, 57. *Newton* a-18-20, 22, 64; c-22. *Staton* a-13, 38, 44, 45. *Sutton* a-19, 23, 25, 45; c-8, 18.

GHOST RIDER (See A-1 Comics, Best of the West, Black Phantom, Bobby Benson, Great Western, Red Mask & Tim Holt)
Magazine Enterprises: 1950 - No. 14, 1954
NOTE: *The character was inspired by Vaughn Monroe's "Ghost Riders in the Sky", and Disney's movie "The Headless Horseman".*

	GD	VG	FN	VF	VF/NM	NM-
1(A-1 #27)-Origin Ghost Rider	110	220	330	688	1144	1600
2-5: 2(A-1 #29), 3(A-1 #34), 4(A-1 #34), 5(A-1 #37)-All Frazetta-c only	72	144	216	450	750	1050
6,7: 6(A-1 #44)-Loco weed story, 7(A-1 #51)	32	64	96	186	293	400
8,9: 8(A-1 #57)-Drug use story, 9(A-1 #69)	27	54	81	158	249	340
10(A-1 #71)-Vs. Frankenstein	29	58	87	170	268	365
11-14: 11(A-1 #75). 12(A-1 #80)-Bondage-c; one-eyed Devil-c 13(A-1 #84). 14(A-1 #112)	24	48	72	139	220	300

NOTE: *Dick Ayers* art in all; c-1, 6-14.

GHOST RIDER, THE (See Night Rider & Western Gunfighters)
Marvel Comics Group: Feb, 1967 - No. 7, Nov, 1967 (Western hero)(12¢)

	GD	VG	FN	VF	VF/NM	NM-
1-Origin & 1st app. Ghost Rider; Kid Colt-reprints begin	8	16	24	56	93	130
2	5	10	15	30	48	65
3-7: 6-Last Kid Colt-r; All Ayers-c/a(p)	4	8	12	26	41	55

GHOST RIDER (See The Champions, Marvel Spotlight #5, Marvel Team-Up #15, 58, Marvel Treasury Edition #18, Marvel Two-In-One #8, The Original Ghost Rider & The Original Ghost Rider Rides Again)
Marvel Comics Group: Sept, 1973 - No. 81, June, 1983 (Super-hero)

	GD	VG	FN	VF	VF/NM	NM-
1-Johnny Blaze, the Ghost Rider begins; 1st brief app. Daimon Hellstrom (Son of Satan)	12	24	36	87	156	225
2-1st full app. Daimon Hellstrom; gives glimpse of costume (1 panel); story continues in Marvel Spotlight #12	5	10	15	35	55	75
3-5: 3-Ghost Rider gains power to make cycle of fire; Son of Satan app.	4	8	12	24	37	50
6-10: 10-Reprints origin/1st app. from Marvel Spotlight #5; Ploog-a	3	6	9	18	27	35
11-16	2	4	6	11	16	20
17,19-(Reg. 25¢ editions)(4,8/76)	2	4	6	10	14	18
17,19-(30¢ variants, limited distribution)	4	8	12	28	44	60
18-(Reg. 25¢ edition)(6/76). Spider-Man-c & app.	2	4	6	11	16	20
18-(30¢-c variant, limited distribution)	5	10	15	32	51	70
20-Daredevil x-over; ties into D.D. #138; Byrne-a	3	6	9	16	22	28
21-30: 22-1st app. Enforcer. 29,30-Vs. Dr. Strange	1	3	4	6	8	10

Ghost Rider #10 © MAR

Ghost Rider (2006 series) #9 © MAR

Ghosts #40 © DC

	GD	VG	FN	VF	VF/NM	NM-
	2.0	4.0	6.0	8.0	9.0	9.2

24-26-(35¢-c variants, limited distribution) — 4 | 8 | 12 | 24 | 37 | 50
31-34,36-49 — 1 | 2 | 3 | 5 | 6 | 8
35-Death Race classic; Starlin-c/a/sty — 2 | 4 | 6 | 8 | 11 | 14
50-Double size — 1 | 3 | 4 | 6 | 8 | 10
51-76,78-80: 80-Brief origin recap. 68,77-Origin retold — 6.00
81-Death of Ghost Rider (Demon leaves Blaze) — 2 | 4 | 6 | 11 | 16 | 20
...Team Up TPB (2007, $15.99) r/#27, 50, Marvel Team-Up #91, Marvel Two-In-One #80, Avengers #214 and Marvel Premiere #28; Night Rider app.; coveer gallery — 16.00

NOTE: **Anderson** c-64p. **Infantino** a(p)-43, 44, 51. **G. Kane** a-21p; c(p)-1, 2, 4, 5, 8, 9, 11-13, 19, 20, 24, 25. **Kirby** c-21-23. **Mooney** a-2-9p, 30i. **Nebres** c-26i. **Newton** a-23i. **Perez** c-26p. **Shores** a-2i. **Sparling** a-62p, 64p, 65p. **Starlin** c(p)-35. **Sutton** a-1p, 44i, 64i, 65i, 66, 67i. **Tuska** a-13p, 14p, 16p.

GHOST RIDER (Volume 2) (Also see Doctor Strange/Ghost Rider Special, Marvel Comics Presents & Midnight Sons Unlimited)
Marvel Comics (Midnight Sons imprint #44 on): V2#1, May, 1990 - No. 93, Feb, 1998 ($1.50/$1.75/$1.95)

1-($1.95, 52 pgs.)-Origin/1st app. new Ghost Rider; Kingpin app. — 6.00
1-2nd printing (not gold) — 2.50
2-5: 3-Kingpin app. 5-Punisher app.; Jim Lee-c — 3.00
5-Gold background 2nd printing — 2.50
6-14,16-24,29,30,32-39: 6-Punisher app. 6,17-Spider-man/Hobgoblin-c/story. 9-X-Factor app. 10-Reintro Ghost Rider on the last pg. 11-Stroman-c/a(p). 12,13-Dr. Strange x-over cont'd in D.S. #28. 13-Painted-c. 14-Johnny Blaze vs. Ghost Rider; origin recap 1st Ghost Rider (Blaze). 18-Painted-c by Nelson. 29-Wolverine-c/story. 32-Dr. Strange x-over; Johnny Blaze app. 34-Williamson-a(i). 36-Daredevil app. 37-Archangel app. — 3.00
15-Glow in the dark-c — 3.00
25-27: 25-($2.75)-Contains pop-up scene insert. 26,27-X-Men x-over; Lee/Williams-c on both — 3.00
28,31-($2.50, 52 pgs.)-Polybagged w/poster; part 1 & part 6 of Rise of the Midnight Sons storyline (see Ghost Rider/Blaze #1) — 3.00
40-Outer-c is Darkhold made of black parchment w/gold ink; Midnight Massacre x-over; Demogoblin app. — 3.00
41-48: 41-Lilith & Centurious app.; begin 1.75-c. 41-43-Neon ink-c. 43-Has free extra 16 pg. insert on Siege of Darkness. 44,45-Siege of Darkness parts 2 & 10. 44-Spot varnish-c. 46-Intro new Ghost Rider. 48-Spider-man app. — 2.50
49,51-60,62-74: 49-Begin $1.95-c; bound-in trading card sheet; Hulk app. 55-Werewolf by Night app. 65-Punisher app. 67,68-Gambit app. 68-Wolverine app. 73,74-Blaze, Vengeance app. — 2.50
50,61: 50-($2.50, 52 pgs.)-Regular edition — 3.00
50-($2.95, 52 pgs.)-Collectors Ed. die cut foil-c — 3.00
75-89: 76-Vs. Vengeance. 77,78-Dr. Strange-app. 78-New costume — 2.50
90-92 — 5.00
93-($2.99)-Last issue; Saltares & Texeira-a — 1 | 2 | 3 | 5 | 6 | 8
(#94, see Ghost Rider Finale for unpublished story)
#(-1) Flashback (7/97) Saltares-a — 2.50
Annual 1,2 ('93, '94, $2.95, 68 pgs.) 1-Bagged w/card — 3.00
...And Cable 1 (9/92, $3.95, stiff-c, 68 pgs.)-Reprints Marvel Comics Presents #90-98 w/new Kieth-a — 4.00
...:Crossroads (11/95, $3.95) Die cut cover; Nord-a — 5.00
...: Finale (2007, $3.99) r/#93 and the story meant for the unpublished #94; Saltares-a — 4.00
Highway to Hell (2001, $3.50) Reprints origin from Marvel Spotlight #5 — 3.50
...:Resurrected TPB (2001, $12.95) r/#1-7 — 13.00

NOTE: **Andy & Joe Kubert** c/a-28-31. **Quesada** c-21. **Williamson** a(i)-33-35; c-33i.

GHOST RIDER (Volume 3)
Marvel Comics: Aug, 2001 - No. 6, Jan, 2002 ($2.99, limited series)

1-6-Grayson-s/Kaniuga-a/c — 3.00
...: The Hammer Lane TPB (6/02, $15.95) r/#1-6 — 16.00

GHOST RIDER
Marvel Comics: Nov, 2005 - No. 6, Apr, 2006 ($2.99, limited series)

1-6-Garth Ennis-s/Clayton Crain-a/c. 1-Origin retold — 3.00
1 (Director's Cut) (2005, $3.99) r/#1 with Ennis pitch and script and Crain art process — 4.00
...: Road to Damnation HC (2006, $19.99, dust jacket) r/#1-6; variant covers & concept-a — 20.00
...: Road to Damnation SC (2007, $14.99) r/#1-6; variant covers & concept-a — 15.00

GHOST RIDER
Marvel Comics: Sept, 2006 - Present ($2.99)

1-11: 11-World War Hulk x-over. 2-4-Dr. Strange app. 6,7-Corben-a — 3.00
12-15: 12,13-World War Hulk x-over; Saltares/Dell'Otto-c — 3.00
...: Vol. 1: Vicious Cycle TPB (2007, $13.99) r/#1-5 — 14.00
...: Vol. 2: The Life and Death of Johnny Blaze TPB (2007, $13.99) r/#6-11 — 14.00

GHOST RIDER/BALLISTIC
Marvel Comics: Feb, 1997 ($2.95, one-shot)

1-Devil's Reign pt. 3 — 3.00

GHOST RIDER/BLAZE: SPIRITS OF VENGEANCE (Also see Blaze)
Marvel Comics (Midnight Sons imprint #17 on): Aug, 1992 - No. 23, June, 1994 ($1.75)

1-($2.75, 52 pgs.)-Polybagged w/poster; part 2 of Rise of the Midnight Sons storyline; Adam Kubert-c/a begins — 3.00
2-11,14-21: 4-Art Adams & Joe Kubert-p. 5,6-Spirits of Venom parts 2 & 4 cont'd from Web of Spider-man #95,96 w/Demogoblin. 14-17-Neon ink-c. 15-Intro Blaze's new costume & power. 17,18-Siege of Darkness parts 8 & 13. 17-Spot varnish-c — 2.50
12-($2.95)-Glow-in-the-dark-c — 2.50
13-($2.25)-Outer-c is Darkhold envelope made of black parchment w/gold ink; Midnight Massacre x-over — 3.00
22,23: 22-Begin $1.95-c; bound-in trading card sheet — 2.50

NOTE: **Adam & Joe Kubert** c-6. **J. Kubert** a-13p(6 pgs.)

GHOST RIDER/CAPTAIN AMERICA: FEAR
Marvel Comics: Oct, 1992 ($5.95, 52 pgs.)

nn-Wraparound gatefold-c; Williamson inks — 6.00

GHOST RIDER: TRAIL OF TEARS
Marvel Comics: Apr, 2007 - No. 6, Sept, 2007 ($2.99, limited series)

1-6-Garth Ennis-s/Clayton Crain-a/c; Civil War era tale — 3.00
HC (2007, $19.99) r/series — 20.00

GHOST RIDER 2099
Marvel Comics: May, 1994 - No. 25, May, 1996 ($1.50/$1.95)

1 ($2.25)-Collector's Edition w/prismatic foil-c — 3.00
1 ($1.50)-Regular Edition; bound-in trading card sheet — 2.50
2-24: 7-Spider-man 2099 app. — 2.50
2-(Variant; polybagged with Sega Sub-Terrania poster) — 5.00
25 ($2.95) — 3.00

GHOST RIDER, WOLVERINE, PUNISHER: THE DARK DESIGN
Marvel Comics: Dec, 1994 ($5.95, one-shot)

nn-Gatefold-c — 6.00

GHOST RIDER; WOLVERINE; PUNISHER: HEARTS OF DARKNESS
Marvel Comics: Dec, 1991 ($4.95, one-shot, 52 pgs.)

1-Double gatefold-c; John Romita, Jr.-c/a(p) — 5.00

GHOSTS (Ghost No. 1)
National Periodical Publications/DC Comics: Sept-Oct, 1971 - No. 112, May, 1982 (No. 1-5: 52 pgs.)

	GD	VG	FN	VF	VF/NM	NM-
	2.0	4.0	6.0	8.0	9.0	9.2
1-Aparo-a	12	24	36	86	153	220
2-Wood-a(i)	7	14	21	47	76	105
3-5-(52 pgs.)	6	12	18	39	62	85
6-10	3	6	9	18	27	35
11-20	2	4	6	13	18	22
21-39	2	4	6	8	11	14
40-(68 pgs.)	3	6	9	15	21	26
41-60	1	2	3	5	7	9
61-96	1	2	3	4	5	7

97-99-The Spectre vs. Dr. 13 by Aparo. 97,98-Spectre-c by Aparo. — 2 | 4 | 6 | 8 | 11 | 14
100-Infinity-c — 2 | 4 | 6 | 8 | 11 | 14
101-112 — 6.00

NOTE: **B. Baily** a-77. **Buckler** c-99. 100. **J. Craig** a-108. **Ditko** a-77. 111. **Giffen** a-104p, 106p, 111p. **Glanzman** a-2. **Golden** a-88. **Infantino** a-8. **Kaluta** c-7, 93, 101. **Kubert** a-8; c-89, 105-108, 111. **Mayer** a-111. **McWilliams** a-99. **Win Mortimer** a-89, 91, 94. **Nasser/Netzer** a-97. **Newton** a-92p, 94p. **Nino** a-35, 37, 57. **Orlando** a-74i; c-80. **Redondo** a-8, 13, 45. **Sparling** a(p)-90, 93, 94. **Spiegle** a-103, 105. **Tuska** a-2i. Dr. 13, the Ghostbreaker back-ups in 95-99, 101.

GHOSTS SPECIAL (See DC Special Series No. 7)

GHOST SPY
Image Comics: May, 2004 - No. 6 ($2.95, limited series)

1-5-Jacob Elijah-s/Steve Albertson-a — 3.00

GHOST STORIES (See Amazing Ghost Stories)

GHOST STORIES
Dell Publ. Co.: Sept-Nov, 1962; No. 2, Apr-June, 1963 - No. 37, Oct, 1973

	GD	VG	FN	VF	VF/NM	NM-
	2.0	4.0	6.0	8.0	9.0	9.2
12-295-211(#1)-Written by John Stanley	6	12	18	41	66	90
2	4	8	12	22	34	45

3-10: Two No. 6's exist with different c/a(12-295-406 & 12-295-503) #12-295-503 is actually #9 with indicia to #6 — 3 | 6 | 9 | 19 | 29 | 38
11-21: 21-Last 12¢ issue — 3 | 6 | 9 | 16 | 23 | 28
22-37 — 2 | 4 | 6 | 11 | 16 | 20

NOTE: #21-34, 36, 37 all reprint earlier issues.

GHOUL TALES (Magazine)
Stanley Publications: Nov, 1970 - No. 5, July, 1971 (52 pgs.) (B&W)

Giant Comics Edition #12 © STJ

Giant-Size Dracula #3 © MAR

Giant-Size Invaders #1 © MAR

	GD	VG	FN	VF	VF/NM	NM-
	2.0	4.0	6.0	8.0	9.0	9.2

1-Aragon pre-code reprints; Mr. Mystery as host; bondage-c
7   14   21   49   80   110
2,3: 2-(1/71)Reprint/Climax #1. 3-(3/71)
4   8   12   26   41   55
4-(5/71)Reprints story "The Way to a Man's Heart" used in **SOTI**
5   10   15   30   48   65
5-ACG reprints
4   8   12   22   34   45
NOTE: *No. 1-4 contain pre-code Aragon reprints.*

GIANT BOY BOOK OF COMICS (Also see Boy Comics)
Newsbook Publications (Gleason): 1945 (240 pgs.), hard-c)
1-Crimebuster & Young Robin Hood; Biro-c
93   186   279   581   966   1350

GIANT COMIC ALBUM
King Features Syndicate: 1972 (59¢, 11x14", 52 pgs., B&W, cardboard-c)
Newspaper reprints: Barney Google, Little Iodine, Katzenjammer Kids, Henry, Beetle Bailey,
  Blondie, & Snuffy Smith   each...
3   6   9   17   25   32
Flash Gordon ('68-69 Dan Barry)
4   8   12   22   34   45
Mandrake the Magician ('59 Falk), Popeye
3   6   9   19   29   38

GIANT COMICS
Charlton Comics: Summer, 1957 - No. 3, Winter, 1957 (25¢, 100 pgs.)
1-Atomic Mouse, Hoppy app.
21   42   63   122   191   260
2,3: 2-Romance. 3-Christmas Book; Atomic Mouse, Atomic Rabbit, Li'l
  Genius, Li'l Tomboy & Atom the Cat stories
15   30   45   88   137   185
NOTE: *The above may be rebound comics; contents could vary.*

GIANT COMICS (See Wham-O Giant Comics)

GIANT COMICS EDITION (See Terry-Toons) (Also see Fox Giants)
St. John Publishing Co.: 1947 - No. 17, 1950 (25¢, 100-164 pgs.)
1-Mighty Mouse
50   100   150   305   503   700
2-Abbie & Slats
27   54   81   158   249   340
3-Terry-Toons Album; 100 pgs.
42   84   126   239   380   520
4-Crime comics; contains Red Seal No. 16, used & illo. in **SOTI**
54   108   162   338   562   785
5-Police Case Book (4/49, 132 pgs.)-Contents varies; contains remaindered St. John books
  - some volumes contain 5 copies rather than 4, with 160 pages; Matt Baker-c
54   108   162   338   557   775
5A-Terry-Toons Album (132 pgs.)-Mighty Mouse, Heckle & Jeckle, Gandy Goose &
  Dinky stories
37   74   111   213   337   460
6-Western Picture Stories; Baker-c/a(3); Tuska-a; The Sky Chief, Blue Monk, Ventrilo app.,
  132 pgs.
52   104   156   317   521   725
7-Contains a teen-age romance plus 3 Mopsy comics
34   68   102   197   311   425
8-The Adventures of Mighty Mouse (10/49)
37   74   111   213   337   460
9-Romance and Confession Stories; Kubert-a(4); Baker-a; photo-c (132 pgs.)
66   132   198   413   682   950
10-Terry-Toons Album (132 pgs.)-Mighty Mouse, Heckle & Jeckle, Gandy Goose stories
37   74   111   213   337   460
11-Western Picture Stories-Baker-c/a(4); The Sky Chief, Desperado, & Blue Monk app.;
  another version with Son of Sinbad by Kubert (132 pgs.)
52   104   156   317   521   725
12-Diary Secrets; Baker prostitute-c; 4 St. John romance comics; Baker-a
172   344   516   1075   1788   2500
13-Romances; Baker, Kubert-a
55   110   165   344   572   800
14-Mighty Mouse Album (132 pgs.)
36   72   108   208   329   450
15-Romances (4 love comics)-Baker-c
62   124   186   388   644   900
16-Little Audrey; Abbott & Costello, Casper
40   80   120   235   368   500
17(nn)-Mighty Mouse Album (nn, no date, but did follow No. 16); 100 pgs.
  on cover but has 148 pgs.
36   72   108   208   329   450
NOTE: *The above books contain remaindered comics and contents could vary with each issue. No. 11, 12 have part photo magazine insides.*

GIANT COMICS EDITIONS
United Features Syndicate: 1940's (132 pgs.)
1-Abbie & Slats, Abbott & Costello, Jim Hardy, Ella Cinders, Iron Vic, Gordo,
  & Bill Bumlin
40   80   120   235   368   500
2-Jim Hardy, Ella Cinders, Elmo & Gordo
27   54   81   158   249   340
NOTE: *Above books contain rebound copies; contents can vary.*

GIANT GRAB BAG OF COMICS (See Archie All-Star Specials under Archie Comics)

GIANTKILLER
DC Comics: Aug, 1999 - No. 6, Jan, 2000 ($2.50, limited series)
1-6-Story and painted art by Dan Brereton   2.50
...A to Z: A Field Guide to Big Monsters (8/99)   2.50
...Vol. 1 TPB (Image Comics, 2006, $14.99) r/#1-6 & A-Z; gallery of concept art   15.00

GIANTS (See Thrilling True Story of the Baseball...)

	GD	VG	FN	VF	VF/NM	NM-
	2.0	4.0	6.0	8.0	9.0	9.2

GIANT-SIZE...
Marvel Comics Group: May, 1974 - Dec, 1975 (35/50¢, 52/68 pgs.)
(Some titles quarterly) (Scarce in strict NM or better due to defective cutting, gluing and binding; warping, splitting and off-center pages are common)
Avengers 1(8/74)-New-a plus G.A. H. Torch-r; 1st modern app. The Whizzer; 1st & only
  modern app. Miss America; 2nd app. Invaders; Kang, Rama-Tut, Mantis app.
5   10   15   30   48   65
Avengers 2,3,5: 2(11/74)-Death of the Swordsman; origin of Rama-Tut. 3(2/75).
  5(12/75)-Reprints Avengers Special #1
3   6   9   19   29   38
Avengers 4 (6/75)-Vision marries Scarlet Witch.
4   8   12   24   37   50
Captain America 1(12/75)-r/stories T.O.S. 59-63 by Kirby (#63 reprints origin)
4   8   12   22   34   45
Captain Marvel 1(12/75)-r/Capt. Marvel #17, 20, 21 by Gil Kane (p)
3   6   9   18   27   35
Chillers 1(6/74, 52 pgs)-Curse of Dracula; origin/1st app. Lilith, Dracula's daughter; Heath-r,
  Colan-c/a(p); becomes Giant-Size Chillers #2 on
5   10   15   32   51   70
Chillers 1(2/75, 50¢, 68 pgs.)-Alcala-a
3   6   9   18   27   35
Chillers 2(5/75)-All-r; Everett-r from Advs. into Weird Worlds
3   6   9   16   22   28
Chillers 3(8/75)-Wrightson-c(new)/a(r); Colan, Kirby, Smith-r
3   6   9   18   27   35
Conan 1(9/74)-B. Smith-r/#3; start adaptation of Howard's "Hour of the
  Dragon" (ends #4); 1st app. Belit; new-a begins
4   8   12   24   37   50
Conan 2(12/74)-B. Smith-r/#5; Sutton-a(i)(#1 also); Buscema-c
3   6   9   16   23   30
Conan 3-5: 3(4/75)-B. Smith-r/#6; Sutton-a(i). 4(6/75)-B. Smith-r/#7.
  5(1975)-B. Smith-r/#14,15; Kirby-a
3   6   9   15   21   26
Creatures 1(5/74, 52 pgs.)-Werewolf app; 1st app. Tigra (formerly Cat);
  Crandall-r; becomes Giant-Size Werewolf w/#2
4   8   12   26   41   55
Daredevil 1(1974)-Reprints Daredevil Annual #1
3   6   9   17   25   32
Defenders 1(7/74)-Silver Surfer app.; Starlin-a; Ditko, Everett & Kirby reprints
4   8   12   24   37   50
Defenders 2(10/74, 68 pgs.)-New G. Kane-a(p); Son of Satan app.; Sub-Mariner-r by Everett;
  Ditko-r/Strange Tales #119 (Dr. Strange); Maneely-r
3   6   9   17   25   32
Defenders 3-5: 3(1/75)-1st app. Korvac.; Newton, Starlin-a; Ditko, Everett-r. 4(4/75)-Ditko,
  Everett-r; G. Kane-c. 5-(7/75)-Guardians app.
3   6   9   16   22   28
Doc Savage 1(1975, 68 pgs.)-r/#1,2; Mooney-r
3   6   9   14   19   24
Doctor Strange 1(11/75)-Reprints stories from Strange Tales #164-168;
  Lawrence, Tuska-r
3   6   9   16   22   28
Dracula 2(9/74, 50¢)-Formerly Giant-Size Chillers
3   6   9   16   23   30
Dracula 3(12/74)-Fox-r/Uncanny Tales #6
3   6   9   17   25   32
Dracula 4(3/75)-Ditko-r(2)
3   6   9   17   25   32
Dracula 5(6/75)-1st byrne art at Marvel
4   8   12   28   44   60
Fantastic Four 2-4: 2(8/74)-Formerly Giant-Size Super-Stars; Ditko-r. 3(11/74).
  4(2/75)-1st Madrox; 2-4-All have Buscema-a
3   6   9   19   29   38
Fantastic Four 5,6: 5(7/75)-All-r; Kirby, G. Kane-r. 6(10/75)-All-r; Kirby-r
3   6   9   16   22   28
Hulk 1(1975) r/Hulk Special #1
3   6   9   16   22   28
Invaders 1(6/75, 50¢, 68 pgs.)-Origin; G.A. Sub-Mariner-r/Sub-Mariner #1; intro Master Man
3   6   9   21   32   42
Iron Man 1(1975)-Ditko reprint
3   6   9   18   27   35
Kid Colt 1-3: 1(1975). 2(4/75). 3(7/75)-new Ayers-a
6   12   18   43   69   95
Man-Thing 1(5/74)-New Ploog-c/a (25 pgs.); Ditko-r/Amazing Adv. #11; Kirby-r/
  Strange Tales Ann. #2 & T.O.S. #15; (#1-5 all have new Man-Thing stories,
  pre-hero-r & are 68 pgs.)
4   8   12   22   34   45
Man-Thing 2,3: 2(11/74)-Buscema-c/a(p); Kirby, Powell-r. 3(2/75)-Alcala-a;
  Ditko, Kirby, Sutton-r; Gil Kane-c
3   6   9   16   23   30
Man-Thing 4,5: 4(5/75)-Howard the Duck by Brunner-c/a; Ditko-r. 5(8/75)-Howard the Duck by
  Brunner (p); Dracula cameo in Howard the Duck; Buscema-a(p); Sutton-a(i); G. Kane-c
3   6   9   16   22   28
Marvel Triple Action 1,2: 1(5/75). 2(7/75)
3   6   9   14   19   24
Master of Kung Fu 1(9/74)-Russell-a; Yellow Claw-r in #1-4; Gulacy-a in #1,2
3   6   9   20   30   40
Master of Kung Fu 2-4: 2(12/74)-r/Yellow Claw #1. 3(3/75)-Gulacy-a; Kirby-a. 4(6/75)-Kirby-a
3   6   9   16   23   30
Power Man 1(1975)
3   6   9   16   22   28
Spider-Man 1(7/74)-Spider-Man /Human Torch-r by Kirby/Ditko; Byrne-r plus new-a
  (Dracula-c/story)
6   12   18   41   66   90
Spider-Man 2,3: 2(10/74)-Shang-Chi-app. 3(1/75)-Doc Savage-c/app.; Daredevil/
  Spider-Man-r w/Ditko-a
4   8   12   24   37   50
Spider-Man 4(4/75)-3rd Punisher app.; Byrne, Ditko-r
10   20   30   68   119   170
Spider-Man 5,6: 5(7/75)-Man-Thing/Lizard-c. 6(9/75)
3   6   9   21   32   42

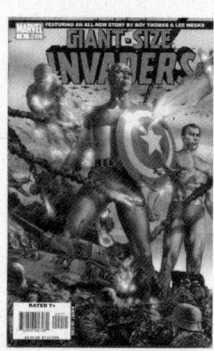

Giant-Size Invaders #2 © MAR

G.I. Combat #25 © QUA

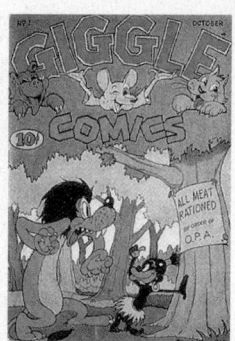

Giggle Comics #1 © ACG

	GD 2.0	VG 4.0	FN 6.0	VF 8.0	VF/NM 9.0	NM- 9.2
Super-Heroes Featuring Spider-Man 1(6/74, 35¢, 52 pgs.)-Spider-Man vs. Man-Wolf; Morbius, the Living Vampire app.; Ditko-r; G. Kane-a(p); Spidey villains app.						
	6	12	18	39	62	85
Super-Stars 1(5/74, 35¢, 52 pgs.)-Fantastic Four; Thing vs. Hulk; Kirbyish-c/a by Buckler/Sinnott; F.F. villains profiled; becomes Giant-Size Fantastic Four #2 on						
	5	10	15	32	51	70
Super-Villain Team-Up 1(3/75, 68 pgs.)-Craig-r(i) (Also see Fantastic Four #6 for 1st super-villain team-up)	3	6	9	18	27	35
Super-Villain Team-Up 2(6/75, 68 pgs.)-Dr. Doom, Sub-Mariner app.; Spider-Man-r from Amazing Spider-Man #8 by Ditko; Sekowsky-a(p)	3	6	9	16	22	28
Thor 1(7/75)	3	6	9	21	32	42
Werewolf 2(10/74, 68 pgs.)-Formerly Giant-Size Creatures; Ditko-r; Frankenstein app.						
	3	6	9	17	25	32
Werewolf 3,5: 3(1/75, 68 pgs.). 5(7/75, 68 pgs.)	3	6	9	17	25	32
Werewolf 4(4/75, 68 pgs.)-Morbius the Living Vampire app.						
	3	6	9	19	29	38
X-Men 1(Summer, 1975, 50¢, 68 pgs.)-1st app. new X-Men; intro. Nightcrawler, Storm, Colossus & Thunderbird; 2nd full app. Wolverine after Incredible Hulk #181						
	52	104	156	442	821	1200
X-Men 2 (11/75)-N. Adams-a (51 pgs)	8	16	24	56	93	130

GIANT-SIZE...
Marvel Comics: 2005 - Present ($4.99/$3.99)

Marvel TPB (2005, $24.99) reprints stories from Giant-Size Avengers #1, G-S Fantastic Four #4, G-S Defenders #4, G-S Super-Heroes #1, G-S Invaders #1, G-S X-Men #1 and Giant-Size Creatures #1 .... 25.00
Hulk 1 (8/06, $4.99)-2 new stories: Planet Hulk (David-s/Santacruz-a) & Hulk vs. The Champions (Pak-s/Lopresti-a); r/Incredible Hulk: The End 5.00
Invaders 1 (12/06, $4.99)-new Thomas-s/Weeks-a; r/Invaders #1&2 & All-Winners #1&2 .... 5.00
Marvel Adventures The Avengers (9/07, $3.99) Agents of Atlas and Kang app.; Kirk-a: reprint of 1st Namora app. from Marvel Mystery Comics #82; reprint from Venus #1 .... 4.00
Spider-Woman ('05, $4.99)-new Bendis-s/Mays-a; r/Marvel Spotlight #32 & S-W #1,37,38 .... 5.00
Wolverine (12/06, $4.99)-new Lapham-s/Aja-a; r/X-Men #6,7 .... 5.00
X-Men 1 ('05, $4.99)-new Whedon-s/N. Adams-a; r/team-ups; Cockrum & Cassaday-c 5.00

GIANT SPECTACULAR COMICS (See Archie All-Star Special under Archie Comics)
GIANT SUMMER FUN BOOK (See Terry-Toons...)

G. I. COMBAT
Quality Comics Group: Oct, 1952 - No. 43, Dec, 1956

1-Crandall-c; Cuidera a-1-43i	72	144	216	450	750	1050
2	37	74	111	213	339	465
3-5,10-Crandall-c/a	32	64	96	186	293	400
6-Crandall-a	28	56	84	162	256	350
7-9	24	48	72	139	220	300
11-20	18	36	54	105	165	225
21-31,33,35-43: 41-1st S.A. issue	16	32	48	94	147	200
32-Nuclear attack-c/story "Atomic Rocket Assault"	19	38	57	109	172	235
34-Crandall-a	17	34	51	100	158	215

G. I. COMBAT (See DC Special Series #22)
National Periodical Publ./DC Comics: No. 44, Jan, 1957 - No. 288, Mar, 1987

44-Grey tone-c	50	100	150	425	788	1150
45	26	52	78	195	348	500
46-50	22	44	66	165	295	425
51-Grey tone-c	26	52	78	195	348	500
52-54,59,60	20	40	60	146	261	375
55-Minor Sgt. Rock prototype by Finger	21	42	64	156	278	400
56-Sgt. Rock prototype by Kanigher/Kubert	24	48	72	180	323	465
57,58-Pre-Sgt. Rock Easy Co. stories	22	44	66	165	295	425
61-65,70-74: 74-American flag-c	15	30	45	107	191	275
66-Pre-Sgt. Rock Easy Co. story	21	42	63	156	278	400
67-1st Tank Killer	26	52	78	187	336	485
68-(1/59) Introduces "The Rock", Sgt. Rock prototype by Kanigher/Kubert; once considered his actual 1st app. (see Our Army at War #82,83)	61	122	183	519	960	1400
69-Grey tone-c	16	32	48	116	206	295
75-80: 75-Grey tone-c begin, end #109	21	42	64	156	278	400
81,82,84-86	16	32	48	118	209	300
83-1st Big Al, Little Al, & Charlie Cigar; grey tone-c	19	38	57	138	244	350
87-(4-5/61) 1st Haunted Tank; series begins; classic Heath washtone-c						
	65	130	195	553	1027	1500
88-(6-7/61) 2nd Haunted Tank	26	52	78	195	348	500
89,90: 90-Last 10¢ issue	16	32	48	118	209	300
91-(12/61-1/62)1st Haunted Tank-c	24	48	72	175	313	450
92-99: 92-95,99-Grey tone-c	13	26	39	93	164	235
100,108: 100-(6-7/63). 108-1st Sgt. Rock x-over	14	28	42	99	175	250

101-107,109: 104,109-Grey tone-c	11	22	33	79	140	200
110-112,115-120: 119-Grey tone-c	10	20	30	70	123	175
113-Grey tone-c	11	22	33	79	140	200
114-Origin Haunted Tank	19	38	57	138	244	350
121-136: 121-1st app. Sgt. Rock's father. 125-Sgt. Rock app. 136-Last 12¢ issue						
	6	12	18	41	66	90
137,139,140	4	8	12	24	37	50
138-Intro. The Losers (Capt. Storm, Gunner/Sarge, Johnny Cloud) in Haunted Tank (10-11/69)						
	9	18	27	60	100	140
141-143	3	6	9	16	23	30
144-148 (68 pgs.)	4	8	12	22	34	45
149,151-154 (52 pgs.): 151-Capt. Storm story. 151,153-Medal of Honor series by Maurer						
	3	6	9	17	25	32
150- (52 pgs.) Ice Cream Soldier story (tells how he got his name); Death of Haunted Tank-c/s						
	4	8	12	22	34	45
155-167,169,170	3	6	9	12	15	18
168-Neal Adams-c	3	6	9	14	19	24
171-192,194-199: 195-Haunted Tank & War That Time Forgot						
	2	4	6	8	10	12
193-(10/76) Haunted Tank meets War That Time Forgot; Dinosaur-c/s; Kubert-a						
	2	4	6	9	13	16
200-(3/77) Haunted Tank-c/s; Sgt. Rock and the Losers app.; Kubert-c						
	2	4	6	11	16	20
201,202 ($1.00 size) Neal Adams-c	2	4	6	11	16	20
203-210 ($1.00 size)	2	4	6	9	12	15
211-230 ($1.00 size)	2	4	6	8	10	12
231-259 ($1.00 size).232-Origin Kana the Ninja. 244-Death of Slim Stryker; 1st app. The Mercenaries. 246-(76 pgs., $1.50)-30th Anniversary issue. 257-Intro. Stuart's Raiders						
	1	2	3	5	7	9
260-281: 260-Begin $1.25, 52 pg. issues, end #281. 264-Intro Sgt. Bullet; origin Kana. 269-Intro. The Bravos of Vietnam. 274-Cameo of Monitor from Crisis on Infinite Earths						6.00
282-288 (75¢): 282-New advs. begin						6.00

NOTE: **N. Adams** c-168, 201, 202. **Check** a-168, 173. **Drucker** a-48, 61, 63, 66, 71, 72, 76, 134, 140, 141, 144, 147, 148, 153. **Evans** a-135, 138, 158, 164, 166, 201, 202, 204, 205, 215, 256. **Giffen** a-267. **Glanzman** a-most issues. **Kubert/Heath** a-most issues; **Kubert** covers most issues. **Morrow** a-159-161(2 pgs.). **Redondo** a-189, 240i, 243i. **Sekowsky** a-162p. **Severin** a-147, 152, 154. **Simonson** c-169. **Thorne** a-152, 156. **Wildey** a-153. Johnny Cloud app.-112, 115, 120. Mlle. Marie app.-123, 132, 200. Sgt. Rock app.-111-113, 115, 120, 125, 141, 146, 147, 149, 200. USS Stevens by **Glanzman**-145, 150-153, 157. **Grandenetti** c-44-48.

GIDGET (TV)
Dell Publishing Co.: Apr, 1966 - No. 2, Dec, 1966

1-Sally Field photo-c	9	18	27	60	100	140
2	6	12	18	43	69	95

GIFT COMICS
Fawcett Publications: 1942 - No. 4, 1949 (50¢/25¢, 324 pgs./152 pgs.)

1-Captain Marvel, Bulletman, Golden Arrow, Ibis the Invincible, Mr. Scarlet, & Spy Smasher begin; not rebound, remaindered comics, printed at same time as originals; 50¢ c & 324 pgs. begin, end #3.

	276	552	828	1725	2863	4000
2-Commando Yank, Phantom Eagle, others app.	166	332	498	1035	1719	2400
3	112	224	336	700	1163	1625
4-(25¢, 152 pgs.)-The Marvel Family, Captain Marvel, etc.; each issue can vary in contents						
	69	138	207	431	716	1000

GIFTS FROM SANTA (See March of Comics No. 137)
GIFTS OF THE NIGHT
DC Comics (Vertigo): Feb, 1999 - No. 4, May, 1999 ($2.95, limited series)

1-4-Bolton-c/a; Chadwick-a 3.00

GIGGLE COMICS (Spencer Spook No. 100) (Also see Ha Ha Comics)
Creston No.1-63/American Comics Group No. 64 on; Oct, 1943 - No. 99, Jan-Feb, 1955

1-Funny animal	34	68	102	197	311	425
2	16	32	48	94	147	200
3-5: 5-Ken Hultgren-a begins	14	28	42	76	108	140
6-10: 9-1st Superkatt (6/44)	11	22	33	60	83	105
11-20	10	20	30	54	72	90
21-40: 32-Patriotic-c. 37,61-X-Mas-c	9	18	27	47	61	75
41-54,56-59,61-99: Spencer Spook app. in many	8	16	24	42	54	65
55,60-Milt Gross-a	10	20	30	54	72	90

G-I IN BATTLE (G-I No. 1 only)
Ajax-Farrell Publ./Four Star: Aug, 1952 - No. 9, July, 1953; Mar, 1957 - No. 6, May, 1958

1	12	24	36	69	97	125
2	8	16	24	40	50	60
3-9	7	14	21	37	46	55
Annual 1(1952, 25¢, 100 pgs.)	25	50	75	145	228	310

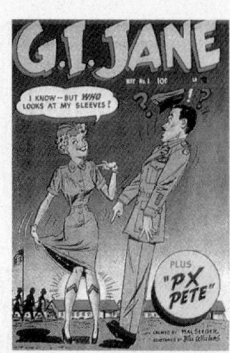

G.I. Jane #1 © Stanhall

G.I. Joe #17 © Z-D

G.I. Joe V2 #12 © Hasbro

	GD	VG	FN	VF	VF/NM	NM-
	2.0	4.0	6.0	8.0	9.0	9.2

	GD 2.0	VG 4.0	FN 6.0	VF 8.0	VF/NM 9.0	NM- 9.2
1(1957-Ajax)	8	16	24	42	54	65
2-6	6	12	18	28	34	40

G. I. JANE
Stanhall/Merit No. 11: May, 1953 - No. 11, Mar, 1955 (Misdated 3/54)

	GD 2.0	VG 4.0	FN 6.0	VF 8.0	VF/NM 9.0	NM- 9.2
1-PX Pete begins; Bill Williams-c/a	14	28	42	76	108	140
2-7(5/54)	8	16	24	44	57	70
8-10(12/54, Stanhall)	8	16	24	40	50	60
11 (3/55, Merit)	7	14	21	37	46	55

G. I. JOE (Also see Advs. of..., Showcase #53, 54 & The Yardbirds)
Ziff-Davis Publ. Co. (Korean War): No. 10, 1950; No. 11, 4-5/51 - No. 51, 6/57(52pgs.: 10-14,6-17?)

	GD 2.0	VG 4.0	FN 6.0	VF 8.0	VF/NM 9.0	NM- 9.2
10(#1, 1950)-Saunders painted-c begin	16	32	48	94	147	200
11-14(#2-5, 10/51): 11-New logo. 12-New logo	11	22	33	64	90	115
V2#6(12/51)-17-(11/52; Last 52 pgs.?)	10	20	30	56	76	95
18-(25¢, 100 pg. Giant, 12-1/52-53)	24	48	72	139	220	300
19-30: 20-22,24,28-31-The Yardbirds app.	9	18	27	50	65	80
31-47,49-51	9	18	27	47	61	75
48-Atom bomb story	9	18	27	50	65	80

NOTE: **Powell** a-V2#7, 8, 11. **Norman Saunders** painted c-10-14, V2#6-14, 26, 30, 31, 35, 38, 39. **Tuska** a-7. Bondage c-29, 35, 38.

G. I. JOE (America's Movable Fighting Man)
Custom Comics: 1967 (1-1/8x8-3/8", 36 pgs.)

	GD	VG	FN	VF	VF/NM	NM-
nn-Schaffenberger-a; based on Hasbro toy	3	6	9	20	30	40

G.I. JOE
Dark Horse Comics: Dec, 1995 - No. 4, Apr, 1996 ($1.95, limited series)

1-4: Mike W. Barr scripts. 1-Three Frank Miller covers with title logos in red, white and blue. 2-Breyfogle-c. 3-Simonson-c						3.00

G.I. JOE
Dark Horse Comics: V2#1, June, 1996 - V2#4, Sept, 1996 ($2.50)

V2#1-4: Mike W. Barr scripts. 4-Painted-c						3.00

G.I. JOE
Image Comics/Devil's Due Publishing: 2001 - No. 43, May, 2005 ($2.95)

	GD	VG	FN	VF	VF/NM	NM-
1-Campbell-c; back-c painted by Beck; Blaylock-s	2	4	6	8	10	12
1-2nd printing with front & back covers switched						6.00
2,3						5.00
4-($3.50)						4.00
5-20,22-44: 6-SuperPatriot preview. 18-Brereton-c. 31-33-Wraith back-up; Caldwell-a						3.00
21-Silent issue; Zeck-a; two covers by Campbell and Zeck						3.00
42,43-($4.50)-Dawn of the Red Shadows; leads into G.I. Joe Vol. 2						4.50
....Cobra Reborn (1/04, $4.95) Bradstreet-c/Jenkins-a						5.00
....G.I. Joe Reborn (2/04, $4.95) Bradstreet-c/Bennett & Saltares-a						5.00
... Malfunction (2003, $15.95) r/#11-15						16.00
... M. I. A. (2002, $4.95) r/#1&2; Beck back-c from #1 on cover						5.00
.... Players & Pawns (11/04, $12.95) r/#28-33; cover gallery						13.00
.... Reborn (2004, $9.99) r/Cobra Reborn & G.I. Joe Reborn						10.00
.... Reckonings (2002, $12.95) r/#6-9; Zeck-c						13.00
.... Reinstated (2002, $14.95) r/#1-4						15.00
.... The Return of Serpentor (9/04, $12.95) r/#16,22-25; cover gallery						13.00
....Vol. 8: The Rise of the Red Shadows (1/06, $14.95) r/#42,43 & prologue pgs. from #37-41						15.00

G.I. JOE (Volume 2) (Also see Snake Eyes: Declassified)
Devil's Due Publishing: No. 0, June, 2005 - Present (25¢/$2.95/$3.50/$4.50)

0-(25¢) Casey-s/Caselli-a						2.50
1-4,7,19 ($2.95): 1-Four covers; Casey-s/Caselli-a. 4-R. Black-c						3.00
5,6-($4.50) 6-Wraparound-c						4.50
20-27-($3.50) 25-Wraparound-c World War III part 1						3.50
...America's Elite Vol. 1: The Newest War TPB ('06, $14.95) r/#0-5; cover gallery						15.00
...America's Elite Vol. 2: The Ties That Bind TPB (8/06, $15.95) r/#6-12; cover gallery						16.00
...America's Elite Vol. 3: In Sheep's Clothing TPB (2007, $18.99) r/#13-18; cover gallery						19.00
... Data Desk Handbook (10/05, $2.95) character profile pages						3.00
...:Scarlett: Declassified (7/06, $4.95) Scarlett's childhood and training; Noto-c/a						5.00
... Special Missions (2/06, $4.95) short stories and profile pages by various						5.00
... Special Missions Antarctica (12/06, $4.95) short stories and profile pages by various						5.00
... Special Missions Brazil (4/07, $5.50) short stories and profile pages by various						5.50
... Special Missions: The Enemy (9/07, $5.50) two stories and profile pages by various						5.50
... Special Missions Tokyo (9/06, $4.95) short stories and profile pages by various						5.00
... The Hunt For Cobra Commander (5/06, 25¢) short story and character profiles						2.50

G. I. JOE AND THE TRANSFORMERS
Marvel Comics Group: Jan, 1987 - No. 4, Apr, 1987 (Limited series)

1-4						6.00

G. I. JOE, A REAL AMERICAN HERO (...Starring Snake-Eyes on-c #135 on)
Marvel Comics Group: June, 1982 - No. 155, Dec, 1994

	GD 2.0	VG 4.0	FN 6.0	VF 8.0	VF/NM 9.0	NM- 9.2
1-Printed on Baxter paper; based on Hasbro toy	3	6	9	16	23	30
2-Printed on regular paper; 1st app. Kwinn	3	6	9	16	22	28
3-10: 6-1st app. Oktober Guard	2	4	6	11	16	20
11-20: 11-Intro Airborne. 13-1st Destro (cameo). 14-1st full app. Destro. 15-1st app. Major Blood. 16-1st app. Cover Girl and Trip-Wire	2	4	6	9	12	15
21-1st app. Storm Shadow; silent issue	3	6	9	16	23	30
22-1st app. Duke and Roadblock	2	4	6	8	11	14
23-25,28-30,60: 25-1st full app. Zartan, 1st app of Cutter, Deep Six, Mutt and Junkyard, and The Dreadnoks. 60-Todd McFarlane-a	1	2	3	5	6	8
26,27-Origin Snake-Eyes parts 1 & 2	2	4	6	10	14	18
31-50: 31-1st Spirit Iron-Knife. 32-1st Blowtorch, Lady J, Recondo, Ripcord. 33-New headquarters. 40-1st app. of Shipwreck, Barbecue. 48-1st app. Sgt. Slaughter. 49-1st app. of Lift-Ticket, Slipstream, Leatherneck, Serpentor						5.00
51-59,61-90						4.00
91,92,94-99: 94-96-Snake Eyes Trilogy						5.00
93-Snake-Eyes' face first revealed	2	4	6	9	13	16
100,135-138: 135-138-($1.75)-Bagged w/trading card. 138-Transformers app.	2	4	6	8	10	12
101-134: 101-New Oktober Guard app. 110-1st Garney-a. 117- Debut G.I. Joe Ninja Force	1	2	3	5	6	8
139-142-New Transformers app.	2	4	6	9	13	16
143,145-149: 145-Intro. G.I. Joe Star Brigade	2	4	6	8	10	12
144-Origin Snake-Eyes	2	4	6	10	14	18
150-Low print thru #155	3	6	9	16	22	28
151-154: 152-30th Anniversary (of doll) issue, original G.I. Joe General Joseph Colton app. (also app. in #151)	3	6	9	15	21	26
155-Last issue	4	8	12	22	34	45
All 2nd printings						2.50
Special #1 (2/95, $1.50) r/#60 w/McFarlane-a. Cover swipe from Spider-Man #1	3	6	9	20	30	40
Special Treasury Edition (1982)-r/#1	3	6	9	16	22	28
Volume 1 TPB (4/02, $24.95) r/#1-10; new cover by Michael Golden						25.00
Volume 2 TPB (6/02, $24.95) r/#11-20; new cover by J. Scott Campbell						25.00
Volume 3 TPB (2002, $24.99) r/#21-30; new cover by J. Scott Campbell						25.00
Volume 4 TPB (2002, $25.99) r/#31-40; new cover by J. Scott Campbell						26.00
Volume 5 TPB (2002, $24.99) r/#42-50; new cover by J. Scott Campbell						25.00
Yearbook 1-4: (3/85-3/88)-r/#1; Golden-c. 2-Golden-c/a						5.00

NOTE: **Garney** a(p)-110. **Golden** c-23, 29, 34, 36. **Heath** a-24. **Rogers** a(p)-75, 77-82, 84, 86; c-77.

G.I. JOE: BATTLE FILES
Image Comics: 2002 - No. 3, 2002 ($5.95)

1-3-Profile pages of characters and history; Beck-c						6.00

G. I. JOE COMICS MAGAZINE
Marvel Comics Group: Dec, 1986 - No. 13, 1988 ($1.50, digest-size)

	GD	VG	FN	VF	VF/NM	NM-
1-13: G.I. Joe-r	1	3	4	6	8	10

G.I. JOE DECLASSIFIED
Devil's Due Publishing: June, 2006 - Present ($4.95, bi-monthly)

1-3-New "early" adventures of the team; Hama-s; Quinn & DeLandro-a; var-c for each						5.00
TPB (1/07, $18.99) r/#1-3; cover gallery						19.00

G.I. JOE DREADNOKS: DECLASSIFIED
Devil's Due Publishing: Nov, 2006 - No. 3, Mar, 2007 ($4.95/$4.99/$5.50, bi-monthly)

1,2-Secret history of the team; Blaylock-s; var-c for each						5.00
3-($5.50)						5.50

G. I. JOE EUROPEAN MISSIONS (Action Force in indicia) (Series reprints Action Force)
Marvel Comics Ltd. (British): Jun, 1988 - No. 15, Dec, 1989 ($1.50/$1.75)

	GD	VG	FN	VF	VF/NM	NM-
1,3-Snake Eyes & Storm Shadow-c/s	1	2	3	5	7	9
2,4-15						6.00

G.I. JOE: FRONT LINE
Image Comics: 2002 - No. 18, Dec, 2003 ($2.95)

1-18: 1-Jurgens-a/Hama-s. 1-Two covers by Dorman & Sharpe. 7,8-Harris-c						3.00
...Vol. 1 - The Mission That Never Was TPB (2003, $14.95) r/ #1-4; script pages						15.00
...Vol. 2 - Icebound TPB (3/04, $12.95) r/ #5-8						13.00
...Vol. 3 - History Repeating TPB (4/04, $9.95) r/#11-14						10.00
...Vol. 4 - One-Shots TPB (5/04, $15.95) r/#9,10,15-18						16.00

G.I. JOE: MASTER & APPRENTICE
Image Comics: May, 2004 - No. 4, Aug, 2004 ($2.95)

1-4-Caselli-a/Jerwa-s						3.00

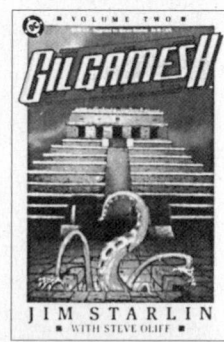

Gilgamesh II #2 © DC

Ginger #10 © AP

Girls #24 © Luna Bros.

	GD	VG	FN	VF	VF/NM	NM-
	2.0	4.0	6.0	8.0	9.0	9.2

G.I. JOE: MASTER & APPRENTICE 2
Image Comics: Feb, 2005 - No. 4, May, 2005 ($2.95, limited series)

1-4: Stevens & Vedder-a/Jerwa-s						3.00

G. I. JOE ORDER OF BATTLE, THE
Marvel Comics Group: Dec, 1986 - No. 4, Mar, 1987 (limited series)

1-4						6.00

G.I. JOE: RELOADED
Image Comics: Mar, 2004 -No. 14, Apr, 2005 ($2.95)

1-14: 1-3-Granov-c/Ney Rieber-s. 5,6-Rieber-s/Saltares-a. 8-Origin of the Baroness						3.00
Vol. 1 In the Name of Patriotism (11/04, $12.95) r/#1-6; cover gallery						13.00

G.I. JOE SIGMA 6 (Based on the cartoon TV series)
Devil's Due Publishing: Dec, 2005 - No. 6, May, 2006 ($2.95, limited series)

1-6-Andrew Daab-s						3.00
TPB Vol. 1 (10/06, $10.95, 8-1/4" x 5-3/4") r/#1-6; cover gallery						11.00

G. I. JOE SPECIAL MISSIONS (Indicia title: Special Missions)
Marvel Comics Group: Oct, 1986 - No. 28, Dec, 1989 ($1.00)

1-20						4.00
21-28						5.00

G.I. JOE VS. THE TRANSFORMERS
Image Comics: Jun, 2003 - No. 6, Nov, 2003 ($2.95, limited series)

1-Blaylock-s/Mike Miller-a; three covers by Miller, Campbell & Andrews						3.00
1-2nd printing; black cover with logo; back-c by Campbell						3.00
2-6: 2-Two covers by Miller & Brooks						3.00
TPB (3/04, $15.95) r/series; sketch pages						16.00

G.I. JOE VS. THE TRANSFORMERS (Volume 2)
Devil's Due Publ.: Sept, 2004 - No. 4, Dec, 2004 ($4.95/$2.95, limited series)

1-($4.95) Three covers; Jolley-s/Su & Seeley-a						5.00
2-4-($2.95) Two covers by Su & Pollina						3.00
Vol. 2 TPB (4/05, $14.95) r/series; interview with creators; sketch pages and covers						15.00

G.I. JOE VS. THE TRANSFORMERS (Volume 3) **THE ART OF WAR**
Devil's Due Publ.: Mar, 2006 - No. 5, July, 2006 ($2.95, limited series)

1-5: 1-Three covers; Seeley-s/Ng-a						3.00
TPB (8/06, $14.95) r/series; cover gallery						15.00

G.I. JOE VS. THE TRANSFORMERS (Volume 4) **BLACK HORIZON**
Devil's Due Publ.: Jan, 2007 - No. 2, 2006 ($5.50, limited series)

1,2: 1-Three covers; Seeley-s/Wildman-a. 2-Two covers						5.50

G. I. JUNIORS (See Harvey Hits No. 86,91,95,98,101,104,107,110,112,114,116,118,120,122)

GILGAMESH II
DC Comics: 1989 - No. 4, 1989 ($3.95, limited series, prestige format, mature)

1-4: Starlin-c/a/scripts						4.00

GIL THORP
Dell Publishing Co.: May-July, 1963

	GD	VG	FN	VF	VF/NM	NM-
1-Caniff-*ish* art	4	8	12	24	37	50

GINGER
Archie Publications: 1951 - No. 10, Summer, 1954

	GD	VG	FN	VF	VF/NM	NM-
1-Teenage humor	15	30	45	83	124	165
2-(1952)	9	18	27	50	65	80
3-6: 6-(Sum/53)	8	16	24	42	54	65
7-10-Katy Keene app.	10	20	30	54	72	90

GINGER FOX (Also see The World of Ginger Fox)
Comico: Sept, 1988 - No. 4, Dec, 1988 ($1.75, limited series)

1-4: Part photo-c on all						2.50

G.I. R.A.M.B.O.T.
Wonder Color Comics/Pied Piper #2: Apr, 1987 - No. 2? ($1.95)

1,2: 2-Exist?						2.50

GIRL
DC Comics (Vertigo Verite): Jul, 1996 - No. 3, 1996 ($2.50, lim. series, mature)

1-3: Peter Milligan scripts; Fegredo-c/a						2.50

GIRL COMICS (Becomes Girl Confessions No. 13 on)
Marvel/Atlas Comics(CnPC): Oct, 1949 - No. 12, Jan, 1952 (#1-4: 52 pgs.)

	GD	VG	FN	VF	VF/NM	NM-
1-Photo-c	23	46	69	130	205	280
2-Kubert-a; photo-c	14	28	42	76	108	140
3-Everett-a; Liz Taylor photo-c	28	56	84	162	256	350
4-11: 4-Photo-c. 10-12-Sol Brodsky-c	11	22	33	62	86	110

	GD	VG	FN	VF	VF/NM	NM-
12-Krigstein-a; Al Hartley-c	12	24	36	67	94	120

GIRL CONFESSIONS (Formerly Girl Comics)
Atlas Comics (CnPC/ZPC): No. 13, Mar, 1952 - No. 35, Aug, 1954

	GD	VG	FN	VF	VF/NM	NM-
13-Everett-a	13	26	39	74	105	135
14,15,19,20	10	20	30	54	72	90
16-18-Everett-a	11	22	33	62	86	110
21-35: Robinson-a	8	16	24	44	57	70

GIRL CRAZY
Dark Horse Comics: May, 1996 - No. 3, July, 1996 ($2.95, B&W, limited series)

1-3: Gilbert Hernandez-a/scripts.						3.00

GIRL FROM U.N.C.L.E., THE (TV) (Also see The Man From…)
Gold Key: Jan, 1967 - No. 5, Oct, 1967

	GD	VG	FN	VF	VF/NM	NM-
1-McWilliams-a; Stephanie Powers photo front/back-c & pin-ups (no ads, 12¢)	9	18	27	58	89	120
2-5-Leonard Swift-Courier No. 5. 4-Back-c pin-up	7	14	21	40	60	80

GIRLS
Image Comics: May, 2005 - No. 24, Apr, 2007 ($2.95/$2.99)

1-Luna Brothers-s/a/c						4.00
2-24						3.00
... Vol. 1: Conception TPB (2005, $14.99) r/#1-6						15.00
... Vol. 2: Emergence TPB (2006, $14.99) r/#7-12						15.00
... Vol. 3: Survival TPB (2006, $14.99) r/#13-18						15.00
... Vol. 4: Extinction TPB (2007, $14.99) r/#19-24						15.00

GIRLS' FUN & FASHION MAGAZINE (Formerly Polly Pigtails)
Parents' Magazine Institute: V5#44, Jan, 1950 - V5#48, Sept., 1950

	GD	VG	FN	VF	VF/NM	NM-
V5#44	7	14	21	35	43	50
45-48	5	10	15	24	30	35

GIRLS IN LOVE
Fawcett Publications: May, 1950 - No. 2, July, 1950

	GD	VG	FN	VF	VF/NM	NM-
1-Photo-c	12	24	36	69	97	125
2-Photo-c	10	20	30	54	72	90

GIRLS IN LOVE (Formerly G. I. Sweethearts No. 45)
Quality Comics Group: No. 46, Sept, 1955 - No. 57, Dec, 1956

	GD	VG	FN	VF	VF/NM	NM-
46	9	18	27	50	65	80
47-53,55,56	7	14	21	37	46	55
54- 'Commie' story	8	16	24	44	57	70
57-Matt Baker-c/a	12	24	36	67	94	120

GIRLS IN WHITE (See Harvey Comics Hits No. 58)

GIRLS' LIFE (Patsy Walker's Own Magazine For Girls!)
Atlas Comics (BFP): Jan, 1954 - No. 6, Nov, 1954

	GD	VG	FN	VF	VF/NM	NM-
1	13	26	39	74	105	135
2-Al Hartley-a	8	16	24	44	57	70
3-6	8	16	24	40	50	60

GIRLS' LOVE STORIES
National Comics(Signal Publ. No. 9-65/Arleigh No. 83-117): Aug-Sept, 1949 - No. 180, Nov-Dec, 1973 (No. 1-13: 52 pgs.)

	GD	VG	FN	VF	VF/NM	NM-
1-Toth, Kinstler-a, 8 pgs. each; photo-c	54	108	162	338	557	775
2-Kinstler-a?	31	62	93	178	282	385
3-10: 1-9-Photo-c	21	42	63	122	191	260
11-20	16	32	48	94	147	200
21-33: 21-Kinstler-a. 33-Last pre-code (1-2/55)	12	24	36	69	97	125
34-50	11	22	33	60	83	105
51-70	10	20	30	54	72	90
71-99: 83-Last 10¢ issue	5	10	15	32	51	70
100	5	10	15	35	55	75
101-146: 113-117-April O'Day app.	3	6	9	20	30	40
147-151- "Confessions" serial. 150-Wood-a	3	6	9	21	32	42
152-160,171-179	3	6	9	16	22	28
161-170 (52 pgs.)	4	8	12	22	34	45
180 Last issue	3	6	9	20	30	40
Ashcan (8-9/49) not distributed to newsstands, only for in house use						(no known sales)

GIRLS' ROMANCES
National Periodical Publ.(Signal Publ. No. 7-79/Arleigh No. 84): Feb-Mar, 1950 - No. 160, Oct, 1971 (No. 1-11: 52 pgs.)

	GD	VG	FN	VF	VF/NM	NM-
1-Photo-c	53	106	159	323	537	750
2-Photo-c; Toth-a	30	60	90	174	275	375
3-10: 3-6-Photo-c	21	42	63	122	191	260

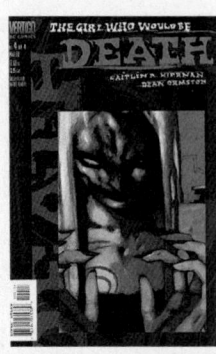
The Girl Who Would Be Death #4 © DC

Glamorous Romances #45 © ACE

Glory #15 © Rob Liefeld

	GD 2.0	VG 4.0	FN 6.0	VF 8.0	VF/NM 9.0	NM- 9.2
11,12,14-20	15	30	45	86	133	180
13-Toth-c	15	30	45	90	140	190
21-31: 31-Last pre-code (2-3/55)	12	24	36	69	97	125
32-50	7	14	21	45	73	100
51-99: 80-Last 10¢ issue	5	10	15	32	51	70
100	5	10	15	35	55	75
101-108,110-120	3	6	9	20	30	40
109-Beatles-c/story	12	24	36	86	153	220
121-133,135-140	3	6	9	18	27	35
134-Neal Adams-c (splash pg. is same as-c)	5	10	15	32	51	70
141-158	3	6	9	16	22	28
159,160-52 pgs.	4	8	12	22	34	45

GIRL WHO WOULD BE DEATH, THE
DC Comics (Vertigo): Dec, 1998 - No. 4, March, 1999 ($2.50, lim. series)

1-4-Kiernan-s/Ormston-a						2.50

G. I. SWEETHEARTS (Formerly Diary Loves; Girls In Love #46 on)
Quality Comics Group: No. 32, June, 1953 - No. 45, May, 1955

	GD	VG	FN	VF	VF/NM	NM-
32	10	20	30	54	72	90
33-45: 44-Last pre-code (3/55)	8	16	24	40	50	60

G.I. TALES (Formerly Sgt. Barney Barker No. 1-3)
Atlas Comics (MCI): No. 4, Feb, 1957 - No. 6, July, 1957

4-Severin-a(4)	10	20	30	54	72	90
5	8	16	24	40	50	60
6-Orlando, Powell, & Woodbridge-a	8	16	24	42	54	65

GIVE ME LIBERTY (Also see Dark Horse Presents Fifth Anniversary Special, Dark Horse Presents #100-4, Happy Birthday Martha Washington, Martha Washington Goes to War, Martha Washington Stranded In Space & San Diego Comicon Comics #2)
Dark Horse Comics: June, 1990 - No. 4, 1991 ($4.95, limited series, 52 pgs.)

1-4: 1st app. Martha Washington; Frank Miller scripts, Dave Gibbons-c/a in all						5.00

G. I. WAR BRIDES
Superior Publishers Ltd.: Apr, 1954 - No. 8, June, 1955

1	10	20	30	54	72	90
2	7	14	21	35	43	50
3-8: 4-Kamenesque-a; lingerie panels	6	12	18	31	38	45

G. I. WAR TALES
National Periodical Publications: Mar-Apr, 1973 - No. 4, Oct-Nov, 1973

1-Reprints all; dinosaur-c/s	3	6	9	16	23	30
2-N. Adams-a(r)	2	4	6	10	14	18
3,4: 4-Krigstein-a(r)	2	4	6	9	13	16

NOTE: Drucker a-3r, 4r. Heath a-4r. Kubert a-2, 3; c-4r.

GIZMO (Also see Domino Chance)
Chance Ent.: May-June, 1985 (B&W, one-shot)

1						6.00

GIZMO
Mirage Studios: 1986 - No. 6, July, 1987 ($1.50, B&W)

1-6						2.50

G.L.A. (Great Lakes Avengers)(Also see GLX-Mas Special)
Marvel Comics: June, 2005 - No. 4, Sept, 2005 ($2.99, limited series)

1-4-Slott-s/Pelletier-a						3.00
...: Misassembled TPB (2005, $14.99) r/#1-4, West Coast Avengers #46 (1st app.) and Marvel Super-Heroes #8 (1st app. Squirrel Girl; Ditko-a)						15.00

GLADSTONE COMIC ALBUM
Gladstone: 1987 - No. 28, 1990 ($5.95/$9.95, 8-1/2x11")(All Mickey Mouse albums are by Gottfredson)

1-10: 1-Uncle Scrooge; Barks-r; Beck-c. 2-Donald Duck; r/F.C. #108 by Barks. 3-Mickey Mouse-r by Gottfredson. 4-Uncle Scrooge; r/F.C. #456 by Barks w/unedited story. 5-Donald Duck Advs.; r/F.C. #199. 6-Uncle Scrooge-r by Barks. 7-Donald Duck-r by Barks. 8-Mickey Mouse-r. 9-Bambi; r/F.C. #186? 10-Donald Duck Advs.; r/F.C. #275						
	1	3	4	6	8	10
11-20: 11-Uncle Scrooge; r/U.S. #4. 12-Donald And Daisy; r/F.C. #1055, WDC&S. 13-Donald Duck Advs.; r/F.C. #408. 14-Uncle Scrooge; Barks-r/U.S #21. 15-Donald And Gladstone; Barks-r 16-Donald Duck Advs.; r/F.C. #238. 17-Mickey Mouse strip-r (The World of Tomorrow, The Pirate Ghost Ship). 18-Donald Duck and the Junior Woodchucks; Barks-r. 19-Uncle Scrooge; r/U.S. #12; Rosa-c. 20-Uncle Scrooge; r/F.C. #386; Barks-c/a(r)						
	1	3	4	6	8	10
21-25: 21-Donald Duck Family; Barks-c/a(r). 22-Mickey Mouse strip-r. 23-Donald Duck; Barks-r/D.D. #26 w/unedited story. 24-Donald Duck; Barks-r; Rosa-c. 25-D. Duck; Barks-c/a-r/F.C. #367						
	1	3	4	6	8	10
26-28: All have $9.95-c. 26-Mickey & Donald; Gottfredson-c/a(r). 27-Donald Duck; r/WDC&S by Barks; Barks painted-c. 28-Uncle Scrooge & Donald Duck; Rosa-c/a (4 stories)						
	1	3	4	6	8	10
Special 1-7: 1 ('89-'90, $9.95/13.95)-1-Donald Duck Finds Pirate Gold; r/F.C. #9. 2 ('89, $8.95)-Uncle Scrooge and Donald Duck; Barks-r/Uncle Scrooge #5; Rosa-c. 3 ('89, $8.95)-Mickey Mouse strip-r. 4 ('89, $11.95)-Uncle Scrooge; Rosa-c/a-r/Son of the Sun from U.S. #219 plus Barks-r/U.S. 5 ('90, $11.95)-Donald Duck Advs.; Barks-r/F.C. #282 & 422 plus Barks painted-c. 6 ('90, $12.95)-Uncle Scrooge; Barks-c/a-r/Uncle Scrooge. 7 ('90, $13.95)-Mickey Mouse; Gottfredson strip-r						
	2	4	6	9	11	14

GLADSTONE COMIC ALBUM (2nd Series)(Also see The Original Dick Tracy)
Gladstone Publishing: 1990 ($5.95, 8-1/2 x 11," stiff-c, 52 pgs.)

1,2-The Original Dick Tracy. 2-Origin of the 2-way wrist radio						6.00
3-D Tracy Meets the Mole-r by Gould ($6.95).	1	2	3	5	6	8

GLAMOROUS ROMANCES (Formerly Dotty)
Ace Magazines (A. A. Wyn): No. 41, July, 1949 - No. 90, Oct, 1956 (Photo-c 68-90)

41-Dotty app.	10	20	30	58	79	160
42-72,74-80: 44-Begin 52 pg. issues. 45,50-61-Painted-c. 80-Last pre-code (2/55)	8	16	24	42	54	65
73-L.B. Cole-a/All Love #27	8	16	24	44	57	70
81-90	8	16	24	40	50	60

GLOBAL FREQUENCY
DC Comics (WildStorm): Dec, 2002 - No. 12, Aug, 2004 ($2.95, limited series)

1-12-Warren Ellis-s. 1-Leach-a. 2-Fabry-a. 3-Dillon-a. 5-Muth-a. 7-Bisley-a. 12-Ha-a						3.00
1-RRP Edition variant-c; promotional giveaway for retailers (200 printed)						10.00
...: Detonation Radio TPB (2005, $14.95) r/#7-12						15.00
...: Planet Ablaze TPB (2003, $14.95) r/#1-6						15.00

GLORY
Image Comics (Extreme Studios)/Maximum Press: Mar, 1995 - No. 22, Apr, 1997 ($2.50)

0-Deodato-c/a, 1-(3/95)-Deodato-a						2.50
1A-Variant-c						4.00
2-11,13-22: 4-Variant-c by Quesada & Palmiotti. 5-Bagged w/Youngblood gaming card. 7,8-Deodato-c/a(p). 8-Babewatch x-over. 9-Cruz-c; Extreme Destroyer Pt. 5; polybagged w/card. 10-Angela-c/app. 11-Deodato-c.						2.50
12-($3.50)-Photo-c						3.50
... & Friends Christmas Special (12/95, $2.50) Deodato-c						2.50
... & Friends Lingerie Special (9/95, $2.95) Pin-ups w/photos; photo-c; varant-c exists						3.00
... /Angela: Angels in Hell (4/96, $2.50) Flip book w/Darkchylde #1						2.50
... /Avengelyne (10/95, $3.95) 1-Chromium-c, 1-Regular-c						4.00
Trade Paperback (1995, $9.95)-r/#1-4						10.00

GLORY
Awesome Comics: Mar, 1999 ($2.50)

0-Liefeld-c; story and sketch pages						2.50

GLORY (ALAN MOORE'S...)
Avatar Press: Dec, 2001 - No. 2 ($3.50)

Preview-(9/01, $1.99) B&W pages and cover art; Alan Moore-s						2.50
0-Four regular covers						3.50
1,2: 1-Alan Moore-s/Mychaels & Gebbie-a; nine covers by various. 2-Five covers						3.50

GLORY & FRIENDS BIKINI FEST
Image Comics (Extreme): Sept, 1995 - No. 2, Oct, 1995 ($2.50, limited series)

1,2: 1-Photo-c; centerfold photo; pin-ups						2.50

GLORY/CELESTINE: DARK ANGEL
Image Comics/Maximum Press (Extreme Studios): Sept, 1996 - No. 3, Nov, 1996 ($2.50, limited series)

1-3						2.50

GLX-MAS SPECIAL (Great Lakes Avengers)
Marvel Comics: Feb, 2006 ($3.99, one-shot)

1-Christmas themed stories by various incl. Haley, Templeton, Grist, Wieringo						4.00

GNOME MOBILE, THE (See Movie Comics)

GOBBLEDYGOOK
Mirage Studios: 1984 - No. 2, 1984 (B&W)(1st Mirage comics, published at same time)

1-(24 pgs.)-(distribution of approx. 50) Teenage Mutant Ninja Turtles app. on full page back-c ad; Teenage Mutant Ninja Turtles do not appear inside. 1st app of Fugitoid						
	48	96	144	384	692	1000
2-(24 pgs.)-Teenage Mutant Ninja Turtles on full page back-c ad						
	32	64	96	240	445	650

NOTE: Counterfeit copies exist. Originals feature both black & white covers and interiors. Signed and numbered copies do not exist.

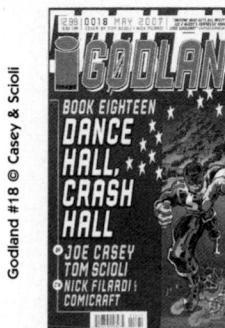

Godland #18 © Casey & Scioli

Go-Go #3 © CC

Golden Arrow #4 © FAW

	GD 2.0	VG 4.0	FN 6.0	VF 8.0	VF/NM 9.0	NM- 9.2		GD 2.0	VG 4.0	FN 6.0	VF 8.0	VF/NM 9.0	NM- 9.2

GOBBLEDYGOOK
Mirage Studios: Dec, 1986 ($3.50, B&W, one-shot, 100 pgs.)

1-New 8 pg. TMNT story plus a Donatello/Michaelangelo 7 pg. story & a Gizmo story;
Corben-i(r)/TMNT #7 ... 1 ... 2 ... 3 ... 4 ... 5 ... 7

GOBLIN, THE
Warren Publishing Co.: June, 1982 - No. 3, Dec, 1982 ($2.25, B&W magazine with 8 pg. color insert comic in all)

1-The Gremlin app. Philo Photon & the Troll Patrol, Micro-Buccaneers & Wizard Wormglow
begin & app. in all. Tin Man app. Golden-a(p). Nebres-c/a in all ... 2 ... 4 ... 6 ... 13 ... 18 ... 22

2,3: 2-1st Hobgoblin. 3-Tin Man app. ... 2 ... 4 ... 6 ... 9 ... 12 ... 15

NOTE: *Bermejo a-1-3. Elias a-1-3. Laxamana a-1-3. Nino a-3.*

GODDESS
DC Comics (Vertigo): June, 1995 - No. 8, Jan, 1996 ($2.95, limited series)

1-Garth Ennis scripts; Phil Winslade-c/a in all ... 5.00

2-8 ... 4.00

TPB (2002, $19.95) r/#1-8; foreword and sketch pages by Winslade ... 20.00

GODFATHERS, THE (See The Crusaders)

GOD IS
Spire Christian Comics (Fleming H. Revell Co.): 1973, 1975 (35-49¢)

nn-(1973) By Al Hartley ... 2 ... 4 ... 6 ... 8 ... 11 ... 14

nn-(1975) ... 1 ... 3 ... 4 ... 6 ... 8 ... 10

GODLAND
Image Comics: July, 2005 - Present ($2.99)

1-15,17-19-Joe Casey-s; Kirby-esque art by Tom Scioli. 13-Var-c by Giffen & Larsen ... 3.00

16-(60¢-c) Re-cap/origin issue ... 2.25

...: Celestial Edition One HC (2007, $34.99) r/#1-12 and story from Image Holiday Special;
intro. by Grant Morrison; cover gallery, developmental art and original story pitches ... 35.00

... Vol. 1: Hello Cosmic! TPB (1/06, $14.99) r/#1-6; sketch development pages ... 15.00

... Vol. 2: Another Sunny Delight TPB (8/06, $14.99) r/#7-12; early Christmas story ... 15.00

... Vol. 3: Proto-Plastic Party TPB (2007, $14.99) r/#13-18 ... 15.00

GOD SAVE THE QUEEN
DC Comics (Vertigo): 2007 ($19.99, hardcover with dustjacket, graphic novel)

nn-Mike Carey-s/John Bolton-painted art ... 20.00

GOD'S COUNTRY (Also see Marvel Comics Presents)
Marvel Comics: 1994 ($6.95)

nn-P. Craig Russell-a; Colossus story; r/Marvel Comics Presents #10-17 ... 7.00

GOD'S HEROES IN AMERICA
Catechetical Guild Educational Society: 1956 (nn) (25¢/35¢, 68 pgs.)

307 ... 3 ... 6 ... 9 ... 16 ... 23 ... 30

GOD'S SMUGGLER (Religious)
Spire Christian Comics/Fleming H. Revell Co.: 1972 (35¢/39¢/40¢)

1-Three variations exist ... 2 ... 4 ... 6 ... 8 ... 11 ... 14

GODWHEEL
Malibu Comics (Ultraverse): No. 0, Jan, 1995 - No. 3, Feb, 1995 ($2.50, limited series)

0-3: 0-Flip-c. 1-1st app. of Primevil; Thor cameo (1 panel). 3-Perez-a in
Chapter 3, Thor app. ... 2.50

GODZILLA (Movie)
Marvel Comics: August, 1977 - No. 24, July, 1979 (Based on movie series)

1-(Regular 30¢ edition)-Mooney-i ... 3 ... 6 ... 9 ... 16 ... 23 ... 30

1-(35¢-c variant, limited distribution) ... 6 ... 12 ... 18 ... 37 ... 59 ... 80

2-(Regular 30¢ edition)-Tuska-i. ... 2 ... 4 ... 6 ... 8 ... 10 ... 12

2,3-(35¢-c variant, limited distribution) ... 3 ... 6 ... 9 ... 20 ... 30 ... 40

3-(30¢-c) Champions app.(w/o Ghost Rider) ... 2 ... 4 ... 6 ... 8 ... 11 ... 14

4-10: 4,5-Sutton-a ... 1 ... 3 ... 4 ... 6 ... 8 ... 10

11-23: 14-Shield app. 20-F.F. app. 21,22-Devil Dinosaur app.
... 1 ... 2 ... 3 ... 5 ... 7 ... 9

24-Last issue ... 2 ... 4 ... 6 ... 8 ... 10 ... 12

GODZILLA (Movie)
Dark Horse Comics: May, 1988 - No. 6, 1988 ($1.95, B&W, limited series) (Based on movie series)

1 ... 6.00

2-6 ... 4.00

...Collection (1990, $10.95)-r/1-6 with new-c ... 11.00

...Color Special 1 (Sum, 1992, $3.50, color, 44 pgs.)-Arthur Adams wraparound-c/a &
part scripts ... 5.00

...King Of The Monsters Special (8/87, $1.50)-Origin; Bissette-c/a ... 4.00

...Vs. Barkley nn (12/93, $2.95, color)-Dorman painted-c ... 4.00

GODZILLA (King of the Monsters) (Movie)
Dark Horse Comics: May, 1995 - No. 16, Sept, 1996 ($2.50) (Based on movies)

0-16: 0-r/Dark Horse Comics #10,11. 1-3-Kevin Maguire scripts. 3-8-Art Adams-c ... 4.00

...Vs. Hero Zero ($2.50) ... 3.00

GOG (VILLAINS) (See Kingdom Come)
DC Comics: Feb, 1998 ($2.95, one-shot)

1-Waid-s/Ordway-a(p)/Pearson-c ... 3.00

GO GIRL!
Image Comics: Aug, 2000 - Present ($3.50, B&W, quarterly)

1-5-Trina Robbins-s/Anne Timmons-a; pin-up gallery ... 3.50

GO-GO
Charlton Comics: June, 1966 - No. 9, Oct, 1967

1-Miss Bikini Luv begins w/Jim Aparo's 1st published work; Rolling Stones, Beatles, Elvis,
Sonny & Cher, Bob Dylan, Sinatra, parody; Herman's Hermits pin-ups;
D'Agostino-c/a in #1-8 ... 8 ... 16 ... 24 ... 52 ... 86 ... 120

2-Ringo Starr, David McCallum & Beatles photos on cover; Beatles story and photos
... 8 ... 16 ... 24 ... 52 ... 86 ... 120

3,4: 3-Blooperman begins, ends #6; 1 pg. Batman & Robin satire; full pg. photo pin-ups
Lovin' Spoonful & The Byrds ... 5 ... 10 ... 15 ... 30 ... 48 ... 65

5,7,9: 5 (2/67)-Super Hero & TV satire by Jim Aparo & Grass Green begins. 6-8-Aparo-a.
7-Photo of Brian Wilson of Beach Boys on-c & Beach Boys photo inside f/b-c. 9-Aparo-c/a
... 5 ... 10 ... 15 ... 30 ... 48 ... 65

6-Parody of JLA & DC heroes vs. Marvel heroes; Aparo-a; Elvis parody; Petula Clark photo-c
... 5 ... 10 ... 15 ... 35 ... 55 ... 75

8-Monkees photo on-c & photo inside f/b-c ... 6 ... 12 ... 18 ... 39 ... 62 ... 85

GO-GO AND ANIMAL (See Tippy's Friends...)

GOING STEADY (Formerly Teen-Age Temptations)
St. John Publ. Co.: No. 10, Dec, 1954 - No. 13, June, 1955; No. 14, Oct, 1955

10(1954)-Matt Baker-c/a ... 24 ... 48 ... 72 ... 139 ... 220 ... 300

11(2/55, last precode), 12(4/55)-Baker-c ... 14 ... 28 ... 42 ... 80 ... 115 ... 150

13(6/55)-Baker-c/a ... 18 ... 36 ... 54 ... 105 ... 165 ... 225

14(10/55)-Matt Baker-c/a, 25 pgs. ... 22 ... 44 ... 66 ... 128 ... 202 ... 275

GOING STEADY (Formerly Personal Love)
Prize Publications/Headline: V3#3, Feb, 1960 - V3#6, Aug, 1960; V4#1, Sept-Oct, 1960

V3#3-6, V4#1 ... 3 ... 6 ... 9 ... 16 ... 22 ... 28

GOING STEADY WITH BETTY (Becomes Betty & Her Steady No. 2)
Avon Periodicals: Nov-Dec, 1949

1 ... 15 ... 30 ... 45 ... 85 ... 130 ... 175

GOLDEN AGE, THE (TPB also reprinted in 2005 as JSA: The Golden Age)
DC Comics (Elseworlds): 1993 - No. 4, 1994 ($4.95, limited series)

1-4: James Robinson scripts; Paul Smith-c/a; gold foil embossed-c ... 6.00

Trade Paperback (1995, $19.95) intro by Howard Chaykin ... 20.00

GOLDEN AGE SECRET FILES
DC Comics: Feb, 2001 ($4.95, one-shot)

1-Origins and profiles of JSA members and other G.A. heroes; Lark-c ... 5.00

GOLDEN ARROW (See Fawcett Miniatures, Mighty Midget & Whiz Comics)

GOLDEN ARROW (...Western No. 6)
Fawcett Publications: Spring, 1942 - No. 6, Spring, 1947 (68 pgs.)

1-Golden Arrow begins . ... 75 ... 150 ... 225 ... 469 ... 760 ... 1050

2-(1943) ... 40 ... 80 ... 120 ... 235 ... 368 ... 500

3-5: 3-(Win/45-46). 4-(Spr/46). 5-(Fall/46) ... 29 ... 58 ... 87 ... 167 ... 259 ... 350

6-Krigstein-a ... 30 ... 60 ... 90 ... 173 ... 267 ... 360

Ashcan (1942) not distributed to newsstands, only for in house use (no known sales)

GOLDEN COMICS DIGEST
Gold Key: May, 1969 - No. 48, Jan, 1976

NOTE: *Whitman editions exist of many titles and are generally valued the same.*

1-Tom & Jerry, Woody Woodpecker, Bugs Bunny ... 5 ... 10 ... 15 ... 30 ... 48 ... 65

2-Hanna-Barbera TV Fun Favorites; Space Ghost, Flintstones, Atom Ant, Jetsons,
Yogi Bear, Banana Splits, others app. ... 6 ... 12 ... 18 ... 41 ... 66 ... 90

3-Tom & Jerry, Woody Woodpecker ... 3 ... 6 ... 9 ... 15 ... 21 ... 26

4-Tarzan; Manning & Marsh-a ... 4 ... 8 ... 12 ... 26 ... 41 ... 55

5,8-Tom & Jerry, W. Woodpecker, Bugs Bunny ... 3 ... 6 ... 9 ... 14 ... 19 ... 24

6-Bugs Bunny ... 3 ... 6 ... 9 ... 14 ... 19 ... 24

7-Hanna-Barbera TV Fun Favorites ... 5 ... 10 ... 15 ... 30 ... 48 ... 65

Golden Comics Digest #23 © GK

Golden Lad #4 © Spark Pub.

Gomer Pyle #1 © GK

	GD 2.0	VG 4.0	FN 6.0	VF 8.0	VF/NM 9.0	NM- 9.2

9-Tarzan — 4, 8, 12, 26, 41, 55

10,12-17: 10-Bugs Bunny. 12-Tom & Jerry, Bugs Bunny, W. Woodpecker Journey to the Sun. 13-Tom & Jerry. 14-Bugs Bunny Fun Packed Funnies. 15-Tom & Jerry, Woody Woodpecker, Bugs Bunny. 16-Woody Woodpecker Cartoon Special. 17-Bugs Bunny — 3, 6, 9, 14, 19, 24

11-Hanna-Barbera TV Fun Favorites — 5, 10, 15, 32, 51, 70

18-Tom & Jerry; Barney Bear-r by Barks — 3, 6, 9, 15, 21, 26

19-Little Lulu — 4, 8, 12, 22, 34, 45

20-22: 20-Woody Woodpecker Falltime Funtime. 21-Bugs Bunny Showtime. 22-Tom & Jerry Winter Wingding — 3, 6, 9, 14, 19, 24

23-Little Lulu & Tubby Fun Fling — 4, 8, 12, 22, 34, 45

24-26,28: 24-Woody Woodpecker Fun Festival. 25-Tom & Jerry. 26-Bugs Bunny Halloween Hulla-Boo-Loo; Dr. Spektor article, also #25. 28-Tom & Jerry — 2, 4, 6, 13, 18, 22

27-Little Lulu & Tubby in Hawaii — 3, 6, 9, 21, 32, 42

29-Little Lulu & Tubby — 3, 6, 9, 21, 32, 42

30-Bugs Bunny Vacation Funnies — 2, 4, 6, 13, 18, 22

31-Turok, Son of Stone; r/4-Color #596,656; c-r/#9 — 4, 8, 12, 23, 36, 48

32-Woody Woodpecker Summer Fun — 2, 4, 6, 13, 18, 22

33,36: 33-Little Lulu & Tubby Halloween Fun; Dr. Spektor app. 36-Little Lulu & Her Friends — 3, 6, 9, 21, 32, 42

34,35,37-39: 34-Bugs Bunny Winter Funnies. 35-Tom & Jerry Snowtime Funtime. 37-Woody Woodpecker County Fair. 39-Bugs Bunny Summer Fun — 2, 4, 6, 13, 18, 22

38-The Pink Panther — 3, 6, 9, 15, 21, 26

40,43: 40-Little Lulu & Tubby Trick or Treat; all by Stanley. 43-Little Lulu in Paris — 3, 6, 9, 21, 32, 42

41,42,44,47: 41-Tom & Jerry Winter Carnival. 42-Bugs Bunny. 44-Woody Woodpecker Family Fun Festival. 47-Bugs Bunny — 2, 4, 6, 11, 16, 20

45-The Pink Panther — 3, 6, 9, 15, 21, 26

46-Little Lulu & Tubby — 3, 6, 9, 19, 29, 38

48-The Lone Ranger — 3, 6, 9, 16, 23, 30

NOTE: #1-30, 164 pgs.; #31 on, 132 pgs..

GOLDEN LAD
Spark/Fact & Fiction Publ.: July, 1945 - No. 5, June, 1946 (#4, 5: 52 pgs.)

1-Origin & 1st app. Golden Lad & Swift Arrow; Sandusky and the Senator begins — 66, 132, 198, 413, 669, 925

2-Mort Meskin-c/a — 34, 68, 102, 192, 296, 400

3,4-Mort Meskin-c/a — 30, 60, 90, 173, 267, 360

5-Origin & 1st app. Golden Girl; Shaman & Flame app. — 34, 68, 102, 192, 296, 400

NOTE: All have Robinson, and Roussos art plus Meskin covers and art.

GOLDEN LEGACY
Fitzgerald Publishing Co.: 1966 - 1972 (Black History) (25¢)

1-12,14-16: 1-Toussaint L'Ouverture (1966), 2-Harriet Tubman (1967), 3-Crispus Attucks & the Minutemen (1967), 4-Benjamin Banneker (1968), 5-Matthew Henson (1969), 6-Alexander Dumas & Family (1969), 7-Frederick Douglass, Part 1 (1969), 8-Frederick Douglass, Part 2 (1970), 9-Robert Smalls (1970), 10-J. Cinque & the Amistad Mutiny (1970), 11-Men in Action: White, Marshall J. Wilkins (1970), 12-Black Cowboys (1972), 14-The Life of Alexander Pushkin (1971), 15-Ancient African Kingdoms (1972), 16-Black Inventors (1972) each.... — 3, 6, 9, 16, 23, 30

13-The Life of Martin Luther King, Jr. (1972) — 3, 6, 9, 20, 30, 40

1-10,12,13,15,16(1976)-Reprints — 1, 2, 3, 5, 7, 9

GOLDEN LOVE STORIES (Formerly Golden West Love)
Kirby Publishing Co.: No. 4, April, 1950

4-Powell-a; Glenn Ford/Janet Leigh photo-c — 15, 30, 45, 90, 140, 190

GOLDEN PICTURE CLASSIC, A
Western Printing Co. (Simon & Shuster): 1956-1957 (Text stories w/illustrations in color; 100 pgs. each)

CL-401: Treasure Island — 10, 20, 30, 58, 79, 100

CL-402,403: 402: Tom Sawyer. 403: Black Beauty — 9, 18, 27, 50, 65, 80

CL-404, 405: CL-404: Little Women. CL-405: Heidi — 9, 18, 27, 50, 65, 80

CL-406: Ben Hur — 8, 16, 24, 40, 50, 60

CL-407: Around the World in 80 Days — 8, 16, 24, 40, 50, 60

CL-408: Sherlock Holmes — 8, 16, 24, 44, 57, 70

CL-409: The Three Musketeers — 8, 16, 24, 40, 50, 60

CL-410: The Merry Advs. of Robin Hood — 8, 16, 24, 40, 50, 60

CL-411,412: 411: Hans Brinker. 412: The Count of Monte Cristo — 8, 16, 24, 44, 57, 70

(Both soft & hardcover editions are valued the same)

NOTE: Recent research has uncovered new information. Apparently #s 1-6 were issued in 1956 and #7-12 in 1957. But they can be found in five different series listings: CL-1 to CL-12 (softbound); CL-401 to CL-412 (also softbound); CL-101 to CL-112 (hardbound); plus two new series discoveries: A Golden Reading Adventure, publ. by Golden

---

	GD 2.0	VG 4.0	FN 6.0	VF 8.0	VF/NM 9.0	NM- 9.2

Press; edited down to 60 pages and reduced in size to 6x9"; only #s discovered so far are #381 (CL-4), #382 (CL-6) & #387 (CL-3). They have no reorder list and some have covers different from GPC. There have also been found British hardbound editions of GPC with dust jackets. Copies of all five listed series vary from scarce to very rare. Some editions of some series have not yet been found at all.

GOLDEN PICTURE STORY BOOK
Racine Press (Western): Dec, 1961 (50¢, Treasury size, 52 pgs.) (All are scarce)

ST-1-Huckleberry Hound (TV); Hokey Wolf, Pixie & Dixie, Quick Draw McGraw, Snooper and Blabber, Augie Doggie app. — 17, 34, 51, 128, 227, 325

ST-2-Yogi Bear (TV); Snagglepuss, Yakky Doodle, Quick Draw McGraw, Snooper and Blabber, Augie Doggie app. — 17, 34, 51, 128, 227, 325

ST-3-Babes in Toyland (Walt Disney's...)-Annette Funicello photo-c — 22, 44, 66, 160, 285, 410

ST-4-(...of Disney Ducks)-Walt Disney's Wonderful World of Ducks (Donald Duck, Uncle Scrooge, Donald's Nephews, Grandma Duck, Ludwig Von Drake, & Gyro Gearloose stories) — 22, 44, 66, 160, 285, 410

GOLDEN RECORD COMIC (See Amazing Spider-Man #1, Avengers #4, Fantastic Four #1, Journey Into Mystery #83)

GOLDEN STORY BOOKS
Western Printing Co. (Simon & Shuster): 1949 (Heavy covers, digest size, 128 pgs.) (Illustrated text in color)

7-Walt Disney's Mystery in Disneyville, a book-length adventure starring Donald and Nephews, Mickey and Nephews, and with Minnie, Daisy and Goofy. Art by Dick Moores & Manuel Gonzales (scarce) — 30, 60, 90, 174, 275, 375

10-Bugs Bunny's Treasure Hunt, a book-length adventure starring Bugs & Porky Pig, with Petunia Pig & Nephew, Cicero. Art by Tom McKimson (scarce) — 21, 42, 63, 122, 191, 260

GOLDEN WEST LOVE (Golden Love Stories No. 4)
Kirby Publishing Co.: Sept-Oct, 1949 - No. 3, Feb, 1950 (All 52 pgs.)

1-Powell-a in all; Roussos-a; painted-c — 22, 44, 66, 126, 198, 270

2,3-Photo-c — 15, 30, 45, 90, 140, 190

GOLDEN WEST RODEO TREASURY (See Dell Giants)

GOLDFISH (See A.K.A. Goldfish)

GOLDILOCKS (See March of Comics No. 1)

GOLD KEY CHAMPION
Gold Key: Mar, 1978 - No. 2, May, 1978 (50¢, 52pgs.)

1,2: 1-Space Family Robinson; half-r. 2-Mighty Samson; half-r — 1, 3, 4, 6, 8, 10

GOLD KEY SPOTLIGHT
Gold Key: May, 1976 - No. 11, Feb, 1978

1-Tom, Dick & Harriet — 2, 4, 6, 8, 10, 12

2-11: 2-Wacky Advs. of Cracky. 3-Wacky Witch. 4-Tom, Dick & Harriet. 5-Wacky Advs. of Cracky. 6-Dagar the Invincible; Santos-a; origin Demonomicon. 7-Wacky Witch & Greta Ghost 1O-O. G. Whiz.11-Tom, Dick & Harriet. 8-The Occult Files of Dr. Spektor, Simbar, Lu-sai; Santos-a. 9-Tragg — 1, 3, 4, 6, 8, 10

GOLD MEDAL COMICS
Cambridge House: 1945 (25¢, one-shot, 132 pgs.)

nn-Captain Truth by Fugitani as well as Stallman and Howie Post, Crime Detector, The Witch of Salem, Luckyman, others app. — 30, 60, 90, 174, 275, 375

GOMER PYLE (TV)
Gold Key: July, 1966 - No. 3, Jan, 1967

1-Photo front/back-c — 8, 16, 24, 54, 90, 125

2,3 — 6, 12, 18, 39, 62, 85

GON
DC Comics (Paradox Press): July, 1996 - No. 4, Oct, 1996; No. 5, 1997 ($5.95, B&W, digest-size, limited series)

1-5: Misadventures of baby dinosaur; 1-Gon. 2-Gon Again. 3-Gon: Here Today, Gone Tomorrow. 4-Gon: Going, Going...Gon. 5-Gon Swimmin'. Tanaka-c/a/scripts in all — 1, 2, 3, 5, 6, 8

GON COLOR SPECTACULAR
DC Comics (Paradox Press): 1998 ($5.95. square-bound)

nn-Tanaka-c/a/scripts — 1, 2, 3, 5, 6, 8

GON ON SAFARI
DC Comics (Paradox Press): 2000 ($7.95, B&W, digest-size)

nn-Tanaka-c/a/scripts — 1, 2, 3, 5, 6, 8

GON UNDERGROUND
DC Comics (Paradox Press): 1999 ($7.95, B&W, digest-size)

nn-Tanaka-c/a/scripts — 1, 2, 3, 5, 6, 8

Good Guys #1 © EEP

Goon Noir #413 © Eric Powell

Gotham Nights #4 © DC

	GD	VG	FN	VF	VF/NM	NM-		GD	VG	FN	VF	VF/NM	NM-
	2.0	4.0	6.0	8.0	9.0	9.2		2.0	4.0	6.0	8.0	9.0	9.2

GON WILD
DC Comics (Paradox Press): 1997 ($9.95, B&W, digest-size)

nn-Tanaka-c/a/scripts in all. (Rep. Gon #3,4)	1	3	4	6	8	10	

GOODBYE, MR. CHIPS (See Movie Comics)

GOOD GIRL ART QUARTERLY
AC Comics: Summer, 1990 - No. 15, Spring, 1994 (B&W/color, 52 pgs.)

1,3-15 ($3.50)-All have one new story (often FemForce) & rest reprints by Baker, Ward & other "good girl" artists 4.00
2 ($3.95) 4.00

GOOD GIRL COMICS (Formerly Good Girl Art Quarterly)
AC Comics: No. 16, Summer, 1994 - No. 18, 1995 (B&W)

16-18 .... 4.00

GOOD GUYS, THE
Defiant: Nov, 1993 - No. 9, July, 1994 ($2.50/$3.25/$3.50)

1-($3.50, 52 pgs.)-Glory x-over from Plasm 3.50
2,3,5-9: 9-Pre-Schism issue 2.50
4-($3.25, 52 pgs.) 3.25

GOOD TRIUMPHS OVER EVIL! (Also see Narrative Illustration)
M.C. Gaines: 1943 (12 pgs., 7-1/4"x10", B&W) (not a comic book) (Rare)

nn-A pamphlet, sequel to Narrative Illustration	97	194	291	606	1003	1400	

NOTE: *Print, A Quarterly Journal of the Graphic Arts* Vol. 3 No. 3 (64 pg. square bound) features 1st printing of Good Triumphs Over Evil! A VG copy sold for $350 in 2005.

GOOFY (Disney)(See Dynabrite Comics, Mickey Mouse Magazine V4#7, Walt Disney Showcase #35 & Wheaties)
Dell Publishing Co.: No. 468, May, 1953 - Sept-Nov, 1962

	GD	VG	FN	VF	VF/NM	NM-
Four Color 468 (#1)	12	24	36	82	146	210
Four Color 562,627,658,702,747,802,857	7	14	21	47	76	105
Four Color 899,952,987,1053,1094,1149,1201	5	10	15	32	51	70
12-308-211(Dell, 9-11/62)	5	10	15	32	51	70

GOOFY ADVENTURES
Disney Comics: June, 1990 - No. 17, 1991 ($1.50)

1-17: Most new stories. 2-Joshua Quagmire-a w/free poster. 7-WDC&S-r plus new-a. 9-Gottfredson-r. 14-Super Goof story. 15-All Super Goof issue. 17-Gene Colan-a(p) 3.00

GOOFY ADVENTURE STORY (See Goofy No. 857)

GOOFY COMICS (Companion to Happy Comics)(Not Disney)
Nedor Publ. Co. No. 1-14/Standard No. 14-48: June, 1943 - No. 48, 1953 (Animated Cartoons)

	GD	VG	FN	VF	VF/NM	NM-
1-Funny animal; Oriolo-c	29	58	87	170	268	365
2	15	30	45	86	133	180
3-10	13	26	39	74	105	135
11-19	10	20	30	58	79	100
20-35-Frazetta text illos in all	11	22	33	64	90	115
36-48	9	18	27	50	65	80

GOOFY SUCCESS STORY (See Goofy No. 702)

GOON, THE
Avatar Press: Mar, 1999 - No. 3, July, 1999 ($3.00, B&W)

1- Eric Powell-s/a 20.00
2 .... 12.00
3 .... 8.00
....: Rough Stuff (Albatross, 1/03, $15.95) r/Avatar Press series #1-3 .... 16.00
....: Rough Stuff (Dark Horse, 2/04, $12.95) r/Avatar Press series #1-3 newly colored 13.00

GOON, THE (2nd series)
Albatross Exploding Funny Books: Oct, 2002 - No. 4, Feb, 2003 ($2.95)

1- Eric Powell-s/a 10.00
2-4 .... 6.00
...Color Special 1 (8/02) 10.00
....: Nothin' But Misery Vol. 1 (Dark Horse, 7/03, $15.95, TPB) - Reprints The Goon #1-4 (Albatross series), Color Special, and story from DHP #157 .... 16.00

GOON, THE (3rd series)
Dark Horse Comics: June, 2003 - Present ($2.99)

1-19-Eric Powell-s/a. 7-Hellboy-c/app; framing seq. by Mignola 14-Two covers 3.00
...25¢ Edition (9/05, 25¢) 2.50
....: Fancy Pants Edition HC (10/05, $24.95, dust jacket) r/#1,2 of 2nd series & #1,3,5,9 of 3rd series; Powell intro.; sketch pages and cover gallery 25.00
....: Heaps of Ruination (5/05, $12.95, TPB) r/#5-8; intro. by Frank Darabont 13.00
....: My Murderous Childhood (And Other Grievous Yarns) (5/04, $13.95, TPB) r/#1-4 and short

story from Drawing on Your Nightmares one-shot; intro. by Frank Cho 14.00
...: Virtue and the Grim Consequences Thereof (2/06, $16.95) r/#9-13 .... 17.00
...: Wicked Inclinations (12/06, $14.95) r/#14-18; intro. by Mike Allred 15.00

GOON NOIR, THE (Dwight T. Albatross's...)
Dark Horse Comics: Sept, 2006 - No. 3, Jan, 2007 ($2.99, B&W, limited series)

1-3-Anthology 1-Oswalt-s/Ploog-a; Sniegoski-s/Powell-a; Morrison-s/a; Niles-s/Sook-a. 2-Nowlan, Barta-a. 3-Ramos, Guy Davis-a; Nelson, Posehn, Thomas Lennon-s 3.00
TPB (7/07, $12.95) r/#1-3; sketch pages; intros by "Dwight" 13.00

GOOSE (Humor magazine)
Cousins Publ. (Fawcett): Sept, 1976 - No. 3, 1976 (75¢, 52 pgs., B&W)

	GD	VG	FN	VF	VF/NM	NM-
1-Nudity in all	2	4	6	13	18	22
2,3: 2-(10/76) Fonz-c/s; Lone Ranger story. 3-Wonder Woman, King Kong, Six Million Dollar Man stories	2	4	6	9	12	15

GORDO (See Comics Revue No. 5 & Giant Comics Edition)

GORGO (Based on M.G.M. movie) (See Return of...)
Charlton Comics: May, 1961 - No. 23, Sept, 1965

	GD	VG	FN	VF	VF/NM	NM-
1-Ditko-a, 22 pgs.	22	44	66	164	292	420
2,3-Ditko-c/a	12	24	36	82	146	210
4-Ditko-c	8	16	24	54	90	125
5-11,13-16: 11,13-16-Ditko-a	7	14	21	47	76	105
12,17-23: 12-Reptisaurus x-over; Montes/Bache-a-No. 17-23. 20-Giordano-c						
	5	10	15	30	48	65
Gorgo's Revenge('62)-Becomes Return of...	6	12	18	37	59	80

GOSPEL BLIMP, THE
Spire Christian Comics (Fleming H. Revell Co.): 1973,1975 (35¢/39¢, 36 pgs.)

	GD	VG	FN	VF	VF/NM	NM-
nn-(1973)	2	4	6	8	11	14
nn-(1975)	2	4	6	8		10

GOTHAM BY GASLIGHT (A Tale of the Batman)(See Batman: Master of...)
DC Comics: 1989 ($3.95, one-shot, squarebound, 52 pgs.)

nn-Mignola/Russell-a; intro by Robert Bloch 4.00

GOTHAM CENTRAL
DC Comics: Early Feb, 2003 - No. 40, Apr, 2006 ($2.50)

1-40-Stories of Gotham City Police. 1-Brubaker & Rucka-s/Lark-c/a. 10-Two-Face app. 13,15-Joker-c. 18-Huntress app. 27-Catwoman-c. 32-Poison Ivy app. 34-Teen Titans-c/app. 38-Crispus Allen killed (becomes The Spectre in Infinite Crisis #5) 2.50
...: Dead Robin (2007, $17.99, TPB) r/#33-40; cover gallery 18.00
...: Half a Life (2005, $14.99, TPB) r/#6-10; Batman Chronicles #16 and Detective #747 .... 15.00
...: In The Line of Duty (2004, $9.95, TPB) r/#1-5, cover gallery & sketch pages 10.00
...: The Quick and the Dead TPB (2006, $14.99) r/#23-25,28-31 .... 15.00
...: Unresolved Targets (2006, $14.99, TPB) r/#12-15,19-22, cover gallery 15.00

GOTHAM GIRLS
DC Comics: Oct, 2002 - No. 5, Feb, 2003 ($2.25, limited series)

1-5-Catwoman, Batgirl, Poison Ivy, Harley Quinn from animated series 2.50

GOTHAM NIGHTS (See Batman: Gotham Nights II)
DC Comics: Mar, 1992 - No. 4, June, 1992 ($1.25, limited series)

1-4: Featuring Batman 2.50

GOTHIC ROMANCES
Atlas/Seaboard Publ.: Dec, 1974 (75¢, B&W, magazine, 76 pgs.)

	GD	VG	FN	VF	VF/NM	NM-
1-Text w/ illos by N. Adams, Chaykin, Heath (2 pgs. ea.); painted cover (scarce)	16	32	48	118	209	300

GOTHIC TALES OF LOVE (Magazine)
Marvel Comics: Apr, 1975 - No. 3, 1975 (B&W, 76 pgs.)

	GD	VG	FN	VF	VF/NM	NM-
1-3-Painted-c/a (scarce)	19	38	57	138	244	350

GOVERNOR & J. J., THE (TV)
Gold Key: Feb, 1970 - No. 3, Aug, 1970 (Photo-c)

	GD	VG	FN	VF	VF/NM	NM-
1	4	8	12	26	41	55
2,3	3	6	9	19	29	38

GRACKLE, THE
Acclaim Comics: Jan, 1997 - No. 4, Apr, 1997 ($2.95, B&W)

1-4: Mike Baron scripts & Paul Gulacy-c/a. 1-4-Doublecross 3.00

GRAFIK MUSIK
Caliber Press: Nov, 1990 - No. 4, Aug, 1991 ($3.50/$2.50)

	GD	VG	FN	VF	VF/NM	NM-
1-($3.50, 48 pgs., color) Mike Allred-c/a/scripts-1st app. in color of Frank Einstein (Madman)	6	9	14	20	25	
2-($2.50, 24 pgs., color)	2	4	6	9	12	15

Gravestone #1 © MAL

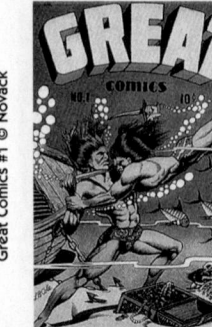

Great Comics #1 © Novack

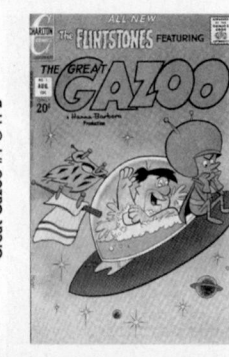

Great Gazoo #1 © H-B

	GD 2.0	VG 4.0	FN 6.0	VF 8.0	VF/NM 9.0	NM- 9.2		GD 2.0	VG 4.0	FN 6.0	VF 8.0	VF/NM 9.0	NM- 9.2

3,4-($2.50, 24 pgs., B&W) — 2 | 4 | 6 | 8 | 10 | 12

GRANDMA DUCK'S FARM FRIENDS(See Walt Disney's C&S 293 & Wheaties)
Dell Publishing Co.: No. 763, Jan, 1957 - No. 1279, Feb, 1962 (Disney)

Four Color 763 (#1) — 8 | 16 | 24 | 52 | 86 | 120
Four Color 873 — 6 | 12 | 18 | 37 | 59 | 80
Four Color 965,1279 — 5 | 10 | 15 | 32 | 51 | 70
Four Color 1010,1073,1161-Barks-a; 1073,1161-Barks c/a — 12 | 24 | 36 | 87 | 156 | 225

GRAND PRIX (Formerly Hot Rod Racers)
Charlton Comics: No. 16, Sept, 1967 - No. 31, May, 1970

16-Features Rick Roberts — 4 | 8 | 12 | 22 | 34 | 45
17-20 — 3 | 6 | 9 | 17 | 26 | 34
21-31 — 3 | 6 | 9 | 16 | 23 | 30

GRAPHIQUE MUSIQUE
Slave Labor Graphics: Dec, 1989 - No. 3, May, 1990 ($2.95, 52 pgs.)

1-Mike Allred-c/a/scripts — 3 | 6 | 9 | 20 | 30 | 40
2,3 — 3 | 6 | 9 | 16 | 23 | 30

GRAVE TALES
Hamilton Comics: Oct, 1991 - No. 3, Feb, 1992 ($3.95, B&W, mag., 52 pgs.)

1-Staton-c/a — 1 | 2 | 3 | 5 | 6 | 8
2,3: 2-Staton-a; Morrow-c — 6.00

GRAVITY (Also see Beyond! limited series)
Marvel Comics: Aug, 2005 - No. 5, Dec, 2005 ($2.99, limited series)

1-5: 1-Intro. Gravity; McKeever-s/Norton-a. 2-Rhino-c/app. 5-Spider-Man app. — 3.00
....: Big-City Super Hero (2005, $7.99, digest) r/#1-5 — 8.00

GRAY AREA, THE
Image Comics: Jun, 2004 - No. 3, Oct, 2004 ($5.95/$3.95, limited series)

1,3-($5.95) Romita, Jr.-a/Brunswick-s; sketch pages and script pages. 3-Pin-up pages — 6.00
2-($3.95) — 4.00
...Vol. 1: All Of This Can Be Yours (2005, $14.95) r/series & sketch,script & pin-up pages — 15.00

GRAY GHOST, THE
Dell Publishing Co.: No. 911, July, 1958; No. 1000, June-Aug, 1959

Four Color 911 (#1), 1000-Photo-c each — 8 | 16 | 24 | 56 | 93 | 130

GREAT ACTION COMICS
I. W. Enterprises: 1958 (Reprints with new covers)

1-Captain Truth reprinted from Gold Medal #1 — 3 | 6 | 9 | 16 | 23 | 30
8,9-Reprints Phantom Lady #15 & 23 — 7 | 14 | 21 | 49 | 80 | 110

GREAT AMERICAN COMICS PRESENTS - THE SECRET VOICE
Peter George 4-Star Publ./American Features Syndicate: 1945 (10¢)

1-Anti-Nazi; "What Really Happened to Hitler" — 36 | 72 | 108 | 208 | 329 | 450

GREAT AMERICAN WESTERN, THE
AC Comics: 1987 - No. 4, 1990? ($1.75/$2.95/$3.50, B&W with some color)

1-4: 1-Western-r plus Bill Black-a. 2-Tribute to ME comics; Durango Kid photo-c 3-Tribute to Tom Mix plus Roy Rogers, Durango Kid; Billy the Kid-r by Severin; photo-c. 4- ($3.50, 52 pgs., 16 pgs. color)-Tribute to Lash LaRue; photo-c & interior photos; Fawcett-r — 4.00
...Presents 1 (1991, $5.00) New Sunset Carson; film history — 5.00

GREAT CAT FAMILY, THE (Disney-TV/Movie)
Dell Publishing Co.: No. 750, Nov, 1956 (one-shot)

Four Color 750-Pinocchio & Alice app. — 6 | 12 | 18 | 43 | 69 | 95

GREAT COMICS
Great Comics Publications: Nov, 1941 - No. 3, Jan, 1942

1-Origin/1st app. The Great Zarro; Madame Strange & Guy Gorham, Wizard of Science & The Great Zarro begin — 124 | 248 | 372 | 775 | 1288 | 1800
2-Buck Johnson, Jungle Explorer app.; X-Mas-c — 65 | 130 | 195 | 406 | 671 | 935
3-Futuro Takes Hitler to Hell-c/s; "The Lost City" movie story (starring William Boyd); continues in Choice Comics #3 — 300 | 600 | 900 | 1931 | 3366 | 4800

GREAT COMICS
Novack Publishing Co./Jubilee Comics/Knockout/Barrel O' Fun: 1945

1-(Four publ. variations: Barrel O-Fun, Jubilee, Knockout & Novack)-The Defenders, Capt. Power app.; L. B. Cole-c — 32 | 64 | 96 | 186 | 293 | 400
1-(Jubilee)-Same cover; Boogey Man, Satanas & The Sorcerer & His Apprentice — 26 | 52 | 78 | 154 | 242 | 330
1-(Barrel O' Fun)-L. B. Cole-c; Barrel O' Fun overprinted in indicia; Li'l Cactus, Cuckoo Sheriff (humorous) — 18 | 36 | 54 | 103 | 162 | 220

GREAT DOGPATCH MYSTERY (See Mammy Yokum & the...)

GREATEST BATMAN STORIES EVER TOLD, THE
DC Comics

Hardcover ($24.95) — 50.00
Softcover ($15.95) "Greatest DC Stories Vol. 2" on spine — 20.00
Vol. 2 softcover (1992, $16.95) "Greatest DC Stories Vol. 7" on spine — 20.00

GREATEST FLASH STORIES EVER TOLD, THE
DC Comics: 1991

nn-Hardcover ($29.95); Infantino-c — 45.00
nn-Softcover ($14.95) — 20.00

GREATEST GOLDEN AGE STORIES EVER TOLD, THE
DC Comics: 1990 ($24.95, hardcover)

nn-Ordway-c — 60.00

GREATEST JOKER STORIES EVER TOLD, THE (See Batman)
DC Comics: 1983

Hardcover ($19.95)-Kyle Baker painted-c — 45.00
Softcover ($14.95) — 20.00
Stacked Deck...Expanded Edition (1992, $29.95)-Longmeadow Press Publ. — 32.00

GREATEST 1950s STORIES EVER TOLD, THE
DC Comics: 1990

Hardcover ($29.95)-Kubert-c — 55.00
Softcover ($14.95) "Greatest DC Stories Vol. 5" on spine — 22.00

GREATEST TEAM-UP STORIES EVER TOLD, THE
DC Comics: 1989

Hardcover ($24.95)-DeVries and Infantino painted-c — 55.00
Softcover ($14.95) "Greatest DC Stories Vol. 4" on spine; Adams-c — 22.00

GREATEST SUPERMAN STORIES EVER TOLD, THE
DC Comics: 1987

Hardcover ($24.95) — 50.00
Softcover ($15.95) — 22.00

GREAT EXPLOITS
Decker Publ./Red Top: Oct, 1957

1-Krigstein-a(2) (re-issue on cover); reprints Daring Advs. #6 by Approved Comics — 6 | 12 | 18 | 31 | 38 | 45

GREAT FOODINI, THE (See Foodini)

GREAT GAZOO, THE (The Flintstones)(TV)
Charlton Comics: Aug, 1973 - No. 20, Jan, 1977 (Hanna-Barbera)

1 — 4 | 8 | 12 | 22 | 34 | 45
2-10 — 2 | 4 | 6 | 13 | 18 | 22
11-20 — 2 | 4 | 6 | 9 | 13 | 16

GREAT GRAPE APE, THE (TV)(See TV Stars #1)
Charlton Comics: Sept, 1976 - No. 2, Nov, 1976 (Hanna-Barbera)

1 — 3 | 6 | 9 | 20 | 30 | 40
2 — 2 | 4 | 6 | 13 | 18 | 22

GREAT LOCOMOTIVE CHASE, THE (Disney)
Dell Publishing Co.: No. 712, Sept, 1956 (one-shot)

Four Color 712-Movie, photo-c — 7 | 14 | 21 | 47 | 76 | 105

GREAT LOVER ROMANCES (Young Lover Romances #4,5)
Toby Press: 3/51; #2, 1951(nd); #3, 1952 (nd); #6, Oct?, 1952 - No. 22, May, 1955 (Photo-c #1-5, 10 ,13, 15, 17) (no #4, 5)

1-Jon Juan story-r/Jon Juan #1 by Schomburg; Dr. Anthony King app. — 17 | 34 | 51 | 98 | 154 | 210
2-Jon Juan, Dr. Anthony King app. — 11 | 22 | 33 | 60 | 83 | 105
3,7,9-14,16-22: 10-Rita Hayworth photo-c. 17-Rita Hayworth & Aldo Ray photo-c — 8 | 16 | 24 | 44 | 57 | 70
6-Kurtzman-a (10/52) — 10 | 20 | 30 | 58 | 79 | 100
8-Five pgs. of "Pin-Up Pete" by Sparling — 10 | 20 | 30 | 58 | 79 | 100
15-Liz Taylor photo-c — 28 | 56 | 84 | 162 | 256 | 350

GREAT RACE, THE (See Movie Classics)

GREAT SCOTT SHOE STORE (See Bulls-Eye)

GREAT SOCIETY COMIC BOOK, THE (Political parody)
Pocket Books Inc./Parallax Pub.: 1966 ($1.00, 36 pgs., 7"x10", one-shot)

nn-Super-LBJ-c/story; 60s politicians app. as super-heroes; Tallarico-a — 3 | 6 | 9 | 16 | 23 | 30

GREAT WEST (Magazine)
M. F. Enterprises: 1969 (B&W, 52 pgs.)

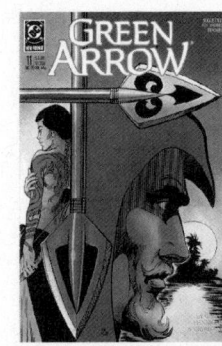

Green Arrow #11 © DC

Green Arrow ('07) #71 © DC

Green Goblin #6 © MAR

	GD 2.0	VG 4.0	FN 6.0	VF 8.0	VF/NM 9.0	NM- 9.2		GD 2.0	VG 4.0	FN 6.0	VF 8.0	VF/NM 9.0	NM- 9.2

V1#1
2 4 6 10 14 18

GREAT WESTERN
Magazine Enterprises: No. 8, Jan-Mar, 1954 - No. 11, Oct-Dec, 1954

8(A-1 93)-Trail Colt by Guardineer; Powell Red Hawk-r/Straight Arrow begins, ends #11; Durango Kid story
18 36 54 103 162 220
9(A-1 105), 11(A-1 127)-Ghost Rider, Durango Kid app. in each. 9-Red Mask-c, but no app.
15 30 45 83 124 165
10(A-1 113)-The Calico Kid by Guardineer-r/Tim Holt #8; Straight Arrow, Durango Kid app.
12 24 36 69 97 125
I.W. Reprint #1,2 9: 1,2-r/Straight Arrow #36,42. 9-r/Straight Arrow #?
3 6 9 16 22 28
I.W. Reprint #8-Origin Ghost Rider(r/Tim Holt #11); Tim Holt app.; Bolle-a
3 6 9 17 25 32

NOTE: *Guardineer* c-8. *Powell* a(r)-8-11 (from Straight Arrow).

GREEN ARROW (See Action #440, Adventure, Brave & the Bold, DC Super Stars #17, Detective #521, Flash #217, Green Lantern #76, Justice League of America #4, Leading Comics, More Fun #73 (1st app.), Showcase '95 #9 & World's Finest Comics)

GREEN ARROW
DC Comics: May, 1983 - No. 4, Aug, 1983 (limited series)

1-Origin; Speedy cameo; Mike W. Barr scripts, Trevor Von Eeden-c/a 5.00
2-4 4.00

GREEN ARROW
DC Comics: Feb, 1988 - No. 137, Oct, 1998 ($1.00-$2.50) (Painted-c #1-3)

1-Mike Grell scripts begin, ends #80
2-49,51-74,76-86: 27,28-Warlord app. 35-38-Co-stars Black Canary; Bill Wray-i. 40-Grell-a. 47-Begin $1.50-c. 63-No longer has mature readers on-c. 63-66-Shado app. 81-Aparo-a begins, ends #100; Nuklon app. 82-Intro & death of Rival. 83-Huntress-c/story. 84-Deathstroke cameo. 85-Deathstroke-c/app. 86-Catwoman-c/story w/Jim Balent layouts
2.50
50,75-($2.50, 52 pgs.): Anniversary issues. 75-Arsenal (Roy Harper) & Shado app. 3.00
0,87-96: 87-$1.95-c begins. 88-Guy Gardner, Martian Manhunter, & Wonder Woman-c/app.; Flash-c. 89-Anarky app. 90-9(94)-Zero Hour tie-in. 0-(10/94)-1st app. Connor Hawke; Aparo-a(p). 91-(11/94). 93-1st app. Camorouge. 95-Hal Jordan cameo. 96-Intro new Force of July; Hal Jordan (Parallax); Oliver Queen learns that Connor Hawke is his son 2.50
97-99,102-109: 97-Begin $2.25-c; no Aparo-a. 97-99-Arsenal app. 102,103-Underworld Unleashed x-over. 104-GL(Kyle Rayner)-c/app. 105-Robin-c/app. 107-109-Thorn app. 109-Lois Lane cameo; Weeks-c.
2.50
100-($3.95)-Foil-c; Superman app. 1 3 4 6 8 10
101-Death of Oliver Queen; Superman app. 3 6 9 16 23 30
110,111-124: 110,111-GL x-over. 110-Intro Hatchet. 114-Final Night. 115-117-Black Canary & Oracle app.
2.50
125-($3.50, 48 pgs)-GL x-over cont. in GL #92 3.50
126-136: 126-Begin $2.50-c. 130-GL & Flash x-over. 132,133-JLA app. 134,135-Brotherhood of the Fist pts. 1,5. 136-Hal Jordan-c/app.
2.50
137-Last issue; Superman app.; last panel cameo of Oliver Queen
2 4 6 9 12 15
#1,000,000 (11/98) 853rd Century x-over 2.50
Annual 1-6 ('88-'94, 68 pgs.)-1-No Grell scripts. 2-No Grell scripts; recaps origin Green Arrow, Speedy, Black Canary & others. 3-Bill Wray-a. 4-50th anniversary issue. 5-Batman, Eclipso app. 6-Bloodlines; Hook app.
3.50
Annual 7-('95, $3.95)-Year One story 4.00
NOTE: *Aparo* a-0, 81-85, 86 (partial),87p, 88p, 91-95, 96i, 98-100p, 109p; c-81,98-100p. *Austin* c-96i. *Balent* layouts-86. *Burchett* c-91-95. *Campanella* a-100-108i, 110-113i; c-99i, 101-108i,110-113i. *Denys Cowan* a-39p, 41-43p, 47p, 48p, 60p; c-41-43. *Damaggio* a(p)-97p, 100-108p, 110-112p; c-97-99p, 101-108p, 110-113p. *Mike Grell* a-1-4, 10p, 11, 39, 40, 44, 45, 47-80, Annual 4, 5. *Nasser/Netzer* a-89, 96. *Sienkiewicz* a-109i. *Springer* a-67, 68. *Weeks* c-109.

GREEN ARROW
DC Comics: Apr, 2001 - No. 75, Aug, 2007 ($2.50/$2.99)

1-Oliver Queen returns; Kevin Smith-s/Hester-a/Wagner-painted-c
2 4 6 9 13 16
1-2nd-4th printings 3.00
2-Batman cameo 1 2 3 4 5 7
2-2nd printing 2.50
3-5: 4-JLA app. 5.00
6-15: 7-Barry Allen & Hal Jordan app. 9,10-Stanley & his Monster app. 10-Oliver regains his soul. 12-Hawkman-c/app.
3.00
16-25: 16-Brad Meltzer's begin; The Shade app. 18-Solomon Grundy-c/app. 19-JLA app. 22-Beatty-s; Count Vertigo app. 23-25-Green Lantern app.; Raab-a/Adlard-a
2.50
26-49: 26-Winick-s begin. 35-37-Riddler app. 43-Mia learns she's HIV+. 45-Mia becomes the new Speedy. 46-Teen Titans app. 49-The Outsiders app.
2.50
50-($3.50) Green Arrow's team and the Outsiders vs. The Riddler and Drakon 3.50
51-59: 51-Anarky app. 52-Zatanna c/app. 55-59-Dr. Light app. 2.50
60-74: 60-One Year Later starts. 62-Begin $2.99-c. 69-Batman app. 3.00

75-($3.50) Ollie proposes to Dinah (see Black Canary mini-series); JLA app. 3.50
...: City Walls SC (2005, $17.95) r/#32, 34-39 18.00
...: Crawling Through the Wreckage SC (2007, $12.99) r/#60-65 13.00
...: Heading Into the Light SC (2006, $12.99) r/#52,54-59 13.00
...: Moving Targets SC (2006, $17.99) r/#40-50 18.00
...: Quiver HC (2002, $24.95) r/#1-10; Smith intro. 25.00
...: Quiver SC (2003, $17.95) r/#1-10; Smith intro. 18.00
...Secret Files & Origins 1-(12/02, $4.95) Origin stories & profiles; Wagner-c 5.00
...: Sounds of Violence HC (2003, $19.95) r/#11-15; Hester intro. & sketch pages 20.00
...: Sounds of Violence SC (2003, $12.95) r/#11-15; Hester intro. & sketch pages 13.00
...: Straight Shooter SC (2004, $12.95) r/#26-31 13.00
...: The Archer's Quest HC (2003, $19.95) r/#16-21; pitch, script and sketch pages 20.00
...: The Archer's Quest SC (2004, $14.95) r/#16-21; pitch, script and sketch pages 15.00

GREEN ARROW: THE LONG BOW HUNTERS
DC Comics: Aug, 1987 - No. 3, Oct, 1987 ($2.95, limited series, mature)

1-Grell-c/a in all 6.00
1,2-2nd printings 3.00
2,3 4.00
Trade paperback (1989, $12.95)-r/#1-3 13.00

GREEN ARROW: THE WONDER YEAR
DC Comics: Feb, 1993 - No. 4, May, 1993 ($1.75, limited series)

1-4: Mike Grell-a(p)/scripts & Gray Morrow-a(i) 2.50

GREEN ARROW: YEAR ONE
DC Comics: Early Sept, 2007 - No. 6, Late Nov, 2007 ($2.99, bi-weekly limited series)

1-4-Origin re-told; Diggle-s/Jock-a 3.00

GREEN BERET, THE (See Tales of the...)

GREEN CANDLES
DC Comics (Paradox Press): Sept, 1995 - No. 3, Dec, 1995 ($5.95, B&W, limited series, digest size)

1-3 6.00
Paperback ($9.95) 10.00

GREEN GIANT COMICS (Also see Colossus Comics)
Pelican Publ. (Funnies, Inc.): 1940 (No price on cover; distributed in New York City only)

1-Dr. Nerod, Green Giant, Black Arrow, Mundoo & Master Mystic app.; origin Colossus (Rare)
1050 2100 3150 8000 13,500 19,000
NOTE: The idea for this book came from George Kapitan. Printed by Moreau Publ. of Orange, N.J. as an experiment to see if they could profitably use the idle time of their 40-page Hoe color press. The experiment failed due to the difficulty of obtaining good quality color registration and Mr. Moreau believes the book never reached the stands. The book has no price or date which lends credence to this. Contains five pages reprinted from Motion Picture Funnies Weekly.

GREEN GOBLIN
Marvel Comics: Oct, 1995 - No. 13, Oct, 1996 ($2.95/$1.95)

1-($2.95)-Scott McDaniel-c/a begins, ends #7; foil-c 3.50
2-13: 2-Begin $1.95-c. 4-Hobgoblin-c/app. Thing app. 6-Daredevil-c/app. 8-Robertson-a; McDaniel-c. 12,13-Onslaught x-over. 13-Green Goblin quits; Spider-Man app.
2.50

GREENHAVEN
Aircel Publishing: 1988 - No. 3, 1988 ($2.00, limited series, 28 pgs.)

1-3 2.50

GREEN HORNET, THE (TV)
Dell Publishing Co./Gold Key: Sept, 1953; Feb, 1967 - No. 3, Aug, 1967

Four Color 496-Painted-c 23 46 69 171 306 440
1-All have Bruce Lee photo-c 17 34 51 126 223 320
2,3 12 24 36 82 146 210

GREEN HORNET, THE (Also see Kato of the... & Tales of the...)
Now Comics: Nov, 1989 - No. 14, Feb, 1991 ($1.75)
V2#1, Sept, 1991 - V2#40, Jan, 1995 ($1.95)

1 ($2.95, double-size)-Steranko painted-c; G.A. Green Hornet 5.00
1,2: 1-2nd printing ('90, $3.95)-New Butler-c 4.00
3-14: 5-Death of original ('30s) Green Hornet. 6-Dave Dorman painted-c. 11-Snyder-c 3.00
V2#1-11,13-21,24-26,28-30,32-37: 1-Butler painted-c. 9-Mayerik-c 2.50
12-($2.50)-Color Green Hornet button polybagged inside 4.00
22,23-($2.95)-Bagged w/color hologravure card 4.00
27-($2.95)-Newsstand ed. polybagged w/multi-dimensional card (1993 Anniversary Special on cover). 27-($2.95)-Direct Sale ed. polybagged w/multi-dimensional card; cover variations
3.00
31,38: 31-($2.50)-Polybagged w/trading card 2.50
39,40-Low print run 6.00
1-($2.50)-Polybagged w/button (same as #12) 3.00
2,3-($1.95)-Same as #13 & 14 2.50

	GD 2.0	VG 4.0	FN 6.0	VF 8.0	VF/NM 9.0	NM- 9.2

Annual 1 (12/92, $2.50), Annual 1994 (10/94, $2.95) 3.50

GREEN HORNET: DARK TOMORROW
Now Comics: Jun, 1993 - No. 3, Aug, 1993 ($2.50, limited series)
1-3: Future Green Hornet 3.00

GREEN HORNET: SOLITARY SENTINEL, THE
Now Comics: Dec, 1992 - No. 3, 1993 ($2.50, limited series)
1-3 3.00

GREEN HORNET COMICS (...Racket Buster #44) (Radio, movies)
Helnit Publ. Co.(Holyoke) No. 1-6/Family Comics(Harvey) No. 7-on:
Dec, 1940 - No. 47, Sept, 1949 (See All New #13,14)(Early issues: 68 pgs.)

	GD 2.0	VG 4.0	FN 6.0	VF 8.0	VF/NM 9.0	NM- 9.2
1-1st app. Green Hornet & Kato; origin of Green Hornet on inside front-c; intro the Black Beauty (Green Hornet's car); painted-c	503	1006	1509	3521	6161	8800
2-Early issues based on radio adventures	214	428	642	1338	2219	3100
3	148	296	444	925	1538	2150
4-6: 6-(8/41)	121	242	363	756	1253	1750
7 (6/42)-Origin The Zebra & begins; Robin Hood, Spirit of '76, Blonde Bomber & Mighty Midgets begin; new logo	98	196	294	613	1019	1425
8,10	85	170	255	531	878	1225
9-Kirby-c	103	206	309	644	1072	1500
11,12-Mr. Q in both	81	162	243	506	841	1175
13-1st Nazi-c; shows Hitler poster on-c	88	176	264	550	913	1275
14-19	64	128	192	400	663	925
20-Classic-c	76	152	228	475	788	1100
21-23,25-30	46	92	138	281	466	650
24-Sci-Fi-c	53	106	159	320	528	735
31-The Man in Black Called Fate begins (11-12/45, early app.)	49	98	147	299	492	685
32-36	36	72	108	208	329	450
37,38: Shock Gibson app. by Powell. 37-S&K Kid Adonis reprinted from Stuntman #3. 38-Kid Adonis app.	36	72	108	208	329	450
39-Stuntman story by S&K	40	80	120	240	383	525
40-47: 42-47-Kerry Drake in all. 45-Boy Explorers on-c only. 46- "Case of the Marijuana Racket" cover/story; Kerry Drake app.	28	56	84	162	256	350

NOTE: *Fuje* a-23, 24, 26. *Henkle* c-7-9. *Kubert* a-20, 30. *Powell* a-7-10, 12, 14, 16-21, 30, 31(2), 32(3), 33, 34(3), 35, 36, 37(2), 38. *Robinson* a-27. *Schomburg* c-15, 17-23. Kirbyish c-7, 15. Bondage c-8, 14, 18, 26, 36.

GREEN JET COMICS, THE (See Comic Books, Series 1)

GREEN LAMA (Also see Comic Books, Series 1, Daring Adventures #17 & Prize Comics #7)
Spark Publications/Prize No. 7 on: Dec, 1944 - No. 8, Mar, 1946

	GD 2.0	VG 4.0	FN 6.0	VF 8.0	VF/NM 9.0	NM- 9.2
1-Intro. Lt. Hercules & The Boy Champions; Mac Raboy-c/a #1-8	114	228	342	713	1182	1650
2-Lt. Hercules borrows the Human Torch's powers for one panel	62	124	186	388	644	900
3-6,8: 4-Dick Tracy take-off in Lt. Hercules story by H. L. Gold (science fiction writer). 5-Lt. Hercules story; Little Orphan Annie, Smilin' Jack & Snuffy Smith take-off (5/45)	50	100	150	305	503	700
7-X-mas-c; Raboy paint tint-c/a (note: a small quantity of NM copies surfaced)	34	68	102	197	311	425

NOTE: *Robinson* a-3-5, 8. *Roussos* a-8. Formerly a pulp hero who began in 1940.

GREEN LANTERN (1st Series) (See All-American, All Flash Quarterly, All Star Comics, The Big All-American & Comic Cavalcade)
National Periodical Publications/All-American: Fall, 1941 - No. 38, May-June, 1949 (#1-18 are quarterly)

	GD 2.0	VG 4.0	FN 6.0	VF 8.0	VF/NM 9.0	NM- 9.2
1-Origin retold; classic Purcell-c	3000	6000	9000	22,000	38,000	60,000
2-1st book-length story	657	1314	1971	4600	8050	11,500
3-Classic German war-c by Mart Nodell	514	1028	1542	3600	6300	9000
4-Green Lantern & Doiby Dickles join the Army	394	788	1182	2561	4531	6500
5	317	634	951	1981	3291	4600
6,8: 8-Hop Harrigan begins; classic-c	235	470	705	1469	2435	3400
7-Robot-c	248	496	744	1550	2575	3600
9,10: 10-Origin/1st app. Vandal Savage	207	414	621	1294	2147	3000
11-15: 12-Origin/1st app. Gambler	155	310	465	969	1610	2250
16-Classic jungle-c (scarce in high grade)	162	324	486	1013	1682	2350
17,19,20	131	262	393	819	1360	1900
18-Christmas-c	172	344	516	1075	1788	2500
21-26,28	119	238	357	744	1235	1725
27-Origin/1st app. Sky Pirate	128	256	384	800	1325	1850
29-All Harlequin issue; classic Harlequin-c	131	262	393	819	1360	1900
30-1st app. Streak the Wonder Dog by Toth (2-3/48) (scarce)	207	414	621	1294	2147	3000
31-35: 35-Kubert-c. 35-38-New logo	103	206	309	644	1072	1500
36-38: 37-Sargon the Sorcerer app.	121	242	363	756	1253	1750

	GD 2.0	VG 4.0	FN 6.0	VF 8.0	VF/NM 9.0	NM- 9.2

NOTE: *Book-length stories #2-7. Mayer/Moldoff c-9. Mayer/Purcell c-8. Purcell c-1. Mart Nodell c-2, 3, 7. Paul Reinman c-11, 12, 15-22. Toth a-28, 30, 31, 34p, 36-38p. Cover to #8 says Fall while the indicia says Summer Issue. Streak the Wonder Dog c-30 (w/Green Lantern), 34, 36, 38.*

GREEN LANTERN (See Action Comics Weekly, Adventure Comics, Brave & the Bold, Day of Judgment, DC Special, DC Special Series, Flash, Guy Gardner, Guy Gardner Reborn, JLA, JSA, Justice League of America, Parallax: Emerald Night, Showcase, Showcase '93 #12 & Tales of The...Corps)

GREEN LANTERN (2nd Series)(Green Lantern Corps #206 on) (See Showcase #22-24)
National Periodical Publ./DC Comics: Jul/Aug. 1960 - No. 89, Apr/May 1972; No. 90, Aug/Sept. 1976 - No. 205, Oct, 1986

	GD 2.0	VG 4.0	FN 6.0	VF 8.0	VF/NM 9.0	NM- 9.2
1-(7-8/60)-Origin retold; Gil Kane-c/a continues; 1st app. Guardians of the Universe	348	696	1044	3132	5916	8700
2-1st Pieface	74	148	222	629	1165	1700
3-Contains readers poll	45	90	135	360	648	935
4,5: 5-Origin/1st app. Hector Hammond	37	74	111	278	507	735
6-Intro Tomar-Re the alien G.L.	32	64	96	240	445	650
7-Origin/1st app. Sinestro (7-8/61)	31	62	93	233	429	625
8-1st 5700 A.D. story; grey tone-c	27	54	81	203	364	525
9,10: 9-1st Jordan Brothers; last 10¢ issue	26	52	78	187	336	485
11,12	18	36	54	134	237	340
13-Flash x-over	30	60	90	220	398	575
14-20: 14-Origin/1st app. Sonar. 16-Origin & 1st app. Star Sapphire. 20-Flash x-over	15	30	45	111	198	285
21-30: 21-Origin & 1st app. Dr. Polaris. 23-1st Tattooed Man. 24-Origin & 1st app. Shark. 29-JLA cameo; 1st Blackhand	12	24	36	84	150	215
31-39: 37-1st app. Evil Star (villain)	10	20	30	73	129	185
40-Origin of Infinite Earths (10/65); 2nd solo G.A. Green Lantern in Silver Age (see Showcase #55); origin The Guardians; Doiby Dickles app.	43	86	129	344	622	900
41-44,46-50: 42-Zatanna x-over. 43-Flash x-over (7-8/61)	9	18	27	63	107	150
45-2nd S.A. app. G.A. Green Lantern in title (6/66)	14	28	42	99	175	250
51,53-58	7	14	21	50	83	115
52-G.A. Green Lantern x-over	9	18	27	61	103	145
59-1st app. Guy Gardner (3/68)	15	30	45	109	195	280
60,62-69: 69-Wood inks; last 12¢ issue	6	12	18	37	59	80
61-G.A. Green Lantern x-over	7	14	21	45	73	100
70-75	5	10	15	30	49	65
76-(4/70)-Begin Green Lantern/Green Arrow series (by Neal Adams #76-89) ends #122 (see Flash #217 for 2nd series)	35	70	105	263	482	700
77	9	18	27	63	107	150
78-80	8	16	24	52	86	120
81-84: 82-Wrightson-i(1 pg.). 83-G.L. reveals i.d. to Carol Ferris. 84-N. Adams/Wrightson-a (22 pgs.); last 15¢-c; partial photo-c	9	18	27	60	100	140
85,86-(52 pgs.)-Anti-drug issues. 86-G.A. Green Lantern-r; Toth-a	9	18	27	60	100	140
87-(52 pgs.): 2nd app. Guy Gardner (cameo); 1st app. John Stewart (12-1/71-72) (becomes 3rd Green Lantern in #182)	6	12	18	41	66	90
88-(2-3/72, 52 pgs.)-Unpubbed G.A. Green Lantern story; Green Lantern-r/Showcase #23. N. Adams-c/a (1 pg.)	5	10	15	30	48	65
89-(4-5/72, 52 pgs.)-G.A. Green Lantern-r; Green Lantern & Green Arrow move to Flash #217 (2nd team-up series)	6	12	18	41	66	90
90 (8-9/76)-Begin 3rd Green Lantern/Green Arrow team-up series; Mike Grell-c/a begins, ends #111	2	4	6	13	18	22
91-99	2	4	6	8	10	12
100-(1/78, Giant)-1st app. Air Wave II	2	4	6	11	16	20
101-107,110,113-115,117-119: 107-1st Tales of the G.L. Corps story	1	2	3	5	7	9
108-110-(44 pgs.)-G.A. Green Lantern back-ups in each. 111-Origin retold; G.A. Green Lantern app.	1	3	4	6	8	10
112-G.A. Green Lantern origin retold	2	4	6	9	13	16
116-1st app. Guy Gardner as a G.L. (5/79)	4	8	12	22	34	45
116-Whitman variant; issue # on cover	4	8	12	28	44	60
117-119,121-(Whitman variants; low print run; none have issue # on cover)	2	4	6	8	11	14

120-122,124-150: 22-Last Green Lantern/Green Arrow team-up. 130-132-Tales of the G.L. Corps. 132-Adam Strange series begins, ends147. 136,137-1st app. Citadel; Space Ranger app. 141-1st app. Omega Men (6/81). 142,143-Omega Men app.;Perez-c. 144-Omega Men cameo. 148-Tales of the G.L. Corps begins, ends #173. 150-Anniversary issue, 52 pgs.; no G.L. Corps 6.00

	GD 2.0	VG 4.0	FN 6.0	VF 8.0	VF/NM 9.0	NM- 9.2
123-Green Lantern back to solo action; 2nd app. Guy Gardner as Green Lantern	1	3	4	6	8	10

151-180,183,184,186,187: 159-Origin Evil Star. 160,161-Omega Men app. 4.00
181,182,185,188: 181-Hal Jordan resigns as G.L. 182-John Stewart becomes new G.L.; origin recap of Hal Jordan as G.L. 185-Origin new G.L. (John Stewart).188-I.D. revealed; Alan Moore back-up scripts. 5.00
189-193,196-199,201-205: 191-Re-intro Star Sapphire (cameo). 192-Re-intro & origin of Star

Green Lantern (3rd) #98 © DC

Green Lantern (4th) #18 © DC

Green Lantern Corps #14 © DC

	GD	VG	FN	VF	VF/NM	NM-		GD	VG	FN	VF	VF/NM	NM-
	2.0	4.0	6.0	8.0	9.0	9.2		2.0	4.0	6.0	8.0	9.0	9.2

Sapphire (1st full app.). 194,198-Crisis x-over. 199-Hal Jordan returns as a member of G.L. Corps (3 G.L.s now). 201-Green Lantern Corps begins (is cover title, says premiere issue); intro. Kilowog — 3.50

194-Hal Jordan/Guy Gardner battle; Guardians choose Guy Gardner to become new Green Lantern — 6.00

195-Guy Gardner becomes Green Lantern; Crisis on Infinite Earths x-over

	2	4	6	8	10	12
						4.00

200-Double-size

Annual 1 (Listed as Tales Of The Green Lantern Corps Annual 1)
Annual 2,3 (See Green Lantern Corps Annual #2,3) — 3.50
Special 1 (1988), 2 (1989)-(Both $1.50, 52 pgs.) — 3.50
NOTE: **N. Adams** a-76, 77-87p, 89; c-63, 76-89. **M. Anderson** a-137i. **Austin** a-93i, 94i, 171i. **Chaykin** c-196. **Greene** a-39-49i, 58-63i; c-54-58i. **Grell** a-90-106, 108-111; c-90-106, 108-112. **Heck** a-120-122p. **Infantino** a-137p, 145-147p, 151, 152p. **Gil Kane** a-1-49p, 50-57, 58-61p, 68-75p, 85p(r), 87p(r), 88p(r), 156, 177, 184p; c-1-52, 54-61p, 67-75, 123, 154, 156, 165-171, 177, 184. **Newton** a-148p, 149p, 181. **Perez** c-132p, 141-144. **Sekowsky** a-65p, 170p. **Simonson** a-200. **Sparling** a-63p. **Starlin** a-129, 133. **Staton** a-117p, 123-127p, 128, 129-131p, 132-139, 140p, 141-146, 147p, 148-150, 151-155p; c-107p, 117p, 135(i), 136p, 145p, 146, 147, 148-152p, 155p. **Toth** a-86r, 171p. **Tuska** a-166-168p, 170p.

GREEN LANTERN (3rd Series)
DC Comics: June, 1990 - No. 181, Nov, 2004 ($1.00/$1.25/$1.50/$1.75/$1.95/$1.99/$2.25)

1-Hal Jordan, John Stewart & Guy Gardner return; Batman & JLA app. — 5.00
2-26: 8-Guy Gardner solo story. 13-($2 pgs.). 18-Guy Gardner solo story. 19-($1.75, 52 pgs.)-50th anniversary issue; Mart Nodell (original G.A. artist) part-p on G.A. Gr.Lantern; G. Kane-c. 25-($1.75, 52 pgs.)-Hal Jordan/Guy Gardner battle — 4.00
27-45,47: 30,31-Gorilla Grodd-c/story(see Flash #69). 38,39-Adam Strange-c/story.
42-Deathstroke-c/s. 47-Green Arrow x-over — 3.00
46,48,49,50: 46-Superman app. cont'd in Superman #82. 48-Emerald Twilight part 1.
50-($2.95, 52 pgs.)-Glow-in-the-dark-c — 6.00
0, 51-62: 51-1st app. New Green Lantern (Kyle Rayner) with new costume.
53-Superman-c/story. 55-(9/94)-Zero Hour. 0-(10/94). 56-(11/94) — 4.00
63,64-Kyle Rayner vs. Hal Jordan. — 4.00
65-80,82-92: 63-Begin $1.75-c. 65-New Titans app. 66,67-Flash app. 71-Batman & Robin app.
72-Shazam!-c/app. 73-Wonder Woman-c/app. 73-75-Adam Strange app. 76,77-Green Arrow x-over. 80-Final Night. 87-JLA app. 91-Genesis x-over. 92-Green Arrow x-over — 3.00
81-(Regular Ed.)-Memorial for Hal Jordan (Parallax); most DC heroes app. — 3.00
81-($3.95, Deluxe Edition)-Embossed prism-c — 6.00
93-99: 93-Begin $1.95-c; Deadman app. 94-Superboy app. 95-Starlin(a(p).
98,99-Legion of Super-Heroes-c/app. — 2.50
100-($2.95) Two covers (Jordan & Rayner); vs. Sinestro — 5.00
101-106: 101-106-Hal Jordan-c/app. 103-JLA-c/app. 104-Green Arrow app.
105,106-Parallax app. — 3.00
107-126: 107-Jade becomes a Green Lantern. 119-Hal Jordan/Spectre app. 125-JLA app.
127-149: 127-Begin $2.25-c. 129-Winick-s begin. 134-136-JLA-c/app. 143-Joker: Last Laugh;
Lee-c. 145-Kyle becomes The Ion. — 2.50
150-($3.50) Jim Lee-c; Kyle becomes Green Lantern again; new costume — 2.50
151-181: 151-155-Jim Lee-c. 154-Terry attacked. 155-Spectre-c/app. 162-164-Crossover with Green Arrow #23-25. 165-Raab-s begin. 169-Kilowog returns — 2.50
#1,000,000 (11/98) 853rd Century x-over; Hitch & Neary-a/c — 3.00
Annual 1-3: ('92-'94, 68 pgs.)-1-Eclipso app. 2 -Intro Nightblade. 3-Elseworlds story — 3.50
Annual 4 (1995, $3.50)-Year One story — 4.00
Annual 5,7,8 ('96, '98, '99, $2.95): 5-Legends of the Dead Earth. 7-Ghosts; Wrightson-c.
8-JLApe; Art Adams-c — 3.00
Annual 6 (1997, $3.95)-Pulp Heroes story — 3.50
Annual 9 (2000, $3.50)-Planet DC — 3.50
...80 Page Giant (12/98, $4.95) Stories by various — 5.00
...80 Page Giant 2 (6/99, $4.95)-Team-ups — 5.00
...80 Page Giant 3 (8/00, $5.95) Darkseid vs. the GL Corps — 6.00
...: 1001 Emerald Nights (2001, $6.95) Elseworlds; Guay-a/c; LaBan-s — 7.00
...-3-D #1 (12/98, $3.95) Jeanty-a — 4.00
...: A New Dawn TPB (1998, $9.95)-r/#50-55 — 10.00
...: Baptism of Fire TPB (1999, $12.95)-r/#59,64,66,67,70-75 — 13.00
...: Brother's Keeper (2003, $12.95)-r/#151-155; Green Lantern Secret Files #3 — 15.00
...: Emerald Allies TPB (2000, $14.95)-r/GL/GA team-ups — 13.00
...: Emerald Knights TPB (1998, $12.95)-r/Hal Jordan's return — 13.00
...: Emerald Twilight nn (1994, $5.95)-r/#48-50 — 6.00
...: Emerald Twilight/New Dawn TPB (2003, $19.95)-r/#48-55 — 20.00
...: Ganthet's Tale nn (1992, $5.95, 68 pgs.)-Silver foil logo; Niven scripts; Byrne-c/a — 6.00
.../Green Arrow Vol. 1 (2004, $12.95) -r/GL #76-82; intro. by O'Neil — 13.00
.../Green Arrow Vol. 2 (2004, $12.95) -r/GL #83-87,89 & Flash #217-219, 226; cover gallery with 1983-84 GL/GA covers #1-7; intro. by Giordano — 13.00
.../Green Arrow Collection, Vol. 2 TPB (1993, $12.95) r/GL #84-87,89 & Flash #217-219 & GL/GA #5-7 by O'Neil/Adams/Wrightson — 13.00
...: New Journey, Old Path TPB (2001, $12.95)-r/#129-136 — 13.00
...: Our Worlds at War (8/01, $2.95) Jae Lee-c; prelude to x-over — 3.00
...: Passing The Torch (2004, $12.95, TPB) r/#156,158-161 & GL Secret Files #2 — 13.00

...Plus 1 (12/1996, $2.95)-The Ray & Polaris-c/app. — 3.00
...Secret Files 1-3 (7/98-7/02, $4.95)1-Origin stories & profiles. 2-Grell-c — 5.00
.../Superman: Legend of the Green Flame (2000, $5.95) 1988 unpub. Neil Gaiman story of Hal Jordan with new art by various; Frank Miller-c — 6.00
...: The Power of Ion (2003, $14.95, TPB) r/#142-150 — 15.00
...The Road Back nn (1992, $8.95)-r/1-8 w/covers — 9.00
...Traitor TPB (2001, $12.95) r/Legends of the DCU #20,21,28,29,37,38 — 13.00
...: Willworld (2001, $24.95, HC) Seth Fisher-a/J.M. DeMatteis-s; Hal Jordan — 25.00
...: Willworld (2003, $17.95, SC) Seth Fisher-a/J.M. DeMatteis-s; Hal Jordan — 18.00
NOTE: **Staton** a(p)-9-12; c-9-12.

GREEN LANTERN (See Tangent Comics/ Green Lantern)

GREEN LANTERN (4th Series) (Follows Hal Jordan's return in Green Lantern: Rebirth)
DC Comics: July, 2005 - Present ($3.50/$2.99)

1-($3.50) Two covers by Pacheco and Ross; Johns-s/Van Sciver and Pacheco-a — 3.50
2-20-($2.99) 2-4-Manhunters app. 6-Bianchi-a. 7,8-Green Arrow app. 8-Bianchi-c.
9-Batman app.; two covers by Bianchi and Van Sciver. 10,11-Reis-a. 17-19-Star Sapphire returns. 18-Acuna-a; Sinestro Corps back-ups begin — 3.00
8-Variant-c by Neal Adams — 5.00
21-Sinestro Corps War pt. 2 — 5.00
21-2nd printing with variant green hued background-c — 3.00
22-Sinestro Corps War pt. 4; green hued-c — 4.00
22-2nd printing with yellow hued-c — 3.00
...Secret Files and Origins 2005 (6/05, $4.99) Johns-s/Cooke & Van Sciver-a; profiles with art by various incl. Chaykin, Gibbons, Gleason, Igle; Pacheco-c — 5.00
...: No Fear HC (2006, $24.99) r/#1-6 & Secret Files and Origins — 25.00
...: Revenge of the Green Lanterns HC (2006, $19.99) r/#7-13; variant cover gallery — 20.00
...: Wanted: Hal Jordan HC (2007, $19.99) r/#14-20 without Sinestro Corps back-ups — 20.00

GREEN LANTERN ANNUAL NO. 1, 1963
DC Comics: 1998 ($4.95, one-shot)

1-Reprints Golden Age & Silver Age stories in 1963-style 80 pg. Giant format; new Gil Kane sketch art — 5.00

GREEN LANTERN: BRIGHTEST DAY; BLACKEST NIGHT
DC Comics: 2002 ($5.95, squarebound, one-shot)

nn-Alan Scott vs. Solomon Grundy in 1944; Snyder III-c/a; Seagle-s — 6.00

GREEN LANTERN: CIRCLE OF FIRE
DC Comics: Early Oct, 2000 - No. 2, Late Oct, 2000 (limited series)

1-($4.95) Intro. other Green Lanterns — 5.00
2-($3.75) — 4.00
Green Lantern (x-overs)- .../Adam Strange; .../Atom; .../Firestorm; ... /Green Lantern, Winick-s; .../Power Girl (all $2.50-c) — 2.50
TPB (2002, $17.95) r/#1,2 & x-overs — 18.00

GREEN LANTERN CORPS, THE (Formerly Green Lantern; see Tales of...)
DC Comics: No. 206, Nov. 1986 - No. 224, May, 1988

206-223: 212-John Stewart marries Katma Tui. 220,221-Millennium tie-ins — 3.00
224-Double-size last issue — 4.00
...Corps Annual 2,3- (12/86,8/87) 1-Formerly Tales of ...Annual #1; Alan Moore scripts.
3-Indicia says Green Lantern Annual #3; Moore scripts; Byrne-a — 3.00
NOTE: **Austin** a-Annual 3i. **Gil Kane** a-223, 224p; c-223, 224, Annual 2. **Russell** a-Annual 3i. **Staton** a-207-213p, 217p, 221p, 222p, Annual 3; c-207-213p, 217p, 221p, 222p. **Willingham** a-213p, 219p, 220p, 218p, 219p, Annual 2, 3p; c-218p, 219p.

GREEN LANTERN CORPS
DC Comics: Aug, 2006 - Present ($2.99)

1-13: 1-6,10,11-Gibbons-s. 9-Darkseid app. — 3.00
14,15-Sinestro Corps War pts. 3,5 — 4.00
,,,: To Be a Lantern TPB (2007, $12.99) r/#1-6 — 13.00

GREEN LANTERN CORPS QUARTERLY
DC Comics: Summer, 1992 - No. 8, Spring, 1994 ($2.50/$2.95, 68 pgs.)

1,7,8: 1-G.A. Green Lantern story; Staton-a(p). 7-Painted-c; Tim Vigil-a. 8-Lobo-c/s — 3.50
2-6: 2-G.A. G.L.-c/story; Austin-c(i); Gulacy-a(p). 3-G.A. G.L. story. 4-Austin-i — 3.00

GREEN LANTERN CORPS: RECHARGE
DC Comics: Nov, 2005 - No. 5, Mar, 2006 ($3.50/$2.99, limited series)

1-($3.50) Kyle Rayner, Guy Gardner & Kilowog app.; Gleason-a — 3.50
2-5-($2.99) — 3.00
TPB (2006, $12.99) r/series — 13.00

GREEN LANTERN: DRAGON LORD
DC Comics: 2001 - No. 3, 2001 ($4.95, squarebound, limited series)

1-3: A G.L. in ancient China; Moench-s/Gulacy-c/a — 5.00

GREEN LANTERN: EMERALD DAWN (Also see Emerald Dawn)

Green Lantern: Rebirth #4 © DC

Green Lantern: Sinestro Corps Special #1 © DC

Grendel: Devil Child #1 © Matt Wagner

	GD 2.0	VG 4.0	FN 6.0	VF 8.0	VF/NM 9.0	NM- 9.2

DC Comics: Dec, 1989 - No. 6, May, 1990 ($1.00, limited series)
1-Origin retold; Giffen plots in all						5.00
2-6: 4-Re-intro. Tomar-Re						4.00

GREEN LANTERN: EMERALD DAWN II (Emerald Dawn II #1 & 2)
DC Comics: Apr, 1991 - No. 6, Sept, 1991 ($1.00, limited series)
1-6						2.50
TPB (2003, $12.95) r/#1-6; Alan Davis-a						13.00

GREEN LANTERN: EVIL'S MIGHT (Elseworlds)
DC Comics: 2002 - No. 3 ($5.95, squarebound, limited series)
1-3-Kyle Rayner in 19th century NYC; Rogers-a; Chaykin & Tischman-s						6.00

GREEN LANTERN: FEAR ITSELF
DC Comics: 1999 (Graphic novel)
Hardcover ($24.95) Ron Marz-s/Brad Parker painted-a						25.00
Softcover ($14.95)						15.00

GREEN LANTERN/FLASH: FASTER FRIENDS (See Flash/Green Lantern...)
DC Comics: 1997 ($4.95, limited series)
1-Marz-s						5.00

GREEN LANTERN GALLERY
DC Comics: Dec, 1996 ($3.50, one-shot)
1-Wraparound-c; pin-ups by various						3.50

GREEN LANTERN/GREEN ARROW (Also see The Flash #217)
DC Comics: Oct, 1983 - No. 7, April, 1984 (52-60 pgs.)
1-7-r-Green Lantern #76-89						4.00

NOTE: Neal Adams r-1-7; c-1-4. Wrightson r-4, 5.

GREEN LANTERN • LEGACY: THE LAST WILL & TESTAMENT OF HAL JORDAN
DC Comics: 2002 ($24.95, hardcover graphic novel)
Hardcover-Anderson & Sienkiewicz-a/c; Kelly-s; Return of Oa						25.00
Softcover (2004, $17.95)						18.00

GREEN LANTERN: MOSAIC (Also see Cosmic Odyssey #2)
DC Comics: June, 1992 - No. 18, Nov, 1993 ($1.25)
1-18: Featuring John Stewart. 1-Painted-c by Cully Hamner						2.50

GREEN LANTERN: REBIRTH
DC Comics: Dec, 2004 - No. 6, May, 2005 ($2.95, limited series)
1-Johns-s/Van Sciver-a; Hal Jordan as The Spectre on-c						8.00
1-2nd printing; Hal Jordan as Green Lantern on-c						4.00
1-3rd printing; B&W-c version of 1st printing						3.00
2-Guy Gardner becomes a Green Lantern again; JLA app.						5.00
2-2nd & 3rd printings						3.00
3-6: 3-Sinestro returns. 4-6-JLA & JSA app.						3.00
HC (2005, $24.99, dust jacket) r/series & Wizard preview; intro. by Brad Meltzer						25.00
SC (2007, $14.99) r/series & Wizard preview; intro. by Brad Meltzer						15.00

GREEN LANTERN/SENTINEL: HEART OF DARKNESS
DC Comics: Mar, 1998 - No. 3, May, 1998 ($1.95, limited series)
1-3-Marz-s/Pelletier-a						3.00

GREEN LANTERN/SILVER SURFER: UNHOLY ALLIANCES
DC Comics: 1995 ($4.95, one-shot)(Prelude to DC Versus Marvel)
nn-Hal Jordan app.						5.00

GREEN LANTERN SINESTRO CORPS SPECIAL (Continues in Green Lantern #21)
DC Comics: Aug, 2007 ($4.99, one-shot)
1-Kyle Rayner becomes Parallax; Cyborg Superman & Earth-Prime Superboy app.; Johns-s; Van Sciver-a/c; back-up story origin of Sinestro; Gibbons-a; Sinestro on cover						8.00
1-(2nd printing) Kyle Rayner as Parallax on cover						6.00
1-(3rd printing) Sinestro cover with muted colors						5.00

GREEN LANTERN: THE GREATEST STORIES EVER TOLD
DC Comics: 2006 ($19.99, TPB)
SC-Reprints Showcase #22; G.L. #1,31,74,87,172; ('90 series) #3, and others; Ross-c						20.00

GREEN LANTERN: THE NEW CORPS
DC Comics: 1999 - No. 2, 1999 ($4.95, limited series)
1,2-Kyle recruits new GLs; Eaton-a						5.00

GREEN LANTERN VS. ALIENS
Dark Horse Comics: Sept, 2000 - No. 4, Dec, 2000 ($2.95, limited series)
1-4: 1-Hal Jordan and GL Corps vs. Aliens; Leonardi-p. 2-4-Kyle Rayner						3.00

GREEN MASK, THE (See Mystery Men)
Summer, 1940 - No. 9, 2/42; No. 10, 8/44 - No. 11, 11/44;

Fox Features Syndicate: V2#1, Spring, 1945 - No. 6, 10-11/46
	GD 2.0	VG 4.0	FN 6.0	VF 8.0	VF/NM 9.0	NM- 9.2
V1#1-Origin The Green Mask & Domino; reprints/Mystery Men #1-3,5-7; Lou Fine-c	333	666	1000	2165	3833	5500
2-Zanzibar The Magician by Tuska	131	262	393	819	1360	1900
3-Powell-a; Marijuana story	83	166	249	519	860	1200
4-Navy Jones begins, ends #6	65	130	195	406	671	935
5	53	106	159	323	537	750
6-The Nightbird begins, ends #9; bondage/torture-c	45	90	135	275	450	625
7-9: 9(2/42)-Becomes The Bouncer #10(nn) on? & Green Mask #10 on	39	78	117	225	355	485
10,11: 10-Origin One Round Hogan & Rocket Kelly	30	60	90	174	275	375
V2#1	23	46	69	132	209	285
2-6	19	38	57	109	172	235

GREEN PLANET, THE
Charlton Comics: 1962 (one-shot) (12¢)
nn-Giordano-c; sci-fi	6	12	18	43	69	95

GREEN TEAM (See Cancelled Comic Cavalcade & 1st Issue Special)

GREETINGS FROM SANTA (See March of Comics No. 48)

GRENDEL (Also see Primer #2, Mage and Comico Collection)
Comico: Mar, 1983 - No. 3, Feb, 1984 ($1.50, B&W)(#1 has indicia to Skrog #1)
1-Origin Hunter Rose	10	20	30	70	123	175
2,3: 2-Origin Argent	7	14	21	50	83	115

GRENDEL
Comico: Oct, 1986 - No. 40, Feb, 1990 ($1.50/$1.95/$2.50, mature)
1	1	2	3	5	7	9
1,2: 2nd printings						3.00
2,3,5-15: 13-15-Ken Steacy-c.						4.00
4,16: 4-Dave Stevens-c(i). 16-Re-intro Mage (series begins, ends #19)						6.00
17-40: 24-25,27-28,30-31-Snyder-c/a						3.00
Devil by the Deed (Graphic Novel, 10/86, $5.95, 52 pgs.)-r/Grendel back-ups/ Mage 6-14; Alan Moore intro.	1	2	3	4	5	7
Devil's Legacy ($14.95, 1988, Graphic Novel)	2	4	6	9	12	15
Devil's Vagary (10/87, B&W & red)-No price; included in Comico Collection	2	4	6	8	10	12

GRENDEL (Title series): **Dark Horse Comics**
--ARCHIVES, 5/07 ($14.95, HC) r/1st apps. in Primer #2 and Grendel #1-3; Wagner intro.						15.00
--BLACK, WHITE, AND RED, 11/98 - No. 4, 2/99 ($3.95, anthology)						
1-Wagner-s in all. Art by Sale, Leon and others						5.00
2-4: 2-Mack, Chadwick-a. 3-Allred, Kristensen-a. 4-Pearson, Sprouse-a						4.00
--CLASSICS, 7/95 - No. 4 ($3.95, mature) 1,2-reprints; new Wagner-c						4.00
--CYCLE, 10/95 ($5.95) 1-nn-history of Grendel by M. Wagner & others						6.00
--DEVIL BY THE DEED, 7/93 ($3.95, varnish-c) 1-nn-M. Wagner-c/a/scripts; r/Grendel back-ups from Mage #6-14						4.00
Reprint (12/97, $3.95) w/pin-ups by various						4.00
Hardcover (2007, $12.95) reprint recolored to B&W&red; includes covers and intros from previously reprinted editions						13.00
--DEVIL CHILD, 6/99 - No. 2, 7/99 ($2.95, mature) 1,2-Sale & Kristiansen-a/Schutz-s						3.00
--DEVIL QUEST, 11/95 ($4.95) 1-nn-Prequel to Batman/Grendel II; M. Wagner story & art; r/back-up story from Grendel Tales series.						5.00
--DEVILS AND DEATHS, 10/94 - 11/94 ($2.95, mature) 1,2						3.00
: DEVIL'S LEGACY, 3/00 - No. 12, 2/01 ($2.95, reprints 1986 series, recolored) 1-12-Wagner-s/c						3.00
: DEVIL'S REIGN, 5/04 - No. 7, 12/04 ($3.50, repr. 1989 series #34-40, recolored) 1-7-Sale-c/a.						3.50
: GOD AND THE DEVIL, No. 0, 1/03 - No. 10, 12/03 ($3.50/$4.99, repr. 1986 series, recolored)						
0-9: 0-Sale-c/a; r/#23. 1-9-Snyder-c						3.50
10-($4.99) Double-sized; Snyder-c						5.00
--RED, WHITE & BLACK, 9/02 - No. 4, 12/02 ($4.99, anthology)						
1-4-Wagner-s in all. 1-Art by Thompson, Sakai, Mahfood and others. 2-Kelley Jones, Watson, Brereton, Hester & Parks-a. 3-Oeming, Noto, Cannon, Ashley Wood, Huddleston-a. 4-Chiang, Dalrymple, Robertson, Snyder III and Zulli-a						5.00
TPB (2005, $19.95) r/#1-4; cover gallery, artist bios						20.00
--TALES: DEVIL'S CHOICES, 3/95 - 6/95 ($2.95, mature) 1-4						3.00
--TALES: FOUR DEVILS, ONE HELL, 8/93 - 1/94 ($2.95, mature)						

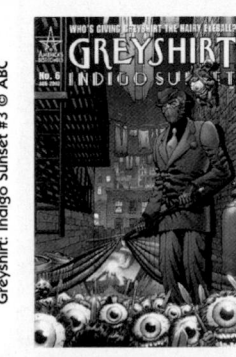

Greyshirt: Indigo Sunset #3 © ABC

Grimm's Ghost Stories #48 © GK

Groo the Wanderer #65 © Sergio Aragonés

	GD 2.0	VG 4.0	FN 6.0	VF 8.0	VF/NM 9.0	NM- 9.2
1-6-Wagner painted-c						3.00
TPB (12/94, $17.95) r/#1-6						18.00
--TALES: HOMECOMING, 12/94 - 2/95 ($2.95, mature) 1-3						3.00
--TALES: THE DEVIL IN OUR MIDST, 5/94 - 9/95 ($2.95, mature) 1-5-Wagner painted-c						3.00
--TALES: THE DEVIL MAY CARE, 12/95 - No. 6, 5/96 ($2.95, mature)						
1-6-Terry LaBan scripts. 5-Batman/Grendel II preview						3.00
--TALES: THE DEVIL'S APPRENTICE, 9/97 - No. 3, 11/97 ($2.95, mature)						
1-3						3.00
: THE DEVIL INSIDE, 9/01 - No. 3, 11/01 ($2.99)						
1-3-r/#13-15 with new Wagner-c						3.00
GRENDEL: WAR CHILD						
Dark Horse Comics: Aug, 1992 - No. 10, Jun, 1993 ($2.50, lim. series, mature)						
1-9: 1-4-Bisley painted-c; Wagner-i & scripts in all						3.00
10-($3.50, 52 pgs.) Wagner-c						4.00
Limited Edition Hardcover ($99.95)						100.00
GREYFRIARS BOBBY (Disney)(Movie)						
Dell Publishing Co.: No. 1189, Nov, 1961 (one-shot)						
Four Color 1189-Photo-c (scarce)	7	14	21	47	76	105
GREYLORE						
Sirius: 12/85 - No. 5, Sept, 1986 ($1.50/$1.75, high quality paper)						
1-5: Bo Hampton-a in all						2.50
GREYSHIRT: INDIGO SUNSET (Also see Tomorrow Stories)						
America's Best Comics: Dec, 2001 - No. 6, Aug, 2002 ($3.50, limited series)						
1-6-Veitch-s/a. 4-Back-up w/John Severin-a. 6-Cho-a						3.50
TPB (2002, $19.95) r/#1-6; preface by Alan Moore						20.00
GRIDIRON GIANTS						
Ultimate Sports Ent.: 2000 - No. 2 ($3.95, cardstock covers)						
1,2-NFL players Sanders, Marino, Plummer, T. Davis battle evil						4.00
GRIFFIN, THE						
DC Comics: 1991 - No. 6, 1991 ($4.95, limited series, 52 pgs.)						
Book 1-6: Matt Wagner painted-c						5.00
GRIFTER (Also see Team 7 & WildC.A.T.S)						
Image Comics (WildStorm Prod.): May, 1995 - No. 10, Mar, 1996 ($1.95)						
1 ($1.95, Newsstand)-WildStorm Rising Pt. 5						2.50
1-10:1 ($2.50, Direct)-WildStorm Rising Pt. 5, bound-in trading card						3.00
...: One Shot (1/95, $4.95) Flip-c						5.00
GRIFTER						
Image Comics (WildStorm Prod.): V2#1, July, 1996 - No. 14, Aug, 1997 ($2.50)						
V2#1-14: Steven Grant scripts						3.00
GRIFTER & MIDNIGHTER						
DC Comics (WildStorm Prod.): May, 2007 - No. 6, Oct, 2007 ($2.99, limited series)						
1-6-Dixon-s/Benjamin-a/c. 1,3-The Authority app.						3.00
GRIFTER AND THE MASK						
Dark Horse Comics: Sept, 1996 - No. 2, Oct, 1996 ($2.50, limited series)						
(1st Dark Horse Comics/Image x-over)						
1,2: Steve Seagle scripts						3.00
GRIFTER/BADROCK (Also see WildC.A.T.S & Youngblood)						
Image Comics (Extreme Studios): Oct, 1995 - No.2, Nov, 1995 ($2.50, unfinished lim. series)						
1,2: 2-Flip book w/Badrock #2						2.50
GRIFTER/SHI						
Image Comics (WildStorm Productions): Apr, 1996 - No. 2, May, 1996 ($2.95, limited series)						
1,2: 1-Jim Lee-c/a(p); Travis Charest-a(p). 2-Billy Tucci-c/a(p); Travis Charest-a(p)						3.00
GRIM GHOST, THE						
Atlas/Seaboard Publ.: Jan, 1975 - No. 3, July, 1975						
1-3: Fleisher-s in all. 1-Origin. 2-Son of Satan; Colan-a. 3-Heath-c	1	2	3	5	7	9
GRIMJACK (Also see Demon Knight & Starslayer)						
First Comics: Aug, 1984 - No. 81, Apr, 1991 ($1.00/$1.95/$2.25)						
1-John Ostrander scripts & Tim Truman-c/a begins						3.00
2-25: 20-Sutton-c/a begins. 22-Bolland-a.						2.50
26-2nd color Teenage Mutant Ninja Turtles						4.00
27-74,76-81 (Later issues $1.95, $2.25): 30-Dynamo Joe x-over; 31-Mandrake-c/a begins. 73,74-Kelley Jones-a						2.50

	GD 2.0	VG 4.0	FN 6.0	VF 8.0	VF/NM 9.0	NM- 9.2
75-($5.95, 52 pgs.)-Fold-out map; coated stock						6.00
The Legend of Grimjack Vol. 1 (IDW Publishing, 2004, $19.99) r/Starslayer #10-18; 8 new pages & art						20.00
The Legend of Grimjack Vol. 2 (IDW, 2005, $19.99) r/#1-7; unpublished art						20.00
The Legend of Grimjack Vol. 3 (IDW, 2005, $19.99) r/#8-14; cover gallery						20.00
The Legend of Grimjack Vol. 4 (IDW, 2005, $24.99) r/#15-21; cover gallery						25.00
The Legend of Grimjack Vol. 5 (IDW, 5/06, $24.99) r/#22-30; cover gallery						25.00
The Legend of Grimjack Vol. 6 (IDW, 1/07, $24.99) r/#31-37; cover gallery						25.00
The Legend of Grimjack Vol. 7 (IDW, 4/07, $24.99) r/#38-46; covers; "Rough Trade"						25.00
NOTE: *Truman* c/a-1-17.						
GRIMJACK CASEFILES						
First Comics: Nov, 1990 - No. 5, Mar, 1991 ($1.95, limited series)						
1-5 Reprints 1st stories from Starslayer #10 on						2.50
GRIMJACK: KILLER INSTINCT						
IDW Publ.: Jan, 2005 - No. 6, June, 2005 ($3.99, limited series)						
1-6-Ostrander-s/Truman-a						4.00
GRIMM'S GHOST STORIES (See Dan Curtis)						
Gold Key/Whitman No. 55 on: Jan, 1972 - No. 60, June, 1982 (Painted-c #1-42,44,46-56)						
1	3	6	9	20	30	40
2-5,8: 5,8-Williamson-a	2	4	6	11	16	20
6,7,9,10	2	4	6	10	14	18
11-20	2	4	6	8	10	12
21-42,45-54: 32,34-Reprints. 45-Photo-c		2	4	5	7	9
43,44,55-60: 43,44--(52 pgs.). 43-Photo-c. 58(2/82). 59(4/82)-Williamson-a(r/#8). 60(6/82)	2	4	6	8	10	12
Mini-Comic No. 1 (3-1/4x6-1/2", 1976)	1	3	4	6	8	10
NOTE: *Reprints-#32?, 34?, 39, 43, 44, 47?, 53; 56-60(1/3). Bolle a-8, 17, 22-25, 27, 29(2), 33, 35, 41, 43r, 45(2), 48(2), 50, 52, 57. Celardo a-17, 26, 28p, 30, 31, 43(2), 45. Lopez a-24, 25. McWilliams a-33, 44r, 48, 54(2), 57, 58. Win Mortimer a-31, 33, 49, 51, 55, 56, 58(2), 59, 60. Roussos a-25, 30. Sparling a-23, 24, 28, 30, 31, 33, 43r, 44, 45, 51(2), 52, 56-58, 59(2), 60. Spiegle a-44.*						
GRIN (The American Funny Book) (Satire)						
APAG House Pubs: Nov, 1972 - No. 3, April, 1973 (Magazine, 52 pgs.)						
1-Parodies-Godfather, All in the Family	3	6	9	16	22	28
2,3	2	4	6	9	13	16
GRIN & BEAR IT (See Gags)						
Dell Publishing Co.: No. 28, 1941						
Large Feature Comic 28	16	32	48	94	147	200
GRIPS (Extreme violence)						
Silverwolf Comics: Sept, 1986 - No. 4, Dec, 1986 ($1.50, B&W, mature)						
1-Tim Vigil-c/a in all						6.00
2-4						4.00
GRIP: THE STRANGE WORLD OF MEN						
DC Comics (Vertigo): Jan, 2002 - No. 5, May, 2002 ($2.50, limited series)						
1-4-Gilbert Hernandez-s/a						2.50
GRIT GRADY (See Holyoke One-Shot No. 1)						
GROO (Sergio Aragonés'...)						
Image Comics: Dec, 1994 - No. 12, Dec, 1995 ($1.95)						
1-12: 2-Indicia reads #1, Jan, 1995; Aragonés-c/a in all						3.50
GROO (Sergio Aragonés'...)						
Dark Horse Comics: Jan, 1998 - No. 4, Apr, 1998 ($2.95)						
1-4: Aragonés-c/a in all						4.00
GROO CHRONICLES, THE (Sergio Aragonés)						
Marvel Comics (Epic Comics): June, 1989 - No. 6, Feb, 1990 ($3.50)						
Book 1-6: Reprints early Pacific issues						3.50
GROO SPECIAL						
Eclipse Comics: Oct, 1984 ($2.00, 52 pgs., Baxter paper)						
1-Aragonés-c/a	3	6	9	14	19	24
GROO THE WANDERER (See Destroyer Duck #1 & Starslayer #5)						
Pacific Comics: Dec, 1982 - No. 8, Apr, 1984						
1-Aragonés-c/a(p) in all; Aragonés bio., photo	2	4	6	11	16	20
2-5: 5-Deluxe paper (1.00-c)	2	4	6	8	11	14
6-8	2	4	6	9	13	16
GROO THE WANDERER (Sergio Aragonés'...) (See Marvel Graphic Novel #32)						
Marvel Comics (Epic Comics): March, 1985 - No. 120, Jan, 1995						
1-Aragonés-c/a in all	2	4	6	8	11	14
2-10	1	2	3	4	5	7

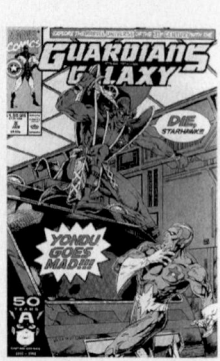
Guardians of the Galaxy #8 © MAR

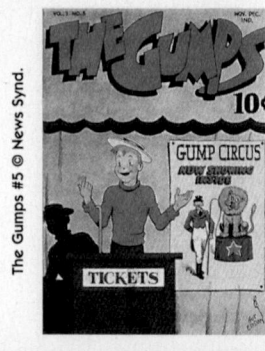
The Gumps #5 © News Synd.

Gunfire #3 © DC

	GD	VG	FN	VF	VF/NM	NM-
	2.0	4.0	6.0	8.0	9.0	9.2

11-20,50-($1.50, double size)						5.00
21-49,51-99: 87-direct sale only, high quality paper						3.00
100-($2.95, 52 pgs.)						5.00
101-120						4.00
Groo Carnival, The (12/91, $8.95)-r/#9-12						11.00
Groo Garden, The (4/94, $10.95)-r/#25-28						11.00

GROOVY (Cartoon Comics - not CCA approved)
Marvel Comics Group: March, 1968 - No. 3, July, 1968

	GD	VG	FN	VF	VF/NM	NM-
1-Monkees, Ringo Starr, Sonny & Cher, Mamas & Papas photos	8	16	24	56	93	130
2,3	6	12	18	37	59	80

GROSS POINT
DC Comics: Aug, 1997 - No. 14, Aug, 1998 ($2.50)

1-14: 1-Waid/Augustyn-s						2.50

GROUNDED
Image Comics: July, 2005 - No. 6, May, 2006 ($2.95/$2.99, limited series)

1-6-Mark Sable-s/Paul Azaceta-a. 1-Mike Oeming-c						3.00
Vol. 1: Powerless TPB (2006, $14.99) r/#1-6; sketch pages and creator bios						15.00

GRRL SCOUTS (Jim Mahfood's...) (Also see 40 oz. Collected)
Oni Press: Mar,1999 - No. 4, Dec, 1999 ($2.95, B&W, limited series)

1-4-Mahfood-s/c/a						3.00
TPB (2003, $12.95) r/#1-4; pin-ups by Warren, Winick, Allred, Fegredo and others						13.00

GRRL SCOUTS: WORK SUCKS
Image Comics: Feb, 2003 - No. 4, May, 2003 ($2.95, B&W, limited series)

1-4-Mahfood-s/c/a						3.00
TPB (2004, $12.95) r/#1-4; pin-ups by Oeming, Dwyer, Tennapel and others						13.00

GUADALCANAL DIARY (See American Library)

GUARDIAN ANGEL
Image Comics: May, 2002 - No. 2, July, 2002 ($2.95)

1,2-Peterson-s/Wiesenfeld-a						3.00

GUARDIANS
Marvel Comics: Sept, 2004 - No. 5, Dec, 2004 ($2.99, limited series)

1-5-Sumerak-s/Casey Jones-a						3.00

GUARDIANS OF JUSTICE & THE O-FORCE
Shadow Comics: 1990 (no date) ($1.50, 7-1/2 x10-1/4)

1-Super-hero group						2.50

GUARDIANS OF METROPOLIS
DC Comics: Nov, 1995 - Feb, 1995 ($1.50, limited series)

1-4: 1-Superman & Granny Goodness app.						2.50

GUARDIANS OF THE GALAXY (Also see The Defenders #26, Marvel Presents #3, Marvel Super-Heroes #18, Marvel Two-In-One #5)
Marvel Comics: June, 1990 - No. 62, July, 1995 ($1.00/$1.25)

1-Valentino-c/a(p) begin.						3.00
2-16: 2-Zeck-c(i). 5-McFarlane-c(i). 7-Intro Malevolence (Mephisto's daughter); Perez-c(i). 8-Intro Rancor (descendant of Wolverine) in cameo. 9-1st full app. Rancor; Rob Liefeld-c(i). 10-Jim Lee-c(i). 13,14-1st app. Spirit of Vengeance (futuristic Ghost Rider). 14-Spirit of Vengeance vs. The Guardians. 15-Starlin-c(i). 16-($1.50, 52 pgs.)-Starlin-c(i)						2.50
17-24,26-38,40-47: 17-20-31st century Punishers storyline. 20-Last $1.00-c. 21-Rancor app. 22-Reintro Starhawk. 24-Silver Surfer-c/story; Ron Lim-c/a. 26-Origin retold. 27-28-Infinity War x-over; 27-Inhumans app. 43-Intro Wooden (son of Thor)						2.50
25-($2.50)-Prism foil-c; Silver Surfer/Galactus-c/s						3.00
25-($2.50)-Without foil-c; newsstand edition						2.50
39-($2.95, 52 pgs.)-Embossed & holo-grafx foil-c; Dr. Doom vs. Rancor						3.00
48,49,51-62: 48-bound-in trading card sheet						2.50
50-($2.00, 52 pgs.)-Newsstand edition						2.75
50-($2.95, 52 pgs.)-Collectors ed. w/foil embossed-c						3.00
Annual 1-4: ('91-'94, 68 pgs.)-1-Origin. 2-Spirit of Vengeance-c/story. 3,4-Bagged w/card						3.00

GUERRILLA WAR (Formerly Jungle War Stories)
Dell Publishing Co.: No. 12, July-Sept, 1965 - No. 14, Mar, 1966

12-14	3	6	9	15	21	26

GUFF
Dark Horse Comics: Apr, 1998 ($1.95, B&W)

1-Flip book; Aragonés-c						2.50

GUILTY (See Justice Traps the Guilty)

GULLIVER'S TRAVELS (See Dell Jr. Treasury No. 3)

	GD	VG	FN	VF	VF/NM	NM-
	2.0	4.0	6.0	8.0	9.0	9.2

Dell Publishing Co.: Sept-Nov, 1965 - No. 3, May, 1966

1	5	10	15	35	55	75
2,3	4	8	12	24	37	50

GUMBY
Wildcard Ink: July, 2006 - Present ($3.99)

1,2-Bob Burden & Rick Geary-s&a						4.00

GUMBY'S SUMMER FUN SPECIAL
Comico: July, 1987 ($2.50)

1-Art Adams-c/a; B. Burden scripts						3.00

GUMBY'S WINTER FUN SPECIAL
Comico: Dec, 1988 ($2.50, 44 pgs.)

1-Art Adams-c/a						3.00

GUMPS, THE (See Merry Christmas..., Popular & Super Comics)
Dell Publ. Co./Bridgeport Herald Corp.: No. 73, 1945; Mar-Apr, 1947 - No. 5, Nov-Dec, 1947

Four Color 73 (Dell)(1945)	12	24	36	82	146	210
1 (3-4/47)	15	30	45	88	137	185
2-5	11	22	33	60	83	105

GUN CANDY (Also see The Ride)
Image Comics: July, 2005 - Present ($5.99)

1,2-Stelfreeze-c/a; flip book with The Ride (1-Pearson-c. 2-Noto-c)						6.00

GUNFIGHTER (Fat & Slat #1-4) (Becomes Haunt of Fear #15 on)
E. C. Comics (Fables Publ. Co.)**:** No. 5, Sum, 1948 - No. 14, Mar-Apr, 1950

5,6-Moon Girl in each	53	106	159	333	549	765
7-14: 14-Bondage-c	40	80	120	240	383	525

NOTE: Craig & H. C. Kiefer art in most issues. Craig c-5, 6, 13, 14. Feldstein/Craig a-10. Feldstein a-7-11. Harrison/Wood a-13, 14. Ingels a-5-14; c-7-12.

GUNFIGHTERS, THE
Super Comics (Reprints): 1963 - 1964

10-12,15,16,18: 10,11-r/Billy the Kid #s? 12-r/The Rider #5(Swift Arrow). 15-r/Straight Arrow #42; Powell-r. 16-r/Billy the Kid #?(Toby). 18-r/The Rider #3; Severin-c	2	4	6	10	14	18

GUNFIGHTERS, THE (Formerly Kid Montana)
Charlton Comics: No. 51, 10/66 - No. 52, 10/67; No. 53, 6/79 - No. 85, 7/84

51,52	2	4	6	11	16	20
53,54,56:53,54-Williamson/Torres-r/Six Gun Heroes #47,49. 56-Williamson/Severin-c; Severin-r/Sheriff of Tombstone #1	1	3	4	6	8	10
55,57-80						6.00
81-84-Lower print run	1	2	3	5	6	8
85-S&K-r/1955 Bullseye	1	3	4	6	8	10

GUNFIRE (See Deathstroke Annual #2 & Showcase 94 #1,2)
DC Comics: May, 1994 - No. 13, June, 1995 ($1.75/$2.25)

1-5,0,6-13: 2-Ricochet-c/story. 5-(9/94). 0-(10/94). 6-(11/94)						2.50

GUN GLORY (Movie)
Dell Publishing Co.: No. 846, Oct, 1957 (one-shot)

Four Color 846-Toth-a, photo-c.	8	16	24	58	97	135

GUNHAWK, THE (Formerly Whip Wilson)(See Wild Western)
Marvel/Atlas (MCI): No. 12, Nov, 1950 - No. 18, Dec, 1951 (Also see Two-Gun Western #5)

12	18	36	54	105	165	225
13-18: 13-Tuska-a. 16-Colan-a. 18-Maneely-c	14	28	42	76	108	140

GUNHAWKS (Gunhawk No. 7)
Marvel Comics Group: Oct, 1972 - No. 7, October, 1973

1,6: 1-Reno Jones, Kid Cassidy; Shores-c/a(p). 6-Kid Cassidy dies	3	6	9	15	21	26
2-5,7: 7-Reno Jones solo	2	4	6	10	14	18

GUNMASTER (Becomes Judo Master #89 on)
Charlton Comics: 9/64 - No. 4, 1965; No. 84. 7/65 - No. 88, 3-4/66; No. 89, 10/67

V1#1	4	8	12	22	34	45
2,4, V5#84-86: 84-Formerly Six-Gun Heroes	3	6	9	16	22	28
V5#87-89	2	4	6	11	16	20

NOTE: Vol. 5 was originally cancelled with #88 (3-4/66). #89 on, became Judo Master, then later in 1967, Charlton issued #89 as a Gunmaster one-shot.

GUN RUNNER
Marvel Comics UK: Oct, 1993 - No. 6, Mar, 1994 ($1.75, limited series)

1-($2.75)-Polybagged w/4 trading cards; Spirits of Vengeance app.						3.00

Guns Against Gangsters #6 © NOVP

Gunwitch: Outskirts of Doom #3 © Dan Brereton

Hack/Slash #4 © Seeley & Caselli

	GD 2.0	VG 4.0	FN 6.0	VF 8.0	VF/NM 9.0	NM- 9.2
2-6: 2-Ghost Rider & Blaze app.						2.50

GUNS AGAINST GANGSTERS (True-To-Life Romances #8 on)
Curtis Publications/Novelty Press: Sept-Oct, 1948 - No. 6, July-Aug, 1949; V2#1, Sept-Oct, 1949

	GD 2.0	VG 4.0	FN 6.0	VF 8.0	VF/NM 9.0	NM- 9.2
1-Toni & Greg Gayle begins by Schomburg; L.B. Cole-c	40	80	120	235	368	500
2-L.B. Cole-c	28	56	84	162	256	350
3-6, V2#1: 6-Toni Gayle-c by Cole	25	50	75	145	228	310

NOTE: *L. B. Cole* c-1-6, V2#1; 2; a-1, 2, 3(2), 4-6.

GUNSLINGER
Dell Publishing Co.: No. 1220, Oct-Dec, 1961 (one-shot)

Four Color 1220-Photo-c	8	16	24	56	93	130

GUNSLINGER (Formerly Tex Dawson...)
Marvel Comics Group: No. 2, Apr, 1973 - No. 3, June, 1973

2,3	2	4	6	11	16	20

GUNSLINGERS
Marvel Comics: Feb, 2000 ($2.99)

1-Reprints stories of Two-Gun Kid, Rawhide Kid and Caleb Hammer						3.00

GUNSMITH CATS: (Title series), **Dark Horse Comics**

--BAD TRIP (Manga), 6/98 - No. 6, 11/98 ($2.95, B&W) 1-6						3.00
--BEAN BANDIT (Manga), 1/99 - No. 9 ($2.95, B&W, limited series) 1-9						3.00
--GOLDIE VS. MISTY (Manga), 11/97 - No. 7, 5/98 ($2.95, B&W) 1-7						3.00
--KIDNAPPED (Manga), 11/99 - No. 10, 8/00 ($2.95, B&W) 1-10						3.00
--MISTER V (Manga), 10/00 - No. 11, 8/01 ($3.50/$2.99), B&W) 1-7,9-11						3.50
8-($2.99)						3.00
--THE RETURN OF GRAY (Manga), 8/96 - No. 7, 2/97 ($2.95, B&W) 1-7						3.00
--SHADES OF GRAY (Manga), 5/97 - No. 5, 9/97 ($2.95, B&W) 1-5						3.00
--SPECIAL (Manga) Nov, 2001 ($2.99, B&W, one-shot)						3.00

GUNSMOKE (Blazing Stories of the West)
Western Comics (Youthful Magazines): Apr-May, 1949 - No. 16, Jan, 1952

1-Gunsmoke & Masked Marvel begin by Ingels; Ingels bondage-c	45	90	135	275	450	625
2-Ingels c/a(2)	29	58	87	170	268	365
3-Ingels bondage-c/a	25	50	75	145	228	310
4-6: Ingels-c	20	40	60	115	180	245
7-10	13	26	39	72	101	130
11-16: 15,16-Western/horror stories	12	24	36	69	97	125

NOTE: *Stallman* a-11, 14. *Wildey* a-15, 16.

GUNSMOKE (TV)
Dell Publishing Co./Gold Key (All have James Arness photo-c): No. 679, Feb, 1956 - No. 27, Feb, 1969 - No. 6, Feb, 1970

Four Color 679(#1)	16	32	48	118	209	300
Four Color 720,769,797,844 (#2-5),6(11-1/57-58)	9	18	27	61	103	145
7,8,9,11,12-Williamson-a in all, 4 pgs. each	9	18	27	63	107	150
10-Williamson/Crandall-a, 4 pgs.	9	18	27	63	107	150
13-27	8	16	24	52	86	120
1 (Gold Key)	6	12	18	41	66	90
2-6('69-70)	4	8	12	22	34	45

GUNSMOKE TRAIL
Ajax-Farrell Publ./Four Star Comic Corp.: June, 1957 - No. 4, Dec, 1957

1	11	22	33	60	83	105
2-4	7	14	21	35	43	50

GUNSMOKE WESTERN (Formerly Western Tales of Black Rider)
Atlas Comics No. 32-35(CPS/NPI); Marvel No. 36 on: No. 32, Dec, 1955 - No. 77, July, 1963

32-Baker & Drucker-a	17	34	51	98	154	210
33,35,36-Williamson-a in each; 5,6 & 4 pgs. plus Drucker-a #33. 33-Kinstler-a?	14	28	42	81	118	155
34-Baker-a, 4 pgs.; Kirby-c	14	28	42	76	108	140
37-Davis-a; Williamson text illo	12	24	36	67	94	120
38,39: 39-Williamson text illo (unsigned)	10	20	30	54	72	90
40-Williamson/Mayo-a (4 pgs.)	10	20	30	58	79	100
41,42,45,46,48,49,52-54,57,58,60: 49,52-Kirby from Texas story. 57-1st Two Gun Kid by Severin. 60-Sam Hawk app. in Kid Colt	8	16	24	57		70
43,44-Torres-a	8	16	24	44	57	70
47,51,59,61: 47,51,59-Kirby-a. 61-Crandall-a	9	18	27	52	69	85
50-Kirby, Crandall-a	10	20	30	58	79	100

	GD 2.0	VG 4.0	FN 6.0	VF 8.0	VF/NM 9.0	NM- 9.2
55,56-Matt Baker-a	10	20	30	56	76	95
62-67,69,71-73,77-Kirby-a. 72-Origin Kid Colt	5	10	15	35	55	75
68,70,74-76: 68-(10¢-c)	4	8	12	28	44	60
68-(10¢ cover price blacked out, 12¢ printed on)	8	16	24	52	86	120

NOTE: *Colan* a-35-37, 39, 72, 76. *Davis* a-37, 52, 54, 55; c-50. 54. *Ditko* a-66; c-56p. *Drucker* a-32-34. *Heath* c-33. *Jack Keller* a-35, 40, 60, 72; c-72. *Kirby* a-47, 50, 51, 59, 62(3), 63-67, 69, 71, 73, 77; c-56(w/Ditko),57, 58, 60, 61(w/Ayers), 62, 63, 66, 68, 69, 71-77. *Robinson* a-35. *Severin* a-35, 59-61; c-34, 35, 39, 42, 43. *Tuska* a-34. *Wildey* a-10, 37, 42, 56, 57. *Kid Colt* in all. Two-Gun Kid in No. 57, 59, 60-63. *Wyatt Earp* in No. 45, 48, 49, 52, 54, 55, 58.

GUNS OF FACT & FICTION (Also see A-1 Comics)
Magazine Enterprises: No. 13, 1948 (one-shot)

A-1 13-Used in SOTI, pg. 19; Ingels & J. Craig-a	27	54	81	158	249	340

GUNS OF THE DRAGON
DC Comics: Oct, 1998 - No. 4, Jan, 1999 ($2.50, limited series)

1-4-DCU in the 1920's; Enemy Ace & Bat Lash app.						2.50

GUN THEORY
Marvel Comics (Epic): Oct, 2003 - No. 4 ($2.50, limited series)

1,2-Daniel Way-s/Jon Proctor-a						2.50

GUNWITCH, THE : OUTSKIRTS OF DOOM (See The Nocturnals)
Oni Press: June, 2001 - No. 3, Oct, 2001 ($2.95, B&W, limited series)

1-3-Brereton-s/painted-c/Naifeh-s						3.00

GUY GARDNER (Guy Gardner: Warrior #17 on)(Also see Green Lantern #59)
DC Comics: Oct, 1992 - No. 44, July, 1996 ($1.25/$1.50/$1.75)

1-24,0,26-30: 1-Staton-c/a(p) begins. 6-Guy vs. Hal Jordan. 8-Vs. Lobo-c/story. 15-JLA x-over, begin $1.50-c. 18-Begin 4-part Emerald Fallout story; splash page x-over GL #50. 18-21-Vs. Hal Jordan. 24-(9/94)-Zero Hour. 0-(10/94)						2.50
25 (11/94), $2.50, 52 pgs.						3.00
29 ($2.95)-Gatefold-c						3.50
29-Variant-c (Edward Hopper's Nighthawks)						2.50
31-44: 31-$1.75-c begins. 40-Gorilla Grodd-c/app. 44-Parallax-app. (1 pg.)						2.50
Annual 1 (1995, $3.50)-Year One story						4.00
Annual 2 (1996, $2.95)-Legends of the Dead Earth story						3.00

GUY GARDNER: COLLATERAL DAMAGE
DC Comics: 2006 - No. 2 ($5.99, square-bound, limited series)

1,2-Howard Chaykin-s/a						6.00

GUY GARDNER REBORN
DC Comics: 1992 - Book 3, 1992 ($4.95, limited series)

1-3: Staton-c/a(p). 1-Lobo-c/cameo. 2,3-Lobo-c/s						5.00

GYPSY COLT
Dell Publishing Co.: No. 568, June, 1954 (one-shot)

Four Color 568--Movie	5	10	15	32	51	70

GYRO GEARLOOSE (See Dynabrite Comics, Walt Disney's C&S #140 &Walt Disney Showcase #18)
Dell Publishing Co.: No. 1047, Nov-Jan/1959-60 - May-July, 1962 (Disney)

Four Color 1047 (No. 1)-All Barks-c/a	17	34	51	128	227	325
Four Color 1095,1184-All by Carl Barks	9	18	27	65	113	160
Four Color 1267-Barks c/a, 4 pgs.	8	16	24	54	90	125
01329-207 (#1, 5-7/62)-Barks-c only (intended as 4-Color 1329?)	6	12	18	41	66	90

HACKER FILES, THE
DC Comics: Aug, 1992 - No. 12, July, 1993 ($1.95)

1-12: 1-Sutton-a(p) begins; computer generated-c						2.50

HACK/SLASH
Devil's Due Publishing: Apr. 2004 - Present ($3.25/$4.95)

1-Seeley-s/Caselli-a/c						5.00
.... Comic Book Carnage (3/05) Manfredi-/Seeley-s; Robert Kirkman & Steve Niles app.						5.00
.... First Cut TPB (10/05, $14.95) r/one-shots with sketch pages , designs, interviews						15.00
.... Girls Gone Dead (10/04, $4.95) Manfredi-/Seeley-s						5.00
.... Land of Lost Toys 1-3 (11/05 - No. 3, 1/06, $3.25) Crossland-a/Seeley-s						3.25
.... The Final Revenge of Evil Ernie (6/05, $4.95) Salman-a/Seeley-s; two covers						5.00
.... Trailers (2/05, $3.25) short stories by Seeley; art by various; three covers						3.25
.... Slice Hard (12/05, $4.95) Seeley-s						5.00
.... Slice Hard Pre-Sliced 25¢ Special (2/06, 25¢) origin story by Seeley; sketch pages						2.25
.... The Series 1-4 (5/07-Present, $3.50) Flashack to Cassie's childhood and origin						3.50
.... Vs Chucky (3/07, $5.50) Seeley-s/Merhoff-a; 3 covers						5.50
.... Vol. 2 Death By Sequel TPB (1/07, $18.99) r/Land of Lost Toys #1-3, Trailers, Slice Hard						19.00

HAGAR THE HORRIBLE (See Comics Reading Libraries in the Promotional Comics section)

Ha-Ha Comics #10 © ACG

Hammer of the Gods #1 © Oeming & Wheatley

Hanna-Barbera Giant Size V2 #1 © H-B

	GD	VG	FN	VF	VF/NM	NM-
	2.0	4.0	6.0	8.0	9.0	9.2

HA HA COMICS (Teepee Tim No. 100 on; also see Giggle Comics)
Scope Mag.(Creston Publ.) No. 1-80/American Comics Group: Oct, 1943 - No. 99, Jan, 1955

	GD	VG	FN	VF	VF/NM	NM-
1-Funny animal	35	70	105	204	322	440
2	17	34	51	98	154	210
3-5: Ken Hultgren-a begins?	14	28	42	78	112	145
6-10	11	22	33	62	86	110
11-20: 14-Infinity-c	9	18	27	52	69	85
21-40	9	18	27	47	61	75
41-94,96-99: 49,61-X-Mas-c	8	16	24	42	54	65
95-3-D effect-c	15	30	45	85	130	175

HAIR BEAR BUNCH, THE (TV) (See Fun-In No. 13)
Gold Key: Feb, 1972 - No. 9, Feb, 1974 (Hanna-Barbera)

1		4	8	12	23	36	48
2-9		3	6	9	16	23	30

HALF DEAD
Marvel Comics (Dabel Brothers Prods.): March, 2007 ($10.99, softcover, graphic novel)
SC-Barb Lien-Cooper & Park Cooper-s/Jimmy Bott-a 11.00

HALLELUJAH TRAIL, THE (See Movie Classics)

HALL OF FAME FEATURING THE T.H.U.N.D.E.R. AGENTS
JC Productions(Archie Comics Group): May, 1983 - No. 3, Dec, 1983
1-3: Thunder Agents-r(Crandall, Kane, Tuska, Wood-a). 2-New Ditko-c 3.00

HALLOWEEN (Movie)
Chaos! Comics: Nov, 2000; Apr, 2001 ($2.95/$2.99, one-shots)
1-Brewer-a; Michael Myers childhood at the Sanitarium 3.00
...II: The Blackest Eyes (4/01, $2.99) Beck-a 3.00
...III: The Devil's Eyes (11/01, $2.99) Justiniano-a 3.00

HALLOWEEN HORROR
Eclipse Comics: Oct, 1987 (Seduction of the Innocent #7)($1.75)
1-Pre-code horror-r 3.00

HALLOWEEN MEGAZINE
Marvel Comics: Dec, 1996 ($3.95, one-shot, 96 pgs.)
1-Reprints Tomb of Dracula 4.00

HALO GRAPHIC NOVEL (Based on video game)
Marvel Publishing Inc.: 2006 ($24.99, hardcover with dust jacket)
HC-Anthology set in the Halo universe; art by Bisley, Moebius and others; pin-up gallery by various incl. Darrow, Pratt, Williams and Van Fleet; Phil Hale painted-c 25.00

HALO: UPRISING (Based on video game) (Also see Marvel Spotlight: Halo)
Marvel Comics: Oct, 2007 - No. 4 ($3.99, limited series)
1-Bendis-s/Maleev-a; takes pllace between the *Halo 2* and *Halo 3* video games 4.00

HALO JONES (See The Ballad of...)

HAMMER, THE
Dark Horse Comics: Oct, 1997 - No. 4, Jan, 1998 ($2.95, limited series)
1-4-Kelley Jones-s/c/a, ...: Uncle Alex (8/98, $2.95) 3.00

HAMMER, THE: THE OUTSIDER
Dark Horse Comics: Feb, 1999 - No. 3, Apr, 1999 ($2.95, limited series)
1-3-Kelley Jones-s/c/a 3.00

HAMMERLOCKE
DC Comics: Sept, 1992 - No. 9, May, 1993 ($1.75, limited series)
1-($2.50, 52 pgs.)-Chris Sprouse-c/a in all 3.00
2-9 .... 2.50

HAMMER OF GOD (Also see Nexus)
First Comics: Feb, 1990 - No. 4, May, 1990 ($1.95, limited series)
1-4 .... 2.50

HAMMER OF GOD: BUTCH
Dark Horse Comics: May, 1994 - No. 4, Aug, 1994 ($2.50, limited series)
1-3 .... 2.50

HAMMER OF GOD: PENTATHLON
Dark Horse Comics: Jan, 1994 ($2.50, one shot)
1-Character from Nexus 2.50

HAMMER OF GOD: SWORD OF JUSTICE
First Comics: Feb 1991 - Mar 1991 ($4.95, lim. series, squarebound, 52 pgs.)
V2#1,2 .... 5.00

HAMMER OF THE GODS
Insight Studio Groups: 2001 - No. 5, 2001 ($2.95, limited series)
1-Michael Oeming & Mark Wheatley-s/a; Frank Cho-c 6.00
2-5: 3-Hughes-c. 5-Dave Johnson-c 3.00
The ColorSaga (2002, $4.95) r/"Enemy of the Gods" internet strip 5.00
Mortal Enemy TPB (2002, $18.95) r/#1-5; intro. by Peter David; afterword by Raven 19.00

HAMMER OF THE GODS: HAMMER HITS CHINA
Image Comics: Feb, 2003 - No. 3, Sept, 2003 ($2.95, limited series)
1-3-Oeming & Wheatley-s/a; Oeming-c. 2-Frankenstein Mobster by Wheatley 3.00

HANDBOOK OF THE CONAN UNIVERSE, THE
Marvel Comics: June, 1985; Jan, 1986 ($1.25, one-shot)
1-(6/85) Kaluta-c (2 printings) 4.00
1-(1/86) Kaluta-c 6.00

nn-(no date, circa '87-88, B&W, 36 pgs.) reprints '86 with changes; new painted cover					
	1	2	3	5	6	8

HAND OF FATE (Formerly Men Against Crime)
Ace Magazines: No. 8, Dec, 1951 - No. 25, Dec, 1954 (Weird/horror stories) (Two #25's)

8-Surrealistic text story	41	82	123	256	416	575
9,10,21-Necronomicon sty; drug belladonna used	25	50	75	145	228	310
11-18,20,22,23	21	42	63	120	188	255
19-Bondage, hypo needle scenes	22	44	66	128	202	275
24-Electric chair-c	31	62	93	178	282	385
25a(11/54), 25b(12/54)-Both have Cameron-a	16	32	48	94	147	200

NOTE: *Cameron a-9, 10, 19-25a, 25b; c-13. Sekowsky a-8, 9, 13, 14.*

HAND OF FATE
Eclipse Comics: Feb, 1988 - No. 3, Apr, 1988 ($1.75/$2.00, Baxter paper)
1-3; 3-B&W 2.50

HANDS OF THE DRAGON
Seaboard Periodicals (Atlas): June, 1975

1-Origin/1st app.; Craig-a(p)/Mooney inks	1	3	4	6	8	10

HANGMAN COMICS (Special Comics No. 1; Black Hood No. 9 on)
(Also see Flyman, Mighty Comics, Mighty Crusaders & Pep Comics)
MLJ Magazines: No. 2, Spring, 1942 - No. 8, Fall, 1943

2-The Hangman, Boy Buddies begin	197	394	591	1231	2041	2850
3-Beheading splash pg.; 1st Nazi war-c	182	262	393	819	1360	1900
4-8: 5-1st Jap war-c. 8-2nd app. Super Duck (ties w/Jolly Jingles #11)	114	228	342	713	1182	1650

NOTE: *Fuje a-7(3), 8(3); c-3. Reinman c/a-3. Bondage c-3. Sahle c-6.*

HANK
Pentagon Publishing Co.: 1946

nn-Coulton Waugh's newspaper reprint	8	16	24	44	57	70

HANNA-BARBERA (See Golden Comics Digest No. 2, 7, 11)

HANNA-BARBERA ALL-STARS
Archie Publications: Oct, 1995 - No. 4, Apr, 1996 ($1.50, bi-monthly)
1-4 .... 3.00

HANNA-BARBERA BANDWAGON (TV)
Gold Key: Oct, 1962 - No. 3, Apr, 1963

1-Giant, 84 pgs. 1-Augie Doggie app.; 1st app. Lippy the Lion, Touché Turtle & Dum Dum, Wally Gator, Snagg de Loop,	12	24	36	87	156	225
2-Giant, 84 pgs.; Mr. & Mrs. J. Evil Scientist (1st app.) in Snagglepuss story; Yakky Doodle, Ruff and Reddy and others app.	9	18	27	60	100	140
3-Regular size; Mr. & Mrs. J. Evil Scientist app. (pre-#1), Snagglepuss, Wally Gator and others app.	7	14	21	47	76	105

HANNA-BARBERA GIANT SIZE
Harvey Comics: Oct, 1992 - No. 3 ($2.25, 68 pgs.)
V2#1-3:Flintstones, Yogi Bear, Magilla Gorilla, Huckleberry Hound, Quick Draw McGraw, Yakky Doodle & Chopper, Jetsons & others 5.00

HANNA-BARBERA HI-ADVENTURE HEROES (See Hi-Adventure...)

HANNA-BARBERA PARADE (TV)
Charlton Comics: Sept, 1971 - No. 10, Dec, 1972

1	7	14	21	49	80	110
2,4-10	4	8	12	26	41	55
3-(52 pgs.)- "Summer Picnic"	6	12	18	37	59	80

NOTE: *No. 4 (1/72) went on sale late in 1972 with the January 1973 issues.*

HANNA-BARBERA PRESENTS
Archie Publications: Nov, 1995 - No. 6 ($1.50, bi-monthly)

Hap Hazard Comics #9 © ACE

Happy Comics #11 © STD

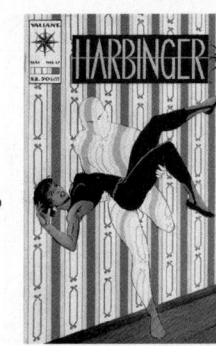

Harbinger #17 © VAL

	GD 2.0	VG 4.0	FN 6.0	VF 8.0	VF/NM 9.0	NM- 9.2

1-8: 1-Atom Ant & Secret Squirrel. 2-Wacky Races. 3-Yogi Bear. 4-Quick Draw McGraw & Magilla Gorilla. 5-A Pup Named Scooby-Doo. 6-Superstar Olympics. 7-Wacky Races. 8-Frankenstein Jr. & the Impossibles ... 3.00

HANNA-BARBERA SPOTLIGHT (See Spotlight)

HANNA-BARBERA SUPER TV HEROES (TV)
Gold Key: Apr, 1968 - No. 7, Oct, 1969 (Hanna-Barbera)

	GD	VG	FN	VF	VF/NM	NM-
1-The Birdman, The Herculoids(ends #6; not in #3), Moby Dick, Young Samson & Goliath (ends #2,4), and The Mighty Mightor begin; Spiegle-a in all	15	30	45	107	191	275
2-The Galaxy Trio app.; Shazzan begins; 12¢ & 15¢ versions exist	10	20	30	70	123	175
3,6,7-The Space Ghost app.	9	18	27	65	113	160
4,5	8	16	24	58	97	135

NOTE: Birdman in #1,2,4,5. Herculoids in #2,4-7. Mighty Mightor in #1,2,4-7. Moby Dick in all. Shazzan in #2-5. Young Samson & Goliath in #1,3.

HANNA-BARBERA TV FUN FAVORITES (See Golden Comics Digest #2,7,11)

HANNA-BARBERA (TV STARS) (See TV Stars)

HANS BRINKER (Disney)
Dell Publishing Co.: No. 1273, Feb, 1962 (one-shot)

	GD	VG	FN	VF	VF/NM	NM-
Four Color 1273-Movie, photo-c	6	12	18	43	69	95

HANS CHRISTIAN ANDERSEN
Ziff-Davis Publ. Co.: 1953 (100 pgs., Special Issue)

	GD	VG	FN	VF	VF/NM	NM-
nn-Danny Kaye (movie)-Photo-c; fairy tales	16	32	48	94	147	200

HANSEL & GRETEL
Dell Publishing Co.: No. 590, Oct, 1954 (one-shot)

	GD	VG	FN	VF	VF/NM	NM-
Four Color 590-Partial photo-c	6	12	18	43	69	95

HANSI, THE GIRL WHO LOVED THE SWASTIKA
Spire Christian Comics (Fleming H. Revell Co.): 1973, 1976 (39¢/49¢)

	GD	VG	FN	VF	VF/NM	NM-
1973 edition with 39¢-c	4	8	12	28	44	60
1976 edition with 49¢-c	3	6	9	18	27	35

HAP HAZARD COMICS (Real Love No. 25 on)
Ace Magazines (Readers' Research): Summer, 1944 - No. 24, Feb, 1949 (#1-6 are quarterly issues)

	GD	VG	FN	VF	VF/NM	NM-
1	15	30	45	84	127	170
2	9	18	27	52	69	85
3-10	8	16	24	44	57	70
11-13,15-24	8	16	24	40	50	60
14-Feldstein-c (4/47)	10	20	30	56	76	95

HAP HOPPER (See Comics Revue No. 2)

HAPPIEST MILLIONAIRE, THE (See Movie Comics)

HAPPI TIM (See March of Comics No. 182)

HAPPY BIRTHDAY MARTHA WASHINGTON (Also see Give Me Liberty, Martha Washington Goes To War, & Martha Washington Stranded In Space)
Dark Horse Comics: Mar, 1995 ($2.95, one-shot)

	GD	VG	FN	VF	VF/NM	NM-
1-Miller script; Gibbons-c/a						3.00

HAPPY COMICS (Happy Rabbit No. 41 on)
Nedor Publ./Standard Comics (Animated Cartoons): Aug, 1943 - No. 40, Dec, 1950 (Companion to Goofy Comics)

	GD	VG	FN	VF	VF/NM	NM-
1-Funny animal	27	54	81	158	249	340
2	15	30	45	84	127	170
3-10	11	22	33	62	86	110
11-19	10	20	30	54	72	90
20-31,34-37-Frazetta text illos in all (2 in #34&35, 3 in #27,28,30). 27-Al Fago-a	11	22	33	62	86	110
32-Frazetta-a, 7 pgs. plus 2 text illos; Roussos-a	20	40	60	117	184	250
33-Frazetta-a(2), 6 pgs. each (Scarce)	28	56	84	162	256	350
38-40	9	18	27	47	61	75

HAPPYDALE: DEVILS IN THE DESERT
DC Comics (Vertigo): 1999 - No. 2, 1999 ($6.95, limited series)

	GD	VG	FN	VF	VF/NM	NM-
1,2-Andrew Dabb-s/Seth Fisher-a						7.00

HAPPY DAYS (TV)(See Kite Fun Book)
Gold Key: Mar, 1979 - No. 6, Feb, 1980

	GD	VG	FN	VF	VF/NM	NM-
1-Photo-c of TV cast; 35¢-c	3	6	9	16	23	50
2-6-(40¢-c)	2	4	6	9	12	15

HAPPY HOLIDAY (See March of Comics No. 181)

HAPPY HOULIHANS (Saddle Justice No. 3 on; see Blackstone, The Magician Detective)
E. C. Comics: Fall, 1947 - No. 2, Winter, 1947-48

	GD	VG	FN	VF	VF/NM	NM-
1-Origin Moon Girl (same date as Moon Girl #1)	54	108	162	338	557	775
2	31	62	93	178	282	385

HAPPY JACK
Red Top (Decker): Aug, 1957 - No. 2, Nov, 1957

	GD	VG	FN	VF	VF/NM	NM-
V1#1,2	5	10	15	22	26	30

HAPPY JACK HOWARD
Red Top (Farrell)/Decker: 1957

	GD	VG	FN	VF	VF/NM	NM-
nn-Reprints Handy Andy story from E. C. Dandy Comics #5, renamed "Happy Jack"	5	10	15	22	26	30

HAPPY RABBIT (Formerly Happy Comics)
Standard Comics (Animated Cartoons): No. 41, Feb, 1951 - No. 48, Apr, 1952

	GD	VG	FN	VF	VF/NM	NM-
41-Funny animal	8	16	24	42	54	65
42-48	6	12	18	31	38	45

HARBINGER (Also see Unity)
Valiant: Jan, 1992 - No. 41, June, 1995 ($1.95/$2.50)

	GD	VG	FN	VF	VF/NM	NM-
0-Prequel to the series; available by redeeming coupons in #1-6; cover image has pink sky; title logo is blue	3	6	9	20	30	40
0-(2nd printing) cover has blue sky & red logo						4.00
1-1st app.	1	3	4	6	8	10
2-4: 4-Low print run	1	2	3	4	5	7
5,6: 5-Solar app. 6-Torque dies						6.00
7-10: 8,9-Unity x-overs. 8-Miller-c. 9-Simonson-c. 10-1st app. H.A.R.D. Corps (10/92)						4.00
11-24,26-41: 14-1st app. Stronghold. 18-Intro Screen. 19-1st app. Stunner. 22-Archer & Armstrong app. 24-Cover similar to #1. 26-Intro New Harbingers. 29-Bound-in trading card. 30-H.A.R.D. Corps app. 32-Eternal Warrior app. 33-Dr. Eclipse app.						2.50
25-($3.50, 52 pgs.)-Harada vs. Sting						3.50
...Files 1,2 (8/94,2/95 $2.50)						2.50
Trade paperback nn (11/92, $9.95)-Reprints #1-4 & comes polybagged with a copy of Harbinger #0 w/new-c. Price for TPB only						10.00

NOTE: Issues 1-6 have coupons with origin of Harada and are redeemable for Harbinger #0.

HARD BOILED
Dark Horse Comics: Sept, 1990 - No. 3, Mar, 1992 ($4.95/$5.95, 8 1/2x11", lim. series)

	GD	VG	FN	VF	VF/NM	NM-
1-3-Miller-s; Darrow-c/a; sexually explicit & violent	1	2	3	4	5	7
TPB (5/93, $15.95)						16.00
Big Damn Hard Boiled (12/97, $29.95, B&W) r/#1-3						30.00

HARDCASE (See Break Thru, Flood Relief & Ultraforce, 1st Series)
Malibu Comics (Ultraverse): June, 1993 - No. 26, Aug, 1995 ($1.95/$2.50)

	GD	VG	FN	VF	VF/NM	NM-
1-Intro Hardcase; Dave Gibbons-c; has coupon for Ultraverse Premiere #0; Jim Callahan-a(p) begin, ends #3						3.00
1-With coupon missing						2.25
1-Platinum Edition						4.00
1-Holographic Cover Edition; 1st full-c holograph tied w/Prime 1 & Strangers 1						7.00
1-Ultra Limited silver foil-c						4.00
2,3-Callahan-a, 2-($2.50)-Newsstand edition bagged w/trading card						2.50
4,6-15, 17-19: 4-Strangers app. 7-Break-Thru x-over. 8-Solution app. 9-Vs. Turf. 12-Silver foil logo, wraparound-c. 17-Prime app.						2.50
5-($2.50, 48 pgs.)-Rune flip-c/story by B. Smith (3 pgs.)						2.50
16 ($3.50, 68 pgs.)-Rune pin-up						3.50
20-26: 23-Loki app.						2.50

NOTE: Perez a-8(2); c-20i.

HARDCORE STATION
DC Comics: July, 1998 - No. 6, Dec, 1998 ($2.50, limited series)

	GD	VG	FN	VF	VF/NM	NM-
1-6-Starlin-s/a(p). 3-Green Lantern-c/app. 5,6-JLA-c/app.						3.00

H.A.R.D. CORPS, THE (See Harbinger #10)
Valiant: Dec, 1992 - No. 30, Feb, 1995 ($2.25) (Harbinger spin-off)

	GD	VG	FN	VF	VF/NM	NM-
1-($2.50)-Gatefold-c by Jim Lee & Bob Layton						3.00
1-Gold variant						5.00
2-30: 5-Bloodshot-c/story cont'd from Bloodshot #3. 5-Variant edition; came w/Comic Defense System. 10-Turok app. 17-vs. Armorines. 18-Bound-in trading card. 20-Harbinger app.						2.50

HARD TIME
DC Comics (Focus): Apr, 2004 - No. 12, Mar, 2005 ($2.50)

	GD	VG	FN	VF	VF/NM	NM-
1-12-Gerber-s/Hurtt-a; 1-Includes previews of other DC Focus series						2.50
....: 50 to Life (2004, $9.95, TPB) r/#1-6; cover gallery with sketches						10.00

HARD TIME: SEASON TWO
DC Comics: Feb, 2006 - No. 7, Aug, 2006 ($2.50/$2.99)

Hardware #21 © Milestone

Harley Quinn #2 © DC

Harvey Comics Library #1 © HARV

	GD 2.0	VG 4.0	FN 6.0	VF 8.0	VF/NM 9.0	NM- 9.2		GD 2.0	VG 4.0	FN 6.0	VF 8.0	VF/NM 9.0	NM- 9.2

1-5-Gerber-s/Hurtt-a ... 2.50
6,7-($2.99) 7-Ethan paroled in 2053 ... 3.00

HARDWARE
DC Comics (Milestone): Apr, 1993 - No. 50, Apr, 1997 ($1.50/$1.75/$2.50)
1-($2.95)-Collector's Edition polybagged w/poster & trading card (direct sale only) ... 4.00
1-Platinum Edition ... 6.00
1-15,17-19: 11-Shadow War x-over. 11,14-Simonson-c. 12-Buckler-a(p). 17-Worlds Collide Pt. 2. 18-Simonson-c; Worlds Collide Pt 9. 15-1st Humberto Ramos DC work ... 2.50
16,50-($3.95, 52 pgs.)-16-Collector's Edition w/gatefold 2nd cover by Byrne; new armor; Icon app. ... 4.00
16,20-24,26-49: 16-($2.50, 52 pgs.)-Newsstand Ed. 49-Moebius-c ... 2.50
25-($2.95, 52 pgs.) ... 3.00

HARDY BOYS, THE (Disney
Dell Publ. Co.: No. 760, Dec, 1956 - No. 964, Jan, 1959 (Mickey Mouse Club)
Four Color 760 (#1)-Photo-c ... 10 | 20 | 30 | 70 | 123 | 175
Four Color 830(8/57), 887(1/58), 964-Photo-c ... 9 | 18 | 27 | 60 | 100 | 140

HARDY BOYS, THE (TV)
Gold Key: Apr, 1970 - No. 4, Jan, 1971
1 ... 4 | 8 | 12 | 28 | 44 | 60
2-4 ... 3 | 6 | 9 | 18 | 27 | 35

HARLAN ELLISON'S DREAM CORRIDOR
Dark Horse Comics: Mar, 1995 - No. 5, July, 1995 ($2.95, anthology)
1-5: Adaptation of Ellison stories. 1-4-Byrne-a. ... 3.00
Special (1/95, $4.95) ... 5.00
Trade paperback-(1996, $18.95, 192 pgs)-r/#1-5 & Special #1 ... 19.00

HARLAN ELLISON'S DREAM CORRIDOR QUARTERLY
Dark Horse Comics: V2#1, Aug, 1996 ($5.95, anthology, squarebound)
V2#1-Adaptations of Ellison's stories w/new material; Neal Adams-a ... 6.00
Volume 2 TPB (3/07, $19.95) r/V2#1 and unpublished material incl. last Swan-a ... 20.00

HARLEM GLOBETROTTERS (TV) (See Fun-In No. 8)
Gold Key: Apr, 1972 - No. 12, Jan, 1975 (Hanna-Barbera)
1 ... 4 | 8 | 12 | 24 | 37 | 50
2-5 ... 3 | 6 | 9 | 14 | 20 | 25
6-12 ... 2 | 4 | 6 | 11 | 16 | 20
NOTE: #4, 8, and 12 contain 16 extra pages of advertising.

HARLEQUIN ROMANCE
Dark Horse Comics: Nov, 2001 ($10.95, hardcover, one-shot)
nn-Neil Gaiman-s; painted-a/c by John Bolton ... 11.00

HARLEY QUINN
DC Comics: Dec, 2000 - No. 38, Jan, 2004 ($2.95/$2.25/$2.50)
1-Joker and Poison Ivy app.; Terry & Rachel Dodson-a/c ... 4.00
2-11-($2.25). 2-Two-Face-c/app. 3-Slumber party. 6,7-Riddler app. ... 2.50
12-($2.95) Batman app. ... 3.00
13-38: 13-Joker: Last Laugh. 17,18-Bizarro-c/app. 23-Begin $2.50-c. 23,24-Martian Manhunter app. 25,32-Joker-c/app. ... 2.50
Harley & Ivy: Love on the Lam (2001, $5.95) Winick-s/Chiodo-c/a ... 6.00
...: Our Worlds at War (10/01, $2.95) Jae Lee-c; art by various ... 3.00

HAROLD TEEN (See Popular Comics, & Super Comics)
Dell Publishing Co.: No. 2, 1942 - No. 209, Jan, 1949
Four Color 2 ... 29 | 58 | 87 | 212 | 381 | 550
Four Color 209 ... 6 | 12 | 18 | 39 | 62 | 85

HARROWERS, THE (See Clive Barker's...)

HARSH REALM (Inspired 1999 TV series)
Harris Comics: 1993- No. 6, 1994 ($2.95, limited series)
1-6: Painted-c. Hudnall-s/Paquette & Ridgway-a ... 3.50
TPB (2000, $14.95) r/series ... 15.00

HARVEY
Marvel Comics: Oct, 1970; No. 2, 12/70; No. 3, 6/72 - No. 6, 12/72
1 ... 9 | 18 | 27 | 63 | 107 | 150
2-6 ... 6 | 12 | 18 | 41 | 66 | 90

HARVEY COLLECTORS COMICS (Titled Richie Rich Collectors Comics on cover of #6-on)
Harvey Publ.: Sept, 1975 - No. 15, Jan, 1978; No. 16, Oct, 1979 (52 pgs.)
1-Reprints Richie Rich #1,2 ... 2 | 4 | 6 | 11 | 16 | 20
2-10: 7-Splash pg. shows cover to Friendly Ghost Casper #1 ... 2 | 4 | 6 | 8 | 10 | 12
11-16: 16-Sad Sack-r ... 1 | 2 | 3 | 5 | 6 | 8

NOTE: All reprints: Casper-#2, 7, Richie Rich-#1, 3, 5, 6, 8-15, Sad Sack-#16. Wendy-#4.

HARVEY COMICS HITS (Formerly Joe Palooka #50)
Harvey Publications: No. 51, Oct, 1951 - No. 62, Apr, 1953
51-The Phantom ... 31 | 62 | 93 | 178 | 282 | 385
52-Steve Canyon's Air Power(Air Force sponsored) 13 | 26 | 39 | 72 | 101 | 130
53-Mandrake the Magician ... 20 | 40 | 60 | 117 | 184 | 250
54-Tim Tyler's Tales of Jungle Terror ... 13 | 26 | 39 | 74 | 105 | 135
55-Love Stories of Mary Worth ... 11 | 22 | 33 | 62 | 86 | 110
56-The Phantom; bondage-c ... 26 | 52 | 78 | 152 | 239 | 325
57-Rip Kirby Exposes the Kidnap Racket; entire book by Alex Raymond ... 15 | 30 | 45 | 85 | 130 | 175
58-Girls in White (nurses stories) ... 11 | 22 | 33 | 62 | 86 | 110
59-Tales of the Invisible featuring Scarlet O'Neil ... 12 | 24 | 36 | 67 | 94 | 120
60-Paramount Animated Comics #1 (9/52) (3rd app. Baby Huey); 2nd Harvey app. Baby Huey & Casper the Friendly Ghost (1st in Little Audrey #25 (8/52)); 1st app. Herman & Catnip (c/story) & Buzzy the Crow ... 41 | 82 | 123 | 256 | 416 | 575
61-Casper the Friendly Ghost #6 (3rd Harvey Casper, 8/52)-Casper-c ... 46 | 92 | 138 | 281 | 466 | 650
62-Paramount Animated Comics #2; Herman & Catnip, Baby Huey & Buzzy the Crow ... 17 | 34 | 51 | 98 | 154 | 210

HARVEY COMICS LIBRARY
Harvey Publications: Apr, 1952 - No. 2, 1952
1-Teen-Age Dope Slaves as exposed by Rex Morgan, M.D.; drug propaganda story; used in SOTI, pg. 27 ... 145 | 290 | 435 | 906 | 1503 | 2100
2-Dick Tracy Presents Sparkle Plenty in "Blackmail Terror" ... 20 | 40 | 60 | 117 | 184 | 250

HARVEY COMICS SPOTLIGHT
Harvey Comics: Sept, 1987 - No. 4, Mar, 1988 (75¢/$1.00)
1-New material; begin 75¢, ends #3; Sand Sack ... 5.00
2-4: 2,4-All new material. 2-Baby Huey. 3-Little Dot; contains reprints w/5 pg. new story.
4-$1.00-c; Little Audrey ... 4.00
NOTE: No. 5 was advertised but not published.

HARVEY HITS (Also see Tastee-Freez Comics in the Promotional Comics section)
Harvey Publications: Sept, 1957 - No. 122, Nov, 1967
1-The Phantom ... 25 | 50 | 75 | 184 | 330 | 475
2-Rags Rabbit (10/57) ... 5 | 10 | 15 | 32 | 51 | 70
3-Richie Rich (11/57)-r/Little Dot; 1st book devoted to Richie Rich; see Little Dot for 1st app. ... 122 | 244 | 366 | 1037 | 1919 | 2800
4-Little Dot's Uncles (12/57) ... 16 | 32 | 48 | 118 | 209 | 300
5-Stevie Mazie's Boy Friend (1/58) ... 4 | 8 | 12 | 26 | 41 | 55
6-The Phantom (2/58); Kirby-c; 2pg. Powell-a ... 17 | 34 | 51 | 122 | 216 | 310
7-Wendy the Good Little Witch (3/58, pre-dates Wendy #1; 1st book devoted to Wendy) ... 25 | 50 | 75 | 184 | 330 | 475
8-Sad Sack's Army Life; George Baker-c ... 8 | 16 | 24 | 51 | 78 | 105
9-Richie Rich's Golden Deeds; (2nd book devoted to Richie Rich) reprints Richie Rich story from Tastee-Freez #1 ... 50 | 100 | 150 | 413 | 757 | 1100
10-Little Lotta's Lunch Box ... 10 | 20 | 30 | 73 | 129 | 185
11-Little Audrey Summer Fun (7/58) ... 8 | 16 | 24 | 58 | 97 | 135
12-The Phantom; Kirby-c; 2pg. Powell-a (8/58) ... 14 | 28 | 42 | 99 | 175 | 250
13-Little Dot's Uncles (9/58); Richie Rich 1pg. ... 10 | 20 | 30 | 73 | 129 | 185
14-Herman & Katnip (10/58, TV/movies) ... 4 | 8 | 12 | 26 | 41 | 55
15-The Phantom (12/58)-1 pg. origin ... 14 | 28 | 42 | 99 | 175 | 250
16-Wendy the Good Little Witch (1/59); Casper app. ... 11 | 22 | 33 | 79 | 140 | 200
17-Sad Sack's Army Life (2/59) ... 6 | 12 | 18 | 39 | 62 | 85
18-Buzzy & the Crow ... 4 | 8 | 12 | 26 | 41 | 55
19-Little Audrey (4/59) ... 6 | 12 | 18 | 37 | 59 | 80
20-Casper & Spooky ... 8 | 16 | 24 | 52 | 86 | 120
21-Wendy the Witch ... 8 | 16 | 24 | 52 | 86 | 120
22-Sad Sack's Army Life ... 5 | 10 | 15 | 30 | 48 | 65
23-Wendy the Witch (8/59) ... 8 | 16 | 24 | 52 | 86 | 120
24-Little Dot's Uncles (9/59); Richie Rich 1pg. ... 9 | 18 | 27 | 60 | 100 | 140
25-Herman & Katnip (10/59) ... 4 | 8 | 12 | 22 | 34 | 45
26-The Phantom (11/59) ... 10 | 20 | 30 | 73 | 129 | 185
27-Wendy the Good Little Witch (12/59) ... 7 | 14 | 21 | 50 | 83 | 115
28-Sad Sack's Army Life (1/60) ... 4 | 8 | 12 | 26 | 41 | 55
29-Harvey-Toon (No.1)('60); Casper, Buzzy ... 5 | 10 | 15 | 35 | 55 | 75
30-Wendy the Witch (3/60) ... 7 | 14 | 21 | 50 | 83 | 115
31-Herman & Katnip (4/60) ... 3 | 6 | 9 | 20 | 30 | 40
32-Sad Sack's Army Life (5/60) ... 4 | 8 | 12 | 22 | 34 | 45
33-Wendy the Witch (6/60) ... 7 | 14 | 21 | 47 | 76 | 105
34-Harvey-Toon (7/60) ... 4 | 8 | 12 | 24 | 37 | 50
35-Funday Funnies (8/60) ... 3 | 6 | 9 | 20 | 30 | 40

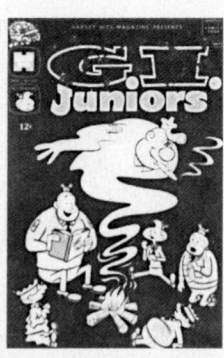
Harvey Hits #107 © HARV

Hate Annual #1 © Peter Bagge

The Haunted #1 © Chaos!

	GD 2.0	VG 4.0	FN 6.0	VF 8.0	VF/NM 9.0	NM- 9.2
36-The Phantom (1960)	10	20	30	68	119	170
37-Casper & Nightmare	6	12	18	37	59	80
38-Harvey-Toon	4	8	12	24	37	50
39-Sad Sack's Army Life (12/60)	3	6	9	21	32	42
40-Funday Funnies (1/61)	3	6	9	17	25	32
41-Herman & Katnip	3	6	9	17	25	32
42-Harvey-Toon (3/61)	3	6	9	19	29	38
43-Sad Sack's Army Life (4/61)	3	6	9	19	29	38
44-The Phantom (5/61)	9	18	27	65	113	160
45-Casper & Nightmare	5	10	15	30	48	65
46-Harvey-Toon (7/61)	3	6	9	17	25	32
47-Sad Sack's Army Life (8/61)	3	6	9	17	25	32
48-The Phantom (9/61)	9	18	27	65	113	160
49-Stumbo the Giant (1st app. in Hot Stuff)	9	18	27	65	113	160
50-Harvey-Toon (11/61)	3	6	9	16	23	30
51-Sad Sack's Army Life (12/61)	3	6	9	16	23	30
52-Casper & Nightmare	4	8	12	28	44	60
53-Harvey-Toons (2/62)	3	6	9	16	23	30
54-Stumbo the Giant	5	10	15	35	55	75
55-Sad Sack's Army Life (4/62)	3	6	9	16	23	30
56-Casper & Nightmare	4	8	12	26	41	55
57-Stumbo the Giant	5	10	15	35	55	75
58-Sad Sack's Army Life	3	6	9	16	23	30
59-Casper & Nightmare (7/62)	4	8	12	26	41	55
60-Stumbo the Giant (9/62)	5	10	15	35	55	75
61-Sad Sack's Army Life	3	6	9	16	22	28
62-Casper & Nightmare	4	8	12	23	36	48
63-Stumbo the Giant	4	8	12	28	44	60
64-Sad Sack's Army Life (1/63)	3	6	9	16	22	28
65-Casper & Nightmare	4	8	12	23	36	48
66-Stumbo The Giant (3/63)	4	8	12	28	44	60
67-Sad Sack's Army Life (4/63)	3	6	9	16	22	28
68-Casper & Nightmare	4	8	12	23	36	48
69-Stumbo the Giant (6/63)	4	8	12	28	44	60
70-Sad Sack's Army Life (7/63)	3	6	9	16	22	28
71-Casper & Nightmare (8/63)	3	6	9	21	32	42
72-Stumbo the Giant	4	8	12	28	44	60
73-Little Sad Sack (10/63)	3	6	9	16	22	28
74-Sad Sack's Muttsy… (11/63)	3	6	9	16	22	28
75-Casper & Nightmare	3	6	9	19	29	38
76-Little Sad Sack	3	6	9	16	22	28
77-Sad Sack's Muttsy…	3	6	9	16	22	28
78-Stumbo the Giant (3/64); JFK caricature	4	8	12	28	44	60

79-87: 79-Little Sad Sack (4/64). 80-Sad Sack's Muttsy… (5/64). 81-Little Sad Sack. 82-Sad Sack's Muttsy… 83-Little Sad Sack(8/64). 84-Sad Sack's Muttsy… 85-Gabby Gob (#1) (10/64). 86-G. I. Juniors (#1)(11/64). 87-Sad Sack's Muttsy… (12/64)

	3	6	9	16	22	28
88-Stumbo the Giant (1/65)	4	8	12	28	44	60

89-122: 89-Sad Sack's Muttsy… 90-Gabby Gob. 91-G. I. Juniors. 92-Sad Sack's Muttsy… (5/65). 93-Sadie Sack (6/65). 94-Gabby Gob. 95-G. I. Juniors (8/65). 96-Sad Sack's Muttsy… (11/65). 97-Gabby Gob (10/65). 98-G. I. Juniors (11/65). 99-Sad Sack's Muttsy… (12/65). 100-Gabby Gob(1/66). 101-G. I. Juniors (2/66). 102-Sad Sack's Muttsy… (3/66). 103-Gabby Gob. 104- G. I. Juniors. 105-Sad Sack's Muttsy… 106-Gabby Gob (7/66). 107-G. I. Juniors (8/66). 108-Sad Sack's Muttsy…109-Gabby Gob. 110-G. I. Juniors (11/66). 111-Sad Sack's Muttsy… (12/66). 112-G. I. Juniors. 113-Sad Sack's Muttsy… 114-G. I. Juniors. 115-Sad Sack's Muttsy… 116-G. I. Juniors (5/67). 117-Sad Sack's Muttsy… 118-G. I. Juniors. 119-Sad Sack's Muttsy… (8/67). 120-G. I. Juniors (9/67). 121-Sad Sack's Muttsy… (10/67). 122-G. I. Juniors (11/67)

	2	4	6	10	14	18

HARVEY HITS COMICS
Harvey Publications: Nov, 1986 - No. 6, Oct, 1987

	GD 2.0	VG 4.0	FN 6.0	VF 8.0	VF/NM 9.0	NM- 9.2
1-Little Lotta, Little Dot, Wendy & Baby Huey	1	2	3	4	5	7
2-6: 3-Xmas-c						4.50

HARVEY POP COMICS (Rock Happening) (Teen Humor)
Harvey Publications: Oct, 1968 - No. 2, Nov, 1969 (Both are 68 pg. Giants)

1-The Cowsills	5	10	15	35	55	75
2-Bunny	5	10	15	30	48	65

HARVEY 3-D HITS (See Sad Sack)

HARVEY-TOON (…S) (See Harvey Hits No. 29, 34, 38, 42, 46, 50, 53)

HARVEY WISEGUYS (…Digest #7 on)
Harvey Comics: Nov, 1987; #2, Nov, 1988; #3, Apr, 1989 - No. 4, Nov, 1989 (98 pgs, digest-size, $1.25/$1.75)

1-Hot Stuff, Spooky, etc.	1	2	3	4	5	7

	GD 2.0	VG 4.0	FN 6.0	VF 8.0	VF/NM 9.0	NM- 9.2
2-4: 2 (68 pgs.)						4.50

HATARI (See Movie Classics)

HATE
Fantagraphics Books: Spr, 1990 - No. 30, 1998 ($2.50/$2.95, B&W/color)

1	2	4	6	10	12	15
2-3	1	2	3	5	6	8
4-10						5.00
11-20: 16- color begins						4.00
21-29						3.00
30-($3.95) Last issue						4.00
Annual 1 (2/01, $3.95) Peter Bagge-s/a						4.00
Annual 2-6 (12/01-Present; $4.95) Peter Bagge-s/a						5.00
Buddy Bites the Bullet! (2001, $16.95) r/Buddy stories in color						17.00
Buddy Go Home! (1997, $16.95) r/Buddy stories in color						17.00
Hate-Ball Special Edition ($3.95, giveaway)-reprints						4.00
Hate Jamboree (10/98, $4.50) old & new cartoons						4.50

HATHAWAYS, THE (TV)
Dell Publishing Co.: No. 1298, Feb-Apr, 1962 (one-shot)

Four Color 1298-Photo-c	5	10	15	30	48	65

HAUNTED (See This Magazine Is Haunted)

HAUNTED (Baron Weirwulf's Haunted Library on-c #21 on)
Charlton Comics: 9/71 - No. 30, 11/76; No. 31, 9/77 - No. 75, 9/84

1-All Ditko issue	4	8	12	28	44	60
2-7-Ditko-c/a	3	6	9	16	23	30
8,12,28-Ditko-a	2	4	6	10	14	18
9,19	2	4	6	8	11	14
10,20,15,18: 10,20-Sutton-a. 15-Sutton-c	2	4	6	8	11	14
11,13,14,16-Ditko-c/a	2	4	6	11	16	20
17-Sutton-c/a; Newton-a	2	4	6	9	12	15
21-Newton-c/a; Sutton-a; 1st Baron Weirwulf	3	6	9	16	22	28
22-Newton-c/a; Sutton-a	2	4	6	9	13	16
23,24-Sutton-c; Ditko-a	2	4	6	9	13	16
25-27,29,32,33	1	3	5	6	8	10
30,41,47,49-52,60,74-Ditko-c/a. 51-Reprints #1	1	3	4	6	8	10
31,35,37,38-Sutton-a	1	3	4	6	8	10
34,36,39,40,42,57-Ditko-a	2	4	6	10	12	14
43-46,48,53-56,58,59,61-73: 59-Newton-a. 64-Sutton-c. 71-73-Low print						
75 (9/84) Last issue; low print	2	4	6	9	13	16

NOTE: **Aparo** c-45. **Ditko** a-1-8, 11-16, 18, 23, 24, 28, 30, 34r, 36r, 39-42r, 47r, 49-52r, 57, 60, 74. c-1-7, 11, 13, 14, 16, 30, 41, 47, 49-52, 74. **Howard** a-6, 9, 18, 22, 25, 32. **Kim** a-9, 19. **Morisi** a-13. **Newton** a-17, 21, 59r; c-21, 22(painted). **Staton** a-11, 12, 18, 21, 22, 30, 33, 35, 38; c-18, 33, 38. **Sutton** a-10, 17, 20-22, 31, 35, 37, 38; c-15, 17, 18, 23(painted), 24(painted), 27, 64r. #49 reprints Tales of the Mysterious Traveler #4.

HAUNTED, THE
Chaos! Comics: Jan, 2002 - No. 4, Apr, 2002 ($2.99, limited series)

1-4-Peter David-s/Nat Jones-a						3.00
…: Gray Matters (7/02, $2.99) David-s/Jones-a						3.00

HAUNTED LOVE
Charlton Comics: Apr, 1973 - No. 11, Sept, 1975

1-Tom Sutton-a (16 pgs.)	5	10	15	30	48	65
2,3,6,7,10,11	3	6	9	16	22	28
4,5-Ditko-a	3	6	9	18	27	35
8,9-Newton-a	3	6	9	16	23	30
Modern Comics #1(1978)	2	4	6	8	11	14

NOTE: **Howard** a-8i. **Kim** a-7-9. **Newton** c-8, 9. **Staton** a-1-6. **Sutton** a-1, 3-5, 10, 11.

HAUNTED MAN, THE
Dark Horse Comics: Mar, 2000 ($2.95, unfinished limited series)

1-Gerald Jones-s/Mark Badger-a						3.00

HAUNTED THRILLS (Tales of Horror and Terror)
Ajax/Farrell Publications: June, 1952 - No. 18, Nov-Dec, 1954

1-r/Ellery Queen #1	55	110	165	344	572	800
2-L. B. Cole-a r/Ellery Queen #1	40	80	120	235	368	500
3-5: 3-Drug use story	34	68	102	197	311	425
6-10,12: 7-Hitler story	30	60	90	172	271	370
11-Nazi death camp story	31	62	93	180	285	390
13-18: 18-Lingerie panels. 14-Jesus Christ apps. in story by Webb. 15-Jo-Jo-r	24	48	72	139	220	300

NOTE: **Kamenish** art in most issues. **Webb** a-12.

HAUNT OF FEAR (Formerly Gunfighter)
E. C. Comics: No. 15, May-June, 1950 - No. 28, Nov-Dec, 1954

Haunt of Fear #15 © WMG

Haven: The Broken City #6 © DC

Hawkgirl #63 © DC

	GD 2.0	VG 4.0	FN 6.0	VF 8.0	VF/NM 9.0	NM- 9.2

15(#1, 1950)(Scarce) — 279 558 837 2232 3491 4750

16-1st app. "The Witches Cauldron" & the Old Witch (by Kamen); begin series as hostess of Haunt of Fear — 119 238 357 952 1489 2025

17-Origin of Crypt of Terror, Vault of Horror, & Haunt of Fear; used in SOTI, pg. 43; last pg. Ingels-a used by N.Y. Legis. Comm.; story "Monster Maker" based on Frankenstein. Old Witch by Feldstein — 119 238 357 952 1489 2025

4-Ingels becomes regular artist for Old Witch. 1st Vault Keeper & Crypt Keeper app. in HOF; begin series — 74 148 222 592 926 1260

5-Injury-to-eye panel, pg. 4 of Wood story — 58 116 174 464 725 985

6,7,9,10: 6-Crypt Keeper by Feldstein begins. 9-Crypt Keeper by Davis begins. 10-Ingels biog. — 43 86 129 344 540 735

8-Classic Feldstein Shrunken Head-c — 46 92 138 368 577 785

11,12: Classic Ingels-c; 11-Kamen biog. 12-Feldstein biog. — 35 70 105 280 440 600

13,15,16,20: 16-Ray Bradbury adaptation. 20-Feldstein-r/Vault of Horror #12 — 33 66 99 264 415 565

14-Origin Old Witch by Ingels; classic-Ingels-c — 48 96 144 384 597 810

17-Classic Ingels-c — 35 70 105 280 440 600

18-Old Witch-c; Ray Bradbury adaptation & biography — 35 70 105 280 440 600

19-Used in SOTI, ill. "A comic book baseball game" & Senate investigation on juvenile delinq. bondage/decapitation-c — 43 86 129 344 540 735

21-27: 23-Used in SOTI, pg. 241. 24-Used in Senate Investigative Report, pg.8. 26-Contains anti-censorship editorial, 'Are you a Red Dupe?' 27-Cannibalism story; Vault Keeper shown reading SOTI — 24 48 72 192 296 400

28-Low distribution — 31 62 93 248 392 535

NOTE: (Canadian reprints known; see Table of Contents). Craig a-15-17, 5, 7, 10, 12, 13; c-15-17, 5-7. Crandall a-20, 21, 26, 27. Davis a-4-26, 28. Evans a-15-19, 22-25, 27. Feldstein a-15-17, 20; c-4, 8-10. Ingels a-16, 17, 4-28; c-11-28. Kamen a-16, 4, 6, 7, 9-11, 13-19, 21-28. Krigstein a-28. Kurtzman a-15(#1), 17(#3). Orlando a-9, 12. Wood a-15, 16, 4-6.

HAUNT OF FEAR, THE
Gladstone Publishing: May, 1991 - No. 2, July, 1991 ($2.00, 68 pgs.)

1,2: 1-Ghastly Ingels-c(r); 2-Craig-c(r) — 3.00

HAUNT OF FEAR
Russ Cochran/Gemstone Publ.: Sept, 1991 - No. 5, 1992 ($2.00, 68 pgs.); Nov, 1992 - No. 28, Aug, 1998 ($1.50/$2.00/$2.50)

1-28: 1-Ingels-c(r). 1-3-r/HOF #15-17 with original-c. 4,5-r/HOF #4,5 with original-c — 2.50
Annual 1-5: 1- r/#1-5. 2- r/#6-10. 3- r/#11-15. 4- r/#16-20. 5- r/#21-25 — 14.00
Annual 6-r/#26-28 — 9.00

HAUNT OF HORROR, THE (Digest)
Marvel Comics: Jun, 1973 - No. 2, Aug, 1973 (164 pgs.; text and art)

1-Morrow painted skull-c; stories by Ellison, Howard, and Leiber; Brunner-a — 4 8 12 22 34 45

2-Kelly Freas painted bondage-c; stories by McCaffrey, Goulart, Leiber, Ellison; art by Simonson, Brunner, and Buscema — 3 6 9 16 23 30

HAUNT OF HORROR, THE (Magazine)
Cadence Comics Publ. (Marvel): May, 1974 - No. 5, Jan, 1975 (75¢) (B&W)

1,2: 2-Origin & 1st app. Gabriel the Devil Hunter; Satana begins — 3 6 9 14 19 24

3-5: 4-Neal Adams-a. 5-Evans-a(2) — 3 6 9 16 23 30
NOTE: Alcala a-2. Colan a-2p. Heath r-1. Krigstein r-3. Reese a-1. Simonson a-1.

HAUNT OF HORROR: EDGAR ALLAN POE
Marvel Comics (MAX): July, 2006 - No. 3, Sept, 2006 ($3.99, B&W, limited series)

1-3- Poe-inspired/adapted stories with Richard Corben-a — 3.00
HC (2006, $19.99) r/series; cover sketches — 20.00

HAVE GUN, WILL TRAVEL (TV)
Dell Publishing Co.: No. 931, 8/58 - No. 14, 7-9/62 (All Richard Boone photo-c)

Four Color 931 (#1) — 13 26 39 95 168 240
Four Color 983,1044 (#2,3) — 9 18 27 60 100 140
4 (1-3/60) - 10 — 8 16 24 54 90 125
11-14 — 8 16 24 52 86 120

HAVEN: THE BROKEN CITY (See JLA/Haven: Arrival and JLA/Haven: Anathema)
DC Comics: Feb, 2002 - No. 9, Oct, 2002 ($2.50, limited series)

1-9-Olivetti-c/a; 1- JLA app. Series concludes in JLA/Haven: Anathema — 2.50

HAVOK & WOLVERINE - MELTDOWN (See Marvel Comics Presents #24)
Marvel Comics (Epic Comics): Mar, 1989 - No. 4, Oct, 1989 ($3.50, mini-series, square-bound, mature)

1-4: Art by Kent Williams & Jon J. Muth; story by Walt & Louise Simonson — 4.00

HAWAIIAN DICK

Image Comics: Dec, 2002 - No. 3, Feb, 2003 ($2.95, limited series)

1-3-B. Clay Moore-s/Steven Griffin-a — 3.00
....: Byrd of Paradise TPB (8/03, $14.95) r/#1-3, script & sketch pages — 15.00

HAWAIIAN DICK: THE LAST RESORT
Image Comics: Aug, 2004 - No. 4, June, 2006 ($2.95/$2.99, limited series)

1-4-B. Clay Moore-s/Steven Griffin-a — 3.00
Vol. 2 TPB (10/06, $14.99) r/#1-4 & the original series pitch — 15.00

HAWAIIAN EYE (TV)
Gold Key: July, 1963 (Troy Donahue, Connie Stevens photo-c)

1 (10073-307) — 5 10 15 35 55 75

HAWAIIAN ILLUSTRATED LEGENDS SERIES
Hogarth Press: 1975 (B&W)(Cover printed w/blue, yellow, and green)

1-Kalelealuaka, the Mysterious Warrior — 5.00

HAWK, THE (Also see Approved Comics #1, 7 & Tops In Adventure)
Ziff-Davis/St. John Publ. Co. No. 4 on: Wint/51 - No. 3, 11-12/52; No. 4, 1-2/53; No. 8, 9/54 - No. 12, 5/55 (Painted c-1-4)(#5-7 don't exist)

1-Anderson-a — 20 40 60 115 180 245
2 (Sum, '52)-Kubert, Infantino-a — 12 24 36 69 97 125
3-4,11: 11-Buckskin Belle & The Texan app. — 10 20 30 56 76 95
8-10,12: 8(9/54)-Reprints #3 w/different-c by Baker. 9-Baker-a(r)/#2. 10-Baker-c/a; r/one story from #2. 12-Baker-c/a; Buckskin Belle app. — 14 28 42 80 115 150
3-D (11/53, 25¢)-Came w/glasses; Baker-c — 32 64 96 186 293 400
NOTE: Baker c-8-12. Larsen a-10. Tuska a-1, 9, 12. Painted c-1, 4, 7.

HAWK AND THE DOVE, THE (See Showcase #75 & Teen Titans) (1st series)
National Periodical Publications: Aug-Sept, 1968 - No. 6, June-July, 1969

1-Ditko-c/a — 8 16 24 54 90 125
2-6: 5-Teen Titans cameo — 5 10 15 32 51 70
NOTE: Ditko c/a-1, 2. Gil Kane a-3p, 4p, 5, 6p; c-3-6.

HAWK AND DOVE (2nd Series)
DC Comics: Oct, 1988 - No. 5, Feb, 1989 ($1.00, limited series)

1-Rob Liefeld-c/a(p) in all — 4.00
2-5 — 3.00
Trade paperback ('93, $9.95)-Reprints #1-5 — 10.00

HAWK AND DOVE
DC Comics: June, 1989 - No. 28, Oct, 1991 ($1.00)

1-28 — 2.50
Annual 1,2 ('90, '91, $2.00) 1-Liefeld pin-up. 2-Armageddon 2001 x-over — 3.00

HAWK AND DOVE
DC Comics: Nov, 1997 - No. 5, Mar, 1998 ($2.50, limited series)

1-5-Baron-s/Zachary & Giordano-a — 2.50

HAWK AND WINDBLADE (See Elflord)
Warp Graphics: Aug, 1997 - No.2, Sept, 1997 ($2.95, limited series)

1,2-Blair-s/Chan-c/a — 3.00

HAWKEYE (See The Avengers #16 & Tales Of Suspense #57)
Marvel Comics Group: Sept, 1983 - No. 4, Dec, 1983 (limited series)

1-4: Mark Gruenwald-a/scripts. 1-Origin Hawkeye. 3-Origin Mockingbird. 4-Hawkeye & Mockingbird elope — 3.00

HAWKEYE
Marvel Comics: Jan, 1994 - No. 4, Apr, 1994 ($1.75, limited series)

1-4 — 2.50

HAWKEYE (Volume 2)
Marvel Comics: Dec, 2003 - No. 8, Aug, 2004 ($2.99)

1-8: 1-6-Nicieza-s/Raffaele-a. 7,8-Bennett-a; Black Widow app. — 3.00

HAWKEYE & THE LAST OF THE MOHICANS (TV)
Dell Publishing Co.: No. 884, Mar, 1958 (one-shot)

Four Color 884-Photo-c — 7 14 21 47 76 105

HAWKEYE: EARTH'S MIGHTIEST MARKSMAN
Marvel Comics: Oct, 1998 ($2.99, one-shot)

1-Justice and Firestar app.; DeFalco-s — 3.00

HAWKGIRL (Title continued from Hawkman #49, Apr, 2006)
DC Comics: No. 50, May, 2006 - No. 66, Sept, 2007 ($2.50/$2.99)

50-66: 50-Chaykin-a/Simonson-s begin; One Year Later. 52-Begin $2.99-c. 57,58-Bennett-a. 59-Blackfire app. 63-Batman app. 64-Superman app. — 3.00

Hawkman #5 © DC

Hawkmoon: The Jewel in the Skull #2 © FC

Headline Comics #4 © PRIZE

	GD 2.0	VG 4.0	FN 6.0	VF 8.0	VF/NM 9.0	NM- 9.2

...: The Maw TPB (2007, $17.99) r/#50-56 — 18.00

HAWKMAN (See Atom & Hawkman, The Brave & the Bold, DC Comics Presents, Detective Comics, Flash Comics, Hawkworld, JSA, Justice League of America #31, Legend of the Hawkman, Mystery in Space, Shadow War Of..., Showcase, & World's Finest #256)

HAWKMAN (1st Series) (Also see The Atom #7 & Brave & the Bold #34-36, 42-44, 51)
National Periodical Publications: Apr-May, 1964 - No. 27, Aug-Sept, 1968

1-(4-5/64)-Anderson-c/a begins, ends #21	50	100	150	425	788	1150
2	22	44	66	164	292	420
3,5: 5-2nd app. Shadow Thief	14	28	42	102	181	260
4-Origin & 1st app. Zatanna (10-11/64)	17	34	51	128	227	325
6	11	22	33	75	133	190
7	9	18	27	65	113	160
8-10: 9-Atom cameo; Hawkman & Atom learn each other's I.D.; 3rd app. Shadow Thief	8	16	24	58	97	135
11-15	7	14	21	45	73	100
16,17-27: 18-Adam Strange x-over (cameo #19). 25-G.A. Hawkman-r by Moldoff. 26-Kirby-a(r). 27-Kubert-c	5	10	15	35	55	75

HAWKMAN (2nd Series)
DC Comics: Aug, 1986 - No. 17, Dec, 1987

1-17: 10-Byrne-c. Special #1 (1986, $1.25)						2.50
Trade paperback (1989, $19.95)-r/Brave and the Bold #34-36,42-44 by Kubert; Kubert-c						20.00

HAWKMAN (4th Series)(See both Hawkworld limited & ongoing series)
DC Comics: Sept, 1993 - No. 33, July, 1996 ($1.75/$1.95/$2.25)

1-($2.50)-Gold foil embossed-c; storyline cont'd from Hawkworld ongoing series; new costume & powers.						3.00
2-13,0,14-33: 2-Green Lantern x-over. 3-Airstryke app. 4,6-Wonder Woman app. 13-(9/94)-Zero Hour. 0-(10/94). 14-(11/94). 15-Aquaman-c & app. 23-Wonder Woman app. 25-Kent Williams-c. 29,30-Chaykin-c. 32-Breyfogle-c						2.50
Annual 1 (1993, $2.50, 68 pgs.)-Bloodlines Earthplague						3.00
Annual 2 (1995, $3.95)-Year One story						4.00

HAWKMAN (Title continues as Hawkgirl #50-on) (See JSA #23 for return)
DC Comics: May, 2002 - No. 49, Apr, 2006 ($2.50)

1-Johns & Robinson-s/Morales-a						5.00
1-2nd printing						2.50
2-40: 2-4-Shadow Thief app. 5,6-Green Arrow-c/app. 8-Atom-c/app. 13-Van Sciver-a. 14-Gentleman Ghost app. 15-Hawkwoman app. 16-Byth returns. 23-25-Black Reign x-over with JSA #56-58. 26-Byrne-c/a. 29,30-Land-c. 37-Golden Eagle returns						2.50
41-49: 41-Hawkman killed. 43-Golden Eagle origin. 46-49-Adam Kubert-c						2.50
...: Allies & Enemies TPB (2004, $14.95) r/#7-14 & pages from Secret Files and Origins						15.00
...: Endless Flight TPB (2003, $12.95) r/#1-6 & Secret Files and Origins						13.00
...: Rise of the Golden Eagle TPB (2006, $17.99) r/#37-45						18.00
... Secret Files and Origins (10/02, $4.95) profiles and pin-ups by various						5.00
... Wings of Fury TPB (2005, $17.99) r/#15-22						18.00

HAWKMOON: THE JEWEL IN THE SKULL
First Comics: May, 1986 - No. 4, Nov, 1986 ($1.75, limited series, Baxter paper)

1-4: Adapts novel by Michael Moorcock						2.50

HAWKMOON: THE MAD GOD'S AMULET
First Comics: Jan, 1987 - No. 4, July, 1987 ($1.75, limited series, Baxter paper)

1-4: Adapts novel by Michael Moorcock						2.50

HAWKMOON: THE RUNESTAFF
First Comics: Jun, 1988 - No. 4, Dec, 1988 ($1.75-$1.95, lim. series, Baxter paper)

1-4: ($1.75) Adapts novel by Michael Moorcock. 3,4 ($1.95)						2.50

HAWKMOON: THE SWORD OF DAWN
First Comics: Sept, 1987 - No. 4, Mar, 1988 ($1.75, lim. series, Baxter paper)

1-4: Dorman painted-c; adapts Moorcock novel						2.50

HAWKS OF THE SEAS (WILL EISNER'S...)
Dark Horse Comics: July, 2003 ($19.95, B&W, hardcover)

nn-Reprints 1937-1939 weekly Pirate serial by Will Eisner; Williamson intro.						20.00

HAWKWORLD
DC Comics: 1989 - No. 3, 1989 ($3.95, prestige format, limited series)

Book 1-3: 1-Tim Truman story & art in all; Hawkman dons new costume; reintro Byth						4.00
TPB (1991, $16.95) r/#1-3						17.00

HAWKWORLD (3rd Series)
DC Comics: June, 1990 - No. 32, May, 1993 ($1.50/$1.75)

1-Hawkman spin-off; story cont'd from limited series.						3.00
2-32: 15,16-War of the Gods x-over. 22-J'onn J'onzz app.						2.50
Annual 1-3 ('90-'92, $2.95, 68 pgs.), 2-2nd printing with silver ink-c						3.00

NOTE: *Truman* a-30-32; c-27-32, Annual 1.

HAYWIRE
DC Comics: Oct, 1988 - No. 13, Sept, 1989 ($1.25, mature)

1-13						2.50

HAZARD
Image Comics (WildStorm Prod.): June, 1996 - No. 7, Nov, 1996 ($1.75)

1-7: 1-Intro Hazard; Jeff Mariotte scripts begin; Jim Lee-c(p)						3.00

HEADHUNTERS
Image Comics: Apr, 1997 - No. 3, June, 1997 ($2.95, B&W)

1-3: Chris Marrinan-s/a						3.00

HEADLINE COMICS
DC Comics: Jan. 1942

nn - Ashcan comic, not distributed to newsstands, only for in-house use. Cover art is More Fun Comics #73 with interior being Star Spangled Comics #2   (no known sales)

HEADLINE COMICS (...For the American Boy) (...Crime No. 32-39)
Prize Publ./American Boys' Comics: Feb, 1943 - No. 22, Nov-Dec, 1946; No. 23, 1947 - No. 77, Oct, 1956

1-Junior Rangers-c/stories begin; Yank & Doodle x-over in Junior Rangers (Junior Rangers are Uncle Sam's nephews)	57	114	171	356	591	825
2	34	68	102	197	311	425
3-Used in **POP**, pg. 84	23	46	69	135	213	290
4-7,9,10: 4,9,10-Hitler stories in each	19	38	57	112	176	240
8-Classic Hitler-c	76	152	228	475	788	1100
11,12	17	34	51	98	154	210
13-15-Blue Streak in all	18	36	54	105	165	225
16-Origin & 1st app. Atomic Man (11-12/45)	27	54	81	158	249	340
17,18,20,21: 21-Atomic Man ends (9-10/46)	15	30	45	86	133	180
19-S&K-a	31	62	93	178	282	385
22-Last Junior Rangers; Kiefer-c	14	28	42	78	112	145
23,24: (All S&K-a). 23-Valentine's Day Massacre story; content changes to true crime. 24-Dope-crazy killer story	30	60	90	172	271	370
25-35-S&K-c/a. 25-Powell-a	27	54	81	158	249	340
36-S&K-a; photo-c begin	21	42	63	120	188	255
37-1 pg. S&K, Severin-a; rare Kirby photo-c app.	21	42	63	120	188	255
38,40-Meskin-a	10	20	30	56	76	95
39,41-43,46-50,52-55: 41-J. Edgar Hoover 26th Anniversary Issue with photo on-c						
43,49-Meskin-a	9	18	27	47	61	75
44-S&K-c; Severin/Elder, Meskin-a	14	28	42	82	121	160
45-Kirby-a	12	24	36	69	97	125
51-Kirby-c	11	22	33	60	83	105
56-S&K-a	14	28	42	80	115	150
57-77: 72-Meskin-c/a(i)	8	16	24	40	50	60

NOTE: *Hollingsworth* a-30. Photo c-36-43. *H. C. Kiefer* c-12-16, 22. Atomic Man c-17-19.

HEADMAN
Innovation Publishing: 1990 ($2.50, mature)

1-Sci/fi						2.50

HEAP, THE
Skywald Publications: Sept, 1971 (52 pgs.)

1-Kinstler-r/Strange Worlds #8; new-s w/Sutton-a	3	6	9	18	27	35

HEART AND SOUL
Mikeross Publications: April-May, 1954 - No. 2, June-July, 1954

1,2	8	16	24	42	54	65

HEARTBREAKERS (Also see Dark Horse Presents)
Dark Horse Comics: Apr, 1996 - No. 4, July, 1996 ($2.95, limited series)

1-4: 1-W/paper doll & pin-up. 2-Alex Ross pin-up. 3-Evan Dorkin pin-ups. 4-Brereton-c; Matt Wagner pin-up						3.00
...Superdigest (7/98, $9.95, digest-size) new stories						10.00

HEARTLAND (See Hellblazer)
DC Comics (Vertigo): Mar, 1997 ($4.95, one-shot, mature)

1-Garth Ennis-s/Steve Dillon-c/a						5.00

HEART OF DARKNESS
Hardline Studios: 1994 ($2.95)

1-Brereton-c						3.00

HEART OF EMPIRE
Dark Horse Comics: Apr, 1999 - No. 9, Dec, 1999 ($2.95, limited series)

1-9-Bryan Talbot-s/a						3.00

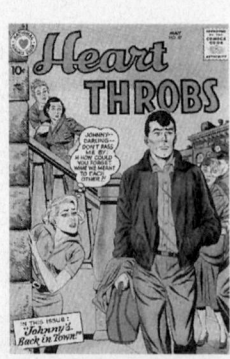

Heart Throbs #47 © DC

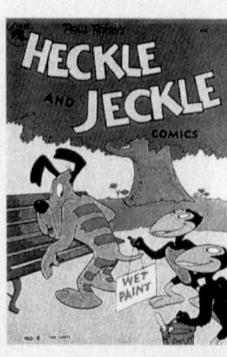

Heckle and Jeckle Comics #6 © CBS

Hedy Devine Comics #29 © MAR

	GD 2.0	VG 4.0	FN 6.0	VF 8.0	VF/NM 9.0	NM- 9.2

HEART OF THE BEAST, THE
DC Comics (Vertigo): 1994 ($19.95, hardcover, mature)

1-Dean Motter scripts						20.00

HEARTS OF DARKNESS (See Ghost Rider; Wolverine; Punisher: Hearts of...)

HEART THROBS (Love Stories No. 147 on)
Quality Comics/National Periodical #47(4-5/57) on (Arleigh #48-101): 8/49 - No. 8, 10/50;
No. 9, 3/52 - No. 146, Oct, 1972

	GD 2.0	VG 4.0	FN 6.0	VF 8.0	VF/NM 9.0	NM- 9.2
1-Classic Ward-c, Gustavson-a, 9 pgs.	42	84	126	258	422	585
2-Ward-c/a (9 pgs); Gustavson-a	26	52	78	152	239	325
3-Gustavson-a	12	24	36	69	97	125
4,6,8-Ward-a, 8-9 pgs.	15	30	45	86	133	180
5,7	10	20	30	56	76	95
9-Robert Mitchum, Jane Russell photo-c	13	26	39	74	105	135
10,15-Ward-a	13	26	39	74	105	135
11-14,16-20: 12 (7/52)	9	18	27	50	65	80
21-Ward-c	12	24	36	67	94	120
22,23-Ward-a(p)	10	20	30	54	72	90
24-33: 33-Last pre-code (3/55)	9	18	27	47	61	75
34-39,41-46 (12/56; last Quality issue): 45-Baker-a	8	16	24	44	57	70
40-Ward-a; r-7 pgs./#21	8	18	27	50	65	80
47-(4-5/57); 1st DC issue)	21	42	63	156	278	400
48-60, 100	8	16	24	58	97	135
61-70	6	12	18	41	66	90
71-99: 74-Last 10 cent issue	5	10	15	35	55	75
101-The Beatles app. on-c	13	26	39	95	168	240
102-120: 102-123-(Serial)-Three Girls, Their Lives, Their Loves						
	3	6	9	19	29	38
121-132,143-146	3	6	9	16	23	30
133-142-(52 pgs.)	3	6	9	21	32	42

NOTE: *Gustavson* a-8. *Tuska* a-128. Photo c-4, 5, 8-10, 15, 17.

HEART THROBS - THE BEST OF DC ROMANCE COMICS (See Fireside Book Series)

HEART THROBS
DC Comics (Vertigo): Jan, 1999 - No. 4, Apr, 1999 ($2.95, lim. series)

1-4-Romance anthology. 1-Timm-c. 3-Corben-a						3.00

HEATHCLIFF (See Star Comics Magazine)
Marvel Comics (Star Comics)/Marvel Comics No. 23 on: Apr, 1985 - No. 56, Feb, 1991
(#16-on, $1.00)

1-Post-a most issues						6.00
2-10,47: 47-Batman parody (Catman vs. the Soaker)						4.00
11-46,48-56: 43-X-Mas issue						3.00
Annual 1 ('87)						3.00

HEATHCLIFF'S FUNHOUSE
Marvel Comics (Star Comics)/Marvel No. 6 on: May, 1987 - No. 10, 1988

1						4.00
2-10						3.00

HEAVEN'S DEVILS
Image Comics: Sept, 2003 - No. 4, July, 2004 ($2.95/$3.50, B&W, limited series)

1-3-($2.95) Jai Nitz-s/Zach Howard-a						3.00
4-($3.50) Kevin Sharpe-a						3.50

HEAVY HITTERS
Marvel Comics (Epic Comics): 1993 ($3.75, 68 pgs.)

1-Bound w/trading card; Lawdog, Feud, Alien Legion, Trouble With Girls, & Spyke						3.75

HEAVY LIQUID
DC Comics (Vertigo): Oct, 1999 - No. 5, Feb, 2000 ($5.95, limited series)

1-5-Paul Pope-s/a; flip covers						6.00
TPB (2001, $29.95) r/#1-5						30.00

HECKLE AND JECKLE (Paul Terry's...)(See Blue Ribbon, Giant Comics Edition #5A & 10,
Paul Terry's, Terry-Toons Comics)
St. John Publ. Co. No. 1-24/Pines No. 25 on: No. 3, 2/52 - No. 24, 10/55; No. 25, Fall/56 - No.
34, 6/59

	GD 2.0	VG 4.0	FN 6.0	VF 8.0	VF/NM 9.0	NM- 9.2
3(#1)-Funny animal	24	48	72	139	220	300
4(6/52), 5	13	26	39	74	105	135
6-10(4/53)	9	18	27	50	65	80
11-20	8	16	24	40	50	60
21-34: 25-Begin CBS Television Presents on-c	7	14	21	35	43	50

HECKLE AND JECKLE (TV) (See New Terrytoons)
Gold Key/Dell Publ. Co.: 11/62 - No. 4, 8/63; 5/66; No. 2, 10/66; No. 3, 8/67

	GD 2.0	VG 4.0	FN 6.0	VF 8.0	VF/NM 9.0	NM- 9.2
1 (11/62; Gold Key)	6	12	18	43	69	95
2-4	4	8	12	22	34	45
1 (5/66; Dell)	4	8	12	26	41	55
2,3	3	6	9	19	29	38

(See March of Comics No. 379, 472, 484)

HECKLE AND JECKLE 3-D
Spotlight Comics: 1987 - No. 2?, 1987 ($2.50)

1,2						5.00

HECKLER, THE
DC Comics: Sept, 1992 - No. 6, Feb, 1993 ($1.25)

1-6-T&M Bierbaum-s/Keith Giffen-c/a						2.50

HECTIC PLANET
Slave Labor Graphics 1998 ($12.95/$14.95)

Book 1,2-r-Dorkin-s/a from Pirate Corp$ Vol. 1 & 2						15.00

HECTOR COMICS (The Keenest Teen in Town)
Key Publications: Nov, 1953 - No. 3, 1954

	GD 2.0	VG 4.0	FN 6.0	VF 8.0	VF/NM 9.0	NM- 9.2
1-Teen humor	6	12	18	31	38	45
2,3	4	8	12	18	22	25

HECTOR HEATHCOTE (TV)
Gold Key: Mar, 1964

	GD 2.0	VG 4.0	FN 6.0	VF 8.0	VF/NM 9.0	NM- 9.2
1 (10111-403)	7	14	21	47	76	105

HECTOR THE INSPECTOR (See Top Flight Comics)

HEDGE KNIGHT, THE
Image Comics: Aug, 2003 - No. 6, Apr, 2004 ($2.95, limited series)

1-6-George R.R. Martin-s/Mike S. Miller-a. 1-Two covers by Kaluta and Miller						3.00
George R.R. Martin's The Hedge Knight HC (Marvel, 2006, $19.99) r/series; 2 covers						20.00
George R.R. Martin's The Hedge Knight SC (Marvel, 2007, $14.99) r/series						15.00
TPB (2004, $14.95) r/series plus one new short story						15.00

HEDGE KNIGHT II: SWORN SWORD
Marvel Comics (Dabel Brothers): Jun, 2007 - No. 6 ($2.99, limited series)

1-3-George R.R. Martin-s/Mike Miller-a. 1-Two covers by Yu & Miller, plus Miller B&W-c						3.00

HEDY DEVINE COMICS (Formerly All Winners #21? or Teen #22?(6/47);
Hedy of Hollywood #36 on; also see Annie Oakley, Comedy & Venus)
Marvel Comics (RCM)/Atlas #50: No. 22, Aug, 1947 - No. 50, Sept, 1952

	GD 2.0	VG 4.0	FN 6.0	VF 8.0	VF/NM 9.0	NM- 9.2
22-1st app. Hedy Devine (for use as Joker #32)	29	58	87	167	264	360
23,24,27-30: 23-Wolverton-a, 1 pg; Kurtzman's "Hey Look", 2 pgs. 24,27-30- "Hey Look" by Kurtzman, 1-3 pgs.	18	36	54	105	165	225
25-Classic "Hey Look" by Kurtzman, "Optical Illusion"	20	40	60	117	184	250
26- "Giggles 'n' Grins" by Kurtzman	15	30	45	86	133	180
31-34,36-50: 32-Anti-Wertham editorial	12	24	36	67	94	120
35-Four pgs. "Rusty" by Kurtzman	15	30	45	88	137	185

HEDY-MILLIE-TESSIE COMEDY (See Comedy Comics)

HEDY WOLFE (Also see Patsy & Hedy & Miss America Magazine V1#2)
Atlas Publishing Co. (Emgee): Aug, 1957

	GD 2.0	VG 4.0	FN 6.0	VF 8.0	VF/NM 9.0	NM- 9.2
1-Patsy Walker's rival; Al Hartley-c	11	22	33	64	90	115

HEE HAW (TV)
Charlton Press: July, 1970 - No. 7, Aug, 1971

	GD 2.0	VG 4.0	FN 6.0	VF 8.0	VF/NM 9.0	NM- 9.2
1	4	8	12	26	41	55
2-7	3	6	9	18	27	35

HEIDI (See Dell Jr. Treasury No. 6)

HELEN OF TROY (Movie)
Dell Publishing Co.: No. 684, Mar, 1956 (one-shot)

	GD 2.0	VG 4.0	FN 6.0	VF 8.0	VF/NM 9.0	NM- 9.2
Four Color 684-Buscema-a, photo-c	9	18	27	65	113	160

HELL
Dark Horse Comics: July, 2003 - No. 4, Mar, 2004 ($2.99, limited series)

1-4-Augustyn-s/Demong-a/Meglia-c						3.00

HELLBLAZER (John Constantine) (See Saga of Swamp Thing #37)
(Also see Books of Magic limited series)
DC Comics (Vertigo #63 on): Jan, 1988 - Present ($1.25-$2.99)

	GD 2.0	VG 4.0	FN 6.0	VF 8.0	VF/NM 9.0	NM- 9.2
1-(44 pgs.)-John Constantine; McKean-c thru #21	2	4	6	8	10	12
2-5	1	2	3	4	5	7
6-8,10: 10-Swamp Thing cameo						5.00
9,19: 9-X-over w/Swamp Thing #76. 19-Sandman app.						6.00

Hellblazer #228 © DC

Hellboy: Conqueror Worm #4 © Mike Mignola

Hellboy: Wake the Devil #3 © Mike Mignola

	GD 2.0	VG 4.0	FN 6.0	VF 8.0	VF/NM 9.0	NM- 9.2		GD 2.0	VG 4.0	FN 6.0	VF 8.0	VF/NM 9.0	NM- 9.2

11-18,20 5.00
21-26,28-30: 22-Williams-c. 24-Contains bound-in Shocker movie poster.
   25,26-Grant Morrison scripts. 5.00
27-Gaiman scripts; Dave McKean-a; low print run 2 4 6 10 12 15
31-39: 36-Preview of World Without End. 4.00
40-($2.25, 52 pgs.)-Dave McKean-a & colors; preview of Kid Eternity 4.00
41-Ennis scripts begin; ends #83 5.00
42-120: 44,45-Sutton-a(i). 50-($3.00, 52 pgs.). 52-Glenn Fabry painted-c begin. 62-Special
   Death insert by McKean. 63-Silver metallic ink on-c. 77-Totleben-c. 84-Sean Phillips-c/a
   begins; Delano story. 85-88-Eddie Campbell story. 75-($2.95, 52 pgs.). 89-Paul Jenkins
   scripts begin. 100,120 ($3.50,48 pgs.). 108-Adlard-a. 3.50
121-199, 201-235: 129-Ennis-s. 141-Bradstreet-a. 146-150-Corben-a 151-Azzarello-s begins.
   175-Carey-s begin; Dillon-a. 176-Begin $2.75-c. 182,183-Bermejo-a. 216-Mina-s begins.
   220-Begin $2.99-c. 229-Carey-s/Leon-a. 234-Initial printing (white title logo) has missing
   text; corrected printing has lt. blue title logo 3.00
200-($4.50) Carey-s/Dillon, Frusin, Manco-a 4.50
Annual 1 (1989, $2.95, 68 pgs.)-Bryan Talbot's 1st work in American comics 5.00
Special 1 (1993, $3.95, 68 pgs.)-Ennis story; w/pin-ups. 4.00
...Black Flowers (2005, $14.99, TPB) r/#181-186 15.00
...Damnation's Flame (1999, $16.95, TPB) r/#72-77 17.00
...Dangerous Habits (1997, $14.95, TPB) r/#41-46 15.00
...Fear and Loathing (1997, $14.95, TPB) r/#62-67 18.00
...Fear and Loathing (2nd printing, $14.95) 18.00
...: Freezes Over (2003, $14.95, TPB) r/#157-163 15.00
...Good Intentions (2002, $12.95, TPB) r/#151-156 13.00
...Hard Time (2001, $9.95, TPB) r/#146-150 10.00
...Haunting (2003, $12.95, TPB) r/#134-139 13.00
...Highwater (2004, $19.95, TPB) r/#164-174 20.00
John Constantine Hellblazer: All His Engines HC (2005, $24.95, with dustjacket)
   new graphic novel; Mike Carey-s/Leonardo Manco-a 25.00
John Constantine Hellblazer: All His Engines SC (2006, $14.99) new graphic novel 15.00
John Constantine Hellblazer: Empathy is the Enemy SC (2006, $14.99) r/#216-222 15.00
John Constantine Hellblazer: The Devil You Know SC (2007, $19.99) r/#10-13, Annual #1
   and The Horrorist miniseries #1,2 20.00
John Constantine Hellblazer: The Red Right Hand SC (2007, $14.99) r/#223-228 20.00
...Original Sins (1993, $19.95, TPB) r/#1-9 20.00
...Rake at the Gates of Hell (2003, $19.95, TPB) r/#78-83; Heartland #1 20.00
...: Rare Cuts (2005, $14.95, TPB) r/#11,25,26,35,56,84 & Vertigo Secret Files: Hellblazer 15.00
...: Reasons To Be Cheerful (2007, $14.99, TPB) r/#201-206 15.00
...: Red Sepulchre (2005, $12.99, TPB) r/#175-180 13.00
...: Setting Sun (2004, $12.95, TPB) r/#140-143 13.00
...: Son of Man (2004, $12.95, TPB) r/#129-133 13.00
...: Stations of the Cross (2006, $14.99, TPB) r/#194-200 15.00
...: Staring At The Wall (2005, $14.99, TPB) r/#187-193 15.00
...Tainted Love (1998, $16.95, TPB) r/#68-71, Vertigo Jam #1 and Hellblazer Special #1 17.00
NOTE: Alcala a-8i, 9i, 18-22i. Gaiman scripts-27. McKean a-27,40; c-1-21. Sutton a-44i, 45i. Talbot a-Annual 1.

HELLBLAZER SPECIAL: BAD BLOOD
DC Comics (Vertigo): Sept, 2000 - No. 4, Dec, 2000 ($2.95, mini-series)
   1-4-Delano-s/Bond-a; Constantine in 2025 London 3.00

HELLBLAZER SPECIAL: LADY CONSTANTINE
DC Comics (Vertigo): Feb, 2003 - No. 4, May, 2003 ($2.95, mini-series)
   1-4-Story of Johanna Constantine in 1785; Diggle-s/Sudzuka-a/Noto-c 3.00

HELLBLAZER/THE BOOKS OF MAGIC
DC Comics (Vertigo): Dec, 1997 - No. 2, Jan, 1998 ($2.50, mini-series)
   1,2-John Constantine and Tim Hunter 2.50

HELLBOY (Also see Danger Unlimited #4, Dark Horse Presents, Gen13 #13B, Ghost/Hellboy, John Byrne's
Next Men, San Diego Comic Con #2, & Savage Dragon)

HELLBOY: ALMOST COLOSSUS
Dark Horse Comics (Legend): Jun, 1997 - No. 2, Jul, 1997 ($2.95, lim. series)
   1,2-Mignola-s/a 3.50

HELLBOY: BOX FULL OF EVIL
Dark Horse Comics (Legend): Aug, 1999 - No. 2, Sept, 1999 ($2.95, lim. series)
   1,2-Mignola-s/a; back-up story w/ Matt Smith-a 3.50

HELLBOY CHRISTMAS SPECIAL
Dark Horse Comics: Dec, 1997 ($3.95, one-shot)
   nn-Christmas stories by Mignola, Gianni, Darrow, Purcell 4.50

HELLBOY: CONQUEROR WORM
Dark Horse Comics: May, 2001 - No. 4, Aug, 2001 ($2.99, lim. series)
   1-4-Mignola-s/a/c 3.00

HELLBOY: DARKNESS CALLS
Dark Horse Comics: Apr, 2007 - No. 6 ($2.99, lim. series)
   1-5-Mignola-s/Fegredo-a 3.00

HELLBOY, JR.
Dark Horse Comics: Oct, 1999 - No. 2, Nov, 1999 ($2.95, limited series)
   1,2-Stories and art by various 3.50
TPB (1/04, $14.95) r/#1&2, Halloween; sketch pages; intro. by Steve Niles; Bill Wray-c 15.00

HELLBOY, JR., HALLOWEEN SPECIAL
Dark Horse Comics: Oct, 1997 ($3.95, one-shot)
   nn-"Harvey" style renditions of Hellboy characters; Bill Wray, Mike Mignola & various-s/a;
   wraparound-c by Wray 4.50

HELLBOY: MAKOMA, OR A TALE TOLD...
Dark Horse Comics: Feb, 2006 - No. 2, Mar, 2006 ($2.99, lim. series)
   1,2-Mignola-s/c; Mignola & Corben-a 3.00

HELLBOY PREMIERE EDITION
Dark Horse Comics (Wizard): 2004 (no price, one-shot)
   nn- Two covers by Mignola & Davis; Mignola-s/a; BPRD story w/Arcudi-s/Davis-a 5.00
   Wizard World Los Angeles-Movie photo-c; Mignola-s/a; BPRD story w/Arcudi-s/Davis-a 10.00

HELLBOY: SEED OF DESTRUCTION
Dark Horse Comics: Mar, 1994 - No. 4, Jun, 1994 ($2.50, lim. series)
   1-4-Mignola-c/a w/Byrne scripts; Monkeyman & O'Brien back-up story
   (origin) by Art Adams. 5.00
Trade paperback (1994, $17.95)-collects all four issues plus r/Hellboy's 1st app. in
   San Diego Comic Con #2 & pin-ups 18.00
Limited edition hardcover (1995, $99.95)-includes everything in trade paperback
   plus additional material. 100.00

HELLBOY STRANGE PLACES
Dark Horse Books: Apr, 2006 ($17.95, TPB)
   SC - Reprints Hellboy: The Third Wish #1,2 and Hellboy: The Island #1,2; sketch pages 18.00

HELLBOY: THE CHAINED COFFIN AND OTHERS
Dark Horse Comics (Legend): Aug, 1998 ($17.95, TPB)
   nn-Mignola-c/a/s; reprints out-of-print one shots; pin-up gallery 18.00

HELLBOY: THE CORPSE
Dark Horse Comics: Mar, 2004 (25¢, one-shot)
   nn-Mignola-c/a/scripts; reprints "The Corpse" serial from Capitol City's Advance Comics
   catalog; development sketches and photos of the Corpse from the Hellboy movie 2.50

HELLBOY: THE CORPSE AND THE IRON SHOES
Dark Horse Comics: Jan, 1996 ($2.95, one-shot)
   nn-Mignola-c/a/scripts; reprints "The Corpse" serial w/new story 3.50

HELLBOY: THE ISLAND
Dark Horse Comics: June, 2005 - No. 2, July, 2005 ($2.99, lim. series)
   1,2: Mignola-c/a & scripts 3.00

HELLBOY: THE RIGHT HAND OF DOOM
Dark Horse Comics (Legend): Apr, 2000 ($17.95, TPB)
   nn-Mignola-c/a/s; reprints 18.00

HELLBOY: THE THIRD WISH
Dark Horse Comics (Maverick): July, 2002 - No. 2, Aug, 2002 ($2.99, limited series)
   1,2-Mignola-c/a/s 3.00

HELLBOY THE TROLL WITCH AND OTHERS
Dark Horse Books: Nov, 2007 ($17.95, TPB)
   SC - Reprints Hellboy: Makoma, Hellboy Premiere Edition and stories from Dark Horse Book
   of Hauntings, DHB of Witchcraft, DHB of the Dead, DHB of Monsters 18.00

HELLBOY: THE WOLVES OF ST. AUGUST
Dark Horse Comics (Legend): 1995 ($4.95, squarebound, one-shot)
   nn-Mignola--c/a/scripts; r/Dark Horse Presents #88-91 with additional story 5.00

HELLBOY: WAKE THE DEVIL (Sequel to Seed of Destruction)
Dark Horse Comics (Legend): Jun, 1996 - No. 5, Oct, 1996 ($2.95, lim. series)
   1-5: Mignola-c/a & scripts; The Monstermen back-up story by Gary Gianni 4.00
TPB (1997, $17.95) r/#1-5 18.00

HELLBOY: WEIRD TALES
Dark Horse Comics: Feb, 2003 - No. 8, April, 2004 ($2.99, limited series, anthology)
   1-8-Hellboy stories from other creators. 1-Cassaday-c/s/a; Watson-s/a. 6-Cho-c 3.00
...Vol. 1 (2004, 17.95) r/#1-4 18.00

Hellspawn #9 © TMP

Helmet of Fate: Black Alice #1 © DC

Henry #2 © KING

	GD 2.0	VG 4.0	FN 6.0	VF 8.0	VF/NM 9.0	NM- 9.2

... Vol. 2 (2004, 17.95) r/#5-8 and Lobster Johnson serial from #1-8 18.00

HELLCAT
Marvel Comics: Sept, 2000 - No. 3, Nov, 2000 ($2.99)
1-3-Englehart-s/Breyfogle-a; Hedy Wolfe app. 3.00

HELLCOP
Image Comics (Avalon Studios): Aug, 1998 - No. 4, Mar, 1999 ($2.50)
1-4: 1-(Oct. on-c) Casey-s 2.50

HELL ETERNAL
DC Comics (Vertigo Verité): 1998 ($6.95, squarebound, one-shot)
1-Delano-s/Phillips-a 7.00

HELLGATE: LONDON (Based on the video game)
Dark Horse Comics: No. 0, May 2006 - No. 3, Mar, 2007 ($2.99)
0-3-Edginton-s/Pugh-a/Briclot-c 3.00

HELLHOUNDS (... Panzer Cops #3-6)
Dark Horse Comics: 1994 - No. 6, July, 1994 ($2.50, B&W, limited series)
1-6: 1-Hamner-c. 3-(4/94). 2-Joe Phillips-c 3.00

HELLHOUND, THE REDEMPTION QUEST
Marvel Comics (Epic Comics): Dec, 1993 - No. 4, Mar, 1994 ($2.25, lim. series, coated stock)
1-4 2.50

HELLO, I'M JOHNNY CASH
Spire Christian Comics (Fleming H. Revell Co.): 1976 (39¢/49¢)
| nn-(39¢-c) | 2 | 4 | 6 | 11 | 16 | 20 |
| nn-(49¢-c) | 2 | 4 | 6 | 8 | 10 | 12 |

HELL ON EARTH (See DC Science Fiction Graphic Novel)

HELLO PAL COMICS (Short Story Comics)
Harvey Publications: Jan, 1943 - No. 3, May, 1943 (Photo-c)
1-Rocketman & Rocketgirl begin; Yankee Doodle Jones app.; Mickey Rooney photo-c
	62	124	186	388	644	900
2-Charlie McCarthy photo-c (scarce)	54	108	162	338	562	785
3-Bob Hope photo-c (scarce)	60	120	180	375	625	875

HELLRAISER/NIGHTBREED – JIHAD (Also see Clive Barker's...)
Epic Comics (Marvel Comics): 1991 - Book 2, 1991 ($4.50, 52 pgs.)
Book 1,2 4.50

HELL-RIDER (Motorcycle themed magazine)
Skywald Publications: Aug, 1971 - No. 2, Oct, 1971 (B&W, 68 pgs.)
1-Origin & 1st app.; Butterfly & the Wild Bunch begin; 1st Hell-Rider by Andru, Esposito
| and Friedrich | 6 | 12 | 18 | 37 | 59 | 80 |
| 2-Andru, Ayers, Buckler, Shores-a | 4 | 8 | 12 | 24 | 37 | 50 |
NOTE: #3 advertised in Psycho #5 but did not come out. Buckler a-1, 2. Rosenbaum c-1,2.

HELL'S ANGEL (Becomes Dark Angel #6 on)
Marvel Comics UK: July, 1992 - No. 5, Nov, 1993 ($1.75)
1-5: X-Men (Wolverine, Cyclops)-c/stories. 1-Origin. 3-Jim Lee cover swipe 2.50

HELLSHOCK
Image Comics: July, 1994 - No. 4, Nov, 1994 ($1.95, limited series)
1-4-Jae Lee-c/a & scripts. 4-Variant-c. 2.50

HELLSHOCK
Image Comics: Jan, 1997 - No. 3, Jan, 1998 ($2.95/$2.50, limited series)
1-($2.95)-Jae Lee-c/s/a, Villarrubia-painted-a 4.00
2-($2.50) 2.50
Book 3: The Science of Faith (1/98, $2.50) Jae Lee-c/s/a, Villarrubia-painted-a 2.50
Vol. 1 HC (2006, $49.99) r/#1-3 re-colored, with unpublished 22 pg. conclusion; cover gallery
and sketches; alternate opening art; intro. by Jim Lee 50.00

HELLSPAWN
Image Comics: Aug, 2000 - No. 16, Apr, 2003 ($2.50)
1-Bendis-s/Ashley Wood-c/a; Spawn and Clown app. 2.50
2-9: 6-Last Bendis-s; Mike Moran (Miracleman app.). 7-Niles-s 2.50
10-16-Templesmith-a 2.50
...: The Ashley Wood Collection Vol. 1 (4/06, $24.95, TPB) r/#1-10; sketch & cover gallery 25.00

HELLSTORM: PRINCE OF LIES (See Ghost Rider #1 & Marvel Spotlight #12)
Marvel Comics: Apr, 1993 - No. 21, Dec, 1994 ($2.00)
1-($2.95)-Parchment-c w/red thermographic ink 3.00
2-21: 16-Bound-in trading card sheet. 18-P. Craig Russell-c 2.50

HELLSTORM: SON OF SATAN
Marvel Comics (MAX): Dec, 2006 - No. 5, Apr, 2007 ($3.99, limited series)

1-5-Suydam-c/Irvine-s/Braun & Janson-a 4.00
... - Equinox TPB (2007, $17.99) r/#1-5; interviews with the creators 18.00

HELMET OF FATE, THE (Series of one-shots following Doctor Fate's helmet)
DC Comics: Mar, 2007 - May 2007 ($2.99, one-shots)
...: Black Alice (5/07) Simone-s/Rouleau-a/c 3.00
...: Detective Chimp (3/07) Willingham-s/McManus-a/Bolland-c 3.00
...: Ibis the Invincible (3/07) Williams-s/Winslade-a; the Ibistick returns 3.00
...: Sargon the Sorcerer (4/07) Niles-s/Scott Hampton-s; debut new Sargon 3.00
...: Zauriel (4/07) Gerber-s/Snejbjerg-a/Kaluta-c; leads into new Doctor Fate series 3.00

HE-MAN (See Masters Of The Universe)

HE-MAN (Also see Tops In Adventure)
Ziff-Davis Publ. Co. (Approved Comics): Fall, 1952
| 1-Kinstler painted-c; Powell-a | 16 | 32 | 48 | 92 | 144 | 195 |

HE-MAN
Toby Press: May, 1954 - No. 2, July, 1954 (Painted-c by B. Safran)
| 1 | 15 | 30 | 45 | 88 | 137 | 185 |
| 2-Shark-c | 15 | 30 | 45 | 85 | 130 | 175 |

HENNESSEY (TV)
Dell Publishing Co.: No. 1200, Aug-Oct, 1961 - No. 1280, Mar-May, 1962
| Four Color 1200-Gil Kane-a, photo-c | 7 | 14 | 21 | 47 | 76 | 105 |
| Four Color 1280-Photo-c | 6 | 12 | 18 | 43 | 69 | 95 |

HENRY (Also see Little Annie Rooney)
David McKay Publications: 1935 (52 pgs.) (Daily B&W strip reprints)(10"x10" cardboard-c)
| 1-By Carl Anderson | 40 | 80 | 120 | 235 | 368 | 500 |

HENRY (See King Comics & Magic Comics)
Dell Publishing Co.: No. 122, Oct, 1946 - No. 65, Apr-June, 1961
Four Color 122-All new stories begin	14	28	42	99	175	250
Four Color 155 (7/47), 1 (1-3/48)-All new stories	9	18	27	65	113	160
2	6	12	18	39	62	85
3-10	5	10	15	32	51	70
11-20: 20-Infinity-c	4	8	12	24	37	50
21-30	3	6	9	20	30	40
31-40	3	6	9	17	25	32
41-65	3	6	9	15	21	26

HENRY (See Giant Comic Album and March of Comics No. 43, 58, 84, 101, 112, 129, 147, 162, 178, 189)

HENRY ALDRICH COMICS (TV)
Dell Publishing Co.: Aug-Sept, 1950 - No. 22, Sept-Nov, 1954
1-Part series written by John Stanley; Bill Williams-a
	9	18	27	63	107	150
2	5	10	15	35	55	75
3-5	4	8	12	28	44	60
6-10	4	8	12	24	37	50
11-22	3	6	9	20	30	40

HENRY BREWSTER
Country Wide (M.F. Ent.): Feb, 1966 - V2#7, Sept, 1967 (All 25¢ Giants)
| 1 | 3 | 6 | 9 | 17 | 25 | 32 |
| 2-6(12/66), V2#7-Powell-a in most | 2 | 4 | 6 | 10 | 14 | 18 |

HEPCATS
Antarctic Press: Nov, 1996 - No. 12 ($2.95, B&W)
0-12-Martin Wagner-c/s/a: 0-color 3.00
0-($9.95) CD Edition 10.00

HERBIE (See Forbidden Worlds & Unknown Worlds)
American Comics Group: April-May, 1964 - No. 23, Feb, 1967 (All 12¢)
| 1-Whitney-c/a in most issues | 16 | 32 | 48 | 118 | 209 | 300 |
| 2-4 | 9 | 18 | 27 | 63 | 107 | 150 |
| 5-Beatles parody (10 pgs.), Dean Martin, Frank Sinatra app. (10-11/64) |
	10	20	30	70	123	175
6,7,9,10	8	16	24	52	86	120
8-Origin & 1st app. The Fat Fury	9	18	27	61	103	145
11-23: 14-Nemesis & Magicman app. 17-r/2nd Herbie from Forbidden Worlds
#94. 23-r/1st Herbie from F.W. #73	6	12	18	41	66	90

HERBIE
Dark Horse Comics: Oct, 1992 - No. 12, 1993 ($2.50, limited series)
1-Whitney-r plus new-c/a in all; Byrne-c/a & scripts 3.00
2-6: 3-Bob Burden-c/a. 4-Art Adams-c 2.50

HERBIE GOES TO MONTE CARLO, HERBIE RIDES AGAIN (See Walt Disney Showcase No. 24, 41)

Hercules: The Legendary Journeys #3 © MCA

Heroes © MAR

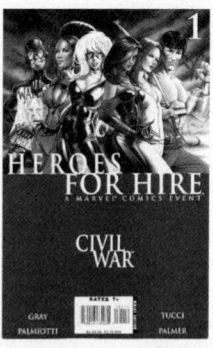

Heroes For Hire #1 © MAR

	GD 2.0	VG 4.0	FN 6.0	VF 8.0	VF/NM 9.0	NM- 9.2		GD 2.0	VG 4.0	FN 6.0	VF 8.0	VF/NM 9.0	NM- 9.2

HERCULES (See Hit Comics #1-21, Journey Into Mystery Annual, Marvel Graphic Novel #37, Marvel Premiere #26 & The Mighty...)

HERCULES (See Charlton Classics)
Charlton Comics: Oct, 1967 - No. 13, Sept, 1969; Dec, 1968

1-Thane of Bagarth begins; Glanzman-a in all	4	8	12	22	34	45
2-13: 1-5,7-10-Aparo-a. 8-(12¢-c)	3	6	9	14	20	25
8-(Low distribution)(12/68, 35¢, B&W); magazine format; new Hercules story plus-r story/#1; Thane-r/#1-3	5	10	15	32	51	70
Modern Comics reprint 10('77), 11('78)						6.00

HERCULES (Prince of Power) (Also see The Champions)
Marvel Comics Group: V1#1, Sept, 1982 - V1#4, Dec, 1982; V2#1, Mar, 1984 - V2#4, Jun, 1984 (color, both limited series)

1-4, V2#1-4: Layton-c/a. 4-Death of Zeus.	3.00

NOTE: *Layton* a-1, 2, 3p, 4p, V2#1-4; c-1-4, V2#1-4.

HERCULES
Marvel Comics: Jun, 2005 - No. 5, Sept, 2005 ($2.99, limited series)

1-5-Texeira-a/c; Tieri-s. 4-Capt. America, Wolverine and New Avengers app.	3.00
...: New Labors of Hercules TPB (2005, $13.99) r/#1-5	14.00

HERCULES: HEART OF CHAOS
Marvel Comics: Aug, 1997 - No. 3, Oct, 1997 ($2.50, limited series)

1-3-DeFalco-s, Frenz-a	2.50

HERCULES: OFFICIAL COMICS MOVIE ADAPTION
Acclaim Books: 1997 ($4.50, digest size)

nn-Adaption of the Disney animated movie	4.50

HERCULES: THE LEGENDARY JOURNEYS (TV)
Topps Comics: June, 1996 - No. 5, Oct, 1996 ($2.95)

1-2: 1-Golden-c.						3.00
3-Xena-c/app.	1	2	3	4	5	7
3-Variant-c	2	4	6	9	12	15
4,5: Xena-c/app.						5.00

HERCULES UNBOUND
National Periodical Publications: Oct-Nov, 1975 - No. 12, Aug-Sept, 1977

1-Wood-i begins	2	4	6	8	11	14
2-12: 7-Adams ad. 10-Atomic Knights x-over	1	2	3	5	6	8

NOTE: *Buckler* c-7p. *Layton* inks-No. 9, 10. *Simonson* a-7-10p, 11, 12; c- 8p, 9-12. *Wood* a-1-8i; c-7i, 8i.

HERCULES (...Unchained #1121) (Movie)
Dell Publishing Co.: No. 1006, June-Aug, 1959 - No.1121, Aug, 1960

Four Color 1006-Buscema-a, photo-c	9	18	27	60	100	140
Four Color 1121-Crandall/Evans-a	9	18	27	60	100	140

HERE COMES SANTA (See March of Comics No. 30, 213, 340)

HERE'S HOWIE COMICS
National Periodical Publications: Jan-Feb, 1952 - No. 18, Nov-Dec, 1954

1	27	54	81	158	249	340
2	15	30	45	84	127	170
3-5: 5-Howie in the Army issues begin (9-10/52)	12	24	36	69	97	125
6-10	10	20	30	58	79	100
11-18	10	20	30	54	72	90
Ashcan (1,2/51) not distributed to newsstands, only for in house use					(no known sales)	

HERETIC, THE
Dark Horse (Blanc Noir): Nov, 1996 - No. 4, Mar, 1997 ($2.95, lim. series)

1-4:-w/back-up story	3.00

HERITAGE OF THE DESERT (See Zane Grey, 4-Color 236)

HERMAN & KATNIP (See Harvey Comics Hits #60 & 62, Harvey Hits #14,25,31,41 & Paramount Animated Comics #1)

HERMES VS. THE EYEBALL KID
Dark Horse Comics: Dec, 1994 - No. 3, Feb, 1995 ($2.95, B&W, limited series)

1-3: Eddie Campbell-c/a/scripts	3.00

H-E-R-O (Dial H For HERO)
DC Comics: Apr, 2003 - No. 22, Jan, 2005 ($2.50)

1-Will Pfeiffer-s/Kano-a/Van Fleet-c	3.00
2-22: 2-6-Kano-a. 7,8-Gleason-a. 12-14-Kirk-a. 15-22-Robby Reed app.	2.50
...: Double Feature (6/03, $4.95) r/#1&2	5.00
...: Powers and Abilities (2003, $9.95) r/#1-6; intro. by Geoff Johns	10.00

HERO (Warrior of the Mystic Realms)
Marvel Comics: May, 1990 - No. 6, Oct, 1990 ($1.50, limited series)

1-6: 1-Portacio-i	2.50

HERO ALLIANCE, THE
Sirius Comics: Dec, 1985 - No. 2, Sept, 1986 (B&W)

1,2: 2-($1.50), Special Edition 1 (7/86, color)	2.50

HERO ALLIANCE
Wonder Color Comics: May, 1987 ($1.95)

1-Ron Lim-a	2.50

HERO ALLIANCE
Innovation Publishing: V2#1, Sept, 1989 - V2#17, Nov, 1991 ($1.95, 28 pgs.)

V2#1-17: 1,2-Ron Lim-a	2.50
Annual 1 (1990, $2.75, 36 pgs.)-Paul Smith-c/a	2.75
Special 1 (1992, $2.50, 32 pgs.)-Stuart Immonen-a (10 pgs.)	2.50

HERO ALLIANCE: END OF THE GOLDEN AGE
Innovation Publ.: July, 1989 - No. 3, Aug, 1989 ($1.75, bi-weekly lim. series)

1-3: Bart Sears & Ron Lim-c/a; reprints & new-a	2.50

HERO BY NIGHT
Platinum Studios Comics: Mar, 2007 - No. 4, Jun, 2007 ($2.99)

1-4-D.J. Coffman-s/a/c	3.00

HEROES
Marvel Comics: Dec, 2001 ($3.50, magazine-size, one-shot)

1-Pin-up tributes to the rescue workers of the Sept. 11 tragedy; art and text by various; cover by Alex Ross	3.50
1-2nd and 3rd printings	3.50

HEROES (Also see Shadow Cabinet & Static)
DC Comics (Milestone): May, 1996 - No. 6, Nov, 1996 ($2.50, limited series)

1-6: 1-Intro Heroes (Iota, Donner, Blitzen, Starlight, Payback & Static)	2.50

HEROES AGAINST HUNGER
DC Comics: 1986 ($1.50; one-shot for famine relief)

1-Superman, Batman app.; Neal Adams-c(p); includes many artists work; Jeff Jones assist (2 pg.) on B. Smith-a; Kirby-a	4.00

HEROES ALL CATHOLIC ACTION ILLUSTRATED
Heroes All Co.: 1943 - V6#3, Mar 10, 1948 (paper covers)

V1#1-(16 pgs., 8x11")	24	48	72	139	220	300
V1#2-(16 pgs., 8x11")	19	38	57	109	172	235
V2#1(1/44)-3(3/44)-(16 pgs., 8x11")	16	32	48	92	144	195
V3#1(1/45)-10(12/45)-(16 pgs., 8x11")	15	30	45	83	124	165
V4#1-35 (12/20/46)-(16 pgs.)	14	28	42	78	112	145
V5#1(1/10/47)-8(2/28/47)-(16 pgs.), V5#9(3/7/47)-20(11/25/47)-(32 pgs.), V6#1(1/10/48)-5(3/10/48)-(32 pgs.)	11	22	33	64	90	115

HEROES ANONYMOUS
Bongo Comics: 2003 - No. 6, 2004 ($2.99, limited series)

1-6-($2.99)-Bill Morrison-c. 2-Guerra-a. 3-Pepoy-a	3.00

HEROES FOR HIRE
Marvel Comics: July, 1997 - No. 19, Jan, 1999 ($2.99/$1.99)

1-($2.99)-Wraparound cover	5.00
2-19: 2-Variant cover. 7-Thunderbolts app. 9-Punisher-c/app. 10,11-Deadpool-c/app. 18,19-Wolverine-c/app.	3.00
.../Quicksilver '98 Annual ($2.99) Siege of Wundagore pt.5	3.00

HEROES FOR HIRE
Marvel Comics: Oct, 2006 - Present ($2.99)

1-5-Tucci-a/c; Black Cat, Shang-Chi, Tarantula, Humbug & Daughters of the Dragon app.	3.00
6-13: 6-8-Sparacio-c. 9,10-Golden-c. 11-13-World War Hulk x-over. 13-Takeda-c	3.00
... Vol. 1: Civil War (2007, $13.99) r/#1-5	14.00
... Vol. 2: Ahead of the Curve (2007, $13.99) r/#6-10	14.00

HEROES FOR HOPE STARRING THE X-MEN
Marvel Comics Group: Dec, 1985 ($1.50, one-shot, 52 pgs., proceeds donated to famine relief)

1-Stephen King scripts; Byrne, Miller, Corben-a; Wrightson/J. Jones-a (3 pgs.); Art Adams-c; Starlin back-a	5.00

HEROES, INC. PRESENTS CANNON
Wally Wood/CPL/Gang Publ.: 1969 - No. 2, 1976 (Sold at Army PX's)

nn-Ditko, Wood-a; Wood-c; Reese-a(p)	2	4	6	9	12	15
2-Wood-c; Ditko, Byrne, Wood-a; 8-1/2x10-1/2"; B&W; $2.00	2	4	6	13	18	22

Heroes Reborn: The Return #2 © MAR

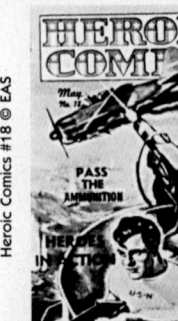

Heroic Comics #18 © EAS

Highlander #0 © Davis•Panzer

	GD 2.0	VG 4.0	FN 6.0	VF 8.0	VF/NM 9.0	NM- 9.2		GD 2.0	VG 4.0	FN 6.0	VF 8.0	VF/NM 9.0	NM- 9.2

NOTE: First issue not distributed by publisher; 1,800 copies were stored and 900 copies were stolen from warehouse. Many copies have surfaced in recent years.

HEROES OF THE WILD FRONTIER (Formerly Baffling Mysteries)
Ace Periodicals: No. 27, Jan, 1956 - No. 2, Apr, 1956

27(#1),2-Davy Crockett, Daniel Boone, Buffalo Bill	6	12	18	29	36	42

HEROES REBORN (one-shots)
Marvel Comics: Jan, 2000 ($1.99)

...:Ashema; ...:Doom; ...:Doomsday; ...:Masters of Evil; ...:Rebel; ...:Remnants;
...:Young Allies 2.50

HEROES REBORN: THE RETURN (Also see Avengers, Fantastic Four, Iron Man & Captain America titles for issues and TPBs)
Marvel Comics: Dec, 1997 - No. 4 ($2.50, weekly mini-series)

1-4-Avengers, Fantastic Four, Iron Man & Captain America rejoin regular Marvel Universe; Peter David-s/Larocca-c/a						4.00
1-4-Variant-c for each						6.00
Wizard 1/2	1	2	3	5	7	9
Return of the Heroes TPB ('98, $14.95) r/#1-4						15.00

HERO FOR HIRE (Power Man No. 17 on; also see Cage)
Marvel Comics Group: June, 1972 - No. 16, Dec, 1973

1-Origin & 1st app. Luke Cage; Tuska-a(p)	8	16	24	54	90	125
2-Tuska-a(p)	4	8	12	24	37	50
3-5: 3-1st app. Mace. 4-1st app. Phil Fox of the Bugle	3	6	9	18	27	35
6-10: 8,9-Dr. Doom app. 9-F.F. app.	2	4	6	13	18	22
11-16: 14-Origin retold. 15-Everett Sub-Mariner-r('53). 16-Origin Stiletto; death of Rackham	2	4	6	8	11	14

HERO HOTLINE (1st app. in Action Comics Weekly #637)
DC Comics: April, 1989 - No. 6, Sept, 1989 ($1.75, limited series)

1-6: Super-hero humor; Schaffenberger-i						2.50

HEROIC ADVENTURES (See Adventures)

HEROIC COMICS (Reg'lar Fellers...#1-15; New Heroic #41 on)
Eastern Color Printing Co./Famous Funnies(Funnies, Inc. No. 1):
Aug, 1940 - No. 97, June, 1955

1-Hydroman (origin) by Bill Everett, The Purple Zombie (origin) & Mann of India by Tarpe Mills begins (all 1st apps.)	190	380	570	1188	1969	2750
2	79	158	237	494	822	1150
3,4	52	104	156	317	521	725
5,6	43	86	129	262	431	600
7-Origin & 1st app. Man O'Metal (1 pg.)	45	90	135	275	455	635
8-10: 10-Lingerie panels	35	70	105	201	318	435
11,13	32	64	96	186	293	400
12-Music Master (origin/1st app.) begins by Everett, ends No. 31; last Purple Zombie & Mann of India	36	72	108	208	329	450
14,15-Hydroman x-over in Rainbow Boy. 14-Origin & 1st app. Rainbow Boy (super hero). 15-1st app. Downbeat	35	70	105	201	318	435
16-20: 16-New logo. 17-Rainbow Boy x-over in Hydroman. 19-Rainbow Boy x-over in Hydroman & vice versa	24	48	72	139	220	300
21-30:25-Rainbow Boy x-over in Hydroman. 28-Last Man O'Metal. 29-Last Hydroman	17	34	51	98	154	210
31,34,38	8	16	24	44	57	70
32,36,37-Toth-a (3-4 pgs. each)	9	18	27	52	69	85
33,35-Toth-a (8 & 9 pgs.)	10	20	30	54	72	90
39-42-Toth, Ingels-a	10	20	30	54	72	90
43,46,47,49-Toth-a (2-4 pgs.). 47-Ingels-a	9	18	27	50	65	80
44,45,50-Toth-a (6-9 pgs.)	9	18	27	52	69	85
48,53,54	8	16	24	54	65	65
51-Williamson-a	9	18	27	52	69	85
52-Williamson-a (3 pg. story)	8	16	24	44	57	70
55-Toth-a	9	18	27	50	65	80
56-60: 60-Everett-a	8	16	24	44	57	70
61-Everett-a	8	16	24	42	54	65
62,64-Everett-c/a	8	16	24	44	57	70
63-Everett-a	8	16	24	42	54	65
65-Williamson/Frazetta-a: Evans-a (2 pgs.)	11	22	33	62	86	110
66,75,94-Frazetta-a (2 pgs. each)	8	16	24	44	57	70
67,73-Frazetta-a (4 pgs. each)	9	18	27	52	69	85
68,74,76-80,84,85,88-93,95-97: 95-Last pre-code	8	16	24	40	50	60
69,72-Frazetta-a (6 & 8 pgs. each); 1st (?) app. Frazetta Red Cross ad	11	22	33	62	86	110
70,71,86,87-Frazetta, 3-4 pgs. each; 1 pg. ad by Frazetta in #70	9	18	27	47	61	75

81,82-Frazetta art (1 pg. each): 81-1st (?) app. Frazetta Boy Scout ad (tied w/ Buster Crabbe #9	8	16	24	42	54	65
83-Frazetta-a (1/2 pg.)	8	16	24	42	54	65

NOTE: **Evans** a-64, 65. **Everett** a-(Hydroman-c/a-No. 1-9), 44, 60-64; c-1-9, 62-64. **Harvey Fuller** c-28-35. **Sid Greene** a-38-43, 46. **Guardineer** a-42(3), 43, 44, 45(2), 49(3), 50, 60, 61(2), 65, 67(2) 70-72. **Ingels** c-41. **Kiefer** a-46, 48; c-19-22, 24, 44, 46, 48, 51-53, 65, 67-69, 71-74, 76, 77, 79, 80, 82, 85, 86, 88, 89, 94, 95. **Mort Lawrence** a-45. **Tarpe Mills** a-2(2), 3(2), 10. **Ed Moore** a-49, 52-54, 56-63, 65-69, 72-74, 76, 77. **H.G. Peter** a-58-74, 76, 77, 87. **Paul Reinman** a-49. **Rico** a-31. Captain Tootsie by **Beck**-31, 32. Painted-c #16 on. Hydroman c-1-11. Music Master c-12, 13, 15. Rainbow Boy c-14.

HERO ZERO (Also see Comics' Greatest World & Godzilla Versus Hero Zero)
Dark Horse Comics: Sept, 1994 ($2.50)

0						2.50

HEX (Replaces Jonah Hex)
DC Comics: Sept, 1985 - No. 18, Feb, 1987 (Story cont'd from Jonah Hex # 92)

1-Hex in post-atomic war world; origin	1	2	3	5	6	8
2-18: 6-Origin Stiletta. 11-13: All contain future Batman storyline. 13-Intro The Dogs of War (origin #15)						5.00

NOTE: **Giffen** a(p)-15-18; c(p)-15,17,18. **Texeira** a-1, 2p, 3p, 5-7p, 9p, 11-14p; c(p)-1, 2, 4-7, 12.

HEXBREAKER (See First Comics Graphic Novel #15)

HEY THERE, IT'S YOGI BEAR (See Movie Comics)

HI-ADVENTURE HEROES (TV)
Gold Key: May, 1969 - No. 2, Aug, 1969 (Hanna-Barbera)

1-Three Musketeers, Gulliver, Arabian Knights	5	10	15	32	51	70
2-Three Musketeers, Micro-Venture, Arabian Knights	4	8	12	28	44	60

HI AND LOIS
Dell Publishing Co.: No. 683, Mar, 1956 - No. 955, Nov, 1958

Four Color 683 (#1)	5	10	15	30	48	65
Four Color 774(3/57),955	4	8	12	24	37	50

HI AND LOIS
Charlton Comics: Nov, 1969 - No. 11, July, 1971

1	3	6	9	14	20	25
2-11	2	4	6	9	12	15

HICKORY (See All Humor Comics)
Quality Comics Group: Oct, 1949 - No. 6, Aug, 1950

1-Sahl-c/a in all; Feldstein?-a	18	36	54	107	169	230
2	11	22	33	64	90	115
3-6	10	20	30	54	72	90

HIDDEN CREW, THE (See The United States Air Force Presents:...)

HIDE-OUT (See Zane Grey, Four Color No. 346)

HIDING PLACE, THE
Spire Christian Comics (Fleming H. Revell Co.): 1973 (39¢/49¢)

nn	2	4	6	8	10	12

HIGH ADVENTURE
Red Top(Decker) Comics (Farrell): Oct, 1957

1-Krigstein-r from Explorer Joe (re-issue on-c)	5	10	15	23	28	32

HIGH ADVENTURE (TV)
Dell Publishing Co.: No. 949, Nov, 1958 - No. 1001, Aug-Oct, 1959 (Lowell Thomas)

Four Color 949 (#1)-Photo-c	6	12	18	37	59	80
Four Color 1001-Lowell Thomas'...(#2)	5	10	15	35	55	75

HIGH CHAPPARAL (TV)
Gold Key: Aug, 1968 (Photo-c)

1 (10226-808)-Tufts-a	5	10	15	32	51	70

HIGHLANDER
Dynamite Entertainment: No. 0, 2006 - Present (25¢)

0-(25¢-c) Takes place after the first movie; photo-c and Dell'Otto painted-c						2.25
1-11: 1-($2.99) Three covers; Moder-a/Jerwa & Oeming-s. 2-Three covers						3.00

HIGH ROADS
DC Comics (Cliffhanger): June, 2002 - No. 6, Nov, 2002 ($2.95, limited series)

1-6-Leinil Yu-c/a; Lobdell-s						3.00
TPB (2003, $14.95) r/#1-6; sketch pages						15.00

HIGH SCHOOL CONFIDENTIAL DIARY (Confidential Diary #12 on)
Charlton Comics: June, 1960 - No. 11, Mar, 1962

1	4	8	12	26	41	55
2-11	3	6	9	17	25	32

Hi-Ho Comics #2 © Four Star

Hit Comics #13 © QUA

Hitman #29 © DC

	GD 2.0	VG 4.0	FN 6.0	VF 8.0	VF/NM 9.0	NM- 9.2

HIGHWAYMEN
DC Comics (WildStorm): Aug, 2007 - Present ($2.99)

	GD 2.0	VG 4.0	FN 6.0	VF 8.0	VF/NM 9.0	NM- 9.2
1-3-Bernardin & Freeman-s/Garbett-a						3.00

HI HI PUFFY AMIYUMI (Based on Cartoon Network animated series)
DC Comics: Apr, 2006 - No. 3 ($2.25, limited series)

1,2-Phil Moy-a						2.50

HI-HO COMICS
Four Star Publications: nd (2/46?) - No. 3, 1946

1-Funny Animal; L. B. Cole-c	38	76	114	219	347	475
2,3: 2-L. B. Cole-c	21	42	63	122	191	260

HI-JINX (Teen-age Animal Funnies)
La Salle Publ. Co./B&I Publ. Co. (American Comics Group)/Creston: 1945; July-Aug, 1947 - No. 7, July-Aug, 1948

nn-(© 1945, 25 cents, 132 Pgs.)(La Salle)	24	48	72	139	220	300
1-Teen-age, funny animal	16	32	48	94	147	200
2,3	11	22	33	62	86	110
4-7-Milt Gross. 4-X-Mas-c	15	30	45	86	133	180

HI-LITE COMICS
E. R. Ross Publishing Co.: Fall, 1945

1-Miss Shady	19	38	57	112	176	240

HILLBILLY COMICS
Charlton Comics: Aug, 1955 - No. 4, July, 1956 (Satire)

1-By Art Gates	9	18	27	50	65	80
2-4	6	12	18	31	38	45

HILLY ROSE'S SPACE ADVENTURES
Astro Comics: May, 1995 - No. 9 ($2.95, B&W)

1	1	2	3	5	7	9
2-5						5.00
6-9						3.00
Trade Paperback (1996, $12.95)-r/#1-5						13.00

HIP FLASK UNNATURAL SELECTION
Active Images: Sept, 2002 ($2.99)

1-Casey & Starkings-s/Ladronn-a; var.-c by Madureira, Campbell, Churchill						3.00

HIP-IT-TY HOP (See March of Comics No. 15)

HIRE, THE (BMWfilms.com's...)
Dark Horse Comics: July, 2004 - No. 6 ($2.99)

1-4: 1-Matt Wagner-s/Wagner & Velasco-a. 2-Bruce Campbell-s/Plunkett-a. 3-Waid-s						3.00
TPB (4/06, $17.95) r/#1-4						18.00

HI-SCHOOL ROMANCE (...Romances No. 41 on)
Harvey Publ./True Love(Home Comics): Oct, 1949 - No. 5, June, 1950; No. 6, Dec, 1950 - No. 73, Mar, 1958; No. 74, Sept, 1958 - No. 75, Nov, 1958

1-Photo-c	15	30	45	88	137	185
2-Photo-c	10	20	30	54	72	90
3-9: 3-5-Photo-c	8	16	24	44	57	70
10-Rape story	10	20	30	54	72	90
11-20	7	14	21	37	46	55
21-31	6	12	18	29	36	42
32- "Unholy passion" story	9	18	27	47	61	75
33-36: 36-Last pre-code (2/55)	6	12	18	28	34	40
37-53,59-72,74,75	5	10	15	23	28	32
54-58,73-Kirby-a	6	12	18	28	34	40

NOTE: **Powell**-a-1-3, 5, 8, 12-16, 18, 21-23, 25-27, 30-34, 36, 37, 39, 45-48, 50-52, 57, 58, 60, 64, 65, 67, 69.

HI-SCHOOL ROMANCE DATE BOOK
Harvey Publications: Nov, 1962 - No. 3, Mar, 1963 (25¢ Giants)

1-Powell, Baker-a	6	12	18	37	59	80
2,3	3	6	9	20	30	40

HIS NAME IS SAVAGE (Magazine format)
Adventure House Press: June, 1968 (35¢, 52 pgs.)

1-Gil Kane-a	5	10	15	30	48	65

HI-SPOT COMICS (Red Ryder No. 1 & No. 3 on)
Hawley Publications: No. 2, Nov, 1940

2-David Innes of Pellucidar; art by J. C. Burroughs; written by Edgar Rice Burroughs						
	128	256	384	800	1325	1850

HISTORY OF THE DC UNIVERSE (Also see Crisis on Infinite Earths)
DC Comics: Sept, 1986 - No. 2, Nov, 1986 ($2.95, limited series)

1,2: 1-Perez-c/a						3.00
Limited Edition hardcover	4	8	12	26	41	55
Softcover (2002, $9.95) new Alex Ross wraparound-c						10.00

HISTORY OF VIOLENCE, A (Inspired the 2005 movie)
DC Comics (Paradox Press) 1997 ($9.95, B&W graphic novel)

nn-Paperback ($9.95) John Wagner-s/Vince Locke-a						10.00

HITCHHIKERS GUIDE TO THE GALAXY (See Life, the Universe and Everything & Restaraunt at the End of the Universe)
DC Comics: 1993 - No. 3, 1993 ($4.95, limited series)

1-3: Adaptation of Douglas Adams book						5.00
TPB (1997, $14.95) r/#1-3						15.00

HIT COMICS
Quality Comics Group: July, 1940 - No. 65, July, 1950

1-Origin/1st app. Neon, the Unknown & Hercules; intro. The Red Bee; Bob & Swab, Blaze Barton, the Strange Twins, X-5 Super Agent, Casey Jones & Jack & Jill (ends #7) begin						
	646	1292	1938	4522	7911	11,300
2-The Old Witch begins, ends #14	269	538	807	1681	2791	3900
3-Casey Jones ends; transvestism story "Jack & Jill"						
	255	510	765	1594	2647	3700
4-Super Agent (ends #17), & Betty Bates (ends #65) begin; X-5 ends						
	228	456	684	1425	2363	3300
5-Classic Lou Fine cover	571	1142	1713	4000	7000	10,000
6-10: 10-Old Witch by Crandall (4 pgs.); 1st work in comics (4/41)						
	193	386	579	1206	2003	2800
11-Classic cover	183	366	549	1144	1897	2650
12-17: 13-Blaze Barton ends. 17-Last Neon; Crandall Hercules in all; Last Lou Fine-c						
	121	242	363	756	1253	1750
18-Origin & 1st app. Stormy Foster, the Great Defender (12/41); The Ghost of Flanders begins; Crandall-c	126	252	378	788	1307	1825
19,20	98	196	294	613	1019	1425
21-24: 21-Last Hercules. 24-Last Red Bee & Strange Twins						
	95	190	285	594	985	1375
25-Origin & 1st app. Kid Eternity and begins by Moldoff (12/42); 1st app. The Keeper (Kid Eternity's aide)	183	366	549	1144	1897	2650
26-Blackhawk x-over in Kid Eternity	97	194	291	606	1003	1400
27-29	49	98	147	299	492	685
30,31- "Bill the Magnificent" by Kurtzman, 11 pgs. in each						
	45	90	135	275	455	635
32-40: 32-Plastic Man x-over. 34-Last Stormy Foster						
	30	60	90	174	275	375
41-50	21	42	63	122	191	260
51-60-Last Kid Eternity	20	40	60	115	180	245
61-63-Crandall-c/a; 61-Jeb Rivers begins	21	42	63	120	188	255
64,65-Crandall-a	20	40	60	115	180	245

NOTE: **Crandall**-a-11-17(Hercules), 23, 24(Stormy Foster); c-18-20, 23, 24. **Fine** c-1-14, 16, 17(most). **Ward** c-33. Bondage c-7, 64. Hercules c-3, 10-17. Jeb Rivers c-61-65. Kid Eternity c-25-60 (w/Keeper- 28-34, 36, 39-43, 45-55). Neon the Unknown c-2, 4, 8, 9. Red Bee c-1, 5-7. Stormy Foster c-18-24.

HITLER'S ASTROLOGER (See Marvel Graphic Novel #35)

HITMAN (Also see Bloodbath #2, Batman Chronicles #4, Demon #43-45 & Demon Annual #2)
DC Comics: May, 1996 - No. 60, Apr, 2001 ($2.25/$2.50)

1-Garth Ennis-s & John McCrea-c/a begin; Batman app.						
	1	2	3	5	7	9
2-Joker-c;Two Face, Mad Hatter, Batman app.						6.00
3-5: 3-Batman-c/app.; Joker app. 4-1st app. Nightfist						4.00
6-20: 8-Final Night x-over. 10-GL cameo. 11-20: 11,12-GL-c/app. 15-20-"Ace of Killers". 16-18-Catwoman app. 17-19-Demon-app.						3.00
21-59: 34-Superman-c/app.						2.50
60-($3.95) Final issue; includes pin-ups by various						4.00
#1,000,000 (11/98) Hitman goes to the 853rd Century						2.50
Annual 1 (1997, $3.95) Pulp Heroes						4.00
.../Lobo: That Stupid Bastich (7/00, $3.95) Ennis-s/Mahnke-a						4.00
TPB-(1997, $9.95) r/#1-3, Demon Ann. #2, Batman Chronicles #4						10.00
Ace of Killers TPB ('00, $17.95) r/#15-22						18.00
Local Heroes TPB ('99, $17.95) r/#9-14 & Annual #1						18.00
10,000 Bullets TPB ('98, $9.95) r/#4-8						10.00
Who Dares Wins TPB ('01, $12.95) r/#23-28						13.00

HI-YO SILVER (See Lone Ranger's Famous Horse... and The Lone Ranger; and March of Comics No. 215 in the Promotional Comics section)

HOBBIT, THE
Eclipse Comics: 1989 - No. 3, 1990 ($4.95, squarebound, 52 pgs.)

Book 1-3: Adapts novel; Wenzel-a						7.00

Holiday Comics #5 © STAR

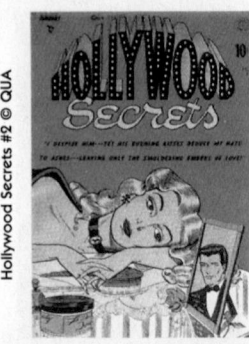
Hollywood Secrets #2 © QUA

Homer Hooper #3 © MAR

	GD 2.0	VG 4.0	FN 6.0	VF 8.0	VF/NM 9.0	NM- 9.2

Book 1-Second printing — 5.00
Graphic Novel (1990, Ballantine)-r/#1-3 — 20.00

HOCUS POCUS (See Funny Book #9)

HOGAN'S HEROES (TV)
Dell Publishing Co.: June, 1966 - No. 8, Sept, 1967; No. 9, Oct, 1969

	GD	VG	FN	VF	VF/NM	NM-
1: #1-7 photo-c	8	16	24	54	90	125
2,3-Ditko-a(p)	5	10	15	35	55	75
4-9: 9-Reprints #1	4	8	12	28	44	60

HOKUM & HEX (See Razorline)
Marvel Comics (Razorline): Sept, 1993 - No. 9, May, 1994 ($1.75/$1.95)

1-($2.50)-Foil embossed-c; by Clive Barker						3.00
2-9: 5-Hyperkind x-over						2.50

HOLIDAY COMICS
Fawcett Publications: 1942 (25¢, 196 pgs.)

1-Contains three Fawcett comics plus two page portrait of Captain Marvel; Capt. Marvel, Jungle Girl #1, & Whiz. Not rebound, remaindered comics; printed at the same time as originals	186	372	558	1163	1932	2700

HOLIDAY COMICS (Becomes Fun Comics #9-12)
Star Publications: Jan, 1951 - No. 8, Oct, 1952

	GD	VG	FN	VF	VF/NM	NM-
1-Funny animal contents (Frisky Fables) in all; L. B. Cole X-Mas-c	34	68	102	195	308	420
2-Classic L. B. Cole-c	36	72	108	208	329	450
3-8: 5,8-X-Mas-c; all L.B. Cole-c	20	40	60	117	184	250
Accepted Reprint 4 (nd)-L.B. Cole-c	10	20	30	58	79	100

HOLIDAY DIGEST
Harvey Comics: 1988 ($1.25, digest-size)

1	1	2	3	5	7	9

HOLIDAY PARADE (Walt Disney's…)
W. D. Publications (Disney): Winter, 1990-91(no year given) - No. 2, Winter, 1990-91 ($2.95, 68 pgs.)

1-Reprints 1947 Firestone by Barks plus new-a						4.00
2-Barks-r plus other stories						4.00

HOLI-DAY SURPRISE (Formerly Summer Fun)
Charlton Comics: V2#55, Mar, 1967 (25¢ Giant)

	GD	VG	FN	VF	VF/NM	NM-
V2#55	3	6	9	21	32	42

HOLLYWOOD COMICS
New Age Publishers: Winter, 1944 (52 pgs.)

1-Funny animal	18	36	54	105	165	225

HOLLYWOOD CONFESSIONS
St. John Publishing Co.: Oct, 1949 - No. 2, Dec, 1949

1-Kubert-c/a (entire book)	32	64	96	186	293	400
2-Kubert-c/a (entire book) (Scarce)	34	68	102	197	311	425

HOLLYWOOD DIARY
Quality Comics Group: Dec, 1949 - No. 5, July-Aug, 1950

1-No photo-c	21	42	63	122	191	260
2-Photo-c	14	28	42	80	115	150
3-5-Photo-c. 5-June Allyson/Peter Lawford photo-c	12	24	36	69	97	125

HOLLYWOOD FILM STORIES
Feature Publications/Prize: April, 1950 - No. 4, Oct, 1950 (All photo-c; "Fumetti" type movie comic)

1-June Allyson photo-c	20	40	60	117	184	250
2-4: 2-Lizabeth Scott photo-c. 3-Barbara Stanwick photo-c. 4-Betty Hutton photo-c	15	30	45	83	124	165

HOLLYWOOD FUNNY FOLKS (Formerly Funny Folks; Becomes Nutsy Squirrel #61 on)
National Periodical Publ.: No. 27, Aug-Sept, 1950 - No. 60, July-Aug, 1954

27	14	28	42	76	108	140
28-40	10	20	30	54	72	90
41-60	9	18	27	47	61	75

NOTE: *Rube Grossman a-most issues. Sheldon Mayer* a-27-35, 37-40, 43-46, 48-51, 53, 56, 57, 60.

HOLLYWOOD LOVE DOCTOR (See Doctor Anthony King…)

HOLLYWOOD PICTORIAL (…Romances on cover)
St. John Publishing Co.: No. 3, Jan, 1950

3-Matt Baker-a; photo-c	24	48	72	139	220	300

(Becomes a movie magazine - Hollywood Pictorial Western with No. 4.)

HOLLYWOOD ROMANCES (Formerly Brides In Love; becomes For Lovers Only #60 on)

Charlton Comics: V2#46, 11/66; #47, 10/67; #48, 11/68;V3#49,11/69-V3#59, 6/71

	GD	VG	FN	VF	VF/NM	NM-
V2#46-Rolling Stones-c/story	9	18	27	60	100	140
V2#47-V3#59: 56- "Born to Heart Break" begins	2	4	6	13	18	22

HOLLYWOOD SECRETS
Quality Comics Group: Nov, 1949 - No. 6, Sept, 1950

1-Ward-c/a (9 pgs.)	34	68	102	197	311	425
2-Crandall-a, Ward-c/a (9 pgs.)	23	46	69	130	205	280
3-6: All photo-c. 5-Lex Barker (Tarzan)-c	13	26	39	74	105	135
…of Romance, I.W. Reprint #9; r/#2 above w/Kinstler-c	2	4	6	10	14	18

HOLLYWOOD SUPERSTARS
Marvel Comics (Epic Comics): Nov, 1990 - No. 5, Apr, 1991 ($2.25)

1-($2.95, 52 pgs.)-Spiegle-c/a in all; Aragones-a, inside front-c plus 2-4 pgs.						3.00
2-5 ($2.25)						2.50

HOLO-MAN (See Power Record Comics)

HOLYOKE ONE-SHOT
Holyoke Publishing Co. (Tem Publ.): 1944 - No. 10, 1945 (All reprints)

	GD	VG	FN	VF	VF/NM	NM-
1,2: 1-Grit Grady (on cover only), Miss Victory, Alias X (origin)-All reprints from Captain Fearless. 2-Rusty Dugan (Corporal); Capt. Fearless (origin), Mr. Miracle (origin) app.	18	36	54	107	169	230
3-Miss Victory; r/Crash #4; Cat Man (origin), Solar Legion by Kirby app.; Miss Victory on cover only (1945)	31	62	93	178	282	385
4,6,8: 4-Mr. Miracle; The Blue Streak app. 6-Capt. Fearless, Alias X, Capt. Stone (splash used as-c to #10); Diamond Jim & Rusty Dugan (splash from cover of #2). 8-Blue Streak, Strong Man (story matches cover to #7)-Crash reprints	16	32	48	92	144	195
5,7: 5-U.S. Border Patrol Comics (Sgt. Dick Carter of the…), Miss Victory (story matches cover to #3), Citizen Smith, & Mr. Miracle app. 7-Secret Agent Z-2, Strong Man, Blue Streak (story matches cover to #8); Reprints from Crash #2	18	36	54	103	162	220
9-Citizen Smith, The Blue Streak, Solar Legion by Kirby & Strongman, the Perfect Human app.; reprints from Crash #4 & 5; Citizen Smith on cover only-from story in #5 (1944-before #3)	21	42	63	120	188	255
10-Captain Stone; r/Crash; Solar Legion by S&K	21	42	63	120	188	255

HOLY TERROR
Image Comics: Aug, 2002 - Present ($2.95)

1,2-Phil Hester-a/c; Jason Caskey-s						3.00

HOMER COBB (See Adventures of…)

HOMER HOOPER
Atlas Comics: July, 1953 - No. 4, Dec, 1953

	GD	VG	FN	VF	VF/NM	NM-
1-Teenage humor	10	20	30	58	79	100
2-4	8	16	24	40	50	60

HOMER, THE HAPPY GHOST (See Adventures of…)
Atlas(ACI/PPI/WPI)/Marvel: 3/55 - No. 22, 11/58; V2#1, 11/69 - V2#4, 5/70

V1#1-Dan DeCarlo-c/a begins, ends #22	22	44	66	126	198	270
2-1st code approved issue	13	26	39	74	105	135
3-10	11	22	33	64	90	115
11-22	10	20	30	56	76	95
V2#1 (11/69)	10	20	30	68	119	170
2-4	6	12	18	39	62	85

HOME RUN (Also see A-1 Comics)
Magazine Enterprises: No. 89, 1953 (one-shot)

A-1 89 (#3)-Powell-a; Stan Musial photo-c	14	28	42	76	108	140

HOMICIDE (Also see Dark Horse Presents)
Dark Horse Comics: Apr, 1990 ($1.95, B&W, one-shot)

1-Detective story						2.50

HONEYMOON (Formerly Gay Comics)
A Lover's Magazine(USA) (Marvel): No. 41, Jan, 1950

41-Photo-c; article by Betty Grable	11	22	33	60	83	105

HONEYMOONERS, THE (TV)
Lodestone: Oct, 1986 ($1.50)

1-Photo-c						4.00

HONEYMOONERS, THE (TV)
Triad Publications: Sept, 1987 - No. 13? ($2.00)

1-13						4.00

HONEYMOON ROMANCE

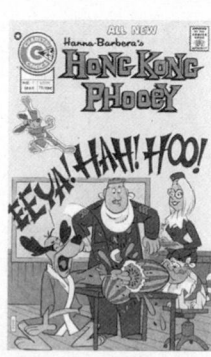

Hong Kong Phooey #1 © H-B

Hopalong Cassidy #15 © FAW

Horrific #5 © Comic Media

	GD 2.0	VG 4.0	FN 6.0	VF 8.0	VF/NM 9.0	NM- 9.2
Artful Publications (Canadian): Apr, 1950 - No. 2, July, 1950 (25¢, digest size)						
1,2-(Rare)	40	80	120	235	368	500
HONEY WEST (TV)						
Gold Key: Sept, 1966 (Photo-c)						
1 (10186-609)	9	18	27	60	100	140
HONG KONG PHOOEY (TV)						
Charlton Comics: June, 1975 - No. 9, Nov, 1976 (Hanna-Barbera)						
1	5	10	15	32	51	70
2	3	6	9	18	27	35
3-9	3	6	9	15	21	26
HONG ON THE RANGE						
Image/Flypaper Press: Dec, 1997 - No. 3, Feb, 1998 ($2.50, lim. series)						
1-3: Wu-s/Lafferty-a						2.50
HOOD, THE						
Marvel Comics (MAX): Jul, 2002 - No. 6, Dec, 2002 ($2.99, limited series)						
1-6-Vaughan-s/Hotz-c/a						3.00
Vol. 1 Blood From Stones HC (2007, $19.99, dustjacket) r/#1-6; production sketch art						20.00
Vol. 1 Blood From Stones TPB (2003, $14.99) r/#1-6						15.00
HOODED HORSEMAN, THE (Formerly Blazing West)						
American Comics Group (Michel Publ.): No. 21, 1-2/52 - No. 27, 1-2/54; No. 18, 12-1/54-55 - No. 22, 8-9/55						
21(1-2/52)-Hooded Horseman, Injun Jones cont.	15	30	45	83	124	165
22	10	20	30	56	76	95
23,24,27(1-2/54)	9	18	27	50	65	80
25 (9-10/53)-Cowboy Sahib on cover only; Hooded Horseman i.d. revealed	9	18	27	52	69	85
26-Origin/1st app. Cowboy Sahib by L. Starr	11	22	33	62	86	110
18(12-1/54-55)(Formerly Out of the Night)	10	20	30	54	72	90
19,21,22: 19-Last precode (1-2/55)	8	16	24	44	57	70
20-Origin Injun Injun	9	18	27	50	65	80

NOTE: *Whitney c/a-21(´52), 20-22.*

	GD 2.0	VG 4.0	FN 6.0	VF 8.0	VF/NM 9.0	NM- 9.2
HOODED MENACE, THE (Also see Daring Adventures)						
Realistic/Avon Periodicals: 1951 (one-shot)						
nn-Based on a band of hooded outlaws in the Pacific Northwest, 1900-1906; reprinted in Daring Advs. #15	48	96	144	293	484	675
HOODS UP (See the Promotional Comics section)						
HOOK (Movie)						
Marvel Comics: Early Feb, 1992 - No. 4, Late Mar, 1992 ($1.00, limited series)						
1-4: Adapts movie; Vess-c; 1-Morrow-a(p)						2.50
nn (1991, $5.95, 84 pgs.)-Contains #1-4; Vess-c						6.00
1 (1991, $2.95, magazine, 84 pgs.)-Contains #1-4; Vess-c (same cover as nn issue)						3.00
HOOT GIBSON'S WESTERN ROUNDUP (See Western Roundup under Fox Giants)						
HOOT GIBSON WESTERN (Formerly My Love Story)						
Fox Features Syndicate: No. 5, May, 1950 - No. 3, Sept, 1950						
5,6(#1,2): 5-Photo-c. 6-Photo/painted-c	23	46	69	130	200	270
3-Wood-a; painted-c	24	48	72	138	214	290
HOPALONG CASSIDY (Also see Bill Boyd Western, Master Comics, Real Western Hero, Six Gun Heroes & Western Hero; Bill Boyd starred as Hopalong Cassidy in movies, radio & TV)						
Fawcett Publications: Feb, 1943; No. 2, Summer, 1946 - No. 85, Nov, 1953						
1 (1943, 68 pgs.)-H. Cassidy & his horse Topper begin (on sale 1/8/43)-Captain Marvel app. on-c	488	976	1464	3416	5858	8300
2-(Sum, '46)	75	150	225	469	760	1050
3,4: 3-(Fall, '46, 52 pgs. begin)	39	78	117	224	350	475
5- "Mad Barber" story mentioned in SOTI, pgs. 308,309; photo-c	29	58	87	167	259	350
6-10: 8-Photo-c	22	44	66	125	193	260
11-19: 11,13,19-Photo-c	16	32	48	92	141	190
20-29 (52 pgs.)-Painted/photo-c	14	28	42	80	115	150
30,31,33,34,37-39,41 (52 pgs.)-Painted-c	11	22	33	64	90	115
32,40 (36pgs.)-Photo-c	10	20	30	58	79	100
35,42,43,45-47,49-51,53,54,56 (52 pgs.)-Photo-c	11	22	33	60	83	105
36,44,48 (36 pgs.)-Photo-c	10	20	30	56	76	95
52,55,57-70 (36 pgs.)-Photo-c	9	18	27	52	69	85
71-84-Photo-c	8	16	24	44	57	70
85-Last Fawcett issue; photo-c	10	20	30	54	72	90

NOTE: *Line-drawn c-1-4, 6, 7, 9, 10, 12.*

	GD 2.0	VG 4.0	FN 6.0	VF 8.0	VF/NM 9.0	NM- 9.2
... & The 5 Men of Evil (AC Comics, 1991, $12.95) r/newspaper strips and Fawcett story "Signature of Death"						13.00
HOPALONG CASSIDY						
National Periodical Publications: No. 86, Feb, 1954 - No. 135, May-June, 1959 (All-36 pgs.)						
86-Gene Colan-a begins, ends #117; photo covers continue	39	78	117	224	355	485
87	21	42	63	122	191	260
88-91: 91-1 pg. Superboy-sty (7/54)	15	30	45	83	124	165
92-99 (98 has #93 on-c; last precode issue, 2/55). 95-Reversed photo-c to #52. 98-Reversed photo-c to #61. 99-Reversed photo-c to #60	14	28	42	76	108	140
100-Same cover as #50	15	30	45	83	124	165
101-108: 105-Same photo-c as #54. 107-Same photo-c to #51. 108-Last photo-c	7	14	21	45	73	100
109-130: 118-Gil Kane-a begins. 123-Kubert-a (2 pgs.). 124-Painted-c	6	12	18	41	66	90
131-135	6	12	18	43	69	95
HOPELESS SAVAGES (Also see Too Much Hopeless Savages; and the Promotional Comics section for Free Comic Book Day edition)						
Oni Press: Aug, 2001 - No. 4, Nov, 2001 ($2.95, B&W, limited series)						
1-4-Van Meter-s/Norrie-a/Clugston-Major-a/Watson-c						3.00
TPB (2002, $13.95, 8" x 5.75") r/#1-4; plus color stories; Watson-c						14.00
HOPELESS SAVAGES: GROUND ZERO						
Oni Press: June, 2002 - No. 4, Oct, 2002 ($2.95, B&W, limited series)						
1-4-Van Meter-s/O'Malley-a/Dodson-c. 1-Watson-a						3.00
TPB (2003, $11.95, 8" x 5.75") r/#1-4; Dodson-c						12.00
HOPE SHIP						
Dell Publishing Co.: June-Aug, 1963						
1	3	6	9	16	22	28
HOPPY THE MARVEL BUNNY (See Fawcett's Funny Animals)						
Fawcett Publications: Dec, 1945 - No. 15, Sept, 1947						
1	28	56	84	164	260	355
2	14	28	42	82	121	160
3-15: 7-Xmas-c	12	24	36	67	94	120
HORACE & DOTTY DRIPPLE (Dotty Dripple No. 1-24)						
Harvey Publications: No. 25, Aug, 1952 - No. 43, Oct, 1955						
25-43	4	8	12	17	21	24
HORIZONTAL LIEUTENANT, THE (See Movie Classics)						
HOROBI						
Viz Premiere Comics: 1990 - No. 8, 1990 ($3.75, B&W, mature readers, 84 pgs.) V2#1, 1990 - No. 7, 1991 ($4.25, B&W, 68 pgs.)						
1-8: Japanese manga, Part Two, #1-7						4.50
HORRIFIC (Terrific No. 14 on)						
Artful/Comic Media/Harwell/Mystery: Sept, 1952 - No. 13, Sept, 1954						
1	57	114	171	356	591	825
2	36	72	108	208	329	450
3-Bullet in head-c	62	124	186	388	644	900
4,5,7,9,10: 4-Shrunken head-c. 7-Guillotine-c	31	62	93	178	282	385
6-Jack The Ripper story	32	64	96	186	293	400
8-Origin & 1st app. The Teller (E.C. parody)	36	72	108	208	329	450
11-13: 11-Swipe/Witches Tales #6,27; Devil-c	24	48	72	139	220	300

NOTE: *Don Heck a-8; c-3-13. Hollingsworth a-4. Morisi a-8. Palais a-5, 7-12.*

	GD 2.0	VG 4.0	FN 6.0	VF 8.0	VF/NM 9.0	NM- 9.2
HORRORCIDE						
IDW Publishing: Sept, 2004 ($6.99)						
1-Steve Niles short stories; art by Templesmith, Medors and Chee						7.00
HORROR FROM THE TOMB (Mysterious Stories No. 2 on)						
Premier Magazine Co.: Sept, 1954						
1-Woodbridge/Torres, Check-a; The Keeper of the Graveyard is host	42	84	126	251	406	560
HORRORIST, THE (Also see Hellblazer)						
DC Comics (Vertigo): Dec, 1995 - No. 2, Jan, 1996 ($5.95, lim. series, mature)						
1,2: Jamie Delano scripts, David Lloyd-c/a; John Constantine (Hellblazer) app.						6.00
HORROR OF COLLIER COUNTY						
Dark Horse Comics: Oct, 1999 - No. 5, Feb, 2000 ($2.95, B&W, limited series)						
1-5-Rich Tommaso-s/a						3.00
HORRORS, THE (Formerly Startling Terror Tales #10)						
Star Publications: No. 11, Jan, 1953 - No. 15, Apr, 1954						

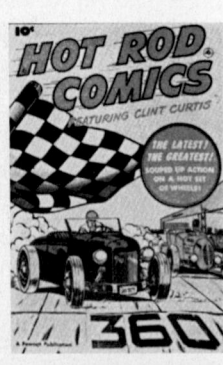

Hot Rod Comics #1 © FAW

Hot Rod Racers #12 © CC

Hourman #12 © DC

	GD 2.0	VG 4.0	FN 6.0	VF 8.0	VF/NM 9.0	NM- 9.2
11-Horrors of War; Disbrow-a(2)	30	60	90	174	275	375
12-Horrors of War; color illo in POP	28	56	84	162	256	350
13-Horrors of Mystery; crime stories	26	52	78	152	239	325
14,15-Horrors of the Underworld; crime stories	28	56	84	162	256	350

NOTE: All have **L. B. Cole** covers; a-12. **Hollingsworth** a-13. **Palais** a-13r.

HORROR TALES (Magazine)
Eerie Publications: V1#7, 6/69 - V6#6, 12/74; V7#1, 2/75; V7#2, 5/76 - V8#5, 1977; V9#1-3, 8/78; V10#1(2/79) (V1-V6: 52 pgs.; V7, V8#2: 112 pgs.; V8#4 on: 68 pgs.) (No V5#3, V8#1,3)

	GD 2.0	VG 4.0	FN 6.0	VF 8.0	VF/NM 9.0	NM- 9.2
V1#7	5	10	15	35	55	75
V1#8,9	4	8	12	24	37	50
V2#1-6('70), V3#1-6('71), V4#1-3,5-7('72)	3	6	9	21	32	42
V4#4-LSD story reprint/Weird V3#5	4	8	12	28	44	60
V5#1,2,4,5(6/73),5(10/73),6(12/73),V6#1-6('74),V7#1,2,4('76),V7#3('76)-Giant issue, V8#2,4,5('77)	3	6	9	21	32	42
V9#1-3(11/78, $1.50), V10#1(2/79)	4	8	12	23	36	48

NOTE: Bondage-c-V6#1, 3, V7#2.

HORSE FEATHERS COMICS
Lev Gleason Publ.: Nov, 1945 - No. 4, July(Summer on-c), 1948 (52 pgs.) (#2,3 are oversized)

	GD 2.0	VG 4.0	FN 6.0	VF 8.0	VF/NM 9.0	NM- 9.2
1-Wolverton's Scoop Scuttle, 2 pgs.	19	38	57	109	172	235
2	11	22	33	60	83	105
3,4: 3-(5/48)	9	18	27	47	61	75

HORSEMAN
Crusade Comics/Kevlar Studios: Mar, 1996 - No. 3, Nov, 1997 ($2.95)

0-1st Kevlar Studios issue, 1-(3/96)-Crusade issue; Shi-c/app., 1-(11/96)-3-(11/97)-Kevlar Studios						3.00

HORSEMASTERS, THE (Disney)(TV Movie)
Dell Publishing Co.: No. 1260, Dec-Feb, 1961/62

	GD 2.0	VG 4.0	FN 6.0	VF 8.0	VF/NM 9.0	NM- 9.2
Four Color 1260-Annette Funicello photo-c	12	24	36	87	156	225

HORSE SOLDIERS, THE
Dell Publishing Co.: No. 1048, Nov-Jan, 1959/60 (John Wayne movie)

	GD 2.0	VG 4.0	FN 6.0	VF 8.0	VF/NM 9.0	NM- 9.2
Four Color 1048-Painted-c, Sekowsky-a	13	26	39	95	168	240

HORSE WITHOUT A HEAD, THE (See Movie Comics)

HOT DOG
Magazine Enterprises: June-July, 1954 - No. 4, Dec-Jan, 1954-55

	GD 2.0	VG 4.0	FN 6.0	VF 8.0	VF/NM 9.0	NM- 9.2
1(A-1 #107)	9	18	27	47	61	75
2,3(A-1 #115),4(A-1 #136)	6	12	18	31	38	45

HOT DOG (See Jughead's Pal, Hotdog)

HOTEL DEPAREE - SUNDANCE (TV)
Dell Publishing Co.: No. 1126, Aug-Oct, 1960 (one-shot)

	GD 2.0	VG 4.0	FN 6.0	VF 8.0	VF/NM 9.0	NM- 9.2
Four Color 1126-Earl Holliman photo-c	6	12	18	43	69	95

HOT ROD AND SPEEDWAY COMICS
Hillman Periodicals: Feb-Mar, 1952 - No. 5, Apr-May, 1953

	GD 2.0	VG 4.0	FN 6.0	VF 8.0	VF/NM 9.0	NM- 9.2
1	27	54	81	158	249	340
2-Krigstein-a	18	36	54	105	165	225
3-5	12	24	36	69	97	125

HOT ROD COMICS (...Featuring Clint Curtis) (See XMas Comics)
Fawcett Publications: Nov, 1951 (no month given) - V2#7, Feb, 1953

	GD 2.0	VG 4.0	FN 6.0	VF 8.0	VF/NM 9.0	NM- 9.2
nn (V1#1)-Powell-c/a in all	29	58	87	167	264	360
2 (4/52)	15	30	45	90	140	190
3-6, V2#7	13	26	39	72	101	130

HOT ROD KING (Also see Speed Smith the Hot Rod King)
Ziff-Davis Publ. Co.: Fall, 1952

	GD 2.0	VG 4.0	FN 6.0	VF 8.0	VF/NM 9.0	NM- 9.2
1-Giacoia-a; Saunders painted-c	25	50	75	148	232	315

HOT ROD RACERS (Grand Prix No. 16 on)
Charlton Comics: Dec, 1964 - No. 15, July, 1967

	GD 2.0	VG 4.0	FN 6.0	VF 8.0	VF/NM 9.0	NM- 9.2
1	8	16	24	54	90	125
2-5	5	10	15	32	51	70
6-15	4	8	12	24	37	50

HOT RODS AND RACING CARS
Charlton Comics (Motor Mag. No. 1): Nov, 1951 - No. 120, June, 1973

	GD 2.0	VG 4.0	FN 6.0	VF 8.0	VF/NM 9.0	NM- 9.2
1-Speed Davis begins; Indianapolis 500 story	28	56	84	162	256	350
2	15	30	45	85	130	175
3-10	12	24	36	67	94	120
11-20	10	20	30	54	72	90
21-33,36-40	8	16	24	44	57	70
34, 35 (? & 6/58, 68 pgs.)	11	22	33	60	83	105

	GD 2.0	VG 4.0	FN 6.0	VF 8.0	VF/NM 9.0	NM- 9.2
41-60	7	14	21	37	46	55
61-80	3	6	9	19	29	38
81-100	3	6	9	16	22	28
101-120	2	4	6	13	18	22

HOT SHOT CHARLIE
Hillman Periodicals: 1947 (Lee Elias)

	GD 2.0	VG 4.0	FN 6.0	VF 8.0	VF/NM 9.0	NM- 9.2
1	11	22	33	60	83	105

HOT SHOTS: AVENGERS
Marvel Comics: Oct, 1995 ($2.95, one-shot)

nn-pin-ups						3.00

HOTSPUR
Eclipse Comics: Jun, 1987 - No. 3, Sep, 1987 ($1.75, lim. series, Baxter paper)

1-3						3.00

HOT STUFF (See Stumbo Tinytown)
Harvey Comics: V2#1, Sept, 1991 - No. 12, June, 1994 ($1.00)

V2#1-Stumbo back-up story						4.00
2-12 ($1.50)						3.00
...Big Book 1 (11/92), 2 (6/93) (Both $1.95, 52 pgs.)						4.00

HOT STUFF CREEPY CAVES
Harvey Publications: Nov, 1974 - No. 7, Nov, 1975

	GD 2.0	VG 4.0	FN 6.0	VF 8.0	VF/NM 9.0	NM- 9.2
1	4	8	12	22	34	45
2-7	3	6	9	15	21	26

HOT STUFF DIGEST
Harvey Comics: July, 1992 - No. 5, Nov, 1993 ($1.75, digest-size)

V2#1-Hot Stuff, Stumbo, Richie Rich stories						6.00
2-5						4.00

HOT STUFF GIANT SIZE
Harvey Comics: Oct, 1992 - No. 3, Oct, 1993 ($2.25, 68 pgs.)

V2#1-Hot Stuff & Stumbo stories						4.50
2,3						3.50

HOT STUFF SIZZLERS
Harvey Publications: July, 1960 - No. 59, Mar, 1974; V2#1, Aug, 1992

	GD 2.0	VG 4.0	FN 6.0	VF 8.0	VF/NM 9.0	NM- 9.2
1- 84 pgs. begin, ends #5; Hot Stuff, Stumbo begin	15	30	45	107	191	275
2-5	8	16	24	54	90	125
6-10: 6-68 pgs. begin, ends #45	6	12	18	41	66	90
11-20	4	8	12	28	44	60
21-45	3	6	9	20	30	40
46-52: 52 pgs. begin	3	6	9	16	23	30
53-59	2	4	6	10	14	18
V2#1-(8/92, $1.25)-Stumbo back-up						5.00

HOT STUFF, THE LITTLE DEVIL (Also see Devil Kids & Harvey Hits)
Harvey Publications (Illustrated Humor): 10/57 - No. 141, 7/77; No. 142, 2/78 - No. 164, 8/82; No. 165, 10/86 - No. 171, 11/87; No. 172, 11/88; No. 173, Sept, 1990 - No. 177, 1/91

	GD 2.0	VG 4.0	FN 6.0	VF 8.0	VF/NM 9.0	NM- 9.2
1	48	96	144	384	692	1000
2-Stumbo-like giant 1st app. (12/57)	24	48	72	175	313	450
3-5: 3-Stumbo the Giant debut (2/58)	17	34	51	128	227	325
6-10	11	22	33	75	133	190
11-20	8	16	24	56	93	130
21-40	6	12	18	37	59	80
41-60	4	8	12	24	37	50
61-80	3	6	9	18	27	35
81-105	3	6	9	14	20	25
106-112: All 52 pg. Giants	3	6	9	17	25	32
113-125	2	4	6	8	11	14
126-141	1	2	3	5	7	9
142-177: 172-177-($1.00)						6.00

HOT WHEELS (TV)
National Periodical Publications: Mar-Apr, 1970 - No. 6, Jan-Feb, 1971

	GD 2.0	VG 4.0	FN 6.0	VF 8.0	VF/NM 9.0	NM- 9.2
1	9	18	27	63	107	150
2,4,5	5	10	15	35	55	75
3-Neal Adams-c	6	12	18	39	62	85
6-Neal Adams-c/a	7	14	21	47	76	105

NOTE: Toth a-1p, 2-5; c-1p, 5.

HOURMAN (Justice Society member, see Adventure Comics #48)

HOURMAN (See JLA and DC One Million)
DC Comics: Apr, 1999 - No. 25, Apr, 2001 ($2.50)
1-25: 1-JLA app.; McDaniel-c. 2-Tomorrow Woman-c/app. 6,7-Amazo app. 11-13-Justice

House of Mystery #2 © DC

House of Mystery #267 © DC

House of Secrets #76 © DC

	GD 2.0	VG 4.0	FN 6.0	VF 8.0	VF/NM 9.0	NM- 9.2

Legion A app. 16-Silver Age flashback. 18,19-JSA-c/app. 22-Harris-c/a. 24-Hourman Vs.
Rex Tyler ... 2.50

HOUSE OF M (Also see miniseries with Fantastic Four, Iron Man and Spider-Man)
Marvel Comics: Aug, 2005 - No. 8, Dec, 2005 ($2.99, limited series)

1-Bendis-s/Coipel-a/Ribic-c; Scarlet Witch changes reality; Quesada variant-c ... 3.00
2-8-Variant covers for each. 3-Hawkeye returns ... 3.00
Secrets Of The House Of M (2005, $3.99, one-shot) profile pages and background info ... 4.00
... Sketchbook (6/05) B&W preview sketches by Coipel, Davis, Hairsine, Quesada ... 2.50
TPB (2006, $24.99) r/#1-8 and The Pulse: House of M Special Edition newspaper ... 25.00
...: Fantastic Four/ Iron Man TPB (2006, $13.99) r/ both House of M mini-series ... 14.00
...: World of M Featuring Wolverine TPB (2006, $13.99) r/2005 x-over issues Wolverine #33-35,
Black Panther #7, Captain America #10 and The Pulse #10 ... 14.00

HOUSE OF MYSTERY
DC Comics: Dec/Jan. 1951
nn - Ashcan comic, not distributed to newsstands, only for in-house use. Cover art is Danger Trail #3 with interior being Star Spangled Comics #109. A VG+ copy sold for $2,357.50 in 2002.

HOUSE OF MYSTERY (See Brave and the Bold #93, Elvira's House of Mystery, Limited Collectors' Edition & Super DC Giant)

HOUSE OF MYSTERY, THE
National Periodical Publications/DC Comics: Dec-Jan, 1951-52 - No. 321, Oct, 1983 (No. 194-203: 52 pgs.)

	GD 2.0	VG 4.0	FN 6.0	VF 8.0	VF/NM 9.0	NM- 9.2
1-DC's first horror comic	241	482	723	1506	2503	3500
2	93	186	279	581	966	1350
3	65	130	195	406	671	935
4,5	52	104	156	317	521	725
6-10	45	90	135	275	450	625
11-15	40	80	120	235	368	500
16(7/53)-25	31	62	93	178	282	385
26-35(2/55)-Last pre-code issue; 30-Woodish-a	24	48	72	139	220	300
36-50: 50-Text story of Orson Welles' War of the Worlds broadcast	13	26	39	95	168	240
51-60: 55-1st S.A. issue	11	22	33	75	133	190
61,63,65,66,69,70,72,76,85-Kirby-a	12	24	36	86	153	220
62,64,67,68,71,73-75,77-83,86-99	9	18	27	65	113	160
84-Prototype of Negative Man (Doom Patrol)	12	24	36	86	153	220
100 (7/60)	10	20	30	70	123	175
101-116: 109-Toth, Kubert-a. 116-Last 10¢ issue	9	18	27	60	100	140
117-130: 117-Swipes-c to HOS #20. 120-Toth-a	8	16	24	54	90	125
131-142	7	14	21	47	76	105
143-J'onn J'onzz, Manhunter begins (6/64), ends #173; story continues from Detective #326; intro. Idol-Head of Diabolu	19	38	57	138	244	350
144	8	16	24	58	97	135
145-155,157-159: 149-Toth-a. 155-The Human Hurricane app. (12/65), Red Tornado prototype. 158-Origin Diabolu Idol-Head	6	12	18	39	62	85
156-Robby Reed begins (origin/1st app.), ends #173	7	14	21	50	83	115
160-(7/66)-Robby Reed becomes Plastic Man in this issue only; 1st S.A. app. Plastic Man; intro Marco Xavier (Martian Manhunter) & Vulture Crime Organization; ends #173						
161-173: 169-Origin/1st app. Gem Girl	4	8	12	28	44	60
174-Mystery format begins.	9	18	27	65	113	160
175-1st app. Cain (House of Mystery host)	7	14	21	45	73	100
176,177	6	12	18	41	66	90
178-Neal Adams-a (2/69)	7	14	21	47	76	105
179-N. Adams/Orlando, Wrightson-a (1st pro work, 3 pgs.)	9	18	27	60	100	140
180,181,183: Wrightson-a (3,10, & 3 pgs.). 180-Last 12¢ issue; Kane/Wood-a(2). 183-Wood-a	6	12	18	41	66	90
182,184: 182-Toth-a. 184-Kane/Wood, Toth-a	4	8	12	28	44	60
185-Williamson/Kaluta-a; Howard-a (3 pgs.)	5	10	15	32	51	70
186-N. Adams-c/a; Wrightson-a (10 pgs.)	6	12	18	41	66	90
187,190: Adams-c. 187-Toth-a. 190-Toth-a(r)	4	8	12	26	41	55
188-Wrightson-a (8 & 3pgs.); Adams-c	5	10	15	35	55	75
189,192,197: Adams-c on all. 189-Wood-a(i). 192-Last 15¢-c	8	12	18	26	41	55
191-Wrightson-a (8 & 3pgs.); Adams-c	5	10	15	35	55	75
193-Wrightson-c	4	8	12	26	41	55
194-Wrightson-c; 52 pgs begin, end #203; Toth,Kirby-a						
	5	10	15	35	55	75
195: Wrightson-c. Swamp creature story by Wrightson similar to Swamp Thing (10 pgs.)(10/71)	7	14	21	45	73	100
196,198	4	8	12	24	37	50
199-Adams-c; Wood-a(8pgs.); Kirby-a	5	10	15	30	48	65

	GD 2.0	VG 4.0	FN 6.0	VF 8.0	VF/NM 9.0	NM- 9.2
200-(25¢, 52 pgs.)-One third-r (3/72)	5	10	15	32	51	70
201-203-(25¢, 52 pgs.)-One third-r	4	8	12	24	37	50
204-Wrightson-c/a, 9 pgs.	4	8	12	22	34	45
205,206,208,210,212,215,216,218	3	6	9	16	22	28
207-Wrightson-c/a; Starlin, Redondo-a	3	6	9	21	32	42
209,211,213,214,217-Wrightson-c	3	6	9	18	27	35
219,220,222,223	3	6	9	14	19	24
221-Wrightson/Kaluta-a(8 pgs.)	3	6	9	21	32	42
224-229: 224-Wrightson-r from Spectre #9; Dillin/Adams-r from House of Secrets #82; begin 100 pg. issues; Phantom Stranger-r. 225,227-(100 pgs.) - 225-Spectre app. 226-Wrightson/Redondo-a Phantom Stranger-r. 228-N. Adams inks; Wrightson-r.						
229-Wrightson-a(r); Toth-r; last 100 pg. issue	5	10	15	32	51	70
230,232-235,237-250	2	4	6	10	14	18
231-Classic Wrightson-c	3	6	9	19	29	38
236-Wrightson-c; Ditko-a(p); N. Adams-i	3	6	9	16	22	28
251-254-(84 pgs.)-Adams-c. 251-Wood-a	3	6	9	16	22	28
255,256-(84 pgs.)-Wrightson-a	3	6	9	16	22	28
257-259-(84 pgs.)	3	6	9	14	20	25
260-289: 282-(68 pgs.)-Has extra story "The Computers That Saved Metropolis" Radio Shack giveaway by Jim Starlin	1	2	3	5	7	9
290-1st "I, Vampire"	3	6	9	14	19	24
291-299: 291,293,295-299- "I, Vampire"	2	4	6	8	11	14
300,319,321: Death of "I, Vampire"	2	4	6	9	13	16
301-318,320: 301-318-"I, Vampire"	2	4	6	8	11	14

Welcome to the House of Mystery (7/98, $5.95) reprints stories with new framing story
by Gaiman and Aragonés ... 6.00

NOTE: *Neal Adams* a-236i: c-175-192, 197, 199, 251-254. *Alcala* a-209, 217, 219, 224, 227. **M. Anderson** a-212; c/a-37. *Aparo* a-209. *Aragonés* a-185, 186, 194, 196, 200, 202, 229, 251. *Baily* a-279p. *Cameron* a-76, 79. *Colan* a-202i. *Craig* a-263, 275, 295, 300. *Dillin/Adams* r-224. *Ditko* a-236p, 247, 253. *Drucker* a-37. *Evans* c-218. *Fradon* a-251. *Giffen* a-284. *Giunta* a-199, 227r. *Golden* a-257, 259. *Heath* a-194r; c-203. *Howard* a-182, 185, 187, 196, 229r, 247r, 254, 279r. *Kaluta* a-195, 200, 250r; c-200-202, 210, 212, 233, 260, 261, 263, 265, 267, 268, 273, 276, 284, 287, 288, 293-295, 300, 302, 304, 305, 309-319, 321. *Bob Kane* a-84. *Gil Kane* a-196p, 253p, 300p. *Kirby* a-194r, 199r; c-65, 76, 78, 79, 85. *Kubert* c-282, 283, 285, 286, 289. *Maneely* a-68, 227r. *Mayer* a-317p. *Meskin* a-52-144 (most), 195r; 224r, 229r; c-63, 66, 124, 127. *Mooney* a-24, 159, 160. *Moreira* a-3, 4, 20-50, 58, 59, 62, 68, 77, 79, 90, 108, 113, 123. *Morrow* a-192, 196, 255, 320i. *Mortimer* a-204(3 pgs.). *Nasser* a-276. *Newton* a-259, 272. *Nino* a-204, 212, 213, 220, 224, 229, 251, 252-256, 283. *Orlando* a-175(2 pgs.), 178, 240i; c-240, 258p, 262, 264p, 270p, 271, 272, 274, 275, 278, 296i. *Redondo* a-194, 195, 197, 202, 203, 207, 211, 214, 217, 219, 220, 227, 259, 283; c-209 (layout), 302p, 303i, 308; c-279 (layout). *Reese* a-195, 200, 205i. *Rogers* a-254, 274, 277. *Roussos* a-65, 84, 224i. *Sekowsky* a-282p. *Sparling* a-203. *Starlin* a-207(2 pgs.), 282p; c-281. *Leonard Starr* a-9. *Staton* a-300p. *Sutton* a-189, 211. *Tuska* a-293p, 294p, 316p. *Wrightson* c-193-195, 204, 207, 209, 211, 213, 214, 217, 219, 221, 231, 236, 255, 256; r-224.

HOUSE OF SECRETS (Combined with The Unexpected after #154)
National Periodical Publications/DC Comics: 11-12/56 - No. 80, 9-10/66; No. 81, 8-9/69 - No. 140, 2-3/76; No. 141, 8-9/76 - No. 154, 10-11/78

	GD 2.0	VG 4.0	FN 6.0	VF 8.0	VF/NM 9.0	NM- 9.2
1-Drucker-a; Moreira-c	109	218	327	927	1714	2500
2-Moreira-c	40	80	120	320	580	840
3-Kirby-c/a	35	70	105	263	482	700
4-Kirby-a	25	50	75	186	333	480
5-7	18	36	54	132	234	335
8-Kirby-a	20	40	60	146	261	375
9-11: 11-Lou Cameron-a (unsigned)	16	32	48	114	202	290
12-Kirby-c/a; Lou Cameron-a	17	34	51	124	220	315
13-15: 14-Flying saucer-c	12	24	36	84	150	215
16-20	11	22	33	75	133	190
21,22,24-30	10	20	30	67	116	165
23-1st app. Mark Merlin & begin series (8/59)	10	20	30	73	129	185
31-50: 48-Toth-a. 50-Last 10¢ issue	9	18	27	61	103	145
51-60: 58-Origin Mark Merlin	7	14	21	50	83	115
61-First Eclipso (7-8/63) and begin series	15	30	45	107	191	275
62	8	16	24	54	90	125
63-65-Toth-a on Eclipso (see Brave and the Bold #64)	6	12	18	43	69	95
66-1st Eclipso-c (also #67,70,78,79); Toth-a	8	16	24	54	90	125
67,73: 67-Toth-a on Eclipso. 73-Mark Merlin becomes Prince Ra-Man (1st app.)	6	12	18	43	69	95
68-72,74-80: 76-Prince Ra-Man vs. Eclipso. 80-Eclipso, Prince Ra-Man end	6	12	18	39	62	85
81-Mystery format begins; 1st app. Abel (House Of Secrets host); (cameo in DC Special #4)	9	18	27	65	113	160
82-84: 82-Neal Adams-c(i)	5	10	15	35	55	75
85,90: 85-N. Adams-a(i). 90-Buckler (early work)/N. Adams-a(i)	6	12	18	37	59	80
86,88,89,91	4	8	12	28	44	60
87-Wrightson & Kaluta-a	6	12	18	39	62	85

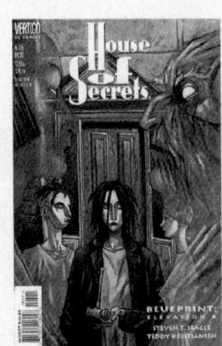

House of Secrets #25
© Seagle & Kristiansen

Howard the Duck #6 © MAR

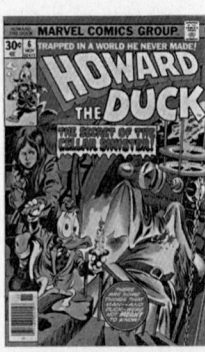

Howdy Doody #10 © Cal. Nat. Prod.

	GD 2.0	VG 4.0	FN 6.0	VF 8.0	VF/NM 9.0	NM- 9.2		GD 2.0	VG 4.0	FN 6.0	VF 8.0	VF/NM 9.0	NM- 9.2

92-1st app. Swamp Thing-c/story (8 pgs.)(6-7/71) by Berni Wrightson(p)
w/JeffJones/Kaluta/Weiss ink assists; classic-c. 48 96 144 384 692 1000
93,94,96-(52 pgs.)-Wrightson-c. 94-Wrightson-a(i); 96-Wood-a

	4	8	12	28	44	60
95,97,98-(52 pgs.)	4	8	12	28	44	60
99-Wrightson splash pg.	4	8	12	24	37	50
100-Classic Wrightson-c	5	10	15	35	55	75
101,102,104,105,108-120: 112-Grey tone-c	3	6	9	14	19	24
103,106,107-Wrightson-c	3	6	9	18	27	36
121-133	2	4	6	9	13	16
134-136,139-Wrightson-a	2	4	6	13	18	22
137,138,141-153	1	3	4	6	8	10

140-1st solo origin of the Patchworkman (see Swamp Thing #3)

	3	6	9	16	22	28
154 (10-11/78, 44 pgs.) Last issue	2	4	6	8	11	14

NOTE: Neal Adams c-81, 82, 84-88, 90, 91. Alcala a-104-107. Anderson a-91. Aparo a-93, 97, 105. B. Bailey a-107. Cameron a-13, 15. Colan a-63. Ditko a-139p; 148. Elias a-58. Evans a-118. Finlay a-7r(Real Fact?). Glanzman a-91. Golden a-151. Heath a-31. Heck a-85. Kaluta a-87, 98, 99; c-98, 99, 101, 102, 105, 149, 151, 154. Bob Kane a-18, 21. G. Kane a-85p. Kirby a-3, 11, 12. Kubert a-39. Meskin a-2-68 (most), 94r; c-55-60. Moreira a-7, 8, 51, 54, 102-104, 106, 108, 113, 116, 118, 121, 123, 127; c-1, 2, 4-10, 13-20. Morrow a-86, 89, 90; c-89, 146-148. Nino a-101, 103, 106, 109, 115, 117, 126, 128, 131, 147, 153. Redondo a-95, 99, 102, 104p, 113, 116, 134, 136, 139, 140. Reese a-85. Severin a-91. Starlin c-150. Sutton a-154. Toth a-63-67, 83, 93r, 94r, 96r-98r, 123. Tuska a-90, 104. Wrightson a-134; c-92-94, 96, 100, 103, 106, 107, 135, 136, 139.

HOUSE OF SECRETS
DC Comics (Vertigo): Oct, 1996 - No. 25, Dec, 1998 ($2.50) (Creator-owned series)

1-Steven Seagle-s/Kristiansen-c/a.						3.50
2-25: 5,7-Kristiansen-c/a. 6-Fegrado-a						3.00
TPB-(1997, $14.95) r/1-5						15.00

HOUSE OF SECRETS: FACADE
DC Comics (Vertigo): 2001 - No. 2, 2001 ($5.95, limited series)

1,2-Steven Seagle-s/Teddy Kristiansen-c/a. 6.00

HOUSE OF TERROR (3-D)
St. John Publishing Co.: Oct, 1953 (25¢, came w/glasses)

1-Kubert, Baker-a 29 58 87 167 264 360

HOUSE OF YANG, THE (See Yang)
Charlton Comics: July, 1975 - No. 6, June, 1976; 1978

1-Sanho Kim-a in all	2	4	6	10	14	18
2-6	1	2	3	5	7	9
Modern Comics #1,2(1978)						4.00

HOUSE ON THE BORDERLAND
DC Comics (Vertigo): 2000 ($29.95, hardcover, one-shot)

HC-Adaptation of William Hope Hodgson book; Corben-a						30.00
SC (2003, $19.95)						20.00

HOUSE II: THE SECOND STORY
Marvel Comics: Oct, 1987 (One-shot)

1-Adapts movie 2.50

HOWARD CHAYKIN'S AMERICAN FLAGG (See American Flagg!)
First Comics: V2#1, May, 1988 - V2#12, Apr, 1989 ($1.75/$1.95, Baxter paper)

V2#1-9,11,12-Chaykin-c(p) in all						2.50
10-Elvis Presley photo-c						3.00

HOWARD THE DUCK (See Bizarre Adventures #34, Crazy Magazine, Fear, Man-Thing, Marvel Treasury Edition & Sensational She-Hulk #14-17)
Marvel Comics Group: Jan, 1976 - No. 31, May, 1979; No. 32, Jan, 1986; No. 33, Sept, 1986

1-Brunner-c/a; Spider-Man x-over (low distr.)	3	6	9	20	30	40
2-Brunner-c/a	2	4	6	10	14	18
3,4-(Regular 25¢ edition). 3-Buscema-a(p), (7/76)	2	4	6	8	10	12
3,4-(30¢-c, limited distribution)	3	6	9	14	19	24
5	2	4	6	8	10	12

6-11: 8-Howard The Duck for president. 9-1st Sgt. Preston Dudley of RCMP.

10-Spider-Man-c/sty	1	2	3	5		6	8
12-1st brief app. Kiss (3/77)	3	6	9	20	30	40

13-(30¢-c) 1st full app. Kiss (6/77); Daimon Hellstrom app. plus cameo of Howard as Son of Satan 8 12 22 34 45
13 (35¢-c, limited distribution) 8 16 24 54 90 125
14-32: 14-17-(Regular 30¢-c). 14-Howard as Son of Satan-c/story; Son of Satan app. 16-Album issue; 3 pgs. comics. 22,23-Man-Thing-c/stories; Star Wars parody. 30,32-P. Smith-a 4.00

14-17-(35¢-c, limited distribution)	2	4	6	11	16	20
33-Last issue; low print run	1	2	3	4	5	7
Annual 1(1977, 52 pgs.)-Mayerik-a	1	2	3	4	5	7

NOTE: Austin c-29i. Bolland c-33. Brunner a-1p, 2p; c-1, 2. Buckler c-3p. Buscema a-3p. Colan a(p)-4-15, 17-20, 24-27, 30, 31; c(p)-4-31, Annual 1p. Leialoha a-1-13i; c(i)-3-5, 8-11. Mayerik a-22, 23, 33. Paul Smith a-30p, 32. Man-Thing app. in #22, 23.

HOWARD THE DUCK (Magazine)
Marvel Comics Group: Oct, 1979 - No. 9, Mar, 1981 (B&W, 68 pgs.)

1-Art by Colan, Janson, Golden. Kidney Lady app.	1	3	4	6	8	10

2,3,5-9 (nudity in most): 2-Mayerick-a. 3-Xmas issue; Jack Davis-c; Duck World flashback. 5-Dracula app. 6-1st Street People back-up story. 7-Has poster by Byrne; Man-Thing-c/s (46 pgs.). 8-Batman parody w/Marshall Rogers-a; Dave Sim-a (1 pg.). 9-Marie Severin-a; John Pound painted-c 5.00
4-Beatles, John Lennon, Elvis, Kiss & Devo cameos; Hitler app.

	2	4	6	8	10	12

NOTE: Buscema a-4p. Colan a-1-5p, 7-9p. Jack Davis c-3. Golden a(p)-1, 5, 6(51pgs.). Rogers a-7, 8. Simonson a-7.

HOWARD THE DUCK (Volume 2)
Marvel Comics: Mar, 2002 - No. 6, Aug, 2002 ($2.99)

1-Gerber-s/Winslade-a/Fabry-c						4.00
2-6: 2,4-6-Gerber-s/Winslade-a/Fabry-c. 3-Fabry-a/c						3.00
TPB (9/02, $14.99) r/#1-6						15.00

HOWARD THE DUCK HOLIDAY SPECIAL
Marvel Comics: Feb, 1997 ($2.50, one-shot)

1-Wraparound-c; Hama-s 2.50

HOWARD THE DUCK: THE MOVIE
Marvel Comics Group: Dec, 1986 - No. 3, Feb, 1987 (Limited series)

1-3: Movie adaptation; r/Marvel Super Special 2.50

HOW BOYS AND GIRLS CAN HELP WIN THE WAR
The Parents' Magazine Institute: 1942 (10¢, one-shot)

1-All proceeds used to buy war bonds 26 52 78 152 239 325

HOWDY DOODY (TV)(See Jackpot of Fun-- & Poll Parrot)
Dell Publishing Co.: 1/50 - No. 38, 7-9/56; No. 761, 1/57; No. 811, 7/57

1-(Scarce)-Photo-c; 1st TV comic	78	156	234	663	1232	1800
2-Photo-c	38	76	114	285	518	750
3-5: All photo-c	22	44	66	160	285	410

6-Used in SOTI, pg. 309; classic-c; painted covers begin

	22	44	66	165	295	425
7-10	14	28	42	103	184	265
11-20: 13-X-Mas-c	12	24	36	86	153	220
21-38, Four Color 761,811	10	20	30	71	126	180

HOW IT BEGAN
United Features Syndicate: No. 15, 1939 (one-shot)

Single Series 15 34 68 102 197 311 425

HOW SANTA GOT HIS RED SUIT (See March of Comics No. 2)

HOW THE WEST WAS WON (See Movie Comics)

HOW TO DRAW FOR THE COMICS
Street and Smith: No date (1942?) (10¢, 64 pgs., B&W & color, no ads)

nn-Art by Robert Winsor McCay (recreating his father's art), George Marcoux (Supersnipe artist), Vernon Greene (The Shadow artist), Jack Binder (with biog.), Thorton Fisher, Jon Small, & Jack Farr; has biographies of each artist
  29 58 87 167 264 360

H. P. LOVECRAFT'S CTHULHU
Millennium Publications: Dec, 1991 - No. 3, May, 1992 ($2.50, limited series)

1-3: 1-Contains trading cards on thin stock 3.00

H. R. PUFNSTUF (TV) (See March of Comics #360)
Gold Key: Oct, 1970 - No. 8, July, 1972

1-Photo-c	15	30	45	107	191	275
2-8-Photo-c on all. 6-8-Both Gold Key and Whitman editions exist	9	18	27	65	113	160

HUBERT AT CAMP MOONBEAM
Dell Publishing Co.: No. 251, Oct. 1949 (one shot)

Four Color 251 6 12 18 39 62 85

HUCK & YOGI JAMBOREE (TV)
Dell Publishing Co.: Mar, 1961 ($1.00, 6-1/4x9", 116 pgs., cardboard-c, high quality paper) (B&W original material)

nn 9 18 27 63 107 150

HUCK & YOGI WINTER SPORTS (TV)
Dell Publishing Co.: No. 1310, Mar, 1962 (Hanna-Barbera) (one-shot)

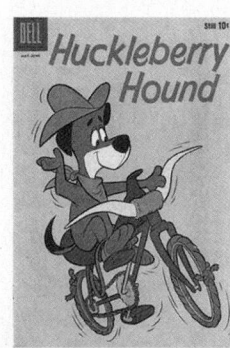

Huckleberry Hound #5 © H-B

Hulk and Power Pack #1 © MAR

Human Fly #3 © MAR

	GD	VG	FN	VF	VF/NM	NM-
	2.0	4.0	6.0	8.0	9.0	9.2

Four Color 1310 ... 8 16 24 56 93 130

HUCK FINN (See The New Adventures of... & Power Record Comics)

HUCKLEBERRY FINN (Movie)
Dell Publishing Co.: No. 1114, July, 1960
Four Color 1114-Photo-c ... 5 10 15 35 55 75

HUCKLEBERRY HOUND (See Dell Giant #31,44, Golden Picture Story Book, Kite Fun Book, March of Comics #199, 214, 235, Spotlight #1 & Whitman Comic Books)

HUCKLEBERRY HOUND (TV)
Dell/Gold Key No. 18 (10/62) on: No. 990, 5-7/59 - No. 43, 10/70 (Hanna-Barbera)
Four Color 990(#1)-1st app. Huckleberry Hound, Yogi Bear, & Pixie & Dixie & Mr. Jinks

	12	24	36	86	153	220
Four Color 1050,1054 (12/59)	8	16	24	56	93	130
3(1-2/60) - 7 (9-10/60), Four Color 1141 (10/60)	8	16	24	52	86	120
8-10	6	12	18	43	69	95
11,13-17 (6-8/62)	5	10	15	32	51	70
12-1st Hokey Wolf & Ding-a-Ling	6	12	18	37	59	80
18,19 (84pgs.; 18-20 titled ...Chuckleberry Tales	8	16	24	52	86	120
20-Titled Chuckleberry Tales	5	10	15	30	48	65
21-30: 28-30-Reprints	4	8	12	24	37	50
31-43: 31,32,35,37-43-Reprints	3	6	9	20	30	40

HUCKLEBERRY HOUND (TV)
Charlton Comics: Nov, 1970 - No. 8, Jan, 1972 (Hanna-Barbera)

1	5	10	15	32	51	70
2-8	3	6	9	18	27	35

HUEY, DEWEY, & LOUIE (See Donald Duck, 1938 for 1st app. Also see Mickey Mouse Magazine V4#2, V5#7 & Walt Disney's Junior Woodchucks Limited Series)

HUEY, DEWEY, & LOUIE BACK TO SCHOOL (See Dell Giant #22, 35, 49 & Dell Giants)

HUEY, DEWEY, AND LOUIE JUNIOR WOODCHUCKS (Disney)
Gold Key No. 1-61/Whitman No. 62 on: Aug, 1966 - No. 81, July, 1984
(See Walt Disney's Comics & Stories #125)

1	6	12	18	39	62	85
2,3(12/68)	4	8	12	22	34	45
4,5(4/70)-r/two WDC&S D.Duck stories by Barks	3	6	9	20	30	40
6-17	3	6	9	18	27	35
18,27-30	3	6	9	15	21	26
19-23,25-New storyboarded scripts by Barks, 13-25 pgs. per issue						
	3	6	9	19	29	38
24,26: 26-r/Barks Donald Duck WDC&S stories	3	6	9	16	23	30
31-57,60,61: 35,41-r/Barks J.W. scripts	2	4	6	8	11	14
58,59: 58-r/Barks Donald Duck WDC&S stories	2	4	6	9	13	16
62-64 (Whitman)	2	4	6	9	13	16
65-(9/80), 66 (Pre-pack? scarce)	3	6	9	20	30	40
67 (1/81),68	2	4	6	9	13	16
69-74: 72(2/82), 73(2-3/82), 74(3/82)	2	4	6	8	11	14
75-81 (all #90183; pre-pack; nd, nd code; scarce): 75(4/83), 76(5/83), 77(7/83), 78(8/83), 79(4/84), 80(5/84), 81(7/84)						
	3	6	9	14	20	25

HUGGA BUNCH (TV)
Marvel Comics (Star Comics): Oct, 1986 - No. 6, Aug, 1987
1-6 ... 4.00

HULK (Magazine)(Formerly The Rampaging Hulk)(Also see The Incredible Hulk)
Marvel Comics: No. 10, Aug., 1978 - No. 27, June, 1981 ($1.50)
10-18: 10-Bill Bixby interview. 11-Moon Knight begins. 12-15,17,18-Moon Knight stories. 12-Lou Ferrigno interview.

	2	4	6	9	13	16

19-27: 20-Moon Knight story. 23-Last full color issue; Banner is attacked. 24-Part color, Lou Ferrigno interview. 25-Part color. 26,27-are B&W

	1	3	4	6	8	10

NOTE: #10-20 have fragile spines which split easily. **Alcala** a(i)-15, 17-20, 22, 24-27. **Buscema** a-23; c-26. **Chaykin** a-21-25. **Colan** a(p)-11, 19, 24-27. **Jusko** painted c-12. **Nebres** a-16. **Severin** a-19i. Moon Knight by **Sienkiewicz** in 13-15, 17, 18, 20. **Simonson** a-27; c-23. Dominic Fortune appears in #21-24.

HULK (Becomes Incredible Hulk Vol. 2 with issue #12) (Also see Marvel Age Hulk)
Marvel Comics: Apr, 1999 - No. 11, Feb, 2000 ($2.99/$1.99)
1-($2.99) Byrne-s/Garney-a ... 5.00
1-Variant-c ... 9.00
1-DFE Remarked-c ... 50.00
1-Gold foil variant ... 10.00
2-7-($1.99): 2-Two covers. 5-Art by Jurgens, Buscema & Texeira. 7-Avengers app. ... 4.00
8-Hulk battles Wolverine ... 7.00
9-11: 11-She-Hulk app. ... 3.00
1999 Annual ($3.50) Chapter One story; Byrne-s/Weeks-a ... 3.50

Hulk Vs. The Thing (12/99, $3.99, TPB) reprints their notable battles ... 4.00

HULK AND POWER PACK (All ages series)
Marvel Comics: May, 2007 - No. 4, Aug, 2007 ($2.99, limited series)
1-4-Sumerak-s. 1,2,4-Williams-a. 1-Absorbing Man app. 3-Kuhn-a; Abomination app. ... 3.00
...: Pack Smash! (2007, $6.99, digest) r/#1-4 ... 7.00

HULK & THING: HARD KNOCKS
Marvel Comics: Nov, 2004 - No. 4, Feb, 2005 ($3.50, limited series)
1-4-Bruce Jones-s/Jae Lee-a/c ... 3.50
TPB (2005, $13.99) r/#1-4 and Giant-Size Super-Stars #1 ... 14.00

HULK: DESTRUCTION
Marvel Comics: Sept, 2005 - No. 4, Dec, 2005 ($2.99, limited series)
1-4-Origin of the Abomination; Peter David-s/Jim Muniz-a ... 3.00

HULK: FUTURE IMPERFECT
Marvel Comics: Jan, 1993 - No. 2, Dec, 1992 (In error) ($5.95, 52 pgs., squarebound, limited series)
1,2: Embossed-c; Peter David story & George Perez-c/a. 1-1st app. Maestro.

	1	2	3		6	8

HULK: GRAY
Marvel Comics: Dec, 2003 - No. 6, Apr, 2004 ($3.50, limited series)
1-6-Hulk's origin & early days; Loeb-s/Sale-a/c ... 3.50
HC (2004, $21.99, with dust jacket) oversized r/#1-6 ... 22.00
SC (2005, $19.99) r/#1-6 ... 20.00

HULK: NIGHTMERICA
Marvel Comics: Aug, 2003 - No. 6, May, 2004 ($2.99, limited series)
1-6-Brian Ashmore painted-a/c ... 3.00

HULK/ PITT
Marvel Comics: 1997 ($5.99, one-shot)
1-David-s/Keown-c/a ... 6.00

HULK SMASH
Marvel Comics: Mar, 2001 - No. 2, Apr, 2001 ($2.99, limited series)
1,2-Ennis-s/McCrea & Janson-a/Nowlan painted-c ... 3.00

HULK: THE MOVIE
Marvel Comics
...Adaptation (8/03, $3.50) Bruce Jones-s/Bagley-a/Keown-c ... 3.50
TPB (2003, $12.99) r/Adaptation, Ultimates #5, Inc. Hulk #34, Ult. Marvel Team-Up #2&3 ... 13.00

HULK 2099
Marvel Comics: Dec, 1994 - No. 10, Sept, 1995 ($1.50/$1.95)
1-($2.50)-Green foil-c ... 3.00
2-10: 2-A. Kubert-c ... 2.50

HULK/WOLVERINE: 6 HOURS
Marvel Comics: Mar, 2003 - No. 4, May, 2003 ($2.99, limited series)
1-4-Bruce Jones-s/Scott Kolins-a; Bisley-c ... 3.00
Hulk Legends Vol. 1: Hulk/Wolverine: 6 Hours (2003, $13.99, TPB) r/#1-4 & 1st Wolverine app. from Incredible Hulk #181 ... 14.00

HUMAN DEFENSE CORPS
DC Comics: Jul, 2003 - No. 6, Dec, 2003 ($2.50, limited series)
1-6-Ty Templeton-s/Sauve, Jr & Vlasco-a. 1-Lois Lane app. ... 2.50

HUMAN FLY
I.W. Enterprises/Super: 1963 - 1964 (Reprints)

	GD	VG	FN	VF	VF/NM	NM-
I.W. Reprint #1-Reprints Blue Beetle #44('46)	2	4	6	13	18	22
Super Reprint #10-R/Blue Beetle #46('47)	2	4	6	13	18	22

HUMAN FLY, THE
Marvel Comics Group: Sept, 1977 - No. 19, Mar, 1979

1,2,9,19: 1,2-(Regular 30¢-c). 1-Origin; Spider-Man x-over. 2-Ghost Rider app. 9-Daredevil x-over; Byrne-c(p). 19-Last issue	1	2	3	5	6	8
1,2-(35¢-c, limited distribution)	3	6	9	16	23	30
3-8,10-18						4.00

NOTE: **Austin** c-4i, 9i. **Elias** a-1, 3p, 4p, 7p, 10-12p, 15p, 18p, 19p. **Layton** c-19.

HUMANKIND
Image Comics (Top Cow): Sept, 2004 - No. 5, Mar, 2005 ($2.99, limited series)
1-5-Tony Daniel-a. 1-Three covers by Daniel, Silvestri, and Land ... 3.00

HUMAN RACE, THE
DC Comics: May, 2005 - No. 7, Nov, 2005 ($2.99, limited series)
1-7-Raab-s/Justiniano-a/c ... 3.00

Human Torch #2 (#1) © MAR

Humdinger #1 © NOVP

The Hunger #1 © Speakeasy

	GD 2.0	VG 4.0	FN 6.0	VF 8.0	VF/NM 9.0	NM- 9.2

HUMAN TARGET
DC Comics (Vertigo): Apr, 1999 - No. 4, July, 1999 ($2.95, limited series)

1-4-Milligan-s/Bradstreet-c/Biukovic-a						3.00
TPB (2000, $12.95) new Bradstreet-c						13.00

HUMAN TARGET
DC Comics (Vertigo): Oct, 2003 - No. 21, June, 2005 ($2.95)

1-21: 1-5-Milligan-s/Pulido-a/c. 6-Chiang-a						3.00
...: Living in Amerika TPB (2004, $14.95) r/#6-10; Chiang sketch pages						15.00
...: Strike Zones TPB (2004, $9.95) r/#1-5						10.00

HUMAN TARGET: FINAL CUT
DC Comics (Vertigo): 2002 ($29.95/$19.95, graphic novel)

Hardcover (2002, $29.95) Milligan-s/Pulido-a/c						30.00
Softcover (2003, $19.95)						20.00

HUMAN TARGET SPECIAL (TV)
DC Comics: Nov, 1991 ($2.00, 52 pgs., one-shot)

1						3.00

HUMAN TORCH, THE (Red Raven #1)(See All-Select, All Winners, Marvel Mystery, Men's Adventures, Mystic Comics (2nd series), Sub-Mariner, USA & Young Men)
Timely/Marvel Comics (TP 2,3/TCI 4-9/SePI 10/SnPC 11-25/CnPC 26-35/Atlas Comics (CPC 36-38)): No. 2, Fall, 1940 - No. 15, Spring, 1944; No. 16, Fall, 1944 - No. 35, Mar, 1949 (Becomes Love Tales #36 on): No. 36, April, 1954 - No. 38, Aug, 1954

	GD 2.0	VG 4.0	FN 6.0	VF 8.0	VF/NM 9.0	NM- 9.2
2(#1)-Intro & Origin Toro; The Falcon, The Fiery Mask, Mantor the Magician, & Microman only app.; Human Torch by Burgos, Sub-Mariner by Everett begin (origin of each in text)	3000	6000	9000	22,500	41,250	60,000
3(#2)-40 pg. H.T. story; H.T. & S.M. battle over who is best artist in text-Everett or Burgos	543	1086	1629	3800	6650	9500
4(#3)-Origin The Patriot in text; last Everett Sub-Mariner; Sid Greene-a	429	858	1287	3000	5250	7500
5(#4)-The Patriot app; Angel x-over in Sub-Mariner (Summer, 1941); 1st Nazi war-c this title	364	728	1092	2366	4183	6000
5-Human Torch battles Sub-Mariner (Fall, '41); 60 pg. story	543	1086	1629	3800	6650	9500
6,9	283	566	849	1769	2935	4100
7-1st Japanese war-c	290	580	870	1813	3007	4200
8-Human Torch battles Sub-Mariner; 52 pg. story; Wolverton-a, 1 pg.	370	740	1110	2405	4253	6100
10-Human Torch battles Sub-Mariner, 45 pg. story; Wolverton-a, 1 pg.	600	900	1970	3485	5000	
11,13-15: 14-1st Atlas Globe logo (Winter, 1943-44; see All Winners #11 also)	214	428	642	1338	2219	3100
12-Classic-c	333	666	1000	2165	3833	5500
16-20: 20-Last War issue	148	296	444	925	1538	2150
21,22,24-30: 27-2nd app. (1st-c) Asbestos Lady (see Capt. America Comics #63 for 1st app.)	131	262	393	819	1360	1900
23 (Sum/46)-Becomes Junior Miss 24? Classic Schomburg Robot-c	155	310	465	969	1610	2250
31,32: 31-Namora x-over in Sub-Mariner (also #30); last Toro. 32-Sungirl, Namora app.; Sungirl-c	110	220	330	688	1144	1600
33-Capt. America x-over	116	232	348	725	1200	1675
34-Sungirl solo	103	206	309	644	1072	1500
35-Captain America & Sungirl app. (1949)	110	220	330	688	1144	1600
36-38(1954)-Sub-Mariner in all	90	180	270	563	932	1300

NOTE: Ayers Human Torch in 36(3). Brodsky c-25, 31-33?, 37, 38, Burgos c-36. Everett a-1-3, 27, 28, 30, 37, 38. Powell a-36(Sub-Mariner). Schomburg c-1-3, 5-8, 10-23. Sekowsky c-28, 34?, 35? Shores c-24, 26, 27, 29, 30. Mickey Spillane text 4-6. Bondage c-2, 12, 19.

HUMAN TORCH, THE (Also see Avengers West Coast, Fantastic Four, The Invaders, Saga of the Original… & Strange Tales #101)
Marvel Comics Group: Sept, 1974 - No. 8, Nov, 1975

	GD 2.0	VG 4.0	FN 6.0	VF 8.0	VF/NM 9.0	NM- 9.2
1: 1-8-r/stories from Strange Tales #101-108	2	4	6	11	16	20
2-8: 1st H.T. title since G.A. 7-vs.-Sub-Mariner	2	4	6	8	10	12

NOTE: Golden Age & Silver Age Human Torch-r #1-8. Ayers r-6, 7. Kirby/Ayers r-1-5, 8.

HUMAN TORCH (From the Fantastic Four)
Marvel Comics: June, 2003 - No. 12, Jun, 2004 ($2.50/$2.99)

1-7-Skottie Young-c/a; Karl Kesel-s						2.50
8-12-($2.99) 8,10-Dodd-a. 9-Young-a. 11-Porter-a. 12-Medina-a						3.00
... Vol. 1: Burn TPB (2005, $7.99, digest size) r/#1-6						8.00

HUMBUG (Satire by Harvey Kurtzman)
Humbug Publications: Aug, 1957 - No. 9, May, 1958; No. 10, June, 1958; No. 11, Oct, 1958

	GD 2.0	VG 4.0	FN 6.0	VF 8.0	VF/NM 9.0	NM- 9.2
1-Wood-a (intro pgs. only)	27	54	81	158	249	340
2	15	30	45	83	124	165

	GD 2.0	VG 4.0	FN 6.0	VF 8.0	VF/NM 9.0	NM- 9.2
3-9: 8-Elvis in Jailbreak Rock	13	26	39	74	105	135
10,11-Magazine format. 10-Photo-c	15	30	45	88	137	185
Bound Volume(#1-9)(extremely rare)	65	130	195	406	671	935

NOTE: Davis a-1-11. Elder a-2-4, 6-9, 11. Heath a-2, 4-8, 10. Jaffee a-2, 4-9. Kurtzman a-11.

HUMDINGER (Becomes White Rider and Super Horse #3 on?)
Novelty Press/Premium Group: May-June, 1946 - V2#2, July-Aug, 1947

	GD 2.0	VG 4.0	FN 6.0	VF 8.0	VF/NM 9.0	NM- 9.2
1-Jerkwater Line, Mickey Starlight by Don Rico, Dink begin	36	72	108	204	315	450
2	16	32	48	89	137	200
3-6, V2#1,2	12	24	36	67	94	125

HUMONGOUS MAN
Alternative Press (Ikon Press): Sept, 1997 -No. 3 ($2.25, B&W)

1-3-Stepp & Harrison-c/s/a.						2.50

HUMOR (See All Humor Comics)

HUMPHREY COMICS (Joe Palooka Presents…; also see Joe Palooka)
Harvey Publications: Oct, 1948 - No. 22, Apr, 1952

	GD 2.0	VG 4.0	FN 6.0	VF 8.0	VF/NM 9.0	NM- 9.2
1-Joe Palooka's pal (r); (52 pgs.)-Powell-a	14	28	42	80	115	150
2,3: Powell-a	9	18	27	47	61	75
4-Boy Heroes app.; Powell-a	9	18	27	50	65	80
5-8,10: 5,6-Powell-a. 7-Little Dot app.	8	16	24	40	50	60
9-Origin Humphrey	9	18	27	47	61	75
11-22	7	14	21	37	46	55

HUNCHBACK OF NOTRE DAME, THE
Dell Publishing Co.: No. 854, Oct, 1957 (one shot)

	GD 2.0	VG 4.0	FN 6.0	VF 8.0	VF/NM 9.0	NM- 9.2
Four Color 854-Movie, photo-c	12	24	36	87	156	225

HUNGER, THE
Speakeasy Comics: May, 2005 - Present ($2.99)

1-Andy Bradshaw-s/a; Eric Powell-c						3.00

HUNGER DOGS, THE (See DC Graphic Novel #4)

HUNK
Charlton Comics: Aug, 1961 - No. 11, 1963

	GD 2.0	VG 4.0	FN 6.0	VF 8.0	VF/NM 9.0	NM- 9.2
1	4	8	12	24	37	50
2-11	3	6	9	14	20	25

HUNTED (Formerly My Love Memoirs)
Fox Features Syndicate: No. 13, July, 1950; No. 2, Sept, 1950

	GD 2.0	VG 4.0	FN 6.0	VF 8.0	VF/NM 9.0	NM- 9.2
13(#1)-Used in SOTI, pg. 42 & illo. "Treating police contemptuously" (lower left); Hollingsworth bondage-c	36	72	108	208	329	450
2	16	32	48	94	147	200

HUNTER-KILLER
Image Comics (Top Cow): Nov, 2004 - No. 12, Mar, 2007 ($2.99)

0-(11/04, 25¢) Prelude with Silvestri sketch page and Waid afterword						2.25
1-12: 1-(3/05, $2.99) Waid-s/Silvestri-a; four covers. 2-Linsner variant-c						3.00
... Collected Edition Vol. 1 (9/05, $4.99) r/#0-3						5.00
...Dossier 1 (9/05, $2.99) character profiles with art by various; Migliari-a						3.00

HUNTER: THE AGE OF MAGIC (See Books of Magic)
DC Comics (Vertigo): Sept, 2001 - No. 25, Sept, 2003 ($2.50/$2.75)

1-25: Horrocks-s/Case-a. 1-8-Bolton-c. 14-Begin $2.75-c. 19-Bachalo-c						2.75

HUNTRESS, THE (See All-Star Comics #69, Batman Family, DC Super Stars #17, Detective #652, Infinity, Inc. #1 & Wonder Woman #271)
DC Comics: Apr, 1989 - No. 19, Oct, 1990 ($1.00, mature)

1-16: Staton-c/a(p) in all						2.50
17-19-Batman-c/stories						3.00
..: Darknight Daughter TPB (2006, $19.99) r/origin & early apps. in DC Super Stars #17, Batman Family #18-20 & Wonder Woman #271-287,289,290,294,295; Bolland-c						20.00

HUNTRESS, THE
DC Comics: June, 1994 - No. 4, Sept, 1994 ($1.50, limited series)

1-4-Netzer-c/a: 2-Batman app.						2.25

HURRICANE COMICS
Cambridge House: 1945 (52 pgs.)

	GD 2.0	VG 4.0	FN 6.0	VF 8.0	VF/NM 9.0	NM- 9.2
1-(Humor, funny animal)	23	46	69	132	209	285

HYBRIDS
Continuity Comics: Jan, 1994 ($2.50, one-shot)

1-Neal Adams-c(p) & part-a(i); embossed-c						3.50

HYBRIDS DEATHWATCH 2000
Continuity Comics: Apr, 1993 - No. 3, Aug, 1993 ($2.50)

Ibis the Invincible #4 © FAW

Ideal #3 © MAR

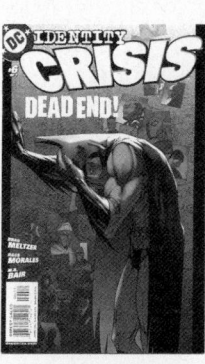

Identity Crisis #6 © DC

	GD 2.0	VG 4.0	FN 6.0	VF 8.0	VF/NM 9.0	NM- 9.2

0-(Giveaway)-Foil-c; Neal Adams-c(i) & plots (also #1,2) — 3.50
1-3: 1-Polybagged w/card; die-cut-c. 2-Thermal-c. 3-Polybagged w/card; indestructible-c; Adams plot — 3.00

HYBRIDS ORIGIN
Continuity Comics: 1993 - No. 5, Jan, 1994 ($2.50)

1-5: 2,3-Neal Adams-c. 4,5-Valeria the She-Bat app. Adams-c(i) — 3.25

HYDE
IDW Publ.: Oct, 2004 ($7.49, one-shot)

1-Steve Niles-s/Nick Stakal — 7.50

HYDE-25
Harris Publications: Apr, 1995 ($2.95, one-shot)

0-coupon for poster; r/Vampirella's 1st app. — 3.00

HYDROMAN (See Heroic Comics)

HYPERKIND (See Razorline)
Marvel Comics: Sept, 1993 - No. 9, May, 1994 ($1.75/$1.95)

1-($2.50)-Foil embossed-c; by Clive Barker — 3.00
2-9 — 2.50

HYPERKIND UNLEASED
Marvel Comics: Aug, 1994 ($2.95, 52 pgs., one-shot)

1 — 3.00

HYPER MYSTERY COMICS
Hyper Publications: May, 1940 - No. 2, June, 1940 (68 pgs.)

1-Hyper, the Phenomenal begins; Calkins-a	207	414	621	1294	2147	3000
2	103	206	309	644	1072	1500

HYPERSONIC
Dark Horse Comics: Nov, 1997 - No. 4, Feb, 1998 ($2.95, limited series)

1-4: Abnett & White/Erskine-a — 3.00

I AIM AT THE STARS (Movie)
Dell Publishing Co.: No. 1148, Nov-Jan/1960-61 (one-shot)

Four Color 1148-The Werner Von Braun Sty-photo-c	7	14	21	47	76	105

I AM COYOTE (See Eclipse Graphic Album Series & Eclipse Magazine #2)

I AM LEGEND
Eclipse Books: 1991 - No. 4, 1991 ($5.95, B&W, squarebound, 68 pgs.)

1-4: Based on 1954 novel by Richard Matheson — 6.00

IBIS, THE INVINCIBLE (See Fawcett Miniatures, Mighty Midget & Whiz)
Fawcett Publications: 1942 (Fall?), #2, Mar.,1943; #3, Wint, 1945 - #5, Fall, 1946; #6, Spring, 1948

1-Origin Ibis; Raboy-c; on sale 1/2/43	228	456	684	1425	2363	3300
2-Bondage-c (on sale 2/5/43)	100	200	300	625	1038	1450
3-Wolverton-a #3-6 (4 pgs. each)	74	148	222	463	769	1075
4-6: 5-Bondage-c	49	98	147	299	492	685

NOTE: *Mac Raboy c(p)-3-5. Schaffenberger c-6.*

I-BOTS (See Isaac Asimov's I-BOTS)

ICE AGE ON THE WORLD OF MAGIC: THE GATHERING (See Magic The Gathering)

ICE KING OF OZ, THE (See First Comics Graphic Novel #13)

ICEMAN (Also see The Champions & X-Men #94)
Marvel Comics Group: Dec, 1984 - No. 4, June, 1985 (Limited series)

1,2,4: Zeck covers on all — 3.50
3-The Defenders, Champions (Ghost Rider) & the original X-Men x-over — 4.00

ICEMAN (X-Men)
Marvel Comics: Dec, 2001 - No. 4, Mar, 2002 ($2.50, limited series)

1-4-Abnett & Lanning/Kerschl-a — 3.00

ICON
DC Comics (Milestone): May, 1993 - No. 42, Feb, 1997($1.50/$1.75/$2.50)

1-($2.95)-Collector's Edition polybagged w/poster & trading card (direct sale only) — 3.00
1-24,30-42: 9-Simonson-c. 15,16-Worlds Collide Pt. 4 & 11. 15-Superboy app. 16-Superman-c/story. 40-Vs. Blood Syndicate — 2.50
25-($2.95, 52 pgs.) — 3.00

IDAHO
Dell Publishing Co.: June-Aug, 1963 - No. 8, July-Sept, 1965

1	3	6	9	17	25	32
2-8: 5-7-Painted-c	2	4	6	9	13	16

IDEAL (… a Classical Comic) (2nd Series) (Love Romances No. 6 on)

Timely Comics: July, 1948 - No. 5, March, 1949 (Feature length stories)

1-Antony & Cleopatra	37	74	111	213	337	460
2-The Corpses of Dr. Sacotti	31	62	93	178	282	385
3-Joan of Arc; used in SOTI, pg. 308 'Boer War'	29	58	87	167	264	360
4-Richard the Lion-hearted; titled "…the World's Greatest Comics"; The Witness app.	40	80	120	240	383	525
5-Ideal Love & Romance; change to love; photo-c	19	38	57	112	176	240

IDEAL COMICS (1st Series) (Willie Comics No. 5 on)
Timely Comics (MgPC): Fall, 1944 - No. 4, Spring, 1946

1-Funny animal; Super Rabbit in all	24	48	72	139	220	300
2	14	28	42	80	115	150
3,4	14	28	42	76	108	140

IDEAL LOVE & ROMANCE (See Ideal, A Classical Comic)

IDEAL ROMANCE (Formerly Tender Romance)
Key Publ.: No. 3, April, 1954 - No. 8, Feb, 1955 (Diary Confessions No. 9 on)

3-Bernard Baily-c	9	18	27	52	69	85
4-8: 4-6-B. Baily-c	7	14	21	35	43	50

IDEALS (Secret Stories)
Ideals Publ., USA: 1981 (68 pgs, graphic novels, 7x10", stiff-c)

Captain America - Star Spangled Super Hero	3	6	9	18	27	35
Fantastic Four - Cosmic Quartet	3	6	9	18	27	35
Incredible Hulk - Gamma Powered Goliath	3	6	9	18	27	35
Spider-Man - World Famous Wall Crawler	4	8	12	22	34	45

IDENTITY CRISIS
DC Comics: Aug, 2004 - No. 7, Feb, 2005 ($3.95, limited series)

1-Meltzer-s/Morales-a/Turner-c in all; Sue Dibny murdered — 6.00
1-(Second printing) black-c with white sketch lines — 4.00
1-(Third printing) Bloody broken photo glass image-c by Morales — 4.00
1-Diamond Retailer Summit Edition with sketch-c — 125.00
2-7: 2-4-Deathstroke app. 5-Firestorm, Jack Drake, Capt. Boomerang killed — 4.00
2-(Second printing) new Morales sketch-c — 4.00
Final printings for all issues with red background variant covers
HC (2005, $24.99, dust jacket) r/series; Director's Cut extras; cover gallery; Whedon intro.; 2 covers: Direct Market-c by Turner, Bookstore-c with Morales-a — 25.00
SC (2006, $14.99) r/series; Director's Cut extras; cover gallery; Whedon intro — 15.00

IDENTITY DISC
Marvel Comics: Aug, 2004 - No. 5, Dec, 2004 ($2.99, limited series)

1-5-Sabretooth, Bullseye, Sandman, Vulture, Deadpool, Juggernaut app.; Higgins-a — 4.00
TPB (2004, $13.99) r/#1-5 — 14.00

I DIE AT MIDNIGHT (Vertigo V2K)
DC Comics (Vertigo): 2000 ($6.95, prestige format, one-shot)

1-Kyle Baker-s/a — 7.00

IDOL
Marvel Comics (Epic Comics): 1992 - No. 3, 1992 ($2.95, mini-series, 52 pgs.)

Book 1-3 — 3.00

I DREAM OF JEANNIE (TV)
Dell Publishing Co.: Apr, 1965 - No. 2, Dec, 1966 (Photo-c)

1-Barbara Eden photo-c, each	14	28	42	102	181	260
2	11	22	33	77	136	195

I FEEL SICK
Slave Labor Graphics: Aug, 1999 - No. 2, May, 2000 ($3.95, limited series)

1,2-Jhonen Vasquez-s/a — 4.00

I (heart) MARVEL
Marvel Comics: Apr, 2006; May, 2006 ($2.99, one-shots)

...: Marvel AI 1 (4/06) Cebulski-s; manga art by various; Vision, Daredevil, Elektra app. — 3.00
...: Masked Intentions 1 (5/06) Squirrel Girl, Speedball, Firestar, Justice app.; Nicieza-s — 3.00
...: My Mutant Heart 1 (4/06) Wolverine, Cannonball, Doop app. — 3.00
...: Outlaw Love 1 (4/06) Bullseye, The Answer, Ruby Thursday app.; Nicieza-s — 3.00
...: Web of Romance 1 (4/06) Spider-Man, Mary Jane, The Avengers app. — 3.00

ILLUMINATOR
Marvel Comics/Nelson Publ.: 1993 - No. 4, 1993 ($4.99/$2.95, 52 pgs.)

1,2-($4.99) Religious themed — 5.00
3,4 — 3.00

ILLUSTRATED GAGS
United Features Syndicate: No. 16, 1940

Single Series 16	16	32	48	94	147	200

I Love Lucy #24 © Desilu

I, Lusiphur #1 © Drew Hayes

Impact #3 © WMG

	GD 2.0	VG 4.0	FN 6.0	VF 8.0	VF/NM 9.0	NM- 9.2

ILLUSTRATED LIBRARY OF..., AN (See Classics Illustrated Giants)

ILLUSTRATED STORIES OF THE OPERAS
Baily (Bernard) Publ. Co.: 1943 (16 pgs., B&W) (25 cents) (cover-B&W & red)

	GD	VG	FN	VF	VF/NM	NM-
nn-(Rare)(4 diff. issues)-Faust (part-r in Cisco Kid #1), nn-Aida, nn-Carmen; Baily-a, nn-Rigoleito	55	110	165	337	556	775

ILLUSTRATED STORY OF ROBIN HOOD & HIS MERRY MEN, THE (See Classics Giveaways, 12/44)

ILLUSTRATED TARZAN BOOK, THE (See Tarzan Book)

I LOVED (Formerly Rulah; Colossal Features Magazine No. 33 on)
Fox Features Syndicate: No. 28, July, 1949 - No. 32, Mar, 1950

	GD	VG	FN	VF	VF/NM	NM-
28	13	26	39	72	101	130
29-32	9	18	27	52	69	85

I LOVE LUCY
Eternity Comics : 6/90 - No. 6, 1990;V2#1, 11/90 - No. 6, 1991 ($2.95, B&W, mini-series)

1-6: Reprints 1950s comic strip; photo-c						4.00
Book II #1-6: Reprints comic strip; photo-c						4.00
...In Full Color 1 (1991, $5.95, 52 pgs.)-Reprints I Love Lucy Comics #4,5,8,16; photo-c with embossed logo (2 versions exist, one with pgs. 18 & 19 reversed, the other corrected)						
...In 3-D 1 (1991, $3.95, w/glasses)-Reprints I Love Lucy Comics; photo-c; bagged						6.00

I LOVE LUCY COMICS (TV) (Also see The Lucy Show)
Dell Publishing Co.: No. 535, Feb, 1954 - No. 35, Apr-June, 1962 (Lucille Ball photo-c on all)

	GD	VG	FN	VF	VF/NM	NM-
Four Color 535(#1)	45	90	135	360	655	950
Four Color 559(#2, 5/54)	30	60	90	217	391	565
3 (8-10/54) - 5	17	34	51	128	227	325
6-10	14	28	42	102	181	260
11-20	10	20	30	71	126	180
21-35	9	18	27	61	103	145

I LOVE NEW YORK
Linsner.com: 2002 ($2.95, B&W, one-shot)

1-Linsner-s/a; benefit book for the Sept. 11 charities						3.00

I LOVE YOU
Fawcett Publications: June, 1950 (one-shot)

	GD	VG	FN	VF	VF/NM	NM-
1-Photo-c	15	30	45	83	124	165

I LOVE YOU (Formerly In Love)
Charlton Comics: No. 7, 9/55 - No. 121, 12/76; No. 122, 3/79 - No. 130, 5/80

	GD	VG	FN	VF	VF/NM	NM-
7-Kirby-c; Powell-a	9	18	27	60	100	140
8-10	5	10	15	30	48	65
11-16,18-20	4	8	12	26	41	55
17-(68 pg. Giant)	7	14	21	47	76	105
21-50: 26-No Torres-a	3	6	9	20	30	40
51-59	3	6	9	16	22	28
60-(1/66)-Elvis Presley line drawn c/story	15	30	45	107	191	275
61-85	2	4	6	10	14	18
86-90,92-110	1	3	4	6	8	10
91-(5/71) Ditko-a (5 pgs.)	2	4	6	10	14	18
111-130: 114-Psychedelic cover	1	2	3	5	6	8

I, LUSIPHUR (Becomes Poison Elves, 1st series #8 on)
Mulehide Graphics: 1991 - No. 7, 1992 (B&W, magazine size)

	GD	VG	FN	VF	VF/NM	NM-
1-Drew Hayes-c/a/scripts	4	8	12	22	34	45
2,4,5	2	4	6	11	16	20
3-Low print run	4	8	12	24	37	50
6,7	2	4	6	8	10	12
Poison Elves: Requiem For An Elf (Sirius Ent., 6/96, $14.95, trade paperback) -Reprints I, Lusiphur #1,2 as text, and 3-6						15.00

I'M A COP
Magazine Enterprises: 1954 - No. 3, 1954

	GD	VG	FN	VF	VF/NM	NM-
1(A-1 #111)-Powell-a in all	15	30	45	88	137	185
2(A-1 #126), 3(A-1 #128)	10	20	30	56	76	95

IMAGE COMICS HARDCOVER
Image Comics: 2005 ($24.99, hardcover with dust jacket)

Vol. 1-New Spawn by McFarlane-s/a; Savage Dragon origin by Larsen; CyberForce by Silvestri; ShadowHawk by Valentino; intro by Marder; Image timeline						25.00

IMAGE FIRST
Image Comics: 2005 ($6.99, TPB)

Vol. 1 (2005) r/Strange Girl #1, Sea of Red #1, The Walking Dead #1 and Girls #1						7.00

IMAGE GRAPHIC NOVEL

Image Int.: 1984 ($6.95)(Advertised as Pacific Comics Graphic Novel #1)

1-The Seven Samuroid; Brunner-c/a						7.00

IMAGE HOLIDAY SPECIAL 2005
Image Comics: 2005 ($9.99, TPB)

nn-Holiday-themed short stories by various incl. Larsen, Kurtz, Kirkman, Valentino						10.00

IMAGE INTRODUCES...
Image Comics: Oct, 2001 - June, 2002 ($2.95, anthology)

Believer #1-Schamberger-s/Thurman & Molder-a; Legend of Isis preview						3.00
Cryptopia #1-Raab-s/Quinn-a						3.00
Dog Soldiers #1-Hunter-s/Pachoumis-a						3.00
Legend of Isis #1-Valdez-a						3.00
Primate #1-Two covers; Beau Smith & Bernhardt-s/Byrd-a						3.00

IMAGES OF A DISTANT SOIL
Image Comics: Feb, 1997 ($2.95, B&W, one-shot)

1-Sketches by various						3.00

IMAGES OF SHADOWHAWK (Also see Shadowhawk)
Image Comics: Sept, 1993 - No. 3, 1994 ($1.95, limited series)

1-3: Keith Giffen-c/a; Trencher app.						2.50

IMAGE TWO-IN-ONE
Image Comics: Mar, 2001 ($2.95, 48 pgs., B&W, one-shot)

1-Two stories; 24 pages produced in 24 hrs. by Larsen and Eliopoulos						3.00

IMAGE ZERO
Image Comics: 1993 (Received through mail w/coupons from Image books)

0-Savage Dragon, StormWatch, Shadowhawk, Strykeforce; 1st app. Troll; 1st app. McFarlane's Freak, Blotch, Sweat and Bludd						5.00

IMAGINARIES, THE
Image Comics: Mar, 2005 - No. 4, June, 2005 ($2.95, limited series)

1-4-Mike S. Miller & Ben Avery-s; Miller & Titus-a						3.00

I'M DICKENS - HE'S FENSTER (TV)
Dell Publishing Co.: May-July, 1963 - No. 2, Aug-Oct, 1963 (Photo-c)

	GD	VG	FN	VF	VF/NM	NM-
1	6	12	18	37	59	80
2	5	10	15	32	51	70

I MET A HANDSOME COWBOY
Dell Publishing Co.: No. 324, Mar, 1951

	GD	VG	FN	VF	VF/NM	NM-
Four Color 324	8	16	24	56	93	130

IMMORTAL DOCTOR FATE, THE
DC Comics: Jan, 1985 - No. 3, Mar, 1985 ($1.25, limited series)

1-3: 1-Simonson-c/a. 2-Giffen-c/a(p)						4.00

IMMORTAL IRON FIST, THE (Also see Iron Fist)
Marvel Comics: Jan, 2007 - Present ($2.99)

1-Brubaker & Fraction-s/Aja-c/a; origin retold; intro. Orson Randall						5.00
1-Variant-c by Dell'Otto						8.00
1-Director's Cut ($3.99) r/#1 and 8-page story from Civil War: Choosing Sides; script excerpt; character designs; sketch and inks art; cover variant and concepts						4.00
2-9: 6-Flashback-a by Heath						3.00
Annual 1 (11/07, $3.99) Brubaker & Fraction-s/Chaykin, Brereton & J. Djurdjevic-a						4.00
... Vol. 1: The Last Iron Fist Story HC (2007, $19.99, dustjacket) r/#1-6, story from Civil War: Choosing Sides; sketch pages						20.00
... Vol. 1: The Last Iron Fist Story SC (2007, $14.99) same content as HC						15.00

IMMORTALIS (See Mortigan Goth: Immortalis)

IMMORTAL II
Image Comics: Apr, 1997 - No. 5, Feb, 1998 ($2.50, B&W&Grey, limited series)

1-5: 1-B&W w/ color pull-out poster						2.50

IMPACT
E. C. Comics: Mar-Apr, 1955 - No. 5, Nov-Dec, 1955

	GD	VG	FN	VF	VF/NM	NM-
1-Not code approved	17	34	51	136	213	290
2	10	20	30	80	125	170
3-5: 4-Crandall-a	9	18	27	72	111	150

NOTE: *Crandall* a-1-4. *Davis* a-2-4; c-1-5. *Evans* a-1, 4, 5. *Ingels* a-in all. *Kamen* a-3. *Krigstein* a-1, 5. *Orlando* a-2, 5.

IMPACT
Gemstone Publishing: Apr, 1999 - No. 5, Aug, 1999 ($2.50)

1-5-Reprints E.C. series						2.50

IMPACT CHRISTMAS SPECIAL

Impulse #50 © DC

Incredible Hulk #4 © MAR

Incredible Hulk #207 © MAR

	GD 2.0	VG 4.0	FN 6.0	VF 8.0	VF/NM 9.0	NM- 9.2

DC Comics (Impact Comics): 1991 ($2.50, 68 pgs.)
1-Gift of the Magi by Infantino/Rogers; The Black Hood, The Fly, The Jaguar, & The Shield stories ... 2.50

IMPERIAL GUARD
Marvel Comics: Jan, 1997 - No. 3, Mar, 1997 ($1.95, limited series)
1-3: Augustyn-s in all; 1-Wraparound-c ... 2.50

IMPOSSIBLE MAN SUMMER VACATION SPECTACULAR, THE
Marvel Comics: Aug, 1990 - No. 2, Sept, 1991 ($2.00, 68 pgs.) (See Fantastic Four#11)
1-Spider Man, Quasar, Dr. Strange, She-Hulk, Punisher & Dr. Doom stories; Barry Crain, Guice-a; Art Adams-c(i) ... 2.50
2-Ka Zar & Thor app.; Cable Wolverine-c app. ... 2.50

IMPULSE (See Flash #92, 2nd Series for 1st app.) (Also see Young Justice)
DC Comics: Apr, 1995 - No. 89, Oct, 2002 ($1.50/$1.75/$1.95/$2.25/$2.50)
1-Mark Waid scripts & Humberto Ramos-c/a(p) begin; brief retelling of origin ... 6.00
2-12: 9-XS from Legion (Impulse's cousin) comes to the 20th Century, returns to the 30th Century in #12. 10-Dead Heat Pt. 3 (cont'd in Flash #110). 11-Dead Heat Pt.4 (cont'd in Flash #111); Johnny Quick dies. ... 3.00
13-25: 14-Trickster app. 17-Zatanna-c/app. 21-Legion-c/app. 22-Jesse Quick-c/app. 24-Origin; Flash app. 25-Last Ramos-a. ... 2.50
26-55: 26-Rousseau-a begins. 28-1st new Arrowette (see World's Finest #113). 30-Genesis x-over. 47-Superman-c/app. 50-Batman & Joker-c/app. Van Sciver-a begins ... 2.50
56-62: 56-Young Justice app. ... 2.50
63-89: 63-Begin $2.50-c. 66-JLA,JSA-c/app. 68,69-Adam Strange, GL app. 77-Our Worlds at War x-over; Young Justice-c/app. 85-World Without Young Justice x-over pt. 2. ... 2.50
#1,000,000 (11/98) John Fox app. ... 2.50
Annual 1 (1996, $2.95)-Legends of the Dead Earth; Parobeck-a ... 4.00
Annual 2 (1997, $3.95)-Pulp Heroes stories; Orbik painted-c ... 4.00
.../Atom Double-Shot 1(2/98, $1.95) Jurgens-s/Mhan-a ... 3.00
....Bart Saves the Universe (4/99, $5.95) JSA app. ... 6.00
...Plus(9/97, $2.95) w/Gross Out (Scare Tactics)-c/app. ... 3.00
...Reckless Youth (1997, $14.95, TPB) r/Flash #92-94, Impulse #1-6 ... 15.00

INCAL, THE
Marvel Comics (Epic): Nov, 1988 - No. 3, Jan, 1989 ($10.95/$12.95, mature)
1-3: Moebius-c/a in all; sexual content ... 16.00

INCOMPLETE DEATH'S HEAD (Also see Death's Head)
Marvel Comics UK: Jan, 1993 - No. 12, Dec, 1993 ($1.75, limited series)
1-($2.95, 56 pgs.)-Die-cut cover ... 3.00
2-11: 2-Re-intro original Death's Head. 3-Original Death's Head vs. Dragon's Claws ... 2.50
12-($2.50, 52 pgs.)-She Hulk app. ... 2.50

INCREDIBLE HULK, THE (See Aurora, The Avengers #1, The Defenders #1, Giant-Size..., Hulk, Marvel Collectors Item Classics, Marvel Comics Presents #26, Marvel Fanfare, Marvel Treasury Edition, Power Record Comics, Rampaging Hulk, She-Hulk & 2099 Unlimited)

INCREDIBLE HULK, THE
Marvel Comics: May, 1962 - No. 6, Mar, 1963; No. 102, Apr, 1968 - No. 474, Mar, 1999

1-Origin & 1st app. (skin is grey colored); Kirby pencils begin, end #5

	1000	2000	3000	10,000	21,000	32,000
2-1st green skinned Hulk; Kirby/Ditko-a	258	516	744	2258	4229	6200
3-Origin retold; 1st app. Ringmaster (9/62)	154	308	462	1348	2524	3700
4,5: 4-Brief origin retold	148	296	444	1258	2329	3400
6-(3/63) Intro. Teen Brigade; all Ditko-a	163	326	489	1426	2663	3900

102-(4/68) (Formerly Tales to Astonish)-Origin retold; story continued from Tales to Astonish #101 ... 20 40 60 146 261 375
103 ... 9 18 27 63 107 150
104-Rhino app. ... 9 18 27 63 107 150
105-108: 105-1st Missing Link. 107-Mandarin app.(9/68). 108-Mandarin & Nick Fury app. (10/68) ... 6 12 18 43 69 95
109,110: 109-Ka-Zar app. ... 5 10 15 35 55 75
111-117: 117-Last 12¢ issue ... 4 8 12 28 44 60
118-Hulk vs. Sub-Mariner ... 4 8 12 38 62 85
119-121,123-125 ... 4 8 12 22 34 45
122-Hulk battles Thing (12/69) ... 7 14 21 49 80 110
126-1st Barbara Norriss (Valkyrie) ... 4 8 12 24 37 50
127-130: 131-Hulk vs. Iron Man; 1st Jim Wilson, Hulk's new sidekick. 136-1st Xeron, The Star-Slayer ... 3 6 9 17 25 32
140-Written by Harlan Ellison; 1st Jarella, Hulk's love ... 3 6 9 18 27 35
140-2nd printing (1994) ... 2 4 6 8 10 12
141-1st app. Doc Samson (7/71) ... 8 16 24 58 97 135
142-144: 144-Last 12¢ issue ... 3 6 9 16 24 30
145-(52 pgs.)-Origin retold ... 4 8 12 24 37 50
146-160: 149-1st app. The Inheritor. 155-1st app. Shaper. 158-Warlock cameo(12/72)

... 3 6 9 14 20 25
161-The Mimic dies; Beast app. ... 4 8 12 22 34 45
162-1st app. The Wendigo (4/73); Beast app. ... 6 12 18 41 66 90
163-171,173-176: 163-1st app. The Gremlin. 164-1st Capt. Omen & Colonel John D. Armbruster. 166-1st Zzzax. 168-1st The Harpy; nudity panels of Betty Brant. 169-1st app. Bi-Beast.176-Warlock cameo (2 panels only); same date as Strange Tales #178 (6/74) ... 2 4 6 11 16 20
172-X-Men cameo; origin Juggernaut retold ... 4 8 12 22 34 45
177-1st actual death of Warlock (last panel only) ... 2 4 6 13 18 22
178-Rebirth of Warlock ... 2 4 6 13 18 22
179 ... 2 4 6 9 12 15
180-(10/74)-1st brief app. Wolverine (last pg.) ... 15 30 45 111 198 285
181-(11/74)-1st full Wolverine story; Trimpe-a ... 90 180 270 700 1075 1450
182-Wolverine cameo; see Giant-Size X-Men #1 for next app.; 1st Crackajack Jackson ... 10 20 30 70 123 175
183-199: 185-Death of Col. Armbruster. 195,196-Abomination app. 197,198-Man-Thing-c/s ... 3 6 9 14 20 25
198,199, 201,202-(30¢-c variants, lim. distribution) ... 3 6 9 16 23 30
200-(25¢-c) Silver Surfer app.; anniversary issue ... 3 6 9 17 25 32
200-(30¢-c variant, limited distribution)(6/76) ... 5 10 15 32 51 70
201-220: 201-Conan swipe-c/sty. 212-1st app. The Constrictor ... 6.00
212-216-(35¢-c variant, limited distribution) ... 3 6 9 20 30 40
221-249: 227-Original Avengers app. 232-Capt. America x-over from C.A. #230. 233-Marvel Man app. 234-(4/79)-1st app. Quasar (formerly called Marvel Man). 243-Cage app. ... 5.00
250-Giant size; Silver Surfer app. ... 6 10 12
251-277,280-299: 271-Rocket Raccoon app. 272-Sasquatch & Wendigo app.; Wolverine & Alpha Flight cameo in flashback. 282-284-She-Hulk app. 293-F.F. app. ... 4.00
278,279-Most Marvel characters app. (Wolverine in both). 279-X-Men & Alpha Flight cameo ... 5.00
300-(11/84, 52 pgs.)-Spider-Man app in new black costume on-c & 2 pg. cameo ... 6.00
301-313: 312-Origin Hulk retold ... 3.00
314-Byrne-a begins, ends #319 ... 5.00
315-319: 319-Bruce Banner & Betty Talbot wed ... 4.00
320-323,325,327-329 ... 3.00
324-1st app. Grey Hulk since #1 (c-swipe of #1) ... 2 4 6 8 10 12
326-Grey vs. Green Hulk ... 5.00
330,331: 330-1st McFarlane ish (4/87); Thunderbolt Ross dies. 331-Grey Hulk series begins ... 3 6 9 14 20 25
332-334,336-339: 336,337-X-Factor app. ... 2 4 6 8 11 14
335-No McFarlane-a ... 5.00
340-Hulk battles Wolverine by McFarlane ... 4 8 12 22 34 45
341-346: 345-($1.50, 52 pgs.). 346-Last McFarlane issue ... 1 2 3 5 6 8
347-349,351-358,360-366: 347-1st app. Marlo ... 3.00
350-Hulk/Thing battle ... 6.00
359-Wolverine app. (illusion only) ... 3.00
367,372,377: 367-1st Dale Keown-a on Hulk (3/90). 372-Green Hulk app.;Keown-c/a. 377-1st all new Hulk; fluorescent-c; Keown-c/a ... 1 2 3 5 6 8
368-371,373-376: 368-Sam Kieth-c/a, 1st app. Pantheon. 369,370-Dale Keown-c/a. 370,371-Original Defenders app. 371,373-376: Keown-c/a. 376-Green vs. Grey Hulk ... 5.00
377-Fluorescent green logo 2nd printing ... 3.00
378,380,389: No Keown-a. 380-Doc Samson app. ... 3.00
379,381-388,390-392-Keown-a. 385-Infinity Gauntlet x-over. 389-Last $1.00-c ... 4.00
392-X-Factor app. ... 4.00
393-(7/92, 52 pgs.)-30th anniversary issue; green foil stamped-c; swipes-c to #1; has pin-ups of classic battles; Keown-c/a ... 5.00
393-2nd printing ... 2.50
394-399: 394-No Keown-c/a; intro Trauma. 395,396-Punisher-c/stories; Keown-c/a. 397-Begin "Ghost of the Past" 4-part sty; Keown c/a. 398-Last Keown-c/a ... 2.50
400-($2.50, 68 pgs.)-Holo-grafx foil-c & r/TTA #63 ... 3.00
400-416: 400-2nd print-Diff. color foil-c. 402-Return of Doc Samson ... 2.50
417-424: 417-Begin $1.50-c; Rick Jones' bachelor party; Hulk returns from "Future Imperfect"; bound-in trading card sheet. 418-(Regular edition)-Rick Jones marries Marlo; includes cameo apps of various Marvel characters as well as DC's Death & Peter David. 420-Death of Jim Wilson ... 2.50
418-($2.50)-Collector's Edition w/gatefold die-cut-c ... 3.00
425-($2.25, 52 pgs.) ... 2.50
425-($3.50, 52 pgs.)-Holographic-c ... 4.00
426-434, 436-442: 426-Begin $1.95-c. 427, 428-Man-Thing app. 431,432-Abomination app. 434-Funeral for Nick Fury. 436-Ghosts of the Future begins, ends #440. 439-Hulk becomes Maestro, Avengers app. 440-Thor-c/app. 441,442-She-Hulk-c/app. ... 2.50
435-($2.50)-Rhino-app; excerpt from "What Savage Beast" ... 2.50
443,446-448: 443-Begin $1.50-c; re-app. of Hulk. 446-w/card insert. 447-Begin Deodato-c/a(p) ... 2.50

Incredible Hulk #467 © MAR

Incredible Hulk (2nd series) #110 © MAR

Independence Day #2 © 20th Century Fox

	GD 2.0	VG 4.0	FN 6.0	VF 8.0	VF/NM 9.0	NM- 9.2

444,445: 444-Cable-c/app.; "Onslaught". 445-"Onslaught" — 4.00
447-Variant cover — 4.00
449-1st app. Thunderbolts — 6.00
450-($2.95)-Thunderbolts app.; 2 stories; Heroes Reborn-c/app. — 5.00
451-470: 455-X-Men-c/app. 460-Bruce Banner returns. 464-Silver Surfer-c/app. 466,467: Betty dies. 467-Last Peter David-s/Kubert-a. 468-Casey/Pulido-c begin — 2.50
471-473 — 3.00
474-($2.99) Last issue; Abomination app. — 4.00
#(-1) Flashback (7/97) Kubert-a — 2.50
Special 1 (10/68, 25¢, 68 pg.)-New 51 pg. story, Hulk battles The Inhumans (early app.); Steranko-c — 10 20 30 67 116 165
Special 2 (10/69, 25¢, 68 pg.)-Origin retold — 6 12 18 37 59 80
Special 3,4: 3-(1/71, 25¢, 68 pg.). 4-(1/72, 52pgs.) — 3 6 9 18 27 35
Annual 5 (1976) — 2 4 6 9 13 16
Annual 6-8 ('77-79)-7-Byrne/Layton-c/a; Iceman & Angel app. in book-length story.
8-Book-length Sasquatch-c/sty — 2 4 6 8 10 12
Annual 9,10: 9('80). 10 ('81) — 6.00
Annual 11('82)-Doc Samson back-up by Miller(p)(5 pgs.); Spider-Man & Avengers app. Buckler-a(p) — 6.00
Annual 12-17: 12 ('83). 14('85). 15('86). 16('90, $2.00, 68 pgs.)-She-Hulk app. 17(1991, $2.00)-Origin retold — 3.50
Annual 18-20 ('92-'94 68 pgs.)-18-Return of the Defenders, Pt. I; no Keown-c/a 19-Bagged w/card — 3.00
...'97 ($2.99) Pollina-c — 3.00
...And Wolverine 1 (10/86, $2.50)-r/1st app. (#180-181) — 1 3 4 6 8 10
...: Beauty and the Behemoth ('98, $19.95, TPB) r/Bruce & Betty stories — 20.00
...Ground Zero ('95, $12.95) r/#340-346 — 13.00
...Hercules Unleashed (10/96, $2.50) David-s/Deodato-c/a — 2.50
...Sub-Mariner '98 Annual ($2.99) — 3.00
...Versus Quasimodo 1 (3/83, one-shot)-Based on Saturday morning cartoon — 4.00
...Vs. Superman 1 (7/99, $5.95, one-shot)-painted-c by Rude — 6.00
...Versus Venom 1 (4/94, $2.50, one-shot)-Embossed-c; red foil logo — 3.00
...Visionaries: Peter David Vol. 1 (2005, $19.99) r/#331-339 written by Peter David — 20.00
...Visionaries: Peter David Vol. 2 (2005, $19.99) r/#340-348 — 20.00
... Visionaries: Peter David Vol. 3 (2006, $19.99) r/#349-354, Web of Spider-Man #44, and Fantastic Four #320 — 20.00
...Visionaries: Peter David Vol. 4 (2007, $19.99) r/#355-363 and Marvel Comics Presents #26,45 — 20.00
Wizard #1 Ace Edition - Reprints #1 with new Andy Kubert-c — 14.00
Wizard #181 Ace Edition - Reprints #181 with new Chen-c — 14.00
(Also see titles listed under **Hulk**)

NOTE: **Adkins** a-111-116i. **Austin** a-350, 351, 353, 354; c-302i, 350i. **Ayers** a-3-5i. **Buckler** a-Annual 5; c-252. **John Buscema** c-202p. **Byrne** a-314-319p; c-314-316, 318, 319, 359, Annual 14. **Colan** c-363. **Ditko** a-2i, 6, 249, Annual 2r(5), 3r, 9p; c-2i, 6, 235, 249. **Everett** c-133i. **Golden** c-248, 251. **Kane** c(p)-193, 194, 196, 198. **Dale Keown** a(p)-367, 369-377, 379, 381-388, 390-393, 395-398; c-369-377p, 381, 382p, 384, 385, 386, 387p, 388, 390p, 391-393, 395p, 396, 397p, 398. **Kirby** a-1-5p, Special 2, 3p, Annual 5p; c-1-5, Annual 5. **McFarlane** a-330-333p, 336-339p, 340-343, 344-346p; c-330p, 340p, 341-343, 344p, 345, 346p. **Mignola** c-313. **Miller** c-258p, 261, 264, 268. **Mooney** a-230p, 287i, 288i. **Powell** a-Special 3r(2). **Romita** a-Annual 17p. **Severin** a(i)-108-113, 101-133, 141-151, 153, 155; c(i)-109, 110, 112, 142, 144-155. **Simonson** c-283, 364-367. **Starlin** a-222p; c-217. **Staton** a(i)-187-189, 191-209. **Tuska** a-102i, 105i, 106i, 218p. **Williamson** a-310i; c-310i, 311i. **Wrightson** c-197.

INCREDIBLE HULK (Vol. 2) (Formerly Hulk #1-11) (Also see World War Hulk)
Marvel Comics: No. 12, Mar, 2000 - Present ($1.99-$3.50)

12-Jenkins-s/Garney & McKone-a — 3.00
13,14-($1.99) Garney & Buscema-a — 2.50
15-24,26-32: 15-Begin $2.25-c. 21-Maximum Security x-over. 24-($1.99-c) — 2.50
25-($2.99) Hulk vs. The Abomination; Romita Jr.-a — 3.00
33-($3.50, 100 pgs.) new Bogdanove-a/Priest-s; reprints — 3.50
34-Bruce Jones begin; Romita Jr.-a — 5.00
35-49,51-54: 35-39-Jones-s/Romita Jr.-a. 40-43-Weeks-a. 44-49-Immonen-a — 3.00
50-($3.50) Deodato-a begins; Abomination app. thru #54 — 3.50
55-74,77-91: 55(25¢-c) Absorbing Man returns; Fernandez-a. 60-65,70-72-Deodato-a. 66-69-Braithwaite-a. 71-74-Iron Man app. 77-($2.99-c) Peter David-s begin/Weeks-a. 80-Wolverine-c. 82-Jae Lee-c/a. 83-86-House of M x-over. 87-Scorpion app. — 3.00
75,76-($3.50) The Leader app. 75-Robertson-a/Frank-c. 76-Braithwaite-a — 3.50
92-Planet Hulk begins; Ladronn-a — 4.00
92-2nd printing with variant-c by Bryan Hitch — 3.00
93-99,101-105 Planet Hulk; Ladronn-a — 3.00
100-($3.99) Planet Hulk continues; back-up w/Frank-a; r/#152,153; Ladronn-a — 4.00
100-($3.99) Green Hulk variant-c by Michael Turner — 10.00
100-($3.99) Gray Hulk variant-c by Michael Turner — 30.00
106-World War Hulk begins; Gary Frank-a/c — 5.00
106-2nd printing with new cover of Hercules and Angel — 3.00
107-110: 107-Hercules vs. Hulk. 108-Rick Jones app. — 3.00
Annual 2000 ($3.50) Texeira-a/Jenkins-s; Avengers app. — 3.50

Annual 2001 ($2.99) Thor-c/app.; Larsen-s/Williams III-c — 3.00
... : Boiling Point (Volume 2, 2002, $8.99, TPB) r/#40-43; Andrews-c — 9.00
Dogs of War (6/01, $19.95, TPB) r/#12-20 — 20.00
House of M (2006, $13.99) r/House of M tie-in issues Incredible Hulk #83-87 — 14.00
Hulk: Planet Hulk HC (2007, $39.99, dustjacket) oversized r/#92-105, Planet Hulk: Gladiator Guidebook, stories from Amazing Fantasy (2004) #15 and Giant-Size Hulk #1 — 40.00
Planet Hulk: Gladiator Guidebook (2006, $3.99) bios of combatants and planet history — 4.00
...: Prelude to Planet Hulk (2006, $13.99, TPB) r/#88-91 & Official Handbook: Hulk 2004 — 14.00
... : Return of the Monster (7/02, $12.99, TPB) r/#34-39 — 13.00
...: The End (8/02, $5.95) David-s/Keown-a; Hulk in the far future — 6.00
...Volume 1 HC (2002, $29.99, oversized) r/#34-43 & Startling Stories: Banner #1-4 — 30.00
...Volume 2 HC (2003, $29.99, oversized) r/#44-54; sketch pages and cover gallery — 30.00
Volume 3: Transfer of Power (2003, $12.99, TPB) r/#44-49 — 13.00
Volume 4: Abominable (2003, $11.99, TPB) r/#50-54; Abomination app.; Deodato-a — 12.00
Volume 5: Hide in Plain Sight (2003, $11.99, TPB) r/#55-59; Fernandez-a — 12.00
Volume 6: Split Decisions (2004, $12.99, TPB) r/#60-65; Deodato-a — 13.00
Volume 7: Dead Like Me (2004, $12.99, TPB) r/#66-69 & Hulk Smash #1&2 — 13.00
Volume 8: Big Things (2004, $17.99, TPB) r/#70-76; Iron Man app. — 18.00
Volume 9: Tempest Fugit (2005, $14.99, TPB) r/#77-82 — 15.00

INCREDIBLE MR. LIMPET, THE (See Movie Classics)

INCREDIBLES, THE
Image Comics: Nov, 2004 - No. 4, Feb, 2005 ($2.99, limited series)

1-4-Adaptation of 2004 Pixar movie; Ricardo Curtis-a — 3.00
TPB (2005, $12.95) r/#1-4; cover gallery — 13.00

INCREDIBLE SCIENCE FICTION (Formerly Weird Science-Fantasy)
E. C. Comics: No. 30, July-Aug, 1955 - No. 33, Jan-Feb, 1956

30-Davis-c begin, end #32 — 39 78 117 312 486 660
31-Williamson/Krenkel-a, Wood-a(2) — 40 80 120 320 498 675
32-Williamson/Krenkel-a — 40 80 120 320 498 675
33-Classic Wood-c; "Judgment Day" story-r/Weird Fantasy #18; final issue & last E.C. comic book — 41 82 123 328 509 690
NOTE: **Davis** a-30, 32, 33; c-30-32. **Krigstein** a-in all. **Orlando** a-30, 32, 33. **Wood** a-30, 31, 33; c-33.

INCREDIBLE SCIENCE FICTION (Formerly Weird Science-Fantasy)
Russ Cochran/Gemstone Publ.: No. 8, Aug, 1994 - No. 11, May, 1995 ($2.00)

8-11: Reprints #30-33 of E.C. series — 2.50

INDEPENDENCE DAY (Movie)
Marvel Comics: No. 0, June, 1996 - No. 2, Aug, 1996 ($1.95, limited series)

0-Special Edition; photo-c — 5.00
0-2 — 2.50

INDEPENDENT VOICES
Peregrine Entertainment: Sept, 1998; Sept, 1999 ($1.95/$2.95, B&W)

1-Sampler of Indy titles for CBLDF — 2.50
2-(9/99, $2.95); 2nd printing-(5/00) — 3.00

INDIA AUTHENTIC
Virgin Comics: May, 2007 - Present ($2.99)

... 1-Ganesha (5/07); 2-Kali (6/07); 3-Indra (6/07); 4-Uma (8/07); 5-Shiva (9/07) foreward by Deepak Chopra in each — 3.00

INDIANA JONES (Title series), Dark Horse Comics

--AND THE ARMS OF GOLD, 2/94 - 5/94 ($2.50) 1-4 — 2.50
--AND THE FATE OF ATLANTIS, 3/91 - 9/91 ($2.50) 1-4-Dorman painted-c on all; contain trading cards (#1 has a 2nd printing, 10/91) — 2.50
--AND THE GOLDEN FLEECE, 6/94 - 7/94 ($2.50) 1,2 — 2.50
--AND THE IRON PHOENIX, 12/94 - 3/95 ($2.50) 1-4 — 2.50

INDIANA JONES AND THE LAST CRUSADE
Marvel Comics: 1989 - No. 4, 1989 ($1.00, limited series, movie adaptation)

1-4: Williamson-i assist — 3.00
1-(1989, $2.95, B&W mag., 80 pgs.) — 4.00

--AND THE SHRINE OF THE SEA DEVIL: Dark Horse, 9/94 ($2.50, one shot)
1-Gary Gianni-a — 2.50
--AND THE SPEAR OF DESTINY: Dark Horse, 4/95 - 8/95 ($2.50) 1-4 — 2.50
--THUNDER IN THE ORIENT: Dark Horse, 9/93 - '94 ($2.50)
1-6: Dan Barry story & art in all; 1-Dorman painted-c — 2.50

INDIANA JONES AND THE TEMPLE OF DOOM
Marvel Comics Group: Sept, 1984 - No. 3, Nov, 1984 (Movie adaptation)

1-3-r/Marvel Super Special; Guice-a — 3.00

INDIAN BRAVES (Baffling Mysteries No. 5 on)

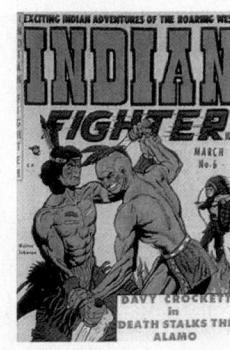

Indian Fighter #6 © YM

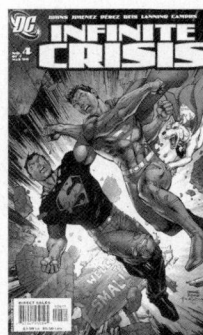

Infinite Crisis #4 © DC

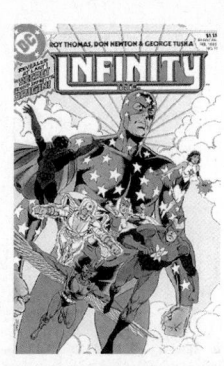

Infinity Inc. #11 © DC

	GD 2.0	VG 4.0	FN 6.0	VF 8.0	VF/NM 9.0	NM- 9.2

Ace Magazines: March, 1951 - No. 4, Sept, 1951

	GD 2.0	VG 4.0	FN 6.0	VF 8.0	VF/NM 9.0	NM- 9.2
1-Green Arrowhead begins, ends #3	14	28	42	82	121	160
2	9	18	27	50	65	80
3,4	8	16	24	44	57	70
I.W. Reprint #1 (nd)-r/Indian Braves #4	2	4	6	9	13	16

INDIAN CHIEF (White Eagle...) (Formerly The Chief, Four Color 290)
Dell Publ. Co.: No. 3, July-Sept, 1951 - No. 33, Jan-Mar, 1959 (All painted-c)

3	5	10	15	35	55	75
4-11: 6-White Eagle app.	4	8	12	28	44	60
12-1st White Eagle(10-12/53)-Not same as earlier character	5	10	15	35	55	75
13-29	4	8	12	23	36	48
30-33-Buscema-a	4	8	12	24	37	50

INDIAN CHIEF (See March of Comics No. 94, 110, 127, 140, 159, 170, 187)

INDIAN FIGHTER, THE (Movie)
Dell Publishing Co.: No. 687, May, 1956 (one-shot)

Four Color 687-Kirk Douglas photo-c	7	14	21	50	83	115

INDIAN FIGHTER
Youthful Magazines: May, 1950 - No. 11, Jan, 1952

1	14	28	42	82	121	160
2-Wildey-a/c(bondage)	10	20	30	58	79	100
3-11: 3,4-Wildey-a	8	16	24	44	57	70

NOTE: *Hollingsworth* a-5. *Walter Johnson* c-1, 3, 4, 6. *Palais* a-10. *Stallman* a-5-8. *Wildey* a-2-4; c-2, 5.

INDIAN LEGENDS OF THE NIAGARA (See American Graphics)

INDIANS
Fiction House Magazines (Wings Publ. Co.): Spring, 1950 - No. 17, Spr, 1953 (1-8: 52 pgs.)

1-Manzar The White Indian, Long Bow & Orphan of the Storm begin	30	60	90	174	275	375
2-Starlight begins	15	30	45	88	137	185
3-5: 5-17-Most-c by Whitman	14	28	42	80	115	150
6-10	12	24	36	69	97	125
11-17	11	22	33	60	83	105

INDIANS OF THE WILD WEST
I. W. Enterprises: Circa 1958? (no date) (Reprints)

9-Kinstler-c; Whitman-a; r/Indians #?	2	4	6	10	14	18

INDIANS ON THE WARPATH
St. John Publishing Co.: No date (Late 40s, early 50s) (132 pgs.)

nn-Matt Baker-c; contains St. John comics rebound. Many combinations possible	37	74	111	213	339	465

INDIAN TRIBES (See Famous Indian Tribes)

INDIAN WARRIORS (Formerly White Rider and Super Horse; becomes Western Crime Cases #9)
Star Publications: No. 7, June, 1951 - No. 8, Sept, 1951

7-White Rider & Superhorse continue; "Last of the Mohicans" serial begins; L.B. Cole-c	18	36	54	105	165	225
8-L. B. Cole-c	17	34	51	98	154	210
3-D 1(12/53, 25¢)-Came w/glasses; L. B. Cole-c	35	70	105	204	322	440
Accepted Reprint(nn)(inside cover shows White Rider & Superhorse #11)-r/cover to #7; origin White Rider &...; L. B. Cole-c	7	14	21	37	46	55
Accepted Reprint #8 (nd); L.B. Cole-c (r-cover to #8)	7	14	21	37	46	55

INDOORS-OUTDOORS (See Wisco)

INDOOR SPORTS
National Specials Co.: nd (6x9", 64 pgs., B&W-r, hard-c)

nn-By Tad	5	10	15	24	30	35

INDUSTRIAL GOTHIC
DC Comics (Vertigo): Dec, 1995 - No. 5, Apr, 1996 ($2.50, limited series)

1-5: Ted McKeever-c/a/scripts						2.50

INFERIOR FIVE, THE (Inferior 5 #11, 12) (See Showcase #62, 63, 65)
National Periodical Publications (#1-10: 12¢): 3-4/67 - No. 10, 9-10/68; No. 11, 8-9/72 - No. 12, 10-11/72

1-(3-4/67)-Sekowsky-a(p); 4th app.	5	10	15	35	55	75
2-5: 2-Plastic Man, F.F. app. 4-Thor app.	3	6	9	19	29	38
6-9: 6-Stars DC staff	3	6	9	16	22	28
10-Superman x-over; F.F., Spider-Man & Sub-Mariner app.	3	6	9	18	27	35
11,12: Orlando-c/a; both r/Showcase #62,63	2	4	6	11	16	20

INFERNO

Caliber Comics: 1995 - No. 5 ($2.95, B&W)

1-5						3.00

INFERNO (See Legion of Super-Heroes)
DC Comics: Oct, 1997 - No. 4, Feb, 1998 ($2.50, limited series)

1-Immonen-s/c/a in all						4.00
2-4						3.00

INFERNO: HELLBOUND
Image Comics (Top Cow): Jan, 2002 - Present ($2.50/$2.99)

1,2: 1-Seven covers; Silvestri-a/Silvestri and Wohl-s						2.50
3-($2.99) Tan-a						3.00
#0 (7/02, $3.00) Tan-a						3.00
Wizard #0- Previews series; bagged with Wizard Top Cow Special mag						2.25

INFINITE CRISIS
DC Comics: Dec, 2005 - No. 7, Jun, 2006 ($3.99, limited series)

1-Johns-s/Jimenez-a; two covers by Jim Lee and George Pérez						5.00
1-RRP Edition with Jim Lee sketch-c						275.00
2-7: 4-New Spectre; Earth-2 returns. 5-Earth-2 Lois dies; new Blue Beetle debut. 6-Superboy killed, new Earth formed. 7-Earth-2 Superman dies						4.00
HC (2006, $24.99, dustjacket) r/#1-7; DiDio intro.; sketch cover gallery; interview/commentary with Johns, Jimenez and editors; sketch art						25.00
... Companion TPB (2006, $14.99) r/Day of Vengeance: Infinite Crisis Special #1, Rann-Thanagar War: ICS #1, The Omac Project: ICS #1, Villains United: ICS #1						15.00
... Secret Files 2006 (4/06, $5.99) tie-in story with Earth-2 Lois and Superman, Earth-Prime Superboy and Alexander Luthor; art by various; profile pages						6.00

INFINITE CRISIS AFTERMATH (See Crisis Aftermath:...)

INFINITY ABYSS (Also see Marvel Universe: The End)
Marvel Comics: Aug, 2002 - No. 6 ($2.99, limited series)

1-5-Starlin-s/a; Thanos, Captain Marvel, Spider-Man, Dr. Strange app.						3.00
6-($3.50)						3.50
Thanos Vol. 2: Infinity Abyss TPB (2003, $17.99) r/ #1-6						18.00

INFINITY CRUSADE
Marvel Comics: June, 1993 - No. 6, Nov, 1993 ($2.50, limited series, 52 pgs.)

1-6: By Jim Starlin & Ron Lim						2.50

INFINITY GAUNTLET (The... #2 on; see Infinity Crusade, The Infinity War & Warlock & the Infinity Watch)
Marvel Comics: July, 1991 - No. 6, Dec, 1991 ($2.50, limited series)

1-6:Thanos-c/stories in all; Starlin scripts in all; 5,6-Ron Lim-c/a						3.00
TPB (4/99, $24.95) r/#1-6						25.00

NOTE: *Lim* a-3p(part), 5p, 6p; c-5i, 6i. *Perez* a-1-3p, 4p(part); c-1(painted), 2-4, 5i, 6i.

INFINITY, INC. (See All-Star Squadron #25)
DC Comics: Mar, 1984 - No. 53, Aug, 1988 ($1.25, Baxter paper, 36 pgs.)

1-Brainwave, Jr., Fury, The Huntress, Jade, Northwind, Nuklon, Obsidian, Power Girl, Silver Scarab & Star Spangled Kid begin						4.00
2-13,38-49,51-53: 2-Dr. Midnite, G.A. Flash, W. Woman, Dr. Fate, Hourman, Green Lantern, Wildcat app. 5-Nudity panels. 46,47-Millennium tie-ins						3.00
14-Todd McFarlane-a (5/85, 2nd full story)	1	2	3	6		9
15-37-McFarlane-a (20,23,24: 5 pgs. only; 33: 2 pgs.); 18-24-Crisis x-over. 21-Intro new Hourman & Dr. Midnight. 26-New Wildcat app. 31-Star Spangled Kid becomes Skyman. 32-Green Fury becomes Green Flame. 33-Origin Obsidian. 35-1st modern app. G.A. Fury						4.00
50 ($2.50, 52 pgs.)						3.00
Annual 1,2: 1(12/85)-Crisis x-over. 2('88, $2.00), Special 1 ('87, $1.50)						3.00

NOTE: *Kubert* r-4. *McFarlane* a-14-37p, Annual 1p; c/p(-14-19, 22, 25, 26, 31-33, 37, Annual 1. *Newton* a-12p, 13p(last work 4/85). *Tuska* a-11p. JSA app. 3-10.

INFINITY, INC. (See 52)
DC Comics: Nov, 2007 - Present ($2.99)

1-Milligan-s; Steel app.						3.00

INFINITY WAR, THE (Also see Infinity Gauntlet & Warlock and the Infinity...)
Marvel Comics: June, 1992 - No. 6, Nov, 1992 ($2.50, mini-series)

1-Starlin scripts, Lim-c/a(p), Thanos app. in all						2.50
2-6: All have wraparound gatefold covers						2.50
TPB (2006, $29.99) r/#1-6, Marvel Comics Presents #108-111, Warlock and the Infinity Watch #7-10; cover gallery and synopses of Infinity War crossovers						30.00

INFORMER, THE
Feature Television Productions: April, 1954 - No. 5, Dec, 1954

1-Sekowsky-a begins	12	24	36	69	97	125
2	9	18	27	47	61	75

Inhumans V2 #3 © MAR

The Inspector #3 © GK

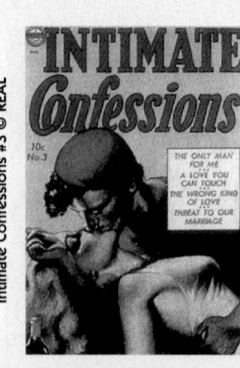

Intimate Confessions #3 © REAL

	GD 2.0	VG 4.0	FN 6.0	VF 8.0	VF/NM 9.0	NM- 9.2
3-5	8	16	24	42	54	65

IN HIS STEPS
Spire Christian Comics (Fleming H. Revell Co.): 1973, 1977 (39/49¢)

	GD 2.0	VG 4.0	FN 6.0	VF 8.0	VF/NM 9.0	NM- 9.2
nn	2	4	6	8	10	12

INHUMANOIDS, THE (TV)
Marvel Comics (Star Comics): Jan, 1987 - No. 4, July 1987

1-4: Based on Hasbro toys	3.00

INHUMANS, THE (See Amazing Adventures, Fantastic Four #54 & Special #5, Incredible Hulk Special #1, Marvel Graphic Novel & Thor #146)
Marvel Comics Group: Oct, 1975 - No. 12, Aug, 1977

	GD 2.0	VG 4.0	FN 6.0	VF 8.0	VF/NM 9.0	NM- 9.2
1: #1-4,6 are 25¢ issues	2	4	6	13	18	22
2-4-Peréz-a	1	3	4	6	8	10
5-12: 9-Reprints Amazing Adventures #1,2('70). 12-Hulk app.	1	2	3	5	7	9
4-(30¢-c variant, limited distribution)(4/76) Peréz-a	2	4	6	10	14	18
6-(30¢-c variant, limited distribution)(8/76)	2	4	6	10	14	18
11,12-(35¢-c variants, limited distribution)	2	4	6	10	14	18
Special 1(4/90, $1.50, 52 pgs.)-F.F. cameo						3.00
....The Great Refuge (5/95, $2.95)						3.00

NOTE: **Buckler** c-2-4p, 5. **Gil Kane** a-5-7p; c-1p, 7p, 8p. **Kirby** a-9r. **Mooney** a-11i. **Perez** a-1-4p, 8p.

INHUMANS (Marvel Knights)
Marvel Comics: Nov, 1998 - No. 12, Oct, 1999 ($2.99, limited series)

1-Jae Lee-c/a; Paul Jenkins-s	10.00
1-($6.95) DF Edition; Jae Lee variant-c	7.00
2-Two covers by Lee and Darrow	4.00
3-12	3.00
TPB (10/00, $24.95) r/#1-12	25.00

INHUMANS (Volume 3)
Marvel Comics: Jun, 2000 - No. 4, Oct, 2000 ($2.99, limited series)

1-4-Ladronn-c/Pacheco & Marin-s. 1-3-Ladronn-a. 4-Lucas-a	3.00

INHUMANS (Volume 6)
Marvel Comics: Jun, 2003 - No. 12, Jun, 2004 ($2.50/$2.99)

1-12: 1-6-McKeever-s/Clark-a. 7-Begin $2.99-c. 7,8-Teranishi-a	3.00
Vol. 1: Culture Shock (2005, $7.99, digest) r/#1-6; story pitch and sketch pages	8.00

INHUMANS 2099
Marvel Comics: Nov, 2004 ($2.99, one-shot)

1-Kirkman-s/Rathburn-a/Pat Lee-c	3.00

INKY & DINKY (See Felix's Nephews...)

IN LOVE (...Magazine on-c; I Love You No. 7 on)
Mainline/Charlton No. 5 (5/55)-on: Aug-Sept, 1954 - No. 6, July, 1955 ('Adult Reading' on-c)

	GD 2.0	VG 4.0	FN 6.0	VF 8.0	VF/NM 9.0	NM- 9.2
1-Simon & Kirby-a; book-length novel in all issues	40	80	120	235	368	500
2,3-S&K-a. 3-Last pre-code (12-1/54-55)	23	46	69	135	213	290
4-S&K-a.(Rare)	26	52	78	150	235	320
5-S&K-c only	13	26	39	72	101	130
6-No S&K-a	9	18	27	47	61	75

INNOVATION SPECTACULAR
Innovation Publishing: 1991 - No. 2, 1991 ($2.95, squarebound, 100 pgs.)

1,2: Contains rebound comics w/o covers	3.00

INNOVATION SUMMER FUN SPECIAL
Innovation Publishing: 1991 ($3.50, B&W/color, squarebound)

1-Contains rebound comics (Power Factory)	3.50

IN SEARCH OF THE CASTAWAYS (See Movie Comics)

INSIDE CRIME (Formerly My Intimate Affair)
Fox Features Syndicate (Hero Books): No. 3, July, 1950 - No. 2, Sept, 1950

	GD 2.0	VG 4.0	FN 6.0	VF 8.0	VF/NM 9.0	NM- 9.2
3-Wood-a (10 pgs.); L. B. Cole-c	30	60	90	174	275	375
2-Used in SOTI, pg. 182,183; r/Spook #24	23	46	69	132	209	285
nn(no publ. listed, nd)	11	22	33	60	83	105

INSPECTOR, THE (TV) (Also see The Pink Panther)
Gold Key: July, 1974 - No. 19, Feb, 1978

	GD 2.0	VG 4.0	FN 6.0	VF 8.0	VF/NM 9.0	NM- 9.2
1	3	6	9	19	29	38
2-5	2	4	6	13	18	22
6-9	2	4	6	10	14	18
10-19: 11-Reprints	2	4	6	8	10	12

INSPECTOR GILL OF THE FISH POLICE (See Fish Police)

INSPECTOR WADE

David McKay Publications: No. 13, May, 1938

	GD 2.0	VG 4.0	FN 6.0	VF 8.0	VF/NM 9.0	NM- 9.2
Feature Books 13	29	58	87	167	264	360

INSTANT PIANO
Dark Horse Comics: Aug, 1994 - No. 4, Feb, 1995 ($3.95, B&W, bimonthly, mature)

1-4	4.00

INTERFACE
Marvel Comics (Epic Comics): Dec, 1989 - No. 8, Dec, 1990 ($1.95, mature, coated paper)

1-8: Cont. from 1st ESPers series; painted-c/a	2.50
Espers: Interface TPB ('98, $16.95) r/#1-6	17.00

INTERNATIONAL COMICS (...Crime Patrol No. 6)
E. C. Comics: Spring, 1947 - No. 5, Nov-Dec, 1947

	GD 2.0	VG 4.0	FN 6.0	VF 8.0	VF/NM 9.0	NM- 9.2
1-Schaffenberger-a begins, ends #4	62	124	186	388	644	900
2	43	86	129	263	431	600
3-5	40	80	120	239	380	520

INTERNATIONAL CRIME PATROL (Formerly International Comics #1-5; becomes Crime Patrol No. 7 on)
E. C. Comics: No. 6, Spring, 1948

	GD 2.0	VG 4.0	FN 6.0	VF 8.0	VF/NM 9.0	NM- 9.2
6-Moon Girl app.	62	124	186	388	644	900

IN THE BLOOD
Boom! Studios: Feb, 2006 - Present ($3.99)

1-Steve Niles-s/Josh Medors-a	3.00

IN THE DAYS OF THE MOB (Magazine)
Hampshire Dist. Ltd. (National): Fall, 1971 (B&W)

	GD 2.0	VG 4.0	FN 6.0	VF 8.0	VF/NM 9.0	NM- 9.2
1-Kirby-a; John Dillinger wanted poster inside (1/2 value if poster is missing)	7	14	21	49	80	110

IN THE PRESENCE OF MINE ENEMIES
Spire Christian Comics/Fleming H. Revell Co.: 1973 (35/49¢)

	GD 2.0	VG 4.0	FN 6.0	VF 8.0	VF/NM 9.0	NM- 9.2
nn	2	4	6	8	10	12

IN THE SHADOW OF EDGAR ALLAN POE
DC Comics (Vertigo): 2002 (Graphic novel)

Hardcover (2002, $24.95) Fuqua-s/Phillips and Parke photo-a	25.00
Softcover (2003, $17.95)	18.00

INTIMATE
Charlton Comics: Dec, 1957 - No. 3, May, 1958

	GD 2.0	VG 4.0	FN 6.0	VF 8.0	VF/NM 9.0	NM- 9.2
1	6	12	18	28	34	40
2,3	4	8	12	18	22	25

INTIMATE CONFESSIONS (See Fox Giants)

INTIMATE CONFESSIONS
Country Press Inc.: 1942

nn-Ashcan comic, not distributed to newsstands, only for in house use. A VF copy sold for $1,000 in 2007, and a VF+ copy sold for $1,525 in 2007.

INTIMATE CONFESSIONS
Realistic Comics: July-Aug, 1951 - No. 7, Aug, 1952; No. 8, Mar, 1953 (All painted-c)

	GD 2.0	VG 4.0	FN 6.0	VF 8.0	VF/NM 9.0	NM- 9.2
1-Kinstler-c/a; c/Avon paperback #222	86	172	258	538	894	1250
2	23	46	69	130	205	280
3-c/Avon paperback #250; Kinstler-c/a	27	54	81	156	246	335
4-8: 4-c/Avon paperback #304; Kinstler-c. 6-c/Avon paperback #120.						
8-c/Avon paperback #375; Kinstler-a	23	46	69	130	205	280

INTIMATE CONFESSIONS
I. W. Enterprises/Super Comics: 1964

	GD 2.0	VG 4.0	FN 6.0	VF 8.0	VF/NM 9.0	NM- 9.2
I.W. Reprint #9,10, Super Reprint #10,12,18	2	4	6	10	14	18

INTIMATE LOVE
Standard Comics: No. 5, 1950 - No. 28, Aug, 1954

	GD 2.0	VG 4.0	FN 6.0	VF 8.0	VF/NM 9.0	NM- 9.2
5-8: 6-8-Severin/Elder-a	10	20	30	54	72	90
9	8	16	24	40	50	60
10-Jane Russell, Robert Mitchum photo-c	13	26	39	74	105	135
11-18,20,23,25,27,28	7	14	21	37	46	55
19,21,22,24,26-Toth-a	8	16	24	44	57	70

NOTE: **Celardo** a-8, 10. **Colletta** a-23. **Moreira** a-13(2). Photo-c-6, 7, 10, 12, 14, 15, 18-20, 24, 26, 27.

INTIMATES, THE
DC Comics (WildStorm): Jan, 2005 - No. 12, Dec, 2005 ($2.95/$2.99)

1-12: 1-Joe Casey-s/Jim Lee-c/Lee and Giuseppe Camuncoli-a	3.00

INTIMATE SECRETS OF ROMANCE
Star Publications: Sept, 1953 - No. 2, Apr, 1954

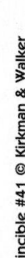
The Invaders #29 © MAR

Invincible #41 © Kirkman & Walker

Invisibles #9 © Grant Morrison

	GD 2.0	VG 4.0	FN 6.0	VF 8.0	VF/NM 9.0	NM- 9.2
1,2-L. B. Cole-c	19	38	57	109	172	235

INTIMIDATORS (Jim Valentino's...)
Image Comics (Shadowline): Dec, 2005 - Present ($3.50)

1-4: 1-Montenegro-a/Kleid-s. 4-Oeming-c						3.50

INTRIGUE
Quality Comics Group: Jan, 1955

1-Horror; Jack Cole reprint/Web of Evil	34	68	102	195	308	420

INTRIGUE
Image Comics: Aug, 1999 - No. 3, Feb, 2000 ($2.50/$2.95)

1,2: 1-Two covers (Andrews, Wieringo); Shum-s/Andrews-a						2.50
3-($2.95)						3.00

INTRUDER
TSR, Inc.: 1990 - No. 10, 1991 ($2.95, 44 pgs.)

1-10						3.00

INVADERS, THE (TV)
Gold Key: Oct, 1967 - No. 4, Oct, 1968 (All have photo-c)

1-Spiegle-a in all	9	18	27	60	100	140
2-4: 2-Pin-up on back-c	6	12	18	41	66	90

INVADERS, THE (Also see The Avengers #71 & Giant-Size Invaders)
Marvel Comics Group: August, 1975 - No. 40, May, 1979; No. 41, Sept, 1979

1-Captain America & Bucky, Human Torch & Toro, & Sub-Mariner begin; cont'd. from Giant Size Invaders #1; #1-7 are 25¢ issues	5	10	15	32	51	70
2-5: 2-1st app. Brain-Drain. 3-Battle issue; Cap vs. Namor vs. Torch; intro U-Man				15	21	26
6-10: 6,7-(Regular 25¢ edition). 6-(7/76) Liberty Legion app. 7-Intro Baron Blood & intro/1st app. Union Jack; Human Torch origin retold. 8-Union Jack-c/story. 9-Origin Baron Blood. 10-G.A. Capt. America-r/C.A #22	2	4	6	9	12	15
6,7-(30¢-c variants, limited distribution)	3	6	9	20	30	40
11-19: 11-Origin Spitfire; intro The Blue Bullet. 14-1st app. The Crusaders. 16-Re-intro The Destroyer. 17-Intro Warrior Woman. 18-Re-intro The Destroyer w/new origin. 19-Hitler-c/story	1	3	4	6	8	10
17-19,21-(35¢-c variants, limited distribution)	4	8	12	24	37	50
20-(Regular 30¢-c) Reprints origin/1st app. Sub-Mariner from Motion Picture Funnies Weekly with color added & brief write-up about MPFW; 1st app. new Union Jack II	2	4	6	9	12	15
20-(35¢-c variant, limited distribution)	4	8	12	28	44	60
21-(Regular 30¢ edition)-r/Marvel Mystery #10 (battle issue)	2	4	6	8	10	12
22-30,34-40: 22-New origin Toro. 24-r/Marvel Mystery #17 (team-up issue; all-r). 25-All new-a begins. 28-Intro new Human Top & Golden Girl. 29-Intro Teutonic Knight. 34-Mighty Destroyer joins. 35-The Whizzer app.	1	2	3	4	5	7
31-33: 31-Frankenstein-c/sty. 32,33-Thor app.	1	3	4	6	8	10
41-Double size last issue	2	4	6	10	14	18
Annual 1 (9/77)-Schomburg, Rico stories (new); Schomburg-c/a (1st for Marvel in 30 years); Avengers app.; re-intro The Shark & The Hyena	4	8	12	26	41	55
... Classic Vol. 1 TPB (2007, $24.99) r/#1-9, Giant-Size Invaders #1 and Marvel Premiere #29,30; cover pencils and cover inks						25.00

NOTE: *Buckler* a-5. *Everett* r-20('39), 21(1940), 24, Annual 1. *Gil Kane* c(p)-13, 17, 18, 20-27. *Kirby* c(p)-3-12, 14-16, 32, 33. *Mooney* a-5i, 16, 22. *Robbins* a-1-4, 6-9, 10(3 pg.), 11-15, 17-21, 23, 25-28; c-28.

INVADERS (See Namor, the Sub-Mariner #12)
Marvel Comics Group: May, 1993 - No. 4, Aug, 1993 ($1.75, limited series)

1-4						2.50

INVADERS (2004 title - see New Invaders)

INVADERS FROM HOME
DC Comics (Piranha Press): 1990 - No. 6, 1990 ($2.50, mature)

1-6						2.50

INVASION
DC Comics: Holiday, 1988-'89 - No. 3, Jan, 1989 ($2.95, lim. series, 84 pgs.)

1-3:1-McFarlane/Russell-a. 2-McFarlane/Russell & Giffen/Gordon-a						3.00

INVINCIBLE (Also see The Pact #4)
Image Comics: Jan, 2003 - Present ($2.95/$2.99)

1-Kirkman/Walker-a						5.00
2-7-Kirkman-s/Walker-a. 4-Preview of The Moth						4.00
8-24,26-41,43,45: 11-Origin of Omni-Man. 14-Cho-c. 33-Tie-in w/Marvel Team-Up #14						3.00
25-($4.95) Science Dog app.; back-up stories w/origins of Science Dog and teammates						5.00
42-($1.99) Includes re-cap of the entire series						2.25
#0-(4/05, 50¢) Origin of Invincible; Ottley-a						2.25

	GD 2.0	VG 4.0	FN 6.0	VF 8.0	VF/NM 9.0	NM- 9.2
Official Handbook of the Invincible Universe 1,2 (11/06, 1/07, $4.99) profile pages						5.00

The Complete Invincible Library Vol. 1 Slipcase HC (2006, $125.00) oversized r/#1-24, #0 and story from Image Comics Summer Special (FCBD 2004); sketch pages; script for #1						125.00
..., Ultimate Collection Vol. 1 HC (2005, $34.95) oversized r/#1-13; sketch pages						35.00
..., Ultimate Collection Vol. 2 HC (2006, $34.99) oversized r/#14-24, #0 and story from Image Comics Summer Special (FCBD 2004); sketch pages and script for #23; intro by Damon Lindelof; afterword by Robert Kirkman						35.00
..., Ultimate Collection Vol. 3 HC (2007, $34.95) oversized r/#25-35 & The Pact #4; sketch pages and script for #28; afterword by Robert Kirkman						35.00
Vol. 1: Family Matters TPB (8/03, $12.95) r/#1-4; intro. by Busiek; sketch pages						13.00
Vol. 2: Eight in Enough TPB (3/04, $12.95) r/#5-8; intro. by Larsen; sketch pages						13.00
Vol. 3: Perfect Strangers TPB (2004, $12.95) r/#9-12; intro. by Brevoort; sketch pages						13.00
Vol. 4: Head of the Class TPB (1/05, $14.95) r/#14-19; intro. by Waid; sketch pages						15.00
Vol. 5: The Facts of Life TPB (2005, $14.99) r/#0,20-24; intro. by Wieringo; sketch pages						15.00
Vol. 6: A Different World TPB (2006, $14.99) r/#25-30; intro. by Brubaker; sketch pages						15.00
Vol. 7: Three's Company TPB (2006, $14.99) r/#31-35 & The Pact #4; sketch pages						15.00
Vol. 8: My Favorite Martian TPB (2007, $14.99) r/#36-41; sketch pages						15.00

INVINCIBLE FOUR OF KUNG FU & NINJA
Leung Publications: April, 1988 - No. 6, 1989 ($2.00)

1-($2.75)						3.00
2-6: 2-Begin $2.00-c						2.50

INVISIBLE BOY (See Approved Comics)

INVISIBLE MAN, THE (See Superior Stories #1 & Supernatural Thrillers #2)

INVISIBLE PEOPLE
Kitchen Sink Press: 1992 (B&W, lim. series)

Book One: Sanctum; Book Two: "The Power": Will Eisner-s/a in all						2.50
Book Three: "Mortal Combat"						4.00
Hardcover ($34.95)						35.00
TPB (DC Comics, 9/00, $12.95) reprints series						13.00

INVISIBLES, THE (1st Series)
DC Comics (Vertigo): Sept, 1994 - No. 25, Oct, 1996 ($1.95/$2.50, mature)

1-($2.95, 52 pg.)-Intro King Mob, Ragged Robin, Boy, Lord Fanny & Dane (Jack Frost); Grant Morrison scripts in all						6.00
2-8: 4-Includes bound-in trading cards. 5-1st app. Orlando; brown paper-c						4.00
9-25: 10-Intro Jim Crow. 13-15-Origin Lord Fanny. 19-Origin King Mob; polybagged. 20-Origin Boy. 21-Mister Six revealed. 25-Intro Division X						2.50
Apocalipstick (2001, $19.95, TPB)-r/#9-16; Bolland-c						20.00
Entropy in the U.K. (2001, $19.95, TPB)-r/#17-25; Bolland-c						20.00
Say You Want A Revolution (1996, $17.50, TPB)-r/#1-8						18.00

NOTE: *Buckingham* a-25p. *Rian Hughes* c-1, 5. *Phil Jimenez* a-17p-19p. *Paul Johnson* a-16, 21. *Sean Phillips* c-2-4, 6-25. *Weston* a-10p. *Yeowell* a-1p-4p, 22p-24p.

INVISIBLES, THE (2nd Series)
DC Comics (Vertigo): V2#1, Feb, 1997 - No. 22, Feb, 1999 ($2.50, mature)

1-Intro Jolly Roger; Grant Morrison scripts, Phil Jimenez-a, & Brian Bolland-c begins						4.00
2-22: 9,14-Weston-a						2.50
Bloody Hell in America TPB ('98, $12.95) r/#1-4						13.00
Counting to None TPB ('99, $19.95) r/#5-13						20.00
Kissing Mr. Quimper TPB ('00, $19.95) r/#14-22						20.00

INVISIBLES, THE (3rd Series) (Issue #'s go in reverse from #12 to #1)
DC Comics (Vertigo): V3#12, Apr, 1999 - No. 1, June, 2000 ($2.95, mature)

1-12-Bolland-c; Morrison-s on all. 1-Quitely-a. 2-4-Art by various. 5-8-Phillips-a. 9-12-Phillip Bond-a.						3.00
The Invisible Kingdom TPB ('02, $19.95) r/#12-1; new Bolland-c						20.00

INVISIBLE SCARLET O'NEIL (Also see Famous Funnies #81 & Harvey Comics Hits #59)
Famous Funnies (Harvey): Dec, 1950 - No. 3, Apr, 1951 (2-3 pgs. of Powell-a in each issue)

1	15	30	45	86	133	180
2,3	12	24	36	67	94	120

ION (Green Lantern Kyle Rayner) (See Countdown)
DC Comics: Jun, 2006 - No. 12, May, 2007 ($2.99)

1-12: 1-Marz-s/Tocchini-a. 3-Mogo app. 9,10-Tangent Green Lantern app. 12-Monitor app.						3.00
...: The Torchbearer TPB (2007, $14.99) r/#1-6						15.00

I, PAPARAZZI
DC Comics (Vertigo): 2001 ($29.95, HC, digitally manipulated photographic art)

nn-Pat McGreal/Steven Parke-digital-a/Stephen John Phillips-photos						30.00

IRON AND THE MAIDEN
Aspen MLT: Sept, 2007 - Present ($3.99)

1,2: 1-Two covers by Manapul and Madureira/Matsuda; Jason Rubin-s						4.00

IRON CORPORAL, THE (See Army War Heroes #22)

Iron Fist #14 © MAR

Iron Man #110 © MAR

Iron Man #286 © MAR

	GD 2.0	VG 4.0	FN 6.0	VF 8.0	VF/NM 9.0	NM- 9.2

Charlton Comics: No. 23, Oct, 1985 - No. 25, Feb, 1986

	GD 2.0	VG 4.0	FN 6.0	VF 8.0	VF/NM 9.0	NM- 9.2
23-25: Glanzman-a(r); low print						5.00

IRON FIST (See Immortal Iron Fist, Deadly Hands of Kung Fu, Marvel Premiere & Power Man)
Marvel Comics: Nov, 1975 - No. 15, Sept, 1977

	GD 2.0	VG 4.0	FN 6.0	VF 8.0	VF/NM 9.0	NM- 9.2
1-Iron Fist battles Iron Man (#1-6: 25¢)	6	12	18	37	59	80
2	3	6	9	20	30	40
3-10: 4-6-(Regular 25¢ edition)(4-6/76). 8-Origin retold	3	6	9	16	23	30
4-6-(30¢-c variant, limited distribution)	5	10	15	32	51	70
11,13: 13-(30¢-c)	3	6	9	14	19	24
12-Capt. America app.	3	6	9	16	23	30
13-(35¢-c variant, limited distribution)	7	14	21	45	73	100
14-1st app. Sabretooth (8/77)(see Power Man)	12	24	36	87	156	225
14-(35¢-c variant, limited distribution)	52	104	156	442	821	1200
15-(Regular 30¢ ed.) X-Men app., Byrne-a	6	12	18	39	62	85
15-(35¢-c variant, limited distribution)	19	38	57	138	244	350

NOTE: *Adkins* a-8p, 10i, 13i; c-8i. *Byrne* a-1-15p; c-8p, 15p. *G. Kane* c-4-6p. *McWilliams* a-1i.

IRON FIST
Marvel Comics: Sept, 1996 - No. 2, Oct, 1996 ($1.50, limited series)

	GD 2.0	VG 4.0	FN 6.0	VF 8.0	VF/NM 9.0	NM- 9.2
1,2						3.00

IRON FIST
Marvel Comics: Jul, 1998 - No. 3, Sept, 1998 ($2.50, limited series)

	GD 2.0	VG 4.0	FN 6.0	VF 8.0	VF/NM 9.0	NM- 9.2
1-3: Jurgens-s/Guice-a						2.50

IRON FIST (Also see Immortal Iron Fist)
Marvel Comics: May, 2004 - No. 6, Oct, 2004 ($2.99)

	GD 2.0	VG 4.0	FN 6.0	VF 8.0	VF/NM 9.0	NM- 9.2
1-6: 1-4,6-Kevin Lau-c/a. 5-Mays-c/a						3.00

IRON FIST: WOLVERINE
Marvel Comics: Nov, 2000 - No. 4, Feb, 2001 ($2.99, limited series)

	GD 2.0	VG 4.0	FN 6.0	VF 8.0	VF/NM 9.0	NM- 9.2
1-4-Igle-c/a; Kingpin app. 2-Iron Man app. 3,4-Capt. America app.						3.00

IRON GHOST
Image Comics: Apr, 2005 - No. 6, Mar, 2006 ($2.95/$2.99, limited series)

	GD 2.0	VG 4.0	FN 6.0	VF 8.0	VF/NM 9.0	NM- 9.2
1-6-Chuck Dixon-s/Sergio Cariello-a; flip cover on each						3.00

IRONHAND OF ALMURIC (Robert E. Howard's...)
Dark Horse Comics: Aug, 1991 - No. 4, 1991 ($2.00, B&W, mini-series)

	GD 2.0	VG 4.0	FN 6.0	VF 8.0	VF/NM 9.0	NM- 9.2
1-4: 1-Conrad painted-c						2.25

IRON HORSE (TV)
Dell Publishing Co.: March, 1967 - No. 2, June, 1967

	GD 2.0	VG 4.0	FN 6.0	VF 8.0	VF/NM 9.0	NM- 9.2
1-Dale Robertson photo covers on both	3	6	9	18	27	35
2	3	6	9	15	21	26

IRONJAW (Also see The Barbarians)
Atlas/Seaboard Publ.: Jan, 1975 - No. 4, July, 1975

	GD 2.0	VG 4.0	FN 6.0	VF 8.0	VF/NM 9.0	NM- 9.2
1,2-Neal Adams-c. 1-1st app. Iron Jaw; Sekowsky-a(p); Fleisher-s	2	4	6	8	10	12
3,4-Marcos. 4-Origin	1	2	3	4	5	7

IRON LANTERN
Marvel Comics (Amalgam): June, 1997 ($1.95, one-shot)

	GD 2.0	VG 4.0	FN 6.0	VF 8.0	VF/NM 9.0	NM- 9.2
1-Kurt Busiek-s/Paul Smith & Al Williamson-a						2.50

IRON MAN (Also see The Avengers #1, Giant-Size…, Marvel Collectors Item Classics, Marvel Double Feature, Marvel Fanfare & Tales of Suspense #39)
Marvel Comics: May, 1968 - No. 332, Sept, 1996

	GD 2.0	VG 4.0	FN 6.0	VF 8.0	VF/NM 9.0	NM- 9.2
1-Origin; Colan-c/a(p); story continued from Iron Man & Sub-Mariner #1	32	64	96	240	445	650
2	12	24	36	86	153	220
3	8	16	24	58	97	135
4,5	7	14	21	49	80	110
6-10: 9-Iron Man battles green Hulk-like android	6	12	18	39	62	85
11-15: 15-Last 12¢ issue	5	10	15	32	51	70
16-20	4	8	12	26	41	55
21-24,26-30: 22-Death of Janice Cord. 27-Intro Firebrand	3	6	9	19	29	38
25-Iron Man battles Sub-Mariner	4	8	12	22	34	45
31-42: 33-1st app. Spymaster. 35-Nick Fury & Daredevil x-over. 42-Last 15¢ issue	3	6	9	15	21	26
43-Intro The Guardsman; 25¢ giant (52 pgs.)	4	8	12	22	34	45
44-46,48-50: 43-Ant-Man back-up by Ayers. 44-Ant-Man by Tuska. 46-The Guardsman dies. 50-Princess Python app.	2	4	6	11	16	20
47-Origin retold; Barry Smith-a(p)	3	6	9	17	25	32

	GD 2.0	VG 4.0	FN 6.0	VF 8.0	VF/NM 9.0	NM- 9.2
51-53: 53-Starlin part pencils	2	4	6	9	13	16
54-Iron Man battles Sub-Mariner; 1st app. Moondragon (1/73) as Madame MacEvil; Everett part-c	4	8	12	24	37	50
55-1st app. Thanos (brief), Drax the Destroyer, Mentor, Starfox & Kronos (2/73); Starlin-c/a	13	26	39	93	164	235
56-Starlin-a	4	8	12	24	37	50
57-65,67-70: 59-Firebrand returns. 65-Origin Dr. Spectrum. 67-Last 20¢ issue. 68-Sunfire & Unicorn app.; origin retold; Starlin-c	2	4	6	9	12	15
66-Iron Man vs. Thor.	3	6	9	16	22	28
71-84: 72-Cameo portraits of N. Adams. 73-Rename Stark Industries to Stark International; Brunner. 76-r/#9.	2	4	6	8	10	12
85-89-(Regular 25¢ editions): 86-1st app. Blizzard. 87-Origin Blizzard. 88-Thanos app. 89-Daredevil app.; last 25¢-c	2	4	6	8	10	12
85-89-(30¢-c variants, limited distribution)(4-8/76)	3	6	9	20	30	40
90-99: 96-1st app. new Guardsman	1	3	4	6	8	10
99,101-103-(35¢-c variants, limited dist.)	4	8	12	26	41	55
100-(7/77)-Starlin-a	3	6	9	16	23	30
100-(35¢-c variant, limited dist.)	8	16	24	56	93	130
101-117: 101-Intro DreadKnight. 109-1st app. new Crimson Dynamo; 1st app. Vanguard. 110-Origin Jack of Hearts retold; death of Count Nefaria. 114-Avengers app.	1	2	3	5	6	8
118-Byrne-a(p); 1st app. Jim Rhodes	2	4	6	8	10	12
119-127: 120,121-Sub-Mariner x-over. 122-Origin. 123-128-Tony Stark treated for alcohol problem. 125-Ant-Man app.	1	3	4	6	8	10
128-Classic Tony Stark alcoholism cover	2	4	6	10	14	18
129,130,133-149						6.00
131,132-Hulk x-over	1	2	3	5	6	8
150-Double size	1	2	3	5	7	9
151-168: 152-New armor. 161-Moon Knight app. 167-Tony Stark alcohol problem resurfaces						4.00
169-New Iron Man (Jim Rhodes replaces Tony Stark)						6.00
170,171						4.00
172-199: 172-Captain America x-over. 186-Intro Vibro. 190-Scarlet Witch app. 191-198-Tony Stark returns as original Iron Man. 192-Both Iron Men battle						3.00
200-(11/85, $1.25, 52 pgs.)-Tony Stark returns as new Iron Man (red & white armor) thru #230						5.00
201-213,215-224: 213-Intro new Dominic Fortune						3.00
214,225,228,231,234,247: 214-Spider-Woman app. in new black costume (1/87). 225-Double size ($1.25). 228-vs. Capt. America. 231-Intro new Iron Man. 234-Spider-Man x-over. 247-Hulk x-over						4.00
226,227,229,230,232,233,235-243,245,246,248,249: 233-Ant-Man app. 243-Tony Stark loses use of legs						2.50
244-($1.50, 52 pgs.)-New Armor makes him walk						3.00
250-($1.50, 52 pgs.)-Dr. Doom-c/story						3.00
251-274,276-281,283,285-287,289,291-299: 258-277-Byrne scripts. 271-Fin Fang Foom app. 276-Black Widow-c/story; last $1.00-c. 281-1st brief app. War Machine.						2.50
275-($1.50, 52 pgs.)						3.00
282-1st full app. War Machine (7/92)						4.00
283-2nd full app. War Machine						2.50
284-Death of Iron Man (Tony Stark)						4.00
288-($2.50, 52pg.)-Silver foil stamped-c; Iron Man's 350th app. in comics						3.00
290-($2.95, 52pg.)-Gold foil stamped-c; 30th ann.						3.00
300-($3.95, 68 pgs.)-Collector's Edition w/embossed foil-c; anniversary issue; War Machine-c/story						4.00
300-($2.50)-Newsstand Edition						2.50
301-303: 302-Venom-c/story (cameo #301)						2.50
304-316,318-324,326-331: 304-Begin $1.50-c; bound-in trading card sheet; Thunderstrike-c/story. 310-Orange logo. 312-w/bound-in Power Ranger Card. 319-Prologue to "The Crossing." 326-New Tony Stark; Pratt-c. 330-War Machine & Stockpile app; return of Morgan Stark						2.50
310,325: 310 ($2.95)-Polybagged w/ 16 pg. Marvel Action Hour preview & acetate print; white logo. 325-($2.95)-Wraparound-c						3.00
317-($2.50)-Flip book						2.50
332-Onslaught x-over						4.00
Special 1 (8/70)-Sub-Mariner x-over; Everett-c	4	8	12	26	41	55
Special 2 (11/71, 52 pgs.)-r/TOS #81,82,91 (all-r)	3	6	9	16	23	30
Annual 3 (1976)-Man-Thing app.	2	4	6	10	14	18
King Size 4 (8/77)-The Champions (w/Ghost Rider) app.; Newton-a(i)	2	4	6	9	12	15
Annual 5 ('82) New-a						6.00
Annual 6-8: ('83-'85) 6-New Iron Man (J. Rhodes) app. 8-X-Factor app.						5.00
Annual 9-15: ('86-'94) 10-Atlantis Attacks x-over; P. Smith-a; Layton/Guice-a; Sub-Mariner app. 11-(1990)-Origin of Mrs. Arbogast by Ditko (p&i). 12-1 pg. origin recap; Ant-Man back-up-s. 13-Darkhawk & Avengers West Coast app.; Colan/Williamson-a. 14-Bagged w/card						3.00

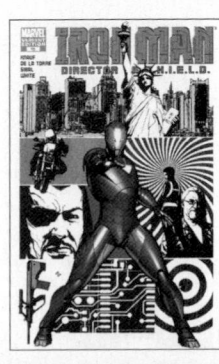

Iron Man (2005 series) #15 © MAR

Iron Man: Enter the Mandarin #1 © MAR

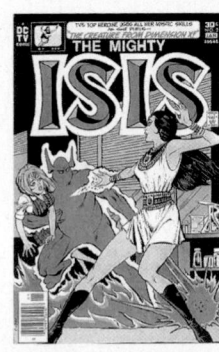

Isis #2 © Filmation

	GD	VG	FN	VF	VF/NM	NM-
	2.0	4.0	6.0	8.0	9.0	9.2

...: Armor Wars TPB (2007, $24.99) r/#225-232; Michelinie intro.   25.00
Manual 1 (1993, $1.75)-Operations handbook   2.50
Graphic Novel: Crash (1988, $12.95, Adults, 72 pgs.)-Computer generated art & color;
    violence & nudity   13.00
...Collector's Preview 1(11/94, $1.95)-wraparound-c; text & illos-no comics   2.50
...: Demon in a Bottle TPB (2006, $24.99) r/#120-128   25.00
...Vs. Dr. Doom (12/94, $12.95)-r/#149-150, 249,250. Julie Bell-c   13.00
NOTE: **Austin** c-105i, 109-111i, 151i. **Byrne** a-118p; c-109p, 197, 253. **Colan** a-1p, 253, Special 1p(3); c-1p. **Craig** a-1i, 2-4, 5-13i, 14, 15-19i, 24p, 25p, 26-28i; c-2-4. **Ditko** a-160p. **Everett** c-29. **Guice** a-233-241p. **G. Kane** c(p)-52-54, 63, 67, 72-75, 77-79, 88, 98. **Kirby** a-Special 1p; c-13, 80p, 90, 92-95. **Mooney** a-40i, 43i, 47i. **Perez** c-103p. **Simonson** a-Annual 8. **B. Smith** a-232p, 243i; c-232. **P. Smith** a-159p, 245p, Annual 10p; c-159. **Starlin** a-53p(part), 55p, 56p; c-55p, 160, 163. **Tuska** a-5-13p, 15-23p, 24i, 32p, 38-46p, 48-54p, 57-61p, 63-69p, 70-72p, 78p, 86-92p, 95-106p, Annual 4p. **Wood** a-Special 1i.

IRON MAN (The Invincible...) (Volume Two)
Marvel Comics: Nov, 1996 - No. 13, Nov, 1997 ($2.95/$1.95/$1.99)
(Produced by WildStorm Productions)

V2#1-3-Heroes Reborn begins; Scott Lobdell scripts & Whilce Portacio-c/a begin;
    new origin Iron Man & Hulk. 2-Hulk app. 3-Fantastic Four app.   4.00
1-Variant-c   5.00
4-11: 4-Two covers. 6-Fantastic Four app.; Industrial Revolution; Hulk app. 7-Return of Rebel.
    11-($1.99) Dr. Doom-c/app.   3.00
12-($1.99) "Heroes Reunited"-pt. 3; Hulk-c/app.   3.50
13-($1.99) "World War 3"-pt. 3, x-over w/Image   3.00
Heroes Reborn: Iron Man (2006, $29.99, TPB) r/#1-12; Heroes Reborn #1/2; pin-ups   30.00

IRON MAN (The Invincible...) (Volume Three)
Marvel Comics: Feb, 1998 - No. 89, Dec, 2004 ($2.99/$1.99/$2.25)

V3#1-($2.99)-Follows Heroes Return; Busiek scripts & Chen-c/a begin; Deathsquad app.   5.00
1-Alternate Ed.   1   2   3   5   6   8
2-12: 2-Two covers. 6-Black Widow-c/app. 7-Warbird-c/app. 8-Black Widow app. 9-Mandarin
    returns   3.00
13-($2.99) battles the Controller   3.50
14-24: 14-Fantastic Four-c/app.   3.00
25-($2.99) Iron Man and Warbird battle Ultimo; Avengers app.   3.00
26-30-Quesada-s. 28-Whiplash killed. 29-Begin $2.25-c.   2.50
31-45,47-49,51-54: 35-Maximum Security x-over; FF-c/app. 41-Grant-a begins.
    44-New armor debut. 48-Ultron-c/app.   2.50
46-($3.50, 100 pgs.) Sentient armor returns; r/V1#78,140,141   3.50
50-($3.50) Grell-s begin; Black Widow app.   3.50
55-($3.50) 400th issue; Asamiya-c; back-up story Stark reveals ID; Grell-a   3.50
56-66: 56-Reis-a. 57,58-Ryan-a. 59-61-Grell-c/a. 62,63-Ryan-a. 64-Davis-a; Thor-c/app.   2.50
67-89: 67-Begin $2.99-c; Gene Ha-c. 75-83-Granov-c. 84-Avengers Disassembled prologue
    85-89-Avengers Disassembled. 85-88-Harris-a. 86-89-Pat Lee-c. 87-Rumiko killed   3.00
.../Captain America '98 Annual ($3.50) vs. Modok   3.50
1999, 2000 Annual ($3.50)   3.00
2001 Annual ($2.99) Claremont-s/Ryan-a   3.00
Avengers Disassembled: Iron Man TPB (2004, $14.99) r/#84-89   15.00
Mask in the Iron Man (5/01, $14.95, TPB) r/#26-30, #1/2   15.00

IRON MAN (The Invincible...)
Marvel Comics: Jan, 2005 - Present ($3.50/$2.99)

1-($3.50-c) Warren Ellis-s/Adi Granov-c/a   3.50
2-14-($2.99) 5-Flashback to origin; Stark gets new abilities. 7-Knauf-s/Zircher-a
    13,14-Civil War   3.00
15-22: 15-Stark becomes Director of S.H.I.E.L.D. 19,20-World War Hulk-over; Guice-a   3.00
Civil War: Iron Man TPB (2007, $11.99) r/#13,14, .../Captain America: Casualties of War,
    and Civil War: The Confession   12.00
.../Captain America: Casualities of War (2/07, $3.99) two covers; flashbacks   4.00
HC (2006, $19.99, dust jacket) r/#1-6 and Granov covers from Iron Man V3 #75-83   20.00
...: Director of S.H.I.E.L.D. TPB (2007, $14.99) r/#15-18; Strange Tales #135 (1965) and Iron
    Man #129; profile pages for Iron Man and S.H.I.E.L.D.; creator interviews   15.00
...: Extremis SC (2007, $14.99) r/#1-6 and Granov covers from Iron Man V3 #75-83   15.00
...: Execute Program SC (2007, $14.99) r/#7-12; cover layouts and sketches   15.00

IRON MAN & SUB-MARINER
Marvel Comics Group: Apr, 1968 (12¢, one-shot) (Pre-dates Iron Man #1 & Sub-Mariner #1)

1-Iron Man story by Colan/Craig continued from Tales of Suspense #99 & continued in
    Iron Man #1; Sub-Mariner story by Colan continued from Tales to Astonish #101 &
    continued in Sub-Mariner #1; Colan/Everett-c   14   28   42   77   175   250

IRON MAN: BAD BLOOD
Marvel Comics: Sept, 2000 - No. 4, Dec, 2000 ($2.99, limited series)

1-4-Micheline-s/Layton-a   3.00

IRON MAN: ENTER THE MANDARIN
Marvel Comics: Nov, 2007 - No. 6 ($2.99, limited series)

1-Casey-s/Canete-a; retells first meeting   3.00

IRON MAN: HOUSE OF M (Also see House of M and related x-overs)
(Reprinted in House of M: Fantastic Four/ Iron Man TPB)
Marvel Comics: Sept, 2005 - No. 3, Nov, 2005 ($2.99, limited series)

1-3-Pat Lee-a/c; Greg Pak-s   3.00

IRON MAN: HYPERVELOCITY
Marvel Comics: Mar, 2007 - No. 6, Aug, 2007 ($2.99, limited series)

1-6-Adam Warren-s/Brian Denham-a/c   3.00
TPB (2007, $14.99) r/#1-6; layout pages and armor design sketches

IRON MAN: INEVITABLE
Marvel Comics: Feb, 2006 - No. 6, July, 2006 ($2.99, limited series)

1-6-Joe Casey-s/Frazer Irving; Spymaster and the Living Laser app.   3.00
TPB (2006, $14.99) r/#1-6; cover sketches   15.00

IRON MAN: THE IRON AGE
Marvel Comics: Aug, 1998 - No. 2, Sept, 1998 ($5.99, limited series)

1,2-Busiek-s; flashback story from gold armor days   6.00

IRON MAN: THE LEGEND
Marvel Comics: Sept, 1996 ($3.95, one-shot)

1-Tribute issue   4.50

IRON MAN 2020 (Also see Machine Man limited series)
Marvel Comics: June, 1994 ($5.95, one-shot)

nn   6.00

IRON MAN/X-O MANOWAR: HEAVY METAL (See X-O Manowar/Iron Man:
In Heavy Metal)
Marvel Comics: Sept, 1996 ($2.50, one-shot) (1st Marvel/Valiant x-over)

1-Pt. II of Iron Man/X-O Manowar x-over; Fabian Nicieza scripts; 1st app. Rand Banion   2.50

IRON MARSHALL
Jademan Comics: July, 1990 - No. 32, Feb, 1993 ($1.75, plastic coated-c)

1,32: Kung Fu stories. 1-Poster centerfold   2.50
2-31-Kung Fu stories in all   2.50

IRON VIC (See Comics Revue No. 3 & Giant Comics Editions)
United Features Syndicate/St. John Publ. Co.: 1940

Single Series 22   34   68   102   195   308   420

IRONWOLF
DC Comics: 1986 ($2.00, one shot)

1-r/Weird Worlds 8-10; Chaykin story & art   2.50

IRONWOLF: FIRES OF THE REVOLUTION (See Weird Worlds #8-10)
DC Comics: 1992 ($29.95, hardcover)

nn-Chaykin/Moore story, Mignola-a w/Russell inks.   30.00

IRREDEEMABLE ANT-MAN, THE
Marvel Comics: Dec, 2006 - No. 12, Nov, 2007 ($2.99)

1-12-Kirkman-s/Hester-a/c; intro. Eric O'Grady as the new Ant-Man. 7-Ms. Marvel app.
    10-World War Hulk x-over   3.00
... Vol. 1: Lowlife (2007, $9.99, digest) r/#1-6   10.00

ISAAC ASIMOV'S I-BOTS
Tekno Comix: Dec, 1995 - No. 7, May, 1996 ($1.95)

1-7: 1-6-Perez-c/a. 2-Chaykin variant-c exists. 3-Polybagged. 7-Lady Justice-c/app.   2.50

ISAAC ASIMOV'S I-BOTS
BIG Entertainment: V2#1, June, 1996 - No. 9, Feb, 1997 ($2.25)

V2#1-9: 1-Lady Justice-c/app. 6-Gil Kane-c   2.50

ISIS (TV) (Also see Shazam)
National Per.l Publ./DC Comics: Oct-Nov, 1976 - No. 8, Dec-Jan, 1977-78

1-Wood inks   2   4   6   9   13   16
2-8: 5-Isis new look. 7-Origin   1   2   3   5   7   9

ISLAND AT THE TOP OF THE WORLD (See Walt Disney Showcase #27)

ISLAND OF DR. MOREAU, THE (Movie)
Marvel Comics Group: Oct, 1977 (52 pgs.)

1-Gil Kane-c   1   2   3   5   6   8

I SPY (TV)
Gold Key: Aug, 1966 - No. 6, Sept, 1968 (All have photo-c)

1-Bill Cosby, Robert Culp photo covers   15   30   45   107   191   275
2-6: 3,4-McWilliams-a. 5-Last 12¢-c   9   18   27   65   113   160

It Girl #1 © Mike Allred

Jackie Gleason #1 © STJ

Jack of Fables #2 © Bill Willingham & DC

	GD 2.0	VG 4.0	FN 6.0	VF 8.0	VF/NM 9.0	NM- 9.2

IT! (See Astonishing Tales No. 21-24 & Supernatural Thrillers No. 1)

ITCHY & SCRATCHY COMICS (The Simpsons TV show)
Bongo Comics: 1993 - No. 3, 1993 ($1.95)

1-3: 1-Bound-in jumbo poster. 3-w/decoder screen trading card						4.00
Holiday Special ('94, $1.95)						4.00

IT GIRL (Also see Atomics, and Madman Comics)
Oni Press: May, 2002 ($2.95, one-shot)

1-Allred-s/Clugston-Major-c/a; Atomics and Madman app.						3.00

IT REALLY HAPPENED
William H. Wise No. 1,2/Standard (Visual Editions): 1944 - No. 11, Oct, 1947

1-Kit Carson & Ben Franklin stories	23	46	69	139	205	280
2	14	28	42	76	108	140
3,4,6,9,11: 6-Joan of Arc story. 9-Captain Kidd & Frank Buck stories						
	11	22	33	64	90	115
5-Lou Gehrig & Lewis Carroll stories	16	32	48	94	147	200
7-Teddy Roosevelt story	14	28	42	76	108	140
8-Story of Roy Rogers	16	32	48	94	147	200
10-Honus Wagner & Mark Twain stories	14	28	42	82	121	160

NOTE: *Guardineer* a-7(2), 8(2), 11. **Schomburg** c-1-7, 9-11.

IT RHYMES WITH LUST (Also see Bold Stories & Candid Tales)
St. John Publishing Co.: 1950 (Digest size, 128 pgs.)

nn (Rare)-Matt Baker & Ray Osrin-a	76	152	228	475	788	1100

IT'S A BIRD...
DC Comics: 2004 ($24.95, hardcover with dust jacket)

HC-Semi-autobiographical story of Steven Seagle writing Superman; Kristiansen-a						25.00
SC-($17.95)						18.00

IT'S ABOUT TIME (TV)
Gold Key: Jan, 1967

1 (10195-701)-Photo-c	4	8	12	28	44	60

IT'S A DUCK'S LIFE
Marvel Comics/Atlas(MMC): Feb, 1950 - No. 11, Feb, 1952

1-Buck Duck, Super Rabbit begin	15	30	45	86	133	180
2	10	20	30	54	72	90
3-11	9	18	27	50	65	80

IT'S GAMETIME
National Periodical Publications: Sept-Oct, 1955 - No. 4, Mar-Apr, 1956

1-(Scarce)-Infinity-c; Davy Crockett app. in puzzle	79	158	237	494	822	1150
2,3 (Scarce): 2-Dodo & The Frog	60	120	180	375	625	875
4 (Rare)	63	126	189	394	657	920

IT'S LOVE, LOVE, LOVE
St. John Publishing Co.: Nov, 1957 - No. 2, Jan, 1958 (10¢)

1,2	6	12	18	31	38	45

IVANHOE (See Fawcett Movie Comics No. 20)

IVANHOE
Dell Publishing Co.: July-Sept, 1963

1 (12-373-309)	3	6	9	21	32	42

IWO JIMA (See Spectacular Features Magazine)

JACE PEARSON OF THE TEXAS RANGERS (Radio/TV)(4-Color #396 is titled Tales of the Texas Rangers; ...'s Tales of ... #11-on)(See Western Roundup under Dell Giants)
Dell Publishing Co.: No. 396, 5/52 - No. 1021, 8-10/59 (No #10) (All-Photo-c)

Four Color 396 (#1)	10	20	30	73	129	185
2(5-7/53) - 9(2-4/55)	7	14	21	47	76	105
Four Color 648(#10, 9/55)	6	12	18	41	66	90
11(11-2/55-56) - 14,17-20(6-8/58)	6	12	18	37	59	80
15,16-Toth-a	6	12	18	39	62	85
Four Color 961,1021: 961-Spiegle-a	6	12	18	37	59	80

NOTE: Joel McCrea photo c-1-9, F.C. 648 (starred on radio show only); Willard Parker photo c-11-on (starred on TV series).

JACK ARMSTRONG (Radio)(See True Comics)
Parents' Institute: Nov. 1947 - No. 9, Sept, 1948; No. 10, Mar, 1949 - No. 13, Sept, 1949

1-(Scarce) (odd size) Cast intro. inside front-c	43	86	129	262	431	600
2	20	40	60	115	180	245
3-5	15	30	45	83	124	165
6-13: 7-Vic Hardy's Crime Lab begins?	13	26	39	72	101	130

JACK CROSS
DC Comics: Oct, 2005 - Present ($2.50)

	GD 2.0	VG 4.0	FN 6.0	VF 8.0	VF/NM 9.0	NM- 9.2

1-4-Warren Ellis-s/Gary Erskine-a						2.50

JACK HUNTER
Blackthorne Publishing: July, 1987 - No. 3 ($1.25)

1-3						2.50

JACKIE CHAN'S SPARTAN X
Topps Comics: May, 1997 - No. 3 ($2.95, limited series)

1-3-Michael Golden-s/a; variant photo-c						3.00

JACKIE CHAN'S SPARTAN X: HELL BENT HERO FOR HIRE
Image Comics (Little Eva Ink): Mar, 1998 - No. 3 ($2.95, B&W)

1-3-Michael Golden-s/a: 1-variant photo-c						3.00

JACKIE GLEASON (TV) (Also see The Honeymooners)
St. John Publishing Co.: Sept, 1955 - No. 4, Dec, 1955

1(1955)(TV)-Photo-c	62	124	186	388	644	900
2-4	41	82	123	256	416	575

JACKIE GLEASON AND THE HONEYMOONERS
National Periodical Publications: June-July, 1956 - No. 12, Apr-May, 1958

1-1st app. Ralph Kramden	90	180	270	563	932	1300
2	53	106	159	323	537	750
3-11	41	82	123	256	416	575
12 (Scarce)	60	120	180	375	625	875

JACKIE JOKERS (Became Richie Rich &...)
Harvey Publications: March, 1973 - No. 4, Sept, 1973 (#5 was advertised, but not published)

1-1st app.	3	6	9	16	22	28
2-4: 2-President Nixon app.	2	4	6	8	11	14

JACKIE ROBINSON (Famous Plays of...) (Also see Negro Heroes #2 & Picture News #4)
Fawcett Publications: May, 1950 - No. 6, 1952 (Baseball hero) (All photo-c)

nn	97	194	291	606	1003	1400
2	55	110	165	344	572	800
3-6	46	92	138	281	466	650

JACK IN THE BOX (Formerly Yellowjacket Comics #1-10; becomes Cowboy Western Comics #17 on)
Frank Comunale/Charlton Comics No. 11 on: Feb, 1946; No. 11, 1946 - No. 16, Nov-Dec, 1947

1-Stitches, Marty Mouse & Nutsy McKrow	17	34	51	98	154	210
11-Yellowjacket (early Charlton comic)	20	40	60	117	184	250
12,14,15	11	22	33	64	90	115
13-Wolverton-a	21	42	63	122	191	260
16-12 pg. adapt. of Silas Marner; Kiefer-a	13	26	39	74	105	135

JACK KIRBY'S FOURTH WORLD (See Mister Miracle & New Gods, 3rd Series)
DC Comics: Mar, 1997 - No. 20, Oct, 1998 ($1.95/$2.25)

1-20: 1-Byrne-a/scripts & Simonson begin; story cont'd from New Gods, 3rd Series #15; retells "The Pact" (New Gods, 1st Series #7); 1st brief DC app. Thor. 2-Thor vs. Big Barda; "Apokolips Then" back-up begins; Kirby-c/swipe (Thor #126) 8-Genesis x-over. 10-Simonson-s/a 13-Simonson back-up story. 20-Superman-c/app.						2.50

JACK KIRBY'S GALACTIC BOUNTY HUNTERS
Marvel Comics (Icon): July, 2006 - No. 6, Nov, 2007 ($3.99)

1-6-Based on a Kirby concept; Mike Thibodeaux-a; Lisa Kirby, Thibodeaux and others-s						4.00
HC (2007, $24.99) r/series						25.00

JACK KIRBY'S SECRET CITY SAGA
Topps Comics (Kirbyverse): No. 0, Apr, 1993; No. 1, May, 1993 - No. 4, Aug, 1993 ($2.95, limited series)

0-(No cover price, 20 pgs.)-Simonson-c/a						3.00
0-Red embossed-c (limited ed.)						5.00
1-4-Bagged w/3 trading cards; Ditko-c/a: 1-Ditko/Art Adams-c. 2-Ditko/Byrne-c; has coupon for Pres. Clinton holo-foil trading card. 3-Dorman poster; has coupon for Gore holo-foil trading card. 4-Ditko/Perez-c						3.00

NOTE: Issues #1-4 contain coupons redeemable for Kirbychrome version of #1

JACK KIRBY'S SILVER STAR (Also see Silver Star)
Topps Comics (Kirbyverse): Oct, 1993 ($2.95)(intended as a 4-issue limited series)

1-Silver ink-c; Austin-c/a(i); polybagged w/3 cards						3.00

JACK KIRBY'S TEENAGENTS (See Satan's Six)
Topps Comics (Kirbyverse): Aug, 1993 - No. 4, Nov, 1993 ($2.95, limited series)

1-4: Bagged with/3 trading cards; Busiek-s/Austin-c(i): 3-Liberty Project app.						3.00

JACK OF FABLES (See Fables)
DC Comics (Vertigo): Sept, 2006 - Present ($2.99)

Jackpot Comics #4 © MLJ

Jane Arden #2 © UFS

Jay and Silent Bob #3 © View Askew

	GD 2.0	VG 4.0	FN 6.0	VF 8.0	VF/NM 9.0	NM- 9.2

1-13: 1-Willingham & Sturges-s/Akins-a ... 3.00
...: The (Nearly) Great Escape TPB (2007, $14.99) r/#1-5; Akins sketch pages ... 15.00

JACK OF HEARTS (Also see The Deadly Hands of Kung Fu #22 & Marvel Premiere #44)
Marvel Comics Group: Jan, 1984 - No. 4, Apr, 1984 (60¢, limited series)
1-4 ... 2.50

JACKPOT COMICS (Jolly Jingles #10 on)
MLJ Magazines: Spring, 1941 - No. 9, Spring, 1943

	GD 2.0	VG 4.0	FN 6.0	VF 8.0	VF/NM 9.0	NM- 9.2
1-The Black Hood, Mr. Justice, Steel Sterling & Sgt. Boyle begin; Biro-c	321	642	963	2087	3694	5300
2-S. Cooper-c	145	290	435	906	1503	2100
3-Hubbell-c	110	220	330	688	1144	1600
4-Archie begins (Win/41; on sale 12/41)-(also see Pep Comics #22); 1st app. Mrs. Grundy, the principal; Novick-c	429	858	1287	3000	5250	7500
5-Hitler, Tojo, Mussolini by Montana; 1st definitive Mr. Weatherbee; 1st brief app. Reggie in 1 panel	172	344	516	1075	1788	2500
6-9: 6,7-Bondage-c by Novick. 8,9-Sahle-c	110	220	330	688	1144	1600

JACK Q FROST (See Unearthly Spectaculars)

JACK STAFF (Vol. 2; previously published in Britain)
Image Comics: Feb, 2003 - Present ($2.95/$3.50)
1-5-Paul Grist-s/a ... 3.00
6-13-($3.50) 6-Flashback to the WW2 Freedom Fighters ... 3.50
The Weird World of Jack Staff King Size Special 1 (7/07, $5.99, B&W) r/story serialized in Comics International magazine; afterword by Grist ... 6.00
Vol. 1: Everything Used to Be Black and White TPB (12/03, $19.95) r/British issues ... 20.00
Vol. 2: Soldiers TPB (2005, $15.95) r/#1-5; cover gallery ... 16.00
Vol. 3: Echoes of Tomorrow TPB (2006, $16.99) r/#6-12; cover gallery ... 17.00

JACK THE GIANT KILLER (See Movie Classics)

JACK THE GIANT KILLER (New Adventures of...)
Bimfort & Co.: Aug-Sept, 1953

	GD 2.0	VG 4.0	FN 6.0	VF 8.0	VF/NM 9.0	NM- 9.2
V1#1-H. C. Kiefer-c/a	24	48	72	139	220	300

JACKY'S DIARY
Dell Publishing Co.: No. 1091, Apr-June, 1960 (one-shot)

	GD 2.0	VG 4.0	FN 6.0	VF 8.0	VF/NM 9.0	NM- 9.2
Four Color 1091	5	10	15	30	48	65

JADEMAN COLLECTION
Jademan Comics: Dec, 1989 - No. 3, 1990 ($2.50, plastic coated-c, 68 pgs.)
1-3: 1-Wraparound-c w/fold-out poster ... 2.50

JADEMAN KUNG FU SPECIAL
Jademan Comics: 1988 ($1.50, 64 pgs.)
1 ... 2.50

JADE WARRIORS (Mike Deodato's...)
Image Comics (Glass House Graphics): Nov, 1999 - No. 3, 2000 ($2.50)
1-3-Deodato-a ... 2.50
1-Variant-c ... 2.50

JAGUAR, THE (Also see The Adventures of...)
Impact Comics (DC): Aug, 1991 - No. 14, Oct, 1992 ($1.00)
1-14: 4-The Black Hood x-over. 7-Sienkiewicz-c. 9-Contains Crusaders trading card ... 2.50
Annual 1 (1992, $2.50, 68 pgs.)-With trading card ... 2.50

JAGUAR GOD
Verotik: Mar, 1995 - No. 7, June, 1997 ($2.95, mature)
0 (2/96, $3.50)-Embossed Frazetta-c; Bisley-a; w/pin-ups. ... 4.00
1-Frazetta-c. ... 4.00
2-7: 2-Frazetta-c. 3-Bisley-c. 4-Emond-c. 7-($2.95)-Frazetta-c ... 3.00

JAKE THRASH
Aircel Publishing: 1988 - No. 3, 1988 ($2.00)
1-3 ... 2.50

JAM, THE (...Urban Adventure)
Slave Labor Nos. 1-5/Dark Horse Comics Nos. 6-8/Caliber Comics No. 9 on:
Nov, 1989 - No. 14, 1997 ($1.95/$2.50/$2.95, B&W)
1-14: Bernie Mireault-c/a/scripts. 6-1st Dark Horse issue. 9-1st Caliber issue ... 3.00

JAMBOREE
Round Publishing Co.: Feb, 1946(no month given) - No. 3, Apr, 1946

	GD 2.0	VG 4.0	FN 6.0	VF 8.0	VF/NM 9.0	NM- 9.2
1-Funny animal	25	50	75	148	232	315
2,3	15	30	45	88	137	185

JAMES BOND 007: A SILENT ARMAGEDDON

Dark Horse Comics/Acme Press: Mar, 1993 - Apr 1993 (limited series)
1,2 ... 3.50

JAMES BOND 007: GOLDENEYE (Movie)
Topps Comics: Jan, 1996 ($2.95, unfinished limited series of 3)
1-Movie adaptation; Stelfreeze-c ... 3.00

JAMES BOND 007: SERPENT'S TOOTH
Dark Horse Comics/Acme Press: July 1992 - Aug 1992 ($4.95, limited series)
1-3-Paul Gulacy-c/a ... 5.00

JAMES BOND 007: SHATTERED HELIX
Dark Horse Comics: Jun 1994 - July 1994 ($2.50, limited series)
1,2 ... 3.00

JAMES BOND 007: THE QUASIMODO GAMBIT
Dark Horse Comics: Jan 1995 - May 1995 ($3.95, limited series)
1-3 ... 4.50

JAMES BOND FOR YOUR EYES ONLY
Marvel Comics Group: Oct, 1981 - No. 2, Nov, 1981
1,2-Movie adapt.; r/Marvel Super Special #19 ... 3.00

JAMES BOND JR. (TV)
Marvel Comics: Jan, 1992 - No. 12, Dec, 1992 (#1: $1.00, #2-on: $1.25)
1-12: Based on animated TV show ... 2.50

JAMES BOND: LICENCE TO KILL (See Licence To Kill)

JAMES BOND: PERMISSION TO DIE
Eclipse Comics/ACME Press: 1989 - No. 3, 1991 ($3.95, lim. series, squarebound, 52 pgs.)
1-3: Mike Grell-c/a/scripts in all. 3-($4.95) ... 5.00

JAM, THE: SUPER COOL COLOR INJECTED TURBO ADVENTURE #1 FROM HELL!
Comico: May, 1988 ($2.50, 44 pgs., one-shot)
1 ... 2.50

JANE ARDEN (See Feature Funnies & Pageant of Comics)
St. John (United Features Syndicate): Mar, 1948 - No. 2, June, 1948

	GD 2.0	VG 4.0	FN 6.0	VF 8.0	VF/NM 9.0	NM- 9.2
1-Newspaper reprints	15	30	45	88	137	185
2	12	24	36	67	94	120

JANN OF THE JUNGLE (Jungle Tales No. 1-7)
Atlas Comics (CSI): No. 8, Nov, 1955 - No. 17, June, 1957

	GD 2.0	VG 4.0	FN 6.0	VF 8.0	VF/NM 9.0	NM- 9.2
8(#1)	36	72	108	208	329	450
9,11-15	20	40	60	115	180	245
10-Williamson/Colletta-c	20	40	60	117	184	250
16,17-Williamson/Mayo-a(3), 5 pgs. each	21	42	63	122	191	260

NOTE: **Everett** c-15-17. **Heck** a-8, 15, 17. **Maneely** c-11. **Shores** a-8.

JASON & THE ARGOBOTS
Oni Press: Aug, 2002 - No. 4, Dec, 2002 ($2.95, B&W, limited series)
1-4-Torres/Norton-c/a ... 3.00
Vol. 1 Birthquake TPB (6/03, $11.95, digest size) r/#1-4, Sunday comic strips ... 12.00
Vol. 2 Machina Ex Deus TPB (9/03, $11.95, digest size) new story ... 12.00

JASON & THE ARGONAUTS (See Movie Classics)

JASON GOES TO HELL: THE FINAL FRIDAY (Movie)
Topps Comics: July, 1993 - No. 3, Sept, 1993 ($2.95, limited series)
1-3: Adaptation of film. 1-Glow-in-the-dark-c ... 3.00

JASON'S QUEST (See Showcase #88-90)

JASON VS. LEATHERFACE
Topps Comics: Oct, 1995 - No. 3, Jan, 1996 ($2.95, limited series)
1-3: Collins scripts; Bisley-c ... 3.00

JAWS 2 (See Marvel Comics Super Special, A)

JAY & SILENT BOB (See Clerks, Oni Double Feature, and Tales From the Clerks)
Oni Press: July, 1998 - No. 4, Oct, 1999 ($2.95, B&W, limited series)
1-Kevin Smith-s/Fegredo-a; photo-c & Quesada/Palmiotti-c ... 8.00
1-San Diego Comic Con variant covers (2 different covers, came packaged with action figures) ... 10.00
1-2nd & 3rd printings, 2-4: 2-Allred-c. 3-Flip-c by Jaime Hernandez ... 3.00
Chasing Dogma TPB (1999, $11.95) r/#1-4; Alanis Morissette intro. ... 12.00
Chasing Dogma TPB (2001, $12.95) r/#1-4 in color; Morissette intro. ... 13.00
Chasing Dogma HC (1999, $69.95, S&N) r/#1-4 in color; Morissette intro. ... 70.00

JCP FEATURES
J.C. Productions (Archie): Feb, 1982-c; Dec, 1981-indicia ($2.00, one-shot, B&W magazine)

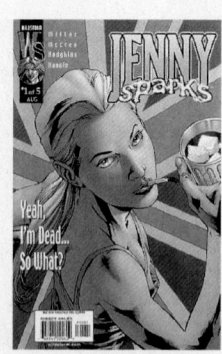

Jenny Sparks: The Secret History of the Authority #1 © WSP

Jet #1 © WSP

The Jetsons #24 © H-B

	GD	VG	FN	VF	VF/NM	NM-
	2.0	4.0	6.0	8.0	9.0	9.2

1-T.H.U.N.D.E.R. Agents; Black Hood by Morrow & Neal Adams; Texeira-a;
2 pgs. S&K-a from Fly #1 .... 1 ... 3 ... 4 ... 6 ... 8 ... 10

JEANIE COMICS (Formerly All Surprise; Cowgirl Romances #28)
Marvel Comics/Atlas(CPC): No. 13, April, 1947 - No. 27, Oct, 1949
13-Mitzi, Willie begin .... 21 ... 42 ... 63 ... 122 ... 191 ... 260
14,15 .... 15 ... 30 ... 45 ... 84 ... 127 ... 170
16-Used in Love and Death by Legman; Kurtzman's "Hey Look"
.... 16 ... 32 ... 48 ... 94 ... 147 ... 200
17-19,21,22-Kurtzman's "Hey Look" (1-3 pgs. each) 14 ... 28 ... 42 ... 76 ... 108 ... 140
20,23-27 .... 12 ... 24 ... 36 ... 69 ... 97 ... 125

JEEP COMICS (Also see G.I. Comics and Overseas Comics)
R. B. Leffingwell & Co.: Winter, 1944 - No. 3, Mar-Apr, 1948
1-Capt. Power, Criss Cross & Jeep & Peep (costumed) begin
.... 59 ... 118 ... 177 ... 369 ... 615 ... 860
2 .... 40 ... 80 ... 120 ... 235 ... 368 ... 500
3-L. B. Cole dinosaur-c .... 47 ... 94 ... 141 ... 287 ... 474 ... 660

JEFF JORDAN, U.S. AGENT
D. S. Publishing Co.: Dec, 1947 - Jan, 1948
1 .... 15 ... 30 ... 45 ... 84 ... 127 ... 170

JEMM, SON OF SATURN
DC Comics: Sept, 1984 - No. 12, Aug, 1985 (Maxi-series, mando paper)
1-12: 3-Origin 2.50
NOTE: *Colan a-1-12p; c-1-5, 7-12p.*

JENNY FINN
Oni Press: June, 1999 - No. 2, Sept, 1999 ($2.95, B&W, unfinished lim. series)
1,2-Mignola & Nixey-s/Nixey-a/Mignola-c 3.00
....: Doom (Atomeka, 2005, $6.99, TPB) r/#1 & 2 with new supplemental material 7.00

JENNY SPARKS:THE SECRET HISTORY OF THE AUTHORITY
DC Comics (WildStorm): Aug, 2000 - No. 5, Mar, 2001 ($2.50, limited series)
1-Millar-s/McCrea & Hodgkins-a/Hitch & Neary-c 3.50
1-Variant-c by McCrea .... 1 ... 3 ... 4 ... 6 ... 8 ... 10
2-5: 2-Apollo & Midnighter. 3-Jack Hawksmoor. 4-Shen. 5-Engineer 3.00
TPB (2001, $14.95) r/#1-5; Ellis intro. 15.00

JEREMIAH HARM
Boom! Studios: Feb, 2006 - Present ($3.99)
1-5: 1-Giffen & Grant-s/Lyra-a 4.00

JERRY DRUMMER (Formerly Soldier & Marine V2#9)
Charlton Comics: V2#10, Apr, 1957 - V3#12, Oct, 1957
V2#10, V3#11,12: 11-Whitman-c/a .... 6 ... 12 ... 18 ... 29 ... 36 ... 42

JERRY IGER'S... (All titles, Blackthorne/First)(Value: cover or less)

JERRY LEWIS (See The Adventures of...)

JESSE JAMES (The True Story Of..., also seeThe Legend of...)
Dell Publishing Co.: No. 757, Dec, 1956 (one shot)
Four Color 757-Movie, photo-c .... 8 ... 16 ... 24 ... 58 ... 97 ... 135

JESSE JAMES (See Badmen of the West & Blazing Sixguns)
Avon Periodicals: 8/50 - No. 9, 11/53; No. 15, 10/53; No. 29, 8-9/56
1-Kubert Alabam-r/Cowpuncher #1 .... 17 ... 34 ... 51 ... 98 ... 154 ... 210
2-Kubert-a(3) .... 14 ... 28 ... 42 ... 80 ... 115 ... 150
3-Kubert Alabam-r/Cowpuncher #2 .... 14 ... 28 ... 42 ... 76 ... 108 ... 140
4,9-No Kubert .... 8 ... 16 ... 24 ... 44 ... 57 ... 70
5,6-Kubert Jesse James-a(3); 5-Wood-a(1pg.) 14 ... 28 ... 42 ... 76 ... 108 ... 140
7-Kubert Jesse James-a(2) .... 12 ... 24 ... 36 ... 67 ... 94 ... 120
8-Kinstler-a(3) .... 9 ... 18 ... 27 ... 50 ... 65 ... 80
15-Kinstler-r/#3 .... 8 ... 16 ... 24 ... 40 ... 50 ... 60
16-Kinstler-r/#3 & story-r/Butch Cassidy #1 .... 8 ... 16 ... 24 ... 42 ... 54 ... 65
17-19,21: 17-Jesse James-r/#4; Kinstler-c idea from Kubert splash in #6. 18-Kubert Jesse
James-r/#5. 19-Kubert Jesse James-r/#6. 21-Two Jesse James-r/#4, Kinstler-r/#4
20-Williamson/Frazetta-a; r/Chief Vic. Apache Massacre; Kubert Jesse James-r/#6; Kit West
story by Larsen .... 14 ... 28 ... 42 ... 80 ... 115 ... 150
22-29: 22,23-No Kubert. 24-New McCarty strip by Kinstler; Kinstler-r. 25-New McCarty Jesse
James strip by Kinstler; Jesse James-r/#7,9. 26,27-New McCarty Jesse James strip plus a
Kinstler/McCann Jesse James-r. 28-Reprints most of Red Mountain, Featuring Quantrells
Raiders .... 7 ... 14 ... 21 ... 37 ... 46 ... 55
Annual nn (1952; 25¢, 100 pgs.) - "...Brings Six-Gun Justice to the West"- 3 earlier issues
rebound; Kubert, Kinstler-a(3) .... 28 ... 56 ... 84 ... 162 ... 256 ... 350
NOTE: *Mostly reprints #10 on. Fawcette c-1, 2. Kida a-5. Kinstler a-3, 4, 7-9, 15r, 16r(2), 21-27; c-3, 4, 9, 17-27.*

Painted c-5-8. 22 has 2 stories r/Sheriff Bob Dixon's Chuck Wagon #1 with name changed to Sheriff Bob Trent.

JESSE JAMES
Realistic Publications: July, 1953
nn-Reprints Avon's #1; same-c, colors different .... 9 ... 18 ... 27 ... 52 ... 69 ... 85

JEST (Formerly Snap; becomes Kayo #12)
Harry 'A' Chesler: No. 10, 1944; No. 11, 1944
10-Johnny Rebel & Yankee Boy app. in text .... 17 ... 34 ... 51 ... 98 ... 154 ... 210
11-Little Nemo in Adventure Land .... 17 ... 34 ... 51 ... 98 ... 154 ... 210

JESTER
Harry 'A' Chesler: No. 10, 1945
10 .... 15 ... 30 ... 45 ... 86 ... 133 ... 180

JESUS
Spire Christian Comics (Fleming H. Revell Co.): 1979 (49¢)
nn .... 2 ... 4 ... 6 ... 9 ... 12 ... 15

JET (See Jet Powers)

JET (Crimson from Wildcore & Backlash)
DC Comics (WildStorm): Nov, 2000 - No. 4, Feb, 2001 ($2.50, limited series)
1-4-Nguyen-a/Abnett & Lanning-s 2.50

JET ACES
Fiction House Magazines: 1952 - No. 4, 1953
1 .... 16 ... 32 ... 48 ... 94 ... 147 ... 200
2-4 .... 11 ... 22 ... 33 ... 60 ... 83 ... 105

JETCAT CLUBHOUSE (Also see Land of Nod, The)
Oni Press: Apr, 2001 - No. 3, Aug, 2001 ($3.25)
1-3-Jay Stephens-s/a. 1-Wraparound-c 3.25
TPB (8/02, $10.95, 8 3/4" x 5 3/4") r/#1-3 & stories from Nickelodeon mag. & other 11.00

JET DREAM (...and Her Stunt-Girl Counterspies)(See The Man from Uncle #7)
Gold Key: June, 1968 (12¢)
1-Painted-c .... 4 ... 8 ... 12 ... 22 ... 34 ... 45

JET FIGHTERS (Korean War)
Standard Magazines: No. 5, Nov, 1952 - No. 7, Mar, 1953
5,7-Toth-a. 5-Toth-c .... 12 ... 24 ... 36 ... 69 ... 97 ... 125
6-Celardo-a .... 8 ... 16 ... 24 ... 40 ... 50 ... 60

JET POWER
I.W. Enterprises: 1963
I.W. Reprint 1,2-r/Jet Powers #1,2 .... 3 ... 6 ... 9 ... 17 ... 25 ... 32

JET POWERS (American Air Forces No. 5 on)
Magazine Enterprises: 1950 - No. 4, 1951
1(A-1 #30)-Powell-c/a begins .... 38 ... 76 ... 114 ... 219 ... 347 ... 475
2(A-1 #32) Classic Powell dinosaur-c/a .... 38 ... 76 ... 114 ... 219 ... 347 ... 475
3(A-1 #35)-Williamson/Evans-a .... 40 ... 80 ... 120 ... 243 ... 389 ... 535
4(A-1 #38)-Williamson/Wood-a; "The Rain of Sleep" drug story
.... 40 ... 80 ... 120 ... 243 ... 389 ... 535

JET PUP (See 3-D Features)

JETSONS, THE (TV) (See March of Comics #276, 330, 348 & Spotlight #3)
Gold Key: Jan, 1963 - No. 36, Oct, 1970 (Hanna-Barbera)
1-1st comic book app. .... 23 ... 46 ... 69 ... 171 ... 306 ... 440
2 .... 12 ... 24 ... 36 ... 82 ... 146 ... 210
3-10 .... 9 ... 18 ... 27 ... 60 ... 100 ... 140
11-22 .... 7 ... 14 ... 21 ... 47 ... 76 ... 105
23-36-Reprints .... 6 ... 12 ... 18 ... 37 ... 59 ... 80

JETSONS, THE (TV) (Also see Golden Comics Digest)
Charlton Comics: Nov, 1970 - No. 20, Dec, 1973 (Hanna-Barbera)
1 .... 8 ... 16 ... 24 ... 56 ... 93 ... 130
2 .... 5 ... 10 ... 15 ... 30 ... 48 ... 65
3-10 .... 3 ... 6 ... 9 ... 21 ... 32 ... 42
11-20 .... 3 ... 6 ... 9 ... 17 ... 25 ... 32
nn (1973, digest, 60¢, 100 pgs.) B&W one page gags 4 ... 8 ... 12 ... 24 ... 37 ... 50

JETSONS, THE (TV)
Harvey Comics: V2#1, Sept, 1992 - No. 5, Nov, 1993 ($1.25/$1.50) (Hanna-Barbera)
V2#1-5 .... 4.00
...Big Book V2#1,2,3 ($1.95, 52 pgs.) 1-(11/92). 2-(4/93). 3-(7/93) 4.00
...Giant Size 1,2,3 ($2.25, 68 pgs): 1-(10/92). 2-(4/93). 3-(10/93) 4.00

JETSONS, THE (TV)

Jetta of the 21st Century #7 © STD

Jimmy Wakely #10 © DC

Jingle Jangle Comics #15 © EAS

	GD 2.0	VG 4.0	FN 6.0	VF 8.0	VF/NM 9.0	NM- 9.2

Archie Comics: Sept, 1995 - No. 8, Apr, 1996 ($1.50)

| 1-8 | | | | | | 3.00 |

JETTA OF THE 21ST CENTURY
Standard Comics: No. 5, Dec, 1952 - No. 7, Apr, 1953 (Teen-age Archie type)

5-Dan DeCarlo-a	23	46	69	135	213	290
6,7: 6-Robot-c	14	28	42	80	121	160
TPB (Airwave Publ., 2006, $9.99) B&W reprint of series; Bill Morrison intro./back-c						10.00

JEZEBEL JADE (Hanna-Barbera)
Comico: Oct, 1988 - No. 3, Dec, 1988 ($2.00, mini-series)

| 1-3: Johnny Quest spin-off | | | | | | 3.00 |

JEZEBELLE (See Wildstorm 2000 Annuals)
DC Comics (WildStorm): Mar, 2001 - No. 6, Aug, 2001 ($2.50, limited series)

| 1-6-Ben Raab-s/Steve Ellis-a | | | | | | 2.50 |

JIGGS & MAGGIE
Dell Publishing Co.: No. 18, 1941 (one shot)

| Four Color 18 (#1)-(1936-38-r) | 48 | 96 | 144 | 293 | 484 | 675 |

JIGGS & MAGGIE
Standard Comics/Harvey Publications No. 22 on: No. 11, 1949(June) - No. 21, 2/53; No. 22, 4/53 - No. 27, 2-3/54

11	14	28	42	80	115	150
12-15,17-21	9	18	27	50	65	80
16-Wood text illos.	10	20	30	54	72	90
22-24-Little Dot app.	10	20	30	54	72	90
25,27	9	18	27	52	69	85
26-Four pgs. partially in 3-D	14	28	42	78	112	145

NOTE: Sunday page reprints by McManus loosely blended into story continuity. Based on Bringing Up Father strip. Advertised on covers as "All New."

JIGSAW (Big Hero Adventures)
Harvey Publ. (Funday Funnies): Sept, 1966 - No. 2, Dec, 1966 (36 pgs.)

| 1-Origin & 1st app.; Crandall-a (5 pgs.) | 3 | 6 | 9 | 20 | 30 | 40 |
| 2-Man From S.R.A.M. | 3 | 6 | 9 | 14 | 20 | 25 |

JIGSAW OF DOOM (See Complete Mystery No. 2)

JIM BOWIE (Formerly Danger?; Black Jack No. 20 on)
Charlton Comics: No. 16, Mar, 1956 - No. 19, Apr, 1957

| 16 | 8 | 16 | 24 | 42 | 54 | 65 |
| 17-19: 18-Giordano-a | 6 | 12 | 18 | 29 | 36 | 42 |

JIM BOWIE (TV, see Western Tales)
Dell Publishing Co.: No. 893, Mar, 1958 - No. 993, May-July, 1959

| Four Color 893 (#1) | 6 | 12 | 18 | 39 | 62 | 85 |
| Four Color 993-Photo-c | 5 | 10 | 15 | 35 | 55 | 75 |

JIM DANDY
Dandy Magazine (Lev Gleason): May, 1956 - No. 3, Sept, 1956 (Charles Biro)

| 1-Biro-c | 9 | 18 | 27 | 47 | 61 | 75 |
| 2,3 | 6 | 12 | 18 | 29 | 36 | 42 |

JIM HARDY (See Giant Comics Eds., Sparkler & Treasury of Comics #2 & 5)
United Features Syndicate/Spotlight Publ.: 1939; 1942; 1947 - No. 2, 1947

Single Series 6 ('39)	41	82	123	256	416	575
Single Series 27('42)	36	72	108	208	329	450
1('47)-Spotlight Publ.	15	30	45	85	130	175
2	10	20	30	54	72	90

JIM HARDY
Spotlight/United Features Synd.: 1944 (25¢, 132 pgs.) (Tip Top, Sparkler-r)

| nn-Origin Mirror Man; Triple Terror app. | 40 | 80 | 120 | 235 | 368 | 500 |

JIMINY CRICKET (Disney,, see Mickey Mouse Mag. V5#3 & Walt Disney Showcase #37)
Dell Publishing Co.: No. 701, May, 1956 - No. 989, May-July, 1959

| Four Color 701 | 8 | 16 | 24 | 56 | 93 | 130 |
| Four Color 795, 897, 989 | 6 | 12 | 18 | 43 | 69 | 95 |

JIM LEE SKETCHBOOK
DC Comics (WildStorm): 2002 (no price, 16 pgs.)

| nn-Various DC and WildStorm character sketches by Lee | | | | | | 2.50 |

JIMMY CORRIGAN (See Acme Novelty Library)

JIMMY DURANTE (Also see A-1 Comics)
Magazine Enterprises: No. 18, 1949 - No. 20, 1949

| A-1 18,20-Photo-c | 42 | 84 | 126 | 256 | 421 | 585 |

JIMMY OLSEN (See Superman's Pal...)

JIMMY OLSEN: ADVENTURES BY JACK KIRBY
DC Comics: 2003, 2004 ($19.95, TPB)

| nn-(2003) Reprints Jack Kirby's early issues of Superman's Pal Jimmy Olsen #133-139,141; Mark Evanier intro.; cover by Kirby and Steve Rude | | | | | | 20.00 |
| Vol. 2 (2004) Reprints #142-148; Evanier intro.; cover gallery and sketch pages | | | | | | 20.00 |

JIMMY WAKELY (Cowboy movie star)
National Per. Publ.: Sept-Oct, 1949 - No. 18, July-Aug, 1952 (1-13: 52pgs.)

1-Photo-c, 52 pgs. begin; Alex Toth-a; Kit Colby Girl Sheriff begins	90	180	270	563	932	1300
2-Toth-a	40	80	120	235	368	500
3,4,6,7-Frazetta-a in all, 3 pgs. each; Toth-a in all. 7-Last photo-c. 4-Kurtzman "Pot-Shot Pete", 1 pg; Toth-a	41	82	123	256	416	575
5,8-15-Toth-a; 12,14-Kubert-a (3 & 2 pgs.)	31	62	93	178	282	385
16-18	26	52	78	152	239	325

NOTE: Gil Kane c-10-19p.

JIM RAY'S AVIATION SKETCH BOOK
Vital Publishers: Mar-Apr, 1946 - No. 2, May-June, 1946

| 1-Picture stories about planes and pilots | 40 | 80 | 120 | 235 | 368 | 500 |
| 2 | 26 | 52 | 78 | 150 | 235 | 320 |

JIM SOLAR (See Wisco/Klarer in the Promotional Comics section)

JINGLE BELLE (Paul Dini's...)
Oni Press: Nov, 1999 - No. 2, Dec, 1999 ($2.95, B&W, limited series)

1,2-Paul Dini-s. 2-Alex Ross flip-c						3.00
Jingle Belle: Dash Away All (12/03, $11.95, digest-size) Dini-s/Garibaldi-a						12.00
Jingle Belle's Cool Yule (11/02, $13.95,TPB) r/All-Star Holiday Hullabaloo, The Mighty Elves, and Jubilee; internet strips and a color section w/DeStefano-a						14.00
Paul Dini's Jingle Belle Jubilee (11/01, $2.95) Dini-s; art by Rolston, DeCarlo, Morrison and Bone; pin-ups by Thompson and Aragonés						3.00
Paul Dini's Jingle Belle's All-Star Holiday Hullabaloo (11/00, $4.95) stories by various including Dini, Aragonés, Jeff Smith, Bill Morrison; Frank Cho-c						5.00
Paul Dini's Jingle Belle: The Fight Before Christmas (12/05, $2.99) Dini-s/Bone & others-a						3.00
Paul Dini's Jingle Belle: The Mighty Elves (7/01, $2.95) Dini-s/Bone-a						3.00
Paul Dini's Jingle Belle Winter Wingding (11/02, $2.95) Dini-s/Clugston-Major-c						3.00
The Bakers Meet Jingle Belle (12/06, $2.99) Dini-s/Kyle Baker-a						3.00
TPB (10/00, $8.95) r/#1&2, and app. from Oni Double Feature #13						9.00

JINGLE BELLE (Paul Dini's...)
Dark Horse Comics: Nov, 2004 - No. 4, Apr, 2005 ($2.99, limited series)

| 1-4-Paul Dini-s/Jose Garibaldi-a | | | | | | 3.00 |
| TPB (9/05, $12.95) r/#1-4 | | | | | | 13.00 |

JINGLE BELLS (See March of Comics No. 65)

JINGLE BELLE CHRISTMAS STOCKING COMICS (See Foodini #2)
Stanhall Publications: V2#1, 1951 (no date listed) (25¢, 100 pgs.; giant-size) (Publ. annually)

| V2#1-Foodini & Pinhead, Silly Pilly plus games & puzzles | 19 | 38 | 57 | 109 | 172 | 235 |

JINGLE JANGLE COMICS (Also see Puzzle Fun Comics)
Eastern Color Printing Co.: Feb, 1942 - No. 42, Dec, 1949

1-Pie-Face Prince of Old Pretzleburg, Jingle Jangle Tales by George Carlson, Hortense, & Benny Bear begin	46	92	138	281	461	640
2-4: 2,3-No Pie-Face Prince. 4-Pie-Face Prince-c	21	42	63	124	195	265
5	19	38	57	112	176	240
6-10: 8-No Pie-Face Prince	15	30	45	85	130	175
11-15	12	24	36	69	97	125
16-30: 17,18-No Pie-Face Prince. 24,30-XMas-c	10	20	30	56	76	95
31-42: 36,42-Xmas-c	9	18	27	52	69	85

NOTE: George Carlson a-(2) in all except No. 2, 3, 8; c-1-6. Carlson 1 pg. puzzles in 9, 10, 12-15, 18, 20. Carlson illustrated a series of Uncle Wiggily books in 1930's.

JING PALS
Victory Publishing Corp.: Feb, 1946 - No. 4, Aug?, 1946 (Funny animal)

| 1-Wishing Willie, Puggy Panda & Johnny Rabbit begin | 15 | 30 | 45 | 84 | 127 | 170 |
| 2-4 | 9 | 18 | 27 | 52 | 69 | 85 |

JINKS, PIXIE, AND DIXIE (See Kite Fun Book & Whitman Comic Books)

JINX
Caliber Press: 1996 - No. 7, 1996 ($2.95, B&W, 32 pgs.)

| 1-7: Brian Michael Bendis-c/a/scripts. 2-Photo-c | | | | | | 3.00 |

JINX (Volume 2)

JLA #100 © DC

JLA 80-Page Giant #1 © DC

JLA: Created Equal #1 © DC

	GD	VG	FN	VF	VF/NM	NM-		GD	VG	FN	VF	VF/NM	NM-
	2.0	4.0	6.0	8.0	9.0	9.2		2.0	4.0	6.0	8.0	9.0	9.2

Image Comics: 1997 - No. 5, 1998 ($2.95, B&W, bi-monthly)

1-4: Brian Michael Bendis-c/a/scripts.						3.00
5-($3.95) Brereton-c						4.00
...Buried Treasures ('98, $3.95) short stories, ...Confessions ('98, $3.95) short stories, ...Pop Culture Hoo-Hah ('98, $3.95) humor shorts						4.00
TPB (1997, $10.95) r/Vol 1,#1-4						11.00
...: The Definitive Collection ('01, $24.95) remastered #1-5, sketch pages, art gallery, script excerpts, Mack intro.						25.00

JINX: TORSO
Image Comics: 1998 - No. 6, 1999 ($3.95/$4.95, B&W)

1-6-Based on Eliot Ness' pursuit of America's first serial killer; Brian Michael Bendis & Marc Andreyko-s/Bendis-a. 3-6-($4.95)						5.00
Softcover (2000, $24.95) r/#1-6; intro. by Greg Rucka; photo essay of the actual murders and police documents						25.00
Hardcover (2000, $49.95) signed & numbered						50.00

JLA (See Justice League of America and Justice Leagues)
DC Comics: Jan, 1997 - No. 125, Apr, 2006 ($1.95/$1.99/$2.25/$2.50)

1-Morrison-s/Porter & Dell-a. The Hyperclan app.	2	4	6	9	12	15
2		1	3	4	6	8	10
3,4		1	2	3	5	7	9
5-Membership drive; Tomorrow Woman app.						6.00
6-9: 8-Green Arrow joins.						6.00
10-21: 10-Rock of Ages begins. 11-Joker and Luthor-c/app. 15-($2.95) Rock of Ages concludes. 16-New members join; Prometheus app. 17,20-Jorgensen-a. 18-21-Waid-s. 20,21-Adam Strange c/app.						5.00
22-40: 22-Begin $1.99-c; Sandman (Daniel) app. 27-Amazo app. 28-31-JSA app. 35-Hal Jordan/Spectre app. 36-40-World War 3						2.50
41-($2.99) Conclusion of World War 3; last Morrison-s						3.00
42-46: 43-Waid-s; Ra's al Ghul app. 44-Begin $2.25-c. 46-Batman leaves						2.50
47-49: 47-Hitch & Neary-a begins; JLA battles Queen of Fables						2.50
50-($3.75) JLA vs. Dr. Destiny; art by Hitch & various						3.75
51-74: 52-55-Hitch-a. 59-Joker: Last Laugh. 61-68-Kelly-s/Mahnke-a. 69-73-Hunt for Aquaman; bi-monthly with alternating art by Mahnke and Guichet						2.50
75-(1/03, $3.95) leads into Aquaman (4th series) #1						4.00
76-93: 76-Firestorm app. 77-Banks-a. 79-Kanjar Ro app. 91-93-O'Neil-s/Hua-a.						2.50
94-99-Byrne & Ordway-s/Claremont-s; Doom Patrol app.						2.50
100-($3.50) Intro. Vera Black; leads into Justice League Elite #1						3.50
101-114: 101-106-Austen-s/Garney-a/c. 107-114-Crime Syndicate app.; Busiek-s						2.25
115-125: 115-Begin $2.50-c; Johns & Heinberg-s;Secret Society of Super-Villains app.						2.50
#1,000,000 (11/98) 853rd Century x-over						2.50
Annual 1 (1997, $3.95) Pulp Heroes; Augustyn-s/Olivetti & Ha-a						4.00
Annual 2 (1998, $2.95) Ghosts; Wrightson-s						4.00
Annual 3 (1999, $2.95) JLApe; Art Adams-c						3.00
Annual 4 (2000, $3.50) Planet DC x-over; Steve Scott-c/a						3.50
... American Dreams (1998, $7.95, TPB) r/#5-9						8.00
...: Crisis of Conscience TPB (2006, $12.99) r/#115-119						13.00
.../ Cyberforce (DC/Top Cow, 2005, $5.99) Kelly-s/Mahnke-a/Silvestri-c						6.00
Divided We Fall (2001, $17.95, TPB) r/#47-54						18.00
...80-Page Giant 1 (7/98, $4.95) stories & art by various						6.00
...80-Page Giant 2 (11/99, $4.95) Green Arrow & Hawkman app. Hitch-c						6.00
...80-Page Giant 3 (10/00, $5.95) Pariah & Harbinger; intro. Moon Maiden						6.00
...Foreign Bodies (1999, $5.95, one-shot) Kobra app.; Semeiks-a						6.00
...Gallery (1997, $2.95) pin-ups by various; Quitely-c						3.00
...God & Monsters (2001, $6.95, one-shot) Benefiel-a/c						7.00
Golden Perfect (2003, $12.95, TPB) r/#61-65						13.00
...: / Haven: Anathema (2002, $6.95) Concludes the Haven: The Broken City series						7.00
...: / Haven: Arrival (2001, $6.95) Leads into the Haven: The Broken City series						7.00
...In Crisis Secret Files 1 (11/98, $4.95) recap of JLA in DC x-overs						5.00
...: Island of Dr. Moreau, The (2002, $6.95, one-shot) Elseworlds; Pugh-c/a; Thomas-s						7.00
...: / JSA Secret Files & Origins (1/03, $4.95) prelude to JLA/JSA: Virtue & Vice; short stories and pin-ups by various; Pacheco-c						5.00
.../ JSA: Virtue and Vice HC (2002, $24.95) Teams battle Despero & Johnny Sorrow; Goyer & Johns-s/Pacheco-a/c						25.00
.../ JSA: Virtue and Vice SC (2003, $17.95)						18.00
Justice For All (1999, $14.95, TPB) r/#24-33						15.00
New World Order (1997, $5.95, TPB) r/#1-4						6.00
...: Obsidian Age Book One, The (2003, $12.95) r/#66-71						13.00
...: Obsidian Age Book Two, The (2003, $12.95) r/#72-76						13.00
One Million (2004, $19.95, TPB) r/#DC One Million #1-4 and other #1,000,000 x-overs						20.00
...: Our Worlds at War (9/01, $2.95) Jae Lee-c; Aquaman presumed dead						3.00
...: Pain of the Gods (2005, $12.99) r/#101-106						13.00
...: Primeval (1999, $5.95, one-shot) Abnett & Lanning-s/Olivetti-a						6.00
...: Riddle of the Beast HC (2001, $24.95) Grant-s/painted-a by various; Sweet-c						25.00

...: Riddle of the Beast SC (2003, $14.95) Grant-s/painted-a by various; Kaluta-c						15.00
Rock of Ages (1998, $9.95, TPB) r/#10-15						10.00
Rules of Engagement (2004, $12.95, TPB) r/#77-82						13.00
...: Seven Caskets (2000, $5.95, one-shot) Brereton-s/painted-c/a						6.00
...: Shogun of Steel (2002, $6.95, one-shot) Elseworlds; Justiniano-c/a						7.00
...Showcase 80-Page Giant (2/00, $4.95) Hitch-c						5.00
Strength in Numbers (1998, $12.95, TPB) r/#16-23, Secret Files #2 and Prometheus #1						13.00
...Superpower (1999, $5.95, one-shot) Arcudi-s/Eaton-a; Mark Antaeus joins						6.00
Syndicate Rules (2005, $17.99, TPB) r/#107-114, Secret Files #4						18.00
Terror Incognita (2002, $12.95, TPB) r/#55-60						13.00
The Tenth Circle (2004, $12.95, TPB) r/#94-99						13.00
...: The Greatest Stories Ever Told TPB (2006, $19.99) r/Justice League of America #19,71,122, 166-168,200, Justice League #1, JLA Secret Files #1 and JLA #61; Alex Ross-c						20.00
Tower of Babel (2001, $12.95, TPB) r/#42-46, Secret Files #3, 80-Page Giant #1						13.00
Trial By Fire (2004, $12.95, TPB) r/#84-89						13.00
...Vs. Predator (DC/Dark Horse, 2000, $5.95, one-shot) Nolan-c/a						6.00
...: Welcome to the Working Week (2003, $6.95, one-shot) Patton Oswalt-s						7.00
...: World War III (2000, $6.95, one-shot)						7.00
...: World Without a Justice League (2006, $12.99, TPB) r/#120-125						13.00
...: Zatanna's Search (2003, $12.95, TPB) rep. Zatanna's early app. & origin; Bolland-c						13.00

JLA: ACT OF GOD
DC Comics: 2000 - No. 3, 2001 ($4.95, limited series)

1-3-Elseworlds; metahumans lose their powers; Moench-s/Dave Ross-a						5.00

JLA: AGE OF WONDER
DC Comics: 2003 - No. 2, 2003 ($5.95, limited series)

1,2-Elseworlds; Superman and the League of Science during the Industrial Revolution						6.00

JLA: A LEAGUE OF ONE
DC Comics: 2000 (Graphic novel)

Hardcover ($24.95) Christopher Moeller-s/painted-a						25.00
Softcover (2002, $14.95)						15.00

JLA/AVENGERS (See Avengers/JLA for #2 & #4)
Marvel Comics: Sept, 2003; No. 3, Dec, 2003 ($5.95, limited series)

1-Busiek-s/Pérez-a; wraparound-c; Krona, Starro, Grandmaster, Terminus app.						6.00
3-Busiek-s/Pérez-a; wraparound-c; Phantom Stranger app.						6.00

JLA: BLACK BAPTISM
DC Comics: May, 2001 - No. 4, Aug, 2001 ($2.50, limited series)

1-4-Saiz-a(p)/Bradstreet-c; Zatanna app.						2.50

JLA: CLASSIFIED
DC Comics: Jan, 2005 - Present ($2.95/$2.99)

1-3-Morrison-s/McGuinness-a/c; Ultramarines app.						3.00
4-9-"I Can't Believe It's Not The Justice League," Giffen & DeMatteis-s/Maguire-a						3.00
10-31,33-41: 10-15-New Maps of Hell; Ellis-s/Guice-a. 16-21-Garcia-Lopez-a. 22-25-Detroit League & Royal Flush Gang app.; Englehart-s. 26-28-Chaykin-s. 37-41-Kid Amazo						3.00
32-($3.99) Dr. Destiny app.; Jurgens-a						
I Can't Believe It's Not the Justice League TPB (2005, $12.99) r/#4-9						13.00
...: New Maps of Hell TPB (2006, $12.99) r/#10-15						13.00

JLA CLASSIFIED: COLD STEEL
DC Comics: 2005 - No. 2, 2006 ($5.99, limited series, prestige format)

1,2-Chris Moeller-s/a; giant robot Justice League						6.00

JLA: CREATED EQUAL
DC Comics: 2000 - No. 2, 2000 ($5.95, limited series, prestige format)

1,2-Nicieza-s/Maguire-a; Elseworlds-Superman as the last man on Earth						6.00

JLA: DESTINY
DC Comics: 2002 - No. 4, 2002 ($5.95, prestige format, limited series)

1-4-Elseworlds; Arcudi-s/Mandrake-a						6.00

JLA: EARTH 2
DC Comics: 2000 (Graphic novel)

Hardcover ($24.95) Morrison/Quitely-a; Crime Syndicate app.						25.00
Softcover ($14.95)						15.00

JLA: GATEKEEPER
DC Comics: 2001 - No. 3, 2001 ($4.95, prestige format, limited series)

1-3-Truman-s/a						5.00

JLA: HEAVEN'S LADDER
DC Comics: 2000 ($9.95, Treasury-size one-shot)

nn-Bryan Hitch & Paul Neary-c/a; Mark Waid-s						10.00

JLA: INCARNATIONS

JLA/Titans #1 © DC

Joe Louis #1 © FAW

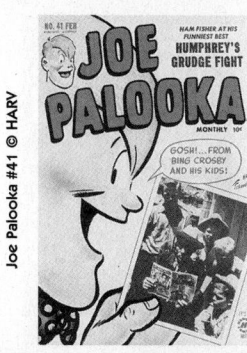

Joe Palooka #41 © HARV

	GD 2.0	VG 4.0	FN 6.0	VF 8.0	VF/NM 9.0	NM- 9.2

DC Comics: Jul, 2001 - No. 7, Feb, 2002 ($3.50, limited series)

1-7-Ostrander-s/Semeiks-a; different eras of the Justice League ... 3.50

JLA: LIBERTY AND JUSTICE
DC Comics: Nov, 2003 ($9.95, Treasury-size one-shot)

nn-Alex Ross-c/a; Paul Dini-s; story of the classic Justice League ... 10.00

JLA PARADISE LOST
DC Comics: Jan, 1998 - No. 3, Mar, 1998 ($1.95, limited series)

1-3-Millar-s/Olivetti-a ... 2.50

JLA: SCARY MONSTERS
DC Comics: May, 2003 - No. 6, Oct, 2003 ($2.50, limited series)

1-6-Claremont-s/Art Adams-c ... 2.50

JLA SECRET FILES
DC Comics: Sept, 1997 - Present ($4.95)

1-Standard Ed. w/origin-s & pin-ups ... 5.00
1-Collector's Ed. w/origin-s & pin-ups; cardstock-c ... 6.00
2,3: 2-(8/98) origin-s of JLA #16's newer members. 3-(12/00) ... 5.00
... 2004 (11/04) Justice League Elite app.; Mahnke & Byrne; Crime Syndicate app. ... 5.00

JLA: SECRET ORIGINS
DC Comics: Nov, 2002 ($7.95, Treasury-size one-shot)

nn-Alex Ross 2-page origins of Justice League members; text by Paul Dini ... 8.00

JLA: SECRET SOCIETY OF SUPER-HEROES
DC Comics: 2000 - No. 2, 2000 ($5.95, limited series, prestige format)

1,2-Elseworlds JLA; Chaykin and Tischman-s/McKone-a ... 6.00

JLA /SPECTRE: SOUL WAR
DC Comics: 2003 - No. 2, 2003 ($5.95, limited series, prestige format)

1,2-DeMatteis-s/Banks & Neary-a ... 6.00

JLA: THE NAIL (Elseworlds) (Also see Justice League of America: Another Nail)
DC Comics: Aug, 1998 - No. 3, Oct, 1998 ($4.95, prestige format)

1-3-JLA in a world without Superman; Alan Davis-s/a(p) ... 5.00
TPB ('98, $12.95) r/series w/new Davis-c ... 13.00

JLA / TITANS
DC Comics: Dec, 1998 - No. 3, Feb, 1999 ($2.95, limited series)

1-3-Grayson-s; P. Jimenez-c/a ... 3.00
....The Technis Imperative ('99, $12.95, TPB) r/#1-3; Titans Secret Files ... 13.00

JLA: TOMORROW WOMAN (Girlfrenzy)
DC Comics: June, 1998 ($1.95, one-shot)

1-Peyer-s; story takes place during JLA #5 ... 2.50

JLA / WILDC.A.T.S
DC Comics: 1997 ($5.95, one-shot, prestige format)

1-Morrison-s/Semeiks & Conrad-a ... 6.00

JLA /WITCHBLADE
DC Comics/Top Cow: 2000 ($5.95, prestige format, one-shot)

1-Pararillo-c/a ... 6.00

JLA / WORLD WITHOUT GROWN-UPS (See Young Justice)
DC Comics: Aug, 1998 - No. 2, Sept, 1998 ($4.95, prestige format)

1,2-JLA, Robin, Impulse & Superboy app.; Ramos & McKone-a ... 6.00
TPB ('98, $9.95) r/series & Young Justice: The Secret #1 ... 10.00

JLA: YEAR ONE
DC Comics: Jan, 1998 - No. 12, Dec, 1998 ($2.95/$1.95, limited series)

1-($2.95)-Waid & Augustyn-s/Kitson-a ... 5.00
1-Platinum Edition ... 10.00
2-8-($1.95): 5-Doom Patrol-c/app. 7-Superman app. ... 4.00
9-12 ... 3.00
TPB ('99, $19.95) r/#1-12; Busiek intro. ... 20.00

JLA-Z
DC Comics: Nov, 2003 - No. 3, Jan, 2004 ($2.50, limited series)

1-3-Pin-ups and info on current and former JLA members and villains; art by various ... 2.50

JLX
DC Comics (Amalgam): Apr, 1996 ($1.95, one-shot)

1-Mark Waid scripts ... 2.50

JLX UNLEASHED
DC Comics (Amalgam): June, 1997 ($1.95, one-shot)

1-Priest-s/ Oscar Jimenez & Rodriquez/a ... 2.50

JOAN OF ARC (Also see A-1 Comics & Ideal a Classical Comic)
Magazine Enterprises: No. 21, 1949 (one shot)

A-1 21-Movie adaptation; Ingrid Bergman photo-covers & interior photos;
Whitney-a ... 29 58 87 170 268 365

JOE COLLEGE
Hillman Periodicals: Fall, 1949 - No. 2, Wint, 1950 (Teen-age humor, 52 pgs.)

1-Powell-a; Briefer-a ... 12 24 36 67 94 120
2-Powell-a ... 10 20 30 54 72 90

JOE JINKS
United Features Syndicate: No. 12, 1939

Single Series 12 ... 31 62 93 178 282 385

JOE LOUIS (See Fight Comics #2, Picture News #6 & True Comics #5)
Fawcett Publications: Sept, 1950 - No. 2, Nov, 1950 (Photo-c) (Boxing champ) (See Dick Cole #10)

1-Photo-c; life story ... 55 110 165 344 572 800
2-Photo-c ... 40 80 120 235 368 500

JOE PALOOKA (1st Series) (Also see Big Shot Comics, Columbia Comics & Feature Funnies)
Columbia Comic Corp. (Publication Enterprises): 1942 - No. 4, 1944

1-1st to portray American president; gov't permission required ... 98 196 294 613 1019 1425
2 (1943)-Hitler-c ... 57 114 171 356 591 825
3-Nazi Sub-c ... 40 80 120 235 368 500
4 ... 34 68 102 195 308 420

JOE PALOOKA (2nd Series) (Battle Adv. #68-74; ...Advs. #75, 77-81, 83-85, 87; Champ of the Comics #76, 82, 86, 89-93) (See All-New)
Harvey Publications: Nov, 1945 - No. 118, Mar, 1961

1 ... 49 98 147 299 492 685
2 ... 25 50 75 145 228 310
3,4,6,7-1st Flyin' Fool, ends #25 ... 15 30 45 90 140 190
5-Boy Explorers by S&K (7-8/46) ... 21 42 63 122 191 260
8-10 ... 14 28 42 80 115 150
11-14,16,18-20: 14-Black Cat text-s(2). 18-Powell-a. 19-Freedom Train-c ... 11 22 33 64 90 115
15-Origin & 1st app. Humphrey (12/47); Super-heroine Atoma app. by Powell ... 15 30 45 90 140 190
17-Humphrey vs. Palooka-c/s; 1st app. Little Max ... 15 30 45 90 140 190
21-26,29,30: 22-Powell-a. 30-Nude female painting ... 10 20 30 56 76 95
27-Little Max app.; Howie Morenz-s ... 10 20 30 58 79 100
28-Babe Ruth 4 pg. sty. ... 10 20 30 58 79 100
31,39,51: 31-Dizzy Dean 4 pg. sty. 39-(12/49) Humphrey & Little Max begin; Sonny Baugh football-s. 51-Babe Ruth 2 pg. sty; Jake Lamotta 1/2 pg. sty. ... 9 18 27 50 65 80
32-38,40-50,52-61: 35-Little Max-c/story(4 pgs.). 36-Humphrey story. 41-Bing Crosby photo on-c. 44-Palooka marries Ann Howe. 50-(11/51)-Becomes Harvey Comics Hits #51 ... 8 16 24 44 57 70
62-S&K Boy Explorers-r ... 9 18 27 50 65 80
63-65,73-80,100: 79-Story of 1st meeting with Ann ... 8 16 24 40 50 60
66,67-'Commie' torture story "Drug-Diet Horror" ... 10 20 30 58 69 85
68,70-72: 68,70-Joe vs. "Gooks"-c. 71-Bloody bayonets-c. 72-Tank-c ... 9 18 27 50 65 80
69-1st "Battle Adventures" issue; torture & bondage ... 9 18 27 52 69 85
81-99,101-115: 104,107-Humphrey & Little Max-s ... 7 14 21 37 46 55
116-S&K Boy Explorers-r (Giant, '60) ... 9 18 27 47 61 75
117-(84 pg. Giant) r/Commie issues #66,67; Powell-a ... 9 18 27 50 65 80
118-(84 pg. Giant) Jack Dempsey 2 pg. sty, Powell-a ... 9 18 27 47 61 75
...**Visits the Lost City** nn (1945)(One Shot)(50¢)-164 page continuous story strip reprint. Has biography & photo of Ham Fisher; possibly the single longest comic book story published in that era (159 pgs.?) ... 179 358 537 1119 1860 2600

NOTE: *Nostrand/Powell* a-73. *Powell* a-7, 8, 10, 12, 14, 17, 19, 26-45, 47-53, 70, 73 at least. Black Cat text stories #8, 12, 13, 19.

JOE PSYCHO & MOO FROG
Goblin Studios: 1996 - No. 5, 1997 ($2.50, B&W)

1-5: 4-Two covers ... 2.50
...Full Color Extravaganzonzo ($2.95, color) ... 3.00

JOE YANK (Korean War)
Standard Comics (Visual Editions): No. 5, Mar, 1952 - No. 16, 1954

5-Toth, Celardo, Tuska-a ... 10 20 30 54 72 90
6-Toth, Severin/Elder-a ... 9 18 27 52 69 85
7-Pinhead Perkins by Dan DeCarlo (in all?) ... 7 14 21 37 46 55
8-Toth-c ... 8 16 24 42 54 65

	GD 2.0	VG 4.0	FN 6.0	VF 8.0	VF/NM 9.0	NM- 9.2
9-16: 9-Andru-c. 12-Andru-a	7	14	21	35	43	50

JOHN BOLTON'S HALLS OF HORROR
Eclipse Comics: June, 1985 - No. 2, June, 1985 ($1.75, limited series)

1,2-British-r; Bolton-c/a						3.00

JOHN BOLTON'S STRANGE WINK
Dark Horse Comics: Mar, 1998 - No. 3, May, 1998 ($2.95, B&W, limited series)

1-3-Anthology; Bolton-s/c/a						3.00

JOHN BYRNE'S NEXT MEN (See Dark Horse Presents #54)
Dark Horse Comics (Legend imprint #19 on): Jan, 1992 - No. 30, Dec, 1994 ($2.50, mature)

1-Silver foil embossed-c; Byrne-c/a/scripts in all						4.00
1-4: 1-2nd printing with gold ink logo						2.50
0-(2/92)-r/chapters 1-4 from DHP w/new Byrne-c						2.50
5-20,22-30: 7-10-MA #1-4 mini-series on flip side. 16-Origin of Mark IV. 17-Miller-c. 19-22-Faith storyline. 23-26-Power storyline. 27-30-Lies storyline Pt. 1-4						2.50
21-(12/93) 1st Hellboy; cover and Hellboy pages by Mike Mignola; Byrne other pages	3	6	9	18	27	35
...Parallel, Book 2 ($16.95)-TPB; r/#7-12						17.00
...Fame, Book 3($16.95)-TPB r/#13-18						17.00
...Faith, Book 4($14.95)-TPB r/#19-22						15.00

NOTE: Issues 1 through 6 contain certificates redeemable for an exclusive Next Men trading card set by Byrne. Prices are for complete books. Cody painted c-23-26. Mignola a-21(part); c-21.

JOHN BYRNE'S 2112
Dark Horse Comics (Legend): Oct, 1994 ($9.95, TPB)

1-Byrne-c/a/s						10.00

JOHN CARTER OF MARS (See The Funnies & Tarzan #207)
Dell Publishing Co.: No. 375, Mar-May, 1952 - No. 488, Aug-Oct, 1953
(Edgar Rice Burroughs)

Four Color 375 (#1)-Origin; Jesse Marsh-a	25	50	75	186	333	480
Four Color 437, 488-Painted-c	15	30	45	111	198	285

JOHN CARTER OF MARS
Gold Key: Apr, 1964 - No. 3, Oct, 1964

1(10104-404)-r/4-Color #375; Jesse Marsh-a	6	12	18	41	66	90
2(407), 3(410)-r/4-Color #437 & 488; Marsh-a	4	8	12	28	44	60

JOHN CARTER OF MARS
House of Greystoke: 1970 (10-1/2x16-1/2", 72 pgs., B&W, paper-c)

1941-42 Sunday strip-r; John Coleman Burroughs-a	3	6	9	20	30	40

JOHN CARTER, WARLORD OF MARS (Also see Weird Worlds)
Marvel Comics: June, 1977 - No. 28, Oct, 1979

1,18: 1-Origin. 18-Frank Miller-a(p)(1st publ. Marvel work)	1	2	3	5	7	9
1-(35¢-c variant, limited dist.)	3	6	9	20	30	40
2-5-(35¢-c variants, limited dist.)	3	6	9	16	23	30
2-17,19-28: 11-Origin Dejah Thoris						4.00
Annuals 1-3: 1(1977). 2(1978). 3(1979)-All 52 pgs. with new book-length stories						5.00

NOTE: Austin c-24i. Gil Kane a-1-10p; c-1p, 2p, 3, 4-9p, 10, 15p. Layton a-17i. Miller c-25, 26p. Nebres a-2-4i, 8-16i; c(j)-6-9, 11-22, 25, Annual 1p. Perez c-24p. Simonson a-15p. Sutton a-7i.

JOHN CONSTANTINE - HELLBLAZER SPECIAL: PAPA MIDNITE
DC Comics (Vertigo): April, 2005 - No. 5, Aug, 2005 ($2.95/$2.99, limited series)

1-5-Origin of Papa Midnite; Akins-a/Johnson-s						3.00

JOHN F. KENNEDY, CHAMPION OF FREEDOM
Worden & Childs: 1964 (no month) (25¢)

nn-Photo-c	7	14	21	49	80	110

JOHN F. KENNEDY LIFE STORY
Dell Publishing Co.: Aug-Oct, 1964; Nov, 1965; June, 1966 (12¢)

12-378-410-Photo-c	6	12	18	41	66	90
12-378-511 (reprint, 11/65)	3	6	9	21	32	42
12-378-606 (reprint, 6/66)	3	6	9	19	29	38

JOHN FORCE (See Magic Agent)

JOHN HIX SCRAP BOOK, THE
Eastern Color Printing Co. (McNaught Synd.): Late 1930's (no date) (10¢, 68 pgs., regular size)

1-Strange As It Seems (resembles Single Series books)	40	80	120	235	368	500
2-Strange As It Seems	26	52	78	152	239	325

JOHN JAKES' MULLKON EMPIRE
Tekno Comix: Sept, 1995 - No. 6, Feb, 1996 ($1.95)

	GD 2.0	VG 4.0	FN 6.0	VF 8.0	VF/NM 9.0	NM- 9.2
1-6						2.50

JOHN LAW DETECTIVE (See Smash Comics #3)
Eclipse Comics: April, 1983 ($1.50, Baxter paper)

1-Three Eisner stories originally drawn in 1948 for the never published John Law #1; original cover pencilled in 1948 & inked in 1982 by Eisner						3.00

JOHNNY APPLESEED (See Story Hour Series)

JOHNNY CASH (See Hello, I'm...)

JOHNNY DANGER (See Movie Comics, 1946)
Toby Press: 1950 (Based on movie serial)

1-Photo-c; Sparling-a	17	34	51	100	158	215

JOHNNY DANGER PRIVATE DETECTIVE
Toby Press: Aug, 1954 (Reprinted in Danger #11 by Super)

1-Photo-c; Opium den story	14	28	42	78	112	145

JOHNNY DELGADO IS DEAD
Image Comics: Sept, 2007 - Present ($3.99)

1-Chris Moreno-a/John Leekley & Michael D. Olmos-s						4.00

JOHNNY DYNAMITE (Formerly Dynamite #1-9; Foreign Intrigues #14 on)
Charlton Comics: No. 10, June, 1955 - No. 12, Oct, 1955

10-12	11	22	33	60	83	105

JOHNNY DYNAMITE
Dark Horse Comics: Sept, 1994 - Dec, 1994 ($2.95, B&W & red, limited series)

1-4: Max Allan Collins scripts in all; Terry Beatty-a						3.00
...: Underworld GN (AiT/Planet Lar, 3/03, $12.95, B&W) r/#1-4 in B&W without red						13.00

JOHNNY HAZARD
Best Books (Standard Comics) (King Features): No. 5, Aug, 1948 - No. 8, May, 1949; No. 35, date?

5-Strip reprints by Frank Robbins (c/a)	18	36	54	105	165	225
6,8-Strip reprints by Frank Robbins	15	30	45	88	137	185
7,35: 7-New art, not Robbins	12	24	36	67	94	120

JOHNNY JASON (...Teen Reporter)
Dell Publishing Co.: Feb-Apr, 1962 - No. 2, June-Aug, 1962

Four Color 1302, 2(01380-208)	4	8	12	24	37	50

JOHNNY LAW, SKY RANGER
Good Comics (Lev Gleason): Apr, 1955 - No. 3, Aug, 1955; No. 4, Nov, 1955

1-Edmond Good-c/a	10	20	30	56	76	95
2-4	7	14	21	35	43	50

JOHNNY MACK BROWN (Western star; see Western Roundup under Dell Giants)
Dell Publishing Co.: No. 269, Mar, 1950 - No. 963, Feb, 1959 (All Photo-c)

Four Color 269(#1)(3/50, 52pgs.)-Johnny Mack Brown & his horse Rebel begin; photo front/back-c begin; Marsh-a in #1-9	22	44	66	160	285	410
2(10-12/50, 52pgs.)	11	22	33	79	140	200
3(1-3/51, 52pgs.)	9	18	27	63	107	150
4-10 (9-11/52)(36pgs.), Four Color 455,493,541,584,618,645,685,722,776,834,963	7	14	21	47	76	105
Four Color 922-Manning-a	7	14	21	45	73	100

JOHNNY NEMO
Eclipse Comics: Sept, 1985 - No. 3, Feb, 1986 (Mini-series)

1-3						2.50

JOHNNY PERIL (See Comic Cavalcade #15, Danger Trail #5, Sensation Comics #107 & Sensation Mystery)

JOHNNY RINGO (TV)
Dell Publishing Co.: No. 1142, Nov-Jan, 1960/61 (one shot)

Four Color 1142-Photo-c	7	14	21	47	76	105

JOHNNY STARBOARD (See Wisco)

JOHNNY THE HOMICIDAL MANIAC (Also see Squee)
Slave Labor Graphics: Aug, 1995 - No. 7, Jan, 1997 ($2.95, B&W, lim. series)

1-Jhonen Vasquez-c/s/a	1	3	4	6	8	10
1-Signed & numbered edition	2	4	6	9	12	15
2,3: 2-(11/95). 3-(2/96)						6.00
4-7: 4-(5-96). 5-(8/96)						4.00
Hardcover-($29.95) r/#1-7						30.00
TPB-($19.95)						20.00

JOHNNY THUNDER
National Periodical Publications: Feb-Mar, 1973 - No. 3, July-Aug, 1973

1-Johnny Thunder & Nighthawk-r. in all	2	4	6	11	16	20

John Wayne
Adventure Comics #12 © TOBY

Joker Comics #1 © MAR

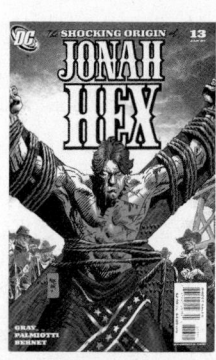

Jonah Hex (2006 series) #13 © DC

	GD 2.0	VG 4.0	FN 6.0	VF 8.0	VF/NM 9.0	NM- 9.2
2,3: 2-Trigger Twins app.	2	4	6	8	10	12

NOTE: All contain 1950s DC reprints from All-American Western. *Drucker* r-2, 3. *G. Kane* r-2, 3. *Moreira* r-1. *Toth* r-1, 3; c-1r, 3r. Also see All-American, All-Star Western, Flash Comics, Western Comics, World's Best & World's Finest.

JOHN PAUL JONES
Dell Publishing Co.: No. 1007, July-Sept, 1959 (one-shot)

	GD	VG	FN	VF	VF/NM	NM-
Four Color 1007-Movie, Robert Stack photo-c	5	10	15	35	55	75

JOHN ROMITA JR. 30TH ANNIVERSARY SPECIAL
Marvel Comics: 2006 ($3.99, one-shot)

nn-r/1st story in Amazing Spider-Man Annual #11; timeline, sketch pages, interviews						4.00

JOHN STEED & EMMA PEEL (See The Avengers, Gold Key series)

JOHN STEELE SECRET AGENT (Also see Freedom Agent)
Gold Key: 1964

	GD	VG	FN	VF	VF/NM	NM-
1-Freedom Agent	6	12	18	37	59	80

JOHN WAYNE ADVENTURE COMICS (Movie star; See Big Tex, Oxydol-Dreft, Tim McCoy, & With The Marines...#1)
Toby Press: Winter, 1949-50 - No. 31, May, 1955 (Photo-c: 1-12,17,25-on)

	GD	VG	FN	VF	VF/NM	NM-
1 (36pgs.)-Photo-c begin (1st time in comics on-c)	162	324	486	1013	1682	2350
2-4: 2-(4/50, 36pgs.)-Williamson/Frazetta-a(2) 6 & 2 pgs. (one story-r/Billy the Kid #1); photo back-c. 3-(36pgs.)-Williamson/Frazetta-a(2), 16 pgs. total; photo back-c. 4-(52pgs.)-Williamson/Frazetta-a(2), 16 pgs. total	142	213	444	735	1025	
5 (52pgs.)-Kurtzman-a(Alfred "E" Newman in Potshot Pete)	52	104	156	317	521	725
6 (52pgs.)-Williamson/Frazetta-a (10 pgs.); Kurtzman-a "Pot-Shot Pete", (5 pgs.) & "Genius Jones", (1 pg.)	61	122	183	381	633	885
7 (52pgs.)-Williamson/Frazetta-a (10 pgs.)	53	106	159	329	545	760
8 (36pgs.)-Williamson/Frazetta-a(2) (12 & 9 pgs.)	66	132	198	413	682	950
9-11: Photo western-c	39	78	117	225	355	485
12,14-Photo war-c. 12-Kurtzman-a(2 pg.) "Genius"	39	78	117	225	355	485
13,15: 13,15-Line-drawn-c begin, end #24	33	66	99	190	300	410
16-Williamson/Frazetta-r/Billy the Kid #1	36	72	108	208	329	450
17-Photo-c	36	72	108	208	329	450
18-Williamson/Frazetta-a (r/#4 & 8, 19 pgs.)	40	80	120	235	368	500
19-24: 23-Evans-a?	29	58	87	170	268	365
25-Photo-c resume; end #31; Williamson/Frazetta-r/Billy the Kid #3	40	80	120	235	368	500
26-28,30-Photo-c	33	66	99	190	300	410
29,31-Williamson/Frazetta-a in each (r/#4, 2)	38	76	114	222	351	480

NOTE: Williamsonish art in later issues by *Gerald McCann*.

JO-JO COMICS (...Congo King #7-29; My Desire #30 on)(Also see Fantastic Fears and Jungle Jo)
Fox Feature Syndicate: 1945 - No. 29, July, 1949 (Two No.7's; no #13)

	GD	VG	FN	VF	VF/NM	NM-
nn(1945)-Funny animal, humor	16	32	48	92	144	195
2(Sum,'46)-6(4-5/47): Funny animal. 2-Ten pg. Electro story (Fall/46)	10	20	30	56	76	95
7(7/47)-Jo-Jo, Congo King begins (1st app.); Bronze Man & Purple Tigress app.	90	180	270	563	932	1300
7(#8) (9/47)	66	132	198	413	682	950
8-10(#9-11): 8-Tanee begins	54	108	162	338	557	775
11,12(#12,13),14,16: 11,16-Kamen bondage-c	48	96	144	293	484	675
15,17: 15-Cited by Dr. Wertham in 5/47 Saturday Review of Literature.						
17-Kamen bondage-c	50	100	150	305	503	700
18-20	48	96	144	293	484	675
21-29: 21-Hollingsworth-a(4 pgs.; 23-1 pg.)	40	80	120	244	392	540

NOTE: Many bondage-c/a by *Baker/Kamen/Feldstein/Good*. No. 7's have Princesses Gwenna, Geesa, Yolda, & Safra before settling down on Tanee.

JOKEBOOK COMICS DIGEST ANNUAL (...Magazine No. 5 on)
Archie Publications: Oct, 1977 - No. 13, Oct, 1983 (Digest Size)

	GD	VG	FN	VF	VF/NM	NM-
1(10/77)-Reprints; Neal Adams-a	2	4	6	13	18	22
2(4/78)-5	2	4	6	9	12	15
6-13	1	3	4	6	8	10

JOKER, THE (See Batman #1, Batman: The Killing Joke, Brave & the Bold, Detective, Greatest Joker Stories & Justice League Annual #2)
National Periodical Publications: May, 1975 - No. 9, Sept-Oct, 1976

	GD	VG	FN	VF	VF/NM	NM-
1-Two-Face app.	5	10	15	32	51	70
2,3: 3-The Creeper app.	3	6	9	18	27	35
4-9: 4-Green Arrow-c/sty. 6-Sherlock Holmes-c/sty. 7-Lex Luthor-c/story. 8-Scarecrow-c/story.						
9-Catwoman-c/story	3	6	9	15	21	26

JOKER, THE (See Tangent Comics/ The Joker)

JOKER COMICS (Adventures Into Terror No. 43 on)

Timely/Marvel Comics No. 36 on (TCI/CDS): Apr, 1942 - No. 42, Aug, 1950

	GD 2.0	VG 4.0	FN 6.0	VF 8.0	VF/NM 9.0	NM- 9.2
1-(Rare)-Powerhouse Pepper (1st app.) begins by Wolverton; Stuporman app. from Daring Comics	297	594	891	1856	3078	4300
2-Wolverton-a; 1st app. Tessie the Typist & begin series	95	190	285	594	985	1375
3-5-Wolverton-a	54	108	162	338	562	785
6-10-Wolverton-a. 6-Tessie-c begin	41	82	123	256	416	575
11-20-Wolverton-a	40	80	120	235	368	500
21,22,24-27,29,30-Wolverton cont'd. & Kurtzman's "Hey Look" in #23-27	34	68	102	197	311	425
23-1st "Hey Look" by Kurtzman; Wolverton-a	36	72	108	208	329	450
28,32,34,37-41: 28-Millie the Model begins. 32-Hedy begins. 41-Nellie the Nurse begins	14	28	42	82	121	160
31-Last Powerhouse Pepper; not in #28	26	52	78	150	235	320
33,35,36-Kurtzman's "Hey Look"	15	30	45	84	127	170
42-Only app. 'Patty Pinup,' clone of Millie the Model	15	30	45	83	124	165

JOKER: DEVIL'S ADVOCATE
DC Comics: 1996 ($24.95/$12.95, one-shot)

nn-(Hardcover)-Dixon scripts/Nolan & Hanna-a						25.00
nn-(Softcover)						13.00

JOKER: LAST LAUGH
DC Comics: Dec, 2001 - No. 6, Jan, 2002 ($2.95, weekly limited series)

1-6: 1,6-Bolland-a						3.00
...Secret Files (12/01, $5.95) Short stories by various; Simonson-c						6.00

JOKER / MASK
Dark Horse Comics: May, 2000 - No. 4, Aug, 2000 ($2.95, limited series)

1-4-Batman, Harley Quinn, Poison Ivy app.						3.00

JOLLY CHRISTMAS, A (See March of Comics No. 269)

JOLLY COMICS: Four Star Publishing Co.: 1947 (Advertised, not published)

JOLLY JINGLES (Formerly Jackpot Comics)
MLJ Magazines: No. 10, Sum, 1943 - No. 16, Wint, 1944/45

	GD	VG	FN	VF	VF/NM	NM-
10-Super Duck begins (1st app.); Woody The Woodpecker begins (not same as Lantz character)	40	80	120	235	368	500
11 (Fall, '43)-2nd Super Duck(see Hangman #8)	20	40	60	117	184	250
12-Hitler-c	28	56	84	162	256	350
13-16: 13-Sahle-c. 15,16-Vigoda-c	14	28	42	80	115	150

JONAH HEX (See All-Star Western, Hex and Weird Western Tales)
National Periodical Pub./DC Comics: Mar-Apr, 1977 - No. 92, Aug, 1985

	GD	VG	FN	VF	VF/NM	NM-
1	18	27	63	107	150	
2	5	10	15	35	55	75
3,4,9: 9-Wrightson-c.	4	8	12	28	44	60
5,6,10: 5-Rep 1st app. from All-Star Western #10	4	8	12	24	37	50
7,8-Explains Hex's face disfigurement (origin)	5	10	15	30	48	65
11-20: 12-Starlin-c	3	6	9	16	23	30
21-32: 31,32-Origin retold	2	4	6	9	13	16
33-50	1	3	4	6	8	10
51-80						6.00
81-91: 89-Mark Teixeira-a. 91-Cover swipe from Superman #243 (hugging a mystery woman)	1	2	3	4	5	7
92-Story cont'd in Hex #1	3	6	9	14	19	24

NOTE: *Ayers* a(p)-35-37, 40, 41, 44-53, 56, 58-82. *Buckler* a-11; c-11, 13-16. *Kubert* c-43-46. *Morrow* a-90-92; c-10. *Spiegle(Tothish)* a-34, 38, 40, 49, 52. *Teixeira* a-89b. Batlash back-ups in 49, 52. El Diablo back-ups in 48, 56-60, 73-75. Scalphunter back-ups in 40, 41, 45-47.

JONAH HEX
DC Comics: Jan, 2006 - Present ($2.99)

1-Justin Gray & Jimmy Palmiotti-s/Luke Ross-a/Quitely-c						5.00
2-21: 5-Bat app. 10,16,17,19,20,22-Noto-a. 11-El Diablo app.; Beck-a. 13-15-Origin retold. 21,23-Bernet-a						3.00
....: Face Full of Violence TPB (2006, $12.99) r/#1-6						13.00
....: Guns of Vengeance TPB (2007, $12.99) r/#7-12						13.00

JONAH HEX AND OTHER WESTERN TALES (Blue Ribbon Digest)
DC Comics: Sept-Oct, 1979 - No. 3, Jan-Feb, 1980 (100 pgs.)

	GD	VG	FN	VF	VF/NM	NM-
1-3: 1-Origin Scalphunter-r, Ayers/Evans, Neal Adams-a.; painted-c. 2-Weird Western Tales-r; Neal Adams, Toth, Aragones-a. 3-Outlaw-r, Scalphunter-r; Gil Kane, Wildey-a	2	4	6	10	14	18

JONAH HEX: RIDERS OF THE WORM AND SUCH
DC Comics (Vertigo): Mar, 1995 - No. 5, July, 1995 ($2.95, limited series)

1-5-Lansdale story, Truman -a						4.00

Jonesy #4 © QUA

Jon Juan #1 © TOBY

Journey into Fear #12 © SUPR

	GD 2.0	VG 4.0	FN 6.0	VF 8.0	VF/NM 9.0	NM- 9.2

JONAH HEX: SHADOWS WEST
DC Comics (Vertigo): Feb, 1999 - No. 3, Apr, 1999 ($2.95, limited series)

1-3-Lansdale-s/Truman -a						4.00

JONAH HEX SPECTACULAR (See DC Special Series No. 16)

JONAH HEX: TWO-GUN MOJO
DC Comics (Vertigo): Aug, 1993 - No. 5, Dec, 1993 ($2.95, limited series)

1-Lansdale scripts in all; Truman/Glanzman-a in all w/Truman-c						6.00
1-Platinum edition with no price on cover						20.00
2-5						4.00
TPB-(1994, $12.95) r/#1-5						13.00

JONESY (Formerly Crack Western)
Comic Favorite/Quality Comics Group: No. 85, Aug, 1953; No. 2, Oct, 1953 - No. 8, Oct, 1954

85(#1)-Teen-age humor	8	16	24	44	57	70
2	6	12	18	27	33	38
3-8	5	10	15	23	28	32

JON JUAN (Also see Great Lover Romances)
Toby Press: Spring, 1950

1-All Schomburg-a (signed Al Reid on-c); written by Siegel; used in SOTI, pg. 38 (Scarce)						
	64	128	192	400	663	925

JONNI THUNDER (…A.K.A. Thunderbolt)
DC Comics: Feb, 1985 - No. 4, Aug, 1985 (75¢, limited series)

1-4: 1-Origin & 1st app.						2.50

JONNY DOUBLE
DC Comics (Vertigo): Sept, 1998 - No. 4, Dec, 1998 ($2.95, limited series)

1-4-Azzarello-s						3.00
TPB (2002, $12.95) r/#1-4; Chiarello-c						13.00

JONNY QUEST (TV)
Gold Key: Dec, 1964 (Hanna-Barbera)

1 (10139-412)	34	68	102	255	465	675

JONNY QUEST (TV)
Comico: June 1986 - No. 31, Dec, 1988 ($1.50/$1.75)(Hanna-Barbera)

1						5.00
2,3,5: 3,5-Dave Stevens-c						4.00
4,6-31: 30-Adapts TV episode						3.00
Special 1(9/88, $1.75), 2(10/88, $1.75)						4.00
NOTE: M. Anderson a-9. Mooney a-Special 1. Pini a-2. Quagmire a-31p. Rude a-1; c-2i. Sienkiewicz c-11. Spiegle a-7, 12, 21; c-21 Staton a-2i, 11p. Steacy c-8. Stevens a-4i; c-3,5. Wildey a-1, c-1, 7, 12. Williamson a-4i; c-4i.

JONNY QUEST CLASSICS (TV)
Comico: May, 1987 - No. 3, July, 1987 ($2.00) (Hanna-Barbera)

1-3: Wildey-c/a; 3-Based on TV episode						3.00

JON SABLE, FREELANCE (Also see Mike Grell's Sable & Sable)
First Comics: 6/83 - No. 56, 2/88 (#1-17, $1; #18-33, $1.25, #34-on, $1.75)

1-Mike Grell-c/a/scripts						3.00
2-56: 3-5-Origin, parts 1-3. 6-Origin, part 4. 11-1st app. of Maggie the Cat. 14-Mando paper begins. 16-Maggie the Cat. app. 25-30-Shatter app. 34-Deluxe format begins ($1.75)						2.50
The Complete Jon Sable, Freelance: Vol. 1 (IDW, 2005, $19.99) r/#1-6						20.00
The Complete Jon Sable, Freelance: Vol. 2 (IDW, 2005, $19.99) r/#7-11						20.00
The Complete Jon Sable, Freelance: Vol. 3 (IDW, 2005, $19.99) r/#12-16						20.00
The Complete Jon Sable, Freelance: Vol. 4 (IDW, 2005, $19.99) r/#17-21						20.00
NOTE: Aragones a-33; c-33(part). Grell a-1-43;c-1-52, 53p, 54-56.

JON SABLE, FREELANCE: BLOODTRAIL
IDW Publ.: Apr, 2005 - No. 6, Nov, 2005 ($3.99, limited series)

1-6-Mike Grell-c/a/scripts						4.00
TPB (4/06, $19.99) r/#1-6; cover gallery						20.00

JOSEPH & HIS BRETHREN (See The Living Bible)

JOSIE (She's… #1-16) (…& the Pussycats #45 on) (See Archie's Pals 'n' Gals #23 for 1st app.) (Also see Archie Giant Series Magazine #528, 540, 551, 562, 571, 584, 597, 610, 622)
Archie Publ./Radio Comics: Feb, 1963; No. 2, Aug, 1963 - No. 106, Oct, 1982

1	15	30	45	109	195	280
2	9	18	27	60	100	140
3-5	6	12	18	43	69	95
6-10	4	8	12	28	44	60
11-20	3	6	9	21	32	42
21, 23-30	3	6	9	17	25	32
22 (9/66)-Mighty Man & Mighty (Josie Girl) app.	4	8	12	23	36	48

	GD 2.0	VG 4.0	FN 6.0	VF 8.0	VF/NM 9.0	NM- 9.2

31-44	3	6	9	15	21	26
45 (12/69)-Josie and the Pussycats begins (Hanna Barbera TV cartoon); 1st app. of the Pussycats	10	20	30	70	123	175
46-2nd app./1st cover Pussycats	7	14	21	49	80	110
47-3rd app. of the Pussycats	5	10	15	32	51	70
48,49-Pussycats band-c/s	6	12	18	37	59	80
50-J&P-c; go to Hollywood, meet Hanna & Barbera	6	12	18	43	69	95
51-54	3	6	9	17	25	32
55-74 (2/74)(52 pg. issues)	3	6	9	17	25	32
75-90(8/76)	2	4	6	10	14	18
91-99	2	4	6	9	12	15
100 (10/79)	2	4	6	11	16	20
101-106	2	4	6	10	14	18

JOSIE & THE PUSSYCATS (TV)
Archie Comics: 1993 - No. 2, 1994 ($2.00, 52 pgs.)(Published annually)

1,2-Bound-in pull-out poster in each. 2-(Spr/94)						5.00

JOURNAL OF CRIME (See Fox Giants)

JOURNEY
Aardvark-Vanaheim #1-14/Fantagraphics Books #15-on: 1983 - No. 14, Sept, 1984; No. 15, Apr, 1985 - No. 27, July, 1986 (B&W)

1						3.00
2-27: 20-Sam Kieth-a						2.50

JOURNEY INTO FEAR
Superior-Dynamic Publications: May, 1951 - No. 21, Sept, 1954

1-Baker-r(2)	66	132	198	413	682	950
2	46	92	138	281	466	640
3,4	40	80	120	235	368	500
5-10,15: 15-Used in SOTI, pg. 389	29	38	87	167	264	360
11-14,16-21	26	52	78	154	242	330
NOTE: Kamenish 'headlight'-a most issues. Robinson a-10.

JOURNEY INTO MYSTERY (1st Series) (Thor Nos. 126-502)
Atlas(CPS No. 1-48/AMI No. 49-68/Marvel No. 69 (6/61) on): 6/52 - No. 48, 8/57; No. 49, 11/58 - No. 125, 2/66; 503, 11/96 - No. 521, June, 1998

1-Weird/horror stories begin	300	600	900	1970	3485	5000
2	109	218	327	681	1128	1575
3,4	81	162	243	506	841	1175
5-11	54	108	162	338	562	785
12-20,22: 15-Atomic explosion panel. 22-Davisesque-a; last pre-code issue (2/55)	44	88	132	268	439	610
21-Kubert-a; Tothish-a by Andru	44	88	132	-273	447	620
23-32,35-38,40: 24-Torres?-a. 38-Ditko-c	34	68	102	195	308	420
33-Williamson-a; Ditko-a (his 1st for Atlas?)	36	72	108	208	329	450
34,39: 34-Krigstein-a. 39-1st S.A. issue; Wood-a	34	68	102	197	311	425
41-Crandall-a; Frazettaesque-a by Morrow	19	38	57	141	251	360
42,46,48: 42,48-Torres-a. 46-Torres & Krigstein-a	19	38	57	138	244	350
43,44-Williamson/Mayo-a in both. 43-Invisible Woman prototype						
	19	38	57	141	251	360
45,47,50,52-54: 50-Davis-a. 54-Williamson-a	18	36	54	134	237	340
49-Matt Fox, Check-a	19	38	57	138	244	350
51-Kirby/Wood-a	20	40	60	150	268	385
55-61,63-65,67-69,71,72,74,75: 74-Contents change to Fantasy. 75-Last 10¢ issue						
	19	38	57	138	244	350
62-Prototype ish. (The Hulk); 1st app. Xemnu (Titan) called "The Hulk"	29	58	87	212	381	550
66-Prototype ish. (The Hulk)-Return of Xemnu "The Hulk"	25	50	75	184	330	475
70-Prototype ish. (The Sandman)(7/61); similar to Spidey villain	24	48	72	175	313	450
73-Story titled "The Spider" where a spider is exposed to radiation & gets powers of a human and shoots webbing; a reverse prototype of Spider-Man's origin						
	36	72	108	270	498	725
76,77,80-82: 80-Anti-communist propaganda story	15	30	45	107	191	275
76-(10¢ cover price blacked out, 12¢ printed on)	36	72	108	270	498	725
78-The Sorcerer (Dr. Strange prototype) app. (3/62)	24	48	72	175	313	450
79-Prototype issue. (Mr. Hyde)	20	40	60	146	261	375
83-Origin & 1st app. The Mighty Thor by Kirby (8/62) and begin series; Thor-c also begin						
	600	1200	1800	5500	10,250	15,000
83-Reprint from the Golden Record Comic Set	15	30	45	109	195	280
With the record (1966)	22	44	66	164	292	420
84-2nd app. Thor	158	316	474	1383	2592	3800
85-1st app. Loki & Heimdall; 1st brief app. Odin (1 panel); 1st app. Asgard						

Journey into Mystery #112 © MAR

Journey into Unknown Worlds #37 © MAR

JSA #50 © DC

	GD 2.0	VG 4.0	FN 6.0	VF 8.0	VF/NM 9.0	NM- 9.2
	102	204	306	867	1609	2350
86-1st full app. Odin	63	126	189	536	993	1450
87-89: 89-Origin Thor retold	50	100	150	413	757	1100
90-No Kirby-a	41	82	123	328	589	850
91,92,94,96-Sinnott-a	34	68	102	255	465	675
93,97-Kirby-a; Tales of Asgard series begins #97 (origin which concludes in #99); origin/1st app. Lava Man	40	80	120	300	550	800
95-Sinnott-a	38	76	114	285	518	750
98,99-Kirby/Heck-a. 98-Origin/1st app. The Human Cobra. 99-1st app. Surtur & Mr. Hyde	29	58	87	212	381	550
100-Kirby/Heck-a; Thor battles Mr. Hyde	29	58	87	212	381	550
101,108: 101-(2/64)-2nd Avengers x-over (w/o Capt. America); see Tales Of Suspense #49 for 1st x-over. 108-(9/64)-Early Dr. Strange & Avengers x-over; ten extra pgs. Kirby-a	19	38	57	138	244	350
102,104-107,110: 102-Intro Sif. 105-109-Ten extra pgs. Kirby-a in each.						
107-1st app. Grey Gargoyle	18	36	54	130	230	330
103-1st app. Enchantress	20	40	60	148	264	380
109-Magneto-c & app. (1st x-over, 10/64)	39	78	117	293	534	775
111,118: 113-Origin Loki	15	30	45	105	188	270
112-Thor Vs. Hulk (1/65); Origin Loki	45	90	135	360	655	950
114-Origin/1st app. Absorbing Man	20	40	60	148	264	380
115-Detailed origin of Loki	18	36	54	134	237	340
116-123,125: 118-1st app. Destroyer. 119-Intro Hogun, Fandral, Volstagg	12	24	36	87	156	225
124-Hercules-c/story	13	26	39	95	168	240
503-521: 503-(11/96, $1.50)-The Lost Gods begin; Tom DeFalco scripts & Deodato Studios-c/a.						
505-Spider-Man-c/app. 509-Loki-c/app. 514-516-Shang-Chi						2.50
#(-1) Flashback (7/97) Tales of Asgard Donald Blake app.						2.50
Annual 1(1965, 25¢, 72 pgs.)-New Thor vs. Hercules(1st app.)-c/story (see Incredible Hulk #3); Kirby-c/a; r/#85,93,95,97	21	42	63	156	278	400

NOTE: *Ayers* a-14, 39, 64i, 71i, 74i, 80i. *Bailey* a-43. *Briefer* a-5, 12. *Cameron* a-35. *Check* a-17. *Colan* a-23, 81; c-14. *Dibby* a-33, 38. 50-No; c-58, 67, 71, 88i. *Kirby/Ditko* a-50-83. *Everett* a-20, 48; c-4-7, 9, 36, 37, 39-42, 44, 45, 47. *Forte* a-19, 35, 40, 53. *Heath* a-4-6, 11, 14; c-1, 8, 11, 15, 51. *Heck* a-53, 73. *Kirby* a(p)-51, 52, 56, 57-60, 62-64, 66-89, 93, 97, 98, 100(w/Heck), 101-125; c-50-57, 59-66, 68-70, 72-82, 88(w/Ditko), 83 & 84(w/Sinnott), 85-96(w/Ayers), 97-125p. *Leiber/Fox* a-93, 98-102. *Maneely* a-20-22. *Morisi* a-42. *Morrow* a-41, 42. *Orlando* a-30, 45, 57. *Mac Pakula* (Tothish) a-9, 35, 41. *Powell* a-26, 27, 34. *Reinman* a-39, 87, 92, 96i. *Robinson* a-9. *Roussos* a-39. *Robert Sale* a-14. *Severin* a-27; c-30. *Sinnott* a-41; c-50. *Tuska* a-11. *Wildey* a-16.

JOURNEY INTO MYSTERY (2nd Series)
Marvel Comics: Oct., 1972 - No. 19, Oct., 1975

1-Robert Howard adaptation; Starlin/Ploog-a	3	6	9	18	27	35
2-5: 2,3,5-Bloch adapt. 4-H. P. Lovecraft adapt.	3	6	9	14	19	24
6-19: Reprints	2	4	6	10	14	18

NOTE: *N. Adams* c-1. *Ditko* r-7, 10, 12, 14, 15, 19; c-10. *Everett* r-9. *G. Kane* a-1p, 2p; c-1-3p. *Kirby* r-7, 13, 15, 18, 19; c-7. *Mort Lawrence* r-2. *Maneely* r-3. *Orlando* r-16. *Reese* a-1, 2i. *Starlin* a-1p, 3p. *Torres* r-16. *Wildey* r-9, 14.

JOURNEY INTO UNKNOWN WORLDS (Formerly Teen)
Atlas Comics (WFP): No. 36, Sept, 1950 - No. 38, Feb, 1951;
No. 4, Apr, 1951 - No. 59, Aug, 1957

36(#1)-Science fiction/weird; "End Of The Earth" c/story						
	255	510	765	1594	2647	3700
37(#2)-Science fiction; "When Worlds Collide" c/story; Everett-c/a; Hitler story	103	206	309	644	1072	1500
38(#3)-Science fiction	88	176	264	550	913	1275
4-6,8,10-Science fiction/weird	54	108	162	338	557	775
7-Wolverton-a "Planet of Terror", 6 pgs; electric chair c-inset/story	90	180	270	563	932	1300
9-Giant eyeball story	66	132	198	415	688	960
11,12-Krigstein-a	43	86	129	243	389	535
13,16,17,20	36	72	108	208	329	450
14-Wolverton-a "One of Our Graveyards Is Missing", 4 pgs; Tuska-a	66	132	198	413	682	950
15-Wolverton-a "They Crawl by Night", 5 pgs.; 2 pg. Maneely s/f story	66	132	198	413	682	950
18,19-Matt Fox-a	43	86	129	243	389	535
21-33-Decapitation-c. 24-Sci/fic story. 26-Atom bomb panel. 27-Sid Check-a. 33-Last pre-code (2/55)	26	52	78	152	239	325
34-Kubert, Torres-a	21	42	63	120	188	255
35-Torres-a	23	46	69	134	107	230
36-45,48,50,53,55,59: 43-Krigstein-a. 44-Davis-a. 45,55,59-Williamson-a in all; with Mayo #55,59. 55-Crandall-a. 48,53-Crandall-a (4 pgs. #48). 48-Check-a. 50-Davis, Crandall-a	18	36	54	103	162	220
46,47,49,52,54,56-58: 54-Torres-a	16	32	48	92	144	195
51-Ditko, Wood-a	20	40	60	115	180	245

NOTE: *Ayers* a-24, 43, *Berg* a-38(#3), 43. *Lou Cameron* a-33. *Colan* a-37(#2), 6, 17, 19, 20, 23, 39. *Ditko* a-45,

	GD 2.0	VG 4.0	FN 6.0	VF 8.0	VF/NM 9.0	NM- 9.2
51. *Drucker* a-35, 58. *Everett* a-37(#2), 11, 14, 41, 55, 56; c-37(#2), 11, 13, 14, 17, 22, 47, 48, 50, 53-55, 59.						
Forte a-49. *Fox* a-21i. *Heath* a-36(#1), 4, 6-8, 17, 20, 22, 36i; c-18. *Keller* a-15. *Mort Lawrence* a-38, 39.						
Maneely a-7, 8, 15, 16, 22, 49, 58; c-19, 25, 52. *Morrow* a-48. *Orlando* a-44, 57. *Pakula* a-36. *Powell* a-42, 53,						
54. *Reinman* a-8. *Rico* a-21. *Robert Sale* a-24, 49. *Sekowsky* a-4, 5, 9. *Severin* a-38, 51; c-38, 48i, 56. *Sinnott*						
a-9, 21, 24. *Tuska* a-38(#3), 14. *Wildey* a-25, 43, 44.						

JOURNEYMAN
Image Comics: Aug, 1999 - No. 3, Oct, 1999 ($2.95, B&W, limited series)

| 1-3-Brandon McKinney-s/a | | | | | | 3.00 |

JOURNEY TO THE CENTER OF THE EARTH (Movie)
Dell Publishing Co.: No. 1060, Nov-Jan, 1959/60 (one-shot)

| Four Color 1060-Pat Boone & James Mason photo-c | 10 | 20 | 30 | 73 | 129 | 185 |

JSA (Justice Society of America) (Also see All Star Comics)
DC Comics: Aug, 1999 - No. 87, Sept, 2006 ($2.50/$2.99)

1-Robinson and Goyer-s; funeral of Wesley Dodds	2	4	6	8	10	12
2-5: 4-Return of Dr. Fate						6.00
6-24: 6-Black Adam-c/app. 11,12-Kobra. 16-20-JSA vs. Johnny Sorrow. 19,20-Spectre app. 22-Hawkgirl origin. 23-Hawkman returns						4.00
25-($3.75) Hawkman rejoins the JSA	1	2	3	5	7	9
26-36, 38-49: 27-Capt. Marvel app. 29-Joker: Last Laugh. 31,32-Snejberg-a. 33-Infinite-Humanite. 34-Intro. new Crimson Avenger and Hourman. 42-G.A. Mr. Terrific and the Freedom Fighters app. 46-Eclipso returns						3.00
37-($3.50) Johnny Thunder merges with the Thunderbolt; intro new Crimson Avenger						3.50
50-($3.95) Wraparound-c by Pacheco; Sentinel becomes Green Lantern again						4.00
51-74,76-82: 51-Kobra killed. 54-JLA app. 55-Ma Hunkle (Red Tornado) app. 56-58-Black Reign x-over with Hawkman #23-25. 64-Sand returns. 67-Identity Crisis tie-in; Gibbons-a. 68,69,72-81-Ross-c. 73,74-Day of Vengeance tie-in. 76-OMAC tie-in. 82-Infinite Crisis x-over; Levitz-s/Perez-a						2.50
75-($2.99) Day of Vengeance tie-in; Alex Ross Spectre-c						3.00
83-87: One Year Later; Pérez-s. 83-85,87-Morales-a; Gentleman Ghost app. 85-Begin $2.99-c; Earth-2 Batman, Atom, Sandman, Mr. Terrific app. 86,87-Ordway-a.						3.00
Annual 1 (10/00, $3.50) Planet DC; intro. Nemesis						3.50
.... Black Reign TPB (2005, $12.99) r/#56-58, Hawkman #23-25; Watson cover gallery						13.00
.... Black Vengeance TPB (2006, $19.99) r/#66-75						20.00
.... Darkness Falls TPB (2002, $19.95) r/#6-15						20.00
.... Fair Play TPB (2003, $14.95) r/#26-31 & Secret Files #2						15.00
.... Ghost Stories TPB (2006, $14.99) r/#82-87						15.00
.... Justice Be Done TPB (2000, $14.95) r/Secret Files & #1-5						15.00
.... Lost TPB (2005, $19.99) r/#59-67						20.00
.... Mixed Signals TPB (2006, $14.99) r/#76-81						15.00
.... Our Worlds At War 1 (9/01, $2.95) Jae Lee-c; Saltares-a						
.... Princes of Darkness TPB (2005, $19.95) r/#46-55						20.00
.... Savage Times TPB (2004, $14.95) r/#39-45						15.00
.... Secret Files 1 (8/99, $4.95) Origin stories and pin-ups; death of Wesley Dodds (G.A. Sandman); intro new Hawkgirl						5.00
.... Secret Files 2 (9/01, $4.95) Short stories and profile pages						5.00
.... Stealing Thunder TPB (2003, $14.95) r/#32-38; JSA vs. The Ultra-Humanite						15.00
.... The Golden Age TPB (2005, $19.99) r/"The Golden Age" Elseworlds mini-series						20.00
.... The Return of Hawkman TPB (2002, $19.95) r/#16-26 & Secret Files #1						20.00

JSA: ALL STARS
DC Comics: July, 2003 - No. 8, Feb, 2004 ($2.50/$3.50, limited series, back-up stories in Golden Age style)

1-6,8-Goyer & Johns-s/Cassaday-c/a. 1-Velluto-a; intro. Legacy. 2-Hawkman by Loeb/Sale 3-Dr. Fate by Cooke. 4-Starman by Robinson/Harris. 5-Hourman by Chaykin. 6-Dr. Mid-nite by Azzarello/Risso						2.50
7-($3.50) Mr. Terrific back-up story by Chabon; Lark-a						3.50
TPB (2004, $14.95) r/#1-8						15.00

JSA: CLASSIFIED (Issues #1-4 reprinted in Power Girl TPB)
DC Comics: Sept, 2005 - Present ($2.50/$2.99)

1-(1st printing) Conner-c/a; origin of Power Girl						3.00
1-(1st printing) Adam Hughes variant-c						5.00
1-(2nd & 3rd printings) 2nd-Hughes B&W sketch-c. 3rd-Close-up of Conner-c						2.50
2-11: 2-LSH app. 4-Leads into Infinite Crisis #2. 5-7-Injustice Society app. 10-13-Vandal Savage origin retold; Gulacy-a/c						2.50
12-29: 12-Begin $2.99-c. 17,18-Bane app. 19,20-Morales-s/a. 21,22-Simonson-s/a						3.00
...: Honor Among Thieves TPB (2007, $14.99) r/#5-9						15.00

JSA STRANGE ADVENTURES
DC Comics: Oct, 2004 - No. 6, Mar, 2005 ($3.50, limited series)

| 1-6-Johnny Thunder as pulp writer; Kitson-a/Watson-c/ Kevin Anderson-s | | | | | | 3.50 |

JSA: THE LIBERTY FILE (Elseworlds)
DC Comics: Feb, 2000 - No. 2, Mar, 2000 ($6.95, limited series)

J2 #10 © MAR

Judomaster #94 © CC

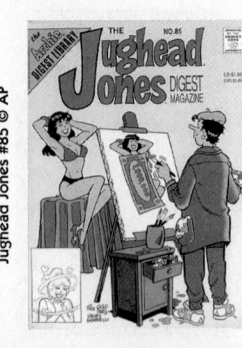

Jughead Jones #85 © AP

	GD 2.0	VG 4.0	FN 6.0	VF 8.0	VF/NM 9.0	NM- 9.2

1,2-Batman, Dr. Mid-Nite and Hourman vs. WW2 Joker; Tony Harris-c/a ... 7.00
JSA: The Liberty Files TPB (2004, $19.95) r/The Liberty File and The Unholy Three series ... 20.00

JSA: THE UNHOLY THREE (Elseworlds)(Sequel to JSA: The Liberty File)
DC Comics: 2003 - No. 2, 2003 ($6.95, limited series)

1,2-Batman, Superman and Hourman; Tony Harris-c/a ... 7.00

J2 (Also see A-Next and Juggernaut)
Marvel Comics: Oct., 1998 - No. 12, Sept, 1999 ($1.99)

1-12:1-Juggernaut's son; Lim-a. 2-Two covers; X-People app. 3-J2 battles the Hulk ... 2.50
Spider-Girl Presents Juggernaut Jr. Vol.1: Secrets & Lies (2006, $7.99, digest) r/#1-6 ... 8.00

JUBILEE (X-Men)
Marvel Comics: Nov, 2004 - No. 6, Apr, 2005 ($2.99)

1-6: 1-Jubilee in a Los Angeles high school; Kirkman-s; Casey Jones-c ... 3.00

JUDE, THE FORGOTTEN SAINT
Catechetical Guild Education Soc.: 1954 (16 pgs.; 8x11"; full color; paper-c)

nn ... 5 ... 10 ... 15 ... 22 ... 26 ... 30

J.U.D.G.E.: THE SECRET RAGE
Image Comics: Mar, 2000 - No. 3, May, 2000 ($2.95)

1-3-Greg Horn-s/c/a ... 3.00

JUDGE COLT
Gold Key: Oct, 1969 - No. 4, Sept, 1970

1 ... 3 ... 6 ... 9 ... 16 ... 23 ... 30
2-4 ... 2 ... 4 ... 6 ... 9 ... 13 ... 16

JUDGE DREDD (...Classics #62 on; also see Batman - Judge Dredd, The Law of Dredd & 2000 A.D. Monthly)
**Eagle Comics/IPC Magazines Ltd./Quality Comics #34-35, V2#1-37/
Fleetway #38 on:** Nov, 1983 - No. 35, 1986; V2#1, Oct, 1986 - No. 77, 1993

1-Bolland-c/a ... 6.00
2-35 ... 3.00
V2#1-77: 1-('86)-New look begins. 20-Begin $1.50-c. 21/22, 23/24-Two issue numbers in one.
28-1st app. Megaman (super-hero). 39-Begin $1.75-c. 51-Begin $1.95-c. 53-Bolland-a.
57-Reprints 1st published Judge Dredd story ... 2.50
Special 1 ... 2.50
NOTE: Bolland a-1-6, 8, 10; c-1-10, 15. Guice c-V2#23/24, 26, 27.

JUDGE DREDD (3rd Series)
DC Comics: Aug, 1994 - No. 18, Jan, 1996 ($1.95)

1-18: 12-Begin $2.25-c ... 2.50
nn ($5.95)-Movie adaptation, Sienkiewicz-c ... 6.00

JUDGE DREDD'S CRIME FILE
Eagle Comics: Aug, 1989 - No. 6, Feb, 1986 ($1.25, limited series)

1-6: 1-Byrne-a ... 2.50

JUDGE DREDD: LEGENDS OF THE LAW
DC Comics: Dec, 1994 - No. 13, Dec, 1995 ($1.95)

1-13: 1-5-Dorman-c ... 2.50

JUDGE DREDD: THE EARLY CASES
Eagle Comics: Feb, 1986 - No. 6, Jul, 1986 ($1.25, Mega-series, Mando paper)

1-6: 2000 A.D.-r ... 2.50

JUDGE DREDD: THE JUDGE CHILD QUEST (Judge Child in indicia)
Eagle Comics: Aug, 1984 - No. 5, Oct, 1984 ($1.25, Lim. series, Baxter paper)

1-5: 2000A.D.-r; Bolland-c/a ... 2.50

JUDGE DREDD: THE MEGAZINE
Fleetway/Quality: 1991 - Present ($4.95, stiff-c, squarebound, 52 pgs.)

1-3 ... 5.00

JUDGE DREDD VS. ALIENS: INCUBUS
Dark Horse Comics: March, 2003 - No. 4, June, 2003 ($2.99, limited series)

1-4-Flint-a/Wagner & Diggle-s ... 3.00

JUDGE PARKER
Argo: Feb, 1956 - No. 2, 1956

1-Newspaper strip reprints ... 7 ... 14 ... 21 ... 35 ... 43 ... 50
2 ... 5 ... 10 ... 15 ... 24 ... 30 ... 35

JUDGMENT DAY
Awesome Entertainment: June, 1997 - No. 3, Oct, 1997 ($2.50, limited series)

1-3: 1 Alpha-Moore-s/Liefeld-c/a(p) flashback art by various in all. 2 Omega.
3 Final Judgment. All have a variant cover by Dave Gibbons ... 2.50
...Aftermath ($3.50) Moore-s/Kane-a; Youngblood, Glory, New Men, Maximage, Allies and

Spacehunter short stories. Also has a variant cover by Dave Gibbons ... 3.50
TPB (Checker Books, 2003, $16.95) r/series ... 17.00

JUDO JOE
Jay-Jay Corp.: Aug, 1953 - No. 3, Dec, 1953 (Judo lessons in each issue)

1-Drug ring story ... 10 ... 20 ... 30 ... 58 ... 79 ... 100
2,3: 3-Hypo needle story ... 8 ... 16 ... 24 ... 40 ... 50 ... 60

JUDOMASTER (Gun Master #84-89) (Also see Crisis on Infinite Earths, Sarge Steel #6 & Special War Series)
Charlton Comics: No. 89, May-June, 1966 - No. 98, Dec, 1967 (Two No. 89's)

89-3rd app. Judomaster ... 4 ... 8 ... 12 ... 24 ... 37 ... 50
90-Origin of Thunderbolt ... 4 ... 8 ... 12 ... 22 ... 34 ... 45
91-Sarge Steel begins ... 3 ... 6 ... 9 ... 21 ... 32 ... 42
92-98: 93-Intro. Tiger ... 3 ... 6 ... 9 ... 20 ... 30 ... 40
93,94,96,98 (Modern Comics reprint, 1977) ... 4.00
NOTE: Morisi Thunderbolt #90. #91 has 1 pg. biography on writer/artist Frank McLaughlin.

JUDY CANOVA (Formerly My Experience) (Stage, screen, radio)
Fox Features Syndicate: No. 23, May, 1950 - No. 3, Sept, 1950

23(#1)-Wood-c,a(p)? ... 23 ... 46 ... 69 ... 130 ... 205 ... 280
24-Wood-a(p) ... 22 ... 44 ... 66 ... 126 ... 198 ... 270
3-Wood-c; Wood/Orlando-a ... 24 ... 48 ... 72 ... 139 ... 220 ... 300

JUDY GARLAND (See Famous Stars)

JUDY JOINS THE WAVES
Toby Press: 1951 (For U.S. Navy)

nn ... 7 ... 14 ... 21 ... 35 ... 43 ... 50

JUGGERNAUT (See X-Men)
Marvel Comics: Apr, 1997, Nov, 1999 ($2.99, one-shots)

1-(4/97) Kelly-s/ Rouleau-a ... 3.00
1-(11/99) Casey-s; Eighth Day x-over; Thor, Iron Man, Spidey app. ... 3.00

JUGHEAD (Formerly Archie's Pal...)
Archie Publications: No. 127, Dec, 1965 - No. 352, June, 1987

127-130: 129-LBJ on cover ... 3 ... 6 ... 9 ... 16 ... 23 ... 30
131,133,135-160(9/68) ... 3 ... 6 ... 9 ... 14 ... 19 ... 24
132,134: 132-Shield-c; The Fly & Black Hood app.; Shield cameo.
    134-Shield-c ... 3 ... 6 ... 9 ... 20 ... 30 ... 40
161-180 ... 2 ... 4 ... 6 ... 10 ... 14 ... 18
181-199 ... 2 ... 4 ... 6 ... 8 ... 11 ... 14
200(1/72) ... 2 ... 4 ... 6 ... 9 ... 13 ... 16
201-240(5/75) ... 1 ... 3 ... 4 ... 6 ... 8 ... 10
241-270(11/77) ... 1 ... 2 ... 3 ... 5 ... 6 ... 8
271-299 ... 1 ... 2 ... 3 ... 4 ... 5 ... 7
300(5/80)-Anniversary issue; infinity-c ... 1 ... 2 ... 3 ... 5 ... 6 ... 8
301-320(1/82) ... 5.00
321-324,326-352 ... 4.00
325-(10/82) Cheryl Blossom app. (not on cover); same month as intro. (cover & story)
    in Archie's Girls, Betty & Veronica #320; Jason Blossom app.; DeCarlo-a
    ... 3 ... 6 ... 9 ... 18 ... 27 ... 35

JUGHEAD (2nd Series) (Becomes Archie's Pal Jughead Comics #46 on)
Archie Enterprises: Aug, 1987 - No. 45, May, 1993 (.75/$1.00/$1.25)

1 ... 1 ... 2 ... 3 ... 4 ... 5 ... 7
2-10 ... 4.00
11-45: 4-X-Mas issue. 17-Colan-c/a ... 3.00

JUGHEAD & FRIENDS DIGEST MAGAZINE
Archie Publ.: June, 2005 - Present ($2.39/$2.49, digest-size)

1-25: 1-That Wilkin Boy app. ... 2.50

JUGHEAD AS CAPTAIN HERO (See Archie as Pureheart the Powerful, Archie Giant Series Magazine #142 & Life With Archie)
Archie Publications: Oct, 1966 - No. 7, Nov, 1967

1-Super hero parody ... 6 ... 12 ... 18 ... 43 ... 69 ... 95
2 ... 4 ... 8 ... 12 ... 28 ... 44 ... 60
3-7 ... 4 ... 8 ... 12 ... 24 ... 37 ... 50

JUGHEAD JONES COMICS DIGEST, THE (...Magazine No. 10-64;
Jughead Jones Digest Magazine #65)
Archie Publ.: June, 1977 - No. 100, May, 1996 ($1.35/$1.50/$1.75, digest-size, 128 pgs.)

1-Neal Adams-a; Capt. Hero-r ... 3 ... 6 ... 9 ... 20 ... 30 ... 40
2(9/77)-Neal Adams-a ... 3 ... 6 ... 9 ... 15 ... 21 ... 26
3-6,8-10 ... 2 ... 4 ... 6 ... 10 ... 14 ... 18
7-Origin Jaguar-r; N. Adams-a. ... 2 ... 4 ... 6 ... 11 ... 16 ... 20

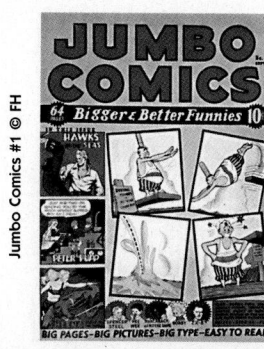

Jughead's Folly #1 © AP

Jumbo Comics #1 © FH

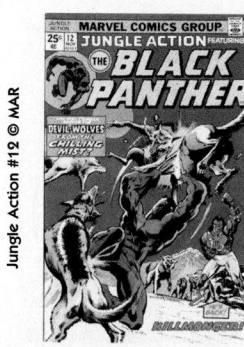

Jungle Action #12 © MAR

	GD 2.0	VG 4.0	FN 6.0	VF 8.0	VF/NM 9.0	NM- 9.2
11-20: 13-r/1957 Jughead's Folly	1	3	4	6	8	10
21-50	1	2	3	4	5	7
51-70						5.00
71-100						3.00

JUGHEAD'S BABY TALES
Archie Comics: Spring, 1994 - No. 2, Wint. 1994 ($2.00, 52 pgs.)

1,2: 1-Bound-in pull-out poster						4.00

JUGHEAD'S DINER
Archie Comics: Apr, 1990 - No. 7, Apr, 1991 ($1.00)

1						4.00
2-7						2.50

JUGHEAD'S DOUBLE DIGEST (...Magazine #5)
Archie Comics: Oct, 1989 - Present ($2.25 - $3.69)

1	2	4	6	8	10	12
2-10: 2,5-Capt. Hero stories	1	2	3	5	6	8
11-25						5.00
26-136: 58-Begin $2.99-c. 66-Begin $3.19-c. 75-Begin $3.29-c. 91-Begin $3.59-c						3.75

JUGHEAD'S EAT-OUT COMIC BOOK MAGAZINE (See Archie Giant Series Magazine No. 170)

JUGHEAD'S FANTASY
Archie Publications: Aug, 1960 - No. 3, Dec, 1960

1	16	32	48	118	209	300
2	10	20	30	71	126	180
3	8	16	24	58	97	135

JUGHEAD'S FOLLY
Archie Publications (Close-Up): 1957 (36 pgs.)(one-shot)

1-Jughead a la Elvis (Rare) (1st reference to Elvis in comics?)	50	100	150	305	503	700

JUGHEAD'S JOKES
Archie Publications: Aug, 1967 - No. 78, Sept, 1982
(No. 1-8, 38 on: reg. size; No. 9-23: 68 pgs.; No. 24-37: 52 pgs.)

1	6	12	18	41	66	90
2	4	8	12	22	34	45
3-8	3	6	9	16	23	30
9,10 (68 pgs.)	3	6	9	18	27	35
11-23(4/71) (68 pgs.)	3	6	9	16	22	28
24-37(1/74) (52 pgs.)	2	4	6	10	14	18
38-50(9/76)	1	2	3	5	7	9
51-78						6.00

JUGHEAD'S PAL HOT DOG (See Laugh #14 for 1st app.)
Archie Comics: Jan, 1990 - No. 5, Oct, 1990 ($1.00)

1						4.00
2-5						2.50

JUGHEAD'S SOUL FOOD
Spire Christian Comics (Fleming H. Revell Co.): 1979 (49¢/59¢)

nn-Low print run	2	4	6	9	13	16

JUGHEAD'S TIME POLICE
Archie Comics: July, 1990 - No. 6, May, 1991 ($1.00, bi-monthly)

1						4.00
2-6: Colan a-3-6p; c-3-6						2.50

JUGHEAD WITH ARCHIE DIGEST (...Plus Betty & Veronica & Reggie Too No. 1,2; ...Magazine #33-?, 101-on; ...Comics Digest Mag.)
Archie Pub.: Mar, 1974 - No. 200, May, 2005 ($1.00-$2.39)

1	5	10	15	32	51	70
2	4	8	12	22	34	45
3-10	3	6	9	17	25	32
11-13,15-17,19,20: Capt. Hero-r in #14-16; Capt. Pureheart #17,19	2	4	6	9	13	16
14,18,21,22-Pureheart the Powerful in #18,21,22	2	4	6	10	14	18
23-30: 29-The Shield-r. 30-The Fly-r	1	3	4	6	8	10
31-50,100	1	2	3	5	6	8
51-99	1	2	3	4	5	7
101-121						4.00
122-200: 156-Begin $2.19-c. 180-Begin $2.39-c						2.50

JUKE BOX COMICS
Famous Funnies: Mar, 1948 - No. 6, Jan, 1949

1-Toth-c/a; Hollingsworth-a	40	80	120	235	368	500
2-Transvestism story	24	48	72	139	220	300

	GD 2.0	VG 4.0	FN 6.0	VF 8.0	VF/NM 9.0	NM- 9.2
3-6: 3-Peggy Lee story. 4-Jimmy Durante line drawn-c. 6-Features Desi Arnaz plus Arnaz line drawn-c	18	36	54	105	165	225

JUMBO COMICS (Created by S.M. Iger)
Fiction House Magazines (Real Adv. Publ. Co.): Sept, 1938 - No. 167, Mar, 1953 (No. 1-3: 68 pgs.; No. 4-8: 52 pgs.)(No. 1-8 oversized-10-1/2x14-1/2"; black & white)

1-(Rare)-Sheena Queen of the Jungle(1st app.) by Meskin, Hawks of the Seas (The Hawk #10 on; see Feature Funnies #3) by Eisner, The Hunchback by Dick Briefer (ends #8), Wilton of the West (ends #24), Inspector Dayton (ends #67) & ZX-5 (ends #140) begin; 1st comic art by Jack Kirby (Count of Monte Cristo & Wilton of the West); Mickey Mouse appears (1 panel) with brief biography of Walt Disney; 1st app. Peter Pupp by Bob Kane. Note: Sheena was created by Iger for publication in England as a newspaper strip. The early issues of Jumbo contain Sheena strip-r; multiple panel-c 1,2,7	2150	4300	6450	21,500	–	–
2-(Rare)-Origin Sheena. Diary of Dr. Hayward by Kirby (also #3) plus 2 other stories; contains strip from Universal Film featuring Edgar Bergen & Charlie McCarthy plus-c (preview of film)	700	1400	2100	7000	–	–
3-Last Kirby issue	500	1000	1500	5000	–	–
4-(Scarce)-Origin The Hawk by Eisner; Wilton of the West by Fine (ends #14)(1st comic work); Count of Monte Cristo by Fine (ends #15); The Diary of Dr. Hayward by Fine (cont'd #8,9)	460	920	1380	4600	–	–
5-Christmas-c	395	790	1185	3950	–	–
6-8-Last B&W issue. #8 was a 1939 N. Y. World's Fair Special Edition; Frank Buck's Jungleland story	355	710	1065	3550	–	–
9-Stuart Taylor begins by Fine (ends #140); Fine-c; 1st color issue (8-9/39)-1st Sheena (jungle) cover; 8-1/4x10-1/4" (oversized in width only)	335	670	1005	3350	–	–
10-Regular size 68 pg. issues begin; Sheena dons new costume w/origin costume; Stuart Taylor scifi-c classic Lou Fine-c.	200	400	600	1250	2075	2900
11-13: 12-The Hawk-c by Eisner. 13-Eisner-c	131	262	393	819	1360	1900
14-Intro. Lightning (super-hero) on-c only	134	268	402	838	1394	1950
15,17-20: 15-1st Lightning story and begins, ends #41. 17-Lightning part-c	83	166	249	519	860	1200
16-Lightning-c	98	196	294	613	1019	1425
21-30: 22-1st Tom, Dick & Harry; origin The Hawk retold. 25-Midnight the Black Stallion begins, ends #65	62	124	186	388	644	900
31-40: 31-(9/41)-1st app. Mars God of War in Stuart Taylor story (see Planet Comics #15). 35-Shows V2#11 (correct number does not appear)	52	104	156	317	521	725
41-50: 42-Ghost Gallery begins, ends #167	40	80	120	244	392	540
51-60: 52-Last Tom, Dick & Harry	36	72	108	208	329	450
61-70: 68-Sky Girl begins, ends #130; not in #79	28	56	84	162	256	350
71-93,95-99: 89-ZX5 becomes a private eye.	23	46	69	132	209	285
94-Used in Love and Death by Legman	25	50	75	145	228	310
100	25	50	75	145	228	310
101-121	21	42	63	122	191	260
121-140,150-158: 155-Used in POP, pg. 98	18	36	54	105	165	225
141-149-Two Sheena stories. 141-Long Bow, Indian Boy begins, ends #160	19	38	57	109	172	235
159-163: Space Comics serial in all. 160-Last jungle-c (6/52). 161-Ghost Gallery covers begin, end #167. 163-Suicide Smith app.	16	32	48	94	147	200
164-The Star Pirate begins, ends #165	16	32	48	94	147	200
165-167: 165,167-Space Rangers app.	16	32	48	94	147	200

NOTE: *Bondage covers, negligee panels, torture, etc. are common in this series. Hawks of the Seas, Inspector Dayton, Spies in Action, Sport Shorts, & Uncle Otto by Eisner, #1-7. Hawk-#10-15. Eisner c-1-8, 12-14. 1pg. Patsy pin-ups in 92-97, 99-101. Sheena by Meskin-#1, 4; by Powell-#2, 3, 5-28; Powell c-14, 16, 17, 19. Powell/Eisner c-15. Sky Girl by Matt Baker-#69-78, 80-130. ZX-5 & Ghost Gallery by Kamen-#90-130. Bailey a-3-8. Briefer a-1-8, 10. Fine a-14; c-9-11. Kamen a-101, 105, 123, 132; c-105, 121-145. Bob Kane a-1-8. Whitman c-146-167(most). Jungle c-9, 13, 15, 17 on.*

JUNGLE ACTION
Atlas Comics (IPC): Oct, 1954 - No. 6, Aug, 1955

1-Leopard Girl begins by Al Hartley (#1,3); Jungle Boy by Forte; Maneely-a in all	37	74	111	214	340	465
2-(3-D effect cover)	37	74	111	214	340	465
3-6: 3-Last precode (2/55)	23	46	69	147	209	285

NOTE: *Maneely c-1, 5; Romita a-3, 6. Shores a-3, 6; c-3, 4?.*

JUNGLE ACTION (...& Black Panther #18-21?)
Marvel Comics Group: Oct, 1972 - No. 24, Nov, 1976

1-Lorna, Jann-r (All reprints in 1-4)	2	4	6	11	16	20
2-4	2	4	6	8	10	12
5-Black Panther begins (r/Avengers #62)	3	6	9	16	23	30
6-New solo Black Panther stories begin	3	6	9	15	21	26
7,9,10: 9-Contains pull-out centerfold ad by Mark Jewelers	2	4	6	8	11	14

	GD 2.0	VG 4.0	FN 6.0	VF 8.0	VF/NM 9.0	NM- 9.2
8-Origin Black Panther	2	4	6	11	16	20
11-20,23,24: 19-23-KKK x-over. 23-r/#22. 24-1st Wind Eagle; story contd in Marvel Premiere #51-#53	1	2	3	5	7	9
21,22-(Regular 25¢ edition)(5,7/76)	1	2	3	5	7	9
21,22-(30¢-c variant, limited distribution)	3	6	9	14	20	25

NOTE: **Buckler** a-6-9p, 22; c-8p, 12p. **Buscema** a-5p; c-22. **Byrne** c-23. **Gil Kane** a-8p; c-2, 4, 10p, 11p, 13-17, 19, 24. **Kirby** c-18. **Maneely** c-1. **Russell** a-13i. **Starlin** c-3p.

JUNGLE ADVENTURES
Super Comics: 1963 - 1964 (Reprints)

	GD 2.0	VG 4.0	FN 6.0	VF 8.0	VF/NM 9.0	NM- 9.2
10,12,15,17,18: 10-r/Terrors of the Jungle #4 & #10(Rulah). 12-r/Zoot #14(Rulah).15-r/Kaanga from Jungle #152 & Tiger Girl. 17-All Jo-Jo-r. 18-Reprints/White Princess of the Jungle #1; no Kinstler-a; origin of both White Princess & Cap'n Courage	3	6	9	19	29	38

JUNGLE ADVENTURES
Skywald Comics: Mar, 1971 - No. 3, June, 1971 (25¢, 52 pgs.) (Pre-code reprints & new-s)

	GD 2.0	VG 4.0	FN 6.0	VF 8.0	VF/NM 9.0	NM- 9.2
1-Zangar origin; reprints of Jo-Jo, Blue Gorilla(origin)/White Princess #3, Kinstler-r/White Princess #2	3	6	9	16	22	28
2,3: 2-Zangar, Sheena-r/Sheena #17 & Jumbo #162, Jo-Jo, origin Slave Girl-r. 3-Zangar, Jo-Jo, White Princess, Rulah-r	2	4	6	10	14	18

JUNGLE BOOK (See King Louie and Mowgli, Movie Comics, Mowgli..., Walt Disney Showcase #45 & Walt Disney's The Jungle Book)

JUNGLE CAT (Disney)
Dell Publishing Co.: No. 1136, Sept-Nov, 1960 (one shot)

	GD 2.0	VG 4.0	FN 6.0	VF 8.0	VF/NM 9.0	NM- 9.2
Four Color 1136-Movie, photo-c	6	12	18	43	69	95

JUNGLE COMICS
Fiction House Magazines: 1/40 - No. 157, 3/53; No. 158, Spr, 1953 - No. 163, Summer, 1954

	GD 2.0	VG 4.0	FN 6.0	VF 8.0	VF/NM 9.0	NM- 9.2
1-Origin The White Panther, Kaanga, Lord of the Jungle, Tabu, Wizard of the Jungle; Wambi, the Jungle Boy, Camilla & Capt. Terry Thunder begin (all 1st app.). Lou Fine-c	457	914	1371	3462	5600	8000
2-Fantomah, Mystery Woman of the Jungle begins, ends #51; The Red Panther begins, ends #26	166	332	498	1038	1719	2400
3,4	134	268	402	838	1394	1950
5-Classic Eisner-c	150	300	450	938	1557	2175
6-10: 7,8-Powell-c	79	158	237	494	822	1150
11-20: 13-Tuska-c	54	108	162	338	557	775
21-30: 25-Shows V2#1 (correct number does not appear).#27-New origin Fantomah, Daughter of the Pharoahs; Camilla dons new costume	45	90	135	275	455	635
31-40	37	74	111	213	337	460
41,43-50	32	64	96	186	293	400
42-Kaanga by Crandall, 12 pgs.	34	68	102	195	308	420
51-60	28	56	84	162	256	350
61-70: 67-Cover swipes Crandall splash pg. in #42	25	50	75	145	228	310
71-80: 79-New origin Tabu	22	44	66	128	202	275
81-97,99	21	42	63	122	191	260
98-Used in SOTI, pg. 185 & illo "In ordinary comic books, there are pictures within pictures for children who know how to look;" used by N.Y. Legis. Comm.	33	66	99	190	300	410
100	25	50	75	145	228	310
101-110: 104-In Camilla story, villain is Dr. Wertham	20	40	60	117	184	250
111-120: 118-Clyde Beatty app.	19	38	57	112	176	240
121-130	18	36	54	105	165	225
131-163: 135-Desert Panther begins in Terry Thunder (origin), not in #137; ends (dies) #138. 139-Last 52 pg. issue. 141-Last Tabu. 143,145-Used in POP, pg. 99. 151-Last Camilla & Terry Thunder. 152-Tiger Girl begins. 158-Last Wambi; Sheena app.	16	32	48	94	147	200
I.W. Reprint #1,9: 1-r/? 9-r/#151	3	6	9	17	25	32

NOTE: Bondage covers, negligee panels, torture, etc. are common to this series. Camilla by **Fran Hopper** #70-92; by **Baker** #69, 100-113, 115, 116; by **Lubbers** #97-99 by **Tuska** #63, 65. Kaanga by **John Celardo** #80-113; by **Larsen** #71, 75-79; by **Moreira** #58, 60, 61, 63-70, 72-74; by **Tuska** #37, 62; by **Whitman** #114-163. Tabu by **Larsen** #59-75, 82-92; by **Whitman** #93-115. Terry Thunder by **Hopper** #71, 72; by **Celardo** #78, 79; by **Lubbers** #80-85. Tiger Girl by **Baker** #152, 153, 155-157, 159. Wambi by **Baker** #62-67, 74. **Astarita** c-45, 46. **Celardo** a-78; c-98-113. **Crandall** c-67 from splash pg. **Eisner** c-2, 5, 6. **Fine** c-1. **Larsen** a-65, 66, 71, 72, 74, 75, 79, 83, 84, 87-90. **Moreira** c-43, 44. **Morisi** a-51. **Powell** c-7, 8. **Sultan** c-3, 4. **Tuska** c-13. **Whitman** c-132-163(most). **Zolnerowich** c-11, 12, 18-41.

JUNGLE COMICS
Blackthorne Publishing: May, 1988 - No. 4 ($2.00, B&W/color)

1-Dave Stevens-c; B. Jones scripts in all.						3.00
2-4: 2-B&W-a begins						2.50

JUNGLE GIRL (See Lorna, the...)

JUNGLE GIRL (Nyoka, Jungle Girl No. 2 on)
Fawcett Publications: Fall, 1942 (one-shot)(No month listed)

	GD 2.0	VG 4.0	FN 6.0	VF 8.0	VF/NM 9.0	NM- 9.2
1-Bondage-c; photo of Kay Aldridge who played Nyoka in movie serial app. on-c. Adaptation of the classic Republic movie serial Perils of Nyoka. 1st comic to devote entire contents to a movie serial adaptation	124	248	372	775	1288	1800

JUNGLE GIRL
Dynamite Entertainment: No. 0, 2007 - Present (25¢/$2.99)

0-(25¢-c) Eight page preview; preview of Superpowers w/Alex Ross-a						2.25
1-Frank Cho-plot/cover; Batista-a/variant-c						3.00

JUNGLE GIRLS
AC Comics: 1989 - No. 16, 1993 (B&W)

1-16: 1-4,10,13-16-New story & "good girl" reprints. 5-9,11,12-All g.g. reprints (Baker, Powell, Lubbers, others)						3.00

JUNGLE JIM (Also see Ace Comics)
Standard Comics (Best Books): No. 11, Jan, 1949 - No. 20, Apr, 1951

	GD 2.0	VG 4.0	FN 6.0	VF 8.0	VF/NM 9.0	NM- 9.2
11	11	22	33	62	86	110
12-20	8	16	24	42	54	65

JUNGLE JIM
Dell Publishing Co.: No. 490, 8/53 - No. 1020, 8-10/59 (Painted-c)

	GD 2.0	VG 4.0	FN 6.0	VF 8.0	VF/NM 9.0	NM- 9.2
Four Color 490(#1)	7	14	21	49	80	110
Four Color 565(#2, 6/54)	5	10	15	30	48	65
3(10-12/54)-5	4	8	12	28	44	60
6-19(1-3/59), Four Color 1020(#20)	4	8	12	26	41	55

JUNGLE JIM
King Features Syndicate: No. 5, Dec, 1967

	GD 2.0	VG 4.0	FN 6.0	VF 8.0	VF/NM 9.0	NM- 9.2
5-Reprints Dell #5; Wood-c	2	4	6	10	14	18

JUNGLE JIM (Continued from Dell series)
Charlton Comics: No. 22, Feb, 1969 - No. 28, Feb, 1970 (#21 was an overseas edition only)

	GD 2.0	VG 4.0	FN 6.0	VF 8.0	VF/NM 9.0	NM- 9.2
22-Dan Flagg begins; Ditko/Wood-a	3	6	9	21	32	42
23-26: 23-Last Dan Flagg; Howard-c. 24-Jungle People begin	3	6	9	15	21	26
27,28: 27-Ditko/Howard-a. 28-Ditko-a	3	6	9	17	25	32

NOTE: Ditko cover of #22 reprints story panels.

JUNGLE JO
Fox Feature Syndicate (Hero Books): Mar, 1950 - No. 3, Sept, 1950

	GD 2.0	VG 4.0	FN 6.0	VF 8.0	VF/NM 9.0	NM- 9.2
nn-Jo-Jo blanked out in titles of interior stories, leaving Congo King; came out after Jo-Jo #29 (intended as Jo-Jo #30?)	48	96	144	293	484	675
1-Tangi begins; part Wood-a	50	100	150	305	503	700
2,3	40	80	120	235	368	500

JUNGLE LIL (Dorothy Lamour #2 on; also see Feature Stories Magazine)
Fox Feature Syndicate (Hero Books): April, 1950

	GD 2.0	VG 4.0	FN 6.0	VF 8.0	VF/NM 9.0	NM- 9.2
1	40	80	120	240	383	525

JUNGLE TALES (Jann of the Jungle No. 8 on)
Atlas Comics (CSI): Sept, 1954 - No. 7, Sept, 1955

	GD 2.0	VG 4.0	FN 6.0	VF 8.0	VF/NM 9.0	NM- 9.2
1-Jann of the Jungle	39	78	117	225	355	485
2-7: 3-Last precode (1/55)	26	52	78	152	239	325

NOTE: **Heath** c-5. **Reck** c-7. **Maneely** a-2; c-1, 3. **Shores** a-5-7; c-4, 6. **Tuska** a-2.

JUNGLE TALES OF TARZAN
Charlton Comics: Dec, 1964 - No. 4, July, 1965

	GD 2.0	VG 4.0	FN 6.0	VF 8.0	VF/NM 9.0	NM- 9.2
1	6	12	18	37	59	80
2-4	4	8	12	24	37	50

NOTE: **Giordano** c-3p. **Glanzman** a-1-3. **Montes/Bache** a-4.

JUNGLE TERROR (See Harvey Comics Hits No. 54)

JUNGLE THRILLS (Formerly Sports Thrills; Terrors of the Jungle #17 on)
Star Publications: No. 16, Feb, 1952; Dec, 1953; No. 7, 1954

	GD 2.0	VG 4.0	FN 6.0	VF 8.0	VF/NM 9.0	NM- 9.2
16-Phantom Lady & Rulah story-reprint/All Top No. 15; used in POP, pg. 98,99; L. B. Cole-c	49	98	147	299	492	685
3-D 1(12/53, 25¢)-Came w/glasses; Jungle Lil & Jungle Jo appear; L. B. Cole-c	49	98	147	299	492	685
7-Titled 'Picture Scope Jungle Adventures,' (1954, 36 pgs, 15¢)-3-D effect c/stories; story & coloring book; Disbrow-a/script; L.B. Cole-c	49	98	147	299	492	685

JUNGLE TWINS, THE (Tono & Kono)
Gold Key/Whitman: No. 18: Apr, 1972 - No. 17, Nov, 1975; No. 18, May, 1982

	GD 2.0	VG 4.0	FN 6.0	VF 8.0	VF/NM 9.0	NM- 9.2
1	3	6	9	14	19	24
2-5	2	4	6	8	10	12
6-18: 18(Whitman, 5/82)-Reprints	1	2	3	5	6	8

NOTE: UFO c/story No. 13. Painted-c No. 1-17. **Spiegle** c-18.

JUNGLE WAR STORIES (Guerrilla War No. 12 on)

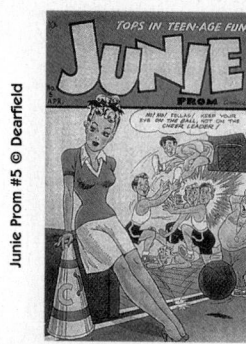

Junie Prom #5 © Dearfield

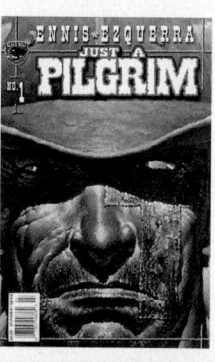

Just a Pilgrim #1 © Black Bull

Justice #12 © DC

	GD 2.0	VG 4.0	FN 6.0	VF 8.0	VF/NM 9.0	NM- 9.2

Dell Publishing Co.: July-Sept, 1962 - No. 11, Apr-June, 1965 (Painted-c)

	GD 2.0	VG 4.0	FN 6.0	VF 8.0	VF/NM 9.0	NM- 9.2
01-384-209 (#1)	4	8	12	22	34	45
2-11	3	6	9	16	23	30

JUNIE PROM (Also see Dexter Comics)
Dearfield Publishing Co.: Winter, 1947-48 - No. 7, Aug, 1949

1-Teen-age	14	28	42	80	115	150
2	9	18	27	47	61	75
3-7	8	16	24	40	50	60

JUNIOR
Fantagraphics Books: June, 2000 - No. 5, Jan, 2001 ($2.95, B&W)

1-5-Peter Bagge-s/a						3.00

JUNIOR CARROT PATROL (Jr. Carrot Patrol #2)
Dark Horse Comics: May, 1989; No. 2, Nov, 1990 ($2.00, B&W)

1,2-Flaming Carrot spin-off. 1-Bob Burden-c(i)						2.50

JUNIOR COMICS (Formerly Li'l Pan; becomes Western Outlaws with #17)
Fox Feature Syndicate: No. 9, Sept, 1947 - No. 16, July, 1948

9-Feldstein-c/a; headlights-c	110	220	330	688	1144	1600
10-16-Feldstein-c/a; headlights-c on all	100	200	300	625	1038	1450

JUNIOR FUNNIES (Formerly Tiny Tot Funnies No. 9)
Harvey Publ. (King Features Synd.): No. 10, Aug, 1951 - No. 13, Feb, 1952

10-Partial reprints in all; Blondie, Dagwood, Daisy, Henry, Popeye, Felix, Katzenjammer Kids	6	12	18	28	34	40
11-13	5	10	15	24	30	35

JUNIOR HOPP COMICS
Stanmor Publ.: Feb, 1952 - No. 3, July, 1952

1-Teenage humor	10	20	30	54	72	90
2,3- 3-Dave Berg-a	6	12	18	31	38	45

JUNIOR MEDICS OF AMERICA, THE
E. R. Squire & Sons: No. 1359, 1957 (15¢)

1359	4	8	12	17	21	24

JUNIOR MISS
Timely/Marvel (CnPC): Wint, 1944; No. 24, Apr, 1947 - No. 39, Aug, 1950

1-Frank Sinatra & June Allyson life story	31	62	93	178	282	385
24-Formerly The Human Torch #23?	15	30	45	84	127	170
25-38: 29,31,34-Cindy-c/stories (others?)	12	24	36	52	69	85
39-Kurtzman-a	11	22	33	60	83	105

NOTE: Painted-c 35-37, 38-all romance. 36, 38-mostly teen humor.

JUNIOR PARTNERS (Formerly Oral Roberts' True Stories)
Oral Roberts Evangelistic Assn.: No. 120, Aug, 1959 - V3#2, Dec, 1961

120(#1)	4	8	12	24	37	50
2(9/59)	3	6	9	17	25	32
3-12(7/60)	2	4	6	13	18	22
V2#1(8/60)-5(12/60)	2	4	6	9	13	16
V3#1(1/61)-12	2	4	6	8	10	12

JUNIOR TREASURY (See Dell Junior...)

JUNIOR WOODCHUCKS GUIDE (Walt Disney's...)
Danbury Press: 1973 (8-3/4"x5-3/4", 214 pgs., hardcover)

nn-Illustrated text based on the long-standing J.W. Guide used by Donald Duck's nephews Huey, Dewey & Louie by Carl Barks. The guidebook was a popular plot device to enable the nephews to solve problems facing their uncle or Scrooge McDuck (scarce)

	5	10	15	35	55	75

JUNIOR WOODCHUCKS LIMITED SERIES (Walt Disney's...)
W. D. Publications (Disney): July, 1991 - No. 4, Oct, 1991 ($1.50, limited series; new & reprint-a)

1-4: 1-The Beagle Boys app.; Barks-r						2.50

JUNIOR WOODCHUCKS (See Huey, Dewey & Louie...)

JUNK CULTURE
DC Comics (Vertigo): July, 1997 - No. 2, Aug, 1997 ($2.50, limited series)

1,2: Ted McKeever-s/a in all						3.00

JURASSIC PARK
Topps Comics: June, 1993 - No. 4, Aug, 1993; No. 5, Oct, 1994 - No. 10, Feb, 1995

1-($2.50)-Newsstand Edition; Kane/Perez-a in all; 1-4: movie adaptation						2.50
1-($2.95)-Collector's Ed.; polybagged w/3 cards						4.00
1-Amberchrome Edition w/no price and ads	1	2	3	4	5	7
2-4-($2.50)-Newsstand Edition						2.50

	GD 2.0	VG 4.0	FN 6.0	VF 8.0	VF/NM 9.0	NM- 9.2
2,3-($2.95)-Collector's Ed.; polybagged w/3 cards						3.00
4-10: 4-($2.95)-Collector's Ed.; polybagged w/1 of 4 different action hologram trading card; Gil Kane/Perez-a. 5-becomes Advs. of						3.00
Annual 1 ($3.95, 5/95)						4.00
Trade paperback (1993, $9.95)-r/#1-4; bagged w/#0						10.00

JURASSIC PARK: RAPTOR
Topps Comics: Nov, 1993 - No. 2, Dec, 1993 ($2.95, limited series)

1,2: 1-Bagged w/3 trading cards & Zorro #0; Golden c-1,2						3.00

JURASSIC PARK: RAPTORS ATTACK
Topps Comics: Mar, 1994 - No. 4, June, 1994 ($2.50, limited series)

1-4-Michael Golden-c/frontispiece						2.50

JURASSIC PARK: RAPTORS HIJACK
Topps Comics: July, 1994 - No. 4, Oct, 1994 ($2.50, limited series)

1-4: Michael Golden-c/front piece						2.50

JUST A PILGRIM
Black Bull Entertainment: May, 2001 - No. 5, Sept, 2001 ($2.99)

Limited Preview Edition (12/00, $7.00) Ennis & Ezquerra interviews						7.00
1-Ennis-s/Ezquerra-a; two covers by Texeira & JG Jones						3.00
2-5: 2-Fabry-c. 3-Nowlan-c. 4-Sienkiewicz-c						3.00
TPB (11/01, $12.99) r/#1-5; Waid intro.						13.00

JUST A PILGRIM: GARDEN OF EDEN
Black Bull Entertainment: May, 2002 - No. 4, Aug, 2002 ($2.99, limited series)

Limited Preview Ed. (1/02, $7.00) Ennis & Ezquerra interviews; Jones-c						7.00
1-4-Ennis-s/Ezquerra-a						3.00
TPB (11/02, $12.99) r/#1-4; Gareb Shamus intro.						13.00

JUSTICE
Marvel Comics Group (New Universe): Nov, 1986 - No. 32, June, 1989

1-32: 26-32-$1.50-c (low print run)						2.50

JUSTICE
DC Comics: Oct, 2005 - No. 12, Aug, 2007 ($2.99/$3.50/$3.99, bi-monthly maxi-series)

1-Classic Justice League vs. The Legion of Doom; Alex Ross & Doug Braithwaite-a; Jim Krueger-s; two covers by Ross; Ross sketch pages						5.00
1-2nd & 3rd printings						4.00
2-($3.50)						4.00
2 (2nd printing), 3-11-($3.50)						3.50
12-($3.99) Two covers (Heroes & Villains)						4.00
...Volume One HC (2006, $19.99, dustjacket) r/#1-4; Krueger intro.; sketch pages						20.00
...Volume Two HC (2007, $19.99, dustjacket) r/#5-8; Krueger intro.; sketch pages						20.00

JUSTICE COMICS (Formerly Wacky Duck; Tales of Justice #53 on)
Marvel/Atlas Comics (NPP 7-9,4-19/CnPC 20-23/MjMC 24-38/Male 39-52): No. 7, Fall/47 - No. 9, 6/48; No. 4, 8/48 - No. 52, 3/55

7(#1, 1947)	30	60	90	174	275	375
8(#2)-Kurtzman-a "Giggles 'n' Grins" (3)	20	40	60	117	184	250
9(#3, 6/48)	18	36	54	103	162	220
4	16	32	48	92	144	195
5(9/48)-9: 8-Anti-Wertham editorial	14	28	42	82	121	160
10-15-Photo-c	12	24	36	69	97	125
16-30	11	22	33	60	83	105
31-40,42-52: 35-Gene Colan-a. 48-Last precode; Pakula & Tuska-a.	10	20	30	56	76	95
41-Electrocution-c	16	32	48	94	147	200

NOTE: Heath a-24. Maneely c-44, 52. Pakula a-43, 45, 48. Louis Ravielli a-39. Robinson a-22, 25, 41. Shores c-7(#1), 8(#2)? Tuska a-48. Wildey a-52.

JUSTICE: FOUR BALANCE
Marvel Comics: Sept, 1994 - No. 4, Dec, 1994 ($1.75, limited series)

1-4: 1-Thing & Firestar app.						2.50

JUSTICE, INC. (The Avenger) (Pulp)
National Periodical Publications: May-June, 1975 - No. 4, Nov-Dec, 1975

1-McWilliams-a, Kubert-c; origin	2	4	6	9	13	16
2-4: 2-4-Kirby-a(p), c-2,3p. 4-Kubert-c	2	4	6	9	12	15

NOTE: Adapted from Kenneth Robeson novel, creator of Doc Savage.

JUSTICE, INC.
DC Comics: 1989 - No. 2, 1989 ($3.95, 52 pgs., squarebound, mature)

1,2: Re-intro The Avenger; Andrew Helfer scripts & Kyle Baker-c/a						4.00

JUSTICE LEAGUE (...International #7-25; ...America #26 on)
DC Comics: May, 1987 - No. 113, Aug, 1996 (Also see Legends #6)

1-Batman, Green Lantern (Guy Gardner), Blue Beetle, Mr. Miracle, Capt. Marvel & Martian						

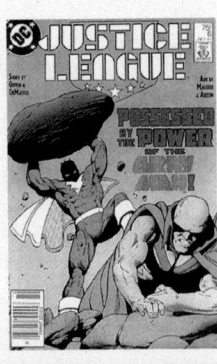

Justice League #6 © DC

Justice League Europe #5 © DC

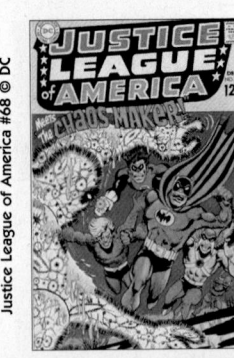

Justice League of America #68 © DC

	GD 2.0	VG 4.0	FN 6.0	VF 8.0	VF/NM 9.0	NM- 9.2
Manhunter begin	1	2	3	4	5	7
2,3: 3-Regular-c (white background)						5.00
3-Limited-c (yellow background, Superman logo)	4	8	12	24	37	50
4-10: 4-Booster Gold joins. 5-Origin Gray Man; Batman vs. Guy Gardner; Creeper app. 7-($1.25, 52 pgs.)-Capt. Marvel & Dr. Fate resign; Capt. Atom & Rocket Red join. 9,10-Millennium x-over						3.00
11-17,22,23,25-49,51-68,71-82: 16-Bruce Wayne-c/story. 31,32-J. L. Europe x-over. 58-Lobo app. 61-New team begins; swipes-c to J.L. of A. #1('60). 70-Newsstand version w/o outer-c. 71-Direct sales version w/black outer-c. 71-Newsstand version w/o outer-c. 80-Intro new Booster Gold. 82,83-Guy Gardner-c/stories						2.50
18-21,24,50: 18-21-Lobo app. 24-($1.50)-1st app. Justice League Europe. 50-($1.75, 52 pgs.)						3.00
69-Doomsday tie-in; takes place between Superman: The Man of Steel #18 & Superman #74						5.00
69,70-2nd printings						2.50
70-Funeral for a Friend part 1; red 3/4 outer-c						4.00
83-99,101-113: 92-(9/94)-Zero Hour x-over; Triumph app. 113-Green Lantern, Flash & Hawkman app.						2.50
100 ($3.95)-Foil-c; 52 pgs.						4.00
100 ($2.95)-Newstand						3.00
#0-(10/94) Zero Hour (publ between #92 & #93); new team begins (Hawkman, Flash, Wonder Woman, Metamorpho, Nuklon, Crimson Fox, Obsidian & Fire)						2.50
Annual 1-8,10 ('87-'94, '96, 68 pgs.): 2-Joker-c/story; Batman cameo. 5-Armageddon 2001 x-over; Silver ink 2nd print. 7-Bloodlines app. 8-Elseworlds story. 10-Legends of the Dead Earth						3.00
Annual 9 (1995, $3.50)-Year One story						3.50
Special 1,2 ('90,'91, 52 pgs.): 1-Giffen plots. 2-Staton-a(p)						3.00
Spectacular 1 (1992, $1.50, 52 pgs.)-Intro new JLI & JLE teams; ties into JLI #61 & JLE #37; two interlocking covers by Jurgens						3.00
A New Beginning Trade Paperback (1989, $12.95)-r/#1-7						13.00

NOTE: **Anderson** c-61i. **Austin** a-1i, 60i; c-1i. **Giffen** a-13; c-21p. **Guice** a-62i. **Maguire** a-1-12, 16-19, 22, 23. **Russell** c-1i; c-54i. **Willingham** a-30p, Annual 2.

JUSTICE LEAGUE ADVENTURES (Based on Cartoon Network series)
DC Comics: Jan, 2002 - No. 34, Oct, 2004 ($1.99/$2.25)

	GD 2.0	VG 4.0	FN 6.0	VF 8.0	VF/NM 9.0	NM- 9.2
1-Timm & Ross-c						3.00
2-32: 3-Nicieza-s. 5-Starro app. 10-Begin $2.25-c. 14-Includes 16 pg. insert for VERB with Haberlin CG-art. 15,29-Amancio-a. 16-McCloud-s. 20-Psycho Pirate app. 25,26-Adam Strange-c/app. 28-Legion of Super-Heroes app. 30-Kamandi app.						2.50
Free Comic Book Day giveaway - (See Promotional Comics section)						
TPB (2003, $9.95) r/#1,3,6,10-13; Timm/Ross-c from #1						10.00
...Vol. 1: The Magnificent Seven (2004, $6.95) digest-size reprints #3,6,10-12						7.00
...Vol. 2: Friends and Foes (2004, $6.95) digest-size reprints #13,14,16,19,20						7.00

JUSTICE LEAGUE: A MIDSUMMER'S NIGHTMARE
DC Comics: Sept, 1996 - No. 3, Nov, 1996 ($2.95, limited series, 38 pgs.)

	GD 2.0	VG 4.0	FN 6.0	VF 8.0	VF/NM 9.0	NM- 9.2
1-3: Re-establishes Superman, Batman, Green Lantern, The Martian Manhunter, Flash, Aquaman & Wonder Woman as the Justice League; Mark Waid & Fabian Nicieza co-scripts; Jeff Johnson & Darick Robertson-a(p); Kevin Maguire-c						5.00
TPB-(1997, $8.95) r/1-3						9.00

JUSTICE LEAGUE ELITE (See JLA #100 and JLA Secret Files 2004)
DC Comics: Sept, 2004 - No. 12, Aug, 2005 ($2.50)

	GD 2.0	VG 4.0	FN 6.0	VF 8.0	VF/NM 9.0	NM- 9.2
1-12-Flash, Green Arrow, Vera Black and others; Kelly-s/Mahnke-a. 5,6-JSA app.						2.50
JL Elite TPB (2005, $19.99) r/#1-4, Action #775, JLA #100, JLA Secret Files 2004						20.00

JUSTICE LEAGUE EUROPE (Justice League International #51 on)
DC Comics: Apr, 1989 - No. 68, Sept., 1994 (75¢/ $1.00/$1.25/$1.50)

	GD 2.0	VG 4.0	FN 6.0	VF 8.0	VF/NM 9.0	NM- 9.2
1-Giffen plots in all, breakdowns in 8,13-30; Justice League #1-c/swipe						3.00
2-10: 7-9-Batman app. 7,8-JLA x-over. 8,9-Superman app.						3.00
11-49: 12-Metal Men app. 20-22-Rogers-c/a(p). 33,34-Lobo vs. Despero. 37-New team begins; swipes-c to JLA #9; see JLA Spectacular						2.50
50-($2.50, 64 pgs.)-Battles Sonar						2.50
51-68: 68-Zero Hour x-over; Triumph joins Justice League Task Force (See JLTF #17)						2.50
Annual 1-5 ('90-'94, 68 pgs.):1-Return of the Global Guardians; Giffen plots/breakdowns. 2-Armageddon 2001; Giffen-a(p); Rogers-a(p); Golden-a(i). 3-Eclipso app. 4-Intro Lionheart. 5-Elseworlds story						3.00

NOTE: **Phil Jimenez** a-6p. **Rogers** a/a-20-22. **Sears** a-1-12, 14-19, 23-29; c-1-10, 14, 19, 23-29.

JUSTICE LEAGUE INTERNATIONAL (See Justice League Europe)

JUSTICE LEAGUE OF AMERICA (See Brave & the Bold #28-30, Mystery In Space #75 & Official... Index) (See Crisis on Multiple Earths TPBs for reprints of JLA/JSA crossovers)
National Periodical Publ./DC Comics: Oct-Nov, 1960 - No. 261, Apr, 1987 (#91-99,139-157: 52 pgs.)

	GD 2.0	VG 4.0	FN 6.0	VF 8.0	VF/NM 9.0	NM- 9.2
1-(10-11/60)-Origin & 1st app. Despero; Aquaman, Batman, Flash, Green Lantern, J'onn J'onzz, Superman & Wonder Woman continue from Brave and the Bold	400	800	1200	3600	6800	10,000
2	100	200	300	850	1575	2300
3-Origin/1st app. Kanjar Ro (see Mystery in Space #75)(scarce in high grade due to black-c)	83	166	249	706	1303	1900
4-Green Arrow joins JLA	52	104	156	442	821	1200
5-Origin & 1st app. Dr. Destiny	50	100	150	400	725	1050
6-8,10: 6-Origin & 1st app. Prof. Amos Fortune. 7-(10-11/61)-Last 10¢ issue. 10-(3/62)-Origin & 1st app. Felix Faust; 1st app. Lord of Time	39	78	117	293	534	775
9-(2/62)-Origin JLA (1st origin)	45	90	135	360	655	950
11-15: 12-(6/62)-Origin & 1st app. Dr. Light. 13-(8/62)-Speedy app. 14-(9/62)-Atom joins JLA.	24	48	72	175	313	450
16-20: 17-Adam Strange flashback	20	40	60	146	261	375
21-(8/63)-"Crisis on Earth-One"; re-intro. of JSA in this title (see Flash #129) (1st S.A. app. Hourman & Dr. Fate)	35	70	105	263	482	700
22- "Crisis on Earth-Two"; JSA x-over (story continued from #21)	30	60	90	225	413	600
23-28: 24-Adam Strange app. 27-Robin app.	15	30	45	107	191	275
29-JSA x-over; 1st S.A. app. Starman; "Crisis on Earth-Three"	17	34	51	128	227	325
30-JSA x-over	16	32	48	118	209	300
31-Hawkman joins JLA, Hawkgirl cameo (11/64)	12	24	36	86	153	220
32,34: 32-Intro & Origin Brain Storm. 34-Joker-c/sty	10	20	30	67	116	150
33,35,36,40,41: 40-3rd S.A. Penguin app. 41-Intro & origin The Key	9	18	27	63	107	150
37-39: 37,38-JSA x-over. 37-1st S.A. app. Mr. Terrific; Batman cameo. 38-"Crisis on Earth-A". 39-Giant G-16; r/B&B #28,30 & JLA #5	11	22	33	79	140	200
42-45: 42-Metamorpho app. 43-Intro. Royal Flush Gang	7	14	21	50	83	115
46-JSA x-over; 1st S.A. app. Sandman; 3rd S.A. app. of G.A. Spectre (8/66)	11	22	33	79	140	200
47-JSA x-over; 4th S.A. app of G.A. Spectre.	8	16	24	58	97	135
48-Giant G-29; r/JLA #2,3 & B&B #29	8	16	24	54	90	125
49-54,57,59,60	6	12	18	43	69	95
55-Intro. Earth 2 Robin (1st S.A.)	8	16	24	56	93	130
56-JLA vs. JSA (1st G.A. Wonder Woman in S.A.)	7	14	21	49	80	110
58-Giant G-41; r/JLA #6,8,1	7	14	21	49	80	110
61-63,66,68-72: 69-Wonder Woman quits. 71-Manhunter leaves. 72-Last 10¢ issue	5	10	15	32	51	70
64,65-JSA story. 64-(8/68)-Origin/1st app. S.A. Red Tornado	6	12	18	37	59	80
67-Giant G-53; r/JLA #4,14,31	7	14	21	47	76	105
73-1st S.A. app. of G.A. Superman	6	12	18	39	62	85
74-Black Canary joins; 1st meeting of G.A. & S.A. Superman; Neal Adams-c	6	12	18	39	62	85
75-2nd app. Green Arrow in new costume (see Brave & the Bold #85)	6	12	18	37	59	80
76-Giant G-65	6	12	18	37	59	80
77-80: 78-Re-intro Vigilante (1st S.A. app?)	4	8	12	32	54	75
81-84,86-90: 82-1st S.A. app. of G.A. Batman (cameo). 83-Apparent death of The Spectre. 90-Last 15¢ issue	3	6	9	20	30	40
85,93-(Giant G-77,G-89; 68 pgs.)	4	8	12	28	44	60
91,92: 91-1st meeting of the G.A. & S.A. Robin; begin 25¢, 52 pgs. issues, ends #99. 92-S.A. Robin tries on costume that is similar to that of G.A. Robin in All Star Comics #58	4	8	12	24	37	50
94-Reprints 1st Sandman story (Adv. #40) & origin/1st app. Starman (Adventure #61); Deadman x-over; N. Adams-a (4 pgs.)	6	12	18	52	86	120
95,96: 95-Origin Dr. Fate & Dr. Midnight -r/ More Fun #67, All-American #25).	4	8	12	26	41	55
96-Origin Hourman (Adv. #48); Wildcat-r	4	8	12	26	41	55
97-99: 97-Origin JLA retold; Sargon, Starman-r. 98-G.A. Sargon, Starman-r. 99-G.A. Sandman, Atom-r; last 52 pg. issue	4	8	12	22	34	45
100-(8/72)-1st meeting of G.A. & S.A. W. Woman	4	8	12	26	41	55
101,102: JSA x-overs. 102-Red Tornado dies	4	8	11	21	32	42
103-106,109: 103-Rutland Vermont Halloween x-over; Phantom Stranger joins. 105-Elongated Man joins. 106-New Red Tornado joins. 109-Hawkman resigns	3	6	9	15	21	26
107,108-JSA x-over; 1st revival app. of G.A. Uncle Sam, Black Condor, The Ray, Dollman, Phantom Lady & The Human Bomb	3	6	9	18	23	30
110-116: All 100 pgs. 111-JLA vs. Injustice Gang; Shining Knight, Green Arrow-r. 112-Amazo app; Crimson Avenger, Vigilante-r; origin Starman-r/Adv. #81. 115-Martian Manhunter app.	4	8	11	24	41	55
117-122,125-134: 117-Hawkman rejoins. 120,121-Adam Strange app. 125,126-Two-Face-app. 128-Wonder Woman rejoins. 129-Destruction of Red Tornado	2	4	6	11	16	20
123-(10/75),124: JLA/JSA x-over. DC editor Julie Schwartz & JLA writers Cary Bates & Elliot						

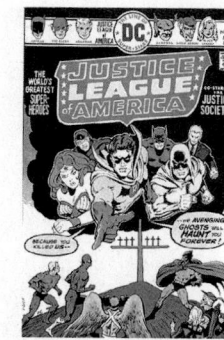

Justice League of America #124 © DC

Justice League of America ('06) #8 © DC

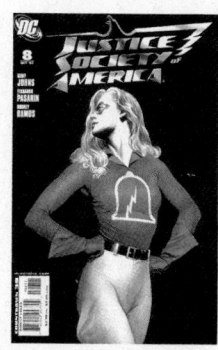

Justice Society of America ('07) #8 © DC

	GD 2.0	VG 4.0	FN 6.0	VF 8.0	VF/NM 9.0	NM- 9.2

	GD 2.0	VG 4.0	FN 6.0	VF 8.0	VF/NM 9.0	NM- 9.2

S! Maggin appear in story as themselves. 1st named app. Earth-Prime (3rd app. after Flash; 1st Series #179 & 228)

	3	6	9	14	19	24

135-136: 135-137-G.A. Bulletman, Bulletgirl, Spy Smasher, Mr. Scarlet, Pinky & Ibis x-over, 1st appearances since G.A.

	3	6	9	14	19	24

137-Superman battles G.A. Capt. Marvel

	3	6	9	16	22	28

138-Adam Strange app. w/c by Neal Adams; 1st app. Green Lantern of the 73rd Century

	2	4	11	16	20

139-157: 139-157-(52 pgs.): 139-Adam Strange app. 144-Origin retold; origin J'onn J'onzz. 145-Red Tornado resurrected. 147,148-Legion of Super-Heroes x-over

	2	4	6	9	13	16

158-160-(44 pgs.)

	2	4	6	8	10	12

158,160-162,169,171,172,173,176-179,181-(Whitman variants; low print run, none show issue # on cover)

	2	4	6	9	13	16

161-165,169-182: 161-Zatanna joins & new costume. 171,172-JSA x-over. 171-Mr. Terrific murdered. 178-Cover similar to #1; J'onn J'onzz app. 179-Firestorm joins.

181-Green Arrow leaves JLA

	2	3	4	5	7

166-168- "Identity Crisis (2004)" precursor; JSA app. vs. Secret Society of Super-Villains

	2	4	6	10	14	18

166-168-Whitman variants (no issue # on covers)

	3	6	9	18	27	35

183-185-JSA/New Gods/Darkseid/Mr. Miracle x-over

	1	2	3	5	7	9

186-194,198,199: 192,193-Real origin Red Tornado. 193-1st app. All-Star Squadron as free 16 pg. insert

	6.00

195-197-JSA app. vs. Secret Society of Super-Villains

	1	2	3	4	5	7

200 ($1.50, Anniversary issue, 76 pgs.)-JLA origin retold; Green Arrow rejoins; Bolland, Aparo, Giordano, Gil Kane, Infantino, Kubert-a; Perez-c/a 1

	2	3	4	5	7

201-206,209-243,246-259: 203-Intro/origin new Royal Flush Gang. 219,220-True origin Black Canary. 228-Re-intro Martian Manhunter. 228-230-War of the Worlds storyline; JLA Satellite destroyed by Martians. 233-Story cont'd from Annual #2. 243-Aquaman leaves. 250-Batman rejoins. 253-Origin Despero. 258-Death of Vibe. 258-261-Legends x-over

	4.00

207,208-JSA, JLA, & All-Star Squadron team-up

	6.00

244,245-Crisis x-over

	5.00

260-Death of Steel

	6.00

261-Last issue

	1	2	3	5	8

Annual 1-3 ('83-'85), 2-Intro new J.L.A. (Aquaman, Martian Manhunter, Steel, Gypsy, Vixen, Vibe, Elongated Man & Zatanna). 3-Crisis x-over

	4.00

... Hereby Elects (2006, $14.99, TPB) reprints issues where new members joined; JLofA #4,75,105,106,146,161,173&174; roster of various incarnations; Ordway-c

	15.00

NOTE: **Neal Adams** c-63, 66, 67, 70, 74, 79, 81, 82, 86-89, 91, 92, 94, 96-98, 138, 139. **M. Anderson** c-1-4, 6, 7, 10, 12-14. **Aparo** a-200. **Austin** a-200i. **Bailly** a-96r. **Bolland** a-200. **Buckler** c-158, 163, 164. **Burnley** r-94, 98, 99. **Greene** a-46-61i, 64-73i, 110(r)i. **Grell** c-117, 122. **Kaluta** c-154p. **Gil Kane** a-200. **Krigstein** a-96(r/Sensation #84). **Kubert** a-200; c-72, 73. **Nino** a-200i, 203i. **Orlando** c-151i. **Perez** a-184-186p, 192-197p, 200p; c-184p, 186, 192-195, 196p, 197p, 199, 200, 201p, 202, 203-205p, 207-209, 212-215, 217, 219, 220. **Reinman** r-97. **Roussos** a-62i. **Sekowsky** a-37, 38, 44-63p, 110-112p(r); c-46-48p, 51p. **Sekowsky/Anderson** c-5, 8, 9, 11, 15. **B. Smith** c-185i. **Starlin** c-178-180, 183, 185p. **Staton** a-244p; c-157p, 244p. **Toth** r-110. **Tuska** a-153, 228p, 241-243p. JSA x-overs-21, 22, 29, 30, 37, 38, 46, 47, 55, 56, 64, 65, 73, 74, 82, 83, 91, 92, 100, 101, 102, 107, 108, 110, 113, 115, 123, 124, 135-137, 147, 148, 159, 160, 171, 172, 183-185, 195-197, 207-209, 219, 220, 231, 232, 244.

JUSTICE LEAGUE OF AMERICA

DC Comics: No. 0, Sept, 2006 - Present ($2.99)

0-Meltzer-s; history of the JLA; art by various incl. Lee, Giordano, Benes; Turner-c	5.00
0-Variant-c by Campbell	12.00
1-($3.99) Two interlocking covers by Benes; Benes-a	5.00
1-Variant-c by Turner	8.00
1-RRP Edition; sideways composite of both Benes covers	80.00
1-Second printing; Benes cover image between black bars	4.00
2-5-($2.99) Turner-c	3.00
2-5: Variant-c 2-Jimenez. 3-Sprouse. 4-JG Jones. 5-Art Adams	5.00
6,7-($3.50) 6-JLA vs. Amazo; covers by Turner and Hughes. 7-Roster picked, new HQs; two Benes covers and Turner cover.	3.50
8-11-($2.99) JLA/JSA team-up; covers by Turner and Jimenez. 10-Wally West returns	3.00
12-($3.50) Two Ross covers; origin retold with Wight-a; Benes-a	3.50
...: The Tornado's Path HC (2007, $24.99, dustjacket) r/#1-7; variant cover gallery; Lindelof intro.; commentary by Meltzer & Benes	25.00

JUSTICE LEAGUE OF AMERICA : ANOTHER NAIL (Elseworlds) (Also see JLA: The Nail)

DC Comics: 2004 - No. 3, 2004 ($5.95, prestige format)

1-3-Sequel to JLA: The Nail; Alan Davis-s/a(p)	6.00
TPB (2004, $12.95) r/series	13.00

JUSTICE LEAGUE OF AMERICA SUPER SPECTACULAR

DC Comics: 1999 ($5.95, mimics format of DC 100 Page Super Spectaculars)

1-Reprints Silver Age JLA and Golden Age JLA	6.00

JUSTICE LEAGUE QUARTERLY (...International Quarterly #6 on)

DC Comics: Winter, 1990-91 - No. 17, Winter, 1994 ($2.95/$3.50, 84 pgs.)

1-12,14-17: 1-Intro The Conglomerate (Booster Gold, Praxis, Gypsy, Vapor, Echo, Maxi-Man,

& Reverb); Justice League #1-c/swipe. 1,2-Giffen plots/breakdowns. 3-Giffen plot; 72 pg. story. 4-Rogers/Russell-a in back-up. 5,6-Waid scripts. 8,17-Global Guardians app.

	3.50

13-Linsner-c

	6.00

NOTE: **Phil Jimenez** a-17p. **Sprouse** a-1p.

JUSTICE LEAGUES...

DC Comics: Mar, 2001 ($2.50, limited series)

JL?, Justice League of Amazons, Justice League of Atlantis, Justice League of Arkham, Justice League of Aliens, JLA: JLA split by the Advance Man; Perez-c in all; s&a by various

	2.50

JUSTICE LEAGUE TASK FORCE

DC Comics: June, 1993 - No. 37, Aug, 1996 ($1.25/$1.50/$1.75)

1-16,0,17-37: Aquaman, Nightwing, Flash, J'onn J'onzz, & Gypsy form team. 5,6-Knight-quest tie-ins (new Batman cameo #5, 1 pg.). 15-Triumph cameo. 16-(9/94)-Zero Hour x-over; Triumph app. 0-(10/94). 17-(11/94)-Triumph becomes part of Justice League Task Force (See JLE #68). 26-Impulse app. 35-Warlord app. 37-Triumph quits team

	2.50

JUSTICE LEAGUE UNLIMITED (Based on Cartoon Network animated series) (Also see Free Comic Book Day Edition in the Promotional Comics section)

DC Comics: Nov, 2004 - Present ($2.25)

1-36: 1-Zatanna app. 2,23-Royal Flush Gang app. 4-Adam Strange app. 10-Creeper app. 17-Freedom Fighters app. 18-Space Cabby app. 27-Black Lightning app. 34-Zod app.	2.50
Jam Packed Action (2005, $7.99, digest) adaptations of two TV episodes	8.00
... Vol. 1: United They Stand (2005, $6.99, digest) r/#1-5	7.00
... Vol. 2: World's Greatest Heroes (2005, $6.99, digest) r/#6-10	7.00
... Vol. 3: Champions of Justice (2006, $6.99, digest) r/#11-15	7.00

JUSTICE MACHINE, THE

Noble Comics: June, 1981 - No. 5, Nov, 1983 ($2.00, nos. 1-3 are mag. size)

	GD	VG	FN	VF	VF/NM	NM-
1-Byrne-c(p)	3	6	9	15	21	26
2-Austin-c(i)	2	4	6	9	12	15
3	1	3	4	6	8	10
4,5, Annual 1: Ann. 1-(1/84, 68 pgs.)(published by Texas Comics); 1st app. The Elementals; Golden-c(p); new Thunder Agents story (43 pgs.)						6.00

JUSTICE MACHINE (Also see The New Justice Machine)

Comico/Innovation Publishing: Jan, 1987 - No. 29, May 1989 ($1.50/$1.75)

1-29	2.50
Annual 1(6/89, $2.50, 36 pgs.)-Last Comico ish.	3.00
Summer Spectacular 1 ('89, $2.75)-Innovation Publ.; Byrne/Gustovich-c	3.00

JUSTICE MACHINE, THE

Innovation Publishing: 1990 - No. 4, 1990 ($1.95/$2.25, deluxe format, mature)

1-4- Gustovich-c/a in all	2.50

JUSTICE MACHINE FEATURING THE ELEMENTALS

Comico: May, 1986 - No. 4, Aug, 1986 ($1.50, limited series)

1-4	2.50

JUSTICE RIDERS

DC Comics: 1997 ($5.95, one-shot, prestige format)

1-Elseworlds; Dixon-s/Williams & Gray-a	6.00

JUSTICE SOCIETY

DC Comics: 2006; 2007 ($14.99, TPB)

Vol. 1 - Rep. from 1976 revival in All Star Comics #58-67 & DC Special #29; Bolland-c	15.00
Vol. 2 - R/All Star Comics #68-74 & Adventure Comics #461-466; new Bolland-c	15.00

JUSTICE SOCIETY OF AMERICA (See Adventure #461 & All-Star #3)

DC Comics: April, 1991 - No. 8, Nov, 1991 ($1.00, limited series)

1-8: 1-Flash. 2-Black Canary. 3-Green Lantern. 4-Hawkman. 5-Flash/Hawkman. 6-Green Lantern/Black Canary. 7-JSA	2.50

JUSTICE SOCIETY OF AMERICA (Also see Last Days of the... Special)

DC Comics: Aug, 1992 - No. 10, May, 1993 ($1.25)

1-10	2.50

JUSTICE SOCIETY OF AMERICA (Follows JSA series)

DC Comics: Feb, 2007 - Present ($3.99/$2.99)

1-($3.99) New team selected; intro. Maxine Hunkle; Alex Ross-c	4.00
1-Variant-c by Eaglesham	6.00
2-8: Covers by Ross and Eaglesham. 3,4-Vandal Savage app. 5,6-JLA/JSA team-up	3.00

JUSTICE SOCIETY OF AMERICA 100-PAGE SUPER SPECTACULAR

DC Comics: 2000 ($6.95, mimics format of DC 100 Page Super Spectaculars)

1-"1975 Issue" reprints Flash team-up and Golden Age JSA	7.00

JUSTICE SOCIETY RETURNS, THE (See All Star Comics (1999) for related titles)

Justice Traps the Guilty #2 © PRIZE

Just Imagine Stan Lee with Joe Kubert Creating Batman © DC

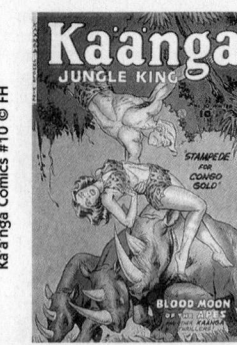
Ka'a'nga Comics #10 © FH

	GD 2.0	VG 4.0	FN 6.0	VF 8.0	VF/NM 9.0	NM- 9.2

DC Comics: 2003 ($19.95, TPB)
TPB-Reprints 1999 JSA x-over from All-Star Comics #1,2 and related one-shots ... 20.00

JUSTICE TRAPS THE GUILTY (Fargo Kid V11#3 on)
Prize/Headline Publications: Oct-Nov, 1947 - V11#3(#92), Apr-May, 1958 (True FBI Cases)

	GD 2.0	VG 4.0	FN 6.0	VF 8.0	VF/NM 9.0	NM- 9.2
V2#1-S&K-c/a; electrocution-c	58	116	174	363	599	835
2-S&K-c/a	35	70	105	204	322	440
3-5-S&K-c/a	32	64	96	186	293	400
6-S&K-c/a; Feldstein-a	34	68	102	197	311	425
7,9-S&K-c/a. 7-9-V2#1-3 in indicia; #7-9 on-c	28	56	84	164	260	355
8-Krigstein-a; S&K-c	27	54	81	158	249	340
10-Krigstein-a; S&K-c/a	28	56	84	164	260	355
11,18,19-S&K-c	15	30	45	86	133	180
12,14-17,20-No S&K. 14-Severin/Elder-a (8pg.)	10	20	30	56	76	95
13-Used in **SOTI**, pg. 110-111	11	22	33	62	86	110
21,30-S&K-c/a	15	30	45	86	133	180
22,23-S&K-c	12	24	36	67	94	120
24-26,27,29,31-50: 32-Meskin story	9	18	27	52	69	85
28-Kirby-c	11	22	33	62	86	110
51-55,57,59-70	9	18	27	47	61	75
56-Ben Oda, Joe Simon, Joe Genola, Mort Meskin & Jack Kirby app. in police line-up on classic-c	12	24	36	69	97	125
58-Illo. in **SOTI**, "Treating police contemptuously" (top left); text on heroin	25	50	75	145	228	310
71-92: 76-Orlando-a	8	16	24	44	50	60

NOTE: *Bailey* a-12, 13. *Elder* a-8. *Kirby* a-19p. *Meskin* a-22, 27, 63, 64; c-45, 46. *Robinson/Meskin* a-5, 19. *Severin* a-8, 11p. Photo c-12, 15-17.

JUST IMAGINE STAN LEE WITH... (Stan Lee re-invents DC icons)
DC Comics: 2001 - 2002 ($5.95, prestige format, one-shots)
(Adam Hughes back-c on all)(Michael Uslan back-up stories in all, diff. artists)

Scott McDaniel Creating **Aquaman**- Back-up w/Fradon-a	6.00
Joe Kubert Creating **Batman**- Back-up w/Kaluta-a	6.00
Chris Bachalo Creating **Catwoman**- Back-up w/Cooke & Allred-a	6.00
John Cassaday Creating **Crisis**- no back-up story	6.00
Kevin Maguire Creating **The Flash**- Back-up w/Aragonés-a	6.00
Dave Gibbons Creating **Green Lantern**- Back-up w/Giordano-a	6.00
Jerry Ordway Creating **JLA**- Back-up w/Kano-a	6.00
John Byrne Creating **Robin**- Back-up w/John Severin-a	6.00
Walter Simonson Creating **Sandman**- Back-up w/Corben-a	6.00
Gary Frank Creating **Shazam!**- Back-up w/Gene Colan-a	6.00
John Buscema Creating **Superman**- Back-up w/Kyle Baker-a	6.00
Jim Lee Creating **Wonder Woman**- Back-up w/Gene Colan-a	6.00
Secret Files and Origins #1 (3/02, $4.95)-Crisis prologue; Jurgens-a	5.00
TPB -Just Imagine Stan Lee Creating the DC Universe: Book One (2002, $19.95) r/Batman, Wonder Woman, Superman, Green Lantern	20.00
TPB -Just Imagine Stan Lee Creating the DC Universe: Book Two (2003, $19.95) r/Flash, JLA, Secret Files and Origins, Robin, Shazam; sketch pages	20.00
TPB -Just Imagine Stan Lee Creating the DC Universe: Book Three (2004, $19.95) r/Aquaman, Catwoman, Sandman, Crisis; profile pages	20.00

JUST MARRIED
Charlton Comics: January, 1958 - No. 114, Dec, 1976

	GD 2.0	VG 4.0	FN 6.0	VF 8.0	VF/NM 9.0	NM- 9.2
1	6	12	18	39	62	85
2	3	6	9	21	32	42
3-10	3	6	9	17	25	32
11-30	3	6	9	14	19	24
31-50	2	4	6	10	14	18
51-70	2	4	6	9	12	15
71-78,80-90: 90-Susan Dey and David Cassidy full page poster	2	4	6	8	10	12
79-Ditko-a (7 pages)	2	4	6	9	13	16
91-114	1	3	4	6	8	10

JUSTY
Viz Comics: Dec 6, 1988 - No. 9, 1989 ($1.75, B&W, bi-weekly mini-series)

1-9: Japanese manga	2.50

KA'A'NGA COMICS (...Jungle King)(See Jungle Comics)
Fiction House Magazines (Glen-Kel Publ. Co.): Spring, 1949 - No. 20, Summer, 1954

	GD 2.0	VG 4.0	FN 6.0	VF 8.0	VF/NM 9.0	NM- 9.2
1-Ka'a'nga, Lord of the Jungle begins	52	104	156	317	521	725
2 (Winter, '49-'50)	30	60	90	170	275	375
3,4	22	44	66	128	202	275
5-Camilla app.	17	34	51	98	154	210
6-10: 7-Tuska-a. 9-Tabu, Wizard of the Jungle app. 10-Used in **POP**, pg. 99	15	30	45	85	130	175

	GD 2.0	VG 4.0	FN 6.0	VF 8.0	VF/NM 9.0	NM- 9.2
11-15: 15-Camilla-r by Baker/Jungle #106	14	28	42	76	108	140
16-Sheena app.	14	28	42	80	115	150
17-20	12	24	36	69	97	125
I.W. Reprint #1,8: 1-r/#18; Kinstler-c. 8-r/#10	3	6	9	14	20	25

NOTE: *Celardo* c-1. *Whitman* c-8-20(most).

KABOOM
Awesome Entertainment: Sept, 1997 - No. 3, Nov, 1997 ($2.50)

1-3: 1-Matsuda-a/Loeb-s; 4 covers exist (Matsuda, Sale, Pollina and McGuinness), 1-Dynamic Forces Edition, 2-Regular, 2-Alicia Watcher variant-c, 2-Gold logo variant-c, 3-Two covers by Liefeld & Matsuda, 3-Dynamic Forces Ed., Prelude Ed.	2.50
Prelude Gold Edition	4.00

KABOOM (2nd series)
Awesome Entertainment: July, 1999 - No. 3, Dec, 1999 ($2.50)

1-3: 1-Grant-a(p); at least 4 variant covers	2.50

KABUKI
Caliber: Nov, 1994 ($3.50, B&W, one-shot)

	GD 2.0	VG 4.0	FN 6.0	VF 8.0	VF/NM 9.0	NM- 9.2
nn-(Fear The Reaper) 1st app.; David Mack-c/a/s	1	2	3	5	6	8
Color Special (1/96, $2.95)-Mack-c/a/scripts; pin-ups by Tucci, Harris & Quesada						4.00
Gallery (8/95, $2.95)- pinups from Mack, Bradstreet, Paul Pope & others						3.00

KABUKI
Image Comics: Oct, 1997 - No. 9, Mar, 2000 ($2.95, color)

	GD 2.0	VG 4.0	FN 6.0	VF 8.0	VF/NM 9.0	NM- 9.2
1-David Mack-c/s/a						5.00
1-($10.00)-Dynamic Forces Edition	1	3	4	6	8	10
2-5						4.00
6-9						3.00
#1/2 (9/01, $2.95) r/Wizard 1/2; Eklipse Mag. article; bio						3.00
...Classics (2/99, $3.95) reprints Fear the Reaper						4.00
...Classics 2 (3/99, $3.95) Reprints Dance of Dance						4.00
...Classics 3-5 (3-6/99, $4.95) Reprints Circle of Blood-Acts 1-3						5.00
...Classics 6-12 (7/99-3/00, $3.25) Various reprints						3.25
...Images (6/98, $4.95) r/#1 with new pin-ups						5.00
...Images 2 (1/99, $4.95) r/#1 with new pin-ups						5.00
...Metamorphosis TPB (10/00, $24.95) r/#1-9; Sienkiewicz intro.; 2nd printing exists						25.00
...Reflections 1-4 (7/98-5/02; $4.95) new story plus art techniques						5.00
...The Ghost Play (11/02, $2.95) new story plus interview						3.00

KABUKI
Marvel Comics (Icon): July, 2004 - Present ($2.99, color)

1-8: 1-David Mack-c/s/a in all; variant-c by Alex Maleev. 4-Variant-c by Adam Hughes. 6-Variant-c by Mignola. 8-Variant-c by Kent Williams	3.00
... Reflections 5-8 (7/05-4/07, $5.99) paintings & sketches of recent work; photos	6.00

KABUKI AGENTS (SCARAB)
Image Comics: Aug, 1999 - No. 8, Aug, 2001 ($2.95, B&W)

1-8-David Mack-s/Rick Mays-a	3.00
Lost in Translation HC (3/02, $29.95) r/#1-8; intro. by Paul Pope	30.00
Lost in Translation SC (3/02, $19.95) r/#1-8; intro. by Paul Pope	20.00

KABUKI: CIRCLE OF BLOOD
Caliber Press: Jan, 1995 - No. 6, Nov, 1995 ($2.95, B&W)

1-David Mack story/a in all	5.00
2-6: 3-#1 on inside indicia.	3.00
6-Variant-c	3.00
TPB ($16.95) r/#1-6, intro. by Steranko	17.00
TPB (1997, $17.95) Image Edition-r/#1-6, intro. by Steranko	18.00
TPB ($24.95) Deluxe Edition	25.00

KABUKI: DANCE OF DEATH
London Night Studios: Jan, 1995 ($3.00, B&W, one-shot)

	GD 2.0	VG 4.0	FN 6.0	VF 8.0	VF/NM 9.0	NM- 9.2
1-David Mack-c/a/scripts	1	2	3	5	6	8

KABUKI: DREAMS
Image Comics: Jan, 1998 ($4.95, TPB)

nn-Reprints Color Special & Dreams of the Dead	5.00

KABUKI: DREAMS OF THE DEAD
Caliber: July, 1996 ($2.95, one-shot)

nn-David Mack-c/a/scripts	3.00

KABUKI FAN EDITION
Gemstone Publ./Caliber: Feb, 1997 (mail-in offer, one-shot)

nn-David Mack-c/a/scripts	4.00

KABUKI: MASKS OF THE NOH
Caliber: May, 1996 - No. 4, Feb, 1997 ($2.95, limited series)

Kamandi, the Last Boy on Earth #11 © DC

Karate Kid #1 © DC

Katy Keene #54 © AP

KA

	GD	VG	FN	VF	VF/NM	NM-
	2.0	4.0	6.0	8.0	9.0	9.2

1-4: 1-Three-c (1A-Quesada, 1B-Buzz, &1C-Mack). 3-Terry Moore pin-up ... 3.00
TPB-(4/98, $10.95) r/#1-4; intro by Terry Moore ... 11.00

KABUKI: SKIN DEEP
Caliber Comics: Oct, 1996 - No. 3, May, 1997 ($2.95)

1-3:David Mack-c/a/scripts. 2-Two-c (1-Mack, 1-Ross) ... 3.00
TPB-(5/98, $9.95) r/#1-3; intro by Alex Ross ... 10.00

KAMANDI: AT EARTH'S END
DC Comics: June, 1993 - No. 6, Nov, 1993 ($1.75, limited series)

1-6: Elseworlds storyline ... 2.50

KAMANDI, THE LAST BOY ON EARTH (Also see Alarming Tales #1, Brave and the Bold #120 & 157 & Cancelled Comic Cavalcade)
National Periodical Publ./DC Comics: Oct-Nov, 1972 - No. 59, Sept-Oct, 1978

	GD	VG	FN	VF	VF/NM	NM-
1-Origin & 1st app. Kamandi	7	14	21	47	76	105
2,3	4	8	12	26	41	55
4,5: 4-Intro. Prince Tuftan of the Tigers	4	8	12	22	34	45
6-10	3	6	9	17	25	32
11-20	2	4	6	13	18	22
21-28,30,31,33-40: 24-Last 20¢ issue. 31-Intro Pyra.	2	4	6	11	16	20
29,32: 29-Superman x-over. 32-(68 pgs.)-r/origin from #1 plus one new story; 4 pg. biog. of Jack Kirby with B&W photos	3	6	9	14	19	24
41-57	2	4	6	9	13	16
58-(44 pgs.)-Karate Kid x-over from LSH	2	4	6	13	18	22
59-(44 pgs.)-Cont'd in B&B #157; The Return of Omac back-up by Starlin-c/a(p)	2	4	6	13	18	22

NOTE: *Ayers* a(p)-48-59 (most). *Giffen* a-44p, 45p. *Kirby* a-1-40p; c-1-33. *Kubert* c-34-41. *Nasser* a-45p, 46p. *Starlin* a-59p; c-57, 59p.

KAMUI (Legend Of...#2 on)
Eclipse Comics/Viz Comics: May 12, 1987 - No. 37, Nov. 15, 1988 ($1.50, B&W, bi-weekly)

1-37: 1-3 have 2nd printings ... 2.50

KAOS MOON (Also see Negative Burn #34)
Caliber Comics: 1996 - No. 4, 1997 ($2.95, B&W)

1-4-David Boller-s/a ... 3.00
3,4-Limited Alternate-c ... 4.00
3,4-Gold Alternate-c, Full Circle TPB ($5.95) r/#1,2 ... 6.00

KARATE KID (See Action, Adventure, Legion of Super-Heroes, & Superboy)
National Periodical Publications/DC Comics: Mar-Apr, 1976 - No. 15, July-Aug, 1978 (Legion of Super-Heroes spin-off)

	GD	VG	FN	VF	VF/NM	NM-
1,15: 1-Meets Iris Jacobs; Estrada/Staton-a. 15-Continued into Kamandi #58	2	4	6	9	11	14
2-14: 2-Major Disaster app. 14-Robin x-over	1	2	3	5	6	8

NOTE: *Grell* c-1-4, 5p, 6p, 7, 8. *Staton* a-1-9i. Legion x-over-No. 1, 2, 4, 6, 10, 12, 13. Princess Projectra x-over-#8, 9.

KATHY
Standard Comics: Sept, 1949 - No. 17, Sept, 1955

	GD	VG	FN	VF	VF/NM	NM-
1-Teen-age	14	28	42	82	121	160
2-Schomburg-c	11	22	33	60	83	105
3-5	8	16	24	44	57	70
6-17: 17-Code approved	8	16	24	40	50	60

KATHY (The Teenage Tornado)
Atlas Comics/Marvel (ZPC): Oct, 1959 - No. 27, Feb, 1964 (most issues contain paper dolls and pin-up pages)

	GD	VG	FN	VF	VF/NM	NM-
1-The Teen-age Tornado; Goldberg-c/a in all	7	14	21	49	80	110
2	4	8	12	28	44	60
3-15	4	8	12	22	34	45
16-23,25,27	3	6	9	16	23	30
24-(8/63) Frank Sinatra, Cary Grant, Ed Sullivan & Liz Taylor-c	3	6	9	18	27	35
26-(12/63) Kathy becomes a model; Millie app.	3	6	9	18	27	35

KAT KARSON
I. W. Enterprises: No date (Reprint)

	GD	VG	FN	VF	VF/NM	NM-
1-Funny animals	2	4	6	10	12	15

KATO OF THE GREEN HORNET (Also see The Green Hornet)
Now Comics: Nov, 1991 - No. 4, Feb, 1992 ($2.50, mini-series)

1-4: Brent Anderson-c/a ... 2.50

KATO OF THE GREEN HORNET II (Also see The Green Hornet)
Now Comics: Nov, 1992 - No. 2, Dec, 1993 ($2.50, mini-series)

1,2-Baron-s/Mayerik & Sherman-a ... 2.50

KATY KEENE (Also see Kasco Komics, Laugh, Pep, Suzie, & Wilbur)
Archie Publ./Close-Up/Radio Comics: 1949 - No. 4, 1951; No. 5, 3/52 - No. 62, Oct, 1961 (50-53-Adventures of...on-c) (Cut and missing pages are common)

	GD	VG	FN	VF	VF/NM	NM-
1-Bill Woggon-c/a begins; swipes-c to Mopsy #1	138	276	414	863	1432	2000
2-(1950)	59	118	177	369	610	850
3-5: 3-(1951). 4-(1951)	46	92	138	281	466	650
6-10	37	74	111	213	337	460
11,13-21: 21-Last pre-code issue (3/55)	30	60	90	174	275	375
12-(Scarce)	36	72	108	208	329	450
22-40	21	42	63	122	191	260
41-60: 54-Wedding Album plus wedding pin-up	16	32	48	94	147	200
61,62: 62-Robot-c	18	36	54	105	165	225
Annual 1('54, 25¢)-All new stories; last pre-code	53	106	159	323	537	750
Annual 2-6('55-59, 25¢)-All new stories	31	62	93	178	282	385
3-D 1(1953, 25¢, large size)-Came w/glasses	39	78	117	224	355	485
Charm 1(9/58)-Woggon-c/a; new stories, and cut-outs	29	58	87	170	268	365
Glamour 1(1957)-Puzzles, games, cut-outs	29	58	87	170	268	365
Spectacular 1('56)	30	60	90	172	271	370

NOTE: *Debby's Diary in #45, 47-49, 52, 57.*

KATY KEENE COMICS DIGEST MAGAZINE
Close-Up, Inc. (Archie Ent.): 1987 - No. 10, July, 1990 ($1.25/$1.35/$1.50, digest size)

	GD	VG	FN	VF	VF/NM	NM-
1	2	4	6	9	13	16
2-10	1	2	3	5	7	9

NOTE: *Many used copies are cut-up inside.*

KATY KEENE FASHION BOOK MAGAZINE
Radio Comics/Archie Publications: 1955 - No. 13, Sum, '56 - N. 23, Wint, '58-59 (nn 3-10)

	GD	VG	FN	VF	VF/NM	NM-
1-Bill Woggon-c/a	52	104	156	317	521	725
2	30	60	90	174	275	375
11-18: 18-Photo Bill Woggon	22	44	66	126	198	270
19-23	18	36	54	103	162	220

KATY KEENE HOLIDAY FUN (See Archie Giant Series Magazine No. 7, 12)

KATY KEENE PINUP PARADE
Radio Comics/Archie Publications: 1955 - No. 15, Summer, 1961 (25¢) (Cut-out and missing pages are common)

	GD	VG	FN	VF	VF/NM	NM-
1-Cut-outs in all?; last pre-code issue	52	104	156	317	521	725
2-(1956)	30	60	90	174	275	375
3-5: 3-(1957)	26	52	78	150	235	320
6-10,12-14: 8-Mardy parody. 10-Bill Woggon photo	21	42	63	122	191	260
11-Story of how comics get CCA approved, narrated by Katy	26	52	78	152	239	325
15(Rare)-Photo artist & family	40	80	120	243	389	535

KATY KEENE SPECIAL (Katy Keene #7; see Laugh Comics Digest)
Archie Ent.: Sept, 1983 - No. 33, 1990 (Later issues published quarterly)

	GD	VG	FN	VF	VF/NM	NM-
1-10: 1-Woggon-r; new Woggon-c. 3-Woggon-r						5.00
11-25: 12-Spider-Man parody						6.00
26-32:(Low print run)	1	2	3	5	7	9
33	2	4	6	8	10	12

KATZENJAMMER KIDS, THE (See Captain & the Kids & Giant Comic Album)
David McKay Publ./Standard No. 12-21(Spring/'50 - 53)/Harvey No. 22, 4/53 on: 1945-1946; Summer, 1947 - No. 27, Feb-Mar, 1954

	GD	VG	FN	VF	VF/NM	NM-
Feature Books 30	20	40	60	117	184	250
Feature Books 32,35('45),41,44('46)	18	36	54	103	162	220
Feature Book 37-Has photos & biography of Harold Knerr	19	38	57	109	172	235
1(1947)-All new stories begin	19	38	57	109	172	235
2	11	22	33	64	90	115
3-11	9	18	27	52	69	85
12-14(Standard)	8	16	24	42	54	65
15-21(Standard)	8	16	24	40	50	60
22-25,27(Harvey): 22-24-Henry app.	7	14	21	35	43	50
26-Half in 3-D	16	32	48	94	147	200

KAYO (Formerly Bullseye & Jest; becomes Carnival Comics)
Harry 'A' Chesler: No. 12, Mar, 1945

	GD	VG	FN	VF	VF/NM	NM-
12-Green Knight, Capt. Glory, Little Nemo (not by McCay)	17	34	51	98	154	210

KA-ZAR (Also see Marvel Comics #1, Savage Tales #6 & X-Men #10)
Marvel Comics Group: Aug, 1970 - No. 3, Mar, 1971 (Giant-Size, 68 pgs.)

1-Reprints earlier Ka-Zar stories; Avengers x-over in Hercules; Daredevil, X-Men app.;

Ka-Zar the Savage #18 © MAR

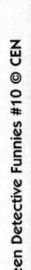

Keen Detective Funnies #10 © CEN

Ken Shannon #7 © QUA

	GD 2.0	VG 4.0	FN 6.0	VF 8.0	VF/NM 9.0	NM- 9.2
hidden profanity-c	3	6	9	21	32	42
2,3-Daredevil- r. 2-r/Daredevil #13 w/Kirby layouts; Ka-Zar origin, Angel-r from X-Men by Tuska. 3-Romita & Heck-a (no Kirby)	3	6	9	16	22	28

NOTE: *Buscema* r-2. *Colan* a-1p(r). *Kirby* c/a-1, 2. #1-Reprints X-Men #10 & Daredevil #24

KA-ZAR
Marvel Comics Group: Jan, 1974 - No. 20, Feb, 1977 (Regular Size)

1	2	4	6	10	14	18
2-10	1	2	3	5	7	9
11-14,16,18-20						6.00
15,17-(Regular 25¢ edition)(8/76)						6.00
15,17-(30¢-c variants, limited distribution)	2	4	6	10	14	18

NOTE: *Alcala* a-6i, 8i. *Brunner* c-4. *J. Buscema* a-6-10p; c-1, 5, 7. *Heath* a-12. *G. Kane* c(p)-3, 5, 8-11, 15, 20. *Kirby* c-12p. *Reinman* a-1p.

KA-ZAR (Volume 2)
Marvel Comics: May, 1997 - No. 20, Dec, 1998 ($1.95/$1.99)

1-Waid-s/Andy Kubert-c/a. thru #4		3.00
1-2nd printing; new cover		2.50
2,4: 2-Two-c		2.50
3-Alpha Flight #1 preview		3.00
5-13,15-20: 8-Includes Spider-Man Cybercomic CD-ROM. 9-11-Thanos app.		
15-Priest-s/Martinez & Rodriguez-a begin; Punisher app.		2.50
14-($2.99) Last Waid/Kubert issue; flip book with 2nd story previewing new creative team of Priest-s/Martinez & Rodriguez-a		3.00
'97 Annual ($2.99)-Wraparound-c		3.00

KA-ZAR OF THE SAVAGE LAND
Marvel Comics: Feb, 1997 ($2.50, one-shot)

1-Wraparound-c		2.50

KA-ZAR: SIBLING RIVALRY
Marvel Comics: July, 1997 ($1.95, one-shot)

(# -1) Flashback story w/Alpha Flight #1 preview		2.50

KA-ZAR THE SAVAGE (See Marvel Fanfare)
Marvel Comics Group: Apr, 1981 - No. 34, Oct, 1984 (Regular size)(Mando paper #10 on)

1		4.00
2-20,24,27,28,30-34: 11-Origin Zabu. 12-One of two versions with panel missing on pg. 10. 20-Kraven the Hunter-c/story (also apps. in #21)		2.50
12-Version with panel on pg. 10 (1600 printed)		6.00
21-23, 25,26-Spider-Man app. 26-Photo-c.		3.00
29-Double size; Ka-Zar & Shanna wed		3.00

NOTE: *B. Anderson* a-1-15p, 18, 19; c-1-17, 18p, 20(back). *G. Kane* a(back-up)-11, 12, 14.

KEEN DETECTIVE FUNNIES (Formerly Detective Picture Stories?)
Centaur Publications: No. 8, July, 1938 - No. 24, Sept, 1940

V1#8-The Clock continues-r/Funny Picture Stories #1; Roy Crane-a (1st?)	241	482	723	1506	2503	3500
9-Tex Martin by Eisner; The Gang Buster app.	88	176	264	550	913	1275
10,11: 11-Dean Denton story (begins)	79	158	237	494	822	1150
V2#1,2-The Eye Sees by Frank Thomas begins; ends #23(Not in V2#3&5). 2-Jack Cole-a						
	73	146	219	456	758	1060
3-6: 3-TNT Todd begins. 4-Gabby Flynn begins. 5,6-Dean Denton story						
	69	138	207	431	716	1000
7-The Masked Marvel by Ben Thompson begins (7/39, 1st app.)(scarce)						
	248	496	744	1550	2575	3600
8-Nudist ranch panel w/four girls	88	176	264	550	913	1275
9-11	78	156	234	488	807	1125
12(12/39)-Origin The Eye Sees by Frank Thomas; death of Masked Marvel's sidekick ZL						
	95	190	285	594	985	1375
V3#1,2	69	138	207	431	716	1000
18,19,21,22: 18-Bondage/torture-c	69	138	207	431	716	1000
20-Classic Eye Sees-c by Thomas	105	210	315	656	1091	1525
23-Air Man begins (intro); Air Man-c	97	194	291	606	1003	1400
24-(scarce) Air Man-c	103	206	309	644	1072	1500

NOTE: *Burgos* a-V2#2. *Jack Cole*-c-V2#2. *Eisner* a-10, V2#6r. *Ken Ernst* a-V2#4-7, 9, 10, 19, 21; c-V2#4. *Everett* a-V2#6, 7, 9, 11, 12, 20. *Guardineer* a-V2#5, 66. *Gustavson* a-V2#4-6. *Simon* c-V3#1. *Thompson* c-V2#7, 9, 10, 22.

KEEN KOMICS
Centaur Publications: V2#1, May, 1939 - V2#3, Nov, 1939

V2#1(Large size)-Dan Hastings (s/f), The Big Top, Bob Phantom the Magician, The Mad Goddess app.	97	194	606	1003	1400	
V2#2(Reg. size)-The Forbidden Idol of Machu Picchu; Cut Carson by Burgos begins						
	62	124	186	388	644	900
V2#3-Saddle Sniffl by Jack Cole, Circus Pays, Kings Revenge app.						
	62	124	186	388	644	900

NOTE: *Binder* a-V2#2. *Burgos* a-V2#2, 3. *Ken Ernst* a-V2#3. *Gustavson* a-V2#2. *Jack Cole* a-V2#3.

KEEN TEENS (Girls magazine)
Life's Romances Publ./Leader/Magazine Ent.: 1945 - No. 6, Aug-Sept, 1947

nn (#1)-14 pgs. Claire Voyant (cont'd. in other nn issue) movie photos, Dotty Dripple, Gertie O'Grady & Sissy; Van Johnson, Frank Sinatra photo-c						
	40	80	120	235	368	500
nn (#2, 1946)-16 pgs. Claire Voyant & 16 pgs. movie photos						
	28	56	84	162	256	350
3-6: 4-Glenn Ford photo-c. 5-Perry Como-c	14	28	42	82	121	160

KELLYS, THE (Formerly Rusty Comics; Spy Cases No. 26 on)
Marvel Comics (HPC): No. 23, Jan, 1950 - No. 25, June, 1950 (52 pgs.)

23-Teenage	13	26	39	74	105	135
24,25: 24-Margie app.	9	18	27	50	65	80

KEN MAYNARD WESTERN (Movie star)(See Wow Comics, 1936)
Fawcett Publ.: Sept, 1950 - No. 8, Feb, 1952 (All 36 pgs; photo front/back-c)

1-Ken Maynard & his horse Tarzan begin	50	100	150	305	490	675
2	30	60	90	173	267	360
3-8: 6-Atomic bomb explosion panel	22	44	66	125	193	260

KEN SHANNON (Becomes Gabby #11 on) (Also see Police Comics #103)
Quality Comics Group: Oct, 1951 - No. 10, Apr, 1953 (A private eye)

1-Crandall-a	40	80	120	235	368	500
2-Crandall-c/a(2)	29	58	87	167	264	360
3-Horror-c; Crandall-a	24	48	72	139	220	300
4,5-Crandall-a	21	42	63	122	191	260
6-Crandall-c/a; "The Weird Vampire Mob"-c/s	24	48	72	139	220	300
7,10: 7-Crandall-a. 10-Crandall-c	18	36	54	103	162	220
8,9: 8-Opium den drug use story	17	34	51	98	154	210

NOTE: *Crandall/Cuidera* c-1-10. *Jack Cole* a-1-9. #1-15 published after title change to Gabby.

KEN STUART
Publication Enterprises: Jan, 1949 (Sea Adventures)

1-Frank Borth-c/a	10	20	30	54	72	90

KENT BLAKE OF THE SECRET SERVICE (Spy)
Marvel/Atlas Comics(20CC): May, 1951 - No. 14, July, 1953

1-Injury to eye, bondage, torture; Brodsky-c	21	42	63	122	191	260
2-Drug use w/hypo scenes; Brodsky-c	15	30	45	85	130	175
3-14: 8-R.Q. Sale-a (2 pgs.)	10	20	30	56	76	95

NOTE: *Heath* c-5, 7, 8. *Infantino* c-12. *Maneely* c-3. *Sinnott* a-2(3). *Tuska* a-8(3pg.).

KENTS, THE
DC Comics: Aug, 1997 - No. 12, July, 1998 ($2.50, limited series)

1-12-Ostrander-s/art by Truman and Bair (#1-8), Mandrake (#9-12)		3.00
TPB ($19.95) r/#1-12		20.00

KERRY DRAKE (Also see A-1 Comics)
Argo: Jan, 1956 - No. 2, March, 1956

1,2-Newspaper-r	8	16	24	44	57	70

KERRY DRAKE DETECTIVE CASES (...Racket Buster No. 32,33)
(Also see Chamber of Clues & Green Hornet Comics #42-47)
Life's Romances/Com/Magazine Ent. No.1-5/Harvey No.6 on: 1944 - No. 5, 1944; No. 6, Jan, 1948 - No. 33, Aug, 1952

nn(1944)(A-1 Comics)(slightly over-size)	30	60	90	174	275	375
2	18	36	54	105	165	225
3-5(1944)	15	30	45	88	137	185
6,8(1948): Lady Crime by Powell. 8-Bondage-c	12	24	36	67	94	120
7-Kubert-a; biog of Andriola (artist)	13	26	39	74	105	135
9,10-Two-part marijuana story; Kerry smokes marijuana in #10						
	15	30	45	88	137	185
11-15	10	20	30	58	79	100
16-33	9	18	27	50	65	80

NOTE: *Andiola* c-6-9. *Berg* a-5. *Powell* a-10-23, 28, 29.

KEWPIES
Will Eisner Publications: Spring, 1949

1-Feiffer-a; Kewpie Doll ad on back cover	46	92	138	281	466	650

KEY COMICS
Consolidated Magazines: Jan, 1944 - No. 5, Aug, 1946

1-The Key, Will-O-The-Wisp begin	41	82	123	256	416	575
2 (3/44)	23	46	69	132	209	285
3,4: 4-(5/46)-Origin John Quincy The Atom (begins); Walter Johnson c-3-5						
	20	40	60	115	180	245
5-4pg. Faust Opera adaptation; Kiefer-a; back-c advertises "Masterpieces Illustrated" by						

Kid Colt (Outlaw) #2 © MAR

Kid Eternity #3 © QUA

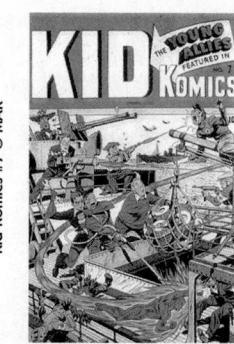

Kid Komics #7 © MAR

	GD 2.0	VG 4.0	FN 6.0	VF 8.0	VF/NM 9.0	NM- 9.2

Lloyd Jacquet after he left Classic Comics (no copies of Masterpieces Illustrated known)

| | 25 | 50 | 75 | 145 | 228 | 310 |

KEY RING COMICS
Dell Publishing Co.: 1941 (16 pgs.; two colors) (sold 5 for 10¢)

| 1-Sky Hawk, 1-Viking Carter, 1-Features Sleepy Samson, 1-Origin Greg Gilday-r/War Comics #2 | 9 | 18 | 27 | 47 | 61 | 75 |
| 1-Radior (Super hero) | 10 | 20 | 30 | 54 | 72 | 90 |

NOTE: Each book has two holes in spine to put in binder.

KID CARROTS
St. John Publishing Co.: September, 1953

| 1-Funny animal | 8 | 16 | 24 | 42 | 54 | 65 |

KID COLT OUTLAW (Kid Colt #1-4; ...Outlaw #5-on)(Also see All Western Winners, Best Western, Black Rider, Giant-Size..., Two-Gun Kid, Two-Gun Western, Western Winners, Wild Western, Wisco)
Marvel Comics(LCC) 1-16; Atlas(LMC) 17-102; Marvel 103-on: 8/48 - No. 139, 3/68; No. 140, 11/69 - No. 229, 4/79

1-Kid Colt & his horse Steel begin.	110	220	330	688	1144	1600
2	53	106	159	323	537	750
3-5: 4-Anti-Wertham editorial; Tex Taylor app. 5-Blaze Carson app.						
	42	84	126	256	421	585
6-8: 6-Tex Taylor app; 7-Nimo the Lion begins, ends #10						
	30	60	90	174	275	375
9,10 (52 pgs.)	30	60	90	174	275	375
11-Origin	35	70	105	201	318	435
12-20	20	40	60	117	184	250
21-32	16	32	48	94	147	200
33-45: Black Rider in all	14	28	42	80	115	150
46,47,49,50	12	24	36	67	94	120
48-Kubert-a	12	24	36	69	97	125
51-53,55,56	10	20	30	56	76	95
54-Williamson/Maneely-c	11	22	33	60	83	105
57-60,66: 4-pg. Williamson-a in all	7	14	21	49	80	110
61-63,67-78,80-86: 70-Severin-a. 69,73-Maneely-c. 86-Kirby-a(r).						
	6	12	18	37	59	80
64,65-Crandall-a	6	12	18	39	62	85
79,87: 79-Origin retold. 87-Davis-a(r)	6	12	18	39	62	85
88,89-Williamson-a in both (4 pgs.) 89-Redrawn Matt Slade #2						
	6	12	18	41	66	90
90-99,101-106,108,109: 91-Kirby/Ayers-c. 95-Kirby/Ayers-c/story. 102-Last 10¢ issue						
	5	10	15	32	51	70
100	5	10	15	35	55	75
107-Only Kirby sci-fi cover of title; Kirby -a.	6	12	18	41	66	90
110-(5/63)-1st app. Iron Mask (Iron Man type villain)	6	12	18	39	62	85
111-120: 114-(1/64)-2nd app. Iron Mask	4	8	12	26	41	55
121-129,133-139: 121-Rawhide Kid x-over. 125-Two-Gun Kid x-over. 139-Last 12¢ issue						
	3	6	9	20	30	40
130-132 (68 pgs.)-one new story each. 130-Origin	4	8	12	28	44	60
140-155: 140-Reprints begin (later issues mostly-r). 155-Last 15¢ issue						
	2	4	6	11	16	20
156-Giant; reprints (52 pgs.)	3	6	9	16	23	30
157-180,200: 170-Origin retold.	2	4	6	9	13	16
181-199	2	4	6	8	10	12
201-229: 201-New material w/Rawhide Kid app; Kane-c. 229-Rawhide Kid-r						
	1	3	4	6	8	10
205-209-(30¢-c variants, limited dist.)	5	10	15	30	48	65
218-220-(35¢-c variants, limited dist.)	7	14	21	47	76	105
...Album (no date; 1950's; Atlas Comics)-132 pgs.: random binding, cardboard cover, B&W stories; contents can vary (Rare)	86	172	258	538	894	1250

NOTE: Ayers a-many. Colan a-52, 53; c(p)-223, 228, 229. Crandall a-140r, 167r. Everett a-90, 137i, 205(1). Heath a-8(2); c-34, 35, 39, 44, 46, 48, 49, 57, 64. Heck a-135, 139. Jack Keller a-25(2), 26-68(3-4), 78, 94p, 98, 99, 108, 110, 130, 132, 140-150r. Kirby a-86r, 93, 96, 107, 119, 176(part); c-87, 92-95, 97, 99-112, 114-117, 121-123, 197r; w/Ditko c-89. Maneely a-12, 68, 81; c-17, 19, 40-43, 47, 52, 53, 62, 65, 68, 78, 81, 142r, 150r. Morrow a-173r, 216r. Rico a-13, 18. Severin a-58, 59, 143, 148, 149. Shores a-39, 41-43, 143r; c-1-10(most), 24. Sutton a-136, 137p, 225p(r). Wildey a-47, 54, 82, 144r. Williamson r-147, 170, 172, 216. Woodbridge a-64, 81. Black Rider in #33-45, 74, 86. Iron Mask in #110, 114, 121. Sam Hawk in #80, 84, 101, 111, 121, 146, 174, 181, 188.

KID COWBOY (Also see Approved Comics #4 & Boy Cowboy)
Ziff-Davis Publ./St. John (Approved Comics) #11,14: 1950 - No. 11, Wint, '52-'53; No. 13, April 1953; No. 14, June, 1954 (No #12) (Painted covers #1-10,13,14)

1-Lucy Belle & Red Feather begin	16	32	48	94	147	200
2-Maneely-c	11	22	33	62	86	110
3-11,13,14: (#3, spr. '51). 5-Berg-a. 14-Code approved						
	10	20	30	56	76	95

KID DEATH & FLUFFY HALLOWEEN SPECIAL

Event Comics: Oct, 1997 ($2.95, B&W, one-shot)

| 1-Variant-c by Cebollero & Quesada/Palmiotti | | | | | | 3.00 |

KID DEATH & FLUFFY SPRING BREAK SPECIAL
Event Comics: July, 1996 ($2.50, B&W, one-shot)

| 1-Quesada & Palmiotti-c/scripts | | | | | | 2.50 |

KIDDIE KAPERS
Kiddie Kapers Co., 1945/Decker Publ. (Red Top-Farrell): 1945?(nd); Oct, 1957; 1963 - 1964

1(nd, 1945-46?, 36 pgs.)-Infinity-c; funny animal	10	20	30	54	72	90
1(10/57)(Decker)-Little Bit-r from Kiddie Karnival	5	10	15	22	26	30
Super Reprint #7, 10('63), 12, 14('63), 15,17('64), 18('64): 10. 14-r/Animal Adventures #1. 15-Animal Advs. #? 17-Cowboys 'N' Injuns #?	2	4	6	8	11	14

KIDDIE KARNIVAL
Ziff-Davis Publ. Co. (Approved Comics): 1952 (25¢, 100 pgs.) (One Shot)

| nn-Rebound Little Bit #1,2; painted-c | 36 | 72 | 108 | 208 | 329 | 450 |

KID ETERNITY (Becomes Buccaneers) (See Hit Comics)
Quality Comics Group: Spring, 1946 - No. 18, Nov, 1949

1	103	206	309	644	1072	1500
2	41	82	123	250	400	550
3-Mac Raboy-a	41	82	123	253	409	565
4-10	25	50	75	145	228	310
11-18	19	38	57	109	172	235

KID ETERNITY
DC Comics: 1991 - No. 3, Nov, 1991 ($4.95, limited series)

| 1-3: Grant Morrison scripts/Duncan Fegredo-a/c | | | | | | 6.00 |
| TPB (2006, $14.99) r/#1-3 | | | | | | 15.00 |

KID ETERNITY
DC Comics (Vertigo): May, 1993 - No. 16, Sept, 1994 ($1.95, mature)

| 1-16: 1-Gold ink-c. 6-Photo-c. All Sean Phillips-c/a except #15 (Phillips-c/i only) | | | | | | 2.50 |

KID FROM DODGE CITY, THE
Atlas Comics (MMC): July, 1957 - No. 2, Sept, 1957

| 1-Don Heck-c | 10 | 20 | 30 | 56 | 76 | 95 |
| 2-Everett-c | 7 | 14 | 21 | 37 | 46 | 55 |

KID FROM TEXAS, THE (A Texas Ranger)
Atlas Comics (CSI): June, 1957 - No. 2, Aug, 1957

| 1-Powell-a; Severin-c | 10 | 20 | 30 | 56 | 76 | 95 |
| 2 | 7 | 14 | 21 | 37 | 46 | 55 |

KID KOKO
I. W. Enterprises: 1958

| Reprint #1,2-(r/M.E.'s Koko & Kola #4, 1947) | 2 | 4 | 6 | 8 | 11 | 14 |

KID KOMICS (Kid Movie Komics)
Timely Comics (USA 1,2/FCI 3-10): Feb, 1943 - No. 10, Spring, 1946

1-Origin Captain Wonder & sidekick Tim Mullrooney, & Subbie; intro the Sea-Going Lad, Pinto Pete, & Trixie Trouble; Knuckles & Whitewash Jones (from Young Allies) app.; Wolverton-a (7 pgs.)	423	846	1269	2855	5028	7200
2-The Young Allies, Red Hawk, & Tommy Tyme begin; last Captain Wonder & Subbie	200	400	600	1250	2075	2900
3-The Vision, Daredevils & Red Hawk app.	152	304	456	950	1575	2200
4-The Destroyer begins; Sub-Mariner app.; Red Hawk & Tommy Tyme end						
	128	256	384	800	1325	1850
5,6: 5-Tommy Tyme begins, ends #10	97	194	291	606	1003	1400
7-10: 7,10-The Whizzer app. Destroyer not in #7,8. 10-Last Destroyer, Young Allies & Whizzer	86	172	258	538	894	1250

NOTE: Brodsky c-5. Schomburg c-2-4, 6-10. Shores c-1. Captain Wonder c-1, 2. The Young Allies c-3-10.

KID MONTANA (Formerly Davy Crockett Frontier Fighter; The Gunfighters No. 51 on)
Charlton Comics: V2#9, Nov, 1957 - No. 50, Mar, 1965

V2#9 (#1)	4	8	12	28	44	60
10	3	6	9	20	30	40
11,12,14-20	3	6	9	16	22	28
13-Williamson-a	3	6	9	20	30	40
21-35: 25,31-Giordano-a/c. 32-Origin Kid Montana. 34-Geronimo-c/s. 35-Snow Monster-c/s						
	2	4	6	11	16	20
36-50: 36-Dinosaur-c/s. 37,48-Giordano-c	2	4	6	9	12	15

NOTE: Title change to Montana Kid on cover #44 & 45; remained Kid Montana on inside. Chasal a-29,30. Giordano c-25,31,37,48. Giordano/Alascia c-12. Mastroserio a-9,11,13,14,22; c-11,14. Masulli/Mastrosrio c-1, 2. Montes/Bache c-42. Morisi c-16,32-34,36?,40,41,44,46; a-13,15,16,31-50. Nicholas/Alascia a-44,48.

KID MOVIE KOMICS (Formerly Kid Komics; Rusty Comics #12 on)
Timely Comics: No. 11, Summer, 1946

The Killers #1 © ME

Kilroy V2 #1 © Joe Pruett

Kinetic #1 © Puckett & Purepop

	GD 2.0	VG 4.0	FN 6.0	VF 8.0	VF/NM 9.0	NM- 9.2

11-Silly Seal & Ziggy Pig; 2 pgs. Kurtzman "Hey Look" plus 6 pg. "Pigtales" story ... 27 | 54 | 81 | 158 | 249 | 340

KIDNAPPED (Robert Louis Stevenson's...also see Movie Comics)(Disney)
Dell Publishing Co.: No. 1101, May, 1960
Four Color 1101-Movie, photo-c ... 6 | 12 | 18 | 43 | 69 | 95

KIDNAP RACKET (See Harvey Comics Hits No. 57)

KID SLADE GUNFIGHTER (Formerly Matt Slade...)
Atlas Comics (SPI): No. 5, Jan, 1957 - No. 8, July, 1957
5-Maneely, Roth, Severin in all; Maneely-c ... 13 | 26 | 39 | 72 | 101 | 130
6,8-Severin-c ... 8 | 16 | 24 | 44 | 57 | 70
7-Williamson/Mayo-a, 4 pgs. ... 10 | 20 | 30 | 56 | 76 | 95

KID SUPREME (See Supreme)
Image Comics (Extreme Studios): Mar, 1996 - No. 3, July, 1996 ($2.50)
1-3: Fraga-a/scripts. 3-Glory-c/app. ... 2.50

KID TERRIFIC
Image Comics: Nov, 1998 ($2.95, B&W)
1-Snyder & Diliberto-s/a ... 3.00

KID ZOO COMICS
Street & Smith Publications: July, 1948 (52 pgs.)
1-Funny Animal ... 29 | 58 | 87 | 170 | 268 | 365

KILLER (...Tales By Timothy Truman)
Eclipse Comics: March, 1985 ($1.75, one-shot, Baxter paper)
1-Timothy Truman-c/a ... 2.50

KILLER INSTINCT (Video game)
Acclaim Comics: June, 1996 - No. 6 ($2.50, limited series)
1-6: 1-Bart Sears-a(p). 4-Special #1. 5-Special #2. 6-Special #3 ... 3.00

KILLER PRINCESSES
Oni Press: Dec, 2001 - No. 3, Apr, 2003 ($2.95, limited series)
1-3-Gail Simone-s/Lea Hernandez-a ... 3.00
TPB (11/04, $9.95, digest size) r/#1-3; intro by Mark Waid ... 10.00

KILLERS, THE
Magazine Enterprises: 1947 - No. 2, 1948 (No month)
1-Mr. Zin, the Hatchet Killer; mentioned in SOTI, pgs. 179,180; used by N.Y. Legis. Comm.; L. B. Cole-c ... 114 | 228 | 342 | 713 | 1182 | 1650
2-(Scarce)-Hashish smoking story; "Dying, Dying, Dead" drug story; Whitney, Ingels-a; Whitney hanging-c ... 93 | 186 | 279 | 581 | 966 | 1350

KILLING GIRL
Image Comics: Aug, 2007 - No. 5 ($2.99, limited series)
1-Frank Espinosa-s/Glen Brunswick-s; covers by Espinosa and Frank Cho ... 3.00

KILLING JOKE, THE (See Batman: The Killing Joke under Batman one-shots)

KILLPOWER: THE EARLY YEARS
Marvel Comics UK: Sept, 1993 - No. 4, Dec, 1993 ($1.75, mini-series)
1-($2.95)-Foil embossed-c ... 3.00
2-4: 2-Genetix app. 3-Punisher app. ... 2.25

KILLRAVEN (See Amazing Adventures #18 (5/73))
Marvel Comics: Feb, 2001 ($2.99, one-shot)
1-Linsner-s/a/c ... 3.00

KILLRAVEN
Marvel Comics: Dec, 2002 - No. 6, May, 2003 ($2.99, limited series)
1-6-Alan Davis-s/a(p)/Mark Farmer-i ... 3.00
HC (2007, $19.99) r/#1-6; cover gallery, pencil art; foreward by Alan Davis ... 20.00

KILLRAZOR
Image Comics (Top Cow Productions): Aug, 1995 ($2.50, one-shot)
1 ... 2.50

KILL YOUR BOYFRIEND
DC Comics (Vertigo): June, 1995 ($4.95, one-shot)
1-Grant Morrison story ... 6.00
1 ($5.95, 1998) 2nd printing ... 6.00

KILROY (Volume 2)
Caliber Press: 1998 ($2.95, B&W)
1-Pruett-s ... 3.00

KILROY IS HERE
Caliber Press: 1995 ($2.95, B&W)

	GD 2.0	VG 4.0	FN 6.0	VF 8.0	VF/NM 9.0	NM- 9.2

1-10 ... 3.00

KILROYS, THE
B&I Publ. Co. No. 1-19/American Comics Group: June-July, 1947 - No. 54, June-July, 1955
1 ... 22 | 44 | 66 | 126 | 198 | 270
2 ... 13 | 26 | 39 | 74 | 105 | 135
3-5: 5-Gross-a ... 11 | 22 | 33 | 62 | 86 | 110
6-10: 8-Milt Gross's Moronica ... 9 | 18 | 27 | 52 | 69 | 85
11-20: 14-Gross-a ... 9 | 18 | 27 | 47 | 61 | 75
21-30 ... 8 | 16 | 24 | 42 | 54 | 65
31-47,50-54 ... 8 | 16 | 24 | 40 | 50 | 60
48,49-(3-D effect-c/stories) ... 17 | 34 | 51 | 98 | 154 | 210

KILROY: THE SHORT STORIES
Caliber Press: 1995 ($2.95, B&W)
1 ... 3.00

KIN
Image Comics (Top Cow): Mar, 2000 - No. 6, Sept, 2000 ($2.95)
1-5-Gary Frank-s/c/a ... 3.00
1-($6.95) DF Alternate footprint cover ... 7.00
6-($3.95) ... 4.00
... Descent of Man TPB (2002, $19.95) r/ #1-6 ... 20.00

KINDRED, THE
Image Comics (WildStorm Productions): Mar, 1994 - No. 4, July, 1995 ($1.95, limited series)
1-($2.50)-Grifter & Backlash app. in all; bound-in trading card ... 2.50
2-4 ... 2.50
2,3: 2-Variant-c. 3-Alternate-c by Portacio, see Deathblow #5 ... 4.00
Trade paperback (2/95, $9.95) ... 10.00
NOTE: Booth c/a-1-4. The first four issues contain coupons redeemable for a Jim Lee Grifter/Backlash print.

KINDRED II, THE
DC Comics (WildStorm): Mar, 2002 - No. 4, June, 2002 ($2.50, limited series)
1-4-Booth-s/Booth & Regla-a ... 2.50

KINETIC
DC Comics (Focus): May, 2004 - No. 8, Dec, 2004 ($2.50)
1-8-Puckett-s/Pleece-a/c ... 2.50
TPB (2005, $9.99) r/#1-8; cover gallery and sketch pages ... 10.00

KING (Magazine)
Skywald Publ.: Mar, 1971 - No. 2, July, 1971
1-Violence; semi-nudity; Boris Vallejo-a (2 pgs.) ... 4 | 8 | 12 | 28 | 44 | 60
2-Photo-c ... 3 | 6 | 9 | 18 | 27 | 35

KING ARTHUR AND THE KNIGHTS OF JUSTICE
Marvel Comics UK: Dec, 1993 - No. 3, Feb, 1994 ($1.25, limited series)
1-3: TV adaptation ... 2.50

KING CLASSICS
King Features : 1977 (36 pgs., cardboard-c) (Printed in Spain for U.S. distr.)
1-Connecticut Yankee, 2-Last of the Mohicans, 3-Moby Dick, 4-Robin Hood, 5-Swiss Family Robinson, 6-Robinson Crusoe, 7-Treasure Island, 8-20,000 Leagues, 9-Christmas Carol, 10-Huck Finn, 11-Around the World in 80 Days, 12-Davy Crockett, 13-Don Quixote, 14-Gold Bug, 15-Ivanhoe, 16-Three Musketeers, 17-Baron Munchausen, 18-Alice in Wonderland, 19-Black Arrow, 20-Five Weeks in a Balloon, 21-Great Expectations, 22-Gulliver's Travels, 23-Prince & Pauper, 24-Lawrence of Arabia (Originals, 1977-78)
each.... ... 2 | 4 | 6 | 9 | 12 | 15
Reprints (1979); HRN-24 ... 1 | 2 | 3 | 5 | 7 | 9
NOTE: The first eight issues were not numbered. Issues No. 25-32 were advertised but not published. The 1977 originals have HRN 32a; the 1978 originals have HRN 32b.

KING COLT (See Luke Short's Western Stories)

KING COMICS (Strip reprints)
David McKay Publications/Standard #156-on: 4/36 - No. 155, 11-12/49; No. 156, Spr/50 - No. 159, 2/52 (Winter on-c)
1-1st app. Flash Gordon by Alex Raymond; Brick Bradford (1st app.), Popeye, Henry (1st app.) & Mandrake the Magician (1st app.) begin; Popeye-c begin ... 1250 | 2500 | 3750 | 10,000 | – | –
2 ... 360 | 720 | 1080 | 1980 | 2790 | 3600
3 ... 245 | 490 | 735 | 1348 | 1899 | 2450
4 ... 190 | 380 | 570 | 1045 | 1473 | 1900
5 ... 140 | 280 | 420 | 770 | 1085 | 1400
6-10: 9-X-Mas-c ... 95 | 190 | 285 | 523 | 737 | 950
11-20 ... 75 | 150 | 225 | 413 | 582 | 750
21-30: 21-X-Mas-c ... 55 | 110 | 165 | 303 | 427 | 550
31-40: 33-Last Segar Popeye ... 45 | 90 | 135 | 248 | 349 | 450

King Comics #23 © DMP

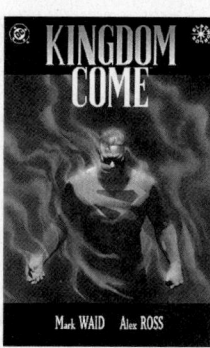

Kingdom Come #4 © DC

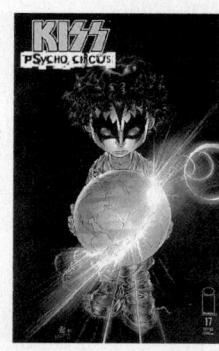

KISS: The Psycho Circus #17 © KISS Catalog

	GD 2.0	VG 4.0	FN 6.0	VF 8.0	VF/NM 9.0	NM- 9.2		GD 2.0	VG 4.0	FN 6.0	VF 8.0	VF/NM 9.0	NM- 9.2

41-50: 46-Text illos by Marge Buell contain characters similar to Lulu, Alvin & Tubby.

	GD	VG	FN	VF	VF/NM	NM-
50-The Lone Ranger begins	32	64	96	186	293	400
51-60: 52-Barney Baxter begins?	23	46	69	132	209	285
61-The Phantom begins	24	48	72	139	220	300
62-80: 76-Flag-c. 79-Blondie begins	17	34	51	98	154	210
81-99	14	28	42	81	118	155
100	16	32	48	92	144	195

101-114: 114-Last Raymond issue (1 pg.); Flash Gordon by Austin Briggs begins, ends #155

	GD	VG	FN	VF	VF/NM	NM-
	14	28	42	76	108	140
115-145: 117-Phantom origin retold	10	20	30	56	76	95
146,147-Prince Valiant in both	9	18	27	50	65	80
148-155: 155-Flash Gordon ends (11-12/49)	9	18	27	50	65	80
156-159: 156-New logo begins (Standard)	9	18	27	47	61	75

NOTE: Marge Buell text illos in No. 24-46 at least.

KING CONAN (Conan The King No. 20 on)
Marvel Comics Group: Mar, 1980 - No. 19, Nov, 1983 (52 pgs.)

1						6.00
2-19: 4-Death of Thoth Amon. 7-1st Paul Smith-a, 1 pg. pin-up (9/81)						4.00

NOTE: **J. Buscema** a-1-9p, 17p; c(p)-1-5, 7-9, 14, 17. **Kaluta** c-19. **Nebres** a-17i, 18, 19i. **Severin** c-18. **Simonson** c-6.

KING DAVID
DC Comics (Vertigo): 2002 ($19.95, 8 1/2" x 11")

nn-Story of King David; Kyle Baker-s/a						20.00

KINGDOM, THE
DC Comics: Feb, 1999 - No. 2, Feb, 1999 ($2.95/$1.99, limited series)

1,2-Waid-s; sequel to Kingdom Come; introduces Hypertime						4.00
...: Kid Flash 1 (2/99, $1.99) Waid-s/Pararillo-a, ...: Nightstar 1 (2/99, $1.99) Waid-s/Haley-a, ...: Offspring 1 (2/99, $1.99) Waid-s/Quitely-a, ...: Planet Krypton 1 (2/99, $1.99) Waid-s/Kitson-a, ...: Son of the Bat 1 (2/99, $1.99) Waid-s/Apthorp-a						2.50

KINGDOM COME
DC Comics: 1996 - No. 4, 1996 ($4.95, painted limited series)

	GD	VG	FN	VF	VF/NM	NM-
1-Mark Waid scripts & Alex Ross-painted c/a in all; tells the last days of the DC Universe; 1st app. Magog	1	2	3	5	6	8
2-Superman forms new Justice League	1	2	3	4	5	7
3-Return of Captain Marvel						5.00
4-Final battle of Superman and Captain Marvel	1	2	3	4	5	7
Deluxe Slipcase Edition-($89.95) w/Revelations companion book, 12 new story pages, foil stamped covers, signed and numbered						120.00
Hardcover Edition-($29.95)-Includes 12 new story pages and artwork from Revelations, new cover artwork with gold foil inlay						35.00
Hardcover 2nd printing						30.00
Softcover Ed.-($14.95)-Includes 12 new story pgs. & artwork from Revelations, new c-artwork						15.00

KINGDOM OF THE WICKED
Dark Horse Books: Dec. 2004 ($15.95, hardcover graphic novel)

nn-Ian Edginton-s/D'Israeli-a						16.00

KING KONG (See Movie Comics)

KING KONG: THE 8TH WONDER OF THE WORLD (Adaptation of 2005 movie)
Dark Horse Comics: Dec, 2005 ($3.99, planned limited series completed in TPB)

1-Photo-c; Dustin Weaver-a/Christian Gossett-s						4.00
TPB (11/06, $12.95) r/#1 and unpublished parts 2&3; photo-c; Dorman paintings						13.00

KING LEONARDO & HIS SHORT SUBJECTS (TV)
Dell Publishing Co./Gold Key: Nov-Jan, 1961-62 - No. 4, Sept, 1963

	GD	VG	FN	VF	VF/NM	NM-
Four Color 1242,1278	12	24	36	84	150	215
01390-207(5-7/62)(Dell)	9	18	27	61	103	145
1 (10/62)	10	20	30	71	126	180
2-4	8	16	24	56	93	130

KING LOUIE & MOWGLI (See Jungle Book under Movie Comics)
Gold Key: May, 1968 (Disney)

	GD	VG	FN	VF	VF/NM	NM-
1 (#10223-805)-Characters from Jungle Book	3	6	9	18	27	35

KING OF DIAMONDS (TV)
Dell Publishing Co.: July-Sept, 1962

	GD	VG	FN	VF	VF/NM	NM-
01-391-209-Photo-c	4	8	12	24	37	50

KING OF KINGS (Movie)
Dell Publishing Co.: No. 1236, Oct-Nov, 1961

	GD	VG	FN	VF	VF/NM	NM-
Four Color 1236-Photo-c	7	14	21	50	83	115

KING OF THE BAD MEN OF DEADWOOD

Avon Periodicals: 1950 (See Wild Bill Hickok #16)

	GD	VG	FN	VF	VF/NM	NM-
nn-Kinstler-c; Kamen/Feldstein-r/Cowpuncher #2	15	30	45	90	140	190

KING OF THE ROYAL MOUNTED (See Famous Feature Stories, King Comics, Red Ryder #3 & Super Book #2, 6)

KING OF THE ROYAL MOUNTED (Zane Grey's...)
David McKay/Dell Publishing Co.: No. 1, May, 1937; No. 9, 1940; No. 207, Dec, 1948 - No. 935, Sept-Nov, 1958

	GD	VG	FN	VF	VF/NM	NM-
Feature Books 1 (5/37)(McKay)	86	172	258	538	894	1250
Large Feature Comic 9 (1940)	47	94	141	287	474	660
Four Color 207(#1, 12/48)	14	28	42	97	175	250
Four Color 265,283	8	16	24	58	97	135
Four Color 310,340	6	12	18	43	69	95
Four Color 363,384, 8(6-8/52)-10	6	12	18	39	62	85
11-20	5	10	15	35	55	75
21-28(3-5/58), Four Color 935(9-11/58)	4	8	12	28	44	60

NOTE: 4-Color No. 207, 265, 283, 310, 340, 363, 384 are all newspaper reprints with **Jim Gary** art. No. 8 on are all Dell originals. Painted c-No. 9-on.

KINGPIN
Marvel Comics: Nov, 1997 ($5.99, squarebound, one-shot)

nn-Spider-Man & Daredevil vs. Kingpin; Stan Lee-s/ John Romita Sr.-a						6.00

KINGPIN
Marvel Comics: Aug, 2003 - No. 7, Jan, 2004 ($2.50/$2.99, limited series)

1-6-Bruce Jones-s/Sean Phillips & Klaus Janson-a						2.50
7-($2.99)						3.00

KING RICHARD & THE CRUSADERS
Dell Publishing Co.: No. 588, Oct, 1954

	GD	VG	FN	VF	VF/NM	NM-
Four Color 588-Movie, Matt Baker-a, photo-c	9	18	27	63	107	150

KINGS OF THE NIGHT
Dark Horse Comics: 1990 - No. 2, 1990 ($2.25, limited series)

1,2-Robert E. Howard adaptation; Bolton-c						2.50

KING SOLOMON'S MINES (Movie)
Avon Periodicals: 1951

	GD	VG	FN	VF	VF/NM	NM-
nn (#1 on 1st page)	40	80	120	235	368	500

KING TIGER & MOTORHEAD
Dark Horse Comics: Aug, 1996 - No. 2, Sept, 1996 ($2.95, limited series)

1,2: Chichester scripts						3.00

KIPLING, RUDYARD (See Mowgli, The Jungle Book)

KISS (See Crazy Magazine, Howard the Duck #12, 13, Marvel Comics Super Special #1, 5, Rock Fantasy Comics #10 & Rock N' Roll Comics #9)

KISS
Dark Horse Comics: June, 2002 - No. 13, Sept, 2003 ($2.99, limited series)

1-Photo-c and J. Scott Campbell-c; Casey-s						4.00
2-13: 2-Photo-c and J. Scott Campbell-c. 3-Photo-c and Leinil Yu-c						3.00
...: Men and Monsters TPB (9/03, $12.95) r/#7-10						13.00
...: Rediscovery TPB (2003, $9.95) r/#1-3						10.00
...: Return of the Phantom TPB (2003, $9.95) r/#4-6						10.00
...: Unholy War TPB (2004, $9.95) r/#11-13						10.00

KISS 4K
Platinum Studios Comics: May, 2007 - Present ($3.99/$2.99)

1-Sprague-s/Crossley & Campos-a/Migliari-c						4.00
1-B&W sketch-c						6.00
1-Destroyer Edition ($50.00, 30"x18", edition of 5000)						50.00
2,3-($2.99)						3.00

KISS: THE PSYCHO CIRCUS
Image Comics: Aug, 1997 - No. 31, June, 2000 ($1.95/$2.25/$2.50)

	GD	VG	FN	VF	VF/NM	NM-
1-Holguin-s/Medina-a(p)	1	2	3	5	6	8
1-2nd & 3rd printings						2.50
2						5.00
3,4: 4-Photo-c						4.00
5-8: 5-Begin $2.25-c						3.00
9-29						2.50
30,31: 30-Begin $2.50-c						2.50
Book 1 TPB ('98, $12.95) r/#1-6						13.00
Book 2 Destroyer TPB (8/99, $9.95) r/#10-13						10.00
Book 3 Whispered Scream TPB ('00, $9.95) r/#7-9,18						10.00
...Magazine 1 ($6.95) r/#1-3 plus interviews						7.00
...Magazine 2-5 ($4.95) 2-r/#4,5 plus interviews. 3-r/#6,7. 4-r/#8,9						5.00

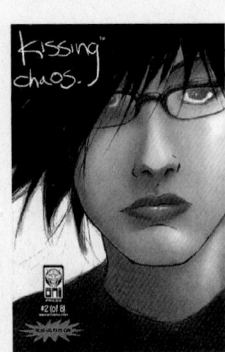

Kissing Chaos #2 © Arthur Dela Cruz

Knockout Adventures #1 © FH

Kobra #7 © DC

	GD 2.0	VG 4.0	FN 6.0	VF 8.0	VF/NM 9.0	NM- 9.2
Wizard Edition ('98, supplement) Bios, tour preview and interviews						2.50

KISSING CHAOS
Oni Press: Sept, 2001 - No. 8, Mar, 2002 ($2.25, B&W, 6" x 9", limited series)

1-8-Arthur Dela Cruz-s/a						2.50
...: Nine Lives (12/03, $2.99, regular comic-sized)						3.00
...: 1000 Words (7/03, $2.99, regular comic-sized)						3.00
TPB (9/02, $17.95) r/#1-8						18.00

KISSING CHAOS: NONSTOP BEAUTY
Oni Press: Oct, 2002 - No. 4, March, 2003 ($2.95, B&W, 6" x 9", limited series)

1-4-Arthur Dela Cruz-s/a						3.00
TPB (9/03, $11.95) r/#1-4						12.00

KISS KISS BANG BANG
CrossGen Comics: Feb, 2004 - No. 5, Jun, 2004 ($2.95)

1-5-Bedard-s/Perkins-a						3.00

KISSYFUR (TV)
DC Comics: 1989 (Sept.) ($2.00, 52 pgs., one-shot)

1-Based on Saturday morning cartoon						4.00

KIT CARSON (Formerly All True Detective Cases No. 4; Fighting Davy Crockett No. 9; see Blazing Sixguns & Frontier Fighters)
Avon Periodicals: 1950; No. 2, 8/51 - No. 3, 12/51; No. 5, 11-12/54 - No. 8, 9/55 (No #4)

nn(#1) (1950)- "...Indian Scout" ; r-Cowboys 'N' Injuns #?	14	28	42	76	108	140
2(8/51)	10	20	30	56	76	95
3(12/51)- "...Fights the Comanche Raiders"	9	18	27	50	65	80
5-6,8(11-12/54-9/55): 5-Formerly All True Detective Cases (last pre-code); titled "...and the Trail of Doom"	9	18	27	47	61	75
7-McCann-a?	9	18	27	47	61	75
I.W. Reprint #10('63)-r/Kit Carson #1; Severin-a	2	4	6	11	16	20
NOTE: *Kinstler* c-1-3, 5-8.

KIT CARSON & THE BLACKFEET WARRIORS
Realistic: 1953

nn-Reprint; Kinstler-c	9	18	27	52	69	85

KIT KARTER
Dell Publishing Co.: May-July, 1962

1	3	6	9	19	29	38

KITTY
St. John Publishing Co.: Oct, 1948

1-Teenage; Lily Renee-c/a	8	16	24	44	57	70

KITTY PRYDE, AGENT OF S.H.I.E.L.D. (Also see Excalibur and Mekanix)
Marvel Comics: Dec, 1997 - No. 3, Feb, 1998 ($2.50, limited series)

1-3-Hama-s						2.50

KITTY PRYDE AND WOLVERINE (Also see Uncanny X-Men & X-Men)
Marvel Comics Group: Nov, 1984 - No. 6, Apr, 1985 (Limited series)

1-6: Characters from X-Men						4.50

KLARER GIVEAWAYS (See Wisco in the Promotional Comics section)

KNIGHTHAWK
Acclaim Comics (Windjammer): Sept, 1995 - No. 6, Nov, 1995 ($2.50, lim. series)

1-6: 6-origin						2.50

KNIGHTMARE
Antarctic Press: July, 1994 - May, 1995 ($2.75, B&W, mature readers)

1-6						2.75

KNIGHTMARE
Image Comics (Extreme Studios): Feb, 1995 - No. 5, June, 1995 ($2.50)

0 ($3.50)						3.50
1-5: 4-Quesada & Palmiotti variant-c, 5-Flip book w/Warcry						2.50

KNIGHTS 4 (See Marvel Knights 4)

KNIGHTS OF PENDRAGON, THE (Also see Pendragon)
Marvel Comics Ltd.: July, 1990 - No. 18, Dec, 1991 ($1.95)

1-18: 1-Capt. Britain app. 2,8-Free poster inside. 9,10-Bolton-c. 11,18-Iron Man app.						2.50

KNIGHTS OF THE ROUND TABLE
Dell Publishing Co.: No. 540, Mar, 1954

Four Color 540-Movie, photo-c		7	14	21	47	76	105

KNIGHTS OF THE ROUND TABLE

Pines Comics: No. 10, April, 1957

10	5	10	15	24	30	35

KNIGHTS OF THE ROUND TABLE
Dell Publishing Co.: Nov-Jan, 1963-64

1 (12-397-401)-Painted-c	3	6	9	21	32	42

KNIGHTSTRIKE (Also see Operation: Knightstrike)
Image Comics (Extreme Studios): Jan, 1996 ($2.50)

1-Rob Liefeld & Eric Stephenson story; Extreme Destroyer Part 6.						2.50

KNIGHT WATCHMAN (See Big Bang Comics & Dr. Weird)
Image Comics: June, 1998 - No. 4, Oct, 1998 ($2.95/$3.50, B&W, lim. series)

1-3-Ben Torres-c/a in all						3.00
4-($3.50)						3.50

KNIGHT WATCHMAN: GRAVEYARD SHIFT
Caliber Press: 1994 ($2.95, B&W)

1,2-Ben Torres-a						3.00

KNOCK KNOCK (...Who's There?)
Dell Publ./Gerona Publications: No. 801, 1936 (52 pgs.) (8x9", B&W)

801-Joke book; Bob Dunn-a	10	20	30	54	72	90

KNOCKOUT ADVENTURES
Fiction House Magazines: Winter, 1953-54

1-Reprints Fight Comics #53 w/Rip Carson-c/s	14	28	42	76	108	140

KNUCKLES (Spin-off of Sonic the Hedgehog)
Archie Publications: Apr, 1997 - Present ($1.50/$1.75/$1.79)

1-29						2.50

KNUCKLES' CHAOTIX
Archie Publications: Jan, 1996 ($2.00, annual)

1						3.00

KOBALT
DC Comics (Milestone): June, 1994 - No. 16, Sept, 1995 ($1.75/$2.50)

1-16: 1-Byrne-c. 4-Intro Page. 16-Kent Williams-c						2.50

KOBRA (Unpublished #8 appears in DC Special Series No. 1)
National Periodical Publications: Feb-Mar, 1976 - No. 7, Mar-Apr, 1977

1-1st app.; Kirby-a redrawn by Marcos; only 25¢-c	1	3	4	6	8	10
2-7: (All 30¢ issues) 3-Giffen-a						6.00
NOTE: *Austin* a-3i. *Buckler* a-5p; c-5p. *Kubert* c-4. *Nasser* a-6p, 7; c-7.

KOKEY KOALA (...and the Magic Button)
Toby Press: May, 1952

1	11	22	33	62	86	110

KOKO AND KOLA (Also see A-1 Comics #16 & Tick Tock Tales)
Com/Magazine Enterprises: Fall, 1946 - No. 5, May, 1947; No. 6, 1950

1-Funny animal	12	24	36	67	94	120
2-X-Mas-c	8	16	24	44	57	70
3-6: 6(A-1 28)	8	16	24	40	50	60

KO KOMICS
Gerona Publications: Oct, 1945 (scarce)

1-The Duke of Darkness & The Menace (hero)	73	146	219	456	758	1060

KOLCHAK: THE NIGHT STALKER (TV)
Moonstone: 2002 - Present ($6.50/$6.95)

1-($6.50) Jeff Rice-s/Gordon Purcell-a						6.50
... Black & White & Read All Over (2005, $4.95) short stories by various; 2 covers						5.00
... Devil in the Details (2003, $6.95) Trevor Von Eeden-a						7.00
... Eve of Terror (2005, $5.95) Gentile-s/Figueroa-a/ Beck-c						6.00
... Fever Pitch (2002, $6.95) Christopher Jones-a						7.00
... Get of Belial (2002, $6.95) Art Nichols-a						7.00
... Lambs to the Slaughter (2003, $6.95) Trevor Von Eeden-a						7.00
... Pain Most Human (2004, $6.95) Greg Scott-a						7.00
... Tales: The Frankenstein Agenda 1 (2007 - No. 3, $3.50) Michelinie-s						3.50
... Tales of the Night Stalker 1-7 (2003-Present, $3.50) two covers by Moore & Ulanski						3.50
TPB (2004, $17.95) r/#1, Get of Belial & Fever Pitch						18.00
Vol. 2: Terror Within TPB (2006, $16.95) r/Pain Most Human, Pain Without Tears & Devil in the Details						17.00

KOMIC KARTOONS
Timely Comics (EPC): Fall, 1945 - No. 2, Winter, 1945

1,2-Andy Wolf, Bertie Mouse	20	40	60	117	184	250

Kong the Untamed #4 © DC

Krazy Komics #8 © MAR

Krypto the Superdog #5 © DC

	GD 2.0	VG 4.0	FN 6.0	VF 8.0	VF/NM 9.0	NM- 9.2		GD 2.0	VG 4.0	FN 6.0	VF 8.0	VF/NM 9.0	NM- 9.2

KOMIK PAGES (Formerly Snap; becomes Bullseye #11)
Harry 'A' Chesler, Jr. (Our Army, Inc.): Apr, 1945 (All reprints)

10(#1 on inside)-Land O' Nod by Rick Yager (2 pgs.), Animal Crackers, Foxy GrandPa, Tom, Dick & Mary, Cheerio Minstrels, Red Starr plus other 1-2 pg. strips; Cole-a	23	46	69	135	213	290

KONA (...Monarch of Monster Isle)
Dell Publishing Co.: Feb-Apr, 1962 - No. 21, Jan-Mar, 1967 (Painted-c)

Four Color 1256 (#1)	9	18	27	60	100	140
2-10: 4-Anak begins. 6-Gil Kane-c	5	10	15	32	51	70
11-21	4	8	12	26	41	55

NOTE: *Glanzman a-all issues.*

KONGA (Fantastic Giants No. 24) (See Return of...)
Charlton Comics: 1960; No. 2, Aug, 1961 - No. 23, Nov, 1965

1(1960)-Based on movie; Giordano-c	23	46	69	169	302	435
2-5: 2-Giordano-c; no Ditko-a	10	20	30	73	129	185
6-15	9	18	27	60	100	140
16-23	6	12	18	39	62	85

NOTE: *Ditko a-1, 3-15; c-4, 6-9. Glanzman a-12. Montes & Bache a-16-23.*

KONGA'S REVENGE (Formerly Return of...)
Charlton Comics: No. 2, Summer, 1963 - No. 3, Fall, 1964; Dec, 1968

2,3: 2-Ditko-c/a	6	12	18	41	66	90
1(12/68)-Reprints Konga's Revenge #3	3	6	9	17	25	32

KONG THE UNTAMED
National Periodical Publications: June-July, 1975 - V2#5, Feb-Mar, 1976

1-1st app. Kong; Wrightson-c; Alcala-a	2	4	6	8	10	12
2-Wrightson-c; Alcala-a	1	2	3	5	7	9
3-5: 3-Alcala-a						6.00

KOOKIE
Dell Publishing Co.: Feb-Apr, 1962 - No. 2, May-July, 1962 (15 cents)

1-Written by John Stanley; Bill Williams-a	8	16	24	54	90	125
2	7	14	21	49	80	110

KOOSH KINS
Archie Comics: Oct, 1991 - No. 3, Feb, 1992 ($1.00, bi-monthly, limited series)

1-3		2.50

NOTE: *No. 4 was planned, but cancelled.*

KORAK, SON OF TARZAN (Edgar Rice Burroughs)(See Tarzan #139)
Gold Key: Jan, 1964 - No. 45, Jan, 1972 (Painted-c No. 1-?)

1-Russ Manning-a	9	18	27	60	100	140
2-5-Russ Manning-a	5	10	15	32	51	70
6-11-Russ Manning-a	4	8	12	28	44	60
12-23: 12,13-Warren Tufts-a. 14-Jon of the Kalahari ends. 15-Mabu, Jungle Boy begins.						
21-Manning-a. 23-Last 12¢ issue	4	8	12	24	37	50
24-30	3	6	9	19	29	38
31-45	3	6	9	16	22	28

KORAK, SON OF TARZAN (Tarzan Family #60 on; see Tarzan #230)
National Periodical Publications: V9#46, May-June, 1972 - V12#56, Feb-Mar, 1974; No. 57, May-June, 1975 - No. 59, Sept-Oct, 1975 (Edgar Rice Burroughs)

46-(52 pgs.)-Carson of Venus begins (origin), ends #56; Pellucidar feature; Weiss-a	3	6	9	13	18	22
47-59: 49-Origin Korak retold	1	3	4	6	8	10

NOTE: *All have covers by Joe Kubert. Manning strip reprints-No. 57-59. Murphy Anderson a-52. Michael Kaluta a-46-56. Frank Thorne a-46-51.*

KORE
Image Comics: Apr, 2003 - No. 5, Sept, 2003 ($2.95)

1-5: 1-Two covers by Capullo and Seeley; Seeley-a (p)		3.00

KORG: 70,000 B. C. (TV)
Charlton Publications: May, 1975 - No. 9, Nov, 1976 (Hanna-Barbera)

1,2: 1-Boyette-c/a. 2-Painted-c; Byrne text illos	2	4	6	10	14	18
3-9	2	4	6	8	10	12

KORNER KID COMICS: Four Star Publications: 1947 (Advertised, not pub.)

KOSMIC KAT ACTIVITY BOOK (See Deity)
Image Comics: Aug, 1999 ($2.95, one-shot)

1-Stories and games by various		3.00

KRAZY KAT
Holt: 1946 (Hardcover)

Reprints daily & Sunday strips by Herriman	56	12	168	350	580	810

dust jacket only	43	86	129	262	431	600

KRAZY KAT (See Ace Comics & March of Comics No. 72, 87)
KRAZY KAT COMICS (...& Ignatz the Mouse early issues)
Dell Publ. Co./Gold Key: May-June, 1951 - F.C. #696, Apr, 1956; Jan, 1964 (None by Herriman)

1(1951)	9	18	27	60	100	140
2-5 (#5, 8-10/52)	5	10	15	35	55	75
Four Color 454,504	5	10	15	32	51	70
Four Color 548,619,696 (4/56)	5	10	15	30	48	65
1(10098-401)(1/64-Gold Key)(TV)	4	8	12	26	41	55

KRAZY KOMICS (1st Series) (Cindy Comics No. 27 on) (Also see Ziggy Pig)
Timely Comics (USA No. 1-21/JPC No. 22-26): July, 1942 - No. 26, Spr, 1947

1-Toughy Tomcat, Ziggy Pig (by Jaffee) & Silly Seal begin	66	132	198	413	682	950
2	30	60	90	174	275	375
3-8,10	21	42	63	122	191	260
9-Hitler parody	22	44	66	126	198	270
11,13,14	15	30	45	90	140	190
12-Timely's entire art staff drew themselves into a Creeper story	26	52	78	152	239	325
15-(8-9/44)-Has "Super Soldier" by Pfc. Stan Lee	15	30	45	90	140	190
16-24,26: 16-(10-11/44). 26-Super Rabbit-c/story	14	28	42	80	115	150
25-Wacky Duck-c/story & begin; Kurtzman-a (6pgs.)	15	30	45	90	140	190

KRAZY KOMICS (2nd Series)
Timely/Marvel Comics: Aug, 1948 - No. 2, Nov, 1948

1-Wolverton (10 pgs.) & Kurtzman (8 pgs.)-a; Eustice Hayseed begins (Li'l Abner swipe)	43	86	129	262	431	600
2-Wolverton-a (10 pgs.); Powerhouse Pepper cameo	32	64	96	186	293	400

KRAZY KROW (Also see Dopey Duck, Film Funnies, Funny Frolics & Movie Tunes)
Marvel Comics (ZPC): Summer, 1945 - No. 3, Wint, 1945/46

1	22	44	66	126	198	270
2,3	14	28	42	82	121	160
I.W. Reprint #1('57), 2('58), 7	2	4	6	11	16	20

KRAZYLIFE (Becomes Nutty Life #2)
Fox Feature Syndicate: 1945 (no month)

1-Funny animal	19	38	57	109	172	235

KREE/SKRULL WAR STARRING THE AVENGERS, THE
Marvel Comics: Sept, 1983 - No. 2, Oct, 1983 ($2.50, 68 pgs., Baxter paper)

1,2		4.00

NOTE: *Neal Adams p-1r, 2. Buscema a-1r, 2r. Simonson a-1p; c-1p.*

KROFFT SUPERSHOW (TV)
Gold Key: Apr, 1978 - No. 6, Jan, 1979

1-Photo-c	3	6	9	16	23	30
2-6: 6-Photo-c	2	4	6	11	16	20

KRULL
Marvel Comics Group: Nov, 1983 - No. 2, Dec, 1983

1,2-Adaptation of film; r/Marvel Super Special. 1-Photo-c from movie		2.50

KRUSTY COMICS (TV)(See Simpsons Comics)
Bongo Comics: 1995 - No. 3, 1995 ($2.25, limited series)

1-3		2.50

KRYPTON CHRONICLES
DC Comics: Sept, 1981 - No. 3, Nov, 1981

1-3: 1-Buckler-c(p)		4.00

KRYPTO THE SUPERDOG (TV)
DC Comics: Nov, 2006 - No. 6, Apr, 2007 ($2.25)

1-6-Based on Cartoon Network series. 1-Origin retold		2.50

KULL AND THE BARBARIANS
Marvel Comics: May, 1975 - No. 3, Sept, 1975 ($1.00, B&W, magazine)

1-(84 pgs.) Andru/Wood-r/Kull #1; 2 pgs. Neal Adams; Gil Kane(p), Marie & John Severin-a(r); Krenkel text illo.	3	6	9	16	22	28
2,3: 2-(84 pgs.) Red Sonja by Chaykin begins; Solomon Kane by Weiss/Adams; Gil Kane-a; Solomon Kane pin-up by Wrightson. 3-(76 pgs.) Origin Red Sonja by Chaykin; Adams-a; Solomon Kane app.	3	6	9	16	22	28

KULL THE CONQUEROR (...the Destroyer #11 on; see Conan #1, Creatures on the Loose #10, Marvel Preview, Monsters on the Prowl)

Kull the Conqueror #4 © MAR

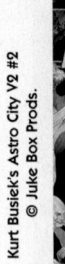

Kurt Busiek's Astro City V2 #2 © Juke Box Prods.

Lady Death #5 © Chaos!

	GD 2.0	VG 4.0	FN 6.0	VF 8.0	VF/NM 9.0	NM- 9.2

Marvel Comics Group: June, 1971 - No. 2, Sept, 1971; No. 3, July, 1972 - No. 15, Aug, 1974; No. 16, Aug, 1976 - No. 29, Oct, 1978

	GD 2.0	VG 4.0	FN 6.0	VF 8.0	VF/NM 9.0	NM- 9.2
1-Andru/Wood-a; 2nd app. & origin Kull; 15¢ issue	5	10	15	30	48	65
2-5: 2-3rd Kull app. Last 15¢ iss. 3-13: 20¢ issues	3	6	9	15	21	26
6-10	2	4	6	8	11	14
11-15: 11-15-Ploog-a. 14,15: 25¢ issues	1	3	4	6	8	10
16-(Regular 25¢ edition)(8/76)	1	2	3	5	6	8
16-(30¢-c variant, limited distribution)	2	4	6	11	16	20
17-29: 21-23-(Reg. 30¢ editions)	1	2	3	5		8
21-23-(35¢-c variants, limited distribution)	3	6	9	20	40	60

NOTE: No. 1, 2, 7-9, 11 are based on Robert E. Howard stories. **Alcala** a-17p, 18-20i; c-24. **Ditko** a-12r, 15r. **Gil Kane** c-15p, 21. **Nebres** a-22i-27i; c-25i, 27i. **Ploog** c-11, 12p, 13. **Severin** a-2-9i; c-2-10i, 19. **Starlin** c-14.

KULL THE CONQUEROR
Marvel Comics Group: Dec, 1982 - No. 2, Mar, 1983 (52 pgs., Baxter paper)

1,2: 1-Buscema-a(p)						4.00

KULL THE CONQUEROR (No. 9,10 titled "Kull")
Marvel Comics Group: 5/83 - No. 10, 6/85 (52 pgs., Baxter paper)

V3#1-10: Buscema-a in #1-3,5-10						3.00

NOTE: Bolton a-4. Golden painted c-3-8. Guice a-4p. Sienkiwicz a-4; c-2.

KUNG FU (See Deadly Hands of..., & Master of...)

KUNG FU FIGHTER (See Richard Dragon...)

KURT BUSIEK'S ASTRO CITY (Limited series) (Also see Astro City: Local Heroes)
Image Comics (Juke Box Productions): Aug, 1995 - No. 6, Jan, 1996 ($2.25)

1-Kurt Busiek scripts, Brent Anderson-a & Alex Ross front & back-c begins; 1st app. Samaritan & Honor Guard (Cleopatra, MHP, Beautie, The Black Rapier, Quarrel & N-Forcer)	2	4	6	8	10	12
2-6: 2-1st app. The Silver Agent, The Old Soldier, & the "original" Honor Guard (Max O'Millions, Starwoman, the "original" Cleopatra, the "original" N-Forcer, The Bouncing Beatnik, Leopardman & Kitkat). 3-1st app. Jack-in-the-Box & The Deacon. 4-1st app. Winged Victory (cameo), The Hanged Man & The First Family. 5-1st app. Crackerjack, The Astro City Irregulars, Nightingale & Sunbird. 6-Origin Samaritan; 1st full app. Winged Victory	1	3	4	6	8	10
Life In The Big City-(8/96, $19.95, trade paperback)-r/Image Comics limited series w/sketchbook & cover gallery; Ross-c						20.00
Life In The Big City-(8/96, $49.95, hardcover, 1000 print run)-r/Image Comics limited series w/sketchbook & cover gallery; Ross-c						50.00

KURT BUSIEK'S ASTRO CITY (1st Homage Comics series)
Image Comics (Homage Comics): V2#1, Sept, 1996 - No. 15, Dec, 1998;
DC Comics (Homage Comics): No. 16, Mar, 1999 - No. 22, Aug, 2000 ($2.50)

1/2-(10/96)-The Hanged Man story; 1st app. The All-American & Slugger, The Lamplighter, The Time-Keeper & Eterneon	1	3	4	6	8	10
1/2-(1/98) 2nd printing w/new cover						2.50
1- Kurt Busiek scripts, Alex Ross-c, Brent Anderson-p & Will Blyberg-i begin; intro The Gentleman, Thunderhead & Helia.	1	2	3	5	6	8
1-(12/97, $4.95) "3-D Edition" w/glasses						5.00
2-Origin The First Family; Astra story	1	2	3	4	5	7
3-5: 4-1st app. The Crossbreed, Ironhorse, Glue Gun & The Confessor (cameo)						6.00
6-10						5.00
11-22: 14-20-Steeljack story arc. 16-(3/99) First DC issue						2.50
TPB-($19.95) Ross-c, r/#4-9, #1/2 w/sketchbook						20.00
Family Album TPB ($19.95) r/#1-3,10-13						20.00
The Tarnished Angel HC ($29.95) r/#14-20; new Ross dust jacket; sketch pages by Anderson & Ross; cover gallery with reference photos						30.00
The Tarnished Angel SC ($19.95) r/#14-20; new Ross-c						20.00

LABMAN
Image Comics: Nov, 1996 ($3.50, one-shot)

1-Allred-c						4.00

LAB RATS
DC Comics: June, 2002 - No. 8, Jan, 2003 ($2.50)

1-8-John Byrne-s/a. 5,6-Superman app.						2.50

LABYRINTH
Marvel Comics Group: Nov, 1986 - No. 3, Jan, 1987 (Limited series)

1-3: David Bowie movie adaptation: r/Marvel Super Special #40						4.00

LA COSA NOSTROID (See Scud: The Disposible Assassin)
Fireman Press: Mar, 1996 - No. 9, 1998 ($2.95, B&W)

1-9-Dan Harmon-s/Rob Schrab-c/a						3.00

LAD: A DOG (Movie)
Dell Publishing Co.: 1961 - No. 2, July-Sept, 1962

	GD 2.0	VG 4.0	FN 6.0	VF 8.0	VF/NM 9.0	NM- 9.2
Four Color 1303	4	8	12	28	44	60
2	4	8	12	24	37	50

LADY AND THE TRAMP (Disney, See Dell Giants & Movie Comics)
Dell Publishing Co.: No. 629, May, 1955 - No. 634, June, 1955

Four Color 629 (#1)-..with Jock	7	14	21	47	76	105
Four Color 634-...Album	5	10	15	32	51	70

LADY COP (See 1st Issue Special)

LADY DEATH (See Evil Ernie)
Chaos! Comics: Jan, 1994 - No. 3, Mar, 1994 ($2.75, limited series)

1/2-S. Hughes-c/a in all, 1/2 Velvet	1	2	3	4	5	7
1/2 Gold	1	3	4	6	8	10
1/2 Signed Limited Edition	2	4	6	8	10	12
1-($3.50)-Chromium-c	2	4	6	10	14	18
1-Commemorative	2	4	6	9	13	16
1-(9/96, $2.95) "Encore Presentation"; r/#1						3.00
2	1	2	3	5	6	8
3						5.00
... And Jade (4/02, $2.99) Augustyn-s/Reis-a						3.00
...And The Women of Chaos! Gallery #1 (11/96, $2.25) pin-ups by various						3.00
...Bad Kitty (9/01, $2.99) Mota-c/a						3.00
...Bedlam (6/02, $2.99) Augustyn-s/Reis-a						3.00
...By Steven Hughes (6/00, $2.95) Tribute issue to Steven Hughes						3.00
...By Steven Hughes Deluxe Edition(6/00, $15.95)						16.00
...Chastity (1/02, $2.99) Mota-c/a; Augustyn-s						3.00
...Death Becomes Her #0 (11/97, $2.95) Hughes-c/a						3.00
...FAN Edition: All Hallow's Eve #1 (1/97, mail-in)						5.00
...In Lingerie #1 (8/95, $2.95) pin-ups, wraparound-c						3.00
...In Lingerie #1-Leather Edition (10,000)						12.00
...In Lingerie #1-Micro Premium Edition; Lady Demon-c (2,000)						35.00
...Love Bites (3/01, $2.99) Kaminski-s/Luke Ross-a						3.00
.../Medieval Witchblade (8/01, $3.50) covers by Molenaar and Silvestri						3.50
.../Medieval Witchblade Preview Ed. (8/01, $1.99) Molenaar-c						2.50
...: Mischief Night (11/01, $2.99) Ostrander-s/Reis-a						3.00
... Re-Imagined (7/02, $2.99) Gossett-c						3.00
... River of Fear (4/01, $2.99) Bennett-a(p)/Cleavenger-c						3.00
...Swimsuit Special #1-($2.50)-Wraparound-c						3.00
...Swimsuit Special #1-Red velvet-c						14.00
...Swimsuit 2001 #1-(2/01, $2.99)-Reis-c; art by various						3.00
...: The Reckoning (7/94, $6.95)-r/#1 #3						7.00
...: The Reckoning (8/95, $12.95)- new printing including Lady Death 1/2 & Swimsuit Special #1						13.00
.../Vampirella (3/99, $3.50) Hughes-c/a						3.50
.../Vampirella 2 (3/00, $3.50) Deodato-c/a						3.50
... Vs. Purgatori (12/99, $3.50) Deodato-a						3.50
... Vs. Vampirella Preview (2/00, $1.00) Deodato-a/c						2.50

LADY DEATH (Ongoing series)
Chaos! Comics: Feb, 1998 - No. 16, May, 1999 ($2.95)

1-16: 1-4: Pulido-s/Hughes-c/a. 5-8,13-16-Deodato-a. 9-11-Hughes-a						3.00
...Retribution (8/98, $2.95) Jadsen-a						3.00
...Retribution Premium Ed.						6.00

LADY DEATH: ALIVE
Chaos! Comics: May, 2001 - No. 4, Aug, 2001 ($2.99, limited series)

1-4-Ivan Reis-a; Lady Death becomes mortal						3.00

LADY DEATH: A MEDIEVAL TALE (Brian Pulido's...)
CG Entertainment: Mar, 2003 - No. 12, Apr, 2004 ($2.95)

1-12: 1-Brian Pulido-s/Ivan Reis-a; Lady Death in the CrossGen Universe						3.00
Vol.1 TPB (2003, $9.95) digest-sized reprint of #1-6						10.00

LADY DEATH: DARK ALLIANCE
Chaos! Comics: July, 2001 - No. 5, ($2.99, limited series)

1-3-Reis-a/Ostrander-s						3.00

LADY DEATH: DARK MILLENNIUM
Chaos! Comics: Feb, 2000 - No. 3, Apr, 2000 ($2.95, limited series)

Preview (6/00, $5.00)						5.00
1-3-Ivan Reis-a						3.00

LADY DEATH: GODDESS RETURNS
Chaos! Comics: Jun, 2002 - No. 2, Aug, 2002 ($2.99, limited series)

1,2-Mota-a/Ostrander-s						3.00

LADY DEATH: HEARTBREAKER

Lady Pendragon V3 #2 © Matt Hawkins

Lana #3 © MAR

Lance O'Casey #2 © FAW

	GD 2.0	VG 4.0	FN 6.0	VF 8.0	VF/NM 9.0	NM- 9.2

Chaos! Comics: Mar, 2002 - No. 4, ($2.99, limited series)
1-Molenaar-a/Ostrander-s ... 3.00

LADY DEATH: JUDGEMENT WAR
Chaos! Comics: Nov, 1999 - No. 3, Jan, 2000 ($2.95, limited series)
Prelude (10/99) two covers ... 3.00
1-3-Ivan Reis-a ... 3.00

LADY DEATH: LAST RITES
Chaos! Comics: Oct, 2001 - No. 4, Feb, 2001 ($2.99, limited series)
1-4-Ivan Reis-a/Ostrander-s ... 3.00

LADY DEATH: THE CRUCIBLE
Chaos! Comics: Nov, 1996 - No. 6, Oct, 1997 ($3.50/$2.95, limited series)
1/2 ... 4.00
1/2 Cloth Edition ... 8.00
1-Wraparound silver foil embossed-c ... 4.00
2-6-($2.95) ... 3.00

LADY DEATH: THE GAUNTLET
Chaos! Comics: Apr, 2002 - No. 2, May, 2002 ($2.99, limited series)
1,2: 1-J. Scott Campbell-c/redesign of Lady Death's outfit; Mota-a ... 3.00

LADY DEATH: THE ODYSSEY
Chaos! Comics: Apr, 1996 - No. 4, Aug, 1996 ($3.50/$2.95)
1-($1.50)-Sneak Peek Preview ... 2.50
1-($1.50)-Sneak Peek Preview Micro Premium Edition (2500 print run)

	2	4	6	8	10	12

1-($3.50)-Embossed, wraparound goil foil-c ... 5.00

1-Black Onyx Edition (200 print run)	6	12	18	37	59	80

1-($19.95)-Premium Edition (10,000 print run) ... 20.00
2-4-($2.95) ... 3.00

LADY DEATH: THE RAPTURE
Chaos! Comics: Jun, 1999 - No. 4, Sept, 1999 ($2.95, limited series)
1-4-Ivan Reis-c/a; Pulido-s ... 3.00

LADY DEATH: THE WILD HUNT (Brian Pulido's...)
CG Entertainment: Apr, 2004 - No. 2, May, 2005 ($2.95)
1-2: 1-Brian Pulido-s/Jim Cheung-a ... 3.00

LADY DEATH: TRIBULATION
Chaos! Comics: Dec, 2000 - No. 4, Mar, 2001 ($2.95, limited series)
1-4-Ivan Reis-a; Kaminski-s ... 3.00

LADY DEATH II: BETWEEN HEAVEN & HELL
Chaos! Comics: Mar, 1995 - No. 4, July, 1995 ($3.50, limited series)
1-Chromium wraparound-c; Evil Ernie cameo ... 5.00

1-Commemorative (4,000), 1-Black Velvet-c	2	4	6	10	14	18
1-Gold	1	3	4	6	8	10
1-"Refractor" edition (5,000)	2	4	6	11	16	20

2-4 ... 3.50

4-Lady Demon variant-c	1	2	3	5	7	9

Trade paperback-($12.95)-r/#1-4 ... 13.00

LADY DEMON
Chaos! Comics: Mar, 2000 - No. 3, May, 2000 ($2.95, limited series)
1-3-Kaminski-s/Brewer-a ... 3.00
1-Premium Edition ... 10.00

LADY FOR A NIGHT (See Cinema Comics Herald)

LADY JUSTICE (See Neil Gaiman's...)

LADY LUCK (Formerly Smash #1-85) (Also see Spirit Sections #1)
Quality Comics Group: No. 86, Dec, 1949 - No. 90, Aug, 1950

86(#1)	91	182	273	569	947	1325
87-90	66	132	198	413	682	950

LADY PENDRAGON
Maximum Press: Mar, 1996 ($2.50)
1-Matt Hawkins script ... 2.50

LADY PENDRAGON
Image Comics: Nov, 1998 - No. 3, Jan, 1999 ($2.50, mini-series)
Preview (6/98) Flip book w/ Deity preview ... 3.00
1-3: 1-Matt Hawkins-s/Stinsman-a ... 3.00
1-($6.95) DF Ed. with variant-c by Jusko ... 7.00
2-($4.95)Variant edition ... 5.00
0-(3/99) Origin; flip book ... 2.50

LADY PENDRAGON (Volume 3)
Image Comics: Apr, 1999 - No. 9, Mar, 2000 ($2.50, mini-series)
1,2,4-6,8-10: 1-Matt Hawkins-s/Stinsman-a. 2-Peterson-c ... 2.50
3-Flip book w/Alley Cat preview (1st app.) ... 3.00
7-($3.95) Flip book; Stinsman-a/Cleavenger painted-a ... 4.00
Gallery Edition (10/99, $2.95) pin-ups ... 3.00
...Merlin (1/00, $2.95) Stinsman-a ... 3.00

LADY PENDRAGON/ MORE THAN MORTAL
Image Comics: May, 1999 ($2.50, one-shot)
Preview (2/99) Diamond Dateline suppl. ... 2.50
1-Scott-s/Norton-a; 2 covers by Norton & Finch ... 2.50

LADY RAWHIDE
Topps Comics: July, 1995 - No. 5, Mar, 1996 ($2.95, bi-monthly, limited series)
1-5: Don McGregor scripts & Mayhew-a. in all. 2-Stelfreeze-c. 3-Hughes-c. 4-Golden-c.
5-Julie Bell-c. ... 3.00
It Can't Happen Here TPB (8/99, $16.95) r/#1-5 ... 17.00
Mini Comic 1 (7/95) Maroto-a; Zorro app. ... 2.50
Special Edition 1 (6/95, $3.95)-Reprints ... 4.00

LADY RAWHIDE (Volume 2)
Topps Comics: Oct, 1996 -No. 5, June, 1997 ($2.95, limited series)
1-5: 1-Julie Bell-c. ... 3.00

LADY RAWHIDE OTHER PEOPLE'S BLOOD (ZORRO'S ...)
Image Comics: Mar, 1999 - No. 5, July, 1999 ($2.95, B&W)
1-5-Reprints Lady Rawhide series in B&W ... 3.00

LADY SUPREME (See Asylum)(Also see Supreme & Kid Supreme)
Image Comics (Extreme): May, 1996 - No. 2, June, 1996 ($2.50, limited series)
1,2-Terry Moore-s: 1-Terry Moore-c. 2-Flip book w/Newmen preview ... 2.50

LAFF-A-LYMPICS (TV)(See The Funtastic World of Hanna-Barbera)
Marvel Comics: Mar, 1978 - No. 13, Mar, 1979 (Newsstand sales only)

1-Yogi Bear, Scooby Doo, Pixie & Dixie, etc.	3	6	9	17	25	32
2-8	2	4	6	13	18	22
9-13: 11-Jetsons x-over; 1 pg. illustrated bio of Mighty Mightor, Herculoids, Shazzan, Galaxy Trio & Space Ghost	3	6	9	16	22	28

LAFFY-DAFFY COMICS
Rural Home Publ. Co.: Feb, 1945 - No. 2, Mar, 1945

1,2-Funny animal	10	20	30	56	76	95

LANA (Little Lana No. 8 on)
Marvel Comics (MjMC): Aug, 1948 - No. 7, Aug, 1949 (Also see Annie Oakley)

1-Rusty, Millie begin	22	44	66	128	202	275
2-Kurtzman's "Hey Look" (1); last Rusty	14	28	42	80	115	150
3-7: 3-Nellie begins	11	22	33	60	83	105

LANCELOT & GUINEVERE (See Movie Classics)

LANCELOT LINK, SECRET CHIMP (TV)
Gold Key: Apr, 1971 - No. 8, Feb, 1973

1-Photo-c	6	12	18	41	66	90
2-8: 2-Photo-c	4	8	12	24	37	50

LANCE O'CASEY (See The Shield)
Fawcett Publications: Spring, 1946 - No. 3, Fall, 1946; No. 4, Summer, 1948

1-Captain Marvel app. on-c	30	60	90	174	275	375
2	19	38	57	112	176	240
3,4	15	30	45	86	133	180

NOTE: The cover for the 1st issue was done in 1942 but was not published until 1946. The cover shows 68 pages but actually has only 36 pages.

LANCER (TV)(Western)
Gold Key: Feb, 1969 - No. 3, Sept, 1969 (All photo-c)

1	4	8	12	24	37	50
2,3	3	6	9	18	27	35

LAND OF NOD, THE
Dark Horse Comics: July, 1997 - No. 3, Feb, 1998 ($2.95, B&W)
1-3-Jetcat; Jay Stephens-s/a ... 3.00

LAND OF OZ
Arrow Comics: 1998 - No. 9 ($2.95, B&W)
1-9-Bishop-s/Bryan-s/a ... 3.00

LAND OF THE DEAD (George A. Romaro's...)

Large Feature Comic #26 © NYNS

Lash LaRue Western #4 © FAW

Lassie #4 © MGM

	GD 2.0	VG 4.0	FN 6.0	VF 8.0	VF/NM 9.0	NM- 9.2

IDW Publishing: Aug, 2005 - No. 5 ($3.99, limited series)

	GD 2.0	VG 4.0	FN 6.0	VF 8.0	VF/NM 9.0	NM- 9.2
1-4-Adaptation of 2005 movie; Ryall-s/Rodriguez-a						4.00
TPB (3/06, $19.99) r/#1-5; cover gallery						20.00

LAND OF THE GIANTS (TV)
Gold Key: Nov, 1968 - No. 5, Sept, 1969 (All have photo-c)

	GD 2.0	VG 4.0	FN 6.0	VF 8.0	VF/NM 9.0	NM- 9.2
1	6	12	18	43	69	95
2-5	4	8	12	26	41	55

LAND OF THE LOST COMICS (Radio)
E. C. Comics: July-Aug, 1946 - No. 9, Spring, 1948

	GD 2.0	VG 4.0	FN 6.0	VF 8.0	VF/NM 9.0	NM- 9.2
1	39	78	117	225	355	485
2	24	48	72	139	220	300
3-9	20	40	60	117	184	250

LAND UNKNOWN, THE (Movie)
Dell Publishing Co.: No. 845, Sept, 1957

	GD 2.0	VG 4.0	FN 6.0	VF 8.0	VF/NM 9.0	NM- 9.2
Four Color 845-Alex Toth-a	11	22	33	79	140	200

LA PACIFICA
DC Comics (Paradox Press): 1994/1995 ($4.95, B&W, limited series, digest size, mature readers)

	GD 2.0	VG 4.0	FN 6.0	VF 8.0	VF/NM 9.0	NM- 9.2
1-3						5.00

LARAMIE (TV)
Dell Publishing Co.: Aug, 1960 - July, 1962 (All photo-c)

	GD 2.0	VG 4.0	FN 6.0	VF 8.0	VF/NM 9.0	NM- 9.2
Four Color 1125-Gil Kane/Heath-a	8	16	24	58	97	135
Four Color 1223,1284, 01-418-207 (7/62)	6	12	18	43	69	95

LAREDO (TV)
Gold Key: June, 1966

	GD 2.0	VG 4.0	FN 6.0	VF 8.0	VF/NM 9.0	NM- 9.2
1 (10179-606)-Photo-c	4	8	12	22	34	45

LARGE FEATURE COMIC (Formerly called Black & White in previous guides)
Dell Publishing Co.: 1939 - No. 13, 1943

Note: See individual alphabetical listings for prices

1 (Series I)-Dick Tracy Meets the Blank
3-Heigh-Yo Silver! The Lone Ranger (text & ill.)(76 pgs.); also exists as a Whitman #710; based on radio
6-Terry & the Pirates & The Dragon Lady; reprints dailies from 1936
8-Dick Tracy the Racket Buster
9-King of the Royal Mounted (Zane Grey's...)
10-(Scarce)-Gang Busters (No. appears on inside front cover); first slick cover (based on radio program)
13-Dick Tracy and Scottie of Scotland Yard
15-Dick Tracy and the Kidnapped Princes
17-Gang Busters (1941)
18-Phantasmo (see The Funnies #45)
20-Donald Duck Comic Paint Book (rarer than #16) (Disney)
21,22: 21-Private Buck. 22-Nuts & Jolts
24-Popeye in "Thimble Theatre" by Segar
26-Smitty
28-Grin and Bear It
30-Tillie the Toiler
2-Winnie Winkle (#1)
3-Dick Tracy
4-Tiny Tim (#1)
6-Terry and the Pirates; Caniff-a
8-Bugs Bunny (#1)('42)
9-Bringing Up Father
10-Popeye (Thimble Theatre)
11-Barney Google and Snuffy Smith
13-(nn)-1001 Hours Of Fun; puzzles & games; by A. W. Nugent. This book was bound as #13 with Large Feature Comics in publisher's files

2-Terry and the Pirates (#1)
4-Dick Tracy Gets His Man
5-Tarzan of the Apes (#1) by Harold Foster (origin); reprints 1st Tarzan dailies from 1929
7-(Scarce, 52 pgs.)-Hi-Yo Silver the Lone Ranger to the Rescue; also exists as a Whitman #715; based on radio program
11-Dick Tracy Foils the Mad Doc Hump
12-Smilin' Jack; no number on-c
14-Smilin' Jack Helps G-Men Solve a Case!
16-Donald Duck; 1st app. Daisy Duck on back cover (6/41-Disney)
19-Dumbo Comic Paint Book (Disney); partial-r from 4-Color #17
23-The Nebbs
25-Smilin' Jack-1st issue to show title on-c
27-Terry and the Pirates; Caniff-c/a
29-Moon Mullins
1 (Series II)-Peter Rabbit by Harrison Cady; arrival date-3/27/42
5-Toots and Casper
7-Pluto Saves the Ship (#1) (Disney)-Written by Carl Barks, Jack Hannah, & Nick George (Barks' 1st comic book work)
12-Private Buck

NOTE: The Black & White Feature Books are oversized 8-1/2x11-3/8" comics with color covers and black and white interiors. The first nine issues all have rough, heavy stock covers and, except for #7, all have 76 pages, including covers. #7 and #10-on all have 52 pages. Beginning with #10 the covers are slick and thin and, because of their size, are difficult to handle without damaging. For this reason, they are seldom found in fine to mint condition. The paper stock, unlike Wow #1 and Capt. Marvel #1, is itself not unstable ...just thin. Issues #2,6 and #10

were reprinted in the early 1980s, identical except for the copyright notice on the first page.

LARRY DOBY, BASEBALL HERO
Fawcett Publications: 1950 (Cleveland Indians)

	GD 2.0	VG 4.0	FN 6.0	VF 8.0	VF/NM 9.0	NM- 9.2
nn-Bill Ward-a; photo-c	76	152	228	475	788	1100

LARRY HARMON'S LAUREL AND HARDY (...Comics)
National Periodical Publ.: July-Aug, 1972 (Digest advertised, not published)

	GD 2.0	VG 4.0	FN 6.0	VF 8.0	VF/NM 9.0	NM- 9.2
1-Low print run	8	16	24	54	90	125

LARS OF MARS
Ziff-Davis Publishing Co.: No. 10, Apr-May, 1951 - No. 11, July-Aug, 1951 (Painted-c) (Created by Jerry Siegel, editor)

	GD 2.0	VG 4.0	FN 6.0	VF 8.0	VF/NM 9.0	NM- 9.2
10-Origin; Anderson-a(3) in each; classic robot-c	83	166	249	519	860	1200
11-Gene Colan-a; classic-c	66	132	198	413	682	950

LARS OF MARS 3-D
Eclipse Comics: Apr, 1987 ($2.50)

	GD 2.0	VG 4.0	FN 6.0	VF 8.0	VF/NM 9.0	NM- 9.2
1-r/Lars of Mars #10,11 in 3-D plus new story						4.00
2-D limited edition (B&W, 100 copies)						6.00

LASER ERASER & PRESSBUTTON (See Axel Pressbutton & Miracle Man 9)
Eclipse Comics: Nov, 1985 - No. 6, 1987 (95¢/$2.50, limited series)

	GD 2.0	VG 4.0	FN 6.0	VF 8.0	VF/NM 9.0	NM- 9.2
1-6: 5,6-(95¢)						2.50
...In 3-D 1 (8/86, $2.50)						4.00
2-D 1 (B&W, limited to 100 copies signed & numbered)						8.00

LASH LARUE WESTERN (Movie star; King of the bullwhip)(See Fawcett Movie Comic, Motion Picture Comics & Six-Gun Heroes)
Fawcett Publications: Sum, 1949 - No. 46, Jan, 1954 (36 pgs., 1-6,9,13,16-on)

	GD 2.0	VG 4.0	FN 6.0	VF 8.0	VF/NM 9.0	NM- 9.2
1-Lash & his horse Black Diamond begin; photo front/back-c begin	89	178	267	556	903	1250
2(11/49)	40	80	120	235	368	500
3-5	34	68	102	192	296	400
6,9: 6-Last photo back-c; intro. Frontier Phantom (Lash's twin brother)	27	54	81	154	237	320
7,8,10 (52pgs.)	28	56	84	161	248	335
11,12,14,15 (52pgs.)	19	38	57	106	163	220
13,16-20 (36pgs.)	17	34	51	96	148	200
21-30: 21-The Frontier Phantom app.	15	30	45	84	127	170
31-45	14	28	42	76	108	140
46-Last Fawcett issue & photo-c	14	28	42	80	115	150

LASH LARUE WESTERN (Continues from Fawcett series)
Charlton Comics: No. 47, Mar-Apr, 1954 - No. 84, June, 1961

	GD 2.0	VG 4.0	FN 6.0	VF 8.0	VF/NM 9.0	NM- 9.2
47-Photo-c	17	34	51	96	148	200
48	14	28	42	80	115	150
49-60, 67,68-(68 pgs.). 68-Check-a	11	22	33	62	86	110
61-66,69,70: 52-r/#8; 53-r/#22	10	20	30	54	72	90
71-83	8	16	24	44	57	70
84-Last issue	10	20	30	54	72	90

LASH LARUE WESTERN
AC Comics: 1990 ($3.50, 44 pgs) (24 pgs. of color, 16 pgs. of B&W)

	GD 2.0	VG 4.0	FN 6.0	VF 8.0	VF/NM 9.0	NM- 9.2
1-Photo covers; r/Lash #6; r/old movie posters						3.50
Annual 1 (1990, $2.95, B&W, 44 pgs.)-Photo covers						3.00

LASSIE (TV)(M-G-M's ... #1-36; see Kite Fun Book)
Dell Publ. Co./Gold Key No. 59 (10/62) on: June, 1950 - No. 70, July, 1969

	GD 2.0	VG 4.0	FN 6.0	VF 8.0	VF/NM 9.0	NM- 9.2
1 (52 pgs.)-Photo-c; inside lists One Shot #282 in error	15	30	45	111	198	285
2-Painted-c begin	8	16	24	58	97	135
3-10	6	12	18	43	69	95
11-19: 12-Rocky Langford (Lassie's master) marries Gerry Lawrence. 15-1st app. Timbu	5	10	15	35	55	75
20-22-Matt Baker-a	6	12	18	39	62	85
23-38: 33-Robinson-a.	5	10	15	32	51	70
39-1st app. Timmy as Lassie picks up her TV family; photo-c	6	12	18	43	69	95
40-50-Photo-c on all	5	10	15	32	51	70
51-58-Photo-c on all	5	10	15	30	48	65
59 (10/62)-1st Gold Key	5	10	15	32	51	70
60-70: 63-Last Timmy (10/63). 64-r/#19. 65-Forest Ranger Corey Stuart begins, ends #69. 70-Forest Rangers Bob Ericson & Scott Turner app. (Lassie's new masters)	4	8	12	26	41	55
11193(1978, $1.95, 224 pgs., Golden Press)-Baker-r (92 pgs.)	4	8	12	28	44	60

NOTE: Also see March of Comics #210, 217, 230, 254, 266, 278, 296, 308, 324,334, 346, 358, 370, 381, 394,

Last American #1 © MAR

Laugh V2 #21 © AP

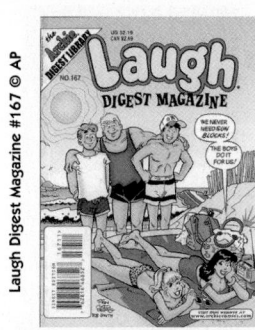

Laugh Digest Magazine #167 © AP

	GD 2.0	VG 4.0	FN 6.0	VF 8.0	VF/NM 9.0	NM- 9.2		GD 2.0	VG 4.0	FN 6.0	VF 8.0	VF/NM 9.0	NM- 9.2

411, 432.

LAST AMERICAN, THE
Marvel Comics (Epic): Dec, 1990 - No. 4, March, 1991 ($2.25, mini-series)
1-4: Alan Grant scripts — 2.50

LAST AVENGERS STORY, THE (Last Avengers #1)
Marvel Comics: Nov, 1995 - No. 2, Dec, 1995 ($5.95, painted, limited series) (Alterniverse)
1,2: Peter David story; acetate-c in all. 1-New team (Hank Pym, Wasp, Human Torch, Cannonball, She-Hulk, Hotshot, Bombshell, Tommy Maximoff, Hawkeye & Mockingbird) forms to battle Ultron 59, Kang the Conqueror, The Grim Reaper & Oddball — 6.00

LAST CHRISTMAS, THE
Image Comics: May, 2006 - No. 5, Oct, 2006 ($2.99, limited series)
1-5-Gerry Duggan & Brian Posehn-s/Rick Remender & Hilary Barta-a — 3.00
TPB (2006, $14.99) r/#1-5; Patton Oswalt intro.; sketch pages and art — 15.00

LAST DAY IN VIETNAM
Dark Horse Books: July, 2000 ($10.95, graphic novel)
nn-Will Eisner-s/a/c — 11.00

LAST DAYS OF THE JUSTICE SOCIETY SPECIAL
DC Comics: 1986 ($2.50, one-shot, 68 pgs.)
1-62 pg. JSA story plus unpubbed G.A. pg. — 1 — 3 — 4 — 6 — 8 — 10

LAST FANTASTIC FOUR STORY, THE
Marvel Comics: Oct, 2007 ($4.99, one-shot)
1-Stan Lee-s/John Romita, Jr.-a/c; Galactus app. — 5.00

LAST GENERATION, THE
Black Tie Studios: 1986 - No. 5, 1989 ($1.95, B&W, high quality paper)
1-5 — 2.50
Book 1 (1989, $6.95)-By Caliber Press — 7.00

LAST HERO STANDING (Characters from Spider-Girl's M2 universe)
Marvel Comics: Aug, 2005 - No. 5, Aug, 2005 ($2.99, weekly limited series)
1-5: 1-DeFalco-s/Olliffe-a. 4-Thor app. 5-Capt. America dies — 3.00
TPB (2005, $13.99) r/#1-5 — 14.00

LAST HUNT, THE
Dell Publishing Co.: No. 678, Feb, 1956
Four Color 678-Movie, photo-c — 7 — 14 — 21 — 50 — 83 — 115

LAST KISS
ACME Press (Eclipse): 1988 ($3.95, B&W, squarebound, 52 pgs.)
1-One story adapts E.A. Poe's The Black Cat — 4.00

LAST OF THE COMANCHES (Movie) (See Wild Bill Hickok #28)
Avon Periodicals: 1953
nn-Kinstler-c/a, 21pgs.; Ravielli-a — 15 — 30 — 45 — 88 — 137 — 185

LAST OF THE ERIES, THE (See American Graphics)

LAST OF THE FAST GUNS, THE
Dell Publishing Co.: No. 925, Aug, 1958
Four Color 925-Movie, photo-c — 7 — 14 — 21 — 47 — 76 — 105

LAST OF THE MOHICANS (See King Classics & White Rider and...)

LAST OF THE VIKING HEROES, THE (Also see Silver Star #1)
Genesis West Comics: Mar, 1987 - No. 12 ($1.50/$1.95)
1-4,5A,5B,6-12: 4-Intro The Phantom Force, 1-Signed edition ($1.50), 5A-Kirby/Stevens-c. 5B,6 ($1.95). 7-Art Adams-c. 8-Kirby back-c. — 4.00
Summer Special 1-3: 1-(1988)-Frazetta-c & illos. 2 (1990, $2.50)-A TMNT app. 3 (1991, $2.50)-Teenage Mutant Ninja Turtles — 4.00
Summer Special 1-Signed edition (sold for $1.95) — 4.00
NOTE: Art Adams c-7. Byrne c-3. Kirby c-1p, 5p. Perez c-2i. Stevens c-5Ai.

LAST ONE, THE
DC Comics (Vertigo): July, 1993 - No. 6, Dec, 1993 ($2.50, lim. series, mature)
1-6 — 2.50

LAST PLANET STANDING
Marvel Comics: July, 2006 - No. 5, Sept, 2006 ($2.99, limited series)
1-5-Galactus threatens Spider-Girl & Fantastic Five's M2 Earth; Avengers app.; Olliffe-a — 3.00
TPB (2006, $13.99) r/series — 14.00

LAST SHOT
Image Comics: Aug, 2001 - No. 4, Mar, 2002 ($2.95, limited series)
1-4: 1-Wraparound-c; by Studio XD — 3.00
...: First Draw (5/01, $2.95) Introductory one-shot — 3.00

LAST STARFIGHTER, THE
Marvel Comics Group: Oct, 1984 - No. 3, Dec, 1984 (75¢, movie adaptation)
1-3: r/Marvel Super Special; Guice-c — 2.50

LAST TEMPTATION, THE
Marvel Comics: 1994 - No. 3, 1994 ($4.95, limited series)
1-3-Alice Cooper story; Neil Gaiman scripts; McKean-c; Zulli-a: 1-Two covers — 5.00
HC (Dark Horse Comics, 2005, $14.95) r/#1-3; Gaiman intro. — 15.00

LAST TRAIN FROM GUN HILL
Dell Publishing Co.: No. 1012, July, 1959
Four Color 1012-Movie, photo-c — 8 — 16 — 24 — 56 — 93 — 130

LAST TRAIN TO DEADSVILLE: A CAL McDONALD MYSTERY (See Criminal Macabre)
Dark Horse Comics: May, 2004 - No. 4, Sept, 2004 ($2.99, limited series)
1-4-Steve Niles-s/Kelley Jones-a/c — 3.00
TPB (2005, $14.95) r/series — 15.00

LATEST ADVENTURES OF FOXY GRANDPA (See Foxy Grandpa)

LATEST COMICS (Super Duper No. 3?)
Spotlight Publ./Palace Promotions (Jubilee): Mar, 1945 - No. 2, 1945?
1-Super Duper — 16 — 32 — 48 — 94 — 147 — 200
2-Bee-29 (nd); Jubilee in indicia blacked out — 14 — 28 — 42 — 76 — 108 — 140

LAUGH
Archie Enterprises: June, 1987 - No. 29, Aug, 1991 (75¢/$1.00)
V2#1 — 5.00
2-10,14,24: 5-X-Mas issue. 14-1st app. Hot Dog. 24-Re-intro Super Duck — 4.00
11-13,15-23,25-29: 19-X-Mas issue — 3.00

LAUGH COMICS (Teenage) (Formerly Black Hood #9-19) (Laugh #226 on)
Archie Publications (Close-Up): No. 20, Fall, 1946 - No. 400, Apr, 1987
20-Archie begins; Katy Keene & Taffy begin by Woggon; Suzie & Wilbur also begin; Archie covers begin — 66 — 132 — 198 — 413 — 682 — 950
21-23,25 — 37 — 74 — 111 — 213 — 337 — 460
24- "Pipsy" by Kirby (6 pgs.) — 38 — 76 — 114 — 216 — 343 — 470
26-30 — 21 — 42 — 63 — 124 — 195 — 265
31-40 — 15 — 30 — 45 — 90 — 140 — 190
41-60: 41,54-Debbi by Woggon — 13 — 26 — 39 — 74 — 105 — 135
61-80: 67-Debbi by Woggon — 10 — 20 — 30 — 54 — 72 — 90
81-99 — 5 — 10 — 15 — 32 — 51 — 70
100 — 5 — 10 — 15 — 35 — 55 — 75
101-126: 106-109,111,113-Neal Adams-a (1 pg.) in each. 125-Debbi app. — 4 — 8 — 12 — 26 — 41 — 55
127-144: Super-hero app. in all (see note) — 5 — 10 — 15 — 30 — 48 — 65
145-(4/63) Josie by DeCarlo begins — 5 — 10 — 15 — 35 — 55 — 75
146-149-early Josie app. by DeCarlo — 4 — 8 — 12 — 24 — 37 — 50
150,162,163,165,167,169,170-No Josie — 3 — 6 — 9 — 17 — 25 — 32
151-161,164,168-Josie app. by DeCarlo — 4 — 8 — 12 — 22 — 34 — 45
166-Beatles-c (1/65) — 5 — 10 — 15 — 32 — 51 — 70
171-180, 200 (12/67) — 3 — 6 — 9 — 16 — 23 — 30
181-199 — 3 — 6 — 9 — 14 — 19 — 24
201-240(3/71) — 2 — 4 — 6 — 9 — 13 — 16
241-280(7/74) — 2 — 4 — 6 — 8 — 11 — 14
281-299 — 1 — 3 — 4 — 6 — 8 — 10
300(3/76) — 2 — 4 — 6 — 8 — 10 — 12
301-340 (7/79) — 1 — 2 — 3 — 5 — 6 — 8
341-370 (1/82) — — — — — — 6.00
371-380,385-399 — — — — — — 5.00
381-384-Katy Keene app.; by Woggon-381,382 — — — — — — 6.00
NOTE: The Fly app. in 128, 129, 132, 134, 138, 139. Flygirl app. in 136, 137, 143. Flyman app. in 137. The Jaguar app. in 127, 130, 131, 133, 135, 140-142, 144. Josie app. in 145-149, 151-161, 166, 168. Katy Keene app. in 120-125, 129, 130, 133. Horror/Sci-Fi covers on 128-135, 137, 139. Many issues contain paper dolls. Al Fagaly c-20-29. Montana c-33, 36, 37, 42. Bill Vigoda c-30, 50.

LAUGH COMICS DIGEST (...Magazine #23-89; Laugh Digest Mag. #90 on)
Archie Publ. (Close-Up No. 1, 3 on): 8/74; No. 2, 9/75; No. 3, 3/76 - No. 200, Apr, 2005 (Digest-size) (Josie and Sabrina app. in most issues)
1-Neal Adams-a — 5 — 10 — 15 — 30 — 48 — 65
2,7,8,19-Neal Adams-a — 3 — 6 — 9 — 18 — 27 — 35
3-6,9,10 — 3 — 6 — 9 — 15 — 21 — 26
11-18,20 — 2 — 4 — 6 — 10 — 14 — 18
21-40 — 2 — 4 — 6 — 9 — 12 — 15
41-60 — 1 — 3 — 4 — 6 — 8 — 10
61-80 — 1 — 2 — 3 — 5 — 6 — 8
81-99 — — — — — — 5.00
100 — — — — — — 6.00

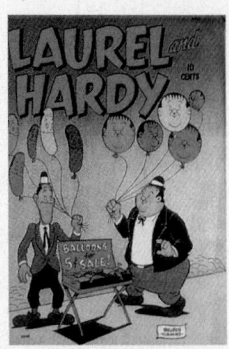

Laurel and Hardy #2 © STJ

Lawbreakers #9 © CC

Leading Comics #7 © DC

	GD 2.0	VG 4.0	FN 6.0	VF 8.0	VF/NM 9.0	NM- 9.2

101-138   3.00
139-200: 139-Begin $1.95-c. 148-Begin $1.99-c. 156-Begin $2.19-c. 180-Begin $2.39-c   2.50
NOTE: Katy Keene in 23, 25, 27, 32-38, 40, 45-48, 50. The Fly-r in 19, 20. The Jaguar-r in 25, 27. Mr. Justice-r in 21. The Web-r in 23.

LAUGH COMIX (Formerly Top Notch Laugh; Suzie Comics No. 49 on)
MLJ Magazines: No. 46, Summer, 1944 - No. 48, Winter, 1944-45

46-Wilbur & Suzie in all; Harry Sahle-c	23	46	69	130	205	280
47,48: 47-Sahle-c. 48-Bill Vigoda-c	15	30	45	88	137	185

LAUGH-IN MAGAZINE (TV)(Magazine)
Laufer Publ. Co.: Oct, 1968 - No. 12, Oct, 1969 (50¢) (Satire)

V1#1	5	10	15	30	48	65
2-12	3	6	9	21	32	42

LAUREL & HARDY (See Larry Harmon's... & March of Comics No. 302, 314)

LAUREL AND HARDY (...Comics)
St. John Publ. Co.: 3/49 - No. 3, 9/49; No. 26, 11/55 - No. 28, 3/56 (No #4-25)

1	72	144	216	450	750	1050
2	40	80	120	240	383	525
3	31	62	93	178	282	385
26-28 (Reprints)	16	32	48	92	144	195

LAUREL AND HARDY (TV)
Dell Publishing Co.: Oct, 1962 - No. 4, Sept-Nov, 1963

12-423-210 (8-10/62)	6	12	18	41	66	90
2-4 (Dell)	4	8	12	28	44	60

LAUREL AND HARDY (Larry Harmon's...)
Gold Key: Jan, 1967 - No. 2, Oct, 1967

1-Photo back-c	4	8	12	28	44	60
2	4	8	12	22	34	45

LAUREL AND HARDY DIGEST: DC Comics. 1972 (Advertised, not published)

L.A.W., THE (LIVING ASSAULT WEAPONS)
DC Comics: Sept, 1999 - No. 6, Feb, 2000 ($2.50, limited series)

1-6-Blue Beetle, Question, Judomaster, Capt. Atom app.; Giordano-a. 5-JLA app.   2.50

LAW AGAINST CRIME (Law-Crime on cover)
Essenkay Publishing Co.: April, 1948 - No. 3, Aug, 1948 (Real Stories from Police Files)

1-(#1-3 are half funny animal, half crime stories)-L. B. Cole-c/a in all; electrocution-c	72	144	216	450	750	1050
2-L. B. Cole-c/a	54	108	162	338	557	775
3-Used in SOTI, pg. 180,181 & illo "The wish to hurt or kill couples in lovers' lanes;" reprinted in All-Famous Crime #9	68	136	204	425	705	985

LAW AND ORDER
Maximum Press: Sept, 1995 - No. 2, 1995 ($2.50, unfinished limited series)

1,2   2.50

LAWBREAKERS (...Suspense Stories No. 10 on)
Law and Order Magazines (Charlton): Mar, 1951 - No. 9, Oct-Nov, 1952

1	40	80	120	244	392	540
2	23	46	69	135	213	290
3,5,6,8,9	19	38	57	109	172	235
4- "White Death" junkie story	24	48	72	139	220	300
7- "The Deadly Dopesters" drug story	24	48	72	139	220	300

LAWBREAKERS ALWAYS LOSE!
Marvel Comics (CBS): Spring, 1948 - No. 10, Oct, 1949

1-2pg. Kurtzman-a, "Giggles 'n' Grins"	36	72	108	208	329	450
2	19	38	57	109	172	235
3-5: 4-Vampire story	15	30	45	86	133	180
6(2/49)-Has editorial defense against charges of Dr. Wertham	16	32	48	94	147	200
7-Used in SOTI, illo "Comic-book philosophy"	31	62	93	178	282	385
8-10: 9,10-Photo-c	14	28	42	80	115	150

NOTE: Brodsky c-4, 5. Shores c-1-3, 6-8.

LAWBREAKERS SUSPENSE STORIES (Formerly Lawbreakers; Strange Suspense Stories No. 16 on)
Capitol Stories/Charlton Comics: No. 10, Jan, 1953 - No. 15, Nov, 1953

10	40	80	120	244	392	540
11 (3/53)-Severed tongues-c/story & woman negligee scene	117	234	351	731	1216	1700
12-14: 13-Giordano-c begin, end #15	26	52	78	152	239	325
15-Acid-in-face-c/story; hands dissolved in acid sty	54	108	162	338	557	775

LAW-CRIME (See Law Against Crime)

LAWDOG
Marvel Comics (Epic Comics): May, 1993 - No. 10, Feb, 1993

1-10   2.50

LAWDOG/GRIMROD: TERROR AT THE CROSSROADS
Marvel Comics (Epic Comics): Sept, 1993 ($3.50)

1   3.50

LAWMAN (TV)
Dell Publishing Co.: No. 970, Feb, 1959 - No. 11, Apr-June, 1962 (All photo-c)

Four Color 970(#1)	12	24	36	87	156	225
Four Color 1035('60), 3(2-4/60)-Toth-a	8	16	24	54	90	125
4-11	6	12	18	43	69	95

LAW OF DREDD, THE (Also see Judge Dredd)
Quality Comics/Fleetway #8 on: 1989 - No. 33, 1992 ($1.50/$1.75)

1-33: Bolland a-1-6,8,10-12,14(2 pg),15,19   2.50

LAWRENCE (See Movie Classics)

LAZARUS CHURCHYARD
Tundra Publishing: June, 1992 - No. 3, 1992 ($3.95, 44 pgs., coated stock)

1-3	4.00
The Final Cut (Image, 1/01, $14.95, TPB) Reprints Ellis/D'Israeli strips	15.00

LAZARUS FIVE
DC Comics: July, 2000 - No. 5, Nov, 2000 ($2.50, limited series)

1-5-Harris-c/Abell-a(p)   2.50

LEADING COMICS
DC Comics: Jan. 1942

nn - Ashcan comic, not distributed to newsstands, only for in-house use. Cover art is Detective Comics #57 with interior being Star Spangled Comics #2   (no known sales)

LEADING COMICS (...Screen Comics No. 42 on)
National Periodical Publications: Winter, 1941-42 - No. 41, Feb-Mar, 1950

1-Origin The Seven Soldiers of Victory; Crimson Avenger, Green Arrow & Speedy, Shining Knight, The Vigilante, Star Spangled Kid & Stripesy begin; The Dummy (Vigilante villain)						
1st app.	446	892	1338	3122	5461	7800
2-Meskin-a; Fred Ray-c	159	318	477	994	1647	2300
3	121	242	363	756	1253	1750
4,5	86	172	258	538	889	1240
6-10	66	132	198	413	682	950
11,12,14(Spring, 1945)	48	96	144	293	484	675
13-Classic robot-c	93	186	279	581	966	1350
15-(Sum,'45)-Contents change to funny animal	28	56	84	162	256	350
16-22,24-30: 16-Nero Fox-c begin, end #22	14	28	42	80	115	150
23-1st app. Peter Porkchops by Otto Feuer & begins	28	56	84	162	256	350
31,32,34-41: 34-41-Leading Screen... on-c only	12	24	36	67	94	120
33-(Scarce)	20	40	60	117	184	250

NOTE: Otto Feuer a most #15-on; Rube Grossman-a most #15-on;c-15-41. Post a-23-37, 39, 41.

LEADING MAN
Image Comics: June, 2006 - No. 5, Feb, 2007 ($3.50, limited series)

1-5-B. Clay Moore-s/Jeremy Haun-a	3.50
TPB (2/07, $14.95) r/#1-5; sketch gallery	15.00

LEADING SCREEN COMICS (Formerly Leading Comics)
National Periodical: No. 42, Apr-May, 1950 - No. 77, Aug-Sept, 1955

42-Peter Porkchops-c/stories continue	12	24	36	67	94	120
43-77	11	22	33	60	83	105

NOTE: Grossman a-most. Mayer a-45-48, 50, 54-57, 60, 62-74, 75(3), 76, 77.

LEAGUE OF CHAMPIONS, THE (Also see The Champions)
Hero Graphics: Dec, 1990 - No. 12, 1992 ($2.95, 52 pgs.)

1-12: 1-Flare app. 2-Origin Malice   3.00

LEAGUE OF EXTRAORDINARY GENTLEMEN, THE
America's Best Comics: Mar, 1999 - No. 6, Sept, 2000 ($2.95, limited series)

1-Alan Moore-s/Kevin O'Neill-a	2	4	6	8	10	12
1-DF Edition ($10.00) O'Neill-c	2	4	6	9	12	15
2,3						6.00
4-6: 5-Revised printing with "Amaze 'Whirling Spray' Syringe" parody ad						4.00
5-Initial printing recalled because of "Marvel Co. Syringe" parody ad						30.00
... Compendium 1,2: 1-r/#1,2. 2-r/#3,4						6.00
Hardcover (2000, $24.95) r/#1-6 plus cover gallery						25.00

LEAGUE OF EXTRAORDINARY GENTLEMEN, THE (Volume 2)

Leave it to Binky #5 © DC

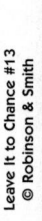

Leave It to Chance #13 © Robinson & Smith

Legend of the Shield #1 © AP

	GD 2.0	VG 4.0	FN 6.0	VF 8.0	VF/NM 9.0	NM- 9.2
America's Best Comics: Sept, 2002 - No. 6, Nov, 2003 ($3.50, limited series)						
1-6-Alan Moore-s/Kevin O'Neill-a						4.00
... Bumper Compendium 1,2: 1-r/#1,2. 2-r/#3,4						6.00
LEAGUE OF JUSTICE						
DC Comics (Elseworlds): 1996 - No. 2, 1996 ($5.95, 48 pgs., squarebound)						
1,2: Magic-based alternate DC Universe story; Giordano-i						6.00
LEATHERFACE						
Arpad Publishing: May (April on-c), 1991 - No. 4, May, 1992 ($2.75, painted-c)						
1-4-Based on Texas Chainsaw movie; Dorman-c						6.00
LEATHERNECK THE MARINE (See Mighty Midget Comics)						
LEAVE IT TO BEAVER (TV)						
Dell Publishing Co.: No. 912, June, 1958; May-July, 1962 (All photo-c)						
Four Color 912	16	32	48	114	202	290
Four Color 999,1103,1191,1285, 01-428-207	13	26	39	95	168	240
LEAVE IT TO BINKY (Binky No. 72 on) (Super DC Giant) (No. 1-22: 52 pgs.)						
National Periodical Publications: 2-3/48 - #60, 10/58; #61, 6-7/68 - #71, 2-3/70 (Teen-age humor)						
1-Lucy wears Superman costume	36	72	108	208	329	450
2	18	36	54	105	165	225
3,4	13	26	39	74	105	135
5-Superman cameo	17	34	51	100	158	215
6-10	11	22	33	62	85	110
11-14,16-22: Last 52 pg. issue	10	20	30	56	76	95
15-Scribbly story by Mayer	11	22	33	64	90	115
23-28,30-45: 45-Last pre-code (2/55)	9	18	27	47	61	75
29-Used in POP, pg. 78	9	18	27	50	65	80
46-60: 60-(10/58)	5	10	15	32	51	70
61 (6-7/68) 1950's reprints with art changes	6	12	18	37	59	80
62-69: 67-Last 12¢ issue	4	8	12	26	41	55
70-7pg. app. Bus Driver who looks like Ralph from Honeymooners	5	10	15	30	48	65
71-Last issue	4	8	12	28	44	60
NOTE: *Aragones-a-61, 62, 67. Drucker a-28. Mayer a-1, 2, 15. Created by Mayer.*						
LEAVE IT TO CHANCE (Also see Promotional Comics section for FCBD Ed.)						
Image Comics (Homage Comics): Sept, 1996 - No. 11, Sept, 1998; No. 13, July, 2002						
DC Comics (Homage Comics): No. 12, Jun, 1999 ($2.50/$2.95/$4.95)						
1-3: 1-Intro Chance Falconer & St. George; James Robinson scripts & Paul Smith-c/a						5.00
4-12: 12-(6/99)						3.00
13-(7/02, $4.95) includes sketch pages and pin-ups						5.00
Shaman's Rain TPB (1997, $9.95) r/#1-4						10.00
Shaman's Rain HC (2002, $14.95, over-sized 8 1/4" x 12") r/#1-4						15.00
Trick or Threat TPB (1997, $12.95) r/#5-8						13.00
Trick or Threat HC (2002, $14.95, over-sized 8 1/4" x 12") r/#5-8						15.00
Vol. 3: Monster Madness and Other Stories HC (2003, $14.95, 8 1/4" x 12") r/#9-11						15.00
LEE HUNTER, INDIAN FIGHTER						
Dell Publishing Co.: No. 779, Mar, 1957; No. 904, May, 1958						
Four Color 779 (#1)	5	10	15	33	55	75
Four Color 904	4	8	12	26	41	55
LEFT-HANDED GUN, THE (Movie)						
Dell Publishing Co.: No. 913, July, 1958						
Four Color 913-Paul Newman photo-c	9	18	27	63	107	150
LEGACY						
Majestic Entertainment: Oct, 1993 - No. 2, Nov, 1993; No. 0, 1994 ($2.25)						
1-2,0: 1-Glow-in-the-dark-c. 0-Platinum						2.50
LEGACY						
Image Comics: May, 2003 - No. 4, Feb, 2004 ($2.95)						
1-4: 1-Francisco-a/Treffiletti-s						3.00
LEGACY OF KAIN (Based on the Eidos video game)						
Top Cow Productions: Oct, 1999; Jan, 2004 ($2.99)						
...Defiance 1 (1/04, $2.99) Cha-c; Kirkham-a						3.00
...Soul Reaver 1 (10/99, Diamond Dateline supplement) Benitez-c						2.50
LEGEND						
DC Comics (WildStorm): Apr, 2005 - No. 4, July, 2005 ($5.95/$5.99, limited series)						
1-4-Howard Chaykin-s/Russ Heath-a; inspired by Philip Wylie's novel "Gladiator"						6.00
LEGEND OF CUSTER, THE (TV)						
Dell Publishing Co.: Jan, 1968						

	GD 2.0	VG 4.0	FN 6.0	VF 8.0	VF/NM 9.0	NM- 9.2
1-Wayne Maunder photo-c	3	6	9	18	27	35
LEGEND OF ISIS						
Alias Entertainment: May, 2005 - Present ($2.99)						
1-5: 1-Three covers; Ottney-s/Fontana-a						3.00
...: Beginnings TPB (5/05, $9.99) Ottney-s						10.00
LEGEND OF JESSE JAMES, THE (TV)						
Gold Key: Feb, 1966						
10172-602-Photo-c	3	6	9	18	27	35
LEGEND OF KAMUI, THE (See Kamui)						
LEGEND OF LOBO, THE (See Movie Comics)						
LEGEND OF MOTHER SARAH (Manga)						
Dark Horse Comics: Apr, 1995 - No. 8, Nov, 1995 ($2.50, limited series)						
1-8: Katsuhiro Otomo scripts						4.00
LEGEND OF MOTHER SARAH: CITY OF THE ANGELS (Manga)						
Dark Horse Comics: Oct, 1996 - No. 9 ($3.95, B&W, limited series)						
1(10/96), 2(12/97),3-9: Otomo scripts						4.00
LEGEND OF MOTHER SARAH: CITY OF THE CHILDREN (Manga)						
Dark Horse Comics: Jan, 1996 - No. 7, July, 1996 ($3.95, B&W, limited series)						
1-7:Otomo scripts						4.00
LEGEND OF SUPREME						
Image Comics (Extreme): Dec, 1994 - No. 3, Feb, 1995 ($2.50, limited series)						
1-3						2.50
LEGEND OF THE ELFORD						
DavDez Arts: July, 1998 - No. 2, Sept, 1998 ($2.95)						
1,2-Barry Blair & Colin Chin-s/a						3.00
LEGEND OF THE HAWKMAN						
DC Comics: 2000 - No. 3, 2000 ($4.95, limited series)						
1-3-Raab-s/Lark-c/a						5.00
LEGEND OF THE SHIELD, THE						
DC Comics (Impact Comics): July, 1991 - No. 16, Oct, 1992 ($1.00)						
1-16: 6,7-The Fly x-over. 12-Contains trading card						2.50
Annual 1 (1992, $2.50, 68 pgs.)-Snyder-a; w/trading card						2.50
LEGEND OF WONDER WOMAN, THE						
DC Comics: May, 1986 - No. 4, Aug, 1986 (75¢, limited series)						
1-4						4.00
LEGEND OF YOUNG DICK TURPIN, THE (Disney)(TV)						
Gold Key: May, 1966						
1 (10176-605)-Photo/painted-c	3	6	9	18	27	35
LEGEND OF ZELDA, THE (Link: The Legend... in indicia)						
Valiant Comics: 1990 - No. 4, 1990 ($1.95, coated stiff-c) V2#1, 1990 - No. 5, 1990 ($1.50)						
1-4: 4-Layton-c(i)						3.00
V2#1-5						3.00
LEGENDS						
DC Comics: Nov, 1986 - No. 6, Apr, 1987 (75¢, limited series)						
1-5: 1-Byrne-c/a(p) in all; 1st app. new Capt. Marvel. 3-1st app. new Suicide Squad; death of Blockbuster						4.00
6-1st app. new Justice League						6.00
LEGENDS OF DANIEL BOONE, THE (...Frontier Scout)						
National Periodical Publications: Oct-Nov, 1955 - No. 8, Dec-Jan, 1956-57						
1 (Scarce)-Nick Cardy c-1-8	56	112	168	350	580	810
2 (Scarce)	41	82	123	252	406	560
3-8 (Scarce)	35	70	105	204	322	440
LEGENDS OF NASCAR, THE						
Vortex Comics: Nov, 1990 - No. 14, 1992? (#1 3rd printing (1/91) says 2nd printing inside)						
1-Bill Elliott biog.; Trimpe-a ($1.50)						5.00
1-2nd printing (11/90, $2.00)						2.50
1-3rd print; contains Maxx racecards ($3.00)						3.00
2-14: 2-Richard Petty. 3-Ken Schrader (7/91). 4-Bobby Allison; Spiegle-a(p); Adkins part-i. 5-Sterling Marlin. 6-Bill Elliott. 7-Junior Johnson; Spiegle-c/a. 8-Benny Parsons; Heck-a						3.00
1-13-Hologram cover versions. 2-Hologram shows Bill Elliott's car by mistake (all are numbered & limited)						5.00
2-Hologram corrected version						5.00
Christmas Special ($5.95)						6.00

	GD 2.0	VG 4.0	FN 6.0	VF 8.0	VF/NM 9.0	NM- 9.2		GD 2.0	VG 4.0	FN 6.0	VF 8.0	VF/NM 9.0	NM- 9.2

LEGENDS OF THE DARK CLAW
DC Comics (Amalgam): Apr, 1996 ($1.95)

1-Jim Balent-c/a — 3.00

LEGENDS OF THE DARK KNIGHT (See Batman: ...)

LEGENDS OF THE DC UNIVERSE
DC Comics: Feb, 1998 - No. 41, June, 2001 ($1.95/$1.99/$2.50)

1-13,15-21: 1-3-Superman; Robinson-s/Semeiks-a/Orbik-painted-c. 4,5-Wonder Woman; Deodato-a/Rude painted-c. 8-GL/GA, O'Neil-s. 10,11-Batgirl; Dodson-a. 12,13-Justice League. 15-17-Flash. 18-Kid Flash; Guice-a. 19-Impulse; prelude to JLApe Annuals. 20,21-Abin Sur — 3.00
14-($3.95) Jimmy Olsen; Kirby-esque-c by Rude — 4.00
22-27,30: 22,23-Superman; Rude-c/Ladronn-a. 26,27-Aquaman/Joker — 2.50
28,29: Green Lantern & the Atom; Gil Kane-s; covers by Kane and Ross — 2.50
31,32: 32-Begin $2.50-c; Wonder Woman; Texeira-a — 2.50
33-36-Hal Jordan as The Spectre; DeMatteis-s/Zulli-a; Hale painted-c — 2.50
37-41: 37,38-Kyle Rayner. 39-Superman. 40,41-Atom; Harris-c — 2.50
... Crisis on Infinite Earths 1 (2/99, $4.95) Untold story during and after Crisis on Infinite Earths #4; Wolfman-s/Ryan-a/Orbik-c — 5.00
... 80 Page Giant 1 (9/98, $4.95) Stories and art by various incl. Ditko, Perez, Gibbons, Mumy; Joe Kubert-c — 5.00
... 80 Page Giant 2 (1/00, $4.95) Stories and art by various incl. Challengers by Art Adams; Sean Phillips-c — 5.00
... 3-D Gallery (12/98, $2.95) Pin-ups w/glasses — 3.00

LEGENDS OF THE LEGION (See Legion of Super-Heroes)
DC Comics: Feb, 1998 - No. 4, May, 1998 ($2.25, limited series)

1-4:1-Origin-s of Ultra Boy. 2-Spark. 3-Umbra. 4-Star Boy — 3.00

LEGENDS OF THE STARGRAZERS (See Vanguard Illustrated #2)
Innovation Publishing: Aug, 1989 - No. 6, 1990 ($1.95, limited series, mature)

1-6: 1-Redondo part inks — 2.50

LEGENDS OF THE WORLD'S FINEST (See World's Finest)
DC Comics: 1994 - No. 3, 1994 ($4.95, squarebound, limited series)

1-3-Simonson scripts; Brereton-c/a; embossed foil logos — 6.00
TPB-(1995, $14.95) r/#1-3 — 15.00

L.E.G.I.O.N. (The # to right of title represents year of print)(Also see Lobo & R.E.B.E.L.S.)
DC Comics: Feb, 1989 - No. 70, Sept, 1994 ($1.50/$1.75)

1-Giffen plots/breakdowns in #1-12,28 — 5.00
2-22,24-47: 3-Lobo app. #3 on. 4-1st Lobo-c this title. 5-Lobo joins L.E.G.I.O.N. 13-Lar Gand app. 16-Lar Gand joins L.E.G.I.O.N., leaves #19. 31-Capt. Marvel app. 35-L.E.G.I.O.N. '92 begins — 3.00
23,70-($2.50, 52 pgs.)-L.E.G.I.O.N. '91 begins. 70-Zero Hour — 4.00
48,49,51-69: 48-Begin $1.75-c. 63-L.E.G.I.O.N. '94 begins; Superman x-over — 3.00
50-($3.50, 68 pgs.) — 4.00
Annual 1-5 ('90-94, 68 pgs.): 1-Lobo, Superman app. 2-Alan Grant scripts. 5-Elseworlds story; Lobo app. — 4.00
NOTE: *Alan Grant scripts in #1-39, 51, Annual 1, 2.*

LEGION, THE (Continued from Legion Lost & Legion Worlds)
DC Comics: Dec, 2001 - No. 38, Oct, 2004 ($2.50)

1-Abnett & Lanning-s; Coipel & Lanning-c/a — 4.00
2-24: 3-8-Ra's al Ghul app. 5-Snejbjerg-a. 9-DeStefano-a. 12-Legion vs. JLA. 16-Fatal Five app.; Walker-a 17,18-Ra's al Ghul app. 20-23-Universo app. — 2.50
25-($3.95) Art by Harris, Cockrum, Rivoche; teenage Clark Kent app.; Harris-c — 4.00
26-38-Superboy in classic costume. 26-30-Darkseid app. 31-Giffen-a. 35-38-Jurgens-a — 2.50
...Secret Files 3003 (1/04, $4.95) Kirk-a, Harris-c/a; Superboy app. — 5.00
...Foundations TPB (2004, $19.95) r/#25-30 & Secret Files 3003; Harris-c — 20.00

LEGION LOST (Continued from Legion of Super-Heroes [4th series] #125)
DC Comics: May, 2000 - No. 12, Apr, 2001 ($2.50, limited series)

1-Abnett & Lanning-s. Coipel and Lanning-c/a	1	2	3	4	5	7	
2-12-Abnett & Lanning-s. Coipel & Lanning-c/a in most. 4,9-Alixe-a						3.00	

LEGIONNAIRES (See Legion of Super-Heroes #40, 41 & Showcase 95 #6)
DC Comics: Apr, 1992 - No. 81, Mar, 2000 ($1.25/$1.50/$2.25)

0-(10/94)-Zero Hour restart of Legion; released between #18 & #19 — 2.50
1-49,51-77: 1-(4/92)-Chris Sprouse-c/a; polybagged w/SkyBox trading card. 11-Kid Quantum joins. 18-(9/94)-Zero Hour. 19(11/94). 37-Valor (Lar Gand) becomes M'onel (5/96). 43-Legion tryouts; reintro Princess Projectra, Shadow Lass & others. 47-Forms one cover image with LSH #91. 60-Karate Kid & Kid Quantum join. 61-Silver Age & 70's Legion app. 76-Return of Wildfire. 79,80-Coipel-c/a; Legion vs. the Blight — 2.50
50-($3.95) Pullout poster by Davis/Farmer — 4.00
#1,000,000 (11/98) Sean Phillips-a — 2.50

Annual 1,3 ('94,'96 $2.95)-1-Elseworlds-s. 3-Legends of the Dead Earth-s — 3.00
Annual 2 (1995, $3.95)-Year One-s — 4.50

LEGIONNAIRES THREE
DC Comics: Jan, 1986 - No. 4, May, 1986 (75¢, limited series)

1-4 — 3.00

LEGION OF MONSTERS (Also see Marvel Premiere #28 & Marvel Preview #8)
Marvel Comics Group: Sept, 1975 ($1.00, B&W, magazine, 76 pgs.)

1-Origin & 1st app. Legion of Monsters; Neal Adams-c; Morrow-a; origin & only app. The Manphibian; Frankenstein by Mayerik; Bram Stoker's Dracula adaptation; Reese-a; painted-c (#2 was advertised with Morbius & Satana, but was never published) — 4 8 12 28 44 60

LEGION OF MONSTERS (One-shots)
Marvel Comics: Apr, 2007 - Sept, 2007 ($2.99)

... Man-Thing (5/07) Huston-s/Janson-a/Land-c; Simon Garth: Zombie by Ted McKeever — 3.00
... Morbius (9/07) Cahill-s/Gaydos-a/Land-c; Dracula w/Finch-c/Cebulski-s — 3.00
... Satana (8/07) Furth-s/Andrasofszky-a/Land-c; Living Mummy by Hickman — 3.00
... Werewolf By Night (4/07) Carey-s/Land-a/c; Monster of Frankenstein by Skottie Young — 3.00

LEGION OF NIGHT, THE
Marvel Comics: Oct, 1991 - No. 2, Oct, 1991 ($4.95, 52 pgs.)

1,2-Whilce Portacio-c/a(p) — 5.00

LEGION OF SUBSTITUTE HEROES SPECIAL (See Adventure Comics #306)
DC Comics: July, 1985 ($1.25, one-shot, 52 pgs.)

1-Giffen-c/a(p) — 3.00

LEGION OF SUPER-HEROES (See Action Comics, Adventure, All New Collectors Edition, Legionnaires, Legends of the Legion, Limited Collectors Edition, Secrets of the…, Superboy & Superman)
National Periodical Publications: Feb, 1973 - No. 4, July-Aug, 1973

1-Legion & Tommy Tomorrow reprints begin	3	9	17	25	32		
2-4: 2-Forte-r. 3-r/Adv. #340. Action r/240. 4-r/Adv. #341, Action #233; Mooney-r	2	4	6	9	13	16	

LEGION OF SUPER-HEROES, THE (Formerly Superboy and…; Tales of The Legion No. 314 on)
DC Comics: No. 259, Jan, 1980 - No. 313, July, 1984

259(#1)-Superboy leaves Legion	2	4	6	8	11	14	
260-270,285-289: 265-Contains 28 pg. insert "Superman & the TRS-80 computer"; origin Tyroc; Tyroc leaves Legion						5.00	
261,263,264,266—(Whitman variants; low print run; no cover #'s)	2	4	6	8	10	12	
271-284: 272-Blok joins; origin; 20 pg. insert-Dial 'H' For Hero. 277-Intro. Reflecto. 280-Superboy re-joins Legion. 282-Origin Reflecto. 283-Origin Wildfire						5.00	
290-294-Great Darkness saga. 294-Double size (52 pgs.)	1	2	3	5	6	8	
295-299,301-313: 297-Origin retold. 298-Free 16 pg. Amethyst preview. 306-Brief origin Star Boy (Swan art). 311-Colan-a						3.00	
300-(68 pg., Mando paper)-Anniversary issue; has c/a by almost everyone at DC						5.00	
Annual 1-3(82-84, 52 pgs.)-1-Giffen-c/a; 1st app./origin new Invisible Kid who joins Legion. 2-Karate Kid & Princess Projectra wed & resign						3.00	
…The Great Darkness Saga (1989, $17.95, 196 pgs.)-r/LSH #287,290-294 & Annual #3; Giffen-c/a	2	4	6	10	14	18	

NOTE: *Aparo c-282, 283, 300(part). Austin c-268i. Buckler c-273p, 274p, 276p. Colan a-311p. Ditko a(p)-267, 268, 272, 274, 276, 281. Giffen a-285-313p, Annual 1p; c-287p, 288p, 289, 290p, 291p, 292, 293, 294-299p, 300, 301-313p, Annual 1p, 2p. Perez c-268p, 277-280, 281p. Starlin a-265. Staton a-259p, 260p, 280. Tuska a-308p.*

LEGION OF SUPER-HEROES (3rd Series) (Reprinted in Tales of the Legion)
DC Comics: Aug, 1984 - No. 63, Aug, 1989 ($1.25/$1.75, deluxe format)

1-Silver ink logo — 5.00
2-36,39-44,46-49,51-62: 4-Death of Karate Kid. 5-Death of Nemesis Kid. 12-Cosmic Boy, Lightning Lad, & Saturn Girl resign. 14-Intro new members: Tellus, Sensor Girl, Quislet. 15-17-Crisis tie-in. 18-Crisis x-over. 25-Sensor Girl i.d. revealed as Princess Projectra. 35-Saturn Girl rejoins. 42,43-Millennium tie-ins. 44-Origin Quislet — 3.00

37,38-Death of Superboy	2	4	6	8	11	14	
45,50: 45 ($2.95, 68 pgs.)-Anniversary ish. 50-Double size ($2.50-c)						4.00	
63-Final issue						4.00	
Annual 1-4 (10/85-'88, 52 pgs.)-1-Crisis tie-in						3.00	

NOTE: *Byrne c-36p. Giffen a(p)-1, 2, 50-55, 57-63, Annual 1p, 2; c-1-5p, 54p, Annual 1. Orlando a-6p. Steacy c-45-50, Annual 3.*

LEGION OF SUPER-HEROES (4th Series)
DC Comics: Nov, 1989 - No. 125, Mar, 2000 ($1.75/$1.95/$2.25)

0-(10/94)-Zero Hour restart of Legion; released between #61 & #62 — 2.50
1-Giffen-c/a(p)/scripts begin (4 pg.-a only #18) — 4.00

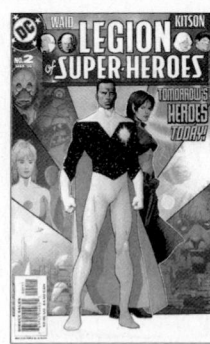

Legion of Super-Heroes #2 © DC

Lenore #11 © Roman Dirge

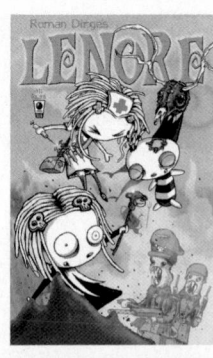

Let's Pretend #1 © DS

	GD 2.0	VG 4.0	FN 6.0	VF 8.0	VF/NM 9.0	NM- 9.2

2-20,26-49,51-53,55-58: 4-Mon-El (Lar Gand) destroys Time Trapper, changes reality. 5-Alt. reality story where Mordru rules all; Ferro Lad app. 6-1st app. of Laurel Gand (Lar Gand's cousin). 8-Origin. 13-Free poster by Giffen showing new costumes. 15-(2/91)-1st reference of Lar Gand as Valor. 26-New map of headquarters. 34-Six pg. preview of Timber Wolf mini-series. 40-Minor Legionnaires app. 41-(3/93)-SW6 Legion renamed Legionnaires w/new costumes and some new code-names 3.00

21-25: 21-24-Lobo & Darkseid storyline. 24-Cameo SW6 younger Legion duplicates. 25-SW6 Legion full intro. 3.50
50-($3.50, 68 pgs.) 4.00
54-($2.95)-Die-cut & foil stamped-c 4.00
59-99: 61-(9/94)-Zero Hour. 62-(11/94). 75-XS travels back to the 20th Century (cont'd in Impulse #9). 77-Origin of Brainiac 5. 81-Reintro Sun Boy. 85-Half of the Legion sent to the 20th century, Superman-c/app. 86-Final Night. 87-Deadman-c/app. 88-Impulse-c/app. Adventure Comics #247 cover swipe. 91-Forms one cover image with Legionnaires #47. 96-Wedding of Ultra Boy and Apparition. 99-Robin, Impulse, Superboy app. 2.50
100-($5.95, 96 pgs.)-Legionnaires return to the 30th Century; gatefold-c;

5 stories-art by Simonson, Davis and others	1	2	3	4	5	7

101-121: 101-Armstrong-a(p) begins. 105-Legion past & present vs. Time Trapper. 109-Moder-a. 110-Thunder joins. 114,115-Bizarro Legion. 120,121-Fatal Five. 2.50
122-124: 122,123-Coipel-c/a. 124-Coipel-c 3.00
125-Leads into "Legion Lost" maxi-series; Coipel-c 5.00
#1,000,000 (11/98) Giffen-a 2.50
Annual 1-5 (1990-1994, $3.50, 68 pgs.): 4-Bloodlines. 5-Elseworlds story 3.50
Annual 6 (1995,$3.95)-Year One story 4.00
Annual 7 (1996, $3.50, 48 pgs.)-Legends of the Dead Earth story; intro 75th Century Legion of Super-Heroes; Wildfire app. 3.50
Legion: Secret Files 1 (1/98, $4.95) Retold origin & pin-ups 5.00
Legion: Secret Files 2 (6/99, $4.95) Story and profile pages 5.00
The Beginning of Tomorrow TPB ('99, $17.95) r/post-Zero Hour reboot 18.00
NOTE: *Giffen* a-1-24; breakdowns-26-32, 34-36; c-1-7, 8(part), 9-24. *Brandon Peterson* a(p)-15(1st for DC), 16, 18, Annual 2(54 pgs.) c-Annual 2p. *Swan/Anderson* c-8(part).

LEGION OF SUPER-HEROES (5th Series) (Title becomes Supergirl and the Legion of Super-Heroes #16-on) (Intro. in Teen Titans/Legion Special)
DC Comics: Feb, 2005 - Present ($2.95/$2.99)

1-15: 1-Waid-s/Kitson-a/c. 4-Kirk & Gibbons-a. 9-Jeanty-a. 15-Dawnstar, Tyroc, Blok-c	3.00
... Death of a Dream TPB ('06, $14.99) r/#7-13 .... 15.00
... Teenage Revolution TPB ('05, $14.99) r/#1-6 & Teen Titans/Legion Spec.; sketch pages 15.00

LEGION OF SUPER-HEROES IN THE 31ST CENTURY (Based on the animated series)
DC Comics: June, 2007 - Present ($2.25)

1-5: 1-Chynna Clugston-a; Fatal Five app. 2.25

LEGION: SCIENCE POLICE (See Legion of Super-Heroes)
DC Comics: Aug, 1998 - No. 4, Nov, 1998 ($2.25, limited series)

1-4-Ryan-a 2.50

LEGION WORLDS (Follows Legion Lost series)
DC Comics: Jun, 2001 - No. 6, Nov, 2001 ($3.95, limited series)

1-6-Abnett & Lanning-s; art by various. 5-Dillon-a. 6-Timber Wolf app. 4.00

LEMONADE KID, THE (See Bobby Benson's B-Bar-B Riders)
AC Comics: 1990 ($2.50, 28 pgs.)

1-Powell-c(r); Red Hawk-r by Powell; Lemonade Kid-r/Bobby Benson by Powell (2 stories) 2.50

LENNON SISTERS LIFE STORY, THE
Dell Publishing Co.: No. 951, Nov, 1958 - No. 1014, Aug, 1959

Four Color 951 (#1)-Toth-a, 32pgs, photo-c	13	26	39	95	168	240
Four Color 1014-Toth-a, photo-c	12	24	36	87	156	225

LENORE
Slave Labor Graphics: Feb, 1998 - Present ($2.95/$3.95, B&W, color #13-on)

1-12: 1-Roman Dirge-s/a. 1,2-2nd printing 3.00
13-($3.95, color) 4.00
....: Noogies TPB ($11.95) r/#1-4 .... 12.00
....: Wedgies TPB (2000, $13.95) r/#5-8 .... 14.00
....: Cooties TPB (3/06, $13.95) r/#9-12; pin-ups by various 14.00

LEONARD NIMOY'S PRIMORTALS
Tekno Comics: Mar, 1995 - No. 15, May, 1996 ($1.95)

1-15: Concept by Leonard Nimoy & Isaac Asimov 1-3-w/bound-in game piece & trading card. 4-w/Teknophage Steel Edition coupon. 13,14-Art Adams-c. 15-Simonson-c 2.50

LEONARD NIMOY'S PRIMORTALS
BIG Entertainment: V2#0, June, 1996 - No. 8, Feb, 1997 ($2.25)

V2#0-8: 0-Includes Pt. 9 of "The Big Bang" x-over. 0,1-Simonson-c/a. 3-Kelley Jones-c 2.50

LEONARD NIMOY'S PRIMORTALS ORIGINS
Tekno Comix: Nov, 1995 - No. 2, Dec, 1995 ($2.95, limited series)

1,2: Nimoy scripts; Art Adams-c; polybagged 3.00

LEONARDO (Also see Teenage Mutant Ninja Turtles)
Mirage Studios: Dec, 1986 ($1.50, B&W, one-shot)

1 .... 6.00

LEO THE LION
I. W. Enterprises: No date(1960s) (10¢)

1-Reprint	2	4	6	9	13	16

LEROY (Teen-age)
Standard Comics: Nov, 1949 - No. 6, Nov, 1950

1	14	28	42	76	108	140
2-Frazetta text illo.	10	20	30	54	72	90
3-6: 3-Lubbers-a	9	18	27	47	61	75

LETHAL (Also see Brigade)
Image Comics (Extreme Studios): Feb, 1996 ($2.50, unfinished limited series)

1-Marat Mychaels-c/a 2.50

LETHAL FOES OF SPIDER-MAN (Sequel to Deadly Foes of Spider-Man)
Marvel Comics: Sept, 1993 - No. 4, Dec, 1993 ($1.75, limited series)

1-4 .... 2.50

LETHAL INSTINCT
Alias Entertainment: Apr, 2005 - Present (75¢/$2.99)

1-(75¢-c) Soares-s/Jadson-a 2.50
2-($2.99-c) Borges-a 3.00

LETHARGIC LAD
Crusade Ent.: June, 1996 - No. 3, Sept, 1996 ($2.95, B&W, limited series)

1,2 .... 3.00
3-Alex Ross-c/swipe (Kingdom Come) 4.00
...Jumbo Sized Annual #1 (Summer 2002, $3.99) prints comic stories from internet 4.00

LETHARGIC LAD ADVENTURES
Crusade Ent./Destination Ent.#3 on: Oct, 1997 - No. 12, Sept./Oct. 1999 ($2.95, B&W)

1-12-Hyland-s/a. 9-Alex Ross sketch page & back-c 3.00

LET'S PRETEND (CBS radio)
D. S. Publishing Co.: May-June, 1950 - No. 3, Sept-Oct, 1950

1	17	34	51	98	154	210
2,3	14	28	42	80	115	150

LET'S READ THE NEWSPAPER
Charlton Press: 1974

nn-Features Quincy by Ted Sheares	1	3	4	6	8	10

LET'S TAKE A TRIP (TV) (CBS Television Presents)
Pines Comics: Spring, 1958

1-Marv Levy-c/a	5	10	15	23	28	32

LETTERS TO SANTA (See March of Comics No. 228)

LEX LUTHOR: MAN OF STEEL
DC Comics: May, 2005 - No. 5, Sept, 2005 ($2.99, limited series)

1-5: 1-Azzarello-s/Bermejo-a/c in all. 3-Batman-c/app. 3.00
TPB (2005, $12.99) r/series 13.00

LEX LUTHOR: THE UNAUTHORIZED BIOGRAPHY
DC Comics: 1989 ($3.95, 52 pgs., one-shot, squarebound)

1-Painted-c; Clark Kent app. 4.00

LEX TALIONIS: A JUNGLE TALE
Image Comics: Jan, 2004 ($5.95, one-shot, reads sideways)

1-Aneurin Wright-s/a 6.00

LIBERTY COMICS (Miss Liberty No. 1)
Green Publishing Co.: No. 5, May, '46 - No. 15, July, 1946 (MLJ & other-r)

5 (5/46)-The Prankster app; Starr-a	21	42	63	122	191	260
10-Hangman & Boy Buddies app.; reprints 3 Hangman stories, incl. Hangman #8	22	44	66	128	202	275
11 (V2#2, 1/46)-Wilbur in women's clothes	17	34	51	100	158	215
12 (V2#4)-Black Hood & Suzie app.; classic Skull-c	57	114	171	356	591	825
14,15-Patty of Airliner; Starr-a in both	15	30	45	85	130	175

LIBERTY COMICS
Heroic Publishing: Sept, 2007 - Present ($4.50)

	GD 2.0	VG 4.0	FN 6.0	VF 8.0	VF/NM 9.0	NM- 9.2

1-Mark Sparacio-c — — — — — 4.50

LIBERTY GIRL
Heroic Publishing: Aug, 2006 - Present ($3.25/$2.99)

1-3-Mark Sparacio-c/a — — — — — 3.25

LIBERTY GUARDS
Chicago Mail Order: No date (1946?)

nn-Reprints Man of War #1 with cover of Liberty Scouts #1; Gustavson-c
35 70 105 201 318 435

LIBERTY MEADOWS
Insight Studios Group/Image Comics #27 on: 1999 - Present ($2.95, B&W)

1-Frank Cho-s/a; reprints newspaper strips 3 6 9 14 20 25
2,3 2 4 6 8 11 14
4-10 1 2 3 4 5 7
11-25,27-37: 20-Adam Hughes-c. 22-Evil Brandy vs. Brandy. 27-1st Image issue, printed sideways — — — — — 3.00
..., Cover Girl HC (Image, 2006, $24.99, with dustjacket) r/color covers of #1-19,21-37 along with B&W inked versions, sketches and pin-up art — — — — — 25.00
...: Eden Book 1 SC (Image, 2002, $14.95) r/#1-9; sketch gallery — — — — — 15.00
...: Eden Book 1 SC 2nd printing (Image, 2004, $19.95) r/#1-9; sketch gallery — — — — — 20.00
...: Eden Book 1 HC (Image, 2003, $24.95, with dustjacket) r/#1-9; sketch gallery — — — — — 25.00
...: Creature Comforts Book 2 HC (Image, 2004, $24.95, with d.j.) r/#10-18; sketch gallery — — — — — 25.00
...: Creature Comforts Book 2 SC (Image, 12/04, $14.95) r/#10-18; sketch gallery — — — — — 15.00
...Book 3: Summer of Love HC (Image, 2004, $24.95) r/#19-27; sketch gallery — — — — — 25.00
...Book 3: Summer of Love SC (Image, 7/05, $14.95) r/#19-27; sketch gallery — — — — — 15.00
...Book 4: Cold, Cold Heart HC (Image, 9/05, $24.95) r/#28-36; sketch gallery — — — — — 25.00
...Book 4: Cold, Cold Heart SC (Image, 2006, $14.99) r/#28-36; sketch gallery — — — — — 15.00
... Sourcebook (5/04, $4.95) character info and unpublished strips — — — — — 5.00
... Wedding Album (#26) (2002, $2.95) — — — — — 3.00

LIBERTY PROJECT, THE
Eclipse Comics: June, 1987 - No. 8, May, 1988 ($1.75, color, Baxter paper)

1-8: 6-Valkyrie app. — — — — — 2.50

LIBERTY SCOUTS (See Liberty Guards & Man of War)
Centaur Publications: No. 2, June, 1941 - No. 3, Aug, 1941

2(#1)-Origin The Fire-Man, of Man of War; Vapo-Man & Liberty Scouts begin; intro Liberty Scouts; Gustavson-c/a in both 128 256 384 800 1325 1850
3(#2)-Origin & 1st app. The Sentinel 90 180 270 563 932 1300

LICENCE TO KILL (James Bond 007) (Movie)
Eclipse Comics: 1989 ($7.95, slick paper, 52 pgs.)

nn-Movie adaptation; Timothy Dalton photo-c 1 2 3 5 6 8
Limited Hardcover ($24.95) — — — — — 25.00

LIDSVILLE (TV)
Gold Key: Oct, 1972 - No. 5, Oct, 1973

1-Photo-c 5 10 15 35 55 75
2-5 4 8 12 22 34 45

LIEUTENANT, THE (TV)
Dell Publishing Co.: April-June, 1964

1-Photo-c 3 6 9 18 27 35

LIEUTENANT BLUEBERRY (Also see Blueberry)
Marvel Comics (Epic Comics): 1991 - No. 3, 1991 (Graphic novel)

1,2 ($8.95)-Moebius-a in all 2 4 6 8 10 12
3 ($14.95) 2 4 6 11 16 20

LT. ROBIN CRUSOE, U.S.N. (See Movie Comics & Walt Disney Showcase #26)

LIFE EATERS, THE
DC Comics (WildStorm): 2003 ($29.95, hardcover with dust jacket)

HC-David Brin-s; Scott Hampton-painted-a/c; Norse Gods team with the Nazis — — — — — 30.00
SC-(2004, $19.95) — — — — — 20.00

LIFE OF CAPTAIN MARVEL, THE
Marvel Comics Group: Aug, 1985 - No. 5, Dec, 1985 ($2.00, Baxter paper)

1-5: 1-All reprint Starlin issues of Iron Man #55, Capt. Marvel #25-34 plus Marvel Feature #12 (all with Thanos). 4-New Thanos back-c by Starlin — — — — — 3.00

LIFE OF CHRIST, THE
Catechetical Guild Educational Society: No. 301, 1949 (35¢, 100 pgs.)

301-Reprints from Topix(1949)-V5#11,12 9 18 27 50 65 80

LIFE OF CHRIST: THE CHRISTMAS STORY, THE
Marvel Comics/Nelson: Feb, 1993 ($2.99, slick stock)

nn — — — — — 5.00

LIFE OF CHRIST: THE EASTER STORY, THE
Marvel Comics/Nelson: 1993 ($2.99, slick stock)

nn — — — — — 5.00

LIFE OF CHRIST VISUALIZED
Standard Publishers: 1942 - No. 3, 1943

1-3: All came in cardboard case, each... 8 16 24 44 57 70
Case only..... 10 20 30 54 72 90

LIFE OF CHRIST VISUALIZED
The Standard Publ. Co.: 1946? (48 pgs. in color)

nn 6 12 18 29 36 42

LIFE OF ESTHER VISUALIZED
The Standard Publ. Co.: No. 2062, 1947 (48 pgs. in color)

2062 6 12 18 29 36 42

LIFE OF JOSEPH VISUALIZED
The Standard Publ. Co.: No. 1054, 1946 (48 pgs. in color)

1054 6 12 18 29 36 42

LIFE OF PAUL (See The Living Bible)

LIFE OF POPE JOHN PAUL II, THE
Marvel Comics Group: Jan, 1983 ($1.50/$1.75)

1 1 2 3 5 7 9

LIFE OF RILEY, THE (TV)
Dell Publishing Co.: No. 917, July, 1958

Four Color 917-Photo-c 10 20 30 70 123 175

LIFE ON ANOTHER PLANET
Kitchen Sink Press: 1978 (B&W, graphic novel, magazine size)

nn-Will Eisner-s/a — — — — — 13.00
Reprint (DC Comics, 5/00, $12.95) — — — — — 13.00

LIFE'S LIKE THAT
Croyden Publ. Co.: 1945 (25¢, B&W, 68 pgs.)

nn-Newspaper Sunday strip-r by Neher 7 14 21 35 43 50

LIFE STORIES OF AMERICAN PRESIDENTS (See Dell Giants)

LIFE STORY
Fawcett Publications: Apr, 1949 - V8#46, Jan, 1953; V8#47, Apr, 1953 (All have photo-c?)

V1#1 14 28 42 82 121 160
2 9 18 27 50 65 80
3-6, V2#7-12 8 16 24 42 54 65
V3#13-Wood-a 14 28 42 82 121 160
V3#14-18, V4#19-24, V5#25-30, V6#31-35 7 14 21 37 46 55
V6#36- "I sold drugs" on-c 9 18 27 52 69 85
V7#37,40-42, V8#44,45 7 14 21 35 43 50
V7#38, V8#43-Evans-a 7 14 21 37 46 55
V7#39-Drug Smuggling & Junkie story 9 18 27 47 61 75
V8#46,47 (Scarce) 9 18 27 47 61 75

NOTE: Powell a-13, 23, 24, 26, 28, 30, 32, 39. Marcus Swayze a-1-3, 10-12, 15, 16, 20, 21, 23-25, 31, 35, 37, 40, 44, 46.

LIFE, THE UNIVERSE AND EVERYTHING (See Hitchhikers Guide to the Galaxy & Restaurant at the End of the Universe)
DC Comics: 1996 - No. 3, 1996 ($6.95, squarebound, limited series)

1-3: Adaptation of novel by Douglas Adams. 1 2 3 4 5 7

LIFE WITH ARCHIE
Archie Publications: Sept, 1958 - No. 286, Sept, 1991

1 25 50 75 184 330 475
2-(9/59) 13 26 39 93 164 235
3-5: 3-(7/60) 9 18 27 63 107 150
6-8,10 7 14 21 49 80 110
9,11-Horror/SciFi-c 8 16 24 52 86 120
12-20 6 12 18 37 59 80
21(7/63)-30 4 8 12 28 44 60
31-34,36-38,40,41 4 8 12 22 34 45
35,39-Horror/Sci-fi-c 4 8 12 26 41 55
42-Pureheart begins (1st app.-c/s, 10/65) 7 14 21 47 76 105
43,44 5 10 15 30 48 65
45(1/66) 1st Man From R.I.V.E.R.D.A.L.E. 6 12 18 39 62 85
46-Origin Pureheart 5 10 15 30 48 65
47-49 4 8 12 23 36 48

	GD 2.0	VG 4.0	FN 6.0	VF 8.0	VF/NM 9.0	NM- 9.2
50-United Three begin: Pureheart (Archie), Superteen (Betty), Captain Hero (Jughead)	5	10	15	30	48	65
51-59: 59-Pureheart ends	4	8	12	23	36	48
60-Archie band begins, ends #66	5	10	15	30	48	65
61-66: 61-Man From R.I.V.E.R.D.A.L.E.-c/s	3	6	9	21	32	42
67-80	3	6	9	14	19	24
81-99	2	4	6	13	18	22
100 (8/70), 113-Sabrina & Salem app.	3	6	9	17	25	32
101-112, 114-130(2/73), 139(11/73)-Archie Band c/s	2	4	6	9	13	16
131,134-138,140-146,148-161,164-170(6/76)	2	4	6	8	10	12
132,133,147,163-all horror-c/s	2	4	6	11	16	20
162-UFO c/s	2	4	6	11	16	20
171,173-175,177-184,186,189,191-194,196	1	2	3	5	6	8
172,185,197 : 172-(9/77)-Bi-Cent. spec. ish, 185-2nd 24th cent.-c/s, 197-Time machine/SF-c/s	1	2	3	5	7	9
176(12/76)-1st app. Capt. Archie of Starship Rivda, in 24th century c/s; 1st app. Stella the Robot	2	4	6	11	16	20
187,188,195,198,199-all horror-c/s	2	4	6	8	10	12
190-1st Dr. Doom-c/s	2	4	6	8	10	12
200 (12/78) Maltese Pigeon-s	1	3	4	6	8	10
201-203,205-237,239,240(1/84): 208-Reintro Veronica.						6.00
204-Flying saucer-c/s	1	2	3	5	6	8
238-(9/83)-25th anniversary issue; Ol' Betsy (jalopy) replaced	1	2	3	4	5	7
241-278,280-285: 250-Comic book convention-s						5.00
279,286: 279-Intro Mustang Sally ($1.00, 7/90)						6.00

NOTE: *Gene Colan* a-272-279, 285, 286. Horror/Sci-Fi c 9, 11, 35, 39, 162.

LIFE WITH MILLIE (Formerly A Date With Millie) (Modeling With Millie #21 on)
Atlas/Marvel Comics Group: No. 8, Dec, 1960 - No. 20, Dec, 1962

	GD 2.0	VG 4.0	FN 6.0	VF 8.0	VF/NM 9.0	NM- 9.2
8-Teenage	8	16	24	52	86	120
9-11	6	12	18	37	59	80
12-20	5	10	15	32	51	70

LIFE WITH SNARKY PARKER (TV)
Fox Feature Syndicate: Aug, 1950

	GD 2.0	VG 4.0	FN 6.0	VF 8.0	VF/NM 9.0	NM- 9.2
1-Early TV comic; photo-c from TV puppet show	27	54	81	158	249	340

LIGHT AND DARKNESS WAR, THE
Marvel Comics (Epic Comics): Oct, 1988 - No. 6, Dec, 1989 ($1.95, lim. series)

1-6   2.50

LIGHT BRIGADE, THE
DC Comics: 2004 - No. 4, 2004 ($5.95, limited series)

1-4-Archangels in World War II; Tomasi-s/Snejbjerg-a   6.00
TPB (2005, $19.99) r/series; cover galery   20.00

LIGHT FANTASTIC, THE (Terry Pratchett's)
Innovation Publishing: June, 1992 - No. 4, Sept, 1992 ($2.50, mini-series)

1-4: Adapts 2nd novel in Discworld series   2.50

LIGHT IN THE FOREST (Disney)
Dell Publishing Co.: No. 891, Mar, 1958

	GD 2.0	VG 4.0	FN 6.0	VF 8.0	VF/NM 9.0	NM- 9.2
Four Color 891-Movie, Fess Parker photo-c	7	14	21	50	83	115

LIGHTNING COMICS (Formerly Sure-Fire Nun 1-3)
Ace Magazines: No. 4, Dec, 1940 - No. 13(V3#1), June, 1942

	GD 2.0	VG 4.0	FN 6.0	VF 8.0	VF/NM 9.0	NM- 9.2
4-Characters continue from Sure-Fire	100	200	300	625	1038	1450
5,6: 6-Dr. Nemesis begins	68	136	204	425	705	985
V2#1-6: 2- "Flash Lightning" becomes "Lash…"	54	108	162	338	557	775
V3#1-Intro. Lightning Girl & The Sword	54	108	162	338	557	775

NOTE: *Anderson* a-V2#5, 6, V2#1-6, V3#1. Bondage c-V2#6. Lightning-c on all.

LIGHTNING COMICS PRESENTS
Lightning Comics: May, 1994 ($3.50)

1-Red foil-c distr. by Diamond Distr., 1-Black/yellow/blue-c distrib. by Capital Distr., 1-Red/yellow-c distributed by H. World, 1-Platinum   3.50

LI'L ... (See Little ...)

LILI
Image Comics: No. 0, 1999 ($4.95, B&W)

0-Bendis & Yanover-s   5.00

LILLITH (See Warrior Nun...)
Antarctic Press: Sept, 1996 - No. 3, Feb, 1997 ($2.95, limited series)

1-3: 1-Variant-c   3.00

LIMITED COLLECTORS' EDITION (See Famous First Edition, Marvel Treasury #28, Rudolph

---

The Red-Nosed Reindeer, & Superman Vs. The Amazing Spider-Man; becomes All-New Collectors' Edition)
National Periodical Publications/DC Comics:
(#21-34,51-59: 84 pgs.; #35-41: 68 pgs.; #42-50: 60 pgs.)
C-21, Summer, 1973 - No. C-59, 1978 ($1.00) (10x13-1/2")

(Rudolph...C-20 (implied), 12/72)-See Rudolph The Red-Nosed Reindeer

	GD 2.0	VG 4.0	FN 6.0	VF 8.0	VF/NM 9.0	NM- 9.2
C-21: Shazam (TV); r/Captain Marvel Jr. #11 by Raboy; C.C. Beck-c, biog. & photo	3	6	9	19	29	38
C-22: Tarzan; complete origin reprinted from #207-210; all Kubert-c/a; Joe Kubert biography & photo inside	3	6	9	13	21	30
C-23: House of Mystery; Wrightson, N. Adams/Orlando, G. Kane/Wood, Toth, Aragones, Sparling reprints	4	8	12	22	34	45
C-24: Rudolph The Red-Nosed Reindeer	6	12	18	43	69	95
C-25: Batman; Neal Adams-c/a(r); G.A. Joker-r; Batman/Enemy Ace-r; Novick-a(r); has photos from TV show	4	8	12	24	37	50
C-26: See Famous First Edition C-26 (same contents)						
C-27,C-29,C-31: C-27: Shazam (TV); G.A. Capt. Marvel & Mary Marvel-r; Beck-r. C-29: Tarzan; reprints "Return of Tarzan" from #219-223 by Kubert; Kubert-c. C-31: Superman; origin-r; Giordano-a; photos of George Reeves from 1950s TV show on inside b/c; Burnley, Boring-r	3	6	9	16	22	28
C-32: Ghosts (new-a)	3	6	9	21	32	42
C-33: Rudolph The Red-Nosed Reindeer(new-a)	6	12	18	39	62	85
C-34: Christmas with the Super-Heroes; unpublished Angel & Ape story by Oksner & Wood; Batman & Teen Titans-r						
C-35: Shazam (TV); photo cover features TV's Captain Marvel, Jackson Bostwick; Beck-r; TV photos inside b/c	3	6	9	14	20	25
C-36: The Bible; all new adaptation beginning with Genesis by Kubert, Redondo & Mayer; Kubert-c	3	6	9	14	20	25
C-37: Batman; r/1946 Sundays; inside b/c photos of Batman TV show villains (all villain issue; r/G.A. Joker, Catwoman, Penguin, Two-Face, & Scarecrow stories plus 1946 Sundays-r)	3	6	9	17	25	32
C-38: Superman; 1 pg. N. Adams; part photo-c; photos from TV show on inside back-c	3	6	9	14	20	25
C-39: Secret Origins of Super-Villains; N. Adams-i(r); collection reprints 1950's Joker origin, Luthor origin from Adv. Comics #271, Captain Cold origin from Showcase #8 among others; G.A. Batman-r; Beck-r	3	6	9	14	20	25
C-40: Dick Tracy by Gould featuring Flattop; newspaper r-from 12/21/43 - 5/17/44; biog. of Chester Gould	3	6	9	14	20	25
C-41: Super Friends (TV); JLA-r(1965); Toth-c/a	3	6	9	16	22	28
C-42: Rudolph	4	8	12	26	41	55
C-43-C-47: C-43: Christmas with the Super-Heroes; Wrightson, S&K, Neal Adams-a. C-44: Batman; N. Adams-p(r) & G.A.-r; painted-c. C-45: More Secret Origins of Super-Villains; Flash-r/#105; G.A. Wonder Woman & Batman/Catwoman-r. C-46: Justice League of America(1963-r); 3 pgs. Toth-a C-47: Superman Salutes the Bicentennial (Tomahawk interior); 2 pgs. new-a	3	6	9	14	19	24
C-48,C-49: C-48: Superman Vs. The Flash (Superman/Flash race); swipes-c to Superman #199; r/Superman #199 & Flash #175; 6 pgs. Neal Adams-a. C-49: Superboy & the Legion of Super-Heroes	3	6	9	16	22	28
C-50: Rudolph The Red-Nosed Reindeer; contains poster (1/2 price if poster is missing)	4	8	12	26	41	55
C-51: Batman; Neal Adams-c/a	3	6	9	16	23	30
C-52,C-57: C-52: The Best of DC; Neal Adams-c/a; Toth, Kubert-a. C-57: Welcome Back, Kotter-r(TV)(5/78) includes unpublished #11	3	6	9	14	20	25
C-53 thru C-56, C-58, C-60 thru C-62 (See All-New Collectors' Edition)						
C-59: Batman's Strangest Cases; N. Adams-r; Wrightson-r/Swamp Thing #7; N. Adams/Wrightson-c	3	6	9	14	20	25

NOTE: All-r with exception of some special features and covers. *Aparo* a-52r; c-37. *Grell* c-49. *Infantino* a-25, 39, 44, 45, 52. *Bob Kane* r-25. *Robinson* r-25, 44. *Sprang* r-44. Issues #21-31, 35-39, 45, 48 have back cover cut-outs.

LINDA (Everybody Loves...) (Phantom Lady No. 5 on)
Ajax-Farrell Publ. Co.: Apr-May, 1954 - No. 4, Oct-Nov, 1954

	GD 2.0	VG 4.0	FN 6.0	VF 8.0	VF/NM 9.0	NM- 9.2
1-Kamenish-a	15	30	45	85	130	175
2-Lingerie panel	13	26	39	72	101	130
3,4	10	20	30	56	76	95

LINDA CARTER, STUDENT NURSE
Atlas Comics (AMI): Sept, 1961 - No. 9, Jan, 1963

	GD 2.0	VG 4.0	FN 6.0	VF 8.0	VF/NM 9.0	NM- 9.2
1-Al Hartley-c	6	12	18	41	66	90
2-9	4	8	12	28	44	60

LINDA LARK
Dell Publishing Co.: Oct-Dec, 1961 - No. 8, Aug-Oct, 1963

	GD 2.0	VG 4.0	FN 6.0	VF 8.0	VF/NM 9.0	NM- 9.2
1	3	6	9	19	29	38
2-8	3	6	9	14	19	24

Lisa Comics #1 © Bongo

Li'l Abner #72 © TOBY

Little Archie #40 © AP

	GD 2.0	VG 4.0	FN 6.0	VF 8.0	VF/NM 9.0	NM- 9.2

LINUS, THE LIONHEARTED (TV)
Gold Key: Sept, 1965

| 1 (10155-509) | 7 | 14 | 21 | 49 | 80 | 110 |

LION, THE (See Movie Comics)

LIONHEART
Awesome Comics: Sept, 1999 - No. 2 ($2.99/$2.50)

| 1-Ian Churchill-story-a, Jeph Loeb/s; Coven app. | | | | | | 3.00 |
| 2-Flip book w/Coven #4 | | | | | | 2.50 |

LION OF SPARTA (See Movie Classics)

LIPPY THE LION AND HARDY HAR HAR (TV)
Gold Key: Mar, 1963 (12¢) (See Hanna-Barbera Band Wagon #1)

| 1 (10049-303) | 9 | 18 | 27 | 63 | 107 | 150 |

LISA COMICS (TV)(See Simpsons Comics)
Bongo Comics: 1995 ($2.25)

| 1-Lisa in Wonderland | | | | | | 3.00 |

LI'L ABNER (See Comics on Parade, Sparkle, Sparkler Comics, Tip Top Comics & Tip Topper)
United Features Syndicate: 1939 - 1940

| Single Series 4 ('39) | 76 | 152 | 228 | 475 | 788 | 1100 |
| Single Series 18 ('40) (#18 on inside, #2 on-c) | 59 | 118 | 177 | 369 | 610 | 850 |

LI'L ABNER (Al Capp's; continued from Comics on Parade #58)
Harvey Publ. No. 61-69 (2/49)/Toby Press No. 70 on: No. 61, Dec, 1947 - No. 97, Jan, 1955
(See Oxydol-Dreft in Promotional Comics section)

61(#1)-Wolverton & Powell-a	32	64	96	184	285	385
62-65: 63-The Wolf Girl app. 65-Powell-a	18	36	54	101	156	210
66,67,69,70	16	32	48	92	141	190
68-Full length Fearless Fosdick-c/story	17	34	51	96	148	200
71-74,76,80	14	28	42	80	115	150
75,77-79,86,91-All with Kurtzman art; 86-Sadie Hawkins Day. 91-r/#77	16	32	48	92	141	190
81-85,87-90,92-94,96,97: 83-Evil-Eye Fleegle & Double Whammy app. 88-Cousin Weakeyes goes hunting. 94-Six lessons from Adam Lazonga. 96-Football issue	14	28	42	76	108	140
95-Full length Fearless Fosdick story	14	28	42	82	121	160

LI'L ABNER
Toby Press: 1951

| 1 | 18 | 36 | 54 | 103 | 162 | 220 |

LI'L ABNER'S DOGPATCH (See Al Capp's...)

LITTLE AL OF THE F.B.I.
Ziff-Davis Publications: No. 10, 1950 (no month) - No. 11, Apr-May, 1951 (Saunders painted-c)

| 10(1950) | 16 | 32 | 48 | 94 | 147 | 200 |
| 11(1951) | 14 | 28 | 42 | 78 | 112 | 145 |

LITTLE AL OF THE SECRET SERVICE
Ziff-Davis Publications: No. 10, 7-8/51; No. 2, 9-10/51; No. 3, Winter, 1951 (Saunders painted-c)

| 10(#1) | 16 | 32 | 48 | 92 | 144 | 195 |
| 2,3 | 14 | 28 | 42 | 76 | 108 | 140 |

LITTLE AMBROSE
Archie Publications: September, 1958

| 1-Bob Bolling-c | 15 | 30 | 45 | 84 | 127 | 170 |

LITTLE ANGEL
Standard (Visual Editions)/Pines: No. 5, Sept, 1954; No. 6, Sept, 1955 - No. 16, Sept, 1959

| 5-Last pre-code issue | 8 | 16 | 24 | 40 | 50 | 60 |
| 6-16 | 5 | 10 | 15 | 24 | 30 | 35 |

LITTLE ANNIE ROONEY (Also see Henry)
David McKay Publ.: 1935 (25¢, B&W dailies, 48 pgs.)(10"x10", cardboard-c)

| Book 1-Daily strip-r by Darrell McClure | 38 | 76 | 114 | 222 | 351 | 480 |

LITTLE ANNIE ROONEY (See King Comics & Treasury of Comics)
David McKay/St. John/Standard: 1938; Aug, 1948 - No. 3, Oct, 1948

Feature Books 11 (McKay, 1938)	39	78	117	225	355	485
1 (St. John)	15	30	45	88	137	185
2,3	10	20	30	54	72	90

LITTLE ARCHIE (The Adventures of... #13-on) (See Archie Giant Series Mag. #527, 534, 538, 545, 549, 556, 560, 566, 570, 583, 594, 596, 607, 609, 619)
Archie Publications: 1956 - No. 180, Feb, 1983 (Giants No. 3-84)

1-(Scarce)	54	108	162	459	855	1250
2 (1957)	24	48	72	175	313	450
3-5: 3-(1958)-Bob Bolling-c & giant issues begin	14	28	42	102	181	260
6-10	10	20	30	71	126	180
11-17,19,21 (84 pgs.)	8	16	24	52	86	120
18,20,22 (84 pgs.)-Horror/Sci-Fi-c	9	18	27	60	100	140
23-39 (68 pgs.)	6	12	18	39	62	85
40 (Fall/66)-Intro. Little Pureheart-c/s (68 pgs.)	6	12	18	43	69	95
41,44-Little Pureheart (68 pgs.)	6	12	18	37	59	80
42-Intro The Little Archies Band, ends #66 (68 pgs.)	6	12	18	41	66	90
43-1st Boy From R.I.V.E.R.D.A.L.E. (68 pgs.)	6	12	18	39	62	85
45-58 (68 pgs.)	4	8	12	28	44	60
59 (68 pgs.)-Little Sabrina begins	7	14	21	50	83	115
60-66 (68 pgs.)	4	8	12	24	37	50
67(9/71)-84: 84-Last 52pg. Giant-Size (2/74)	3	6	9	16	23	30
85-99	2	4	6	9	12	15
100	2	4	6	10	14	18
101-112,114-116,118-129	1	2	3	5	7	9
113,117,130: 113-Halloween Special issue(12/76). 117-Donny Osmond-c cameo	2	4	6	8	10	12
130-UFO cover (5/78)						
131-150(1/80), 180(Last issue, 2/83)	1	2	3	4	5	7
151-179						5.00
...In Animal Land 1 (1957)	12	24	36	86	153	220
...In Animal Land 17 (Winter, 1957-58)-19 (Summer,1958)-Formerly Li'l Jinx	7	14	21	49	80	110
Archie Classics - The Adventures of Little Archie Vol. 1 TPB (2004, $10.95) reprints						11.00
NOTE: Little Archie Band app. 42-66. Little Sabrina in 59-78,80-180

LITTLE ARCHIE CHRISTMAS SPECIAL (See Archie Giant Series #581)

LITTLE ARCHIE COMICS DIGEST ANNUAL (...Magazine #5 on)
Archie Publications: 10/77 - No. 48, 5/91 (Digest-size, 128 pgs., later issues $1.35-$1.50)

1(10/77)-Reprints	3	6	9	19	29	38
2(4/78,3(11/78)-Neal Adams-a. 3-The Fly-r by S&K	3	6	9	14	19	24
4(4/79) - 10	2	4	6	9	13	16
11-20	1	3	4	6	8	10
21-30: 28-Christmas-c	1	2	3	4	5	7
31-48: 40,46-Christmas-c						5.00
NOTE: Little Jinx, Little Jughead & Little Sabrina in most issues.

LITTLE ARCHIE DIGEST MAGAZINE
Archie Comics: July, 1991 - No. 21, Mar, 1998 ($1.50/$1.79/$1.89, digest size, bi-annual)

V2#1						6.00
2-10						3.50
11-21						2.50

LITTLE ARCHIE MYSTERY
Archie Publications: Aug, 1963 - No. 2, Oct, 1963 (12¢ issues)

| 1 | 10 | 20 | 30 | 71 | 126 | 180 |
| 2 | 6 | 12 | 18 | 41 | 66 | 90 |

LITTLE ASPIRIN (See Little Lenny & Wisco)
Marvel Comics (CnPC): July, 1949 - No. 3, Dec, 1949 (52 pgs.)

1-Oscar app.; Kurtzman-a (4 pgs.)	17	34	51	98	154	210
2-Kurtzman-a (4 pgs.)	11	22	33	60	83	105
3-No Kurtzman-a	9	18	27	47	61	75

LITTLE AUDREY (Also see Playful...)
St. John Publ.: Apr, 1948 - No. 24, May, 1952

1-1st app. Little Audrey	48	96	144	293	484	675
2	26	52	78	150	235	320
3-5	17	34	51	98	154	210
6-10	14	28	42	80	115	150
11-20: 16-X-Mas-c	10	20	30	58	79	100
21-24	9	18	27	52	69	85

LITTLE AUDREY (See Harvey Hits #11, 19)
Harvey Publications: No. 25, Aug, 1952 - No. 53, April, 1957

25-(Paramount Pictures Famous Star... on-c); 1st Harvey Casper and Baby Huey (1 month earlier than Harvey Comic Hits #60(9/52)	13	26	39	93	164	235
26-30: 26-28-Casper app.	7	14	21	50	83	115
31-40: 32-35-Casper app.	6	12	18	43	69	95
41-53	5	10	15	32	51	70
...Clubhouse 1 (9/61, 68 pg. Giant)-New stories & reprints	8	16	24	58	97	135

LITTLE AUDREY
Harvey Comics: Aug, 1992 - No. 8, July, 1994 ($1.25/$1.50)

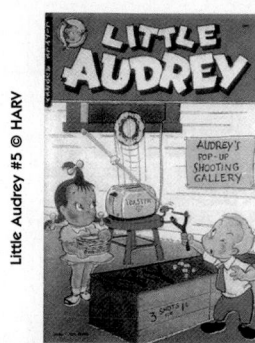
Little Audrey #5 © HARV

Little Dot #11 © HARV

Little Endless Story Book © DC

	GD 2.0	VG 4.0	FN 6.0	VF 8.0	VF/NM 9.0	NM- 9.2
V2#1						3.00
2-8						2.50

LITTLE AUDREY (…Yearbook)
St. John Publishing Co.: 1950 (50¢, 260 pgs.)

Contains 8 complete 1949 comics rebound; Casper, Alice in Wonderland, Little Audrey, Abbott & Costello, Pinocchio, Moon Mullins, Three Stooges (from Jubilee), Little Annie Rooney app. (Rare)

	GD 2.0	VG 4.0	FN 6.0	VF 8.0	VF/NM 9.0	NM- 9.2
	79	158	237	494	822	1150

(Also see All Good & Treasury of Comics)
NOTE: *This book contains remaindered St. John comics; many variations possible.*

LITTLE AUDREY & MELVIN (Audrey & Melvin No. 62)
Harvey Publications: May, 1962 - No. 61, Dec, 1973

	GD 2.0	VG 4.0	FN 6.0	VF 8.0	VF/NM 9.0	NM- 9.2
1	9	18	27	65	113	160
2-5	6	12	18	37	59	80
6-10	4	8	12	28	44	60
11-20	3	6	9	18	27	35
21-40: 22-Richie Rich app.	3	6	9	14	19	24
41-50,55-61	2	4	6	10	14	18
51-54: All 52 pg. Giants	3	6	9	14	19	24

LITTLE AUDREY TV FUNTIME
Harvey Publ.: Sept, 1962 - No. 33, Oct, 1971 (#1-31: 68 pgs.; #32,33: 52 pgs.)

	GD 2.0	VG 4.0	FN 6.0	VF 8.0	VF/NM 9.0	NM- 9.2
1-Richie Rich app.	9	18	27	65	113	160
2,3: Richie Rich app.	6	12	18	37	59	80
4,5: 5-25¢ & 35¢ issues exist	5	10	15	30	48	65
6-10	3	6	9	20	30	40
11-20	3	6	9	15	21	26
21-33	2	4	6	13	18	22

LITTLE BAD WOLF (Disney; seeWalt Disney's C&S #52, Walt Disney Showcase #21 & Wheaties)
Dell Publishing Co.: No. 403, June, 1952 - No. 564, June, 1954

	GD 2.0	VG 4.0	FN 6.0	VF 8.0	VF/NM 9.0	NM- 9.2
Four Color 403 (#1)	7	14	21	47	76	105
Four Color 473 (6/53), 564	5	10	15	32	51	70

LITTLE BEAVER
Dell Publishing Co.: No. 211, Jan, 1949 - No. 870, Jan, 1958 (All painted-c)

	GD 2.0	VG 4.0	FN 6.0	VF 8.0	VF/NM 9.0	NM- 9.2
Four Color 211('49)-All Harman-a	8	16	24	56	93	130
Four Color 267,294,332(5/51)	5	10	15	35	55	75
3(10-12/51)-8(1-3/53)	5	10	15	32	51	70
Four Color 483(8-10/53),529	5	10	15	30	48	65
Four Color 612,660,695,744,817,870	5	10	15	30	48	65

LITTLE BIT
Jubilee/St. John Publishing Co.: Mar, 1949 - No. 2, June, 1949

	GD 2.0	VG 4.0	FN 6.0	VF 8.0	VF/NM 9.0	NM- 9.2
1	9	18	27	52	69	85
2	7	14	21	37	46	55

LITTLE DOT (See Humphrey, Li'l Max, Sad Sack, and Tastee-Freez Comics)
Harvey Publications: Sept, 1953 - No. 164, Apr, 1976

	GD 2.0	VG 4.0	FN 6.0	VF 8.0	VF/NM 9.0	NM- 9.2
1-Intro./1st app. Richie Rich & Little Lotta	241	482	723	1506	2503	3500
2-1st app. Freckles & Pee Wee (Richie Rich's poor friends)						
	86	172	258	538	894	1250
3	54	108	162	338	557	775
4	48	96	144	293	484	675
5-Origin dots on Little Dot's dress	54	108	162	338	557	775
6-Richie Rich, Little Lotta, & Little Dot all on cover; 1st Richie Rich cover featured						
	54	108	162	338	557	775
7-10: 9-Last pre-code issue (1/55)	34	68	102	197	311	425
11-20	24	48	72	139	220	300
21-30	15	30	45	88	137	185
31-40	12	24	36	69	97	125
41-50	10	20	30	54	72	90
51-60	8	16	24	42	54	65
61-80	4	8	12	24	37	50
81-100	3	6	9	18	27	35
101-141	3	6	9	15	21	26
142-145: All 52 pg. Giants	3	6	9	16	23	30
146-164	2	4	6	10	14	18

NOTE: *Richie Rich & Little Lotta in all.*

LITTLE DOT
Harvey Comics: Sept, 1992 - No. 7, June, 1994 ($1.25/$1.50)

	GD 2.0	VG 4.0	FN 6.0	VF 8.0	VF/NM 9.0	NM- 9.2
V2#1-Little Dot, Little Lotta, Richie Rich in all						3.00
2-7 ($1.50)						2.50

LITTLE DOT DOTLAND (Dot Dotland No. 62, 63)
Harvey Publications: July, 1962 - No. 61, Dec, 1973

	GD 2.0	VG 4.0	FN 6.0	VF 8.0	VF/NM 9.0	NM- 9.2
1-Richie Rich begins	11	22	33	79	140	200
2,3	7	14	21	45	73	100
4,5	6	12	18	37	59	80
6-10	4	8	12	28	44	60
11-20	3	6	9	20	30	40
21-30	3	6	9	16	23	30
31-50	3	6	9	14	20	25
51-54: All 52 pg. Giants	3	6	9	16	23	30
55-61	2	4	6	9	13	16

LITTLE DOT'S UNCLES & AUNTS (See Harvey Hits No. 4, 13, 24)
Harvey Enterprises: Oct, 1961; No. 2, Aug, 1962 - No. 52, Apr, 1974

	GD 2.0	VG 4.0	FN 6.0	VF 8.0	VF/NM 9.0	NM- 9.2
1-Richie Rich begins; 68 pgs. begin	13	26	39	97	171	245
2,3	8	16	24	52	86	120
4,5	6	12	18	37	59	80
6-10	5	10	15	30	48	65
11-20	4	8	12	22	34	45
21-37: Last 68 pg. issue	3	6	9	17	25	32
38-52: All 52 pg. Giants	3	6	9	15	21	26

LITTLE DRACULA
Harvey Comics: Jan, 1992 - No. 3, May, 1992 ($1.25, quarterly, mini-series)

	GD 2.0	VG 4.0	FN 6.0	VF 8.0	VF/NM 9.0	NM- 9.2
1-3						3.00

LITTLE ENDLESS STORYBOOK, THE (See The Sandman titles)
DC Comics: 2001 ($5.95, Prestige format, one-shot)

	GD 2.0	VG 4.0	FN 6.0	VF 8.0	VF/NM 9.0	NM- 9.2
nn-Jill Thompson-s/painted-a/c; puppy Barnabas searches for Delirium						20.00

LITTLE EVA
St. John Publishing Co.: May, 1952 - No. 31, Nov, 1956

	GD 2.0	VG 4.0	FN 6.0	VF 8.0	VF/NM 9.0	NM- 9.2
1	15	30	45	90	140	190
2	10	20	30	54	72	90
3-5	8	16	24	44	57	70
6-10	8	16	24	40	50	60
11-31	7	14	21	35	43	50
3-D 1,2(10/53, 11/53, 25¢)-Both came w/glasses. 1-Infinity-c						
	18	36	54	107	169	230
I.W. Reprint #1-3,6-8: 1-r/Little Eva #28. 2-r/Little Eva #29. 3-r/Little Eva #24						
	2	4	6	8	11	14
Super Reprint #10,12('63),14,16,18('64): 18-r/Little Eva #25.						
	2	4	6	8	11	14

LI'L GENIUS (Formerly Super Brat; Summer Fun No. 54) (See Blue Bird & Giant Comics #3)
Charlton Comics: 1954 - No. 52, 1/65; No. 53, 10/65; No. 54, 10/85 - No. 55, 1/86

	GD 2.0	VG 4.0	FN 6.0	VF 8.0	VF/NM 9.0	NM- 9.2
5(#1?)	11	22	33	62	86	110
6-10	7	14	21	37	46	55
11-15,19,20	6	12	18	29	36	42
16,17-(68 pgs.)	8	16	24	40	50	60
18-(100 pgs.), 10/58	11	22	33	60	83	105
21-35	3	6	9	16	22	28
36-53	2	4	6	10	14	18
54,55 (Low print)						5.00

LI'L GHOST
St. John Publ. Co./Fago No. 1 on: 2/58; No. 2,1/59 - No. 3, Mar, 1959

	GD 2.0	VG 4.0	FN 6.0	VF 8.0	VF/NM 9.0	NM- 9.2
1(St. John)	9	18	27	50	65	80
2,3	6	12	18	28	34	40

LITTLE GIANT COMICS
Centaur Publications: 7/38 - No. 3, 10/38; No. 4, 2/39 (132 pgs.) (6-3/4x4-1/2")

	GD 2.0	VG 4.0	FN 6.0	VF 8.0	VF/NM 9.0	NM- 9.2
1-B&W with color-c; stories, puzzles, magic	93	186	279	581	966	1350
2,3-B&W with color-c	62	124	186	388	644	900
4 (6-5/8x9-3/8")(68 pgs., B&W inside)	62	124	186	388	644	900

NOTE: *Filchock c-2, 4. Gustavson a-1. Pinajian a-4. Bob Wood a-1.*

LITTLE GIANT DETECTIVE FUNNIES
Centaur Publ.: Oct, 1938 - No. 4, Jan, 1939 (6-3/4x4-1/2", 132 pgs., B&W)

	GD 2.0	VG 4.0	FN 6.0	VF 8.0	VF/NM 9.0	NM- 9.2
1-B&W with color-c	93	186	279	581	966	1350
4(1/39, B&W; color-c; 68 pgs., 6-1/2x9-1/2")-Eisner-r						
	62	124	186	388	644	900

LITTLE GIANT MOVIE FUNNIES
Centaur Publications: Aug, 1938 - No. 2, Oct, 1938 (6-3/4x4-1/2", 132 pgs., B&W)

	GD 2.0	VG 4.0	FN 6.0	VF 8.0	VF/NM 9.0	NM- 9.2
1-Ed Wheelan's "Minute Movies" reprints	93	186	279	581	966	1350
2-Ed Wheelan's "Minute Movies" reprints	62	124	186	388	644	900

LITTLE GROUCHO (…the Red-Headed Tornado; …Grouchy No. 2)

Little Iodine #33 © DELL

Li'l Jinx #3 © AP

Little Lotta #2 © HARV

	GD 2.0	VG 4.0	FN 6.0	VF 8.0	VF/NM 9.0	NM- 9.2

Reston Publ. Co.: No. 16; Feb-Mar, 1955 - No. 2, June-July, 1955 (See Tippy Terry)

	GD 2.0	VG 4.0	FN 6.0	VF 8.0	VF/NM 9.0	NM- 9.2
16, 1 (2-3/55)	8	16	24	42	54	65
2(6-7/55)	6	12	18	27	33	38

LITTLE HIAWATHA (Disney; see Walt Disney's C&S #143)
Dell Publishing Co.: No. 439, Dec, 1952 - No. 988, May-July, 1959

	GD	VG	FN	VF	VF/NM	NM-
Four Color 439 (#1)	6	12	18	39	62	85
Four Color 787 (4/57), 901 (5/58), 988	5	10	15	30	48	65

LITTLE IKE
St. John Publishing Co.: April, 1953 - No. 4, Oct, 1953

	GD	VG	FN	VF	VF/NM	NM-
1	10	20	30	54	72	90
2	6	12	18	31	38	45
3,4	5	10	15	24	30	35

LITTLE IODINE (See Giant Comic Album)
Dell Publ. Co.: No. 224, 4/49 - No. 257, 1949: 3-5/50 - No. 56, 4-6/62 (1-4-52pgs.)

	GD	VG	FN	VF	VF/NM	NM-
Four Color 224-By Jimmy Hatlo	11	22	33	79	140	200
Four Color 257	8	16	24	56	93	130
1(3-5/50)	9	18	27	65	113	160
2-5	6	12	18	37	59	80
6-10	4	8	12	28	44	60
11-20	4	8	12	22	34	45
21-30: 27-Xmas-c	3	6	9	20	30	40
31-40	3	6	9	18	27	35
41-56	3	6	9	16	23	30

LITTLE JACK FROST
Avon Periodicals: 1951

	GD	VG	FN	VF	VF/NM	NM-
1	11	22	33	62	86	110

LI'L JINX (Little Archie in Animal Land #17) (Also see Pep Comics #62)
Archie Publications: No. 1(#11), Nov, 1956 - No. 16, Sept, 1957

	GD	VG	FN	VF	VF/NM	NM-
1(#11)-By Joe Edwards; "First Issue" on cover	14	28	42	76	108	140
12(1/57)-16	10	20	30	54	72	90

LI'L JINX (See Archie Giant Series Magazine No. 223)

LI'L JINX CHRISTMAS BAG (See Archie Giant Series Mag. No. 195, 206, 219)

LI'L JINX GIANT LAUGH-OUT (See Archie Giant Series Mag. No. 176, 185)
Archie Publications: No. 33, Sept, 1971 - No. 43, Nov, 1973 (52 pgs.)

	GD	VG	FN	VF	VF/NM	NM-
33-43 (52 pgs.)	2	4	6	11	16	20

LITTLE JOE (See Popular Comics & Super Comics)
Dell Publishing Co.: No. 1, 1942

	GD	VG	FN	VF	VF/NM	NM-
Four Color 1	50	100	150	400	725	1050

LITTLE JOE
St. John Publishing Co.: Apr, 1953

	GD	VG	FN	VF	VF/NM	NM-
1	5	10	15	24	30	35

LI'L KIDS (Also see Li'l Pals)
Marvel Comics Group: 8/70 - No. 2, 10/70; No. 3, 11/71 - No. 12, 6/73

	GD	VG	FN	VF	VF/NM	NM-
1	7	14	21	45	73	100
2-9	4	8	12	24	37	50
10-12-Calvin app.	4	8	12	26	41	55

LITTLE KING
Dell Publishing Co.: No. 494, Aug, 1953 - No. 677, Feb, 1956

	GD	VG	FN	VF	VF/NM	NM-
Four Color 494 (#1)	9	18	27	60	100	140
Four Color 597, 677	5	10	15	30	55	75

LITTLE LANA (Formerly Lana)
Marvel Comics (MjMC): No. 8, Nov, 1949; 9, Mar, 1950

	GD	VG	FN	VF	VF/NM	NM-
8,9	11	22	33	60	83	105

LITTLE LENNY
Marvel Comics (CDS): June, 1949 - No. 3, Nov, 1949

	GD	VG	FN	VF	VF/NM	NM-
1-Little Aspirin app.	13	26	39	72	101	130
2,3	8	16	24	44	57	70

LITTLE LIZZIE
Marvel Comics (PrPI)/Atlas (OMC): 6/49 - No. 5, 4/50; 9/53 - No. 3, Jan, 1954

	GD	VG	FN	VF	VF/NM	NM-
1	14	28	42	80	115	150
2-5	9	18	27	47	61	75
1 (9/53, 2nd series by Atlas)-Howie Post-c	10	20	30	54	72	90
2,3	8	16	24	40	50	60

LITTLE LOTTA (See Harvey Hits No. 10)

Harvey Publications: 11/55 - No. 110, 11/73; No. 111, 9/74 - No. 120, 5/76
V2#1, Oct, 1992 - No. 4, July, 1993 ($1.25)

	GD	VG	FN	VF	VF/NM	NM-
1-Richie Rich (r) & Little Dot begin	35	70	105	263	482	700
2,3	16	32	48	118	209	300
4,5	10	20	30	71	126	180
6-10	8	16	24	52	86	120
11-20	6	12	18	37	59	80
21-40	4	8	12	22	34	45
41-60	3	6	9	18	27	35
61-80: 62-1st app. Nurse Jenny	3	6	9	14	20	25
81-99	2	4	6	10	14	18
100-103: All 52 pg. Giants	2	4	6	13	18	22
104-120	1	3	4	6	8	10
V2#1-4 (1992-93)						3.00

NOTE: No. 121 was advertised, but never released.

LITTLE LOTTA FOODLAND
Harvey Publications: 9/63 - No. 14, 10/67; No. 15, 10/68 - No. 29, Oct, 1972

	GD	VG	FN	VF	VF/NM	NM-
1-Little Lotta, Little Dot, Richie Rich, 68 pgs. begin	12	24	36	86	153	220
2,3	8	16	24	56	93	130
4,5	6	12	18	41	66	90
6-10	5	10	15	30	48	65
11-20	3	6	9	19	29	38
21-26: 26-Last 68 pg. issue	3	6	9	16	22	28
27,28: Both 52 pgs.	2	4	6	13	18	22
29-(36 pgs.)	2	4	6	8	11	14

LITTLE LULU (Formerly Marge's Little Lulu)
Gold Key 207-257/Whitman 258 on: No. 207, Sept, 1972 - No. 268, Mar, 1984

	GD	VG	FN	VF	VF/NM	NM-
207,209,220-Stanley-r. 207-1st app. Henrietta	2	4	6	11	16	20
208,210-219: 208-1st app. Snobbly, Wilbur's butler	2	4	6	9	12	15
221-240,242-249, 250(r/#166), 251-254(r/#206)	1	2	3	5	7	9
241,263-Stanley-r	1	3	4	6	8	10
255-257(Gold Key): 256-r/#212	1	2	3	5	6	8
258,259,262,264(2/82),265(3/82) (Whitman)	2	4	6	8	10	12
260-(9/80)(Whitman pre-pack only - low distribution)	14	28	42	99	175	250
261-(11/80)(Whitman pre-pack only)	8	12	24	37	50	
266-268 (All #90028 on-c; no date, no date code; 3-pack): 266(7/83). 267(8/83).						
268(3/84)-Stanley-r	3	6	9	15	21	26

LITTLE LULU
Dark Horse Books: Nov, 2004 - Present ($9.95/$10.95, B&W, digest-size TPB)

	Price
Vol. 1 -B&W reprints of Marge's Little Lulu #6-12; John Stanley-s/a & Irving Tripp-a	10.00
...: (Vol. 2) Lulu Takes a Trip (2/05) -B&W r/Marge's Little Lulu #13-16	10.00
...: (Vol. 3) My Dinner With Lulu (4/05) -B&W r/Four Color #74,97,110,115,120	10.00
...: (Vol. 4) Sunday Afternoon (6/05) -B&W r/Four Color #131,139,146,158	10.00
...: (Vol. 5) Lulu in the Doghouse (8/05) -B&W r/Four Color #165 & Marge's Little Lulu #1-5	10.00
...: (Vol. 6) Letters to Santa (10/05) -B&W r/Marge's Little Lulu #18-22	10.00
...: (Vol. 7) Lulu's Umbrella Service (12/05) -B&W r/Marge's Little Lulu #23-27	10.00
...: (Vol. 8) Late For School (2/06) -B&W r/Marge's Little Lulu #28-32	10.00
...: (Vol. 9) Lucky Lulu (4/06) -B&W r/Marge's Little Lulu #33-37	10.00
...: (Vol. 10) All Dressed Up (6/06) -B&W r/Marge's Little Lulu #38-42	10.00
...: (Vol. 11) April Fools (8/06) -B&W r/Marge's Little Lulu #43-48	10.00
...: (Vol. 12) Leave It to Lulu (10/06) -B&W r/Marge's Little Lulu #49-53	10.00
...: (Vol. 13) Too Much Fun (12/06) -B&W r/Marge's Little Lulu #54-58	10.00
...: (Vol. 14) Queen Lulu (2/07) -B&W r/Marge's Little Lulu #59-63	10.00
...: (Vol. 15) The Explorers (4/07) -B&W r/Marge's Little Lulu #64-68	10.00
...: (Vol. 16) A Handy Kid (7/07, $10.95) -B&W r/Marge's Little Lulu #69-74	11.00
Color Special (9/06, $13.95, standard size) r/various stories from Marge's Little Lulu	14.00

LITTLE MARY MIXUP (See Comics On Parade)
United Features Syndicate: No. 10, 1939, - No. 26, 1940

	GD	VG	FN	VF	VF/NM	NM-
Single Series 10, 26	34	68	102	197	311	425

LITTLE MAX COMICS (Joe Palooka's Pal; see Joe Palooka)
Harvey Publications: Oct, 1949 - No. 73, Nov, 1961

	GD	VG	FN	VF	VF/NM	NM-
1-Infinity-c; Little Dot begins; Joe Palooka on-c	22	44	66	126	198	270
2-Little Dot app.; Joe Palooka on-c	13	26	39	74	105	135
3-Little Dot app.; Joe Palooka on-c	10	20	30	56	76	95
4-10: 5-Little Dot app., 1pg.	8	16	24	44	57	70
11-20	8	16	24	40	50	60
21-40: 23-Little Dot app. 38-r/#20	6	12	18	31	38	45
41-62,66	3	6	9	18	27	35
63-65,67-73-Include new five pg. Richie Rich stories. 70-73-Little Lotta app.	3	6	9	19	29	38

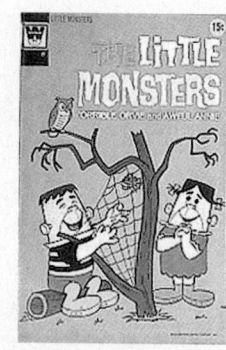

Little Monsters #18 © GK

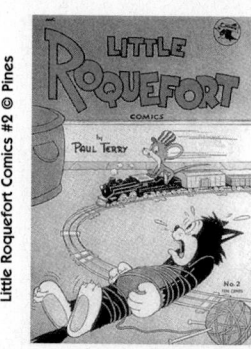

Little Roquefort Comics #2 © Pines

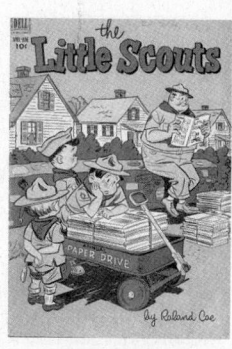

Little Scouts #4 © DELL

	GD 2.0	VG 4.0	FN 6.0	VF 8.0	VF/NM 9.0	NM- 9.2

LI'L MENACE
Fago Magazine Co.: Dec, 1958 - No. 3, May, 1959

	GD 2.0	VG 4.0	FN 6.0	VF 8.0	VF/NM 9.0	NM- 9.2
1-Peter Rabbit app.	8	16	24	44	57	70
2-Peter Rabbit (Vincent Fago's)	7	14	21	35	43	50
3	6	12	18	28	34	40

LITTLE MERMAID, THE (Walt Disney's...; also see Disney's...)
W. D. Publications (Disney): 1990 (no date given)($5.95, no ads, 52 pgs.)

nn-Adapts animated movie	1	2	3	4	5	7
nn-Comic version ($2.50)						3.00

LITTLE MERMAID, THE
Disney Comics: 1992 - No. 4, 1992 ($1.50, mini-series)

1-4: Based on movie						3.00
1-4: 2nd printings sold at Wal-Mart w/different-c						2.25

LITTLE MISS MUFFET
Best Books (Standard Comics)/King Features Synd.: No. 11, Dec, 1948 - No. 13, March, 1949

11-Strip reprints; Fanny Cory-c/a	9	18	27	50	65	80
12,13-Strip reprints; Fanny Cory-c/a	7	14	21	35	43	50

LITTLE MISS SUNBEAM COMICS
Magazine Enterprises/Quality Bakers of America: June-July, 1950 - No. 4, Dec-Jan, 1950-51

1	16	32	48	94	147	200
2-4	10	20	30	56	76	95
...Advs. In Space ('55)	7	14	21	35	43	50

LITTLE MONSTERS, THE (See March of Comics #423, Three Stooges #17)
Gold Key: Nov, 1964 - No. 44, Feb, 1978

1	6	12	18	37	59	80
2	3	6	9	20	30	40
3-10	3	6	9	17	25	32
11-20	3	6	9	15	21	26
21-30: 19-21-Reprints	2	4	6	11	16	20
31-44: 34-39,43-Reprints	2	4	6	8	11	14

LITTLE MONSTERS (Movie)
Now Comics: 1989 - No. 6, June, 1990 ($1.75)

1-6: Photo-c from movie						2.50

LITTLE NEMO (See Cocomalt, Future Comics, Help, Jest, Kayo, Punch, Red Seal, & Superworld; mostly by Winsor McCay Jr., son of famous artist) (Other McCay books: see Little Sammy Sneeze & Dreams of the Rarebit Fiend)

LITTLE NEMO (...in Slumberland)
McCay Features/Nostalgia Press('69): 1945 (11x7-1/4", 28 pgs., B&W)

1905 & 1911 reprints by Winsor McCay	10	20	30	56	76	95
1969-70 (Exact reprint)	2	4	6	9	12	15

LITTLE ORPHAN ANNIE (See Annie, Famous Feature Stories, Marvel Super Special, Merry Christmas..., Popular Comics, Super Book #7, 11, 23 & Super Comics)

LITTLE ORPHAN ANNIE
David McKay Publ./Dell Publishing Co.: No. 7, 1937 - No. 3, Sept-Nov, 1948; No. 206, Dec, 1948

Feature Books(McKay) 7-(1937) (Rare)	97	194	291	606	1003	1400
Four Color 12(1941)	57	114	171	356	591	825
Four Color 18(1943)-Flag-c	34	68	102	255	465	675
Four Color 52(1944)	26	52	78	211	348	485
Four Color 76(1945)	21	42	63	156	278	400
Four Color 107(1946)	18	36	54	134	237	340
Four Color 152(1947)	12	24	36	87	156	225
1(3-5/48)-r/strips from 5/7/44 to 7/30/44	12	24	36	86	153	220
2-r/strips from 7/21/40 to 9/9/40	9	18	27	60	100	140
3-r/strips from 9/10/40 to 11/9/40	9	18	27	60	100	140
Four Color 206(12/48)	8	16	24	54	90	125

LI'L PALS (Also see Li'l Kids)
Marvel Comics Group: Sept, 1972 - No. 5, May, 1973

1	6	12	18	37	59	80
2-5	4	8	12	24	37	50

LI'L PAN (Formerly Rocket Kelly; becomes Junior Comics with #9)
Fox Features Syndicate: No. 6, Dec-Jan, 1946-47 - No. 8, Apr-May, 1947
(Also see Wotalife Comics)

6	10	20	30	56	76	95
7,8: 7-Atomic bomb story; robot-c	8	16	24	42	54	65

LITTLE PEOPLE (Also see Darby O'Gill & the...)

Dell Publishing Co.: No. 485, Aug-Oct, 1953 - No. 1062, Dec, 1959 (Walt Scott's)

Four Color 485 (#1)	8	16	24	52	86	120
Four Color 573(7/54), 633(6/55)	5	10	15	32	51	70
Four Color 692(3/56),753(11/56),809(7/57),868(12/57),908(5/58), 959(12/58), 1062						
	5	10	15	32	51	70

LITTLE RASCALS
Dell Publishing Co.: No. 674, Jan, 1956 - No. 1297, Mar-May, 1962

Four Color 674 (#1)	9	18	27	60	100	140
Four Color 778(3/57),825(8/57)	6	12	18	39	62	85
Four Color 883(3/58),936(9/58),974(3/59),1030(9/59),1079(2-4/60),1137(9-11/60)						
	6	12	18	37	59	80
Four Color 1174(3-5/61),1224(10-12/61),1297	5	10	15	30	48	65

LI'L RASCAL TWINS (Formerly Nature Boy)
Charlton Comics: No. 6, 1957 - No. 18, Jan, 1960

6-Li'l Genius & Tomboy in all	6	12	18	29	36	42
7-18: 7-Timmy the Timid Ghost app.	4	8	12	18	22	25

LITTLE RED HOT: (CHANE OF FOOLS)
Image Comics: Feb, 1999 - No. 3, Apr, 1999 ($2.95/$3.50, B&W, limited series)

1-3-Dawn Brown-s/a. 2,3-($3.50-c)						3.50
The Foolish Collection TPB ($12.95) r/#1-3						13.00

LITTLE RED HOT: BOUND
Image Comics: July, 2001 - No. 3, Nov, 2001 ($2.95, color, limited series)

1-3-Dawn Brown-s/a.						3.00

LITTLE ROQUEFORT COMICS (See Paul Terry's Comics #105)
St. John Publishing Co.(all pre-code)/Pines No. 10: June, 1952 - No. 9, Oct, 1953; No. 10, Summer, 1958

1-By Paul Terry	10	20	30	54	72	90
2	6	12	18	31	38	45
3-10: 10-CBS Television Presents on-c	5	10	15	24	30	35

LITTLE SAD SACK (See Harvey Hits No. 73, 76, 79, 81, 83)
Harvey Publications: Oct, 1964 - No. 19, Nov, 1967

1-Richie Rich app. on cover only	5	10	15	30	48	65
2-10	3	6	9	17	25	32
11-19	3	6	9	14	20	25

LITTLE SCOUTS
Dell Publishing Co.: No. 321, Mar, 1951 - No. 587, Oct, 1954

Four Color 321 (#1)	4	8	12	28	44	60
2(10-12/51) - 6 (10-12/52)	4	8	12	22	34	45
Four Color 462,506,550,587	4	8	12	22	34	45

LITTLE SHOP OF HORRORS SPECIAL (Movie)
DC Comics: Feb, 1987 ($2.00, 68 pgs.)

1-Colan-c/a						4.00

LITTLE SPUNKY
I. W. Enterprises: No date (1963?) (10¢)

1-r/Frisky Fables #1	2	4	6	8	11	14

LITTLE STAR
Oni Press: Feb, 2005 - No. 6, Dec, 2005 ($2.99, B&W, limited series)

1-6-Andi Watson-s/a						3.00
TPB (4/06, $19.95) r/#1-6						20.00

LITTLE STOOGES, THE (The Three Stooges' Sons)
Gold Key: Sept, 1972 - No. 7, Mar, 1974

1-Norman Maurer cover/stories in all	3	6	9	18	27	35
2-7	2	4	6	11	16	20

LITTLEST OUTLAW (Disney)
Dell Publishing Co.: No. 609, Jan, 1955

Four Color 609-Movie, photo-c	6	12	18	43	69	95

LITTLEST SNOWMAN, THE
Dell Publishing Co.: No. 755, 12/56; No. 864, 12/57; 12-2/1963-64

Four Color 755,864, 1(1964)	5	10	15	32	51	70

LI'L TOMBOY (Formerly Fawcett's Funny Animals; see Giant Comics #3)
Charlton Comics: V14#92, Oct, 1956; No. 93, Mar, 1957 - No. 107, Feb, 1960

V14#92	5	10	15	24	30	35
93-107: 97-Atomic Bunny app.	5	10	14	20	24	28

Living Bible #2 © Living Bible Corp.

Lobo #24 © DC

Lone Eagle #4 © AJAX

	GD	VG	FN	VF	VF/NM	NM-
	2.0	4.0	6.0	8.0	9.0	9.2

LI'L WILLIE COMICS (Formerly & becomes Willie Comics #22 on)
Marvel Comics (MgPC): No. 20, July, 1949 - No. 21, Sept, 1949

	GD	VG	FN	VF	VF/NM	NM-
20,21: 20-Little Aspirin app.	12	24	36	69	97	125

LITTLE WOMEN (See Power Record Comics)

LIVE IT UP
Spire Christian Comics (Fleming H. Revell Co.): 1973, 1974 (39-49 cents)

nn-1973 Edition	2	4	6	8	11	14
nn-1974 Edition	1	3	4	6	8	10

LIVEWIRES
Marvel Comics: Apr, 2005 - No. 6, Sept, 2005 ($2.99, limited series)

1-6-Adam Warren-s/c; Rick Mays-a 3.00
...: Clockwork Thugs, Yo (2005, $7.99, digest) r/#1-6 8.00

LIVING BIBLE, THE
Living Bible Corp.: Fall, 1945 - No. 3, Spring, 1946

1-The Life of Paul; all have L. B. Cole-c	39	78	117	224	355	485
2-Joseph & His Brethren; Jonah & the Whale	27	54	81	158	249	340
3-Chaplains At War (classic-c)	40	80	120	240	383	525

LOADED BIBLE
Image Comics: Apr, 2006; May, 2007 ($4.99)

...: Jesus vs. Vampires (4/06) Tim Seeley-s/Nate Bellegarde-a 5.00
...2 : Blood of Christ (5/07) Seeley-s/Mike Norton-a 5.00

LOBO
Dell Publishing Co.: Dec, 1965; No. 2, Oct, 1966

1-1st black character to have his own title	4	8	12	24	37	50
2	3	6	9	18	27	35

LOBO (Also see Action #650, Adventures of Superman, Demon (2nd series), Justice League, L.E.G.I.O.N., Mister Miracle, Omega Men #3 & Superman #41)
DC Comics: Nov, 1990 - No. 4, Feb, 1991 ($1.50, color, limited series)

1-(99¢)-Giffen plots/Breakdowns in all 4.00
1-2nd printing 2.50
2-4: 2-Legion '89 spin-off. 1-4 have Bisley painted covers & art 2.50
...: Blazing Chain of Love 1 (9/92, $1.50)-Denys Cowan-c/a; Alan Grant scripts, ...Convention
Special 1 (1993, $1.75), ...Paramilitary Christmas Special 1 (1991, $2.39, 52 pgs.)
-Bisley-c/a, ...: Portrait of a Victim 1 (1993, $1.75) 2.50

LOBO (Also see Showcase '95 #9)
DC Comics: Dec, 1993 - No. 64, Jul, 1999 ($1.75/$1.95/$2.25/$2.50, mature)

1 ($2.95)-Foil enhanced-c; Alan Grant scripts begin 3.00
2-9,0,10-64: 2-7-Alan Grant scripts. 9-(9/94). 0-(10/94)-Origin retold. 50-Lobo
vs. the DCU. 58-Giffen-a 2.50
#1,000,000 (11/98) 853rd Century x-over 2.50
Annual 1 (1993, $3.50, 68 pgs.)-Bloodlines x-over 3.50
Annual 2 (1994, $3.50)-21 artists (20 listed on-c); Alan Grant script; Elseworlds story 3.50
Annual 3 (1995, $3.95)-Year One story 4.00
.../Authority: Holiday Hell TPB (2006, $17.99) r/Lobo Paramilitary Christmas Special;
Authority/Lobo: Jingle Hell and Spring Break Massacre; WildStorm Winter Special 18.00
...Big Babe Spring Break Special (Spr, '95, $1.95)-Balent-a 2.50
...Bounty Hunting for Fun and Profit ('95)-Bisley-c/a 5.00
... Chained (5/97, $2.50)-Alan Grant story 2.50
.../Deadman: The Brave And The Bald (2/95, $3.50) 3.50
.../Demon: Helloween (12/96, $2.25)-Giarrano-a 2.50
...Fragtastic Voyage 1 ('97, $5.95)-Mejia painted-c/a 6.00
... Gallery (9/95, $3.50)-pin-ups. 3.50
... In the Chair 1 (8/94, $1.95, 36 pgs.), ...I Quit-(12/95, $2.25) 2.50
.../Judge Dredd ('95, $4.95). 5.00

LOBO: (Title Series), DC Comics

--A CONTRACT ON GAWD, 4/94 - 7/94 (mature) 1-4: Alan Grant scripts. 3-Groo cameo 2.50
--DEATH AND TAXES, 10/96 - No. 4, 1/97, 1-4-Giffen/Grant scripts 2.50
--GOES TO HOLLYWOOD, 8/96 ($2.25), 1-Grant scripts 2.50
--INFANTICIDE, 10/92 - 1/93 ($1.50, mature), 1-4-Giffen-c/a; Grant scripts 2.50
--/ MASK, 2/97 - No. 2, 3/97 ($5.95), 1,2 6.00
--'S BACK, 5/92 - No. 4, 11/92 ($1.50, mature), 1-4: 1-Has 4 outer covers. Bisley
painted-c; a1-3. 3-Sam Kieth-c; all have Giffen plots/breakdown & Grant scripts 2.50
Trade paperback (1993, $9.95)-r/1-4 10.00
--THE DUCK, 6/97 ($1.95), 1-A. Grant-s/V. Semeiks & R. Kryssing-a 2.50
--UNAMERICAN GLADIATORS, 6/93 - No. 4, 9/93 ($1.75, mature), 1-4-Mignola-c;

Grant/Wagner scripts 2.50
--UNBOUND, 8/03 - No. 6, 5/04 ($2.95), 1-6-Giffen-s/Horley-c/a. 4-6-Ambush Bug app.3.00

LOBSTER JOHNSON: THE IRON PROMETHEUS (See B.P.R.D. and Hellboy titles)
Dark Horse Comics: Sept, 2007 - No. 5 ($2.99, limited series)

1-Mignola-s/c; Armstrong-a 3.00

LOCO (Magazine) (Satire)
Satire Publications: Aug, 1958 - V1#3, Jan, 1959

V1#1-Chic Stone-a	9	18	27	47	61	75
V1#2,3-Severin-a, 2 pgs. Davis; 3-Heath-a	7	14	21	35	43	50

LOGAN: PATH OF THE WARLORD
Marvel Comics: Feb, 1996 ($5.95, one-shot)

1-John Paul Leon-a 6.00

LOGAN: SHADOW SOCIETY
Marvel Comics: 1996 ($5.95, one-shot)

1 6.00

LOGAN'S RUN
Marvel Comics Group: Jan, 1977 - No. 7, July, 1977

1: 1-5-Based on novel & movie	1	3	4	6	8	10
2-5,7: 6,7-New stories adapted from novel						6.00
6-1st Thanos (also see Iron Man #55) solo story (back-up) by Zeck (6/77)	3	6	9	18	24	30
6-(35¢-c variant, limited distribution)	5	10	15	35	55	75
7-(35¢-c variant, limited distribution)	3	6	9	18	27	35

NOTE: *Austin* a-6i. *Gulacy* c-6. *Kane* c-7p. *Perez* a-1-5p; c-1-5p. *Sutton* a-6p, 7p.

LOIS & CLARK, THE NEW ADVENTURES OF SUPERMAN
DC Comics: 1994 ($9.95, one-shot)

1-r/Man of Steel #2, Superman Ann. 1, Superman #9 & 11, Action #600 & 655,
Adventures of Superman #445, 462 & 466 1 3 4 6 8 10

LOIS LANE (Also see Daring New Adventures of Supergirl, Showcase #9,10 & Superman's Girlfriend...)
DC Comics: Aug, 1986 - No. 2, Sept, 1986 ($1.50, 52 pgs.)

1,2-Morrow-c/a in each 4.00

LOKI (Thor)
Marvel Comics: Sept, 2004 - No. 4, Nov, 2004 ($3.50)

1-4-Rodi-s/Ribic-a/c 3.50
HC (2005, $17.99, with dustjacket) oversized r/#1-4; original proposal and sketch pages 18.00
SC (2007, $12.99) r/#1-4; original proposal and sketch pages 13.00

LOLLY AND PEPPER
Dell Publishing Co.: No. 832, Sept, 1957 - July, 1962

Four Color 832(#1)	5	10	15	30	48	65
Four Color 940,978,1086,1206	4	8	12	22	34	45
01-459-207 (7/62)	3	6	9	18	27	35

LOMAX (See Police Action)

LONDON'S DARK
Escape/Titan: 1989 ($8.95, B&W, graphic novel)

nn-James Robinson script; Paul Johnson-c/a 1 2 3 5 7 9

LONE
Dark Horse Comics: Sept, 2003 - No. 6, Mar, 2004 ($2.99)

1-6-Stuart Moore-s/Jerome Opeña-a/Templesmith-c 3.00

LONE EAGLE (The Flame No. 5 on)
Ajax/Farrell Publications: Apr-May, 1954 - No. 4, Oct-Nov, 1954

1	13	26	39	74	105	135
2-4: 3-Bondage-c	9	18	27	50	65	80

LONE GUNMEN, THE (From the X-Files)
Dark Horse Comics: June, 2001 ($2.99, one-shot)

1-Paul Lee-a; photo-c 3.00

LONELY HEART (Formerly Dear Lonely Hearts; Dear Heart #15 on)
Ajax/Farrell Publ. (Excellent Publ.): No. 9, Mar, 1955 - No. 14, Feb, 1956

9-Kamenesqe-a; (Last precode)	10	20	30	54	72	90
10-14	7	14	21	37	46	55

LONE RANGER, THE (See Ace Comics, Aurora, Dell Giants,Future Comics, Golden Comics Digest #48, King Comics, Magic Comics & March of Comics #165, 174, 193, 208, 225, 238, 310, 322, 338, 350)

LONE RANGER, THE
Dell Publishing Co.: No. 3, 1939 - No. 167, Feb, 1947

Lone Ranger #13 © KING

Lone Ranger #1 © Classic Media

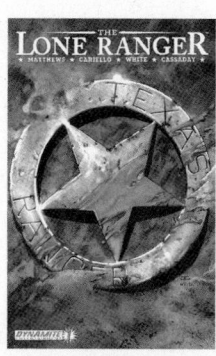

Lone Rider #18 © SUPR

	GD	VG	FN	VF	VF/NM	NM-
	2.0	4.0	6.0	8.0	9.0	9.2

Large Feature Comic 3(1939)-Heigh-Yo Silver; text with illus. by Robert Weisman; also exists
as a Whitman #710 ... 153 ... 304 ... 456 ... 950 ... 1575 ... 2200
Large Feature Comic 7(1939)-Illustr. by Henry Vallely; Hi-Yo Silver the Lone Ranger to the
Rescue; also exists as a Whitman #715 ... 145 ... 290 ... 435 ... 906 ... 1503 ... 2100
Feature Book 21(1940), 24(1941) ... 86 ... 172 ... 258 ... 538 ... 894 ... 1250
Four Color 82(1945) ... 38 ... 76 ... 114 ... 285 ... 518 ... 750
Four Color 98(1945),118(1946) ... 29 ... 58 ... 87 ... 212 ... 381 ... 550
Four Color 125(1946),136(1947) ... 20 ... 40 ... 60 ... 150 ... 268 ... 385
Four Color 151,167(1947) ... 17 ... 34 ... 51 ... 128 ... 227 ... 325

LONE RANGER, THE (Movie, radio & TV; Clayton Moore starred as Lone Ranger in the
movies; No. 1-37: strip reprints)(See Dell Giants)
Dell Publishing Co.: Jan-Feb, 1948 - No. 145, May-July, 1962

1 (36 pgs.)-The Lone Ranger, his horse Silver, companion Tonto & his horse Scout begin
... 52 ... 104 ... 156 ... 442 ... 821 ... 1200
2 (52 pgs. begin, end #41) ... 27 ... 54 ... 81 ... 203 ... 364 ... 525
3-5 ... 20 ... 40 ... 60 ... 150 ... 268 ... 385
6,7,9,10 ... 17 ... 34 ... 51 ... 126 ... 223 ... 320
8-Origin retold; Indian back-c begin, end #35 ... 20 ... 40 ... 60 ... 146 ... 261 ... 375
11-20: 11- "Young Hawk" Indian boy serial begins, ends #145
... 12 ... 24 ... 36 ... 87 ... 156 ... 225
21,22,24-31: 51-Reprint. 31-1st Mask logo ... 10 ... 20 ... 30 ... 70 ... 123 ... 175
23-Origin retold ... 13 ... 26 ... 39 ... 90 ... 160 ... 230
32-37: 32-Painted-c begin. 36-Animal photo back-c begin, end #49. 37-Last newspaper-r
issue; new outfit; red shirt becomes blue; most known copies show the blue shirt on-c &
inside ... 18 ... 27 ... 61 ... 103 ... 145
37-Variant issue; Long Ranger wears a red shirt on-c and inside. A few copies of the red shirt
outfit were printed before catching the mistake and changing the color to blue (rare)
... 16 ... 32 ... 48 ... 114 ... 202 ... 290
38-41 (All 52 pgs.) 38-Paul S. Newman-s (wrote most of the stories #38-on)
... 9 ... 18 ... 27 ... 60 ... 100 ... 140
42-50 (36 pgs.) ... 7 ... 14 ... 21 ... 50 ... 83 ... 115
51-74 (52 pgs.): 56-One pg. origin story of Lone Ranger & Tonto. 71-Blank inside-c
... 7 ... 14 ... 21 ... 49 ... 80 ... 110
75,77-99: 79-X-mas-c ... 7 ... 14 ... 21 ... 45 ... 73 ... 100
76-Classic flag-c ... 7 ... 14 ... 21 ... 49 ... 80 ... 110
100 ... 8 ... 16 ... 24 ... 52 ... 86 ... 120
101-111: Last painted-c ... 6 ... 12 ... 18 ... 43 ... 69 ... 95
112-Clayton Moore photo-c begin, end #145 ... 17 ... 34 ... 51 ... 128 ... 227 ... 325
113-117: 117-10¢ &15¢-c exist ... 10 ... 20 ... 30 ... 70 ... 123 ... 175
118-Origin Lone Ranger, Tonto, & Silver retold; Special anniversary issue
... 22 ... 44 ... 66 ... 160 ... 285 ... 410
119-140: 139-Fran Striker-s ... 9 ... 18 ... 27 ... 65 ... 113 ... 155
141-145 ... 10 ... 20 ... 30 ... 67 ... 116 ... 165
NOTE: **Hank Hartman** painted c(signed)-65, 66, 70, 75, 82; unsigned-64?, 67-69?, 71, 72, 73?, 74?, 76-78, 80,
81, 83-91, 92?, 93-111. **Ernest Nordli** painted c(signed)-42, 50, 52, 53, 56, 59, 60; unsigned-39-41, 44-49, 51,
54, 55, 57, 58, 61-63?

LONE RANGER, THE
Gold Key (Reprints in #13-20): 9/64 - No. 16, 12/69; No. 17, 11/72; No. 18, 9/74 - No. 28, 3/77

1-Retells origin ... 6 ... 12 ... 18 ... 41 ... 66 ... 90
2 ... 4 ... 8 ... 12 ... 22 ... 34 ... 45
3-10: Small Bear-r in #6-12. 10-Last 12¢ issue ... 3 ... 6 ... 9 ... 20 ... 30 ... 40
11-17 ... 3 ... 6 ... 9 ... 16 ... 22 ... 28
18-28 ... 2 ... 4 ... 6 ... 11 ... 16 ... 20
Golden West 1(30029-610, 10/66)-Giant; r/most Golden West #3 including Clayton Moore
photo front/back-c ... 7 ... 14 ... 21 ... 45 ... 73 ... 100

LONE RANGER
Dynamite Entertainment: 2006 - Present ($2.99)

1-Retells origin; Carriello-a/Matthews-s; badge cover by Cassaday ... 3.00
1-Variant mask cover by Cassaday ... 5.00
1-Baltimore Comic-Con 2006 variant cover with masked face and horse silhouette ... 12.00
1-Directors' Cut ($4.99) r/#1 with comments at page bottoms, script and sketches ... 5.00
2-8: Origin continues; Tonto app. ... 3.00
... Volume 1: Now and Forever TPB (2007, $19.99) r/#1-6; sketch pages ... 20.00

LONE RANGER AND TONTO, THE
Topps Comics: Aug, 1994 - No. 4, Nov, 1994 ($2.50, limited series)

1-4: 3-Origin of Lone Ranger; Tonto leaves; Lansdale story, Truman-c/a in all. ... 2.50
1-4: Silver logo. 1-Signed by Lansdale and Truman ... 6.00
Trade paperback (1/95, $9.95) ... 10.00

LONE RANGER'S COMPANION TONTO, THE (TV)
Dell Publishing Co.: No. 312, Jan, 1951 - No. 33, Nov-Jan/58-59 (All painted-c)

Four Color 312(#1, 1/51) ... 11 ... 22 ... 33 ... 75 ... 133 ... 190

	GD	VG	FN	VF	VF/NM	NM-
	2.0	4.0	6.0	8.0	9.0	9.2

2(8-10/51),3: (#2 titled "Tonto") ... 6 ... 12 ... 18 ... 43 ... 69 ... 95
4-10 ... 6 ... 12 ... 18 ... 37 ... 59 ... 80
11-20 ... 5 ... 10 ... 15 ... 32 ... 51 ... 70
21-33 ... 4 ... 8 ... 12 ... 28 ... 44 ... 60
NOTE: **Ernest Nordli** painted c(signed)-2, 7; unsigned-3-6, 8-11, 12?, 13, 14, 18?, 22-24?
See Aurora Comic Booklets.

LONE RANGER'S FAMOUS HORSE HI-YO SILVER, THE (TV)
Dell Publishing Co.: No. 369, Jan, 1952 - No. 36, Oct-Dec, 1960 (All painted-c, most by Sam
Savitt) (Lone Ranger appears in most issues)

Four Color 369(#1)-Silver's origin as told by The Lone Ranger
... 10 ... 20 ... 30 ... 71 ... 126 ... 180
Four Color 392(#2, 4/52) ... 6 ... 12 ... 18 ... 41 ... 66 ... 90
3(7-9/52)-10(4-6/53) ... 5 ... 10 ... 15 ... 35 ... 55 ... 75
11-36 ... 4 ... 8 ... 12 ... 28 ... 44 ... 60

LONE RIDER (Also see The Rider)
Superior Comics(Farrell Publ.): Apr, 1951 - No. 26, Jul, 1955 (#3-on: 36 pgs.)

1 (52 pgs.)-The Lone Rider & his horse Lightning' begin; Kamenish-a begins
... 31 ... 62 ... 93 ... 178 ... 282 ... 385
2 (52 pgs.)-The Golden Arrow begins (origin) ... 15 ... 30 ... 45 ... 90 ... 140 ... 190
3-6: 6-Last Golden Arrow ... 15 ... 30 ... 45 ... 86 ... 133 ... 180
7-Golden Arrow becomes Swift Arrow; origin of his shield
... 15 ... 30 ... 45 ... 90 ... 140 ... 190
8-Origin Swift Arrow ... 16 ... 32 ... 48 ... 94 ... 147 ... 200
9,10 ... 11 ... 22 ... 33 ... 62 ... 86 ... 110
11-14 ... 9 ... 18 ... 27 ... 52 ... 69 ... 85
15-Golden Arrow origin-r from #2, changing name to Swift Arrow
... 10 ... 20 ... 30 ... 56 ... 76 ... 95
16-20,22-26: 23-Apache Kid app. ... 9 ... 18 ... 27 ... 47 ... 61 ... 75
21-3-D effect-c ... 15 ... 30 ... 45 ... 88 ... 137 ... 185

LONERS, THE
Marvel Comics: June, 2007 - No. 6 ($2.99, limited series)

1-5-Cebulski-s/Moline-a/Pearson-c; Lightspeed, Spider-Woman, Ricochet app. ... 3.00

LONE WOLF AND CUB
First Comics: May, 1987 - No. 45, Apr, 1991 ($1.95-$3.25, B&W, deluxe size)

1-Frank Miller-c & intro.; reprints manga series by Koike & Kojima
... 1 ... 2 ... 3 ... 6 ... 8 ... 10
1-2nd print, 3rd print, 2-2nd print ... 3.25
2-12: 6-72 pgs. origin issue ... 5.50
13-38,40: 40-Ploog-c ... 4.00
39-($5.95, 120 pgs.)-Ploog-c ... 6.50
41-44: 41-($3.95, 84 pgs.)-Ploog-c. 42-Ploog-c ... 6.00
45-Last issue; low print ... 1 ... 2 ... 3 ... 5 ... 6 ... 8
Deluxe Edition ($19.95, B&W) ... 20.00
NOTE: **Sienkiewicz** c-13-24. **Matt Wagner** c-25-30.

LONE WOLF AND CUB (Trade paperbacks)
Dark Horse Comics: Aug, 2000 - No. 28 ($9.95, B&W, 4" x 6", approx. 300 pgs.)

1-Collects First Comics reprint series; Frank Miller-c ... 18.00
1-(2nd printing) ... 12.00
1-(3rd-5th printings) ... 10.00
2,3-(1st printings) ... 12.00
2,3-(2nd printings) ... 10.00
4-28 ... 10.00

LONE WOLF 2100 (Also see Reveal)
Dark Horse Comics: May, 2002 - No. 11, Dec, 2003 ($2.99, color)

1-New homage to Lone Wolf and Cub; Kennedy-s/Velasco-a ... 4.00
2-11 ... 3.00
...: The Red File (1/03, $2.99) character and story background files ... 3.00
... Vol. 1 - Shadows on Saplings TPB (2003, $12.95, 6" x 9") r/#1-4 ... 13.00
... Vol. 2 - The Language of Chaos TPB (2003, $12.95, 6" x 9") r/#5-8, Dirty Tricks short story
from Reveal ... 13.00

LONG BOW (...Indian Boy)(See Indians & Jumbo Comics #141)
Fiction House Mag. (Real Adventures Publ.): 1951 - No. 9, Wint, 1952/53

1-Most covers by Maurice Whitman ... 17 ... 34 ... 51 ... 98 ... 154 ... 210
2 ... 11 ... 22 ... 33 ... 60 ... 83 ... 105
3-9 ... 10 ... 20 ... 30 ... 54 ... 72 ... 90

LONG HOT SUMMER, THE
DC Comics (Milestone): Jul, 1995 - No. 3, Sept, 1995 ($2.95/$2.50, lim. series)

1-3: 1-($2.95-c). 2,3-($2.50-c) ... 3.00

LONG JOHN SILVER & THE PIRATES (Formerly Terry & the Pirates)

Looney Tunes #136 © WB

Looney Tunes and Merrie Melodies #27 © WB

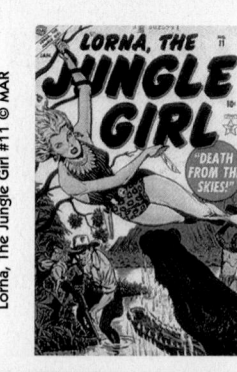

Lorna, The Jungle Girl #11 © MAR

	GD 2.0	VG 4.0	FN 6.0	VF 8.0	VF/NM 9.0	NM- 9.2

Charlton Comics: No. 30, Aug, 1956 - No. 32, March, 1957 (TV)

30-32: Whitman-c	10	20	30	54	72	90

LONGSHOT (Also see X-Men, 2nd Series #10)
Marvel Comics: Sept, 1985 - No. 6, Feb, 1986 (60¢, limited series)

1-6: 1-Art Adams/Whilce Portacio-c/a in all. 4-Spider-Man app. 6-Double size	1	2	3	4	5	7
Trade Paperback (1989, $16.95)-r/#1-6						17.00

LONGSHOT
Marvel Comics: Feb, 1998 ($3.99, one-shot)

1-DeMatteis-s/Zulli-a						4.00

LOOKING GLASS WARS: HATTER M
Image Comics (Desperado): Dec, 2005 - No. 4, Nov, 2006 ($3.99)

1-4-Templesmith-a/c						4.00

LOONEY TUNES (2nd Series) (TV)
Gold Key/Whitman: April, 1975 - No. 47, June, 1984

1-Reprints	3	6	9	20	30	40
2-10: 2,4-reprints	2	4	6	11	16	20
11-20: 16-reprints	2	4	6	8	11	14
21-30	1	2	3	5	7	9
31,32,36-42(2/82)	1	2	3	4	5	7
33-(8/80)-35 (Whitman pre-pack only, scarce)	3	6	9	16	23	30
43(4/82),44(6/83) (low distribution)	2	4	6	8	11	14
45-47 (All #90296 on-c; nd, nd code, pre-pack) 45(8/83), 46(3/84), 47(6/84)	3	6	9	14	19	24

LOONEY TUNES (3rd Series) (TV)
DC Comics: Apr, 1994 - Present ($1.50/$1.75/$1.95/$1.99/$2.25)

1-10,120: 1-Marvin Martian-c/sty; Bugs Bunny, Roadrunner, Daffy begin. 120-($2.95-C)						3.00
11-119,121-153: 23-34-($1.75-c). 35-43-($1.95-c). 44-Begin $1.99-c. 93-Begin $2.25-c. 100-Art by various incl. Kyle Baker, Marie Severin, Darwyn Cooke, Jill Thompson						2.50
...Back In Action Movie Adaptation (12/03, $3.95) photo-c						4.00

LOONEY TUNES AND MERRIE MELODIES COMICS ("Looney Tunes" #166(8/55) on) (Also see Porky's Duck Hunt)
Dell Publishing Co.: 1941 - No. 246, July-Sept, 1962

1-Porky Pig, Bugs Bunny, Daffy Duck, Elmer Fudd, Mary Jane & Sniffles, Pat Patsy and Pete begin (1st comic book app. of each). Bugs Bunny story by Win Smith (early Mickey Mouse artist)	1050	2100	3150	8000	14,000	20,000
2 (11/41)	152	304	456	1292	2396	3500
3-Kandi the Cave Kid begins by Walt Kelly; also in #4-6,8,11,15	109	218	327	927	1714	2500
4-Kelly-a	109	218	327	927	1714	2500
5-Bugs Bunny The Super-Duper Rabbit story (1st funny animal super hero, 3/42; also see Coo Coo); Kelly-a	83	166	249	706	1303	1900
6,8-Kelly-a	63	126	189	536	993	1450
7,9,10: 9-Painted-c. 10-Flag-c	51	102	153	408	742	1075
11,15-Kelly-a; 15-X-Mas-c	50	100	150	400	725	1050
12-14,16-19	39	78	117	293	534	775
20-25: Pat, Patsy & Pete by Walt Kelly in all	32	64	96	240	445	650
26-30	25	50	75	184	330	475
31-40: 33-War Bonds-c. 39-X-Mas-c	20	40	60	150	268	385
41-50: 45-War Bonds-c	15	30	45	111	198	285
51-60	12	24	36	87	156	225
61-80	9	18	27	63	107	150
81-99: 87-X-Mas-c	8	16	24	54	90	125
100	8	16	24	58	97	135
101-120	7	14	21	45	73	100
121-150	6	12	18	39	62	85
151-200: 159-X-Mas-c	5	10	15	35	55	75
201-240	5	10	15	32	51	70
241-246	5	10	15	35	55	75

LOONY SPORTS (Magazine)
3-Strikes Publishing Co.: Spring, 1975 (68 pgs.)

1-Sports satire	2	4	6	8	11	14

LOOSE CANNON (Also see Action Comics Annual #5 & Showcase '94 #5)
DC Comics: June, 1995 - No. 4, Sept, 1995 ($1.75, limited series)

1-4: Adam Pollina-a. 1-Superman app.						2.50

LOOY DOT DOPE
United Features Syndicate: No. 13, 1939

Single Series 13	30	60	90	174	275	375

LORD JIM (See Movie Comics)

LORD PUMPKIN
Malibu Comics (Ultraverse): Oct, 1994 ($2.50, one-shot)

0-Two covers						2.50

LORD PUMPKIN/NECROMANTRA
Malibu Comics (Ultraverse): Apr, 1995 - No. 4, July, 1995 ($2.95, limited series, flip book)

1-4						3.00

LORNA THE JUNGLE GIRL (...Jungle Queen #1-5)
Atlas Comics (NPI 1/OMC 2-11/NPI 12-26): July, 1953 - No. 26, Aug, 1957

1-Origin & 1st app.	40	80	120	235	368	500
2-Intro. & 1st app. Greg Knight	19	38	57	112	176	240
3-5	16	32	48	94	147	200
6-11: 11-Last pre-code (1/55)	14	28	42	82	121	160
12-17,19-26: 14-Colletta & Maneely-c	13	26	39	72	101	130
18-Williamson/Colletta-c	14	28	42	76	108	140

NOTE: **Brodsky** c-1-3, 5, 9. **Everett** c-21, 23-26. **Heath** c-6, 7. **Maneely** c-12, 15. **Romita** a-20, 22, 24, 26. **Shores** a-14-18, 24, 26; c-11, 13, 16. **Tuska** a-6.

LOSERS
DC Comics (Vertigo): Aug, 2003 - No. 32, Mar, 2006 ($2.95/$2.99)

1-Andy Diggle-s/Jock-a						4.00
2-32: 15-Bagged with Sky Captain CD. 20-Oliver-a. 27-Wilson-a						3.00
...: Ante Up TPB (2004, $9.95) r/#1-6						10.00
...: Close Quarters TPB (2005, $14.99) r/#20-25						15.00
...: Double Down TPB (2004, $12.95) r/#7-12						13.00
...: Endgame TPB (2006, $14.99) r/#26-32						15.00
...: Trifecta TPB (2005, $14.99) r/#13-19						15.00

LOSERS SPECIAL (See Our Fighting Forcers #123)(Also see G.I. Combat & Our Fighting Forces)
DC Comics: Sept, 1985 ($1.25, one-shot)

1-Capt. Storm, Gunner & Sarge; Crisis x-over						5.00

LOST, THE
Chaos! Comics: Dec, 1997 - No. 3 ($2.95, B&W, unfinished limited series)

1-3-Andreyko-script: 1-Russell back-c						3.00

LOST CONTINENT
Eclipse Int'l: Sept, 1990 - No. 6, 1991 ($3.50, B&W, squarebound, 60 pgs.)

1-6: Japanese story translated to English						3.50

LOST HEROES
Davdez Arts: Mar, 1998 - No. 4 ($2.95)

0-4-Rob Prior-s/painted-a						3.00

LOST IN SPACE (Movie)
Dark Horse Comics: Apr, 1998 - No. 3, July, 1998 ($2.95, limited series)

1-3-Continuation of 1998 movie; Erskine-a						3.00

LOST IN SPACE (TV)(Also see Space Family Robinson)
Innovation Publishing: Aug, 1991 - No. 12, Jan, 1993 ($2.50, limited series)

1-12: Bill Mumy (Will Robinson) scripts in #1-9. 9-Perez-c						3.00
1,2-Special Ed.: r/#1,2 plus new art & new-c						3.00
Annual 1,2 (1991, 1992, $2.95, 52 pgs.)						3.00
...: Project Robinson (11/93, $2.50) 1st & only part of intended series						3.00

LOST IN SPACE: VOYAGE TO THE BOTTOM OF THE SOUL
Innovation Publishing: No. 13, Aug, 1993 - No. 18, 1994 ($2.50, limited series)

13(V1#1, $2.95)-Embossed silver logo edition; Bill Mumy scripts begin; painted-c						3.00
13(V1#1, $4.95)-Embossed gold logo edition bagged w/poster						5.00
14-18: Painted-c						3.00

NOTE: Originally intended to be a 12 issue limited series.

LOST ONES, THE
Image Comics: Mar, 2000 ($2.95)

1-Ken Penders-s/a						3.00

LOST PLANET
Eclipse Comics: 5/87 - No. 5, 2/88; No. 6, 3/89 (Mini-series, Baxter paper)

1-6-Bo Hampton-c/a in all						2.50

LOST WAGON TRAIN, THE (See Zane Grey Four Color 583)

LOST WORLD, THE
Dell Publishing Co.: No. 1145, Nov-Jan, 1960-61

Four Color 1145-Movie, Gil Kane-a, photo-c; 1pg. Conan Doyle biography by Torres	9	18	27	64	110	155

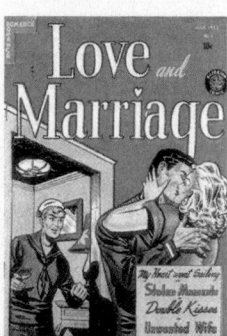

Love and Marriage #3 © SUPR

Love Confessions #2 © QUA

Love Diary #2 © QUA

	GD 2.0	VG 4.0	FN 6.0	VF 8.0	VF/NM 9.0	NM- 9.2

LOST WORLD, THE (See Jurassic Park)
Topps Comics: May, 1997 - No. 4, Aug, 1997 ($2.95, limited series)

	GD	VG	FN	VF	VF/NM	NM-
1-4-Movie adaption						3.00

LOST WORLDS (Weird Tales of the Past and Future)
Standard Comics: No. 5, Oct, 1952 - No. 6, Dec, 1952

	GD	VG	FN	VF	VF/NM	NM-
5- "Alice in Terrorland" by Alex Toth; J. Katz-a	43	86	129	262	431	600
6-Toth-a	36	72	108	208	329	450

LOTS 'O' FUN COMICS
Robert Allen Co.: 1940's? (5¢, heavy stock, blue covers)

nn-Contents can vary; Felix, Planet Comics known; contents would determine value.
Similar to Up-To-Date Comics. Remainders - re-packaged.

LOU GEHRIG (See The Pride of the Yankees)

LOVE ADVENTURES (Actual Confessions #13)
Marvel (IPS)/Atlas Comics (MPI): Oct, 1949; No. 2, Jan, 1950; No. 3, Feb, 1951 - No. 12, Aug, 1952

	GD	VG	FN	VF	VF/NM	NM-
1-Photo-c	17	34	51	98	154	210
2-Powell-a; Tyrone Power, Gene Tierney photo-c	15	30	45	84	127	170
3-8,10-12: 8-Robinson-a	10	20	30	54	72	90
9-Everett-a	10	20	30	56	76	95

LOVE AND MARRIAGE
Superior Comics Ltd. (Canada): Mar, 1952 - No. 16, Sept, 1954

	GD	VG	FN	VF	VF/NM	NM-
1	14	28	42	82	121	160
2	9	18	27	47	61	75
3-10	8	16	24	42	54	65
11-16	7	14	21	37	46	55
I.W. Reprint #1,2,8,11,14: 8-r/Love and Marriage #3. 11-r/Love and Marriage #11	2	4	6	9	13	16
Super Reprint #10('63),15,17('64):15-Love and Marriage #?						
	2	4	6	9	13	16

NOTE: All issues have Kamenish art.

LOVE AND ROCKETS
Fantagraphics Books: July, 1982 - No. 50, May, 1996 ($2.95/$2.50/$4.95, B&W, mature)

	GD	VG	FN	VF	VF/NM	NM-
1-B&W-c (6/82, $2.95; small size, publ. by Hernandez Bros.)(800 printed)						
	5	10	15	32	51	70
1 (Fall, '82; color-c)	3	6	9	20	30	40
1-2nd & 3rd printing, 2-11,29-31: 2nd printings						3.00
2	2	4	6	8	11	14
3-10	1	2	3	5	7	9
11-49: 30 ($2.95, 52 pgs.)						5.00
50-($4.95)						6.00

LOVE AND ROCKETS (Volume 2)
Fantagraphics Books: Spring, 2001 - Present ($3.95-$7.99, B&W, mature)

	GD	VG	FN	VF	VF/NM	NM-
1-9-Gilbert, Jaime and Mario Hernandez-s/a						4.00
10-($5.95)						6.00
11-19-($4.50)						4.50
20-($7.99)						8.00

LOVE AND ROMANCE
Charlton Comics: Sept, 1971 - No. 24, Sept, 1975

	GD	VG	FN	VF	VF/NM	NM-
1	3	6	9	17	25	32
2-10	2	4	6	9	13	16
11-24: 12-Susan Dey poster	1	3	4	6	8	10

LOVE AT FIRST SIGHT
Ace Magazines (RAR Publ. Co./Periodical House): Oct, 1949 - No. 43, Nov, 1956 (Photo-c: 18-42)

	GD	VG	FN	VF	VF/NM	NM-
1-Painted-c	15	30	45	86	133	180
2-Painted-c	10	20	30	54	72	90
3-10: 4,7-Painted-c	8	16	24	44	57	70
11-20	8	16	24	42	54	65
21-33: 33-Last pre-code	8	16	24	40	50	60
34-43	7	14	21	37	46	55

LOVE BUG, THE (See Movie Comics)
LOVEBUNNY AND MR. HELL
Devil's Due Publ./Image Comics: 2002 - Present ($2.95, B&W, one-shots)

	GD	VG	FN	VF	VF/NM	NM-
1-Tim Seeley-s						3.00
...: A Day in the Lovelife (Image, 2003) Blaylock-a						3.00
...: Savage Love (Image, 2003) Seeley-s/a; Savage Dragon app.; Seeley & Larsen-c						3.00
TPB (4/04, $9.95, digest-sized) reprints						10.00

	GD 2.0	VG 4.0	FN 6.0	VF 8.0	VF/NM 9.0	NM- 9.2

LOVE CLASSICS
A Lover's Magazine/Marvel: Nov, 1949 - No. 2, Feb, 1950 (Photo-c, 52 pgs.)

	GD	VG	FN	VF	VF/NM	NM-
1,2: 2-Virginia Mayo photo-c; 30 pg. story "I Turned Into a Small-Town Flirt"						
	15	30	45	85	130	175

LOVE CONFESSIONS
Quality Comics: Oct, 1949 - No. 54, Dec, 1956 (Photo-c: 3,4,6,7,9,11-18,21,24,25)

	GD	VG	FN	VF	VF/NM	NM-
1-Ward-c/a, 9 pgs; Gustavson-a	31	62	93	178	282	385
2-Gustavson-a; Ward-c	15	30	45	86	133	180
3	10	20	30	58	79	100
4-Crandall-a	11	22	33	64	90	115
5-Ward-a, 7 pgs.	13	26	39	74	105	135
6,7,9,11-13,15,16,18: 7-Van Johnson photo-c. 8-Robert Mitchum & Jane Russell photo-c						
	9	18	27	47	61	75
8,10-Ward-a (2 stories in #10)	13	26	39	74	105	135
14,17,19,22-Ward-a; 17-Faith Domerque photo-c	12	24	36	69	97	125
20-Ward-a(2)	13	26	39	74	105	135
21,23-28,30-38,40-42: Last precode, 4/55	8	16	24	40	50	60
29-Ward-a	11	22	33	64	90	115
39,53-Matt Baker-a	10	20	30	54	72	90
43,44,46,47,50-52,54: 47-Ward-c	7	14	21	37	46	55
45,48-Ward-a	9	18	27	47	61	75
49-Baker-c/a	11	22	33	60	83	105

LOVECRAFT
DC Comics: 2003 (graphic novel)

	GD	VG	FN	VF	VF/NM	NM-
Hardcover ($24.95) Rodionoff & Giffen-s/Breccia-a; intro. by John Carpenter					25.00	
Softcover ($17.95)					18.00	

LOVE DIARY
Our Publishing Co./Toytown/Patches: July, 1949 - No. 48, Oct, 1955 (Photo-c: 1-24,27-29) (52 pgs.#1-11?)

	GD	VG	FN	VF	VF/NM	NM-
1-Krigstein-a	20	40	60	117	184	250
2,3-Krigstein & Mort Leav-a in each	14	28	42	80	115	150
4-8	10	20	30	54	72	90
9,10-Everett-a	10	20	30	56	76	95
11-15,17-20	9	18	27	47	61	75
16- Mort Leav-a, 3 pg. Baker-sty. Leav-a	9	18	27	50	65	80
21-30,32-48: 45-Leav-a. 47-Last precode(12/54)	8	16	24	44	57	70
31-John Buscema headlights-c	9	18	27	52	69	85

LOVE DIARY (Diary Loves #2 on; title change due to previously published title)
Quality Comics Group: Sept, 1949

	GD	VG	FN	VF	VF/NM	NM-
1-Ward-c/a, 9 pgs.	31	62	93	178	282	385

LOVE DIARY
Charlton Comics: July, 1958 - No. 102, Dec, 1976

	GD	VG	FN	VF	VF/NM	NM-
1	10	20	30	56	76	95
2	7	14	21	35	43	50
3-5,7-10: 10-Photo-c	6	12	18	28	34	40
6-Torres-a	6	12	18	31	38	45
11-20: 20-Photo-c	3	6	9	16	23	30
21-40	3	6	9	14	19	24
41-60	2	4	6	10	14	18
61-80,100-102	2	4	6	8	11	14
81-99: 82-Partridge Family poster. 85-Danny poster	1	3	4	6	8	10

LOVE DOCTOR (See Dr. Anthony King...)
LOVE DRAMAS (True Secrets No. 3 on?)
Marvel Comics (IPS): Oct, 1949 - No. 2, Jan, 1950

	GD	VG	FN	VF	VF/NM	NM-
1-Jack Kamen-a; photo-c	18	36	54	107	169	230
2-Photo-c	14	28	42	78	112	145

LOVE EXPERIENCES (Challenge of the Unknown No. 6)
Ace Periodicals (A.A. Wyn/Periodical House): Oct, 1949 - No. 5, June, 1950; No. 6, Apr, 1951 - No. 38, June, 1956

	GD	VG	FN	VF	VF/NM	NM-
1-Painted-c	15	30	45	84	127	170
2	9	18	27	52	69	85
3-5: 5-Painted-c	8	16	24	44	57	70
6-10	8	16	24	42	54	65
11-30: 30-Last pre-code (2/55)	7	14	21	37	46	55
31-38: 38-Indicia date-6/56; c-date-8/56	6	12	18	31	38	45

NOTE: Anne Brewster a-15. Photo c-4, 15-35, 38.

LOVE FIGHTS (Also see Free Comic Book Day Edition in the Promotional Comics section)
Oni Press: June, 2003 - No. 12, Aug, 2004 ($2.99, B&W)

Love Journals #10 © Our Publ. Co.

Love Letters #29 © QUA

Lovers' Lane #1 © LEV

	GD 2.0	VG 4.0	FN 6.0	VF 8.0	VF/NM 9.0	NM- 9.2
1-12-Andi Watson-s/a						3.00
Vol.1 TPB (4/04, $14.95, digest-size) r/#1-6						15.00

LOVE JOURNAL
Our Publishing Co.: No. 10, Oct, 1951 - No. 25, July, 1954

	GD 2.0	VG 4.0	FN 6.0	VF 8.0	VF/NM 9.0	NM- 9.2
10	12	24	36	67	94	120
11-25: 16-Buscema headlight-c. 19-Mort Leav-a	8	16	24	44	57	70

LOVELAND
Mutual Mag./Eye Publ. (Marvel): Nov, 1949 - No. 2, Feb, 1950 (52 pgs.)

1,2-Photo-c	12	24	36	69	97	125

LOVELESS
DC Comics: Dec, 2005 - Present ($2.99)

1-19: 1-Azzarello-s/Frusin-a. 6-8,15-Zezelj-a. 11,12,16-19-Dell'Edera-a						3.00
...: A Kin of Homecoming TPB (2006, $9.99) r/#1-5						10.00
...: Thicker Than Blackwater TPB (2007, $14.99) r/#6-12						15.00

LOVE LESSONS
Harvey Comics/Key Publ. No. 5: Oct, 1949 - No. 5, June, 1950

1-Metallic silver-c printed over the cancelled covers of Love Letters #1; indicia title is "Love Letters"	15	30	45	85	130	175
2-Powell-a; photo-c	9	18	27	52	69	85
3-5: 3,4-Photo-c	8	16	24	42	54	65

LOVE LETTERS (10/49, Harvey; advertised but never published; covers were printed before cancellation and were used as the cover to Love Lessions #1)

LOVE LETTERS (Love Secrets No. 32 on)
Quality Comics: 11/49 - #6, 9/50; #7, 3/51 - #31, 6/53; #32, 2/54 - #51, 12/56

1-Ward-c, Gustavson-a	25	50	75	145	228	310
2-Ward-c, Gustavson-a	20	40	60	115	180	245
3-Gustavson-a	14	28	42	82	121	160
4-Ward-a, 9 pgs.; photo-c	18	36	54	107	169	230
5-8,10	10	20	30	54	72	90
9-One pg. Ward "Be Popular with the Opposite Sex"; Robert Mitchum photo-c	11	22	33	60	83	105
11-Ward-r/Broadway Romances #2 & retitled	11	22	33	60	83	105
12-15,18-20	9	18	27	47	61	75
16,17-Ward-a; 16-Anthony Quinn photo-c. 17-Jane Russell photo-c	14	28	42	80	115	150
21-29	8	16	24	44	57	70
30,31(6/53)-Ward-a	10	20	30	54	72	90
32(2/54)-39: 37-Ward-a. 38-Crandall-a. 39-Last precode (4/55)	8	16	24	40	50	60
40-48	7	14	21	37	46	55
49,50-Baker-a	11	22	33	62	86	110
51-Baker-c	10	20	30	58	79	100

NOTE: Photo-c on most 3-28.

LOVE LIFE
P. L. Publishing Co.: Nov, 1951

1	10	20	30	56	76	95

LOVELORN (Confessions of the Lovelorn #52 on)
American Comics Group (Michel Publ./Regis Publ.): Aug-Sept, 1949 - No. 51, July, 1954 (No. 1-26: 52 pgs.)

1	15	30	45	90	140	190
2	10	20	30	56	76	95
3-10	9	18	27	47	61	75
11-20,22-48: 18-Drucker-a(2 pgs.). 46-Lazarus-a	8	16	24	40	50	60
21-Prostitution story	9	18	27	50	65	80
49-51-Has 3-D effect-c/stories	15	30	45	90	140	190

LOVE MEMORIES
Fawcett Publications: 1949 (no month) - No. 4, July, 1950 (All photo-c)

1	15	30	45	88	137	185
2-4: 2-(Win/49-50)	10	20	30	56	76	95

LOVE ME TENDERLOIN: A CAL McDONALD MYSTERY
Dark Horse Comics: Jan, 2004 ($2.99, one-shot)

1-Niles-s/Templesmith-a/c						3.00

LOVE MYSTERY
Fawcett Publications: June, 1950 - No. 3, Oct, 1950 (All photo-c)

1-George Evans-a	22	44	66	128	202	275
2,3-Evans-a. 3-Powell-a	16	32	48	92	144	195

LOVE PROBLEMS (See Fox Giants)

LOVE PROBLEMS AND ADVICE ILLUSTRATED (see True Love...)

LOVE ROMANCES (Formerly Ideal #5)
Timely/Marvel/Atlas(TCI No. 7-71/Male No. 72-106): No. 6, May, 1949 - No. 106, July, 1963

6-Photo-c	16	32	48	94	147	200
7-Photo-c; Kamen-a	11	22	33	62	86	110
8-Kubert-a; photo-c	11	22	33	62	86	110
9-20: 9-12-Photo-c	10	20	30	56	76	95
21,24-Krigstein-a	10	20	30	58	79	100
22,23,25-35,37,39,40	10	20	30	54	72	90
36,38-Krigstein-a	10	20	30	56	76	95
41-44,46,47: Last precode (2/55)	9	18	27	52	69	85
45,57-Matt Baker-a	11	22	33	60	83	105
48,50-52,54-56,58-74	5	10	15	32	51	70
49,53-Toth-a, 6 & ? pgs.	6	12	18	37	59	80
75,77,82-Matt Baker-a	6	12	18	43	69	95
76,78-81,86,88-90,92-95: 80-Heath-a. 95-Last 10¢-c?	5	10	15	30	48	65
83,84,87,91-Kirby-a. 83-Severin-a	6	12	18	41	66	90
85,96,97,99-106-Kirby-c/a. 97-10¢ cover price blacked out, 12¢ printed on cover	7	14	21	49	80	110
98-Kirby-c/a	7	14	21	50	83	115

NOTE: Anne Brewster a-67, 72. Colletta a-37, 40, 42, 44, 67(2); c-42, 44, 49, 54, 80. Everett c-70. Hartley c-20, 21, 30, 31. Heath a-87. Robinson a-29.

LOVERS (Formerly Blonde Phantom)
Marvel Comics No. 23,24/Atlas No. 25 on (ANC): No. 23, May, 1949 - No. 86, Aug?, 1957

23-Photo-c begin, end #29	17	34	51	98	154	210
24-Toth-ish plus Robinson-a	11	22	33	60	83	105
25,30-Kubert-a; 7, 10 pgs.	11	22	33	62	86	110
26-29,31-36,39,40: 35-Maneely-a	10	20	30	54	72	90
37,38-Krigstein-a	11	22	33	60	83	105
41-Everett-a(2)	11	22	33	60	83	105
42,44-65: 65-Last pre-code (1/55)	8	16	24	44	57	70
43-Frazetta 1 pg. ad	9	18	27	47	61	75
66,68-80,82-86	8	16	24	42	54	65
67-Toth-a	9	18	27	47	61	75
81-Baker-a	9	18	27	47	61	75

NOTE: Anne Brewster a-86. Colletta a-54, 59, 62, 64, 65, 69, 85; c-61, 64, 65, 75. Hartley c-37, 53, 54. Heath a-61. Maneely a-57. Powell a-27, 30. Robinson a-42, 54, 56.

LOVERS' LANE
Lev Gleason Publications: Oct, 1949 - No. 41, June, 1954 (No. 1-18: 52 pgs.)

1-Biro-c	14	28	42	80	115	150
2-Biro-c	9	18	27	50	65	80
3-20: 3,4-Painted-c. 20-Frazetta 1 pg. ad	8	16	24	44	57	70
21-38,40,41	7	14	21	37	46	55
39-Story narrated by Frank Sinatra	8	16	24	47	61	80

NOTE: Briefer a-6, 13, 21. Esposito a-5. Fuje a-4, 16; c-many. Guardineer a-1, 3. Kinstler c-41. Sparling a-3. Tuska a-6. Painted c-3-18. Photo c-19-22, 26-28.

LOVE SCANDALS
Quality Comics: Feb, 1950 - No. 5, Oct, 1950 (Photo-c #2-5) (All 52 pgs.)

1-Ward-c/a, 9 pgs.	26	52	78	152	239	325
2,3: 2-Gustavson-a	13	26	39	72	101	130
4-Ward-a, 18 pgs; Gil Fox-a	20	40	60	117	184	250
5-C. Cuidera-a; tomboy story "I Hated Being a Woman"	13	26	39	72	101	130

LOVE SECRETS
Marvel Comics(IPC): Oct, 1949 - No. 2, Jan, 1950 (52 pgs., photo-c)

1	15	30	45	90	140	190
2	11	22	33	62	86	110

LOVE SECRETS (Formerly Love Letters #31)
Quality Comics Group: No. 32, Aug, 1953 - No. 56, Dec, 1956

32	12	24	36	67	94	120
33,35-39	8	16	24	44	57	70
34-Ward-a	12	24	36	67	94	120
40-Matt Baker-c	10	20	30	58	79	100
41-43: 43-Last precode (3/55)	8	16	24	44	57	70
44,47-50,53,54	7	14	21	37	46	55
45-Ward-a	10	20	30	54	72	90
46-Ward-a; Baker-a	10	20	30	58	79	100
51,52-Ward(r). 52-r/Love Confessions #17	8	16	24	44	57	70
55,56: 55-Baker-a. 56-Baker-c	9	18	27	52	69	85

LOVE STORIES (See Top Love Stories)

Love Stories of Mary Worth #3 © HARV

Lucifer #11 © DC

The Lucy Show #2 © Desilu

	GD 2.0	VG 4.0	FN 6.0	VF 8.0	VF/NM 9.0	NM- 9.2

LOVE STORIES (Formerly Heart Throbs)
National Periodical Publ.: No. 147, Nov, 1972 - No. 152, Oct-Nov, 1973

| 147-152 | 2 | 4 | 6 | 13 | 18 | 22 |

LOVE STORIES OF MARY WORTH (See Harvey Comics Hits #55 & Mary Worth)
Harvey Publications: Sept, 1949 - No. 5, May, 1950

| 1-1940's newspaper reprints-#1-4 | 9 | 18 | 27 | 47 | 61 | 75 |
| 2-5: 3-Kamen/Baker-a? | 6 | 12 | 18 | 31 | 38 | 45 |

LOVE TALES (Formerly The Human Torch #35)
Marvel/Atlas Comics (ZPC No. 36-50/MMC No. 67-75): No. 36, 5/49 - No. 58, 8/52; No. 59, date? - No. 75, Sept, 1957

36-Photo-c	16	32	48	94	147	200
37	10	20	30	56	79	100
38-44,46-50: 39-41-Photo-c	10	20	30	54	72	90
45,51,52,69: 45-Powell-a. 51,69-Everett-a. 52-Krigstein-a	10	20	30	56	76	95
53-60: 60-Last pre-code (2/55)	8	16	24	44	57	70
61-68,70-75: 75-Brewster, Cameron, Colletta-a	8	16	24	42	54	65

LOVE THRILLS (See Fox Giants)

LOVE TRAILS (Western romance)
A Lover's Magazine (CDS)(Marvel): Dec, 1949 - No. 2, Mar, 1950 (52 pgs.)

| 1,2: 1-Photo-c | 15 | 30 | 45 | 85 | 130 | 175 |

LOWELL THOMAS' HIGH ADVENTURE (See High Adventure)

LT. (See Lieutenant)

LUCIFER (See The Sandman #4)
DC Comics (Vertigo): Jun, 2000 - No. 75, Aug, 2006 ($2.50/$2.75)

1-Carey-s/Weston-a/Fegredo-c						8.00
2,3-Carey-s/Weston-a/Fegredo-c						5.00
4-10: 4-Pleece-a. 5-Gross-a						4.00
11-49,51-73: 16-Moeller-a begin. 25,26-Death app. 45-Naifeh-a. 53-Kaluta-a begin. 62-Doran-a. 63-Begin $2.75-c						2.75
50-($3.50) P. Craig Russell-a; Mazikeen app.						3.50
74-($3.99) Kaluta-a						3.00
75-($3.99) Last issue; Lucifer's origins retold; Morpheus app.; Gross-a/Moeller-c						4.00
Preview-16 pg. flip book w/Swamp Thing Preview						3.00
...: A Dalliance With the Damned TPB ('02, $14.95) r/#14-20						15.00
...: Children and Monsters TPB ('01, $17.95) r/#5-13						18.00
...: Crux TPB (2006, $14.99) r/#55-61						15.00
...: Devil in the Gateway TPB ('01, $14.95) r/#1-4 & Sandman Presents:..#1-3						15.00
...: Evensong TPB (2007, $14.99) r/#70-75 & Lucifer: Nirvana one-shot						15.00
...: Exodus TPB (2005, $14.95) r/#42-44,46-49						15.00
...: Inferno TPB (2003, $14.95) r/#29-35						15.00
...: Mansions of the Silence TPB (2004, $14.95) r/#36-41						15.00
...: Morningstar TPB (2006, $14.99) r/#62-69						15.00
...: Nirvana (2002, $5.95) Carey-s/Muth-painted-c/a; Daniel app.						6.00
...: The Divine Comedy TPB (2003, $17.95) r/#21-28						18.00
...: The Wolf Beneath the Tree TPB (2005, $14.99) r/#45,50-54						15.00

LUCIFER'S HAMMER (Larry Niven & Jerry Pournelle's...)
Innovation Publishing: Nov, 1993 - No. 6, 1994 ($2.50, painted, limited series)

| 1-6: Adaptatin of novel, painted-c & art | | | | | | 2.50 |

LUCKY COMICS
Consolidated Magazines: Jan, 1944; No. 2, Sum, 1945 - No. 5, Sum, 1946

| 1-Lucky Starr & Bobbie begin | 22 | 44 | 66 | 126 | 198 | 270 |
| 2-5: 5-Devil-c by Walter Johnson | 14 | 28 | 42 | 76 | 108 | 140 |

LUCKY DUCK
Standard Comics (Literary Ent.): No. 5, Jan, 1953 - No. 8, Sept, 1953

| 5-Funny animal; Irving Spector-a | 11 | 22 | 33 | 60 | 83 | 105 |
| 6-8-Irving Spector-a | 10 | 20 | 30 | 54 | 72 | 90 |

NOTE: *Harvey Kurtzman tried to hire Spector for Mad #1.*

LUCKY "7" COMICS
Howard Publishers Ltd.: 1944 (No date listed)

| 1-Pioneer, Sir Gallagher, Dick Royce, Congo Raider, Punch Powers; bondage-c | 40 | 80 | 120 | 235 | 368 | 500 |

LUCKY STAR (Western)
Nation Wide Publ. Co.: 1950 - No. 7, 1951; No. 8, 1953 - No. 14, 1955 (5x7-1/4"; full color, 5¢)

nn (#1)-(5¢, 52 pgs.)-Davis-a	17	34	51	98	154	210
2,3-(5¢, 52 pgs.)-Davis-a	11	22	33	64	90	115
4-7-(5¢, 52 pgs.)-Davis-a	10	20	30	58	79	100

| 8-14-(36 pgs.)(Exist?) | 9 | 18 | 27 | 47 | 61 | 75 |

Given away with Lucky Star Western Wear by the Juvenile Mfg. Co.

| | 7 | 14 | 21 | 35 | 43 | 50 |

LUCY SHOW, THE (TV) (Also see I Love Lucy)
Gold Key: June, 1963 - No. 5, June, 1964 (Photo-c: 1,2)

1	12	24	36	87	156	225
2	7	14	21	49	80	110
3-5: Photo back c-1,2,4,5	6	12	18	43	69	95

LUCY, THE REAL GONE GAL (Meet Miss Pepper #5 on)
St. John Publishing Co.: June, 1953 - No. 4, Dec, 1953

1-Negligee panels	14	28	42	82	121	160
2	9	18	27	50	65	80
3,4: 3-Drucker-a	8	16	24	44	57	70

LUDWIG BEMELMAN'S MADELEINE & GENEVIEVE
Dell Publishing Co.: No. 796, May, 1957

| Four Color 796 | 4 | 8 | 12 | 24 | 37 | 50 |

LUDWIG VON DRAKE (TV)(Disney)(See Walt Disney's C&S #256)
Dell Publishing Co.: Nov-Dec, 1961 - No. 4, June-Aug, 1962

| 1 | 7 | 14 | 21 | 45 | 73 | 100 |
| 2-4 | 5 | 10 | 15 | 32 | 51 | 70 |

LUFTWAFFE: 1946 (Volume 1)
Antarctic Press: July, 1996 - No. 4, Jan, 1997 ($2.95, B&W, limited series)

| 1-4-Ben Dunn & Ted Nomura-s/a, ...Special Ed. | | | | | | 3.00 |

LUFTWAFFE: 1946 (Volume 2)
Antarctic Press: Mar, 1997 - No. 18 ($2.95/$2.99, B&W, limited series)

1-18: 8-Reviews Tigers of Terra series						3.00
Annual 1 (4/98, $2.95)-Reprints early Nomura pages						3.00
...Color Special (4/98)						3.00
...Technical Manual 1,2 (2/98, 4/99)						4.00

LUGER
Eclipse Comics: Oct, 1986 - No. 3, Feb, 1987 ($1.75, miniseries, Baxter paper)

| 1-3: Bruce Jones scripts; Yeates-c/a | | | | | | 2.50 |

LUKE CAGE (See Cage & Hero for Hire)

LUKE SHORT'S WESTERN STORIES
Dell Publishing Co.: No. 580, Aug, 1954 - No. 927, Aug, 1958

| Four Color 580(8/54), 651(9/55)-Kinstler-a | 4 | 8 | 12 | 28 | 44 | 60 |
| Four Color 739,771,807,848,875,927 | 4 | 8 | 12 | 26 | 41 | 55 |

LUNATIC FRINGE, THE
Innovation Publishing: July, 1989 - No. 2, 1989 ($1.75, deluxe format)

| 1,2 | | | | | | 2.50 |

LUNATICKLE (Magazine) (Satire)
Whitstone Publ.: Feb, 1956 - No. 2, Apr, 1956

| 1,2-Kubert-a (scarce) | 8 | 16 | 24 | 40 | 50 | 60 |

LUNATIK
Marvel Comics: Dec, 1995 - No. 3, Feb, 1996 ($1.95, limited series)

| 1-3 | | | | | | 2.50 |

LURKERS, THE
IDW Publ.: Oct, 2004 - No. 4, Jan, 2005 ($3.99)

| 1-4-Niles-s/Casanova-a | | | | | | 4.00 |

LUST FOR LIFE
Slave Labor Graphics: Feb, 1997 - No. 4, Jan, 1998 ($2.95, B&W)

| 1-4: 1-Jeff Levin-s/a | | | | | | 3.00 |

LYCANTHROPE LEO
Viz Communications: 1994 - No. 7($2.95, B&W, limited series, 44 pgs.)

| 1-7 | | | | | | 3.00 |

LYNCH (See Gen [13])
Image Comics (WildStorm Productions): May, 1997 ($2.50, one-shot)

| 1-Helmut-c/app. | | | | | | 2.50 |

LYNCH MOB
Chaos! Comics: June, 1994 - No. 4, Sept, 1994 ($2.50, limited series)

| 1-4 | | | | | | 2.50 |
| 1-Special edition full foil-c | | | | | | 5.00 |

LYNDON B. JOHNSON

Machine Man #1 © MAR

Mad #15 © EC

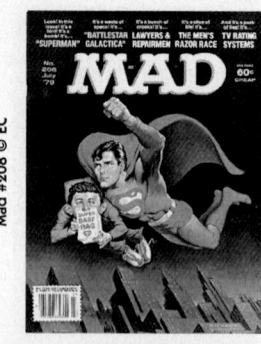

Mad #208 © EC

	GD 2.0	VG 4.0	FN 6.0	VF 8.0	VF/NM 9.0	NM- 9.2

Dell Publishing Co.: Mar, 1965

12-445-503-Photo-c	3	6	9	20	30	40

M
Eclipse Books: 1990 - No. 4, 1991 ($4.95, painted, 52 pgs.)

1-Adapts movie; contains flexi-disc ($5.95)						6.00
2-4						5.00

MACE GRIFFIN BOUNTY HUNTER (Based on video game)
Image Comics (Top Cow): May, 2003 ($2.99, one-shot)

1-Nocon-a						3.00

MACHINE, THE
Dark Horse Comics: Nov, 1994 - No. 4, Feb, 1995 ($2.50, limited series)

1-4						2.50

MACHINE MAN (Also see 2001, A Space Odyssey)
Marvel Comics Group: Apr, 1978 - No. 9, Dec, 1978; No. 10, Aug, 1979 - No. 19, Feb, 1981

1-Jack Kirby-c/a/scripts begin; end #9	2	4	6	9	13	16
2-9-Kirby-c/a/s. 9-(12/78)	1	2	3	5	6	8
10-17: 10-(8/79) Marv Wolfman scripts and Ditko-a begins						5.00
18-Wendigo, Alpha Flight-ties into X-Men #140	2	4	6	11	16	20
19-Intro/1st app. Jack O'Lantern (Macendale), later becomes 2nd Hobgoblin	2	4	6	9	13	16

NOTE: **Austin** c-7i, 19i. **Buckler** c-17p, 18p. **Byrne** c-14p. **Ditko** a-10-19; c-10-13, 14i, 15, 16. **Kirby** a-1-9p; c-1-5, 7-9p. **Layton** c-7i. **Miller** c-19p. **Simonson** c-6.

MACHINE MAN (Also see X-51)
Marvel Comics Group: Oct, 1984 - No. 4, Jan, 1985 (limited series)

1-4-Barry Smith-c/a(i) & colors in all						4.00
TPB (1988, $6.95) r/ #1-4; Barry Smith-c						7.00
.../Bastion '98 Annual ($2.99) wraparound-c						3.00

MACHINE MAN 2020
Marvel Comics: Aug, 1994 - Nov, 1994 ($2.00, 52 pgs., limited series)

1-4: Reprints Machine Man limited series; Barry Windsor-Smith-c/i(r)						2.50

MACHINE TEEN
Marvel Comics: July, 2005 - No. 5, Nov, 2005 ($2.99, limited series)

1-5-Sumerak-s/Hawthorne-a. 1-James Jean-c						3.00
...: History (2005, $7.99, digest) r/#1-5						7.99

MACK BOLAN: THE EXECUTIONER (Don Pendleton's...)
Innovation Publishing: July, 1993 ($2.50)

1-3-($2.50)						2.50
1-($3.95)-Indestructible Cover Edition						4.00
1-($2.95)-Collector's Gold Edition; foil stamped						3.00
1-($3.50)-Double Cover Edition; red foil outer-c						3.50

MACKENZIE'S RAIDERS (Movie, TV)
Dell Publishing Co.: No. 1093, Apr-June, 1960

Four Color 1093-Richard Carlson photo-c from TV show						
	6	12	18	43	69	95

MACROSS (Becomes Robotech: The Macross Saga #2 on)
Comico: Dec, 1984 ($1.50)(Low print run)

1-Early manga app.	3	6	9	14	20	25

MACROSS II
Viz Select Comics: 1992 - No. 10, 1993 ($2.75, B&W, limited series)

1-10: Based on video series						2.75

MAD (Tales Calculated to Drive You...)
E. C. Comics (Educational Comics): Oct-Nov, 1952 - Present (No. 24-on are magazine format) (Kurtzman editor No. 1-28, Feldstein No. 29 - No. ?)

1-Wood, Davis, Elder start as regulars	412	824	1236	3296	5148	7000
2-Dick Tracy cameo	109	218	327	872	1361	1850
3,4: 3-Stan Lee mentioned. 4-Reefer mention story "Flob Was a Slob" by Davis; Superman parody	75	150	225	600	938	1275
5-Low distr.; W.M. Gaines biog.	153	306	459	1224	1912	2600
6-11: 6-Popeye cameo. 7,8- "Hey Look" reprints by Kurtzman. 11-Wolverton-a; Davis story was-r/Crime Suspenstories #12 w/new Kurtzman dialogue	59	118	177	472	736	1000
12-15: 15,18-Pot Shot Pete-r by Kurtzman	47	94	141	376	588	800
16-23(5/55): 18-Alice in Wonderland by Jack Davis. 21-1st app. Alfred E. Neuman on-c in fake ad. 22-All by Elder plus photo-montages by Kurtzman.						
23-Special cancel announcement	40	80	120	320	503	685
24(7/55)-1st magazine issue (25¢); Kurtzman logo & border on-c; 1st "What? Me Worry?"						

	GD 2.0	VG 4.0	FN 6.0	VF 8.0	VF/NM 9.0	NM- 9.2
on-c; 2nd printing exists	94	188	282	752	1176	1600
25-Jaffee starts as regular writer	44	88	132	352	551	750
26,27: 27-Jaffee starts as story artist; new logo	39	78	117	312	489	665
28-Last issue edited by Kurtzman; (three cover variations exist with different wording on contents banner on lower right of cover; value of each the same)	37	74	111	231	353	475
29-Kamen-a; Don Martin starts as regular; Feldstein editing begins	37	74	111	231	353	475
30-1st A. E. Neuman cover by Mingo; last Elder-a; Bob Clarke starts as regular; Disneyland & Elvis Presley spoof	56	112	168	350	538	725
31-Freas starts as regular; last Davis-a until #99	33	66	99	206	316	425
32,33: 32-Orlando, Drucker, Woodbridge start as regulars; Wood back-c. 33-Orlando back-c	28	56	84	175	268	360
34-Berg starts as regular	22	44	66	138	214	290
35-Mingo wraparound-c; Crandall-a	22	44	66	138	214	290
36-40 (7/58): 39-Beall-c	17	34	51	106	161	215
41-50: 42-Danny Kaye-s. 44-Xmas-c. 47-49-Sid Caesar-s. 48-Uncle Sam-c. 50 (10/59)-Peter Gunn-s	14	28	42	88	137	185
51-59: 52-Xmas-c; 77 Sunset Strip. 53-Rifleman-s. 54-Jaffee-s begins. 55-Sid Caesar-s. 59-Strips of Superman, Flash Gordon, Donald Duck & others. 59-Halloween/Headless Horseman-c	12	24	36	75	113	150
60 (1/61)-JFK/Nixon flic-c; 1st Spy vs. Spy by Prohias, who starts as regular	14	28	42	88	132	175
61-70: 64-Rickard starts as regular. 65-JFK-s. 66-JFK-c. 68-Xmas-c by Martin. 70-Route 66-s	9	18	27	56	83	110
71-75,77,80 (7/63): 72-10th Anniv. special; 1/3 pg. strips of Superman, Tarzan & others. 73-Bonanza-s. 74-Dr. Kildare-s	5	10	15	35	55	75
76-Aragonés starts in all	6	12	18	39	62	85
81-85: 81-Superman strip. 82-Castro-c. 85-Lincoln-c	5	10	15	30	48	65
86-1st Fold-in; commonly creased back covers makes these and later issues scarcer in NM	6	12	18	37	59	80
87,88	5	10	15	35	55	75
89,90: 89-One strip by Walt Kelly; Frankenstein-c; Fugitive-s. 90-Ringo back-c by Frazetta; Beatles app.	6	12	18	37	59	80
91,94,96,100: 94-King Kong-c. 96-Man From U.N.C.L.E. 100-(1/66)-Anniversary issue	5	10	15	30	48	65
92,93,95,97-99: 99-Davis-a resumes	4	8	12	28	44	60
101,104,106,108,114,115,119,121: 101-Infinity-c; Voyage to the Bottom of the Sea-s. 104-Lost in Space-s. 106-Tarzan back-c by Frazetta; 2 pg. Batman by Aragonés. 108-Hogan's Heroes by Davis. 114-Rat Patrol-s. 115-Star Trek. 119-Invaders (TV). 121-Beatles-c; Ringo pin-up; flic-c of Sik-Teen; Flying Nun-s	3	6	9	21	32	42
102,103,107,109-113,116-118,120(7/68): 118-Beatles cameo	3	6	9	19	29	38
105-Batman-c/s, TV show parody (9/66)	4	8	12	24	37	50
122,124,126,128,129,131-134,136,137,139,140: 122-Ronald Reagan photo inside; Drucker & Mingo-c. 126-Family Affair-s. 128-Last Orlando. 131-Reagan photo back-c. 132-Xmas-c. 133-John Wayne/True Grit. 136-Room 222	3	6	9	16	23	30
123-Four different covers	3	6	9	16	23	30
125,127,130,135,138: 125-2001 Space Odyssey; Hitler back-c. 127-Mod Squad-s. 130-Land of the Giants-s. 135-Easy Rider-c by Davis. 138-Snoopy-s; MASH-s	3	6	9	17	25	32
141-149,151-156,158-165,167-170: 141-Hawaii Five-0. 147-All in the Family-s. 153-Dirty Harry-s. 156-Columbo-s. 159-Clockwork Orange-c/s. 161-Tarzan-s. 164-Kung Fu (TV)-s. 165-James Bond-s; Dean Martin-c. 169-Drucker-c; McCloud-s. 170-Exorcist-s	3	6	9	14	19	24
150-(4/72) Partridge Family-s	3	6	9	15	21	26
157-(3/73) Planet of the Apes-c/s	3	6	9	16	23	30
166-(4/74) Classic finger-c	3	6	9	16	23	30
171-185,187,189-192,194,195,198,199: 172-Six Million Dollar Man-s; Hitler back-c. 178-Godfather II-c/s. 180-Jaws-c/s (1/76). 182-Bob Jones starts as regular.185-Starsky & Hutch-s. 187-Fonz/Happy Days-c/s; Harry North starts as regular. 189-Travolta/Kotter-c/s. 190-John Wayne-c/s. 192-King Kong-c/s. 194-Rocky-c/s; Laverne & Shirley-s. 199-James Bond-s	3	6	9	14	19	24
186,188,197,200: 186-Star Trek-c/s. 188-Six Million Dollar Man/ Bionic Woman. 197-Spock-s; Star Wars-s. 200-Close Encounters	2	4	6	13	18	22
193,196: 193-Farrah/Charlie's Angels-c/s. 196-Star Wars-c/s	2	4	6	13	18	22
201,203,205,220: 201-Sat. Night Fever-c/s. 203-Star Wars. 205-Travolta/Grease. 220-Yoda-c/s; Empire Strikes Back-s	3	6	9	13	16	
202,204,206,207,209,211-219,221-227,229,230: 204-Hulk TV show. 206-Tarzan. 208-Superman movie. 209-Mork & Mindy. 212-Spider-Man-s; Alien (movie)-s. 213-James Bond, Dracula, Rocky II-s 216-Star Trek. 219-Martin-c. 221-Shining-s. 223-Dallas-c/s. 225-Popeye. 226-Superman II. 229-James Bond. 230-Star Wars	1	3	4	6	8	10

Mad #283 © EC

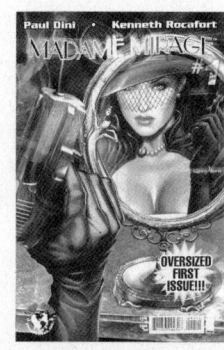

Madame Mirage #1 © Dini & TCOW

Madman Atomic Comics #1 © Mike Allred

	GD 2.0	VG 4.0	FN 6.0	VF 8.0	VF/NM 9.0	NM- 9.2

208,228: 208-Superman movie-c/s; Battlestar Galactica-s. 228-Raiders of the Lost Ark-c/s
 2 4 6 9 12 15

210-Lord of the Rings
 2 4 6 9 13 16

231-235,237-241,243-249,251-260: 233-Pac-Man-c. 234-MASH-c/s. 235-Flip-c with Rocky III & Conan; Boris-a. 239-Mickey Mouse-c. 241-Knight Rider-a. 243-Superman III. 245- Last Rickard-a. 247-Seven Dwarfs-c. 253-Supergirl movie-s; Prince/Purple Rain-s. 254-Rock stars-s. 255-Reagan-c; Cosby-s. 256-Last issue edited by Feldstein; Dynasty, Bev. Hills Cop. 259-Rambo. 260-Back to the Future-c/s; Honeymooners-s
 1 2 3 5 6 8

236,242,250: 236-E.T.-c/s;Star Trek II-s. 242-Star Wars/A-Team-c/s. 250-Temple of Doom-c/s; Tarzan-s
 1 2 3 5 7 9

261-267,269-276,278-288,290-297: 261-Miami Vice. 262-Rocky IV-c/s, Leave It To Beaver-s. 263-Young Sherlock Holmes-s. 264-Hulk Hogan-c; Rambo-s. 267-Top Gun. 271-Star Trek IV-c/s. 272-ALF-c; Get Smart-s. 273-Pee Wee Herman-c/s. 274-Last Martin-a. 281-California Raisins-c. 282-Star Trek:TNG-s; ALF-s. 283-Rambo III-c/s. 284-Roger Rabbit-s. 285-Hulk Hogan-c. 287-3 pgs. Eisner-a. 291-TMNT-c; Indiana Jones-s. 292-Super Mario Bros.-c; Married with Children-s. 295-Back to the Future II. 297-Mike Tyson-c
 1 2 3 4 5 7

268,277,289,298-300: 268-Aliens-c/s. 277-Michael Jackson-c/s. 289-Batman movie parody. 298-Gremlins II-c/s; Robocop II. Batman-s. 299-Simpsons-c/story; Total Recall-s. 300(1/91) Casablanca-s, Dick Tracy-s, Wizard of Oz-s, Gone With The Wind-s
 1 2 3 5 6 8

300-303 (1/91-6/91)-Special Hussein Asylum Editions; only distributed to the troops in the Middle East (see Mad Super Spec.)
 2 4 6 13 18 22

301-304,310,312,313,315-320,322,324,326-334,337-349: 303-Home Alone-c/s. 305-Simpsons-s. 306-TMNT II movie. 308-Terminator II. 315-Tribute to William Gaines. 316-Photo-c. 319-Dracula-c/s. 320-Disney's Aladdin-s. 322-Batman Animated series-s. 327-Seinfeld-s; X-Men-s. 331-Flintstones-c/s. 332-O.J. Simpson-c/s; Simpsons app. in Lion King. 334-Frankenstein-c/s. 338-Judge Dredd-c by Frazetta. 341-Pocahontas-s. 345-Beatles app. (1 pg.) 347-Broken Arrow & Mission Impossible 5.00

311,314,321,323,325,335,336,350,354,358: 311-Addams Family-c/story, Home Improvement-s. 314-Batman Returns-c/story. 321-Star Trek DS9-c/s. 323-Jurassic Park-s. 325,336-Beavis & Butthead-s. 335-X-Files-s; Pulp Fiction-s; Interview with the Vampire-s. 336-Lois & Clark-s. 350-Polybagged w/CD Rom. 354-Star Wars; Beavis & Butthead-s. 358-X-Files-s 6.00

351-353,355-357,359-400 4.00
401-475 4.00
Mad About Super Heroes (2002, $9.95) r/super hero app.; Alex Ross-c 10.00

NOTE: *Aragones* a-210, 293. *Beall* c-39. *Davis* c-2, 27, 135, 139, 173, 178, 212, 213, 219, 246, 260, 296, 308. *Drucker* a-35-62; c-122, 169, 176, 225, 234, 264, 266, 274, 280, 285, 297, 299, 303, 314, 315, 321. *Elder* c-5, 259, 261, 268. *Elder/Kurtzman* a-258-274. *Jules Feiffer* a(r)-42. *Freas* c-40-59, 62-67, 69-70, 72, 74. *Heath* a-14, 27. *Jaffee* c-199, 217, 224, 258. *Kamen* a-29. *Krigstein* a-12, 17, 24, 26. *Kurtzman* a-1, 3, 4, 6-10, 13, 16, 18. *Martin* a-29-62; c-68, 165, 229. *Mingo* c-30-37, 61, 71, 75-80, 82-114, 117-124, 126, 129, 131, 133, 134, 136, 140, 143-148, 150-162, 164, 166-168, 171, 172, 174, 175, 177, 179, 181, 183, 185, 198, 206, 209, 211, 214, 218, 221, 222, 300. *John Severin* a-1-6, 9, 10. *Wolverton* c-11; a-11, 17, 29, 34. *Wood* a-1-21, 23-62; c-26, 28, 29. *Woodbridge* a-35-62. Issues 1-23 are 36 pgs.; 24-28 are 58 pgs.; 29 on are 52 pgs.

MAD (See Mad Follies, ...Special, More Trash from..., and The Worst from...)

MAD ABOUT MILLIE (Also see Millie the Model)
Marvel Comics Group: April, 1969 - No. 16, Nov, 1970
1-Giant issue 8 16 24 56 93 130
2,3 (Giants) 6 12 18 37 59 80
4-10 4 8 12 24 37 50
11-16: 16-r 4 8 12 22 34 45
Annual 1(11/71, 52 pgs.) 4 8 12 24 37 50

MADAME MIRAGE
Image Comics (Top Cow): June, 2007 - Present ($2.99)
1,2: 1-Paul Dini-s/Kenneth Rocafort-a; two covers by Horn and Rocafort 3.00
... First Look (5/07, 99¢) preview of series; Dini interview; cover gallery 2.25

MADAME XANADU
DC Comics: July, 1981 ($1.00, no ads, 36 pgs.)
1-Marshall Rogers-a(25 pgs.); Kaluta-c/a(2pgs.); pin-up 5.00

MADBALLS
Star Comics/Marvel Comics #9 on: Sept, 1986 - No. 3, Nov, 1986; No. 4, June, 1987 - No. 10, June, 1988
1-10: Based on toys. 9-Post-a 4.00

MAD DISCO
E.C. Comics: 1980 (one-shot, 36 pgs.)
1-Includes 30 minute flexi-disc of Mad disco music 2 4 6 11 16 20

MAD-DOG
Marvel Comics: May, 1993 - No. 6, Oct, 1993 ($1.25)
1-6-Flip book w/2nd story "created" by Bob Newhart's character from his TV show "Bob" set at a comic book company; actual s/a-Ty Templeton 2.50

MAD DOGS
Eclipse Comics: Feb, 1992 - No. 3, July, 1992 ($2.50, B&W, limited series)
1-3 2.50

MAD 84 (Mad Extra)
E.C. Comics: 1984 (84 pgs.)
1 1 3 4 6 8 10

MAD FOLLIES (Special)
E.C. Comics: 1963 - No. 7, 1969
nn(1963)-Paperback book covers 22 44 66 160 285 410
2(1964)-Calendar 17 34 51 122 216 310
3(1965)-Mischief Stickers 13 26 39 97 171 245
4(1966)-Mobile; Frazetta-r/back-c Mad #90 10 20 30 67 116 165
5,6: 5(1967)-Stencils. 6(1968)-Mischief Stickers 8 16 24 52 86 120
7(1969)-Nasty Cards 8 16 24 52 86 120
(If bonus is missing, issue is half price)
NOTE: *Clarke* c-4. *Frazetta* r-4, 6 (1 pg. ea.). *Mingo* c-1-3. *Orlando* a-5.

MAD HATTER, THE (Costumed Hero)
O. W. Comics Corp.: Jan-Feb, 1946 - No. 2, Sept-Oct, 1946
1-Freddy the Firefly begins; Giunta-c/a 76 152 228 475 788 1100
2-Has ad for E.C.'s Animal Fables #1 40 80 120 240 383 525

MADHOUSE
Ajax/Farrell Publ. (Excellent Publ./4-Star): 3-4/54 - No. 4, 9-10/54; 6/57 - No. 4, Dec?, 1957
1(1954) 31 62 93 178 282 385
2,3 16 32 48 94 147 200
4-Surrealistic-c 23 46 69 135 213 290
1(1957, 2nd series) 14 28 42 80 115 150
2-4 (#4 exist?) 10 20 30 54 72 90

MAD HOUSE (Formerly Madhouse Glads; ...Comics #104? on)
Red Circle Productions/Archie Publications: No. 95, 9/74 - No. 97, 1/75; No. 98, 8/75 - No. 130, 10/82
95,96-Horror stories through #97; Morrow-c 2 4 6 9 13 16
97-Intro. Henry Hobson; Morrow-a/c, Thorne-a 2 4 6 8 10 12
98,99,101-120-Satire/humor stories. 110-Sabrina app.,1pg.
 1 2 3 5 7 9
100 1 3 4 6 8 10
121-129 1 3 4 5 6 8
130 2 4 6 9 12 15
Annual 8(1970-71)-Formerly Madhouse Ma-ad Annual; Sabrina app. (6 pgs.) 4 8 12 22 34 45
Annual 9-12(1974-75): 11-Wood-a(r) 2 4 6 11 16 20
...Comics Digest 1('75-76) 2 4 6 10 14 18
2-8(8/82)(...Mag. #5 on)-Sabrina in many 2 4 6 8 11 14
NOTE: *B. Jones* a-96. *McWilliams* a-97. *Wildey* a-95, 96. See Archie Comics Digest #1, 13.

MADHOUSE GLADS (Formerly ...Ma-ad; Madhouse #95 on)
Archie Publ.: No. 73, May, 1970 - No. 94, Aug, 1974 (No. 78-92: 52 pgs.)
73-77,93,94: 74-1 pg. Sabrina 2 4 6 9 13 16
78-92 (52 pgs.) 2 4 6 11 16 20

MADHOUSE MA-AD (...Jokes #67-70; ...Freak-Out #71-74)
(Formerly Archie's Madhouse) (Becomes Madhouse Glads #73 on)
Archie Publications: No. 67, April, 1969 - No. 72, Jan, 1970
67-71: 70-1 pg. Sabrina 2 4 6 13 18 22
72-6 pgs. Sabrina 2 4 6 14 23 45
...Annual 7(1969-70)-Formerly Archie's Madhouse Annual; becomes Madhouse Annual; 6 pgs. Sabrina 4 8 12 22 34 45

MADMAN (See Creatures of the Id #1)
Tundra Publishing: Mar, 1992 - No. 3, 1992 ($3.95, duotone, high quality, lim. series, 52 pgs.)
1-Mike Allred-c/a in all 2 4 6 8 10 12
1-2nd printing 4.00
2,3 6.00

MADMAN ADVENTURES
Tundra Publishing: 1992 - No. 3, 1993 ($2.95, limited series)
1-Mike Allred-c/a in all 1 2 3 5 7 9
2,3 5.00
TPB (Oni Press, 2002, $14.95) r/#1-3 & first app. of Frank Einstein from Creatures of the Id in color; gallery pages 15.00

MADMAN ATOMIC COMICS (Also see The Atomics)
Image Comics: Apr, 2007 - Present ($2.99)
1-4-Mike Allred-s/c/a. 1-Origin re-told; pin-ups by Rivoche and Powell. 3-Sale back-c 3.00

Madman/The Jam #1 © Allred & Mireault

Mage #9 © Matt Wagner

Magic Comics #11 © DMP

	GD 2.0	VG 4.0	FN 6.0	VF 8.0	VF/NM 9.0	NM- 9.2

MADMAN COMICS (Also see The Atomics)
Dark Horse Comics (Legend No. 2 on): Apr, 1994 - No. 20, Dec, 2000 ($2.95/$2.99):

1-Allred-c/a; F. Miller back-c.	1	2	3	5	6	8
2-3: 3-Alex Toth back-c.						5.00
4-11: 4-Dave Stevens back-c. 6,7-Miller/Darrow's Big Guy app. 6-Bruce Timm back-c. 7-Darrow back-c. 8-Origin?; Bagge back-c. 10-Allred/Ross-c; Ross back-c.						
11-Frazetta back-c						4.00
12-16: 12-(4/99)						3.00
17-20: 17-The G-Men From Hell #1 on cover; Brereton back-c. 18-(#2). 19,20-($2.99-c). 20-Clowes back-c						3.00
... Boogaloo TPB (6/99, $8.95) r/Nexus Meets Madman & Madman/The Jam						9.00
... Gargantua! (2007, $125.00, HC with dustjacket) r/Madman#1-3, Madman Adventures #1-3, Madman Comics #1-20 and Madman King-Size Super Groovy Special; pin-ups						125.00
Ltd. Ed. Slipcover (1997, $99.95, signed and numbered) w/Vol.1 & Vol. 2. Vol.1- reprints #1-5; Vol. 2- reprints #6-10						100.00
The Complete Madman Comics: Vol. 2 (11/96, $17.95, TPB) r/#6-10 plus new material						18.00
Madman King-Size Super Groovy Special (Oni Press, 7/03, $6.95) new short stories by Allred, Derington, Krall and Weissman						7.00
Madman Picture Exhibition No. 1-4 (4-7/02, $3.95) pin-ups by various						4.00
Madman Picture Exhibition Limited Edition (10/02, $29.95) Hardcover collects MPE #1-4						30.00
Yearbook '95 (1996, $17.95, TPB)-r/#1-5, intro by Teller						18.00

MADMAN / THE JAM
Dark Horse Comics: Jul, 1998 - No. 2, Aug, 1998 ($2.95, mini-series)

1,2-Allred & Mireault-s/a						3.00

MAD MONSTER PARTY (See Movie Classics)

MADNESS IN MURDERWORLD
Marvel Comics: 1989 (Came with computer game from Paragon Software)

V1#1-Starring The X-Men						2.50

MADRAVEN HALLOWEEN SPECIAL
Hamilton Comics: Oct, 1995 ($2.95, one-shot)

nn-Morrow-a						3.00

MADROX (from X-Factor)
Marvel Comics (Marvel Knights): Nov, 2004 - No. 5, Mar, 2005 ($2.99)

1-5-Peter David-s/Pablo Raimondi-a; Strong Guy app.						3.00
...: Multiple Choice TPB (2005, $13.99) r/#1-5						14.00

MAD SPECIAL (...Super Special)
E. C. Publications, Inc.: Fall, 1970 - Present (84 - 116 pgs.)
(If bonus is missing, issue is one half price)

Fall 1970(#1)-Bonus-Voodoo Doll; contains 17 pgs. new material	10	20	30	68	119	170
Spring 1971(#2)-Wall Nuts; 17 pgs. new material	6	12	18	37	59	80
3-Protest Stickers	6	12	18	37	59	80
4-8: 4-Mini Posters. 5-Mad Flag. 6-Mad Mischief Stickers. 7-Presidential candidate posters, Wild Shocking Message posters. 8-TV Guise	5	10	15	32	51	70
9(1972)-Contains Nostalgic Mad #1 (28 pgs.)	4	8	12	26	41	55
10-13: 10-Nonsense Stickers (Don Martin). 13-Sickie Stickers; 3 pgs. Wolverton-r/Mad #137.						
11-Contains 33-1/3 RPM record. 12-Contains Nostalgic Mad #2 (36 pgs.); Davis, Wolverton-a	3	6	9	20	30	40
14,16-21,24: 4-Vital Message posters & Art Depreciation paintings. 16-Mad-hesive Stickers. 17-Don Martin posters. 20-Martin Stickers. 18-Contains Nostalgic Mad #4 (36 pgs.). 21,24-Contains Nostalgic Mad #5 (28 pgs.) & #6 (28 pgs.)	3	6	9	16	23	30
15-Contains Nostalgic Mad #3 (28 pgs.)	3	6	9	17	25	32
22,23,25,27-29,30: 22-Diplomas. 23-Martin Stickers. 25-Martin Posters. 27-Mad Shock-Sticks. 28-Contains Nostalgic Mad #7 (36 pgs.). 29-Mad Collectable-Connectables Posters.						
30-The Movies	2	4	6	9	13	16
26-Has 33-1/3 RPM record	2	4	6	13	18	22
31,33,35,37-50	2	4	6	9	11	14
32-Contains Nostalgic Mad #8. 36-Has 96 pgs. of comic book & comic strip spoofs: titles "The Comics" on-c	2	4	6	9	13	16
51-70	1	3	4	6	8	10
71-88,90-100: 71-Batman parodies-r by Wood, Drucker. 72-Wolverton-c r-from 1st panel in Mad #11; Wolverton-s r/new dialogue. 83-All Star Trek spoof issue	1	2	3	5	6	8
76-(Fall, 1991)-Special Hussein Asylum Edition; distributed only to the troops in the Middle East (see Mad #300-303)	2	4	6	13	18	22
89-($3.95)-Polybagged w/1st of 3 Spy v. Spy hologram trading cards (direct sale only issue) (other cards came w/card set)	1	3	4	6	8	10
101-135: 117-Sci-Fi parodies-r.						4.00

NOTE: #28-30 have no number on cover. Freas c-76. Mingo c-9, 11, 15, 19, 23.

MAGDALENA, THE (See The Darkness #15-18)
Image Comics (Top Cow): Apr, 2000 - No. 3, Jan, 2001 ($2.50)

Preview Special ('00, $4.95) Flip book w/Blood Legacy preview						5.00
1-Benitez-c/a; variant covers by Silvestri & Turner						2.50
2,3: 2-Two covers						2.50
...Angelus #1/2 (11/01, $2.95) Benitez-c/Ching-a						3.00
...Blood Divine (2002, $9.95) r/#1-3 & #1/2; cover gallery						10.00
...Vampirella (7/03, $2.99) Wohl-s/Benitez-a; two covers						3.00

MAGDALENA, THE (Volume 2)
Image Comics (Top Cow): Aug, 2003 - No. 4 ($2.99)

Preview (6/03) B&W preview; Wizard World East logo on cover						2.50
1-4-Holguin-s/Basaldua-a						3.00
1-Variant-c by Jim Silke benefitting ACTOR charity						5.00
TPB Volume 1 (12/06, $19.99) r/both series, Darkness #15-18 & Magdalena/Angelus						20.00
...Vampirella (12/04, $2.99) Kirkman-s/Manapul-a; two covers by Manapul and Bachalo						3.00
... Vs. Dracula Monster War 2005 (6/05, $2.99) four covers; Joyce Chin-a						3.00

MAGE (The Hero Discovered...; also see Grendel #16)
Comico: Feb, 1984 (no month) - No. 15, Dec, 1986 ($1.50, Mando paper)

1-Comico's 1st color comic	2	4	6	8	11	14
2-5: 3-Intro Edsel						6.00
6-Grendel begins (1st in color)	3	6	9	14	20	25
7-1st new Grendel story	2	4	6	8	10	12
8-14: 13-Grendel dies. 14-Grendel story ends						6.00
15-($2.95) Double size w/pullout poster	1	2	3	5	6	8
TPB Volume 1-4 (Image, $5.95) 1- r/#1,2. 2- r/#3,4. 3- r/#5,6. 4- r/#7,8						7.00
TPB Volume 5-7 (Image, $6.95) 5- r/#9,10. 6- r/#11,12. 7- r/#13,14						7.00
TPB Volume 8 (Image, 9/99, $7.50) r/#15						7.50
..., Vol. 1 TPB (Image, 2004, $29.99) r/#1-15; cover gallery, promo artwork, bonus art						30.00

MAGE (The Hero Defined) (Volume 2)
Image Comics: July, 1997 - No. 15, Oct, 1999 ($2.50)

0-(7/97, $5.00) American Ent. Ed.						5.00
1-14:Matt Wagner-c/s/a in all. 13-Three covers						2.50
1-"3-D Edition" (2/98, $4.95) w/glasses						5.00
15-($5.95) Acetate cover						6.00
Volume 1,2 TPB ('98,'99, $9.95) 1- r/#1-4. 2-r/#5-8						10.00
Volume 3 TPB ('00, $12.95) r/#9-12						13.00
Volume 4 TPB ('01, $14.95) r/#13-15						15.00
Hardcover Vol. 2 (2005, $49.95) r/#1-15; cover gallery, character design & sketch pages						50.00

MAGE KNIGHT: STOLEN DESTINY (Based on the fantasy game Mage Knight)
Idea + Design Works: Oct, 2002 - No. 5, Feb, 2003 ($3.50, limited series)

1-5: 1-J. Scott Campbell-c; Cabrera-a/Dezago-s, 2-Dave Johnson-c						3.50

MAGGIE AND HOPEY COLOR SPECIAL (See Love and Rockets)
Fantagraphics Books: May, 1997 ($3.50, one-shot)

1						3.50

MAGGIE THE CAT (Also see Jon Sable, Freelance #11 & Shaman's Tears #12)
Image Comics (Creative Fire Studio): Jan, 1996 - No. 2, Feb, 1996 ($2.50, unfinished limited series)

1,2: Mike Grell-c/a/scripts						2.50

MAGICA DE SPELL (See Walt Disney Showcase #30)

MAGIC AGENT (See Forbidden Worlds & Unknown Worlds)
American Comics Group: Jan-Feb, 1962 - No. 3, May-June, 1962

1-Origin & 1st app. John Force	4	8	12	24	37	50
2,3	3	6	9	18	27	35

MAGICAL POKÉMON JOURNEY
Viz Comics: 2000 - Present ($4.95, B&W, magazine-size)

1-4						5.00
Part 2: 1-3; Part 3: 1-4: 1-Includes color poster; Part 4: 1-4; Part 5: 1-4; Part 6: 1-4						5.00

MAGIC COMICS
David McKay Publications: Aug, 1939 - No. 123, Nov-Dec, 1949

1-Mandrake the Magician, Henry, Popeye , Blondie, Barney Baxter, Secret Agent X-9 (not by Raymond), Bunky by Billy DeBeck & Thornton Burgess text stories illustrated by Harrison Cady begin; Henry covers begin	347	694	1041	1943	2922	3900
2	124	248	372	694	1047	1400
3	91	182	273	510	768	1025
4	71	142	213	398	599	800
5	58	116	174	325	488	650
6-10: 8-11,21-Mandrake/Henry-c	47	94	141	263	394	525
11-16,18,20: 12-Mandrake-c begin	39	78	117	218	329	440

Magician: Apprentice #5 © Feist

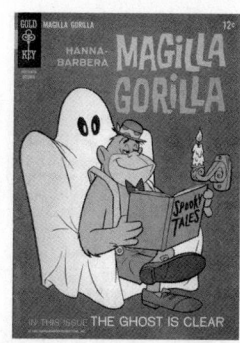

Magilla Gorilla #9 © H-B

Magnus, Robot Fighter #20 © GK

	GD	VG	FN	VF	VF/NM	NM-
	2.0	4.0	6.0	8.0	9.0	9.2

	GD 2.0	VG 4.0	FN 6.0	VF 8.0	VF/NM 9.0	NM- 9.2
17-The Lone Ranger begins	43	86	129	241	361	480
19-Classic robot-c	60	120	180	336	506	675
21-30: 25-Only Blondie-c. 26-Dagwood-c begin	26	52	78	150	235	320
31-40: 36-Flag-c	18	36	54	103	162	220
41-50	15	30	45	83	124	165
51-60	13	26	39	72	101	130
61-70	11	22	33	60	83	105
71-99, 107,108-Flash Gordon app; not by Raymond	9	18	27	52	69	85
100	10	20	30	56	76	95
101-106,109-123: 123-Last Dagwood-c	9	18	27	47	61	75

MAGIC FLUTE, THE (See Night Music #9-11)

MAGICIAN: APPRENTICE
Dabel Brothers/Marvel Comics (Dabel Brothers) #3 on: Mar, 2007 - No. 12 ($2.95/$2.99)

1-9-Adaptation of the Raymond E. Feist Riftwar Saga series		3.00
1,2-($5.95) 1-Wraparound variant-c by Maitz. 2-Wraparound variant-c by Booth		6.00
Collected Edition (10/06, $3.99) r/#1&2		4.00
Vol. 1 HC (2007, $19.99, dustjacket) r/#1-6; foreword by Feist		20.00

MAGIC PICKLE
Oni Press: Sept, 2001 - No. 4, Dec, 2001 ($2.95, limited series)

1-4-Scott Morse-s/a; Mahfood-a (2 pgs.)		3.00

MAGIC SWORD, THE (See Movie Classics)

MAGIC THE GATHERING (Title Series), Acclaim Comics (Armada)

...ANTIQUITIES WAR,11/95 - 2/96 ($2.50), 1-4-Paul Smith-a(p)		2.50
...ARABIAN NIGHTS, 12/95 - 1/96 ($2.50), 1,2		2.50
...COLLECTION ,'95 ($4.95), 1,2-polybagged		5.00
...CONVOCATIONS, '95 ($2.50), 1-nn-pin-ups		2.50
...ELDER DRAGONS, '95 ($2.50), 1,2-Doug Wheatley-a		2.50
...FALLEN ANGEL, '95 ($5.95), nn		6.00
...FALLEN EMPIRES ,9/95 - 10/95 ($2.75), 1,2		3.00
...Collection ($4.95)-polybagged		5.00
...HOMELANDS ,'95 ($5.95), nn-polybagged w/card; Hildebrandts-c		6.00
...ICE AGE (On The World of...) ,7/5 -11/95 ($2.50), 1-4: 1,2-bound-in Magic Card. 3,4-bound-in insert		2.50
...LEGEND OF JEDIT OJANEN, '96 ($2.50), 1,2		2.50
...NIGHTMARE, '95 ($2.50, one shot), 1		2.50
...THE SHADOW MAGE, 7/95 - 10/95 ($2.50), 1-4-bagged w/Magic The Gathering card		2.50
...Collection 1,2 (1995, $4.95)-Trade paperback; polybagged		5.00
...SHANDALAR ,'96 ($2.50), 1,2		2.50
...WAYFARER ,11/95 - 2/96 ($2.50), 1-5		2.50

MAGIC: THE GATHERING: GERRARD'S QUEST
Dark Horse Comics: Mar, 1998 - No. 4, June, 1998 ($2.95, limited series)

1-4- Grell-s/Mhan-a		3.00

MAGIK (Illyana and Storm Limited Series)
Marvel Comics Group: Dec, 1983 - No. 4, Mar, 1984 (60¢, limited series)

1-4: 1-Characters from X-Men; Inferno begins; X-Men cameo (Buscema pencils in #1,2; c-1p. 2-4: 2-Nightcrawler app. & X-Men cameo		3.00

MAGIK (See Black Sun mini-series)
Marvel Comics: Dec, 2000 - No. 4, Mar, 2001 ($2.99, limited series)

1-4-Liam Sharp-a/Abnett & Lanning-s; Nightcrawler app.		3.00

MAGILLA GORILLA (TV) (See Kite Fun Book)
Gold Key: May, 1964 - No. 10, Dec, 1968 (Hanna-Barbera)

	GD	VG	FN	VF	VF/NM	NM-
1-1st comic app.	9	18	27	63	107	150
2-4: 3-Vs. Yogi Bear for President. 4-1st Punkin Puss & Mushmouse, Ricochet Rabbit & Droop-a-Long	5	10	15	35	55	75
5-10: 10-Reprints	4	8	12	28	44	60

MAGILLA GORILLA (TV)(See Spotlight #4)
Charlton Comics: Nov, 1970 - No. 5, July, 1971 (Hanna-Barbera)

	GD	VG	FN	VF	VF/NM	NM-
1	5	10	15	32	51	70
2-5	3	6	9	20	30	40

MAGNETIC MEN FEATURING MAGNETO
Marvel Comics (Amalgam): June, 1997 ($1.95, one-shot)

1-Tom Peyer-s/Barry Kitson & Dan Panosian-a		2.50

MAGNETO (See X-Men #1)

Marvel Comics: nd (Sept, 1993) (Giveaway) (one-shot)

0-Embossed foil-c by Sienkiewicz; r/Classic X-Men #19 & 12 by Bolton		5.00

MAGNETO
Marvel Comics: Nov, 1996 - No. 4, Feb, 1997 ($1.95, limited series)

1-4: Peter Milligan scripts & Kelley Jones-a(p)		2.50

MAGNETO AND THE MAGNETIC MEN
Marvel Comics (Amalgam): Apr, 1996 ($1.95, one-shot)

1-Jeff Matsuda-a(p)		2.50

MAGNETO ASCENDANT
Marvel Comics: May, 1999 ($3.99, squarebound one-shot)

1-Reprints early Magneto appearances		4.00

MAGNETO: DARK SEDUCTION
Marvel Comics: Jun, 2000 - No. 4, Sept, 2000 ($2.99, limited series)

1-4: Nicieza-s/Cruz-a. 3,4-Avengers-c/app.		3.00

MAGNETO REX
Marvel Comics: Apr, 1999 - No. 3, July, 1999 ($2.50, limited series)

1-3-Rogue, Quicksilver app.; Peterson-a(p)		2.50

MAGNUS, ROBOT FIGHTER (...4000 A.D.)(See Doctor Solar)
Gold Key: Feb, 1963 - No. 46, Jan, 1977 (All painted covers except #5,30,31)

	GD	VG	FN	VF	VF/NM	NM-
1-Origin & 1st app. Magnus; Aliens (1st app.) series begins	22	44	66	164	292	420
2,3	10	20	30	70	123	175
4-10: 10-Simonson fan club illo (5/65, 1st-a?)	7	14	21	47	76	105
11-20	5	10	15	32	51	70
21,24-28: 28-Aliens ends	4	8	12	22	34	45
22,23: 22-Origin-r/#1; last 12¢ issue	4	8	12	23	36	48
29-46-Mostly reprints	2	4	6	11	16	20

Russ Manning's Magnus Robot Fighter - Vol. 1 HC (Dark Horse, 2004, $49.95) r/#1-7		50.00
Russ Manning's Magnus Robot Fighter - Vol. 2 HC (DH, 6/05, $49.95) r/#8-14; forward by Steve Rude		50.00
Russ Manning's Magnus Robot Fighter - Vol. 3 HC (Dark Horse, 10/06, $49.95) r/#15-21		50.00

NOTE: **Manning** a-1-22, 28-43(r). **Spiegle** a-23, 44r.

MAGNUS ROBOT FIGHTER (Also see Vintage Magnus)
Valiant/Acclaim Comics: May, 1991 - No. 64, Feb, 1996 ($1.75/$1.95/$2.25/$2.50)

	GD	VG	FN	VF	VF/NM	NM-
1-Nichols/Layton-c/a; 1-8 have trading cards	1	2	3	5	6	8
2-8: 4-Rai cameo. 5-Origin & 1st full app. Rai (10/91); 5-8 are in flip book format and back-c & half of book are Rai #1-4 mini-series. 6-1st Solar x-over. 7-Magnus vs. Rai-c/story; 1st X-O Armor						6.00
0-Origin issue; Layton-a; ordered through mail w/coupons from 1st 8 issues plus 50¢; B. Smith trading card	2	4	6	11	16	20
0-Sold thru comic shops without trading card	2	4	6	8	10	12
9-11						3.00
12-(3.25, 44 pgs.)-Turok-c/story (1st app. in Valiant universe, 5/92); has 8 pg. Magnus story insert	1	3	4	6	8	10
13-24,26-48: 14-1st app. Isak. 15,16-Unity x-overs. 15-Miller-c. 16-Birth of Magnus. 21-New direction & new logo. 21-Gold ink variant. 22-Story cont'd in Rai & the Future Force #9. 33-Timewalker app.36-Bound-in trading cards. 37-Rai & Starwatchers app. 44-Bound-in sneak peek card.						2.50
25-($2.95)-Embossed silver foil-c; new costume						3.00
49-63						3.00
64-($2.50): 64-Magnus dies?						4.00
...Invasion (1994, $9.95)-r/Rai #1-4 & Magnus #5-8						10.00
Magnus Steel Nation (1994, $9.95) r/#1-4						10.00
Yearbook (1994, $3.95, 52 pgs.)						4.00

NOTE: **Ditko/Reese** a-18. **Layton** a(i)-5; c-6-9i, 25; back(i)-5-8. **Reese** a(i)-22, 25, 28; c(i)-22, 24, 28. **Simonson** c-16. Prices for issues 1-8 are for trading cards and coupons intact.

MAGNUS ROBOT FIGHTER
Acclaim Comics (Valiant Heroes): V2#1, May, 1997 - No. 18, Jun, 1998 ($2.50)

1-18: 1-Reintro Magnus; Donavon Wylie (X-O Manowar) cameo; Tom Peyer scripts & Mike McKone-c/a begin; painted variant-c exists		2.50

MAGNUS ROBOT FIGHTER/NEXUS
Valiant/Dark Horse Comics: Dec, 1993 - No. 2, Apr, 1994 ($2.95, lim. series)

1,2: Steve Rude painted-c & pencils in all		3.00

MAID OF THE MIST (See American Graphics)

MAI, THE PSYCHIC GIRL
Eclipse Comics: May, 1987 - No. 28, July, 1989 ($1.50, B&W, bi-weekly, 44pgs.)

1-28, 1,2-2nd print		2.50

Major Victory Comics #1 © CHES

Man-Bat #3 © DC

Man Comics #10 © MAR

	GD 2.0	VG 4.0	FN 6.0	VF 8.0	VF/NM 9.0	NM- 9.2

MAJESTIC (Mr. Majestic from WildCATS)
DC Comics: Oct, 2004 - No. 4, Jan, 2005 ($2.95, limited series)

1-4-Kerschl-a/Abnett & Lanning-s. 1-Superman app.; Superman #1 cover swipe						3.00
...: Strange New Visitor TPB (2005, $14.99) r/#1-4 & Action #811, Advs. of Superman #624 & Superman #201						15.00

MAJESTIC (Mr. Majestic from WildCATS)
DC Comics (WildStorm): Mar, 2005 - No. 17, July, 2006 ($2.95/$2.99)

1-17: 1-Googe-a/Abnett & Lanning-s; 9-Jeanty-a; Zealot app.						3.00
...: Meanwhile, Back on Earth... TPB (2006, $14.99) r/#8-12						13.00
...: The Final Cut TPB (2007, $14.99) r/#13-17 & story fro WildStorm Winter Special						15.00
...: While You Were Out TPB (2006, $12.99) r/#1-7						13.00

MAJOR BUMMER
DC Comics: Aug, 1997 - No. 15, Oct, 1998 ($2.50)

1-15: 1-Origin and 1st app. Major Bummer						2.50

MAJOR HOOPLE COMICS (See Crackajack Funnies)
Nedor Publications: nd (Jan, 1943)

1-Mary Worth, Phantom Soldier app. by Moldoff	39	78	117	224	355	485

MAJOR VICTORY COMICS (Also see Dynamic Comics)
H. Clay Glover/Service Publ./Harry 'A' Chesler: 1944 - No. 3, Summer, 1945

1-Origin Major Victory (patriotic hero) by C. Sultan (reprint from Dynamic #1); 1st app. Spider Woman	64	128	192	400	663	925
2-Dynamic Boy app.	40	80	120	235	368	500
3-Rocket Boy app.	37	74	111	213	337	460

MALIBU ASHCAN: RAFFERTY (See Firearm #12)
Malibu Comics (Ultraverse): Nov, 1994 (99¢, B&W w/color-c; one-shot)

1-Previews "The Rafferty Saga" storyline in Firearm; Chaykin-c						2.50

MALTESE FALCON
David McKay Publications: No. 48, 1946

Feature Books 48-by Dashiell Hammett	81	162	243	506	841	1175

MALU IN THE LAND OF ADVENTURE
I. W. Enterprises: 1964 (See White Princess of Jungle #2)

1-r/Avon's Slave Girl Comics #1; Severin-c	5	10	15	30	48	65

MAMMOTH COMICS
Whitman Publishing Co.(K. K. Publ.): 1938 (84 pgs.) (B&W, 8-1/2x11-1/2")

1-Alley Oop, Terry & the Pirates, Dick Tracy, Little Orphan Annie, Wash Tubbs, Moon Mullins, Smilin' Jack, Tailspin Tommy, Don Winslow, Dan Dunn, Smokey Stover & other reprints (scarce)	200	400	600	1250	2075	2900

MAN AGAINST TIME
Image Comics (Motown Machineworks): May, 1996 - No. 4, Aug, 1996 ($2.25, limited series)

1-4: 1-Simonson-c. 2,3-Leon-c. 4-Barreto & Leon-c						2.50

MAN-BAT (See Batman Family, Brave & the Bold, & Detective #400)
National Periodical Publ./DC Comics: Dec-Jan, 1975-76 - No. 2, Feb-Mar, 1976; Dec, 1984

1-Ditko-a(p); Aparo-c; Batman app.; 1st app. She-Bat?	2	4	6	11	16	20
2-Aparo-c	2	4	6	8	10	12
1 (12/84)-N. Adams-r(3)/Det.(Vs. Batman on-c)						4.00

MAN-BAT
DC Comics: Feb, 1996 - No. 3, Apr, 1996 ($2.25, limited series)

1-3: Dixon scripts in all. 2-Killer Croc-c/app.						2.50

MAN-BAT
DC Comics: Jun, 2006 - No. 5, Oct, 2006 ($2.99, limited series)

1-5: Bruce Jones-s/Mike Huddleston-a/c. 1-Hush app.						3.00

MAN CALLED A-X, THE
Malibu Comics (Bravura): Nov, 1994 - No. 4, Jun, 1995 ($2.95, limited series)

0-4: Marv Wolfman scripts & Shawn McManus-c/a. 0-(2/95). 1-"1A" on cover						3.00

MAN CALLED A-X, THE
DC Comics: Oct, 1997 - No. 8, May, 1998 ($2.50)

1-8: Marv Wolfman scripts & Shawn McManus-c/a.						2.50

MAN CALLED KEV, A (See The Authority)
DC Comics (WildStorm): Sept, 2006 - No. 5, Feb, 2007 ($2.99, limited series)

1-5-Ennis-s/Ezquerra-a/Fabry-c						3.00
TPB (2007, $14.99) r/#1-5; cover gallery						15.00

MAN COMICS
Marvel/Atlas Comics (NPI): Dec, 1949 - No. 28, Sept, 1953 (#1-6: 52 pgs.)

1-Tuska-a	23	46	69	135	213	290
2-Tuska-a	14	28	42	81	118	155
3-6	11	22	33	64	90	115
7,8	11	22	33	60	83	105
9-13,15: 9-Format changes to war	9	18	27	50	65	80
14-Henkel (3 pgs.)/Pakula-a	9	18	27	52	69	85
16-21,23-28: 28-Crime issue (Bob Brant)	8	16	24	44	57	70
22-Krigstein-a, 5 pgs.	10	20	30	54	72	90

NOTE: **Berg** a-14, 15, 19. **Colan** a-9, 21. **Everett** a-8, 22; c-22, 25. **Heath** a-11, 17, 21. **Kubertish** a-by **Bob Brown**-3. **Maneely** a-11; c-10, 11. **Reinman** a-11. **Robinson** a-7, 10, 14. **Robert Sale** a-9, 11. **Sinnott** a-22, 23. **Tuska** a-14, 23.

MANDRAKE THE MAGICIAN (See Defenders Of The Earth, 123, 46, 52, 55, Giant Comic Album, King Comics, Magic Comics, The Phantom #21, Tiny Tot Funnies & Wow Comics, '36)

MANDRAKE THE MAGICIAN (See Harvey Comics Hits #53)
David McKay Publ./Dell/King Comics (All 12¢): 1938 - 1948; Sept, 1966 - No. 10, Nov, 1967

Feature Books 18,19,23 (1938)	65	130	195	406	671	935
Feature Books 46	45	90	135	275	450	625
Feature Books 52,55	38	76	114	219	347	475
Four Color 752 (11/56)	10	20	30	70	123	175
1-Begin S.O.S. Phantom, ends #3	5	10	15	35	55	75
2-7,9: 4-Girl Phantom app. 5-Flying Saucer-c/story. 5,6-Brick Bradford app. 7-Origin Lothar. 9-Brick Bradford app.	3	6	9	20	30	40
8-Jeff Jones-a (4 pgs.)	4	8	12	22	34	45
10-Rip Kirby app.; Raymond-a (14 pgs.)	4	8	12	26	41	55

MANDRAKE THE MAGICIAN
Marvel Comics: Apr, 1995 - No. 2, May, 1995 ($2.95, unfinished limited series)

1,2: Mike Barr scripts						3.00

MAN-EATING COW (See Tick #7,8)
New England Comics: July, 1992 - No. 10, 1994? ($2.75, B&W, limited series)

1-10						3.00
Man-Eating Cow Bonanza (6/96, $4.95, 128 pgs.)-r/#1-4.						5.00

MAN FROM ATLANTIS (TV)
Marvel Comics: Feb, 1978 - No. 7, Aug, 1978

1-(84 pgs.)-Sutton-a(p), Buscema; origin & cast photos	1	3	4	6	8	10
2-7						4.00

MAN FROM PLANET X, THE
Planet X Productions: 1987 (no price; probably unlicensed)

1-Reprints Fawcett Movie Comic						2.50

MAN FROM U.N.C.L.E., THE (TV) (Also see The Girl From Uncle)
Gold Key: Feb, 1965 - No. 22, Apr, 1969 (All photo-c)

1	13	26	39	95	168	240
2-Photo back c-2-8	7	14	21	50	83	115
3-10: 7-Jet Dream begins (1st app., also see Jet Dream) (all new stories)	6	12	18	37	59	80
11-22: 19-Last 12¢ issue. 21,22-Reprint #10 & 7	5	10	15	32	51	70

MAN FROM U.N.C.L.E., THE (TV)
Entertainment Publishing: 1987 - No. 11 ($1.50/$1.75, B&W)

1-7 ($1.50). 8-11 ($1.75)						3.00

MAN FROM WELLS FARGO (TV)
Dell Publishing Co.: No. 1287, Feb-Apr, 1962 - May-July, 1962 (Photo-c)

Four Color 1287, #01-495-207	6	12	18	37	59	80

MANGA DARKCHYLDE (Also see Darkchylde titles)
Dark Horse Comics: Feb, 2005 - No. 5 ($2.99, limited series)

1,2-Randy Queen-s/a; manga-style pre-teen Ariel Chylde						3.00

MANGA SHI (See Tomoe)
Crusade Entertainment: Aug, 1996 ($2.95)

1-Printed backwards (manga-style)						3.00

MANGA SHI 2000
Crusade Entertainment: Feb, 1997 - No. 3, June, 1997 ($2.95, mini-series)

1-3: 1-Two covers						3.00

MANGA ZEN (Also see Zen Intergalactic Ninja)
Zen Comics (Fusion Studios): 1996 - No. 3, 1996 ($2.50, B&W)

1-3						2.50

MANGAZINE
Antarctic Press: Aug, 1985 - No. 4, Sept, 1986 (B&W)

1-Soft paper-c	2	4	6	10	14	18

Manhunt #8 © ME

Manhunter #28 © DC

Man-Thing #1 © MAR

	GD 2.0	VG 4.0	FN 6.0	VF 8.0	VF/NM 9.0	NM- 9.2		GD 2.0	VG 4.0	FN 6.0	VF 8.0	VF/NM 9.0	NM- 9.2

2-4	2	4	6	8	10	12

MANGLE TANGLE TALES
Innovation Publishing: 1990 ($2.95, deluxe format)

1-Intro by Harlan Ellison						3.00

MANHUNT! (Becomes Red Fox #15 on)
Magazine Enterprises: 10/47 - No. 11, 8/48; #13,14, 1953 (no #12)

	GD	VG	FN	VF	VF/NM	NM-
1-Red Fox by L. B. Cole, Undercover Girl by Whitney, Space Ace begin (1st app.); negligee panels	50	100	150	305	503	700
2-Electrocution-c	40	80	120	235	368	500
3-6: 6-Bondage-c	32	64	96	186	293	400
7-10: 7-Space Ace ends. 8-Trail Colt begins (intro/1st app., 5/48) by Guardineer; Trail Colt-c. 10-G. Ingels-a	28	56	84	162	256	350
11(8/48)-Frazetta-a, 7 pgs.; The Duke, Scotland Yard begin	42	84	126	239	380	520
13(A-1 #63)-Frazetta, r-/Trail Colt #1, 7 pgs.	40	80	120	235	368	500
14(A-1 #77)-Bondage/hypo-c; last L. B. Cole Red Fox; Ingels-a	40	80	120	235	368	500

NOTE: *Guardineer* a-1-5; c-8. *Whitney* a-2-14; c-1-6, 10. Red Fox by *L. B. Cole* #1-14. #15 was advertised but came out as Red Fox #15.

MANHUNTER (See Adventure #58, 73, Brave & the Bold, Detective Comics, 1st Issue Special, House of Mystery #143 and Justice League of America)
DC Comics: 1984 ($2.50, 76 pgs; high quality paper)

1-Simonson-c/a(r)/Detective; Batman app.						3.50

MANHUNTER
DC Comics: July, 1988 - No. 24, Apr, 1990 ($1.00)

1-24: 8,9-Flash app. 9-Invasion. 17-Batman-c/sty						2.50

MANHUNTER
DC Comics: No. 0, Nov, 1994 - No. 12, Nov, 1995 ($1.95/$2.25)

0-12						2.50

MANHUNTER
DC Comics: Oct, 2004 - Present ($2.50/$2.99)

1-21: 1-Intro. Kate Spencer; Saiz-a/Jae Lee-a/Andreyko-s. 2,3 Shadow Thief app. 13,14-Omac x-over. 20-One Year Later						2.50
22-30: 22-Begin $2.99-c. 23-Sandra Knight app. 27-Chaykin-c. 28-Batman app.						3.00
...: Street Justice (2005, $12.99) r/#1-5; Andreyko intro.						13.00
...: Trial By Fire (2007, $17.99) r/#6-14						18.00

MANHUNTER: THE SPECIAL EDITION
DC Comics: 1999 ($9.95)

TPB-Reprints Detective Comics stories by Goodwin and Simonson						10.00

MANIFEST ETERNITY
DC Comics: Aug, 2006 - No. 6, Jan, 2007 ($2.99)

1-6-Lobdell-s/Nguyen-a/c						3.00

MAN IN BLACK (See Thrill-O-Rama) (Also see All New Comics, Front Page, Green Hornet #31, Strange Story & Tally-Ho Comics)
Harvey Publications: Sept, 1957 - No. 4, Mar, 1958

	GD	VG	FN	VF	VF/NM	NM-
1-Bob Powell-c/a	18	36	54	105	165	225
2-4-Powell-c/a	14	28	42	80	115	150

MAN IN BLACK
Lorne-Harvey Publications (Recollections): 1990 - No. 2, July, 1991 (B&W)

1,2						3.00

MAN IN FLIGHT (Disney, TV)
Dell Publishing Co.: No. 836, Sept, 1957

	GD	VG	FN	VF	VF/NM	NM-
Four Color 836	7	14	21	47	76	105

MAN IN SPACE (Disney, TV, see Dell Giant #27)
Dell Publishing Co.: No. 716, Aug, 1956 - No. 954, Nov, 1958

	GD	VG	FN	VF	VF/NM	NM-
Four Color 716-A science feat. from Tomorrowland	8	16	24	56	93	130
Four Color 954-Satellites	7	14	21	47	76	105

MANKIND (WWF Wrestling)
Chaos Comics: Sept, 1999 ($2.95, one-shot)

1-Regular and photo-c						3.00
1-Premium Edition ($10.00) Dwayne Turner & Danny Miki-c						10.00

MANN AND SUPERMAN
DC Comics: 2000 ($5.95, prestige format, one-shot)

nn-Michael T. Gilbert-s/a						6.00

MAN OF STEEL, THE (Also see Superman: The Man of Steel)

DC Comics: 1986 (June release) - No. 6, 1986 (75¢, limited series)

1-6: 1-Silver logo; Byrne-c/a/scripts in all; origin, 1-Alternate-c for newsstand sales,1-Distr. to toy stores by So Much Fun, 2-6: 2-Intro. Lois Lane, Jimmy Olsen. 3-Intro/origin Magpie; Batman-c/story. 4-Intro. new Lex Luthor						4.00
1-6-Silver Editions (1993, $1.95)-r/1-6						3.00
...The Complete Saga nn-Contains #1-6, given away in contest						35.00

Limited Edition, softcover	4	8	12	28	44	60

NOTE: Issues 1-6 were released between Action #583 (9/86) & Action #584 (1/87) plus Superman #423 (9/86) & Advs. of Superman #424 (1/87).

MAN OF THE ATOM (See Solar, Man of the Atom Vol. 2)

MAN OF WAR (See Liberty Guards & Liberty Scouts)
Centaur Publications: Nov. 1, Jan, 1942

	GD	VG	FN	VF	VF/NM	NM-
1-The Fire-Man, Man of War, The Sentinel, Liberty Guards, & Vapo-Man begin; Gustavson-c/a; Flag-c	166	332	498	1038	1719	2400
2-Intro The Ferret; Gustavson-c/a	121	242	363	756	1258	1760

MAN OF WAR
Eclipse Comics: Aug, 1987 - No. 3, Feb, 1988 ($1.75, Baxter paper)

1-3: Bruce Jones scripts						2.50

MAN OF WAR (See The Protectors)
Malibu Comics: 1993 - No, 8, Feb, 1994 $1.95/$2.50/$2.25)

1-5 ($1.95)-Newsstand Editions w/different-c						2.50
1-8: 1-5-Collector's Edi. w/poster. 6-8 ($2.25): 6-Polybagged w/Skycap. 8-Vs. Rocket Rangers						3.00

MAN O' MARS
Fiction House Magazines: 1953; 1964

	GD	VG	FN	VF	VF/NM	NM-
1-Space Rangers; Whitman-c	45	90	135	275	450	625
I.W. Reprint #1-r/Man O'Mars #1 & Star Pirate; Murphy Anderson-a	5	10	15	35	55	75

MANTECH ROBOT WARRIORS
Archie Enterprises, Inc.: Sept, 1984 - No. 4, Apr, 1985 (75¢)

1-4: Ayers-c/a(p). 1-Buckler-c(i)						3.00

MAN-THING (See Fear, Giant-Size..., Marvel Comics Presents, Marvel Fanfare, Monsters Unleashed, Power Record Comics & Savage Tales)
Marvel Comics Group: Jan, 1974 - No. 22, Oct, 1975; V2#1, Nov, 1979 - V2#11, July, 1981

	GD	VG	FN	VF	VF/NM	NM-
1-Howard the Duck(2nd app.) cont'd/Fear #19	5	10	15	32	51	70
2	3	6	9	14	20	25
3-1st app. original Foolkiller	2	4	6	11	16	20
4-Origin Foolkiller; last app. 1st Foolkiller	2	4	6	10	14	18
5-11-Ploog-a. 11-Foolkiller cameo (flashback)	2	4	6	10	14	18
12-22: 19-1st app. Scavenger. 20-Spidey cameo. 21-Origin Scavenger, Man-Thing. 22-Howard the Duck cameo	1	3	4	6	8	10
V2#1(1979)	1	2	3	5	6	8
V2#2-11: 4-Dr. Strange-c/app. 11-Mayerik-a						4.00

NOTE: *Alcala* a-14. *Brunner* c-1. *J. Buscema* a-12p, 13p, 16p. *Gil Kane* c-4p, 10p, 12-20p, 21. *Mooney* a-17, 18, 19p, 20-22, V2#1-3p. *Ploog* Man-Thing-5p, 6p, 7, 8, 9-11p; c-5, 6, 8, 9, 11. *Sutton* a-13i. No. 19 says #10 in indicia.

MAN-THING (Volume Three, continues in Strange Tales #1 (9/98))
Marvel Comics: Dec, 1997 - No. 8, July, 1998 ($2.99)

1-8-DeMatteis-s/Sharp-a. 2-Two covers. 6-Howard the Duck-c/app.						3.00

MAN-THING (Prequel to 2005 movie)
Marvel Comics: Sept, 2004 - No. 3, Nov, 2004 ($2.99, limited series)

1-3-Hans Rodionoff-s/Kyle Hotz-a						3.00
...: Whatever Knows Fear... (2005, $12.99, TPB) r/#1-3, Savage Tales #1, Adv. Into Fear #16						13.00

MANTRA
Malibu Comics (Ultraverse): July, 1993 - No. 24, Aug, 1995 ($1.95/$2.50)

	GD	VG	FN	VF	VF/NM	NM-
1-Polybagged w/trading card & coupon						3.00
1-Newsstand edition w/o trading card or coupon						2.50
1-Full cover holographic edition	1	3	4	6	8	10
1-Ultra-limited silver foil-c						5.00
2-9,11-24: 3-Intro Warstrike & Kismet. 6-Break-Thru x-over. 2-($2.50-Newsstand edition bagged w/card. 4-($2.50, 48 pgs.) 6-Rune flip-c/story by B. Smith (3 pgs.). 7-Prime app.; origin Prototype by Jurgens/Austin (2 pgs.). 11-New costume. 17-Intro NecroMantra & Pinnacle; prelude to Godwheel						2.50
10-($3.50, 68 pgs.)-Flip-c w/Ultraverse Premiere #2						3.50
Giant Size 1 (7/94, $2.50, 44 pgs.)						2.50
...Spear of Destiny 1,2 (4/95, $2.50, 36pgs.)						2.50

MANTRA (2nd Series) (Also See Black September)
Malibu Comics (Ultraverse): Infinity, Sept, 1995 - No. 7, Apr, 1996 ($1.50)

Many Loves of Dobie Gillis #9 © DC

Marco Polo © CC

Marge's Tubby #10 © WEST

	GD 2.0	VG 4.0	FN 6.0	VF 8.0	VF/NM 9.0	NM- 9.2

Infinity (9/95, $1.50)-Black September x-over, Intro new Mantra ... 2.50
1-7: 1-(10/95). 5-Return of Eden (original Mantra). 6,7-Rush app. ... 2.50

MAN WITH THE SCREAMING BRAIN (Based on screenplay by Bruce Campbell & David Goodman)
Dark Horse Comics: Apr, 2005 - No. 4, July, 2005 ($2.99, limited series)
1-4-Campbell & Goodman-s; Remender-a/c. 1-Variant-c by Noto. 3-Powell var-c.
4-Mignola var-c ... 3.00
TPB (11/05, $13.95) r/#1-4; David Goodman intro.; cover gallery ... 14.00

MAN WITH THE X-RAY EYES, THE (See X,... under Movie Comics)

MANY GHOSTS OF DR. GRAVES, THE (Doctor Graves #73 on)
Charlton Comics: 5/67 - No. 60, 12/76; No. 61, 9/77 - No. 62, 10/77; No. 63, 2/78 - No. 65, 4/78; No. 66, 6/81 - No. 72, 5/82

	GD 2.0	VG 4.0	FN 6.0	VF 8.0	VF/NM 9.0	NM- 9.2
1-Ditko-a; Palais-a; early issues 12¢-c	5	10	15	35	55	75
2-6,8,10	3	6	9	17	25	32
7,9-Ditko-a	3	6	9	19	29	38
11-13,16-18-Ditko-c/a	3	6	9	16	22	28
14,19,23,25	2	4	6	8	11	14
15,20,21-Ditko-a	2	4	6	10	14	18
22,24,26,27,29-35,38,40-Ditko-c/a	2	4	6	11	16	20
28-Ditko-c	2	4	6	10	14	18
36,46,56,57,59,61,66,67,69,71	1	2	3	5	7	9
37,41,43,51,60-Ditko-a	2	4	6	8	10	12
39,58-Ditko-a. 39-Sutton-a. 58-Ditko-a	2	4	6	8	10	12
42,44,53-Sutton-c; Ditko-a. 42-Sutton-a	2	4	6	8	10	12
45-(5/74) 2nd Newton comic work (8 pgs.); new logo; Sutton-c	2	4	6	9	13	16
47-Newton, Sutton, Ditko-a	2	4	6	8	11	14
48-Ditko, Sutton-a	2	4	6	8	10	12
49-Newton-c/a; Sutton-a.	1	3	4	6	8	10
50-Sutton-a	1	2	3	5	7	9
52-Newton-c; Ditko-a	2	4	6	8	10	12
54-Early Byrne-c; Ditko-a	2	4	6	8	10	12
55-Ditko-c; Sutton-a	2	4	6	8	10	12
62-65,68-Ditko-c/a. 65-Sutton-a	2	4	6	9	13	16
70,72-Ditko-a	2	4	6	8	11	14
Modern Comics Reprint 12,25 (1978)						4.00

NOTE: Aparo a-4, 5, 7, 8, 66r, 69r; c-8, 14, 19, 66r, 67r. Byrne c-54. Ditko a-1, 7, 9, 11-13, 15-18, 20-22, 24, 26, 27, 29, 30-35, 37, 38, 40-44, 47, 48, 51-54, 58, 60r-65r, 70, 72; c-11-13, 16-18, 22, 24, 26-35, 38, 40, 55, 58, 62-65. Howard a-38, 39, 45i, 65; c-48. Kim a-36, 46, 52. Larson a-58. Morisi a-13, 14, 23, 26. Newton a-45, 47p, 49p; c-49, 52. Staton a-36, 37, 41, 43. Sutton a-39, 42, 47-50, 55, 65; c-42, 44, 45; painted c-53. Zeck a-56, 59.

MANY LOVES OF DOBIE GILLIS, THE (TV)
National Periodical Publications: May-June, 1960 - No. 26, Oct, 1964

	GD 2.0	VG 4.0	FN 6.0	VF 8.0	VF/NM 9.0	NM- 9.2
1-Most covers by Bob Oskner	22	44	66	164	292	420
2-5	12	24	36	87	156	225
6-10: 10-Last 10¢-c	9	18	27	60	100	140
11-26: 20-Drucker-a. 24-(3-4/64). 25-(9/64)	8	16	24	54	90	125

MANY WORLDS OF TESLA STRONG, THE (Also see Tom Strong)
America's Best Comics: July, 2003 ($5.95, one-shot)
1-Two covers by Timm & Art Adams; art by various incl. Campbell, Cho, Noto, Hughes ... 6.00

MARAUDER'S MOON (See Luke Short, Four Color #848)

MARCH OF COMICS (See Promotional Comics section)

MARCH OF CRIME (Formerly My Love Affair #1-6) (See Fox Giants)
Fox Features Synd.: No. 7, July, 1950 - No. 2, Sept, 1950; No. 3, Sept, 1951

	GD 2.0	VG 4.0	FN 6.0	VF 8.0	VF/NM 9.0	NM- 9.2
7(#1)(7/50)-True crime stories; Wood-a	42	84	126	239	380	520
2(9/50)-Wood-a (exceptional)	40	80	120	235	368	500
3(9/51)	18	36	54	107	169	230

MARCO POLO
Charlton Comics Group: 1962 (Movie classic)

	GD 2.0	VG 4.0	FN 6.0	VF 8.0	VF/NM 9.0	NM- 9.2
nn (Scarce)-Glanzman-c/a (25 pgs.)	10	20	30	67	116	165

MARC SILVESTRI SKETCHBOOK
Image Comics (Top Cow): Jan, 2004 ($2.99, one-shot)
1-Character sketches, concept artwork, storyboards of Witchblade, Darkness & others ... 3.00

MARC SPECTOR: MOON KNIGHT (Also see Moon Knight)
Marvel Comics: June, 1989 - No. 60, March, 1994 ($1.50/$1.75, direct sales)
1-24,26-49,51-54,58,59: 4-Intro new Midnight. 8,9-Punisher app. 15-Silver Sable app. 19-21-Gambit & Punisher app. 25-(52 pgs.)-Ghost Rider app. 32,33-Hobgoblin II (Macendale) & Spider-Man (in black costume) app. 35-38-Punisher story. 42-44-Infinity War x-over. 46-Demogoblin app. 51,53-Gambit app. 55-New look. 57-Moon Knight-c/story. 60-Moon Knight dies ... 2.50

50-(56 pgs.)-Special die-cut-c ... 3.00
55-57,60-Platt a ... 3.50
...: Divided We Fall ($4.95, 52 pgs.) ... 5.00
Special 1 (1992, $2.50) ... 2.50
NOTE: Cowan c(p) 20-23. Guice c-20. Heath c/a-4. Platt -a 55-57,60; c-55-60.

MARGARET O'BRIEN (See The Adventures of...)

MARGE'S LITTLE LULU (Continues as Little Lulu from #207 on)
Dell Publishing Co./Gold Key #165-206: No. 74, 6/45 - No. 164, 7-9/62; No. 165, 10/62 - No. 206, 8/72

Marjorie Henderson Buell, born in Philadelphia, Pa., in 1904, created Little Lulu, a cartoon character that appeared weekly in the Saturday Evening Post from Feb. 23, 1935 through Dec. 30, 1944. She was not responsible for any of the comic books. John Stanley did pencils only on all Little Lulu comics through at least #135 (1959). He did pencils and inks on Four Color #74 & 97. Irving Tripp began handling stories from #1 on, and remained the comic's illustrator throughout its entire run. Stanley did storyboards (layouts), pencils, and scripts in all cases and inking only on covers. His word balloons were written in cursive. Tripp and occasionally other artists at Western Publ. in Poughkeepsie, N.Y. blew up the pencilled pages, inked the blowups, and lettered them. Arnold Drake did storyboards, pencils and scripts starting with #197 (1970), amidst reprinted issues. Buell sold her rights exclusively to Western Publ. in Dec., 1971. The earlier issues had to be approved by Buell prior to publication.

	GD 2.0	VG 4.0	FN 6.0	VF 8.0	VF/NM 9.0	NM- 9.2
Four Color 74('45)-Intro Lulu, Tubby & Alvin	115	230	345	961	1781	2600
Four Color 97(2/46)	51	102	153	408	742	1075

(Above two books are all John Stanley - cover, pencils, and inks.)

	GD 2.0	VG 4.0	FN 6.0	VF 8.0	VF/NM 9.0	NM- 9.2
Four Color 110('46)-1st Alvin Story Telling Time; 1st app. Willy; variant cover exists	36	72	108	270	498	725
Four Color 115-1st app. Boys' Clubhouse	35	70	105	263	482	700
Four Color 120, 131: 120-1st app. Eddie	30	60	90	225	413	600
Four Color 139('47),146,158	30	60	90	220	398	575
Four Color 165 (10/47)-Smokes doll hair & has wild hallucinations. 1st Tubby detective story	30	60	90	220	398	575
1(1-2/48)-Lulu's Diary feature begins	59	118	177	502	926	1350
2-1st app. Gloria; 1st Tubby story in a L.L. comic; 1st app. Miss Feeny	30	60	90	220	398	575
3-5	27	54	81	203	364	525
6-10: 7-1st app. Annie; Xmas-c	22	44	66	165	295	425
11-20: 18-X-mas-c. 19-1st app. Wilbur. 20-1st app. Mr. McNabbem	18	36	54	132	234	335
21-30: 26-r/F.C. 110. 30-Xmas-c	15	30	45	111	198	285
31-38,40: 35-1st Mumday story	12	24	36	87	156	225
39-Intro. Witch Hazel in "That Awful Witch Hazel"	13	26	39	95	168	240
41-60: 42-Xmas-c. 45-2nd Witch Hazel app. 49-Gives Stanley & others credit	11	22	33	79	140	200
61-80: 63-1st app. Chubby (Tubby's cousin). 68-1st app. Prof. Cleff. 78-Xmas-c. 80-Intro. Little Itch (2/55)	9	18	27	63	107	150
81-99: 90-Xmas-c	8	16	24	52	86	120
100	8	16	24	56	93	130
101-130: 123-1st app. Fifi	6	12	18	41	66	90
131-164: 135-Last Stanley-p	5	10	15	35	55	75
165-Giant; ...in Paris ('62)	10	20	30	71	126	180
166-Giant; ...Christmas Diary (1962 - '63)	10	20	30	71	126	180
167-169	4	8	12	28	44	60
170,171,175,176,178-196,198-200-Stanley-r. 182-1st app. Little Scarecrow Boy	3	6	9	16	23	30
171,173,174,177,197	3	6	9	14	19	24
201,203,206-Last issue to carry Marge's name	2	4	6	13	18	22
202,204,205-Stanley-r	3	6	9	14	19	24
...& Tubby in Japan (12¢)(5-7/62) 01476-207	7	14	21	49	80	110
...Summer Camp 1(8/67-G.K.-Giant) '57-58-r	6	12	18	39	62	85
...Trick 'N' Treat 1(12¢)(12/62-Gold Key)	6	12	18	43	69	95

NOTE: See Dell Giant Comics #23, 29, 36, 42, 50, & Dell Giants for annuals. All Giants not by Stanley from L.L. on Vacation (7/54) on. Irving Tripp a-#1-on. Christmas c-7, 18, 30, 42, 78, 90, 126, 166, 250. Summer Camp issues #173, 177, 181, 189, 197, 201, 206.

MARGE'S LITTLE LULU (See Golden Comics Digest #19, 23, 27, 29, 33, 36, 40, 43, 46, & March of Comics #251, 267, 275, 293, 307, 323, 335, 349, 355, 369, 385, 406, 417, 427, 439, 456, 468, 475, 488)

MARGE'S TUBBY (Little Lulu)(See Dell Giants)
Dell Publishing Co./Gold Key: No. 381, Aug, 1952 - No. 49, Dec-Feb, 1961-62

	GD 2.0	VG 4.0	FN 6.0	VF 8.0	VF/NM 9.0	NM- 9.2
Four Color 381(#1)-Stanley script; Irving Tripp-a	20	40	60	146	261	375
Four Color 430,444-Stanley-a	12	24	36	82	146	210
Four Color 461 (4/53)-1st Tubby & Men From Mars story; Stanley-a	10	20	30	71	126	180
5 (7-9/53)-Stanley-a	9	18	27	60	100	140
6-10	7	14	21	50	83	115
11-20	6	12	18	37	59	80
21-30	5	10	15	30	48	65
31-49	4	8	12	26	41	55
...& the Little Men From Mars No. 30020-410(10/64-G.K.)-25¢, 68 pgs.	8	16	24	52	86	120

Marine War Heroes #1 © CC

Mark Trail #5 © Hall Synd.

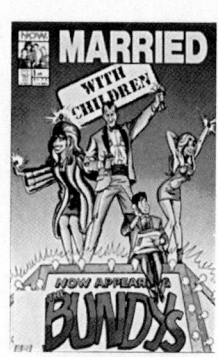

Married With Children #1 © 20th Century Fox

	GD	VG	FN	VF	VF/NM	NM-
	2.0	4.0	6.0	8.0	9.0	9.2

NOTE: **John Stanley** did all storyboards & scripts through at least #35 (1959). **Lloyd White** did all art except F.C. 381, 430, 444, 461 & #5.

MARGIE (See My Little...)
MARGIE (TV)
Dell Publ. Co.: No. 1307, Mar-May, 1962 - No. 2, July-Sept, 1962 (Photo-c)

| Four Color 1307(#1) | 6 | 12 | 18 | 37 | 59 | 80 |
| 2 | 5 | 10 | 15 | 30 | 48 | 65 |

MARGIE COMICS (Formerly Comedy Comics; Reno Browne #50 on)
(Also see Cindy Comics & Teen Comics)
Marvel Comics (ACI): No. 35, Winter, 1946-47 - No. 49, Dec, 1949

35	17	34	51	98	154	210
36-38,42,45,47-49	11	22	33	60	83	105
39,41,43(2),44,46-Kurtzman's "Hey Look"	12	24	36	67	94	120
40-Three "Hey Looks", three "Giggles 'n' Grins" by Kurtzman	14	28	42	76	108	140

MARINES (See Tell It to the...)
MARINES ATTACK
Charlton Comics: Aug, 1964 - No. 9, Feb-Mar, 1966

| 1-Glanzman-a begins | 4 | 8 | 12 | 22 | 34 | 45 |
| 2-9 | 3 | 6 | 9 | 14 | 19 | 24 |

MARINES AT WAR (Formerly Tales of the Marines #4)
Atlas Comics (OPI): No. 5, Apr, 1957 - No. 7, Aug, 1957

| 5-7 | 9 | 18 | 27 | 52 | 69 | 85 |

NOTE: **Colan** a-5. **Drucker** a-5. **Everett** a-5. **Maneely** a-5. **Orlando** a-7. **Severin** c-5.

MARINES IN ACTION
Atlas News Co.: June, 1955 - No. 14, Sept, 1957

| 1-Rock Murdock, Boot Camp Brady begin | 11 | 22 | 33 | 64 | 90 | 125 |
| 2-14 | 9 | 18 | 27 | 50 | 65 | 85 |

NOTE: **Berg** a-2, 8, 9, 11, 14. **Heath** c-2, 9. **Maneely** c-1. **Severin** a-4; c-7-11, 14.

MARINES IN BATTLE
Atlas Comics (ACI No. 1-12/WPI No. 13-25): Aug, 1954 - No. 25, Sept, 1958

1-Heath-c; Iron Mike McGraw by Heath; history of U.S. Marine Corps begins	21	42	63	122	191	260
2-Heath-c	13	26	39	72	101	130
3-6,8-10: 4-Last precode (2/55)	10	20	30	56	76	95
7-Kubert/Moskowitz-a (6 pgs.)	10	20	30	58	79	100
11-16,18-21,24	9	18	27	52	69	85
17-Williamson-a (3 pgs.)	11	22	33	60	83	105
22,25-Torres-a	10	20	30	54	72	90
23-Crandall-a; Mark Murdock app.	10	20	30	56	76	95

NOTE: **Berg** a-22. **G. Colan** a-22, 23. **Drucker** a-6. **Everett** a-4, 15; c-21. **Heath** c-1, 2, 4. **Maneely** c-23, 24. **Orlando** a-14. **Pakula** a-16. **Severin** a-2; c-12. **Sinnott** a-23. **Tuska** a-15.

MARINE WAR HEROES (Charlton Premiere #19 on)
Charlton Comics: Jan, 1964 - No. 18, Mar, 1967

| 1-Montes/Bache-c/a | 4 | 8 | 12 | 22 | 34 | 45 |
| 2-18: 14,18-Montes/Bache-a | 3 | 6 | 9 | 14 | 19 | 24 |

MARK, THE (Also see Mayhem)
Dark Horse Comics: Dec, 1993 - No. 4, Mar, 1994 ($2.50, limited series)

| 1-4 | | | | | | 2.50 |

MARK HAZZARD: MERC
Marvel Comics Group: Nov, 1986 - No. 12, Oct, 1987 (75¢)

| 1-12: Morrow-a, Annual 1 (11/87, $1.25) | | | | | | 2.50 |

MARK OF CHARON (See Negation)
CG Entertainment: Apr, 2003 - No. 5, Aug, 2003 ($2.95, limited series)

| 1-5-Bedard-s/Bennett-a | | | | | | 3.00 |

MARK OF ZORRO (See Zorro, Four Color #228)
MARK 1 COMICS (Also see Shaloman)
Mark 1 Comics: Apr, 1988 - No. 3, Mar, 1989 ($1.50)

| 1-3: Early Shaloman app. 2-Origin | | | | | | 2.50 |

MARKSMAN, THE (Also see Champions)
Hero Comics: Jan, 1988 - No. 5, 1988 ($1.95)

| 1-5: 1-Rose begins. 1-3-Origin The Marksman | | | | | | 2.50 |
| Annual 1 ('88, $2.75, 52pgs)-Champions app. | | | | | | 2.75 |

MARK TRAIL
Standard Magazines (Hall Syndicate)/Fawcett Publ. No. 5: Oct, 1955; No. 5, Summer, 1959

| 1(1955)-Sunday strip-r | 7 | 14 | 21 | 37 | 46 | 55 |

| 5(1959) | 5 | 10 | 15 | 22 | 26 | 30 |
| ...Adventure Book of Nature 1 (Summer, 1958, 25¢, Pines)-100 pg. Giant; Special Camp Issue; contains 78 Sunday strip-r | 9 | 18 | 27 | 52 | 69 | 85 |

MARMADUKE MONK
I. W. Enterprises/Super Comics: No date; 1963 (10¢)

| I.W. Reprint 1 (nd) | 2 | 4 | 6 | 8 | 11 | 14 |
| Super Reprint 14 (1963)-r/Monkeyshines Comics #? | 2 | 4 | 6 | 8 | 10 | 12 |

MARMADUKE MOUSE
Quality Comics Group (Arnold Publ.): Spring, 1946 - No. 65, Dec, 1956 (Early issues: 52 pgs.)

1-Funny animal	17	34	51	98	154	210
2	11	22	33	60	83	105
3-10	9	18	27	47	61	75
11-30	7	14	21	35	43	50
31-65: Later issues are 36 pgs.	6	12	18	28	34	40
Super Reprint #14(1963)	2	4	6	9	12	15

MARQUIS, THE
Oni Press

| ...: A Sin of One ($2.99, 5/03) Guy Davis-s/a; Michael Gaydos-c | | | | | | 3.00 |
| ...: Intermezzo TPB ($11.95, 12/03) r/A Sin of One and Hell's Courtesan #1,2 | | | | | | 12.00 |

MARQUIS, THE: DANSE MACABRE
Oni Press: May, 2000 - No. 5, Feb, 2001 ($2.95, B&W, limited series)

| 1-5-Guy Davis-s/a. 1-Wagner-c. 2-Mignola-c. 3-Vess-c. 5-K. Jones-c | | | | | | 3.00 |
| TPB (8/2001, $18.95) r/1-5 & Les Preludes; Seagle intro. | | | | | | 19.00 |

MARQUIS, THE: DEVIL'S REIGN: HELL'S COURTESAN
Oni Press: Feb, 2002 - No. 2, Apr, 2002 ($2.95, B&W, limited series)

| 1,2-Guy Davis-s/a | | | | | | 3.00 |

MARRIAGE OF HERCULES AND XENA, THE
Topps Comics: July, 1998 ($2.95, one-shot)

| 1-Photo-c; Lopresti-a; Alex Ross pin-up, 1-Alex Ross painted-c | | | | | | 3.00 |
| 1-Gold foil logo-c | | | | | | 5.00 |

MARRIED ... WITH CHILDREN (TV)(Based on Fox TV show)
Now Comics: June, 1990 - No. 7, Feb, 1991(12/90 inside) ($1.75)
V2#1, Sept, 1991 - No. 12, 1992 ($1.95)

1-7: 2-Photo-c, 1,2-2nd printing, V2#1-12: 1,4,5,9-Photo-c						2.50
...Buck's Tale (6/94, $1.95)						2.50
...1994 Annual nn (2/94, $2.50, 52 pgs.)-Flip book format						3.00
Special 1 (7/92, $1.95)-Kelly Bundy photo-c/poster						2.50

MARRIED ... WITH CHILDREN: KELLY BUNDY
Now Comics: Aug, 1992 - No. 3, Oct, 1992 ($1.95, limited series)

| 1-3: Kelly Bundy photo-c & poster in each | | | | | | 2.50 |

MARRIED ... WITH CHILDREN: QUANTUM QUARTET
Now Comics: Oct, 1993 - No. 4, 1994, ($1.95, limited series)

| 1-4: Fantastic Four parody | | | | | | 2.50 |

MARRIED ... WITH CHILDREN: 2099
Now Comics: June, 1993 - No. 3, Aug, 1993 ($1.95, limited series)

| 1-3 | | | | | | 2.50 |

MARS
First Comics: Jan, 1984 - No. 12, Jan, 1985 ($1.00, Mando paper)

| 1-12: Marc Hempel & Mark Wheatley story & art. 2-The Black Flame begins. 10-Dynamo Joe begins | | | | | | 2.50 |
| TPB (IDW Publ., 8/05, $39.99) r/#1-12, creator commentary; bonus art; new Hempel-c | | | | | | 40.00 |

MARS & BEYOND (Disney, TV)
Dell Publishing Co.: No. 866, Dec, 1957

| Four Color 866-A Science feat. from Tomorrowland | 8 | 16 | 24 | 56 | 93 | 130 |

MARS ATTACKS
Topps Comics: May, 1994 - No. 5, Sept, 1994 ($2.95, limited series)

1-5-Giffen story; flip books						4.50
Special Edition	2	4	6	8	10	12
Trade paperback (12/94, $12.95)-r/limited series plus new 8 pg. story						13.00

MARS ATTACKS
Topps Comics: V2#1, 8/95 - V2#3, 10/95; V2#4, 1/96 - No. 7, 5/96($2.95, bi-monthly #6 on)

| V2#1-7: 1-Counterstrike storyline begins. 4-(1/96). 5-(1/96). 5,7-Brereton-c. 6-(3/96)-Simonson-c. 7-Story leads into Baseball Special #1 | | | | | | 3.00 |
| Baseball Special 1 (6/96, $2.95)-Bisley-c. | | | | | | 3.00 |

Martian Manhunter #5 © DC

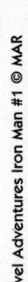

Marvel Adventures Iron Man #1 © MAR

Marvel Adventures Spider-Man #13 © MAR

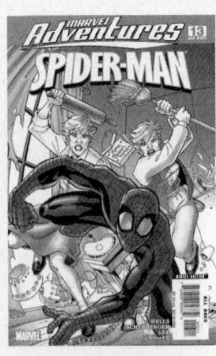

	GD	VG	FN	VF	VF/NM	NM-		GD	VG	FN	VF	VF/NM	NM-
	2.0	4.0	6.0	8.0	9.0	9.2		2.0	4.0	6.0	8.0	9.0	9.2

MARS ATTACKS HIGH SCHOOL
Topps Comics: May, 1997 - No. 2, Sept, 1997 ($2.95, B&W, limited series)
1,2-Stelfreeze-c 3.00

MARS ATTACKS IMAGE
Topps Comics: Dec, 1996 - No. 4, Mar, 1997 ($2.50, limited series)
1-4-Giffen-s/Smith/Sienkiewicz-a 3.00

MARS ATTACKS THE SAVAGE DRAGON
Topps Comics: Dec, 1996 - No. 4, Mar, 1997 ($2.95, limited series)
1-4: 1-w/bound-in card 3.00

MARSHAL BLUEBERRY (See Blueberry)
Marvel Comics (Epic Comics): 1991 ($14.95, graphic novel)

1-Moebius-a	2	4	6	11	16	20

MARSHAL LAW (Also see Crime And Punishment: Marshall Law...)
Marvel Comics (Epic Comics): Oct, 1987 - No. 6, May, 1989 ($1.95, mature)
1-6 .... 2.50

M.A.R.S. PATROL TOTAL WAR (Formerly Total War #1,2)
Gold Key: No. 3, Sept, 1966 - No. 10, Aug, 1969 (All-Painted-c except #7)

3-Wood-a; aliens invade USA	6	12	18	39	62	85
4-10	4	8	12	23	36	48

Wally Wood's M.A.R.S. Patrol Total War TPB (Dark Horse, 9/04, $12.95) r/#3 & Total War #1&2;
foreward by Batton Lash; afterword by Dan Adkins 13.00

**MARTHA WASHINGTON (Also see Dark Horse Presents Fifth Anniversary Special, Dark Horse Presents
#100-4, Give Me Liberty, Happy Birthday Martha Washington & San Diego Comicon Comics #2)**

MARTHA WASHINGTON... (one-shots)
Dark Horse Comics (Legend): ($2.95/$3.50, one-shots)
... Dies (7/07, $3.50) Miller-s/Gibbons-a; r/Miller's original outline for Give Me Liberty ... 3.50
... Stranded in Space (11/95, $2.95) Miller-s/Gibbons-a; Big Guy app. 3.00

MARTHA WASHINGTON GOES TO WAR
Dark Horse Comics (Legend): May, 1994 - No. 5, Sep, 1994 ($2.95, lim. series)
1-5-Miller scripts; Gibbons-c/a 3.00
TPB ($17.95) r/#1-5 .... 18.00

MARTHA WASHINGTON SAVES THE WORLD
Dark Horse Comics: Dec, 1997 - No. 3, Feb, 1998 ($2.95/$3.95, lim. series)
1,2-Miller scripts; Gibbons-c/a in all 3.00
3-($3.95) 4.00

MARTHA WAYNE (See The Story of...)

MARTIAN MANHUNTER (See Detective Comics & Showcase '95 #9)
DC Comics: May, 1988 - No. 4, Aug,. 1988 ($1.25, limited series)
1-4: 1,4-Batman app. 2-Batman cameo 2.50
Special 1-(1996, $3.50) 3.50

MARTIAN MANHUNTER (See JLA)
DC Comics: No. 0, Oct, 1998 - No. 36, Nov, 2001 ($1.99)
0-(10/98) Origin retold; Ostrander/Mandrake-c/a 3.00
1-36: 1-(12/98). 6-9-JLA app. 18,19-JSA app. 24-Mahnke-a 2.50
#1,000,000 (11/98) 853rd Century x-over 2.50
Annual 1,2 (1998,1999; $2.95) 1-Ghosts; Wrightson-c. 2-JLApe ... 3.00

MARTIAN MANHUNTER (See DCU Brave New World)
DC Comics: Oct, 2006 - No. 8, May, 2007 ($2.99, limited series)
1-8-Lieberman-s/Barrionuevo-a 3.00
...: The Others Among Us TPB (2007, $19.99) r/#1-8 & story from DCU Brave New World ... 20.00

MARTIAN MANHUNTER: AMERICAN SECRETS
DC Comics: 1992 - Book Three, 1992 ($4.95, limited series, prestige format)
1-3: Barreto-a 5.00

MARTIN KANE (William Gargan as... Private Eye)(Stage/Screen/Radio/TV)
Fox Features Syndicate (Hero Books): No. 4, June, 1950 - No. 2, Aug, 1950 (Formerly My
Secret Affair)

4(#1)-True crime stories; Wood-c/a(2); used in SOTI, pg. 160; photo back-c	31	62	93	178	282	385
2-Wood/Orlando story. 5 pgs: Wood-a(2)	23	46	69	135	213	290

MARTIN MYSTERY
Dark Horse (Bonelli Comics): Mar, 1999 - No. 6, Aug, 1999 ($4.95, B&W, digest size)
1-6-Reprints Italian series in English; Gibbons-c on #1-3 .... 5.00

MARTY MOUSE
I. W. Enterprises: No date (1958?) (10¢)

1-Reprint

	2	4	6	9	12	15

MARVEL ACTION HOUR FEATURING IRON MAN (TV cartoon)
Marvel Comics: Nov, 1994 - No. 8, June, 1995 ($1.50/$2.95)
1-8: Based on cartoon series 2.50
1 ($2.95)-Polybagged w/16 pg Marvel Action Hour Preview & acetate print ... 3.00

MARVEL ACTION HOUR FEATURING THE FANTASTIC FOUR (TV cartoon)
Marvel Comics: Nov, 1994 - No. 8, June, 1995 ($1.50/$2.95)
1-8: Based on cartoon series 2.50
1-($2.95)-Polybagged w/ 16 pg. Marvel Action Hour Preview & acetate print ... 3.00

MARVEL ACTION UNIVERSE (TV cartoon)
Marvel Comics: Jan, 1989 ($1.00, one-shot)
1-r/Spider-Man And His Amazing Friends 4.00

MARVEL ADVENTURES
Marvel Comics: Apr, 1997 - No. 18, Sept, 1998 ($1.50)
1-18-"Animated style": 1,4,7-Hulk-c/app. 2,11-Spider-Man. 3,8,15-X-Men. 5-Spider-Man &
X-Men. 6-Spider-Man & Human Torch. 9,12-Fantastic Four. 10,16-Silver Surfer.
13-Spider-Man & Silver Surfer. 14-Hulk & Dr. Strange. 18-Capt. America 2.50

MARVEL ADVENTURES FANTASTIC FOUR (All ages title)
Marvel Comics: No. 0, July, 2005 - Present ($1.99/$2.50/$2.99)
0-($1.99) Movie version characters; Dr. Doom app.; Eaton-a 2.50
1-10-($2.50) 1-Skrulls app.; Pagulayan-a. 7-Namor app. 2.50
11-28-($2.99) 12-Dr. Doom app. 24-Namor app. 26,28-Silver Surfer app. ... 3.00
... Vol. 1: Family of Heroes (2005, $6.99, digest) r/#1-4 .... 7.00
... Vol. 2: Fantastic Voyages (2006, $6.99, digest) r/#5-8 .... 7.00
... Vol. 3: World's Greatest (2006, $6.99, digest) r/#9-12 .... 7.00
... Vol. 4: Cosmic Threats (2006, $6.99, digest) r/#13-16 .... 7.00
... Vol. 5: All 4 One, 4 For All (2007, $6.99, digest) r/#17-20 .... 7.00
... Vol. 6: Monsters & Mysteries (2007, $6.99, digest) r/#21-24 ... 7.00

MARVEL ADVENTURES FLIP MAGAZINE (All ages title)
Marvel Comics: Aug, 2005 - Present ($3.99/$4.99)
1-11: 1-10-Rep. Marvel Advs. Fantastic Four and Marvel Advs. Spider-Man in flip format ... 4.00
12-14-Reprints Marvel Advs. Spider-Man & X-Men/Power Pack in flip format ... 5.00
15-26-Rep. Marvel Advs. Fantastic Four and Marvel Advs. Spider-Man in flip format ... 5.00

MARVEL ADVENTURES HULK (All ages title)
Marvel Comics: Sept, 2007 - Present ($2.99)
1-3: 1-New version of Hulk's origin; Pagulayan-a. 2-Jamie Madrox app. ... 3.00

MARVEL ADVENTURES IRON MAN (All ages title)
Marvel Comics: July, 2007 - Present ($2.99)
1-5: 1-4-Michael Golden-c. 1-New version of Iron Man's origin. 2-Intro. the Mandarin ... 3.00
... Vol. 1: Heart of Steel (2007, $6.99, digest) r/#1-4 .... 7.00

MARVEL ADVENTURES SPIDER-MAN (All ages title)
Marvel Comics: May, 2005 - Present ($2.50/$2.99)
1-13-Lee & Ditko stories retold with new art. 13-Conner-c 2.50
14-31: 14-Begin $2.99-c. 16-Conner-c. 16-Lizard app. 22,23-Black costume ... 2.99
... Vol. 1 HC (2006, $19.99, with dustjacket) r/#1-8; plot for #7; sketch pages from #6,8 ... 20.00
... Vol. 1: The Sinister Six (2005, $6.99, digest) r/#1-4 .... 7.00
... Vol. 2: Power Struggle (2005, $6.99, digest) r/#5-8 .... 7.00
... Vol. 3: Doom With a View (2006, $6.99, digest) r/#9-12 .... 7.00
... Vol. 4: Concrete Jungle (2006, $6.99, digest) r/#13-16 .... 7.00
... Vol. 5: Monsters on the Prowl (2007, $6.99, digest) r/#17-20 .. 7.00
... Vol. 6: The Black Costume (2007, $6.99, digest) r/#21-24 ...... 7.00
... Vol. 7: Secret Identity (2007, $6.99, digest) r/#25-28 .... 7.00

MARVEL ADVENTURES STARRING DAREDEVIL (...Adventure #3 on)
Marvel Comics Group: Dec, 1975 - No. 6, Oct, 1976

1	1	3	4	6	8	10
2-6-r/Daredevil #22-27 by Colan. 3-5-(25¢-c)						6.00
3-5-(30¢-c variants, limited distribution)(4,6,8/76)	2	4	6	11	16	20

MARVEL ADVENTURES THE AVENGERS (All ages title)
Marvel Comics: July, 2006 - Present ($2.99)
1-16-Spider-Man, Wolverine, Hulk, Iron Man, Capt. America, Storm, Giant-Girl app. ... 3.00
... Vol. 1: Heroes Assembled (2006, $6.99, digest) r/#1-4 .... 7.00
... Vol. 2: Mischief (2006, $6.99, digest) r/#5-8 .... 7.00
... Vol. 3: Bizarre Adventures (2007, $6.99, digest) r/#9-12 ...... 7.00
... Vol. 4: The Dream Team (2007, $6.99, digest) r/#13-15 & Giant-Size #1 ... 7.00

MARVEL ADVENTURES TWO-IN-ONE
Marvel Comics: Oct, 2007 - Present ($4.99, bi-weekly)

Marvel Boy #4 © MAR

Marvel Collectors' Item Classics #8 © MAR

Marvel Comics Presents #3 © MAR

			GD	VG	FN	VF	VF/NM	NM-					GD	VG	FN	VF	VF/NM	NM-
			2.0	4.0	6.0	8.0	9.0	9.2					2.0	4.0	6.0	8.0	9.0	9.2

1-3-Reprints Marvel Adventures Spider-Man and Fantastic Four stories   5.00

MARVEL AGE FANTASTIC FOUR (All ages title)
Marvel Comics: Jun, 2004 - No. 12, Mar, 2005 ($2.25)

1-12-Lee & Kirby stories retold with new art by various. 11-Impossible Man app.   2.50
...Tales (4/05, $2.25) retells first meeting with the Black Panther; O'Hare & Lim-a   2.50
Vol. 1: All For One TPB (2004, $5.99, digest size) r/#1-4   6.00
Vol. 2: Doom TPB (2004, $5.99, digest size) r/#5-8   6.00
Vol. 3: The Return of Doctor Doom TPB (2005, $5.99, digest size) r/#9-12   6.00

MARVEL AGE HULK (All ages title)
Marvel Comics: Nov, 2004 - No. 4, Feb, 2005 ($1.75)

1-3-Lee & Kirby stories retold with new art by various   2.50
Vol. 1: Incredible TPB (2005, $5.99, digest size) r/#1-4   6.00

MARVEL AGE SPIDER-MAN (All ages title) (Also see Free Comic Book Day edition in the Promotional Comics section)
Marvel Comics: May, 2004 - No. 20, Mar, 2005 ($2.25)

1-20-Lee & Ditko stories retold with new art. 4-Doctor Doom app. 5-Lizard app.   2.50
Vol. 1 TPB (2004, $5.99, digest) 1-r/#1-4   6.00
Vol. 2: Everyday Hero TPB (2004, $5.99, digest) r/#5-8   6.00
Vol. 3: Swingtime TPB (2004, $5.99, digest) r/#9-12   6.00
Spidey Strikes Back TPB (2005, 5.99, digest) r/#17-20   6.00

MARVEL AGE TEAM-UP (All ages Spider-Man team-ups) (Also see Free Comic Book Day edition in the Promotional Comics section)
Marvel Comics: Nov, 2004 - No. 5, Apr, 2005 ($1.75)

1-5-Stories retold with new art by various. 1-Fantastic Four app. 3-Kitty Pryde app.   2.50
... Vol. 1: A Little Help From My Friends (2005, $7.99, digest) r/#1-5   8.00

MARVEL AND DC PRESENT FEATURING THE UNCANNY X-MEN AND THE NEW TEEN TITANS
Marvel Comics/DC Comics: 1982 ($2.00, 68 pgs., one-shot, Baxter paper)

													GD	VG	FN	VF	VF/NM	NM-
1-3rd app. Deathstroke the Terminator; Darkseid app.; Simonson/Austin-c/a													2	4	6	11	16	20

MARVEL BOY (Astonishing #3 on; see Marvel Super Action #4)
Marvel Comics (MPC): Dec, 1950 - No. 2, Feb, 1951

	GD	VG	FN	VF	VF/NM	NM-
1-Origin Marvel Boy by Russ Heath	110	220	330	688	1144	1600
2-Everett-a	78	156	234	488	807	1125

MARVEL BOY (Marvel Knights)
Marvel Comics: Aug, 2000 - No. 6, Mar, 2001 ($2.99, limited series)

1-Intro. Marvel Boy; Morrison-s/J.G. Jones-c/a   3.50
1-DF Variant-c   5.00
2-6   3.00
TPB (6/01, $15.95)   16.00

MARVEL CHILLERS (Also see Giant-Size Chillers)
Marvel Comics Group: Oct, 1975 - No. 7, Oct, 1976 (All 25¢ issues)

	GD	VG	FN	VF	VF/NM	NM-
1-Intro. Modred the Mystic, ends #2; Kane-c(p)	2	4	6	9	12	15
2,4,5,7: 4-Kraven app. 5,6-Red Wolf app. 7-Kirby-c; Tuska-(p)	1	2	3	5	7	9
3-Tigra, the Were-Woman begins (origin), ends #7 (see Giant-Size Creatures #1). Chaykin/Wrightson-c.	2	4	6	13	18	22
4-6-(30¢ variants, limited distribution)(4-8/76)	3	6	9	16	23	30
6-Byrne-a(p); Buckler-c(p)	2	4	8	10	12	12

NOTE: *Bolle* a-1. *Buckler* c-2. *Kirby* c-7.

MARVEL CLASSICS COMICS SERIES FEATURING...
(Also see Pendulum Illustrated Classics)
Marvel Comics Group: 1976 - No. 36, Dec, 1978 (52 pgs., no ads)

	GD	VG	FN	VF	VF/NM	NM-
1-Dr. Jekyll and Mr. Hyde	2	4	6	10	14	18
2-10,28: 28-1st Golden-c/a; Pit and the Pendulum	2	4	6	8	10	12
11-27,29-36	1	2	3	5	7	9

NOTE: *Adkins* c-1i, 4i, 12i. *Alcala* a-34i; c-34. *Bolle* a-35. *Buscema* c-17p, 19p, 26p. *Golden* c/a-28. *Gil Kane* c-1-16p, 21p, 22p, 24p, 32p. *Nebres* a-5; c-24i. *Nino* a-2, 8, 12. *Redondo* a-1, 9. No. 1-12 were reprinted from Pendulum Illustrated Classics.

MARVEL COLLECTIBLE CLASSICS: AVENGERS
Marvel Comics: 1998 ($10.00, reprints with chromium wraparound-c)

1-Reprints Avengers Vol.3, #1; Perez-c   10.00

MARVEL COLLECTIBLE CLASSICS: SPIDER-MAN
Marvel Comics: 1998 ($10.00, reprints with chromium wraparound-c)

1-Reprints Amazing Spider-Man #300; McFarlane-c   10.00
2-Reprints Spider-Man #1; McFarlane-c   10.00

MARVEL COLLECTIBLE CLASSICS: X-MEN

Marvel Comics: 1998 ($10.00, reprints with chromium wraparound-c)

1-6: 1-Reprints (Uncanny) X-Men #1 & 2; Adam Kubert-c. 2-Reprints Uncanny X-Men #141 & 142; Byrne-c. 3-Reprints (Uncanny) X-Men #137; Larroca-c. 4-Reprints X-Men #25; Andy Kubert-c. 5-Reprints Giant Size X-Men #1; Gary Frank-c. 6-Reprints X-Men V2#1; Ramos-c   10.00

MARVEL COLLECTOR'S EDITION
Marvel Comics: 1992 (Ordered thru mail with Charleston Chew candy wrapper)

1-Flip-book format; Spider-Man, Silver Surfer, Wolverine (by Sam Kieth), & Ghost Rider stories; Wolverine back-c by Kieth   3.00

MARVEL COLLECTORS' ITEM CLASSICS (Marvel's Greatest #23 on)
Marvel Comics Group(ATF): Feb, 1965 - No. 22, Aug, 1969 (25¢, 68 pgs.)

	GD	VG	FN	VF	VF/NM	NM-
1-Fantastic Four, Spider-Man, Thor, Hulk, Iron Man-r begin	10	20	30	68	119	170
2 (4/66)	6	12	18	39	62	85
3,4	5	10	15	30	48	65
5-10	4	8	12	26	41	55
11-22: 22-r/The Man in the Ant Hill/TTA #27	4	8	12	22	34	45

NOTE: *All reprints; Ditko, Kirby* art in all.

MARVEL COMICS (Marvel Mystery Comics #2 on)
Timely Comics (Funnies, Inc.): Oct, Nov, 1939

NOTE: The first issue was originally dated October 1939. Most copies have a black circle stamped over the date (on cover and inside) with "November" printed over it. However, some copies do not have the November overprint and could have a higher value. Most No. 1's have printing defects, i.e., tilted pages which caused trimming into the panels usually on right side and bottom. Covers exist with and without glossy finish.

	GD	VG	FN	VF	VF/NM	NM-
1-Origin Sub-Mariner by Bill Everett(1st newsstand app.); 1st 8 pgs. were produced for Motion Picture Funnies Weekly #1 which was probably not distributed outside of advance copies; intro Human Torch by Carl Burgos, Kazar the Great (1st Tarzan clone), & Jungle Terror(only app.); intro. The Angel by Gustavson, The Masked Raider & his horse Lightning (ends #12); cover by sci/fi pulp illustrator Frank R. Paul	22,000	44,000	66,000	147,000	260,000	440,000

MARVEL COMICS PRESENTS
Marvel Comics (Midnight Sons imprint #143 on): Early Sept, 1988 - No. 175, Feb, 1995 ($1.25/$1.50/$1.75, bi-weekly)

	GD	VG	FN	VF	VF/NM	NM-
1-Wolverine by Buscema in #1-10						6.00
2-5						4.00
6-10: 6-Sub-Mariner app. 10-Colossus begins						3.00

11-47,51-71: 17-Cyclops begins. 19-1st app. Damage Control. 24-Havok begins. 25-Origin/1st app. Nth Man. 26-Hulk begins by Rogers. 29-Quasar app. 31-Excalibur begins by Austin (i). 32-McFarlane-a(p). 33-Capt. America; Jim Lee-a. 37-Devil-Slayer app. 38-Wolverine begins by Buscema; Hulk app. 39-Spider-Man app. 46-Liefeld Wolverine-c. 51-53-Wolverine by Rob Liefeld. 54-61-Wolverine/Hulk story. 54-Werewolf by Night begins; The Shroud by Ditko. 58-Iron Man by Ditko. 59-Punisher. 62-Deathlok & Wolverine stories 63-Wolverine. 64-71-Wolverine/Ghost Rider 8-part story. 70-Liefeld Ghost Rider/Wolverine-c   2.50

48-50-Wolverine & Spider-Man team-up by Erik Larsen-a. 48-Wasp app. 49,50-Savage Dragon prototype app. by Larsen. 50-Silver Surfer. 50-53-Comet Man; Mumy scripts   4.00
72-Begin 13-part Weapon-X story (Wolverine origin) by B. Windsor-Smith (prologue)   5.00
73-Weapon-X part 1; Black Knight, Sub-Mariner   4.00
74-84: 74-Weapon-X part 2; Black Knight, Sub-Mariner. 76-Death's Head story. 77-Mr. Fantastic story. 78-Iron Man by Steacy. 80,81-Capt. America by Ditko/Austin. 81-Daredevil by Rogers/Williamson. 82-Power Man. 83-Human Torch by Ditko(a&scripts); $1.00-c direct, $1.25 newsstand. 84-Last Weapon-X (24 pg. conclusion)   3.00
85-Begin 8-part Wolverine story by Sam Kieth (c/a); 1st Kieth-a on Wolverine; begin 8-part Ghost Rider story by Jae Lee(p) with Liefeld part pencils #85,86; 1st Jae Lee-a (assisted w/Liefeld, 1991)   4.00
86-90: 86-89-Wolverine, Beast stories continue. 90-Begin 8-part Ghost Rider & Cable story, ends #97; begin flip book format   3.00
91-175: 93-Begin 6-part Wolverine story, ends #98. 98-Begin 2-part Ghost Rider story. 99-Spider-Man story. 100-Full-length Ghost Rider/Wolverine story by Sam Kieth w/Tim Vigil assists; anniversary issue, non flip-book. 101-Begin 6-part Ghost Rider/Dr. Strange story & begin 8-part Wolverine/Nightcrawler story by Colan/Williamson; Punisher story. 107-Begin 6-part Ghost Rider/Werewolf by Night story. 109-Begin 8-part Wolverine/Typhoid Mary story. 111-Iron Fist. 113-Begin 6-part Giant-Man & begin 6-part Ghost Rider/Iron Fist stories. 117-Preview of Ravage 2099 (1st app.); begin 6-part Wolverine/Venom story w/Kieth-a. 118-Preview of Doom 2099 (1st app.). 119-Begin Ghost Rider/Cloak & Dagger by Colan. 120,136,138-Spider-Man story. 123-Begin 6-part Ghost Rider/Typhoid Mary story; begin 4-part She Hulk story; begin 8-part Wolverine/Lynx story. 125-Begin 6-part Iron Fist story. 130-Begin 6-part Ghost Rider; begin 6-part Wolverine/ Cage story. 136-Daredevil. 137-Begin 6-part Wolverine story & 6-part Ghost Rider story. 147-Begin 2-part story w/new Ghost Rider. 149-Vengeance-c/story w/new Ghost Rider. 150-Silver ink-c; begin 2-part Bloody Mary story w/Typhoid Mary,Wolverine, Daredevil, new Ghost Rider; intro Steel

Marvel Double Feature #15 © MAR

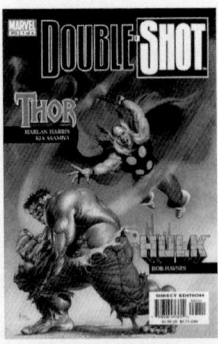

Marvel Double Shot #1 © MAR

Marvel Family #7 © FAW

	GD 2.0	VG 4.0	FN 6.0	VF 8.0	VF/NM 9.0	NM- 9.2

Raven. 152-Begin 4-part Wolverine, 4-part War Machine, 4-part Vengeance, 3-part Moon Knight stories; same date as War Machine #1. 143-146: Siege of Darkness parts 3,6,11,14; all have spot-varnished-c. 143-Ghost Rider/Scarlet Witch; intro new Werewolf. 144-Begin 2-part Morbius story. 145-Begin 2-part Nightstalkers story. 153-155-Bound-in Spider-Man trading card sheet 2.50

...Colossus: God's Country (1994, $6.95) r/#10-17 1 2 3 4 5 7

...: Wolverine Vol. 1 TPB (2005, $12.99) r/Wolverine stories from #1-10 .... 13.00
...: Wolverine Vol. 2 TPB (2006, $12.99) r/from #39-50 and Marvel Age Annual #4 .... 13.00
...: Wolverine Vol. 3 TPB (2006, $12.99) r/from #51-61 .... 13.00
...: Wolverine Vol. 4 TPB (2006, $12.99) r/from #62-71 .... 13.00
NOTE: *Austin* a-31-37i; c(i)-48, 50, 99, 122. *Buscema* a-1-10, 38-47; c-6. *Byrne* a-79; c-71. *Colan* a(p)-36, 37. *Colan/Williamson* a-101-108. *Ditko* a-7p, 10, 56p, 58, 80, 81, 83. *Guice* a-62. *Sam Kieth* a-85-92, 117-122; c-85-98, 99p, 100-108, 117, 118, 120-122; back c-109-113, 117. *Jae Lee* c-129(back). *Liefeld* a-51, 52, 53p(2), 85p; c-46, 70. *McFarlane* c-32. *Mooney* a-73. *Rogers* a-26, 38, 46i, 81p. *Russell* a-10-14,16,17i; c-4,19, 30,31i. *Saltares* a-8p(early), 38-45p. *Simonson* c-1. *B. Smith* a-72-84; c-72-84. *P. Smith* c-34. *Sparling* a-33. *Starlin* a-89i. *Staton* a-74. *Steacy* a-78. *Sutton* a-101-105. *Williamson* c-62i. Two Gun Kid by *Gil Kane* in #116, 122.

MARVEL COMICS PRESENTS
Marvel Comics: Nov, 2007 - Present ($3.99)

1-Short stories by various; wraparound-c by Campbell 4.00

MARVEL COMICS SUPER SPECIAL, A (Marvel Super Special #5 on)
Marvel Comics: Sept, 1977 - No. 41(?), Nov, 1986 (nn 7) ($1.50, magazine)

1-Kiss, 40 pgs. comics plus photos & features; John Buscema-a(p); also see Howard the Duck #12; ink contains real KISS blood; Dr. Doom, Spider-Man, Avengers, Fantastic Four, Mephisto app. 11 22 33 77 136 195
2-Conan (1978) 2 4 6 13 18 22
3-Close Encounters of the Third Kind (1978); Simonson-a 2 4 6 9 12 15
4-The Beatles Story (1978)-Perez/Janson-a; has photos & articles 4 8 12 28 44 60
5-Kiss (1978)-Includes poster 11 22 33 77 136 195
6-Jaws II (1978) 2 4 6 9 12 15
7-Sgt. Pepper; Beatles movie adaptation; withdrawn from U.S. distribution (French ed. exists)
8-Battlestar Galactica; tabloid size ($1.50, 1978); adapts TV show 2 4 6 11 16 20
8-Modern-r of tabloid size 2 4 6 10 14 18
8-Battlestar Galactica; publ. in regular magazine format; low distribution ($1.50, 8-1/2x11") 2 4 6 13 18 22
9-Conan 2 4 6 10 14 18
10-Star-Lord 2 4 6 8 11 14
11-13-Weirdworld begins #11; 25 copy special press run of each with gold seal and signed by artists (Proof quality), Spring-June, 1979 7 14 21 50 83 115
11-15: 11-13-Weirdworld (regular issues): 11-Fold-out centerfold. 14-Miller-c(p); adapts movie "Meteor." 15-Star Trek with photos & pin-ups ($1.50-c) 1 3 4 6 8 10
15-With $2.00 price; the price was changed at tail end of a 200,000 press run 2 4 6 8 10 12
16-Empire Strikes Back adaption; Williamson-a 2 4 6 8 11 14
17-20 (Movie adaptations):17-Xanadu. 18-Raiders of the Lost Ark. 19-For Your Eyes Only (James Bond). 20-Dragonslayer 6.00
21-26,28-30 (Movie adaptations): 21-Conan. 22-Blade Runner; Williamson-a; Steranko-c. 23-Annie. 24-The Dark Crystal. 25-Rock and Rule-w/photos; artwork is from movie. 26-Octopussy (James Bond). 28-Krull; photo-c. 29-Tarzan of the Apes (Greystoke movie). 30-Indiana Jones and the Temple of Doom 1 2 3 4 5 6
27,31-41: 27-Return of the Jedi. 31-The Last Star Fighter. 32-The Muppets Take Manhattan. 33-Buckaroo Banzai. 34-Sheena. 35-Conan The Destroyer. 36-Dune. 37-2010. 38-Red Sonja. 39-Santa Claus:The Movie. 40-Labyrinth. 41-Howard The Duck 1 2 3 4 5 6
NOTE: *J. Buscema* a-1, 2, 9, 11-13, 18p, 21, 35, 40; c-11(part), 13. *Chaykin* a-9, 19p; c-18, 19. *Colan* a(p)-6, 10, 14. *Morrow* a-34; c-1i, 34. *Nebres* a-11. *Spiegle* a-29. *Stevens* a-27. *Williamson* a-27. #22-28 contain photos from movies.

MARVEL COMICS: 2001
Marvel Comics: 2001 (no cover price, one-shot)

1-Previews new titles for Fall 2001; Wolverine-c 2.50

MARVEL DABEL BROTHERS SAMPLER
Marvel Comics: Dec, 2006 (no cover price, one-shot)

1-Profiles and sample pages of Anita Blake, Magician: Apprentice, Red Prophet, Ptolus 2.50

MARVEL DOUBLE FEATURE
Marvel Comics Group: Dec, 1973 - No. 21, Mar, 1977

1-Capt. America, Iron Man-r/T.O.S. begin 2 4 6 9 13 16
2-10: 3-Last 20¢ issue 1 3 4 6 8 10
11-17,20,21:17-Story-r/Iron Man & Sub-Mariner #1; last 25¢ issue 6.00
15-17-(30¢-c variants, limited distribution)(4,6,8/76) 1 3 4 6 8 10

18,19-Colan/Craig-r from Iron Man #1 in both 1 2 3 5 6 8
NOTE: *Colan* r-1-19p. *Craig* a-17-19i. *G. Kane* r-15p; c-15p. *Kirby* r-1-16p, 20, 21; c-17-20.

MARVEL DOUBLE SHOT
Marvel Comics: Jan, 2003 - No. 4, April, 2003 ($2.99, limited series)

1-4: 1-Hulk by Haynes; Thor w/Asamiya-a; Jusko-c. 2-Dr. Doom by Rivera; Simpsons-style Avengers by Bill Morrison 3.00

MARVEL FAMILY (Also see Captain Marvel Adventures No. 18)
Fawcett Publications: Dec, 1945 - No. 89, Jan, 1954

1-Origin Captain Marvel, Captain Marvel Jr., Mary Marvel, & Uncle Marvel retold; origin/1st app. Black Adam 179 358 537 1119 1860 2600
2-The 3 Lt. Marvels & Uncle Marvel app. 78 156 234 488 807 1125
3 54 108 162 338 557 775
4,5 45 90 135 275 450 625
6-10: 7-Shazam app. 39 78 117 224 355 485
11-20 29 58 87 167 264 360
21-30 25 50 75 145 228 310
31-40 20 40 60 117 184 250
41-46,48-50 16 32 48 94 147 200
47-Flying Saucer-c/story (5/50) 23 46 69 135 213 290
51-76 15 30 45 88 137 185
77-Communist Threat-c 26 52 78 150 235 320
78,81-Used in **POP**, pg. 92,93. 18 36 54 103 162 220
79,80,82-89: 79-Horror satire-c 17 34 51 98 154 210

MARVEL FANFARE (1st Series)
Marvel Comics Group: Mar, 1982 - No. 60, Jan, 1992 ($1.25/$2.25, slick paper, direct sales)

1-Spider-Man/Angel team-up; 1st Paul Smith-a (1st full story); see King Conan #7); Daredevil app. (many copies were printed missing the centerfold) 1 2 3 5 6 8
2-Spider-Man, Ka-Zar, The Angel. F.F. origin retold 6.00
3,4-X-Men & Ka-Zar. 4-Deathlok, Spidey app. 5.00
5-14: 5-Dr. Strange, Capt. America. 6-Spider-Man, Scarlet Witch. 7-Incredible Hulk; D.D. back-up(also 15). 8-Dr. Strange; Wolf Boy begins. 9-Man-Thing. 10-13-Black Widow. 14-The Vision 3.00
15,24,33: 15-The Thing by Barry Smith, c/a. 24-Weirdworld; Wolverine back-up. 33-X-Men, Wolverine app.; Punisher cameo. 4.00
16-23,25-32,34,44,46-50: 16,17-Skywolf. 16-Sub-Mariner back-up. 17-Hulk back-up. 18-Capt. America by Miller. 19-Cloak and Dagger. 20-Thing/Dr. Strange. 21-Thing/Dr. Strange /Hulk. 22,23-Iron Man vs. Dr. Octopus. 25,26-Weirdworld. 27-Daredevil/Spider-Man. 28-Alpha Flight. 29-Hulk. 30-Moon Knight. 31,32-Captain America. 34-37-Warriors Three. 38-Moon Knight/Dazzler. 39-Moon Knight/Hawkeye. 40-Angel/Rogue & Storm. 41-Dr. Strange. 42-Spider-Man. 43-Sub-Mariner/Human Torch. 44-Iron Man vs. Dr. Doom by Ken Steacy. 46-Fantastic Four. 47-Hulk. 48-She-Hulk/Vision. 49-Dr. Strange/Nick Fury. 50-X-Factor 2.50
45-All pin-up issue by Steacy, Art Adams & others 4.00
51-($2.95, 52 pgs.)-Silver Surfer; Fantastic Four & Capt. Marvel app.; 51,52-Colan/Williamson back-up (Dr. Strange) 3.00
52,53,56-60: 52,53-Black Knight; 53-Iron Man back up. 56-59-Shanna the She-Devil. 58-Vision & Scarlet Witch back-up. 60-Black Panther/Rogue/Daredevil stories 2.50
54,55-Wolverine back-ups. 54-Black Knight. 55-Power Pack 4.00
NOTE: *Art Adams* c-13. *Austin* a-1i, 4i, 33i, 38i; c-8i, 33i. *Buscema* a-51p. *Byrne* a-1p, 29, 48; c-29. *Chiodo* painted c-56-59. *Colan* a-51p. *Cowan/Simonson* c/a-60. *Golden* a-1, 2, 4p, 47; c-1, 2, 47. *Infantino* c/a(p)-8. *Gil Kane* a-8-11p. *Miller* a-18; c-1(Back-c), 18. *Perez* a-10, 11p, 12, 13p; c-10-13p. *Rogers* a-5p; c-5p. *Russell* a-5i, 6i, 8-11i, 43i; c-5i, 6. *Paul Smith* a-1p, 4p, 32, 60; c-4p. *Staton* a-7a(50(p). *Williamson* a-30i, 51i.

MARVEL FANFARE (2nd Series)
Marvel Comics: Sept, 1996 - No. 6, Feb, 1997 (99¢)

1-6: 1-Capt. America & The Falcon-c/story; Deathlok app. 2-Wolverine & Hulk-c/app. 3-Ghost Rider & Spider-Man-c/app. 5-Longshot-c/app. 6-Sabretooth, Power Man, & Iron Fist-c/app 2.50

MARVEL FEATURE (See Marvel Two-In-One)
Marvel Comics Group: Dec, 1971 - No. 12, Nov, 1973 (1,2: 25¢, 52 pg. giants) (#1-3: quarterly)

1-Origin/1st app. The Defenders (Sub-Mariner, Hulk & Dr. Strange); see Sub-Mariner #34,35 for prequel; Dr. Strange solo story (predates Dr.Strange #1) plus 1950s Sub-Mariner-r; Neal Adams-c 15 30 45 107 191 275
2-2nd app. Defenders; 1950s Sub-Mariner-r. Rutland, Vermont Halloween x-over 8 16 24 54 90 125
3-Defenders ends 6 12 18 39 62 85
4-Re-intro Antman (1st app. since 1960s), begin series; brief origin; Spider-Man app. 4 8 12 18 27 35
5-7,9,10: 6-Wasp app. & begins team-ups. 9-Iron Man app. 10-Last Antman 2 4 6 11 16 18
8-Origin Antman & Wasp/TTA #44; Kirby-a 2 4 6 13 18 22
11-Thing vs. Hulk; 1st Thing solo book (9/73); origin Fantastic Four retold

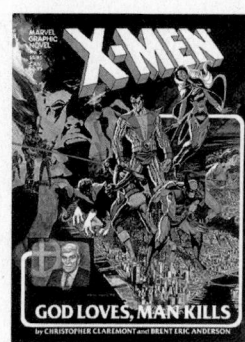

Marvel Graphic Novel #5 © MAR

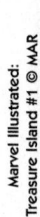

Marvel Illustrated: Treasure Island #1 © MAR

Marvel Knights #5 © MAR

	GD 2.0	VG 4.0	FN 6.0	VF 8.0	VF/NM 9.0	NM- 9.2
	6	12	18	39	62	85

12-Thing/Iron Man; early Thanos app.; occurs after Capt. Marvel #33; Starlin-a(p)

| | 4 | 8 | 12 | 24 | 37 | 50 |

NOTE: *Bolle* a-9i. *Everett* a-1i, 3i. *Hartley* r-10. *Kane* c-3p, 7p. *Russell* a-7-10p. *Starlin* a-8, 11, 12; c-8.

MARVEL FEATURE (Also see Red Sonja)
Marvel Comics: Nov, 1975 - No. 7, Nov, 1976 (Story cont'd in Conan #68)

1,7: 1-Red Sonja begins (pre-dates Red Sonja #1); adapts Howard short story; Adams-r/Savage Sword of Conan #1. 7-Battles Conan

| | 1 | 3 | 4 | 6 | 8 | 10 |

2-6: Thorne-c/a in #2-7. 4,5-(Regular 25¢ edition)(5,7/76)

| | | | | | | 6.00 |

4,5-(30¢-c variants, limited distribution)

| | 2 | 4 | 6 | 11 | 16 | 20 |

MARVEL FRONTIER COMICS UNLIMITED
Marvel Frontier Comics: Jan, 1994 ($2.95, 68 pgs.)

1-Dances with Demons, Immortalis, Children of the Voyager, Evil Eye, The Fallen stories 3.00

MARVEL FUMETTI BOOK
Marvel Comics Group: Apr, 1984 ($1.00, one-shot)

1-All photos; Stan Lee photo-c; Art Adams touch-ups 4.00

MARVEL FUN & GAMES
Marvel Comics Group: 1979/80 (color comic for kids)

1,11: 1-Games, puzzles. etc. 11-X-Men-c

| | 1 | 2 | 3 | 5 | 7 | 9 |

2-10,12,13: (beware marked pages)

| | | | | | | 6.00 |

MARVEL GRAPHIC NOVEL
Marvel Comics Group (Epic Comics): 1982 - No. 38, 1990? ($5.95/$6.95)

1-Death of Captain Marvel (2nd Marvel graphic novel); Capt. Marvel battles Thanos by Jim Starlin (c/a/scripts)

| | 3 | 6 | 9 | 14 | 19 | 24 |

1 (2nd & 3rd printings)

| | 1 | 2 | 3 | 5 | 6 | 9 |

2-Elric: The Dreaming City

| | 2 | 4 | 6 | 8 | 10 | 12 |

3-Dreadstar; Starlin-c/a, 52 pgs.

| | 2 | 4 | 6 | 8 | 11 | 14 |

4-Origin/1st app. The New Mutants (1982)

| | 2 | 4 | 6 | 8 | 11 | 14 |

4,5-2nd printings

| | 1 | 2 | 3 | 4 | 5 | 7 |

5-X-Men; book-length story (1982)

| | 2 | 4 | 6 | 9 | 14 | 20 |

6-15,20,23,25,30,31: 6-The Star Slammers. 7-Killraven. 8-Super Boxers; Byrne scripts. 9-The Futurians. 10-Heartburst. 11-Void Indigo. 12-Dazzler. 13-Starstruck. 14-The Swords Of The Swashbucklers. 15-The Raven Banner (a Tale of Asgard). 20-Greenberg the Vampire. 23-Dr. Strange. 25-Alien Legion. 30-A Sailor's Story. 31-Wolfpack

| | 1 | 2 | 3 | 5 | 7 | 9 |

16,17,21,29: 16-The Aladdin Effect (Storm, Tigra, Wasp, She-Hulk). 17-Revenge Of The Living Monolith (Spider-Man, Avengers, FF app.). 21-Marada the She-Wolf. 29-The Big Chance (Thing vs. Hulk)

| | 1 | 2 | 3 | 5 | 7 | 9 |

18,19,26-28: 18-She Hulk. 19-Witch Queen of Acheron (Conan). 26-Dracula. 27-Avengers (Emperor Doom). 28-Conan the Reaver

| | 2 | 4 | 6 | 9 | 11 | 13 |

22-Amaz. Spider-Man in Hooky by Wrightson

| | 2 | 4 | 6 | 9 | 12 | 15 |

24-Love and War (Daredevil); Miller scripts

| | 2 | 4 | 6 | 8 | 11 | 14 |

32-Death of Groo

| | 2 | 4 | 6 | 9 | 12 | 15 |

32-2nd printing ($5.95)

| | 1 | 2 | 3 | 5 | 5 | 6 |

33,34,36,37: 33-Thor. 34-Predator & Prey (Cloak & Dagger). 36-Willow (movie adapt.). 37-Hercules

| | 1 | 3 | 4 | 6 | 8 | 10 |

35-Hitler's Astrologer (The Shadow, $12.95, HC)

| | 2 | 4 | 6 | 9 | 13 | 16 |

35-Soft-c reprint (1990, $10.95)

| | 2 | 4 | 6 | 8 | 10 | 12 |

38-Silver Surfer (Judgement Day)($14.95, HC)

| | 2 | 4 | 6 | 10 | 14 | 18 |

38-Silver Surfer reprint (1990, $10.95)

| | 2 | 4 | 6 | 8 | 11 | 14 |

nn-Absolom Dalak Killer (1990, $8.95) Dr. Who

| | 1 | 3 | 4 | 6 | 8 | 10 |

nn-Arena by Bruce Jones (1989, $5.95) Dinosaurs

| | 1 | 2 | 3 | 5 | 6 | 8 |

nn- A-Team Storybook Comics Illustrated (1983) r/ A-Team mini-series #1-3

| | 1 | 3 | 4 | 6 | 8 | 10 |

nn-Ax (1988, $5.95) Ernie Colan-s/a

| | 1 | 3 | 4 | 6 | 8 | 10 |

nn-Black Widow Coldest War (4/90, $9.95)

| | 2 | 4 | 6 | 8 | 10 | 12 |

nn-Chronicles of Genghis Grimtoad (1990, $8.95)-Alan Grant-s

| | 1 | 3 | 4 | 6 | 8 | 10 |

nn-Conan the Barbarian in the Horn of Azoth (1990, $8.95)

| | 2 | 4 | 6 | 8 | 11 | 16 |

nn-Conan of Isles ($8.95)

| | 2 | 4 | 6 | 8 | 11 | 16 |

nn-Conan Ravagers of Time (1992, $9.95) Kull & Red Sonja app.

| | 2 | 4 | 6 | 8 | 11 | 16 |

nn-Conan -The Skull of Set

| | 2 | 4 | 6 | 8 | 11 | 16 |

nn-Doctor Strange and Doctor Doom Triumph and Torment (1989, $17.95, HC)

| | 3 | 6 | 9 | 13 | 18 | 22 |

nn-Dreamwalker (1989, $6.95)-Morrow-a

| | 1 | 2 | 3 | 5 | 7 | 9 |

nn-Excalibur Weird War III (1990, $9.95)

| | 2 | 4 | 6 | 8 | 10 | 12 |

nn-G.I. Joe - The Trojan Gambit (1983, 68 pgs.)

| | 2 | 4 | 6 | 8 | 10 | 12 |

nn-Harvey Kurtzman Strange Adventures (Epic, $19.95, HC) Aragonés, Crumb

---

	GD 2.0	VG 4.0	FN 6.0	VF 8.0	VF/NM 9.0	NM- 9.2

nn-Hearts and Minds (1990, $8.95) Heath-a

| | 3 | 6 | 9 | 14 | 20 | 25 |

nn-Inhumans (1988, $7.95)-Williamson-i

| | 1 | 3 | 4 | 6 | 8 | 10 |

nn-Jhereg (Epic, 1990, $8.95)

| | 1 | 2 | 3 | 5 | 7 | 9 |

nn-Kazar-Guns of the Savage Land (7/90, $8.95)

| | 1 | 3 | 4 | 6 | 8 | 10 |

nn-Kull-The Vale of Shadow ('89, $6.95)

| | 2 | 4 | 6 | 8 | 10 | 12 |

nn-Last of the Dragons (1988, $6.95) Austin-a(i)

| | 1 | 2 | 3 | 4 | 5 | 7 |

nn-Nightraven: House of Cards (1991, $14.95)

| | 2 | 4 | 6 | 9 | 12 | 15 |

nn-Nightraven: The Collected Stories (1990, $9.95) Bolton-r/British Hulk mag.; David Lloyd-c/a

| | 2 | 4 | 6 | 8 | 10 | 12 |

nn-Original Adventures of Cholly and Flytrap (Epic, 1991, $9.95) Suydam-s/c/a

| | 2 | 4 | 6 | 9 | 12 | 15 |

nn-Rick Mason Agent (1989, $9.95)

| | 1 | 3 | 4 | 6 | 8 | 10 |

nn-Roger Rabbit In The Resurrection Of Doom (1989, $8.95)

| | 1 | 3 | 4 | 6 | 8 | 10 |

nn-A Sailor's Story Book II: Winds, Dreams and Dragons ('86, $6.95, softcover) Glansman-s/c/a

| | 1 | 3 | 4 | 6 | 8 | 10 |

nn-Squadron Supreme: Death of a Universe (1989, $9.95) Gruenwald-s; Ryan & Williamson-a

| | 3 | 6 | 9 | 14 | 20 | 25 |

nn-Who Framed Roger Rabbit (1989, $6.95)

| | 1 | 3 | 4 | 6 | 8 | 10 |

NOTE: *Aragones* a-27, 32. *Buscema* a-38. *Byrne* c/a-18. *Heath* a-35i. *Kaluta* a-13, 35p; c-13. *Miller* a-24p. *Simonson* a-6; c-26. *Starlin* c/a-1,3. *Williamson* a-34. *Wrightson* c-29i.

MARVEL-HEROES & LEGENDS
Marvel Comics: Oct, 1996; 1997 ($2.95)

nn-Wraparound-c, ...1997 ($2.99) -Original Avengers story 3.00

MARVEL HEROES FLIP MAGAZINE
Marvel Comics: Aug, 2005 - No. 26, Sept, 2007 ($3.99/$4.99)

1-11-Reprints New Avengers and Captain America (2005 series) in flip format thru #13 4.00
12-26: 14-19-Reprints New Avengers and Young Avengers in flip format. 20-Ghost Rider 5.00

MARVEL HOLIDAY SPECIAL
Marvel Comics: No. 1, 1991 ($2.25, 84 pgs.) - Present

1-X-Men, Fantastic Four, Punisher, Thor, Capt. America, Ghost Rider, Capt. Ultra, Spidey stories; Art Adams-c/a 3.00
nn (1/93)-Wolverine, Thanos (by Starlin/Lim/Austin) 3.00
nn (1994)-Capt. America, X-Men, Silver Surfer 3.00
...1996-Spider-Man by Waid & Olliffe; X-Men, Silver Surfer 3.00
...2004-Spider-Man by DeFalco & Miyazawa; X-Men, Fantastic Four 3.00
...2004 TPB ($15.99) r/M.H.S. 2004 & past Christmas-themed stories 16.00
1 (1/06, $3.99) new Christmas-themed stories by various; Immonen-c 4.00
....2006 (2/07, $3.99) Fin Fang Foom, Hydra, AIM app.; gallery of past covers; Irving-c 4.00
Marvel Holiday (2006, $7.99, digest) reprints from M.H.S. 2004, 2006 & TPB 8.00
NOTE: *Art Adams* c-'93. *Golden* a-'93. *Perez* c-'94.

MARVEL ILLUSTRATED...
Marvel Comics: 2007 ($2.99)

...Jungle Book - reprints from Marvel Fanfare #8-11; Gil Kane-s/a(p); P. Craig Russell-i 3.00

MARVEL ILLUSTRATED: LAST OF THE MOHICANS
Marvel Comics: July, 2007 - No. 6 ($2.99, limited series)

1-5-Adaptation of the Cooper novel; Roy Thomas-s/Steve Kurth-a. 1-Jo Chen-c 3.00

MARVEL ILLUSTRATED: SWIMSUIT ISSUE (Also see Marvel Swimsuit Special)
Marvel Comics: 1991 ($3.95, magazine, 52 pgs.)

V1#1-Parody of Sports Illustrated swimsuit issue; Mary Jane Parker centerfold pin-up by Jusko; 2nd print exists

| | 1 | 3 | 4 | 6 | 8 | 10 |

MARVEL ILLUSTRATED: THE MAN IN THE IRON MASK
Marvel Comics: Sept, 2007 - No. 6 ($2.99, limited series)

1-3-Adaptation of the Dumas novel; Roy Thomas-s/Hugo Petrus-a. 1-Djurdjevic-c 3.00

MARVEL ILLUSTRATED: TREASURE ISLAND
Marvel Comics: Aug, 2007 - No. 6 ($2.99, limited series)

1-4-Adaptation of the Stevenson novel; Roy Thomas-s/Mario Gully-a/Greg Hildebrandt-c 3.00

MARVEL KNIGHTS (See Black Panther, Daredevil, Inhumans, & Punisher)
Marvel Comics: 1998 (Previews for upcoming series)

Sketchbook-Wizard suppl.; Quesada & Palmiotti-c 3.00
Tourbook-($2.99) Interviews and art previews 3.00

MARVEL KNIGHTS
Marvel Comics: July, 2000 - No. 15, Sept, 2001 ($2.99)

1-Daredevil, Punisher, Black Widow, Shang-Chi, Dagger app. 4.00
2-15: 2-Two covers by Barreto & Quesada 3.00
.../Marvel Boy Genesis Edition (6/00) Sketchbook preview 2.50
...: Millennial Visions (2/02, $3.99) Pin-ups by various; Harris-c 4.00

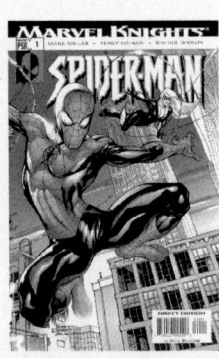

Marvel Knights: Spider-Man #1 © MAR

Marvel Mangaverse #3 © MAR

Marvel Monsters: Monsters on the Prowl #1 © MAR

	GD	VG	FN	VF	VF/NM	NM-		GD	VG	FN	VF	VF/NM	NM-
	2.0	4.0	6.0	8.0	9.0	9.2		2.0	4.0	6.0	8.0	9.0	9.2

MARVEL KNIGHTS (Volume 2)
Marvel Comics: May, 2002 - No. 6, Oct, 2002 ($2.99)

1-6-Daredevil, Punisher, Black Widow app.; Ponticelli-a   3.00

MARVEL KNIGHTS: DOUBLE SHOT
Marvel Comics: June, 2002 - No. 4 ($2.99, limited series)

1-5: 1-Punisher by Ennis & Quesada; Daredevil by Haynes; Fabry-c   3.00

MARVEL KNIGHTS 4 (Fantastic Four) (Issues #1&2 are titled **Knights 4**) (#28-30 titled **Four**)
Marvel Comics: Apr, 2004 - No. 30, July, 2006 ($2.99)

1-30: 1-7-McNiven-c/a; Aguirre-Sacasa-a. 8,9-Namor app. 13-Cho-c. 14-Land-c.
  21-Flashback meeting with Black Panther. 30-Namor app.   3.00
...Vol. 1: The Wolf at the Door (2004, $16.99, TPB) r/#1-7   17.00
...Vol. 2: The Stuff of Nightmares (2005, $13.99, TPB) r/#8-12   14.00
...Vol. 3: Divine Time (2005, $14.99, TPB) r/#13-18   15.00
...Vol. 4: Impossible Things Happen Every Day (2006, $14.99, TPB) r/#19-24 15.00
Fantastic Four: The Resurrection of Nicholas Scratch TPB (2006, $14.99) r/#25-30 15.00

MARVEL KNIGHTS MAGAZINE
Marvel Comics: May, 2001 - No. 6, Oct, 2001 ($3.99, magazine size)

1-6-Reprints of recent Daredevil, Punisher, Black Widow, Inhumans   4.00

MARVEL KNIGHTS SPIDER-MAN (Title continues in Sensational Spider-Man #23)
Marvel Comics: Jun, 2004 - No. 22, Mar, 2006 ($2.99)

1-Wraparound-c by Dodson; Millar-s/Dodson-a; Green Goblin app.   3.00
2-12: 2-Avengers app. 2,3-Vulture & Electro app. 5,8-Cho-c/a. 6-8-Venom app. 3.00
13-18-Reginald Hudlin-s/Billy Tan-a. 13,14,18-New Avengers app. 15-Punisher app. 3.00
19-22-The Other x-over pts. 2,5,8,11; Pat Lee-a
19-22-var-c: 19-Black costume. 20-Scarlet Spider. 21-Spider-Armor. 22-Peter Parker 5.00
... Vol. 1 HC (2005, $29.99, over-sized with d.j.) r/#1-12; Stan Lee intro.; Dodson & Cho
  sketch pages   30.00
... Vol. 1: Down Among the Dead Men (2004, $9.99, TPB) r/#1-4   10.00
... Vol. 2: Venomous (2005, $9.99, TPB) r/#5-8   10.00
... Vol. 3: The Last Stand (2005, $9.99, TPB) r/#9-12   10.00
... Vol. 4: Wild Blue Yonder (2005, $14.99, TPB) r/#13-18   15.00

MARVEL KNIGHTS 2099
Marvel Comics: 2005 ($13.99, TPB)

nn-Reprints one shots: Daredevil 2099, Punisher 2099, Black Panther 2099, Inhumans 2099
  and Mutant 2099; Pat Lee-c   14.00

MARVEL LEGACY: ...
Marvel Comics: 2006, 2007 ($4.99, one-shots)

... The 1970s Handbook - Profiles of 1970s iconic and minor characters; info thru 1979 5.00
... The 1980s Handbook - Profiles of 1980s iconic and minor characters; info thru 1989 5.00
... The 1990s Handbook - Profiles of 1990s iconic and minor characters; Lim-c 5.00

MARVEL MANGAVERSE:... (one-shots)
Marvel Comics: March, 2002 ($2.25, manga-inspired one-shots)

Avengers Assemble! - Udon Studio-s/a   2.50
Eternity Twilight ($3.50) - Ben Dunn-s/a/wrap-around-c   3.50
Fantastic Four - Adam Warren-s/Keron Grant-a   2.50
Ghost Riders - Chuck Austen-s/a   2.50
Punisher - Peter David-s/Lea Hernandez-a   2.50
Spider-Man - Kaare Andrews-s/a   2.50
X-Men - C.B. Cebulski-s/Jeff Matsuda-a   2.50

MARVEL MANGAVERSE (Manga series)
Marvel Comics: June, 2002 - No. 6, Nov., 2002 ($2.25)

1-6: 1-Ben Dunn-s/a; intro. manga Captain Marvel   2.50
Vol. 1 TPB (2002, $24.95) r/one-shots   25.00
Vol. 2 TPB (2002, $12.99) r/#1-6   13.00
Vol. 3: Spider-Man-Legend of the Spider-Clan (2003, $11.99, TPB) r/series 12.00

MARVEL MASTERPIECES COLLECTION, THE
Marvel Comics: May, 1993 - No. 4, Aug, 1993 ($2.95, coated paper, lim. series)

1-4-Reprints Marvel Masterpieces trading cards w/ new Jusko paintings in each;
  Jusko painted-c/a   3.00

MARVEL MASTERPIECES 2 COLLECTION, THE
Marvel Comics: July, 1994 - No. 3, Sept, 1994 ($2.95, limited series)

1-3: 1-Kaluta-c; r/trading cards; new Steranko centerfold   3.00

MARVEL MILESTONE EDITION
Marvel Comics: 1991 - 1999 ($2.95, coated stock)(r/originals with original ads w/silver ink-c)

...: X-Men #1-Reprints X-Men #1 (1991)   3.00
...: Giant Size X-Men #1-(1991, $3.95, 68 pgs.)   4.00
...: Fantastic Four #1 (11/91), ...: Incredible Hulk #1 (3/92, says 3/91 by error), ...: Amazing

Fantasy #15 (3/92), ...: Fantastic Four #5 (11/92), ...: Amazing Spider-Man #129 (11/92),
  ...: Iron Man #55 (11/92), ...: Iron Fist #14 (11/92), ...: Amazing Spider-Man #1 (1/93),
  ...: Amazing Spider-Man #1 (1/93) variation- no price on-c, ...: Tales of Suspense #39
  (3/93), ...: Avengers #1 (9/93), ...: X-Men #9 (10/93), ...: Avengers #16 (10/93), ...:Amazing
  Spider-Man #149 (11/94, $2.95), ...:X-Men #28 (11/94, $2.95)   3.00
...:Captain America #1 (3/95, $3.95)   4.00
...:Amazing Spider-Man #3 (3/95, $2.95), ...:Avengers #4 (3/95, $2.95),
  ...:Strange Tales-r/Dr. Strange stories from #110, 111, 114, & 115 3.00
.....:Hulk #181 (8/99, $2.99)   3.00

MARVEL MILESTONES
Marvel Comics: 2005 - Present ($3.99, coated stock)(r/originals w/silver ink-c)

...: Beast & Kitty Pryde-r/from Amazing Adventures #11 & Uncanny X-Men #153 4.00
...: Black Panther, Storm & Ka-Zar-r/from Black Panther #26, Marvel Team-Up #100 and
  Marvel Mystery Comics #7   4.00
...: Blade, Man-Thing & Satana-r/from Tomb of Dracula #10, Adv. Into Fear #16 and
  Vampire Tales #2   4.00
...: Captain Britain, Psylocke & Sub-Mariner-r/from Spect. Spidey #114, Uncanny X-Men #213
  and Human Torch #2   4.00
...: Doom, Sub-Mariner & Red Skull -r/from FF Ann. #2, Sub-Mariner Comics #1, Captain
  America Comics #1   4.00
...: Dragon Lord, Silver Surfer, Sub-Mariner, & Hulk -r/from Marvel Spotlight #5, Speedball #1
  and Amazing Adult Fantasy #14; Ditko-a on all   4.00
...: Dr. Strange, Silver Surfer, Sub-Mariner, & Hulk -r/from Marvel Premiere #3, FF Ann. #5,
  Marvel Comics #1, Incredible Hulk #3   4.00
...: Ghost Rider, Black Widow & Iceman -r/from Marvel Spotlight #5, Daredevil #81, X-Men #47 4.00
...: Iron Man, Ant-Man & Captain America -r/from TOS #39,40, TTA #27, Capt. America #1 4.00
...: Legion of Monsters, Spider-Man and Brother Voodoo -r/Marvel Premiere #28 & others 4.00
...: Millie the Model & Patsy Walker-r/from Millie the Model #100, Defenders #65 4.00
...: Onslaught -r/Onslaught: Marvel; wraparound-c   4.00
...: Rawhide Kid & Two-Gun Kid-r/Two-Gun Kid #60 and Rawhide Kid #17 4.00
...: Special: Bloodstone, X-51 & Captain Marvel II ($4.99) -r/from Marvel Presents #1, Machine
  Man #1, Amazing Spider-Man Ann. #19, and Bloodstone #1   5.00
...: Star Brand & Quasar -r/from Star Brand #1 & Quasar #1   4.00
...: Ultimate Spider-Man, Ult. X-Men, Microman & Mantor -r/from Ultimate Spider-Man #1/2,
  Ultimate X-Men #1/2 and Human Torch #2   4.00
...: Venom & Hercules -r/Marvel S-H Secret Wars #8, Journey Into Mystery Ann. #1 4.00
...: Wolverine, X-Men & Tuk: Caveboy -r/from Marvel Comics Presents #1, Uncanny X-Men
  #201, Capt. America Comics #1,2   4.00
...: (Jim Lee and Chris Claremont) X-Men and the Starjammers Pt. 1 -r/r/Unc. X-Men #275 4.00
...: X-Men and the Starjammers Pt. 2 -r/Unc. X-Men #276,277   4.00

MARVEL MINI-BOOKS (See Promotional Comics section)

MARVEL MONSTERS:... (one-shots)
Marvel Comics: Dec, 2005 ($3.99)

...Devil Dinosaur 1 - Hulk app.; Eric Powell-c/a; Sniegoski-s; r/Journey Into Mystery #62 4.00
...Fin Fang Four 1 - FF app.; Powell-c; Langridge-s/Gray-a; r/Strange Tales #89 4.00
...From the Files of Ulysses Bloodstone 1 - Guide to classic Marvel monsters; Powell-c 4.00
...Monsters on the Prowl 1 - Niles-s/Fegredo-a/Powell-c; Thing, Hulk, Giant-Man & Beast app. 4.00
...Where Monsters Dwell 1 - Giffen-s/a; David-s/Pander-a; Parker-s/Braun-s; Powell-c 4.00
HC (2006, $20.99, dust jacket) r/one-shots   21.00

MARVEL MOVIE PREMIERE (Magazine)
Marvel Comics Group: Sept, 1975 (B&W, one-shot)

1-Burroughs' "The Land That Time Forgot" adapt.   2   4   6   8   11   14

MARVEL MOVIE SHOWCASE FEATURING STAR WARS
Marvel Comics Group: Nov, 1982 - No. 2, Dec, 1982 ($1.25, 68 pgs.)

1,2-Star Wars movie adaptation; reprints Star Wars #1-6 by Chaykin;
  1-Reprints-c to Star Wars #1. 2-Stevens-r   4.00

MARVEL MOVIE SPOTLIGHT FEATURING RAIDERS OF THE LOST ARK
Marvel Comics Group: Nov, 1982 ($1.25, 68 pgs.)

1-Edited-r/Raiders of the Lost Ark #1-3; Buscema-c/a(p); movie adapt. 3.00

MARVEL MUST HAVES (Reprints of recent sold-out issues)
Marvel Comics: Dec, 2001 - Present ($2.99/$3.99/$4.99)

1,2,4-6: 1-r/Wolverine: Origin #1, Startling Stories: Banner #1, Tangled Web #4 and
  Cable #97. 2-Amazing Spider-Man #36 and others. 4-Truth #1, Capt. America V4 #1, and
  The Ultimates #1. 5-r/Ultimate War #1, Ult. X-Men #26, Ult Spider-Man #33.
6-Ult. Spider-Man #33-36   4.00
3-r/Call of Duty: The Brotherhood #1 & Daredevil #32,33   3.00
Amazing Spider-Man #30-32; Incredible Hulk #34-36; The Ultimates #1-3; Ultimate Spider-Man
  #1-3; Ultimate X-Men #1-3; (New) X-Men #114-116 each....   4.00
NYX #1-3; NYX #4-5 with sketch & cover gallery; Ultimates 2 #1-3 each... 5.00
Spider-Man and the Black Cat #1-3; preview of #4   5.00

Marvel Mystery Comics #9 © MAR

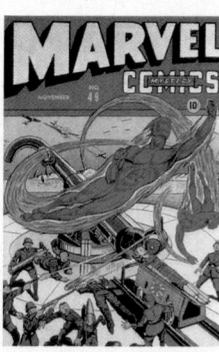

Marvel Mystery Comics #49 © MAR

Marvel Premiere #42 © MAR

	GD	VG	FN	VF	VF/NM	NM-
	2.0	4.0	6.0	8.0	9.0	9.2

MARVEL MYSTERY COMICS (Formerly Marvel Comics) (Becomes Marvel Tales No. 93 on)
Timely /Marvel Comics (TP #2-17/TCI #18-54/MCI #55-92): No. 2, Dec, 1939 - No. 92, June, 1949 (Some material from #8-10 reprinted in 2004's Marvel 65th Anniversary Special #1)

2-(Rare)-American Ace begins, ends #3; Human Torch (blue costume) by Burgos, Sub-Mariner by Everett continue; 2 pg. origin recap of Human Torch
| | 2750 | 5500 | 8250 | 20,500 | 37,750 | 55,000 |

3-New logo from Marvel pulp begins; 1st app. of television in comics? in Human Torch story (1/40)
| | 1525 | 3050 | 4575 | 11,500 | 20,750 | 30,000 |

4-Intro. Electro, the Marvel of the Age (ends #19), The Ferret, Mystery Detective (ends #9); 1st Sub-Mariner-c by Schomburg; 2nd German swastika on-c of a comic (2/40); one month after Top-Notch Comics #2
| | 1233 | 2466 | 3700 | 9250 | 16,625 | 24,000 |

5 Classic Schomburg-c (Scarce)
| | 2300 | 4600 | 6900 | 17,250 | 31,625 | 46,000 |

6,7: 6-Gustavson Angel story
| | 770 | 1540 | 2310 | 5390 | 9045 | 14,500 |

8-1st Human Torch & Sub-Mariner battle(6/40)
| | 1120 | 2240 | 3360 | 7850 | 13,925 | 20,000 |

9-(Scarce)-Human Torch & Sub-Mariner battle (cover/story); classic-c
| | 2600 | 5200 | 7800 | 19,500 | 35,750 | 52,000 |

10-Human Torch & Sub-Mariner battle, conclusion; Terry Vance, the Schoolboy Sleuth begins, ends #57
| | 943 | 1886 | 2829 | 6600 | 11,550 | 16,500 |

11
| | 376 | 752 | 1128 | 2444 | 4322 | 6200 |

12-Classic Kirby-c
| | 423 | 846 | 1269 | 2855 | 5028 | 7200 |

13-Intro. & 1st app. The Vision by S&K (11/40); Sub-Mariner dons new costume, ends #15
| | 537 | 1074 | 1611 | 3759 | 6580 | 9400 |

14-16: 14-Shows-c to Human Torch #1 on-c (12/40). 15-S&K Vision, Gustavson Angel story
| | 300 | 600 | 900 | 1881 | 3141 | 4400 |

17-Human Torch & Sub-Mariner team-up by Burgos/Everett; pin-up on back-c; shows-c to Human Torch #2 on-c
| | 328 | 656 | 984 | 2050 | 3400 | 4750 |

18
| | 283 | 566 | 849 | 1769 | 2935 | 4100 |

19,20: 19-Origin Toro in text; shows-c to Sub-Mariner #1 on-c. 20-Origin The Angel in text
| | 290 | 580 | 870 | 1813 | 3007 | 4200 |

21-The Patriot begins, (intro. in Human Torch #4 (#3)); not in #46-48; pin-up on back-c (7/41)
| | 283 | 566 | 849 | 1769 | 2935 | 4100 |

22-25: 23-Last Gustavson Angel; origin The Vision in text. 24-Injury-to-eye story
| | 269 | 538 | 807 | 1681 | 2791 | 3900 |

26-30: 27-Ka-Zar ends; last S&K Vision who battles Satan. 28-Jimmy Jupiter in the Land of Nowhere begins, ends #48; Sub-Mariner vs. The Flying Dutchman. 30-1st Japanese war-c
| | 241 | 482 | 723 | 1506 | 2503 | 3500 |

31-33,35,36,38,39: 31-Sub-Mariner by Everett ends, resumes #84. 32-1st app. The Boboes
| | 214 | 428 | 642 | 1338 | 2219 | 3100 |

34-Everett, Burgos, Martin Goodman, Funnies, Inc. office appear in story & battles Hitler; last Burgos Human Torch
| | 241 | 482 | 723 | 1506 | 2503 | 3500 |

37-Classic Hitler-c
| | 245 | 490 | 735 | 1531 | 2541 | 3550 |

40-Classic Zeppelin-c
| | 241 | 482 | 723 | 1506 | 2503 | 3500 |

41-43,45,47,48: 48-Last Vision; flag-c
| | 179 | 358 | 537 | 1119 | 1860 | 2600 |

44-Classic Super Plane-c
| | 210 | 420 | 630 | 1313 | 2182 | 3050 |

46-Classic Hitler-c
| | 207 | 414 | 621 | 1294 | 2147 | 3000 |

49-Origin Miss America
| | 207 | 414 | 621 | 1294 | 2147 | 3000 |

50-Mary becomes Miss Patriot (origin)
| | 179 | 358 | 537 | 1119 | 1860 | 2600 |

51-60: 54-Bondage-c
| | 155 | 310 | 465 | 969 | 1610 | 2250 |

61,62,64-Last German war-c
| | 148 | 296 | 444 | 925 | 1538 | 2150 |

63-Classic Hitler War-c; The Villainess Cat-Woman only app.
| | 176 | 352 | 528 | 1100 | 1825 | 2550 |

65,66-Last Japanese War-c
| | 148 | 296 | 444 | 925 | 1538 | 2150 |

67-78: The Last Patriot. 75-Young Allies begin. 76-Ten Chapter Miss America serial begins, ends #85
| | 124 | 248 | 372 | 775 | 1288 | 1800 |

79-New cover format; Super Villains begin on cover; last Angel
| | 129 | 258 | 387 | 806 | 1341 | 1875 |

80-1st app. Capt. America in Marvel Comics
| | 148 | 296 | 444 | 925 | 1538 | 2150 |

81-Captain America app.
| | 124 | 248 | 366 | 763 | 1269 | 1775 |

82-Origin & 1st app. Namora (5/47); 1st Sub-Mariner/Namora team-up; Captain America app.
| | 290 | 580 | 870 | 1813 | 3007 | 4200 |

83,85: 83-Last Young Allies. 85-Last Miss America; Blonde Phantom app.
| | 109 | 218 | 327 | 681 | 1128 | 1575 |

84-Blonde Phantom begins (on-c of #84,88,89); Sub-Mariner by Everett begins; Captain America app.
| | 148 | 296 | 444 | 925 | 1538 | 2150 |

86-Blonde Phantom i.d. revealed; Captain America app.; last Bucky app.
| | 116 | 232 | 348 | 725 | 1200 | 1675 |

87-1st Capt. America/Golden Girl team-up; last Toro line (8/48)
| | 126 | 252 | 378 | 788 | 1307 | 1825 |

88-Golden Girl, Namora, & Sun Girl (1st in Marvel Comics) x-over; Captain America, Blonde Phantom app.
| | 116 | 232 | 348 | 725 | 1205 | 1685 |

89-1st Human Torch/Sun Girl team-up; 1st Captain America solo; Blonde Phantom app.
| | 116 | 232 | 348 | 725 | 1200 | 1675 |

90,91: 90-Blonde Phantom un-masked; Captain America app. 91-Capt. America app.; Blonde Phantom & Sub-Mariner end; early Venus app. (4/49)-(scarce)

| | 152 | 304 | 456 | 950 | 1575 | 2200 |

92-Feature story on the birth of the Human Torch and the death of Professor Horton (his creator); 1st app. The Witness in Marvel Comics; Captain America app. (scarce)
| | 315 | 630 | 945 | 2048 | 3624 | 5200 |

132 Pg. issue, B&W, 25¢ (1943-44)-printed in N. Y.; square binding, blank inside covers; has Marvel No. 33-c in color; contains Capt. America #18 & Marvel Mystery Comics #33; same contents as Captain America Annual (Less than 5 copies known to exist)
| | 5000 | 10,000 | 15,000 | 30,000 | – | – |

132 Pg. issue (with variant contents), B&W, 25¢ (1942-'43)- square binding, blank inside covers; has same Marvel No. 33-c in color but contains Capt. America #22 & Marvel Mystery Comics #41 instead (possibly scarcer than other version)
(a VG+ copy sold in 2007 for $29,000)

NOTE: **Brodsky** c-49, 72, 86, 88-92. **Crandall** a-26i. **Everett** c-7-9, 27, 84. **Gabrielle** c-30-32. **Schomburg** c-3-11, 13-29, 33-36, 39-48, 50-59, 63-69, 74, 76, 132 pg. issue. **Shores** c-37, 38, 75p, 77, 78p, 79p, 80, 81p, 82-84, 85p, 87p. **Sekowsky** c-73. Bondage covers-3, 4, 7, 12, 28, 29, 49, 50, 52, 56, 57, 58, 59, 65. Angel c-2, 3, 8, 12. Remember Pearl Harbor issues-#30-32.

MARVEL MYSTERY COMICS
Marvel Comics: Dec, 1999 ($3.95, reprints)

1-Reprints original 1940s stories; Schomburg-c from #74
| | | | | | | 4.00 |

MARVEL NEMESIS: THE IMPERFECTS (EA Games characters)
Marvel Comics: July, 2005 - No. 6, Dec, 2005 ($2.99, limited series)

1-6-Jae Lee-c/Greg Pak-s/Renato Arlem-a; Spider-Man, Thing, Wolverine, Elektra app.
| | | | | | | 3.00 |
Digest (2005, $7.99) r/#1-6
| | | | | | | 3.00 |

MARVEL NO-PRIZE BOOK, THE (The Official... on-c)
Marvel Comics Group: Jan, 1983 (one-shot, direct sales only)

1-Golden-c; Kirby-a
| | | | | | | 4.00 |

MARVELOUS ADVENTURES OF GUS BEEZER
Marvel Comics: May, 2003; Feb, 2004 ($2.99, one-shots)

...: Gus Beezer & Spider-Man 1 - (5/03) Gurihiru-a
| | | | | | | 3.00 |
...: Hulk 1 - (5/03) Simone-s/Lethcoe-a; She-Hulk app.
| | | | | | | 3.00 |
...: Spider-Man 1 - (5/03) Simone-s/Lethcoe-a; The Lizard & Dr. Doom app.
| | | | | | | 3.00 |
...: X-Men 1 - (5/03) Simone-s/Lethcoe-a
| | | | | | | 3.00 |

MARVEL PREMIERE
Marvel Comics Group: April, 1972 - No. 61, Aug, 1981 (A tryout book for new characters)

1-Origin Warlock (pre-#1) by Gil Kane/Adkins; origin Counter-Earth; Hulk & Thor cameo (#1-14 are 20¢-c)
| | 6 | 12 | 18 | 41 | 66 | 90 |
2-Warlock ends; Kirby Yellow Claw-r
| | 3 | 6 | 9 | 20 | 30 | 40 |
3-Dr. Strange series begins (pre #1, 7/72), B. Smith-c/a(p)
| | 6 | 12 | 18 | 37 | 59 | 80 |
4-Smith/Brunner-a
| | 3 | 6 | 9 | 17 | 25 | 32 |
5-9: 8-Starlin-c/a(p)
| | 2 | 4 | 6 | 13 | 18 | 22 |
10-Death of the Ancient One
| | 3 | 6 | 9 | 16 | 22 | 28 |
11-14: 11-Dr. Strange origin-r by Ditko. 14-Last Dr. Strange (3/74), gets own title 3 months later
| | 2 | 4 | 6 | 8 | 11 | 14 |
15-Origin/1st app. Iron Fist (5/74), ends #25
| | 8 | 16 | 24 | 52 | 86 | 120 |
16,25: 16-2nd app. Iron Fist; origin cont'd from #15; Hama's 1st Marvel-a. 25-1st Byrne Iron Fist (moves to own title next)
| | 4 | 8 | 12 | 22 | 34 | 45 |
17-24: Iron Fist in all
| | 3 | 6 | 9 | 16 | 22 | 28 |
26-Hercules.
| | 1 | 2 | 3 | 5 | 6 | 8 |
27-Satana
| | 1 | 3 | 4 | 6 | 8 | 10 |
28-Legion of Monsters (Ghost Rider, Man-Thing, Morbius, Werewolf)
| | 3 | 6 | 9 | 15 | 19 | 24 |
29-46,49: 29,30-The Liberty Legion. 29-1st modern app. Patriot. 31-1st app. Woodgod; last 25¢ issue. 32-1st app. Monark Starstalker. 33,34-1st solo app. Solomon Kane (Robert E. Howard adaptation "Red Shadows"). 35-Origin/1st app. 3-D Man. 36,37-3-D Man. 38-1st Weirdworld. 39,40-Torpedo. 41-1st Seeker 3000! 42-Tigra. 43-Paladin. 44-Jack of Hearts (1st solo book, 1/78). 45,46-Man-Wolf. 49-The Falcon (1st solo book, 8/79)
| | | | | | | 4.00 |
29-31-(30¢-c variants, limited distribution)(4,6,8/76)
| | 2 | 4 | 6 | 10 | 14 | 18 |
36-38-(35¢-c variants, limited distribution)(6,8,10/77)
| | 3 | 6 | 9 | 16 | 23 | 30 |
47,48-Byrne-a: 47-Origin/1st app. new Ant-Man. 48-Ant-Man
| | 2 | 4 | 6 | 8 | 10 | 12 |
50-1st app. Alice Cooper; co-plotted by Alice
| | 2 | 4 | 6 | 9 | 12 | 15 |
51-56,58-61: 51-53-Black Panther. 54-1st Caleb Hammer. 55-Wonder Man. 56-1st color app. Dominic Fortune. 58-60-Dr. Who. 61-Star Lord
| | | | | | | 4.00 |
57-Dr. Who (2nd U.S. app.-see Movie Classics)
| | | | | | | 6.00 |

NOTE: **N. Adams** (Crusty Bunkers) part inks-10, 12, 13. **Austin** a-50i, 56i; c-46i, 50i, 56i, 58. **Brunner** a-4i, 6p, 9-14p; c-9-14. **Byrne** a-47p, 48p. **Chaykin** a-32-34; c-32, 33, 56. **Giffen** a-31p, 44p; c-44. **Gil Kane** a(p)-1, 2, 15; c(p)-1, 2, 15, 16, 22-24, 27, 36, 37. **Kirby** c-26, 29-31, 35. **Layton** a-47i, 48i; c-47. **McWilliams** a-25i. **Miller** c-49p, 53p, 58p. **Nebres** a-44i; c-38i. **Nino** a-38i. **Perez** c/a-38p, 45p, 46p. **Ploog** a-38; c-5-7. **Russell** a-7p. **Simonson** a-60(2pgs.); c-57. **Starlin** a-8p; c-8. **Sutton** a-41, 43, 50p, 61; c-50p, 61. #57-60 publ'd w/two different prices on-c

MARVEL PRESENTS

Marvel Preview #20 © MAR

Marvel 1602 #2 © MAR

Marvel Special Edition Featuring... #1 © MAR

	GD 2.0	VG 4.0	FN 6.0	VF 8.0	VF/NM 9.0	NM- 9.2

Marvel Comics: October, 1975 - No. 12, Aug, 1977 (#1-6 are 25¢ issues)

	GD 2.0	VG 4.0	FN 6.0	VF 8.0	VF/NM 9.0	NM- 9.2
1-Origin & 1st app. Bloodstone	2	4	6	8	10	12
2-Origin Bloodstone continued; Kirby-c	1	2	3	4	5	7
3-Guardians of the Galaxy (1st solo book, 2/76) begins, ends #12	2	4	6	9	13	16
4-7,9-12: 9,10-Origin Starhawk	1	2	3	5	6	8
4-6-(30¢-c variants, limited distribution)(4-8/76)	2	4	6	11	16	20
8-r/story from Silver Surfer #2 plus 4 pgs. new-a	1	2	3	5	6	8
11,12-(35¢-c variants, limited distribution)(6,8/77)	3	6	9	20	30	40

NOTE: Austin a-6i. Buscema r-8p. Chaykin a-5p. Kane c-1p. Starlin layouts-10.

MARVEL PREVIEW (Magazine) (Bizarre Adventures #25 on)
Marvel Comics: Feb (no month), 1975 - No. 24, Winter, 1980 (B&W) ($1.00)

1-Man-Gods From Beyond the Stars; Crusty Bunkers (Neal Adams)-a(i) & cover; Nino-a	2	4	6	13	18	22
2-1st origin The Punisher (see Amaz. Spider-Man #129 & Classic Punisher); 1st app. Dominic Fortune; Morrow-c	9	18	27	63	107	150
3,8,10: 3-Blade the Vampire Slayer. 8-Legion of Monsters; Morbius app. 10-Thor the Mighty; Starlin frontispiece	3	6	9	15	21	26
4,5: 4-Star-Lord & Sword in the Star (origins & 1st app.). 5,6-Sherlock Holmes.	2	4	6	11	16	20
6,9: 6-Sherlock Holmes; N. Adams frontispiece. 9-Man-God; origin Star Hawk, ends #20	2	4	6	10	13	16
7-Satana, Sword in the Star app.	2	4	6	9	14	18
11,12,16,19: 11-Star-Lord; Byrne-a; Starlin frontispiece. 12-Haunt of Horror. 16-Masters of Terror. 19-Kull	1	2	3	5	7	9
13-15,17,18,20-24: 14,15-Star-Lord. 14-Starlin painted-c. 17-Blackmark by G. Kane (see SSOC #1-3). 18-Star-Lord; Sienkiewicz-a; Veitch & Bissette-a. 20-Bizarre Advs. 21-Moon Knight (Spr/80)-Predates Moon Knight #1; The Shroud by Ditko. 22-King Arthur. 23-Bizarre Advs.; Miller-a. 24-Debut Paradox						6.00

NOTE: N. Adams (C. Bunkers) r-20i. Buscema a-22, 23. Byrne a-11. Chaykin a-20. Colan a-8, 16p(3), 18p, 23p; c-16p. Elias a-18. Giffen a-7. Infantino a-14p. Kaluta a-12; c-15. Miller a-23. Morrow a-8i; c-2-4. Perez a-20p. Ploog a-8. Starlin c-13, 14. Nudity in some issues

MARVEL RIOT
Marvel Comics: Dec, 1995 ($1.95, one-shot)

1-"Age of Apocalypse" spoof; Lobdell script						2.50

MARVEL ROMANCE
Marvel Comics: 2006 ($19.99, TPB)

nn-Reprints romance stories from 1960-1972; art by Kirby, Buscema, Colan, Romita						20.00

MARVEL ROMANCE REDUX (Humor stories using art reprinted from Marvel romance comics)
Marvel Comics: Apr, 2006 - Present ($2.99, one-shots)

....: But I Thought He Loved Me Too (4/06) art by Kirby, Colan, Buscema & Romita; Giffen-c						3.00
....: Guys & Dolls (5/06) art by Starlin, Heck, Colan & Buscema; Conner-c						3.00
....: I Should Have Been a Blonde (7/06) art by Brodsky Colletta & Colan; Cho-c						3.00
....: Love is a Four Letter Word (8/06) art by Kirby, Buscema, Colan & Heck; Land-c						3.00
....: Restraining Orders are For Other Girls (6/06) art by Giordano, Kirby; Baker-c						3.00
....: Another Kind of Love TPB (2007, $13.99) r/one-shots						14.00

MARVELS
Marvel Comics: Jan, 1994 - No. 4, Apr, 1994 ($5.95, painted lim. series)
No. 1 (2nd Printing), Apr, 1996 - No. 4 (2nd Printing), July, 1996 ($2.95)

1-4: Kurt Busiek scripts & Alex Ross painted-c/a in all; double-c w/acetate overlay	2	3	5	6		8
Marvel Classic Collectors Pack ($11.90)-Issues #1 & 2 boxed (1st printings).	2	4	6	9	13	16
0-(8/94, $2.95)-no acetate overlay.						4.00
1-4-(2nd printing): r/original limited series w/o acetate overlay						3.00
Hardcover (1994, $59.95)-r/#0-4: w/intros by Stan Lee, John Romita, Sr., Kurt Busiek & Scott McCloud.						60.00
...: 10th Anniversary Edition (2004, $49.99, hardcover w/dustjacket) r/#0-4; scripts and commentaries; Ross sketch pages, cover gallery, behind the scenes art						50.00
Trade paperback ($19.95)						20.00

MARVEL SAGA, THE
Marvel Comics Group: Dec, 1985 - No. 25, Dec, 1987

1,21-25						2.50
2-20						2.50

NOTE: Williamson a(i)-9, 10; c(i)-7, 10-12, 14, 16.

MARVELS COMICS: ... (Marvel-type comics read in the Marvel Universe)
Marvel Comics: Jul, 2000 ($2.25, one-shots)

...Captain America #1 -Frenz & Sinnott-a; ...Daredevil #1 -Isabella-s/Newell-a; ...Fantastic Four #1 -Kesel-s/Paul Smith-a; Spider-Man #1 -Oliff-a; ...Thor #1 -Templeton-s/Aucoin-a						2.50
...X-Men #1 -Millar-s/ Sean Phillips & Duncan Fegredo-a						2.50

The History of Marvels Comics (no cover price)-Faux history; previews titles — 2.50

MARVEL SELECT FLIP MAGAZINE
Marvel Comics: Aug, 2005 - Present ($3.99/$4.99)

1-11-Reprints Astonishing X-Men and New X-Men: Academy X in flip format						4.00
12-24-($4.99) Reprints recent X-Men mini-series in flip format						5.00

MARVEL SELECTS:
Marvel Comics: Jan, 2000 - No. 6, June, 2000 ($2.75/$2.99, reprints)

...Fantastic Four 1-6: Reprints F.F. #107-112; new Davis-c						2.75
...Spider-Man 1,2,4-6: Reprints AS-M #100,101,103,104,93; Wieringo-c						2.75
...Spider-Man 3 ($2.99): Reprints AS-M #102; new Wieringo-c						3.00

MARVEL'S GREATEST COMICS (Marvel Collectors' Item Classics #1-22)
Marvel Comics Group: No. 23, Oct, 1969 - No. 96, Jan, 1981

23-34 (Giants). Begin Fantastic Four-r/#30s?-116	3	6	9	14	19	24
35-37-Silver Surfer-r/Fantastic Four #48-50	2	4	6	8	10	12
38-50: 42-Silver Surfer-r/F.F.(others?)	1	2	3	5	6	8
51-70: 63,64-(25¢ editions)						5.00
63,64-(30¢-c variants, limited distribution)(5,7/76)	2	4	6	11	16	20
71-96: 71-73-(30¢ editions)						4.00
71-73-(35¢-c variants, limited distribution)(7,9-10/77)	3	6	9	14	20	25
...: Fantastic Four #52 (2006, $2.99) reprints entire comic with ads and letter column						3.00

NOTE: Dr. Strange, Fantastic Four, Iron Man, Watcher-#23, 24. Capt. America, Dr. Strange, Iron Man, Fantastic Four-#25-28. Fantastic Four-#38-96. Buscema r-85-92; c-87-92t. Ditko r-23-28. Kirby r-23-82; c-75, 77p, 80p. #81 reprints Fantastic Four #100.

MARVEL'S GREATEST SUPERHERO BATTLES (See Fireside Book Series)

MARVEL: SHADOWS AND LIGHT
Marvel Comics: Feb, 1997 ($2.95, B&W, one-shot)

1-Tony Daniel-c						3.00

MARVEL 1602
Marvel Comics: Nov, 2003 - No. 8, June, 2004 ($3.50, limited series)

1-8-Neil Gaiman-s; Andy Kubert & Richard Isanove-a						3.50
HC (2004, $24.99) r/series; script pages for #1, sketch pages and Gaiman afterword						25.00
SC (2005, $19.99)						20.00

MARVEL 1602: FANTASTICK FOUR
Marvel Comics: Nov, 2006 - No. 5, Mar, 2007s ($3.50, limited series)

1-5-Peter David-s/Pascal Alixe-a/Leinil Yu-c						3.50
TPB (2007, $14.99) r/#1-5; sketch page						15.00

MARVEL 1602: NEW WORLD
Marvel Comics: Oct, 2005 - No. 5, Jan, 2006 ($3.50, limited series)

1-5-Greg Pak-s/Greg Tocchini-a; "Hulk" and "Iron Man" app.						3.50
TPB (2006, $14.99) r/#1-5						15.00

MARVEL 65TH ANNIVERSARY SPECIAL
Marvel Comics: 2004 ($4.99, one-shot)

1-Reprints Sub-Mariner & Human Torch battle from Marvel Mystery Comics #8-10						5.00

MARVELS OF SCIENCE
Charlton Comics: March, 1946 - No. 4, June, 1946

1-A-Bomb story	23	46	69	130	205	280
2-4	14	28	42	80	115	150

MARVEL SPECIAL EDITION FEATURING... (Also see Special Collectors' Ed.)
Marvel Comics Group: 1975 - 1978 (84 pgs.) (Oversized)

1-The Spectacular Spider-Man ($1.50); r/Amazing Spider-Man #6,35, Annual 1; Ditko-a(r)	3	6	9	16	23	30
1,2-Star Wars ('77,78; r/Star Wars #1-3 & #4-6; regular edition and Whitman variant exist	2	4	6	10	14	18
3-Star Wars ('78, $2.50, 116 pgs.) r/S. Wars #1-6; regular edition and Whitman variant exist	3	6	9	14	19	24
3-Close Encounters of the Third Kind (1978, $1.50, 56 pgs.)-Movie adaptation; Simonson-a(p)	2	4	6	9	13	16
V2#2(Spring, 1980, $2.00, oversized)- "Star Wars: The Empire Strikes Back"; r/Marvel Comics Super Special #16	3	6	9	16	22	28

NOTE: Chaykin c/a(r)-1(1977), 2, 3. Stevens a(r)-2i, 3i. Williamson a(r)-V2#2.

MARVEL SPECTACULAR
Marvel Comics: Aug, 1973 - No. 19, Nov, 1975

1-Thor-r from mid-sixties begin by Kirby	2	4	6	8	10	12
2-19						6.00

MARVELS: PORTRAITS
Marvel Comics: Mar, 1995 - No. 4, June, 1995 ($2.95, limited series)

1-4: Different artists renditions of Marvel characters						3.00

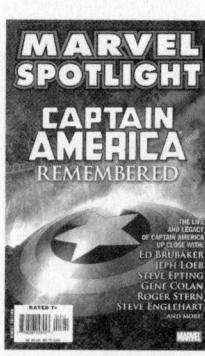

Marvel Spotlight: Captain America Remembered © MAR

Marvel Super Action #11 © MAR

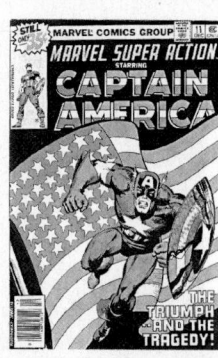

Marvel Super-Heroes #74 © MAR

	GD	VG	FN	VF	VF/NM	NM-
	2.0	4.0	6.0	8.0	9.0	9.2

MARVEL SPOTLIGHT (...& Son of Satan #19, 20, 23, 24)
Marvel Comics Group: Nov, 1971 - No. 33, Apr, 1977; V2#1, July, 1979 - V2#11, Mar, 1981 (A try-out book for new characters)

1-Origin Red Wolf (western hero)(1st solo book, pre-#1); Wood inks, Neal Adams-c; only 15¢ issue	5	10	15	32	51	70
2-(25¢, 52 pgs.)-Venus-r by Everett; origin/1st app. Werewolf By Night (begins) by Ploog; N. Adams-c	19	38	57	138	244	350
3,4: 4-Werewolf By Night ends (6/72); gets own title 9/72	6	12	18	41	66	90
5-Origin/1st app. Ghost Rider (8/72) & begins	21	42	63	156	278	400
6-8: 6-Origin G.R. retold. 8-Last Ploog issue	6	12	18	41	66	90
9-11-Last Ghost Rider (gets own title next mo.)	5	10	15	30	48	65
12-Origin & 2nd full app. The Son of Satan (10/73); story cont'd from Ghost Rider #2 & into #3; series begins, ends #24	4	8	12	22	34	45
13-24: 13-Partial origin Son of Satan. 14-Last 20¢ issue. 22-Ghost Rider-c & cameo (5 panels). 24-Last Son of Satan (10/75); gets own title 12/75	2	4	6	8	10	12
25,27,30,31: 27-(Regular 25¢-c), Sub-Mariner app. 30-The Warriors Three. 31-Nick Fury						6.00
26-Scarecrow	2	4	6	8		10
27-(30¢-c variant, limited distribution)	2	4	6	13	18	22
28-(Regular 25¢-c) 1st solo Moon Knight app.	3	6	9	18	27	35
28-(30¢-c variant, limited distribution)	7	14	21	50	83	115
29,32: 29-(Regular 25¢-c) (8/76) Moon Knight app.; last 25¢ issue. 32-1st app./partial origin Spider-Woman (2/77); Nick Fury app.	3	6	9	14	19	24
29-(30¢-c variant, limited distribution)	6	12	18	37	59	80
33-Deathlok; 1st app. Devil-Slayer	1	2	3	5	6	8
V2#1-7,9-11: 1-4-Capt. Marvel. 5-Dragon Lord. 6,7-StarLord; origin #6. 9-11-Capt. Universe (see Micronauts #8)						3.00
1-Variant copy missing issue #1 on cover	2	4	6	8	10	12
8-Capt. Marvel; Miller-c/a(p)						6.00

NOTE: Austin c-V2#2l. 8. J. Buscema c/a-30p. Chaykin a-31; c-26, 31. Colan a-18p, 19p. Ditko a-V2#4, 5, 9-11; c-V2#4, 9-11. Kane c-21p, 32p. Kirby c-29p. McWilliams a-20i. Miller a-V2#9p; c(p)-V2#2, 5, 7, 8. Mooney a-8i, 10i, 14p, 15i, 16p, 17p, 24p, 27, 32i. Nasser a-33p. Ploog a-2-5, 6-8p; c-3-9. Romita c-13. Sutton a-V2#6, 7. #29-25¢ & 30¢ issues exist.

MARVEL SPOTLIGHT (Most issues spotlight one Marvel artist and one Marvel writer)
Marvel Comics: 2005 - Present ($2.99)

...Brian Bendis/Mark Bagley; Daniel Way/Olivier Coipel; David Finch/Roberto Aguirre-Sacasa; Ed Brubaker/Billy Tan; John Cassaday/Sean McKeever; Joss Whedon/Michael Lark; Neil Gaiman/Salvador Larroca; Robert Kirkman/Greg Land; Stan Lee/Jack Kirby; Warren Ellis/Jim Cheung each...						3.00
...Steve McNiven/Mark Millar - Civil War						10.00
.... Captain America Remembered (2007) character features; creator interviews						3.00
.... Civil War Aftermath (2007) Top 10 Moments, casualty list, previews of upcoming series						3.00
.... Dark Tower (2007) previews the Stephen King adaptation; creator interviews						5.00
.... Fantastic Four and Silver Surfer (2007) character features; creator interviews						3.00
.... Ghost Rider (2007) character and movie features; creator interviews						3.00
.... Halo (2007) a World of Halo feature; Bendis & Maleev interviews						3.00
...: Heroes Reborn/Onslaught Reborn (2006)						3.00
...: Spider-Man (2007) character features; creator interviews; Ditko art showcase						3.00
...: Thor (2007) character features; Straczynski interview; Romita Jr. art showcase						3.00
.... World War Hulk (2007) character features; creator interviews; early art showcase						3.00

MARVEL SUPER ACTION (Magazine)
Marvel Comics Group: Jan, 1976 (B&W, 76 pgs.)

1-2nd app. Dominic Fortune (see Marvel Preview); early Punisher app.; Weird World & The Huntress; Evans, Ploog-a	6	12	18	43	69	95

MARVEL SUPER ACTION
Marvel Comics: May, 1977 - No. 37, Nov, 1981

1-Reprints Capt. America #100 by Kirby	2	4	6	8	10	12
2-13: 2,3,5-13 reprint Capt. America #101,102,103-111. 4-Marvel Boy-r(origin)/M. Boy #1. 11-Origin-r. 12,13-Classic Steranko-c/a(r).	1	2	3	4	5	7
2,3-(35¢-c variants, limited distribution)(6,8/77)	3	6	9	20	30	40
14-20: Marvel Boy-r; r/Avengers #55,56, Annual 2, others						4.00
21-37: 30-r/Hulk #6 from U.K.						3.50

NOTE: Buscema a(r)-14p, 15p; c-18-20, 22, 35r-37. Everett a-4. Heath a-4r. Kirby r-1-3, 5-11. B. Smith a-27r, 28r. Steranko a(r)-12p, 13p; c-12r, 13r.

MARVEL SUPER HERO CONTEST OF CHAMPIONS
Marvel Comics Group: June, 1982 - No. 3, Aug, 1982 (Limited series)

1-3: Features nearly all Marvel characters currently appearing in their comics; 1st Marvel limited series	1	2	3	5	6	8

MARVEL SUPER HEROES
Marvel Comics Group: October, 1966 (25¢, 68 pgs.) (1st Marvel one-shot)

1-r/origin Daredevil from D.D. #1; r/Avengers #2; G.A. Sub-Mariner-r/Marvel Mystery #8	

(Human Torch app.). Kirby-a	10	20	30	71	126	180

MARVEL SUPER-HEROES (Formerly Fantasy Masterpieces #1-11)
(Also see Giant-Size Super Heroes) (#12-20: 25¢, 68 pgs.)
Marvel Comics: No. 12, 12/67 - No. 31, 11/71; No. 32, 9/72 - No. 105, 1/82

12-Origin & 1st app. Capt. Marvel of the Kree; G.A. Human Torch, Destroyer, Capt. America, Black Knight, Sub-Mariner-r (#12-20 all contain new stories and reprints)	12	24	36	82	146	210
13-2nd app. Capt. Marvel; G.A. Black Knight, Torch, Vision, Capt. America, Sub-Mariner-r	7	14	21	45	73	100
14-Amazing Spider-Man (5/68, new-a by Andru/Everett); G.A. Sub-Mariner, Torch, Mercury (1st Kirby-a at Marvel), Black Knight, Capt. America reprints	9	18	27	63	107	150
15-17: 15-Black Bolt cameo in Medusa (new-a); Black Knight, Sub-Mariner, Black Marvel, Capt. America-r. 16-Origin & 1st app. S. A. Phantom Eagle; G.A. Torch, Capt. America, Black Knight, Patriot, Sub-Mariner-r. 17-Origin Black Knight (new-a); G.A. Torch, Sub-Mariner-r; reprint from All-Winners Squad #21 (cover & story)	8	16	26	41	55	
18-Origin/1st app. Guardians of the Galaxy (1/69); G.A. Sub-Mariner, All-Winners Squad-r	6	12	18	39	62	85
19-Ka-Zar (new-a); G.A. Torch, Marvel Boy, Black Knight, Sub-Mariner reprints; Smith-c(p); Tuska-a(r)	4	8	12	24	37	50
20-Doctor Doom (5/69); r/Young Men #24 w/-c	4	8	12	24	37	50
21-31: All-r issues. 21-X-Men, Daredevil, Iron Man-r begin, end #31. 31-Last Giant issue	2	4	6	11	16	20
32-50: 32-Hulk/Sub-Mariner-r begin from TTA.	1	2	3	5	6	8
51-70,100: 56-r/origin Hulk/Inc. Hulk #102; Hulk-r begin						5.00
57,58-(30¢-c variants, limited distribution)(5,7/76)	2	4	6	10	14	18
65,66-(35¢-c variants, limited distribution)(7,9/77)	3	6	9	16	23	30
71-99,101-105						4.00

NOTE: Austin a-104. Colan a(p)-12, 13, 15, 18; c-12, 13, 15. Everett a-14i(new); r-14, 15i, 18, 19, 33; c-85(r). New Kirby c-22, 27, 54. Maneely r-14, 15, 19. Severin r-83-85i, 100-102; c-100-102r. Starlin c-47. Tuska a-19p. Black Knight-r by Maneely in 12-16, 19. Sub-Mariner-r by Everett in 12-20.

MARVEL SUPER-HEROES
Marvel Comics: May, 1990 - V2#15, Oct, 1993 ($2.95/$2.50, quart., 68-84 pgs.)

1-Moon Knight, Hercules, Black Panther, Magik, Brother Voodoo, Speedball (by Ditko) & Hellcat; Hembeck-a						3.00
2,4,5,V2#3,6-15: 2-Summer Special(7/90), Rogue, Speedball (by Ditko), Iron Man, Falcon, Tigra & Daredevil. 4-Spider-Man/Nick Fury, Daredevil,Speedball, Wonder Man, Spitfire & Black Knight; Byrne-c. 5-Thor, Dr. Strange, Thing & She-Hulk; Speedball by Ditko(p). V2#3-Retells origin Capt. America w/new facts; Blue Shield, Capt. Marvel,Speedball, Wasp; Hulk by Ditko/Rogers V2#6-9: 6-8-$2.25-c. 6,7-X-Men, Cloak & Dagger, The Shroud (by Ditko) & Marvel Boy in each. 8-X-Men, Namor & Iron Man (by Ditko); Larsen-c. 9-West Coast Avengers, Iron Man app.; Keith-c(p). V2#10-Ms. Marvel/Sabretooth-c/story (intended for Ms. Marvel #24); shows-c to #24); Namor, Vision, Scarlet Witch stories. V2#11,12 :11-Original Ghost Rider-c/story; Giant-Man, Ms. Marvel stories. 12-Dr. Strange, Falcon, Iron Man. V2#13-15 ($2.75, 84 pg.): 13-All Iron Man 30th anniversary. 15-Iron Man/Thor/Volstagg/Dr. Druid						2.75

MARVEL SUPER-HEROES MEGAZINE
Marvel Comics: Oct, 1994 - No. 6, Mar, 1995 ($2.95, 100 pgs.)

1-6: 1-r/FF #232, DD #159, Iron Man #115, Incred. Hulk #314		3.00

MARVEL SUPER-HEROES SECRET WARS (See Secret Wars II)
Marvel Comics Group: May, 1984 - No. 12, Apr, 1985 (limited series)

1	1	2	3	5	6	8
1-3-(2nd printings, sold in multi-packs)						2.50
2-6,9-11: 6-The Wasp dies						6.00
7,12: 7-Intro. new Spider-Woman. 12-($1.00, 52 pgs.)	1	2	3	4	5	7
8-Spider-Man's new black costume explained as alien costume (1st app. Venom as alien costume)	4	8	12	21	26	30

NOTE: Zeck a-1-12; c-1,3,8-12. Additional artists (John Romita Sr., Art Adams and others) had uncredited art in #12.

MARVEL SUPER SPECIAL, A (See Marvel Comics Super...)

MARVEL SWIMSUIT SPECIAL (Also see Marvel Illustrated...)
Marvel Comics: 1992 - No. 4, 1995 ($3.95/$4.50, magazine, 52 pgs.)

1-4-Silvestri-c; pin-ups by diff. artists. 2-Jusko-c. 3-Hughes-c						
	1	2	3	5	7	9

MARVEL TAILS STARRING PETER PORKER THE SPECTACULAR SPIDER-HAM
(Also see Peter Porker...)
Marvel Comics Group: Nov, 1983 (one-shot)

1-Peter Porker, the Spectacular Spider-Ham, Captain Americat, Goose Rider, Hulk Bunny app.	
	4.00

Marvel Tales #125 © MAR

Marvel Tales (2nd) #247 © MAR

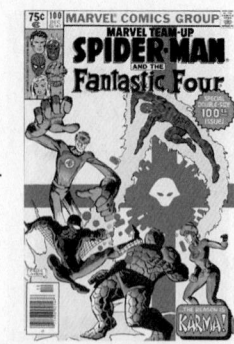

Marvel Team-Up #100 © MAR

	GD 2.0	VG 4.0	FN 6.0	VF 8.0	VF/NM 9.0	NM- 9.2

MARVEL TALES (Formerly Marvel Mystery Comics #1-92)
Marvel/Atlas Comics (MCI): No. 93, Aug, 1949 - No. 159, Aug, 1957

	GD 2.0	VG 4.0	FN 6.0	VF 8.0	VF/NM 9.0	NM- 9.2
93-Horror/weird stories begin	145	290	435	906	1503	2100
94-Everett-a	93	186	279	581	966	1350
95-New logo	69	138	207	431	716	1000
96,99,101,103,105	59	118	177	369	610	850

97-Sun Girl, 2 pgs; Kirbyish-a; one story used in N.Y. State Legislative document

	76	152	228	475	788	1100
98,100: 98-Krigstein-a	60	120	180	375	625	875
102-Wolverton-a "The End of the World", (6 pgs.)	83	166	249	519	860	1200
104-Wolverton-a "Gateway to Horror", (6 pgs.)	83	166	249	519	860	1200
106,107-Krigstein-a. 106-Decapitation story	48	96	144	293	484	675

108-120: 118-Hypo-c/panels in End of World story. 120-Jack Katz-a

	36	72	108	208	329	450

121,123-131: 128-Flying Saucer-c. 131-Last precode (2/55)

	28	56	84	162	256	350
122-Kubert-a	29	58	87	167	264	360
132,133,135-141,143,145	21	42	63	122	191	260
134-Krigstein, Kubert-a; flying saucer-c	23	46	69	132	209	285
142-Krigstein-a	22	44	66	126	198	270
144-Williamson/Krenkel-a, 3 pgs.	22	44	66	126	198	270

146,148-151,154-156,158: 150-1st S.A. issue. 156-Torres-a

	16	32	48	94	147	200
200						
147,152: 147-Ditko-a. 152-Wood, Morrow-a	19	38	57	109	172	235
153-Everett End of World c/story	21	42	63	124	195	265
157,159-Krigstein-a	17	34	51	100	158	215

NOTE: Andru a-103. Briefer a-118. Check a-147. Colan a-102, 105, 107, 118, 120, 127, 131. Drucker a-127, 135, 141, 146, 150. Everett a-98, 104, 106(2), 108(2), 131, 148, 151, 153, 155; c-107, 109, 111, 112, 114, 117, 127, 143, 147-151, 153, 155, 156. Forte a-119, 143. Heath a-110, 113, 118, 119; c-104-106, 110, 130. Gil Kane a-117. Lawrence a-130. Maneely a-111, 126, 129; c-108, 116, 120, 129, 152. Mooney a-114. Morisi a-153. Morrow a-150, 152, 156. Orlando a-149, 151, 157. Pakula a-119, 121, 135, 144, 150, 152. Powell a-136, 137, 150, 154. Ravielli a-117. Rico a-97, 99. Romita a-108. Sekowsky a-96-98. Shores a-110; c-96. Sinnott a-105, 116. Tuska a-114. Whitney a-107. Wildey a-126, 138.

MARVEL TALES (...Annual #1,2; ...Starring Spider-Man #123 on)
Marvel Comics Group (NPP earlier issues): 1964 - No. 291, Nov, 1994 (No. 1-32: 72 pgs.)
(#1-3 have Canadian variants; back & inside-c are blank, same value)

1-Reprints origins of Spider-Man/Amazing Fantasy #15, Hulk/Inc. Hulk#1, Ant-Man/T.T.A. #35, Giant Man/T.T.A. #49, Iron Man/T.O.S. #39,48, Thor/J.I.M. #83 & r/Sgt. Fury #1

	29	58	87	212	381	550

2 ('65)-r/X-Men #1(origin), Avengers #1(origin), origin Dr. Strange/Strange Tales #115 & origin Hulk(Hulk #3)

	10	20	30	70	123	175

3 (7/66)-Spider-Man, Strange Tales (H. Torch), Journey into Mystery (Thor), Tales to Astonish (Ant-Man)-r begin (r/Strange Tales #101)

	6	12	18	41	66	90
4,5	4	8	12	28	44	60
6-8,10: 10-Reprints 1st Kraven/Amaz. S-M #15	3	6	9	18	27	35
9-r/Amazing Spider-Man #14 w/cover	3	6	9	20	30	40

11-33: 11-Spider-Man battles Daredevil-r/Amaz. Spider-Man #16. 13-Origin Marvel Boy-r from M. Boy #1. 22-Green Goblin-c/story-r/Amaz. Spider-Man #27. 30-New Angel story (x-over w/Ka-Zar #2,3). 32-Last 72 pg. iss. 33-(52 pgs.) Kraven-r

	3	6	9	14	19	24
34-50: 34-Begin regular size issues	1	2	3	5	6	8
51-65						5.00
66-70-(Regular 25¢ editions)(4-8/76)						4.00
66-70-(30¢-c variants, limited distribution)	2	4	6	9	12	15

71-105: 75-Origin Spider-Man-r. 77-79-Drug issues-r/Amaz. Spider-Man #96-98. 98-Death of Gwen Stacy-r/Amaz. Spider-Man #121 (Green Goblin). 99-Death Green Goblin-r/Amaz. Spider-Man #122. 100-(52 pgs.)-New Hawkeye/Two Gun Kid story.

101-105-All Spider-Man-r						3.00
80-84-(35¢-c variants, limited distribution)(6-10/77)	3	6	9	14	20	25
106-r/1st Punisher-Amazing Spider-Man #129	1	2	3	5	6	8

107-136: 107-133-All Spider-Man-r. 111,112-r/Spider-Man #134,135 (Punisher). 113,114-r/Spider-Man #136,137(Green Goblin). 126-128-r/clone story from Amazing Spider-Man #149-151. 134-136-Dr. Strange-r begin; SpM stories continue.

134-Dr. Strange-r/Strange Tales #110						3.00

137-Origin-r Dr. Strange; shows original unprinted-c & origin Spider-Man/Amazing Fantasy #15

						6.00
137-Nabisco giveaway	1	2	3	4	5	7

138-Reprints all Amazing Spider-Man #1; begin reprints of Spider-Man with covers similar to originals

						5.00
139-144: r/Amazing Spider-Man #2-7						3.00

145-149,151-190,193-199: Spider-Man-r continue w/#8 on 149-Contains skin "Tattooz" decals. 153-r/1st Kraven/Spider-Man #15. 155-r/2nd Green Goblin/Spider-Man #17. 161,164,165-Gr. Goblin-c/stories-r/Spider-Man #23,26,27. 178,179-Green Goblin-c/story-r/

Spider-Man #39,40. 187,189-Kraven-r. 193-Byrne-r/Marvel Team-Up begin w/scripts

						2.50

150,191,192,200: 150-($1.00, 52pgs.)-r/Spider-Man Annual #1(Kraven app.). 191-($1.50, 68 pgs.)-r/Spider-Man #96-98. 192-($1.25, 52 pgs.)-r/Spider-Man #121,122. 200-Double size ($1.25)-Miller-c & r/Annual #14

						4.00

201-257: 208-Last Byrne-r. 210,211-r/Spidey #134,135. 212,213-r/Giant-Size Spidey #4. 213-r/1st solo Silver Surfer story/F.F. Annual #5. 214,215-r/Spidey #161,162. 222-Reprints origin Punisher/Spectacular Spider-Man #83; last Punisher reprint. 209-Reprints 1st app. The Punisher/Amazing Spider-Man #129; Punisher reprints begin w/#222. 223-McFarlane-c begins, end #239. 233-Spider-Man/X-Men team-ups begin; r/X-Men #35. 234-r/Marvel Team-Up #4. 235,236-r/M. Team-Up Annual #1. 237,238-r/M. Team-Up #150. 239,240-r/M. Team-Up #38,90(Beast). 242-r/M.Team-Up #89. 243-r/M. Team-Up #117 (Wolverine). 250-($1.50, 52pgs.)-r/1st Karma/M. Team-Up #100. 251-r/Spider-Man #100 (Green Goblin-c/story). 252-r/1st app. Morbius/Amaz. Spider-Man #101. 253-($1.50, 52 pgs.) -r/Amaz. S-M #102254-r/M. Team-Up #15(Ghost Rider); new painted-c. 255,256-Spider-Man & Ghost Rider/Marvel Team-Up #58,91. 257-Hobgoblin-r begin (r/Amazing Spider-Man #238)

						2.50

258-291: 258-261-r/A. Spider-Man #239,249-251(Hobgoblin). 262,263-r/Marv. Team-Up #53,54. 262-New X-Men vs. Sunstroke story. 263-New Woodgod origin story. 264,265-r/Amazing Spider-Man Annual 5. 266-273-Reprints alien costume stories/A. S-M 252-259. 277-r/1st Silver Sable/A. S-M 265. 283-r/A. S-M 275 (Hobgoblin). 284-r/A. S-M 276 (Hobgoblin)

						2.50
285-variant w/Wonder-Con logo on c-no price-giveaway						2.50
286-($2.95)-p/bagged w/16 page insert & animation print						3.00

NOTE: All contain reprints; some have new art. #89-97-r/Amazing Spider-Man #110-118; #98-136-r/#121-159; #137-150-r/Amazing Fantasy #15, #1-12 & Annual 1; #151-167-r/#13-28 & Annual 2; #168-186-r/#29-46. Austin a-100i; c-272i, 273i. Byrne a(r)-193-198p, 201-208p. Ditko a-1-30, 83, 100, 137-155. G. Kane a-71, 81, 98-101p, 249r; c-125-127p, 130p, 137-155. Sam Kieth c-255, 262, 263. Ron Lim c-266p-281p, 283p-285p. McFarlane c-223-239. Mooney a-63, 95-97i, 103(i). Nasser a-100p. Nebres a-242i. Perez c-259-261. Rogers c-240, 241, 243-252.

MARVEL TALES FLIP MAGAZINE
Marvel Comics: Sept, 2005 - No. 25, Sept, 2007 ($3.99/$4.99)

1-6-Reprints Amazing Spider-Man #30-up and Amazing Fantasy (2004) in flip format						4.00
7-10-Reprints Amazing Spider-Man #36-up and Runaways Vol. 2 in flip format						4.00
11-25-($4.99) Reprints Amazing Spider-Man #36-up and Runaways Vol. 2 in flip format						5.00

MARVEL TAROT, THE
Marvel Comics: 2007 ($3.99, one-shot)

1-Marvel characters featured in Tarot deck images; Djurdjevic-c						4.00

MARVEL TEAM-UP (See Marvel Treasury Edition #18 & Official Marvel Index To...)
(Replaced by Web of Spider-Man)
Marvel Comics Group: March, 1972 - No. 150, Feb, 1985
NOTE: Spider-Man team-ups in all but Nos. 18, 23, 26, 29, 32, 35, 97, 104, 105, 137.

1-Human Torch	12	24	36	87	156	225
2-Human Torch	5	10	15	35	55	75
3-Spider-Man/Human Torch vs. Morbius (part 1); 3rd app. of Morbius (7/72)						
	6	12	18	41	66	90
4-Spider-Man/X-Men vs. Morbius (part 2 of story); 4th app. of Morbius						
	6	12	18	41	66	90
5-10: 5-Vision. 6-Thing. 7-Thor. 8-The Cat (4/73, came out between The Cat #3 & 4). 9-Iron Man. 10-H-T						
	3	6	9	17	25	35
11,13,14,16-20: 11-Inhumans. 13-Capt. America. 14-Sub-Mariner. 16-Capt. Marvel. 17-Mr. Fantastic. 18-H-T/Hulk. 19-Ka-Zar. 20-Black Panther; last 20¢ issue						
	2	4	6	9	13	16
12-Werewolf (By Night) (8/73)	3	6	9	18	27	35
15-1st Spider-Man/Ghost Rider team-up (11/73)	3	6	9	18	27	35
21-30: 21-Dr. Strange. 22-Hawkeye. 23-H-T/Iceman (X-Men cameo). 24-Brother Voodoo. 25-Daredevil. 26-H-T/Thor. 27-Hulk. 28-Hercules. 29-H-T/Iron Man. 30-Falcon						
	3	6	8	8	8	10
31-45,47-50: 31-Iron Fist. 32-H-T/Son of Satan. 33-Nighthawk. 34-Valkyrie. 35-H-T/Dr. Strange. 36-Frankenstein. 37-Man-Wolf. 38-Beast. 39-H-T. 40-Sons of the Tiger/H-T. 41-Scarlet Witch. 42-The Vision. 43-Dr. Doom; retells origin. 44-Moondragon. 45-Killraven. 47-Thing. 48-Iron Man; last 25¢ issue. 49-Dr. Strange; Iron Man app. 50-Iron Man; Dr. Strange app.						
	1	2	3	4	5	7
44-48-(30¢-c variants, limited distribution)(4-8/76)	3	6	9	20	30	40
46-Spider-Man/Deathlok team-up	1	2	3	5	6	8
51,52,56,57: 51-Iron Man; Dr. Strange app. 52-Capt. America. 56-Daredevil. 57-Black Widow						
						6.00
53-Hulk; Woodgod & X-Men app., 1st Byrne-a on X-Men (1/77)						
	3	6	9	17	25	32
54,55,58-60: 54,59,60: 54-Hulk; Woodgod app. 59-Yellowjacket/The Wasp. 60-The Wasp (Byrne-a in all). 55-Warlock-c/story; Byrne-a. 58-Ghost Rider						
	1	2	3	5	6	9
58-62-(35¢-c variants, limited distribution)(6-10/77)	4	8	12	26	41	55
61-70: All Byrne-a. 61-H-T. 62-Ms. Marvel; last 30¢ issue. 63-Iron Fist. 64-Daughters of the Dragon. 65-Capt. Britain (1st U.S. app.). 66-Capt. Britain; 1st app. Arcade. 67-Tigra; Kraven						

Marvel Team-Up #8 © MAR

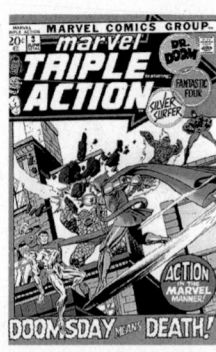

Marvel Triple Action #3 © MAR

Marvel Two-In-One #44 © MAR

	GD	VG	FN	VF	VF/NM	NM-
	2.0	4.0	6.0	8.0	9.0	9.2

the Hunter app. 68-Man-Thing. 69-Havok (from X-Men). 70-Thor

| | 1 | 2 | 3 | 4 | 5 | 7 |

71-74,76-78,80: 71-Falcon. 72-Iron Man. 73-Daredevil. 74-Not Ready for Prime Time Players (Belushi). 76-Dr. Strange. 77-Ms. Marvel. 78-Wonder Man. 80-Dr. Strange/Clea; last 35¢ issue — 4.00

75,79,81: Byrne-a(p). 75-Power Man; Cage app. 79-Mary Jane Watson as Red Sonja; Clark Kent cameo (1 panel, 3/79). 81-Death of Satana — 6.00

82-99: 82-Black Widow. 83-Nick Fury. 84-Shang-Chi. 86-Guardians of the Galaxy. 89-Nightcrawler (from X-Men). 91-Ghost Rider. 92-Hawkeye. 93-Werewolf by Night. 94-Spider-Man vs. The Shroud. 95-Mockingbird (intro.); Nick Fury app. 96-Howard the Duck; last 40¢ issue. 97-Spider-Woman/ Hulk. 98-Black Widow. 99-Machine Man. 85-Shang-Chi/ Black Widow/Nick Fury. 87-Black Panther. 88-Invisible Girl. 90-Beast — 3.00

100-(Double-size)-Fantastic Four/Storm/Black Panther; origin/1st app. Karma, one of the New Mutants; origin Storm; X-Men x-over; Miller-c/a(p); Byrne-a (on X-Men app. only)

| | 1 | 2 | 3 | 4 | 5 | 7 |

101-116: 101-Nighthawk(Ditko-a). 102-Doc Samson. 103-Ant-Man. 104-Hulk/Ka-Zar. 105-Hulk/Powerman/Iron Fist. 106-Capt. America. 107-She-Hulk. 108-Paladin; Dazzler cameo. 109-Dazzler; Paladin app. 110-Iron Man. 111-Devil-Slayer. 112-King Kull; last 50¢ issue. 113-Quasar. 114-Falcon. 115-Thor. 116-Valkyrie — 3.00

117-Wolverine-c/story

| | 1 | 3 | 4 | 6 | 8 | 10 |

118-140,142-149: 118-Professor X; Wolverine app. (4 pgs.); X-Men cameo. 119-Gargoyle. 120-Dominic Fortune. 121-Human Torch. 122-Man-Thing. 123-Daredevil. 124-The Beast. 125-Tigra. 126-Hulk & Powerman/Son of Satan. 127-The Watcher. 128-Capt. America; Spider-Man/Capt. America photo-c. 129-The Vision. 130-Scarlet Witch. 131-Frogman. 132-Mr. Fantastic. 133-Fantastic Four. 134-Jack of Hearts. 135-Kitty Pryde; X-Men cameo. 136-Wonder Man. 137-Aunt May/Franklin Richards. 138-Sandman. 139-Nick Fury. 140-Black Widow. 142-Capt. Marvel. 143-Starfox. 144-Moon Knight. 145-Iron Man. 146-Nomad. 147-Human Torch; Spider-Man back to old costume. 148-Thor. 149-Cannonball — 2.50

141-Daredevil; SpM/Black Widow app. (Spidey in new black costume; ties w/ Amazing Spider-Man #252 for 1st black costume)

| | 1 | 3 | 4 | 6 | 8 | 10 |

150-X-Men ($1.00, double-size); B. Smith-c — 5.00

Annual 1 (1976)-Spider-Man/X-Men (early app.)

| | 3 | 6 | 9 | 18 | 27 | 35 |

Annual 2 (1979)-Spider-Man/Hulk

| | 1 | 2 | 3 | 5 | 7 | 9 |

Annuals 3,4: 3 (1980)-Hulk/Power Man/Machine Man/Iron Fist; Miller-c(p). 4 (1981)-Spider-Man /Daredevil/Moon Knight/Power Man/Iron Fist; brief origins of each; Miller-c; Miller scripts on Daredevil — 6.00

Annuals 5-7: 5 (1982)-SpM/The Thing/Scarlet Witch/Dr. Strange/Quasar. 6 (1983)-Spider-Man/ New Mutants (early app.). Cloak & Dagger. 7(1984)-Alpha Flight; Byrne-c(i) — 5.00

NOTE: Art Adams c-141p. Austin a-79; c-76i, 79i, 96i, 101i, 112i, 130i. Bolle a-9i. Byrne a(p)-53-55, 59-70, 75, 79, 100; c-68p, 70p, 72p, 75, 76p, 79p, 129i, 133i. Colan a-87p. Ditko a-101. Kane a(r)-4-6, 13, 14, 16-19, 23; c(p)-4, 13, 14, 17-19, 23, 25, 26, 32-35, 37, 41, 44, 45, 47, 53, 54. Miller a-100p; c-95p, 99p, 100p, 102p, 106. Mooney a-2i, 7i, 8, 10p, 11p, 16i, 24-31p, 72, 93i. Annual 5i. Nasser a-89p; c-101p. Simonson c-99i, 148. Paul Smith c-131, 132. Starlin c-27. Sutton a-93p. "H-T" means Human Torch; "SpM" means Spider-Man; "S-M" means Sub-Mariner.

MARVEL TEAM-UP (2nd Series)
Marvel Comics: Sept, 1997 - No. 11, July, 1998 ($1.99)

1-11: 1-Spider-Man team-ups begin, Generation x-app. 2-Hercules-c/app.; two covers. 3-Sandman. 4-Man-Thing. 5-Blade. 6-Namor team-ups begin, Dr. Strange app. 9-Capt. America. 10-Thing. 11-Iron Man — 2.50

MARVEL TEAM-UP
Marvel Comics: Jan, 2005 - No. 25, Dec, 2006 ($2.25/$2.99)

1-7,9: 1,2-Spider-Man & Wolverine; Kirkman-s/Kolins-a. 5,6-X-23 app. — 2.50
8,10-25 ($2.99-c) 10-Spider-Man & Daredevil. 12-Origin of Titannus. 14-Invincible app. — 3.00
... Vol. 1: The Golden Child TPB (2005, $12.99) r/#1-6 — 13.00
... Vol. 2: Master of the Ring TPB (2005, $17.99) r/#7-13 — 18.00
... Vol. 3: League of Losers TPB (2006, $13.99) r/#14-18 — 14.00
... Vol. 4: Freedom Ring TPB (2007, $17.99) r/#19-25 — 18.00

MARVEL: THE LOST GENERATION
Marvel Comics: No. 12, Mar, 2000 - No. 1, Feb, 2001 ($2.99, issue #s go in reverse)

1-12-Stern-s/Byrne-s/a; untold story of The First Line. 5-Thor app. — 3.00

MARVEL/ TOP COW CROSSOVERS
Image Comics (Top Cow): Nov, 2005 ($24.99, TPB)

Vol. 1-Reprints crossovers with Wolverine, Witchblade, Hulk, Darkness; Devil's Reign — 25.00

MARVEL TREASURY EDITION
Marvel Comics Group/Whitman #17,18: 1974; #2, Dec, 1974 - #28, 1981 ($1.50/$2.50, 100 pgs., oversized, new-a &-r)(Also see Amazing Spider-Man, The, Marvel Spec. Ed. Feat.--, Savage Fists of Kung Fu, Superman Vs. & 2001, A Space Odyssey)

1-Spectacular Spider-Man; story-r/Marvel Super-Heroes #14; Romita-c/a(r); G. Kane, Ditko-r; Green Goblin/Hulk-r

| | 5 | 10 | 15 | 32 | 51 | 70 |

1-1,000 numbered copies signed by Stan Lee & John Romita on front-c & sold thru mail for $5.00; these were the 1st 1,000 copies off the press

| | 10 | 20 | 30 | 68 | 119 | 170 |

2-10: 2-Fantastic Four-r/F.F. 6,11,48-50(Silver Surfer). 3-The Mighty Thor-r/Thor #125-130. 4-Conan the Barbarian; Barry Smith-c/a(r)/Conan #11. 5-The Hulk (origin-r/Hulk #3). 6-Dr. Strange. 7-Mighty Avengers. 8-Giant Superhero Holiday Grab-Bag; Spider-Man, Hulk, Nick Fury. 9-Giant; Super-hero team-up. 10-Thor; r/Thor #154-157

| | 3 | 6 | 9 | 16 | 22 | 28 |

11-20: 11-Fantastic Four. 12-Howard the Duck (r/#H. the Duck #1 & G.S. Man-Thing #4,5) plus new Defenders story. 13-Giant Super-Hero Holiday Grab-Bag. 14-The Sensational Spider-Man; r/1st Morbius from Amazing S-M #101,102 plus #100 & r/Not Brand Echh #6. 15-Conan; B. Smith, Neal Adams-i; r/Conan #24. 16-The Defenders (origin) & Valkyrie; r/Defenders #1,4,13,14. 17-The Hulk. 18-The Astonishing Spider-Man; r/Spider-Man's 1st team-ups with Iron Fist, The X-Men, Ghost Rider & Werewolf by Night; inside back-c has photos from 1978 Spider-Man TV show. 19-Conan the Barbarian. 20-Hulk

| | 2 | 4 | 6 | 10 | 14 | 18 |

21-24,27: 21-Fantastic Four. 22-Spider-Man. 23-Conan. 24-Rampaging Hulk. 27-Spider-Man

| | 2 | 4 | 6 | 10 | 14 | 18 |

25-Spider-Man vs. The Hulk new story

| | 3 | 6 | 9 | 14 | 19 | 24 |

26-The Hulk; 6 pg. new Wolverine/Hercules-s

| | 2 | 4 | 6 | 13 | 18 | 22 |

28-Spider-Man/Superman; (origin of each)

| | 4 | 8 | 12 | 26 | 41 | 55 |

NOTE: Reprints-2, 3, 5, 7-9, 13, 14, 16, 17. Neal Adams a(i)-6, 15. Brunner a-6, 12; c-6. Buscema a-15, 19, 28; c-28. Colan a-6r; c-12p. Ditko a-1, 6. Gil Kane c-16p. Kirby a-1-3, 5, 7, 9-11; c-7. Perez a-26. Romita c-1, 5. B. Smith a-4, 15, 19; c-4, 19.

MARVEL TREASURY OF OZ FEATURING THE MARVELOUS LAND OF OZ
Marvel Comics Group: 1975 ($1.50, oversized) (See MGM's Marvelous…)

1-Roy Thomas-s/Alfredo Alcala-a; Romita-c & bk-c

| | 3 | 6 | 9 | 15 | 21 | 26 |

MARVEL TREASURY SPECIAL (Also see 2001: A Space Odyssey)
Marvel Comics Group: 1974; 1976 ($1.50, oversized, 84 pgs.)

Vol. 1-Spider-Man, Torch, Sub-Mariner, Avengers "Giant Superhero Holiday Grab-Bag"; Wood, Colan/Everett, plus 2 Kirby-r; reprints Hulk vs. Thing from Fantastic Four #25,26

| | 3 | 6 | 9 | 15 | 21 | 26 |

Vol. 1-... Featuring Captain America's Bicentennial Battles (6/76)-Kirby-a; B. Smith inks, 11 pgs.

| | 3 | 6 | 9 | 16 | 22 | 28 |

MARVEL TRIPLE ACTION (See Giant-Size…)
Marvel Comics Group: Feb, 1972 - No. 24, Mar, 1975; No. 25, Aug, 1975 - No. 47, Apr, 1979

1-(25¢ giant, 52 pgs.)-Dr. Doom, Silver Surfer, The Thing begin, end #4 ('66 reprints from Fantastic Four)

	3	6	9	18	27	35
2-5	2	4	6	9	12	15
6-10	1	2	3	5	6	8
11-47: 45-r/X-Men #45. 46-r/Avengers #53(X-Men)						4.00
29,30-(30¢-c variants, limited distribution)(5,7/76)	2	4	6	10	14	18
36,37-(35¢-c variants, limited distribution)(7,9/77)	3	6	9	16	23	30

NOTE: #5-44, 46, 47 reprint Avengers #11 thru ?. #40-r/Avengers #48(1st Black Knight). Buscema a(r)-35p, 36p, 38p, 39p, 41, 42, 43p, 44p, 46p, 47p. Ditko a-2r; c-47. Kirby a(r)-1-4p; c-1-4, 9-19, 22, 24, 29. Starlin c-7. Tuska a(r)-40p, 43i, 46i, 47i. #2 through #17 are 20¢-c.

MARVEL TWO-IN-ONE (…Featuring … #82 on; also see The Thing)
Marvel Comics Group: January, 1974 - No. 100, June, 1983

1-Thing team-ups begin; Man-Thing	6	12	18	39	62	85
2,3: 2-Sub-Mariner; last 20¢ issue. 3-Daredevil	3	6	9	16	23	30
4-6: 4-Capt. America. 5-Guardians of the Galaxy (9/74, 2nd app.?). 6-Dr. Strange (11/74)	2	4	6	11	16	20
7,9,10	2	4	6	11	14	14
8-Early Ghost Rider app. (3/75)	2	4	6	13	18	22
11-14,19,20: 13-Power Man. 14-Son of Satan (early app.)						
	1	2	3	5	6	8
15-18: (Regular 25¢ editions)(5-7/76) 17-Spider-Man.	1	2	3	5	6	8
15-18-(30¢-c variants, limited distribution)	3	6	9	16	23	30
21-29: 27-Deathlok. 29-Master of Kung Fu; Spider-Woman cameo						6.00
28,29,31-(35¢-c variants, limited distribution)	3	6	9	20	30	40
30-2nd full app. Spider-Woman (see Marvel Spotlight #32 for 1st app.)						
	1	3	4	6	8	10
30-(35¢-c variant, limited distribution)(8/77)	4	8	12	28	44	60
31-33-Spider-Woman app.	1	2	3	5	6	8
34-40: 39-Vision						6.00
41,42,44,45,47,49: 42-Capt. America. 45-Capt. Marvel						4.00
43,50,53,55-Byrne-a(p). 53-Quasar(7/79, 2nd app.)						6.00
46-Thing battles Hulk-c/story	1	3	4	6	8	10
51-The Beast, Nick Fury, Ms. Marvel; Miller-p	1	2	3	4	5	7
52-Moon Knight app.						3.00
54-Death of Deathlok: Byrne-a	1	3	4	6	8	10
56-60,64-74,76-79,81,82: 60-Intro. Impossible Woman. 68-Angel. 69-Guardians of the Galaxy. 71-1st app. Maelstrom. 76-Iceman						3.00
61-63: 61-Starhawk (from Guardians); "The Coming of Her" storyline begins, ends #63; cover similar to F.F. #67 (Him-c). 62-Moondragon; Thanos & Warlock cameo in flashback;						

Marvel Visionaries: John Buscema © MAR

Marvel Zombies #3 © MAR

Mary Marvel Comics #28 © FAW

	GD 2.0	VG 4.0	FN 6.0	VF 8.0	VF/NM 9.0	NM- 9.2

Starhawk app. 63-Warlock revived shortly; Starhawk & Moondragon app. 4.00
75-Avengers (52 pgs.) 4.00
80,90,100: 80-Ghost Rider. 90-Spider-Man. 100-Double size, Byrne-s 4.00
83-89,91-99: 83-Sasquatch. 84-Alpha Flight app. 93-Jocasta dies. 96-X-Men-c & cameo 3.00

Annual 1(1976, 52 pgs.)-Thing/Liberty Legion; Kirby-c	2	4	6	8	10	12

Annual 2(1977, 52 pgs.)-Thing/Spider-Man; 2nd death of Thanos; end of Thanos saga;

Warlock app.; Starlin-c/a	4	8	12	24	37	50

Annual 3,4 (1978-79, 52 pgs.): 3-Nova. 4-Black Bolt 6.00
Annual 5-7 (1980-82, 52 pgs.): 5-Hulk. 6-1st app. American Eagle. 7-The Thing/Champion;
   Sasquatch, Colossus app.; X-Men cameo (1 pg.) 4.00
NOTE: Austin c(i)-42, 54, 56, 58, 61, 63, 66. John Buscema a-30p, 45; c-30p. Byrne (p)-43, 50, 53-55; c-43,
53p, 56p, 98i, 99i. Gil Kane a-1p, 2p; c(p)-1-3, 9, 11, 14, 28. Kirby c-10, 12, 19p, 20, 25, 27. Mooney a-18i, 38i,
90i. Nasser a-70p. Perez a(p)-56-58, 60, 64, 65; c(p)-32, 33, 42, 50-52, 54, 55, 57, 58, 61-66, 70. Roussos a-
Annual 1i. Simonson c-43i, 97p, Annual 6i. Starlin c-6, Annual 1. Tuska a-6p.

MARVEL TWO-IN-ONE
Marvel Comics: Sept, 2007 - Present ($4.99, 64 pgs.)
1-3-Reprints Marvel Adventures Avengers and X-Men: First Class stories 5.00

MARVEL UNIVERSE (See Official Handbook Of The...)

MARVEL UNIVERSE (Title on variant covers for newsstand editions of some 2001 Marvel titles. See indicia
for actual titles and issue numbers)

MARVEL UNIVERSE
Marvel Comics: June, 1998 - No. 7, Dec, 1998 ($2.99/$1.99)
1-($2.99)-Invaders stories from WW2; Stern-s 3.00
2-7-($1.99): 2-Two covers. 4-7-Monster Hunters; Manley-a/Stern-s 2.50

MARVEL UNIVERSE: MILLENNIAL VISIONS
Marvel Comics: Feb, 2002 ($3.99, one-shot)
1-Pin-ups by various; wraparound-c by JH Williams & Gray 4.00

MARVEL UNIVERSE: THE END (Also see Infinity Abyss)
Marvel Comics: May, 2003 - No. 6, Aug, 2003 ($3.50/$2.99, limited series)
1-($3.50)-Thanos, X-Men, FF, Avengers, Spider-Man, Daredevil app.; Starlin-s/a(p) 3.50
2-6-($2.99) Akhenaten, Eternily, Living Tribunal app. 3.00
Thanos Vol. 3: Marvel Universe - The End (2003, $16.99) r/#1-6 17.00

MARVEL UNLIMITED (Title on variant covers for newsstand editions of some 2001 Daredevil issues.
See indicia for actual titles and issue numbers)

MARVEL VALENTINE SPECIAL
Marvel Comics: Mar, 1997 ($2.99, one-shot)
1-Valentine stories w/Spider-Man, Daredevil, Cyclops, Phoenix 3.00

MARVEL VERSUS DC (See DC Versus Marvel) (Also see Amazon, Assassins, Bruce Wayne:
Agent of S.H.I.E.L.D., Bullets & Bracelets, Doctor Strangefate, JLX, Legend of the Dark Claw,
Magneto & The Magnetic Men, Speed Demon, Spider-Boy, Super Soldier, & X-Patrol)
Marvel Comics: No. 2, 1996 - No. 3, 1996 ($3.95, limited series)
2,3: 2-Peter David script. 3-Ron Marz script; Dan Jurgens-a(p). 1st app. of Super Soldier,
   Spider-Boy, Dr. Doomsday, Doctor Strangefate, The Dark Claw, Nightcreeper, Amazon,
   Wraith & others. Storyline continues in Amalgam books. 4.00

MARVEL VISIONARIES
Marvel Comics: 2002 - Present (various prices, HC and TPB)
...: Chris Claremont (2005, $29.99) r/X-Men #137, Uncanny X-Men #153,205,268 & Ann. #12,
   Iron Fist #14, Wolverine #3, New Mutants #21 and other highlights 30.00
...: Gil Kane (8/02, $24.95) r/Amazing Spider-Man #99, Marvel Premiere #1,#15, TOA #76 &
   others; plus sketch pages and a cover gallery 25.00
...: Jack Kirby HC (2004, $29.99) r/career highlights- Red Raven Comics #1 (1st work),
   Captain America Comics #1, Avengers #4, Fantastic Four #48-50 and more 30.00
...: Jack Kirby Vol. 2 HC (2006, $34.99) r/career highlights- Captain America, Two-Gun Kid,
   Fantastic Four, Thor, Fin Fang Foom, Devil Dinosaur, romance and more 35.00
...: Jim Steranko (9/02, $14.95) r/Captain America #110,111,113; X-Men #50,51 and stories
   from Tower of Shadows #1 and Our Love Story #5; plus a cover gallery 15.00
...: John Buscema (2007, $34.99) r/career highlights-Avengers, Silver Surfer, Thor, FF, Hulk,
   Wolverine and others; Roy Thomas intro.; sketch pages and pin-up art 35.00
...: John Romita Jr. (2005, $29.99) r/various stories 1977-2002; debut in AS-M Ann. #11; Iron
   Man #128, AS-M V2 #36, issues of Hulk, Daredevil: The Man Without Fear, Punisher;
   sketch pages; intro. by John Romita Sr. 30.00
....: John Romita Sr. (2005, $29.99) r/various stories 1951-1997 including Young Men #24&26,
   Daredevil #16, ASM #39,42,50; sketch pages; intro. by John Romita Jr. 30.00
...: Roy Thomas (2006, $34.99) r/various career highlights; intro. by Stan Lee 35.00
...: Steve Ditko (2005, $29.99) r/various stories 1961-1992; intro. by Blake Bell 30.00
...: Stan Lee HC (2005, $29.99) r/career highlights- Captain America Comics #3 (1st work),
   and various Spider-Man, FF, Thor, Daredevil stories; 1940-1995; Roy Thomas intro. 30.00

MARVEL WEDDINGS
Marvel Comics: 2005 ($19.99, TPB)

TPB-Reprints weddings of Peter & Mary Jane, Reed & Sue, Scott & Jean, and others 20.00

MARVEL WESTERNS: ...
Marvel Comics: 2006 ($3.99, one-shots)
... Kid Colt and the Arizona Girl 1 (9/06) 2 short stories & 3 Kirby/Ayers reps.; Powell-c 4.00
... Outlaw Files-Profiles and essays about Marvel western characters 4.00
... Strange Westerns Starring The Black Rider 1 (10/06) Englehart-s/Rogers-a & 2 Kirby
   Rawhide Kid reprints; Rogers-c 4.00
... The Two-Gun Kid 1 (8/06) 2 short stories & a Kirby/Ayers reprint; Powell-c 4.00
... Western Legends 1 (9/06) 2 short stories & r/Rawhide Kid origin by Kirby; Powell-c 4.00
HC (2006, $20.99, dustjacket) r/one-shots 21.00

MARVEL X-MEN COLLECTION, THE
Marvel Comics: Jan, 1994 - No. 3, Mar, 1994 ($2.95, limited series)
1-3-r/X-Men trading cards by Jim Lee 3.00

MARVEL - YEAR IN REVIEW (Magazine)
Marvel Comics: 1989 - No. 3, 1991 (52 pgs.)
1-3: 1-Spider-Man-c by McFarlane. 2-Capt. America-c. 3-X-Men/Wolverine-c 5.00

MARVEL ZOMBIES (See Ultimate Fantastic Four #21-23, 30-32)
Marvel Comics: Feb, 2006 - No. 5, June, 2006 ($2.99, limited series)
1-Zombies vs. Magneto; Kirkman-s/Phillips-a/Suydam-c swipe of A.F. #15 15.00
1-(2nd-4th printings) Variant Suydam-c swipes of Spider-Man #1, Amazing Spider-Man #50
   and Incredible Hulk #1 5.00
2-Avengers #4 cover swipe by Suydam 8.00
3-5: 3-Inc. Hulk #340 c-swipe. 4-X-Men #1 c-swipe. 5-AS-M Ann. #21 c-swipe 5.00
3-5-(2nd printings) 3-Daredevil #179 c-swipe. 4-AS-M #39 c-swipe. 5-Silver Surfer #1 3.00
...: Dead Days (7/07, $3.99) Early days of the plague; Kirkman-s/Phillips-a/Suydam-c 4.00
...: The Book of Angels, Demons and Various Monstrosities (2007, $3.99) profile pages 4.00
HC (2006, $19.99) r/#1-5; Kirkman foreword; cover gallery with variants 20.00

MARVEL ZOMBIES / ARMY OF DARKNESS
Marvel Comics/Dynamite Entertainment: May, 2007 - No. 5, Aug, 2007($2.99, limited series)
1-Zombies vs. Ash during the start of the plague; Layman-s/Neves-a/Suydam-c 5.00
1-Second printing with Suydam zombie-fied Captain America Comics #1 cover swipe 3.00
2-5-Suydam zombie-fied cover swipes on all 3.00
HC (2007, $19.99) r/#1-5; cover gallery with variants and non-zombied original covers 20.00

MARVILLE
Marvel Comics: Nov, 2002 - No. 7, Jul, 2003 ($2.25, limited series)
1-6-Satire on DC/AOL-Time-Warner; Jemas-a/Bright-a/Horn-c 2.50
1-($3.95) Variant foil cover by Udon Studios; bonus sketch pages and Jemas afterword 4.00
7-($2.99) Intro. to Epic Comics line with submission guidelines 3.00

MARVIN MOUSE
Atlas Comics (BPC): September, 1957

1-Everett-c/a; Maneely-a	14	28	42	80	115	150

MARY JANE (Spider-Man) (Also see Spider-Man Loves Mary Jane)
Marvel Comics: Aug, 2004 - No. 4, Nov, 2004 ($2.25, limited series)
1-4-Marvel Age series with teen-age MJ Watson; Miyazawa-c/a; McKeever-s 2.50
... Vol. 1: Circle of Friends (2004, $5.99, digest-size) r/#1-4 6.00

MARY JANE & SNIFFLES (See Looney Tunes)
Dell Publishing Co.: No. 402, June, 1952 - No. 474, June, 1953

Four Color 402 (#1)	7	14	21	50	83	115
Four Color 474	7	14	21	47	76	105

MARY JANE: HOMECOMING (Spider-Man)
Marvel Comics: May, 2005 - No. 4, Aug, 2005 ($2.99, limited series)
1-4-Teen-age MJ Watson in high school; Miyazawa-c/a; McKeever-s 3.00
... Vol. 2 (2006, $6.99, digest-size) r/#1-4 7.00

MARY MARVEL COMICS (Monte Hale #29 on) (Also see Captain Marvel #18, Marvel Family,
Shazam, & Wow Comics)
Fawcett Publications: Dec, 1945 - No. 28, Sept, 1948

1-Captain Marvel introduces Mary on-c; intro/origin Georgia Sivana	221	442	663	1381	2291	3200
2	79	158	237	494	822	1150
3,4: 3-New logo	53	106	159	323	537	750
5-8: 8-Bulletgirl x-over in Mary Marvel; X-Mas-c	40	80	120	240	383	525
9,10	37	74	111	214	340	465
11-20	25	50	75	148	232	315
21-28: 28-Western-c	21	42	63	122	191	260

MARY POPPINS (See Movie Comics & Walt Disney Showcase No. 17)

MARY SHELLEY'S FRANKENSTEIN

The Mask #4 © DH

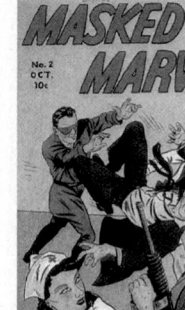

Masked Marvel #2 © CEN

Master Comics #23 © FAW

	GD 2.0	VG 4.0	FN 6.0	VF 8.0	VF/NM 9.0	NM- 9.2		GD 2.0	VG 4.0	FN 6.0	VF 8.0	VF/NM 9.0	NM- 9.2

Topps Comics: Oct, 1994 - Jan, 1995 ($2.95, limited series)

1-4-polybagged w/3 trading cards — — — — — 3.00
1-4 ($2.50)-Newstand ed. — — — — — 2.50

MARY WORTH (See Harvey Comics Hits #55 & Love Stories of...)
Argo: March, 1956 (Also see Romantic Picture Novelettes)

1 — 8 16 24 42 54 65

MASK (TV)
DC Comics: Dec, 1985 - No. 4, Mar, 1986; Feb, 1987 - No. 9, Oct, 1987

1-4; 1-9 (2nd series)-Sat. morning TV show. — — — — — 2.50

MASK, THE (Also see Mayhem)
Dark Horse Comics: Aug, 1991 - No. 4, Oct, 1991; No. 0, Dec, 1991 ($2.50, 36 pgs., limited series)

1-4: 1-1st app. Lt. Kellaway as The Mask (see Dark Horse Presents #10 for 1st app.) — — — — — 5.00
0-(12/91, B&W, 56 pgs.)-r/Mayhem #1-4 — — — — — 4.00

...: HUNT FOR GREEN OCTOBER July, 1995 - Oct, 1995 ($2.50, lim. series)

1-4-Evan Dorkin scripts — — — — — 2.50

.../ MARSHALL LAW Feb, 1998 - No. 2, Mar, 1998 ($2.95, lim. series)

1,2-Mills-s/O'Neill-a — — — — — 3.00

...: OFFICIAL MOVIE ADAPTATION July, 1994 - Aug, 1994 ($2.50, lim. series)

1,2 — — — — — 2.50

... RETURNS Oct, 1992 - No. 4, Mar, 1993 ($2.50, limited series)

1-4 — — — — — 4.00

... SOUTHERN DISCOMFORT Mar, 1996 - No. 4, July, 1996 ($2.50, lim. series)

1-4 — — — — — 2.50

... STRIKES BACK Feb, 1995 - No. 5, Jun, 1995 ($2.50, limited series)

1-5 — — — — — 2.50

... SUMMER VACATION July, 1995 ($10.95, one shot, hard-c)

1-nn-Rick Geary-c/a — — — — — 11.00

... TOYS IN THE ATTIC Aug, 1998 - No. 4, Nov, 1998 ($2.95, limited series)

1-4-Fingerman-s — — — — — 3.00

... VIRTUAL SURREALITY July, 1997 ($2.95, one shot)

nn-Mignola, Aragonés, and others-s/a — — — — — 3.00

... WORLD TOUR Dec, 1995 - No. 4, Mar, 1996 ($2.50, limited series)

1-4: 3-X & Ghost-c/app. — — — — — 2.50

MASK COMICS
Rural Home Publ.: Feb-Mar, 1945 - No. 2, Apr-May, 1945; No. 2, Fall, 1945

1-Classic L. B. Cole Satan-c/a; Palais-a 300 600 900 1881 3141 4400
2-(Scarce)-Classic L. B. Cole Satan-c; Black Rider, The Boy Magician, & The Collector app.
  183 366 549 1144 1897 2650
2-(Fall, 1945)-No publ.-same as regular #2; L. B. Cole-c
  145 290 435 906 1503 2100

MASKED BANDIT, THE
Avon Periodicals: 1952

nn-Kinstler-a 16 32 48 94 147 200

MASKED MAN, THE
Eclipse Comics: 12/84 - #10, 4/86; #11, 10/87; #12, 4/88 ($1.75/$2.00, color/B&W #9 on, Baxter paper)

1-12: 1-Origin retold. 3-Origin Aphid-Man; begin $2.00-c — — — — — 2.50

MASKED MARVEL (See Keen Detective Funnies)
Centaur Publications: Sept, 1940 - No. 3, Dec, 1940

1-The Masked Marvel begins 166 332 498 1038 1719 2400
2,3: 2-Gustavson, Tarpe Mills-a 110 220 330 688 1144 1600

MASKED RAIDER, THE (Billy The Kid #9 on; Frontier Scout, Daniel Boone #10-13)
(Also see Blue Bird)
Charlton Comics: June, 1955 - No. 8, July, 1957; No. 14, Aug, 1958 - No. 30, June, 1961

1-Masked Raider & Talon the Golden Eagle begin; painted-c
  13 26 39 72 101 130
2 8 16 24 42 54 65
3-8,15: 8-Billy The Kid app. 15-Williamson-a, 7 pgs. 6 12 18 31 38 45
14,16-30: 22-Rocky Lane app. 5 10 15 24 30 35

MASKED RANGER
Premier Magazines: Apr, 1954 - No. 9, Aug, 1955

1-The Masked Ranger, his horse Streak, & The Crimson Avenger (origin) begin, end #9; Woodbridge/Frazetta-a 42 84 126 239 380 520
2,3 15 30 45 85 130 175

4-8-All Woodbridge-a. 5-Jesse James by Woodbridge. 6-Billy The Kid by Woodbridge. 7-Wild Bill Hickok by Woodbridge. 8-Jim Bowie's Life Story
  15 30 45 86 133 180
9-Torres-a; Wyatt Earp by Woodbridge; Says Death of Masked Ranger on-c
  16 32 48 92 144 195
NOTE: *Check a-1. Woodbridge c/a-1, 4-9.*

MASK OF DR. FU MANCHU, THE (See Dr. Fu Manchu)
Avon Periodicals: 1951

1-Sax Rohmer adapt.; Wood-c/a (26 pgs.); Hollingsworth-a
  93 186 279 581 966 1350

MASK OF ZORRO, THE
Image Comics: Aug, 1998 - No. 4, Dec, 1998 ($2.95, limited series)

1-4-Movie adapt. Photo variant-c — — — — — 3.00

MASKS: TOO HOT FOR TV!
DC Comics (WildStorm): Feb, 2004 ($4.95)

1-Short stories by various incl. Thompson, Brubaker, Mahnke, Conner; Fabry-c — — — — — 5.00

MASQUE OF THE RED DEATH (See Movie Classics)

MASTER COMICS (Combined with Slam Bang Comics #7 on)
Fawcett Publications: Mar, 1940 - No. 133, Apr, 1953 (No. 1-6: oversized issues) (#1-3: 15¢, 52 pgs.; #4-6: 10¢, 36 pgs.; #7-Begin 68 pg. issues)

1-Origin & 1st app. Master Man; The Devil's Dagger, El Carim, Master of Magic, Rick O'Say, Morton Murch, White Rajah, Shipwreck Roberts, Frontier Marshal, Streak Sloan, Mr. Clue begin (all features end #6) 771 1542 2313 5397 9449 13,500
2 241 482 723 1506 2503 3500
3-6: 6-Last Master Man 172 344 516 1075 1788 2500
NOTE: *#1-6 rarely found in near mint or very fine condition due to large-size format.*
7-(10/40)-Bulletman, Zoro, the Mystery Man (ends #22), Lee Granger, Jungle King, & Buck Jones begin; only app. The War Bird & Mark Swift & the Time Retarder; Zoro, Lee Granger, Jungle King & Mark Swift all continue from Slam Bang; Bulletman moves from Nickel
  293 586 879 1831 3041 4250
8-The Red Gaucho (ends #13), Captain Venture (ends #22) & The Planet Princess begin
  155 310 465 969 1610 2250
9,10: 10-Lee Granger ends 121 242 363 756 1253 1750
11-Origin & 1st app. Minute-Man (2/41) 262 524 786 1638 2719 3800
12 128 256 384 800 1325 1850
13-Origin & 1st app. Bulletgirl; Hitler-c 200 400 600 1250 2075 2900
14-16: 14-Companions Three begins, ends #31 109 218 327 681 1128 1575
17-20: 17-Raboy-a on Bulletman begins. 20-Captain Marvel cameo app. in Bulletman
  100 200 300 625 1038 1450
21-(12/41; Scarce)-Captain Marvel & Bulletman team up against Capt. Nazi; origin & 1st app. Capt. Marvel Jr's most famous nemesis Captain Nazi who will cause creation of Capt. Marvel Jr. in Whiz #25. Part I of trilogy origin of Capt. Marvel, Jr.; 1st Mac Raboy-c for Fawcett; Capt. Nazi-c 503 1006 1509 3521 6161 8800
22-(1/42)-Captain Marvel Jr. moves over from Whiz #25 & teams up with Bulletman against Captain Nazi; part III of trilogy origin of Capt. Marvel Jr. & his 1st cover and adventure
  451 902 1353 3157 5529 7900
23-Capt. Marvel Jr. c/stories begin (1st solo story); fights Capt. Nazi by himself.
  286 572 858 1788 2969 4150
24,25 100 200 300 625 1038 1450
26-28,30-Captain Marvel Jr. vs. Capt. Nazi. 28-Liberty Bell-c. 30-Flag-c
  91 182 273 569 947 1325
29-Hitler & Hirohito-c 117 234 351 731 1216 1700
31-33,35: 32-Last El Carim & Buck Jones; intro Balbo, the Boy Magician in El Carim story; classic Eagle-c by Raboy. 33-Balbo, the Boy Magician (ends #47), Hopalong Cassidy (ends #49) begins 66 132 198 413 682 950
34-Capt. Marvel Jr. vs. Capt. Nazi-c/story 74 148 222 463 769 1075
36-40: 40-Flag-c 60 120 180 375 620 865
41-(8/43)-Bulletman, Capt. Marvel Jr. & Bulletgirl x-over in Minute-Man; only app. Crime Crusaders Club (Capt. Marvel, Jr., Minute-Man, Bulletman & Bulletgirl)
  64 128 192 400 663 925
42-47,49: 47-Hitler becomes Corpl. Hitler Jr. 49-Last Minute-Man
  40 80 120 244 392 540
48-Intro. Bulletboy; Capt. Marvel cameo in Minute-Man
  46 92 138 281 461 640
50-Intro Radar & Nyoka the Jungle Girl & begin series (5/44); Radar also intro in Captain Marvel #35 (same date); Capt. Marvel x-over in Radar; Capt. Marvel & Capt. Marvel, Jr. introduce Radar on-c 42 84 126 254 410 565
51-58 24 48 72 139 220 300
59-62: Nyoka serial "Terrible Tiara" in all; 61-Capt. Marvel Jr. 1st meets Uncle Marvel
  26 52 78 152 239 325
63-80 18 36 54 107 169 230
81,83-87,89-91,95-99: 88-Hopalong Cassidy begins (ends #94). 95-Tom Mix begins

Master of Kung Fu #71 © MAR

Masters of the Universe #1 © DC

Maverick #6 © MAR

	GD 2.0	VG 4.0	FN 6.0	VF 8.0	VF/NM 9.0	NM- 9.2
(cover only in #123, ends #133)	16	32	48	94	147	200
82,88,92-94-Krigstein-a	17	34	51	98	154	210
100	17	34	51	98	154	210
101-106-Last Bulletman (not in #104)	15	30	45	90	140	190
107-120: 118-Mary Marvel	15	30	45	86	133	180
121-131-(lower print run): 123-Tom Mix-c only	16	32	48	92	144	195
132-B&W and color illos in POP; last Nyoka	16	32	48	94	147	200
133-Bill Battle app.	22	44	66	128	202	275

NOTE: Mac Raboy a-15-39, 40(part), 42, 58, c-21-49, 51, 52, 54, 56, 58, 68(part), 69(part). Bulletman c-7-11, 13(half), 15, 18(part), 19, 20, 21(w/Capt. Marvel & Capt. Nazi), 22(w/Capt. Marvel, Jr.). Capt. Marvel, Jr. c-23-133. Master Man c-1-6. Minute Man c-12, 13(half), 14, 16, 17, 18(part).

MASTER DARQUE
Acclaim Comics (Valiant): Feb, 1998 ($3.95)

1-Manco-a/Christina Z.-s						4.00

MASTER DETECTIVE
Super Comics: 1964 (Reprints)

17-r/Criminals on the Loose V4 #2; r/Young King Cole #?; McWilliams-r						
	2	4	6	8	11	14

MASTER OF KUNG FU (Formerly Special Marvel Edition; see Deadly Hands of Kung Fu & Giant-Size...)
Marvel Comics Group: No. 17, April, 1974 - No. 125, June, 1983

17-Starlin-a; intro Black Jack Tarr; 3rd Shang-Chi (ties w/Deadly Hands #1)						
	3	6	9	18	27	35
18,20	2	4	6	10	14	18
19-Man-Thing-c/story	2	4	6	11	16	20
21-23,25-30	2	4	6	8	10	12
24-Starlin, Simonson-a	2	4	6	8	11	14
31-50: 33-1st Leiko Wu. 43-Last 25¢ issue	1	2	3	4	5	7
39-43-(30¢-c variants, limited distribution)(5-7/76)	3	6	9	14	20	25
51-99						4.00
53-57-(35¢-c variants, limited distribution)(6-10/77)	3	6	9	15	21	26
100,118,125-Double size						5.00
101-117,119-124						3.00
Annual 1(4/76)-Iron Fist app.	3	6	9	14	20	25

NOTE: Austin c-63i, 74i. Buscema c-44p. Gulacy a(p)-18-20, 22, 25, 29-31, 33-35, 38, 39, 40(p&i), 42-50, 53r(#20); c-51, 55, 64, 67. Gil Kane c(p)-20, 38, 39, 42, 45, 59, 63. Nebres c-73i. Starlin a-17p, 24; c-54. Sutton a-42i. #53 reprints #20.

MASTER OF KUNG-FU, SHANG-CHI:... (2002 series, see Shang Chi:...)

MASTER OF KUNG-FU: BLEEDING BLACK
Marvel Comics: Feb, 1991 ($2.95, 84 pgs., one-shot)

1-The Return of Shang-Chi						3.00

MASTER OF THE WORLD
Dell Publishing Co.: No. 1157, July, 1961

Four Color 1157-Movie based on Jules Verne's "Master of the World" and "Robur the Conqueror" novels; with Vincent Price & Charles Bronson	6	12	18	41	66	90

MASTERS OF TERROR (Magazine)
Marvel Comics Group: July, 1975 - No. 2, Sept, 1975 (B&W) (All reprints)

1-Brunner, Barry Smith-a; Morrow/Steranko-a; Starlin-a(p); Gil Kane-a						
	3	6	9	14	19	24
2-Reese, Kane, Mayerik-a; Adkins/Steranko-a	2	4	6	9	13	16

MASTERS OF THE UNIVERSE (See DC Comics Presents #47 for 1st app.)
DC Comics: Dec, 1982 - No. 3, Feb, 1983 (Mini-series)

1						6.00
2,3: 2-Origin He-Man & Ceril						4.00

NOTE: Alcala a-1i,, 2i. Tuska a-1-3p; c-1-3p. #2 has 75 & 95 cent cover price.

MASTERS OF THE UNIVERSE (Comic Album)
Western Publishing Co.: 1984 (8-1/2x11", $2.95, 64 pgs.)

11362-Based on Mattel toy & cartoon	2	4	6	10	13	16

MASTERS OF THE UNIVERSE
Star Comics/Marvel #7 on: May 1986 - No. 13, May, 1988 (75¢/$1.00)

1						6.00
2-11: 8-Begin $1.00-c						4.00
12-Death of He-Man (1st Marvel app.)	1	3	4	6	8	10
13-Return of He-Man & death of Skeletor	1	3	4	6	8	10
The Motion Picture (11/87, $2.00)-Tuska-p						5.00

MASTERS OF THE UNIVERSE
Image Comics: Nov, 2002 - No. 4, March, 2003 ($2.95, limited series)

1-($2.95) Two covers by Santalucia and Campbell; Santalucia-a						3.00

1-($5.95) Variant-c by Norem w/gold foil logo						6.00
2-4($2.95) 2-Two covers by Santalucia and Manapul. 3,4-Two covers						3.00
TPB (CrossGen, 2003, $9.95, 8-1/4" x 5-1/2") digest-sized reprints #1-4						10.00

MASTERS OF THE UNIVERSE (Volume 2)
Image Comics: March, 2003 - No. 6, Aug, 2003 ($2.95)

1-6-($2.95) 1-Santalucia-c. 2-Two covers by Santalucia & JJ Kirby						3.00
1-($5.95) Wraparound variant-c by Struzan w/silver foil logo						6.00
3,4-($5.95) Wraparound variant holofoil-c. 3-By Edwards 4-By Boris Vallejo & Julie Bell						6.00
Volume 2 Dark Reflections TPB (2004, $18.95) r/#1-6						19.00

MASTERS OF THE UNIVERSE (Volume 3)
MVCreations: Apr, 2004 - No. 8, Dec, 2004 ($2.95)

1-8: 1-Santalucia-c						3.00

MASTERS OF THE UNIVERSE...
CrossGen Comics

...Rise of the Snake-Men (Nov, 2003 - No. 3, $2.95) Meyers-a						3.00
...The Power of Fear (12/03, $2.95, one-shot) Santalucia-a						3.00

MASTERS OF THE UNIVERSE, ICONS OF EVIL
Image Comics/CrossGen Comics: 2003 ($4.95, one-shots)

...Beastman -(Image) Origin of Beast Man; Tony Moore-a						5.00
...Mer-Man -(CrossGen)						5.00
...Trapjaw -(CrossGen)						5.00
...Tri-Klops -(CrossGen) Walker-c						5.00
TPB (3/04, $18.95, MVCreations) r/one-shots; sketch pages						19.00

MASTERWORKS SERIES OF GREAT COMIC BOOK ARTISTS, THE
Sea Gate Dist./DC Comics: May, 1983 - No. 3, Dec, 1983 (Baxter paper)

1-3: 1,2-Shining Knight by Frazetta r-/Adventure. 2-Tomahawk by Frazetta r. 3-Wrightson-c/a(r)						5.00

MATADOR
DC Comics (WildStorm): July, 2005 - No. 6, May, 2006 ($2.99, limited series)

1-6-Devin Grayson-s/Brian Stelfreeze-a/c						3.00

MATRIX COMICS, THE (Movie)
Burlyman Entertainment: 2003; 2004 ($21.95, trade paperback)

nn-Short stories by various incl. Wachowskis, Darrow, Gaiman, Sienkiewicz, Bagge						22.00
...Volume One Preview (7/03, no cover price) bios of creators; Chadwick-s/a						2.50
Volume 2-(2004) Short stories by various incl. Wachowskis, Sale, McKeever, Dorman						22.00

MATT SLADE GUNFIGHTER (Kid Slade Gunfighter #5 on; See Western Gunfighters)
Atlas Comics (SPI): May, 1956 - No. 4, Nov, 1956

1-Intro Matt & horse Eagle; Williamson/Torres-a	18	36	54	107	169	230
2-Williamson-a	13	26	39	74	105	135
3,4	10	20	30	56	76	95

NOTE: Maneely a-1i, 3, 4; c-1, 2, 4. Roth a-2-4. Severin a-1, 3, 4. Maneely c/a-1. Issue #s stamped on cover after printing.

MAUS: A SURVIVOR'S TALE (First graphic novel to win a Pulitzer Prize)
Pantheon Books: 1986, 1991 (B&W)

Vol. 1-(...: My Father Bleeds History)(1986) Art Spiegelman-s/a; recounts stories of Spiegelman's father in 1930s-40s Nazi-occupied Poland; collects first six stories serialized in Raw Magazine from 1980-1985						20.00
Vol. 2-(...: And Here My Troubles Began)(1991)						20.00
Complete Maus Survivor's Tale -HC Vols. 1& 2 w/slipcase						35.00
Hardcover Vol. 1 (1991)						24.00
Hardcover Vol. 2 (1991)						24.00
TPB (1992, $14.00) Vols. 1& 2						14.00

MAVERICK (TV)
Dell Publishing Co.: No. 892, 4/58 - No. 19, 4-6/62 (All have photo-c)

Four Color 892 (#1)-James Garner photo-c begin	22	44	66	165	295	425
Four Color 930,945,962,980,1005 (6-8/59): 945-James Garner/Jack Kelly photo-c begin						
	11	22	33	75	133	190
7 (10-12/59) - 14: Last Garner/Kelly-c	9	18	27	63	109	150
15-18: Jack Kelly Roger Moore photo-c	8	16	24	52	86	120
19-Jack Kelly photo-c (last issue)	8	16	24	54	90	125

MAVERICK (See X-Men)
Marvel Comics: Jan, 1997 ($2.95, one-shot)

1-Hama-s						3.00

MAVERICK (See X-Men)
Marvel Comics: Sept, 1997 - No. 12, Aug, 1998 ($2.99/$1.99)

1,12: 1-($2.99)-Wraparound-c. 12-($2.99) Battles Omega Red						4.00
2-11: 2-Two covers. 4-Wolverine app. 6,7-Sabretooth app.						3.00

The Maxx #11 © I Before E

MD #4 © WMG

Measles #8 © Fantagraphics

	GD 2.0	VG 4.0	FN 6.0	VF 8.0	VF/NM 9.0	NM- 9.2		GD 2.0	VG 4.0	FN 6.0	VF 8.0	VF/NM 9.0	NM- 9.2

MAVERICK MARSHAL
Charlton Comics: Nov, 1958 - No. 7, May, 1960

1	6	12	18	31	38	45
2-7	5	10	15	22	26	30

MAVERICKS
Daggar Comics Group: Jan, 1994 - No. 5, 1994 (#1-$2.75, #2-5-$2.50)

1-5: 1-Bronze. 1-Gold. 1-Silver — 2.75

MAX BRAND (See Silvertip)

MAX HAMM FAIRY TALE DETECTIVE
Nite Owl Comix: 2002 - 2004 ($4.95, B&W, 6 1/2" x 8")

1-(2002) Frank Cammuso-s/a — 5.00
Vol. 2 #1-3 (2003-2004) Frank Cammuso-s/a — 5.00

MAXIMAGE
Image Comics (Extreme Studios): Dec, 1995 - No. 7, June 1996 ($2.50)

1-7: 1-Liefeld-c. 2-Extreme Destroyer Pt. 2; polybagged w/card. 4-Angela & Glory-c/app. — 2.50

MAXIMO
Dreamwave Prods.: Jan, 2004 ($3.95, one-shot)

1-Based on the Capcom video game — 4.00

MAXIMUM SECURITY (Crossover)
Marvel Comics: Oct, 2000 - No. 3, Jan, 2001 ($2.99)

1-3-Busiek-s/Ordway-a; Ronan the Accuser, Avengers app. — 3.00
...Dangerous Planet 1: Busiek-s/Ordway-a; Ego, the Living Planet — 3.00
Thor vs. Ego (11/00, $2.99) Reprints Thor #133,160,161; Kirby-a — 3.00

MAXX (Also see Darker Image, Primer #5, & Friends of Maxx)
Image Comics (I Before E): Mar, 1993 - No. 35, Feb, 1998 ($1.95)

1/2	1	3	4	6	8	10
1/2 (Gold)						20.00
1-Sam Kieth-c/a/scripts						4.00
1-Glow-in-the-dark variant	2	4	6	8	10	12
1-"3-D Edition" (1/98, $4.95) plus new back-up story						5.00
2-12: 6-Savage Dragon cameo(1 pg.). 7,8-Pitt-c & story						2.50
13-16						2.50
17-35: 21-Alan Moore-s						2.50
Volume 1 TPB (DC/WildStorm, 2003, $17.95) r/#1-6						18.00
Volume 2 TPB (DC/WildStorm, 2004, $17.95) r/#7-13						18.00
Volume 3 TPB (DC/WildStorm, 2004, $17.95) r/#14-20						18.00
Volume 4 TPB (DC/WildStorm, 2005, $17.95) r/#21-27						18.00
Volume 5 TPB (DC/WildStorm, 2005, $19.99) r/#28-35						20.00
Volume 6 TPB (DC/WildStorm, 2006, $19.99) r/Friends of Maxx #1-3 & The Maxx 3-D						20.00

MAYA (See Movie Classics)
Gold Key: Mar, 1968

1 (10218-803)(TV)	3	6	9	17	25	32

MAYHEM
Dark Horse Comics: May, 1989 - No. 4, Sept, 1989 ($2.50, B&W, 52 pgs.)

1- Four part Stanley Ipkiss/Mask story begins; Mask-c

	1	3	4	6	8	10
2-4: 2-Mask 1/2 back-c. 4-Mask-c	1	2	3	5	7	9

MAZE AGENCY, THE
Comico/Innovation Publ. #8 on: Dec, 1988 - No. 20, 1991 ($1.95-$2.50, color)

1-20: 9-Ellery Queen app. 7 ($2.50)-Last Comico issue — 2.50
Annual 1 (1990, $2.75)-Ploog-c; Spirit tribute ish — 2.75
Special 1 (1989, $2.75)-Staton-p (Innovation) — 2.75
TPB (IDW Publ., 11/05, $24.99) r/#1-5 — 25.00

MAZE AGENCY, THE (Vol. 2)
Caliber Comics: July, 1997 - No. 3, 1998 ($2.95, B&W)

1-3: 1-Barr-s/Gonzales-a(p). 3-Hughes-c — 3.00

MAZE AGENCY, THE
Caliber Comics: Nov, 2005 - No. 3, Jan, 2006 ($3.99, limited series)

1-3-Barr-s/Padilla-a(p)/c — 4.00

MAZIE (...& Her Friends) (See Flat-Top, Mortie, Stevie & Tastee-Freez)
Mazie Comics(Magazine Publ.)/Harvey Publ. No. 13-on: 1953 - #12, 1954; #13, 12/54 - #22, 9/56; #23, 9/57 - #28, 8/58

1-(Teen-age)-Stevie's girlfriend	10	20	30	54	72	90
2	6	12	18	31	38	45
3-10	6	12	18	28	34	40
11-28	5	10	15	22	26	30

MAZIE
Nation Wide Publishers: 1950 - No. 7, 1951 (5¢) (5x7-1/4"-miniature)(52 pgs.)

1-Teen-age	15	30	45	90	140	190
2-7	10	20	30	56	76	95

MAZINGER (See First Comics Graphic Novel #17)

'MAZING MAN
DC Comics: Jan, 1986 - No. 12, Dec, 1986

1-11: 7,8-Hembeck-a — 2.50
12-Dark Knight part-c by Miller — 3.00
Special 1 ('87), 2 (4/88), 3 ('90)-All $2.00, 52pgs. — 2.50

McCANDLESS & COMPANY
Mandalay Books: 2001 ($7.95)

...: Dead Razor - J.C. Vaughn-s/Busch & Sheehan-a; 3 covers — 8.00
Crime Scenes: A McCandless & Company Reader TPB (Spring 2006, $17.95) Vaughn-s — 18.00

McHALE'S NAVY (TV) (See Movie Classics)
Dell Publ. Co.: May-July, 1963 - No. 3, Nov-Jan, 1963-64 (All have photo-c)

1	7	14	21	45	73	100
2,3	5	10	15	32	51	70

McKEEVER & THE COLONEL (TV)
Dell Publishing Co.: Feb-Apr, 1963 - No. 3, Aug-Oct, 1963

1-Photo-c	6	12	18	39	62	85
2,3	5	10	15	30	48	65

McLINTOCK (See Movie Comics)

MD
E. C. Comics: Apr-May, 1955 - No. 5, Dec-Jan, 1955-56

1-Not approved by code; Craig-c	14	28	42	112	176	240
2-5	9	18	27	72	116	160

NOTE: Crandall, Evans, Ingels, Orlando art in all issues; Craig c-1-5.

MD
Russ Cochran/Gemstone Publishing: Sept, 1999 - No. 5, Jan, 2000 ($2.50)

1-5-Reprints original EC series — 2.50
Annual 1 (1999, $13.50) r/#1-5 — 14.00

MEASLES
Fantagraphics Books: Christmas 1998 - Present ($2.95, B&W, quarterly)

1-8-Anthology - Love & Rockets-s by Hernandez — 3.00

MECHA (Also see Mayhem)
Dark Horse Comics: June, 1987 - No. 6, 1988 ($1.50/$1.95, color/B&W)

1-6: 1,2 ($1.95, color), 3,4-($1.75, B&W), 5,6-($1.50, B&W) — 2.50

MECHANIC, THE
Image Comics: 1998 ($5.95, one-shot, squarebound)

1-Chiodo-painted art; Peterson-s — 6.00
1-($10.00) DF Alternate Cover Ed. — 10.00

MECHA SPECIAL
Dark Horse Comics: May, 1995 ($2.95, one-shot)

1 — 3.00

MECH DESTROYER
Image Comics: Apr, 2001 - No. 4, Sept, 2001 ($2.95, limited series)

1-4-Jae Kim-c/a; Robert Chong-s — 3.00

MEDAL FOR BOWZER, A
American Visuals: 1966 (8 pgs.)

nn-Eisner-c/script	27	54	81	156	246	335

MEDAL OF HONOR COMICS
A. S. Curtis: Spring, 1946

1-War stories	13	26	39	74	105	135

MEDAL OF HONOR SPECIAL
Dark Horse Comics: 1994 ($2.50, one-shot)

1-Kubert-c/a (first story) — 2.50

MEDIA STARR
Innovation Publ.: July, 1989 - No. 3, Sept, 1989 ($1.95, mini-series, 28 pgs.)

1-3: Deluxe format — 2.50

MEDIEVAL SPAWN/WITCHBLADE
Image Comics (Top Cow Productions): May, 1996 - No. 3, June, 1996 ($2.95, limited series)

1-3-Garth Ennis scripts in all — 6.00

Meet Merton #2 © TOBY

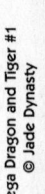

Mega Dragon and Tiger #1 © Jade Dynasty

Menace #1 © MAR

	GD 2.0	VG 4.0	FN 6.0	VF 8.0	VF/NM 9.0	NM- 9.2
1-Platinum foil-c (500 copies from Pittsburgh Con)						35.00
1-Gold						10.00
1-ETM Exclusive Edition; gold foil logo						7.00
TPB ($9.95) r/#1-3						10.00

MEET ANGEL (Formerly Angel & the Ape)
National Periodical Publications: No. 7, Nov-Dec, 1969

	GD 2.0	VG 4.0	FN 6.0	VF 8.0	VF/NM 9.0	NM- 9.2
7-Wood-a(i)	3	6	9	18	27	35

MEET CORLISS ARCHER (Radio/Movie)(My Life #4 on)
Fox Features Syndicate: Mar, 1948 - No. 3, July, 1948

1-(Teen-age)-Feldstein-c/a; headlight-c	103	206	309	644	1072	1500
2	55	110	165	344	572	800
3-Part Feldstein-c only	52	104	156	317	521	725

NOTE: No. 1-3 used in Seduction of the Innocent, pg. 39.

MEET HERCULES (See Three Stooges)

MEET MERTON
Toby Press: Dec, 1953 - No. 4, June, 1954

1-(Teen-age)-Dave Berg-c/a	9	18	27	52	69	85
2-Dave Berg-c/a	6	12	18	29	36	42
3,4-Dave Berg-c/a	6	12	18	27	33	38
I.W. Reprint #9, Super Reprint #11('63), 18	2	4	6	8	11	14

MEET MISS BLISS (Becomes Stories Of Romance #5 on)
Atlas Comics (LMC): May, 1955 - No. 4, Nov, 1955

1-Al Hartley-c/a	14	28	42	80	115	150
2-4	9	18	27	52	69	85

MEET MISS PEPPER (Formerly Lucy, The Real Gone Gal)
St. John Publishing Co.: No. 5, April, 1954 - No. 6, June, 1954

5-Kubert/Maurer-a	21	42	63	122	191	260
6-Kubert/Maurer-a; Kubert-c	17	34	51	98	154	210

MEGACITY909
Devil's Due Publ.: Sept, 2004 - No. 8, Aug, 2005 ($2.95)

1-8-Kano Kang & Zack Suh-a						3.00

MEGA DRAGON & TIGER
Image Comics: Mar, 1999 - No. 5 ($2.95)

1-5-Tony Wong-s/a						3.00

MEGAHURTZ
Image Comics: Aug, 1997 - No. 3, Oct, 1997 ($2.95, B&W)

1-3-St. Pierre-s						3.00

MEGALITH (Megalith Deathwatch 2000 #1,2 of second series)
Continuity: 1989 - No. 9, Mar, 1992; No. 0, Apr, 1993 - No. 7, Jan, 1994

1-9-($2.00-c) 1-Neal Adams & Mark Texiera-c/Texiera & Nebres-a						3.00
2nd series: 0-(4/93)-Foil-c; no c-price, giveaway; Adams plot						3.00
1-7: 1-Bagged w/card: 1-Gatefold-c by Nebres; Adams plot. 2-Fold-out-c; Adams plot.						
3-Indestructible-c. 4-7-Embossed-c: 4-Adams/Nebres-c; 5-Sienkiewicz-i.						
6-Adams part-i. 7-Adams-c(p); Adams plot						3.00

MEGAMAN
Dreamwave Productions: Sept, 2003 - No. 4, Dec, 2003 ($2.95)

1-4-Brian Augustyn-s/Mic Fong-a						3.00
1-($5.95) Chromium wraparound variant-c						6.00

MEGA MORPHS
Marvel Comics: Oct, 2005 - No. 4, Dec, 2005 ($2.99, limited series)

1-4-Giant robots based on action figures; McKeever-s; Kang-a						3.00
Digest (2006, $7.99) r/#1-4 plus mini-comics						8.00

MEGATON (A super hero)
Megaton Publ.: Nov, 1983; No. 2, Oct, 1985 - No. 8, Aug, 1987 (B&W)

1-($2.00, 68 pgs.)-Erik Larsen's 1st pro work; Vanguard by Larsen begins (1st app.), ends #4; 1st app. Megaton, Berzerker, & Ethrian; Guice-c/a(p); Gustovich-a(p) in #1,2	2	4	6	9	12	15
2-($2.00, 68 pgs.)-1st brief app. The Dragon (1 pg.) by Larsen (later The Savage Dragon in Image Comics); Guice-c/a(p)	3	6	9	8	10	12
3-(44 pgs.)-1st full app. Savage Dragon-c/story by Larsen; 1st comic book work by Angel Medina (pin-up)	2	4	6	10	14	18
4-(52 pgs.)-2nd full app. Savage Dragon by Larsen; 4,5-Wildman by Grass Green	2	4	6	8	10	10
5-1st Liefeld published-a (inside f/c, 6/86)	1	2	3	4	5	7
6,7: 6-Larsen-c						6.00
8-1st Liefeld story-a (7 pg. super hero story) plus 1 pg. Youngblood ad						

	GD 2.0	VG 4.0	FN 6.0	VF 8.0	VF/NM 9.0	NM- 9.2
	1	2	3	5	7	9
...Explosion (6/87, 16 pg. color giveaway)-1st app. Youngblood by Rob Liefeld (2 pg. spread); shows Megaton heroes	2	4	6	13	18	22
...Holiday Special 1 (1994, $2.95, color, 40 pgs., publ. by Entity Comics)-Gold foil logo; bagged w/Kelley Jones card; Vanguard, Megaton plus shows unpublished-c to 1987 Youngblood #1 by Liefeld/Ordway						4.00

NOTE: Copies of Megaton Explosion were also released in early 1992 all signed by Rob Liefeld and were made available to retailers.

MEGATON MAN (See Don Simpson's Bizarre Heroes)
Kitchen Sink Enterprises: Nov, 1984 - No. 10, Dec, 1986

1-10, 1-2nd printing (1989)						3.00
...Meets The Uncategorizable X-Thems 1 (4/89, $2.00)						3.00

MEGATON MAN: BOMB SHELL
Image Comics: Jul, 1999 - No. 2 ($2.95, B&W, mini-series)

1-Reprints stories from Megaton Man internet site						3.00

MEGATON MAN: HARD COPY
Image Comics: Feb, 1999 - No. 2, Apr, 1999 ($2.95, B&W, mini-series)

1,2-Reprints stories from Megaton Man internet site						3.00

MEGATON MAN VS. FORBIDDEN FRANKENSTEIN
Fiasco Comics: Apr, 1996 ($2.95, B&W, one-shot)

1-Intro The Tomb Team (Forbidden Frankenstein, Drekula, Bride of the Monster, & Moon Wolf)						3.00

MEK (See Reload/Mek flipbook for TPB reprint)
DC Comics (Homage): Jan, 2003 - No. 3, Mar, 2003 ($2.95, limited series)

1-3-Warren Ellis-s/Steve Rolston-a						3.00

MEKANIX (See X-Men titles) (See X-Treme X-Men Vol. 4 for TPB)
Marvel Comics: Dec, 2002 - No. 6, May, 2003 ($2.99, limited series)

1-6-Kitty Pryde in college; Claremont-s/Bobillo & Sosa-a						3.00

MEL ALLEN SPORTS COMICS (The Voice of the Yankees)
Standard Comics: No. 5, Nov, 1949; No. 6, June, 1950

5(#1 on inside)-Tuska-a	23	46	69	130	205	280
6(#2)-Lou Gehrig story	15	30	45	88	137	185

MELTDOWN
Image Comics: Dec, 2006 - No. 2, Jan, 2007 ($5.95, squarebound, limited series)

1,2-Schwartz-s/Wang-a. 1-Bachalo-c. 2-Horn-c						6.00

MELVIN MONSTER
Dell Publishing Co.: Apr-June, 1965 - No. 10, Oct, 1969

1-By John Stanley	9	18	27	65	113	160
2-10-All by Stanley. #10-r/#1	7	14	21	49	80	110

MELVIN THE MONSTER (See Peter, the Little Pest & Dexter The Demon #7)
Atlas Comics (HPC): July, 1956 - No. 6, July, 1957

1-Maneely-c/a	14	28	42	78	112	145
2-6: 4-Maneely-c/a	10	20	30	54	72	90

MENACE
Atlas Comics (HPC): Mar, 1953 - No. 11, May, 1954

1-Horror & sci/fi stories begin; Everett-c/a	69	138	207	431	716	1000
2-Post-atom bomb disaster by Everett; anti-Communist propaganda/torture scenes; Sinnott sci/fi story "Rocket to the Moon"	47	94	141	287	474	660
3,4,6-Everett-a. 4-Sci/fi story "Escape to the Moon". 6-Romita sci/fi story "Science Fiction"	40	80	120	240	383	525
5-Origin & 1st app. The Zombie by Everett (reprinted in Tales of the Zombie #1)(7/53);	54	108	162	338	562	785
5-Sci/fi story "Rocket Ship"						
7,8,10,11: 7-Frankenstein story. 8-End of world story; Heath 3-D art(3 pgs.). 10-H-Bomb panels	32	64	96	186	293	400
9-Everett-a r-in Vampire Tales #1	36	72	108	208	329	450

NOTE: Brodsky c-7, 8, 11. Colan a-6; c-9. Everett a-1-6, 9; c-1-6. Heath a-11; c-10. Katz a-11. Maneely a-3, 5, 7-9. Powell a-11. Romita a-3, 6, 8, 11. Shelly a-10. Shores a-7. Sinnott a-2, 7. Tuska a-1, 2, 5.

MENACE
Awesome-Hyperwerks: Nov, 1998 ($2.50)

1 Jada Pinkett Smith-s/Fraga-a						2.50

MEN AGAINST CRIME (Formerly Mr. Risk; Hand of Fate #8 on)
Ace Magazines: No. 3, Feb, 1951 - No. 7, Oct, 1951

3-Mr. Risk app.	11	22	33	60	83	105
4-7: 4-Colan-a; entire book-r is Trapped! #4. 5-Meskin-a	8	16	24	44	57	70

MEN, GUNS, & CATTLE (See Classics Illustrated Special Issue)

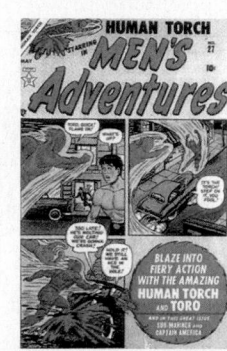

Men's Adventures #27 © MAR

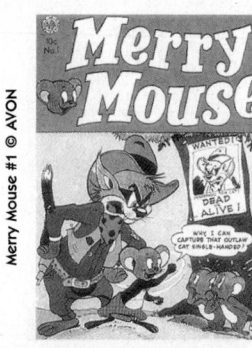

Merry Mouse #1 © AVON

Meta 4 #3 © FC

	GD 2.0	VG 4.0	FN 6.0	VF 8.0	VF/NM 9.0	NM- 9.2		GD 2.0	VG 4.0	FN 6.0	VF 8.0	VF/NM 9.0	NM- 9.2

MEN IN ACTION (Battle Brady #10 on)
Atlas Comics (IPS): April, 1952 - No. 9, Dec, 1952 (War stories)

	GD	VG	FN	VF	VF/NM	NM-
1-Berg, Reinman-a	17	34	51	98	154	210
2,3: 3-Heath-c/a	11	22	33	60	83	105
4-6,8,9	10	20	30	54	72	90
7-Krigstein-a; Heath-c	11	22	33	60	83	105

NOTE: *Brodsky* c-1, 4-6. *Maneely* c-5. *Pakula* a-1, 6. *Robinson* c-8. *Shores* c-9.

MEN IN ACTION
Ajax/Farrell Publications: April, 1957 - No. 6, 1958

	GD	VG	FN	VF	VF/NM	NM-
1	9	18	27	52	69	85
2	6	12	18	33	41	48
3-6	6	12	18	28	34	40

MEN IN BLACK, THE (1st series)
Aircel Comics (Malibu): Jan, 1990 - No. 3 Mar, 1990 ($2.25, B&W, lim. series)

	GD	VG	FN	VF	VF/NM	NM-
1-Cunningham-s/a in all	4	8	12	24	37	50
2,3	3	6	9	16	22	28
Graphic Novel (Jan, 1991) r/#1-3	3	6	9	14	20	25

MEN IN BLACK (2nd series)
Aircel Comics (Malibu): May, 1991 - No. 3, Jul, 1991 ($2.50, B&W, lim. series)

	GD	VG	FN	VF	VF/NM	NM-
1-Cunningham-s/a in all	3	6	9	16	22	28
2,3	2	4	6	8	11	14

MEN IN BLACK: FAR CRY
Marvel Comics: Aug, 1997 ($3.99, color, one-shot)

	NM-
1-Cunningham	4.00

MEN IN BLACK: RETRIBUTION
Marvel Comics: Dec, 1997 ($3.99, color, one-shot)

	NM-
1-Cunningham; continuation of the movie	4.00

MEN IN BLACK: THE MOVIE
Marvel Comics: Oct, 1997 ($3.99, one-shot, movie adaption)

	NM-
1-Cunningham-s	4.00

MEN INTO SPACE
Dell Publishing Co.: No. 1083, Feb-Apr, 1960

	GD	VG	FN	VF	VF/NM	NM-
Four Color 1083-Anderson-a, photo-c	5	10	15	35	55	75

MEN OF BATTLE (Also see New Men of Battle)
Catechetical Guild: V1#5, March, 1943 (Hardcover)

	GD	VG	FN	VF	VF/NM	NM-
V1#5-Topix reprints	6	12	18	28	34	40

MEN OF WAR
DC Comics, Inc.: August, 1977 - No. 26, March, 1980 (#9,10: 44 pgs.)

	GD	VG	FN	VF	VF/NM	NM-
1-Enemy Ace, Gravedigger (origin #1,2) begin	2	4	6	11	16	20
2-4,8-10,12-14,19,20: All Enemy Ace stories. 4-1st Dateline Frontline. 9-Unknown Soldier app.	1	3	4	6	8	10
5-7,11,15-18,21-25: 17-1st app. Rosa	1	2	3	5	6	8
26-Sgt. Rock & Easy Co.-c/s	2	4	6	19	12	15

NOTE: *Chaykin* a-9, 10, 12-14, 19, 20. *Evans* a-25. *Kubert* c-2-23, 24p, 26.

MEN'S ADVENTURES (Formerly True Adventures)
Marvel/Atlas Comics (CCC): No. 4, Aug, 1950 - No. 28, July, 1954

	GD	VG	FN	VF	VF/NM	NM-
4(#1)(52 pgs.)	32	64	96	186	293	400
5-Flying Saucer story	21	42	63	120	188	255
6-8: 7-Buried alive story. 8-Sci/fic story	18	36	54	107	169	230
9-20: All war format	13	26	39	74	105	135
21,22,24,26: All horror format	21	42	63	124	195	265
23-Crandall-a; Fox-a(i); horror format	22	44	66	128	202	275
25-Shrunken head-c	34	68	102	197	311	425
27,28-Human Torch & Toro-c/stories; Captain America & Sub-Mariner stories in each (also see Young Men #24-28)	107	214	321	669	1110	1550

NOTE: *Ayers* a-27(H. Torch). *Berg* a-15, 16. *Brodsky* c-4-9, 11, 12, 16-18, 24. *Burgos* c-27, 28(Human Torch). *Colan* a-14, 19. *Everett* a-10, 14, 22, 25, 28; c-14, 21-23. *Heath* a-8, 11, 24; c-13, 20, 26. *Lawrence* a-21. *Mac Pakula* a-15, 23. *Maneely* a-24; c-10, 15. *Post* a-23. *Powell* a-27(Sub-Mariner). *Reinman* a-11, 12. *Robinson* c-19. *Romita* a-22. *Shores* c-25. *Sinnott* a-21. *Tuska* a-24. Adventure-#4-8; War-#9-20; Weird/Horror-#21-26.

MENZ INSANA
DC Comics (Vertigo): 1997 ($7.95, one-shot)

	GD	VG	FN	VF	VF/NM	NM-
nn-Fowler-s/Bolton painted art	1	2	3	5	6	8

MEPHISTO VS... (See Silver Surfer #3)
Marvel Comics Group: Apr, 1987 - No. 4, July, 1987 ($1.50, mini-series)

	NM-
1-4: 1-Fantastic Four; Austin-i. 2-X-Factor. 3-X-Men. 4-Avengers	3.00

MERC (See Mark Hazzard: Merc)

MERCHANTS OF DEATH
Acme Press (Eclipse): Jul, 1988 - No. 4, Nov, 1988 ($3.50, B&W/16 pgs. color, 44 pg. mag.)

	NM-
1-4: 4-Toth-c	3.50

MERCY
DC Comics (Vertigo): 1993 ($5.95, 68 pgs., mature)

	NM-
nn	6.00

MERIDIAN
CrossGeneration Comics: Jul, 2000 - No. 44, Apr, 2004 ($2.95)

	NM-
1-44: Barbara Kesel-s	3.00
Flying Solo Vol. 1 TPB (2001, $19.95) r/#1-7; cover by Steve Rude	20.00
Going to Ground Vol. 2 TPB (2002, $19.95) r/#8-14	20.00
Taking the Skies Vol. 3 TPB (2002, $15.95) r/#15-20	16.00
Vol. 4: Coming Home (12/02, $15.95) r/#21-26	16.00
Vol. 5: Minister of Cadador (7/03, $15.95) r/#27-32	16.00
Vol. 6: Changing Course (1/04, $15.95) r/#33-38	16.00
Traveler Vol. 1-4 ($9.95): Digest-size reprints of TPBs	10.00

MERLIN JONES AS THE MONKEY'S UNCLE (See Movie Comics and The Misadventures of... under Movie Comics)

MERRILL'S MARAUDERS (See Movie Classics)

MERRY CHRISTMAS (See A Christmas Adventure, Donald Duck..., Dell Giant #39, & March of Comics #153 in the Promotional Comics section)

MERRY COMICS
Carlton Publishing Co.: Dec, 1945 (10¢)

	GD	VG	FN	VF	VF/NM	NM-
nn-Boogeyman app.	20	40	60	117	184	250

MERRY COMICS: Four Star Publications: 1947 (Advertised, not published)

MERRY-GO-ROUND COMICS
LaSalle Publ. Co./Croyden Publ./Rotary Litho.: 1944 (25¢, 132 pgs.); 1946; 9-10/47 - No. 2, 1948

	GD	VG	FN	VF	VF/NM	NM-
nn(1944)(LaSalle)-Funny animal; 29 new features	18	36	54	105	165	225
21 (Publisher?)	9	18	27	47	61	75
1(1946)(Croyden)-Al Fago-c; funny animal	11	22	33	60	83	105
V1#1,2(1947-48; 52 pgs.)(Rotary Litho. Co. Ltd., Canada); Ken Hultgren-a	9	18	27	47	61	75

MERRY MAILMAN (See Fawcett's Funny Animals #87-89)

MERRY MOUSE (Also see Funny Tunes & Space Comics)
Avon Periodicals: June, 1953 - No. 4, Jan-Feb, 1954

	GD	VG	FN	VF	VF/NM	NM-
1-1st app.; funny animal; Frank Carin-c/a	10	20	30	54	72	90
2-4	7	14	21	35	43	50

MERV PUMPKINHEAD, AGENT OF D.R.E.A.M. (See The Sandman)
DC Comics (Vertigo): 2000 ($5.95, one-shot)

	NM-
1-Buckingham-a(p); Nowlan painted-c	6.00

MESSENGER, THE
Image Comics: July, 2000 ($5.95, one-shot)

	NM-
1-Ordway-s/c/a	6.00

META-4
First Comics: Feb, 1991 - No. 4, 1991 ($2.25)

	NM-
1-($3.95, 52pgs.)	4.00
2-4	2.50

METAL GEAR SOLID (Based on the video game)
IDW Publ.: Sept, 2004 - No. 12, Aug, 2005 ($3.99)

	NM-
1-12: 1-Two covers; Ashley Wood-a/Kris Oprisko-s	4.00
1-Retailer edition with foil cover	20.00

METAL GEAR SOLID: SONS OF LIBERTY
IDW Publ.: Sept, 2005 - Present ($3.99)

	NM-
#0 (9/05) profile pages on characters; Ashley Wood-a	4.00
1-9: 1-Two covers; Ashley Wood-a/Alex Garner-s	4.00

METALLIX
Future Comics: Dec, 2002 - No. 6, June, 2003 ($3.50)

	NM-
0-6-Ron Lim-a. 0-(6/03) Origin. 1-Layton-c	3.50
1-Collector's Edition with variant cover by Lim	3.50
1-Free Comic Book Day Edition (4/03) Layton-c	2.50

METAL MEN (See Brave & the Bold, DC Comics Presents, and Showcase #37-40)
National Periodical Publications/DC Comics: 4-5/63 - No. 41, 12-1/69-70; No. 42, 2-3/73 - No. 44, 7-8/73; No. 45, 4-5/76 - No. 56, 2-3/78

	GD	VG	FN	VF	VF/NM	NM-
1-(4-5/63)-5th app. Metal Men	50	100	150	425	788	1150

Metal Men #1 © DC

Mice Templar #1 © Glass & Oeming

Mickey Finn #4 © McNaught Synd.

	GD 2.0	VG 4.0	FN 6.0	VF 8.0	VF/NM 9.0	NM- 9.2
2	20	40	60	150	268	385
3-5	14	28	42	99	175	250
6-10	9	18	27	63	107	150
11-20: 12-Beatles cameo (2-3/65)	7	14	21	49	80	110
21-Batman, Robin & Flash x-over	6	12	18	39	62	85
22-26,28-30	5	10	15	35	55	75
27-Origin Metal Men retold	7	14	21	47	76	105
31-41(1968-70): 38-Last 12¢ issue. 41-Last 15¢	5	10	15	30	48	65
42-44(1973)-Reprints	2	4	6	9	12	15
45('76)-49-Simonson-a in all: 48,49-Re-intro Eclipso	1	2	3	6	8	10
50-56: 50-Part-r. 54,55-Green Lantern x-over	1	2	3	6	8	10

NOTE: **Andru/Esposito** c-1-30. **Aparo** c-53-56. **Giordano** c-45, 46. **Kane/Esposito** a-30, 31; c-31. **Simonson** a-45-49; c-47-52. **Staton** a-50-56.

METAL MEN (Also see Tangent Comics/ Metal Men)
DC Comics: Oct, 1993 - No. 4, Jan, 1994 ($1.25, mini-series)

1-($2.50)-Multi-colored foil-c						4.00
2-4: 2-Origin						2.50

METAL MEN (Also see 52)
DC Comics: Oct, 2007 - No. 8 ($2.99, limited series)

1,2-Duncan Rouleau-s/a; origin re-told						3.00

METAMORPHO (See Action Comics #413, Brave & the Bold #57,58, 1st Issue Special, & World's Finest #217)
National Periodical Publications: July-Aug, 1965 - No. 17, Mar-Apr, 1968 (All 12¢ issues)

1-(7-8/65)-3rd app. Metamorpho	12	24	36	82	146	210
2,3	7	14	21	45	73	100
4-6,10:10-Origin & 1st app. Element Girl (1-2/67)	6	12	18	37	59	80
7-9	5	10	15	32	51	70
11-17: 17-Sparling-c/a	4	8	12	28	44	60

NOTE: **Ramona Fradon** a-B&B 57, 58, 1-4. **Orlando** a-5, 6; c-5-9, 11. **Trapani** a(p)-7-16; i-16.

METAMORPHO
DC Comics: Aug, 1993 - No. 4, Nov, 1993 ($1.50, mini-series)

1-4						2.50

METAPHYSIQUE
Malibu Comics (Bravura): Apr, 1995 - No. 6, Oct, 1995 ($2.95, limited series)

1-6: Norm Breyfogle-c/a/scripts						3.00

METEOR COMICS
L. L. Baird (Croyden): Nov, 1945

1-Captain Wizard, Impossible Man, Race Wilkins app.; origin Baldy Bean, Capt. Wizard's sidekick; bare-breasted mermaids story	40	80	120	235	368	500

METEOR MAN
Marvel Comics: Aug, 1993 - No. 6, Jan, 1994 ($1.25, limited series)

1-6: 1-Regular unbagged. 4-Night Thrasher-c/story. 6-Terry Austin-c(i)						2.50
1-Polybagged w/button & rap newspaper						4.00
...: The Movie (4/93 [7/93 on cover], $2.25) movie adaptation						2.50

METROPOL (See Ted McKeever's...)

METROPOL A.D. (See Ted McKeever's...)

METROPOLIS S.C.U. (Also see Showcase '96 #1)
DC Comics: Nov, 1995 - No. 4, Feb, 1996 ($1.50, limited series)

1-4:1-Superman-c & app.						2.50

MEZZ: GALACTIC TOUR 2494 (Also See Nexus)
Dark Horse Comics: May, 1994 ($2.50, one-shot)

1						2.50

MGM'S MARVELOUS WIZARD OF OZ (See Marvel Treasury of Oz)
Marvel Comics Group/National Periodical Publications: 1975 ($1.50, 84 pgs.; oversize)

1-Adaptation of MGM's movie; J. Buscema-a	3	6	9	15	21	26

M.G.M.'S MOUSE MUSKETEERS (Formerly M.G.M.'s The Two Mouseketeers)
Dell Publishing Co.: No. 670, Jan, 1956 - No. 1290, Mar-May, 1962

Four Color 670 (#4)	5	10	15	35	55	75
Four Color 711,728,764	4	8	12	26	41	55
8 (4-6/57) - 21 (3-5/60)	4	8	12	24	37	50
Four Color 1135,1175,1290	4	8	12	24	37	50

M.G.M.'S SPIKE AND TYKE (also see Tom & Jerry #79)
Dell Publishing Co.: No. 499, Sept, 1953 - No. 1266, Dec-Feb, 1961-62

Four Color 499 (#4)	6	12	18	41	66	90
Four Color 577,638	4	8	12	26	41	55
4(12-2/55-56)-10	4	8	12	22	34	45
11-24(12-2/60-61)	3	6	9	19	29	38
Four Color 1266	4	8	12	22	34	45

M.G.M.'S THE TWO MOUSKETEERS
Dell Publishing Co.: No. 475, June, 1953 - No. 642, July, 1955

Four Color 475 (#1)	8	16	24	52	86	120
Four Color 603 (11/54), 642	6	12	18	37	59	80

MICE TEMPLAR, THE
Image Comics: Sept, 2007 - Present ($3.99)

1-Bryan Glass-s/Michael Avon Oeming-a/c						4.00

MICHAELANGELO CHRISTMAS SPECIAL (See Teenage Mutant Ninja Turtles Christmas Special)

MICHAELANGELO, TEENAGE MUTANT NINJA TURTLE
Mirage Studios: 1986 (One shot) ($1.50, B&W)

1						5.00
1-2nd printing ('89, $1.75)-Reprint plus new-a						2.50

MICHAEL CHABON PRESENTS THE AMAZING ADVENTURES OF THE ESCAPIST
Dark Horse Comics: Feb, 2004 - Present ($8.95, squarebound)

1-5,7,8-Short stories by Chabon and various incl. Chaykin, Starlin, Brereton, Baker						9.00
6-Includes 6 pg. Spirit & Escapist story (Will Eisner's last work); Spirit on cover						9.00
... Vol. 1 (5/04, $17.95, digest-size) r/#1&2; wraparound-c by Chris Ware						18.00
... Vol. 2 (11/04, $17.95, digest-size) r/#3&4; wraparound-c by Matt Kindt						18.00
... Vol. 3 (4/06, $14.95, digest-size) r/#5&6; Tim Sale-c						15.00

MICHAEL MOORCOCK'S ELRIC: THE MAKING OF A SORCERER
DC Comics: 2004 - No. 4, 2006 ($5.95, prestige format, limited series)

1-4-Moorcock-s/Simonson-a						6.00
TPB (2007, $19.99) r/#1-4						20.00

MICHAEL MOORCOCK'S MULTIVERSE
DC Comics (Helix): Nov, 1997 - No. 12, Oct, 1998 ($2.50, limited series)

1-12: Simonson, Reeve & Ridgway-a						2.50
TPB (1999, $19.95) r/#1-12						20.00

MICHAEL TURNER PRESENTS: ASPEN (See Aspen)

MICKEY AND DONALD (See Walt Disney's...)

MICKEY AND DONALD IN VACATIONLAND (See Dell Giant No. 47)

MICKEY & THE BEANSTALK (See Story Hour Series)

MICKEY & THE SLEUTH (See Walt Disney Showcase #38, 39, 42)

MICKEY FINN (Also see Big Shot Comics #74 & Feature Funnies)
Eastern Color 1-4/McNaught Synd. #5 on (Columbia)/Headline V3#2:
Nov?, 1942 - V3#2, May, 1952

1	30	60	90	172	271	370
2	15	30	45	88	137	185
3-Charlie Chan story	12	24	36	67	94	120
4	10	20	30	54	72	90
5-10	9	18	27	47	61	75
11-15(1949): 12-Sparky Watts app.	8	16	24	40	50	60
V3#1,2(1952)	6	12	18	31	38	45

MICKEY MALONE
Hale Nass Corp.: 1936 (Color, punchout-c) (B&W-a on back)

nn-1pg. of comics	190	380	760	-	-	-

MICKEY MANTLE (See Baseball's Greatest Heroes #1)

MICKEY MOUSE (See Adventures of Mickey Mouse, The Best of Walt Disney Comics, Cheerios giveaways, Donald and ..., Dynabrite Comics, 40 Big Pages..., Gladstone Comic Album, Merry Christmas From..., Walt Disney's Mickey and Donald, Walt Disney's Comics & Stories, Walt Disney's..., & Wheaties)

MICKEY MOUSE (...Secret Agent #107-109; Walt Disney's... #148-205?)
(See Dell Giants for annuals) (#204 exists from both G.K. & Whitman)
Dell Publ. Co./Gold Key #85-204/Whitman #204-218/Gladstone #219 on:
#16, 1941 - #84, 7-9/62; #85, 11/62 - #218, 6/84; #219, 10/86 - #256, 4/90

Four Color 16(1941)-1st Mickey Mouse comic book; "...vs. the Phantom Blot" by Gottfredson	1250	2500	3750	14,500	-	-
Four Color 27(1943)- "7 Colored Terror"	76	152	228	646	1198	1750
Four Color 79(1945)-By Carl Barks (1 story)	91	182	273	774	1437	2100
Four Color 116(1946)	26	52	78	211	348	485
Four Color 141,157(1947)	21	42	63	156	278	400
Four Color 170,181,194('48)	18	36	54	134	237	340
Four Color 214('49),231,248,261	14	28	42	99	175	250
Four Color 268-Reprints/WDC&S #22-24 by Gottfredson ("Surprise Visitor")	13	26	39	95	168	240
Four Color 279,286,296	10	20	30	70	123	175

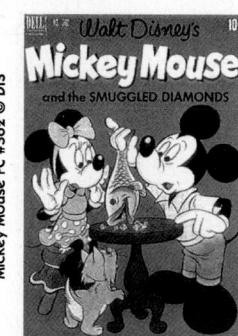

Mickey Mouse FC #362 © DIS

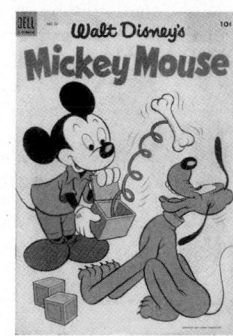

Mickey Mouse #34 © DIS

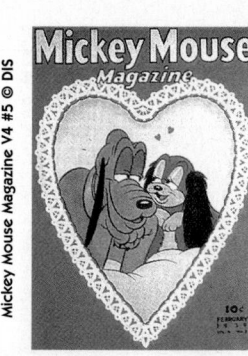

Mickey Mouse Magazine V4 #5 © DIS

	GD 2.0	VG 4.0	FN 6.0	VF 8.0	VF/NM 9.0	NM- 9.2
Four Color 304,313(#1),325(#2),334	9	18	27	63	107	150
Four Color 343,352,362,371,387	8	16	24	54	90	125
Four Color 401,411,427(10-11/52)	6	12	18	43	69	95
Four Color 819-Mickey Mouse in Magicland	6	12	18	37	59	80
Four Color 1057,1151,1246(1959-61)-Album; #1057 has 10¢ & 12¢ editions; back covers are different	5	10	15	32	51	70
28(12-1/52-53)-32,34	5	10	15	35	55	75
33-(Exists with 2 dates, 10-11/53 & 12-1/54)	5	10	15	35	55	75
35-50	5	10	15	30	48	65
51-73,75-80	4	8	12	24	37	50
74-Story swipe "The Rare Stamp Search" from 4-Color #422- "The Gilded Man"	4	8	12	26	41	55
81-105: 93,95-titled "Mickey Mouse Club Album". 100-105: Reprint 4-Color #427,194,279, 170,343,214 in that order	3	6	9	20	30	40
106-120	3	6	9	16	23	30
121-130	2	4	6	13	18	22
131-146	2	4	6	11	16	20
147,148: 147-Reprints "The Phantom Fires" from WDC&S #200-202.148-Reprints "The Mystery of Lonely Valley" from WDC&S #208-210	2	4	6	11	16	20
149-158	2	4	6	8	11	14
159-Reprints "The Sunken City" from WDC&S #205-207	2	4	6	8	11	14
160-178: 162-165,167-170-r	2	4	6	9	13	16
179-(52 pgs.)	1	3	4	6	8	10
180-203: 200-r/Four Color #371	1	2	3	5	7	9
204-(Whitman or G.K.), 205,206	2	4	6	8	11	14
207(8/80), 209(pre-pack?)	4	8	12	22	34	45
208-(8-12/80)-Only distr. in Whitman 3-pack	8	16	24	52	86	120
210(2/81),211-214	2	4	6	8	11	14
215-218: 215(2/82), 216(4/82), 217(3/84), 218(misdated 8/82; actual date 7/84)	2	4	6	9	13	16
219-1st Gladstone issue; The Seven Ghosts serial-r begins by Gottfredson		4	6	10	14	18
220,221	1	2	3	5	7	9
222-225: 222-Editor-in Grief strip-r						4.00
226-230						4.00
231-243,246-254: 240-r/March of Comics #27. 245-r/F.C. #279. 250-r/F.C. #248						3.00
244 (1/89, $2.95, 100 pgs.)-Squarebound 60th anniversary issue; gives history of Mickey						4.00
245,256: 245-r/F.C. #279. 256-$1.95, 68 pgs.						4.00
255 ($1.95, 68 pgs.)						3.00

NOTE: Reprints #195-197, 198(2/3), 199(1/3), 200-208, 211(1/2), 212, 213, 215(1/3), 216-on. **Gottfredson** Mickey Mouse serials in #219-239, 241-244, 246-249, 251-253, 255.

	GD 2.0	VG 4.0	FN 6.0	VF 8.0	VF/NM 9.0	NM- 9.2
Album 01-518-210(Dell), 1(10082-309)(9/63-Gold Key)	3	6	9	20	30	40
...Club 1(1/64-Gold Key)(TV)	3	6	9	21	32	42
Mini Comic 1(1976)(3-1/4x6-1/2")-Reprints 158	1	2	3	5	6	8
Surprise Party 1(30037-901, G.K.)(1/69)-40th Anniversary (see Walt Disney Showcase #47)	3	6	9	21	32	42
Surprise Party 1(1979)-r/1969 issue	1	2	3	5	6	8

MICKEY MOUSE ADVENTURES
Disney Comics: June, 1990 - No. 18, Nov, 1991 ($1.50)

						NM- 9.2
1,8,9: 1-Bradbury, Murry-r/M.M. #45,73 plus new-a. 8-Byrne-c. 9-Fantasia 50th ann. issue w/new adapt. of movie						3.00
2-7,10,18: 2-Begin all new stories. 10-r/F.C. #214						2.50

MICKEY MOUSE CLUB FUN BOOK
Golden Press: 1977 (1.95, 228 pgs.)(square bound)

	GD 2.0	VG 4.0	FN 6.0	VF 8.0	VF/NM 9.0	NM- 9.2
11190-1950s-r; 20,000 Leagues, M. Mouse Silly Symphonys, The Reluctant Dragon, etc.	4	8	12	24	37	50

MICKEY MOUSE CLUB MAGAZINE (See Walt Disney...)

MICKEY MOUSE COMICS DIGEST
Gladstone: 1986 - No. 5, 1987 (96 pgs.)

	GD 2.0	VG 4.0	FN 6.0	VF 8.0	VF/NM 9.0	NM- 9.2
1 ($1.25-c)	1	2	3	5	6	8
2-5: 3-5 ($1.50-c)						5.00

MICKEY MOUSE IN COLOR
Another Rainbow/Pantheon: 1988 (Deluxe, 13"x17", hard-c, $250.00)
(Trade, 9-7/8"x11-1/2", hard-c, $39.95)

	GD 2.0	VG 4.0	FN 6.0	VF 8.0	VF/NM 9.0	NM- 9.2
Deluxe limited edition of 3,000 copies signed by Floyd Gottfredson and Carl Barks, designated as the "Official Mickey Mouse 60th Anniversary" book. Mickey Sunday and daily reprints, plus Barks "Riddle of the Red Hat" from Four Color #79. Comes with 45 r.p.m. record interview with Gottfredson and Barks. 240 pgs.	15	30	45	107	191	275
Deluxe, limited to 100 copies, as above, but with a unique colored pencil original drawing of Mickey Mouse by Carl Barks. Add value of art to book price.						800.00

	GD 2.0	VG 4.0	FN 6.0	VF 8.0	VF/NM 9.0	NM- 9.2
Pantheon trade edition, edited down & without Barks, 192 pgs.	3	6	9	20	30	40

MICKEY MOUSE MAGAZINE (Becomes Walt Disney's Comics & Stories)(Also see 40 Big Pages of Mickey Mouse)
K. K. Publ./Western Publishing Co.: Summer, 1935 (June-Aug, indicia) - V5#12, Sept, 1940; V1#1-5, V3#11,12, V4#1-3 are 44 pgs; V2#3-100 pgs; V5#12-68 pgs; rest are 36 pgs.(No V3#1, V4#6)

	GD 2.0	VG 4.0	FN 6.0	VF 8.0	VF/NM 9.0	NM- 9.2
V1#1 (Large size, 13-1/4x10-1/4"; 25¢)-Contains puzzles, games, cels, stories & comics of Disney characters. Promotional magazine for Disney cartoon movies and paraphernalia	1375	2750	4125	8800	18,000	–

Note: Some copies were autographed by the editors & given away with all early one year subscriptions.

	GD 2.0	VG 4.0	FN 6.0	VF 8.0	VF/NM 9.0	NM- 9.2
2 (Size change, 11-1/2x8-1/2"; 10/35; 10¢)-High quality paper begins; Messmer-a	259	518	777	2200	–	–
3,4: 3-Messmer-a	141	282	423	1200	–	–
5-1st Donald Duck solo-c; 2nd cover app. ever; last 44 pg. & high quality paper issue	247	494	741	2100	–	–
6-9: 6-36 pg. issues begin; Donald becomes editor. 8-2nd Donald solo-c.	129	258	387	1100	–	–
9-1st Mickey/Minnie-c	129	258	387	1100	–	–
10-12, V2#1,2: 11-1st Pluto/Mickey-c; Donald fires himself and appoints Mickey as editor	124	248	372	1050	–	–
V2#3-Special 100 pg. Christmas issue (25¢); Messmer-a; Donald becomes editor of Wise Quacks	412	824	1236	3500	–	–
4-Mickey Mouse Comics & Roy Ranger (adventure strip) begin; both end V2#9; Messmer-a	103	206	309	875	–	–
5-9: 5-Ted True (adventure strip, ends V2#9) & Silly Symphony Comics (ends V3#3) begin. 6-1st solo Minnie-c. 6-9-Mickey Mouse Movies cut-out in each	53	106	159	323	537	750
10-1st full color issue; Mickey Mouse (by Gottfredson; ends V3#12) & Silly Symphony (ends V3#3) full color Sunday-r, Peter The Farm Detective (ends V5#8) & Ole Of The North (ends V3#3) begins	79	158	237	494	822	1150
11-13: 12-Hiawatha-c & feature story	52	104	156	317	521	725
V3#2-Big Bad Wolf Halloween-c	60	120	180	375	620	865
3 (12/37)-1st app. Snow White & The Seven Dwarfs (before release of movie) (possibly 1st in print); Mickey X-mas-c	107	214	321	669	1110	1550
4 (1/38)-Snow White & The Seven Dwarfs serial begins (on stands before release of movie); Ducky Symphony (ends V3#11) begins	88	176	264	550	913	1275
5-1st Snow White & Seven Dwarfs-c (St. Valentine's Day)	107	214	321	669	1110	1550
6-Snow White serial ends; Lonesome Ghosts app. (2 pp.)	59	118	177	369	615	860
7-Seven Dwarfs Easter-c	55	110	165	344	572	800
8-10: 9-Dopey-c. 10-1st solo Goofy-c	48	96	144	293	484	675
11,12 (44 pgs; 8 more pgs. color added). 11-Mickey the Sheriff serial (ends V4#3) & Donald Duck strip-r (ends V4#12) begin. Color feature on Snow White's Forest Friends	52	104	156	317	521	725
V4#1 (10/38; 44 pgs.)-Brave Little Tailor-c/feature story, nominated for Academy Award; Bobby & Chip by Otto Messmer (ends V4#2) & The Practical Pig (ends V4#2) begin	52	104	156	317	521	725
2 (44 pgs.)-1st Huey, Dewey & Louie-c	53	106	159	323	537	750
3 (12/38, 44 pgs.)-Ferdinand The Bull-c/feature story, Academy Award winner; Mickey Mouse & The Whalers serial begins, ends V4#12	52	104	156	317	521	725
4-Spotty, Mother Pluto strip-r begin; and V4#8	48	96	144	293	484	675
5-St. Valentine's day-c. 1st Pluto solo-c	53	106	157	334	550	765
7 (3/39)-The Ugly Duckling-c/feature story, Academy Award winner	52	104	156	317	521	725
7 (4/39)-Goofy & Wilbur The Grasshopper classic-c/feature story from 1st Goofy solo cartoon movie; Timid Elmer begins, ends V5#5	52	104	156	317	521	725
8-Big Bad Wolf-c from Practical Pig movie poster; Practical Pig feature story	52	104	156	317	521	725
9-Donald Duck & Mickey Mouse Sunday-r begin; The Pointer feature story, nominated for Academy Award	52	104	156	317	521	725
10-Classic July 4th drum & fife-c; last Donald Sunday-r	62	124	186	388	644	900
11-1st slick-c; last over-sized issue	48	96	144	293	484	675
12 (9/39; format change, 10-1/4x8-1/4")-1st full color, cover to cover issue; Donald's Penguin-c/feature story	55	110	165	344	572	800
V5#1-Black Pete-c; Officer Duck-c/feature story; Autograph Hound feature story; Robinson Crusoe serial begins	54	108	162	338	562	785
2-Goofy-c; 1st brief app. Pinocchio	71	142	213	444	735	1025

3 (12/39)-Pinocchio Christmas-c (Before movie release). 1st app. Jiminy Cricket;

Micronauts #59 © MEGO

Midnighter #7 © WSP

Mighty Avengers #3 © MAR

	GD 2.0	VG 4.0	FN 6.0	VF 8.0	VF/NM 9.0	NM- 9.2

Pinocchio serial begins — 83 166 249 519 860 1200
4,5: 5-Jiminy Cricket-c; Pinocchio serial ends; Donald's Dog Laundry feature story
    54 108 162 338 562 785
6,7: 6-Tugboat Mickey feature story; Rip Van Winkle feature begins, ends V5#8.
    7-2nd Huey, Dewey & Louie-c — 53 106 159 329 545 760
8-Last magazine size issue; 2nd solo Pluto-c; Figaro & Cleo feature story
    54 108 162 338 562 785
9-11: 9 (6/40; change to comic book size)-Jiminy Cricket feature story; Donald-c &
    Sunday-r begin. 10-Special Independence Day issue. 11-Hawaiian Holiday & Mickey's
    Trailer feature stories; last 36 pg. issue 59 118 177 369 615 860
12 (Format change)-The transition issue (68 pgs.) becoming a comic book.
    With only a title change to follow, becomes Walt Disney's Comics & Stories #1
    with the next issue 457 914 1371 3200 5600 8000
NOTE: **Otto Messmer**-a is in many issues of the first two-three years. The following story titles and issues have gags created by **Carl Barks:** V4#3(12/38)-'Donald's Better Self' & 'Donald's Golf Game;' V4#4(1/39)-'Donald's Lucky Day;' V4#7(3/39)-'Hockey Champ;' V4#8(4/39)-'Donald's Cousin Gus;' V4#9(6/39)-'Sea Scouts;' V4#12(9/39)-'Donald's Penguin;' V5#9 (6/40)-'Donald's Vacation;' V5#10(7/40)-'Bone Trouble;' V5#12(9/40)-'Window Cleaners.'

MICKEY MOUSE MAGAZINE (Russian Version)
May 16, 1991 (1st Russian premiere of a modern comic book)
    1-Bagged w/gold label commemoration in English 10.00

MICKEY MOUSE MARCH OF COMICS (See March of Comics #8,27,45,60,74)

MICKEY MOUSE'S SUMMER VACATION (See Story Hour Series)

MICKEY MOUSE SUMMER FUN (See Dell Giants)

MICKEY SPILLANE'S MIKE DANGER
Tekno Comix: Sept, 1995 - No. 11, May, 1996 ($1.95)
    1-11: 1-Frank Miller-c. 7-polybagged; Simonson-c. 8,9-Simonson-c 2.50

MICKEY SPILLANE'S MIKE DANGER
Big Entertainment: V2#1, June, 1996 - No. 10, Apr, 1997 ($2.25)
    V2#1-10: Max Allan Collins scripts 2.50

MICKEY'S TWICE UPON A CHRISTMAS (Disney)
Gemstone Publishing: 2004 ($3.95, square-bound, one-shot)
    nn-Christmas short stories with Mickey, Minnie, Donald, Uncle Scrooge, Goofy and others 4.00

MICROBOTS, THE
Gold Key: Dec, 1971 (one-shot)
    1 (10271-112) 3 6 9 15 21 26

MICRONAUTS (Toys)
Marvel Comics Group: Jan, 1979 - No. 59, Aug, 1984 (Mando paper #53 on)
    1-Intro/1st app. Baron Karza 5.00
    2-10,35,37,57: 7-Man-Thing app. 8-1st app. Capt. Universe (8/79). 9-1st app. Cilicia.
      35-Double size; origin Microverse; intro Death Squad; Dr. Strange app. 37-Nightcrawler
      app.; X-men cameo (p.). 57-(52 pgs.) 2.50
    11-34,36,38-56,58,59: 13-1st app. Jasmine. 15-Death of Microtron. 15-17-Fantastic Four app.
      17-Death of Jasmine. 20-Ant-Man app. 25-Microverse series begins. 25-Origin Baron Karza.
      25-29-Nick Fury app. 27-Death of Biotron. 34-Dr. Strange app. 38-First direct sale.
      40-Fantastic Four app. 48-Early Guice-a begins. 59-Golden painted-c 2.50
    nn-Blank UPC; diamond on top 2.50
    Annual 1,2 (12/79,10/80)-Ditko-c/a 3.00
NOTE: **#38**-on distributed only through comic shops. **N. Adams** a-7i. **Chaykin** a-13-18p. **Ditko** a-39p. **Giffen** a-36p, 37p(part). **Golden** a-1-12p; c-2-7p, 8-23, 24p, 38, 39, 59. **Guice** a-48-58p; c-49-58. **Gil Kane** a-38, 40-45p; c-40-45. **Layton** c-33-37. **Miller** c-31.

MICRONAUTS (Toys)
Marvel Comics Group: Oct, 1984 - No. 20, May, 1986
    V2#1-20 2.50
NOTE: **Kelley Jones** a-1; c-1, 6. **Guice** a-4p; c-2p.

MICRONAUTS
Image Comics: 2002 - No. 11, Sept, 2003 ($2.95)
    2002 Convention Special (no cover price, B&W) previews series 2.50
    1-11: 1-3-Hanson-a; Dave Johnson-c. 4-Su-a; 2 covers by Linsner & Hanson 3.00
    ...Vol. 1: Revolution (2003, $12.95, digest size) r/#1-5 13.00

MICRONAUTS (Volume 2)
Devil's Due Publishing: Mar, 2004 - No. 3, May, 2004 ($2.95)
    1-3-Jolley-s/Broderick-a 3.00

MICRONAUTS: KARZA
Image Comics: Feb, 2003 - No. 4, May, 2003 ($2.95)
    1-4-Krueger-s/Kurth-a 3.00

MICRONAUTS SPECIAL EDITION
Marvel Comics Group: Dec, 1983 - No. 5, Apr, 1984 ($2.00, limited series, Baxter paper)

1-5: r-/original series 1-12; Guice-c(p)-all 3.00

MIDGET COMICS (Fighting Indian Stories)
St. John Publishng Co.: Feb, 1950 - No. 2, Apr, 1950 (5-3/8x7-3/8", 68 pgs.)
    1-Fighting Indian Stories; Matt Baker-c 18 36 54 103 162 220
    2-Tex West, Cowboy Marshal (also in #1) 10 20 30 56 76 95

MIDNIGHT (See Smash Comics #18)

MIDNIGHT
Ajax/Farrell Publ. (Four Star Comic Corp.): Apr, 1957 - No. 6, June, 1958
    1-Reprints from Voodoo & Strange Fantasy with some changes
      15 30 45 83 124 165
    2-6 10 20 30 54 72 90

MIDNIGHT (See The Authority)
DC Comics (WildStorm): Jan, 2007 - Present ($2.99)
    1-11: 1-Ennis-s/Sprouse-a/c. 6-Fabry-a. 7-Vaughan-s. 8-Gage-s. 9-Stelfreeze-a 3.00
    1-Variant cover by Michael Golden 5.00

MIDNIGHT EYE
Viz Premiere Comics: 1991 - No. 6, 1992 ($4.95, 44 pgs., mature)
    1-6: Japanese stories translated into English 5.00

MIDNIGHT MASS
DC Comics (Vertigo): Jun, 2002 - No. 8, Jan, 2003 ($2.50)
    1-8-Rozum-s/Saiz & Palmiotti-a 2.50

MIDNIGHT MASS: HERE THERE BE MONSTERS
DC Comics (Vertigo): March, 2004 - No. 6, Aug, 2004 ($2.95, limited series)
    1-6-Rozum-s/Paul Lee-a 3.00

MIDNIGHT MEN
Marvel Comics (Epic Comics/Heavy Hitters): June, 1993 - No. 4, Sept, 1993 ($2.50/$1.95, limited series)
    1-($2.50)-Embossed-c; Chaykin-c/a & scripts in all 3.00
    2-4 2.50

MIDNIGHT MYSTERY
American Comics Group: Jan-Feb, 1961 - No. 7, Oct, 1961
    1-Sci/Fi story 8 16 24 52 86 120
    2-7: 7-Gustavson-a 4 8 12 28 44 60
NOTE: **Reinman** a-1, 3. **Whitney** a-1, 4-6; c-1-3, 5, 7.

MIDNIGHT NATION
Image Comics (Top Cow): Oct, 2000 - No. 12, July, 2002 ($2.50/$2.95)
    1-Straczynski-s/Frank-a; 2 covers 3.00
    2-11-9-Twin Towers cover 2.50
    12-($2.95)Last issue 3.00
    Wizard #1/2 (2001) Michael Zulli-a; two covers by Frank 3.00
    Vol. 1 ('03, $29.99, TPB) r/#1-12 & Wizard #1/2; cover gallery; afterword by Straczynski 30.00

MIDNIGHT SONS UNLIMITED
Marvel Comics (Midnight Sons imprint #4 on): Apr, 1993 - No. 9, May, 1995 ($3.95, 68 pgs.)
    1-9: Blaze, Darkhold (by Quesada #1), Ghost Rider, Morbius & Nightstalkers in all.
      1-Painted-c. 3-Spider-man app. 4-Siege of Darkness part 17; new Dr. Strange & new
      Ghost Rider app.; spot varnish-c 4.00
NOTE: **Sears** a-2.

MIDNIGHT TALES
Charlton Press: Dec, 1972 - No. 18, May, 1976
    V1#1 2 4 6 13 18 22
    2-10 2 4 6 8 11 14
    11-18: 11-14-Newton-a(p) 1 3 4 6 8 10
    12,17(Modern Comics reprint, 1977) 5.00
NOTE: **Adkins** a-12i. **Ditko** a-12. **Howard** (Wood imitator) a-1-15, 17, 18; c-1-18. **Don Newton** a-11-14p. **Staton** a-1, 3-11, 13. **Sutton** a-3-10.

MIGHTY ATOM, THE (...& the Pixies #6) (Formerly The Pixies #1-5)
Magazine Enterprises: No. 6, 1949; Nov, 1957 - No. 6, Aug-Sept, 1958
    6(1949-M.E.)-no month (1st Series) 7 14 21 35 43 50
    1-6(2nd Series)-Pixies-r 4 8 12 18 22 25
    I.W. Reprint #1(nd) 2 4 6 8 11 14

MIGHTY AVENGERS
Marvel Comics: May, 2007 - Present ($3.99/$2.99)
    1-($3.99) Iron Man, Ms. Marvel select new team; Bendis-s/Cho-a/c; Mole Man app. 5.00
    2-4-($2.99) Ultron returns 3.00
    ...: Most Wanted Files (2007, $3.99) profiles of members, accomplices & adversaries 4.00

Mighty Crusaders #8 © AP

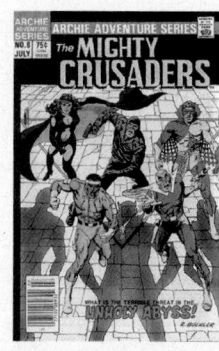

Mighty Marvel Western #22 © MAR

Mighty Mouse #9 © Paul Terry

	GD 2.0	VG 4.0	FN 6.0	VF 8.0	VF/NM 9.0	NM- 9.2
MIGHTY BEAR (Formerly Fun Comics; becomes Unsane #15)						
Star Publ. No. 13,14/Ajax-Farrell (Four Star): No. 13, Jan, 1954 - No. 14, Mar, 1954; 9/57 - No. 3, 2/58						
13,14-L. B. Cole-c	18	36	54	103	162	220
1-3('57-58)Four Star; becomes Mighty Ghost #4	7	14	21	35	43	50
MIGHTY COMICS (...Presents) (Formerly Flyman)						
Radio Comics (Archie): No. 40, Nov, 1966 - No. 50, Oct, 1967 (All 12¢ issues)						
40-Web	4	8	12	22	34	45
41-50: 41-Shield, Black Hood. 42-Black Hood. 43-Shield, Web & Black Hood. 44-Black Hood, Steel Sterling & The Shield. 45-Shield & Hangman; origin Web retold. 46-Steel Sterling, Web & Black Hood. 47-Black Hood & Mr. Justice. 48-Shield & Hangman; Wizard x-over in Shield. 49-Steel Sterling & Fox; Black Hood x-over in Steel Sterling. 50-Black Hood & Web; Inferno x-over in Web	3	6	9	20	30	40

NOTE: *Paul Reinman* a-40-50.

	GD 2.0	VG 4.0	FN 6.0	VF 8.0	VF/NM 9.0	NM- 9.2
MIGHTY CRUSADERS, THE (Also see Adventures of the Fly, The Crusaders & Fly Man)						
Mighty Comics Group (Radio Comics): Nov, 1965 - No. 7, Oct, 1966 (All 12¢)						
1-Origin The Shield	6	12	18	41	66	90
2-Origin Comet	4	8	12	23	36	48
3,5-7: 3-Origin Fly-Man. 5-Intro. Ultra-Men (Fox, Web, Capt. Flag) & Terrific Three (Jaguar, Mr. Justice, Steel Sterling). 7-Steel Sterling feature; origin Fly-Girl	4	8	12	22	34	45
4-1st S.A. app. Fireball, Inferno & Fox; Firefly, Web, Bob Phantom, Blackjack, Hangman, Zambini, Kardak, Steel Sterling, Mr. Justice, Wizard, Capt. Flag, Jaguar x-over	4	8	12	24	37	50
Volume 1: Origin of a Super Team TPB (2003, $12.95) r/#1 & Fly Man #31-33						13.00

NOTE: *Reinman* a-6.

	GD 2.0	VG 4.0	FN 6.0	VF 8.0	VF/NM 9.0	NM- 9.2
MIGHTY CRUSADERS, THE (All New Advs. of...#2)						
Red Circle Prod./Archie Ent. No. 6 on: Mar, 1983 - No. 13, Sept, 1985 ($1.00, 36 pgs, Mando paper)						
1-Origin Black Hood, The Fly, Fly Girl, The Shield, The Wizard, The Jaguar, Pvt. Strong & The Web.						6.00
2-10: 2-Mister Midnight begins. 4-Darkling replaces Shield. 5-Origin Jaguar, Shield begins. 7-Untold origin Jaguar. 10-Veitch-a						4.00
11-13-Lower print run						5.00

NOTE: *Buckler* a-1-3, 4i, 5p, 7p, 8i, 9i; c-1-10p.

	GD 2.0	VG 4.0	FN 6.0	VF 8.0	VF/NM 9.0	NM- 9.2
MIGHTY GHOST (Formerly Mighty Bear #1-3)						
Ajax/Farrell Publ.: No. 4, June, 1958						
4	6	12	18	31	38	45
MIGHTY HERCULES, THE (TV)						
Gold Key: July, 1963 - No. 2, Nov, 1963						
1 (10072-307)	14	28	42	100	178	255
2 (10072-311)	13	26	39	95	168	240
MIGHTY HEROES, THE (TV) (Funny)						
Dell Publishing Co.: Mar, 1967 - No. 4, July, 1967						
1-Also has a 1957 Heckle & Jeckle-r	13	26	39	95	168	240
2-4: 4-Has two 1958 Mighty Mouse-r	9	18	27	63	107	150
MIGHTY HEROES						
Spotlight Comics: 1987 (B&W, one-shot)						
1-Heckle & Jeckle backup						5.00
MIGHTY HEROES						
Marvel Comics: Jan, 1998 ($2.99, one-shot)						
1-Origin of the Mighty Heroes						3.00
MIGHTY LOVE						
DC Comics: 2003 ($24.99/$17.95, graphic novel)						
HC-($24.95) Howard Chaykin-s/a; intro. Skylark and the Iron Angel						25.00
SC-($17.95)						18.00
MIGHTY MAN (From Savage Dragon titles)						
Image Comics: Dec, 2004 ($7.95, one-shot)						
1-Reprints seriaziedl back-up from Savage Dragon #109-118						8.00
MIGHTY MARVEL TEAM-UP THRILLERS						
Marvel Comics: 1983 ($5.95, trade paperback)						
1-Reprints team-up stories						38.00
MIGHTY MARVEL WESTERN, THE						
Marvel Comics Group (LMC earlier issues): Oct, 1968 - No. 46, Sept, 1976 (#1-14: 68 pgs.; #15,16: 52 pgs.)						
1-Begin Kid Colt, Rawhide Kid, Two-Gun Kid-r	5	10	15	32	51	70

	GD 2.0	VG 4.0	FN 6.0	VF 8.0	VF/NM 9.0	NM- 9.2
2-5: (2-14 are 68 pgs.)	4	8	12	22	34	45
6-16: (15,16 are 52 pgs.)	3	6	9	20	30	40
17-20	2	4	6	11	16	20
21-30,32,37: 24-Kid Colt-r end. 25-Matt Slade-r begin. 32-Origin-r/Rawhide Kid #23; Williamson-r/Kid Slade #7. 37-Williamson, Kirby-r/Two-Gun Kid 51	2	4	6		12	15
31,33-36,38-46: 31-Baker-r.	2	4	6	8	10	12
45-(30¢-c variant, limited distribution)(6/76)	3	6	9	20	30	40

NOTE: *Jack Davis* a(r)-21-24. *Keller* r-1-13, 22. *Kirby* a(r)-1-3, 6, 9, 12-14, 16, 25-29, 32-38, 40, 41, 43-46; c-29. *Maneely* a(r)-22. *Severin* c-3i, 9. No Matt Slade-#43.

	GD 2.0	VG 4.0	FN 6.0	VF 8.0	VF/NM 9.0	NM- 9.2
MIGHTY MIDGET COMICS, THE (Miniature)						
Samuel E. Lowe & Co.: No date; circa 1942-1943 (Sold 2 for 5¢, B&W and red, 36 pgs, approx. 5x4")						
Bulletman #11(1943)-r/cover/Bulletman #3	18	36	54	107	169	230
Captain Marvel Adventures #11	18	36	54	107	169	230
Captain Marvel #11 (Same as above except for full color ad on back cover; this issue was glued to cover of Captain Marvel #20 and is not found in fine-mint condition)	340	680	1020	–	–	–
Captain Marvel Jr. #11 (Same-c as Master #27)	18	36	54	107	169	230
Captain Marvel Jr. #11 (Same as above except for full color ad on back-c; this issue was glued to cover of Captain Marvel #21 and is not found in fine-mint condition)	340	680	1020	–	–	–
Golden Arrow #11	16	32	48	92	144	200
Golden Arrow #11 (Same as above except for full color ad on back-c; this issue was glued to cover of Captain Marvel #21 and is not found in fine-mint condition)	280	560	840	–	–	–
Ibis the Invincible #11(1942)-Origin; reprints cover to Ibis #1 (Predates Fawcett's Ibis the Invincible #1).	18	36	54	107	169	230
Spy Smasher #11(1942)	18	36	54	107	169	230

NOTE: *The above books came in a box called "box full of books" and was distributed with other Samuel Lowe puzzles, paper dolls, coloring books, etc. They are not titled Mighty Midget Comics. All have a war bond seal on back cover which is otherwise blank. These books came in a "Mighty Midget" flat cardboard counter display rack.*

	GD 2.0	VG 4.0	FN 6.0	VF 8.0	VF/NM 9.0	NM- 9.2
Balbo, the Boy Magician #12 (1943)-1st book devoted entirely to character.	11	22	33	62	86	110
Bulletman #12	14	28	42	81	118	155
Commando Yank #12 (1943)-Only comic devoted entirely to character.	11	22	33	62	86	110
Dr. Voltz the Human Generator (1943)-Only comic devoted entirely to character.	11	22	33	64	90	115
Lance O'Casey #12 (1943)-1st comic devoted entirely to character (Predates Fawcett's Lance O'Casey #1).	11	22	33	62	86	110
Leatherneck the Marine (1943)-Only comic devoted entirely to character.	11	22	33	62	86	110
Minute Man #12	14	28	42	80	115	150
Mister "Q" (1943)-Only comic devoted entirely to character.	11	22	33	62	86	110
Mr. Scarlet and Pinky #12 (1943)-Only comic devoted entirely to character.	13	26	39	72	101	130
Pat Wilton and His Flying Fortress (1943)-1st comic devoted entirely to character.	11	22	33	62	86	110
The Phantom Eagle #12 (1943)-Only comic devoted entirely to character.	11	22	33	62	86	110
State Trooper Stops Crime (1943)-Only comic devoted entirely to character.	11	22	33	62	86	110
Tornado Tom (1943)-Origin, r/from Cyclone #1-3; only comic devoted entirely to character.	11	22	33	62	86	110
MIGHTY MORPHIN' POWER RANGERS: THE MOVIE (Also see Saban's Mighty Morphin' Power Rangers)						
Marvel Comics: Sept, 1995 ($3.95, one-shot)						
nn-adaptation of movie						4.00
MIGHTY MOUSE (See Adventures of..., Dell Giant #43, Giant Comics Edition, March of Comics #205, 237, 247, 257, 447, 459, 471, 483, Oxydol-Dreft, Paul Terry's, & Terry-Toons Comics)						
MIGHTY MOUSE (1st Series)						
Timely/Marvel Comics (20th Century Fox): Fall, 1946 - No. 4, Summer, 1947						
1	155	310	465	969	1610	2250
2	64	128	192	400	663	925
3,4	41	82	123	252	406	560
MIGHTY MOUSE (2nd Series) (Paul Terry's... #62-71)						
St. John Publishing Co./Pines No. 68 (3/56) on (TV issues #72 on): Aug, 1947 - No. 67, 11/55; No. 68, 3/56 - No. 83, 6/59						
5(#8)	40	80	120	235	368	500
6-10: 10-Over-sized issue	20	40	60	117	184	250

Mighty Samson #3 © GK

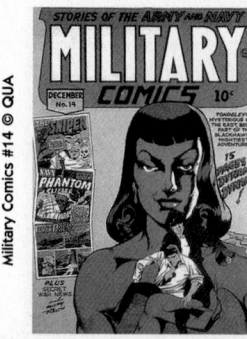

Military Comics #14 © QUA

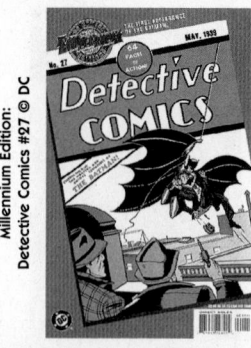

Millennium Edition:
Detective Comics #27 © DC

	GD 2.0	VG 4.0	FN 6.0	VF 8.0	VF/NM 9.0	NM- 9.2
11-19	14	28	42	80	115	150
20 (11/50) - 25-(52 pg. editions)	11	22	33	62	86	110
20-25-(36 pg. editions)	10	20	30	54	72	90
26-37: 35-Flying saucer-c	9	18	27	50	65	80
38-45-(100 pgs.)	18	36	54	107	169	230
46-83: 62-64,67-Painted-c. 82-Infinity-c	9	18	27	47	61	75
Album nn (nd, 1952/53?, St. John)(100 pgs.)(Rebound issues w/new cover)						
	22	44	66	128	202	275
Album 1(10/52, 25¢, 100 pgs., St. John)-Gandy Goose app.						
	28	56	84	162	256	350
Album 2,3(11/52 & 12/52, St. John) (100 pgs.)	22	44	66	128	202	275
Fun Club Magazine 1(Fall, 1957-Pines, 25¢, 100 pgs.) (CBS TV)-Tom Terrific, Heckle & Jeckle, Dinky Duck, Gandy Goose	15	30	45	90	140	190
Fun Club Magazine 2-6(Winter, 1958-Pines)	11	22	33	62	86	110
3-D 1-(1st printing-9/53, 25¢)(St. John)-Came w/glasses; stiff covers; says World's First! on-c; 1st 3-D comic	28	56	84	162	256	350
3-D 1-(2nd printing-10/53, 25¢)-Came w/glasses; slick, glossy covers, slightly smaller						
	20	40	60	117	184	250
3-D 2,3(11/53, 12/53, 25¢)-(St. John)-With glasses	20	40	60	117	184	250
MIGHTY MOUSE (TV)(3rd Series)(Formerly Adventures of Mighty Mouse)						
Gold Key/Dell Publ. Co. No. 166-on: No. 161, Dec., 1964 - No. 172, Oct, 1968						
161(10/64)-165(9/65)-(Becomes Adventures of... No. 166 on)						
	5	10	15	30	48	65
166(3/66), 167(6/66)-172	3	6	9	21	32	42
MIGHTY MOUSE (TV)						
Spotlight Comics: 1987 - No. 2, 1987 ($1.50, color)						
1,2-New stories						3.00
...And Friends Holiday Special (11/87, $1.75)						3.00
MIGHTY MOUSE (TV)						
Marvel Comics: Oct, 1990 - No. 10, July, 1991 ($1.00)(Based on Sat. cartoon)						
1-10: 1-Dark Knight-c parody. 2-10: 3-Intro Bat-Bat; Byrne-c. 4,5-Crisis-c/story parodies w/Perez-c. 6-Spider-Man-c parody. 7-Origin Bat-Bat						2.50
MIGHTY MOUSE ADVENTURE MAGAZINE						
Spotlight Comics: 1987 ($2.00, B&W, 52 pgs., magazine size, one-shot)						
1-Deputy Dawg, Heckle & Jeckle backup stories						5.00
MIGHTY MOUSE ADVENTURES (Adventures of... #2 on)						
St. John Publishing Co.: November, 1951						
1	34	68	102	197	311	425
MIGHTY MOUSE ADVENTURE STORIES (Paul Terry's... on-c only)						
St. John Publishing Co.: 1953 (50¢, 384 pgs.)						
nn-Rebound issues	43	86	129	262	431	600
MIGHTY MUTANIMALS (See Teenage Mutant Ninja Turtles Adventures #19)						
May, 1991 - No. 3, July, 1991 ($1.00, limited series)						
Archie Comics: Apr, 1992 - No. 8, June, 1993 ($1.25)						
1-3: 1-Story cont'd from TMNT Advs. #19.						2.25
1-9 (1992): 7-1st app. Merdude						2.25
MIGHTY SAMSON (Also see Gold Key Champion)						
Gold Key/Whitman #32: July, 1964 - No. 20, Nov, 1969; No. 21, Aug, 1972; No. 22, Dec, 1973 - No. 31, Mar, 1976; No. 32, 1982 (Painted-c #1-31)						
1-Origin/1st app.; Thorne-a begins	8	16	24	52	86	120
2-5	5	10	15	30	48	65
6-10: 7-Tom Morrow begins, ends #20	3	6	9	20	30	40
11-20	3	6	9	16	23	30
21-31: 21,22-r	2	4	6	11	16	20
32(Whitman, 8/82)-r	2	4	6	8	10	12
MIGHTY THOR (See Thor)						
MIKE BARNETT, MAN AGAINST CRIME (TV)						
Fawcett Publications: Dec, 1951 - No. 6, Oct, 1952						
1	19	38	57	109	172	235
2	13	26	39	72	101	130
3,4,6	10	20	30	58	79	100
5- "Market for Morphine" cover/story	14	28	42	80	115	150
MIKE DANGER (See Mickey Spillane's...)						
MIKE DEODATO'S...						
Caliber Comics: 1996, ($2.95, B&W)						
...FALLOUT 3000 #1, ...JONAS (mag. size) #1,...PRIME CUTS (mag. size) #1, ...PROTHEUS #1,2, ...RAMTHAR #1,...RAZOR NIGHTS #1						
						3.00

	GD 2.0	VG 4.0	FN 6.0	VF 8.0	VF/NM 9.0	NM- 9.2
MIKE GRELL'S SABLE (Also see Jon Sable & Sable)						
First Comics: Mar, 1990 - No. 10, Dec, 1990 ($1.75)						
1-10: r/Jon Sable Freelance #1-10 by Grell						2.50
MIKE MIST MINUTE MIST-ERIES (See Ms. Tree/Mike Mist in 3-D)						
Eclipse Comics: April, 1981 ($1.25, B&W, one-shot)						
1						2.50
MIKE SHAYNE PRIVATE EYE						
Dell Publishing Co.: Nov-Jan, 1962 - No. 3, Sept-Nov, 1962						
1	4	8	12	22	34	45
2,3	3	6	9	16	23	30
MILITARY COMICS (Becomes Modern Comics #44 on)						
Quality Comics Group: Aug, 1941 - No. 43, Oct, 1945						
1-Origin/1st app. Blackhawk by C. Cuidera (Eisner scripts); Miss America, The Death Patrol by Jack Cole (also #2-7,27-30), & The Blue Tracer by Guardineer; X of the Underground, The Yankee Eagle, Q-Boat & Shot & Shell, Archie Atkins, Loops & Banks by Bud Ernest (Bob Powell)(ends #13) begin	800	1600	2400	5600	9800	14,000
2-Secret War News begins (by McWilliams #2-16); Cole-a; new uniform with yellow circle & hawk's head for Blackhawk	235	470	705	1469	2435	3400
3-Origin/1st app. Chop Chop (9/41)	200	400	600	1250	2075	2900
4	162	324	486	1013	1682	2350
5-The Sniper begins; Miss America in costume #4-7						
	138	276	414	863	1432	2000
6-9: 8-X of the Underground begins (ends #13). 9-The Phantom Clipper begins (ends #16)						
	97	194	291	606	1003	1400
10-Classic Eisner-c	110	220	330	688	1144	1600
11-Flag-c	83	166	249	519	860	1200
12-Blackhawk by Crandall begins, ends #22	93	186	279	581	966	1350
13-15: 14-Private Dogtag begins (ends #83)	72	144	216	450	750	1050
16-20: 16-Blue Tracer ends. 17-P.T. Boat begins	62	124	186	388	644	900
21-31: 22-Last Crandall Blackhawk. 23-Shrunken head-c. 27-Death Patrol revived						
	53	106	159	323	537	750
32-43	45	90	135	275	450	625
NOTE: *Berg a-6. Al Bryant c-31-34, 38, 40-43. J. Cole a-1-3, 27-32. Crandall a-12-22; c-13-20. Cuidera c-2-9. Eisner c-1, 2(part), 9, 10. Kotsky c-21-29, 35, 37, 39. McWilliams a-2-16. Powell a-1-13. Ward Blackhawk-30, 31(15 pgs. each); c-30.*						
MILK AND CHEESE (Also see Cerebus Bi-Weekly #20)						
Slave Labor: 1991 - Present ($2.50, B&W)						
1-Evan Dorkin story & art in all	4	8	12	24	37	50
1-2nd-6th printings						4.00
2- "Other #1"	3	6	9	16	23	30
2-reprint						3.00
3- "Third #1"	2	4	6	11	16	20
4- "Fourth #1", 5- "First Second Issue"	1	3	4	6	8	10
6,7: 6- "#666"						5.00
NOTE: *Multiple printings of all issues exist and are worth cover price unless listed here.*						
MILKMAN MURDERS, THE						
Dark Horse Comics: Jun, 2004 - No. 4, Aug, 2004 ($2.99, limited series)						
1-4-Casey-s/Parkhouse-a						3.00
MILLENNIUM						
DC Comics: Jan, 1988 - No. 8, Feb, 1988 (Weekly limited series)						
1-Staton c/a(p) begins						3.00
2-8						2.50
MILLENNIUM EDITION:... (Reprints of classic DC issues)						
DC Comics: Feb, 2000 - Feb, 2001 (gold foil cover stamps)						
Action Comics #1, Adventure Comics #61, All Star Comics #3, All Star Comics #8, Batman #1, Detective Comics #1, Detective Comics #27, Detective Comics #38, Flash Comics #1, Military Comics #1, More Fun Comics #73, Police Comics #1, Sensation Comics #1, Superman #1, Whiz Comics #2, Wonder Woman #1 -($3.95-c)						4.00
Action Comics #252, Adventure Comics #247, Brave and the Bold #28, Brave and the Bold #85, Crisis on Infinte Earths #1, Detective #225, Detective #327, Detective #359, Detective #395, Flash #123, Gen13 #1, Green Lantern #1, House of Mystery #1, House of Secrets #92, JLA #1, Justice League #1, Mad #1, Man of Steel #1, Mysterious Suspense #1, New Gods #1, New Teen Titans #1, Our Army at War #81, Plop! #1, Saga of the Swamp Thing #21, Shadow #1, Showcase #4, Showcase #9, Showcase #22, Superman #233, Superman (2nd) #75, Superman's Pal Jimmy Olsen #1, Watchmen #1, WildC.A.T.s #1, Wonder Woman #1, World's Finest #71 -($2.50-c)						2.50
All-Star Western #10, Hellblazer #1, More Fun Comics #101, Preacher #1, Sandman #1, Spirit #1, Superboy #1, Superman #76, Young Romance #1-($2.95-c)						3.00
Batman: The Dark Knight Returns #1, Kingdom Come #1 -($5.95-c)						6.00
All Star Comics #3, Batman #1, Justice League #1: Chromium cover						10.00

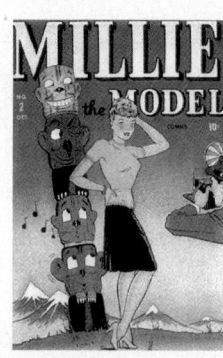

Millie the Model #2 © MAR

Minute Man #2 © FAW

Miracleman #15 © ECL

	GD	VG	FN	VF	VF/NM	NM-
	2.0	4.0	6.0	8.0	9.0	9.2

Crisis on Infinite Earths #1 Chromium cover ... 20.00

MILLENNIUM FEVER
DC Comics (Vertigo): Oct, 1995 - No.4, Jan, 1996 ($2.50, limited series)
1-4: Duncan Fregedo-c/a ... 2.50

MILLENNIUM INDEX
Independent Comics Group: Mar, 1988 - No. 2, Mar, 1988 ($2.00)
1,2 ... 2.50

MILLENNIUM 2.5 A.D.
ACG Comics: No. 1, 2000 ($2.95)
1-Reprints 1934 Buck Rogers daily strips #1-48 ... 3.00

MILLIE, THE LOVABLE MONSTER
Dell Publishing Co.: Sept-Nov, 1962 - No. 6, Jan, 1973

	GD	VG	FN	VF	VF/NM	NM-
12-523-211	5	10	15	32	51	70
2(8-10/63)-Bill Woggon c/a	4	8	12	28	44	60
3(8-10/64)	4	8	12	24	37	50
4(7/72), 5(10/72), 6(1/73)	2	4	6	13	18	22

NOTE: *Woggon* a-3-6; c-3-6. 4 reprints 1; 5 reprints 2; 6 reprints 3.

MILLIE THE MODEL (See Comedy Comics, A Date With..., Joker Comics #28, Life With..., Mad About..., Marvel Mini-Books, Misty & Modeling With...)
Marvel/Atlas/Marvel Comics(CnPC #1)(SPI/Male/VPI):1945 - No. 207, Dec, 1973

	GD	VG	FN	VF	VF/NM	NM-
1-Origin	90	180	270	563	932	1300
2 (10/46)-Millie becomes The Blonde Phantom to sell Blonde Phantom perfume; a pre-Blonde Phantom app. (see All-Select #11, Fall, 1946)	41	82	123	256	416	575
3-8,10: 4-7-Willie app. 7-Willie smokes extra strong tobacco. 8,10-Kurtzman's "Hey Look".						
8-Willie & Rusty app.	31	62	93	178	282	385
9-Powerhouse Pepper by Wolverton, 4 pgs.	35	70	105	201	318	435
11-Kurtzman-a, "Giggles 'n' Grins"	21	42	63	122	191	260
12,15,17,19,20: 12-Rusty & Hedy Devine app.	15	30	45	90	140	190
13,14,16,18: 13,14,16-Kurtzman's "Hey Look". 13-Hedy Devine app. 18-Dan DeCarlo-a begins	16	32	48	94	147	200
21-30	13	26	39	74	105	135
31-40	7	14	21	49	80	110
41-60	6	12	18	41	66	90
61-99	5	10	15	32	51	70
100	6	12	18	37	59	80
101-130: 107-Jack Kirby app. in story	4	8	12	28	44	60
131-134,136,138-153: 141-Groovy Gears-c/s	4	8	12	23	34	45
135-(2/66) 1st app. Groovy Gears	4	8	12	28	44	60
137-2nd app. Groovy Gears	4	8	12	24	37	50
154-New Millie begins (10/67)	5	10	15	32	51	70
155-190	4	8	12	23	34	45
191,193-199,201-206	3	6	9	18	27	35
192-(52 pgs.)	4	8	12	23	36	48
200,207(Last issue)	4	8	12	23	36	48
(Beware: cut-up pages are common in all Annuals)						
Annual 1(1962)-Early Marvel annual (2nd?)	19	38	57	138	244	350
Annual 2(1963)	13	26	39	93	164	235
Annual 3-5 (1964-1966)	9	18	27	60	100	140
Annual 6-10(1967-11/71)	7	14	21	47	76	105
Queen-Size 11(9/74), 12(1975)	6	12	18	41	66	90

NOTE: *Dan DeCarlo* a-18-93.

MILLION DOLLAR DIGEST (Richie Rich... #23 on; also see Richie Rich...)
Harvey Publications: 11/86 - No. 7, 11/87; No. 8, 4/88 - No. 34, Nov, 1994 ($1.25/$1.75, digest size)

	1	2	3	4	5	7
2-8: 8-(68 pgs.)						5.00
9-34: 9-Begin $1.75-c. 14-May not exist						3.50

MILT GROSS FUNNIES (Also see Picture News #1)
Milt Gross, Inc. (ACG?): Aug, 1947 - No. 2, Sept, 1947

	GD	VG	FN	VF	VF/NM	NM-
1	21	42	63	122	191	260
2	15	30	45	84	127	170

MILTON THE MONSTER & FEARLESS FLY (TV)
Gold Key: May, 1966

	GD	VG	FN	VF	VF/NM	NM-
1 (10175-605)	9	18	27	63	107	150

MINIMUM WAGE
Fantagraphics Books: V1#1, July, 1995 ($9.95, B&W, graphic novel, mature)
V2#1, 1995 - Present ($2.95, B&W, mature)

	GD	VG	FN	VF	VF/NM	NM-
	2.0	4.0	6.0	8.0	9.0	9.2

	GD	VG	FN	VF	VF/NM	NM-
V1#1-Bob Fingerman story & art	1	3	4	6	8	10
V2#1-9($2.95): Bob Fingerman story & art. 2-Kevin Nowlan back-c. 4-w/pin-ups.						
5-Mignola back-c						3.00
Book Two TPB ('97, $12.95) r/V2#1-5						13.00

MINISTRY OF SPACE
Image Comics: Apr, 2001 - No. 3, Apr, 2004 ($2.95, limited series)
1-3-Warren Ellis-s/Chris Weston-a ... 3.00
...Vol. 1 Omnibus (3/04, $4.95) r/1&2 ... 5.00
TPB (12/04, $12.95) r/series; sketch & design pages; intro by Mark Millar ... 13.00

MINOR MIRACLES
DC Comics: 2000 ($12.95, B&W, squarebound)
nn-Will Eisner-s/a ... 13.00

MINUTE MAN (See Master Comics & Mighty Midget Comics)
Fawcett Publications: Summer, 1941 - No. 3, Spring, 1942 (68 pgs.)

	GD	VG	FN	VF	VF/NM	NM-
1	207	414	621	1294	2147	3000
2,3	122	244	366	763	1269	1775

MINX, THE
DC Comics (Vertigo): Oct, 1998 - No. 8, May, 1999 ($2.50, limited series)
1-8-Milligan-s/Phillips-c/a ... 3.00

MIRACLE COMICS
Hillman Periodicals: Feb, 1940 - No. 4, Mar, 1941

	GD	VG	FN	VF	VF/NM	NM-
1-Sky Wizard Master of Space, Dash Dixon, Man of Might, Pinkie Parker, Dusty Doyle, The Kid Cop, K-7, Secret Agent, The Scorpion, & Blandu, Jungle Queen begin; Masked Angel only app. (all 1st app.)	186	372	558	1163	1932	2700
2	93	186	279	581	966	1350
3,4: 3-Bill Colt, the Ghost Rider begins. 4-The Veiled Prophet & Bullet Bob (by Burnley) app.	80	160	240	500	830	1160

MIRACLEMAN
Eclipse Comics: Aug, 1985 - No. 15, Nov, 1988; No. 16, Dec, 1989 - No. 24, 1994
1-r/British Marvelman series; Alan Moore scripts in #1-16

	1	2	3	5	7	9
1-Gold variant (edition of 400, signed by Alan Moore, came with signed & #'d certificate of authenticity)	65	130	195	553	1027	1500
1-Blue variant (edition of 600, came with signed certificate of authenticity)	40	80	120	300	550	800
2-12: 8-Airboy preview. 9,10-Origin Miracleman. 9-Shows graphic scenes of childbirth.						
10-Snyder-c	1	2	3	5	6	8
13,14	2	4	6	9	12	15
15-($1.75-c, scarce) end of Kid Miracleman	5	10	15	32	51	70
16-Last Alan Moore-s; 1st $1.95-c (low print)	2	4	6	13	18	22
17,18-($1.95): 17-"The Golden Age" begins, ends #22. Dave McKean-c begins, end #22; Neil Gaiman scripts in #17-24	2	4	6	11	14	
19-23-($2.50): 23-"The Silver Age" begins; BWS-c	1	2	3	5	7	9
24-Last issue; B. Smith-c	2	4	6	9	12	15
3-D 1 (12/85)	1	2	3	5	6	9

NOTE: *Miracleman 3-D #1 (12/85) (2D edition) Interior is the same as the 3-D version except in non 3-D format. Indicia are the same for both versions of the book with only the non 3-D art distinguishing this book from the standard 3-D version. Standard 3-D edition has noise ad mentioning the non 3-D edition. One known copy exists in the Michigan State University Special Collection Department. (No known sales)*

Book One: A Dream of Flying (1988, $9.95, TPB) r/#1-5; Leach-c						22.00
Book One: A Dream of Flying-Hardcover (1988, $29.95) r/#1-5						70.00
Book Two: The Red King Syndrome (1990, $12.95, TPB) r/#6-10; Bolton-c						22.00
Book Two: The Red King Syndrome-Hardcover (1990, $30.95) r/#6-10						85.00
Book Three: Olympus (1990, $12.95, TPB) r/#11-16						120.00
Book Three: Olympus-Hardcover (1990, $30.95) r/#11-16						250.00
Book Four: The Golden Age (1992, $15.95, TPB) r/#17-22						30.00
Book Four: The Golden Age Hardcover (1992, $33.95) r/#17-22						50.00
Book Four: The Golden Age (1993, $12.99, TPB) new McKean-c						15.00

NOTE: *Eclipse archive copies exist for #4,5,8,17,23. Each has a small Miracleman image foil-stamped on the cover. Chaykin c-3. Gulacy c-7. McKean c-17-22. B. Smith c-23, 24. Starlin c-4. Totleben a-11-13; c-9, 11-13. Truman c-6.*

MIRACLEMAN: APOCRYPHA
Eclipse Comics: Nov, 1991 - No. 3, Feb, 1992 ($2.50, limited series)
1-3: 1-Stories by Neil Gaiman, Mark Buckingham, Alex Ross & others. 3-Stories by James Robinson, Kelley Jones, Matt Wagner, Neil Gaiman, Mark Buckingham and others

	1	2	3	4	5	7
TPB (12/92, $15.95) r/#1-3; Buckingham-c						20.00

MIRACLEMAN FAMILY
Eclipse Comics: May, 1988 - No. 2, Sept, 1988 ($1.95, lim. series, Baxter paper)
1,2: 2-Gulacy-c ... 5.00

Miss America Magazine V7 #24 © MAR

Miss Fury Comics #5 © MAR

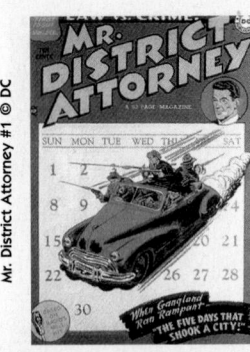

Mr. District Attorney #1 © DC

	GD	VG	FN	VF	VF/NM	NM-		GD	VG	FN	VF	VF/NM	NM-
	2.0	4.0	6.0	8.0	9.0	9.2		2.0	4.0	6.0	8.0	9.0	9.2

MIRACLE OF THE WHITE STALLIONS, THE (See Movie Comics)
MIRACLE SQUAD, THE
Upshot Graphics (Fantagraphics Books): Aug, 1986 - No. 4, 1987 ($2.00)

1-4						2.50

MIRACLE SQUAD: BLOOD AND DUST, THE
Apple Comics: Jan, 1989 - No. 4, July, 1989 ($1.95, B&W, limited series)

1-4						2.50

MISADVENTURES OF MERLIN JONES, THE (See Movie Comics & Merlin Jones as the Monkey's Uncle under Movie Comics)
MISPLACED
Image Comics: May, 2003 - No. 4, Dec, 2004 ($2.95)

1-4: 1-Three covers by Blaylock, Green and Clugston-Major; Blaylock-s/a						3.00
... @17 (12/04, $4.95) Nara from "Dead @17 " app.; Blaylock-s/a						5.00
Somewhere Under the Rainbow TPB (12/04, $10.99, digest size) r/#1-4						11.00

MISS AMERICA COMICS (Miss America Magazine #2 on; also see Blonde Phantom & Marvel Mystery Comics)
Marvel Comics (20CC): 1944 (one-shot)

	GD	VG	FN	VF	VF/NM	NM-
1-2 pgs. pin-ups	183	366	549	1144	1897	2650

MISS AMERICA MAGAZINE (Formerly Miss America; Miss America #51 on)
Miss America Publ. Corp./Marvel/Atlas (MAP): V1#2, Nov, 1944 - V7#24, Nov, 1958

	GD	VG	FN	VF	VF/NM	NM-
V1#2-Photo-c of teenage girl in Miss America costume; Miss America, Patsy Walker (intro.) comic stories plus movie reviews & stories; intro. Buzz Baxter & Hedy Wolfe:						
1 pg. origin Miss America	136	272	408	850	1413	1975
3-5-Miss America & Patsy Walker stories	53	106	159	323	537	750
6-Patsy Walker only	24	48	72	139	220	300
V2#1(4/45)-6(9/45)-Patsy Walker continues	13	26	39	72	101	130
V3#1(10/45)-6(4/46)	11	22	33	64	90	115
V4#1(5/46),2,5(9/46)	11	22	33	60	83	105
V4#3(7/46)-Liz Taylor photo-c	26	52	78	152	239	325
V4#4 (8/46; 68 pgs.), V4#6 (10/46; 92 pgs.)	10	20	30	56	76	95
V5#1(11/46)-6(4/47), V6#1(5/47)-3(7/47)	10	20	30	56	76	95
V7#1(8/47)-23(#56, 6/49)	10	20	30	54	72	90
V7#24(#57, 7/49)-Kamen-a (becomes Best Western #58 on?)						
	10	20	30	56	76	95
V7#25(8/49), 27-44(3/52), VII,nn(5/52)	9	18	27	52	69	85
V7#26(9/49)-All comics	10	20	30	56	76	95
V1,nn(7/52)-V1,nn(1/53)(#46-49), V7#50(Spring '53), V1#51-V7?#54(7/53), 55-93	9	18	27	50	65	80

NOTE: Photo-c #1, 4, V2#1, 4, 5, V3#5, V4#3, 4, 6, V7#15, 16, 24, 26, 34, 37, 38. Painted c-3. *Powell a-V7#31.

MISS BEVERLY HILLS OF HOLLYWOOD (See Adventures of Bob Hope)
National Periodical Publ.: Mar-Apr, 1949 - No. 9, July-Aug, 1950 (52 pgs.)

	GD	VG	FN	VF	VF/NM	NM-
1 (Meets Alan Ladd)	60	120	180	375	625	875
2-William Holden photo on-c	44	88	132	268	444	620
3-5: 2-9-Part photo-c. 5-Bob Hope photo on-c	40	80	120	239	380	520
6,7,9: 6-Lucille Ball photo on-c	36	72	108	208	329	450
8-Reagan photo on-c	40	80	120	244	392	540

NOTE: Beverly meets Alan Ladd in #1, Eve Arden #2, Betty Hutton #4, Bob Hope #5.

MISS CAIRO JONES
Croyden Publishers: 1945

	GD	VG	FN	VF	VF/NM	NM-
1-Bob Oksner daily newspaper-r (1st strip story); lingerie panels	20	40	60	115	180	245

MISS FURY COMICS (Newspaper strip reprints)
Timely Comics (NPI 1/CmPl 2/MPC 3-8): Winter, 1942-43 - No. 8, Winter, 1946 (Published twice a year)

	GD	VG	FN	VF	VF/NM	NM-
1-Origin Miss Fury by Tarpe' Mills (68 pgs.) in costume w/paper dolls with cut-out costumes						
	388	776	1164	2522	4461	6400
2-(60 pgs.)-In costume w/paper dolls	200	400	600	1250	2075	2900
3-(60 pgs.)-In costume w/paper dolls; Hitler-c	155	310	465	969	1610	2250
4-(52 pgs.)-In costume, 2 pgs. w/paper dolls	121	242	363	756	1253	1750
5-(52 pgs.)-In costume w/paper dolls	103	206	309	644	1072	1500
6-(52 pgs.)-Not in costume on inside stories, w/paper dolls						
	93	186	279	581	966	1350
7,8-(36 pgs.)-In costume 1 pg. each; no paper dolls	81	162	243	506	841	1175

NOTE: *Schomburg c-1, 5, 6.*

MISS FURY
Adventure Comics: 1991 - No. 4, 1991 ($2.50, limited series)

1-4: 1-Origin; granddaughter of original Miss Fury						3.00
1-Limited ed. ($4.95)						5.00

MISSION IMPOSSIBLE (TV)
Dell Publ. Co.: May, 1967 - No. 4, Oct, 1968; No. 5, Oct, 1969 (All have photo-c)

	GD	VG	FN	VF	VF/NM	NM-
1	8	16	24	58	97	135
2-5: 5-Reprints #1	6	12	18	41	66	90

MISSION IMPOSSIBLE (Movie)
Marvel Comics (Paramount Comics): May, 1996 ($2.95, one-shot)
(1st Paramount Comics book)

1-Liefeld-c & back-up story						3.00

MISS LIBERTY (Becomes Liberty Comics)
Burten Publishing Co.: 1945 (MLJ reprints)

	GD	VG	FN	VF	VF/NM	NM-
1-The Shield & Dusty, The Wizard, & Roy, the Super Boy app.; r/Shield-Wizard #13						
	28	56	84	162	256	350

MISS MELODY LANE OF BROADWAY (See The Adventures of Bob Hope)
National Periodical Publ.: Feb-Mar, 1950 - No. 3, June-July, 1950 (52 pgs.)

	GD	VG	FN	VF	VF/NM	NM-
1-Movie stars photos app. on all-c.	60	120	180	375	625	875
2,3: 3-Ed Sullivan photo on-c.	40	80	120	235	368	500

MISS PEACH
Dell Publishing Co.: Oct-Dec, 1963; 1969

	GD	VG	FN	VF	VF/NM	NM-
1-Jack Mendelsohn-a/script	8	16	24	52	86	120
...Tells You How to Grow (1969; 25¢)-Mel Lazarus-a; also given away (36 pgs.)						
	5	10	15	30	48	65

MISS PEPPER (See Meet Miss Pepper)
MISS SUNBEAM (See Little Miss....)
MISS VICTORY (See Captain Fearless #1,2, Holyoke One-Shot #3, Veri Best Sure Fire & Veri Best Sure Shot Comics)
MISTER AMERICA
Endeavor Comics: Apr, 1994 - No. 2, May, 1994 ($2.95, limited series)

1,2						3.00

MR. & MRS. BEANS
United Features Syndicate: No. 11, 1939

	GD	VG	FN	VF	VF/NM	NM-
Single Series 11	35	70	105	201	318	435

MR. & MRS. J. EVIL SCIENTIST (TV)(See The Flintstones & Hanna-Barbera Band Wagon #3)
Gold Key: Nov, 1963 - No. 4, Sept, 1966 (Hanna-Barbera, all 12¢)

	GD	VG	FN	VF	VF/NM	NM-
1	6	12	18	41	66	90
2-4	4	8	12	24	37	50

MR. ANTHONY'S LOVE CLINIC (Based on radio show)
Hillman Periodicals: Nov, 1949 - No. 5, Apr-May, 1950 (52 pgs.)

	GD	VG	FN	VF	VF/NM	NM-
1-Photo-c	15	30	45	86	133	180
2	10	20	30	58	79	100
3-5: 5-Photo-c	10	20	30	54	72	90

MISTER BLANK
Amaze Ink: No. 0, Jan, 1996 - No. 14, May, 2000 ($1.75/$2.95, B&W)

0-($1.75, 16 pgs.) Origin of Mr. Blank						2.25
1-14-($2.95) Chris Hicks-s/a						3.00

MR. DISTRICT ATTORNEY (Radio/TV)
National Per. Publ.: Jan-Feb, 1948 - No. 67, Jan-Feb, 1959 (1-23: 52 pgs.)

	GD	VG	FN	VF	VF/NM	NM-
1-Howard Purcell c-5-23 (most)	86	172	258	538	894	1250
2	41	82	123	250	400	550
3-5	29	58	87	167	264	360
6-10	23	46	69	132	209	285
11-20	17	34	51	98	154	210
21-43: 43-Last pre-code (1-2/55)	14	28	42	76	108	140
44-67	11	22	33	62	86	110

MR. DISTRICT ATTORNEY (See The Funnies #35)
Dell Publishing Co.: No. 13, 1942

	GD	VG	FN	VF	VF/NM	NM-
Four Color 13-See The Funnies #35 for 1st app.	27	54	81	203	364	525

MISTER E (Also see Books of Magic limited series)
DC Comics: Jun, 1991 - No. 4, Sept, 1991($1.75, limited series)

1-4-Snyder III-c/a; follow-up to Books of Magic limited series						3.00

MISTER ED, THE TALKING HORSE (TV)
Dell Publishing Co./Gold Key: Mar-May, 1962 - No. 6, Feb, 1964 (All photo-c; photo back-c: 1-6)

	GD	VG	FN	VF	VF/NM	NM-
Four Color 1295	12	24	36	87	156	225

Mister Miracle #25 © DC

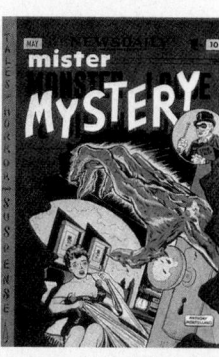
Mister Mystery #5 © Media Publ.

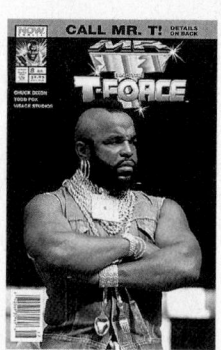
Mr. T and the T-Force #8 © NOW

	GD 2.0	VG 4.0	FN 6.0	VF 8.0	VF/NM 9.0	NM- 9.2
1(11/62) (Gold Key)-Photo-c	9	18	27	60	100	140
2-6: Photo-c	6	12	18	37	59	80

(See March of Comics #244, 260, 282, 290)

MR. GUM (From The Atomics)
Oni Press: April, 2003 ($2.99, one-shot)

1-Mike Allred-s/J. Bone-a; Madman & The Atomics app.						3.00

MR. HERO, THE NEWMATIC MAN (See Neil Gaiman's...)

MR. MAGOO (TV) (The Nearsighted..., ...& Gerald McBoing Boing 1954 issues; formerly Gerald McBoing-Boing And ...)
Dell Publishing Co.: No. 6, Nov-Jan, 1953-54; 5/54 - 3-5/62; 9-11/63 - 3-5/65

	GD 2.0	VG 4.0	FN 6.0	VF 8.0	VF/NM 9.0	NM- 9.2
6	10	20	30	68	119	170
Four Color 561(5/54),602(11/54)	10	20	30	68	119	170
Four Color 1235(#1, 12-2/62),1305(#2, 3-5/62)	8	16	24	56	93	130
3(9-11/63) - 5	7	14	21	50	83	115
Four Color 1235(12-536-505)(3-5/65)-2nd Printing	6	12	18	41	66	90

MR. MAJESTIC (See WildC.A.T.S.)
DC Comics (WildStorm): Sept, 1999 - No. 9, May, 2000 ($2.50)

1-9: 1-McGuinness-a/Casey & Holguin-s. 2-Two covers						2.50
TPB (2002, $14.95) r/#1-6 & Wildstorm Spotlight #1						

MISTER MIRACLE (1st series) (See Cancelled Comic Cavalcade)
National Periodical Publications/DC Comics: 3-4/71 - V4#18, 2-3/74; V5#19, 9/77 - V6#25, 8-9/78; 1987 (Fourth World)

	GD 2.0	VG 4.0	FN 6.0	VF 8.0	VF/NM 9.0	NM- 9.2
1-1st app. Mr. Miracle (#1-3 are 15¢)	7	14	21	49	80	110
2,3: 2-Intro. Granny Goodness. 3-Last 15¢ issue	4	8	12	26	41	55
4-8: 4-Intro. Barda; Boy Commandos begin; all 52 pgs.						
	4	8	12	26	41	55
9-18: 9-Origin Mr. Miracle; Darkseid cameo. 15-Intro/1st app. Shilo Norman. 18-Barda & Scott Free wed; New Gods app. & Darkseid cameo; Last Kirby issue.						
	3	6	9	15	21	26
19-25 (1977-78)	1	2	3	5	7	9
Special 1(1987, $1.25, 52 pgs.)						3.00
Jack Kirby's Fourth World TPB ('01, $12.95) B&W&Grey-toned reprint of #11-18; Mark Evanier intro.						13.00
Jack Kirby's Mister Miracle TPB ('98, $12.95) B&W&Grey-toned reprint of #1-10; David Copperfield intro.						13.00

NOTE: **Austin** a-19i. **Ditko** a-6r. **Golden** a-23-25p; c-25p. **Heath** a-24i, 25i; c-25i. **Kirby** a(p)/c-1-18. **Nasser** a-19i. **Rogers** a-19-22p; c-19, 20p, 21p, 22-24. 4-8 contain **Simon & Kirby** Boy Commandos reprints from Detective 82,76, Boy Commandos 1, 3 & Detective 64 in that order.

MISTER MIRACLE (2nd Series) (See Justice League)
DC Comics: Jan, 1989 - No. 28, June, 1991 ($1.00/$1.25)

1-28: 13,14-Lobo app. 22-1st new Mr. Miracle w/new costume						2.50

MISTER MIRACLE (3rd Series)
DC Comics: Apr, 1996 - No. 7, Oct, 1996 ($1.95)

1-7: 2-Vs. JLA. 6-Simonson-c						2.50

MR. MIRACLE (See Capt. Fearless #1 & Holyoke One-Shot #4)

MR. MONSTER (1st Series) (Doc Stearn... #7 on; See Airboy-Mr. Monster Special, Dark Horse Presents, Super Duper Comics & Vanguard Illustrated #7)
Eclipse Comics: Jan, 1985 - No. 10, June, 1987 ($1.75, Baxter paper)

1-3: 1-1st story-r from Vanguard III. #7(1st app.). 2-Dave Stevens-c. 3-Alan Moore scripts; Wolverton-r/Weird Mysteries #5.						5.00
4-10: 6-Ditko-r/Fantastic Fears #5 plus new Giffen-a. 10- "6-D" issue						4.00

MR. MONSTER
Dark Horse Comics: Feb, 1988 - No. 8, July, 1991 ($1.75, B&W)

1-7						3.00
8-($4.95, 60 pgs.)-Origins conclusion						5.00

MR. MONSTER ATTACKS! (Doc Stearn...)
Tundra Publ.: Aug, 1992 - No. 3, Oct, 1992 ($3.95, limited series, 32 pgs.)

1-3: Michael T. Gilbert-a/scripts; Gilbert/Dorman painted-c						4.00

MR. MONSTER PRESENTS (CRACK-A-BOOM!)
Caliber Comics: 1997 - No. 3, 1997 ($2.95, B&W&Red, limited series)

1-3: Michael T. Gilbert-a/scripts: 1-Wraparound-c						3.00

MR. MONSTER'S GAL FRIDAY...KELLY!
Image Comics: Jan, 2000 - No. 3, May, 2004 ($3.50, B&W)

1-3-Michael T. Gilbert-c; story & art by various. 3-Alan Moore-s						3.50

MR. MONSTER'S SUPER-DUPER SPECIAL
Eclipse Comics: May, 1986 - No. 8, July, 1987

	GD 2.0	VG 4.0	FN 6.0	VF 8.0	VF/NM 9.0	NM- 9.2
1-(5/86)...3-D High Octane Horror #1						5.00
1-(5/86)...2-D version, 100 copies	2	4	6	9	13	16
2-(8/86)...High Octane Horror #1, 3-(9/86)...True Crime #1, 4-(11/86)...True Crime #2, 5-(1/87)...Hi-Voltage Super Science #1, 6-(3/87)...High Shock Schlock #1, 7-(5/87)...High Shock Schlock #2, 8-(7/87)...Weird Tales Of The Future #1						4.00

NOTE: **Jack Cole** r-3, 4. **Evans** a-2r. **Kubert** a-1r. **Powell** a-5r. **Wolverton** a-2r, 7r, 8r.

MR. MONSTER VS. GORZILLA
Image Comics: July, 1998 ($2.95, one-shot)

1-Michael T. Gilbert-a						3.00

MR. MONSTER: WORLDS WAR TWO
Atomeka Press: 2004 ($6.99, one-shot)

nn-Michael T. Gilbert-s/George Freeman-a; two covers by Horley & Dorman						7.00

MR. MUSCLES (Formerly Blue Beetle #18-21)
Charlton Comics: No. 22, Mar, 1956; No. 23, Aug, 1956

	GD 2.0	VG 4.0	FN 6.0	VF 8.0	VF/NM 9.0	NM- 9.2
22,23	8	16	24	44	57	70

MR. MXYZPTLK (VILLAINS)
DC Comics: Feb, 1998 ($1.95, one-shot)

1-Grant-s/Morgan-a/Pearson-c						2.50

MISTER MYSTERY (Tales of Horror and Suspense)
Mr. Publ. (Media Publ.) No. 1-3/SPM Publ./Stanmore (Aragon): Sept, 1951 - No. 19, Oct, 1954

	GD 2.0	VG 4.0	FN 6.0	VF 8.0	VF/NM 9.0	NM- 9.2
1-Kurtzmanesque horror story	91	182	273	569	947	1325
2,3-Kurtzmanesque story. 3-Anti-Wertham edit.	60	120	180	375	625	875
4,6: Bondage-c; 6-Torture	60	120	180	375	625	875
5,8,10	54	108	162	338	562	785
7- "The Brain Bats of Venus" by Wolverton; partially re-used in Weird Tales of the Future #7	122	244	366	763	1269	1775
9-Nostrand-a	54	108	162	338	562	785
11-Wolverton "Robot Woman" story/Weird Mysteries #2, cut up, rewritten & partially redrawn	82	164	246	513	849	1185
12-Classic injury to eye-c	128	256	384	800	1325	1850
13-17,19: 15- "Living Dead" junkie story. 17-Severed heads-c. 19-Reprints	42	84	126	256	421	585
18- "Robot Woman" by Wolverton reprinted from Weird Mysteries #2; decapitation, bondage-c	61	122	183	381	633	885

NOTE: **Andru** a-1, 2p, 3p. **Andru/Esposito** c-1-3. **Baily** c-10-18(most). **Mortellaro** c-5-7. Bondage c-7. Some issues have graphic dismemberment scenes.

MR. PUNCH
DC Comics (Vertigo): 1994 ($24.95, one-shot)

nn (Hard-c)-Gaiman scripts; McKean-c/a						40.00
nn (Soft-c)						15.00

MISTER Q (See Mighty Midget Comics & Our Flag Comics #5)

MR. RISK (Formerly All Romances; Men Against Crime #3 on)(Also see Our Flag Comics & Super-Mystery Comics)
Ace Magazines: No. 7, Oct, 1950; No. 2, Dec, 1950

	GD 2.0	VG 4.0	FN 6.0	VF 8.0	VF/NM 9.0	NM- 9.2
7,2	9	18	27	50	65	80

MR. SCARLET & PINKY (See Mighty Midget Comics)

MR. T
APComics: May, 2005 ($3.50)

1-Chris Bunting-s/Neil Edwards-a						3.50

MR. T AND THE T-FORCE
Now Comics: June, 1993 - No. 10, May, 1994 ($1.95, color)

1-10-Newsstand editions: 1-7-polybagged with photo trading card in each. 1,2-Neal Adams-c/a(p). 3-Dave Dorman painted-c						2.50
1-10-Direct Sale editions polybagged w/line drawn trading cards. 1-Contains gold foil trading card by Neal Adams						2.50

MISTER UNIVERSE (Professional wrestler)
Mr. Publications Media Publ. (Stanmor, Aragon): July, 1951; No. 2, Oct, 1951 - No. 5, April, 1952

	GD 2.0	VG 4.0	FN 6.0	VF 8.0	VF/NM 9.0	NM- 9.2
1	22	44	66	126	198	270
2- "Jungle That Time Forgot", (24 pg. story); Andru/Esposito-c	14	28	42	80	115	150
3-Marijuana story	14	28	42	80	115	150
4,5- "Goes to War" cover/stories	11	22	33	60	83	105

MISTER X (See Vortex)
Mr. Publications/Vortex Comics/Caliber V3#1 on: 6/84 - No. 14, 8/88 ($1.50/$2.25, direct sales, coated paper);V2#1, Apr, 1989 - V2#12, Mar, 1990 ($2.00/$2.50, B&W, newsprint) V3#1, 1996 - Present ($2.95, B&W)

Mitzi's Romances #10 © MAR

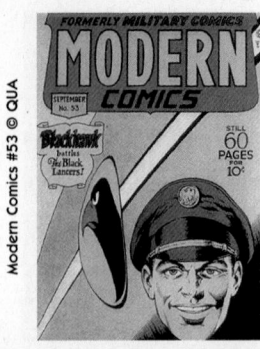

Modern Comics #53 © QUA

Molly O'Day #1 © AVON

	GD 2.0	VG 4.0	FN 6.0	VF 8.0	VF/NM 9.0	NM- 9.2
1-14: 11-Dave McKean story & art (6 pgs.)						4.00
V2 #1-12: 1-11 (Second Coming, B&W): 1-Four diff.-c. 10-Photo-c						3.00
V3 #1-4						3.00
Return of... ($11.95, graphic novel)-r/V1#1-4						12.00
Return of... ($34.95, hardcover limited edition)-r/1-4						35.00
Special (no date, 1990?)						3.00

MISTY
Marvel Comics (Star Comics): Dec, 1985 - No. 6, May, 1986 (Limited series)

1-6: Millie The Model's niece						3.00

MITZI COMICS (Becomes Mitzi's Boy Friend #2-7)(See All Teen)
Timely Comics: Spring, 1948 (one-shot)

	GD 2.0	VG 4.0	FN 6.0	VF 8.0	VF/NM 9.0	NM- 9.2
1-Kurtzman's "Hey Look" plus 3 pgs. "Giggles 'n' Grins"	26	52	78	154	242	330

MITZI'S BOY FRIEND (Formerly Mitzi Comics; becomes Mitzi's Romances)
Marvel Comics (TCI): No. 2, June, 1948 - No. 7, April, 1949

	GD 2.0	VG 4.0	FN 6.0	VF 8.0	VF/NM 9.0	NM- 9.2
2	14	28	42	82	121	160
3-7	12	24	36	69	97	125

MITZI'S ROMANCES (Formerly Mitzi's Boy Friend)
Timely/Marvel Comics (TCI): No. 8, June, 1949 - No. 10, Dec, 1949

	GD 2.0	VG 4.0	FN 6.0	VF 8.0	VF/NM 9.0	NM- 9.2
8-Becomes True Life Tales #8 (10/49) on?	13	26	39	74	105	135
9,10: 10-Painted-c	11	22	33	60	83	105

MNEMOVORE
DC Comics (Vertigo): Jun, 2005 - No. 6, Nov, 2005 ($2.99, limited series)

1-6-Rodionoff & Fawkes-s/Huddleston-a/c						3.00

MOBY DICK (See Feature Presentations #6, and King Classics)
Dell Publishing Co.: No. 717, Aug, 1956

	GD 2.0	VG 4.0	FN 6.0	VF 8.0	VF/NM 9.0	NM- 9.2
Four Color 717-Movie, Gregory Peck photo-c	8	16	24	56	93	130

MOBY DUCK (See Donald Duck #112 & Walt Disney Showcase #2,11)
Gold Key (Disney): Oct, 1967 - No. 11, Oct, 1970; No. 12, Jan, 1974 - No. 30, Feb, 1978

	GD 2.0	VG 4.0	FN 6.0	VF 8.0	VF/NM 9.0	NM- 9.2
1	3	6	9	21	32	42
2-5	2	4	6	11	16	20
6-11	2	4	6	9	13	16
12-30: 21,30-r	1	3	4	6	8	10

MODEL FUN (With Bobby Benson)
Harle Publications: No. 2, Fall, 1954 - No. 5, July, 1955

	GD 2.0	VG 4.0	FN 6.0	VF 8.0	VF/NM 9.0	NM- 9.2
2-Bobby Benson	7	14	21	35	43	50
3-5-Bobby Benson	5	10	15	23	28	32

MODELING WITH MILLIE (Formerly Life With Millie)
Atlas/Marvel Comics (Male Publ.): No. 21, Feb, 1963 - No. 54, June, 1967

	GD 2.0	VG 4.0	FN 6.0	VF 8.0	VF/NM 9.0	NM- 9.2
21	8	16	24	52	86	120
22-30	5	10	15	30	48	65
31-53	4	8	12	24	37	50
54-Last issue; Gears-c & 6 pg. story; Beatles swipe imitators; FF #63 comic appears in story; "Millie the Marvel" 6 pg. story as super-hero	4	8	12	26	41	55

MODERN COMICS (Formerly Military Comics #1-43)
Quality Comics Group: No. 44, Nov, 1945 - No. 102, Oct, 1950

	GD 2.0	VG 4.0	FN 6.0	VF 8.0	VF/NM 9.0	NM- 9.2
44-Blackhawk continues	53	106	159	334	550	765
45-52: 49-1st app. Fear, Lady Adventuress	40	80	120	237	374	510
53-Torchy by Ward begins (9/46)	42	84	126	256	421	585
54-60: 55-J. Cole-a	35	70	105	201	318	435
61-Classic-c	34	68	102	197	311	425
62-77,79,80: 73-J. Cole-a	33	66	99	190	300	410
78-1st app. Madame Butterfly	36	72	108	208	329	450
81-99,101: 82,83-One pg. J. Cole-a. 83-Last 52 pg. issue						
99-Blackhawks on the moon-c/story	31	62	93	178	282	385
100	33	66	99	190	300	410
102-(Scarce)-J. Cole-a; Spirit by Eisner app.	39	78	117	224	355	485

NOTE: *Al Bryant* c-44-51, 54, 55, 66, 69. *Jack Cole* a-55, 73. *Crandall* Blackhawk-#46, 47, 50, 51, 54, 56, 58-60, 64, 67-70, 73, 74, 76-78, 80-83; c-60-65, 67, 68, 70-95. *Crandall/Cuidera* c-56-59, 96-102. *Gustavson* a-47, 49. *Ward* Blackhawk-#52, 53, 55 (15 pgs. each). Torchy in #53-102; by *Ward* only in #53-89(9/49); by *Gil Fox* #92, 93, 102.

MODERN LOVE
E. C. Comics: June-July, 1949 - No. 8, Aug-Sept, 1950

	GD 2.0	VG 4.0	FN 6.0	VF 8.0	VF/NM 9.0	NM- 9.2
1-Feldstein, Ingels-a	74	148	222	463	769	1075
2-Craig/Feldstein-c/s	48	96	144	293	484	675
3	43	86	129	262	431	600
4-6 (Scarce): 4-Bra/panties panels	54	108	162	338	557	775
7,8	43	86	129	262	431	600

NOTE: *Craig* a-3. *Feldstein* a-in most issues; c-1, 2i, 3-8. *Harrison* a-4. *Iger* a-6-8. *Ingels* a-1, 2, 4-7. *Palais* a-5. *Wood* a-3. *Wood/Harrison* a-5-7. (Canadian reprints known; see Table of Contents.)

MOD LOVE
Western Publishing Co.: 1967 (50¢, 36 pgs.)

	GD 2.0	VG 4.0	FN 6.0	VF 8.0	VF/NM 9.0	NM- 9.2
1-(Low print)	5	10	15	32	51	70

MODNIKS, THE
Gold Key: Aug, 1967 - No. 2, Aug, 1970

	GD 2.0	VG 4.0	FN 6.0	VF 8.0	VF/NM 9.0	NM- 9.2
10206-708(#1)	3	6	9	20	30	40
2	3	6	9	15	21	26

MOD SQUAD (TV)
Dell Publishing Co.: Jan, 1969 - No. 3, Oct, 1969 - No. 8, April, 1971

	GD 2.0	VG 4.0	FN 6.0	VF 8.0	VF/NM 9.0	NM- 9.2
1-Photo-c	7	14	21	45	73	100
2-4: 2-4-Photo-c	4	8	12	28	44	60
5-8: 8-Photo-c; Reprints #2	4	8	12	24	37	50

MOD WHEELS
Gold Key: Mar, 1971 - No. 19, Jan, 1976

	GD 2.0	VG 4.0	FN 6.0	VF 8.0	VF/NM 9.0	NM- 9.2
1	4	8	12	26	41	55
2-9	3	6	9	16	23	30
10-19: 11,15-Extra 16 pgs. ads	3	6	9	14	19	24

MOE & SHMOE COMICS
O. S. Publ. Co.: Spring, 1948 - No. 2, Summer, 1948

	GD 2.0	VG 4.0	FN 6.0	VF 8.0	VF/NM 9.0	NM- 9.2
1	9	18	27	47	61	75
2	6	12	18	31	38	45

MOEBIUS (Graphic novel)
Marvel Comics (Epic Comics): Oct, 1987 - No. 6, 1988; No. 7, 1990; No. 8, 1991 ($9.95, 8x11", mature)

	GD 2.0	VG 4.0	FN 6.0	VF 8.0	VF/NM 9.0	NM- 9.2
1,2,4-6,8: (#2, 2nd printing, $9.95)	2	4	6	10	14	18
3,7,0: 3-(1st & 2nd printings, $12.95). 0 (1990, $12.95)	2	4	6	13	18	22
Moebius I-Signed & #'d hard-c ($45.95, Graphitti Designs, 1,500 copies printed)-r/#1-3	4	8	12	28	44	60

MOEBIUS COMICS
Caliber: May, 1996 - No. 6 ($2.95, B&W)

1-6: Moebius-c/a. 1-William Stout-a						3.00

MOEBIUS: THE MAN FROM CIGURI
Dark Horse Comics: 1996 ($7.95, digest-size)

nn-Moebius-c/a						8.00

MOLLY MANTON'S ROMANCES (Romantic Affairs #3)
Marvel Comics (SePI): Sept, 1949 - No. 2, Dec, 1949 (52 pgs.)

	GD 2.0	VG 4.0	FN 6.0	VF 8.0	VF/NM 9.0	NM- 9.2
1-Photo-c (becomes Blaze the Wonder Collie #2 (10/49) on? & Molly Manton's Romances #2	16	32	48	94	147	200
2-Titled "Romances of..."; photo-c	12	24	36	69	97	125

MOLLY O'DAY (Super Sleuth)
Avon Periodicals: February, 1945 (1st Avon comic)

	GD 2.0	VG 4.0	FN 6.0	VF 8.0	VF/NM 9.0	NM- 9.2
1-Molly O'Day, The Enchanted Dagger by Tuska (r/Yankee #1), Capt'n Courage, Corporal Grant app.	54	108	162	338	562	785

MOMENT OF SILENCE
Marvel Comics: Feb, 2002 ($3.50, one-shot)

1-Tributes to the heroes and victims of Sept. 11; s/a by various						3.50

MONARCHY, THE (Also see The Authority and StormWatch)
DC Comics (WildStorm): Apr, 2001 - No. 12, May, 2002 ($2.50)

1-12: 6-Leach & Young-s/a						2.50
Bullets Over Babylon TPB (2001, $12.95) r/#1-4, Authority #21						13.00

MONKEES, THE (TV)(Also see Circus Boy, Groovy, Not Brand Echh #3, Teen-Age Talk, Teen Beam & Teen Beat)
Dell Publishing Co.: March, 1967 - No. 17, Oct, 1969

	GD 2.0	VG 4.0	FN 6.0	VF 8.0	VF/NM 9.0	NM- 9.2
1-Photo-c	10	20	30	68	119	170
2-17: All photo-c. 17-Reprints #1	6	12	18	41	66	90

MONKEY AND THE BEAR, THE
Atlas Comics (ZPC): Sept, 1953 - No. 3, Jan, 1954

	GD 2.0	VG 4.0	FN 6.0	VF 8.0	VF/NM 9.0	NM- 9.2
1-Howie Post-c/a in all; funny animal	9	18	27	52	69	85
2,3	7	14	21	37	46	55

MONKEYMAN AND O'BRIEN (Also see Dark Horse Presents #80, 100-5, Gen[13]/..., Hellboy: Seed of Destruction, & San Diego Comic Con #2)
Dark Horse Comics (Legend): Jul, 1996 - No. 3, Sept, 1996 ($2.95, lim. series)

Monster Hunters #7 © CC

Monsters on the Prowl #9 © MAR

Monte Hale Western #46 © FAW

	GD 2.0	VG 4.0	FN 6.0	VF 8.0	VF/NM 9.0	NM- 9.2
1-3: New stories; Art Adams-c/a/scripts						3.50
nn-(2/96, $2.95)-r/back-up stories from Hellboy: Seed of Destruction; Adams-c/a/scripts						3.50

MONKEYSHINES COMICS
Ace Periodicals/Publishers Specialists/Current Books/Unity Publ.: Summer, 1944 - No. 27, July, 1949

	GD	VG	FN	VF	VF/NM	NM-
1-Funny animal	14	28	42	82	121	160
2-(Aut/44)	9	18	27	50	65	80
3-10: 3-(Win/44)	8	16	24	44	57	70
11-18,20-27: 23,24-Fago-c/a	8	16	24	40	50	60
19-Frazetta-a	9	18	27	50	65	80

MONKEY'S UNCLE, THE (See Merlin Jones As... under Movie Comics)

MONOLITH, THE
DC Comics: Apr, 2004 - Present ($3.50/$2.95)

1-($3.50) Palmiotti & Gray-s/Winslade-a						3.50
2-12-($2.95): 6-8-Batman app.; Coker-a						3.00

MONROES, THE (TV)
Dell Publishing Co.: Apr, 1967

1-Photo-c	3	6	9	18	27	35

MONSTER
Fiction House Magazines: 1953 - No. 2, 1953

1-Dr. Drew by Grandenetti; reprint from Rangers Comics #48; Whitman-c	52	104	156	317	521	725
2-Whitman-c	40	80	120	235	368	500

MONSTER CRIME COMICS (Also see Crime Must Stop)
Hillman Periodicals: Oct, 1952 (15¢, 52 pgs.)

1 (Scarce)	131	262	393	819	1360	1900

MONSTER HOUSE (Companion to the 2006 movie)
IDW Publishing: June, 2006 ($7.99, one-shot)

nn-Two stories about Bones and Skull by Joshua Dysart and Simeon Wilkins						8.00

MONSTER HOWLS (Magazine)
Humor-Vision: December, 1966 (Satire) (35¢, 68 pgs.)

1	6	12	18	37	59	80

MONSTER HUNTERS
Charlton Comics: Aug, 1975 - No. 9, Jan, 1977; No. 10, Oct, 1977 - No. 18, Feb, 1979

1-Howard-a; Newton-c; 1st Countess Von Bludd and Colonel Whiteshroud	3	6	9	16	23	30
2-Sutton-c/a; Ditko-a	2	4	6	11	16	20
3,4,5,7: 4-Sutton-c/a	2	4	6	8	10	12
6,8,10: 6,8,10-Ditko-a	2	4	6	9	12	15
9,11,12	1	2	3	5	7	9
13,15,18-Ditko-c/a. 18-Sutton-a	2	4	6	9	12	15
14-Special all-Ditko-a/c	3	6	9	16	22	28
16,17-Sutton-a	1	2	3	5	7	9
1,2 (Modern Comics reprints, 1977)						4.00

NOTE: *Ditko* a-2, 6, 8, 10, 13-15r, 18r; c-13-15, 18. *Howard* a-1, 3, 17; r-13. *Morisi* a-1. *Staton* a-1. *Sutton* a-2, 4; c-2, 4; r-16-18. *Zeck* a-4-9. Reprints in #12-18.

MONSTER MADNESS (Magazine)
Marvel Comics: 1972 - No. 3, 1973 (60¢, B&W)

1-3: Stories by "Sinister" Stan Lee	4	8	12	24		50

MONSTER MAN
Image Comics (Action Planet): Sept, 1997 ($2.95, B&W)

1-Mike Manley-c/s/a						3.00

MONSTER MASTERWORKS
Marvel Comics: 1989 ($12.95, TPB)

nn-Reprints 1960's monster stories; art by Kirby, Ditko, Ayers, Everett						13.00

MONSTER MATINEE
Chaos! Comics: Oct, 1997 - No. 3, Oct, 1997 ($2.50, limited series)

1-3: pin-ups						2.50

MONSTER MENACE
Marvel Comics: Dec, 1993 - No. 4, Mar, 1994 ($1.25, limited series)

1-4: Pre-code Atlas horror reprints.						6.00

NOTE: *Ditko*-r & *Kirby*-r in all.

MONSTER OF FRANKENSTEIN (See Frankenstein and Essential Monster of Frankenstein)

MONSTERS ATTACK (Magazine)
Globe Communications Corpse: Sept, 1989 - No. 5, Dec, 1990 (B&W)

	GD 2.0	VG 4.0	FN 6.0	VF 8.0	VF/NM 9.0	NM- 9.2
1-5-Ditko, Morrow, J. Severin-a. 5-Toth, Morrow-a	1	2	3	4	5	7

MONSTERS ON THE PROWL (Chamber of Darkness #1-8)
Marvel Comics Group (No. 13,14: 52 pgs.): No. 9, 2/71 - No. 27, 11/73; No. 28, 6/74 - No. 30, 10/74

9-Barry Smith inks	3	6	9	20	30	40
10-12,15: 12-Last 15¢ issue	3	6	9	14	19	24
13,14-(52 pgs.)	3	6	9	16	23	30
16-(4/72)-King Kull 4th app.; Severin-c	3	6	9	16	23	30
17-30	2	4	6	10	14	18

NOTE: *Ditko*-r-9, 14, 16. *Kirby*-r-10-11, 21, 23, 25, 27, 28, 30; c-9, 25. *Kirby/Ditko*-r-14, 17-20, 22, 24, 26, 29. *Marie/John Severin* a-16(Kull). 9-13, 15 contain one new story. Woodish art by *Reese*-11. King Kull created by Robert E. Howard.

MONSTERS TO LAUGH WITH (Magazine) (Becomes Monsters Unlimited #4)
Marvel Comics Group: 1964 - No. 3, 1965 (B&W)

1-Humor by Stan Lee	7	14	21	45	73	100
2,3	4	8	12	26	41	55

MONSTERS UNLEASHED (Magazine)
Marvel Comics Group: July, 1973 - No. 11, Apr, 1975; Summer, 1975 (B&W)

1-Soloman Kane sty; Werewolf app.	4	8	12	26	41	55
2-4: 2-The Frankenstein Monster begins, ends #10. 3-Neal Adams-c/a; The Man-Thing begins (origin-r); Son of Satan preview. 4-Werewolf app.	4	8	12	22	34	45
5-7: Werewolf in all. 7-Williamson-a(r)	3	6	9	17	25	32
8-11: 8-Man-Thing; N. Adams-r. 9-Man-Thing; Wendigo app. 10-Origin Tigra	3	6	9	17	25	32
Annual 1 (Summer,1975, 92 pgs.)-Kane-a	3	6	9	18	27	35

NOTE: *Boris* c-2, 6. *Brunner* a-2; c-11. *J. Buscema* a-2p, 4p, 5p. *Colan* a-1, 4r. *Davis* a-3r. *Everett* a-2r. *G. Kane* a-3, *Krigstein* r-4. *Morrow* a-3; c-1. *Perez* a-8. *Ploog* a-5. *Reese* a-1, 7. *Tuska* a-3p. *Wildey* a-1r.

MONSTERS UNLIMITED (Magazine) (Formerly Monsters To Laugh With)
Marvel Comics Group: No. 4, 1965 - No. 7, 1966 (B&W)

4-7	4	8	12	24	37	50

MONSTER WORLD
DC Comics (WildStorm): Jul, 2001 - No. 4, Oct, 2001 ($2.50, limited series)

1-4-Lobdell-s/Meglia-c/a						2.50

MONTANA KID, THE (See Kid Montana)

MONTE HALE WESTERN (Movie star; Formerly Mary Marvel #1-28; also see Fawcett Movie Comic, Motion Picture Comics, Picture News #8, Real Western Hero, Six-Gun Heroes, Western Hero & XMas Comics)
Fawcett Publ./Charlton No. 83 on: No. 29, Oct, 1948 - No. 88, Jan, 1956

29-(#1, 52 pgs.)-Photo-c begin, end #82; Monte Hale & his horse Pardner begin	40	80	120	235	368	500
30-(52 pgs.)-Big Bow and Little Arrow begin, end #34; Captain Tootsie by Beck	19	38	57	108	167	225
31-36,38-40-(52 pgs.): 34-Gabby Hayes begins, ends #80. 39-Captain Tootsie by Beck	15	30	45	83	124	165
37,41,45,49-(36 pgs.)	12	24	36	66	97	125
42-44,46-48,50-(52 pgs.): 47-Big Bow & Little Arrow app.	14	28	42	76	108	140
51,52,54-56,58,59-(52 pgs.)	11	22	33	64	90	115
53,57-(36 pgs.): 53-Slim Pickens app.	10	20	30	54	72	90
60-81: 36 pgs. #60-on. 80-Gabby Hayes ends	9	18	27	52	69	85
82-Last Fawcett issue (6/53)	11	22	33	60	83	105
83-1st Charlton issue (2/55); B&W photo back-c begin. Gabby Hayes returns, ends #86	12	24	36	69	97	125
84 (4/55)	10	20	30	54	72	90
85-86	9	18	27	52	69	85
87,88: 87-Wolverton-r, 1/2 pg. 88-Last issue	10	20	30	54	72	90

NOTE: *Gil Kane* a-33?, 34? *Rocky Lane* 1 pg. (Carnation ad)-38, 40, 41, 43, 44, 46, 55.

MONTY HALL OF THE U.S. MARINES (See With the Marines...)
Toby Press: Aug, 1951 - No. 11, Apr, 1953

1	12	24	36	67	94	120
2	8	16	24	40	50	60
3-5	7	14	21	37	46	55
6-11	7	14	21	35	43	50

NOTE: *Full page pin-ups (Pin-Up Pete) by Jack Sparling* in #1-9.

MOON, A GIRL...ROMANCE, A (Becomes Weird Fantasy #13 on; formerly Moon Girl #1-8)
E. C. Comics: No. 9, Sept-Oct, 1949 - No. 12, Mar-Apr, 1950

9-Moon Girl cameo	76	152	228	475	788	1100
10,11	62	124	186	388	644	900
12-(Scarce)	76	152	228	475	788	1100

NOTE: *Feldstein, Ingels* art in all. *Feldstein* c-9-12. *Wood/Harrison* a-10-12. Canadian reprints known; see

Moon Knight #11 © MAR

Moonshadow #1 © DeMatteis & Muth

Morbius, The Living Vampire #18 © MAR

	GD	VG	FN	VF	VF/NM	NM-		GD	VG	FN	VF	VF/NM	NM-
	2.0	4.0	6.0	8.0	9.0	9.2		2.0	4.0	6.0	8.0	9.0	9.2

MOON GIRL AND THE PRINCE (#1) (Moon Girl #2-6; Moon Girl Fights Crime #7, 8; becomes A Moon, A Girl, Romance #9 on)(Also see Animal Fables #7, Int. Crime Patrol #6, Happy Houlihans & Tales From The Crypt #22)
E. C. Comics: Fall, 1947 - No. 8, Summer, 1949

1-Origin Moon Girl (see Happy Houlihans #1). Intro Santana, Queen of the Underworld	102	204	306	638	1057	1475
2-Moon Girl battles Futureman	58	116	174	363	602	840
3,4: 3-Santana, Queen of the Underworld returns. 4-Moon Girl vs. a vampire	51	102	153	311	513	715
5-E.C.'s 1st horror story, "Zombie Terror"	112	224	336	700	1163	1625
6-8 (Scarce): 7-Origin Star (Moongirl's sidekick)	58	116	174	363	602	840

NOTE: **Craig** a-2, 5; c-1, 2. **Moldoff** a-1-8; c-3-8 (Shelly). **Wheelan's** Fat and Slat app. in #3, 4, 6. #2 & #3 are 52 pgs., #4 on, 36 pgs. Canadian reprints known; (see Table of Contents.)

MOON KNIGHT (Also see The Hulk, Marc Spector..., Marvel Preview #21, Marvel Spotlight & Werewolf by Night #32)
Marvel Comics Group: Nov, 1980 - No. 38, Jul, 1984 (Mando paper #33 on)

1-Origin resumed in #4		5.00
2-15,25,35: 4-Intro Midnight Man. 25-Double size. 35-($1.00, 52 pgs.)-X-Men app.; F.F. cameo		3.00
16-24,26-28,30,34,36-38: 16-The Thing app.		2.50
29,30-Werewolf By Night app.		4.00

NOTE: **Austin** c-27i, 31i. **Cowan** a-16; c-16, 17. **Kaluta** c-36-38; back c-35. **Miller** c-9, 12p, 13p, 15p, 27p. **Ploog** back c-35. **Sienkiewicz** a-1-15, 17-20, 22-26, 28-30, 33i, 36(4), 37; c-1-5, 7, 8, 10, 11, 14-16, 18-26, 28-30, 31p, 33, 34.

MOON KNIGHT
Marvel Comics Group: June, 1985 - V2#6, Dec, 1985

V2#1-6: 1-Double size; new costume. 6-Sienkiewicz painted-c		2.50

MOON KNIGHT
Marvel Comics: Jan, 1998 - No. 4, Apr, 1998 ($2.50, limited series)

1-4-Moench-s/Edwards-c/a		2.50

MOON KNIGHT (Volume 3)
Marvel Comics: Jan, 1999 - No. 4, Feb, 1999 ($2.99, limited series)

1-4-Moench-s/Texeira-a(p)		3.00

MOON KNIGHT (Fourth series)
Marvel Comics: June, 2006 - Present ($2.99, limited series)

1-Finch-a/c; Huston-s		4.00
1-B&W sketch variant-c		8.00
2-12: 7-Spider-Man app. 9,10-Punisher app.		3.00
... Vol. 1: The Bottom HC (2006, $19.99) r/#1-6; Huston afterword; 2 covers		20.00
... Vol. 1: The Bottom SC (2007, $14.99) r/#1-6; Huston afterword		15.00

MOON KNIGHT: DIVIDED WE FALL
Marvel Comics: 1992 ($4.95, 52 pgs.)

nn-Denys Cowan-c/a(p)		5.00

MOON KNIGHT SPECIAL
Marvel Comics: Oct, 1992 ($2.50, 52 pgs.)

1-Shang Chi, Master of Kung Fu-c/story		2.50

MOON KNIGHT SPECIAL EDITION
Marvel Comics Group: Nov, 1983 - No. 3, Jan, 1984 ($2.00, limited series, Baxter paper)

1-3: Reprints from Hulk mag. by Sienkiewicz		3.00

MOON MULLINS (See Popular Comics, Super Book #3 & Super Comics)
Dell Publishing Co.: 1941 - 1945

Four Color 14(1941)	45	90	135	275	450	625
Large Feature Comic 29(1941)	36	72	108	208	329	450
Four Color 31(1943)	17	34	51	128	227	325
Four Color 81(1945)	10	20	30	73	129	185

MOON MULLINS
Michel Publ. (American Comics Group)#1-6/St. John #7,8: Dec-Jan, 1947-48 - No. 8, 1949 (52 pgs.)

1-Alternating Sunday & daily strip-r	22	44	66	126	198	270
2	13	26	39	74	105	135
3-8: 7,8-St. John Publ. 8-...Featuring Kayo on-c	12	24	36	69	97	125

NOTE: **Milt Gross** a-2-6, 8. **Frank Willard** r-all.

MOON PILOT
Dell Publishing Co.: No. 1313, Mar-May, 1962

Four Color 1313-Movie, photo-c	7	14	21	47	76	105

MOONSHADOW (Also see Farewell, Moonshadow)

Marvel Comics (Epic Comics): 5/85 - #12, 2/87 ($1.50/$1.75, mature)
(1st fully painted comic book)

1-Origin; J. M. DeMatteis scripts & Jon J. Muth painted-c/a.		6.00
2-12: 11-Origin		4.00
Trade paperback (1987?)-r/#1-12		14.00

Signed & numbered hard-c ($39.95, 1,200 copies)-r/#1-12						
	4	8	12	28	44	60

MOONSHADOW
DC Comics (Vertigo): Oct, 1994 - No. 12, Aug, 1995 ($2.25/$2.95)

1-11: Reprints Epic series.		2.50
12 ($2.95)-w/expanded ending		3.00
The Complete Moonshadow TPB ('98, $39.95) r/#1-12 and Farewell Moonshadow; new Muth painted-c		40.00

MOON-SPINNERS, THE (See Movie Comics)

MOONSTONE MONSTERS
Moonstone: 2003 - 2005 ($2.95, B&W)

...: Demons ($2.95) - Short stories by various; Frenz-c		3.00
...: Ghosts ($2.95) - Short stories by various; Frenz-c		3.00
...: Sea Creatures ($2.95) - Short stories by various; Frenz-c		3.00
...: Witches ($2.95) - Short stories by various; Frenz-c		3.00
...: Zombies ($2.95) - Short stories by various; Frenz-c		3.00
Volume 1 (2004, $16.95, TPB) r/short stories from series; Wolak-c		17.00

MOONSTONE NOIR
Moonstone: 2003 - Present ($2.95/$4.95/$5.50, B&W)

...: Bulldog Drummond (2004, $4.95) - Messner-Loebs-s/Barkley-a		5.00
...: Johnny Dollar ($4.95) - Gallaher-s/Theriault-a		5.00
...: Mr. Keen, Tracer of Lost Persons 1,2 ($2.95, limited series) - Ferguson-a		3.00
...: Mysterious Traveler (2003, $5.50) - Trevor Von Eeden-a/Joe Gentile-s		5.50
...: Mysterious Traveler Returns (2004, $4.95) - Trevor Von Eeden-a/Joe Gentile-s		5.00
...: The Lone Wolf ($4.95) - Jolley-s/Croall-a		5.00

MOPSY (See Pageant of Comics & TV Teens)
St. John Publ. Co.: Feb, 1948 - No. 19, Sept, 1953

1-Part-r; reprints "Some Punkins" by Neher	18	36	54	103	162	220
2	11	22	33	62	86	110
3-10(1953): 8-Lingerie panels	10	20	30	56	76	95
11-19: 19-Lingerie-c	9	18	27	52	69	85

NOTE: #1-7, 13, 18, 19 have paper dolls.

MORBIUS REVISITED
Marvel Comics: Aug, 1993 - No. 5, Dec, 1993 ($1.95, mini-series)

1-5-Reprints Fear #27-31		2.50

MORBIUS: THE LIVING VAMPIRE (Also see Amazing Spider-Man #101,102, Fear #20, Marvel Team-Up #3, 4, Midnight Sons Unl. & Vampire Tales)
Marvel Comics (Midnight Sons imprint #16 on): Sep, 1992 - No. 32, Apr, 1995 ($1.75/$1.95)

1-($2.75, 52 pgs.)-Polybagged w/poster; Ghost Rider & Johnny Blaze x-over (part 3 of Rise of the Midnight Sons)		3.00
2-11,13-24,26-32: 3,4-Vs. Spider-Man-c.15-Ghost Rider app. 16-Spot varnish-c. 16,17-Siege of Darkness,parts 5 &13. 18-Deathlok app. 21-Bound-in Spider-Man trading card sheet; Spider-Man app.		2.50
12-($2.25)-Outer-c is a Darkhold envelope made of black parchment w/gold ink; Midnight Massacre x-over		2.50
25-($2.50, 52 pgs.)-Gold foil logo		2.50

MORE FUN COMICS (Formerly New Fun Comics #1-6)
National Periodical Publications: No. 7, Jan, 1936 - No. 127, Nov-Dec, 1947 (No. 7,9-11: paper-c)

7(1/36)-Oversized, paper-c; 1 pg. Kelly-a	787	1574	2361	6000	–	–
8(2/36)-Oversized (10x12"), paper-c; 1 pg. Kelly-a; Sullivan-c	787	1574	2361	6000	–	–
9(3-4/36)(Very rare, 1st standard-sized comic book with original material)-Last multiple panel-c	947	1894	2841	7200	–	–
10,11(7/36): 10-Last Henri Duval by Siegel & Shuster; new classic logo begins	547	1094	1641	4200	–	–
12(8/36)-Slick-c begin	433	866	1299	3300	–	–
V2#1(9/36, #13) 1 pg. Fred Astaire photo/bio	397	794	1191	3000	–	–
2(10/36, #14)-Dr. Occult in costume (1st in color)(Superman proto-type; 1st DC appearance) continues from The Comics Magazine, ends #17	1867	3734	5601	14,000	–	–
V2#3(11/36, #15), 17(V2#5)	760	1520	2280	5750	–	–
16(V2#4)-Cover numbering begins; ties with New Comics #11 as 1st DC Christmas-c; last Superman tryout issue	775	1550	2325	5900	–	–

NOTE: The 10,11(7/36)-Last "Calling All Cars" by Siegel & Shuster; new classic logo begins

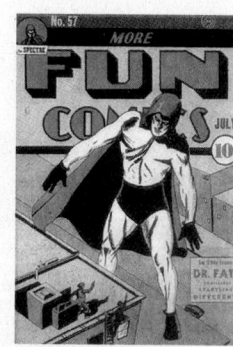

More Fun Comics #57 © DC

More Than Mortal #1 © Liar

Mortie #2 © Magazine Publ.

	GD	VG	FN	VF	VF/NM	NM-
	2.0	4.0	6.0	8.0	9.0	9.2

	GD	VG	FN	VF	VF/NM	NM-
	2.0	4.0	6.0	8.0	9.0	9.2

18-20(V2#8, 5/37) — 300 / 600 / 900 / 2300 / – / –
21(V2#9)-24(V2#12, 9/37) — 276 / 552 / 828 / 1518 / 2159 / 2800
25(V3#1, 10/37)-27(V3#3, 12/37): 27-Xmas-c — 276 / 552 / 828 / 1518 / 2159 / 2800
28-30: 30-1st non-funny cover — 250 / 500 / 750 / 1375 / 1938 / 2500
31-Has ad for Action Comics #1 — 265 / 530 / 795 / 1458 / 2054 / 2650
32-35: 32-Last Dr. Occult — 250 / 500 / 750 / 1375 / 1938 / 2500
36-40: 36-(10/38)-The Masked Ranger & sidekick Pedro begins; Ginger Snap
by Bob Kane (2 pgs.; 1st-a?). 39-Xmas-c — 250 / 500 / 750 / 1375 / 1938 / 2500
41-50: 41-Last Masked Ranger — 212 / 424 / 636 / 1166 / 1708 / 2250
51-The Spectre app. (in costume) in one panel ad at end of Buccaneer story — 741 / 1482 / 2223 / 4076 / 5788 / 7500
52-(2/40)-Origin/1st app. The Spectre (in costume splash panel only), part 1 by Bernard Baily
(parts 1 & 2 written by Jerry Siegel; Spectre's costume changes color from purple & blue to
green & grey; last Wing Brady; Spectre-c — 6000 / 12,000 / 18,000 / 45,000 / 80,000 / 115,000
53-Origin The Spectre (in costume at end of story), part 2; Capt. Desmo begins;
Spectre-c — 2850 / 5700 / 8550 / 20,000 / 40,000 / 60,000
54-The Spectre in costume; last King Carter; classic-Spectre-c — 1367 / 2734 / 4100 / 10,000 / 18,000 / 26,000
55-(Scarce, 5/40)-Dr. Fate begins (1st app.); last Bulldog Martin; Spectre-c — 1425 / 2850 / 4275 / 10,500 / 18,750 / 27,000
56-1st Dr. Fate-c (classic), origin continues. Congo Bill begins (6/40), 1st app. — 714 / 1428 / 2142 / 5000 / 8750 / 12,500
57-60-All Spectre-c — 412 / 824 / 1236 / 2678 / 4739 / 6800
61,65: 61-Classic Dr. Fate-c. 65-Classic Spectre-c — 382 / 764 / 1146 / 2483 / 4392 / 6300
62-64,66: 63-Last Lt. Bob Neal. 64-Lance Larkin begins; all Spectre-c — 300 / 600 / 900 / 1970 / 3485 / 5000
67-(5/41)-Origin (1st) Dr. Fate; last Congo Bill & Biff Bronson (Congo Bill continues in
Action Comics #37, 6/41)-Spectre-c — 729 / 1458 / 2187 / 5103 / 8927 / 12,750
68-70: 68-Clip Carson begins. 70-Last Lance Larkin; all Dr. Fate-c — 269 / 538 / 807 / 1681 / 2791 / 3900
71-Origin & 1st app. Johnny Quick by Mort Weisinger (9/41); classic sci/fi Dr. Fate-c — 526 / 1052 / 1578 / 3682 / 6441 / 9200
72-Dr. Fate's new helmet; last Sgt. Carey, Sgt. O'Malley & Captain Desmo;
German submarine-c (only German war-c) — 762 / 524 / 786 / 1638 / 2719 / 3800
73-Origin & 1st app. Aquaman (11/41) by Paul Norris; intro. Green Arrow & Speedy;
Dr. Fate-c — 1367 / 2734 / 4100 / 10,000 / 18,000 / 26,000
74-2nd Aquaman; 1st Percival Popp, Supercop; Dr. Fate-c — 300 / 600 / 900 / 1881 / 3141 / 4400
75,76: 75-New origin Spectre; Nazi spy ring cover w/Hitler's photo. 76-Last Dr. Fate-c;
Johnny Quick (by Meskin #76-97) begins, ends #107; last Clip Carson — 252 / 504 / 756 / 1575 / 2613 / 3650
77-80: 77-Green Arrow-c begin — 200 / 400 / 600 / 1250 / 2075 / 2900
81-83,85,88,90: 81-Last large logo. 82-1st small logo. — 134 / 268 / 402 / 838 / 1394 / 1950
84-Green Arrow Japanese war-c — 138 / 276 / 414 / 863 / 1432 / 2000
86,87-Johnny Quick-c. 87-Last Radio Squad — 134 / 268 / 402 / 838 / 1394 / 1950
89-Origin Green Arrow & Speedy Team-up — 143 / 286 / 429 / 894 / 1485 / 2075
91,97,99: 91-1st bi-monthly issue. 93-Dover & Clover begin (1st app., 9-10/43).
97-Kubert-a — 90 / 180 / 270 / 563 / 932 / 1300
98-Last Dr. Fate (scarce) — 110 / 220 / 330 / 688 / 1144 / 1600
100 (11-12/44)-Johnny Quick-c — 121 / 242 / 363 / 756 / 1253 / 1750
101-Origin & 1st app. Superboy (1-2/45)(not by Siegel & Shuster); last Spectre issue;
Green Arrow-c — 857 / 1714 / 2571 / 6000 / 10,500 / 15,000
102-2nd Superboy app; 1st Dover & Clover-c — 138 / 276 / 414 / 863 / 1432 / 2000
103-3rd Superboy app; last Green Arrow-c — 100 / 200 / 300 / 625 / 1038 / 1450
104-1st Superboy c w/Dover & Clover — 86 / 172 / 258 / 538 / 894 / 1250
105,106-Superboy-c — 79 / 158 / 237 / 494 / 822 / 1150
107-Last Johnny Quick & Superboy — 79 / 158 / 237 / 494 / 822 / 1150
108-120: 108-Genius Jones begins; 1st c-app. (3-4/46; cont'd from Adventure Comics #102) — 25 / 50 / 75 / 145 / 228 / 310
121-124,126: 121-123,126-Post funny animal (Jimminy & the Magic Book)-c — 23 / 46 / 69 / 132 / 209 / 285
125-Superman c-app.w/Jimminy — 79 / 158 / 237 / 494 / 822 / 1150
127-(Scarce)-Post-c/a — 38 / 76 / 114 / 219 / 347 / 475

NOTE: All issues are scarce to rare. Cover features: The Spectre-#52-55, 57-60, 62-67. Dr. Fate-#56, 61, 68-76.
The Green Arrow & Speedy-#77-85, 88-97, 99, 101 (w/Dover & Clover-#98, 100). Johnny Quick-#86, 87, 100.
Dover & Clover-#102, (104, 106 w/Superboy), 107, 108(w/Genius Jones), 110, 112, 114, 117, 119. Genius Jones-
#109, 113, 115, 116, 118, 120. Baily a-45, 52-on; c-52-55, 57-60, 62-67. Al Capp a-45(signed Koppy).
Ellsworth c-7. Creig Flessel c-30, 31, 35-48(most). Guardineer c-47, 49, 50. Kiefer a-20. Meskin c-86, 87, 100?
Moldoff c-55. George Papp c-77-85. Post c-121-127. Vincent Sullivan c-8-28, 32-34.

MORE FUND COMICS (Benefit book for the Comic Book Legal Defense Fund)
(Also see Even More Fund Comics)
Sky Dog Press: Sept, 2003 ($10.00, B&W, trade paperback)
nn-Anthology of short stories and pin-ups by various; Hulk-c by Pérez — 10.00

MORE SEYMOUR (See Seymour My Son)
Archie Publications: Oct, 1963
1-DeCarlo-a? — 3 / 6 / 9 / 18 / 27 / 35
MORE THAN MORTAL (Also see Lady Pendragon/...)
Liar Comics: June, 1997 - No. 4, Apr, 1998 ($2.95, limited series)
Image Comics: No. 5, Dec, 1999 - Present ($2.95)
1-Blue forest background-c, 1-Variant-c — 4.00
1-White-c — 6.00
1-2nd printing; purple sky cover — 3.00
2-4-Silvestri-c, 2-Two-c, one by Randy Queen — 3.00
5,6: 5-1st Image Comics issue — 3.00
MORE THAN MORTAL: OTHERWORLDS
Image Comics: July, 1999 - No. 4, Dec, 1999 ($2.95, limited series)
1-4-Firchow-a. 1-Two covers — 3.00
MORE THAN MORTAL SAGAS
Liar Comics: Jun, 1998 - No. 3, Dec, 1998 ($2.95, limited series)
1,2-Painted art by Romano. 2-Two-c, one by Firchow — 3.00
1-Variant-c by Linsner — 5.00
MORE THAN MORTAL TRUTHS AND LEGENDS
Liar Comics: Aug, 1998 - No. 6, Apr, 1999 ($2.95)
1-6-Firchow-a(p) — 3.00
1-Variant-c by Dan Norton — 4.50
MORE TRASH FROM MAD (Annual)
E. C. Comics: 1958 - No. 12, 1969
(Note: Bonus missing = half price)
nn(1958)-8 pgs. color Mad reprint from #20 — 19 / 38 / 57 / 138 / 244 / 350
2(1959)-Market Product Labels — 14 / 28 / 42 / 99 / 175 / 250
3(1960)-Text book covers — 12 / 24 / 36 / 84 / 156 / 225
4(1961)-Sing Along with Mad booklet — 12 / 24 / 36 / 84 / 156 / 225
5(1962)-Window Stickers; r/from Mad #39 — 9 / 18 / 27 / 63 / 107 / 150
6(1963)-TV Guise booklet — 9 / 18 / 27 / 63 / 107 / 150
7(1964)-Alfred E. Neuman commemorative stamps — 8 / 16 / 24 / 52 / 86 / 120
8(1965)-Life size poster-Alfred E. Neuman — 6 / 12 / 18 / 41 / 66 / 90
9-12: 9,10(1966-67)-Mischief Sticker. 11(1968)-Campaign poster & bumper sticker.
12(1969)-Pocket medals — 6 / 12 / 18 / 41 / 66 / 90
NOTE: Kelly Freas c-1, 2, 4. Mingo c-3, 5-9, 12.
MORGAN THE PIRATE (Movie)
Dell Publishing Co.: No. 1227, Sept-Nov, 1961
Four Color 1227-Photo-c — 7 / 14 / 21 / 50 / 83 / 115
MORLOCKS
Marvel Comics: June, 2002 - No. 4, Sept, 2002 ($2.50, limited series)
1-4-Johns-s/Martinbrough-c/a — 2.50
MORLOCK 2001
Atlas/Seaboard Publ.: Feb, 1975 - No. 3, July, 1975
1,2: 1-(Super-hero)-Origin & 1st app.; Milgrom-c — 1 / 2 / 3 / 6 / — / 8
3-Ditko/Wrightson-a; origin The Midnight Man & The Mystery Men — 1 / 3 / 4 / 6 / 8 / 10
MORNINGSTAR SPECIAL
Comico: Apr, 1990 ($2.50)
1-From the Elementals; Willingham-c/a/scripts — 3.00
MORTAL KOMBAT
Malibu Comics: July, 1994 - No. 6, Dec, 1994 ($2.95)
1-6: 1-Two diff. covers exist — 3.00
1-Limited edition gold foil embossed-c — 4.00
0 (12/94), Special Edition 1 (11/94) — 3.00
Tournament Edition I(12/94, $3.95), II('95)($3.95) — 4.00
...: BARAKA ,June, 1995 ($2.95, one-shot) #1; ...BATTLEWAVE ,2/95 - No. 6, 7/95, #1-6;
...GORO, PRINCE OF PAIN ,9/94 - No. 3, 11/94, #1-3; ...KITANA AND MILEENA ,8/95 ,
...KUNG LAO ,7/95 , #1; ...RAYDON & KANO ,3/95 - No. 3, 5/95, #1-3: ...(all $2.95-c)
— 3.00
...: U.S. SPECIAL FORCES ,1/95 - No. 2, ($3.50), #1,2 — 3.50
MORTIE (Mazie's Friend; also see Flat-Top)
Magazine Publishers: Dec, 1952 - No. 4, June, 1953?
1 — 9 / 18 / 27 / 50 / 65 / 80
2-4 — 6 / 12 / 18 / 28 / 34 / 40
MORTIGAN GOTH: IMMORTALIS (See Marvel Frontier Comics Unlimited)

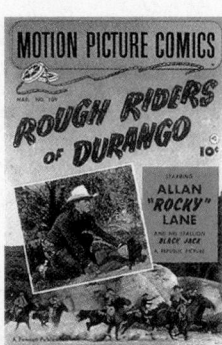

Motion Picture Comics #109 © FAW

Motormouth #9 © MAR

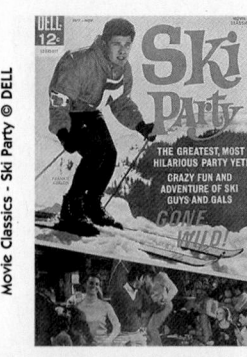

Movie Classics - Ski Party © DELL

	GD	VG	FN	VF	VF/NM	NM-
	2.0	4.0	6.0	8.0	9.0	9.2

Marvel Comics: Sept, 1993 - No. 4, Mar, 1994 ($1.95, mini-series)

1-($2.95)-Foil-c					3.00
2-4					2.50

MORT THE DEAD TEENAGER
Marvel Comics: Nov, 1993 - No. 4, Mar, 1994 ($1.75, mini-series)

1-4					2.50

MORTY MEEKLE
Dell Publishing Co.: No. 793, May, 1957

	GD	VG	FN	VF	VF/NM	NM-
Four Color 793	4	8	12	22	34	45

MOSES & THE TEN COMMANDMENTS (See Dell Giants)

MOSTLY WANTED
DC Comics (WildStorm): Jul, 2000 - No. 4, Nov, 2000 ($2.50, limited series)

1-4-Lobdell-s/Flores-a					2.50

MOTH, THE
Dark Horse Comics: Apr, 2004 - No. 4 ($2.99)

1-4-Steve Rude-c/a; Gary Martin-s					3.00
... Special (3/04, $4.95)					5.00
TPB (5/05, $12.95) r/#1-4 and Special; gallery of extras					13.00

MOTHER GOOSE AND NURSERY RHYME COMICS (See Christmas With Mother Goose)
Dell Publishing Co.: No. 41, 1944 - No. 862, Nov, 1957

	GD	VG	FN	VF	VF/NM	NM-
Four Color 41-Walt Kelly-c/a	22	44	66	165	295	425
Four Color 59, 68-Kelly c/a	18	36	54	134	237	340
Four Color 862-The Truth About..., Movie (Disney)	7	14	21	49	80	110

MOTHER TERESA OF CALCUTTA
Marvel Comics Group: 1984

1-(52 pgs.) No ads					4.00

MOTION PICTURE COMICS (See Fawcett Movie Comics)
Fawcett Publications: No. 101, 1950 - No. 114, Jan, 1953 (All-photo-c)

	GD	VG	FN	VF	VF/NM	NM-
101- "Vanishing Westerner"; Monte Hale (1950)	24	48	72	136	211	285
102- "Code of the Silver Sage"; Rocky Lane (1/51)	21	42	63	121	186	250
103- "Covered Wagon Raid"; Rocky Lane (3/51)	21	42	63	121	186	250
104- "Vigilante Hideout"; Rocky Lane (5/51)-Book length Powell-a	21	42	63	121	186	250
105- "Red Badge of Courage"; Audie Murphy; Bob Powell-a (7/51)	27	54	81	155	240	325
106- "The Texas Rangers"; George Montgomery (9/51)	21	42	63	121	186	250
107- "Frisco Tornado"; Rocky Lane (11/51)	19	38	57	108	167	225
108- "Mask of the Avenger"; John Derek	15	30	45	85	130	175
109- "Rough Rider of Durango"; Rocky Lane	15	30	45	84	112	174	235
110- "When Worlds Collide"; George Evans-a (5/52); Williamson & Evans drew themselves in story; (also see Famous Funnies 72-88)	96	192	288	600	975	1350
111- "The Vanishing Outpost"; Lash LaRue	24	48	72	136	211	285
112- "Brave Warrior"; Jon Hall & Jay Silverheels	15	30	45	83	124	165
113- "Walk East on Beacon"; George Murphy; Schaffenberger-a	12	24	36	69	97	125
114- "Cripple Creek"; George Montgomery (1/53)	13	26	39	74	105	135

MOTION PICTURE FUNNIES WEEKLY (See Promotional Comics section)

MOTORHEAD (See Comic's Greatest World)
Dark Horse Comics: No. 101, 1994 - No. 6, Jan, 1996 ($2.50)

1-6: Bisley-c on all. 1-Predator app.					2.50
Special 1 (3/94, $3.95, 52pgs.)-Jae Lee-c; Barb Wire, The Machine & Wolf Gang app.					4.00

MOTORMOUTH (... & Killpower #7? on)
Marvel Comics UK: June, 1992 - No. 12, May, 1993 ($1.75)

1-13: 1,2-Nick Fury app. 3-Punisher-c/story. 5,6-Nick Fury & Punisher app. 6-Cable cameo. 7-9-Cable app.					2.50

MOUNTAIN MEN (See Ben Bowie)

MOUSE MUSKETEERS (See M.G.M.'s...)

MOUSE ON THE MOON, THE (See Movie Classics)

MOVIE CARTOONS
DC Comics: Dec, 1944 (cover only ashcan)

nn-Ashcan comic, not distributed to newsstands, only for in house use. Covers were produced, but not the rest of the book. A copy sold in 2006 for $400.

MOVIE CLASSICS
Dell Publishing Co.: Apr, 1956; May-Jul, 1962 - Dec, 1969

	GD	VG	FN	VF	VF/NM	NM-
	2.0	4.0	6.0	8.0	9.0	9.2

(Before 1963, most movie adaptations were part of the 4-Color series)
(Disney movie adaptations after 1970 are in Walt Disney Showcase)

	GD	VG	FN	VF	VF/NM	NM-
Around the World Under the Sea 12-030-612 (12/66)	3	6	9	20	30	40
Bambi 3(4/56)-Disney; r/4-Color #186	4	8	12	23	36	48
Battle of the Bulge 12-056-606 (6/66)	3	6	9	21	32	42
Beach Blanket Bingo 12-058-509	7	14	21	47	76	105
Bon Voyage 01-068-212 (12/62)-Disney; photo-c	4	8	12	22	34	45
Castilian, The 12-110-401	3	6	9	20	30	40
Cat, The 12-109-612 (12/66)	3	6	9	19	29	38
Cheyenne Autumn 12-112-506 (4-6/65)	5	10	15	35	55	75
Circus World, Samuel Bronston's 12-115-411; John Wayne app.; John Wayne photo-c	9	18	27	65	113	160
Countdown 12-150-710 (10/67)-James Caan photo-c	3	6	9	21	32	42
Creature, The 1 (12-142-302) (12-2/62-63)	8	16	24	54	90	125
Creature, The 12-142-410 (10/64)	5	10	15	30	48	65
David Ladd's Life Story 12-173-212 (10-12/62)-Photo-c	7	14	21	47	76	105
Die, Monster, Die 12-175-603 (3/66)-Photo-c	5	10	15	35	55	75
Dirty Dozen 12-180-710 (10/67)	4	8	12	28	44	60
Dr. Who & the Daleks 12-190-612 (12/66)-Peter Cushing photo-c; 1st U.S. app. of Dr. Who	10	20	30	70	123	175
Dracula 12-231-212 (10-12/62)	7	14	21	49	80	110
El Dorado 12-240-710 (10/67)-John Wayne; photo-c	11	22	33	79	140	200
Ensign Pulver 12-257-410 (8-10/64)	3	6	9	19	29	38
Frankenstein 12-283-305 (3-5/63)(see Frankenstein 8-10/64 for 2nd printing)	7	14	21	50	83	115
Great Race, The 12-299-603 (3/66)-Natallie Wood, Tony Curtis photo-c	4	8	12	28	44	60
Hallelujah Trail, The 12-307-602 (2/66) (Shows 1/66 inside); Burt Lancaster, Lee Remick photo-c	5	10	15	30	48	65
Hatari 12-340-301 (1/63)-John Wayne	8	16	24	52	86	120
Horizontal Lieutenant, The 01-348-210 (10/62)	3	6	9	19	29	38
Incredible Mr. Limpet, The 12-370-408; Don Knotts photo-c	4	8	12	28	44	60
Jack the Giant Killer 12-374-301 (1/63)	7	14	21	50	83	115
Jason & the Argonauts 12-376-310 (8-10/63)-Photo-c	9	18	27	60	100	140
Lancelot & Guinevere 12-416-310 (10/63)	5	10	15	32	51	70
Lawrence 12-426-308 (8/63)-Story of Lawrence of Arabia; movie ad on back-c; not exactly it	5	10	15	32	51	70
Lion of Sparta 12-439-301 (1/63)	4	8	12	22	34	45
Mad Monster Party 12-460-801 (9/67)-Based on Kurtzman's screenplay	8	16	24	54	90	125
Magic Sword, The 01-496-209 (9/62)	5	10	15	35	55	75
Masque of the Red Death 12-490-410 (8-10/64)-Vincent Price photo-c	6	12	18	41	66	90
Maya 12-495-612 (12/66)-Clint Walker & Jay North part photo-c	4	8	12	24	37	50
McHale's Navy 12-500-412 (10-12/64)	4	8	12	28	44	60
Merrill's Marauders 12-510-301 (1/63)-Photo-c	3	6	9	19	29	38
Mouse on the Moon, The 12-530-312 (10/12/63)-Photo-c	4	8	12	22	34	45
Mummy, The 12-537-211 (9-11/62) 2 versions with different back-c	8	16	24	52	86	120
Music Man, The 12-538-301 (1/63)	3	6	9	20	30	40
Naked Prey, The 12-545-612 (12/66)-Photo-c	5	10	15	35	55	75
Night of the Grizzly, The 12-558-612 (12/66)-Photo-c	4	8	12	24	37	45
None But the Brave 12-565-506 (4-6/65)	5	10	15	35	55	75
Operation Bikini 12-597-310 (10/63)-Photo-c	3	6	9	20	30	40
Operation Crossbow 12-590-512 (10/66)-Photo-c	3	6	9	20	30	40
Prince & the Pauper, The 01-654-207 (5-7/62)-Disney	4	8	12	22	34	45
Raven, The 12-680-309 (9/63)-Vincent Price photo-c	6	12	18	39	62	85
Ring of Bright Water 01-701-910 (10/69) (inside shows #12-701-909)	4	8	12	22	34	45
Runaway, The 12-707-412 (10-12/64)	3	6	9	19	29	38
Santa Claus Conquers the Martians #? (1964)-Photo-c	9	18	27	65	113	160
Santa Claus Conquers the Martians 12-725-603 (3/66, 12¢)-Reprints 1964 issue: photo-c	7	14	21	47	76	105
Another version given away with a Golden Record, SLP 170, nn, no price (3/66)-Complete with record	12	24	36	87	156	225
Six Black Horses 12-750-301 (1/63)-Photo-c	3	6	9	20	30	40
Ski Party 12-743-511 (9-11/65)-Frankie Avalon photo-c; photo inside-c; Adkins-a						

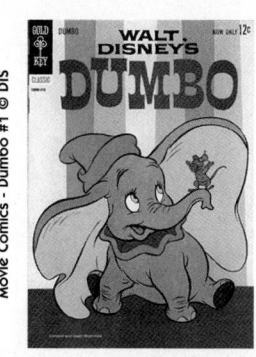

Movie Classics - Twice Told Tales © DELL — Movie Comics - Dumbo #1 © DIS

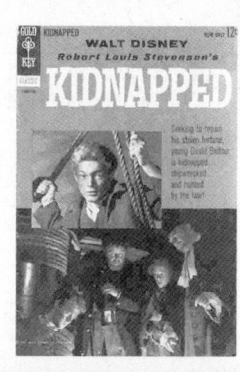

Movie Comics - Kidnapped © DIS

	GD 2.0	VG 4.0	FN 6.0	VF 8.0	VF/NM 9.0	NM- 9.2
Smoky 12-746-702 (2/67)	5	10	15	30	48	65
Sons of Katie Elder 12-748-511 (9-11/65); John Wayne app.; photo-c	3	6	9	19	29	38
	12	24	36	86	153	200
Tales of Terror 12-793-302 (2/63)-Evans-a	5	10	15	35	55	75
Three Stooges Meet Hercules 01-828-208 (8/62)-Photo-c	9	18	27	60	100	140
Tomb of Ligeia 12-830-506 (4-6/65)	5	10	15	35	55	75
Treasure Island 01-845-211 (7-9/62)-Disney; r/4-Color #624	3	6	9	20	30	40
Twice Told Tales (Nathaniel Hawthorne) 12-840-401 (11-1/63-64); Vincent Price photo-c	6	12	18	37	59	80
Two on a Guillotine 12-850-506 (4-6/65)	4	8	12	22	34	45
Valley of Gwangi 01-880-912 (12/69)	9	18	27	60	100	140
War Gods of the Deep 12-900-509 (7-9/65)	3	6	9	20	30	40
War Wagon, The 12-533-709 (9/67); John Wayne app.	8	16	24	54	90	125
Who's Minding the Mint? 12-924-708 (8/67)	3	6	9	19	29	38
Wolfman, The 12-922-308 (6-8/63)	7	14	21	50	83	115
Wolfman, The 1(12-922-410)(8-10/64)-2nd printing; r/#12-922-308	4	8	12	23	36	48
Zulu 12-950-410 (8-10/64)-Photo-c	7	14	21	49	80	110

MOVIE COMICS (See Cinema Comics Herald & Fawcett Movie Comics)

MOVIE COMICS
National Periodical Publications/Picture Comics: April, 1939 - No. 6, Sept-Oct, 1939 (Most all photo-c)

	GD 2.0	VG 4.0	FN 6.0	VF 8.0	VF/NM 9.0	NM- 9.2
1- "Gunga Din", "Son of Frankenstein", "The Great Man Votes", "Fisherman's Wharf", & "Scouts to the Rescue" part 1; Wheelan "Minute Movies" begin	345	690	1035	2243	3972	5700
2- "Stagecoach", "The Saint Strikes Back", "King of the Turf","Scouts to the Rescue" part 2, "Arizona Legion", Andy Devine photo-c	241	482	723	1506	2503	3500
3- "East Side of Heaven", "Mystery in the White Room", "Four Feathers", "Mexican Rose" with Gene Autry, "Spirit of Culver", "Many Secrets", "The Mikado" (1st Gene Autry photo cover)	172	344	516	1075	1788	2500
4- "Captain Fury", Gene Autry in "Blue Montana Skies", "Streets of N.Y." with Jackie Cooper, "Oregon Trail" part 1 with Johnny Mack Brown, "Big Town Czar" with Barton MacLane, & "Star Reporter" with Warren Hull	145	290	435	906	1503	2100
5- "The Man in the Iron Mask", "Five Came Back", "Wolf Call", "The Girl & the Gambler", "The House of Fear", "The Family Next Door", "Oregon Trail" part 2	159	318	477	994	1647	2300
6- "The Phantom Creeps", "Chumps at Oxford", & "The Oregon Trail" part 3; 2nd Robot-c	197	394	591	1231	2041	2850

NOTE: Above books contain many original movie stills with dialogue from movie scripts. All issues are scarce.

MOVIE COMICS
Fiction House Magazines: Dec, 1946 - No. 4, 1947

	GD 2.0	VG 4.0	FN 6.0	VF 8.0	VF/NM 9.0	NM- 9.2
1-Big Town (by Lubbers), Johnny Danger begin; Celardo-a; Mitzi of the Movies by Fran Hopper	46	92	138	281	466	650
2-(2/47)- "White Tie & Tails" with William Bendix; Mitzi of the Movies begins	36	72	108	208	329	450
3-(6/47)-Andy Hardy starring Mickey Rooney	36	72	108	208	329	450
4-Mitzi In Hollywood by Matt Baker; Merton of the Movies with Red Skelton; Yvonne DeCarlo & George Brent in "Slave Girl"	41	82	123	250	400	550

MOVIE COMICS
Gold Key/Whitman: Oct, 1962 - 1984

	GD 2.0	VG 4.0	FN 6.0	VF 8.0	VF/NM 9.0	NM- 9.2
Alice in Wonderland 10144-503 (3/65)-Disney; partial reprint of 4-Color #331	4	8	12	22	34	45
Alice In Wonderland #1 (Whitman pre-pack, 3/84)	2	4	6	10	14	18
Aristocats, The 1 (30045-103)(3/71)-Disney; with pull-out poster (25¢) (No poster = half price)	7	14	21	47	76	105
Bambi 1 (10087-309)(9/63)-Disney; r/4-C #186	4	8	12	24	37	50
Bambi 2 (10087-607)(7/66)-Disney; r/4-C #186	3	6	9	20	30	40
Beneath the Planet of the Apes 30044-012 (12/70)-with pull-out poster; photo-c (No poster = half price)	9	18	27	60	100	140
Big Red 10026-211 (11/62)-Disney; photo-c	3	6	9	20	30	40
Big Red 10026-503 (3/65)-Disney; reprints 10026-211; photo-c	3	6	9	16	23	30
Blackbeard's Ghost 10222-806 (6/68)-Disney	3	6	9	19	29	38
Bullwhip Griffin 10181-706 (6/67)-Disney; Spiegle-a; photo-c	4	8	12	22	34	45
Captain Sindbad 10077-309 (9/63)-Manning-a; photo-c	6	12	18	41	66	90
Chitty Chitty Bang Bang 1 (30038-902)(2/69)-with pull-out poster; Disney; photo-c (No poster = half price)	6	12	18	43	69	95
Cinderella 10152-508 (8/65)-Disney; r/4-C #786	4	8	12	26	41	55
Darby O'Gill & the Little People 10251-001(1/70)-Disney; reprints 4-Color #1024 (Toth-a); photo-c	5	10	15	30	48	65
Dumbo 1 (10090-310)(10/63)-Disney; r/4-C #668	3	6	9	21	32	42
Emil & the Detectives 10120-502 (11/64)-Disney; photo-c	3	6	9	20	30	40
Escapade in Florence 1 (10043-301)(1/63)-Disney; starring Annette Funicello	8	16	24	52	86	120
Fall of the Roman Empire 10118-407 (7/64); Sophia Loren photo-c	4	8	12	24	37	50
Fantastic Voyage 10178-702 (2/67)-Wood/Adkins-a; photo-c	6	12	18	37	59	80
55 Days at Peking 10081-309 (9/63)-Photo-c	3	6	9	20	30	40
Fighting Prince of Donegal, The 10193-701 (1/67)-Disney	3	6	9	19	29	38
First Men in the Moon 10132-503 (3/65)-Fred Fredericks-a; photo-c	4	8	12	24	37	50
Gay Purr-ee 30017-301(1/63, 84 pgs.)	5	10	15	32	51	70
Gnome Mobile, The 10207-710 (10/67)-Disney	4	8	12	22	34	45
Goodbye, Mr. Chips 10246-006 (6/70)-Peter O'Toole photo-c	3	6	9	20	30	40
Happiest Millionaire, The 10221-804 (4/68)-Disney	4	8	12	22	34	45
Hey There, It's Yogi Bear 10122-409 (9/64)-Hanna-Barbera	6	12	18	43	69	95
Horse Without a Head, The 10109-401 (1/64)-Disney	3	6	9	19	29	38
How the West Was Won 10074-307 (7/63)-Based on the L'Amour novel; Tufts-a	4	8	12	28	44	60
In Search of the Castaways 10048-303 (3/63)-Disney; Hayley Mills photo-c	6	12	18	43	69	95
Jungle Book, The 1 (6022-801)(1/68-Whitman)-Disney; large size (10x13-1/2"); 59¢	6	12	18	43	69	95
Jungle Book, The 1 (30033-803)(3/68, 68 pgs.)-Disney; same contents as Whitman #1	4	8	12	24	37	50
Jungle Book, The 1 (6/78, $1.00 tabloid)	3	6	9	16	23	30
Jungle Book (7/84)-r/Giant; Whitman pre-pack	2	4	6	10	14	18
Kidnapped 10080-306 (6/63)-Disney; reprints 4-Color #1101; photo-c	3	6	9	20	30	40
King Kong 30036-809(9/68-68 pgs.)-painted-c	8	16	26	41		55
King Kong nn-Whitman Treasury($1.00, 68 pgs.,1968), same cover as Gold Key issue	5	10	15	35	55	75
King Kong 11299(#1-786, 10x13-1/4", 68 pgs., $1.00, 1978)	3	6	9	18	27	35
Lady and the Tramp 10042-301 (1/63)-Disney; r/4-Color #629	3	6	9	21	32	42
Lady and the Tramp 1 (1967-Giant; 25¢)-Disney; reprints part of Dell #1	5	10	15	35	55	75
Lady and the Tramp 2 (10042-203)(3/72)-Disney; r/4-Color #629	3	6	9	16	23	30
Legend of Lobo, The 1 (10059-303)(3/63)-Disney; photo-c	3	6	9	16	23	30
Lt. Robin Crusoe, U.S.N. 10191-610 (10/66)-Disney; Dick Van Dyke photo-c	3	6	9	18	27	35
Lion, The 10035-301 (1/63)-Photo-c	3	6	9	17	25	32
Lord Jim 10156-509 (9/65)-Photo-c	3	6	9	17	25	32
Love Bug, The 10237-906 (6/69)-Disney; Buddy Hackett photo-c	4	8	12	22	34	45
Mary Poppins 10136-501 (1/65)-Disney; photo-c	5	10	15	30	48	65
Mary Poppins 30023-501 (1/65-68 pgs.)-Disney; photo-c	7	14	21	47	76	105
McLintock 10110-403 (3/64); John Wayne app.; John Wayne & Maureen O'Hara photo-c	12	24	36	82	146	210
Merlin Jones as the Monkey's Uncle 10115-510 (10/65)-Disney; Annette Funicello front/back photo-c	6	12	18	39	62	85
Miracle of the White Stallions, The 10065-306 (6/63)-Disney	3	6	9	19	29	38
Misadventures of Merlin Jones, The 10115-405 (5/64)-Disney; Annette Funicello photo front/back-c	6	12	18	39	62	85
Moon-Spinners, The 10124-410 (10/64)-Disney; Hayley Mills photo-c	6	12	18	43	69	95
Mutiny on the Bounty 1 (10040-302)(2/63)-Marlon Brando photo-c	4	8	12	22	34	45
Nikki, Wild Dog of the North 10141-412 (12/64)-Disney; reprints 4-Color #1226	3	6	9	16	23	30

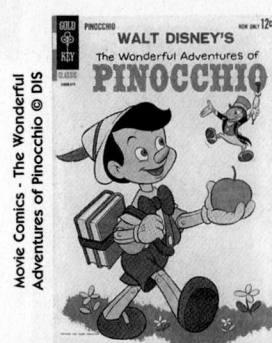

Movie Comics - The Wonderful Adventures of Pinocchio © DIS

Movie Love #12 © FF

Ms. Marvel #4 © MAR

	GD 2.0	VG 4.0	FN 6.0	VF 8.0	VF/NM 9.0	NM- 9.2

Old Yeller 10168-601 (1/66)-Disney; reprints 4-Color #869; photo-c

| | 3 | 6 | 9 | 16 | 23 | 30 |

One Hundred & One Dalmations 1 (10247-002) (2/70)-Disney; reprints Four Color #1183

| | 3 | 6 | 9 | 18 | 27 | 35 |

Peter Pan 1 (10086-309)(9/63)-Disney; reprints Four Color #442

| | 3 | 6 | 9 | 21 | 32 | 42 |

Peter Pan 2 (10086-909)(9/69)-Disney; reprints Four Color #442

| | 3 | 6 | 9 | 16 | 23 | 30 |

Peter Pan 1 (3/84)-r/4-Color #442; Whitman pre-pack

| | 2 | 4 | 6 | 11 | 16 | 20 |

P.T. 109 10123-409 (9/64)-John F. Kennedy

| | 5 | 10 | 15 | 30 | 48 | 65 |

Rio Conchos 10143-503(3/65)

| | 4 | 8 | 12 | 22 | 34 | 45 |

Robin Hood 10163-506 (6/65)-Disney; reprints Four Color #413

| | | | | 9 | 17 | 25 | 32 |

Shaggy Dog & the Absent-Minded Professor 30032-708 (8/67-Giant, 68 pgs.) Disney; reprints 4-Color #985,1199

| | 5 | 10 | 15 | 32 | 51 | 70 |

Sleeping Beauty 1 (30042-009)(9/70)-Disney; with pull-out poster (No poster = half price)

| | 6 | 12 | 18 | 43 | 69 | 95 |

Snow White & the Seven Dwarfs 1 (10091-310)(10/63)-Disney; reprints Four Color #382

| | 3 | 6 | 9 | 20 | 30 | 40 |

Snow White & the Seven Dwarfs 10091-709 (9/67)-Disney; reprints Four Color #382

| | 3 | 6 | 9 | 16 | 23 | 30 |

Snow White & the Seven Dwarfs 90091-204 (2/84)-Reprints Four Color #382; Whitman pre-pack

| | 2 | 4 | 6 | 11 | 16 | 20 |

Son of Flubber 1 (10057-304)(4/63)-Disney; sequel to "The Absent-Minded Professor"

| | 4 | 8 | 12 | 22 | 34 | 45 |

Summer Magic 10076-309 (9/63)-Disney; Hayley Mills photo-c; Manning-a

| | 6 | 12 | 18 | 43 | 69 | 95 |

Swiss Family Robinson 10236-904 (4/69)-Disney; reprints Four Color #1156; photo-c

| | 3 | 6 | 9 | 18 | 27 | 35 |

Sword in the Stone, The 30019-402 (2/64-Giant, 68 pgs.)-Disney (see March of Comics #258 & Wart and the Wizard

| | 6 | 12 | 18 | 43 | 69 | 95 |

That Darn Cat 10171-602 (2/66)-Disney; Hayley Mills photo-c

| | 6 | 12 | 18 | 43 | 69 | 95 |

Those Magnificent Men in Their Flying Machines 10162-510 (10/65); photo-c

| | 3 | 6 | 9 | 20 | 30 | 40 |

Three Stooges in Orbit 30016-211 (11/62-Giant, 32 pgs.)-All photos from movie; stiff-cover

| | 18 | 27 | 65 | 113 | 160 |

Tiger Walks, A 10117-406 (6/64)-Disney; Torres?, Tufts-a; photo-c

| | 4 | 8 | 12 | 24 | 37 | 50 |

Toby Tyler 10142-502 (2/65)-Disney; reprints Four Color #1092; photo-c

| | 3 | 6 | 9 | 18 | 27 | 35 |

Treasure Island 1 (10200-703)(3/67)-Disney; reprints Four Color #624; photo-c

| | 3 | 6 | 9 | 16 | 23 | 30 |

20,000 Leagues Under the Sea 1 (10095-312)(12/63)-Disney; reprints Four Color #614

| | 3 | 6 | 9 | 18 | 27 | 35 |

Wonderful Adventures of Pinocchio, The 1 (10089-310)(1/63)-Disney; reprints Four Color #545 (see Wonderful Advs. of…)

| | 3 | 6 | 9 | 21 | 32 | 42 |

Wonderful Adventures of Pinocchio, The 10089-109 (9/71)-Disney; reprints Four Color #545

| | 3 | 6 | 9 | 16 | 23 | 30 |

Wonderful World of the Brothers Grimm 1 (10008-210)(10/62)

| | 4 | 8 | 12 | 28 | 44 | 60 |

X, the Man with the X-Ray Eyes 10083-309 (9/63)-Ray Milland photo on-c

| | | | 21 | 49 | 80 | 110 |

Yellow Submarine 35000-902 (2/69-Giant, 68 pgs.)-With pull-out poster; The Beatles cartoon movie; Paul S. Newman-s

| | 21 | 42 | 63 | 156 | 278 | 400 |

Without poster

| | 9 | 18 | 27 | 61 | 103 | 145 |

MOVIE FABLES
DC Comics: Dec, 1944 (cover only ashcan)

nn-Ashcan comic, not distributed to newsstands, only for in house use. Covers were produced, but not the rest of the book. A copy sold in 2006 for $400.

MOVIE GEMS
DC Comics: Dec, 1944 (cover only ashcan)

nn-Ashcan comic, not distributed to newsstands, only for in house use. Covers were produced, but not the rest of the book. A copy sold in 2006 for $400.

MOVIE LOVE (Also see Personal Love)
Famous Funnies: Feb, 1950 - No. 22, Aug, 1953 (All photo-c)

1-Dick Powell, Evelyn Keyes, & Mickey Rooney photo-c

| | 16 | 32 | 48 | 94 | 147 | 200 |

2-Myrna Loy photo-c

| | 10 | 20 | 30 | 58 | 79 | 100 |

3-7,9: 6-Ricardo Montalban photo-c. 9-Gene Tierney, John Lund, Glenn Ford, & Rhonda Fleming photo-c.

| | 10 | 20 | 30 | 54 | 72 | 90 |

8-Williamson/Frazetta-a, 6 pgs.

| | 45 | 90 | 135 | 275 | 450 | 625 |

10-Frazetta-a, 6 pgs.

| | 45 | 90 | 135 | 277 | 456 | 635 |

11,14-16: 14-Janet Leigh photo-c

| | 9 | 18 | 27 | 52 | 69 | 85 |

12-Dean Martin & Jerry Lewis photo-c (12/51, pre-dates Advs. of Dean Martin & Jerry Lewis comic)

| | 18 | 36 | 54 | 103 | 162 | 220 |

13-Ronald Reagan photo-c with 1 pg. biog.

| | 25 | 50 | 75 | 145 | 228 | 310 |

17-Leslie Caron & Ralph Meeker photo-c; 1 pg. Frazetta ad

| | 10 | 20 | 30 | 54 | 72 | 90 |

18-22: 19-John Derek photo-c. 20-Donald O'Connor & Debbie Reynolds photo-c. 21-Paul Henreid & Patricia Medina photo-c. 22-John Payne & Coleen Gray photo-c

| | 9 | 18 | 27 | 50 | 65 | 80 |

NOTE: *Each issue has a full-length movie adaptation with photo covers.*

MOVIE THRILLERS (Movie)
Magazine Enterprises: 1949

1-Adaptation of "Rope of Sand" w/Burt Lancaster; Burt Lancaster photo-c

| | 28 | 56 | 84 | 162 | 256 | 350 |

MOVIE TOWN ANIMAL ANTICS (Formerly Animal Antics; becomes Raccoon Kids #52 on)
National Periodical Publ.: No. 24, Jan-Feb, 1950 - No. 51, July-Aug, 1954

24-Raccoon Kids continue

| | 12 | 24 | 36 | 67 | 94 | 120 |

25-51

| | 10 | 20 | 30 | 54 | 72 | 90 |

NOTE: *Sheldon Mayer a-28-33, 35, 37-41, 43, 44, 47, 49-51.*

MOVIE TUNES COMICS (Formerly Animated…; Frankie No. 4 on)
Marvel Comics (MgPC): No. 3, Fall, 1946

3-Super Rabbit, Krazy Krow, Silly Seal & Ziggy Pig

| | 14 | 28 | 42 | 80 | 115 | 150 |

MOWGLI JUNGLE BOOK (Rudyard Kipling's…)
Dell Publ. Co.: No. 487, Aug-Oct, 1953 - No. 620, Apr, 1955

Four Color 487 (#1)

| | 6 | 12 | 18 | 37 | 59 | 80 |

Four Color 582 (8/54), 620

| | 5 | 10 | 15 | 30 | 48 | 65 |

MR. (See Mister)

M. REX
Image Comics: July, 1999 - No. 2, Dec, 1999 ($2.95)

Preview ($5.00) B&W pages and sketchbook; Rouleau-a ... 5.00

1,2-($2.95) 1-Joe Kelly-s/Rouleau-a/c. 2-Rouleau-c ... 3.00

MS. MARVEL (Also see The Avengers #183)
Marvel Comics Group: Jan, 1977 - No. 23, Apr, 1979

1-1st app. Ms. Marvel; Scorpion app. in #1,2

| | 2 | 4 | 6 | 8 | 10 | 12 |

2-10: 2-Origin. 5-Vision app. 6-10-(Reg. 30¢-c). 10-Last 30¢ issue ... 6.00

6-10-(35¢-c variants, limited dist.)(6/77)

| | 3 | 6 | 9 | 18 | 27 | 35 |

11-15,19-23: 19-Capt. Marvel app. 20-New costume. 23-Vance Astro (leader of the Guardians) app. ... 5.00

16,17-1st brief app. Mystique

| | 2 | 4 | 6 | 13 | 18 | 22 |

18-1st full app. Mystique; Avengers x-over

| | 4 | 8 | 12 | 22 | 34 | 45 |

NOTE: *Austin c-14i, 16i, 17i, 22i. Buscema a-1-3p; c(p)-2, 4, 6, 7, 15. Infantino a-14p, 19p. Gil Kane c-8. Mooney a-4-8p, 13p, 15-18p. Starlin c-12.*

MS. MARVEL (Also see New Avengers)
Marvel Comics: May, 2006 - Present ($2.99)

1-19: 1-Cho-c/Reed-s/De La Torre-a; Stilt-Man app. 4,5-Dr. Strange app. 6,7-Araña app. ... 3.00

1-Variant cover by Michael Turner ... 5.00

... Special (3/07, $2.99) Reed-s/Camuncoli-a/c ... 3.00

... Vol. 1: Best of the Best HC (2006, $19.99) r/#1-5 & Giant-Size Ms. Marvel #1 ... 20.00

... Vol. 1: Best of the Best SC (2007, $14.99) r/#1-5 & Giant-Size Ms. Marvel #1 ... 15.00

... Vol. 2: Civil War HC (2007, $19.99) r/#6-10 & Ms. Marvel Special #1 ... 20.00

... Vol. 2: Civil War SC (2007, $14.99) r/#6-10 & Ms. Marvel Special #1 ... 15.00

MS. MYSTIC
Pacific Comics: Oct, 1982 - No. 2, Feb, 1984 ($1.00/$1.50)

1,2: Neal Adams-c/a/script. 1-Origin; intro Erth, Ayre, Fyre & Watr ... 4.00

MS. MYSTIC
Continuity Comics: 1988 - No. 9, May, 1992 ($2.00)

1-9: 1-Reprint Pacific Comics issues ... 3.00

MS. MYSTIC
Continuity Comics: V2#1, Oct, 1993 - V2#4, Jan, 1994 ($2.50)

V2#1-4: 1-Adams-c(i)/part-i. 2-4-Embossed-c. 2-Nebres part-i. 3-Adams-c(i)/plot. 4-Adams-c(p)/plot ... 2.50

MS. MYSTIC DEATHWATCH 2000 (Ms. Mystic #3)
Continuity: May, 1993 - No. 3, Aug, 1993 ($2.50)

1-3-Bagged w/card; Adams plots ... 2.50

MS. TREE QUARTERLY / SPECIAL
DC Comics: Summer, 1990 -No. 10, 1992 ($3.95/$3.50, 84 pgs, mature)

Ms. Tree Quarterly #3 © DC

Murder Incorporated #6 © FOX

Murderous Gangsters #3 © REAL

	GD 2.0	VG 4.0	FN 6.0	VF 8.0	VF/NM 9.0	NM- 9.2
1-10: 1-Midnight story; Batman text story, Grell-a. 2,3-Midnight stories; The Butcher text stories						4.00

NOTE: **Cowan** c-2. **Grell** c-1, 6. **Infantino** a-8.

MS. TREE'S THRILLING DETECTIVE ADVS (Ms. Tree #4 on; also see The Best of Ms. Tree) (Baxter paper #4-9)
Eclipse Comics/Aardvark-Vanaheim 10-18/Renegade Press 19 on: 2/83 - #9, 7/84; #10, 8/84 - #18, 5/85; #19, 6/85 - #50, 6/89

	GD 2.0	VG 4.0	FN 6.0	VF 8.0	VF/NM 9.0	NM- 9.2
1						3.00
2-49: 2-Scythe begins. 9-Last Eclipse & last color issue. 10,11-two-tone						2.50
50-Contains flexi-disc ($3.95, 52pgs.)						4.00
Summer Special 1 (8/86)						3.00
1950s 3-D Crime (7/87, no glasses)-Johnny Dynamite in 3-D						3.00
Mike Mist in 3-D (8/85)-With glasses						3.00

NOTE: **Miller** pin-up 1-4. Johnny Dynamite-r begin #36 by **Morisi**.

MS. VICTORY SPECIAL(Also see Capt. Paragon & Femforce)
Americomics: Jan, 1985 (nd)

	GD	VG	FN	VF	VF/NM	NM-
1						2.50

MUCHA LUCHA (Based on Kids WB animated TV show)
DC Comics: Jun, 2003 - No. 3, Aug, 2003 ($2.25, limited series)

	GD	VG	FN	VF	VF/NM	NM-
1-3-Rikochet, Buena Girl and The Flea app.						2.50

MUGGSY MOUSE (Also see Tick Tock Tales)
Magazine Enterprises: 1951 - No. 3, 1951; No. 4, 1954 - No. 5, 1954; 1963

	GD	VG	FN	VF	VF/NM	NM-
1(A-1 #33)	9	18	27	50	65	80
2(A-1 #36)-Racist-c	12	24	36	67	94	120
3(A-1 #39), 4(A-1 #95), 5(A-1 #99)	7	14	21	37	46	55
Super Reprint #14(1963), I.W. Reprint #1,2 (nd)	2	4	6	8	11	14

MUGGY-DOO, BOY CAT
Stanhall Publ.: July, 1953 - No. 4, Jan, 1954

	GD	VG	FN	VF	VF/NM	NM-
1-Funny animal; Irving Spector-a	9	18	27	47	61	75
2-4	6	12	18	27	33	38
Super Reprint #12('63), 16('64)	2	4	6	8	11	14

MULLKON EMPIRE (See John Jake's...)

MUMMY, THE (See Universal Presents... under Dell Giants & Movie Classics)

MUMMY, THE: VALLEY OF THE GODS (Movie adaption)
Chaos! Comics: May, 2001 - No. 3 ($2.99, limited series)

	GD	VG	FN	VF	VF/NM	NM-
1-Based on "The Mummy Returns" movie; Broome-a; Broome & photo-c						3.00

MUNDEN'S BAR ANNUAL
First Comics: Apr, 1988; 1989 ($2.95/$5.95)

	GD	VG	FN	VF	VF/NM	NM-
1-($2.95)-r/from Grimjack; Fish Police story; Ordway-c						3.00
2-($5.95)-Teenage Mutant Ninja Turtles app.						6.00

MUNSTERS, THE (TV)
Gold Key: Jan, 1965 - No. 16, Jan, 1968 (All photo-c)

	GD	VG	FN	VF	VF/NM	NM-
1 (10134-501)	17	34	51	126	223	320
2	9	18	27	65	113	160
3-5	8	16	24	54	90	125
6-16	7	14	21	47	76	105

MUNSTERS, THE (TV)
TV Comics!: Aug, 1997 - No. 4 ($2.95, B&W)

	GD	VG	FN	VF	VF/NM	NM-
1-4-All have photo-c						3.00
1,4-($7.95)-Variant-c						8.00
2-Variant-c w/Beverly Owens as Marilyn						3.00
Special Comic Con Ed. (7/97, $9.95)						10.00

MUPPET BABIES, THE (TV)(See Star Comics Magazine)
Marvel Comics (Star Comics)/Marvel #18 on: Aug, 1985 - No. 26, July, 1989 (Children's book)

	GD	VG	FN	VF	VF/NM	NM-
1-26						3.00

MUPPETS TAKE MANHATTAN, THE
Marvel Comics (Star Comics): Nov, 1984 - No. 3, Jan, 1985

	GD	VG	FN	VF	VF/NM	NM-
1-3-Movie adapt. r/Marvel Super Special						3.00

MURCIELAGA, SHE-BAT
Heroic Publishing: Jan, 1993 - No. 2, 1993 (B&W)

	GD	VG	FN	VF	VF/NM	NM-
1-($1.50, 28 pgs.)						2.50
2-($2.95, 36 pgs.)-Coated-c						3.00

MURDER CAN BE FUN
Slave Labor Graphics: Feb, 1996 - No. 12 ($2.95, B&W)

	GD 2.0	VG 4.0	FN 6.0	VF 8.0	VF/NM 9.0	NM- 9.2
1-12: 1-Dorkin-c. 2-Vasquez-c.						3.00

MURDER INCORPORATED (My Private Life #16 on)
Fox Feature Syndicate: 1/48 - No. 15, 12/49; (2 No.9's); 6/50 - No. 3, 8/51

	GD 2.0	VG 4.0	FN 6.0	VF 8.0	VF/NM 9.0	NM- 9.2
1 (1st Series); 1,2 have 'For Adults Only' on-c	50	100	150	305	503	700
2-Electrocution story	40	80	120	235	368	500
3-7,9(4/49),10(5/49),11-15	23	46	69	132	209	285
8-Used in **SOTI**, pg. 150	25	50	75	148	232	315
9(3/49)-Possible use in **SOTI**, pg. 145; r/Blue Beetle #56('48)	23	46	69	132	209	285
5(#1, 6/50)(2nd Series)-Formerly My Desire #4; bondage-c	18	36	54	107	169	230
2(8/50)-Morisi-a	16	32	48	94	147	200
3(8/51)-Used in **POP**, pg. 81; Rico-a; lingerie-c/panels	18	36	54	103	162	220

MURDER ME DEAD
El Capitán Books: July, 2000 - No. 9, Oct, 2001 ($2.95/$4.95, B&W)

	GD	VG	FN	VF	VF/NM	NM-
1-8-David Lapham-s/a						3.00
9-($4.95)						5.00

MURDEROUS GANGSTERS
Avon Per./Realistic No. 3 on: Jul, 1951; No. 2, Dec, 1951 - No. 4, Jun, 1952

	GD	VG	FN	VF	VF/NM	NM-
1-Pretty Boy Floyd, Leggs Diamond; 1 pg. Wood-a	45	90	135	275	455	635
2-Baby-Face Nelson; 1 pg. Wood-a; painted-c	29	58	87	170	268	365
3-Painted-c	24	48	72	139	220	300
4- "Murder by Needle" drug story; Mort Lawrence-a; Kinstler-c	30	60	90	174	275	375

MURDER MYSTERIES (Neil Gaiman's...)
Dark Horse Comics: 2002 ($13.95, HC, one-shot)

	GD	VG	FN	VF	VF/NM	NM-
HC-Adapts Gaiman story; P. Craig Russell-script/art						14.00

MURDER TALES (Magazine)
World Famous Publications: V1#10, Nov, 1970 - V1#11, Jan, 1971 (52 pgs.)

	GD	VG	FN	VF	VF/NM	NM-
V1#10-One pg. Frazetta ad	4	8	12	24	37	50
11-Guardineer-r; bondage-c	3	6	9	20	30	40

MUSHMOUSE AND PUNKIN PUSS (TV)
Gold Key: September, 1965 (Hanna-Barbera)

	GD	VG	FN	VF	VF/NM	NM-
1 (10153-509)	8	16	24	58	97	135

MUSIC MAN, THE (See Movie Classics)

MUTANT CHRONICLES (Video game)
Acclaim Comics (Armada): May, 1996 - No. 4, Aug, 1996 ($2.95, lim. series)

	GD	VG	FN	VF	VF/NM	NM-
1-4: Simon Bisley-c on all, Sourcebook (#5)						3.00

MUTANT EARTH (Stan Winston's...)
Image Comics: April, 2002 - No. 4, Jan, 2003 ($2.95)

	GD	VG	FN	VF	VF/NM	NM-
1-4-Flip book w/Realm of the Claw						3.00
Trakk...His Adventures in Mutant Earth TPB (2003, $16.95) r/#1-4; Winston interview						17.00

MUTANT MISADVENTURES OF CLOAK AND DAGGER, THE
(Becomes Cloak and Dagger #14 on)
Marvel Comics: Oct, 1988 - No. 19, Aug, 1991 ($1.25/$1.50)

	GD	VG	FN	VF	VF/NM	NM-
1-8,10-15: 1-X-Factor app. 10-Painted-c. 12-Dr. Doom app. 14-Begin new direction						2.50
9,16-19: 9-(52 pgs.) The Avengers x-over; painted-c. 16-18-Spider-Man x-over. 18-Infinity Gauntlet x-over; Thanos cameo; Ghost Rider app. 19-(52 pgs.) Origin Cloak & Dagger						3.00

NOTE: **Austin** a-12i; c(i)-4, 12, 13; scripts-all. **Russell** a-2i. **Williamson** a-14i-16i; c-15i.

MUTANTS & MISFITS
Silverline Comics (Solson): 1987 - No. 3, 1987 ($1.95)

	GD	VG	FN	VF	VF/NM	NM-
1-3						2.50

MUTANTS VS. ULTRAS
Malibu Comics (Ultraverse): Nov, 1995 ($6.95, one-shot)

	GD	VG	FN	VF	VF/NM	NM-
1-r/Exiles vs. X-Men, Night Man vs. Wolverine, Prime vs. Hulk						7.00

MUTANT, TEXAS: TALES OF SHERIFF IDA RED (Also see Jingle Belle)
Oni Press: May, 2002 - No. 4, Nov, 2002 ($2.95, B&W, limited series)

	GD	VG	FN	VF	VF/NM	NM-
1-4-Paul Dini-s/J. Bone-c/a						3.00
TPB (2003, $11.95) r/#1-4; intro. by Joe Lansdale						12.00

MUTANT 2099
Marvel Comics (Marvel Knights): Nov, 2004 ($2.99, one-shot)

	GD	VG	FN	VF	VF/NM	NM-
1-Kirkman-s/Pat Lee-c						3.00

MUTANT X (See X-Factor)
Marvel Comics: Nov, 1998 - No. 32, June, 2001 ($2.99/$1.99/$2.25)

Mutant X #2 © MAR

Mutt and Jeff #9 © DC

My Greatest Adventure #7 © DC

	GD 2.0	VG 4.0	FN 6.0	VF 8.0	VF/NM 9.0	NM- 9.2
1-($2.99) Alex Summers with alternate world's X-Men						3.00
2-11,13-19-($1.99): 2-Two covers. 5-Man-Spider-c/app.						2.50
12,25-($2.99): 12-Pin-up gallery by Kaluta, Romita, Byrne						3.00
20-24,26-32: 20-Begin $2.25-c. 28-31-Logan-c/app. 32-Last issue						2.50
Annual '99, '00 (5/99,'00, $3.50) '00-Doran-a(p)						3.50
Annual 2001 ($2.99) Story oocurs between #31 & #32; Dracula app.						3.00

MUTANT X (Based on TV show)
Marvel Comics: May, 2002 - Present ($3.50)

	GD 2.0	VG 4.0	FN 6.0	VF 8.0	VF/NM 9.0	NM- 9.2
...: Dangerous Decisions (6/02) -Kuder-s/Immonen-a						3.50
...: Origin (5/02) -Tischman & Chaykin-s/Ferguson-a						3.50

MUTATIS
Marvel Comics (Epic Comics): 1992 - No. 3, 1992 ($2.25, mini-series)

	GD 2.0	VG 4.0	FN 6.0	VF 8.0	VF/NM 9.0	NM- 9.2
1-3: Painted-c						2.50

MUTIES
Marvel Comics: Apr, 2002 - No. 6, Sept, 2002 ($2.50)

	GD 2.0	VG 4.0	FN 6.0	VF 8.0	VF/NM 9.0	NM- 9.2
1-6: 1-Bollars-s/Ferguson-a. 2-Spaziante-a. 3-Haspiel-a. 4-Kanuiga-a						2.50

MUTINY (Stormy Tales of the Seven Seas)
Aragon Magazines: Oct, 1954 - No. 3, Feb, 1955

	GD 2.0	VG 4.0	FN 6.0	VF 8.0	VF/NM 9.0	NM- 9.2
1	16	32	48	92	144	195
2,3: 2-Capt. Mutiny. 3-Bondage-c	14	28	42	76	108	140

MUTINY ON THE BOUNTY (See Classics Illustrated #100 & Movie Comics)

MUTOPIA X (Also see House of M and related titles)
Marvel Comics: Sept, 2005 - No. 5, Jan, 2006 ($2.99, limited series)

	GD 2.0	VG 4.0	FN 6.0	VF 8.0	VF/NM 9.0	NM- 9.2
1-5-Medina-a/Hine-s						3.00
House of M: Mutopia X (2006, $13.99, TPB) r/series						14.00

MUTT AND JEFF (See All-American, All-Flash #18, Cicero's Cat, Comic Cavalcade, Famous Feature Stories, The Funnies, Popular & Xmas Comics)
All American/National 1-103(6/58)/Dell 104(10/58)-115 (10-12/59)/
Harvey 116(2/60)-148: Summer, 1939 (nd) - No. 148, Nov, 1965

	GD 2.0	VG 4.0	FN 6.0	VF 8.0	VF/NM 9.0	NM- 9.2
1(nn)-Lost Wheels	138	276	414	863	1432	2000
2(nn)-Charging Bull (Summer, 1940, nd; on sale 6/20/40)						
	68	136	204	425	705	985
3(nn)-Bucking Broncos (Summer, 1941, nd)	49	98	147	299	492	685
4(Winter, '41), 5(Summer, '42)	45	90	135	275	450	625
6-10: 6-Includes Minute Man Answers the Call	26	52	78	152	239	325
11-20: 20-X-Mas-c	18	36	54	105	165	225
21-30	14	28	42	82	121	160
31-50: 32-X-Mas-c	12	24	36	67	94	120
51-75-Last Fisher issue. 53-Last 52 pgs.	10	20	30	54	72	90
76-99,101-103: 76-Last pre-code issue(1/55)	5	10	15	32	51	70
100	5	10	15	35	55	75
104-115,132-148	4	8	12	26	41	55
116-131-Richie Rich app.	4	8	12	28	44	60
...Jokes 1-3(8/60-61, Harvey)-84 pgs.; Richie Rich in all; Little Dot in #2,3; Lotta in #2						
	4	8	12	28	44	60
...New Jokes 1-4(10/63-11/65, Harvey)-68 pgs.; Richie Rich in #1-3; Stumbo in #1						
	4	8	12	22	34	45

NOTE: *Most all issues by **Al Smith**. Issues from 1963 on have **Fisher** reprints. Clarification: early issues signed by Fisher are mostly drawn by Smith.*

MY BROTHERS' KEEPER
Spire Christian Comics (Fleming H. Revell Co.): 1973 (35/49¢, 36 pgs.)

	GD 2.0	VG 4.0	FN 6.0	VF 8.0	VF/NM 9.0	NM- 9.2
nn	2	4	6	8	10	12

MY CONFESSIONS (My Confession #7&8; formerly Western True Crime; A Spectacular Feature Magazine #11)
Fox Feature Syndicate: No. 7, Aug, 1949 - No. 10, Jan-Feb, 1950

	GD 2.0	VG 4.0	FN 6.0	VF 8.0	VF/NM 9.0	NM- 9.2
7-Wood-a (10 pgs.)	24	48	72	139	220	300
8,9: 8-Harrison/Wood-a (19 pgs.). 9-Wood-a	22	44	66	126	198	270
10	12	24	36	67	94	120

MY DATE COMICS (Teen-age)
Hillman Periodicals: July, 1947 - V1#4, Jan, 1948 (2nd Romance comic; see Young Romance)

	GD 2.0	VG 4.0	FN 6.0	VF 8.0	VF/NM 9.0	NM- 9.2
1-S&K-c/a	38	76	114	219	347	475
2-4-S&K-c/a; Dan Barry-a	26	52	78	150	235	320

MY DESIRE (Formerly Jo-Jo Comics; becomes Murder, Inc. #5 on)
Fox Feature Syndicate: No. 30, Aug, 1949 - No. 4, April, 1950

	GD 2.0	VG 4.0	FN 6.0	VF 8.0	VF/NM 9.0	NM- 9.2
30(#1)	17	34	51	98	154	210
31 (#2, 10/49),3(2/50),4	13	26	39	74	105	135
31 (Canadian edition)	8	16	24	44	57	70
32(12/49)-Wood-a	21	42	63	120	188	255

MY DIARY (Becomes My Friend Irma #3 on?)
Marvel Comics (A Lovers Mag.): Dec, 1949 - No. 2, Mar, 1950

	GD 2.0	VG 4.0	FN 6.0	VF 8.0	VF/NM 9.0	NM- 9.2
1,2-Photo-c	15	30	45	85	130	175

MY EXPERIENCE (Formerly All Top; becomes Judy Canova #23 on)
Fox Feature Syndicate: No. 19, Sept, 1949 - No. 22, Mar, 1950

	GD 2.0	VG 4.0	FN 6.0	VF 8.0	VF/NM 9.0	NM- 9.2
19,21: 19-Wood-a. 21-Wood-a(2)	26	52	78	150	235	320
20	14	28	42	76	108	140
22-Wood-a (9 pgs.)	22	44	66	126	198	270

MY FAITH IN FRANKIE
DC Comics (Vertigo): March, 2004 - No. 4, June, 2004 ($2.95, limited series)

	GD 2.0	VG 4.0	FN 6.0	VF 8.0	VF/NM 9.0	NM- 9.2
1-4-Mike Carey-s/Sonny Liew & Marc Hempel-a						3.00
TPB (2004, $6.95, digest-size) r/series in B&W; Dead Boy Detectives preview						7.00

MY FAVORITE MARTIAN (TV)
Gold Key: 1/64; No.2, 7/64 - No. 9, 10/66 (No. 1,3-9 have photo-c)

	GD 2.0	VG 4.0	FN 6.0	VF 8.0	VF/NM 9.0	NM- 9.2
1-Russ Manning-a	12	24	36	87	156	225
2	7	14	21	49	80	110
3-9	6	12	18	41	66	90

MY FRIEND IRMA (Radio/TV) (Formerly My Diary? and/or Western Life Romances?)
Marvel/Atlas Comics (BFP): No. 3, June, 1950 - No. 47, Dec, 1954; No. 48, Feb, 1955

	GD 2.0	VG 4.0	FN 6.0	VF 8.0	VF/NM 9.0	NM- 9.2
3-Dan DeCarlo-a in all; 52 pgs. begin, end ?	18	36	54	105	165	225
4-Kurtzman-a (10 pgs.)	18	36	54	107	169	230
5- "Egghead Doodle" by Kurtzman (4 pgs.)	15	30	45	85	130	175
6,8-10: 9-Paper dolls, 1 pg.; Millie app. (5 pgs.)	12	24	36	69	97	125
7-One pg. Kurtzman-a	13	26	39	72	101	130
11-23: 23-One pg. Frazetta-a	9	18	27	52	69	85
24-48: 41,48-Stan Lee & Dan DeCarlo app.	8	16	24	44	57	70

MY GIRL PEARL
Atlas Comics: 4/55 - #4, 10/55; #5, 7/57 - #6, 9/57; #7, 8/60 - #11, ?/61

	GD 2.0	VG 4.0	FN 6.0	VF 8.0	VF/NM 9.0	NM- 9.2
1-Dan DeCarlo-c/a in #1-6	15	30	45	85	130	175
2	9	18	27	52	69	85
3-6	8	16	24	42	54	65
7-11	4	8	12	26	41	55

MY GREATEST ADVENTURE (Doom Patrol #86 on)
National Periodical Publications: Jan-Feb, 1955 - No. 85, Feb, 1964

	GD 2.0	VG 4.0	FN 6.0	VF 8.0	VF/NM 9.0	NM- 9.2
1-Before CCA	125	250	375	875	1788	2700
2	46	92	138	368	672	975
3-5	34	68	102	255	465	675
6-10: 6-Science fiction format begins	28	56	84	227	384	540
11-14: 12-1st S.A. issue	20	40	60	150	268	385
15-17: Kirby-a in all	22	44	66	164	292	420
18-Kirby-c/a	25	50	75	186	333	480
19,22-25	17	34	51	126	223	320
20,21,28-Kirby-a	20	40	60	150	268	385
26,27,29,30	13	26	39	93	164	235
31-40	11	22	33	75	133	190
41,42,44-57,59	9	18	27	64	110	155
43-Kirby-a	10	20	30	68	119	170
58,60,61-Toth-a; Last 10¢ issue	9	18	27	65	113	160
62-76,78,79: 79-Promotes "Legion of the Strange" for next issue; renamed Doom Patrol for #80	7	14	21	48	80	110
77-Toth-a; Robotman prototype	7	14	21	50	83	115
80-(6/63)-Intro/origin Doom Patrol and begin series; origin & 1st app. Negative Man, Elasti-Girl & S.A. Robotman	45	90	135	360	655	950
81,85-Toth-a	17	34	51	128	227	325
82-84	16	32	48	118	209	300

NOTE: **Anderson** a-42. **Cameron** a-24. **Colan** a-77. **Meskin** a-25, 26, 32, 39, 45, 50, 56, 57, 61, 64, 70, 73, 74, 76, 79; c-76. **Moreira** a-11, 12, 15, 17, 20, 23, 25, 27, 37, 40-43, 46, 48, 55-57, 59, 60, 62-65, 67, 69, 70; c-1-4, 7-10. **Roussos** c/a-71-73. **Wildey** a-32.

MY GREAT LOVE (Becomes Will Rogers Western #5)
Fox Feature Syndicate: Oct, 1949 - No. 4, Apr, 1950

	GD 2.0	VG 4.0	FN 6.0	VF 8.0	VF/NM 9.0	NM- 9.2
1	15	30	45	88	137	185
2-4	10	20	30	56	76	95

MY INTIMATE AFFAIR (Inside Crime #3)
Fox Feature Syndicate: Mar, 1950 - No. 2, May, 1950

	GD 2.0	VG 4.0	FN 6.0	VF 8.0	VF/NM 9.0	NM- 9.2
1	15	30	45	88	137	185
2	10	20	30	56	76	95

MY LIFE (Formerly Meet Corliss Archer)
Fox Feature Syndicate: No. 4, Sept, 1948 - No. 15, July, 1950

My Life #8 © FOX

My Love #10 © MAR

My Own Romance #76 © MAR

	GD 2.0	VG 4.0	FN 6.0	VF 8.0	VF/NM 9.0	NM- 9.2
4-Used in **SOTI**, pg. 39; Kamen/Feldstein-a	40	80	120	240	383	525
5-Kamen-a	24	48	72	139	220	300
6-Kamen/Feldstein-a	26	52	78	152	239	325
7-Wood-a; wash cover	21	42	63	124	195	265
8,9,11-15	12	24	36	69	97	125
10-Wood-a	19	38	57	112	176	240

MY LITTLE MARGIE (TV)
Charlton Comics: July, 1954 - No. 54, Nov, 1964

1-Photo front/back-c	37	74	111	213	339	465
2-Photo front/back-c	18	36	54	103	162	220
3-7,10	12	24	36	67	94	120
8,9-Infinity-c	12	24	36	69	97	125
11-14: Part-photo-c (#13, 8/56)	10	20	30	58	79	100
15-19	10	20	30	54	72	90
20-(25¢, 100 pg. issue)	15	30	45	85	130	175
21-40: 40-Last 10¢ issue	5	10	15	32	51	70
41-53	4	8	12	28	44	60
54-(11/64) Beatles on cover; lead story spoofs the Beatle haircut craze of the 1960's; Beatles app. (scarce)	16	32	48	118	209	300

NOTE: Doll cut-outs in 32, 33, 40, 45, 50.

MY LITTLE MARGIE'S BOY FRIENDS (TV) (Freddy V2#12 on)
Charlton Comics: Aug, 1955 - No. 11, Apr?, 1958

1-Has several Archie swipes	15	30	45	84	127	170
2	9	18	27	52	69	85
3-11	8	16	24	44	57	70

MY LITTLE MARGIE'S FASHIONS (TV)
Charlton Comics: Feb, 1959 - No. 5, Nov, 1959

1	14	28	42	76	108	140
2-5	8	16	24	44	57	70

MY LOVE (Becomes Two Gun Western #5 (11/50) on)
Marvel Comics (CLDS): July, 1949 - No. 4, Apr, 1950 (All photo-c)

1	15	30	45	88	137	185
2,3	11	22	33	60	83	105
4-Bettie Page photo-c (see Cupid #2)	39	78	117	225	355	485

MY LOVE
Marvel Comics Group: Sept, 1969 - No. 39, Mar, 1976

1	6	12	18	41	66	90
2-9: 4-6-Colan-a	4	8	12	22	34	45
10-Williamson-r/My Own Romance #71; Kirby-a	4	8	12	23	36	48
11-13,15-19	3	6	9	18	27	35
14-(52 pgs.)-Woodstock-c/sty; Morrow-c/a; Kirby/Colletta-r	5	10	15	30	48	65
20-Starlin-a	3	6	9	20	30	40
21,22,24-27,29-38: 38-Reprints	3	6	9	16	23	30
23-Steranko-r/Our Love Story #5	3	6	9	20	30	40
28-Kirby-a	3	6	9	18	27	35
39-Last issue; reprints	3	6	9	18	27	35
Special 1 (12/71)(52 pgs.)	4	8	12	28	44	60

NOTE: **John Buscema** a-1-7, 10, 18-21, 22(2), 24r, 25r, 29r, 34r, 36r, 37r, Spec. (r)(4); c-13, 15, 25, 27, Spec. **Colan** a-4, 5, 6, 8, 9, 16, 17, 20, 21, 22, 24r, 27r, 30r, 35r, 39r. **Colan/Everett** a-13, 15, 16, 27(r#13). **Kirby** a-(r)-10, 14, 26, 28. **Romita** a-13, 19, 20, 25, 34, 38; c-1-3, 15.

MY LOVE AFFAIR (March of Crime #7 on)
Fox Feature Syndicate: July, 1949 - No. 6, May, 1950

1	15	30	45	88	137	185
2	10	20	30	56	76	95
3-6-Wood-a. 5-(3/50)-Becomes Love Stories #6	18	36	54	107	169	230

MY LOVE LIFE (Formerly Zegra)
Fox Feature Synd.: No. 6, June, 1949 - No. 13, Aug, 1950; No. 13, Sept, 1951

6-Kamenish-a	15	30	45	88	137	185
7-13	10	20	30	58	79	100
13 (9/51)(Formerly My Story #12)	10	20	30	54	72	90

MY LOVE MEMOIRS (Formerly Women Outlaws; Hunted #13 on)
Fox Feature Syndicate: No. 9, Nov, 1949 - No. 12, May, 1950

9,11,12-Wood-a	18	36	54	107	169	230
10	10	20	30	58	79	100

MY LOVE SECRET (Formerly Phantom Lady; Animal Crackers #31)
Fox Feature Syndicate/M. S. Distr.: No. 24, June, 1949 - No. 30, June, 1950; No. 53, 1954

24-Kamen/Feldstein-a	19	38	57	109	172	235
25-Possible caricature of Wood on-c?	13	26	39	74	105	135

	GD 2.0	VG 4.0	FN 6.0	VF 8.0	VF/NM 9.0	NM- 9.2
26,28-Wood-a	18	36	54	107	169	230
27,29,30: 30-Photo-c	11	22	33	62	86	110
53-(Reprint, M.S. Distr.) 1954? nd given; formerly Western Thrillers; becomes Crimes by Women #54; photo-c	7	14	21	35	43	50

MY LOVE STORY (Hoot Gibson Western #5 on)
Fox Feature Syndicate: Sept, 1949 - No. 4, Mar, 1950

1	15	30	45	88	137	185
2	10	20	30	56	76	95
3,4-Wood-a	18	36	54	107	169	230

MY LOVE STORY
Atlas Comics (GPS): April, 1956 - No. 9, Aug, 1957

1	14	28	42	76	108	140
2	8	16	24	44	57	70
3,7: Matt Baker-a. 7-Toth-a	10	20	30	58	79	100
4-6,8,9	8	16	24	42	54	65

NOTE: **Brewster** a-3. **Colletta** a-1(2), 3, 4(2), 5; c-3.

MY NAME IS CHAOS
DC Comics: 1992 - No. 4, 1992 ($4.95, limited series, 52 pgs.)

Book 1-4: Tom Veitch scripts; painted-c						5.00

MY NAME IS HOLOCAUST
DC Comics: May, 1995 - No. 5, Sept, 1995 ($2.50, limited series)

1-5						2.50

MY ONLY LOVE
Charlton Comics: July, 1975 - No. 9, Nov, 1976

1	3	6	9	14	19	24
2,4-9	2	4	6	9	13	16
3-Toth-a	2	4	6	11	16	20

MY OWN ROMANCE (Formerly My Romance; Teen-Age Romance #77 on)
Marvel/Atlas (MjPC/RCM No. 4-59/ZPC No. 60-76): No. 4, Mar, 1949 - No. 76, July, 1960

4-Photo-c	15	30	45	90	140	190
5-10: 5,6,8-10-Photo-c	11	22	33	60	83	105
11-20: 14-Powell-a	10	20	30	54	72	90
21-42,55: 42-Last precode (2/55). 55-Toth-a	9	18	27	50	65	80
43-54,56-60	5	10	15	30	48	65
61-70,72,73,75,76	4	8	12	26	41	55
71-Williamson-a	5	10	15	32	51	70
74-Kirby-a	5	10	15	32	51	70

NOTE: **Brewster** a-59. **Colletta** a-45(2), 48, 50, 55, 57(2), 59; c-58i, 59, 61. **Everett** a-25; c-58p. **Kirby** c-71, 75, 76. **Morisi** a-18. **Orlando** a-61. **Romita** a-36. **Tuska** a-10.

MY PAL DIZZY (See Comic Books, Series I)

MY PAST (...Confessions) (Formerly Western Thrillers)
Fox Feature Syndicate: No. 7, Aug, 1949 - No. 11, Apr, 1950 (Crimes Inc. #12)

7	15	30	45	88	137	185
8-10	10	20	30	56	76	95
11-Wood-a	18	36	54	107	169	230

MY PERSONAL PROBLEM
Ajax/Farrell/Steinway Comic: 11/55; No. 2, 2/56; No. 3, 9/56 - No. 4, 11/56; 10/57 - No. 3, 5/58

1	9	18	27	52	69	85
2-4	7	14	21	35	43	50
1-3('57-'58)-Steinway	6	12	18	28	34	40

MY PRIVATE LIFE (Formerly Murder, Inc.; becomes Pedro #18)
Fox Feature Syndicate: No. 16, Feb, 1950 - No. 17, April, 1950

16,17	14	28	42	78	112	145

MYRA NORTH (See The Comics, Crackajack Funnies & Red Ryder)
Dell Publishing Co.: No. 3, Jan, 1940

Four Color 3	95	190	285	594	985	1375

MY REAL LOVE
Standard Comics: No. 5, June, 1952 (Photo-c)

5-Toth-a, 3 pgs.; Tuska, Cardy, Vern Greene-a	14	28	42	76	108	140

MY ROMANCE (Becomes My Own Romance #4 on)
Marvel Comics (RCM): Sept, 1948 - No. 3, Jan, 1949

1	18	36	54	103	162	220
2,3: 2-Anti-Wertham editorial (11/48)	12	24	36	67	94	120

MY ROMANTIC ADVENTURES (Formerly Romantic Adventures)
American Comics Group: No. 68, 8/56 - No. 115, 12/60; No. 116, 7/61 - No. 138, 3/64

My Secret #3 © SUPR

Mysteries Weird and Strange #7 © SUPR

Mysterious Adventures #3 © Story

	GD 2.0	VG 4.0	FN 6.0	VF 8.0	VF/NM 9.0	NM- 9.2
68	8	16	24	40	50	60
69-85	6	12	18	31	38	45
86-Three pg. Williamson-a (2/58)	8	16	24	42	54	65
87-100	3	6	9	18	27	35
101-138	3	6	9	15	21	26

NOTE: *Whitney* art in most issues.

MY SECRET (Becomes Our Secret #4 on)
Superior Comics, Ltd.: Aug, 1949 - No. 3, Oct, 1949

1	15	30	45	83	124	165
2,3	11	22	33	62	86	110

MY SECRET AFFAIR (Becomes Martin Kane #4)
Hero Book (Fox Feature Syndicate): Dec, 1949 - No. 3, April, 1950

1-Harrison/Wood-a (10 pgs.)	23	46	69	130	205	280
2,3-Wood-a	18	36	54	107	169	230

MY SECRET CONFESSION
Sterling Comics: September, 1955

1-Sekowsky-a	9	18	27	50	65	80

MY SECRET LIFE (Formerly Western Outlaws; Romeo Tubbs #26 on)
Fox Feature Syndicate: No. 22, July, 1949 - No. 27, July, 1950; No. 27, 9/51

22	13	26	39	72	101	130
23,26-Wood-a, 6 pgs.	18	36	54	107	169	230
24,25,27	11	22	33	62	86	110
27 (9/51)	10	20	30	54	72	90

NOTE: The title was changed to Romeo Tubbs after #25 even though #26 & 27 did come out.

MY SECRET LIFE (Formerly Young Lovers; Sue & Sally Smith #48)
Charlton Comics: No. 19, Aug, 1957 - No. 47, Sept, 1962

19	4	8	12	22	34	45
20-35	3	6	9	15	21	26
36-47: 44-Last 10¢ issue	2	4	6	13	18	22

MY SECRET MARRIAGE
Superior Comics, Ltd.: May, 1953 - No. 24, July, 1956 (Canadian)

1	14	28	42	76	108	140
2	8	16	24	44	57	70
3-24	7	14	21	37	46	55
I.W. Reprint #9	2	4	6	8	11	14

NOTE: Many issues contain **Kamen-ish** art.

MY SECRET ROMANCE (Becomes A Star Presentation #3)
Hero Book (Fox Feature Syndicate): Jan, 1950 - No. 2, March, 1950

1	15	30	45	86	133	180
2-Wood-a	18	36	54	107	169	230

MY SECRETS (Magazine)
Atlas/Seaboard: Feb, 1975 (B&W, 68 pgs.)

Vol. 1 #1	5	10	15	35	55	75

MY SECRET STORY (Formerly Captain Kidd #25; Sabu #30 on)
Fox Feature Syndicate: No. 26, Oct, 1949 - No. 29, April, 1950

26	15	30	45	84	127	170
27-29	10	20	30	54	72	90

MYSTERIES (...Weird & Strange)
Superior/Dynamic Publ. (Randall Publ. Ltd.): May, 1953 - No. 11, Jan, 1955

1-All horror stories	41	82	123	250	400	550
2-A-Bomb blast story	26	52	78	152	239	325
3-11: 10-Kamenish-c/a reprinted from Strange Mysteries #2; cover is based on a panel in Strange Mysteries #2	23	46	69	132	209	285

MYSTERIES IN SPACE (See Fireside Book Series)

MYSTERIES OF SCOTLAND YARD (Also see A-1 Comics)
Magazine Enterprises: No. 121, 1954 (one shot)

A-1 121-Reprinted from Manhunt (5 stories)	15	30	45	85	130	175

MYSTERIES OF UNEXPLORED WORLDS (See Blue Bird)(Becomes Son of Vulcan V2#49 on)
Charlton Comics: Aug, 1956; No. 2, Jan, 1957 - No. 48, Sept, 1965

1	37	74	111	214	340	465
2-No Ditko	15	30	45	88	137	185
3,4,8,9 Ditko-a. 3-Diko c/a (4). 4-Ditko c/a (2).	29	58	87	170	268	365
5,6,10,11: 5,6-Ditko-c/a (all). 10-Ditko-c/a(4). 11-Ditko-c/a(3); signed J. Kotdi	31	62	93	178	282	385
7-(2/58, 68 pgs.) 4 stories w/Ditko-a	34	68	102	197	311	425

12,19,21-24,26-Ditko-a. 12-Ditko sty (3); Baker story "The Charm Bracelet."

	GD 2.0	VG 4.0	FN 6.0	VF 8.0	VF/NM 9.0	NM- 9.2
	23	46	69	130	205	280
13-18,20	10	20	30	56	76	95
25,27-30	5	10	15	32	51	70
31-45	4	8	12	26	41	55
46(5/65)-Son of Vulcan begins (origin/1st app.)	4	8	12	28	44	60
47,48	4	8	12	23	34	45

NOTE: *Ditko* c-3-6, 10, 11, 19, 21-24. Covers to #19, 21-24 reprint story panels.

MYSTERIOUS ADVENTURES
Story Comics: Mar, 1951 - No. 24, Mar, 1955; No. 25, Aug, 1955

1-All horror stories	68	136	204	425	705	985
2	40	80	120	235	368	500
3,4,6,10	37	74	111	214	340	465
5-Bondage-c	40	80	120	235	368	500
7-Dagger in eye panel; dismemberment stories	42	84	126	258	422	585
8-Eyeball story	49	98	147	299	492	685
9-Extreme violence (8/52)	40	80	120	240	383	525
11(12/52)-Used in SOTI, pg. 84	40	80	120	240	383	525
12,14: 14-E.C. Old Witch swipe	37	74	111	214	340	465
13-Classic skull-c	42	84	126	258	422	585
15-21: 18-Used in Senate Investigative report, pgs. 5,6; E.C. swipe/TFTC #35; The Coffin-Keeper & Corpse (hosts). 20-Used by Wertham in the Senate hearings. 21-Bondage/beheading-c	41	82	123	250	400	550
22- "Cinderella" parody	37	74	111	214	340	465
23-Disbrow-a (6 pgs.); E.C. swipe "The Mystery Keeper's Tale" (host) and "Mother Ghoul's Nursery Tale"	37	74	111	214	340	465
24,25	26	52	78	152	239	325

NOTE: *Tothish* art by *Ross Andru*-22, 23. *Bache* a-8. *Cameron* a-5-7. *Harrison* a-12. *Hollingsworth* a-3-8, 12. *Schaffenberger* a-24, 25. *Wildey* a-15, 17.

MYSTERIOUS ISLAND
Dell Publishing Co.: No. 1213, July-Sept, 1961

Four Color 1213-Movie, photo-c	8	16	24	56	93	130

MYSTERIOUS ISLE
Dell Publishing Co.: Nov-Jan, 1963/64 (Jules Verne)

1	3	6	9	20	30	40

MYSTERIOUS RIDER, THE (See Zane Grey, 4-Color 301)

MYSTERIOUS STORIES (Formerly Horror From the Tomb #1)
Premier Magazines: No. 2, Dec-Jan, 1954-1955 - No. 7, Dec, 1955

2-Woodbridge-c; last pre-code issue	48	96	144	293	484	675
3-Woodbridge-c/a	34	68	102	195	308	420
4-7: 5-Cinderella parody. 6-Woodbridge-c	31	62	93	178	282	385

NOTE: *Hollingsworth* a-2, 4.

MYSTERIOUS STRANGER
DC Comics: Aug/Sept. 1952

nn - Ashcan comic, not distributed to newsstands, only for in-house use. Cover art is All Star Western #60 with interior being Sensation Comic #100. A FN/VF copy sold for $2,357.50 in 2002.

MYSTERIOUS SUSPENSE (Also see Blue Beetle #1 (1967))
Charlton Comics: Oct, 1968 (12¢)

1-Return of the Question by Ditko (c/a)	6	12	18	43	69	95

MYSTERIOUS TRAVELER (See Tales of the...)

MYSTERIOUS TRAVELER COMICS (Radio)
Trans-World Publications: Nov, 1948

1-Powell-c/a(2), Poe adaptation, "Tell Tale Heart"	57	114	171	356	591	825

MYSTERY COMICS
William H. Wise & Co.: 1944 - No. 4, 1944 (No months given)

1-The Magnet, The Silver Knight, Brad Spencer, Wonderman, Dick Devins, King of Futuria, & Zudo the Jungle Boy begin (all 1st app.); Schomburg-c on all	121	242	363	756	1253	1750
2-Bondage-c	69	138	207	431	716	1000
3,4: 3-Lance Lewis, Space Detective begins (1st app.); Robot-c. 4(V2#1 inside)	62	124	186	388	644	900

MYSTERY COMICS DIGEST
Gold Key/Whitman?: Mar, 1972 - No. 26, Oct, 1975

1-Ripley's Believe It or Not; reprint of Ripley's #1 origin Ra-Ka-Tep the Mummy; Wood-a	4	8	12	23	36	48

2-9: 2-Boris Karloff Tales of Mystery; Wood-a; 1st app. Werewolf Count Wulfstein. 3-Twilight Zone (TV); Crandall, Toth & George Evans-a; 1st app. Tragg & Simbar the Lion Lord; (2) Crandall/Frazetta-r/Twilight Zone #1 4-Ripley's Believe It or Not; 1st app. Baron Tibor, the Vampire. 5-Boris Karloff Tales of Mystery; 1st app. Dr. Spektor. 6-Twilight Zone

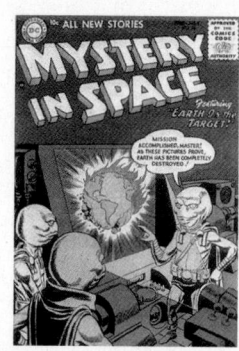

Mystery in Space #26 © DC

Mystery Tales #9 © MAR

Mystic #10 © CRO

	GD 2.0	VG 4.0	FN 6.0	VF 8.0	VF/NM 9.0	NM- 9.2		GD 2.0	VG 4.0	FN 6.0	VF 8.0	VF/NM 9.0	NM- 9.2

(TV); 1st app. U.S. Marshal Reid & Sir Duane; Evans-r. 7-Ripley's Believe It or Not; origin
The Lurker in the Swamp; 1st app. Duroc. 8-Boris Karloff Tales of Mystery; McWilliams-r;
Orlando-r. 9-Twilight Zone (TV); Williamson, Crandall, McWilliams-a; 2nd Tragg app.;Torres,
Evans, Heck/Tuska-r
| | | | 3 | 6 | 9 | 18 | 27 | 35 |

10-26: 10,13-Ripley's Believe It or Not: 13-Orlando-r. 11,14-Boris Karloff Tales of Mystery.
14-1st app. Xorkon. 12,15-Twilight Zone (TV). 16,19,22,25-Ripley's Believe It or Not.
17-Boris Karloff Tales of Mystery; Williamson-r; Orlando-r. 18,21,24-Twilight Zone (TV).
20,23,26-Boris Karloff Tales of Mystery
| | | | 3 | 6 | 9 | 15 | 21 | 26 |

NOTE: Dr. Spektor app.-#5, 10-12, 21. Durak app.-#15. Duroc app.-#14 (later called Durak). King George 1st app.-#8.

MYSTERY IN SPACE (Also see Fireside Book Series and Pulp Fiction Library: ...)
National Periodical Pub.: 4-5/51 - No. 110, 9/66; No. 111, 9/80 - No. 117, 3/81 (#1-3: 52 pgs.)

1-Frazetta-a, 8 pgs.; Knights of the Galaxy begins, ends #8
	238	476	714	2083	3892	5700
2	85	170	255	723	1337	1950
3	67	134	201	570	1060	1550
4,5	55	110	165	468	872	1275
6-10: 7-Toth-a	44	88	132	352	639	925
11-15	35	70	105	263	482	700

16-18,20-25: Interplanetary Insurance feature by Infantino in all. 21-1st app. Space Cabbie.
| 24-Last pre-code issue | 30 | 60 | 90 | 225 | 413 | 600 |
| 19-Virgil Finlay-a | 32 | 64 | 96 | 240 | 445 | 650 |

26-40: 26-Space Cabbie feature begins. 34-1st S.A. issue
	25	50	75	184	330	475
41-52: 47-Space Cabbie feature ends	19	38	57	141	251	360
53-Adam Strange begins (8/59, 10pg. sty); robot-c	152	304	456	1315	2458	3600
54	44	88	132	352	639	925
55-Grey tone-c	40	80	120	300	550	800
56-60: 59-Kane/Anderson-a	22	44	66	165	295	425

61-71: 61-1st app. Adam Strange foe Ulthoon. 62-1st app. A.S. foe Mortan. 63-Origin Vandor.
66-Star Rovers begin (1st app.). 68-1st app. Dust Devils (6/61). 69-1st Mailbag. 70-2nd
app. Dust Devils. 71-Last 10¢ issue
	17	34	51	128	227	325
72-74,76-80	12	24	36	86	153	220
75-JLA x-over in Adam Strange (5/62)(sequel to J.L.A. #3)						
	23	46	69	169	302	435
81-86	10	20	30	68	119	170

87-(11/63)-Adam Strange/Hawkman double feat begins; 3rd Hawkman tryout series
	17	34	51	126	223	320
88-Adam Strange & Hawkman stories	15	30	45	111	198	285
89-Adam Strange & Hawkman stories	15	30	45	107	191	275

90-Adam Strange & Hawkman team-up for 1st time (3/64); Hawkman moves to own title
next month
| | 17 | 34 | 51 | 126 | 223 | 320 |

91-102: 91-End Infantino art on Adam Strange; double-length Adam Strange story. 92-Space
Ranger begins (6/64), ends #103. 92-94,96,98-Space Ranger-c. 94,98-Adam Strange/
Space Ranger team-up. 102-Adam Strange ends (no Space Ranger)
	6	12	18	43	69	95
103-Origin Ultra, the Multi-Alien; last Space Ranger	6	12	18	39	62	85
104-110: 110-(9/66)-Last 12¢ issue	5	10	15	30	48	65
V17#111(9/80)-117: 117-Newton-a(3 pgs.)	1	3	4	6	8	10

NOTE: Anderson-a-2, 4, 8-10, 12-17, 19, 45-48, 51, 57. Bondage-c-3, 7, 8, 25, 27-29, 31. Blue Beetle c-7, 8, 10-31. D-13 Secret Agent c-6.
108, 110. Aparo-a-111. Austin-a-112i. Bolland-a-115. Craig-a-114, 116. Ditko-a-111, 114-116. Drucker-a-19, 32.
Elias-a-98, 102, 103. Golden-a-113p. Sid Greene-a-78, 91. Infantino-a-1-8, 11, 14-25, 27-46, 48, 49, 51, 53-91,
103, 117; c-60-86, 88, 90, 91, 105, 107. Gil Kane-a-14p, 15p, 18p, 19p, 26p, 29-59p(most); c-61-65, 69. Kirby-a-
Kubert-a-113; c-111-115. Moreira-a-27, 28. Rogers-a-111. Sekowsky-a-52. Simon & Kirby-a-4(2 pgs.). Spiegle-
a-111, 114. Starlin-c-116. Sutton-a-113. Tuska-a-115p, 117p.

MYSTERY IN SPACE
DC Comics: Nov, 2006 - No. 8, Jul, 2007 ($3.99, limited series)

| 1-8: 1-Captain Comet's rebirth; Starlin-s/Shane Davis-a; The Weird by Starlin | | | | | | 4.00 |
| 1-Variant cover by Neal Adams | | | | | | 10.00 |

MYSTERY MEN COMICS
Fox Features Syndicate: Aug, 1939 - No. 31, Feb, 1942

1-Intro. & 1st app. The Blue Beetle, The Green Mask, Rex Dexter of Mars by Briefer, Zanzibar
by Tuska, Lt. Drake, D-13-Secret Agent by Powell, Chen Chang, Wing Turner, & Captain
Denny Scott
	1000	2000	3000	7000	12,250	17,500
2-Robot & sci/fi-c (2nd Robot-c w/Movie #6)	333	666	1000	2165	3833	5500
3 (10/39)-Classic Lou Fine-c	423	846	1269	2907	5104	7300
4,5: 4-Capt. Savage begins (11/39)	262	524	786	1638	2719	3800
5-Tuska-c	221	442	663	1381	2291	3200
7-1st Blue Beetle-c app.	276	552	828	1725	2863	4000
8-Lou Fine-c	248	496	744	1550	2575	3600
9-The Moth begins; Lou Fine-c	124	248	372	775	1288	1800
10-12: All Joe Simon-c. 10-Wing Turner by Kirby; Simon-c. 11-Intro. Domino						
	102	204	306	638	1057	1475
13-Intro. Lynx & sidekick Blackie (8/40)	66	132	198	413	682	950

14-18	62	124	186	388	644	900
19-Intro. & 1st app. Miss X (ends #21)	66	132	198	413	682	950
20-31: 26-The Wraith begins	60	120	180	375	625	875

NOTE: Briefer a-1-15, 20, 24; c-9. Cuidera a-22. Lou Fine c-1-5,8,9. Powell a-1-15, 24. Simon c-10-12. Tuska
a-1-16, 22, 24, 27; c-6. Bondage-c 1, 3, 7, 8, 25, 27-29, 31. Blue Beetle c-7, 8, 10-31. D-13 Secret Agent c-6.
Green Mask c-1, 3-5. Rex Dexter of Mars c-2, 9.

MYSTERY MEN MOVIE ADAPTION
Dark Horse Comics: July, 1999 - No. 2, Aug, 1999 ($2.95, mini-series)

| 1,2-Fingerman-s; photo-c | | | | | | 3.00 |

MYSTERY PLAY, THE
DC Comics (Vertigo): 1994 ($19.95, one-shot)

| nn-Hardcover-Morrison-s/Muth-painted art | | | | | | 25.00 |
| Softcover ($9.95)-New Muth cover | | | | | | 10.00 |

MYSTERY TALES
Atlas Comics (20CC): Mar, 1952 - No. 54, Aug, 1957

| 1-Horror/weird stories in all | 88 | 176 | 264 | 550 | 913 | 1275 |
| 2-Krigstein-a | 46 | 92 | 138 | 281 | 466 | 650 |

3-10: 6-A-Bomb panel. 10-Story similar to "The Assassin" from Shock SuspenStories
| | 41 | 82 | 123 | 256 | 416 | 575 |

11,13-21: 14-Maneely s/f story. 20-Electric chair issue. 21-Matt Fox-a;
decapitation story
	30	60	90	174	275	375
12,22: 12-Matt Fox-a. 22-Forte/Matt Fox-c; a(i)	34	68	102	195	308	420
23-26 (2/55)-Last precode issue	24	48	72	139	220	300

27,29-35,37,38,41-43,48,49: 43-Morisi story contains Frazetta art swipes from Untamed Love
	19	38	57	109	172	235
28,36,39,40,45: 28-Jack Katz-a. 36,39-Krigstein-a. 40,45-Ditko-a (#45 is 3 pgs. only)						
	20	40	60	115	180	245
44,51-Williamson/Krenkel-a	21	42	63	122	191	260
46-Williamson/Krenkel-a; Crandall text illos	21	42	63	122	191	260
47-Crandall, Ditko, Powell-a	21	42	63	122	191	260
50,52,53: 50-Torres, Morrow-a	19	38	57	109	172	235
54-Crandall, Check-a	20	40	60	115	180	245

NOTE: Ayers a-18, 49, 52. Berg a-17, 51. Colan a-1, 3, 18, 35, 43. Colletta a-18. Drucker a-41. Everett a-2, 29,
33, 35, 41; c-8-11, 14, 38, 39, 41, 43, 44, 48-51, 53. Fass a-16. Forte a-21, 22, 43, 46, 49. Matt Fox a-12?, 21,
22; c-22. Heath a-3; c-3, 15, 17, 26. Heck a-25. Kinstler a-15. Mort Lawrence a-26, 32, 34. Maneely a-1, 9, 14,
22; c-12, 23, 24, 27. Mooney a-3, 40. Morisi a-43, 49, 52. Morrow a-50. Orlando a-51. Pakula a-16. Powell a-
21, 29, 37, 38, 47. Reinman a-1, 14, 17. Robinson a-7p, 42. Romita a-37. Roussos a-4, 44. R.Q. Sale a-45, 46,
49. Severin c-52. Shores a-17, 45. Tuska a-10, 12, 14. Whitney a-2. Wildey a-37.

MYSTERY TALES
Super Comics: 1964

Super Reprint #16,17('64): 16-r/Tales of Horror #2. 17-r/Eerie #14(Avon),
18-Kubert-r/Strange Terrors #4
| | 3 | 6 | 9 | 14 | 20 | 25 |

MYSTERY TRAIL
DC Comics: Feb/Mar 1950

nn - Ashcan comic, not distributed to newsstands, only for in-house use. Cover art is Danger
Trail #3 with interior being Star Spangled Comics #109. A FN/VF copy sold for $2,357.50
in 2002.

MYSTIC (3rd Series)
Marvel/Atlas Comics (CLDS 1/CSI 2-21/OMC 22-35/CSI 35-61): March, 1951 - No. 61, Aug,
1957

1-Atom bomb panels; horror/weird stories in all	93	186	279	581	966	1350
2	50	100	150	305	503	700
3-Eyes torn out	45	90	135	275	450	625
4- "The Devil Birds" by Wolverton (6 pgs.)	79	158	237	494	822	1150
5,7-10	35	70	105	201	318	435
6- "The Eye of Doom" by Wolverton (7 pgs.)	79	158	237	494	822	1150
11-20: 16-Bondage/torture c/story	29	58	87	167	264	360
21-25,27-36-Last precode (3/55). 25-E.C. swipe	24	48	72	139	220	300
26-Atomic War story; severed head story/cover	26	52	78	154	242	330
37-51,53-56,61	20	40	60	115	180	245
52-Wood-a; Crandall-a?	22	44	66	126	198	270

57-Story "Trapped in the Ant-Hill" (1957) is very similar to "The Man in the Ant Hill" in TTA #27
	23	46	69	130	205	280
58,59-Krigstein-a	20	40	60	117	184	250
60-Williamson/Mayo-a (4 pgs.)	20	40	60	117	184	250

NOTE: Andru a-23, 25. Ayers a-35, 53; c-8. Berg a-49. Cameron a-49, 51. Check a-31, 60. Colan a-3, 12, 21,
37, 60. Colletta a-29. Drucker a-46, 52, 56. Everett a-8, 9, 17, 40, 44, 57; c-13, 18, 21, 42, 47, 49, 51-55, 57-59,
61. Forte a-35, 52, 58. Fox a-24i. Al Hartley a-35. Heath a-10; c-10, 20, 22, 23, 25, 30. Infantino a-12. Kane a-8,
24p. Jack Katz a-31, 33. Mort Law.rence a-19, 37. Maneely a-22, 24, 58; c-7, 15, 28, 29, 31. Moldoff a-29.
Morisi a-48, 49, 52. Morrow a-51. Orlando a-57, 61. Pakula a-52, 57, 59. Powell a-52, 54-56. Robinson a-2.
Romita a-11, 15, 49, 53, 58. Sekowsky a-1, 2, 4, 5. Severin c-56, 60. Tuska a-15. Whitney a-1.
Wildey a-28, 30. Ed Win a-17, 20. Canadian reprints known-title 'Startling.'

MYSTIC (Also see CrossGen Chronicles)

Mystical Tales #1 © MAR

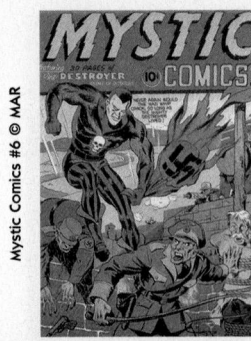

Mystic Comics #6 © MAR

Mythos: Hulk #1 © MAR

	GD 2.0	VG 4.0	FN 6.0	VF 8.0	VF/NM 9.0	NM- 9.2

CrossGeneration Comics: Jul, 2000 - No. 43, Jan, 2004 ($2.95)

1-43: 1-Marz-s/Peterson & Dell-a. 15-Cameos by DC & Marvel characters					3.00
...: Rite of Passage Vol. 1 TPB (5/01, $19.95) r/#1-7; Linsner-c					20.00
...: The Demon Queen Vol. 2 TPB (2002, $19.95) r/#8-14					20.00
...: Siege of Scales Vol. 3 TPB (2002, $15.95) r/#15-20					16.00
...: Out All Night Vol.4 TPB (2003, $15.95) r/#21-26					16.00
Vol. 5: Master Class (2003, $15.95) r/#27-32					16.00

MYSTICAL TALES
Atlas Comics (CCC 1/EPI 2-8): June, 1956 - No. 8, Aug, 1957

1-Everett-c/a	48	96	144	293	484	675
2-4: 2-Berg-a. 3,4-Crandall-a.	26	52	78	152	239	325
5-Williamson-a (4 pgs.)	28	56	84	162	256	350
6-Torres, Krigstein-a	25	50	75	145	228	310
7-Bolle, Forte, Torres, Orlando-a	24	48	72	139	220	300
8-Krigstein, Check-a	25	50	75	145	228	310

NOTE: *Everett* a-1; c-1-4, 6, 7. *Orlando* a-1, 2, 7. *Pakula* a-3. *Powell* a-1, 4.

MYSTIC ARCANA
Marvel Comics: Aug, 2007 - Present ($2.99)

1-Magik on-c; art by Scott and Nguyen; Ian McNee and Dani Moonstar app.					3.00
(#2)...: Black Knight 1 (9/07, $2.99) Djurdjevic-c/Grummett & Hanna-a; origin retold					3.00
3-("Scarlet Witch" on cover)(10/07, $2.99) Djurdjevic-c/Santacruz-a; childhood					3.00
...: The Book of Marvel Magic ('07, $3.99) Official Handbook profiles of the magic-related					4.00

MYSTIC COMICS (1st Series)
Timely Comics (TPI 1-5/TCI 8-10): March, 1940 - No. 10, Aug, 1942

1-Origin The Blue Blaze, The Dynamic Man, & Flexo the Rubber Robot; Zephyr Jones, 3X's & Deep Sea Demon app.; The Magician begins (all 1st app.); c-from Spider pulp V18#1, 6/39	1340	2680	4020	10,100	17,800	25,500
2-The Invisible Man & Master Mind Excello begin; Space Rangers, Zara of the Jungle, Taxi Taylor app. (scarce)	469	938	1407	3283	5742	8200
3-Origin Hercules, who last appears in #4	339	678	1017	2204	3902	5600
4-Origin The Thin Man & The Black Widow; Merzak the Mystic app.; last Flexo, Dynamic Man, Invisible Man & Blue Blaze (some issues have date sticker on cover; others have July w/August overprint in silver color); Roosevelt assassination-c	364	728	1092	2366	4183	6000
5-(3/41)-Origin The Black Marvel, The Blazing Skull, The Sub-Earth Man, Super Slave & The Terror; The Moon Man & Black Widow app.; 5-German war-c begin, end #10	339	678	1017	2204	3902	5600
6-(10/41)-Origin The Challenger & The Destroyer (1st app.?; also see All-Winners #2, Fall, 1941)	406	812	1218	2639	4670	6700
7-The Witness begins (12/41, origin & 1st app.); origin Davey & the Demon; last Black Widow; Hitler opens his trunk of terror-c by Simon & Kirby (classic-c)	423	846	1269	2750	4875	7000
8,10: 10-Father Time, World of Wonder, & Red Skeleton app.; last Challenger & Terror	255	510	765	1594	2647	3700
9-Gary Gaunt app.; last Black Marvel, Mystic & Blazing Skull; Hitler-c	276	552	828	1725	2863	4000

NOTE: *Gabrielle* c-8-10. *Kirby/Schomburg* c-6. *Rico* a-9(2). *Schomburg* a-1-4; c-1-5. *Sekowsky* a-9. *Sekowsky/Klein* a-8(Challenger). Bondage c-1, 2, 9.

MYSTIC COMICS (2nd Series)
Timely Comics (ANC): Oct, 1944 - No. 3, Win, 1944-45; No. 4, Mar, 1945

1-The Angel, The Destroyer, The Human Torch, Terry Vance the Schoolboy Sleuth, & Tommy Tyme begin	269	538	807	1681	2791	3900
2-(Fall/44)-Last Human Torch & Terry Vance; bondage/hypo-c	138	276	414	863	1432	2000
3-Last Angel (two stories) & Tommy Tyme	126	252	378	788	1307	1825
4-The Young Allies-c & app.; Schomburg-c	114	228	342	713	1182	1650

MYSTIC EDGE (Manga)
Antarctic Press: Oct, 1998 ($2.95, one-shot)

1-Ryan Kinnaird-s/a/c					3.00

MYSTIQUE (See X-Men titles)
Marvel Comics: June, 2003 - No. 24, Apr, 2005 ($2.99)

1-24: 1-6-Linsner-c/Vaughan-s/Lucas-a. 7-Ryan-a begins. 8-Horn-c. 9-24-Mayhew-c 23-Wolverine & Rogue app.					3.00
... Vol. 1: Drop Dead Gorgeous TPB (2004, $14.99) r/#1-6					15.00
... Vol. 2: Tinker, Tailor, Mutant, Spy TPB (2004, $17.99) r/#7-13					18.00
... Vol. 3: Unnatural TPB (2004, $13.99) r/#14-18					14.00

MYSTIQUE & SABRETOOTH (Sabretooth and Mystique on-c)
Marvel Comics: Dec, 1996 - No. 4, Mar, 1997 ($1.95, limited series)

1-4: Characters from X-Men					3.00

MY STORY (...True Romances in Pictures #5,6; becomes My Love Life #13) (Formerly Zago)
Hero Books (Fox Features Syndicate): No. 5, May, 1949 - No. 12, Aug, 1950

5-Kamen/Feldstein-a	21	42	63	124	195	265
6-8,11,12: 12-Photo-c	12	24	36	67	94	120
9,10-Wood-a	18	36	54	107	169	230

MYTHOS
Marvel Comics: Mar, 2006; Oct, 2006; Mar, 2007 ($3.99)

1-Retelling of X-Men #1 with painted-a by Paolo Rivera; Paul Jenkins-s					4.00
...: Ghost Rider 1 (3/07) Retelling of Marvel Spotlight #5; painted-a by Rivera; Jenkins-s					4.00
...: Hulk 1 (10/06) Retelling of Incredible Hulk #1; painted-a by Rivera; Jenkins-s					4.00
...: Spider-Man 1 (8/07) Retelling of Amazing Fantasy #15; painted-a by Rivera; Jenkins-s					4.00

MYTHOS: THE FINAL TOUR
DC Comics/Vertigo: Dec, 1996 - No. 3, Feb, 1997 ($5.95, limited series)

1-3: 1-Ney Rieber-s/Amaro-a. 2-Snejberg-a; Constantine-app. 3-Kristiansen-a; Black Orchid-app.					6.00

MYTHSTALKERS
Image Comics: Mar, 2003 - No. 8, Mar, 2004 ($2.95)

1-8-Jiro-a					3.00

MY TRUE LOVE (Formerly Western Killers #64; Frank Buck #70 on)
Fox Features Syndicate: No. 65, July, 1949 - No. 69, March, 1950

65	16	32	48	94	147	200
66,68,69: 69-Morisi-a	12	24	36	67	94	120
67-Wood-a	18	36	54	107	169	230

NAIL, THE
Dark Horse Comics: June, 2004 - No. 4, Oct, 2004 ($2.99, limited series)

1-4-Rob Zombie & Steve Niles-s/Nat Jones-a/Simon Bisley-c					3.00
TPB (2005, $12.95) r/series					13.00

NAKED BRAIN (Marc Hempel's...)
Insight Studios Group: 2002 - No. 3, 2002 ($2.95, B&W, limited series)

1-3-Marc Hempel cartoons and sketches; Tug & Buster app.					3.00

NAKED PREY, THE (See Movie Classics)

'NAM, THE (See Savage Tales #1, 2nd series & Punisher Invades...)
Marvel Comics Group: Dec, 1986 - No. 84, Sept, 1993

1-Golden a(p)/c begins, ends #13					5.00
1 (2nd printing)					2.50
2-7,9-19,21-66,70-74: 7-Golden-a (2 pgs.). 32-Death R. Kennedy. 52,53-Frank Castle (The Punisher) app. 52,53-Gold 2nd printings. 58-Silver logo. 65-Heath-c/a. 70-Lomax scripts begin					3.00
8-1st app. Fudd Verzyl, Tunnel Rat					4.00
20-2nd app. Fudd Verzyl, Tunnel Rat					3.50
67-69,76-84: 67-69-Punisher 3 part story					3.00
75-($2.25, 52 pgs.)					3.50
Trade Paperback 1,2: 1-r/#1-4. 2-r/#5-8					5.00
TPB ('99, $14.95) r/#1-4; recolored					15.00

'NAM MAGAZINE, THE
Marvel Comics: Aug, 1988 - No. 10, May, 1989 ($2.00, B&W, 52pgs.)

1-10: Each issue reprints 2 issues of the comic					2.50

NAMELESS, THE
Image Comics: May, 1997 - No. 5, Sept, 1997 ($2.95, B&W)

1-5: Pruett/Hester-s/a					3.00
...: The Director's Cut TPB (2006, $15.99) r/#1-5; original proposal by Pruett					16.00

NAMES OF MAGIC, THE (Also see Books of Magic)
DC Comics (Vertigo): Feb, 2001 - No. 5, June, 2001 ($2.50, limited series)

1-5: Bolton painted-c on all; Case-a; leads into Hunter: The Age of Magic					2.50
TPB (2002, $14.95) r/#1-5					15.00

NAME OF THE GAME, THE
DC Comics: 2001 ($29.95, graphic novel)

Hardcover ($29.95) Will Eisner-s/a					30.00

NAMOR (Volume 2)
Marvel Comics: June, 2003 - No. 12, May, 2004 (25¢/$2.25/$2.99)

1-(25¢-c)Young Namor in the 1920s; Larroca-c/a					2.50
2-6-($2.25) Larroca-a					2.50
7-12-($2.99): 7-Olliffe-a begins					3.00

NAMORA (See Marvel Mystery Comics #82 & Sub-Mariner Comics)
Marvel Comics (PrPI): Fall, 1948 - No. 3, Dec, 1948

Namor, The Sub-Mariner #1 © MAR

NASCAR Heroes #1 © NASCAR

National Comics #16 © QUA

	GD 2.0	VG 4.0	FN 6.0	VF 8.0	VF/NM 9.0	NM- 9.2

1-Sub-Mariner x-over in Namora; Namora by Everett(2), Sub-Mariner by
Rico (10 pgs.) 269 538 807 1681 2791 3900
2-The Blonde Phantom & Sub-Mariner story; Everett-a
. . . . 138 276 414 863 1432 2000
3-(Scarce)-Sub-Mariner app.; Everett-a 145 290 435 906 1503 2100

NAMOR, THE SUB-MARINER (See Prince Namor & Sub-Mariner)
Marvel Comics: Apr, 1990 - No. 62, May, 1995 ($1.00/$1.25/$1.50)

1-Byrne-c/a/scripts in 1-25 (scripts only #26-32) 4.00
2-5: 5-Iron Man app. 3.00
6-11,13-23,25,27-49,51-62: 16-Re-intro Iron Fist (8-cameo only). 18-Punisher cameo
(1 panel); 21-23,25-Wolverine cameos. 22,23-Iron Fist app. 28-Iron Fist-c/story.
31-Dr. Doom-c/story. 33,34-Iron Fist cameo. 35-New Tiger Shark-c/story.
37-Aqua holografx foil-c. 48-The Thing app. 2.50
12,24: 12-(52pgs.)-Re-intro. The Invaders. 24-Namor vs. Wolverine . . . 3.00
26-Namor w/new costume; 1st Jae Lee-c/a this title (5/92) & begins . . 3.50
50-($1.75, 52 pgs.)-Newsstand ed.; w/bound-in S-M trading card sheet (both versions) 2.50
50-($2.95, 52 pgs.)-Collector edition w/foil-c 3.00
Annual 1-4 ('91-94, 68 pgs.): 1-3 pg. origin recap. 2-Return/Defenders. 3-Bagged w/card.
4-Painted-c 3.00
NOTE: *Jae Lee* a-26-30p, 31-37, 38p, 39, 40; c-26-40.

NANCY AND SLUGGO (See Comics On Parade & Sparkle Comics)
United Features Syndicate: No. 16, 1949 - No. 23, 1954

16(#1) 10 20 30 58 79 100
17-23 . . . . 8 16 24 40 50 60

NANCY & SLUGGO (Nancy #146-173; formerly Sparkler Comics)
St. John/Dell #146-187/Gold Key #188 on: No. 121, Apr, 1955-No. 192, Oct, 1963

121(4/55)(St. John) 10 20 30 54 72 90
122-145(7/57)(St. John) 8 16 24 44 57 70
146(9/57)-Peanuts begins, ends #192 (Dell) . . 7 14 21 45 73 100
147-161 (Dell) Peanuts in all 6 12 18 39 62 85
162-165,177-180-John Stanley-a 7 14 21 49 80 110
166-176-Oona & Her Haunted House series; Stanley-a
. . . . 8 16 24 54 90 125
181-187(3-5/62)(Dell) 5 10 15 35 55 75
188(10/62)-192 (Gold Key) 5 10 15 35 55 75
Four Color 1034(9-11/59)-Summer Camp 5 10 15 32 51 70
(See Dell Giant #34, 45 & Dell Giants)

NANNY AND THE PROFESSOR (TV)
Dell Publishing Co.: Aug, 1970 - No. 2, Oct, 1970 (Photo-c)

1-(01-546-008) 5 10 15 32 51 70
2 . . . . 4 8 12 26 41 55

NAPOLEON
Dell Publishing Co.: No. 526, Dec, 1953

Four Color 526 . . . . 4 8 12 24 37 50

NAPOLEON & SAMANTHA (See Walt Disney Showcase No. 10)

NAPOLEON & UNCLE ELBY (See Clifford McBride's…)
Eastern Color Printing Co.: July, 1942 (68 pgs.) (One Shot)

1 . . . . 43 86 129 262 431 600
1945-American Book-Strafford Press (128 pgs.) (8x10-1/2"; B&W reprints; hardcover)
. . . . 15 30 45 83 124 165

NARRATIVE ILLUSTRATION, THE STORY OF THE COMICS (Also see Good Triumphs
Over Evil!)
M.C. Gaines: Summer, 1942 (32 pgs., 7-1/4"x10", B&W w/color inserts)

nn-16 pgs. text with illustrations of ancient art, strips and comic covers; 4 pg. WWII War Bond
promo, "The Minute Man Answers the Call" color comic drawn by Shelly and a special
8-page color comic insert of "The Story of Saul" (from *Picture Stories from the Bible* #10 or
soon to appear in PS #10) or "Noah and His Ark" or "The Story of Ruth". Insert has
special title page indicating it was part of a Sunday newspaper supplement insert series
that had already run in a New England "Sunday Herald." Another version exists
with insert from *Picture Stories from the Bible* #7.
(very rare) . . . . Estimated value... 1500.00
NOTE: *Print, A Quarterly Journal of the Graphic Arts* Vol. 3 No. 2 (88 pg., saddle bound) features the 1st printing of Narrative Illustration, The Story of The Comics. A VG+ copy sold for $750 in 2005.

NASCAR HEROES
Starbridge Media: 2007 ($3.95)

1-Origin of fictional racer Jimmy Dash 4.00

NASH (WCW Wrestling)
Image Comics: July, 1999 - No. 2, July, 1999 ($2.95)

1,2-Regular and photo-c 3.00
1-($6.95) Photo-split-cover Edition 7.00

NATHANIEL DUSK
DC Comics: Feb, 1984 - No. 4, May, 1984 ($1.25, mini-series, direct sales, Baxter paper)

1-4: 1-Intro/origin; Gene Colan-c/a in all 2.50

NATHANIEL DUSK II
DC Comics: Oct, 1985 - No. 4, Jan, 1986 ($2.00, mini-series, Baxter paper)

1-4: Gene Colan-c/a in all 2.50

NATIONAL COMICS
Quality Comics Group: July, 1940 - No. 75, Nov, 1949

1-Uncle Sam begins (1st app.); origin sidekick Buddy by Eisner; origin Wonder Boy &
Kid Dixon; Merlin the Magician (ends #45); Cyclone, Kid Patrol, Sally O'Neil Policewoman,
Pen Miller (by Klaus Nordling; ends #22), Prop Powers (ends #26), & Paul Bunyan (ends
#22) begin 514 1028 1542 3600 6300 9000
2 . . . . 241 482 723 1506 2503 3500
3-Last Eisner Uncle Sam 167 334 501 1044 1735 2425
4-Last Cyclone 131 262 393 819 1360 1900
5-(11/40)-Quicksilver begins (1st app.; 3rd w/lightning speed?; re-intro'd by DC in 1993 as
Max Mercury in Flash #76, 2nd series); origin Uncle Sam; bondage-c
. . . . 150 300 450 938 1557 2175
6,8-11: 8-Jack & Jill begins (ends #22). 9-Flag-c 124 248 372 775 1288 1800
7-Classic Lou Fine-c 241 482 723 1506 2503 3500
12 . . . . 85 170 255 531 878 1225
13-16-Lou Fine-a 86 172 258 538 894 1250
17,19-22: 21-Classic Nazi swastika cover. 22-Last Pen Miller (moves to Crack #23)
. . . . 67 134 201 419 697 975
18-(12/41)-Shows Asians attacking Pearl Harbor; on stands one month before actual event
. . . . 128 256 384 800 1325 1850
23-The Unknown & Destroyer 171 begin 68 136 204 425 705 985
24-Japanese WW-II 68 136 204 425 705 985
25-30: 25-Nazi drug usage/hypodermic needle in story. 26-Wonder Boy ends. 27- G-2 the
Unknown begins (ends #46). 29-Origin The Unknown
. . . . 47 94 141 287 474 660
31-33: 33-Chic Carter begins (ends #47) 43 86 129 262 431 600
34-37,40: 35-Last Kid Patrol 39 78 117 225 355 485
38-Hitler, Tojo, Mussolini-c 52 104 156 317 521 725
39-Hitler-c 53 106 159 323 537 750
41,43-50: 48-Origin The Whistler . . 25 50 75 145 228 310
42-The Barker begins (1st app?, 5/44); The Barker covers begin
. . . . 34 68 102 197 311 425
51-Sally O'Neil by Ward, 8 pgs. (12/45) 29 58 87 167 264 360
52-60 . . . . 20 40 60 115 180 245
61-67: 67-Format change; Quicksilver app. 15 30 45 86 133 180
68-75: The Barker ends 14 28 42 80 115 150
NOTE: *Cole* Quicksilver-13; *Barker*-43; c-43, 46, 47, 49-51. *Crandall* Uncle Sam-11-13 (with *Fine*), 25, 26; c-24-
26, 30-33, 43. *Crandall* The Barker-13 (w/Crandall), 17, 18; c-1-14, 16, 18, 21. *Gill Fox*
c-69-74. *Guardineer* Quicksilver-27, 35. *Gustavson* Quicksilver-14-26. *McWilliams* a-23-28, 55, 57. *Uncle Sam*
c-1-41. Barker c-42-75.

NATIONAL COMICS (Also see All Star Comics 1999 crossover titles)
DC Comics: May, 1999 ($1.99, one-shot)

1-Golden Age Flash and Mr. Terrific; Waid/s-Lopresti-a 2.50

NATIONAL CRUMB, The (Magazine-Size)
Mayfair Publications: August, 1975 (52 pgs., B&W) (Satire)

1-Grandenetti-c/a, Ayers-a 2 4 6 11 16 20

NATIONAL VELVET (TV)
Dell Publishing Co./Gold Key: May-July, 1961 - No. 2, Mar, 1963 (All photo-c)

Four Color 1195 (#1) 7 14 21 49 80 110
Four Color 1312, 01-556-207, 12-556-210 (Dell) 4 8 12 28 44 60
1,2: 1(12/62) (Gold Key). 2(3/63) 4 8 12 28 44 60

NATION OF SNITCHES
Piranha Press (DC): 1990 ($4.95, color, 52 pgs.)

nn 5.00

NATURE BOY (Formerly Danny Blaze; Li'l Rascal Twins #6 on)
Charlton Comics: No. 3, March, 1956 - No. 5, Feb, 1957

3-Origin; Blue Beetle story; Buscema-c/a 23 46 69 130 205 280
4,5 . . . . 16 32 48 92 144 195
NOTE: *John Buscema* a-3, 4p, 5; c-3. *Powell* a-4.

NATURE OF THINGS (Disney, TV/Movie)
Dell Publishing Co.: No. 727, Sept, 1956 - No. 842, Sept, 1957

Navy Combat #6 © MAR

Negation #5 © CRO

Negative Burn V2 #8 © Image

	GD 2.0	VG 4.0	FN 6.0	VF 8.0	VF/NM 9.0	NM- 9.2
Four Color 727 (#1), 842-Jesse Marsh-a	5	10	15	35	55	75

NAUSICAA OF THE VALLEY OF WIND
Viz Comics: 1988 - No. 7, 1989; 1989 - No. 4, 1990 ($2.50, B&W, 68pgs.)

Book 1-7: 1-Contains Moebius poster		3.25
Part II, Book 1-4 ($2.95)		3.25

NAVY ACTION (Sailor Sweeney #12-14)
Atlas Comics (CDS): Aug, 1954 - No. 11, Apr, 1956; No. 15, 1/57 - No. 18, 8/57

	GD 2.0	VG 4.0	FN 6.0	VF 8.0	VF/NM 9.0	NM- 9.2
1-Powell-a	18	36	54	107	169	230
2-Lawrence-a	11	22	33	64	90	115
3-11: 4-Last precode (2/55)	9	18	27	52	69	85
15-18	9	18	27	50	65	80

NOTE: *Berg* a-7, 9. *Colan* a-8. *Drucker* a-7, 17. *Everett* a-3, 7, 16; c-16, 17. *Heath* c-1, 2, 6. *Maneely* a-7, 8, 18; c-9, 11. *Pakula* a-2, 3, 9. *Reinman* a-17.

NAVY COMBAT
Atlas Comics (MPI): June, 1955 - No. 20, Oct, 1958

	GD 2.0	VG 4.0	FN 6.0	VF 8.0	VF/NM 9.0	NM- 9.2
1-Torpedo Taylor begins by Don Heck	18	36	54	107	169	230
2	11	22	33	64	90	115
3-10	9	18	27	52	69	85
11,13-16,18-20: 14-Torres-a	9	18	27	50	65	80
12-Crandall-a	10	20	30	56	76	95
17-Williamson-a, 4 pgs.; Torres-a	10	20	30	54	72	90

NOTE: *Berg* a-10, 11. *Colan* a-11. *Drucker* a-7. *Everett* a-3, 20; c-8 & 9 w/Tuska, 10, 13-16. *Heck* a-11(2). *Maneely* c-1, 6, 11, 17. *Morisi* a-8. *Pakula* a-7. *Powell* a-20.

NAVY HEROES
Almanac Publishing Co.: 1945

	GD 2.0	VG 4.0	FN 6.0	VF 8.0	VF/NM 9.0	NM- 9.2
1-Heavy in propaganda	13	26	39	74	105	135

NAVY PATROL
Key Publications: May, 1955 - No. 4, Nov, 1955

	GD 2.0	VG 4.0	FN 6.0	VF 8.0	VF/NM 9.0	NM- 9.2
1	8	16	24	44	57	70
2-4	6	12	18	28	34	40

NAVY TALES
Atlas Comics (CDS): Jan, 1957 - No. 4, July, 1957

	GD 2.0	VG 4.0	FN 6.0	VF 8.0	VF/NM 9.0	NM- 9.2
1-Everett-c; Berg, Powell-a	16	32	48	90	147	200
2-Williamson/Mayo-a(5 pgs); Crandall-a	14	28	42	80	115	150
3,4-Reinman-a; Severin-a. 4-Crandall-a	12	24	36	69	97	125

NOTE: *Colan* a-4. *Maneely* c-2. *Sinnott* a-4.

NAVY TASK FORCE
Stanmor Publications/Aragon Mag. No. 4-8: Feb, 1954 - No. 8, April, 1956

	GD 2.0	VG 4.0	FN 6.0	VF 8.0	VF/NM 9.0	NM- 9.2
1	9	18	27	50	65	80
2	6	12	18	28	34	40
3-8: #8-r/Navy Patrol #1	5	10	15	24	30	35

NAVY WAR HEROES
Charlton Comics: Jan, 1964 - No. 7, Mar-Apr, 1965

	GD 2.0	VG 4.0	FN 6.0	VF 8.0	VF/NM 9.0	NM- 9.2
1	3	6	9	20	30	40
2-7	3	6	9	14	19	24

NAZA (Stone Age Warrior)
Dell Publishing Co.: Nov-Jan, 1963-64 - No. 9, March, 1966

	GD 2.0	VG 4.0	FN 6.0	VF 8.0	VF/NM 9.0	NM- 9.2
12-555-401 (#1)-Painted-c	5	10	15	32	51	70
2-9: 2-4-Painted-c	4	8	12	22	34	45

NAZZ, THE
DC Comics: 1990 - No. 4, 1991 ($4.95, 52 pgs., mature)

1-4		5.00

NEBBS, THE (Also see Crackajack Funnies)
Dell Publishing Co./Croydon Publishing Co.: 1941; 1945

	GD 2.0	VG 4.0	FN 6.0	VF 8.0	VF/NM 9.0	NM- 9.2
Large Feature Comic 23(1941)	21	42	63	122	191	260
1(1945, 36 pgs.)-Reprints	13	26	39	74	105	135

NECROMANCER
Image Comics (Top Cow): Sept, 2005 - No. 6, July 2006 ($2.99)

1-6: 1-Manapul-a/Ortega-s; three covers by Manapul, Horn & Bachalo		3.00

NECROMANCER: THE GRAPHIC NOVEL
Marvel Comics (Epic Comics): 1989 ($8.95)

nn		9.00

NECROWAR
Dreamwave Productions: July, 2003 - No. 3, Sept, 2003 ($2.95)

1-3-Furman-s/Granov-digital art		3.00

NEGATION
CrossGeneration Comics: Dec, 2001 - No. 27, Mar, 2004 ($2.95)

Prequel (12/01)		3.00
1-27: 1-(1/02) Pelletier-a/Bedard & Waid-s		3.00
... Lawbringer (11/02, $2.95) Nebres-a		3.00
Vol. 1: Bohica! (10/02, $19.95, TPB) r/ Prequel & #1-6		20.00
Vol. 2: Baptism of Fire (5/03, $15.95, TPB) r/#7-12		16.00
Vol. 3: Hounded (12/03, $15.95, TPB) r/#13-18		16.00

NEGATION WAR
CrossGeneration Comics: Apr, 2004 - No. 6 ($2.95)

1-4-Bedard-s/Pelletier-a		3.00

NEGATIVE BURN
Caliber: 1993 - No. 50, 1997 ($2.95, B&W, anthology)

	GD 2.0	VG 4.0	FN 6.0	VF 8.0	VF/NM 9.0	NM- 9.2
1,2,4-12,14-47: Anthology by various including Bolland, Burden, Doran, Gaiman, Moebius, Moore, & Pope						4.00
3,13: 3-Bone story. 13-Strangers in Paradise story	2	4	6	8	10	12
48,49-($4.95)						5.00
50-($6.95, 96 pgs.)-Gaiman, Robinson, Bolland						7.00
...Summer Special 2005 (Image, 2005, $9.99) new short stories by various						10.00
... The Best From 1993-1998 (Image, 1/05, $19.95) r/short stories by various						20.00
...Winter Special 2005 (Image, 2005, $9.95) new short stories by various						10.00

NEGATIVE BURN
Image Comics (Desperado): May, 2006 - Present ($5.99, B&W, anthology)

1-11: 1-Art by Bolland, Powell, Luna, Smith, Hester. 2-Milk & Cheese by Dorkin		6.00

NEGRO (See All-Negro)

NEGRO HEROES (Calling All Girls, Real Heroes, & True Comics reprints)
Parents' Magazine Institute: Spring, 1947 - No. 2, Summer, 1948

	GD 2.0	VG 4.0	FN 6.0	VF 8.0	VF/NM 9.0	NM- 9.2
1	93	186	279	581	966	1350
2-Jackie Robinson-c/story	100	200	300	625	1038	1450

NEGRO ROMANCE (Negro Romances #4)
Fawcett Publications: June, 1950 - No. 3, Oct, 1950 (All photo-c)

	GD 2.0	VG 4.0	FN 6.0	VF 8.0	VF/NM 9.0	NM- 9.2
1-Evans-a	121	242	363	756	1253	1750
2,3	93	186	279	581	966	1350

NEGRO ROMANCES (Formerly Negro Romance; Romantic Secrets #5 on)
Charlton Comics: No. 4, May, 1955

	GD 2.0	VG 4.0	FN 6.0	VF 8.0	VF/NM 9.0	NM- 9.2
4-Reprints Fawcett #2	67	134	201	419	697	975

NEIL GAIMAN AND CHARLES VESS' STARDUST
DC Comics (Vertigo): 1997 - No. 4, 1998 ($5.95/$6.95, square-bound, lim. series)

1-4: Gaiman text with Vess paintings in all		7.00
Hardcover (1998, $29.95) r/series with new sketches		35.00
Softcover (1999, $19.95) oversized; new Vess-c		20.00

NEIL GAIMAN'S LADY JUSTICE
Tekno Comix: Sept, 1995 - No. 11, May, 1996 ($1.95/$2.25)

1-11: 1-Sienkiewicz-c; pin-ups. 1-5-Brereton-c. 7-Polybagged. 11-The Big Bang Pt. 7		2.50

NEIL GAIMAN'S LADY JUSTICE
BIG Entertainment: V2#1, June, 1996 - No. 9, Feb, 1997 ($2.25)

V2#1-9: Dan Brereton-c on all. 6-8-Dan Brereton script		2.50

NEIL GAIMAN'S MIDNIGHT DAYS
DC Comics (Vertigo): 1999 ($17.95, trade paperback)

nn-Reprints Gaiman's short stories; new Swamp Thing w/ Bissette-a		18.00

NEIL GAIMAN'S MR. HERO-THE NEWMATIC MAN
Tekno Comix: Mar, 1995 - No. 17, May, 1996 ($1.95/$2.25)

1-17: 1-Intro Mr. Hero & Teknophage; bound-in game piece and trading card. 4-w/Steel edition Neil Gaiman's Teknophage #1 coupon. 13-Polybagged		2.50

NEIL GAIMAN'S MR. HERO-THE NEWMATIC MAN
BIG Entertainment: V2#1, June, 1996 ($2.25)

V2#1-Teknophage destroys Mr. Hero; includes The Big Bang Pt. 10		2.50

NEIL GAIMAN'S NEVERWHERE
DC Comics (Vertigo): Aug, 2005 - No. 9, Sept, 2006 ($2.99, limited series)

1-9-Adaptation of Gaiman novel; Carey-s/Fabry-a/c		3.00
TPB (2007, $19.99) r/series; intro. by Carey		20.00

NEIL GAIMAN'S PHAGE-SHADOWDEATH
BIG Entertainment: June, 1996 - No. 6, Nov, 1996 ($2.25, limited series)

1-6: Bryan Talbot-c & scripts in all. 1-1st app. Orlando Holmes		2.50

Nellie the Nurse #4 © MAR

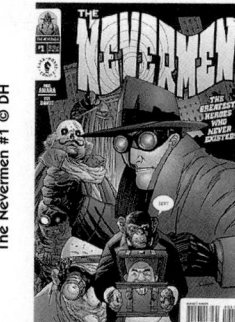

The Nevermen #1 © DH

New Avengers #4 © MAR

	GD 2.0	VG 4.0	FN 6.0	VF 8.0	VF/NM 9.0	NM- 9.2

NEIL GAIMAN'S TEKNOPHAGE
Tekno Comix: Aug, 1995 - No. 10, Mar, 1996 ($1.95/$2.25)

1-6-Rick Veitch scripts & Bryan Talbot-c/a.		2.50
1-Steel Edition		4.00
7-10: Paul Jenkins scripts in all. 8-polybagged		2.50

NEIL GAIMAN'S WHEEL OF WORLDS
Tekno Comix: Apr, 1995 - No. 1, May, 1996 ($2.95/$3.25)

0-1st app. Lady Justice; 48 pgs.; bound-in poster		3.25
0-Regular edition		2.50
1 ($3.25, 5/96)-Bruce Jones scripts; Lady Justice & Teknophage app.; CGI photo-c		3.25

NEIL THE HORSE (See Charlton Bullseye #2)
Aardvark-Vanaheim #1-10/Renegade Press #11 on: 2/83 - No. 10, 12/84; No. 11, 4/85 - #15, 1985 (B&W)

1($1.40)		4.00
1-2nd print		2.50
2-13: Double-size; 11,13-w/paperdolls		2.50
14,15: Double size ($3.00). 15 is a flip book(2-c)		3.00

NELLIE THE NURSE (Also see Gay Comics & Joker Comics)
Marvel/Atlas Comics (SPI/LMC): 1945 - No. 36, Oct, 1952; 1957

	GD	VG	FN	VF	VF/NM	NM-
1-(1945)	41	82	123	256	416	575
2-(Spring/46)	21	42	63	124	195	265
3,4: 3-New logo (9/46)	16	32	48	94	147	200
5-Kurtzman's "Hey Look" (3); Georgie app.	17	34	51	100	158	215
6-8,10: 7,8-Georgie app. 10-Millie app.	15	30	45	88	137	185
9-Wolverton-a (1 pg.); Mille the Model app.	15	30	45	90	140	190
11,14-16,18-Kurtzman's "Hey Look"	16	32	48	92	144	195
12- "Giggles 'n' Grins" by Kurtzman	15	30	45	88	137	185
13,17,19,20: 17-Annie Oakley app.	13	26	39	74	105	135
21-30: 28-Mr. Nexdoor-r (3 pgs.) by Kurtzman/Rusty #22	11	22	33	64	90	115
31-36: 36-Post-c	10	20	30	56	76	95
1('57)-Leading Mag. (Atlas)-Everett-a, 20 pgs	11	22	33	60	83	105

NELLIE THE NURSE
Dell Publishing Co.: No. 1304, Mar-May, 1962

	GD	VG	FN	VF	VF/NM	NM-
Four Color 1304-Stanley-a	7	14	21	47	76	105

NEMESIS THE WARLOCK (Also see Spellbinders)
Eagle Comics: Sept, 1984 - No. 7, Mar, 1985 (limited series, Baxter paper)

1-7: 2000 A.D. reprints		2.50

NEMESIS THE WARLOCK
Quality Comics/Fleetway Quality #2 on: 1989 - No. 19, 1991 ($1.95, B&W)

1-19		2.50

NEUTRO
Dell Publishing Co.: Jan, 1967

	GD	VG	FN	VF	VF/NM	NM-
1-Jack Sparling-c/a (super hero); UFO-s	4	8	12	26	41	55

NEVADA (See Zane Grey's Four Color 412, 996 & Zane Grey's Stories of the West #1)

NEVADA (Also see Vertigo Winter's Edge #1)
DC Comics (Vertigo): May, 1998 - No. 6, Oct, 1998 ($2.50, limited series)

1-6-Gerber-s/Winslade-c/a		2.50
TPB (1999, $14.95) r/#1-6 & Vertigo Winter's Edge preview		15.00

NEVER AGAIN (War stories; becomes Soldier & Marine V2#9)
Charlton Comics: Aug, 1955 - No. 8, July, 1956 (No #2-7)

	GD	VG	FN	VF	VF/NM	NM-
1	9	18	27	50	65	80
8-(Formerly Foxhole?)	6	12	18	28	34	40

NEVERMEN, THE (See Dark Horse Presents #148-150)
Dark Horse Comics: May, 2000 - No. 4, Aug, 2000 ($2.95, limited series)

1-4-Phil Amara-s/Guy Davis-a		3.00

NEVERMEN, THE: STREETS OF BLOOD
Dark Horse Comics: Jan, 2003 - No. 3, Apr, 2003 ($2.99, limited series)

1-3-Phil Amara-s/Guy Davis-a		3.00
TPB (7/03, $9.95) r/#1-3; Paul Jenkins intro.; Davis sketch pages		10.00

NEW ADVENTURE COMICS (Formerly New Comics; becomes Adventure Comics #32 on; V1#12 indicia says NEW COMICS #12)
National Periodical Publications: V1#12, Jan, 1937 - No. 31, Oct, 1938

	GD	VG	FN	VF	VF/NM	NM-
V1#12-Federal Men by Siegel & Shuster continues; Jor-L mentioned; Whitney Ellsworth-c begin, end #14	533	1066	1600	4000	–	–
V2#1(2/37, #13)-(Rare)	507	1014	1521	3800	–	–

	GD	VG	FN	VF	VF/NM	NM-
V2#2 (#14)	450	900	1350	3400	–	–
15(V2#3)-20(V2#8): 15-1st Adventure logo; Creig Flessel-c begin, end #31. 16-1st non-funny cover. 17-Nadir, Master of Magic begins, ends #30	360	720	1080	1980	2940	3900
21(V2#9),22(V2#10, 2/37): 22-X-Mas-c	320	640	960	1760	2630	3500
23-25,27-31: 27(6/38) has house ad for Action Comics #1 showing B&W image of cover (early published image of Superman)	270	540	810	1485	2243	3000
26(5/38) (scarce) has house ad for Action Comics #1 showing B&W image of cover (early published image of Superman)(prices vary widely on this book) (A CGC 5.0 sold in 2006 for $5377.50)						

NEW ADVENTURES OF ABRAHAM LINCOLN, THE
Image Comics (Homage): 1998 ($19.95, one-shot)

1-Scott McCloud-s/computer art		20.00

NEW ADVENTURES OF CHARLIE CHAN, THE (TV)
National Periodical Publications: May-June, 1958 - No. 6, Mar-Apr, 1959

	GD	VG	FN	VF	VF/NM	NM-
1 (Scarce)-John Broome-s/Sid Greene-a in all	72	144	216	450	750	1050
2 (Scarce)	46	92	138	281	466	650
3-6 (Scarce)-Greene/Giella-a	40	80	120	240	383	525

NEW ADVENTURES OF HUCK FINN, THE (TV)
Gold Key: December, 1968 (Hanna-Barbera)

	GD	VG	FN	VF	VF/NM	NM-
1- "The Curse of Thut"; part photo-c	4	8	12	22	34	45

NEW ADVENTURES OF PINOCCHIO (TV)
Dell Publishing Co.: Oct-Dec, 1962 - No. 3, Sept-Nov, 1963

	GD	VG	FN	VF	VF/NM	NM-
12-562-212(#1)	8	16	24	56	93	130
2,3	7	14	21	45	73	100

NEW ADVENTURES OF ROBIN HOOD (See Robin Hood)

NEW ADVENTURES OF SHERLOCK HOLMES (Also see Sherlock Holmes)
Dell Publishing Co.: No. 1169, Mar-May, 1961 - No. 1245, Nov, 1961/62

	GD	VG	FN	VF	VF/NM	NM-
Four Color 1169(#1)	14	28	42	102	181	260
Four Color 1245	13	26	39	90	160	230

NEW ADVENTURES OF SPEED RACER
Now Comics: Dec, 1993 - No. 7, 1994? ($1.95)

1-7		2.50
0-(Premiere)-3-D cover		3.00

NEW ADVENTURES OF SUPERBOY, THE (Also see Superboy)
DC Comics: Jan, 1980 - No. 54, June, 1984

1		5.00
2-6,8-10		4.00
11-49,51-54: 11-Superboy gets new power. 14-Lex Luthor app. 15-Superboy gets new parents. 28-Dial "H" For Hero begins, ends #49. 45-47-1st app. Sunburst. 48-Begin 75¢-c.		3.00

	1	2	3	5	7	9
1,2,5,6,8 (Whitman variants; low print run; no issue # shown on cover)						
7,50: 7-Has extra story "The Computers That Saved Metropolis" by Starlin (Radio Shack giveaway w/indicia). 50-Legion app.						5.00

NOTE: *Buckler* a-9p; c-36p. *Giffen* a-50; c-50. 40i. *Gil Kane* c-32p, 33p, 35, 39, 41-49.
Miller c-51. *Starlin* a-7. Krypto back-ups in 17, 22. Superbaby in 11, 14, 19, 24.

NEW ADVENTURES OF THE PHANTOM BLOT, THE (See The Phantom Blot)

NEW AMERICA
Eclipse Comics: Nov, 1987 - No. 4, Feb, 1988 ($1.75, Baxter paper)

1-4: Scout limited series		2.50

NEW ARCHIES, THE (TV)
Archie Comic Publications: Oct, 1987 - No. 22, May, 1990 (75¢)

1		5.00
2-10: 3-Xmas issue		4.00
11-22: 17-22 (95¢-$1.00): 21-Xmas issue		3.00

NEW ARCHIES DIGEST (TV)(...Comics Digest Magazine #4?-10; ...Digest Magazine #11 on)
Archie Comics: May, 1988 - No. 14, July, 1991 ($1.35/$1.50, quarterly)

1		6.00
2-14: 6-Begin $1.50-c		3.50

NEW AVENGERS, THE (Also see Promotional section for military giveaway)
Marvel Comics: Jan, 2005 - Present ($2.25/$2.50/$2.99)

1-Bendis-s/Finch-a; Spider-Man app.; re-intro The Sentry; 4 covers by McNiven, Quesada & Finch; variants from #1-6 combine for one team image		5.00
1-Director's Cut ($3.99) includes alternate covers, script, villain gallery		4.00
2-20: 2-6-Finch-a. 5-Wolverine app. 7-10-Origin of the Sentry; McNiven-a. 11-Debut of Ronin. 14,15-Cho-c/a. 17-20-Deodato-a		3.00

New Avengers: Illuminati © MAR

New Excalibur #16 © MAR

New Gods #8 © DC

	GD	VG	FN	VF	VF/NM	NM-
	2.0	4.0	6.0	8.0	9.0	9.2

21-34: 21-Civil War. 21-Chaykin-a/c. 26-Maleev-a. 27-31-Yu-a; Echo & "Elektra" app. 33,34-The Hood app. 3.00
Annual 1 (6/06, $3.99) Wedding of Luke Cage and Jessica Jones; Bendis-s/Coipel-a 4.00
...: Illuminati (5/06, $3.99) Bendis-s/Maleev-a; leads into Planet Hulk; Civil War preview 4.00
... Most Wanted Files (2006, $3.99) profile pages of Avenger villains 4.00
... Vol. 1: Breakout HC (2005, $19.99) r/#1-6; gallery of variant covers 20.00
... Vol. 1: Breakout SC (2006, $14.99) r/#1-6; gallery of variant covers 15.00
... Vol. 2: Sentry HC (2006, $19.99) r/#7-10 & ... Most Wanted Files 20.00
... Vol. 2: Sentry SC (2006, $14.99) r/#7-10 & ... Most Wanted Files 15.00
... Vol. 3: Secrets and Lies HC (2006, $19.99) r/#11-15 & Giant-Size Spider-Woman #1 20.00
... Vol. 3: Secrets and Lies SC (2006, $14.99) r/#11-15 & Giant-Size Spider-Woman #1 15.00
... Vol. 4: The Collective HC (2006, $19.99) r/#16-20 20.00
... Vol. 4: The Collective SC (2007, $14.99) r/#16-20 15.00
... Vol. 5: Civil War HC (2007, $19.99) r/#21-25 20.00
... Vol. 5: Civil War SC (2007, $14.99) r/#21-25 15.00
... Vol. 6: Revolution HC (2007, $19.99) r/#26-31 20.00
... Vol. 6: Revolution SC (2007, $14.99) r/#26-31 15.00

NEW AVENGERS: ILLUMINATI (Also see Civil War)
Marvel Comics: Feb, 2007 - No. 5 ($2.99, limited series)
1-4-Bendis & Reed-s/Cheung-a. 3-Origin of The Beyonder 3.00

NEW AVENGERS/TRANSFORMERS
Marvel Comics: Sept, 2007 - No. 4 ($2.99, limited series)
1-3-Kirkham-a; Capt. America app. 1-Cheung-c. 2-Pearson-c 3.00

NEW BOOK OF COMICS (Also see Big Book Of Fun)
National Periodical Publ.: 1937; No. 2, Spring, 1938 (100 pgs. each) (Reprints)
1(Rare)-1st regular size comic annual; 2nd DC annual; contains r/New Comics #1-4 & More Fun #9; r/Federal Men (8 pgs.), Henri Duval (1 pg.) & Dr. Occult in costume (1 pg.) by Siegel & Shuster; Moldoff, Sheldon Mayer (15 pgs.)-a
1850 3700 5550 12,000 21,000 29,000
2-Contains-r/More Fun #15 & 16; r/Dr. Occult in costume (a Superman prototype), & Calling All Cars (4 pgs.) by Siegel & Shuster 950 1900 2850 6175 11,069 15,500

NEW COMICS (New Adventure #12 on)
National Periodical Publ.: 12/35 - No. 11, 12/36 (No. 1-6: paper cover) (No. 1-5: 84 pgs.)
V1#1-Billy the Kid, Sagebrush 'n' Cactus, Jibby Jones, Needles, The Vikings, Sir Loin of Beef, Now-When I Was a Boy, & other 1-2 pg. strips; 2 pgs. Kelly art(1st)-(Gulliver's Travels); Sheldon Mayer-a(1st)(2 pgs. strips); Vincent Sullivan-c(1st)
2714 5428 8142 19,000 – –
2-1st app. Federal Men by Siegel & Shuster & begins (also see The Comics Magazine #2); Mayer, Kelly-a (Rare)(1/36) 1143 2286 3429 8000 – –
3-6: 3,4-Sheldon Mayer-a which continues in The Comics Magazine #1. 3-Vincent Sullivan-c. 4-Dickens' "A Tale of Two Cities" adaptation begins. 5-Junior Federal Men Club; Kiefer-a.
6- "She" adaptation begins 800 1600 2400 5600 – –
7-10 571 1142 1713 4000 – –
11-Ties with More Fun #16 as DC's 1st Christmas-c 600 1200 1800 4200 – –
NOTE: #1-6 rarely occur in mint condition. Whitney Ellsworth c-4-11.

NEW DEFENDERS (See Defenders)

NEW DNAGENTS, THE (Formerly DNAgents)
Eclipse Comics: V2#1, Oct, 1985 - V2#17, Mar, 1987 (Whole #s 25-40; Mando paper)
V2#1-17: 1-Origin recap. 7-Begin 95 cent-c. 9,10-Airboy preview 2.50
3-D 1 (1/86, $2.25) 2.50
2-D 1 (1/86)-Limited ed. (100 copies) 10.00

NEW ETERNALS: APOCALYPSE NOW (Also see Eternals, The)
Marvel Comics: Feb, 2000 ($3.99, one-shot)
1-Bennett & Hanna-a; Ladronn-c 4.00

NEW EXCALIBUR
Marvel Comics: Jan, 2006 - Present ($2.99)
1-23: 1-Claremont-s/Ryan-a; Dazzler app. 3-Juggernaut app. 4-Lionheart app. 3.00
... Vol. 1: Defenders of the Realm TPB (2006, $17.99) r/#1-7 18.00
... Vol. 2: Last Days of Camelot TPB (2007, $19.99) r/#8-15 20.00

NEWFORCE (Also see Newmen)
Image Comics (Extreme Studios): Jan, 1996-No. 4, Apr, 1996 ($2.50, lim. series)
1-4: 1-"Extreme Destroyer" Pt. 8; polybagged w/gaming card. 4-Newforce disbands 2.50

NEW FUN COMICS (More Fun #7 on; see Big Book of Fun Comics)
National Periodical Publications: Feb, 1935 - No. 6, Oct, 1935 (10x15", No. 1-4,: slick-c) (No. 1-5: 36 pgs; 40 pgs. No. 6)
V1#1 (1st DC comic); 1st app. Oswald The Rabbit; Jack Woods (cowboy) begins
7000 14,000 21,000 49,000 – –
2(3/35)-(Very Rare) 3000 6000 9000 21,000 – –

3-5(8/35): 3-Don Drake on the Planet Soro-c/story (sci/fi, 4/35); early (maybe 1st) DC letter column. 5-Soft-c 1650 3300 4950 11,500 – –
6(10/35)-1st Dr. Occult by Siegel & Shuster (Leger & Reuths); last "New Fun" title. "New Comics" #1 begins in Dec. which is reason for title change to More Fun; Henri Duval (ends #10) by Siegel & Shuster; paper-c
3300 6600 9900 23,000 – –

NEW FUNNIES (The Funnies #1-64; Walter Lantz...#109 on; New TV... #259, 260, 272, 273; TV Funnies #261-271)
Dell Publishing Co.: No. 65, July, 1942 - No. 288, Mar-Apr, 1962
65(#1)-Andy Panda in a world of real people, Raggedy Ann & Andy, Oswald the Rabbit (with Woody Woodpecker x-overs), Li'l Eight Ball & Peter Rabbit begin; Bugs Bunny and Elmer app. 67 134 201 570 1060 1550
66-70: 66-Felix the Cat begins. 67-Billy & Bonny Bee by Frank Thomas begins. 69-Kelly-a (2 pgs.); The Brownies begin (not by Kelly) 32 64 96 240 438 635
71-75: 72-Kelly illos. 75-Brownies by Kelly? 21 42 63 156 278 400
76-Andy Panda (Carl Barks & Pabian-a); Woody Woodpecker x-over in Oswald ends 73 146 219 621 1148 1675
77,78: 77-Kelly-c. 78-Andy Panda in a world with real people ends 21 42 63 156 278 400
79-81 14 28 42 103 184 265
82-Brownies by Kelly begins; Homer Pigeon begins 15 30 45 111 198 285
83-85-Brownies by Kelly in ea. 83-X-mas-c; Homer Pigeon begins. 85-Woody Woodpecker, 1 pg. strip begins 15 30 45 109 195 280
86-90: 87-Woody Woodpecker stories begin 11 22 33 79 140 200
91-99 9 18 27 63 107 150
100 (6/45) 9 18 27 65 113 160
101-120: 119-X-mas-c 7 14 21 49 80 110
121-150: 131,143-X-mas-c 6 12 18 43 69 95
151-200: 155-X-mas-c. 167-X-mas-c. 182-Origin & 1st app. Knothead & Splinter.
191-X-mas-c 6 12 18 37 59 80
201-240 5 10 15 32 51 70
241-288: 270,271-Walter Lantz c-app. 281-1st story swipes/WDC&S #100
4 8 12 28 44 60

NOTE: Early issues written by John Stanley.

NEW GODS, THE (1st Series)(New Gods #12 on)(See Adventure #459, DC Graphic Novel #4, 1st Issue Special #13 & Super-Team Family)
National Periodical Publications/DC Comics: 2-3/71 - V2#11, 10-11/72; V3#12, 7/77 - V3#19, 7-8/78 (Fourth World)
1-Intro/1st app. Orion; 4th app. Darkseid (cameo; 3 weeks after Forever People #1) (#1-3 are 15¢ issues) 8 16 24 56 93 130
2-Darkseid-c/story (2nd full app., 4-5/71) 4 8 12 28 44 60
3-1st app. Black Racer; last 15¢ issue 3 6 9 20 30 40
4-9: (25¢, 52 pg. giants): 4-Darkseid cameo; origin Manhunter-r. 5,7,8-Young Gods feature. 7-Darkseid app. (2-3/72); origin Orion; 1st origin of all New Gods as a group.
9-1st app. Forager 3 6 9 20 30 40
10,11-11-Last Kirby issue. 3 6 9 16 23 30
12-19: Darkseid storyline w/minor apps. 12-New costume Orion (see 1st Issue Special #13 for 1st new costume). 19-Story continued in Adventure Comics #459,460
1 2 3 5 7 9
Jack Kirby's New Gods TPB ('98, $11.95, B&W&Grey) r/#1-11 plus cover gallery of original series and '84 reprints 12.00
NOTE: #4-9(25¢, 52 pgs.) contain Manhunter-r by Simon & Kirby from Adventure #73, 74, 75, 76, 77, 78 with covers in that order. Adkins i-12-14, 17-19. Buckler a(p)-15. Kirby c/a-1-11p. Newton a(p)-12-14, 16-19. Starlin c-17. Staton c-19p.

NEW GODS (Also see DC Graphic Novel #4)
DC Comics: June, 1984 - No. 6, Nov, 1984 ($2.00, Baxter paper)
1-5: New Kirby-c; r/New Gods #1-10. 4.00
6-Reprints New Gods #11 w/48 pgs of new Kirby story & art; leads into DC Graphic Novel #4 2 4 6 8 10 12

NEW GODS (2nd Series)
DC Comics: Feb, 1989 - No. 28, Aug, 1991 ($1.50)
1-28 2.50

NEW GODS (3rd Series) (Becomes Jack Kirby's Fourth World) (Also see Showcase '94 #1 & Showcase '95 #7)
DC Comics: Oct, 1995 - No. 15, Feb, 1997 ($1.95)
1-11,13-15: 9-Giffen-a(p). 10,11-Superman app. 13-Takion, Mr. Miracle & Big Barda app. 13-15-Byrne-a(p)/scripts & Simonson-c. 15-Apokolips merged w/ New Genesis; story cont'd in Jack Kirby's Fourth World 2.50
12-(11/96, 99¢)-Byrne-a(p)/scripts & Simonson-c begin; Takion cameo; indicia reads October 1996 2.50
...Secret Files 1 (9/98, $4.95) Origin-s 5.00

New Love #6 © Gilbert Hernandez

New Mutants #93 © MAR

New Talent Showcase #13 © DC

	GD 2.0	VG 4.0	FN 6.0	VF 8.0	VF/NM 9.0	NM- 9.2

NEW GUARDIANS, THE
DC Comics: Sept, 1988 - No. 12, Sept, 1989 ($1.25)

1-($2.00, 52 pgs)-Staton-c/a in #1-9						3.00
2-12						2.50

NEW HEROIC (See Heroic)

NEW INVADERS (Titled Invaders for #0 & #1) (See Avengers V3#83,84)
Marvel Comics: No. 0, Aug, 2004 - No. 9, June, 2005 ($2.99)

0-9-Roster of U.S. Agent, Sub-Mariner, Blazing Skull and others. 0-Avengers app.						3.00

NEW JUSTICE MACHINE, THE (Also see The Justice Machine)
Innovation Publishing: 1989 - No. 3, 1989 ($1.95, limited series)

1-3						2.50

NEW KIDS ON THE BLOCK, THE (Also see Richie Rich and...)
Harvey Comics: Dec, 1990 - No. 8, Dec, 1991 ($1.25)

1-8						2.50
...Back Stage Pass 1(12/90) - 7(11/91) Chillin' 1(12/90) - 7(12/91): 1-Photo-c						
...Comic Tour '90/91 1 (12/90) - 7(12/91) Digest 1(1/91) - 5(1/92) Hanging Tough 1 (2/91)						
Magic Summer Tour 1 (Fall/90) Magic Summer Tour nn (Fall/90, sold at concerts)						
Step By Step 1 (Fall/90, one-shot) Valentine Girl 1 (Fall/90, one-shot)-Photo-c						2.50

NEW LINE CINEMA'S TALES OF HORROR (Anthology)
DC Comics (WildStorm): Nov, 2007 - Present ($2.99)

1-Freddy Krueger and Leatherface app.; Darick Robertson-c						3.00

NEW LOVE (See Love & Rockets)
Fantagraphics Books: Aug, 1996 - No. 6, Dec, 1997 ($2.95, B&W, lim. series)

1-6: Gilbert Hernandez-s/a						3.00

NEWMAN
Image Comics (Extreme Studios): Jan, 1996 - No. 4, Apr, 1996 ($2.50, lim. series)

1-4: 1-Extreme Destroyer Pt. 3; polybagged w/card. 4-Shadowhunt tie-in; Eddie Collins becomes new Shadowhawk						2.50

NEW MANGAVERSE (Also see Marvel Mangaverse)
Marvel Comics: Mar, 2006 - No. 5, July, 2006 ($2.99, lim. series)

1-5: Cebulski-s/Ohtsuka-a; The Hand and Elektra app.						3.00
...: The Rings of Fate (2006, $7.99, digest) r/#1-5						8.00

NEWMEN (becomes The Adventures Of The...#22)
Image Comics (Extreme Studios): Apr, 1994 - No. 20, Nov, 1995; No. 21, Nov, 1996 ($1.95/$2.50)

1-21: 1-5: Matsuda-c/a. 10-Polybagged w/trading card. 11-Polybagged. 20-Has a variant-c; Babewatch! x-over. 21-(11/96)-Series relaunch; Chris Sprouse-a begins; pin-up. 16-Has a variant-c by Quesada & Palmiotti						2.50
TPB-(1996, $12.95) r/#1-4 w/pin-ups						13.00

NEW MEN OF BATTLE, THE
Catechetical Guild: 1949 (nn) (Carboard-c)

nn(V8#1-3,5,6)-192 pgs.; contains 5 issues of Topix rebound	9	18	27	47	61	75
nn(V8#7-V8#11)-160 pgs.; contains 5 iss. of Topix	9	18	27	47	61	75

NEW MUTANTS, THE (See Marvel Graphic Novel #4 for 1st app.)(Also see X-Force & Uncanny X-Men #167)
Marvel Comics Group: Mar, 1983 - No. 100, Apr, 1991

1						5.00
2-10: 3,4-Ties into X-Men #167. 10-1st app. Magma						3.00
11-17,19,20: 13-Kitty Pryde app. 16-1st app. Warpath (w/out costume); see X-Men #193						2.50
18,21: 18-Intro. new Warlock. 21-Double size; origin new Warlock; newsstand version has cover price written in by Sienkiewicz						3.00
22-24,27-30: 23-25-Cloak & Dagger app.						2.50
25,26: 25-1st brief app. Legion. 26-1st full Legion app.						4.00
31-58: 35-Magneto intro'd as new headmaster. 43-Portacio-i. 50-Double size. 58-Contains pull-out mutant registration form						2.50
59-61: Fall of The Mutants series. 60(52 pgs.)						3.00
62-85: 68-Intro Spyder. 63-X-Men & Wolverine clones app. 73-(52 pgs.). 76-X-Factor & X-Terminator app. 85-Liefeld-c begins						2.50
86-Rob Liefeld-a begins; McFarlane-c/(i) swiped from Ditko splash pg.; 1st brief app. Cable (last page teaser)						6.00
87-1st full app. Cable (3/90)	2	4	6	11	16	20
87-2nd printing; gold metallic ink-c ($1.00)						2.50
88-2nd app. Cable	1	2	3	4	5	7
92-No Liefeld-a; Liefeld-c						4.00
89,90,91,93-100: 89-3rd app. Cable. 90-New costumes. 90,91-Sabretooth app. 93,94-Cable						

vs. Wolverine. 95-97-X-Tinction Agenda x-over. 95-Death of new Warlock. 97-Wolverine & Cable-c, but no app. 98-1st app. Deadpool, Gideon & Domino (2/91); 2nd Shatterstar (cameo). 99-1st app. of Feral (of X-Force); Byrne-c/swipe (X-Men, 1st Series #138).						
100-(52 pgs.)-1st brief app. X-Force.						5.00
95,100-Gold 2nd printing. 100-Silver ink 3rd printing						2.50
Annual 1 (1984)						4.00
Annual 2 (1986, $1.25)-1st Psylocke	1	2	3	5	6	8
Annual 3,4,6,7 ('87, '88,'90,'91, 68 pgs.): 4-Evolutionary War x-over. 6-1st new costumes by Liefeld (3 pgs.); 1st brief app. Shatterstar (of X-Force). 7-Liefeld pin-up only; X-Terminators back-up story; 2nd app. X-Force (cont'd in New Warriors Annual #1)						3.00
Annual 5 (1989, $2.00, 68 pgs.)-Atlantis Attacks; 1st Liefeld-a on New Mutants						4.00
...Classic Vol. 1 TPB (2006, $24.99) r/#1-7, Marvel Graphic Novel #4, Uncanny X-Men #167						25.00
...Classic Vol. 2 TPB (2007, $24.99) r/#8-17						25.00
Special 1-Special Edition ('85, 68 pgs.)-Ties in w/X-Men Alpha Flight limited series; cont'd in X-Men Annual #9; Art Adams/Austin-a						5.00
Summer Special 1(Sum/90, $2.95, 84 pgs.)						3.00

NOTE: **Art Adams** c-38, 39. **Austin** c-57i. **Byrne** c/a-75p. **Liefeld** a-86-91p, 93-96p, 98-100, Annual 5p, 6(3 pgs.); c-85-91p, 92, 93p, 94, 95, 96p, 97-100, Annual 5, 6p. **McFarlane** c-85-89i, 93i. **Portacio** a(i)-43. **Russell** a-48i. **Sienkiewicz** a-18-31, 35-38i; c-17-31, 35i, 37i, Annual 1. **Simonson** c-11p. **B. Smith** c-36, 40-48. **Williamson** a(i)-69, 71-73, 78-80, 82, 83; c(i)-69, 72, 73, 78i.

NEW MUTANTS (Continues as New X-Men (Academy X))
Marvel Comics: July, 2003 - No. 13, June, 2004 ($2.50/$2.99)

1-7: 1-6-Josh Middleton-c. 7-Bachalo-c						2.50
8-13 ($2.99) 8-11-Bachalo-c						3.00
...Vol. 1: Back To School TPB (2005, $16.99) r/#1-6; new Middleton-c						17.00

NEW MUTANTS, THE: TRUTH OR DEATH
Marvel Comics: Nov, 1997 - No. 3, Jan, 1998 ($2.50, limited series)

1-3-Raab/Chang-a(p)						2.50

NEW ORDER, THE
CFD Publishing: Nov, 1994 ($2.95)

1						3.00

NEW PEOPLE, THE (TV)
Dell Publishing Co.: Jan, 1970 - No. 2, May, 1970

1	3	6	9	17	25	32
2	3	6	9	15	21	26

NEW ROMANCES
Standard Comics: No. 5, May, 1951 - No. 21, May, 1954

5-Photo-c	15	30	45	84	127	170
6-9: 6-Barbara Bel Geddes, Richard Basehart "Fourteen Hours" photo-c. 7-Ray Milland & Joan Fontaine photo-c. 9-Photo-c from '50s movie	10	20	30	54	72	90
10,14,16,17-Toth-a	10	20	30	58	79	100
11-Toth-a; Liz Taylor, Montgomery Clift photo-c	26	52	78	152	239	325
12,13,15,18-21	9	18	27	50	65	80

NOTE: **Celardo** a-9. **Moreira** a-6. **Tuska** a-7, 20. Photo c-5-16.

NEW SHADOWHAWK, THE (Also see Shadowhawk & Shadowhunt)
Image Comics (Shadowline Ink): June, 1995 - No. 7, Mar, 1996 ($2.50)

1-7: Kurt Busiek scripts in all						3.00

NEW STATESMEN, THE
Fleetway Publications (Quality Comics): 1989 - No. 5, 1990 ($3.95, limited series, mature readers, 52pgs.)

1-5: Futuristic; squarebound; 3-Photo-c						4.00

NEWSTRALIA
Innovation Publ.: July, 1989 - No. 5, 1989 ($1.75, color)(#2 on, $2.25, B&W)

1-5: 1,2: Timothy Truman-c/a; Gustovich-i						2.50

NEW TALENT SHOWCASE (Talent Showcase #16 on)
DC Comics: Jan, 1984 - No. 19, Oct, 1985 (Direct sales only)

1-19: Features new strips & artists. 18-Williamson-c(i)						2.50

NEW TEEN TITANS, THE (See DC Comics Presents #26, Marvel and DC Present & Teen Titans; Tales of the Teen Titans #41 on)
DC Comics: Nov, 1980 - No. 40, Mar, 1984

1-Robin, Kid Flash, Wonder Girl, The Changeling (1st app.), Starfire, The Raven, Cyborg begin; partial origin	2	4	6	9	12	15
2-1st app. Deathstroke the Terminator	3	6	9	18	27	35
3-10: 3-Origin Starfire; Intro The Fearsome Five. 4-Origin continues; J.L.A. app. 6-Origin Raven. 7-Cyborg origin. 8-Origin Kid Flash retold. 9-Minor app. Deathstroke on last pg. 10-2nd app. Deathstroke the Terminator (see Marvel & DC Present for 3rd app.); origin Changeling retold						6.00

New Teen Titans #28 © DC

New Warriors #25 © MAR

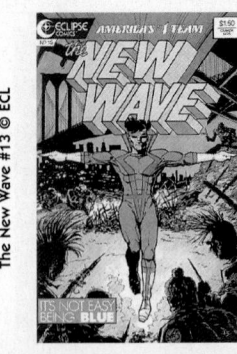

The New Wave #13 © ECL

	GD 2.0	VG 4.0	FN 6.0	VF 8.0	VF/NM 9.0	NM- 9.2

11-20: 13-Return of Madame Rouge & Capt. Zahl; Robotman revived. 14-Return of Mento; origin Doom Patrol. 15-Death of Madame Rouge & Capt. Zahl; intro. new Brotherhood of Evil. 16-1st app. Captain Carrot (free 16 pg. preview). 18-Return of Starfire. 19-Hawkman teams-up — 5.00

21-40: 21-Intro Night Force in free 16 pg. insert; intro Brother Blood. 23-1st app. Vigilante (not in costume), & Blackfire. 24-Omega Men app. 25-Omega Men cameo; free 16 pg. preview Masters of the Universe. 26-1st app. Terra. 27-Free 16 pg. preview Atari Force. 29-The New Brotherhood of Evil & Speedy app. 30-Terra joins the Titans. 34-4th app. Deathstroke the Terminator.37-Batman & The Outsiders x-over. 38-Origin Wonder Girl. 39-Last Dick Grayson as Robin; Kid Flash quits — 4.00
Annual 1(11/82)-Omega Men app. — 5.00
Annual V2#2(9/83)-1st app. Vigilante in costume; 1st app. Lyla — 4.00
Annual 3 (See Tales of the Teen Titans Annual #3)
...: Terra Incognito TPB (2006, $19.99) r/#26,28-34 & Annual #2 — 20.00
...: The Judas Contract TPB (2003, $19.95) r/#39,40 plus Tales of the Teen Titans #41-44 & Annual #3 — 20.00
...: Who is Donna Troy? TPB (2005, $19.99) r/#38,Tales of the Teen Titans #50, New Titans #50-55 and Teen Titans/Outsiders Secret Files 2003 — 20.00
NOTE: Perez a-1-4p, 6-34p, 37-40p, Annual 1p, 2p; c-1-12, 13-17p, 18-21, 22p, 23p, 24-37, 38, 39(painted), 40, Annual 1, 2.

NEW TEEN TITANS, THE (Becomes The New Titans #50 on)
DC Comics: Aug, 1984 - No. 49, Nov, 1988 ($1.25/$1.75; deluxe format)

1-New storyline; Perez-c/a begins — 6.00
2,3: 2-Re-intro Lilith — 5.00
4-10: 5-Death of Trigon. 7-9-Origin Lilith. 8-Intro Kole. 10-Kole joins — 4.00
11-49: 13,14-Crisis x-over. 20-Robin (Jason Todd) joins; original Teen Titans return. 38-Infinity, Inc. x-over. 47-Origin of all Titans; Titans (East & West) pin-up by Perez — 3.00
Annual 1-4 (9/85-'88): 1-Intro. Vanguard. 2-Byrne (Jason Todd) c/a(p); origin Brother Blood; intro new Dr. Light. 3-Intro. Danny Chase. 4-Perez-c — 3.50
.... The Terror of Trigon TPB (2003, $17.95) r/#1-5; new cover by Phil Jimenez — 18.00
NOTE: Buckler c-10. Kelley Jones a-47, Annual 4. Erik Larsen a-33. Orlando c-33p. Perez a-1-5; c-1-7, 19-23, 43. Steacy c-47.

NEW TERRYTOONS (TV)
Dell Publishing Co./Gold Key: 6-8/60 - No. 8, 3-5/62; 10/62 - No. 54, 1/79

1(1960-Dell)-Deputy Dawg, Dinky Duck & Hashimoto-San begin (1st app. of each)
	8	16	24	54	90	125
2-8(1962)
	5	10	15	30	48	65
1(30010-210)(10/62-Gold Key, 84 pgs.)-Heckle & Jeckle begin
	8	16	24	58	97	135
2(30010-301)-84 pgs.
	8	16	24	52	86	120
3-5
	4	8	12	24	37	50
6-10
	3	6	9	20	30	40
11-20
	3	6	9	16	22	28
21-30
	2	4	6	9	13	16
31-43
	1	3	4	6	8	10
44-54: Mighty Mouse-c/s in all
	2	4	6	8	11	14
NOTE: Reprints: #4-12, 38, 40, 47. (See March of Comics #379, 393, 412, 435)

NEW TESTAMENT STORIES VISUALIZED
Standard Publishing Co.: 1946 - 1947

"New Testament Heroes–Acts of Apostles Visualized, Book I"
"New Testament Heroes–Acts of Apostles Visualized, Book II"
"Parables Jesus Told" Set....
	16	32	48	94	147	200
NOTE: All three are contained in a cardboard case, illustrated on front and into about the set.

NEW THUNDERBOLTS (Continues in Thunderbolts #100)
Marvel Comics: Jan, 2005 - No. 18, Apr, 2006 ($2.99)

1-18: 1-Grummett-a/Nicieza-s. 1-Captain Marvel app. 2-Namor app. 4-Wolverine app. — 3.00
... Vol. 1: One Step Forward (2005, $14.99) r/#1-6 — 15.00
... Vol. 2: Modern Marvels (2005, $14.99) r/#7-12 — 15.00
... Vol. 3: Right of Power (2006, $17.99) r/#13-18 & Thunderbolts #100 — 18.00

NEW TITANS, THE (Formerly The New Teen Titans)
DC Comics: No. 50, Dec, 1988 - No. 130, Feb, 1996 ($1.75/$2.25)

50-Perez-c/a begins; new origin Wonder Girl — 6.00
51-59: 50-55-Painted-c. 55-Nightwing (Dick Grayson) forces Danny Chase to resign; Batman app. in flashback, Wonder Girl becomes Troia — 3.00
60,61: 60-A Lonely Place of Dying Part 2 continues from Batman #440; new Robin tie-in; Timothy Drake app. 61-A Lonely Place of Dying Part 4 — 3.00
62-99,101-124,126-130: 62-65: Deathstroke the Terminator app. 65-Tim Drake (Robin) app. 70-1st Deathstroke solo cover/sty. 71-(44 pgs.)-10th anniversary issue; Deathstroke cameo. 72-79-Deathstroke in all: 74-Intro. Pantha. 79-Terra brought back to life; 1 panel cameo Team Titans (1st app.). Deathstroke in #80-84,86. 80-2nd full app. Team Titans. 83,84-Deathstroke kills his son, Jericho. 85-Team Titans app. 86-Deathstroke vs. Nightwing-c/story; last Deathstroke app. 87-New costume Nightwing. 90-92-Parts 2,5,8

Total Chaos (Team Titans). 115-(11/94) — 2.50
100-($3.50, 52 pgs.)-Holo-grafx foil-c — 3.50
125 (3.50)-wraparound-c — 3.50
#0-(10/94) Zero Hour, released between #114 & 115 — 2.50
Annual 5-10 ('89-'94, 68 pgs.. 7-Armageddon 2001 x-over; 1st full app. Teen (Team) Titans (new group). 8-Deathstroke app.; Eclipso app. (minor). 10-Elseworlds story — 3.50
Annual 11 (1995, $3.95)-Year One story — 4.00
NOTE: Perez a-50-55p, 57,60p, 58,59,61(layouts); c-50-61, 62-67i, Annual 5i; co-plots-66.

NEW TV FUNNIES (See New Funnies)

NEW TWO-FISTED TALES, THE
Dark Horse Comics/Byron Preiss:1993 ($4.95, limited series, 52 pgs.)

1-Kurtzman-r & new-a — 5.00
NOTE: Eisner c-1i. Kurtzman c-1p, 2.

NEWUNIVERSAL
Marvel Comics: Feb, 2007 - Present ($2.99)

1-6-Warren Ellis-s/Salvador Larroca-a. 1,2-Variant covers by Ribic — 3.00
...: Everything Went White HC (2007, $19.99) r/#1-6; sketch pages — 20.00

NEW WARRIORS, THE (See Thor #411,412)
Marvel Comics: July, 1990 - No. 75, 1996 ($1.00/$1.50)

1-Williamson-i; Bagley-c/a(p) in 1-13, Annual 1 — 5.00
1-Gold 2nd printing (7/91) — 2.50
2-5: 1,3-Guice-c(i). 2-Williamson-c/a(i). — 3.00
6-24,26-49,51-75: 7-Punisher cameo (last pg.). 8,9-Punisher app. 14-Darkhawk & Namor x-over. 17-Fantastic Four & Silver Surfer x-over. 19-Gideon (of X-Force) app. 28-Intro Turbo & Cardinal. 31-Cannonball & Warpath app. 42-Nova vs. Firelord. 46-Photo-c. 47-Bound-in S-M trading card sheet. 52-12 pg. ad insert. 62-Scarlet Spider-c/app. 70-Spider-Man-c/app. 72-Avengers-c/app. — 2.50
25-($2.50, 52 pgs.)-Die-cut cover — 3.00
40,60: 40-($2.25)-Gold foil collector's edition — 3.00
50-($2.95, 52 pgs.)-Glow in the dark-c — 3.00
Annual 1-4('91-'94,68 pgs.)-1-Origins all members; 3rd app. X-Force (cont'd from New Mutants Ann. #7 & cont'd in X-Men Ann. #15); x-over before X-Force #1. 3-Bagged w/card — 3.00

NEW WARRIORS, THE
Marvel Comics: Oct, 1999 - No. 10, July, 2000 ($2.99/$2.50)

0-Wizard supplement; short story and preview sketchbook — 2.25
1-($2.99) — 3.00
2-10: 2-Two covers. 5-Generation X app. 9-Iron Man-c — 2.50

NEW WARRIORS (See Civil War #1)
Marvel Comics: Aug, 2005 - No. 6, Feb, 2006 ($2.99, limited series)

1-6-Scottie Young-a — 3.00
...: Reality Check TPB (2006, $14.99) r/#1-6 — 15.00

NEW WARRIORS (The Initiative)
Marvel Comics: Aug, 2007 - Present ($2.99)

1-4: 1-Medina-a; new team is formed. 2-4-Jubilee app. — 3.00

NEW WAVE, THE
Eclipse Comics: 6/10/86 - No. 13, 3/87 (#1-8: bi-weekly, 20pgs; #9-13: monthly)

1-13:1-Origin, concludes #5. 6-Origin Megabyte. 8,9-The Heap returns. 13-Snyder-c — 2.50
...Versus the Volunteers 3-D #1,2(4/87): 1-Snyder-c — 3.00

NEW WEST, THE
Black Bull Comics: Mar, 2005 - No. 2, Jun, 2005 ($4.99, limited series)

1,2-Phil Noto-a/c; Jimmy Palmiotti-s — 5.00

NEW WORLD (See Comic Books, series I)

NEW WORLDS
Caliber: 1996 - No. 6 ($2.95/$3.95, 80 pgs., B&W, anthology)

1-6: 1-Mister X & other stories — 4.00

NEW X-MEN (See X-Men 2nd series #114-156)

NEW X-MEN (Academy X) (Continued from New Mutants)
Marvel Comics: July, 2004 - Present ($2.99)

1-42: 1,2-Green-c/a. 16-19-House of M. 20,21-Decimation. 40-Endangered Species back-ups begin — 3.00
Yearbook 1 (12/05, $3.99) new story and profile pages — 4.00
...: Childhood's End Vol. 1 TPB (2006, $10.99) r/#20-23 — 11.00
...: Childhood's End Vol. 2 TPB (2006, $10.99) r/#24-27 — 11.00
...: Childhood's End Vol. 3 TPB (2006, $10.99) r/#28-32 — 11.00
...: Childhood's End Vol. 4 TPB (2007, $10.99) r/#33-36 — 11.00
House of M: New X-Men TPB (2006, $13.99) r/#16-19 and selections from Secrets Of The House of M one-shot — 14.00

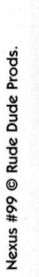

New York World's Fair 1940 © DC

Nexus #99 © Rude Dude Prods.

Nickel Comics #4 © FAW

	GD	VG	FN	VF	VF/NM	NM-
	2.0	4.0	6.0	8.0	9.0	9.2

... Vol. 1: Choosing Sides TPB (2004, $14.99) r/#1-6 — 15.00
... Vol. 2: Haunted TPB (2005, $14.99) r/#7-12 — 15.00
... Vol. 3: X-Posed TPB (2006, $14.99) r/#12-15 & Yearbook Special — 15.00

NEW X-MEN: HELLIONS
Marvel Comics: July, 2005 - No. 4, Oct, 2005 ($2.99, limited series)
1-4-Henry-a/Weir & DeFilippis-s — 3.00
TPB (2006, $9.99) r/#1-4 — 10.00

NEW YORK GIANTS (See Thrilling True Story of the Baseball Giants)

NEW YORK STATE JOINT LEGISLATIVE COMMITTEE TO STUDY THE PUBLICATION OF COMICS, THE
N.Y. State Legislative Document: 1951, 1955

This document was referenced by Wertham for *Seduction of the Innocent*. Contains numerous repros from comics showing violence, sadism, torture, and sex. 1955 version (196p, No. 37, 2/23/55) - Sold for $180 in 1986.

NEW YORK, THE BIG CITY
Kitchen Sink Press: 1986 ($10.95, B&W); **DC Comics:** July, 2000 ($12.95, B&W)
nn-Will Eisner-s/a — 13.00

NEW YORK WORLD'S FAIR (Also see Big Book of Fun & New Book of Fun)
National Periodical Publ.: 1939, 1940 (100 pgs.; cardboard covers)
(DC's 4th & 5th annuals)
1939-Scoop Scanlon, Superman (blond haired Superman on-c), Sandman, Zatara, Slam Bradley, Ginger Snap by Bob Kane begin; 1st published app. The Sandman (see Adventure #40 for his 1st drawn story); Vincent Sullivan-c; cover background by Guardineer
| | 1900 | 3800 | 5700 | 14,000 | 31,000 | — |
1940-Batman, Hourman, Johnny Thunderbolt, Red, White & Blue & Hanko (by Creig Flessel) app.; Superman, Batman & Robin-c (1st time they all appear together); early Robin app.; 1st Burnley-c/a (per page)
| | 1000 | 2000 | 3000 | 7500 | 16,800 | — |
NOTE: The 1939 edition was published 4/29/39 and released 4/30/39, the day the fair opened, at 25¢, and was first sold only at the fair. Since all other comics were 10¢, it didn't sell. Remaining copies were advertised beginning in the August issues of most DC comics for 25¢, but soon the price was dropped to 15¢. Everyone that sent a quarter through the mail for it received a free Superman #1 or a #2 to make up the dime difference. 15¢ stickers were placed over the 25¢ price. Four variations on the 15¢ stickers are known. The 1940 edition was published 5/11/40 and was priced at 15¢. It was a precursor to World's Best #1.

NEW YORK: YEAR ZERO
Eclipse Comics: July, 1988 - No. 4, Oct, 1988 ($2.00, B&W, limited series)
1-4 — 2.50

NEXT, THE
DC Comics: Sept, 2006 - No. 6, Feb, 2007 ($2.99, limited series)
1-6-Tad Williams-s/Dietrich Smith-a; Superman app. — 3.00

NEXT MEN (See John Byrne's...)

NEXT NEXUS, THE
First Comics: Jan, 1989 - No. 4, April, 1989 ($1.95, limited series, Baxter paper)
1-4 Mike Baron scripts & Steve Rude-c/a — 2.50
TPB (10/89, $9.95) r/series — 10.00

NEXTWAVE: AGENTS OF H.A.T.E
Marvel Comics: March, 2006 - No. 12, Mar, 2007 ($2.99)
1-12-Warren Ellis-s/Stuart Immonen-a. 2-Fin Fang Foom app. 12-Devil Dinosaur app. — 3.00
Vol. 1 - This Is What They Want HC (2006, $19.99) r/#1-6; Ellis original pitch — 20.00
Vol. 1 - This Is What They Want SC (2007, $14.99) r/#1-6; Ellis original pitch — 15.00
Vol. 2 - I Kick Your Face HC (2007, $19.99) r/#7-12 — 20.00

NEXUS (See First Comics Graphic Novel #4, 19 & The Next Nexus)
Capital Comics/First Comics No. 7 on: June, 1981 - No. 6, Mar, 1984; No. 7, Apr, 1985 - No. 80?, May, 1991 (Direct sales only, 36 pgs.; V2#1(`83)-printed on Baxter paper)
1-B&W version; mag. size: w/double size poster
| | 3 | 6 | 9 | 14 | 19 | 24 |
1-B&W 1981 limited edition; 500 copies printed and signed; same as above except this version has a 2-pg. poster & a pencil sketch on paperboard by Steve Rude
| | 3 | 6 | 20 | 30 | 40 | |
2-B&W, magazine size
| | 2 | 4 | 6 | 10 | 14 | 18 |
3-B&W, magazine size; Brunner back-c; contains 33-1/3 rpm record ($2.95 price)
| | 2 | 4 | 6 | 8 | 11 | 14 |
V2#1-Color version — 4.00
2-49,51-80: 2-Nexus' origin begins. 67-Snyder-c/a — 2.50
50-($3.50, 52 pgs.) — 3.50
Hardcover Volume One (Dark Horse Books, 11/05, $49.95) r/#1-3 & V2 #1-4; creator bios — 50.00
Hardcover Volume Two (Dark Horse Books, 3/06, $49.95) r/V2 #5-11; creator bios — 50.00
Hardcover Volume Three (Dark Horse Books, 5/06, $49.95) r/V2 #12-18; Marz forward — 50.00
Hardcover Volume Four (Dark Horse Books, 8/06, $49.95) r/V2 #19-25; Powell forward — 50.00
Hardcover Volume Five (Dark Horse Books, 2/07, $49.95) r/V2 #26-32; Brubaker forward — 50.00
Hardcover Volume Six (Dark Horse Books, 2/07, $49.95) r/V2 #33-39; Evanier forward — 50.00
NOTE: *Bissette* c-V2#29. *Giffen* c/a-V2#23. *Gulacy* c-1 (B&W), 2(B&W). *Mignola* c/a-V2#28. *Rude* c-3(B&W).

V2#1-22, 24-27, 33-36, 39-42, 45-48, 50, 58-60, 75; a-1-3, V2#1-7, 8-16p, 18-22p, 24-27p, 33-36p, 39-42p, 45-48p, 50, 58, 59p, 60. **Paul Smith** a-V2#37, 38, 43, 44, 51-55p; c-V2#37, 38, 43, 44, 51-55.

NEXUS
Rude Dude Productions: No. 99, July, 2007 - Present ($2.99)
99-Mike Baron scripts & Steve Rude-c/a — 3.00

NEXUS: ALIEN JUSTICE
Dark Horse Comics: Dec, 1992 - No. 3, Feb, 1993 ($3.95, limited series)
1-3 Mike Baron scripts & Steve Rude-c/a — 4.00

NEXUS: EXECUTIONER'S SONG
Dark Horse Comics: June, 1996 - No. 4, Sept, 1996 ($2.95, limited series)
1-4 Mike Baron scripts & Steve Rude-c/a — 3.00

NEXUS FILES
First Comics: 1989 ($4.50, color/16pgs. B&W, one-shot, squarebound, 52 pgs.)
1-New Rude-a; info on Nexus — 4.50

NEXUS: GOD CON
Dark Horse Comics: Apr, 1997 - No. 2, May, 1997 ($2.95, limited series)
1,2-Baron-s/Rude-c/a — 3.00

NEXUS LEGENDS
First Comics: May, 1989 - No. 23, Mar, 1991 ($1.50, Baxter paper)\\
1-23: R/1-3(Capital) & early First Comics issues w/new Rude covers #1-6,9,10 — 2.50

NEXUS MEETS MADMAN (...Special)
Dark Horse Comics: May, 1996 ($2.95, one-shot)
nn-Mike Baron & Mike Allred scripts, Steve Rude-c/a. — 3.00

NEXUS: NIGHTMARE IN BLUE
Dark Horse Comics: July, 1997 - No. 4, Oct, 1997 ($2.95, limited series)
1-4: 1,2,4-Adam Hughes-c — 3.00

NEXUS: THE LIBERATOR
Dark Horse Comics: Aug, 1992 - No. 4, Nov, 1992 ($2.95, limited series)
1-4 — 3.00

NEXUS: THE ORIGIN
Dark Horse Comics: July, 1996 ($3.95, one-shot)
nn-Mike Baron- scripts, Steve Rude-c/a. — 4.00

NEXUS: THE WAGES OF SIN
Dark Horse Comics: Mar, 1995 - No. 4, June, 1995 ($2.95, limited series)
1-4 — 3.00

NFL SUPERPRO
Marvel Comics: Oct, 1991 - No. 12, Sept, 1992 ($1.00)
1-12: 1-Spider-Man-c/app. — 2.50
Special Edition (9/91, $2.00) Jusko painted-c — 3.00
Super Bowl Edition (3/91, squarebound) Jusko painted-c — 4.00

NICKEL COMICS
Dell Publishing Co.: 1938 (Pocket size - 7-1/2x5-1/2")(68 pgs.)
1- "Bobby & Chip" by Otto Messmer, Felix the Cat artist. Contains some English reprints
| | 79 | 158 | 237 | 494 | 822 | 1150 |

NICKEL COMICS
Fawcett Publications: Feb 1940
nn - Ashcan comic, not distributed to newsstands, only for in-house use. A CGC certified 9.6 copy sold for $7,200 in 2003.

NICKEL COMICS
Fawcett Publications: May, 1940 - No. 8, Aug, 1940 (36 pgs.; Bi-Weekly; 5¢)
1-Origin/1st app. Bulletman
| | 364 | 728 | 1092 | 2366 | 4183 | 6000 |
2
| | 114 | 228 | 342 | 713 | 1182 | 1650 |
3
| | 83 | 166 | 249 | 519 | 860 | 1200 |
4-The Red Gaucho begins
| | 67 | 134 | 201 | 419 | 697 | 975 |
5-7
| | 66 | 132 | 198 | 413 | 682 | 950 |
8-World's Fair-c; Bulletman moved to Master Comics #7 in October (scarce)
| | 86 | 172 | 258 | 538 | 894 | 1250 |
NOTE: *Beck* c-5-8. *Jack Binder* c-1-4. Bondage c-5. Bulletman c-1-8.

NICK FURY, AGENT OF SHIELD (See Fury, Marvel Spotlight #31 & Shield)
Marvel Comics Group: 6/68 - No. 15, 11/69; No. 16, 11/70 - No. 18, 3/71
1
| | 10 | 20 | 30 | 71 | 126 | 180 |
2-4: 4-Origin retold
| | 6 | 12 | 18 | 41 | 66 | 90 |
5-Classic-c
| | 7 | 14 | 21 | 45 | 73 | 100 |
6,7: 7-Salvador Dali painting swipe
| | 6 | 12 | 18 | 37 | 59 | 80 |

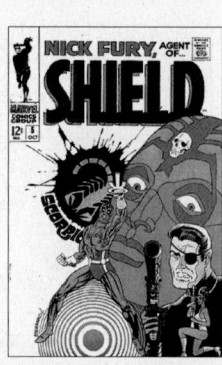

Nick Fury, Agent of SHIELD #5 © MAR

Night Force #8 © DC

Night Man #8 © MAL

	GD 2.0	VG 4.0	FN 6.0	VF 8.0	VF/NM 9.0	NM- 9.2

	GD 2.0	VG 4.0	FN 6.0	VF 8.0	VF/NM 9.0	NM- 9.2

8-11,13: 9-Hate Monger begins, ends #11. 10-Smith layouts/pencil. 11-Smith-c.

13-1st app. Super-Patriot; last 12¢ issue	4	8	12	22	34	45
12-Smith-c/a	4	8	12	23	36	48
14-Begin 15¢ issues	3	6	9	19	29	38

15-1st app. & death of Bullseye-c/story(11/69); Nick Fury shot & killed; last 15¢ issue

	7	14	21	45	73	100
16-18-(25¢, 52 pgs.)-r/Str. Tales #135-143	3	6	9	16	23	30
TPB (May 2000, $19.95) r/ Strange Tales #150-168						20.00
...: Who is Scorpio? TPB (11/00, $12.95) r/#1-3,5; Steranko-c						13.00

NOTE: **Adkins** a-3i. **Craig** a-10i. **Sid Greene** a-12i. **Kirby** a-16-18r. **Springer** a-4, 6, 7, 8p, 9, 10p, 11; c-8, 9. **Steranko** a(p)-1-3, 5; c-1-7.

NICK FURY AGENT OF SHIELD (Also see Strange Tales #135)
Marvel Comics: Dec, 1983 - No. 2, Jan, 1984 (2.00, 52 pgs., Baxter paper)

1,2-r/Nick Fury #1-4; new Steranko-c						3.50

NICK FURY, AGENT OF S.H.I.E.L.D.
Marvel Comics: Sept, 1989 - No. 47, May, 1993 ($1.50/$1.75)

V2#1-26,30-47: 10-Capt. America app. 13-Return of The Yellow Claw. 15-Fantastic Four app. 30,31-Deathlok app. 36-Cage app. 37-Woodgod c/story. 38-41-Flashes back to pre-Shield days after WWII. 44-Capt. America-c/s. 45-Viper-c/s. 46-Gideon x-over ... 2.25
27-29-Wolverine-c/stories ... 2.50

NOTE: **Alan Grant** scripts-11. **Guice** a(p)-20-23, 25, 26; c-20-28.

NICK FURY'S HOWLING COMMANDOS
Marvel Comics: Dec, 2005 - No. 6, May, 2006 ($2.99)

1-6: 1-Giffen-s/Francisco-a						3.00
1-Director's Cut ($3.99) r/#1 with original script and sketch design pages						4.00

NICK FURY VS. S.H.I.E.L.D.
Marvel Comics: June, 1988 - No. 6, Nov, 1988 ($3.50, 52 pgs, deluxe format)

1,2: 1-Steranko-c. 2-(Low print run) Sienkiewicz-c						5.00
3-6						4.00

NICK HALIDAY (Thrill of the Sea)
Argo: May, 1956

1-Daily & Sunday strip-r by Petree	8	16	24	44	57	70

NIGHT AND THE ENEMY (Graphic Novel)
Comico: 1988 (8-1/2x11") ($11.95, color, 80 pgs.)

1-Harlan Ellison scripts/Ken Steacy-c/a; r/Epic Illustrated & new-a (1st & 2nd printings)						12.00
1-Limited edition ($39.95)						40.00

NIGHT BEFORE CHRISTMAS, THE (See March of Comics No. 152 in the Promotional Comics section)

NIGHT BEFORE CHRISTMASK, THE
Dark Horse Comics: Nov, 1994 ($9.95, one-shot)

nn-Hardcover book; The Mask; Rick Geary-c/a						10.00

NIGHTBREED (See Clive Barker's Nightbreed)

NIGHT CLUB
Image Comics: Apr, 2005 - No. 4, Dec, 2006 ($2.95/$2.99, limited series)

1-4: 1-Mike Baron-s/Mike Norton-a						3.00

NIGHTCRAWLER (X-Men)
Marvel Comics Group: Nov, 1985 - No. 4, Feb, 1986 (Mini-series from X-Men)

1-4: 1-Cockrum-c/a						3.50

NIGHTCRAWLER (Volume 2)
Marvel Comics: Feb, 2002 - No. 4, May, 2002 ($2.50, limited series)

1-4-Matt Smith-a						2.50

NIGHTCRAWLER
Marvel Comics: Nov, 2004 - No. 12, Jan, 2006 ($2.99)

1-12: 1-6-Robertson-a/Land-c. 2-Magik app. 8-Wolverine app. 10-Man-Thing app.						3.00
...: The Devil Inside TPB (2005, $14.99) r/#1-6						15.00
...: The Winding Way TPB (2006, $14.99) r/#7-12						15.00

NIGHTFALL: THE BLACK CHRONICLES
DC Comics (Homage): Dec, 1999 - No. 3, Feb, 2000 ($2.95, limited series)

1-3-Coker-a/Gilmore-s						3.00

NIGHT FORCE, THE (See New Teen Titans #21)
DC Comics: Aug, 1982 - No. 14, Sept, 1983 (60¢)

1						4.00
2-14: 13-Origin Baron Winter. 14-Nudity panels						3.00

NOTE: **Colan** c/a-1-14p. **Giordano** c-1i, 2i, 4i, 5i, 7i, 12i.

NIGHT FORCE
DC Comics: Dec, 1996 - No. 12, Nov, 1997 ($2.25)

1-12: 1-3-Wolfman-s/Anderson-a(p). 8-"Convergence" part 2						2.50

NIGHT GLIDER
Topps Comics (Kirbyverse): April, 1993 ($2.95, one-shot)

1-Kirby c-1, Heck-a; polybagged w/Kirbychrome trading card						3.00

NIGHTHAWK
Marvel Comics: Sept, 1998 - No. 3, Nov, 1998 ($2.99, mini-series)

1-3-Krueger-s; Daredevil app.						3.00

NIGHTINGALE, THE
Henry H. Stansbury Once-Upon-A-Time Press, Inc.: 1948 (10¢, 7-1/4x10-1/4", 14 pgs., 1/2 B&W)

(Very Rare)-Low distribution; distributed to Westchester County & Bronx, N.Y. only; used in **Seduction of the Innocent**, pg. 312,313 as the 1st and only "good" comic book ever published. Ill. by Dong Kingman; 1,500 words of text, printed on high quality paper & no word balloons. Copyright registered 10/22/48, distributed week of 12/5/48. (By Hans Christian Andersen)

Estimated value........						$250

NIGHT MAN, THE (See Sludge #1)
Malibu Comics (Ultraverse): Oct, 1993 - No. 23, Aug, 1995 ($1.95/$2.50)

1-($2.50, 48 pgs.)-Rune flip-c/story by B. Smith (3 pgs.)						2.50
1-Ultra-Limited silver foil-c						6.00
2-15, 17: 3-Break-Thru x-over; Freex app. 4-Origin Firearm (2 pgs.) by Chaykin. 6-TNTNT app. 8-1st app. Teknight						2.50
16 ($3.50)-flip book (Ultraverse Premiere #11)						3.50
...: The Pilgrim Conundrum Saga (1/95, $3.95, 68 pgs.)-Strangers app.						4.00
18-23: 22-Loki-c/a						2.50
Infinity ($1.50)						2.50
...Vs. Wolverine #0-Kelley Jones-c; mail in offer	1	3	4	6	8	10

NOTE: **Zeck** a-16.

NIGHT MAN, THE
Malibu Comics (Ultraverse): Sept, 1995 - No.4, Dec, 1995 ($1.50, lim. series)

1-4: Post Black September storyline						2.50

NIGHT MAN, THE /GAMBIT
Malibu Comics (Ultraverse): Mar, 1996 - No. 3, May, 1996 ($1.95, lim. series)

0-Limited Premium Edition						4.00
1-3: David Quinn scripts in all. 3-Rhiannon discovered to be The Night Man's mother						2.50

NIGHTMARE
Ziff-Davis (Approved Comics)/St. John No. 3: Summer, 1952 - No. 3, Winter, 1952, 53 (Painted-c)

1-1 pg. Kinstler-a; Tuska-a(2)	54	108	162	338	557	775
2-Kinstler-a-Poe's "Pit & the Pendulum"	40	80	120	235	368	500
3-Kinstler-a	34	68	102	197	311	425

NIGHTMARE (Weird Horrors #1-9) (Amazing Ghost Stories #14 on)
St. John Publishing Co.: No. 10, Dec, 1953 - No. 13, Aug, 1954

10-Reprints Ziff-Davis Weird Thrillers #2 w/new Kubert-a plus 2 pgs. Kinstler-a; Anderson, Colan & Toth-a	53	106	159	323	537	750
11-Krigstein-a; painted-c; Poe adapt., "Hop Frog"	40	80	120	235	368	500
12-Kubert bondage-c; adaptation of Poe's "The Black Cat;" Cannibalism story	38	76	114	222	351	480
13-Reprints Z-D Weird Thrillers #3 with new cover; Powell-a(2), Tuska-a; Baker-c	26	52	78	152	239	325

NIGHTMARE (Magazine) (Also see Psycho)
Skywald Publishing Corp.: Dec, 1970 - No. 23, Feb, 1975 (B&W, 68 pgs.)

1-Everett-a; Heck-a; Shores-a	8	16	24	56	93	130
2-5,8,9: 2,4-Decapitation story. 5-Nazi-s; Boris Karloff 4 pg. photo/text-s. 8-Features E.C. movie "Tales From the Crypt"; reprints some E.C. comics panels. 9-Wrightson-a; bondage-c; 1st Lovecraft Saggoth Chronicles/Cthulhu	5	10	15	30	48	65
6-Kaluta-a; Jeff Jones-c, photo & interview; 1st Living Gargoyle; Love Witch-s w/nudity; Boris Karloff-s	5	10	15	32	51	70
7	4	8	12	24	37	50
10-Wrightson-a (1 pg.); Princess of Earth-c/s; Edward & Mina Sartyros, the Human Gargoyles series continues from Psycho #8	5	10	15	32	51	70
11-19: 12-Excessive gore, severed heads. 13-Lovecraft-s. 15-Dracula-c/s. 17-Vampires issue; Autobiography of a Vampire series begins	3	6	9	21	32	42
20-John Byrne's 1st artwork (2 pgs.)(8/74); severed head-c; Hitler app.	6	12	18	43	69	95
21-23: 21-(1974 Summer Special)-Kaluta-a. 22-Tomb of Horror issue. 23-(1975 Winter Special)	4	8	12	23	36	48
Annual 1(1972)-Squarebound; B. Jones-a	4	8	12	23	36	48
Winter Special 1(1973)-All new material	3	6	9	21	32	42
Yearbook nn(1974)-B. Jones, Reese, Wildey-a	3	6	9	21	32	42

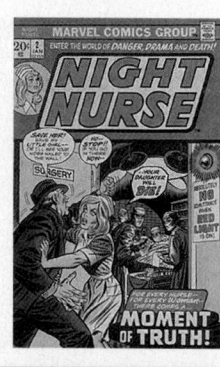

Night Nurse #2 © MAR

Nightside #1 © MAR

Nightwing #41 © DC

	GD	VG	FN	VF	VF/NM	NM-		GD	VG	FN	VF	VF/NM	NM-
	2.0	4.0	6.0	8.0	9.0	9.2		2.0	4.0	6.0	8.0	9.0	9.2

NOTE: **Adkins** a-5. **Boris** c-2, 3, 5 (#4 is not by Boris). **Buckler** a-3, 15. **Byrne** a-20p. **Everett** a-1, 2, 4, 5, 12. **Jeff Jones** a-6, 21(Psycho #6); c-6. **Katz** a-3, 5, 21. **Reese** a-4, 5. **Wildey** a-4, 5, 6, 21, '74 Yearbook. **Wrightson** a-9, 10.

NIGHTMARE (Alex Nino's)
Innovation Publishing: 1989 ($1.95)

1-Alex Nino-a 2.50

NIGHTMARE
Marvel Comics: Dec, 1994 - No. 4, Mar, 1995 ($1.95, limited series)

1-4 ..... 2.50

NIGHTMARE & CASPER (See Harvey Hits #71) (Casper & Nightmare #6 on)
(See Casper The Friendly Ghost #19)
Harvey Publications: Aug, 1963 - No. 5, Aug, 1964 (25¢)

1-All reprints?	8	16	24	52	86	120
2-5: All reprints?	5	10	15	30	48	65

NIGHTMARE ON ELM STREET, A (Also see Freddy Krueger's...)
DC Comics (WildStorm): Dec, 2006 - Present ($2.99)

1-8: 1-Two covers by Harris & Bradstreet; Dixon-s/West-a 3.00

NIGHTMARES (See Do You Believe in Nightmares)

NIGHTMARES
Eclipse Comics: May, 1985 - No. 2, May, 1985 ($1.75, Baxter paper)

1,2 ..... 3.00

NIGHTMARE THEATER
Chaos! Comics: Nov, 1997 - No. 4, Nov, 1997 ($2.50, mini-series)

1-4-Horror stories by various; Wrightson-a 2.50

NIGHTMARK: BLOOD & HONOR
Alpha Productions: 1994 - No. 3, 1994 ($2.50, B&W, mini-series)

1,2 ..... 2.50

NIGHTMARK MYSTERY SPECIAL
Alpha Productions: Jan, 1994 ($2.50, B&W)

1 ..... 2.50

NIGHTMASK
Marvel Comics Group: Nov, 1986 - No. 12, Oct, 1987

1-12 ..... 2.50

NIGHT MASTER
Silverwolf: Feb, 1987 ($1.50, B&W)

1-Tim Vigil-c/a 3.00

NIGHT MUSIC (See Eclipse Graphic Album Series, The Magic Flute)
Eclipse Comics: Dec, 1984 - No. 11, 1990 ($1.75/$3.95/$4.95, Baxter paper)

1-7: 3-Russell's Jungle Book adapt. 4,5-Pelleas And Melisande (double titled)
6-Salomé (double titled). 7-Red Dog #1 ..... 2.50
8-($3.95) Ariane and Bluebeard 4.00
9-11-($4.95) The Magic Flute; Russell adapt. 5.00

NIGHT NURSE
Marvel Comics Group: Nov, 1972 - No. 4, May, 1973

1	10	20	30	73	129	185
2-4	8	16	24	54	90	125

NIGHT OF MYSTERY
Avon Periodicals: 1953 (no month) (one-shot)

nn-1 pg. Kinstler-a, Hollingsworth-c	45	90	135	275	450	625

NIGHT OF THE GRIZZLY, THE (See Movie Classics)

NIGHTRAVEN (See Marvel Graphic Novel)

NIGHT RIDER (Western)
Marvel Comics Group: Oct, 1974 - No. 6, Aug, 1975

1: 1-6 reprint Ghost Rider #1-6 (#1-origin)	2	4	6	9	13	16
2-6	1	3	4	6	8	10

NIGHT'S CHILDREN: THE VAMPIRE
Millenium: July, 1995 - No. 2, Aug, 1995 ($2.95, B&W)

1,2: Wendy Snow-Lang story & art 3.00

NIGHTSIDE
Marvel Comics: Dec, 2001 - No. 4, Mar, 2002 ($2.99)

1-4: 1-Weinberg-s/Derenick-a; intro Sydney Taine 3.00

NIGHTS INTO DREAMS (Based on video game)
Archie Comics: Feb, 1998 -No. 6, Oct, 1998 ($1.75, limited series)

1-6 ..... 2.50

NIGHTSTALKERS (Also see Midnight Sons Unlimited)
Marvel Comics (Midnight Sons #14 on): Nov, 1992 - No. 18, Apr, 1994 ($1.75)

1-($2.75, 52 pgs.)-Polybagged w/poster; part 5 of Rise of the Midnight Sons storyline;
Garney/Palmer-c/a; Hannibal King, Blade & Frank Drake begin (see Tomb of Dracula
for & Dr. Strange) 3.00
2-9,11-18: 5-Punisher app. 7-Ghost Rider app. 8,9-Morbius app. 14-Spot varnish-c.
14,15-Siege of Darkness Pts 1 & 9 ..... 2.50
10-($2.25)-Outer-c is a Darkhold envelope made of black parchment w/gold ink;
Midnight Massacre part 1 ..... 2.75

NIGHT TERRORS, THE
Chanting Monks Studios: 2000 ($2.75, B&W)

1-Bernie Wrightson-c; short stories, one by Wrightson-s/a 2.75

NIGHT THRASHER (Also see The New Warriors)
Marvel Comics: Aug, 1993 - No. 21, Apr, 1995 ($1.75/$1.95)

1-($2.95, 52 pgs.)-Red holo-grafx foil-c; origin 3.00
2-21: 2-Intro Tantrum. 3-Gideon (of X-Force) app. 10-Bound-in trading card sheet; Iron Man
app. 15-Hulk app. 2.50

NIGHT THRASHER: FOUR CONTROL
Marvel Comics: Oct, 1992 - No. 4, Jan, 1993 ($2.00, limited series)

1-4: 2-Intro Tantrum. 3-Gideon (of X-Force) app. 2.50

NIGHT TRIBES
DC Comics (WildStorm): July, 1999 ($4.95, one-shot)

1-Golden & Sniegoski-s/Chin-a 5.00

NIGHTVEIL (Also see Femforce)
Americomics/AC Comics: Nov, 1984 - No. 7, 1987 ($1.75)

1-7 ..... 2.50
...'s Cauldron Of Horror 1 (1989, B&W)-Kubert, Powell, Wood-r plus new Nightveil story 3.00
...'s Cauldron Of Horror 2 (1990, $2.95, B&W)-Pre-code horror-r by Kubert & Powell 3.00
...'s Cauldron Of Horror 3 (1991) 3.00
Special 1 ('88, $1.95)-Kaluta-c 2.50
One Shot ('96, $5.95)-Flip book w/ Colt 6.00

NIGHTWATCH
Marvel Comics: Apr, 1994 - No. 12, Mar, 1995 ($1.50)

1-($2.95)-Collectors edition; foil-c; Ron Lim-c/a begins; Spider-Man app. 3.00
1-12-Regular edition. 2-Bound-in S-M trading card sheet; 5,6-Venom-c & app.
7,11-Cardiac app. 2.50

NIGHTWING (Also see New Teen Titans, New Titans, Showcase '93 #11,12,
Tales of the New Teen Titans & Teen Titans Spotlight)
DC Comics: Sept, 1995 - No. 4, Dec, 1995 ($2.25, limited series)

1-Dennis O'Neil story/Greg Land-a in all 5.00
2-4 ..... 4.00
...: Alfred's Return (7/95, $3.50) Giordano-a 4.00
...Ties That Bind (1997, $12.95, TPB) r/mini-series & Alfred's Return 13.00

NIGHTWING
DC Comics: Oct, 1996 - Present ($1.95/$1.99/$2.25/$2.50/$2.99)

1-Chuck Dixon scripts & Scott McDaniel-c/a	2	4	6	9	11	12
2,3						6.00
4-10: 6-Robin-c/app.						4.00
11-20: 13-15-Batman app. 19,20-Cataclysm pts. 2,11						3.00

21-49,51-64: 23-Green Arrow app. 26-29-Huntress-c/app. 30-Superman-c/app.
35-39-No Man's Land. 41-Land/Geraci-a begins. 46-Begin $2.25-c. 47-Texiera-c.
52-Catwoman-c/app. 54-Shrike app. 2.50
50-($3.50) Nightwing battles Torque 3.50
65-74,76-99: 65,66-Bruce Wayne: Murderer x-over pt. 3,9. 68,69: B.W.: Fugitive pt. 6,9.
70-Last Dixon-s. 71-Devin Grayson-s begin. 81-Batgirl vs. Deathstroke.
93-Blockbuster killed. 94-Copperhead app. 96-Bagged w/CD. 96-98-War Games 2.50
75-(1/03, $2.95) Intro. Tarantula 3.00
100-(2/05, $2.95) Tarantula app. 3.00
101-117: 101-Year One begins. 103-Jason Todd & Deadman app. 107-110-Hester-a.
109-Begin $2.50-c. 109,110-Villains United tie-in. 112-Deathstroke app. 2.50
118-136: 118-One Year Later; Jason Todd as 2nd Nightwing. 120-Begin $2.99-c 3.00
#1,000,000 (11/98) teams with future Batman 2.50
Annual 1(1997, $3.95) Pulp Heroes 4.00
Annual 2 (6/07, $3.99) Dick Grayson and Barbara Gordon's shared history 4.00
...Eighty Page Giant 1 (12/00, $5.95) Intro. of Hella; Dixon-s/Haley-c 6.00
.... Big Guns (2004, $14.95, TPB) r/#47-50; Secret Files 1, Eighty Page Giant 1 ..... 15.00
.... Brothers in Blood (2007, $14.99, TPB) r/#118-124 ..... 15.00

Nightwing and Huntress #1 © DC

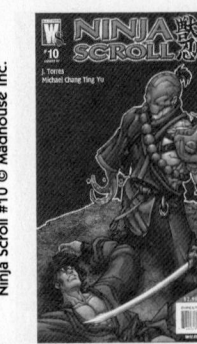
Ninja Scroll #10 © Madhouse Inc.

Nocturnals: The Dark Forever #1 © Dan Brereton

	GD	VG	FN	VF	VF/NM	NM-
	2.0	4.0	6.0	8.0	9.0	9.2

...: A Darker Shade of Justice (2001, $19.95, TPB) r/#30-39, Secret Files #1 ... 20.00
...: A Knight in Blüdhaven (1998, $14.95, TPB) r/#1-8 ... 15.00
...: Love and Bullets (2000, $17.95, TPB) r/#1/2, 19,21,22,24-29 ... 18.00
...: On the Razor's Edge (2005, $14.99, TPB) r/#52,54-60 ... 15.00
...: Our Worlds at War (9/01, $2.95) Jae Lee-c ... 3.00
...: Renegade TPB (2006, $17.95) r/#112-117 ... 18.00
...: Rough Justice (1999, $17.95, TPB) r/#9-18 ... 18.00
Secret Files 1 (10/99, $4.95) Origin-s and pin-ups ... 5.00
...: The Hunt for Oracle (2003, $14.95, TPB) r/#41-46 & Birds of Prey #20,21 ... 15.00
...: The Target (2001, $5.95) McDaniel-c/a ... 6.00
Wizard 1/2 (Mail offer) ... 5.00
...: Year One (2005, $14.99) r/#101-106 ... 15.00

NIGHTWING (See Tangent Comics/ Nightwing)

NIGHTWING AND HUNTRESS
DC Comics: May, 1998 - No. 4, Aug, 1998 ($1.95, limited series)
1-4-Grayson-s/Land & Sienkiewicz-a ... 2.50
TPB (2003, $9.95) r/#1/4; cover gallery ... 10.00

NIGHTWINGS (See DC Science Fiction Graphic Novel)

NIKKI, WILD DOG OF THE NORTH (Disney, see Movie Comics)
Dell Publishing Co.: No. 1226, Sept, 1961
Four Color 1226-Movie, photo-c ... 5 10 15 35 55 75

9-11 - ARTISTS RESPOND
Dark Horse Comics: 2002 ($9.95, TPB, proceeds donated to charities)
Volume 1-Short stories about the September 11 tragedies by various Dark Horse, Chaos! and Image writers and artists; Eric Drooker-c ... 10.00

9-11: EMERGENCY RELIEF
Alternative Comics: 2002 ($14.95, TPB, proceeds donated to the Red Cross)
nn-Short stories by various inc. Pekar, Eisner, Hester, Oeming, Noto; Cho-c ... 15.00

9-11 - THE WORLD'S FINEST COMIC BOOK WRITERS AND ARTISTS TELL STORIES TO REMEMBER
DC Comics: 2002 ($9.95, TPB, proceeds donated to charities)
Volume 2-Short stories about the September 11 tragedies by various DC, MAD, and WildStorm writers and artists ; Alex Ross-c ... 10.00

NINE RINGS OF WU-TANG
Image Comics: July, 1999 - No. 5, July, 2000 ($2.95)
Preview (7/99, $5.00, B&W) ... 5.00
1-5: 1-(11/99, $2.95) Clayton Henry-a ... 3.00
Tower Records Variant-c ... 5.00
Wizard #0 Prelude ... 2.50
TPB (1/01, $19.95) r/#1-5, Preview & Prelude; sketchbook & cover gallery ... 20.00

1963
Image Comics (Shadowline Ink): Apr, 1993 - No. 6, Oct, 1993 ($1.95, lim. series)
1-6: Alan Moore scripts; Veitch, Bissette & Gibbons-a(p) ... 2.50
1-Gold ... 3.00
NOTE: *Bissette a-2-4; Gibbons a-1i, 2i, 6i; c-2.*

1984 (Magazine) (1994 #11 on)
Warren Publishing Co.: June, 1978 - No. 10, Jan, 1980 ($1.50, B&W with color inserts, mature content with nudity; 84 pgs. except #4 has 92 pgs.)
1-Nino-a in all; Mutant World begins by Corben ... 3 6 9 14 19 24
2-10: 4-Rex Havoc begins. 7-1st Ghita of Alizarr by Thorne. 9-1st Starfire ... 2 4 6 9 13 16
NOTE: *Alcala a-1-3,5,7i. Corben a-1-8; c-1,2. Nebres a-1-8,10. Thorne a-7,8,10. Wood a-1,2,5i.*

1994 (Formerly 1984) (Magazine)
Warren Publishing Co.: No. 11, Feb, 1980 - No. 29, Feb, 1983 (B&W with color; mature; #11-(84 pgs.); #12-16,18-21,24-(76 pgs.); #17,22,23,25-29-(68 pgs.)
11,17,18,20,22,23,29: 11,17-8 pgs. color insert. 18-Giger-c. 20-1st Diana Jacklighter Manhuntress by Maroto. 22-1st Sigmund Pavlov by Nino; 1st Ariel Hart by Hsu. 23-All Nino issue ... 2 4 6 8 11 14
12-16,19,21,24-28: 21-1st app. Angel by Nebres. 27-The Warhawks return ... 1 3 4 6 8 10
NOTE: *Corben c-26. Maroto a-20, 21-24. Nebres a-11-13, 15, 16, 18, 21, 22, 25, 28. Nino a-11-19, 20(2), 21, 25, 26, 28; c-21. Redondo c-20. Thorne a-11-14, 17-21, 24-26, 28, 29.*

NINJA BOY
DC Comics (WildStorm): Oct, 2001 - No. 6, Mar, 2002 ($3.50/$2.95)
1-($3.50) Ale Garza-a/c ... 3.50
2-6:($2.95) ... 3.00
...: Faded Dreams TPB (2003, $14.95) r/#1-6; sketch pages ... 15.00

NINJA HIGH SCHOOL (1st series)
Antarctic Press: 1986 - No. 3, Aug, 1987 (B&W)
1-Ben Dunn-s/c/a; early Manga series ... 2 4 6 9 12 15
2,3 ... 1 3 4 6 8 10

NINJAK (See Bloodshot #6, 7 & Deathmate)
Valiant/Acclaim Comics (Valiant) No. 16 on: Feb, 1994 - No. 26, Nov, 1995 ($2.25/$2.50)
1 ($3.50)-Chromium-c; Quesada-c/a(p) in #1-3 ... 3.50
1-Gold ... 5.00
2-13: 3-Batman, Spawn & Random (from X-Factor) app. as costumes at party (cameo). 4-w/bound-in trading card. 5,6-X-O app. ... 2.50
0,00,14-26: 14-(4/95)-Begin $2.50-c. 0-(6/95, $2.50). 00-(6/95, $2.50) ... 2.50
Yearbook 1 (1994, $3.95) ... 4.00

NINJAK
Acclaim Comics (Valiant Heroes): V2#1, Mar, 1997 -No. 12, Feb, 1998 ($2.50)
V2#1-12: 1-Intro new Ninjak; 1st app. Brutakon; Kurt Busiek scripts begin; painted variant-c exists. 2-1st app. Karnivor & Zeer. 3-1st app. Gigantik, Shurikai, & Nixie. 4-Origin; 1st app. Yasuiti Motomiya; intro The Dark Dozen; Colin King cameo. 9-Copycat-c ... 2.50

NINJA SCROLL
DC Comics (WildStorm): Nov, 2006 - Present ($2.99)
1-12: 1-J. Torres-s/Michael Chang Ting Yu-a/c. 11-Puckett-s/Meyers-a ... 3.00
1-3-Variant covers by Jim Lee ... 5.00

NINTENDO COMICS SYSTEM (Also see Adv. of Super Mario Brothers)
Valiant Comics: Feb, 1990 - No. 9, Oct, 1991 ($4.95, card stock-c, 68pgs.)
1-9: 1-Featuring Game Boy, Super Mario, Clappwall. 3-Layton-a. 5-8-Super Mario Bros. 9-Dr. Mario 1st app. ... 5.00

NOAH'S ARK
Spire Christian Comics/Fleming H. Revell Co.: 1973 (35/49¢)
nn-By Al Hartley ... 2 4 6 8 10 12

NOBLE CAUSES
Image Comics: July, 2001; Jan, 2002 - No. 4, May, 2002 ($2.95)
...First Impressions (7/01) Intro. the Noble family; Faerber-s ... 3.00
1-4: 1-(1/02) Back-ups with Conner-a. 2-Igle back-up-a. 2,4-Two covers ... 3.00
...: Extended Family (5/03, $6.95) short stories by various ... 7.00
...: Extended Family 2 (6/04, $7.95) short stories by various ... 8.00
Vol. 1: In Sickness and in Health (2003, $12.95) r/#1-4 & ...First Impresssions ... 13.00

NOBLE CAUSES (Volume 3)
Image Comics: July, 2004 - Present ($3.50)
1-24,26-31-Faerber-s. 1-Two covers. 2-Venture app. 5-Invincible app. ... 3.50
25-($4.99) Art by various; Randolph-c ... 5.00
Vol. 4: Blood and Water (2005, $14.95) r/#1-6 ... 15.00
Vol. 5: Betrayals (2006, $14.99) r/#7-12 & The Pact V2 #2 ... 15.00
Vol. 6: Hidden Agendas (2006, $15.99) r/#13-18 and Image Holiday Spec. 2005 story ... 16.00

NOBLE CAUSES: DISTANT RELATIVES
Image Comics: Jul, 2003 - No. 4, Oct, 2003 ($2.95, B&W, limited series)
1-4-Faerber-s/Richardson & Ponce-a ... 3.00
Vol. 3: Distant Relatives (1/05, $12.95) r/#1-4; intro. by Joe Casey ... 13.00

NOBLE CAUSES: FAMILY SECRETS
Image Comics: Oct, 2002 - No. 4, Jan, 2003 ($2.95, limited series)
1-4-Faerber-s/Oeming-a. 1-Variant cover by Walker. 2,3-Valentino var-c. 4-Hester var-c ... 3.00
Vol. 2: Family Secrets (2004, $12.95) r/#1-4; sketch pages ... 13.00

NOBODY (Amado, Cho & Adlard's...)
Oni Press: Nov, 1998 - No. 4, Feb, 1999 ($2.95, B&W, mini-series)
1-4 ... 3.00

NOCTURNALS, THE
Malibu Comics (Bravura): Jan, 1995 - No. 6, Aug, 1995 ($2.95, limited series)
1-6: Dan Brereton painted-c/a & scripts ... 3.00
1-Glow-in-the-Dark premium edition ... 5.00

NOCTURNALS, THE
Dark Horse Comics/Oni Press: one-shots and trade paperbacks
Black Planet TPB (Oni Press, 1998, $19.95) r/#1-6 (Malibu Comics series) ... 20.00
Troll Bridge (Oni Press, 2000, $4.95, B&W & orange) Brereton-s/painted-c; art by Brereton, Chin, Art Adams, Sakai, Timm, Warren, Thompson, Purcell, Stephens and others ... 5.00
Unhallowed Eve TPB (Oni Press, 10/02, $9.95) r/Witching Hour & Troll Bridge one-shots ... 10.00
Witching Hour (Dark Horse, 5/98, $4.95) Brereton-s/a; reprints DHP stories + 8 new pgs. ... 5.00

NOCTURNALS: THE DARK FOREVER
Oni Press: Jul, 2001 -No. 3, Feb, 2002 ($2.95, limited series)

No Honor #1 © TCOW

Nomad V2 #4 © MAR

Nova ('07) #1 © MAR

	GD 2.0	VG 4.0	FN 6.0	VF 8.0	VF/NM 9.0	NM- 9.2

1-3-Brereton-s/painted-a/c ... 3.00
TPB (5/02, $9.95) r/#1-3; afterword & pin-ups by Alex Ross ... 10.00

NOCTURNE
Marvel Comics: June, 1995 - No. 4, Sept. 1995 ($1.50, limited series)
1-4 ... 2.50

NO ESCAPE (Movie)
Marvel Comics: June, 1994 - No. 3, Aug, 1994 ($1.50)
1-3: Based on movie ... 2.50

NO HONOR
Image Comics (Top Cow): Feb, 2001 - No. 4, July, 2001 ($2.50)
Preview (12/00, B&W) Silvestri-c ... 2.50
1-4-Avery-s/Crain-a ... 2.50
TPB (8/03, $12.99) r/#1-4; intro. by Straczynski ... 13.00

NOMAD (See Captain America #180)

NOMAD
Marvel Comics: Nov, 1990 - No. 4, Feb, 1991 ($1.50, limited series)
1-4: 1,4-Captain America app. ... 2.50

NOMAD
Marvel Comics: V2#1, May, 1992 - No. 25, May, 1994 ($1.75)
V2#1-25: 1-Has gatefold-c w/map/wanted poster. 4-Deadpool x-over. 5-Punisher vs. Nomad-c/story. 6-Punisher & Daredevil-c/story cont'd in Punisher War Journal #48. 7-Gambit-c/story. 10-Red Wolf app. 21-Man-Thing-c/story. 25-Bound-in trading card sheet ... 2.50

NOMAN (See Thunder Agents)
Tower Comics: Nov, 1966 - No. 2, March, 1967 (25¢, 68 pgs.)

	GD 2.0	VG 4.0	FN 6.0	VF 8.0	VF/NM 9.0	NM- 9.2
1-Wood/Williamson-a; Lightning begins; Dynamo cameo; Kane-a(p) & Whitney-a	8	16	24	58	97	135
2-Wood-a only; Dynamo x-over; Whitney-a	5	10	15	35	55	75

NONE BUT THE BRAVE (See Movie Classics)

NOODNIK COMICS (See Pinky the Egghead)
Comic Media/Mystery/Biltmore: Dec, 1953; No. 2, Feb, 1954 - No. 5, Aug, 1954

	GD 2.0	VG 4.0	FN 6.0	VF 8.0	VF/NM 9.0	NM- 9.2
3-D(1953, 25¢; Comic Media)(#1)-Came w/glasses	29	58	87	170	268	365
2-5	9	18	27	50	65	80

NORMALMAN (See Cerebus the Aardvark #55, 56)
Aardvark-Vanaheim/Renegade Press #6 on: Jan, 1984 - No. 12, Dec, 1985 ($1.70/$2.00)
1-12: 1-Jim Valentino-c/a in all. 6-12 ($2.00, B&W): 10-Cerebus cameo; Sim-a (2 pgs.) ... 2.50
...- Megaton Man Special 1 (Image Comics, 8/94, $2.50) ... 3.00
...-3-D 1 (Annual, 1986, $2.25) ... 2.50
...-Twentieth Anniversary Special (7/04, $2.95) ... 3.00

NORTH AVENUE IRREGULARS (See Walt Disney Showcase #49)

NORTHSTAR
Marvel Comics: Apr, 1994 - No. 4, July, 1994 ($1.75, mini-series)
1-4: Character from Alpha Flight ... 2.50

NORTH TO ALASKA
Dell Publishing Co.: No. 1155, Dec, 1960

	GD 2.0	VG 4.0	FN 6.0	VF 8.0	VF/NM 9.0	NM- 9.2
Four Color 1155-Movie, John Wayne photo-c	16	32	48	114	202	290

NORTHWEST MOUNTIES (Also see Approved Comics #12)
Jubilee Publications/St. John: Oct, 1948 - No. 4, July, 1949

	GD 2.0	VG 4.0	FN 6.0	VF 8.0	VF/NM 9.0	NM- 9.2
1-Rose of the Yukon by Matt Baker; Walter Johnson-a; Lubbers-c	46	92	138	281	466	650
2-Baker-a; Lubbers-c	38	76	114	219	347	475
3-Bondage-c, Baker-a; Sky Chief, K-9 app.	40	80	120	235	368	500
4-Baker-c/a(2 pgs.); Blue Monk & The Desperado app.	40	80	120	240	383	525

NO SLEEP 'TIL DAWN
Dell Publishing Co.: No. 831, Aug, 1957

	GD 2.0	VG 4.0	FN 6.0	VF 8.0	VF/NM 9.0	NM- 9.2
Four Color 831-Movie, Karl Malden photo-c	6	12	18	43	69	95

NOSTALGIA ILLUSTRATED
Marvel Comics: Nov, 1974 - V2#8, Aug, 1975 (B&W, 76 pgs.)

	GD 2.0	VG 4.0	FN 6.0	VF 8.0	VF/NM 9.0	NM- 9.2
V1#1	3	6	9	17	25	32
V1#2, V2#1-8	2	4	6	11	16	20

NOT BRAND ECHH (Brand Echh #1-4; See Crazy, 1973)
Marvel Comics Group (LMC): Aug, 1967 - No. 13, May, 1969
(1st Marvel parody book)

	GD 2.0	VG 4.0	FN 6.0	VF 8.0	VF/NM 9.0	NM- 9.2
1: 1-8 are 12¢ issues	6	12	18	37	59	80

2-8: 3-Origin Thor, Hulk & Capt. America; Monkees, Alfred E. Neuman cameo. 4-X-Men app. 5-Origin/intro. Forbush Man. 7-Origin Fantastical-4 & Stuporman. 8-Beatles cameo; X-Men

	GD 2.0	VG 4.0	FN 6.0	VF 8.0	VF/NM 9.0	NM- 9.2
satire; last 12¢-c	3	6	9	20	30	40
9-13 (25¢, 68 pgs., all Giants) 9-Beatles cameo. 10-All-r; The Old Witch, Crypt Keeper & Vault Keeper cameos. 12,13-Beatles cameo	4	8	12	26	41	55

NOTE: *Colan* a(p)-4, 5, 8, 9, 13. *Everett* a-1i. *Kirby* a(p)-1, 3, 5-7, 10r; c-1p. *J. Severin* a-1; c-3, 6-8, 11. *M. Severin* a-1-13; c-2, 9, 10, 12, 13. *Sutton* a-3, 4, 5i, 6i, 8, 9, 10r, 11-13; c-5. Archie satire in #9. Avengers satire in #8, 12.

NOTHING CAN STOP THE JUGGERNAUT
Marvel Comics: 1989 ($3.95)
1-r/Amazing Spider-Man #229 & 230 ... 4.00

NO TIME FOR SERGEANTS (TV)
Dell Publ. Co.: No. 914, July, 1958; Feb-Apr, 1965 - No. 3, Aug-Oct, 1965

	GD 2.0	VG 4.0	FN 6.0	VF 8.0	VF/NM 9.0	NM- 9.2
Four Color 914 (Movie)-Toth-a; Andy Griffith photo-c	9	18	27	65	113	160
1(2-4/65) (TV): Photo-c	6	12	18	39	62	85
2,3 (TV): Photo-c	5	10	15	30	48	65

NOVA (The Man Called... No. 22-25)(See New Warriors)
Marvel Comics Group: Sept, 1976 - No. 25, May, 1979

	GD 2.0	VG 4.0	FN 6.0	VF 8.0	VF/NM 9.0	NM- 9.2
1-Origin/1st app. Nova	2	4	6	10	14	18
2-4,12: 4-Thor x-over. 12-Spider-Man x-over.	1	2	3	5	7	9
5-11						6.00
10,11-(35¢-c variants, limited distribution)(6,7/77)	3	6	9	20	30	40
12-(35¢-c variant, limited distribution)(8/77)	4	8	12	24	37	50
13,14-(Regular 30¢ editions)(9/77) 13-Intro Crime-Buster.						5.00
13,14-(35¢-c variants, limited distribution)	3	6	9	18	27	35
15-24: 18-Yellow Claw app. 19-Wally West (Kid Flash) cameo						5.00
25-Last issue	1	2	3	5	6	8

NOTE: *Austin* c-21i, 23i. *John Buscema* a(p)-1-3, 8, 21; c-1p, 2, 15. *Infantino* a(p)-15-20, 22-25; c-17-20, 21p, 23p, 24p. *Kirby* c-4p, 5, 7. *Nebres* c-25i. *Simonson* a-23i.

NOVA
Marvel Comics: Jan, 1994 - June, 1995 ($1.75/$1.95)
(Started as 4-part mini-series)
1-($2.95, 52 pgs.)-Collector's Edition w/gold foil-c; new Nova costume ... 3.00
1-($2.25, 52 pgs.)-Newsstand Edition w/o foil-c ... 2.50
2-18: 3-Spider-Man-c/story. 5-Stan Lee app. 5-Bound-in card sheet. 13-Firestar & Night Thrasher app.14-Darkhawk ... 2.50

NOVA
Marvel Comics: May, 1999 - No. 7, Nov, 1999 ($2.99/$1.99)
1-($2.99) Larsen-s/Bennett-a; wraparound-c by Larsen ... 3.00
2-7-($1.99): 2-Two covers; Capt. America app. 5-Spider-Man. 7-Venom ... 2.50

NOVA
Marvel Comics: June, 2007 - Present ($2.99)
1-6: 1-Sean Chen-a/Granov-c. 2,3-Iron Man app. 3-Thunderbolts app. ... 3.00

NOW AGE ILLUSTRATED (See Pendulum Illustrated Classics)

NOW AGE BOOKS ILLUSTRATED (See Pendulum Illustrated Classics)

NTH MAN THE ULTIMATE NINJA (See Marvel Comics Presents #25)
Marvel Comics: Aug, 1989 - No. 16, Sept, 1990 ($1.00)
1-16-Ninja mercenary. 8-Dale Keown's 1st Marvel work (1/90, pencils) ... 2.50

NUCLEUS (Also see Cerebus)
Heiro-Graphic Publications: May, 1979 ($1.50, B&W, adult fanzine)

	GD 2.0	VG 4.0	FN 6.0	VF 8.0	VF/NM 9.0	NM- 9.2
1-Contains "Demonhorn" by Dave Sim; early app. of Cerebus The Aardvark (4 pg. story)	5	10	15	30	48	65

NUKLA
Dell Publishing Co.: Oct-Dec, 1965 - No. 4, Sept, 1966

	GD 2.0	VG 4.0	FN 6.0	VF 8.0	VF/NM 9.0	NM- 9.2
1-Origin & 1st app. Nukla (super hero)	4	8	12	28	44	60
2,3	3	6	9	19	29	38
4-Ditko-a, c(p)	4	8	12	23	36	48

NURSE BETSY CRANE (Formerly Teen Secret Diary) (Also see Registered Nurse for reprints)
Charlton Comics: V2#12, Aug, 1961 - V2#27, Mar, 1964 (See Soap Opera Romances)

	GD 2.0	VG 4.0	FN 6.0	VF 8.0	VF/NM 9.0	NM- 9.2
V2#12-27	3	6	9	16	23	30

NURSE HELEN GRANT (See The Romances of...)

NURSE LINDA LARK (See Linda Lark)

NURSERY RHYMES
Ziff-Davis Publ. Co. (Approved Comics): No. 10, July-Aug, 1951 - No. 2, Winter, 1951 (Painted-c)

	GD 2.0	VG 4.0	FN 6.0	VF 8.0	VF/NM 9.0	NM- 9.2
10 (#1), 2: 10-Howie Post-a	16	32	48	94	147	200

NURSES, THE (TV)
Gold Key: April, 1963 - No. 3, Oct, 1963 (Photo-c: #1,2)

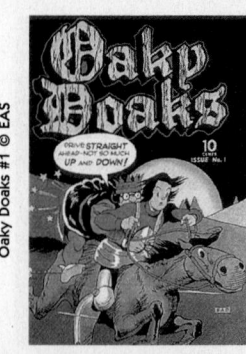
	GD 2.0	VG 4.0	FN 6.0	VF 8.0	VF/NM 9.0	NM- 9.2
1	4	8	12	24	37	50
2,3	3	6	9	18	27	35

NUTS! (Satire)
Premiere Comics Group: March, 1954 - No. 5, Nov, 1954

1-Hollingsworth-a	30	60	90	174	275	375
2,4,5: 5-Capt. Marvel parody	20	40	60	117	184	250
3-Drug "reefers" mentioned	20	40	60	117	184	250

NUTS (Magazine) (Satire)
Health Knowledge: Feb, 1958 - No. 2, April, 1958

1	9	18	27	52	69	85
2	7	14	21	35	43	50

NUTS & JOLTS
Dell Publishing Co.: No. 22, 1941

Large Feature Comic 22	17	34	51	98	154	210

NUTSY SQUIRREL (Formerly Hollywood Funny Folks)(See Comic Cavalcade)
National Periodical Publications: #61, 9-10/54 - #69, 1-2/56; #70, 8-9/56 - #71, 10-11/56; #72, 11/57

61-Mayer-a; Grossman-a in all	14	28	42	76	108	140
62-72: Mayer a-62,65,67-72	10	20	30	54	72	90

NUTTY COMICS
Fawcett Publications: Winter, 1946 (Funny animal)

1-Capt. Kidd story; 1 pg. Wolverton-a	14	28	42	80	115	150

NUTTY COMICS
Home Comics (Harvey Publications): 1945; No. 4, May-June, 1946 - No. 8, June-July, 1947 (No #2,3)

nn-Helpful Hank, Bozo Bear & others (funny animal)	9	18	27	50	65	80
4	7	14	21	37	46	55
5-Rags Rabbit begins(1st app.); infinity-c	8	16	24	40	50	60
6-8	6	12	18	31	38	45

NUTTY LIFE (Formerly Krazy Life #1; becomes Wotalife Comics #3 on)
Fox Features Syndicate: No. 2, Summer, 1946

2	15	30	45	83	124	165

NYC MECH
Image Comics: Apr, 2004 - No. 6, Sept, 2004 ($2.95)

1-6: 1-MacDonald-a/Brandon & Gunter-s. 1-Dave Johnson-c						3.00

NYC MECH: BETA LOVE
Image Comics: Apr, 2005 - No. 6, Apr, 2006 ($2.95/$2.99)

1-6: 1-MacDonald-a/Brandon & Gunter-s. 1-Canete-c						3.00

NYOKA, THE JUNGLE GIRL (Formerly Jungle Girl; see The Further Adventures of..., Master Comics #50 & XMas Comics)
Fawcett Publications: No. 2, Winter, 1945 - No. 77, June, 1953 (Movie serial)

2	54	108	162	338	562	785
3	32	64	96	186	293	400
4,5	26	52	78	152	239	325
6-11,13,14,16-18-Krigstein-a: 17-Sam Spade ad by Lou Fine	19	38	57	109	172	235
12,15,19,20	17	34	51	98	154	210
21-30: 25-Clayton Moore photo-c?	14	28	42	76	108	140
31-40	11	22	33	62	86	110
41-50	10	20	30	56	76	95
51-60	9	18	27	50	65	80
61-77	8	16	24	44	57	70

NOTE: Photo-c from movies 25, 30-70, 72, 75-77. Bondage c-4, 5, 7, 8, 14, 24.

NYOKA, THE JUNGLE GIRL (Formerly Zoo Funnies; Space Adventures #23 on)
Charlton Comics: No. 14, Nov, 1955 - No. 22, Nov, 1957

14	11	22	33	62	86	110
15-22	9	18	27	52	69	85

NYX (Also see X-23 title)
Marvel Comics: Nov, 2003 - No. 7, Oct, 2005 ($2.99)

1,2: 1-Quesada-s/Middleton-a/c; intro. Kiden Nixon						3.00
3-1st app. X-23	1	3	4	6	8	10
4-6: 5,6-Teranishi-a						3.00
7-($3.99) Teranishi-a						4.00
NYX X-23 (2005, $34.99, oversized with d.j.) r/X-23 #1-6 & NYX #1-7; intro by Craig Kyle; sketch pages, development art and unused covers						35.00
...: Wannabe TPB (2006, $19.99) r/#1-7; development art and unused covers						20.00

OAKLAND PRESS FUNNYBOOK, THE
The Oakland Press: 9/17/78 - 4/13/80 (16 pgs.) (Weekly)
Full color in comic book form; changes to tabloid size 4/20/80-on
Contains Tarzan by Manning, Marmaduke, Bugs Bunny, etc. (low distribution);
9/23/79 - 4/13/80 contain Buck Rogers by Gray Morrow & Jim Lawrence 2.50

OAKY DOAKS (See Famous Funnies #190)
Eastern Color Printing Co.: July, 1942 (One Shot)

1	35	70	105	201	318	435

OBERGEIST: RAGNAROK HIGHWAY
Image Comics (Top Cow/Minotaur): May, 2001 - No. 6, Nov, 2001 ($2.95, limited series)

Preview ('01, B&W, 16 pgs.) Harris painted-c						2.25
1-6-Harris-c/a/Jolley-s. 1-Three covers						3.00
... :The Directors' Cut (2002, $19.95, TPB) r/#1-6; Bruce Campbell intro.						20.00
... :The Empty Locket (3/02, $2.95, B&W) Harris & Snyder-a						3.00

OBIE
Store Comics: 1953 (6¢)

1	6	12	18	28	34	40

OBJECTIVE FIVE
Image Comics: July, 2000 - No. 6, Jan, 2001($2.95)

1-6-Lizalde-a						3.00

OBLIVION
Comico: Aug, 1995 - No. 3, May, 1996.($2.50)

1-3: 1-Art Adams-c. 2-(1/96)-Bagged w/gaming card. 3-(5/96)-Darrow-c						2.50

OBNOXIO THE CLOWN (Character from Crazy Magazine)
Marvel Comics Group: April, 1983 (one-shot)

1-Vs. the X-Men						3.00

OCCULT CRIMES TASKFORCE
Image Comics: July, 2006 - No. 4, May, 2007 ($2.99, limited series)

1-4-Rosario Dawson & David Atchison-s/Tony Shasteen-a						3.00
... Vol. 1 TPB (2007, $14.99) r/#1-4; sketch and cover development art						15.00

OCCULT FILES OF DR. SPEKTOR, THE
Gold Key/Whitman No. 25: Apr, 1973 - No. 24, Feb, 1977; No. 25, May, 1982 (Painted-c #1-24)

1-1st app. Lakota; Baron Tibor begins	4	8	12	26	41	55
2-5: 3-Mummy-c/s. 5-Jekyll & Hyde-c/s	3	6	9	16	22	28
6-10: 6,9-Frankenstein. 8,9-Dracula c/s. 9.-Jekyll & Hyde c/s. 10-Mummy-c/s						
	2	4	6	10	14	18
11-13,15-17,19-22,24: 11-1st app. Spektor as Werewolf. 11-13-Werewolf c/s. 12,16-Frankenstein c/s. 17-Zombie/Voodoo-c. 19-Sea monster-c/s. 20-Mummy-s. 21-Swamp monster-c/s. 24-Dragon-c/s	2	4	6	8	10	12
14-Dr. Solar app.	3	6	9	14	19	24
18,23-Dr. Solar cameo	2	4	6	9	12	15
25(Whitman, 5/82)-r/#1 with line drawn-c	2	4	6	9	12	15
	1	3	4	6	8	10

NOTE: Also see Dan Curtis, Golden Comics Digest 33, Gold Key Spotlight, Mystery Comics Digest 5, & Spine Tingling Tales.

OCEAN
DC Comics (WildStorm): Dec, 2005 - No. 6, Sept, 2005 ($2.95/$2.99/$3.99, limited series)

1-5-Warren Ellis-s/Chris Sprouse-a						3.00
6-($3.99) Conclusion						4.00

ODELL'S ADVENTURES IN 3-D (See Adventures in 3-D)

OFFCASTES
Marvel Comics (Epic Comics/Heavy Hitters): July, 1993 - No. 3, Sept, 1993 ($1.95, limited series)

1-3: Mike Vosburg-c/a/scripts in all						2.50

OFFICIAL CRISIS ON INFINITE EARTHS INDEX, THE
Independent Comics Group (Eclipse): Mar, 1986 ($1.75)

1						5.00

OFFICIAL CRISIS ON INFINITE EARTHS CROSSOVER INDEX, THE
Independent Comics Group (Eclipse): July, 1986 ($1.75)

1-Perez-c.						5.00

OFFICIAL DOOM PATROL INDEX, THE
Independent Comics Group (Eclipse): Feb, 1986 - No. 2, Mar, 1986 ($1.50, limited series)

1,2: Byrne-c.						4.00

OFFICIAL HANDBOOK OF THE CONAN UNIVERSE (See Handbook of...)

OFFICIAL HANDBOOK OF THE MARVEL UNIVERSE, THE

Official Handbook of the Marvel Universe #2 © MAR

The Official Marvel Index to the Amazing Spider-Man #1 © MAR

Oh My Goddess pt. 2 #8 © Fujishima

	GD 2.0	VG 4.0	FN 6.0	VF 8.0	VF/NM 9.0	NM- 9.2		GD 2.0	VG 4.0	FN 6.0	VF 8.0	VF/NM 9.0	NM- 9.2

Marvel Comics Group: Jan, 1983 - No. 15, May, 1984 (Limited series)

1-Lists Marvel heroes & villains (letter A) — 5.00
2-15: 2 (B-C), 3-(C-D). 4-(D-G). 5-(H-J), 6-(K-L). 7-(M). 8-(N-P); Punisher-c. 9-(Q-S), 10-(S). 11-(S-U). 12-(V-Z); Wolverine-c. 13,14-Book of the Dead. 15-Weaponry catalogue — 4.00
NOTE: *Bolland* a-8. *Byrne* c/a(p)-1-14; c-15p. *Grell* a-6, 9. *Kirby* a-1, 3. *Layton* a-2, 5, 7. *Mignola* a-3, 4, 5, 6, 8, 12. *Miller* a-4-6, 8, 10. *Nebres* a-3, 4, 8. *Redondo* a-3, 4, 8, 13, 14. *Simonson* a-1, 4, 6-13. *Paul Smith* a-1-12. *Starlin* a-5, 7, 8, 10, 13, 14. *Steranko* a-8p. *Zeck*-2-14.

OFFICIAL HANDBOOK OF THE MARVEL UNIVERSE, THE
Marvel Comics: Dec, 1985 - No. 20, Feb, 1988 ($1.50, maxi-series)

V2#1-Byrne-c — 4.00
2-20: 2,3-Byrne-c — 3.00
Trade paperback Vol. 1-10 ($6.95) — 1 3 4 6 8 10
NOTE: *Art Adams* a-7, 8, 11, 12, 14. *Bolland* a-8, 10, 13. *Buckler* a-1, 3, 5, 10. *Buscema* a-1, 5, 8, 9, 10, 13, 14. *Byrne* a-1-14; c-1-11. *Ditko* a-1, 2, 4, 6, 7, 11. *Mignola* a-2, 4, 9, 11, 13. *Miller* a-2, 12. *Simonson* a-1, 2, 4-13, 15. *Paul Smith* a-1-5, 7-12, 14. *Starlin* a-6, 8, 9, 12, 16. *Zeck* a-1-4, 6, 7, 9-14, 16.

OFFICIAL HANDBOOK OF THE MARVEL UNIVERSE, THE
Marvel Comics: July, 1989 - No. 8, Mid-Dec, 1990 ($1.50, lim. series, 52 pgs.)

V3#1-8: 1-McFarlane-a (2 pgs.) — 3.00

OFFICIAL HANDBOOK OF THE MARVEL UNIVERSE, THE (Also see Spider-Man)
Marvel Comics: 2004 - Present ($3.99, one-shots)

...: Alternate Universes 2005 - Profile pages of 1602, MC2, 2099, Earth X, Mangaverse, Days of Future Past, Squadron Supreme, Spider-Ham's Larval Earth and others — 4.00
...: Avengers 2004 - Profile pages; art by various; lists of character origins and 1st apps. — 4.00
...: Avengers 2005 - Profile pages and info for New Avengers, Young Avengers & others — 4.00
...: Book of the Dead 2004 - Profile pages of deceased Marvel characters; art by various; — 4.00
...: Daredevil 2004 - Profile pages; art by various; lists of character origins and 1st apps. — 4.00
...: Fantastic Four 2005 - Profile pages of members, friends & enemies — 4.00
...: Golden Age 2005 - Profile pages; art by various; lists of character origins and 1st apps. — 4.00
...: Horror 2005 - Profile pages; art by various; lists of character origins and 1st apps. — 4.00
...: Hulk 2004 - Profile pages; art by various; lists of character origins and 1st apps. — 4.00
...: Marvel Knights 2005 - Profile pages of characters from Marvel Knights line — 4.00
...: Spider-Man 2004 - Profile pages; art by various; lists of character origins and 1st apps. — 4.00
...: Spider-Man 2005 - Profile pages of Spidey's friends and foes, emphasizing the recent — 4.00
...: Wolverine 2004 - Profile pages; art by various; lists of character origins and 1st apps. — 4.00
...: Teams 2005 - Profile pages of Avengers, X-Men and other teams — 4.00
...: Women of Marvel 2005 - Profile pages; art by various; Greg Land-c — 4.00
...: X-Men 2004 - Profile pages; art by various; lists of character origins and 1st apps. — 4.00
...: X-Men 2005 - Profile pages; art by various; lists of character origins and 1st apps. — 4.00
...: X-Men: The Age of Apocalypse 2005 - Profile pages of characters plus Exiles — 4.00

OFFICIAL HANDBOOK OF THE ULTIMATE MARVEL UNIVERSE, THE
Marvel Comics: 2005 ($3.99, one-shots)

... 2005: The Fantastic Four and Spider-Man - Profile pages; art by various — 4.00
... The Ultimates and X-Men 2005 - Profile pages; art by various; Bagley-c — 4.00

OFFICIAL HAWKMAN INDEX, THE
Independent Comics Group: Nov, 1986 - No. 2, Dec, 1986 ($2.00)

1,2 — 4.00

OFFICIAL JUSTICE LEAGUE OF AMERICA INDEX, THE
Independent Comics Group (Eclipse): April, 1986 - No. 8, Mar, 1987 ($2.00, Baxter paper)

1-8: 1,2-Perez-c. — 6.00

OFFICIAL LEGION OF SUPER-HEROES INDEX, THE
Independent Comics Group (Eclipse): Dec, 1986 - No. 5, 1987 ($2.00, limited series)
(No Official in Title #2 on)

1-5: 4-Mooney-c — 6.00

OFFICIAL MARVEL INDEX TO MARVEL TEAM-UP
Marvel Comics Group: Jan, 1986 - No. 6, 1987 ($1.25, limited series)

1-6 — 4.00

OFFICIAL MARVEL INDEX TO THE AMAZING SPIDER-MAN
Marvel Comics Group: Apr, 1985 - No. 9, Dec, 1985 ($1.25, limited series)

1 ($1.00)-Byrne-c. — 4.00
2-9: 5,6,8,9-Punisher-c. — 3.00

OFFICIAL MARVEL INDEX TO THE AVENGERS, THE
Marvel Comics: Jun, 1987 - No. 7, Aug, 1988 ($2.95, limited series)

1-7 — 5.00

OFFICIAL MARVEL INDEX TO THE AVENGERS, THE
Marvel Comics: V2#1, Oct, 1994 - V2#6, 1995 ($1.95, limited series)

V2#1-#6 — 3.00

OFFICIAL MARVEL INDEX TO THE FANTASTIC FOUR

Marvel Comics Group: Dec, 1985 - No. 12, Jan, 1987 ($1.25, limited series)

1-12: 1-Byrne-c. 1,2-Kirby back-c (unpub. art) — 3.00

OFFICIAL MARVEL INDEX TO THE X-MEN, THE
Marvel Comics: May, 1987 - No. 7, July, 1988 ($2.95, limited series)

1-7 — 5.00

OFFICIAL MARVEL INDEX TO THE X-MEN, THE
Marvel Comics: V2#1, Apr, 1994 - V2#5, 1994 ($1.95, limited series)

V2#1-5: 1-Covers X-Men #1-51. 2-Covers #52-122,Special #1,2,Giant-Size #1,2. 3-Byrne-c; covers #123-177, Annuals 3-7, Spec. Ed. #1. 4-Covers Uncanny X-Men #178-234, Annuals 8-12. 5-Covers #235-287, Annuals 13-15 — 3.00

OFFICIAL SOUPY SALES COMIC (See Soupy Sales)

OFFICIAL TEEN TITANS INDEX, THE
Indep. Comics Group (Eclipse): Aug, 1985 - No. 5, 1986 ($1.50, lim. series)

1-5 — 4.00

OFFICIAL TRUE CRIME CASES (Formerly Sub-Mariner #23; All-True Crime Cases #26 on)
Marvel Comics (OCI): No. 24, Fall, 1947 - No. 25, Winter, 1947-48

24(#1)-Burgos-a; Syd Shores-c — 23 46 69 132 209 285
25-Syd Shores-c; Kurtzman's "Hey Look" — 18 36 54 105 165 225

OF SUCH IS THE KINGDOM
George A. Pflaum: 1955 (15¢, 36 pgs.)

nn-Reprints from 1951 Treasure Chest — 4 7 10 14 17 20

O.G. WHIZ (See Gold Key Spotlight #10)
Gold Key: 2/71 - No. 6, 5/72; No. 7, 5/78 - No. 11, 1/79 (No. 7: 52 pgs.)

1-John Stanley script — 5 10 15 35 55 75
2-John Stanley script — 4 8 12 24 37 50
3-6(1972) — 3 6 9 18 27 35
7-11(1978-79)-Part-r: 9-Tubby issue — 2 4 6 9 12 15

OH, BROTHER! (Teen Comedy)
Stanhall Publ.: Jan, 1953 - No. 5, Oct, 1953

1-By Bill Williams — 8 16 24 42 54 65
2-5 — 6 12 18 27 33 38

OH MY GODDESS! (Manga)
Dark Horse Comics: Aug, 1994 - Present ($2.50-$3.99, B&W)

1-6-Kosuke Fujishima-s/a in all — 3.00
... PART II 2/95 - No. 9, 9/95 ($2.50, B&W, lim.series) #1-9 — 3.00
... PART III 11/95 - No. 11, 9/96 ($2.95, B&W, lim. series) #1-11 — 3.00
... PART IV 12/96 - No. 8, 7/97 ($2.95, B&W, lim. series) #1-8 — 3.00
... PART V 9/97 - No. 12, 8/98 ($2.95, B&W, lim. series) — 3.00
1,2,5,8: 5-Ninja Master pt. 1 — 3.00
3,4,6,7,10-12-($3.95, 48 pgs.) 10-Fallen Angel. 11-Play The Game — 4.00
9-($3.50) "It's Lonely At The Top" — 3.50
... PART VI 10/98 - No. 5, 3/99 ($3.50/$2.95, B&W, lim. series) — 3.50
1-($3.50) — 3.50
2-5-($2.95)-6-Super Urd one-shot — 3.00
... PART VII 5/99 - No. 8, 12/99 ($2.95, B&W, lim. series) #1-3 — 3.00
4-8-($3.50) — 3.50
... PART VIII 1/00 - No. 6, 6/00 ($3.50, B&W, lim. series) #1-3,5,7 — 3.50
4-($2.95) "Hail To The Chief" begins — 3.00
... PART IX 7/00 - No. 7, 1/01 ($3.50/$2.99) #1-4: 3-Queen Sayoko — 3.50
5-7-($2.99) — 3.00
... PART X 2/01 - No. 5, 6/01 ($3.50) #1-5 — 3.50
... PART XI 10/01 - No. 10, 3/02 ($3.50) #1,2,7,8 — 3.50
3-6,9-($2.99) Mystery Child — 3.00
10-($3.99) — 4.00
(Series adapts new numbering) 88-90-($3.50) Learning to Love — 3.50
91-94,96-103,105,107-110: 91-94 ($2.99) Traveler. 96-98-The Phantom Racer — 3.00
95,104,106-($3.50) 95-Traveler pt. 5 — 3.50
111,112-($3.99) — 4.00

OH SUSANNA (TV)
Dell Publishing Co.: No. 1105, June-Aug, 1960 (Gale Storm)

Four Color 1105-Toth-a, photo-c — 11 22 33 77 136 195

OKAY COMICS
United Features Syndicate: July, 1940

1-Captain & the Kids & Hawkshaw the Detective reprints — 45 90 135 275 450 625

O.K. COMICS
Hit Publications: May, 1940 (ashcan)

O.K. Comics #2 © UFS

Omac #1 © DC

Omega Flight #1 © MAR

	GD 2.0	VG 4.0	FN 6.0	VF 8.0	VF/NM 9.0	NM- 9.2

nn-Ashcan comic, not distributed to newsstands, only for in house use. A CGC certified 8.0 copy sold in 2003 for $1,000.

O.K. COMICS
United Features Syndicate/Hit Publications: July, 1940 - No. 2, Oct, 1940

	GD	VG	FN	VF	VF/NM	NM-
1-Little Giant (w/super powers), Phantom Knight, Sunset Smith, & The Teller Twins begin	73	146	219	456	758	1060
2 (Rare)-Origin Mister Mist by Chas. Quinlan	75	150	225	469	777	1085

OKLAHOMA KID
Ajax/Farrell Publ.: June, 1957 - No. 4, 1958

1	11	22	33	60	83	105
2-4	7	14	21	37	46	55

OKLAHOMAN, THE
Dell Publishing Co.: No. 820, July, 1957

Four Color 820-Movie, photo-c	8	16	24	58	97	135

OKTANE
Dark Horse Comics: Aug, 1995 - Nov, 1995 ($2.50, color, limited series)

1-4-Gene Ha-a 2.50

OKTOBERFEST COMICS
Now & Then Publ.: Fall 1976 (75¢, Canadian, B&W, one-shot)

1-Dave Sim-s/a; Gene Day-a; 1st app. Uncle Hans & Natter P. Bombast; The Beavers sty; 1st Cap'n Riverrat, Sim-s/Day-a	2	4	6	13	18	22

OLD GLORY COMICS
DC Comics: 1941

nn - Ashcan comic, not distributed to newsstands, only for in-house use. Cover art is Flash Comics #12 with interior being Action Comics #37 (no known sales)

OLD IRONSIDES (Disney)
Dell Publishing Co.: No. 874, Jan, 1958

Four Color 874-Movie w/Johnny Tremain	6	12	18	43	69	95

OLD YELLER (Disney, see Movie Comics, and Walt Disney Showcase #25)
Dell Publishing Co.: No. 869, Jan, 1958

Four Color 869-Movie, photo-c	5	10	15	35	55	75

OMAC (One Man Army; ...Corps. #4 on; also see Kamandi #59 & Warlord)
(See Cancelled Comic Cavalcade)
National Periodical Publications: Sept-Oct, 1974 - No. 8, Nov-Dec, 1975

1-Origin	5	10	15	30	48	65
2-8: 8-2 pg. Neal Adams ad	3	6	9	15	21	26

NOTE: *Kirby* a-1-8p; c-1-7p. *Kubert* c-8.

OMAC (See DCU Brave New World)
DC Comics: Sept, 2006 - No. 8, Apr, 2007 ($2.99, limited series)

1-8: 1-Bruce Jones-s/Renato Guedes-a. 1-3-Firestorm & Cyborg app. 8-Superman app. 3.00

OMAC: ONE MAN ARMY CORPS
DC Comics: 1991 - No. 4, 1991 ($3.95, B&W, mini-series, mature, 52 pgs.)

Book One - Four: John Byrne-c/a & scripts 4.00

OMAC PROJECT, THE
DC Comics: June, 2005 - No. 6, Nov, 2005 ($2.50, limited series)

1-6-Prelude to Infinite Crisis x-over; Rucka-s/Saiz-a 2.50
...: Infinite Crisis Special 1 (5/06, $4.99) Rucka-s/a; follows destruction of satellite 5.00
TPB (2005, $14.99) r/#1-6, Countdown to Infinite Crisis, Wonder Woman #219 .... 15.00

O'MALLEY AND THE ALLEY CATS
Gold Key: April, 1971 - No. 9, Jan, 1974 (Disney)

1	3	6	9	16	23	30
2-9	2	4	6	9	13	16

OMEGA ELITE
Blackthorne Publishing: 1987 ($1.25)

1-Starlin-c 3.00

OMEGA FLIGHT
Marvel Comics: Jun, 2007 - No. 5, Oct, 2007 ($2.99, limited series)

1-Oeming-s/Kolins-a; Wrecking Crew app. 4.00
1-Second printing with Sasquatch variant-c 3.00
2-5: 5-Beta Ray Bill app. 3.00

OMEGA MEN, THE (See Green Lantern #141)
DC Comics: Dec, 1982 - No. 38, May, 1986 ($1.00/$1.25/$1.50; Baxter paper)

1,20: 20-2nd full Lobo story 3.00
2,4-9,11-19,21-25,28-30,32,33,36,38: 2-Origin Broot. 5,9-2nd & 3rd app. Lobo (cameo, 2 pgs.

each). 7-Origin The Citadel. 19-Lobo cameo. 30-Intro new Primus 2.50

3-1st app. Lobo (5 pgs.)(6/83); Lobo-c	1	2	3	4	5	7

10-1st full Lobo story 5.00
26,27,31,34,35: 26,27-Alan Moore scripts. 31-Crisis x-over. 34,35-Teen Titans x-over 3.00
37-1st solo Lobo story (8 pg. back-up by Giffen) 4.00
Annual 1(11/84, 52 pgs.), 2(11/85) 3.00

NOTE: *Giffen* c/a-1-6p. *Morrow* a-24r. *Nino* c/a-16, 21; a-Annual 1i.

OMEGA MEN, THE
DC Comics: Dec, 2006 - No. 6, May, 2007 ($2.99, limited series)

1-6: 1-Superman, Wonder Girl, Green Lantern app.; Flint-a/Gabrych-s 3.00

OMEGA THE UNKNOWN
Marvel Comics Group: March, 1976 - No. 10, Oct, 1977

1-1st app. Omega	2	4	6	8	10	12
2,3-(Regular 25¢ editions). 2-Hulk-c/story. 3-Electro-c/story.	1	2	3	4	5	7
2,3-(30¢-c variants, limited distribution)	3	6	9	15	21	26

4-10: 8-1st brief app. 2nd Foolkiller (Greg Salinger), 1 panel only. 9,10-(Reg. 30¢ editions). 9-1st full app. 2nd Foolkiller 6.00

9,10-(35¢-c variants, limited distribution)	3	6	9	18	27	35

... Classic TPB (2005, $29.99) r/#1-10 .... 30.00

NOTE: *Kane* c(p)-3, 5, 8, 9. *Mooney* a-1-3, 4p, 5, 6p, 7, 8i, 9, 10.

OMEN
Northstar Publishing: 1989 - No. 3, 1989 ($2.00, B&W, mature)

1-Tim Vigil-c/a in all	1	2	3	5	7	9

1, (2nd printing) 3.00
2,3 .... 6.00

OMEN, THE
Chaos! Comics: May, 1998 - No. 5, Sept, 1998 ($2.95, limited series)

1-5: 1-Six covers, ...: Vexed (10/98, $2.95) Chaos! characters appear 3.00

OMNI MEN
Blackthorne Publishing: 1987 - No. 3, 1987 ($1.25)

1-3 .... 2.50
Graphic Novel (1989, $3.50) 3.50

ONE, THE
Marvel Comics (Epic Comics): July, 1985 - No. 6, Feb, 1986 (Limited series, mature)

1-6: Post nuclear holocaust super-hero. 2-Intro The Other 2.50

ONE-ARM SWORDSMAN, THE
Victory Prod./Lueng's Publ. #4 on: 1987 - No. 12, 1990 ($2.75/$1.80, 52 pgs.)

1-3 ($2.75) 2.75
4-12: 4-6-$1.80-c. 7-12-$2.00-c 2.50

ONE HUNDRED AND ONE DALMATIANS (Disney, see Cartoon Tales, Movie Comics, and Walt Disney Showcase #9, 51)
Dell Publishing Co.: No. 1183, Mar, 1961

Four Color 1183-Movie	9	18	27	65	113	160

101 DALMATIONS (Movie)
Disney Comics: 1991 (52 pgs., graphic novel)

nn-($4.95, direct sales)-r/movie adaptation & more 5.00
1-($2.95, newsstand edition) 3.00

101 WAYS TO END THE CLONE SAGA (See Spider-Man)
Marvel Comics: Jan, 1997 ($2.50, one-shot)

1 .... 2.50

100 BULLETS
DC Comics (Vertigo): Aug, 1999 - Present ($2.50/$2.75)

1-Azzarello-s/Risso-a/Dave Johnson-c 4.00
2-5 .... 3.00
6-49,51-61: 26-Series summary; art by various. 45-Preview of Losers 2.50
50-($3.50) History of the Trust 3.50
62-71: 62-Begin $2.75-c. 64-Preview of Loveless 2.75
72-84: 72-Begin $2.99-c 3.00
...: A Foregone Tomorrow TPB (2002, $17.95) r/#20-30 .... 18.00
...: Decayed TPB (2006, $14.99) r/#68-75; Darwyn Cooke intro. 15.00
...: First Shot, Last Call TPB (2000, $9.95) r/#1-5, Vertigo Winter's Edge #3 .... 10.00
...: Hang Up on the Hang Low TPB (2001, $9.95) r/#15-19; Jim Lee intro. 10.00
...: Once Upon a Crime TPB (2007, $12.99) r/#76-83 .... 13.00
...: Samurai TPB (2003, $12.95) r/#43-49 .... 13.00
...: Six Feet Under the Gun TPB (2003, $12.95) r/#37-42 .... 13.00
...: Split Second Chance TPB (2001, $14.95) r/#6-14 .... 15.00

100 Bullets #36 © Azzarello & Risso

On the Spot nn © FAW

Operation Peril #15 © ACG

	GD 2.0	VG 4.0	FN 6.0	VF 8.0	VF/NM 9.0	NM- 9.2

...: Strychnine Lives TPB (2006, $14.99) r/#59-67; Manuel Ramos intro. — 15.00
...: The Counterfifth Detective TPB (2003, $12.95) r/#31-36 — 13.00
...: The Hard Way TPB (2005, $14.99) r/#50-58 — 15.00

100 GREATEST MARVELS OF ALL TIME
Marvel Comics: Dec, 2001 ($7.50/$3.50, limited series)

1-5-Reprints top #6-#25 stories voted by poll for Marvel's 40th ann. — 7.50
6-($3.50) (#5 on-c) Reprints X-Men (2nd series) #1 — 3.50
7-($3.50) (#4 on-c) Reprints Giant-Size X-Men #1 — 3.50
8-($3.50) (#3 on-c) Reprints (Uncanny) X-Men #137 (Death of Jean Grey) — 3.50
9-($3.50) (#2 on-c) Reprints Fantastic Four #1 — 3.50
10-($3.50) (#1 on-c) Reprints Amazing Fantasy #15 (1st app. Spider-Man) — 3.50

100 PAGES OF COMICS
Dell Publishing Co.: 1937 (Stiff covers, square binding)

101(Found on back cover)-Alley Oop, Wash Tubbs, Capt. Easy, Og Son of Fire, Apple Mary, Tom Mix, Dan Dunn, Tailspin Tommy, Doctor Doom — 145 290 435 906 1503 2100

100 PAGE SUPER SPECTACULAR (See DC 100 Page Super Spectacular)

100%
DC Comics (Vertigo): Aug, 2002 - No. 5, July, 2003 ($5.95, B&W, limited series)

1-5-Paul Pope-s/a — 6.00
TPB (2005, $24.99) r/#1-5; sketch pages and background info — 25.00

100% TRUE?
DC Comics (Paradox Press): Summer 1996 - No. 2 ($4.95, B&W)

1,2-Reprints stories from various Paradox Press books. — 5.00

$1,000,000 DUCK (See Walt Disney Showcase #5)

ONE MILLION YEARS AGO (Tor #2 on)
St. John Publishing Co.: Sept, 1953

1-Origin & 1st app. Tor; Kubert-c/a; Kubert photo inside front cover — 18 36 54 105 165 225

ONE PLUS ONE
Oni Press: Sept, 2002 - No. 5, March, 2003 ($2.95, B&W, limited series)

1-5-Shaffer-s/Krall-a — 3.00
TPB (9/03, $14.95, digest-size) r/#1-5 & story from Oni Press Color Special 2002 — 15.00

ONE SHOT (See Four Color...)

1001 HOURS OF FUN
Dell Publishing Co.: No. 13, 1943

Large Feature Comic 13 (nn)-Puzzles & games; by A.W. Nugent. This book was bound as #13 w/Large Feature Comics in publisher's files — 28 56 84 162 256 350

ONE TRICK RIP OFF, THE (See Dark Horse Presents)

ONI (Adaption of video game)
Dark Horse Comics: Feb, 2001 - No. 3, Apr, 2001 ($2.99, limited series)

1-3-Sunny Lee-a(p) — 3.00

ONI DOUBLE FEATURE (See Clerks: The Comic Book and Jay & Silent Bob)
Oni Press: Jan, 1998 - No. 13, Sept, 1999 ($2.95, B&W)

1-Jay & Silent Bob; Kevin Smith-s/Matt Wagner-a — 1 3 4 6 8 10
1-2nd printing — 3.00
2-11,13: 2,3-Paul Pope-s/a. 3,4-Nixey-s/a. 4,5-Sienkewicz-s/a. 6,7-Gaiman-s. 9-Bagge-s. 13-All Paul Dini-s; Jingle Belle — 3.00
12-Jay & Silent Bob as Bluntman & Chronic; Smith-s/Allred-a — 5.00

ONI PRESS COLOR SPECIAL
Oni Press: Jun, 2001; Jul, 2002 ($5.95, annual)

...2001-Oeming "Who Killed Madman?" cover; stories & art by various — 6.00
...2002-Allred wraparound-c; stories & art by various — 6.00

ONSLAUGHT: EPILOGUE
Marvel Comics: Feb, 1997 ($2.95, one-shot)

1-Hama-s/Green-a; Xavier-c; Bastion-app. — 3.00

ONSLAUGHT: MARVEL
Marvel Comics: Oct, 1996 ($3.95, one-shot)

1-Conclusion to Onslaught x-over; wraparound-c — 1 2 3 4 5 7

ONSLAUGHT REBORN
Marvel Comics: Jan, 2007 - No. 5 ($2.99, limited series)

1-4-Loeb-s/Liefeld-a; female Bucky app. 3-McGuiness variant-c. 4-Campbell var-c — 3.00
1-Variant-c by Michael Turner — 4.00
2-Variant-c by Joe Madureira — 3.00

ONSLAUGHT: X-MEN
Marvel Comics: Aug, 1996 ($3.95, one-shot)

1-Waid & Lobdell script; Fantastic Four & Avengers app.; Xavier as Onslaught — 5.00
1-Variant-c — 2 4 6 8 10 12

ON STAGE
Dell Publishing Co.: No. 1336, Apr-June, 1962

Four Color 1336-Not by Leonard Starr — 5 10 15 30 48 65

ON THE DOUBLE (Movie)
Dell Publishing Co.: No. 1232, Sept-Nov, 1961

Four Color 1232 — 5 10 15 30 48 65

ON THE ROAD TO PERDITION (Movie)
DC Comics (Paradox Press): 2003 - Book 3, 2004 ($7.95, 8"x5 1/2", B&W, limited series)

...: Oasis, Book 1-Max Allan Collins-s/José Luis García-López-a/David Beck-c — 8.00
...: Sanctuary, Book 2-Max Allan Collins-s/Steve Lieber-a/José Luis García-López-c — 8.00
...: Detour, Book 3-Max Allan Collins-s/José Luis García-López-a/Steve Lieber-c/a(i) — 8.00
Road to Perdition 2: On the Road (2004, $14.95) r/series; Collins intro. — 15.00

ON THE ROAD WITH ANDRAE CROUCH
Spire Christian Comics (Fleming H. Revell): 1973, 1974 (39¢)

nn-1973 Edition — 2 4 6 8 11 14
nn-1974 Edition — 1 3 4 6 8 10

ON THE SCENE PRESENTS:...
Warren Publishing Co.: Oct, 1966 - No. 2, 1967 (B&W magazine, two #1 issues)

#1 "Super Heroes" (68 pgs.) Batman 1966 movie photo-c/s; has articles/photos/comic art from serials on Superman, Flash Gordon, Capt. America, Capt. Marvel and The Phantom — 8 12 26 41 55
#1 "Freak Out, USA" (Fall/1966, 60 pgs.) (lower print run) articles on musicians like Zappa, Jefferson Airplane, Supremes — 4 8 12 28 44 60
#2 "Freak Out, USA" (2/67, 52 pgs.) Beatles, Country Joe, Doors/Jim Morrison, Bee Gees — 4 8 12 28 44 60

ON THE SPOT (Pretty Boy Floyd...)
Fawcett Publications: Fall, 1948

nn-Pretty Boy Floyd photo on-c; bondage-c — 34 68 102 197 311 425

ONYX OVERLORD
Marvel Comics (Epic): Oct, 1992 - No. 4, Jan, 1993 ($2.75, mini-series)

1-4: Moebius scripts — 2.75

OPEN SPACE
Marvel Comics: Mid-Dec, 1989 - No. 4, Aug, 1990 ($4.95, bi-monthly, 68 pgs.)

1-4: 1-Bill Wray-a; Freas-c — 5.00
0-(1999) Wizard supplement; unpubl. early Alex Ross-a; new Ross-c — 2.50

OPERATION BIKINI (See Movie Classics)

OPERATION BUCHAREST (See The Crusaders)

OPERATION CROSSBOW (See Movie Classics)

OPERATION: KNIGHTSTRIKE (See Knightstrike)
Image Comics (Extreme Studios): May, 1995 - No.3, July, 1995 ($2.50)

1-3 — 2.50

OPERATION PERIL
American Comics Group (Michel Publ.): Oct-Nov, 1950 - No. 16, Apr-May, 1953 (#1-5: 52 pgs.)

1-Time Travelers, Danny Danger (by Leonard Starr) & Typhoon Tyler (by Ogden Whitney) begin — 40 80 120 235 368 500
2-War-c — 23 46 69 132 209 285
3-War-c; horror story — 20 40 60 117 184 250
4,5-Sci/fi-c/story — 23 46 69 132 209 285
6-10: 6,8,9,10-Sci/fi-c. 6-Dinosaur-c. 7-Sabretooth-c — 19 38 57 112 176 240
11,12-War-c; last Time Travelers — 14 28 42 80 115 150
13-16: All war format — 10 20 30 56 76 95
NOTE: Starr a-2, 5. Whitney a-1, 2, 5-10, 12; c-1, 3, 5, 8, 9.

OPERATION: STORMBREAKER
Acclaim Comics (Valiant Heroes): Aug, 1997 ($3.95, one-shot)

1-Waid/Augustyn-s, Braithwaite-a — 4.00

OPTIC NERVE
Drawn and Quarterly: Apr, 1995 - Present ($2.95-$3.95, bi-annual)

1-7: Adrian Tomine-c/a/scripts in all — 3.00
8-11: 8-($3.50). 9-11-($3.95) — 4.00
32 Stories-($9.95, trade paperback)-r/Optic Nerve mini-comics — 10.00
32 Stories-($29.95, hardcover)-r/Optic Nerve mini-comics; signed & numbered — 30.00

The Order #1 © MAR

The Originals SC © Dave Gibbons

Oscar Comics #4 © MAR

	GD	VG	FN	VF	VF/NM	NM-		GD	VG	FN	VF	VF/NM	NM-
	2.0	4.0	6.0	8.0	9.0	9.2		2.0	4.0	6.0	8.0	9.0	9.2

ORAL ROBERTS' TRUE STORIES (Junior Partners #120 on)
TelePix Publ. (Oral Roberts' Evangelistic Assoc./Healing Waters): 1956 (no month) - No. 119, 7/59 (15¢)(No. 102: 25¢)

V1#1(1956)-(Not code approved)- "The Miracle Touch"	19	38	57	109	172	235
102-(Only issue approved by code, 10/56) "Now I See"	13	26	39	74	105	135
103-119: 115-(114 on inside)	10	20	30	54	72	90

NOTE: Also see Happiness & Healing For You.

ORANGE BIRD, THE
Walt Disney Educational Media Co.: No date (1980) (36 pgs.; in color; slick cover)

nn-Included with educational kit on foods, ...in Nutrition Adventures nn (1980)
...and the Nutrition Know-How Revue nn (1983) ... 3.00

ORB (Magazine)
Orb Publishing: 1974 - No. 6, Mar/Apr 1976 (B&W/color)

1-1st app. Northern Light & Kadaver, both series begin	4	8	12	22	34	45
2,3 (72 pgs.)	3	6	9	14	19	24
4-6 (60 pgs.)- 4,5-origin Northern Light	2	4	6	9	13	16

NOTE: Allison a-1-3. Gene Day a-1-6. P. Hsu a-4-6. Steacy s/a-3,4.

ORBIT
Eclipse Books: 1990 - No. 3, 1990 ($4.95, 52 pgs., squarebound)

1-3: Reprints from Isaac Asimov's Science Fiction Magazine; 1-Dave Stevens-c, Bolton-a.
3-Bolton-c/a, Yeates-a ... 5.00

ORBITER
DC Comics (Vertigo): 2003 ($24.95, hardcover with dust jacket)

HC-Warren Ellis-s/Colleen Doran-a ... 25.00
SC-(2004, $17.95) Warren Ellis-s/Colleen Doran-a ... 18.00

ORDER, THE (cont'd from Defenders V2#12)
Marvel Comics: Apr, 2002 - No. 6, Sept, 2002 ($2.25, limited series)

1-6: 1-Haley-a/Duffy & Busiek-s. 3-Avengers-c/app. 4-Jurgens-a ... 2.50

ORDER, THE (The Initiative following Civil War)
Marvel Comics: Sept, 2007 - Present ($2.99)

1-3-California's Initiative team; Fraction-s/Kitson-a/c ... 3.00

ORIENTAL HEROES
Jademan Comics: Aug, 1988 - No. 55, Feb, 1993 ($1.50/$1.95, 68 pgs.)

1,55 ... 2.50
2-54 ... 2.50

ORIGINAL ADVENTURES OF CHOLLY & FLYTRAP, THE
Image Comics: Feb, 2006 - No. 2, June, 2006 ($5.99, limited series)

1,2-Arthur Suydam-s/a; interview with Suydam and art pages ... 6.00

ORIGINAL ASTRO BOY, THE
Now Comics: Sept, 1987 - No. 20, Jun, 1989 ($1.50/$1.75)

1-20-All have Ken Steacy painted-c/a ... 3.00

ORIGINAL BLACK CAT, THE
Recollections: Oct. 6, 1988 - No. 9, 1992 ($2.00, limited series)

1-9: Elias-r; 1-Bondage-c. 2-Murphy Anderson-c ... 4.00

ORIGINAL DICK TRACY, THE
Gladstone Publishing: Sept, 1990 - No. 5, 1991 ($1.95, bi-monthly, 68pgs.)

1-5: 1-Vs. Pruneface. 2-& the Evil influence; begin $2.00-c ... 2.50
NOTE: #1 reprints strips 7/16/43 - 9/30/43. #2 reprints strips 12/1/46 - 2/2/47. #3 reprints 8/31/46 - 11/14/46. #4 reprints 9/17/45 - 12/23/45. #5 reprints 6/10/46 - 8/28/46.

ORIGINAL DOCTOR SOLAR, MAN OF THE ATOM, THE
Valiant: Apr, 1995 ($2.95, one-shot)

1-Reprints Doctor Solar, Man of the Atom #1,5; Bob Fugitani-r; Paul Smith-c;
afterword by Seaborn Adamson ... 4.00

ORIGINAL E-MAN AND MICHAEL MAUSER, THE
First Comics: Oct, 1985 - No. 7, April, 1986 ($1.75, Baxter paper)

1-7: 1-Has r-/Charlton's E-Man, Vengeance Squad. 2-Shows #4 in indicia by mistake.
7-($2.00, 44pgs.)-Staton-a ... 2.50

ORIGINAL GHOST RIDER, THE
Marvel Comics: July, 1992 - No. 20, Feb, 1994 ($1.75)

1-20: 1-7-r/Marvel Spotlight #5-11 by Ploog w/new-c. 3-New Phantom Rider (former Night
Rider) back-ups begin by Ayers. 4-Quesada-c(p). 8-Ploog-c. 8,9-r/Ghost Rider #1,2.
10-r/Marvel Spotlight #12. 11-18,20-r/Ghost Rider #3-12. 19-r/Marvel Two-in-One #8 ... 2.50

ORIGINAL GHOST RIDER RIDES AGAIN, THE
Marvel Comics: July, 1991 - No. 7, Jan, 1992, ($1.50, limited series, 52 pgs.)

1-7: 1-r/Ghost Rider #68(origin),69 w/covers. 2-7: R/ G.R. #70-81 w/covers ... 2.50

ORIGINAL MAGNUS ROBOT FIGHTER, THE
Valiant: Apr, 1995 ($2.95, one-shot)

1-Reprints Magnus, Robot Fighter 4000 #2; Russ Manning-r; Rick Leonardi-c;
afterword by Seaborn Adamson ... 4.00

ORIGINAL NEXUS GRAPHIC NOVEL (See First Comics Graphic Novel #19)

ORIGINALS, THE
DC Comics (Vertigo): 2004 ($24.95/$17.99, B&W graphic novel)

HC (2004, $24.95) Dave Gibbons-s/a ... 25.00
SC (2005, $17.99) ... 18.00

ORIGINAL SHIELD, THE
Archie Enterprises, Inc.: Apr, 1984 - No. 4, Oct, 1984

1-4: 1,2-Origin Shield; Ayers p-1-4, Nebres c-1,2 ... 4.00

ORIGINAL SWAMP THING SAGA, THE (See DC Special Series #2, 14, 17, 20)

ORIGINAL TUROK, SON OF STONE, THE
Valiant: Apr, 1995 - No. 2, May, 1995 ($2.95, limited series)

1,2: 1-Reprints Turok, Son of Stone #24,25,42; Alberto Gioletti-r; Rags Morales-c; afterword
by Seaborn Adamson. 2-Reprints Turok, Son of Stone #24,33; Gioletti-r; McKone-c ... 4.00

ORIGIN OF GALACTUS (See Fantastic Four #48-50)
Marvel Comics: Feb, 1996 ($2.50, one-shot)

1-Lee & Kirby reprints w/pin-ups ... 2.50

ORIGIN OF THE DEFIANT UNIVERSE, THE
Defiant Comics: Feb, 1994 ($1.50, 20 pgs., one-shot)

1-David Lapham, Adam Pollina & Alan Weiss-a; Weiss-c ... 5.00
NOTE: The comic was originally published as Defiant Genesis and was distributed at the 1994 Philadelphia
ComicCon.

ORIGINS OF MARVEL COMICS (See Fireside Book Series)

ORION (Manga)
Dark Horse Comics: Sept, 1992 - No. 6, July, 1993 ($2.95/$3.95, B&W, bimonthly, lim. series)

1-6:1,2,6-Squarebound): 1-Masamune Shirow-c/a/s in all ... 4.00

ORION (See New Gods)
DC Comics: June, 2000 - No. 25, June, 2002 ($2.50)

1-14-Simonson-s/a. 3-Back-up story w/Miller-a. 4-Gibbons-a back-up. 7-Chaykin back-up.
8-Loeb/Liefeld back-up. 10-A. Adams back-up-a 12-Jim Lee back-up-a. 13-JLA-c/app.;
Byrne-a ... 2.50
15-($3.95) Black Racer app.; back-up story w/J.P. Leon-a ... 4.00
16-24-Simonson-s/a. 19-Joker: Last Laugh x-over ... 2.50
25-($3.95) Last issue; Mister Miracle-c/app. ... 4.00
The Gates of Apocalypse (2001, $12.95, TPB) r/#1-5 & various short-s ... 13.00

ORORO: BEFORE THE STORM (Storm from X-Men)
Marvel Comics: Aug, 2005 - No. 4, Nov, 2005 ($2.99, limited series)

1-4-Barberi-a/Sumerak-s; young Storm in Egypt ... 3.00
... Digest (2006, $6.99) r/#1-4 ... 7.00

OSBORNE JOURNALS (See Spider-Man titles)
Marvel Comics: Feb, 1997 ($2.95, one-shot)

1-Hotz-c/a ... 3.00

OSCAR COMICS (Formerly Funny Tunes; Awful...#11 & 12) (Also see Cindy Comics)
Marvel Comics: No. 24, Spring, 1947 - No. 10, Apr, 1949; No. 13, Oct, 1949

24(#1, Spring, 1947)	18	36	54	107	169	230
25(#2, Sum, 1947)-Wolverton-a plus Kurtzman's "Hey Look"	20	40	60	117	184	250

26(#3)-Same as regular #3 except #26 was printed over in black ink with #3 appearing on-c
below the over print	14	28	42	76	108	140
3-9,13: 8-Margie app.	14	28	42	76	108	140
10-Kurtzman's "Hey Look"	14	28	42	82	121	160

OSWALD THE RABBIT (Also see New Fun Comics #1)
Dell Publishing Co.: No. 21, 1943 - No. 1268, 12-2/61-62 (Walter Lantz)

Four Color 21(1943)	42	84	126	336	606	875
Four Color 39(1943)	29	58	87	212	381	550
Four Color 67(1944)	17	34	51	126	223	320
Four Color 102(1946)-Kelly-a, 1 pg.	14	28	42	102	181	260
Four Color 143,183	9	18	27	63	107	150
Four Color 225,273	7	14	21	45	73	100

Our Army at War #9 © DC

Our Army at War #159 © DC

Our Fighting Forces #11 © DC

	GD 2.0	VG 4.0	FN 6.0	VF 8.0	VF/NM 9.0	NM- 9.2
Four Color 315,388	6	12	18	39	62	85
Four Color 458,507,549,593	5	10	15	32	51	70
Four Color 623,697,792,894,979,1268	4	8	12	28	44	60

OSWALD THE RABBIT (See The Funnies, March of Comics #7, 38, 53, 67, 81, 95, 111, 126, 141, 156, 171, 186, New Funnies & Super Book #8, 20)

OTHER SIDE, THE
DC Comics (Vertigo): Dec, 2006 - No. 5, Apr, 2007 ($2.99, limited series)

1-5-Soldiers from both sides of the Vietnam War; Aaron-s/Stewart-a/c		3.00
TPB (2007, $12.99) r/#1-5; sketch pages, Stewart's travelogue to Saigon		13.00

OTHERWORLD
DC Comics (Vertigo): May, 2005 - No. 7, Nov, 2005 ($2.99)

1-7-Phil Jimenez-s/a(p)		3.00
...: Book One TPB (2006, $19.99) r/#1-7; cover gallery		20.00

OUR ARMY AT WAR (Becomes Sgt. Rock #302 on; also see Army At War)
National Periodical Publications: Aug, 1952 - No. 301, Feb, 1977

	GD 2.0	VG 4.0	FN 6.0	VF 8.0	VF/NM 9.0	NM- 9.2
1	152	304	456	1292	2396	3500
2	65	130	195	553	1027	1500
3,4: 4-Krigstein-a	50	100	150	413	757	1100
5-7	42	84	126	336	606	875
8-11,14-Krigstein-a	40	80	120	300	550	800
12,15-20	33	66	99	248	454	660
13-Krigstein-c/a; flag-c	40	80	120	309	567	825
21-31: Last precode (2/55)	22	44	66	165	295	425
32-40	19	38	57	138	244	350
41-60: 51-1st S.A. issue	16	32	48	118	209	300
61-70: 67-Minor Sgt. Rock prototype	14	28	42	102	181	260
71-80	12	24	36	87	156	225
81- (4/59)-Sgt. Rocky of Easy Co. app. by Andru & Esposito-a/ Haney-s; (the last Sgt. Rock prototype)	208	416	624	1820	3410	5000
82-1st Sgt. Rock app., in name only, in Easy Co. story (6 panels) by Kanigher & Drucker	52	104	156	442	821	1200
83-(6/59)-1st true Sgt. Rock app. in "The Rock and the Wall" by Kubert & Kanigher; (most similar to prototype in G.I. Combat #68)	167	334	501	1461	2731	4000
84-Kubert-a	31	62	93	233	429	625
85-Origin & 1st app. Ice Cream Soldier	39	78	117	293	539	785
86,87-Early Sgt. Rock; Kubert-a	30	60	90	225	413	600
88-1st Sgt. Rock-c; Kubert-c/a	35	70	105	263	482	700
89	26	52	78	195	348	500
90-Kubert-c/a; How Rock got his stripes	34	68	102	255	465	675
91-All-Sgt. Rock issue; Grandenetti-c/Kubert-a	65	130	195	553	1027	1500
92,94,96-99: 97-Regular Kubert-c begin	17	34	51	128	227	325
93-1st Zack Nolan	18	36	54	134	237	340
95,100: 95-1st app. Bulldozer	19	38	57	138	244	350
101,105,108,113,115: 101-1st app. Buster. 105-1st app. Wildman & Jackie Johnson. 115-Rock revealed as orphan; 1st x-over Mlle. Marie. 1st Sgt. Rock's battle family	14	28	42	102	181	260
102-104,106,107,109,110,114,116-120: 104-Nurse Jane-c/s. 109-Pre Easy Co. Sgt. Rock-s. 118-Sunny injured	12	24	36	87	156	225
111-1st app. Wee Willie & Sunny	16	32	48	118	209	300
112-Classic Easy Co. roster-c	17	34	51	128	227	325
121-125,130-133,135-139,141-150: 138-1st Sparrow. 141-1st Shaker. 147,148-Rock becomes a General	9	18	27	63	107	150
126,129,134: 126-1st app. Canary; grey tone-c	9	18	27	65	113	160
127-2nd all-Sgt. Rock issue; 1st app. Little Sure Shot	12	24	36	87	156	225
128-Training & origin Sgt. Rock; 1st Sgt. Krupp	26	52	78	195	348	500
140-3rd all-Sgt. Rock issue	10	20	30	70	123	175
151-Intro. Enemy Ace by Kubert (2/65), black-c	38	76	114	285	518	750
152-4th all-Sgt. Rock issue	10	20	30	67	116	165
153-2nd app. Enemy Ace (4/65)	17	34	51	122	216	310
154,156,157,159-161,165-167: 157-2 pg. pin-up: 159-1st Nurse Wendy Winston-c/s. 165-2nd Iron Major	7	14	21	49	80	110
155-3rd app. Enemy Ace (6/65)(see Showcase)	12	24	36	82	146	210
158-Origin & 1st app. Iron Major(9/65), formerly Iron Captain	9	18	27	60	100	140
162,163-Viking Prince x-over in Sgt. Rock	8	16	24	56	93	130
164-Giant G-19	13	26	39	93	164	235
168-1st Unknown Soldier app.; referenced in Star-Spangled War Stories #157; (Sgt. Rock x-over) (6/66)	12	24	36	87	156	225
169,170	6	12	18	43	69	95
171-176,178-181: 171-1st Mad Emperor	6	12	18	39	62	85
177-(80 pg. Giant G-32)	8	16	24	58	97	135
182,183,186-Neal Adams-a. 186-Origin retold	6	12	18	43	69	95

	GD 2.0	VG 4.0	FN 6.0	VF 8.0	VF/NM 9.0	NM- 9.2
184-Wee Willie dies	7	14	21	49	80	110
185,187,188,193-195,197-199	5	10	15	32	51	70
189,191,192,196: 189-Intro. The Teen-age Underground Fighters of Unit 3. 196-Hitler cameo	5	10	15	35	55	75
190-(80 pg. Giant G-44)	7	14	21	47	76	105
200-12 pg. Rock story told in verse; Evans-a	6	12	18	37	59	80
201,202,204-207: 201-Krigstein-r/#14. 204,205-All reprints; no Sgt. Rock. 207-Last 12¢ cover	4	8	12	24	37	50
203-(80 pg. Giant G-56)-All-r, Sgt. Rock story	6	12	18	41	66	90
208-215	3	6	9	19	29	38
216,229-(80 pg. Giants G-68, G-80): 216-Has G-58 on-c by mistake	6	12	18	37	59	80
217-219: 218-1st U.S.S. Stevens	3	6	9	17	25	32
220-Classic dinosaur/Sgt. Rock-c/s	3	6	9	19	29	38
221-228,230-234: 231-Intro/death Rock's brother. 234-Last 15¢ issue	3	6	9	15	21	26
235-239,241: 52 pg. Giants	3	6	9	19	29	38
240-Neal Adams-a; 52 pg. Giant	4	8	12	24	37	50
242-Also listed as DC 100 Page Super Spectacular #9; see for price						
243-246: (All 52 pgs.) 244-No Adams-a	3	6	9	18	27	35
247-250,254-268,270: 247-Joan of Arc	2	4	6	11	16	20
251-253-Return of Iron Major	3	6	9	14	19	24
269,275-(100 pgs.)	4	8	12	26	41	55
271-274,276-279: 273-Crucifixion-c	2	4	6	10	14	18
280-(68 pgs.)-200th app. Sgt. Rock; reprints Our Army at War #81,83	3	6	9	18	27	35
281-299,301: 295-Bicentennial cover	3	6	9	13	16	19
300-Sgt. Rock-s by Kubert (2/77)	2	4	6	11	16	20

NOTE **Alcala** a-251. **Drucker** a-27, 67, 68, 79, 82, 83, 96, 164, 177, 203, 212, 243r, 244, 269r, 275r, 280r. **Evans** a-165-175, 200, 266, 269, 270, 274, 276, 278, 280. **Glanzman** a-218, 220, 222, 223, 225, 227, 230-232, 238-241, 244, 247, 248, 256-259, 261, 265-267, 271, 282, 283, 298. **Grandenetti** c-91,120. **Grell** a-287. **Heath** a-50, 164, & most 176-281. **Kubert** a-38, 59, 67, 68 & most issues from 83-165, 171, 233, 236, 267, 275, 300; c-84, 280. **Maurer** a-233, 237, 239, 240, 45, 280, 284, 288, 290, 291, 295. **Severin** a-236, 252, 265, 267, 269r, 272. **Toth** a-235, 241, 254. **Wildey** a-283-285, 287p. **Wood** a-249.

OUR FIGHTING FORCES
National Per. Publ./DC Comics: Oct-Nov, 1954 - No. 181, Sept-Oct, 1978

	GD 2.0	VG 4.0	FN 6.0	VF 8.0	VF/NM 9.0	NM- 9.2
1-Grandenetti-c/a	100	200	300	850	1575	2300
2	42	84	126	336	606	875
3-Kubert-c; last precode issue (3/55)	35	70	105	263	482	700
4,5	29	58	87	212	381	550
6-9: 7-1st S.A. issue	24	48	72	175	313	450
10-Wood-a	24	48	72	179	320	460
11-19	20	40	60	146	261	375
20-Grey tone-c (4/57)	25	50	75	184	330	475
21-30	15	30	45	107	191	275
31-40	14	28	42	99	175	250
41-Unknown Soldier tryout	16	32	48	118	209	300
42-44	12	24	36	87	156	225
45-Gunner & Sarge begins, end #94	40	80	120	311	568	825
46	16	32	48	118	209	300
47	12	24	36	87	156	225
48,50	11	22	33	79	140	200
49-1st Pooch	15	30	45	107	191	275
51-Grey tone-c	12	24	36	87	156	225
52-64: 64-Last 10¢ issue	9	18	27	63	107	150
65-70	7	14	21	49	80	110
71-Grey tone-c	8	16	24	58	97	135
72-80	6	12	18	41	66	90
81-90	5	10	15	35	55	75
91-98: 95-Devil-Dog begins, ends #98	4	8	12	26	41	55
99-Capt. Hunter begins, ends #106	4	8	12	28	44	60
100	4	8	12	28	44	60
101-105,107-120: 116-Mlle. Marie app. 120-Last 12¢ issue	4	8	12	22	34	45
106-Hunters Hellcats begin	4	8	12	24	37	50
121,122: 121-Intro. Heller	3	6	9	19	29	38
123-The Losers (Capt. Storm, Gunner & Sarge, Johnny Cloud) begin	6	12	18	39	62	85
124-132: 132-Last 15¢ issue	3	6	9	15	21	26
133-137 (Giants). 134-Toth-a	3	6	9	17	26	35
138-145,147-150: 146-Toth-a	4	8	12	10	14	18
146-Classic Toth & Goodwin-a	2	4	6	13	18	22
151-162-Kirby a(p)	3	6	9	14	19	24
163-180	2	4	6	11	14	18
181-Last issue	2	4	6	10	14	18

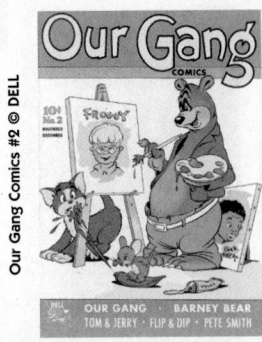

Our Gang Comics #2 © DELL

Our Secret #8 © SUPR

Outlaw Nation #12 © Delano & Sudzuka

	GD	VG	FN	VF	VF/NM	NM-
	2.0	4.0	6.0	8.0	9.0	9.2

NOTE: **N. Adams** c-147. **Drucker** a-28, 37, 39, 42-44, 49, 53, 133r. **Evans** a-149, 164-174, 177-181. **Glanzman** a-125-128, 132, 134, 138-141, 143, 144. **Heath** a-2, 16, 18, 28, 41, 44, 49, 114, 135-138r; c-51. **Kirby** a-151-162r; c-152-159. **Kubert** c/a in many issues. **Maurer** a-135. **Redondo** a-166. **Severin** a-123-130, 131i, 132-150.

OUR FIGHTING MEN IN ACTION (See Men In Action)

OUR FLAG COMICS
Ace Magazines: Aug, 1941 - No. 5, April, 1942

1-Captain Victory, The Unknown Soldier (intro.) & The Three Cheers begin						
	255	510	765	1594	2647	3700
2-Origin The Flag (patriotic hero); 1st app?	110	220	330	688	1144	1600
3-5: 5-Intro & 1st app. Mr. Risk	83	166	249	519	860	1200

NOTE: **Anderson** a-1, 4. **Mooney** a-1; c-2.

OUR GANG COMICS (With Tom & Jerry #39-59; becomes Tom & Jerry #60 on; based on film characters)
Dell Publishing Co.: Sept-Oct, 1942 - No. 59, June, 1949

1-Our Gang & Barney Bear by Kelly, Tom & Jerry, Pete Smith, Flip & Dip, The Milky Way begin (all 1st app.)	70	140	210	595	1098	1600
2-Benny Burro begins (#2 by Kelly)	37	74	111	278	509	740
3-5	26	52	78	187	336	485
6-Bumbazine & Albert only app. by Kelly	34	68	102	255	465	675
7-No Kelly story	19	38	57	141	251	360
8-Benny Burro begins by Barks	43	86	129	344	622	900
9-Barks-a(2): Benny Burro & Happy Hound; no Kelly story	40	80	120	300	550	800
10-Benny Burro by Barks	30	60	90	220	398	575
11-1st Barney Bear & Benny Burro by Barks (5-6/44); Happy Hound by Barks	40	80	120	300	550	800
12-20	19	38	57	141	251	360
21-30: 30-X-Mas-c	14	28	42	100	178	255
31-36-Last Barks issue	11	22	33	77	136	195
37-40	8	16	24	52	86	120
41-50	7	14	21	45	73	100
51-57	6	12	18	41	66	90
58,59-No Kelly art or Our Gang stories	6	12	18	37	59	80
Our Gang Volume 1 (Fantagraphics Books, 2006, $12.95, TPB) r/Our Gang stories written and by Walt Kelly from #1-8; Leonard Maltin intro.; Jeff Smith-c						13.00
Our Gang Volume 2 (Fantagraphics Books, 2007, $12.95, TPB) r/Our Gang stories written and by Walt Kelly from #9-15; Steve Thompson intro.; Jeff Smith-c						13.00

NOTE: **Barks** art in part only. **Barks** did not write Barney Bear stories #30-34. (See March of Comics #3, 26). Early issues have photo back-c.

OUR LADY OF FATIMA
Catechetical Guild Educational Society: 3/11/55 (15¢) (36 pgs.)

395	6	12	18	28	34	40

OUR LOVE (True Secrets #3 on? or Romantic Affairs #3 on?)
Marvel Comics (SPC): Sept, 1949 - No. 2, Jan, 1950

1-Photo-c	15	30	45	86	133	180
2-Photo-c	11	22	33	60	83	105

OUR LOVE STORY
Marvel Comics Group: Oct, 1969 - No. 38, Feb, 1976

1	6	12	18	41	66	90
2-4,6-8,10,11	3	6	9	20	30	40
5-Steranko-a	8	16	24	56	93	130
9,12-Kirby-a	4	8	12	22	34	45
13-(10/71, 52 pgs.)	4	8	12	26	41	55
14-New story by Gary Fredrich & Tarpe' Mills	4	8	12	22	34	45
15-20,27;27-Colan/Everett-a(r?); Kirby/Colletta-r	3	6	9	16	23	30
21-26,28-37	3	6	9	14	19	24
38-Last issue	3	6	9	17	25	32

NOTE: **J. Buscema** a-1-3, 5-7, 9, 13r, 16r, 19r(2), 21r, 22r(2), 23r, 34r, 35r; c-11, 13, 16, 22, 23, 24, 27, 35. **Colan** a-3-6, 21r(#6), 22r, 23r(#3), 24r(#4), 27; c-19. **Katz** a-17. **Maneely** a-13r. **Romita** a-13r; c-1, 2, 4-6. **Weiss** a-16, 17, 29r(#17).

OUR MEN AT WAR
DC Comics: Aug/Sept 1952

nn - Ashcan comic, not distributed to newsstands, only for in-house use. Cover art is All Star Western #60 with interior being Detective Comics #181 (no known sales)

OUR MISS BROOKS
Dell Publishing Co.: No. 751, Nov, 1956

Four Color 751-Photo-c	7	14	21	50	83	115

OUR SECRET (Exciting Love Stories)(Formerly My Secret)
Superior Comics Ltd.: No. 4, Nov, 1949 - No. 8, Jun, 1950

4-Kamen-a; spanking scene	18	36	54	103	162	220

	GD	VG	FN	VF	VF/NM	NM-
	2.0	4.0	6.0	8.0	9.0	9.2

5,6,8	11	22	33	62	86	110
7-Contains 9 pg. story intended for unpublished Ellery Queen #5; lingerie panels						
	12	24	36	67	94	120

OUTBREED 999
Blackout Comics: May, 1994 - No. 6, 1994 ($2.95)

1-6: 4-1st app. of Extreme Violet in 7 pg. backup story						3.00

OUTCAST, THE
Valiant: Dec, 1995 ($2.50, one-shot)

1-Breyfogle-a.						2.50

OUTCASTS
DC Comics: Oct, 1987 - No. 12, Sept, 1988 ($1.75, limited series)

1-12: John Wagner & Alan Grant scripts in all						2.50

OUTER LIMITS, THE (TV)
Dell Publishing Co.: Jan-Mar, 1964 - No. 18, Oct, 1969 (Most painted-c)

1	12	24	36	86	153	220
2-5	7	14	21	49	80	110
6-10	6	12	18	41	66	90
11-18: 17-Reprints #1. 18-r/#2	5	10	15	35	55	75

OUTER SPACE (Formerly This Magazine Is Haunted, 2nd Series)
Charlton Comics: No. 17, May, 1958 - No. 25, Dec, 1959; Nov, 1968

17-Williamson/Wood style art; not by them (Sid Check?)						
	14	28	42	80	115	150
18-20-Ditko-a	23	46	69	130	205	280
21-Ditko-c	16	32	48	94	147	200
22-25	14	28	42	80	115	150
V2#1(11/68)-Ditko-a, Boyette-c	5	10	15	32	51	70

OUT FOR BLOOD
Dark Horse: Sept, 1999 - No. 4, Dec, 1999 ($2.95, B&W, limited series)

1-4-Kelley Jones-c; Erskine-a						3.00

OUTLANDERS (Manga)
Dark Horse Comics: Dec, 1988 - No. 33, Sept,1991 ($2.00-$2.50, B&W, 44 pgs.)

1-33: Japanese Sci-fi manga						2.50

OUTLAW (See Return of the...)

OUTLAW FIGHTERS
Atlas Comics (IPC): Aug, 1954 - No. 5, Apr, 1955

1-Tuska-a	14	28	42	76	108	140
2-5: 5-Heath-c/a, 7 pgs.	9	18	27	50	65	80

NOTE: **Heath** c/a-5. **Maneely** c-2. **Pakula** a-2. **Reinman** a-2. **Tuska** a-1, 3.

OUTLAW KID, THE (1st Series; see Wild Western)
Atlas Comics (CCC No. 1-11/EPI No. 12-29): Sept, 1954 - No. 19, Sept, 1957

1-Origin; The Outlaw Kid & his horse Thunder begin; Black Rider app.						
	27	54	81	158	249	340
2-Black Rider app.	14	28	42	80	115	150
3-7,9: 3-Wildey-a(3)	12	24	36	69	97	125
8-Williamson/Woodbridge-a, 4 pgs.	13	26	39	74	105	135
10-Williamson-a	13	26	39	74	105	135
11-17,19: 13-Baker text illo. 15-Williamson text illo (unsigned)						
	9	18	27	52	69	85
18-Williamson/Mayo-a	10	20	30	56	76	95

NOTE: **Berg** a-4, 7, 13. **Maneely** c-1-3, 5-8, 11-13, 15, 16, 18. **Pakula** a-3. **Severin** c-10, 17, 19. **Shores** a-1. **Wildey** a-1(3), 2-8, 10, 11, 12(4), 13(4), 15-19(4 each); c-4.

OUTLAW KID, THE (2nd Series)
Marvel Comics Group: Aug, 1970 - No. 30, Oct, 1975

1-Reprints; 1-Orlando-r, Wildey-r(3)	3	6	9	18	27	35
2,3,9: 2-Reprints. 3,9-Williamson-a(r)	2	4	6	10	14	18
4-7: 7-Last 15¢ issue	2	4	6	9	13	16
8-Double size (52 pgs.); Crandall-r	2	4	6	16	22	28
10-Origin	3	6	9	18	27	35
11-20: new-a in #10-16	2	4	6	10	14	18
21-30: 27-Origin-r/#10	2	4	6	8	10	12

NOTE: **Ayers** a-10, 27r. **Berg** a-7, 25r. **Everett** a-2(2 pgs.). **Gil Kane** c-10, 11, 15, 27r, 28. **Roussos** a-10i, 27(r). **Severin** c-1, 9, 20, 25. **Wildey** r-1-4, 6-9, 19-22, 25, 26. **Williamson** a-28r. **Woodbridge/Williamson** a-9r.

OUTLAW NATION
DC Comics (Vertigo): Nov, 2000 - No. 19, May, 2002 ($2.50)

1-19-Fabry painted-c/Delano-s/Sudzuka-a						2.50
TPB (Image Comics, 11/06, $15.99) B&W reprint of #1-19; Delano intro.						16.00

OUTLAWS

Out of the Night #7 © ACG

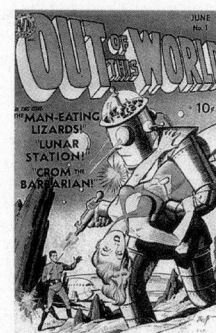

Out of This World #1 © AVON

Outsiders #9 © DC

	GD 2.0	VG 4.0	FN 6.0	VF 8.0	VF/NM 9.0	NM- 9.2
D. S. Publishing Co.: Feb-Mar, 1948 - No. 9, June-July, 1949						
1-Violent & suggestive stories	34	68	102	195	308	420
2-Ingels-a; Baker-a	34	68	102	195	308	420
3,5,6: 3-Not Frazetta. 5-Sky Sheriff by Good app. 6-McWilliams-a						
	15	30	45	88	137	185
4-Orlando-a	16	32	48	94	147	200
7,8-Ingels-a in each	24	48	72	139	220	300
9-(Scarce)-Frazetta-a (7 pgs.)	46	92	138	281	466	650
NOTE: *Another #3 was printed in Canada with Frazetta art "Prairie Jinx," 7 pgs.*						
OUTLAWS, THE (Formerly Western Crime Cases)						
Star Publishing Co.: No. 10, May, 1952 - No. 13, Sep, 1953; No. 14, Apr, 1954						
10-L. B. Cole-c	21	42	63	120	188	255
11-14-L. B. Cole-c. 14-Reprints Western Thrillers #4 (Fox) w/new L.B. Cole-c; Kamen, Feldstein-r	16	32	48	92	144	195
OUTLAWS						
DC Comics: Sept, 1991 - No. 8, Apr, 1992 ($1.95, limited series)						
1-8: Post-apocalyptic Robin Hood.						2.50
OUTLAWS OF THE WEST (Formerly Cody of the Pony Express #10)						
Charlton Comics: No. 11, 7/57 - No. 81, 5/70; No. 82, 7/79 - No. 88, 4/80						
11	8	16	24	42	54	65
12,13,15-17,19,20	5	10	15	24	30	35
14-(68 pgs., 2/58)	9	18	27	47	61	75
18-Ditko-a	10	20	30	54	72	90
21-30	3	6	9	16	22	28
31-50: 34-Gunmaster app.	2	4	6	11	16	20
51-63,65,67-70: 54-Kid Montana app.	2	4	6	9	13	16
64,66: 64-Captain Doom begins (1st app.). 68-Kid Montana series begins	2	4	6	11	16	20
71-79: 73-Origin & 1st app. The Sharp Shooter, last app. #74. 75-Last Capt. Doom	2	4	6	8	11	14
80,81-Ditko-a	2	4	6	11	16	20
82-88						5.00
64,79(Modern Comics-r, 1977, '78)						4.00
OUTLAWS OF THE WILD WEST						
Avon Periodicals: 1952 (25¢, 132 pgs.) (4 rebound comics)						
1-Wood back-c; Kubert-a (3 Jesse James-r)	34	68	102	197	311	425
OUTLAW TRAIL (See Zane Grey 4-Color 511)						
OUT OF SANTA'S BAG (See March of Comics #10 in the Promotional Comics section)						
OUT OF THE NIGHT (The Hooded Horseman #18 on)						
Amer. Comics Group (Creston/Scope): Feb-Mar, 1952 - No. 17, Oct-Nov, 1954						
1-Williamson/LeDoux-a (9 pgs.)	66	132	198	413	682	950
2-Williamson-a (5 pgs.)	47	94	141	287	474	660
3,5-10: 9-Sci/Fic story	29	58	87	170	268	365
4-Williamson-a (7 pgs.)	40	80	120	240	383	525
11-17: 13-Nostrand-a? 17-E.C. Wood swipe	22	44	66	126	198	270
NOTE: *Landau a-14, 16, 17. Shelly a-12.*						
OUT OF THE SHADOWS						
Standard Comics/Visual Editions: No. 5, July, 1952 - No. 14, Aug, 1954						
5-Toth-p; Moreira, Tuska; Roussos-c	54	108	162	338	557	775
6-Toth/Celardo-a; Katz-a(2)	40	80	120	235	368	500
7,9: 7-Jack Katz-c/a(2). 9-Crandall-a(2)	31	62	93	178	282	385
8-Katz shrunken head-c	50	100	150	305	503	700
10-Spider-c; Sekowsky-a	31	62	93	178	282	385
11-Toth-a, 2 pgs.; Katz-a; Andru-c	31	62	93	178	282	385
12-Toth/Peppe-a(2); Katz-a	40	80	120	235	368	500
13-Cannabalism story; Sekowsky-a; Roussos-a	37	74	111	213	337	460
14-Toth-a	31	62	93	178	282	385
OUT OF THE VORTEX (Comics' Greatest World:... #1-4)						
Dark Horse Comics: Oct., 1993 - No. 12, Oct, 1994 ($2.00, limited series)						
1-11: 1-Foil logo. 4-Dorman-c(p). 6-Hero Zero x-over						2.50
12 ($2.50)						2.50
NOTE: *Art Adams c-7. Golden c-8. Mignola c-2. Simonson c-3. Zeck c-10.*						
OUT OF THIS WORLD						
Charlton Comics: Aug, 1956 - No. 16, Dec, 1959						
1	26	52	78	150	235	320
2	14	28	42	81	118	155
3-6-Ditko-c/a (3) each	31	62	93	180	285	390
7-(2/58, 15¢, 68 pgs.)-Ditko-c/a(4)	33	66	99	190	300	410
8-(5/58, 15¢, 68 pgs.)-Ditko-a(2)	29	58	87	170	268	365

	GD 2.0	VG 4.0	FN 6.0	VF 8.0	VF/NM 9.0	NM- 9.2
9,10,12,16-Ditko-a	22	44	66	128	202	275
11-Ditko c/a (3)	26	52	78	152	239	325
13-15	11	22	33	64	90	115
NOTE: *Ditko c-3-12, 16. Reinman a-10.*						
OUT OF THIS WORLD						
Avon Periodicals: June, 1950; Aug, 1950						
1-Kubert-a(2) (one reprinted/Eerie #1, 1947) plus Crom the Barbarian by Gardner Fox & John Giunta (origin); Fawcette-c	69	138	207	431	716	1000
1-(8/50) Reprint; no month on cover	43	86	129	262	431	600
OUT OF THIS WORLD ADVENTURES						
Avon Periodicals: July, 1950 - No. 2, Dec, 1950 (25¢ pulp)						
1-Kubert-a	66	132	198	413	682	950
2-Kubert-a plus The Spider God of Akka by Gardner Fox & John Giunta pulp magazine w/comic insert	45	90	135	275	450	625
NOTE: *Out of This World Adventures is a sci-fi pulp magazine w/32 pgs. of color comics.*						
OUT OUR WAY WITH WORRY WART						
Dell Publishing Co.: No. 680, Feb, 1956						
Four Color 680	4	8	12	24	37	50
OUTPOSTS						
Blackthorne Publishing: June, 1987 - No. 4, 1987 ($1.25)						
1-4: 1-Kaluta-c(p)						2.50
OUTSIDERS, THE						
DC Comics: Nov, 1985 - No. 28, Feb, 1988						
1						3.00
2-17						2.50
18-28: 18-26-Batman returns. 21-Intro. Strike Force Kobra; 1st app. Clayface IV 22-E.C. parody; Orlando-a. 21- 25-Atomic Knight app. 27,28-Millennium tie-ins						2.50
Annual 1 (12/86, $2.50), Special 1 (7/87, $1.50)						2.50
NOTE: *Aparo a-1-7, 9-14, 17-22, 25, 26; c-1-7, 9-14, 17, 19-26. Byrne a-11. Bolland a-6; 18; c-16. Ditko a-13p. Erik Larsen a-24, 27 28; c-27, 28. Morrow a-13.*						
OUTSIDERS						
DC Comics: Nov, 1993 - No. 24, Nov, 1995 ($1.75/$1.95/$2.25)						
1-11,0,12-24: 1-Alpha; Travis Charest-c. 1-Omega; Travis Charest-c. 5-Atomic Knight app. 8-New Batman-c/story. 11-(9/94)-Zero Hour. 0-(10/94).12-(11/94). 21-Darkseid cameo. 22-New Gods app.						2.50
OUTSIDERS (See Titans/Young Justice: Graduation Day)						
DC Comics: Aug, 2003 - Present ($2.50/$2.99)						
1-Nightwing, Arsenal, Metamorpho app.; Winick-s/Raney-a						5.00
2-Joker and Grodd app.						3.00
3-33: 3-Joker-c. 5,6-ChrisCross-a. 8-Huntress app. 9,10-Capt. Marvel Jr. app. 24,25-X-over with Teen Titans. 26,27-Batman & old Outsiders						2.50
34-49: 34-One Year Later. 36-Begin $2.99-c. 37-Superman app. 44-Red Hood app.						3.00
Annual 1 (6/07, $3.99) McDaniel-a; Black Lightning app.						4.00
...: Double Feature (10/03, $4.95) r/#1,2						5.00
...: Crisis Intervention TPB (2006, $12.99) r/#29-33						13.00
...: Looking For Trouble TPB (2004, $12.95) r/#1-7 & Teen Titans/Outsiders Secret Files & Origins 2003; intro. by Winick						13.00
...: Pay As You Go TPB (2007, $14.99) r/#42-46 & Annual 1						15.00
...: Sum of All Evil TPB (2004, $14.95) r/#8-15						15.00
...: The Good Fight TPB (2006, $14.99) r/#34-41						15.00
...: Wanted TPB (2005, $14.99) r/#16-23						15.00
OUTSIDERS: FIVE OF A KIND (Bridges Outsiders #49 & 50)						
DC Comics: Oct, 2007 ($2.99, weekly limited series)						
...Katana/Shazam! (part 2 of 5) - Barr-s/Sharpe-a						3.00
...Metamorpho/Aquaman (part 4 of 5) - Wilson-s/Middleton-a						3.00
...Nightwing/Captain Boomerang (part 1 of 5) - DeFilippis & Weir-s/Willams-a						3.00
...Thunder/Martian Manhunter (part 3 of 5) - Bedard-s/Turnbull-a; Grayven app.						3.00
...Wonder Woman/Grace (part 5 of 5) - Andreyko-s/Richards-a						3.00
OUT THERE						
DC Comics(Cliffhanger): July, 2001 - No. 18, Aug, 2003 ($2.50/$2.95)						
1-Humberto Ramos-c/a; Brian Augustyn-s						3.00
1-Variant-c by Carlos Meglia						4.00
2-8: 3-Variant-c by Bruce Timm						2.50
9-18: 9-Begin $2.95-c						3.00
...: The Evil Within TPB (2002, $12.95) r/#1-6; Ramos sketch pages						13.00
OVERKILL: WITCHBLADE/ ALIENS/ DARKNESS/ PREDATOR						
Image Comics/Dark Horse Comics: Dec, 2000 - No. 2, 2001 ($5.95)						
1,2-Jenkins-s/Lansing, Ching & Benitez-a						6.00

Ozark Ike #15 © KING

Ozzie and Harriet #1 © DC

Painkiller Jane V2 #1 © Q&P

	GD 2.0	VG 4.0	FN 6.0	VF 8.0	VF/NM 9.0	NM- 9.2

OVER THE EDGE
Marvel Comics: Nov, 1995 - No. 10, Aug, 1996 (99¢)

1-10: 1,6,10-Daredevil-c/story. 2,7-Dr. Strange-c/story. 3-Hulk-c/story. 4,9-Ghost Rider-c/story. 5-Punisher-c/story. 8-Elektra-c/story ... 2.50

OWL, THE (See Crackajack Funnies #25, Popular Comics #72 and Occult Files of Dr. Spektor #22)
Gold Key: April, 1967; No. 2, April, 1968

	GD	VG	FN	VF	VF/NM	NM-
1-Written by Jerry Siegel; '40s super hero	6	12	18	39	62	85
2	5	10	15	30	48	65

OZ (See First Comics Graphic Novel, Marvel Treaury Of Oz & MGM's Marvelous...)

OZ
Caliber Press: 1994 - 1997 ($2.95, B&W)

0-20: 0-Released between #10 & #11 ... 3.00
1 ($5.95)-Limited Edition; double-c ... 6.00
...Specials: Freedom Fighters. Lion. Scarecrow. Tin Man ... 3.00

OZARK IKE
Dell Publishing Co./Standard Comics B11 on: Feb, 1948; Nov, 1948 - No. 24, Dec, 1951; No. 25, Sept, 1952

	GD	VG	FN	VF	VF/NM	NM-
Four Color 180(1948-Dell)	10	20	30	67	116	165
B11, B12, 13-15	10	20	30	54	72	90
16-25	9	18	27	47	61	75

OZ: DAEMONSTORM
Caliber Press: 1997 ($3.95, B&W, one-shot)

1 ... 4.00

OZ: ROMANCE IN RAGS
Caliber Press: 1996 ($2.95, B&W, limited series)

1-3, ..Special ... 3.00

OZ SQUAD
Brave New Worlds/Patchwork Press: 1992 - No. 4, 1994 ($2.50/$2.75, B&W)

1-4-Patchwork Press ... 3.00

OZ SQUAD
Patchwork Press: Dec, 1995 - No. 10, 1996 ($3.95/$2.95, B&W)

1-($3.95) ... 4.00
2-10 ... 3.00

OZ: STRAW AND SORCERY
Caliber Press: 1997 ($2.95, B&W, limited series)

1-3 ... 3.00

OZ-WONDERLAND WARS, THE
DC Comics: Jan, 1986 - No. 3, March, 1986 (Mini-series)(Giants)

1-3-Capt. Carrot app.; funny animals ... 4.00

OZZIE & BABS (TV Teens #14 on)
Fawcett Publications: Dec, 1947 - No. 13, Fall, 1949

	GD	VG	FN	VF	VF/NM	NM-
1-Teen-age	10	20	30	54	72	90
2	6	12	18	31	38	45
3-13	6	12	18	27	33	38

OZZIE AND HARRIET (The Adventures of... on cover) (Radio)
National Periodical Publications: Oct-Nov, 1949 - No. 5, June-July, 1950

	GD	VG	FN	VF	VF/NM	NM-
1-Photo-c	93	186	279	581	966	1350
2	46	92	138	281	466	650
3-5	40	80	120	235	368	500

OZZY OSBOURNE (Todd McFarlane Presents)
Image Comics (Todd McFarlane Prod.): June, 1999 ($4.95, magazine-sized)

1-Bio, interview and comic story; Ormston painted-a; Ashley Wood-c ... 5.00

PACIFIC COMICS GRAPHIC NOVEL (See Image Graphic Novel)

PACIFIC PRESENTS (Also see Starslayer #2, 3)
Pacific Comics: Oct, 1982 - No. 2, Apr, 1983; No. 3, Mar, 1984 - No. 4, Jun, 1984

1-Chapter 3 of The Rocketeer; Stevens-c/a; Bettie Page model		1	2	3	4	5	7
2-Chapter 4 of The Rocketeer (4th app.); nudity; Stevens-c/a		1	2	3	4	5	7
3,4: 3-1st app. Vanity							3.00

NOTE: **Conrad** a-3, 4; c-3. **Ditko** a-1-3; c-1(1/2). **Dave Stevens** a-1, 2; c-1(1/2), 2.

PACT, THE
Image Comics: Feb, 1994 - No. 3, June, 1994 ($1.95, limited series)

1-3: Valentino co-scripts & layouts ... 2.50

PACT, THE
Image Comics: Apr, 2005 - No. 4, Jan, 2006 ($2.99/$2.95)

1-4: Invincible, Shadowhawk, Firebreather & Zephyr team-up. 1-Valentino-s/a ... 3.00

PAGEANT OF COMICS (See Jane Arden & Mopsy)
Archer St. John: Sept, 1947 - No. 2, Oct, 1947

	GD	VG	FN	VF	VF/NM	NM-
1,2: 1-Mopsy strip-r. 2-Jane Arden strip-r	10	20	30	54	72	90

PAINKILLER JANE
Event Comics: June, 1997 - No. 5, Nov, 1997 ($3.95/$2.95)

1-Augustyn/Waid-s/Leonardi/Palmiotti-a, variant-c ... 4.00
2-5: Two covers (Quesada, Leonardi) ... 3.00
0-(1/99, $3.95): Retells origin; two covers ... 4.00
Essential Painkiller Jane TPB (2007, $19.99) r/#0-5; cover gallery and pin-ups ... 20.00

PAINKILLER JANE
Dynamite Entertainment: 2006 - No. 3, 2006 ($2.99)

1-3-Quesada & Palmiotti-s/Moder-a. 1-Four covers by Q&P, Moder, Tan and Conner ... 3.00
Volume #1 TPB (2007, $9.99) r/#1-3; cover gallery and Palmiotti interview ... 10.00

PAINKILLER JANE
Dynamite Entertainment: No. 0, 2007 - Present ($3.50)

0-(25¢) Quesada & Palmiotti-s/Moder-a ... 2.25
1-3-($3.50) 1-Continued from #0; 5 covers ... 3.50

PAINKILLER JANE / DARKCHYLDE
Event Comics: Oct, 1998 ($2.95, one-shot)

Preview-($6.95) DF Edition, 1-($6.95) DF Edition ... 7.00
1-Three covers; J.G. Jones-a ... 3.00

PAINKILLER JANE / HELLBOY
Event Comics: Aug, 1998 ($2.95, one-shot)

1-Leonardi & Palmiotti-a ... 3.00

PAINKILLER JANE VS. THE DARKNESS
Event Comics: Apr, 1997 ($2.95, one-shot)

1-Ennis-s; four variant-c (Conner, Hildebrandts, Quesada, Silvestri) ... 3.50

PAKKINS' LAND
Caliber Comics (Tapestry): Oct, 1996 - No. 6, July, 1997 ($2.95, B&W)

1-Gary and Rhoda Shipman-s/a ... 6.00
2,3 ... 4.00
1-3-2nd printing ... 3.00
4-6 ... 3.00
0-(6/97, $1.95) ... 3.00

PAKKINS' LAND
Alias Enterprises: Apr, 2005 - No. 2 ($2.99)

1,2-Gary Shipman-s/a ... 3.00

PAKKINS' LAND: FORGOTTEN DREAMS
Caliber Comics/Image Comics #4: Apr, 1998 - No. 4, Mar, 2000 ($2.95, B&W)

1-4-Gary and Rhoda Shipman-s/a ... 3.00

PAKKINS' LAND: QUEST FOR KINGS
Caliber Comics: Aug, 1997 - No. 6, Mar, 1998 ($2.95, B&W)

1-6: 1-Gary and Rhoda Shipman-s/a; Jeff Smith var-c ... 3.00

PANCHO VILLA
Avon Periodicals: 1950

	GD	VG	FN	VF	VF/NM	NM-
nn-Kinstler-c	23	46	69	130	205	280

PANHANDLE PETE AND JENNIFER (TV) (See Gene Autry #20)
J. Charles Laue Publishing Co.: July, 1951 - No. 3, Nov, 1951

	GD	VG	FN	VF	VF/NM	NM-
1	10	20	30	54	72	90
2,3: 2-Interior photo-cvrs	7	14	21	37	46	55

PANIC (Companion to Mad)
E. C. Comics (Tiny Tot Comics): Feb-Mar, 1954 - No. 12, Dec-Jan, 1955-56

	GD	VG	FN	VF	VF/NM	NM-
1-Used in Senate Investigation hearings; Elder draws entire E. C. staff; Santa Claus & Mickey Spillane parody	31	62	93	248	387	525
2	15	30	45	120	185	250
3,4: 3-Senate Subcommittee parody; Davis draws Gaines, Feldstein & Kelly, 1 pg.; Old King Cole smokes marijuana. 4-Infinity-c; John Wayne parody	12	24	36	96	148	200

5-11: 8-Last pre-code issue (5/55). 9-Superman, Smilin' Jack & Dick Tracy app. on-c; has photo of Walter Winchell on-c. 11-Wheedies cereal box-c

Panic #5 © WMG

Paradise X #4 © MAR

Patches #10 © Patches Publ.

	GD 2.0	VG 4.0	FN 6.0	VF 8.0	VF/NM 9.0	NM- 9.2
	11	22	33	88	137	185
12 (Low distribution; thousands were destroyed)	14	28	42	112	176	240

NOTE: *Davis* a-1-12; c-12. *Elder* a-1-12. *Feldstein* c-1-3, 5. *Kamen* a-1. *Orlando* a-1-9. *Wolverton* c-4, panel-3. *Wood* a-2-9, 11, 12.

PANIC (Magazine) (Satire)
Panic Publ.: July, 1958 - No. 6, July, 1959; V2#10, Dec, 1965 - V2#12, 1966

	GD 2.0	VG 4.0	FN 6.0	VF 8.0	VF/NM 9.0	NM- 9.2
1	13	26	39	74	105	135
2-6	9	18	27	47	61	75
V2#10-12: Reprints earlier issues	3	6	9	16	23	30

NOTE: *Davis* a-3(2 pgs.), 4, 5, 10; c-10. *Elder* a-5. *Powell* a-V2#10, 11. *Torres* a-1-5. *Tuska* a-V2#11.

PANIC
Gemstone Publishing: March, 1997 - No. 12, Dec, 1999 ($2.50, quarterly)
1-12: E.C. reprints 2.50

PANTHA (See Vampirella-The New Monthly #16,17)

PANTHA: HAUNTED PASSION (Also see Vampirella Monthly #0)
Harris Comics: May, 1997 ($2.95, B&W, one-shot)
1-r/Vampirella #30,31 ..... 3.00

PAPA MIDNITE (See John Constantine - Hellblazer Special:...)

PARADE (See Hanna-Barbera...)

PARADE COMICS (See Frisky Animals on Parade)

PARADE OF PLEASURE
Derric Verschoyle Ltd., London, England: 1954 (192 pgs.) (Hardback book)
By Geoffrey Wagner. Contains section devoted to the censorship of American comic books with illustrations in color and black and white. (Also see *Seduction of the Innocent*).

	GD 2.0	VG 4.0	FN 6.0	VF 8.0	VF/NM 9.0	NM- 9.2
Distributed in USA by Library Publishers, N.Y.	50	100	150	275	413	550
with dust jacket....	105	210	315	578	839	1100

PARADISE TOO!
Abstract Studios: 2000 - No. 14, 2003 ($2.95, B&W)
1-14-Terry Moore's unpublished newspaper strips and sketches 3.00
...: Checking For Weirdos TPB (4/03, $14.95) r/#8-12 ..... 15.00
...: Drunk Ducks! TPB (7/02, $15.95) r/#1-7 ..... 16.00

PARADISE X (Also see Earth X and Universe X)
Marvel Comics: Apr, 2002 - No. 11, July, 2003 ($4.50/$2.99)
0-Ross-c; Braithwaite-a 4.50
1-11-($2.99) Ross-c; Braithwaite-a. 7-Punisher on-c. 10-Kingpin on-c 3.00
...:A (10/03, $2.99) Braithwaite-a; Ross-c 3.00
...:Devils (11/02, $4.50) Sadowski-a; Ross-c 4.50
...:Ragnarok 1,2 (3/02, 4/03, $2.99) Yeates-a; Ross-c 3.00
...:X (11/03, $2.99) Braithwaite-a; Ross-c; conclusion of story 3.00
...:Xen (7/02, $4.50) Yeowell & Sienkiewicz-c; Ross-c 4.50
Earth X Vol. 4: Paradise X Book 1 (2003, $29.99, TPB) r/#0,1-5, ...: Xen; Heralds #1-3 ..... 30.00
Vol. 5: Paradise X Book 2 (2004, $29.99, TPB) r/#6-12, Ragnarok #1&2; Devils, A & X 30.00

PARADISE X: HERALDS (Also see Earth X and Universe X)
Marvel Comics: Dec, 2001 - No. 3, Feb, 2002 ($3.50)
1-3-Prelude to Paradise X series; Ross-c; Pugh-a 3.50
Special Edition (Wizard preview) Ross-c 2.50

PARADOX
Dark Visions Publ.: June, 1994 - No. 2, Aug, 1994 ($2.95, B&W, mature)
1,2: 1-Linsner-a. 2-Boris-c. 3.00

PARALLAX: EMERALD NIGHT (See Final Night)
DC Comics: Nov, 1996 ($2.95, one-shot)
1-Final Night tie-in; Green Lantern (Kyle Rayner) app. 4.00

PARAMOUNT ANIMATED COMICS (See Harvey Comics Hits #60, 62)
Harvey Publications: No. 3, Feb, 1953 - No. 22, July, 1956
3-Baby Huey, Herman & Katnip, Buzzy the Crow begin

	GD 2.0	VG 4.0	FN 6.0	VF 8.0	VF/NM 9.0	NM- 9.2
	23	46	69	130	205	280
4-6	-13	26	39	72	101	130

7-Baby Huey becomes permanent cover feature; cover title becomes Baby Huey with #9

	GD 2.0	VG 4.0	FN 6.0	VF 8.0	VF/NM 9.0	NM- 9.2
	22	44	66	126	198	270
8-10: 9-Infinity-c	12	24	36	69	97	125
11-22	10	20	30	54	72	90

PARENT TRAP, THE (Disney)
Dell Publishing Co.: No. 1210, Oct-Dec, 1961

	GD 2.0	VG 4.0	FN 6.0	VF 8.0	VF/NM 9.0	NM- 9.2
Four Color 1210-Movie, Haley Mills photo-c	9	18	27	60	100	140

PARLIAMENT OF JUSTICE
Image Comics: Mar, 2003 ($5.95, B&W, one-shot, square-bound)

	GD 2.0	VG 4.0	FN 6.0	VF 8.0	VF/NM 9.0	NM- 9.2

1-Michael Avon Oeming-c/s; Neil Vokes-a 6.00

PARODY
Armour Publishing: Mar, 1977 - No. 3, Aug, 1977 (B&W humor magazine)

	GD 2.0	VG 4.0	FN 6.0	VF 8.0	VF/NM 9.0	NM- 9.2
1	2	4	6	11	16	20
2,3: 2-King Kong, Happy Days. 3-Charlie's Angels, Rocky	2	4	6	9	12	15

PAROLE BREAKERS
Avon Periodicals/Realistic #2 on: Dec, 1951 - No. 3, July, 1952
1(#2 on inside)-r/c-Avon paperback #283 (painted-c)

	GD 2.0	VG 4.0	FN 6.0	VF 8.0	VF/NM 9.0	NM- 9.2
	43	86	129	262	431	600
2-Kubert-a; r-c/Avon paperback #114 (photo-c)	30	60	90	174	275	375
3-Kinstler-c	27	54	81	158	249	340

PARTRIDGE FAMILY, THE (TV)(Also see David Cassidy)
Charlton Comics: Mar, 1971 - No. 21, Dec, 1973

	GD 2.0	VG 4.0	FN 6.0	VF 8.0	VF/NM 9.0	NM- 9.2
1-(2 versions: B&W photo-c & tinted color photo-c)	6	12	18	41	66	90
2-4,6-10	4	8	12	22	34	45

5-Partridge Family Summer Special (52 pgs.); The Shadow, Lone Ranger, Charlie McCarthy, Flash Gordon, Hopalong Cassidy, Gene Autry & others app.

	GD 2.0	VG 4.0	FN 6.0	VF 8.0	VF/NM 9.0	NM- 9.2
	7	14	21	47	76	105
11-21	3	6	9	19	29	38

PARTS OF A HOLE
Caliber Press: 1991 ($2.50, B&W)
1-Short stories & cartoons by Brian Michael Bendis 3.00

PARTS UNKNOWN
Eclipse Comics/FX: July, 1992 - No. 4, Oct, 1992 ($2.50, B&W, mature)
1-4: All contain FX gaming cards 2.50

PARTS UNKNOWN
Image Comics: May, 2000 - Present ($2.95, B&W)
...: Killing Attractions 1 (5/00) Beau Smith-s/Brad Gorby-a 3.00
...: Hostile Takeover 1-4 (6-9/00) 3.00

PASSION, THE
Catechetical Guild: No. 394, 1955

	GD 2.0	VG 4.0	FN 6.0	VF 8.0	VF/NM 9.0	NM- 9.2
394	6	12	18	27	33	38

PASSOVER (See Avengelyne)
Maximum Press: Dec, 1996 ($2.99, one-shot)
1 ..... 3.00

PAT BOONE (TV)(Also see Superman's Girlfriend Lois Lane #9)
National Per. Publ.: Sept-Oct, 1959 - No. 5, May-Jun, 1960 (All have photo-c)

	GD 2.0	VG 4.0	FN 6.0	VF 8.0	VF/NM 9.0	NM- 9.2
1	45	90	135	275	450	625

2-5: 3-Fabian, Connie Francis & Paul Anka photos on-c. 4-Previews "Journey To The Center Of The Earth". 4-Johnny Mathis & Bobby Darin photos on-c. 5-Dick Clark & Frankie Avalon photos on-c

	GD 2.0	VG 4.0	FN 6.0	VF 8.0	VF/NM 9.0	NM- 9.2
	36	72	108	208	329	450

PATCHES
Rural Home/Patches Publ. (Orbit): Mar-Apr, 1945 - No. 11, Nov, 1947

	GD 2.0	VG 4.0	FN 6.0	VF 8.0	VF/NM 9.0	NM- 9.2
1-L. B. Cole-c	40	80	120	240	383	525
2	15	30	45	88	137	185

3,4,6,8-11: 6-Henry Aldrich story. 8-Smiley Burnette-c/s (6/47); pre-dates Smiley Burnette #1. 9-Mr. District Attorney story (radio). Leav/Keigstein-a (16 pgs.). 9-11-Leav-c. 10-Jack Carson (radio) c/story; Leav-c. 11-Red Skelton story

	GD 2.0	VG 4.0	FN 6.0	VF 8.0	VF/NM 9.0	NM- 9.2
	15	30	45	85	130	175
5-Danny Kaye-c/story; L.B. Cole-c.	21	42	63	120	188	255
7-Hopalong Cassidy-c/story	18	36	54	103	162	220

PATH, THE (Also see Negation War)
CrossGeneration Comics: Apr, 2002 - No. 23, Apr, 2004 ($2.95)
1-23: 1-Ron Marz-s/Bart Sears-a. 13-Matthew Smith-a begins 3.00
Vol. 1: Crisis of Faith (2002, $15.95, TPB) r/#1-6 ..... 16.00
Vol. 2: Blood on Snow (5/03, $15.95, TPB) r/#7-12 ..... 16.00
Vol. 3: Death and Dishonor ('03, $15.95, TPB) r/#13-18 ..... 16.00

PATHWAYS TO FANTASY
Pacific Comics: July, 1984
1-Barry Smith-c/a; Jeff Jones-a (4 pgs.) 4.00

PATIENT ZERO
Image Comics: Mar, 2004 - No. 4, Jun, 2004 ($2.95, limited series)
1-4-Brent White/John McLean-Foreman-s 3.00

PATORUZU (See Adventures of...)

PATRIOTS, THE

Patsy and Hedy #64 © MAR

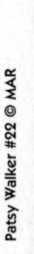

Patsy Walker #22 © MAR

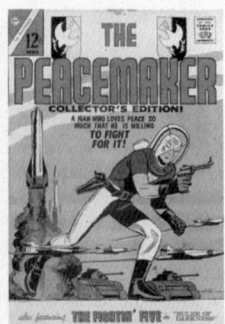

Peacemaker #1 © CC

	GD 2.0	VG 4.0	FN 6.0	VF 8.0	VF/NM 9.0	NM- 9.2
DC Comics (WildStorm): Jan, 2000 - No. 10, Oct, 2000 ($2.50)						
1-10-Choi and Peterson-s/Ryan-a						2.50
PATSY & HEDY (Teenage)(Also see Hedy Wolfe)						
Atlas Comics/Marvel (GPI/Male): Feb, 1952 - No. 110, Feb, 1967						
1-Patsy Walker & Hedy Wolfe; Al Jaffee-c	23	46	69	132	209	285
2	14	28	42	78	112	145
3-10: 3,7,8,9-Al Jaffee-c	11	22	33	62	86	110
11-20: 17,19,20-Al Jaffee-c	10	20	30	54	72	90
21-40	8	16	24	44	57	70
41-50	5	10	15	30	48	65
51-60	4	8	12	28	44	60
61-80,100: 88-Lingerie panel	4	8	12	24	37	50
81-87,89-99,101-110	4	8	12	22	34	45
Annual 1(1963)-Early Marvel annual	9	18	27	60	100	140
PATSY & HER PALS (Teenage)						
Atlas Comics (PPI): May, 1953 - No. 29, Aug, 1957						
1-Patsy Walker	18	36	54	105	165	225
2	11	22	33	62	86	110
3-10	10	20	30	56	76	95
11-29: 24-Everett-a	9	18	27	47	61	75
PATSY WALKER (See All Teen, A Date With Patsy, Girls' Life, Miss America Magazine, Patsy & Hedy, Patsy & Her Pals & Teen Comics)						
Marvel/Atlas Comics (BPC): 1945 (no month) - No. 124, Dec, 1965						
1-Teenage	53	106	159	323	537	750
2	29	58	87	167	264	360
3,4,6-10	23	46	69	132	209	285
5-Injury-to-eye-c	26	52	78	150	235	320
11,12,15,16,18	15	30	45	83	124	165
13,14,17,19-22-Kurtzman's "Hey Look"	15	30	45	85	130	175
23,24	12	24	36	69	97	125
25-Rusty by Kurtzman; painted-c	15	30	45	85	130	175
26-29,31: 26-31: 52 pgs.	11	22	33	60	83	105
30(52 pgs.)-Egghead Doodle by Kurtzman (1 pg.)	11	22	33	64	90	115
32-57: Last precode (3/55)	9	18	27	50	65	80
58-80,100	4	8	12	28	44	60
81-99: 92,98-Millie x-over. 99-Linda Carter x-over	4	8	12	24	37	50
101-124	4	8	12	22	34	45
Fashion Parade 1(1966, 68 pgs.) (Beware cut-out & marked pages)						
	8	16	24	54	90	125
NOTE: Painted c-25-28. Anti-Wertham editorial in #21. Georgie app. in #8, 11. Millie app. in #10, 92, 98. Mitzi app. in #11. Rusty app. in #12, 25. Willie app. in #12. *Al Jaffee* c-44, 47, 49, 57, 58.						
PAT THE BRAT (Adventures of Pipsqueak #34 on)						
Archie Publications (Radio): June, 1953; Summer, 1955 - No. 4, 5/56; No. 15, 7/56 - No. 33, 7/59						
nn(6/53)	14	28	42	76	108	140
1(Summer, 1955)	10	20	30	54	72	90
2-4-(5/56) (#5-14 not published)	7	14	21	37	46	55
15-(7/56)-33	4	8	12	24	34	45
PAT THE BRAT COMICS DIGEST MAGAZINE						
Archie Publications: October, 1980						
1-Li'l Jinx & Super Duck app.	2	4	6	9	12	15
PATTY CAKE						
Permanent Press: Mar, 1995 - No. 9, Jul, 1996 ($2.95, B&W)						
1-9: Scott Roberts-s/a						3.00
PATTY CAKE						
Caliber Press (Tapestry): Oct, 1996 - No. 3, Apr, 1997 ($2.95, B&W)						
1-3: Scott Roberts-s/a, ...Christmas (12/96)						3.00
PATTY CAKE & FRIENDS						
Slave Labor Graphics: Nov, 1997 - Present ($2.95, B&W)						
Here There Be Monsters (10/97), 1-14: Scott Roberts-s/a						3.00
Volume 2 #1 (11/00, $4.95)						5.00
PATTY POWERS (Formerly Della Vision #3)						
Atlas Comics: No. 4, Oct, 1955 - No. 7, Oct, 1956						
4	10	20	30	58	79	100
5-7	7	14	21	35	43	50
PAT WILTON (See Mighty Midget Comics)						
PAUL						
Spire Christian Comics (Fleming H. Revell Co.): 1978 (49¢)						

	GD 2.0	VG 4.0	FN 6.0	VF 8.0	VF/NM 9.0	NM- 9.2
nn	2	4	6	8	10	12
PAULINE PERIL (See The Close Shaves of...)						
PAUL REVERE'S RIDE (TV, Disney, see Walt Disney Showcase #34)						
Dell Publishing Co.: No. 822, July, 1957						
Four Color 822-w/Johnny Tremain, Toth-a	8	16	24	58	97	135
PAUL TERRY (See Heckle and Jeckle)						
PAUL TERRY'S ADVENTURES OF MIGHTY MOUSE (See Adventures of...)						
PAUL TERRY'S COMICS (Formerly Terry-Toons Comics; becomes Adventures of Mighty Mouse No. 126 on)						
St. John Publishing Co.: No. 85, Mar, 1951 - No. 125, May, 1955						
85,86-Same as Terry-Toons #85, & 86 with only a title change; published at same time?; Mighty Mouse, Heckle & Jeckle & Gandy Goose continue from Terry-Toons						
	12	24	36	67	94	120
87-99	9	18	27	50	65	80
100	10	20	30	54	72	90
101-104,107-125: 121,122,125-Painted-c	9	18	27	47	61	75
105,106-Giant Comics Edition (25¢, 100 pgs.) (9/53 & ?). 105-Little Roquefort-c/story						
	18	36	54	105	165	225
PAUL TERRY'S MIGHTY MOUSE (See Mighty Mouse)						
PAUL TERRY'S MIGHTY MOUSE ADVENTURE STORIES (See Mighty Mouse Adventure Stories)						
PAUL THE SAMURAI (See The Tick #4)						
New England Comics: July, 1992 - No. 6, July, 1993 ($2.75, B&W)						
1-6						2.75
PAWNEE BILL						
Story Comics (Youthful Magazines?): Feb, 1951 - No. 3, July, 1951						
1-Bat Masterson, Wyatt Earp app.	13	26	39	72	101	130
2,3: 3-Origin Golden Warrior; Cameron-a	8	16	24	42	54	65
PAY-OFF (This Is the..., ...Crime, ...Detective Stories)						
D. S. Publishing Co.: July-Aug, 1948 - No. 5, Mar-Apr, 1949 (52 pgs.)						
1-True Crime Cases #1,2	26	52	78	152	239	325
2	16	32	48	94	147	200
3-5-Thrilling Detective Stories	14	28	42	82	121	160
PEACEMAKER, THE (Also see Fightin' Five)						
Charlton Comics: V3#1, Mar, 1967 - No. 5, Nov, 1967 (All 12¢ cover price)						
1-Fightin' Five begins	5	10	15	32	51	70
2,3,5	3	6	9	20	30	40
4-Origin The Peacemaker	4	8	12	24	37	50
1,2(Modern Comics reprint, 1978)						5.00
PEACEMAKER (Also see Crisis On Infinite Earths & Showcase '93 #7,9,10)						
DC Comics: Jan, 1988 - No. 4, Apr, 1988 ($1.25, limited series)						
1-4						2.50
PEANUTS (Charlie Brown) (See Fritzi Ritz, Nancy & Sluggo, Sparkle & Sparkler, Tip Top, Tip Topper & United Comics)						
United Features Syndicate/Dell Publishing Co./Gold Key: 1953-54; No. 878, 2/58 - No. 13, 5-7/62; 5/63 - No. 4, 2/64						
1(U.F.S.)(1953-54)-Reprints United Features' Strange As It Seems, Willie, Ferdnand						
	12	24	36	82	146	210
Four Color 878(#1) (Dell) Schulz-s/a, with assistance from Dale Hale and Jim Sasseville thru #4	19	38	57	138	244	350
Four Color 969,1015('59)	12	24	36	82	146	210
4(2-4/60) Schulz-s/a; one story by Anthony Pocrnich, Schulz's assistant cartoonist						
	10	20	30	68	119	170
5-13-Schulz-c only; s/a by Pocrnich	8	16	24	58	97	135
1(Gold Key, 5/63)	10	20	30	70	123	175
2-4	7	14	21	47	76	105
PEBBLES & BAMM BAMM (TV) (See Cave Kids #7, 12)						
Charlton Comics: Jan, 1972 - No. 36, Dec, 1976 (Hanna-Barbera)						
1-From the Flintstones; "Teen Age..." on cover	5	10	15	30	48	65
2-10	3	6	9	17	25	32
11-20	2	4	6	13	18	22
21-36	2	4	6	9	13	16
nn (1973, digest, 100 pgs.) B&W one page gags	3	6	9	18	27	35
PEBBLES & BAMM BAMM (TV)						
Harvey Comics: Nov, 1993 - No. 3, Mar, 1994 ($1.50) (Hanna-Barbera)						
V2#1-3						3.00
...Giant Size 1 (10/93, $2.25, 68 pgs.)("Summer Special" on-c)						4.00

Pedro #1 © FOX

Penny #3 © AVON

Pep Comics #3 © AP

	GD 2.0	VG 4.0	FN 6.0	VF 8.0	VF/NM 9.0	NM- 9.2
PEBBLES FLINTSTONE (TV) (See The Flintstones #11)						
Gold Key: Sept, 1963 (Hanna-Barbera)						
1 (10088-309)-Early Pebbles app.	9	18	27	60	100	140
PEDRO (Formerly My Private Life #17; also see Romeo Tubbs)						
Fox Features Syndicate: No. 18, June, 1950 - No. 2, Aug, 1950?						
18(#1)-Wood-c/a(p)	22	44	66	128	202	275
2-Wood-a?	15	30	45	88	137	185
PEE-WEE PIXIES (See The Pixies)						
PELLEAS AND MELISANDE (See Night Music #4, 5)						
PENALTY (See Crime Must Pay the...)						
PENANCE (See Civil War, Thunderbolts and related titles)						
Marvel Comics: Nov, 2007 - No. 5 (2007)						
1-Speedball/Penance; Jenkins-s/Gulacy-a						3.00
PENDRAGON (Knights of... #5 on; also see Knights of...)						
Marvel Comics UK, Ltd.: July, 1992 - No. 15, Sept, 1993 ($1.75)						
1-15: 1-4-Iron Man app. 6-8-Spider-Man app.						2.50

PENDULUM ILLUSTRATED BIOGRAPHIES
Pendulum Press: 1979 (B&W)

19-355x-George Washington/Thomas Jefferson, 19-3495-Charles Lindbergh/Amelia Earhart, 19-3509-Harry Houdini/Walt Disney, 19-3517-Davy Crockett/Daniel Boone-Redondo-a, 19-3525-Elvis Presley/Beatles, 19-3533-Benjamin Franklin/Martin Luther King Jr, 19-3541-Abraham Lincoln/Franklin D. Roosevelt, 19-3568-Marie Curie/Albert Einstein-Redondo-a, 19-3576-Thomas Edison/Alexander Graham Bell-Redondo-a, 19-3584-Vince Lombardi/Pele, 19-3592-Babe Ruth/Jackie Robinson, 19-3606-Jim Thorpe/Althea Gibson

Softback						3.00
Hardback						5.00

NOTE: Above books still available from publisher.

PENDULUM ILLUSTRATED CLASSICS (Now Age Illustrated)
Pendulum Press: 1973 - 1978 (75¢, 62pp, B&W, 5-3/8x8")
(Also see Marvel Classics)

64-100x(1973)-Dracula-Redondo art, 64-131x-The Invisible Man-Nino art, 64-0968-Dr. Jekyll and Mr. Hyde-Redondo art, 64-1005-Black Beauty, 64-1010-Call of the Wild, 64-1020-Frankenstein, 64-1025-Huckleberry Finn, 64-1030-Moby Dick-Nino-a, 64-1040-Red Badge of Courage, 64-1045-The Time Machine-Nino-a, 64-1050-Tom Sawyer, 64-1055-Twenty Thousand Leagues Under the Sea, 64-1328(1974)-Kidnapped, 64-1336-Three Musketeers-Nino art, 64-1344-A Tale of Two Cities, 64-1352-Journey to the Center of the Earth, 64-1360-The War of the Worlds-Nino-a, 64-1379-The Greatest Advs. of Sherlock Holmes-Redondo art, 64-1387-Mysterious Island, 64-1395-Hunchback of Notre Dame, 64-1409-Helen Keller-story of my life, 64-1417-Scarlet Letter, 64-1425-Gulliver's Travels, 64-2618(1977)-Around the World in Eighty Days, 64-2626-Captains Courageous, 64-2634-Connecticut Yankee, 64-2642-The Hound of the Baskervilles, 64-2650-The House of Seven Gables, 64-2669-Jane Eyre, 64-2677-The Last of the Mohicans, 64-2685-The Best of O'Henry, 64-2693-The Best of Poe-Redondo-a, 64-2707-Two Years Before the Mast, 64-2715-White Fang, 64-2723-Wuthering Heights, 64-3126(1978)-Ben Hur-Redondo art, 64-3134-A Christmas Carol, 64-3142-The Food of the Gods, 64-3150-Ivanhoe, 64-3169-The Man in the Iron Mask, 64-3177-The Prince and the Pauper, 64-3185-The Prisoner of Zenda, 64-3193-The Return of the Native, 64-3207-Robinson Crusoe, 64-3215-The Scarlet Pimpernel, 64-3223-The Sea Wolf, 64-3231-The Swiss Family Robinson, 64-3851-Billy Budd, 64-386x-Crime and Punishment, 64-3878-Don Quixote, 64-3886-Great Expectations, 64-3894-Heidi, 64-3908-The Iliad, 64-3916-Lord Jim, 64-3924-The Mutiny on Board H.M.S. Bounty, 64-3932-The Odyssey, 64-3940-Oliver Twist, 64-3959-Pride and Prejudice, 64-3967-The Turn of the Screw

Softback						3.00
Hardback						5.00

NOTE: All of the above books can be ordered from the publisher; some were reprinted as Marvel Classic Comics #1-12. In 1972 there was another brief series of 12 titles which contained Classics III. artwork. They were entitled *Now Age Books* Illustrated, but can be easily distinguished from later series by the small Classics Illustrated logo at the top of the front cover. The format is the same as the later series. The 48 pg. C.I. art was stretched out to make 62 pgs. After Twin Circle Publ. terminated the Classics III. series in 1971, they made a one year contract with Pendulum Press to print these twelve titles of C.I. art. Pendulum was unhappy with the contract, and at the end of 1972 began their own art series, utilizing the talents of the Filipino artist group. One detail which makes this rather confusing is that when they redid the art in 1973, they gave it the same identifying no. as the 1972 series. All 12 of the 1972 C.I. editions have new covers, taken from internal art panels. In spite of their recent age, all of the 1972 C.I. series are very rare. Mint copies would fetch at least $50. Here is a list of the 1972 series, with C.I. title no counterpart:

64-1005 (CI#60-A2) 64-1010 (CI#91) 64-1015 (CI-Jr #503) 64-1020 (CI#26)
64-1025 (CI#19-A2) 64-1030 (CI#5-A2) 64-1035 (CI#169) 64-1040 (CI#98)
64-1045 (CI#133) 64-1050 (CI#50-A2) 64-1055 (CI#47) 64-1060 (CI-Jr#535)

PENDULUM ILLUSTRATED ORIGINALS
Pendulum Press: 1979 (In color)

94-4254-Solarman: The Beginning (See Solarman)						6.00

PENDULUM'S ILLUSTRATED STORIES
Pendulum: 1990 - No. 72, 1990? (No cover price ($4.95), squarebound, 68 pgs.)

1-72: Reprints Pendulum III. Classics series						5.00

PENNY
Avon Comics: 1947 - No. 6, Sept-Oct, 1949 (Newspaper reprints)

	GD 2.0	VG 4.0	FN 6.0	VF 8.0	VF/NM 9.0	NM- 9.2
1-Photo & biography of creator	15	30	45	86	133	180
2-5	9	18	27	52	69	85
6-Perry Como photo on-c	10	20	30	56	76	95

PENNY CENTURY (See Love and Rockets)
Fantagraphics Books: Dec, 1997 - Present ($2.95, B&W, mini-series)

1-7-Jaime Hernandez-s/a						3.00

PEP COMICS (See Archie Giant Series #576, 589, 601, 614, 624)
MLJ Magazines/Archie Publications No. 56 (3/46) on: Jan, 1940 - No. 411, Mar, 1987

	GD 2.0	VG 4.0	FN 6.0	VF 8.0	VF/NM 9.0	NM- 9.2
1-Intro. The Shield (1st patriotic hero) by Irving Novick; origin & 1st app. The Comet by Jack Cole, The Queen of Diamonds & Kayo Ward; The Rocket, The Press Guardian; The Falcon (#1 only), Sergeant Boyle, Fu Chang, & Bentley of Scotland Yard; Robot-c; Shield-c begin						
	971	1942	2913	6800	11,900	17,000
2-Origin The Rocket	259	518	777	1619	2685	3750
3	193	386	579	1206	2003	2800
4-Wizard cameo; early robot-s	152	304	456	950	1575	2200
5-Wizard cameo in Shield story	152	304	456	950	1575	2200
6-10: 8-Last Cole Comet; no Cole-a in #6,7	122	244	366	763	1269	1775
11-Dusty, Shield's sidekick begins (1st app.); last Press Guardian, Fu Chang	126	252	378	788	1307	1825
12-Origin & 1st app. Fireball (2/41); last Rocket & Queen of Diamonds; Danny in Wonderland begins	145	290	435	906	1503	2100
13-15	100	200	300	625	1038	1450
16-Origin Madam Satan; blood drainage-c	159	318	477	994	1647	2300
17-Origin/1st app. The Hangman (7/41); death of The Comet; Comet is revealed as Hangman's brother	364	728	1092	2366	4183	6000
18,19,21: 21-Last Madam Satan	93	186	279	581	966	1350
20-Classic Nazi swastika-c; last Fireball	100	200	300	625	1038	1450
22-Intro. & 1st app. Archie, Betty, & Jughead(12/41); (also see Jackpot)	1737	3474	5211	13,028	23,014	33,000
23	221	442	663	1381	2291	3200
24,25: 24-Coach Kleets app. (unnamed until Archie #94); bondage/torture-c. 25-1st app. Archie's jalopy; 1st skinny Mr. Weatherbee prototype	145	290	435	906	1503	2100
26-1st app. Veronica Lodge (4/42); "Remember Pearl Harbor!" cover caption	228	456	684	1425	2363	3300
27,29,30: 27-Bill of Rights-c. 29-Origin Shield retold; 30-Capt. Commando begins; bondage/torture-c; 1st Miss Grundy (definitive version); see Jackpot #4	114	228	342	713	1182	1650
28-Classic swastika/Hangman-c	121	242	363	756	1253	1750
31-35: 31-MLJ offices & artists are visited in Sgt. Boyle story; 1st app. Mr. Lodge. 32-Shield dons new costume. 34-Bondage/Hypo-c. 33-Pre-Moose tryout (see Jughead #1)	93	186	279	581	966	1350
36-1st Archie-c (2/43) w/Shield & Hangman	248	496	744	1550	2575	3600
37-40	64	128	192	400	665	930
41-50: 41-Archie-c begin. 47-Last Hangman issue; infinity-c. 48-Black Hood begins (5/44); ends #51,59,60	51	102	153	275	453	630
51-60: 52-Suzie begins; 1st Mr Weatherbee-c. 56-Last Capt. Commando. 59-Black Hood not in costume; lingerie panels; Archie dresses as his aunt; Suzie ends. 60-Katy Keene begins(3/47)	30	60	90	176	278	380
61-65-Last Shield. 62-1st app. Li'l Jinx (7/47)	25	50	75	148	232	315
66-80: 66-G-Man Club becomes Archie Club (2/48); Nevada Jones by Bill Woggon. 78-1st app. Dilton	15	30	45	88	137	185
81-99	14	28	42	76	108	140
100	15	30	45	86	133	180
101-130	9	18	27	50	65	80
131(2/59)-140: 138-140-Neal Adams-a (1 pg.) in each	5	10	15	30	48	65
141-149(9/61)	4	8	12	24	37	50
150-160-Super-heroes app. in each (see note). 150 (10/61?)-2nd or 3rd app. The Jaguar?						
151-154,156-158-Horror/Sci/Fi-c. 157-Li'l Jinx	5	10	15	35	55	75
161(3/63)-167,169-180: 161-Early Josie stories w/DeCarlo-a begin (see Note for others)	3	6	9	18	27	35
168,200: 168-(1/64)-Jaguar app. 200-(12/66)	3	6	9	20	30	40
181(5/65)-199: 187-Pureheart tryout story. 192-UFO-c. 198-Giantman-c(only)	3	6	9	16	22	28
201-217,219-226,228-240(4/70)	2	4	6	13	18	22
218,227-Archies Band-c only	3	6	9	14	19	24
241-270(10/72)	2	4	6	9	13	16
271-297,299	1	3	4	6	8	10
298, 300: 298-Josie and the Pussycats-c. 300(4/75)	2	4	6	9	12	15
301-340(8/78)	1	2	3	5	6	8
341-382						5.00
383(4/82),393(3/84): 383-Marvelous Maureen begins (Sci/fi). 393-Thunderbunny begins						6.00
384-392,394-399,401-410						4.00
400(5/85),411: 400-Story featuring Archie staff (DeCarlo-a)						6.00

NOTE: *Biro* a-2, 4, 5. *Jack Cole* a-1-5, 8. *Al Fagaly* c-55-72. *Fuje* a-39, 45, 47; c-34. *Meskin* a-2, 4, 5, 11(2). *Montana* c-30, 32, 33, 36, 73-87(most). *Novick* c-1-28, 29(w/Schomburg), 31i. *Harry Sahle* c-35, 39-50.

Perfect Crime #28 © Cross Pub.

Personal Love #13 © FF

Peter Parker: Spider-Man #10 © MAR

	GD	VG	FN	VF	VF/NM	NM-
	2.0	4.0	6.0	8.0	9.0	9.2

Schomburg c-38. **Bob Wood** *a-2, 4-6, 11. The Fly app. in 151, 154, 160. Flygirl app. in 153, 155, 156, 158. Jaguar app. in 150, 152, 157, 159, 168. Josie by* **DeCarlo** *in 161-166, 168-171, 173, 175-177, 179, 181-on. Katy Keene by* **Bill Woggon** *in 73-126. Bondage c-7, 12, 13, 15, 18, 21, 31, 32. Cover features: Shield #1-16; Shield/Hangman #17-27, 29-41; Hangman #28. Archie #36, 41-on.*

PEPE
Dell Publishing Co.: No. 1194, Apr, 1961

Four Color 1194-Movie, photo-c	4	8	12	22	34	45

PERFECT CRIME, THE
Cross Publications: Oct, 1949 - No. 33, May, 1953 (#2-12, 52 pgs.)

1-Powell-a(2)	35	70	105	201	318	435
2 (4/50)	19	38	57	109	172	235
3-10: 7-Steve Duncan begins, ends #30. 10-Flag-c	16	32	48	94	147	200
11-Used in SOTI, pg. 159	18	36	54	105	165	225
12-14	15	30	45	88	137	185
15- "The Most Terrible Menace" 2 pg. drug editorial	16	32	48	94	147	200
16,17,19-25,27-29,31-33	13	26	39	74	105	135
18-Drug cover, heroin drug propaganda story, plus 2 pg. anti-drug editorial	25	50	75	148	232	315
26-Drug-c with hypodermic needle; drug propaganda story	26	52	78	154	242	330
30-Strangulation cover	26	52	78	150	235	320

NOTE: *Powell-a-No. 1, 2, 4. Wildey a-1, 5. Bondage c-11.*

PERFECT LOVE
Ziff-Davis(Approved Comics)/St. John No. 9 on: #10, 8-9/51 (cover date; 5-6/51 indicia date); #2, 10-11/51 - #10, 12/53

10(#1)(8-9/51)-Painted-c	21	42	63	122	191	260
2(10-11/51)	15	30	45	83	124	165
3,5-7: 3-Painted-c. 5-Photo-c	13	26	39	72	101	130
4,8 (Fall, 1952)-Kinstler-a; last Z-D issue	13	26	39	74	105	135
9,10 (10/53, 12/53, St. John): 9-Painted-c. 10-Photo-c	12	24	36	69	97	125

PERHAPANAUTS, THE
Dark Horse Comics: Nov, 2005 - No. 4, Feb, 2006 ($2.99, limited series)

1-4-Todd Dezago-s/Craig Rousseau-a/c						3.00

PERHAPANAUTS: SECOND CHANCES, THE
Dark Horse Comics: Oct, 2006 - No. 4, Jan, 2007 ($2.99, limited series)

1-4-Todd Dezago-s/Craig Rousseau-a/c						3.00

PERRI (Disney)
Dell Publishing Co.: No. 847, Jan, 1958

Four Color 847-Movie, w/2 diff-c publ.	5	10	15	35	55	75

PERRY MASON
David McKay Publications: No. 49, 1946 - No. 50, 1946

Feature Books 49, 50-Based on Gardner novels	31	62	93	178	282	385

PERRY MASON MYSTERY MAGAZINE (TV)
Dell Publishing Co.: June-Aug, 1964 - No. 2, Oct-Dec, 1964

1	6	12	18	37	59	80
2-Raymond Burr photo-c	5	10	15	30	48	65

PERSONAL LOVE (Also see Movie Love)
Famous Funnies: Jan, 1950 - No. 33, June, 1955

1-Photo-c	20	40	60	117	184	250
2-Kathryn Grayson & Mario Lanza photo-c	12	24	36	69	97	125
3-7,10: 7-Robert Walker & Joanne Dru photo-c. 10-Loretta Young & Joseph Cotton photo-c	13	26	33	62	86	110
8,9: 8-Esther Williams & Howard Keel photo-c. 9-Debra Paget & Louis Jourdan photo-c	11	22	33	64	90	115
11-Toth-a; Glenn Ford & Gene Tierney photo-c	14	28	42	76	108	140
12,16,17-One pg. Frazetta each. 17-Rock Hudson & Yvonne DeCarlo photo-c	11	22	33	62	86	110
13-15,18 & 23: 12-Jane Greer & William Lundigan photo-c. 14-Kirk Douglas photo-c. 15-Dale Robertson & Joanne Dru photo-c. 18-Gregory Peck & Susan Hayworth photo-c. 19-Anthony Quinn & Suzan Ball photo-c. 20-Robert Wagner & Kathleen Crowley photo-c. 21-Roberta Peters & Byron Palmer photo-c. 22-Dale Robertson photo-c.						
23-Rhonda Fleming-c	10	20	30	58	79	100
24,27,28-Frazetta-a in each (8,8&6 pgs.). 27-Rhonda Fleming & Fernando Lamas photo-c. 28-Mitzi Gaynor photo-c	43	86	129	262	431	600
25-Frazetta-a (tribute to Betty Page, 7 pg. story); Tyrone Power/Terry Moore photo-c from "House of the Khyber Rifles"	53	106	159	323	537	750
26,29,30,33: 26-Constance Smith & Byron Palmer photo-c. 29-Charlton Heston & Nicol Morey photo-c. 30-Johnny Ray & Mitzi Gaynor photo-c. 33-Dana Andrews & Piper Laurie photo-c.						

	10	20	30	58	79	100
31-Marlon Brando & Jean Simmons photo-c; last pre-code (2/55)	13	26	39	72	101	130
32-Classic Frazetta-a (8 pgs.); Kirk Douglas & Bella Darvi photo-c	57	114	171	356	591	825

NOTE: *All have photo-c. Many feature movie stars.* **Everett** *a-5, 9, 10, 24.*

PERSONAL LOVE (Going Steady V3#3 on)
Prize Publ. (Headline): V1#1, Sept, 1957 - V3#2, Nov-Dec, 1959

V1#1	9	18	27	52	69	85
2	6	12	18	31	38	45
3-6(7-8/58)	6	12	18	28	34	40
V2#1(9-10/58)-V2#6(7-8/59)	5	10	15	24	30	35
V3#1-Wood?/Orlando-a	6	12	18	29	36	42
2	5	10	15	23	28	32

PETER CANNON - THUNDERBOLT (See Crisis on Infinite Earths)(Also see Thunderbolt)
DC Comics: Sept, 1992 - No. 12, Aug, 1993 ($1.25)

1-12						2.50

PETER COTTONTAIL
Key Publications: Jan, 1954; Feb, 1954 - No. 2, Mar, 1954 (Says 3/53 in error)

1(1/54)-Not 3-D	9	18	27	50	65	80
1(2/54)-(3-D, 25¢)-Came w/glasses; written by Bruce Hamilton	21	42	63	120	188	255
2-Reprints 3-D #1 but not in 3-D	6	12	18	31	38	45

PETER GUNN (TV)
Dell Publishing Co.: No. 1087, Apr-June, 1960

Four Color 1087-Photo-c	8	16	24	58	97	135

PETE ROSE: HIS INCREDIBLE BASEBALL CAREER
Masstar Creations Inc.: 1995

1-John Tartaglione-a						2.50

PETER PAN (Disney) (See Hook, Movie Classics & Comics, New Adventures of… & Walt Disney Showcase #36)
Dell Publishing Co.: No. 442, Dec, 1952 - No. 926, Aug, 1958

Four Color 442 (#1)-Movie	10	20	30	70	123	175
Four Color 926-Reprint of 442	4	8	12	28	44	60

PETER PAN
Disney Comics: 1991 ($5.95, graphic novel, 68 pgs.)(Celebrates video release)

nn-r/Peter Pan Treasure Chest from 1953						7.00

PETER PANDA
National Periodical Publications: Aug-Sept, 1953 - No. 31, Aug-Sept, 1958

1-Grossman-c/a in all	45	90	135	275	450	625
2	24	48	72	139	220	300
3,4,6-8,10	20	40	60	117	184	250
5-Classic-c (scarce)	46	92	138	281	466	650
9-Robot-c	25	50	75	145	228	310
11-31	14	28	42	80	115	150

PETER PAN TREASURE CHEST (See Dell Giants)

PETER PARKER (See The Spectacular Spider-Man)

PETER PARKER: SPIDER-MAN
Marvel Comics: Jan, 1999 - No. 57, Aug, 2003 ($2.99/$1.99/$2.25)

1-Mackie-s/Romita Jr.-a; wraparound-c						3.00
1-($6.95) DF Edition w/variant cover by the Romitas						7.00
2-11,13-17-($1.99): 2-Two covers; Thor app. 3-Iceman-c/app. 4-Marrow-c/app. 5-Spider-Woman app. 7,8-Blade app. 9,10-Venom app. 11-Iron Man & Thor-c/app.						2.50
12-($2.99) Sinister Six and Venom app.						3.00
18-24,26-43: 18-Begin $2.25-c. 20-Jenkins-s/Buckingham-a start. 23-Intro Typeface. 24-Maximum Security x-over. 29-Rescue of MJ. 30-Ramos-c. 42,43-Mahfood-a						2.50
25-($2.99) Two covers; Spider-Man & Green Goblin						3.00
44-47-Humberto Ramos-c/a; Green Goblin-c/app.						3.00
48,49,51-57: 48,49-Buckingham-c/a. 51,52-Herrera-a. 56,57-Kieth-a; Sandman returns						2.50
50-($3.50) Buckingham-c/a						3.50
...99 Annual (8/99, $3.50) Man-Thing app.						3.50
...'00 Annual ($3.50) Bounty app.; Joe Bennett-a; Black Cat back-up story						3.50
...'01 Annual ($2.99) Avery-s						3.00
...: A Day in the Life TPB (5/01, $14.95) r/#20-22,26; Webspinners #10-12						15.00
...: One Small Break TPB (2002, $16.95) r/#27,28,30-34; Andrews-c						17.00
Spider-Man: Return of the Goblin TPB (2002, $8.99) r/#44-47; Ramos-c						9.00
...Vol. 4: Trials & Tribulations TPB (2003, $11.99) r/#35,37,48-50; Cho-c						12.00

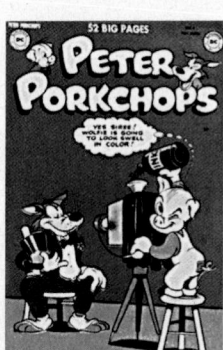

Peter Porkchops #4 © DC

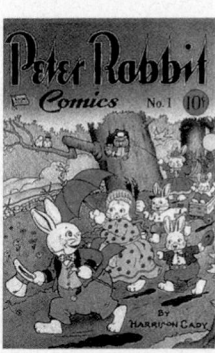

Peter Rabbit #1 © AVON

The Phantom #22 © KING

	GD 2.0	VG 4.0	FN 6.0	VF 8.0	VF/NM 9.0	NM- 9.2

PETER PAT
United Features Syndicate: No. 8, 1939

| Single Series 8 | 36 | 72 | 108 | 208 | 329 | 450 |

PETER PAUL'S 4 IN 1 JUMBO COMIC BOOK
Capitol Stories (Charlton): No date (1953)

| 1-Contains 4 comics bound; Space Adventures, Space Western, Crime & Justice, Racket Squad in Action | 40 | 80 | 120 | 230 | 355 | 480 |

PETER PIG
Standard Comics: No. 5, May, 1953 - No. 6, Aug, 1953

| 5,6 | 7 | 14 | 21 | 35 | 43 | 50 |

PETER PORKCHOPS (See Leading Comics #23)
National Periodical Publications: 11-12/49 - No. 61, 9-11/59; No. 62, 10-12/60 (1-11: 52 pgs.)

1	34	68	102	195	308	420
2	15	30	45	90	140	190
3-10: 6- "Peter Rockets to Mars!" c/story	13	26	39	74	105	135
11-30	10	20	30	56	76	95
31-62	9	18	27	47	61	75
NOTE: Otto Feuer a-all. Rube Grossman-a most issues. Sheldon Mayer a-30-38, 40-44, 46-52, 61.

PETER PORKER, THE SPECTACULAR SPIDER-HAM
Star Comics (Marvel): May, 1985 - No. 17, Sept, 1987 (Also see Marvel Tails)

| 1-Michael Golden-c | | | | | | 5.00 |
| 2-17: 12-Origin/1st app. Bizarro Phil. 13-Halloween issue | | | | | | 4.00 |
NOTE: Back-up features: 2-X-Bugs. 3-Iron Mouse. 4-Croctor Strange. 5-Thrr, Dog of Thunder.

PETER POTAMUS (TV)
Gold Key (Hanna-Barbera)

| 1-1st app. Peter Potamus & So-So, Breezly & Sneezly | 9 | 18 | 27 | 63 | 107 | 150 |

PETER RABBIT (See New Funnies #65 & Space Comics)
Dell Publishing Co.: No. 1, 1942

| Large Feature Comic 1 | 60 | 120 | 180 | 375 | 625 | 875 |

PETER RABBIT (Adventures of…; New Advs. of… #9 on)(Also see Funny Tunes & Space Comics)
Avon Periodicals: 1947 - No. 34, Aug-Sept, 1956

1(1947)-Reprints 1943-44 Sunday strips; contains a biography & drawing of Cady	35	70	105	201	318	435
2 (4/48)	24	48	72	139	220	300
3 ('48) - 6(7/49)-Last Cady issue	21	42	63	124	195	265
7-10(1950-8/51): 9-New logo	10	20	30	58	79	100
11(11/51)-34('56)-Avon's character	9	18	27	50	65	80
…Easter Parade (1952, 25¢, 132 pgs.)	19	38	57	112	176	240
…Jumbo Book (1954-Giant Size, 25¢)-Jesse James by Kinstler (6 pgs.); space ship-c	23	46	69	135	213	290

PETER RABBIT 3-D
Eternity Comics: April, 1990 ($2.95, with glasses; sealed in plastic bag)

| 1-By Harrison Cady (reprints) | | | | | | 3.00 |

PETER, THE LITTLE PEST (#4 titled Petey)
Marvel Comics Group: Nov, 1969 - No. 4, May, 1970

| 1 | 6 | 12 | 18 | 39 | 62 | 85 |
| 2-4-r-Dexter the Demon & Melvin the Monster | 4 | 8 | 12 | 26 | 41 | 55 |

PETE'S DRAGON (See Walt Disney Showcase #43)

PETE THE PANIC
Stanmor Publications: November, 1955

| nn-Code approved | 5 | 10 | 15 | 23 | 28 | 32 |

PETEY (See Peter, the Little Pest)

PETTICOAT JUNCTION (TV, inspired Green Acres)
Dell Publ. Co.: Oct-Dec, 1964 - No. 5, Oct-Dec, 1965 (#1-3, 5 have photo-c)

| 1 | 7 | 14 | 21 | 47 | 76 | 105 |
| 2-5 | 5 | 10 | 15 | 32 | 51 | 70 |

PETUNIA (Also see Looney Tunes and Porky Pig)
Dell Publishing Co.: No. 463, Apr, 1953

| Four Color 463 | 4 | 8 | 12 | 26 | 41 | 55 |

PHAGE (See Neil Gaiman's Teknophage & Neil Gaiman's Phage-Shadowdeath)

PHANTACEA
McPherson Publishing Co.: Sept, 1977 - No. 6, Summer, 1980 (B&W)

1-Early Dave Sim-a (32 pgs.)	3	6	9	18	27	35
2-Dave Sim-a(10 pgs.)	2	4	6	11	16	20
3-6: 3-Flip-c w/Damnation Bridge. 4-Gene Day-a	2	4	6	8	11	14

PHANTASMO (See The Funnies #45)
Dell Publishing Co.: No. 18, 1941

| Large Feature Comic 18 | 38 | 76 | 114 | 219 | 347 | 475 |

PHANTOM, THE
David McKay Publishing Co.: 1939 - 1949

Feature Books 20	90	180	270	563	932	1300
Feature Books 22	65	130	195	406	671	935
Feature Books 39	50	100	150	305	503	700
Feature Books 53,56,57	40	80	120	244	392	540

PHANTOM, THE (See Ace Comics, Defenders Of The Earth, Eat Right To Work and Win, Future Comics, Harvey Comics Hits #51,56, Harvey Hits #1, 6, 12, 15, 26, 36, 44, 48, & King Comics)

PHANTOM, THE (nn (#29)-Published overseas only) (Also see Comics Reading Libraries in the Promotional Comics section)
Gold Key(#1-17)/King(#18-28)/Charlton(#30 on): Nov, 1962 - No. 17, Jul, 1966; No. 18, Sept, 1966 - No. 28, Dec, 1967; No. 30, Feb, 1969 - No. 74, Jan, 1977

1-Origin revealed on inside-c & back-c	15	30	45	111	198	285
2-King, Queen & Jack begins, ends #11	9	18	27	60	100	140
3-5	7	14	21	50	83	115
6-10	6	12	18	41	66	90
11-17: 12-Track Hunter begins	5	10	15	32	51	70
18-Flash Gordon begins; Wood-a	4	8	12	26	41	55
19-24: 20-Flash Gordon ends (both by Gil Kane). 21-Mandrake begins. 20,24-Girl Phantom app.	4	8	12	24	37	50
25-28: 25-Jeff Jones-a(4 pgs.); 1 pg. Williamson ad. 26-Brick Bradford app. 28(nn)-Brick Bradford app.	3	6	9	20	30	40
30-33: 33-Last 12¢ issue	3	6	9	16	23	30
34-40: 36,39-Ditko-a	3	6	9	16	22	28
41-66: 46-Intro. The Piranha. 62-Bolle-c	2	4	6	13	18	22
67-Origin retold; Newton-c/a	3	6	9	16	23	30
68-73-Newton-c/a	2	4	6	11	16	20
74-Classic flag-c by Newton; Newton-a;	3	6	9	16	22	28
NOTE: Aparo a-31-34, 36-38; c-31-38, 60, 61. Painted c-1-17.

PHANTOM, THE
DC Comics: May, 1988 - No. 4, Aug, 1988 ($1.25, mini-series)

| 1-4: Orlando-c/a in all | | | | | | 3.00 |

PHANTOM, THE
DC Comics: Mar, 1989 - No. 13, Mar, 1990 ($1.50)

| 1-13: 1-Brief origin | | | | | | 3.00 |

PHANTOM, THE
Wolf Publishing: 1992 - No. 8, 1993 ($2.25)

| 1-8 | | | | | | 2.50 |

PHANTOM, THE
Moonstone: 2003 - Present ($3.50)

| 1-17: 1-Cassaday-c/Raab-s/Quinn-a | | | | | | 3.50 |
| ... Annual #1 (2007, $6.50) Blevins-c; stroy and art by various incl. Nolan | | | | | | 6.50 |

PHANTOM BLOT, THE (#1 titled New Adventures of…)
Gold Key: Oct, 1964 - No. 7, Nov, 1966 (Disney)

1 (Meets The Mysterious Mr. X)	6	12	18	37	59	80
2-1st Super Goof	5	10	15	32	51	70
3-7	3	6	9	20	30	40

PHANTOM EAGLE (See Mighty Midget, Marvel Super Heroes #16 & Wow #6)

PHANTOM FORCE
Image Comics/Genesis West #0, 3-7: 12/93 - #2, 1994; #0, 3/94; #3, 5/94 - #8, 10/94 ($2.50/$3.50, limited series)

0 (3/94, $2.50)-Kirby/Jim Lee-c; Kirby-p pgs. 1,5,24-29.						3.00
1 (12/93, $2.50)-Polybagged w/trading card; Kirby Liefeld-c; Kirby plots/pencils w/inks by Liefeld, McFarlane, Jim Lee, Silvestri, Larsen, Williams, Ordway & Miki						3.00
2 ($3.50)-Kirby-a(p); Kirby/Larson-c						3.50
3-8: 3-(5/94, $2.50)-Kirby/McFarlane-c 4-(5/94)-Kirby-c(p). 5-(6/94)						3.00

PHANTOM GUARD
Image Comics (WildStorm Productions): Oct, 1997 - No. 6, Mar, 1998 ($2.50)

| 1-6: 1-Two covers | | | | | | 3.00 |
| 1-($3.50)-Voyager Pack w/Wildcore preview | | | | | | 3.50 |

PHANTOM JACK
Image Comics: Mar, 2004 - No. 5, July, 2004 ($2.95)

Phantom Lady #14 © FOX

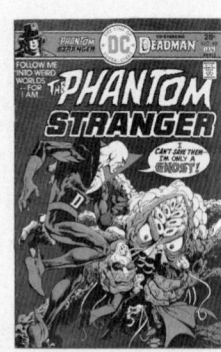

Phantom Stranger #40 © DC

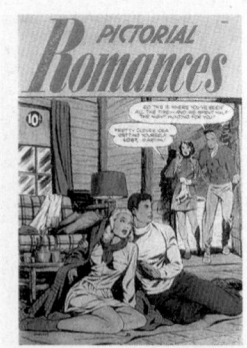

Pictorial Romances #5 © STJ

	GD 2.0	VG 4.0	FN 6.0	VF 8.0	VF/NM 9.0	NM- 9.2		GD 2.0	VG 4.0	FN 6.0	VF 8.0	VF/NM 9.0	NM- 9.2

1-5-Mike San Giacomo-s/Mitchell Breitweiser-a. 4-Initial printings with errors exist 3.00
The Collected Edition (Speakeasy Comics, 2005, $17.99) r/series; Bendis intro 18.00

PHANTOM LADY (1st Series) (My Love Secret #24 on) (Also see All Top, Daring Adventures, Freedom Fighters, Jungle Thrills, & Wonder Boy)
Fox Features Syndicate: No. 13, Aug, 1947 - No. 23, Apr, 1949

13(#1)-Phantom Lady by Matt Baker begins (see Police Comics #1 for 1st app.); Blue Beetle
  story 423 846 1269 2855 5028 7200
14-16: 14(#2)-Not Baker-c. 15-P.L. injected with experimental drug. 16-Negligee-c, panels;
  true crime stories begin 259 518 777 1619 2685 3750
17-Classic bondage cover; used in SOTI, illo "Sexual stimulation by combining 'headlights'
  with the sadist's dream of tying up a woman" 600 1200 1800 4200 7350 10,500
18,19 179 358 537 1119 1860 2600
20-22 148 296 444 925 1538 2150
23-Bondage-c 159 318 477 994 1647 2300
NOTE: **Matt Baker** a-in all; c-13, 15-21. **Kamen** a-22, 23.

PHANTOM LADY (2nd Series) (See Terrific Comics) (Formerly Linda)
Ajax/Farrell Publ.: V1#5, Dec-Jan, 1954/1955 - No. 4, June, 1955

V1#5(#1)-By Matt Baker 116 232 348 725 1200 1675
V1#2-Last pre-code 86 172 258 538 894 1250
3,4-Red Rocket. 3-Heroin story 68 136 204 425 705 985

PHANTOM LADY
Verotik Publications: 1994 ($9.95)

1-Reprints G. A. stories from Phantom Lady and All Top Comics; Adam Hughes-c 10.00

PHANTOM PLANET, THE
Dell Publishing Co.: No. 1234, 1961

Four Color 1234-Movie 7 14 21 47 76 105

PHANTOM STRANGER, THE (1st Series) (See Saga of Swamp Thing)
National Periodical Publications: Aug-Sept, 1952 - No. 6, June-July, 1953

1(Scarce)-1st app. 200 400 600 1250 2075 2900
2 (Scarce) 110 220 330 688 1144 1600
3-6 (Scarce) 95 190 285 594 985 1375
Ashcan (8,9/52) Not distributed to newsstands, only for in house use (no known sales)

PHANTOM STRANGER, THE (2nd Series) (See Showcase #80) (See Showcase Presents for B&W reprints)
National Periodical Publications: May-June, 1969 - No. 41, Feb-Mar, 1976

1-2nd S.A. app. P. Stranger; only 12¢ issue 10 20 30 71 126 180
2,3 6 12 18 37 59 80
4-1st new look Phantom Stranger; N. Adams-a 6 12 18 39 62 85
5-7 4 8 12 28 44 60
8-14: 14-Last 15¢ issue 3 6 9 19 29 38
15-19: All 25¢ giants (52 pgs.) 3 6 9 21 32 42
20-Dark Circle begins, ends #24. 3 6 9 14 19 24
21,22 2 4 6 10 14 18
23-Spawn of Frankenstein begins by Kaluta 3 6 9 21 32 42
24,25,27-30-Last Spawn of Frankenstein 3 6 9 17 25 32
26- Book-length story featuring Phantom Stranger, Dr. 13 & Spawn of Frankenstein
  3 6 9 18 27 35
31-The Black Orchid begins (6-7/74). 3 6 9 17 25 32
32,34-38: 34-Last 20¢ issue (#35 on are 25¢) 2 4 6 10 14 18
33,39-41: 33-Deadman-c/story. 39-41-Deadman app. 2 4 6 13 18 22
NOTE: **N. Adams** a-4; c-3-19. **Anderson** a-4, 5i. **Aparo** a-7-17, 19-26; c-20-24, 33-41. **B. Bailey** a-27-30. **DeZuniga** a-12-16, 18, 19, 21, 22, 31, 34. **Grell** a-33. **Kaluta** a-23-25; c-26. **Meskin** r-15, 16, 18, 19. **Redondo** a-32, 35, 36. **Sparling** a-20. **Starr** a-17r. **Toth** a-15r. Black Orchid by **Carrillo**-38-41. Dr. 13 solo in-13, 18, 19, 20, 21, 34. Frankenstein by **Kaluta**-23-25; by **Baily**-27-30. No Black Orchid-33, 34, 37.

PHANTOM STRANGER (See Justice League of America #103)
DC Comics: Oct, 1987 - No. 4, Jan, 1988 (75¢, limited series)

1-4-Mignola/Russell-c/a & Eclipso app. in all. 3,4-Eclipso-c 3.00

PHANTOM STRANGER (See Vertigo Visions-The Phantom Stranger)

PHANTOM: THE GHOST WHO WALKS
Marvel Comics: Feb, 1995 - No. 3, Apr, 1995 ($2.95, limited series)

1-3 4.00

PHANTOM: THE GHOST WHO WALKS
Moonstone: 2003 ($16.95, TPB)

nn-Three new stories by Raab, Goulart, Collins, Blanco and others; Klauba painted-c 17.00

PHANTOM 2040 (TV cartoon)
Marvel Comics: May, 1995 - No. 4, Aug, 1995 ($1.50)

1-4-Based on animated series; Ditko-a(p) in all 3.00

PHANTOM WITCH DOCTOR (Also see Durango Kid #8 & Eerie #8)

Avon Periodicals: 1952

1-Kinstler-c/a (7 pgs.) 47 94 141 287 474 660

PHANTOM ZONE, THE (See Adventure #283 & Superboy #100, 104)
DC Comics: January, 1982 - No. 4, April, 1982

1-4-Superman app. in all. 2-4: Batman, Green Lantern app. 3.00
NOTE: **Colan** a-1-4p; c-1-4p. **Giordano** c-1-4i.

PHAZE
Eclipse Comics: Apr, 1988 - No. 2, Oct, 1988 ($2.25)

1,2: 1-Sienkiewicz-c. 2-Gulacy painted-c 2.50

PHIL RIZZUTO (Baseball Hero) (See Sport Thrills, Accepted reprint)
Fawcett Publications: 1951 (New York Yankees)

nn-Photo-c 69 138 207 431 716 1000

PHOENIX
Atlas/Seaboard Publ.: Jan, 1975 - No. 4, Oct, 1975

1-Origin; Rovin-s/Amendola-a 1 3 4 6 8 10
2-4: 3-Origin & only app. The Dark Avenger. 4-New origin/costume The Protector
  (formerly Phoenix) 1 2 3 5 7 9
NOTE: **Infantino** appears in #1, 2. **Austin** a-3i. **Thorne** c-3.

PHOENIX (...The Untold Story)
Marvel Comics Group: April, 1984 ($2.00, one-shot)

1-Byrne/Austin-r/X-Men #137 with original unpublished ending
  2 4 6 8 10 12

PHOENIX RESURRECTION, THE
Malibu Comics (Ultraverse): 1995 - 1996 ($3.95)

Genesis #1 (12/95)-X-Men app; wraparound-c, Revelations #1 (12/95)-X-Men app;
  wraparound-c, Aftermath #1 (1/96)-X-Men app. 4.00
0-($1.95)-r/series 2.50
0-American Entertainment Ed. 4.00

PICNIC PARTY (See Dell Giants)

PICTORIAL CONFESSIONS (Pictorial Romances #4 on)
St. John Publishing Co.: Sept, 1949 - No. 3, Dec, 1949

1-Baker-c/a(3) 41 82 123 250 400 550
2-Baker-a; photo-c 23 46 69 132 209 285
3-Kubert, Baker-a; part Kubert-c 24 48 72 139 220 300

PICTORIAL LOVE STORIES (Formerly Tim McCoy)
Charlton Comics: No. 22, Oct, 1949 - No. 26, July, 1950 (all photo-c)

22-26: All have "Me-Dan Cupid". 25-Fred Astaire-c 19 38 57 112 176 240

PICTORIAL LOVE STORIES
St. John Publishing Co.: October, 1952

1-Baker-c 31 62 93 178 282 385

PICTORIAL ROMANCES (Formerly Pictorial Confessions)
St. John Publ. Co.: No. 4, Jan, 1950; No. 5, Jan, 1951 - No. 24, Mar, 1954

4-Baker-a; photo-c 30 60 90 174 275 375
5,10-All Matt Baker issues. 5-Reprints all stories from #4 w/new Baker-c
  26 52 78 152 239 325
6-9,12,13,15,16-Baker-c, 2-3 stories 19 38 57 112 176 240
11-Baker-c/a(3); Kubert-r/Hollywood Confessions #1
  24 48 72 139 220 300
14,21-24: Baker-c/a each. 21,24-Each has signed story by Estrada
  20 40 60 117 184 250
17-20(7/53, 25¢, 100 pgs.): Baker-c/a; each has two signed stories by Estrada
  40 80 120 235 368 500
NOTE: **Matt Baker** art in most issues. **Estrada** a-17-20(2), 21, 24.

PICTURE NEWS
Lafayette Street Corp.: Jan, 1946 - No. 10, Jan-Feb, 1947

1-Milt Gross begins, ends No. 6; 4 pg. Kirby-a; A-Bomb-c/story
  41 82 123 250 400 550
2-Atomic explosion panels; Frank Sinatra/Perry Como story
  22 44 66 126 198 270
3-Atomic explosion panels; Frank Sinatra, June Allyson, Benny Goodman
  stories 18 36 54 107 169 230
4-Atomic explosion panels; "Caesar and Cleopatra" movie adapt. w/Claude Raines &
  Vivian Leigh; Jackie Robinson story 21 42 63 120 188 255
5-7: 5-Hank Greenberg story. 6-Joe Louis-c/story 15 30 45 90 140 190
8,10: 8-Monte Hale story (9-10/46; 1st?). 10-Dick Quick; A-Bomb story; Krigstein, Gross-a
  16 32 48 94 147 200
9-A-Bomb story; "Crooked Mile" movie adaptation; Joe DiMaggio story.

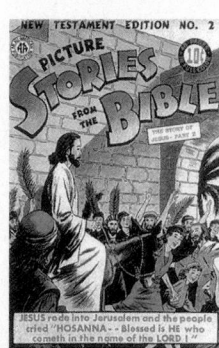

Picture Stories From the Bible #2 © WMG

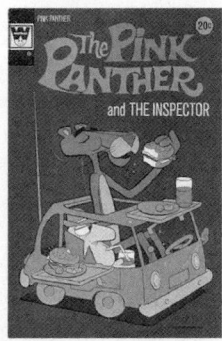

Pink Panther #13 © GK

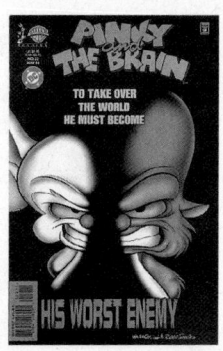

Pinky and the Brain #22 © WB

	GD	VG	FN	VF	VF/NM	NM-			GD	VG	FN	VF	VF/NM	NM-
	2.0	4.0	6.0	8.0	9.0	9.2			2.0	4.0	6.0	8.0	9.0	9.2

	GD	VG	FN	VF	VF/NM	NM-
	18	36	54	107	169	230

PICTURE PARADE (Picture Progress #5 on)
Gilberton Company (Also see A Christmas Adventure): Sept, 1953 - V1#4, Dec, 1953 (28 pgs.)
V1#1-Andy's Atomic Adventures; A-bomb blast-c; (Teachers version distributed to schools

	GD	VG	FN	VF	VF/NM	NM-
exists)	20	40	60	117	184	250
2-Around the World with the United Nations	12	24	36	69	97	125
3-Adventures of the Lost One(The American Indian), 4-A Christmas Adventure (r-under same title in 1969)	12	24	36	69	97	125

PICTURE PROGRESS (Formerly Picture Parade)
Gilberton Corp.: V1#5, Jan, 1954 - V3#2, Oct, 1955 (28-36 pgs.)
V1#5-9,V2#1-9: 5-News in Review 1953. 6-The Birth of America. 7-The Four Seasons. 8-Paul Revere's Ride. 9-The Hawaiian Islands(5/54). V2#1-The Story of Flight(9/54). 2-Vote for Crazy River (The Meaning of Elections). 3-Louis Pasteur. 4-The Star Spangled Banner. 5-News in Review 1954. 6-Alaska: The Great Land. 7-Life in the Circus. 8-The

	GD	VG	FN	VF	VF/NM	NM-
Time of the Cave Man. 9-Summer Fun(5/55)	9	18	27	47	61	75
V3#1,2: 1-The Man Who Discovered America. 2-The Lewis & Clark Expedition	8	16	24	44	57	70

PICTURE SCOPE JUNGLE ADVENTURES (See Jungle Thrills)

PICTURE STORIES FROM AMERICAN HISTORY
National/All-American/E. C. Comics: 1945 - No. 4, Sum, 1947 (#1,2: 10¢, 56 pgs.; #3,4: 15¢, 52 pgs.)

	GD	VG	FN	VF	VF/NM	NM-
1	30	60	90	174	275	375
2-4	24	48	72	139	220	300

PICTURE STORIES FROM SCIENCE
E.C. Comics: Spring, 1947 - No. 2, Fall, 1947

	GD	VG	FN	VF	VF/NM	NM-
1-(15¢)	30	60	90	174	275	375
2-(10¢)	24	48	72	139	220	300

PICTURE STORIES FROM THE BIBLE (See Narrative Illustration, the Story of the Comics by M.C. Gaines)
National/All-American/E.C. Comics: 1942 - No. 4, Fall, 1943; 1944-46

	GD	VG	FN	VF	VF/NM	NM-
1-4('42-Fall, '43)-Old Testament (DC)	50	100	150	325	562	800

Complete Old Testament Edition, (12/43-DC, 232 pgs.);-1st printing; contains #1-4; 2nd - 8th (1/47) printings exist; later printings by E.C. some with 65¢-c

	GD	VG	FN	VF	VF/NM	NM-
	27	54	81	158	249	340

Complete Old Testament Edition (1945-publ. by Bible Pictures Ltd.)-232 pgs., hardbound, in color with dust jacket

	GD	VG	FN	VF	VF/NM	NM-
	27	54	81	158	249	340

NOTE: Both Old and New Testaments published in England by Bible Pictures Ltd. in hardback, 1943, in color, 376 pgs. (2 vols.: O.T. 232 pgs. & N.T. 144 pgs.), and were also published by Scarf Press in 1979 (Old Test., $9.95) and in 1980 (New Test., $7.95)

	GD	VG	FN	VF	VF/NM	NM-
1-3(New Test.; 1944-46, DC)-52 pgs. ea.	18	36	54	105	165	225

The Complete Life of Christ Edition (1945, 25¢, 96 pgs.)-Contains #1&2 of the New Testament Edition

	GD	VG	FN	VF	VF/NM	NM-
	27	54	81	158	249	340
1,2(Old Testament-r in comic book form)(E.C., 1946; 52 pgs.)	18	36	54	105	165	225
1(DC),2(AA),3(EC)(New Testament-r in comic book form)(E.C., 1946; 52 pgs.)	18	36	54	105	165	225

Complete New Testament Edition (1945-E.C., 40¢, 144 pgs.)-Contains #1-3

	GD	VG	FN	VF	VF/NM	NM-
1946 printing has 50¢-c	37	54	81	158	249	340

NOTE: Another British series entitled **The Bible Illustrated** from 1947 has recently been discovered, with the same internal artwork. This eight edition series (5-OT, 3-NT) is of particular interest to Classics Ill. collectors because it exactly copied the Classics Ill. logo format. The British publisher was Thorpe & Porter, who in 1951 began publishing the British Classics Ill. series. All editions of The Bible Ill. have new British painted covers. While this market is still new, and not all editions have as yet been found, current market value is about the same as the first U.S. editions of Picture Stories From The Bible.

PICTURE STORIES FROM WORLD HISTORY
E.C. Comics: Spring, 1947 - No. 2, Summer, 1947 (52, 48 pgs.)

	GD	VG	FN	VF	VF/NM	NM-
1-(15¢)	30	60	90	174	275	375
2-(10¢)	24	48	72	139	220	300

PINHEAD
Marvel Comics (Epic Comics): Dec, 1993 - No. 6, May, 1994 ($2.50)

	GD	VG	FN	VF	VF/NM	NM-
1-($2.95)-Embossed foil-c by Kelley Jones; Intro Pinhead & Disciples (Snakeoil, Hangman, Fan Dancer & Dixie)						3.00
2-6						2.50

PINHEAD & FOODINI (TV)(Also see Foodini & Jingle Dingle Christmas...)
Fawcett Publications: July, 1951 - No. 4, Jan, 1952 (Early TV comic)

	GD	VG	FN	VF	VF/NM	NM-
1-(52 pgs.)-Photo-c; based on TV puppet show	32	64	96	186	293	400
2,3-Photo-c	16	32	48	92	144	195
4	14	28	42	78	112	145

PINHEAD VS. MARSHALL LAW (Law in Hell)
Marvel Comics (Epic): Nov, 1993 - No. 2, Dec, 1993 ($2.95, lim. series)

	GD	VG	FN	VF	VF/NM	NM-
1,2: 1-Embossed red foil-c. 2-Embossed silver foil-c						3.00

PINK DUST
Kitchen Sink Press: 1998 ($3.50, B&W, mature)

	GD	VG	FN	VF	VF/NM	NM-
1-J. O'Barr-s/a						3.50

PINK PANTHER, THE (TV)(See The Inspector & Kite Fun Book)
Gold Key #1-70/Whitman #71-87: April, 1971 - No. 87, Mar, 1984

	GD	VG	FN	VF	VF/NM	NM-
1-The Inspector begins	5	10	15	32	51	70
2-5	3	6	9	16	23	30
6-10	2	4	6	13	18	22
11-30: Warren Tufts-a #16-on	2	4	6	9	12	15
31-60	2	4	6	8	10	12
61-70	1	2	3	5	6	8
71-74,81-83: 81(2/82), 82(3/82), 83(4/82)	1	3	4	6	8	10
75(8/80)-77 (Whitman pre-pack) (scarce)	3	6	9	18	27	35
78(1/81)-80 (Whitman pre-pack) (not as scarce)	2	4	6	9	13	16
78 (1/81, 40¢-c) Cover price error variant	3	6	9	14	19	24
84-87(All #90266 on-c, no date or date code): 84(6/83), 85(8/83), 87(3/84)						
	3	6	9	14	19	24
Mini-comic No. 1(1976)(3-1/4x6-1/2")	1	3	4	6	8	10

NOTE: Pink Panther began as a movie cartoon. (See Golden Comics Digest #38, 45 and March of Comics #376, 384, 390, 409, 418, 429, 441, 449, 461, 473, 486); #37, 72, 80-85 contain reprints.

PINK PANTHER SUPER SPECIAL (TV)
Harvey Comics: Oct, 1993 ($2.25, 68 pgs.)

	GD	VG	FN	VF	VF/NM	NM-
V2#1-The Inspector & Wendy Witch stories also						4.00

PINK PANTHER, THE
Harvey Comics: Nov, 1993 - No. 9, July, 1994 ($1.50)

	GD	VG	FN	VF	VF/NM	NM-
V2#1-9						3.00

PINKY & THE BRAIN (See Animaniacs)
DC Comics: July, 1996 - No. 27, Nov, 1998 ($1.75/$1.95/$1.99)

	GD	VG	FN	VF	VF/NM	NM-
1-27, ...Christmas Special (1/96, $1.50)						3.00

PINKY LEE (See Adventures of...)

PINKY THE EGGHEAD
I.W./Super Comics: 1963 (Reprints from Noodnik)

	GD	VG	FN	VF	VF/NM	NM-
I.W. Reprint #1,2(nd)	2	4	6	8	11	14
Super Reprint #14-r/Noodnik Comics #4	2	4	6	8	11	14

PINOCCHIO (See 4-Color #92, 252, 545, 1203, Mickey Mouse Mag. V5#3, Movie Comics under Wonderful Advs. of..., New Advs. of..., Thrilling Comics #2, Walt Disney Showcase, Walt Disney's..., Wonderful Advs. of..., & World's Greatest Stories #2)
Dell Publishing Co.: No. 92, 1945 - No. 1203, Mar, 1962 (Disney)
Four Color 92-The Wonderful Adventures of...; 16 pg. Donald Duck story ;

	GD	VG	FN	VF	VF/NM	NM-
entire book by Kelly	50	100	150	406	741	1075
Four Color 252 (10/49)-Origin, not by Kelly	10	20	30	73	129	185
Four Color 545 (3/54)-The Wonderful Advs. of...; part-r of 4-Color #92; Disney-movie	7	14	21	47	76	105
Four Color 1203 (3/62)	5	10	15	35	55	75

PINOCCHIO AND THE EMPEROR OF THE NIGHT
Marvel Comics: Mar, 1988 ($1.25, 52 pgs.)

	GD	VG	FN	VF	VF/NM	NM-
1-Adapts film						3.00

PINOCCHIO LEARNS ABOUT KITES (See Kite Fun Book)

PIN-UP PETE (Also see Great Lover Romances & Monty Hall...)
Toby Press: 1952

	GD	VG	FN	VF	VF/NM	NM-
1-Jack Sparling pin-ups	18	36	54	103	162	220

PIONEER MARSHAL (See Fawcett Movie Comics)

PIONEER PICTURE STORIES
Street & Smith Publications: Dec, 1941 - No. 9, Dec, 1943

	GD	VG	FN	VF	VF/NM	NM-
1-The Legless Air Ace begins	31	62	93	178	282	385
2 -True life story of Errol Flynn	15	30	45	90	140	190
3-9	14	28	42	82	121	160

PIONEER WEST ROMANCES (Firehair #1,2,7-11)
Fiction House Magazines: No. 3, Spring, 1950 - No. 6, Winter, 1950-51

	GD	VG	FN	VF	VF/NM	NM-
3-(52 pgs.)-Firehair continues	19	38	57	109	172	235
4-6	19	38	57	109	172	235

PIPSQUEAK (See The Adventures of...)

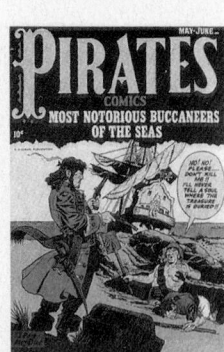

Pirates Comics #2 © HILL

Pitt #14 © Dale Keown

Planet Comics #31 © FH

	GD 2.0	VG 4.0	FN 6.0	VF 8.0	VF/NM 9.0	NM- 9.2

PIRACY
E. C. Comics: Oct-Nov, 1954 - No. 7, Oct-Nov, 1955

	GD 2.0	VG 4.0	FN 6.0	VF 8.0	VF/NM 9.0	NM- 9.2
1-Williamson/Torres-a	27	54	81	216	333	450
2-Williamson/Torres-a	17	34	51	136	213	290
3-7: 5-7-Comics Code symbol on cover	13	26	39	104	165	225

NOTE: **Crandall** a-in all; c-2-4. **Davis** a-1, 2, 6. **Evans** a-3-7; c-7. **Ingels** a-3-7. **Krigstein** a-3-5, 7; c-5, 6. **Wood** a-1, 2; c-1.

PIRACY
Gemstone Publishing: March, 1998 - No. 7, Sept, 1998 ($2.50)

1-7: E.C. reprints		2.50
Annual 1 ($10.95) Collects #1-4		11.00
Annual 2 ($7.95) Collects #5-7		8.00

PIRANA (See The Phantom #46 & Thrill-O-Rama #2, 3)

PIRATE CORP$, THE (See Hectic Planet)
Eternity Publishing: 1987 - No. 4, 1988 ($1.95)

1-4: 1,2-Color. 3,4-B&W		2.50
Special 1 ('89, B&W)-Slave Labor Publ.		2.50

PIRATE CORP$, THE (Volume 2)
Slave Labor Graphics: 1989 - No. 6, 1992 ($1.95)

1-6-Dorkin-s/a		2.50

PIRATE OF THE GULF, THE (See Superior Stories #2)

PIRATES COMICS
Hillman Periodicals: Feb-Mar, 1950 - No. 4, Aug-Sept, 1950 (All 52 pgs.)

	GD	VG	FN	VF	VF/NM	NM-
1	24	48	72	139	220	300
2-Dave Berg-a	17	34	51	98	154	210
3,4-Berg-a	15	30	45	88	137	185

PIRATES OF CONEY ISLAND, THE
Image Comics: Oct, 2006 - No. 8 ($2.99)

1-5-Rick Spears-s/-s;Vasilis Lolos-a; two covers. 2-Cloonan var-c		3.00

PIRATES OF DARK WATER, THE (Hanna Barbera)
Marvel Comics: Nov, 1991 - No. 9, Aug, 1992 ($1.95)

1-9: 9-Vess-c		3.00

P.I.'S: MICHAEL MAUSER AND MS. TREE, THE
First Comics: Jan, 1985 - No. 3, May, 1985 ($1.25, limited series)

1-3: Staton-c/a(p)		2.50

PITT, THE (Also see The Draft & The War)
Marvel Comics: Mar, 1988 ($3.25, 52 pgs., one-shot)

1-Ties into Starbrand, D.P.7		3.50

PITT (See Youngblood #4 & Gen 13 #3,#4)
Image Comics #1-9/Full Bleed #1/2,10-on: Jan, 1993 - No. 20 ($1.95, intended as a four part limited series)

1/2-(12/95)-1st Full Bleed issue		4.00
1-Dale Keown-c/a. 1-1st app. The Pitt		4.00
2-13: All Dale Keown-c/a. 3 (Low distribution). 10 (1/96)-Indicia reads "January 1995"		3.00
14-20: 14-Begin $2.50-c, pullout poster		2.50
TPB-(1997, $9.95) r/#1/2, 1-4		10.00
TPB 2-(1999, $11.95) r/#5-9		12.00

PITT CREW
Full Bleed Studios: Aug, 1998 - No. 5, Dec, 1999 ($2.50)

1-5: 1-Richard Pace-s/Ken Lashley-a. 2-4-Scott Lee-a		2.50

PITT IN THE BLOOD
Full Bleed Studios: Aug, 1996 ($2.50, one-shot)

nn-Richard Pace-a/script		2.50

PIXIE & DIXIE & MR. JINKS (TV)(See Jinks, Pixie and Dixie & Whitman Comic Books)
Dell Publishing Co./Gold Key: July-Sept, 1960 - Feb, 1963 (Hanna-Barbera)

	GD	VG	FN	VF	VF/NM	NM-
Four Color 1112	7	14	21	50	83	115
Four Color 1196,1264, 01-631-207 (Dell, 7/62)	6	12	18	37	59	80
1(2/63-Gold Key)	6	12	18	43	69	95

PIXIE PUZZLE ROCKET TO ADVENTURELAND
Avon Periodicals: Nov, 1952

	GD	VG	FN	VF	VF/NM	NM-
1	14	28	42	80	115	150

PIXIES, THE (Advs. of...)(The Mighty Atom and ...#6 on)(See A-1 Comics #16)
Magazine Enterprises: Winter, 1946 - No. 4, Fall?, 1947!; No. 5, 1948

	GD	VG	FN	VF	VF/NM	NM-
1-Mighty Atom	9	18	27	50	65	80
2-5-Mighty Atom	6	12	18	28	34	40
I.W. Reprint #1(1958), 8-(Pee-Wee Pixies), 10-I.W. on cover, Super on inside	2	4	6	8	10	12

PIZZAZZ
Marvel Comics: Oct, 1977 - No. 16, Jan, 1979 (slick-color kids mag. w/puzzles, games, comics)

	GD	VG	FN	VF	VF/NM	NM-
1-Star Wars photo-c/article; origin Tarzan; KISS photos/article; Iron-On bonus; 2 pg. pin-up calendars thru #8	3	6	9	17	25	32
2-Spider-Man-c; Beatles pin-up calendar	2	4	6	10	14	18
3-8: 3-Close Encounters-s; Bradbury-s. 4-Alice Cooper, Travolta; Charlie's Angels/Fonz/Hulk/Spider-Man-c. 5-Star Trek quiz. 6-Asimov-s. 7-James Bond; Spock/Darth Vader-c.						
8-TV Spider-Man photo-c/article	2	4	6	9	13	16
9-14: 9-Shaun Cassidy-c. 10-Sgt. Pepper-c/s. 12-Battlestar Galactica-s; Spider-Man app.						
13-TV Hulk-c/s. 14-Meatloaf-c/s	2	4	6	8	11	14
15,16: 15-Battlestar Galactica-s. 16-Movie Superman photo-c/s, Hulk.	2	4	6	9	13	16

NOTE: **Star Wars** comics in all (1-6:Chaykin-a, 7-9: DeZuniga-a, 10-13:Simonson/Janson-a. 14-16:Cockrum-a). **Tarzan** comics, 1pg.-#1-8. 1pg. "Hey Look" by Kurtzman #12-16.

PLANETARY (See Preview in flip book Gen13 #33)
DC Comics (WildStorm Prod.): Apr, 1999 - Present ($2.50/$2.95/$2.99)

	GD	VG	FN	VF	VF/NM	NM-
1-Ellis-s/Cassaday-a/c	1	3	4	6	8	10
2-5						6.00
6-10						5.00
11-15: 12-Fourth Man revealed						4.00
16-26: 16-Begin $2.95-c. 23-Origin of The Drummer						3.00
...: All Over the World and Other Stories (2000, $14.95) r/#1-6 & Preview						15.00
...: All Over the World and Other Stories-Hardcover (2000, $24.95) r/#1-6 & Preview; with dustjacket						25.00
.../Batman: Night on Earth 1 (8/03, $5.95) Ellis-s/Cassaday-a						6.00
...: Crossing Worlds (2004, $14.95) r/Batman, JLA, and The Authority x-overs						15.00
.../JLA: Terra Occulta (11/02, $5.95) Elseworlds; Ellis-s/Ordway-a						6.00
...: Leaving the 20th Century -HC (2004, $24.95) r/#13-18						25.00
...: Leaving the 20th Century -SC (2004, $14.99) r/#13-18						25.00
.../The Authority: Ruling the World (8/00, $5.95) Ellis-s/Phil Jimenez-a						6.00
...: The Fourth Man -Hardcover (2001, $24.95) r/#7-12						25.00
...: The Planetary Reader (8/03, $5.95) r/#13-15						6.00

PLANETARY BRIGADE (Also see Hero Squared)
Boom Studios: Feb, 2006 - Present ($2.99)

1,2-Giffen & DeMatteis-s/art by various; Haley-c		3.00
... Origins 1-3 (10/06-4/07, $3.99) Giffen & DeMatteis-s/Julia Bax-a		4.00

PLANET COMICS
Fiction House Magazines: 1/40 - No. 62, 9/49; No. 63, Wint, 1949-50; No. 64, Spring, 1950; No. 65, 1951(nd); No. 66-68, 1952(nd); No. 69, Wint, 1952-53; No. 70-72, 1953(nd); No. 73, Winter, 1953-54

	GD	VG	FN	VF	VF/NM	NM-
1-Origin Auro, Lord of Jupiter by Briefer (ends #61); Flint Baker & The Red Comet begin; Eisner/Fine-c	1150	2300	3450	8600	15,300	22,000
2-Lou Fine-c (Scarce)	423	846	1269	2961	5181	7400
3-Eisner-c	300	600	900	1931	3366	4800
4-Gale Allen and the Girl Squadron begins	283	566	849	1769	2935	4100
5,6-(Scarce): 5-Eisner/Fine-c	269	538	807	1681	2791	3900
7-12: 8-Robot-c. 12-The Star Pirate begins	207	414	621	1294	2147	3000
13,14: 13-Reff Ryan begins	152	304	456	950	1575	2200
15-(Scarce)-Mars, God of War begins (11/41); see Jumbo Comics #31 for 1st app.	300	600	900	1931	3366	4800
16-20,22	138	276	414	863	1432	2000
21-The Lost World & Hunt Bowman begin	145	290	435	906	1503	2100
23-26: 26-Space Rangers begin (9/43), end #71	128	256	384	800	1325	1850
27-30	103	206	309	644	1072	1500
31-35: 33-Origin Star Pirates Wonder Boots, reprinted in #52. 35-Mysta of the Moon begins, ends #62	88	176	264	550	913	1275
36-45: 38-1st Mysta of the Moon-c. 41-New origin of "Auro, Lord of Jupiter". 42-Last Gale Allen. 43-Futura begins	81	162	243	506	841	1175
46-60: 48-Robot-c. 53-Used in **SOTI**, pg. 32	64	128	192	400	663	925
61-68,70: 64,70-Robot-c. 65-70-All partial-r of earlier issues. 70-r/stories from #41	48	96	144	293	484	675
69-Used in **POP**, pgs. 101,102	48	96	144	293	484	675
71-73-No series stories. 71-Space Rangers strip	40	80	120	235	368	500
I.W. Reprint 1,8,9: 1(nd)-r/#70; cover-r from Attack on Planet Mars 8 (r/#72), 9-r/#73	7	14	21	50	83	115

NOTE: **Anderson** a-33-38, 40-51 (Star Pirate). **Matt Baker** a-53-59 (Mysta of the Moon). **Celardo** c-12. **Bill Discount** a-71 (Space Rangers). **Elias** c-70. **Evans** a-46-49 (Auro, Lord of Jupiter), 50-64 (Lost World). **Fine** c-2, 5. **Hopper** a-31, 35 (Gale Allen), 41, 42, 48, 49 (Mysta of the Moon). **Ingels** a-24-31 (Lost World), 56-61 (Auro, Lord of Jupiter). **Lubbers** a-44-47 (Space Rangers); c-40, 41. **Moreira** a-43, 44 (Mysta of the Moon). **Renee** a-40-

Planet of the Apes #1 © DH

Plastic Man #38 © QUA

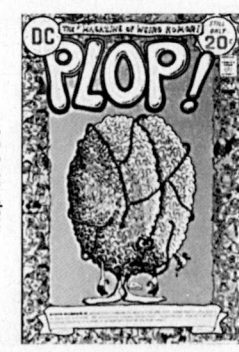

Plop! #7 © DC

	GD	VG	FN	VF	VF/NM	NM-
	2.0	4.0	6.0	8.0	9.0	9.2

49 (Lost World); c-33, 35, 39. Tuska a-30 (Star Pirate). M. Whitman a-50-52 (Mysta of the Moon), 53-58 (Star Pirate); c-71-73. Starr a-59. Zolnerwich c-10. 13-25. Bondage c-53.

PLANET COMICS
Pacific Comics: 1984 ($5.95)

1-Reprints Planet Comics #1(1940)	1	2	3	5	6	8

PLANET COMICS
Blackthorne Publishing: Apr, 1988 - No. 3 ($2.00, color/B&W #3)

1-3: New stories. 1-Dave Stevens-c		3.00

PLANET HULK (See Incredible Hulk and Giant-Size Hulk #1 (2006))

PLANET OF THE APES (Magazine) (Also see Adventures on the… & Power Record Comics)
Marvel Comics Group: Aug, 1974 - No. 29, Feb, 1977 (B&W) (Based on movies)

1-Ploog-a	3	6	9	20	30	40
2-Ploog-a	3	6	9	15	21	26
3-10	2	4	6	11	16	20
11-20	2	4	6	13	18	22
21-28 (low distribution)	3	6	9	15	21	26
29 (low distribution)	4	8	12	28	44	60

NOTE: Alcala a-7-11, 17-22, 24. Ploog a-1-4, 6, 8, 11, 13, 14, 19. Sutton a-11, 12, 15, 17, 19, 20, 23, 24, 29. Tuska a-1-6.

PLANET OF THE APES
Adventure Comics: Apr, 1990 - No. 24, 1992 ($2.50, B&W)

1-New movie tie-in; comes w/outer-c (3 colors)	4.00
1-Limited serial numbered edition ($5.00)	5.00
1-2nd printing (no outer-c, $2.50)	2.50
2-24	3.00
Annual 1 ($3.50)	4.00
…Urchak's Folly 1-4 ($2.50, mini-series)	3.00

PLANET OF THE APES (The Human War)
Dark Horse Comics: Jun, 2001 - No. 3, Aug, 2001 ($2.99, limited series)

1-3-Follows the 2001 movie; Edginton-s	3.00

PLANET OF THE APES
Dark Horse Comics: Sept, 2001 - No. 6, Feb, 2002 ($2.99, ongoing series)

1-6: 1-3-Edginton-s. 1-Photo & Wagner covers. 2-Plunkett & photo-c	3.00

PLANET OF VAMPIRES
Seaboard Publications (Atlas): Feb, 1975 - No. 3, July, 1975

1-Neal Adams-c(i); 1st Broderick c/a(p); Hama-s	2	4	6	8	10	12
2,3: 2-Neal Adams-c. 3-Heath-c/a	1	2	3	5	7	9

PLANET TERRY
Marvel Comics (Star Comics)/Marvel: April, 1985 - No. 12, March, 1986 (Children's comic)

1-12	3.00
1-Variant with "Star Chase" game on last page & inside back-c	10.00

PLASM (See Warriors of Plasm)
Defiant Comics: June, 1993

0-Came bound into Diamond Previews V3#6 (6/93); price is for complete Previews with comic still attached	3.00
0-Comic only removed from Previews	2.50

PLASMER
Marvel Comics UK: Nov, 1993 - No. 4, Feb, 1994 ($1.95, limited series)

1-($2.50)-Polybagged w/4 trading cards	2.75
2-4: Capt. America & Silver Surfer app.	2.50

PLASTIC FORKS
Marvel Comis (Epic Comics): 1990 - No. 5, 1990 ($4.95, 68 pgs., limited series, mature)

Book 1-5: Squarebound	5.00

PLASTIC MAN (Also see Police Comics & Smash Comics #17)
Vital Publ. No. 1,2/Quality Comics No. 3 on: Sum, 1943 - No. 64, Nov, 1956

nn(#1)- "In The Game of Death"; Skull-c; Jack Cole-c/a begins; ends-#64?

	GD	VG	FN	VF	VF/NM	NM-
	423	846	1269	2750	4875	7000
nn(#2, 2/44)- "The Gay Nineties Nightmare"	179	358	537	1119	1860	2600
3 (Spr, '46)	117	234	351	731	1216	1700
4 (Sum, '46)	91	182	273	569	922	1275
5 (Aut, '46)	72	144	216	450	750	1050
6-10	59	118	177	369	610	850
11-15,17-20	53	106	159	323	537	750
16-Classic-c	55	110	165	344	572	800
21-30: 26-Last non-r issue?	41	82	123	250	400	550
31-40: 40-Used in POP, pg. 91	34	68	102	197	311	425
41-64: 53-Last precode issue. 54-Robot-c	26	52	78	152	239	325

Super Reprint 11,16,18: 11('63)-r/#16. 16-r/#18 & #21; Cole-a, 18('64)-Spirit-r by Eisner from Police #95

	4	8	12	24	37	50

NOTE: Cole r-44, 49, 56, 58, 59 at least. Cuidera c-32-64i.

PLASTIC MAN (See DC Special #15 & House of Mystery #160)
National Periodical Publications/DC Comics: 11-12/66 - No. 10, 5-6/68; V4#11, 2-3/76 - No. 20, 10-11/77

1-Real 1st app. Silver Age Plastic Man (House of Mystery #160 is actually tryout); Gil Kane-c/a; 12¢ issues begin	9	18	27	63	107	150
2-5: 4-Infantino-c; Mortimer-a	5	10	15	30	48	65
6-10('68): 7-G.A. Plastic Man & Woozy Winks (1st S.A. app.) app.; origin retold. 10-Sparling-a; last 12¢ issue	4	8	12	24	37	50
V4#11('76)-20: 11-20-Fradon-p. 17-Origin retold	1	2	3	5	7	9
…80-Page Giant (2003, $6.95) reprints origin and other stories in 80-Pg. Giant format						7.00
…Special 1 (8/99, $3.95)						4.00

PLASTIC MAN
DC Comics: Nov, 1988 - No. 4, Feb, 1989 ($1.00, mini-series)

1-4: 1-Origin; Woozy Winks app.	2.50

PLASTIC MAN
DC Comics: Feb, 2004 - No. 20, Mar, 2006 ($2.95/$2.99)

1-20-Kyle Baker-s/a in most. 1-Retells origin. 7,12-Scott Morse-s/a. 8-JLA cameo	3.00
…: On the Lam TPB (2004, $14.95) r/#1-6	15.00
…: Rubber Bandits TPB (2005, $14.99) r/#8-11,13,14	15.00

PLASTRON CAFE
Mirage Studios: Dec, 1992 - No. 4, July, 1993 ($2.25, B&W)

1-4: 1-Teenage Mutant Ninja Turtles app.; Kelly Freas-c. 2-Hildebrandt painted-c. 4-Spaced & Alien Fire stories	2.50

PLAYFUL LITTLE AUDREY (TV)(Also see Little Audrey #25)
Harvey Publications: 6/57 - No. 110, 11/73; No. 111, 8/74 - No. 121, 4/76

1	22	44	66	165	295	425
2	11	22	33	79	140	200
3-5	8	16	24	58	97	135
6-10	7	14	21	45	73	100
11-20	5	10	15	32	51	70
21-40	4	8	12	24	37	50
41-60	3	6	9	19	29	38
61-84: 84-Last 12¢ issue	3	6	9	16	22	28
85-99	2	4	6	11	16	20
100-52 pg. Giant	3	6	9	16	23	30
101-103: 52 pg. Giants	3	6	9	14	20	25
104-121	1	3	4	6	8	10
…In 3-D (Spring, 1988, $2.25, Blackthorne #66)						4.00

PLOP! (Also see The Best of DC #60)
National Periodical Publications: Sept-Oct, 1973 - No. 24, Nov-Dec, 1976

1-Sergio Aragonés-a begins; Wrightson-a	3	6	9	21	32	42
2-4,6-20	2	4	6	13	18	22
5-Wrightson-a	3	6	9	19	24	24
21-24 (52 pgs.). 23-No Aragonés-a	3	6	9	15	21	26

NOTE: Alcala a-13. Anderson a-5. Aragonés a-1-22, 24. Ditko a-16p. Evans a-19. Mayer a-1. Orlando a-21, 22; c-21. Sekowsky a-5, 6p. Toth a-11. Wolverton r-4, 22-24(1 pg.ea.); c-1-12, 14, 17, 18. Wood a-14, 16i, 18-24; c-13, 15, 16, 19.

PLUTO (See Cheerios Premiums, Four Color #537, Mickey Mouse Magazine, Walt Disney Showcase #4, 7, 13, 20, 23, 33 & Wheaties)
Dell Publ. Co.: No. 7, 1942; No. 429, 10/52 - No. 1248, 11-1/61-62 (Disney)

Large Feature Comic 7(1942)-Written by Carl Barks, Jack Hannah, & Nick George

(Barks' 1st comic book work)	159	318	477	994	1647	2300
Four Color 429 (#1)	9	18	27	64	110	155
Four Color 509	6	12	18	41	66	90
Four Color 595,654,736,853	5	10	15	32	51	70
Four Color 941,1039,1143,1248	4	8	12	28	44	60

POCKET CLASSICS
Academic Inc. Publications: 1984 (B&W, 4 1/4" x 6 3/4", 68 pages)

C1(Black Beauty. C2(The Call of the Wild. C3(Dr. Jekyll and Mr. Hyde). C4(Dracula). C5(Frankenstein). C6(Huckleberry Finn. C7(Moby Dick). C8(The Red Badge of Courage). C9(The Time Machine). C10(Tom Sawyer). C11(Treasure Island). C12(20,000 Leagues Under the Sea). C13(The Great Adventures of Sherlock Holmes). C14(Gulliver's Travels). C15(The Hunchback of Notre Dame). C16(The Invisible Man). C17(Journey to the Center of the Earth). C18(Kidnapped). C19(The Mysterious Island). C20(The Scarlet Letter). C21(The Story of My Life). C22(A Tale of Two Cities). C23(The Three Musketeers). C24(The War of the Worlds). C25(Around the World in Eighty Days). C26(Captains Courageous). C27(A Connecticut Yankee in King Arthur's Court). C28(Sherlock Holmes - The Hound of the

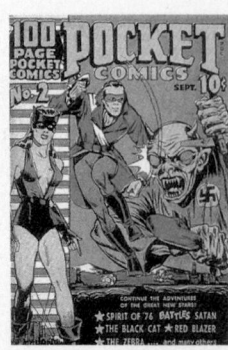

Pocket Comics #2 © HARV

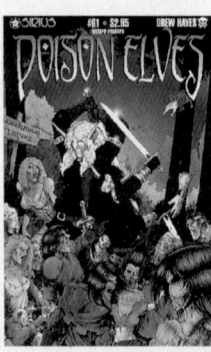

Poison Elves #61 © Drew Hayes

Police Action #1 © MAR

	GD	VG	FN	VF	VF/NM	NM-
	2.0	4.0	6.0	8.0	9.0	9.2

Baskervilles). C29(The House of the Seven Gables). C30(Jane Eyre). C31(The Last of the Mohicans). C32(The Best of O. Henry). C33(The Best of Poe). C34(Two Years Before the Mast). C35(White Fang). C36(Wuthering Heights). C37(Ben Hur). C38(A Christmas Carol). C39(The Food of the Gods). C40(Ivanhoe). C41(The Man in the Iron Mask). C42(The Prince and the Pauper). C43(The Prisoner of Zenda). C44(The Return of the Native). C45(Robinson Crusoe). C46(The Scarlet Pimpernel). C47(The Sea Wolf). C48(The Swiss Family Robinson). C49(Billy Budd). C50(Crime and Punishment). C51(Don Quixote). C52(Great Expectations). C53(Heidi). C54(The Illiad). C55(Lord Jim). C56(The Mutiny on Board H.M.S. Bounty). C57(The Odyssey). C58(Oliver Twist). C59(Pride and Prejudice). C60(The Turn of the Screw)

each...						8.00

Shakespeare Series:
S1(As You Like It). S2(Hamlet). S3(Julius Caesar). S4(King Lear). S5(Macbeth). S6(The Merchant of Venice). S7(A Midsummer Night's Dream). S8(Othello). S9(Romeo and Juliet). S10(The Taming of the Shrew). S11(The Tempest). S12(Twelfth Night). each... 9.00

POCKET COMICS (Also see Double Up)
Harvey Publications: Aug, 1941 - No. 4, Jan, 1942 (Pocket size; 100 pgs.)
(1st Harvey comic)

	GD	VG	FN	VF	VF/NM	NM-
1-Origin & 1st app. The Black Cat, Cadet Blakey the Spirit of '76, The Red Blazer, The Phantom, Sphinx, & The Zebra; Phantom Ranger, British Agent #99, Spin Hawkins, Satan, Lord of Evil begin (1st app. of each); Simon-c/a in #1-3	97	194	291	606	1003	1400
2 (9/41)-Black Cat on-c #2-4	65	130	195	406	671	935
3,4	50	100	150	305	503	700

POE
Cheese Comics: Sept, 1996 - No. 6, Apr, 1997 ($2.00, B&W)

1-6-Jason Asala-s/a						3.00

POE
Sirius Entertainment (Dogstar Press): Oct, 1997 - No. 24 ($2.50/$2.95, B&W)

1-24-Jason Asala-s/a. 20-24 ($2.95)						3.00
... Color Special (12/98, $2.95) Linsner-c						3.00

POGO PARADE (See Dell Giants)

POGO POSSUM (Also see Animal Comics & Special Delivery)
Dell Publishing Co.: No. 105, 4/46 - No. 148, 5/47; 10-12/49 - No. 16, 4-6/54

	GD	VG	FN	VF	VF/NM	NM-
Four Color 105(1946)-Kelly-c/a	51	102	153	434	805	1175
Four Color 148-Kelly-c/a	43	86	129	344	622	900
1-(10-12/49)-Kelly-c/a in all	38	76	114	285	518	750
2	26	52	78	195	348	500
3-5	19	38	57	138	244	350
6-10: 10-Infinity-c	16	32	48	118	209	300
11-16: 11-X-Mas-c	12	24	36	87	156	225

NOTE: #1-4, 9-13: 52 pgs.; #5-8, 14-16: 36 pgs.

POINT BLANK (See Wildcats)
DC Comics (WildStorm): Oct, 2002 - No. 5, Feb, 2003 ($2.95, limited series)

1-5-Brubaker-s/Wilson-a/Bisley-c. 1-Variant-c by Wilson; Grifter and John Lynch app.						3.00
TPB (2003, $14.95) r/#1-5						15.00

POISON ELVES (Formerly I, Lusiphur)
Mulehide Graphics: No. 8, 1993- No. 20, 1995 (B&W, magazine/comic size, mature readers)

	GD	VG	FN	VF	VF/NM	NM-
8-Drew Hayes-c/a/scripts.	2	4	6	8	10	12
9-11: 11-1st comic size issue	2	4	6	8	10	12
12,14,16	1	2	3	5	6	8
13,15-(low print)	2	4	6	8	11	14
15-2nd print						4.00
17-20	1	2	3	5	6	8
...Desert of the Third Sin-(1997, $14.95, TPB)-r/#13-18						15.00
...Patrons-($4.95, TPB)-r/#19,20						5.00
...Traumatic Dogs-(1996, $14.95,TPB)-Reprints I, Lusiphur #7, Poison Elves #8-12						15.00

POISON ELVES (See I, Lusiphur)
Sirius Entertainment: June, 1995 - No. 79, Sept, 2004 ; No. 80, 2007 ($2.50/$2.95, B&W, mature readers)

	GD	VG	FN	VF	VF/NM	NM-
1-Linsner-c; Drew Hayes-a/scripts in all.						5.00
1-2nd print						2.50
2-25: 12-Purple Marauder-c/app.						3.00
26-45, 47-49						2.50
46,50-79: 61-Fillbäch Brothers-s/a. 74-Art by Crilley (3 pgs.)						3.00
... Baptism By Fire-(2003, $19.95, TPB)-r/#48-59						20.00
... Color Special #1 (12/98, $2.95)						5.00
... Companion (12/02, $3.50) Back-story and character bios						3.50
... : Dark Wars TPB Vol. 1 (2005, $15.95) r/#60,62-68						16.00
... FAN Edition #1 mail-in offer; Drew Hayes-c/s/a	1	2	3	5	6	8

...Rogues-(2002, $15.95, TPB)-r/#40-47 — 16.00
...Salvation-(2001, $19.95, TPB)-r/#26-39 — 20.00
...Sanctuary-(1999, $14.95, TPB)-r/#1-12 — 15.00

POISON ELVES: DOMINION
Sirius Entertainment: Sept, 2005 - No. 6, Sept, 2006 ($3.50, B&W, limited series)

1-6-Keith Davidsen-s/Scott Lewis-a						3.50

POISON ELVES: HYENA
Sirius Entertainment: Sept, 2004 - No. 4, Feb, 2005 ($2.95, B&W, limited series)

1-4-Keith Davidsen-s/Scott Lewis-a						3.00
Ventures TPB Vol. 1: The Hyena Collection (2006, $14.95) r/#1-4 & 2 short stories						15.00

POISON ELVES: LOST TALES
Sirius Entertainment: Jan, 2006 - Present ($2.95, B&W, limited series)

1-11-Aaron Bordner-a; Bordner & Davidsen-s						3.00

POISON ELVES: LUSIPHUR & LIRILITH
Sirius Entertainment: 2001 - No. 4, 2001 ($2.95, B&W, limited series)

1-4-Drew Hayes-s/Jason Alexander-a						3.00
TPB (2002, $11.95) r/#1-4						12.00

POISON ELVES: PARINTACHIN
Sirius Entertainment: 2001 - No. 3, 2002 ($2.95, B&W, limited series)

1-3-Drew Hayes-c/Fillbäch Brothers-s/a						3.00
TPB (2003, $8.95) r/#1-3						9.00

POISON ELVES VENTURES
Sirius Entertainment: May, 2005 - No. 4, Apr, 2006 ($3.50, B&W, limited series)

... #1: Cassanova; ...#2: Lynn; ...#3: The Purple Marauder; #4: Jace - Bordner-a						3.50

POKÉMON (TV) (Also see Magical Pokémon Journey)
Viz Comics: Nov, 1998 - Present ($3.25/$3.50, B&W)

...Part 1: The Electric Tale of Pikachu

	GD	VG	FN	VF	VF/NM	NM-
1-Toshiro Ono-s/a	1	3	4	6	8	10
1-4 (2nd through current printings)						3.50
2						6.00
3,4						4.00
TPB ($12.95)						13.00

...Part 2: Pikachu Strikes Back

1						5.00
2-4						4.00
TPB						13.00

...Part 3: Electric Pikachu Boogaloo

1						4.00
2-4 ($2.95-c)						3.50
TPB						13.00

...Part 4: Surf's Up Pikachu

1,3,4						4.00
2 ($2.95-c)						3.50
TPB						13.00

NOTE: Multiple printings exist for most issues

POKÉMON ADVENTURES
Viz Comics: Sept, 1999 - No. 4 ($5.95, B&W, magazine-size)

1-4-Includes stickers bound in						6.00

POKÉMON ADVENTURES
Viz Comics: 2000 - Present ($2.95/$4.95, B&W)

Part 2 (2/00-7/00) 1-6-Includes stickers bound in						3.50
Part 3 (8/00-2/01) 1-7						3.50
Part 4 (3/00-6/01) 1-4						5.00
Part 5 (7/01-10/01) 1-4						5.00
Part 6 - 1-4, Part 7 1-5						5.00

POKÉMON: THE FIRST MOVIE
Viz Comics: 1999 ($3.95)

Mewtwo Strikes Back 1-4						4.00
Pikachu's Vacation						4.00

POKÉMON: THE MOVIE 2000
Viz Comics: 2000 ($3.95)

1-Official movie adaption						4.00
Pikachu's Rescue Adventure						4.00
...:The Power of One (mini-series) 1-3						4.00

POLICE ACADEMY (TV)
Marvel Comics: Nov, 1989 - No. 6, Feb, 1990 ($1.00)

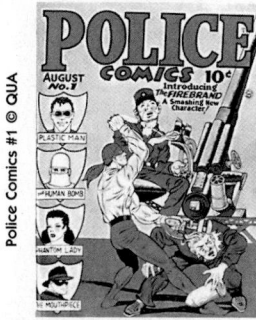

Police Comics #1 © QUA

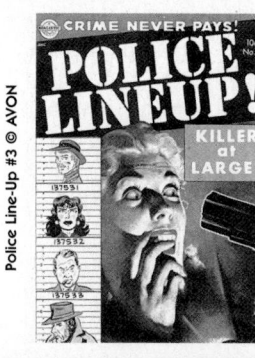

Police Line-Up #3 © AVON

Polly Pigtails #3 © PMI

	GD 2.0	VG 4.0	FN 6.0	VF 8.0	VF/NM 9.0	NM- 9.2
1-6: Based on TV cartoon; Post-c/a(p) in all						2.50

POLICE ACTION
Atlas News Co.: Jan, 1954 - No. 7, Nov, 1954

	GD 2.0	VG 4.0	FN 6.0	VF 8.0	VF/NM 9.0	NM- 9.2
1-Violent-a by Robert Q. Sale	21	42	63	120	188	255
2	12	24	36	67	94	120
3-7: 7-Powell-a	11	22	33	60	83	105

NOTE: *Ayers* a-4, 5. *Colan* a-1. *Forte* a-1, 2. *Mort Lawrence* a-5. *Maneely* a-3; c-1, 5. *Reinman* a-6, 7.

POLICE ACTION
Atlas/Seaboard Publ.: Feb, 1975 - No. 3, June, 1975

	GD	VG	FN	VF	VF/NM	NM-
1-3: 1-Lomax, N.Y.P.D., Luke Malone begin; McWilliams-a. 2-Origin Luke Malone, Manhunter; Ploog-a	1	2	3	5	7	9

NOTE: *Ploog* art in all. *Sekowsky/McWilliams* a-1-3. *Thorne* c-3.

POLICE AGAINST CRIME
Premiere Magazines: April, 1954 - No. 9, Aug, 1955

	GD	VG	FN	VF	VF/NM	NM-
1-Disbrow-a; extreme violence (man's face slashed with knife); Hollingsworth-a	27	54	81	156	246	335
2-Hollingsworth-a	15	30	45	85	130	175
3-9	13	26	39	74	105	135

POLICE BADGE #479 (Formerly Spy Thrillers #1-4)
Atlas Comics (PrPl): No. 5, Sept, 1955

	GD	VG	FN	VF	VF/NM	NM-
5-Maneely-c/a (6 pgs.); Heck-a	11	22	33	60	83	105

POLICE CASE BOOK (See Giant Comics Editions)

POLICE CASES (See Authentic... & Record Book of...)

POLICE COMICS
Quality Comics Group (Comic Magazines): Aug, 1941 - No. 127, Oct, 1953

	GD	VG	FN	VF	VF/NM	NM-
1-Origin/1st app. Plastic Man by Jack Cole (r-in DC Special #15), The Human Bomb by Gustavson, & No. 711; intro. The Firebrand by Reed Crandall, The Mouthpiece by Guardineer, Phantom Lady, & The Sword; Chic Carter by Eisner app.; Firebrand-c 1-4	771	1542	2313	5397	9449	13,500
2-Plastic Man smuggles opium	300	600	900	1970	3485	5000
3	224	448	672	1400	2325	3250
4	190	380	570	1188	1969	2750
5-Plastic Man-c begin; Plastic Man forced to smoke marijuana; Plastic Man covers begin, end #102	207	414	621	1294	2147	3000
6,7	167	334	501	1044	1735	2425
8-Manhunter begins (origin/1st app.) (3/42)	193	386	579	1206	2003	2800
9,10	133	266	399	831	1378	1925
11-The Spirit strip reprints begin by Eisner (origin-strip #1); 1st comic book app. The Spirit & 1st cover app. (9/42)	255	510	765	1594	2647	3700
12-Intro. Ebony	145	290	435	906	1503	2100
13-Intro. Woozy Winks; last Firebrand	141	282	423	881	1466	2050
14-19: 15-Last No. 711; Destiny begins	95	190	285	594	985	1375
20-The Raven x-over in Phantom Lady; features Jack Cole himself	95	190	285	594	985	1375
21,22: 21-Raven & Spider Widow x-over in Phantom Lady (cameo in #22)	79	158	237	494	822	1150
23-30: 23-Last Phantom Lady. 24-26-Flatfoot Burns by Kurtzman in all	74	148	222	463	769	1075
31-41: 37-1st app. Candy by Sahle & begins (12/44). 41-Last Spirit-r by Eisner	52	104	156	317	521	725
42,43-Spirit-r by Eisner/Fine	51	102	153	311	513	715
44-Fine Spirit-r begin, end #88,90,92	51	102	153	310	510	710
45-50: 50-(#50 on-c, #49 on inside, 1/46)	40	80	120	243	389	535
51-60: 58-Last Human Bomb	33	66	99	190	300	410
61-88,90,92: 63-(Some issues have #65 printed on cover, but #63 on inside) Kurtzman-a, 6 pgs. 90,92-Spirit by Fine	25	50	75	145	228	310
89,91,93-No Spirit stories	23	46	69	130	205	280
94-99,101,102: Spirit by Eisner in all; 101-Last Manhunter. 102-Last Spirit & Plastic Man by Jack Cole	32	64	96	186	293	400
100	38	76	114	222	351	480
103-Content change to crime; Ken Shannon & T-Man 1st app. of each, 12/50)	27	54	81	158	249	340
104-112,114-127: Crandall-a most issues (not in 104,105,122,125-127). 109-Atomic bomb story. 112-Crandall-a	19	38	57	109	172	235
113-Crandall-c/a(2), 9 pgs. each	21	42	63	120	188	255

NOTE: *Most Spirit stories signed by Eisner are not by him; all are reprints. Crandall Firebrand-1-8. Spirit by Eisner 1-41, 94-102; by Eisner/Fine-42, 43; by Fine-44-88, 90, 92, 103, 109. Al Bryant c-33, 34. Cole c-17-32, 35-102(most). Crandall c-13, 14. Crandall/Cuidera c-105-127. Eisner c-4i. Gill Fox c-1-3, 4p, 5-12, 15. Bondage c-103, 109, 125.*

POLICE LINE-UP

Avon Periodicals/Realistic Comics #3,4: Aug, 1951 - No. 4, July, 1952 (Painted-c #1-3)

	GD	VG	FN	VF	VF/NM	NM-
1-Wood-a, 1 pg. plus part-c; spanking panel-r/Saint #5	39	78	117	225	355	485
2-Classic story "The Religious Murder Cult", drugs, perversion; r/Saint #5; c-r/Avon paperback #329	27	54	81	156	246	335
3,4: 3-Kubert-a(r?)/part-c; Kinstler-a (inside-c only)	20	40	60	117	184	250

POLICE TRAP (Public Defender In Action #7 on)
Mainline #1-4/Charlton #5,6: 8-9/54 - No. 4, 2-3/55; No. 5, 7/55 - No. 6, 9/55

	GD	VG	FN	VF	VF/NM	NM-
1-S&K covers-all issues; Meskin-a; Kirby scripts	31	62	93	178	282	385
2-4	19	38	57	112	176	240
5,6-S&K-c/a	25	50	75	145	228	310

POLICE TRAP
Super Comics: No. 11, 1963; No. 16-18, 1964

	GD	VG	FN	VF	VF/NM	NM-
Reprint #11,16-18: 11-r/Police Trap #3. 16-r/Justice Traps the Guilty #? 17-r/Inside Crime #3 & r/Justice Traps The Guilty #83; 18-r/Inside Crime #3	2	4	6	9	13	16

POLLY & HER PALS (See Comic Monthly #1)

POLLY & THE PIRATES
Oni Press: Sept, 2005 - No. 6, June, 2006 ($2.99, B&W, limited series)

	GD	VG	FN	VF	VF/NM	NM-
1-6-Ted Naifeh-s/a; Polly is shanghaied by the pirate ship Titania						3.00
TPB (7/06, $11.95, digest) r/#1-6						12.00

POLLYANNA (Disney)
Dell Publishing Co.: No. 1129, Aug-Oct, 1960

	GD	VG	FN	VF	VF/NM	NM-
Four Color 1129-Movie, Haley Mills photo-c	7	14	21	50	83	115

POLLY PIGTAILS (Girls' Fun & Fashion Magazine #44 on)
Parents' Magazine Institute/Polly Pigtails: Jan, 1946 - V4#43, Oct-Nov, 1949

	GD	VG	FN	VF	VF/NM	NM-
1-Infinity-c; photo-c	14	28	42	82	121	160
2-Photo-c	9	18	27	50	65	80
3-5: 3,4-Photo-c	8	16	24	44	57	70
6-10: 7-Photo-c	8	16	24	40	50	60
11-30: 22-Photo-c	7	14	21	35	43	50
31-43	6	12	18	28	34	40

PONY EXPRESS (See Tales of the...)

PONYTAIL (Teen-age)
Dell Publishing Co./Charlton No. 13 on: 7-9/62 - No. 12, 10-12/65; No. 13, 11/69 - No. 20, 1/71

	GD	VG	FN	VF	VF/NM	NM-
12-641-209(#1)	4	8	12	22	34	45
2-12	3	6	9	16	23	30
13-20	2	4	6	11	16	20

POP COMICS
Modern Store Publ.: 1955 (36 pgs.; 5x7"; in color) (7¢)

	GD	VG	FN	VF	VF/NM	NM-
1-Funny animal	6	12	18	28	34	40

POPEYE (See Comic Album #7, 11, 15, Comics Reading Libraries *in the Promotional Comics section*, Eat Right to Work and Win, Giant Comic Album, King Comics, Kite Fun Book, Magic Comics, March of Comics #37,52, 66, 80, 96, 117, 134, 148, 157, 169, 194, 246, 264, 274, 294, 453, 465, 477 & Wow Comics, 1st series)

POPEYE
David McKay Publications: 1937 - 1939 (All by Segar)

	GD	VG	FN	VF	VF/NM	NM-
Feature Books nn (100 pgs.) (Very Rare)	650	1300	1950	4700	7600	10,500
Feature Books 2 (52 pgs.)	90	180	270	563	932	1300
Feature Books 3 (100 pgs.)-r/nn issue with a new-c	83	166	249	519	860	1200
Feature Books 5,10 (76 pgs.)	74	148	222	463	769	1075
Feature Books 14 (76 pgs.) (Scarce)	81	162	243	506	841	1175

POPEYE (Strip reprints through 4-Color #70)
Dell #1-65/Gold Key #66-80/King #81-92/Charlton #94-138/Gold Key #139-155/Whitman #156 on: 1941 - 1947; #1, 2-4/48 - #65, 7-9/62; #66, 10/62 - #80, 5/66; #81, 8/66 - #92, 12/67; #94, 2/69 - #138, 1/77; #139, 5/78 - #171, 6/84 or #93,160,161)

	GD	VG	FN	VF	VF/NM	NM-
Large Feature Comic 24('41)-Half by Segar	68	136	204	425	705	985
Four Color 25('41)-by Segar	83	166	249	519	860	1200
Large Feature Comic 10('43)	55	110	165	344	572	800
Four Color 17('43),26('43)-by Segar	42	84	126	336	606	875
Four Color 43('44)	31	62	93	222	404	585
Four Color 70('45)-Title: ...& Wimpy	22	44	66	165	295	425
Four Color 113('46-original strips begin),127,145('47),168	14	28	42	102	181	260
1(2-4/48)(Dell)-All new stories continue	26	52	78	195	348	500
2	14	28	42	99	175	250
3-10: 5-Popeye on moon w/rocket-c	11	22	33	79	140	200

Popular Comics #43 © DELL

Popular Romance #10 © STD

Porky Pig #73 © WB

	GD 2.0	VG 4.0	FN 6.0	VF 8.0	VF/NM 9.0	NM- 9.2
11-20	9	18	27	60	115	150
21-40,46: 46-Origin Swee' Pee	8	16	24	52	86	120
41-45,47-50	6	12	18	43	69	95
51-60	6	12	18	37	59	80
61-65 (Last Dell issue)	5	10	15	32	51	70
66,67-Both 84 pgs. (Gold Key)	6	12	18	43	69	95
68-80	4	8	12	23	36	48
81-92,94-97 (no #93): 97-Last 12¢ issue	3	6	9	19	29	38
98,99,101-138	2	4	6	13	18	22
100	3	6	9	17	25	32
139-155: 144-50th Anniversary issue	1	3	4	6	8	10
156,157,162-167(Whitman)(no #160,161).167(3/82)	2	4	6	9	13	16
158(9/80),159(11/80)-pre-pack only	3	6	9	21	32	42
168-171:(All #90069 on-c; pre-pack) 168(6/83). 169(#168 on-c)(8/83). 170(3/84).						
171(6/84)	3	6	9	15	21	26

NOTE: Reprints-#145, 147, 149, 151, 153, 155, 157, 163-168(1/3), 170.

POPEYE
Harvey Comics: Nov, 1993 - No. 7, Aug, 1994 ($1.50)

V2#1-7						3.00
...Summer Special V2#1-(10/93, $2.25, 68 pgs.)-Sagendorf-r & others						4.00

POPEYE SPECIAL
Ocean Comics: Summer, 1987 - No. 2, Sept, 1988 ($1.75/$2.00)

1,2: 1-Origin						4.00

POPPLES (TV, movie)
Star Comics (Marvel): Dec, 1986 - No. 5, Aug, 1987

1-5-Based on toys						4.00

POPPO OF THE POPCORN THEATRE
Fuller Publishing Co. (Publishers Weekly): 10/29/55 - No. 13, 1956 (weekly)

1	9	18	27	50	65	80
2-5	7	14	21	35	43	50
6-13	6	12	18	28	34	40

NOTE: By Charles Biro. 10¢ cover, given away by supermkets such as IGA.

POP-POP COMICS
R. B. Leffingwell Co.: No date (Circa 1945) (52 pgs.)

1-Funny animal	13	26	39	72	101	130

POPULAR COMICS
Dell Publishing Co.: Feb, 1936 - No. 145, July-Sept, 1948

1-Dick Tracy (1st comic book app.), Little Orphan Annie, Terry & the Pirates, Gasoline Alley, Don Winslow (1st app.), Harold Teen, Little Joe, Skippy, Moon Mullins, Mutt & Jeff, Tailspin Tommy, Smitty, Smokey Stover, Winnie Winkle & The Gumps begin (all strip-r)						
	771	1542	2313	5400	–	–
2	257	514	771	1800	–	–
3	193	386	579	1350	–	–
4-6(7/36): 5-Tom Mix begins. 6-1st app. Scribbly	150	300	450	1050	–	–
7-10: 8,9-Scribbly & Reglar Fellers app.	121	242	363	850	–	–
11-20: 12-X-Mas-c	83	166	249	477	739	1000
21-27: 27-Last Terry & the Pirates, Little Orphan Annie, & Dick Tracy	63	126	189	362	556	750
28-37: 28-Gene Autry app. 31,32-Tim McCoy app. 35-Christmas-c; Tex Ritter app.	49	98	147	282	434	585
38-43: Tarzan in text only. 38-(4/39)-Gang Busters (Radio, 2nd app.) & Zane Grey's Tex Thorne begins? 43-The Masked Pilot app.; 1st non-funny-c?	47	94	141	270	415	560
44,45: 45-Hurricane Kid-c	36	72	108	207	321	435
46-Origin/1st app. Martan, the Marvel Man(12/39)	46	92	138	265	408	550
47-50	35	70	105	201	311	420
51-Origin The Voice (The Invisible Detective) strip begins (5/40)	37	74	111	213	327	440
52-Robot-c	42	84	126	242	371	500
53-59: 55-End of World story	33	66	99	190	295	400
60-Origin/1st app. Professor Supermind and Son (2/41)	34	68	102	196	303	410
61-71: 63-Smilin' Jack begins	26	52	78	150	230	310
72-The Owl & Terry & the Pirates begin (2/42); Smokey Stover reprints begin	42	84	126	242	371	500
73-75	29	58	87	167	259	350
76-78-Capt. Midnight in all (see The Funnies #57)	40	80	120	230	358	485
79-85-Last Owl	27	54	81	155	238	320
86-99: 98-Felix the Cat, Smokey Stover-r begin	18	36	54	104	157	210
100	20	40	60	115	175	235
101-130	10	20	30	58	89	120

	GD 2.0	VG 4.0	FN 6.0	VF 8.0	VF/NM 9.0	NM- 9.2
131-145: 142-Last Terry & the Pirates	9	18	27	52	79	105

NOTE: Martan, the Marvel Man c-47-49, 52, 57-59. Professor Supermind c-60-63, 64(1/2), 65, 66. The Voice c-53.

POPULAR FAIRY TALES (See March of Comics #6, 18)

POPULAR ROMANCE
Better-Standard Publications: No. 5, Dec, 1949 - No. 29, July, 1954

5	13	26	39	72	101	130
6-9: 7-Palais-a; lingerie panels	10	20	30	54	72	90
10-Wood-a (2 pgs.)	11	22	33	60	83	105
11,12,14-16,18-21,28,29	8	16	24	44	57	70
13,17-Severin/Elder-a (3&8 pgs.)	9	18	27	50	65	80
22-27-Toth-a	10	20	30	56	76	95

NOTE: All have photo-c. Tuska art in most issues.

POPULAR TEEN-AGERS (Secrets of Love) (School Day Romances #1-4)
Star Publications: No. 5, Sept, 1950 - No. 23, Nov, 1954

5-Toni Gay, Midge Martin & Eve Adams continue from School Day Romances; Ginger Bunn (formerly Ginger Snapp & becomes Honey Bunn #6 on) begins; all features end #8	27	54	81	158	249	340
6-8 (7/51)-Honey Bunn begins; all have L. B. Cole-c; 6-Negligee panels	22	44	66	128	202	275
9-(...Romances; 1st romance issue, 10/51)	18	36	54	105	165	225
10-(...Secrets of Love thru #23)	17	34	51	98	154	210
11,16,18,19,22,23	15	30	45	83	124	165
12,13,17,20,21-Disbrow-a	15	30	45	88	137	185
14-Harrison/Wood-a	21	42	63	122	191	260
15-Wood?, Disbrow-a	16	32	48	94	147	200
Accepted Reprint 5,6 (nd); L.B. Cole-c	9	18	27	47	61	75

NOTE: All have L. B. Cole covers.

PORKY PIG (See Bugs Bunny &..., Kite Fun Book, Looney Tunes, March of Comics #42, 57, 71, 89, 99, 113, 130, 143, 164, 175, 192, 209, 218, 367, and Super Book #6, 18, 30)

PORKY PIG (...& Bugs Bunny #40-69)
Dell Publishing Co./Gold Key No. 1-93/Whitman No. 94 on: No. 16, 1942 - No. 81, Mar-Apr, 1962; Jan, 1965 - No. 109, June, 1984

Four Color 16(#1, 1942)	80	160	240	680	1265	1850
Four Color 48(1944)-Carl Barks-a	87	174	261	740	1370	2000
Four Color 78(1945)	26	52	78	195	348	500
Four Color 112(7/46)	16	32	48	118	209	300
Four Color 156,182,191('49)	12	24	36	82	146	210
Four Color 226,241('49),260,271,277,284,295	10	20	30	67	116	165
Four Color 303,311,322,330: 322-Sci/fi-c/story	7	14	21	50	83	115
Four Color 342,351,360,370,385,399,410,426	6	12	18	39	62	85
25 (11-12/52)-30	5	10	15	32	51	70
31-40	4	8	12	28	44	60
41-60	4	8	12	22	34	45
61-81(3-4/62)	3	6	9	18	27	35
1(1/65-Gold Key)(2nd Series)	5	10	15	30	48	65
2,4,5-r/4-Color 226,284 & 271 in that order	3	6	9	14	21	28
3,6-10: 3-r/Four Color #342	3	6	9	16	22	28
11-30	2	4	6	11	16	20
31-54	2	4	6	9	12	15
55-70	1	3	4	6	8	10
71-93(Gold Key)	1	2	3	5	6	8
94-96	1	2	3	5	7	9
97(9/80),98-pre-pack only (99 known not to exist)	3	6	9	19	29	38
100	2	4	6	9	12	15
101-105: 104(2/82). 105(4/82)	1	3	4	6	8	10
106-109 (All #90140 on-c, no date or date code): 106(7/83), 107(8/83), 108(2/84), 109(6/84) low print run						
	6	12	18			22

NOTE: Reprints-#1-8, 9-35(2/3); 36-46(1/4-1/2), 58, 67, 69-74, 76, 78, 102-109(1/3-1/2).

PORKY PIG'S DUCK HUNT
Saalfield Publishing Co.: 1938 (12pgs.)(large size)(heavy linen-like paper)

2178-1st app. Porky Pig & Daffy Duck by Leon Schlesinger. Illustrated text story book written in verse.1st comic book ever devoted to these characters. (see Looney Tunes #1 for their 1st comic book app.)	74	148	222	463	769	1075

PORTENT, THE
Image Comics: Feb, 2006 - No. 4, Aug, 2006 ($2.99)

1-4-Peter Bergting-s/a						3.00
Vol. 1: Duende TPB (2006, 12.99) r/#1-4; pin-up art; intro. by Kaluta						13.00

PORTIA PRINZ OF THE GLAMAZONS
Eclipse Comics: Dec, 1986 - No. 6, Oct, 1987 ($2.00, B&W, Baxter paper)

Power and Glory #4
© Howard Chaykin

Power Man #54 © MAR

Power Pack #15 © MAR

	GD	VG	FN	VF	VF/NM	NM-		GD	VG	FN	VF	VF/NM	NM-
	2.0	4.0	6.0	8.0	9.0	9.2		2.0	4.0	6.0	8.0	9.0	9.2

1-6 .... 2.50

POSSESSED, THE
DC Comics (Cliffhanger): Sept, 2003 - No. 6, March, 2004 ($2.95, limited series)

1-6-Johns & Grimminger-s/Sharp-a 3.00
TPB (2004, $14.95) r/#1-6; promo art and sketch pages 15.00

POST GAZETTE (See Meet the New... in the Promotional Comics section)

POWDER RIVER RUSTLERS (See Fawcett Movie Comics)

POWER & GLORY (See American Flagg! & Howard Chaykin's American Flagg!)
Malibu Comics (Bravura): Feb, 1994 - No. 4, May, 1994 ($2.50, limited series, mature)

1A, 1B-By Howard Chaykin; w/Bravura stamp
1-Newsstand ed. (polybagged w/children's warning on bag), Gold ed., Silver-foil ed., Blue-foil
  ed.(print run of 10,000), Serigraph ed. (print run of 3,000)($2.95)-Howard Chaykin-c/a
  begin 3.00
2-4-Contains Bravura stamp 2.50
Holiday Special (Win '94, $2.95) 3.00

POWER COMICS
Holyoke Publ. Co./Narrative Publ.: 1944 - No. 4, 1945

1-L. B. Cole-c	138	276	414	863	1432	2000
2-Hitler, Hirohito-c (scarce)	138	276	414	863	1432	2000
3-Classic L.B. Cole-c; Dr. Mephisto begins?	166	332	498	1038	1719	2400
4-L.B. Cole-c; Miss Espionage app. #3,4; Leav-a	138	276	414	863	1432	2000

POWER COMICS
Power Comics Co.: 1977 - No. 5, Dec, 1977 (B&W)

1- "A Boy And His Aardvark" by Dave Sim; first Dave Sim aardvark (not Cerebus)	2	4	6	13	18	22
1-Reprint (3/77, black-c)	1	2	3	5	6	8
2-Cobalt Blue by Gustovich	1	3	4	6	8	10
3-5: 3-Nightwitch. 4-Northern Light. 5-Bluebird	1	3	4	6	8	10

POWER COMICS
Eclipse Comics (Acme Press): Mar, 1988 - No. 4, Sept, 1988 ($2.00, B&W, mini-series)

1-4: Bolland, Gibbons-r in all 2.50

POWER COMPANY, THE
DC Comics: Apr, 2002 - No. 18, Sept, 2003 ($2.50/$2.75)

1-6-Busiek-s/Grummett-a. 6-Green Arrow & Black Canary-c/app. ... 2.50
7-18: 7-Begin $2.75-c. 8,9-Green Arrow app. 11-Firestorm joins. 15-Batman app. ... 2.75
...Bork (3/02) Busiek-s/Dwyer-a; Batman & Flash (Barry Allen) app. ... 2.50
...Josiah Power (3/02) Busiek-s/Giffen-a; Superman app. 2.50
...Manhunter (3/02) Busiek-s/Jurgens-a; Nightwing app. 2.50
...Sapphire (3/02) Busiek-s/Bagley-a; JLA & Kobra app. 2.50
...Skyrocket (3/02) Busiek-s/Staton-a; Green Lantern (Hal Jordan) app. ... 2.50
...Striker Z (3/02) Busiek-s/Bachs-a; Superboy app. 2.50
...Witchfire (3/02) Busiek-s/Haley-a; Wonder Woman app. 2.50

POWER FACTOR
Wonder Color Comics #1/Pied Piper #2: May, 1987 - No. 2, 1987 ($1.95)

1,2: Super team. 2-Infantino-c 2.50

POWER FACTOR
Innovation Publishing: Oct, 1990 - No. 3, 1991 ($1.95/$2.25)

1-3: 1-R-/1st story + new-a. 2-r/2nd story + new-a. 3-Infantino-a ... 2.50

POWER GIRL (See All-Star #58, Infinity, Inc., JSA Classified, Showcase #97-99)
DC Comics: June, 1988 - No. 4, Sept, 1988 ($1.00, color, limited series)

1-4 .... 3.00
TPB (2006, $14.99) r/Showcase #97-99; Secret Origins #11; JSA Classified #1-4 and pages
  from JSA #32,39; cover gallery 15.00

POWERHOUSE PEPPER COMICS (See Gay Comics, Joker Comics & Tessie the Typist)
Marvel Comics (20CC): No. 1, 1943; No. 2, May, 1948 - No. 5, Nov, 1948

1-(60 pgs.)-Wolverton-a in all; c-2,3	207	414	621	1294	2147	3000
2	88	176	264	550	913	1275
3,4	81	162	243	506	841	1175
5-(Scarce)	93	186	279	581	966	1350

POWERLESS
Marvel Comics: Aug, 2004 - No. 6, Jan, 2005 ($2.99, limited series)

1-6-Peter Parker, Matt Murdock and Logan without powers; Gaydos-a ... 3.00
TPB (2005, $14.99) r/series; sketch page by Gaydos 15.00

POWER LINE
Marvel Comics (Epic Comics): May, 1988 - No. 8, Sept, 1989 ($1.25/$1.50)

1-8: 2-Williamson-i. 3-Dr. Zero app. 4-7-Morrow-a. 8-Williamson-i ... 2.50

POWER LORDS
DC Comics: Dec, 1983 - No. 3, Feb, 1984 (Limited series, Mando paper)

1-3: Based on Revell toys 2.50

POWER MAN (Formerly Hero for Hire; ...& Iron Fist #50 on; see Cage & Giant-Size...)
Marvel Comics Group: No. 17, Feb, 1974 - No. 125, Sept, 1986

17-Luke Cage continues; Iron Man app.	2	4	6	10	14	18
18-20: 18-Last 20¢ issue	2	4	6	8	10	12
21-30	1	2	3	5	6	8
30-(30¢-c variant, limited distribution)(4/76)	3	6	9	15	20	30
31-46: 31-Part Neal Adams-i. 34-Last 25¢ issue. 36-r/Hero for Hire #12.						
41-1st app. Thunderbolt. 45-Starlin-c.	1	2	3	4	5	7
31-34-(30¢-c variants, limited distribution)(5-8/76)	3	6	9	16	23	30
44-46-(35¢-c variants, limited distribution)(6-8/77)	3	6	9	20	30	40
47-Barry Smith-a	1	2	3	5	7	9
47-(35¢-c variant, limited distribution)(10/77)	4	8	12	24	37	50
48-50-Byrne-a(p); 48-Power Man/Iron Fist 1st meet. 50-Iron Fist joins Cage				8	10	12
51-56,58-60,65,67-77: 58-Intro El Aguila. 75-Double size. 77-Daredevil app.				6		4.00
57-New X-Men app. (6/79)	3	6	9	18	27	35
66-2nd app. Sabretooth (see Iron Fist #14)	4	8	12	26	41	55
78,84: 78-3rd app. Sabretooth (cameo under cloak). 84-4th app. Sabretooth	3	6	9	16	23	30
79-83,85-99,101-124: 87-Moon Knight app. 109-The Reaper app.						3.00
100,125-Double size: 100-Origin K'un Lun. 125-Death of Iron Fist						4.00
Annual 1(1976)-Punisher cameo in flashback	2	4	6	9	13	16

NOTE: *Austin* c-102i. *Byrne* a-48-50; c-102, 104, 106, 107, 112-116. *Kane* c(p)-24, 25, 28, 48. *Miller* a-68, 76(2
pgs.); c-66-68, 70-74, 80i. *Mooney* a-38i, 53i, 55i. *Nebres* a-76p. *Nino* a-42i, 43i. *Perez* a-27. *B. Smith* a-47i.
Tuska a(p)-17, 20, 24, 26, 28, 29, 36, 47. Painted c-75, 100.

POWER OF PRIME
Malibu Comics (Ultraverse): July, 1995 - No. 4, Nov, 1995 ($2.50, lim. series)

1-4 .... 2.50

POWER OF SHAZAM!, THE (See SHAZAM!)
DC Comics: 1994 (Painted graphic novel) (Prequel to new series)

Hardcover-($19.95)-New origin of Shazam!; Ordway painted-c/a & script	3	6	9	14	20	25
Softcover-($7.50), Softcover-($9.95)-New-c.	2	4	6	8	10	12

POWER OF SHAZAM!, THE
DC Comics: Mar, 1995 - No. 47, Mar, 1999 ($1.50/$1.75/$1.95/$2.50)

1-Jerry Ordway scripts begin 4.00
2-20: 4-Begin $1.75-c. 6-Re-intro of Capt. Nazi. 8-Re-intro of Spy Smasher, Bulletman &
  Minuteman; Swan-a (7 pgs.). 11-Re-intro of Ibis, Swan-a(2 pgs.). 14-Gil Kane-a(p).
  20-Superman-c/app.; "Final Night" 3.00
21-47: 21-Plastic Man-c/app. 22-Batman-c/app. 35,36-X-over w/Starman #39,40.
  38-41-Mr. Mind. 45-JLA-c/app. 2.50
#1,000,000 (11/98) 853rd Century x-over; Ordway-c/s/a 3.00
Annual 1 (1996, $2.95)-Legends of the Dead Earth story; Jerry Ordway-c; Mike Manley-a 4.00

POWER OF STRONGMAN, THE (Also see Strongman)
AC Comics: 1989 ($2.95)

1-Powell G.A.-r 3.00

POWER OF THE ATOM (See Secret Origins #29)
DC Comics: Aug, 1988 - No. 18, Nov, 1989 ($1.00)

1-18: 6-Chronos returns; Byrne-p. 9-JLI app. 2.50

POWER PACHYDERMS
Marvel Comics: Sept, 1989 ($1.25, one-shot)

1-Elephant super-heroes; parody of X-Men, Elektra, & 3 Stooges ... 2.50

POWER PACK
Marvel Comics Group: Aug, 1984 - No. 62, Feb, 1991

1-($1.00, 52 pgs.)-Origin & 1st app. Power Pack 3.00
2-18,20-26,28,30-45,47-62 .... 2.50
19-(52 pgs.)-Cloak & Dagger, Wolverine app. 3.00
27-Mutant massacre; Wolverine & Sabretooth app. 5.00
29,46: 29-Spider-Man & Hobgoblin app. 46-Punisher app. 2.75
Graphic Novel: Power Pack & Cloak & Dagger: Shelter From the Storm ('89, SC, $7.95)
  Velluto/Farmer-a 10.00
...Holiday Special 1 (2/92, $2.25, 68 pgs.) 2.50

NOTE: *Austin* scripts-43. *Mignola* c-20. *Morrow* a-51. *Spiegle* a-55i. *Williamson* a(i)-43, 50, 52.

POWER PACK (Volume 2)
Marvel Comics: Aug, 2000 - No. 4, Nov, 2000 ($2.99, lim. series)

1-4-Doran & Austin-c/a 3.00

Powerpuff Girls #6 © Cartoon Network

Powers V2 #22 © Jinxworld

Preacher #37 © Ennis & Dillon

	GD 2.0	VG 4.0	FN 6.0	VF 8.0	VF/NM 9.0	NM- 9.2

POWER PACK
Marvel Comics: June, 2005 - No. 4, Aug, 2005 ($2.99, limited series)

1-4-Sumerak-s/Gurihiru-a; back-up Franklin Richards story. 3-Fantastic Four app.						3.00
... Digest (2006, $6.99) r/#1-4						7.00

POWERPUFF GIRLS, THE (Also see Cartoon Network Starring... #1)
DC Comics: May, 2000 - No. 70, Mar, 2006 ($1.99/$2.25)

1						4.00
2-55,57-70: 25-Pin-ups by Allred, Byrne, Baker, Mignola, Hernandez, Warren						2.50
56-($2.95) Bonus pages; Mojo Jojo-c						3.00
...Double Whammy (12/00, $3.95) r/#1,2 & a Dexter's Lab story						3.95
...Movie: The Comic (9/02, $2.95) Movie adaptation; Phil Moy & Chris Cook-a						3.00

POWER RANGERS ZEO (TV)(Saban's...)(Also see Saban's Mighty Morphin Power Rangers)
Image Comics (Extreme Studios): Aug, 1996 ($2.50)

1-Based on TV show						2.50

POWER RECORD COMICS
Marvel Comics/Power Records: 1974 - 1978 ($1.49, 7x10" comics, 20 pgs. with 45 R.P.M. record) (Clipped corners - reduce value 20%) (Comic alone - 50%; record alone - 50%)

PR10-Spider-Man-r/from #124,125; Man-Wolf app. PR18-Planet of the Apes-r. PR19-Escape From the Planet of the Apes-r. PR20-Beneath the Planet of the Apes-r. PR21-Battle for the Planet of the Apes-r. PR24-Spider-Man II-New-a begins. PR27-Batman "Stacked Cards"; N. Adams-a(p). PR30-Batman; N. Adams-r./Det.(7 pgs.).

With record; each...	4	8	12	44		60

PR11-Hulk-r. PR12-Captain America-r/#168. PR13-Fantastic Four-r/#126. PR14-Frankenstein-Ploog-r/#1. PR15-Tomb of Dracula-Colan-r/#2. PR16-Man-Thing-Ploog-r/#5. PR17-Werewolf By Night-Ploog-r/Marvel Spotlight #2. PR28-Superman "Alien Creatures". PR29-Space: 1999 "Breakaway". PR31-Conan-N. Adams-a; reprinted in Conan #116. PR32-Space: 1999 "Return to the Beginning". PR33-Superman-G.A. origin, Buckler-a(p). PR34-Superman. PR35-Wonder Woman-Buckler-a(p)

With record; each...	4	8	12	24		50

PR25-Star Trek "Passage to Moauv" PR26-Star Trek "Crier in Emptiness." PR36-Holo-Man. PR37-Robin Hood. PR39-Huckleberry Finn. PR40-Davy Crockett. PR41-Robinson Crusoe. PR42-20,000 Leagues Under the Sea. PR46-Star Trek "The Robot Masters". PR47-Little Women

With record; each...	3	6	9	20	30	40

POWERS
Image Comics: 2000 - No. 37, Feb, 2004 ($2.95)

1-Bendis-s/Oeming-a; murder of Retro Girl	1	3	4	6	8	10
2-6: 6-End of Retro Girl arc.						5.00
7-14: 7-Warren Ellis app. 12-14-Death of Olympia						3.50
15-37: 31-36-Origin of the Powers						3.00
Annual 1 (2001, $3.95)						3.95
...: Anarchy TPB (11/03, $14.95) r/#21-24; interviews, sketchbook, cover gallery						15.00
...Coloring/Activity Book (2001, $1.50, B&W, 8 x 10.5") Oeming-a						2.50
...: Forever TPB (2005, $19.95) r/#31-37; script for #31, sketchbook, cover gallery						20.00
...: Little Deaths TPB (2002, $19.95) r/#7,12-14, Ann. #1, Coloring/Activity Book; sketch pages, cover gallery						20.00
...: Roleplay TPB (2001, $13.95) r/#8-11; sketchbook, cover gallery						14.00
...: Scriptbook (2001, $19.95) scripts for #1-11; Oeming sketches						20.00
...: Supergroup TPB (2003, $19.95) r/#15-20; sketchbook, cover gallery						20.00
...: The Definitive Collection Vol. 1 HC (2006, $29.99, dust jacket) r/#1-11 & Coloring/Activity Book, script for #1, sketch pages and covers, interviews, letter column highlights						30.00
...: Who Killed Retro Girl TPB (2000, $21.95) r/#1-6; sketchbook, cover gallery, and promotional strips from Comic Shop News						22.00

POWERS
Marvel Comics (Icon): Jul, 2004 - Present ($2.95)

1-11,13-24-Bendis-s/Oeming-a. 14-Cover price error						3.00
12-($3.95, 64 pages) 2 covers; Bendis & Oeming interview						4.00
25-($3.95, 64 pages) 2 covers; Bendis interview						4.00
...: Legends TPB (2005, $17.95) r/#1-6; sketchbook, cover gallery						18.00
...: Psychotic TPB (1/06, $19.95) r/#7-12; Bendis & Oeming interview, cover gallery						20.00

POWERS THAT BE (Becomes Star Seed No.7 on)
Broadway Comics: Nov, 1995 - No. 6, June, 1996 ($2.50)

1-6: 1-Intro of Fatale & Star Seed. 6-Begin $2.95-c.						3.00
Preview Editions 1-3 (9/95 - 11/95, B&W)						2.50

POW MAGAZINE (Bob Sproul's) (Satire Magazine)
Humor-Vision: Aug, 1966 - No. 3, Feb, 1967 (30¢)

1,2: 2-Jones-a	4	8	12	26	41	55
3-Wrightson-a	5	10	15	32	51	70

PREACHER
DC Comics (Vertigo): Apr, 1995 - No. 66, Oct, 2000 ($2.50, mature)

nn-Preview	2	4	6	11	16	20
1 ($2.95)-Ennis scripts, Dillon-a & Fabry-c in all; 1st app. Jesse, Tulip, & Cassidy						

2,3: 2-1st app. Saint of Killers.	2	4	6	8	11	14
4,5	1	2	3	5	7	9
	1	2	3	4	5	7
6-10						5.00
11-20: 12-Polybagged w/videogame w/Ennis text. 13-Hunters storyline begins; ends #17. 19-Saint of Killers app.; begin "Crusaders", ends #24						4.00
21-25: 21-24-Saint of Killers app. 25-Origin of Cassidy.						3.00
26-49,52-64: 52-Tulip origin						2.50
50-($3.75) Pin-ups by Jim Lee, Bradstreet, Quesada and Palmiotti						3.75
51-Includes preview of 100 Bullets; Tulip origin						4.00
65,66-($3.75) 65-Almost everyone dies. 66-Final issue						5.00
Alamo (2001, $17.95, TPB) r/#59-66; Fabry-c						18.00
All Hell's a-Coming (2000, $17.95, TPB) r/#51-58, ...:Tall in the Saddle						18.00
...: Dead or Alive HC (2000, $29.95) Gallery of Glenn Fabry's cover paintings for every Preacher issue; commentary by Fabry & Ennis						30.00
...: Dead or Alive SC (2003, $19.95)						20.00
Dixie Fried (1998, $14.95, TPB)-r/#27-33, Special: Cassidy						15.00
Gone To Texas (1996, $14.95, TPB)-r/#1-7; Fabry-c						15.00
Proud Americans (1997, $14.95, TPB)-r/#18-26; Fabry-c						15.00
Salvation (1999, $14.95, TPB)-r/#41-50; Fabry-c						15.00
Until the End of the World (1996, $14.95, TPB)-r/#8-17; Fabry-c						15.00
War in the Sun (1999, $14.95, TPB)-r/#34-40						15.00

PREACHER SPECIAL: CASSIDY: BLOOD & WHISKEY
DC Comics (Vertigo): 1998 ($5.95, one-shot)

1-Ennis-scripts/Fabry-c /Dillon-a						6.00

PREACHER SPECIAL: ONE MAN'S WAR
DC Comics (Vertigo): Mar, 1998 ($4.95, one-shot)

1-Ennis-scripts/Fabry-c /Snejbjerg-a						5.00

PREACHER SPECIAL: SAINT OF KILLERS
DC Comics (Vertigo): Aug, 1996 - No. 4, Nov, 1996 ($2.50, lim. series, mature)

1-4: Ennis-scripts/Fabry-c. 1,2-Pugh-a. 3,4-Ezquerra-a						3.00
1-Signed & numbered						20.00

PREACHER SPECIAL: THE GOOD OLD BOYS
DC Comics (Vertigo): Aug, 1997 ($4.95, one-shot, mature)

1-Ennis-scripts/Fabry-c /Esquerra-a						5.00

PREACHER SPECIAL: THE STORY OF YOU-KNOW-WHO
DC Comics (Vertigo): Dec, 1996 ($4.95, one-shot, mature)

1-Ennis-scripts/Fabry-c/Case-a						5.00

PREACHER: TALL IN THE SADDLE
DC Comics (Vertigo): 2000 ($5.95, one-shot)

1-Ennis-scripts/Fabry-c/Dillon-a; early romance of Tulip and Jesse						6.00

PREDATOR (Also see Aliens Vs. ..., Batman vs. ..., Dark Horse Comics, & Dark Horse Presents)
Dark Horse Comics: June, 1989 - No. 4, Mar, 1990 ($2.25, limited series)

1-Based on movie; 1st app. Predator	1	2	3	4	5	7
1-2nd printing						3.00
2						5.00
3,4						4.00
Trade paperback (1990, $12.95)-r/#1-4						13.00
... Omnibus Volume 1 (8/07, $24.95, 6" x 9") r/#1-4, ... Cold War, ... Dark River, ...Bloody Sands of Time mini-series and stories from Dark Horse Comics #1,2,4-7,10-12						25.00

PREDATOR: (title series) **Dark Horse Comics**

--BAD BLOOD, 12/93 - No. 4, 1994 ($2.50) 1-4						3.00
--BIG GAME, 3/91 - No. 4, 6/91 ($2.50) 1-4: 1-3 Contain 2 Dark Horse trading cards						3.00
--BLOODY SANDS OF TIME, No. 2, 2/92 ($2.50) 1,2-Dan Barry-c/a(p)/scripts						3.00
--CAPTIVE, 4/98 ($2.95, one-shot) 1						3.00
--COLD WAR, 9/91 - No. 4, 12/91 ($2.50) 1-4: All have painted-c						3.00
--DARK RIVER, 7/96 - No.4, 10/96 ($2.95)1-4: Miran Kim-c						3.00
--HELL & HOT WATER, 6/97 - No. 3, 6/97 ($2.95) 1-3						3.00
--HELL COME A WALKIN', 2/98 - No. 2, 3/98 ($2.95) 1,2-In the Civil War						3.00
--HOMEWORLD, 3/99 - No. 4, 6/99 ($2.95) 1-4						3.00
--INVADERS FROM THE FOURTH DIMENSION, 7/94 ($3.95, one-shot, 52 pgs.) 1						4.00
--JUNGLE TALES. 3/95 ($2.95t) 1-r/Dark Horse Comics						3.00
--KINDRED, 12/96 - No. 4, 3/97 ($2.50) 1-4						3.00
--NEMESIS, 12/97 - No. 2, 1/98 ($2.95) 1,2-Predator in Victorian England; Taggart-c						3.00
--PRIMAL, 7/97 - No. 2, 8/97 ($2.95) 1,2						3.00

Pride & Joy #4 © Ennis & Higgins

Prime #6 © MAL

Prince Valiant #2 © KING

	GD	VG	FN	VF	VF/NM	NM-
	2.0	4.0	6.0	8.0	9.0	9.2

--RACE WAR (See Dark Horse Presents #67), 2/93 - No. 4,10/93 ($2.50, color)
1-4,0: 1-4-Dorman painted-c #1-4, 0(4/93) 3.00
--STRANGE ROUX, 11/96 ($2.95, one-shot) 1 .... 3.00
--XENOGENESIS (Also see Aliens Xenogenesis), 8/99 - No. 4, 11/99 ($2.95)
1,2-Edginton-s 3.00
PREDATOR 2
Dark Horse Comics: Feb, 1991 - No. 2, June, 1991 ($2.50, limited series)
1,2: 1-Adapts movie; both w/trading cards & photo-c 3.00
PREDATOR VS. JUDGE DREDD
Dark Horse Comics: Oct, 1997 - No. 3 ($2.50, limited series)
1-3-Wagner-s/Alcatena-a/Bolland-c 3.00
PREDATOR VS. MAGNUS ROBOT FIGHTER
Dark Horse/Valiant: Oct, 1992 - No. 2, 1993 ($2.95, limited series)
(1st Dark Horse/Valiant x-over)
1,2: (Reg.)-Barry Smith-c; Lee Weeks-a. 2-w/trading cards 3.00
1 (Platinum edition, 11/92)-Barry Smith-c 10.00
PREHISTORIC WORLD (See Classics Illustrated Special Issue)
PRELUDE TO INFINITE CRISIS
DC Comics: 2005 ($5.99, squarebound)
nn-Reprints stories and panels with commentary leading into Infinite Crisis series 6.00
PREMIERE (See Charlton Premiere)
PRESTO KID, THE (See Red Mask)
PRETTY BOY FLOYD (See On the Spot)
PREZ (See Cancelled Comic Cavalcade, Sandman #54 & Supergirl #10)
National Periodical Publications: Aug-Sept, 1973 - No. 4, Feb-Mar, 1974
1-Origin; Joe Simon scripts | 3 | 6 | 9 | 16 | 23 | 30
2-4 | 2 | 4 | 6 | 10 | 14 | 18
PRICE, THE (See Eclipse Graphic Album Series)
PRIDE & JOY
DC Comics (Vertigo): July, 1997 - No. 4, Oct, 1997 ($2.50, limited series)
1-4-Ennis-s 2.50
TPB (2004, $14.95) r/#1-4 .... 15.00
PRIDE AND THE PASSION, THE
Dell Publishing Co.: No. 824, Aug, 1957
Four Color 824-Movie, Frank Sinatra & Cary Grant photo-c | 9 | 18 | 27 | 63 | 107 | 150
PRIDE OF BAGHDAD
DC Comics (Vertigo): 2006 ($19.99, hardcover with dustjacket)
HC-A pride of lions escaping from the Baghdad zoo in 2003; Vaughan-s/Henrichon-a 20.00
PRIDE OF THE YANKEES, THE (See Real Heroes & Sport Comics)
Magazine Enterprises: 1949 (The Life of Lou Gehrig)
nn-Photo-c; Ogden Whitney-a | 81 | 162 | 243 | 506 | 841 | 1175
PRIEST (Also see Asylum)
Maximum Press: Aug, 1996 - No. 2, Oct, 1996 ($2.99)
1,2 .... 3.00
PRIMAL FORCE
DC Comics: No. 0, Oct, 1994 - No. 14, Dec, 1995 ($1.95/$2.25)
0-14: 0- Teams Red Tornado, Golem, Jack O'Lantern, Meridian & Silver Dragon. 9-begin $2.25-c 2.50
PRIMAL MAN (See The Crusaders)
PRIMAL RAGE
Sirius Entertainment: 1996 ($2.95)
1-Dark One-c; based of video game 3.00
PRIME (See Break-Thru, Flood Relief & Ultraforce)
Malibu Comics (Ultraverse): June, 1993 - No. 26, Aug, 1995 ($1.95/$2.50)
1-1st app. Prime; has coupon for Ultraverse Premiere #0 .... 3.00
1-With coupon missing 2.00
1-Full cover holographic edition; 1st of kind w/Hardcase #1 & Strangers #1 .... 6.00
1-Ultra 5,000 edition w/silver ink-c 4.00
2-11,14-26: 2-Polybagged w/card & coupon for U. Premiere #0. 3,4-Prototype app. 4-Direct sale w/o card.4-($2.50)-Newsstand ed. polybagged w/card. 5-($2.50, 48 pgs.)-Rune flip-c/ story part B by Barry Smith; see Sludge #1 for 1st app. Rune; 3-pg. Night Man preview. 6-Bill & Chelsea Clinton app. 7-Break-Thru x-over. 8-Mantra app.; 2-pg. origin Freex by

Simonson. 10-Firearm app.15-Intro Papa Verite; Perez-c/a. 16-Intro Turbo Charge 2.50
12-($3.50, 68 pgs.)-Flip book w/Ultraverse Premiere #3; silver foil logo 3.50
13-($2.95, 52 pgs.)-Variant covers 3.00
...: Gross and Disgusting 1 (10/94, $3.95)-Boris-c; "Annual" on cover, published monthly in indicia 4.00
...Month "Ashcan" (8/94, 75¢)-Boris-c 2.50
... Time: A Prime Collection (1994, $9.95)-r/1-4 .... 10.00
...Vs. The Incredible Hulk (1995)-mail away limited edition 10.00
...Vs. The Incredible Hulk Premium edition 10.00
...Vs. The Incredible Hulk Super Premium edition 15.00
NOTE: *Perez* a-15; c-15, 16.
PRIME (Also see Black September)
Malibu Comics (Ultraverse): Infinity, Sept, 1995 - V2#15, Dec, 1996 ($1.50)
Infinity, V2#1-8: Post Black September storyline. 6-8-Solitaire app. 9-Breyfogle-c/a. 10-12-Ramos-c. 15-Lord Pumpkin app. 2.50
Infinity Signed Edition (2,000 printed) 5.00
PRIME/CAPTAIN AMERICA
Malibu Comics: Mar, 1996 ($3.95, one-shot)
1-Norm Breyfogle-a 4.00
PRIME8: CREATION
Two Morrows Publishing: July, 2001 ($3.95, B&W)
1-Neal Adams-c 4.00
PRIMER (Comico...)
Comico: Oct (no month), 1982 - No. 6, Feb, 1984 (B&W)
1 (52 pgs.) | 2 | 4 | 6 | 8 | 11 | 14
2-1st app. Grendel & Argent by Wagner | 8 | 16 | 24 | 56 | 93 | 130
3,4 | 1 | 3 | 4 | 6 | 8 | 10
5-1st Sam Kieth art in comics ('83) & 1st The Maxx | 3 | 6 | 9 | 19 | 29 | 38
6-Intro & 1st app. Evangeline | 2 | 4 | 6 | 9 | 12 | 15
PRIMORTALS (Leonard Nimoy's...)
PRIMUS (TV)
Charlton Comics: Feb, 1972 - No. 7, Oct, 1972
1-Staton-a in all | 2 | 4 | 6 | 11 | 16 | 20
2-7: 6-Drug propaganda story | 2 | 4 | 6 | 8 | 11 | 14
PRINCE NAMOR, THE SUB-MARINER (Also see Namor ...)
Marvel Comics Group: Sept, 1984 - No. 4, Dec, 1984 (Limited-series)
1-4 .... 2.50
PRINCESS NATASHA (Video game)
DC Comics: Aug, 2006 - No. 4, Nov, 2006 ($2.25, limited series)
1-4-Character from AOL For Kids 2.50
PRINCESS SALLY (Video game)
Archie Publications: Apr, 1995 - No. 3, June, 1995 ($1.50, limited series)
1-3: Spin-off from Sonic the Hedgehog 4.00
PRINCE VALIANT (See Ace Comics, Comics Reading Libraries *in the Promotional Comics section*, & King Comics #146, 147)
David McKay Publ./Dell: No. 26, 1941; No. 67, June, 1954 - No. 900, May, 1958
Feature Books 26 ('41)-Harold Foster-c/a; newspaper strips reprinted, pgs. 1-28,30-63; color & 68 pgs; Foster cover is only original comic book artwork by him | 97 | 194 | 291 | 606 | 1003 | 1400
Four Color 567 (6/54)(#1)-By Bob Fuje-Movie, photo-c | 10 | 20 | 30 | 73 | 129 | 185
Four Color 650 (9/55), 699 (4/56), 719 (8/56),-Fuje-a | 7 | 14 | 21 | 50 | 83 | 115
Four Color 788 (4/57), 849 (1/58), 900-Fuje-a | 7 | 14 | 21 | 47 | 76 | 105
PRINCE VALIANT
Marvel Comics: Dec, 1994 - No. 4, Mar, 1995 ($3.95, limited series)
1-4; Kaluta-c in all. 4.00
PRINCE VANDAL
Triumphant Comics: Nov, 1993 - Apr?, 1994 ($2.50)
1-6: 1,2-Triumphant Unleashed x-over 2.50
PRIORITY: WHITE HEAT
AC Comics: 1986 - No. 2, 1986 ($1.75, mini-series)
1,2-Bill Black-a 3.00
PRISCILLA'S POP
Dell Publishing Co.: No. 569, June, 1954 - No. 799, May, 1957
Four Color 569 (#1), 630 (5/55), 704 (5/56),799 | 4 | 8 | 12 | 26 | 41 | 55

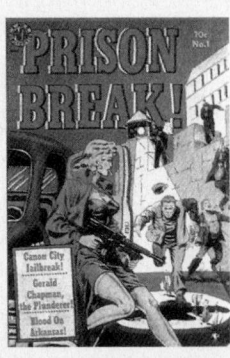
Prison Break! #1 © AVON

Prize Comics #25 © Prize

Promethea #9 © ABC

	GD	VG	FN	VF	VF/NM	NM-			GD	VG	FN	VF	VF/NM	NM-
	2.0	4.0	6.0	8.0	9.0	9.2			2.0	4.0	6.0	8.0	9.0	9.2

PRISON BARS (See Behind...)

PRISON BREAK!
Avon Per./Realistic No. 3 on: Sept, 1951 - No. 5, Sept, 1952 (Painted c-3)

1-Wood-c & 1 pg.; has-r/Saint #7 retitled Michael Strong Private Eye
	41	82	123	254	410	565
2-Wood-c; Kubert-a; Kinstler inside front-c	30	60	90	174	275	375
3-Orlando, Check-a; c-/Avon paperback #179	24	48	72	139	220	300
4,5: 4-Kinstler-c & inside f/c; Lawrence, Lazarus-a. 5-Kinstler-c; Infantino-a						
	21	42	63	124	195	265

PRISONER, THE (TV)
DC Comics: 1988 - No. 4, 1989 ($3.50, squarebound, mini-series)

1-4 (Books a-d) 3.50

PRISON RIOT
Avon Periodicals: 1952

1-Marijuana Murders-1 pg. text; Kinstler-c; 2 Kubert illos on text pages
	28	56	84	162	256	350

PRISON TO PRAISE
Logos International: 1974 (35¢) (Religious, Christian)

nn-True Story of Merlin R. Carothers
	2	4	6	9	12	15

PRIVATE BUCK
Dell Publishing Co.: No. 21, 1941 - No. 12, 1942

Large Feature Comic 21 (#1)(1941)(Series I), 22 (1941)(Series I), 12 (1942)(Series II)
	17	34	51	98	154	210

PRIVATE EYE (Cover title: Rocky Jorden...#6-8)
Atlas Comics (MCI): Jan, 1951 - No. 8, March, 1952

1-Cover title: Crime Cases... #1-5	21	42	63	122	191	260
2,3-Tuska c/a(3)	14	28	42	76	108	140
4-8	11	22	33	60	83	105
NOTE: *Henkel* a-6(3), 7; c-7. *Sinnott* a-6.

PRIVATE EYE (See Mike Shayne...)

PRIVATE SECRETARY
Dell Publishing Co.: Dec-Feb, 1962-63 - No. 2, Mar-May, 1963

1	3	6	9	21	32	42
2	3	6	9	17	25	32

PRIVATE STRONG (See The Double Life of...)

PRIZE COMICS (...Western #69 on) (Also see Treasure Comics)
Prize Publications: March, 1940 - No. 68, Feb-Mar, 1948

1-Origin Power Nelson, The Futureman & Jupiter, Master Magician; Ted O'Neil, Secret Agent
M-11, Jaxon of the Jungle, Bucky Brady & Storm Curtis begin (1st app. of each)
	269	538	807	1681	2791	3900
2-The Black Owl begins (1st app.)	117	234	351	731	1216	1700
3	103	206	309	644	1072	1500
4-Classic robot-c	110	220	330	688	1144	1600
5,6: Dr. Dekkar, Master of Monsters app. in each	90	180	270	563	932	1300
7-(Scarce)-1st app. The Green Lama (12/40); Black Owl by S&K; origin/1st app. Dr. Frost & Frankenstein; Capt. Gallant, The Great Voodini & Twist Turner begin;						
	214	428	642	1338	2219	3100
8,9-Black Owl & Ted O'Neil by S&K	100	200	300	625	1038	1450
10-12,14,15: 11-Origin Bulldog Denny. 14-War-c	72	144	216	450	750	1050
13-Yank & Doodle begin (8/41), origin/1st app.)	79	158	237	494	822	1150
16-20: 16-Spike Mason begins	66	132	198	413	682	950
21-24: 21-War-c. 22-Statue of Liberty jap attack war-c. 23-Uncle Sam patriotic war-c.						
24-Lincoln statue patriotic-c	50	100	150	305	503	700
25-30: 25-28 War-c. 26-Liberty Bell-c	36	72	108	208	329	450
31-33: 31-Jap war-c	30	60	90	174	275	375
34-Origin Airmale, Yank & Doodle; The Black Owl joins army, Yank & Doodle's father assumes Black Owl's role	34	68	102	195	308	420
35-36,38,40: 35-Flying Fist & Bingo begin	24	48	72	139	220	300
37-Intro. Stampy, Airmale's sidekick; Hitler-c	40	80	120	235	368	500
41-50: 45-Yank & Doodle learn Black Owl's I.D. (their father). 48-Prince Ra begins						
	19	38	57	109	172	235
51-62,64,67,68: 53-Transvestism story. 55-No Frankenstein. 57-X-Mas-c. 64-Black Owl retires	15	30	45	88	137	185
63-Simon & Kirby c/a	18	36	54	107	169	230
65,66-Frankenstein-c by Briefer	16	32	48	94	147	200
NOTE: *Briefer* a-7-on; c-65, 66. *J. Binder* a-16; c-21-29. *Guardineer* a-62. *Kiefer* c-62. *Palais* c-68. *Simon & Kirby* c-63, 75, 83.

PRIZE COMICS WESTERN (Formerly Prize Comics #1-68)

Prize Publications (Feature): No. 69(V7#2), Apr-May, 1948 - No. 119, Nov-Dec, 1956 (No. 69-84: 52 pgs.)

69(V7#2)	14	28	42	80	115	150
70-75: 74-Kurtzman-a (8 pgs.)	12	24	36	67	94	120
76-Randolph Scott photo-c; "Canadian Pacific" movie adaptation						
	13	26	39	72	101	130
77-Photo-c; Severin/Elder, Mart Bailey-a; "Streets of Laredo" movie adaptation						
	12	24	36	67	94	120
78-Photo-c; S&K-a, 10 pgs.; Severin, Mart Bailey-a; "Bullet Code", & "Roughshod" movie adaptations	15	30	45	90	140	190
79-Photo-c; Kurtzman-a, 8 pgs.; Severin/Elder, Severin, Mart Bailey-a; "Stage To Chino" movie adaptation w/George O'Brien	15	30	45	90	140	190
80-82-Photo-c; 80,81-Severin/Elder-a(2). 82-1st app. The Preacher by Mart Bailey; Severin/Elder-a(3)	13	26	39	72	101	130
83,84	10	20	30	58	79	100
85-1st app. American Eagle by John Severin & begins (V9#6, 1-2/51)						
	19	38	57	112	176	240
86,101-105, 109-Severin/Williamson-a	11	22	33	64	90	115
87-99,110,111-Severin/Elder-a(2-3) each	12	24	36	69	97	125
100	13	26	39	74	105	135
106-108,112	9	18	27	47	61	75
113-Williamson/Severin-a(2)/Frazetta?	12	24	36	69	97	125
114-119: Drifter series in all; by Mort Meskin #114-118						
	8	16	24	42	54	65
NOTE: *Fass* a-81. *Severin & Elder* c-84-99. *Severin* a-72, 75, 77-79, 83-86, 96, 97, 100-105; c-92,100-109(most), 110-119. *Simon & Kirby* c-75, 83.

PRIZE MYSTERY
Key Publications: May, 1955 - No. 3, Sept, 1955

1	11	22	33	60	83	105
2,3	8	16	24	44	57	70

PRO, THE
Image Comics: July, 2002 ($5.95, squarebound, one-shot)

1-Ennis-s/Conner & Palmiotti-a; prostitute gets super-powers 8.00
1-Second printing with different cover 6.00
Hardcover Edition (10/04, $14.95) oversized reprint plus new 8 pg. story; sketch pages 15.00

PROFESSIONAL FOOTBALL (See Charlton Sport Library)

PROFESSOR COFFIN
Charlton Comics: No. 19, Oct, 1985 - No. 21, Feb, 1986

19-21: Wayne Howard-a(r); low print run	1	2	3	5	6	8

PROFESSOR OM
Innovation Publishing: May, 1990 - No. 2, 1990 ($2.50, limited series)

1,2-East Meets West spin-off 2.50

PROFESSOR XAVIER AND THE X-MEN (Also see X-Men, 1st series)
Marvel Comics: Nov, 1995 - No. 18 (99¢)

1-18: Stories featuring the Original X-Men. 2-vs. the Blob. 5-Vs. the Original Brotherhood of Evil Mutants. 10-Vs. the Avengers 2.50

PROGRAMME, THE
DC Comics (WildStorm): Sept, 2007 - No. 12 ($2.99, limited series)

1,2: 1-Milligan-s/C.P. Smith-a; covers by Smith & Van Sciver 3.00

PROJECT A-KO (Manga)
Malibu Comics: Mar, 1994 - No. 4, June, 1994 ($2.95)

1-4-Based on anime film 3.00

PROJECT A-KO 2 (Manga)
CPM Comics: May, 1995 - No. 3, Aug, 1995 ($2.95, limited series)

1-3 .... 3.00

PROJECT A-KO VERSUS THE UNIVERSE (Manga)
CPM Comics: Oct, 1995 - No. 5, June, 1996 ($2.95, limited series, bi-monthly)

1-5 .... 3.00

PROMETHEA
America's Best Comics: Aug, 1999 - No. 32, Apr, 2005 ($3.50/$2.95)

1-Alan Moore-s/Williams III & Gray-a; Alex Ross painted-c 3.50
1-Variant-c by Williams III & Gray 3.50
2-31-($2.95): 7-Villarrubia photo-a. 10-"Sex, Stars & Serpents". 26-28-Tom Strong app. 27-Cover swipe of Superman vs. Spider-Man treasury ed. ... 3.00
32-($3.95) Final issue; pages can be cut & assembled into a 2-sided poster 4.00
32-Limited edition of 1000; variant issue printed as 2-sided poster, signed by Moore and Williams; each came with a 48 page book of Promethea covers 120.00

Prophet #2 © Liefeld

Prototype #15 © MAL

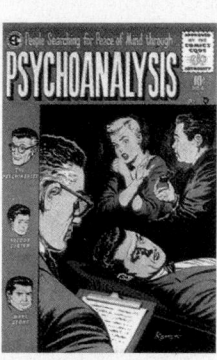

Psychoanalysis #4 © WMG

	GD 2.0	VG 4.0	FN 6.0	VF 8.0	VF/NM 9.0	NM- 9.2

	NM-
Book 1 Hardcover ($24.95, dust jacket) r/#1-6	25.00
Book 1 TPB ($14.95) r/#1-6	15.00
Book 2 Hardcover ($24.95, dust jacket) r/#7-12	25.00
Book 2 TPB ($14.95) r/#7-12	15.00
Book 3 Hardcover ($24.95, dust jacket) r/#13-18	25.00
Book 3 TPB ($14.95) r/#13-18	15.00
Book 4 Hardcover ($24.95, dust jacket) r/#19-25	25.00
Book 4 TPB ($14.99) r/#19-25	15.00
Book 5 Hardcover ($24.95, d.j.) r/#26-32; includes 2-sided poster image from #32	25.00
Book 5 TPB ($14.99) r/#26-32; includes 2-sided poster image from #32	15.00

PROMETHEUS (VILLAINS) (Leads into JLA #16,17)
DC Comics: Feb, 1998 ($1.95, one-shot)

	NM-
1-Origin & 1st app.; Morrison-s/Pearson-c	3.00

PROPELLERMAN
Dark Horse Comics: Jan, 1993 - No. 8, Mar, 1994 ($2.95, limited series)

	NM-
1-8: 2,4,8-Contain 2 trading cards	3.00

PROPHET (See Youngblood #2)
Image Comics (Extreme Studios): Oct, 1993 - No. 10, 1995 ($1.95)

	NM-
1-($2.50)-Liefeld/Panosian-c/a; 1st app. Mary McCormick; Liefeld scripts in 1-4; #1-3 contain coupons for Prophet #0	2.50
1-Gold foil embossed-c edition rationed to dealers	4.00
2-10: 2-Liefeld-c(p). 3-1st app. Judas. 4-1st app. Omen; Black and White Pt. 3 by Thibert. 4-Alternate-c by Stephen Platt. 5,6-Platt-c/a. 7-(9/94, $2.50)-Platt-c/a. 8-Bloodstrike intro. 10-Polybagged w/trading card; Platt-c.	2.50
0-(7/94, $2.50)-San Diego Comic Con ed. (2200 copies)	3.00

PROPHET
Image Comics (Extreme Studios): V2#1, Aug, 1995 - No. 8 ($3.50)

	NM-
V2#1-8: Dixon scripts in all. 1-4-Platt-a. 1-Boris-c; F. Miller variant-c. 4-Newmen app. 5,6-Wraparound-c	3.50
Annual 1 (9/95, $2.50)-Bagged w/Youngblood gaming card; Quesada-c	2.50
Babewatch Special 1 (12/95, $2.50)-Babewatch tie-in	2.50
1995 San Diego Edition-B&W preview of V2#1.	3.00
TPB-(1996, $12.95) r/#1-7	13.00

PROPHET (Volume 3)
Awesome Comics: Mar, 2000 ($2.99)

	NM-
1-Flip-c by Jim Lee and Liefeld	3.00

PROPHET/CABLE
Image Comics (Extreme): Jan, 1997 - No. 2, Mar, 1997 ($3.50, limited series)

	NM-
1,2-Liefeld-c/a: 2-#1 listed on cover	3.50

PROPHET/CHAPEL: SUPER SOLDIERS
Image Comics (Extreme): May, 1996 - No. 2, June, 1996 ($2.50, limited series)

	NM-
1,2: 1-Two covers exist	2.50
1-San Diego Edition; B&W-c	2.50

PROPOSITION PLAYER
DC Comics (Vertigo): Dec, 1999 - No. 6, May, 2000 ($2.50, limited series)

	NM-
1-6-Willingham-s/Guinan-a/Bolton-c	2.50
TPB (2003, $14.95) r/#1-6; intro. by James McManus	15.00

PROTECTORS (Also see The Ferret)
Malibu Comics: Sept, 1992 - No. 20, May, 1994 ($1.95-$2.95)

	NM-
1-20 ($2.50, direct sale)-With poster & diff-c: 1-Origin; has 3/4 outer-c. 3-Polybagged w/Skycap	2.50
1-12 ($1.95, newsstand)-Without poster	2.25

PROTOTYPE (Also see Flood Relief & Ultraforce)
Malibu Comics (Ultraverse): Aug, 1993 - No. 18, Feb, 1995 ($1.95/$2.50)

	NM-
1-Holo-c	6.00
1-Ultra Limited silver foil-c	4.00
1-12,0,14-18: 3-($2.50, 48 pgs.)-Rune flip-c/story by B. Smith (3 pgs.). 4-Intro Wrath. 5-Break-Thru & Strangers x-over. 6-Arena cameo. 7,8-Arena-c/story. 12-(7/94). 0-(8/94, $2.50, 44 pgs.), 14(10/94)	2.50
13 (8/94, $3.50)-Flip book(Ultraverse Premiere #6)	3.50
Giant Size 1 (10/94, $2.50, 44 pgs.)	2.50

PROWLER (Also see Revenge of the...)
Eclipse Comics: July, 1987 - No. 4, Oct, 1987 ($1.75)

	NM-
1-4: Snyder-c/a. 3,4-Origin	2.50

PROWLER, THE
Marvel Comics: Nov, 1994 ($1.75)

	NM-
1-4: 1-Spider-Man app.	2.50

PROWLER IN "WHITE ZOMBIE", THE
Eclipse Comics: Oct, 1988 ($2.00, B&W, Baxter paper)

	NM-
1-Adapts Bela Lugosi movie White Zombie	2.50

PROXIMITY EFFECT
Image Comics (Top Cow): Aug, 2004 ($9.99, graphic novel, one shot)

	NM-
nn-Nakayama-a/Silvestri-c	10.00

PRUDENCE & CAUTION (Also see Dogs of War & Warriors of Plasm)
Defiant: May, 1994 - No. 2, June, 1994 ($3.50/$2.50)(Spanish versions exist)

	NM-
1-($3.50, 52 pgs.)-Chris Claremont scripts in all	3.50
2-($2.50)	2.50

PRYDE AND WISDOM (Also see Excalibur)
Marvel Comics: Sept, 1996 - No. 3, Nov, 1996 ($1.95, limited series)

	NM-
1-3: Warren Ellis scripts; Terry Dodson & Karl Story-c/a	2.50

PSCYTHE (Mark Texeira's ...)
Image Comics: Sept, 2004 - No. 2, Oct, 2004 ($3.95, B&W)

	NM-
1,2-Mark Texeira-s/a; Industry of War back-up by Jordan Raskin	4.00

PSI-FORCE
Marvel Comics Group: Nov, 1986 - No. 32, June, 1989 (75¢/$1.50)

	NM-
1-25: 11-13-Williamson-i	2.50
26-32	2.50
Annual 1 (10/87)	3.00

PSI-JUDGE ANDERSON
Fleetway Publications (Quality): 1989 - No. 15, 1990 ($1.95, B&W)

	NM-
1-15	2.50

PSI-LORDS
Valiant: Sept, 1994 - No. 10, June, 1995 ($2.25)

	NM-
1-($3.50)-Chromium wraparound-c	3.50
1-Gold	5.00
2-10: 3-Chaos Effect Epsilon Pt. 2	2.50

PSYBA-RATS (Also see Showcase '94 #3,4)
DC Comics: Apr, 1995-No. 3, June, 1995 ($2.50, limited series)

	NM-
1-3	2.50

PSYCHO (Magazine) (Also see Nightmare)
Skywald Publ. Corp.: Jan, 1971 - No. 24, Mar, 1975 (68 pgs.; B&W)

	GD 2.0	VG 4.0	FN 6.0	VF 8.0	VF/NM 9.0	NM- 9.2
1-All reprints	8	16	24	54	90	125
2-Origin & 1st app. The Heap, series begins	6	12	18	37	59	80
3-Frankenstein series by Adkins begins	5	10	15	35	55	75
4,7,9,10: 4-7-Squarebound. 4-1st app Out of Chaos/Satan-c/s	5	10	15	30	48	65
8-(Squarebound)1st app. Edward & Mina Sartyros, the Human Gargoyles	6	12	18	35	55	75
11-18: 13-Cannabalism; 3 pgs of Christopher Lee as Dracula photos. 18-Injury to eye-c.	4	8	12	23	36	48
19-Origin Dracula	4	8	12	24	37	50
20-Severed Head-c	4	8	12	28	44	60
21-24: 22-1974 Fall Special; Reese, Wildey-a(r). 24-1975 Winter Special; Dave Sim scripts (1st pro work)	4	8	12	26	41	55
Annual 1 (1972)(68 pgs.) Dracula & the Heap app.	4	8	12	26	41	55
Yearbook (1974-nn)-Everett, Reese-a	4	8	12	22	34	45

NOTE: **Boris** c-3, 5. **Buckler** a-2, 4, 5. **Gene Day** a-21, 23, 24. **Everett** a-3-6. **B. Jones** a-4. **Jeff Jones** a-6, 7, 9; c-12. **Kaluta** a-13. **Katz/Buckler** a-3. **Kim** a-24. **Morrow** a-1. **Reese** a-5. **Dave Sim** s-24. **Sutton** a-3. **Wildey** a-5.

PSYCHO, THE
DC Comics: 1991 - No. 3, 1991 ($4.95, squarebound, limited series)

	NM-
1-3-Hudnall-s/Brereton painted-a/c	5.00
TPB (Image Comics, 2006, $17.99) r/series; Brereton sketch pages; Hudnall afterword	18.00

PSYCHOANALYSIS
E. C. Comics: Mar-Apr, 1955 - No. 4, Sept-Oct, 1955

	GD 2.0	VG 4.0	FN 6.0	VF 8.0	VF/NM 9.0	NM- 9.2
1-All Kamen-c/a; not approved by code	19	38	57	152	241	330
2-4-Kamen-c/a in all	13	26	39	104	162	220

PSYCHOANALYSIS
Gemstone Publishing: Oct, 1999 - No. 4, Jan, 2000 ($2.50)

	NM-
1-4-Reprints E.C. series	2.50
Annual 1 (2000, $10.95) r/#1-4	11.00

PSYCHOBLAST
First Comics: Nov, 1987 - No. 9, July, 1988 ($1.75)

Public Enemies #6 © DS

The Pulse #11 © MAR

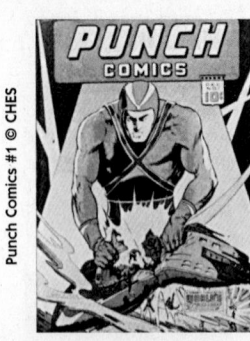

Punch Comics #1 © CHES

	GD 2.0	VG 4.0	FN 6.0	VF 8.0	VF/NM 9.0	NM- 9.2

PSYCHONAUTS
Marvel Comics (Epic Comics): Oct, 1993 - No. 4, Jan, 1994 ($4.95, lim. series)

1-4: American/Japanese co-produced comic						5.00

PSYLOCKE & ARCHANGEL CRIMSON DAWN
Marvel Comics: Aug, 1997 - No. 4, Nov, 1997 ($2.50, limited series)

1-4-Raab-s/Larroca-a(p)						2.50

PTOLUS: CITY BY THE SPIRE
Dabel Brothers Productions/Marvel Comics (Dabel Brothers) #2 on: June, 2006 - No. 6, Mar, 2007 ($2.99)

1-(1st printing, Dabel) Adaptation of the Monte Cook novel; Cook-s						3.00
1-(2nd printing, Marvel), 2-6						3.00
Monte Cooke's Ptolus: City By the Spire TPB (2007, $14.99) r/#1-6						15.00

P.T. 109 (See Movie Comics)

PUBLIC DEFENDER IN ACTION (Formerly Police Trap)
Charlton Comics: No. 7, Mar, 1956 - No. 12, Oct, 1957

	GD	VG	FN	VF	VF/NM	NM-
7	10	20	30	58	79	100
8-12	8	16	24	40	50	60

PUBLIC ENEMIES
D. S. Publishing Co.: 1948 - No. 9, June-July, 1949

	GD	VG	FN	VF	VF/NM	NM-
1-True Crime Stories	26	52	78	152	239	325
2-Used in **SOTI**, pg. 95	22	44	66	128	202	275
3-5: 5-Arrival date of 10/1/48	15	30	45	85	130	175
6,8,9	15	30	45	83	124	165
7-McWilliams-a; injury to eye panel	15	30	45	85	130	175

PUBO
Dark Horse Comics: Dec, 2002 - No. 3, Mar, 2003 ($3.50, B&W, limited series)

1-3-Leland Purvis-s/a						3.50

PUDGY PIG
Charlton Comics: Sept, 1958 - No. 2, Nov, 1958

	GD	VG	FN	VF	VF/NM	NM-
1,2	3	6	9	17	25	32

PUFFED
Image Comics: Jul, 2003 - No. 3, Sept, 2003 ($2.95, B&W)

1-3-Layman-s/Crosland-a. 1-Two covers by Crosland & Quitely						3.00

PULP FANTASTIC (Vertigo V2K)
DC Comics (Vertigo): Feb, 2000 - No. 3, Apr, 2000 ($2.50, limited series)

1-3-Chaykin & Tischman-s/Burchett-a						2.50

PULP FICTION LIBRARY: MYSTERY IN SPACE
DC Comics: 1999 ($19.95, TPB)

nn-Reprints classic sci-fi stories from Mystery in Space, Strange Adventures, Real Fact Comics and My Greatest Adventure						20.00

PULSE, THE (Also see Alias and Deadline)
Marvel Comics: Apr, 2004 - No. 14, May, 2006 ($2.99)

1-14: 1-5-Bendis-s/Bagley-a; Jessica Jones, Ben Urich, Kat Farrell app. 3-5-Green Goblin app. 6,7-Brent Anderson-a 9-Wolverine app. 10-House of M. 11-14-Gaydos-a						3.00
...: House of M Special (9/05, 50¢) tabloid newspaper format; Mayhew- "photos"						2.50
Vol. 1: Thin Air (2004, $13.99) r/#1-5, gallery of cover layouts and sketches						14.00
Vol. 2: Secret War (2005, $11.99) r/#6-9						12.00
Vol. 3: Fear (2006, $14.99) r/#11-14 and New Avengers Annual #1						15.00

PUMA BLUES
Aardvark One International/Mirage Studios #21 on: 1986 - No. 26, 1990 ($1.70-$1.75, B&W)

1-19, 21-26: 1-1st & 2nd printings. 25,26-$1.75-c						2.50
20 ($2.25)-By Alan Moore, Miller, Grell, others						5.00
Trade Paperback (12/88, $14.95)						15.00

PUMPKINHEAD: THE RITES OF EXORCISM (Movie)
Dark Horse Comics: 1993 - No. 2, 1993 ($2.50, limited series)

1,2: Based on movie; painted-c by McManus						2.50

PUNCH & JUDY COMICS
Hillman Per.: 1944; No. 2, Fall, 1944 - V3#2, 12/47; V3#3, 6/51 - V3#9, 12/51

	GD	VG	FN	VF	VF/NM	NM-
V1#1-(60 pgs.)	23	46	69	130	205	280
2	14	28	42	76	108	140
3-12(7/46)	11	22	33	62	86	110
V2#1(8/49),3-9	9	18	27	47	61	75
V2#2,10-12, V3#1-Kirby-a(2) each	21	42	63	122	191	260
V3#2-Kirby-a	18	36	54	107	169	230

PUNCH COMICS
Harry 'A' Chesler: 12/41; #2, 2/42; #9, 7/44 - #19, 10/46; #20, 7/47 - #23, 1/48

	GD	VG	FN	VF	VF/NM	NM-
3-9	8	16	24	44	57	70
1-Mr. E, The Sky Chief, Hale the Magician, Kitty Kelly begin	145	290	435	906	1503	2100
2-Captain Glory app.	90	180	270	563	932	1300
9-Rocketman & Rocket Girl & The Master Key begin	86	172	258	538	894	1250
10-Sky Chief app.; J. Cole-a; Master Key-r/Scoop #3	62	124	186	388	644	900
11-Origin Master Key-r/Scoop #1; Sky Chief, Little Nemo app.; Jack Cole-a; Fine-ish art by Sultan	57	114	171	356	591	825
12-Rocket Boy & Capt. Glory app; classic Skull-c	255	510	765	1594	2647	3700
13-Cover has list of 4 Chesler artists' names on tombstone	62	124	186	388	644	900
14,15,19,21: 21-Hypo needle story	54	108	162	338	557	775
16,17-Gag-c	42	84	126	256	421	585
18-Bondage-c; hypodermic panels	67	134	201	419	697	975
20-Unique cover with bare-breasted women. Rocket Girl-c	103	206	309	644	1072	1500
22,23-Little Nemo-not by McCay. 22-Intro Baxter (teenage)(68 pgs.)	23	46	69	132	209	285

PUNCHY AND THE BLACK CROW
Charlton Comics: No. 10, Oct, 1985 - No. 12, Feb, 1986

10-12: Al Fago funny animal-r; low print run						6.00

PUNISHER (See Amazing Spider-Man #129, Blood and Glory, Born, Captain America #241, Classic Punisher, Daredevil #182-184, 257, Daredevil and the..., Ghost Rider V2#5, 6, Marc Spector #8 & 9, Marvel Preview #2, Marvel Super Action, Marvel Tales, Power Pack #46, Spectacular Spider-Man #81-83, 140, 141, 143 & new Strange Tales #13 & 14)

PUNISHER (The...)
Marvel Comics Group: Jan, 1986 - No. 5, May, 1986 (Limited series)

	GD	VG	FN	VF	VF/NM	NM-
1-Double size	2	4	6	11	16	20
2-5	1	3	4	6	8	10
Trade Paperback (1988)-r/#1-5						11.00
Circle of Blood TPB (8/01, $15.95) Zeck-c						16.00

NOTE: **Zeck** a-1-4; c-1-5.

PUNISHER (The...) (Volume 2)
Marvel Comics: July, 1987 - No. 104, July, 1995

	GD	VG	FN	VF	VF/NM	NM-
1	1	3	4	6	8	10
2-9: 8-Portacio/Williams-c/a begins, ends #18. 9-Scarcer, low dist.						6.00
10-Daredevil app; ties in w/Daredevil #257	1	3	4	6	8	10
11-74,76-85,87-89: 13-18-Kingpin app. 19-Stroman-c/a. 20-Portacio-c(p). 24-1st app. Shadowmasters. 25,50:($1.50,52 pgs.). 25-Shadowmasters app. 57-Photo-c; came w/outer-c (newsstand ed. w/o outer-c). 59-Punisher is severely cut & has skin grafts (has black skin). 60-62-Luke Cage app. 62-Punisher back to white skin. 68-Tarantula-c/story. 85-Prequel to Suicide Run Pt. 0. 87,88-Suicide Run Pt. 6 & 9						2.50
75-($2.75, 52 pgs.)-Embossed silver foil-c						3.00
86-($2.95, 52 pgs.)-Embossed & foil stamped-c; Suicide Run part 3						3.00
90-99: 90-bound-in cards. 99-Cringe app.						2.50
100,104: 100-($2.95, 68 pg.). 104-Last issue						4.00
100-($3.95, 68 pgs.)-Foil cover						5.00
101-103: 102-Bullseye						3.50
"Ashcan" edition (75¢)-Joe Kubert-c						3.00
Annual 1-7 ('88-'94, 68 pgs.) 1-Evolutionary War x-over. 2-Atlantis Attacks x-over; Jim Lee-a(p) (back-up story, 6 pgs.). Moon Knight app. 4-Golden-c(p). 6-Bagged w/card.						3.00
...: A Man Named Frank (1994, $6.95, TPB)						7.00
...and Wolverine in African Saga nn (1989, $5.95, 52 pgs.)-Reprints Punisher War Journal #6 & 7; Jim Lee-c/a(r)						6.00
... Assassin Guild (1988, $6.95, graphic novel)						10.00
Back to School Special 1-3 (11/92-10/94, $2.95, 68 pgs.)						3.00
.../Batman: Deadly Knights (10/94, $4.95)						5.00
.../Black Widow: Spinning Doomsday's Web (1992, $9.95, graphic novel)						12.00
...Bloodlines nn (1991, $5.95, 68 pgs.)						6.00
... Die Hard in the Big Easy nn ('92, $4.95, 52 pgs.)						5.00
...: Empty Quarter nn ('94, $6.95)						7.00
...G-Force nn (1992, $4.95, 52 pgs.)-Painted-c						5.00
...Holiday Special 1-3 (1/93-1/95,, 52 pgs.,68pgs.)-1-Foil-c						3.00
...Intruder Graphic Novel (1989, $14.95, hardcover)						20.00
...Intruder Graphic Novel (1991, $9.95, softcover)						12.00
...Invades the 'Nam: Final Invasion nn (2/94, $6.95)-J. Kubert-c & chapter break art; reprints The 'Nam #84 & unpublished #85,86						7.00
...Kingdom Gone Graphic Novel (1990, $16.95, hardcover)						20.00

Punisher #75 © MAR

Punisher V4 #12 © MAR

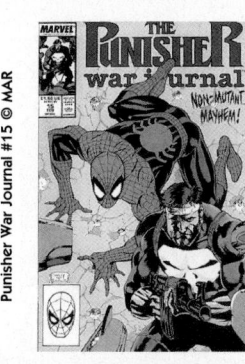

Punisher War Journal #15 © MAR

	GD 2.0	VG 4.0	FN 6.0	VF 8.0	VF/NM 9.0	NM- 9.2		GD 2.0	VG 4.0	FN 6.0	VF 8.0	VF/NM 9.0	NM- 9.2

...Meets Archie (8/94, $3.95, 52 pgs.)-Die cut-c; no ads; same contents as
Archie Meets The Punisher — 5.00
...Movie Special 1 (6/90, $5.95, squarebound, 68 pgs.) painted-c; Brent Anderson-a;
contents intended for a 3 issue series which was advertised but not published — 6.00
...: No Escape nn (1990, $4.95, 52 pgs.)-New-a — 5.00
...Return to Big Nothing Graphic Novel (Epic, 1989, $16.95, hardcover) — 25.00
...Return to Big Nothing Graphic Novel (Marvel, 1989, $12.95, softcover) — 15.00
...The Prize nn (1990, $4.95, 68 pgs.)-New-a — 5.00
Summer Special 1-4(8/91-7/94, 52 pgs.):1-No ads. 2-Bisley-c; Austin-a(i). 3-No ads — 3.00
NOTE: *Austin* c(i)-47, 48. *Cowan* c-39. *Golden* c-50, 85, 86, 100. *Heath* a-26, 27, 89, 90, 91; c-26, 27. *Quesada* c-56p, 62p. *Sienkiewicz* c-Back to School 1.*Stroman* a-76p(9 pgs.). *Williamson* a(i)-25, 60-62i, 64-70, 74, Annual 5; c(i)-62, 65-68.

PUNISHER (Also see Double Edge)
Marvel Comics: Nov, 1995 - No. 18, Apr, 1997 ($2.95/$1.95/$1.50)

1 ($2.95)-Ostrander scripts begin; foil-c. — 3.00
2-18: 7-Vs. S.H.I.E.L.D. 11-"Onslaught." 12-17-X-Cutioner-c/app. 17-Daredevil,
Spider-Man-c/app. — 2.50

PUNISHER (Marvel Knights)
Marvel Comics: Nov, 1998 - No. 4, Feb, 1999 ($2.99, limited series)

1-4: 1-Wrightson-a; Wrightson & Jusko-c — 3.00
1-($6.95) DF Edition; Jae Lee variant-c — 7.00

PUNISHER (Marvel Knights) (Volume 3)
Marvel Comics: Apr, 2000 - No. 12, Mar, 2001 ($2.99, limited series)

1-Ennis-s/Dillon & Palmiotti-a/Bradstreet-c — 5.00
1-Bradstreet white variant-c — 10.00
1-($6.95) DF Edition; Jurgens & Ordway variant-c — 7.00
2-Two covers by Bradstreet & Dillon — 3.00
3-($3.99) Bagged with Marvel Knights Genesis Edition; Daredevil app. — 4.00
4-12: 9-11-The Russian app. — 3.00
HC (6/02, $34.95) r/#1-12, Punisher Kills the Marvel Universe, and Marvel Knights
Double Shot #1 — 35.00
.../Painkiller Jane (1/01, $3.50) Jusko-c; Ennis-s/Jusko and Dave Ross-a(p) — 3.50
...: Welcome Back Frank TPB (4/01, $19.95) r/#1-12 — 20.00

PUNISHER (Marvel Knights) (Volume 4)
Marvel Comics: Aug, 2001 - No. 37, Feb, 2004 ($2.99)

1-Ennis-s/Dillon & Palmiotti-a/Bradstreet-c; The Russian app. — 4.00
2-Two covers (Dillon & Bradstreet) Spider-Man-c/app. — 3.00
3-37: 3-7-Ennis-s/Dillon-a. 9-12-Peyer-s/Gutierrez-a. 13,14-Ennis-s/Dilllon-a.
16,17-Wolverine app.; Robertson-a. 18-23,32-Dillon-a. 24-27-Mandrake-a. 27-Elektra app.
33-37-Spider-Man, Daredevil, & Wolverine app. 36,37-Hulk app. — 3.00
...Army of One TPB (2/02, $15.95) r/#1-7; Bradstreet-c — 16.00
Vol. 2 HC (2003, $29.95) r/#1-7,13-18; intro. by Mike Millar — 30.00
Vol. 3 HC (2004, $29.95) r/#19-27; script pages for #19 — 30.00
Vol. 3: Business as Usual TPB (2003, $14.99) r/#13-18; Bradstreet-c — 15.00
Vol. 4: Full Auto TPB (2003, $17.99) r/#20-26; Bradstreet-c — 18.00
Vol. 5: Streets of Laredo TPB (2003, $17.99) r/#19,27-32 — 18.00
Vol. 6: Confederacy of Dunces TPB (2004, $13.99) r/#33-37 — 14.00

PUNISHER (Marvel MAX)
Marvel Comics: Mar, 2004 - Present ($2.99)

1-49: 1-Ennis-s/LaRosa-a/Bradstreet-c; flashback to his family's murder; Micro app.
6-Micro killed. 7-12,19-25-Fernandez-a. 13-18-Braithwaite-a. 31-36-Barracuda.
43-49-Medina-a. — 3.00
50-($3.99) Barracuda returns; Chaykin-a — 4.00
Annual (11/07, $3.99) Mike Benson-s/Laurence Campbell-a — 4.00
...: Bloody Valentine (4/06, $3.99) Palmiotti & Gray-s/Gulacy & Palmiotti-a; Gulacy-c — 4.00
...: Red X-Mas (2/05, $3.99) Palmiotti & Gray-s/Texeira & Palmiotti-a; Texeira-c — 4.00
...: Silent Night (2/06, $3.99) Diggle-s/Hotz-a/Deodato-c — 4.00
...: The Cell (7/05, $4.99) Ennis-s/LaRosa-a/Bradstreet-c — 5.00
...: The Tyger (2/06, $4.99) Ennis-s/Severin-a/Bradstreet-c; Castle's childhood — 5.00
...: Very Special Holidays TPB ('06, $12.99) r/Red X-Mas, Bloody Valentine and Silent Night — 13.00
...: X-Mas Special (1/07, $3.99) Stuart Moore-s/CP Smith-a — 4.00
... MAX: From First to Last HC (2006, $19.99) r/The Tyger, The Cell and The End 1-shots — 20.00
... MAX Vol. 1 (2005, $29.99) oversized r/#1-12; gallery of Fernandez art from #7 shown from
layout to colored pages — 30.00
... MAX Vol. 2 (2006, $29.99) oversized r/#13-24; gallery of Fernandez pencil art — 30.00
... MAX Vol. 3 (2007, $29.99) oversized r/#25-36; gallery of Fernandez and Parlov art — 30.00
Vol. 1: In the Beginning TPB (2004, $14.99) r/#1-6 — 15.00
Vol. 2: Kitchen Irish TPB (2004, $14.99) r/#7-12 — 15.00
Vol. 3: Mother Russia TPB (2005, $14.99) r/#13-18 — 15.00
Vol. 4: Up is Down and Black is White TPB (2005, $14.99) r/#19-24 — 15.00
Vol. 5: The Slavers TPB (2006, $15.99) r/#25-30; Fernandez pencil pages — 16.00

Vol. 6: Barracuda TPB (2006, $15.99) r/#31-36; Parlov sketch page — 16.00
Vol. 7: Man of Stone TPB (2007, $15.99) r/#37-42 — 16.00
Vol. 8: Widowmaker TPB (2007, $17.99) r/#43-49 — 18.00

PUNISHER AND WOLVERINE: DAMAGING EVIDENCE (See Wolverine and...)

PUNISHER ARMORY, THE
Marvel Comics: 7/90 ($1.50); No. 2, 6/91; No. 3, 4/92 - 10/94($1.75/$2.00)

1-10: 1-r/weapons pgs. from War Journal. 1,2-Jim Lee-c. 3-10- All new material.
3-Jusko painted-c — 2.50

PUNISHER KILLS THE MARVEL UNIVERSE
Marvel Comics: Nov, 1995 ($5.95, one-shot)

1-Garth Ennis script/Doug Braithwaite-a — 7.00
1-2nd printing (3/00) Steve Dillon-c — 6.00

PUNISHER MAGAZINE, THE
Marvel Comics: Oct, 1989 - No. 16, Nov, 1990 ($2.25, B&W, Magazine, 52 pgs.)

1-16: 1-r/Punisher #1('86). 2,3-r/Punisher 2-5. 4-16: 4-7-r/Punisher V2#1-8. 8-Chiodo-c.
8-r/Punisher #10 & Daredevil #257; Portacio & Lee-c. 14-r/Punisher War Journal #1,2
w/new Lee-c. 16-r/Punisher W. J. #3,8 — 3.00
NOTE: *Chiodo* painted c-4, 7, 16. *Jusko* painted c-6, 8. *Jim Lee* r-8, 14-16; c-14. *Portacio/Williams* r-7-12.

PUNISHER: OFFICIAL MOVIE ADAPTATION
Marvel Comics: May, 2004 - No. 3, May, 2004 ($2.99, limited series)

1-3-Photo-c of Thomas Jane; Milligan-s/Olliffe-a — 3.00

PUNISHER: ORIGIN OF MICRO CHIP, THE
Marvel Comics: July, 1993 - No. 2, Aug, 1993 ($1.75, limited series)

1,2 — 2.50

PUNISHER: P.O.V.
Marvel Comics: 1991 - No. 4, 1991 ($4.95, painted, limited series, 52 pgs.)

1-4: Starlin scripts & Wrightson painted-c/a in all. 2-Nick Fury app. — 5.00

PUNISHER PRESENTS: BARRACUDA MAX
Marvel Comics (MAX): Apr, 2007 - No. 5, Aug, 2007 ($3.99, limited series)

1-5-Ennis-s/Parlov-a — 4.00
SC (2007, $17.99) r/series; sketch pages — 18.00

PUNISHER: THE END
Marvel Comics: June, 2004 ($4.50, one-shot)

1-Ennis-s/Corben-a/c — 4.50

PUNISHER: THE GHOSTS OF INNOCENTS
Marvel Comics: Jan, 1993 - No. 2, Jan, 1993 ($5.95, 52 pgs.)

1,2-Starlin scripts — 6.00

PUNISHER: THE MOVIE
Marvel Comics: 2004 ($12.99,TPB)

nn-Reprints Amazing Spider-Man #129; Official Movie Adaptation and Punisher V3 #1 — 13.00

PUNISHER 2099 (See Punisher War Journal #50)
Marvel Comics: Feb, 1993 - No. 34, Nov, 1995 ($1.25/$1.50/$1.95)

1-24,26-34: 1-Foil stamped-c. 1-Second printing. 13-Spider-Man 2099 x-over; Ron Lim-c(p).
16-bound-in card sheet — 2.50
25 ($2.95, 52 pgs.)-Deluxe edition; embossed foil-cover — 3.00
25 ($2.25, 52 pgs.) — 2.50
(Marvel Knights) #1 (11/04, $2.99) Kirkman-s/Mhan/Pat Lee-c — 3.00

PUNISHER VS. BULLSEYE
Marvel Comics: Jan, 2006 - No. 5, May, 2006 ($2.99, limited series)

1-5-Daniel Way-s/Steve Dillon-a — 4.00
TPB (2006, $13.99) r/#1-5; cover sketch pages — 14.00

PUNISHER VS. DAREDEVIL
Marvel Comics: Jun, 2000 ($3.50, one-shot)

1-Reprints Daredevil #183,#184 & #257 — 3.50

PUNISHER WAR JOURNAL, THE
Marvel Comics: Nov, 1988 - No. 80, July, 1995 ($1.50/$1.75/$1.95)

1-Origin The Punisher; Matt Murdock cameo; Jim Lee inks begin — 5.00
2-7: 2,3-Daredevil x-over; Jim Lee-c(i). 4-Jim Lee c/a begins. 6-Two part Wolverine story
begins. 7-Wolverine-c, story ends — 4.00
8-49,51-60,62,63,65: 13-16,20-22: No Jim Lee-a. 13-Lee-c only. 13-15-Heath-i.
14,15-Spider-Man x-over. 19-Last Jim Lee-c/a.29,30-Ghost Rider app. 31-Andy & Joe
Kubert art. 36-Photo-c. 47,48-Nomad/Daredevil-c/stories; see Nomad. 57,58-Daredevil &
Ghost Rider-c/stories. 62,63-Suicide Run Pt. 4 & 7. — 3.00
50,61,64($2.95, 52 pgs.): 50-Preview of Punisher 2099 (1st app.); embossed-c. 61-Embossed
foil cover; Suicide Run Pt. 1. 64-Die-cut-c; Suicide Run Pt. 10 — 3.00

Punisher War Journal ('07) #5 © MAR

Purgatori #6 © Chaos!

PvP #2 © Scott R. Kurtz

	GD 2.0	VG 4.0	FN 6.0	VF 8.0	VF/NM 9.0	NM- 9.2

	GD 2.0	VG 4.0	FN 6.0	VF 8.0	VF/NM 9.0	NM- 9.2

64-($2.25, 52 pgs.)-Regular cover edition   2.50
66-74,76-80: 66-Bound-in card sheet   2.50
75 ($2.50, 52 pgs.)   2.75
NOTE: *Golden* c-25-30, 40, 61, 62. *Jusko* painted c-31, 32. *Jim Lee* a-1i-3i, 4p-13p, 17p-19p; c-2i, 3i, 4p-15p, 17p, 18p, 19p. Painted c-40.

PUNISHER WAR JOURNAL (Frank Castle back in the regular Marvel Universe)
Marvel Comics: Jan, 2007 - Present ($2.99)

1-Civil War tie-in; Spider-Man app; Fraction-s/Olivetti-a   5.00
1-B&W edition (11/06)   5.00
2-5: 2,3-Civil War tie-in. 4-Deodato-a   4.00
6-11: 6-10-Punisher dons Captain America-*esque* outfit. 7-Two covers. 11-Winter Soldier app.
... Vol. 1: Civil War HC (2007, $19.99) r/#1-4 and #1 B&W edition; Olivetti sketch pages   20.00
... Vol. 1: Civil War SC (2007, $14.99) r/#1-4 and #1 B&W edition; Olivetti sketch pages   15.00

PUNISHER: WAR ZONE, THE
Marvel Comics: Mar, 1992 - No. 41, July, 1995 ($1.75/$1.95)

1-($2.25, 40 pgs.)-Die cut-c; Romita, Jr.-c/a begins   3.00
2-22,24,26,27-41: 8-Last Romita, Jr.-c/a. 19-Wolverine app. 24-Suicide Run Pt. 5.
   27-Bound-in card sheet. 31-36-Joe Kubert-a   2.50
23-($2.95, 52 pgs.)-Embossed foil-c; Suicide Run part 2; Buscema-a(part)   3.00
25-($2.25, 52 pgs.)-Suicide Run part 8; painted-c   2.50
Annual 1,2 ('93, 94, $2.95, 68 pgs.)-1-Bagged w/card; John Buscema-a   3.00
...: River Of Blood TPB (2006, $15.99) r/#31-36; Joe Kubert-a   16.00
NOTE: *Golden* c-23. *Romita, Jr.* c/a-1-8.

PUNISHER: YEAR ONE
Marvel Comics: Dec, 1994 - No. 4, Apr, 1995 ($2.50, limited series)

1-4   2.50

PUNX
Acclaim (Valiant): Nov, 1995 - No. 3, Jan, 1996 ($2.50, unfinished lim. series)

1-3: Giffen story & art in all. 2-Satirizes Scott McCloud's Understanding Comics   2.50
(Manga) Special 1 (3/96, $2.50)-Giffen scripts   2.50

PUPPET COMICS
George W. Dougherty Co.: Spring, 1946 - No. 2, Summer, 1946

1-Funny animal in both	14	28	42	76	108	140
2	11	22	33	60	83	105

PUPPETOONS (See George Pal's...)

PUREHEART (See Archie as...)

PURGATORI
Chaos! Comics: Prelude #-1, 5/96 ($1.50, 16 pgs.); 1996 - No. 3 Dec, 1996 ($3.50/$2.95, limited series)

Prelude #-1-Pulido story; Balent-c/a; contains sketches & interviews   2.25
0-(2/01, $2.99) Prelude to "Love Bites"; Rio-c/a   3.00
1/2 (12/00, $2.95) Al Rio-c/a   3.00
1-($3.50)-Wraparound cover; red foil embossed-c; Jim Balent-a   5.00
1-($19.95)-Premium Edition (1000 print run)   20.00
2-($3.00)-Wraparound-c   3.00
2-Variant-c   5.00
...: Heartbreaker 1 (3/02, $2.99) Jolley-s   3.00
...: Love Bites 1 (3/01, $2.99) Turnbull-a/Kaminski-s   3.00
...: Mischief Night 1 (11/01, $2.99)   3.00
...: Re-Imagined 1 (7/02, $2.99) Jolley-s/Neves-a   3.00
...The Dracula Gambit-($2.95)   3.00
...The Dracula Gambit Sketchbook-($2.95)   3.00
...The Vampire's Myth 1 ($19.95) Premium Ed. (10,000)   20.00
...Vs. Chastity (7/00, $2.95) Two versions (Alpha and Omega) with different endings; Rio-a   3.00
...Vs. Lady Death (1/01, $2.95) Kaminski-s   3.00
...Vs. Vampirella (4/00, $2.95) Zanier-a; Chastity app.   3.00

PURGATORI
Chaos! Comics: Oct, 1998 - No. 7, Apr, 1999 ($2.95)

1-7-Quinn-s/Rio-c/a. 2-Lady Death-c   3.00

PURGATORI: DARKEST HOUR
Chaos! Comics: Sept, 2001 - No. 2, Oct, 2001 ($2.99, limited series)

1,2   3.00

PURGATORI: EMPIRE
Chaos! Comics: May, 2000 - No. 3, July, 2000 ($2.95, limited series)

1-3-Cleavenger-c   3.00

PURGATORI: GODDESS RISING
Chaos! Comics: July, 1999 - No. 4, Oct, 1999 ($2.95, limited series)

1-4-Deodato-c/a   3.00

PURGATORI: GOD HUNTER
Chaos! Comics: Apr, 2002 - No. 2, May, 2002 ($2.99, limited series)

1,2-Molenaar-a/Jolley-s   3.00

PURGATORI: GOD KILLER
Chaos! Comics: Jun, 2002 - No. 2, July, 2002 ($2.99, limited series)

1,2-Molenaar-a/Jolley-s   3.00

PURGATORI: THE HUNTED
Chaos! Comics: Jun, 2001 - No. 2, Aug, 2001 ($2.99, limited series)

1,2   3.00

PURPLE CLAW, THE (Also see Tales of Horror)
Minoan Publishing Co./Toby Press: Jan, 1953 - No. 3, May, 1953

1-Origin; horror/weird stories in all	32	64	96	186	293	400
2,3: 1-3 r-in Tales of Horror #9-11	23	46	69	132	209	285
I.W. Reprint #8-Reprints #1	3	6	9	16	23	30

PUSSYCAT (Magazine)
Marvel Comics Group: Oct, 1968 (B&W reprints from Men's magazines)

1-(Scarce)-Ward, Everett, Wood-a; Everett-c	17	34	51	128	227	325

PUZZLE FUN COMICS (Also see Jingle Jangle)
George W. Dougherty Co.: Spring, 1946 - No. 2, Summer, 1946 (52 pgs.)

1-Gustavson-a	23	46	69	130	205	280
2	15	30	45	88	137	185

NOTE: #1 & 2('46) each contain a *George Carlson* cover plus a 6 pg. story "Alec in Fumbleland"; also many puzzles in each.

PvP (Player vs. Player)
Image Comics: Mar, 2003 - Present ($2.95/$2.99, B&W, reads sideways)

1-34-Scott Kurtz-s/a. 1,16-Frank Cho-c. 11-Savage Dragon-c/app. 14-Invincible app.
   19-Jonathan Luna-c. 25-Cho-a (2 pgs.)   3.00
#0 (7/05, 50¢) Secret Origin of Skull   2.25
...: At Large TPB (7/04, $11.95) r/#1-6   12.00
... Vol. 2: Reloaded TPB (12/04, $11.95) r/#7-12   12.00
... Vol. 3: Rides Again TPB (2005, $11.99) r/#13-18   12.00
... Vol. 4: PVP Goes Bananas TPB (2007, $12.99) r/#19-24   13.00
...: The Dork Ages TPB (2/04, $11.95) r/#1-6 from Dork Storm Press   12.00

QUACK!
Star Reach Productions: July, 1976 - No. 6, 1977? ($1.25, B&W)

1-Brunner-c/a on Duckaneer (Howard the Duck clone); Dave Stevens, Gilbert, Shaw-a		2	4	6	8	10	12
1-2nd printing (10/76)						4.00

2-6: 2-Newton the Rabbit Wonder by Aragonés/Leialoha; Gilbert, Shaw-a; Leialoha-c.
   3-The Beavers by Dave Sim begin, end #5; Gilbert, Shaw-a; Sim/Leialoha-c. 6-Brunner-a

(Duckeneer); Gilbert-a	1	2	3	5	6	8

QUADRANT
Quadrant Publications: 1983 - No. 8, 1986 (B&W, nudity, adults)

1-Peter Hsu-c/a in all	2	4	6	8	11	14
2-8	1	2	3	5	6	8

QUANTUM & WOODY
Acclaim Comics: June, 1997 - No. 17, No. 32 (9/99), No. 18 - No. 21, Feb, 2000 ($2.50)

1-17: 1st app.; two covers. 6-Copycat-c. 9-Troublemakers app.   2.50
32-(9/99); 18-(10/99),19-21   2.50
The Director's Cut TPB ('97, $7.95) r/#1-4 plus extra pages   8.00

QUANTUM LEAP (TV) (See A Nightmare on Elm Street)
Innovation Publishing: Sept, 1991 - No. 12, Jun, 1993 ($2.50, painted-c)

1-12: Based on TV show; all have painted-c. 8-Has photo gallery   3.00
Special Edition 1 (10/92)-r/#1 w/8 extra pgs. of photos & articles   3.00
Time and Space Special 1 (#13) ($2.95)-Foil logo   3.00

QUANTUM TUNNELER, THE
Revolution Studio: Oct, 2001 (no cover price, one-shot)

1-Prequel to "The One" movie; Clayton Henry-a   2.50

QUASAR (See Avengers #302, Captain America #217, Incredible Hulk #234, Marvel Team-Up #113 & Marvel Two-in-One #53)
Marvel Comics: Oct, 1989 - No. 60, Jul, 1994 ($1.00/$1.25, Direct sales #17 on)

1-Origin; formerly Marvel Boy/Marvel Man   3.00
2-49,51-60: 3-Human Torch app. 6-Venom cameo (2 pgs.). 7-Cosmic Spidey. 11-Excalibur
   x-over. 14-McFarlane-c. 16-($1.50, 52 pgs.). 17-Flash parody (Buried Alien). 20-Fantastic
   Four app. 23-Ghost Rider x-over. 25-($1.50, 52 pgs.)-New costume Quasar. 26-Infinity

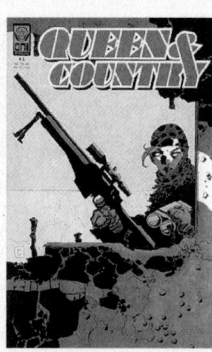

Queen & Country #1 © Greg Rucka

Quick Draw McGraw #1 © H-B

Quicksilver #5 © MAR

	GD	VG	FN	VF	VF/NM	NM-		GD	VG	FN	VF	VF/NM	NM-
	2.0	4.0	6.0	8.0	9.0	9.2		2.0	4.0	6.0	8.0	9.0	9.2

Gauntlet x-over; Thanos-c/story. 27-Infinity Gauntlet x-over. 30-Thanos cameo in flashback; last $1.00-c. 31-Begin $1.25-c; D.P. 7 guest stars. 38-40-Infinity War x-overs. 38-Battles Warlock. 39-Thanos-c & cameo. 40-Thanos app. 42-Punisher-c/story.

53-Warlock & Moondragon app. 58-w/bound-in card sheet						2.50
50-($2.95, 52 pgs.)-Holo-grafx foil-c; Silver Surfer, Man-Thing, Ren & Stimpy app.						3.00
Special #1-3 ($1.25, newsstand)-Same as #32-34						2.50

QUEEN & COUNTRY (See Whiteout)
Oni Press: Mar, 2001 - No. 32, Aug, 2007 ($2.95/$2.99, B&W)

1-Rucka-s in all. Rolston-a/Sale-c	1	2	3	4	5	7
2-5: 2-4-Rolston-a/Sale-c. 5-Snyder-c/Hurtt-a						4.00
6-24,26-32: 6,7-Snyder-c/Hurtt-a. 13-15-Alexander-a. 16-20-McNeil-a. 21-24-Hawthorne-a						
26-28-Norton-a						3.00
25-($5.99) Rolston-a						6.00
Free Comic Book Day giveaway (5/02) r/#1 with "Free Comic Book Day" banner on-c						2.25
Operation: Blackwall (10/03, $8.95, TPB) r/#13-15; John Rogers intro.						9.00
Operation: Broken Ground (2002, $11.95, TPB) r/#1-4; Ellis intro.						12.00
Operation: Crystal Ball (1/03, $14.95, TPB) r/#8-12; Judd Winick intro.						15.00
Operation: Dandelion HC (8/04, $25.00) r/#21-24; Jamie S. Rich intro.						25.00
Operation: Dandelion (8/04, $11.95, TPB) r/#21-24; Jamie S. Rich intro.						12.00
Operation: Morningstar (9/02, $8.95, TPB) r/#5-7; Stuart Moore intro.						9.00
Operation: Storm Front (3/04, $14.95, TPB) r/#16-20; Geoff Johns intro.						15.00

QUEEN & COUNTRY: DECLASSIFIED
Oni Press: Nov, 2002 - No. 3, Jan, 2003 ($2.95, B&W, limited series)

1-3-Rucka-s/Hurtt-a/Morse-c						3.00
TPB (7/03, $8.95) r/#1-3; intro. by Micah Wright						9.00

QUEEN & COUNTRY: DECLASSIFIED (Volume 2)
Oni Press: Jan, 2005 - No. 3, Feb, 2006 ($2.95/$2.99, B&W, limited series)

1-3-Rucka-s/Burchett-a/c						3.00
TPB (3/06, $8.95) r/#1-3						9.00

QUEEN & COUNTRY: DECLASSIFIED (Volume 3)
Oni Press: Jun, 2005 - No. 3, Aug, 2005 ($2.95, B&W, limited series)

1-3- "Sons & Daughters;" Johnston-s/Mitten-a/c						3.00
TPB (3/06, $8.95) r/#1-3						9.00

QUEEN OF THE WEST, DALE EVANS (TV)(See Dale Evans Comics, Roy Rogers & Western Roundup under Dell Giants)
Dell Publ. Co.: No. 479, 7/53 - No. 22, 1-3/59 (All photo-c; photo back c-4-8,15)

Four Color 479(#1, '53)	19	38	57	141	251	360
Four Color 528(#2, '54)	10	20	30	70	123	175
3,4: 3(4-6/54)-Toth-a. 4-Toth, Manning-a	8	16	24	54	90	125
5-10-Manning-a. 5-Marsh-a	7	14	21	47	76	105
11,19,21-No Manning 21-Tufts-a	5	10	15	35	55	75
12-18,20,22-Manning-a	6	12	18	39	62	85

QUENTIN DURWARD
Dell Publishing Co.: No. 672, Jan, 1956

Four Color 672-Movie, photo-c	7	14	21	45	73	100

QUESTAR ILLUSTRATED SCIENCE FICTION CLASSICS
Golden Press: 1977 (224 pgs.) ($1.95)

11197-Stories by Asimov, Sturgeon, Silverberg & Niven; Starstream-r						
	3	6	9	19	29	38

QUEST FOR CAMELOT
DC Comics: July, 1998 ($4.95)

1-Movie adaption						5.00

QUEST FOR DREAMS LOST (Also see Word Warriors)
Literacy Volunteers of Chicago: July 4, 1987 ($2.00, B&W, 52 pgs.)(Proceeds donated to help fight illiteracy)

1-Teenage Mutant Ninja Turtles by Eastman/Laird, Trollords, Silent Invasion, The Realm, Wordsmith, Reacto Man, Eb'nn, Aniverse						2.50

QUESTION, THE (See Americomics, Blue Beetle (1967), Charlton Bullseye & Mysterious Suspense)
QUESTION, THE (Also see Showcase '95 #3)
DC Comics: Feb, 1987 - No. 36, Mar, 1990 ($1.50)

1-36: Denny O'Neil scripts in all						2.50
Annual 1 (1988, $2.50)						2.50
Annual 2 (1989, $3.50)						3.50

QUESTION, THE
DC Comics: Jan, 2005 - No. 6, Jun, 2005 ($2.95, limited series)

1-6-Rick Veitch-s/Tommy Lee Edwards-a. 4,6-Superman app.						3.00

QUESTION QUARTERLY, THE
DC Comics: Summer, 1990 - No. 5, Spring, 1992 ($2.50, 52pgs.)

1-5						2.50
NOTE: *Cowan* a-1, 2, 4, 5; c-1-3, 5. *Mignola* a-5i. *Quesada* a-3-5.						

QUESTION RETURNS, THE
DC Comics: Feb, 1997 ($3.50, one-shot)

1-Brereton-c						3.50

QUESTPROBE
Marvel Comics: 8/84; No. 2, 1/85; No. 3, 11/85 (lim. series)

1-3: 1-The Hulk app. by Romita. 2-Spider-Man; Mooney-a(i). 3-Human Torch & Thing						3.00

QUICK DRAW McGRAW (TV) (Hanna-Barbera)(See Whitman Comic Books)
Dell Publishing Co./Gold Key No. 12 on: No. 1040, 12-2/59-60 - No. 11, 7-9/62; No. 12, 11/62; No. 13, 2/63; No. 14, 4/63; No. 15, 6/69 (1st show aired 9/29/59)

Four Color 1040(#1) 1st app. Quick Draw & Baba Looey, Augie Doggie & Doggie Daddy and Snooper & Blabber	13	26	39	95	168	240
2(4-6/60)-4,6: 2-Augie Doggie & Snooper & Blabber stories (8 pgs. each); pre-dates both of their #1 issues. 4-Augie Doggie & Snooper & Blabber stories.						
	6	12	18	41	66	90
5-1st Snagglepuss app.; last 10¢ issue	7	14	21	45	73	100
7-11	5	10	15	32	51	70
12,13-Title change to ...Fun-Type Roundup (84pgs.)	7	14	21	45	73	100
14,15: 15-Reprints	4	8	12	28	44	60

QUICK DRAW McGRAW (TV)(See Spotlight #2)
Charlton Comics: Nov, 1970 - No. 8, Jan, 1972 (Hanna-Barbera)

1.	5	10	15	32	51	70
2-8	3	6	9	19	29	38

QUICKSILVER (See Avengers)
Marvel Comics: Nov, 1997 - No. 13, Nov, 1998 ($2.99/$1.99)

1-($2.99)-Peyer-s/Casey Jones-a; wraparound-c						3.00
2-11: 2-Two covers-variant by Golden. 4-6-Inhumans app.						2.50
12-($2.99) Siege of Wundagore pt. 4						3.00
13-Magneto-c/app.; last issue						2.50

QUICK-TRIGGER WESTERN (...Action #12; Cowboy Action #5-11)
Atlas Comics (ACI #12/WPI #13-19): No. 12, May, 1956 - No. 19, Sept, 1957

12-Baker-a	15	30	45	90	140	190
13-Williamson-a, 5 pgs.	15	30	45	84	127	170
14-Everett, Crandall, Torres-a; Heath-c	14	28	42	81	118	155
15,16: 15-Torres, Crandall-a. 16-Orlando, Kirby-a	12	24	36	69	97	125
17,18: 18-Baker-a	12	24	36	67	94	120
19	10	20	30	54	72	90
NOTE: *Ayers* a-17. *Colan* a-16. *Maneely* a-15, 17; c-15, 18. *Morrow* a-18. *Powell* a-14. *Severin* a-19; c-12, 13, 16, 17, 19. *Shores* a-16. *Tuska* a-17.						

QUINCY (See Comics Reading Libraries in the Promotional Comics section)

QUITTER, THE
DC Comics (Vertigo): 2005 ($19.99, B&W graphic novel)

HC ($19.99) Autobiography of Harvey Pekar; Pekar-s/Daen Haspiel-a						20.00
SC (2006, $12.99)						13.00

RACCOON KIDS, THE (Formerly Movietown Animal Antics)
National Periodical Publications (Arleigh No. 63,64): No. 52, Sept-Oct, 1954 - No. 62, Oct-Nov, 1956; No. 63, Sept, 1957; No. 64, Nov, 1957

52-Doodles Duck by Mayer	15	30	45	83	124	165
53-64: 53-62-Doodles Duck by Mayer	11	22	33	62	86	110
NOTE: *Otto Feuer*-a most issues. *Rube Grossman*-a most issues.						

RACE FOR THE MOON
Harvey Publications: Mar, 1958 - No. 3, Nov, 1958

1-Powell-a(5); 1/2-pg. S&K-a; cover redrawn from Galaxy Science Fiction pulp (5/53)						
	15	30	45	88	137	185
2-Kirby/Williamson-c(r)/a(3); Kirby-p 7 more stys	26	52	78	152	239	325
3-Kirby/Williamson-c/a(4); Kirby-p 6 more stys	28	56	84	162	256	350

RACE OF SCORPIONS
Dark Horse Comics: 1990 - No. 2, 1990 ($4.50/$4.95, 52pgs.)

1,2: 1-1st/stories from Dark Horse Presents #23-27. 2-($4.95-c)						5.00

RACER-X
Now Comics: 8/88 - No. 11, 8/89; V2#1, 9/89 - V2#10, 1990 ($1.75)

0-Deluxe ($3.50)						3.50
1 (9/88) - 11, V2#1-10						2.50

RACER X (See Speed Racer)

Racket Squad in Action #5 © CC

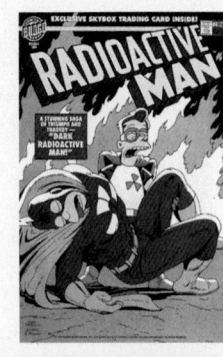

Radioactive Man #412 © Bongo

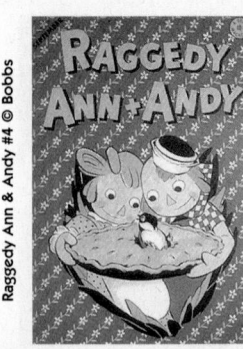

Raggedy Ann & Andy #4 © Bobbs

	GD 2.0	VG 4.0	FN 6.0	VF 8.0	VF/NM 9.0	NM- 9.2		GD 2.0	VG 4.0	FN 6.0	VF 8.0	VF/NM 9.0	NM- 9.2

DC Comics (WildStorm): Oct, 2000 - No. 3, Dec, 2000 ($2.95, limited series)
1-3: 1-Tommy Yune-s/Jo Chen-a; 2 covers by Yune. 2,3-Kabala app. — 3.50

RACING PETTYS
STP Corp.: 1980 ($2.50, 68 pgs., 10 1/8" x 13 1/4")
1-Bob Kane-a. Kane bio on inside back-c. — 10.00

RACK & PAIN
Dark Horse Comics: Mar, 1994 - No. 4, June, 1994 ($2.50, limited series)
1-4: Brian Pulido scripts in all. 1-Greg Capullo-c — 3.00

RACK & PAIN: KILLERS
Chaos! Comics: Sept, 1996 - No. 4, Jan, 1997 ($2.95, limited series)
1-4: Reprints Dark Horse series; Jae Lee-c — 3.00

RACKET SQUAD IN ACTION
Capitol Stories/Charlton Comics: May-June, 1952 - No. 29, Mar, 1958

	GD	VG	FN	VF	VF/NM	NM-
1	28	56	84	162	256	350
2-4,6: 3,4,6-Dr. Neff, Ghost Breaker app.	15	30	45	84	127	170
5-Dr. Neff, Ghost Breaker app; headlights-c	21	42	63	124	195	265
7-10: 10-Explosion-c	14	28	42	80	115	150
11-Ditko-c/a	30	60	90	174	275	375
12-Ditko explosion-c (classic); Shuster-a(2)	52	104	156	317	521	725
13-Shuster-c(p)/a.	12	24	36	69	97	125
14-Marijuana story "Shakedown"; Giordano-a	14	28	42	82	121	160
15-28: 15,20,22,23-Giordano-c	11	22	33	60	83	105
29-(15¢, 68 pgs.)	14	28	42	76	108	140

RADIANT LOVE (Formerly Daring Love #1)
Gilmor Magazines: No. 2, Dec, 1953 - No. 6, Aug, 1954

	GD	VG	FN	VF	VF/NM	NM-
2	11	22	33	62	86	110
3-6	8	16	24	40	50	60

RADICAL DREAMER
Blackball Comics: No. 0, May, 1994 - No. 4, Nov, 1994 ($1.99, bi-monthly)
(1st poster format comic)
0-4: 0-($1.99, poster format): 0-1st app. Max Wrighter. 3,4-($2.50-c) — 3.00

RADICAL DREAMER
Mark's Giant Economy Size Comics: V2#1, June, 1995 - V2#6, Feb, 1996 ($2.95, B&W, limited series)
V2#1-6 — 3.00
Prime (5/96, $2.95) — 3.00
Dreams Cannot Die!-(1996, $20.00, softcover)-Collects V1#0-4 & V2#1-6; intro by Kurt Busiek; afterward by Mark Waid — 20.00
Dreams Cannot Die!-(1996, $60.00, hardcover)-Signed & limited edition; collects V1#0-4 & V2#1-6; intro by Kurt Busiek; afterward by Mark Waid — 60.00

RADIOACTIVE MAN (Simpsons TV show)
Bongo Comics: 1993 - No. 6, 1994 ($1.95/$2.25, limited series)
1-($2.95)-Glow-in-the-dark-c; bound-in jumbo poster; origin Radioactive Man; (cover dated Nov. 1952) — 5.00
2-6: 2-Says #88 on-c & inside & dated May 1962; cover parody of Atlas Kirby monster-c; Superior Squad app. origin Fallout Boy. 3-($1.95)-Cover "dated" Aug 1972 #216.
4-($2.25)-Cover "dated" Oct 1986 #412; w/trading card. 5-Cover "dated" Jan 1986 #679; w/trading card. 6-(Jan 1995 #1000) — 4.00
Colossal #1-($4.95) — 7.00
#4 (2001, $2.50) Faux 1953 issue; Murphy Anderson-i (6 pgs.) — 2.50
#100 (2001, $2.50) Comic Book Guy-c/app.; faux 1963 issue inside — 2.50
#136 (2001, $2.50) Dan DeCarlo-c/a — 2.50
#222 (2001, $2.50) Batton Lash-s; Radioactive Man in 1972-style — 2.50
#575 (2002, $2.50) Chaykin-c; Radioactive Man in 1984-style — 2.50
1963-106 (2002, $2.50) Radioactive Man in 1960s Gold Key-style; Groening-c — 2.50
#7 Bongo Super Heroes Starring... (2003, $2.50) Marvel Silver Age-style Superior Squad — 2.50
#8 Official Movie Adaptation (2004, $2.99) starring Rainier Wolfcastle and Milhouse — 3.00
#9 (#197 on-c) (2004, $2.50) Kirby-esque New Gods spoof; Golden Age Radio Man app. — 2.50

RADIO FUNNIES
DC Comics: Mar. 1931
nn - Ashcan comic, not distributed to newsstands, only for in-house use. Cover art is Adventure Comics #39 with interior being Detective Comics #19 (no known sales)

RADISKULL & DEVIL DOLL
Image Comics: Nov, 2002 - Present ($2.50/$2.95, B&W, one-shots)
...: Radiskull Hate Christmas (11/02, $2.50) Josh Blaylock & Tim Seeley-s/Mike Norton-a — 2.50
...: Radiskull Hate Love (3/03, $2.95) Josh Blaylock & Tim Seeley-s/Jamar Nicholas-a — 3.00

RADIX

Image Comics: Dec, 2001 - No. 3, Apr, 2002 ($2.95)
1-3-Ray & Ben Lai-s/a — 3.00

RAGAMUFFINS
Eclipse Comics: Jan, 1985 ($1.75, one shot)
1-Eclipse Magazine-r, w/color; Colan-a — 2.50

RAGGEDY ANN AND ANDY (See Dell Giants, March of Comics #23 & New Funnies)
Dell Publishing Co.: No. 5, 1942 - No. 533, 2/54; 10-12/64 - No. 4, 3/66

	GD	VG	FN	VF	VF/NM	NM-
Four Color 5(1942)	45	90	135	360	655	950
Four Color 23(1943)	34	68	102	255	465	675
Four Color 45(1943)	29	58	87	216	388	560
Four Color 72(1945)	24	48	72	179	320	460
1(6/46)-Billy & Bonnie Bee by Frank Thomas	32	64	96	240	445	650
2,3: 3-Egbert Elephant by Dan Noonan begins	17	34	51	128	227	325
4-Kelly-a, 16 pgs.	18	36	54	134	237	340
5,6,8-10	14	28	42	99	175	250
7-Little Black Sambo, Black Mumbo & Black Jumbo only app; Christmas-c	16	32	48	114	202	290
11-20	11	22	33	79	140	200
21-Alice In Wonderland cover/story	14	28	42	99	175	250
22-27,29-39(8/49), Four Color 262(1/50): 34-"...In Candyland"	10	20	30	67	116	165
28-Kelly-c	10	20	30	70	123	175
Four Color 306,354,380,452,533	7	14	21	50	83	115
1(10-12/64-Dell)	4	8	12	24	37	50
2,3(10-12/65), 4(3/66)	3	6	9	16	23	30

NOTE: *Kelly* art ("Animal Mother Goose")-#1-34, 36, 37; c-28. Peterkin Pottle by *John Stanley* in 32-38.

RAGGEDY ANN AND ANDY
Gold Key: Dec, 1971 - No. 6, Sept, 1973

	GD	VG	FN	VF	VF/NM	NM-
1	3	6	9	19	29	38
2-6	3	6	9	15	21	26

RAGGEDY ANN & THE CAMEL WITH THE WRINKLED KNEES (See Dell Jr. Treasury #8)

RAGMAN (See Batman Family #20, The Brave & The Bold #196 & Cancelled Comic Cavalcade)
National Per. Publ./DC Comics No. 5: Aug-Sept, 1976 - No. 5, Jun-Jul, 1977

	GD	VG	FN	VF	VF/NM	NM-
1-Origin & 1st app.	2	4	6	8	11	14
2-5: 2-Origin ends; Kubert-c. 4-Drug use story	1	2	3	5	6	8

NOTE: *Kubert* a-4, 5; c-1-5. *Redondo* studios a-1-4.

RAGMAN (2nd Series)
DC Comics: Oct, 1991 - No. 8, May, 1992 ($1.50, limited series)
1-8: 1-Giffen plots/breakdowns. 3-Origin. 8-Batman-c/story — 3.00

RAGMAN: CRY OF THE DEAD
DC Comics: Aug, 1993 - No. 6, Jan, 1994 ($1.75, limited series)
1-6: Joe Kubert-c — 3.00

RAGS RABBIT (Formerly Babe Ruth Sports #10 or Little Max #10?; also see Harvey Hits #2, Harvey Wiseguys & Tastee Freez)
Harvey Publications: No. 11, June, 1951 - No. 18, March, 1954 (Written & drawn for little folks)

	GD	VG	FN	VF	VF/NM	NM-
11-(See Nutty Comics #5 for 1st app.)	6	12	18	31	38	45
12-18	5	10	15	24	30	35

RAI (Rai and the Future Force #9-23) (See Magnus #5-8)
Valiant: Mar, 1992 - No. 0, Oct, 1992; No. 9, May, 1993 - No. 33, Jun, 1995 ($1.95/$2.25)

	GD	VG	FN	VF	VF/NM	NM-
1-Valiant's 1st original character	2	4	6	8	11	14
2-4,0: 4-Low print run. 0-(11/92)-Origin/1st app. new Rai (Rising Spirit) & 1st full app. & partial origin Bloodshot; also see Eternal Warrior #4; tells future of all characters	3	4	6	8		10
5-10: 6,7-Unity x-overs. 7-Death of Rai. 9-($2.50)-Gatefold-c; story cont'd from Magnus #24; Magnus, Eternal Warrior & X-O app.						5.00
11-33: 15-Manowar Armor app. 17-19-Magnus x-over. 21-1st app. The Starwatchers (cameo); trading card. 22-Death of Rai. 26-Chaos Effect Epsilon Pt. 3						2.50

NOTE: *Layton* c-2i, 9i. *Miller* c-6. *Simonson* c-7.

RAIDERS OF THE LOST ARK (Movie)
Marvel Comics Group: Sept, 1981 - No. 3, Nov, 1981 (Movie adaptation)
1-3: 1-r/Marvel Comics Super Special #18 — 3.00
NOTE: *Buscema* a(p)-1-3; c(p)-1. *Simonson* a-3i; scripts-1-3.

RAINBOW BRITE AND THE STAR STEALER
DC Comics: 1985

	GD	VG	FN	VF	VF/NM	NM-
nn-Movie adaptation	2	4	6	8	10	12

RAISE THE DEAD

Rampaging Hulk #9 © MAR

Range Romances #1 © QUA

Rann-Thanagar War: Infinite Crisis Special © DC

	GD 2.0	VG 4.0	FN 6.0	VF 8.0	VF/NM 9.0	NM- 9.2

Dynamite Entertainment: 2007 - Present ($3.50)
1-3-Arthur Suydam-c/Leah Moore & John Reppion-s/Hugo Petrus-a. 3-Phillips var-c 3.50

RALPH KINER, HOME RUN KING
Fawcett Publications: 1950 (Pittsburgh Pirates)
nn-Photo-c; life story 59 118 177 369 610 850

RALPH SNART ADVENTURES
Now Comics: June, 1986 - V2#9, 1987; V3#1 - #26, Feb, 1991; V4#1, 1992 - #4, 1992
1-3, V2#1-7,V3#1-23,25,26:1-($1.00, B&W)-1(B&W),V2#1(11/86), B&W), 8,9-color.
V3#1(9/88)-Color begins 2.50
V3#24-($2.50)-3-D issue, V4#1-3-Direct sale versions w/cards 2.50
V4#1-3-Newsstand versions w/random cards 2.50
Book 1 1 2 3 5 6 8
3-D Special (11/92, $3.50)-Complete 12-card set w/3-D glasses 3.50

RAMAR OF THE JUNGLE (TV)
Toby Press No. 1/Charlton No. 2 on: 1954 (no month); No. 2, Sept, 1955 - No. 5, Sept, 1956
1-Jon Hall photo-c; last pre-code issue 21 42 63 122 191 260
2-5-Jon Hall photo-c 15 30 45 84 127 170

RAMAYAN 3392 A.D.
Virgin Comics: Sept, 2006 - Present ($2.99)
1-8: 1-Alex Ross-c; re-imagining of the Indian myth of Ramayana; poster of cover inside 3.00
... Reloaded (8/07, $2.99) two covers by Kang and Oeming 3.00

RAMM
Megaton Comics: May, 1987 - No. 2, Sept, 1987 ($1.50, B&W)
1,2-Both have 1 pg. Youngblood ad by Liefeld 2.50

RAMPAGING HULK (The Hulk #10 on; also see Marvel Treasury Edition)
Marvel Comics Group: Jan, 1977 - No. 9, June, 1978 ($1.00, B&W magazine)
1-Bloodstone story w/Buscema & Nebres-a. Origin re-cap w/Simonson-a; Gargoyle,
UFO story; Ken Barr-c 3 6 9 17 25 32
2-Old X-Men app; origin old w/Simonson-a & new X-Men in text w/Cockrum illos;
Bloodstone story w/Brown & Nebres-a 3 6 9 14 19 24
3-9: 3-Iron Man app. 4-Gallery of villains w/Giffen-a. 5,6-Hulk vs. Sub-Mariner. 7-Man-Thing
story. 8-Original Avengers app. 9-Thor vs. Hulk battle; Shanna the She-Devil story
w/DeZuniga-a 2 4 6 10 14 18
NOTE: Alcala a-1-3i, 5i, 8i. Buscema a-1. Giffen a-4. Nino a-4i. Simonson a-1-3p. Starlin a-4(w/Nino), 7; c-4, 5, 7.

RAMPAGING HULK
Marvel Comics: Aug, 1998 - No. 6, Jan, 1999 ($2.99/$1.99)
1-($2.99) Flashback stories of Savage Hulk; Leonardi-a 3.00
2-6-($1.99)-Two covers 2.50

RANDOLPH SCOTT (Movie star)(See Crack Western #67, Prize Comics Western #76, Western Hearts #8, Western Love #1 & Western Winners #7)

RANGE BUSTERS
Fox Features Syndicate: Sept, 1950 (One shot)
1 (Exist?) 20 40 60 115 180 245

RANGE BUSTERS (Formerly Cowboy Love?; Wyatt Earp, Frontier Marshall #11 on)
Charlton Comics: No. 8, May, 1955 - No. 10, Sept, 1955
8 8 16 24 42 54 65
9,10 6 12 18 28 34 40

RANGELAND LOVE
Atlas Comics (CDS): Dec, 1949 - No. 2, Mar, 1950 (52 pgs.)
1-Robert Taylor & Arlene Dahl photo-c 17 34 51 98 154 210
2-Photo-c 14 28 42 80 115 150

RANGER, THE (See Zane Grey, Four Color #255)

RANGE RIDER, THE (TV)(See Flying A's...)

RANGE ROMANCES
Comic Magazines (Quality Comics): Dec, 1949 - No. 5, Aug, 1950 (#5: 52 pg)
1-Gustavson-c/a 26 52 78 150 235 320
2-Crandall-c/a 26 52 78 150 235 320
3-Crandall, Gustavson-a; photo-c 22 44 66 128 202 275
4-Crandall-a; photo-c 19 38 57 112 176 240
5-Gustavson-a; Crandall-a(p); photo-c 19 38 57 112 176 240

RANGERS COMICS (...of Freedom #1-7)
Fiction House Magazines: 10/41 - No. 67, 10/52; No. 68, Fall, 1952; No. 69, Winter, 1952-53 (Flying stories)
1-Intro. Ranger Girl & The Rangers of Freedom; ends #7, cover app. only #5

	GD 2.0	VG 4.0	FN 6.0	VF 8.0	VF/NM 9.0	NM- 9.2
	315	630	945	2048	3624	5200
2	95	190	285	594	985	1375
3	69	138	207	431	716	1000
4,5	62	124	186	388	644	900
6-10: 8-U.S. Rangers begin	50	100	150	305	503	700
11,12-Commando Rangers app.	46	92	138	281	466	650

13-Commando Ranger begins-not same as Commando Rangers 45 90 135 275 450 625
14-20 40 80 120 240 383 525
21-Intro/origin Firehair (begins, 2/45) 41 82 123 253 407 560
22-30: 23-Kazanda begins, ends #28. 28-Tiger Man begins (origin/1st app., 4/46), ends #46.
30-Crusoe Island begins, ends #40 31 62 93 178 282 385
31-40: 33-Hypodermic panels 26 52 78 152 239 325
41-46: 41-Last Werewolf Hunter 22 44 66 126 198 270
47-56: "Eisnerish" Dr. Drew by Grandenetti. 48-Last Glory Forbes. 53-Last 52 pg. issue.
55-Last Sky Rangers 21 42 63 122 191 260
57-60-Straight run of Dr. Drew by Grandenetti 15 30 45 90 140 190
61-69: 64-Suicide Smith begins. 63-Used in POP, pgs. 85, 99. 67-Space Rangers begin,
end #69 14 28 42 82 121 160
NOTE: Bondage, discipline covers, lingerie panels are common. Crusoe Island by **Larsen**-#30-36. Firehair by **Lubbers**-#30-49. Glory Forbes by Baker-#36-45, 47; by Whitman-#34, 35. I Confess in #41-53. Jan of the Jungle in #42-58. King of the Congo in #49-53. Tiger Man by Celardo-#30-39. **M. Anderson** a-30? Baker a-36-38, 42, 44. John Celardo a-34, 36-39. Lee Elias a-21-28. Evans a-19, 38-46, 48-52. Hopper a-25, 26. Ingels a-13-16. **Larsen** a-30-44. **Bob Lubbers** a-30-38, 40-44; c-40-45. Moreira a-41-47. Tuska a-16, 17, 19, 22. **M. Whitman** c-61-66. Zolnerwich c-1-17.

RANGO (TV)
Dell Publishing Co.: Aug, 1967
1-Photo-c of comedian Tim Conway 4 8 12 22 34 45

RANN-THANAGAR WAR (See Adam Strange 2004 mini-series)(Prelude to Infinite Crisis)
DC Comics: July, 2005 - No. 6, Dec, 2005 ($2.50, limited series)
1-6-Adam Strange, Hawkman and Green Lantern (Kyle Rayner) app.; Gibbons-s/Reis-a 2.50
...: Infinite Crisis Special (4/06, $4.99) Kyle Rayner becomes Ion again; Jade dies 5.00
TPB (2005, $12.99) r/#1-6; cover gallery; new Bolland-c 13.00

RAPHAEL (See Teenage Mutant Ninja Turtles)
Mirage Studios: 1985 ($1.50, 7-1/2x11", B&W w/2 color cover, one-shot)
1-1st Turtle one-shot spin-off; contains 1st drawing of the Turtles as a group from 1983 6.00
1-2nd printing (11/87); new-c & 8 pgs. art 2.50

RAPHAEL BAD MOON RISING (See Teenage Mutant Ninja Turtles)
Mirage Publishing: July, 2007 - No. 4 ($3.25, B&W, limited series)
1,2-Continued from Tales of the TMNT #7; Lawson-a 3.25

RASCALS IN PARADISE
Dark Horse Comics: Aug, 1994 - No. 3, Dec, 1994 ($3.95, magazine size)
1-3-Jim Silke-a/story 4.00
Trade paperback-($16.95)-r/#1-3 17.00

RATFINK (See Frantic, Zany, & Ed "Big Daddy" Roth's Ratfink Comix)
Canrom, Inc.: Oct, 1964
1-Woodbridge-a 6 12 18 43 69 95

RAT PATROL, THE (TV)
Dell Publishing Co.: Mar, 1967 - No. 5, Nov, 1967; No. 6, Oct, 1969
1-Christopher George photo-c 7 14 21 47 76 105
2-6: 3-6-Photo-c 4 8 12 28 44 60

RAVAGE 2099 (See Marvel Comics Presents #117)
Marvel Comics: Dec, 1992 - No. 33, Aug, 1995($1.25/$1.50)
1-($1.75)-Gold foil stamped-c; Stan Lee scripts 3.00
1-($1.75)-2nd printing 2.50
2-24,26-33: 5-Last Ryan-a. 6-Last Ryan-a. 14-Punisher 2099 x-over. 15-Ron Lim-c(p).
18-Bound-in card sheet 2.50
25 ($2.25, 52 pgs.) 2.50
25 ($2.95, 52 pgs.)-Silver foil embossed-c 3.00

RAVEN, THE (See Movie Classics)

RAVEN CHRONICLES
Caliber (New Worlds): 1995 - No. 16 ($2.95, B&W)
1-16: 10-Flip book w/Wordsmith #6. 15-Flip book w/High Caliber #4 3.00

RAVENS AND RAINBOWS
Pacific Comics: Dec, 1983 (Baxter paper)(Reprints fanzine work in color)
1-Jeff Jones-c/a(r); nudity scenes 3.00

RAWHIDE (TV)
Dell Publishing Co./Gold Key: Sept-Nov, 1959 - June-Aug, 1962; July, 1963 - No. 2, Jan, 1964

Rawhide Kid #49 © MAR

The Ray #1 © DC

Real Clue Crime Stories V2 #6 © HILL

	GD 2.0	VG 4.0	FN 6.0	VF 8.0	VF/NM 9.0	NM- 9.2
Four Color 1028 (#1)	22	44	66	160	285	410
Four Color 1097,1160,1202,1261,1269	14	28	42	102	181	260
01-684-208 (8/62, Dell)	12	24	36	87	156	225
1(10071-307) (7/63, Gold Key)	12	24	36	87	156	225
2-(12¢)	11	22	33	79	140	200

NOTE: All have Clint Eastwood photo-c. **Tufts** a-1028.

RAWHIDE KID
Atlas/Marvel Comics (CnPC No. 1-16/AMI No. 17-30): Mar, 1955 - No. 16, Sept, 1957; No. 17, Aug, 1960 - No. 151, May, 1979

	GD 2.0	VG 4.0	FN 6.0	VF 8.0	VF/NM 9.0	NM- 9.2
1-Rawhide Kid, his horse Apache & sidekick Randy begin; Wyatt Earp app.; #1 was not code approved; Maneely splash pg.	91	182	273	569	947	1325
2	40	80	120	235	368	500
3-5	30	60	90	174	275	375
6-10: 7-Williamson-a (4 pgs.)	23	46	69	130	205	280
11-16: 16-Torres-a	18	36	54	105	165	225
17-Origin by Jack Kirby; Kirby-a begins	42	84	126	258	422	585
18-21,24-30	11	22	33	79	140	200
22-Monster-c/story by Kirby/Ayers	14	28	42	103	184	265
23-Origin retold by Jack Kirby	17	34	51	128	227	325
31-35,40: 31,32-Kirby-a. 33-35-Davis-a. 34-Kirby-a. 35-Intro & death of The Raven. 40-Two-Gun Kid x-over.	9	18	27	65	113	160
36,37,39,41,42-No Kirby. 42-1st Larry Lieber issue	8	16	24	58	97	135
38-Red Raven-c/story; Kirby-c (2/64).	10	20	30	71	126	180
43-Kirby-a (beware: pin-up often missing)	10	20	30	71	126	180
44,46: 46-Toth-a. 46-Doc Holliday-c/s	8	16	24	54	90	125
45-Origin retold, 17 pgs.	9	18	27	65	113	160
47-49,51-60	5	10	15	35	55	75
50-Kid Colt x-over; vs. Rawhide Kid	5	10	15	39	62	85
61-70: 64-Kid Colt story. 66-Two-Gun Kid story. 67-Kid Colt story. 70-Last 12¢ issue	4	8	12	26	41	55
71-78,80-83,85	3	6	9	17	25	32
79,84,86,95: 79-Williamson-a(r). 84,86: Kirby-a. 86-Origin-r; Williamson-r/Ringo Kid #13 (4 pgs.)	3	6	9	18	27	35
87-91: 90-Kid Colt app. 91-Last 15¢ issue	3	6	9	16	22	28
92,93 (52 pg.Giants). 92-Kirby-a	3	6	9	21	32	42
94,96-99	3	6	9	14	19	24
100 (6/72)-Origin retold & expanded	3	6	9	18	27	35
101-120: 115-Last new story	2	4	6	10	14	18
121-151	2	4	6	8	10	12
133,134-(30¢-c variants, limited distribution)(5,7/76)	3	6	9	21	32	42
140,141-(35¢-c variants, limited distribution)(7,9/77)	5	10	15	30	48	65
Special 1(9/71, 25¢, 68 pgs.)-All Kirby/Ayers-r	4	8	12	26	41	55

NOTE: **Ayers** a-13, 14, 16. **Colan** a-35, 37; c-145p, 148p, 149p. **Davis** a-125r. **Everett** a-54i, 65, 66, 88, 96i, 148i(r). **Gulacy** c-147. **Heath** c-4. **G. Kane** c-101, 144. **Keller** a-5, 144r. **Kirby** a-17-32, 34, 42, 43, 84, 86, 92, 109r, 112r, 116r, 117r, 137r, Spec. 1; c-17-35, 37, 38, 40, 41, 43-47, 137r. **Maneely** c-1, 2, 5, 6, 14. **Morisi** a-13. **Morrow/Williamson** r-111. **Roussos** a-146i, 147i, 149-151i. **Severin** a-16; c-8, 13. **Sutton** a-93. **Torres** a-99r. **Tuska** a-14. **Wildey** r-146-151(Outlaw Kid). **Williamson** r-79, 86, 95.

RAWHIDE KID
Marvel Comics Group: Aug, 1985 - No. 4, Nov, 1985 (Mini-series)

1-4 .... 5.00

RAWHIDE KID
Marvel Comics (MAX): Apr, 2003 - No. 5, June, 2003 ($2.99, limited series)

1-John Severin-a/Ron Zimmerman-s; Dave Johnson-c 3.00
2-5: 3-Dodson-a. 4-Darwyn Cooke-c. 5-J. Scott Campbell-c 3.00
Vol. 1: Slap Leather TPB (2003, $12.99) r/#1-5 .... 13.00

RAY, THE (See Freedom Fighters & Smash Comics #14)
DC Comics: Feb, 1992 - No. 6, July, 1992 ($1.00, mini-series)

1-Sienkiewicz-c; Joe Quesada-a(p) in 1-5 .... 5.00
2-6: 3-6-Quesada-c(p). 6-Quesada layouts only 3.00
...In a Blaze of Power (1994, $12.95)-r/#1-6 w/new Quesada-c 13.00

RAY, THE
DC Comics: May, 1994 - No. 28, Oct, 1996 ($1.75/$1.95/$2.25)

1-Quesada-c(p); Superboy app. 3.00
1-($2.95)-Collectors Edition w/diff. Quesada-c; embossed foil-c 4.00
2-5,0,6-24,26-28: 2-Quesada-c(p); Superboy app. 5-(9/94). 0-(10/94) 2.50
25-($3.50)-Future Flash (Bart Allen)-c/app; double size 3.50
Annual 1 ($3.95, 68 pgs.)-Superman app. 4.00

RAY BRADBURY COMICS
Topps Comics: Feb, 1993 - V4#1, June, 1994 ($2.95)

1-5-Polybagged w/3 trading cards each. 1-All dinosaur issue; Corben-a; Williamson/Torres/Krenkel-r/Weird Science-Fantasy #25. 3-All dinosaur issue; Steacy painted-c; Stout-a 3.00

Special Edition 1 (1994, $2.95)-The Illustrated Man 3.00
...Special: Tales of Horror #1 ($2.50), ...Trilogy of Terror V3#1 (5/94, $2.50), ...Martian Chronicles V4#1 (6/94, $2.50)-Steranko-c 2.50

NOTE: **Kelley Jones** a-Trilogy of Terror V3#1. **Kaluta** a-Martian Chronicles V4#1. **Kurtzman/Matt Wagner** c-2. **McKean** c-4. **Mignola** a-4. **Wood** c-Trilogy of Terror V3#1.

RAZORLINE
Marvel Comics: Sept, 1993 (75¢, one-shot)

1-Clive Barker super-heroes: Ectokid, Hokum & Hex, Hyperkind & Saint Sinner (all 1st app.) 2.50

RAZOR'S EDGE, THE
DC Comics (WildStorm): Dec, 2004 - No. 5, Apr, 2005 ($2.95)

1-5-Warblade; Bisley-c/a; Ridley-s 3.00

REAL ADVENTURE COMICS (Action Adventure #2 on)
Gillmor Magazines: Apr, 1955

	GD 2.0	VG 4.0	FN 6.0	VF 8.0	VF/NM 9.0	NM- 9.2
1	9	18	27	47	61	75

REAL ADVENTURES OF JONNY QUEST, THE
Dark Horse Comics: Sept, 1996 - No. 12, Sept, 1997 ($2.95)

1-12 .... 3.00

REAL CLUE CRIME STORIES (Formerly Clue Comics)
Hillman Periodicals: V2#4, June, 1947 - V8#3, May, 1953

	GD 2.0	VG 4.0	FN 6.0	VF 8.0	VF/NM 9.0	NM- 9.2
V2#4(#1)-S&K c/a(3); Dan Barry-a	48	96	144	293	484	675
5-7-S&K c/a(3-4). 7-Iron Lady app.	40	80	120	235	368	500
8-12	13	26	39	74	105	135
V3#1-8,10-12, V4#1-3,5-8,11,12	11	22	33	62	86	110
V3#9-Used in SOTI, pg. 102	14	28	42	76	108	140
V4#4-S&K-a	14	28	42	80	115	150
V4#9,10-Krigstein-a	11	22	33	64	90	115
V5#1-5,7,8,10,12	10	20	30	54	72	90
6,9,11(1/54)-Krigstein-a	10	20	30	58	79	100
V6#1-5,8,9,11	9	18	27	50	65	80
6,7,10,12-Krigstein-a. 10-Bondage-c	10	20	30	58	79	100
V7#1-3,5-11, V8#1-3: V7#6-1 pg. Frazetta ad "Prayer" - 1st app.?	9	18	27	50	65	90
4,12-Krigstein-a	10	20	30	58	79	100

NOTE: **Barry** a-9, 10; c-V2#8. **Briefer** a-V6#6. **Fuje** a-V2#7(2), 8, 11. **Infantino** a-V2#8; c-V2#11. **Lawrence** a-V3#8, V5#7. **Powell** a-V4#11, 12. V5#4, 5, 7 are 68 pgs.

REAL EXPERIENCES (Formerly Tiny Tessie)
Atlas Comics (20CC): No. 25, Jan, 1950

	GD 2.0	VG 4.0	FN 6.0	VF 8.0	VF/NM 9.0	NM- 9.2
25-Virginia Mayo photo-c from movie "Red Light"	10	20	30	56	76	95

REAL FACT COMICS
National Periodical Publications: Mar-Apr, 1946 - No. 21, July-Aug, 1949

	GD 2.0	VG 4.0	FN 6.0	VF 8.0	VF/NM 9.0	NM- 9.2
1-S&K-c/a; Harry Houdini story; Just Imagine begins (w/no by Finlay); Fred Ray-a	54	108	162	338	562	785
2-S&K-a; Rin-Tin-Tin & P. T. Barnum stories	34	68	102	197	311	425
3-H.G. Wells, Lon Chaney stories; early DC letter column (New Fun Comics #3 from 1935 may be the 1st)	32	64	96	186	293	400
4-Virgil Finlay-a on 'Just Imagine' begins, ends #12 (2 pgs. each); Jimmy Stewart & Jack London stories; Joe DiMaggio 1 pg. biography	35	70	105	204	322	440
5-Batman/Robin-c taken from cover of Batman #9; 5 pg. story about creation of Batman & Robin; Tom Mix story	179	358	537	1119	1860	2600
6-Origin & 1st app. Tommy Tomorrow by Weisinger and Sherman (1-2/47); Flag-c; 1st writing by Harlan Ellison (letter column, non-professional); "First Man to Reach Mars" epic-c/story	103	206	309	644	1072	1500
7-(No. 6 on inside)-Roussos-a; D. Fairbanks sty.	18	36	54	105	165	225
8-2nd app. Tommy Tomorrow by Finlay (5-6/47)	59	118	177	369	610	850
9-S&K-a; Glenn Miller, Indianapolis 500 stories	25	50	75	145	228	310
10-Vigilante by Meskin (based on movie serial); 4 pg. Finlay s/f story	24	48	72	139	220	300
11,12: 11-Annie Oakley, G-Men stories; Kinstler-a	15	30	45	86	133	180
13-Dale Evans and Tommy Tomorrow-c/stories	43	86	129	262	431	600
14,17,18: 14-Will Rogers story	15	30	45	83	124	165
15-Nuclear explosion part-c "Last War on Earth" story); Clyde Beatty story	18	36	54	105	165	225
16-Tommy Tomorrow app.; 1st Planeteers?	41	82	123	250	400	550
19-Sir Arthur Conan Doyle story	15	30	45	88	137	185
20-Kubert-a, 4 pgs; Daniel Boone story	17	34	51	98	154	210
21-Kubert-a, 2 pgs; Kit Carson story	15	30	45	83	124	165
Ashcan (2/46) Not distributed to newsstands, only for in house use				(no known sales)		

NOTE: **Barry** c-16. **Virgil Finlay** c-6, 8. **Meskin** c-10. **Roussos** a-1-4, 6.

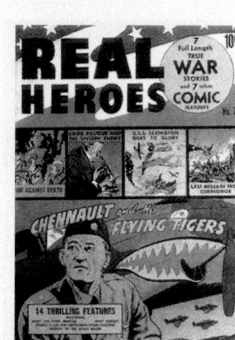

Real Heroes Comics #7 © PMI

Realistic Romances #2 © AVON

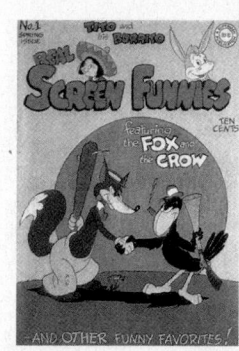

Real Screen Funnies #1 © DC

	GD 2.0	VG 4.0	FN 6.0	VF 8.0	VF/NM 9.0	NM- 9.2

REAL FUNNIES
Nedor Publishing Co.: Jan, 1943 - No. 3, June, 1943

	GD 2.0	VG 4.0	FN 6.0	VF 8.0	VF/NM 9.0	NM- 9.2
1-Funny animal, humor; Black Terrier app. (clone of The Black Terror)						
	32	64	96	186	293	400
2,3	16	32	48	94	147	200

REAL GHOSTBUSTERS, THE (Also see Slimer)
Now Comics: Aug, 1988 - No. 32, 1991 ($1.75/$1.95)

	GD	VG	FN	VF	VF/NM	NM-
1-32: 1-Based on Ghostbusters movie. #29-32 exist?						3.00

REAL HEROES COMICS
Parents' Magazine Institute: Sept, 1941 - No. 16, Oct, 1946

	GD	VG	FN	VF	VF/NM	NM-
1-Roosevelt-c/story	32	64	96	186	293	400
2-J. Edgar Hoover-c/story	15	30	45	83	124	165
3-5,7-10: 4-Churchill, Roosevelt stories	14	28	42	76	108	140
6-Lou Gehrig-c/story	20	40	60	115	180	245
11-16: 13-Kiefer-a	10	20	30	54	72	90

REALISTIC ROMANCES
Realistic Comics/Avon Periodicals: July-Aug, 1951 - No. 17, Aug-Sept, 1954 (No #9-14)

	GD	VG	FN	VF	VF/NM	NM-
1-Kinstler-a; c/-Avon paperback #211	26	52	78	152	239	325
2	14	28	42	80	115	150
3,4	14	28	42	76	108	140
5,8-Kinstler-a	14	28	42	78	112	145
6-c/-Diversey Prize Novels #6; Kinstler-a	14	28	42	80	115	150
7-Evans-a?; c/-Avon paperback #360	14	28	42	80	115	150
15,17: 17-Kinstler-c	13	26	39	72	101	130
16-Kinstler marijuana story-r/Romantic Love #6	14	28	42	78	112	145
I.W. Reprint #1,8,9: #1-r/Realistic Romances #4; Astarita-a. 9-r/Women To Love #1	2	4	6	9	13	16

NOTE: *Astarita* a-2-4, 7, 8, 17. Photo c-1, 2. Painted c-3, 4.

REAL LIFE COMICS
Nedor/Better/Standard Publ./Pictorial Magazine No. 13: Sept, 1941 - No. 59, Sept, 1952

	GD	VG	FN	VF	VF/NM	NM-
1-Uncle Sam-c/story; Daniel Boone story	57	114	171	356	591	825
2	29	58	87	167	264	360
3-Hitler cover	124	248	372	775	1288	1800
4,5: 4-Story of American flag "Old Glory"	18	36	54	103	162	220
6-10: 6-Wild Bill Hickok story	17	34	51	98	154	210
11-20: 17-Albert Einstein story	15	30	45	90	140	190
21-23,25,26,28-30: 29-A-Bomb story	14	28	42	82	121	160
24-Story of Baseball (Babe Ruth)	21	42	63	120	188	255
27-Schomburg A-Bomb-c; story of A-Bomb	20	40	60	115	180	245
31-33,35,36,42-44,48,49: 49-Baseball issue	14	28	42	76	108	140

34,37-41,45-47: 34-Jimmy Stewart story. 37-Story of motion pictures; Bing Crosby story. 38-Jane Froman story. 39-"1,000,000 A.D." story. 40-Bob Feller. 41-Jimmie Foxx story ("Jimmy" on-c); "Home Run" Baker story. 45-Story of Olympic games; Burl Ives & Kit Carson story. 46-Douglas Fairbanks Jr. & Sr. story. 47-George Gershwin story

	GD	VG	FN	VF	VF/NM	NM-
	14	28	42	82	121	160
50-Frazetta-a (5 pgs.)	30	60	90	174	275	375
51-Jules Verne "Journey to the Moon" by Evans; Severin/Elder-a						
	20	40	60	115	180	245
52-Frazetta-a (4 pgs.); Severin/Elder-a(2); Evans-a	33	66	99	190	300	410
53-57-Severin/Elder-a. 54-Bat Masterson-c/story	15	30	45	88	137	185
58-Severin/Elder-a(2)	15	30	45	90	140	190
59-1 pg. Frazetta; Severin/Elder-a	15	30	45	88	137	185

NOTE: Some issues had two titles. *Guardineer* a-40(2), 44. *Meskin* a-52. *Roussos* a-50. *Schomburg* c-1, 2, 4, 5, 7, 11, 13-21, 23, 24, 26, 28, 30-32, 34-40, 42, 44-47, 55. *Tuska* a-53. Photo c-5, 6.

REAL LIFE SECRETS (Real Secrets #2 on)
Ace Periodicals: Sept, 1949 (one-shot)

	GD	VG	FN	VF	VF/NM	NM-
1-Painted-c	14	28	42	76	108	140

REAL LIFE STORY OF FESS PARKER (Magazine)
Dell Publishing Co.: 1955

	GD	VG	FN	VF	VF/NM	NM-
1	9	18	27	61	103	145

REAL LIFE TALES OF SUSPENSE (See Suspense)

REAL LOVE (Formerly Hap Hazard)
Ace Periodicals (A. A. Wyn): No. 25, April, 1949 - No. 76, Nov, 1956

	GD	VG	FN	VF	VF/NM	NM-
25	14	28	42	76	108	140
26	10	20	30	56	76	95
27-L. B. Cole-a	12	24	36	67	94	120
28-35	9	18	27	50	65	80
36-66: 66-Last pre-code (2/55)	8	16	24	44	57	70
67-76	7	14	21	37	46	55

NOTE: Photo c-50-76. Painted c-46.

REALM, THE
Arrow Comics/WeeBee Comics #13/Caliber Press #14 on: Feb, 1986 - No. 21, 1991 ($1.50/$1.95/$2.50, B&W)

	GD	VG	FN	VF	VF/NM	NM-
1-21: 4-1st app. Deadworld (9/86)						2.50
Book 1 ($4.95, B&W)						5.00

REAL McCOYS, THE (TV)
Dell Publ. Co.: No. 1071, 1-3/60 - 5-7/1962 (All have Walter Brennan photo-c)

	GD	VG	FN	VF	VF/NM	NM-
Four Color 1071,1134-Toth-a in both	9	18	27	60	100	140
Four Color 1193,1265	8	16	24	56	93	130
01-689-207 (5-7/62)	7	14	21	50	83	115

REALM OF THE CLAW (Also see Mutant Earth as part of a flipbook)
Image Comics: Oct, 2003 - Present ($2.95)

	GD	VG	FN	VF	VF/NM	NM-
0-(7/03, $5.95) Convention Special; cover has gold-foil title logo						6.00
1,2-Two covers by Yardin						3.00
Vol. 1 TPB (2006, $16.99) r/series; concept art & sketch pages						17.00

REAL SCREEN COMICS (#1 titled Real Screen Funnies; TV Screen Cartoons #129-138)
National Periodical Publications: Spring, 1945 - No. 128, May-June, 1959 (#1-40: 52 pgs.)

	GD	VG	FN	VF	VF/NM	NM-
1-The Fox & the Crow, Flippity & Flop, Tito & His Burrito begin						
	98	196	294	613	1019	1425
2	46	92	138	281	466	650
3-5	32	64	96	186	293	400
6-10 (2-3/47)	21	42	63	122	191	260
11-20 (10-11/48): 13-The Crow x-over in Flippity & Flop						
	16	32	48	92	144	195
21-30 (6-7/50)	13	26	39	74	105	135
31-50	11	22	33	60	83	105
51-99	10	20	30	54	72	90
100	10	20	30	56	76	95
101-128	8	16	24	44	57	70

REAL SCREEN FUNNIES
DC Comics: Spring 1945

1-Ashcan comic, not distributed to newsstands, only for in-house use. Cover art is Real Screen Funnies #1 with interior being Detective Comics #92. Only ashcan cover to be produced using the regular production first issue art and only using the color yellow.
(no known sales)

REAL SECRETS (Formerly Real Life Secrets)
Ace Periodicals: No. 2, Nov, 1950 - No. 5, May, 1950

	GD	VG	FN	VF	VF/NM	NM-
2-Painted-c	10	20	30	56	76	95
3-5: 3-Photo-c	8	16	24	42	54	65

REAL SPORTS COMICS (All Sports Comics #2 on)
Hillman Periodicals: Oct-Nov, 1948 (52 pgs.)

	GD	VG	FN	VF	VF/NM	NM-
1-Powell-a (12 pgs.)	40	80	120	235	368	500

REAL WAR STORIES
Eclipse Comics: July, 1987; No. 2, Jan, 1991 ($2.00, 52 pgs.)

	GD	VG	FN	VF	VF/NM	NM-
1-Bolland-a(p), Bissette-a, Totleben-a(i); Alan Moore scripts (2nd printing exists, 2/88)						3.00
2-($4.95)						5.00

REAL WESTERN HERO (Formerly Wow #1-69; Western Hero #76 on)
Fawcett Publications: No. 70, Sept, 1948 - No. 75, Feb, 1949 (All 52 pgs.)

	GD	VG	FN	VF	VF/NM	NM-
70(#1)-Tom Mix, Monte Hale, Hopalong Cassidy, Young Falcon begin						
	28	56	84	162	256	350
71-75: 71-Gabby Hayes begins. 71,72-Captain Tootsie by Beck. 75-Big Bow and Little Arrow begin	17	34	51	98	154	210

NOTE: Painted/photo c-70-73; painted c-74, 75.

REAL WEST ROMANCES
Crestwood Publishing Co./Prize Publ.: 4-5/49 - V1#6, 3/50; V2#1, Apr-May, 1950 (All 52 pgs. & photo-c)

	GD	VG	FN	VF	VF/NM	NM-
V1#1-S&K-a(p)	26	52	78	150	235	320
2	14	28	42	80	115	150
3-Kirby-a(p) only	14	28	42	82	121	160
4-S&K-a; Whip Wilson, Reno Browne photo-c	19	38	57	112	176	240
5-Audie Murphy, Gale Storm photo-c; S&K-a	18	36	54	98	154	210
6-Produced by S&K, no S&K-a; Robert Preston & Cathy Downs photo-c						
	14	28	42	78	112	145
V2#1-Kirby-a(p)	12	24	36	69	97	125

NOTE: *Meskin* a-V1#5, 6. *Severin/Elder* a-V1#3-6, V2#1. *Meskin* a-V1#6. *Leonard Starr* a-1-3. Photo c-V1#1-6, V2#1.

REALWORLDS :...
DC Comics: 2000 ($5.95, one-shots, prestige format)

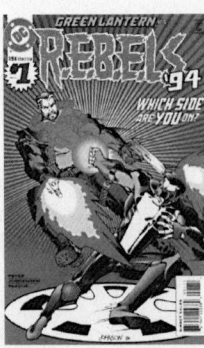

R.E.B.E.L.S. '94 #1 © DC

Red Circle Comics #4 © Enwil

Red Dragon Comics #5 © S&S

	GD 2.0	VG 4.0	FN 6.0	VF 8.0	VF/NM 9.0	NM- 9.2

Batman - Marshall Rogers-a/Golden & Sniegoski-s; Justice League of America -Dematteis-s/
Barr-painted art; Superman -Vance-s/García-López & Rubenstein-a; Wonder Woman -
Hanson & Neuwirth-s/Sam-a 6.00

RE-ANIMATOR IN FULL COLOR
Adventure Comics: Oct, 1991 - No. 3, 1992 ($2.95, mini-series)
1-3: Adapts horror movie. 1-Dorman painted-c 3.00

REAP THE WILD WIND (See Cinema Comics Herald)

REBEL, THE (TV)
Dell Publishing Co.: No. 1076, Feb-Apr, 1960 - No. 1262, Dec-Feb, 1961-62

	GD	VG	FN	VF	VF/NM	NM-
Four Color 1076 (#1)-Sekowsky-a, photo-c	9	18	27	65	113	160
Four Color 1138 (9-11/60), 1207 (9-11/61), 1262-Photo-c	8	16	24	56	93	130

R.E.B.E.L.S. '94 (Becomes R.E.B.E.L.S. '95 & R.E.B.E.L.S. '96)
DC Comics: No. 0, Oct, 1994 - No. 17, Mar, 1996 ($1.95/$2.25)
0-17: 8-$2.25-c begins. 15-R.E.B.E.L.S '96 begins. 2.50

RECORD BOOK OF FAMOUS POLICE CASES
St. John Publishing Co.: 1949 (25¢, 132 pgs.)

	GD	VG	FN	VF	VF/NM	NM-
nn-Kubert-a(3); r/Son of Sinbad; Baker-c	40	80	120	235	368	500

RED
DC Comics (Homage): Sept, 2003 - No. 3, Feb, 2004 ($2.95, limited series)
1-3-Warren Ellis-s/Cully Hamner-a/c 3.00
Red/Tokyo Storm Warning TPB (2004, $14.95) Flip book r/both series 15.00

RED ARROW
P. L. Publishing Co.: May-June, 1951 - No. 3, Oct, 1951

	GD	VG	FN	VF	VF/NM	NM-
1	11	22	33	60	83	105
2,3	9	18	27	47	61	75

RED BAND COMICS
Enwil Associates: Nov, 1944 - No. 4, May, 1945

	GD	VG	FN	VF	VF/NM	NM-
1	40	80	120	235	368	500
2-Origin Bogeyman & Santanas; c-reprint/#1	28	56	84	162	256	350
3,4-Captain Wizard app. in both (1st app.); each has identical contents/cover	26	52	78	152	239	325

REDBLADE
Dark Horse Comics: Apr, 1993 - No. 3, July, 1993 ($2.50, mini-series)
1-3: Double gatefold-c 3.00

RED CIRCLE COMICS (Also see Blazing Comics & Blue Circle Comics)
Rural Home Publications (Enwil): Jan, 1945 - No. 4, April, 1945

	GD	VG	FN	VF	VF/NM	NM-
1-The Prankster & Red Riot begin	40	80	120	240	383	525
2-Starr-a; The Judge (costumed hero) app.	29	58	87	170	268	365
3,4-Starr-c/a. 3-The Prankster not in costume	23	46	69	135	213	290
4-(Dated 4/45)-Leftover covers to #4 were later restapled over early 1950s coverless comics; variations in the coverless comics used are endless; Woman Outlaws, Dorothy Lamour, Crime Does Not Pay, Sabu, Diary Loves, Love Confessions & Young Love V3#3 known	16	32	48	94	147	200

RED CIRCLE SORCERY (Chilling Adventures in Sorcery #1-5)
Red Circle Prod. (Archie): No. 6, Apr, 1974 - No. 11, Feb, 1975 (All 25¢ iss.)

	GD	VG	FN	VF	VF/NM	NM-
6,8,9,11: 6-Early Chaykin-a. 7-Pino-a. 8-Only app. The Cobra	2	4	6	8	10	12
7-Bruce Jones-a with Wrightson, Kaluta, Jeff Jones	2	4	6	10	14	18
10-Wood-a(i)	2	4	6	8	11	14

NOTE: *Chaykin* a-6, 10. *McWilliams* a-10(2 & 3 pgs.) *Mooney* a-11p. *Morrow* a-6-8, 9(int illos), 10, 11i; c-6-11. *Thorne* a-8, 10. *Toth* a-8, 9.

RED DOG (See Night Music #7)

RED DRAGON
Comico: June, 1996 ($2.95)
1-Bisley-c 3.00

RED DRAGON COMICS (1st Series) (Formerly Trail Blazers; see Super Magician V5#7, 8)
Street & Smith Publications: No. 5, Jan, 1943 - No. 9, Jan, 1944

	GD	VG	FN	VF	VF/NM	NM-
5-Origin Red Rover, the Crimson Crimebuster; Rex King, Man of Adventure, Captain Jack Commando, & The Minute Man begin; text origin Red Dragon; Binder-c	97	194	291	606	1003	1400
6-Origin The Black Crusader & Red Dragon (3/43); 1st story app. Red Dragon & 1st cover (classic-c)	255	510	765	1594	2647	3700
7-Classic-c	207	414	621	1294	2147	3000
8-The Red Knight app.	76	152	228	475	788	1100
9-Origin Chuck Magnon, Immortal Man	76	152	228	475	788	1100

RED DRAGON COMICS (2nd Series) (See Super Magician V2#8)
Street & Smith Publications: Nov, 1947 - No. 6, Jan, 1949; No. 7, July, 1949

	GD	VG	FN	VF	VF/NM	NM-
1-Red Dragon begins; Elliman, Nigel app.; Edd Cartier-c/a	93	186	279	581	966	1350
2-Cartier-c	65	130	195	406	671	935
3-1st app. Dr. Neff Ghost Breaker by Powell; Elliman, Nigel app.	54	108	162	338	557	775
4-Cartier c/a	76	152	228	475	788	1100
5-7	40	80	120	240	383	525

NOTE: *Maneely* a-5, 7. *Powell* a-2-7; c-3, 5, 7.

RED EAGLE
David McKay Publications: No. 16, Aug, 1938

	GD	VG	FN	VF	VF/NM	NM-
Feature Books 16	26	52	78	152	239	325

REDEYE (See Comics Reading Libraries in the Promotional Comics section)

RED FOX (Formerly Manhunt!; #1-14; also see Extra Comics)
Magazine Enterprises: No. 15, 1954

	GD	VG	FN	VF	VF/NM	NM-
15(A-1 #108)-Undercover Girl story; L.B. Cole-c/a (Red Fox); r-from Manhunt; Powell-a	19	38	57	109	172	235

RED GOOSE COMIC SELECTIONS (See Comic Selections)

RED HAWK (See A-1 Comics, Bobby Benson's ..#14-16 & Straight Arrow #2)
Magazine Enterprises: No. 90, 1953

	GD	VG	FN	VF	VF/NM	NM-
A-1 90-Powell-c/a	13	26	39	72	101	130

RED MASK (Formerly Tim Holt; see Best Comics, Blazing Six-Guns)
Magazine Enterprises No. 42-53/Sussex No. 54 (M.E. on-c): No. 42, June-July, 1954 - No. 53, May, 1956; No. 54, Sept, 1957

	GD	VG	FN	VF	VF/NM	NM-
42-Ghost Rider by Ayers continues, ends #50; Black Phantom continues; 3-D effect c/stories begin	21	42	63	124	195	265
43- 3-D effect-c/stories	19	38	57	109	172	235
44-52: 3-D effect stories only. 47-Last pre-code issue. 50-Last Ghost Rider. 51-The Presto Kid begins by Ayers (1st app.); Presto Kid-c begins; last 3-D effect story.						
52-Origin The Presto Kid	17	34	51	98	154	210
53,54-Last Black Phantom; last Presto Kid-c	15	30	45	83	124	165
I.W. Reprint #1 (r-/#52). 2 (nd, r/#51 w/diff.-c). 3, 8 (nd; Kinstler-c); 8-r/Red Mask #52	3	6	9	16	22	28

NOTE: *Ayers* art on Ghost Rider & Presto Kid. *Bolle* art in all (Red Mask); c-43, 44, 49. *Guardineer* a-52. *Black Phantom* in #42-44, 47-50, 53, 54.

REDMASK OF THE RIO GRANDE
AC Comics: 1990 ($2.50, 28pgs.) (Has photos of movie posters)
1-Bolle-c/a(r); photo inside-c 2.50

RED MENACE
DC Comics (WildStorm): Jan, 2007 - No. 6, Jun, 2007 ($2.99, limited series)
1-6-Ordway-a/c; Bilson, DeMeo & Brody-s 3.00

RED MOUNTAIN FEATURING QUANTRELL'S RAIDERS (Movie) (Also see Jesse James #28)
Avon Periodicals: 1952

	GD	VG	FN	VF	VF/NM	NM-
nn-Alan Ladd; Kinstler-c	27	54	81	158	249	340

RED PROPHET: THE TALES OF ALVIN MAKER
Dabel Brothers Prods./Marvel Comics (Dabel Brothers): Mar, 2006 - Present ($2.99)
1-10-Adaptation of Orson Scott Card novel. 1-Miguel Montenegro-a 3.00
... Vol. 1 HC (2007, $19.99, dustjacket) r/#1-6 ...... 20.00
... Vol. 1 SC (2007, $15.99) r/#1-6 ...... 16.00

"RED" RABBIT COMICS
Dearfield Comic/J. Charles Laue Publ. Co.: Jan, 1947 - No. 22, Aug-Sep, 1951

	GD	VG	FN	VF	VF/NM	NM-
1	14	28	42	76	108	140
2	8	16	24	44	57	70
3-10	7	14	21	37	46	55
11-17,19-22	7	14	21	35	43	50
18-Flying Saucer-c (1/51)	8	16	24	44	57	70

RED RAVEN COMICS (Human Torch #2 on) (Also see X-Men #44 & Sub-Mariner #26, 2nd series)
Timely Comics: August, 1940

	GD	VG	FN	VF	VF/NM	NM-
1-Origin & 1st app. Red Raven; Comet Pierce & Mercury by Kirby, The Human Top & The Eternal Brain; intro. Magar, the Mystic & only app.; Kirby-c (his 1st signed work)	1150	2300	3450	8600	15,300	22,000

RED ROCKET 7
Dark Horse Comics: Aug, 1997 - No. 7, June, 1998 ($3.95, square format, limited series)
1-7-Mike Allred-c/s/a 4.00

Red Ryder Comics #8 © DELL

Red Sonja #6 © Red Sonja Corp.

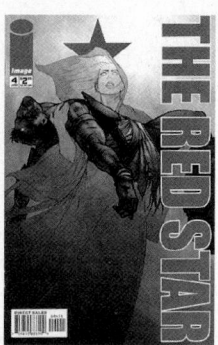
The Red Star #4 © Christian Gossett

	GD 2.0	VG 4.0	FN 6.0	VF 8.0	VF/NM 9.0	NM- 9.2

RED RYDER COMICS (Hi Spot #2)(Movies, radio)(See Crackajack Funnies & Super Book of Comics)
Hawley Publ. No. 1/Dell Publishing Co.(K.K.) No. 3 on: 9/40; No. 3, 8/41 - No. 5, 12/41; No. 6, 4/42 - No. 151, 4-6/57

	GD 2.0	VG 4.0	FN 6.0	VF 8.0	VF/NM 9.0	NM- 9.2
1-Red Ryder, his horse Thunder, Little Beaver & his horse Papoose strip reprints begin by Fred Harman; 1st meeting of Red & Little Beaver; Harman line-drawn-c #1-85	276	552	828	1725	2863	4000
3-(Scarce)-Alley Oop, Capt. Easy, Dan Dunn, Freckles & His Friends, King of the Royal Mtd., Myra North strip-r begin	70	140	210	595	1098	1600
4-6: 6-1st Dell issue (4/42)	35	70	105	263	482	700
7-10	30	60	90	220	398	575
11-20	21	42	63	156	278	400
21-32-Last Alley Oop, Dan Dunn, Capt. Easy, Freckles	15	30	45	107	191	275
33-40 (52 pgs.): 40-Photo back-c begin, end #57	11	22	33	75	133	190
41 (52 pgs.)-Rocky Lane photo back-c	11	22	33	79	140	200
42-46 (52 pgs.): 46-Last Red Ryder strip-r	9	18	27	64	110	155
47-53 (52 pgs.): 47-New stories on Red Ryder begin. 49,52-Harman photo back-c	8	16	24	56	93	130
54-92: 54-73 (36 pgs.). 59-Harmon photo back-c. 73-Last King of the Royal Mtd; strip-r by Jim Gary. 74-85 (52 pgs.)-Harman line-drawn-c. 86-92 (52 pgs.)-Harman painted-c	7	14	21	47	76	105
93-99,101-106: 94-96 (36 pgs.)-Harman painted-c. 97,98,(36 pgs.)-Harman line-drawn-c. 99,101-106 (36 pgs.)-Jim Bannon Photo-c	6	12	18	41	66	90
100 (36 pgs.)-Bannon photo-c	6	12	18	43	69	95
107-118 (52 pgs.)-Harman line-drawn-c	6	12	18	39	62	85
119-129 (52 pgs.): 119-Painted-c begin, not by Harman, end #151	6	12	18	37	59	80
130-151 (36 pgs.): 145-Title change to Red Ryder Ranch Magazine						
149-Title change to Red Ryder Ranch Comics	5	10	15	35	55	75
Four Color 916 (7/58)	5	10	15	35	55	75

NOTE: *Fred Harman a-1-99; c-1-98, 107-118. Don Red Barry, Allan Rocky Lane, Wild Bill Elliott & Jim Bannon starred as Red Ryder in the movies. Robert Blake starred as Little Beaver.*

RED RYDER PAINT BOOK
Whitman Publishing Co.: 1941 (8-1/2x11-1/2", 148 pgs.)

	GD 2.0	VG 4.0	FN 6.0	VF 8.0	VF/NM 9.0	NM- 9.2
nn-Reprints 1940 daily strips	76	152	228	475	788	1100

RED SEAL COMICS (Formerly Carnival Comics, and/or Spotlight Comics?)
Harry 'A' Chesler/Superior Publ. No. 19 on: No. 14, 10/45 - No. 18, 10/46; No. 19, 6/47 - No. 22, 12/47

	GD 2.0	VG 4.0	FN 6.0	VF 8.0	VF/NM 9.0	NM- 9.2
14-The Black Dwarf begins (continued from Spotlight?); Little Nemo app; bondage/hypo-c; Tuska-a	76	152	228	475	788	1100
15-Torture story; funny-c	41	82	123	250	400	550
16-Used in **SOTI**, pg. 181, illo "Outside the forbidden pages of de Sade, you find draining a girl's blood only in children's comics;" drug club story r-later in Crime Reporter #1; Veiled Avenger & Barry Kuda app; Tuska-a; funny-c	62	124	186	388	644	900
17,18,20: Lady Satan, Yankee Girl & Sky Chief app; 17-Tuska-a	49	98	147	299	492	685
19-No Black Dwarf (on-c only); Zor, El Tigre app.	43	86	129	262	431	600
21-Lady Satan & Black Dwarf app.	32	64	96	186	293	400
22-Zor, Rocketman app. (68 pgs.)	32	64	96	186	293	400

REDSKIN (Thrilling Indian Stories)(Famous Western Badmen #13 on)
Youthful Magazines: Sept, 1950 - No. 12, Oct, 1952

	GD 2.0	VG 4.0	FN 6.0	VF 8.0	VF/NM 9.0	NM- 9.2
1-Walter Johnson-a (7 pgs.)	17	34	51	98	154	210
2	11	22	33	62	86	110
3-12: 3-Daniel Boone story. 6-Geronimo story	10	20	30	54	72	90

NOTE: *Walter Johnson c-3, 4. Palais a-11. Wildey a-5, 11. Bondage c-6, 12.*

RED SONJA (Also see Conan #23, Kull & The Barbarians, Marvel Feature & Savage Sword Of Conan #1)
Marvel Comics Group: 1/77 - No. 15, 5/79; V1#1, 2/83 - V2#2, 3/83; V3#1, 8/83 - V3#4, 2/84; V3#5, 1/85 - V3#13, 5/86

	GD 2.0	VG 4.0	FN 6.0	VF 8.0	VF/NM 9.0	NM- 9.2
1-Created by Robert E. Howard	2	4	6	9	12	15
2-10: 5-Last 30¢ issue	1	2	3	4	5	7
4,5-(35¢-c variants, limited distribution)(7,9/77)	3	6	9	18	27	35
11-15, V1#1,V2#2: 14-Last 35¢ issue						6.00
V3#1-13: #1-$1.00, 52 pgs.)						3.50

NOTE: *Brunner c-12-14. J. Buscema a(p)-12, 13, 15; c-V#1. Nebres a-V3#3i(part). N. Redondo a-8i, V3#2i, 3i. Simonson a-V3#1. Thorne c/a-1-11.*

RED SONJA
Dynamite Entertainment: No. 0, Apr, 2005 - Present (25¢/$2.99)

	GD 2.0	VG 4.0	FN 6.0	VF 8.0	VF/NM 9.0	NM- 9.2
0-(4/05, 25¢) Greg Land-a/Mel Rubi-a/Oeming & Carey-s						2.25
1-(6/05, $2.99) Five covers by Ross, Linsner, Cassaday, Turner, Rivera; Rubi-a						3.00

	GD 2.0	VG 4.0	FN 6.0	VF 8.0	VF/NM 9.0	NM- 9.2
2-25-Multiple covers on all						3.00
5-RRP Edition with Red Foil logo and Isonove-a						10.00
Annual #1 (2007, $3.50) Oeming-s/Sadowski-a; Red Sonja Comics Chronology						3.50
... Cover Showcase Vol. 1 (2007, $5.99) gallery of variant covers; Cho sketches						6.00
Giant Size Red Sonja #1 (2007, $4.99) Chaykin-c; new story and reprints and pin-ups						5.00
... Goes East ($4.99) three covers; Joe Ng-a						5.00
...: Monster Isle ($4.99) two covers; Pablo Marcos-a/Roy Thomas-s						5.00
... One More Day ($4.99) two covers; Liam Sharp-a						5.00
... Vacant Shell ($4.99) two covers; Remender-a/Renaud-a						5.00
The Adventures of Red Sonja TPB (2005, $19.99) r/Marvel Feature #1-7						20.00
... Vol. 1 TPB (2006, $19.99) r/#0-6; gallery of covers and variants; creators interview						20.00

RED SONJA/CLAW: THE DEVIL'S HANDS (See Claw the Unconquered)
DC Comics (WildStorm)/Dynamite Ent.: May, 2006 - No. 4, Aug, 2006 ($2.99, limited series)

	GD 2.0	VG 4.0	FN 6.0	VF 8.0	VF/NM 9.0	NM- 9.2
1-4-Covers by Jim Lee & Dell'Otto.; Andy Smith-a 1-Alex Ross var-c. 2-Dell'Otto var-c. 3-Bermejo var-c. 4-Andy Smith var-c						3.00
TPB (2007, $12.99) r/#1-4; cover gallery						13.00

RED SONJA: SCAVENGER HUNT
Marvel Comics: Dec, 1995 ($2.95, one-shot)

	GD 2.0	VG 4.0	FN 6.0	VF 8.0	VF/NM 9.0	NM- 9.2
1						3.00

RED SONJA: THE MOVIE
Marvel Comics Group: Nov, 1985 - No. 2, Dec, 1985 (Limited series)

	GD 2.0	VG 4.0	FN 6.0	VF 8.0	VF/NM 9.0	NM- 9.2
1,2-Movie adapt-r/Marvel Super Spec. #38						3.00

RED SONJA VS. THULSA DOOM
Dynamite Entertainment: 2005 - No. 4, 2006 ($3.50)

	GD 2.0	VG 4.0	FN 6.0	VF 8.0	VF/NM 9.0	NM- 9.2
1-4-Conrad-a; Conrad & Dell'Otto covers						3.50
..., Volume 1 TPB (2006, $14.99) r/series; cover gallery						15.00

RED STAR, THE
Image Comics/Archangel Studios: June, 2000 - No. 9, June, 2002 ($2.95)

	GD 2.0	VG 4.0	FN 6.0	VF 8.0	VF/NM 9.0	NM- 9.2
1-Christian Gossett-s/a(p)						4.00
2-9: 9-Beck-c						3.00
#(7.5) Reprints Wizard #1/2 story with new pages						3.00
Annual 1 (Archangel Studios, 11/02, $3.50) "Run Makita Run"						3.50
TPB (4/01, $24.95, 9x12") oversized r/#1-4; intro. by Bendis						25.00
Nokgorka TPB (8/02, $24.95, 9x12") oversized r/#6-9; w/sketch pages						25.00
Wizard 1/2 (mail order)						10.00

RED STAR, THE (Volume 2)
CrossGen Comics #1,2/Archangel Studios #3 on: Feb, 2003 - No. 5, July, 2004 ($2.95/$2.99)

	GD 2.0	VG 4.0	FN 6.0	VF 8.0	VF/NM 9.0	NM- 9.2
1-5-Christian Gossett-s/a(p)						3.00
Prison of Souls TPB (8/04, $24.95, 9x12") oversized r/#1-5; w/sketch pages						25.00

RED STAR, THE: SWORD OF LIES
Archangel Studios: Aug, 2006 ($4.50)

	GD 2.0	VG 4.0	FN 6.0	VF 8.0	VF/NM 9.0	NM- 9.2
1-Christian Gossett-s/a(p); origin of the Red Star team						4.50

RED TORNADO (See All-American #20 & Justice League of America #64)
DC Comics: July, 1985 - No. 4, Oct, 1985 (Limited series)

	GD 2.0	VG 4.0	FN 6.0	VF 8.0	VF/NM 9.0	NM- 9.2
1-4: Kurt Busiek scripts in all. 1-3-Superman & Batman cameos						3.00

RED WARRIOR
Marvel/Atlas Comics (TCI): Jan, 1951 - No. 6, Dec, 1951

	GD 2.0	VG 4.0	FN 6.0	VF 8.0	VF/NM 9.0	NM- 9.2
1-Red Warrior & his horse White Wing; Tuska-a	16	32	48	92	144	195
2-Tuska-c	10	20	30	56	76	95
3-6: 4-Origin White Wing. 6-Maneely-c	9	18	27	47	61	75

RED, WHITE & BLUE COMICS
DC Comics: 1941

	GD 2.0	VG 4.0	FN 6.0	VF 8.0	VF/NM 9.0	NM- 9.2
nn - Ashcan comic, not distributed to newsstands, only for in-house use. Cover art is All-American Comics #20 with interior being Flash Comics #17 (no known sales)						

RED WOLF (See Avengers #80 & Marvel Spotlight #1)
Marvel Comics Group: May, 1972 - No. 9, Sept, 1973

	GD 2.0	VG 4.0	FN 6.0	VF 8.0	VF/NM 9.0	NM- 9.2
1-(Western hero); Gil Kane/Severin-c; Shores-a	3	6	9	16	23	30
2-9: 2-Kane-c; Shores-a. 6-Tuska-r in back-up. 7-Red Wolf as super hero begins.						
9-Origin sidekick, Lobo (wolf)	2	4	6	10	14	18

REESE'S PIECES
Eclipse Comics: Oct, 1985 - No.2, Oct, 1985 ($1.75, Baxter paper)

	GD 2.0	VG 4.0	FN 6.0	VF 8.0	VF/NM 9.0	NM- 9.2
1,2-B&W-r in color						2.50

REFORM SCHOOL GIRL!
Realistic Comics: 1951

	GD 2.0	VG 4.0	FN 6.0	VF 8.0	VF/NM 9.0	NM- 9.2
nn-Used in **SOTI**, pg. 358, & cover ill. with caption "Comic books are supposed to be like fairy tales"	300	600	900	1894	3197	4500

Re-Gex Preview © Awesome Ent.

WIZARD WORLD SPECIAL EDITION

Reggie's Wise Guy Jokes #40 © AP

Relative Heroes #3 © Grayson & Guichet

	GD	VG	FN	VF	VF/NM	NM-		GD	VG	FN	VF	VF/NM	NM-
	2.0	4.0	6.0	8.0	9.0	9.2		2.0	4.0	6.0	8.0	9.0	9.2

(Prices vary widely on this book)

NOTE: The cover and title originated from a digest-sized book published by Diversey Publishing Co. of Chicago in 1948. The original book "House of Fury", Doubleday, came out in 1941. The girl's real name which appears on the cover of the digest and comic is Marty Collins, Canadian model and ice skating star who posed for this special color photograph for the Diversey novel.

REGENTS ILLUSTRATED CLASSICS
Prentice Hall Regents, Englewood Cliffs, NJ 07632: 1981 (Plus more recent reprintings) (48 pgs., B&W-a with 14 pgs. of teaching helps)

NOTE: This series contains Classics Ill. art, and was produced from the same illegal source as **Cassette Books**. But when Twin Circle sued to stop the sale of the Cassette Books, they decided to permit this series to continue. This series was produced as a teaching aid. The 20 title series is divided into four levels based upon number of basic words used therein. There is also a teacher's manual for each level. All of the titles are still available from the publisher for about $5 each retail. The number to call for mail order purchases is (201)767-5937. Almost all of the issues have new covers taken from some interior art panel. Here is a list of the series by Regents ident. no. and the Classics Ill. counterpart.

16770(CI#24-A2)18333(CI#3-A2)21668(CI#13-A2)32224(CI#21)33051(CI#26)35788(CI#84)37153(CI#16)44460 (CI#19-A2)44808(CI#18-A2)52395(CI#4-A2)58627(CI#5-A2)60067(CI#30)68405(CI#23A1)70302(CI#29)78192 (CI#7-A2)78193(CI#10-A2)79679(CI#85)92046(CI#1-A2)93062(CI#64)93512(CI#8).

RE: GEX
Awesome-Hyperwerks: Jul, 1998 - No. 0, Dec, 1998; ($2.50)

Preview (7/98) Wizard Con Edition						3.00
0-(12/98) Loeb-s/Liefeld-a/Pat Lee-c, 1-(9/98) Loeb-s/Liefeld-a/c						2.50

REGGIE (Formerly Archie's Rival...; Reggie & Me #19 on)
Archie Publications: No. 15, Sept, 1963 - No. 18, Nov, 1965

15(9/63), 16(10/64), 17(8/65), 18(11/65)	4	8	12	28	44	60

NOTE: Cover title No. 15 & 16 is Archie's Rival Reggie.

REGGIE AND ME (Formerly Reggie)
Archie Publ.: No. 19, Aug, 1966 - No. 126, Sept, 1980 (No. 50-68: 52 pgs.)

19-Evilheart app.	4	8	12	22	34	45
20-23-Evilheart app.; with Pureheart #22	3	6	9	18	27	35
24-40(3/70)	2	4	6	13	18	22
41-49(7/71)	2	4	6	9	13	16
50(9/71)-68 (1/74, 52 pgs.)	2	4	6	11	16	20
69-99	1	2	3	5	7	9
100(10/77)	2	4	6	8	10	12
101-126	1	2	3	4	5	7

REGGIE'S JOKES (See Reggie's Wise Guy Jokes)

REGGIE'S REVENGE!
Archie Comic Publications, Inc.: Spring, 1994 - No. 3 ($2.00, 52 pgs.) (Published semi-annually)

1-Bound-in pull-out poster						3.00
2,3						2.50

REGGIE'S WISE GUY JOKES
Archie Publications: Aug, 1968 - No. 55, 1980 (#5-28 are Giants)

1	4	8	12	26	41	55
2-4	3	6	9	14	19	24
5-16 (1/71)(68 pg. Giants)	3	6	9	16	23	30
17-28 (52 pg. Giants)	2	4	6	11	16	20
29-40(1/77)	1	2	3	5	7	9
41-55						6.00

REGISTERED NURSE
Charlton Comics: Summer, 1963

1-r/Nurse Betsy Crane & Cynthia Doyle	3	6	9	16	22	28

REG'LAR FELLERS
Visual Editions (Standard): No. 5, Nov, 1947 - No. 6, Mar, 1948

5,6	9	18	27	47	61	75

REG'LAR FELLERS HEROIC (See Heroic Comics)

REID FLEMING, WORLD'S TOUGHEST MILKMAN
Eclipse Comics/ Deep Sea Comics: 8/86; V2#1, 12/86 - V2#3, 12/88; V2#4, 11/89; V2#5, 11/90 (B&W)

1 (3rd print, large size, 8/86, $2.50)-1-4th & 5th printings ($2.50)						3.00
V2#1 (10/86, regular size, $2.00), 1-2nd print, 3rd print ($2.00, 2/89)						2.50
2-8 , V2#2-2nd & 3rd printings, V2#4-2nd printing, V2#5 ($2.00)						2.50

REIGN OF THE ZODIAC
DC Comics: Oct, 2003 - No. 8, May, 2004 ($2.75)

1-8: 1-6,8-Giffen-s/Doran-a/Harris-c. 7-Byrd-a						2.75

RELATIVE HEROES
DC Comics: Mar, 2000 - No. 6, Aug, 2000 ($2.50, limited series)

1-6-Grayson-s/Guichet & Sowd-a. 6-Superman-c/app.   2.50

RELOAD
DC Comics (Homage): May, 2003 - No. 3, Sept, 2003 ($2.95, limited series)

1-3-Warren Ellis-s/Paul Gulacy & Jimmy Palmiotti-a						3.00
.../Mek TPB (2004, $14.95, flip book) r/Reload #1-3 & Mek #1-3						15.00

RELUCTANT DRAGON, THE (Walt Disney's...)
Dell Publishing Co.: No. 13, 1940

Four Color 13-Contains 2 pgs. of photos from film; 2 pg. foreword to Fantasia by Leopold Stokowski; Donald Duck, Goofy, Baby Weems & Mickey Mouse (as the Sorcerer's Apprentice) app.	214	428	642	1338	2219	3100

REMAINS
IDW Publishing: May, 2004 - No. 5, Sept, 2004 ($3.99)

1-5-Steve Niles-s/Kieron Dwyer-a   4.00

REMARKABLE WORLDS OF PROFESSOR PHINEAS B. FUDDLE, THE
DC Comics (Paradox Press): 2000 - No. 4, 2000 ($5.95, limited series)

1-4-Boaz Yakin-s/Erez Yakin-a						6.00
TPB (2001, $19.95) r/series						20.00

REMEMBER PEARL HARBOR
Street & Smith Publications: 1942 (68 pgs.) (Illustrated story of the battle)

nn-Uncle Sam-c; Jack Binder-a	92	138	281	466	650

REN & STIMPY SHOW, THE (TV) (Nicklodeon cartoon characters)
Marvel Comics: Dec, 1992 - No. 44, July, 1996 ($1.75/$1.95)

1-($2.25)-Polybagged w/scratch & sniff Ren or Stimpy air fowler (equal numbers of each were made)		6.00
1-2nd & 3rd printing; different dialogue on-c		2.50
2-6: 4-Muddy Mudskipper back-up. 5-Bill Wray painted-c. 6-Spider-Man vs. Powdered Toast Man		4.00
7-17: 12-1st solo back-up story w/Tank & Brenner		2.50
18-44: 18-Powered Toast Man app.		2.50
25 ($2.95) Deluxe edition w/die cut cover		3.00
...Don't Try This at Home (3/94, $12.95, TPB)-r/#9-12		13.00
...Eenteractive Special ('95, $2.95)		3.00
...Holiday Special 1994 (2/95, $2.95, 52 pgs.)		3.00
...Mini Comic (1995)		5.00
...Pick of the Litter nn (1993, $12.95, TPB)-r/#1-4		13.00
...Radio Daze (11/95, $1.95)		2.50
...Running Joke nn (1993, $12.95, TPB)-r/#1-4 plus new-a		13.00
...Seeck Little Monkeys (1/95, $12.95)-r/#17-20		13.00
...Special 2 (7/94, $2.95, 52 pgs.), ...Special 3 (10/94, $2.95, 52 pgs.)-Choose adventure, ...Special: Around the World in a Daze ($2.95), ...Special: Four Swerks (1/95, $2.95, 52 pgs.)-FF #1 cover swipe; cover reads "Four Swerks w/5 pg. coloring book.", ...Special: Powdered Toast Man 1 (4/94, $2.95, 52 pgs.), ...Special: Powdered Toast Man's Cereal Serial (4/95, $2.95), ...Special: Sports (10/95, $2.95)		3.00
...Tastes Like Chicken nn (11/93,$12.95,TPB)-r/#5-8		13.00
...Your Pals (1994, $12.95, TPB)-r/#13-16		13.00

RENFIELD
Caliber Press:1994 - No. 3, 1995 ($2.95, B&W, limited series)

1-3   3.00

RENO BROWNE, HOLLYWOOD'S GREATEST COWGIRL (Formerly Margie Comics; Apache Kid #53 on; also see Western Hearts, Western Life Romances & Western Love)
Marvel Comics (MPC): No. 50, April, 1950 - No. 52, Sept, 1950 (52 pgs.)

50-Reno Browne photo-c on all	31	62	93	178	282	385
51,52	26	52	78	152	239	325

REPLACEMENT GOD
Amaze Ink: June, 1995 - No. 8 ($2.95, B&W)

1-8-Zander Cannon-s/a   3.00

REPLACEMENT GOD
Image Comics: May, 1997 - No. 5 ($2.95, B&W)

1-5: 1-Flip book w/"Knute's Escapes", r/original series. 2-Flip book w/"Harris Thermidor".		
3-5: 3-Flip book w/"Myth and Legend"		3.00

REPTILICUS (Becomes Reptisaurus #3 on)
Charlton Comics: Aug, 1961 - No. 2, Oct, 1961

1 (Movie)	19	38	57	138	244	350
2	10	20	30	70	123	175

REPTISAURUS (Reptilicus #1,2)
Charlton Comics: V2#3, Jan, 1962 - No. 8, Dec, 1962; Summer, 1963

Resurrection Man #10 © DC

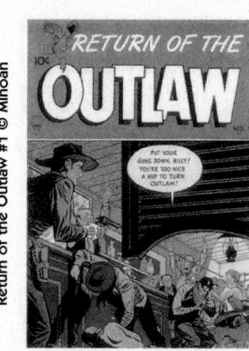
Return of the Outlaw #1 © Minoan

Rex Allen Comics #4 © DELL

	GD 2.0	VG 4.0	FN 6.0	VF 8.0	VF/NM 9.0	NM- 9.2
V2#3-8: 8-Montes/Bache-c/a	6	12	18	41	66	90
Special Edition 1 (Summer, 1963)	6	12	18	39	62	85

REQUIEM FOR DRACULA
Marvel Comics: Feb, 1993 ($2.00, 52 pgs.)
nn-r/Tomb of Dracula #69,70 by Gene Colan ... 2.50

RESCUERS, THE (See Walt Disney Showcase #40)

RESIDENT EVIL (Based on video game)
Image Comics (WildStorm): Mar, 1998 - No. 5 ($4.95, quarterly magazine)
1 ... 7.00
2-5 ... 5.00
...Code: Veronica 1-4 (2002, $14.95) English reprint of Japanese comics ... 15.00
...Collection One ('99, $14.95, TPB) r/#1-4 ... 15.00

RESIDENT EVIL: FIRE AND ICE
DC Comics (WildStorm): Dec, 2000 - No. 4, May, 2001 ($2.50, limited series)
1-4-Bermejo-c ... 2.50

RESISTANCE, THE
DC Comics (WildStorm): Nov, 2002 - No. 8, June, 2003 ($2.95)
1-8-Palmiotti & Gray-s/Santacruz-a ... 3.00

RESTAURANT AT THE END OF THE UNIVERSE, THE (See Hitchhiker's Guide to the Galaxy & Life, the Universe & Everything)
DC Comics: 1994 - No. 3, 1994 ($6.95, limited series)
1-3 ... 7.00

RESTLESS GUN (TV)
Dell Publishing Co.: No. 934, Sept, 1958 - No. 1146, Nov-Jan, 1960-61
Four Color 934 (#1)-Photo-c ... 10 20 30 71 126 180
Four Color 986 (5/59), 1045 (11-1/60), 1089 (3/60), 1146-Wildey-a; all photo-c ... 8 16 24 52 86 120

RESURRECTION MAN
DC Comics: May, 1997 - No. 27, Aug, 1999 ($2.50)
1-Lenticular disc on cover ... 5.00
2-5: 2-JLA app. ... 4.00
6-10: 6-Genesis-x-over. 7-Batman app. 10-Hitman-c/app. ... 3.00
11-27: 16,17-Supergirl x-over. 18-Deadman & Phantom Stranger-c/app. 21-JLA-c/app. ... 2.50
#1,000,000 (11/98) 853rd Century x-over ... 2.50

RETIEF (Keith Laumer's)
Adventure Comics (Malibu): Dec, 1989 - Vol. 2, No.6, ($2.25, B&W)
1-6,Vol. 2, #1-6,Vol. 3 (...of The CDT) #1-6 ... 2.50
...and The Warlords #1-6, ...: Diplomatic Immunity #1 (4/91), ...: Giant Killer #1 (9/91), ...: Crime & Punishment #1 (11/91) ... 2.50

RETURN FROM WITCH MOUNTAIN (See Walt Disney Showcase #44)

RETURN OF ALISON DARE: LITTLE MISS ADVENTURES, THE (Also see Alison Dare: Little Miss Adventures)
Oni Press: Apr, 2001 - No. 3, Sept, 2001 ($2.95, B&W, limited series)
1-3-J. Torres-s/J.Bone-c/a ... 3.00

RETURN OF GORGO, THE (Formerly Gorgo's Revenge)
Charlton Comics: No. 2, Aug, 1963; No. 3, Fall, 1964 (12¢)
2,3-Ditko-c/a; based on M.G.M. movie ... 7 14 21 49 80 110

RETURN OF KONGA, THE (Konga's Revenge #2 on)
Charlton Comics: 1962
nn ... 7 14 21 49 80 110

RETURN OF MEGATON MAN
Kitchen Sink Press: July, 1988 - No. 3, 1988 ($2.00, limited series)
1-3: Simpson-c/a ... 2.50

RETURN OF THE OUTLAW
Toby Press (Minoan): Feb, 1953 - No. 11, 1955
1-Billy the Kid ... 10 20 30 54 72 90
2 ... 7 14 21 35 43 50
3-11 ... 6 12 18 31 38 45

RETURN TO JURASSIC PARK
Topps Comics: Apr, 1995 - No. 9, Feb, 1996 ($2.50/$2.95)
1-9: 3-Begin $2.95-c. 9-Artist's Jam issue ... 3.00

RETURN TO THE AMALGAM AGE OF COMICS: THE MARVEL COMICS COLLECTION
Marvel Comics: 1997 ($12.95, TPB)
nn-Reprints Amalgam one-shots: Challengers of the Fantastic #1, The Exciting X-Patrol #1,

Iron Lantern #1, The Magnetic Men Featuring Magneto #1, Spider-Boy Team-Up #1 & Thorion of the New Asgods #1 ... 13.00

REVEAL
Dark Horse Comics: Nov, 2002 ($6.95, squarebound)
1-Short stories of Dark Horse characters by various; Lone Wolf 2100, Buffy, Spyboy app. ... 7.00

REVEALING LOVE STORIES (See Fox Giants)

REVEALING ROMANCES
Ace Magazines: Sept, 1949 - No. 6, Aug, 1950
1 ... 14 28 42 80 115 150
2 ... 9 18 27 47 61 75
3-6 ... 8 16 24 42 54 65

REVELATIONS
Dark Horse Comics: Aug, 2005 - No. 6, Jan, 2006 ($2.99, limited series)
1-6-Paul Jenkins-s/Humberto Ramos-a/c ... 3.00

REVENGE OF THE PROWLER (Also see The Prowler)
Eclipse Comics: Feb, 1988 - No. 4, June, 1988 ($1.75/$1.95)
1,3,4: 1-$1.75. 3,4-$1.95-c; Snyder III-a(p) ... 2.50
2 ($2.50)-Contains flexi-disc ... 2.75

REVOLUTION ON THE PLANET OF THE APES
Mr. Comics: Dec, 2005 - No. 6, Aug, 2006 ($3.95)
1-6: 1,2-Salgood Sam-a ... 4.00

REX ALLEN COMICS (Movie star)(Also see Four Color #877 & Western Roundup under Dell Giants)
Dell Publ. Co.: No. 316, Feb, 1951 - No. 31, Dec-Feb, 1958-59 (All-photo-c)
Four Color 316(#1)(52 pgs.)-Rex Allen & his horse Koko begin; Marsh-a ... 14 28 42 102 181 260
2 (9-11/51, 36 pgs.) ... 9 18 27 63 107 150
3-10 ... 7 14 21 45 73 100
11-20 ... 6 12 18 39 62 85
21-23,25-31 ... 5 10 15 35 55 75
24-Toth-a ... 6 12 18 39 62 85
NOTE: **Manning** a-20, 27-30. Photo back-c F.C. #316, 2-12, 20, 21.

REX DEXTER OF MARS (See Mystery Men Comics)
Fox Features Syndicate: Fall, 1940 (68 pgs.)
1-Rex Dexter, Patty O'Day, & Zanzibar (Tuska)-a) app.; Briefer-c/a ... 193 386 579 1206 2003 2800

REX HART (Formerly Blaze Carson; Whip Wilson #9 on)
Timely/Marvel Comics (USA): No. 6, Aug, 1949 - No. 8, Feb, 1950 (All photo-c)
6-Rex Hart & his horse Warrior begin; Black Rider app; Captain Tootsie by Beck ... 26 52 78 154 242 330
7,8: 18 pg. Thriller in each. 8-Blaze the Wonder Collie app. in text ... 18 36 54 103 162 220

REX MORGAN, M.D. (Also see Harvey Comics Library)
Argo Publ.: Dec, 1955 - No. 3, Apr?, 1956
1-r/Rex Morgan daily newspaper strips & daily panel-r of "These Women" by D'Alessio & "Timeout" by Jeff Keate ... 14 28 42 76 108 140
2,3 ... 10 20 30 54 72 90

REX MUNDI (Latin for "King of the World")
Image Comics: No. 0, Aug, 2002 - No. 18, Apr, 2006 ($2.95/$2.99)
0-18-Arvid Nelson-s. 0-13-Eric Johnson-a. 14,15-Jim DiBartolo-a. 18-Ramos-c ... 3.00
Book 1: The Guardian of the Temple TPB (Dark Horse, 11/06, $16.95) r/#0-5 & Brother Matthew web comic; Dysart intro. ... 17.00
Book 2: The River Underground (Dark Horse, 2006, $16.95) r/#6-11 ... 17.00
Vol. 1: The Guardian of the Temple TPB (1/04, $14.95) r/#0-5 ... 15.00
Vol. 2: The River Underground TPB (4/05, $14.95) r/#6-11 ... 15.00
Vol. 3: The Lost Kings TPB (Dark Horse, 9/06, $16.95) r/#12-17 ... 17.00

REX MUNDI (Volume 2)
Dark Horse Comics: July, 2006 - Present ($2.99)
1-7-Arvid Nelson-s. 1-JH Williams-c ... 3.00

REX THE WONDER DOG (See The Adventures of...)

RHUBARB, THE MILLIONAIRE CAT
Dell Publishing Co.: No. 423, Sept-Oct, 1952 - No. 563, June, 1954
Four Color 423 (#1) ... 6 12 18 39 62 85
Four Color 466(5/53),563 ... 5 10 15 35 55 75

RIB

Ribtickler #2 © FOX

Richard Dragon Kung-Fu Fighter #1 © DC

Richie Rich #32 © HARV

	GD 2.0	VG 4.0	FN 6.0	VF 8.0	VF/NM 9.0	NM- 9.2

Dilemma Productions: Oct, 1995 - April, 1996 ($1.95, B&W)

Ashcan, 1						3.00

RIB
Bookmark Productions: 1996 ($2.95, B&W)

1-Sakai-c; Andrew Ford-s/a						3.00

RIB
Caliber Comics: May, 1997 - No. 5, 1998 ($2.95, B&W)

1-5: 1-"Beginnings" pts. 1 & 2						3.00

RIBIT! (Red Sonja imitation)
Comico: Jan, 1989 - No. 4, April?, 1989 ($1.95, limited series)

1-4: Frank Thorne-c/a/scripts						3.00

RIBTICKLER (Also see Fox Giants)
Fox Feature Synd./Green Publ. (1957)/Norlen (1959): 1945 - No. 9, Aug, 1947; 1957; 1959

	GD	VG	FN	VF	VF/NM	NM-
1-Funny animal	15	30	45	90	140	190
2-(1946)	10	20	30	54	72	90
3-9; 3,7-Cosmo Cat app.	9	18	27	47	61	75
3,7,8 (Green Publ.-1957), 3,7,8 (Norlen Mag.-1959)	3	6	9	16	23	30

RICHARD DRAGON
DC Comics: July, 2004 - No. 12, Jun, 2005 ($2.50)

1-12: 1-Dixon-s/McDaniel-a/c; Ben Turner app. 2,3-Nightwing app. 4-6,11,12-Lady Shiva						2.50

RICHARD DRAGON, KUNG-FU FIGHTER (See The Batman Chronicles #5, Brave & the Bold, & The Question)
National Periodical Publ./DC Comics: Apr-May, 1975 - No. 18, Nov-Dec, 1977

	GD	VG	FN	VF	VF/NM	NM-
1-Intro Richard Dragon, Ben Stanley & O-Sensei; 1st app. Barney Ling; adaptation of Jim Dennis novel "Dragon's Fists" begins, ends #4	2	4	6	10	14	18
2,3: 2-Intro Carolyn Woosan; Starlin/Weiss-c/a; bondage-c. 3-Kirby-a(p); Giordano bondage-c	1	3	4	6	8	10
4-8-Wood inks. 4-Carolyn Woosan dies. 5-1st app. Lady Shiva	1	2	3	4	5	7
9-13,15-18: 9-Ben Stanley becomes Ben Turner; intro Preying Mantis. 16-1st app. Prof Ojo. 18-1st app. Ben Turner as The Bronze Tiger	1	2	3	4	5	7
14-"Spirit of Bruce Lee"	2	4	6	10	14	18

NOTE: Buckler a-14. c-15, 18. Chua c-13. Estrada a-9, 13-18. Estrada/Abel a-10-12. Estrada/Wood a-4-8. Giordano c-1, 3-11. Weiss a-2(partial) c-2i.

RICHARD THE LION-HEARTED (See Ideal a Classical Comic)

RICHIE RICH (See Harvey Collectors Comics, Harvey Hits, Little Dot, Little Lotta, Little Sad Sack, Million Dollar Digest, Mutt & Jeff, Super Richie & 3-D Dolly; also Tastee-Freez Comics in the Promotional Comics section)

RICHIE RICH (...the Poor Little Rich Boy) (See Harvey Hits #3, 9)
Harvey Publ.: Nov, 1960 - #218, Oct, 1982; #219, June 1987, 1986 - #254, Jan, 1991

	GD	VG	FN	VF	VF/NM	NM-
1-(See Little Dot #1 for 1st app.)	200	400	600	1750	3275	4800
2	67	134	201	570	1060	1550
3-5	43	86	129	344	622	900
6-10: 8-Christmas-c	26	52	78	195	348	500
11-20	17	34	51	128	227	325
21-30	12	24	36	82	146	210
31-40	10	20	30	67	116	165
41-50: 42(2/66)-X-mas-c	8	16	24	52	86	120
51-55,57-60: 59-Buck, prototype of Dollar the Dog	6	12	18	37	59	80
56-1st app. Super Richie	7	14	21	45	73	100
61-64,66-80: 71-Nixon & Robert Kennedy caricatures; outer space-c	4	8	12	28	44	60
65-Buck the Dog (Dollar prototype) on cover	6	12	18	41	66	90
81-99	3	6	9	20	30	40
100(12/70)-1st app. Irona the robot maid	4	8	12	24	37	50
101-111,117-120	3	6	9	14	19	24
112-116: All 52 pg. Giants	3	6	9	16	23	30
121-140: 137-1st app. Mr. Cheepers and Professor Keenbean	2	4	6	9	13	16
141-160: 145-Infinity-c. 155-3rd app. The Money Monster	2	4	6	8	10	12
161-180	1	3	4	6	8	10
181-199	1	2	3	5	6	8
200	1	3	4	6	8	10
201-218: 210-Stone-Age Riches app	1	2	3	4	5	7
219-254: 237-Last original material						6.00

RICHIE RICH
Harvey Comics: Mar, 1991 - No. 28, Nov, 1994 ($1.00, bi-monthly)

1-28: Reprints best of Richie Rich						2.50

Giant Size 1-4 (10/91-10/93, $2.25, 68 pgs.)						3.00

RICHIE RICH ADVENTURE DIGEST MAGAZINE
Harvey Comics: 1992 - No. 7, Sept, 1994 ($1.25, quarterly, digest-size)

1-7						4.00

RICHIE RICH AND...
Harvey Comics: Oct, 1987 - No. 11, May, 1990 ($1.00)

1-Professor Keenbean						4.00
2-11: 2-Casper. 3-Dollar the Dog. 4-Cadbury. 5 Mayda Munny. 6-Irona. 7-Little Dot. 8-Professor Keenbean. 9-Little Audrey. 10-Mayda Munny. 11-Cadbury						3.00

RICHIE RICH AND BILLY BELLHOPS
Harvey Publications: Oct, 1977 (52 pgs., one-shot)

	GD	VG	FN	VF	VF/NM	NM-
1	2	4	6	9	12	15

RICHIE RICH AND CADBURY
Harvey Publ.: 10/77; #2, 9/78 - #23, 7/82; #24, 7/90 - #29, 1/91 (1-10: 52pgs.)

	GD	VG	FN	VF	VF/NM	NM-
1-(52 pg. Giant)	2	4	6	11	16	20
2-10-(52 pg. Giant)	2	4	6	8	10	12
11-23						6.00
24-29: 24-Begin $1.00-c						4.00

RICHIE RICH AND CASPER
Harvey Publications: Aug, 1974 - No. 45, Sept, 1982

	GD	VG	FN	VF	VF/NM	NM-
1	3	6	9	20	30	40
2-5	2	4	6	13	18	22
6-10: 10-Xmas-c	2	4	6	9	13	16
11-20	1	3	4	6	8	10
21-45: 22-Xmas-c						6.00

RICHIE RICH AND DOLLAR THE DOG (See Richie Rich #65)
Harvey Publications: Sept, 1977 - No. 24, Aug, 1982 (#1-10: 52 pgs.)

	GD	VG	FN	VF	VF/NM	NM-
1-(52 pg. Giant)	2	4	6	11	16	20
2-10-(52 pg. Giant)	2	4	6	8	10	12
11-24						6.00

RICHIE RICH AND DOT
Harvey Publications: Oct, 1974 (one-shot)

	GD	VG	FN	VF	VF/NM	NM-
1	3	6	9	16	22	28

RICHIE RICH AND GLORIA
Harvey Publications: Sept, 1977 - No. 25, Sept, 1982 (#1-11: 52 pgs.)

	GD	VG	FN	VF	VF/NM	NM-
1-(52 pg. Giant)	2	4	6	11	16	20
2-11-(52 pg. Giant)	2	4	6	8	10	12
12-25						6.00

RICHIE RICH AND HIS GIRLFRIENDS
Harvey Publications: April, 1979 - No. 16, Dec, 1982

	GD	VG	FN	VF	VF/NM	NM-
1-(52 pg. Giant)	2	4	6	9	13	16
2-(52 pg. Giant)	1	3	4	6	8	10
3-10	1	2	3	5	6	8
11-16						6.00

RICHIE RICH AND HIS MEAN COUSIN REGGIE
Harvey Publications: April, 1979 - No. 3, 1980 (50¢) (#1,2: 52 pgs.)

	GD	VG	FN	VF	VF/NM	NM-
1	2	4	6	9	13	16
2-3:	1	3	4	6	8	10

NOTE: No. 4 was advertised, but never released.

RICHIE RICH AND JACKIE JOKERS (Also see Jackie Jokers)
Harvey Publications: Nov, 1973 - No. 48, Dec, 1982

	GD	VG	FN	VF	VF/NM	NM-
1: 52 pg. Giant; contains material from unpublished Jackie Jokers #5	4	8	12	24	37	50
2,3-(52 pg. Giants). 2-R.R. & Jackie 1st meet	3	6	9	16	22	28
4,5	2	4	6	13	18	22
6-10	2	4	6	9	13	16
11-20,26: 11-1st app. Kool Katz. 26-Star Wars parody	1	3	4	6	8	10
21-25,27-40	1	2	3	4	5	7
41-48						6.00

RICHIE RICH AND PROFESSOR KEENBEAN
Harvey Comics: Sept, 1990 - No. 2, Nov, 1990 ($1.00)

1,2						3.00

RICHIE RICH AND THE NEW KIDS ON THE BLOCK
Harvey Publications: Feb, 1991 - No. 3, June, 1991 ($1.25, bi-monthly)

1-3: 1,2-New Richie Rich stories						3.00

RICHIE RICH AND TIMMY TIME

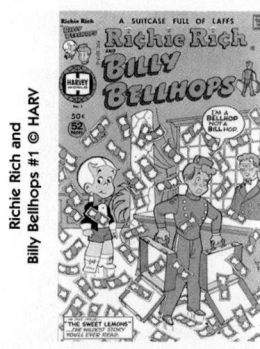

Richie Rich and Billy Bellhops #1 © HARV

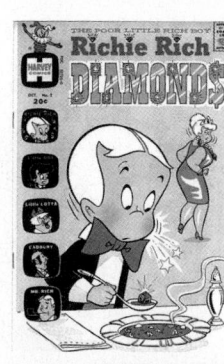

Richie Rich Diamonds #2 © HARV

Richie Rich Giant Size #1 © HARV

	GD 2.0	VG 4.0	FN 6.0	VF 8.0	VF/NM 9.0	NM- 9.2

Harvey Publications: Sept, 1977 (50¢, 52 pgs, one-shot)

	GD 2.0	VG 4.0	FN 6.0	VF 8.0	VF/NM 9.0	NM- 9.2
1	2	4	6	9	12	15

RICHIE RICH BANK BOOK
Harvey Publications: Oct, 1972 - No. 59, Sept, 1982

	GD 2.0	VG 4.0	FN 6.0	VF 8.0	VF/NM 9.0	NM- 9.2
1	5	10	15	30	48	65
2-5: 2-2nd app. The Money Monster	3	6	9	16	23	30
6-10	2	4	6	11	16	20
11-20: 18-Super Richie app.	2	4	6	8	10	12
21-30	1	2	3	5	7	9
31-40	1	2	3	4	5	7
41-59						6.00

RICHIE RICH BEST OF THE YEARS
Harvey Publications: Oct, 1977 - No. 6, June, 1980 (128 pgs., digest-size)

	GD 2.0	VG 4.0	FN 6.0	VF 8.0	VF/NM 9.0	NM- 9.2
1(10/77)-Reprints	2	4	6	9	12	15
2-6(11/79-6/80, 95¢). #2(10/78)-Rep.. #3(6/79, 75¢)	1	2	3	5	7	9

RICHIE RICH BIG BOOK
Harvey Publications: Nov, 1992 - No. 2, May, 1993 ($1.50, 52 pgs.)

	NM- 9.2
1,2	3.00

RICHIE RICH BIG BUCKS
Harvey Publications: Apr, 1991 - No. 8, July, 1992 ($1.00, bi-monthly)

	NM- 9.2
1-8	3.00

RICHIE RICH BILLIONS
Harvey Publications: Oct, 1974 - No. 48, Oct, 1982 (#1-33: 52 pgs.)

	GD 2.0	VG 4.0	FN 6.0	VF 8.0	VF/NM 9.0	NM- 9.2
1	4	8	12	22	34	45
2-5: 2-Christmas issue	3	6	9	14	20	25
6-10	2	4	6	10	14	18
11-20	2	4	6	8	10	12
21-33	1	2	3	5	6	8
34-48: 35-Onion app.						6.00

RICHIE RICH CASH
Harvey Publications: Sept, 1974 - No. 47, Aug, 1982

	GD 2.0	VG 4.0	FN 6.0	VF 8.0	VF/NM 9.0	NM- 9.2
1-1st app. Dr. N-R-Gee	3	6	9	20	30	40
2-5	2	4	6	13	18	22
6-10	2	4	6	9	13	16
11-20	1	3	4	6	8	10
21-30	1	2	3	4	5	7
31-47: 33-Dr. Blemish app.						6.00

RICHIE RICH CASH MONEY
Harvey Comics: May, 1992 - No. 2, Aug, 1992 ($1.25)

	NM- 9.2
1,2	3.00

RICHIE RICH, CASPER AND WENDY - NATIONAL LEAGUE
Harvey Comics: June, 1976 (50¢)

	GD 2.0	VG 4.0	FN 6.0	VF 8.0	VF/NM 9.0	NM- 9.2
1-Newsstand version of the baseball giveaway	2	4	6	13	18	22

RICHIE RICH COLLECTORS COMICS (See Harvey Collectors Comics)

RICHIE RICH DIAMONDS
Harvey Publications: Aug, 1972 - No. 59, Aug, 1982 (#1, 23-45: 52 pgs.)

	GD 2.0	VG 4.0	FN 6.0	VF 8.0	VF/NM 9.0	NM- 9.2
1-(52 pg. Giant)	5	10	15	32	51	70
2-5	3	6	9	16	23	30
6-10	2	4	6	11	16	20
11-22	2	4	6	8	10	12
23-30-(52 pg. Giants)	2	4	6	8	11	14
31-45: 39-r/Origin Little Dot	1	2	3	5	7	9
46-50	1	2	3	4	5	7
51-59						6.00

RICHIE RICH DIGEST
Harvey Publications: Oct, 1986 - No. 42, Oct, 1994 ($1.25/$1.75, digest-size)

	GD 2.0	VG 4.0	FN 6.0	VF 8.0	VF/NM 9.0	NM- 9.2
1	1	3	4	6	8	10
2-10						6.00
11-20						5.00
21-42						4.00

RICHIE RICH DIGEST STORIES (...Magazine #?-on)
Harvey Publications: Oct, 1977 - No., 17, Oct, 1982 (75¢/95¢, digest-size)

	GD 2.0	VG 4.0	FN 6.0	VF 8.0	VF/NM 9.0	NM- 9.2
1-Reprints	2	4	6	9	12	15
2-10: Reprints	1	2	3	5	7	9
11-17: Reprints						6.00

RICHIE RICH DIGEST WINNERS

Harvey Publications: Dec, 1977 - No. 16, Sept, 1982 (75¢/95¢, 132 pgs., digest-size)

	GD 2.0	VG 4.0	FN 6.0	VF 8.0	VF/NM 9.0	NM- 9.2
1	2	4	6	9	12	15
2-5	1	2	3	5	7	9
6-16						6.00

RICHIE RICH DOLLARS & CENTS
Harvey Publications: Aug, 1963 - No. 109, Aug, 1982 (#1-43: 68 pgs.; 44-60, 71-94: 52 pgs.)

	GD 2.0	VG 4.0	FN 6.0	VF 8.0	VF/NM 9.0	NM- 9.2
1: (#1-64 are all reprint issues)	18	36	54	134	237	340
2	10	20	30	68	119	170
3-5: 5-r/1st app. of R.R. from Little Dot #1	9	18	27	63	107	150
6-10	7	14	21	47	76	105
11-20	5	10	15	30	48	65
21-30: 25-r/1st app. Nurse Jenny (Little Lotta #62)	4	8	12	22	34	45
31-43: 43-Last 68 pg. issue	3	6	9	18	27	35
44-60: All 52 pgs.	3	6	9	14	19	25
61-71	1	3	4	6	8	10
72-94: All 52 pgs.	2	4	6	8	10	12
95-99,101-109						6.00
100-Anniversary issue	1	2	3	5	7	9

RICHIE RICH FORTUNES
Harvey Publications: Sept, 1971 - No. 63, July, 1982 (#1-15: 52 pgs.)

	GD 2.0	VG 4.0	FN 6.0	VF 8.0	VF/NM 9.0	NM- 9.2
1	6	12	18	39	62	85
2-5	3	6	9	20	30	40
6-10	2	4	6	13	18	22
11-15: 11-r/1st app. The Onion	2	4	6	9	12	15
16-30	1	2	3	5	7	9
31-40	1	2	3	4	5	7
41-63: 62-Onion app.						6.00

RICHIE RICH GEMS
Harvey Publications: Sept, 1974 - No. 43, Sept, 1982

	GD 2.0	VG 4.0	FN 6.0	VF 8.0	VF/NM 9.0	NM- 9.2
1	3	6	9	20	30	40
2-5	2	4	6	13	18	22
6-10	2	4	6	9	13	16
11-20	1	3	4	6	8	10
21-30	1	2	3	4	5	7
31-43: 36-Dr. Blemish, Onion app. 38-1st app. Stone-Age Riches						6.00

RICHIE RICH GOLD AND SILVER
Harvey Publications: Sept, 1975 - No. 42, Oct, 1982 (#1-27: 52 pgs.)

	GD 2.0	VG 4.0	FN 6.0	VF 8.0	VF/NM 9.0	NM- 9.2
1	3	6	9	18	27	35
2-5	2	4	6	11	16	20
6-10	2	4	6	8	11	14
11-27	1	2	3	5	7	9
28-42: 34-Stone-Age Riches app.						6.00

RICHIE RICH GOLD NUGGETS DIGEST
Harvey Publications: Dec., 1990 - No. 4, June, 1991 ($1.75, digest-size)

	NM- 9.2
1-4	3.00

RICHIE RICH HOLIDAY DIGEST MAGAZINE (...Digest #4)
Harvey Publications: Jan, 1980 - #3, Jan, 1982; #4, 3/88; #5, 2/89 (annual)

	VG 4.0	FN 6.0	VF 8.0	VF/NM 9.0	NM- 9.2
1-X-Mas-c	2	4	6	8	10
2-5: 2,3; All X-Mas-c. 4-(3/88, $1.25), 5-(2/89, $1.75)	1 2	3	4	5	7

RICHIE RICH INVENTIONS
Harvey Publications: Oct, 1977 - No. 26, Oct, 1982 (#1-11: 52 pgs.)

	GD 2.0	VG 4.0	FN 6.0	VF 8.0	VF/NM 9.0	NM- 9.2
1	2	4	6	11	16	20
2-5	2	4	6	8	10	12
6-11	1	2	3	5	6	8
12-26						6.00

RICHIE RICH JACKPOTS
Harvey Publications: Oct, 1972 - No. 58, Aug, 1982 (#41-43: 52 pgs.)

	GD 2.0	VG 4.0	FN 6.0	VF 8.0	VF/NM 9.0	NM- 9.2
1-Debut of Cousin Jackpots	5	10	15	30	48	65
2-5	3	6	9	16	23	30
6-10	2	4	6	11	16	20
11-15,17-20	2	4	6	8	10	12
16-Super Richie app.	2	4	6	9	12	15
21-30	1	2	3	5	7	9
31-40,44-50: 37-Caricatures of Frank Sinatra, Dean Martin, Sammy Davis, Jr. 45-Dr. Blemish app.	1	2	3	4	5	7
41-43 (52 pgs.)	1	3	4	6	8	10
51-58						6.00

RICHIE RICH MILLION DOLLAR DIGEST (...Magazine #?-on)(See Million Dollar Digest)

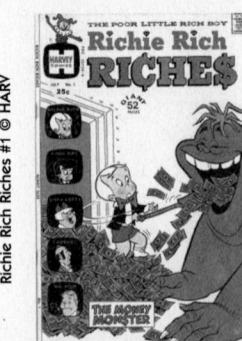

Richie Rich Millions #10 © HARV

Richie Rich Riches #1 © HARV

The Rifleman #2 © DELL

	GD 2.0	VG 4.0	FN 6.0	VF 8.0	VF/NM 9.0	NM- 9.2

Harvey Publications: Oct, 1980 - No. 10, Oct, 1982 ($1.50)

1	1	3	4	6	8	10
2-10						6.00

RICHIE RICH MILLIONS
Harvey Publ.: 9/61; #2, 9/62 - #113, 10/82 (#1-48: 68 pgs.; 49-64, 85-97: 52 pgs.)

1: (#1-3 are all reprint issues)	21	42	63	156	278	400
2	11	22	33	77	136	195
3-5: All other giants are new & reprints. 5-1st 15 pg. Richie Rich story						
	9	18	27	65	113	160
6-10	8	16	24	58	97	135
11-20	6	12	18	41	66	90
21-30	4	8	12	28	44	60
31-48: 31-1st app. The Onion. 48-Last 68 pg. Giant	3	6	9	20	30	40
49-64: 52 pg. Giants	3	6	9	14	20	25
65-67,69-73,75-84	2	4	6	8	10	12
68-1st Super Richie-c (11/74)	2	4	6	13	18	22
74-1st app. Mr. Woody; Super Richie app.	2	4	6	8	11	14
85-97: 52 pg. Giants	2	4	6	8	11	14
98,99	1	2	3	4	5	7
100	1	2	3	5	7	9
101-113						6.00

RICHIE RICH MONEY WORLD
Harvey Publications: Sept, 1972 - No. 59, Sept, 1982

1-(52 pg. Giant)-1st app. Mayda Munny	6	12	18	37	59	80
2-Super Richie app.	3	6	9	18	27	35
3-5	3	6	9	16	23	30
6-10: 9,10-Richie Rich mistakenly named Little Lotta on covers						
	2	4	6	11	16	20
11-20: 16,20-Dr. N-R-Gee	2	4	6	8	10	12
21-30	1	2	3	5	7	9
31-50	1	2	3	4	5	7
51-59						6.00
Digest 1 (2/91, $1.75)						5.00
2-8 (12/93, $1.75)						3.00

RICHIE RICH PROFITS
Harvey Publications: Oct, 1974 - No. 47, Sept, 1982

1	3	6	9	20	30	40
2-5	2	4	6	13	18	22
6-10: 10-Origin of Dr. N-R-Gee	2	4	6	9	13	16
11-20: 15-Christmas-c	1	3	4	6	8	10
21-30	1	2	3	4	5	7
31-47						6.00

RICHIE RICH RELICS
Harvey Comics: Jan, 1988 - No.4, Feb, 1989 (75¢/$1.00, reprints)

1-4						3.00

RICHIE RICH RICHES
Harvey Publications: July, 1972 - No. 59, Aug, 1982 (#1, 2, 41-45: 52 pgs.)

1-(52 pg. Giant)-1st app. The Money Monster	6	12	18	37	59	80
2-(52 pg. Giant)	3	6	9	20	30	40
3-5	3	6	9	16	23	30
6-10: 7-1st app. Aunt Novo	2	4	6	11	16	20
11-20: 17-Super Richie app. (3/75)	2	4	6	8	10	12
21-40	1	2	3	5	6	8
41-45: 52 pg. Giants	1	3	4	6	8	10
46-59: 56-Dr. Blemish app.						6.00

RICHIE RICH SUCCESS STORIES
Harvey Publications: Nov, 1964 - No. 105, Sept, 1982 (#1-38: 68 pgs., 39-55, 67-90: 52 pgs.)

1	17	34	51	128	227	325
2	9	18	27	65	113	160
3-5	8	16	24	58	97	135
6-10	6	12	18	39	62	85
11-20	5	10	15	32	51	70
21-30: 27-1st Penny Van Dough (8/69)	4	8	12	24	37	50
31-38: 38-Last 68 pg. Giant	3	6	9	20	30	40
39-55-(52 pgs.): 44-Super Richie app.	3	6	9	14	20	25
56-66	2	4	6	8	10	12
67-90: 52 pgs.	2	4	6	8	11	14
91-99,101-105: 91-Onion app. 101-Dr. Blemish app.						6.00
100	1	2	3	5	7	9

RICHIE RICH SUMMER BONANZA

Harvey Comics: Oct, 1991 ($1.95, one-shot, 68 pgs.)

1-Richie Rich, Little Dot, Little Lotta						3.00

RICHIE RICH TREASURE CHEST DIGEST (...Magazine #3)
Harvey Publications: Apr, 1982 - No. 3, Aug, 1982 (95¢, Digest Mag.)
(#4 advertised but not publ.)

1	1	2	3	5	7	9
2,3	1	2	3	4	5	7

RICHIE RICH VACATION DIGEST
Harvey Comics: Oct, 1991; Oct, 1992; Oct, 1993 ($1.75, digest-size)

1-(10/91), 1-(10/92), 1-(10/93)						4.00

RICHIE RICH VACATIONS DIGEST
Harvey Publ.: 11/77; No. 2, 10/78 - No. 7, 10/81; No. 8, 8/82; No. 9, 10/82 (Digest, 132 pgs.)

1-Reprints	2	4	6	9	12	15
2-6	1	2	3	5	7	9
7-9						6.00

RICHIE RICH VAULT OF MYSTERY
Harvey Publications: Nov, 1974 - No. 47, Sept, 1982

1	3	6	9	20	30	40
2-5: 5-The Condor app.	2	4	6	13	18	22
6-10	2	4	6	9	13	16
11-20	1	3	4	6	8	10
21-30	1	2	3	4	5	7
31-47						6.00

RICHIE RICH ZILLIONZ
Harvey Publ.: Oct, 1976 - No. 33, Sept, 1982 (#1-4: 68 pgs.; #5-18: 52 pgs.)

1	3	6	9	18	27	35
2-4: 4-Last 68 pg. Giant	2	4	6	11	16	20
5-10	2	4	6	8	10	12
11-18: 18-Last 52 pg. Giant	1	2	3	5	6	8
19-33						6.00

RICKY
Standard Comics (Visual Editions): No. 5, Sept, 1953

5-Teenage humor	6	12	18	28	34	40

RICKY NELSON (TV)(See Sweethearts V2#42)
Dell Publishing Co.: No. 956, Dec, 1958 - No. 1192, June, 1961 (All photo-c)

Four Color 956,998	17	34	51	126	223	320
Four Color 1115, 1192: 1192-Manning-a	14	28	42	100	178	255

RIDE, THE (Also see Gun Candy flip-book)
Image Comics: June, 2004 - No. 2, July, 2004 ($2.95, B&W, anthology)

1,2: Hughes-c/Wagner-s. 1-Hamner & Stelfreeze-a. 2-Jeanty & Pearson-a.						3.00
... Die Valkyrie 1,2 (6/07 - No. 3, $2.99) Stelfreeze-a/Wagner-s/Pearson-c						3.00
... Foreign Parts 1 (1/05, $2.95) Dixon-s/Haynes-a; Marz-s/Brunner-a; Pearson-c						3.00
... Savannah 1 (4/07, $4.99) s/a by students of Savannah College of Art						5.00
... 2 For the Road 1 (10/04, $2.95) Dixon-s/Hamner & Gregory-a/Johnson-c						3.00
Vol. 1 TPB (2005, $9.99) r/#1,2, Foreign Parts, 2 For the Road, Chaykin intro.						10.00

RIDER, THE (Frontier Trail #6; also see Blazing Sixguns I.W. Reprint #10, 11)
Ajax/Farrell Publ. (Four Star Comic Corp.): Mar, 1957 - No. 5, 1958

1-Swift Arrow, Lone Rider begin	13	26	39	72	101	130
2-5	8	16	24	42	54	65

RIDERS OF THE PURPLE SAGE (See Zane Grey & Four Color #372)

RIFLEMAN, THE (TV)
Dell Publ. Co./Gold Key No. 13 on: No. 1009, 7-9/59 - No. 12, 7-9/62; No. 13, 11/62 - No. 20, 10/64

Four Color 1009 (#1)	21	42	63	156	278	400
2 (1-3/60)	11	22	33	79	140	200
3-Toth-a (4 pgs.)	11	22	33	79	140	200
4-10: 6-Toth-a (4 pgs.)	10	20	30	70	123	175
11-20	8	16	24	54	90	125

NOTE: *Warren Tufts a-2-9. All have Chuck Connors photo-c. Photo back c-13-15.*

RIMA, THE JUNGLE GIRL
National Periodical Publications: Apr-May, 1974 - No. 7, Apr-May, 1975

1-Origin, part 1 (#1-5: 20¢; 6,7: 25¢)	2	4	6	9	13	16
2-7: 2-4-Origin, parts 2-4. 7-Origin & only app. Space Marshal						
	1	2	3	5	6	8

NOTE: *Kubert c-1-7. Nino a-1-7. Redondo a-1-7.*

RING OF BRIGHT WATER (See Movie Classics)

Rin Tin Tin #8 © DELL

Riot #6 © MAR

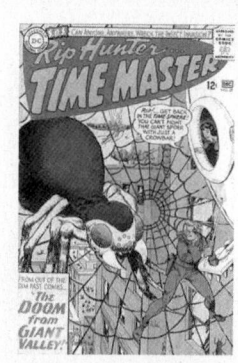

Rip Hunter Time Master #29 © DC

	GD 2.0	VG 4.0	FN 6.0	VF 8.0	VF/NM 9.0	NM- 9.2

RING OF THE NIBELUNG, THE
DC Comics: 1989 - No. 4, 1990 ($4.95, squarebound, 52 pgs., mature readers)
1-4: Adapts Wagner cycle of operas, Gil Kane-c/a ... 5.00

RING OF THE NIBELUNG, THE
Dark Horse Comics: Feb, 2000 - Sept, 2001 ($2.95/$2.99/$5.99, limited series)
Vol. 1 (The Rhinegold) 1-4: Adapts Wagner; P. Craig Russell-s/a ... 3.00
Vol. 2,3: Vol. 2 (The Valkyrie) 1-3: 1-(8/00). Vol. 3 (Siegfried) 1-3: 1-(12/00) ... 3.00
Vol. 4 (The Twilight of the Gods) 1-3: 1-(6/01) ... 3.00
4-(9/01, $5.99, 64 pgs.) Conclusion with sketch pages ... 6.00

RINGO KID, THE (2nd Series)
Marvel Comics Group: Jan, 1970 - No. 23, Nov, 1973; No. 24, Nov, 1975 - No. 30, Nov, 1976

	GD 2.0	VG 4.0	FN 6.0	VF 8.0	VF/NM 9.0	NM- 9.2
1-Williamson-a r-from #10, 1956.	3	6	9	16	23	30
2-11: 2-Severin-c. 11-Last 15¢ issue	2	4	6	9	13	16
12 (52 pg. Giant)	3	6	9	14	19	24
13-20: 13-Wildey-r. 20-Williamson-r/#1	2	4	6	8	10	12
21-30	1	2	3	5	7	9
27,28-(30¢-c variant, limited distribution)(5,7/76)	3	6	9	18	27	35

RINGO KID WESTERN, THE (1st Series) (See Wild Western & Western Trails)
Atlas Comics (HPC)/Marvel Comics: Aug, 1954 - No. 21, Sept, 1957

	GD 2.0	VG 4.0	FN 6.0	VF 8.0	VF/NM 9.0	NM- 9.2
1-Origin; The Ringo Kid begins	30	60	90	174	275	375
2-Black Rider app.; origin/1st app. Ringo's Horse Arab	15	30	45	88	137	185
3-5	12	24	36	67	94	120
6-8-Severin-a(3) each	13	26	39	72	101	130
9,11,12,14-21: 12-Orlando-a (4 pgs.)	10	20	30	54	72	90
10,13-Williamson-a (4 pgs.)	10	20	30	58	79	100

NOTE: Berg a-8. Maneely a-1-5, 15, 16(text illos only), 17(4), 18, 20, 21; c-1-6, 8, 13, 15-18, 20. J. Severin c-10, 11. Sinnott a-1. Wildey a-16-18.

RIN TIN TIN (See March of Comics #163,180,195)

RIN TIN TIN (TV) (…& Rusty #21 on; see Western Roundup under Dell Giants)
Dell Publishing Co./Gold Key: Nov, 1952 - No. 38, May-July, 1961; Nov, 1963 (All Photo-c)

	GD 2.0	VG 4.0	FN 6.0	VF 8.0	VF/NM 9.0	NM- 9.2
Four Color 434 (#1)	14	28	42	102	181	260
Four Color 476,523	8	16	24	56	93	130
4(3-5/54)-10	7	14	21	45	73	100
11-17,19,20	6	12	18	43	69	95
18-(4-5/57) 1st app. of Rusty and the Cavalry of Fort Apache; photo-c	7	14	21	45	73	100
21-38: 36-Toth-a (4 pgs.)	5	10	15	35	55	75
… & Rusty 1 (11/63-Gold Key)	6	12	18	37	59	80

RIO (Also see Eclipse Monthly)
Comico: June, 1987 ($8.95, 64 pgs.)
1-Wildey-c/a ... 9.00

RIO AT BAY
Dark Horse Comics: July, 1992 - No. 2, Aug, 1992 ($2.95, limited series)
1,2-Wildey-c/a ... 3.00

RIO BRAVO (Movie) (See 4-Color #1018)
Dell Publishing Co.: June, 1959

	GD 2.0	VG 4.0	FN 6.0	VF 8.0	VF/NM 9.0	NM- 9.2
Four Color 1018-Toth-a; John Wayne, Dean Martin, & Ricky Nelson photo-c.	22	44	66	160	285	410

RIO CONCHOS (See Movie Comics)

RIOT (Satire)
Atlas Comics (ACI No. 1-5/WPI No. 6): Apr, 1954 - No. 3, Aug, 1954; No. 4, Feb, 1956 - No. 6, June, 1956

	GD 2.0	VG 4.0	FN 6.0	VF 8.0	VF/NM 9.0	NM- 9.2
1-Russ Heath-a	32	64	96	186	293	400
2-Li'l Abner satire by Post	23	46	69	130	205	280
3-Last precode (8/54)	20	40	60	115	180	245
4-Infinity-c; Marilyn Monroe "7 Year Itch" movie satire; Mad Rip-off ads	26	52	78	150	235	320
5-Marilyn Monroe, John Wayne parody; part photo-c	26	52	78	152	239	325
6-Lorna of the Jungle satire by Everett; Dennis the Menace satire-c/story; part photo-c	20	40	60	115	180	245

NOTE: Berg a-3. Burgos c-1, 2. Colan a-1. Everett a-1, 4, 6. Heath a-1. Maneely a-1, 2, 4-6; c-3, 4, 6. Post a-1-4. Reinman a-2. Severin a-4-6.

RIOT GEAR
Triumphant Comics: Sept, 1993 - No. 11, July, 1994 ($2.50, serially numbered)
1-11: 1-2nd app. Riot Gear. 2-1st app. Rabin. 3,4-Triumphant Unleashed x-over. 3-1st app. Surzar. 4-Death of Captain Tich ... 2.50

Violent Past 1,2: 1-(2/94, $2.50) ... 2.50

R.I.P.
TSR, Inc.:1990 - No. 8, 1991 ($2.95, 44 pgs.)
1-8-Based on TSR game ... 3.00

RIPCLAW (See Cyberforce)
Image Comics (Top Cow Prod.): Apr, 1995 - No. 3, June, 1995 (Limited series)

	GD 2.0	VG 4.0	FN 6.0	VF 8.0	VF/NM 9.0	NM- 9.2
1/2-Gold, 1/2-San Diego ed., 1/2-Chicago ed.	1	3	4	6	8	10

1-3: Brandon Peterson-a(p) ... 3.00
Special 1 (10/95, $2.50) ... 2.50

RIPCLAW
Image Comics (Top Cow Prod.): V2#1, Dec, 1995 - No. 6, June, 1996 ($2.50)
V2#1-6: 5-Medieval Spawn/Witchblade Preview ... 2.50
…: Pilot Season 1 (2007, $2.99) Jason Aaron-s/Jorge Lucas-a/Tony Moore-c ... 3.00

RIPCORD (TV)
Dell Publishing Co.: Mar-May, 1962

	GD 2.0	VG 4.0	FN 6.0	VF 8.0	VF/NM 9.0	NM- 9.2
Four Color 1294	7	14	21	47	76	105

R.I.P.D.
Dark Horse Comics: Oct, 1999 - No. 4, Jan, 2000 ($2.95, limited series)
1-4 ... 3.00
TPB (2003, $12.95) r/#1-4 ... 13.00

RIP HUNTER TIME MASTER (See Showcase #20, 21, 25, 26 & Time Masters)
National Periodical Publications: Mar-Apr, 1961 - No. 29, Nov-Dec, 1965

	GD 2.0	VG 4.0	FN 6.0	VF 8.0	VF/NM 9.0	NM- 9.2
1-(3-4/61)	50	100	150	400	725	1050
2	24	48	72	180	323	465
3-5: 5-Last 10¢ issue	15	30	45	109	195	280
6,7-Toth-a in each	10	20	30	71	126	180
8-15	8	16	24	58	97	135
16-20: 20-Hitler c/s	7	14	21	45	73	100
21-29: 29-Gil Kane-c	6	12	18	39	62	85

RIP IN TIME (Also see Teenage Mutant Ninja Turtles #5-7)
Fantagor Press: Aug, 1986 - No.5, 1987 ($1.50, B&W)
1-5: Corben-c/a in all ... 3.00

RIP KIRBY (Also see Harvey Comics Hits #57, & Street Comix)
David McKay Publications: 1948

	GD 2.0	VG 4.0	FN 6.0	VF 8.0	VF/NM 9.0	NM- 9.2
Feature Books 51,54: Raymond-c; 51-Origin	35	70	105	201	318	435

RIPLEY'S BELIEVE IT OR NOT! (See Ace Comics, All-American Comics, Mystery Comics Digest #1, 4, 7, 10, 13, 16, 19, 22, 25)

RIPLEY'S BELIEVE IT OR NOT!
Harvey Publications: Sept, 1953 - No. 4, March, 1954

	GD 2.0	VG 4.0	FN 6.0	VF 8.0	VF/NM 9.0	NM- 9.2
1-Powell-a	14	28	42	76	108	140
2-4	10	20	30	54	72	90

RIPLEY'S BELIEVE IT OR NOT! (Continuation of Ripleys'…True Ghost Stories & Ripley's…True War Stories)
Gold Key: No. 4, April, 1967 - No. 94, Feb, 1980

	GD 2.0	VG 4.0	FN 6.0	VF 8.0	VF/NM 9.0	NM- 9.2
4-Photo-c; McWilliams-a	4	8	12	24	37	50
5-Subtitled "True War Stories"; Evans-a; 1st Jeff Jones-a in comics? (2 pgs.)	4	8	12	24	37	50
6-10: 6-McWilliams-a. 10-Evans-a(2)	3	6	9	20	30	40
11-20: 15-Evans-a	3	6	9	16	23	30
21-30	2	4	6	13	18	22
31-38,40-60	2	4	6	9	13	16
39-Crandall-a	2	4	6	10	14	18
61-73	1	3	4	6	8	10
74,77-83-(52 pgs.)	2	4	6	9	13	16
75,76,84-94	1	2	3	5	6	8
Story Digest Mag. 1(6/70)-4-3/4x6-1/2", 148pp.	5	10	15	32	51	70

NOTE: Evanish art by Luiz Dominguez #22-25, 27, 30, 31, 40. Jeff Jones a-5(2 pgs.). McWilliams a-65, 66, 70, 89. Orlando a-8. Sparling c-68. Reprints-74, 77-84, 87 (part); 91, 93 (all). Williamson, Wood a-80r/#1.

RIPLEY'S BELIEVE IT OR NOT!
Dark Horse Comics: May, 2002 - No. 4 ($2.99, B&W, limited series)
1-3-Nord-c/a. 1-Stories of Amelia Earhart & D.B. Cooper ... 3.00

RIPLEY'S BELIEVE IT OR NOT! TRUE GHOST STORIES (Along with Ripley's…True War Stories, the three issues together precede the 1967 series that starts its numbering with #4) (Also see Dan Curtis)
Gold Key: June, 1965 - No. 2, Oct, 1966

	GD 2.0	VG 4.0	FN 6.0	VF 8.0	VF/NM 9.0	NM- 9.2
1-Williamson, Wood & Evans-a; photo-c	7	14	21	47	76	105

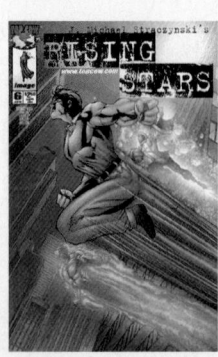

Rising Stars #6 © Straczynski & TCOW

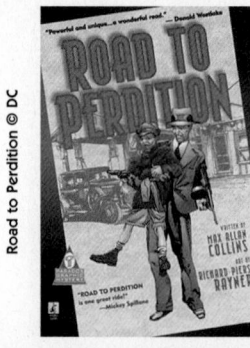

Road to Perdition © DC

Robin #159 © DC

	GD 2.0	VG 4.0	FN 6.0	VF 8.0	VF/NM 9.0	NM- 9.2
2-Orlando, McWilliams-a; photo-c	4	8	12	26	41	55
Mini-Comic 1(1976-3-1/4x6-1/2")	2	4	6	8	11	14
11186(1977)-Golden Press; ($1.95, 224 pgs.)-All-r	4	8	12	24	37	50
11401(3/79)-Golden Press; ($1.00, 96 pgs.)-All-r	3	6	9	15	21	26

RIPLEY'S BELIEVE IT OR NOT! TRUE WAR STORIES (Along with Ripley's...True Ghost Stories, the three issues together precede the 1967 series that starts its numbering with #4)
Gold Key: Nov, 1965 (Aug, 1965 in indicia)

	GD	VG	FN	VF	VF/NM	NM-
1-No Williamson-a	4	8	12	26	41	55

RIPLEY'S BELIEVE IT OR NOT! TRUE WEIRD
Ripley Enterprises: June, 1966 - No. 2, Aug, 1966 (B&W Magazine)

	GD	VG	FN	VF	VF/NM	NM-
1,2-Comic stories & text	3	6	9	16	23	30

RISE OF APOCALYPSE
Marvel Comics: Oct, 1996 - No. 4, Jan, 1997 ($1.95, limited series)

1-4: Adam Pollina-c/a						2.50

RISING STARS
Image Comics (Top Cow): Mar, 1999 - No. 24, Mar, 2005 ($2.50/$2.99)

	GD	VG	FN	VF	VF/NM	NM-
Preview-(3/99, $5.00) Straczynski-s						6.00
0-(6/00, $2.50) Gary Frank-a/c						2.50
1/2-(8/01, $2.95) Anderson-c; art & sketch pages by Zanier						3.00
1-Four covers; Keu Cha-c/a	1	2	3	5	7	9
1-($10.00) Gold Editions-four covers						10.00
1-($50.00) Holofoil-c						50.00
2-7: 5-7-Zanier & Lashley-a(p)	1	2	3	5	7	9
8-23: 8-13-Zanier & Lashley-a(p). 14-Immonen-a. 15-Flip book B&W preview of Universe.						
15-23-Brent Anderson-a						3.00
24-($3.99) Series finale; Anderson-a(c)						4.00
Born In Fire TPB (11/00, $19.95) r/#1-8; foreword by Neil Gaiman						20.00
Power TPB (2002, $19.95) r/#9-16						20.00
Prelude-(10/00, $2.95) Cha-a/Lashley-c						3.00
...: Visitations (2002, $8.99) r/#0, 1/2, Preview; new Anderson-c; cover gallery						9.00
Vol. 3: Fire and Ash TPB (2005, $19.99) r/#17-24; design pages & cover gallery						20.00
Vol. 4 TPB (2006, $19.99) r/Rising Stars Bright #1-3 and Voices of the Dead #1-6						20.00
Wizard #0-(3/99) Wizard supplement; Straczynski-s						2.50
Wizard #1/2						10.00

RISING STARS BRIGHT
Image Comics (Top Cow): Mar, 2003 - No. 3, May, 2003 ($2.99, limited series)

1-3-Avery-s/Jurgens & Gorder-a/Beck-c						3.00

RISING STARS: UNTOUCHABLE
Image Comics (Top Cow): Mar, 2006 - No. 5, July, 2006 ($2.99, limited series)

1-5-Avery-s/Anderson-a						3.00

RISING STARS: VOICES OF THE DEAD
Image Comics (Top Cow): June, 2005 - No. 6, Dec, 2005 ($2.99, limited series)

1-6-Avery-s/Staz Johnson-a						3.00

RIVERDALE HIGH (Archie's... #7,8)
Archie Comics: Aug, 1990 - No. 8, Oct, 1991 ($1.00, bi-monthly)

1						4.00
2-8						3.00

RIVER FEUD (See Zane Grey & Four Color #484)

RIVETS
Dell Publishing Co.: No. 518, Nov, 1953

	GD	VG	FN	VF	VF/NM	NM-
Four Color 518	4	8	12	24	37	50

RIVETS (A dog)
Argo Publ.: Jan, 1956 - No. 3, May, 1956

	GD	VG	FN	VF	VF/NM	NM-
1-Reprints Sunday & daily newspaper strips	6	12	18	31	38	45
2,3	5	10	15	22	26	30

ROACHMILL
Blackthorne Publ.: Dec, 1986 - No. 6, Oct, 1987 ($1.75, B&W)

1-6						2.50

ROACHMILL
Dark Horse Comics: May, 1988 - No. 10, Dec, 1990 ($1.75, B&W)

1-10: 10-Contains trading cards						2.50

ROAD RUNNER (See Beep Beep, the...)

ROAD TO PERDITION (Inspired the 2002 Tom Hanks/Paul Newman movie)
(Also see On the Road to Perdition)
DC Comics/Paradox Press: 1998, 2002 ($13.95, B&W paperback graphic novel)

nn-(1st printing) Max Allan Collins-s/Richard Piers Rayner-a						30.00
2nd & 3rd printings (2002, $13.95)						14.00
Movie photo cover edition (2002)						14.00

ROADTRIP
Oni Press: Aug, 2000 ($2.95, B&W, one-shot)

1-Reprints Judd Winick's back-up stories from Oni Double Feature #9,10						3.00

ROADWAYS
Cult Press: May, 1994 ($2.75, B&W, limited series)

1						2.75

ROARIN' RICK'S RARE BIT FIENDS
King Hell Press: July, 1994 - No. 21, Aug, 1996 ($2.95, B&W, mature)

1-21: Rick Veitch-c/a/scripts in all. 20-(5/96). 21-(8/96)-Reads Subtleman #1 on cover						3.00
Rabid Eye: The Dream Art of Rick Veitch ($14.95, B&W, TPB)-r/#1-8 & the appendix from #12						15.00
Pocket Universe (6/96, $14.95, B&W, TPB)-Reprints						15.00

ROBERT E. HOWARD'S CONAN THE BARBARIAN
Marvel Comics: 1983 ($2.50, 68 pgs., Baxter paper)

1-r/Savage Tales #2,3 by Smith, c-r/Conan #21 by Smith.						4.00

ROBERT LOUIS STEVENSON'S KIDNAPPED (See Kidnapped)

ROBIN (See Aurora, Birds of Prey, Detective Comics #38, New Teen Titans, Robin II, Robin III, Robin 3000, Star Spangled Comics #65, Teen Titans & Young Justice)

ROBIN (See Batman #457)
DC Comics: Jan, 1991 - No. 5, May, 1991 ($1.00, limited series)

1-Free poster by N. Adams; Bolland-c on all						4.00
1-2nd & 3rd printings (without poster)						2.50
2-5						3.00
2-2nd printing						2.50
Annual 1,2 (1992-93, $2.50, 68 pgs.): 1-Grant/Wagner scripts; Sam Kieth-c.						
2-Intro Razorsharp; Jim Balent-c(p)						3.00

ROBIN (See Detective #668)
DC Comics: Nov, 1993 - Present ($1.50/$1.95/$1.99/$2.25)

1-($2.95)-Collector's edition w/foil embossed-c; 1st app. Robin's car, The Redbird; Azrael as Batman app.						4.00
1-Newsstand ed.						2.50
0,2-49,51-66-Regular editions: 3-5-The Spoiler app. 6-The Huntress-c/story cont'd from Showcase '94 #5. 7-Knightquest: The Conclusion w/new Batman (Azrael) vs. Bruce Wayne. 8-KnightsEnd Pt. 5. 9-KnightsEnd Aftermath; Batman-c & app. 10-(9/94)-Zero Hour. 0-(10/94). 11-(11/94). 25-Green Arrow-c/app. 26-Batman app. 27-Contagion Pt. 3; Catwoman-c/app. 32-Legacy Pt. 1. 35-Final Night. 46-Genesis. 52,53-Cataclysm pt. 7, conclusion. 55-Green Arrow app. 62-64-Flash-c/app.						2.50
14 ($2.50)-Embossed-c; Troika Pt. 4						3.00
50-($2.95)-Lady Shiva & King Snake app.						3.00
67-74,76-78: 67-72-No Man's Land						2.50
75-($2.95)						3.00
79-97: 79-Begin $2.25-c; Green Arrow app. 86-Pander Bros.-a						2.50
98,99-Bruce Wayne: Murderer x-over pt. 6, 11						2.50
100-($3.50) Last Dixon-s						3.50
101-147: 101-Young Justice x-over. 106-Kevin Lau-c. 121,122-Willingham-s/Mays-a. 125-Tim Drake quits. 126-Spoiler becomes the new Robin. 129-131-War Games. 132-Robin moves to Bludhaven, Batgirl app. 138-Begin $2.50-c. 139-McDaniel-a begins. 146-147-Teen Titans app.						2.50
148-165: 148-One Year Later; new costume. 150-Begin $2.99-c. 152,153-Boomerang app.						3.00
#1,000,000 (11/98) 853rd Century x-over						2.50
Annual 3-5: 3-(1994, $2.95)-Elseworlds story. 4-(1995, $2.95)-Year One story. 5-(1996, $2.95)-Legends of the Dead Earth story						3.00
Annual 6 (1997, $3.95)-Pulp Heroes story.						4.00
...:Argent 1 (2/98, $1.95) Argent (Teen Titans) app.						2.50
...:/Batgirl: Fresh Blood TPB (2005, $12.99) r/#132,133 & Batgirl #58,59						13.00
...: Days of Fire and Madness (2006, $12.99, TPB) r/#140-145						13.00
...:Eighty-Page Giant 1 (9/00, $5.95) Chuck Dixon-s/Diego Barreto-a						6.00
...: Flying Solo (2000, $12.95, TPB) r/#1-6, Showcase '94 #5,6						13.00
...Plus 1 (12/96, $2.95) Impulse-c/app.; Waid-s						3.00
...Plus 2 (12/97, $2.95) Fang (Scare Tactics) app.						3.00
...: Unmasked (2004, $12.99, TPB) r/#121-125; Pearson-c						13.00
...: Wanted (2007, $12.99, TPB) r/#148-153						13.00

ROBIN: A HERO REBORN
DC Comics: 1991 ($4.95, squarebound, trade paperback)

nn-r/Batman #455-457 & Robin #1-5; Bolland-c						5.00

Robin Hood Tales #7 © DC

Robin III #3 © DC

Robocop #1 © Avatar

	GD 2.0	VG 4.0	FN 6.0	VF 8.0	VF/NM 9.0	NM- 9.2		GD 2.0	VG 4.0	FN 6.0	VF 8.0	VF/NM 9.0	NM- 9.2

ROBIN HOOD (See The Advs. of..., Brave and the Bold, Four Color #413, 669, King Classics, Movie Comics & Power Record Comics)

ROBIN HOOD (...& His Merry Men, The Illustrated Story of...) (See Classic Comics #7 & Classics Giveaways, 12/44)

ROBIN HOOD (Disney)
Dell Publishing Co.: No. 413, Aug, 1952; No. 669, Dec, 1955

Four Color 413-(1st Disney movie Four Color book)(8/52)-Photo-c

| | 9 | 18 | 27 | 65 | 113 | 160 |
| Four Color 669 (12/55)-Reprints #413 plus photo-c | 6 | 12 | 18 | 37 | 59 | 80 |

ROBIN HOOD (Adventures of... #7, 8)
Magazine Enterprises (Sussex Pub. Co.): No. 52, Nov, 1955 - No. 6, Jun, 1957

52 (#1)-Origin Robin Hood & Sir Gallant of the Round Table

	15	30	45	85	130	175
53 (#2), 3-6: 6-Richard Greene photo-c (TV)	12	24	36	67	94	120
I.W. Reprint #1,2,9: 1-r/#3. 2-r/#4. 9-r/#52 (1963)	2	4	6	9	13	16
Super Reprint #10,15: 10-r/#53. 15-r/#5	2	4	6	9	13	16

NOTE: *Bolle* a-in all; c-52. *Powell* a-6.

ROBIN HOOD (Not Disney)
Dell Publishing Co.: May-July, 1963 (one-shot)

| 1 | 3 | 6 | 9 | 16 | 23 | 30 |

ROBIN HOOD (Disney) (Also see Best of Walt Disney)
Western Publishing Co.: 1973 ($1.50, 8-1/2x11", 52 pgs., cardboard-c)

96151- "Robin Hood", based on movie, 96152- "The Mystery of Sherwood Forest", 96153- "In King Richard's Service", 96154- "The Wizard's Ring"

| each.... | 3 | 6 | 9 | 16 | 22 | 28 |

ROBIN HOOD
Eclipse Comics: July, 1991 - No. 3, Dec, 1991 ($2.50, limited series)

| 1-3: Timothy Truman layouts | | | | | | 2.50 |

ROBIN HOOD AND HIS MERRY MEN (Formerly Danger & Adventure)
Charlton Comics: No. 28, Apr, 1956 - No. 38, Aug, 1958

28	10	20	30	54	72	90
29-37	8	16	24	42	54	65
38-Ditko-a (5 pgs.); Rocke-c	14	28	42	76	108	140

ROBIN HOOD TALES (Published by National Periodical #7 on)
Quality Comics Group (Comic Magazines): Feb, 1956 - No. 6, Nov-Dec, 1956

| 1-All have Baker/Cuidera-c | 32 | 64 | 96 | 186 | 293 | 400 |
| 2-6-Matt Baker-a | 30 | 60 | 90 | 174 | 275 | 375 |

ROBIN HOOD TALES (Cont'd from Quality series)(See Brave & the Bold #5)
National Periodical Publ.: No. 7, Jan-Feb, 1957 - No. 14, Mar-Apr, 1958

| 7-All have Andru/Esposito-c | 36 | 72 | 108 | 208 | 329 | 450 |
| 8-14 | 30 | 60 | 90 | 174 | 275 | 375 |

ROBINSON CRUSOE (See King Classics & Power Record Comics)
Dell Publishing Co.: Nov-Jan, 1963-64

| 1 | 3 | 6 | 9 | 15 | 21 | 26 |

ROBIN II (The Joker's Wild)
DC Comics: Oct, 1991 - No. 4, Dec, 1991 ($1.50, mini-series)

1-(Direct sales, $1.50)-With 4 diff.-c; same hologram on each						3.00
1-(Newsstand, $1.00)-No hologram; 1 version						2.50
1-Collector's set ($10.00)-Contains all 5 versions bagged with hologram trading card inside						12.00
2-(Direct sales, $1.50)-With 3 different-c						2.50
2-4-(Newsstand, $1.00)-1 version of each						2.50
2-Collector's set ($8.00)-Contains all 4 versions bagged with hologram trading card inside						9.00
3-(Direct sale, $1.50)-With 2 different-c						2.50
3-Collector's set ($6.00)-Contains all 3 versions bagged with hologram trading card inside						7.00
4-(Direct sales, $1.50)-Only one version						2.50
4-Collector's set ($4.00)-Contains both versions bagged with Bat-Signal hologram trading card						5.00
Multi-pack (All four issues w/hologram sticker)						8.00
Deluxe Complete Set ($30.00)-Contains all 14 versions of #1-4 plus a new hologram trading card; numbered & limited to 25,000; comes with slipcase & 2 acid free backing boards						35.00

ROBIN III: CRY OF THE HUNTRESS
DC Comics: Dec, 1992 - No. 6, Mar, 1993 (Limited series)

1-6 ($2.50, collector's ed.)-Polybagged w/movement enhanced-c plus mini-poster of

newsstand-c by Zeck | | | | | | 3.00 |
1-6 ($1.25, newsstand ed.): All have Zeck-c | | | | | | 2.50 |

ROBIN 3000
DC Comics (Elseworlds): 1992 - No. 2, 1992 ($4.95, mini-series, 52 pgs.)

| 1,2-Foil logo; Russell-c/a | | | | | | 5.00 |

ROBIN: YEAR ONE
DC Comics: 2000 - No. 4, 2001 ($4.95, square-bound, limited series)

| 1-4: Earliest days of Robin's career; Javier Pulido-c/a. 2,4-Two-Face app. | | | | | | 5.00 |
| TPB (2002, $14.95) r/#1-4 | | | | | | 15.00 |

ROBOCOP
Marvel Comics: Oct, 1987 ($2.00, B&W, magazine, one-shot)

| 1-Movie adaptation | | | | | | 4.00 |

ROBOCOP (Also see Dark Horse Comics)
Marvel Comics: Mar, 1990 - No. 23, Jan, 1992 ($1.50)

1-Based on movie						3.00
2-23						2.50
nn (7/90, $4.95, 52 pgs.)-r/B&W magazine in color; adapts 1st movie						5.00

ROBOCOP (FRANK MILLER'S...) (Also see Promotional Comics section for FCBD Ed.)
Avatar Press: July, 2003 - No. 9, Jan, 2006 ($3.50/$3.99, limited series)

| 1-9-Frank Miller-s/Juan Ryp-a. 1-Three covers by Miller, Ryp, and Barrows. 2-Two covers | | | | | | 4.00 |

ROBOCOP: MORTAL COILS
Dark Horse Comics: Sept, 1993 - No. 4, Dec, 1993 ($2.50, limited series)

| 1-4: 1,2-Cago painted-c | | | | | | 2.50 |

ROBOCOP: PRIME SUSPECT
Dark Horse Comics: Oct, 1992 - No. 4, Jan, 1993 ($2.50, limited series)

| 1-4: 1,3-Nelson painted-c. 2,4-Bolton painted-c | | | | | | 2.50 |

ROBOCOP: ROULETTE
Dark Horse Comics: Dec, 1993 - No. 4, 1994 ($2.50, limited series)

| 1-4: 1,3-Nelson painted-c. 2,4-Bolton painted-c | | | | | | 2.50 |

ROBOCOP 2
Marvel Comics: Aug, 1990 ($2.25, B&W, magazine, 68 pgs.)

| 1-Adapts movie sequel | | | | | | 2.50 |

ROBOCOP 2
Marvel Comics: Aug, 1990; Late Aug, 1990 - #3, Late Sept, 1990 ($1.00, limited series)

nn-(8/90, $4.95, 68 pgs., color)-Same contents as B&W magazine						5.00
1: #1-3 reprint no number issue						3.00
2,3: 2-Guice-c(i)						2.50

ROBOCOP 3
Dark Horse Comics: July, 1993 - No. 3, Nov, 1993 ($2.50, limited series)

| 1-3: Nelson painted-c; Nguyen-a(p) | | | | | | 2.50 |

ROBOCOP VERSUS THE TERMINATOR
Dark Horse Comics: Sept, 1992 - No. 4, 1992 (Dec.) ($2.50, limited series)

| 1-4: Miller scripts & Simonson-c/a in all | | | | | | 3.00 |
| 1-Platinum Edition | | | | | | 6.00 |

NOTE: *All contain a different Robocop cardboard cut-out stand-up.*

ROBO DOJO
DC Comics (WildStorm): Apr, 2002 - No. 6, Sept, 2002 ($2.95, limited series)

| 1-6-Wolfman-s | | | | | | 3.00 |

ROBO-HUNTER (Also see Sam Slade...)
Eagle Comics: Apr, 1984 - No. 5, 1984 ($1.00)

| 1-5-2000 A.D. | | | | | | 2.50 |

R.O.B.O.T. BATTALION 2050
Eclipse Comics: Mar, 1988 ($2.00, B&W, one-shot)

| 1 | | | | | | 2.50 |

ROBOT COMICS
Renegade Press: No. 0, June, 1987 ($2.00, B&W, one-shot)

| 0-Bob Burden story & art | | | | | | 2.50 |

ROBOTECH
Antarctic Press: Mar, 1997 - No. 11, Nov, 1998 ($2.95)

1-11, Annual 1 (4/98, $2.95)						3.00
...Class Reunion (12/98, $3.95, B&W)						4.00
...Escape (5/98, $2.95, B&W), ...Final Fire (12/98, $2.95, B&W)						3.00

ROBOTECH

Robotech #9 © Harmony Gold USA

The Rock #1 © WWE Ent.

Rocket Kelly #2 © FOX

	GD 2.0	VG 4.0	FN 6.0	VF 8.0	VF/NM 9.0	NM- 9.2

DC Comics (WildStorm): No. 0, Feb, 2003 - No. 6, Jul, 2003 ($2.50/$2.95, limited series)

0-Tommy Yune-s; art by Jim Lee, Garza, Bermejo and others; pin-up pages by various						2.50
1-6 ($2.95)-Long Vo-a						3.00
...: From the Stars (2003, $9.95, digest-size) r/#0-6 & Sourcebook						10.00
... Sourcebook (3/03, $2.95) pin-ups and info on characters and mecha; art by various						3.00

ROBOTECH: COVERT-OPS
Antarctic Press: Aug, 1998 - No. 2, Sept, 1998 ($2.95, B&W, limited series)

1,2-Gregory Lane-s/a						3.00

ROBOTECH DEFENDERS
DC Comics: Mar, 1985 - No. 2, Apr, 1985 (Mini-series)

1,2						3.00

ROBOTECH IN 3-D (TV)
Comico: Aug, 1987 ($2.50)

1-Steacy painted-c						4.00

ROBOTECH: INVASION
DC Comics (WildStorm): Feb, 2004 - No. 5, July, 2004 ($2.95, limited series)

1-5-Faerber & Yune-s/Miyazawa & Dogan-a						3.00

ROBOTECH: LOVE AND WAR
DC Comics (WildStorm): Aug, 2003 - No. 6, Jan, 2004 ($2.95, limited series)

1-6-Long Vo & Charles Park-a/Faerber & Yune-s. 2-Variant-c by Warren						3.00

ROBOTECH MASTERS (TV)
Comico: July, 1985 - No. 23, Apr, 1988 ($1.50)

1-23						3.00

ROBOTECH: PRELUDE TO THE SHADOW CHRONICLES
DC Comics (WildStorm): Dec, 2005 - No. 5, Mar, 2006 ($3.50, limited series)

1-5-Yune-s/Dogan & Udon Studios-a						3.50

ROBOTECH: SENTINELS - RUBICON
Antarctic Press: July, 1998 ($2.95, B&W)

1						3.00

ROBOTECH SPECIAL
Comico: May, 1988 ($2.50, one-shot, 44 pgs.)

1-Steacy wraparound-c; partial photo-c						4.00

ROBOTECH THE GRAPHIC NOVEL
Comico: Aug, 1986 ($5.95, 8-1/2x11", 52 pgs.)

1-Origin SDF-1; intro T.R. Edwards, Steacy-c/a; 2nd printing also exists (12/86)						7.00

ROBOTECH: THE MACROSS SAGA (TV)(Formerly Macross)
Comico: No. 2, Feb, 1985 - No. 36, Feb, 1989 ($1.50)

2-10						4.00
11-36: 12,17-Ken Steacy painted-c. 26-Begin $1.75-c. 35,36-($1.95)						3.00
Volume 1-4 TPB (WildStorm, 2003, $14.95, 5-3/4" x 8-1/4")1-Reprints #2-6 & Macross #1. 2- r/#7-12. 3-r/#13-18. 4-r/#19-24						15.00

ROBOTECH: THE NEW GENERATION
Comico: July, 1985 - No. 25, July, 1988

1-25						3.00

ROBOTECH: VERMILION
Antarctic Press: Mar, 1997 - No. 4, ($2.95, B&W, limited series)

1-4						3.00

ROBOTECH: WINGS OF GIBRALTAR
Antarctic Press: Aug, 1998 - No. 2, Sept, 1998 ($2.95, B&W, limited series)

1,2-Lee Duhig-s/a						3.00

ROBOTIX
Marvel Comics: Feb, 1986 (75¢, one-shot)

1-Based on toy						3.00

ROBOTMEN OF THE LOST PLANET (Also see Space Thrillers)
Avon Periodicals: 1952 (Also see Strange Worlds #19)

1-McCann-a (3 pgs.); Fawcette-a	110	220	330	688	1144	1600

ROB ROY
Dell Publishing Co.: 1954 (Disney-Movie)

Four Color 544-Manning-a, photo-c	7	14	21	50	83	115

ROCK, THE (WWF Wrestling)
Chaos! Comics: June, 2001 ($2.99, one-shot)

1-Photo-c; Grant-s/Neves-a						3.00

ROCK & ROLL HIGH SCHOOL
Roger Corman's Cosmic Comics: Oct, 1995 ($2.50)

1-Bob Fingerman scripts						2.50

ROCK AND ROLLO (Formerly TV Teens)
Charlton Comics: V2#14, Oct, 1957 - No. 19, Sept, 1958

V2#14-19	6	12	18	29	36	42

ROCK COMICS
Landgraphic Publ.: Jul/Aug, 1979 ($1.25, tabloid size, 28 pgs.)

1-N. Adams-c; Thor(not Marvel's) story by Adams	2	4	6	13	18	22

ROCKET COMICS
Hillman Periodicals: Mar, 1940 - No. 3, May, 1940

1-Rocket Riley, Red Roberts the Electro Man (origin), The Phantom Ranger, The Steel Shark, The Defender, Buzzard Barnes and his Sky Devils, Lefty Larson, & The Defender, the Man with a Thousand Faces begin (1st app. of each); all have Rocket Riley-c	255	510	765	1594	2647	3700
2,3	124	248	372	775	1288	1800

ROCKETEER, THE (See Eclipse Graphic Album Series, Pacific Presents & Starslayer)

ROCKETEER ADVENTURE MAGAZINE, THE
Comico/Dark Horse Comics No. 3: July, 1988 ($2.00); No. 2, July, 1989 ($2.75); No. 3, Jan, 1995 ($2.95)

1-(7/88, $2.00)-Dave Stevens-c/a in all; Kaluta back-up-a; 1st app. Jonas (character based on The Shadow)	1	2	3	5	7	9
2-(7/89, $2.75)-Stevens/Dorman painted-c						6.00
3-(1/95, $2.95)-Includes pinups by Stevens, Gulacy, Plunkett, & Mignola						3.50
Volume 2-(9/96, $9.95, magazine size TPB)-Reprints #1-3						10.00

ROCKETEER SPECIAL EDITION, THE
Eclipse Comics: Nov, 1984 ($1.50, Baxter paper)(Chapter 5 of Rocketeer serial)

1-Stevens-c/a; Kaluta back-c; pin-ups inside	2	4	6	8	10	12

NOTE: *Originally intended to be published in Pacific Presents.*

ROCKETEER: THE OFFICIAL MOVIE ADAPTATION, THE
W. D. Publications (Disney): 1991

nn-($5.95, 68 pgs.)-Squarebound deluxe edition						6.00
nn-($2.95, 68 pgs.)-Stapled regular edition						3.00
3-D Comic Book (1991, $7.98, 52 pgs.)						8.00

ROCKET KELLY (See The Bouncer, Green Mask #10); becomes Li'l Pan #6)
Fox Feature Syndicate: 1944; Fall, 1945 - No. 5, Oct-Nov, 1946

nn (1944), 1	35	70	105	201	318	435
2-The Puppeteer app. (costumed hero)	24	48	72	139	220	300
3-5:-(#5 on cover, #4 inside)	21	42	63	124	195	265

ROCKETMAN (Strange Fantasy #2 on) (See Hello Pal & Scoop Comics)
Ajax/Farrell Publications: June, 1952-(Strange Stories of the Future)

1-Rocketman & Cosmo	40	80	120	239	380	520

ROCKET RACCOON (Also see Incredible Hulk #271)
Marvel Comics: May, 1985 - No. 4, Aug, 1985 (color, limited series)

1-4: Mignola-a						2.50

ROCKET SHIP X
Fox Features Syndicate: September, 1951; 1952

1	61	122	183	381	633	885
1952 (nn, nd, no publ.)-Edited 1951-c (exist?)	39	78	117	224	355	485

ROCKET TO ADVENTURE LAND (See Pixie Puzzle...)

ROCKET TO THE MOON
Avon Periodicals: 1951

nn-Orlando-c/a; adapts Otis Adelbert Kline's "Maza of the Moon"	110	220	330	688	1144	1600

ROCK FANTASY COMICS
Rock Fantasy Comics: Dec, 1989 - No. 16?, 1991 ($2.25/$3.00, B&W)(No cover price)

1-Pink Floyd part 1						5.00
1-2nd printing ($3.00-c)						3.00
2,3: 2-Rolling Stones #1. 3-Led Zeppelin #1						4.00
2,3: 2nd printings ($3.00-c, 1/90 & 2/90)						3.00
4-Stevie Nicks Not published						
5-Monstrosities of Rock #1; photo back-c						4.00
5-2nd printing ($3.00, 3/90 indicia, 2/90-c)						3.00
6-9,11-15,17,18: 6-Guns n' Roses #1 (1st & 2nd printings, 3/90)-Begin $3.00-c.						
7-Sex Pistols #1. 8-Alice Cooper; not published. 9-Van Halen #1; photo back-c						

Rocko's Modern Life #5 © Nickelodeon

Rocky Lane Western #5 © FAW

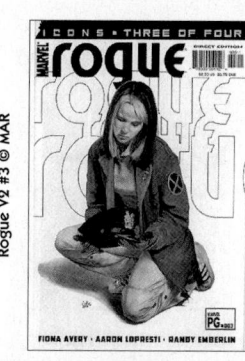

Rogue V2 #3 © MAR

	GD 2.0	VG 4.0	FN 6.0	VF 8.0	VF/NM 9.0	NM- 9.2
11-Jimi Hendrix #1; wraparound-c						3.00
10-Kiss #1; photo back-c	2	4	6	8	10	12
16-($5.00, 68 pgs.)-The Great Gig in the Sky(Floyd)						5.00

ROCK HAPPENING (See Bunny and Harvey Pop Comics:...)

ROCK N' ROLL COMICS
DC Comics: Dec./Jan 1956 (ashcan)

nn-Ashcan comic, not distributed to newsstands, only for in house use					(no known sales)	

ROCK N' ROLL COMICS
Revolutionary Comics: Jun, 1989 - No. 65 ($1.50/$1.95/$2.50, B&W/col. #15 on)

1-Guns N' Roses	1	2	3	5	6	8
1-2nd thru 7th printings. 7th printing (full color w/new-c/a)						2.50
2-Metallica	1	3	4	6	8	10
2-2nd thru 6th printings (6th in color)						2.50
3-Bon Jovi (no reprints)	1	2	3	5	6	8
4-8,10-65: 4-Motley Crue(2nd printing only, 1st destroyed). 5-Def Leppard (2 printings). 6-Rolling Stones(4 printings). 7-The Who (3 printings). 8-Skid Row; not published. 10-Warrant/Whitesnake(2 printings; 1st has 2 diff.-c). 11-Aerosmith (2 printings?). 12-New Kids on the Block(2 printings). 12-3rd printing; rewritten & titled NKOTB Hate Book. 13-Led Zeppelin. 14-Sex Pistols. 15-Poison; 1st color issue. 16-Van Halen. 17-Madonna. 18-Alice Cooper. 19-Public Enemy/2 Live Crew. 20-Queensryche/Tesla. 21-Prince? 22-AC/DC; begin $2.50.-c. 23-Living Colour. 24-Anthrax. 29-Ozzy. 45,46-Grateful Dead. 49-Metal. 50,51-Bob Dylan. 56-David Bowie						5.00
9-Kiss	2	4	6	8	10	12
9-2nd & 3rd printings						2.50

NOTE: Most issues were reprinted except #3. Later reprints are in color. #8 was not released.

ROCKO'S MODERN LIFE (TV)
Marvel Comics: June, 1994 - No. 7, Dec, 1994 ($1.95) (Nickelodeon cartoon)

1-7						2.50

ROCKY AND HIS FIENDISH FRIENDS (TV)(Bullwinkle)
Gold Key: Oct, 1962 - No. 5, Sept, 1963 (Jay Ward)

1 (25¢, 80 pgs.)	15	30	45	107	191	275
2,3 (25¢, 80 pgs.)	10	20	30	73	129	185
4,5 (Regular size, 12¢)	8	16	24	52	86	120

ROCKY AND HIS FRIENDS (See Kite Fun Book & March of Comics #216 in the Promotional Comics section)

ROCKY AND HIS FRIENDS (TV)
Dell Publishing Co.: No. 1128, 8-10/60 - No.1311,1962 (Jay Ward)

Four Color #1128 (#1) (8-10/60)	29	58	87	212	381	550
Four Color #1152 (12-2/61), 1166, 1208, 1275, 1311('62)	19	38	57	138	244	350

ROCKY HORROR PICTURE SHOW THE COMIC BOOK, THE
Caliber Press: Jul, 1990 - No. 3, Jan, 1991 ($2.95, mini-series, 52 pgs.)

1-3: 1-Adapts cult film plus photos, etc., 1-2nd printing						3.00
...Collection ($4.95)						5.00

ROCKY JONES SPACE RANGER (See Space Adventures #15-18)

ROCKY JORDEN PRIVATE EYE (See Private Eye)

ROCKY LANE WESTERN (Allan Rocky Lane starred in Republic movies & TV for a short time as Allan Lane, Red Ryder & Rocky Lane) (See Black Jack Fawcett Movie Comics, Motion Picture Comics & Six-Gun Heroes)
Fawcett Publications/Charlton No. 56 on: May, 1949 - No. 87, Nov, 1959

1 (36 pgs.)-Rocky, his stallion Black Jack, & Slim Pickens begin; photo-c begin, end #57; photo back-c	83	166	249	519	860	1200
2 (36 pgs.)-Last photo back-c	34	68	102	197	311	425
3-5 (52 pgs.): 4-Captain Tootsie by Beck	24	48	72	139	220	300
6,10 (36 pgs.): 10-Complete western novelette "Badman's Reward"	16	32	48	94	147	200
7-9 (52 pgs.)	17	34	51	105	165	225
11-13,15-17,19,20 (52 pgs.): 15-Black Jack's Hitching Post begins, ends #25.						
20-Last Slim Pickens	14	28	42	82	121	160
14,18 (36 pgs.)	13	26	39	74	105	135
21,23,24 (52 pgs.): 21-Dee Dickens begins, ends #55,57,65-68	13	26	39	74	105	135
22,25-28,30 (36 pgs. begin)	12	24	36	69	97	125
29-Classic complete novel "The Land of Missing Men" with hidden land of ancient temple ruins (r-in #65)	16	32	48	94	147	200
31-40	12	24	36	67	94	120
41-54	10	20	30	58	79	100
55-Last Fawcett issue (1/54)	12	24	36	67	94	120
56-1st Charlton issue (2/54)-Photo-c	18	36	54	103	162	220

	GD 2.0	VG 4.0	FN 6.0	VF 8.0	VF/NM 9.0	NM- 9.2
57,60-Photo-c	12	24	36	67	94	120
58,59,61-64,66-78,80-86: 59-61-Young Falcon app. 64-Slim Pickens app.						
66-68: Reprints #30,31,32	10	20	30	56	76	95
65-r/#29, "The Land of Missing Men"	11	22	33	62	86	110
79-Giant Edition (68 pgs.)	12	24	36	69	97	125
87-Last issue	11	22	33	64	90	115

NOTE: Complete novels in #10, 14, 18, 22, 25, 30-32, 36, 38, 39, 49. Captain Tootsie in #4, 12, 20. Big Bow and Little Arrow in #11, 28, 63. Black Jack's Hitching Post in #15-25, 64, 73.

ROCKY LANE WESTERN
AC Comics: 1989 ($2.50, B&W, one-shot?)

1-Photo-c; Giordano reprints						4.00
Annual 1 (1991, $2.95, B&W, 44 pgs.)-photo front/back & inside-c; reprints						4.00

ROD CAMERON WESTERN (Movie star)
Fawcett Publications: Feb, 1950 - No. 20, Apr, 1953

1-Rod Cameron, his horse War Paint, & Sam The Sheriff begin; photo front/back-c begin	41	82	123	256	416	575
2	21	42	63	124	195	265
3-Novel length story "The Mystery of the Seven Cities of Cibola"	19	38	57	109	172	235
4-10: 9-Last photo back-c	15	30	45	88	137	185
11-19	14	28	42	80	115	150
20-Last issue & photo-c	14	28	42	82	121	160

NOTE: Novel length stories in No. 1-8, 12-14.

RODEO RYAN (See A-1 Comics #8)

ROEL
Sirius: Feb, 1997 ($2.95, B&W, one-shot)

1						3.00

ROGAN GOSH
DC Comics (Vertigo): 1994 ($6.95, one-shot)

nn-Peter Milligan scripts						7.00

ROGER DODGER (Also in Exciting Comics #57 on)
Standard Comics: No. 5, Aug, 1952

5-Teen-age	6	12	18	28	34	40

ROGER RABBIT (Also see Marvel Graphic Novel)
Disney Comics: June, 1990 - No. 18, Nov, 1991 ($1.50)

1-18-All new stories						3.00
In 3-D 1 (1992, $2.50)-Sold at Wal-Mart?; w/glasses						4.00

ROGER RABBIT'S TOONTOWN
Disney Comics: Aug, 1991 - No. 5, Dec, 1991 ($1.50)

1-5						2.50

ROGER ZELAZNY'S AMBER: THE GUNS OF AVALON
DC Comics: 1996 - No. 3, 1996 ($6.95, limited series)

1-3: Based on novel						7.00

ROG 2000
Pacific Comics: June, 1982 ($2.95, 44 pgs., B&W, one-shot, magazine)

nn-Byrne-c/a (r)	2	4	6	8	10	12
2nd printing (7/82)	1	2	3	4	5	7

ROG 2000
Fantagraphics Books: 1987 - No. 2, 1987 ($2.00, limited series)

1,2-Byrne-r						3.00

ROGUE (From X-Men)
Marvel Comics: Jan, 1995 - No. 4, Apr, 1995 ($2.95, limited series)

1-4: 1-Gold foil logo						4.00
TPB-($12.95) r/#1-4						13.00

ROGUE (Volume 2)
Marvel Comics: Sept, 2001 - No. 4, Dec, 2001 ($2.50, limited series)

1-4-Julie Bell painted-c/Lopresti-a; Rogue's early days with X-Men						2.50

ROGUE (From X-Men)
Marvel Comics: Jan, 2004 - No. 12, Aug, 2005 ($2.99)

1-12: 1-Richards-a. 4-Gambit app. 11-Sunfire dies, Rogue absorbs his powers						3.00
...: Going Rogue TPB (2005, $14.99) r/#1-6						15.00
...: Forget-Me-Not TPB (2006, $14.99) r/#7-12						15.00

ROGUES GALLERY
DC Comics: 1996 ($3.50, one-shot)

1-Pinups of DC villains by various artists						3.50

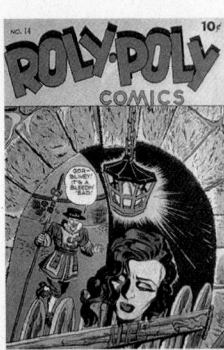

Roly Poly Comic Book #14 © Green Pub.

Rom #25 © Parker Brothers

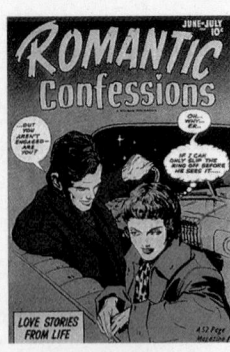

Romantic Confessions #9 © HILL

	GD 2.0	VG 4.0	FN 6.0	VF 8.0	VF/NM 9.0	NM- 9.2

ROGUES, THE (VILLAINS) (See The Flash)
DC Comics: Feb, 1998 ($1.95, one-shot)

	GD	VG	FN	VF	VF/NM	NM-
1-Augustyn-s/Pearson-c						2.50

ROKKIN
DC Comics (WildStorm): Sept, 2006 - No. 6, Feb, 2007 ($2.99, limited series)

1-6-Hartnell-s/Bradshaw-a						3.00

ROLLING STONES: VOODOO LOUNGE
Marvel Comics: 1995 ($6.95, Prestige format, one-shot)

nn-Dave McKean-script/design/art						7.00

ROLY POLY COMIC BOOK
Green Publishing Co.: 1945 - No. 15, 1946 (MLJ reprints)

	GD	VG	FN	VF	VF/NM	NM-
1-Red Rube & Steel Sterling begin; Sahle-c	31	62	93	178	282	385
6-The Blue Circle & The Steel Fist app.	19	38	57	109	172	235
10-Origin Red Rube retold; Steel Sterling story (Zip #41)						
	27	54	81	156	246	335
11,12: The Black Hood app. in both	18	36	54	107	169	230
14-Classic decapitation-c; the Black Hood app.	43	86	129	262	431	600
15-The Blue Circle & The Steel Fist app.; cover exact swipe from Fox Blue Beetle #1						
	32	64	96	186	293	400

ROM (Based on the Parker Brothers toy)
Marvel Comics Group: Dec, 1979 - No. 75, Feb, 1986

	GD	VG	FN	VF	VF/NM	NM-
1-Origin/1st app.	2	4	6	9	12	15
2-16,19-23,28-30: 5-Dr. Strange. 13-Saga of the Space Knights begins. 19-X-Men cameo. 23-Powerman & Iron Fist app.						5.00
17,18-X-Men app.	1	3	4	6	8	10
24-27: 24-F.F. cameo; Skrulls, Nova & The New Champions app. 25-Double size. 26,27-Galactus app.						6.00
31-49,51-60: 31,32-Brotherhood of Evil Mutants app. 32-X-Men cameo. 34,35-Sub-Mariner app. 41,42-Dr. Strange app. 56,57-Alpha Flight app. 58,59-Ant-Man app.						3.00
50-Skrulls app. (52 pgs.) Pin-ups by Konkle, Austin						4.00
61-74: 65-West Coast Avengers & Beta Ray Bill app. 65,66-X-Men app.						3.00
75-Last issue						3.00
Annual 1-4: (1982-85, 52 pgs.)						3.00

NOTE: *Austin* c-3i, 18i, 61i. *Byrne* a-74i; c-56, 57, 74. *Ditko* a-59-75p, Annual 4. *Golden* c-7-12, 19. *Guice* a-61i; c-55, 58, 60p, 70p. *Layton* a-59i, 72i; c-15, 59i, 69. *Miller* c-2p?, 3p, 17p, 18p. *Russell* a(i)-64, 65, 67, 69, 71, 75; c-64, 65i, 66, 71i, 75. *Severin* c-41p. *Sienkiewicz* a-53i; c-46, 47, 52-54, 68, 71p, Annual 2. *Simonson* c-18. *P. Smith* c-59p. *Starlin* c-67. *Zeck* c-50.

ROMANCE (See True Stories of...)

ROMANCE AND CONFESSION STORIES (See Giant Comics Edition)
St. John Publishing Co.: No date (1949) (25¢, 100 pgs.)

	GD	VG	FN	VF	VF/NM	NM-
1-Baker-c/a; remaindered St. John love comics	43	86	129	262	431	600

ROMANCE DIARY
Marvel Comics (CDS)(CLDS): Dec, 1949 - No. 2, Mar, 1950

	GD	VG	FN	VF	VF/NM	NM-
1,2	15	30	45	85	130	175

ROMANCE OF FLYING, THE
David McKay Publications: 1942

	GD	VG	FN	VF	VF/NM	NM-
Feature Books 33 (nn)-WW II photos	15	30	45	85	130	175

ROMANCES OF MOLLY MANTON (See Molly Manton)

ROMANCES OF NURSE HELEN GRANT, THE
Atlas Comics (VPI): Aug, 1957

	GD	VG	FN	VF	VF/NM	NM-
1	9	18	27	47	61	75

ROMANCES OF THE WEST (Becomes Romantic Affairs #3?)
Marvel Comics (SPC): Nov, 1949 - No. 2, Mar, 1950 (52 pgs.)

	GD	VG	FN	VF	VF/NM	NM-
1-Movie photo-c of Yvonne DeCarlo & Howard Duff (Calamity Jane & Sam Bass)	23	46	69	135	213	290
2-Photo-c	15	30	45	85	130	175

ROMANCE STORIES OF TRUE LOVE (Formerly True Love Problems & Advice Illustrated)
Harvey Publications: No. 45, 5/57 - No. 50, 3/58; No. 51, 9/58 - No. 52, 11/58

	GD	VG	FN	VF	VF/NM	NM-
45-51: 45,46,48-50-Powell-a	6	12	18	31	38	45
52-Matt Baker-a	9	18	27	47	61	75

ROMANCE TALES (Formerly Western Winners #6?)
Marvel Comics (CDS): No. 7, Oct, 1949 - No. 9, Mar, 1950 (7,8: photo-c)

	GD	VG	FN	VF	VF/NM	NM-
7	14	28	42	80	115	150
8,9: 8-Everett-a	10	20	30	54	72	90

ROMANCE TRAIL
National Periodical Publications: July-Aug, 1949 - No. 6, May-June, 1950

	GD	VG	FN	VF	VF/NM	NM-
(All photo-c & 52 pgs.)						
1-Kinstler, Toth-a; Jimmy Wakely photo-c	59	118	177	369	610	850
2-Kinstler-a; Jim Bannon photo-c	33	66	99	190	300	410
3-Photo-c; Kinstler, Toth-a	35	70	105	201	318	435
4-Photo-c; Toth-a	26	52	78	150	235	320
5,6: Photo-c on both. 5-Kinstler-a	23	46	69	135	213	290

ROMAN HOLIDAYS, THE (TV)
Gold Key: Feb, 1973 - No. 4, Nov, 1973 (Hanna-Barbera)

	GD	VG	FN	VF	VF/NM	NM-
1	4	8	12	28	44	60
2-4	3	6	9	18	27	35

ROMANTIC ADVENTURES (My... #49-67, covers only)
American Comics Group (B&I Publ. Co.): Mar-Apr, 1949 - No. 67, July, 1956 (Becomes My... #68 on)

	GD	VG	FN	VF	VF/NM	NM-
1	18	36	54	103	162	220
2	11	22	33	62	86	110
3-10	9	18	27	50	65	80
11-20 (4/52)	8	16	24	42	54	65
21-45,51,52: 52-Last Pre-code (2/55)	7	14	21	37	46	55
46-49-3-D effect-c/stories (TrueVision)	12	24	36	69	97	125
50-Classic cover/story "Love of A Lunatic"	11	22	33	62	86	110
53-67	7	14	21	35	43	50

NOTE: #1-23, 52 pgs. *Shelly* a-40. *Whitney* c/art in many issues.

ROMANTIC AFFAIRS (Formerly Molly Manton's Romances #2 and/or Romances of the West #2 and/or Our Love #2?)
Marvel Comics (SPC): No. 3, Mar, 1950

	GD	VG	FN	VF	VF/NM	NM-
3-Photo-c from Molly Manton's Romances #2	10	20	30	54	72	90

ROMANTIC CONFESSIONS
Hillman Periodicals: Oct, 1949 - V3#1, Apr-May, 1953

	GD	VG	FN	VF	VF/NM	NM-
V1#1-McWilliams-a	15	30	45	90	140	190
2-Briefer-a; negligee panels	10	20	30	56	76	95
3-12	9	18	27	47	61	75
V2#1,2,4-8,10-12: 2-McWilliams-a	8	16	24	42	54	65
3-Krigstein-a	9	18	27	50	65	80
9-One pg. Frazetta ad	8	16	24	42	54	65
V3#1	8	16	24	40	50	60

ROMANTIC HEARTS
Story Comics/Master/Merit Pubs.: Mar, 1951 - No. 10, Oct, 1952; July, 1953 - No. 12, July, 1955

	GD	VG	FN	VF	VF/NM	NM-
1(3/51) (1st Series)	14	28	42	80	115	150
2	9	18	27	47	61	75
3-10: Cameron-a	8	16	24	42	54	65
1(7/53) (2nd Series)-Some say #11 on-c	9	18	27	52	69	85
2	8	16	24	40	50	60
3-12	7	14	21	35	43	50

ROMANTIC LOVE
Avon Periodicals/Realistic (No #14-19): 9-10/49 - #3, 1-2/50; #4, 2-3/51 - #13, 10/52; #20, 3-4/54 - #23, 9-10/54

	GD	VG	FN	VF	VF/NM	NM-
1-c/Avon paperback #252	27	54	81	158	249	340
2-5: 3-c/paperback Novel Library #12. 4-c/paperback Diversey Prize Novel #5.						
5-c/paperback Novel Library #34	16	32	48	94	147	200
6- "Thrill Crazy" marijuana story; c-/Avon paperback #207; Kinstler-a						
	23	46	69	132	209	285
7,8: 8-Astarita-a(2)	15	30	45	90	140	190
9-12: 9-c/paperback Novel Library #41; Kinstler-a. 10-c-/Avon paperback #212.						
11-c/paperback Novel Library #17; Kinstler-a. 12-c/paperback Novel Library #13						
	16	32	48	94	147	200
13,21-23: 22,23-Kinstler-c	15	30	45	88	137	185
20-Kinstler-c/a	15	30	45	90	140	190
nn(1-3/53)(Realistic-r)	11	22	33	60	83	105

NOTE: *Astarita* a-7, 10, 11, 21. Painted c-1-3, 5, 7-11, 13. Photo c-4, 6.

ROMANTIC LOVE
Quality Comics Group: 1963-1964

	GD	VG	FN	VF	VF/NM	NM-
I.W. Reprint #2,3,8: 2-r/Romantic Love #2	2	4	6	9	12	15

ROMANTIC MARRIAGE (Cinderella Love #25 on)
Ziff-Davis/St. John No. 18 on (#1-8: 52 pgs.): #1-3 (1950, no months); #4, 5-6/51 - #17, 9/52; #18, 9/53 - #24, 9/54

	GD	VG	FN	VF	VF/NM	NM-
1-Photo-c; Cary Grant/Betsy Drake photo back-c.	21	42	63	122	191	260
2-Painted-c; Anderson-a (also #15)	14	28	42	82	121	160
3-9: 3,4,8,9-Painted-c; 5-7-Photo-c	14	28	42	76	108	140

Romantic Western #1 © FAW

Ronin #4 © Frank Miller

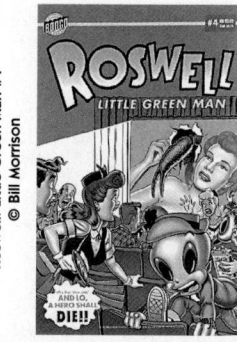

Roswell: Little Green Man #4 © Bill Morrison

	GD 2.0	VG 4.0	FN 6.0	VF 8.0	VF/NM 9.0	NM- 9.2		GD 2.0	VG 4.0	FN 6.0	VF 8.0	VF/NM 9.0	NM- 9.2

10-Unusual format; front-c is a painted-c; back-c is a photo-c complete with logo, price, etc.

	19	38	57	109	172	235
11-17 13-Photo-c. 15-Signed story by Anderson. 17-(9/52)-Last Z-D issue						
	12	24	36	69	97	125
18-22,24: 20-Photo-c	12	24	36	69	97	125
23-Baker-c; all stories are reprinted from #15	14	28	42	80	115	150

ROMANTIC PICTURE NOVELETTES
Magazine Enterprises: 1946

1-Mary Worth-r; Creig Flessel-c	16	32	48	92	144	195

ROMANTIC SECRETS (Becomes Time For Love)
Fawcett/Charlton Comics No. 5 (10/55) on: Sept, 1949 - No. 39, 4/53; No. 5, 10/55 - No. 52, 11/64 (#1-5: photo-c)

1-(52 pg. issues begin, end #?)	16	32	48	92	144	195
2,3	10	20	30	58	79	100
4,9-Evans-a	11	22	33	62	86	110
5-8,10	9	18	27	47	61	75
11-23	8	16	24	42	54	65
24-Evans-a	9	18	27	47	61	75
25-39('53)	8	16	24	40	50	60
5 (Charlton, 2nd Series)(10/55, formerly Negro Romances #4)						
	10	20	30	54	72	90
6-10	8	16	24	42	54	65
11-20	3	6	9	21	32	42
21-35: Last 10¢ issue?	3	6	9	18	27	35
36-52('64)	3	6	9	16	22	28

NOTE: *Bailey* a-20. *Powell* a(1st series)-5, 7, 10, 12, 16, 17, 20, 26, 33, 34, 36, 37. *Sekowsky* a-26. Photo c(1st series)-1-5, 16, 25, 27, 33. *Swayze* a(1st series)-16, 18, 19, 23, 26-28, 31, 32, 39.

ROMANTIC STORY (Cowboy Love #28 on)
Fawcett/Charlton Comics No. 23 on: 11/49 - #22, Sum, 1953; #23, 5/54 - #27, 12/54; #28, 8/55 - #130, 11/73

1-Photo-c begin, end #24; 52 pgs. begins	18	36	54	103	162	220
2	11	22	33	62	86	110
3-5	10	20	30	54	72	90
6-14	9	18	27	50	65	80
15-Evans-a	10	20	30	54	72	90
16-22(Sum, '53; last Fawcett issue). 21-Toth-a?	8	16	24	42	54	65
23-39: 26,29-Wood swipes	7	14	21	37	46	55
40-(100 pgs.)	11	22	33	64	90	115
41-50	3	6	9	21	32	42
51-80: 57-Hypo needle story	3	6	9	16	23	30
81-99	2	4	6	10	14	18
100	2	4	6	13	28	22
101-130	2	4	6	9	12	15

NOTE: *Jim Aparo* a-94. *Powell* a-7, 8, 16, 20, 30. *Marcus Swayze* a-2, 12, 20, 32.

ROMANTIC THRILLS (See Fox Giants)

ROMANTIC WESTERN
Fawcett Publications: Winter, 1949 - No. 3, June, 1950 (All Photo-c)

1	22	44	66	128	202	275
2-(Spr/50)-Williamson, McWilliams-a	20	40	60	115	180	245
3	15	30	45	85	130	175

ROMEO TUBBS (...That Lovable Teenager; formerly My Secret Life)
Fox Feature Syndicate/Green Publ. Co. No. 27: No. 26, 5/50 - No. 28, 7/50; No. 1, 1950; No. 27, 12/52

26-Teen-age	11	22	33	64	90	115
28 (7/50)	10	20	30	58	79	100
27 (12/52)-Contains Pedro on inside; Wood-a (exist?)						
	15	30	45	84	127	170

RONALD McDONALD (TV)
Charlton Press (King Features Synd.): Sept, 1970 - No. 4, March, 1971

1	8	16	24	56	93	130
2-4	5	10	15	30	48	65
V2#1,3-Special reprint for McDonald systems; "Not for resale" on cover						
	6	12	18	37	59	80

RONIN
DC Comics: July, 1983 - No. 6, Aug, 1984 ($2.50, limited series, 52 pgs.)

1-5-Frank Miller-c/a/scripts in all						5.00
6-Scarcer; has fold-out poster.	1	2	3	5	6	8
Trade paperback (1987, $12.95)-Reprints #1-6						13.00

RONNA

Knight Press: Apr, 1997 ($2.95, B&W, one-shot)

1-Beau Smith-s						3.00

ROOK (See Eerie Magazine & Warren Presents: The Rook)
Warren Publications: Oct, 1979 - No. 14, April, 1982 (B&W magazine)

1-Nino-a/Corben-c; with 8 pg. color insert	3	6	9	16	23	30
2-4,6,7: 2-Voltar by Alcala begins. 3,4-Toth-a	2	4	6	9	13	16
5,8-14: 11-Zorro-s. 12-14-Eagle by Severin	2	4	6	9	13	16

ROOK
Harris Comics: No. 0, Jun, 1995 - No. 4, 1995 ($2.95)

0-4: 0-short stories (3) w/preview. 4-Brereton-c.						3.00

ROOKIE COP (Formerly Crime and Justice?)
Charlton Comics: No. 27, Nov, 1955 - No. 33, Aug, 1957

27	9	18	27	47	61	75
28-33	6	12	18	31	38	45

ROOM 222 (TV)
Dell Publishing Co.: Jan, 1970; No. 2, May, 1970 - No. 4, Jan, 1971

1	5	10	15	35	55	75
2-4: 2,4-Photo-c. 3-Marijuana story. 4 r/#1	4	8	12	22	34	45

ROOTIE KAZOOTIE (TV)(See 3-D-ell)
Dell Publishing Co.: No. 415, Aug, 1952 - No. 6, Oct-Dec, 1954

Four Color 415 (#1)	9	18	27	65	113	160
Four Color 459,502(#2,3), 4(4-6/54)-6	7	14	21	47	76	105

ROOTS OF THE SWAMP THING
DC Comics: July, 1986 - No.5, Nov, 1986 ($2.00, Baxter paper, 52 pgs.)

1-5: r/Swamp Thing #1-10 by Wrightson & House of Mystery-r. 1-new Wrightson-c (2-5 reprinted covers).						4.00

ROSE (See Bone)
Cartoon Books: Nov, 2000 - No. 3, Feb, 2002 ($5.95, lim. series, square-bound)

1-3-Prequel to Bone; Jeff Smith-s/Charles Vess painted-a/c						6.00
HC (2001, $29.95) r/#1-3; new Vess cover painting						30.00
SC (2002, $19.95) r/#1-3; new Vess cover painting						20.00
1-($6.00)-Blood & Glory Edition						6.00

ROSE AND THORN
DC Comics: Feb, 2004 - No. 6, July, 2004 ($2.95, limited series)

1-6-Simone-s/Melo-a/Hughes-c						3.00

ROSWELL: LITTLE GREEN MAN (See Simpsons Comics #19-22)
Bongo Comics: 1996 - No. 6 ($2.95, quarterly)

1-6						3.50
...Walks Among Us ('97, $12.95, TPB) r/ #1-3 & Simpsons flip books						13.00

ROUND TABLE OF AMERICA: PERSONALITY CRISIS (See Big Bang Comics)
Image Comics: Aug, 2005 ($3.50, one-shot)

1-Carlos Rodriguez-a/Pedro Angosto-s						3.50

ROUNDUP (...Western Crime Stories)
D. S. Publishing Co.: July-Aug, 1948 - No. 5, Mar-Apr, 1949 (All 52 pgs.)

1-Kiefer-a	18	36	54	107	169	230
2-5: 2-Marijuana drug mention story	14	28	42	82	121	160

ROUTE 666
CrossGeneration Comics: July, 2002 - No. 22, Jun, 2004 ($2.95)

1-22-Bedard-s/Moline-a in most. 5-Richards-a. 15-McCrea-a						3.00
...: Highway to Horror (4/03, $15.95, TPB) r/#1-6						16.00
Vol. 2: Three-Ring Circus (2003, $15.95) r/#7-12						16.00

ROYAL ROY
Marvel Comics (Star Comics): May, 1985 - No.6, Mar, 1986 (Children's book)

1-6						4.00

ROY CAMPANELLA, BASEBALL HERO
Fawcett Publications: 1950 (Brooklyn Dodgers)

nn-Photo-c; life story	59	118	177	369	610	850

ROY ROGERS (See March of Comics #17, 35, 47, 62, 68, 73, 77, 86, 91, 100, 105, 116, 121, 131, 136, 146, 151, 161, 167, 176, 206, 221, 236, 250)

ROY ROGERS AND TRIGGER
Gold Key: Apr, 1967

1-Photo-c; reprints	4	8	12	28	44	60

ROY ROGERS ANNUAL
Wilson Publ. Co., Toronto/Dell: 1947 ("Giant Edition" on-c)(132 pgs., 50¢)

Roy Rogers Comics #15 © Roy Rogers

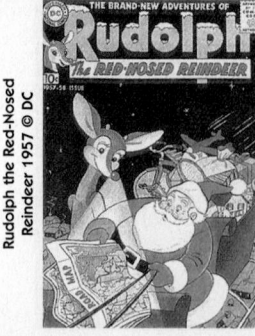
Rudolph the Red-Nosed Reindeer 1957 © DC

Runaways V2 #25 © MAR

	GD 2.0	VG 4.0	FN 6.0	VF 8.0	VF/NM 9.0	NM- 9.2

nn-Less than 5 known copies. Front and back cover art are from Roy Rogers #2. Stories reprinted from Roy Rogers #2, Four Color #137 and Four Color #153. (A copy in VG/FN was sold in 1986 for $400, in 1996 for $1200 & in 2000 for $1500; a FN+ sold for $1,650.)

ROY ROGERS COMICS (See Western Roundup under Dell Giants)
Dell Publishing Co.: No. 38, 4/44 - No. 177, 12/47 (#38-166: 52 pgs.)

Four Color 38 (1944)-49 pg. story; photo front/back-c on all 4-Color issues (1st western comic with photo-c)	167	334	501	1461	2731	4000
Four Color 63 (1945)-Color photos on all four-c	41	82	123	328	589	850
Four Color 86,95 (1945)	31	62	93	222	404	585
Four Color 109 (1946)	23	46	69	171	306	440
Four Color 117,124,137,144	19	38	57	138	244	350
Four Color 153,160,166: 166-48 pg. story	17	34	51	124	220	315
Four Color 177 (36 pgs.)-32 pg. story	16	32	48	118	209	300

ROY ROGERS COMICS (...& Trigger #92(8/55)-on)(Roy starred in Republic movies, radio & TV) (Singing cowboy) (Also see Dale Evans, It Really Happened #8, Queen of the West Dale Evans, & Roy Rogers' Trigger)
Dell Publishing Co.: Jan, 1948 - No. 145, Sept-Oct, 1961 (#1-19: 36 pgs.)

1-Roy, his horse Trigger, & Chuck Wagon Charley's Tales begin; photo-c begin, end #145	67	134	201	570	1060	1550
2	24	48	72	180	323	465
3-5	17	34	51	128	227	325
6-10	14	28	42	103	184	265
11-19: 19-Chuck Wagon Charley's Tales ends	12	24	36	86	153	220
20 (52 pgs.)-Trigger feature begins, ends #46	12	24	36	87	156	225
21-30 (52 pgs.)	10	20	30	71	126	180
31-46 (52 pgs.): 37-X-mas-c	9	18	27	60	100	140
47-56 (36 pgs.): 47-Chuck Wagon Charley's Tales returns, ends #133. 49-X-mas-c.						
55-Last photo back-c	7	14	21	47	76	105
57 (52 pgs.)-Heroin drug propaganda story	7	14	21	49	80	110
58-70 (52 pgs.): 58-Heroin drug use/dealing story. 61-X-Mas-c						
	7	14	21	47	76	105
71-80 (52 pgs.): 73-X-mas-c	6	12	18	41	66	90
81-91 (36 pgs. #81-on): 85-X-mas-c	6	14	18	39	62	85
92-99,101-110,112-118: 92-Title changed to Roy Rogers and Trigger (8/55)						
	6	12	18	37	59	80
100-Trigger feature returns, ends #131	6	12	18	43	69	95
111,119-124-Toth-a	7	14	21	45	73	100
125-131: 125-Toth-a (1 pg.)	5	10	15	35	55	75
132-144-Manning-a. 132-1st Dale Evans-sty by Russ Manning. 138,144-Dale Evans featured						
	6	12	18	39	62	85
145-Last issue	7	14	21	47	76	105

NOTE: *Buscema* a-74-108(2 stories each). *Manning* a-123, 124, 132-144. *Marsh* a-110. Photo back-c No. 1-9, 11-35, 38-55.

ROY ROGERS' TRIGGER
Dell Publishing Co.: No. 329, May, 1951 - No. 17, June-Aug, 1955

Four Color 329 (#1)-Painted-c	14	28	42	103	184	265
2 (9-11/51)-Photo-c	11	22	33	77	136	195
3-5: 3-Painted-c begin, end #17, most by S. Savitt	6	12	18	43	69	95
6-17: Title merges with Roy Rogers after #17	5	10	15	35	55	75

ROY ROGERS WESTERN CLASSICS
AC Comics: 1989 - No. 4 ($2.95/$3.95, 44pgs.) (24 pgs. color, 16 pgs. B&W)

1-4: 1-Dale Evans-r by Manning, Trigger-r by Buscema; photo covers & interior photos by Roy & Dale. 2-Buscema-r (3); photo-c & B&W photos inside. 3-Dale Evans-r by Manning; Trigger-r by Buscema plus other Buscema-r; photo-c						4.00

RUDOLPH, THE RED-NOSED REINDEER
National Per. Publ.: 1950 - No. 13, Winter, 1962-63 (Issues are not numbered)

1950 issue (#1); Grossman-c/a in all	21	42	63	122	191	260
1951-53 issues (3 total)	13	26	39	74	105	135
1954/55, 55/56, 56/57	11	22	33	64	90	115
1957/58, 58/59, 59/60, 60/61, 61/62	7	14	21	45	73	100
1962/63 (rare)/(84 pgs.)(shows "Annual" in indicia)	10	20	30	73	129	185

NOTE: 13 total issues published. Has games & puzzles also.

RUDOLPH, THE RED-NOSED REINDEER (Also see Limited Collectors' Edition C-20, C-24, C-33, C-42, C-50; and All-New Collectors' Edition C-53 & C-60)
National Per. Publ.: Christmas 1972 (Treasury-size)

nn-Precursor to Limited Collectors' Edition title (scarce) (implied to be Lim. Coll .Ed. C-20)	20	40	60	148	264	380

RUFF AND REDDY (TV)
Dell Publ. Co.: No. 937, 9/58 - No. 12, 1-3/62 (Hanna-Barbera)(#9 on: 15¢)

Four Color 937(#1)(1st Hanna-Barbera comic book)	12	24	36	84	150	215

Four Color 981,1038	8	16	24	52	86	120
4(1-3/60)-12: 8-Last 10¢ issue	7	14	21	45	73	100

RUGGED ACTION (Strange Stories of Suspense #5 on)
Atlas Comics (CSI): Dec, 1954 - No. 4, June, 1955

1-Brodsky-c	14	28	42	76	108	140
2-4: 2-Last precode (2/55)	10	20	30	54	72	90

NOTE: *Ayers* a-2, 3. *Maneely* c-2, 3. *Severin* a-2.

RUINS
Marvel Comics (Alterniverse): July, 1995 - No. 2, Sept, 1995 ($5.00, painted, limited series)

1,2: Phil Sheldon from Marvels; Warren Ellis scripts; acetate-c						5.00

RULAH JUNGLE GODDESS (Formerly Zoot; I Loved #28 on) (Also see All Top Comics & Terrors of the Jungle)
Fox Features Syndicate: No. 17, Aug, 1948 - No. 27, June, 1949

17	100	200	300	625	1038	1450
18-Classic girl-fight interior splash	68	136	204	425	705	985
19,20	66	132	198	413	682	950
21-Used in SOTI, pg. 388,389	67	134	201	419	697	975
22-Used in SOTI, pg. 22,23	66	132	198	413	682	950
23-27	52	104	156	317	521	725

NOTE: *Kamen* c-17-19, 21, 22.

RUNAWAY, THE (See Movie Classics)

RUNAWAYS
Marvel Comics: July, 2003 - No. 18, Nov, 2004 ($2.95/$2.25/$2.99)

1-($2.95) Vaughan-s/Alphona-a/Jo Chen-c						3.00
2-9-($2.50)						2.50
10-18-($2.99) 11,12-Miyazawa-a; Cloak and Dagger app. 16-The mole revealed						3.00
Hardcover (2005, $34.99) oversized r/#1-18; proposal & sketch pages; Vaughan intro.						35.00
Marvel Age Runaways Vol. 1: Pride and Joy (2004, $7.99, digest size) r/#1-6						8.00
...Vol. 2: Teenage Wasteland (2004, $7.99, digest size) r/#7-12						8.00
...Vol. 3: The Good Die Young (2004, $7.99, digest size) r/#13-18						8.00

RUNAWAYS (Also see X-Men/Runaways 2006 FCBD Edition in the Promotional Section)
Marvel Comics: Apr, 2005 - Present ($2.99)

1-24: 1-6-Vaughan-s/Alphona-a/Jo Chen-c. 7,8-Miyazawa-a/Bachalo-c. 11-Spider-Man app. 12-New Avengers app. 18-Gert killed						3.00
25-27: 25-Whedon-s/Ryan-a begin; Punisher app.						3.00
... Saga (2007, $3.99) re-caps the 2 series thru #24; 4 new pages w/Ramos-a; Ramos-c						4.00
Hardcover (2006, $24.99) oversized r/#1-12 & X-Men/Runaways; script & sketch pages						25.00
Hardcover Vol. 3 (2007, $24.99) oversized r/#13-24; sketch pages						25.00
...Vol. 4: True Believers (2006, $7.99, digest size) r/#1-6						8.00
...Vol. 5: Escape To New York (2006, $7.99, digest size) r/#7-12						8.00
...Vol. 6: Parental Guidance (2006, $7.99, digest size) r/#13-18						8.00

RUN BABY RUN
Logos International: 1974 (39¢, Christian religious)

nn-By Tony Tallarico from Nicky Cruz's book	2	4	6	8	11	14

RUN, BUDDY, RUN (TV)
Gold Key: June, 1967 (Photo-c)

1 (10204-706)	3	6	9	18	27	35

RUNE (See Curse of Rune, Sludge & all other Ultraverse titles for previews)
Malibu Comics (Ultraverse): 1994 - No. 9, Apr, 1995 ($1.95)

0-Obtained by sending coupons from 11 comics; came w/Solution #0, poster, temporary tattoo, card	1	2	3	5	6	8
1,2,4-9: 1-Barry Windsor-Smith-c/a/stories begin, ends #6. 5-1st app. of Gemini. 6-Prime & Mantra app.						2.50
1-(1/94)-"Ashcan" edition flip book w/Wrath #1						2.50
1-Ultra 5000 Limited silver foil edition						4.00
3-(3/94, $3.50, 68 pgs.)-Flip book w/Ultraverse Premiere #1						3.50
Giant Size 1 ($2.50, 44 pgs.)-B.Smith story & art.						2.50

RUNE (2nd Series)(Formerly Curse of Rune)(See Ultraverse Unlimited #1)
Malibu Comics (Ultraverse): Infinity. Sept, 1995 - V2#7, Apr, 1996 ($1.50)

Infinity, V2#1-7: Infinity-Black September tie-in; black-c & painted-c exist. 1,3-7-Marvel's Adam Warlock app; regular & painted-c exist. 2-Flip book w/ "Phoenix Resurrection" Pt. 6						2.50
...Vs. Venom 1 (12/95, $3.95)						4.00

RUNE: HEARTS OF DARKNESS
Malibu Comics (Ultraverse): Sept, 1996 - No. 3, Nov, 1996 ($1.50, lim. series)

1-3: Moench scripts & Kyle Hotz-c/a; flip books w/6 pg. Rune story by the Pander Bros.						2.50

RUNE/SILVER SURFER
Marvel Comics/Malibu Comics (Ultraverse): Apr, 1995 ($5.95/$2.95, one-shot)

Rush City #5 © DC

Sabretooth: Mary Shelley Overdrive #1 © MAR

Sabrina the Teenage Witch V2 #74 © AP

	GD 2.0	VG 4.0	FN 6.0	VF 8.0	VF/NM 9.0	NM- 9.2
1 ($5.95, direct market)-BWS-c						6.00
1 ($2.95, newstand)-BWS-c						3.00
1-Collector's limited edition						6.00

RUSE (Also see Archard's Agents)
CrossGeneration Comics: Nov, 2001 - No. 26, Jan, 2004 ($2.95)

	GD 2.0	VG 4.0	FN 6.0	VF 8.0	VF/NM 9.0	NM- 9.2
1-Waid-s/Guice & Perkins-a						5.00
2-26: 6-Jeff Johnson-a. 11,15-Paul Ryan-a. 12-Last Waid-s						3.00
Enter the Detective Vol. 1 TPB (2002, $15.95) r/#1-6; Guice-c						16.00
...: The Silent Partner Vol. 2 (3/03, $15.95, TPB) r/#7-12						16.00
...: Criminal Intent Vol. 3 ('03, $15.95, TPB) r/#13-18						16.00
Traveler 1,2 ($9.95): Digest-size editions of the TPBs						10.00

RUSH CITY
DC Comics: Sept, 2006 - No. 6, May, 2007 ($2.99, limited series)

1-6: 1-Dixon-s/Green-a/Jock-c. 2,3-Black Canary app.						3.00

RUSTLERS, THE (See Zane Grey Four Color 532)

RUSTY, BOY DETECTIVE
Good Comics/Lev Gleason: Mar-April, 1955 - No. 5, Nov, 1955

	GD 2.0	VG 4.0	FN 6.0	VF 8.0	VF/NM 9.0	NM- 9.2
1-Bob Wood, Carl Hubbell-a begins	9	18	27	47	61	75
2-5	6	12	18	31	38	45

RUSTY COMICS (Formerly Kid Movie Comics; Rusty and Her Family #21, 22; The Kelleys #23 on; see Millie The Model)
Marvel Comics (HPC): No. 12, Apr, 1947 - No. 22, Sept, 1949

	GD 2.0	VG 4.0	FN 6.0	VF 8.0	VF/NM 9.0	NM- 9.2
12-Mitzi app.	21	42	63	122	191	260
13	21	39	74	105	135	
14-Wolverton's Powerhouse Pepper (4 pgs.) plus Kurtzman's "Hey Look"	22	44	66	128	202	275
15-17-Kurtzman's "Hey Look"	15	30	45	90	140	190
18,19	12	24	36	67	94	120
20-Kurtzman-a (5 pgs.)	16	32	48	94	147	200
21,22-Kurtzman-a (17 & 22 pgs.)	21	42	63	124	195	265

RUSTY DUGAN (See Holyoke One-Shot #2)

RUSTY RILEY
Dell Publishing Co.: No. 418, Aug, 1952 - No. 554, April, 1954 (Frank Godwin strip reprints)

	GD 2.0	VG 4.0	FN 6.0	VF 8.0	VF/NM 9.0	NM- 9.2
Four Color 418 (...a Boy, a Horse, and a Dog #1)	5	10	15	32	51	70
Four Color 451(2/53), 486 ('53), 554	4	8	12	26	41	50

RUULE
Beckett Comics: Dec, 2003 - No. 5, Apr, 2004 ($2.99)

1-5-David Mack-c/Mike Hawthorne-a						3.00

RUULE: KISS & TELL
Beckett Comics: Jun, 2004 - No. 8 ($1.99)

1-7: 1-Amano-s/c; Rousseau-a. 4-Maleev-c						2.00
TPB (2005, $19.99) r/#1-8						20.00

SAARI ("The Jungle Goddess")
P. L. Publishing Co.: November, 1951

	GD 2.0	VG 4.0	FN 6.0	VF 8.0	VF/NM 9.0	NM- 9.2
1	45	90	135	275	450	625

SABAN POWERHOUSE (TV)
Acclaim Books: 1997 ($4.50, digest size)

1,2-Power Rangers, BeetleBorgs, and others						4.50

SABAN PRESENTS POWER RANGERS TURBO VS. BEETLEBORGS METALLIX (TV)
Acclaim Books: 1997 ($4.50, digest size, one-shot)

nn						4.50

SABAN'S MIGHTY MORPHIN POWER RANGERS
Hamilton Comics: Dec, 1994 - No. 6, May, 1995 ($1.95, limited series)

1-6: 1-w/bound-in Power Ranger Barcode Card						2.50

SABAN'S MIGHTY MORPHIN POWER RANGERS (TV)
Marvel Comics: 1995 - No. 8, 1996 ($1.75)

1-8						2.50

SABLE (Formerly Jon Sable, Freelance; also see Mike Grell's...)
First Comics: Mar, 1988 - No. 27, May, 1990 ($1.75/$1.95)

1-27: 10-Begin $1.95-c						2.50

SABLE & FORTUNE (Also see Silver Sable and the Wild Pack)
Marvel Comics: Mar, 2006 - No. 4, June, 2006 ($2.99, limited series)

1-4-John Burns-a/Brendan Cahill-s						3.00

SABRE (See Eclipse Graphic Album Series)

Eclipse Comics: Aug, 1982 - No. 14, Aug, 1985 (Baxter paper #4 on)

	GD 2.0	VG 4.0	FN 6.0	VF 8.0	VF/NM 9.0	NM- 9.2
1-14: 1-Sabre & Morrigan Tales begin. 4-6-Incredible Seven origin						2.50

SABRETOOTH (See Iron Fist, Power Man, X-Factor #10 & X-Men)
Marvel Comics: Aug, 1993 - No. 4, Nov, 1993 ($2.95, lim. series, coated paper)

1-4: 1-Die-cut-c. 3-Wolverine app.						4.00
...Special 1 "In the Red Zone" (1995, $4.95) Chromium wraparound-c						6.00
V2 #1 (1/98, $5.95, one-shot) Wildchild app.						6.00
Trade paperback (12/94, $12.95) r/#1-4						13.00

SABRETOOTH
Marvel Comics: Dec, 2004 - No. 4, Feb, 2005 ($2.99, limited series)

1-4-Sears-a. 3,4-Wendigo app.						3.00
...: Open Season TPB (2005, $9.99) r/#1-4						10.00

SABRETOOTH AND MYSTIQUE (See Mystique and Sabretooth)

SABRETOOTH CLASSIC
Marvel Comics: May, 1994 - No. 15, July, 1995 ($1.50)

1-15: 1-3-r/Power Man & Iron Fist #66,78,84. 4-r/Spec. S-M #116. 9-Uncanny X-Men #212, 10-r/Uncanny X-Men #213. 11-r/ Daredevil #238. 12-r/Classic X-Men #10						3.00

SABRETOOTH: MARY SHELLEY OVERDRIVE
Marvel Comics: Aug, 2002 - No. 4, Nov, 2002 ($2.99, limited series)

1-4-Jolley-s; Harris-c						3.00

SABRINA (Volume 2) (Based on animated series)
Archie Publications: Jan, 2000 - Present ($1.79/$1.99/$2.19/$2.25)

1-Teen-age Witch magically reverted to 12 years old						4.00
2-10: 4-Begin $1.99-c						3.00
11-90: 38-Sabrina aged back to 16 years old. 39-Begin $2.19-c. 58-Manga-style begins; Tania Del Rio-a. 67-Josie and the Pussycats app.						2.50

SABRINA'S CHRISTMAS MAGIC (See Archie Giant Series Magazine #196, 207, 220, 231, 243, 455, 467, 479, 491, 503, 515)

SABRINA'S HALLOWEEN SPOOOKTACULAR
Archie Publications: 1993 - 1995 ($2.00, 52 pgs.)

	GD 2.0	VG 4.0	FN 6.0	VF 8.0	VF/NM 9.0	NM- 9.2
1-Neon orange ink-c; bound-in poster	1	2	3	5	6	8
2,3						5.00

SABRINA'S HOLIDAY SPECTACULAR
Archie Publications: 1993 - 1995 ($2.00, 52 pgs.)

	GD 2.0	VG 4.0	FN 6.0	VF 8.0	VF/NM 9.0	NM- 9.2
1	1	2	3	5	6	8
2,3						5.00

SABRINA, THE TEEN-AGE WITCH (TV)(See Archie Giant Series, Archie's Madhouse 22, Archie's TV..., Chilling Advs. In Sorcery, Little Archie #59)
Archie Publications: April, 1971 - No. 77, Jan, 1983 (52 pg.Giants No. 1-17)

	GD 2.0	VG 4.0	FN 6.0	VF 8.0	VF/NM 9.0	NM- 9.2
1-52 pgs. begin, end #17	14	28	42	102	181	260
2-Archie's group x-over	8	16	24	54	90	125
3-5: 3,4-Archie's Group x-over	6	12	18	37	59	80
6-10	5	10	15	32	51	70
11-17(2/74)	4	8	12	24	37	50
18-30	3	6	9	18	27	35
31-40(8/77)	3	6	9	14	19	24
41-60(6/80)	2	4	6	9	13	16
61-70	2	4	6	8	10	12
71-76-low print run	2	4	6	9	13	16
77-Last issue; low print run	2	4	6	13	18	22

SABRINA, THE TEEN-AGE WITCH
Archie Publications: 1996 ($1.50, 32 pgs., one-shot)

1-Updated origin						5.00

SABRINA, THE TEEN-AGE WITCH (Continues in Sabrina, Vol. 2)
Archie Publications: May, 1997 - No. 32, Dec, 1999 ($1.50/$1.75/$1.79)

	GD 2.0	VG 4.0	FN 6.0	VF 8.0	VF/NM 9.0	NM- 9.2
1-Photo-c with Melissa Joan Hart	1	2	3	5	6	8
2-10: 9-Begin $1.75-c						5.00
11-20						4.00
21-32: 24-Begin $1.79-c. 28-Sonic the Hedgehog-c/app.						3.00

SABU, "ELEPHANT BOY" (Movie; formerly My Secret Story)
Fox Features Syndicate: No. 30, June, 1950 - No. 2, Aug, 1950

	GD 2.0	VG 4.0	FN 6.0	VF 8.0	VF/NM 9.0	NM- 9.2
30(#1)-Wood-a; photo-c from movie	26	52	78	152	239	325
2-Photo-c from movie; Kamen-a	19	38	57	109	172	235

SACHS & VIOLENS
Marvel Comics (Epic Comics): Nov, 1993 - No. 4, July, 1994 ($2.25, limited series, mature)

The Sadhu #7 © Virgin Comics

Sad Sack Comics #7 © HARV

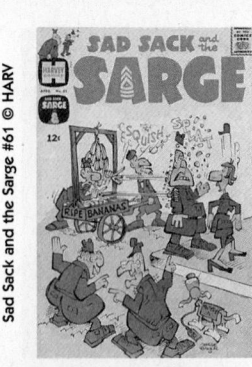

Sad Sack and the Sarge #61 © HARV

	GD	VG	FN	VF	VF/NM	NM-
	2.0	4.0	6.0	8.0	9.0	9.2

	GD	VG	FN	VF	VF/NM	NM-
	2.0	4.0	6.0	8.0	9.0	9.2

1-($2.75)-Embossed-c w/bound-in trading card 2.75
1-($3.50)-Platinum edition (1 for each 10 ordered) 4.00
2-4: Perez-c/a; bound-in trading card: 2-(5/94) 2.50
TPB (DC, 2006, $14.99) r/series; intro. by Peter David; creator bios. 15.00

SACRAMENTS, THE
Catechetical Guild Educational Society: Oct, 1955 (25¢)

304	5	10	15	23	28	32

SACRED AND THE PROFANE, THE (See Eclipse Graphic Album Series #9 & Epic Illustrated #20)

SADDLE JUSTICE (Happy Houlihans #1,2) (Saddle Romances #9 on)
E. C. Comics: No. 3, Spring, 1948 - No. 8, Sept-Oct, 1949

3-The 1st E.C. by Bill Gaines to break away from M. C. Gaines' old Educational Comics format. Craig, Feldstein, H. C. Kiefer, & Stan Asch-a; mentioned in Love and Death

	52	104	156	317	521	725
4-1st Graham Ingels a-for E.C.	45	90	135	275	450	635
5-8-Ingels-a in all	42	84	126	256	408	560

NOTE: *Craig* and *Feldstein* art in most issues. Canadian reprints known; see Table of Contents. *Craig* c-3, 4. *Ingels* c-5-8. #4 contains a biography of *Craig*.

SADDLE ROMANCES (Saddle Justice #3-8; Weird Science #12 on)
E. C. Comics: No. 9, Nov-Dec, 1949 - No. 11, Mar-Apr, 1950

9,11: 9-Ingels-c/a. 11-Ingels-a; Feldstein-c	46	92	138	281	461	640
10-Wally Wood's 1st work at E. C.; Ingels-a; Feldstein-c						
	46	92	138	281	466	650

NOTE: Canadian reprints known; see Table of Contents. *Wood/Harrison* a-10, 11.

SADHU
Virgin Comics: July, 2006 - No. 8, June, 2007 ($2.99)

1-8: 1,2-Gotham Chopra-s/Jeevan Kang-a 3.00
...: The Silent Ones 1 (8/07 - No. 5, $2.99) 3.00

SADIE SACK (See Harvey Hits #93)

SAD SACK AND THE SARGE
Harvey Publications: Sept, 1957 - No. 155, June, 1982

1	13	26	39	95	168	240
2	7	14	21	50	83	115
3-10	6	12	18	39	62	85
11-20	5	10	15	30	48	65
21-30	3	6	9	20	30	40
31-50	3	6	9	14	20	25
51-70	2	4	6	9	13	16
71-90,97-99	1	3	4	6	8	10
91-96: All 52 pg. Giants	2	4	6	9	13	16
100	2	4	6	8	10	12
101-120	1	2	3	4	5	7
121-155						5.00

SAD SACK COMICS (See Harvey Collector's Comics #16, Little Sad Sack, Tastee Freez Comics #4 & True Comics #55)
Harvey Publications/Lorne-Harvey Publications (Recollections) #288 On: Sept, 1949 - No. 287, Oct, 1982; No. 288, 1992 - No. 291, 1993

1-Infinity-c; Little Dot begins (1st app.); civilian issues begin, end #21; based on comic strip

	65	130	195	553	1027	1500
2-Flying Fool by Powell	26	52	78	195	348	500
3	15	30	45	107	191	275
4-10	11	22	33	79	140	200
11-21	8	16	24	54	90	125
22-("Back In The Army Again" on covers #22-36); "The Specialist" story about Sad Sack's return to Army	9	18	27	63	107	150
23-30	6	12	18	37	59	80
31-50	4	8	12	28	44	60
51-80,100: 62-"The Specialist" reprinted	3	6	9	20	30	40
81-99	3	6	9	16	23	30
101-140	3	6	9	14	19	24
141-170,200	2	4	6	11	16	20
171-199	2	4	6	9	13	16
201-207: 207-last 12¢ issue	2	4	6	8	11	14
208-222	1	2	3	5	6	8
223-228 (25¢ Giants, 52 pgs.)	2	4	6	8	11	14
229-250	1	3	4	6	8	10
251-285						6.00
286,287-Limited distribution	1	2	3	5	7	9
288,289 ($2.75, 1992): 289-50th anniversary issue						6.00
290,291 ($1.00, 1993, B&W)						3.00

3-D 1 (1/54, 25¢)-Came with 2 pairs of glasses; titled "Harvey 3-D Hits"

	16	32	48	118	209	300
...At Home for the Holidays 1 (1993, no-c price)-Publ. by Lorne-Harvey' X-Mas issue						4.00

NOTE: *The Sad Sack Comics comic book was a spin-off from a Sunday Newspaper strip launched through John Wheeler's Bell Syndicate. The previous Sunday page and the first 21 comics depicted the Sad Sack in civvies. Unpopularity caused the Sunday page to be discontinued in the early '50s. Meanwhile Sad Sack returned to the Army, by popular demand, in issue No. 22, remaining there ever since. Incidentally, relatively few of the first 21 issues were ever collected and remain scarce due to this.*

SAD SACK FUN AROUND THE WORLD
Harvey Publications: 1974 (no month)

1-About Great Britain	2	4	6	11	16	20

SAD SACK GOES HOME
Harvey Publications: 1951 (16 pgs. in color, no cover price)

nn-By George Baker	5	10	15	35	55	75

SAD SACK LAUGH SPECIAL
Harvey Publications: Winter, 1958-59 - No. 93, Feb, 1977 (#1-9: 84 pgs.; #10-60: 68 pgs.; #61-76: 52 pgs.)

1-Giant 25¢ issues begin	10	20	30	71	126	180
2	6	12	18	41	66	90
3-10	5	10	15	32	51	70
11-30	4	8	12	26	41	55
31-60: 31-Hi-Fi Tweeter app. 60-Last 68 pg. Giant	3	6	9	16	23	30
61-76-(All 52 pg. issues)	2	4	6	10	14	18
77-93	1	2	3	5	6	8

SAD SACK NAVY, GOBS 'N' GALS
Harvey Publications: Aug, 1972 - No. 8, Oct, 1973

1: 52 pg. Giant	3	6	9	16	23	30
2-8	2	4	6	9	12	15

SAD SACK'S ARMY LIFE (See Harvey Hits #8, 17, 22, 28, 32, 39, 43, 47, 51, 55, 58, 61, 64, 67, 70)

SAD SACK'S ARMY LIFE (...Parade #1-57, ...Today #58 on)
Harvey Publications: Oct, 1963 - No. 60, Nov, 1975; No. 61, May, 1976

1-(68 pg. issues begin)	8	16	24	52	86	120
2-10	4	8	12	28	44	60
11-20	3	6	9	20	30	40
21-34: Last 68 pg. issue	3	6	9	16	23	30
35-51: All 52 pgs.	2	4	6	10	14	18
52-61	1	3	4	6	8	10

SAD SACK'S FUNNY FRIENDS (See Harvey Hits #75)
Harvey Publications: Dec, 1955 - No. 75, Oct, 1969

1	10	20	30	71	126	180
2-10	6	12	18	41	66	90
11-20	4	8	12	24	37	50
21-30	3	6	9	18	27	35
31-50	3	6	9	14	20	25
51-75	2	4	6	9	13	16

SAD SACK'S MUTTSY (See Harvey Hits #74, 77, 80, 82, 84, 87, 89, 92, 96, 99, 102, 105, 108, 111, 113, 115, 117, 119, 121)

SAD SACK USA (...Vacation #8)
Harvey Publications: Nov, 1972 - No. 7, Nov, 1973; No. 8, Oct, 1974

1	3	6	9	14	20	25
2-8	2	4	6	8	10	12

SAD SACK WITH SARGE & SADIE
Harvey Publications: Sept, 1972 - No. 8, Nov, 1973

1-(52 pg. Giant)	3	6	9	14	20	25
2-8	2	4	6	8	10	12

SAD SAD SACK WORLD
Harvey Publ.: Oct, 1964 - No. 46, Dec, 1973 (#1-31: 68 pgs.; #32-38: 52 pgs.)

1	7	14	21	49	80	110
2-10	4	8	12	26	41	55
11-20	3	6	9	20	30	40
21-31: 31-Last 68 pg. issue	3	6	9	16	23	30
32-39-(All 52 pgs)	2	4	6	10	14	18
40-46	1	3	4	6	8	10

SAFEST PLACE IN THE WORLD, THE
Dark Horse Comics: 1993 ($2.50, one-shot)

1-Steve Ditko-c/a/scripts 2.50

SAFETY-BELT MAN
Sirius Entertainment: June, 1994 - No. 6, 1995 ($2.50, B&W)

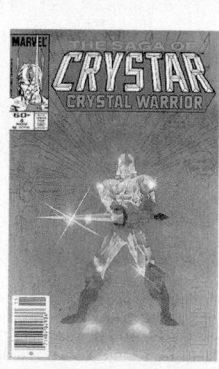

Saga of Crystar, Crystal Warrior #4 © MAR

The Saint #9 © AVON

Samson #5 © FOX

	GD 2.0	VG 4.0	FN 6.0	VF 8.0	VF/NM 9.0	NM- 9.2

	GD 2.0	VG 4.0	FN 6.0	VF 8.0	VF/NM 9.0	NM- 9.2

1-6: 1-Horan-s/Dark One-a/Sprouse-c. 2,3-Warren-c. 4-Linsner back-up story.
5,6-Crilley-a 3.00

SAFETY-BELT MAN ALL HELL
Sirius Entertainment: June, 1996 - No. 6, Mar, 1997 ($2.95, color)
1-6-Horan-s/Fillbach Bros.-a 3.00

SAGA OF BIG RED, THE
Omaha World-Herald: Sept, 1976 ($1.25) (In color)
nn-by Win Mumma; story of the Nebraska Cornhuskers (sports) 6.00

SAGA OF CRYSTAR, CRYSTAL WARRIOR, THE
Marvel Comics: May, 1983 - No. 11, Feb, 1985 (Remco toy tie-in)
1,6: 1-(Baxter paper). 6-Nightcrawler app; Golden-c 4.00
2-5,7-11: 3-Dr. Strange app. 3-11-Golden-c (painted-4,5). 11-Alpha Flight app. 3.00

SAGA OF RA'S AL GHUL, THE
DC Comics: Jan, 1988 - No. 4, Apr, 1988 ($2.50, limited series)
1-4-r/N. Adams Batman 6.00

SAGA OF SABAN'S MIGHTY MORPHIN POWER RANGERS (Also see
Saban's Mighty Morphin Power Rangers)
Hamilton Comics: 1995 - No. 4, 1995 ($1.95, limited series)
1-4 .... 2.50

SAGA OF SEVEN SUNS, THE : VEILED ALLIANCES
DC Comics (WildStorm): 2004 ($24.95, hardcover graphic novel with dustjacket)
HC-Kevin J. Anderson-s/Robert Teranishi-a 25.00
SC-(2004, $17.95) 18.00

SAGA OF THE SWAMP THING, THE (See Swamp Thing)

SAGA OF THE ORIGINAL HUMAN TORCH
Marvel Comics: Apr, 1990 - No. 4, July, 1990 ($1.50, limited series)
1-4: 1-Origin; Buckler-c/a(p). 4-Hitler-c 2.50

SAGA OF THE SUB-MARINER, THE
Marvel Comics: Nov, 1988 - No. 12, Oct, 1989 ($1.25/$1.50 #5 on, maxi-series)
1-12: 9-Original X-Men app. 3.00

SAILOR MOON (Manga)
Mixx Entertainment Inc.: 1998 - Present ($2.95)

	GD	VG	FN	VF	VF/NM	NM-
1	2	4	6	10	14	18
1-(San Diego edition)	2	4	6	11	16	20
2-5	2	4	6	8	10	12
6-25						5.00
26-35						3.00
... Rini's Moon Stick 1						15.00

SAILOR ON THE SEA OF FATE (See First Comics Graphic Novel #11)

SAILOR SWEENEY (Navy Action #1-11, 15 on)
Atlas Comics (CDS): No. 12, July, 1956 - No. 14, Nov, 1956

	GD	VG	FN	VF	VF/NM	NM-
12-14: 12-Shores-a. 13,14-Severin-c	9	18	27	52	69	85

SAINT, THE (Also see Movie Comics(DC) #2 & Silver Streak #18)
Avon Periodicals: Aug, 1947 - No. 12, Mar, 1952

	GD	VG	FN	VF	VF/NM	NM-
1-Kamen bondage-c/a	83	166	249	519	860	1200
2	43	86	129	243	389	535
3-5: 4-Lingerie panels	36	72	108	208	329	450
6-Miss Fury app. by Tarpe Mills (14 pgs.)	45	90	135	275	450	625
7-c/Avon paperback #118	29	58	87	167	264	360
8,9(12/50): Saint strip-r in #8-12; 9-Kinstler-c	26	52	78	152	239	325
10-Wood-a, 1 pg; c/Avon paperback #289	26	52	78	152	239	325
11	19	38	57	112	176	240
12-c/Avon paperback #123	22	44	66	126	198	270

NOTE: Lucky Dale, Girl Detective in #1,2,4,6. Hollingsworth a-4, 6. Painted-c 7, 8, 10-12.

SAINT ANGEL
Image Comics: Mar, 2000 - No. 4, Mar, 2001 ($2.95/$3.95)
0-Altstaetter & Napton-s/Altstaetter-a 3.00
1-4-($3.95) Flip book w/Deity. 1-(6/00). 2-(10/00) 4.00

ST. GEORGE
Marvel Comics (Epic Comics): June, 1988 - No.8, Oct, 1989 ($1.25,/$1.50)
1-8: Sienkiewicz-c. 3-begin $1.50-c 2.50

SAINT GERMAINE
Caliber Comics: 1997 - No. 8, 1998 ($2.95)
1-8: 1,5-Alternate covers 3.00

ST. SWITHIN'S DAY
Trident Comics: Apr, 1990 ($2.50, one-shot)
1-Grant Morrison scripts 3.00

ST. SWITHIN'S DAY
Oni Press: Mar, 1998 ($2.95, B&W, one-shot)
1-Grant Morrison-s/Paul Grist-a 3.00

SALOMÉ (See Night Music #6)

SAM AND MAX, FREELANCE POLICE SPECIAL
Fishwrap Prod./Comico: 1987 ($1.75, B&W); Jan, 1989 ($2.75, 44 pgs.)
1 ($1.75, B&W, Fishwrap) 3.00
2 ($2.75, color, Comico) 2.75

SAM AND TWITCH (See Spawn and Case Files:...)
Image Comics (Todd McFarlane Prod.): Aug, 1999 - No. 26, Feb, 2004 ($2.50)
1-26: 1-19-Bendis-s. 1-14-Medina-a. 15-19-Maleev-a. 20-24-McFarlane-s/Maleev-a 2.50
Book One: Udaku (2000, $21.95, TPB) B&W reprint of #1-8 .... 22.00
...: The Brian Michael Bendis Collection Vol. 1 (2/06, $24.95) r/#1-9 in color; sketch pages 25.00
...: The Brian Michael Bendis Collection Vol. 2 (6/07, $24.95) r/#10-19; cover gallery 25.00

SAM HILL PRIVATE EYE
Close-Up (Archie): 1950 - No. 7, 1951

	GD	VG	FN	VF	VF/NM	NM-
1	16	32	48	92	144	195
2	10	20	30	56	76	95
3-7	10	20	30	54	72	90

SAMSON (1st Series) (Captain Aero #7 on; see Big 3 Comics)
Fox Features Syndicate: Fall, 1940 - No. 6, Sept, 1941 (See Fantastic Comics)

	GD	VG	FN	VF	VF/NM	NM-
1-Samson begins, ends #6; Powell-a, signed 'Rensie'; Wing Turner by Tuska app; Fine-c?	221	442	663	1381	2291	3200
2-Dr. Fung by Powell; Fine-c?	79	158	237	494	822	1150
3-Navy Jones app.; Joe Simon-c	60	120	180	375	620	865
4-Yarko the Great, Master Magician begins	53	106	159	323	537	750
5,6: 6-Origin The Topper	43	86	129	262	431	600

SAMSON (2nd Series) (Formerly Fantastic Comics #10, 11)
Ajax/Farrell Publications (Four Star): No. 12, April, 1955 - No. 14, Aug, 1955

	GD	VG	FN	VF	VF/NM	NM-
12-Wonder Boy	30	60	90	174	275	375
13,14: 13-Wonder Boy, Rocket Man	26	52	78	152	239	325

SAMSON (See Mighty Samson)

SAMSON & DELILAH (See A Spectacular Feature Magazine)

SAMUEL BRONSTON'S CIRCUS WORLD (See Circus World under Movie Classics)

SAMURAI (Also see Eclipse Graphic Album Series #14)
Aircel Publications: 1985 - No. 23, 1987 ($1.70, B&W)
1, 14-16-Dale Keown-a 3.00
1-(reprinted),2-12,17-23: 2 (reprinted issue exists) 2.50
13-Dale Keown's 1st published artwork (1987) 5.00

SAMURAI
Warp Graphics: May, 1997 ($2.95, B&W)
1 .... 3.00

SAMURAI CAT
Marvel Comics (Epic Comics): June, 1991 - No. 3, Sept, 1991 ($2.25, limited series)
1-3: 3-Darth Vader-c/story parody 2.50

SAMURAI: HEAVEN & EARTH
Dark Horse Comics: Dec, 2004 - No. 5, Dec, 2005 ($2.99)
1-5-Luke Ross-a/Ron Marz-s 3.00
TPB (4/06, $14.95) r/#1-5; sketch pages and cover and pin-up gallery 15.00

SAMURAI: HEAVEN & EARTH (Volume 2)
Dark Horse Comics: Nov, 2006 - No. 5, June, 2007 ($2.99)
1-5-Luke Ross-a/Ron Marz-s 3.00

SAMURAI JACK SPECIAL (TV)
DC Comics: Sept, 2002 ($3.95, one-shot)
1-Adaptation of pilot episode with origin story; Tartakovsky-s 4.00

SAMUREE
Continuity Comics: May, 1987 - No. 9, Jan, 1991
1-9 .... 3.00

SAMUREE
Continuity Comics: V2#1, May, 1993 - V2#4, Jan,1994 ($2.50)

	GD	VG	FN	VF	VF/NM	NM-			GD	VG	FN	VF	VF/NM	NM-
	2.0	4.0	6.0	8.0	9.0	9.2			2.0	4.0	6.0	8.0	9.0	9.2

V2#1-4-Embossed-c: 2,4-Adams plot, Nebres-i. 3-Nino-c(i) 2.50

SAMUREE
Acclaim Comics (Windjammer): Oct, 1995 - No. 2, Nov,1995 ($2.50, lim. series)
1,2 .... 2.50

SAN DIEGO COMIC CON COMICS
Dark Horse Comics: 1992 - No.4, 1995 (B&W, promo comic for the San Diego Comic Con)
1-(1992)-Includes various characters published from Dark Horse including Concrete, The Mask, RoboCop and others; 1st app. of Sprint from John Byrne's Next Men; art by Quesada, Byrne, Rude, Burden, Moebius & others; pin-ups by Rude, Dorkin, Allred & others; Chadwick-c 1 2 3 4 5 7
2-(1993)-Intro of Legend imprint; 1st app. of John Byrne's Danger Unlimited, Mike Mignola's Hellboy, Art Adams' Monkeyman & O'Brien; contains stories featuring Concrete, Sin City, Martha Washington & others; Grendel, Madman, & Big Guy pin-ups; Don Martin-c. 1 3 4 5 8 10
3-(1994)-Contains stories featuring Barb Wire, The Mask, The Dirty Pair, & Grendel by Matt Wagner; contains pin-ups of Ghost, Predator & Rascals In Paradise; The Mask-c. 6.00
4-(1995)-Contains Sin City story by Miller (3pg.), Star Wars, The Mask, Tarzan, Foot Soldiers; Sin City & Star Wars flip-c 6.00

SANDMAN, THE (1st Series) (Also see Adventure Comics #40, New York World's Fair & World's Finest #3)
National Periodical Publ.: Winter, 1974; No. 2, Apr-May, 1975 - No. 6, Dec-Jan, 1975-76
1-1st app. Bronze Age Sandman by Simon & Kirby (last S&K collaboration) 6 12 18 39 62 85
2-6: 6-Kirby/Wood-c/a 3 6 9 18 27 35
NOTE: Kirby a-1p, 4-6p; c-1-5, 6p.

SANDMAN (2nd Series) (See Books of Magic, Vertigo Jam & Vertigo Preview)
DC Comics (Vertigo imprint on #47 on): Jan, 1989 - No. 75, Mar, 1996 ($1.50-$2.50, mature)
1 ($2.00, 52 pgs.)-1st app. Modern Age Sandman (Morpheus); Neil Gaiman scripts begin; Sam Kieth-a(p) in #1-5; Wesley Dodds (G.A. Sandman) cameo. 3 6 9 20 30 40
2-Cain & Abel app. (from HOM & HOS) 2 4 6 10 14 18
3-5: 3-John Constantine app. 2 4 6 9 12 15
6,7 .... 1 3 4 6 8 10
8-Death-c/story (1st app.)-Regular ed. has Jeanette Kahn publishorial & American Cancer Society ad w/no indicia on inside front-c 2 4 6 13 18 22
8-Limited ed. (600+ copies?); has Karen Berger editorial and next issue teaser on inside covers (has indicia) 4 8 12 28 44 60
9-14: 10-Has explaination about #8 mixup; has bound-in Shocker movie poster.
14-(52 pgs.)-Bound-in Nightbreed fold-out 1 2 3 5 7 9
15-20: 16-Photo-c. 17,18-Kelley Jones-a. 19-Vess-a. 6.00
18-Error version w/1st 3 panels on pg. 1 in blue ink 3 6 9 14 20 25
19-Error version w/pages 18 & 20 facing each other 2 4 6 11 16 20
21,23-27: Seasons of Mist storyline. 22-World Without End preview. 24-Kelley Jones/Russell-a 6.00
22-1st Daniel (Later becomes new Sandman) 2 4 6 8 10 12
28-30 .... 5.00
31-49,51-74: 36-(52 pgs.). 41,44-48-Metallic ink on-c. 48-Cerebus appears as a doll. 54-Re-intro Prez; Death app.; Belushi, Nixon & Wildcat cameos. 57-Metallic ink on c. 65-w/bound-in trading card. 69-Death of Sandman. 70-73-Zulli-a. 74-Jon J. Muth-a. 4.00
50-($2.95, 52 pgs.)-Black-c w/metallic ink by McKean; Russell-a; McFarlane pin-up 5.00
50-($2.95)-Signed & limited (5,000) Treasury Edition w/sketch of Neil Gaiman 1 2 3 4 6 8
50-Platinum 20.00
75-($3.95)-Vess-a. 5.00
Special 1 (1991, $3.50, 68 pgs.)-Glow-in-the-dark-c 5.00
Absolute Sandman Special Edition #1 (2006, 50¢) sampling from HC; recolored r/#1 .... 2.50
Absolute Sandman Volume One (2006, $99.00, slipcased hardcover) recolored r/#1-20; Gaiman's original proposal; script and pencils from #19; character sketch gallery 100.00
...: A Gallery of Dreams ($2.95)-Intro by N. Gaiman 3.00
...: Preludes & Nocturnes ($29.95, HC)-r/#1-8. .... 30.00
...: The Doll's House (1990, $29.95, HC)-r/#8-16. .... 30.00
...: Dream Country ($29.95, HC)-r/#17-20. .... 30.00
...: Season of Mists ($29.95, Leatherbound HC)-r/#21-28. .... 50.00
...: A Game of You ($29.95, HC)-r/#32-37, ...: Fables and Reflections ($29.95, HC)-r/Vertigo Preview #1, Sandman Special #1, #29-31, #38-40 & #50. ...: Brief Lives ($29.95, HC)-r/#41-49. ...: World's End ($29.95, HC)-r/#51-56 .... 30.00
...: The Kindly Ones (1996, $34.95, HC)-r/#57-69 & Vertigo Jam #1 .... 35.00
...: The Wake ($29.95, HC)-r/#70-75. .... 30.00
NOTE: A new set of hardcover printings with new covers was introduced in 1998-99. Multiple printings exist of softcover collections. Bachalo a-12; Kelley Jones a-17, 18, 22, 23, 26, 27. Vess a-19, 75.

SANDMAN: ENDLESS NIGHTS

DC Comics (Vertigo): 2003 ($24.95, hardcover, with dust jacket)
HC-Neil Gaiman stories of Morpheus and the Endless illustrated by Fabry, Manara, Prado, Quitely, Russell, Sienkiewicz, and Storey; McKean-c 25.00
...Special (11/03, $2.95) Previews hardcover; Dream story w/Prado-a; McKean-c 3.00
SC (2004, $17.95) 18.00

SANDMAN MIDNIGHT THEATRE
DC Comics (Vertigo): Sept, 1995 ($6.95, squarebound, one-shot)
nn-Modern Age Sandman (Morpheus) meets G.A. Sandman; Gaiman & Wagner story; McKean-c; Kristiansen-a 7.00

SANDMAN MYSTERY THEATRE (Also see Sandman (2nd Series) #1)
DC Comics (Vertigo): Apr, 1993 - No. 70, Feb, 1999 ($1.95/$2.25/$2.50)
1-G.A. Sandman advs. begin; Matt Wagner scripts begin 4.50
2-49: 5-Neon ink logo. 29-32-Hourman app. 38-Ted Knight (G.A. Starman) app. 42-Jim Corrigan (Spectre) app. 45-48-Blackhawk app. 2.50
50-($3.50, 48 pgs.) w/bonus story of S.A. Sandman, Torres-a 3.50
51-70 .... 2.50
Annual 1 (10/94, $3.95, 68 pgs.)-Alex Ross, Bolton & others-a 5.00
...: Dr. Death and the Night of the Butcher (2007, $19.99) r/#21-28 .... 20.00
...: The Face and the Brute (2004, $19.95) r/#5-12 .... 20.00
...: The Scorpion (2006, $12.99) r/#17-20 .... 13.00
...: The Tarantula (1995, $14.95) r/#1-4 .... 15.00
...: The Vamp (2005, $12.99) r/#13-16 .... 13.00

SANDMAN MYSTERY THEATRE (2nd Series)
DC Comics (Vertigo): Feb, 2007 - No. 5, Jun, 2007 ($2.99, limited series)
1-5-Wesley Dodds and Dian in 1997; Rieber-s/Nguyen-a 3.00

SANDMAN PRESENTS...
DC Comics (Vertigo)
Taller Tales TPB (2003, $19.95) r/S.P.: The Thessaliad #1-4; Merv Pumpkinhead, Agent...; The Dreaming #55; S.P. Everything You Always...; new McKean-c; intro by Willingham 20.00

SANDMAN PRESENTS: BAST
DC Comics (Vertigo): Mar, 2003 - No. 3, May, 2003 ($2.95, limited series)
1-3-Kiernan-s/Bennett-a/McKean-c 3.00

SANDMAN PRESENTS: DEADBOY DETECTIVES (See Sandman #21-28)
DC Comics (Vertigo): Aug, 2001 - No. 4, Nov, 2001 ($2.50, limited series)
1-4:Talbot-a/McKean-c/Brubaker-s 2.50

SANDMAN PRESENTS: EVERYTHING YOU ALWAYS WANTED TO KNOW ABOUT DREAMS...BUT WERE AFRAID TO ASK
DC Comics (Vertigo): Jul, 2001 ($3.95, one-shot)
1-Short stories by Willingham; art by various; McKean-c 4.00

SANDMAN PRESENTS: LOVE STREET
DC Comics (Vertigo): Jul, 1999 - No. 3, Sept, 1999 ($2.95, limited series)
1-3: Teenage Hellblazer in 1968 London; Zulli-a 3.00

SANDMAN PRESENTS: LUCIFER
DC Comics (Vertigo): Mar, 1999 - No. 3, May, 1999 ($2.95, limited series)
1-3: Scott Hampton painted-c/a 3.00

SANDMAN PRESENTS: PETREFAX
DC Comics (Vertigo): Mar, 2000 - No. 4, Jun, 2000 ($2.95, limited series)
1-4-Carey-s/Leialoha-a 3.00

SANDMAN PRESENTS: THE CORINTHIAN
DC Comics (Vertigo): Dec, 2001 - No. 3, Feb, 2002 ($2.95, limited series)
1-3-Macan-s/Zezelj-a/McKean-c 3.00

SANDMAN PRESENTS, THE: THE FURIES
DC Comics (Vertigo): 2002 ($24.95, one-shot)
Hardcover-Mike Carey-s/John Bolton-painted art; Lyta Hall's reunion with Daniel 30.00
Softcover-(2003, $17.95) 18.00

SANDMAN PRESENTS, THE: THESSALY: WITCH FOR HIRE
DC Comics (Vertigo): Apr, 2004 - No. 4, July, 2004 ($2.95, limited series)
1-4-Willingham-s/McManus-a/McPherson-c 3.00
TPB-(2005, $12.99) r/#1-4 .... 13.00

SANDMAN PRESENTS, THE: THE THESSALIAD
DC Comics (Vertigo): Mar, 2002 - No. 4, Jun, 2002 ($2.95, limited series)
1-4-Willingham-s/McManus-a/McKean-c 3.00

SANDMAN, THE: THE DREAM HUNTERS
DC Comics (Vertigo): Oct, 1999 ($29.95/$19.95, one-shot)

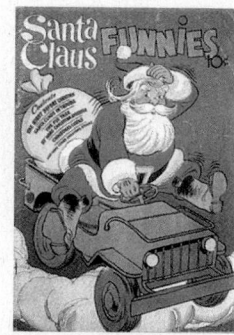

Santa Claus Funnies nn © DELL

Satan's Six #4 © Jack Kirby

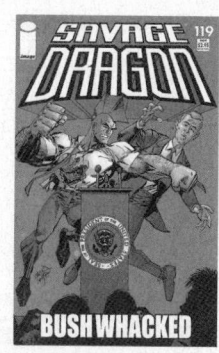

Savage Dragon #119 © Erik Larsen

	GD 2.0	VG 4.0	FN 6.0	VF 8.0	VF/NM 9.0	NM- 9.2
Hardcover-Neil Gaiman-s/Yoshitaka Amano-painted art						30.00
Softcover-(2000, $19.95) new Amano-c						20.00

SANDSCAPE
Dreamwave Productions: Jan, 2003 - No. 4, May, 2003 ($2.95)

	GD 2.0	VG 4.0	FN 6.0	VF 8.0	VF/NM 9.0	NM- 9.2
1-4: 1-Gatefold wraparound-c						3.00

SANDS OF THE SOUTH PACIFIC
Toby Press: Jan, 1953

	GD 2.0	VG 4.0	FN 6.0	VF 8.0	VF/NM 9.0	NM- 9.2
1	21	42	63	120	188	255

SANTA AND HIS REINDEER (See March of Comics #166)

SANTA AND THE ANGEL (See Dell Junior Treasury #7)
Dell Publishing Co.: Dec, 1949 (Combined w/Santa at the Zoo) (Gollub-a condensed from FC#128)

	GD 2.0	VG 4.0	FN 6.0	VF 8.0	VF/NM 9.0	NM- 9.2
Four Color 259	5	10	15	35	55	75

SANTA AT THE ZOO (See Santa And The Angel)

SANTA CLAUS AROUND THE WORLD (See March of Comics #241 in Promotional Comics section)

SANTA CLAUS CONQUERS THE MARTIANS (See Movie Classics)

SANTA CLAUS FUNNIES (Also see Dell Giants)
Dell Publishing Co.: Dec?, 1942 - No. 1274, Dec, 1961

	GD 2.0	VG 4.0	FN 6.0	VF 8.0	VF/NM 9.0	NM- 9.2
nn(#1)(1942)-Kelly-a	35	70	105	263	482	700
2(12/43)-Kelly-a	23	46	69	169	302	435
Four Color 61(1944)-Kelly-a	22	44	66	165	295	425
Four Color 91(1945)-Kelly-a	17	34	51	128	227	325
Four Color 128('46),175('47)-Kelly-a	14	28	42	102	181	260
Four Color 205,254-Kelly-a	13	26	39	93	164	235
Four Color 302,361,525,607,666,756,867	7	14	21	45	73	100
Four Color 958,1063,1154,1274	6	12	18	41	66	90

NOTE: Most issues contain only one Kelly story.

SANTA CLAUS PARADE
Ziff-Davis (Approved Comics)/St. John Publishing Co.: 1951; No. 2, Dec, 1952; No. 3, Jan, 1955 (25¢)

	GD 2.0	VG 4.0	FN 6.0	VF 8.0	VF/NM 9.0	NM- 9.2
nn(1951-Ziff-Davis)-116 pgs.(Xmas Special 1,2)	29	58	87	167	264	360
2(12/52-Ziff-Davis)-100 pgs.; Dave Berg-a	22	44	66	126	198	270
V1#3(1/55-St. John)-100 pgs.; reprints-c/#1	19	38	57	109	172	235

SANTA CLAUS' WORKSHOP (See March of Comics #50,168 in Promotional Comics section)

SANTA IS COMING (See March of Comics #197 in Promotional Comics section)

SANTA IS HERE (See March of Comics #49 in Promotional Comics section)

SANTA'S BUSY CORNER (See March of Comics #31 in Promotional Comics section)

SANTA'S CANDY KITCHEN (See March of Comics #14 in Promotional Comics section)

SANTA'S CHRISTMAS BOOK (See March of Comics #123 in Promotional Comics section)

SANTA'S CHRISTMAS COMICS
Standard Comics (Best Books): Dec, 1952 (100 pgs.)

	GD 2.0	VG 4.0	FN 6.0	VF 8.0	VF/NM 9.0	NM- 9.2
nn-Supermouse, Dizzy Duck, Happy Rabbit, etc.	18	36	54	105	165	225

SANTA'S CHRISTMAS LIST (See March of Comics #255 in Promotional Comics section)

SANTA'S HELPERS (See March of Comics #64, 106, 198 in Promotional Comics section)

SANTA'S LITTLE HELPERS (See March of Comics #270 in Promotional Comics section)

SANTA'S SHOW (See March of Comics #311 in Promotional Comics section)

SANTA'S SLEIGH (See March of Comics #298 in Promotional Comics section)

SANTA'S SURPRISE (See March of Comics #13 in Promotional Comics section)

SANTA'S TINKER TOTS
Charlton Comics: 1958

	GD 2.0	VG 4.0	FN 6.0	VF 8.0	VF/NM 9.0	NM- 9.2
1-Based on "The Tinker Tots Keep Christmas"	4	8	12	22	34	45

SANTA'S TOYLAND (See March of Comics #242 in Promotional Comics section)

SANTA'S TOYS (See March of Comics #12 in Promotional Comics section)

SANTA'S VISIT (See March of Comics #283 in Promotional Comics section)

SANTA THE BARBARIAN
Maximum Press: Dec, 1996 ($2.99, one-shot)

	GD 2.0	VG 4.0	FN 6.0	VF 8.0	VF/NM 9.0	NM- 9.2
1-Fraga/Mhan-s/a						3.00

SANTIAGO (Movie)
Dell Publishing Co.: Sept, 1956 (Alan Ladd photo-c)

	GD 2.0	VG 4.0	FN 6.0	VF 8.0	VF/NM 9.0	NM- 9.2
Four Color 723-Kinstler-a	9	18	27	63	107	150

SARGE SNORKEL (Beetle Bailey)
Charlton Comics: Oct, 1973 - No. 17, Dec, 1976

	GD 2.0	VG 4.0	FN 6.0	VF 8.0	VF/NM 9.0	NM- 9.2
1	2	4	6	11	16	20
2-10	2	4	6	8	10	12
11-17	1	2	3	5	7	9

SARGE STEEL (Becomes Secret Agent #9 on; also see Judomaster)
Charlton Comics: Dec, 1964 - No. 8, Mar-Apr, 1966 (All 12¢ issues)

	GD 2.0	VG 4.0	FN 6.0	VF 8.0	VF/NM 9.0	NM- 9.2
1-Origin & 1st app.	4	8	12	24	37	50
2-5,7,8	3	6	9	16	23	30
6-2nd app. Judomaster	3	6	9	20	30	40

SATAN'S SIX
Topps Comics (Kirbyverse): Apr, 1993 - No. 4, July, 1993 ($2.95, lim. series)

	GD 2.0	VG 4.0	FN 6.0	VF 8.0	VF/NM 9.0	NM- 9.2
1-4: 1-Polybagged w/Kirbychrome trading card; Kirby/McFarlane-c plus 8 pgs. Kirby-a(p); has coupon for Kirbychrome ed. of Secret City Saga #0. 2-4-Polybagged w/3 cards. 4-Teenagents preview						3.00

NOTE: Ditko a-1. Miller a-1.

SATAN'S SIX: HELLSPAWN
Topps Comics (Kirbyverse): June, 1994 - No. 3, July, 1994 ($2.50, limited series)

	GD 2.0	VG 4.0	FN 6.0	VF 8.0	VF/NM 9.0	NM- 9.2
1-3: 1-(6/94)-Indicia incorrectly shows "Vol 1 #2". 2-(6/94)						2.50

SAURIANS: UNNATURAL SELECTION (See Sigil)
CrossGeneration Comics: Feb, 2002 - No. 2, Mar, 2002 ($2.95, limited series)

	GD 2.0	VG 4.0	FN 6.0	VF 8.0	VF/NM 9.0	NM- 9.2
1,2-Waid-s/DiVito-a						3.00

SAVAGE COMBAT TALES
Atlas/Seaboard Publ.: Feb, 1975 - No. 3, July, 1975

	GD 2.0	VG 4.0	FN 6.0	VF 8.0	VF/NM 9.0	NM- 9.2
1,3: 1-Sgt. Stryker's Death Squad begins (origin); Goodwin-s	1	2	3	5	7	9
2-Toth-a; only app. War Hawk; Goodwin-s	2	4	6	8	10	12

NOTE: Buckler c-3. McWilliams a-1-3; c-1. Sparling a-1, 3.

SAVAGE DRAGON, THE (See Megaton #3 & 4)
Image Comics (Highbrow Entertainment): July, 1992 - No. 3, Dec, 1992 ($1.95, lim. series)

	GD 2.0	VG 4.0	FN 6.0	VF 8.0	VF/NM 9.0	NM- 9.2
1-Erik Larsen-c/a/scripts & bound-in poster in all; 4 cover color variations w/4 different posters; 1st Highbrow Entertainment title						4.00
2-Intro SuperPatriot-c/story (10/92)						3.00
3-Contains coupon for Image Comics #0						3.00
3-With coupon missing						2.50
...Vs. Savage Megaton Man 1 (3/93, $1.95)-Larsen & Simpson-c/a						3.00
TPB-('93, $9.95) r/#1-3						10.00

SAVAGE DRAGON, THE
Image Comics (Highbrow Entertainment): June, 1993 - Present ($1.95/$2.50/$2.99)

	GD 2.0	VG 4.0	FN 6.0	VF 8.0	VF/NM 9.0	NM- 9.2
1-Erik Larsen-c/a/scripts						4.00
2-30: 2-(Wondercon Exclusive): 2-($2.95, 52 pgs.)-Teenage Mutant Ninja Turtles-c/story; flip book features Vanguard #0 (See Megaton for 1st app.). 3-7: Erik Larsen-c/a/scripts. 3-Mighty Man back-up story w/Austin-a(i). 4-Flip book w/Ricochet. 5-Mighty Man flip-c & back-up plus poster. 6-Jae Lee poster. 7-Vanguard poster. 8-Deadly Duo poster by Larsen. 13A (10/94)-Jim Lee-c/a; 1st app. Max Cash (Condition Red). 13B (6/95)-Larsen story. 15-Dragon poster by Larsen. 22-TMNT-c/a; Bisley pin-up. 27-"Wondercon Exclusive" new-c. 28-Maxx-c/app. 29-Wildstar-c/app. 30-Spawn app.						3.00
25 ($3.95)-variant-c exists.						4.00
31-49,51-71: 31-God vs. The Devil; alternate version exists w/o expletives (has "God Is Good" inside Image logo) 33-Birth of Dragon/Rapture's baby. 34,35-Hellboy-c/app. 51-Origin of She-Dragon. 70-Ann Stevens killed						2.50
50-($5.95, 100 pgs. Kaboom and Mighty Man app.; Matsuda back-c; pin-ups by McFarlane, Simonson, Capullo and others						6.00
72-74: 72-Begin $2.95-c						3.00
75-($5.95)						6.00
76-99,101-106,108-114,116-124,126-127,129-131: 76-New direction starts. 83,84-Madman-c/app. 84-Atomics app. 97-Dragon returns home; Mighty Man app.						3.00
100-($8.95) Larsen-s/a; inked by various incl. Sienkiewicz, Timm, Austin, Simonson, Royer; plus pin-ups by Timm, Silvestri, Miller, Cho, Art Adams, Pacheco						9.00
107-($3.95) Firebreather, Invincible, Major Damage-c/app.; flip book w/Major Damage						4.00
115-($7.95, 100 pgs.) Wraparound-c; Larsen & Englert-a						8.00
125-($4.99, 64 pgs.) new story, The Fly, & various Mr. Glum reprints						5.00
128-Wesley and the villains from Wanted app.; J.G. Jones-c						4.00
132-($6.99, 80 pgs.) new story with Larsen-a; back-up story with Fosco-a						7.00
#0-(7/06, $1.95) reprints origin story from 2005 Image Comics Hardcover						2.50
...Archives Vol. 1 (12/06, $19.99) B&W rep. 1st mini-series #1-3 & #1-21						20.00
...Archives Vol. 2 (2007, $19.99) B&W rep. #22-50; roster pages of Dragon's fellow cops						20.00
...Companion (7/02, $2.95) guide to issues #1-100, character backgrounds						
...Endgame (2/04, $15.95, TPB) r/#47-52						16.00
The Fallen (11/97, $12.95, TPB) r/#7-11, ...Possessed (9/98, $12.95, TPB) r/#12-16, ...Revenge (1998, $12.95, TPB) r/#17-21						13.00
...Gang War (4/00, $16.95, TPB) r/#22-26						17.00

Savage She-Hulk #2 © MAR

Savage Sword of Conan #92 © Conan Props.

Scarab #7 © DC

	GD 2.0	VG 4.0	FN 6.0	VF 8.0	VF/NM 9.0	NM- 9.2

.../Hellboy (10/02, $5.95) r/#34 & #35; Mignola-c ... 6.00
...Team-Ups (10/98, $19.95, TPB) r/team-ups ... 20.00
...: Terminated HC (2/03, $28.95) r/#34-40 & #1/2 ... 29.00
...: This Savage World HC (2002, $24.95) r/#76-81; intro. by Larsen ... 25.00
...: This Savage World SC (2003, $15.95) r/#76-81; intro. by Larsen ... 16.00
...: Worlds at War SC (2004, $16.95) r/#41-46; intro. by Larsen; sketch pages ... 17.00

SAVAGE DRAGON ARCHIVES (Also see Dragon Archives, The)

SAVAGE DRAGONBERT: FULL FRONTAL NERDITY
Image Comics: Oct, 2002 ($5.95, B&W, one-shot)
1-Reprints of the Savage Dragon/Dilbert spoof strips ... 6.00

SAVAGE DRAGON/DESTROYER DUCK, THE
Image Comics/ Highbrow Entertainment: Nov, 1996 ($3.95, one-shot)
1 ... 4.00

SAVAGE DRAGON: GOD WAR
Image Comics: July, 2004 - No. 4, Oct, 2005 ($2.95, limited series)
1-4-Kirkman-s/Englert-a ... 3.00

SAVAGE DRAGON/MARSHALL LAW
Image Comics: July, 1997 - No. 2, Aug, 1997 ($2.95, B&W, limited series)
1,2-Pat Mills-s, Kevin O'Neill-a ... 3.00

SAVAGE DRAGON: SEX & VIOLENCE
Image Comics: Aug, 1997 - No. 2, Sept, 1997 ($2.50, limited series)
1,2-T&M Bierbaum-s, Mays, Lupka, Adam Hughes-a ... 3.00

SAVAGE DRAGON/TEENAGE MUTANT NINJA TURTLES CROSSOVER
Mirage Studios: Sept, 1993 ($2.75, one-shot)
1-Erik Larsen-c(i) only ... 3.00

SAVAGE DRAGON: THE RED HORIZON
Image Comics/ Highbrow Entertainment: Feb, 1997 - No. 3 ($2.50, lim. series)
1-3 ... 3.00

SAVAGE FISTS OF KUNG FU
Marvel Comics: 1975 (Marvel Treasury)
1-Iron Fist, Shang Chi, Sons of Tiger; Adams, Starlin-a   3   6   9   17   25   32

SAVAGE HULK, THE (Also see Incredible Hulk)
Marvel Comics: Jan, 1996 ($6.95, one-shot)
1-Bisley-c; David, Lobdell, Wagner, Loeb, Gibbons, Messner-Loebs scripts; McKone, Kieth, Ramos & Sale-a. ... 7.00

SAVAGE RAIDS OF GERONIMO (See Geronimo #4)

SAVAGE RANGE (See Luke Short, Four Color 807)

SAVAGE RED SONJA: QUEEN OF THE FROZEN WASTES
Dynamite Entertainment: 2006 - No. 4, 2006 ($3.50, limited series)
1-4: 1-Three covers by Cho, Texeira & Homs; Cho & Murray-s/Homs-a ... 3.50

SAVAGE RETURN OF DRACULA
Marvel Comics: 1992 ($2.00, 52 pgs.)
1-r/Tomb of Dracula #1,2 by Gene Colan ... 3.00

SAVAGE SHE-HULK, THE (See The Avengers, Marvel Graphic Novel #18 & The Sensational She-Hulk)
Marvel Comics Group: Feb, 1980 - No. 25, Feb, 1982
1-Origin & 1st app. She-Hulk   2   4   6   8   10   12
2-5,25: 25-(52 pgs.) ... 6.00
6-24: 6-She-Hulk vs. Iron Man. 8-Vs. Man-Thing ... 5.00
NOTE: *Austin* a-25i; c-23-25i. *J. Buscema* a-1p; c-1, 6p. *Golden* c-8-11.

SAVAGE SWORD OF CONAN (The... #41 on; ...The Barbarian #175 on)
Marvel Comics Group: Aug, 1974 - No. 235, July, 1995 ($1.00/$1.25/$2.25, B&W magazine, mature)
1-Smith-r; J. Buscema/N. Adams/Krenkel-a; origin Blackmark by Gil Kane (part 1, ends #3); Blackmark's 1st app. in magazine form-r/from paperback) & Red Sonja (3rd app.)   9   18   27   65   113   160
2-Neal Adams-c; Chaykin/N. Adams-a   5   10   15   32   51   70
3-Severin/B. Smith-a; N. Adams-a   4   8   12   24   37   50
4-Neal Adams/Kane-a(r)   3   6   9   20   30   40
5-10: 5-Jeff Jones frontispiece (r)   3   6   9   16   23   30
11-20   2   4   6   11   16   20
21-30   2   4   6   8   13   16
31-50: 34-3 pg. preview of Conan newspaper strip. 35-Cover similar to Savage Tales #1. 45-Red Sonja returns; begin $1.25-c   2   4   6   8   11   14

51-99: 63-Toth frontispiece. 65-Kane-a w/Chaykin/Miller/Simonson/Sherman finishes. 70-Article on movie. 83-Red Sonja-r by Neal Adams from #1   1   2   3   5   7   9
100   1   3   4   6   8   10
101-176: 163-Begin $2.25-c. 169-King Kull story. 171-Soloman Kane by Williamson (i). 172-Red Sonja story ... 6.00
177-199: 179,187,192-Red Sonja app. 190-193-4 part King Kull story. 196-King Kull story ... 5.00
200-220: 200-New Buscema-a; Robert E. Howard app. with Conan in story. 202-King Kull story. 204-60th anniversary (1932-92). 211-Rafael Kayanan's 1st Conan-a. 214-Sequel to Red Nails by Howard ... 6.00
221-230   1   2   3   5   7   9
231-234   2   4   6   8   10   12
235-Last issue   2   4   6   10   14   18
Special 1(1975, B&W)-B. Smith-r/Conan #10,13   3   6   9   16   23   30
NOTE: *N. Adams* a-14p, 60, 83p(r). *Alcala* a-2, 4, 7, 12, 15-20, 23, 24, 28, 59, 67, 69, 75, 76i, 80i, 82i, 83i, 89, 180i, 184i, 187i, 189i, 216p. *Austin* a-78i. *Boris* painted c-1, 4, 5, 7, 9, 10, 12, 15. *Brunner* a-30; c-8, 30. *Buscema* a-1-5, 7, 10-12, 15-24, 26-28, 31, 32, 36-43, 45, 47-58p, 60-67p, 70, 71-74p, 76-81p, 87-96p, 98, 99-101p, 190-204p; painted c-40. *Chaykin* c-31. *Chiodo* painted c-71, 76, 79, 81, 84, 85, 178. *Conrad* c-215, 217. *Corben* a-4, 16, 29. *Finlay* a-16. *Golden* a-98, 101; c-98, 101, 105, 106, 117, 124, 150. *Kaluta* a-11, 18; c-3, 91, 93. *Gil Kane* a-2, 3, 8, 13r, 29, 47, 64, 65, 67, 85p, 86p. *Rafael Kayanan* a-211-213, 215, 217. *Krenkel* a-9, 11, 14, 16, 24. *Morrow* a-7. *Nebres* a-93i, 101i, 107, 114. *Newton* a-6. *Nino* c/a-6. *Redondo* painted c-48-50, 52, 56, 57, 85i, 90, 96i. *Marie & John Severin* a-Special 1. *Simonson* a-7, 8, 12, 15-17. *Barry Smith* a-7, 16, 24, 82r, Special 1r. *Starlin* c-26. *Toth* a-64. *Williamson* a(i)-162, 171, 186. No. 8, 10 & 16 contain a Robert E. Howard Conan adaptation.

SAVAGE TALES (...Featuring Conan #4 on)(Magazine)
Marvel Comics Group: May, 1971; No. 2, 10/73; No. 3, 2/74 - No. 12, Summer, 1975 (B&W)
1-Origin/1st app. The Man-Thing by Morrow; Conan the Barbarian by Barry Smith (1st Conan x-over outside his own title); Femizons by Romita-r/in #3; Ka-Zar story by Buscema   16   32   48   118   209   300
2-B. Smith, Brunner, Morrow, Williamson-a; Wrightson King Kull reprint/ Creatures on the Loose #10   6   12   18   37   59   80
3-B. Smith, Brunner, Steranko, Williamson-a   4   8   12   28   44   60
4,5-N. Adams-c; last Conan (Smith-r/#4) plus Kane/N. Adams-a. 5-Brak the Barbarian begins, ends #8   4   8   12   24   37   50
6-Ka-Zar begins; Williamson-r; N. Adams-c   3   6   9   17   25   32
7-N. Adams-i   2   4   6   13   18   22
8,9,11: 8-Shanna, the She-Devil app. thru #10; Williamson-r   2   4   6   11   16   20
10-Neal Adams-a(i), Williamson-r   2   4   6   13   18   22
...Featuring Ka-Zar Annual 1 (Summer, '75, B&W)(#12 on inside)-Ka-Zar origin by Gil Kane; B. Smith-r/Astonishing Tales   3   6   9   15   21   26
NOTE: *Boris* c-7, 10. *Buscema* a-5r, 6p, 8p; c-2. *Colan* a-1p. *Fabian* c-8. *Golden* a-1, 4; c-1. *Heath* a-10p, 11p. *Kaluta* c-9. *Maneely* r-2, 4(The Crusader in both). *Morrow* a-1, 2, Annual 1. *Reese* a-2. *Severin* a-1-7. *Starlin* a-5. Robert E. Howard adaptations-1-4.

SAVAGE TALES
Marvel Comics Group: Nov, 1985 - No. 8, Dec, 1986 ($1.50, B&W, magazine, mature)
1-1st app. The Nam; Golden, Morrow-a ... 5.00
2-8: 2,7-Morrow-a. 4-2nd Nam story; Golden-a ... 3.00

SAVAGE TALES
Dynamite Entertainment: 2007 - Present ($4.99)
1-3: 1-Anthology; Red Sonja app.; three covers ... 5.00

SAVANT GARDE (Also see WildC.A.T.S...)
Image Comics/WildStorm Productions: Mar, 1997 - No. 7, Sept, 1997 ($2.50)
1-7 ... 2.50

SAVED BY THE BELL (TV)
Harvey Comics: Mar, 1992 - No. 5, May, 1993 ($1.25, limited series)
1-5, Holiday Special 1 (9/92), Special 1 (9/92, $1.50)-photo-c; Summer Break 1 (10/92) ... 2.50

SAW: REBIRTH (Based on 2004 movie Saw)
IDW Publ.: Oct, 2005 ($3.99, one-shot)
1-Guedes-a ... 4.00

SCALPED
DC Comics (Vertigo): Mar, 2007 - Present ($2.99, limited series)
1-9-Aaron-s/Guera-a/Jock-c ... 3.00
...: Indian Country TPB (2007, $9.99) r/#1-5; intro. by Brian K. Vaughan ... 10.00

SCAMP (Walt Disney)(See Walt Disney's Comics & Stories #204)
Dell Publ.: No. 703, 5/56 - No. 1204, 8-10/61; 11/67 - No. 45, 1/79
Four Color 703(#1)   8   16   24   58   97   135
Four Color 777,806('57),833   6   12   18   43   69   95
5(3-5/58)-10(6-8/59)   5   10   15   35   55   75
11-16(12-2/60-61), Four Color 1204(1961)   4   8   12   28   44   60
1(12/67-Gold Key)-Reprints begin   4   8   12   26   41   55

Scary Godmother #2
© Jill Thompson

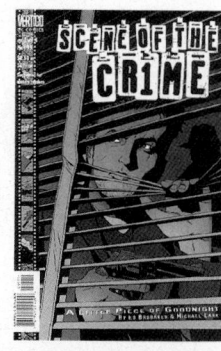

Scene of the Crime #1
© Brubaker & Lark

Science Comics #5 © FOX

	GD 2.0	VG 4.0	FN 6.0	VF 8.0	VF/NM 9.0	NM- 9.2
2(3/69)-10	2	4	6	13	18	22
11-20	2	4	6	8	11	14
21-45	1	2	3	4	5	7

NOTE: New stories-#20(in part), 22-25, 27, 29-31, 34, 36-40, 42-45. New covers-#11, 12, 14, 15, 17-25, 27, 29-31, 34, 36-38.

SCARAB
DC Comics (Vertigo): Nov, 1993 - No. 8, June, 1994 ($1.95, limited series)

1-8-Glenn Fabry painted-c: 1-Silver ink-c. 2-Phantom Stranger app.						2.50

SCARECROW OF ROMNEY MARSH, THE (See W. Disney Showcase #53)
Gold Key: April, 1964 - No. 3, Oct, 1965 (Disney TV Show)

10112-404 (#1)	4	8	12	28	44	60
2,3	3	6	9	20	30	40

SCARECROW (VILLAINS) (See Batman)
DC Comics: Feb, 1998 ($1.95, one-shot)

1-Fegredo-a/Milligan-s/Pearson-c						2.50

SCARE TACTICS
DC Comics: Dec, 1996 - No. 12, Mar, 1998 ($2.25)

1-12: 1-1st app.						2.50

SCAR FACE (See The Crusaders)

SCARFACE: SCARRED FOR LIFE (Based on the 1983 movie)
IDW Publishing: Dec, 2006 - No. 5, Apr, 2007 ($3.99, limited series)

1-5-Tony Montana survives his shooting; Layman-s/Crosland-a						4.00

SCARLET O'NEIL (See Harvey Comics Hits #59 & Invisible...)

SCARLET CRUSH
Awesome Entertainment: Jan, 1998 - No. 2, Feb, 1998 ($2.50)

1-Five covers by Liefeld, Stinsman(wraparound), Churchill, Skroce, and Sprouse; Stinsman-s/a(p)						2.50
1-American Entertainment Ed.; Stinsman-c						5.00
2-Three covers by Stinsman, McGuinness & Peterson						2.50

SCARLET SPIDER
Marvel Comics: Nov, 1995 - No. 2, Jan, 1996 ($1.95, limited series)

1,2: Replaces Spider-Man						2.50

SCARLET SPIDER UNLIMITED
Marvel Comics: Nov, 1995 ($3.95, one-shot)

1-Replaces Spider-Man						4.00

SCARLET WITCH (See Avengers #16, Vision &... & X-Men #4)
Marvel Comics: Jan, 1994 - No. 4, Apr, 1994 ($1.75, limited series)

1-4						2.50

SCARY GODMOTHER (Hardcover story books)
Sirius: 1997 - Present ($19.95, HC with dust jackets, one-shots)

Volume 1 (9/97) Jill Thompson-s/a; first app. of Scary Godmother						20.00
Vol. 2 - The Revenge of Jimmy (9/98, $19.95)						20.00
Vol. 3 - The Mystery Date (10/99, $19.95)						20.00
Vol. 4 - The Boo Flu (9/02, $19.95)						20.00

SCARY GODMOTHER
Sirius: 2001 - No. 6, 2002 ($2.95, B&W, limited series)

1-6-Jill Thompson-s/a						3.00
...: Activity Book (12/00, $2.95, B&W) Jill Thompson-s/a						3.00
...: Bloody Valentine Special (2/98, $3.95, B&W) Jill Thompson-s/a; pin-ups by Ross, Mignola, Russell						4.00
...: Ghoul's Out For Summer (2002,$14.95, B&W) r/#1-6						15.00
...: Holiday Spooktakular (11/98, $2.95, B&W) Jill Thompson-s/a; pin-ups by Brereton, LaBan, Dorkin, Fingerman						3.00

SCARY GODMOTHER: WILD ABOUT HARRY
Sirius: 2000 - No. 3 ($2.95, B&W, limited series)

1-3-Jill Thompson-s/a						3.00
TPB (2001, $9.95) r/series						10.00

SCARY TALES
Charlton Comics: 8/75 - #9, 1/77; #10, 9/77 - #20, 6/79; #21, 8/80 - #46, 10/84

1-Origin/1st app. Countess Von Bludd, not in #2	3	6	9	16	23	30
2,4,6,9,10: 4-Sutton-a. 9-Sutton-c/a	2	4	6	8	10	12
3-Sutton painted-c; Ditko-a	2	4	6	9	13	16
5,11-Ditko-a/c-a	2	4	6	10	14	18
7,8-Ditko-a	2	4	6	8	11	14
12,15,16,19,21,39-Ditko-a	2	4	6	8	10	12

	GD 2.0	VG 4.0	FN 6.0	VF 8.0	VF/NM 9.0	NM- 9.2
13,17,20	1	2	3	5	7	9
14,18,30,32-Ditko-c/a	2	4	6	9	12	15
22-29,33-37,39,40: 37,38,40-New-a. 39-Reprints	1	2	3	5	6	8
31,38: 31-Newton-c/a. 38-Mr. Jigsaw app.	1	2	3	5	6	8
41-45-New-a. 41-Ditko-a(3). 42-45-(Low print)	1	2	3	5	7	9
46-Reprints (Low print)	2	4	6	8	11	14
1(Modern Comics reprint, 1977)						4.00

NOTE: Adkins a-31l; c-31l. Ditko a-3, 5, 7, 8(2), 11, 12, 14-16r, 18(3)r, 19r, 21r, 30r, 32, 39r, 41(3); c-5, 11, 14, 18, 30, 32. Newton a-31p; c-31p. Powell a-18r. Staton a-1(2 pgs.), 4, 20r; c-1, 20. Sutton a-9; c-4, 9.

SCATTERBRAIN
Dark Horse Comics: Jun, 1998 - No. 4, Sept, 1998 ($2.95, limited series)

1-4-Humor anthology by Aragonés, Dorkin, Stevens and others						3.00

SCAVENGERS
Quality Comics: Feb, 1988 - No. 14, 1989 ($1.25/$1.50)

1-14: 9-13-Guice-c						2.50

SCAVENGERS
Triumphant Comics: 1993(nd, July) - No. 11, May, 1994 ($2.50, serially numbered)

1-9,0,10,11: 5,6-Triumphant Unleashed x-over. 9-(3/94). 0-Retail edition (3/94, $2.50, 36 pgs.). 0-Giveaway edition (3/94, 20 pgs.). 0-Coupon redemption edition. 10-(4/94)						2.50

SCENE OF THE CRIME (Also see Vertigo: Winter's Edge #2)
DC Comics (Vertigo): May, 1999 - No. 4, Aug, 1999 ($2.50, limited series)

1-4-Brubaker-s/Lark-a						2.50
...: A Little Piece of Goodnight TPB ('00, $12.95) r/#1-4; Winter's Edge #2						13.00

SCHOOL DAY ROMANCES (...of Teen-Agers #4; Popular Teen-Agers #5 on)
Star Publications: Nov-Dec, 1949 - No. 4, May-June, 1950 (Teenage)

1-Toni Gayle (later Toni Gay), Ginger Snapp, Midge Martin & Eve Adams begin	28	56	84	162	256	350
2,3: 3-Jane Powell photo on-c & true life story	20	40	60	117	184	250
4-Ronald Reagan photo on-c; L.B. Cole-c	31	62	93	178	282	385

NOTE: All have L. B. Cole covers.

SCHWINN BICYCLE BOOK (...Bike Thrills, 1959)
Schwinn Bicycle Co.: 1949; 1952; 1959 (10¢)

1949	6	12	18	28	34	40
1952-Believe It or Not facts; comic format; 36 pgs.	5	10	14	20	24	28
1959	3	6	8	11	13	15

SCIENCE COMICS (1st Series)
Fox Features Syndicate: Feb, 1940 - No. 8, Sept, 1940

1-Origin Dynamo (1st app., called Electro in #1), The Eagle (1st app.), & Navy Jones; Marga, The Panther Woman (1st app.), Cosmic Carson & Perisphere Payne, Dr. Doom begin; bondage/hypo-c; Electro-c	423	846	1269	2855	5028	7200
2-Classic Lou Fine Dynamo-c	228	456	684	1425	2363	3300
3-Classic Lou Fine Dynamo-c	186	372	558	1163	1932	2700
4-Kirby-a; Cosmic Carson-c by Joe Simon	166	332	498	1038	1719	2400
5-8: 5,8-Eagle-c. 6,7-Dynamo-c	100	200	300	625	1038	1450

NOTE: Cosmic Carson by Tuska-#1-3; by Kirby-#4. Lou Fine c-1-3 only.

SCIENCE COMICS (2nd Series)
Humor Publications (Ace Magazines?): Jan, 1946 - No. 5, 1946

1-Palais-c in #1-3; A-Bomb-c	19	38	57	109	172	235
2	11	22	33	62	86	110
3-Feldstein-a (6 pgs.)	15	30	45	88	137	185
4,5: 4-Palais-c	9	18	27	50	65	80

SCIENCE COMICS
Ziff-Davis Publ. Co.: May, 1947 (8 pgs. in color)

nn-Could be ordered by mail for 10¢; like the nn Amazing Adventures (1950) & Boy Cowboy (1950); used to test the market	40	80	120	235	368	500

SCIENCE COMICS (True Science Illustrated)
Export Publication Ent., Toronto, Canada: Mar, 1951 (Distr. in U.S. by Kable News Co.)

1-Science Adventure stories plus some true science features; man on moon story	12	24	36	67	94	120

SCIENCE FICTION SPACE ADVENTURES (See Space Adventures)

SCION (Also see CrossGen Chronicles)
CrossGeneration Comics: July, 2000 - No. 43, Apr, 2004 ($2.95)

1-43: 1-Marz-s/Cheung-a						3.00
...: Conflict of Conscience Vol. 1 TPB (5/01, $19.95) r/#1-7; Adam Hughes-c						20.00
...: Blood For Blood Vol. 2 TPB (2002, $19.95) r/#8-14 & CrossGen Chronicles #2						20.00
...: Divided Loyalties Vol. 3 TPB (2002, $15.95) r/#15-21						16.00
...: Sanctuary Vol. 4 TPB (2003, $15.95) r/#22-27						16.00

Scooby Doo #113 © H-B

Scoop Comics #3 © CHES

Scorpion King #1 © Universal Studios

	GD 2.0	VG 4.0	FN 6.0	VF 8.0	VF/NM 9.0	NM- 9.2

Vol. 5: The Far Kingdom (2003, $15.95) r/#28-33 ... 16.00
Vol. 6: The Royal Wedding (2004, $15.95) r/#34-39 ... 16.00
Traveler Vol. 1-3 ($9.95) Digest-sized reprints of TPBs ... 10.00

SCI-SPY
DC Comics (Vertigo): Apr, 2002 - No. 6, Sept, 2002 ($2.50, limited series)
1-6-Moench-s/Gulacy-c/a ... 2.50

SCI-TECH
DC Comics (WildStorm): Sept, 1999 - No. 4, Dec, 1999 ($2.50, limited series)
1-4-Benes-a/Choi & Peterson-s ... 2.50

SCOOBY DOO (TV)(...Where are you? #1-16,26; ...Mystery Comics #17-25, 27 on)
(See March Of Comics #356, 368, 382, 391 in the Promotional Comics section)
Gold Key: Mar, 1970 - No. 30, Feb, 1975 (Hanna-Barbera)

	GD	VG	FN	VF	VF/NM	NM-
1	12	24	36	87	156	225
2-5	7	14	21	49	80	110
6-10	6	12	18	41	66	90
11-20: 11-Tufts-a	5	10	15	32	51	70
21-30	4	8	12	24	37	50

SCOOBY DOO (TV)
Charlton Comics: Apr, 1975 - No. 11, Dec, 1976 (Hanna-Barbera)

	GD	VG	FN	VF	VF/NM	NM-
1	6	12	18	37	59	80
2-5	4	8	12	23	36	48
6-11	3	6	9	19	29	38
nn-(1976, digest, 68 pgs., B&W)	4	8	12	22	34	45

SCOOBY-DOO (TV)(Newsstand sales only) (See Dynamutt & Laff-A-Lympics)
Marvel Comics Group: Oct, 1977 - No. 9, Feb, 1979 (Hanna-Barbera)

	GD	VG	FN	VF	VF/NM	NM-
1,6,9: 1-Dyno-Mutt begins	3	6	9	17	25	32
1-(35¢-c variant, limited distribution)(10/77)	7	14	21	45	73	100
2-5	3	6	9	14	19	24

SCOOBY-DOO (TV)
Harvey Comics: Sept, 1992 - No. 3, May, 1993 ($1.25)

	GD	VG	FN	VF	VF/NM	NM-
V2#1,2						6.00
Big Book 1,2 (11/92, 4/93, $1.95, 52 pgs.)	1	2	3	4	5	7
Giant Size 1,2 (10/92, 3/93, $2.25, 68 pgs.)	1	2	3	4	5	7

SCOOBY DOO (TV)
Archie Comics: Oct, 1995 -No. 21, June, 1997 ($1.50)
1 ... 6.00
2-21: 12-Cover by Scooby Doo creative designer Iwao Takamoto ... 4.00

SCOOBY DOO (TV)
DC Comics: Aug, 1997 - Present ($1.75/$1.95/$1.99/$2.25)
1 ... 6.00
2-10: 5-Begin-$1.95-c ... 4.00
11-45: 14-Begin $1.99-c ... 2.50
46-89,91-123: 63-Begin $2.25-c. 75-With 2 Garbage Pail Kids stickers. 100-Wray-c ... 2.50
90-($2.95) Bonus stories ... 3.00
...Spooky Spectacular 1 (10/99, $3.95) Comic Convention story ... 4.00
...Spooky Spectacular 2000 (10/00, $3.95) ... 4.00
...Spooky Summer Special 2001 (8/01, $3.95) Staton-a ... 4.00
...Super Scarefest (8/02, $3.95) r/#20,25,30-32 ... 4.00
Vol. 1: You Meddling Kids (2003, $6.95, digest-size) r/#1-5 ... 7.00
Vol. 2: Ruh-Roh! (2003, $6.95, digest-size) r/#6-10 ... 7.00
Vol. 3: All Wrapped Up! (2005, $6.95, digest-size) r/#11-15 ... 7.00
Vol. 4: The Big Squeeze! (2005, $6.95, digest-size) r/#16-20 ... 7.00
Vol. 5: Surf's Up! (2006, $6.99, digest-size) r/#21-25 ... 7.00
Vol. 5: Space Fright! (2006, $6.99, digest-size) r/#26-30 ... 7.00

SCOOP COMICS (Becomes Yankee Comics #4-7, a digest sized cartoon book; then after #8
it becomes Snap #9)
Harry 'A' Chesler (Holyoke): November, 1941 - No. 3, Mar, 1943; No. 8, 1944

	GD	VG	FN	VF	VF/NM	NM-
1-Intro. Rocketman & Rocketgirl & begins; origin The Master Key & begins; Dan Hastings begins; Charles Sultan-c/a	152	304	456	950	1575	2200
2-Rocket Boy begins; injury to eye story (reprinted in Spotlight #3); classic-c	166	332	498	1038	1719	2400
3-Injury to eye story-r from #2; Rocket Boy	72	114	216	450	750	1050
8-Formerly Yankee Comics; becomes Snap	45	90	135	275	450	625

SCOOTER (See Swing With...)

SCOOTER COMICS
Rucker Publ. Ltd. (Canadian): Apr, 1946

	GD	VG	FN	VF	VF/NM	NM-
1-Teen-age/funny animal	11	22	33	60	83	105

SCOOTER GIRL
Oni Press: May, 2003 - No. 6, Feb, 2004 ($2.99, B&W, limited series)
1-6-Chynna Clugston-Major-s/a ... 3.00
TPB (5/04, $14.95, digest size) r/series; sketch pages ... 15.00

SCORPION
Atlas/Seaboard Publ.: Feb, 1975 - No. 3, July, 1975

	GD	VG	FN	VF	VF/NM	NM-
1-Intro.; bondage-c by Chaykin	2	4	6	8	10	12
2-Chaykin-a w/Wrightson, Kaluta, Simonson assists(p)	2	4	6	8	10	12
3-Jim Craig-c/a	1	2	3	5	7	9

NOTE: *Chaykin a-1, 2; c-1. Colon c-2. Craig c/a-3.*

SCORPION KING, THE (Movie)
Dark Horse Comics: March, 2002 - No. 2, Apr, 2002 ($2.99, limited series)
1,2-Photo-c of the Rock; Richards-a ... 3.00

SCORPIO ROSE
Eclipse Comics: Jan, 1983 - No. 2, Oct, 1983 ($1.25, Baxter paper)
1,2: Dr. Orient back-up story begins. 2-origin. ... 4.00

SCOTLAND YARD (Inspector Farnsworth of)(Texas Rangers in Action #5 on?)
Charlton Comics Group: June, 1955 - No. 4, Mar, 1956

	GD	VG	FN	VF	VF/NM	NM-
1-Tothish-a	14	28	42	80	115	150
2-4: 2-Tothish-a	10	20	30	54	72	90

SCOUT (See Eclipse Graphic Album #16, New America & Swords of Texas)
(Becomes Scout: War Shaman)
Eclipse Comics: Dec, 1985 - No. 24, Oct, 1987($1.75/$1.25, Baxter paper)
1-15,17,18,20-24: 19-Airboy preview. 10-Bissette-a. 11-Monday, the Eliminator begins. 15-Swords of Texas ... 2.50
16,19: 16-Scout 3-D Special ($2.50), 16-Scout 2-D Limited Edition, 19-contains flexidisk ($2.50) ... 3.00
...Handbook 1 (8/87, $1.75, B&W) ... 2.50
Mount Fire (1989, $14.95, TPB) r/#8-14 ... 15.00

SCOUT: WAR SHAMAN (Formerly Scout)
Eclipse Comics: Mar, 1988 - No. 16, Dec, 1989 ($1.95)
1-16 ... 2.50

SCRATCH
DC Comics: Aug, 2004 - No. 5, Dec, 2004 ($2.50, limited series)
1-5-Sam Kieth-s/a/c; Batman app. ... 2.50

SCREAM (...Comics) (Andy Comics #20 on)
Humor Publications/Current Books(Ace Magazines): Autumn, 1944 - No. 19, Apr, 1948

	GD	VG	FN	VF	VF/NM	NM-
1-Teenage humor	16	32	48	92	144	195
2	10	20	30	56	76	95
3-16: 11-Racist humor (Indians). 16-Intro. Lily-Belle	9	18	27	47	61	75
17,19	8	16	24	42	54	65
18-Hypo needle story	9	18	27	47	61	75

SCREAM (Magazine)
Skywald Publ. Corp.: Aug, 1973 - No. 11, Feb, 1975 (68 pgs., B&W) (Painted-c on all)

	GD	VG	FN	VF	VF/NM	NM-
1-Nosferatu-c/1st app. (series thru #11); Morrow-a. Cthulhu/Necronomicon-s	6	12	18	41	66	90
2,3: 2-(10/73) Lady Satan 1st app. & series begins; Edgar Allan Poe adaptations begin (thru #11); Phantom of the Opera-s. 3-(12/73) Origin Lady Satan	4	8	12	28	44	60
4-1st Cannibal Werewolf and 1st Lunatic Mummy	4	8	12	24	37	50
5,7,8: 5,7-Frankenstein app. 8-Buckler-a; Werewolf-s; Slither-Slime Man-s	4	8	12	24	37	50
6, 9,10: 6-(6/74) Saga of The Victims/ I Am Horror, classic GGA Hewetson series begins (thru #11); Frankenstein 2073-s. 9-Severed head-c; Marcos-a. 9,10-Werewolf-s.	4	8	12	26	41	55
10-Dracula-c/s						
11- (1975 Winter Special) "Mr. Poe and the Raven" story	4	8	12	28	44	60

NOTE: *Buckler a-8. Hewetson s-1-11. Marcos a-9. Miralles c-2. Morrow a-1. Poe s-2-11. Segrelles a-7; c-1.*

SCREEN CARTOONS
DC Comics: Dec, 1944 (cover only ashcan)
nn-Ashcan comic, not distributed to newsstands, only for in house use. Covers were produced, but not the rest of the book. A copy sold in 2006 for $400.

SCREEN COMICS
DC Comics: Dec, 1944 (cover only ashcan)
nn-Ashcan comic, not distributed to newsstands, only for in house use. Covers were produced, but not the rest of the book. A copy sold in 2006 for $400.

SCREEN FABLES

Scribbly #15 © DC

Sea Devils #28 © DC

Second Life of Doctor Mirage #4 © VAL

	GD 2.0	VG 4.0	FN 6.0	VF 8.0	VF/NM 9.0	NM- 9.2

DC Comics: Dec, 1944 (cover only ashcan)

nn-Ashcan comic, not distributed to newsstands, only for in house use. Covers were produced, but not the rest of the book. A copy sold in 2006 for $400.

SCREEN FUNNIES
DC Comics: Dec, 1944 (cover only ashcan)

nn-Ashcan comic, not distributed to newsstands, only for in house use. Covers were produced, but not the rest of the book. A copy sold in 2006 for $400.

SCREEN GEMS
DC Comics: Dec, 1944 (cover only ashcan)

nn-Ashcan comic, not distributed to newsstands, only for in house use. Covers were produced, but not the rest of the book. A copy sold in 2006 for $400.

SCREWBALL SQUIRREL
Dark Horse Comics: July, 1995 - No. 3, Sept, 1995 ($2.50, limited series)

1-3: Characters created by Tex Avery						2.50

SCRIBBLY (See All-American Comics, Buzzy, The Funnies, Leave It To Binky & Popular Comics)
National Periodical Publ.: 8-9/48 - No. 13, 8-9/50; No. 14, 10-11/51 - No. 15, 12-1/51-52

	GD	VG	FN	VF	VF/NM	NM-
1-Sheldon Mayer-c/a in all; 52 pgs. begin	93	186	279	581	966	1350
2	59	118	177	369	610	850
3-5	48	96	144	293	484	675
6-10	39	78	117	225	355	485
11-15: 13-Last 52 pgs.	33	66	99	192	304	415

SCUD: TALES FROM THE VENDING MACHINE
Fireman Press: 1998 - No. 5 ($2.50, B&W)

1-5: 1-Kaniuga-a. 2-Ruben Martinez-a						2.50

SCUD: THE DISPOSABLE ASSASSIN
Fireman Press: Feb, 1994 - No. 19, 1997 ($2.95, B&W)

1		6.00
1-2nd printing in color		2.50
2,3		4.00
4-9		3.00
10-19		2.50
Heavy 3PO ($12.95, TPB) r/#1-4		13.00
Programmed For Damage ($14.95, TPB) r/#5-9		15.00
Solid Gold Bomb ($17.95, TPB) r/#10-15		18.00

SEA DEVILS (See Limited Collectors' Edition #39,45, & Showcase #27-29)
National Periodical Publications: Sept-Oct, 1961 - No. 35, May-June, 1967

	GD	VG	FN	VF	VF/NM	NM-
1-(9-10/61)	50	100	150	425	788	1150
2-Last 10¢ issue	29	58	87	212	381	550
3-Begin 12¢ issues thru #35	19	38	57	138	244	350
4,5	16	32	48	118	209	300
6-10	11	22	33	77	136	195
11,12,14-20	8	16	24	56	93	130
13-Kubert, Colan-a; Joe Kubert app. in story	8	16	24	58	97	135
21-35: 22-Intro. International Sea Devils; origin & 1st app. Capt. X & Man Fish	6	12	18	41	66	90

NOTE: Heath a-Showcase 27-29, 1-10; c-Showcase 27-29, 1-10, 14-16. Moldoff a-16.

SEA DEVILS (See Tangent Comics/ Sea Devils)

SEADRAGON (Also see the Epsilon Wave)
Elite Comics: May, 1986 - No. 8, 1987 ($1.75)

1-8: 1-1st & 2nd printings exist		2.50

SEAGUY
DC Comics (Vertigo): July, 2004 - No. 3, Sept, 2004 ($2.95, limited series)

1-3-Grant Morrison-s/Cameron Stewart-a/c		3.00
TPB (2005, $9.95) r/#1-3		10.00

SEA HOUND, THE (Captain Silver's Log Of The...)
Avon Periodicals: 1945 (no month) - No. 2, Sept-Oct, 1945

	GD	VG	FN	VF	VF/NM	NM-
nn (#1)-29 pg. novel length sty-"The Esmeralda's Treasure"	18	36	54	105	165	225
2	13	26	39	74	105	135

SEA HOUND, THE (Radio)
Capt. Silver Syndicate: No. 3, July, 1949 - No. 4, Sept, 1949

	GD	VG	FN	VF	VF/NM	NM-
3,4	10	20	30	54	72	90

SEA HUNT (TV)
Dell Publishing Co.: No. 928, 8/58 - No. 1041, 10-12/59; No. 4, 1-3/60 - No. 13, 4-6/62 (All have Lloyd Bridges photo-c)

	GD	VG	FN	VF	VF/NM	NM-
Four Color 928(#1)	11	22	33	79	140	200

	GD	VG	FN	VF	VF/NM	NM-
Four Color 994(#2), 4-13: Manning-a #4-6,8-11,13	8	16	24	54	90	125
Four Color 1041(#3)-Toth-a	8	16	24	54	90	125

SEA OF RED
Image Comics: Mar, 2005 - No. 13, Nov, 2006 ($2.95/$2.99/$3.50)

1-12-Vampirates at sea; Remender & Dwyer-s/Dwyer & Sam-a		3.00
13-($3.50)		3.50
Vol. 1: No Grave But The Sea (9/05, $8.95) r/#1-4		9.00
Vol. 2: No Quarter (2006, $11.99) r/#5-8		12.00
Vol. 3: The Deadlights (2006, $14.99) r/#9-13		15.00

SEAQUEST (TV)
Nemesis Comics: Mar, 1994 ($2.25)

1-Has 2 diff-c stocks (slick & cardboard); Alcala-i		2.50

SEARCH FOR LOVE
American Comics Group: Feb-Mar, 1950 - No. 2, Apr-May, 1950 (52 pgs.)

	GD	VG	FN	VF	VF/NM	NM-
1	12	24	36	69	97	125
2	9	18	27	47	61	75

SEARCHERS, THE (Movie)
Dell Publishing Co.: No. 709, 1956

	GD	VG	FN	VF	VF/NM	NM-
Four Color 709-John Wayne photo-c	23	46	69	171	306	440

SEARCHERS, THE
Caliber Comics: 1996 - No. 4, 1996 ($2.95, B&W)

1-4		3.00

SEARCHERS, THE : APOSTLE OF MERCY
Caliber Comics: 1997 - No. 2, 1997 ($2.95/$3.95, B&W)

1-($2.95)		3.00
2-($3.95)		4.00

SEARS (See Merry Christmas From...)

SEASON'S GREETINGS
Hallmark (King Features): 1935 (6-1/4x5-1/4", 32 pgs. in color)

nn-Cover features Mickey Mouse, Popeye, Jiggs & Skippy. "The Night Before Christmas" told one panel per page, each panel by a famous artist featuring their character. Art by Alex Raymond, Gottfredson, Swinnerton, Segar, Chic Young, Milt Gross, Sullivan (Messmer), Herriman, McManus, Percy Crosby & others (22 artists in all)

Estimated value...		950.00

SEBASTIAN O
DC Comics (Vertigo): May, 1993 - No. 3, July, 1993 ($1.95, limited series)

1-3-Grant Morrison scripts; Steve Yeowell-a		2.50
TPB (2004, $9.95) r/#1-3; intro. chronology by Morrison		10.00

SECOND LIFE OF DOCTOR MIRAGE, THE (See Shadowman #16)
Valiant: Nov, 1993 - No. 18, May, 1995 ($2.50)

1-18: 1-With bound-in poster. 5-Shadowman x-over. 7-Bound-in trading card		2.50
1-Gold ink logo edition; no price on-c		3.00

SECRET AGENT (Formerly Sarge Steel)
Charlton Comics: V2#9, Oct, 1966; V2#10, Oct, 1967

	GD	VG	FN	VF	VF/NM	NM-
V2#9-Sarge Steel part-r begins	3	6	9	17	25	32
10-Tiffany Sinn, CIA app. (from Career Girl Romances #39); Aparo-a	3	6	9	14	19	24

SECRET AGENT (TV) (See Four Color #1231)
Gold Key: Nov, 1966; No. 2, Jan, 1968

	GD	VG	FN	VF	VF/NM	NM-
1-Photo-c	8	16	24	58	97	135
2-Photo-c	6	12	18	41	66	90

SECRET AGENT X-9 (See Flash Gordon #4 by King)
David McKay Publ.: 1934 (Book 1: 84 pgs.; Book 2: 124 pgs.) (8x7-1/2")

Book 1-Contains reprints of the first 13 weeks of the strip by Alex Raymond; complete except for 2 dailies

Book 2-Contains reprints immediately following contents of Book 1, for 20 weeks by Alex Raymond; complete except for two dailies. Note: Raymond mis-dated the last five strips from 6/34, and while the dating sequence is confusing, the continuity is correct

	GD	VG	FN	VF	VF/NM	NM-
	43	86	129	262	431	600
	39	78	117	225	355	485

SECRET AGENT X-9 (See Magic Comics)
Dell Publishing Co.: Dec, 1937 (Not by Raymond)

	GD	VG	FN	VF	VF/NM	NM-
Feature Books 8	46	92	138	281	466	650

SECRET AGENT Z-2 (See Holyoke One-Shot No. 7)

SECRET CITY SAGA (See Jack Kirby's Secret City Saga)

Secret Defenders #19 © MAR

Secret Mysteries #16 © Ribage

Secret Origins (3rd series) #28 © DC

	GD 2.0	VG 4.0	FN 6.0	VF 8.0	VF/NM 9.0	NM- 9.2

SECRET DEFENDERS (Also see The Defenders & Fantastic Four #374)
Marvel Comics: Mar, 1993 - No. 25, Mar, 1995 ($1.75/$1.95)

1-($2.50)-Red foil stamped-c; Dr. Strange, Nomad, Wolverine, Spider Woman & Darkhawk begin   3.00
2-11,13-24: 9-New team w/Silver Surfer, Thunderstrike, Dr. Strange & War Machine. 13-Thanos replaces Dr. Strange as leader; leads into Cosmic Powers limited series; 14-Dr. Druid. 15-Bound in card sheet. 18-Giant Man & Iron Fist app.   2.50
12,25: 12-($2.50)-Prismatic foil-c. 25 ($2.50, 52 pgs.)   2.75

SECRET DIARY OF EERIE ADVENTURES
Avon Periodicals: 1953 (25¢ giant, 100 pgs., one-shot)

nn-(Rare)-Kubert-a; Hollingsworth-c; Sid Check back-c   200 400 600 1250 2075 2900

SECRET FILES & ORIGINS GUIDE TO THE DC UNIVERSE
DC Comics: Mar, 2000; Feb, 2002 ($6.95/$4.95)

2000 (3/00, $6.95)-Overview of DC characters; profile pages by various   7.00
2001-2002 (2/02, $4.95) Olivetti-c   5.00

SECRET FILES PRESIDENT LUTHOR
DC Comics: Mar, 2001 ($4.95, one-shot)

1-Short stories & profile pages by various; Harris-c   5.00

SECRET HEARTS
National Periodical Publications (Beverly)(Arleigh No. 50-113):
9-10/49 - No. 6, 7/8-50; No. 7, 12-1/51-52 - No. 153, 7/71

1-Kinstler-a; photo-c begin, end #6	55	110	165	344	572	800
2-Toth-a (1 pg.); Kinstler-a	30	60	90	174	275	375
3,6 (1950)	26	52	78	150	235	320
4,5-Toth-a	26	52	78	154	242	330
7(12-1/51-52) (Rare)	40	80	120	240	383	525
8-10 (1952)	19	38	57	109	172	235
11-20	15	30	45	85	130	175
21-26: 26-Last precode (2-3/55)	14	28	42	80	115	150
27-40	7	14	21	47	76	105
41-50	5	10	15	35	55	75
51-60	5	10	15	30	48	65
61-75,100: 75-Last 10¢ issue	4	8	12	28	44	60
76-99,101-109	4	8	12	22	34	45
110-"Reach for Happiness" serial begins, ends #138	4	8	12	24	37	50
111-119,121-126	3	6	9	17	25	32
120,134-Neal Adams-c	4	8	12	24	37	50
127 (4/68)-Beatles cameo	4	8	12	24	37	50
128-133,135-142: 141,142- "20 Miles to Heartbreak", Chapter 2 & 3 (see Young Love for Chapters 1 & 4); Toth, Colletta-a	3	6	9	16	23	30
143-148,150-152: 144-Morrow-a	3	6	9	14	19	24
149,153: 149-Toth-a. 153-Kirby-i	3	6	9	15	21	26

SECRET ISLAND OF OZ, THE (See First Comics Graphic Novel)

SECRET LOVE (See Fox Giants & Sinister House of...)

SECRET LOVE
Ajax-Farrell/Four Star Comic Corp. No. 2 on: 12/55 - No. 3, 8/56; 4/57 - No. 5, 2/58; No. 6, 6/58

1(12/55-Ajax, 1st series)	10	20	30	54	72	90
2,3	7	14	21	35	43	50
1(4/57-Ajax, 2nd series)	8	16	24	44	57	70
2-6: 6-Bakerish-a	6	12	18	31	38	45

SECRET LOVE STORIES (See Fox Giants)

SECRET LOVES
Comic Magazines/Quality Comics Group: Nov, 1949 - No. 6, Sept, 1950

1-Ward-c	25	50	75	148	232	315
2-Ward-c	21	42	63	122	191	260
3-Crandall-a	14	28	42	81	118	155
4,6	11	22	33	64	90	115
5-Suggestive art "Boom Town Babe"; photo-c	14	28	42	81	118	155

SECRET MISSIONS (Admiral Zacharia's...)
St. John Publishing Co.: February, 1950

1-Joe Kubert-c; stories of U.S. foreign agents   20 40 60 117 184 250

SECRET MYSTERIES (Formerly Crime Mysteries & Crime Smashers)
Ribage/Merit Publications No. 17 on: No. 16, Nov, 1954 - No. 19, July, 1955

16-Horror, Palais-a; Myron Fass-c	28	56	84	162	256	350
17-19-Horror. 17-Fass-c; mis-dated 3/54?	19	38	57	112	176	240

	GD 2.0	VG 4.0	FN 6.0	VF 8.0	VF/NM 9.0	NM- 9.2

SECRET ORIGINS (1st Series) (See 80 Page Giant #8)
National Periodical Publications: Aug-Oct, 1961 (Annual) (Reprints)

1-Origin Adam Strange (Showcase #17), Green Lantern (Green Lantern #1), Challengers (partial-r/Showcase #6, 6 pgs. Kirby-a), J'onn J'onzz (Det. #225), The Flash (Showcase #4), Green Arrow (1 pg. text), Superman-Batman team (World's Finest #94), Wonder Woman (Wonder Woman #105)   46 92 138 368 664 960
Replica Edition (1998, $4.95) r/entire book and house ads   5.00
Even More Secret Origins (2003, $6.95) reprints origins of Hawkman, Eclipso, Kid Flash, Blackhawks, Green Lantern's oath, and Jimmy Olsen-Robin team in 80 pg. Giant style 7.00

SECRET ORIGINS (2nd Series)
National Periodical Publications: Feb-Mar, 1973 - No. 6, Jan-Feb, 1974; No. 7, Oct-Nov, 1974 (All 20¢ issues) (All origin reprints)

1-Superman(r/1 pg. origin/Action #1, 1st time since G.A.), Batman(Detective #33), Ghost(Flash #88), The Flash(Showcase #4)	4	8	12	28	44	60
2-7: 2-Green Lantern & The Atom(Showcase #22 & 34), Supergirl(Action #252). 3-Wonder Woman (W.W. #1), Wildcat(Sensation #1). 4-Vigilante (Action #42) by Meskin, Kid Eternity(Hit #25). 5-The Spectre by Baily (More Fun #52,53). 6-Blackhawk(Military #1) & Legion of Super-Heroes(Superboy #147). 7-Robin (Detective #38), Aquaman (More Fun #73)	3	6	9	17	25	32

NOTE: *Infantino a-1. Kane a-2. Kubert a-1.*

SECRET ORIGINS (3rd Series)
DC Comics: 4/86 - No. 50, 8/90 (All origins)(52 pgs. #6 on)(#27 on: $1.50)

1-Origin Superman   6.00
2-6: 2-Blue Beetle. 3-Shazam. 4-Firestorm. 5-Crimson Avenger. 6-Halo/G.A. Batman   3.00
7-9,11,12,14-20,22-26: 7-Green Lantern(Guy Gardner)/G.A. Sandman. 8-Shadow Lass/Doll Man. 9-G.A. Flash/Skyman.11-G.A. Hawkman/Power Girl. 12-Challengers of Unknown/ G.A. Fury (2nd modern app.). 14-Suicide Squad; Legends spin-off. 15-Spectre/Deadman. 16-G.A. Hourman/Warlord. 17-Adam Strange story by Carmine Infantino; Dr. Occult. 18-G.A. Gr. Lantern/The Creeper. 19-Uncle Sam/The Guardian. 20-Batgirl/G.A. Dr. Mid-Nite. 22-Manhunters. 23-Floronic Man/Guardians of the Universe. 24-Blue Devil/Dr. Fate. 25-LSH/Atom. 26-Black Lightning/Miss America   2.50
10-Phantom Stranger w/Alan Moore scripts; Legends spin-off   2.50
13-Origin Nightwing; Johnny Thunder app.   2.50
21-Jonah Hex/Black Condor   2.50
27-30,36-38,40-49: 27-Zatara/Zatanna. 28-Midnight/Nightshade. 29-Power of the Atom/Mr. America; new 3 pg. Red Tornado story by Mayer (last app. of Scribbly, 8/88). 30-Plastic Man/Elongated Man. 36-Poison Ivy by Neil Gaiman & Mark Buckingham/Green Lantern. 37-Legion Of Substitute Heroes/Doctor Light. 38-Green Arrow/Speedy; Grell scripts. 40-All Ape issue. 41-Rogues Gallery of Flash. 42-Phantom Girl/GrimGhost. 43-Original Hawk & Dove/Cave Carson/Chris KL-99. 44-Batman app.; story based on Det. #40. 45-Blackhawk/ El Diablo. 46-JLA/LSH/New Titans. 47-LSH. 48-Ambush Bug/Stanley & His Monster/Rex the Wonder Dog/Trigger Twins. 49-Newsboy Legion/Silent Knight/Bouncing Boy   2.50
31-35,39: 31-JSA. 32-JLA. 33-35-JLI. 39-Animal Man-c/story continued in Animal Man #10; Grant Morrison scripts; Batman app.   3.00
50-($3.95, 100 pgs.)-Batman & Robin in text, Flash of Two Worlds, Johnny Thunder, Dolphin, Black Canary & Space Museum   5.00
Annual 1 (8/87)-Capt. Comet/Doom Patrol   3.00
Annual 2 ('88, $2.95)-Green Flash II & Flash III   3.00
Annual 3 ('89, $2.95, 84 pgs.)-Teen Titans; 1st app. new Flamebird who replaces original Bat-Girl   3.00
Special 1 (10/89, $2.00)-Batman villains: Penguin, Riddler, & Two-Face; Bolland-c; Sam Kieth-a; Neil Gaiman scripts   3.00

NOTE: *Art Adams a-33i(part). M. Anderson 8, 19, 21, 25i; c-19i(part). Aparo c/a-10. Bissette c-23. Bolland c-7. Byrne c/a-Annual 1. Colan c/a-5p. Forte a-37. Giffen a-18p, 44p, 48. Infantino a-17, 50p. Kaluta c-39. Gil Kane a-2, 28; c-2p. Kirby c-19i(part). Erik Larsen a-13. Mayer a-29. Morrow a-21. Orlando a-10. Perez a-50i, Annual 3i; c- Annual 3. Rogers a-6p. Russell a-27i. Simonson c-22. Staton a-36, 50p. Steacy a-35. Tuska a-4p, 9p.*

SECRET ORIGINS 80 PAGE GIANT (Young Justice)
DC Comics: Dec, 1998 ($4.95, one-shot)

1-Origin-s of Young Justice members; Ramos-a (Impulse)   5.00

SECRET ORIGINS FEATURING THE JLA
DC Comics: 1999 ($14.95, TPB)

1-Reprints recent origin-s of JLA members; Cassaday-c   15.00

SECRET ORIGINS OF SUPER-HEROES (See DC Special Series #10, 19)

SECRET ORIGINS OF SUPER-VILLAINS 80 PAGE GIANT
DC Comics: Dec, 1999 ($4.95, one-shot)

1-Origin-s of Sinestro, Amazo and others; Gibbons-c   5.00

SECRET ORIGINS OF THE WORLD'S GREATEST SUPER-HEROES
DC Comics: 1989 ($4.95, 148 pgs.)

nn-Reprints Superman, JLA origins; new Batman origin-s; Bolland-c   1 2 3 4 5 7

Secret Six #3 © DC

Secrets of Haunted House #40 © DC

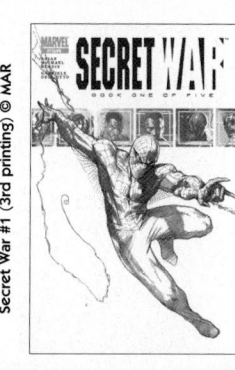

Secret War #1 (3rd printing) © MAR

	GD 2.0	VG 4.0	FN 6.0	VF 8.0	VF/NM 9.0	NM- 9.2
SECRET ROMANCE						
Charlton Comics: Oct, 1968 - No. 41, Nov, 1976; No. 42, Mar, 1979 - No. 48, Feb, 1980						
1-Begin 12¢ issues, ends #?	3	6	9	16	22	28
2-10: 9-Reese-a	2	4	6	9	13	16
11-30: 17-Susan Dey poster. 18-Shirley Jones poster	2	4	6	8	10	12
31-48	1	2	3	5	7	9
NOTE: *Beyond the Stars app.-No. 9, 11, 12, 14.*						
SECRET ROMANCES (Exciting Love Stories)						
Superior Publications Ltd.: Apr, 1951 - No. 27, July, 1955						
1	15	30	45	85	130	175
2	11	22	33	60	83	105
3-10	9	18	27	47	61	75
11-13,15-18,20-27	8	16	24	40	50	60
14,19-Lingerie panels	8	16	24	42	54	65
SECRET SERVICE (See Kent Blake of the...)						
SECRET SIX (See Action Comics Weekly)						
National Periodical Publications: Apr-May, 1968 - No. 7, Apr-May, 1969 (12¢)						
1-Origin/1st app.	6	12	18	41	66	90
2-7	4	8	12	22	34	45
SECRET SIX (See Tangent Comics/ Secret Six)						
SECRET SIX (See Villains United)						
DC Comics: Jul, 2006 - No. 6, Jan, 2007 ($2.99, limited series)						
1-6-Gail Simone-s/Brad Walker-a. 4-Doom Patrol app.						3.00
...: Six Degrees of Devastation TPB (2007, $14.99) r/#1-6						15.00
SECRET SKULL						
IDW Publ.: Aug, 2004 - No. 4, Nov, 2004 ($3.99)						
1-4-Steve Niles-s/Chuck BB-a						4.00
SECRET SOCIETY OF SUPER-VILLAINS						
National Per. Publ./DC Comics: May-June, 1976 - No. 15, June-July, 1978						
1-Origin; JLA cameo & Capt. Cold app.	2	4	6	11	16	20
2-5,15: 2-Re-intro/origin Capt. Comet; Green Lantern x-over. 5-Green Lantern, Hawkman x-over; Darkseid app. 15-G.A. Atom, Dr. Midnite, & JSA app.	2	4	6	8	10	12
6-14: 9,10-Creeper x-over. 11-Capt. Comet; Orlando-i	1	2	3	5	7	9
SECRET SOCIETY OF SUPER-VILLAINS SPECIAL (See DC Special Series #6)						
SECRETS OF HAUNTED HOUSE						
National Periodical Publications/DC Comics: 4-5/75 - #5, 12-1/75-76; #6, 6-7/77 - #14, 10-11/78; #15, 8/79 - #46, 3/82						
1	5	10	15	30	48	65
2-4	3	6	9	16	22	28
5-Wrightson-c	3	6	9	19	29	38
6-14	2	4	6	9	13	16
15-30	1	3	4	6	8	10
31,44: 31-(12/80) Mr. E series begins (1st app.), ends #41. 44-Wrightson-c	2	4	6	8	10	12
32-(1/81) Origin of Mr. E	1	3	4	5	6	7
33-43,45,46: 34,35-Frankenstein Monster app.	1	2	3	4	5	7
NOTE: *Aparo c-7. Aragones a-1. B. Bailey a-8. Bissette a-46. Buckler c-32-40p. Ditko a-1, 12, 41, 45. Golden a-10. Howard a-13i. Kaluta c-8, 10, 11, 14, 16, 29. Kubert c-41, 42. Sheldon Mayer a-43p. McWilliams a-35. Nasser a-24. Newton a-30p. Nino a-1, 13, 19. Orlando c-13, 30, 43, 45i. N. Redondo a-4, 5, 29. Rogers c-26. Spiegle a-31-41. Wrightson c-5, 44.*						
SECRETS OF HAUNTED HOUSE SPECIAL (See DC Special Series #12)						
SECRETS OF LIFE (Movie)						
Dell Publishing Co.: 1956 (Disney)						
Four Color 749-Photo-c	5	10	15	32	51	70
SECRETS OF LOVE (See Popular Teen-Agers...)						
SECRETS OF LOVE AND MARRIAGE						
Charlton Comics: V2#1, Aug, 1956 - V2#25, June, 1961						
V2#1	4	8	12	26	41	55
V2#2-6	3	6	9	18	27	35
V2#7-9-(All 68 pgs.)	4	8	12	28	44	60
10-25	3	6	9	16	22	28
SECRETS OF MAGIC (See Wisco)						
SECRETS OF SINISTER HOUSE (Sinister House of Secret Love #1-4)						
National Periodical Publ.: No. 5, June-July, 1972 - No. 18, June-July, 1974						
5-(52 pgs.).	5	10	15	30	48	65
6-9: 7-Redondo-a	3	6	9	19	29	38

	GD 2.0	VG 4.0	FN 6.0	VF 8.0	VF/NM 9.0	NM- 9.2
10-Neal Adams-a(i)	3	6	9	21	32	42
11-18: 15-Redondo-a. 17-Barry-a; early Chaykin 1 pg. strip	3	6	9	14	19	24
NOTE: *Alcala a-6, 13, 14. Glanzman a-7. Kaluta c-6, 7. Nino a-8, 11-13. Ambrose Bierce adapt.-#14.*						
SECRETS OF THE LEGION OF SUPER-HEROES						
DC Comics: Jan, 1981 - No. 3, Mar, 1981 (Limited series)						
1-3: 1-Origin of the Legion. 2-Retells origins of Brainiac 5, Shrinking Violet, Sun-Boy, Bouncing Boy, Ultra-Boy, Matter-Eater Lad, Mon-El, Karate Kid & Dream Girl						4.00
SECRETS OF TRUE LOVE						
St. John Publishing Co.: Feb, 1958						
1	7	14	21	37	46	55
SECRETS OF YOUNG BRIDES						
Charlton Comics: No. 5, Sept, 1957 - No. 44, Oct, 1964; July, 1975 - No. 9, Nov, 1976						
5	4	8	12	28	44	60
6-10: 8-Negligee panel	3	6	9	20	30	40
11-20	3	6	9	18	27	35
21-30: Last 10¢ issue?	3	6	9	16	23	30
31-44(10/64)	2	4	6	11	16	20
1-(2nd series) (7/75)	2	4	6	13	18	22
2-9	2	4	6	8	10	12
SECRET SQUIRREL (TV)(See Kite Fun Book)						
Gold Key: Oct, 1966 (12¢) (Hanna-Barbera)						
1-1st Secret Squirrel and Morocco Mole, Squiddly Diddly, Winsome Witch	10	20	30	73	129	185
SECRET STORY ROMANCES (Becomes True Tales of Love)						
Atlas Comics (TCI): Nov, 1953 - No. 21, Mar, 1956						
1-Everett-a; Jay Scott Pike-c	15	30	45	86	133	180
2	10	20	30	54	72	90
3-11: 11-Last pre-code (2/55)	9	18	27	47	61	75
12-21	8	16	24	42	54	65
NOTE: *Colletta a-10, 14, 15, 17, 21; c-10, 14, 17.*						
SECRET VOICE, THE (See Great American Comics Presents...)						
SECRET WAR						
Marvel Comics: Apr, 2004 - No. 5, Dec, 2005 ($3.99, limited series)						
1-Bendis-s/Dell'Otto painted-a/c;						5.00
1-2nd printing with gold logo on white cover and full-color Spider-Man						4.00
1-3rd printing with white cover and B&W sketched Spider-Man						4.00
2-5: 2-Wolverine-c. 3-Capt. America-c. 4-Black Widow-c. 5-Daredevil-c.						4.00
2-2nd printing with white cover and B&W sketched Wolverine						4.00
... : From the Files of Nick Fury (2005, $3.99) Fury's journal entries; profiles of characters						4.00
HC (2005, $29.99, dust jacket) r/#1-5 & ...From the Files of Nick Fury; additional art						30.00
SC (2006, $24.99) r/#1-5 & ...From the Files of Nick Fury; additional art						25.00
SECRET WARS II (Also see Marvel Super Heroes...)						
Marvel Comics Group: July, 1985 - No. 9, Mar, 1986 (Maxi-series)						
1,9: 9-(52 pgs.) X-Men app., Spider-Man app.						4.00
2-8: 2,8-X-Men app. 5-1st app. Boom Boom. 5,8-Spider-Man app.						3.00
SECRET WEAPONS						
Valiant: Sept, 1993 - No. 21, May, 1995 ($2.25)						
1-10,12-21: 3-Reese-a(i). 5-Ninjak app. 9-Bound-in trading card. 12-Bloodshot app.						2.50
11-(Sept. on envelope, Aug on-c, $2.50)-Enclosed in manilla envelope; Bloodshot app; intro new team.						2.50
SECTAURS						
Marvel Comics: June, 1985 - No. 8, Sept, 1986 (75¢) (Based on Coleco Toys)						
1-8, 1-Giveaway; same-c with "Coleco 1985 Toy Fair Collectors' Edition"						3.00
SECTION ZERO						
Image Comics (Gorilla): June, 2000 - No. 3, Sept, 2000 ($2.50)						
1-3-Kesel-s/Grummett-a						2.50
SEDUCTION OF THE INNOCENT (Also see New York State Joint Legislative Committee to Study...)						
Rinehart & Co., Inc., N. Y.: 1953, 1954 (400 pgs.) (Hardback, $4.00)(Written by Fredric Wertham, M.D.)(Also printed in Canada by Clarke, Irwin & Co. Ltd.)						
(1st Version)-with bibliographical note intact (pages 399 & 400)(several copies got out before the comic publishers forced the removal of this page)						
	55	110	165	344	572	800
Dust jacket only	34	68	102	197	311	425
(1st Version)-without bibliographical note	34	68	102	197	311	425
Dust jacket only	16	32	48	94	147	200

Seekers into the Mystery #12 © J.M. DeMatteis

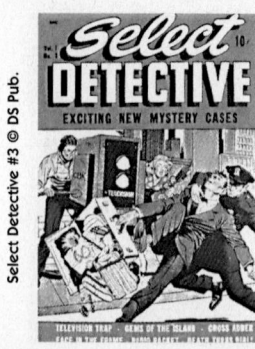
Select Detective #3 © DS Pub.

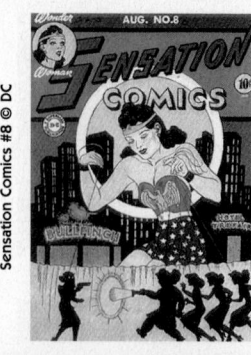
Sensation Comics #8 © DC

	GD	VG	FN	VF	VF/NM	NM-
	2.0	4.0	6.0	8.0	9.0	9.2

(2nd Version)-Published in England by Kennikat Press, 1954, 399 pgs. has

bibliographical page	14	28	42	76	108	140

1972 r-/of 2nd version; 400 pgs. w/bibliography page; Kennikat Press

	4	8	12	22	34	45

NOTE: Material from this book appeared in the November, 1953(Vol.70, pp50-53,214) issue of the **Ladies' Home Journal** under the title "What Parents Don't Know About Comic Books". With the release of this book, Dr. Wertham reveals seven years of research attempting to link juvenile delinquency to comic books. Many illustrations showing excessive violence, sex, sadism, and torture are shown. This book was used at the Kefauver Senate hearings which led to the Comics Code Authority. Because of the influence this book had on the comic industry and the collector's interest in it, we feel this listing is justified. Also see **Parade of Pleasure**.

SEDUCTION OF THE INNOCENT! (Also see Halloween Horror)
Eclipse Comics: Nov, 1985 - 3-D#2, Apr, 1986 ($1.75)

1-6: Double listed under cover title from #7 on						3.00
3-D 1 (10/85, $2.25, 36 pgs.)-contains unpublished Advs. Into Darkness #15 (pre-code); Dave Stevens-c						4.00
2-D 1 (100 copy limited signed & #ed edition)(B&W)	1	2	3		6	8
3-D 2 (4/86)-Baker, Toth, Wrightson-c						5.00
2-D 1 (100 copy limited signed & #ed edition)(B&W)	1	2	3		7	9

NOTE: **Anderson** r-2, 3. **Crandall** c/a(r)-1. **Meskin** c/a(r)-3, 3-D 1. **Moreira** r-2. **Toth** a-1-6r; c-4r. **Tuska** r-6.

SEEKER
Sky Comics: Apr, 1994 ($2.50, one-shot)

1						2.50

SEEKERS INTO THE MYSTERY
DC Comics (Vertigo): Jan, 1996 - No. 15, Apr, 1997 ($2.50)

1-14: J.M. DeMatteis scripts in all. 1-4-Glenn Barr-a. 5,10-Muth-c/a. 6-9-Zulli-c/a.						
11-14-Bolton-c; Jill Thompson-a						2.50
15-($2.95)-Muth-c/a						3.00

SEEKER 3000 (See Marvel Premiere #41)
Marvel Comics: Jun, 1998 - No. 4, Sept, 1998 ($2.99/$2.50, limited series)

1-($2.99)-Set 25 years after 1st app.; wraparound-c						3.00
2-4-($2.50)						2.50
...Premiere 1 (6/98, $1.50) Reprints 1st app. from Marvel Premiere #41; wraparound-c						2.50

SELECT DETECTIVE (Exciting New Mystery Cases)
D. S. Publishing Co.: Aug-Sept, 1948 - No. 3, Dec-Jan, 1948-49

1-Matt Baker-a	29	58	87	170	268	365
2-Baker, McWilliams-a	18	36	54	107	169	230
3	15	30	45	88	137	185

SEMPER FI (Tales of the Marine Corp)
Marvel Comics: Dec, 1988- No.9, Aug, 1989 (75¢)

1-9: Severin-c/a						2.50

SENSATIONAL POLICE CASES (Becomes Captain Steve Savage, 2nd Series)
Avon Periodicals: 1952; No. 2, 1954 - No. 4, July-Aug, 1954

nn-(1952, 25¢, 100 pgs.)-Kubert-a?; Check, Larsen, Lawrence & McCann-a; Kinstler-c	40	80	120	235	368	500
2-4: 2-Kirbyish-a (3-4/54). 4-Reprint/Saint #5	15	30	45	85	130	175
I.W. Reprint #5-(1963?, nd)-Reprints Prison Break #5(1952-Realistic); Infantino-a	3	6	9	16	23	30

SENSATIONAL SHE-HULK, THE (She-Hulk #21-23) (See Savage She-Hulk)
Marvel Comics: V2#1, 5/89 - No. 60, Feb, 1994 ($1.50/$1.75, deluxe format)

V2#1-Byrne-c/a(p)/scripts begin, end #8						3.00
2,3,5-8: 3-Spider-Man app.						2.50
4,14-17,21-23: 4-Reintro G.A. Blonde Phantom. 14-17-Howard the Duck app. 21-23-Return of the Blonde Phantom. 22-All Winners Squad app.						2.50
9-13,18-20,24-49,51-60: 25-Thor app. 26-Excalibur app. 27-Wolverine app. (3 pgs.). 30-Hobgoblin-c & cameo. 31-Byrne-c/a/scripts begin again. 35-Last $1.50-c. 37-Wolverine/Punisher/Spidey-c, but no app. 39-Thing app. 56-War Zone app.; Hulk cameo. 57-Vs. Hulk-c/story. 58-Electro-c/story. 59-Jack O'Lantern app.						2.50
50-($2.95, 52 pgs.)-Embossed green foil-c; Byrne app.; last Byrne-c/a; Austin, Chaykin, Simonson-a; Miller-a(2 pgs.)						3.00

NOTE: **Dale Keown** c(p)-13, 15-22.

SENSATIONAL SHE-HULK IN CEREMONY, THE
Marvel Comics: 1989 - No. 2, 1989 ($3.95, squarebound, 52 pgs.)

nn-Part 1, nn-Part 2						4.00

SENSATIONAL SPIDER-MAN
Marvel Comics: Apr, 1989 ($5.95, squarebound, 80 pgs.)

1-r/Amazing Spider-Man Annual #14,15 by Miller & Annual #8 by Kirby & Ditko						6.00

SENSATIONAL SPIDER-MAN, THE
Marvel Comics: Jan, 1996 - No. 33, Nov, 1998 ($1.95/$1.99)

0 ($4.95)-Lenticular-c; Jurgens-a/scripts						5.00
1						5.00
1-($2.95) variant-c; polybagged w/cassette	1	2	3	5	6	8
2-5: 2-Kaine & Rhino app. 3-Giant-Man app.						4.00
6-18: 9-Onslaught tie-in; revealed that Peter & Mary Jane's unborn baby is a girl.						
11-Revelations. 13-15-Ka-Zar app. 14,15-Hulk app.						3.00
19-24: Living Pharoah app. 22,23-Dr. Strange app.						2.50
25-($2.99) Spiderhunt pt. 1; Normie Osborne kidnapped						4.00
25-Variant-c	1	2	3	5	6	8
26-33: 26-Nauck-a. 27-Double-c with "The Sensational Hornet #1"; Vulture app. 28-Hornet vs. Vulture. 29,30-Black Cat-c/app. 33-Last issue; Gathering of Five concludes						2.50
#(-1) Flashback(7/97) Dezago-s/Wieringo-a						3.00
'96 Annual ($2.95)						3.00

SENSATIONAL SPIDER-MAN, THE (Previously Marvel Knights Spider-Man #1-22)
Marvel Comics: No. 23, Apr, 2006 - Present ($2.99)

23-40: 23-25-Aguirre-Sacasa-s/Medina-a. 23-Wraparound-c. 24,34,37-Black Cat app. 26-New costume. 28-Unmasked; Dr. Octopus app.; Crain-a. 35-Black costume resumes						3.00
... Annual 1 (2007, $3.99) Flashbacks of Peter & MJ's relationship; Larroca-a/Fraction-s						4.00
... Feral HC (2006, $19.99, dustjacket) r/#23-27; sketch pages						20.00
Civil War: Peter Parker, Spider-Man TPB (2007, $17.99) r/#28-34; Crain cover concepts						18.00

SENSATION COMICS (Sensation Mystery #110 on)
National Per. Publ./All-American: Jan, 1942 - No. 109, May-June, 1952

1-Origin Mr. Terrific(1st app.), Wildcat(1st app.), The Gay Ghost, & Little Boy Blue; Wonder Woman (cont'd from All Star #8), The Black Pirate begin; intro. Justice & Fair Play Club	2850	5700	8550	21,000	40,500	60,000

1-Reprint, Oversize 13-1/2x10". WARNING: This comic is an exact duplicate reprint of the original except for its size. DC published it in 1974 with a second cover titling it as a Famous First Edition. There have been many reported cases of the outer cover being removed and the interior sold as the original edition. The reprint with the new outer cover removed is practically worthless. See Famous First Edition for value.

2-Etta Candy begins	457	914	1371	3200	5600	8000
3-W. Woman gets secretary's job	290	580	870	1813	3007	4200
4-1st app. Stretch Skinner in Wildcat	200	400	600	1250	2075	2900
5-Intro. Justin, Black Pirate's son	159	318	477	994	1647	2300
6-Origin/1st app. Wonder Woman's magic lasso	162	324	486	1013	1682	2350
7-10	116	232	348	725	1200	1675
11,12,14-20	100	200	300	625	1038	1450
13-Hitler, Tojo, Mussolini-c (as bowling pins)	145	290	435	906	1503	2100
21-30	79	158	237	494	822	1150
31-33	58	116	174	363	599	835
34-Sargon, the Sorcerer begins (10/44), ends #36; begins again #52	61	122	183	381	633	885
35-40: 38-X-Mas-c	53	106	159	324	542	760
41-50: 43-The Whip app.	51	102	153	311	511	710
51-60: 51-Last Black Pirate. 56,57-Sargon by Kubert	49	98	147	299	492	685
61-67,69-80: 63-Last Mr. Terrific. 66-Wildcat by Kubert	41	82	123	256	416	575
68-Origin & 1st app. Huntress (8/47)	46	92	138	281	466	650
81-Used in SOTI, pg. 33,34; Krigstein-a	45	90	135	275	450	625
82-93: 83-Last Sargon. 86-The Atom app. 90-Last Wildcat. 91-Streak begins by Alex Toth. 92-Toth-a (2 pgs.)	80	160	240	383	525
94-1st all girl issue	55	110	165	344	572	800
95-99,101-106: 95-Unmasking of Wonder Woman-c/story. 99-1st app. Astra, Girl of the Future, ends #106. 103-Robot-c. 105-Last 52 pgs. 106-Wonder Woman ends	50	100	150	300	503	700
100-(11-12/50)	60	120	180	375	625	875
107-(Scarce, 1-2/52)-1st mystery issue; Johnny Peril by Toth(p), 8 pgs. & begins; continues from Danger Trail #5 (3-4/51)(see Comic Cavalcade #15 for 1st app.)	68	136	204	425	705	985
108-(Scarce)-Johnny Peril by Toth(p)	57	114	171	356	591	825
109-(Scarce)-Johnny Peril by Toth(p)	68	136	204	425	705	985

NOTE: **Krigstein** a-(Wildcat)-81, 83, 84. **Moldoff** Black Pirate-1-25; Black Pirate not in 34-36, 43-48. **Oskner** c(i)-89-91, 94-106. **Wonder Woman** by H. G. Peter, all issues except #8, 17-19, 21; c-4-7, 9-18, 20-88, 92, 93. **Toth** a-91, 98; c-107. Wonder Woman c-1-106.

SENSATION COMICS (Also see All Star Comics 1999 crossover titles)
DC Comics: May, 1999 ($1.99, one-shot)

1-Golden Age Wonder Woman and Hawkgirl; Robinson-s						2.50

SENSATION MYSTERY (Formerly Sensation Comics #1-109)
National Periodical Publ.: No. 110, July-Aug, 1952 - No. 116, July-Aug, 1953

110-Johnny Peril	45	90	135	275	450	625
111-116-Johnny Peril in all. 116-M. Anderson-a	45	90	135	275	450	625

NOTE: **M. Anderson** c-110. **Colan** a-114p. **Glunta** a-112. **G. Kane** c(p)-108, 109, 111-115.

The Sentry #4 © MAR

Serenity #1 © Universal Studios

Sgt. Rock #329 © DC

	GD 2.0	VG 4.0	FN 6.0	VF 8.0	VF/NM 9.0	NM- 9.2

SENSUOUS STREAKER
Marvel Publ.: 1974 (B&W magazine, 68pgs.)

	GD 2.0	VG 4.0	FN 6.0	VF 8.0	VF/NM 9.0	NM- 9.2
1	4	8	12	2	34	45

SENTINEL
Marvel Comics: June, 2003 - No. 12, April, 2004 ($2.99/$2.50)

1-Sean McKeever-s/Udon Studios-a	3.00
2-12	3.00
Marvel Age Sentinel Vol. 1: Salvage (2004, $7.99, digest size) r/#1-6	8.00
Vol. 2: No Hero (2004, $7.99, digest size) r/#7-12; sketch pages	8.00

SENTINEL (2nd series)
Marvel Comics: Jan, 2006 - No. 5, May, 2006 ($2.99, limited series)

1-5-Sean McKeever-s/Joe Vriens-a	3.00
Vol. 3: Past Imperfect (2006, $7.99, digest size) r/#1-5	8.00

SENTINELS OF JUSTICE, THE (See Americomics & Captain Paragon &...)

SENTINEL SQUAD O*N*E
Marvel Comics: Mar, 2006 - No. 5, July, 2006 ($2.99)

1-5-Lopresti-a/Layman-s	3.00
Decimation: Sentinel Squad O*N*E (2006, $13.99, TPB) r/series; sketch pg. by Caliafore	14.00

SENTRY (Also see New Avengers)
Marvel Comics: Sept, 2000 - No. 5, Jan, 2001 ($2.99, limited series)

1-5-Paul Jenkins-s/Jae Lee-a. 3-Spider-Man-c/app. 4-X-Men, FF app.	3.00
.../Fantastic Four (2/01, $2.99) Continues story from #5; Winslade-a	3.00
.../Hulk (2/01, $2.99) Sienkiewicz-c/a	3.00
.../Spider-Man (2/01, $2.99) back story of the Sentry; Leonardi-a	3.00
.../The Void (2/01, $2.99) Conclusion of story; Jae Lee-a	3.00
.../X-Men (2/01, $2.99) Sentry and Archangel; Texeira-a	3.00
TPB (10/01, $24.95) r/#1-5 & all one-shots; Stan Lee interview	25.00
TPB (2nd edition, 2005, $24.99)	25.00

SENTRY (Follows return in New Avengers #10)
Marvel Comics: Nov, 2005 - No. 8, Jun, 2006 ($2.99, limited series)

1-8-Paul Jenkins-s/John Romita Jr.-a. 1-New Avengers app. 3-Hulk app.	3.00
1-(Rough Cut) (12/05, $3.99) Romita sketch art and Jenkins script; cover sketches	4.00
...: Reborn TPB (2006, $21.99) r/#1-8	22.00

SENTRY SPECIAL
Innovation Publishing: 1991 ($2.75, one-shot)(Hero Alliance spin-off)

1-Lost in Space preview (3 pgs.)	2.75

SERAPHIM
Innovation Publishing: May, 1990 ($2.50, mature readers)

1	2.50

SERENITY (Based on 2005 movie Serenity and 2003 TV series Firefly)
Dark Horse Comics: July, 2005 - No. 3, Sept, 2005 ($2.99, limited series)

1-3: Whedon & Matthews-s/Conrad-a. Three covers for each issue by various	4.00
...: Those Left Behind HC (11/07, $19.95, dustjacket) r/series; intro. by Nathan Fillion; pre-production art for the movie; Hughes-c	20.00
...: Those Left Behind TPB (1/06, $9.95) r/series; intro. by Nathan Fillion; Hughes-c	10.00

SERGEANT BARNEY BARKER (Becomes G. I. Tales #4 on)
Atlas Comics (MCI): Aug, 1956 - No. 3, Dec, 1956

	GD 2.0	VG 4.0	FN 6.0	VF 8.0	VF/NM 9.0	NM- 9.2
1-Severin-c/a(4)	18	36	54	105	165	225
2,3: 2-Severin-c/a(4). 3-Severin-c/a(5)	14	28	42	76	108	140

SERGEANT BILKO (Phil Silvers Starring as...) (TV)
National Periodical Publications: May-June, 1957 - No. 18, Mar-Apr, 1960

	GD 2.0	VG 4.0	FN 6.0	VF 8.0	VF/NM 9.0	NM- 9.2
1-All have Bob Oskner-c	62	124	186	388	644	900
2	34	68	102	195	308	420
3-5	28	56	84	162	256	350
6-18: 11,12,15,17-Photo-c	23	46	69	130	205	280

SGT. BILKO'S PVT. DOBERMAN (TV)
National Periodical Publications: June-July, 1958 - No. 11, Feb-Mar, 1960

	GD 2.0	VG 4.0	FN 6.0	VF 8.0	VF/NM 9.0	NM- 9.2
1-Bob Oskner c-1-4,7,11	26	52	78	195	348	500
2	14	28	42	102	181	260
3-5: 5-Photo-c	10	20	30	71	126	180
6-11: 6,9-Photo-c	8	16	24	52	86	120

SGT. DICK CARTER OF THE U.S. BORDER PATROL (See Holyoke One-Shot)

SGT. FURY (& His Howling Commandos)(See Fury & Special Marvel Edition)
Marvel Comics Group (BPC earlier issues): May, 1963 - No. 167, Dec, 1981

1-1st app. Sgt. Nick Fury (becomes agent of Shield in Strange Tales #135); Kirby/Ayers-c/a;

	GD 2.0	VG 4.0	FN 6.0	VF 8.0	VF/NM 9.0	NM- 9.2
1st Dum-Dum Dugan & the Howlers	152	304	456	1315	2458	3600
2-Kirby-a	40	80	120	311	568	825
3-5: 3-Reed Richards x-over. 4-Death of Junior Juniper. 5-1st Baron Strucker app.; Kirby-a	24	48	72	175	313	450
6-10: 8-Baron Zemo, 1st Percival Pinkerton app. 9-Hitler-c & app. 10-1st app. Capt. Savage (the Skipper)(9/64)	14	28	42	99	175	250
11,12,14-20: 14-1st Blitz Squad. 18-Death of Pamela Hawley	8	16	24	54	90	125
13-Captain America & Bucky app.(12/64); 2nd solo Capt. America x-over outside The Avengers; Kirby-a	34	68	102	255	465	675
13-2nd printing (1994)	2	4	6	8	10	12
21-24,26,28-30	5	10	15	35	55	75
25,27: 25-Red Skull app. 27-1st app. Eric Koenig; origin Fury's eye patch	6	12	18	37	59	80
31-33,35-50: 35-Eric Koenig joins Howlers. 43-Bob Hope, Glen Miller app. 44-Flashback on Howlers' 1st mission	3	6	9	21	32	42
34-Origin Howling Commandos	4	8	12	22	34	45
51-60	3	6	9	18	27	35
61-67: 64-Capt. Savage & Raiders x-over; peace symbol-c. 67-Last 12c issue; flag-c	3	6	9	16	22	28
68-80: 76-Fury's Father app. in WWI story	3	6	9	14	19	24
81-91: 91-Last 15¢ issue	2	4	6	11	16	20
92-(52 pgs.)	3	6	9	15	21	26
93-99: 98-Deadly Dozen x-over	2	4	6	10	14	18
100-Capt. America, Fantastic 4 cameos; Stan Lee, Martin Goodman & others app.	3	6	9	15	21	26
101-120: 101-Origin retold	2	4	6	9	12	15
121-130: 121-123-r/#19-21	1	3	4	6	8	10
131-167: 167-Reprints (from 1963)	1	2	3	5	6	8
133,134-(30¢-c variants, limited dist.)(5,7/76)	3	6	9	16	22	28
141,142-(35¢-c variants, limited dist.)(7,9/77)	4	8	12	22	34	45
Annual 1(1965, 25¢, 72 pgs.)-r/#4,5 & new-a	14	28	42	99	175	250
Special 2(1966)	6	12	18	39	62	85
Special 3(1967) All new material	4	8	12	24	37	50
Special 4(1968)	3	6	9	18	27	35
Special 5-7(1969-11/71)	3	6	9	15	21	26

NOTE: *Ayers* a-8, Annual 1. *Ditko* a-15i. *Gil Kane* c-37, 96. *Kirby* a-1-7, 13p, 167p(r). Special 5: c-1-8, 10-20, 25,
167p. *Severin* a-44-46, 48, 162, 164; inks-69-72, 75, 78, 80; c-4i, 5, 6, 44, 46, 110, 149i, 155i, 162-166. *Sutton*
a-57p. Reprints in #80, 82, 85, 87, 89, 91, 93, 95, 99, 101, 103, 105, 107, 109, 111, 121-123, 145-155, 167.

SGT. FURY AND HIS HOWLING DEFENDERS (See The Defenders #147)

SERGEANT PRESTON OF THE YUKON (TV)
Dell Publishing Co.: No. 344, Aug, 1951 - No. 29, Nov-Jan, 1958-59

	GD 2.0	VG 4.0	FN 6.0	VF 8.0	VF/NM 9.0	NM- 9.2
Four Color 344(#1)-Sergeant Preston & his dog Yukon King begin; painted-c begin, end #18	12	24	36	82	146	210
Four Color 373,397,419('52)	8	16	24	52	86	120
5(11-1/52-53)-10(2-4/54): 6-Bondage-c.	6	12	18	41	66	90
11,12,14-17	6	12	18	37	59	80
13-Origin Sgt. Preston	6	12	18	41	66	90
18-Origin Yukon King; last painted-c	6	12	18	41	66	90
19-29: All photo-c	7	14	21	49	80	110

SGT. ROCK (Formerly Our Army at War; see Brave & the Bold #52 & Showcase #45)
National Periodical Publications/DC Comics: No. 302, Mar, 1977 - No. 422, July, 1988

	GD 2.0	VG 4.0	FN 6.0	VF 8.0	VF/NM 9.0	NM- 9.2
302	3	6	9	20	30	40
303-310	2	4	6	11	16	20
311-320: 318-Reprints	2	4	6	8	10	12
321-350	1	2	3	5	7	9
329-Whitman variant (scarce)	1	3	4	6	8	10
351-399,401-421						6.00
400,422: 422-1st Joe, Adam, Andy Kubert-a team	1	2	3	5	7	9
Annual 2-4: 2(1982)-Formerly Sgt. Rock's Prize Battle Tales #1. 3(1983). 4(1984)	1	2	3	5	7	9

NOTE: *Estrada* a-322, 327, 331, 336, 337, 341, 342i. *Glanzman* a-384, 421. *Kubert* a-302, 303, 305i, 306, 328,
351, 356, 368, 373, 422; c-317, 318r, 319-323, 325-333-on, Annual 2, 3. *Severin* a-347. *Spiegle* a-382, Annual 2,
3. *Thorne* a-384. *Toth* a-385r. *Wildey* a-307, 311, 313, 314.

SGT. ROCK: BETWEEN HELL AND A HARD PLACE
DC Comics (Vertigo): 2003 ($24.95, hardcover one-shot)

HC-Joe Kubert-a/c; Brian Azzarello-s	25.00
SC (2004, $17.95)	18.00

SGT. ROCK'S COMBAT TALES
DC Comics: 2005 - Present ($9.99, digest)

Vol. 1-Reprints early app. in Our Army at War, G.I. Combat, Star Spangled War Stories	10.00

SGT. ROCK SPECIAL (Sgt. Rock #14 on; see DC Special Series #3)

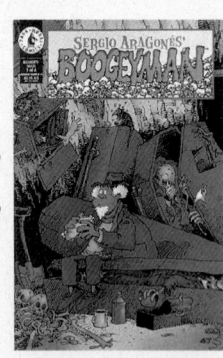

Sergio Aragonés' Boogeyman #1 © Sergio Aragonés

Seven Seas Comics #5 © Universal Phoenix

Seven Soldiers: Bulleteer #4 © DC

	GD 2.0	VG 4.0	FN 6.0	VF 8.0	VF/NM 9.0	NM- 9.2

DC Comics: Oct, 1988 - No. 21, Feb, 1992; No. 1, 1992; No. 2, 1994 ($2.00, quarterly/monthly, 52 pgs)

1-Reprint begin	1	3	4	6	8	10

2-21: All-r; 5-r/early Sgt. Rock/Our Army at War #81. 7-Tomahawk-r by Thorne. 9-Enemy Ace-r by Kubert. 10-All Rock issue. 11-r/1st Haunted Tank story. 12-All Kubert issue; begins monthly. 13-Dinosaur story by Heath(r). 14-Enemy Ace-r (22 pgs.) by Adams/Kubert. 15-Enemy Ace (22 pgs.) by Kubert. 16-Iron Major-c/story. 16,17-Enemy Ace-r.

19-r/Batman/Sgt. Rock team-up/B&B #108 by Aparo						6.00
1 (1992, $2.95, 68 pgs.)-Simonson-c; unpubbed Kubert-a; Glanzman, Russell, Pratt, & Wagner-a						5.00
2 (1994, $2.95) Brereton painted-c						4.00

NOTE: *Neal Adams* i-1, 8, 14p. *Chaykin* a-2; r-3, 9(2pgs.); c-3. *Drucker* r-6. *Glanzman* r-20. *Golden* a-1. *Heath* a-2; r-5, 9-13, 16, 19, 21. *Krigstein* r-4, 8. *Kubert* r-1-17, 20, 21; c-1p, 2, 8, 14-21. *Miller* r-6p. *Severin* r-3, 6, 10. *Simonson* r-2, 4; c-4. *Thorne* r-7. *Toth* r-2, 8, 11. *Wood* r-4.

SGT. ROCK SPECTACULAR (See DC Special Series #13)

SGT. ROCK'S PRIZE BATTLE TALES (Becomes Sgt. Rock Annual #2 on; see DC Special Series #18 & 80 Page Giant #7)
National Periodical Publications: Winter, 1964 (Giant - 80 pgs., one-shot)

1-Kubert, Heath-r; new Kubert-c	30	60	90	222	404	585
... Replica Edition (2000, $5.95) Reprints entire issue						6.00

SGT. ROCK: THE PROPHECY
DC Comics: Mar, 2006 - No. 6, Aug, 2006 ($2.99, limited series)

1-6-Joe Kubert-s/a/c. 1-Variant covers by Andy and Adam Kubert						3.00
TPB (2007, $17.99) r/#1-6						18.00

SGT. STRYKER'S DEATH SQUAD (See Savage Combat Tales)

SERGIO ARAGONÉS' ACTIONS SPEAK
Dark Horse Comics: Jan, 2001 - No. 6, Jun, 2001 ($2.99, B&W, limited series)

1-6-Aragonés-c/a; wordless one-page cartoons						3.00

SERGIO ARAGONÉS' BLAIR WHICH?
Dark Horse Comics: Dec, 1999 ($2.95, B&W, one-shot)

nn-Aragonés-c/a; Evanier-s. Parody of "Blair Witch Project" movie						3.00

SERGIO ARAGONÉS' BOOGEYMAN
Dark Horse Comics: June, 1998 - No. 4, Sept, 1998 ($2.95, B&W, lim. series)

1-4-Aragonés-c/a						3.00

SERGIO ARAGONÉS DESTROYS DC
DC Comics: June, 1996 ($3.50, one-shot)

1-DC Superhero parody book; Aragonés-c/a; Evanier scripts						3.50

SERGIO ARAGONÉS' DIA DE LOS MUERTOS
Dark Horse Comics: Oct, 1998 ($2.95, one-shot)

1-Aragonés-c/a; Evanier scripts						3.00

SERGIO ARAGONÉS' GROO & RUFFERTO
Dark Horse Comics: Dec, 1998 - No. 4, Mar, 1999 ($2.95, lim. series)

1-3-Aragonés-c/a						3.00

SERGIO ARAGONÉS' GROO: DEATH AND TAXES
Dark Horse Comics: Dec, 2001 - No. 4, Apr, 2002 ($2.99, lim. series)

1-4-Aragonés-c/a; Evanier-s						3.00

SERGIO ARAGONÉS' GROO: MIGHTIER THAN THE SWORD
Dark Horse Comics: Jan, 2000 - No. 4, Apr, 2000 ($2.95, lim. series)

1-4-Aragonés-c/a; Evanier-s						3.00

SERGIO ARAGONÉS' GROO THE WANDERER (See Groo...)

SERGIO ARAGONÉS' LOUDER THAN WORDS
Dark Horse Comics: July, 1997 - No. 6, Dec, 1997 ($2.95, B&W, limited series)

1-6-Aragonés-c/a						3.00

SERGIO ARAGONÉS MASSACRES MARVEL
Marvel Comics: June, 1996 ($3.50, one-shot)

1-Marvel Superhero parody book; Aragonés-c/a; Evanier scripts						3.50

SERGIO ARAGONÉS STOMPS STAR WARS
Marvel Comics: Jan, 2000 ($2.95, one-shot)

1-Star Wars parody; Aragonés-c/a; Evanier scripts						3.00

SEVEN BLOCK
Marvel Comics (Epic Comics): 1990 ($4.50, one-shot, 52 pgs.)

1-Dixon-s/Zaffinoa						4.50
nn-(IDW Publ., 2004, $5.99) reprints #1						6.00

SEVEN BROTHERS (John Woo's...)

	GD 2.0	VG 4.0	FN 6.0	VF 8.0	VF/NM 9.0	NM- 9.2

Virgin Comics: Oct, 2006 - No. 5, Feb, 2007 ($2.99)

1-5-Garth Ennis-s/Jeevan Kang-a. 1-Two covers by Amano & Horn. 2-Kang var-c						3.00
TPB (6/07, $14.99) r/#1-5; cover gallery, deleted scenes and concept art						15.00
Volume 2 (9/07 - Present) 1-Edison George-a						3.00

SEVEN DEAD MEN (See Complete Mystery #1)

SEVEN DWARFS (Also see Snow White)
Dell Publishing Co.: No. 227, 1949 (Disney-Movie)

Four Color 227	9	18	27	65	113	160

SEVEN MILES A SECOND
DC Comics (Vertigo Verité): 1996 ($7.95, one-shot)

nn-Wojnarowicz-s/Romberg-a						8.00

SEVEN SAMUROID, THE (See Image Graphic Novel)

SEVEN SEAS COMICS
Universal Phoenix Features/Leader No. 6: Apr, 1946 - No. 6, 1947(no month)

1-South Sea Girl by Matt Baker, Capt. Cutlass begin; Tugboat Tessie by Baker app.

	88	176	264	550	913	1275
2-Swashbuckler-c	67	134	201	419	697	975
3,5,6: 3-Six pg. Feldstein-a	66	132	198	413	682	950
4-Classic Baker-c	83	166	249	519	860	1200

NOTE: *Baker* a-1-6; c-3-6.

SEVEN SOLDIERS OF VICTORY (Book-ends for seven related mini-series)
DC Comics: No. 0, Apr, 2005; No. 1, Dec, 2006 ($2.95/$3.99)

0-Grant Morrison-s/J.H. Williams-a						3.00
1-($3.99) Series conclusion; Grant Morrison-s/J.H. Williams-a						4.00
... Volume One (2006, $14.99) r/#0, Shining Knight #1,2; Zatanna #1,2; Guardian #1,2; and Klarion the Witch Boy #1; intro. by Morrison; character design sketches						15.00
... Volume Two (2006, $14.99) r/Shining Knight #3,4; Zatanna #3; Guardian #3,4; and Klarion the Witch Boy #2,3						15.00
... Volume Three ('06, $14.99) r/Zatanna #4; Mister Miracle #1,2; Bulleteer #1,2; Frankenstein #1 and Klarion the Witch Boy #4;						15.00
... Volume Four ('07, $14.99) r/Mister Miracle #3,4; Bulleteer #3,4; Frankenstein #2-4 and Seven Soldiers of Victory #1; script pages						15.00

SEVEN SOLDIERS: BULLETEER
DC Comics: Jan, 2006 - No. 4, May, 2006 ($2.99, limited series)

1-4-Grant Morrison-s/Yanick Paquette-a/c						3.00

SEVEN SOLDIERS: FRANKENSTEIN
DC Comics: Jan, 2006 - No. 4, May, 2006 ($2.99, limited series)

1-4-Grant Morrison-s/Doug Mahnke-a/c						3.00

SEVEN SOLDIERS: GUARDIAN
DC Comics: May, 2005 - No. 4, Nov, 2005 ($2.99, limited series)

1-4-Grant Morrison-s/Cameron Stewart-a; Newsboy Army app.						3.00

SEVEN SOLDIERS: KLARION THE WITCH BOY
DC Comics: June, 2005 - No. 4, Dec, 2005 ($2.99, limited series)

1-4-Grant Morrison-s/Frazer Irving-a						3.00

SEVEN SOLDIERS: MISTER MIRACLE
DC Comics: Nov, 2005 - No. 4, May, 2006 ($2.99, limited series)

1-4: 1-Grant Morrison-s/Pasqual Ferry-a/c. 3,4-Freddie Williams II-a/c						3.00

SEVEN SOLDIERS: SHINING KNIGHT
DC Comics: May, 2005 - No. 4, Oct, 2005 ($2.99, limited series)

1-4-Grant Morrison-s/Simone Bianchi-a						3.00

SEVEN SOLDIERS: ZATANNA
DC Comics: June, 2005 - No. 4, Dec, 2005 ($2.99, limited series)

1-4-Grant Morrison-s/Ryan Sook-a						3.00

1776 (See Charlton Classic Library)

7TH VOYAGE OF SINBAD, THE (Movie)
Dell Publishing Co.: Sept, 1958 (photo-c)

Four Color 944-Buscema-a	12	24	36	87	156	225

77 SUNSET STRIP (TV)
Dell Publ. Co./Gold Key: No. 1066, Jan-Mar, 1960 - No. 2, Feb, 1963 (All photo-c)

Four Color 1066-Toth-a	10	20	30	71	126	180
Four Color 1106,1159-Toth-a	8	16	24	58	97	135
Four Color 1211,1263,1291, 01-742-209(7-9/62)-Manning-a in all						125
	8	16	24	54	90	125
1,2: Manning-a. 1(11/62-G.K.)	8	16	24	54	90	125

Shade, the Changing Man #14 © DC

Shadow Cabinet #8 © Milestone

Shadow Comics #4 © S&S

	GD	VG	FN	VF	VF/NM	NM-		GD	VG	FN	VF	VF/NM	NM-
	2.0	4.0	6.0	8.0	9.0	9.2		2.0	4.0	6.0	8.0	9.0	9.2

77TH BENGAL LANCERS, THE (TV)
Dell Publishing Co.: May, 1957

	GD	VG	FN	VF	VF/NM	NM-
Four Color 791-Photo-c	7	14	21	47	76	105

SEYMOUR, MY SON (See More Seymour)
Archie Publications (Radio Comics): Sept, 1963

1-DeCarlo-a?	3	6	9	20	30	40

SHADE, THE (See Starman)
DC Comics: Apr, 1997 - No. 4, July, 1997 ($2.25, limited series)

1-4-Robinson-s/Harris-a: 1-Gene Ha-a. 2-Williams/Gray-a 3-Blevins-a. 4-Zulli-a		3.00

SHADE, THE CHANGING MAN (See Cancelled Comic Cavalcade)
National Per. Publ./DC Comics: June-July, 1977 - No. 8, Aug-Sept, 1978

1-1st app. Shade; Ditko-c/a in all	2	4	6	9	12	15
2-8	1	2	3	5	7	9

SHADE, THE CHANGING MAN (2nd series) (Also see Suicide Squad #16)
DC Comics (Vertigo imprint #33 on): July, 1990 - No. 70, Apr, 1996 ($1.50-$2.25, mature)

1-($2.50, 52 pgs.)-Peter Milligan scripts in all		4.00
2-41,45-49,51-59: 6-Preview of World Without End. 17-Begin $1.75-c. 33-Metallic ink on-c.		2.50
  41-Begin $1.95-c
42-44-John Constantine app.		3.00
50-($2.95, 52 pgs.)		3.50
60-70: 60-begin $2.25-c		2.50
...: The American Scream (2003, $17.95) r/#1-6		18.00
NOTE: *Bachalo a-1-9, 11-13, 15-21, 23-26, 33-39, 42-45, 47, 49, 50; c-30, 33-41.*

SHADO: SONG OF THE DRAGON (See Green Arrow #63-66)
DC Comics: 1992 - No. 4, 1992 ($4.95, limited series, 52 pgs.)

Book One - Four: Grell scripts; Morrow-a(i)		5.00

SHADOW, THE (See Batman #253, 259 & Marvel Graphic Novel #35)

SHADOW, THE (Pulp, radio)
Archie Comics (Radio Comics): Aug, 1964 - No. 8, Sept, 1965 (All 12¢)

1-Jerrry Siegel scripts in all; Shadow-c.	8	16	24	52	86	120
2-8: 2-App. in super-hero costume on-c only; Reinman-a(backup). 3-Superhero begins;						
Reinman-a (book-length novel). 3,4,6,7-The Fly 1 pg. strips. 4-8-Reinman-a. 5-8-Siegel						
scripts. 7-Shield app.	5	10	15	30	48	65

SHADOW, THE
National Periodical Publications: Oct-Nov, 1973 - No. 12, Aug-Sept, 1975

1-Kaluta-a begins	5	10	15	32	51	70
2	3	6	9	17	25	32
3-Kaluta/Wrightson-a	3	6	9	19	29	38
4,6-Kaluta-a ends. 4-Chaykin, Wrightson part-i	3	6	9	16	22	28
5,7-12: 11-The Avenger (pulp character) x-over	2	4	6	9	13	16
NOTE: *Craig a-10. Cruz a-10-12. Kaluta a-1, 2, 3p, 4, 6; c-1-4, 6, 10-12. Kubert c-9. Robbins a-5, 7-9; c-5, 7, 8.*

SHADOW, THE
DC Comics: May, 1986 - No. 4, Aug, 1986 (limited series)

1-4: Howard Chaykin art in all		3.00
Blood & Judgement ($12.95)-r/1-4		13.00

SHADOW, THE
DC Comics: Aug, 1987 - No. 19, Jan, 1989 ($1.50)

1-19: Andrew Helfer scripts in all.		3.00
Annual 1,2 (12/87, '88,)-2-The Shadow dies; origin retold (story inspired by the movie		4.00
  "Citizen Kane").
NOTE: *Kyle Baker a-7i, 8-19, Annual 1. Chaykin c-Annual 1. Helfer scripts in all.
Orlando a-Annual 1. Rogers c-7. Sienkiewicz c/a-1-6.*

SHADOW, THE (Movie)
Dark Horse Comics: June, 1994 - No. 2, July, 1994 ($2.50, limited series)

1,2-Adaptation from Universal Pictures film		3.00
NOTE: *Kaluta c/a-1, 2.*

SHADOW AND DOC SAVAGE, THE
Dark Horse Comics: July, 1995 - No. 2, Aug, 1995 ($2.95, limited series)

1,2		3.50

SHADOW AND THE MYSTERIOUS 3, THE
Dark Horse Comics: Sept, 1994 ($2.95, one-shot)

1-Kaluta co-scripts.		3.00
NOTE: *Stevens c-1.*

SHADOW CABINET (See Heroes)
DC Comics (Milestone): Jan, 1994 - No. 17, Oct, 1995 ($1.75/$2.50)

0,1-17: 0-($2.50, 52 pgs.)-Silver ink-c; Simonson-c. 1-Byrne-c		2.50

SHADOW COMICS (Pulp, radio)
Street & Smith Publications: Mar, 1940 - V9#5, Aug-Sept, 1949

NOTE: *The Shadow first appeared on radio in 1929 and was featured in pulps beginning in April, 1931, written by Walter Gibson. The early covers of this series were reprinted from the pulp covers.*

	GD	VG	FN	VF	VF/NM	NM-
V1#1-Shadow, Doc Savage, Bill Barnes, Nick Carter (radio), Frank Merriwell, Iron Munro,						
the Astonishing Man begin	457	914	1371	3200	5600	8000
2-The Avenger begins, ends #6; Capt. Fury only app.						
	204	408	612	1275	2113	2950
3(nn-5/40)-Norgil the Magician app.; cover is exact swipe of Shadow pulp from 1/33						
	145	290	435	906	1503	2100
4,5: 4-The Three Musketeers begins, ends #8. 5-Doc Savage ends						
	110	220	330	688	1144	1600
6,8,9: 9-Norgil the Magician app.	93	186	279	581	966	1350
7-Origin/1st app. The Hooded Wasp & Wasplet (11/40); series ends V3#8;						
Hooded Wasp/Wasplet app. on-c thru #9	98	196	294	613	1019	1425
10-Origin The Iron Ghost, ends #11; The Dead End Kids begins, ends #14						
	93	184	279	581	966	1350
11-Origin Hooded Wasp & Wasplet retold	93	184	279	581	966	1350
12-Dead End Kids app.	86	172	258	538	894	1250
V2#1(11/41)	83	166	249	519	860	1200
2-(Rare) Giant ant-c; Dead End Kids story	152	304	456	950	1575	2200
3-Origin & 1st app. Supersnipe (3/42); series begins; Little Nemo story						
	134	268	402	838	1394	1950
4,5: 4,8-Little Nemo story	72	144	216	450	750	1050
6-9: 6-Blackstone the Magician story	69	138	207	431	716	1000
10,12: 10-Supersnipe app.	67	134	201	419	697	975
11-Classic Devil Kyoti World War 2 sunburst-c	74	148	222	463	769	1075
V3#1-5,7-12: 10-Doc Savage begins, not in V5#5, V6#10-12, V8#4						
	66	132	198	413	682	950
6-Classic underwater-c	72	144	216	450	750	1050
V4#1-12	46	92	138	281	466	650
V5#1-12	41	82	123	256	416	575
V6#1-11: 9-Intro. Shadow, Jr. (12/46)	40	80	120	235	368	500
12-Powell-c/a; atom bomb panels	41	82	123	256	416	575
V7#1,2,5,7-9,12: 2,5-Shadow, Jr. app.; Powell-c/a	40	80	120	235	368	500
3,6,11-Powell-c/a	43	86	129	262	431	600
4-Powell-c/a; Atom bomb panels	45	90	135	275	450	625
10(1/48)-Flying Saucer-c/story (2nd of this theme; see The Spirit 9/28/47); Powell-c/a						
	57	114	171	356	591	825
V8#1-12-Powell-a. 8-Powell Spider-c/a	43	86	129	262	431	600
V9#1,5-Powell-a	41	82	123	256	416	575
2-4-Powell-c/a	43	86	129	262	431	600
NOTE: *Binder c-V3#1. Powell art in most issues beginning V6#12. Painted c-1-6.*

SHADOWDRAGON
DC Comics: 1995 ($3.50, annual)

Annual 1-Year One story		3.50

SHADOW EMPIRES: FAITH CONQUERS
Dark Horse Comics: Aug, 1994 - No. 4, Nov, 1994 ($2.95, limited series)

1-4		3.00

SHADOWHAWK (See Images of Shadowhawk, New Shadowhawk, Shadowhawk II, Shadowhawk III & Youngblood #2)
Image Comics (Shadowline Ink): Aug, 1992 - No. 4, Mar, 1993; No. 12, Aug, 1994 - No. 18, May, 1995 ($1.95/$2.50)

1-($2.50)-Embossed silver foil stamped-c; Valentino/Liefeld-c; Valentino-c/a/		4.00
  scripts in all; has coupon for Image #0; 1st Shadowline Ink title
1-With coupon missing		2.00
1-($1.95)-Newsstand version w/o foil stamp		2.00
2-13,0,1418: 2-Shadowhawk poster w/McFarlane-i; brief Spawn app.; wraparound-c w/silver		2.50
  ink highlights. 3-($2.50)-Glow-in-the-dark-c. 4-Savage Dragon-c/story; Valentino/Larsen-c.
  5-11-(See Shadowhawk II and III). 12-Cont'd from Shadowhawk III; pull-out poster by
  Texeira.13-w/ShadowBone poster; WildC.A.T.s app. 0 (10/94)-Liefeld c/a/story; ShadowBart
  poster. 14-(10/94, $2.50)-The Others app. 17-Spawn app.; story cont'd
  from Badrock & Co. #6. 18-Shadowhawk dies; Savage Dragon & Brigade app.
Special 1(12/94, $3.50, 52 pgs.)-Silver Age Shadowhawk flip book		3.50
Gallery (4/94, $1.95)		2.50
Out of the Shadows ($19.95)-r/Youngblood #2, Shadowhawk #1-4, Image Zero #0,		20.00
  Operation: Urban Storm (Never published)
.../Vampirella (2/95, $4.95)-Pt.2 of x-over (See Vampirella/Shadowhawk for Pt. 1)		5.00
NOTE: *Shadowhawk was originally a four issue limited series. The story continued in Shadowhawk II, Shadowhawk III & then became Shadowhawk again with issue #12.*

SHADOWHAWK II (Follows Shadowhawk #4)
Image Comics (Shadowline Ink): V2#1, May, 1993 - V2#3, Aug, 1993 ($3.50/$1.95/$2.95,

Shadowman #1 © VAL

Shadowpact #1 © DC

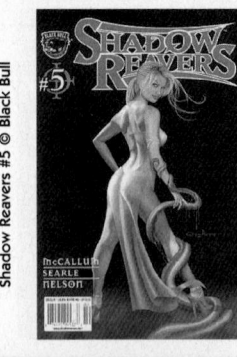

Shadow Reavers #5 © Black Bull

	GD 2.0	VG 4.0	FN 6.0	VF 8.0	VF/NM 9.0	NM- 9.2

limited series)
V2#1 ($3.50)-Cont'd from Shadowhawk #4; die-cut mirricard-c ... 3.50
2 ($1.95)-Foil embossed logo; reveals identity; gold-c variant exists ... 2.50
3 ($2.95)-Pop-up-c w/Pact ashcan insert ... 3.00

SHADOWHAWK III (Follows Shadowhawk II #3)
Image Comics (Shadowline Ink): V3#1, Nov, 1993 - V3#4, Mar, 1994 ($1.95, limited series);
V3#1-4: 1-Cont'd from Shadowhawk II; intro Valentine; gold & red foil stamped-c variations.
2-(52 pgs.)-Shadowhawk contracts HIV virus; U.S. Male by M. Anderson (p) in free
16 pg.insert. 4-Continues in Shadowhawk #12 ... 2.50

SHADOWHAWK (Volume 2) (Also see New Man #4)
Image Comics: May, 2005 - Present ($2.99/$3.50)
1-4-Eddie Collins as Shadowhawk; Rodríguez-a; Valentino-co-plotter ... 3.00
5-15-($3.50) 5-Cover swipe of Superman Vs. Spider-Man treasury edition ... 3.50
...One Shot #1 (7/06, $1.99) r/Return of Shadowhawk ... 2.50
Return of Shadowhawk (12/04, $2.99) Valentino-s/a/c; Eddie Collins origin retold ... 3.00

SHADOWHAWKS OF LEGEND
Image Comics (Shadowline Ink): Nov, 1995 ($4.95, one-shot)
nn-Stories of past Shadowhawks by Kurt Busiek, Beau Smith & Alan Moore ... 5.00

SHADOW, THE: HELL'S HEAT WAVE (Movie, pulp, radio)
Dark Horse Comics: Apr, 1995 - No. 3, June, 1995 ($2.95, limited series)
1-3: Kaluta story ... 3.00

SHADOWHUNT SPECIAL
Image Comics (Extreme Studios): Apr, 1996 ($2.50)
1-Retells origin of past Shadowhawks; Valentino script; Chapel app. ... 2.50

SHADOW, THE: IN THE COILS OF THE LEVIATHAN (Movie, pulp, radio)
Dark Horse Comics: Oct, 1993 - No. 4, Apr, 1994 ($2.95, limited series)
1-4-Kaluta-c & co-scripter ... 3.00
Trade paperback (10/94, $13.95)-r/1-4 ... 14.00

SHADOWLINE SAGA: CRITICAL MASS, A
Marvel Comics (Epic): Jan, 1990 - No. 7, July, 1990 ($4.95, lim. series, 68 pgs)
1-6: Dr. Zero, Powerline, St. George ... 5.00
7 ($5.95, 84 pgs.)-Morrow-a, Williamson-c(i) ... 6.00

SHADOWMAN (See X-O Manowar #4)
Valiant/Acclaim Comics (Valiant): May, 1992 - No. 43, Dec, 1995 ($2.50)
1-Partial origin ... 5.00
2-5: 3-1st app. Sousa the Soul Eater ... 4.00
6-43: 8-1st app. Master Darque. 16-1st app. Dr. Mirage (8/93). 15-Minor Turok app.
17,18-Archer & Armstrong x-over. 19-Aerosmith-c/story. 23-Dr. Mirage x-over. 24-(4/94).
25-Bound-in trading card. 29-Chaos Effect. 43-Shadowman jumps to his death ... 2.50
0-($2.50, 4/94)-Regular edition ... 2.50
0-($3.50)-Wraparound chromium-c edition ... 3.50
0-Gold ... 15.00
Yearbook 1 (12/94, $3.95) ... 4.00

SHADOWMAN (Volume 2)
Acclaim Comics (Valiant Heroes): Mar, 1997 - No. 20 ($2.50, mature)
1-20: 1-1st app. Zero; Garth Ennis scripts begin, end #4. 2-Zero becomes new Shadowman.
4-Origin; Jack Boniface (original Shadowman) rises from the grave. 5-Jamie Delano scripts
begin. 9-Copycat-c ... 2.50
1-Variant painted cover ... 2.50
#0 Gold ... 5.00

SHADOWMAN (Volume 3)
Acclaim Comics: July, 1999 - No. 5, Nov, 1999 ($3.95/$2.50)
1-($3.95)-Abnett & Lanning-s/Broome & Benjamin-a ... 4.00
2-5-($2.50): 3,4-Flip book with Unity 2000 ... 2.50

SHADOWMASTERS
Marvel Comics: Oct, 1989 - No.4, Jan, 1990 ($3.95, squarebound, 52 pgs.)
1-4: Heath-a(i). 1-Jim Lee-c; story cont'd from Punisher ... 4.00

SHADOW OF THE BATMAN
DC Comics: Dec, 1985 - No. 5, Apr, 1986 ($1.75, limited series)

	GD	VG	FN	VF	VF/NM	NM-
1-Detective-r (all have wraparound-c)	1	2	3	4	5	7

2,3,5: 2-Penguin-c & cameo. 5-Clayface app. ... 5.00
4-Joker-c/story ... 6.00
NOTE: *Austin* a(new)-2i, 3i; r-2-4i. *Rogers* a(new)-1, 2p, 3p, 4, 5; r-1-5p; c-1-5. *Simonson* a-1r.

SHADOW OF THE TORTURER, THE
Innovation: July, 1991 - No. 3, 1992 ($2.50, limited series)

1-3: Based on Pocket Books novel ... 2.50

SHADOW ON THE TRAIL (See Zane Grey & Four Color #604)

SHADOWPACT (See Day of Vengeance)
DC Comics: Jul, 2006 - Present ($2.99)
1-16-Bill Willingham-s; Detective Chimp, Ragman, Blue Devil, Nightshade, Enchantress
and Nightmaster app. 1-Superman app. 13-Zauriel app.; S. Hampton-a ... 3.00
...: The Pentacle Plot TPB (2007, $14.99) r/#1-3,5-8 ... 15.00

SHADOW PLAY (Tales of the Supernatural)
Whitman Publications: June, 1982

	GD	VG	FN	VF	VF/NM	NM-
1-Painted-c	1	2	3	4	5	7

SHADOWPLAY
IDW Publ.: Sept, 2005 - No. 4, Dec, 2005 ($3.99)
1-4-Benson-s/Templesmith-a; Christina Z-s/Wood-a; 2 covers by Templesmith & Wood ... 4.00
TPB (3/06, $17.99) r/series; flip book format ... 18.00

SHADOW REAVERS
Black Bull Ent.: Oct, 2001 - No. 5, Mar, 2002 ($2.99)
1-5-Nelson-a; two covers for each issue ... 3.00
Limited Preview Edition (5/01, no cover price) ... 2.50

SHADOW RIDERS
Marvel Comics UK, Ltd.: June, 1993 - No. 4, Sept, 1993 ($1.75, limited series)
1-($2.50)-Embossed-c; Cable-c/story ... 2.75
2-4-Cable app. 2-Ghost Rider app. ... 2.50

SHADOWS
Image Comics: Feb, 2003 - No. 4, Nov, 2003 ($2.95)
1-4-Jade Dodge-s/Matt Camp-a/c ... 3.00

SHADOWS & LIGHT
Marvel Comics: Feb, 1998 - No. 3, July, 1998 ($2.99, B&W, quarterly)
1-3: 1-B&W anthology of Marvel characters; Black Widow art by Gene Ha, Hulk
by Wrightson, Iron Man by Ditko & Daredevil by Stelfreeze; Stelfreeze painted-c. 2-Weeks,
Sharp, Starlin, Thompson-a. 3-Buscema, Grindberg, Giffen, Layton-a. ... 3.00

SHADOW'S FALL
DC Comics (Vertigo): Nov, 1994 - No. 6, Apr, 1995 ($2.95, limited series)
1-6: Van Fleet-c/a in all. ... 3.00

SHADOWS FROM BEYOND (Formerly Unusual Tales)
Charlton Comics: V2#50, October, 1966

	GD	VG	FN	VF	VF/NM	NM-
V2#50-Ditko-c	3	6	9	20	30	30
40						

SHADOW SLASHER
Pocket Change Comics: No. 0, 1994 - No. 6, 1995? ($2.50, B&W)
0-6 ... 2.50

SHADOW STATE
Broadway Comics: Dec, 1995 - No. 5, Apr, 1996 ($2.50)
1-5: 1,2-Fatale back-up story; Cockrum-a(p) ... 2.50
Preview Edition 1,2 (10-11/95, $2.50, B&W) ... 2.50

SHADOW STRIKES!, THE (Pulp, radio)
DC Comics: Sept, 1989 - No.31, May, 1992 ($1.75)
1-4,7-31: 31-Mignola-c ... 2.50
5,6-Doc Savage x-over ... 4.00
Annual 1 (1989, $3.50, 68 pgs.)-Spiegle-a; Kaluta-c ... 3.50

SHADOW WAR OF HAWKMAN
DC Comics: May, 1985 - No. 4, Aug, 1985 (limited series)
1-4 ... 2.50

SHAGGY DOG & THE ABSENT-MINDED PROFESSOR (See Four Color #1199,
Movie Comics & Walt Disney Showcase #46)(Disney-Movie)
Dell Publ. Co.: No. 985, May, 1959

	GD	VG	FN	VF	VF/NM	NM-
Four Color 985	7	14	21	50	83	115

SHALOMAN
Al Wiesner/ Mark 1 Comics: 1989 - Present (B&W)
V1#1-Al Wiesner-s/a in all ... 4.50
2-9 ... 2.50
V2 #1(The New Adventures)-4,6-10, V3 (The Legend of...) #1-12 ... 2.75
V2 #5 (Color)-Shows Vol 2, No. 4 in indicia ... 3.00
V4 (The Saga of ...) #1(2004), 2-7 ... 2.75

SHAMAN'S TEARS (Also see Maggie the Cat)

Shanna, The She-Devil: Survival of the Fittest #1 © MAR

Shaun of the Dead #1 © Universal Studios

Shazam!: The Monster Society of Evi #1 © DC

	GD 2.0	VG 4.0	FN 6.0	VF 8.0	VF/NM 9.0	NM- 9.2

Image Comics (Creative Fire Studio): 5/93 - No. 2, 8/93; No. 3, 11/94 - No. 0, 1/96 ($2.50/$1.95)

0-2: 0-(DEC-c, 1/96)-Last Issue. 1-(5/93)-Embossed red foil-c; Grell-c/a & scripts in all.
2-Cover unfolds into poster (8/93-c, 7/93 inside) — 2.50
3-12: 3-Begin $1.95-c. 5-Re-intro Jon Sable. 12-Re-intro Maggie the Cat (1 pg.) — 2.50

SHANG-CHI: MASTER OF KUNG-FU ("Master of Kung Fu" on cover for #1&2)
Marvel Comics: Nov, 2002 - No. 6, Apr, 2003 ($2.99, limited series)

1-6-Moench-s/Gulacy-c/a — 3.00
... Vol. 1: The Hellfire Apocalypse TPB (2003, $14.99) r/#1-6 — 15.00

SHANGRI-LA
Image Comics: Jan, 2004 ($7.95, B&W, square-bound graphic novel)

1-Marc Bryant-s/Shepherd Hendrix-a — 8.00

SHANNA, THE SHE-DEVIL (See Savage Tales #8)
Marvel Comics Group: Dec, 1972 - No. 5, Aug, 1973 (All are 20¢ issues)

	GD 2.0	VG 4.0	FN 6.0	VF 8.0	VF/NM 9.0	NM- 9.2
1-1st app. Shanna; Steranko-c; Tuska-a(p)	3	6	9	17	25	32
2-Steranko-c; heroin drug story	3	6	9	14	19	24
3-5	2	4	6	9	13	16

SHANNA, THE SHE-DEVIL
Marvel Comics: Apr, 2005 - No. 7, Oct, 2005 ($3.50, limited series)

1-7-Reintro of Shanna; Frank Cho-s/a/c in all — 3.50
HC (2005, $24.99, dust jacket) r/#1-7 — 25.00
SC (2006, $16.99) r/#1-7 — 17.00

SHANNA, THE SHE-DEVIL: SURVIVAL OF THE FITTEST
Marvel Comics: Oct, 2007 - No. 4 ($2.99, limited series)

1,2-Khari Evans-a/c; Gray & Palmiotti-s — 3.00

SHAOLIN COWBOY
Burlyman Entertainment: Dec, 2004 - Present ($3.50)

1-7-Geof Darrow-s/a. 3-Moebius-c — 3.50

SHARK FIGHTERS, THE (Movie)
Dell Publishing Co.: Jan, 1957

	GD 2.0	VG 4.0	FN 6.0	VF 8.0	VF/NM 9.0	NM- 9.2
Four Color 762-Buscema-a; photo-c	7	14	21	50	83	115

SHARKY
Image Comics: Feb, 1998 - No. 4, 1998 ($2.50, bi-monthly)

1-4: 1-Mask app.; Elliot-s/a. Horley painted-c. 3-Three covers by Horley, Bisley, & Horley/Elliot. 4-Two covers (swipe of Avengers #4 and wraparound) — 2.50
1-($2.95) "$1,000,000" variant — 3.00
2-($2.50) Savage Dragon variant-c — 2.50

SHARP COMICS (Slightly large size)
H. C. Blackerby: Winter, 1945-46 - V1#2, Spring, 1946 (52 pgs.)

	GD 2.0	VG 4.0	FN 6.0	VF 8.0	VF/NM 9.0	NM- 9.2
V1#1-Origin Dick Royce Planetarian	40	80	120	240	383	525
2-Origin The Pioneer; Michael Morgan, Dick Royce, Sir Gallagher, Planetarian, Steve Hagen, Weeny and Pop app.	36	72	108	208	329	450

SHARPY FOX (See Comic Capers & Funny Frolics)
I. W. Enterprises/Super Comics: 1958; 1963

	GD 2.0	VG 4.0	FN 6.0	VF 8.0	VF/NM 9.0	NM- 9.2
1,2-I.W. Reprint (1958): 2-r/Kiddie Kapers #1	2	4	6	8	10	12
14-Super Reprint (1963)	2	4	6	8	10	14

SHATTER (See Jon Sable #25-30)
First Comics: June, 1985; Dec, 1985 - No. 14, Apr, 1988. ($1.75, Baxter paper/deluxe paper)

1 (6/85)-1st computer generated-a in a comic book (1st printing) — 3.00
1-(2nd print.); 1(12/85)-14: computer generated-a & lettering in all — 2.50
Special 1 (1988) — 2.50

SHATTERED IMAGE
Image Comics (WildStorm Productions): Aug, 1996 - No. 4, Dec, 1996 ($2.50, limited series)

1-4: 1st Image company-wide x-over; Kurt Busiek scripts in all. 1-Tony Daniel-c/a(p). 2-Alex Ross-c/swipe (Kingdom Come) by Ryan Benjamin & Travis Charest — 2.50

SHAUN OF THE DEAD (Movie)
IDW Publishing: June, 2005 - No. 4, Sept, 2005 ($3.99, limited series)

1-4-Adaptation of 2004 movie; Zach Howard-a — 4.00
TPB (12/05, $17.99) r/series; sketch pages and cover gallery — 18.00

SHAZAM (See Giant Comics to Color, Limited Collectors' Edition, Power Of Shazam!and Trials of Shazam!)

SHAZAM! (TV)(See World's Finest #253 for story from unpublished #36)
National Periodical Publ./DC Comics: Feb, 1973 - No. 35, May-June, 1978

1-1st revival of original Captain Marvel since G.A. (origin retold), by C.C. Beck; Mary Marvel

	GD 2.0	VG 4.0	FN 6.0	VF 8.0	VF/NM 9.0	NM- 9.2

& Captain Marvel Jr. app.; Superman-c — 5 10 15 30 48 65

	GD 2.0	VG 4.0	FN 6.0	VF 8.0	VF/NM 9.0	NM- 9.2
2-5: 2-Infinity photo-c.; re-intro Mr. Mind & Tawny. 3-Capt. Marvel-r. (10/46). 4-Origin retold; Capt. Marvel-r. (1949). 5-Capt. Marvel Jr. origin retold; Capt. Marvel-r. (1948, 7 pgs.)	2	4	6	13	18	22
6,7,9-11: 6-photo-c; Capt. Marvel-r (1950, 6 pgs.). 9-Mr. Mind app. 10-Last C.C. Beck issue. 11-Schaffenberger-a begins.	2	4	6	10	14	18
8 (100 pgs.). 8-r/Capt. Marvel Jr. by Raboy; origin/C.M. #80; origin Mary Marvel/C.M.A. #18; origin Mr. Tawny/C.M.A. #79	5	10	15	32	51	70
12-17-(All 100 pgs.). 15-vs. Lex Luthor & Mr. Mind	4	8	12	24	37	50
18-24,26-30: 21-24-All reprints. 26-Sivana app. (10/76). 27-Kid Eternity teams up w/Capt. Marvel. 28-1st S.A. app. of Black Adam. 30-1st DC app. 3 Lt. Marvels	2	4	6	8	10	12
25-1st app. Isis	2	4	6	9	13	16
31-35: 31-1st DC app. Minuteman. 34-Origin Capt. Nazi & Capt. Marvel Jr. retold	2	4	6	9	13	16

NOTE: Reprints in #1-8, 10, 12-17, 21-24. **Beck** a-1-10, 12-17r, 21-24r; c-1, 3-9. **Nasser** c-35p. **Newton** a-35p. **Raboy** a-5r, 8r, 17r. **Schaffenberger** a-11, 14-20, 25, 26, 27p, 28, 29-31p, 33i, 35i; c-20, 22, 23, 25, 26l, 27i, 28-33.

SHAZAM! AND THE SHAZAM FAMILY! ANNUAL
DC Comics: 2002 ($5.95, squarebound, one-shot)

1-Reprints Golden Age stories including 1st Mary Marvel and 1st Black Adam — 6.00

SHAZAM!: POWER OF HOPE
DC Comics: Nov, 2000 ($9.95, treasury size, one-shot)

nn-Painted art by Alex Ross; story by Alex Ross and Paul Dini — 10.00

SHAZAM!: THE MONSTER SOCIETY OF EVIL
DC Comics: 2007 - No. 4, 2007 ($5.99, square-bound, limited series)

1-3: Jeff Smith-s/a/c in all. 1-Retelling of origin. 2-Mary Marvel & Dr. Sivana app. — 6.00

SHAZAM: THE NEW BEGINNING
DC Comics: Apr, 1987 - No. 4, July, 1987 (Legends spin-off) (Limited series)

1-4: 1-New origin & 1st modern app. Captain Marvel; Marvel Family cameo. 2-4-Sivana & Black Adam app. — 3.00

SHEA THEATRE COMICS
Shea Theatre: No date (1940's) (32 pgs.)

	GD 2.0	VG 4.0	FN 6.0	VF 8.0	VF/NM 9.0	NM- 9.2
nn-Contains Rocket Comics; MLJ cover in one color	10	20	30	56	76	95

SHE-BAT (See Murcielaga, She-Bat & Valeria the She-Bat)

SHE-DRAGON (See Savage Dragon #117)
Image Comics: July, 2006 ($5.99, one-shot)

nn- She-Dragon in Dimension-X; origin retold; Franchesco-a/Larsen-s; sketch pages — 6.00

SHEENA (Movie)
Marvel Comics: Dec, 1984 - No. 2, Feb, 1985 (limited series)

1,2-r/Marvel Comics Super Special #34; Tanya Roberts movie — 3.00

SHEENA, QUEEN OF THE JUNGLE (See Jerry Iger's Classic..., Jumbo Comics, & 3-D Sheena)
Fiction House Magazines: Spr, 1942; No. 2, Wint, 1942-43; No. 3, Spr, 1943; No. 4, Fall, 1948; No. 5, Sum, 1949; No. 6, Spr, 1950; No. 7-10, 1950(nd); No. 11, Spr, 1951 - No. 18, Wint, 1952-53 (#1-3: 68 pgs.; #4-7: 52 pgs.)

	GD 2.0	VG 4.0	FN 6.0	VF 8.0	VF/NM 9.0	NM- 9.2
1-Sheena begins	269	538	807	1681	2791	3900
2 (Winter, 1942-43)	114	228	342	713	1182	1650
3 (Spring, 1943)	83	166	249	519	860	1200
4,5 (Fall, 1948, Sum, 1949): 4-New logo; cover swipe from Jumbo #20	52	104	156	317	521	725
6,7 (Spring, 1950, 1950)	44	88	132	268	444	620
8-10(1950 - Win/50, 36 pgs.)	40	80	120	244	392	540
11-18: 15-Cover swipe from Jumbo #43. 18-Used in POP, pg. 98	35	70	105	201	318	435
I.W. Reprint #9-r/#18; c-r/White Princess #3	4	8	12	28	44	60

NOTE: **Baker** c-5-10? **Whitman** c-11-18(most).

SHEENA, QUEEN OF THE JUNGLE
Devil's Due Publishing: Mar, 2007 - Present (99¢/$3.50)

1-3: 1-Rodi-s/Merhoff-a; 5 covers — 3.50
... 99¢ Special (3/07) Revival of the character; Rodi-s/Cummings-a; sketch pages; history — 2.25

SHEENA 3-D SPECIAL (Also see Blackthorne 3-D Series #1)
Eclipse Comics: Jan, 1985 ($2.00)

1-Dave Stevens-c — 5.00

SHE-HULK (Also see The Savage She-Hulk & The Sensational She-Hulk)
Marvel Comics: May, 2004 - No. 12, Apr, 2005 ($2.99)

1-4-Bobillo-a/Slott-s/Granov-c. 1-Avengers app. 4-Spider-Man-c/app. — 3.00

She-Hulk #4 © MAR

Shield-Wizard Comics #4 © MLJ

Ship of Fools #2 © Michael Oeming

	GD 2.0	VG 4.0	FN 6.0	VF 8.0	VF/NM 9.0	NM- 9.2		GD 2.0	VG 4.0	FN 6.0	VF 8.0	VF/NM 9.0	NM- 9.2

5-12: Mayhew-c. 9-12-Pelletier-a. 10-Origin of Titania   3.00
Vol. 1: Single Green Female TPB (2004, $14.99) r/#1-6   15.00
Vol. 2: Superhuman Law TPB (2005, $14.99) r/#7-12   15.00

SHE-HULK (2nd series)
Marvel Comics: Dec, 2005 - Present ($2.99)

1,2,4-7,9-21: 1-Bobillo-a/Slott-s/Horn-c. 1-New Avengers app. 2-Hawkeye-c/app.
  9-Jen marries John Jameson. 12-Thanos app. 16-Wolverine app.   3.00
3-($3.99) 100th She-Hulk issue; new story w/art by various incl. Bobillo, Conner, Mayhew &
  Powell; r/Savage She-Hulk #1 and r/Sensational She-Hulk #1   4.00
8-Civil War   15.00
8-2nd printing with variant Bobillo-c   3.00
Vol. 3: Time Trials (2006, $14.99) r/#1-5; Bobillo sketch page   15.00
Vol. 4: Laws of Attraction (2007, $19.99) r/#6-12; Paul Smith sketch page   20.00

SHERIFF BOB DIXON'S CHUCK WAGON (TV) (See Wild Bill Hickok #22)
Avon Periodicals: Nov, 1950

1-Kinstler-c/a(3)   14   28   42   76   108   140

SHERIFF OF TOMBSTONE
Charlton Comics: Nov, 1958 - No. 17, Sept, 1961

V1#1-Giordano-c; Severin-a   6   12   18   41   66   90
2   4   8   12   22   34   45
3-10   3   6   9   17   25   32
11-17   3   6   9   14   20   25

SHERLOCK HOLMES (See Marvel Preview, New Adventures of..., & Spectacular Stories)

SHERLOCK HOLMES (All New Baffling Adventures of...)(Young Eagle #3 on?)
Charlton Comics: Oct, 1955 - No. 2, Mar, 1956

1-Dr. Neff, Ghost Breaker app.   40   80   120   243   389   535
2   36   72   108   208   329   450

SHERLOCK HOLMES (Also see The Joker)
National Periodical Publications: Sept-Oct, 1975

1-Cruz-a; Simonson-c   3   6   9   16   22   28

SHERRY THE SHOWGIRL (Showgirls #4)
Atlas Comics: July, 1956 - No. 3, Dec, 1956; No. 5, Apr, 1957 - No. 7, Aug, 1957

1-Dan DeCarlo-c/a in all   16   32   48   94   147   200
2   12   24   36   67   94   120
3,5-7   10   20   30   58   79   100

SHE'S JOSIE (See Josie)

SHEVA'S WAR
DC Comics (Helix): Oct, 1998 - No. 5, Feb, 1999 ($2.95, mini-series)

1-5-Christopher Moeller-s/painted-a/c   3.00

SHI (one-shots and TPBs)
Crusade Comics

...: Akai (2001, $2.99)-Intro. Victoria Cross; Tucci-a/c; J.C. Vaughn-s   3.00
...: Akai Victoria Cross Ed. ($5.95, edition of 2000) variant Tucci-c   6.00
...: C.G.I. (2001, $4.99) preview of unpublished series   5.00
.../ Cyblade: The Battle for the Independents (9/95, $2.95) Tucci-c; Hellboy, Bone app.   3.00
.../ Cyblade: The Battle for the Independents (9/95, $2.95) Silvestri variant-c   3.00
.../ Daredevil: Honor Thy Mother (1/97, $2.95) Flip book   3.00
...: Judgment Night (200, $3.99) Wolverine app.; Battlebook card and pages; Tucci-a   4.00
...: Kaidan (10/96, $2.95) Two covers; Tucci-c; Jae Lee wraparound-c   3.00
...: Masquerade (3/98, $3.50) Painted art by Lago, Texeira, and others   3.50
...: Nightstalkers (9/97, $3.50) Painted art by Val Mayerik   3.50
...: Rekishi (1/97, $2.95) Character bios and story summaries of Shi: The Way of the Warrior
  told in Detective Joe Labianca's point of view; Christopher Golden script; Tucci-c;
  J.G. Jones-a; flip book w/Shi: East Wind Rain preview   3.00
...: The Art of War Tourbook (1998, $4.95) Blank cover for sketches; early Tucci-a inside   5.00
.../ Vampirella (10/97, $2.95) Ellis-s/Lau-a   3.00
... Vs. Tomoe (8/96, $3.95) Tucci-a/scripts; wraparound foil-c   4.00
... Vs. Tomoe (6/96, $5.00. B&W)-Preview Ed.; sold at San Diego Comic Con   5.00
The Definitive Shi Vol. 1 (2006-2007, $24.99, TPB) B&W r/Way of the Warrior, Tomoe, Rekishi,
  and Senryaku series; cover gallery with sketches; Tucci & Sparacio-a   25.00

SHI: BLACK, WHITE AND RED
Crusade Comics: Mar, 1998 - No. 2, May, 1998 ($2.95, B&W&Red, mini-series)

1,2-J.G. Jones-painted art   3.00
...- Year of the Dragon Collected Edition (2000, $5.95) r/#1&2   6.00

SHIDIMA
Image Comics: Jan, 2001 - No. 7, Nov, 2002 ($2.95, limited series)

1-7-Prequel to Warlands   3.00

#0-(10/01, $2.25) Short story and sketch pages   2.50

SHI: EAST WIND RAIN
Crusade Comics: Nov, 1997 - No. 2, Feb, 1998 ($3.50, limited series)

1,2-Shi at WW2 Pearl Harbor   3.50

S.H.I.E.L.D. (Nick Fury & His Agents of...) (Also see Nick Fury)
Marvel Comics Group: Feb, 1973 - No. 5, Oct, 1973 (All 20¢ issues)

1-All contain reprint stories from Strange Tales #146-155; new Steranko-c
     2   4   6   10   14   18
2-New Steranko flag-c   2   4   6   8   11   14
3-5: 3-Kirby/Steranko-c(r). 4-Steranko-c(r)   1   2   3   5   7   9
NOTE: *Buscema* a-3p(r). *Kirby* layouts 1-5; c-3 (w/Steranko). *Steranko* a-3r, 4r(2).

SHIELD, THE (Becomes Shield-Steel Sterling #3; #1 titled Lancelot Strong; also see Advs. of
the Fly, Double Life of Private Strong, Fly Man, Mighty Comics, The Mighty Crusaders,
The Original... & Pep Comics #1)
Archie Enterprises, Inc.: June, 1983 - No. 2, Aug, 1983

1,2-Kaniger app. 2-Kaniger-s   4.00
America's 1st Patriotic Comic Book Hero, The Shield (2002, $12.95, TPB) r/Pep Comics #1-5,
  Shield-Wizard Comics #1; foreward by Robert M. Overstreet   13.00

SHIELD, THE: SPOTLIGHT (TV)
IDW Publishing: Jan, 2004 - No. 5, May, 2004 ($3.99)

1-5-Jeff Marriote-s/Jean Diaz-a/Tommy Lee Edwards-c   4.00
TPB (7/04, $19.99) r/#1-5; Michael Chiklis photo-c   20.00

SHIELD-STEEL STERLING (Formerly The Shield)
Archie Enterprises, Inc.: No. 3, Dec, 1983 (Becomes Steel Sterling No. 4)

3-Nino-a; Steel Sterling by Kaniger & Barreto   3.00

SHIELD WIZARD COMICS (Also see Pep Comics & Top-Notch Comics)
MLJ Magazines: Summer, 1940 - No. 13, Spring, 1944

1-(V1#5 on inside)-Origin The Shield by Irving Novick & The Wizard by Ed Ashe, Jr; Flag-c
     503   1006   1509   3521   6161   8800
2-(Winter/40)-Origin The Shield retold; Wizard's sidekick, Roy the Super Boy begins
  (see Top-Notch #8 for 1st app.)   259   518   777   1619   2685   3750
3,4   162   324   486   1013   1682   2350
5-Dusty, the Boy Detective begins   136   272   408   850   1413   1975
6,7: 6-Roy the Super Boy app. 7-Shield dons new costume (Summer, 1942); S & K-c?
     133   266   399   831   1378   1925
8-Bondage-c; Hitler photo on-c   136   272   408   850   1413   1975
9-13: 9,13-Bondage-c   91   182   273   569   947   1325
NOTE: *Bob Montana* c-13. *Novick* c-1-6,8-11. *Harry Sahle* c-12.

SHI: FAN EDITIONS
Crusade Comics: 1997

1-3-Two covers polybagged in FAN #19-21   3.00
1-3-Gold editions   4.00

SHI: HEAVEN AND EARTH
Crusade Comics: June, 1997 - No. 4, Apr, 1998 ($2.95)

1-4   3.00
4-($4.95) Pencil-c variant   5.00
Rising Sun Edition-signed by Tucci in FanClub Starter Pack   4.00
"Tora No Shi" variant-c   3.00

SHI: JU-NEN
Dark Horse Comics: July, 2004 - No. 4, May, 2005 ($2.99, mini-series)

1-4-Tucci-a/Tucci & Vaughn-s; variant covers   3.00
TPB (2/06, $12.95) r/#1-4; Tucci and Sparacio-c   13.00

SHINING KNIGHT (See Adventure Comics #66)

SHINOBI (Based on Sega video game)
Dark Horse Comics: Aug, 2002 ($2.99, one-shot)

1-Medina-a/c   3.00

SHIP AHOY
Spotlight Publishers: Nov, 1944 (52 pgs.)

1-L. B. Cole-c   19   38   57   109   172   235

SHIP OF FOOLS
Image Comics: Aug, 1997 - No. 3 ($2.95, B&W)

0-3-Glass-s/Oeming-a   3.00

SHI: POISONED PARADISE
Avatar Press: July, 2002 - No. 2, Aug, 2002 ($3.50, limited series)

1,2-Vaughn and Tucci-s/Waller-a; 1-Four covers   3.50

Shi: The Way of the Warrior #2
© Billy Tucci

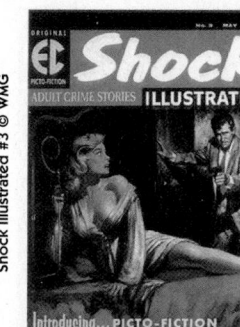

Shock Illustrated #3 © WMG

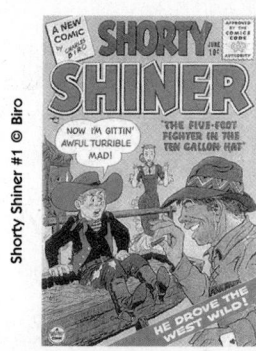

Shorty Shiner #1 © Biro

	GD 2.0	VG 4.0	FN 6.0	VF 8.0	VF/NM 9.0	NM- 9.2

SHIPWRECKED! (Disney-Movie)
Disney Comics: 1990 ($5.95, graphic novel, 68 pgs.)

nn-adaptation; Spiegle-a						6.00

SHI: SEMPO
Avatar Press: Aug, 2003 - No. 2, ($3.50, B&W, limited series)

1,2-Vaughn and Tucci-s/Alves-a; Four covers						3.50

SHI: SENRYAKU
Crusade Comics: Aug, 1995 - No. 3, Nov, 1995 ($2.95, limited series)

1-3: 1-Tucci-s/c; Quesada, Darrow, Sim, Lee, Smith-a. 2-Tucci-c; Silvestri, Balent, Perez, Mack-a. 3-Jusko-c; Hughes, Ramos, Bell, Moore-a						3.00
1-variant-c (no logo)						4.00
Hardcover ($24.95)-r/#1-3; Frazetta-c.						25.00
Trade Paperback ($13.95)-r/#1-3; Frazetta-c.						14.00

SHI: THE ILLUSTRATED WARRIOR
Crusade Comics: 2002 - No. 7, 2003 ($2.99, B&W)

1-7-Story text with Tucci full page art						3.00

SHI: THE SERIES
Crusade Comics: Aug, 1997 - No. 13 ($2.95, color #1-10, B&W #11)

1-10						3.00
11-13: 11-B&W. 12-Color; Lau-a						3.00
#0 Convention Edition						5.00

SHI: THE WAY OF THE WARRIOR
Crusade Comics: Mar, 1994 - No. 12, Apr, 1997 ($2.50/$2.95)

1/2						4.00
1	2	4	6	8	10	12
1-Commemorative ed., B&W, new-c; given out at 1994 San Diego Comic Con	2	4	6	10	14	18
1-Fan appreciation edition -r/#1						2.50
1-Fan appreciation edition (variant)						6.00
1- 10th Anniversary Edition (2004, $2.99)						3.00
2						5.00
2-Commemorative edition (3,000)	2	4	6	9	13	16
2-Fan appreciation edition -r/#2						2.50
3						4.00
4-7: 4-Silvestri poster. 7-Tomoe app.						2.50
5,6: 5-Silvestri variant-c. 6-Tomoe #1 variant-c						3.00
5-Gold edition						12.00
6,8-12: 6-Fan appreciation edition						2.50
8-Combo Gold edition						6.00
8-Signed Edition-(5000)						3.00
Trade paperback (1995, $12.95)-r/#1-4						13.00
Trade paperback (1995, $14.95)-r/#1-4 revised; Julie Bell-c						15.00

SHI: YEAR OF THE DRAGON
Crusade Comics: 2000 - No. 3, 2000 ($2.99, limited series)

1-3: 1-Two covers; Tucci-a/c; flashback to teen-aged Ana						3.00

SHMOO (See Al Capp's... & Washable Jones &...)

SHOCK (Magazine)
Stanley Publ.: May, 1969 - V3#4, Sept, 1971 (B&W reprints from horror comics, including some pre-code) (No V2#1,3)

V1#1-Cover-r/Weird Tales of the Future #7 by Bernard Baily; r/Weird Chills #1	6	12	18	41	66	90
2-Wolverton-r/Weird Mysteries 5; r-Weird Mysteries #7 used in SOTI; cover reprints cover to Weird Chills #1	5	10	15	32	51	70
3,5,6	4	8	12	22	34	45
4-Harrison/Williamson-r/Forbid. Worlds #6	4	8	12	24	37	50
V2#2(5/70), V1#8(7/70), V2#4(9/70)-6(1/71), V3#1-4: V2#4-Cover swipe from Weird Mysteries #6	3	6	9	20	30	40

NOTE: Disbrow r-V2#4; Bondage c-V1#4, V2#6, V3#1.

SHOCK DETECTIVE CASES (Formerly Crime Fighting Detective)
(Becomes Spook Detective Cases No. 22)
Star Publications: No. 20, Sept, 1952 - No. 21, Nov, 1952

20,21-L.B. Cole-c; based on true crime cases	23	46	69	132	209	285

NOTE: Palais a-20. 21-Fox-r.

SHOCK ILLUSTRATED (...Adult Crime Stories; Magazine format)
E. C. Comics: Sept-Oct, 1955 - No. 3, Spring, 1956 (Adult Entertainment on-c #1,2)(All 25¢)

1-All by Kamen; drugs, prostitution, wife swapping	17	34	51	98	154	210
2-Williamson-a redrawn from Crime SuspenStories #13 plus Ingels, Crandall, Evans & part Torres-i; painted-c	18	36	54	103	162	220

3-Only 100 known copies bound & given away at E.C. office; Crandall, Evans-a; painted-c; shows May, 1956 on-c

	110	220	330	688	1144	1600

SHOCKING MYSTERY CASES (Formerly Thrilling Crime Cases)
Star Publications: No. 50, Sept, 1952 - No. 60, Oct, 1954 (All crime reprints?)

50-Disbrow "Frankenstein" story	42	84	126	256	421	585
51-Disbrow-a	27	54	81	156	246	335
52-60: 56-Drug use story	25	50	75	148	232	315

NOTE: L. B. Cole covers on all; a-60(2 pgs.). Hollingsworth a-52. Morisi a-55.

SHOCKING TALES DIGEST MAGAZINE
Harvey Publications: Oct, 1981 (95¢)

1-1957-58-r; Powell, Kirby, Nostrand-a	2	4	6	8	11	14

SHOCK ROCKETS
Image Comics (Gorilla): Apr, 2000 - No. 6, Oct, 2000 ($2.50)

1-6-Busiek-s/Immonen & Grawbadger-a. 6-Flip book w/Superstar preview						2.50
...: We Have Ignition TPB (Dark Horse, 8/04, $14.95, 6" x 9") r/#1-6						15.00

SHOCK SUSPENSTORIES (Also see EC Archives • Shock SuspenStories)
E. C. Comics: Feb-Mar, 1952 - No. 18, Dec-Jan, 1954-55

1-Classic Feldstein electrocution-c	82	162	243	648	1012	1375
2	45	90	135	360	560	760
3,4: 4-Used in SOTI, pg. 387,388	33	66	99	264	415	565
5-Hanging-c	38	76	114	304	477	650
6-Classic hooded vigilante bondage-c	47	94	141	376	588	800
7-Classic face melting-c	49	98	147	392	609	825
8-Williamson-a	32	64	96	256	403	550
9-11: 9-Injury to eye panel. 10-Junkie story	28	56	84	224	350	475
12- "The Monkey" classic junkie cover/story; anti-drug propaganda issue	35	70	105	280	440	600
13-Frazetta's only solo story for E.C., 7 pgs.	38	76	114	304	477	650
14-Used in Senate Investigation hearings	23	46	69	184	285	385
15-Used in 1954 Reader's Digest article, "For the Kiddies to Read"	21	42	63	168	259	350
16-18: 16- "Red Dupe" editorial; rape story	19	38	57	152	241	330

NOTE: Ray Bradbury adaptations-1, 7, 9. Craig a-13; c-11. Crandall a-9-13, 15-18. Davis a-1-5. Evans a-7, 8, 14-18; c-16-18. Feldstein c-1, 7-9, 12. Ingels a-1, 2, 6. Kamen a-in all; c-10, 13, 15. Krigstein a-14, 18. Orlando a-1, 3-7, 9, 10, 12, 16, 17. Wood a-2-15; c-2-6, 14.

SHOCK SUSPENSTORIES (Also see EC Archives • Shock SuspenStories)
Russ Cochran/Gemstone Publishing: Sept, 1992 - No. 18, Dec, 1996 ($1.50/$2.00/$2.50, quarterly)

1-18: 1-3: Reprints with original-c. 17-r/HOF #17						2.50

SHOGUN WARRIORS
Marvel Comics Group: Feb, 1979 - No. 20, Sept, 1980 (Based on Mattel toys of the classic Japanese animation characters) (1-3: 35¢; 4-19: 40¢; 20: 50¢)

1-Raydeen, Combatra, & Dangard Ace begin; Trimpe-a	2	4	6	8	10	12
2-20: 2-Lord Maurkon & Elementals of Evil app.; Rok-Korr app. 6-Shogun vs. Shogun. 7,8-Cerberus. 9-Starchild. 11-Austin-c. 12-Simonson-a. 14-16-Doctor Demonicus. 17-Juggernaut. 19,20-FF x-over	1	2	3	5	6	8

SHOOK UP (Magazine) (Satire)
Dodsworth Publ. Co.: Nov, 1958

V1#1	4	8	12	26	41	55

SHORT RIBS
Dell Publishing Co.: No. 1333, Apr - June, 1962

Four Color 1333	5	10	15	35	55	75

SHORTSTOP SQUAD (Baseball)
Ultimate Sports Ent. Inc.: 1999 ($3.95, one-shot)

1-Ripken Jr., Larkin, Jeter, Rodriguez app.; Edwards-c/a						4.00

SHORT STORY COMICS (See Hello Pal,...)

SHORTY SHINER (The Five-Foot Fighter in the Ten Gallon Hat)
Dandy Magazine (Charles Biro): June, 1956 - No. 3, Oct, 1956

1	7	14	21	37	46	55
2,3	5	10	15	24	30	35

SHOTGUN SLADE (TV)
Dell Publishing Co.: No. 1111, July-Sept, 1960

Four Color 1111-Photo-c	6	12	18	41	66	90

SHOWCASE (See Cancelled Comic Cavalcade & New Talent...)
National Per. Publ./DC Comics: 3-4/56 - No. 93, 9/70; No. 94, 8-9/77 - No. 104, 9/78

1-Fire Fighters; w/Fireman Farrell	270	540	810	2363	4432	6500

Showcase #14 © DC

Showcase #76 © DC

Showcase '94 #2 © DC

	GD 2.0	VG 4.0	FN 6.0	VF 8.0	VF/NM 9.0	NM- 9.2
2-Kings of the Wild; Kubert-a (animal stories)	83	166	249	706	1303	1900
3-The Frogmen by Russ Heath; Heath greytone-a (early DC example, 7-8/56)						
	83	166	249	706	1303	1900
4-Origin/1st app. The Flash (1st DC Silver Age hero, Sept-Oct, 1956); Kanigher-s; Infantino & Kubert-c/a; 1st app. Iris West and The Turtle; r/in Secret Origins #1 ('61 & '73); Flash shown reading G.A. Flash Comics #13; back-up story w/Broome-s/Infantino & Kubert-a						
	1333	2666	4000	15,000	30,000	45,000
5-Manhunters	80	160	240	680	1265	1850
6-Origin/1st app. Challengers of the Unknown by Kirby, partly r/in Secret Origins #1 & Challengers #64,65 (1st S.A. hero team & 1st original concept S.A. series)(1-2/57)						
	300	1500	2100	2625	4913	7200
7-Challengers of the Unknown by Kirby (2nd app.) reprinted in Challengers of the Unknown #75	152	304	456	1292	2396	3500
8-The Flash (5-6/57, 2nd app.); origin & 1st app. Captain Cold						
	820	1640	2460	7500	12,750	18,000
9-Lois Lane (Pre-#1, 7-8/57) (1st Showcase character to win own series) Superman app. on-c	650	1300	1950	5200	9100	13,000
10-Lois Lane; Jor-el cameo; Superman app. on-c	238	476	714	2083	3892	5700
11-Challengers of the Unknown by Kirby (3rd)	139	278	417	1182	2191	3200
12-Challengers of the Unknown by Kirby (4th)	139	278	417	1182	2191	3200
13-The Flash (3rd app.); origin Mr. Element	320	640	960	2880	5440	8000
14-The Flash (4th app.); origin Dr. Alchemy, former Mr. Element (rare in NM)	332	664	996	2988	5644	8300
15-Space Ranger (7-8/58, 1st app.)	152	304	456	1315	2458	3600
16-Space Ranger (9-10/58, 2nd app.)	75	150	225	638	1182	1725
17-(11-12/58)-Adventures on Other Worlds; origin/1st app. Adam Strange by Gardner Fox & Mike Sekowsky	183	366	549	1600	3000	4400
18-Adventures on Other Worlds (2nd A. Strange)	93	186	279	791	1471	2150
19-Adam Strange; 1st Adam Strange logo	102	204	306	867	1609	2350
20-Rip Hunter; origin & 1st app. (5-6/59); Moreira-a	79	158	237	672	1249	1825
21-Rip Hunter (7-8/59, 2nd app.); Sekowsky-c/a	44	88	132	352	639	925
22-Origin & 1st app. Silver Age Green Lantern by Gil Kane and John Broome (9-10/59); reprinted in Secret Origins #2	372	744	1116	3348	6324	9300
23-Green Lantern (11-12/59, 2nd app.); nuclear explosion-c	130	260	390	1105	2053	3000
24-Green Lantern (1-2/60, 3rd app.)	130	260	390	1105	2053	3000
25,26-Rip Hunter by Kane. 25-Grey tone-c	36	72	108	270	498	725
27-Sea Devils (7-8/60, 1st app.); Heath-c/a	40	140	210	595	1098	1600
28-Sea Devils (9-10/60, 2nd app.); Heath-c/a	38	76	114	285	518	750
29-Sea Devils; Heath-c/a; grey tone c-27-29	41	82	123	328	589	850
30-Origin Silver Age Aquaman (1-2/61) (see Adventure #260 for 1st S.A. origin)	74	148	222	629	1165	1700
31,32-Aquaman	40	80	120	300	550	800
33-Aquaman	40	80	120	300	550	800
34-Origin & 1st app. Silver Age Atom by Gil Kane & Murphy Anderson (9-10/61); reprinted in Secret Origins #2	117	234	351	995	1848	2700
35-The Atom by Gil Kane (2nd); last 10¢ issue	54	108	162	459	855	1250
36-The Atom by Gil Kane (1-2/62, 3rd app.)	44	88	132	352	639	925
37-Metal Men (3-4/62, 1st app.)	57	114	171	485	893	1300
38-Metal Men (5-6/62, 2nd app.)	35	70	105	263	482	700
39-Metal Men (7-8/62, 3rd app.)	27	54	81	219	365	510
40-Metal Men (9-10/62, 4th app.)	24	48	72	179	320	460
41,42-Tommy Tomorrow (parts 1 & 2). 42-Origin	15	30	45	111	198	285
43-Dr. No (James Bond); Nodel-a; originally published as British Classics Illustrated #158A & as #6 in a European Classics series, all with diff. painted-c. This Showcase #43 version is actually censored, deleting all racial skin color and dialogue thought to be racially demeaning (1st DC S.A. movie adaptation)(based on Ian Fleming novel & movie)						
	43	86	129	344	622	900
44-Tommy Tomorrow	11	22	33	75	133	190
45-Sgt. Rock (7-8/63); pre-dates B&B #52; origin retold; Heath-c						
	30	60	90	225	413	600
46,47-Tommy Tomorrow	10	20	30	67	116	165
48,49-Cave Carson (3rd tryout series; see B&B)	8	16	24	58	97	135
50,51-I Spy (Danger Trail-r by Infantino), King Faraday story (#50 has new 4 pg. story)						
	8	16	24	52	86	120
52-Cave Carson	8	16	24	52	86	120
53,54-G.I. Joe (11-12/64, 1-2/65); Heath-a	11	22	33	75	133	190
55-Dr. Fate & Hourman (3-4/65); origin of each in text; 1st solo app. G.A. Green Lantern in Silver Age (pre-dates Gr. Lantern #40); 1st S.A. app. Solomon Grundy						
	24	48	72	175	313	450
56-Dr. Fate & Hourman	14	28	42	102	181	260
57-Enemy Ace by Kubert (7-8/65, 4th app. after Our Army at War #155)						
	20	40	60	146	261	375
58-Enemy Ace by Kubert (5th app.)	17	34	51	128	227	325
59-Teen Titans (11-12/65, 3rd app.)	14	28	42	99	175	250
60-1st S. A. app. The Spectre; Anderson-a (1-2/66); origin in text						
	27	54	81	203	364	525
61-The Spectre by Anderson (2nd app.)	14	28	42	102	181	260
62-Origin & 1st app. Inferior Five (5-6/66)	9	18	27	61	103	145
63,65-Inferior Five. 63-Hulk parody. 65-X-Men parody (11-12/66)						
	6	12	18	41	66	90
64-The Spectre by Anderson (5th app.)	14	28	42	99	175	250
66,67-B'wana Beast	5	10	15	32	51	70
68-Maniaks (1st app., spoof of The Monkees)	5	10	15	35	55	75
69,71-Maniaks. 71-Woody Allen-c/app.	5	10	15	32	51	70
70-Binky (9-10/67)-Tryout issue; 1950's Leave It To Binky reprints with art changes						
	6	12	18	39	62	85
72-Top Gun (Johnny Thunder-r)-Toth-a	5	10	15	32	51	70
73-Origin/1st app. Creeper; Ditko-c/a (3-4/68)	12	24	36	87	156	225
74-Intro/1st app. Anthro; Post-c/a (5/68)	8	16	24	56	93	130
75-Origin/1st app. Hawk & the Dove; Ditko-c/a	11	22	33	79	140	200
76-1st app. Bat Lash (8/68)	7	14	21	49	80	110
77-1st app. Angel & The Ape (9/68)	7	14	21	45	73	100
78-1st app. Jonny Double (11/68)	5	10	15	30	48	65
79-1st app. Dolphin (12/68); Aqualad origin-r	6	12	18	41	66	90
80-1st S.A. app. Phantom Stranger (1/69); Neal Adams-c						
	9	18	27	63	107	150
81-Windy & Willy; r/Many Loves of Dobie Gillis #26 with art changes						
	5	10	15	35	55	75
82-1st app. Nightmaster (5/69) by Grandenetti & Giordano; Kubert-c						
	6	12	18	43	69	95
83,84-Nightmaster by Wrightson w/Jones/Kaluta ink assist in each; Kubert-c. 83-Last 12¢ issue 84-Origin retold; begin 15¢	6	12	18	41	66	90
85-87-Firehair; Kubert-a	3	6	9	16	23	30
88-90-Jason's Quest: 90-Manhunter 2070 app.	3	6	9	14	20	25
91-93-Manhunter 2070: 92-Origin. 93-(9/70) Last 12¢ issue						
	3	6	9	14	20	25
94-Intro/origin new Doom Patrol & Robotman(8-9/77)	2	4	6	10	14	18
95,96-The Doom Patrol. 95-Origin Celsius	1	2	3	5	7	9
97-99-Power Girl; origin-97,98; JSA cameos	1	2	3	5	7	9
100-(52 pgs.)-Most Showcase characters featured	1	2	3	6	9	12
101-103-Hawkman; Adam Strange x-over	1	2	3	5	7	9
104-(52 pgs.)-O.S.S. Spies at War	1	2	3	5	7	9

NOTE: **Anderson** a-22-24i, 34-36i, 55, 56, 60, 61, 64, 101-103i; c-50i, 51i, 55, 56, 60, 61, 64. **Aparo** c-94-96. **Boring** c-10. **Estrada** a-104. **Fraden** c(p)-30, 31, 33. **Heath** c-5, 27-29. **Infantino** c/a(p)-4, 8, 13, 14; c-50p, 51p. **Gil Kane** a-22-24p, 34-36p; c-17-19, 22-24p(w/Giella), 31. **Kane/Anderson** c-34-36. **Kirby** c-11, 12. **Kirby/Stein** c-6, 7. **Kubert** a-2, 4i, 25, 26, 45, 53, 54, 72; c-25, 26, 53, 54, 57, 58, 82-87, 101-104; c-2, 4i. **Moreira** c-5. **Orlando** a-62p, 63p, 97i; c-62, 63, 97i. **Sekowsky** a-65p. **Sparling** a-78. **Staton** a-94, 95-99p, 100; c-97-100p.

SHOWCASE '93
DC Comics: Jan, 1993 - No. 12, Dec, 1993 ($1.95, limited series, 52 pgs.)

1-12: 1-Begin 4 part Catwoman story & 6 part Blue Devil story; begin Cyborg story; Art Adams/Austin-c. 3-Flash by Charest (p). 6-Azrael in Bat-costume (2 pgs.). 7,8-Knightfall parts 13 & 14. 6-10-Deathstroke app. (6,10-cameo). 9,10-Austin-i. 10-Azrael as Batman in new costume app.) Gulacy-c. 11-Perez-c. 12-Creeper app.; Alan Grant scripts						3.00

NOTE: **Chaykin** c-9. **Fabry** c-8. **Giffen** c-3. **Golden** c-3. **Zeck** c-6.

SHOWCASE '94
DC Comics: Jan, 1994 - No. 12, Dec, 1994 ($1.95, limited series, 52 pgs.)

1-12: 1,2-Joker & Gunfire stories. 1-New Gods. 4-Riddler story. 5-Huntress-c/story w/app. new Batman. 6-Huntress-c/story w/app. Robin; Atom story. 7-Penguin story by Peter David, P. Craig Russell, & Michael T. Gilbert; Penguin-c by Jae Lee. 8,9-Scarface origin story by Alan Grant, John Wagner,& Teddy Kristiansen; Prelude to Zero Hour. 10-Zero Hour tie-in story. 11-Man-Bat.						3.00

NOTE: **Alan Grant** scripts-3, 4. **Kelley Jones** c-12. **Mignola** c-3. **Nebres** a(i)-2. **Quesada** c-10. **Russell** a-7p. **Simonson** c-5.

SHOWCASE '95
DC Comics: Jan, 1995 - No. 12, Dec, 1995 ($2.50/$2.95, limited series)

1-4-Supergirl story. 3-Eradicator-c. 4-Thorn c/story						3.00
5-12-Thorn-c/story; begin $2.95-c. 8-Spectre story. 12-The Shade story by James Robinson & Wade Von Grawbadger; Maitresse story by Claremont & Alan Davis						3.00

SHOWCASE '96
DC Comics: Jan, 1996 - No. 12, Dec, 1996 ($2.95, limited series)

1-12: 1-Steve Geppi cameo. 3-Black Canary & Lois Lane-c/story; Deadman story by Jamie Delano & Wade Von Grawbadger, Gary Frank-c. 4-Firebrand & Guardian-c/story; The Shade & Dr. Fate "Times Past" story by James Robinson & Matt Smith begins, ends #5. 6-Superboy-c/story; Atom app.; Capt. Marvel (Mary Marvel)-c/app. 8-Supergirl by David & Dodson. 11-Scare Tactics app. 11,12-Legion of Super-Heroes vs. Brainiac.						
12-Jesse Quick app.						3.00

Showcase Presents: Batgirl Vol. 1 © DC

The Shroud #1 © MAR

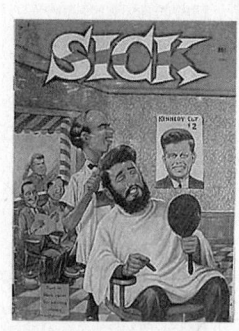

Sick #5 © Feature Pub.

	GD 2.0	VG 4.0	FN 6.0	VF 8.0	VF/NM 9.0	NM- 9.2

SHOWCASE PRESENTS... (B&W archive reprints of DC Silver Age stories)
DC Comics: 2005 - Present ($9.99/$16.99, B&W, over 500 pgs., squarebound)

Adam Strange Vol. 1 (2007, $16.99) r/Showcase #17-19 & Mystery in Space #53-84						17.00
Aquaman Vol. 1 (2007, $16.99) r/Aquaman #1-6 & other early app.						17.00
The Atom Vol. 1 (2007, $16.99) r/Showcase #34-36 & The Atom #1-17						17.00
Batgirl Vol. 1 (2007, $16.99) r/early apps. from Detective #359 (1967) thru 1975						17.00
Batman Vol. 1 (2006, $16.99) r/"new look" from Detective #327-342, Batman #164-174						17.00
Batman Vol. 2 (2007, $16.99) r/"new look" from Detective #343-358, Batman #175-188						17.00
The Brave and the Bold Batman team-ups Vol. 1 (2007, $16.99) r/#59,64,67-71,74-87						17.00
Challengers of the Unknown Vol. 1 (2006, $16.99) r/#1-17 & Showcase #6,7,11,12						17.00
The Elongated Man Vol. 1 ('06, $16.99) r/early apps. in Flash & Detective ('60-'68)						17.00
The Flash Vol. 1 (2007, $16.99) r/Flash Comics #104 (last G.A. issue), Showcase #4,8,13,14 & The Flash #105-119						17.00
Green Arrow Vol. 1 (2006, $16.99) r/Adventure #250-269, Brave and the Bold #50,71,85; Justice League of America #4; World's Finest #95-134,136,138,140						17.00
Green Lantern Vol. 1 (2005, $9.99) r/Showcase #22-24 & Green Lantern #1-17						10.00
Green Lantern Vol. 2 (2007, $16.99) r/Green Lantern #18-38						17.00
Haunted Tank Vol. 1 (2006, $16.99) r/G.I. Combat #87-119, Brave & The Bold #52 and Our Army at War #155; Russ Heath-c						17.00
Hawkman Vol. 1 ('07, $16.99) r/Brave&Bold #34-36,42-44, Mystery in Space #87-90, Hawkman #1-11, and The Atom #7						17.00
The House of Mystery Vol. 1 ('06, $16.99) r/House of Mystery #174-194 ('68-'71)						17.00
The House of Mystery Vol. 2 ('07, $16.99) r/House of Mystery #195-211 ('71-'73)						17.00
Jonah Hex Vol. 1 (2005, $16.99) r/All Star Western #10-12, Weird Western Tales #13,14, 16-33; plus the complete adventures of Outlaw from All Star Western #2-8						17.00
Justice League of America Vol. 1 ('05, $16.99) r/Brave & the Bold #28-30, J.L. of A. #1-16 and Mystery in Space #75						17.00
Justice League of America Vol. 2 ('07, $16.99) r/Justice League of America #17-36						17.00
Legion of Super-Heroes Vol. 1 ('07, $16.99) r/Adventure #247 & early app. thru 1964						17.00
Martian Manhunter Vol. 1 (2007, $16.99) r/Detective #225-304 & Batman #78 (prototype)						17.00
Metamorpho Vol. 1 ('05, $16.99) r/Brave&Bold #57,58,66,68; Metamorpho #1-17;JLA #42						17.00
Phantom Stranger Vol. 1 (2006, $16.99) r/#1-21 (2nd series) & Showcase #80						17.00
Shazam! Vol. 1 ('06, $16.99) r/#1-33						17.00
Superman Vol. 1 (2005, $9.99) r/Action #241-257 & Superman #122-134 (1958-59)						10.00
Superman Vol. 2 ('06, $16.99) r/Action #258-275 & Superman #134-145 (1959-61)						17.00
Superman Vol. 3 ('07, $16.99) r/Action #279-292 & Superman #146-156 & Annual #3,4						17.00
Superman Family Vol. 1 ('06, $16.99) r/Superman's Pal Jimmy Olsen #1-22; Showcase #9 and Superman #22						17.00
The Unknown Soldier Vol. 1 ('06, $16.99) r/Star Spangled War Stories #158-188						17.00
The War That Time Forgot Vol. 1 ('07, $16.99) r/S.S.W.S. #90,92,94-125,127,128						17.00

SHOWGIRLS (Formerly Sherry the Showgirl #3)
Atlas Comics (MPC No. 2): No. 4, 2/57; June, 1957 - No. 2, Aug, 1957

	GD 2.0	VG 4.0	FN 6.0	VF 8.0	VF/NM 9.0	NM- 9.2
4-(2/57) Dan DeCarlo-c/a begins	10	20	30	58	79	100
1-(6/57) Millie, Sherry, Chili, Pearl & Hazel begin	13	26	39	74	105	135
2	10	20	30	58	79	100

SHREK (Movie)
Dark Horse Comics: Sept, 2003 - No. 3, Dec, 2003 ($2.99, limited series)

1-3-Takes place after 1st movie; Evanier-s/Bachs-a; CGI cover						3.00

SHROUD, THE (See Super-Villain Team-Up #5)
Marvel Comics: Mar, 1994 - No. 4, June, 1994 ($1.75, mini-series)

1-4: 1,2,4-Spider-Man & Scorpion app.						2.50

SHROUD OF MYSTERY
Whitman Publications: June, 1982

1	1	2	3	4	5	7

SHRUGGED
Aspen MLT, Inc.: No. 0, June, 2006 - Present ($2.50/$2.99)

0-($2.50) Turner & Mastromauro-s/Gunnell-a; intro. story and character profiles						2.50
1-6-($2.99) 1-Six covers. 2-Three covers						3.00
... : Beginnings (5/06, $1.99) Prequel intro. to Ange and Dev; Gunnell-a; development art						2.50

SHUT UP AND DIE
Image Comics/Halloween: 1998 - No. 3, 1998 ($2.95,B&W, bi-monthly)

1-3: Hudnall-s						3.00

SICK (Sick Special #131) (Magazine) (Satire)
Feature Publ./Headline Publ./Crestwood Publ. Co./Hewfred Publ./ Pyramid Comm./Charlton Publ. No. 109 (4/76) on: Aug, 1960 - No. 134, Fall, 1980

	GD 2.0	VG 4.0	FN 6.0	VF 8.0	VF/NM 9.0	NM- 9.2
V1#1-Jack Paar photo on-c; Torres-a; Untouchables; Ben Hur movie photo-s	16	32	48	118	209	300
2-Torres-a; Elvis app.; Lenny Bruce app.	10	20	30	70	123	175
3-5-Torres-a in all. 3-Khruschev-c; Hitler-s. 4-Newhart-s; Castro-s; John Wayne.						
5-JFK/Castro-c; Elvis pin-up; Hitler.	9	18	27	63	107	150
6-Photo-s of Ricky Nelson & Marilyn Monroe; JFK	9	18	27	65	113	160
V2#1,2,4-8 (#7,8,10-14): 1-(#7) Hitler-s; Brando photo-s. 2-(#8) Dick Clark-s. 4-(#10) Untouchables-c; Candid Camera-s. 5-(#11) Nixon-c; Lone Ranger-s; JFK-s. 6-(#12) Beatnik-c/s. 8-(#14) Liz Taylor pin-up, JFK-s; Dobie Gillis-s; Sinatra & Dean Martin photo-s	8	16	24	58	97	135
3-(#9) Marilyn Monroe/JFK-c; Kingston Trio-s	9	18	27	63	107	150
V3#1-7 (#15-21): 1-(#15) JFK app.; Liz Tayor/Richard Burton-s. 2-(#16) Ben Casey/ Frankenstein-c/s; Hitler photo-s. 5-(#19) Nixon back-c/s; Sinatra photo-s. 6-(#20) 1st Huckleberry Fink-c	5	10	15	35	55	75
8-(#22) Cassius Clay vs. Liston-s; 1st Civil War Blackouts-/Pvt. Bo Reargard w/ Jack Davis-a	6	12	18	39	62	85
V4#1-5 (#23-27): Civil War Blackouts-/Pvt. Bo Reargard w/ Jack Davis-a in all. 1-(#23) Smokey Bear-c; Tarzan-s. 2-(#24) Goldwater & Paar-s; Castro-s. 3-(#25) Frankenstein-c; Cleopatra/Liz Taylor-s; Steve Reeves photo-s. 4-(#26) James Bond-s; Hitler-s. 5-(#27) Taylor/Burton pin-up; Sinatra, Martin, Andress, Ekberg photo-s	6	12	18	26	41	55
28,31,36,39: 31-Pink Panther movie photo-s; Burke's Law-s. 39-Westerns; Elizabeth Montgomery photo-s; Beat mag-s	4	8	12	22	34	45
29,34,37,38: 29-Beatles-c by Jack Davis. 34-Two pg. Beatles-s & photo pin-up. 37-Playboy parody issue. 38-Addams Family-s	4	8	12	26	41	55
30,32,35,40: 30-Beatles photo pin-up; James Bond photo-s. 32-Ian Fleming-s; LBJ-s; Tarzan-s. 35-Beatles cameo; Three Stooges parody. 40-Tarzan-s; Crosby/Hope-s; Beatles parody	4	8	12	28	44	60
33-Ringo Starr photo-c & spoof on "A Hard Day's Night"; inside-c has Beatles photos	6	12	18	39	62	85
41,50,51,53,54,60: 41-Sports Illustrated parody-s. 50-Mod issue; flip-c w/1967 calendar w/Bob Taylor-a. 51-Get Smart-s. 53-Beatles cameo; nudity panels. 54-Monkees-c. 60-TV Daniel Boone-s	3	6	9	19	28	38
42-Fighting American-c revised from Simon/Kirby-s; "Good girl" art by Sparling; profile on Bob Powell; superhero parodies	5	10	15	35	55	75
43-49,52,55-59: 43-Sneaker set begins by Sparling. 45-Has #44 on-c & #45 on inside; TV Westerns-s; Beatles cameo. 46-Hell's Angels-s; NY Mets-s. 47-UFO/Space-c. 49-Men's Adventure mag. parody issue; nudity. 52-LBJ-s. 55-Underground culture spread. 56-Alfred E. Neuman-c; inventors issue. 58-Hippie issue-c/s. 59-Hippie-s	3	6	9	17	22	30
61-64,66-69,71,73,75-80: 63-Tiny Tim-c & poster; Monkees-s. 64-Flip-c. 66-Flip-c; Mod Squad-s. 69-Beatles cameo; Peter Sellers photo-s. 71-Flip-c; Clint Eastwood0s. 76-Nixon-s; Marcus Welby-s. 78-Ma Barker-s; Courtship of Eddie's Father-s; Abbie Hoffman-s	3	6	9	15	21	26
65,70,74: 65-Cassius Clay/Brando/J. Wayne-c; Johnny Carson-s. 70-(9/69) John & Yoko-c, 1/2 pg. story. 74-Clay, Agnew, Namath & others as superheroes-c/s; Easy Rider-s; Ghost and Mrs. Muir-s	3	6	9	16	23	30
72-(84 pgs.) Xmas issue w/2 pg. slick color poster; Tarzan-s; 2 pg. Superman & superheroes-s	4	8	12	20	30	40
81-85,87-95,98,99: 81-(2/71) Woody Allen photo-s. 85 Monster Mag. parody-s; Nixon-s w/Ringo & John cameo. 88-Klute photo-s. 92-Lily Tomlin; Archie Bunker pin-up. 93-Woody Allen	2	4	6	11	16	20
86,96,97,100: 86-John & Yoko, Tiny Tim-c; Love Story movie photo-s. 96-Kung Fu-c; Mummy-s, Dracula & Frankenstein app. 97-Superman-s; 1974 Calendar; Charlie Brown & Snoopy pin-up. 100-Serpico-s; Cosell-s; Jacques Cousteau-s	2	4	6	13	18	22
101-103,105-114,116,119,120: 101-Three Musketeers-s; Dick Tracy-s. 102-Young Frankenstein-s. 103-Kojak-s; Evel Knievel-s. 105-Towering Inferno-s; Peanuts/Snoopy-s. 106-Cher-c/s. 10 7-Jaws-c/s. 108-Pink Panther-c/s; Archie-s. 109-Adam & Eve-s(nudity). 110-Welcome Back Kotter-s. 111-Sonny & Cher-s. 112-King Kong-c/s. 120-Star Trek-s	3	6	9	13	15	16
104,115,117,118: 104-Muhammad Ali-c/s. 115-Charlie's Angels-s. 117-Bionic Woman & Six Million $ Man-c/s; Cher D'Flower begins by Sparling (nudity). 118-Star Wars-s; Popeye-s	2	4	6	11	16	20
121,125,128-130: 122-Darth Vader-s. 123-Jaws II-s. 128-Superman-c/movie parody. 130-Alien movie-s	2	4	6	10	14	18
126,127: 126-(68 pgs.) Battlestar Galactica-c/s; Star Wars-s; Wonder Woman-s. 127-Mork & Mindy-s; Lord of the Rings-s	2	4	6	12	15	18
131-(1980 Special) Star Wars/Star Trek/Flash Gordon wraparound-c/s; Superman parody; Battlestar Galactica-s	2	4	6	13	19	24
132,133: 132-1980 Election-c/s; Apocalypse Now-s. 133-Star Trek-s; Chips-s; Superheroes parody	2	4	6	13	18	22
134 (scarce)(68 pg. Giant)-Star Wars-c; Alien-s; WKRP-s; Taxi-s; MASH-s	4	8	12	21	30	40
Annual 1- 7th Annual Yearbook (1967)-Davis-a, 2 pg. glossy poster insert						
Annual 2- Birthday Annual (1967)-3 pg. Huckleberry Fink fold out	6	12	18	23	34	50

Sigil #22 © CRO

Silent War #1 © MAR

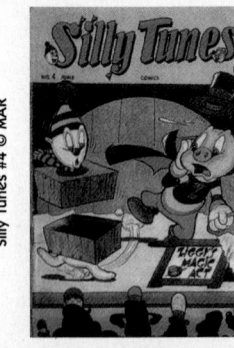

Silly Tunes #4 © MAR

	GD 2.0	VG 4.0	FN 6.0	VF 8.0	VF/NM 9.0	NM- 9.2

	GD 2.0	VG 4.0	FN 6.0	VF 8.0	VF/NM 9.0	NM- 9.2

	4	8	12	20	29	40
Annual 3 (1968) "Big Sick Laff-in" on-c (84 pgs.)-w/psychedelic posters; Frankenstein poster						
	3	6	9	18	27	35
Annual 1969, 1970, 1971	3	6	9	17	25	32
Annual 12,13-(1972,1973, 84 pgs.) 13-Monster-c	3	6	9	17	25	32
Annual 14 (1974, 84 pgs.) Hitler photo-s	3	6	9	17	25	32
Annual 2-4 (1980)	2	4	6	9	13	16
Special 1 (1980) Buck Rogers-c/s; MASH-s	3	6	9	14	19	24
Special 2 (1980) Wraparound Star Wars:Empire Strikes Back-c; Charlie's Angels/Farrah-s; Rocky-s; plus reprints	3	6	9	14	19	24
Yearbook 15(1975, 84 pgs.) Paul Revere-c	3	6	9	16	23	30

NOTE: **Davis** a-42, 87; c-22, 23, 25, 29, 31, 32. **Powell** a-7, 31, 57. **Simon** a-1-3, 10, 41, 42, 87, 99; c-1, 47, 57, 59, 69, 91, 95-97, 99, 100, 102, 107, 112. **Torres** a-1-3, 29, 31, 47, 49. **Tuska** a-14, 41-43. Civil War Blackouts-23, 24. #42 has biography of Bob Powell.

SIDEKICK (Paul Jenkins'...)
Image Comics (Desperado): June, 2006 - No. 5, May, 2007 ($3.50, limited series)

1-5-Paul Jenkins-s/Chris Moreno-a	3.50
... Super Summer Sidekick Spectacular 1 (7/07, $2.99)	3.00

SIDEKICKS
Fanboy Ent., Inc.: Jun, 2000 - No. 3, Apr, 2001 ($2.75, B&W, lim. series)

1-3-J.Torres-s/Takesi Miyazawa-a. 3-Variant-c by Wieringo	2.75
...: Super Fun Summer Special (Oni Press, 7/03, $2.99) art by various incl. Wieringo	3.00
...: The Substitute (Oni Press, 7/02, $2.95)	3.00
...: The Transfer Student TPB (Oni Press, 6/02, $8.95, 9" x 6") r/#1-3	9.00
...: The Transfer Student TPB 2nd Ed. (10/03, $11.95, 9" x 6") r/#1-3; The Substitute	12.00

SIDESHOW
Avon Periodicals: 1949 (one-shot)

	GD	VG	FN	VF	VF/NM	NM-
1-(Rare)-Similar to Bachelor's Diary	36	72	108	208	329	450

SIEGEL AND SHUSTER: DATELINE 1930s
Eclipse Comics: Nov, 1984 - No. 2, Sept, 1985 ($1.50/$1.75, Baxter paper #1)

1,2: 1-Unpublished samples of strips from the '30s; includes 'Interplanetary Police'; Shuster-c. 2 ($1.75, B&W)-unpublished strips; Shuster-c	2.50

SIGIL (Also see CrossGen Chronicles)
CrossGeneration Comics: Jul, 2000 - No. 43, Jan, 2004 ($2.95)

1-43: 1-Barbara Kesel-s/Ben & Ray Lai-a. 12-Waid-s begin. 21-Chuck Dixon-s begin	3.00
...: Mark of Power TPB (5/01, $19.95) r/#1-7; Moeller painted-c	20.00
...: The Marked Man Vol. 2 TPB (2002, $19.95) r/#8-14	20.00
...: The Lizard God Vol. 3 TPB (2002, $15.95) r/#15-20	16.00
Vol. 4: Hostage Planet (4/03, $15.95) r/#21-26	16.00
Vol. 5: Death Match (2003, $15.95) r/#27-32	16.00

SIGMA
Image Comics (WildStorm): March, 1996 - No. 3, June, 1996 ($2.50, limited series)

1-3: 1-"Fire From Heaven" prelude #2; Coker-a. 2-"Fire From Heaven" pt. 6. 3-"Fire From Heaven" pt. 14.	2.50

SILENT DRAGON
DC Comics (WildStorm): Sept, 2005 - No. 6, Feb, 2006 ($2.99, limited series)

1-6-Tokyo 2066 A.D.; Leinil Yu-a/c; Andy Diggle-s	3.00
TPB (2006, $19.99) r/series; sketch page	20.00

SILENT HILL: DEAD/ALIVE
IDW Publishing: Dec, 2005 - No. 5, Apr, 2006 ($3.99, limited series)

1-5-Stakal-a/Ciencin-s. 1-Four covers. 2-5-Two covers	4.00

SILENT HILL: DYING INSIDE
IDW Publishing: Feb, 2004 - No. 5, June, 2004 ($3.99, limited series)

1-5-Based on the Konami computer game. 1-Templesmith-a; Ashley Wood-c	4.00
...: Paint It Black (2/05, $7.49) Ciencin-s/Thomas-a	7.50
...: The Grinning Man 5/05, $7.49) Ciencin-s/Stakal-a	7.50
TPB (8/04, $19.99) r/#1-5; Ashley Wood-c	20.00

SILENT INVASION, THE
Rengade Press: Apr, 1986 - No.12, Mar, 1988 ($1.70/$2.00, B&W)

1-12-UFO sightings of the '50s	3.00
Book 1- reprints ($7.95)	8.00

SILENT MOBIUS
Viz Select Comics: 1991 - No. 5, 1992 ($4.95, color, squarebound, 44 pgs.)

1-5: Japanese stories translated to English	5.00

SILENT SCREAMERS (Based on the Aztech Toys figures)
Image Comics: Oct, 2000 ($4.95)

Nosferatu Issue - Alex Ross front & back-c	5.00

SILENT WAR
Marvel Comics: Mar, 2007 - No. 6, Aug, 2007 ($2.99, limited series)

1-6-Inhumans, Black Bolt and Fantastic Four app.; Hine-s/Irving-a/Watson-c	3.00
TPB (2007, $14.99) r/series	15.00

SILKE
Dark Horse Comics: Jan, 2001 - No. 4, Sept, 2001 ($2.95)

1-4-Tony Daniel-s/a	3.00

SILKEN GHOST
CrossGen Comics: June, 2003 - No. 5, Oct, 2003 ($2.95, limited series)

1-5-Dixon-s/Rosado-a	3.00
Traveler Vol. 1 (2003, $9.95) digest-sized reprint #1-5	10.00

SILLY PILLY (See Frank Luther's...)

SILLY SYMPHONIES (See Dell Giants)

SILLY TUNES
Timely Comics: Fall, 1945 - No. 7, June, 1947

1-Silly Seal, Ziggy Pig begin	22	44	66	126	198	270
2-(2/46)	14	28	42	76	108	140
3-7: 6-New logo	11	22	33	62	86	110

SILVER (See Lone Ranger's Famous Horse...)

SILVER AGE
DC Comics: July, 2000 ($3.95, limited series)

1-Waid-s/Dodson-a; "Silver Age" style x-over; JLA & villains switch bodies	4.00
...: Challengers of the Unknown ($2.50) Joe Kubert-c; vs. Chronos	2.50
...: Dial H For Hero ($2.50) Jim Mooney-c; vs. Martian Manhunter	2.50
...: Doom Patrol ($2.50) Ramona Fradon/Peyer-s	2.50
...: Flash ($2.50) Carmine Infantino-c; Kid Flash and Elongated Man app.	2.50
...: Green Lantern ($2.50) Gil Kane-c/Busiek-s/Anderson-a; vs. Sinestro	2.50
...: Justice League of America ($2.50) Ty Templeton-c	2.50
...: Showcase ($2.50) Dick Giordano-c/a; Batgirl, Adam Strange app.	2.50
...: Secret Files ($4.95) Intro. Agamemno; short stories & profile pages	5.00
...: Teen Titans ($2.50) Nick Cardy-c; vs. Penguin, Mr. Element, Black Manta	2.50
...: The Brave and the Bold ($2.50) Jim Aparo-c; Batman & Metal Men	2.50
...: 80-Page Giant ($5.95) Conclusion of x-over; "lost" Silver Age stories	6.00

SILVERBACK
Comico: 1989 - No. 3, 1990 ($2.50, color, limited series, mature readers)

1-3-Character from Grendel: Matt Wagner-a	2.50

SILVERBLADE
DC Comics: Sept, 1987 - No. 12, Sept, 1988

1-12-Colan-c/a in all	3.00

SILVERHAWKS
Star Comics/Marvel Comics #6: Aug, 1987 - No. 6, June, 1988 ($1.00)

1-6	3.00

SILVERHEELS
Pacific Comics: Dec, 1983 - No. 3, May, 1984 ($1.50)

1-3	2.50

SILVER KID WESTERN
Key/Stanmor Publications: Oct, 1954 - No. 5, July, 1955

1	10	20	30	54	72	90
2	6	12	18	31	38	45
3-5	6	12	18	28	34	40
I.W. Reprint #1,2-Severin-c: 1-r/#? 2-r/#1	2	4	6	8	11	14

SILVER SABLE AND THE WILD PACK (See Amazing Spider-Man #265 and Sable & Fortune)
Marvel Comics: June, 1992 - No. 35, Apr, 1995 ($1.25/$1.50

1-($2.00)-Embossed & foil stamped-c; Spider-Man app.	3.00
2-35: 4,5-Dr. Doom-c/story. 6,7-Deathlok-c/story. 9-Origin Silver Sable. 10-Punisher-c/s. 15-Capt. America-c/s. 16,17-Intruders app. 18,19-Venom-c/s. 19-Siege of Darkness x-over. 23-Daredevil (in new costume) & Deadpool app. 24-Bound-in card sheet. Li'l Sylvie backup story. 25-($2.00, 52 pgs.)-Li'l Sylvie backup story	2.50

SILVER STAR (Also see Jack Kirby's...)
Pacific Comics: Feb, 1983 - No. 6, Jan, 1984 ($1.00)

1-6: 1-1st app. Last of the Viking Heroes. 1-5-Kirby-c/a. 2-Ditko-a	5.00
...: Graphite Edition TPB (TwoMorrows Publ., 3/06, $19.95) r/series in B&W including Kirby's original pencils; sketch pages; original screenplay	20.00
Jack Kirby's Silver Star, Volume 1 HC (Image Comics, 2007, $34.99) r/series in color; sketch pages; original screenplay	35.00

Silver Streak Comics #7 © LEV

Silver Surfer #141 © MAR

Silver Surfer: Parable © MAR

	GD	VG	FN	VF	VF/NM	NM-
	2.0	4.0	6.0	8.0	9.0	9.2

SILVER STREAK COMICS (Crime Does Not Pay #22 on)
Your Guide Publs. No. 1-7/New Friday Publs. No. 8-17/Comic House Publ./
Newsbook Publ.: Dec, 1939 - No. 21, May, 1942; No. 23, 1946; No # 22 (Silver logo-#1-5)

	GD	VG	FN	VF	VF/NM	NM-
1-(Scarce)-Intro The Claw by Cole (r-/in Daredevil #21), Red Reeves, Boy Magician, &
Captain Fearless; The Wasp, Mister Midnight begin; Spirit Man app. Silver metallic-c begin,
end #5; Claw c-1,2,6-8 | 1075 | 2150 | 3225 | 7600 | 12,800 | 18,000
2-The Claw by Cole; Simon-c/a | 388 | 776 | 1164 | 2522 | 4461 | 6400
3-1st app. & origin Silver Streak (2nd with lightning speed); Dickie Dean the Boy Inventor,
Lance Hale, Ace Powers, Bill Wayne, & The Planet Patrol begin | 327 | 654 | 981 | 2126 | 3763 | 5400
4-Sky Wolf begins; Silver Streak by Jack Cole (new costume); 1st app. Jackie,
Lance Hale's sidekick | 166 | 332 | 498 | 1038 | 1719 | 2400
5-Jack Cole c/a(2) | 193 | 386 | 579 | 1206 | 2003 | 2800
6-(Scarce, 9/40)-Origin & 1st app. Daredevil (blue & yellow costume) by Jack Binder;
The Claw returns; classic Cole Claw-c | 1250 | 2500 | 3750 | 9375 | 16,688 | 24,000
7-Claw vs. Daredevil (new costume-blue & red) by Jack Cole & 3 other Cole stories (38 pgs.)
2nd app. Daredevil & 1st Daredevil-c | 726 | 1452 | 2178 | 5082 | 8891 | 12,700
8-Claw vs. Daredevil by Cole; last Cole Silver Streak | 327 | 654 | 981 | 2126 | 3763 | 5400
9-Claw vs. Daredevil by Cole | 190 | 380 | 570 | 1188 | 1969 | 2750
10-Origin & 1st app. Captain Battle (5/41); Claw vs. Daredevil by Cole; Robot-c | 169 | 338 | 507 | 1056 | 1753 | 2450
11-Intro. Mercury by Bob Wood, Silver Streak's sidekick; conclusion Claw vs. Daredevil by
Rico; in 'Presto Martin,' 2nd pg., newspaper says 'Roussos does it again' | 117 | 234 | 351 | 731 | 1216 | 1700
12-14: 13-Origin Thun-Dohr | 85 | 170 | 255 | 531 | 878 | 1225
15, 17-Last Daredevil issue. | 79 | 158 | 237 | 494 | 822 | 1150
16-Hitler-c | 97 | 194 | 291 | 606 | 1003 | 1400
18-The Saint begins (2/42, 1st app.) by Leslie Charteris (see Movie Comics #2 by DC);
The Saint | 67 | 134 | 201 | 419 | 697 | 975
19-21(1942): 20,21 have Wolverton's Scoop Scuttle. 21-Hitler app. in strip on cover | 48 | 96 | 144 | 293 | 484 | 675
23(1946(An Atomic Comic)-Reprints; bondage-c | 48 | 96 | 144 | 293 | 484 | 675
nn(11/46)(Newsbook Publ.)-R-/S.S. story from #4-7 plus 2 Captain Fearless stories,
all in color; bondage/torture-c (scarce) | 55 | 110 | 165 | 344 | 572 | 800
NOTE: Binder c-3, 4, 13-15, 17. Jack Cole a-(Daredevil)-#6-10, (Dickie Dean)-#3-10, (Pirate Prince)-#7, (Silver Streak)-#4-8, nn; c-5 (Silver Streak), 6 (Claw), 7, 8 (Daredevil). Everett Red Reed begins #20. Guardineer a-#8-13. Don Rico a-11-17 (Daredevil); c-11, 12, 16. Simon a-3 (Silver Streak). Bob Wood c-9, 10. Captain Battle c-11, 13-15, 17. Claw c-#1, 2, 6-8. Daredevil c-7, 8, 12. Dickie Dean c-19. Ned of the Navy c-20 (war). The Saint c-18. Silver Streak c-5, 9, 10, 16, 23.

SILVER SURFER (See Fantastic Four, Fantasy Masterpieces V2#1, Fireside Book Series, Marvel Graphic Novel, Marvel Presents #8, Marvel's Greatest Comics & Tales To Astonish #92)

SILVER SURFER, THE (Also see Essential Silver Surfer)
Marvel Comics Group: Aug, 1968 - No. 18, Sept, 1970; June, 1982

1-More detailed origin by John Buscema (p); The Watcher back-up stories begin (origin),
end #7; (No. 1-7: 25¢, 68 pgs.) | 40 | 80 | 120 | 311 | 568 | 825
2 | 17 | 34 | 51 | 128 | 227 | 325
3-1st app. Mephisto | 15 | 30 | 45 | 111 | 198 | 285
4-Lower distribution; Thor & Loki app. | 36 | 72 | 108 | 270 | 498 | 725
5-7-Last giant size. 5-The Stranger app.; Fantastic Four app. 6-Brunner inks. 7-(8/69)-Early
cameo Frankenstein's monster (see X-Men #40) | 10 | 20 | 30 | 73 | 129 | 185
8-10: 8-18-(15¢ issues) | 8 | 16 | 24 | 58 | 97 | 135
11-13,15-18: 15-Silver Surfer vs. Human Torch; Fantastic Four app. 17-Nick Fury app. 18-Vs.
The Inhumans; Kirby-c/a | 8 | 16 | 24 | 52 | 86 | 120
14-Spider-Man x-over | 11 | 22 | 33 | 79 | 140 | 200
... Omnibus Vol. 1 Hardcover (2007, $74.99, dustjacket) r/#1-18 re-colored with original letter
pages, Fantastic Four Annual #5 & Not Brand Echh #13; Lee and Buscema bios | | | | | | 75.00
V2#1 (6/82, 52 pgs.)-Byrne-c/a | 1 | 3 | 4 | 6 | 8 | 10
NOTE: Adkins a-8-15i. Brunner a-6i. J. Buscema a-1-17p. Colan a-1-3p. Reinman a-1-4i. #1-14 were reprinted in Fantasy Masterpieces V2#1-14.

SILVER SURFER (Volume 3) (See Marvel Graphic Novel #38)
Marvel Comics Group: V3#1, July, 1987 - No. 146, Nov, 1998

1-Double size ($1.25) | 1 | 2 | 3 | 5 | 7 | 9
2-17: 15-Ron Lim-c/a begins (9/88) | | | | | | 4.00
18-33,39-43: 25,31 ($1.50, 52 pgs.). 25-Skrulls app. 32,39-No Ron Lim-c/a.
39-Alan Grant scripts | | | | | | 3.00
34-Thanos returns (cameo); Starlin scripts begin | | | | | | 5.00
35-38: 35-1st full Thanos app. in Silver Surfer (3/90); reintro Drax the Destroyer on last pg.
(cameo). 36-Recaps history of Thanos; Capt. Marvel & Warlock app. in recap. 37-1st full
app. Drax the Destroyer; Drax-c. 38-Silver Surfer battles Thanos | | | | | | 6.00
44,45,49-Thanos stories (c-44,45) | | | | | | 4.00
46-48: 46-Return of Adam Warlock (2/91); re-intro Gamora & Pip the Troll. 47-Warlock battles
Drax. 48-Last Starlin scripts (also #50) | | | | | | 4.00
50-($1.50, 52 pgs.)-Embossed & silver foil-c; Silver Surfer has brief battle w/Thanos;

story cont'd in Infinity Gauntlet #1 | 1 | 2 | 3 | 4 | 5 | 7
50-2nd & 3rd printings | | | | | | 2.50
51-59: 51-53: Infinity Gauntlet x-over. 54-57: Infinity Gauntlet x-overs. 54-Rhino app.
55,56-Thanos-c & app. 57-Thanos-c & cameo. 58,59-Infinity Gauntlet x-overs; 58-Lim-c
only. 59-Thanos battles Silver Surfer-c/story; Thanos joins | | | | | | 3.00
60-74,76-99,101-124,126-139: 63-Capt. Marvel app. 67-69-Infinity War x-overs. 76-78-Jack of
Hearts-c/s. 83-85-Infinity Crusade x-over; 83,84-Thanos cameo. 85-Storm, Wonder Man
x-over. 86-Thor-c/s. 87-Dr. Strange & Warlock app. 88-Thanos-c/s. 82 (52 pgs.). 95-FF app.
96-Hulk & FF app. 97-Terrax & Nova app. 101-Bound in card sheet. 106-Doc Doom app.
121-Quasar & Beta Ray Bill app. 123-w/card insert; begin Garney-a. 126-Dr. Strange-c/app.
128-Spider-Man & Daredevil-c/app. 138-Thing-c | | | | | | 2.50
75-($2.50, 52 pgs.)-Embossed foil-c; Lim-c/a | | | | | | 3.00
100 ($2.25, 52 pgs.)-Wraparound-c | | | | | | 2.50
100 ($3.95, 52 pgs.)-Enhanced-c | | | | | | 4.00
125 ($2.95)-Wraparound-c; Vs. Hulk-c/app. | | | | | | 3.00
140-146: 140-142,144,145-Muth-c/a. 143,146-Cowan-a. 146-Last issue | | | | | | 2.50
#(-1) Flashback (7/97) | | | | | | 2.50
Annual 1 (1988, $1.75)-Evolutionary War app.; 1st Ron Lim-a on Silver Surfer (20 pg. back-up
story & pin-ups) | | | | | | 5.00
Annual 2-7 ('89-'94, 68 pgs.): 2-Atlantis Attacks. 4-3 pg. origin story; Silver Surfer battles
Guardians of the Galaxy. 5-Return of the Defenders, part 3; Lim-c/a (3 pgs. of pin-ups only).
6-Polybagged w/trading card; 1st app. Legacy; card is by Lim/Austin | | | | | | 3.00
Annual '97 ($2.99), .../Thor Annual '98 ($2.99) | | | | | | 3.00
Ashcan (1995, 75¢) reprints part of V1#3; Lim-c | | | | | | 2.50
...Dangerous Artifacts-(1996, $3.95)-Ron Marz scripts; Galactus-c/app. | | | | | | 4.00
Graphic Novel (1988, HC, $14.95) Judgment Day; Lee-s/Buscema-a | | | | | | 15.00
The Enslavers Graphic Novel (1990, $16.95) | | | | | | 17.00
Homecoming Graphic Novel (1991, $12.95, softcover) Starlin-s | | | | | | 15.00
Inner Demons TPB (4/98, $3.50)r/#123,125,126 | | | | | | 3.50
...: Rebirth of Thanos TPB (2006, $24.99) r/#34-38, Thanos Quest #1,2; Logan's Run #6 | | | | | | 25.00
...: The First Coming of Galactus nn (11/92, $5.95, 68 pgs.)-Reprints Fantastic Four #48-50
with new Lim-c | | | | | | 6.00
Wizard 1/2 | 1 | 2 | 6 | 9 | 12 | 15
NOTE: Austin c(i)-7, 8, 71, 73, 74, 76, 79. Cowan a-143,146. Cully Hamner a-83p. Ron Lim a(p)-15-31, 33-38, 40-55, (56, 57-part-p), 60-65, 73-82, Annual 2, 4; c(p)-15-31, 32-38, 40-84, 86-92, Annual 2, 4-6. Muth c/a-140-142,144,145. M. Rogers a-1-10, 12, 19, 21; c-1-9, 11, 12, 21.

SILVER SURFER (Volume 4)
Marvel Comics: Sept, 2003 - No. 14, Dec, 2004 ($2.25/$2.99)

1-6: 1-Milx-a; Jusko-c. 2-Jae Lee-c | | | | | | 2.50
7-14-($2.99) | | | | | | 3.00
...Vol. 1: Communion (2004, $14.99) r/#1-6 | | | | | | 15.00

SILVER SURFER, THE
Marvel Comics (Epic): Dec, 1988 - No. 2, Jan, 1989 ($1.00, lim. series)

1,2: By Stan Lee scripts & Moebius-c/a | | | | | | 4.00
...: Parable ('98, $5.99) r/#1&2 | | | | | | 6.00

SILVER SURFER: LOFTIER THAN MORTALS
Marvel Comics: Oct, 1999 - No. 2, Oct, 1999 ($2.50, limited series)

1,2-Remix of Fantastic Four #57-60; Velluto-a | | | | | | 2.50

SILVER SURFER: REQUIEM
Marvel Comics: July, 2007 - No. 4 ($3.99, limited series)

1-4-Straczynski-s/Ribic-a. 1-Origin retold; Fantastic Four app. | | | | | | 4.00

SILVER SURFER/SUPERMAN
Marvel Comics: 1996 ($5.95,one-shot)

1-Perez-s/Lim-c/a(p) | | | | | | 6.00

SILVER SURFER VS. DRACULA
Marvel Comics: Feb, 1994 ($1.75, one-shot)

1-r/Tomb of Dracula #50; Everett Vampire-r/Venus #19; Howard the Duck back-up by
Brunner; Lim-c(p) | | | | | | 2.50

SILVER SURFER/WARLOCK: RESURRECTION
Marvel Comics: Mar, 1993 - No. 4, June, 1993 ($2.50, limited series)

1-4: Starlin-c/a & scripts | | | | | | 2.50

SILVER SURFER/WEAPON ZERO
Marvel Comics: Apr, 1997 ($2.95, one-shot)

1-"Devil's Reign" pt. 8 | | | | | | 3.00

SILVERTIP (Max Brand)
Dell Publishing Co.: No. 491, Aug, 1953 - No. 898, May, 1958

Four Color 491 (#1); all painted-c | 8 | 16 | 24 | 52 | 86 | 120
Four Color 572,608,637,667,731,789,898-Kinstler-a | 5 | 10 | 15 | 30 | 48 | 65
Four Color 835 | 5 | 10 | 15 | 30 | 48 | 65

Simpsons Comics #102 © Bongo

Sin City: Lost, Lonely & Lethal © Frank Miller

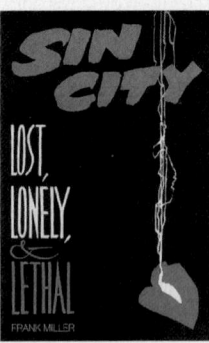

Single Series #14 © UFS

	GD 2.0	VG 4.0	FN 6.0	VF 8.0	VF/NM 9.0	NM- 9.2

SIMPSONS COMICS (See Bartman, Futurama, Itchy & Scratchy & Radioactive Man)
Bongo Comics Group: 1993 - Present ($1.95/$2.50/$2.99)

1-($2.25)-FF#1-c swipe; pull-out poster; flip book	1	2	3	5	6	8

2-5: 2-Patty & Selma flip-c/sty. 3-Krusty, Agent of K.L.O.W.N. flip-c/story. 4-Infinity-c; flip-c of Busman #1; w/trading card. 5-Wraparound-c w/trading card 5.00
6-40: All Flip Books. 6-w/Chief Wiggum's "Crime Comics". 7-w/"McBain Comics". 8-w/"Edna, Queen of the Congo". 9-w/"Barney Gumble". 10-w/"Apu". 11-w/"Homer". 12-w/"White Knuckled War Stories". 13-w/"Jimbo Jones' Wedgie Comics". 14-w/"Grampa". 15-w/"Itchy & Scratchy". 16-w/"Bongo Grab Bag". 17-w/"Headlight Comics". 18-w/"Milhouse". 19,20-w/"Roswell". 21,22-w/"Roswell". 23-w/"Hellfire Comics". 24-w/"Lil' Homey". 36-39-Flip book w/Radioactive Man 4.00
41-49,51-99: 43-Flip book w/Poochie. 52-Dini-s. 77-Dixon-s. 85-Begin $2.99-c 3.00
50-($5.95) Wraparound-c; 80 pgs.; square-bound 1 2 3 4 5 7
100-($6.99) 100 pgs.; square-bound; clip issue of past highlights 7.00
101-134: 102-Barks Ducks homage. 117-Hank Scorpio app. 122-Archie spoof. 132-Movie poster enclosed. 132-133-Two-parter 3.00
... A Go-Go (1999, $11.95)-r/#32-35; ...Big Bonanza (1998, $11.95)-r/#28-31, ...Extravaganza (1994, $10.00)-r/#1-4; infinity-c, ...On Parade (1998, $11.95)-r/#24-27, ...Simpsorama (1996, $10.95)-r/#11-14 12.00
Simpsons Classics 1-13 (2004-Present, $3.99, magazine-size, quarterly) reprints 4.00
Simpsons Comics Barn Burner ('04, $14.95) r/#57-61,63 15.00
Simpsons Comics Beach Blanket Bongo ('07, $14.95) r/#71-75,77 15.00
Simpsons Comics Belly Buster ('04, $14.95) r/#49,51,53-56 15.00
Simpsons Comics Jam-Packed Jamboree ('06, $14.95) r/#64-69 15.00
Simpsons Comics Madness ('03, $14.95) r/#43-48 15.00
Simpsons Comics Royale ('01, $14.95) r/various Bongo issues 15.00
Simpsons Summer Shindig ('07, $4.99) Summer anthology; 8 pg. Batman/Ripken insert 5.00
Simpsons Winter Wing Ding ('06, $4.99) Holiday anthology; Dini-s 5.00

SIMPSONS COMICS AND STORIES
Welsh Publishing Group: 1993 ($2.95, one-shot)

1-(Direct Sale)-Polybagged w/Bartman poster 6.00
1-(Newsstand Edition)-Without poster 4.00

SIMPSONS COMICS PRESENTS BART SIMPSON
Bongo Comics: 2000 - Present ($2.50/$2.99, quarterly)

1-37: 7-9-Dan DeCarlo-layouts. 13-Begin $2.99-c. 17,37-Bartman app. 3.00
The Big Book of Bart Simpson TPB (2002, $12.95) r/#1-4 13.00
The Big Bad Book of Bart Simpson TPB (2003, $12.95) r/#5-8 13.00
The Big Bratty Book of Bart Simpson TPB (2004, $12.95) r/#9-12 13.00
The Big Beefy Book of Bart Simpson TPB (2005, $13.95) r/#13-16 14.00
The Big Bouncy Book of Bart Simpson TPB (2006, $13.95) r/#17-20 14.00

SIMPSONS FUTURAMA CROSSOVER CRISIS II (TV) (Also see Futurama/Simpsons Infinitely Secret Crossover Crisis)
Bongo Comics: 2005 - No. 2, 2005 ($3.00, limited series)

1,2-The Professor brings the Simpsons' Springfield crew to the 31st century 3.00

SIMPSONS SUPER SPECTACULAR (TV)
Bongo Comics: 2006 - Present ($2.99)

1-5: 2-Bartman, Stretch Dude and The Cupcake Kid team up; back-up story Brereton-a. 5-Ramona Fradon-a on Metamorpho spoof 3.00

SIMULATORS, THE
Neatly Chiseled Features: 1991 ($2.50, stiff-c)

1-Super hero group 2.50

SINBAD, JR (TV Cartoon)
Dell Publishing Co.: Sept-Nov, 1965 - No. 3, May, 1966

1	4	8	12	24	37	50
2,3	3	6	9	18	27	35

SIN CITY (See Dark Horse Presents, A Decade of Dark Horse, & San Diego Comic Con Comics #2,4)
Dark Horse Comics (Legend)
TPB ($15.00) Reprints early DHP stories 15.00
Booze, Broads & Bullets TPB ($15.00) 15.00

SIN CITY (FRANK MILLER'S...) (Reissued TPBs to coincide with the April 2005 movie)
Dark Horse Books: Feb, 2005 ($17.00/$19.00, 6" x 9" format with new Miller covers)
Volume 1: The Hard Goodbye ($17.00) reprints stories from Dark Horse Presents #51-62 and DHP Fifth Anniv. Special; covers and publicity pieces 17.00
Volume 2: A Dame to Kill For ($17.00) r/Sin City: A Dame to Kill For #1-6 17.00
Volume 3: The Big Fat Kill ($17.00) r/Sin City: The Big Fat Kill #1-5; pin-up gallery 17.00
Volume 4: That Yellow Bastard ($19.00) r/Sin City: That Yellow Bastard #1-6; pin-up gallery by Mike Allred, Kyle Baker, Jeff Smith and Bruce Timm; cover gallery 19.00
Volume 5: Family Values ($12.00) r/Sin City: Family Values GN 12.00

Volume 6: Booze, Broads & Bullets ($15.00) r/Sin City: The Babe Wore Red and Other Stories; Silent Night; story from A Decade of Dark Horse; Lost, Lonely & Lethal; Sex & Violence; and Just Another Saturday Night 15.00
Volume 7: Hell and Back ($28.00) r/Sin City: Hell and Back #1-9; pin-up gallery 28.00

SIN CITY: A DAME TO KILL FOR
Dark Horse Comics (Legend): Nov, 1993 - No. 6, May, 1994 ($2.95, B&W, limited series)

1-6: Frank Miller-c/a & story in all. 1-1st app. Dwight. 6.00
Limited Edition Hardcover 85.00
Hardcover 25.00
TPB ($15.00) 15.00

SIN CITY: FAMILY VALUES
Dark Horse Comics (Legend): Oct, 1997 ($10.00, B&W, squarebound, one-shot)

nn-Miller-c/a & story 10.00
Limited Edition Hardcover 75.00

SIN CITY: HELL AND BACK
Dark Horse (Maverick): Jul, 1999 - No. 9 ($2.95/$4.95, B&W, limited series)

1-8-Miller-c/a & story. 7-Color 4.00
9-($4.95) 6.00

SIN CITY: JUST ANOTHER SATURDAY NIGHT
Dark Horse Comics (Legend): Aug, 1997 (Wizard 1/2 offer, B&W, one-shot)

1/2-Miller-c/a & story	1	2	3	5	6	8

nn (10/98, $2.50) r/#1/2 2.50

SIN CITY: LOST, LONELY & LETHAL
Dark Horse Comics (Legend): Dec, 1996 ($2.95, B&W and blue, one-shot)

nn-Miller-c/s/a; w/pin-ups 5.00

SIN CITY: SEX AND VIOLENCE
Dark Horse Comics (Legend): Mar, 1997 ($2.95, B&W and blue, one-shot)

nn-Miller-c/a & story 5.00

SIN CITY: SILENT NIGHT
Dark Horse Comics (Legend): Dec, 1995 ($2.95, B&W, one-shot)

1-Miller-c/a & story; Marv app. 5.00

SIN CITY: THAT YELLOW BASTARD (Second Ed. TPB listed under Sin City (Frank Miller's...)
Dark Horse Comics (Legend): Feb, 1996 - No. 6, July, 1996 ($2.95/$3.50, B&W and yellow, limited series)

1-5: Miller-c/a & story in all. 1-1st app. Hartigan. 5.00
6-($3.50) Error & corrected 5.00
Limited Edition Hardcover 25.00
TPB ($15.00) 15.00

SIN CITY: THE BABE WORE RED AND OTHER STORIES
Dark Horse Comics (Legend): Nov, 1994 ($2.95, B&W and red, one-shot)

1-r/serial run in Previews as well as other stories; Miller-c/a & scripts; Dwight app. 4.00

SIN CITY: THE BIG FAT KILL (Second Edition TPB listed under Sin City (Frank Miller's...)
Dark Horse Comics (Legend): Nov, 1994 - No. 5, Mar, 1995 ($2.95, B&W, limited series)

1-5-Miller story & art in all; Dwight app. 5.00
Hardcover 25.00
TPB ($15.00) 15.00

SIN CITY: THE FRANK MILLER LIBRARY
Dark Horse Books: Set 1, Nov, 2005; Set 2, Mar, 2006 ($150, slipcased hardcover, 8" x 12")

Set 1 - Individual hardcovers for Volume 1: The Hard Goodbye, Volume 2: A Dame to Kill For, Volume 3: The Big Fat Kill, Volume 4: That Yellow Bastard; new red foil stamped covers; slipcase box is black with red foil graphics 150.00
Set 2 - Individual hardcovers for Volume 5: Family Values, Volume 6: Booze, Broads & Bullets, Volume 7: Hell and Back, new red foil stamped covers; The Art of Sin City red hardcover; slipcase box is black with red foil graphics 150.00

SINDBAD (See Capt. Sindbad under Movie Comics, and Fantastic Voyages of Sindbad)

SINGING GUNS (See Fawcett Movie Comics)

SINGLE SERIES (Comics on Parade #30 on)(Also see John Hix...)
United Features Syndicate: 1938 - No. 28, 1942 (All 68 pgs.)

Note: See Individual Alphabetical Listings for prices

1-Captain and the Kids (#1)	2-Broncho Bill (1939) (#1)
3-Ella Cinders (1939)	4-Li'l Abner (1939) (#1)
5-Fritzi Ritz (#1)	6-Jim Hardy by Dick Moores (#1)
7-Frankie Doodle	8-Peter Pat (On sale 7/14/39)
9-Strange As It Seems	10-Little Mary Mixup
11-Mr. and Mrs. Beans	12-Joe Jinks

Siren Special #1 © MAL

Six Million Dollar Man (2nd series) #1 © CC

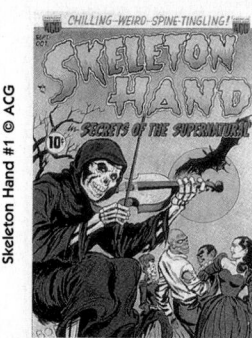

Skeleton Hand #1 © ACG

	GD	VG	FN	VF	VF/NM	NM-
	2.0	4.0	6.0	8.0	9.0	9.2

13-Looy Dot Dope
15-How It Began (1939)
17-Danny Dingle
18-Li'l Abner (#2 on-c)
19-Broncho Bill (#2 on-c)
21-Ella Cinders (#2 on-c; on sale 3/19/40)
23-Tailspin Tommy by Hal Forrest (#1)
25-Abbie and Slats
27-Jim Hardy by Dick Moores (1942)
14-Billy Make Believe
16-Illustrated Gags (1940)-Has ad for Captain and the Kids #1 reprint listed below
20-Tarzan by Hal Foster
22-Iron Vic
24-Alice in Wonderland (#1)
26-Little Mary Mixup (#2 on-c, 1940)
28-Ella Cinders & Abbie and Slats (1942)
1-Captain and the Kids (1939 reprint)-2nd Edition
1-Fritzi Ritz (1939 reprint)-2nd ed.

NOTE: Some issues given away at the 1939-40 New York World's Fair (#6).

SINGULARITY 7
IDW Publ.: July, 2004 - No. 4, Oct, 2004 ($3.99, limited series)

1-4-Templesmith-s/a						4.00

SINISTER HOUSE OF SECRET LOVE, THE (Becomes Secrets of Sinister House No. 5 on)
National Periodical Publ.: Oct-Nov, 1971 - No. 4, Apr-May, 1972

1 (all 52 pgs.)	15	30	45	111	198	285
2,4: 2-Jeff Jones-c	8	16	24	52	86	120
3-Toth-a; greytone-c	8	16	24	54	90	125

SINS OF YOUTH... (Also see Young Justice: Sins of Youth)
DC Comics: May 2000 ($4.95/$2.50, limited series)

Secret Files 1 ($4.95) Short stories and profile pages; Nauck-c 5.00
...Aquaboy/Lagoon Man; Batboy and Robin; JLA Jr.; Kid Flash/Impulse; Starwoman and the JSA, Superman, Jr./Superboy, Sr.; The Secret/ Deadboy, Wonder Girls ($2.50-c) Old and young heroes switch ages 2.50

SIR CHARLES BARKLEY AND THE REFEREE MURDERS
Hamilton Comics: 1993 ($9.95, 8-1/2" x 11", 52 pgs.)

nn-Photo-c; Sports fantasy comic book fiction (uses real names of NBA superstars). Script by Alan Dean Foster, art by Joe Staton. Comes with bound-in sheet of 35 gummed "Moods of Charles Barkley" stamps. Photo/story on Barkley

	2	4	6	8	10	12

Special Edition of 100 copies for charity signed on an affixed book plate by Barkley, Foster & Staton 150.00
Ashcan edition given away to dealers, distributors & promoters (low distribution).
Four pages in color, balance of story in b&w

	2	4	6	8	10	12

SIREN (Also see Eliminator & Ultraforce)
Malibu Comics (Ultraverse): Sept, 1995 - No. 3, Dec, 1995 ($1.50)

Infinity, 1-3: Infinity-Black-c & painted-c exists. 1-Regular-c & painted-c; War Machine app.
2-Flip book w/Phoenix Resurrection Pt. 3 ..... 2.50
Special 1-(2/96, $1.95, 28 pgs.)-Origin Siren; Marvel Comic's Juggernaut-c/app. 2.50

SIREN: SHAPES
Image Comics: May, 1998 - No. 3, Nov, 1998 ($2.95, B&W, limited series)

1-3-J. Torres -s 3.00

SIR LANCELOT (TV)
Dell Publishing Co.: No. 606, Dec, 1954 - No. 775, Mar, 1957

Four Color 606 (not TV)	7	14	21	49	80	110
Four Color 775(...and Brian)-Buscema-a; photo-c	9	18	27	65	113	160

SIR WALTER RALEIGH (Movie)
Dell Publishing Co.: May, 1955 (Based on movie "The Virgin Queen")

Four Color 644-Photo-c	7	14	21	45	73	100

SISTERHOOD OF STEEL (See Eclipse Graphic Adventure Novel #13)
Marvel Comics (Epic Comics): Dec, 1984 -No. 8, Feb, 1986 ($1.50, Baxter paper, mature)

1-8 ..... 3.00

SIX
Image Comics: Aug, 2004 ($5.99, B&W)

1-Oeming-s/c; Beavers-a 6.00

6 BLACK HORSES (See Movie Classics)

SIX FROM SIRIUS
Marvel Comics (Epic Comics): July, 1984 - No. 4, Oct, 1984 ($1.50, limited series, mature)

1-4: Moench scripts; Gulacy-c/a in all 2.50

SIX FROM SIRIUS II
Marvel Comics (Epic Comics): Feb, 1986 - No. 4, May, 1986 ($1.50, limited series, mature)

1-4: Moench scripts; Gulacy-c/a in all 2.50

SIX-GUN HEROES
Fawcett Publications: March, 1950 - No. 23, Nov, 1953 (Photo-c #1-23)

	GD	VG	FN	VF	VF/NM	NM-
	2.0	4.0	6.0	8.0	9.0	9.2

1-Rocky Lane, Hopalong Cassidy, Smiley Burnette begin (same date as Smiley Burnette #1)						
	43	86	129	262	419	575
2	24	48	72	136	211	285
3-5: 5-Lash LaRue begins	17	34	51	96	148	200
6-15	14	28	42	80	115	150
16-22: 17-Last Smiley Burnette. 18-Monte Hale begins						
	12	24	36	67	94	120
23-Last Fawcett issue	13	26	39	72	101	130

NOTE: Hopalong Cassidy photo c-1-3. Monte Hale photo c-18. Rocky Lane photo c-4, 5, 7, 9, 11, 13, 15, 17, 20, 21, 23. Lash LaRue photo c-6, 8, 10, 12, 14, 16, 19, 22.

SIX-GUN HEROES (Cont'd from Fawcett; Gunmasters #84 on) (See Blue Bird)
Charlton Comics: No. 24, Jan, 1954 - No. 83, Mar-Apr, 1965 (All Vol. 4)

24-Lash LaRue, Hopalong Cassidy, Rocky Lane & Tex Ritter begin; photo-c						
	19	38	57	109	172	235
25	11	22	33	64	90	115
26-30: 26-Rod Cameron story. 28-Tom Mix begins?	10	20	30	56	76	95
31-40: 38-Jingles & Wild Bill Hickok (TV)	9	18	27	50	65	80
41-46,48,50	9	18	27	47	61	75
47-Williamson-a, 2 pgs; Torres-a	9	18	27	50	65	80
49-Williamson-a (5 pgs.)	10	20	30	56	76	95
51-56,58-60: 58-Gunmaster app.	4	8	12	24	37	50
57-Origin & 1st app. Gunmaster	5	10	15	30	48	65
61,63-70	3	6	9	18	27	35
62-Origin Gunmaster	4	8	12	22	34	45
71-75,77,78,80-83	3	6	9	14	19	24
76,79: 76-Gunmaster begins. 79-1st app. & origin of Bullet, the Gun-Boy						
	3	6	9	16	22	28

SIXGUN RANCH (See Luke Short & Four Color #580)

SIX-GUN WESTERN
Atlas Comics (CDS): Jan, 1957 - No. 4, July, 1957

1-Crandall-a; two Williamson text illos	18	36	54	105	165	225
2,3-Williamson-a in both	14	28	42	80	115	150
4-Woodbridge-a	10	20	30	58	79	100

NOTE: Ayers a-2, 3. Maneely a-1; c-2, 3. Orlando a-2. Pakula a-2. Powell a-3. Romita a-1, 4. Severin c-1, 4. Shores a-2.

SIX MILLION DOLLAR MAN, THE (TV)
Charlton Comics: 6/76 - No. 4, 12/76; No. 5, 10/77; No. 6, 2/78 - No. 9, 6/78

1-Staton-c/a; Lee Majors photo on-c	3	6	9	14	20	25
2-9: 2-Neal Adams-c; Staton-a	2	4	6	10	14	18

SIX MILLION DOLLAR MAN, THE (TV)(Magazine)
Charlton Comics: July, 1976 - No. 7, Nov, 1977 (B&W)

1-Neal Adams-c/a	3	6	9	18	27	35
2-Neal Adams-c/a	3	6	9	14	20	25
3-N. Adams part inks; Chaykin-a	2	4	6	11	16	20
4-7	2	4	6	9	13	16

SIX STRING SAMURAI
Awesome-Hyperwerks: Sept, 1998 ($2.95)

1-Stinsman & Fraga-a 3.00

67 SECONDS
Marvel Comics (Epic Comics): 1992 ($15.95, 54 pgs., graphic novel)

nn-James Robinson scripts; Steve Yeowell-c/a	2	4	6	11	14	18

SKATEMAN
Pacific Comics: Nov, 1983 (Baxter paper, one-shot)

1-Adams-c/a 4.00

SKELETON HAND (...In Secrets of the Supernatural)
American Comics Gr. (B&M Dist. Co.): Sept-Oct, 1952 - No. 6, Jul-Aug, 1953

1	45	90	135	275	450	625
2	33	66	99	190	300	410
3-6	26	52	78	152	239	325

SKELETON KEY
Amaze Ink: July, 1995 - No. 30, Jan, 1998 ($1.25/$1.50/$1.75, B&W)

1-30 ..... 3.00
Special #1 (2/98, $4.95) Unpublished short stories 5.00
Sugar Kat Special (10/98, $2.95) Halloween stories 3.00
Beyond The Threshold TPB (6/96. $11.95)-r/#1-6 ..... 12.00
Cats and Dogs TPB ($12.95)-r/#25-30 ..... 13.00
The Celestial Calendar TPB ($19.95)-r/#7-18 ..... 20.00
Telling Tales TPB ($12.95)-r/#19-24 ..... 13.00

Skull, The Slayer #3 © MAR

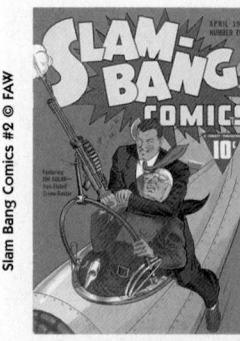

Slam Bang Comics #2 © FAW

Sleepwalker #7 © MAR

	GD 2.0	VG 4.0	FN 6.0	VF 8.0	VF/NM 9.0	NM- 9.2

SKELETON KEY (Volume 2)
Amaze Ink: 1999 - No. 4, 1999 ($2.95, B&W)

1-4-Andrew Watson-s/a — 3.00

SKELETON WARRIORS
Marvel Comics: Apr, 1995 - No. 4, July, 1995 ($1.50)

1-4: Based on animated series. — 2.50

SKIN GRAFT: THE ADVENTURES OF A TATTOOED MAN
DC Comics (Vertigo): July, 1993 - No. 4, Oct, 1993 ($2.50, lim. series, mature)

1-4 — 2.50

SKINWALKER
Oni Press: May, 2002 - No. 4, Sept, 2002 ($2.95, limited series)

1-4-Hurtt & Dela Cruz-a; Talon-c — 3.00
1-(5/05) Free Comic Book Day Edition — 2.50

SKI PARTY (See Movie Classics)

SKREEMER
DC Comics: May, 1989 - No. 6, Oct, 1989 ($2.00, limited series, mature)

1-6: Contains graphic violence; Milligan-s — 2.50
TPB (2002, $19.95) r/#1-6 — 20.00

SKRULL KILL KREW
Marvel Comics: Sept, 1995 - No. 5, Dec, 1995 ($2.95, limited series)

1-5: Grant Morrison & Mark Millar scripts; Steve Yeowell-a. 2,3-Cap America app. — 3.00
TPB (2006, $16.99) r/#1-5 — 17.00

SKUL, THE
Virtual Comics (Byron Preiss Multimedia): Oct, 1996 - No. 3, Dec, 1996 ($2.50, lim. series)

1-3: Ron Lim & Jimmy Palmiotti-a — 2.50

SKULL & BONES
DC Comics: 1992 - No. 3, 1992 ($4.95, limited series, 52 pgs.)

Book 1-3: 1-1st app. — 5.00

SKULL, THE SLAYER
Marvel Comics Group: Aug, 1975 - No. 8, Nov, 1976 (20¢/25¢)

1-Origin & 1st app.; Gil Kane-c	2	4	6	8	10	12
2-8: 2-Gil Kane-c. 5,6-(Regular 25¢-c). 8-Kirby-c	1	2	3	4	5	7
5,6-(30¢-c variants, limited distribution)(5,7/76)	3	6	9	18	27	35

SKY BLAZERS (CBS Radio)
Hawley Publications: Sept, 1940 - No. 2, Nov, 1940

1-Sky Pirates, Ace Archer, Flying Aces begin	60	120	180	375	625	875
2-WWII aerial battle-c	39	78	117	225	355	485

SKYE RUNNER
DC Comics (WildStorm): June, 2006 - No. 6, Mar, 2007 ($2.99)

1-6: 1-Three covers; Warner-s/Garza-a. 2-Three covers, incl. Campbell — 3.00

SKYMAN (See Big Shot Comics & Sparky Watts)
Columbia Comics Gr.: Fall?, 1941 - No. 2, Fall?, 1942; No. 3, 1948 - No. 4, 1948

1-Origin Skyman, The Face, Sparky Watts app.; Whitney-c/a; 3rd story-r from Big Shot #1; Whitney c-1-4	122	244	366	763	1269	1775
2 (1942)-Yankee Doodle	59	118	177	369	610	850
3,4 (1948)	40	80	120	235	368	500

SKYPILOT
Ziff-Davis Publ. Co.: No. 10, 1950(nd) - No. 11, Apr-May, 1951

10,11-Frank Borth-a; Saunders painted-c	15	30	45	83	124	165

SKY RANGER (See Johnny Law...)

SKYROCKET
Harry 'A' Chesler: 1944

nn-Alias the Dragon, Dr. Vampire, Skyrocket & The Desperado app.; WWII Jap zero-c	32	64	96	186	293	400

SKY SHERIFF (Breeze Lawson...) (Also see Exposed & Outlaws)
D. S. Publishing Co.: Summer, 1948

1-Edmond Good-c/a	14	28	42	76	108	140

SKY WOLF (Also see Airboy)
Eclipse Comics: Mar, 1988 - No. 3, Oct, 1988 ($1.25/$1.50/$1.95, lim. series)

1-3 — 2.50

SLAINE, THE BERSERKER (Slaine the King #21 on)
Quality: July, 1987 - No. 28, 1989 ($1.25/$1.50)

1-28 — 2.50

SLAINE, THE HORNED GOD
Fleetway: 1998 - No. 3 ($6.99)

1-3-Reprints series from 2000 A.D.; Bisley-a — 7.00

SLAM BANG COMICS (Western Desperado #8)
Fawcett Publications: Mar, 1940 - No. 7, Sept, 1940 (Combined with Master Comics #7)

1-Diamond Jack, Mark Swift & The Time Retarder, Lee Granger, Jungle King begin & continue in Master	207	414	621	1294	2147	3000
2	83	166	249	519	860	1200
3-Classic-c	155	310	465	969	1610	2250
4-7: 6-Intro Zoro, the Mystery Man (also in #7)	66	132	198	413	682	950

Ashcan (1940) Not distributed to newsstands, only for in house use. A copy sold in 2006 for $4,500.

SLAPSTICK
Marvel Comics: Nov, 1992 - No. 4, Feb, 1993 ($1.25, limited series)

1-4: Fry/Austin-c/a. 4-Ghost Rider, D.D., F.F. app. — 2.50

SLAPSTICK COMICS
Comic Magazines Distributors: nd (1946?) (36 pgs.)

nn-Firetop feature; Post-a(2)	25	50	75	145	228	310

SLASH-D DOUBLECROSS
St. John Publishing Co.: 1950 (Pocket-size, 132 pgs.)

nn-Western comics	21	42	63	120	188	255

SLAUGHTERMAN
Comico: Feb, 1983 - No. 2, 1983 ($1.50, B&W)

1,2 — 3.00

SLAVE GIRL COMICS (See Malu... & White Princess of the Jungle #2)
Avon Periodicals/Eternity Comics (1989): Feb, 1949 - No. 2, Apr, 1949 (52 pgs.); Mar, 1989 (B&W, 44 pgs)

1-Larsen-c/a	97	194	291	606	1003	1400
2-Larsen-a	69	138	207	431	716	1000
1-(3/89, $2.25, B&W, 44 pgs.)-r/#1						3.00

SLEDGE HAMMER (TV)
Marvel Comics: Feb, 1988 - No. 2, Mar,1988 ($1.00, limited series)

1,2 — 3.00

SLEEPER
DC Comics (WildStorm): Mar, 2003 - No. 12, Mar, 2004 ($2.95)

1-12-Brubaker-s/Phillips-c/a. 3-Back-up preview of The Authority: High Stakes pt. 2 — 3.00
...: All False Moves TPB (2004, $17.95) r/#7-12 — 18.00
...: Out in the Cold TPB (2004, $17.95) r/#1-6 — 18.00

SLEEPER: SEASON TWO
DC Comics (WildStorm): Aug, 2004 - No. 12, July, 2005 ($2.95/$2.99)

1-12-Brubaker-s/Phillips-c/a. — 3.00
...: A Crooked Line TPB (2005, $17.99) r/#1-6 — 18.00
...: The Long Way Home TPB (2005, $14.99) r/#7-12 — 15.00

SLEEPING BEAUTY (See Dell Giants & Movie Comics)
Dell Publishing Co.: May, 1959 - No. 984, June, 1959 (Disney)

Four Color 973 (...and the Prince)	10	20	30	71	126	180
Four Color 984 (...Fairy Godmother's)	8	16	24	58	97	135

SLEEPWALKER
Marvel Comics: June, 1991 - No. 33, Feb, 1994 ($1.00/$1.25)

1-1st app. Sleepwalker — 3.00
2-33: 4-Williamson-i. 5-Spider-Man-c/stor. 7-Infinity Gauntlet x-over. 8-Vs. Deathlok-c/story. 11-Ghost Rider-c/story. 12-Quesada-c/a(p) 14-Intro Spectra. 15-F.F.-c/story. 17-Darkhawk & Spider-Man x-over; Quesada/Williamson-c. 21,22-Hobgoblin app. — 2.50
19-($2.00)-Die-cut Sleepwalker mask-c — 2.50
25-($2.95, 52 pgs.)-Holo-grafx foil-c; origin — 3.00
Holiday Special 1 (1/93, $2.00, 52 pgs.)-Quesada-c(p) — 2.50

SLEEPWALKING
Hall of Heroes: Jan, 1996 ($2.50, B&W)

1-Kelley Jones-c — 2.50

SLEEPY HOLLOW (Movie Adaption)
DC Comics (Vertigo): 2000 ($7.95, one-shot)

1-Kelley Jones-a/Seagle-s — 8.00

SLEEZE BROTHERS, THE
Marvel Comics (Epic Comics): Aug, 1989 - No. 6, Jan, 1990 ($1.75, mature)

1-6: 4-6 (9/89 - 11/89 indicia dates) — 2.50
nn-(1991, $3.95, 52 pgs.) — 4.00

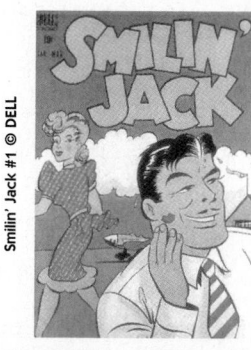

Sludge #7 © MAL

Smash Comics #14 © QUA

Smilin' Jack #1 © DELL

	GD 2.0	VG 4.0	FN 6.0	VF 8.0	VF/NM 9.0	NM- 9.2

SLICK CHICK COMICS
Leader Enterprises: 1947(nd) - No. 3, 1947(nd)

	GD 2.0	VG 4.0	FN 6.0	VF 8.0	VF/NM 9.0	NM- 9.2
1-Teenage humor	14	28	42	76	108	140
2,3	10	20	30	54	72	90

SLIDERS (TV)
Acclaim Comics (Armada): June, 1996 - No. 2, July, 1996 ($2.50, lim. series)
1,2: D.G. Chichester scripts; Dick Giordano-a. ... 2.50

SLIDERS: DARKEST HOUR (TV)
Acclaim Comics (Armada): Oct, 1996 - No. 3, Dec, 1996 ($2.50, limited series)
1-3 ... 2.50

SLIDERS SPECIAL
Acclaim Comics (Armada): Nov, 1996 - No 3, Mar, 1997 ($3.95, limited series)
1-3: 1-Narcotica-Jerry O'Connell-s. 2-Blood and Splendor. 3-Deadly Secrets ... 4.00

SLIDERS: ULTIMATUM (TV)
Acclaim Comics (Armada): Sept, 1996 - No. 2, Sept, 1996 ($2.50, lim. series)
1,2 ... 2.50

SLIMER! (TV cartoon) (Also see the Real Ghostbusters)
Now Comics: 1989 - No. 19, Feb?, 1991 ($1.75)
1-19: Based on animated cartoon ... 3.00

SLIM MORGAN (See Wisco)

SLINGERS (See Spider-Man: Identity Crisis issues)
Marvel Comics: Dec, 1998 - No. 12, Nov, 1999 ($2.99/$1.99)
0-(Wizard #88 supplement) Prelude story ... 2.50
1-($2.99) Four editions w/different covers for each hero, 16 pages common to all, the other pages from each hero's perspective ... 3.00
2-12: 2-Two-c. 12-Saltares-a ... 2.50

SLUDGE
Malibu Comics (Ultraverse): Oct, 1993 - No. 12, Dec, 1994 ($2.50/$1.95)
1-($2.50, 48 pgs.)-Intro/1st app. Sludge; Rune flip-c/story Pt. 1 (1st app., 3 pgs.) by Barry Smith; The Night Man app. (3 pg. preview); The Mighty Magnor 1 pg strip begins by Aragonés (cont. in other titles) ... 3.00
1-Ultra 5000 Limited silver foil ... 4.00
2-11: 3-Break-Thru x-over. 4-2 pg. Mantra origin. 8-Bloodstorm app. ... 2.50
12 ($3.50)-Ultraverse Premiere #8 flip book; Alex Ross poster ... 3.50
...:-Red Xmas (12/94, $2.50, 44 pgs.) ... 2.50

SLUGGER (Little Wise Guys Starring...)(Also see Daredevil Comics)
Lev Gleason Publications: April, 1956

	GD 2.0	VG 4.0	FN 6.0	VF 8.0	VF/NM 9.0	NM- 9.2
1-Biro-c	7	14	21	35	43	50

SMALL GODS
Image Comics: Jun, 2004 - No. 12, Nov, 2005 ($2.95/$2.99, B&W)
1-12-Rand-s/Ferreyra-a ... 3.00
... Special #1 (6/05, $2.95) flip cover ... 3.00
Vol. 1: Killing Grin (1/05, $9.95, TPB) r/#1-4; sketch pages, cover gallery & script page ... 10.00

SMALLVILLE (Based on TV series)
DC Comics: May, 2003 - No. 11 ($3.50/$3.95, bi-monthly)
1-6-Photo-c. 1-Plunkett-a; interviews with cast; season 1 episode guide begins ... 3.50
7-11-($3.95) 7-Chloe Chronicles begin; season 2 episode guide begins ... 4.00
Vol. 1 TPB (2004, $9.95) r/#1-4 & Smallville: The Comic; photo-c ... 10.00

SMALLVILLE: THE COMIC (Based on TV series)
DC Comics: Nov, 2002 ($3.95, 64 pages, one-shot)
1-Photo-c; art by Martinez and Leon; interviews with cast; season 2 preview ... 4.00

SMASH COMICS (Becomes Lady Luck #86 on)
Quality Comics Group: Aug, 1939 - No. 85, Oct, 1949

	GD 2.0	VG 4.0	FN 6.0	VF 8.0	VF/NM 9.0	NM- 9.2
1-Origin Hugh Hazard & His Iron Man, Bozo the Robot, Espionage, Starring Black X by Eisner, & Hooded Justice (Invisible Justice #2 on); Chic Carter & Wings Wendall begin; 1st Robot on the cover of a comic book (Bozo)	315	630	945	2048	3624	5200
2-The Lone Star Rider app; Invisible Hood gains power of invisibility; bondage/torture-c	131	262	393	819	1360	1900
3-Captain Cook & Eisner's John Law begin	68	136	204	425	705	985
4,5: 4-Flash Fulton begins	64	128	192	400	663	925
6-12: 12-One pg. Fine-a	57	114	171	356	591	825
13-Magno begins (8/40); last Eisner issue; The Ray app. in full page ad; The Purple Trio begins	58	116	174	363	599	835
14-Intro. The Ray (9/40) by Lou Fine & others	300	600	900	1894	3197	4500
15,16: 16-The Scarlet Seal begins	124	248	372	775	1288	1800
17-Wun Cloo becomes plastic super-hero by Jack Cole (9-months before Plastic Man)	128	256	384	800	1330	1860
18-Midnight by Jack Cole begins (origin & 1st app., 1/41)	162	324	486	1013	1682	2350
19-22: Last Ray by Fine; The Jester begins-#22	86	172	258	538	894	1250
23,24: 24-The Sword app.; last Chic Carter; Wings Wendall dons new costume #24,25	67	134	201	419	697	975
25-Origin/1st app. Wildfire; Rookie Rankin begins	74	148	222	463	769	1075
26-30: 28-Midnight-c begin, end #85	64	128	192	400	663	925
31,32,34: The Ray by Rudy Palais; also #33	54	108	162	338	562	785
33-Origin The Marksman	62	124	186	388	644	900
35-37	49	98	147	299	492	685
38-The Yankee Eagle begins; last Midnight by Jack Cole; classic-c by Cole	97	194	291	606	1003	1400
39,40-Last Ray issue	50	100	150	305	503	700
41,44-50	40	80	120	244	392	540
42-Lady Luck begins by Klaus Nordling	131	262	393	819	1360	1900
43-Lady Luck-c (1st & only in Smash)	60	120	180	375	620	865
51-60	30	60	90	174	275	375
61-70	23	46	69	135	213	290
71-85: 79-Midnight battles the Men from Mars-c/s	21	42	63	122	191	260

NOTE: Al Bryant c-54, 63-68. Cole a-17-38, 68, 69, 72, 73, 78, 80, 83, 85; c-38, 60-62, 69-84. Crandall a-(Ray)-23-29, 35-38; c-36, 39, 40, 42-44, 46. Fine a(Ray)-14, 15, 16(w/Tuska), 17-22. Fox c-24-35. Fuje Ray-30. Gil Fox a-6-7, 9, 11-13. Guardineer a-(The Marksman)-39-?, 49, 52. Gustavson a-4-7, 9, 11-13 (The Jester)-22-46; (Magno)-13-21; (Midnight)-39(Cole inks), 49, 52, 63-65. Kotzky a-(Espionage)-33-38; c-45, 47-53. Nordling a-49, 52, 63-65. Powell a-11, 12, (Abdul the Arab)-13-24. Black X c-2, 6, 9, 11, 13, 16. Bozo the Robot c-1, 3, 5, 8, 10, 12, 14, 18, 20, 22, 24, 26. Midnight c-28-85. The Ray c-15, 17, 19, 21, 23, 25, 27. Wings Wendall c-4, 7.

SMASH COMICS (Also see All Star Comics 1999 crossover titles)
DC Comics: May, 1999 ($1.99, one-shot)
1-Golden Age Doctor Mid-nite and Hourman ... 2.50

SMASH HIT SPORTS COMICS
Essankay Publications: V2#1, Jan, 1949

	GD 2.0	VG 4.0	FN 6.0	VF 8.0	VF/NM 9.0	NM- 9.2
V2#1-L.B. Cole-c/a	28	56	84	162	256	350

SMAX (Also see Top Ten)
America's Best Comics: Oct, 2003 - No. 5, May, 2004 ($2.95, limited series)
1-5-Alan Moore-s/Zander Cannon-a ... 3.00
... Collected Edition (2004, $19.95, HC with dustjacket) r/#1-5 ... 20.00
... Collected Edition SC (2005, $12.99) r/#1-5 ... 13.00

SMILE COMICS (Also see Gay Comics, Tickle, & Whee)
Modern Store Publ.: 1955 (52 pgs.; 5x7-1/4") (7¢)

	GD 2.0	VG 4.0	FN 6.0	VF 8.0	VF/NM 9.0	NM- 9.2
1	6	12	18	31	38	45

SMILEY BURNETTE WESTERN (Also see Patches #8 & Six-Gun Heroes)
Fawcett Publ.: March, 1950 - No. 4, Oct, 1950 (All photo front & back-c)

	GD 2.0	VG 4.0	FN 6.0	VF 8.0	VF/NM 9.0	NM- 9.2
1-Red Eagle begins	38	76	114	216	333	450
2-4	25	50	75	144	222	300

SMILEY (THE PSYCHOTIC BUTTON) (See Evil Ernie)
Chaos! Comics: July, 1998 - Present ($2.95, one-shots)
1-Ivan Reis-a ... 3.00
... Holiday Special (1/99), ...'s Spring Break (4/99), ...Wrestling Special (5/99) ... 3.00

SMILIN' JACK (See Famous Feature Stories and Popular Comics) (Also see Super Book of Comics #1&2 and Super-Book of Comics #7&19 in the Promotional Comics section)
Dell Publishing Co.: No. 5, 1940 - No. 8, Oct-Dec, 1949

	GD 2.0	VG 4.0	FN 6.0	VF 8.0	VF/NM 9.0	NM- 9.2
Four Color 5	71	142	213	444	735	1025
Four Color 10 (1940)	61	122	183	381	633	885
Large Feature Comic 12,14,25 (1941)	58	116	174	363	602	840
Four Color 4 (1942)	38	76	114	285	518	750
Four Color 14 (1943)	30	60	90	225	413	600
Four Color 36,58 (1943-44)	22	44	66	160	285	410
Four Color 80 (1945)	14	28	42	103	184	265
Four Color 149 (1947)	10	20	30	68	119	170
1 (1-3/48)	10	20	30	70	123	175
2	6	12	18	41	66	90
3-8 (10-12/49)	5	10	15	32	51	70

SMILING SPOOK SPUNKY (See Spunky)

SMITTY (See Popular Comics, Super Book #2, 4 & Super Comics)
Dell Publishing Co.: No. 11, 1940 - No. 7, Aug-Oct, 1949; No. 909, Apr, 1958

	GD 2.0	VG 4.0	FN 6.0	VF 8.0	VF/NM 9.0	NM- 9.2
Four Color 11 (1940)	45	90	135	275	450	625
Large Feature Comic 26 (1941)	36	72	108	208	329	450
Four Color 6 (1942)	21	42	63	156	278	400
Four Color 32 (1943)	15	30	45	111	198	285
Four Color 65 (1945)	13	26	39	90	160	230

Smokey the Bear FC #708 © DELL

Snake Woman #10 © Virgin Comics

Sojourn #10 © CRO

	GD 2.0	VG 4.0	FN 6.0	VF 8.0	VF/NM 9.0	NM- 9.2
Four Color 99 (1946)	10	20	30	73	129	185
Four Color 138 (1947)	9	18	27	64	110	155
1 (2-4/48)	9	18	27	63	107	150
2-(5-7/48)	5	10	15	32	51	70
3,4: 3-(8-10/48), 4-(11-1/48-49)	4	8	12	28	44	60
5-7, Four Color 909 (4/58)	4	8	12	24	37	50

SMOKEY BEAR (TV) (See March Of Comics #234, 362, 372, 383, 407)
Gold Key: Feb, 1970 - No. 13, Mar, 1973

1	3	6	9	19	29	38
2-5	2	4	6	10	14	18
6-13	2	4	6	8	10	12

SMOKEY STOVER (See Popular Comics, Super Book #5,17,29 & Super Comics)
Dell Publishing Co.: No. 7, 1942 - No. 827, Aug, 1957

Four Color 7 (1942)-Reprints	28	56	84	227	384	540
Four Color 35 (1943)	16	32	48	118	209	300
Four Color 64 (1944)	13	26	39	93	164	235
Four Color 229 (1949)	6	12	18	41	66	90
Four Color 730,827	5	10	15	32	51	70

SMOKEY THE BEAR (See Forest Fire for 1st app.)
Dell Publ. Co.: No. 653, 10/55 - No. 1214, 8/61 (See March of Comics #234)

Four Color 653 (#1)	10	20	30	71	126	180
Four Color 708,754,818,932	6	12	18	41	66	90
Four Color 1016,1119,1214	4	8	12	28	44	60

SMOKY (See Movie Classics)

SMURFS (TV)
Marvel Comics: 1982 (Dec) - No. 3, 1983

1-3	1	3	4	6	8	10
...Treasury Edition 1 (64 pgs.)-r/#1-3	3	6	9	16	23	30

SNAFU (Magazine)
Atlas Comics (RCM): Nov, 1955 - V2#2, Mar, 1956 (B&W)

V1#1-Heath/Severin-a; Everett, Maneely-a	14	28	42	82	121	160
V2#1,2-Severin-a	11	22	33	62	86	110

SNAGGLEPUSS (TV)(See Hanna-Barbera Band Wagon, Quick Draw McGraw #5 & Spotlight #4)
Gold Key: Oct, 1962 - No. 4, Sept, 1963 (Hanna-Barbera)

1	8	16	24	58	97	135
2-4	6	12	18	43	69	95

SNAKE EYES (G.I. Joe)
Devil's Due Publ.: Aug, 2005 - No. 6, Jan, 2006 ($2.95)

1-6-Santalucia-a	3.00
...: Declassified TPB (4/06, $18.95) r/series; source guide	19.00

SNAKE PLISSKEN CHRONICLES, (John Carpenter's...)
Hurricane Entertainment: June, 2003 - No. 4 ($2.99)

Preview Issue (8/02, no cover price) B&W preview; John Carpenter interview	2.50
1-4: 1-Three covers; Rodriguez-a	3.00

SNAKES AND LADDERS
Eddie Campbell Comics: 2001 ($5.95, B&W, one-shot)

nn-Alan Moore-s/Eddie Campbell-a	6.00

SNAKES ON A PLANE (Adaptation of the 2006 movie)
Virgin Comics: Oct, 2006 - No. 2, Nov, 2006 ($2.99, limited series)

1,2: 1-Dixon-s/Purcell-a. JG Jones and photo-c. 2-Klebs, Jr.-a; Moore & photo-c	3.00

SNAKE WOMAN (Shekhar Kapur's...)
Virgin Comics: July, 2006 - Present ($2.99)

1-10-Michael Gaydos-a/Zeb Wells-s. 1-Two covers by Gaydos & Singh	3.00
#0 (5/07, 99¢) origin of the Snake Goddess; background info; Gaydos-a/c	2.25
... Tale of the Snake Charmer 1-3 (6/07-8/07, $2.99) Vivek Shinde-a	3.00
... Vol. 1 TPB (6/07, $14.99) r/#1-5; Gaydos sketch pages; creator commentary	15.00

SNAP (Formerly Scoop #8; becomes Jest #10,11 & Komik Pages #10)
Harry 'A' Chesler: No. 9, 1944

9-Manhunter, The Voice	22	44	66	128	202	275

SNAPPY COMICS
Cima Publ. Co. (Prize Publ.): 1945

1-Airmale app.; 9 pg. Sorcerer's Apprentice adapt.; Kiefer-a	33	66	99	190	300	410

SNARKY PARKER (See Life With...)

SNIFFY THE PUP
Standard Publ. (Animated Cartoons): No. 5, Nov, 1949 - No. 18, Sept, 1953

5-Two Frazetta text illos	10	20	30	58	79	100
6-10	7	14	21	35	43	50
11-18	6	12	18	28	34	40

SNOOPER AND BLABBER DETECTIVES (TV) (See Whitman Comic Books)
Gold Key: Nov, 1962 - No. 3, May, 1963 (Hanna-Barbera)

1	7	14	21	49	80	110
2,3	6	12	18	37	59	80

SNOW WHITE (See Christmas With... (in Promotional Comics section), Mickey Mouse Magazine, Movie Comics & Seven Dwarfs)
Dell Publishing Co.: No. 49, July, 1944 - No. 382, Mar, 1952 (Disney-Movie)

Four Color 49 (...& the Seven Dwarfs)	50	100	150	402	731	1060
Four Color 382 (1952)-origin; partial reprint of Four Color 49	9	18	27	65	113	160

SNOW WHITE
Marvel Comics: Jan, 1995 ($1.95, one-shot)

1-r/1937 Sunday newspaper pages	2.50

SNOW WHITE AND THE SEVEN DWARFS
Whitman Publications: April, 1982 (60¢)

nn-r/Four Color 49	1	2	3	5	6	8

SNOW WHITE AND THE SEVEN DWARFS GOLDEN ANNIVERSARY
Gladstone: Fall, 1987 ($2.95, magazine size, 52 pgs.)

1-Contains poster	2	4	6	8	11	14

SOAP OPERA LOVE
Charlton Comics: Feb, 1983 - No. 3, June, 1983

1-3-Low print run	3	6	9	18	27	35

SOAP OPERA ROMANCES
Charlton Comics: July, 1982 - No. 5, March, 1983

1-5-Nurse Betsy Crane-r; low print run	3	6	9	18	27	35

SOCK MONKEY
Dark Horse Comics: Sept, 1998 - No. 2, Oct, 1998 ($2.95/$2.99, B&W)

1,2-Tony Millionaire-s/a	4.00
Vol. 2 (Tony Millionaire's Sock Monkey) July, 1999 - No. 2, Aug, 1999	
1,2	3.00
Vol. 3 (Tony Millionaire's Sock Monkey) Nov, 2000 - No. 2, Dec, 2000	
1,2	3.00
Vol. 4 (Tony Millionaire's Sock Monkey) May, 2003 - No. 2, Aug, 2003	
1,2	3.00
...The Inches Incident (Sept, 2006 - No. 4, Apr, 2007) 1-4-Tony Millionaire-s/a	3.00

SOJOURN
White Cliffs Publ. Co.: Sept, 1977 - No. 2, 1978 ($1.50, B&W & color, tabloid size)

1,2: 1-Tor by Kubert, Eagle by Severin, E. V. Race, Private Investigator by Doug Wildey, T. C. Mars by Aragonés begin plus other strips	2	4	6	8	10	12

NOTE: Most copies came folded. Unfolded copies are worth 50% more.

SOJOURN
CrossGeneration Comics: July, 2001 - No. 34, May, 2004 ($2.95)

Prequel -Ron Marz-s/Greg Land-c/a; preview pages	3.00
1-Ron Marz-s/Greg Land-c/a in most	6.00
2,3	5.00
4-24: 7-Immonen-a. 12-Brigman-a. 17-Lopresti-a. 21-Luke Ross-a	3.25
25-34: 25-$1.00-c. 34-Cariello-a	3.00
...: From the Ashes TPB (2001, $19.95) r/#1-6; Land painted-c	20.00
...: The Dragon's Tale TPB (2002, $15.95) r/#7-12; Jusko painted-c	16.00
...: The Warrior's Tale TPB (2003, $15.95) r/#13-18	16.00
Vol. 4: The Thief's Tale (2003, $15.95) r/#19-24	16.00
Vol. 5: The Sorcerer's Tale (Checker Book Publ.,2007, $17.95) r/#25-30	18.00
Traveler Vol.1,2 ($9.95) digest-sized reprints of TPBs	10.00

SOLAR (...Man of the Atom) (Also see Doctor Solar)
Valiant/Acclaim Comics (Valiant): Sept, 1991 - No. 60, Apr, 1996 ($1.75-$2.50, 44 pgs.)

1-Layton-a(i) on Solar; Barry Windsor-Smith-c/a	1	3	4	6	8	10
2-9: 2-Layton-a(i) on Solar, B. Smith-a. 3-1st app. Harada (11/91). 7-vs. X-O Armor						6.00
10-(6/92, $3.95)-1st app. Eternal Warrior (6 pgs.); black embossed-c; origin & 1st app. Geoff McHenry (Geomancer)	1	3	4	6	8	11
10-($3.95)-2nd printing						4.00
11-15: 11-1st full app. Eternal Warrior. 12,13-Unity x-overs. 14-1st app. Fred Bender (becomes Dr. Eclipse). 15-2nd Dr. Eclipse						3.00

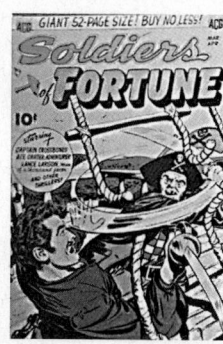

Soldiers of Fortune #1 © ACG

The Solution #11 © MAL

Sonic the Hedgehog #6 © SEGA

	GD 2.0	VG 4.0	FN 6.0	VF 8.0	VF/NM 9.0	NM- 9.2

16-60: 17-X-O Manowar app. 23-Solar splits. 29-1st Valiant Vision book. 33-Valiant Vision;
bound-in trading card. 38-Chaos Effect Epsilion Pt.1. 46-52-Dan Jurgens-a(p)/scripts
w/Giordano-i. 53,54-Jurgens scripts only. 60-Giffen scripts; Jeff Johnson-a(p) ... 2.50
0-($9.95, trade paperback) r/Alpha and Omega origin story; polybagged w/poster ... 10.00
...:Second Death (1994, $9.95)-r/issues #1-4. ... 10.00
NOTE: #1-10 all have free 8 pg. insert "Alpha and Omega" which is a 10 chapter Solar origin story. All 10 center-
folds can pieced together to show climax of story. Ditko a-11p, 14p. Giordano a-46, 47, 48, 49, 50, 51, 52i.
Johnson a-60p. Jurgens a-46, 47, 48, 49, 50 , 51, 52p. Layton a-1-3i; c-2i, 11i, 17i, 25i. Miller c-12. Quesada c-
17p, 20-23p, 29p. Simonson c-13. B. Smith a-1-10; c-1, 3, 5, 7, 19i. Thibert c-22i, 23i.

SOLAR LORD
Image Comics: Mar, 1999 - No. 7, Sept, 1999 ($2.50)
1-7-Khoo Fuk Lung-s/a ... 2.50

SOLARMAN (See Pendulum Ill. Originals)
Marvel Comics: Jan, 1989 - No. 2, May, 1990 ($1.00, limited series)
1,2 ... 2.50

SOLAR, MAN OF THE ATOM (Man of the Atom on cover)
Acclaim Comics (Valiant Heroes): Vol. 2, May, 1997 ($3.95, one-shot, 46 pgs)
(1st Valiant Heroes Special Event)
Vol. 2-Reintro Solar; Ninjak cameo; Warren Ellis scripts; Darick Robertson-a ... 4.00

SOLAR, MAN OF THE ATOM: HELL ON EARTH
Acclaim Comics (Valiant Heroes): Jan, 1998 - No. 4 ($2.50, limited series)
1-4-Priest-s/ Zircher-a(p) ... 2.50

SOLAR, MAN OF THE ATOM: REVELATIONS
Acclaim Comics (Valiant Heroes): Nov, 1997 ($3.95, one-shot, 46 pgs.)
1-Krueger-s/ Zircher-a(p) ... 4.00

SOLDIER & MARINE COMICS (Fightin' Army #16 on)
Charlton Comics (Toby Press of Conn. V1#11): No. 11, Dec, 1954 - No. 15, Aug, 1955;
V2#9, Dec, 1956

V1#11 (12/54)-Bob Powell-a	9	18	27	50	65	80
V1#12(2/55)-15: 12-Photo-c. 14-Photo-c; Colan-a	6	12	18	31	38	45
V2#9(Formerly Never Again; Jerry Drummer V2#10 on)	6	12	18	28	34	40

SOLDIER COMICS
Fawcett Publications: Jan, 1952 - No. 11, Sept, 1953

1	14	28	42	76	108	140
2	8	16	24	44	57	70
3-5	8	16	24	42	54	65
6-11: 8-Illo. in POP	8	16	24	40	50	60

SOLDIERS OF FORTUNE
American Comics Group (Creston Publ. Corp.): Mar-Apr, 1951 - No. 13, Feb-Mar, 1953

1-Capt. Crossbones by Shelly, Ace Carter, Lance Larson begin	23	46	69	130	205	280
2	14	28	42	78	112	145
3-10: 6-Bondage-c	12	24	36	69	97	125
11-13 (War format)	9	18	27	47	61	75

NOTE: Shelly a-1-3, 5. Whitney a-6, 8-11, 13; c-1-3, 5, 6.

SOLDIERS OF FREEDOM
Americomics: 1987 - No. 2, 1987 ($1.75)
1,2 ... 3.00

SOLDIER X (Continued from Cable)
Marvel Comics: Sept, 2002 - No. 12, Aug, 2003 ($2.99/$2.25)
1,10,11,12-($2.99) 1-Kordey-a/Macan-s. 10-Bollers-s/Ranson-a ... 3.00
2-9-($2.25) ... 2.50

SOLITAIRE (Also See Prime V2#6-8)
Malibu Comics (Ultraverse): Nov, 1993 - No. 12, Dec, 1994 ($1.95)
1-($2.50)-Collector's edition bagged w/playing card ... 3.00
1-12: 1-Regular edition w/o playing card. 2,4-Break-Thru x-over. 3-2 pg. origin
The Night Man. 4-Gatefold-c. 5-Two pg. origin the Strangers ... 2.50

SOLO
Marvel Comics: Sept, 1994 - No. 4, Dec, 1994 ($1.75, limited series)
1-4: Spider-Man app. ... 2.50

SOLO (Movie)
Dark Horse Comics: July, 1996 - No. 2, Aug, 1996 ($2.50, limited series)
1,2: Adaptation of film; photo-c ... 2.50

SOLO (Anthology showcasing individual artists)
DC Comics: Dec, 2004 - No. 12, Oct, 2006 ($4.95/$4.99)

1-11: 1-Tim Sale-a; stories by Sale and various. 2-Richard Corben-a; stories by Corben and
Arcudi. 3-Paul Pope. 4-Howard Chaykin. 5-Darwyn Cooke. 6-Jordi Bernet.
7-Michael Allred; Teen Titans & Doom Patrol app. 8-Teddy Kristiansen. 9-Scott Hampton.
10-Damion Scott. 11-Sergio Aragonés. 12-Brendan McCarthy ... 5.00

SOLO AVENGERS (Becomes Avenger Spotlight #21 on)
Marvel Comics: Dec, 1987 - No. 20, July, 1989 (75¢/$1.00)
1-Jim Lee-a on back-up story ... 3.00
2-20: 11-Intro Bobcat ... 2.50

SOLOMON AND SHEBA (Movie)
Dell Publishing Co.: No. 1070, Jan-Mar, 1960

Four Color 1070-Sekowsky-a; photo-c	8	16	24	58	97	135

SOLOMON KANE (Based on the Robert E. Howard character. Also see Blackthorne 3-D
Series #60 & Marvel Premiere)
Marvel Comics: Sept, 1985 - No. 6, July, 1986 (Limited series)
1-6: 1-Double size. 3-6-Williamson-a(i) ... 3.00

SOLUS
CG Entertainment, Inc.: Apr, 2003 - No. 8, Jan, 2004 ($2.95)
1-8: 1-4,6,7-George Pérez-a/c; Barbara Kesel-s. 5-Ryan-a. 8-Kirk-a ... 3.00
Vol. 1: Genesis (1/04, $15.95) r/#1-6 ... 16.00

SOLUTION, THE
Malibu Comics (Ultraverse): Sept, 1993 - No. 17, Feb, 1995 ($1.95)
1,3-15: 1-Intro Meathook, Deathdance, Black Tiger, Tech. 4-Break-Thru x-over; gatefold-c.
5-2 pg. origin The Strangers. 11-Brereton-c ... 2.50
1-($2.50)-Newsstand ed. polybagged w/trading card ... 2.50
1-Ultra 5000 Limited silver foil ... 4.00
0-Obtained w/Rune #0 by sending coupons from 11 comics ... 3.00
2-($2.50, 48 pgs.)-Rune flip-c/story by B. Smith; The Mighty Magnor 1 pg. strip
by Aragonés ... 2.50
16 ($3.50)-Flip-c Ultraverse Premiere #10 ... 3.50
17 ($2.50) ... 2.50

SOMERSET HOLMES (See Eclipse Graphic Novel Series)
Pacific Comics/ Eclipse Comics No. 5, 6: Sept, 1983 - No. 6, Dec, 1984 ($1.50, Baxter
paper)
1-6: 1-Brent Anderson-c/a. Cliff Hanger by Williamson in all ... 3.00

SONG OF THE SOUTH (See Brer Rabbit)

SONIC & KNUCKLES
Archie Comics: Aug, 1995 ($2.00)
1 ... 6.00

SONIC DISRUPTORS
DC Comics: Dec, 1987 - No. 7, July, 1988 ($1.75, unfinished limited series)
1-7 ... 3.00

SONIC'S FRIENDLY NEMESIS KNUCKLES
Archie Publications: July, 1996 - No. 3, Sept, 1996 ($1.50, limited series)
1-3 ... 4.00

SONIC SUPER SPECIAL
Archie Publications: 1997 - Present ($2.00/$2.25/$2.29, 48 pgs)
1-3 ... 4.00
4-6,8-15: 10-Sabrina-c/app. 15-Sin City spoof ... 3.00
7-(w/Image) Spawn, Maxx, Savage Dragon-c/app.; Valentino-a ... 3.00

SONIC THE HEDGEHOG (TV, video game)
Archie Comics: No. 0, Feb, 1993 - No. 3, May, 1993 ($1.25, mini-series)

0(2/93),1: Shaw-a(p) & covers on all	3	6	9	16	22	28
2,3	2	4	6	10	14	18
Beginnings TPB (2003, $10.95) r/#0-3						11.00
...: The Beginning TPB (2006, $10.95) r/#0-3						11.00

SONIC THE HEDGEHOG (TV, video game)
Archie Comics: July, 1993 - Present ($1.25/$1.50/$1.75/$1.79/$1.99/$2.19/$2.25)

1	3	6	9	18	27	35
2,3	2	4	6	13	18	22
4-10: 8-Neon ink-c	2	4	6	10	14	18
11-20	2	4	6	9	12	15
21-30 ($1.50): 25-Silver ink-c	1	3	4	6	8	10
31-50	1	2	3	4	5	7
51-93						3.50
94-183: 117-Begin $2.19-c. 152-Begin $2.25-c. 157-Shadow app.						2.25
Triple Trouble Special (10/95, $2.00, 48 pgs.)						4.50

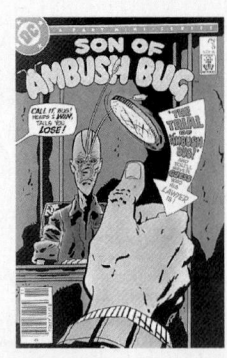

Son of Ambush Bug #5 © DC

Soul Saga #4 © Platt & Lichtner

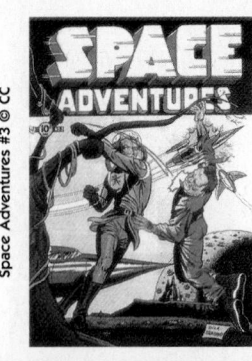

Space Adventures #3 © CC

	GD 2.0	VG 4.0	FN 6.0	VF 8.0	VF/NM 9.0	NM- 9.2

SONIC VS. KNUCKLES "BATTLE ROYAL" SPECIAL
Archie Publications: 1997 ($2.00, one-shot)

1						4.00

SONIC X (Sonic the Hedgehog)
Archie Publications: Nov, 2005 - Present ($2.25)

1-28: 1-Sam Speed app.						2.25

SON OF AMBUSH BUG (See Ambush Bug)
DC Comics: July, 1986 - No. 6, Dec, 1986 (75¢)

1-6: Giffen-c/a in all. 5-Bissette-a.						2.50

SON OF BLACK BEAUTY (Also see Black Beauty)
Dell Publishing Co.: No. 510, Oct, 1953 - No. 566, June, 1954

Four Color 510, 566	4	8	12	26	41	55

SON OF FLUBBER (See Movie Comics)

SON OF M (Also see House of M series)
Marvel Comics: Feb, 2006 - No. 6, July, 2006 ($2.99, limited series)

1-6: 1-Powerless Quicksilver; Martinez-a. 2-Quicksilver regains powers; Inhumans app.						3.00
Decimation: Son of M (2006, $13.99, TPB) r/series; Martinez sketch pages						14.00

SON OF MUTANT WORLD
Fantagor Press: 1990 - No. 5, 1990? ($2.00, bi-monthly)

1-5: 1-3: Corben-c/a. 4,5 ($1.75, B&W)						3.00

SON OF ORIGINS OF MARVEL COMICS (See Fireside Book Series)

SON OF SATAN (Also see Ghost Rider #1 & Marvel Spotlight #12)
Marvel Comics Group: Dec, 1975 - No. 8, Feb, 1977 (25¢)

1-Mooney-a; Kane-c(p), Starlin splash(p)	3	6	9	16	23	30
2,6-8: 2-Origin The Possessor. 8-Heath-a	2	4	6	9	12	15
3-5-(Regular 25¢ editions)(4-8/76): 5-Russell-a	2	4	6	9	12	15
3-5-(30¢-c variants, limited distribution)	2	4	6	13	18	22

SON OF SINBAD (Also see Abbott & Costello & Daring Adventures)
St. John Publishing Co.: Feb, 1950

1-Kubert-c/a	40	80	120	235	368	500

SON OF SUPERMAN (Elseworlds)
DC Comics: 1999 ($14.95, prestige format, one-shot)

nn-Chaykin & Tischman-s/Williams III & Gray-a						15.00

SON OF TOMAHAWK (See Tomahawk)

SON OF VULCAN (Formerly Mysteries of Unexplored Worlds #1-48; Thunderbolt V3#51 on)
Charlton Comics: V2#49, Nov, 1965 - V2#50, Jan, 1966

V2#49,50: 50-Roy Thomas scripts (1st pro work)	3	6	9	17	25	32

SONS OF KATIE ELDER (See Movie Classics)

SORCERY (See Chilling Adventures in... & Red Circle...)

SORORITY SECRETS
Toby Press: July, 1954

1	9	18	27	52	69	85

SOULFIRE (MICHAEL TURNER PRESENTS:...)
Aspen MLT, Inc.: No. 0, 2004 - Present ($2.50/$2.99)

0-($2.50) Turner-a/c; Loeb-s; intro. to characters & development sketches						2.50
1-($2.99) Two covers						3.00
1-Diamond Previews Exclusive						5.00
2-7: 2,3-Two covers. 4-Four covers						3.00
...: The Collected Edition Vol. 1 (5/05, $6.99) r/#1,2; cover gallery						7.00
Hardcover Volume 1 (12/05, $24.99) r/#0-5 & preview from Wizard Magazine; Johns intro.						25.00

SOULFIRE: CHAOS REIGN
Aspen MLT, Inc.: No. 0, June, 2006 - No. 3, Jan, 2007 ($2.50/$2.99)

0-($2.50) Three covers; Marcus To-a; J.T. Krul-s						2.50
1-3-($2.99) 1-Three covers						3.00
...: Beginnings (7/06, $1.99) Marcus To-a; J.T. Krul-s						2.25

SOULFIRE: DYING OF THE LIGHT
Aspen MLT, Inc.: No. 0, 2004 - Present ($2.50/$2.99)

0-($2.50) Three covers; Gunnell-a; Krul-s; back-story to the Soulfire universe						2.50
1-5-($2.99) 1-Five covers						3.00
... Vol. 1 TPB (2007, $14.99) r/#0-5; Gunnell sketch pages, cover gallery						15.00

SOULFIRE: NEW WORLD ORDER
Aspen MLT, Inc.: No. 0, July, 2007 - Present ($2.50/$2.99)

0-($2.50) Two covers; Herrera-a/Krul-s						2.50

SOULQUEST
Innovation: Apr, 1989 ($3.95, squarebound, 52 pgs.)

1-Blackshard app.						4.00

SOUL SAGA
Image Comics (Top Cow): Feb, 2000 - No. 5, Apr, 2001 ($2.50)

1-5: 1-Madureira-c; Platt & Batt-a						2.50

SOULSEARCHERS AND COMPANY
Claypool Comics: June, 1995 - No. 82, Jan, 2007 ($2.50, B&W)

1-10: Peter David scripts						5.00
11-25						3.00
26-82						2.50

SOULWIND
Image Comics: Mar, 1997 - No. 8 ($2.95, B&W, limited series)

1-8: 5-"The Day I Tried To Live" pt. 1						3.00
Book Five; The August Ones (Oni Press, 3/01, $8.50)						8.50
...The Kid From Planet Earth (1997, $9.95, TPB)						10.00
...The Kid From Planet Earth (Oni Press, 1/00, $8.50, TPB)						8.50
...The Day I Tried to Live (Oni Press, 4/00, $8.50, TPB)						8.50
The Complete Soulwind TPB ($29.95, 11/03, 8" x 5 1/2") r/Oni Books #1-5						30.00

SOUPY SALES COMIC BOOK (TV)(The Official...)
Archie Publications: 1965

1	9	18	27	60	100	140

SOUTHERN KNIGHTS, THE (See Crusaders #1)
Guild Publ/Fictioneer Books: No. 2, 1983 - No. 41, 1993 (B&W)

2-Magazine size	1	2	3	5	6	8
3-35, 37-41						3.00
36-($3.50-c)						3.50
Dread Halloween Special 1, Primer Special 1 (Spring, 1989, $2.25)						2.50
Graphic Novels #1-4						4.00

SOVEREIGN SEVEN (Also see Showcase '95 #12)
DC Comics: July, 1995 - No. 36, July, 1998 ($1.95) (1st creator-owned mainstream DC comic)

1-1st app. Sovereign Seven (Reflex, Indigo, Cascade, Finale, Cruiser, Network & Rampart); 1st app. Maitresse; Darkseid app.; Chris Claremont-s & Dwayne Turner-c/a begins						3.00
1-Gold						8.00
1-Platinum						40.00
2-25: 2-Wolverine cameo. 4-Neil Gaiman cameo. 5,8-Batman app. 7-Ramirez cameo (from the movie Highlander). 9-Humphrey Bogart cameo from Casablanca. 10-Impulse app; Manoli Wetherell & Neal Conan cameo from Uncanny X-Men #226. 11-Robin app. 16-Final Night. 24-Superman app. 25-Power Girl app.						2.50
26-36: 26-Begin $2.25-c. 28-Impulse-c/app.						2.50
Annual 1 (1995, $3.95)-Year One story; Big Barda & Lobo app.; Jeff Johnson-c/a						4.00
Annual 2 (1996, $2.95)-Legends of the Dead Earth; Leonardi-c/a						3.50
...Plus 1 (2/97, $2.95)-Legion-c/app.						3.50
TPB-($12.95) r/#1-5, Annual #1 & Showcase '95 #12						13.00

SPACE: ABOVE AND BEYOND (TV)
Topps Comics: Jan, 1996 - No. 3, Mar, 1996 ($2.95, limited series)

1-3: Adaptation of pilot episode; Steacy-c.						3.00

SPACE: ABOVE AND BEYOND--THE GAUNTLET (TV)
Topps Comics: May, 1996 - No. 2, June, 1996 ($2.95, limited series)

1,2						3.00

SPACE ACE (Also see Manhunt!)
Magazine Enterprises: No. 5, 1952

5(A-1 #61)-Guardineer-a	53	106	159	323	537	750

SPACE ACE: DEFENDER OF THE UNIVERSE (Based on the Don Bluth video game)
CrossGen Comics: Oct, 2003 - No. 6 ($2.95, limited series)

1,2-Kirkman-s/Borges-a						3.00

SPACE ACTION
Ace Magazines (Junior Books): June, 1952 - No. 3, Oct, 1952

1-Cameron-a in all (1 story)	75	150	225	469	777	1085
2,3	53	106	159	323	529	735

SPACE ADVENTURES (War At Sea #22 on)
Capitol Stories/Charlton Comics: 7/52 - No. 21, 8/56; No. 23, 5/58 - No. 59, 11/64; V3#60, 10/67; V1#2, 7/68 - V1#8, 7/69; No. 9, 5/78 - No. 13, 3/79

1	53	106	159	323	537	750
2	27	54	81	158	249	340

Space Busters #1 © Z-D

Spaced #12 © ECL

Space Ghost (2005 series) TPB © H-B

	GD 2.0	VG 4.0	FN 6.0	VF 8.0	VF/NM 9.0	NM- 9.2
3-5: 4,6-Flying saucer-c/stories	22	44	66	126	198	270
6-9: 7-Sex change story "Transformation". 8-Robot-c. 9-A-Bomb panel						
	20	40	60	115	180	245
10,11-Ditko-c/a. 10-Robot-c. 11-Two Ditko stories	52	104	156	317	521	725
12-Ditko-c (classic)	68	136	204	425	705	985
13-(Fox-r, 10-11/54); Blue Beetle-c/story	16	32	48	92	144	195
14,15,17,18: 14-Blue Beetle-c/story; Fox-r (12-1/54-55, last pre-code).						
15,17,18-Rocky Jones-c/s.(TV); 15-Part photo-c	20	40	60	117	184	250
16-Krigstein-a; Rocky Jones-c/story (TV)	22	44	66	128	202	275
19	15	30	45	85	130	175
20-Reprints Fawcett's "Destination Moon"	26	52	78	152	239	325
21-(8/56) (no #22)(Becomes War At Sea)	15	30	45	85	130	175
23-(5/58; formerly Nyoka, The Jungle Girl)-Reprints Fawcett's "Destination Moon"						
	23	46	69	132	209	285
24,25,31,32-Ditko-a. 24-Severin-a(signed "LePoer")	20	40	60	117	184	250
26,27-Ditko-a(4) each. 26,28-Flying saucer-c	21	42	63	124	195	265
28-30	11	22	33	60	83	105
33-Origin/1st app. Capt. Atom by Ditko (3/60)	50	100	150	305	503	700
34-40,42-All Captain Atom by Ditko	21	42	63	124	195	265
41,43,45-59: 45-Mercury Man app.	5	10	15	30	48	65
44-1st app. Mercury Man	5	10	15	32	51	70
V3#60(#1, 10/67)-Origin & 1st app. Paul Mann & The Saucers From the Future						
	5	10	15	30	48	65
2,5,6,8 (1968-69)-Ditko-a: 2-Aparo-c/a	3	6	9	19	29	38
3,4,7: 4-Aparo-c/a	3	6	9	16	22	28
9-13(1978-79)-Capt. Atom-r/Space Adventures by Ditko; 9-Reprints origin/1st app. Capt. Atom from #33						5.00

NOTE: *Aparo* a-V3#60. c-V3#8. *Ditko* c-12, 31-42. *Giordano* c-3, 4, 7-9, 18p. *Krigstein* c-15. *Shuster* a-11. Issues 13 & 14 have Blue Beetle logos; #15-18 have Rocky Jones logos.

SPACE ARK
AmeriComics (AC Comics)/ Apple Comics #3 on: June, 1985 - No. 5, Sept, 1987 ($1.75)

1-5: Funny animal (#1,2-color; #3-5-B&W)						2.50

SPACE BUSTERS
Ziff-Davis Publ. Co.: Spring, 1952 - No. 2, Fall, 1952

	GD	VG	FN	VF	VF/NM	NM-
1-Krigstein-a(3); Painted-a by Norman Saunders	80	160	240	500	830	1160
2-Kinstler-a(2 pgs.); Saunders painted-c	61	122	183	381	633	885

NOTE: *Anderson* a-2. Bondage c-2.

SPACE CADET (See Tom Corbett,...)

SPACE CIRCUS
Dark Horse Comics: July, 2000 - No. 4, Oct, 2000 ($2.95, limited series)

1-4-Aragonés-a/Evanier-s						3.00

SPACE COMICS (Formerly Funny Tunes)
Avon Periodicals: No. 4, Mar-Apr, 1954 - No. 5, May-June, 1954

	GD	VG	FN	VF	VF/NM	NM-
4,5-Space Mouse, Peter Rabbit, Super Pup (formerly Spotty the Pup), & Merry Mouse continue from Funny Tunes	8	16	24	40	50	60
I.W. Reprint #8 (nd)-Space Mouse-r	2	4	6	8	10	12

SPACED
Anthony Smith Publ. #1,2/Unbridled Ambition/Eclipse Comics #10 on: 1982 - No. 13, 1988 ($1.25/$1.50, B&W, quarterly)

1-($1.25-c)						3.00
2-13, Special Edition (1983, Mimeo)						2.50

SPACE DETECTIVE
Avon Periodicals: July, 1951 - No. 4, July, 1952

	GD	VG	FN	VF	VF/NM	NM-
1-Rod Hathway, Space Detective begins, ends #4; Wood-c/a(3)-23 pgs.; "Opium Smugglers of Venus" drug story; Lucky Dale-r/Saint #4	110	220	330	688	1144	1600
2-Tales from the Shadow Squad story; Wood/Orlando-c; Wood inside layouts; "Slave Ship of Saturn" story	85	170	255	531	878	1225
3,4: 3-Kinstler-a. 4-Kinstlerish-a by McCann	42	84	123	256	421	585
I.W. Reprint #1(Reprints #2), 8(Reprints cover #1 & part Famous Funnies #191)						
	4	8	12	22	34	45
I.W. Reprint #9-Exist?	4	8	12	22	34	45

SPACE EXPLORER (See March of Comics #202)

SPACE FAMILY ROBINSON (TV)(...Lost in Space #15-37, ...Lost in Space On Space Station One #38 on)(See Gold Key Champion)
Gold Key: Dec, 1962 - No. 36, Oct, 1969; No. 37, 10/73 - No. 54, 11/78; No. 55, 3/81 - No. 59, 5/82 (All painted covers)

	GD	VG	FN	VF	VF/NM	NM-
1-(Low distribution); Spiegle-a in all	21	42	63	156	278	400
2(3/63)-Family becomes lost in space	11	22	33	79	140	200
3-5	8	16	24	52	86	120
6-10: 6-Captain Venture back-up stories begin	6	12	18	43	70	95

	GD 2.0	VG 4.0	FN 6.0	VF 8.0	VF/NM 9.0	NM- 9.2
11-20: 14-(10/65). 15-Title change (1/66)	5	10	15	30	48	65
21-36: 28-Last 12¢ issue. 36-Captain Venture ends	4	8	12	23	36	45
37-48: 37-Origin retold	2	4	6	10	14	18
49-59: Reprints #49,50,55-59	2	4	6	8	10	12

NOTE: *The TV show first aired on 9/15/65. Title changed after TV show debuted.*

SPACE FAMILY ROBINSON (See March of Comics #320, 328, 352, 404, 414)

SPACE GHOST (TV) (Also see Golden Comics Digest #2 & Hanna-Barbera Super TV Heroes #3-7)
Gold Key: March, 1967 (Hanna-Barbera) (TV debut was 9/10/66)

	GD	VG	FN	VF	VF/NM	NM-
1 (10199-703)-Spiegle-a	29	58	87	212	381	550

SPACE GHOST (TV cartoon)
Comico: Mar, 1987 ($3.50, deluxe format, one-shot) (Hanna-Barbera)

	GD	VG	FN	VF	VF/NM	NM-
1-Steve Rude-c/a	1	2	3	5	6	8

SPACE GHOST (TV cartoon)
DC Comics: Jan, 2005 - No. 6, June, 2005 ($2.95/$2.99, limited series)

1-6-Alex Ross-c/Ariel Olivetti-a/Joe Kelly-s; origin of Space Ghost						3.00
TPB (2005, $14.99) r/series; cover gallery						15.00

SPACE GIANTS, THE (TV cartoon)
FBN Publications: 1979 (51¢, B&W, one-shots)

	GD	VG	FN	VF	VF/NM	NM-
1-Based on Japanese TV series	2	4	6	9	12	15

SPACEHAWK
Dark Horse Comics: 1989 - No. 3, 1990 ($2.00, B&W)

1-3-Wolverton-c/a(r) plus new stories by others.						4.00

SPACE JAM
DC Comics: 1996 ($5.95, one-shot, movie adaption)

	GD	VG	FN	VF	VF/NM	NM-
1-Wraparound photo cover of Michael Jordan	1	2	3	5	6	8

SPACE KAT-ETS (...in 3-D)
Power Publishing Co.: Dec, 1953 (25¢, came w/glasses)

	GD	VG	FN	VF	VF/NM	NM-
1	30	60	90	174	275	375

SPACEKNIGHTS
Marvel Comics: Oct, 2000 - No. 5, Feb, 2001 ($2.99, limited series)

1-5-Starlin-s/Batista-a						3.00

SPACEMAN (Speed Carter...)
Atlas Comics (CnPC): Sept, 1953 - No. 6, July, 1954

	GD	VG	FN	VF	VF/NM	NM-
1-Grey tone-c	68	136	204	425	705	985
2	43	86	129	262	431	600
3-6: 4-A-Bomb explosion-c	40	80	120	235	368	500

NOTE: *Everett* c-1, 3. *Heath* a-1. *Maneely* a-1(3), 2(4), 3(3), 4-6; c-5, 6. *Romita* a-1. *Sekowsky* c-4. *Sekowsky/Abel* a-4(3). *Tuska* a-5(3).

SPACE MAN
Dell Publ. Co.: No. 1253, 1-3/62 - No. 8, 3-5/64; No. 9, 7/72 - No. 10, 10/72

	GD	VG	FN	VF	VF/NM	NM-
Four Color 1253 (#1)(1-3/62)(15¢-c)	7	14	21	49	80	110
2,3: 2-(15¢-c). 3-(12¢-c)	4	8	12	28	44	60
4-8-(12¢-c)	4	8	12	22	34	45
9,10-(15¢-c): 9-Reprints #1253. 10-Reprints #2	2	4	6	9	12	15

SPACEMAN (From the Atomics)
Oni Press: July, 2002 ($2.95, one-shot)

1-Mike Allred-s/a; Lawrence Marvit additional art						3.00

SPACE MOUSE (Also see Funny Tunes & Space Comics)
Avon Periodicals: April, 1953 - No. 5, Apr-May, 1954

	GD	VG	FN	VF	VF/NM	NM-
1	10	20	30	54	72	90
2	7	14	21	35	43	50
3-5	6	12	18	28	34	40

SPACE MOUSE (Walter Lantz...#1; see Comic Album #17)
Dell Publishing Co./Gold Key: No. 1132, Aug-Oct, 1960 - No. 5, Nov, 1963 (Walter Lantz)

	GD	VG	FN	VF	VF/NM	NM-
Four Color 1132,1244, 1 (11/62)(G.K.)	4	8	12	28	44	60
2-5	4	8	12	24	37	50

SPACE MYSTERIES
I.W. Enterprises: 1964 (Reprints)

	GD	VG	FN	VF	VF/NM	NM-
1-r/Journey Into Unknown Worlds #4 w/new-c	3	6	9	16	22	28
8,9: 9-r/Planet Comics #73	3	6	9	16	22	28

SPACE: 1999 (TV) (Also see Power Record Comics)
Charlton Comics: Nov, 1975 - No. 7, Nov, 1976

	GD	VG	FN	VF	VF/NM	NM-
1-Origin Moonbase Alpha; Staton-c/a	2	4	6	13	18	22

Space Squadron #4 © MAR

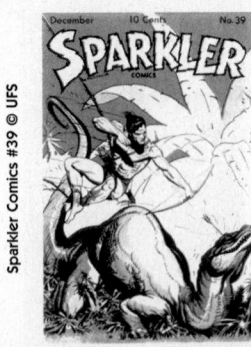

Sparkler Comics #39 © UFS

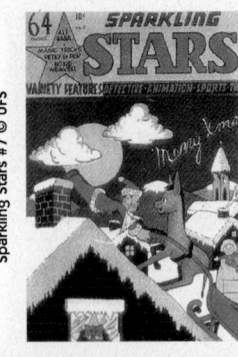

Sparkling Stars #7 © UFS

	GD 2.0	VG 4.0	FN 6.0	VF 8.0	VF/NM 9.0	NM- 9.2
2,7: 2-Staton-a	2	4	6	9	13	16
3-6: All Byrne-a; c-3,5,6	2	4	6	13	18	22
nn (Charlton Press, digest, 100 pgs., B&W, no cover price) new stories & art						
	3	6	9	16	23	30

SPACE: 1999 (TV)(Magazine)
Charlton Comics: Nov, 1975 - No. 8, Nov, 1976 (B&W) (#7 shows #6 inside)

1-Origin Moonbase Alpha; Morrow-c/a	3	6	9	14	19	24
2-8: 2,3-Morrow-c/a. 4-6-Morrow-c. 5,8-Morrow-c	2	4	6	10	14	18

SPACE PATROL (TV)
Ziff-Davis Publishing Co. (Approved Comics): Summer, 1952 - No. 2, Oct-Nov, 1952 (Painted-c by Norman Saunders)

1-Krigstein-a	89	178	267	556	921	1285
2-Krigstein-a(3)	65	130	195	406	671	935

SPACE PIRATES (See Archie Giant Series #533)
SPACE RANGER (See Mystery in Space #92, Showcase #15 & Tales of the Unexpected)
SPACE SQUADRON (In the Days of the Rockets)(Becomes Space Worlds #6)
Marvel/Atlas Comics (ACI): June, 1951 - No. 5, Feb, 1952

1-Space team; Brodsky c-1,5	67	134	201	419	697	975
2- Tuska c-2-4	54	108	162	338	557	775
3-5: 3-Capt. Jet Dixon by Tuska(3). 4-Weird advs. begin						
	46	92	138	281	466	650

SPACE THRILLERS
Avon Periodicals: 1954 (25¢ Giant)

nn-(Scarce)-Robotmen of the Lost Planet; contains 3 rebound comics of The Saint & Strange Worlds. Contents could vary	117	234	351	731	1216	1700

SPACE TRIP TO THE MOON (See Space Adventures #23)
SPACE USAGI
Mirage Studios: June, 1992 - No. 3, 1992 ($2.00, B&W, mini-series) V2#1, Nov, 1993 - V2#3, Jan, 1994 ($2.75)

1-3: Stan Sakai-c/a/scripts, V2#1-3						3.00

SPACE USAGI
Dark Horse Comics: Jan, 1996 - No. 3, Mar, 1996 ($2.95, B&W, limited series)

1-3: Stan Sakai-c/a/scripts						3.00

SPACE WAR (Fightin' Five #28 on)
Charlton Comics: Oct, 1959 - No. 27, Mar, 1964; No. 28, Mar, 1978 - No. 34, 3/79

V1#1-Giordano-c begin, end #3	13	26	39	90	160	235
2,3	7	14	21	50	83	115
4-6,8,10-Ditko-c/a	13	26	39	90	160	235
7,9,11-15: Last 10¢ issue?	6	12	18	37	59	80
16-27 (3/64): 18,19-Robot-c	5	10	15	30	48	65
28(3/78),29-31,33,34-Ditko-c/a(r): 30-Staton, Sutton/Wood-a. 31-Ditko-c/a(3); same-c as Strange Suspense Stories #2 (1968); atom blast-c						
	1	3	4	6	8	10
32-r/Charlton Premiere V2#2; Sutton-a						5.00

SPACE WESTERN (Formerly Cowboy Western Comics; becomes Cowboy Western Comics #46 on)
Charlton Comics (Capitol Stories): No. 40, Oct, 1952 - No. 45, Aug, 1953

40-Intro Spurs Jackson & His Space Vigilantes; flying saucer story						
	55	110	135	344	572	800
41,43-45: 41-Flying saucer-c. 45-Hitler app.	41	82	123	253	407	560
42-Atom bomb explosion-c	43	86	129	262	431	600

SPACE WORLDS (Formerly Space Squadron #1-5)
Atlas Comics (Male): No. 6, April, 1952

6-Sol Brodsky-c	43	86	129	262	431	600

SPAGHETTI WESTERN
Oni Press: June, 2004 ($11.95, digest-size, widescreen, sepia & white)

nn-Scott Morse-s/a; outer wraparound-c						12.00

SPANKY & ALFALFA & THE LITTLE RASCALS (See The Little Rascals)
SPANNER'S GALAXY
DC Comics: Dec, 1984 - No. 6, May, 1985 (limited series)

1-6: Mandrake-c/a in all.						2.50

SPARKIE, RADIO PIXIE (Radio)(Becomes Big Jon & Sparkie #4)
Ziff-Davis Publ. Co.: No. 1 - No. 3, July-Aug, 1952 (Painted-c)(Sparkie #2,3; #1?)

1-Based on children's radio program	27	54	81	158	249	340
2,3: 3-Big Jon and Sparkie on-c only	18	36	54	105	165	225

SPARKLE COMICS
United Features Synd.: Oct-Nov, 1948 - No. 33, Dec-Jan, 1953-54

1-Li'l Abner, Nancy, Captain & the Kids, Ella Cinders (#1-3: 52 pgs.)						
	15	30	45	83	124	165
2	9	18	27	50	65	80
3-10	8	16	24	40	50	60
11-20	7	14	21	35	43	50
21-32	6	12	18	28	34	40
33-(2-3/54) 2 pgs. early Peanuts by Schulz	9	18	27	47	61	75

SPARKLE PLENTY (See Harvey Comics Library #2 & Dick Tracy)
SPARKLER COMICS (1st series)
United Feature Comic Group: July, 1940 - No. 2, 1940

1-Jim Hardy	40	80	120	235	368	500
2-Frankie Doodle	29	58	87	167	264	360

SPARKLER COMICS (2nd series)(Nancy & Sluggo #121 on)(Cover title becomes Nancy and Sluggo #101? on)
United Features Syndicate: July, 1941 - No. 120, Jan, 1955

1-Origin 1st app. Sparkman; Tarzan (by Hogarth in all issues), Captain & the Kids, Ella Cinders, Danny Dingle, Dynamite Dunn, Nancy, Abbie & Slats, Broncho Bill, Frankie Doodle, begin; Spark Man c-1-9,11,12; Hap Hopper c-10,13						
	238	476	714	1488	2469	3450
2	78	156	234	488	812	1135
3,4	59	118	177	369	615	860
5-9: 9-Spark Man's new costume	54	108	162	338	562	785
10-Origin Spark Man?	54	108	162	338	562	785
11,12-Spark Man war-c. 12-Spark Man's new costume (color change)						
	43	86	129	262	431	600
13-Hap Hopper war-c	41	82	123	250	400	550
14-Tarzan-c by Hogarth	53	106	159	323	537	750
15,17: 15-Capt & Kids-c. 17-Nancy & Sluggo-c	36	72	108	208	329	450
16,18-Spark Man war-c	41	82	123	250	416	575
19-1st Race Riley and the Commandos-c/s	41	82	123	250	400	550
20-Nancy war-c	36	72	108	208	329	450
21,25,28,31,34,37,39-Tarzan-c by Hogarth	45	90	135	275	455	635
22-24,26,27,29,30: 22-Race Riley & the Commandos strips begin, ends #44						
	31	62	93	178	282	385
32,33,35,36,38,40	18	36	54	105	165	225
41,43,45,46,48,49	14	28	42	80	115	150
42,44,47,50-Tarzan-c (42,47,50 by Hogarth)	28	56	84	164	260	355
51,52,54-70: 57-Li'l Abner begins (not in #58); Fearless Fosdick app. in #58						
	14	28	42	76	108	140
53-Tarzan-c by Hogarth	24	48	72	139	220	300
71-80	10	20	30	54	72	90
81,82,84-86: 86 Last Tarzan; lingerie panels	9	18	27	47	61	75
83-Tarzan-c; Li'l Abner ends	13	26	39	74	105	135
87-96,98-99	8	16	24	44	57	70
97-Origin Casey Ruggles by Warren Tufts	13	26	39	72	101	130
100	9	18	27	50	65	80
101-107,109-112,114-119	7	14	21	37	46	55
108,113-Toth-a	9	18	27	50	65	80
120-(10-11/54) 2 pgs. early Peanuts by Schulz	9	18	27	50	65	80

SPARKLING LOVE
Avon Periodicals/Realistic (1953): June, 1950; 1953

1(Avon)-Kubert-a; photo-c	23	46	69	135	213	290
nn(1953)-Reprint; Kubert-a	9	18	27	52	69	85

SPARKLING STARS
Holyoke Publishing Co.: June, 1944 - No. 33, March, 1948

1-Hell's Angels, FBI, Boxie Weaver, Petey & Pop, & Ali Baba begin						
	20	40	60	115	180	245
2-Speed Spaulding story	12	24	36	67	94	120
3-Actual FBI case photos & war photos	10	20	30	54	72	90
4-10: 7-X-Mas-c	9	18	27	50	65	80
11-19: 13-Origin/1st app. Jungo the Man-Beast-c/s	8	16	24	44	57	70
20-Intro Fangs the Wolf Boy	9	18	27	50	65	80
21-33: 29-Bondage-c. 31-Sid Greene-a	8	16	24	42	54	65

SPARK MAN (See Sparkler Comics)
Frances M. McQueeny: 1945 (36 pgs., one-shot)

1-Origin Spark Man r/Sparkler #1-3; female torture story; cover redrawn from Sparkler #1						
	32	64	96	186	293	400

SPARKY WATTS (Also see Big Shot Comics & Columbia Comics)

Spawn #117 © TMP

Spawn: The Dark Ages #1 © TMP

Special Marvel Edition #7 © MAR

	GD 2.0	VG 4.0	FN 6.0	VF 8.0	VF/NM 9.0	NM- 9.2

Columbia Comic Corp.: Nov?, 1942 - No. 10, 1949

	GD 2.0	VG 4.0	FN 6.0	VF 8.0	VF/NM 9.0	NM- 9.2
1(1942)-Skyman & The Face app; Hitler-c	71	142	213	444	735	1025
2(1943)	29	58	87	170	268	365
3(1944)	21	42	63	122	191	260
4(1944)-Origin	18	36	54	105	165	225
5(1947)-Skyman app.; Boody Rogers-c/a	15	30	45	88	137	185
6,7,9,10: 6(1947),10(1949)	11	22	33	60	83	105
8(1948)-Surrealistic-c	14	28	42	76	108	140

NOTE: *Boody Rogers c-1-8.*

SPARTACUS (Movie)
Dell Publishing Co.: No. 1139, Nov, 1960 (Kirk Douglas photo-c)

	GD 2.0	VG 4.0	FN 6.0	VF 8.0	VF/NM 9.0	NM- 9.2
Four Color 1139-Buscema-a	12	24	36	87	156	225

SPARTAN: WARRIOR SPIRIT (Also see WildC.A.T.S: Covert Action Teams)
Image Comics (WildStorm Productions): July, 1995 - No. 4, Nov, 1995 ($2.50, limited series)

1-4: Kurt Busiek scripts; Mike McKone-c/a ... 2.50

SPAWN (Also see Curse of the Spawn and Sam & Twitch)
Image Comics (Todd McFarlane Prods.): May, 1992 - Present ($1.95/$2.50)

	GD 2.0	VG 4.0	FN 6.0	VF 8.0	VF/NM 9.0	NM- 9.2
1-1st app. Spawn; McFarlane/a begins; McFarlane/Steacy-c; 1st Todd McFarlane Productions title.	1	3	4	6	8	10
1-Black & white edition	2	4	6	11	16	20
2,3: 2-1st app. Violator; McFarlane/Steacy-c	1	2	3	5	7	9
4-Contains coupon for Image Comics #0	1	2	3	5	7	9

4-With coupon missing ... 3.00
4-Newsstand edition w/o poster or coupon ... 3.00
5-Cerebus cameo (1 pg.) as stuffed animal; Spawn mobile poster #1 ... 6.00
6-8,10: 7-Spawn Mobile poster #2. 8-Alan Moore scripts; Miller poster. 10-Cerebus app.; Dave Sim scripts; 1 pg. cameo app. by Superman ... 4.00
9-Neil Gaiman scripts; Jim Lee poster; 1st Angela. ... 6.00
11-17,19,20,22-30: 11-Miller script; Darrow poster. 12-Bloodwulf poster by Liefeld. 14,15-Violator app. 16,17-Grant Morrison scripts; Capullo-c/a(p). 23,24-McFarlane-a/stories. 25-(10/94). 19-(10/94). 20-(11/94) ... 3.00

	GD 2.0	VG 4.0	FN 6.0	VF 8.0	VF/NM 9.0	NM- 9.2
18-Grant Morrison script, Capullo-c/a(p); low distr.	1	2	3	5	7	9
21-low distribution	1	2	3	5	7	9

31-49: 31-1st app. The Redeemer; new costume (brief). 32-1st full app. new costume. 38-40,42,44,46,48-Tony Daniel-c/a(p). 38-1st app. Cy-Gor. 40,41-Cy-Gor & Curse app. ... 4.00
50-($3.95, 48 pgs.) ... 3.00
51-66: 52-Savage Dragon app. 56-w/ Darkchylde preview. 57-Cy-Gor-c/app. 64-Polybagged w/McFarlane Toys catalog. 65-Photo-c of movie Spawn and McFarlane ... 3.00
67-97: 81-Billy Kincaid returns. 97-Angela-c/app. ... 2.50
98,99,101-149:($2.50): 98,99-Angela app. ... 2.50
100-($4.95) Angela dies; 6 covers by McFarlane, Ross, Miller, Capullo, Wood, Mignola ... 5.00
150-($4.95) 4 covers by McFarlane, Capullo, Tan, Jim Lee ... 5.00
151-171: 151-($2.95) Wraparound-c by Tan. 166-Haberline-a. 167-Clown app. ... 3.00
Annual 1-Blood & Shadows ('99, $4.95) Ashley Wood-c/a; Jenkins-a ... 5.00
...: Armageddon Complete Collection TPB ('07, $29.95) r/#150-163 ... 30.00
...: Armageddon, Part 1 TPB (10/06, $14.99) r/#150-155 ... 15.00
...: Armageddon, Part 2 TPB (2/07, $15.95) r/#156-164 ... 16.00
...Bible-(8/96, $1.95)-Character bios ... 4.00
Book 1 TPB($9.95) r/#1-5; Book 2-r/#6-9,11; Book 3 -r/#12-15, Book 4- r/#16-20; Book 5-r/#21-25; Book 6- r/#26-30; Book 7-r/#31-34; Book 8-r/#35-38; Book 9-r/#39-42; Book 10-r/#43-47 ... 11.00
Book 11 TPB ($10.95) Book 12-r/#51-54 ... 11.00
... Collection Vol. 1 (10/05, $19.95) r/#1-8,11,12; intro. by Frank Miller ... 20.00
... Collection Vol. 2 HC (7/07, $49.95) r/#13-33 ... 50.00
... Collection Vol. 2 SC (9/06, $29.95) r/#13-33 ... 30.00
... Collection Vol. 3 (3/07, $29.95) r/#34-54 ... 30.00
... Collection Vol. 4 (9/07, $29.95) r/#55-75 ... 30.00
... Godslayer Vol. 1 (9/06, $6.99) Anacleto-c/a; Holguin-s; sketch pages ... 7.00
... New Flesh TPB ('07, $14.95) r/#166-169 ... 15.00
...Simony (5/04, $7.95) English translation of French Spawn story; Briclot-a ... 8.00

NOTE: *Capullo a-16p-18p; c-16p-18p. Daniel a-38-40, 42, 44, 46. McFarlane a-1-15; c-1-15p. Thibert a-16(part). Posters come with issues 1, 4, 7-9, 11, 12. #25 was released after #19 & 20.*

SPAWN-BATMAN (Also see Batman/Spawn: War Devil under Batman: One-Shots)
Image Comics (Todd McFarlane Prods.): 1994 ($3.95, one-shot)

1-Miller scripts; McFarlane-c/a ... 6.00

SPAWN: BLOOD FEUD
Image Comics (Todd McFarlane Prods.): June, 1995 - No. 4, Sept, 1995 ($2.25, lim. series)

1-4-Alan Moore scripts, Tony Daniel-a ... 3.50

SPAWN FAN EDITION
Image Comics (Todd McFarlane Productions): Aug, 1996 - No. 3, Oct, 1996 (Giveaway, 12 pgs.) (Polybagged w/Overstreet's FAN)

	GD 2.0	VG 4.0	FN 6.0	VF 8.0	VF/NM 9.0	NM- 9.2
1-3: Beau Smith scripts; Brad Gorby-a(p). 1-1st app. Nordik, the Norse Hellspawn. 2-1st app. McFallon. 3-1st app. Mercy	1	2	3	5	6	8

1-3-(Gold): All retailer incentives ... 16.00

	GD 2.0	VG 4.0	FN 6.0	VF 8.0	VF/NM 9.0	NM- 9.2
1-3-Variant-c	1	2	3	5	6	8

2-(Platinum)-Retailer incentive ... 25.00

SPAWN GODSLAYER
Image Comics (Todd McFarlane Prods.): May, 2007 - Present ($2.99)

1-4-Holguin-s/Tan-a/Anacleto-c ... 3.00

SPAWN: THE DARK AGES
Image Comics (Todd McFarlane Productions): Mar, 1999 - No. 28, Oct, 2001 ($2.50)

1-Fabry-c; Holguin-s/Sharp-a; variant-c by McFarlane ... 2.50
2-28 ... 2.50

SPAWN THE IMPALER
Image Comics (Todd McFarlane Prods.): Oct, 1996 - No. 3, Dec, 1996 ($2.95, limited series)

1-3-Mike Grell scripts, painted-a ... 3.00

SPAWN: THE UNDEAD
Image Comics (Todd McFarlane Prod.): Jun, 1999 - No. 9, Feb, 2000 ($1.95/$2.25)

1-9-Dwayne Turner-c/a; Jenkins-s. 7-9-($2.25-c) ... 2.50

SPAWN/WILDC.A.T.S
Image Comics (WildStorm): Jan, 1996 - No. 4, Apr, 1996 ($2.50, lim. series)

1-4: Alan Moore scripts in all. ... 3.00

SPECIAL AGENT (Steve Saunders...)(Also see True Comics #68)
Parents' Magazine Institute (Commended Comics No. 2): Dec, 1947 - No. 8, Sept, 1949 (Based on true FBI cases)

	GD 2.0	VG 4.0	FN 6.0	VF 8.0	VF/NM 9.0	NM- 9.2
1-J. Edgar Hoover photo on-c	12	24	36	67	94	120
2	8	16	24	40	50	60
3-8	7	14	21	35	43	50

SPECIAL COLLECTORS' EDITION (See Savage Fists of Kung-Fu)

SPECIAL COMICS (Becomes Hangman #2 on)
MLJ Magazines: Winter, 1941-42

	GD 2.0	VG 4.0	FN 6.0	VF 8.0	VF/NM 9.0	NM- 9.2
1-Origin The Boy Buddies (Shield & Wizard x-over); death of The Comet retold (see Pep #17); origin The Hangman retold; Hangman-c	317	634	951	1981	3291	4600

SPECIAL EDITION (See Gorgo and Reptisaurus)

SPECIAL EDITION COMICS
Fawcett Publications: 1940 (August) (68 pgs., one-shot)

	GD 2.0	VG 4.0	FN 6.0	VF 8.0	VF/NM 9.0	NM- 9.2
1-1st book devoted entirely to Captain Marvel; C.C. Beck-c/a; only app. of Captain Marvel with belt buckle; Capt. Marvel appears with button-down flap; 1st story (came out before Captain Marvel #1)	743	1486	2229	5200	9100	13,000

NOTE: *Prices vary widely on this book. Since this book is all Captain Marvel stories, it is actually a pre-Captain Marvel #1. There is speculation that this book almost became Captain Marvel #1. After Special Edition was published, there was an idea or name change at Fawcett. The new editor commissioned Kirby to do a nn Captain Marvel book early in 1941. This book was followed by a 2nd book several months later. This 2nd book was advertised as a #3 (making Special Edition the #1, & the nn book the #2). However, the 2nd book did come out as a #2.*

SPECIAL EDITION: SPIDER-MAN VS. THE HULK (See listing under The Amazing Spider-Man)

SPECIAL EDITION X-MEN
Marvel Comics Group: Feb, 1983 ($2.00, one-shot, Baxter paper)

	GD 2.0	VG 4.0	FN 6.0	VF 8.0	VF/NM 9.0	NM- 9.2
1-r/Giant-Size X-Men #1 plus one new story	2	4	6	8	10	12

SPECIAL MARVEL EDITION (Master of Kung Fu #17 on)
Marvel Comics Group: Jan, 1971 - No. 16, Feb, 1974 (#1-3: 25¢, 68 pgs.; #4: 52 pgs.; #5-16: 20¢, regular ed.)

	GD 2.0	VG 4.0	FN 6.0	VF 8.0	VF/NM 9.0	NM- 9.2
1-Thor-r by Kirby; 68 pgs.	3	6	9	18	27	35
2-4: Thor-r by Kirby; 11-$2,3-68 pg. Giant. 4-(52 pgs.)	2	4	6	11	16	20
5-14: Sgt. Fury-r; 11-r/Sgt. Fury #13 (Capt. America)	1	3	4	6	8	10
15-Master of Kung Fu (Shang-Chi) begins (1st app., 12/73); Starlin-a; origin/1st app. Nayland Smith & Dr. Petrie	10	20	30	70	123	175
16-1st app. Midnight; Starlin-a (2nd Shang-Chi)	10	15	32	51	70	

NOTE: *Kirby c-10-14.*

SPECIAL MISSIONS (See G.I. Joe...)

SPECIAL WAR SERIES (Attack V4#3 on?)
Charlton Comics: Aug, 1965 - No. 4, Nov, 1965

	GD 2.0	VG 4.0	FN 6.0	VF 8.0	VF/NM 9.0	NM- 9.2
V4#1-D-Day (also see D-Day listing)	4	8	12	22	34	45
2-Attack!	3	6	9	14	20	25
3-War & Attack (also see War & Attack)	2	4	6	11	16	20
4-Judomaster (intro/1st app.; see Sarge Steel)	7	14	21	49	80	110

SPECIES (Movie)
Dark Horse Comics: June, 1995 - No. 4, Sept, 1995 ($2.50, limited series)

Spectacular Spider-Man #21 © MAR

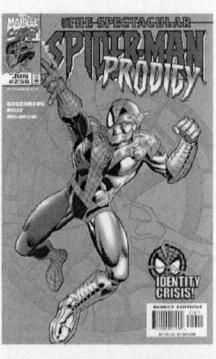

Spectacular Spider-Man #258 © MAR

The Spectre #62 © DC

	GD 2.0	VG 4.0	FN 6.0	VF 8.0	VF/NM 9.0	NM- 9.2

	GD 2.0	VG 4.0	FN 6.0	VF 8.0	VF/NM 9.0	NM- 9.2
1-4: Adaptation of film						3.00
SPECIES: HUMAN RACE (Movie)						
Dark Horse Comics: Nov, 1996 - No. 4, Feb, 1997 ($2.95, limited series)						
1-4						3.00
SPECTACULAR ADVENTURES (See Adventures)						
SPECTACULAR FEATURE MAGAZINE, A (Formerly My Confessions)						
(Spectacular Features Magazine #12)						
Fox Feature Syndicate: No. 11, April, 1950						
11 (#1)-Samson and Delilah	27	54	81	156	246	335
SPECTACULAR FEATURES MAGAZINE (Formerly A Spectacular Feature Magazine)						
Fox Feature Syndicate: No. 12, June, 1950 - No. 3, Aug, 1950						
12 (#2)-Iwo Jima; photo flag-c	27	54	81	156	246	335
3-True Crime Cases From Police Files	22	44	66	126	198	270
SPECTACULAR SCARLET SPIDER						
Marvel Comics: Nov, 1995 - No. 2, Dec, 1995 ($1.95, limited series)						
1,2: Replaces Spectacular Spider-Man						2.50
SPECTACULAR SPIDER-MAN, THE (See Marvel Special Edition and Marvel Treasury Edition)						
SPECTACULAR SPIDER-MAN, THE (Magazine)						
Marvel Comics Group: July, 1968 - No. 2, Nov, 1968 (35¢)						
1-(B&W)-Romita/Mooney 52 pg. story plus updated origin story with Everett-a(i)	11	22	33	75	113	190
1-Variation w/single c-price of 40¢	11	22	33	75	133	190
2-(Color)-Green Goblin-c & 58 pg. story; Romita painted-c (story reprinted in King Size Spider-Man #9); Romita/Mooney-a	12	24	36	82	146	210
SPECTACULAR SPIDER-MAN, THE (Peter Parker…#54-132, 134)						
Marvel Comics Group: Dec, 1976 - No. 263, Nov 1998						
1-Origin recap in text; return of Tarantula	5	10	15	35	55	75
2-Kraven the Hunter app.	3	6	9	16	22	28
3-5: 3-Intro Lightmaster. 4-Vulture app.	2	4	6	11	16	20
6-8-Morbius app.; 6-r/Marvel Team-Up #3 w/Morbius						
	2	4	6	13	18	22
7,8-(35¢-c variants, limited distribution)(6,7/77)	5	10	15	35	55	75
9-20: 9,10-White Tiger app. 11-Last 30¢-c. 17,18-Angel & Iceman app. (from Champions); Ghost Rider cameo. 18-Gil Kane-c	2	4	6	8	10	12
9-11-(35¢-c variants, limited distribution)(8-10/77)	3	6	9	20	30	40
21,24-26: 21-Scorpion app. 26-Daredevil app.	1	2	3	5	7	9
22,23-Moon Knight app.	1	3	4	6	8	10
27-Miller's 1st art on Daredevil (2/79); also see Captain America #235						
	4	8	12	26	41	55
28-Miller Daredevil (p)	4	8	12	22	34	45
29-55,57,59: 33-Origin Iguana. 38-Morbius app.						5.00
56-2nd app. Jack O'Lantern (Macendale) & 1st Spidey/Jack O'Lantern battle (7/81)						6.00
58-Byrne-a(p)						6.00
60-Double size; origin retold with new facts revealed						6.00
61,63,65,68,71-74: 65-Kraven the Hunter app.						4.00
64-1st app. Cloak & Dagger (3/82)	2	4	6	9	12	15
69,70-Cloak & Dagger app.	1	2	3	5	6	8
75-Double size						5.00
76-80: 78,79-Punisher cameo						4.00
81,82-Punisher, Cloak & Dagger app.						6.00
83-Origin Punisher retold (10/83)	1	3	4	6	8	10
84,86-89,91-99: 94-96-Cloak & Dagger app. 98-Intro The Spot						4.00
85-Hobgoblin (Ned Leeds) app. (12/83); gains powers of original Green Goblin (see Amazing Spider-Man #238)	1	3	4	6	8	10
90-Spider-Man's new black costume, last panel (ties w/Amazing Spider-Man #252 & Marvel Team-Up #141 for 1st app.)						5.00
100-(3/85)-Double size						5.00
101-115,117,118,120-129: 107-110-Death of Jean DeWolff. 111-Secret Wars II tie-in. 128-Black Cat new costume						3.00
116,119-Sabretooth-c/story	1	3	4	5	6	8
130-132: 30-Hobgoblin app. 131-Six part Kraven tie-in. 132-Kraven tie-in						
	1	2	3	4	5	7
133-140: 138-1st full app. Tombstone (origin #139). 140-Punisher cameo						3.00
141-143-Punisher app.						5.00
144-146,148-157: 151-Tombstone returns						3.00
147-1st brief app. new Hobgoblin (Macendale), 1 page; continued in Web of Spider-Man #48						
	2	4	6	8	10	12
158-Spider-Man gets new powers (1st Cosmic Spidey, cont'd in Web of Spider-Man #59)						
	1	2	3	4	5	7
159-Cosmic Spider-Man app.						6.00
160-170: 161-163-Hobgoblin app. 168-170-Avengers x-over. 169-1st app. The Outlaws						2.50
171-188,190-199: 180,181,183,184-Green Goblin app. 197-199-Original X-men-c/story						2.50
189-($2.95, 52 pgs.)-Silver hologram on-c; battles Green Goblin; origin Spidey retold; Vess poster w/Spidey & Hobgoblin						4.00
189-(2nd printing)-Gold hologram on-c						3.00
195-(Deluxe ed.)-Polybagged w/"Dirt" magazine #2 & Beastie Boys/Smithereens music cassette						4.00
200-($2.95)-Holo-grafx foil-c; Green Goblin-c/story						4.00
201-219,221,222,224,226-228,230-247: 212-w/card sheet. 203-Maximum Carnage x-over. 204-Begin 4 part death of Tombstone story. 207,208-The Shroud-c/story. 208-Siege of Darkness x-over (#207 is a tie-in). 209-Black Cat back-up. 215,216-Scorpion app. 217-Power & Responsibility Pt. 4. 231-Return of Kaine; Spider-Man corpse discovered. 232-New Doc Octopus app. 233-Carnage-c/app. 235-Dragon Man cameo. 236-Dragon Man-c/app; Lizard app.; Peter Parker regains powers. 238,239-Lizard app. 239-w/card insert. 240-Revelations storyline begins. 241-Flashback						2.50
213-Collectors ed. polybagged w/16 pg. preview & animation cel; 1st meeting Spidey & Typhoid Mary						3.00
213-Version polybagged w/Gamepro #7; no-c date, price						2.50
217,219 ($2.95)-Deluxe edition foil-c: flip book						3.00
220 ($2.25, 52 pgs.)-Flip book, Mary Jane reveals pregnancy						3.00
223,229: ($2.50) 229-Spidey quits						3.00
223,225: ($2.95)-223-Die Cut-c. 225-Newsstand ed.						3.00
225,229: ($3.95) 225-Direct Market Holodisk-c (Green Goblin). 229-Acetate-c, Spidey quits						4.00
240-Variant-c						3.00
248,249,251-254,256: 249-Return of Norman Osborn 256-1st app. Prodigy						2.50
250-($3.25) Double gatefold-c						3.25
255-($2.99) Spiderhunt pt. 4						3.00
257-262: 257-Double cover with "Spectacular Prodigy #1"; battles Jack O'Lantern. 258-Spidey is cleared. 259,260-Green Goblin & Hobgoblin app. 262-Byrne-s						2.50
263-Final issue; Byrne-c; Aunt May returns						4.00
#(-1) Flashback						2.50
Annual 1 (1979)-Doc Octopus-c & 46 pg. story	2	4	6	8	10	12
Annual 2 (1980)-Origin/1st app. Rapier	1	2	3	4	5	7
Annual 3-5: ('81-'83) 3-Last Man-Wolf						5.00
Annual 6-14: 8 ('88,$ 1.75)-Evolutionary War x-over; Daydreamer returns Gwen Stacy "clone" back to real self (not Gwen Stacy). 9 ('89, $2.00, 68 pgs.)-Atlantis Attacks. 10 ('90, $2.00, 68 pgs.)-McFarlane-a. 11 ('91, $2.00, 68 pgs.)-Iron Man app. 12 ('92, $2.25, 68 pgs.)-Venom app.; w/bound in trading card from Amazing Spider-Man Annual #26. 13 ('93, $2.95, 68 pgs.)-Polybagged w/trading card; John Romita, Sr. back-up-a						3.00
Special 1 (1995, $3.95)-Flip book						4.00
NOTE: *Austin* c-21i, Annual 11i. *Buckler* a-103, 107-111, 116, 117, 119, 122, Annual 1, Annual 10; c-103, 107-111, 113, 116-119, 122, Annual 1. *Buscema* a-121. *Byrne* c(p)-17, 43, 58, 101, 102. *Giffen* a-120p. *Hembeck* c/a-86p. *Larsen* c-Annual 11p. *Miller* c-46p, 48p, 50, 51p, 52p, 54p, 55, 56p, 57, 60. *Mooney* a-7i, 11i, 21p, 23p, 25p, 26p, 29-34p, 36p, 37p, 39i, 41, 42i, 49p, 50i, 51i, 53p, 54-57i, 59-66i, 68i, 71i, 73-79i, 81-83i, 85i, 87-99i, 102i, 125p, Annual 1i, 2p. *Nasser* c-37p. *Perez* c-10. *Simonson* c-54i. *Zeck* a-22, 118, 131, 132; c-131, 132.						
SPECTACULAR SPIDER-MAN (2nd series)						
Marvel Comics: Sept, 2003 - No. 27, June, 2005 ($2.25/$2.99)						
1-Jenkins-s/Ramos-a/c; Venom-c/app.						3.00
2-22: 2-5-Venom app. 6-9-Dr. Octopus app. 11-13-The Lizard app. 14-Rivera painted-c. 15,16-Capt. America app. 17,18-Ramos-a. 20-Spider-Man gets organic webshooters 21,22-Caldwell-a. 23-26-Sarah & Gabriel app.; Land-c						2.25
27-($2.99) Last issue; Uncle Ben app. in flashback; Buckingham-a						3.00
... Vol. 1: The Hunger TPB (2003, $11.99) r/#1-5						12.00
... Vol. 2: Countdown TPB (2004, $11.99) r/#6-10						12.00
... Vol. 3: Here There Be Monsters TPB (2004, $9.99) r/#11-14						10.00
... Vol. 4: Disassembled TPB (2004, $14.99) r/#15-20						15.00
... Vol. 5: Sins Remembered (2005, $9.99) r/#23-26						10.00
... Vol. 6: The Final Curtain (2005, $14.99) r/#21,22,27 & Peter Parker: Spider-Man #39-41						15.00
SPECTACULAR STORIES MAGAZINE (Formerly A Star Presentation)						
Fox Feature Syndicate (Hero Books): No. 4, July, 1950 - No. 3, Sept, 1950						
4-Sherlock Holmes (true crime stories)	36	72	108	208	329	450
3-The St. Valentine's Day Massacre (true crime)	24	48	72	139	220	300
SPECTRE, THE (1st Series) (See Adventure Comics #431-440. More Fun & Showcase)						
National Periodical Publ.: Nov-Dec, 1967 - No. 10, May-June, 1969 (All 12¢)						
1-(11-12/67)-Anderson-c/a	13	26	39	93	164	235
2-5-Neal Adams-c/a; 3-Wildcat x-over	9	18	27	60	100	140
6-8,10: 6-8-Anderson inks. 7-Hourman app.	6	12	18	41	66	90
9-Wrightson-a	6	12	18	43	69	95
SPECTRE, THE (2nd Series) (See Saga of the Swamp Thing #58, Showcase '95 #8 & Wrath of the…)						
DC Comics: Apr, 1987 - No. 31, Oct, 1989 ($1.00, new format)						

864

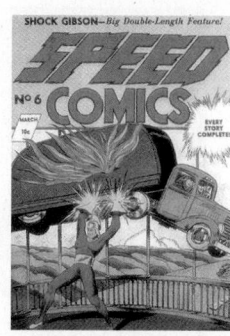

Speed Comics #6 © HARV

Speed Force #1 © DC

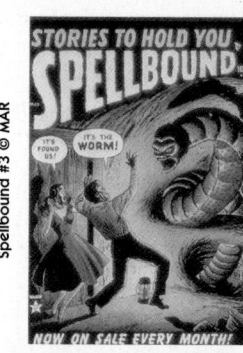

Spellbound #3 © MAR

	GD 2.0	VG 4.0	FN 6.0	VF 8.0	VF/NM 9.0	NM- 9.2
1-Colan-a begins						4.00
2-32: 9-Nudity panels. 10-Batman cameo. 10,11-Millennium tie-ins						3.00
Annual 1 (1988, $2.00)-Deadman app.						3.00

NOTE: **Art Adams** c-Annual 1. **Colan** a-1-6. **Kaluta** c-1-3. **Mignola** c-7-9. **Morrow** a-9-15. **Sears** c/a-22. **Vess** c-13-15.

SPECTRE, THE (3rd Series) (Also see Brave and the Bold #72, 75, 116, 180, 199 & Showcase '95 #8)
DC Comics: Dec, 1992 - No. 62, Feb, 1998 ($1.75/$1.95/$2.25/$2.50)

	GD 2.0	VG 4.0	FN 6.0	VF 8.0	VF/NM 9.0	NM- 9.2
1-($1.95)-Glow-in-the-dark-c; Mandrake-a begins						5.00
2,3						3.00
4-7,9-12,14-20: 10-Kaluta-c. 11-Hildebrandt painted-c. 16-Aparo/K. Jones-a. 19-Snyder III-c. 20-Sienkiewicz-c						2.50
8,13-($2.50)-Glow-in-the-dark-c						3.00
21-62: 22-(9/94)-Superman-c & app. 23-(11/94) 43-Kent Williams-c. 44-Kaluta-c. 47-Final Night x-over. 49-Begin Bolton-c. 51-Batman-c/app. 52-Gianni-c. 54-Corben-c. 60-Harris-c						2.50
#0 (10/94) Released between #22 & #23						2.50
Annual 1 (1995, $3.95)-Year One story						4.00

NOTE: **Bisley** c-27. **Fabry** c-2. **Kelley Jones** c-31. **Vess** c-5.

SPECTRE, THE (4th Series) (Hal Jordan; also see Day of Judgment #5 and Legends of the DC Universe #33-36)
DC Comics: Mar, 2001 - No. 27, May, 2003 ($2.50/$2.75)

	GD 2.0	VG 4.0	FN 6.0	VF 8.0	VF/NM 9.0	NM- 9.2
1-DeMatteis-s/Ryan Sook-c/a						3.00
2-27: 3,4-Superman & Batman-c/app. 5-Two-Face-c/app. 20-Begin $2.75-c. 21-Sinestro returns. 24-JLA app.						2.75

SPECTRE, THE (See Crisis Aftermath: The Spectre)

SPEEDBALL (See Amazing Spider-Man Annual #12, Marvel Super-Heroes & The New Warriors)
Marvel Comics: Sept, 1988(10/88-inside) - No. 11, July, 1989 (75¢)

	GD 2.0	VG 4.0	FN 6.0	VF 8.0	VF/NM 9.0	NM- 9.2
1-11: Ditko/Guice a-1-4, c-1; Ditko a-1-10; c-1-11p						2.25

SPEED BUGGY (TV)(Also see Fun-In #12, 15)
Charlton Comics: July, 1975 - No. 9, Nov, 1976 (Hanna-Barbera)

	GD 2.0	VG 4.0	FN 6.0	VF 8.0	VF/NM 9.0	NM- 9.2
1		3	6	9	16	22	28
2-9		2	4	6	10	14	18

SPEED CARTER SPACEMAN (See Spaceman)

SPEED COMICS (New Speed)(Also see Double Up)
Brookwood Publ./Speed Publ./Harvey Publications No. 14 on:
10/39 - #11, 8/40; #12, 3/41 - #44, 1-2/47 (#14-16: pocket size, 100 pgs.)

	GD	VG	FN	VF	VF/NM	NM-
1-Origin & 1st app. Shock Gibson; Ted Parrish, the Man with 1000 Faces begins; Powell-a; becomes Champion #2 on?; has earliest? full page panel in comics	339	678	1017	2204	3902	5600
2-Powell-a	116	232	348	725	1200	1675
3	66	132	198	413	687	960
4,5: 4-Powell-a? 5-Dinosaur-c	54	108	162	338	557	775
6-11: 7-Mars Mason begins, ends #11	50	100	150	305	503	700
12 (3/41; shows #11 in indicia)-The Wasp begins; Major Colt app. (Capt. Colt #12)	53	106	159	323	537	750
13-Intro. Captain Freedom & Young Defenders; Girl Commandos, Pat Parker (costumed heroine), War Nurse begins; Major Colt app.	59	118	177	369	615	860
14-16 (100 pg. pocket size, 1941): 14-2nd Harvey comic (See Pocket); Shock Gibson dons new costume. 15-Pat Parker dons costume, last in costume #23; no Girl Commandos	74	148	222	463	769	1075
17-Black Cat begins (4/42, early app.; see Pocket #1; origin Black Cat-r/Pocket #1; not in #40,41; S&K-c	76	152	228	475	788	1100
18-20-S&K-c	62	124	186	388	644	900
21-Hitler, Tojo-c; Kirby-c	79	158	237	494	822	1150
22-Kirby-c	62	124	186	388	644	900
23-Origin Girl Commandos; Kirby-c	61	122	183	381	633	885
24-Pat Parker team-up with Girl Commandos; Hitler, Tojo, & Mussolini-c	62	124	186	388	644	900
25-30: 26-Flag-c	48	96	144	293	484	675
31-Schomburg Hitler & Hirohito-c	76	152	228	475	788	1100
32-36-Schomburg-c	53	106	159	324	542	760
37,39-42, 44	41	82	123	252	406	560
38-Iwo-Jima Flag-c	43	86	129	262	431	600
43-Robot-c	43	86	129	262	431	600

NOTE: **Al Avison** c-14-16, 30, 43. **Briefer** a-6, 7. **Jon Henri** (Kirbyesque) c-17-20. **Kubert** a-37, 38, 42-44. **Kirby/Caseneuve** c-21-23. **Cecelia Munson** a-7-11(Mars Mason). **Palais** c-37, 39-42. **Powell** a-1, 2, 4-7, 28, 31, 44. **Schomburg** c-31-36. **Tuska** a-3, 6, 7. **Bondage** c-18, 35. Captain Freedom c-16-24, 25(part), 26-44(w/Black Cat #27, 29, 31, 32-40). Shock Gibson c-1-15.

SPEED DEMON (Also see Marvel Versus DC #3 & DC Versus Marvel #4)

	GD 2.0	VG 4.0	FN 6.0	VF 8.0	VF/NM 9.0	NM- 9.2
Marvel Comics (Amalgam): Apr, 1996 ($1.95, one-shot)						
1						2.50

SPEED DEMONS (Formerly Frank Merriwell at Yale #1-4?; Submarine Attack #11 on)
Charlton Comics: No. 5, Feb, 1957 - No. 10, 1958

	GD 2.0	VG 4.0	FN 6.0	VF 8.0	VF/NM 9.0	NM- 9.2
5-10	7	14	21	35	43	50

SPEED FORCE (See The Flash 2nd Series #143-Cobalt Blue)
DC Comics: Nov, 1997 ($3.95, one-shot)

	GD 2.0	VG 4.0	FN 6.0	VF 8.0	VF/NM 9.0	NM- 9.2
1-Flash & Kid Flash vs. Cobalt Blue; Waid-s/Aparo & Sienkiewicz-a; Flash family stories and pin-ups by various						4.00

SPEED RACER (Also see The New Adventures of...)
Now Comics: July, 1987 - No. 38, Nov, 1990 ($1.75)

	GD 2.0	VG 4.0	FN 6.0	VF 8.0	VF/NM 9.0	NM- 9.2
1-38, 1-2nd printing						2.50
Special 1 (1988, $2.00)						2.50
Special 2 (1988, $3.50)						3.50

SPEED RACER (Also see Racer X)
DC Comics (WildStorm): Oct, 1999 - No. 3, Dec, 1999 ($2.50, limited series)

	GD 2.0	VG 4.0	FN 6.0	VF 8.0	VF/NM 9.0	NM- 9.2
1-3-Nimura-s/a; origin of the Mach 5						2.50
...: Born To Race (2000, $9.95, TPB) r/series & conceptual art						10.00
...: The Original Manga Vol. 1 ('00, $9.95, TPB) r/1950s B&W manga						10.00

SPEED RACER FEATURING NINJA HIGH SCHOOL
Now Comics: Aug, 1993 - No. 2, 1993 (mini-series)

	GD 2.0	VG 4.0	FN 6.0	VF 8.0	VF/NM 9.0	NM- 9.2
1,2: 1-Polybagged w/card. 2-Exists?						2.50

SPEED RACER: RETURN OF THE GRX
Now Comics: Mar, 1994 - No. 2, Apr, 1994 ($1.95, limited series)

	GD 2.0	VG 4.0	FN 6.0	VF 8.0	VF/NM 9.0	NM- 9.2
1,2						2.50

SPEED SMITH-THE HOT ROD KING (Also see Hot Rod King)
Ziff-Davis Publishing Co.: Spring, 1952

	GD 2.0	VG 4.0	FN 6.0	VF 8.0	VF/NM 9.0	NM- 9.2
1-Saunders painted-c	23	46	69	132	209	285

SPEEDY GONZALES
Dell Publishing Co.: No. 1084, Mar, 1960

	GD 2.0	VG 4.0	FN 6.0	VF 8.0	VF/NM 9.0	NM- 9.2
Four Color 1084	5	10	15	35	55	75

SPEEDY RABBIT (See Television Puppet Show)
Realistic/I. W. Enterprises/Super Comics: nd (1953); 1963

	GD 2.0	VG 4.0	FN 6.0	VF 8.0	VF/NM 9.0	NM- 9.2
nn (1953)-Realistic Reprint?	2	4	6	9	13	16
I.W. Reprint #1 (2 versions w/diff. c/stories exist)-Peter Cottontail #?						
Super Reprint #14(1963)	2	4	6	8	10	12

SPELLBINDERS
Quality: Dec, 1986 - No. 12, Jan, 1988 ($1.25)

	GD 2.0	VG 4.0	FN 6.0	VF 8.0	VF/NM 9.0	NM- 9.2
1-12: Nemesis the Warlock, Amadeus Wolf						2.50

SPELLBINDERS
Marvel Comics: May, 2005 - No. 6, Oct, 2005 ($2.99, limited series)

	GD 2.0	VG 4.0	FN 6.0	VF 8.0	VF/NM 9.0	NM- 9.2
1-6-Carey-s/Perkins-a						3.00
....: Signs and Wonders TPB (2006, $7.99, digest) r/#1-6						8.00

SPELLBOUND (See The Crusaders)

SPELLBOUND (Tales to Hold You... #1, Stories to Hold You...)
Atlas Comics (ACI 1-15/Male 16-23/BPC 24-34): Mar, 1952 - #23, June, 1954; #24, Oct, 1955 - #34, June, 1957

	GD 2.0	VG 4.0	FN 6.0	VF 8.0	VF/NM 9.0	NM- 9.2
1-Horror/weird stories in all	68	136	204	425	705	985
2-Edgar A. Poe app.	40	80	120	235	368	500
3-5: 3-Whitney-a; cannibalism story	34	68	102	197	311	425
6-Krigstein-a	34	68	102	197	311	425
7-10: 8-Ayers-a	30	60	90	172	271	370
11-16,18-20: 14-Ed Win-a	25	50	75	145	228	310
17-Krigstein-a	25	50	75	148	232	315
21-23: 23-Last precode (6/54)	20	40	60	117	184	250
24-28,30,31,34: 25-Orlando-a	18	36	54	105	165	225
29-Ditko-a (4 pgs.)	20	40	60	117	184	250
32,33-Torres-a	18	36	54	105	165	225

NOTE: **Brodsky** a-5; c-1, 5-7, 10, 11, 13, 15, 25-27, 32. **Colan** a-17. **Everett** a-2, 5, 31, 34, 28, 31; c-2, 8, 9, 14, 17-19, 28, 30. **Forgione/Abel** a-29. **Forte/Fox** a-16. **Al Hartley** a-2. **Heath** a-2, 4, 8, 9, 12, 14, 16; c-3, 4, 12, 16, 20, 21. **Infantino** a-15. **Keller** a-5. **Kida** a-2, 14, 27; c-24, 29, 31. **Mooney** a-23. **Pakula** a-22, 32. **Post** a-8. **Powell** a-19, 20, 32. **Robinson** a-1. **Romita** a-24, 26, 27. **R.Q. Sale** a-29. **Sekowsky** a-5. **Severin** c-29. **Sinnott** a-8, 16, 17.

SPELLBOUND
Marvel Comics: Jan, 1988 - Apr, 1988 ($1.50, bi-weekly, Baxter paper)

	GD 2.0	VG 4.0	FN 6.0	VF 8.0	VF/NM 9.0	NM- 9.2
1-5						2.50

Spider-Girl #1 © MAR

Spider-Man #12 © MAR

Spider-Man Annual '98 © MAR

	GD 2.0	VG 4.0	FN 6.0	VF 8.0	VF/NM 9.0	NM- 9.2

6 ($2.25, 52 pgs.) ... 2.50

SPELLJAMMER (Also see TSR Worlds Comics Annual)
DC Comics: Sept, 1990 - No. 15, Nov, 1991 ($1.75)
1-15: Based on TSR game. 11-Heck-a. ... 2.50

SPENCER SPOOK (Formerly Giggle Comics; see Adventures of...)
American Comics Group: No. 100, Mar-Apr, 1955 - No. 101, May-June, 1955
100,101 ... 7 14 21 37 46 55

SPIDER, THE
Eclipse Books: 1991 - Book 3, 1991 ($4.95, 52 pgs., limited series)
Book 1-3-Truman-c/a ... 5.00

SPIDER-BOY (Also see Marvel Versus DC #3)
Marvel Comics (Amalgam): Apr, 1996 ($1.95)
1-Mike Wieringo-c/a; Karl Kesel story; 1st app. of Bizarnage, Insect Queen, Challengers of the Fantastic, Sue Storm: Agent of S.H.I.E.L.D., & King Lizard ... 2.50

SPIDER-BOY TEAM-UP
Marvel Comics (Amalgam): June, 1997 ($1.95, one-shot)
1-Karl Kesel & Roger Stern-s/Jo Ladronn-a(p) ... 2.50

SPIDER-GIRL (See What If #105)
Marvel Comics: Oct, 1998 - No. 100, Sept, 2006 ($1.99/$2.25/$2.99)
0-($2.99)-r/1st app. Peter Parker's daughter from What If #105; previews regular series, Avengers-Next and J2 ... 1 2 3 4 5 7
1-DeFalco-s/Olliffe & Williamson-s ... 1 2 3 4 5 7
2-Two covers ... 4.00
3-16,18-20: 3-Fantastic Five-c/app. 10,11-Spider-Girl time-travels to meet teenaged Spider-Man ... 2.50
17-($2.99) Peter Parker suits up ... 3.00
21-24,26-49,51-59: 21-Begin $2.25-c. 31-Avengers app. ... 2.50
25-($2.99) Spider-Girl vs. the Savage Six ... 3.00
50-($3.50) ... 3.50
59-99-($2.99) 59-Avengers app.; Ben Parker born. 75-May in Black costume. 82-84-Venom bonds with Normie Osborn. 93-Venom-c. 95-Tony Stark app. ... 3.00
100-($3.99) Last issue; story plus Rogues Gallery, profile pages; r/#27,53 ... 4.00
1999 Annual ($3.99) ... 4.00
Wizard #1/2 (1999) ... 3.00
... A Fresh Start (1/99,$5.99, TPB) r/#1&2 ... 6.00
... Presents The Buzz and Darkdevil (2007, $7.99, digest) r/mini-series ... 8.00
TPB (10/01, $19.95) r/#0-8; new Olliffe-c ... 20.00
Marvel Age Spider-Girl Vol. 1: Legacy (2004, $7.99, digest size) r/#0-5 ... 8.00
Marvel Age Spider-Girl Vol. 2: Like Father, Like Daughter (2004, $7.99, digest) r/#6-11 ... 8.00
Spider-Girl Vol. 3: Avenging Allies (2005, $7.99, digest) r/#12-16 & 1999 Annual ... 8.00
Spider-Girl Vol. 4: Turning Point (2005, $7.99, digest) r/#17-21 & #1/2 ... 8.00
Spider-Girl Vol. 5: Endgame (2006, $7.99, digest) r/#22-27 ... 8.00
Spider-Girl Vol. 6: Too Many Spiders! (2006, $7.99, digest) r/#28-33 ... 8.00
Spider-Girl Vol. 7: Betrayed (2006, $7.99, digest) r/#34-38 & #51 ... 8.00
Spider-Girl Vol. 8: Duty Calls (2007, $7.99, digest) r/#39-44 ... 8.00
Spider-Girl Vol. 9: Secret Lives (2007, $7.99, digest) r/#45-50 ... 8.00

SPIDER-MAN (See Amazing..., Friendly Neighborhood..., Giant-Size..., Marvel Age..., Marvel Knights..., Marvel Tales, Marvel Team-Up, Spectacular..., Spidey Super Stories, Ultimate Marvel Team-Up, Ultimate..., Venom, & Web Of...)

SPIDER-MAN (Peter Parker Spider-Man on cover but not indicia #75-on)
Marvel Comics: Aug, 1990 - No. 98, Nov, 1998 ($1.75/$1.95/ $1.99)
1-Silver edition, direct sale only (unbagged) ... 1 2 3 5 6 8
1-Silver bagged edition; direct sale, no price on comic, but $2.00 on plastic bag (125,000 print run) ... 20.00
1-Regular edition w/Spidey face in UPC area (unbagged); green-c ... 6.00
1-Regular bagged edition w/Spidey face in UPC area; green cover (125,000) ... 12.00
1-Newsstand bagged w/UPC code ... 8.00
1-Gold edition, 2nd printing (unbagged) with Spider-Man in box (400,000-450,000) ... 5.00
1-Gold 2nd printing w/UPC code; (less than 10,000 print run) intended for Wal-Mart; much scarcer than originally believed ... 120.00
1-Platinum ed. mailed to retailers only (10,000 print run); has new McFarlane-a & editorial material instead of ads; stiff-c, no cover price ... 130.00
2-26: 2-McFarlane-c/a/scripts continue. 6,7-Ghost Rider & Hobgoblin app. 8-Wolverine cameo; Wolverine storyline begins. 12-Wolverine storyline ends. 13-Spidey's black costume returns; Morbius app. 14-Morbius app. 15-Erik Larsen-c/a; Beast c/s. 16-X-Force-c/story w/Liefeld assists; continues in X-Force #4; reads sideways; last McFarlane issue. 17-Thanos-c/app.; Leonardi/Williamson-a. 13,14-Spidey in black costume. 18-Ghost Rider-c/story.
18-23-Sinister Six storyline w/Erik Larsen-c/a/scripts. 19-Hulk & Hobgoblin app.
20-22-Deathlok app. 22,23-Ghost Rider, Hulk, Hobgoblin app. 23-Wrap-around gatefold-c.
24-Infinity War x-over w/Demogoblin & Hobgoblin-c/story. 24-Demogoblin dons new

	GD 2.0	VG 4.0	FN 6.0	VF 8.0	VF/NM 9.0	NM- 9.2

costume & battles Hobgoblin-c/story. 26-($3.50, 52 pgs.)-Silver hologram on-c w/gatefold poster by Ron Lim; Spidey retells his origin. ... 4.00
26-2nd printing; gold hologram on-c ... 3.50
27-45: 32-34-Punisher-c/story. 37-Maximum Carnage x-over. 39,40-Electro-c/s (cameo #38). 41-43-Iron Fist-c/stories w/Jae Lee-a. 42-Intro Platoon. 44-Hobgoblin app. ... 3.00
46-49,51-53, 55, 56,58-74,76-81: 46-Begin $1.95-c; bound-in card sheet. 51-Power & Responsibility Pt. 3. 52,53-Venom app. 60-Kaine revealed. 61-Origin Kaine. 65-Mysterio app. 66-Kaine-c/app.; Peter Parker app. 67-Carnage-c/app. 68,69-Hobgoblin-c/app. 72-Onslaught x-over; Spidey vs. Sentinels. 74-Daredevil-c/app. 77-80-Morbius-c/app. ... 2.50
46-($2.95)-Polybagged; silver ink-c w/16 pg. preview of cartoon series & animation style print; bound-in trading card sheet ... 3.00
50-($2.50)-Newsstand edition ... 2.50
50-($3.95)-Collectors edition w/holographic-c ... 4.00
51-($2.95)-Deluxe edition foil-c; flip book ... 3.00
54-($2.75, 52 pgs.)-Flip book ... 2.75
57-($2.50) ... 2.50
57-($2.50)-Die cut-c ... 3.00
65-($2.95)-Variant-c; polybagged w/cassette ... 3.00
75-($2.95)-Wraparound-c; return of the Green Goblin; death of Ben Reilly (who was the clone) ... 4.00
82-97: 84-Juggernaut app. 91-Double cover with "Dusk #1"; battles the Shocker. 93-Ghost Rider app. ... 2.50
98-Double cover; final issue ... 3.00
#(-1) Flashback (7/97) ... 2.50
Annual '97 ($2.99), '98 ($2.99)-Devil Dinosaur-c/app. ... 3.00
NOTE: *Erik Larsen* c/a-15, 18-23. *M. Rogers/Keith Williams* c/a-27, 28.

SPIDER-MAN (one-shots, hardcovers and TPBs)
...& Arana Special: The Hunter Revealed (5/06, $3.99) Del Rio-s; art by Del Rio & various ... 3.00
...and Batman ('95, $5.95) DeMatteis-s; Joker, Carnage app. ... 6.00
...and Daredevil ('84, $2.00) 1-r/Spectacular Spider-Man #26-28 by Miller ... 3.00
.... Back in Black Handbook (2007, $3.99) Official Handbook format; Lopresti-c ... 4.00
...: Birth of Venom TPB (2007, $29.99) r/Secret Wars #8, AS-M #252-259,298-300,315-317, AS-M Annual #25, Fantastic Four #274 and Web of Spider-Man #1 ... 30.00
...: Carnage (6/93, $6.95, TPB) r/Amazing S-M #344,345,359-363; spot varnish-c ... 7.00
.../Daredevil (10/02, $2.99) Vatche Mavlian-c/a; Brett Matthews-s ... 3.00
...: Dead Man's Hand 1 (4/97, $2.99) ... 3.00
...: Death of the Stacys HC (2007, $19.99, dustjacket) r/Amazing Spider-Man #88-92 and #121,122; intro. by Gerry Conway; afterword by Romita; cover gallery incl. reprints 20.00
.../Dr. Strange: "The Way to Dusty Death" nn (1992, $6.95, 68 pgs.) ... 7.00
.../Elektra '98-($2.99) vs. The Silencer ... 3.00
... Family (2005, $4.99, 100 pgs.) new story and reprints; Spider-Ham app. ... 5.00
... Fear Itself Graphic Novel (2/92, $12.95) ... 18.00
Giant-Sized Spider-Man (12/98, $3.99) r/team-ups ... 4.00
Holiday Special 1995 ($2.95) ... 3.00
... Hot Shots nn (1/96, $2.95) fold out posters by various, inc. Vess and Ross ... 3.00
Identity Crisis (9/98, $19.95, TPB) ... 20.00
...: Kraven's Last Hunt HC (2006, $19.99) r/Amaz. S-M #293,294; Web of S-M #31,32 and Spect. S-M #131-132; intro. by DeMatteis; Zeck-a; cover pencils and interior pencils 20.00
... Legacy of Evil 1 (6/96, $3.95) Kurt Busiek script & Mark Texeira-c/a ... 4.00
...: Legends Vol. 1: Todd McFarlane ('03, $19.99, TPB)-r/Amaz. S-M #298-305 ... 20.00
...: Legends Vol. 2: Todd McFarlane ('03, $19.99, TPB)-r/Amaz. S-M #306-314, & Spec. Spider-Man Annual #10 ... 20.00
...: Legends Vol. 3: Todd McFarlane ('04, $24.99, TPB)-r/Amaz. S-M #315-323,325,328 ... 25.00
...: Legends Vol. 4: Spider-Man & Wolverine ('03, $13.95, TPB) r/Spider-Man & Wolverine #1-4 and Spider-Man/Daredevil #1 ... 14.00
.../Marrow (2/01, $2.99) Garza-a ... 3.00
..., Punisher, Sabretooth: Designer Genes (1993, $8.95) ... 9.00
...: Return of the Goblin TPB (See Peter Parker: Spider-Man)
...: Revelations ('97, $14.99, TPB) r/end of Clone Saga plus 14 new pages by Romita Jr. ... 15.00
...: Saga of the Sandman TPB (2007, $19.99) r/1st app. Amazing S-M #4 and other app. ... 20.00
...: Son of the Goblin (2004, $15.99, TPB) r/AS-M#136-137,312 & Spec. S-M #189,200 16.00
...: Special: Black and Blue and Read All Over 1 (11/06, $3.99) new story and r/ASM #12 ... 4.00
Special Edition 1 (12/92-c, 11/92 inside)-The Trial of Venom; ordered thru mail with $5.00 donation or more to UNICEF; embossed metallic ink; came bagged w/bound-in poster; Daredevil app. ... 1 3 4 6 8 10
Super Special (7/95, $3.95)-Planet of the Symbiotes ... 4.00
The Best of Spider-Man Vol. 2 (2003, $29.99, HC with dust jacket) r/AS-M V2 #37-45, Peter Parker: S-M #44-47, and S-M's Tangled Web #10,11; Pearson-c ... 30.00
The Best of Spider-Man Vol. 3 (2004, $29.99, HC with d.j.) r/AS-M V2 #46-58, 500 ... 30.00
The Best of Spider-Man Vol. 4 (2005, $29.99, HC with d.j.) r/#501-514; sketch pages ... 30.00
The Best of Spider-Man Vol. 5 (2005, $29.99, HC with d.j.) r/#515-524; sketch pages ... 30.00
The Complete Frank Miller Spider-Man (2002, $29.95, HC) r/Miller-s/a ...
The Death of Captain Stacy ($3.50) r/AS-M#88-90 ... 3.50
The Death of Gwen Stacy ($14.95) r/AS-M#96-98,121,122 ... 15.00

Spider-Man and Power Pack #4 © MAR

Spider-Man/Doctor Octopus: Year One #1 © MAR

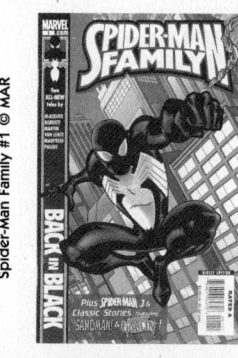

Spider-Man Family #1 © MAR

	GD 2.0	VG 4.0	FN 6.0	VF 8.0	VF/NM 9.0	NM- 9.2

...: The Movie ($12.95) adaptation by Stan Lee-s/Alan Davis-a; plus r/Ultimate
  Spider-Man #8, Peter Parker #35, Tangled Web #10; photo-c — 13.00
...: The Official Movie Adaptation ($5.95) Stan Lee-s/Alan Davis-a — 6.00
.... : The Other HC (2006, $29.99, dust jacket) r/Amazing S-M #525-528, Friendly Neighborhood
  S-M #1-4 and Marvel Knights S-M #19-22; gallery of variant covers — 30.00
...: The Other SC (2006, $24.99) r/crossover; gallery of variant covers — 25.00
...: The Other Sketchbook (2005, $2.99) sketch page preview of 2005-6 x-over — 3.00
Torment TPB (5/01 $15.95) r/#1-5, Spec. S-M #10 — 16.00
... Vs. Doctor Octopus ($17.95) reprints early battles; Sean Chen-c — 18.00
... Vs. Punisher (7/00, $2.99) Michael Lopez-c/a — 3.00
...Vs. Silver Sable (2006, $15.99, TPB)-r/Amazing Spider-Man #265,279-281 & Peter Parker,
  The Spectacular Spider-Man #128,129 — 16.00
...Vs. The Black Cat (2005, $14.99, TPB)-r/Amaz. S-M #194,195,204,205,226,227 — 15.00
...Vs. Venom (1990, $8.95, TPB)-r/Amaz. S-M #300,315-317 w/new McFarlane-c — 9.00
...Visionaries (10/01, $19.95, TPB)-r/Amaz. S-M #298-305; McFarlane-a — 20.00
...Visionaries: John Romita (8/01, $19.95, TPB)-r/Amaz. S-M #39-42, 50,68,69,108,109;
  new Romita-c — 20.00
...Visionaries: Kurt Busiek (2006, $19.99, TPB)-r/Untold Tales of Spider-Man #1-8 — 20.00
...Visionaries: Roger Stern (2007, $24.99, TPB)-r/Amazing Spider-Man #206 & Spectacular
  Spider-Man #43-52,54; Stern interview — 25.00
Wizard 1/2 ($10.00) Leonardi-a; Green Goblin app. — 10.00

SPIDER-MAN ADVENTURES
Marvel Comics: Dec, 1994 - No. 15, Mar, 1996 ($1.50)

1-15 ($1.50)-Based on animated series — 2.50
1-($2.95)-Foil embossed-c — 3.00

SPIDER-MAN AND HIS AMAZING FRIENDS (See Marvel Action Universe)
Marvel Comics Group: Dec, 1981 (one-shot)

1-Adapted from NBC TV cartoon show; Green Goblin-c/story; 1st Spidey, Firestar, Iceman
  team-up; Spiegle-p — 5.00

SPIDER-MAN AND POWER PACK
Marvel Comics: Jan, 2007 - No. 4, Apr, 2007 ($2.99, limited series)

1-4-Sumerak-s/Gurihiru-a; Sandman app. 3,4-Venom app. — 3.00
...: Big City Heroes (2007, $6.99, digest) r/#1-4 — 7.00

SPIDER-MAN AND THE FANTASTIC FOUR
Marvel Comics: Jun, 2007 - No. 4, Sept, 2007 ($2.99, limited series)

1-4-Mike Wieringo-a/c; Jeff Parker-s. 1,4-Impossible Man app. — 3.00

SPIDER-MAN AND THE INCREDIBLE HULK (See listing under Amazing...)

SPIDER-MAN AND THE UNCANNY X-MEN
Marvel Comics: Mar, 1996 ($16.95, trade paperback)

nn-r/Uncanny X-Men #27, Uncanny X-men #35, Amazing Spider-Man #92, Marvel Team-Up
  Annual #1, Marvel Team-Up #150, & Spectacular Spider-Man #197-199 — 17.00

SPIDER-MAN & WOLVERINE (See Spider-Man Legends Vol. 4 for TPB reprint)
Marvel Comics: Aug, 2003 - No. 4, Nov, 2003 ($2.99, limited series)

1-4-Matthews-s/Mavlian-a — 3.00

SPIDER-MAN AND X-FACTOR
Marvel Comics: May, 1994 - No. 3, July, 1994 ($1.95, limited series)

1-3 — 2.50

SPIDER-MAN /BADROCK
Maximum Press: Mar, 1997 ($2.99, mini-series)

1A, 1B(#2)-Jurgens-a — 3.00

SPIDER-MAN/BLACK CAT: THE EVIL THAT MEN DO (Also see Marvel Must Haves)
Marvel Comics: Aug, 2002 - No. 6, Mar, 2006 ($2.99, limited series)

1-6-Kevin Smith-s/Terry Dodson-c/a — 3.00
HC (2006, $19.99, dust jacket) r/#1-6; script to #6 with sketches — 20.00

SPIDER-MAN: BLUE
Marvel Comics: July, 2002 - No. 6, Apr, 2003 ($3.50, limited series)

1-6: Jeph Loeb-s/Tim Sale-a/c; flashback to early MJ and Gwen Stacy — 3.50
HC (2003, $21.99, with dust jacket) over-sized r/#1-6; intro. by John Romita — 22.00
SC (2004, $14.99) r/#1-6; cover gallery — 15.00

SPIDER-MAN: BREAKOUT (See New Avengers #1)
Marvel Comics: June, 2005 - No. 5, Oct, 2005 ($2.99, limited series)

1-5-Bedard-s/Garcia-a. 1-U-Foes app. 5-New Avengers app. — 3.00
TPB (2006, $13.99) r/#1-5 — 14.00

SPIDER-MAN: CHAPTER ONE
Marvel Comics: Dec, 1998 - No. 12, Oct, 1999 ($2.50, limited series)

1-Retelling/updating of origin; John Byrne-s/c/a — 2.50

1-($6.95) DF Edition w/variant-c by Jae Lee — 7.00
2-11: 2-Two covers (one is swipe of ASM #1); Fantastic Four app. 9-Daredevil.
  11-Giant-Man-c/app. — 2.50
12-($3.50) Battles the Sandman — 3.50
0-(5/99) Origins of Vulture, Lizard and Sandman — 2.50

SPIDER-MAN CLASSICS
Marvel Comics: Apr, 1993 - No. 16, July, 1994 ($1.25)

1-14,16: 1-r/Amaz. Fantasy #15 & Strange Tales #115. 2-16-r/Amaz. Spider-Man #1-15.
  6-Austin-c(i) — 2.50
15-($2.95)-Polybagged w/16 pg. insert & animation style print; r/Amazing Spider-Man #14
  (1st Green Goblin) — 3.00

SPIDER-MAN COLLECTOR'S PREVIEW
Marvel Comics: Dec, 1994 ($1.50, 100 pgs., one-shot)

1-wraparound-c; no comics — 3.00

SPIDER-MAN COMICS MAGAZINE
Marvel Comics Group: Jan, 1987 - No. 13, 1988 ($1.50, digest-size)

1-13-Reprints — 6.00

SPIDER-MAN: DEATH AND DESTINY
Marvel Comics: Aug, 2000 - No. 3, Oct, 2000 ($2.99, limited series)

1-3-Aftermath of the death of Capt. Stacy — 3.00

SPIDER-MAN/ DOCTOR OCTOPUS: OUT OF REACH
Marvel Comics: Jan, 2004 - No. 5, May, 2004 ($2.99, limited series)

1-5: 1-Keron Grant-a/Colin Mitchell-s — 3.00
Marvel Age... TPB (2004, $5.99, digest size) r/#1-5 — 6.00

SPIDER-MAN/ DOCTOR OCTOPUS: YEAR ONE
Marvel Comics: Aug, 2004 - No. 5, Dec, 2004 ($2.99, limited series)

1-5-Kaare Andrews-a/Zeb Wells-s — 3.00

SPIDER-MAN FAIRY TALES
Marvel Comics: July, 2007 - No. 4, Oct, 2007 ($2.99, limited series)

1-4: 1-Cebulski-s/Tercio-a. 2-Henrichon-a. 3-Kobayashi-a. 4-Dragotta-p/Allred-i — 3.00
TPB (2007, $10.99) r/#1-4 — 11.00

SPIDER-MAN FAMILY
Marvel Comics: Apr, 2007 - Present ($4.99, anthology)

1-4-New tales and reprints. 1-Black costume, Sandman, Black Cat app. 4-Agents of Atlas
  app., Kirk-a; Puppet Master by Eliopoulos — 5.00
... Featuring Spider-Clan 1 (1/07, $4.99) new Spider-Clan story; reprints w/Spider-Man
  2099 and Amazing Spider-Man #252 (black costume) — 5.00
... Featuring Spider-Man's Amazing Friends 1 (10/06, $4.99) new story with Iceman
  and Firestar; Mini Marvels w/Giarrusso-a; reprints w/Spider-Man 2099 — 5.00
...: Back In Black (2007, $7.99, digest) r/new content from #1-3 — 8.00

SPIDER-MAN: FRIENDS AND ENEMIES
Marvel Comics: Jan, 1995 - No. 4, Apr, 1995 ($1.95, limited series)

1-4-Darkhawk, Nova & Speedball app. — 2.50

SPIDER-MAN: FUNERAL FOR AN OCTOPUS
Marvel Comics: Mar, 1995 - No. 3, May, 1995 ($1.50, limited series)

1-3 — 2.50

SPIDER-MAN/ GEN 13
Marvel Comics: Nov, 1996 ($4.95, one-shot)

nn-Peter David-s/Stuart Immonen-a — 5.00

SPIDER-MAN: GET KRAVEN
Marvel Comics: Aug, 2002 - No. 6, Jan, 2003 ($2.99/$2.25, limited series)

1-($2.99) McCrea-a/Quesada-c; back-up story w/Rio-a — 3.00
2-6-($2.25) 2-Sub-Mariner app. — 2.50

SPIDER-MAN: HOBGOBLIN LIVES
Marvel Comics: Jan, 1997 - No. 3, Mar, 1997 ($2.50, limited series)

1-3-Wraparound-c — 2.50
TPB (1/98, $14.99) r/#1-3 plus timeline — 15.00

SPIDER-MAN: HOUSE OF M (Also see House of M and related x-overs)
Marvel Comics: June, 2005 - No. 5, Dec, 2005 ($2.99, limited series)

1-5-Waid & Peyer-s/Larroca-a; rich and famous Peter Parker in mutant-ruled world — 3.00
House of M: Spider-Man TPB (2006, $13.99) r/series — 14.00

SPIDER-MAN/ HUMAN TORCH
Marvel Comics: Mar, 2005 - No. 5, July, 2005 ($2.99, limited series)

1-5-Ty Templeton-a/Dan Slott-s; team-ups from early days to the present — 3.00

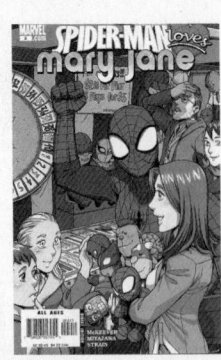

Spider-Man Loves Mary Jane #5 © MAR

Spider-Man: Quality of Life #1 © MAR

Spider-Man's Tangled Web #11 © MAR

	GD 2.0	VG 4.0	FN 6.0	VF 8.0	VF/NM 9.0	NM- 9.2		GD 2.0	VG 4.0	FN 6.0	VF 8.0	VF/NM 9.0	NM- 9.2

...: I'm With Stupid (2006, $7.99, digest) r/#1-5   8.00

SPIDER-MAN: INDIA
Marvel Comics: Jan, 2005 - No. 4, Apr, 2005 ($2.99, limited series)

1-4-Pavitr Prabhakar gains spider powers; Kang-a/Seetharaman-s   3.00

SPIDER-MAN: LEGEND OF THE SPIDER-CLAN (See Marvel Mangaverse for TPB)
Marvel Comics: Dec, 2002 - No. 5, Apr, 2003 ($2.25, limited series)

1-5-Marvel Mangaverse Spider-Man; Kaare Andrews-s/Skottie Young-c/a   2.50

SPIDER-MAN: LIFELINE
Marvel Comics: Apr, 2001 - No. 3, June, 2001 ($2.99, limited series)

1-3-Nicieza-s/Rude-c/a; The Lizard app.   3.00

SPIDER-MAN LOVES MARY JANE (Also see Mary Jane limited series)
Marvel Comics: Feb, 2006 - No. 20, Sept, 2007 ($2.99)

1-20-Mary Jane & Peter in high school; McKeever-s/Miyazawa-a/c. 5-Gwen Stacy app.
16-18,20-Firestar app. 17-Felicia Hardy app.   3.00
... Vol. 1: Super Crush (2006, $7.99, digest) r/#1-5; cover concepts page   8.00
... Vol. 2: The New Girl (2006, $7.99, digest) r/#6-10; sketch pages   8.00
... Vol. 3: My Secret Life (2007, $7.99, digest) r/#11-15; sketch pages   8.00
... Vol. 4: Still Friends (2007, $7.99, digest) r/#16-20   8.00
Hardcover Vol.1 (2007, $24.99) oversized reprints of r/1-5, Mary Jane #1-4 and Mary Jane:
Homecoming #1-4; series proposals, sketch pages and covers; coloring process   25.00

SPIDER-MAN: MADE MEN
Marvel Comics: Aug, 1998 ($5.99, one-shot)

1-Spider-Man & Daredevil vs. Kingpin   6.00

SPIDER-MAN MAGAZINE
Marvel Comics: 1994 - No. 3, 1994 ($1.95, magazine)

1-3: 1-Contains 4 S-M promo cards & 4 X-Men Ultra Fleer cards; Spider-Man story by
Romita, Sr.; X-Men story; puzzles & games. 2-Doc Octopus & X-Men stories   3.00

SPIDER-MAN: MAXIMUM CLONAGE
Marvel Comics: 1995 ($4.95)

Alpha #1-Acetate-c, Omega #1-Chromium-c.   5.00

SPIDER-MAN MEGAZINE
Marvel Comics: Oct, 1994 - No. 6, Mar, 1995 ($2.95, 100 pgs.)

1-6: 1-r/ASM #16,224,225, Marvel Team-Up #1   3.00

SPIDER-MAN: POWER OF TERROR
Marvel Comics: Jan, 1995 - No. 4, Apr, 1995 ($1.95, limited series)

1-4-Silvermane & Deathlok app.   2.50

SPIDER-MAN/PUNISHER: FAMILY PLOT
Marvel Comics: Feb, 1996 - No. 2, Mar, 1996 ($2.95, limited series)

1,2   3.00

SPIDER-MAN: QUALITY OF LIFE
Marvel Comics: Jul, 2002 - No. 4, Oct, 2002 ($2.99, limited series)

1-4-All CGI art by Scott Sava; Rucka-s; Lizard app.   3.00
TPB (2002, $12.99) r/#1-4; a "Making of..." section detailing the CGI process   13.00

SPIDER-MAN: REDEMPTION
Marvel Comics: Sept, 1996 - No. 4, Dec, 1996 ($1.50, limited series)

1-4: DeMatteis scripts; Zeck-a   2.50

SPIDER-MAN/ RED SONJA
Marvel Comics: Oct, 2007 - No. 5 ($2.99, limited series)

1,2-Rubi-a/Oeming-s/Turner-c; Venom & Kulan Gath app.   3.00

SPIDER-MAN: REIGN
Marvel Comics: Feb, 2007 - No. 4, May, 2007 ($3.99, limited series)

1-Kaare Andrews-s/a; red costume on cover   4.00
1-Variant cover with black costume   10.00
2-4   4.00
HC (2007, $19.99, dustjacket) r/#1-4; sketch pages and cover variant gallery   20.00
HC 2nd printing (2007, $19.99, dustjacket) with variant black cover   20.00

SPIDER-MAN: REVENGE OF THE GREEN GOBLIN
Marvel Comics: Oct, 2000 - No. 3, Dec, 2000 ($2.99, limited series)

1-3-Frenz-a/Olliffe-a; continues in AS-M #25 & PP:S-M #25   3.00

SPIDER-MAN SAGA
Marvel Comics: Nov, 1991 - No. 4, Feb, 1992 ($2.95, limited series)

1-4: Gives history of Spider-Man: text & illustrations   3.00

SPIDER-MAN: SWEET CHARITY

Marvel Comics: Aug, 2002 ($4.95, one-shot)

1-The Scorpion-c/app.; Campbell-c/Zimmerman-s/Robertson-a   5.00

SPIDER-MAN'S TANGLED WEB (Titled "Tangled Web" in indicia for #1-4)
Marvel Comics: Jun, 2001 - No. 22, Mar, 2003 ($2.99)

1-3: "The Thousand" on-c; Ennis-s/McCrea-a/Fabry-c.   4.00
4-"Severance Package" on-c; Rucka-s/Risso-a; Kingpin-c/app.   5.00
5,6-Flowers for Rhino; Milligan-s/Fegredo-a   3.00
7-10,12,15-20,22: 7-9-Gentlemen's Agreement; Bruce Jones-s/Lee Weeks-a. 10-Andrews-a.
12-Fegredo-a. 15-Paul Pope-s/a. 18-Ted McKeever-s/a. 19-Mahfood-a. 20-Haspiel-a.   3.00
11,13,21-($3.50) 11-Darwyn Cooke-s/a. 13-Phillips-a. 21-Christmas-s by Cooke & Bone   3.50
14-Azzarello & Scott Levy (WWE's Raven)-s about Crusher Hogan   4.00
TPB (10/01, $15.95) r/#1-6   16.00
Volume 2 TPB (4/02, $14.95) r/#7-11   15.00
Volume 3 TPB (2002, $15.99) r/#12-17; Jason Pearson-c   16.00
Volume 4 TPB (2003, $15.99) r/#18-22; Frank Cho-c   16.00

SPIDER-MAN TEAM-UP
Marvel Comics: Dec, 1995 - No. 7, June, 1996 ($2.95)

1-7: 1-w/ X-Men. 2-w/Silver Surfer. 3-w/Fantastic Four. 4-w/Avengers.
5-Gambit & Howard the Duck-c/app. 7-Thunderbolts-c/app.   3.00
... Special 1 (5/05, $4.99) Fantastic Four app.; Todd Dezago-s/Shane Davis-a   3.00

SPIDER-MAN: THE ARACHNIS PROJECT
Marvel Comics: Aug, 1994 - No. 6, Jan, 1995 ($1.75, limited series)

1-6-Venom, Styx, Stone & Jury app.   2.50

SPIDER-MAN: THE CLONE JOURNAL
Marvel Comics: Mar, 1995 ($2.95, one-shot)

1   3.00

SPIDER-MAN: THE FINAL ADVENTURE
Marvel Comics: Nov, 1995 - No. 4, Feb, 1996 ($2.95, limited series)

1-4: 1-Nicieza scripts; foil-c   3.00

SPIDER-MAN: THE JACKAL FILES
Marvel Comics: Aug, 1995 ($1.95, one-shot)

1   2.50

SPIDER-MAN: THE LOST YEARS
Marvel Comics: Aug, 1995-No. 3, Oct, 1995; No. 0, 1996 ($2.95/$3.95,lim. series)

0-(1/96, $3.95)-Reprints.   4.00
1-3-DeMatteis scripts, Romita, Jr.-c/a   3.00
NOTE: **Romita** c-0i. **Romita, Jr.** a-0r, 1-3p. c-0-3p. **Sharp** a-0r.

SPIDER-MAN: THE MANGA
Marvel Comics: Dec, 1997 - No. 31, June, 1999 ($3.99/$2.99, B&W, bi-weekly)

1-($3.99)-English translation of Japanese Spider-Man   4.00
2-31-($2.99)   3.00

SPIDER-MAN: THE MUTANT AGENDA
Marvel Comics: No. 0, Feb, 1994; No. 1, Mar, 1994 - No. 3, May, 1994 ($1.75, limited series)

0-(2/94, $1.25, 52 pgs.)-Crosses over w/newspaper strip; has empty pages to paste
in newspaper strips; gives origin of Spidey   2.50
1-3: Beast & Hobgoblin app. 1-X-Men app.   2.50

SPIDER-MAN: THE MYSTERIO MANIFESTO (Listed as "Spider-Man and Mysterio" in indicia)
Marvel Comics: Jan, 2001 - No. 3, Mar, 2001 ($2.99, limited series)

1-3-Daredevil-c/app.; Weeks & McLeod-a   3.00

SPIDER-MAN: THE PARKER YEARS
Marvel Comics: Nov, 1995 ($2.50, one-shot)

1   2.50

SPIDER-MAN 2: THE MOVIE
Marvel Comics: Aug, 2004 ($3.50/$12.99, one-shot)

1-($3.50) Movie adaptation; Johnson, Lim & Olliffe-a   3.50
TPB-($12.99) Movie adaptation; r/Amazing Spider-Man #50, Ultimate Spider-Man #14,15   13.00

SPIDER-MAN 2099 (See Amazing Spider-Man #365)
Marvel Comics: Nov, 1992 - No. 46, Aug, 1996 ($1.25/$1.50/$1.95)

1-(stiff-c)-Red foil stamped-c; begins origin of Miguel O'Hara (Spider-Man 2099);
Leonardi/Williamson-c/a begins   3.00
1-2nd printing, 2-24,26-40: 2-Origin continued, ends #3. 4-Doom 2099 app. 13-Extra 16 pg.
insert on Midnight Sons. 19-Bound-in trading cards. 35-Variant-c. 36-Two-c; Jae Lee-a.
37,38-Two-c   2.50
25-($2.25, 52 pgs.)-Newsstand edition   2.50

Spider-Man Unlimited #11 © MAR

Spider-Woman #26 © MAR

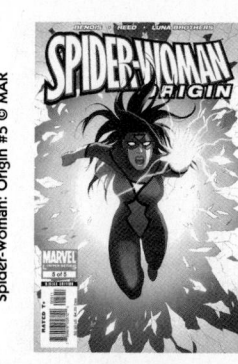

Spider-Woman: Origin #5 © MAR

	GD 2.0	VG 4.0	FN 6.0	VF 8.0	VF/NM 9.0	NM- 9.2

	GD 2.0	VG 4.0	FN 6.0	VF 8.0	VF/NM 9.0	NM- 9.2
25-($2.95, 52 pgs.)-Deluxe edition w/embossed foil-c						3.00
41-46: 46-The Vulture app; Mike McKone-a(p)						3.00
Annual 1 (1994, $2.95, 68 pgs.)						3.00
Special 1 (1995, $3.95)						4.00

NOTE: *Chaykin c-37. Ron Lim a(p)-18; c(p)-13, 16, 18. Kelley Jones c/a-9. Leonardi/Williamson a-1-8, 10-13, 15-17, 19, 20, 22-25; c-1-13, 15, 17-19, 20, 22-25, 35.*

SPIDER-MAN 2099 MEETS SPIDER-MAN
Marvel Comics: 1995 ($5.95, one-shot)

nn-Peter David script; Leonardi/Williamson-c/a.						6.00

SPIDER-MAN UNIVERSE
Marvel Comics: Mar, 2000 - No. 7, Oct, 2000 ($4.95/$3.99, reprints)

1-5-Reprints recent issues from the various Spider-Man titles						5.00
6,7-($3.99)						4.00

SPIDER-MAN UNLIMITED
Marvel Comics: May, 1993 - No. 22, Nov, 1998 ($3.95, quarterly, 68 pgs.)

1-Begin Maximum Carnage storyline, ends; Carnage-c/story						5.00
2-12: 2-Venom & Carnage-c/story; Lim-c/a(p) in #2-6. 10-Vulture app.						4.00
13-22: 13-Begin $2.99-c; Scorpion-c/app. 15-Daniel-c; Puma-c/app. 19-Lizard-c/app. 20-Hannibal King and Lilith app. 21,22-Deodato-a						3.00

SPIDER-MAN UNLIMITED (Based on the TV animated series)
Marvel Comics: Dec, 1999 - No. 5, Apr, 2000 ($2.99/$1.99)

1-($2.99) Venom and Carnage app.						3.00
2-5- 2-($1.99) Green Goblin app.						2.50

SPIDER-MAN UNLIMITED (3rd series)
Marvel Comics: Mar, 2004 - No. 15, July, 2006 ($2.99)

1-16: 1-Short stories by various incl. Miyazawa & Chen-a. 2-Mays-a. 6-Allred-c. 14-Finch-c/a; Black Cat app.						3.00

SPIDER-MAN UNMASKED
Marvel Comics: Nov, 1996 ($5.95, one-shot)

nn-Art w/text						6.00

SPIDER-MAN: VENOM AGENDA
Marvel Comics: Jan, 1998 ($2.99, one-shot)

1-Hama-s/Lyle-c/a						3.00

SPIDER-MAN VS. DRACULA
Marvel Comics: Jan, 1994 ($1.75, 52 pgs., one-shot)

1-r/Giant-Size Spider-Man #1 plus new Matt Fox-a						2.50

SPIDER-MAN VS. WOLVERINE
Marvel Comics Group: Feb, 1987; V2#1, 1990 (68 pgs.)

			GD 2.0	4	6	12	16	20
1-Williamson-c/a(i); intro Charlemagne; death of Ned Leeds (old Hobgoblin)			2	4	6	12	16	20
V2#1 (1990, $4.95)-Reprints #1 (2/87)								5.00

SPIDER-MAN: WEB OF DOOM
Marvel Comics: Aug, 1994 - No. 3, Oct, 1994 ($1.75, limited series)

1-3						2.50

SPIDER-MAN: YEAR IN REVIEW
Marvel Comics: Feb, 2000 ($2.99)

1-Text recaps of 1999 issues						3.00

SPIDER REIGN OF THE VAMPIRE KING, THE (Also see The Spider)
Eclipse Books: 1992 - No. 3, 1992 ($4.95, limited series, coated stock, 52 pgs.)

Book One - Three: Truman scripts & painted-c						5.00

SPIDER'S WEB, THE (See G-8 and His Battle Aces)

SPIDER-WOMAN (Also see The Avengers #240, Marvel Spotlight #32, Marvel Super Heroes Secret Wars #7, Marvel Two-In-One #29 and New Avengers)
Marvel Comics Group: April, 1978 - No. 50, June, 1983 (New logo #47 on)

		GD 2.0	4	6	11	14	18
1-New complete origin & mask added	2	4	6	11	14	18
2-5,7-18: 2-Excalibur app. 3,11,12-Brother Grimm app. 13,15-The Shroud-c/s. 16-Sienkiewicz-c						5.00
6,19,20,28,29,32: 6-Morgan LeFay app. 6,19,32-Werewolf by Night-c/s. 20,28,29-Spider-Man app. 32-Universal Monsters photo/Miller-c						6.00
21-27,30,31,33-36						5.00
37,38-X-Men x-over: 37-1st app. Siryn of X-Force; origin retold	1	3	4	6	8	10
39-49: 46-Kingpin app. 49-Tigra-c/story						4.00
50-(52 pgs.)-Death of Spider-Woman; photo-c	2	4	6	8	11	14

NOTE: *Austin a-37i. Byrne c-26p. Infantino a-1-19. Layton c-19. Miller c-32p.*

SPIDER-WOMAN
Marvel Comics: Nov, 1993 - No. 4, Feb, 1994 ($1.75, mini-series)

V2#1-4: 1,2-Origin; U.S. Agent app.						2.50

SPIDER-WOMAN
Marvel Comics: July, 1999 - No. 18, Dec, 2000 ($2.99/$1.99/$2.25)

1-($2.99) Byrne-s/Sears-a						3.00
2-18: 2-11-($1.99). 2-Two covers. 12-Begin $2.25-c. 15-Capt. America-c/app.						2.50

SPIDER-WOMAN: ORIGIN (Also see New Avengers)
Marvel Comics: Feb, 2006 - No. 5, June, 2006 ($2.99, limited series)

1-5-Bendis & Reed-s/Jonathan & Joshua Luna-a/c						3.00
1-Variant cover by Olivier Coipel						3.00
HC (2006, $19.99) r/series						20.00
SC (2007, $13.99) r/series						14.00

SPIDEY SUPER STORIES (Spider-Man) (Also see Fireside Books)
Marvel/Children's TV Workshop: Oct, 1974 - No. 57, Mar, 1982 (35¢, no ads)

	GD 2.0	VG 4.0	FN 6.0	VF 8.0	VF/NM 9.0	NM- 9.2
1-Origin (stories simplified for younger readers)	4	8	12	26	41	55
2-Kraven	3	6	9	16	23	30
3-10,15: 6-Iceman. 15-Storm-c/sty	2	4	6	13	18	22
11-14,16-20: 19,20-Kirby-c	2	4	6	11	16	20
21-30: 24-Kirby-c	2	4	6	10	14	18
31-53: 31-Moondragon-c/app.; Dr. Doom app. 33-Hulk. 34-Sub-Mariner. 38-F.F. 39-Thanos-c/story. 44-Vision. 45-Silver Surfer & Dr. Doom app.	2	4	6	9	13	16
54-57: 56-Battles Jack O'Lantern-c/sty (exactly one year after 1st app. in Machine Man #19)	2	4	6	13	18	22

SPIKE AND TYKE (See M.G.M.'s...)

SPIKE... (Also see Buffy the Vampire Slayer and related titles)
IDW Publ.: Aug, 2005; Jan, 2006; Apr, 2006 ($7.49, squarebound, one-shots)

...: Lost & Found (4/06, $7.49) Scott Tipton-s/Fernando Goni-a						8.00
...: Old Times (8/05, $7.49) Peter David-s/Fernando Goni-a; Cecily/Halfrek app.						8.00
...: Old Wounds (1/06, $7.49) Tipton-s/Goni-a; flashback to Black Dahlia murder case						8.00
TPB (7/06, $19.99) r/one-shots						20.00

SPIKE: ASYLUM (Buffy the Vampire Slayer)
IDW Publ.: Sept, 2006 - No. 5, Jan, 2007 ($3.99, limited series)

1-5-Lynch-s/Urru-a; multiple covers on each						4.00

SPIKE: SHADOW PUPPETS (Buffy the Vampire Slayer)
IDW Publ.: June, 2007 - Present ($3.99, limited series)

1-Lynch-s/Urru-a; multiple covers on each						4.00

SPIKE VS. DRACULA (Buffy the Vampire Slayer)
IDW Publ.: Feb, 2006 - No. 5, Mar, 2006 ($3.99, limited series)

1-5: 1-Peter David-s/Joe Corroney-a; Dru and Bela Lugosi app.						4.00

SPIN & MARTY (TV) (Walt Disney's)(See Walt Disney Showcase #32)
Dell Publishing Co. (Mickey Mouse Club): No. 714, June, 1956 - No. 1082, Mar-May, 1960 (All photo-c)

	GD 2.0	VG 4.0	FN 6.0	VF 8.0	VF/NM 9.0	NM- 9.2
Four Color 714 (#1)	12	24	36	87	156	225
Four Color 767,808 (#2,3)	9	18	27	63	107	150
Four Color 826 (#4)-Annette Funicello photo-c	22	44	66	160	285	410
5(3-5/58) - 9(6-8/59)	8	16	24	52	86	120
Four Color 1026,1082	8	16	24	52	86	120

SPINE-TINGLING TALES (Doctor Spektor Presents...)
Gold Key: May, 1975 - No. 4, Jan, 1976 (All 25¢ issues)

	GD 2.0	VG 4.0	FN 6.0	VF 8.0	VF/NM 9.0	NM- 9.2
1-1st Tragg-r/Mystery Comics Digest #3	2	4	6	9	12	15
2-4: 2-Origin Ra-Ka-Tep-r/Mystery Comics Digest #1; Dr. Spektor #12. 3-All Durak-r issue; 4-Baron Tibor's 1st app.-r/Mystery Comics Digest #4; painted-c	1	2	3	5	6	8

SPINWORLD
Amaze Ink (Slave Labor Graphics): July, 1997 - No. 4, Jan, 1998 ($2.95/$3.95, B&W, mini-series)

1-3-Brent Anderson-a(p)						3.00
4-($3.95)						4.00

SPIRAL PATH, THE
Eclipse Comics: July, 1986 - No. 2 ($1.75, Baxter paper, limited series)

1,2						2.50

SPIRAL ZONE
DC Comics: Feb, 1988 - No. 4, May, 1988 ($1.00, mini-series)

1-4-Based on Tonka toys						2.50

The Spirit (1952 series) #4 © Will Eisner

The Spirit (2007 series) #8 © Will Eisner

Spirit of the Tao #3 © TCOW

	GD	VG	FN	VF	VF/NM	NM-
	2.0	4.0	6.0	8.0	9.0	9.2

SPIRIT, THE (Newspaper comics - see Promotional Comics section)

SPIRIT, THE (1st Series)(Also see Police Comics Comics #11 and The Best of the Spirit TPB)
Quality Comics Group (Vital): 1944 - No. 22, Aug, 1950

nn(#1)- "Wanted Dead or Alive"	91	182	273	569	947	1325
nn(#2)- "Crime Doesn't Pay"	46	92	138	281	466	650
nn(#3)- "Murder Runs Wild"	40	80	120	240	383	525
4,5: 4-Flatfoot Burns begins, ends #22. 5-Wertham app.	32	64	96	186	293	400
6-10	27	54	81	156	246	335
11	25	50	75	148	232	315
12-17-Eisner-c. 19-Honeybun app.	36	72	108	208	329	450
18-21-Strip-r by Eisner; Eisner-c	41	82	123	252	406	560
22-Used by N.Y. Legis. Comm; classic Eisner-c	83	166	249	519	860	1200
Super Reprint #11-r/Quality Spirit #19 by Eisner	3	6	9	18	27	35
Super Reprint #12-r/Spirit #17 by Fine; Sol Brodsky-c	3	6	9	18	27	35

SPIRIT, THE (2nd Series)
Fiction House Magazines: Spring, 1952 - No. 5, 1954

1-Not Eisner	40	80	120	244	392	540
2-Eisner-c/a(2)	40	80	120	240	383	525
3-Eisner/Grandenetti-c	34	68	102	197	311	425
4-Eisner/Grandenetti-c; Eisner-a	35	70	105	204	322	440
5-Eisner-c/a(4)	40	80	120	235	368	500

SPIRIT, THE
Harvey Publications: Oct, 1966 - No. 2, Mar, 1967 (Giant Size, 25¢, 68 pgs.)

1-Eisner-r plus 9 new pgs.(origin Denny Colt, Take 3, plus 2 filler pgs.) (#3 was advertised, but never published)	8	16	24	52	86	120
2-Eisner-r plus 9 new pgs.(origin of the Octopus)	6	12	18	41	66	90

SPIRIT, THE (Underground)
Kitchen Sink Enterprises (Krupp Comics): Jan, 1973 - No. 2, Sept, 1973 (Black & White)

1-New Eisner-c & 4 pgs. new Eisner-a plus-r (titled Crime Convention)	2	4	6	13	18	22
2-New Eisner-c & 4 pgs. new Eisner-a plus-r (titled Meets P'Gell)	3	6	9	15	21	26

SPIRIT, THE (Magazine)
Warren Publ. Co./Krupp Comic Works No. 17 on: 4/74 - No. 16, 10/76; No. 17, Winter, 1977 - No. 41, 6/83 (B&W w/color) (#6-14,16 are squarebound)

1-Eisner-r begin; 8 pg. color insert	5	10	15	32	51	70
2-5: 2-Powder Pouf-s; UFO-s. 4-Silk Satin-s	3	6	9	19	29	38
6-9,11-15: 7-All Ebony issue. 8-Female Foes issue. 8,12-Sand Seref-s. 9-P'Gell & Octopus-s. 12-X-Mas issue	3	6	9	17	25	32
10-Giant Summer Special ($1.50)-Origin	3	6	9	20	30	40
16-Giant Summer Special ($1.50)-Olga Bustle-c/s	3	6	9	18	27	35
17,18(8/78): 17-Lady Luck-r	2	4	6	10	14	18
19-21-New Eisner-a. 20,21-Wood-r (#21-r/A DP on the Moon by Wood). 20-Outer Space-r	2	4	6	10	14	18

22-41: 22,23-Wood-r (#22-r/Mission the Moon by Wood). 28-r/last story (10/5/52).
30-(7/81)-Special Spirit Jam issue w/Caniff, Corben, Bolland, Byrne, Miller, Kurtzman, Rogers, Sinkiewicz-a & 40 others. 36-Begin Spirit Section-r; r/1st story (6/2/40) in color; new Eisner-c/a(18 pgs.)($2.95). 37-r/2nd story in color plus 18 pgs. new Eisner-a.
38-41: r/3rd - 6th stories in color. 41-Lady Luck Mr. Mystic in color

	2	4	6	9	12	15
Special 1(1975)-All Eisner-a (mail only, 1500 printed, full color)	7	14	21	47	76	105

NOTE: Covers pencilled/inked by Eisner only #1-9,12-16; painted by Eisner & Ken Kelly #10 & 11; painted by Eisner #17-up; one color story reprinted in #1-10. **Austin** a-30i. **Byrne** a-30p. **Miller** a-30p.

SPIRIT, THE
Kitchen Sink Enterprises: Oct, 1983 - No. 87, Jan, 1992 ($2.00, Baxter paper)

1-60: 1-Origin-r/12/23/45 Spirit. 2-r/ 1/20/46-2/10/46. 3-r/2/17/46-3/10/46. 4-r/3/17/46-4/7/46. 11-Last color issue. 54-r/section 2/19/50						4.00
61-87: 85-87-Reprint the Outer Space Spirit stories by Wood. 86-r/A DP on the Moon by Wood from 1952						4.00

SPIRIT, THE (Also see Batman/The Spirit in Batman one-shots)
DC Comics: Feb, 2007 - Present ($2.99)

1-9: 1-6,8,9-Darwyn Cooke-s/a/c. 2-P'Gell app. 3-Origin re-told. 7-Short stories by Baker, Bernet, Palmiotti, Simonson & Sprouse; Cooke-c						3.00

SPIRIT JAM
Kitchen Sink Press: Aug, 1998 ($5.95, B&W, oversized, square-bound)

nn-Reprints Spirit (Magazine) #30 by Eisner & 50 others; and "Cerebus Vs. The Spirit" from Cerebus Jam #1						6.00

SPIRIT, THE: THE NEW ADVENTURES
Kitchen Sink Press: 1997 - No. 8, Nov, 1998 ($3.50, anthology)

1-Moore-s/Gibbons-c/a						4.00
2-8: 2-Gaiman-s/Eisner-c. 3-Moore-s/Bolland-c/Moebius back-c. 4-Allred-s/a; Busiek-s/Anderson-a. 5-Chadwick-s/c/a(p); Nyberg-i. 6-S.Hampton & Mandrake-a						3.50

SPIRIT: THE ORIGIN YEARS
Kitchen Sink Press: May, 1992 - No. 10, Dec, 1993 ($2.95, B&W)

1-10: 1-r/sections 6/2/40(origin)-6/23/40 (all 1940s)						3.00

SPIRITMAN (Also see Three Comics)
No publisher listed: No date (1944) (10¢)
(Triangle Sales Co. ad on back cover)

1-Three 16pg. Spirit sections bound together, (1944, 10¢, 52 pgs.)	21	42	63	122	191	260
2-Two Spirit sections (3/26/44, 4/2/44) bound together; by Lou Fine	19	38	57	109	172	235

SPIRIT OF THE BORDER (See Zane Grey & Four Color #197)

SPIRIT OF THE TAO
Image Comics (Top Cow): Jun, 1998 - No. 15, May, 2000 ($2.50)

Preview						5.00
1-14: 1-D-Tron-s/Tan & D-Tron-a						2.50
15-($4.95)						5.00

SPIRIT OF WONDER (Manga)
Dark Horse Comics: Apr, 1996 - No. 5, Aug, 1996 ($2.95, B&W, limited series)

1-5						3.00

SPIRIT WORLD (Magazine)
National Periodical Publications: Fall, 1971 (B&W)

1-New Kirby-a; Neal Adams-c; poster inside	7	14	21	45	73	100
(1/2 price without poster)						

SPITFIRE
Malverne Herald (Elliot)(J. R. Mahon): No. 132, 1944 (Aug) - No. 133, 1945
(Female undercover runner)

132,133: Both have Classics Gift Box ads on b/c with checklist to #20	25	50	75	148	232	315

SPITFIRE AND THE TROUBLESHOOTERS
Marvel Comics: Oct, 1986 - No. 9, June, 1987 (Codename: Spitfire #10 on)

1-3,5-9						2.50
4-McFarlane-a						3.00

SPITFIRE COMICS (Also see Double Up)
Harvey Publications: Aug, 1941 - No. 2, Oct, 1941 (Pocket size; 100 pgs.)

1-Origin The Clown, The Fly-Man, The Spitfire & The Magician From Bagdad	76	152	228	475	788	1100
2-(Scarce)	69	138	207	431	716	1000

SPLITTING IMAGE
Image Comics: Mar, 1993 - No. 2, 1993 ($1.95)

1,2-Simpson-c/a; parody comic						2.50

SPOOF
Marvel Comics Group: Oct, 1970; No. 2, Nov, 1972 - No. 5, May, 1973

1-Infinity-c; Dark Shadows-c & parody	3	6	9	18	27	35
2-5: 2-All in the Family. 3-Beatles, Osmond's, Jackson 5, David Cassidy, Nixon & Agnew-c.	3	6	9	14	19	24
5-Rod Serling, Woody Allen, Ted Kennedy-c						

SPOOK (Formerly Shock Detective Cases)
Star Publications: No. 22, Jan, 1953 - No. 30, Oct, 1954

22-Sgt. Spook-r; acid in face story; hanging-c	40	80	120	235	368	500
23,25,27: 25-Jungle Lil-r. 27-Two Sgt. Spook-r	28	56	84	164	260	355
24-Used in SOTI, pgs. 182,183-r/Inside Crime #2; Transvestism story	29	58	87	170	268	365
26,28-30: 26-Disbrow-a. 28,29-Rulah app. 29-Jo-Jo app. 30-Disbrow-a(2); only Star-c	28	56	84	164	260	355

NOTE: **L. B. Cole** covers-all issues except #30; a-28(1 pg.). **Disbrow** a-26(2), 28, 29(2), 30(2). No. 30 r/Blue Bolt Weird Tales #114.

SPOOK COMICS
Baily Publications/Star: 1946

1-Mr. Lucifer story	30	60	90	174	275	375

SPOOKY (The Tuff Little Ghost; see Casper The Friendly Ghost)
Harvey Publications: 11/55 - 139, 11/73; No. 140, 7/74 - No. 155, 3/77; No. 156, 12/77 - No. 158, 4/78; No. 159, 9/78; No. 160, 10/79; No. 161, 9/80

Spooky Mysteries #1 © Your Guide

Sports Action #8 © MAR

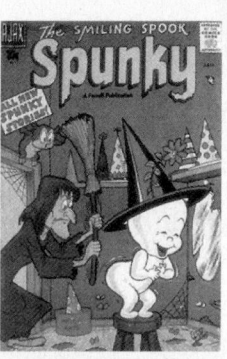
Spunky the Smiling Spook #3 © AJAX

	GD 2.0	VG 4.0	FN 6.0	VF 8.0	VF/NM 9.0	NM- 9.2
1-Nightmare begins (see Casper #19)	41	82	123	328	589	850
2	20	40	60	150	268	385
3-10(1956-57)	12	24	36	87	156	225
11-20(1957-58)	8	16	24	52	86	120
21-40(1958-59)	6	12	18	37	59	80
41-60	4	8	12	28	44	60
61-80,100	3	6	9	20	30	40
81-99	3	6	9	17	25	32
101-120	2	4	6	11	16	20
121-126,133-140	2	4	6	8	11	14
127-132: All 52 pg. Giants	2	4	6	11	16	20
141-161	1	2	3	5	7	9

SPOOKY
Harvey Comics: Nov, 1991 - No. 4, Sept, 1992 ($1.00/$1.25)

1						4.00
2-4: 3-Begin $1.25-c						3.00
...Digest 1-3 (10/92, 6/93, 10/93, $1.75, 100 pgs.)-Casper, Wendy, etc.						4.00

SPOOKY HAUNTED HOUSE
Harvey Publications: Oct, 1972 - No. 15, Feb, 1975

1	3	6	9	18	27	35
2-5	2	4	6	10	14	18
6-10	2	4	6	8	10	12
11-15	1	2	3	5	7	9

SPOOKY MYSTERIES
Your Guide Publ. Co.: No date (1946) (10¢)

1-Mr. Spooky, Super Snooper, Pinky, Girl Detective app.	20	40	60	115	180	245

SPOOKY SPOOKTOWN
Harvey Publ.: 9/61; No. 2, 9/62 - No. 52, 12/73; No. 53, 10/74 - No. 66, 12/76

1-Casper, Spooky; 68 pgs. begin	16	32	48	118	209	300
2	9	18	27	63	107	150
3-5	7	14	21	45	73	100
6-10	5	10	15	35	55	75
11-20	4	8	12	24	37	50
21-39: 39-Last 68 pg. issue	3	6	9	20	30	40
40-45: All 52 pgs.	2	4	6	11	16	20
46-66: 61-Hot Stuff/Spooky team-up story	1	2	3	5	7	9

SPORT COMICS (Becomes True Sport Picture Stories #5 on)
Street & Smith Publications: Oct, 1940 (No mo.) - No. 4, Nov, 1941

1-Life story of Lou Gehrig	54	108	162	338	557	775
2	31	62	93	178	282	385
3,4	27	54	81	156	246	335

SPORT LIBRARY (See Charlton Sport Library)

SPORTS ACTION (Formerly Sport Stars)
Marvel/Atlas Comics (ACI No. 2,3/SAI No. 4-14): No. 2, Feb, 1950 - No. 14, Sept, 1952

2-Powell painted-c; George Gipp life story	43	86	129	262	431	600
1-(nd,no price, no publ., 52pgs, #1 on-c; has same-c as #2; blank inside-c (giveaway)	22	44	66	128	202	275
3-Everett-a	24	48	72	139	220	300
4-11,14: Weiss-a	21	42	63	124	195	265
12,13: 12-Everett-c. 13-Krigstein-a	23	46	69	132	209	285

NOTE: Title may have changed after No. 3, to Crime Must Lose No. 4 on, due to publisher change. *Sol Brodsky* c-4-7, 13, 14. *Maneely* c-3, 8-11.

SPORT STARS
Parents' Magazine Institute (Sport Stars): Feb-Mar, 1946 - No. 4, Aug-Sept, 1946 (Half comic, half photo magazine)

1- "How Tarzan Got That Way" story of Johnny Weissmuller	40	80	120	239	380	520
2-Baseball greats	26	52	78	152	239	325
3,4	23	46	69	132	209	285

SPORT STARS (Becomes Sports Action #2 on)
Marvel Comics (ACI): Nov, 1949 (52 pgs.)

1-Knute Rockne; painted-c	45	90	135	275	450	625

SPORT THRILLS (Formerly Dick Cole; becomes Jungle Thrills #16)
Star Publications: No. 11, Nov, 1950 - No. 15, Nov, 1951

11-Dick Cole begins; Ted Williams & Ty Cobb life stories	29	58	87	170	268	365
12-Joe DiMaggio, Phil Rizzuto stories & photos on-c; L.B. Cole-c/a						

	GD 2.0	VG 4.0	FN 6.0	VF 8.0	VF/NM 9.0	NM- 9.2
	24	48	72	137	216	295
13-15-All L. B. Cole-c. 13-Jackie Robinson, Pee Wee Reese stories & photo on-c.						
14-Johnny Weissmuler life story	24	48	72	137	216	295
Accepted Reprint #11 (#15 on-c, nd); L.B. Cole-c	10	20	30	54	72	90
Accepted Reprint #12 (nd); L.B. Cole-c; Joe DiMaggio & Phil Rizzuto life stories-r/#12	10	20	30	54	72	90

SPOTLIGHT (TV) (newsstand sales only)
Marvel Comics Group: Sept, 1978 - No. 4, Mar, 1979 (Hanna-Barbera)

1-Huckleberry Hound, Yogi Bear; Shaw-a	3	6	9	20	30	40
2,4: 2-Quick Draw McGraw, Augie Doggie, Snooper & Blabber. 4-Magilla Gorilla, Snagglepuss	3	6	9	18	23	30
3-The Jetsons; Yakky Doodle	3	6	9	20	30	40

SPOTLIGHT COMICS
Country Press Inc.: Sept, 1940
nn-Ashcan, not distributed to newsstands, only for in house use. A copy sold in 2006 for $2,225.

SPOTLIGHT COMICS (Becomes Red Seal Comics #14 on?)
Harry 'A' Chesler (Our Army, Inc.): Nov, 1944 - No. 3, 1945

1-The Black Dwarf (cont'd in Red Seal?), The Veiled Avenger, & Barry Kuda begin; Tuska-c	85	170	255	531	878	1225
2	54	108	162	338	562	785
3-Injury in eye story (reprinted from Scoop #3)	57	114	171	356	591	825

SPOTTY THE PUP (Becomes Super Pup #4, see Television Puppet Show)
Avon Periodicals/Realistic Comics: No. 2, Oct-Nov, 1953 - No. 3, Dec-Jan, 1953-54 (Also see Funny Tunes)

2,3	7	14	21	35	43	50
nn (1953, Realistic-r)	4	7	9	14	16	18

SPUNKY (...Junior Cowboy)(...Comics #2 on)
Standard Comics: April, 1949 - No. 7, Nov, 1951

1-Text illos by Frazetta	11	22	33	62	86	110
2-Text illos by Frazetta	9	18	27	47	61	75
3-7	6	12	18	31	38	45

SPUNKY THE SMILING SPOOK
Ajax/Farrell (World Famous Comics/Four Star Comic Corp.): Aug, 1957 - No. 4, May, 1958

1-Reprints from Frisky Fables	10	20	30	54	72	90
2-4	6	12	18	31	38	45

SPY AND COUNTERSPY (Becomes Spy Hunters #3 on)
American Comics Group: Aug-Sept, 1949 - No. 2, Oct-Nov, 1949 (52 pgs.)

1-Origin, 1st app. Jonathan Kent, Counterspy	27	54	81	158	249	340
2	17	34	51	98	154	210

SPYBOY
Dark Horse Comics: Oct, 1999 - No. 17, May, 2001 ($2.50/$2.95/$2.99)

1-17: 1-6-Peter David-s/Pop Mhan-a. 7,8-Meglia-a. 9-17-Mhan-a						3.00
13.1-13.3 (4/03-8/03, $2.99), 13.2,13.3-Mhan-a						3.00
... Special (5/02, $4.99) David-s/Mhan-a						5.00

SPYBOY: FINAL EXAM
Dark Horse Comics: May, 2004 - No. 4, Aug, 2004 ($2.99, limited series)

1-4-Peter David-s/Pop Mhan-a/c						3.00
TPB (2005, $12.95) r/series						13.00

SPYBOY/ YOUNG JUSTICE
Dark Horse Comics: Feb, 2002 - No. 3, Apr, 2002 ($2.99, limited series)

1-3: 1-Peter David-s/Todd Nauck-a/Pop Mhan-c. 2-Mhan-a						3.00

SPY CASES (Formerly The Kellys)
Marvel/Atlas Comics (Hercules Publ.): No. 26, Sept, 1950 - No. 19, Oct, 1953

26 (#1)	23	46	69	132	209	285
27(#2),28(#3, 2/51): 27-Everett-a; bondage-c	14	28	42	80	115	150
4(4/51) - 7,9,10	12	24	36	69	97	125
8-A-Bomb-c/story	14	28	42	78	112	150
11-19: 10-14-War format	14	28	42	50	76	95

NOTE: *Sol Brodsky* c-1-5, 8, 9, 11-14, 17, 18. *Maneely* a-8; c-7, 10. *Tuska* a-7.

SPY FIGHTERS
Marvel/Atlas Comics (CSI): March, 1951 - No. 15, July, 1953
(Cases from official records)

1-Clark Mason begins; Tuska-a; Brodsky-c	25	50	75	145	228	310
2-Tuska-a	14	28	42	81	118	155
3-13: 3-5-Brodsky-c. 7-Heath-c	14	28	42	76	108	140
14,15-Pakula-a(3), Ed Win-a. 15-Brodsky-c	14	28	42	78	112	145

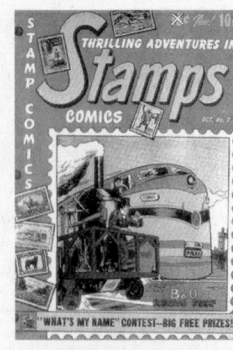

Spy Smasher #9 © FAW   Squeeks #2 © LEV   Stamp Comics #7 © YM

	GD 2.0	VG 4.0	FN 6.0	VF 8.0	VF/NM 9.0	NM- 9.2		GD 2.0	VG 4.0	FN 6.0	VF 8.0	VF/NM 9.0	NM- 9.2

SPY-HUNTERS (Formerly Spy & Counterspy)
American Comics Group: No. 3, Dec-Jan, 1949-50 - No. 24, June-July, 1953 (#3-14: 52 pgs.)

	GD	VG	FN	VF	VF/NM	NM-
3-Jonathan Kent continues, ends #10	23	46	69	135	213	290
4-10: 4,8,10-Starr-a	14	28	42	80	115	150
11-15,17-22,24: 18-War-c begin. 21-War-c/stories begin	10	20	30	56	76	95
16-Williamson-a (9 pgs.)	15	30	45	88	137	185
23-Graphic torture, injury to eye panel	20	40	60	117	184	250

NOTE: *Drucker* a-12. *Whitney* a-many issues; c-7, 8, 10-12, 15, 16.

SPYMAN (Top Secret Adventures on cover)
Harvey Publications (Illustrated Humor): Sept, 1966 - No. 3, Feb, 1967 (12¢)

	GD	VG	FN	VF	VF/NM	NM-
1-Origin and 1st app. of Spyman. Steranko(p)-1st pro work; 1 pg. Neal Adams ad; Tuska-c/a, Crandall-a(i)	7	14	21	45	73	100
2-Simon-c; Steranko-a(p)	4	8	12	28	44	60
3-Simon-c	4	8	12	26	41	55

SPY SMASHER (See Mighty Midget, Whiz & Xmas Comics) (Also see Crime Smasher)
Fawcett Publications: Fall, 1941 - No. 11, Feb, 1943

	GD	VG	FN	VF	VF/NM	NM-
1-Spy Smasher begins; silver metallic-c	327	654	981	2126	3763	5400
2-Raboy-c	152	304	456	950	1575	2200
3,4: 3-Bondage-c. 4-Irvin Steinberg-c	102	204	306	638	1057	1475
5-7: Raboy-c; 6-Raboy-c/a. 7-Part photo-c (movie)	86	172	258	538	894	1250
8,11: War-c	72	144	216	450	750	1050
9-Hitler, Tojo, Mussolini-c.	100	200	300	625	1038	1450
10-Hitler-c	91	182	273	569	947	1325

SPY THRILLERS (Police Badge No. 479 #5)
Atlas Comics (PrPI): Nov, 1954 - No. 4, May, 1955

	GD	VG	FN	VF	VF/NM	NM-
1-Brodsky c-1,2	21	42	63	122	191	260
2-Last precode (1/55)	14	28	42	76	108	140
3,4	11	22	33	60	83	105

SQUADRON SUPREME (Also see Marvel Graphic Novel - ...: Death of a Universe)
Marvel Comics Group: Aug, 1985 - No. 12, Aug, 1986 (Maxi-series)

1-Double size	3.00
2-12	2.50
TPB ($24.99) r/#1-12; Alex Ross painted-c; printing inks contain some of the cremated remains of late writer Mark Gruenwald	25.00
TPB-2nd printing ($24.99) Inks contain no ashes	25.00
...Death of a Universe TPB (2006, $24.99) r/Marvel Graphic Novel, Thor #280, Avengers #5,6; Avengers/Squadron Supreme Annual and Squadron Supreme: New World Order	25.00

SQUADRON SUPREME (Also see Supreme Power)
Marvel Comics: May, 2006 - Present ($2.99)

1-7-Straczynski-s/Frank-a/c	3.00
Saga of Squadron Supreme (2006, $3.99) summary of Supreme Power #1-18; plus Hyperion and Nighthawk limited series; wraparound-c; preview of Squadron Supreme #1	4.00
... Vol. 1: The Pre-War Years (2006, $20.99, dustjacket) r/#1-5 & Saga of S.S.	21.00

SQUADRON SUPREME: HYPERION VS. NIGHTHAWK
Marvel Comics: Mar, 2007 - No. 4, June, 2007 ($2.99, limited series)

1-4-Hyperion and Nighthawk in Darfur; Gulacy-a/c; Guggenheim-s	3.00
TPB (2007, $10.99) r/#1-4	11.00

SQUADRON SUPREME: NEW WORLD ORDER
Marvel Comics: Sept, 1998 ($5.99, one-shot)

1-Wraparound-c; Kaminski-s	6.00

SQUALOR
First Comics: Dec, 1989 - Aug, 1990 ($2.75, limited series)

1-4: Sutton-a	2.75

SQUEE (Also see Johnny The Homicidal Maniac)
Slave Labor Graphics: Apr, 1997 - No. 4, May, 1998 ($2.95, B&W)

1-4: Jhonen Vasquez-s/a in all	3.00

SQUEEKS (Also see Boy Comics)
Lev Gleason Publications: Oct, 1953 - No. 5, June, 1954

	GD	VG	FN	VF	VF/NM	NM-
1-Funny animal; Biro-c; Crimebuster's pet monkey "Squeeks" begins	10	20	30	54	72	90
2-Biro-a	6	12	18	31	38	45
3-5: 3-Biro-a	6	12	18	28	34	40

S.R. BISSETTE'S SPIDERBABY COMIX
SpiderBaby Grafix: Aug, 1996 - No. 2 ($3.95, B&W, magazine size)

Preview-(8/96, $3.95)-Graphic violence & nudity; Laurel & Hardy app.	4.00
1,2	4.00

S.R. BISSETTE'S TYRANT
SpiderBaby Grafix: Sept, 1994 - No. 4 ($2.95, B&W)

1-4	4.00

STAINLESS STEEL RAT
Eagle Comics: Oct, 1985 - No. 6, Mar, 1986 (Limited series)

1 (52 pgs.; $2.25-c)	3.00
2-6 ($1.50)	2.50

STALKER (Also see All Star Comics 1999 and crossover issues)
National Periodical Publications: June-July, 1975 - No. 4, Dec-Jan, 1975-76

	GD	VG	FN	VF	VF/NM	NM-
1-Origin & 1st app; Ditko/Wood-c/a	2	4	6	8	11	14
2-4-Ditko/Wood-c/a	1	2	3	5	6	8

STALKERS
Marvel Comics (Epic Comics): Apr, 1990 - No. 12, Mar, 1991 ($1.50)

1-12: 1-Chadwick-c	2.50

STAMP COMICS (Stamps... on-c; Thrilling Adventures In...#8)
Youthful Magazines/Stamp Comics, Inc.: Oct, 1951 - No. 7, Oct, 1952

	GD	VG	FN	VF	VF/NM	NM-
1-(15¢) ('Stamps' on indicia No. 1-3,5,7)	27	54	81	156	246	335
2	15	30	45	86	133	180
3-6: 3,4-Kiefer, Wildey-a	14	28	42	81	118	155
7-Roy Krenkel (4 pgs.)	17	34	51	98	154	210

NOTE: *Promotes stamp collecting; gives stories behind various commemorative stamps. No. 2, 10¢ printed over 15¢ c-price.* **Kiefer** a-1-7. **Kirkel** a-1-6. **Napoli** a-2-7. **Palais** a-2-4, 7.

STAN LEE MEETS...
Marvel Comics: Nov, 2006 - Jan, 2007 ($3.99, series of one-shots)

Doctor Doom 1 (12/06) Lee-s/Larroca-a/c; Loeb-s/McGuinness-a; r/Fantastic Four #87	4.00
Doctor Strange 1 (11/06) Lee-s/Davis-a/c; Bendis-s/Bagley-a; r/Marvel Premiere #3	4.00
Silver Surfer 1 (1/07) Lee-s/Wieringo-a/c; Jenkins-s/Buckingham-a; r/S.S. #14	4.00
Spider-Man 1 (11/06) Lee-s/Coipel-a/c; Whedon-s/Gaydos-a; r/AS-M #87	4.00
The Thing 1 (12/06) Lee-s/Weeks-a/c; Thomas-s/Kolins-a; r/FF #79; FF #51 cover swipe	4.00
HC (2007, $24.99, dustjacket) r/one-shots; interviews and features	25.00

STANLEY & HIS MONSTER (Formerly The Fox & the Crow)
National Periodical Publ.: No. 109, Apr-May, 1968 - No. 112, Oct-Nov, 1968

	GD	VG	FN	VF	VF/NM	NM-
109-112	4	8	12	20	30	40

STANLEY & HIS MONSTER
DC Comics: Feb, 1993 - No. 4, May, 1993 ($1.50, limited series)

1-4	2.50

STAN SHAW'S BEAUTY & THE BEAST
Dark Horse Comics: Nov, 1993 ($4.95, one-shot)

1	5.00

STAR
Image Comics (Highbrow Entertainment): June, 1995 - No. 4, Oct, 1995 ($2.50, lim. series)

1-4	2.50

STARBLAST
Marvel Comics: Jan, 1994 - No. 4, Apr, 1994 ($1.75, limited series)

1-4: 1-($2.00, 52 pgs.)-Nova, Quasar, Black Bolt; painted-c	2.50

STAR BLAZERS
Comico: Apr, 1987 - No. 4, July, 1987 ($1.75, limited series)

1-4	3.00

STAR BLAZERS
Comico: 1989 ($1.95/$2.50, limited series)

1-5- Steacy wraparound painted-c on all	3.00

STAR BLAZERS (The Magazine of Space Battleship Yamato)
Argo Press: No. 0, Aug, 1995 - No. 3, Dec, 1995 ($2.95)

0-3	3.00

STAR BRAND
Marvel Comics (New Universe): Oct, 1986 - No. 19, May, 1989 (75¢/$1.25)

1-15: 14-begin $1.25-c	2.50
16-19-Byrne story & art; low print run	4.00
Annual 1 (10/87)	2.50
... Classic Vol. 1 TPB (2006, $19.99) r/#1-7	20.00

STARCHILD
Tailspin Press: 1992 - No. 12($2.25/$2.50, B&W)

1,2-('92),0(4/93),3-12: 0-Illos by Chadwick, Eisner, Sim, M. Wagner. 3-(7/93). 4-(11/93). 6-(2/94)	3.00

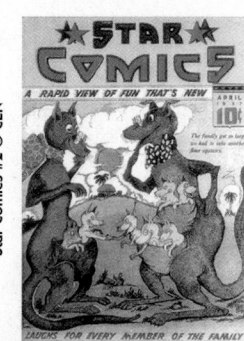

Star Comics #2 © CEN

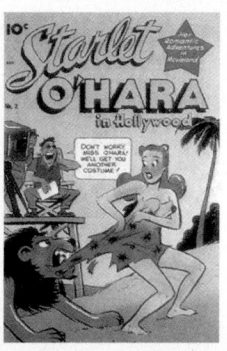

Starlet O'Hara in Hollywood #2 © STD

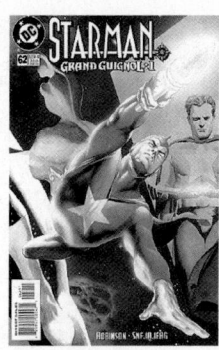

Starman (2nd series) #62 © DC

	GD 2.0	VG 4.0	FN 6.0	VF 8.0	VF/NM 9.0	NM- 9.2

STARCHILD: MYTHOPOLIS
Image Comics: No. 0, July, 1997 - No. 4, Apr, 1998 ($2.95, B&W, limited series)

0-4-James Owen-s/a						3.00

STAR COMICS
Ultem Publ. (Harry `A' Chesler)/Centaur Publications: Feb, 1937 - V2#7 (No. 23), Aug, 1939 (#1-6: large size)

	GD	VG	FN	VF	VF/NM	NM-
V1#1-Dan Hastings (s/f) begins	207	414	621	1294	2147	3000
2	90	180	270	563	932	1300
3-Classic Black Americana cover (rare)	121	242	363	756	1253	1750
4-6 (#6, 9/37): 4,5-Little Nemo-c/stories	76	152	228	475	788	1100

7-9: 8-Severed head centerspread; Impy & Little Nemo by Winsor McCay Jr, Popeye app. by Bob Wood; Mickey Mouse & Popeye app. as toys in Santa's bag on-c;

X-Mas-c	67	134	201	419	697	975

10 (1st Centaur; 3/38)-Impy by Winsor McCay Jr; Don Marlow by Guardineer begins

	88	176	264	550	913	1275
11-1st Jack Cole comic-a, 1 pg. (4/38)	67	134	201	419	697	975

12-15: 12-Riders of the Golden West begins; Little Nemo app. 15-Speed Silvers by Gustavson & The Last Pirate by Burgos begins

	54	108	162	338	562	785

16 (12/38)-The Phantom Rider & his horse Thunder begins, ends V2#6

	57	114	171	356	588	820

V2#1(#17, 2/39)-Phantom Rider-c (only non-funny-c)

	60	120	180	375	623	870

2-7(#18-23): 2-Diana Deane by Tarpe Mills app. 3-Drama of Hollywood by Mills begins.

7-Jungle Queen app.	49	98	147	299	492	685

NOTE: Biro c-6, 9, 10. Burgos a-15, 16, V2#1-7. Ken Ernst a-10, 12, 14. Filchock c-15, 18, 22. Gill Fox c-14, 19. Guardineer a-6, 8-14. Gustavson a-13-16, V2#1-7. Winsor McCay c-4, 5. Tarpe Mills a-15, V2#1-7. Schwab c-20, 23. Bob Wood a-10, 12, 13; c-7, 8.

STAR COMICS MAGAZINE
Marvel Comics (Star Comics): Dec, 1986 - No. 13, 1988 ($1.50, digest-size)

	GD	VG	FN	VF	VF/NM	NM-
1,9-Spider-Man-c/s	2	4	6	8	10	12
2-8-Heathcliff, Ewoks, Top Dog, Madballs-r in #1-13	1	2	3	5	6	8
10-13	1	3	4	6	8	10

S.T.A.R. CORPS
DC Comics: Nov, 1993 - No. 6, Apr, 1994 ($1.50, limited series)

1-6: 1,2-Austin-(i). 1-Superman app.						2.50

STAR CROSSED
DC Comics (Helix): June, 1997 - No. 3, Aug, 1997 ($2.50, limited series)

1-3-Matt Howarth-s/a						2.50

STARDUST (See Neil Gaiman and Charles Vess' Stardust)

STARDUST KID, THE
Image Comics/Boom! Studios #4-on: May, 2005 - Present ($3.50)

1-4-J.M. DeMatteis-s/Mike Ploog-a						3.50

STAR FEATURE COMICS
I. W. Enterprises: 1963

	GD	VG	FN	VF	VF/NM	NM-
Reprint #9-Stunt-Man Stetson-r/Feat. Comics #141	2	4	6	10	13	16

STARFIRE (Not the Teen Titans character)
National Periodical Publ./DC Comics: Aug-Sept, 1976 - No. 8, Oct-Nov, 1977

1-Origin (CCA stamp fell off cover art; so it was approved by code)						
	2	4	6	8	10	12
2-8	1	2	3	4	5	7

STAR HUNTERS (See DC Super Stars #16)
National Periodical Publ./DC Comics: Oct-Nov, 1977 - No. 7, Oct-Nov, 1978

1,7: 1-Newton-a(p). 7-44 pgs.	1	3	4	6	8	10
2-6						6.00

NOTE: Buckler a-4-7p; c-1-7p. Layton a-1-5i; c-1-6i. Nasser a-3p. Sutton a-6i.

STARJAMMERS (See X-Men Spotlight on Starjammers)

STARJAMMERS (Also see Uncanny X-Men)
Marvel Comics: Oct, 1995 - No. 4, Jan, 1996 ($2.95, limited series)

1-4: Foil-c; Ellis scripts						3.00

STARJAMMERS
Marvel Comics: Sept, 2004 - No. 6, Jan, 2005 ($2.99, limited series)

1-6-Kevin J. Anderson-s. 1-Garza-a. 2-6-Lucas-a.						3.00

STARK TERROR
Stanley Publications: Dec, 1970 - No. 5, Aug, 1971 (B&W, magazine, 52 pgs.) (1950s Horror reprints, including pre-code)

	GD	VG	FN	VF	VF/NM	NM-
1-Bondage, torture-c	6	12	18	39	62	85

	GD 2.0	VG 4.0	FN 6.0	VF 8.0	VF/NM 9.0	NM- 9.2
2-4 (Gillmor/Aragon-r)	4	8	12	23	36	48
5 (ACG-r)	3	6	9	19	29	38

STARLET O'HARA IN HOLLYWOOD (Teen-age) (Also see Cookie)
Standard Comics: Dec, 1948 - No. 4, Sept, 1949

	GD	VG	FN	VF	VF/NM	NM-
1-Owen Fitzgerald-a in all	26	52	78	150	235	320
2	15	30	45	85	130	175
3,4	14	28	42	76	108	140

STAR-LORD THE SPECIAL EDITION (Also see Marvel Comics Super Special #10, Marvel Premiere & Preview & Marvel Spotlight V2#6,7)
Marvel Comics Group: Feb, 1982 (one-shot, direct sales) (1st Baxter paper comic)

1-Byrne/Austin-a; Austin-c; 8 pgs. of new-a by Golden (p); Dr. Who story by Dave Gibbons; 1st deluxe format comic						6.00

STARLORD
Marvel Comics: Dec, 1996 - No. 3, Feb, 1997 ($2.50, limited series)

1-3-Timothy Zahn-s						2.50

STARLORD MEGAZINE
Marvel Comics: Nov, 1996 ($2.95, one-shot)

1-Reprints w/preview of new series						3.00

STARMAN (1st Series) (Also see Justice League & War of the Gods)
DC Comics: Oct, 1988 - No. 45, Apr, 1992 ($1.00)

1-25,29-45: 1-Origin. 4-Intro The Power Elite. 9,10,34-Batman app. 14-Superman app. 17-Power Girl app. 38-War of the Gods x-over. 42-45-Eclipso-c/stories						2.50
26-1st app. David Knight (G.A.Starman's son).						5.00
27,28: 27-Starman (David Knight) app. 28-Starman disguised as Superman; leads into Superman #50						5.00

STARMAN (2nd Series) (Also see The Golden Age, Showcase 95 #12, Showcase 96 #4,5)
DC Comics : No. 0, Oct, 1994 - No. 80, Aug, 2001 ($1.95/$2.25/$2.50)

0,1: 0-James Robinson scripts, Tony Harris-c/a(p) & Wade Von Grawbadger-a(i) begins; Sins of the Father storyline begins, ends #3; 1st app. new Starman (Jack Knight); reintro of the G.A. Mist & G.A. Shade; 1st app. Nash; David Knight dies

	1	2	3	4	5	7

2-7: 2-Reintro Charity from Forbidden Tales of Dark Mansion. 3-Reintro/2nd app. "Blue" Starman (1st app. in 1st Issue Special #12); Will Payton app. (both cameos). 5-David Knight app. 6-The Shade "Times Past" story; Kristiansen-a. 7-The Black Pirate cameo 5.00

8-17: 8-Begin $2.25-c. 10-1st app. new Mist (Nash). 11-JSA "Times Past" story; Matt Smith-a. 12-16-Sins of the Child. 17-The Black Pirate app. 4.00

18-37: 18-G.A. Starman "Times Past" story; Watkiss-a. 19-David Knight app. 20-23-G.A. Sandman app. 24-26-Demon Quest; all 3 covers make-up triptych. 33-36-Batman-c/app. 37-David Knight and deceased JSA members app. 3.00

38-49,51-56: 38-Nash vs. Justice League Europe. 39,40-Crossover w/ Power of Shazam! #35,36; Bulletman app. 42-Demon-c/app. 43-JLA-c/app. 44-Phantom Lady-c/app. 46-Gene Ha-a. 51-Jor-el app. 52,53-Adam Strange-c/app.

						2.50
50-($3.95) Gold foil logo on-c; Star Boy (LSH) app.						4.00
57-79: 57-62-Painted covers by Harris and Alex Ross. 72-Death of Ted Knight						2.50
80-($3.95) Final issue; cover by Harris & Robinson						4.00
#1,000,000 (11/98) 853rd Century x-over; Snejbjerg-a						2.50
Annual 1 (1996, $3.50)-Legends of the Dead Earth story; Prince Gavyn & G.A. Starman stories; J.H. Williams III, Bret Blevins, Craig Hamilton-c/a(p)						4.00
Annual 2 (1997, $3.95)-Pulp Heroes story;						4.00
...80 Page Giant (1/99, $4.95) Harris-c						5.00
...Secret Files 1 (4/98, $4.95)-Origin stories and profile pages						5.00
...The Mist (6/98, $1.95) Girlfrenzy; Mary Marvel app.						2.50
A Starry Knight-($17.95, TPB) r/#47-53						18.00
Grand Guignol-(2004, $19.95, TPB)-r/#61-73						20.00
Infernal Devices-($17.95, TPB) r/#29-35,37,38						18.00
Night and Day-($14.95, TPB)-r/#7-10,12-16						15.00
Sins of the Father-($12.95, TPB)-r/#0-5						13.00
Sons of the Father-($14.99, TPB)-r/#75-80						15.00
Stars My Destination-(2003, $14.95, TPB)-r/#55-60						15.00
Times Past-($17.95, TPB)-r/stories of other Starmen						18.00

STARMASTERS
Marvel Comics: Dec, 1995 - No. 3, Feb, 1996 ($1.95, limited series)

1-3-Continues in Cosmic Powers Unlimited #4						2.50

STAR PRESENTATION, A (Formerly My Secret Romance #1,2; Spectacular Stories #4 on) (Also see This Is Suspense)
Fox Features Syndicate (Hero Books): No. 3, May, 1950

3-Dr. Jekyll & Mr. Hyde by Wood & Harrison (reprinted in Startling Terror Tales #10); "The Repulsing Dwarf" by Wood; Wood-c

	54	108	162	338	562	785

STAR QUEST COMIX (Warren Presents... on cover)

Star Ranger #2 © CEN

Stars and S.T.R.I.P.E. #12 © DC

Star Spangled Comics #11 © DC

	GD 2.0	VG 4.0	FN 6.0	VF 8.0	VF/NM 9.0	NM- 9.2			GD 2.0	VG 4.0	FN 6.0	VF 8.0	VF/NM 9.0	NM- 9.2

Warren Publications: Oct, 1978 ($1.50, B&W magazine, 84 pgs., square-bound)

1-Corben, Maroto, Neary-a; Ken Kelly-c; Star Wars	2	4	6	9	12	15

STAR RAIDERS (See DC Graphic Novel #1)

STAR RANGER (Cowboy Comics #13 on)
Chesler Publ./Centaur Publ.: Feb, 1937 - No. 12, May, 1938 (Large size: No. 1-6)

1-(1st Western comic)-Ace & Deuce, Air Plunder; Creig Flessel-a						
	207	414	621	1294	2147	3000
2	91	182	273	569	947	1325
3-6	79	158	237	494	822	1150
7-9: 8(12/37)-Christmas-c; Air Patrol, Gold coast app.; Guardineer centerfold						
	57	114	171	356	591	825
V2#10 (1st Centaur; 3/38)	90	180	270	563	932	1300
11,12	66	132	198	413	682	950

NOTE: *J. Cole* a-10, 12; c-12. *Ken Ernst* a-11. *Gill Fox* a-8(illo), 9, 10. *Guardineer* a-1, 3, 6, 7, 8(illos), 9, 10, 12. *Gustavson* a-8-10, 12. *Fred Schwab* c-2-11. *Bob Wood* a-8-10.

STAR RANGER FUNNIES (Formerly Cowboy Comics)
Centaur Publications: V1#15, Oct, 1938 - V2#5, Oct, 1939

V1#15-Lyin Lou, Ermine, Wild West Junior, The Law of Caribou County by Eisner, Cowboy Jake, The Plugged Dummy, Spurs by Gustavson, Red Coat, Two Buckaroos & Trouble Hunters begin	97	194	291	606	1003	1400
V2#1 (1/39)	72	144	216	450	750	1050
2-5: 2-Night Hawk by Gustavson. 4-Kit Carson app.						
	60	120	180	375	625	875

NOTE: *Jack Cole* a-V2#1, 3; c-V2#1. *Filchock* c-V2#2, 3. *Guardineer* a-V2#3. *Gustavson* a-V2#2. *Pinajian* c/a-V2#5.

STAR REACH (Mature content)
Star Reach Publ.: Apr, 1974 - No. 18, Oct, 1979 (B&W, #12-15 w/color)

1-(75¢, 52 pgs.) Art by Starlin, Simonson. Chaykin-c/a; origin Death. Cody Starbuck-sty						
	2	4	6	13	18	22
1-2nd, 3rd, and 4th printings ($1.00-$1.50-c)						6.00
2-11: 2-Adams, Giordano-a; 1st Stephanie Starr-c/s. 3-1st Linda Lovecraft. 4-1st Sherlock Duck. 5-1st Gideon Faust by Chaykin. 6-Elric-c. 7-BWS-c. 9-14-Sacred & Profane-c/s by Steacy. 11-Samurai	1	3	4	6	8	10
2-2nd printing						4.00
12-15 (44 pgs.): 12-Zelazny-s. Nasser-a, Brunner-c	2	4	6	8	10	12
16-18-Magazine size: 17-Poe's Raven-c/s	2	4	6	8	10	12

NOTE: *Adams* c-2. *Bonivert* a-17. *Brunner* a-3.5; c-3,10,12. *Chaykin* a-1,4,5; c-1(1st ed),4,5; back-c-1(2nd,3rd,4th ed). *Gene Day* a-6,8,9,11,15. *Friedrich* s-2,3,8,10. *Gasbarri* a-7. *Gilbert* a-9,12. *Giordano* a-2. *Gould* a-6. *Hirota/Mukaide* s/a-7. *Jones* c-6. *Konz* a-17. *Leialoha* a-3,4,6-i, 13,15; c-13,15. *Lyda* a-6,12-15. *Marrs* a-2-5,7,10,14,15,16,18; c-18; back-c-2. *Mukaide* a-18. *Nasser* a-12. *Nino* a-6,7. *Russell* a-8,10; c-8. *Dave Sim* s-7; lettering-9. *Simonson* a-1. *Skeates* a-1,2. *Starlin* a-1(x2), 2(x2); back-c-1(1st ed); c-1(2nd,3rd,4th ed). *Barry Smith* c-7. *Staton* a-5,6,7. *Steacy* a-8-14; c-9,11,14,16,18. *Vosburg* a-2-5,7,10. *Workman* a-2-5,8. Nudity panels in most. Wraparound-c: 3-5,7-11,13-16,18.

STAR REACH CLASSICS
Eclipse Comics: Mar, 1984 - No. 6, Aug, 1984 ($1.50, Baxter paper)

1-6: 1-Neal Adams-r/Star Reach #1						3.00

NOTE: *Dave Sim* a-1. *Starlin* a-1.

STARR FLAGG, UNDERCOVER GIRL (See Undercover...)

STARRIORS
Marvel Comics: Aug, 1984 - Feb, 1985 (Limited series) (Based on Tomy toys)

1-4						3.00

STARS AND S.T.R.I.P.E. (Also see JSA)
DC Comics: July, 1999 - No. 14, Sept, 2000 ($2.95/$2.50)

0-($2.95) Moder and Weston-a; Starman app.						3.00
1-Johns and Robinson-s/Moder-a; origin new Star Spangled Kid						2.50
2-14: 4-Marvel Family app. 9-Seven Soldiers of Victory-c/app.						2.50
JSA Presents: Stars and S.T.R.I.P.E. Vol. 1 TPB (2007, $17.99) r/#1-8; Johns intro.						18.00

STARS AND STRIPES COMICS
Centaur Publications: No. 2, May, 1941 - No. 6, Dec, 1941

2(#1)-The Shark, The Iron Skull, A-Man, The Amazing Man, Mighty Man, Minimidget begin; The Voice & Dash Dartwell, the Human Meteor, Reef Kinkaid app.; Gustavson Flag-c						
	221	442	663	1381	2291	3200
3-Origin Dr. Synthe; The Black Panther app.	121	242	363	756	1253	1750
4-Origin/1st app. The Stars and Stripes; injury to eye-c						
	103	206	309	644	1072	1500
5(#5 on cover & inside)	72	144	216	450	745	1040
5(#6)-(#5 on cover, #6 on inside)	72	144	216	450	745	1040

NOTE: *Gustavson* c/a-3. *Myron Strauss* c-4, 5(#5), 5(#6).

STAR SEED (Formerly Powers That Be)
Broadway Comics: No. 7, 1996 - No. 9 ($2.95)

7-9						3.00

STARSHIP TROOPERS
Dark Horse Comics: 1997 - No. 2, 1997 ($2.95, limited series)

1,2-Movie adaption						3.00

STARSHIP TROOPERS: BRUTE CREATIONS
Dark Horse Comics: 1997 ($2.95, one-shot)

1						3.00

STARSHIP TROOPERS: DOMINANT SPECIES
Dark Horse Comics: Aug, 1998 - No. 4, Nov, 1998 ($2.95, limited series)

1-4-Strnad-s/Bolton-c						3.00

STARSHIP TROOPERS: INSECT TOUCH
Dark Horse Comics: 1997 - No. 3, 1997 ($2.95, limited series)

1-3						3.00

STAR SLAMMERS (See Marvel Graphic Novel #6)
Malibu Comics (Bravura): May, 1994 - No. 4, Aug, 1994 ($2.50, unfinished limited series)

1-4: W. Simonson-a/stories; contain Bravura stamps						2.50

STAR SLAMMERS SPECIAL
Dark Horse Comics (Legend): June, 1996 ($2.95, one-shot)

nn-Simonson-c/a/scripts; concludes Bravura limited series.						3.00

STARSLAYER
Pacific Comics/First Comics No. 7 on: Feb, 1982 - No. 6, Apr, 1983; No. 7, Aug, 1983 - No. 34, Nov, 1985

1-Origin & 1st app.; excessive blood & gore; 1 pg. Rocketeer brief app. which continues in #2						5.00
2-Origin/1st full app. the Rocketeer (4/82) by Dave Stevens (Chapter 1 of Rocketeer saga; see Pacific Presents #1,2)	1	2	3	5	6	8
3-Chapter 2 of Rocketeer saga by Stevens						6.00
4,6,7: 7-Grell-a ends						3.00
5-2nd app. Groo the Wanderer by Aragones	1	2	3	4	5	7
8-34: 10-1st app. Grimjack (11/83, ends #17). 18-Starslayer meets Grimjack. 20-The Black Flame begins (9/84, 1st app.), ends #33. 27-Book length Black Flame story						2.50

NOTE: *Grell* a-1-7; c-1-8. *Stevens* back c-2, 3. *Sutton* a-17p, 20-22p, 24-27p, 29-33p.

STARSLAYER (The Director's Cut)
Acclaim Comics (Windjammer): June, 1994 - No. 8, Dec, 1995 ($2.50)

1-8: Mike Grell-c/a/scripts						2.50

STAR SPANGLED COMICS (Star Spangled War Stories #131 on)
National Periodical Publications: Oct, 1941 - No. 130, July, 1952

1-Origin/1st app. Tarantula; Captain X of the R.A.F., Star Spangled Kid (see Action #40), Armstrong of the Army begin; Robot-c	486	972	1458	3400	5950	8500
2	162	324	486	1013	1682	2350
3-5	102	204	306	638	1057	1475
6-Last Armstrong/Army; Penniless Palmer begins	62	124	186	388	644	900
7-(4/42)-Origin/1st app. The Guardian by S&K & Robotman (by Paul Cassidy & created by Siegel);The Newsboy Legion (1st app.), Robotman & TNT begin; last Captain X						
	657	1314	1971	4599	8050	11,500
8-Origin TNT & Dan the Dyna-Mite	231	462	693	1444	2397	3350
9,10	164	328	492	1025	1700	2375
11-17	119	238	357	744	1235	1725
18-Origin Star Spangled Kid	150	300	450	938	1557	2175
19-Last Tarantula	119	238	357	744	1235	1725
20-Liberty Belle begins (5/43)	134	264	402	838	1394	1950
21-29-Last S&K issue; 23-Last TNT. 25-Robotman by Jimmy Thompson begins.						
29-Intro Robbie the Robotdog	101	202	303	631	1046	1460
30-40: 31-S&K-c	59	118	177	369	610	850
41-51: 41,49-Kirby-a. 51-Robot-c by Kirby	53	106	159	323	537	750
52-64: 53 by S&K. 64-Last Newsboy Legion & The Guardian						
	48	96	144	293	484	675
65-Robin begins with c/app. (2/47); Batman cameo in 1 panel; Robin-c begins, end #95						
	162	324	486	1013	1682	2350
66-Batman cameo in Robin story	82	164	246	513	849	1185
67,68,70-80: 68-Last Liberty Belle? 72-Burnley Robin-c						
	67	134	201	419	692	965
69-Origin/1st app. Tomahawk by F. Ray; atom bomb story & splash (6/47)						
	128	256	384	800	1325	1850
81-Origin Merry, Girl of 1000 Gimmicks in Star Spangled Kid story						
	57	114	171	356	591	825
82,85: 82-Last Robotman? 85-Last Star Spangled Kid?						
	52	104	156	317	521	725

Star Spangled Comics #124 © DC

Star Spangled War Stories #92 © DC

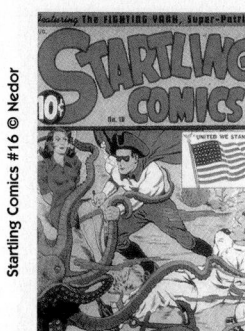

Startling Comics #16 © Nedor

	GD 2.0	VG 4.0	FN 6.0	VF 8.0	VF/NM 9.0	NM- 9.2

83-Tomahawk enters the lost valley, a land of dinosaurs; Capt. Compass begins, ends #130
| | 52 | 104 | 156 | 317 | 521 | 735 |

84,87 (Rare): 87-Batman cameo in Robin
| | 81 | 162 | 243 | 506 | 841 | 1175 |

86-Batman cameo in Robin story
| | 58 | 116 | 174 | 363 | 599 | 835 |

88(1/49)-94: Batman-c/stories in all. 91-Federal Men begin, end #93. 94-Manhunters Around the World begin, end #121
| | 59 | 118 | 177 | 369 | 615 | 860 |

95-Batman story; last Robin-c
| | 53 | 106 | 159 | 323 | 529 | 735 |

96,98-Batman cameo in Robin stories. 96-1st Tomahawk-c (also #97-121)
| | 40 | 80 | 120 | 235 | 368 | 500 |

97,99
| | 34 | 68 | 102 | 197 | 311 | 425 |

100 (1/50)-Pre-Bat-Hound tryout in Robin story (pre-dates Batman #92).
| | 40 | 80 | 120 | 240 | 383 | 525 |

101-109,118,119,121: 121-Last Tomahawk-c
| | 34 | 64 | 96 | 186 | 293 | 400 |

110,111,120-Batman cameo in Robin stories. 120-Last 52 pg. issue
| | 34 | 68 | 102 | 195 | 308 | 420 |

112-Batman & Robin story
| | 36 | 72 | 108 | 208 | 329 | 450 |

113-Frazetta-a (10 pgs.)
| | 41 | 82 | 123 | 256 | 416 | 575 |

114-Retells origin (3/51); Batman & Robin story
| | 43 | 86 | 129 | 262 | 431 | 600 |

115,117-Batman app. in Robin stories
| | 35 | 70 | 105 | 204 | 322 | 440 |

116-Flag-c
| | 35 | 70 | 105 | 204 | 322 | 440 |

122 (11/51)-Ghost Breaker-c/stories begin (origin/1st app.), ends #130 (Ghost Breaker covers #122-130)
| | 43 | 86 | 129 | 262 | 431 | 600 |

123-126,128,129
| | 31 | 62 | 93 | 178 | 282 | 385 |

127-Batman app.
| | 33 | 66 | 99 | 190 | 300 | 410 |

130-Batman cameo in Robin story
| | 35 | 70 | 105 | 201 | 318 | 435 |

NOTE: Most all issues after #29 signed by Simon & Kirby are both by them. Bill Ely c-122-130. Mortimer c-65-74(most), 76-95(most). Fred Ray c-96-106, 109, 110, 112, 113, 115-120. S&K c-7-31, 33, 34, 36, 37, 39, 40, 48, 49, 50-54, 56-58. Hal Sherman c-1-6. Dick Sprang c-75.

STAR SPANGLED COMICS (Also see All Star Comics 1999 crossover titles)
DC Comics: May, 1999 ($1.99, one-shot)

1-Golden Age Sandman and the Star Spangled Kid ... 2.50

STAR SPANGLED KID (See Action #40, Leading Comics & Star Spangled Comics)

STAR SPANGLED WAR STORIES
DC Comics: Aug/Sept 1952

nn - Ashcan comic, not distributed to newsstands, only for in-house use. Cover art is Western Comics #28 with interior being Western Comics #13 (no known sales)

STAR SPANGLED WAR STORIES (Formerly Star Spangled Comics #1-130; Becomes The Unknown Soldier #205 on) (See Showcase)
National Periodical Publications: No. 131, 8/52 - No. 133, 10/52; No. 3, 11/52 - No. 204, 2-3/77

131(#1)
| | 107 | 214 | 321 | 669 | 1110 | 1550 |

132
| | 67 | 134 | 201 | 419 | 697 | 975 |

133-Used in POP, pg. 94
| | 57 | 114 | 171 | 356 | 591 | 825 |

3-6: 4-Devil Dog Dugan app. 6-Evans-a
| | 41 | 82 | 123 | 253 | 407 | 560 |

7-10
| | 24 | 48 | 72 | 175 | 313 | 450 |

11-20
| | 19 | 38 | 57 | 142 | 254 | 365 |

21-30: 30-Last precode (2/55)
| | 17 | 34 | 51 | 126 | 223 | 320 |

31-33,35-40
| | 13 | 26 | 39 | 90 | 160 | 230 |

34-Krigstein-a
| | 13 | 26 | 39 | 95 | 168 | 240 |

41-44,46-50: 50-1st S.A. issue
| | 12 | 24 | 36 | 86 | 153 | 220 |

45-1st DC grey tone war-c (5/56)
| | 19 | 38 | 57 | 138 | 244 | 350 |

51,52,54-63,65,66, 68-83
| | 10 | 20 | 30 | 70 | 123 | 175 |

53-"Rock Sergeant," 3rd Sgt. Rock prototype; inspired "P.I. & The Sand Fleas" in G.I. Combat #56 (1/57)
| | 14 | 28 | 42 | 102 | 181 | 260 |

64-Pre-Sgt. Rock Easy Co. story (12/57)
| | 12 | 24 | 36 | 86 | 153 | 220 |

67-Two Easy Co. stories without Sgt. Rock
| | 13 | 26 | 39 | 90 | 160 | 230 |

84-Origin Mlle. Marie
| | 17 | 34 | 51 | 126 | 223 | 320 |

85-89-Mlle. Marie in all
| | 11 | 22 | 33 | 79 | 140 | 200 |

90-1st app. "War That Time Forgot" series; dinosaur issue-c/story (4-5/60) (also see Weird War Tales #94 & #99)
| | 37 | 74 | 111 | 278 | 507 | 735 |

91,93-No dinosaur stories
| | 10 | 20 | 30 | 73 | 129 | 185 |

92-2nd dinosaur-c/s
| | 15 | 30 | 45 | 107 | 191 | 275 |

94 (12/60)- "Ghost War" story; Baron Von Richter as The Enemy Ace (predates Our Army at War #151)
| | 19 | 38 | 57 | 138 | 244 | 350 |

95-99: Dinosaur-c/s
| | 13 | 26 | 39 | 97 | 171 | 245 |

100-Dinosaur-c/story.
| | 15 | 30 | 45 | 107 | 191 | 275 |

101-115: All dinosaur issues
| | 11 | 22 | 33 | 75 | 133 | 190 |

116-125,127-133,135-137-Last dinosaur story; Heath Birdman-#129,131
| | 9 | 18 | 27 | 65 | 113 | 160 |

126-No dinosaur story
| | 8 | 16 | 24 | 58 | 97 | 135 |

134-Dinosaur story; Neal Adams-a
| | 11 | 22 | 33 | 75 | 133 | 190 |

138-New Enemy Ace-c/stories begin by Joe Kubert (4-5/68), end #150 (also see Our Army at War #151 and Showcase #57)
| | 11 | 22 | 33 | 79 | 140 | 200 |

139-Origin Enemy Ace (7/68)
| | 9 | 18 | 27 | 60 | 100 | 140 |

140-143,145: 145-Last 12¢ issue (6-7/69)
| | 6 | 12 | 18 | 43 | 69 | 95 |

144-Neal Adams/Kubert-a
| | 7 | 14 | 21 | 49 | 80 | 110 |

146-Enemy Ace-c/app.
| | 5 | 10 | 15 | 30 | 48 | 65 |

147,148-New Enemy Ace stories
| | 6 | 12 | 18 | 37 | 59 | 80 |

149,150-Last new Enemy Ace by Kubert. Viking Prince by Kubert
| | 5 | 10 | 15 | 35 | 55 | 75 |

151-1st solo app. Unknown Soldier (6-7/70); Enemy Ace-r begin (from Our Army at War, Showcase & SSWS); end #161
| | 14 | 28 | 42 | 99 | 175 | 250 |

152-Reprints 2nd Enemy Ace app.
| | 4 | 8 | 12 | 28 | 44 | 60 |

153,155-Enemy Ace reprints; early Unknown Soldier stories
| | 4 | 8 | 12 | 24 | 37 | 50 |

154-Origin Unknown Soldier
| | 10 | 20 | 30 | 70 | 123 | 175 |

156-1st Battle Album; Unknown Soldier story; Kubert-c/a
| | 4 | 8 | 12 | 22 | 34 | 45 |

157-Sgt. Rock x-over in Unknown Soldier story.
| | 3 | 6 | 9 | 20 | 30 | 40 |

158-163 (52 pgs.): New Unknown Soldier stories; Kubert-c/a. 161-Last Enemy Ace-r
| | 3 | 6 | 9 | 16 | 23 | 30 |

164-183,200: 181-183-Enemy Ace vs. Balloon Buster serial app; Frank Thorne-a. 200-Enemy Ace back-up
| | 2 | 4 | 6 | 10 | 14 | 18 |

184-199,201-204
| | 2 | 4 | 6 | 8 | 11 | 14 |

NOTE: Anderson a-28. Chaykin a-167. Drucker a-59, 61, 64, 66, 67, 73-84. Estrada a-149. John Giunta a-72. Glanzman a-167, 171, 172, 174. Heath a-122, 132, 133; c-67, 122, 132-134. Kaluta a-197l; c-167. G. Kane a-169. Kubert a-6-163(most later issues), 200. Maurer a-160, 165. Severin a-65, 162. S&K c-7-31, 33, 34, 37, 40. Simonson a-170, 172, 174, 180. Sutton a-168. Thorne a-183. Toth a-164. Wildey a-161. Suicide Squad in 110, 116-118, 120, 121, 127.

STARSTREAM (Adventures in Science Fiction)(See Questar illustrated)
Whitman/Western Publishing Co.: 1976 (79¢, 68 pgs, cardboard-c)

1-4: 1-Bolle-a. 2-4-McWilliams & Bolle-a
| | 2 | 4 | 6 | 9 | 13 | 16 |

STARSTRUCK
Marvel Comics (Epic Comics): Feb, 1985 - No. 6, Feb, 1986 ($1.50, mature)

1-6: Kaluta-a ... 3.00

STARSTRUCK
Dark Horse Comics: Aug, 1990 - No. 4, Nov?, 1990 ($2.95, B&W, 52pgs.)

1-3:Kaluta-r/Epic series plus new-c/a in all ... 3.00
4 (68 pgs.)-contains 2 trading cards ... 3.00

STAR STUDDED
Cambridge House/Superior Publishers: 1945 (25¢, 132 pgs.); 1945 (196 pgs.)

nn-Captain Combat by Giunta, Ghost Woman, Commandette, & Red Rogue app.; Infantino-a
| | 34 | 68 | 102 | 197 | 311 | 425 |

nn-The Cadet, Edison Bell, Hoot Gibson, Jungle Lil (196 pgs.); copies vary; Blue Beetle in some
| | 28 | 56 | 84 | 162 | 256 | 350 |

STARTLING COMICS
Better Publications (Nedor): June, 1940 - No. 53, Sept, 1948

1-Origin Captain Future-Man Of Tomorrow, Mystico (By Sansone), The Wonder Man; The Masked Rider & his horse Pinto begins; Masked Rider formerly in pulps; drug use story
| | 276 | 552 | 828 | 1725 | 2863 | 4000 |

2 -Don Davis, Espionage Ace begins
| | 98 | 196 | 294 | 613 | 1019 | 1425 |

3
| | 83 | 166 | 249 | 519 | 860 | 1200 |

4
| | 60 | 120 | 180 | 375 | 625 | 875 |

5-9
| | 51 | 102 | 153 | 311 | 516 | 720 |

10-The Fighting Yank begins (9/41, origin/1st app.)
| | 388 | 776 | 1164 | 2522 | 4461 | 6400 |

11-2nd app. Fighting Yank
| | 117 | 234 | 351 | 731 | 1216 | 1700 |

12-Hitler, Hirohito, Mussolini-c
| | 107 | 214 | 321 | 669 | 1110 | 1550 |

13-15
| | 64 | 128 | 192 | 400 | 663 | 925 |

16-Origin The Four Comrades; not in #32,35
| | 66 | 132 | 198 | 413 | 682 | 950 |

17-Last Masked Rider & Mystico
| | 49 | 98 | 147 | 299 | 492 | 685 |

18-Pyroman begins (12/42, origin); not in America's Best Comics #3 for 1st app., 11/42)
| | 102 | 204 | 306 | 638 | 1057 | 1475 |

19
| | 49 | 98 | 147 | 299 | 492 | 685 |

20,21: 20-The Oracle begins (3/43); not in issues 26,28,33,34. 21-Origin The Ape, Oracle's enemy
| | 52 | 104 | 156 | 317 | 521 | 725 |

22-34: 34-Origin The Scarab & only app.
| | 50 | 100 | 150 | 305 | 503 | 700 |

35-Hypodermic syringe attacks Fighting Yank in drug story
| | 52 | 104 | 156 | 317 | 521 | 725 |

36-43: 36-Last Four Comrades. 38-Bondage/torture-c. 40-Last Capt. Future & Oracle. 41-Front Page Peggy begins; A-Bomb-c. 43-Last Pyroman
| | 44 | 88 | 132 | 268 | 439 | 610 |

44,45: 44-Lance Lewis, Space Detective begins; Ingels-c; sci/fi-c begin. 45-Tygra begins

Startling Terror Tales #13 © STAR

Star Trek #59 © Paramount

Star Trek: Deep Space Nine #22 © Paramount

	GD 2.0	VG 4.0	FN 6.0	VF 8.0	VF/NM 9.0	NM- 9.2			GD 2.0	VG 4.0	FN 6.0	VF 8.0	VF/NM 9.0	NM- 9.2

(intro/origin, 5/47); Ingels-c/a (splash pg. & inside f/c B&W ad)

	68	136	204	425	705	985
46-Classic Ingels-c; Ingels-a	110	220	330	688	1144	1600
47,48,50-53: 50,51-Sea-Eagle app.	65	130	195	406	671	935
49-Classic Schomburg Robot-c; last Fighting Yank	412	824	1236	2678	4739	6800

NOTE: **Ingels** a-44, 45; c-44, 45, 46(wash). **Schomburg** (Xela) c-21-43; 47-53 Bondage c-16, 21, 37, 46-49. Captain Future c-1-9, 13, 14. Fighting Yank c-10-12, 15-17, 21, 22, 24, 26, 28, 30, 32, 34, 36, 38, 40, 42. Pyroman c-18-20, 23, 25, 27, 29, 31, 33, 35, 37, 39, 41, 43.

STARTLING STORIES: BANNER
Marvel Comics: July, 2001 - No. 4, Oct, 2001 ($2.99, limited series)

1-4-Hulk story by Azzarello; Corben-c/a						3.00
TPB (11/01, $12.95) r/1-4						13.00

STARTLING STORIES: FANTASTIC FOUR - UNSTABLE MOLECULES (See Fantastic Four - ...)

STARTLING STORIES: THE MEGALOMANIACAL SPIDER-MAN
Marvel Comics: Jun, 2002 ($2.99, one-shot)

1-Spider-Man spoof; Peter Bagge-s/a						3.00

STARTLING STORIES: THE THING
Marvel Comics: 2003 ($3.50, one-shot)

1-Zimmerman-s/Kramer-a; Inhumans and the Hulk app.						3.50

STARTLING STORIES: THE THING - NIGHT FALLS ON YANCY STREET
Marvel Comics: Jun, 2003 - No. 4, Sept, 2003 ($3.50, limited series)

1-4-Dorkin-s/Haspiel-a. 2,3-Frightful Four app.						3.50

STARTLING TERROR TALES
Star Publications: No. 10, May, 1952 - No. 14, Feb, 1953; No. 4, Apr, 1953 - No. 11, 1954

10-(1st Series)-Wood/Harrison-a (r/A Star Presentation #3) Disbrow/Cole-c; becomes 4 different titles after #10; becomes Confessions of Love #11 on, The Horrors #11 on, Terrifying Tales #11 on, Terrors of the Jungle #11 on & continues w/Startling Terror #11	74	148	222	463	769	1075
11-(8/52)-L. B. Cole Spider-c; r-Fox's "A Feature Presentation" #5 (blue-c)	152	304	456	950	1575	2200
11-Black-c (variant; believed to be a pressrun change) (Unique)	159	318	477	994	1647	2300
12,14	32	64	96	186	293	400
13-Jo-Jo-r; Disbrow-a	34	68	102	195	308	420
4-9,11(1953-54) (2nd Series): 11-New logo	29	58	87	167	264	360
10-Disbrow-a	35	70	105	204	322	440

NOTE: **L. B. Cole** covers-all issues. Palais a-V2#8r, V2#11r.

STAR TREK (TV) (See Dan Curtis Giveaways, Dynabrite Comics & Power Record Comics)
Gold Key: 7/67; No. 2, 6/68; No. 3, 12/68; No. 4, 6/69 - No. 61, 3/79

1-Photo-c begin, end #9	41	82	123	328	589	850
1 (rare variation w/photo back-c)	50	100	150	413	757	1100
2	22	44	66	160	285	410
2 (rare variation w/photo back-c)	31	62	93	233	422	610
3-5	15	30	45	107	191	275
3 (rare variation w/photo back-c)	23	46	69	171	306	440
6-9	12	24	36	82	146	210
10-20	6	12	18	43	69	95
21-30	6	12	18	37	59	80
31-40	4	8	12	28	44	60
41-61: 52-Drug propaganda story	4	8	12	22	34	45
...the Enterprise Logs nn (8/76)-Golden Press, ($1.95, 224 pgs.)-r/#1-8 plus 7 pgs. by McWilliams (#11185)-Photo-c	5	10	15	35	55	75
...the Enterprise Logs Vol. 2 ('76)-r/#9-17 (#11187)-Photo-c	5	10	15	30	48	65
...the Enterprise Logs Vol. 3 ('77)-r/#18-26 (#11188); McWilliams-a (4 pgs.)-Photo-c	5	10	15	30	48	65
Star Trek Vol. 4 (Winter '77)-Reprints #27,28,30-34,36,38 (#11189) plus 3 pgs. new art	5	10	15	30	48	65
... : The Key Collection (Checker Book Publ. Group, 2004, $22.95) r/#1-8						23.00
... : The Key Collection Volume 2 (Checker, 2004, $22.95) r/#9-16						23.00
... : The Key Collection Volume 3 (Checker, 2005, $22.95) r/#17-24						23.00
... : The Key Collection Volume 4 (Checker, 2005, $22.95) r/#25-33						23.00
... : The Key Collection Volume 5 (Checker, 2006, $22.95) r/#34,36,38,39,40-43						23.00

NOTE: **McWilliams** a-38, 40-44, 46-61. #29 reprints #1; #35 reprints #4; #37 reprints #5; #45 reprints #7. The tabloids have photo covers and blank inside covers. Painted covers #10-44, 46-59.

STAR TREK
Marvel Comics Group: April, 1980 - No. 18, Feb, 1982

1: 1-3-r/Marvel Super Special; movie adapt.	2	4	6	9	12	15
2-16: 5-Miller-a	1	2	3	5	6	8
17-Low print run	2	4	6	8	10	12

18-Last issue; low print run	2	4	6	10	14	18

NOTE: **Austin** c-18i. **Buscema** a-13. **Gil Kane** a-15. **Nasser** a-7. **Simonson** c-17.

STAR TREK (Also see Who's Who In Star Trek)
DC Comics: Feb, 1984 - No. 56, Nov, 1988 (75¢, Mando paper)

1-Sutton-a(p) begins	1	3	4	6	8	10
2-5						6.00
6-10: 7-Origin Saavik						5.00
11-20: 19-Walter Koenig story						4.00
21-32						3.50
33-($1.25, 52 pgs.)-20th anniversary issue						4.00
34-49: 37-Painted-c						3.00
50-($1.50, 52 pgs.)						4.00
51-56, Annual 1-3: 1(1985). 2(1986). 3(1988, $1.50)						3.00
...: To Boldly Go TPB (Titan Books, 7/05, $19.95) r/#1-6; Koenig foreward; cast interviews						20.00
...: The Trial of James T. Kirk TPB (Titan Books, 6/06, $19.95) r/#7-12; cast interviews						20.00
...: The Return of the Worthy TPB (Titan Books, 12/06, $19.95) r/#13-18; cast interviews						20.00

NOTE: **Morrow** a-28, 35, 36, 56. **Orlando** c-8i. **Perez** c-1-3. **Spiegle** a-19. **Starlin** c-24, 25. **Sutton** a-1-6p, 8-18p, 20-27p, 29p, 31-34p, 39-52p, 55p; c-4-6p, 8-22p, 46p.

STAR TREK
DC Comics: Oct, 1989 - No. 80, Jan, 1996 ($1.50/$1.75/$1.95/$2.50)

1-Capt. Kirk and crew						6.00
2,3						4.00
4-23,25-30: 10-12-The Trial of James T. Kirk. 21-Begin $1.75-c						3.00
24-($2.95, 68 pgs.)-40 pg. epic w/pin-ups						3.50
31-49,51-60						2.50
50-($3.50, 68 pgs.)-Painted-c						3.50
61-74,76-80						2.50
75 ($3.95)						4.00
Annual 1-6('90-'95, 68 pgs.): 1-Morrow-a. 3-Painted-c						4.00
Special 1-3 ('9-'95, 68 pgs.)-1-Sutton-a.						4.00
...: The Ashes of Eden (1995, $14.95, 100 pgs.)-Shatner story						15.00
...Generations (1994, $3.95, 68 pgs.)-Movie adaptation						4.00
...Generations (1994, $5.95, 68 pgs.)-Squarebound						6.00

STAR TREK...(TV)
DC Comics (WildStorm): one-shots

All of Me (4/00, $5.95, prestige format) Lopresti-a						6.00
Enemy Unseen TPB (2001, $17.95) r/Perchance to Dream, Embrace the Wolf, The Killing Shadows; Struzan-c						18.00
Enter the Wolves (2001, $5.95) Crispin & Weinstein-s; Mota-a/c						6.00
New Frontier - Double Time (11/00, $5.95)-Captain Calhoun's USS Excalibur; Peter David-s; Stelfreeze-c						6.00
Other Realities TPB (2001, $14.95) r/All of Me, New Frontier - Double Time, and DS9-N-Vector; Van Fleet-c						15.00
Special (2001, $6.95) Stories from all 4 series by various; Van Fleet-c						7.00

STAR TREK: DEBT OF HONOR
DC Comics: 1992 ($24.95/$14.95, graphic novel)

Hardcover ($24.95) Claremont-s/Hughes-a(p)						25.00
Softcover ($14.95)						15.00

STAR TREK: DEEP SPACE NINE (TV)
Malibu Comics: Aug, 1993 - No. 32, Jan, 1996 ($2.50)

1-Direct Sale Edition w/line drawn-c						4.00
1-Newsstand Edition with photo-c						3.00
0-(1/95, $2.95)-Terok Nor						3.00
2-30: 2-Polybagged w/trading card. 9-4 pg. prelude to Hearts & Minds						2.50
31-($3.95)						4.00
32-($3.50)						3.50
Annual 1 (1/95, $3.95, 68 pgs.)						4.00
Special 1 (1995, $3.50)						3.50
Ultimate Annual 1 (12/95, $5.95)						6.00
...:Lightstorm (12/94, $3.50)						3.50

STAR TREK: DEEP SPACE NINE (TV)
Marvel Comics (Paramount Comics): Nov, 1996 - No. 15, Mar, 1998 ($1.95/$1.99)

1-15: 12,13-"Telepathy War" pt. 2,3						2.50

STAR TREK: DEEP SPACE NINE -- N-VECTOR (TV)
DC Comics (WildStorm): Aug, 2000 - No. 4, Nov, 2000 ($2.50, limited series)

1-4-Cypress-a						2.50

STAR TREK DEEP SPACE NINE-THE CELEBRITY SERIES
Malibu Comics: May, 1995 ($2.95)

1-Blood and Honor; Mark Lenard script						3.00

Star Trek: Klingons: Blood Will Tell #1 © Paramount

Star Trek: The Next Generation #24 © Paramount

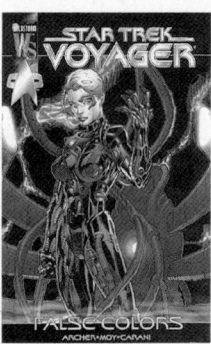

Star Trek: Voyager - False Colors © Paramount

	GD	VG	FN	VF	VF/NM	NM-
	2.0	4.0	6.0	8.0	9.0	9.2

	GD	VG	FN	VF	VF/NM	NM-
	2.0	4.0	6.0	8.0	9.0	9.2

1-Rules of Diplomacy; Aron Eisenberg script   3.00

STAR TREK: DEEP SPACE NINE HEARTS AND MINDS
Malibu Comics: June, 1994 - No. 4, Sept, 1994 ($2.50, limited series)

1-4   2.50
1-Holographic-c   4.00

STAR TREK: DEEP SPACE NINE, THE MAQUIS
Malibu Comics: Feb, 1995 - No. 3, Apr, 1995 ($2.50, limited series)

1-3-Newsstand-c, 1-Photo-c   2.50

STAR TREK: DEEP SPACE NINE/THE NEXT GENERATION
Malibu Comics: Oct, 1994 - No. 2, Nov, 1994 ($2.50, limited series)

1,2: Parts 2 & 4 of x-over with Star Trek: TNG/DS9 from DC Comics   2.50

STAR TREK: DEEP SPACE NINE WORF SPECIAL
Malibu Comics: Dec, 1995 ($3.95, one-shot)

1-Includes pinups   4.00

STAR TREK: DIVIDED WE FALL
DC Comics (WildStorm): July, 2001 - No. 4, Oct, 2001 ($2.95, limited series)

1-4: Ordover & Mack-s; Lenara Kahn, Verad and Odan app.   3.00

STAR TREK EARLY VOYAGES(TV)
Marvel Comics (Paramount Comics): Feb, 1997 - No. 17, Jun, 1998 ($2.95/$1.95/$1.99)

1-($2.95)   3.00
2-17   2.50

STAR TREK: FIRST CONTACT (Movie)
Marvel Comics (Paramount Comics): Nov, 1996 ($5.95, one-shot)

nn-Movie adaption   6.00

STAR TREK: KLINGONS: BLOOD WILL TELL
IDW Publishing: Apr, 2007 - Present ($3.99, limited series)

1-3-Star Trek TOS episodes from the Klingon viewpoint; Messina-a. 2-Tribbles   4.00
1-($4.99) Klingon Language Variant; comic with Kliingon text; English script   5.00

STAR TREK: MIRROR MIRROR
Marvel Comics (Paramount Comics): Feb, 1997 ($3.95, one-shot)

1-DeFalco-s   4.00

STAR TREK MOVIE SPECIAL
DC Comics: 1984 (June) - No. 2, 1987 ($1.50); No. 1, 1989 ($2.00, 52 pgs)

nn-(#1)-Adapts Star Trek III; Sutton-p (68 pgs.)   3.00
2-Adapts Star Trek IV; Sutton-a; Chaykin-c. (68 pgs.)   3.00
1 (1989)-Adapts Star Trek V; painted-c   3.00

STAR TREK: OPERATION ASSIMILATION
Marvel Comics (Paramount Comics): Dec, 1996 ($2.95, one-shot)

1   3.00

STAR TREK VI: THE UNDISCOVERED COUNTRY (Movie)
DC Comics: 1992

1-($2.95, regular edition, 68 pgs.)-Adaptation of film   3.00
nn-($5.95, prestige edition)-Has photos of movie not included in regular edition; painted-c by Palmer; photo back-c   6.00

STAR TREK: STARFLEET ACADEMY
Marvel Comics (Paramount Comics): Dec, 1996 - No. 19, Jun, 1998 ($1.95/$1.99)

1-19: Begin new series. 12-"Telepathy War" pt. 1. 18-English and Klingon language editions   2.50

STAR TREK: TELEPATHY WAR
Marvel Comics (Paramount Comics): Nov, 1997 ($2.99, 48 pgs., one-shot)

1-"Telepathy War" x-over pt. 6   3.00

STAR TREK - THE MODALA IMPERATIVE
DC Comics: Late July, 1991 - No. 4, Late Sept, 1991 ($1.75, limited series)

1-4   2.50
TPB ($19.95) r/series and ST:TNG - The Modala Imperative   20.00

STAR TREK: THE NEXT GENERATION (TV)
DC Comics: Feb, 1988 - No. 6, July, 1988 (limited series)

1 ($1.50, 52 pgs.)-Sienkiewicz painted-c   6.00
2-6 ($1.00)   4.00

STAR TREK: THE NEXT GENERATION (TV)
DC Comics: Oct, 1989 -No. 80, 1995 ($1.50/$1.75/$1.95)

1-Capt. Picard and crew from TV show	1	2	3	5	7	9
2,3						5.00

4-10   4.00
11-23,25-49,51-60   3.00
24,50: 24-($2.50, 52 pgs.). 50-($3.50, 68 pgs.)-Painted-c   5.00
61-74,76-80   2.50
75-($3.95, 50 pgs.)   4.00
Annual 1-6 ('90-'95, 68 pgs.)   4.00
Special 1 -3('93-'95, 68 pgs.)-1-Contains 3 stories   4.00
...-The Series Finale (1994, $3.95, 68 pgs.)   4.00

STAR TREK: THE NEXT GENERATION (TV)
DC Comics (WildStorm): one-shots

Embrace the Wolf (6/00, $5.95, prestige format) Golden & Sniegoski-s   6.00
Forgiveness (2001, $24.95, HC) David Brin-s/Scott Hampton painted-a; dust jacket-c   30.00
Forgiveness (2002, $17.95, SC)   18.00
The Gorn Crisis (1/01, $29.95, HC) Kordey painted-a/dust jacket-c   30.00
The Gorn Crisis (1/01, $17.95, SC) Kordey painted-a   18.00

STAR TREK: THE NEXT GENERATION/DEEP SPACE NINE (TV)
DC Comics: Dec, 1994 - No. 2, Jan, 1995 ($2.50, limited series)

1,2-Parts 1 & 3 of x-over with Star Trek: DS9/TNG from Malibu Comics   2.50

STAR TREK: THE NEXT GENERATION - ILL WIND
DC Comics: Nov, 1995 - No. 4, Feb, 1996 ($2.50, limited series)

1-4: Hugh Fleming painted-c on all   2.50

STAR TREK: THE NEXT GENERATION - PERCHANCE TO DREAM
DC Comics/WildStorm: Feb, 2000 - No. 4, May, 2000 ($2.50, limited series)

1-4-Bradstreet-c   2.50

STAR TREK: THE NEXT GENERATION - RIKER
Marvel Comics (Paramount Comics): July, 1998 ($3.50, one-shot)

1-Riker joins the Maquis   3.50

STAR TREK: THE NEXT GENERATION - SHADOWHEART
DC Comics: Dec, 1994 - No. 4, Mar, 1995 ($1.95, limited series)

1-4   2.50

STAR TREK: THE NEXT GENERATION - THE KILLING SHADOWS
DC Comics/WildStorm: Nov, 2000 - No. 4, Feb, 2001 ($2.50, limited series)

1-4-Scott Ciencin-s; Sela app.   2.50

STAR TREK: THE NEXT GENERATION - THE MODALA IMPERATIVE
DC Comics: Early Sept, 1991 - No. 4, Late Oct, 1991 ($1.75, limited series)

1-4   2.50

STAR TREK: THE NEXT GENERATION: THE SPACE BETWEEN
IDW Publishing: Jan, 2007 - No. 6, June, 2007 ($3.99)

1-6-Single issue stories from various seasons; photo & art covers   4.00

STAR TREK UNLIMITED
Marvel Comics (Paramount Comics): Nov, 1996 - No. 10, July, 1998 ($2.95/$2.99)

1,2-Stories from original series and Next Generation   4.00
3-10: 3-Begin $2.99-c. 6-"Telepathy War" pt. 4. 7-Q & Trelane swap Kirk & Picard   3.50

STAR TREK UNTOLD VOYAGES
Marvel Comics (Paramount Comics): May, 1998 - No. 5, July, 1998 ($2.50)

1-5-Kirk's crew after the 1st movie   2.50

STAR TREK: VOYAGER
Marvel Comics (Paramount Comics): Nov, 1996 - No. 15, Mar, 1998 ($1.95/$1.99)

1-15: 13-"Telepathy War" pt. 5. 14-Seven of Nine joins crew   3.00

STAR TREK: VOYAGER
DC Comics/WildStorm: one-shots and trade paperbacks

- Elite Force (7/00, $5.95) The Borg app.; Abnett & Lanning-s   6.00
... Encounters With the Unknown TPB (2001, $19.95) reprints   20.00
- False Colors (1/00, $5.95) Photo-c and Jim Lee-c; Jeff Moy-a   6.00

STAR TREK: VOYAGER-- THE PLANET KILLER
DC Comics/WildStorm: Mar, 2001 - No. 3, May, 2001 ($2.95, limited series)

1-3-Voyager vs. the Planet Killer from the ST:TOS episode; Teranishi-a   3.00

STAR TREK: VOYAGER SPLASHDOWN
Marvel Comics (Paramount Comics): Apr, 1998 - No. 4, July, 1998 ($2.50, limited series)

1-4-Voyager crashes on a water planet   3.00

STAR TREK/ X-MEN
Marvel Comics (Paramount Comics): Dec, 1996 ($4.99, one-shot)

1-Kirk's crew & X-Men; art by Silvestri, Tan, Winn & Finch; Lobdell-s   5.00

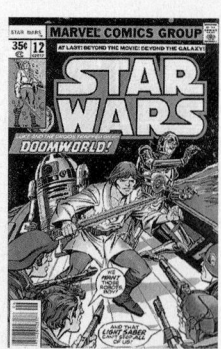

Star Wars #12 © Lucasfilm

Star Wars: Dark Times #2 © Lucasfilm

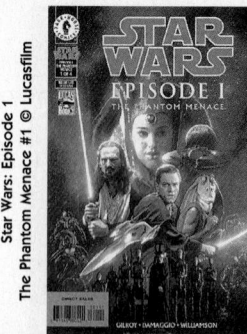

Star Wars: Episode 1 The Phantom Menace #1 © Lucasfilm

	GD 2.0	VG 4.0	FN 6.0	VF 8.0	VF/NM 9.0	NM- 9.2

STAR TREK/ X-MEN: 2ND CONTACT
Marvel Comics (Paramount Comics): May, 1998 ($4.99, 64 pgs., one-shot)
1-Next Gen. crew & X-Men battle Kang, Sentinels & Borg following First Contact movie 5.00
1-Painted wraparound variant cover 5.00

STAR WARS (Movie) (See Classic…, Contemporary Motivators, Dark Horse Comics, The Droids, The Ewoks, Marvel Movie Showcase, Marvel Special Ed.)
Marvel Comics Group: July, 1977 - No. 107, Sept, 1986
1-(Regular 30¢ edition)-Price in square w/UPC code; #1-6 adapt first movie;
    first issue on sale before movie debuted 6 12 18 39 62 85
1-(35¢-c; limited distribution - 1500 copies?)- Price in square w/UPC code
    (Prices vary widely on this book. In 2005 a CGC certified 9.4 sold for $6,500, a CGC
    certified 9.2 sold for $3,403, and a CGC certified 6.0 sold for $610)
                                        87 174 261 740 1370 2000
NOTE: *The rare 35¢ edition has the cover price in a square box, and the UPC box in the lower left hand corner has the UPC code lines running through it.*
2-4-(30¢ issues). 4-Battle with Darth Vader 3 6 9 20 30 40
2-4-(35¢ with UPC code; not reprints) 9 18 27 60 100 140
5,6- 5-Begin 35¢-c on all editions. 6-Stevens-a(i). 2 4 6 13 18 22
7-20 2 4 6 8 10 12
21-70: 39-44-The Empire Strikes Back-r by Al Williamson in all. 50-Giant.
    68-Reintro Boba Fett. 1 2 3 5 7 9
71-80 1 3 4 6 8 10
81-90: 81-Boba Fett app. 2 4 6 8 10 12
91,93-99: 98-Williamson-a 2 4 6 9 12 15
92,100-106: 92,100-($1.00, 52 pgs.). 2 4 6 11 16 20
107(low dist.); Portacio-a(i) 5 10 15 35 55 75
1-9: Reprints; has "reprint" in upper lefthand corner of cover or on inside or price and number
    inside a diamond with no date or UPC on cover; 30¢ and 35¢ issues published 4.00
Annual 1 (12/79, 52 pgs.)-Simonson-c 2 4 6 8 10 12
Annual 2 (11/82, 52 pgs.), 3(12/83, 52 pgs.) 1 3 4 6 8 10
... A Long Time Ago...Vol. 1 TPB (Dark Horse Comics, 6/02, $29.95) r/#1-14 30.00
... A Long Time Ago...Vol. 2 TPB (Dark Horse Comics, 7/02, $29.95) r/#15-28 30.00
... A Long Time Ago...Vol. 3 TPB (Dark Horse Comics, 11/02, $29.95) r/#39-53 30.00
... A Long Time Ago...Vol. 4 TPB (Dark Horse Comics, 1/03, $29.95) r/#54-67 & Ann. 2 30.00
... A Long Time Ago...Vol. 5 TPB (Dark Horse Comics, 3/03, $29.95) r/#68-81 & Ann. 3 30.00
... A Long Time Ago...Vol. 6 TPB (Dark Horse Comics, 5/03, $29.95) r/#82-93 30.00
... A Long Time Ago...Vol. 7 TPB (Dark Horse Comics, 6/03, $29.95) r/#96-107 30.00
Austin a-11-15i, 21i, 38; c-12-15i, 21i. Byrne c-13p. Chaykin a-1-10p; c-1. Golden c/a-38. Miller c-2,9, pin-up-43. Nebres c/a-Annual 2i. Portacio a-107i. Sienkiewicz c-92i, 98. Simonson a-16p, 49p, 51-63p, 65p, 66p; c-16, 49-51, 52p, 53-62, Annual 1. Steacy painted a-105i, 106i; c-105. Williamson a-39-44p, 50p, 98; c-39, 40, 41-44p. Painted c-81, 87, 92, 95, 98, 100, 105.

STAR WARS (Monthly series) (Becomes Star Wars Republic #46-on)
Dark Horse Comics: Dec, 1998 - No. 45, Aug, 2005 ($2.50/$2.95/$2.99)
1-12: 1-6-Prelude To Rebellion; Strnad-s. 4-Brereton-s. 7-12-Outlander 3.00
5,6 (Holochrome-c variants) 6.00
13, 17-18-($2.95): 13-18-Emissaries to Malastare; Truman-s 3.00
14-16-($2.50) Schultz-a 3.00
19-45: 19-22-Twilight; Duursema-a. 23-26-Infinity's End. 42-45-Rite of Passage 3.00
#0 AnotherUniverse.com Ed.($10.00) r/serialized pages from Pizzazz Magazine;
    new Dorman painted-a 10.00
... A Valentine Story (2/03, $3.50) Leia & Han Solo on Hoth; Winick-s/Chadwick-a/c 3.50
...: Rite of Passage (2004, $12.95) r/#42-45 13.00
...: The Stark Hyperspace War (903, $12.95) r/#36-39 13.00

STAR WARS: A NEW HOPE- THE SPECIAL EDITION
Dark Horse Comics: Jan, 1997 - No. 4, Apr, 1997 ($2.95, limited series)
1-4-Dorman-c 4.00

STAR WARS: BOBA FETT
Dark Horse Comics: Dec, 1995 - No. 3 ($3.95) (Originally intended as a one-shot)
1-Kennedy-c/a 6.00
2,3 5.00
Death, Lies, & Treachery TPB (1/98, $12.95) r/#1-3 13.00
... - Agent of Doom (11/00, $2.99) Ostrander-s/Cam Kennedy-a 3.00
... - Overkill (3/06, $2.99) Hughes-c/Andrews-s/Velasco-a 3.00
Twin Engines of Destruction (1/97, $2.95) 3.00

STAR WARS: BOBA FETT: ENEMY OF THE EMPIRE
Dark Horse Comics: Jan, 1999 - No. 4, Apr, 1999 ($2.95, limited series)
1-4-Recalls 1st meeting of Fett and Vader 3.00

STAR WARS: CHEWBACCA
Dark Horse Comics: Jan, 2000 - No. 4, Apr, 2000 ($2.95, limited series)
1-4-Macan-s/art by various incl. Anderson, Kordey, GIbbons; Phillips-c 3.00

	GD 2.0	VG 4.0	FN 6.0	VF 8.0	VF/NM 9.0	NM- 9.2

STAR WARS: CLONE WARS ADVENTURES
Dark Horse Comics: 2004 - Present ($6.95, digest-sized)
1-6-Short stories inspired by Clone Wars animated series 7.00

STAR WARS: CRIMSON EMPIRE
Dark Horse Comics: Dec, 1997 - No. 6, May, 1998 ($2.95, limited series)
1-Richardson-s/Gulacy-a 1 2 3 4 5 7
2-6 5.00

STAR WARS: CRIMSON EMPIRE II: COUNCIL OF BLOOD
Dark Horse Comics: Nov, 1998 - No. 6, Apr, 1999 ($2.95, limited series)
1-6-Richardson & Stradley-s/Gulacy-a 3.00

STAR WARS: DARK EMPIRE
Dark Horse Comics: Dec, 1991 - No. 6, Oct, 1992 ($2.95, limited series)
Preview-(99¢) 3.00
1-All have Dorman painted-c 1 2 3 5 7 9
1-3-2nd printing 4.00
2-Low print run 2 4 6 8 10 12
3 6.00
4-6 4.00
Gold Embossed Set (#1-6)-With gold embossed foil logo (price is for set) 90.00
Platinum Embossed Set (#1-6) 120.00
Trade paperback (4/93, 16.95) 17.00
Dark Empire 1 - TPB 3rd printing (2003, $16.95) 17.00
Ltd. Ed. Hardcover ($99.95) Signed & numbered 100.00

STAR WARS: DARK EMPIRE II
Dark Horse Comics: Dec, 1994 - No. 6, May, 1995 ($2.95, limited series)
1-Dave Dorman painted-c 5.00
2-6- Dorman-c in all. 4.00
Platinum Embossed Set (#1-6) 35.00
Trade paperback ($17.95) 18.00
TPB Second Edition (9/06, $19.95) r/#1-6 and Star Wars: Empire's End #1,2 20.00

STAR WARS: DARK FORCE RISING
Dark Horse Comics: May, 1997 - No. 6, Oct, 1997 ($2.95, limited series)
1-6 4.00
TPB (2/98, $17.95) r/#1-6 18.00

STAR WARS: DARK TIMES (Continued from Star Wars Republic #84)
Dark Horse Comics: Oct, 2006 - Present ($2.99)
1-4-Nineteen years before Episode IV; Doug Wheatley-a 3.00

STAR WARS: DARTH MAUL
Dark Horse Comics: Sept, 2000 - No. 4, Dec, 2000 ($2.95, limited series)
1-4-Photo-c and Struzan painted-c; takes place 6 months before Ep. 1 3.00

STAR WARS: DROIDS (See Dark Horse Comics #17-19)
Dark Horse Comics: Apr, 1994 - #6, Sept, 1994; V2#1, Apr, 1995 - V2#8, Dec, 1995 ($2.50, limited series)
1-($2.95)-Embossed-c 4.00
2-6, Special 1 (1/95, $2.50), V2#1-8 3.00

STAR WARS: EMPIRE
Dark Horse Comics: Sept, 2002 - No. 40, Feb, 2006 ($2.99)
1-40: 1-Benjamin-a; takes place weeks before SW: A New Hope. 7,28-Boba Fett-c. 14-Vader
    after the destruction of the Death Star. 15-Death of Biggs; Wheatley-a 3.00
... Volume 1 (2003, $12.95, TPB) r/#1-4 13.00
... Volume 2 (2004, $17.95, TPB) r/#8-12,15 18.00
... Volume 3: The Imperial Perspective (2004, $17.95, TPB) r/#13,14,16-19 18.00
... Volume 4: The Heart of the Rebellion (2005, $17.95, TPB) r/#5,6,20-22 &
    Star Wars: A Valentine Story 18.00
... Volume 5 (2006, $14.95, TPB) r/#23-27 18.00
... Volume 6: In the Shadows of Their Fathers (10/06, $17.95, TPB) r/#29-34 18.00
... Volume 7: The Wrong Side of the War (1/07, $17.95, TPB) r/#34-40 18.00

STAR WARS: EMPIRE'S END
Dark Horse Comics: Oct, 1995 - No. 2, Nov, 1995 ($2.95, limited series)
1,2-Dorman-c 3.00

STAR WARS: EPISODE 1 THE PHANTOM MENACE
Dark Horse Comics: May, 1999 - No. 4 ($2.95, movie adaptation)
1-4-Regular and photo-c; Damaggio & Williamson-a 3.00
TPB ($12.95) r/#1-4 13.00
...Anakin Skywalker-Photo-c & Bradstreet-c, ...Obi-Wan Kenobi-Photo-c & Egeland-c,
...Queen Amidala-Photo-c & Bradstreet-c, ...Qui-Gon Jinn-Photo-c & Bradstreet-c 3.00
Gold foil covers; Wizard 1/2 10.00

Star Wars: Infinities - A New Hope #4 © Lucasfilm

Star Wars: Legacy #1 © Lucasfilm

Star Wars: Rebellion #1 © Lucasfilm

	GD 2.0	VG 4.0	FN 6.0	VF 8.0	VF/NM 9.0	NM- 9.2

STAR WARS: EPISODE II - ATTACK OF THE CLONES
Dark Horse Comics: Apr, 2002 - No. 4, May, 2002 ($3.99, movie adaptation)

1-4-Regular and photo-c; Duursema-a ... 4.00
TPB ($17.95) r/#1-4; Struzan-c ... 18.00

STAR WARS: EPISODE III - REVENGE OF THE SITH
Dark Horse Comics: May, 2005 - No. 4, May, 2005 ($2.99, movie adaptation)

1-4-Wheatley-a/Dorman-c ... 3.00
TPB ($12.95) r/#1-4; Dorman-c ... 13.00

STAR WARS: GENERAL GRIEVOUS
Dark Horse Comics: Mar, 2005 - No. 4, June, 2005 ($2.99, limited series)

1-4-Leonardi-a/Dixon-s ... 3.00
TPB (2005, $12.95) r/#1-4 ... 13.00

STAR WARS HANDBOOK
Dark Horse Comics: July, 1998 - Present ($2.95, one-shots)

...X-Wing Rogue Squadron (7/98)-Guidebook to characters and spacecraft ... 3.00
...Crimson Empire (7/99) Dorman-c ... 3.00
...Dark Empire (3/00) Dorman-c ... 3.00

STAR WARS: HEIR TO THE EMPIRE
Dark Horse Comics: Oct, 1995 - No.6, Apr, 1996 ($2.95, limited series)

1-6: Adaptation of Zahn novel ... 3.00

STAR WARS: INFINITIES - A NEW HOPE
Dark Horse Comics: May, 2001 - No. 4, Oct, 2001 ($2.99, limited series)

1-4: "What If..." the Death Star wasn't destroyed in Episode 4 ... 3.00
TPB (2002, $12.95) r/ #1-4 ... 13.00

STAR WARS: INFINITIES - THE EMPIRE STRIKES BACK
Dark Horse Comics: July, 2002 - No. 4, Oct, 2002 ($2.99, limited series)

1-4: "What If..." Luke died on the ice planet Hoth; Bachalo-c ... 3.00
TPB (2/03, $12.95) r/ #1-4 ... 13.00

STAR WARS: INFINITIES - RETURN OF THE JEDI
Dark Horse Comics: Nov, 2003 - No. 4, Mar, 2004 ($2.99, limited series)

1- 4:"What If..." ; Benjamin-a ... 3.00

STAR WARS: JABBA THE HUTT
Dark Horse Comics: Apr, 1995 ($2.50, one-shots)

nn, ...The Betrayal, ...The Dynasty Trap, ...The Hunger of Princess Nampi ... 3.00

STAR WARS: JANGO FETT - OPEN SEASONS
Dark Horse Comics: Apr, 2002 - No. 4, July, 2002 ($2.99, limited series)

1-4: 1-Bachs & Fernandez-a ... 3.00

STAR WARS: JEDI
Dark Horse Comics: Feb, 2003 - Jun, 2004 ($4.99, one-shots)

... - Aayla Secura (8/03) Ostrander-s/Duursema-a ... 5.00
... - Count Dooku (11/03) Duursema-a ... 5.00
... - Mace Windu (2/03) Duursema-a ... 5.00
... - Shaak Ti (5/03) Ostrander-s/Duursema-a ... 5.00
... - Yoda (6/04) Barlow-s/Hoon-a ... 5.00

STAR WARS: JEDI ACADEMY - LEVIATHAN
Dark Horse Comics: Oct, 1998 - No. 4, Jan, 1999 ($2.95, limited series)

1-4: 1-Lago-c. 2-4-Chadwick-c ... 3.00

STAR WARS: JEDI COUNCIL: ACTS OF WAR
Dark Horse Comics: Jun, 2000 - No. 4, Sept, 2000 ($2.95, limited series)

1-4-Stradley-s; set one year before Episode 1 ... 3.00

STAR WARS: JEDI QUEST
Dark Horse Comics: Sept, 2001 - No. 4, Dec, 2001 ($2.95, limited series)

1-4-Anakin's Jedi training; Windham-s/Mhan-a ... 3.00

STAR WARS: JEDI VS. SITH
Dark Horse Comics: Apr, 2001 - No. 6, Sept, 2001 ($2.99, limited series)

1-6: Macan-s/Bachs & Robinson-c ... 3.00

STAR WARS: KNIGHTS OF THE OLD REPUBLIC
Dark Horse Comics: Jan, 2006 - Present ($2.99)

1-19-Takes place 3,964 years before Episode IV. 1-6-Brian Ching-a/Travis Charest-c ... 3.00
.../Rebellion #0 (3/06, 25¢) flip book preview of both series ... 2.50
... Vol. 1 Commencement TPB (11/06, $18.95) r/#0-6 ... 19.00

STAR WARS: LEGACY
Dark Horse Comics: No. 0, June, 2006 - Present ($2.99)

0-(25¢) Dossier of characters, settings, ships and weapons; Duursema-c ... 2.50
1-15: 1-Takes place 130 years after Episode IV; Hughes-c/Duursema-a. 4-Duursema-c
7-Luke Skywalker on-c ... 3.00
...: Broken Vol. 1 TPB (4/07, $17.95) r/#1-3,5,6 ... 18.00

STAR WARS: MARA JADE
Dark Horse Comics: Aug, 1998 - No. 6, Jan, 1999 ($2.95, limited series)

1-6-Ezquerra-a ... 3.00

STAR WARS: OBSESSION (Clone Wars)
Dark Horse Comics: Nov, 2004 - No. 5, Apr, 2005 ($2.99, limited series)

1-5-Blackman-s/Ching-a/c; Anakin & Obi-Wan 5 months before Episode III ... 3.00
...: Clone Wars Vol. 7 (2005, $17.95) r/#1-5 and 2005 Free Comic Book Day edition ... 18.00

STAR WARS: PURGE
Dark Horse Comics: Dec, 2005 ($2.99, one-shot)

nn-Vader vs. remaining Jedi one month after Episode III; Hughes-c/Wheatley-a ... 5.00

STAR WARS: QUI-GON & OBI-WAN - LAST STAND ON ORD MANTELL
Dark Horse Comics: Dec, 2000 - No. 3, Mar, 2001 ($2.99, limited series)

1-3: 1-Three covers (photo, Tony Daniel, Bachs) Windham-s ... 3.00

STAR WARS: QUI-GON & OBI-WAN - THE AURORIENT EXPRESS
Dark Horse Comics: Feb, 2002 - No. 2, Mar, 2002 ($2.99, limited series)

1,2-Six years prior to Phantom Menace; Marangon-a ... 3.00

STAR WARS: REBELLION (Also see Star Wars: Knights of the Old Republic flip book)
Dark Horse Comics: Apr, 2006 - No. 5, Aug, 2007 ($2.99)

1-9-Takes place 9 months after Episode IV; Luke Skywalker app. 1-Badeaux-a/c ... 3.00
Vol. 1 TPB (2/07, $14.95) r/#0 (flip book) & #1-5 ... 15.00

STAR WARS: REPUBLIC (Formerly Star Wars monthly series)
Dark Horse Comics: No. 46, Sept, 2002 - No. 83, Feb, 2006 ($2.99)

46-83-Events of the Clone Wars ... 3.00
...: Clone Wars Vol. 1 (2003, $14.95) r/#46-50 ... 15.00
...: Clone Wars Vol. 2 (2003, $14.95) r/#51-53 & Star Wars: Jedi - Shaak Ti ... 15.00
...: Clone Wars Vol. 3 (2004, $14.95) r/#55-59 ... 15.00
...: Clone Wars Vol. 4 (2004, $16.95) r/#54, 63 & Star Wars: Jedi - Aayla Secura & Dooku ... 17.00
...: Clone Wars Vol. 5 (2004, $17.95) r/#60-62, 64 & Star Wars: Jedi - Yoda ... 17.00
...: Clone Wars Vol. 6 (2005, $17.95) r/#65-71 ... 18.00
(Clone Wars Vol. 7 - see Star Wars: Obsession)
...: Clone Wars Vol. 8 (2006, $17.95) r/#72-78 ... 18.00
...: Clone Wars Vol. 9 (2006, $17.95) r/#79-83 & Star Wars: Purge ... 18.00
...: Honor and Duty TPB (5/06, $12.95) r/#46-48,78 ... 13.00

STAR WARS: RETURN OF THE JEDI (Movie)
Marvel Comics Group: Oct, 1983 - No. 4, Dec, 1984 (limited series)

	GD 2.0	VG 4.0	FN 6.0	VF 8.0	VF/NM 9.0	NM- 9.2
1-4-Williamson-p in all; r/Marvel Super Special #27	1	3	4	6	8	10
Oversized issue (1983, $2.95, 10-3/4x8-1/4", 68 pgs., cardboard-c)-r/#1-4	2	4	6	10	13	16

STAR WARS: RIVER OF CHAOS
Dark Horse Comics: June, 1995 - No. 4, Sept, 1995 ($2.95, limited series)

1-4: Louise Simonson scripts ... 3.00

STAR WARS: SHADOWS OF THE EMPIRE
Dark Horse Comics: May, 1996 - No. 6, Oct, 1996 ($2.95, limited series)

1-6: Story details events between The Empire Strikes Back & Return of the Jedi; Russell-a(i). ... 3.00

STAR WARS: SHADOWS OF THE EMPIRE - EVOLUTION
Dark Horse Comics: Feb, 1998 - No. 5, June, 1998 ($2.95, limited series)

1-5: Perry-s/Fegredo-c. ... 3.00

STAR WARS: SHADOW STALKER
Dark Horse Comics: Sept, 1997 ($2.95, one-shot)

nn-Windham-a. ... 3.00

STAR WARS: SPLINTER OF THE MIND'S EYE
Dark Horse Comics: Dec, 1995 - No. 4, June, 1996 ($2.50, limited series)

1-4: Adaption of Alan Dean Foster novel ... 3.00

STAR WARS: STARFIGHTER
Dark Horse Comics: Jan, 2002 - No. 3, March, 2002 ($2.99, limited series)

1-3-Williams & Gray-c ... 3.00

STAR WARS: TAG & BINK ARE DEAD
Dark Horse Comics: Oct, 2001 - No. 2, Nov, 2001($2.99, limited series)

1,2-Rubio-s ... 3.00

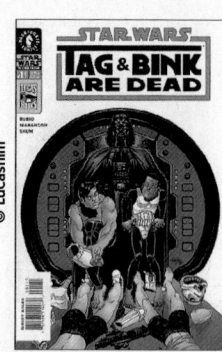

Star Wars: Tag & Bink Are Dead #1 © Lucasfilm

Static Shock: Rebirth of the Cool #1 © DC

Steel #51 © DC

	GD 2.0	VG 4.0	FN 6.0	VF 8.0	VF/NM 9.0	NM- 9.2

	GD 2.0	VG 4.0	FN 6.0	VF 8.0	VF/NM 9.0	NM- 9.2

Star Wars: Tag & Bink Were Here TPB (11/06, $14.95) r/both SW: Tag & Bink series ... 15.00

STAR WARS: TAG & BINK II
Dark Horse Comics: Mar, 2006 - No. 2, Apr, 2006($2.99, limited series)
1-Tag & Bink invade Return of the Jedi; Rubio-s. 2-T&B as Jedi younglings during Ep II ... 3.00

STAR WARS TALES
Dark Horse Comics: Sept, 1999 - No. 24, Jun, 2005 ($4.95/$5.95/$5.99, anthology)
1-4-Short stories by various ... 5.00
5-24 ($5.95/$5.99-c) Art and photo-c on each ... 6.00
Volume 1-6 ($19.95) 1-(1/02) r/#1-4. 2-('02) r/#5-8. 3-(1/03) r/#9-12. 4-(1/04) r/#13-16
5-(1/05) r/#17-20; introduction pages from #1-20. 6-(1/06) r/#21-24 ... 20.00

STAR WARS: TALES - A JEDI'S WEAPON (See Promotional Comics section)

STAR WARS: TALES FROM MOS EISLEY
Dark Horse Comics: Mar, 1996 ($2.95, one-shot)
nn-Bret Blevins-a. ... 3.00

STAR WARS: TALES OF THE JEDI (See Dark Horse Comics #7)
Dark Horse Comics: Oct, 1993 - No. 5, Feb, 1994 ($2.50, limited series)
1-5: All have Dave Dorman painted-c. 3-r/Dark Horse Comics #7-9 w/new coloring & some
    panels redrawn ... 3.00
1-5-Gold foil embossed logo; limited # printed-7500 (set) ... 50.00

STAR WARS: TALES OF THE JEDI-DARK LORDS OF THE SITH
Dark Horse Comics: Oct, 1994 - No. 6, Mar, 1995 ($2.50, limited series)
1-6: 1-Polybagged w/trading card ... 3.00

STAR WARS: TALES OF THE JEDI-REDEMPTION
Dark Horse Comics: July, 1998 - No. 5, Nov, 1998 ($2.95, limited series)
1-5: 1-Kevin J. Anderson-s/Kordey-c ... 3.00

STAR WARS: TALES OF THE JEDI-THE FALL OF THE SITH
Dark Horse Comics: June, 1997 - No. 5, Oct, 1997 ($2.95, limited series)
1-5 ... 3.00

STAR WARS: TALES OF THE JEDI-THE FREEDON NADD UPRISING
Dark Horse Comics: Aug, 1994 - No. 2, Nov, 1994 ($2.50, limited series)
1,2 ... 3.00

STAR WARS: TALES OF THE JEDI-THE GOLDEN AGE OF THE SITH
Dark Horse Comics: July, 1996 - No. 5, Feb, 1997 (99¢/$2.95, limited series)
0-(99¢)-Anderson-s ... 3.00
1-5-Anderson-s ... 3.00

STAR WARS: TALES OF THE JEDI-THE SITH WAR
Dark Horse Comics: Aug, 1995 - No. 6, Jan, 1996 ($2.50, limited series)
1-6: Anderson scripts ... 3.00

STAR WARS: THE BOUNTY HUNTERS
Dark Horse Comics: July, 1999 - Oct, 1999 ($2.95, one-shots)
...Aurra Sing (7/99), ...Kenix Kil (10/99), ...Scoundrel's Wages (8/99) Lando Calrissian app. ... 3.00

STAR WARS: THE JABBA TAPE
Dark Horse Comics: Dec, 1998 ($2.95, one-shot)
nn-Wagner-s/Plunkett-a ... 3.00

STAR WARS: THE LAST COMMAND
Dark Horse Comics: Nov, 1997 - No. 6, July, 1998 ($2.95, limited series)
1-6: Based on the Timothy Zaun novel ... 4.00

STAR WARS: THE PROTOCOL OFFENSIVE
Dark Horse Comics: Sept, 1997 ($4.95, one-shot)
nn-Anthony Daniels & Ryder Windham-s ... 5.00

STAR WARS: UNDERWORLD - THE YAVIN VASSILIKA
Dark Horse Comics: Dec, 2000 - No. 5, June, 2001 ($2.99, limited series)
1-5-(Photo and Robinson covers) ... 3.00

STAR WARS: UNION
Dark Horse Comics: Nov, 1999 - No. 4, Feb, 2000 ($2.95, limited series)
1-4-Wedding of Luke and Mara Jade; Teranishi-a/Stackpole-s ... 3.00

STAR WARS: VADER'S QUEST
Dark Horse Comics: Feb, 1999 - No. 4, May, 1999 ($2.95, limited series)
1-4-Follows destruction of 1st Death Star; Gibbons-a ... 3.00

STAR WARS: VISIONARIES
Dark Horse Comics: Apr, 2005 ($17.95, TPB)
nn-Short stories from the concept artists for Revenge of the Sith movie ... 18.00

STAR WARS: X-WING ROGUE SQUADRON (Star Wars: X-Wing Rogue
Squadron-The Phantom Affair #5-8 appears on cover only)
Dark Horse Comics: July, 1995 - No. 35, Nov, 1998 ($2.95)
1/2 ... 8.00
1-24,26-35: 1-4-Baron scripts. 5-20-Stackpole scripts ... 3.00
25-($3.95) ... 4.00
The Phantom Affair TPB ($12.95) r/#5-8 ... 13.00

STAR WARS: X-WING ROGUE SQUADRON: ROGUE LEADER
Dark Horse Comics: Sept, 2005 - No. 3, Nov, 2005 ($2.99)
1-3-Takes place one week after the Batttle of Endor ... 3.00

S.T.A.T.
Majestic Entertainment: Dec, 1993 ($2.25)
1 ... 2.50

STATIC (Also see Eclipse Monthly)
Charlton Comics: No, 11, Oct, 1985 - No. 12, Dec, 1985
11,12-Ditko-c/a; low print run ... 6.00

STATIC (See Heroes)
DC Comics (Milestone): June, 1993 - No. 45, Mar, 1997 ($1.50/$1.75/$2.50)
1-($2.95)-Collector's Edition; polybagged w/poster & trading card & backing board
    (direct sales only) ... 4.00
1-24,26-45: 2-Origin. 8-Shadow War; Simonson silver ink-c. 14-($2.50, 52 pgs.)-
    Worlds Collide Pt. 14. 27-Kent Williams-c ... 2.50
25 ($3.95) ... 4.00
...: Trial by Fire (2000, $9.95) r/#1-4; Leon-c ... 10.00

STATIC SHOCK!: REBIRTH OF THE COOL (TV)
DC Comics: Jan, 2001 - No. 4, Sept, 2001 ($2.50, limited series)
1-4: McDuffie-s/Leon-c/a ... 2.50

STATIC-X
Chaos! Comics: Aug, 2002 ($5.99)
1-Polybagged with music CD; metal band as super-heroes; Pulido-s ... 6.00

STEAMPUNK
DC/WildStorm (Cliffhanger): Apr, 2000 - No. 12, Aug, 2002 ($2.50/$3.50)
Catechism (1/00) Prologue -Kelly-s/Bachalo-a ... 2.50
1-4,6-11: 4-Four covers by Bachalo, Madureira, Ramos, Campbell ... 2.50
5,12-($3.50) ... 3.50
....: Drama Obscura ('03, $14.95) r/#6-12 ... 15.00
....: Manimatron ('01, $14.95) r/#1-5, Catechism, Idiosincratica ... 15.00

STEED AND MRS. PEEL (TV)(Also see The Avengers)
Eclipse Books/ ACME Press: 1990 - No. 3, 1991 ($4.95, limited series)
Books One - Three: Grant Morrison scripts ... 5.00

STEEL (Also see JLA)
DC Comics: Feb, 1994 - No. 52, July, 1998 ($1.50/$1.95/$2.50)
1-8,0,9-52: 1-From Reign of the Supermen storyline. 6,7-Worlds Collide Pt. 5 &12.
    8-(9/94). 0-(10/94). 9-(11/94). 46-Superboy-c/app. 50-Millennium Giants x-over ... 2.50
Annual 1 (1994, $2.95)-Elseworlds story ... 3.00
Annual 2 (1995, $3.95)-Year One story ... 4.00
...Forging of a Hero TPB (1997, $19.95) r/ early app. ... 20.00

STEEL: THE OFFICIAL COMIC ADAPTION OF THE WARNER BROS. MOTION PICTURE
DC Comics: 1997 ($4.95, Prestige format, one-shot)
nn-Movie adaption; Bogdanove & Giordano-a ... 5.00

STEELGRIP STARKEY
Marvel Comics (Epic Comics): June, 1986 - No. 6, July, 1987 ($1.50, limited series, Baxter paper)
1-6 ... 2.50

STEEL STERLING (Formerly Shield-Steel Sterling; see Blue Ribbon, Jackpot,
Mighty Comics, Mighty Crusaders, Roly Poly & Zip Comics)
Archie Enterprises, Inc.: No. 4, Jan, 1984 - No. 7, July, 1984
4-7: 4-6-Kanigher-s; Barreto-a. 5,6-Infantino-a. 6-McWilliams-a ... 4.00

STEEL, THE INDESTRUCTIBLE MAN (See All-Star Squadron #8 and J.L. of A. Annual #2)
DC Comics: Mar, 1978 - No. 5, Oct-Nov, 1978

1	1	3	4	6	8	10
2-5: 5-44 pgs.						6.00

STEELTOWN ROCKERS
Marvel Comics: Apr, 1987 - No. 6, Sept, 1990 ($1.00, limited series)

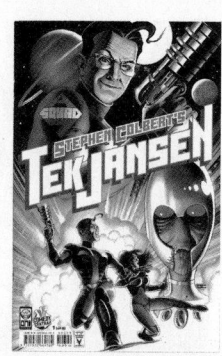

Stephen Colbert's Tek Jansen #1 © Comedy Partners

Steve Roper #2 © FF

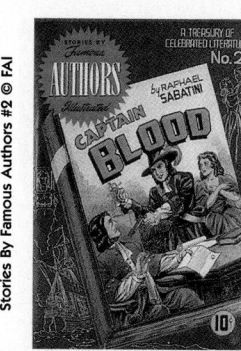

Stories By Famous Authors #2 © FAI

	GD	VG	FN	VF	VF/NM	NM-
	2.0	4.0	6.0	8.0	9.0	9.2

1-6: Small town teens form rock band ... 2.50

STEPHEN COLBERT'S TEK JANSEN (From the animated shorts on The Colbert Report)
Oni Press: July, 2007 - No. 5 ($3.99, limited series)

1-Chantier-a/Layman & Peyer-s; back-up story by Massey-s/Rodriguez-a; Chantier-c						4.00
1-Variant-c by John Cassaday						6.00

STEVE AUSTIN (See Stone Cold Steve Austin)

STEVE CANYON (See Harvey Comics Hits #52)
Dell Publishing Co.: No. 519, 11/53 - No. No. 1033, 9/59 (All Milton Caniff-a except #519, 939, 1033)

	GD	VG	FN	VF	VF/NM	NM-
Four Color 519 (1, '53)	8	16	24	56	93	130
Four Color 578 (8/54), 641 (7/55), 737 (10/56), 804 (5/57), 939 (10/58), 1033 (9/59) (photo-c)	5	10	15	35	55	75

STEVE CANYON
Grosset & Dunlap: 1959 (6-3/4x9", 96 pgs., B&W, no text, hardcover)

100100-Reprints 2 stories from strip (1953, 1957)	6	12	18	31	38	45
100100 (softcover edition)	5	10	15	24	30	35

STEVE CANYON COMICS
Harvey Publ.: Feb, 1948 - No. 6, Dec, 1948 (Strip reprints, No. 4,5: 52pgs.)

1-Origin; has biography of Milton Caniff; Powell-c, 2 pgs.; Caniff-a	21	42	63	120	188	255
2-Caniff, Powell-a in #2-6	14	28	42	80	115	150
3-6: 6-Intro Madame Lynx-c/story	14	28	42	76	108	140

STEVE CANYON IN 3-D
Kitchen Sink Press: June, 1986 ($2.25, one-shot)

1-Contains unpublished story from 1954						5.00

STEVE DITKO'S STRANGE AVENGING TALES
Fantagraphics Books: Feb, 1997 ($2.95, B&W)

1-Ditko-c/s/a						3.00

STEVE DONOVAN, WESTERN MARSHAL (TV)
Dell Publishing Co.: No. 675, Feb, 1956 - No. 880, Feb, 1958 (All photo-c)

Four Color 675-Kinstler-a	8	16	24	52	86	120
Four Color 768-Kinstler-a	6	12	18	43	69	95
Four Color 880	5	10	15	30	48	65

STEVE ROPER
Famous Funnies: Apr, 1948 - No. 5, Dec, 1948

1-Contains 1944 daily newspaper-r	12	24	36	69	97	125
2	9	18	27	47	61	75
3-5	8	16	24	40	50	60

STEVE SAUNDERS SPECIAL AGENT (See Special Agent)

STEVE SAVAGE (See Captain...)

STEVE ZODIAC & THE FIRE BALL XL-5 (TV)
Gold Key: Jan, 1964

10108-401 (#1)	8	16	24	52	86	120

STEVIE (Mazie's boy friend)(Also see Flat-Top, Mazie & Mortie)
Mazie (Magazine Publ.): Nov, 1952 - No. 6, Apr, 1954

1-Teenage humor; Stevie, Mortie & Mazie begin	8	16	24	44	57	70
2-6	6	12	18	28	34	40

STEVIE MAZIE'S BOY FRIEND (See Harvey Hits #5)

STEWART THE RAT (See Eclipse Graphic Album Series)

ST. GEORGE (See listing under Saint...)

STIG'S INFERNO
Vortex/Eclipse: 1985 - No. 7, Mar, 1987 ($1.95, B&W)

1-7 ($1.95)						2.50
Graphic Album (1988, $6.95, B&W, 100 pgs.)						7.00

STING OF THE GREEN HORNET (See The Green Hornet)
Now Comics: June, 1992 - No. 4, 1992 ($2.50, limited series)

1-4: Butler-c/a						2.50
1-4 ($2.75)-Collectors Ed.; polybagged w/poster						3.00

STOKER'S DRACULA (Reprints unfinished Dracula story from 1974-75 with new ending)
Marvel Comics: 2004 - No. 4, May, 2005 ($3.99, B&W)

1-4: 1-Reprints from Dracula Lives! #5-8; Roy Thomas-s/Dick Giordano-a. 2-R/#10,11 & Legion of Monsters #1. 3,4-New story/artwork to finish story. 4-Giordano afterword						4.00
HC (2005, $24.99) r/#1-4; foreward by Thomas; Giordano afterword; bonus art & covers						25.00

STONE
Avalon Studios: Aug, 1998 - No. 4, Apr, 1999 ($2.50, limited series)

1-4-Portacio-a/Haberlin-s						2.50
1-Alternate-c						5.00
2-($14.95) DF Stonechrome Edition						15.00

STONE (Volume 2)
Avalon Studios: Aug, 1999 - No. 4, May, 2000 ($2.50)

1-4-Portacio-a/Haberlin-s						2.50
1-Chrome-c						5.00

STONE COLD STEVE AUSTIN (WWF Wrestling)
Chaos! Comics: Oct, 1999 - No. 4, Feb, 2000 ($2.95)

1-4-Reg. & photo-c; Steven Grant-s						3.00
1-Premium Ed. ($10.00)						10.00
Preview ($5.00)						5.00

STONE PROTECTORS
Harvey Pubications: May, 1994 - No. 3, Sept, 1994

1-3-Ace Novelty a ction figures						
4.00						

STONEY BURKE (TV)
Dell Publishing Co.: June-Aug, 1963 - No. 2, Sept-Nov, 1963

	GD	VG	FN	VF	VF/NM	NM-
1,2-Jack Lord photo-c on both	3	6	9	17	25	32

STONY CRAIG
Pentagon Publishing Co.: 1946 (No #)

nn-Reprints Bell Syndicate's "Sgt. Stony Craig" newspaper strips	8	16	24	40	50	60

STORIES BY FAMOUS AUTHORS ILLUSTRATED (Fast Fiction #1-5)
Seaboard Publ./Famous Authors Ill.: No. 6, Aug, 1950 - No. 13, Mar, 1951

	GD	VG	FN	VF	VF/NM	NM-
1-Scarlet Pimpernel-Baroness Orczy	29	58	87	170	268	365
2-Capt. Blood-Raphael Sabatini	28	56	84	162	256	350
3-She, by Haggard	32	64	96	186	293	400
4-The 39 Steps-John Buchan	18	36	54	107	169	230
5-Beau Geste-P. C. Wren	18	36	54	107	169	230

NOTE: The above five issues are exact reprints of Fast Fiction #1-5 except for the title change and new Kiefer covers on #1 and 2. Kiefer c(r)-3-5. The above 5 issues were released before Famous Authors #6.

6-Macbeth, by Shakespeare; Kiefer art (8/50); used in SOTI, pg. 22,143; Kiefer-c; 36 pgs.	26	52	78	152	239	325
7-The Window, by Shakespeare; Kiefer-c/a; 52 pgs.	18	36	54	107	169	230
8-Hamlet, by Shakespeare; Kiefer-c/a; 36 pgs.	23	46	69	132	209	285
9,10: 9-Nicholas Nickleby, by Dickens; G. Schrotter-a; 52 pgs. 10-Romeo & Juliet, by Shakespeare; Kiefer-c/a; 36 pgs.	18	36	54	107	169	230
11-13: 11-Ben-Hur; Schrotter-a; 52 pgs. 12-La Svengali; Schrotter-a; 36 pgs. 13-Scaramouche; Kiefer-c/a; 36 pgs.	18	36	54	103	162	220

NOTE: Artwork was prepared/advertised for #14, The Red Badge Of Courage. Gilberton bought out Famous Authors, Ltd. and used that story as C.I. #98. Famous Authors, Ltd. then published the Classics Junior series. The Famous Authors Ltd. series were published as part of the regular Classics Ill. Series in Brazil starting in 1952.

STORIES FROM THE TWILIGHT ZONE
Skylark Pub: Mar, 1979, 68pgs. (B&W comic digest, 5-1/4x7-5/8")

	GD	VG	FN	VF	VF/NM	NM-
15405-2: Pfevfer-a, 56 pgs, new comics	3	6	9	16	23	30

STORIES OF ROMANCE (Formerly Meet Miss Bliss)
Atlas Comics (LMC): No. 5, Mar, 1956 - No. 13, Aug, 1957

	GD	VG	FN	VF	VF/NM	NM-
5-Baker-a?	10	20	30	56	76	95
6-10,12,13	7	14	21	37	46	55
11-Baker, Romita-a; Colletta-c/a	9	18	27	50	65	80

NOTE: **Ann Brewster** a-13. **Colletta** a-9(2), 11; c-5, 11.

STORM
Marvel Comics: Feb, 1996 - No. 4, May, 1996 ($2.95, limited series)

1-4-Foil-c; Dodson-a(p); Ellis-s: 2-4-Callisto app.						3.50

STORM
Marvel Comics: Apr, 2006 - No. 6, Sept, 2006 ($2.99, limited series)

1-6: Ororo and T'Challa meet as teens; Eric Jerome Dickey-s						3.00
HC (2007, $19.99, dustjacket) r/#1-6						20.00

STORMBREAKER: THE SAGA OF BETA RAY BILL (Also see Thor)
Marvel Comics: Mar, 2005 - No. 6, Aug, 2005 ($2.99, limited series)

1-6-Oeming & Berman-s/DiVito-a; Galactus app. 6-Spider-Man app.						3.00
TPB (2006, $16.99) r/#1-6						17.00

STORM SHADOW (G.I. Joe character)
Devil's Due Publishing: May, 2007 - Present ($3.50)

Stormwatch #44 © WSP

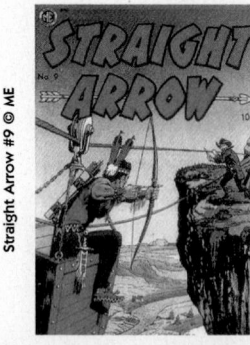
Straight Arrow #9 © ME

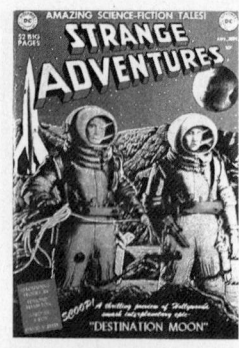
Strange Adventures #1 © DC

	GD	VG	FN	VF	VF/NM	NM-		GD	VG	FN	VF	VF/NM	NM-
	2.0	4.0	6.0	8.0	9.0	9.2		2.0	4.0	6.0	8.0	9.0	9.2

1-3-Larry Hama-s ... 3.50

STORMWATCH (Also see The Authority)
Image Comics (WildStorm Prod.): May, 1993 - No. 50, Jul, 1997 ($1.95/$2.50)

1-8,0,9-36: 1-Intro StormWatch (Battalion, Diva, Winter, Fuji, & Hellstrike); 1st app. Weatherman; Jim Lee-c & part scripts; Lee plots in all. 1-Gold edition.1-3-Includes coupon for limited edition StormWatch trading card #00 by Lee. 3-1st brief app. Backlash. 0-($2.50)-Polybagged w/card; 1st full app. Backlash. 9-(4/94, $2.50)-Intro Defile. 10-(6/94),11,12-Both (8/94). 13,14-(9/94). 15-(10/94). 21-Reads #1 on-c. 22-Direct Market; Wildstorm Rising Pt. 9, bound-in card. 23-Spartan joins team. 25-(6/94, June 1995 on-c, $2.50). 35-Fire From Heaven Pt. 5. 36-Fire From Heaven Pt. 12 ... 2.50
10-Alternate Portacio-c, see Deathblow #5 ... 2.50
22-($1.95)-Newsstand, Wildstorm Rising Pt. 9 ... 2.50
37-(7/96, $3.50, 38 pgs.)-Weatherman forms new team; 1st app. Jenny Sparks, Jack Hawksmoor & Rose Tattoo; Warren Ellis scripts begin; Justice League #1-c/swipe ... 3.50
38-49: 44-Three covers. ... 3.50
50-($4.50) ... 4.50
Special 1 ,2(1/94, 5/95, $3.50, 52 pgs.) ... 3.50
Sourcebook 1 (1/94, $2.50) ... 2.50
Forces of Nature ('99, $14.95, TPB) r/V1 #37-42 ... 15.00
Lightning Strikes ('00, $14.95, TPB) r/V1 #43-47 ... 15.00

STORMWATCH (Also see The Authority)
Image Comics (WildStorm): Oct, 1997 - No. 11, Sept, 1998 ($2.50)

1-Ellis-s/Jimenez-a(p); two covers by Bennett ... 2.50
1-($3.50)-Voyager Pack bagged w/Gen 13 preview ... 3.50
2-4: 4-1st app. Midnighter and Apollo ... 2.50
5-11: 7,8-Freefall app. 9-Gen13 & DV8 app. ... 2.50
A Finer World ('99, $14.95, TPB) r/V2 #4-9 ... 15.00
Change or Die ('99, $14.95, TPB) r/V1 #48-50 & V2 #1-3 ... 15.00
Final Orbit ('01, $9.95, TPB) r/V2 #10,11 & WildC.A.T.S./Aliens; Hitch-c ... 10.00

STORMWATCHER
Eclipse Comics (Acme Press): Apr, 1989 - No. 4, Dec, 1989 ($2.00, B&W)

1-4 ... 2.50

STORMWATCH: P.H.D. (Post Human Division)
DC Comics (WildStorm): Jan, 2007 - Present ($2.99)

1-10: 1-Two covers by Mahnke & Hairsine; Gage-s/Mahnke-a. 2-Var-c by Dell'Otto ... 3.00
TPB (2007, $17.99) r/#1-4,6,7 & story from Worldstorm #1 ... 18.00

STORMWATCH: TEAM ACHILLES
DC Comics (WildStorm): Sept, 2002 - No. 23, Aug, 2004 ($2.95)

1-8: 1-Two covers by Portacio; Portacio-a/Wright-s. 5,6-The Authority app. ... 3.00
9-23-Back-up preview of The Authority: High Stakes pt. 1 ... 3.00
TPB (2003, $14.95) r/Wizard Preview and #1-6; Portacio art pages ... 15.00
Book 2 (2004, $14.95) r/#7-11 & short story from Eye of the Storm Annual ... 15.00

STORMY (Disney) (Movie)
Dell Publishing Co.: No. 537, Feb, 1954

Four Color 537 (...the Thoroughbred)-on top 2/3 of each page; Pluto story on bottom 1/3 ... 5 10 15 30 48 65

STORY OF JESUS (See Classics Illustrated Special Issue)

STORY OF MANKIND, THE (Movie)
Dell Publishing Co.: No. 851, Jan, 1958

Four Color 851-Vincent Price/Hedy Lamarr photo-c ... 7 14 21 47 76 105

STORY OF MARTHA WAYNE, THE
Argo Publ.: April, 1956

1-Newspaper strip-r ... 6 12 18 29 36 42

STORY OF RUTH, THE
Dell Publishing Co.: No. 1144, Nov-Jan, 1961 (Movie)

Four Color 1144-Photo-c ... 8 16 24 58 97 135

STORY OF THE COMMANDOS, THE (Combined Operations)
Long Island Independent: 1943 (15¢, B&W, 68 pgs.) (Distr. by Gilberton)

nn-All text (no comics); photos & illustrations; ad for Classic Comics on back cover (Rare) ... 32 64 96 186 293 400

STORY OF THE GLOOMY BUNNY, THE (See March of Comics #9)

STRAIGHT ARROW (Radio)(See Best of the West & Great Western)
Magazine Enterprises: Feb-Mar, 1950 - No. 55, Mar, 1956 (All 36 pgs.)

1-Straight Arrow (alias Steve Adams) & his palomino Fury begin; 1st mention of Sundown Valley & the Secret Cave. ... 46 92 138 281 461 640
2-Red Hawk begins (1st app?) by Powell (origin), ends #55

3-Frazetta-c ... 23 46 69 132 209 285
4,5: 4-Secret Cave-c ... 31 62 93 178 282 385
6-10 ... 21 42 63 120 188 255
 ... 16 32 48 94 147 200
11-Classic story "The Valley of Time", with an ancient civilization made of gold ... 22 44 66 128 202 275
12-19 ... 14 28 42 82 121 160
20-Origin Straight Arrow's Shield ... 16 32 48 92 144 195
21-Origin Fury ... 19 38 57 109 172 235
22-Frazetta-c ... 25 50 75 145 228 310
23,25-30: 25-Secret Cave-c. 28-Red Hawk meets The Vikings ... 11 22 33 60 83 105
24-Classic story "The Dragons of Doom!" with prehistoric pteradactyls ... 14 28 42 80 115 150
31-38: 36-Red Hawk drug story by Powell ... 9 18 27 52 69 85
39-Classic story "The Canyon Beast", with a dinosaur egg hatching a Tyranosaurus Rex ... 13 26 39 74 105 135
40-Classic story "Secret of The Spanish Specters", with Conquistadors' lost treasure ... 11 22 33 64 90 115
41,42,44-54: 45-Secret Cave-c ... 9 18 27 47 61 75
43-Intro & 1st app. Blaze, S. Arrow's Warrior dog ... 10 20 30 56 76 95
55-Last issue ... 11 22 33 60 83 105

NOTE: **Fred Meagher** a 1-55; c-1, 2, 4-21, 23-55. **Powell** a 2-55. **Whitney** a-1. Many issues advertise the radio premiums associated with Straight Arrow.

STRAIGHT ARROW'S FURY (Also see A-1 Comics)
Magazine Enterprises: No. 119, 1954 (one-shot)

A-1 119-Origin; Fred Meagher-c/a ... 15 30 45 85 130 175

STRANGE (Tales You'll Never Forget)
Ajax-Farrell Publ. (Four Star Comic Corp.): March, 1957 - No. 6, May, 1958

1 ... 21 42 63 124 195 265
2-Censored r/Haunted Thrills ... 13 26 39 72 101 130
3-6 ... 10 20 30 56 76 95

STRANGE (Dr. Strange)
Marvel Comics (Marvel Knghts): Nov, 2004 - No. 6, July, 2005 ($3.50)

1-6-Straczynski & Barnes-s/Peterson-a; Dr. Strange's origin retold ... 3.50
....: Beginnings and Endings TPB (2006, $17.99) r/#1-6 ... 18.00

STRANGE ADVENTURES
DC Comics: July/Aug 1950

nn - Ashcan comic, not distributed to newsstands, only for in-house use. Cover art is All Star Comics #47 with interior being Detective Comics #140. A second example has the interior of Detective Comics #146. A third example has an unidentified issue of Detective Comics as the interior. This is the only ashcan with multiple interiors. A FN+ copy sold for $1,000 in 2007.

STRANGE ADVENTURES
National Periodical Publ.: Aug-Sept, 1950 - No. 244, Oct-Nov, 1973 (No. 1-12: 52 pgs.)

1-Adaptation of "Destination Moon"; preview of movie w/photo-c from movie (also see Fawcett Movie Comic #2); adapt. of Edmond Hamilton's "Chris KL-99" in #1-3; Darwin Jones begins ... 225 450 675 1969 3685 5400
2 ... 102 204 306 867 1609 2350
3,4 ... 71 142 213 604 1115 1625
5-8,10: 7-Origin Kris KL-99 ... 61 122 183 519 960 1400
9-(6/51)-Origin/1st app. Captain Comet (c/story) ... 141 282 423 1199 2225 3250
11-20: 12,13,17,18-Toth-a. 14-Robot-c ... 41 82 123 328 597 865
21-30: 28-Atomic explosion panel. 30-Robot-c ... 33 66 99 248 454 660
31,34-38 ... 30 60 90 225 413 600
32,33-Krigstein-a ... 31 62 93 233 422 610
39-Ill. in SOTI "Treating police contemptuously" (top right) ... 35 70 105 263 482 700
40-49-Last Capt. Comet; not in 45,47,48 ... 30 60 90 222 404 585
50-53-Last precode issue (2/55) ... 22 44 66 160 285 410
54-70 ... 16 32 48 118 209 300
71-99 ... 13 26 39 93 164 235
100 ... 14 28 42 103 184 265
101-110: 104-Space Museum begins by Sekowsky ... 10 20 30 70 123 175
111-116,118,119: 114-Star Hawkins begins, ends #185; Heath-a in Wood E.C. style ... 10 20 30 67 116 165
117-(6/60)-Origin/1st app. Atomic Knights. ... 46 92 138 368 672 975
120-2nd app. Atomic Knights ... 22 44 66 164 292 420
121,122,125,127,128,130,131,133,134: 134-Last 10¢ issue ... 9 18 27 60 100 140
123,126-3rd & 4th app. Atomic Knights ... 12 24 36 87 156 225
124-Intro/origin Faceless Creature ... 9 18 27 64 110 155

Strange Adventures #231 © DC

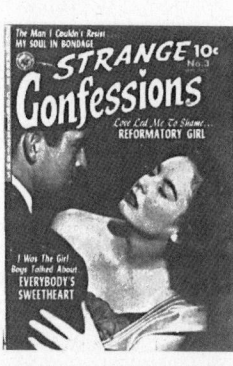

Strange Confessions #3 © Z-D

Strange Mysteries #2 © SUPR

	GD 2.0	VG 4.0	FN 6.0	VF 8.0	VF/NM 9.0	NM- 9.2
129,132,135,138,141,147-Atomic Knights app.	9	18	27	65	113	160
136,137,139,140,143,145,146,148,149,151,152,154,155,157-159: 159-Star Rovers app.; Gil Kane/Anderson-a.	6	12	18	43	69	95
142-2nd app. Faceless Creature	7	14	21	50	83	115
144-Only Atomic Knights-c (by M. Anderson)	10	20	30	70	123	175
150,153,156,160: Atomic Knights in each. 153-(6/63)-3rd app. Faceless Creature. 160-Last Atomic Knights explosion-c.	7	14	21	49	80	110
161-179: 161-Last Space Museum. 163-Star Rovers app. 170-Infinity-c. 177-Intro/origin Immortal Man	5	10	15	35	55	75
180-Origin/1st app. Animal Man	16	32	48	114	202	290
181-183,185-189: 187-Intro/origin The Enchantress	4	8	12	28	44	60
184-2nd app. Animal Man by Gil Kane	10	20	30	70	123	175
190-1st app. Animal Man in costume	13	26	39	90	160	230
191-194,196-200,202-204	4	8	12	24	37	50
195-1st full app. Animal Man	7	14	21	47	76	105
201-Last Animal Man; 2nd full app.	5	10	15	32	51	70
205-(10/67)-Intro/origin Deadman by Infantino & begin series, ends #216	12	24	36	86	153	220
206-Neal Adams-a begins	9	18	27	63	107	150
207-210	8	16	24	56	93	130
211-216: 211-Space Museum-r. 216-(1-2/69)-Deadman story finally concludes in Brave & the Bold #86 (10-11/69); secret message panel by Neal Adams (pg. 13); tribute to Steranko	7	14	21	49	80	110
217-r/origin & 1st app. Adam Strange from Showcase #17, begin-r; Atomic Knights-r begin	3	6	9	14	19	24
218-221,223-225: 218-Last 12¢ issue. 225-Last 15¢ issue	2	4	6	13	18	22
222-New Adam Strange story; Kane/Anderson-a	3	6	9	18	27	36
226,227,230-236-(68-52 pgs.): 226, 227-New Adam Strange text story w/illos by Anderson (8,6 pgs.) 231-Last Atomic Knights-r. 235-JLA-c/s	2	4	6	13	18	22
228,229 (68 pgs.)	3	6	9	16	22	28
237-243	2	4	6	8	11	14
244-Last issue	2	4	6	9	13	16

NOTE: **Neal Adams** a-206-216; c-207-216, 228, 235. **Anderson** a-8-52, 94, 96, 99, 115, 117, 119-163, 217r, 218r, 222, 223-225r, 226, 229r, 242i(r); c-18, 19, 21, 23, 24, 27, 30, 32-44(most); c/r-157i, 190i, 217r-224, 228-231, 233, 235-239, 241-243. **Ditko** a-188, 189. **Drucker** a-42, 43, 45. **Elias** a-212. **Finlay** a-2, 3, 6, 7, 210r, 229r. **Giunta** a-237r. **Heath** a-116. **Infantino** a-10-101, 106-151, 154, 157-163, 180, 190, 218-221r; 223-244p(r); c-50; c(r)-190p, 197, 199-211, 218-221, 223-244. **Kaluta** c-232. **Kubert** a-55(2 pgs.), 226; c-219, 220, 225-227, 232, 234. **Moreira** c-26, 28, 29, 71. **Morrow** c-230. **Mortimer** c-8. **Powell** a-54, 124, 125, 130, 138, 146-157, 173-186, 204, 222r, 227-231r; c(p)-111-17, 125, 114, 146-157. **Gil Kane** a-8-116, 124, 125, 130, 138, 146-157, 173-186, 204, 222r, 227-231r; c(p)-111-17, 125, 114, 146-157. **Sekowsky** a-71p, 97-162p, 217p(r), 218p(r); c-206, 217-219r. **Simon & Kirby** a-2r (2 pgs) **Sparling** a-201. **Toth** a-8, 12, 13, 17-19. **Wood** a-154. Atomic Knights in #117, 120, 123, 126, 129, 132, 135, 138, 141, 144, 147, 150, 153, 156, 160. Atomic Knights reprints by Anderson in 217-221, 223-231. Chris KL99 in 1-3, 5, 7, 9, 11, 15. Capt. Comet covers 9-14, 17-19, 24, 26, 27, 32-44.

STRANGE ADVENTURES
DC Comics (Vertigo): Nov, 1999 - No. 4 ($2.50, limited series)

1-3: 1-Bolland-c; art by Bolland, Gibbons, Quitely						2.50

STRANGE AS IT SEEMS (See Famous Funnies-A Carnival of Comics, Feature Funnies #1, The John Hix Scrap Book & Peanuts)

STRANGE AS IT SEEMS
United Features Syndicate: 1939

	GD 2.0	VG 4.0	FN 6.0	VF 8.0	VF/NM 9.0	NM- 9.2
Single Series 9, 1, 2	35	70	105	204	322	440

STRANGE ATTRACTORS
RetroGraphix: 1993 - No. 15, Feb, 1997 ($2.50, B&W)

1-15: 1-(5/93), 2-(8/93), 3-(11/93), 4-(2/94)						2.50
Volume One-($14.95, trade paperback)-r/#1-7						15.00

STRANGE ATTRACTORS: MOON FEVER
Caliber Comics: Feb, 1997 - No. 3, June, 1997 ($2.95, B&W, mini-series)

1-3						3.00

STRANGE COMBAT TALES
Marvel Comics (Epic Comics): Oct, 1993 - No. 4, Jan, 1994 ($2.50, limited series)

1-4						2.50

STRANGE CONFESSIONS
Ziff-Davis Publ. Co.: Jan-Mar (Spring on-c), 1952 - No. 4, Fall, 1952 (All have photo-c)

	GD 2.0	VG 4.0	FN 6.0	VF 8.0	VF/NM 9.0	NM- 9.2
1(Scarce)-Kinstler-a	53	106	159	323	529	735
2(Scarce, 7-8/52)	38	76	114	219	347	475
3(Scarce, 9-10/52)-#3 on-c, #2 on inside; Reformatory girl story; photo-c	37	74	111	213	337	460
4(Scarce)	35	70	105	204	322	440

STRANGE DAYS
Eclipse Comics: Oct, 1984 - No. 3, Apr, 1985 ($1.75, Baxter paper)

1-3: Freakwave, Johnny Nemo, & Paradax from Vanguard Illustrated; nudity, violence & strong language						2.50

STRANGE DAYS (Movie)
Marvel Comics: Dec, 1995 ($5.95, squarebound, one-shot)

1-Adaptation of film						6.00

STRANGE FANTASY (Eerie Tales of Suspense!)(Formerly Rocketman #1)
Ajax-Farrell: Aug, 1952 - No. 14, Oct-Nov, 1954

	GD 2.0	VG 4.0	FN 6.0	VF 8.0	VF/NM 9.0	NM- 9.2
2(#1, 8/52)-Jungle Princess story; Kamenish-a; reprinted from Ellery Queen #1	46	92	138	281	466	650
2(10/52)-No Black Cat or Rulah; Bakerish, Kamenish-a; hypo/meathook-c	40	80	120	237	376	515
3-Rulah story, called Pulah	40	80	120	235	368	500
4-Rocket Man app. (2/53)	38	76	114	219	347	475
5,6,8,10,12,14	27	54	81	156	246	335
7-Madam Satan/Slave story	38	76	114	219	347	475
9(w/Black Cat), 9(w/Boy's Ranch; S&K-a), 9(w/War)(A rebinding of Harvey interiors; not publ. by Ajax)	34	68	102	197	311	425
9-Regular issue; Steve Ditko's 3rd published work (tied with Captain 3D)	45	90	135	275	455	635
11-Jungle story	35	70	105	201	318	435
13-Bondage-c; Rulah (Kolah) story	35	70	105	201	318	435

STRANGE GALAXY
Eerie Publications: V1#8, Feb, 1971 - No. 11, Aug, 1971 (B&W, magazine)

	GD 2.0	VG 4.0	FN 6.0	VF 8.0	VF/NM 9.0	NM- 9.2
V1#8-Reprints-c/Fantastic V19#3 (2/70) (a pulp)	3	6	9	20	30	40
9-11	3	6	9	16	23	30

STRANGE GIRL
Image Comics: June, 2005 - Present ($2.95/$2.99/$3.50)

1-12: 1-Rick Remender-s/Eric Nguyen-a						3.00
13-17-($3.50)						3.50
.... Vol. 1: Girl Afraid TPB (2005, $12.99) r/#1-4; sketch pages and pin-ups						13.00

STRANGE JOURNEY
America's Best (Steinway Publ.) (Ajax/Farrell): Sept, 1957 - No. 4, Jun, 1958 (Farrell reprints)

	GD 2.0	VG 4.0	FN 6.0	VF 8.0	VF/NM 9.0	NM- 9.2
1	20	40	60	117	184	250
2-4: 2-Flying saucer-c. 3-Titanic-c	15	30	45	83	124	165

STRANGE LOVE (See Fox Giants)

STRANGE MYSTERIES
Superior/Dynamic Publications: Sept, 1951 - No. 21, Jan, 1955

	GD 2.0	VG 4.0	FN 6.0	VF 8.0	VF/NM 9.0	NM- 9.2
1-Kamenish-a & horror stories begin	66	132	198	413	682	950
2	38	76	114	219	347	475
3-5	35	70	105	201	318	435
6-8	30	60	90	174	275	375
9-Bondage 3-D effect-c	36	72	108	208	329	450
10-Used in SOTI, pg. 181	26	52	78	152	239	325
11-18	23	46	69	132	209	285
19-r/Journey Into Fear #1; cover is a splash from one story; Baker-r(2)	24	48	72	139	220	300
20,21-Reprints; 20-r/#1 with new-c	17	34	51	98	154	210

STRANGE MYSTERIES
I. W. Enterprises/Super Comics: 1963 - 1964

	GD 2.0	VG 4.0	FN 6.0	VF 8.0	VF/NM 9.0	NM- 9.2
I.W. Reprint #9: Rulah-r/Spook #28; Disbrow-a	3	6	9	20	30	40
Super Reprint #10-12,15-17(1963-64): 10,11-r/Strange #2,1. 12-r/Tales of Horror #5 (3/53) less-c. 15-r/Dark Mysteries #23. 16-r/The Dead Who Walk. 17-r/Dark Mysteries #22	3	6	9	20	30	40
Super Reprint #18-r/Witchcraft #1; Kubert-a	3	6	9	20	30	40

STRANGE PLANETS
I. W. Enterprises/Super Comics: 1958; 1963-64

	GD 2.0	VG 4.0	FN 6.0	VF 8.0	VF/NM 9.0	NM- 9.2
I.W. Reprint #1(nd)-Reprints E. C. Incredible S/F #30 plus-c/Strange Worlds #3	6	12	18	39	62	85
I.W. Reprint #9-Orlando/Wood-r/Strange Worlds #4; cover-r from Flying Saucers #1	7	14	21	49	80	110
Super Reprint #10-Wood-r (22 pg.) from Space Detective #1; cover-r/Attack on Planet Mars	7	14	21	49	80	110
Super Reprint #11-Wood-r (25 pg.) from An Earthman on Venus	8	16	24	54	90	125
Super Reprint #12-Orlando-r/Rocket to the Moon	7	14	21	49	80	110
Super Reprint #15-Reprints Journey Into Unknown Worlds #8; Heath, Colan-r	4	8	12	28	44	60
Super Reprint #16-Reprints Avon's Strange Worlds #6; Kinstler, Check-a						

The Strangers #14 © MAL

Strangers in Paradise #90 © Terry Moore

Strange Suspense Stories #62 © CC

	GD 2.0	VG 4.0	FN 6.0	VF 8.0	VF/NM 9.0	NM- 9.2

	GD 2.0	VG 4.0	FN 6.0	VF 8.0	VF/NM 9.0	NM- 9.2
	5	10	15	30	48	65
Super Reprint #18-r/Great Exploits #1 (Daring Adventures #6); Space Busters, Explorer Joe, The Son of Robin Hood; Krigstein-a	4	8	12	24	37	50

STRANGERS
Image Comics: Mar, 2003 - No. 6, Sept, 2003 ($2.95)
1-6-Randy & Jean-Marc Lofficier-s; two covers. 2-Nexus back-up story   3.00

STRANGERS, THE
Malibu Comics (Ultraverse): June, 1993 - No. 24, May, 1995 ($1.95/$2.50)
1-4,6-12,14-20: 1-1st app. The Strangers; has coupon for Ultraverse Premiere #0; 1st app. the Night Man (not in costume). 2-Polybagged w/trading card. 7-Break-Thru x-over. 8-2 pg. origin Solution. 12-Silver foil logo; wraparound-c. 17-Rafferty app.   2.50
1-With coupon missing   2.50
1-Full cover holographic edition, 1st of kind w/Hardcase #1 & Prime #1   6.00
1-Ultra 5000 limited silver foil   4.00
4-($2.50)-Newsstand edition bagged w/card   2.50
5-($2.50, 52 pgs.)-Rune flip-c/story by B. Smith (3 pgs.); The Mighty Magnor 1 pg. strip by Aragones; 3-pg. Night Man preview   2.50
13-($3.50, 68 pgs.)-Mantra app.; flip book w/Ultraverse Premiere #4   3.50
21-24 ($2.50)   2.50
...:The Pilgrim Conundrum Saga (1/95, $3.95, 68pgs.)   4.00

STRANGERS IN PARADISE
Antarctic Press: Nov, 1993 - No. 3, Feb, 1994 ($2.75, B&W, limited series)

	GD 2.0	VG 4.0	FN 6.0	VF 8.0	VF/NM 9.0	NM- 9.2
1	5	10	15	30	48	65
1-2nd/3rd prints	1	2	3	5	6	8
2 (2300 printed)	4	8	12	22	34	45
3	3	6	9	16	23	30

Trade paperback (Antarctic Press, $6.95)-Red -c (5000 print run)   10.00
Trade paperback (Abstract Studios, $6.95)-Red (2000 print run)   15.00
Trade paperback (Abstract Studios, $6.95, 1st-4th printing)-Blue-   7.00
Hardcover ('98, $29.95) includes first draft pages   30.00
Gold Reprint Series ($2.75) 1-3-r/#1-3   2.75

STRANGERS IN PARADISE
Abstract Studios: Sept, 1994 - No. 14, July, 1996 ($2.75, B&W)

	GD 2.0	VG 4.0	FN 6.0	VF 8.0	VF/NM 9.0	NM- 9.2
1	2	4	6	9	13	16
1,3- 2nd printings						4.00
2,3: 2-Color dream sequence	1	2	3	5	6	8
4-10						4.00
4-6-2nd printings						2.75
11-14: 14-The Letters of Molly & Poo						3.00

Gold Reprint Series ($2.75) 1-13-r/#1-13   2.75
I Dream Of You ($16.95, TPB) r/#1-9   17.00
It's a Good Life ($8.95, TPB) r/#10-13   9.00

STRANGERS IN PARADISE (Volume Three)
Homage Comics #1-8/Abstract Studios #9-on: Oct, 1996 - No. 90, May, 2007 ($2.75-$2.99, color #1-5, B&W #6-on)
1-Terry Moore-c/s/a in all; dream seq. by Jim Lee-a   4.00

	GD 2.0	VG 4.0	FN 6.0	VF 8.0	VF/NM 9.0	NM- 9.2
1-Jim Lee variant-c	1	2	3	6	7	8

2-5   3.50
6-16: 6-Return to B&W. 13-15-High school flashback. 16-Xena Warrior Princess parody; two covers   3.00
17-89: 33-Color issue. 46-Molly Lane. 49-Molly & Poo. 86-David dies   3.00
90-Last issue; 3 covers of Katchoo, Francine and David forming a triptych   3.00
...Lyrics and Poems   2.75
...Source Book (2003, $2.95) Background on characters & story arcs, checklists   3.00
Brave New World ('02, $8.95, TPB) r/#44,45,47,48   9.00
Child of Rage ($15.95, TPB) r/#31-38   16.00
David's Story (6/04, $8.95, TPB) r/#61-63   9.00
Ever After ('07, $15.95, TPB) r/#83-90   16.00
Flower to Flame ('03, $15.95, TPB) r/#55-60   16.00
Heart in Hand ('03, $12.95, TPB) r/#50-54   13.00
High School ('98, $8.95, TPB) r/#13-16   9.00
Immortal Enemies ('98, $14.95, TPB) r/#6-12   15.00
Love & Lies (2006, $14.95, TPB)r/#77-82   15.00
Love Me Tender ($12.95, TPB) r/#1-5 in B&W w/ color Lee seq.   13.00
Molly & Poo (2005, $8.95, TPB)r/#46,49,73   9.00
My Other Life ($14.95, TPB) r/#25-30   15.00
Pocket Book 1-5 ($17.95, 5 1/2" x 8", TPB) 1-r/Vol.1 & 2. 2-r/#1-17 in B&W 3-r/#18-24,26-32,34-38. 4-r/#41-45,47,48,50-60. 5-r/#46,49,61-76   18.00
Sanctuary ($15.95, TPB) r/#17-24   16.00
Tattoo ($14.95, TPB) r/#70-76; sketch pages and fan tattoo photos   15.00
Tomorrow Now (11/04, $14.95, TPB) r/#64-69   15.00

	GD 2.0	VG 4.0	FN 6.0	VF 8.0	VF/NM 9.0	NM- 9.2

Tropic of Desire ($12.95, TPB) r/#39-43   13.00
The Complete... : Volume 3 Part 1 HC ($49.95) r/#1-12   50.00
The Complete... : Volume 3 Part 2 HC ($49.95) r/#13-15,17-25   50.00
The Complete... : Volume 3 Part 3 HC ('01, $49.95) r/#26-38   50.00
The Complete... : Volume 3 Part 4 HC ('02, $39.95) r/#39-46,49   40.00
The Complete... : Volume 3 Part 5 HC ('03, $49.95) r/#47,48,50-57   50.00
The Complete... : Volume 3 Part 6 HC ('04, $49.95) r/#58-69   50.00
The Complete... : Volume 3 Part 7 HC ('06, $49.95) r/#70-80   50.00

STRANGE SPORTS STORIES (See Brave & the Bold #45-49, DC Special, and DC Super Stars #10)
National Periodical Publications: Sept-Oct, 1973 - No. 6, July-Aug, 1974

	GD 2.0	VG 4.0	FN 6.0	VF 8.0	VF/NM 9.0	NM- 9.2
1	3	6	9	16	23	30
2-6: 2-Swan/Anderson-a	2	4	6	9	13	16

STRANGE STORIES FROM ANOTHER WORLD (Unknown World #1)
Fawcett Publications: No. 2, Aug, 1952 - No. 5, Feb, 1953

	GD 2.0	VG 4.0	FN 6.0	VF 8.0	VF/NM 9.0	NM- 9.2
2-Saunders painted-c	50	100	150	305	503	700
3-5-Saunders painted-c	40	80	120	235	368	500

STRANGE STORIES OF SUSPENSE (Rugged Action #1-4)
Atlas Comics (CSI): No. 5, Oct, 1955 - No. 16, Aug, 1957

	GD 2.0	VG 4.0	FN 6.0	VF 8.0	VF/NM 9.0	NM- 9.2
5(#1)	40	80	120	240	383	525
6,9	25	50	75	145	228	310
7-E. C. swipe cover/Vault of Horror #32	26	52	78	150	235	320
8-Morrow/Williamson-a; Pakula-a	27	54	81	156	246	335
10-Crandall, Torres, Meskin-a	26	52	78	150	235	320
11-13: 12-Torres, Pakula-a. 13-E.C. art swipes	21	42	63	122	191	260
14-16: 14-Williamson/Mayo-a. 15-Krigstein-a. 16-Fox, Powell-a	23	46	69	132	209	285

NOTE: Everett a-6, 7, 13; c-8, 9, 11-14. Heath a-5. Maneely c-5. Morisi a-11. Morrow a-13. Powell a-8. Severin c-7. Wildey a-14.

STRANGE STORY (Also see Front Page)
Harvey Publications: June-July, 1946 (52 pgs.)

	GD 2.0	VG 4.0	FN 6.0	VF 8.0	VF/NM 9.0	NM- 9.2
1-The Man in Black Called Fate by Powell	32	64	96	186	293	400

STRANGE SUSPENSE STORIES (Lawbreakers Suspense Stories #10-15; This Is Suspense #23-26; Captain Atom V1#78 on)
Fawcett Publications/Charlton Comics No. 16 on: 6/52 - No. 5, 2/53; No. 16, 1/54 - No. 22, 11/54; No. 27, 10/55 - No. 77, 10/65; V3#1, 10/67 - V1#9, 9/69

	GD 2.0	VG 4.0	FN 6.0	VF 8.0	VF/NM 9.0	NM- 9.2
1-(Fawcett)-Powell, Sekowsky-a	81	162	243	506	841	1175
2-George Evans horror story	48	96	144	293	484	675
3-5 (2/53)-George Evans horror stories	40	80	120	244	392	540
16(1-2/54)-Formerly Lawbreakers S.S.	29	58	87	170	268	365
17,21: 21-Shuster-a	23	46	69	135	212	290
18-E.C. swipe/HOF 7; Ditko-c/a(2)	40	80	120	239	380	520
19-Ditko electric chair-c; Ditko-a	52	104	156	317	521	725
20-Ditko-c/a(2)	40	80	120	239	380	520
22(11/54)-Ditko-c, Shuster-a; last pre-code issue; becomes This Is Suspense	35	70	105	201	318	435
27(10/55)-(Formerly This Is Suspense #26)	15	30	45	85	130	175
28-30,38	12	24	36	67	94	120
31-33,35,37,40-Ditko-c/a(2-3 each)	21	42	63	124	195	260
34-Story of ruthless business man, Wm. B. Gaines; Ditko-c/a	46	92	138	281	466	650
36-(15¢, 68 pgs.); Ditko-a(4)	26	52	78	150	235	320
39,41,52,53-Ditko-a	18	36	54	103	162	220
42-44,46,49,54-60	6	12	18	37	59	80
45,47,48,50,51-Ditko-c/a	13	26	39	95	168	240
61-74	4	8	12	28	44	60
75(6/65)-Reprints origin/1st app. Captain Atom by Ditko from Space Advs. #33; r/Severin-a/Space Advs. #24 (75-77: 12¢ issues)	12	24	36	82	146	210
76,77-Captain Atom-r by Ditko/Space Advs.	6	12	18	43	69	95
V3#1 (10/67): 12¢ issues begin	3	6	9	20	30	40
V1#2-Ditko-c/a; atom bomb-c	3	6	9	20	30	40
V1#3-9: All 12¢ issues	2	4	6	13	18	22

NOTE: Alascia a-19. Aparo a-60, V3#1, 2, 4; c-V1#4, 8, 9. Baily a-1-3; c-2, 5. Evans c-3, 4. Giordano c-16. 17p. 24p, 25p. Montes/Bache c-66. Powell a-4. Shuster a-19, 21. Marcus Swayze a-27.

STRANGE TALES (...Featuring Warlock #178-181; Doctor Strange #169 on)
Atlas (CCPC #1-67/ZPC #68-79/VPI #80-85)/Marvel #86(7/61) on:
June, 1951 - No. 168, May, 1968; No. 169, Sept, 1973 - No. 188, Nov, 1976

	GD 2.0	VG 4.0	FN 6.0	VF 8.0	VF/NM 9.0	NM- 9.2
1-Horror/weird stories begin	300	600	900	1931	3366	4800
2	103	206	309	644	1072	1500
3,5: 3-Atom bomb panels	79	158	237	494	822	1150
4-Cosmic eyeball story "The Evil Eye"	83	166	249	519	860	1200

Strange Tales #11 © MAR

Strange Tales #102 © MAR

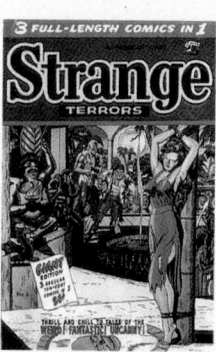

Strange Terrors #6 © STJ

	GD 2.0	VG 4.0	FN 6.0	VF 8.0	VF/NM 9.0	NM- 9.2
6-9: 6-Heath-c/a. 7-Colan-a	57	114	171	356	591	825
10-Krigstein-a	60	120	180	375	625	875
11-14,16-20	41	82	123	253	407	560
15-Krigstein-a	41	82	123	256	416	575
21,23-27,29-34: 27-Atom bomb panels. 33-Davis-a. 34-Last pre-code issue (2/55)	36	72	108	208	329	450
22-Krigstein, Forte/Fox-a	37	74	111	213	337	460
28-Jack Katz story used in Senate Investigation report, pgs. 7 & 169	37	74	111	213	337	460
35-41,43,44: 37-Vampire story by Colan	19	38	57	138	244	350
42,45,59,61-Krigstein-a; #61 (2/58)	19	38	57	142	254	365
46-57,60: 51-(10/56) 1st S.A. issue. 53,56-Crandall-a. 60-(8/57)	17	34	51	128	227	325
58,64-Williamson-a in each, with Mayo-a#58	18	36	54	132	234	335
62,63,65,66: 62-Torres-a. 66-Crandall-a	17	34	51	124	220	315
67-Prototype ish. (Quicksilver)	18	36	54	134	237	340
68,71,72,74,77,80: Ditko/Kirby-a in #67-80	17	34	51	128	227	325
69,70,73,75,76,78,79: 69-Prototype ish. (Prof. X). 70-Prototype ish. (Giant Man). 73-Prototype ish. (Ant-Man). 75-Prototype ish. (Iron Man). 76-Prototype ish. (Human Torch). 78-Prototype ish. (Ant-Man). 79-Prototype ish. (Dr. Strange) (12/60)	21	42	63	156	278	400
81-83,85-88,90,91-Ditko/Kirby-a in all: 86-Robot-c. 90-(11/61)-Atom bomb blast panel	16	32	48	118	209	300
84-Prototype ish. (Magneto)(5/61); has powers like Magneto of X-Men, but two years earlier; Ditko/Kirby-a	20	40	60	144	257	370
89-1st app. Fin Fang Foom (10/61) by Kirby	43	86	129	344	622	900
92-Prototype ish. (Ancient One & Ant-Man); last 10¢ issue	17	34	51	128	227	325
93,95,96,98-100: Kirby-a	15	30	45	107	191	275
94-Creature similar to The Thing; Kirby-a	17	34	51	128	227	325
97-1st app. Aunt May & Uncle Ben by Ditko (6/62), before Amazing Fantasy #15; (see Tales Of Suspense #7); Kirby-a	36	72	108	274	498	725
101-Human Torch begins by Kirby (10/62); origin recap Fantastic Four & Human Torch; Human Torch-c begin	100	200	300	850	575	2300
102-1st app. Wizard; robot-c	38	76	114	285	518	750
103-105: 104-1st app. Trapster. 105-2nd Wizard	30	60	90	220	398	575
106,108,109: 106-Fantastic Four guests (3/63)	21	42	63	156	278	400
107-(4/63)-Human Torch/Sub-Mariner battle; 4th S.A. Sub-Mariner app. & 1st x-over outside of Fantastic Four	29	58	87	212	381	550
110-(7/63)-Intro Doctor Strange, Ancient One & Wong by Ditko	120	240	360	1020	1885	2750
111-2nd Dr. Strange	32	64	96	240	445	650
112,113	15	30	45	109	195	280
114-Acrobat disguised as Captain America, 1st app. since the G.A.; intro. & 1st app. Victoria Bentley; 3rd Dr. Strange app. & begin series (11/63)	38	76	114	285	518	750
115-Origin Dr. Strange; Human Torch vs. Sandman (Spidey villain; 2nd app. & brief origin); early Spider-Man x-over, 12/63	45	90	135	360	648	935
116-(1/64)-Human Torch battles The Thing; 1st Thing x-over	13	26	39	93	164	235
117,118,120: 120-1st Iceman x-over (from X-Men)	10	20	30	70	123	175
119-Spider-Man x-over (2 panel cameo)	11	22	33	79	140	200
121,122,124,126-134: Thing/Torch team-up in 121-134. 126-Intro Clea. 128-Quicksilver & Scarlet Witch app. (1/65). 130-The Beatles cameo. 134-Last Human Torch; The Watcher-c/story; Wood-a(i)	8	16	24	54	90	125
123-1st app. The Beetle (see Amazing Spider-Man #21 for next app.); 1st Thor x-over (8/64); Loki app.	9	18	27	63	107	150
125-Torch & Thing battle Sub-Mariner (10/64)	9	18	27	65	113	160
135-Col. (formerly Sgt.) Nick Fury becomes Nick Fury Agent of Shield (origin/1st app.) by Kirby (8/65); series begins	14	28	42	99	175	250
136-140: 138-Intro Eternity	6	12	18	41	66	90
141-147,149: 145-Begins alternating-c features w/Nick Fury (odd #'s) & Dr. Strange (even #'s). 146-Last Ditko Dr. Strange in consecutive stories since #113; only full Ditko Dr. Strange-c this title. 147-Dr. Strange by Everett (#147-152) continues thru #168, then Dr. Strange #169	6	12	18	41	66	90
148-Origin Ancient One	7	14	21	47	76	105
150(11/66)-John Buscema's 1st work at Marvel	6	12	18	37	59	80
151-Kirby/Steranko-c/a; 1st Marvel work by Steranko	8	16	24	52	86	120
152,153-Kirby/Steranko-a	6	12	18	37	59	80
154-158-Steranko-a/script	6	12	18	37	59	80
159-Origin Nick Fury retold; Intro Val; Captain America-c/story; Steranko-a						
160-162-Steranko-a/scripts; Capt. America app.	6	14	18	43	69	95
163-166,168-Steranko-a(p). 168-Last Nick Fury (gets own book next month) & last	6	12	18	37	59	80

	GD 2.0	VG 4.0	FN 6.0	VF 8.0	VF/NM 9.0	NM- 9.2
Dr. Strange who also gets own book	5	10	15	35	55	75
167-Steranko pen/script; classic flag-c	6	12	18	43	69	95
169-1st app. Brother Voodoo(origin in #169,170) & begin series, ends #173.	2	4	6	13	18	22
170-174: 174-Origin Golem	2	4	6	9	12	15
175-177: 177-Brunner-c	2	4	6	8	10	12
178-(2/75)-Warlock by Starlin begins; origin Warlock & Him retold; 1st app. Magus; Starlin-c/a/scripts in #178-181 (all before Warlock #9)	3	6	9	16	23	30
179-181-All Warlock. 179-Intro/1st app. Pip the Troll. 180-Intro Gamora. 181-(8/75)-Warlock story continued in Warlock #9	2	4	6	11	16	20
182-188: 185,186-(Regular 25¢ editions)						6.00
185,186-(30¢ variants; limited distribution)(5,7/76)	2	4	6	11	16	20
Annual 1(1962)-Reprints from Strange Tales #73,76,78, Tales of Suspense #7,9, Tales to Astonish #1,6,7, & Journey Into Mystery #53,55,59; (1st Marvel annual?)	47	94	141	387	686	985
Annual 2(7/63)-Reprints from Strange Tales #67, Strange Worlds (Atlas) #1-3, World of Fantasy #16; new Human Torch vs. Spider-Man story by Kirby/Ditko (1st Spidey x-over; 4th app.); Kirby-c	70	140	210	595	1098	1600

NOTE: Briefer a-17. Burgos a-123p. J. Buscema a-174p. Colan a-7, 11, 20, 37, 53, 169-173p, 188p. Davis c-71. Ditko a-46, 50, 67-122, 123-125p, 126-146, 175r, 182-188r; c-51, 93, 115, 121, 146. Everett a-4, 21, 40-42, 73, 147-152, 164; c-8, 10, 11, 13, 15, 24, 45, 49-54, 56, 58, 60, 61, 63, 148, 150, 152, 158i. Forte a-27, 45, 62, 73, 54, 60. Heath a-2, 6; c-6, 18-20. Kamen a-45. G. Kane c-170-173, 182p. Kirby Human Torch-101-105, 108, 109, 114, 120; Nick Fury-135p, 141-143p; (Layouts)-135-153; other Kirby a-67-100p; c-68-70, 72-74, 76-92, 94, 95, 101-114, 116-123, 125-130, 132-135, 136p, 138-145, 147, 149, 151p. Kirby/Ayers c-101-106, 108-110. Kirby/Ditko a-80, 88, 121; c-75, 93, 97, 100, 139. Lawrence a-80, 97. Leiber/ Fox a-110-113. Maneely a-3, 37, 42; c-33, 40. Moldoff a-20. Mooney a-174i. Morisi a-53, 56. Morrow a-54. Orlando a-41, 44, 46, 49, 52. Powell a-42, 44, 49, 54, 130-134p; c-131p. Reinman a-151, 160. R.Q. Sale a-56; c-16. Sekowski a-3, 11. Severin a(i)-136-138; c-137. Starlin a-178, 179, 180p, 181p; c-178-180, 181p. Steranko a-151-161, 162-168p; c-151i, 153, 155, 157, 159, 161, 163, 165, 167. Torres a-53, 62. Tuska a-14, 166p. Whitney a-149. Wildey a-60. Woodbridge a-59. Fantastic Four cameos #101-134. Jack Katz app.-26.

STRANGE TALES
Marvel Comics Group: Apr, 1987 - No. 19, Oct, 1988

V2#1-19	2.50

STRANGE TALES
Marvel Comics: Nov, 1994 ($6.95, one-shot)

V3#1-acetate-c	7.00

STRANGE TALES (Anthology; continues stories from Man-Thing #8 and Werewolf By Night #6)
Marvel Comics: Sept, 1998 - No. 2, Oct, 1998 ($4.99)

1,2: 1-Silver Surfer app. 2-Two covers	5.00

STRANGE TALES: DARK CORNERS
Marvel Comics: May, 1998 ($3.99, one-shot)

1-Anthology; stories by Baron & Maleev, McGregor & Dringenberg, DeMatteis & Badger; Estes painted-c	4.00

STRANGE TALES OF THE UNUSUAL
Atlas Comics (ACI No. 1-4/WPI No. 5-11): Dec, 1955 - No. 11, Aug, 1957

	GD 2.0	VG 4.0	FN 6.0	VF 8.0	VF/NM 9.0	NM- 9.2
1-Powell-a	45	90	135	275	450	625
2	28	56	84	164	260	355
3-Williamson-a (4 pgs.)	30	60	90	172	271	370
4,6,8,11	21	42	63	122	191	260
5-Crandall, Ditko-a	26	52	78	150	235	320
7,9: 7-Kirby, Orlando-a. 9-Krigstein-a	23	46	69	132	209	285
10-Torres, Morrow-a	21	42	63	122	191	260

NOTE: Baily a-6. Brodsky c-2-4. Everett a-2; c-6, 9, 11. Heck a-1. Maneely c-1. Orlando a-7. Pakula a-10. Romita a-1. R.Q. Sale a-3. Wildey a-3.

STRANGE TERRORS
St. John Publishing Co.: June, 1952 - No. 7, Mar, 1953

	GD 2.0	VG 4.0	FN 6.0	VF 8.0	VF/NM 9.0	NM- 9.2
1-Bondage-c; Zombies spelled Zoombies on-c; Fine-esque -a	55	110	165	344	572	800
2	34	68	102	197	311	425
3-Kubert-a; painted-c	41	82	123	250	400	550
4-Kubert-a (reprinted in Mystery Tales #18); Ekgren painted-c; Fine-esque -a; Jerry Iger caricature	52	104	156	317	521	725
5-Kubert-a; painted-c	41	82	123	250	400	550
6-Giant (25¢, 100 pgs.).(1/53); bondage-c	53	106	159	323	537	750
7-Giant (25¢, 100 pgs.); Kubert-c/a	54	108	162	338	562	785

NOTE: Cameron a-6, 7. Morisi a-6.

STRANGE WORLD OF YOUR DREAMS
Prize Publications: Aug, 1952 - No. 4, Jan-Feb, 1953

	GD 2.0	VG 4.0	FN 6.0	VF 8.0	VF/NM 9.0	NM- 9.2
1-Simon & Kirby	64	128	192	400	663	925
2,3-Simon & Kirby-c/a. 2-Meskin-a	50	100	150	305	503	700

Strange Worlds #7 © AVON

Stray Bullets #25 © David Lapham

Strikeback #4 © Peterson & Maguire

	GD 2.0	VG 4.0	FN 6.0	VF 8.0	VF/NM 9.0	NM- 9.2
4-S&K-c; Meskin-a	41	82	123	250	400	550

STRANGE WORLDS (#18 continued from Avon's Eerie #1-17)
Avon Periodicals: 11/50 - No. 9, 11/52; No. 18, 10-11/54 - No. 22, 9-10/55
(No #11-17)

	GD 2.0	VG 4.0	FN 6.0	VF 8.0	VF/NM 9.0	NM- 9.2
1-Kenton of the Star Patrol by Kubert (r/Eerie #1 from 1947); Crom the Barbarian by John Giunta	131	262	393	819	1360	1900
2-Wood-a; Crom the Barbarian by Giunta; Dara of the Vikings app.; used in SOTI, pg. 112; injury to eye panel	117	234	351	731	1216	1700
3-Wood/Orlando-a (Kenton), Wood/Williamson/Frazetta/Krenkel/Orlando-a (7 pgs.); Malu Slave Girl Princess app.; Kinstler-c	228	456	684	1425	2363	3300
4-Wood-c/a (Kenton); Orlando-a; origin The Enchanted Daggar; Sultan-a; classic cover	128	256	384	800	1325	1850
5-Orlando/Wood-a (Kenton); Wood-c	68	136	204	425	705	985
6-Kinstler-a(2); Orlando/Wood-c; Check-a	46	92	138	281	466	650
7-Fawcette & Becker/Alascia-a	40	80	120	243	389	535
8-Kubert, Kinstler, Hollingsworth & Lazarus-a; Lazarus Robot-c	40	80	120	243	389	535
9-Kinstler, Fawcette, Alascia-a	40	80	120	237	376	515
18-(Formerly Eerie #17)-Reprints "Attack on Planet Mars" by Kubert	32	64	96	186	293	400
19-r/Avon's "Robotmen of the Lost Planet"; last pre-code issue; Robot-c	32	64	96	186	293	400
20-War-c/story; Wood-c(r)/U.S. Paratroops #1	10	20	30	56	76	95
21,22-War-c/stories. 22-New logo	9	18	27	47	61	75
I.W. Reprint #5-Kinstler-a(r)/Avon's #9	4	8	12	24	37	50

STRANGE WORLDS
Marvel Comics (MPI No. 1,2/Male No. 3,5): Dec, 1958 - No. 5, Aug, 1959

	GD 2.0	VG 4.0	FN 6.0	VF 8.0	VF/NM 9.0	NM- 9.2
1-Kirby & Ditko-a; flying saucer issue	88	176	264	550	913	1275
2-Ditko-c/a	50	100	150	305	503	700
3-Kirby-a(2)	41	82	123	250	400	550
4-Williamson-a	40	80	120	240	383	525
5-Ditko-a	35	70	105	204	322	440

NOTE: **Buscema** a-3, 4. **Ditko** a-1-5; c-2.. **Heck** a-2. **Kirby** a-1, 3. **Kirby/Brodsky** c-1, 3-5.

STRAWBERRY SHORTCAKE
Marvel Comics (Star Comics): Jun, 1985 - No. 6, Feb, 1986 (Children's comic)

	GD 2.0	VG 4.0	FN 6.0	VF 8.0	VF/NM 9.0	NM- 9.2
1-6: Howie Post-a	1	2	3	5	6	8

STRAY
DC Comics (Homage Comics): 2001 ($5.95, prestige format, one-shot)

1-Pollina-c/a; Lobdell & Palmiotti-s						6.00

STRAY BULLETS (Also see Promotional Comics section for Free Comic Book Day edition)
El Capitan Books: 1995 - Present ($2.95/$3.50, B&W, mature readers)

	GD 2.0	VG 4.0	FN 6.0	VF 8.0	VF/NM 9.0	NM- 9.2
1-David Lapham-c/a/scripts	2	4	6	8	10	12
2,3						6.00
4-8						3.50
9-21,31,32-($2.95)						3.00
22-30,33-40-($3.50) 22-Includes preview to Murder Me Dead						3.50
Innocence of Nihilism Volume 1 HC ($29.95, hardcover) r/#1-7						30.00
Somewhere Out West Volume 2 HC ($34.95, hardcover) r/#8-14						35.00
Other People Volume 3 HC ($34.95, hardcover) r/#15-22						35.00
Volume 1-3 TPB ($11.95, softcover) 1-r/#1-4. 2-r/#5-8. 3-r/ #9-12						12.00
Volume 4-7 TPB ($14.95) 4- r/#13-16. 5- r/#17-20. 6- r/#21-24. 7-r/#25-28						15.00

NOTE: Multiple printings of most issues exist & are worth cover price.

STRAY TOASTERS
Marvel Comics (Epic Comics): Jan, 1988 - No. 4, April, 1989 ($3.50, squarebound, limited series)

1-4: Sienkiewicz-c/a/scripts						3.50

STREET COMIX
Street Enterprises/King Features: 1973 (50¢, B&W, 36 pgs.)(20,000 print run)

	GD 2.0	VG 4.0	FN 6.0	VF 8.0	VF/NM 9.0	NM- 9.2
1-Rip Kirby	2	4	6	8	11	14
2-Flash Gordon	2	4	6	10	14	18

STREETFIGHTER
Ocean Comics: Aug, 1986 - No. 4, Spr, 1987 ($1.75, limited series)

1-4: 2-Origin begins						3.00

STREET FIGHTER
Malibu Comics: Sept, 1993 - No. 3, Nov, 1993 ($2.95)

1-3: 3-Includes poster; Ferret x-over						3.00

STREET FIGHTER
Image Comics: Sept, 2003 - No. 14, Feb, 2005 ($2.95)

1-Back-up story w/Madureira-a; covers by Madureira and Tsang						3.00
2-6,8-14: 2-Two covers by Campbell and Warren; back-up story w/Warren-a						3.00
7-($4.50) Larocca-c						4.50
... Vol. 1 (3/04, $9.99, digest-size) r/main stories from #1-6						10.00

STREET FIGHTER: THE BATTLE FOR SHADALOO
DC Comics/CAP Co. Ltd.: 1995 ($3.95, one-shot)

1-Polybagged w/trading card & Tattoo						4.00

STREET FIGHTER II
Tokuma Comics (Viz): Apr, 1994 - No. 8, Nov, 1994 ($2.95, limited series)

1-8						3.00

STREET FIGHTER II
UDON Comics: No. 0, Oct, 2005 - Present ($1.99/$3.95/$2.95)

0-(10/05, $1.99) prelude to series; Alvin Lee-a						2.50
1-($3.95) Two covers by Alvin Lee & Ed McGuinness						4.00
2-5-($2.95)						3.00

STREET FIGHTER LEGENDS
UDON Comics: Aug, 2006 - Present ($3.95)

1-Spotlight on Sakura; two covers						4.00

STREETS
DC Comics: 1993 - No. 3, 1993 ($4.95, limited series, 52 pgs.)

Book 1-3-Estes painted-c						5.00

STREET SHARKS
Archie Publications: Jan, 1996 - No. 3, Mar, 1996 ($1.50, limited series)

1-3						2.50

STREET SHARKS
Archie Publications: May, 1996 - No. 6 ($1.50, published 8 times a year)

1-6						2.50

STRICTLY PRIVATE (You're in the Army Now)
Eastern Color Printing Co.: July, 1942 (#1 on sale 6/15/42)

	GD 2.0	VG 4.0	FN 6.0	VF 8.0	VF/NM 9.0	NM- 9.2
1,2: Private Peter Plink. 2-Says 128 pgs. on-c	23	46	69	132	209	285

STRIKE!
Eclipse Comics: Aug, 1987 - No. 6, Jan, 1988 ($1.75)

1-6, ...Vs. Sgt. Strike Special 1 (5/88, $1.95)						2.50

STRIKEBACK! (The Hunt For Nikita)
Malibu Comics (Bravura): Oct, 1994 - No. 3, Jan, 1995 ($2.95, unfinished limited series)

1-3: Jonathon Peterson script, Kevin Maguire-c/a						3.00
1-Gold foil embossed-c						5.00

STRIKEBACK!
Image Comics (WildStorm Productions): Jan, 1996 - No. 5, May, 1996 ($2.50, limited series)

1-5: Reprints original Bravura series w/additional story & art by Kevin Maguire & Jonathon Peterson; new Maguire-c in all. 4,5-New story & art						2.50

STRIKEFORCE: AMERICA
Comico: Dec, 1995 ($2.95)

V2#1-Polybagged w/gaming card; S. Clark-a(p)						3.00

STRIKEFORCE: MORITURI
Marvel Comics Group: Dec, 1986 - No. 31, July, 1989

1-31: 14-Williamson-i. 13-Double size. 25-Heath-c						2.50

STRIKEFORCE MORITURI: ELECTRIC UNDERTOW
Marvel Comics: Dec, 1989 - No. 5, Mar, 1990 ($3.95, 52 pgs., limited series)

1-5 Squarebound						4.00

STRONG GUY REBORN (See X-Factor)
Marvel Comics: Sept, 1997 ($2.99, one-shot)

1-Dezago-s/Andy Smith, Art Thibert-a						3.00

STRONG MAN (Also see Complimentary Comics & Power of...)
Magazine Enterprises: Mar-Apr, 1955 - No. 4, Sept-Oct, 1955

	GD 2.0	VG 4.0	FN 6.0	VF 8.0	VF/NM 9.0	NM- 9.2
1(A-1 #130)-Powell-c/a	23	46	69	132	209	285
2-4: (A-1 #132,134,139)-Powell-a. 2-Powell-c	18	36	54	105	165	225

STRONTIUM DOG
Eagle Comics: Dec, 1985 - No. 4, Mar, 1986 ($1.25, limited series)

1-4, Special 1: 4-Moore script. Special 1 (1986)-Moore script						2.50

STRYFE'S STRIKE FILE
Marvel Comics: Jan, 1993 ($1.75, one-shot, no ads)

SU

Sub-Mariner #4 © MAR

Sub-Mariner (2007 series) #1 © MAR

Sub-Mariner Comics #4 © MAR

	GD 2.0	VG 4.0	FN 6.0	VF 8.0	VF/NM 9.0	NM- 9.2

1-Stroman, Capullo, Andy Kubert, Brandon Peterson-a; silver metallic ink-c; X-Men tie-in to X-Cutioner's Song — 3.00
1-Gold metallic ink 2nd printing — 2.50

STRYKEFORCE
Image Comics (Top Cow): May, 2004 - No. 5, Oct, 2004 ($2.99)
1-5-Faerber-s/Kirkham-a. 4,5-Preview of HumanKind — 3.00
Vol. 1 TPB (2005, $16.99) r/#1-5 & Codename: Strykeforce #0-3; sketch pages — 17.00

STUMBO THE GIANT (See Harvey Hits #49,54,57,60,63,66,69,72,78,88 & Hot Stuff #2)

STUMBO TINYTOWN
Harvey Publications: Oct, 1963 - No. 13, Nov, 1966 (All 25¢ giants)

	GD 2.0	VG 4.0	FN 6.0	VF 8.0	VF/NM 9.0	NM- 9.2
1-Stumbo, Hot Stuff & others begin	15	30	45	107	191	275
2	9	18	27	61	103	145
3-5	7	14	21	45	73	100
6-13	6	12	18	37	59	80

STUNT DAWGS
Harvey Comics: Mar, 1993 ($1.25, one-shot)
1 — 2.50

STUNTMAN COMICS (Also see Thrills Of Tomorrow)
Harvey Publ.: Apr-May, 1946 - No. 2, June-July, 1946; No. 3, Oct-Nov, 1946

	GD	VG	FN	VF	VF/NM	NM-
1-Origin Stuntman by S&K reprinted in Black Cat #9; S&K-c	114	228	342	713	1182	1650
2-S&K-c/a; The Duke of Broadway story	68	136	204	425	705	985
3-Small size (5-1/2x8-1/2"; B&W; 32 pgs.); distributed to mail subscribers only; S&K-a; Kid Adonis by S&K reprinted in Green Hornet #37	79	158	237	494	822	1150

(Also see All-New #15, Boy Explorers #2, Flash Gordon #5 & Thrills of Tomorrow)

STUPID COMICS (Also see 40 oz. Collected)
Oni Press/Image Comics: July, 2000; Sept, 2002 - Present ($2.95, B&W)
1-(Oni Press, 7/00) Jim Mahfood 1 page satire strips reprinted from JAVA magazine — 3.00
1-3-(Image Comics, 9/02; 10/03) Jim Mahfood 1 page and 2 page satire strips — 3.00
TPB (4/06, $12.99) r/#1(Oni) and #1-3(Image); Phoenix New Times strips — 13.00

STUPID HEROES
Mirage Studios: Sept, 1993 - No. 3, Dec, 1994 ($2.75, unfinished limited series)
1-3-Laird-c/a & scripts; 2 trading cards bound in — 2.75

STUPID, STUPID RAT TAILS (See Bone)
Cartoon Books: Dec, 1999 - No. 3, Feb, 2000 ($2.95, limited series)
1-3-Jeff Smith-s/Tom Sniegoski-s — 3.00

SUBHUMAN
Dark Horse Comics: Nov, 1998 - No. 4, Feb, 1999 ($2.95, limited series)
1-4-Mark Schultz-c — 3.00

SUBMARINE ATTACK (Formerly Speed Demons)
Charlton Comics: No. 11, May, 1958 - No. 54, Feb-Mar, 1966

	GD	VG	FN	VF	VF/NM	NM-
11	4	8	12	24	37	50
12-20	3	6	9	17	25	32
21-30	3	6	9	16	23	30
31-54	3	6	9	14	19	24

NOTE: Glanzman c/a-25. Montes/Bache a-38, 40, 41.

SUB-MARINER (See All-Select, All-Winners, Blonde Phantom, Daring, The Defenders, Fantastic Four #4, Human Torch, The Invaders, Iron Man &..., Marvel Mystery, Marvel Spotlight #27, Men's Adventures, Motion Picture Funnies Weekly, Namora, Namor, The..., Prince Namor, The Sub-Mariner, Saga Of The..., Tales to Astonish #70 & 2nd series, USA & Young Men)

SUB-MARINER, THE (2nd Series)(Sub-Mariner #31 on)
Marvel Comics Group: May, 1968 - No. 72, Sept, 1974 (No. 43: 52 pgs.)

	GD	VG	FN	VF	VF/NM	NM-
1-Origin Sub-Mariner; story continued from Iron Man & Sub-Mariner #1	16	32	48	118	209	300
2-Triton app.	8	16	24	52	86	120
3-5-5-1st Tiger Shark (9/68)	6	12	18	37	59	80
6,7,9,10: 6-Tiger Shark-c & 2nd app., cont'd from #5. 7-Photo-c (1968).						
9-1st app. Serpent Crown (origin in #10 & 12)	4	8	12	28	44	60
8-Sub-Mariner vs. Thing	8	16	24	54	90	125
8-2nd printing (1978)	2	4	6	8	10	12
11-13,15: 15-Last 12¢ issue	4	8	12	22	34	45
14-Sub-Mariner vs. G.A. Human Torch; death of Toro (1st modern app. & only app. Toro, 6/69)	5	10	15	32	51	70
16-20: 19-1st Sting Ray (11/69); Stan Lee, Romita, Heck, Thomas, Everett & Kirby cameos.						
20-Dr. Doom app.	3	6	9	16	23	30
21,23-33,37-39,41,42: 25-Origin Atlantis. 30-Capt. Marvel x-over. 37-Death of Lady Dorma.						
38-Origin retold. 42-Last 15¢ issue.	3	6	9	14	19	24

	GD	VG	FN	VF	VF/NM	NM-
22,40: 22-Dr. Strange x-over. 40-Spider-Man x-over	3	6	9	15	21	26
34-Prelude (w/#35) to 1st Defenders story; Hulk & Silver Surfer x-over	7	14	21	45	73	100
35-Namor/Hulk/Silver Surfer team-up to battle The Avengers-c/story (3/71); hints at teaming up again	5	10	15	35	55	75
36-Wrightson-a(i)	3	6	9	17	25	32
43-King Size Special (52 pgs.)	3	6	9	17	25	32
44,45-Sub-Mariner vs. Human Torch	3	6	9	16	22	28
46-49,56,62,64-72: 47,48-Dr. Doom app. 49-Cosmic Cube story. 62-1st Tales of Atlantis, ends #66. 64-Hitler cameo. 67-New costume; F.F. x-over. 69-Spider-Man x-over (6 panels)	1	3	4	6	8	10
50-1st app. Nita, Namor's niece (later Namorita in New Warriors)	2	4	6	9	12	15
51-55,57,58,60,61,63-Everett issues: 61-Last artwork by Everett; 1st 4 pgs. completed by Mortimer; pgs. 5-20 by Mooney	2	4	6	8	11	14
59-1st battle with Thor; Everett-a	3	6	9	16	23	30
Special 1 (1/71)-r/Tales to Astonish #70-73	3	6	9	17	25	32
Special 2 (1/72)-(52 pgs.)-r/T.T.A. #74-76; Everett-a	3	6	9	14	19	24

NOTE: Bolle a-67. Buscema a(p)-1-8, 20, 24. Colan a(p)-10, 11, 40, 43, 46-49, Special 1, 2; c(p)-10, 11, 40. Craig a-17i, 19-23i. Everett a-45r, 50-55, 57, 58, 59-61(plot), 63(plot); c-47, 48i, 55, 57-59i, 61, Spec. 2. G. Kane c(p)-42-52, 58, 66, 70, 71. Mooney a-24i, 25i, 32-35i, 39i, 42i, 44i, 45i, 60i, 61i, 65p, 66p, 68i. Severin c/a-38i. Starlin c-59p. Tuska a-41p, 42p, 69-71p. Wrightson a-36i. #36, 54-r/stories Sub-Mariner Comics #41 & 39.

SUB-MARINER (The Initiative, follows Civil War series)
Marvel Comics: Aug, 2007 - No. 6 ($2.99, limited series)
1-4: 1-Turner-c/Briones-a/Cherniss & Johnson-s; Iron Man app. 3-Yu-c; Venom app. — 3.00

SUB-MARINER COMICS (1st Series) (The Sub-Mariner #1, 2, 33-42)(Official True Crime Cases #24 on; Amazing Mysteries #32 on; Best Love #33 on)
Timely/Marvel Comics (TCI 1-7/SePI 8/MPI 9-32/Atlas Comics (CCC 33-42)): Spring, 1941 - No. 23, Sum, 1947; No. 24, Wint, 1947 - No. 31, 4/49; No. 32, 7/49; No. 33, 4/54 - No. 42, 10/55

	GD	VG	FN	VF	VF/NM	NM-
1-The Sub-Mariner by Everett & The Angel begin	2850	5700	8550	22,000	41,000	60,000
2-Everett-a	543	1086	1629	3800	6650	9500
3-Churchill assassination-c; 40 pg. S-M story	457	914	1371	3200	5600	8000
4-Everett-a, 40 pgs.; 1 pg. Wolverton-a	364	728	1092	2366	4183	6000
5-Gabrielle/Klein-c	300	600	900	1894	3197	4500
6-10: 9-Wolverton-a, 3 pgs.; flag-c	276	552	828	1725	2863	4000
11-Classic Schomburg-c	283	566	849	1769	2935	4100
12-15	197	394	591	1231	2041	2850
16-20	159	318	477	994	1647	2300
21-Last Angel; Everett-a	121	242	363	756	1253	1750
22-Young Allies app.	121	242	363	756	1253	1750
23-The Human Torch, Namora x-over (Sum/47); 2nd app. Namora after Marvel Mystery #82	138	276	414	863	1432	2000
24-Namora x-over (3rd app.)	122	244	366	763	1269	1775
25-The Blonde Phantom begins (Spr/48), ends No. 31; Kurtzman-a; Namora x-over; last quarterly issue	141	282	423	881	1466	2050
26-28: 28-Namora cover; Everett-a	121	242	363	756	1253	1750
29-31 (4/49): 29-The Human Torch app. 31-Capt. America app.	121	242	363	756	1253	1750
32 (7/49, Scarce)-Origin Sub-Mariner	179	358	537	1119	1860	2600
33 (4/54)-Origin Sub-Mariner; The Human Torch app.; Namora x-over in Sub-Mariner #33-42	103	206	309	644	1072	1500
34,35-Human Torch in each	81	162	243	506	841	1175
36,37,39-41: 36,39-41-Namora app.	79	158	237	494	822	1150
38-Origin Sub-Mariner's wings; Namora app.; last pre-code (2/55)	88	176	264	550	913	1275
42-Last issue	90	180	270	563	932	1300

NOTE: Angel by Gustavson-a, 8. Brodsky c-34-36, 42. Everett a-1-4, 22-24, 26-42; c-32, 33, 40. Maneely a-38; c-37, 39-41. Rico c-27-31. Schomburg c-1-4, 6, 8-18, 20. Sekowsky c-24, 25, 26(w/Rico). Shores c-21-23, 38. Bondage c-13, 22, 24, 25, 34.

SUBSPECIES
Eternity Comics: May, 1991 - No. 4, Aug, 1991 ($2.50, limited series)
1-4: New stories based on horror movie — 2.50

SUBTLE VIOLENTS
CFD Productions: 1991 ($2.50, B&W, mature)

	GD	VG	FN	VF	VF/NM	NM-
1-Linsner-c & story	1	3	4	8	10	12
San Diego Limited Edition	4	8	12	24	37	50

SUE & SALLY SMITH (Formerly My Secret Life)
Charlton Comics: V2#48, Nov, 1962 - No. 54, Nov, 1963 (Flying Nurses)

	GD	VG	FN	VF	VF/NM	NM-
V2#48	3	6	9	17	25	32
49-54	2	4	6	13	18	22

Sugar and Spike #12 © DC

Sunny, America's Sweetheart #12 © FOX

Super Bad James Dynomite #1 © 5-D Comics

	GD 2.0	VG 4.0	FN 6.0	VF 8.0	VF/NM 9.0	NM- 9.2

SUGAR & SPIKE (Also see The Best of DC & DC Silver Age Classics)
National Periodical Publications: Apr-May, 1956 - No. 98, Oct-Nov, 1971

	GD 2.0	VG 4.0	FN 6.0	VF 8.0	VF/NM 9.0	NM- 9.2
1 (Scarce)	300	600	900	1897	3197	4500
2	109	218	327	681	1128	1575
3-5: 3-Letter column begins	71	142	213	444	735	1025
6-10	44	88	132	268	439	610
11-20	37	74	111	213	339	465
21-29: 26-Christmas-c	26	52	78	150	235	320
30-Scribbly & Scribbly, Jr. x-over	26	52	78	154	242	330
31-40	20	40	60	117	184	250
41-60	9	18	27	60	100	140
61-80: 69-1st app. Tornado-Tot-c/story. 72-Origin & 1st app. Bernie the Brain	7	14	21	47	76	105
81-84,86-95: 84-Bernie the Brain apps. as Superman in 1 panel (9/69)	6	12	18	37	59	80
85 (68 pgs.)-r/#72	6	12	18	41	66	90
96 (68 pgs.)	7	14	21	45	73	100
97,98 (52 pgs.)	6	12	18	41	66	90
No. 1 Replica Edition (2002, $2.95) reprint of #1						3.00

NOTE: All written and drawn by Sheldon Mayer.

SUGAR BOWL COMICS (Teen-age)
Famous Funnies: May, 1948 - No. 5, Jan, 1949

	GD 2.0	VG 4.0	FN 6.0	VF 8.0	VF/NM 9.0	NM- 9.2
1-Toth-c/a	15	30	45	83	124	165
2,4,5	9	18	27	50	65	80
3-Toth-a	10	20	30	56	76	95

SUGARFOOT (TV)
Dell Publishing Co.: No. 907, May, 1958 - No. 1209, Oct-Dec, 1961

	GD 2.0	VG 4.0	FN 6.0	VF 8.0	VF/NM 9.0	NM- 9.2
Four Color 907 (#1)-Toth-a, photo-c	12	24	36	84	150	215
Four Color 992 (5-7/59), Toth-a, photo-c	11	22	33	77	136	195
Four Color 1059 (11-1/60), 1098 (5-7/60), 1147 (11-1/61), 1209-all photo-c	8	16	24	58	97	135

SUICIDE SQUAD (See Brave & the Bold and Doom Patrol & Suicide Squad Spec., Legends #3 & note under Star Spangled War stories)
DC Comics: May, 1987 - No. 66, June, 1992 (Direct sales only #32 on)

	GD 2.0	VG 4.0	FN 6.0	VF 8.0	VF/NM 9.0	NM- 9.2
1-66: 9-Millennium x-over. 10-Batman-c/story. 13-JLI app. (Batman). 13-1st Oracle. 27-34,36,37-Snyder-a. 40-43-"The Phoenix Gambit" Batman storyline. 40-Free Batman/Suicide Squad poster						2.50
Annual 1 (1988, $1.50)-Chaykin x-over						2.50

NOTE: Chaykin c-1.

SUICIDE SQUAD (2nd series)
DC Comics: Nov, 2001 - No. 12, Oct, 2002 ($2.50)

	GD 2.0	VG 4.0	FN 6.0	VF 8.0	VF/NM 9.0	NM- 9.2
1-12-Giffen-s/Medina-a; Sgt. Rock app. 4-Heath-a. 10-J. Severin-a. 12-JSA app.						2.50

SUMMER FUN (See Dell Giants)

SUMMER FUN (Formerly Li'l Genius; Holiday Surprise #55)
Charlton Comics: No. 54, Oct, 1966 (Giant)

	GD 2.0	VG 4.0	FN 6.0	VF 8.0	VF/NM 9.0	NM- 9.2
54	4	8	12	22	34	45

SUMMER FUN (Walt Disney's...)
Disney Comics: Summer, 1991 ($2.95, annual, 68 pgs.)

	GD 2.0	VG 4.0	FN 6.0	VF 8.0	VF/NM 9.0	NM- 9.2
1-D. Duck, M. Mouse, Brer Rabbit, Chip 'n' Dale & Pluto, Li'l Bad Wolf, Super Goof, Scamp stories						4.00

SUMMER LOVE (Formerly Brides in Love?)
Charlton Comics: V2#46, Oct, 1965; V2#47, Oct, 1966; V2#48, Nov, 1968

	GD 2.0	VG 4.0	FN 6.0	VF 8.0	VF/NM 9.0	NM- 9.2
V2#46-Beatles-c & 8 pg. story	13	26	39	95	168	240
47-(68 pgs.) Beatles-c & 12 pg. story	9	18	27	65	113	160
48	3	6	9	15	21	26

SUMMER MAGIC (See Movie Comics)

SUNDANCE (See Hotel Deparee...)

SUNDANCE KID (Also see Blazing Six-Guns)
Skywald Publications: June, 1971 - No. 3, Sept, 1971 (52 pgs.)(Pre-code reprints and new-s)

	GD 2.0	VG 4.0	FN 6.0	VF 8.0	VF/NM 9.0	NM- 9.2
1-Durango Kid; Two Kirby Bullseye-r	3	6	9	14	19	24
2,3: 2-Swift Arrow, Durango Kid, Bullseye by S&K; Meskin plus 1 pg. origin						
3-Durango Kid, Billy the Kid, Red Hawk-r	2	4	6	9	13	16

SUNDAY PIX (Christian religious)
David C. Cook Pub/USA Weekly Newsprint Color Comics: V1#1, Mar,1949 - V16#26, July 19, 1964 (7x10", 12 pgs., mail subscription only)

	GD 2.0	VG 4.0	FN 6.0	VF 8.0	VF/NM 9.0	NM- 9.2
V1#1	7	14	21	37	46	55
V1#2-up	5	10	15	24	30	35

	GD 2.0	VG 4.0	FN 6.0	VF 8.0	VF/NM 9.0	NM- 9.2
V2#1-52 (1950)	5	10	15	22	26	30
V3-V6 (1951-1953)	4	8	12	17	21	24
V7-V11#1-7,23-52 (1954-1959)	2	4	6	11	16	20
V11#8-22 (2/22-5/31/59) H.G. Wells First Men in the Moon serial	2	4	6	13	18	22
V12#1-19,21-52; V13-V15#1,2,9-52; V16#1-26(7/19/64)	2	4	6	9	13	16
V12#20 (5/15/60) 2 page interview with Peanuts' Charles Schulz	4	8	12	22	34	45
V15#3-8 (2/24/63) John Glenn, Christian astronaut	2	4	6	13	18	22

SUN DEVILS
DC Comics: July, 1984 - No. 12, June, 1985 ($1.25, maxi series)

	GD 2.0	VG 4.0	FN 6.0	VF 8.0	VF/NM 9.0	NM- 9.2
1-12: 6-Death of Sun Devil						2.50

SUNDIATA: A LEGEND OF AFRICA
NBM Publishing Inc.: 2002 ($15.95, hardcover with dustjacket)

	GD 2.0	VG 4.0	FN 6.0	VF 8.0	VF/NM 9.0	NM- 9.2
nn-Will Eisner-s/a; adaptation of an African folk tale						16.00

SUN FUN KOMIKS
Sun Publications: 1939 (15¢, B&W & red)

	GD 2.0	VG 4.0	FN 6.0	VF 8.0	VF/NM 9.0	NM- 9.2
1-Satire on comics (rare)	59	118	177	369	610	850

SUNFIRE & BIG HERO SIX (See Alpha Flight)
Marvel Comics: Sept, 1998 - No. 3, Nov, 1998 ($2.50, limited series)

	GD 2.0	VG 4.0	FN 6.0	VF 8.0	VF/NM 9.0	NM- 9.2
1-3-Lobdell-s						2.50

SUN GIRL (See The Human Torch & Marvel Mystery Comics #88)
Marvel Comics (CCC): Aug, 1948 - No. 3, Dec, 1948

	GD 2.0	VG 4.0	FN 6.0	VF 8.0	VF/NM 9.0	NM- 9.2
1-Sun Girl begins; Miss America app.	169	338	507	1056	1753	2450
2,3: 2-The Blonde Phantom begins	116	232	348	725	1200	1675

SUNNY, AMERICA'S SWEETHEART (Formerly Cosmo Cat #1-10)
Fox Features Syndicate: No. 11, Dec, 1947 - No. 14, June, 1948

	GD 2.0	VG 4.0	FN 6.0	VF 8.0	VF/NM 9.0	NM- 9.2
11-Feldstein-c/a	103	206	309	644	1072	1500
12-14-Feldstein-c/a; 13,14-Lingerie panels. 13-L.B. Cole-a	76	152	228	475	788	1100
I.W. Reprint #8-Feldstein-a; r/Fox issue	10	20	30	73	129	185

SUN-RUNNERS (Also see Tales of the...)
Pacific Comics/Eclipse Comics/Amazing Comics: 2/84 - No. 3, 5/84; No. 4, 11/84 - No. 7, 1986 (Baxter paper)

	GD 2.0	VG 4.0	FN 6.0	VF 8.0	VF/NM 9.0	NM- 9.2
1-7: P. Smith-a in #2-4						2.50
Christmas Special 1 (1987, $1.95)-By Amazing						2.50

SUNSET CARSON (See also Cowboy Western)
Charlton Comics: Feb, 1951 - No. 4, 1951 (No month) (Photo-c on each)

	GD 2.0	VG 4.0	FN 6.0	VF 8.0	VF/NM 9.0	NM- 9.2
1-Photo/retouched-c (Scarce, all issues)	72	144	216	450	750	1050
2-Kit Carson story; adapts "Kansas Raiders" w/Brian Donlevy, Audie Murphy & Margaret Chapman	53	106	159	323	537	750
3,4	41	82	123	250	400	550

SUNSET PASS (See Zane Grey & 4-Color #230)

SUPER ANIMALS PRESENTS PIDGY & THE MAGIC GLASSES
Star Publications: Dec, 1953 (25¢, came w/glasses)

	GD 2.0	VG 4.0	FN 6.0	VF 8.0	VF/NM 9.0	NM- 9.2
1-(3-D Comics)-L. B. Cole-a	41	82	123	250	400	550

SUPER BAD JAMES DYNOMITE
5-D Comics: Dec, 2005 - No. 5, Feb, 2007 ($3.99)

	GD 2.0	VG 4.0	FN 6.0	VF 8.0	VF/NM 9.0	NM- 9.2
1-5-Created by the Wayans brothers						4.00

SUPERBOY
DC Comics: Jan, 1942

nn-Ashcan comic, not distributed to newsstands, only for in house use. Covers were produced, but not the rest of the book. A CGC certified 9.2 copy sold in 2003 for $6,600.

SUPERBOY (See Adventure, Aurora, DC Comics Presents, DC 100 Page Super Spectacular #15, DC Super Stars, 80 Page Giant #10, More Fun Comics, The New Advs. of... & Superman Family #191, Young Justice)

SUPERBOY (1st Series)(...& the Legion of Super-Heroes with #231)
(Becomes The Legion of Super-Heroes No. 259 on)
National Periodical Publ./DC Comics: Mar-Apr, 1949 - No. 258, Dec, 1979 (#1-16: 52 pgs.)

	GD 2.0	VG 4.0	FN 6.0	VF 8.0	VF/NM 9.0	NM- 9.2
1-Superman cover; intro in More Fun #101 (1-2/45)	829	1658	2487	5803	10,152	14,500
2-Used in SOTI, pg. 35-36,226	228	456	684	1425	2363	3300
3	172	344	516	1075	1788	2500
4,5: 5-1st pre-Supergirl tryout (c/story, 11-12/49)	117	234	351	731	1216	1700
6-9: 8-1st Superbaby	102	204	306	638	1057	1475
10-1st app. Lana Lang	110	220	330	688	1144	1600

Superboy #69 © DC

Superboy #226 © DC

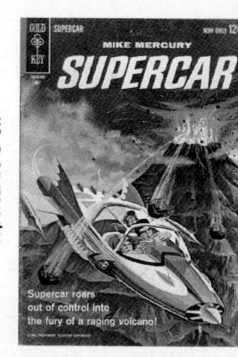

Supercar #3 © GK

	GD 2.0	VG 4.0	FN 6.0	VF 8.0	VF/NM 9.0	NM- 9.2
11-15: 2nd Lana Lang app.; 1st Lana cover	76	152	228	475	788	1100
16-20: 20-2nd Jor-El cover	53	106	159	323	537	750
21-26,28-30: 21-Lana Lang app.	43	86	129	262	431	600
27-Low distribution	45	90	135	275	450	625
31-38: 38-Last pre-code issue (1/55)	38	76	114	219	347	475
39-48,50 (7/56)	34	68	102	195	308	420
49 (6/56)-1st app. Metallo (Jor-El's robot)	36	72	108	208	329	450
51-60: 52-1st S.A. issue. 56-Krypto-c	24	48	72	139	220	300
61-67	20	40	60	117	184	250
68-Origin/1st app. original Bizarro (10-11/58)	59	118	177	369	610	850
69-77,79: 76-1st Supermonkey	16	32	48	94	147	200
78-Origin Mr. Mxyzptlk & Superboy's costume	24	48	72	139	220	300
80-1st meeting Superboy/Supergirl (4/60)	22	44	66	128	202	275
81,83-85,87,88: 83-Origin/1st app. Kryptonite Kid	10	20	30	71	126	180
82-1st Bizarro Krypto	11	22	33	75	133	190
86-(1/61)-4th Legion app; Intro Pete Ross	17	34	51	128	227	325
89-(6/61)-1st app. Mon-el; 2nd Phantom Zone	26	52	78	211	348	485
90-92: 90-Pete Ross learns Superboy's I.D. 92-Last 10¢ issue	10	20	30	68	119	170
93-10th Legion app.(12/61); Chameleon Boy app.	10	20	30	71	126	180
94-97,99: 94-1st app. Superboy Revenge Squad	9	18	27	60	100	140
98-(7/62)-18th Legion app; origin & 1st app. Ultra Boy; Pete Ross joins Legion	11	22	33	79	140	200
100-(10/62)-Ultra Boy app; 1st app. Phantom Zone villains, Dr. Xadu & Erndine. 2 pg. map of Krypton; origin Superboy retold; r-cover of Superman #1	18	36	54	132	234	335
101-160: 104-Origin Phantom Zone. 115-Atomic bomb-c. 117-Legion app.	8	16	24	54	90	125
121-128: 124-(10/65)-1st app. Insect Queen (Lana Lang). 125-Legion cameo. 126-Origin Krypto the Super Dog retold with new facts	7	14	21	47	76	105
129-(80-pg. Giant G-22)-Reprints origin Mon-el	8	16	24	58	97	135
130-137,139,140: 131-Legion statues cameo in Dog Legionnaires story. 132-1st app. Supremo. 133-Superboy meets Robin	6	12	18	39	62	85
138 (80-pg. Giant G-35)	7	14	21	47	76	105
141-146,148-155,157: 145-Superboy's parents regain their youth. 148-Legion app. 157-Last 12¢ issue	5	10	15	30	48	65
147(6/68)-Giant G-47; 1st origin of L.S.H. (Saturn Girl, Lightning Lad, Cosmic Boy); origin Legion of Super-Pets-r/Adv. #293	6	12	18	41	66	90
147 Replica Edition (2003, $6.95) reprints entire issue; cover recreation by Ordway						7.00
156,165,174 (Giants G-59,71,83): 165-r/1st app. Krypto the Superdog from Adventure Comics #210	5	10	15	30	48	65
158-164,166-171,175: 171-1st app. Aquaboy	3	6	9	16	23	30
172,173,176-Legion app.: 172-1st app. & origin Yango (The Super Ape). 176-Partial photo-c; last 15¢ issue	3	6	9	17	25	32
177-184,186,187 (All 52 pgs.): 182-All new origin of the classic World's Finest team (Superman & Batman) as teenagers (2/72, 22pgs.). 184-Origin Dial H for Hero-r	3	6	9	18	27	35
185-Also listed as DC 100 Pg. Super Spectacular #12; Legion-c/story; Teen Titans, Kid Eternity(r/Hit #46), Star Spangled Kid-r(S.S. #55) (see DC 100 Pg. Super Spectacular #12 for price)						
188-190,192,194,196: 188-Origin Karkan. 196-Last Superboy solo story	2	4	6	10	14	18
191,193,195: 191-Origin Sunboy retold; Legion app. 193-Chameleon Boy & Shrinking Violet get new costumes. 195-1st app. Erg-1/Wildfire; Phantom Girl gets new costume	2	4	6	11	16	20
197-Legion series begins; Lightning Lad's new costume	3	6	9	19	28	38
198,199: 198-Element Lad & Princess Projectra get new costumes	3	6	9	14	19	24
200-Bouncing Boy & Duo Damsel marry; J'onn J'onzz cameo	3	6	9	16	22	28
201,204,206,207,209: 201-Re-intro Erg-1 as Wildfire. 204-Supergirl resigns from Legion. 206-Ferro Lad & Invisible Kid app. 209-Karate Kid gets new costume	2	4	6	10	14	18
202,205-(100 pgs.): 202-Light Lass gets new costume; Mike Grell's 1st comic work-i (5-6/74)	4	8	12	28	44	60
203-Invisible Kid killed by Validus	3	6	9	15	21	26
208,210: 208-(68 pgs.). 208-Legion of Super-Villains app. 210-Origin Karate Kid	3	6	9	14	19	24
211-220: 212-Matter-Eater Lad resigns. 216-1st app. Tyroc, who joins the Legion in #218	2	4	6	8	11	14
221-230,246-249: 226-Intro. Dawnstar. 228-Death of Chemical King	1	3	4	6	8	10
231-245: (Giants). 240-Origin Dawnstar. 242-(52 pgs.). 243-Legion of Substitute Heroes app.						
243-245-(44 pgs.)	2	4	6	9	13	16
244,245-(Whitman variants; low print run, no issue# shown on cover)	3	6	9	14	19	24
246-248-(Whitman variants; low ...)	2	4	6	10	14	18
250-258: 253-Intro Blok. 257-Return of Bouncing Boy & Duo Damsel by Ditko	1	2	3	5	6	8
251-258-(Whitman variants; low print run)	2	4	6	8	11	14
Annual 1 (Sum/64, 84 pgs.)-Origin Krypto-r	17	34	51	128	227	325
Spectacular 1 (1980, Giant)-1st comic distributed only through comic stores; mostly-r	1	2	3	5	7	9

NOTE: **Neal Adams** c-143, 145, 146, 148-155, 157-161, 163, 164, 166-168, 172, 173, 175, 176, 178. **M. Anderson** a-178,179, 245i. Ditko a-257p. **Grell** a-202i, 203-219, 220-224p, 235p; c-207-232, 235, 236p, 237, 239p, 240p, 243p, 246, 258. **Nasser** a(p)-222, 225, 226, 230, 231, 233, 236. **Simonson** a-237p. **Starlin** a(p)-239, 250, 251; c-238. **Staton** a-227p, 243-249p, 252-258p; c-247-251p. **Swan/Moldoff** c-109. **Tuska** a-172, 173, 176, 183, 235p. **Wood** inks-153-155, 157-161. Legion app.-172, 173, 176, 177, 183, 184, 188, 190, 191, 193, 195, 197-258.

SUPERBOY (TV)(2nd Series)(The Adventures of...#19 on)
DC Comics: Feb., 1990 - No. 22, Dec, 1991 ($1.00/$1.25)

1-22: Mooney-a(p) in 1-8,18-20; 1-Photo-c from TV show. 8-Bizarro-c/story; Arthur Adams-a(i). 9-12,14-17-Swan-p						3.00
...Special 1 (1992, $1.75) Swan-a						3.00

SUPERBOY (3rd Series)
DC Comics: Feb., 1994 - No. 100, Jul, 2002 ($1.50/$1.95/$1.99/$2.25)

1-Metropolis Kid from Reign of the Supermen						4.00
2-8,0,9-24,26-76: 6,7-Worlds Collide Pts. 3 & 8. 8-(9/94)-Zero Hour x-over. 0-(10/94). 9-(11/94)-King Shark app. 21-Legion app. 33-Final Night. 38-41-"Meltdown". 45-Legion-c/app. 47-Green Lantern-c/app. 50-Last Boy on Earth begins. 60-Crosses Hypertime. 68-Demon-c/app.						2.50
25-($2.95)-New Gods & Female Furies app.; w/pin-ups						3.50
77-99: 77-Begin $2.25-c. 79-Superboy's powers return. 80,81-Titans app. 83-New costume. 85-Batgirl app. 90,91-Our Worlds at War x-over						2.50
100-($3.50) Sienkiewicz-c; Grummett & McCrea-a; Superman cameo						3.50
#1,000,000 (11/98) 853rd Century x-over						2.50
Annual 1 (1994, $2.95, 68 pgs.)-Elseworlds story, Pt. 2 of The Super Seven (see Adventures Of Superman Annual #6)						3.00
Annual 2 (1995, $3.95)-Year One story						4.00
Annual 3 (1996, $2.95)-Legends of the Dead Earth						3.00
Annual 4 (1997, $3.95)-Pulp Heroes story						4.00
...Plus 1 (Jan, 1997, $2.95) w/Capt. Marvel Jr.						3.00
...Plus 2 (Fall, 1997, $2.95) w/Slither (Scare Tactics)						3.00
...Risk Double-Shot 1 (Feb, 1998, $1.95) w/Risk (Teen Titans)						2.50

SUPERBOY & THE RAVERS
DC Comics: Sept., 1996 - No. 19, March, 1998 ($1.95)

1-19: 4-Adam Strange app. 7-Impulse-c/app. 9-Superman-c/app.						2.50

SUPERBOY COMICS
DC Comics: Jan. 1942

nn - Ashcan comic, not distributed to newsstands, only for in-house use. Cover art is Detective Comics #57 with interior being Action Comics #38. A CGC certified 9.2 copy sold for $6,600 in 2003.

SUPERBOY/ROBIN: WORLD'S FINEST THREE
DC Comics: 1996 - No. 2, 1996 ($4.95, squarebound, limited series)

1,2: Superboy & Robin vs. Metallo & Poison Ivy; Karl Kesel & Chuck Dixon scripts; Tom Grummett-c(p)/a(p)						5.00

SUPERBOY'S LEGION (Elseworlds)
DC Comics: 2001 - No. 2, 2001 ($5.95, squarebound, limited series)

1,2-31st century Superboy forms Legion; Farmer-s/i; Davis-a(p)/c						6.00

SUPER BRAT (Li'l Genius #5 on)
Toby Press: Jan, 1954 - No. 4, July, 1954

	GD 2.0	VG 4.0	FN 6.0	VF 8.0	VF/NM 9.0	NM- 9.2
1	8	16	24	42	54	65
2-4: 4-Li'l Teevy by Mel Lazarus	5	10	15	24	30	35
I.W. Reprint #1,2,3,7,8('58): 1-r/#1	2	4	6	8	10	12
I.W. (Super) Reprint #10('63)	2	4	6	8	10	12

SUPERCAR (TV)
Gold Key: Nov., 1962 - No. 4, Aug, 1963 (All painted-c)

	GD 2.0	VG 4.0	FN 6.0	VF 8.0	VF/NM 9.0	NM- 9.2
1	16	32	48	118	209	300
2,3	9	18	27	63	107	150
4-Last issue	10	20	30	73	129	185

SUPER CAT (Formerly Frisky Animals; also see Animal Crackers)
Star Publications #56-58/Ajax/Farrell Publ. (Four Star Comic Corp.):
No. 56, Nov, 1953 - No. 58, May, 1954; Aug, 1957 - No. 4, May, 1958

Super Comics #74 © DELL

Super Friends #13 © DC

Supergirl #3 © DC

	GD	VG	FN	VF	VF/NM	NM-
	2.0	4.0	6.0	8.0	9.0	9.2
56-58-L.B. Cole-c on all	20	40	60	115	180	245
1(1957-Ajax)-"The Adventures of…" c-only	10	20	30	54	72	90
2-4	7	14	21	35	43	50

SUPER CIRCUS (TV)
Cross Publishing Co.: Jan, 1951 - No. 5, Sept, 1951 (Mary Hartline)

	GD	VG	FN	VF	VF/NM	NM-
1-(52 pgs.)-Cast photos on-c	15	30	45	85	130	175
2-Cast photos on-c	10	20	30	58	79	100
3-5	9	18	27	50	65	80

SUPER CIRCUS (TV)
Dell Publ. Co.: No. 542, Mar, 1954 - No. 694, Mar, 1956 (Mary Hartline)

	GD	VG	FN	VF	VF/NM	NM-
Four Color 542: Mary Hartline photo-c	7	14	21	47	76	105
Four Color 592,694: Mary Hartline photo-c	6	12	18	43	69	95

SUPER COMICS
Dell Publishing Co.: May, 1938 - No. 121, Feb-Mar, 1949

	GD	VG	FN	VF	VF/NM	NM-
1-Terry & The Pirates, The Gumps, Dick Tracy, Little Orphan Annie, Little Joe, Gasoline Alley, Smilin' Jack, Smokey Stover, Smitty, Tiny Tim, Moon Mullins, Harold Teen, Winnie Winkle begin	292	584	876	1679	2590	3500
2	106	212	318	610	943	1275
3	94	188	282	541	833	1125
4,5: 4-Dick Tracy-c; also #8-10,17,26(part),31	73	146	219	420	648	875
6-10	58	116	174	334	517	700
11-20: 20-Smilin' Jack-c (also #29,32)	46	92	138	265	408	550
21-29: 21-Magic Morro begins (origin & 1st app., 2/40). 22,27-Ken Ernst-c (also #25?); Magic Morro c-22,25,27,34	36	72	108	208	329	450
30- "Sea Hawk" movie adaptation-c/story with Errol Flynn	38	76	114	216	343	470
31-40: 34-Ken Ernst-c	30	60	90	174	275	375
41-50: 41-Intro Lightning Jim. 43-Terry & The Pirates ends	25	50	75	148	232	315
51-60	19	38	57	109	172	235
61-70: 62-Flag-c. 65-Brenda Starr-r begin? 67-X-mas-c	17	34	51	98	154	210
71-80	14	28	42	80	115	150
81-99	13	26	39	74	105	135
100	14	28	42	78	112	145
101-115-Last Dick Tracy (moves to own title)	10	20	30	56	76	
116-121: 116,118-All Smokey Stover. 117-All Gasoline Alley. 119-121-Terry & The Pirates app. in all	9	18	27	50	65	80

SUPER COPS, THE
Red Circle Productions (Archie): July, 1974 (one-shot)

	GD	VG	FN	VF	VF/NM	NM-
1-Morrow-c/a; art by Pino, Hack, Thorne	1	3	4	6	8	10

SUPER COPS
Now Comics: Sept, 1990 - No. 4, Dec?, 1990 ($1.75)

	NM-
1-($2.75, 52 pgs.)-Dave Dorman painted-c (both printings)	2.75
2-4	2.50

SUPER CRACKED (See Cracked)

SUPER DC GIANT (25-50¢, all 68-52 pg. Giants)
National Per. Publ.: No. 13, 9-10/70 - No. 26, 7-8/71; V3#27, Summer, 1976 (No #1-12)

	GD	VG	FN	VF	VF/NM	NM-
S-13-Binky	10	20	30	73	129	185
S-14-Top Guns of the West; Kubert-c; Trigger Twins, Johnny Thunder, Wyoming Kid-r; Moreira-r (9-10/70)	5	10	15	32	51	70
S-15-Western Comics; Kubert-c; Pow Wow Smith, Vigilante, Buffalo Bill-r; new Gil Kane-a (9-10/70)	5	10	15	32	51	70
S-16-Best of the Brave & the Bold; Batman-r & Metamorpho origin-r from Brave & the Bold; Spectre pin-up.	4	8	12	24	37	50
S-17-Love 1970 (scarce)	24	48	72	175	313	450
S-18-Three Mouseketeers; Dizzy Dog, Doodles Duck, Bo Bunny-r; Sheldon Mayer-a	9	18	27	61	103	145
S-19-Jerry Lewis; Neal Adams pin-up	9	18	27	65	113	160
S-20-House of Mystery; N. Adams-c; Kirby-r(3)	6	12	18	43	69	95
S-21-Love 1971 (scarce)	29	58	87	216	388	560
S-22-Top Guns of the West; Kubert-c	4	8	12	22	34	45
S-23-The Unexpected	4	8	12	26	41	55
S-24-Supergirl	4	8	12	22	34	45
S-25-Challengers of the Unknown; all Kirby/Wood-r	3	6	9	21	32	42
S-26-Aquaman (1971)-r/S.A. Aquaman origin story from Showcase #30	3	6	9	21	32	42
27-Strange Flying Saucers Adventures (Sum, 1976)	3	6	9	21	30	40

NOTE: *Sid Greene* r-27p(2), *Heath* r-27. *G. Kane* a-14(2), 15, 27(p). *Kubert* r-16.

SUPER-DOOPER COMICS

Able Mfg. Co./Harvey: 1946 - No. 8, 1946 (10¢, 32 pgs., paper-c)

	GD	VG	FN	VF	VF/NM	NM-
	2.0	4.0	6.0	8.0	9.0	9.2
1-The Clock, Gangbuster app.	21	42	63	122	191	260
2	14	28	42	80	115	150
3,4,6	13	26	39	72	101	130
5-Capt. Freedom	14	28	42	80	115	150
7,8-Shock Gibson. 7-Where's Theres A Will by Ed Wheelan, Steve Case Crime Rover, Penny & Ullysses Jr. 8-Sam Hill app.	14	28	42	80	115	150

SUPER DUCK COMICS (The Cockeyed Wonder) (See Jolly Jingles)
MLJ Mag. No. 1-4(9/45)/Close-Up No. 5 on (Archie): Fall, 1944 - No. 94, Dec, 1960 (Also see Laugh #24)(#1-5 are quarterly)

	GD	VG	FN	VF	VF/NM	NM-
1-Origin; Hitler & Hirohito-c	57	114	171	356	591	825
2-Bill Vigoda-c	26	52	78	152	239	325
3-5: 4-20-Al Fagaly-c (most)	17	34	51	98	154	210
6-10	14	28	42	80	115	150
11-20(6/48)	10	20	30	58	79	100
21,23-40 (10/51)	9	18	27	52	69	85
22-Used in SOTI, pg. 35,307,308	10	20	30	56	76	95
41-60 (2/55)	8	16	24	42	54	65
61-94	7	14	21	35	43	50

SUPER DUPER (Formerly Pocket Comics #1-4?)
Harvey Publications: No. 5, 1941 - No. 11, 1941

	GD	VG	FN	VF	VF/NM	NM-
5-Captain Freedom & Shock Gibson app.	32	64	96	186	293	400
8,11	20	40	60	117	184	250

SUPER DUPER COMICS (Formerly Latest Comics?)
F. E. Howard Publ.: No. 3, May-June, 1947

	GD	VG	FN	VF	VF/NM	NM-
3-1st app. Mr. Monster	15	30	45	90	140	190

SUPER FRIENDS (TV) (Also see Best of DC & Limited Collectors' Edition)
National Periodical Publications/DC Comics: Nov, 1976 - No. 47, Aug, 1981 (#14 is 44 pgs.)

	GD	VG	FN	VF	VF/NM	NM-
1-Superman, Batman, Robin, Wonder Woman, Aquaman, Atom, Wendy, Marvin & Wonder Dog begin (1st Super Friends)	4	8	12	24	37	50
2-Penquin-c/sty	2	4	6	13	18	22
3-5	2	4	6	11	16	20
6-10,14: 7-1st app. Wonder Twins & The Seraph. 8-1st app. Jack O'Lantern.	2	4	6	9	13	16
9-1st app. Icemaiden. 14-Origin Wonder Twins	2	4	6	9	13	16
11-13,15-30: 13-1st app. Dr. Mist. 25-1st app. Fire as Green Fury. 28-Bizarro app.	1	2	3	4	6	10
13-16,20-23,25,26,29-(Whitman variants; low print run, no issue# on cover)	2	4	6	8	10	12
31,47: 31-Black Orchid app. 47-Origin Fire & Green Fury	2	4	6	8	10	12
32-46: 36,43-Plastic Man app.	1	2	3	5	7	9
TBP (2001, $14.95) r/#1,6-9,14,21,27 & L.C.E. C-41; Alex Ross-c						15.00
…: Truth, Justice and Peace TPB (2003, $14.95) r/#10,12,13,25,28,29,31,36,37						15.00

NOTE: *Estrada* a-1p, 2p. *Orlando* a-1p. *Staton* a-43, 45.

SUPER FUN
Gillmor Magazines: Jan, 1956 (By A.W. Nugent)

	GD	VG	FN	VF	VF/NM	NM-
1-Comics, puzzles, cut-outs by A.W. Nugent	7	14	21	35	43	50

SUPER FUNNIES (…Western Funnies #3,4)
Superior Comics Publishers Ltd. (Canada): Dec, 1953 - No. 4, Sept, 1954

	GD	VG	FN	VF	VF/NM	NM-
1-(3-D, 10¢)-…Presents Dopey Duck; make your own 3-D glasses cut-out inside front-c; did not come w/glasses	35	70	105	204	322	440
2-Horror & crime satire	14	28	42	76	108	140
3-Phantom Ranger-c/s; Geronimo, Billy the Kid app.	9	18	27	47	61	75
4-Phantom Ranger-c/story	9	18	27	47	61	75

SUPERGIRL
DC Comics: Feb. 1944

nn - Ashcan comic, not distributed to newsstands, only for in-house use. Cover art is Boy Commandos #1 with interior being Action Comics #80   (no known sales)

SUPERGIRL (See Action, Adventure #281, Brave & the Bold, Crisis on Infinite Earths #7, Daring New Advs. of…, Super DC Giant, Superman Family, & Super-Team Family)

SUPERGIRL
National Periodical Publ.: Nov, 1972 - No. 9, Dec-Jan, 1973-74; No. 10, Sept-Oct, 1974 (1st solo title)(20¢)

	GD	VG	FN	VF	VF/NM	NM-
1-Zatanna back-up stories begin, end #5	6	12	18	41	66	90
2-4,6,7,9	3	6	9	20	30	40
5,8,10: 5-Zatanna origin-r. 8-JLA x-over; Batman cameo. 10-Prez	3	6	9	21	32	42

NOTE: *Zatanna* in #1-5, 7(Guest); Prez app. in #10. #1-10 are 20¢ issues.

Supergirl (1996 series) #60 © DC

Supergirl (2005 series) #18 © DC

Super Magician Comics #8 © CN

	GD 2.0	VG 4.0	FN 6.0	VF 8.0	VF/NM 9.0	NM- 9.2

SUPERGIRL (Formerly Daring New Adventures of...)
DC Comics: No. 14, Dec, 1983 - No. 23, Sept, 1984

14-23: 16-Ambush Bug app. 20-JLA & New Teen Titans app.						3.00
...Movie Special (1985)-Adapts movie; Morrow-a; photo back-c						4.00

SUPERGIRL
DC Comics: Feb, 1994 - No. 4, May, 1994 ($1.50, limited series)

1-4: Guice-a(i)						3.00

SUPERGIRL (See Showcase '96 #8)
DC Comics: Sept, 1996 - No. 80, May, 2003 ($1.95/$1.99/$2.25/$2.50)

	GD	VG	FN	VF	VF/NM	NM-
1-Peter David scripts & Gary Frank-c/a	1	2	3	5	6	8
1-2nd printing						3.00
2,4-9: 4-Gorilla Grodd-c/app. 6-Superman-c/app. 9-Last Frank-a						4.00
3-Final Night, Gorilla Grodd app.						5.00
10-19: 14-Genesis x-over. 16-Power Girl app.						3.50
20-35: 20-Millennium Giants x-over; Superman app. 23-Steel-c/app. 24-Resurrection Man x-over. 25-Comet ID revealed; begin $1.99-c						3.00
36-46: 36,37-Young Justice x-over						2.50
47-49,51-74: 47-Begin $2.25-c. 51-Adopts costume from animated series. 54-Green Lantern app. 59-61-Our Worlds at War x-over. 62-Two-Face-c/app. 66,67-Demon-c/app. 68-74-Mary Marvel app. 70-Nauck-a. 73-Begin $2.50-c						2.50
50-($3.95) Supergirl's final battle with the Carnivore						4.00
75-80: 75-Re-intro. Kara Zor-El; cover swipe of Action #252 by Haynes; Benes-a. 78-Spectre app. 80-Last issue; Romita-c						2.50
#1,000,000 (11/98) 853rd Century x-over						3.00
Annual 1 (1996, $2.95)-Legends of the Dead Earth						3.00
Annual 2 (1997, $3.95)-Pulp Heroes; LSH app.; Chiodo-c						4.00
...: Many Happy Returns TPB (2003, $14.95) r/#75-80; intro. by Peter David						15.00
...Plus (2/97, $2.95) Capt.(Mary) Marvel-c/app.; David-s/Frank-a						3.00
.../Prysm Double-Shot 1 (Feb, 1998, $1.95) w/Prysm (Teen Titans)						2.50
...: Wings (2001, $5.95) Elseworlds; DeMatteis-s/Talagson-a						6.00
TPB-('98, $14.95) r/Showcase '96 #8 & #1-9						15.00

SUPERGIRL (See Superman/Batman #8 & #19)
DC Comics: No. 0, Oct 2005 - Present ($2.99)

0-Reprints Superman/Batman #19 with white variant of that cover						3.00
1-Loeb/s-Churchill-a; two covers by Churchill & Turner; Power Girl app.						5.00
1-2nd printing with B&W sketch variant of Turner-c						3.00
1-3rd printing with variant-c homage to Adventure #252 by Churchill						3.00
2-4: 2-Teen Titans app. 3-Outsiders app.; covers by Turner & Churchill						3.00
5-($3.99) Supergirl vs. Supergirl; Churchill & Turner-c						4.00
6-20: 6-9-One Year Later; Power Girl app. 11-Intro. Powerboy. 12-Terra debut; Conner-a 20-Amazons Attack x-over						3.00
...: Candor TPB (2007, $14.99) r/#6-9; and pages from JSA Classified #2, Superman #223, Superman/Batman #27 and JLA #122,123						15.00
...: Power TPB (2006, $14.99) r/#1-5 and Superman/Batman #19; variant-c gallery						15.00

SUPERGIRL AND THE LEGION OF SUPER-HEROES (Continues from Legion of Super-Heroes #15, Apr, 2006)
DC Comics: No. 16, May, 2006 - Present ($2.99)

16-Supergirl appears in the 31st century						4.00
16-2nd printing						3.00
17-33: 23-Mon-el cameo. 24,25-Mon-el returns						3.00
...: Adult Education TPB (2007, $14.99) r/#20-25 & LSH #6,9,13-15						15.00
...: Strange Visitor From Another Century TPB (2006, $14.99) r/#16-19 & LSH #11,12,15						15.00

SUPERGIRL/LEX LUTHOR SPECIAL (Supergirl and Team Luthor on-c)
DC Comics: 1993 ($2.50, 68 pgs., one-shot)

1-Pin-ups by Byrne & Thibert						2.50

SUPER GOOF (Walt Disney) (See Dynabrite & The Phantom Blot)
Gold Key No. 1-57/Whitman No. 58 on: Oct, 1965 - No. 74, July, 1984

	GD	VG	FN	VF	VF/NM	NM-
1	4	8	12	28	44	60
2-5	3	6	9	16	23	30
6-10	3	6	9	14	19	24
11-20	2	4	6	8	11	14
21-30	1	3	4	6	8	10
31-50	1	2	3	4	5	7
51-57						6.00
58,59 (Whitman)	1	2	3	5	6	8
60(8/80), 62(11/80) 2-pack only (scarce)	3	6	9	20	30	40
61(9-10/80) 3-pack only (rare)	4	8	12	22	34	45
63-66('81)	1	2	3	5	6	8
63 (1/81, 40¢-c) Cover price error variant (scarce)	2	4	6	10	14	18
67-69: 67(2/82), 68(2-3/82), 69(3/82)						6.00

	GD	VG	FN	VF	VF/NM	NM-
70-74 (#90180 on-c; pre-pack, nd, nd code): 70(5/83), 71(8/83), 72(5/84), 73(6/84), 74(7/84)	3	6	9	14	19	24

NOTE: Reprints in #16, 24, 28, 29, 37, 38, 43, 45, 46, 54(1/2), 56-58, 65(1/2), 72(r-#2).

SUPER GREEN BERET (Tod Holton...)
Lightning Comics (Milson Publ. Co.): Apr, 1967 - No. 2, Jun, 1967

	GD	VG	FN	VF	VF/NM	NM-
1-(25¢, 68 pgs)	5	10	15	30	48	65
2-(25¢, 68 pgs)	4	8	12	21	32	42

SUPER HEROES (See Giant-Size... & Marvel...)

SUPER HEROES
Dell Publishing Co.: Jan, 1967 - No. 4, June, 1967

	GD	VG	FN	VF	VF/NM	NM-
1-Origin & 1st app. Fab 4	4	8	12	24	37	50
2-4	3	6	9	17	25	32

SUPER-HEROES BATTLE SUPER-GORILLAS (See DC Special #16)
National Periodical Publications: Winter, 1976 (52 pgs., all reprints, one-shot)

	GD	VG	FN	VF	VF/NM	NM-
1-Superman, Batman, Flash stories; Infantino-a(p)	2	4	6	9	12	15

SUPER HEROES VERSUS SUPER VILLAINS
Archie Publications (Radio Comics): July, 1966 (no month given)(68 pgs.)

	GD	VG	FN	VF	VF/NM	NM-
1-Flyman, Black Hood, Web, Shield-r; Reinman-a	6	12	18	41	66	90

SUPERHERO WOMEN, THE - FEATURING THE FABULOUS FEMALES OF MARVEL COMICS (See Fireside Book Series)

SUPERICHIE (Formerly Super Richie)
Harvey Publications: No. 5, Oct, 1976 - No. 18, Jan, 1979 (52 pgs. giants)

	GD	VG	FN	VF	VF/NM	NM-
5-Origin/1st app. new costumes for Rippy & Crashman	2	4	6	9	13	16
6-18	2	4	6	8	10	12

SUPERIOR STORIES
Nesbit Publishers, Inc.: May-June, 1955 - No. 4, Nov-Dec, 1955

	GD	VG	FN	VF	VF/NM	NM-
1-The Invisible Man by H.G. Wells	23	46	69	132	209	285
2-4: 2-The Pirate of the Gulf by J.H. Ingrahams. 3-Wreck of the Grosvenor by William Clark Russell. 4-The Texas Rangers by O'Henry	11	22	33	62	86	110

NOTE: Morisi c/a in all. Kiwanis stories in #3 & 4. #4 has photo of Gene Autry on-c.

SUPER MAGIC (Super Magician Comics #2 on)
Street & Smith Publications: May, 1941

	GD	VG	FN	VF	VF/NM	NM-
V1#1-Blackstone the Magician-c/story; origin/1st app. Rex King (Black Fury); Charles Sultan-c; Blackstone-c begin	166	332	498	1038	1719	2400

SUPER MAGICIAN COMICS (Super Magic #1)
Street & Smith Publications: No. 2, Sept, 1941 - V5#8, Feb-Mar, 1947

	GD	VG	FN	VF	VF/NM	NM-
V1#2-Blackstone the Magician continues; Rex King, Man of Adventure app.	64	128	192	400	663	925
3-Tao-Anwar, Boy Magician begins	40	80	120	244	392	540
4-7,9-12: 4-Origin Transo. 11-Supersnipe app.	39	78	117	224	355	485
8-Abbott & Costello story (1st app?, 11/42)	40	80	120	236	373	510
V2#1-The Shadow app.	40	80	120	242	389	535
2-12: 5-Origin Tigerman. 8-Red Dragon begins	20	40	60	117	184	250
V3#1-12: 5-Origin Mr. Twilight	20	40	60	117	184	250
V4#1-12: 11-Nigel Elliman Ace of Magic begins (3/46)						
V5#1-6	16	32	48	92	144	195
7,8-Red Dragon by Edd Cartier-c/a	16	32	48	92	144	195
	39	78	117	224	355	485

NOTE: Jack Binder c-1-14(most). Red Dragon c-V5#7, 8.

SUPERMAN (See Action Comics, Advs. of..., All-New Coll. Ed., All-Star Comics, Best of DC, Brave & the Bold, Cosmic Odyssey, DC Comics Presents, Heroes Against Hunger, JLA, The Kents, Krypton Chronicles, Limited Coll. Ed., Man of Steel, Phantom Zone, Power Record Comics, Special Edition, Steel, Super Friends, Superman: The Man of Steel, Superman: The Man of Tomorrow, Taylor's Christmas Tabloid, Three-Dimension Advs., World of Krypton, World Of Metropolis, World Of Smallville & World's Finest)

SUPERMAN (Becomes Adventures of...#424 on)
National Periodical Publ./DC Comics: Summer, 1939 - No. 423, Sept, 1986
(#1-5 are quarterly)

	GD	VG	FN	VF	VF/NM	NM-
1(nn)-1st four Action stories reprinted; origin Superman by Siegel & Shuster; has a new 2 pg. origin plus 4 pgs. omitted in Action story; see The Comics Magazine #1 & More Fun #14-17 for Superman prototype app.; cover r/splash page from Action #10; 1st pin-up Superman on back-c - 1st pin-up in comics	21,000	42,000	63,000	160,000	280,000	400,000

1-Reprint, Oversize 13-1/2x10". WARNING: This comic is an exact duplicate reprint of the original except for its size. DC published in 1978 with a second cover titling it as a Famous First Edition. There have been many reported cases of the outer cover being removed and the interior sold as the original edition. The reprint with the new outer cover removed is practically worthless. Famous First Edition for value.

	GD	VG	FN	VF	VF/NM	NM-
2-All daily strip-r; full pg. ad for N.Y. World's Fair	1350	2700	4050	10,200	18,600	27,000
3-2nd story-r from Action #5; 3rd story-r from Action #6	857	1714	2571	6000	10,500	15,000

Superman #40 © DC

Superman #96 © DC

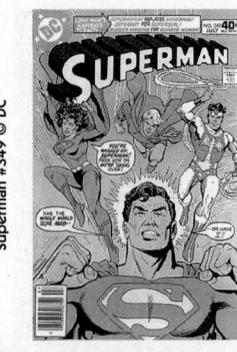

Superman #349 © DC

	GD 2.0	VG 4.0	FN 6.0	VF 8.0	VF/NM 9.0	NM- 9.2

4-2nd mention of Daily Planet (Spr/40); also see Action #23; 2nd & 3rd app. Luthor (red-headed; also see Action #23) — 629 1258 1887 4400 7700 11,000

5-4th Luthor app. (red hair) — 497 994 1491 3479 6090 8700

6,7: 6-1st splash pg. in a Superman comic. 7-1st Perry White? (11-12/40) — 339 678 1017 2204 3902 5600

8-10: 10-5th app. Luthor (1st bald Luthor, 5-6/41) — 315 630 945 2048 3624 5200

11-13,15: 13-Jimmy Olsen & Luthor app. — 262 524 786 1638 2719 3800

14-Patriotic Shield-c classic by Fred Ray — 412 824 1236 2678 4739 6800

16,18-20: 16-1st Lois Lane-c this title (5-6/42); 2nd Lois-c after Action #29 — 207 414 621 1294 2147 3000

17-Hitler, Hirohito-c — 300 600 900 1893 3366 4800

21,22,25: 25-Clark Kent's only military service; Fred Ray's only super-hero story — 152 304 456 950 1575 2200

23-Classic periscope-c — 179 358 537 1119 1860 2600

24-Classic Jack Burnley flag-c — 248 496 744 1550 2575 3600

26-Classic war-c — 235 470 705 1469 2435 3400

27-29: 27,29-Lois Lane-c. 28-Lois Lane Girl Reporter series begins, ends #40,42 — 138 276 414 863 1432 2000

28-Overseas edition for Armed Forces; same as reg. #28 — 138 276 414 863 1432 2000

30-Origin & 1st app. Mr. Mxyztplk (9-10/44)(pronounced "Mix-it-plk") in comic books; name later became Mxyzptlk ("Mix-yez-pit-l-ick") & the character was inspired by a combination of the name of Al Capp's Joe Blyfstyk (the little man with the black cloud over his head) & the devilish antics of Bugs Bunny; he 1st app. in newspapers 3/7/44; Superman flies for the first time — 262 524 786 1638 2719 3800

31-40: 33-(3-4/45)-3rd app. Mxyztplk. 35,36-Lois Lane-c. 38-Atomic bomb story (1-2/46); delayed because of gov't censorship; Superman shown reading Batman #32 on cover. 40-Mxyztplk — 116 232 348 725 1200 1675

41-50: 42-Lois Lane-c. 45-Lois Lane as Superwoman (see Action #60 for 1st app.). 46-(5-6/47)-1st app. Superboy this title? 48-1st time Superman travels thru time — 93 186 279 581 966 1350

51,52: 51-Lois Lane-c — 78 156 234 488 807 1125

53-Third telling of Superman origin; 10th anniversary issue ('48); classic origin-c by Boring — 317 634 951 1981 3291 4600

54,56-60: 57-Lois Lane as Superwoman-c. 58-Intro Tiny Trix — 78 156 234 488 807 1125

55-Used in SOTI, pg. 33 — 79 158 237 494 822 1150

61-Origin Superman retold; origin Green Kryptonite (1st Kryptonite story); Superman returns to Krypton for 1st time & sees his parents for 1st time since infancy, discovers he's not an Earth man — 152 304 456 950 1575 2200

62-70: 62-Orson Welles-c/story. 65-1st Krypton Foes: Mala, Kizo, & U-Ban. 66-2nd Superbaby story. 67-Perry Como-c/story. 68-1st Lana Lang this title (see Action Comics) — 76 152 228 475 788 1100

71-75: 74-2nd Luthor-c this title. 75-Some have #74 on-c — 72 144 216 450 750 1050

76-Batman x-over; Superman & Batman learn each other's I.D. for the 1st time (5-6/52) (also see World's Finest #71) — 214 428 642 1338 2219 3100

77-81: 78-Last 52 pg. issue. 81-Used in POP, pg. 88 — 66 132 198 413 682 950

82-87,89,90: 89-1st Curt Swan-c in title — 59 118 177 369 610 850

88-Prankster, Toyman & Luthor team-up — 64 128 192 400 663 925

91-95: 95-Last precode issue (2/55) — 52 104 156 317 521 725

96-99: 96-Mr. Mxyztplk-c/story — 45 90 135 275 450 625

100 (9-10/55)-Shows cover to #1 on-c — 221 442 663 1381 2291 3200

101-105,107-110: 109-1st S.A. issue — 41 82 123 256 416 575

106 (7/56)-Retells origin — 43 86 129 262 431 600

111-120 — 40 80 120 235 368 500

121,122,124-127,129: 127-Origin/1st app. Titano. 129-Intro Lori Lemaris, The Mermaid — 34 68 102 195 308 420

123-Pre-Supergirl tryout-c/story (8/58). — 40 80 120 244 392 540

128-(4/59)-Red Kryptonite used. Bruce Wayne x-over who protects Superman's i.d. (3rd story) — 36 72 108 208 329 450

130-(7/59)-2nd app, Krypto, the Superdog with Superman (see Sup.'s Pal Jimmy Olsen #29) (all other previous app. w/Superboy) — 36 72 108 208 329 450

131-139: 135-2nd Lori Lemaris app. 139-Lori Lemaris app. — 26 52 78 154 242 330

140-1st Blue Kryptonite & Bizarro Supergirl; origin Bizarro Jr. #1 — 27 54 81 158 249 340

141-145,148: 142-2nd Batman x-over — 22 44 66 128 202 275

146-(7/61)-Imaginary life story; back-up hints at Earth II. Classic-c — 30 60 90 174 275 375

147(8/61)-7th Legion app; 1st app. Legion of Super-Villains; 1st app. Adult Legion; swipes-c to Adv.#247 — 28 56 84 162 256 350

149(11/61)-8th Legion app. (cameo); "The Death of Superman" imaginary story;

last 10¢ issue — 24 48 72 139 220 300

150,151,153,154,157,159,160: 157-Gold Kryptonite used (see Adv. #299); Mon-el app.; Lightning Lad cameo (11/62) — 10 20 30 71 126 180

152,155,156,158,162: 152(4/62)-15th Legion app. Lightning Man & Cosmic Man, & Adult Legion app. 156,162-Legion app. 158-1st app. Flamebird & Nightwing & Nor-Kan of Kandor (12/62) — 11 22 33 75 133 190

161-1st told death of Ma and Pa Kent — 11 22 33 75 133 190

161-2nd printing (1987, $1.25)-New DC logo; sold thru So Much Fun Toy Stores (cover title: Superman Classic) — 4.00

163-166,168-180: 166-Xmas-c. 168-All Luthor issue; JFK tribute/memorial. 169-Bizarro Invasion of Earth-c/story; last Sally Selwyn. 170-Pres. Kennedy story is finally published after delay from #168 due to assassination. 172,173-Legion cameos. 174-Super-Mxyztplk; Bizarro app. — 9 18 27 63 107 150

167-New origin Braniac, text reference of Brainiac 5 descending from adopted human son Braniac II; intro Tharla (later Luthor's wife) — 10 20 30 71 126 180

181,182,184-186,188-190,194-196,198,200: 181-1st 2465 story/series. 182-1st S.A. app. of The Toyman (1/66). 189-Origin/destruction of Krypton II. — 7 14 21 50 83 115

183 (Giant G-18) — 9 18 27 65 113 160

187,193,197 (Giants G-23,G-31,G-36) — 8 16 24 56 93 130

199-1st Superman/Flash race (8/67); also see Flash #175 & World's Finest #198,199 (r-in Limited Coll. Ed. C-48) — 26 52 78 195 348 500

201,203-206,208-211,213-216: 213-Braniac-5 app. 216-Last 12¢ issue — 10 15 30 48 65

202 (80-pg. Giant G-42)-All Bizarro issue — 6 12 18 39 62 85

207,212,217 (Giants G-48,G-54,G-60): 207-30th anniversary Superman (6/68) — 6 12 18 39 62 85

218-221,223-226,228-231 — 4 8 12 26 41 55

222,239(Giants, G-66,G-84) — 6 12 18 37 59 80

227,232(Giants, G-72,G-78)-All Krypton issues — 5 10 15 35 55 75

233-2nd app. Morgan Edge; Clark Kent switches from newspaper reporter to TV newscaster; all Kryptonite on earth destroyed; classic Neal Adams-c — 7 14 21 47 76 105

234-238 — 4 8 12 26 41 55

240-Kaluta-a; last 15¢ issue — 3 6 9 20 30 40

241-244 (All 52 pgs.): 241-New Wonder Woman app. 243-G.A.-r/#38 — 4 8 12 22 34 45

245-Also listed as DC 100 Pg. Super Spectacular #7; Air Wave, Kid Eternity, Hawkman-r; Atom-r/Atom #3 (see DC 100 Pg. Super Spectacular #7 for price)

246-248,250,251,253 (All 52 pgs.): 246-G.A.-r/#40. 248-World of Krypton story. 251-G.A.-r/#45. 253-Finlay-a, 2 pgs., G.A.-r/#1 — 4 8 12 22 34 45

249,254-Neal Adams-a. 249-(52 pgs.); 1st app. Terra-Man (Swan-a) & origin-s by Dick Dillin (p) & Neal Adams (inks) — 5 10 15 32 51 70

252-Also listed as DC 100 Pg. Super Spectacular #13; Ray(r/Smash #17), Black Condor, (r/Crack #18), Hawkman(r/Flash #24); Starman-r/Adv. #67; Dr. Fate & Spectre-r/More Fun #57; N. Adams-c (see DC 100 Pg. Super Spectacular #13 for price)

255-271,273-277,279-283: 263-Photo-c. 264-1st app. Steve Lombard. 276-Intro Capt. Thunder. 279-Batman, Batgirl app. — 2 4 6 10 14 18

272,278,284-All 100 pgs. G.A.-r in all. 272-r/2nd app. Mr. Mxyztplk from Action #80 — 4 8 12 28 44 60

285-299: 289-Partial photo-c. 292-Origin Lex Luthor retold — 4 6 8 10 12

300-(6/76) Superman in the year 2001 — 4 6 8 17 26 35

301-350: 301,320-Solomon Grundy app. 323-Intro. Atomic Skull. 327-329-(44 pgs.). 327-Kobra app. 330-More facts revealed about I.D. 338-The bottled city of Kandor enlarged. 344-Frankenstein & Dracula app. — 6.00

321-323,325-327,329-332,335-345,348,350 (Whitman variants; low print run; no issue # on cover) — 1 3 4 6 8 10

351-399: 353-Brief origin. 354,355,357-Superman 2020 stories (354-Debut of Superman III). 356-World of Krypton story (also #360,367,375). 366-Fan letter by Todd McFarlane. 372-Superman 2021 story. 376-Free 16 pg. preview Daring New Advs. of Supergirl. 377-Free 16 pg. preview Masters of the Universe — 5.00

400 (10/84, $1.50, 68 pgs.)-Many top artists featured; Chaykin painted cover, Miller back-c; Steranko-s/a (10 pages) — 6.00

401-422: 405-Super-Batman story. 408-Nuclear Holocaust-c/story. 411-Special Julius Schwartz tribute issue. 414,415-Crisis x-over. 422-Horror-c — 4.00

409-(7/85) Variant-c with Superman/Superhombre logo — (no reported sales)

423-Alan Moore scripts; Perez-a(i); last Earth I Superman story, cont'd in Action #583 — 1 3 4 6 8 10

Annual 1(10/60, 84 pgs.)-Reprints 1st Supergirl story/Action #252; r/Lois Lane #1; Krypto-r (1st Silver Age DC annual) — 83 166 249 706 1303 1900

Annual 2(Win, 1960-61)-Super-villain issue; Braniac, Titano, Metallo, Bizarro origin-r — 38 76 114 285 518 765

Annual 3(Sum, 1961)-Strange Lives of Superman — 25 50 75 186 333 480

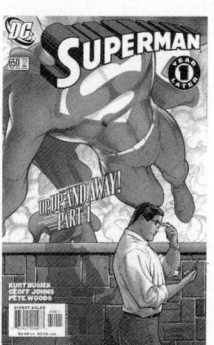

Superman (2nd series) #7 © DC

Superman (2nd series) #161 © DC

Superman #650 © DC

	GD 2.0	VG 4.0	FN 6.0	VF 8.0	VF/NM 9.0	NM- 9.2
Annual 4(Win, 1961-62)-11th Legion app; 1st Legion origins (text & pictures); advs. in time, space & on alien worlds	21	42	63	156	278	400
Annual 5(Sum, 1962)-All Krypton issue	17	34	51	126	223	320
Annual 6(Win, 1962-63)-Legion-r/Adv. #247	15	30	45	111	198	285
Annual 7(Sum, 1963)-Origin-r/Superman-Batman team/Adv. 275; r/1955 Superman dailies	12	24	36	84	150	215
Annual 8(Win, 1963-64)-All origins issue	11	22	33	75	133	190
Annual 9(1983)-Toth/Austin-a						6.00
Annuals 10-12: 10(1984, $1.25)-M. Anderson inks. 11(1985)-Moore scripts.						
12(1986)-Bolland-c						4.00
Special 1-3('83-'85): 1-G. Kane-c/a; contains German-r						4.00

The Amazing World of Superman "Official Metropolis Edition" (1973, $2.00, treasury-size)-
Origin retold; Wood-r(i) from Superboy #153,161; poster incl. (half price if poster missing)

		4	8	12	24	37	50
11195 (2/79, $1.95, 224 pgs.)-Golden Press		3	6	9	20	30	40

NOTE: N. Adams a-249i, 254p; c-204-206, 210, 212-215, 219, 231i, 233-237, 240-243, 249-252, 254, 263, 307, 308, 313, 314, 317. Adkins a-323i. Austin c-368i. Wayne Boring art-late 1940's to early 1960's. Buckler a(p)-352, 363, 364, 369; c(p)-324-327, 356, 363, 368, 369, 373, 376, 378. Burnley a-252r; c-19-25, 30, 33, 34, 35p, 38p, 39p, 45p. Fine a-252r. Kaluta a-400. Gil Kane a-272r; 367, 372, 375, Special 2; c-374p, 375p, 377, 381, 382, 384-390, 392. Annual 9, Special 2. Joe Kubert c-216. Morrow a-238. Mortimer a-250r. Perez c-364p. Fred Ray a-25; c-6, 8-18. Starlin c-355. Staton a-354i, 355i. Swan/Moldoff c-149. Williamson a(i)-408-410, 412-416; c-408i, 409i. Wrightson a-400, 416.

SUPERMAN (2nd Series) (Title continues numbering from Adventures of Superman #649)
DC Comics: Jan, 1987 - No. 226, Apr, 2006; No. 650, May, 2006 - Present (75¢-$2.99)

0-(10/94) Zero Hour; released between #93 & #94						2.50
1-Byrne-c/a begins; intro new Metallo						
2-8,10: 3-Legends x-over; Darkseid-c & app. 7-Origin/1st app. Rampage. 8-Legion app.						3.00
9-Joker-c						4.50
11-15,17-20,22-49,51,52,54-56,58-67: 11-1st new Mr. Mxyzptlk. 12-Lori Lemaris revived. 13-1st app. new Toyman. 17a,18-Millennium x-over. 20-Doom Patrol app.; Supergirl cameo. 31-Mr. Mxyzptlk app. 37-Newsboy Legion app. 41-Lobo app. 44-Batman storyline, part 1. 45-Free extra 8 pgs. 54-Newsboy Legion story. 63-Aquaman x-over. 67-Last $1.00-c						2.50
16,21: 16-1st app. new Supergirl (4/88). 21-Supergirl-c/story; 1st app. Matrix who becomes new Supergirl						4.00
50-($1.50, 52 pgs.)-Clark Kent proposes to Lois						5.00
50-2nd printing						2.50
53-Clark reveals i.d. to Lois (Cont'd from Action #662)						3.00
53-2nd printing						2.50
57-($1.75, 52 pgs.)						3.00
68-72: 65,66,68-Deathstroke-c/stories. 70-Superman & Robin team-up						2.50
73-Doomsday cameo						5.00
74-Doomsday Pt. 2 (Cont'd from Justice League #69); Superman battles Doomsday						6.00
73,74-2nd printings						2.50
75-($2.50)-Collector's Ed.; Doomsday Pt. 6; Superman dies; polybagged w/poster of funeral, obituary from Daily Planet, postage stamp & armband premiums (direct sales only)						
		2	4	6	10	14	18
75-Direct sales copy (no upc code, 1st print)	1	2	3	5	6	8
75-Direct sales copy (no upc code, 2nd-4th prints)						2.50
75-Newsstand copy w/upc code	1	2	3	5	6	8
75-Platinum Edition; given away to retailers						60.00
76,77-Funeral For a Friend parts 4 & 8						3.00
78-($1.95)-Collector's Edition with die-cut outer-c & mini poster; Doomsday cameo						3.00
78-($1.50)-Newsstand Edition w/poster and different-c; Doomsday-c & cameo						2.50
79-81,83-89: 83-Funeral for a Friend epilogue; new Batman (Azrael) cameo. 87,88-Bizarro-c/story						2.50
82-($2.50)-Collector's Edition w/all chromium-c; real Superman revealed; Green Lantern x-over from G.L. #46; no ads						6.00
82-($2.00, 44 pgs.)-Regular Edition w/different-c						2.50
90-99: 93-(9/94)-Zero Hour. 94-(11/94). 95-Atom app. 96-Brainiac returns						2.50
100-Death of Clark Kent foil-c						4.00
100-Newsstand						3.00
101-122: 101-Begin $1.95-c; Black Adam app. 105-Green Lantern app. 110-Plastic Man-c/app. 114-Brainiac app. Dwyer-c. 115-Lois leaves Metropolis. 116-(10/96)-1st app. Teen Titans by Jurgens & Perez in 8 pg. preview. 117-Final Night. 118-Wonder Woman app. 119-Legion app. 122-New powers						2.50
123-Collector's Edition w/glow in the dark-c, new costume						6.00
123-Standard ed., new costume						4.00
124-149: 128-Cyborg-c/app. 131-Birth of Lena Luthor. 132-Superman Red/Superman Blue. 134-Millennium Giants. 136,137-Superman 2999. 139-Starlin-a. 140-Grindberg-a						2.50
150-($2.95) Standard Ed.; Brainiac 2.0 app.; Jurgens-s						3.00
150-($3.95) Collector's Ed. w/holo-foil enhanced variant-c						4.00
151-158: 151-Loeb/s begins; Daily Planet reopens						2.50
159-174: 159-$2.25-c begin. 161-Joker-c/app. 162-Aquaman-c/app. 163-Young Justice app. 165-JLA app.; Ramos; Madureira, Liefeld, A. Adams, Wieringo, Churchill-a. 166-Collector's						

and reg. editions. 167-Return to Krypton. 168-Batman-c/app.(cont'd in Detective #756).

171-173-Our Worlds at War. 173-Sienkiewicz-a (2 pgs.). 174-Adopts black & red "S" logo						2.50
175-($3.50) Joker: Last Laugh x-over; Doomsday-c/app.						3.50
176-189,191-199: 176,180-Churchill-a. 180-Dracula app. 181-Bizarro-c/app. 184-Return to Krypton II. 189-Van Fleet-c. 192,193,195,197-199-New Supergirl app.						2.50
190-($2.25) Regular edition						2.50
190-($3.95) Double-Feature Issue; included reprint of Superman: The 10¢ Adventure						4.00
200-($3.50) Gene Ha-c/art by various; preview art by Yu & Bermejo						3.50
201-Mr Majestic-c/app.; cover swipe of Action #1						2.50
202,203-Godfall parts 3,6; Turner-c; Caldwell-a(p). 203-Jim Lee sketch pages						2.50
204-Jim Lee-c/a begins; Azzarello-s						3.00
204-Diamond Retailer Summit edition with sketch cover						125.00
205-214: 205-Two covers by Jim Lee and Michael Turner. 208-JLA app. 211-Battles Wonder Woman						2.50
215-($2.99) Conclusion to Azzarello/Lee arc						3.00
216-218,220-226: 216-Captain Marvel app. 221-Bizarro & Zoom app. 226-Earth-2 Superman story; Chaykin,Sale, Benes, Ordway-a						2.50
219-Omac/Sacrifice pt. 1; JLA app.						3.00
219-2nd printing with red background variant-c						2.50
(Title continues numbering from Adventures of Superman #649)						
650-(5/06) One Year Later; Clark powerless after Infinite Crisis						3.00
651-665: 652-Begin $2.99-c. 654-658,662-664-Pacheco-a. 665-Origin of Jimmy Olsen						3.00
666-($3.99) Simonson-a						4.00
#1,000,000 (11/98) 853rd Century x-over; Gene Ha-c						2.50
Annual 1,2: 1 (1987)-No Byrne-a. 2 (1988)-Byrne-a; Newsboy Legion; Guardian returns						4.00
Annual 3,4 ('91-'94 68 pgs.): 1-Armageddon 2001 x-over; Batman app.; Austin-c(i) & part inks. 4-Eclipso app. 6-Elseworlds story						3.00
Annual 3-2nd & 3rd printings; 3rd has silver ink						2.50
Annual 7 (1995, $3.95, 69 pgs.)-Year One story						4.00
Annual 8 (1996, $2.95)-Legends of the Dead Earth story						3.00
Annual 9 (1997, $3.95)-Pulp Heroes story						4.00
Annual 10 (1998, $2.95)-Ghosts; Wrightson-c						3.00
Annual 11 (1999, $2.95)-JLApe; Art Adams-c						3.00
Annual 12 (2000, $3.50)-Planet DC						3.50
...: 80 Page Giant (2/99, $4.95) Jurgens-c						5.00
...: 80 Page Giant 2 (6/99, $4.95) Nowlan-c						5.00
...: 80 Page Giant 3 (11/00, $5.95) Nowlan-c; art by various						6.00
Special 1 (1992, $3.50, 68 pgs.)-Simonson-c/a						5.00

SUPERMAN (Hardcovers and Trade Paperbacks)

.... Back in Action TPB (2007, $14.99) r/Action Comics #841-843 and DC Comics Presents #4,17,24; commentary by Busiek						15.00
.... Camelot Falls HC (2007, $19.99, dustjacket) r/Superman #654-658						20.00
.: Chronicles Vol. 1 ('06, $14.99, TPB) r/early Superman app. in Action Comics #1-13, New York World's Fair 1939 and Superman #1						15.00
.: Chronicles Vol. 2 ('07, $14.99, TPB) r/early Superman app. in Action Comics #14-20 and Superman #2						15.00
.: Chronicles Vol. 3 ('07, $14.99, TPB) r/early Superman app. in Action Comics #21-25, Superman #3,4 and New York World's Fair 1940						15.00
.... Critical Condition ('03, $14.95, TPB) r/2000 Kryptonite poisoning storyline						15.00
.: Doomsday: The Collection Edition (2006, $19.99) r/Superman/Doomsday: Hunter/Prey #1-3, Doomsday Ann. #1, Superman: The Doomsday Wars #1-3, Advs. of Superman #594 and Superman #175; intro. by Dan Jurgens						20.00
.... Daily Planet (2006, $19.99, SHB)-reprints stories of Daily Planet staff						20.00
.... Emperor Joker TPB (2007, $14.99) reprints 2000 x-over from Superman titles						15.00
.... Endgame ('04, $14.95, TPB)-reprints Y2K and Brainiac story line						15.00
.... Eradication! The Origin of the Eradicator (1996, $12.95, TPB)						13.00
.... Exile (1998, $14.95, TPB)-Reprints space exile following execution of Kryptonian criminals; 1st Eradicator						15.00
.... For Tomorrow Volume 1 HC (2005, $24.99, dustjacket) r/#204-209; intro by Azzarello; new cover and sketch section by Lee						25.00
.... For Tomorrow Volume 1 SC (2005, $14.99) r/#204-209; foil-stamped S emblem-c						15.00
.... For Tomorrow Volume 2 HC (2005, $24.99, dustjacket) r/#210-215; afterword and sketch section by Lee; new Lee-c with foil-stamped S emblem						25.00
.... For Tomorrow Volume 2 SC (2005, $14.99) r/#210-215; foil-stamped S emblem-c						15.00
.... Godfall HC (2004, $19.95, dustjacket) r/Action #812-813, Advs. of Superman #625-626, Superman #202-203; Caldwell sketch pages; Turner cover gallery; new Turner-c						20.00
.... Godfall SC (2004, $9.99) r/Action #812-813, Advs. of Superman #625-626, Superman #202-203; Caldwell sketch pages; Turner cover gallery; new Turner-c						10.00
.... Infinite Crisis TPB (2006, $12.99) r/Infinite Crisis #5, I.C. Secret Files and Origins 2006, Action Comics #836, Superman #226 and Advs. of Superman #649						13.00
... In the Forties ('05, $19.99, TPB) Intro. by Bob Hughes						20.00
... In the Fifties ('02, $19.95, TPB) Intro. by Mark Waid						20.00
... In the Sixties ('01, $19.95, TPB) Intro. by Mark Waid						20.00

Superman Adventures #21 © DC

Superman & Batman Generations #1 © DC

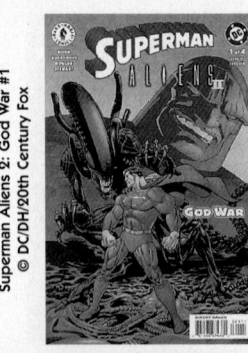

Superman Aliens 2: God War #1 © DC/DH/20th Century Fox

	GD 2.0	VG 4.0	FN 6.0	VF 8.0	VF/NM 9.0	NM- 9.2
... In the Seventies ('00, $19.95, TPB) Intro. by Christopher Reeve						20.00
... In the Eighties ('06, $19.99, TPB) Intro. by Jerry Ordway						20.00
... In the Name of Gog ('05, $17.99, TPB) r/Action 820-825						18.00
... No Limits ('00, $14.95, TPB) Reprints early 2000 stories						15.00
...: Our Worlds at War Book 1 ('02, $19.95, TPB) r/1st half of x-over						20.00
...: Our Worlds at War Book 2 ('02, $19.95, TPB) r/2nd half of x-over						20.00
...: Our Worlds at War - The Complete Collection ('06, $24.99, TPB) r/entire x-over						25.00
...: President Lex TPB (2003, $17.95) r/Luthor's run for the White House; Harris-c						18.00
...: Return to Krypton (2004, $17.95, TPB) r/2001-2002 x-over						18.00
...: Sacrifice (2005, $14.99, TPB) prelude x-over to Infinite Crisis; r/Superman #218-220, Advs. of Superman #642,643; Action #829, Wonder Woman #219,220						15.00
: Strange Attractors (2006, $14.99, TPB) r/Action Comics #827,828,830-835						15.00
...: That Healing Touch TPB (2005, $14.99) r/Advs. of Superman #633-638 & Superman Secret Files 2004						15.00
The Death of Clark Kent (1997, $19.95, TPB)-Reprints Man of Steel #43 (1 page), Superman #99 (1 page),#100-102, Action #709 (1 page), #710,711, Advs. of Superman #523-525, Superman:The Man of Tomorrow #1						20.00
The Death of Superman (1993, $4.95, TPB)-Reprints Man of Steel #17-19, Superman #73-75, Advs. of Superman #496,497, Action #683,684, & Justice League #69	1	2	3	5	6	8
The Death of Superman, 2nd & 3rd printings						
The Death of Superman Platinum Edition						15.00
...: The Greatest Stories Ever Told ('04, $19.95, TPB) Ross-c, Uslan intro.						20.00
...: The Greatest Stories Ever Told Vol. 2 ('06, $19.99, TPB) Ross-c, Greenberger intro.						20.00
...: The Journey ('06, $14.99, TPB) r/Action Comics #831 & Superman #217,221-225						15.00
...: The Man of Steel Vol. 2 ('03, $19.95, TPB) r/Superman #1-3, Action #584-586, Advs. of Superman #424-426 & Who's Who Update '87						20.00
...: The Man of Steel Vol. 3 ('04, $19.95, TPB) r/Superman #4-6, Action #587-589, Advs. of Superman #427-429; intro. by Ordway; new Ordway-c						20.00
...: The Man of Steel Vol. 4 ('05, $19.99, TPB) r/Superman #7,8; Action #590,591; Advs. of Superman #430,431; Legion of Super-Heroes #37,38; new Ordway-c						20.00
...: The Man of Steel Vol. 5 ('06, $19.99, TPB) r/Superman #9-11, Action #592-593, Advs. of Superman #432-435; intro. by Mike Carlin; new Ordway-c						20.00
The Trial of Superman ('97, $14.95, TPB) reprints story arc						15.00
The Wrath of Gog ('05, $14.99, TPB) reprints Action Comics #812-819						15.00
...: They Saved Luthor's Brain ('00, $14.95, TPB) r/ "death" and return of Luthor						15.00
...: 'Til Death Do Us Part ('01, $17.95) reprints; Mahnke-c						18.00
...: Time and Time Again (1994, $7.50, TPB)-Reprints						8.00
...: Transformed ('98, $12.95, TPB) r/post Final Night powerless Superman to Electric Superman						13.00
...: Unconventional Warfare (2005, $14.95, TPB) r/Adventures of Superman #625-632 and pages from Superman Secret Files 2004						15.00
...: Up, Up and Away! (2006, $14.99, TPB) r/Superman #650-653 and Action #837-840						15.00
...: Vs. Lex Luthor (2006, $19.99, TPB) reprints 1st meeting in Action #23 and 11 other classic duels 1940-2001						20.00
...: Vs. The Flash (2005, $19.99, TPB) reprints their races from Superman #199, Flash #175, World's Finest #198, DC Comics Presents #1&2, Advs. of Superman #463 & DC First: Flash/Superman; new Alex Ross-c						20.00
...: Vs. The Revenge Squad (1999, $12.95, TPB)						13.00
NOTE: *Austin* a(i)-1-3. *Byrne* a-1-16p, 17, 19-21p, 22; c-1-17, 20-22; scripts-1-22. *Guice* c/a-64. *Kirby* c-37p. *Joe Quesada* c-Annual 4. *Russell* c/a-23i. *Simonson* c-69i. #19-21 2nd printings sold in multi-packs.						
SUPERMAN (one-shots)						
Daily News Magazine Presents DC Comics' Superman nn-(1987, 8 pgs.)-Supplement to New York Daily News; Perez-c/a						5.00
...: A Nation Divided (1999, $4.95)-Elseworlds Civil War story						5.00
... & Savage Dragon: Chicago (2002, $5.95) Larsen-a; Ross-c						6.00
... & Savage Dragon: Metropolis (11/99, $4.95) Bogdanove-a						5.00
...: At Earth's End (1995, $4.95)-Elseworlds story						5.00
...: Blood of My Ancestors (2003, $6.95)-Gil Kane & John Buscema-a						7.00
...: Distant Fires (1998, $5.95)-Elseworlds; Chaykin-s						6.00
...: Emperor Joker (10/00, $3.50)-Follows Action #769						3.50
...: End of the Century (2000, $24.95, HC)-Immonen-s/a						25.00
...: End of the Century (2003, $17.95, SC)-Immonen-s/a						18.00
... For Earth (1991, $4.95, 52 pgs, printed on recycled paper)-Ordway wraparound-c						5.00
...IV Movie Special (1987, $2.00)-Movie adaptation; Heck-a						3.00
...Gallery, The 1 (1993, $2.95)-Poster-a						3.00
..., Inc. (1999, $6.95)-Elseworlds Clark as a sports hero; Garcia-Lopez-a						7.00
...: Infinite City HC (2005, $24.99, dustjacket) Mike Kennedy-s/Carlos Meglia-a						25.00
...: Infinite City SC (2006, $17.99) Mike Kennedy-s/Carlos Meglia-a						18.00
...: Kal (1995, $5.95)-Elseworlds story						6.00
...: Lex 2000 (1/01, $3.50)-Election night for the Luthor Presidency						3.50
...: Monster (1999, $5.95)-Elseworlds story; Anthony Williams-a						6.00
... Movie Special-(9/83)-Adaptation of Superman III; other versions exist with store logos on bottom 1/3 of-c						4.00

	GD 2.0	VG 4.0	FN 6.0	VF 8.0	VF/NM 9.0	NM- 9.2
...: Our Worlds at War Secret Files 1-(8/01, $5.95)-Stories & profile pages						6.00
... Plus 1(2/97, $2.95)-Legion of Super-Heroes-c/app.						3.00
...'s Metropolis-(1996, $5.95, prestige format)-Elseworlds; McKeever-c/a						6.00
...: Speeding Bullets-(1993, $4.95, 52 pgs.)-Elseworlds						5.00
.../Spider-Man-(1995, $3.95)-r/DC and Marvel Presents...						4.00
...: 10-Cent Adventure 1 (3/02, 10¢) McDaniel-a; intro. Cir-El Supergirl						2.25
...: The Earth Stealers 1-(1988, $2.95, 52 pg., prestige format) Byrne script; painted-c						4.00
...: The Earth Stealers 1-2nd printing						3.00
...: The Legacy of Superman 1 (3/93, $2.50, 68 pgs.)-Art Adams-c; Simonson-a						4.00
...: The Last God of Krypton ('99,$4.95) Hildebrandt Bros.-a/Simonson-s						5.00
...: The Odyssey ('99, $4.95) Clark Kent's post-Smallville journey						5.00
...: 3-D (12/98, $3.95)-with glasses						6.00
.../Thundercats (1/04, $5.95) Winick-s/Garza-a; two covers by Garza & McGuinness						6.00
...Through the Ages (2006, $3.99) r/Action #1, Superman ('87) #7; origins and pin-ups						4.00
.../Toyman-(1996, $1.95)						2.50
...: True Brit (2004, $24.95, HC w/dust jacket) Elseworlds; Kal-El's rocket lands in England; co-written by John Cleese and Kim Howard Johnson; John Byrne-a						25.00
...: True Brit (2005, $17.99, TPB) Elseworlds; Kal-El's rocket lands in England						18.00
...: Under A Yellow Sun (1994, $5.95, 68 pgs.)-A Novel by Clark Kent; embossed-c						6.00
...: Vs. Darkseid: Apokolips Now! 1 (3/03, $2.95) McKone-a; Kara (Supergirl #75) app.						3.00
...: War of the Worlds (1999, $5.95)-Battles Martians						6.00
...: Where is thy Sting? (2001, $6.95)-McCormack-Sharp-c/a						7.00
...: Y2K (2/00, $4.95)-1st Brainiac 13 app.; Guice-c/a						5.00
SUPERMAN ADVENTURES, THE (Based on animated series)						
DC Comics: Oct. 1996 - No. 66, Apr. 2002 ($1.75/$1.95/$1.99)						
1-Rick Burchett-a/begins; Paul Dini script; Lex Luthor app.; silver ink, wraparound-c						3.00
2-20,22: 2-McCloud scripts begin; Metallo-c/app. 3-Brainiac-c/app. 6-Mxyzptlk-c/app.						2.50
21-($3.95) 1st animated Supergirl						5.00
23-66: 23-Begin $1.99-c; Livewire app. 25-Batgirl-c/app. 28-Manley-a.						
54-Retells Superman #233 "Kryptonite Nevermore" 58-Ross-c						2.25
Annual 1 (1997, $3.95)-Zatanna and Bruce Wayne app.						4.00
Special 1 (2/98, $2.95) Superman vs. Lobo						3.00
TPB (1998, $7.95) r/#1-6						8.00
... Vol 1: Up, Up and Away (2004, $6.95, digest) r/#16,19,22-24; Amancio-a						7.00
... Vol 2: The Never-Ending Battle (2004, $6.95) r/#25-29						7.00
... Vol 3: Last Son of Krypton (2006, $6.99) r/#30-34						7.00
... Vol 4: The Man of Steel (2006, $6.99) r/#35-39						7.00
SUPERMAN ALIENS 2: GOD WAR (Also see Superman Vs. Aliens)						
DC Comics/Dark Horse Comics: May, 2002 - No. 4, Nov, 2002 ($2.99, limited series)						
1-4-Bogdanove & Nowlan-a; Darkseid & New Gods app.						3.00
TPB (6/03, $12.95) r/#1-4						13.00
SUPERMAN & BATMAN: GENERATIONS (Elseworlds)						
DC Comics: 1999 - No. 4, 1999 ($4.95, limited series)						
1-4-Superman & Batman team-up from 1939 to the future; Byrne-c/s/a						5.00
TPB (2000, $14.95) r/series						15.00
SUPERMAN & BATMAN: GENERATIONS II (Elseworlds)						
DC Comics: 2001 - No. 4, 2001 ($5.95, limited series)						
1-4-Superman, Batman & others team-up from 1942-future; Byrne-c/s/a						6.00
TPB (2003, $19.95) r/series						20.00
SUPERMAN & BATMAN: GENERATIONS III (Elseworlds)						
DC Comics: Mar, 2003 - No. 12, Feb, 2004 ($2.95, limited series)						
1-12-Superman & Batman through the centuries; Byrne-c/s/a						3.00
SUPERMAN & BATMAN VS. ALIENS AND PREDATOR						
DC Comics: 2007 - No. 2, 2007 ($5.99, squarebound, limited series)						
1,2-Schultz-s/Olivetti-a						6.00
TPB (2007, $12.99) r/#1,2; pencil breakdown pages						13.00
SUPERMAN & BATMAN: WORLD'S FUNNEST (Elseworlds)						
DC Comics: 2000 ($6.95, square-bound, one-shot)						
nn-Mr. Mxyzptlk and Bat-Mite destroy each DC Universe; Dorkin-s; art by various incl. Ross, Timm, Miller, Allred, Moldoff, Gibbons, Cho, Jimenez						7.00
SUPERMAN & BUGS BUNNY						
DC Comics: Jul, 2000 - No. 4, Oct, 2000 ($2.50, limited series)						
1-4-JLA & Looney Tunes characters meet						2.50
SUPERMAN/BATMAN						
DC Comics: Oct, 2003 - Present ($2.95/$2.99)						
1-Two covers (Superman or Batman in foreground) Loeb-s/McGuinness-a; Metallo app.						3.00
1-2nd printing (Batman cover)						3.00
1-3rd printing; new McGuinness cover						3.00

Superman/Batman #7 © DC

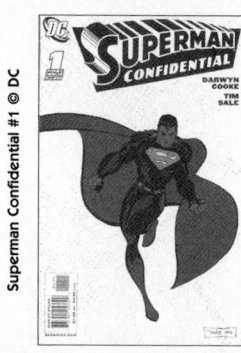

Superman Confidential #1 © DC

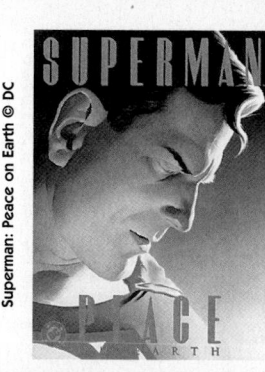

Superman: Peace on Earth © DC

	GD	VG	FN	VF	VF/NM	NM-		GD	VG	FN	VF	VF/NM	NM-
	2.0	4.0	6.0	8.0	9.0	9.2		2.0	4.0	6.0	8.0	9.0	9.2

1-Diamond/Alliance Retailer Summit Edition-variant cover 100.00

2-6: 2,5-Future Superman app. 6-Luthor in battlesuit 3.00

7-Pat Lee-c/a; Superboy & Robin app. 3.00

8-Michael Turner-c/a; intro. new Kara Zor-El 3.00

8-Second printing with sketch cover

8-Third printing with new Turner cover 3.00

9-13-Michael Turner-c/a; Wonder Woman app. 10,13-Variant-c by Jim Lee 3.00

14-25: 14-18-Pacheco-a; Lightning Lord, Saturn Queen & Cosmic King app. 19-Supergirl app.; leads into Supergirl #1. 21-25-Bizarro app. 25-Superman & Batman covers; 2nd printing with white bkgrd cover 3.00

26-($3.99) Sam Loeb tribute issue; 2 covers by Turner; story & art by 26 various; back-up by Loeb & Sale 5.00

27-39: 27-Flashback to Earth-2 Power Girl & Huntress; Maguire-a. 34-36-Metal Men app. 3.00

Annual #1 (12/06, $3.99) Re-imaging of 1st meeting from World's Finest #71 4.00

...Absolute Power HC (2005, $19.99) r/#14-18 20.00

...Absolute Power SC (2006, $12.99) r/#14-18 13.00

...Public Enemies HC (2004, $19.95) r/#1-6 & Secret Files 2003 20.00

...Public Enemies SC (2005, $12.99) r/#1-6 & Secret Files 2003 13.00

...Secret Files 2003 (11/03, $4.95) Reis-a; pin-ups by various; Loeb/Sale short-s 5.00

... :Supergirl HC (2004, $19.95) r/#8-13; intro by Loeb, cover gallery, sketch pages 20.00

... :Supergirl SC (2005, $12.99) r/#8-13; intro by Loeb, cover gallery, sketch pages 13.00

... :Vengeance HC (2006, $19.99) r/#20-25; sketch pages 20.00

SUPERMAN/BATMAN: ALTERNATE HISTORIES
DC Comics: 1996 ($14.95, trade paperback)

nn-Reprints Detective Comics Annual #7, Action Comics Annual #6, Steel Annual #1, Legends of the Dark Knight Annual #4 15.00

SUPERMAN: BIRTHRIGHT
DC Comics: Sept, 2003 - No. 12, Sept, 2004 ($2.95, limited series)

1-12-Waid-s/Leinil Yu-a; retelling of origin and early Superman years 3.00

HC (2004, $29.95, dustjacket) r/series; cover gallery; Waid proposal with Yu concept art 30.00

SC (2005, $19.95) r/series; cover gallery; Waid proposal with Yu concept art 20.00

SUPERMAN COMICS
DC Comics: 1939

nn-Ashcan comic, not distributed to newsstands, only for in-house use. Cover art is Action Comics #7 with interior being Action Comics #8. A CGC certified 9.0 copy sold for $37,375 in 2005 and for $90,000 in 2007.

SUPERMAN CONFIDENTIAL
DC Comics: Jan, 2007 - Present ($2.99)

1-5-Darwyn Cooke-s/Tim Sale-a/c; origin of Kryptonite re-told 3.00

SUPERMAN: DAY OF DOOM
DC Comics: Jan, 2003 - No. 4, Feb, 2003 ($2.95, weekly limited series)

1-4-Jurgens-s/Jurgens & Sienkiewicz-a 3.00

TPB (2003, $9.95) r/#1-4 10.00

SUPERMAN/DOOMSDAY: HUNTER/PREY
DC Comics: 1994 - No. 3, 1994 ($4.95, limited series, 52 pgs.)

1-3 5.00

SUPERMAN FAMILY, THE (Formerly Superman's Pal Jimmy Olsen)
National Per. Publ./DC Comics: No. 164, Apr-May, 1974 - No. 222, Sept, 1982

164-(100 pgs.) Jimmy Olsen, Supergirl, Lois Lane begin

		4	8	12	28	44	60
165-169 (100 pgs.)		3	6	9	18	27	35
170-176 (68 pgs.)		2	4	6	13	18	22

177-190 (52 pgs.): 177-181-52 pgs. 182-Marshall Rogers-a; $1.00 issues begin; Krypto begins, ends #192. 183-Nightwing-Flamebird begins, ends #194.

189-Braniac 5, Mon-el app.		2	4	6	9	12	15
191-193,195-199: 191-Superboy begins, ends #198	1	2	3	5	7	9
194,200: 194-Rogers-a. 200-Book length sty	1	3	4	6	8	10
201-222: 211-Earth II Batman & Catwoman marry	1	2	3	4	5	7

NOTE: **N. Adams** c-182-185. **Anderson** a-186i. **Buckler** c(p)-190, 191, 209, 210, 215, 217, 220. **Jones** a-191-193. **Gil Kane** c(p)-221, 222. **Mortimer** a(p)-193, 197, 199, 201-222. **Orlando** a(i)-186, 187. **Rogers** a-182, 194. **Staton** a-191-194, 196p. **Tuska** a(p)-203, 207-209.

SUPERMAN/FANTASTIC FOUR
DC Comics/Marvel Comics: 1999 ($9.95, tabloid size, one-shot)

1-Battle Galactus and the Cyborg; wraparound-c by Alex Ross and Dan Jurgens; Jurgens-s/a; Thibert-a 10.00

SUPERMAN FOR ALL SEASONS
DC Comics: 1998 - No. 4, 1998 ($4.95, limited series, prestige format)

1-Loeb-s/Sale-a/c; Superman's first year in Metropolis 6.00

2-4 5.00

Hardcover (1999, $24.95) r/#1-4 25.00

SUPERMAN FOR EARTH (See Superman one-shots)

SUPERMAN FOREVER
DC Comics: Jun, 1998 ($5.95, one-shot)

1-($5.95)-Collector's Edition with a 7-image lenticular-c by Alex Ross; Superman returns to normal; s/a by various 7.00

1-($4.95) Standard Edition with single image Ross-c 5.00

SUPERMAN/GEN13
DC Comics (WildStorm): Jun, 2000 - No. 3, Aug, 2000 ($2.50, limited series)

1-3-Hughes-s/ Bermejo-a; Campbell variant-c for each 2.50

TPB (2001, $9.95) new Bermejo-c; cover gallery 10.00

SUPERMAN: KING OF THE WORLD
DC Comics: June, 1999 ($3.95/$4.95, one-shot)

1-($3.95) Regular Ed. 4.00

1-($4.95) Collectors' Ed. with gold foil enhanced-c 5.00

SUPERMAN: LAST SON OF EARTH
DC Comics: 2000 - No. 2, 2000 ($5.95, limited series, prestige format)

1,2-Elseworlds; baby Clark rockets to Krypton; Gerber-s/Wheatley-a 6.00

SUPERMAN: LAST STAND ON KRYPTON
DC Comics: 2003 ($6.95, one-shot, prestige format)

1-Sequel to Superman: Last Son of Earth; Gerber-s/Wheatley-a 7.00

SUPERMAN: LOIS LANE (Girlfrenzy)
DC Comics: Jun, 1998 ($1.95, one shot)

1-Connor & Palmiotti-a 2.50

SUPERMAN/MADMAN HULLABALOO!
Dark Horse Comics: June, 1997 - No. 3, Aug, 1997 ($2.95, limited series)

1-3-Mike Allred-c/s/a 3.00

TPB (1997, $8.95) 9.00

SUPERMAN: METROPOLIS
DC Comics: Apr, 2003 - No. 12, Mar, 2004 ($2.95, limited series)

1-12-Focus on Jimmy Olsen; Austen-s. 1-6-Zezelj-a. 7-12-Kristiansen-a. 8,9-Creeper app. 3.00

SUPERMAN METROPOLIS SECRET FILES
DC Comics: Jun, 2000 ($4.95, one shot)

1-Short stories, pin-ups and profile pages; Hitch and Neary-c 5.00

SUPERMAN: PEACE ON EARTH
DC Comics: Jan, 1999 ($9.95, Treasury-sized, one-shot)

1-Alex Ross painted-c/a; Paul Dini-s 12.00

SUPERMAN: RED SON
DC Comics: 2003 - No. 3, 2003 ($5.95, limited series, prestige format)

1-Elseworlds; Superman's rocket lands in Russia; Mark Millar-s/Dave Johnson-c/a 10.00

2,3 6.00

TPB (2004, $17.95) r/#1-3; intro. by Tom DeSanto; sketch pages 18.00

SUPERMAN RED/ SUPERMAN BLUE
DC Comics: Feb, 1998 ($4.95, one shot)

1-Polybagged w/3-D glasses and reprint of Superman 3-D (1955); Jurgens-plot/3-D cover; script and art by various 5.00

1-($3.95)-Standard Ed.; comic only, non 3-D cover 4.00

SUPERMAN RETURNS... (2006 movie)
DC Comics: Aug, 2006 ($3.99, movie tie-in stories by Singer, Dougherty and Harris)

Prequel 1 - Krypton to Earth; Olivetti-a/Hughes-c; retells Jor-el's story 6.00

Prequel 2 - Ma Kent; Kerschl-a/Hughes-c; Ma Kent during Clark childhood and absence 4.00

Prequel 3 - Lex Luthor; Leonardi-a/Hughes-c; Luthor's 5 years in prison 4.00

Prequel 4 - Lois Lane; Dias-a/Hughes-c; Lois during Superman's absence 4.00

The Movie and Other Tales of the Man of Steel (2006, $12.99, TPB) adaptation; origin from Amazing World of Superman; Action #810, Superman #185; Advs. of Superman #575 13.00

The Official Movie Adaptation (2006, $6.99) Pasko-s/Haley-a; photo-c 7.00

...: The Prequels TPB (2006, $12.99) r/the 4 prequels

SUPERMAN: SAVE THE PLANET
DC Comics: Oct, 1998 ($2.95, one-shot)

1-($2.95) Regular Ed.; Luthor buys the Daily Planet 3.00

1-($3.95) Collector's Ed. with acetate cover 4.00

SUPERMAN SCRAPBOOK (Has blank pages; contains no comics)

SUPERMAN: SECRET FILES
DC Comics: Jan, 1998; May 1999 ($4.95)

Superman's Girlfriend Lois Lane #11 © DC

Superman: Silver Banshee #1 © DC

Superman's Pal Jimmy Olsen #135 © DC

	GD	VG	FN	VF	VF/NM	NM-
	2.0	4.0	6.0	8.0	9.0	9.2

1,2: 1-Retold origin story, "lost" pages & pin-ups ... 5.00
... & Origins 2004 (8/04) pin-ups by Lee, Turner and others ... 5.00
... & Origins 2005 (1/06) short stories and pin-ups by various ... 5.00

SUPERMAN: SECRET IDENTITY
DC Comics: 2004 - No. 4, 2004 ($5.95, squarebound, mini-series)

1-4-Busiek-s/Immonen-a/c ... 6.00

SUPERMAN'S GIRLFRIEND LOIS LANE (See Action Comics #1, 80 Page Giant #3, 14, Lois Lane, Showcase #9, 10, Superman #28 & Superman Family)

SUPERMAN'S GIRLFRIEND LOIS LANE (See Showcase #9,10)
National Periodical Publ.: Mar-Apr, 1958 - No. 136, Jan-Feb, 1974; No. 137, Sept-Oct, 1974

	GD	VG	FN	VF	VF/NM	NM-
1-(3-4/58)	320	640	960	2880	5440	8000
2	83	166	249	706	1303	1900
3	52	104	156	442	821	1200
4,5	43	86	129	344	622	900
6,7	34	68	102	255	465	675
8-10: 9-Pat Boone-c/story	29	58	87	216	388	560
11-13,15-19: 12-(10/59)-Aquaman app. 17-(5/60) 2nd app. Brainiac.	18	36	54	132	234	335
14-Supergirl x-over/ Batman app. on-c only	19	38	57	138	244	350
20-Supergirl/sty	18	36	54	134	237	340
21-28: 23-1st app. Lena Thorul, Lex Luthor's sister; 1st Lois as Elastic Lass.						
27-Bizarro-c/sty	14	28	42	99	175	250
29-Aquaman, Batman, Green Arrow cover app. and cameo; last 10¢ issue	14	28	42	103	184	265
30-32,34-46,48,49	9	18	27	60	100	140
33(5/62)-Mon-el app.	9	18	27	63	107	150
47-Supergirl app.	9	18	27	63	107	150
50(7/64)-Triplicate Girl, Phantom Girl & Shrinking Violet app.	9	18	27	63	107	150
51-55,57-67,69: 59-Jor-el app.; Batman back-up sty	7	14	21	45	73	100
56-Saturn Girl app.	7	14	21	47	76	105
68-(Giant G-26)	8	16	24	56	93	130
70-Penguin & Catwoman app. (1st S.A. Catwoman, 11/66; also see Detective #369 for 3rd app.); Batman & Robin cameo	24	48	72	173	313	450
71-Batman & Robin cameo (3 panels); Catwoman story cont'd from #70 (2nd app.); see Detective #369 for 3rd app	14	28	42	99	175	250
72,73,75,76,78	5	10	15	35	55	75
74-1st Bizarro Flash (5/67); JLA cameo	6	12	18	37	59	80
77-(Giant G-39)	7	14	21	47	76	105
79-Neal Adams-c or c(i) begin, end #95,108	6	12	18	37	59	80
80-85,87,88,90-92: 92-Last 12¢ issue	4	8	12	24	37	50
86,95 (Giants G-51, G-63)-Both have Neal Adams-c	6	12	18	39	62	85
89,93: 89-Batman x-over; all N. Adams-c. 93-Wonder Woman x-over/story	4	8	12	26	41	55
94,96-99,101-103,107-110	3	6	9	20	30	40
100	4	8	12	22	34	45
104-(Giant G-75)	5	10	15	35	55	75
105-Origin/1st app. The Rose & the Thorn.	5	10	15	34	55	75
106-"Black Like Me" sty; Lois changes her skin color to black	6	12	18	37	59	80
111-Justice League-c/s; Morrow-a; last 15¢ issue	4	8	12	22	34	45
112,114-123 (52 pgs.): 122-G.A. Lois Lane-r/Superman #30. 123-G.A. Batman-r/Batman #35 (w/Catwoman)	3	6	9	21	32	42
113-(Giant G-87) Kubert-a (previously unpublished G.A. story)(scarce in NM)	6	12	18	39	62	85
124-135: 130-Last Rose & the Thorn. 132-New Zatanna story	3	6	9	15	21	26
136,137: 136-Wonder Woman x-over	3	6	9	16	23	30
Annual 1(Sum, 1962)-r/L. Lane #12; Aquaman app.	20	40	60	146	261	375
Annual 2(Sum, 1963)	14	28	42	99	175	250

NOTE: Buckler a-117-121p. Curt Swan or Kurt Schaffenberger a-1-81(most); c(p)-1-15.

SUPERMAN/SHAZAM: FIRST THUNDER
DC Comics: Nov, 2005 - No. 4, Feb, 2006 ($3.50, limited series)

1-4-Retells first meeting; Winick-s/Middleton-a. Dr. Sivana app. ... 3.50

SUPERMAN: SILVER BANSHEE
DC Comics: Dec, 1998 - No. 2, Jan, 1999 ($2.25, mini-series)

1,2-Brereton-s/c; Chin-a ... 2.50

SUPERMAN'S NEMESIS: LEX LUTHOR
DC Comics: Mar, 1999 - No. 4, Jun, 1999 ($2.50, mini-series)

1-4-Semeiks-a ... 2.50

SUPERMAN'S PAL JIMMY OLSEN (Superman Family #164 on)

(See Action Comics #6 for 1st app. & 80 Page Giant)
National Periodical Publ.: Sept-Oct, 1954 - No. 163, Feb-Mar, 1974 (Fourth World #133-148)

	GD	VG	FN	VF	VF/NM	NM-
1	460	920	1380	4140	7820	11,500
2	130	260	390	1105	2053	3000
3-Last pre-code issue	74	148	222	629	1165	1700
4,5	50	100	150	425	788	1150
6-10	38	76	114	285	518	750
11-20: 15-1st S.A. issue	26	52	78	211	348	485
21-30: 29-(6/58) 1st app. Krypto with Superman	16	32	48	118	209	300
31-Origin & 1st app. Elastic Lad (Jimmy Olsen)	14	28	42	103	184	265
32-40: 33-One pg. biography of Jack Larson (TV Jimmy Olsen). 36-Intro Lucy Lane.						
37-2nd app. Elastic Lad & 1st cover app.	12	24	36	82	146	210
41-50: 41-1st J.O. Robot. 48-Intro/origin Superman Emergency Squad	10	20	30	67	116	165
51-56: 56-Last 10¢ issue	8	16	24	56	93	130
57-62,64-70: 57-Olsen marries Supergirl. 62-Mon-el & Elastic Lad app. but not as Legionnaires. 70-Element Boy (Lad) app.	6	12	18	41	66	90
63(9/62)-Legion of Super-Villains app.	6	12	18	43	69	95
71,74,75,78,80-84,86,89,90: 86-Jimmy Olsen Robot becomes Congorilla						
	5	10	15	32	51	70
72,73,76,77,79,85,87,88: 72(10/63)-Legion app.; Elastic Lad (Olsen) joins. 73-Ultra Boy app. 76,85-Legion app. 76-Legion app. 77-Olsen with Colossal Boy's powers & costume; origin Titano retold. 79-(9/64)-Titled The Red-headed Beatle of 1000 B.C. 85-Legion app.						
87-Legion of Super-Villains app. 88-Star Boy app.	5	10	15	35	55	75
91-94,96-98	4	8	12	28	44	60
95 (Giant G-25)	7	14	21	45	73	100
99-Olsen w/powers & costumes of Lightning Lad, Sun Boy & Element Lad						
	5	10	15	30	48	65
100-Legion cameo	5	10	15	32	51	70
101-103,105-112,114-120: 106-Legion app. 110-Infinity-c. 117-Batman & Legion cameo	4	8	12	22	34	45
120-Last 12¢ issue	6	12	18	37	59	80
104 (Giant G-38)	5	10	15	32	51	70
113,122,131,140 (Giants G-50,G-62,G-74,G-86)	4	8	12	20	30	40
121,123-130,132						
133-(10/70)-Jack Kirby story & art begins; re-intro Newsboy Legion; 1st app. Morgan Edge	6	12	18	39	62	85
134-1st app. Darkseid (1 panel, 12/70)	7	14	21	45	73	100
135-2nd app. Darkseid (1 pg. cameo; see New Gods & Forever People); G.A. Guardian app.	4	8	12	28	44	60
136-139: 136-Origin new Guardian. 138-Partial photo-c. 139-Last 15¢ issue	4	8	12	22	34	45
141-150: (25¢,52 pgs.). 141-Photo-c; Newsboy Legion-r by S&K begin; full pg. self-portrait of Jack Kirby; Don Rickles cameo. 149,150-G.A. Plastic Man-r in both; 150-Newsboy Legion app.	3	6	9	20	30	40
151-163	3	6	9	14	19	24

Superman: The Amazing Transformations of Jimmy Olsen TPB (2007, $14.99) reprints Olsen's transformations into Wolf-Man, Elastic Lad, Turtle Boy and others; new Bolland-c ... 15.00
NOTE: Issues #141-148 contain Simon & Kirby Newsboy Legion reprints from Star Spangled #7, 8, 9, 10, 11, 12, 13, 14 in that order. N. Adams c-109-112, 115, 117, 118, 120, 121, 132, 134-136, 147, 148. Kirby a-133-139p, 141-148p; c-133, 137, 139, 142, 145p. Kirby/N. Adams c-138, 141-144, 146. Curt Swan c-1-14(most), 140.

SUPERMAN SPECTACULAR (Also see DC Special Series #5)
DC Comics: 1982 (Magazine size, 52 pgs., square binding)

	GD	VG	FN	VF	VF/NM	NM-
1-Saga of Superman Red/ Superman Blue; Luthor and Terra-Man app.; Gonzales & Colletta-a	1	3	4	6	8	10

SUPERMAN: STRENGTH
DC Comics: 2005 - No. 3, 2005 ($5.95, limited series)

1-3: Alex Ross-c/Scott McCloud-s/Aluir Amancio-a ... 6.00

SUPERMAN / SUPERHOMBRE
DC Comics: Apr, 1945

nn - Ashcan comic, not distributed to newsstands, only for in-house use ... (no known sales)

SUPERMAN / TARZAN: SONS OF THE JUNGLE
Dark Horse Comics: Oct, 2001 - No. 3, May, 2002 ($2.99, limited series)

1-3-Elseworlds; Tarzan lands in the jungle; Dixon-s/Meglia-a/Ramos-c ... 3.00

SUPERMAN: THE DARK SIDE
DC Comics: 1998 - No. 3, 1998 ($4.95, squarebound, mini-series)

1-3: Elseworlds; Kal-El lands on Apokolips ... 5.00

SUPERMAN: THE DOOMSDAY WARS
DC Comics: 1998 - No. 3, 1999 ($4.95, squarebound, mini-series)

1-3: Superman & JLA vs. Doomsday; Jurgens-s/a(p) ... 5.00

SUPERMAN: THE KANSAS SIGHTING

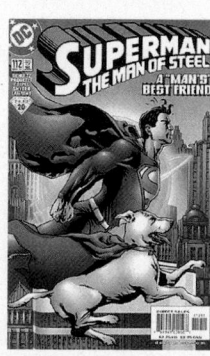

Superman: The Man of Steel #112 © DC

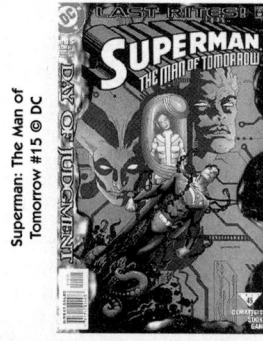

Superman: The Man of Tomorrow #15 © DC

Super-Mystery Comics V4 #3 © ACE

	GD 2.0	VG 4.0	FN 6.0	VF 8.0	VF/NM 9.0	NM- 9.2

DC Comics: 2003 - No. 2, 2003 ($6.95, squarebound, mini-series)

1,2-DeMatteis-s/Tolagson-a 7.00

SUPERMAN: THE MAN OF STEEL (Also see Man of Steel, The)
DC Comics: July, 1991 - No. 134, Mar, 2003 ($1.00/$1.25/$1.50/$1.95/$2.25)

0-(10/94) Zero Hour; released between #37 & #38 .... 2.50
1-($1.75, 52 pgs.)-Painted-c 5.00
2-16: 3-War of the Gods x-over. 5-Reads sideways. 10-Last $1.00-c.
14-Superman & Robin team-up 3.00

17-1st brief app. Doomsday .... 1 ... 2 ... 3 ... 4 ... 5 ... 7
17,18: 17-2nd printing. 18-2nd & 3rd printings 2.50
18-1st full app. Doomsday .... 1 ... 2 ... 3 ... 5 ... 7 ... 9
19-Doomsday battle issue (c/story) 6.00
20-22: 20,21-Funeral for a Friend. 22-($1.95)-Collector's Edition w/die-cut outer-c &
  bound-in poster; Steel-c/story 2.50
22-($1.50)-Newsstand Ed. w/poster & different-c 2.50
23-49,51-99: 30-Regular edition. 32-Bizarro-c/story. 35,36-Worlds Collide Pt. 1 & 10.
  37-(9/94)-Zero Hour x-over. 38-(11/94). 48-Aquaman app. 54-Spectre-c/app; Lex Luthor app.
  56-Mxyzptlk-c/app. 57-G.A. Flash app. 58-Supergirl app. 59-Parasite-c/app.; Steel app.
  60-Reintro Bottled City of Kandor. 62-Final Night. 64-New powers. 67-New powers.
  75-"Death" of Mxyzptlk. 78,79-Millennium Giants. 80-Golden Age style. 92-JLA app.
  98-Metal Men app. 2.50
30-($2.50)-Collector's Edition; polybagged with Superman & Lobo vinyl clings
  that stick to wraparound-c; Lobo-c/story 3.00
50 ($2.95)-The Trial of Superman 4.00
100-($2.99) New Fortress of Solitude revealed 3.00
100-($3.99) Special edition with fold out cardboard-c 4.00
101,102-101-Batman app. 2.50
103-133: 103-Begin $2.25. 105-Batman-c/app. 111-Return to Krypton. 115-117-Our Worlds
  at War. 117-Maxima killed. 121-Royal Flush Gang app. 128-Return to Krypton II. 2.50
134-($2.75) Last issue; Steel app.; Bogdanove-c 2.75
#1,000,000 (11/98) 853rd Century x-over; Gene Ha-c 2.50
Annual 1-5 ('92-'96,68 pgs.): 1-Eclipso app.; Joe Quesada-c(p). 2-Intro Edge. 3 -Elseworlds;
  Mignola-c; Batman app. 4-Year One story. 5-Legends of the Dead Earth story 3.00
Annual 6 (1997, $3.95)-Pulp Heroes story 3.00
...Gallery (1995, $3.50) Pin-ups by various 3.50

SUPERMAN: THE MAN OF TOMORROW
DC Comics: 1995 - No. 15, Fall, 1999 ($1.95, quarterly)

1-15: 1-Lex Luthor app. 3-Lex Luthor-c/app; Joker app. 4-Shazam! app.
  5-Wedding of Lex Luthor. 10-Maxima-c/app. 13-JLA-c/app. 2.50
#1,000,000 (11/98) 853rd Century x-over; Gene Ha-c 2.50

SUPERMAN: THE SECRET YEARS
DC Comics: Feb, 1985 - No. 4, May, 1985 (limited series)

1-4-Miller-c on all 3.00

SUPERMAN: THE WEDDING ALBUM
DC Comics: Dec, 1996 ($4.95, 96 pgs, one-shot)

1-Standard Edition-Story & art by past and present Superman creators; gatefold back-c.
  Byrne-a 5.00
1-Collector's Edition-Embossed cardstock variant-c w/ metallic silver ink and matte and
  gloss varnishes 5.00
Retailer Rep. Program Edition (#'d to 250, signed by Bob Rozakis on back-c) 50.00
TPB ('97, $14.95) r/Wedding and honeymoon stories 15.00

SUPERMAN 3-D (See Three-Dimension Adventures)

SUPERMAN-TIM (See Promotional Comics section)

SUPERMAN VILLAINS SECRET FILES
DC Comics: Jun, 1998 ($4.95, one shot)

1-Origin stories, "lost" pages & pin-ups 5.00

SUPERMAN VS. ALIENS (Also see Superman Aliens 2: God War)
DC Comics/Dark Horse Comics: July, 1995 - No. 3, Sept, 1995 ($4.95, limited series)

1-3: Jurgens/Nowlan-a 5.00

SUPERMAN VS. MUHAMMAD ALI (See All-New Collectors' Edition C-56)

SUPERMAN VS. PREDATOR
DC Comics/Dark Horse Comics: 2000 - No. 3, 2000 ($4.95, limited series)

1-3-Micheline-s/Maleev-a 5.00
TPB (2001, $14.95) r/series 15.00

SUPERMAN VS. THE AMAZING SPIDER-MAN (Also see Marvel Treasury Edition No. 28)
National Periodical Publications/Marvel Comics Group: 1976
($2.00, Treasury sized, 100 pgs.)

1-Superman and Spider-Man battle Lex Luthor and Dr. Octopus; Andru/Giordano-a;

	GD 2.0	VG 4.0	FN 6.0	VF 8.0	VF/NM 9.0	NM- 9.2

1st Marvel/DC x-over. .... 7 ... 14 ... 21 ... 49 ... 80 ... 110
1-2nd printing; 5000 numbered copies signed by Stan Lee & Carmine Infantino on
  front cover & sold through mail .. 12 ... 24 ... 36 ... 86 ... 153 ... 220
nn-(1995, $5.95)-r/#1 .... 6.00

SUPERMAN VS. THE TERMINATOR: DEATH TO THE FUTURE
Dark Horse/DC Comics: Dec, 1999 - No. 4, Mar, 2000 ($2.95, limited series)

1-4-Grant-s/Pugh-a/c: Steel and Supergirl app. 3.00

SUPERMAN/WONDER WOMAN: WHOM GODS DESTROY
DC Comics: 1997 ($4.95, prestige format, limited series)

1-4-Elseworlds; Claremont-s 5.00

SUPERMAN WORKBOOK
National Periodical Publ./Juvenile Group Foundation: 1945 (B&W, reprints, 68 pgs)

nn-Cover-r/Superman #14 .... 162 ... 324 ... 486 ... 1013 ... 1682 ... 2350

SUPER MARIO BROS. (Also see Adventures of the…, Blip, Gameboy, and Nintendo Comics System)
Valiant Comics: 1990 - No. 5?, 1991 ($1.95, slick-c) V2#1, 1991 - No. 5, 1991

1-Wildman-a 4.00
2-5, V2#1-5-($1.50) 3.00
Special Edition 1 (1990, $1.95)-Wildman-a 3.00

SUPER MARKET COMICS
Fawcett Publications: No date (1950s)

nn - Ashcan comic, not distributed to newsstands, only for in-house use ... (no known sales)

SUPER MARKET VARIETIES
Fawcett Publications: No date (1950s)

nn - Ashcan comic, not distributed to newsstands, only for in-house use ... (no known sales)

SUPERMEN OF AMERICA
DC Comics: Mar, 1999 ($3.95/$4.95, one-shot)

1-($3.95) Regular Ed.; Immonen-s/art by various 4.00
1-($4.95) Collectors' Ed. with membership kit 5.00

SUPERMEN OF AMERICA (Mini-series)
DC Comics: Mar, 2000 - No. 6, Aug, 2000 ($2.50)

1-6-Nicieza-s/Braithwaite-a 2.50

SUPERMOUSE (…the Big Cheese; see Coo Coo Comics)
Standard Comics/Pines No. 35 on (Literary Ent.): Dec, 1948 - No. 34, Sept, 1955; No. 35,
Apr, 1956 - No. 45, Fall, 1958

	GD 2.0	VG 4.0	FN 6.0	VF 8.0	VF/NM 9.0	NM- 9.2
1-Frazetta text illos (3)	28	56	84	162	256	350
2-Frazetta text illos	15	30	45	84	127	170
3,5,6-Text illos by Frazetta in all	13	26	39	74	105	135
4-Two pg. text illos by Frazetta	14	28	42	78	112	145
7-10	9	18	27	47	61	75
11-20: 13-Racist humor (Indians)	7	14	21	37	46	55
21-45	6	12	18	31	38	45
1-Summer Holiday issue (Summer, 1957, 25¢, 100 pgs.)-Pines	14	28	42	78	112	145
2-Giant Summer issue (Summer, 1958, 25¢, 100 pgs.)-Pines; has games, puzzles & stories	10	20	30	56	76	95

SUPER-MYSTERY COMICS
Ace Magazines (Periodical House): July, 1940 - V8#6, July, 1949

	GD 2.0	VG 4.0	FN 6.0	VF 8.0	VF/NM 9.0	NM- 9.2
V1#1-Magno, the Magnetic Man & Vulcan begins (1st app.); Q-13, Corp. Flint, & Sky Smith begin	300	600	900	1970	3485	5000
2	102	204	306	638	1057	1475
3-The Black Spider begins (1st app.)	80	160	240	500	830	1160
4-Origin Davy	56	112	168	350	580	810
5-Intro. The Clown & begin series (12/40)	60	120	180	375	625	875
6(2/41)	52	104	156	317	521	725
V2#1(4/41)-Origin Buckskin	50	100	150	305	503	700
2-6(2/42): 6-Vulcan begins again	47	94	141	287	474	660
V3#1(4/42),2: 1-Black Ace begins	41	82	123	256	416	575
3-Intro. The Lancer; Dr. Nemesis & The Sword begin; Kurtzman-c/a(2)						
(Mr. Risk & Paul Revere Jr.); Robot-c	53	106	159	323	532	740
4-Kurtzman-c/a; classic-c	83	166	249	519	860	1200
5-Kurtzman-a(2); L.B. Cole-a; Mr. Risk app.	51	102	153	311	511	710
6(10/43)-Mr. Risk app.; Kurtzman's Paul Revere Jr.; L.B. Cole-a						
	51	102	153	311	511	710
V4#1(1/44)-L.B. Cole-a	45	90	135	275	455	635
2-6(4/45): 2,5,6-Mr. Risk app.	32	64	96	186	293	400
V5#1(7/45)-6	32	64	96	186	293	400
V6#1-6: 3-Torture c-story. 4-Last Magno. Mr. Risk app. in #2,4-6. 6-New logo						

Supernatural: Origins #1 © WB

Superpatriot #3 © Image

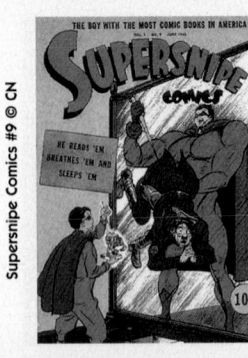

Supersnipe Comics #9 © CN

	GD 2.0	VG 4.0	FN 6.0	VF 8.0	VF/NM 9.0	NM- 9.2
	26	52	78	150	235	320
V7#1-6, V8#1-4,6	24	48	72	134	207	280
V8#5-Meskin, Tuska, Sid Greene-a	23	46	69	132	209	285

NOTE: *Sid Greene* a-V7#4. *Mooney* c-V1#5, 6, V2#1-6. *Palais* a-V5#3, 4; c-V4#6-V5#4, V6#2, V8#4. Bondage c-V2#5, 6, V3#2, 5. *Magno* c-V1#1-V3#6, V4#2-V5#5, V6#2. The Sword c-V4#1, 6(w/Magno).

SUPERNATURAL FREAK MACHINE: A CAL MCDONALD MYSTERY
IDW Publishing: Mar, 2005 - No. 3 ($3.99)

1-3-Steve Niles-s/Kelley Jones-a		4.00

SUPERNATURAL LAW (Formerly Wolff & Byrd, Counselors of the Macabre)
Exhibit A Press: No. 24, Oct, 1999 - Present ($2.50/$2.95, B&W)

24-35-Batton Lash-s/a. 29-Marie Severin-c. 33-Cerebus spoof		2.50
36-39-($2.95). 37-Frank Cho pin-up and story panels		3.00
#1 (2005, $2.95) r/Wolff & Byrd with redrawn and re-toned art; relettered		3.00
#1 At the Box Office (2006, $3.50) new stories and pin-ups		3.50
#1 With a Bullet (2006, $3.50) new stories and pin-ups		3.50
...First Amendment Issue (2005, $3.50) anti-censorship story; CBLDF info		3.50

SUPERNATURAL LAW SECRETARY MAVIS
Exhibit A Press: 2001 - Present ($2.95/$3.50, B&W)

1-3: 3-DeCarlo-c		3.00
4-($3.50) Jaime Hernandez-c		3.50

SUPERNATURAL: ORIGINS (Based on the CW television series)
DC Comics (WildStorm): July, 2007 - Present ($2.99)

1-4: 1-Bradstreet-c; Johnson-s/Smith-a; back-up w/Johns-s/Hester-a		3.00

SUPERNATURALS
Marvel Comics: Dec, 1998 - No. 4, Dec, 1998 ($3.99, weekly limited series)

1-4-Pulido-s/Balent-c; bound-in Halloween masks		4.00
1-4-With bound-in Ghost Rider mask (1 in 10)		4.00

SUPERNATURAL THRILLERS
Marvel Comics Group: Dec, 1972 - No. 6, Nov, 1973; No. 7, Jun, 1974 - No. 15, Oct, 1975

	GD 2.0	VG 4.0	FN 6.0	VF 8.0	VF/NM 9.0	NM- 9.2
1-It!; Sturgeon adap. (see Astonishing Tales #21)	3	6	9	17	25	32
2-4,6: 2-The Invisible Man; H.G. Wells adapt. 3-The Valley of the Worm; R.E. Howard adapt. 4-Dr. Jekyll & Mr. Hyde; R.L. Stevenson adapt.. 6-The Headless Horseman; last 20¢ issue	2	4	6	11	16	20
5-1st app. The Living Mummy	6	12	18	37	59	80
7-15: 7-The Living Mummy begins	3	6	9	15	21	26

NOTE: *Brunner* c-11. *Buckler* a-5p. *Ditko* a-7, 9p, 15p. *G. Kane* a-3p; c-3, 9p, 15p. *Mayerik* a-2p, 7, 8, 9p, 10p, 11. *McWilliams* a-14i. *Mortimer* a-4. *Steranko* c-9, 2. *Sutton* a-15. *Tuska* a-6p.

SUPERPATRIOT (Also see Freak Force & Savage Dragon #2)
Image Comics (Highbrow Entertainment): July, 1993 - No. 4, Dec, 1993 ($1.95, lim. series)

1-4: Dave Johnson-c/a; Larsen scripts; Giffen plots		2.50

SUPERPATRIOT: AMERICA'S FIGHTING FORCE
Image Comics: July, 2002 - No. 4, Oct, 2002 ($2.95, limited series)

1-4-Cory Walker-a/c; Savage Dragon app.		3.00

SUPERPATRIOT: LIBERTY & JUSTICE
Image Comics (Highbrow Entertainment): July, 1995 - No. 4, Oct, 1995 ($2.50, lim. series)

1-4: Dave Johnson-c/a. 1-1st app. Liberty & Justice		2.50
TPB (2002, $12.95) r/#1-4; new cover by Dave Johnson; sketch pages		13.00

SUPERPATRIOT: WAR ON TERROR
Image Comics: July, 2004 - No. 4, May, 2007 ($2.95/$2.99, limited series)

1-4-Kirkman-s/Su-a		3.00

SUPER POWERS (1st Series)
DC Comics: July, 1984 - No. 5, Nov, 1984

1-5: 1-Joker/Penguin-c/story; Batman app.; all Kirby-c. 5-Kirby c/a		5.00

SUPER POWERS (2nd Series)
DC Comics: Sept, 1985 - No. 6, Feb, 1986

1-6: Kirby-c/a; Capt. Marvel & Firestorm join; Batman cameo; Darkseid storyline in all. 4-Batman cameo. 5,6-Batman app.		5.00

SUPER POWERS (3rd Series)
DC Comics: Sept, 1986 - No. 4, Dec, 1986

1-4: 1-Cyborg joins; 1st app. Samurai from Super Friends TV show. 1-4-Batman cameos; Darkseid storyline in #1-4		4.00

SUPER PUP (Formerly Spotty The Pup) (See Space Comics)
Avon Periodicals: No. 4, Mar-Apr, 1954 - No. 5, 1954

	GD 2.0	VG 4.0	FN 6.0	VF 8.0	VF/NM 9.0	NM- 9.2
4,5: 5-Robot-c	6	12	18	31	38	45

SUPER RABBIT (See All Surprise, Animated Movie Tunes, Comedy Comics, Comic Capers,

---

Ideal Comics, It's A Duck's Life, Movie Tunes & Wisco)
Timely Comics (CmPI): Fall, 1944 - No. 14, Nov, 1948

	GD 2.0	VG 4.0	FN 6.0	VF 8.0	VF/NM 9.0	NM- 9.2
1-Hitler & Hirohito-c; war effort paper recycling PSA by S&K; Ziggy Pig & Silly begin?	76	152	228	475	788	1100
2	38	76	114	219	347	475
3-5	23	46	69	135	213	290
6-Origin	25	50	75	145	228	310
7-10: 9-Infinity-c	15	30	45	86	133	180
11-Kurtzman's "Hey Look"	15	30	45	90	140	190
12-14	15	30	45	86	133	180
I.W. Reprint #1,2('58),7,10('63): 1-r/#13. 2-r/#10.	2	4	6	9	13	16

SUPER RICHIE (Superichie #5 on) (See Richie Rich Millions #68)
Harvey Publications: Sept, 1975 - No. 4, Mar, 1976 (All 52 pg. Giants)

	GD 2.0	VG 4.0	FN 6.0	VF 8.0	VF/NM 9.0	NM- 9.2
1	3	6	9	16	23	30
2-4	2	4	6	11	16	20

SUPER SLUGGERS (Baseball)
Ultimate Sports Ent. Inc.: 1999 ($3.95, one-shot)

1-Bonds, Piazza, Caminiti, Griffey Jr. app.; Martinbrough-c/a		4.00

SUPERSNIPE COMICS (Formerly Army & Navy #1-5)
Street & Smith Publications: V1#6, Oct, 1942 - V5#1, Aug-Sept, 1949
(See Shadow Comics V2#3)

	GD 2.0	VG 4.0	FN 6.0	VF 8.0	VF/NM 9.0	NM- 9.2
V1#6-Rex King - Man of Adventure (costumed hero, see Super Magic/Magician) by Jack Binder begins; Supersnipe by George Marcoux continues from Army & Navy #5; Bill Ward-a	110	220	330	688	1144	1600
7,10-12: 10,11-Little Nemo app.	52	104	156	317	521	725
8-Hitler, Tojo, Mussolini in Hell with Devil-c	86	172	258	538	894	1250
9-Doc Savage x-over in Supersnipe; Hitler-c	97	194	291	606	1003	1400
V2 #1: Both V2#1(2/44) & V2#2(4/44) have V2#1 on outside-c; Huck Finn by Clare Dwiggins begins, ends V3#5 (rare)	76	152	228	475	788	1100
V2#2 (4/44) has V2#1 on outside-c; classic shark-c	44	88	132	268	439	610
3-12	39	78	117	224	355	485
V3#1-12: 8-Bobby Crusoe by Dwiggins begins, ends V3#12. 9-X-Mas-c	32	64	96	186	293	400
V4#1-12, V5#1: V4#10-X-Mas-c	23	46	69	130	205	280

NOTE: *George Marcoux* c-V1#6-V3#4. Doc Savage app. in some issues.

SUPER SOLDIER (See Marvel Versus DC #3)
DC Comics (Amalgam): Apr, 1996 ($1.95, one-shot)

1-Mark Waid script & Dave Gibbons-c/a.		2.50

SUPER SOLDIER: MAN OF WAR
DC Comics (Amalgam): June, 1997 ($1.95, one-shot)

1-Waid & Gibbons-s/Gibbons & Palmiotti-c/a.		2.50

SUPER SOLDIERS
Marvel Comics UK: Apr, 1993 - No. 8, Nov, 1993 ($1.75)

1-($2.50)-Embossed silver foil logo		2.50
2-8: 5-Capt. America app. 6-Origin; Nick Fury app.; neon ink-c		2.50

SUPERSPOOK (Formerly Frisky Animals on Parade)
Ajax/Farrell Publications: No. 4, June, 1958

	GD 2.0	VG 4.0	FN 6.0	VF 8.0	VF/NM 9.0	NM- 9.2
4	8	16	24	44	57	70

SUPER SPY (See Wham Comics)
Centaur Publications: Oct, 1940 - No. 2, Nov, 1940 (Reprints)

	GD 2.0	VG 4.0	FN 6.0	VF 8.0	VF/NM 9.0	NM- 9.2
1-Origin The Sparkler	90	180	270	563	932	1300
2-The Inner Circle, Dean Denton, Tim Blain, The Drew Ghost, The Night Hawk by Gustavson, & S.S. Swanson by Glanz app.	54	108	162	338	562	785

SUPERSTAR: AS SEEN ON TV
Image Comics (Gorilla): 2001 ($5.95)

1-Busiek-s/Immonen-a		6.00

SUPER STAR HOLIDAY SPECIAL (See DC Special Series #21)

SUPER-TEAM FAMILY
National Periodical Publ./DC Comics: Oct-Nov, 1975 - No. 15, Mar-Apr, 1978

	GD 2.0	VG 4.0	FN 6.0	VF 8.0	VF/NM 9.0	NM- 9.2
1-Reprints by Neal Adams & Kane/Wood; 68 pgs. begin, ends #4. New Gods app.	2	4	6	13	18	22
2,3: New stories	2	4	6	9	13	16
4-7: Reprints. 4-G.A. JSA-r & Superman/Batman/Robin-r from World's Finest. 5-52 pgs. begin	2	4	6	8	10	12
8-14: 8-10-New Challengers of the Unknown stories. 9-Kirby-a. 11-14: New stories	2	4	6	9	13	16
15-New Gods app. New stories	2	4	6	10	14	18

Super-Villain Team-Up #6 © MAR

Supreme Power: Nighthawk #1 © MAR

Supreme: The Return #1 © Awesome

	GD 2.0	VG 4.0	FN 6.0	VF 8.0	VF/NM 9.0	NM- 9.2

NOTE: *Neal Adams* r-1-3. *Brunner* c-3. *Buckler* c-8p. *Tuska* a-7r. *Wood* a-1i(r), 3.

SUPER TV HEROES (See Hanna-Barbera...)

SUPER-VILLAIN CLASSICS
Marvel Comics Group: May, 1983

1-Galactus -The Origin; Kirby-a						6.00

SUPER-VILLAIN TEAM-UP (See Fantastic Four #6 & Giant-Size...)
Marvel Comics Group: 8/75 - No. 14, 10/77; No. 15, 11/78; No. 16, 5/79; No. 17, 6/80

	GD	VG	FN	VF	VF/NM	NM-
1-Giant-Size Super-Villain Team-Up #2; Sub-Mariner & Dr. Doom begin, end #10	4	8	12	22	34	45
2-5: 5-1st app. The Shroud	2	4	6	9	13	16
5-(30¢-c variant, limited distribution)(4/76)	4	8	12	22	34	45
6,7-(25¢ editions) 6-(6/76)-F.F., Shroud app. 7-Origin Shroud	1	2	3	5	7	9
6,7-(30¢-c, limited distribution)(6,8/76)	3	6	9	20	30	40
8-17: 9-Avengers app. 11-15-Dr. Doom & Red Skull app.	1	2	3	5	7	9
12-14-(35¢-c variants, limited distribution)(6,8,10/77)	4	8	12	24	37	50

NOTE: *Buckler* c-4p, 5p, 7p. *Buscema* c-14. *Byrne/Austin* c-14. *Evans* a-1p, 3p. *Everett* a-1p. *Giffen* a-8p, 13p; c-13p. *Kane* c-2p, 9p. *Mooney* a-4i. *Starlin* c-6. *Tuska* r-1p, 15p. *Wood* r-15p.

SUPER-VILLAIN TEAM-UP/ MODOK'S 11
Marvel Comics: Sept, 2007 - No. 5 ($2.99, limited series)

1-3: 1-MODOK's origin re-told; Portela-a/Powell-c; Purple Man & Mentallo app.						3.00

SUPER WESTERN COMICS (Also see Buffalo Bill)
Youthful Magazines: Aug, 1950 (One shot)

	GD	VG	FN	VF	VF/NM	NM-
1-Buffalo Bill begins; Wyatt Earp, Calamity Jane & Sam Slade app; Powell-c/a	14	28	42	82	121	160

SUPER WESTERN FUNNIES (See Super Funnies)

SUPERWOMAN
DC Comics: Jan 1942

nn - Ashcan comic, not distributed to newsstands, only for in-house use. Cover art is More Fun Comics #73 with interior being Action Comics #38   (no known sales)

SUPERWORLD COMICS
Hugo Gernsback (Komos Publ.): Apr, 1940 - No. 3, Aug, 1940 (68 pgs.)

	GD	VG	FN	VF	VF/NM	NM-
1-Origin & 1st app. Hip Knox, Super Hypnotist; Mitey Powers & Buzz Allen, the invisible Avenger, Little Nemo begin; cover by Frank R. Paul (all have sci-fi-c) (Scarce)	731	1462	2193	5117	8959	12,800
2-Marvo 1-2 Go+, the Super Boy of the Year 2680 (1st app.); Paul-c (Scarce)	423	846	1269	2750	4875	7000
3 (Scarce)	333	666	1000	2165	3833	5500

SUPREME (Becomes ...The New Adventures at #43-48)(See Youngblood #3)
(Also see Bloodwulf Special, Legend of Supreme, & Trencher #3)
Image Comics (Extreme Studios)/ Awesome Entertainment #49 on:
V2#1, Nov, 1992 - V2#42, Sept, 1996; V3#49 - No. 56, Feb, 1998

V2#1-Liefeld-a(i) & scripts; embossed foil logo						4.00
1-Gold Edition						6.00
2-(3/93)-Liefeld co-plots & inks; 1st app. Grizlock						3.00
3-42: 3-Intro Bloodstrike; 1st app. Khrome. 5-1st app. Thor. 6-1st brief app. The Starguard. 7-1st full app. The Starguard. 10-Black and White Pt 1 (Art Thibert (2 pgs. ea. installment). 25-(5/94)-Platt-c. 11-Coupon #4 for Extreme Prejudice #0; Black and White Pt. 7 by Thibert. 12-(4/94)-Platt-c. 13,14-(6/94). 15 (7/94). 16 (7/94)-Stormwatch app. 18-Kid Supreme Sneak Preview; Pitt app.19,20-Polybagged w/trading card. 20-1st app. Woden & Loki (as a dog); Overtkill app. 21-1st app. Loki (in true form). 21-23-Poly-bagged trading card. 32-Lady Supreme cameo. 33-Origin & 1st full app. of Lady Supreme (Probe from the Starguard); Babewatch! tie-in. 37-Intro Loki; Fraga-c. 40-Retells Supreme's past advs. 41-Alan Moore scripts begin; Supreme revised; intro The Supremacy; Jerry Ordway-c (Joe Bennett variant-c exists). 42-New origin w/Rick Veitch-a; intro Radar, The Hound Supreme & The League of Infinity						3.00
28-Variant-c by Quesada & Palmiotti						3.00
(#43-48-See Supreme: The New Adventures)						
V3#49,51: 49-Begin $2.99-c						3.00
50-($3.95)-Double sized, 2 covers, pin-up gallery						4.00
52a,52b-($3.50)						3.50
53-56: 53-Sprouse-a begins. 56-McGuinness-c						3.00
Annual 1-(1995, $2.95)						3.00
...: Supreme Sacrifice (3/06, $3.99) Flip book with Suprema; Kirkman-s/Malin-a						4.00
...: The Return TPB (Checker Book Publ., 2003, $24.95) r/#53-56 & Supreme; The Return #1-6; Ross-c; additional sketch pages by Ross						25.00
...: The Story of the Year TPB (Checker Book Publ., 2002, $26.95) r/#41-52; Ross-c						27.00

NOTE: *Rob Liefeld* a(i)-1, 7; co-plots-2-4; scripts-1, 5, 6. *Ordway* c-41. *Platt* c-12, 25. *Thibert* c(i)-7-9.

SUPREME: GLORY DAYS
Image Comics (Extreme Studios): Oct, 1994 - No. 2, Dec, 1994 ($2.95/$2.50, limited series)

1,2: 2-Diehard, Roman, Superpatriot, & Glory app.						3.00

SUPREME POWER (Also see Squadron Supreme 2006 series)
Marvel Comics (MAX): Oct, 2003 - No. 18, Oct, 2005 ($2.99)

1-($2.99) Straczynski-s/Frank-a; Frank-c						3.00
1-($4.99) Special Edition with variant Quesada-c; includes r/early Squadron Supreme apps.						5.00
2-18: 4-Intro. Nighthawk. 6-The Blur debuts. 10-Princess Zarda returns. 17-Hyperion revealed as alien. 18-Continues in mini-series						3.00
Vol. 1: Contact TPB (2004, $14.99) r/#1-6						15.00
Vol. 2: Powers & Principalities TPB (2004, $14.99) r/#7-12						15.00
Vol. 3: High Command TPB (2005, $14.99) r/#13-18						15.00
Vol. 1 HC (2005, $29.99, 7 1/2" x 11" with dustjacket) r/#1-12; Avengers #85 & 86, Straczynski intro, Frank cover sketches and character design pages						30.00
Vol. 2 HC (2005, $29.99, 7 1/2" x 11" with dustjacket) r/#13-18; ...: Hyperion #1-5; character design pages						30.00

SUPREME POWER: HYPERION
Marvel Comics (MAX): Nov, 2005 - No. 5, Mar, 2006 ($2.99, limited series)

1-5: 1-Straczynski-s/Jurgens-a/Dodson-c						3.00
TPB (2006, $14.99) r/#1-5						15.00

SUPREME POWER: NIGHTHAWK
Marvel Comics (MAX): Nov, 2005 - No. 6, Apr, 2006 ($2.99, limited series)

1-6-Daniel Way-s/Steve Dillon-a; origin of Whiteface						3.00
TPB (2006, $16.99) r/#1-6; cover concept art						17.00

SUPREME: THE NEW ADVENTURES (Formerly Supreme)
Maximum Press: V3#43, Oct, 1996 - V3#48, May, 1997 ($2.50)

V3#43-48: 43-Alan Moore scripts begin; Joe Bennett-a; Rick Veitch-a (8 pgs.); Dan Jurgens-a (1 pg.); intro Citadel Supreme & Suprematons; 1st Allied Supermen of America						3.00

SUPREME: THE RETURN
Awesome Entertainment: May, 1999 - No. 6, June, 2000 ($2.99)

1-6: Alan Moore-s. 1,2-Sprouse & Gordon-a/c. 2,4-Liefeld-c. 6-Kirby app.						3.00

SURE-FIRE COMICS (Lightning Comics #4 on)
Ace Magazines: June, 1940 - No. 4, Oct, 1940 (Two No. 3's)

	GD	VG	FN	VF	VF/NM	NM-
V1#1-Origin Flash Lightning & begins; X-The Phantom Fed, Ace McCoy, Buck Steele, Marvo the Magician, The Raven, Whiz Wilson (Time Traveler) begin (all 1st app.); Flash Lightning c-1-4	179	358	537	1119	1860	2600
2	82	164	246	513	849	1185
3(9/40), 3(#4)(10/40)-nn on-c, #3 on inside	60	120	180	375	620	865

SURF 'N' WHEELS
Charlton Comics: Nov, 1969 - No. 6, Sept, 1970

	GD	VG	FN	VF	VF/NM	NM-
1	3	6	9	20	30	40
2-6	3	6	9	14	19	24

SURGE
Eclipse Comics: July, 1984 - No. 4, Jan, 1985 ($1.50, lim. series, Baxter paper)

1-4-Ties into DNAgents series						2.50

SURPRISE ADVENTURES (Formerly Tormented)
Sterling Comic Group: No. 3, Mar, 1955 - No. 5, July, 1955

	GD	VG	FN	VF	VF/NM	NM-
3-5: 3,5-Sekowsky-a	9	18	27	47	61	75

SUSIE Q. SMITH
Dell Publishing Co.: No. 323, Mar, 1951 - No. 553, Apr, 1954

	GD	VG	FN	VF	VF/NM	NM-
Four Color 323 (#1)	5	10	15	32	51	70
Four Color 377, 453 (2/53), 553	4	8	12	26	41	55

SUSPENSE (Radio/TV issues #1-11; Real Life Tales of... #1-4) (Amazing Detective Cases #3 on?)
Marvel/Atlas Comics (CnPC No. 1-10/BFP No. 11-29): Dec, 1949 - No. 29, Apr, 1953 (#1-8, 17-23: 52 pgs.)

	GD	VG	FN	VF	VF/NM	NM-
1-Powell-a; Peter Lorre, Sidney Greenstreet photo-c from Hammett's "The Verdict"	59	118	177	369	610	850
2-Crime stories; Dennis O'Keefe & Gale Storm photo-c from Universal movie "Abandoned"	35	70	105	201	318	435
3-Change to horror	40	80	120	240	383	525
4,7-10: 7-Dracula-sty	31	62	93	178	282	385
5-Krigstein, Tuska, Everett-a	33	66	99	190	300	410
6-Tuska, Everett, Morisi-a	32	64	96	186	293	400
11-13,15-17,19,20	25	50	75	145	228	310
14-Clasic Heath Hypo-c; A-Bomb panels	36	72	108	208	329	450
18-Krigstein-a	26	52	78	150	235	320
21,23,24,26-29: 24-Tuska-a	22	44	66	128	202	275

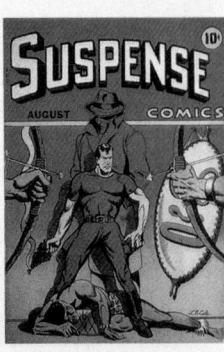

Suspense Comics #5 © Continental

Swamp Thing #13 © DC

Sweetheart Diary #2 © FAW

	GD 2.0	VG 4.0	FN 6.0	VF 8.0	VF/NM 9.0	NM- 9.2
25-Electric chair-c/story	31	62	93	178	282	385

NOTE: *Ayers a*-20. *Briefer a*-5, 7, 27. *Brodsky c*-4, 6-9, 11, 16, 17, 25. *Colan a*-8(2), 9. *Everett a*-5, 6(2), 19, 23, 28; c-21-23, 26. *Fuje a*-29. *Heath a*-5, 6, 8, 10, 12, 14; c-14, 19, 24. *Maneely a*-12, 23, 24, 28, 29; c-5, 6p, 10, 13, 15, 18. *Mooney a*-24, 28. *Morisi a*-6, 12. *Palais a*-10. *Rico a*-7-9. *Robinson a*-29. *Romita a*-20(2), 25. *Sekowsky a*-11, 13, 14. *Sinnott a*-23, 25. *Tuska a*-5(2); 12; c-12. *Whitney a*-15, 16, 22. *Ed Win a*-27.

SUSPENSE COMICS
Continental Magazines: Dec, 1943 - No. 12, Sept, 1946

1-The Grey Mask begins; bondage/torture-c; L. B. Cole-a (7 pgs.)						
	388	776	1164	2522	4461	6400
2-Intro. The Mask; Rico, Giunta, L. B. Cole-a (7 pgs.)						
	276	552	828	1725	2863	4000
3-L.B. Cole-a; classic Schomburg-c (Scarce)	2500	5000	7500	15,000	22,500	30,000
4-6: 4-L. B. Cole begin	207	414	621	1294	2147	3000
7,9,10,12: 9-L.B. Cole eyeball-c	159	318	477	994	1647	2300
8-Classic L. B. Cole spider-c	388	776	1164	2522	4461	6400
11-Classic Devil-c	300	600	900	1970	3485	5000

NOTE: *L. B. Cole c*-4-12. *Fuje a*-8. *Larsen a*-11. *Palais a*-10, 11. *Bondage c*-1, 3, 4.

SUSPENSE DETECTIVE
Fawcett Publications: June, 1952 - No. 5, Mar, 1953

1-Evans-a (11 pgs)	45	90	135	275	450	625
2-Evans-a (10 pgs.)	27	54	81	156	246	335
3-5	23	46	69	130	205	280

NOTE: *Baily a*-4, 5; c-1-3. *Sekowsky a*-2, 4, 5; c-5.

SUSPENSE STORIES (See Strange Suspense Stories)

SUSSEX VAMPIRE, THE (Sherlock Holmes)
Caliber Comics: 1996 ($2.95, 32 pgs., B&W, one-shot)

nn-Adapts Sir Arthur Conan Doyle's story; Warren Ellis scripts						3.00

SUZIE COMICS (Formerly Laugh Comix; see Laugh Comics, Liberty Comics #10, Pep Comics & Top-Notch Comics #28)
Close-Up No. 49,50/MLJ Mag./Archie No. 51 on: No. 49, Spring, 1945 - No. 100, Aug, 1954

49-Ginger begins	24	48	72	139	220	300
50-55: 54-Transvestism story. 55-Woggon-a	15	30	45	86	133	180
56-Katy Keene begins by Woggon	15	30	45	88	137	185
57-65	12	24	36	67	94	120
66-80	11	22	33	62	86	110
81-87,89-99	10	20	30	56	76	95
88,100: 88-Used in **POP**, pgs. 76,77; Bill Woggon draws himself in story.						
100-Last Katy Keene	11	22	33	62	86	110

NOTE: *Al Fagaly c*-49-67. *Katy Keene app. in 53-82, 85-100.*

SWAMP FOX, THE (TV, Disney)(See Walt Disney Presents #2)
Dell Publishing Co.: No. 1179, Dec, 1960

Four Color 1179-Leslie Nielsen photo-c	8	16	24	56	93	130

SWAMP THING (See Brave & the Bold, Challengers of the Unknown #82, DC Comics Presents #8 & 85, DC Special #2, 14, 17, 20, House of Secrets #92, Limited Collectors' Edition C-59, & Roots of the...)

SWAMP THING
National Per. Publ./DC Comics: Oct-Nov, 1972 - No. 24, Aug-Sept, 1976

1-Wrightson-c/a begins; origin	14	28	42	99	175	250
2-1st brief app. Patchwork Man (1 panel)	7	14	21	47	76	105
3-1st full app. Patchwork Man (see House of Secrets #140)						
	5	10	15	35	55	75
4-6,	4	8	12	28	44	60
7-Batman-c/story	5	10	15	30	48	65
8-10: 10-Last Wrightson issue	4	8	12	24	37	50
11-20: 11-19-Redondo-a. 13-Origin retold (1 pg.)	3	6	9	14	20	25
21-24: 23,24-Swamp Thing reverts back to Dr. Holland. 23-New logo						
	3	6	9	14	20	25
Secret of the Swamp Thing (2005, $9.99, digest) r/#1-10						10.00

NOTE: *J. Jones a*-9i(assist). *Kaluta a*-9i. *Redondo c*-12-19, 21. *Wrightson issues (#1-10) reprinted in DC Special Series #2, 14, 17, 20 & Roots of the Swamp Thing.*

SWAMP THING (Saga Of The... #1-38,42-45) (See Essential Vertigo:...)
DC Comics (Vertigo imprint #129 on): May, 1982 - No. 171, Oct, 1996
(Direct sales #65 on)

1-Origin retold; Phantom Stranger series begins; ends #13; Yeates-c/a begins						6.00
2-15: 2-Photo-c from movie. 13-Last Yeates-a						4.00
16-19: Bissette-a.						5.00
20-1st Alan Moore issue	3	4	6	13	18	22
21-New moving vision	2	4	6	10	14	18
22,23,25: 25-John Constantine 1-panel cameo	2	4	6	8	10	12
24-JLA x-over; Last Yeates-c.	2	4	6	8	11	14
26-30	1	2	3	4	5	7
31-33,35,36: 33-r/1st app. from House of Secrets #92						5.00

	GD 2.0	VG 4.0	FN 6.0	VF 8.0	VF/NM 9.0	NM- 9.2
34	1	2	3	5	6	8
37-1st app. John Constantine (Hellblazer) (6/85)	2	4	6	9	12	15
38-40: John Constantine app.	1	2	3	5	6	8
41-52,54-64: 44-Batman cameo. 44-51-John Constantine app. 46-Crisis x-over; Batman cameo. 49-Spectre app. 50-($1.25, 52 pgs.)-Deadman, Dr. Fate, Demon. 52-Arkham Asylum-c/story; Joker-c/cameo. 58-Spectre preview. 64-Last Moore issue						3.50
53-($1.25, 52 pgs.)-Arkham Asylum; Batman-c/story						4.50
65-83,85-99,101-124,126-149,151-153: 65-Direct sales only begins. 66-Batman & Arkham Asylum story. 70,76-John Constantine x-over; 76-X-over w/Hellblazer #9. 79-Superman-c/story. 85-Jonah Hex app. 102-Preview of World Without End. 116-Photo-c. 129-Metallic ink on-c. 140-Millar scripts begin, end #171						3.00
84-Sandman (Morpheus) cameo.						4.00
100,125,150: 100 ($2.50, 52 pgs.). 125-($2.95, 52 pgs.)-20th anniversary issue. 150 (52 pgs.)-Anniversary issue						3.00
154-171: 154-$2.25-c begins. 165-Curt Swan-a(p). 166,169,171-John Constantine & Phantom Stranger app. 168-Arcane returns						2.50
Annual 1,3-6('82-91): 1-Movie Adaptation; painted-c. 3-New format; Bolland-c. 4-Batman-c/story. 5-Batman app. since 1968						4.00
Annual 2 (1985)-Moore scripts; Bissette-a(p); Deadman, Spectre app.						7.00
Annual 7(1993, $3.95)-Children's Crusade						4.00
...A Murder of Crows (2001, $19.95)-r/#43-50; Moore-s						20.00
...: Earth To Earth (2002, $17.95)-r/#51-56; Batman app.						18.00
...: Infernal Triangles (2006, $19.99, TPB) r/#77-81 & Annual #3; cover gallery						20.00
...Love and Death (1990, $17.95)-r/#28-34 & Annual #2; Totleben painted-c						18.00
...: Regenesis (2004, $17.95, TPB) r/#65-70; Veitch-s						18.00
...: Reunion (2003, $19.95, TPB) r/#57-64; Moore-s						20.00
...: Roots (1998, $7.95) Jon J Muth-s/painted-a/c						8.00
Saga of the Swamp Thing ('87, '89)-r/#21-27 (1st & 2nd print)						13.00
...: Spontaneous Generation (2005, $19.99) r/#71-76						20.00
...: The Curse (2000, $19.95, TPB) r/#35-42; Bisley-c						20.00

NOTE: *Bissette a(p)-16-19, 21-27, 29, 30, 34-36, 39-42, 44, 46, 50, 64; c-17i, 24-32p, 35-37p, 40p, 44p, 46-50p, 51-58, 61, 62, 63p. Kaluta c/a-74. Spiegle a-1-3, 6. Sutton a-98p. Totleben a(i)-10, 16-27, 29, 31, 34-40, 42, 44, 46, 48, 50, 53, 55i; c-25-32i, 33, 35-40i, 42i, 44i, 46-50i, 53, 55i, 59p, 64, 65, 68, 73, 76, 80, 82, 84, 89, 91-100, Annual 4, 5. Vess painted-c-151; a-139, Annual 7. Williamson 86i. Wrightson a-18i(r), 33r. John Constantine appears in #37-40, 44-51, 65-67, 70-77, 80-90, 99, 114, 115, 130, 134-138.*

SWAMP THING
DC Comics (Vertigo): May, 2000 - No. 20, Dec, 2001 ($2.50)

1-3-Tefé Holland's return; Vaughan-s/Petersen-a; Hale painted-c						3.00
4-20: 7-9-Bisley-c. 10-John Constantine-c/app. 10-12-Fabry-c. 13-15-Mack-c. 18-Swamp Thing app.						2.50
Preview-16 pg. flip book w/Lucifer Preview						2.25

SWAMP THING
DC Comics (Vertigo): May, 2004 - No. 29, Sept, 2006 ($2.95/$2.99)

1-29: 1-Diggle-s/Breccia-a; Constantine app. 2-6-Sargon app. 7,8,20-Corben-c/a. 21-29-Eric Powell-c						3.00
...: Bad Seed (2004, $9.99) r/#1-6						10.00
...: Healing the Breach (2006, $17.99) r/#15-20						18.00
...: Love in Vain (2005, $14.99) r/#9-14						15.00

SWAT MALONE (America's Home Run King)
Swat Malone Enterprises: Sept, 1991

V1#1-Hy Fleishman-a	11	22	33	62	86	110

SWEATSHOP
DC Comics: Jun, 2003 - No. 6, Nov, 2003 ($2.95)

1-6-Peter Bagge-s/a; Destefano-a						3.00

SWEENEY (Formerly Buz Sawyer)
Standard Comics: No. 4, June, 1949 - No. 5, Sept, 1949

4,5: 5-Crane-a	9	18	27	47	61	75

SWEE'PEA (Also see Popeye #46)
Dell Publishing Co.: No. 219, Mar, 1949

Four Color 219	8	16	24	56	93	130

SWEET CHILDE
Advantage Graphics Press: 1995 - No. 2, 1995 ($2.95, B&W, mature)

1,2						3.00

SWEETHEART DIARY (Cynthia Doyle #66-on)
Fawcett Publications/Charlton Comics No. 32 on: Wint, 1949; #2, Spr, 1950; #3, 6/50 - #5, 10/50; #6, 1951(nd); #7, 9/51 - #14, 1/53; #32, 10/55; #33, 4/56 - #65, 8/62 (#1-14: photo-c)

1	19	38	57	112	176	240
2	12	24	36	67	94	120
3,4-Wood-a	15	30	45	85	130	175
5-10: 8-Bailey-a	10	20	30	54	72	90

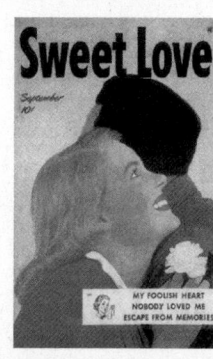

Sweet Love #1 © HARV

Swift Arrow #1 © AJAX

Swords of Texas #1 © ECL

	GD 2.0	VG 4.0	FN 6.0	VF 8.0	VF/NM 9.0	NM- 9.2
11-14: 13-Swayze-a. 14-Last Fawcett issue	8	16	24	44	57	70
32 (10/55; 1st Charlton issue)(Formerly Cowboy Love #31)						
	9	18	27	47	61	75
33-40: 34-Swayze-a	6	12	18	31	38	45
41-(68 pgs.)	7	14	21	35	43	50
42-60	3	6	9	18	27	35
61-65	3	6	9	17	25	32

SWEETHEARTS (Formerly Captain Midnight)
Fawcett Publications/Charlton No. 122 on: #68, 10/48 - #121, 5/53; #122, 3/54; V2#23, 5/54 - #137, 12/73

	GD 2.0	VG 4.0	FN 6.0	VF 8.0	VF/NM 9.0	NM- 9.2
68-Photo-c begin	17	34	51	98	154	210
69,70	11	22	33	60	83	105
71-80	9	18	27	50	65	80
81-84,86-93,95-99,105	8	16	24	44	57	70
85,94,103,110,117-George Evans-a	9	18	27	52	69	85
100	9	18	27	50	65	80
101,107-Powell-a	9	18	27	44	61	75
102,104,106,108,109,112-116,118	8	16	24	42	54	65
111-1 pg. Ronald Reagan biography	10	20	30	54	72	90
119-Marilyn Monroe & Richard Widmark photo-c (1/54?); also appears in story; part Wood-a	53	106	159	323	537	750
120-Atom Bomb story	11	22	33	64	90	115
121-Liz Taylor/Fernanado Lamas photo-c	24	48	72	139	220	300
122-(1st Charlton? 3/54)-Marijuana story	12	24	36	67	94	120
V2#23 (5/54)-28: 28-Last precode issue (2/55)	8	16	24	40	50	60
29-39,41,43-45,47-50	4	8	12	24	37	50
40-Photo-c; Tommy Sands story	4	8	12	26	41	55
42-Ricky Nelson photo-c/story	8	16	24	56	93	130
46-Jimmy Rodgers photo-c/story	4	8	12	26	41	55
51-60	3	6	9	20	30	40
61-80,100	3	6	9	18	27	35
81-99	3	6	9	17	25	32
101-110	2	4	6	13	18	22
111-137	2	4	6	10	14	18

NOTE: Photo c-68-121(Fawcett), 40, 42, 46(Charlton). *Swayze* a(Fawcett)-70-118(most).

SWEETHEART SCANDALS (See Fox Giants)

SWEETIE PIE
Dell Publishing Co.: No. 1185, May-July, 1961 - No. 1241, Nov-Jan, 1961/62

	GD 2.0	VG 4.0	FN 6.0	VF 8.0	VF/NM 9.0	NM- 9.2
Four Color 1185 (#1)	5	10	15	30	48	65
Four Color 1241	4	8	12	24	37	50

SWEETIE PIE
Ajax-Farrell/Pines (Literary Ent.): Dec, 1955 - No. 15, Fall, 1957

	GD 2.0	VG 4.0	FN 6.0	VF 8.0	VF/NM 9.0	NM- 9.2
1-By Nadine Seltzer	9	18	27	52	69	85
2 (5/56; last Ajax?)	6	12	18	31	38	45
3-15	5	10	15	24	30	35

SWEET LOVE
Home Comics (Harvey): Sept, 1949 - No. 5, May, 1950 (All photo-c)

	GD 2.0	VG 4.0	FN 6.0	VF 8.0	VF/NM 9.0	NM- 9.2
1	10	20	30	58	79	100
2	7	14	21	37	46	55
3,4: 3-Powell-a	6	12	18	31	38	45
5-Kamen, Powell-a	9	18	27	47	61	75

SWEET ROMANCE
Charlton Comics: Oct, 1968

	GD 2.0	VG 4.0	FN 6.0	VF 8.0	VF/NM 9.0	NM- 9.2
1	3	6	9	14	20	25

SWEET SIXTEEN (…Comics and Stories for Girls)
Parents' Magazine Institute: Aug-Sept, 1946 - No. 13, Jan, 1948 (All have movie stars photos on covers)

	GD 2.0	VG 4.0	FN 6.0	VF 8.0	VF/NM 9.0	NM- 9.2
1-Van Johnson's life story; Dorothy Dare, Queen of Hollywood Stunt Artists begins (in all issues); part photo-c	22	44	66	128	202	275
2-Jane Powell, Roddy McDowall "Holiday in Mexico" photo on-c; Alan Ladd story	15	30	45	86	133	180
3,5,6,8-11: 5-Ann Francis photo on-c; Gregory Peck story. 6-Dick Haymes story. 8-Shirley Jones photo on-c. 10-Jean Simmons photo on-c; James Stewart story	12	24	36	69	97	125
4-Elizabeth Taylor photo on-c	24	48	72	139	220	300
7-Ronald Reagan's life story	22	44	66	128	202	275
12-Bob Cummings, Vic Damone story	13	26	39	74	105	135
13-Robert Mitchum's life story	14	28	42	76	108	140

SWEET XVI
Marvel Comics: May, 1991 - No. 5, Sept, 1991($1.00, color)

	GD 2.0	VG 4.0	FN 6.0	VF 8.0	VF/NM 9.0	NM- 9.2
1-5: Barbara Slate story & art						3.00

SWIFT ARROW (Also see Lone Rider & The Rider)
Ajax/Farrell Publications: Feb-Mar, 1954 - No. 5, Oct-Nov, 1954; Apr, 1957 - No. 3, Sept, 1957

	GD 2.0	VG 4.0	FN 6.0	VF 8.0	VF/NM 9.0	NM- 9.2
1(1954) (1st Series)	16	32	48	92	144	195
2	10	20	30	56	76	95
3-5: 5-Lone Rider story	9	18	27	50	65	80
1 (2nd Series) (Swift Arrow's Gunfighters #4)	9	18	27	50	65	80
2,3: 2-Lone Rider begins	8	16	24	40	50	60

SWIFT ARROW'S GUNFIGHTERS (Formerly Swift Arrow)
Ajax/Farrell Publ. (Four Star Comic Corp.): No. 4, Nov, 1957

	GD 2.0	VG 4.0	FN 6.0	VF 8.0	VF/NM 9.0	NM- 9.2
4	8	16	24	40	50	60

SWING WITH SCOOTER
National Periodical Publ.: June-July, 1966 - No. 35, Aug-Sept, 1971; No. 36, Oct-Nov, 1972

	GD 2.0	VG 4.0	FN 6.0	VF 8.0	VF/NM 9.0	NM- 9.2
1	8	16	24	56	93	130
2,6-10: 9-Alfred E. Newman swipe in last panel	5	10	15	30	48	65
3-5: 3-Batman cameo on-c. 4-Batman cameo inside. 5-JLA cameo	5	10	15	32	51	70
11-13,15-19: 18-Wildcat of JSA 1pg. text. 19-Last 12¢-c	3	6	9	19	29	38
14-Alfred E. Neuman cameo	3	6	9	20	30	40
20 (68 pgs.)	4	8	12	28	44	60
21-23,25-31	3	6	9	16	23	30
24-Frankenstein-c.	3	6	9	19	29	38
32-34 (68 pgs.). 32-Batman cameo. 33-Interview with David Cassidy. 34-Interview with Rick Ely (The Rebels)	4	8	12	26	41	55
35-(52 pgs.). 1 pg. app. Clark Kent and 4 full pgs. of Superman	7	14	21	47	76	105
36-Bat-signal refererence to Batman	3	6	9	19	29	38

NOTE: *Aragonés* a-13 (1pg.), 18(1pg.), 30(2pgs.) *Orlando* a-1-11, 13. #20, 33, 34; 68 pgs.; #35: 52 pgs.

SWISS FAMILY ROBINSON (Walt Disney's..; see King Classics & Movie Comics)
Dell Publishing Co.: No. 1156, Dec, 1960

	GD 2.0	VG 4.0	FN 6.0	VF 8.0	VF/NM 9.0	NM- 9.2
Four Color 1156-Movie-photo-c	7	14	21	49	80	110

SWORD & THE DRAGON, THE
Dell Publishing Co.: No. 1118, June, 1960

	GD 2.0	VG 4.0	FN 6.0	VF 8.0	VF/NM 9.0	NM- 9.2
Four Color 1118-Movie, photo-c	7	14	21	50	83	115

SWORD & THE ROSE, THE (Disney)
Dell Publishing Co.: No. 505, Oct, 1953 - No. 682, Feb, 1956

	GD 2.0	VG 4.0	FN 6.0	VF 8.0	VF/NM 9.0	NM- 9.2
Four Color 505-Movie, photo-c	8	16	24	56	93	130
Four Color 682-When Knighthood Was in Flower-Movie, reprint of #505; Renamed the Sword & the Rose for the novel; photo-c	7	14	21	47	76	105

SWORD IN THE STONE, THE (See March of Comics #258 & Movie Comics & Wart and the Wizard)

SWORD OF DAMOCLES
Image Comics (WildStorm Productions): Mar, 1996 - No. 2, Apr, 1996 ($2.50, limited series)

1,2: Warren Ellis scripts. 1-Prelude to "Fire From Heaven" x-over; 1st app. Sword	2.50

SWORD OF DRACULA
Image Comics: Oct, 2003 - No. 6, Sept, 2004 ($2.95, B&W, limited series)

1-6-Tony Harris-c. 1,2-Greg Scott-a	3.00
TPB (IDW, 2/05, $14.99) r/series	15.00

SWORD OF SORCERY
National Periodical Publications: Feb-Mar, 1973 - No. 5, Nov-Dec, 1973 (20¢)

	GD 2.0	VG 4.0	FN 6.0	VF 8.0	VF/NM 9.0	NM- 9.2
1-Leiber Fafhrd & The Grey Mouser; Chaykin/Neal Adams (Crusty Bunkers) art; Kaluta-c	2	4	6	13	18	22
2,3: 2-Wrightson-c(i); Adams-a(i). 3-Wrightson-i(5 pgs.)	2	4	6	8	10	12
4,5: 5-Starlin-a(p); Conan cameo	1	2	3	5	7	9

NOTE: *Chaykin* a-1-4p; c-2p, 3-5. *Kaluta* a-3i. *Simonson* a-3i, 4i, 5p; c-5.

SWORD OF THE ATOM
DC Comics: Sept, 1983 - No. 4, Dec, 1983 (Limited series)

1-4: Gil Kane-c/a in all	3.00
Special 1-3('84, '85, '88): 1,2-Kane-c/a each	3.00

SWORDS OF TEXAS (See Scout #15)
Eclipse Comics: Oct, 1987 - No. 4, Jan, 1988 ($1.75, color, Baxter paper)

1-4: Scout app.	2.50

SWORDS OF THE SWASHBUCKLERS (See Marvel Graphic Novel)
Marvel Comics (Epic Comics): May, 1985 - No. 12, Jun, 1987 ($1.50; mature)

1-12-Butch Guice-c/a (Cont'd from Marvel G.N.)	2.50

Taffy #11 © Orbit

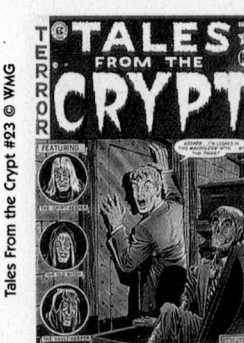
Tales From the Crypt #23 © WMG

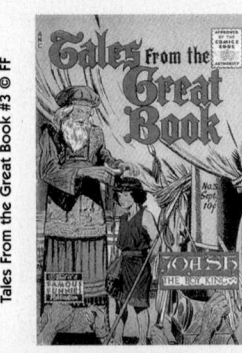
Tales from the Great Book #3 © FF

	GD 2.0	VG 4.0	FN 6.0	VF 8.0	VF/NM 9.0	NM- 9.2

SWORN TO PROTECT
Marvel Comics: Sept, 1995 ($1.95) (Based on card game)
nn-Overpower Game Guide; Jubilee story ... 2.50

SYN
Dark Horse Comics: Aug, 2003 - No. 5, Feb, 2004 ($2.99, limited series)
1-5-Giffen-s/Titus-a ... 3.00

SYPHONS
Now Comics: V2#1, May, 1994 - V2#3, 1994 ($2.50, limited series)
V2#1-3: 1-Stardancer, Knightfire, Raze & Brigade begin ... 2.50
TPB (9/04, $15.95) B&W reprints #1-3; intro. by Tony Caputo ... 16.00

SYSTEM, THE
DC Comics (Vertigo Verite): May, 1996 - No. 3, July, 1996 ($2.95, lim. series)
1-3: Kuper-c/a ... 3.00
TPB (1997, $12.95) r/#1-3 ... 13.00

TAFFY COMICS
Rural Home/Orbit Publ.: Mar-Apr, 1945 - No. 12, 1948
1-L.B. Cole-c; origin & 1st app. of Wiggles The Wonderworm plus 7 chapter
WWII funny animal adventures ... 60 120 180 375 625 875
2-L.B. Cole-c with funny animal Hitler; Wiggles-c/stories in #1-4 ... 32 64 96 186 293 400
3,4,6-12: 6-Perry Como-c/story. 7-Duke Ellington, 2 pgs. 8-Glenn Ford-c/story. 9-Lon
McCallister part photo-c & story. 10-Mort Leav-c. 11-Mickey Rooney-c/story ... 14 28 42 82 121 160
5-L.B. Cole-c; Van Johnson-c/story ... 22 44 66 126 198 270

TAILGUNNER JO
DC Comics: Sept, 1988 - No. 6, Jan, 1989 ($1.25)
1-6 ... 2.50

TAILS
Archie Publications; Dec, 1995 - No. 3, Feb, 1996 ($1.50, limited series)
1-3: Based on Sonic, the Hedgehog video game ... 4.00

TAILSPIN
Spotlight Publishers: November, 1944
nn-Firebird app.; L.B. Cole-c ... 28 56 84 162 256 350

TAILSPIN TOMMY (Also see Popular Comics)
United Features Syndicate/Service Publ. Co.: 1940; 1946
Single Series 23(1940) ... 40 80 120 239 380 520
Best Seller (nd, 1946)-Service Publ. Co. ... 15 30 45 86 133 180

TAINTED
DC Comics (Vertigo): Jan, 1995 ($4.95, one-shot)
1-Jamie Delano scripts; Al Davison-c/a; reads February '95 on-c ... 5.00

TAKION
DC Comics: June, 1996 - No. 7, Dec, 1996 ($1.75)
1-7: Lopresti-c/a(p). 1-Origin; Green Lantern app. 6-Final Night x-over ... 2.50

TALENT SHOWCASE (See New Talent Showcase)

TALE OF ONE BAD RAT, THE
Dark Horse Comics: Oct, 1994 - No. 4, Jan, 1995 ($2.95, limited series)
1-4: Bryan Talbot-c/a/scripts ... 3.00
HC ($69.95, signed and numbered) R/#1-4 ... 70.00

TALES CALCULATED TO DRIVE YOU BATS
Archie Publications: Nov, 1961 - No. 7, Nov, 1962; 1966 (Satire)
1-Only 10¢ issue; has cut-out Werewolf mask (price includes mask) ... 12 24 36 86 153 220
2-Begin 12¢ issues ... 7 14 21 49 80 110
3-6: 3-UFO cover ... 6 12 18 37 59 80
7-Storyline change ... 5 10 15 35 55 75
1(1966, 25¢, 44 pg. Giant)-r/#1; UFO cover ... 5 10 15 35 55 75

TALES CALCULATED TO DRIVE YOU MAD
E.C. Publications: Summer, 1997 - No. 8, Winter, 1999 ($3.99/$4.99, satire)
1-6-Full color reprints of Mad: 1-(#1-3), 2-(#4-6), 3-(#7-9), 4-(#10-12)
5-(#13-15), 6-(#16-18) ... 5.00
7,8-($4.99-c): 7-(#19-21), 8-(#22,23) ... 5.00

TALES FROM RIVERDALE DIGEST
Archie Publ.: June, 2005 - Present ($2.39/$2.49, digest-size)
1-26: 1-Sabrina and Josie & the Pussycats app. 11-Begin $2.49-c ... 2.50

TALES FROM THE AGE OF APOCALYPSE
Marvel Comics: 1996 ($5.95, prestige format, one-shots)
1, ...: Sinister Bloodlines (1997, $5.95) ... 6.00

TALES FROM THE BOG
Aberration Press: Nov, 1995 - No. 7, Nov, 1997 ($2.95/$3.95, B&W)
1-7 ... 4.00
Alternate #1 (Director's Cut) (1998, $2.95) ... 3.00

TALES FROM THE BULLY PULPIT
Image Comics: Aug, 2004 ($6.95, square-bound)
1-Teddy Roosevelt and Edison's ghost with a time machine; Cereno-s/MacDonald-a ... 7.00

TALES FROM THE CLERKS (See Jay and Silent Bob, Clerks and Oni Double Feature)
Graphitti Designs, Inc.: 2006 ($29.95, TPB)
nn-Reprints all the Kevin Smith Clerks and Jay and Silent Bob stories; new Clerks II story
with Mahfood-a; cover gallery, sketch pages, Mallrats credits covers; Smith intro. ... 30.00

TALES FROM THE CRYPT (Formerly The Crypt Of Terror; see Three Dimensional...)
(Also see EC Archives • Tales From the Crypt)
E.C. Comics: No. 20, Oct-Nov, 1950 - No. 46, Feb-Mar, 1955
20-See Crime Patrol #15 for 1st Crypt Keeper ... 115 230 345 920 1435 1950
21-Kurtzman-r/Haunt of Fear #15(#1) ... 94 188 282 752 1176 1600
22-Moon Girl costume at costume party, one panel ... 75 150 225 600 938 1275
23-25: 24-E. A. Poe adaptation ... 58 116 174 464 725 985
26-30: 26-Wood's 2nd EC-c ... 46 92 138 368 577 785
31-Williamson-a(1st at E.C.); B&W and color illos. in POP; Kamen draws himself,
Gaines & Feldstein; Ingels, Craig & Davis draw themselves in this story ... 47 94 141 376 588 800
32,35-39: 38-Censored-c ... 41 82 123 328 514 700
33-Origin The Crypt Keeper ... 64 128 192 512 799 1085
34-Used in POP, pg. 83; lingerie panels ... 42 84 126 336 526 715
40-Used in Senate hearings & in Hartford Cournat anti-comics editorials-1954 ... 41 82 123 328 514 700
41-45: 45-2 pgs. showing E.C. staff ... 40 80 120 320 500 680
46-Low distribution; pre-advertised cover for unpublished 4th horror title
"Crypt of Terror" used on this book ... 47 94 141 376 588 800
NOTE: *Ray Bradbury* adaptations-34, 36. *Craig* a-20, 22-24; c-20. *Crandall* a-38, 44. *Davis* a-24-46; c-29-46. *Elder* a-37, 38. *Evans* a-32-34, 36, 40, 41, 43, 46. *Feldstein* a-20-23; c-21-25, 28. *Ingels* a-in all. *Kamen* a-20, 22, 25, 27-31, 33-36, 39, 41-45. *Krigstein* a-40, 42, 45. *Kurtzman* a-21. *Orlando* a-27-30, 35, 37, 39, 41-45. *Wood* a-21, 24, 25; c-26, 27. Canadian reprints known; see Table of Contents.

TALES FROM THE CRYPT (Magazine)
Eerie Publications: No. 10, July, 1968 (35¢, B&W)
10-Contains Farrell reprints from 1950s ... 4 8 12 28 44 60

TALES FROM THE CRYPT
Gladstone Publishing: July, 1990 - No. 6, May, 1991 ($1.95/$2.00, 68 pgs.)
1-r/TFTC #33 & Crime S.S. #17; Davis-c(r) ... 3.00
2-6: 2,3,5,6-Davis-c(r). 4-Begin $2.00-c; Craig-c(r) ... 3.00

TALES FROM THE CRYPT
Extra-Large Comics (Russ Cochran)/Gemstone Publishing: Jul, 1991 - No. 6 ($3.95, 10 1/4 x13 1/4", 68 pgs.)
1-Davis-c(r); Craig back-c(r); E.C. reprints ... 4.00
2-6 ($2.00, comic sized) ... 3.00

TALES FROM THE CRYPT
Russ Cochran: Sept, 1991 - No. 7, July, 1992 ($2.00, 64 pgs.)
1-7 ... 3.00

TALES FROM THE CRYPT (Also see EC Archives • Tales From the Crypt)
Russ Cochran/Gemstone: Sept, 1992 - No. 30, Dec, 1999 ($1.50, quarterly)
1-4-r/Crypt of Terror #17-19, TFTC #20 w/original-c ... 3.00
5-30: 5-15 ($2.00)-r/TFTC #21-23 w/original-c. 16-30 ($2.50) ... 3.00
Annual 1-6('93-'99) 1-r/#1-5. 2- r/#6-10. 3- r/#11-15. 4- r/#16-20. 5-r/#21-25. 6- r/#26-30 ... 14.00

TALES FROM THE CRYPT
Papercutz: July, 2007 - Present ($3.95)
1,2: 1-New stories in the same vein as the originals; Cryptkeeper app. Kyle Baker-c ... 4.00

TALES FROM THE GREAT BOOK
Famous Funnies: Feb, 1955 - No. 4, Jan, 1956 (Religious themes)
1-Story of Samson; John Lehti-a in all ... 9 18 27 50 65 80
2-4: 2-Joshua. 3-Joash the Boy King. 4-David ... 7 14 21 35 43 50

TALES FROM THE HEART OF AFRICA (The Temporary Natives)
Marvel Comics (Epic Comics): Aug, 1990 ($3.95, 52 pgs.)
1 ... 4.00

Tales of Evil #1 © Atlas

Tales of Horror #6 © Minoan

Tales of Suspense #20 © MAR

	GD 2.0	VG 4.0	FN 6.0	VF 8.0	VF/NM 9.0	NM- 9.2

TALES FROM THE TOMB (Also see Dell Giants)
Dell Publishing Co.: Oct, 1962 (25¢ giant)

	GD 2.0	VG 4.0	FN 6.0	VF 8.0	VF/NM 9.0	NM- 9.2
1(02-810-210)-All stories written by John Stanley	15	30	45	120	205	290

TALES FROM THE TOMB (Magazine)
Eerie Publications: V1#6, July, 1969 - V7#3, 1975 (52 pgs.)

V1#6	6	12	18	43	69	95
V1#7,8	5	10	15	33	55	75
V2#1-6: 4-LSD story-r/Weird V3#5. 6-Rulah-r	4	8	12	28	44	60
V3#1-Rulah-r	4	8	12	28	44	60
2-6('71),V4#1-5('72),V5#1-6('73),V6#1-6('74),V7#1-3('75)						
	4	8	12	26	41	55

TALES OF ASGARD
Marvel Comics Group: Oct, 1968 (25¢, 68 pgs.); Feb, 1984 ($1.25, 52 pgs.)

1-Reprints Tales of Asgard (Thor) back-up stories from Journey into Mystery #97-106; new Kirby-c; Kirby-a	5	10	15	30	48	65
V2#1 (2/84)-Thor-r; Simonson-c						5.00

TALES OF ARMY OF DARKNESS
Dynamite Entertainment: 2006 ($5.95, one-shot)

1-Short stories by Kuhoric, Kirkman, Bradshaw, Sablik, Ottley, Acs, O'Hare and others						6.00

TALES OF EVIL
Atlas/Seaboard Publ.: Feb, 1975 - No. 3, July, 1975 (All 25¢ issues)

1-3: 1-Werewolf w/Sekowsky-a 2-Intro. The Bog Beast; Sparling-a. 3-Origin The Man-Monster; Buckler-a(p)	1	2	3	6	8	10

NOTE: *Grandenetti a-1, 2. Lieber c-1. Sekowsky a-1. Sutton a-2. Thorne c-2.*

TALES OF GHOST CASTLE
National Periodical Publications: May-June, 1975 - No. 3, Sept-Oct, 1975 (All 25¢ issues)

1-Redondo-a; 1st app. Lucien the Librarian from Sandman (1989 series)	3	6	9	14	20	25
2,3: 2-Nino-a. 3-Redondo-a.	2	4	6	8	11	14

TALES OF G.I. JOE
Marvel Comics: Jan, 1988 - No. 15, Mar, 1989

1 ($2.25, 52 pgs.)						3.00
2-15 ($1.50): 1-15-r/G.I. Joe #1-15						2.50

TALES OF HORROR
Toby Press/Minoan Publ. Corp.: June, 1952 - No. 13, Oct, 1954

1	40	80	120	240	383	525
2-Torture scenes	32	64	96	186	293	400
3-13: 9-11-Reprints Purple Claw #1-3	22	44	66	126	198	270
12-Myron Fass-c/a; torture scenes	23	46	69	130	205	280

NOTE: *Andru a-5. Baily a-5. Myron Fass a-2, 3, 12; c-1-3, 12. Hollingsworth a-2. Sparling a-6; c-9.*

TALES OF JUSTICE
Atlas Comics(MjMC No. 53-66/Male No. 67): No. 53, May, 1955 - No. 67, Aug, 1957

53	15	30	45	83	124	165
54-57: 54-Powell-a	11	22	33	60	83	105
58,59-Krigstein-a	12	24	36	67	94	120
60-63,65: 60-Powell-a	10	20	30	54	72	90
64,66,67: 64,67-Crandall-a. 66-Torres, Orlando-a	10	20	30	56	76	95

NOTE: *Everett a-53, 60. Orlando a-65, 66. Severin a-64; c-58, 60, 65. Wildey a-64.*

TALES OF LEONARDO BLIND SIGHT (See Tales of the TMNT Vol. 2 #5)
Mirage Publishing: June, 2006 - No. 4, Sept, 2006 ($3.25, B&W, limited series)

1-4-Jim Lawson-s/a						3.25

TALES OF SUSPENSE (Becomes Captain America #100 on)
Atlas (WPI No. 1,2/Male No. 3-12/VPI No. 13-18)/Marvel No. 19 on: Jan, 1959 - No. 99, Mar, 1968

1-Williamson-a (5 pgs.); Heck-c; #1-4 have sci-fi-c	143	286	429	1216	2258	3300
2,3: 2-Robot-a. 3-Flying saucer-c/story	50	100	150	425	788	1150
4-Williamson-a (4 pgs.); Kirby/Everett-c/a	43	86	129	344	622	900
5,6,8,10: 5-Kirby monster-c begin	32	64	96	240	445	650
7-Prototype ish. (Lava Man); 1 panel app. Aunt May (see Str. Tales #97)						
	36	72	108	270	490	710
9-Prototype ish. (Iron Man)	37	74	111	278	507	735
11,12,15,17-19: 12-Crandall-a.	26	52	78	195	348	500
13-Elektro-c/story	27	54	81	198	354	510
14-Intro/1st app. Colossus-c/sty	34	68	102	255	465	675
16-1st Metallo-c/story (4/61, Iron Man prototype)	31	62	93	233	429	625
20-Colossus-c/story (2nd app.)	27	54	81	203	364	525
21-25: 25-Last 10¢ issue	20	40	60	150	268	385
26,27,29,30,33,34,36-38: 33-(9/62)-Hulk 1st x-over cameo (picture on wall)						

	GD 2.0	VG 4.0	FN 6.0	VF 8.0	VF/NM 9.0	NM- 9.2
28-Prototype ish. (Stone Men)	18	36	54	130	230	330
31-Prototype ish. (Dr. Doom)	18	36	54	134	237	340
32-Prototype ish. (Dr. Strange)(8/62)-Sazzik The Sorcerer app.; "The Man and the Beehive" story, 1 month before TTA #35 (2nd Antman), came out after "The Man in the Ant Hill" in TTA #27 (1/62) (1st Antman)-Characters from both stories were tested to see which got best fan response	20	40	60	150	268	385
	30	60	90	220	398	575
35-Prototype issue (The Watcher)	20	40	60	150	268	385
39 (3/63)-Origin/1st app. Iron Man & begin series; 1st Iron Man story has Kirby layouts						
	500	1000	1500	4500	8500	12,500
40-2nd app. Iron Man (in new armor)	148	296	444	1258	2329	3400
41-3rd app. Iron Man; Dr. Strange (villain) app.	87	174	261	740	1370	2000
42-45: 45-Intro. & 1st app. Happy & Pepper	50	100	150	413	757	1100
46,47: 46-1st app. Unicorn	40	80	120	300	550	800
48-New Iron Man armor by Ditko	45	90	135	360	655	950
49-1st X-Men x-over (same date as X-Men #3, 1/64); 1st Avengers x-over (w/o Captain America); 1st Tales of the Watcher back-up story & begins (2nd app. Watcher; see F.F. #13)	54	108	162	459	855	1250
50-1st app. Mandarin	27	54	81	203	364	525
51-1st Scarecrow	21	42	63	156	278	400
52-1st app. The Black Widow (4/64)	30	60	90	225	413	600
53-Origin The Watcher; 2nd Black Widow app.	21	42	63	156	278	400
54-56: 56-1st app. Unicorn	15	30	45	111	198	285
57-Origin/1st app. Hawkeye (9/64)	30	60	90	225	413	600
58-Captain America battles Iron Man (10/64)-Classic-c; 2nd Kraven app. (Cap's 1st app. in this title)	34	68	102	255	470	685
59-Iron Man plus Captain America double feature begins (11/64); 1st S.A. Captain America solo story; intro Jarvis, Avenger's butler; classic-c	34	68	102	255	470	685
60-2nd app. Hawkeye (#64 is 3rd app.)	19	38	57	138	244	350
61,62,64: 62-Origin Mandarin (2/65)	11	22	33	79	140	200
63-1st Silver Age origin Captain America (3/65)	25	50	75	184	330	475
65-G.A. Red Skull in WWII stories(also in #66);-1st Silver Age Red Skull (5/65).						
	19	38	57	138	244	350
66-Origin Red Skull	14	28	42	103	184	265
67-70: 69-1st app. Titanium Man. 70-Begin alternating-c features w/Capt. America (even #'s) & Iron Man (odd #'s)	8	16	24	54	90	125
71-75, 77,78,81-98: 75-1st app. Agent 13 later named Sharon Carter. 78-Col. Nick Fury app. 82-Intro the Adaptoid by Kirby (also in #83,84). 88-Mole Man app. in Iron Man story. 92-1st Nick Fury x-over (cameo, as Agent of S.H.I.E.L.D., 8/67). 94-Intro Modok. 95-Capt. America's i.d. revealed. 97-1st Whiplash. 98-1st brief app. new Zemo (son?) #99 is 1st full app.	6	12	18	39	62	85
76-Intro Batroc & Sharon Carter, Agent 13 of S.H.I.E.L.D.						
	6	12	18	43	69	95
79-Begin 3 part Iron Man Sub-Mariner battle story; Iron Man-c & cameo; 1st app. Cosmic Cube; 1st modern Red Skull	7	14	21	49	80	110
80-Iron Man battles Sub-Mariner story cont'd in Tales to Astonish #82; classic Red Skull-c	7	14	21	49	80	110
99-Captain America story cont'd in Captain America #100; Iron Man story cont'd in Iron Man & Sub-Mariner #1	7	14	21	50	83	115

NOTE: *Abel a-73-81(as Gary Michaels), J. Buscema a-1; c-3. Colan a-39, 73-99p; c(p)-73, 75, 77, 79, 81, 83, 85-87, 89, 91, 93, 95, 97, 99. Crandall a-12. Davis a-38. Ditko a-1-15, 17-44, 46, 47-49p; c-2, 10i, 13i, 23i. Kirby/Ditko a-7; c-10, 13, 22, 28, 34. Everett a-8. Forte a-5, 9. Giacoia a-82. Heath a-2, 10. Gil Kane a-88p, 89-91; c-88, 89-91p. Kirby a(p)-2-4, 6-35, 40, 41, 43, 59-75, 77-86, 92-99; layouts-69-75, 77; c(p)4-28(most), 29-56, 58-72, 74, 76, 78, 80, 82, 84, 86, 92, 94, 96, 98. Leiber/Fox a-42, 43, 45, 51. Reinman a-26, 44i, 49i, 52i, 53i. Tuska a-58, 70-74i. Wood c/a-71i.*

TALES OF SUSPENSE
Marvel Comics: V2#1, Jan, 1995 ($6.95, one-shot)

V2#1-James Robinson script; acetate-c.						7.00

TALES OF SUSPENSE: CAPTAIN AMERICA & IRON MAN #1 COMMEMORATIVE EDITION
Marvel Comics: 2004 ($3.99, one-shot)

nn-Reprints Captain America (2004) #1 and Iron Man (2004) #1						4.00

TALES OF SWORD & SORCERY (See Dagar)

TALES OF TELLOS (See Tellos)
Image Comics: Oct, 2004 - No. 3, ($3.50, anthology)

1-3: 1-Dezago-s; art by Yates & Rousseau; Wieringo-c. 3-Porter-a						3.50

TALES OF TERROR
Toby Press Publications: 1952 (no month)

1-Fawcette-c; Ravielli-a	26	52	78	150	235	320

NOTE: *This title was cancelled due to similarity to the E.C. title.*

TALES OF TERROR (See Movie Classics)

TALES OF TERROR (Magazine)
Eerie Publications: Summer, 1964

Tales of the Darkness #3 © TCOW

Tales of the Teen Titans #68 © DC

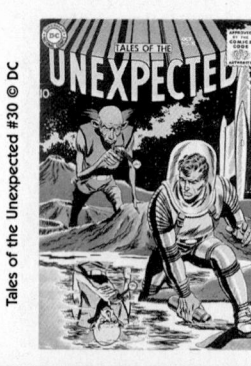
Tales of the Unexpected #30 © DC

	GD 2.0	VG 4.0	FN 6.0	VF 8.0	VF/NM 9.0	NM- 9.2
1	5	10	15	35	55	75

TALES OF TERROR
Eclipse Comics: July, 1985 - No. 13, July, 1987 ($2.00, Baxter paper, mature)

1-13: 5-1st Lee Weeks-a. 7-Sam Kieth-a. 10-Snyder-a. 12-Vampire story						3.00

TALES OF TERROR (IDW's...)
IDW Publishing: Sept, 2004 ($16.99, hardcover)

1-Anthology of short graphic stories and text stories; incl. 30 Days of Night						17.00

TALES OF TERROR ANNUAL
E.C. Comics: 1951 - No. 3, 1953 (25¢, 132 pgs., 16 stories each)

	GD	VG	FN	VF	VF/NM	NM-
nn(1951)(Scarce)-Feldstein infinity-c	650	1300	1950	5200	–	–
2(1952)-Feldstein-c	241	482	723	1808	2654	3500
3(1953)-Feldstein bondage/torture-c	186	372	558	1395	2048	2700

NOTE: No. 1 contains three horror and one science fiction comic which came out in 1950. No. 2 contains a horror, crime, and science fiction book which generally had cover dates in 1951, and No. 3 had horror, crime, and shock books that generally appeared in 1952. All E.C. annuals contain four complete books that did not sell on the stands which were rebound in the annual format, minus the covers, and sold from the E.C. office and on the stands in key cities. The contents of each annual may vary in the same year. Crypt Keeper, Vault Keeper, Old Witch app. on all-c.

TALES OF TERROR ILLUSTRATED (See Terror Illustrated)

TALES OF TEXAS JOHN SLAUGHTER (See Walt Disney Presents, 4-Color #997)

TALES OF THE BEANWORLD
Beanworld Press/Eclipse Comics: Feb, 1985 - No. 19, 1991; No. 20, 1993 - No. 21, 1993 ($1.50/$2.00, B&W)

1-21						3.00

TALES OF THE BIZARRO WORLD
DC Comics: 2000 ($14.95, TPB)

nn-Reprints early Bizarro stories; new Jaime Hernandez-c						15.00

TALES OF THE DARKNESS
Image Comics (Top Cow): Apr, 1998 - No. 4, Dec, 1998 ($2.95)

1-4: 1,2-Portacio-c/a(p). 3,4-Lansing & Nocon-a(p)						3.00
1-American Entertainment Ed.						3.00
#1/2 (1/01, $2.95)						3.00

TALES OF THE GREEN BERET
Dell Publishing Co.: Jan, 1967 - No. 5, Oct, 1969

	GD	VG	FN	VF	VF/NM	NM-
1-Glanzman-a in 1-4 & 5r	4	8	12	20	30	40
2-5: 5-Reprints #1	3	6	9	16	23	30

TALES OF THE GREEN HORNET
Now Comics: Sept, 1990 - No. 2, 1990; V2#1, Jan, 1992 - No.4, Apr, 1992; V3#1, Sept, 1992 - No. 3, Nov, 1992

1,2						2.50
V2#1-4 ($1.95)						2.50
V3#1 ($2.75)-Polybagged w/hologram trading card						3.00
V3#2,3 ($2.50)						2.50

TALES OF THE GREEN LANTERN CORPS (See Green Lantern #107)
DC Comics: May, 1981 - No. 3, July, 1981 (Limited series)

1-3: 1-Origin of G.L. & the Guardians, Annual 1 (1/85)-Gil Kane-c/a						3.50

TALES OF THE INVISIBLE SCARLET O'NEIL (See Harvey Comics Hits #59)

TALES OF THE KILLERS (Magazine)
World Famous Periodicals: V1#10, Dec, 1970 - V1#11, Feb, 1971 (B&W, 52 pg)

	GD	VG	FN	VF	VF/NM	NM-
V1#10-One pg. Frazetta; r/Crime Does Not Pay	4	8	12	28	44	60
11-similar-c to Crime Does Not Pay #47; contains r/Crime Does Not Pay	4	8	12	24	37	50

TALES OF THE LEGION (Formerly Legion of Super-Heroes)
DC Comics: No. 314, Aug, 1984 - No. 354, Dec, 1987

314-354: 326-r-begin						2.50
Annual 4,5 (1986, 1987)-Formerly LSH Annual						3.50

TALES OF THE MARINES (Formerly Devil-Dog Dugan #1-3)
Atlas Comics (OPI): No. 4, Feb, 1957 (Marines At War #5 on)

	GD	VG	FN	VF	VF/NM	NM-
4-Powell-a; Severin-c	8	16	24	44	57	70

TALES OF THE MARVELS
Marvel Comics: 1995/1996 (all acetate, painted-c)

...Blockbuster 1 (1995, $5.95, one-shot), ...Inner Demons 1 (1996, $5.95, one shot), ...Wonder Years 1,2 (1995, $4.95, limited series)						6.00

TALES OF THE MARVEL UNIVERSE
Marvel Comics: Feb, 1997 ($2.95, one-shot)

1-Anthology; wraparound-c; Thunderbolts, Ka-Zar app.						3.00

TALES OF THE MYSTERIOUS TRAVELER (See Mysterious...)
Charlton Comics: Aug, 1956 - No. 13, June, 1959; V2#14, Oct, 1985 - No. 15, Dec, 1985

	GD 2.0	VG 4.0	FN 6.0	VF 8.0	VF/NM 9.0	NM- 9.2
1-No Ditko-a; Giordano/Alascia-c	49	98	147	299	492	685
2-Ditko-a(1)	41	82	123	250	400	550
3-Ditko-c/a(1)	41	82	123	256	416	575
4-7-Ditko-c/a(3-4 stories each)	48	96	144	293	484	675
8,9-Ditko-a(1-3 each). 8-Rocke-c	40	80	120	243	389	535
10,11-Ditko-c/a(3-4 each)	44	88	132	268	439	610
12	18	36	54	103	162	220
13-Baker-a (r?)	19	38	57	109	172	235
V2#14,15 (1985)-Ditko-c/a-low print run	1	2	3	5	7	9

TALES OF THE NEW TEEN TITANS
DC Comics: June, 1982 - No. 4, Sept, 1982 (Limited series)

1-4						4.00

TALES OF THE PONY EXPRESS (TV)
Dell Publishing Co.: No. 829, Aug, 1957 - No. 942, Oct, 1958

	GD	VG	FN	VF	VF/NM	NM-
Four Color 829 (#1)--Painted-c	5	10	15	30	48	65
Four Color 942-Title -Pony Express	5	10	15	30	48	65

TALES OF THE REALM
CrossGen Comics/MVCreations #4-on: Oct, 2003 - No. 5, May, 2004 ($2.95, limited series)

1-5-Robert Kirkman-s/Matt Tyree-a						3.00
Volume 1 HC (8/04, $39.95, dust jacket) r/#1-5; sketch pages and concept art						40.00

TALES OF THE SUN RUNNERS
Sirius Comics/Amazing Comics No. 3: V2#1, July, 1986 - V2#3, 1986? ($1.50)

V2#1-3, Christmas Special 1(12/86)						2.50

TALES OF THE TEENAGE MUTANT NINJA TURTLES (See Teenage Mutant...)
Mirage Studios: May, 1987 - No. 7, Aug (Apr-c), 1989 (B&W, $1.50)

1-7: 2-Title merges w/Teenage Mutant Ninja...						2.50

TALES OF THE TEEN TITANS (Formerly The New Teen Titans)
DC Comics: No. 41, Apr, 1984 - No. 91, July, 1988 (75¢)

41,45-49: 46-Aqualad & Aquagirl join						3.00
42-44: The Judas Contract part 1-3 with Deathstroke the Terminator in all; concludes in Annual #3. 44-Dick Grayson becomes Nightwing (3rd to be Nightwing) & joins Titans; Jericho (Deathstroke's son) joins; origin Deathstroke						3.50
50,53-55: 50-Double size; app. Betty Kane (Bat-Girl) out of costume. 53-1st full app. Azrael; Deathstroke cameo. 54,55-Deathstroke-c/stories						3.50
51,52,56-91: 52-1st brief app. Azrael (not same as newer character). 56-Intro Jinx. 57-Neutron app. 59-r/DC Comics Presents #26. 60-91-r/New Teen Titans Baxter series. 68-B. Smith-c. 70-Origin Kole						2.50
Annual 3(1984, $1.25)-Part 4 of The Judas Contract; Deathstroke-c/story; Death of Terra; indicia says Teen Titans Annual; previous annuals listed as New Teen Titans Annual #1,2						4.00
Annual 4-(1986, $1.25)						2.50

TALES OF THE TEXAS RANGERS (See Jace Pearson...)

TALES OF THE THING (Fantastic Four)
Marvel Comics: May, 2005 - No. 3, July, 2005 ($2.50, limited series)

1-3-Dr. Strange app; Randy Green-c						2.50

TALES OF THE TMNT (Also see Teenage Mutant Ninja Turtles)
Mirage Studios: Jan, 2004 - Present ($2.95/$3.25, B&W)

1-7: 1-Brizuela-a						3.00
8-36: 8-Begin $3.25-c						3.25

TALES OF THE UNEXPECTED (Becomes The Unexpected #105 on)(See Adventure #75, Super DC Giant)
National Periodical Publications: Feb-Mar, 1956 - No. 104, Dec-Jan, 1967-68

	GD	VG	FN	VF	VF/NM	NM-
1	96	192	288	816	1508	2200
2	43	86	129	344	622	900
3-5	31	62	93	233	429	625
6-10: 6-1st Silver Age issue	26	52	78	211	348	485
11,14,19,20	17	34	51	128	227	325
12,13,15,18,21-24: All have Kirby-a. 15,17-Grey tone-c. 16-Character named 'Thor' with a magic hammer by Kirby (8/57, unlike later Thor)	21	42	63	156	278	400
25-30	15	30	45	107	191	275
31-39	13	26	39	93	164	235
40-Space Ranger begins (8/59, 3rd ap.), ends #82	96	192	288	816	1508	2200
41,42-Space Ranger stories	36	72	108	270	498	725
43-1st Space Ranger-c this title; grey tone-c	64	128	192	544	1010	1475
44-46	24	48	72	175	313	450
47-50	19	38	57	138	244	350

Tales of the Unexpected #3 © DC

Tales to Astonish #99 © MAR

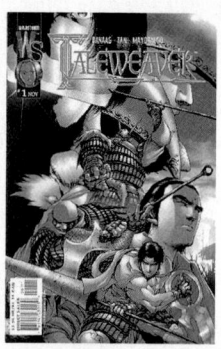

Taleweaver #1 © Agimat

	GD 2.0	VG 4.0	FN 6.0	VF 8.0	VF/NM 9.0	NM- 9.2
51-60: 54-Dinosaur-c/story	15	30	45	111	198	285
61-67: 67-Last 10¢ issue	13	26	39	93	164	235
68-82: 82-Last Space Ranger	8	16	24	52	86	120
83-90,92-99	6	12	18	37	59	80
91,100: 91-1st Automan (also in #94,97)	6	12	18	39	62	85
101-104	5	10	15	32	51	70

NOTE: Neal Adams c-104. Anderson a-50. Brown a-50-82(Space Ranger); c-19, 40, & many Space Ranger-c. Cameron a-24, 27, 29; c-24. Heath a-49. Bob Kane a-24, 48. Kirby a-12, 13, 15-18, 21-24; c-13, 18, 22. Meskin a-15, 18, 26, 27, 35, 66. Moreira a-16, 20, 29, 38, 44, 62, 71; c-38. Roussos c-10. Wildey a-31.

TALES OF THE UNEXPECTED (See Crisis Aftermath: The Spectre)
DC Comics: Dec, 2006 - No. 8, Jul, 2007 ($3.99, limited series)

1-8-The Spectre, Lapham-s/Battle-a; Dr. 13, Azzarello-s/Chiang-a. 4-Wrightson-c						4.00
1-Variant Spectre cover by Neal Adams						5.00

TALES OF THE VAMPIRES (Also see Buffy the Vampire Slayer and related titles)
Dark Horse Comics: 2003 - No. 5, Apr, 2004 ($2.99, limited series)

1-Short stories by Joss Whedon and others. 1-Totleben-c. 3-Powell-c. 4-Edlund-c						3.00
TPB (11/04, $15.95) r/#1-5; afterword by Marv Wolfman						16.00

TALES OF THE WEST (See 3-D...)

TALES OF THE WITCHBLADE
Image Comics (Top Cow Productions): Nov, 1996 - No. 9 ($2.95)

	GD	VG	FN	VF	VF/NM	NM-
1/2	1	2	3	5	7	9
1/2 Gold						15.00
1-Daniel-c/a(p)	1	3	4	6	8	10
1-Variant-c by Turner	2	4	6	9	12	15
1-Platinum Edition						30.00
2,3						6.00
4-6: 6-Green-c						5.00
7-9: 9-Lara Croft-c						3.00
7-Variant-c by Turner	1	2	3	5	6	8
Witchblade: Distinctions (4/01, $14.95, TPB) r/#1-6; Green-c						15.00

TALES OF THE WITCHBLADE COLLECTED EDITION
Image Comics (Top Cow): May, 1998 - No. 2 ($4.95/$5.95, square-bound)

1,2: 1-r/#1,2. 2-($5.95) r/#3,4						6.00

TALES OF THE WIZARD OF OZ (See Wizard of OZ, 4-Color #1308)

TALES OF THE ZOMBIE (Magazine)
Marvel Comics Group: Aug, 1973 - No. 10, Mar, 1975 (75¢, B&W)

	GD	VG	FN	VF	VF/NM	NM-
V1#1-Reprint/Menace #5; origin	4	8	12	28	44	60
2,3: 2-Everett biog. & memorial	4	8	12	22	34	45
V2#1(#4)-Photos & text of James Bond movie "Live & Let Die"	3	6	9	18	27	35
5-10: 8-Kaluta-a	3	6	9	16	23	30
Annual 1(Summer,'75)(#11)-B&W; Everett, Buscema-a	3	6	9	18	27	35

NOTE: Brother Voodoo app. 2, 5, 6, 10. Alcala a-7-9. Boris c-1-4. Colan a-2r, 6. Heath a-5r. Reese a-2. Tuska a-2r.

TALES OF THUNDER
Deluxe Comics: Mar, 1985

1-Dynamo, Iron Maiden, Menthor app.; Giffen-a						2.50

TALES OF VOODOO
Eerie Publications: V1#11, Nov, 1968 - V7#6, Nov, 1974 (Magazine)

	GD	VG	FN	VF	VF/NM	NM-
V1#11	6	12	18	37	59	80
V2#1(3/69)-V2#4(9/69)	4	8	12	26	41	55
V3#1-6('70): 4- "Claws of the Cat" redrawn from Climax #1	3	6	9	21	32	42
V4#1-6('71), V5#1-7('72), V6#1-7('73), V7#1-6('74)	3	6	9	21	32	42
Annual 1	4	8	12	23	36	48

NOTE: Bondage-c-V1#10, V2#4, V3#4.

TALES OF WELLS FARGO (TV)(See Western Roundup under Dell Giants)
Dell Publishing Co.: No. 876, Feb, 1958 - No. 1215, Oct-Dec, 1961

	GD	VG	FN	VF	VF/NM	NM-
Four Color 876 (#1)-Photo-c	9	18	27	60	100	140
Four Color 968 (2/59), 1023, 1075 (3/60), 1113 (7-9/60)-All photo-c	8	16	24	56	93	130
Four Color 1167 (3-5/61), 1215-Photo-c	8	16	24	52	86	120

TALESPIN (Also see Cartoon Tales & Disney's Talespin Limited Series)
Disney Comics: June, 1991 - No. 7, Dec, 1991 ($1.50)

1-7						2.50

TALES TO ASTONISH (Becomes The Incredible Hulk #102 on)
Atlas (MAP No. 1/ZPC No. 2-14/VPI No. 15-21/Marvel No. 22 on: Jan, 1959 - No. 101, Mar,

---

1968

	GD 2.0	VG 4.0	FN 6.0	VF 8.0	VF/NM 9.0	NM- 9.2
1-Jack Davis-a; monster-c.	143	286	429	1216	2258	3300
2-Ditko flying saucer-c (Martians); #2-4 have sci/fi-c.	58	116	174	493	909	1325
3,4	43	86	129	344	622	900
5-Prototype issue (Stone Men); Williamson-a (4 pgs.); Kirby monster-c begin	45	90	135	360	648	935
6-Prototype issue (Stone Men)	35	70	105	263	482	700
7-Prototype issue (Toad Men)	35	70	105	263	482	700
8-10	32	64	96	240	438	635
11-14,17-20: 13-Swipes story from Menace #8	26	52	78	195	348	500
15-Prototype issue (Electro)	32	64	96	240	445	650
16-Prototype issue (Stone Men)	28	56	84	227	384	540
21-(7/61)-Hulk prototype	28	56	84	227	384	540
22-26,28-34: 32-Sandman prototype	20	40	60	150	268	385
27-1st Ant-Man app. (1/62); last 10¢ issue (see Strange Tales #73,78 & Tales of Suspense #32)	368	736	1104	3312	6256	9200
35-(9/62)-2nd app. Ant-Man, 1st in costume; begin series & Ant-Man-c	154	308	462	1348	2524	3700
36-3rd app. Ant-Man	70	140	210	595	1098	1600
37-40: 38-1st app. Egghead	40	80	120	311	568	825
41-43	32	64	96	240	445	650
44-Origin & 1st app. The Wasp (6/63)	42	84	126	336	606	875
45-48: 48-Origin & 1st app. The Porcupine	20	40	60	146	261	375
49-Ant-Man becomes Giant Man (11/63)	24	48	72	180	323	465
50,51,53-56,58: 50-Origin/1st app. Human Top (alias Whirlwind). 53-Origin Colossus	13	26	39	93	164	235
52-Origin/1st app. Black Knight (2/64)	15	30	45	111	198	285
57-Early Spider-Man app. (7/64)	30	60	90	223	404	585
59-Giant Man vs. Hulk feature story (9/64); Hulk's 1st app. this title	29	58	87	216	388	560
60-Giant Man & Hulk double feature begins	20	40	60	146	261	375
61-69: 61-All Ditko issue; 1st mailbag. 62-1st app./origin The Leader; new Wasp costume; Hulk pin-up page missing from many copies. 63-Origin Leader; 65-New Giant Man costume.						
68-New Human Top costume. 69-Last Giant Man	10	20	30	70	123	175
70-Sub-Mariner & Incredible Hulk begins (8/65)	11	22	33	79	140	200
71-81,83-91,94-99: 72-Begin alternating-c features w/Sub-Mariner (even #'s) & Hulk (odd #'s). 79-Hulk vs. Hercules-c/story. 81-1st app. Boomerang. 90-1st app. The Abomination.	7	14	21	47	72	105
97-X-Men cameo (brief)	6	12	18	37	59	80
82-Iron Man battles Sub-Mariner (1st Iron Man x-over outside The Avengers & TOS); story cont'd from Tales of Suspense #80	7	14	21	47	76	105
92-1st Silver Surfer x-over (outside of Fantastic Four, 6/67); 1 panel cameo only	6	12	18	37	59	80
93-Hulk battles Silver Surfer-c/story (1st full x-over)	12	24	36	87	156	225
100-Hulk battles Sub-Mariner full-length story	7	14	21	47	76	105
101-Hulk story cont'd in Incredible Hulk #102; Sub-Mariner story continued in Iron Man & Sub-Mariner #1	7	14	21	50	83	115

NOTE: Ayers c(i)-9-12, 16, 18, 19. Berg a-1. Burgos a-62-64p. Buscema a-85-87p. Colan a(p)-70-76, 78-82, 84, 85, 101; c(p)-71-76, 78, 80, 82, 84, 86, 88, 90. Ditko a-1, 3-48, 50i, 60-67p; c-2, 7i, 8i, 14i, 17i. Everett a-78, 79i, 80-84, 85-90i, 94i, 95, 96; c(i)-79-81, 83, 86, 88. Forte a-1, 5-34-40, 44, 49-51, 68-70, 82, 83; layouts-71-84; c(p)-1, 3-48, 50-70, 72, 73, 75, 77, 78, 79, 81, 85, 90. Kirby/Ditko a-7, 8, 12, 13, 50; c-7, 8, 10, 13. Leiber/Fox a-47, 48, 50, 51. Powell a-65-69p, 73, 74. Reinman a-6, 36, 45, 46, 54i, 56-60i.

TALES TO ASTONISH (2nd Series)
Marvel Comics Group: Dec, 1979 - No. 14, Jan, 1981

V1#1-Reprints Sub-Mariner #1 by Buscema						6.00
2-14: Reprints Sub-Mariner #2-14						4.00

TALES TO ASTONISH
Marvel Comics: V3#1, Oct, 1994 ($6.95, one-shot)

V3#1-Peter David scripts; acetate, painted-c						7.00

TALES TO HOLD YOU SPELLBOUND (See Spellbound)

TALES TO OFFEND
Dark Horse Comics: July, 1997 ($2.95, one-shot)

1-Frank Miller-s/a, EC-style cover						3.50

TALES TOO TERRIBLE TO TELL (Becomes Terrology #10, 11)
New England Comics: Wint, 1989-90 - No. 11, Nov-Dec.1993 ($2.95/$3.50, B&W with card-stock covers)

1-($2.95) Reprints of non-EC pre-code horror; EC-style cover by Bisette						4.00
2-8-($3.50) Story reprints, history of the pre-code titles and creators; cover galleries (B&W) inside & on back-c (color)						4.00
9-11-($2.95) 10,11-"Terrology" on cover						4.00

TALEWEAVER

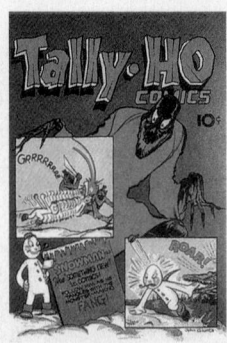

Tally-Ho Comics nn © Baily Pub. Co.

Tangent Comics/The Superman #1 © DC

Target Comics V6 #3 © NOVP

	GD 2.0	VG 4.0	FN 6.0	VF 8.0	VF/NM 9.0	NM- 9.2

DC Comics (WildStorm): Nov, 2001 - No. 6, Apr, 2002 ($3.50, limited series)
1-6-Philip Tan-a/Leonard Banaag-s. 2-Variant-c by Anacleto 3.50

TALKING KOMICS
Belda Record & Publ. Co.: 1947 (20 pgs, slick-c)
Each comic contained a record that followed the story - much like the Golden Record sets.
Known titles: Chirpy Cricket, Lonesome Octopus, Sleepy Santa, Grumpy Shark,
Flying Turtle, Happy Grasshopper
with records... 3 6 9 16 23 30

TALLY-HO COMICS
Swappers Quarterly (Baily Publ. Co.): Dec, 1944
nn-Frazetta's 1st work as Giunta's assistant; Man in Black horror story; violence;
Giunta-c 45 90 135 275 450 625

TALULLAH (See Comic Books Series I)

TAMMY, TELL ME TRUE
Dell Publishing Co.: No. 1233, 1961
Four Color 1233-Movie 6 12 18 43 69 95

TANGENT COMICS
.../ THE ATOM, DC Comics: Dec, 1997 ($2.95, one-shot)
1-Dan Jurgens-s/Jurgens & Paul Ryan-a 3.00
.../ THE BATMAN, DC Comics: Sept, 1998 ($1.95, one-shot)
1-Dan Jurgens-s/Klaus Janson-a 3.00
.../ DOOM PATROL, DC Comics: Dec, 1997 ($2.95, one-shot)
1- Dan Jurgens-s/Sean Chen & Kevin Conrad-a 3.00
.../ THE FLASH, DC Comics: Dec, 1997 ($2.95, one-shot)
1-Todd Dezago-s/Gary Frank & Cam Smith-a 3.00
.../ GREEN LANTERN, DC Comics: Dec, '97 ($2.95, one-shot)
1-James Robinson-s/J.H. Williams III & Mick Gray-a 3.00
.../ JLA, DC Comics: Sept, 1998 ($1.95, one-shot)
1-Dan Jurgens-s/Banks & Rapmund-a 3.00
.../ THE JOKER, DC Comics: Dec, 1997 ($2.95, one-shot)
1-Karl Kesel-s/Matt Haley & Tom Simmons-a 3.00
.../ THE JOKER'S WILD, DC Comics: Sept, 1998 ($1.95, one-shot)
1-Kesel & Simmons-s/Phillips & Rodriguez-a 2.25
.../ METAL MEN, DC Comics: Dec, 1997 ($2.95, one-shot)
1-Ron Marz-s/Mike McKone & Mark McKenna-a 3.00
.../ NIGHTWING, DC Comics: Dec, 1997 ($2.95, one-shot)
1-John Ostrander-s/Jan Duursema-a 3.00
.../ NIGHTWING: NIGHTFORCE, DC Comics: Sept, 1998 ($1.95, one-shot)
1-John Ostrander-s/Jan Duursema-a 2.50
.../ POWERGIRL, DC Comics: Sept, 1998 ($1.95, one-shot)
1-Marz-s/Abell & Vines-a 2.50
.../ SEA DEVILS, DC Comics: Dec, 1997 ($2.95, one-shot)
1-Kurt Busiek-s/Vince Giarrano & Tom Palmer-a 3.00
.../ SECRET SIX, DC Comics: Dec, 1997 ($2.95, one-shot)
1-Chuck Dixon-s/Tom Grummett & Lary Stucker-a 3.00
.../ THE SUPERMAN, DC Comics: Sept, 1998 ($1.95, one-shot)
1-Millar-s/Guice-a 3.00
.../ TALES OF THE GREEN LANTERN, DC Comics: Sept, 1998 ($1.95, one-shot)
1-Story & art by various 3.00
.../ THE TRIALS OF THE FLASH, DC Comics: Sept, 1998 ($1.95, one-shot)
1-Dezago-s/Pelletier & Lanning-a 2.50
.../ WONDER WOMAN DC Comics: Sept, 1998 ($1.95, one-shot),
1-Peter David-s/Unzueta & Mendoza-a 3.00

TANGLED WEB (See Spider-Man's Tangled Web)

TANK GIRL
Dark Horse Comics: May, 1991 - No. 4, Aug, 1991 ($2.25, B&W, mini-series)
1-Contains Dark Horse trading cards 6.00
2-4 4.00

TANK GIRL: APOCALYPSE
DC Comics: Nov, 1995 - No. 4, Feb, 1996 ($2.25, limited series)
1-4 3.00

TANK GIRL: MOVIE ADAPTATION
DC Comics: 1995 ($5.95, 68 pgs., one-shot)

nn-Peter Milligan scripts 6.00

TANK GIRL: THE GIFTING
IDW Publishing: May, 2007 - Present ($3.99)
1,2: 1-Ashley Wood-a/c; Alan Martin-s; 3 covers 4.00

TANK GIRL: THE ODYSSEY
DC Comics: May, 1995 - No.4, Oct, 1995 ($2.25, limited series)
1-4: Peter Milligan scripts; Hewlett-a 3.00

TANK GIRL 2
Dark Horse Comics: June, 1993 - No. 4, Sept, 1993 ($2.50, lim. series, mature)
1-4: Jamie Hewlett & Alan Martin-s/a 3.00
TPB (2/95, $17.95) r/#1-4 18.00

TAPPAN'S BURRO (See Zane Grey & 4-Color #449)

TAPPING THE VEIN (Clive Barker's...)
Eclipse Comics: 1989 - No. 5, 1992 ($6.95, squarebound, mature, 68 pgs.)
Book 1-5: 1-Russell-a, Bolton-c. 2-Bolton-a. 4-Die-cut-c 7.00
TPB (2002, $24.95, Checker Book Publ. Group) r/#1-5 25.00

TARANTULA (See Weird Suspense)

TARGET: AIRBOY
Eclipse Comics: Mar, 1988 ($1.95)
1 2.50

TARGET COMICS (...Western Romances #106 on)
Funnies, Inc./Novelty Publications/Star Publ.: Feb, 1940 - V10#3 (#105), Aug-Sept, 1949

	GD 2.0	VG 4.0	FN 6.0	VF 8.0	VF/NM 9.0	NM- 9.2
V1#1-Origin & 1st app. Manowar, The White Streak by Burgos, & Bulls-Eye Bill by Everett; City Editor (ends #5); High Grass Twins by Jack Cole (ends #4), T-Men by Joe Simon (ends #9), Rip Rory (ends #4), Fantastic Feature Films by Tarpe Mills (ends #39), & Calling 2-R (ends #14) begin; marijuana use story	497	994	1491	3479	6090	8700
2-Everett-c/a	252	504	756	1575	2613	3650
3,4-Everett, Jack Cole-a	152	304	456	950	1575	2200
5-Origin The White Streak in text; Space Hawk by Wolverton begins (6/40) (see Blue Bolt & Circus)	423	846	1269	2961	5181	7400
6-The Chameleon by Everett begins (7/40, 1st app.); White Streak origin cont'd. in text; early mention of comic collecting in letter column; 1st letter column in comics? (7/40)	214	428	642	1338	2219	3100
7-Wolverton Spacehawk-c/story (Scarce)	600	1200	1800	4200	7350	10,500
8-Classic sci-fi cover	176	352	528	1100	1825	2550
9,12: 12-(1/41)	141	282	423	881	1466	2050
10-Intro/1st app. The Target (11/40); Simon-c; Spacehawk-s; text piece by Wolverton	228	456	684	1425	2363	3300
11-Origin The Target & The Targeteers	178	356	534	1113	1844	2575
V2#1-Target by Bob Wood; Uncle Sam flag-c	86	172	258	538	894	1250
2-Ten part Treasure Island serial begins; Harold Delay-a; reprinted in Catholic Comics V3#1-10 (see Key Comics #5)	78	156	234	488	807	1125
3-5: 4-Kit Carter, The Cadet begins	61	122	183	381	633	885
6-9: Red Seal with White Streak in #6-10	58	116	174	363	602	840
10-Classic-c	102	204	306	638	1057	1475
11,12: 12-10-part Last of the Mohicans serial begins; Delay-a	57	114	171	356	591	825
V3#1-3,5-7,9,10: 10-Last Wolverton issue	54	108	162	338	562	785
4-V for Victory-c	60	120	180	375	625	875
8-Hitler, Tojo, Flag-c; 6-part Gulliver Travels serial begins; Delay-a	76	152	228	475	788	1100
11,12	18	36	54	105	165	225
V4#1-4,7-12: 8-X-mas-c	14	28	42	76	108	140
5-Classic Statue of Liberty-c	15	30	45	83	124	165
6-Targetoons by Wolverton	15	30	45	83	124	165
V5#1-8	12	24	36	67	94	120
V6#1-4,6-10	11	22	33	64	90	115
5-Tojo-c	15	30	45	84	127	170
V7#1-12	10	20	30	58	79	100
V8#1,3-5,8,9,11,12	10	20	30	56	76	95
2,6,7-Krigstein-a	11	22	33	62	86	110
10-L.B. Cole-c	34	68	102	197	311	425
V9#1,4,6,8,10-L.B. Cole-c	33	66	99	192	304	415
2,3,5,7,9,11, V10#1	10	20	30	56	76	95
12-Classic L.B. Cole-c	38	76	114	216	343	470
V10#2,3-L.B. Cole-c	32	64	96	186	293	400

NOTE: *Certa* c-V8#9, 11, 12, V9#5, 9, 11, V10#1. *Jack Cole* a-1-8. *Everett* a-1-9; c(signed Blake)-1, 2. *Al Fago* c-V6#8. *Sid Greene* c-V2#9, 12, V3#3. *Walter Johnson* c-V5#6, V6#4. *Tarpe Mills* a-1-4, 6, 8, 11, V3#1. *Rico* a-V7#4, 10, V8#5, 6, V9#3; c-V7#6, 8, 10, V8#2, 4, 6, 7. *Simon* a-1, 2. *Bob Wood* c-V2#2, 3, 5, 6.

Tarzan #17 © ERB

Tarzan #235 © ERB

Tarzan #20 © ERB

	GD 2.0	VG 4.0	FN 6.0	VF 8.0	VF/NM 9.0	NM- 9.2

TARGET: THE CORRUPTORS (TV)
Dell Publishing Co.: No. 1306, Mar-May, 1962 - No. 3, Oct-Dec, 1962
(All have photo-c)

Four Color 1306(#1), #2,3	6	12	18	37	59	80

TARGET WESTERN ROMANCES (Formerly Target Comics; becomes Flaming Western Romances #3)
Star Publications: No. 106, Oct-Nov, 1949 - No. 107, Dec-Jan, 1949-50

106(#1)-Silhouette nudity panel; L.B. Cole-c	36	72	108	208	329	450
107(#2)-L.B. Cole-c; lingerie panels	30	60	90	174	275	375

TARGITT
Atlas/Seaboard Publ.: March, 1975 - No. 3, July, 1975

1-3: 1-Origin; Nostrand-a in all. 2-1st in costume. 3-Becomes Man-Stalker	1	2	3	5	7	9

TARZAN (See Aurora, Comics on Parade, Crackajack, DC 100-Page Super Spec., Edgar Rice Burroughs'..., Famous Feature Stories #1, Golden Comics Digest #4, 9, Jeep Comics #1-29, Jungle Tales of..., Limited Collectors' Edition, Popular, Sparkler, Sport Stars #1, Tip Top & Top Comics)

TARZAN
Dell Publishing Co./United Features Synd.: No. 5, 1939 - No. 161, Aug, 1947

Large Feature Comic 5('39)-(Scarce)-By Hal Foster; reprints 1st dailies from 1929	172	344	516	1075	1788	2500
Single Series 20(:40)-By Hal Foster	114	228	342	713	1182	1650
Four Color 134(2/47)-Marsh-c/a	52	104	156	442	821	1150
Four Color 161(8/47)-Marsh-c/a	48	96	144	384	692	1000

TARZAN (...of the Apes #138 on)
Dell Publishing Co./Gold Key No. 132 on: No. 1-2/48 - No. 131, 7-8/62; No. 132, 11/62 - No. 206, 2/72

1-Jesse Marsh-a begins	96	192	288	816	1508	2200
2	43	86	129	344	622	900
3-5	31	62	93	233	429	625
6-10: 6-1st Tantor the Elephant. 7-1st Valley of the Monsters						
	26	52	78	211	348	485
11-15: 11-Two Against the Jungle begins, ends #24. 13-Lex Barker photo-c begin						
	21	42	63	156	278	400
16-20	17	34	51	126	223	320
21-24,26-30	14	28	42	102	181	260
25-1st "Brothers of the Spear" episode; series ends #156,160,161,196-206						
	16	32	48	114	202	290
31-40	11	22	33	75	133	190
41-54: Last Barker photo-c	9	18	27	61	103	145
55-60: 56-Eight pg. Boy story	8	16	24	52	86	120
61,62,64-70	7	14	21	45	73	100
63-Two Tarzan stories, 1 by Manning	7	14	21	47	76	105
71-79	6	12	18	41	66	90
80-99: 80-Gordon Scott photo-c begin	6	12	18	37	59	80
100	6	12	18	41	66	90
101-109	5	10	15	35	55	75
110 (Scarce)-Last photo-c	6	12	18	41	66	90
111-120	5	10	15	32	51	70
121-131: Last Dell issue	5	10	15	30	48	65
132-1st Gold Key issue	5	10	15	32	51	70
133-138,140-154	4	8	12	24	37	50
139-(12/63)-1st app. Korak (Boy); leaves Tarzan & gets own book (1/64)						
	6	12	18	41	66	90
155-Origin Tarzan	4	8	12	30	48	65
156-161: 157-Banlu, Dog of the Arande begins, ends #159, 195. 169-Leopard Girl app.						
	3	6	9	21	32	42
162,165,168,171 (TV)-Ron Ely photo covers	4	8	12	22	34	45
163,164,166,167,169,170: 169-Leopard Girl app.	3	6	9	20	30	40
172-199,201-206: 178-Tarzan origin-r/#155; Leopard Girl app., also in #179, 190-193						
	3	6	9	18	27	35
200	3	6	9	21	32	42
Story Digest 1-(6/70, G.K., 148pp.)(scarce)	7	14	21	49	80	110

NOTE: #162, 165, 168, 171 are TV issues. #1-153 all have **Marsh** art on Tarzan. #154-161, 163, 164, 166, 167, 172-177 all have **Manning** art on Tarzan. #178, 202 have **Manning** Tarzan reprints. No "Brothers of the Spear" in #1-24, 157-159, 162-195. #39-126, 128-156 all have **Russ Manning** art on "Brothers of the Spear". #196-201, 203-205 all have **Manning** B.O.T.S. reprints. #25-38, 127 all have Jesse **Marsh** on B.O.T.S. #206 has a Marsh B.O.T.S. reprint. **Gollub** c-8-12. **Marsh** c-1-7. **Doug Wildey** a-162, 179-187. Many issues have front and back photo covers.

TARZAN (Continuation of Gold Key series)
National Periodical Publications: No. 207, Apr, 1972 - No. 258, Feb, 1977

207-Origin Tarzan by Joe Kubert, part 1; John Carter begins (origin); 52 pg. issues thru #209						
	5	10	15	32	51	70

208,209-(52 pgs.): 208-210-Parts 2-4 of origin. 209-Last John Carter						
	3	6	9	18	27	35
210-220: 210-Kubert-a. 211-Hogarth, Kubert-a. 212-214: Adaptations from "Jungle Tales of Tarzan". 213-Beyond the Farthest Star begins, ends #218. 215-218-224,225-All by Kubert. 215-part Foster-r. 219-223: Adapts "The Return of Tarzan" by Kubert						
	2	4	6	13	18	22
221-229: 221-223-Continues adaptation of "The Return of Tarzan". 226-Manning-a						
	2	4	6	9	13	16
230-DC 100 Page Super Spectacular; Kubert, Kaluta-a(p); Korak begins ends #234; Carson of Venus app.						
	4	8	12	23	36	48
231-235-New Kubert-a.: 231-234-(All 100 pgs.)-Adapts "Tarzan and the Lion Man"; Rex, the Wonder Dog r-#232, 233. 235-(100 pgs.)-Last Kubert issue.						
	4	8	12	22	34	45
236,237,239-258: 240-243 adapts "Tarzan & the Castaways". 250-256 adapts "Tarzan the Untamed". 252,253-r/#213						
	1	3	4	6	8	10
238-(68 pgs.)	2	4	6	11	16	20
Comic Digest 1-(Fall, 1972, 50¢, 164 pgs.)(DC)-Digest size; Kubert-c; Manning-a						
	2	4	6	26	41	55
Edgar Rice Burroughs' Tarzan The Joe Kubert Years - Volume One HC (Dark Horse Books, 10/05, $49.95, dust jacket) recolored r/#207-214; intro. by Joe Kubert						50.00
Edgar Rice Burroughs' Tarzan The Joe Kubert Years - Volume Two HC (Dark Horse Books, 2/06, $49.95, dust jacket) recolored r/#215-224; intro. by Joe Kubert						50.00
Edgar Rice Burroughs' Tarzan The Joe Kubert Years - Volume Three HC (Dark Horse Books, 6/06, $49.95, dust jacket) recolored r/#225,227-235; Kubert intro. and sketch pages 50.00						

NOTE: **Anderson** a-207, 209, 217, 218. **Chaykin** a-216. **Finlay** a(r)-212. **Foster** strip-r #207-209, 211, 212, 221. **Heath** a-230i. **G. Kane** a(r)-232p, 233p. **Kubert** a-207-225, 227-235, 257r, 258r; c-207-249, 253. **Lopez** a-250-255p; c-250p, 251, 252, 254. **Manning** strip-r 230-235, 238. **Morrow** a-208. **Nino** a-231-234. **Sparling** a-230, 231. **Starr** a-233r.

TARZAN (Lord of the Jungle)
Marvel Comics Group: June, 1977 - No. 29, Oct, 1979

1-New adaptions of Burroughs stories; Buscema-a	1	3	4	6	8	10
1-(35¢-c variant, limited distribution)(6/77)	4	8	12	24	37	50
2-29: 2-Origin by John Buscema. 9-Young Tarzan. 12-14-Jungle Tales of Tarzan. 25-29-New stories						5.00
2-5-(35¢-c variants, limited distribution)(7-10/77)	3	6	9	16	23	30
Annual 1-3: 1-(1977). 2-(1978). 3-(1979)						5.00

NOTE: **N. Adams** c-11i, 12i. **Alcala** a-9i, 10i; c-8i, 9i. **Buckler** c-25-27p, Annual 3p. **John Buscema** a-1-3, 4-18p, Annual 1; c-1-7, 8p, 9p, 10, 11p, 12p, 13, 14-19p, 21p, 22, 23p, 24p, 28p, Annual 1. **Mooney** a-22i. **Nebres** a-22i. **Russell** a-29i.

TARZAN
Dark Horse Comics: July, 1996 - No. 20, Mar, 1998 ($2.95)

1-20: 1-6-Suydam-c						3.00

TARZAN / CARSON OF VENUS
Dark Horse Comics: May, 1998 - No. 4, Aug, 1998 ($2.95, limited series)

1-4-Darko Macan-s/Igor Korday-a						3.00

TARZAN FAMILY, THE (Formerly Korak, Son of Tarzan)
National Periodical Publications: No. 60, Nov-Dec, 1975 - No. 66, Nov-Dec, 1976

60-62-(68 pgs.): 60-Korak begins; Kaluta-r	2	4	6	9	13	16
63-66 (52 pgs.)	2	4	6	8	10	12

NOTE: Carson of Venus-r 60-65. New John Carter-62-64, 65r, 66r. New Korak-60-65. Pellucidar feature-66. Foster strip r-60(9/4/32-10/16/32), 62(6/29/32-7/31/32), 63(10/11/31-12/13/31). **Kaluta** Carson of Venus-60-65. **Kubert** a-61, 64; c-60-64. **Manning** strip-r 60-62, 64. **Morrow** a-66r.

TARZAN/JOHN CARTER: WARLORDS OF MARS
Dark Horse Comics: Jan, 1996 - No. 4, June, 1996 ($2.50, limited series)

1-4: Bruce Jones begins in all. 1,2,4-Bret Blevins-c/a. 2-(4/96)-Indicia reads #3						3.00

TARZAN KING OF THE JUNGLE (See Dell Giant #37, 51)

TARZAN, LORD OF THE JUNGLE
Gold Key: Sept, 1965 (Giant) (25¢, soft paper-c)

1-Marsh-r	8	16	24	54	90	125

TARZAN: LOVE, LIES AND THE LOST CITY (See Tarzan the Warrior)
Malibu Comics: Aug. 10, 1992 - No. 3, Sept, 1992 ($2.50, limited series)

1-($3.95, 68 pgs.)-Flip book format; Simonson & Wagner scripts						4.00
2,3-No Simonson or Wagner scripts						3.00

TARZAN MARCH OF COMICS (See March of Comics #82, 98, 114, 125, 144, 155, 172, 185, 204, 223, 240, 252, 262, 272, 286, 300, 332, 342, 354, 366)

TARZAN OF THE APES
Metropolitan Newspaper Service: 1934? (Hardcover, 4x12", 68 pgs.)

1-Strip reprints	25	50	75	145	228	310

TARZAN OF THE APES
Marvel Comics Group: July, 1984 - No. 2, Aug, 1984 (Movie adaptation)

	GD 2.0	VG 4.0	FN 6.0	VF 8.0	VF/NM 9.0	NM- 9.2

1,2: Origin-r/Marvel Super Spec. — 3.00

TARZAN'S JUNGLE ANNUAL (See Dell Giants)

TARZAN'S JUNGLE WORLD (See Dell Giant #25)

TARZAN: THE BECKONING
Malibu Comics: 1992 - No. 7, 1993 ($2.50, limited series)
1-7 — 3.00

TARZAN: THE LOST ADVENTURE (See Edgar Rice Burroughs' ...)

TARZAN-THE RIVERS OF BLOOD
Dark Horse Comics: Nov, 1999 - No. 8 ($2.95, limited series)
1-4: Korday-c/a — 3.00

TARZAN THE SAVAGE HEART
Dark Horse Comics: Apr, 1999 - No. 4, July, 1999 ($2.95, limited series)
1-4: Grell-c/a — 3.00

TARZAN THE WARRIOR (Also see Tarzan: Love, Lies and the Lost City)
Malibu Comics: Mar, 19, 1992 - No. 5, 1992 ($2.50, limited series)
1-5: 1-Bisley painted pack-c (flip book format-c) — 3.00
1-2nd printing w/o flip-c by Bisley — 2.50

TARZAN VS. PREDATOR AT THE EARTH'S CORE
Dark Horse Comics: Jan, 1996 - No. 4, June, 1996 ($2.50, limited series)
1-4: Lee Weeks-c/a; Walt Simonson scripts — 3.00

TASK FORCE ONE
Image Comics: July, 2006 - Present ($3.50)
1-4-Carlos Rodriguez-a/Jeff Stevenson-s — 3.50

TASKMASTER
Marvel Comics: Apr, 2002 - No. 4, July, 2002 ($2.99, limited series)
1-4-Udon Studio-s/a. 1-Iron Man app. — 3.00

TASMANIAN DEVIL & HIS TASTY FRIENDS
Gold Key: Nov, 1962 (12¢)
1-Bugs Bunny & Elmer Fudd x-over — 14 — 28 — 42 — 102 — 181 — 260

TATTERED BANNERS
DC Comics (Vertigo): Nov, 1998 - No. 4, Feb, 1999 ($2.95, limited series)
1-4-Grant & Giffen-s/McMahon-a — 3.00

TEAM AMERICA (See Captain America #269)
Marvel Comics Group: June, 1982 - No. 12, May, 1983
1-12:1-Origin; Ideal Toy motorcycle characters. 9-Iron Man app. 11-Ghost Rider app. 12-Double size — 2.50

TEAM HELIX
Marvel Comics: Jan, 1993 - No. 4, Apr, 1993 ($1.75, limited series)
1-4: Teen Super Group. 1,2-Wolverine app. — 2.50

TEAM ONE: STORMWATCH (Also see StormWatch)
Image Comics (WildStorm Productions): June, 1995 - No. 2, Aug, 1995 ($2.50, lim. series)
1,2: Steven T. Seagle scripts — 2.50

TEAM ONE: WILDC.A.T.S (Also see WildC.A.T.S)
Image Comics (WildStorm Productions): July, 1995 - No. 2, Aug, 1995 ($2.50, lim. series)
1,2: James Robinson scripts — 2.50

TEAM 7
Image Comics (WildStorm): Oct, 1994 - No.4, Feb, 1995 ($2.50, limited series)
1-4: Dixon scripts in all, 1-Portacio variant-c — 2.50

TEAM 7-DEAD RECKONING
Image Comics (WildStorm): Jan, 1996 - No. 4, Apr, 1996 ($2.50, limited series)
1-4: Dixon scripts in all — 2.50

TEAM 7-OBJECTIVE HELL
image Comics (WildStorm): May, 1995 - No. 3, July, 1995 ($1.95/$2.50, limited series)
1-($1.95)-Newstand; Dixon scripts in all; Barry Smith-c — 2.50
1-3: 1-($2.50)-Direct Market; Barry Smith-c, bound-in card — 2.50

TEAM SUPERMAN
DC Comics: July, 1999 ($2.95, one-shot)
1-Jeanty-a/Stelfreeze-c — 3.00
...Secret Files 1 (5/98, $4.95)Origin-s and pin-ups of Superboy, Supergirl and Steel — 5.00

TEAM TITANS (See Deathstroke & New Titans Annual #7)
DC Comics: Sept, 1992 - No. 24, Sept, 1994 ($1.75/$1.95)

	GD 2.0	VG 4.0	FN 6.0	VF 8.0	VF/NM 9.0	NM- 9.2

1-Five different #1s exist w/origins in 1st half & the same 2nd story in each: Kilowat, Mirage, Nightrider w/Netzer/Perez-a, Redwing, & Terra w/part Perez-p; Total Chaos Pt. 3 — 3.00
2-24: 2-Total Chaos Pt 6. 11-Metallik app. 24-Zero Hour x-over — 2.50
Annual 1,2 ('93, '94, $3.50, 68 pgs.): 2-Elseworlds tory — 3.50

TEAM X/TEAM 7
Marvel Comics: Nov, 1996 ($4.95, one-shot)
1 — 5.00

TEAM X 2000
Marvel Comics: Feb, 1999 ($3.50, one-shot)
1-Kevin Lau-a; Bishop vs. Shi'ar Empire — 3.50

TEAM YANKEE
First Comics: Jan, 1989 - No. 6, Feb, 1989 ($1.95, weekly limited series)
1-6 — 2.50

TEAM YOUNGBLOOD (Also see Youngblood)
Image Comics (Extreme Studios): Sept, 1993 - No. 22, Sept, 1995 ($1.95/$2.50)
1-22: 1-9-Liefeld scripts in all: 1,2,4,6,8-Thibert-c(i). 1-1st app. Dutch & Masada. 3-Spawn cameo. 5-1st app. Lynx. 7,8-Coupons 1 & 4 for Extreme Prejudice #0; Black and White Pt. 4 & 8 by Thibert. 8-Coupon #4 for E. P. #0. 9-Liefeld wraparound-c &(p)/a(p) on Pt. I. 16,17-Bagged w/trading card. 21-Angela & Glory-app. — 2.50

TEAM ZERO
DC Comics (WildStorm Productions): Feb, 2006 - No. 6, Jul, 2006 ($2.99, limited series)
1-6-Dixon-s/Mahnke-a — 3.00

TECH JACKET
Image Comics: Nov, 2002 - No. 6, Apr, 2003 ($2.95)
1-6-Kirkman-s/Su-a — 3.00
Vol. 1: Lost and Found TPB (7/03, $12.95, 7-3/4" x 5-1/4") B&W r/#1-6; Valentino intro. — 13.00

TEDDY ROOSEVELT & HIS ROUGH RIDERS (See Real Heroes #1)
Avon Periodicals: 1950
1-Kinstler-c; Palais-a; Flag-c — 18 — 36 — 54 — 105 — 165 — 225

TEDDY ROOSEVELT ROUGH RIDER (See Battlefield #22 & Classics Illustrated Special Issue)

TED McKEEVER'S METROPOL (See Transit)
Marvel Comics (Epic Comics): Mar, 1991 - No. 12, Mar, 1992 ($2.95, limited series)
V1#1-12: Ted McKeever-c/a/scripts — 3.50

TED McKEEVER'S METROPOL A.D.
Marvel Comics (Epic Comics): Oct, 1992 - No. 3, Dec, 1992 ($3.50, limited series)
V2#1-3: Ted McKeever-c/a/scripts — 3.50

TEENA
Magazine Enterprises/Standard Comics No. 20 on: No. 11, 1948 - No. 15, 1948; No. 20, Aug, 1949 - No. 22, Oct, 1950

	GD 2.0	VG 4.0	FN 6.0	VF 8.0	VF/NM 9.0	NM- 9.2
A-1 #11-Teen-age; Ogden Whitney-c	10	20	30	54	72	90
A-1 #12, 15	9	18	27	47	61	75
20-22 (Standard)	7	14	21	35	43	50

TEEN-AGE BRIDES (True Bride's Experiences #8 on)
Harvey/Home Comics: Aug, 1953 - No. 7, Aug, 1954

	GD 2.0	VG 4.0	FN 6.0	VF 8.0	VF/NM 9.0	NM- 9.2
1-Powell-a	11	22	33	62	86	110
2-Powell-a	8	16	24	44	57	70
3-7; 3,6-Powell-a	8	16	24	40	50	60

TEEN-AGE CONFESSIONS (See Teen Confessions)

TEEN-AGE CONFIDENTIAL CONFESSIONS
Charlton Comics: July, 1960 - No. 22, 1964

	GD 2.0	VG 4.0	FN 6.0	VF 8.0	VF/NM 9.0	NM- 9.2
1	4	8	12	24	37	50
2-10	3	6	9	16	23	30
11-22	2	4	6	13	18	22

TEEN-AGE DIARY SECRETS (Formerly Blue Ribbon Comics; becomes Diary Secrets #10 on)
St. John Publishing Co.: No. 4, 9/49; nn (#5), 9/49 - No. 7, 11/49; No. 8, 2/50; No. 9, 8/50

	GD 2.0	VG 4.0	FN 6.0	VF 8.0	VF/NM 9.0	NM- 9.2
4(9/49)-Oversized; part mag., part comic	30	60	90	174	275	375
nn(#5)(no indicia)-Oversized, all comics; contains sty "I Gave Boys the Green Light."	26	52	78	150	235	320
6,8: (Reg. size) -Photo-c; Baker-a(2-3) in each	28	56	84	162	256	350
7,9-Digest size (Pocket Comics); Baker-a(5); both have same contents; diff.-c	31	62	93	178	282	385

TEEN-AGE DOPE SLAVES (See Harvey Comics Library #1)

TEENAGE HOTRODDERS (Top Eliminator #25 on; see Blue Bird)
Charlton Comics: Apr, 1963 - No. 24, July, 1967

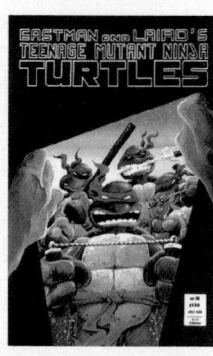

Teenage Mutant Ninja Turtles #16 © MS

Teenage Mutant Ninja Turtles Adventures #4 © MS

Teen-Age Romances #2 © STJ

	GD 2.0	VG 4.0	FN 6.0	VF 8.0	VF/NM 9.0	NM- 9.2
1	6	12	18	37	59	80
2-10	3	6	9	20	30	40
11-24	3	6	9	17	25	32

TEEN-AGE LOVE (See Fox Giants)

TEEN-AGE LOVE (Formerly Intimate)
Charlton Comics: V2#4, July, 1958 - No. 96, Dec, 1973

	GD 2.0	VG 4.0	FN 6.0	VF 8.0	VF/NM 9.0	NM- 9.2
V2#4	4	8	12	28	44	60
5-9	3	6	9	20	30	40
10(9/59)-20	3	6	9	17	25	32
21-35	3	6	9	16	22	28
36-70	2	4	6	13	18	22
71-96: 61&62-Jonnie Love begins (origin)	2	4	6	10	14	18

TEENAGE MUTANT NINJA TURTLES (Also see Anything Goes, Donatello, First Comics Graphic Novel, Gobbledygook, Grimjack #26, Leonardo, Michaelangelo, Raphael & Tales Of The...)
Mirage Studios: 1984 - No. 62, Aug, 1993 ($1.50/$1.75, B&W; all 44-52 pgs.)

1-1st printing (3000 copies)-Origin and 1st app. of the Turtles and Splinter. Only printing to have ad for Gobbledygook #1 & 2; Shredder app. (#1-4: 7-1/2x11") (Prices vary widely on this book. In 2005 a CGC certified 9.4 sold for $8,300, a CGC certified 9.2 sold for $2,850, and a CGC certified 6.0 sold for $1,300)

	GD 2.0	VG 4.0	FN 6.0	VF 8.0	VF/NM 9.0	NM- 9.2
1-2nd printing (6/84)(15,000 copies)	2	4	6	11	16	20
1-3rd printing (2/85)(36,000 copies)	2	4	6	8	10	12
1-4th printing, new-c (50,000 copies)						5.00
1-5th printing, new-c (8/88-c, 11/88 inside)						4.00

1-Counterfeit. **Note:** Most counterfeit copies have a half inch wide white streak or scratch marks across the center of back cover. Black part of cover is a bluish black instead of a deep black. Inside paper is very white & inside cover is bright white (no value)

	GD 2.0	VG 4.0	FN 6.0	VF 8.0	VF/NM 9.0	NM- 9.2
2-1st printing (1984; 15,000 copies)	8	16	24	54	90	125
2-2nd printing	1	3	4	6	8	10
2-3rd printing; new Corben-c (2/85)						5.00

2-Counterfeit with glossy cover stock (no value).

	GD 2.0	VG 4.0	FN 6.0	VF 8.0	VF/NM 9.0	NM- 9.2
3-1st printing (1985, 44 pgs.)	5	10	15	35	55	75

3-Variant, 500 copies, given away in NYC. Has 'Laird's Photo' in white rather than light blue

	GD 2.0	VG 4.0	FN 6.0	VF 8.0	VF/NM 9.0	NM- 9.2
	8	16	24	51	90	125
3-2nd printing; contains new back-up story						3.00
4-1st printing (1985, 44 pgs.)	4	8	12	24	37	50
4,5-2nd printing (5/87, 11/87)						2.50
5-Fugitoid begins, ends #7; 1st full color-c (1985)	3	6	9	14	20	25
6-1st printing (1986)		3	6	9	12	15
6-2nd printing (4/88-c, 5/88 inside)						2.50
7-4 pg. Eastman/Corben color insert; 1st color TMNT (1986, $1.75-c); Bade Biker back-up story	1	3	4	6	8	10
7-2nd printing (1/89) w/o color insert						2.50
8-Cerebus-c/story with Dave Sim-a (1986)	1	2	3	5	6	8
9,10: 9 (9/86)-Rip In Time by Corben						6.00
11-15						4.00
16-18: 18-Mark Bode'-a						3.00
18-2nd printing ($2.25, color, 44 pgs.)-New-c						2.50
19-34: 19-Begin $1.75-c. 24-26-Veitch-c/a.						2.50
32-2nd printing ($2.75, 52 pgs., full color)						3.00
35-49,51: 35-Begin $2.00-c.						2.50
50-Features pin-ups by Larsen, McFarlane, Simonson, etc.						3.00
52-62: 52-Begin $2.25-c						2.50
nn (1990, $5.95, B&W)-Movie adaptation						6.00
Book 1,2($1.50, B&W): 2-Corben-c						2.50

...Christmas Special 1 (12/90, $1.75, B&W, 52 pgs.)-Cover title: Michaelangelo Christmas Special; r/Michaelangelo one-shot plus new Raphael story ... 2.50
...Special (The Maltese Turtle) nn (1/93, $2.95, color, 44 pgs.) ... 3.00
...Special: "Times" Pipeline nn (9/92, $2.95, color, 44 pgs.)-Mark Bode-c/a ... 3.00
Hardcover ($100)-r/#1-10 plus one-shots w/dust jackets - limited to 1000 w/letter of authenticity ... 100.00
Softcover ($40)-r/#1-10 ... 40.00

TEENAGE MUTANT NINJA TURTLES
Mirage Studios: V2#1, Oct, 1993 - V2#13, Oct, 1995 ($2.75)
V2#1-13: 1-Wraparound-c ... 2.75

TEENAGE MUTANT NINJA TURTLES
Image Comics (Highbrow Ent.): June, 1996 - No. 23, Oct, 1999 ($1.95-$2.95)
1-23: 1-8: Eric Larsen-c(i) on all. 10-Savage Dragon-c/app. ... 3.00

TEENAGE MUTANT NINJA TURTLES
Mirage Publishing: V4#1, Dec, 2001 - Present ($2.95, B&W)
V4#1-9,11-28-Laird-s/a(i)/Lawson-a(p). ... 3.00

10-($3.95) Splinter dies ... 4.00

TEENAGE MUTANT NINJA TURTLES
Dreamwave Productions: June 2003 - Present ($2.95, color)
1-7-Animated style; Peter David-s/Lesean-a ... 3.00
Vol. 1 TPB (2003, $9.95) r/#1-4; cover gallery and sketch pages ... 10.00

TEENAGE MUTANT NINJA TURTLES (Adventures)
Archie Publications: Jan, 1996 - No. 3, Mar, 1996 ($1.50, limited series)
1-3 ... 2.50

TEENAGE MUTANT NINJA TURTLES ADVENTURES (TV)
Archie Comics: 8/88 - No. 3, 12/88; 3/89 - No. 72, Oct, 1995 ($1.00/$1.25/$1.50/$1.75)
1-Adapts TV cartoon; not by Eastman/Laird ... 4.00
2,3 (Mini-series), 1 (2nd on-going series), 1-2nd printing ... 2.50
2-18,20-30: 5-Begins original stories not based on TV. 14-Simpson-a(p). 22-Colan-a/c ... 3.00
2-11: 2nd printings ... 2.50
19-1st Mighty Mutanimals (also in #20, 51-54) ... 5.00
31-49 ... 4.00
50-Poster by Eastman/Laird ... 6.00

	GD 2.0	VG 4.0	FN 6.0	VF 8.0	VF/NM 9.0	NM- 9.2
51-54: Mighty Mutanimals	1	2	3	5	6	8
55-60						5.00
61-70: 62-w/poster	1	2	3	5	6	8
71	1	2	3	5	7	9
72- Last issue	2	4	6	8	10	12

nn (1990, $2.50)-Movie adaptation ... 2.50
nn (Spring, 1991, $2.50, 68 pgs.)-(Meet Archie) ... 2.50
nn (Sum, 1991, $2.50, 68 pgs.)-Adapts movie sequel ... 2.50
...Meet the Conservation Corps 1 (1992, $2.50, 68 pgs.) ... 2.50
...III The Movie: The Turtles are Back...In Time (1993, $2.50, 68 pgs.)-1-Bill Wray-c ... 2.50
Special 1,4,5 (Sum/92, Spr/93, Sum/93, 68 pgs.) ... 2.50
Giant Size Special 6 (Fall/93, $1.95, 52 pgs.) ... 2.50
Special 7-10 (Win/93-Fall/94, 52 pgs.): 9-Jeff Smith-c ... 2.50
NOTE: There are 2nd printings of #11-11 w/B&W inside covers. Originals are color.

TEENAGE MUTANT NINJA TURTLES CLASSICS DIGEST (TV)
Archie Comics: Aug, 1993 - No. 8, Mar, 1995? ($1.75)
1-8: Reprints TMNT Advs. ... 3.00

TEENAGE MUTANT NINJA TURTLES/FLAMING CARROT CROSSOVER
Mirage Publishing: Nov, 1993 - No. 4, Feb, 1994 ($2.75, limited series)
1-4: Bob Burden story ... 3.00

TEENAGE MUTANT NINJA TURTLES PRESENTS: APRIL O'NEIL
Archie Comics: Mar, 1993 - No. 3, June, 1993 ($1.25, limited series)
1-3 ... 2.50

TEENAGE MUTANT NINJA TURTLES PRESENTS: DONATELLO AND LEATHERHEAD
Archie Comics: July, 1993 - No. 3, Sept, 1993 ($1.25, limited series)
1-3 ... 2.50

TEENAGE MUTANT NINJA TURTLES PRESENTS: MERDUDE
Archie Comics: Oct, 1993 - No. 3, Dec, 1993 ($1.25, limited series)
1-3-See Mighty Mutanimals #7 for 1st app. Merdude ... 2.50

TEENAGE MUTANT NINJA TURTLES/SAVAGE DRAGON CROSSOVER
Mirage Studios: Aug, 1995 ($2.75, one-shot)
1 ... 3.00

TEEN-AGE ROMANCE (Formerly My Own Romance)
Marvel Comics (ZPC): No. 77, Sept, 1960 - No. 86, Mar, 1962

	GD 2.0	VG 4.0	FN 6.0	VF 8.0	VF/NM 9.0	NM- 9.2
77-83	4	8	12	24	37	50
84-86-Kirby-a. 84-Kirby-a(2 pgs.). 85,86-(3 pgs.)	4	8	12	28	44	60

TEEN-AGE ROMANCES
St. John Publ. Co. (Approved Comics): Jan, 1949 - No. 45, Dec, 1955 (#3,7,10-18,21 are 1/2 inch taller than other issues)

	GD 2.0	VG 4.0	FN 6.0	VF 8.0	VF/NM 9.0	NM- 9.2
1-Baker-c/a(1)	46	92	138	281	466	650
2,3: 2-Baker-c/a. 3-Baker-c/a(3)	32	64	96	186	293	400
4,5,7,8-Photo-c; Baker-a(2-3) each	24	48	72	139	220	300
6-Photo-c; part magazine; Baker-a (10/49)	26	52	78	150	235	320
9-Baker-a; Kubert-a	32	64	96	186	293	400
10-12,20-Baker-c/a(2-3) each	26	52	78	150	235	320
13-19,21,22-Complete issues by Baker	32	64	96	186	293	400
23-25-Baker-c/a(2-3) each	24	48	72	139	220	300

26,27,33,34,36-40,42: 36-Baker-c/a. 33,40-Signed story by Estrada. 38-Suggestive-c.

	GD 2.0	VG 4.0	FN 6.0	VF 8.0	VF/NM 9.0	NM- 9.2
42-r/Cinderella Love #9; Last pre-code (3/55)	16	32	48	94	147	200
28-30-No Baker-a	10	20	30	54	72	90

Teen Love Stories #2 © WP

Teen Titans #26 © DC

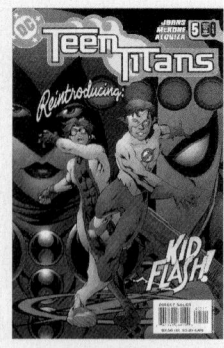

Teen Titans (2005 series) #5 © DC

	GD 2.0	VG 4.0	FN 6.0	VF 8.0	VF/NM 9.0	NM- 9.2
31,32-Baker-c. 31-Estrada-s	14	28	42	80	115	150
35-Baker-c/a (16 pgs.)	16	32	48	94	147	200
41-Baker-c; Infantino-a(r); all stories are Ziff-Davis-r	14	28	42	80	115	150
43-45-Baker-c/a	16	32	48	94	147	200

TEEN-AGE TALK
I.W. Enterprises: 1964

Reprint #1	2	4	6	10	14	18

Reprint #5,8,9: 5-r/Hector #? 9-Punch Comics #?; L.B. Cole-c reprint from School Day

| Romances #1 | 2 | 4 | 6 | 9 | 13 | 16 |

TEEN-AGE TEMPTATIONS (Going Steady #10 on)(See True Love Pictorial)
St. John Publishing Co.: Oct, 1952 - No. 9, Aug, 1954

1-Baker-c/a; has story "Reform School Girl" by Estrada						
	54	108	162	338	557	775
2,4-Baker-c	22	44	66	128	202	275
3,5-7,9-Baker-c/a	30	60	90	174	275	375
8-Teenagers smoke reefer; Baker-c/a	32	64	96	186	293	400

NOTE: *Estrada* a-1, 3-5.

TEEN BEAM (Formerly Teen Beat #1)
National Periodical Publications: No. 2, Jan-Feb, 1968

2-Superman cameo; Herman's Hermits, Yardbirds, Simon & Garfunkel, Lovin Spoonful,

Young Rascals app.; Orlando, Drucker-a(r); Monkees photo-c;						
	12	24	36	87	156	225

TEEN BEAT (Becomes Teen Beam #2)
National Periodical Publications: Nov-Dec, 1967

1-Photos & text only; Monkees photo-c; Beatles, Herman's Hermits, Animals,

| Supremes, Byrds app. | 14 | 28 | 42 | 99 | 175 | 250 |

TEEN COMICS (Formerly All Teen; Journey Into Unknown Worlds #36 on)
Marvel Comics (WFP): No. 21, Apr, 1947 - No. 35, May, 1950

21-Kurtzman's "Hey Look"; Patsy Walker, Cindy (1st app.?), Georgie, Margie app.;

Syd Shores-a begins, end #23	15	30	45	90	140	190
22,23,25,27,29,31-35: 22-(6/47)-Becomes Hedy Devine #22 (8/47) on?						
	14	28	42	76	108	140
24,26,28,30-Kurtzman's "Hey Look"	14	28	42	80	115	150

TEEN CONFESSIONS
Charlton Comics: Aug, 1959 - No. 97, Nov, 1976

1	8	16	24	52	86	120
2	4	8	12	28	44	60
3-10	4	8	12	22	34	45
11-30	3	6	9	18	27	35
31-Beatles-c	11	22	33	79	140	200
32-36,38-55	3	6	9	15	21	26
37 (1/66)-Beatles Fan Club story; Beatles-c	11	22	33	79	140	200
56-58,60-97: 77-Partridge Family poster. 89,90-Newton-c						
	2	4	6	10	14	18
59-Kaluta's 1st pro work? (12/69)	3	6	9	19	29	38

TEENIE WEENIES, THE (America's Favorite Kiddie Comic)
Ziff-Davis Publishing Co.: No. 10, 1950 - No. 11, Apr-May, 1951 (Newspaper reprints)

| 10,11-Painted-c | 20 | 40 | 60 | 115 | 180 | 245 |

TEEN-IN (Tippy Teen)
Tower Comics: Summer, 1968 - No. 4, Fall, 1969

nn(#1, Summer, 1968)(25¢) Has 3 full pg. B&W photos of Sonny & Cher, Donovan and

Herman's Hermits; interviews and photos of Eric Clapton, Jim Morrison and others						
	9	18	27	60	100	140
nn(#2, Spring, 1969),3,4	5	10	15	35	55	75

TEEN LIFE (Formerly Young Life)
New Age/Quality Comics Group: No. 3, Winter, 1945 - No. 5, Fall, 1945 (Teenage magazine)

3-June Allyson photo on-c & story	14	28	42	76	108	140
4-Duke Ellington photo on-c & story	11	22	33	64	90	115
5-Van Johnson, Woody Herman & Jackie Robinson articles; Van Johnson &						
Woody Herman photos on-c	14	28	42	78	112	145

TEEN LOVE STORIES (Magazine)
Warren Publ. Co.: Sept, 1969 - No. 3, Jan, 1970 (68 pgs., photo covers, B&W)

1-Photos & articles plus 36-42 pgs. new comic stories in all; Frazetta-a						
	6	12	18	41	66	90
2,3: 2-Anti-marijuana story	4	8	12	28	44	60

TEEN ROMANCES
Super Comics: 1964

| 10,11,15-17-Reprints | 2 | 4 | 6 | 8 | 11 | 14 |

TEEN SECRET DIARY (Nurse Betsy Crane #12 on)
Charlton Comics: Oct, 1959 - No. 11, June, 1961; No. 1, 1972

1	5	10	15	32	51	70
2	3	6	9	21	32	42
3-11	3	6	9	18	27	35
1 (1972)(exist?)	3	6	9	15	21	26

TEEN TALK (See Teen)

TEEN TITANS (See Brave & the Bold #54,60, DC Super-Stars #1, Marvel & DC Present,
New Teen Titans, New Titans, Official...Index and Showcase #59)
National Periodical Publications/DC Comics: 1-2/66 - No. 43, 1-2/73; No. 44, 11/76 - No. 53, 2/78

1-(1-2/66)-Titans join Peace Corps; Batman, Flash, Aquaman, Wonder Woman cameos

	29	58	87	212	381	550
2	13	26	39	93	164	235
3-5: 4-Speedy app.	8	16	24	58	97	135

6-10: 6-Doom Patrol app.; Beast Boy x-over; readers polled on him joining Titans

	7	14	21	47	76	105
11-18: 11-Speedy app. 13-X-Mas-c	6	12	18	37	59	80
19-Wood-i; Speedy begins as regular	6	12	18	39	62	85
20-22: All Neal Adams-a. 21-Hawk & Dove app.; last 12¢ issue. 22-Origin Wonder Girl						
	7	14	21	50	83	115
23-Wonder Girl dons new costume	4	8	12	28	44	60

24-31: 25-Flash, Aquaman, Batman, Green Arrow, Green Lantern, Superman, & Hawk &
Dove cameos; 1st app. Lilith who joins T.T. West in #50. 29-Hawk & Dove & Ocean Master
app. 30-Aquagirl app. 31-Hawk & Dove app.; last 15¢ issue

	4	8	12	26	41	55
32-34,40-43	3	6	9	17	25	32
35-39-(52 pgs.): 36,37-Superboy-r. 38-Green Arrow/Speedy-r; Aquaman/Aqualad story.						
39-Hawk & Dove-r.	3	6	9	19	29	38
44-(11/76) Dr. Light app.; Mal becomes the Guardian	2	4	6	11	16	20
45,47,49,51,52	2	4	6	10	14	18
46,48: 46-Joker's daughter begins (see Batman Family). 48-Intro Bumblebee;						
Joker's daughter becomes Harlequin	3	6	9	15	21	26
50-1st revival original Bat-Girl; intro. Teen Titans West						
	3	6	9	16	22	28
53-Origin retold	2	4	6	13	18	22

NOTE: *Aparo* a-36. *Buckler* c-46-53. *Cardy* c-1-16. *Kane* a(p)-19, 22-24, 39r. *Tuska* a(p)-31, 36, 38, 39. DC Super-Stars #1 (3/76) was released before #44.

TEEN TITANS (Also see Titans Beat in the Promotional Comics section)
DC Comics: Oct, 1996 - No. 24, Sept, 1998 ($1.95)

1-Dan Jurgens-c/a(p)/scripts & George Pérez-c/a(i) begin; Atom forms new team (Risk,

Argent, Prysm, & Joto); 1st app. Loren Jupiter & Omen; no indicia. 1-3-Origin.						4.00
2-24: 4,5-Robin, Nightwing, Supergirl, Capt. Marvel Jr. app. 12-"Then and Now" begins						
w/original Teen Titans-c/app. 15-Death of Joto. 17-Capt. Marvel Jr. and Fringe join.						
19-Millennium Giants x-over. 23,24-Superman app.						3.00
Annual 1 (1997, $3.95)-Pulp Heroes story						4.00

TEEN TITANS (Also see Titans/Young Justice: Graduation Day)
DC Comics: Sept, 2003 - Present ($2.50/$2.99)

1-McKone-c/a;Johns-s						4.00
1-Variant-c by Michael Turner						5.00
1-2nd and 3rd printings						2.50
2-Deathstroke app.						5.00
2-2nd printing						2.50
3-15: 4-Impulse becomes Kid Flash. 5-Raven returns. 6-JLA app.						2.50
16-33: Titans go to 31st Century; Future Flash app. 17-19-Future Titans app.						
21-23-Dr. Light. 24,25-Outsiders #24,25 x-over. 27,28-Liefeld-a. 32,33-Infinite Crisis						2.50
34-49: 34-One Year Later begins; two covers by Daniel and Benes. 36-Begin $2.99-c.						
40-Zatanna returns. 42-Kid Devil origin; Snejbjerg-a. 43-Titans East. 48,49-Amazons Attack						
x-over; Supergirl app.						3.00
50-($3.99) Art by Pérez (4 pgs.), McKone (6 pgs.), Nauck and Green; future Titans app.						4.00
Annual 1 (4/06, $4.99) Infinite Crisis x-over; Benes-c						5.00
... And Outsiders Secret Files and Origins 2005 (10/05, $4.99) Daniel-c						5.00
.../Legion Special (11/04, $3.50) (cont'd from #16) Reis-a; leads into 2005 Legion of						
Super-Heroes series; LSH preview by Waid & Kitson						3.50
#1/2 (Wizard mail order) origin of Ravager; Reis-a						8.00
.../Outsiders Secret Files 2003 (12/03, $5.95) Reis & Jimenez-a; pin-ups by various						6.00
...: A Kid's Game TPB (2004, $9.95) r/#1-7; Turner-c from #1; McKone sketch pages						10.00
...: Beast Boys and Girls TPB (2005, $9.99) r/#13-15 and Beast Boy #1-4						10.00
...: Family Lost TPB (2004, $9.95) r/#8-12 & #1/2						10.00
...: Life and Death TPB (2006, $14.99) r/#29-33 and pages from Infinite Crisis x-over						15.00
.../ Outsiders: The Death and Return of Donna Troy (2006, $14.99) r/Titans/Young Justice:						

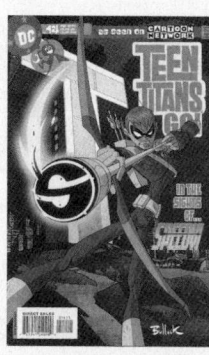

Teen Titans Go! #14 © DC

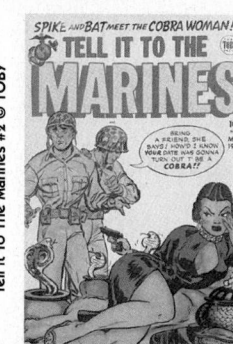

Tell It To The Marines #2 © TOBY

Tellos #9 © Dezago & Wieringo

	GD	VG	FN	VF	VF/NM	NM-
	2.0	4.0	6.0	8.0	9.0	9.2

Graduation Day #1-3, Teen Titans/Outsiders Secret Files 2003 and DC Special: The
Return of Donna Troy #1-4; cover gallery | 15.00
.../ Outsiders: The Insiders (2006, $14.99) r/Teen Titans/ #24-26 & Outsiders #24,25,28 | 15.00
...: The Future is Now (2005, $9.99) r/#15-23 & Teen Titans/Legion Special | 10.00
...: Titans Around the World TPB (2007, $14.99) r/#34-41 | 15.00

TEEN TITANS GO! (Based on Cartoon Network series) (Also see Free Comic Book Day
Edition in the Promotional Comics section)
DC Comics: Jan, 2004 - Present ($2.25)

1-12,14-46: 1,2-Nauck-a/Bullock-c/J. Torres-s. 8-Mad Mod app. 14-Speedy-c. 28-Doom
Patrol app. 31-Nightwing app. 36-Wonder Girl. 38-Mad Mod app.; Clugston-a | 2.25
13-($2.95) Bonus pages with Shazam! reprint | 3.00
Jam Packed Action (2005, $7.99, digest) adaptations of two TV episodes | 8.00
... Vol 1: Truth, Justice, Pizza! (2004, $6.95, digest-size) r/#1-5 | 7.00
... Vol 2: Heroes on Patrol (2005, $6.99, digest-size) r/#6-10 | 7.00
... Vol 3: Bring It On! (2005, $6.99, digest-size) r/#11-15 | 7.00
... Vol 4: Ready For Action! (2006, $6.99, digest-size) r/#16-20 | 7.00
... Vol 5: On The Move! (2006, $6.99, digest-size) r/#21-25 | 7.00

TEEN TITANS SPOTLIGHT
DC Comics: Aug, 1986 - No. 21, Apr, 1988

1-21: 7-Guice's 1st work at DC. 14-Nightwing; Batman app. 15-Austin-c(i).
18,19-Millennium x-over. 21-($1.00-c)-Original Teen Titans; Spiegle-a | 3.00
Note: Guice a-7p, 8p; c-7,8. Orlando c/a-11p. Perez c-1, 17i, 19. Sienkiewicz c-10

TEEPEE TIM (...Heap Funny Indian Boy)(Formerly Ha Ha Comics)
American Comics Group: No. 100, Feb-Mar, 1955 - No. 102, June-July, 1955

100-102 | 6 | 12 | 18 | 31 | 38 | 45

TEGRA JUNGLE EMPRESS (Zegra Jungle Empress #2 on)
Fox Features Syndicate: August, 1948

1-Blue Beetle, Rocket Kelly app.; used in **SOTI**, pg. 31
| 57 | 114 | 171 | 356 | 591 | 825

TEK JANSEN (See Stephen Colbert's...)

TEKNO COMIX HANDBOOK
Tekno Comix: May, 1996 ($3.95, one-shot)

1-Guide to the Tekno Universe | 4.00

TEKNOPHAGE (See Neil Gaiman's...)

TEKNOPHAGE VERSUS ZEERUS
BIG Entertainment: July, 1996 ($3.25, one-shot)

1-Paul Jenkins script | 3.25

TEKWORLD (William Shatner's... on-c only)
Epic Comics (Marvel): Sept, 1992 - Aug, 1994 ($1.75)

1-Based on Shatner's novel, TekWar, set in L.A. in the year 2120 | 3.00
2-24 | 2.50

TELEVISION (See TV)

TELEVISION COMICS (Early TV comic)
Standard Comics (Animated Cartoons): No. 5, Feb, 1950 - No. 8, Nov, 1950

5-1st app. Willy Nilly | 10 | 20 | 30 | 54 | 72 | 90
6-8: 6 has #2 on inside | 8 | 16 | 24 | 42 | 54 | 65

TELEVISION PUPPET SHOW (Early TV comic) (See Spotty the Pup)
Avon Periodicals: 1950 - No. 2, Nov, 1950

1-1st app. Speedy Rabbit, Spotty The Pup | 19 | 38 | 57 | 112 | 176 | 240
2 | 14 | 28 | 42 | 80 | 115 | 150

TELEVISION TEENS MOPSY (See TV Teens)

TELL IT TO THE MARINES
Toby Press Publications: Mar, 1952 - No. 15, July, 1955

1-Lover O'Leary and His Liberty Belles (with pin-ups), ends #6; Spike & Bat
begin, end #6 | 19 | 38 | 57 | 112 | 176 | 240
2-Madame Cobra-c/story | 12 | 24 | 36 | 67 | 94 | 120
3-5 | 10 | 20 | 30 | 54 | 72 | 90
6-12,14,15: 7-9,14,15-Photo-c | 8 | 16 | 24 | 42 | 54 | 65
13-John Wayne photo-c | 15 | 30 | 45 | 83 | 124 | 165
I.W. Reprint #9-r/#1 above | 2 | 4 | 6 | 8 | 10 | 12
Super Reprint #16(1964)-r/#4 above | 2 | 4 | 6 | 8 | 10 | 12

TELLOS
Image Comics: May, 1999 - No. 10 ($2.50)

1-Dezago-s/Wieringo-a | 3.00
1-Variant-c ($7.95) | 8.00
2-10: 4-Four covers | 2.50

	GD	VG	FN	VF	VF/NM	NM-
	2.0	4.0	6.0	8.0	9.0	9.2

...: Maiden Voyage (3/01, $5.95) Didier Crispeels-a/c | 6.00
...: Sons & Moons (2002, $5.95) Nick Cardy-c | 6.00
...: The Last Heist (2001, $5.95) Rousseau-a/c | 6.00
Prelude ($5.00, AnotherUniverse.com) | 5.00
Prologue ($3.95, Dynamic Forces) | 4.00
...Collected Edition 1 (12/99, $8.95) r/#1-3 | 9.00
...: Kindred Spirits (2/01, $17.95) r/#6-10, Section Zero #1 (Scatterjack-s) | 18.00
...: Reluctant Heroes (2/01, $17.95) r/#1-5, Prelude, Prologue; sketchbook | 18.00

TEMPEST (See Aquaman, 3rd Series)
DC Comics: Nov, 1996 - No. 4, Feb, 1997 ($1.75, limited series)

1-4: Formerly Aqualad; Phil Jimenez-c/a/scripts in all | 2.50

TEMPUS FUGITIVE
DC Comics: 1990 - No. 4, 1991 ($4.95, squarebound, 52 pgs.)

Book 1,2: Ken Steacy painted-c/a & scripts | 6.00
Book 3,4-($5.95-c) | 6.00
TPB (Dark Horse Comics, 1/97, $17.95) | 18.00

TEN COMMANDMENTS (See Moses & the... and Classics Illustrated Special)

TENDER LOVE STORIES
Skywald Publ. Corp.: Feb, 1971 - No. 4, July, 1971 (Pre-code reprints and new stories)

1 (All 25¢, 52 pgs.) | 3 | 6 | 9 | 20 | 30 | 40
2-4 | 3 | 6 | 9 | 16 | 23 | 30

TENDER ROMANCE (Ideal Romance #3 on)
Key Publications (Gilmour Magazines): Dec, 1953 - No. 2, Feb, 1954

1-Headlight & lingerie panels; B. Baily-c | 18 | 36 | 54 | 103 | 162 | 220
2-Bernard Baily-c | 11 | 22 | 33 | 62 | 86 | 110

TENSE SUSPENSE
Fago Publications: Dec, 1958 - No. 2, Feb, 1959

1 | 10 | 20 | 30 | 54 | 72 | 90
2 | 8 | 16 | 24 | 40 | 50 | 60

TEN STORY LOVE (Formerly a pulp magazine with same title)
Ace Periodicals: V29#3, June-July, 1951 - V36#5(#209), Sept, 1956 (#3-6: 52 pgs.)

V29#3(#177)-Part comic, part text; painted-c | 14 | 28 | 42 | 80 | 115 | 150
4-6(1/52) | 9 | 18 | 27 | 50 | 65 | 80
V30#1(3/52)-6(1/53) | 9 | 18 | 27 | 47 | 61 | 75
V31#1(2/53), V32#2(4/53)-6(12/53) | 8 | 16 | 24 | 44 | 57 | 70
V33#1(1/54)-3(5#54, #195), V34#4(7/54, #196)-6(10/54, #198)
| 8 | 16 | 24 | 42 | 54 | 65
V35#1(12/54, #199)-3(4/55, #201)-Last precode | 8 | 16 | 24 | 40 | 50 | 60
V35#4-6(9/55, #201-204), V36#1(11/55, #205)-3, 5(9/56, #209)
| 7 | 14 | 21 | 37 | 46 | 55
V36#4-L.B. Cole-a | 10 | 20 | 30 | 56 | 76 | 95

TENTH, THE
Image Comics: Jan, 1997 - No. 4, June, 1997 ($2.50, limited series)

1-4-Tony Daniel-c/a, Beau Smith-s | 5.00
Abuse of Humanity TPB (10/98, $10.95) r/#1-4 | 11.00
Abuse of Humanity TPB (10/98, $11.95) r/#1-4 & 0(8/97) | 12.00

TENTH, THE
Image Comics: Sept, 1997 - No. 14, Jan, 1999 ($2.50)

0-(8/97, $5.00) American Ent. Ed. | 6.00
1-Tony Daniel-c/a, Beau Smith-s | 6.00
2-9: 3,7-Variant-c | 4.00
10-14 | 3.00
...Configuration (8/98) Re-cap and pin-ups | 2.50
...Collected Edition 1 ('98, $4.95, square-bound) r/#1,2 | 5.00
...Special (4/00, $2.95) r/#0 and Wizard #1/2 | 3.00
Wizard #1/2-Daniel-s/Steve Scott-a | 10.00

TENTH, THE (Volume 3) (The Black Embrace)
Image Comics: Mar, 1999 - No. 4, June, 1999 ($2.95)

1-4-Daniel-c/a | 3.00
TPB (1/00, $12.95) r/#1-4 | 13.00

TENTH, THE (Volume 4) (Evil's Child)
Image Comics: Sept, 1999 - No. 4, Mar, 2000 ($2.95, limited series)

1-4-Daniel-c/a | 3.00

TENTH, THE (Darkk Dawn)
Image Comics: July, 2005 ($4.99, one-shot)

1-Kirkham-a/Bonny-s | 5.00

10th Muse #1 © Tidal Wave Studios

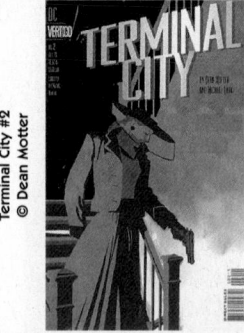

Terminal City #2 © Dean Motter

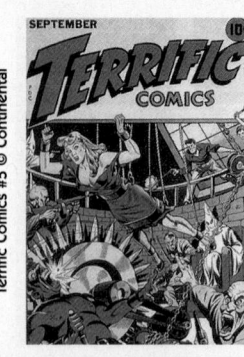

Terrific Comics #5 © Continental

	GD 2.0	VG 4.0	FN 6.0	VF 8.0	VF/NM 9.0	NM- 9.2		GD 2.0	VG 4.0	FN 6.0	VF 8.0	VF/NM 9.0	NM- 9.2

TENTH, THE : RESURRECTED
Dark Horse Comics: July, 2001 - No. 4, Feb, 2002 ($2.99, limited series)

1-4: 1-Two covers; Daniel-s/c; Romano-a   3.00

10th MUSE
Image Comics (TidalWave Studios): Nov, 2000 - No. 9, Jan, 2002 ($2.95)

1-Character based on wrestling's Rena Mero; regular & photo covers   3.00
2-9: 2-Photo and 2 Lashley covers; flip book Dollz preview. 5-Savage Dragon app.;
   2 covers by Lashley and Larsen. 6-Tellos x-over   3.00

10th MUSE (Volume 2)
Avatar Press: July, 2002 ($3.50)

1-Wolfman-s; Cruz-a. 1-Five homage covers by various   3.50

TENTH MUSE
Alias Enterprises: Apr, 2005 - Present ($2.99)

1,2-Amezcua-a. 2-Two covers plus Cindy Margolis photo-c   3.00

TEN WHO DARED (Disney)
Dell Publishing Co.: No. 1178, Dec, 1960

| Four Color 1178-Movie, painted-c; cast member photo on back-c | 7 | 14 | 21 | 49 | 80 | 110 |

TERMINAL CITY
DC Comics (Vertigo): July, 1996 - No. 9, Mar, 1997 ($2.50, limited series)

1-9: Dean Motter scripts, 7,8-Matt Wagner-c   2.50
TPB ('97, $19.95) r/series   20.00

TERMINAL CITY: AERIAL GRAFFITI
DC Comics (Vertigo): Nov, 1997 - No. 5, Mar, 1998 ($2.50, limited series)

1-5: Dean Motter-s/Lark-a/Chiarello-c   2.50

TERMINATOR, THE (See Robocop vs. ... & Rust #12 for 1st app.)
Now Comics: Sept, 1988 - No. 17, 1989 ($1.75, Baxter paper)

1-Based on movie	1	3	4	6	8	10
2-5						6.00
6-17: 12-($2.95, 52 pgs.)-Intro. John Connor						3.00
Trade paperback (1989, $9.95)						10.00

TERMINATOR, THE
Dark Horse Comics: Aug, 1990 - No. 4, Nov, 1990 ($2.50, limited series)

1-Set 39 years later than the movie   4.00
2-4   3.00

TERMINATOR, THE
Dark Horse Comics: 1998 - No. 4, Dec, 1998 ($2.95, limited series)

1-4-Alan Grant-s/Steve Pugh-a/c   3.00
...Special (1998, $2.95) Darrow-c/Grant-s   3.00

TERMINATOR, THE: ALL MY FUTURES PAST
Now Comics: V3#1, Aug, 1990 - V3#2, Sept, 1990 ($1.75, limited series)

V3#1,2   3.00

TERMINATOR, THE: ENDGAME
Dark Horse Comics: Sept, 1992 - No. 3, Nov, 1992 ($2.50, limited series)

1-3: Guice-a(p); painted-c   3.00

TERMINATOR, THE: HUNTERS AND KILLERS
Dark Horse Comics: Mar, 1992 - No. 3, May, 1992 ($2.50, limited series)

1-3   3.00

TERMINATOR, THE: ONE SHOT
Dark Horse Comics: July, 1991 ($5.95, 56 pgs.)

nn-Matt Wagner-a; contains stiff pop-up inside   6.00

TERMINATOR, THE: SECONDARY OBJECTIVES
Dark Horse Comics: July, 1991 - No. 4, Oct, 1991 ($2.50, limited series)

1-4: Gulacy-c/a(p) in all   3.00

TERMINATOR, THE: THE BURNING EARTH
Now Comics: V2#1, Mar, 1990 - V2#5, July, 1990 ($1.75, limited series)

V2#1: Alex Ross painted art (1st published work)	2	4	6	9	12	15
2-5: Ross-c/a in all	1	3	4	6	8	10
Trade paperback (1990, $9.95)-Reprints V2#1-5						12.00
Trade paperback (ibooks, 2003, $17.95)-Digitally remastered reprint						18.00

TERMINATOR, THE: THE DARK YEARS
Dark Horse Comics: Aug, 1999 - No. 4, Dec, 1999 ($2.95, limited series)

1-4-Alan Grant-s/Mel Rubi-a; Jae Lee-c   3.00

TERMINATOR: THE ENEMY FROM WITHIN, THE
Dark Horse Comics: Nov, 1991 - No. 4, Feb, 1992 ($2.50, limited series)

1-4: All have Simon Bisley painted-c   3.00

TERMINATOR 2: CYBERNETIC DAWN
Malibu: Nov, 1995 - No.4, Feb, 1996; No. 0. Apr, 1996 ($2.50, lim. series)

0 (4/96, $2.95)-Erskine-c/a; flip book w/Terminator 2: Nuclear Twilight   3.00
1-4: Continuation of film.   3.00

TERMINATOR 2: INFINITY
Dynamite Entertainment: 2007 - Present ($3.50)

1-3-Furman-s/Raynor-a; 3 covers   3.50

TERMINATOR 2: JUDGEMENT DAY
Marvel Comics: Early Sept, 1991 - No. 3, Early Oct, 1991 ($1.00, lim. series)

1-3: Based on movie sequel; 1-3-Same as nn issues   3.00
nn (1991, $4.95, squarebound, 68 pgs.)-Photo-c   5.00
nn (1991, $2.25, B&W, magazine, 68 pgs.)   3.00

TERMINATOR 2: NUCLEAR TWILIGHT
Malibu: Nov, 1995 - No.4, Feb, 1996; No. 0, Apr, 1996 ($2.50, lim. series)

0 (4/96, $2.95)-Erskine-c/a; flip book w/Terminator 2: Cybernetic Dawn   3.00
1-4:Continuation of film.   3.00

TERMINATOR 3: RISE OF THE MACHINES (... BEFORE THE RISE on cover)
Beckett Comics: July, 2003 - No. 6, Jan, 2004 ($5.95, limited series)

1-6: 1,2-Leads into movie; 2 covers on each. 3-6-Movie adaptation   6.00

TERRAFORMERS
Wonder Color Comics: April, 1987 - No. 2, 1987 ($1.95, limited series)

1,2-Kelley Jones-a   2.50

TERRANAUTS
Fantasy General Comics: Aug, 1986 - No. 2, 1986 ($1.75, limited series)

1,2   2.50

TERRA OBSCURA (See Tom Strong)
America's Best Comics: Aug, 2003 - No. 6, Feb, 2004 ($2.95)

1-6-Alan Moore & Peter Hogan-s/Paquette-a   3.00
TPB (2004, $14.95) r/#1-6   15.00

TERRA OBSCURA VOLUME 2 (See Tom Strong)
America's Best Comics: Oct, 2004 - No. 6, May, 2005 ($2.95)

1-6-Alan Moore & Peter Hogan-s/Paquette-a; Tom Strange app.   3.00
TPB (2005, $14.99) r/#1-6   15.00

TERRARISTS
Marvel Comics (Epic): Nov, 1993 - No. 4, Feb, 1994 ($2.50, limited series)

1-4-Bound-in trading cards in all   2.50

TERRIFIC COMICS (Also see Suspense Comics)
Continental Magazines: Jan, 1944 - No. 6, Nov, 1944

1-Kid Terrific; opium story	315	630	945	2048	3624	5200
2-1st app. The Boomerang by L.B. Cole & Ed Wheelan's "Comics" McCormick,						
called the world's #1 comic book fan begins	228	456	684	1425	2363	3300
3-Diana becomes Boomerang's costumed aide; L.B. Cole-c						
	228	456	684	1425	2363	3300
4-Classic war-c (Scarce)	400	800	1200	2600	4600	6600
5-The Reckoner begins; Boomerang & Diana by L.B. Cole; Classic Schomburg						
bondage & hooded vigilante-c (Scarce)	725	1450	2175	4350	6925	9500
6-L.B. Cole-c/a	207	414	621	1294	2147	3000

NOTE: L.B. Cole a-1, 2(2), 3-6. Fuje a-5, 6. Rico a-2; c-1. Schomburg c-2, 5.

TERRIFIC COMICS (Formerly Horrific; Wonder Boy #17 on)
Mystery Publ.(Comic Media)/(Ajax/Farrell): No. 14, Dec, 1954; No. 16, Mar, 1955 (No #15)

14-Art swipe/Advs. into the Unknown #37; injury-to-eye-c; pg. 2, panel 5 swiped from						
Phantom Stranger #4; surrealistic Palais-a; Human Cross story; classic-c						
	60	120	180	375	625	875
16-Wonder Boy-c/story (last pre-code)	27	54	81	156	246	335

TERRIFYING TALES (Formerly Startling Terror Tales #10)
Star Publications: No. 11, Jan, 1953 - No. 15, Apr, 1954

11-Used in POP, pgs. 99,100; all Jo-Jo	49	98	147	299	492	685
12-Reprints Jo-Jo #19 entirely; L.B. Cole splash	47	94	141	287	474	660
13-All Rulah-r; classic devil-c	53	106	159	323	537	750
14-All Rulah reprints	44	88	132	268	439	610
15-Rulah, Zago-r; used in SOTI-r/Rulah #22	44	88	132	268	439	610

NOTE: All issues have L.B. Cole covers; bondage covers-No. 12-14.

Terrors of the Jungle #9 © STAR

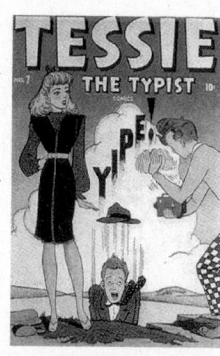

Tessie the Typist #7 © MAR

Testament #7 © Rushkoff & Sharp

	GD 2.0	VG 4.0	FN 6.0	VF 8.0	VF/NM 9.0	NM- 9.2

TERROR ILLUSTRATED (Adult Tales of…)
E.C. Comics: Nov-Dec, 1955 - No. 2, Spring (April on-c), 1956 (Magazine, 25¢)

	GD 2.0	VG 4.0	FN 6.0	VF 8.0	VF/NM 9.0	NM- 9.2
1-Adult Entertainment on-c	21	42	63	122	191	260
2-Charles Sultan-a	15	30	45	86	133	180

NOTE: Craig, Evans, Ingels, Orlando art in each. Crandall c-1, 2.

TERROR INC. (See A Shadowline Saga #3)
Marvel Comics: July, 1992 - No. 13, July, 1993 ($1.75)

1-8,11-13: 6,7-Punisher-c/story. 13-Ghost Rider app.						2.50
9,10-Wolverine-c/story						3.00

TERROR INC.
Marvel Comics (MAX): Oct, 2007 - No. 5 ($3.99, limited series)

1,2: 1-Lapham-s/Zircher-a; origin of Mr. Terror retold						4.00

TERRORS OF DRACULA (Magazine)
Modern Day Periodical/Eerie Publ.: Vol. 1 #3, May, 1979 - Vol. 3 #2, Sept, 1981 (B&W)

	GD 2.0	VG 4.0	FN 6.0	VF 8.0	VF/NM 9.0	NM- 9.2
Vol. 1 #3 (5/79, 1st issue)	4	8	12	22	34	45
#4(8/79), #5(11/79)	3	6	9	18	27	35
Vol. 2 #1-3: 1-(2/80). 2-(5/80). 3-(8/80)	3	6	9	16	22	28
Vol. 3 #1 (5/81), #2 (9/81)	3	6	9	17	25	32

TERRORS OF THE JUNGLE (Formerly Jungle Thrills)
Star Publications: No. 17, 5/52 - No. 21, 2/53; No. 4, 4/53 - No. 10, 9/54

	GD 2.0	VG 4.0	FN 6.0	VF 8.0	VF/NM 9.0	NM- 9.2
17-Reprints Rulah #21, used in SOTI; L.B. Cole bondage-c	47	94	141	287	474	660
18-Jo-Jo-r	36	72	108	208	329	450
19,20(1952)-Jo-Jo-r; Disbrow-a	34	68	102	197	311	425
21-Jungle Jo, Tangi-r; used in POP, pg. 100 & color illos.	38	76	114	219	347	475
4-10: All Disbrow-a. 5-Jo-Jo-r. 8-Rulah, Jo-Jo-r. 9-Jo-Jo-r; Disbrow-a; Tangi by Orlando10-Rulah-r	38	76	114	219	347	475

NOTE: L.B. Cole c-all; bondage c-17, 19, 21, 5, 7.

TERROR TALES (See Beware Terror Tales)

TERROR TALES (Magazine)
Eerie Publications: V1#7, 1969 - V6#6, Dec, 1974; V7#1, Apr, 1976 - V10, 1979? (V1-V6: 52 pgs.; V7 on: 68 pgs.)

	GD 2.0	VG 4.0	FN 6.0	VF 8.0	VF/NM 9.0	NM- 9.2
V1#7	6	12	18	39	62	85
V1#8-11('69): 9-Bondage-c	4	8	12	26	41	55
V2#1-6('70), V3#1-6('71), V4#1-7('72), V5#1-6('73), V6#1-6('74), V7#1,4('76) (no V7#2), V8#1-3('77)	4	8	12	23	36	48
V7#3-7('76) LSD story-r/Weird V3#5	4	8	12	23	36	48
V9#2-4, V10	4	8	12	24	37	50

TERRY AND THE PIRATES (See Famous Feature Stories, Merry Christmas From Sears Toyland, Popular Comics, Super Book #3,5,9,16,28, & Super Comics)

TERRY AND THE PIRATES
Dell Publishing Co.: 1939 - 1953 (By Milton Caniff)

	GD 2.0	VG 4.0	FN 6.0	VF 8.0	VF/NM 9.0	NM- 9.2
Large Feature Comic 2(1939)	86	172	258	538	894	1250
Large Feature Comic 6(1938)-r/1936 dailies	71	142	213	444	735	1025
Four Color 9(1940)	67	134	201	419	692	965
Large Feature Comic 27('41), 6('42)	57	114	171	356	591	825
Four Color 44('43)	34	68	102	255	465	675
Four Color 101('45)	22	44	66	165	295	425
Family Album(1942)	19	38	57	112	176	240

TERRY AND THE PIRATES (Formerly Boy Explorers; Long John Silver & the Pirates #30 on)
(Daily strip-r) (Two #26's)
Harvey Publications/Charlton No. 26-28: No. 3, 4/47 - No. 26, 4/51; No. 26, 6/55 - No. 28, 10/55

	GD 2.0	VG 4.0	FN 6.0	VF 8.0	VF/NM 9.0	NM- 9.2
3(#1)-Boy Explorers by S&K; Terry & the Pirates begin by Caniff; 1st app. The Dragon Lady	40	80	120	235	368	500
4-S&K Boy Explorers	23	46	69	132	209	285
5-11: 11-Man in Black app. by Powell	13	26	39	72	101	130
12-20: 16-Girl threatened with red hot poker	10	20	30	56	76	95
21-26(4/51)-Last Caniff issue & last pre-code issue	10	20	30	54	72	90
26-28('55)(Formerly This Is Suspense)-No Caniff-a	9	18	27	47	61	75

NOTE: Powell a (Tommy Tween)-5-10, 12, 14; 15-17(1/2 to 2 pgs. each).

TERRY BEARS COMICS (TerryToons, The… #4)
St. John Publishing Co.: June, 1952 - No. 3, Mar, 1953

	GD 2.0	VG 4.0	FN 6.0	VF 8.0	VF/NM 9.0	NM- 9.2
1-By Paul Terry	10	20	30	54	72	90
2,3	7	14	21	35	43	50

TERRY-TOONS ALBUM (See Giant Comics Edition)

TERRY-TOONS COMICS (1st Series) (Becomes Paul Terry's Comics #85 on; later issues titled "Paul Terry's…")
Timely/Marvel No. 1-59 (8/47)(Becomes Best Western No. 58 on?, Marvel)/St. John No. 60 (9/47) on: Oct, 1942 - No. 86, May, 1951

	GD 2.0	VG 4.0	FN 6.0	VF 8.0	VF/NM 9.0	NM- 9.2
1 (Scarce)-Features characters that 1st app. on movie screen; Gandy Goose & Sourpuss begin; war-c; Gandy Goose c-1-37	186	372	558	1163	1932	2700
2	66	132	198	413	682	950
3-5	46	92	138	281	466	650
6,8-10: 9,10-World War II gag-c	36	72	108	208	329	450
7-Hitler, Hirohito, Mussolini-c	50	100	150	305	503	700
11-20	22	44	66	128	202	275
21-37	15	30	45	90	140	190
38-Mighty Mouse begins (1st app., 11/45); Mighty Mouse-c begin, end #86; Gandy, Sourpuss welcome Mighty Mouse on-c	152	304	456	950	1575	2200
39-2nd app. Mighty Mouse	48	96	144	293	484	675
40-49: 43-Infinity-c	23	46	69	132	209	285
50-1st app. Heckle & Jeckle (11/46)	41	82	123	256	416	575
51-60: 55-Infinity-c. 60-(9/47)-Atomic explosion panel; 1st St. John issue	14	28	42	82	121	160
61-86: 85,86-Same book as Paul Terry's Comics #85,86 with only a title change; published at same time?	13	26	39	74	105	135

TERRY-TOONS COMICS (2nd Series)
St. John Publishing Co./Pines: June, 1952 - No. 9, Nov, 1953; 1957; 1958

	GD 2.0	VG 4.0	FN 6.0	VF 8.0	VF/NM 9.0	NM- 9.2
1-Gandy Goose & Sourpuss begin by Paul Terry	18	36	54	105	165	225
2	10	20	30	56	76	95
3-9	9	18	27	52	69	85
Giant Summer Fun Book 101,102-(Sum, 1957, Sum, 1958, 25¢, Pines)(TV) CBS Television Presents…; Tom Terrific, Mighty Mouse, Heckle & Jeckle Gandy Goose app.	14	28	42	80	115	150

TERRYTOONS, THE TERRY BEARS (Formerly Terry Bears Comics)
Pines Comics: No. 4, Summer, 1958 (CBS Television Presents…)

	GD 2.0	VG 4.0	FN 6.0	VF 8.0	VF/NM 9.0	NM- 9.2
4	7	14	21	35	43	50

TESSIE THE TYPIST (Tiny Tessie #24; see Comedy Comics, Gay Comics & Joker Comics)
Timely/Marvel Comics (20CC): Summer, 1944 - No. 23, Sept, 1949

	GD 2.0	VG 4.0	FN 6.0	VF 8.0	VF/NM 9.0	NM- 9.2
1-Doc Rockblock & others by Wolverton	69	138	207	431	716	1000
2-Wolverton's Powerhouse Pepper	40	80	120	237	374	510
3-(3/45)-No Wolverton	16	32	48	94	147	200
4,5,7,8-Wolverton-a. 4-(Fall/45)	30	60	90	174	275	375
6-Kurtzman's "Hey Look", 2 pgs. Wolverton-a	30	60	90	174	275	375
9-Wolverton's Powerhouse Pepper (8 pgs.) & 1 pg. Kurtzman's "Hey Look"	33	66	99	190	300	410
10-Wolverton's Powerhouse Pepper (4 pgs.)	31	62	93	178	282	385
11-Wolverton's Powerhouse Pepper (8 pgs.)	33	66	99	190	300	410
12-Wolverton's Powerhouse Pepper (4 pgs.) & 1 pg. Kurtzman's "Hey Look"	31	62	93	178	282	385
13-Wolverton's Powerhouse Pepper (4 pgs.)	31	62	93	178	282	385
14,15: 14-Wolverton's Dr. Whackyhack (1 pg.); 1-1/2 pgs. Kurtzman's "Hey Look". 15-Kurtzman's "Hey Look" (3 pgs.) & 3 pgs. Giggles 'n' Grins	23	46	69	135	213	290
16-18-Kurtzman's "Hey Look" (?, 2 & 1 pg.)	16	32	48	94	147	200
19-Annie Oakley story (8 pgs.)	14	28	42	76	108	140
20-23: 20-Anti-Wertham editorial (2/49)	12	24	36	69	97	125

NOTE: Lana app.-21. Millie the Model app.-13, 15, 17, 21. Rusty app.-10, 11, 13, 15, 17.

TESTAMENT
DC Comics (Vertigo): Feb, 2006 - Present ($2.99)

1-19: 1-5-Rushkoff-s/Sharp-a. 6,7-Gross & Erskine-a						3.00
…: Akedah TPB (2006, $9.99) r/#1-5; Rushkoff intro.						10.00
…: West of Eden TPB (2007, $12.99) r/#6-10; Rushkoff commentary						13.00

TEXAN, THE (Fightin' Marines #15 on; Fightin' Texan #16 on)
St. John Publishing Co.: Aug, 1948 - No. 15, Oct, 1951

	GD 2.0	VG 4.0	FN 6.0	VF 8.0	VF/NM 9.0	NM- 9.2
1-Buckskin Belle	16	32	48	94	147	200
2	10	20	30	58	79	100
3,10: 10-Oversized issue	10	20	30	54	72	90
4,5,7,15-Baker-c/a	18	36	54	105	165	225
6,9-Baker-c	14	28	42	76	108	140
8,11,13,14-Baker-c/a(2-3) each	20	40	60	117	184	250
12-All Matt Baker-c/a; Peyote story	27	54	81	156	246	335

NOTE: Matt Baker a-4-9, 11-15. Larsen a-4-6, 8-10, 15. Tuska a-1, 2, 7-9.

TEXAN, THE (TV)
Dell Publishing Co.: No. 1027, Sept-Nov, 1959 - No. 1096, May-July, 1960

	GD 2.0	VG 4.0	FN 6.0	VF 8.0	VF/NM 9.0	NM- 9.2
Four Color 1027 (#1)-Photo-c	8	16	24	56	93	130

Texas Kid #10 © MAR

Tex Morgan #6 © MAR

Tex Taylor #7 © MAR

	GD 2.0	VG 4.0	FN 6.0	VF 8.0	VF/NM 9.0	NM- 9.2
Four Color 1096-Rory Calhoun photo-c	8	16	24	52	86	120

TEXAS CHAINSAW MASSACRE
DC Comics (WildStorm): Jan, 2007 - No. 6, Jun, 2007 ($2.99, limited series)

1-6: 1-Two covers by Bermejo & Bradstreet; Abnett & Lanning-s						3.00
...: About a Boy #1 (9/07, $2.99) Abnett & Lanning-s/Gomez-a/Robertson-c						3.00
...: B y Himself #1 (10/07, $2.99) Abnett & Lanning-s/Craig-a/Robertson-c						3.00
...: Cut! #1 (8/07, $2.99) Pfeiffer-s/Raffaele-a/Robertson-c						3.00

TEXAS JOHN SLAUGHTER (See Walt Disney Presents, 4-Color #997, 1181 & #2)

TEXAS KID (See Two-Gun Western, Wild Western)
Marvel/Atlas Comics (LMC): Jan, 1951 - No. 10, July, 1952

1-Origin; Texas Kid (alias Lance Temple) & his horse Thunder begin; Tuska-a	23	46	69	130	205	280
2	13	26	39	74	105	135
3-10	10	20	30	56	76	95

NOTE: Maneely a-1-4; c-1, 3, 5-10.

TEXAS RANGERS, THE (See Jace Pearson of... and Superior Stories #4)

TEXAS RANGERS IN ACTION (Formerly Captain Gallant or Scotland Yard?)
Charlton Comics: No. 5, Jul, 1956 - No. 79, Aug, 1970 (See Blue Bird Comics)

5	8	16	24	44	57	70
6,7,9,10	6	12	18	28	34	40
8-Ditko-a (signed)	10	20	30	54	72	90
11-Williamson-a(5&8 pgs.); Torres/Williamson-a (5 pgs.)	10	20	30	54	72	90
12,14-20	5	10	15	23	28	32
13-Williamson-a (5 pgs); Torres, Morisi-a	8	16	24	42	54	65
21-30	3	6	9	16	22	28
31-59: 32-Both 10¢-c & 15¢-c exist	2	4	6	13	18	22
60-Riley's Rangers begin	3	6	9	14	19	24
61-65,68-70	2	4	6	8	11	14
66,67: 66-1st app. The Man Called Loco. 67-Origin	2	4	6	9	13	16
71-79	1	3	4	6	8	10
76 (Modern Comics-r, 1977)						4.00

TEXAS SLIM (See A-1 Comics)

TEX DAWSON, GUN-SLINGER (Gunslinger #2 on)
Marvel Comics Group: Jan, 1973 (20¢)(Also see Western Kid, 1st series)

1-Steranko-c; Williamson-r (4 pgs.); Tex Dawson by Romita(3) from 1955; Tuska-r	3	6	9	14	20	25

TEX FARNUM (See Wisco)

TEX FARRELL (...Pride of the Wild West)
D. S. Publishing Co.: Mar-Apr, 1948

1-Tex Farrell & his horse Lightning; Shelly-c	15	30	45	88	137	185

TEX GRANGER (Formerly Calling All Boys; see True Comics)
Parents' Magazine Inst./Commended: No. 18, Jun, 1948 - No. 24, Sept, 1949

18-Tex Granger & his horse Bullet begin	12	24	36	67	94	120
19	10	20	30	54	72	90
20-24: 22-Wild Bill Hickok story. 23-Vs. Billy the kid; Tim Holt app.	8	16	24	44	57	70

TEX MORGAN (See Blaze Carson and Wild Western)
Marvel Comics (CCC): Aug, 1948 - No. 9, Feb, 1950

1-Tex Morgan, his horse Lightning & sidekick Lobo begin	28	56	84	164	260	355
2	18	36	54	103	162	220
3-6: 3,4-Arizona Annie app.	13	26	39	74	105	135
7-9: photo-c. 8-18 pg. story "The Terror of Rimrock Valley"; Diablo app.	18	36	54	103	162	220

NOTE: Tex Taylor app.-6, 7, 9. Brodsky c-6. Syd Shores c-2, 5.

TEX RITTER WESTERN (Movie star; singing cowboy; see Six-Gun Heroes and Western Hero)
Fawcett No. 1-20 (1/54)/Charlton No. 21 on: Oct. 1950 - No. 46, May, 1959 (Photo-c: 1-21)

1-Tex Ritter, his stallion White Flash & dog Fury begin; photo front/back-c begin	57	114	171	356	578	800
2	29	58	87	167	259	350
3-5: 5-Last photo back-c	21	42	63	121	186	250
6-10	16	32	48	89	137	185
11-19	12	24	36	69	97	125
20-Last Fawcett issue (1/54)	13	26	39	74	105	135
21-1st Charlton issue; photo-c (3/54)	16	32	48	89	137	185
22-B&W photo back-c begin, end #32	11	22	33	60	83	105
23-30: 23-25-Young Falcon app.	10	20	30	56	76	95

31-38,40-45	9	18	27	50	65	80
39-Williamson-a; Whitman-c (1/58)	10	20	30	56	76	95
46-Last issue	10	20	30	54	72	90

TEX TAYLOR (...The Fighting Cowboy on-c #1, 2)(See Blaze Carson, Kid Colt, Tex Morgan, Wild West, Wild Western, & Wisco)
Marvel Comics (HPC): Sept, 1948 - No. 9, March, 1950

1-Tex Taylor & his horse Fury begin	29	58	87	167	264	360
2	15	30	45	88	137	185
3	14	28	42	82	121	160
4-6: All photo-c. 4-Anti-Wertham editorial. 5,6-Diablo Carson app.	16	32	48	92	147	195
7-9: 7-Photo-c;18 pg. Movie-Length Thriller "Trapped in Time's Lost Land!" with sabretoothed tigers, dinosaurs; Diablo app. 8-Photo-c; 18 pg. Movie-Length Thriller "The Mystery of Devil-Tree Plateau!" with dwarf horses, dwarf people & a lost miniature Inca type village; Diablo app. 9-Photo-c; 18 pg. Movie-Length Thriller "Guns Along the Border!" Captain Tootsie by Schreiber; Nimo the Mountain Lion app.	19	38	57	109	172	235

NOTE: Syd Shores c-1-3.

THANE OF BAGARTH (Also see Hercules, 1967 series)
Charlton Comics: No. 24, Oct, 1985 - No. 25, Dec, 1985

24,25-Low print run						5.00

THANOS
Marvel Comics: Dec, 2003 - No. 12, Sept, 2004 ($2.99)

1-12: 1-6-Starlin-s/a(p)/Milgrom-i; Galactus app. 7-12-Giffen-s/Lim-a						3.00
Vol. 4: Epiphany TPB (2004, $14.99) r/#1-6						15.00
Vol. 5: Samaritan TPB (2004, $14.99) r/#7-12						15.00

THANOS QUEST, THE (See Capt. Marvel #25, Infinity Gauntlet, Iron Man #55, Logan's Run, Marvel Feature #12, Marvel Universe: The End, Silver Surfer #34 & Warlock #9)
Marvel Comics: 1990 - No. 2, 1990 ($4.95, squarebound, 52 pgs.)

1,2-Both have Starlin scripts & covers (both printings)	1	2	3	4	5	7
1-(3/2000, $3.99) r/material from #1&2						4.00

THAT DARN CAT (See Movie Comics & Walt Disney Showcase #19)

THAT'S MY POP! GOES NUTS FOR FAIR
Bystander Press: 1939 (76 pgs., B&W)

nn-by Milt Gross	30	60	90	174	275	375

THAT WILKIN BOY (Meet Bingo...)
Archie Publications: Jan, 1969 - No. 52, Oct, 1982

1-1st app. Bingo's Band, Samantha & Tough Teddy	4	8	12	26	41	55
2-5	3	6	9	16	22	28
6-11	2	4	6	11	16	20
12-26-Giants. 12-No # on-c	3	6	9	14	19	24
27-40(1/77)	1	3	4	6	8	10
41-49						5.00
50-52 (low print)	1	2	3	5	6	8

THB
Horse Press: Oct, 1994 - Present ($5.50/$2.50/$2.95, B&W)

1 ($5.50) Paul Pope-s/a in all	1	2	3	5	6	8
1 (2nd Printing)-r/#1 w/new material						3.00
2 ($2.50)						5.00
3						5.00
69 (1995, no price, low distribution, 12 pgs.)-story reprinted in #1 (2nd Printing)						3.00
Giant THB-($4.95)						5.00
Giant THB 1 V2-(2003, $6.95)						7.00
...M3/THB: Mars' Mightiest Mek #1 (2000, $3.95)						4.00
...6A: Mek-Power #1, 6B: Mek-Power #2, 6C: Mek-Power #3 (2000, $3.95)						4.00
...6D: Mek-Power #4 (2002, $4.95)						5.00

T.H.E. CAT (TV)
Dell Publishing Co.: Mar, 1967 - No. 4, Oct, 1967 (All have photo-c)

1	4	8	12	22	34	45
2-4	3	6	9	17	25	32

THERE'S A NEW WORLD COMING
Spire Christian Comics/Fleming H. Revell Co.: 1973 (35/49¢)

nn	2	4	6	8	10	12

THEY ALL KISSED THE BRIDE (See Cinema Comics Herald)

THIEF OF BAGHDAD
Dell Publishing Co.: No. 1229, Oct-Dec, 1961 (one-shot)

Four Color 1229-Movie, Crandall/Evans-a, photo-c	7	14	21	45	73	100

Thimk #1 © Counterpoint

The Thing: Freakshow #1 © MAR

This is War #8 © STD

	GD 2.0	VG 4.0	FN 6.0	VF 8.0	VF/NM 9.0	NM- 9.2

THIMK (Magazine) (Satire)
Counterpoint: May, 1958 - No. 6, May, 1959

	GD 2.0	VG 4.0	FN 6.0	VF 8.0	VF/NM 9.0	NM- 9.2
1	10	20	30	54	72	90
2-6	7	14	21	37	46	55

THING!, THE (Blue Beetle #18 on)
Song Hits No. 1,2/Capitol Stories/Charlton: Feb, 1952 - No. 17, Nov, 1954

1-Weird/horror stories in all; shrunken head-c	88	176	264	550	913	1275
2,3	58	116	174	363	602	840
4-6,8,10: 5-Severed head-c; headlights	53	106	159	323	529	735
7-Injury to eye-c & inside panel	69	138	207	431	716	1000
9-Used in SOTI, pg. 388 & illo "Stomping on the face is a form of brutality which modern children learn early"	81	162	243	506	841	1175
11-Necronomicon story; Hansel & Gretel parody; Injury-to-eye panel; Check-a	64	128	192	400	663	925
12-1st published Ditko-c; "Cinderella" parody; lingerie panels. Ditko-a	88	176	264	550	913	1275
13,15-Ditko-c/a(3 & 5)	88	176	264	550	913	1275
14-Extreme violence/torture; Rumpelstiltskin story; Ditko-c/a(4)	90	180	270	563	932	1300
16-Injury to eye panel	31	62	93	178	282	385
17-Ditko-c/a; classic parody "Through the Looking Glass"; Powell-r/Beware Terror Tales #1 & recolored	79	158	237	494	822	1150

NOTE: Excessive violence, severed heads, injury to eye are common No. 5 on. Al Fago c-4. Forgione c-1i, 2, 6, 8, 9. All Ditko issues #14, 15. Giordano a-6.

THING, THE (See Fantastic Four, Marvel Fanfare, Marvel Feature #11,12, Marvel Two-In-One and Startling Stories:...- Night Falls on Yancy Street)
Marvel Comics Group: July, 1983 - No. 36, June, 1986

1-Life story of Ben Grimm; Byrne scripts begin						3.00
2-36: 5-Spider-Man, She-Hulk app.						2.50

NOTE: Byrne a-2i, 7; c-1, 7, 36i; scripts-1-13, 19-22. Sienkiewicz c-13i.

THING, THE (Fantastic Four)
Marvel Comics: Jan, 2006 - No. 8 ($2.99)

1-8: 1-DiVito-a/Slott-s. 4-Lockjaw app. 6-Spider-Man app. 8-Super-Hero poker game						3.00
...: Idol of Millions TPB (2006, $20.99) r/#1-8; Divito sketch page						21.00

THING & SHE-HULK: THE LONG NIGHT (Fantastic Four)
Marvel Comics: May, 2002 ($2.99, one-shot)

1-Hitch-c/a(pg. 1-25); Reis-a(pg. 26-39); Dezago-s						3.00

THING, THE (From Another World)
Dark Horse Comics: 1991 - No. 2, 1992 ($2.95, mini-series, stiff-c)

1,2-Based on Universal movie; painted-c/a						3.00

THING, THE: FREAKSHOW (Fantastic Four)
Marvel Comics: Aug, 2002 - No. 4, Nov, 2002 ($2.99, limited series)

1-4-Geoff Johns-s/Scott Kolins-a						3.00
TPB (2005, $17.99) r/#1-4 & Thing & She-Hulk: The Long Night one-shot						18.00

THING FROM ANOTHER WORLD: CLIMATE OF FEAR, THE
Dark Horse Comics: July, 1992 - No. 4, Dec, 1992 ($2.50, mini-series)

1-4: Painted-c						3.00

THING FROM ANOTHER WORLD: ETERNAL VOWS
Dark Horse Comics: Dec, 1993 - No. 4, 1994 ($2.50, mini-series)

1-4-Gulacy-c/a						3.00

THIRD WORLD WAR
Fleetway Publ. (Quality): 1990 - No. 6, 1991 ($2.50, thick-c, mature)

1-6						2.50

THIRTEEN (...Going on 18)
Dell Publishing Co.: 11-1/61-62 - No. 25, 12/67; No. 26, 7/69 - No. 29, 1/71

1	6	12	18	39	62	85
2-10	5	10	15	30	48	65
11-25	4	8	12	24	37	50
26-29-r	4	8	12	22	34	45

NOTE: John Stanley script-No. 3-29; art?

13: ASSASSIN
TSR, Inc.: 1990 - No. 8, 1991 ($2.95, 44 pgs.)

1-8: Agent 13; Alcala-a(i); Springer back-up-a						3.00

13th SON, THE
Dark Horse Comics: Nov, 2005 - No. 4, Feb, 2006 ($2.99, limited series)

1-4-Kelley Jones-s/a/c						3.00

30 DAYS OF NIGHT
Idea + Design Works: June, 2002 - No. 3, Oct, 2002 ($3.99, limited series)

1-Vampires in Alaska; Steve Niles-s/Ben Templesmith-a/Ashley Wood-c						30.00
1-2nd printing						10.00
2						12.00
3						6.00
Annual 2004 (1/04, $4.99) Niles-s/art by Templesmith and others						5.00
Annual 2005 (12/05, $7.49) Niles-s/art by Nat Jones						7.50
... Three Tales TPB (7/06, $19.99) r/Annual 2005, ...: Dead Space #1-3, and short story from Tales of Terror (IDW's...)						20.00
TPB (2003, $17.99) r/#1-3, foreward by Clive Barker; script for #1						18.00
The Complete 30 Days of Night (2004, $75.00, oversized hardcover with slipcase) r/#1-3; prequel; script pages for #1-3; original cover and promotional materials						75.00

30 DAYS OF NIGHT: BLOODSUCKER TALES
IDW Publishing: Oct, 2004 - No. 8, May, 2005 ($3.99, limited series)

1-8-Niles-s/Chamberlain-a; Fraction-s/Templesmith-a/c						4.00
HC (8/05, $49.99) r/#1-8; cover gallery						50.00
SC (8/05, $24.99) r/#1-8; cover gallery						25.00

30 DAYS OF NIGHT: DEAD SPACE
IDW Publishing: Jan, 2006 - No. 3, Mar, 2006 ($3.99, limited series)

1-3-Niles and Wickline-s/Milx-a/c						4.00

30 DAYS OF NIGHT: EBEN & STELLA
IDW Publishing: May, 2007 - Present ($3.99, limited series)

1,2-Niles and DeConnick-s/Randall-a/c						4.00

30 DAYS OF NIGHT: RETURN TO BARROW
IDW Publishing: Mar, 2004 - No. 6, Aug, 2004 ($3.99, limited series)

1-6-Steve Niles-s/Ben Templesmith-a/c						4.00
TPB (2004, $19.99) r/#1-6; cover gallery						20.00

30 DAYS OF NIGHT: SPREADING THE DISEASE
IDW Publishing: Dec, 2006 - No. 5, Apr, 2007 ($3.99, limited series)

1-5: 1-Wickline-s/Sanchez-a. 3-5-Sandoval-a						4.00

THIRTY SECONDS OVER TOKYO (See American Library)

THIS IS SUSPENSE! (Formerly Strange Suspense Stories; Strange Suspense Stories #27 on)
Charlton Comics: No. 23, Feb, 1955 - No. 26, Aug, 1955

23-Wood-a(r)/A Star Presentation #3 "Dr. Jekyll & Mr. Hyde"; last pre-code issue	24	48	72	139	220	300
24-Censored Fawcett-r; Evans-a (r/Suspense Detective #1)	14	28	42	80	115	150
25,26: 26-Marcus Swayze-a	10	20	30	56	76	95

THIS IS THE PAYOFF (See Pay-Off)

THIS IS WAR
Standard Comics: No. 5, July, 1952 - No. 9, May, 1953

5-Toth-a	14	28	42	76	108	140
6,9-Toth-a	11	22	33	60	83	105
7,8: 8-Ross Andru-c	8	16	24	44	57	70

THIS IS YOUR LIFE, DONALD DUCK (See Donald Duck..., Four Color #1109)

THIS MAGAZINE IS CRAZY (Crazy #? on)
Charlton Publ. (Humor Magazines): V3#2, July, 1957 - V4#8, Feb, 1959 (25¢, magazine, 68 pgs.)

V3#2-V4#7: V4#5-Russian Sputnik-c parody	10	20	30	54	72	90
V4#8-Davis-a (8 pgs.)	10	20	30	58	79	100

THIS MAGAZINE IS HAUNTED (Danger and Adventure #22 on)
Fawcett Publications/Charlton No. 15(2/54) on: Oct, 1951 - No. 14, 12/53; No. 15, 2/54 - V3#21, Nov, 1954

1-Evans-a; Dr. Death as host begins	64	128	192	400	663	925
2,5-Evans-a	44	88	132	268	444	620
3,4: 3-Vampire-c/story	35	70	105	204	322	440
6-9,11,12,14	26	52	78	152	239	325
10-Severed head-c	41	82	123	250	400	550
13-Severed head-c/story	40	80	120	239	380	520
15,20: 15-Dick Giordano-c. 20-Cover is swiped from panel in The Thing #16	21	42	63	124	195	265
16,19-Ditko-c. 19-Injury-to-eye panel; story-r/#1	40	80	120	243	389	535
17-Ditko-c/a(4); blood drainage story	47	94	141	287	474	660
18-Ditko-c/a(1 story); E.C. swipe/Haunt of Fear #5; injury-to-eye panel; reprints "Caretaker of the Dead" from Beware Terror Tales & recolored						

	GD 2.0	VG 4.0	FN 6.0	VF 8.0	VF/NM 9.0	NM- 9.2

	GD 2.0	VG 4.0	FN 6.0	VF 8.0	VF/NM 9.0	NM- 9.2
	41	82	123	256	416	575
21-Ditko-c, Evans-r/This Magazine Is Haunted #1	38	76	114	219	347	475

NOTE: **Baily** a-1, 3, 4, 21r#1. **Moldoff** c/a-1-13. **Powell** a-3-5, 11, 12, 17. **Shuster** a-18-20. Issues 19-21 have reprints which have been recolored from This Magazine Is Haunted #1.

THIS MAGAZINE IS HAUNTED (2nd Series) (Formerly Zaza the Mystic; Outer Space #17 on)
Charlton Comics: V2#12, July, 1957 - V2#16, May, 1958

	GD 2.0	VG 4.0	FN 6.0	VF 8.0	VF/NM 9.0	NM- 9.2
V2#12-14-Ditko-c/a in all	40	80	120	239	380	520
15-No Ditko-c/a	12	24	36	67	94	120
16-Ditko-a(4).	27	54	81	158	249	340

THIS MAGAZINE IS WILD (See Wild)

THIS WAS YOUR LIFE (Religious)
Jack T. Chick Publ.: 1964 (3 1/2 x 5 1/2", 40 pgs., B&W and red)

	GD 2.0	VG 4.0	FN 6.0	VF 8.0	VF/NM 9.0	NM- 9.2
nn, Another version (5x2 3/4", 26 pgs.)	2	4	6	10	14	18

THOR (See Avengers #1, Giant-Size..., Marvel Collectors Item Classics, Marvel Graphic Novel #33, Marvel Preview, Marvel Spectacular, Marvel Treasury Edition, Special Marvel Edition & Tales of Asgard)
THOR (Journey Into Mystery #1-125, 503-on)(The Mighty Thor #413-490)
Marvel Comics Group: No. 126, Mar, 1966 - No. 502, Sept, 1996

	GD 2.0	VG 4.0	FN 6.0	VF 8.0	VF/NM 9.0	NM- 9.2
126-Thor continues (#125-130 Thor vs. Hercules)	18	36	54	134	237	340
127-130: 127-1st app. Pluto	8	16	24	58	97	135
131-133,135-140: 132-1st app. Ego	7	14	21	47	76	105
134-Intro High Evolutionary	7	14	21	49	80	110

141-150: 146-Inhumans begin (early app.), end #151 (see Fantastic Four #45 for 1st app.)

	GD 2.0	VG 4.0	FN 6.0	VF 8.0	VF/NM 9.0	NM- 9.2
146,147-Origin The Inhumans. 148,149-Origin Black Bolt in each. 149-Origin Medusa, Crystal, Maximus, Gorgon, Karnak	6	12	18	41	66	90
151-157,159,160	5	10	15	35	55	75
158-Origin-r/#83; 158,159-Origin Dr. Blake (Thor)	8	16	24	54	90	125
161,167,170-179: 179-Last Kirby issue	4	8	12	26	41	55
162,168,169-Origin Galactus; Kirby-a	5	10	15	32	51	70
163,164-2nd & 3th brief app. Warlock (Him)	4	8	12	26	41	55
165-1st full app. Warlock (Him) (6/69, see Fantastic Four #67); last 12¢ issue; Kirby-a	8	18	43	69	95	
166-2nd full app. Warlock (Him); battles Thor	6	12	18	37	59	80
180,181-Neal Adams-a	5	10	15	30	48	65
182-192: 192-Last 15¢ issue	3	6	9	17	25	32
193-(25¢, 52 pgs.); Silver Surfer x-over	7	14	21	45	73	100
194-199	3	6	9	15	21	26
200	3	6	9	18	27	35
201-206,208-224	2	4	6	8	11	14
207-Rutland, Vermont Halloween x-over	2	4	6	10	14	18
225-Intro. Firelord	3	6	9	14	19	24
226-245: 226-Galactus app.	1	3	4	6	8	10
246-250:(Regular 25¢ editions)(4-8/76)	1	3	4	6	8	10
246-250-(30¢-c variants, limited distribution)	3	6	9	20	30	40
251-280: 271-Iron Man x-over. 274-Death of Balder the Brave						6.00
260-264-(35¢-c variants, limited distribution)(6-10/77)	3	6	9	20	30	40
281-299: 294-Origin Asgard & Odin						5.00

300-(12/80)-End of Asgard; origin of Odin & The Destroyer

		1	2	3	5	6	8

301-336,338-373,375-381,383: 316-Iron Man x-over. 332,333-Dracula app. 340-Donald Blake returns as Thor. 341-Clark Kent & Lois Lane cameo. 373-X-Factor tie-in 3.00
337-Simonson-c/a begins, ends #382; Beta Ray Bill becomes new Thor

		1	2	3	5	7	9

374-Mutant Massacre; X-Factor app. 4.00
382-($1.25)-Anniversary issue; last Simonson-a 4.00
384-Intro. new Thor 4.00
385-399,401-410,413-428: 385-Hulk x-over. 391-Spider-Man x-over; 1st Eric Masterson. 395-Intro Earth Force. 408-Eric Masterson becomes Thor. 427,428-Excalibur x-over 2.50
400,411: 400-($1.75, 68 pgs.)-Origin Loki. 411-Intro New Warriors (appears in costume in last panel); Juggernaut-c/story 4.00
412-1st full app. New Warriors (Marvel Boy, Kid Nova, Namorita, Night Thrasher, Firestar & Speedball) 6.00
429-431,434-443: 429,430-Ghost Rider x-over. 434-Capt. America x-over. 437-Thor vs. Quasar; Hercules app.;Tales of Asgard back-up stories begin. 443-Dr. Strange & Silver Surfer x-over; last $1.00-c 2.50
432,433: 432-($1.25)-Thor's 300th app. (vs. Loki); reprints origin & 1st app. from Journey into Mystery #83. 433-Intro new Thor 3.00
444-449,451-473: 448-Spider-Man-c/story. 455,456-Dr. Strange back-up. 457-Old Thor returns (3 pgs.). 459-Intro Thunderstrike. 460-Starlin scripts begin. 465-Super Skrull app. 466-Drax app. 469,470-Infinity Watch x-over. 472-Intro the Godlings 2.50
450-($2.50, 68 pgs.)-Flip-book format; r/story JIM #87 (1st Loki) plus-c plus a gallery of past-c; gatefold-c 3.00
474,476-481,483-499: 474-Begin $1.50-c; bound-in trading cards. 459-Intro Thunderstrike,

460-Starlin scripts begin. 472-Intro the Godlings. 490-The Absorbing Man app. 491-Warren Ellis scripts begins, ends #494; Deodato-c/a begins. 492-Reintro The Enchantress; Beta Ray Bill dies. 495-Wm. Messner-Loebs scripts begin; Isherwood-c/a. 2.50
475 ($2.00, 52 pgs.)-Regular edition 2.50
475 ($2.50, 52 pgs.)-Collectors edition w/foil embossed-c 3.00
482 ($2.95, 84 pgs.)-400th issue 3.00
500 ($2.50)-Double-size; wraparound-c; Deodato-c/a; Dr. Strange app. 5.00
501-Reintro Red Norvell 3.00
502-Onslaught tie-in; Red Norvell, Jane Foster & Hela app. 4.00
Special 2(9/66)-(See Journey Into Mystery for 1st annual)

		GD 2.0	VG 4.0	FN 6.0	VF 8.0	VF/NM 9.0	NM- 9.2
		8	16	24	52	86	120
Special 2 (2nd printing, 1994)		2	4	6	8	10	12
King Size Special 3(1/71)		3	6	9	19	29	38
Special 4(12/71)-r/Thor #131,132 & JIM #113		3	6	9	16	22	28

Annual 5,6: 5(11/76). 6(10/77)-Guardians of the Galaxy app.

		2	4	6	9	12	15
Annual 7,8: 7(1978). 8(1979)-Thor vs. Zeus-c/story	1	3	4	6	8	10

Annual 9-12: 9('81). 10('82). 11('83). 12('84) 6.00
Annual 13-19('85-'94, 68 pgs.):14-Atlantis Attacks. 16-3 pg. origin; Guardians of the Galaxy x-over.18-Polybagged w/card 3.00
...Alone Against the Celestials nn (6/92, $5.95)-r/Thor #387-389 6.00
...Legends Vol. 2: Walter Simonson Book 2 TPB (2003, $24.99) r/#349-355,357-359 25.00
...Legends Vol. 3: Walter Simonson Book 3 TPB (2004, $24.99) r/#360-369 25.00
...: The Eternals Saga TPB (2006, $24.99) r/#283-291 & Annual #7; profile pages 25.00
...: The Eternals Saga Vol. 2 TPB ('07, $24.99) r/#292-301; Thomas & Gruenwald essays 25.00
...Visionaries: Mike Deodato Jr. TPB (2004, $19.99) r/#491-494,498-500 20.00
...Visionaries: Walter Simonson (Vol.1) TPB (5/01, $24.95) r/#337-348 25.00
...Visionaries: Walter Simonson Vol. 4 TPB (2007, $24.99) r/#371-373 & Balder the Brave #1-4 25.00
...: Worldengine (8/96, $9.95)-r/#491-494; Deodato-c/a; story & new intermission by Warren Ellis 10.00
NOTE: **Neal Adams** a-180,181; c-179-181. **Austin** a-342i, 346i; c-312i. **Buscema** a(p)-178, 182-213, 215-226, 231-238, 241-253, 254r, 256-259, 272-278, 283-285, 370, Annual 6, 8, 11; c(p)-175, 182-196, 198-200, 202-204, 206, 211, 212, 215, 219, 221, 226, 256, 259, 261, 262, 272-278, 283, 289, 370, Annual 6. **Everett** a(i)-143, 170-175; c(i)-171, 172, 174, 176, 241. **Gil Kane** a-318p; c(p)-201, 205, 207-210, 216, 220, 222, 223, 231, 233-240, 242, 243, 318. **Kirby** a(p)-126-177, 179, 194r, 254r; a(i)-278, 283, Annual 5, Special 2-4. **Mooney** a(i)-201, 204, 214-216, 218, 322i, 324i, 325i, 327i. **Sienkiewicz** c-332, 333, 335. **Simonson** a-260-271p, 337-354, 357-367, 380, Annual 7p; c-260, 263-271, 337-355, 357-369, 371, 373-382, Annual 7. **Starlin** c-213.

THOR (Volume 2)
Marvel Comics: July, 1998 - No. 85, Dec, 2004 ($2.99/$1.99/$2.25)
1-($2.99)-Follows Heroes Return; Jurgens-s/Romita Jr. & Janson-a; wraparound-c; battles the Destroyer 5.00

		1	2	3	5	6	8
1-Variant-c		1	2	3	5	6	8

1-Rough Cut-($2.99) Features original script and pencil pages 3.00
1-Sketch cover 20.00
2-($1.99) Two covers; Avengers app. 3.00
3-11,13-23: 3-Assumes Jake Olson ID. 4-Namor-c/app. 8-Spider-Man-c/app. 14-Iron Man c/app. 17-Juggernaut-c 2.50
12-($2.99) Wraparound-c; Hercules appears 3.00
12-($10.00) Variant-c by Jusko 10.00
24,26-31,33,34: 24-$2.25-c. 26-Mignola-c/Larsen-a. 29-Andy Kubert-a. 30-Maximum Security x-over; Beta Ray Bill-c/app. 33-Intro. Thor Girl 2.50
25-($2.99) Regular edition 3.00
25-($3.99) Gold foil enhanced cover 4.00
32-$3.50, 100 pgs.) new story plus reprints w/Kirby-a; Simonson-a 3.50
35-($2.99) Thor battles The Gladiator; Andy Kubert-a 3.50
36-49,51-61: 37-Starlin-a. 38,39-BWS-c. 38-42-Immonen-a. 40-Odin killed. 41-Orbik-c. 44-'Nuff Said silent issue. 51-Spider-Man app. 57-Art by various. 58-Davis-a; x-over with Iron Man #64. 60-Brereton-c 2.50
50-($4.95) Raney-c/a; back-ups w/Nuckols-a & Armenta-s/Bennett-a 5.00
62-84: 62-Regular $2.99-c. 64-Loki-c/app. 80-Oeming-s begins; Avengers app. 3.00
85-Last issue; Thor dies; Oeming-s/DiVito-a/Epting-c 3.00
...1999 Annual ($3.50) Jurgens-s/a(p) 3.50
...2000 Annual ($3.50) Jurgens-s/Ordway-a(p); back-up stories 3.50
...2001 Annual ($3.50) Jurgens-s/Grummett-a(p); Lightle-c 3.50
...Across All Worlds (9/01, $19.95, TPB) r/#28-35 20.00
Avengers Disassembled: Thor TPB (2004, $16.99) r/#80-85; afterword by Oeming 17.00
...Resurrection ($5.99, TPB) r/#1,2 6.00
...: The Dark Gods (7/00, $15.95, TPB) r/#9-13 16.00
...Vol. 1: The Death of Odin (7/02, $12.99, TPB) r/#39-44 13.00
...Vol. 2: Lord of Asgard (9/02, $15.99, TPB) r/#45-50 16.00
...Vol. 3: Gods on Earth (2003, $21.99, TPB) r/#51-58, Avengers #63, Iron Man #64, Marvel Double-Shot #1; Beck-c 22.00
...Vol. 4: Spiral (2003, $19.99, TPB) r/#59-67; Brereton-c 20.00

Thor (2007 series) #1 © MAR

3-D Action #1 © MAR

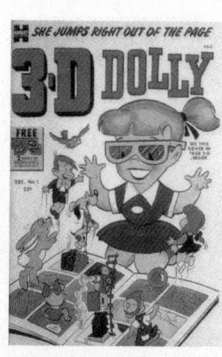

3-D Dolly #1 © HARV

	GD 2.0	VG 4.0	FN 6.0	VF 8.0	VF/NM 9.0	NM- 9.2

...Vol. 5: The Reigning (2004, $17.99, TPB) r/#68-74 — 18.00
...Vol. 6: Gods and Men (2004, $13.99, TPB) r/#75-79 — 14.00

THOR (Also see Fantastic Four #538)
Marvel Comics: Sept, 2007 - Present ($2.99)

1-Straczynski-s/Coipel-a/c — 4.00
1-Variant-c by Michael Turner — 5.00
1-Zombie variant-c by Suydam — 5.00
1-Non-zombie variant-c by Suydam — 5.00
2,3: 2-Two covers by Dell'Otto and Coipel. 3-Iron Man app. — 3.00
2-2nd printing with wraparound-c — 3.00

THOR: BLOOD OATH
Marvel Comics: Nov, 2005 - No. 6, Feb, 2006 ($2.99, limited series)

1-6-Oeming-s/Kolins-a/c — 3.00
HC (2006, $19.99, dust jacket) r/series; afterword by Oeming — 20.00
SC (2006, $14.99) r/series; afterword by Oeming — 15.00

THOR CORPS
Marvel Comics: Sept, 1993 - No. 4, Jan, 1994 ($1.75, limited series)

1-4: 1-Invaders cameo. 2-Invaders app. 3-Spider-Man 2099, Rawhide Kid, Two-Gun Kid & Kid Colt app. 4-Painted-c — 2.50

THOR: GODSTORM
Marvel Comics: Nov, 2001 - No. 3, Jan, 2002 ($3.50)

1-3-Steve Rude-c/a; Busiek; Avengers app. — 3.50

THORION OF THE NEW ASGODS
Marvel Comics (Amalgam): June, 1997 ($1.95, one-shot)

1-Keith Giffen-s/John Romita Jr.-c/a — 2.50

THOR: SON OF ASGARD
Marvel Comics: May, 2004 - No. 12, Mar, 2005 ($2.99, limited series)

1-12: Teenaged Thor, Sif, and Balder; Tocchini-a. 1-6-Granov-c. 7-12-Jo Chen-c — 3.00
...Vol. 1: The Warriors Teen (2004, $7.99, digest) r/#1-6 — 8.00
...Vol. 2: Worthy (2005, $7.99, digest) r/#7-12 — 8.00

THOR: THE LEGEND
Marvel Comics: Sept, 1996 ($3.95, one-shot)

nn-Tribute issue — 4.00

THOR: VIKINGS
Marvel Comics (MAX): Sept, 2003 - No. 5, Jan, 2004 ($3.50, limited series)

1-5-Garth Ennis-s/Glenn Fabry-a/c — 3.50
TPB (2004, $13.99) r/series — 14.00

THOSE MAGNIFICENT MEN IN THEIR FLYING MACHINES (See Movie Comics)

THRAX
Event Comics: Nov, 1996 ($2.95, one-shot)

1 — 3.00

THREE CABALLEROS (Walt Disney's...)
Dell Publishing Co.: No. 71, 1945

Four Color 71-by Walt Kelly, c/a — 62 | 124 | 186 | 310 | 868 | 1425

THREE CHIPMUNKS, THE (TV) (Also see Alvin)
Dell Publishing Co.: No. 1042, Oct-Dec, 1959

Four Color 1042 (#1)-(Alvin, Simon & Theodore) — 7 | 14 | 21 | 47 | 76 | 105

THREE COMICS (Also see Spiritman)
The Penny King Co.: 1944 (10¢, 52 pgs.) (2 different covers exist)

1,3,4-Lady Luck, Mr. Mystic, The Spirit app. (3 Spirit sections bound together); Lou Fine-a — 26 | 52 | 78 | 150 | 235 | 320

NOTE: No. 1 contains Spirit Sections 4/9/44 - 4/23/44, and No. 4 is also from 4/44.

3-D (NOTE: The prices of all the 3-D comics listed include glasses. Deduct 40-50 percent if glasses are missing, and reduce slightly if glasses are loose.)

3-D ACTION
Atlas Comics (ACI): Jan, 1954 (Oversized, 15¢)(2 pairs of glasses included)

1-Battle Brady; Sol Brodsky-c — 38 | 76 | 114 | 219 | 347 | 475

3-D ADVENTURE COMICS
Stats, Etc.: Aug, 1986 (one shot)

1-Promo material — 4.00

3-D ALIEN TERROR
Eclipse Comics: June, 1986 ($2.50)

1-Old Witch, Crypt-Keeper, Vault Keeper cameo; Morrow, John Pound-a, Yeates-c — 6.00
...in 2-D: 100 copies signed, numbered(B&W) — 1 | 3 | 4 | 8 | 10 | 12

	GD 2.0	VG 4.0	FN 6.0	VF 8.0	VF/NM 9.0	NM- 9.2

3-D ANIMAL FUN (See Animal Fun)

THREE DAYS IN EUROPE
Oni Press: Nov, 2002 - No. 5, Apr, 2003 ($2.95, B&W, limited series)

1-5-Johnston-s/Hawthorne-a — 3.00
TPB (11/03, $14.95, digest-sized) r/#1-5 — 15.00

3-D BATMAN (Also see Batman 3-D)
National Periodical Publications: 1953 (Reprinted in 1966)

1953-(25¢)-Reprints Batman #42 & 48 (Penguin-c/story); Tommy Tomorrow story; came with pair of 3-D Bat glasses — 103 | 206 | 309 | 644 | 1072 | 1500
1966-Reprints 1953 issue; new cover by Infantino/Anderson; has inside-c photos of Batman & Robin from TV show (50¢) — 22 | 44 | 66 | 165 | 295 | 425

3-D CIRCUS
Fiction House Magazines (Real Adventures Publ.): 1953 (25¢, w/glasses)

1 — 32 | 64 | 96 | 186 | 293 | 400

3-D COMICS (See Mighty Mouse, Tor and Western Fighters)

3-D DOLLY
Harvey Publications: December, 1953 (25¢, came with 2 pairs of glasses)

1-Richie Rich story redrawn from his 1st app. in Little Dot #1; shows cover in 3-D on inside — 68 | 136 | 204 | 425 | 705 | 985

3-D-ELL
Dell Publishing Co.: No. 1, 1953; No. 3, 1953 (3-D comics) (25¢, came w/glasses)

1-Rootie Kazootie (#2 does not exist) — 34 | 68 | 102 | 197 | 311 | 425
3-Flukey Luke — 32 | 64 | 96 | 186 | 293 | 400

3-D EXOTIC BEAUTIES
The 3-D Zone: Nov, 1990 ($2.95, 28 pgs.)

1-L.B. Cole-c — 1 | 2 | 3 | 5 | 6 | 8

3-D FEATURES PRESENTS JET PUP
Dimensions Publications: Oct-Dec (Winter on-c), 1953 (25¢, came w/glasses)

1-Irving Spector-a(2) — 34 | 68 | 102 | 197 | 311 | 425

3-D FUNNY MOVIES
Comic Media: 1953 (25¢, came w/glasses)

1-Bugsey Bear & Paddy Pelican — 34 | 68 | 102 | 197 | 311 | 425

THREE-DIMENSION ADVENTURES (Superman)
National Periodical Publications: 1953 (25¢, large size, came w/glasses)

nn-Origin Superman (new art) — 103 | 206 | 309 | 644 | 1072 | 1500

THREE DIMENSIONAL ALIEN WORLDS (See Alien Worlds)
Pacific Comics: July, 1984 (1st Ray Zone 3-D book)(one-shot)

1-Bolton-a(p); Stevens-a(i); Art Adams 1st published-a(p) — 6.00

THREE DIMENSIONAL DNAGENTS (See New DNAgents)

THREE DIMENSIONAL E. C. CLASSICS (Three Dimensional Tales From the Crypt No. 2)
E. C. Comics: Spring, 1954 (Prices include glasses; came with 2 pair)

1-Stories by Wood (Mad #3), Krigstein (W.S. #7), Evans (F.C. #13), & Ingels (CSS #5); Kurtzman-c (rare in high grade due to unstable paper) — 93 | 186 | 279 | 581 | 966 | 1350

NOTE: Stories redrawn to 3-D format. Original stories not necessarily by artists listed. CSS: Crime SuspenStories; F.C.: Frontline Combat; W.S.: Weird Science.

THREE DIMENSIONAL TALES FROM THE CRYPT (Formerly Three Dimensional E. C. Classics)(Cover title: ...From the Crypt of Terror)
E. C. Comics: No. 2, Spring, 1954 (Prices include glasses; came with 2 pair)

2-Davis (TFTC #25), Elder (VOH #14), Craig (TFTC #24), & Orlando (TFTC #22) stories; Feldstein-c (rare in high grade) — 91 | 182 | 273 | 569 | 947 | 1325

NOTE: Stories redrawn to 3-D format. Original stories not necessarily by artists listed. TFTC: Tales From the Crypt; VOH: Vault of Horror.

3-D LOVE
Steriographic Publ. (Mikeross Publ.): Dec, 1953 (25¢, came w/glasses)

1 — 34 | 68 | 102 | 197 | 311 | 425

3-D NOODNICK (See Noodnick)

3-D ROMANCE
Steriographic Publ. (Mikeross Publ.): Jan, 1954 (25¢, came w/glasses)

1 — 34 | 68 | 102 | 197 | 311 | 425

3-D SHEENA, JUNGLE QUEEN (Also see Sheena 3-D)
Fiction House Magazines: 1953 (25¢, came w/glasses)

1-Maurice Whitman-c — 68 | 136 | 204 | 425 | 705 | 985

3-D SUBSTANCE

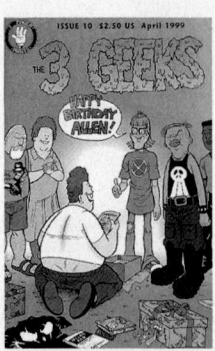
3 Geeks #10 © 3 Finger Prints

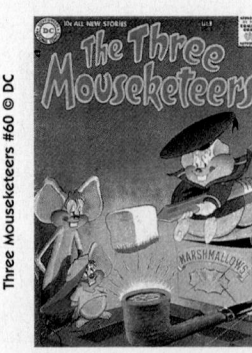
Three Mouseketeers #60 © DC

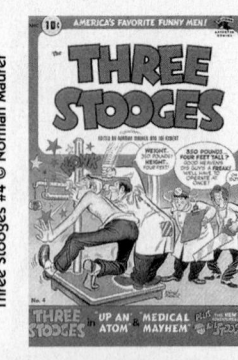
Three Stooges #4 © Norman Maurer

	GD 2.0	VG 4.0	FN 6.0	VF 8.0	VF/NM 9.0	NM- 9.2

The 3-D Zone: July, 1990 ($2.95, 28 pgs.)
1-Ditko-c/a(r)						4.00

3-D TALES OF THE WEST
Atlas Comics (CPS): Jan, 1954 (Oversized) (15¢, came with 2 pair of glasses)
| 1 (3-D)-Sol Brodsky-c | 36 | 72 | 108 | 208 | 329 | 450 |

3-D THREE STOOGES (Also see Three Stooges)
Eclipse Comics: Sept, 1986 - No. 2, Nov, 1986; No. 3, Oct, 1987; No. 4, 1989 ($2.50)
| 1-4: 3-Maurer-r. 4-r-/"Three Missing Links" | | | | | | 5.00 |
| 1-3 (2-D) | | | | | | 5.00 |

3-D WHACK (See Whack)

3-D ZONE, THE
The 3-D Zone (Renegade Press)/Ray Zone: Feb, 1987 - No. 20, 1989 ($2.50)
1,3,4,7-9,11,12,14,15,17,19,20: 1-r/A Star Presentation. 3-Picture Scope Jungle Advs. 4-Electric Fear. 7-Hollywood 3-D Jayne Mansfield photo-c. 8-High Seas 3-D, 9-Redmask-r. 11-Danse Macabre; Matt Fox c/a(r). 12-3-D Presidents. 14-Tyranostar, 15-3-Dementia Comics; Kurtzman-c, Kubert, Maurer-a. 17-Thrilling Love. 19-Cracked Classics.
20-Commander Battle and His Atomic Submarine
2,5,6,10,13,16,18: 2-Wolverton-a. 5-Krazy Kat-r. 6-Ratfink. 10-Jet 3-D; Powell & Williamson-r. 13-Flash Gordon. 16-Space Vixens; Dave Stevens-c/a. 18-Spacehawk; Wolverton-r 6.00
NOTE: *Davis* r-19. *Ditko* r-19. *Elder* r-19. *Everett* r-19. *Feldstein* r-17. *Frazetta* r-19. *Heath* r-19. *Kamen* r-17. *Severin* r-19. *Ward* r-17,19. *Wolverton* r-2,18,19. *Wood* r-1,17. Photo c-12

3 GEEKS, THE (Also see Geeksville)
3 Finger Prints: 1996 - No. 11, Jun, 1999 (B&W)
1,2 -Rich Koslowski-s/a in all	1	2	3		5	6
1-(2nd printing)						2.50
3-7, 9-11						2.50
8-(48 pgs.)						4.00
10-Variant-c						3.50
...48 Page Super-Sized Summer Spectacular (7/04, $4.95)						5.00
...Full Circle (7/03, $4.95) Origin story of the 3 Geeks; "Buck Rodinski" app.						5.00
How to Pick Up Girls If You're a Comic Book Geek (color)(7/97)						4.00
When the Hammer Falls TPB (2001, $14.95) r/#8-11						15.00

300 (Adapted for 2007 movie)
Dark Horse Comics: May, 1998 - No. 5, Sept, 1998 ($2.95/$3.95, limited series)
1-Frank Miller-s/c/a; Spartans vs. Persians war						15.00
1-Second printing						5.00
2-4						8.00
5-($3.95-c)						12.00
HC ($30.00) -oversized reprint of series						30.00

3 LITTLE KITTENS
BroadSword Comics: Aug, 2002 - No. 3, Dec, 2002 ($2.95, limited series)
| 1-3-Jim Balent-s/a; two covers | | | | | | 3.00 |

3 LITTLE PIGS (Disney)(...and the Wonderful Magic Lamp)
Dell Publishing Co.: No. 218, Mar, 1949
| Four Color 218 (#1) | 10 | 20 | 30 | 71 | 126 | 180 |

3 LITTLE PIGS, THE (See Walt Disney Showcase #15 & 21)
Gold Key: May, 1964; No. 2, Sept, 1968 (Walt Disney)
| 1-Reprints Four Color #218 | 3 | 6 | 9 | 20 | 30 | 40 |
| 2 | 3 | 6 | 9 | 15 | 21 | 26 |

THREE MOUSEKETEERS, THE (1st Series)(See Funny Stuff #1)
National Per. Publ.: 3-4/56 - No. 24, 9-10/59; No. 25, 8-9/60 - No. 26, 10-12/60
1	16	32	48	118	209	300
2	9	18	27	63	107	150
3-5,7,9,10	7	14	21	49	80	110
6,8-Grey tone-c	8	16	24	52	86	120
11-26: 24-Cover says 11/59, inside says 9-10/59	6	12	18	43	69	95
NOTE: *Rube Grossman* a-1-26. *Sheldon Mayer* a-1-8; c-1-7.

THREE MOUSEKETEERS, THE (2nd Series) (See Super DC Giant)
National Periodical Publications: May-June, 1970 - No. 7, May-June, 1971 (#5-7: 68 pgs.)
1-Mayer-r in all	5	10	15	35	55	75
2-4: 4-Doodles Duck begins (1st app.)	4	8	12	22	34	45
5-7:(68 pgs.). 5-Dodo & the Frog, Bo Bunny begin	5	10	15	32	51	70

THREE MUSKETEERS, THE (Also see Disney's The Three Musketeers)
Gemstone Publishing: 2004 ($3.95, squarebound, one-shot)
| nn-Adaptation of the 2004 DVD movie; Petrossi-c/a | | | | | | 4.00 |

THREE NURSES (Confidential Diary #12-17; Career Girl Romances #24 on)

Charlton Comics: V3#18, May, 1963 - V3#23, Mar, 1964
| V3#18-23 | 3 | 6 | 9 | 17 | 25 | 32 |

THREE RASCALS
I. W. Enterprises: 1958; 1963
I.W. Reprint #1,2,10: 1-(Says Super Comics on inside)-(M.E.'s Clubhouse Rascals) DeCarlo-a.
| #2-(1958). 10-(1963)-r/#1 | 2 | 4 | 6 | 8 | 10 | 12 |

THREE RING COMICS
Spotlight Publishers: March, 1945
| 1-Funny animal | 16 | 32 | 48 | 92 | 144 | 195 |

THREE RING COMICS (Also see Captain Wizard & Meteor Comics)
Century Publications: April, 1946
1-Prankster-c; Captain Wizard, Impossible Man, Race Wilkins, King O'Leary, & Dr. Mercy app.
| | 35 | 70 | 135 | 201 | 318 | 435 |

THREE ROCKETEERS (See Blast-Off)

THREE STOOGES (See Comic Album #18, Top Comics, The Little Stooges, March of Comics #232, 248, 268, 280, 292, 304, 316, 336, 373, Movie Classics & Comics & 3-D Three Stooges)

THREE STOOGES
Jubilee No. 1/St. John No. 1 (9/53) on: Feb, 1949 - No. 2, May, 1949; Sept, 1953 - No. 7, Oct, 1954
1-(Scarce, 1949)-Kubert-a; infinity-c	114	228	342	713	1182	1650
2-(Scarce)-Kubert, Maurer-a	79	158	237	494	822	1150
1(9/53)-Hollywood Stunt Girl by Kubert (7 pgs.)	68	136	204	425	705	985
2(3-D, 10/53, 25¢)-Came w/glasses; Stunt Girl story by Kubert						
	48	96	144	293	484	675
3(3-D, 10/53, 25¢)-Came w/glasses; has 3-D c	90	135	275	455	635	
4(3/54)-7(10/54): 4- 1st app. Li'l Stooge?	42	84	126	248	384	520
NOTE: *All issues have Kubert-Maurer art & Maurer covers. 6, 7-Partial photo-c.*

THREE STOOGES
Dell Publishing Co./Gold Key No. 10 (10/62) on: No. 1043, Oct-Dec, 1959 - No. 55, June, 1972
Four Color 1043 (#1)	25	50	75	184	330	475
Four Color 1078,1127,1170,1187	13	26	39	95	168	240
6(9-11/61) - 10: 6-Professor Putter begins; ends #16						
	10	20	30	73	129	185
11-14,16,18-20	9	18	27	63	107	150
15-Go Around the World in a Daze (movie scenes)	9	18	27	65	113	160
17-The Little Monsters begin (5/64)(1st app.?)	9	18	27	65	113	160
21,23-30	8	16	24	54	90	125
22-Movie scenes from "The Outlaws Is Coming"	8	16	24	58	97	135
31-55	6	12	18	41	66	90
NOTE: *All Four Colors, 6-50, 52-55 have photo-c.*

THREE STOOGES IN 3-D, THE
Eternity Comics: 1991 ($3.95, high quality paper, w/glasses)
| 1-Reprints Three Stooges by Gold Key; photo-c | | | | | | 5.00 |

THREE STRIKES
Oni Press: Apr, 2003 - No. 5, Oct, 2003 ($2.99, B&W, limited series)
| 1-5-Brian Hurtt-a/DeFilippis & Weir-s | | | | | | 3.00 |
| TPB (3/04, $14.95, digest-size) r/#1-5; Ed Brubaker intro. | | | | | | 15.00 |

3 WORLDS OF GULLIVER
Dell Publishing Co.: No. 1158, July, 1961 (2 issues exist with diff. covers)
| Four Color 1158-Movie, photo-c | 7 | 14 | 21 | 45 | 73 | 100 |

THRILL COMICS (See Flash Comics, Fawcett)

THRILLER
DC Comics: Nov, 1983 - No. 12, Nov, 1984 ($1.25, Baxter paper)
| 1-12: 1-Intro Seven Seconds; Von Eeden-a begins. 2-Origin. 5,6-Elvis satire | | | | | | 2.50 |

THRILLING ADVENTURES IN STAMPS COMICS (Formerly Stamp Comics)
Stamp Comics, Inc. (Very Rare): V1#8, Jan, 1953 (25¢, 100 pgs.)
| V1#8-Harrison, Wildey, Kiefer, Napoli-a | 74 | 148 | 222 | 463 | 769 | 1075 |

THRILLING ADVENTURE STORIES (See Tigerman)
Atlas/Seaboard Publ.: Feb, 1975 - No. 2, Aug, 1975 (B&W, 68 pgs.)
| 1-Tigerman, Kromag the Killer begin; Heath, Thorne-a; Doc Savage movie photos of Ron Ely | 3 | 6 | 9 | 14 | 20 | 25 |
| 2-Heath, Toth, Severin, Simonson-a; Adams-c | 3 | 6 | 9 | 18 | 27 | 35 |

THRILLING COMICS
Better Publ./Nedor/Standard Comics: Feb, 1940 - No. 80, April, 1951

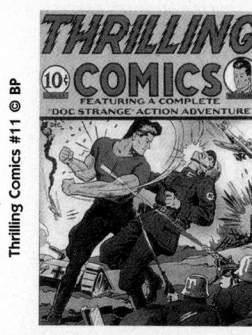

Thrilling Comics #11 © BP

Thrilling Romances #10 © STD

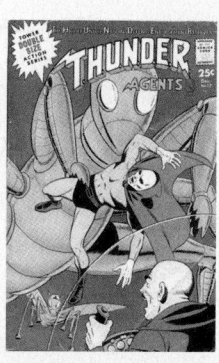

Thunder Agents #17 © TC

	GD 2.0	VG 4.0	FN 6.0	VF 8.0	VF/NM 9.0	NM- 9.2
1-Origin & 1st app. Dr. Strange (37 pgs.), ends #?; Nickie Norton of the Secret Service begins	317	634	951	1981	3291	4600
2-The Rio Kid, The Woman in Red, Pinocchio begins	131	262	393	819	1360	1900
3-The Ghost & Lone Eagle begin	85	170	255	531	878	1225
4-6,8-10 (11/40): 5-Dr. Strange changed to Doc Strange. 10-1st WWII-c (Nazi)	66	132	198	413	682	950
7-Classic-c	86	172	258	538	894	1250
11-18,20	57	114	171	356	591	825
19-Origin & 1st app. The American Crusader (8/41), ends #39,41	664	128	192	400	663	925
21-30: 24-Intro. Mike, Doc Strange's sidekick (1/42). 27-Robot-c. 29-Last Rio Kid	52	104	156	317	521	725
31-40: 36-Commando Cubs begin (7/43, 1st app.)	46	92	138	281	466	650
41-Classic Hitler & Mussolini WWII-c	110	220	330	665	1145	1600
42,43,45-51: 45-Hitler pict. on-c. 51(12/45)-Last WWII-c (Japanese)	40	80	120	240	383	525
44-Hitler WWII-c	100	200	300	625	1038	1450
52-Classic Schomburg hooded bondage-c; the Ghost ends	60	120	180	375	625	875
53,54: 53-The Phantom Detective begins. The Cavalier app. in both; no Commando Cubs in either	40	80	120	235	368	500
55-The Lone Eagle ends	37	74	111	213	337	460
56 (10/46)-Princess Pantha begins (not on-c), 1st app.	48	96	144	293	484	675
57-Doc Strange-c; 2nd Princess Pantha	41	82	123	256	416	575
58-66: All Princess Pantha jungle-c, w/Doc Strange #59, his last-c. 61-Ingels-a; The Lone Eagle app. 65-Last Phantom Detective & Commando Cubs. 66-Frazetta text illo	40	80	120	240	383	525
67,70,71-Last jungle-c; Frazetta-a(5-7 pgs.) in each	46	92	138	281	466	650
68,69-Frazetta-a(2), 8 & 6 pgs.; 9 & 7 pgs.	50	100	150	305	503	700
72,73: 72-Buck Ranger, Cowboy Detective c/stys begin (western theme), and #80; Frazetta-a(5-7 pgs.) in each	43	86	129	262	431	600
74-Last Princess Pantha; Tara app.	34	68	102	195	308	420
75-78: 75-All western format begins	14	28	42	81	118	155
79-Krigstein-a	15	30	45	83	124	165
80-Severin & Elder, Celardo, Moreira-a	15	30	45	83	124	165

NOTE: Bondage c-5, 9, 13, 20, 22, 27-30, 38, 41, 52, 54, 70. Kinstler a-45. Leo Morey a-7. Schomburg sometimes signed as Xela) c-7, 9-19, 36-80 (airbrush 62-71). Tuska a-62, 63. Woman in Red not in #19, 23, 31-33, 39-45. No. 45 exists as a Canadian reprint but numbered #48. No. 72 exists as a Canadian reprint with no Frazetta story. American Crusader c-20-24. Buck Ranger c-72-80. Commando Cubs c-37, 39, 41, 43, 45, 47, 49, 51. Doc Strange c-1-19, 25-36, 38, 40, 42, 44, 46, 48, 50, 52-57, 59. Princess Pantha c-58, 60-71.

THRILLING COMICS (Also see All Star Comics 1999 crossover titles)
DC Comics: May, 1999 ($1.99, one-shot)

1-Golden Age Hawkman and Wildcat; Russ Heath-a						2.50

THRILLING CRIME CASES (Formerly 4Most; becomes Shocking Mystery Cases #50 on)
Star Publications: No. 41, June-July, 1950 - No. 49, July, 1952

	GD 2.0	VG 4.0	FN 6.0	VF 8.0	VF/NM 9.0	NM- 9.2
41	28	56	84	162	256	350
42-45: 42-L.B. Cole-c/a (1); Chameleon story (Fox-r)	25	50	75	145	228	310
46-48: 47-Used in POP, pg. 84	24	48	72	139	220	300
49-(7/52)-Classic L. B. Cole-c	45	90	135	275	450	625

NOTE: L. B. Cole c-all; a-43p, 45p, 46p, 49(2 pgs.). Disbrow a-48. Hollingsworth a-48.

THRILLING ROMANCES
Standard Comics: No. 5, Dec, 1949 - No. 26, June, 1954

	GD 2.0	VG 4.0	FN 6.0	VF 8.0	VF/NM 9.0	NM- 9.2
5	14	28	42	80	115	150
6,8	9	18	27	52	69	85
7-Severin/Elder-a (7 pgs.)	11	22	33	62	86	110
9,10-Severin/Elder-a; photo-c	10	20	30	56	76	95
11,14-21,26: 12-Tyrone Power/ Susan Hayward photo-c.14-Gene Tierney & Danny Kaye photo-c from movie "On the Riviera". 15-Tony Martin/Janet Leigh photo-c	9	18	27	47	61	75
12-Wood-a (2 pgs.)	11	22	33	64	90	115
13-Severin-a	9	18	27	52	69	85
22-25-Toth-a	10	20	30	58	79	100

NOTE: All photo-c. Celardo a-9, 16. Colletta a-23, 24(2). Toth text illos-19. Tuska a-9.

THRILLING SCIENCE TALES
AC Comics: 1989 - No. 2 ($3.50, 2/3 color, 52 pgs.)

1,2: 1-r/Bob Colt #6(saucer); Frazetta, Guardineer (Space Ace), Wood, Krenkel, Orlando, Williamson-r; Kaluta-c. 2-Capt. Video-r by Evans, Capt. Science-r by Wood, Star Pirate-r by Whitman & Mysta of the Moon-r by Moreira						4.00

THRILLING TRUE STORY OF THE BASEBALL...

Fawcett Publications: 1952 (Photo-c, each)

	GD 2.0	VG 4.0	FN 6.0	VF 8.0	VF/NM 9.0	NM- 9.2
...Giants-photo-c; has Willie Mays rookie photo-biography; Willie Mays, Eddie Stanky & others photos on-c	68	136	204	425	705	985
...Yankees-photo-c; Yogi Berra, Joe DiMaggio, Mickey Mantle & others photos on-c	66	132	198	413	682	950

THRILLING WONDER TALES
AC Comics : 1991 ($2.95, B&W)

1-Includes a Bob Powell Thun'da story						3.00

THRILLKILLER
DC Comics : Jan, 1997 - No. 3, Mar, 1997($2.50, limited series)

1-3-Elseworlds Robin & Batgirl; Chaykin-s/Brereton-c/a						3.00
...'62 ('98, $4.95, one-shot) Sequel; Chaykin-s/Brereton-c/a						5.00

TPB-(See Batman: Thrillkiller)

THRILLOGY
Pacific Comics: Jan, 1984 (One-shot, color)

1-Conrad-c/a						3.00

THRILL-O-RAMA
Harvey Publications (Fun Films): Oct, 1965 - No. 3, Dec, 1966

	GD 2.0	VG 4.0	FN 6.0	VF 8.0	VF/NM 9.0	NM- 9.2
1-Fate (Man in Black) by Powell app.; Doug Wildey-a(2); Simon-c	5	10	15	35	55	75
2-Pirana begins (see Phantom #46); Williamson 2 pgs.; Fate (Man in Black) app.; Tuska/Simon-c	4	8	12	22	34	45
3-Fate (Man in Black) app.; Sparling-c	3	6	9	19	29	38

THRILLS OF TOMORROW (Formerly Tomb of Terror)
Harvey Publications: No. 17, Oct, 1954 - No. 20, April, 1955

	GD 2.0	VG 4.0	FN 6.0	VF 8.0	VF/NM 9.0	NM- 9.2
17-Powell-a (horror); r/Witches Tales #7	15	30	45	83	124	165
18-Powell-a (horror); r/Tomb of Terror #11	14	28	42	76	108	140
19,20-Stuntman-c/stories by S&K (r/from Stuntman #1 & 2); 19 has origin & is last pre-code (2/55)	31	62	93	178	282	385

NOTE: Kirby c-19, 20. Palais a-17. Simon c-18?

THROBBING LOVE (See Fox Giants)

THROUGH GATES OF SPLENDOR
Spire Christian Comics (Flemming H. Revell Co.): 1973, 1974 (36 pages) (39-49 cents)

	GD 2.0	VG 4.0	FN 6.0	VF 8.0	VF/NM 9.0	NM- 9.2
nn-1973 Edition	2	4	6	8	11	14
nn-1974 Edition	1	3	4	6	8	10

THUMPER (Disney)
Dell Publishing Co.: No. 19, 1942 - No. 243, Sept, 1949

	GD 2.0	VG 4.0	FN 6.0	VF 8.0	VF/NM 9.0	NM- 9.2
Four Color 19-Walt Disney's...Meets the Seven Dwarfs; reprinted in Silly Symphonies	46	92	138	368	672	975
Four Color 243-...Follows His Nose	11	22	33	79	140	200

THUN'DA (...King of the Congo)
Magazine Enterprises: 1952 - No. 6, 1953

	GD 2.0	VG 4.0	FN 6.0	VF 8.0	VF/NM 9.0	NM- 9.2
1(A-1 #47)-Origin; Frazetta c/a; only comic done entirely by Frazetta; all Thun'da stories, no Cave Girl	148	296	444	925	1538	2150
2(A-1 #56)-Powell-c/a begins, ends #6; Intro/1st app. Cave Girl in filler strip (also app. in 3-6)	23	46	69	132	209	285
3(A-1 #73), 4(A-1 #78)	16	32	48	94	147	200
5(A-1 #83), 6(A-1 #86)	15	30	45	90	140	190

THUN'DA TALES (See Frank Frazetta's...)

THUNDER AGENTS (See Dynamo, Noman & Tales Of Thunder)
Tower Comics: 11/65 - No. 17, 12/67; No. 18, 9/68, No. 19, 11/68, No. 20, 11/69 (No. 1-16: 68 pgs.; No. 17 on: 52 pgs.)(All are 25¢)

	GD 2.0	VG 4.0	FN 6.0	VF 8.0	VF/NM 9.0	NM- 9.2
1-Origin & 1st app. Dynamo, Noman, Menthor, & The Thunder Squad; 1st app. The Iron Maiden	18	36	54	132	234	335
2-Death of Egghead; A-bomb blast panel	10	20	30	68	119	170
3-5: 4-Guy Gilbert becomes Lightning who joins Thunder Squad; Iron Maiden app.	8	16	24	52	86	120
6-10: 7-Death of Menthor. 8-Origin & 1st app. The Raven	6	12	18	43	69	95
11-15: 13-Undersea Agent app.; no Raven story	6	12	18	39	62	85
16-19	6	12	18	37	59	80
20-Special Collectors Edition; all reprints	4	8	12	26	41	55
...Archives Vol. 1 (DC Comics, 2003, $49.95, HC) r/#1-4, restored and recolored						50.00
...Archives Vol. 2 (DC Comics, 2003, $49.95, HC) r/#5-7, Dynamo #1						50.00
...Archives Vol. 3 (DC Comics, 2003, $49.95, HC) r/#8-10, Dynamo #2						50.00
...Archives Vol. 4 (DC Comics, 2003, $49.95, HC) r/#11, Noman #1,2 & Dynamo #3						50.00

NOTE: Crandall a-1, 4p, 5p, 18, 20r; c-18. Ditko a-6, 7p, 12p, 13?, 14p, 16, 18. Giunta a-9. Kane a-1, 5p, 6p?, 14, 16p; c-14, 15. Reinman a-13. Sekowsky a-6. Tuska a-1p, 7, 8, 10, 13-17, 19. Whitney a-9p, 10, 13, 15, 17,

Thunderbolts #11 © MAR

Thundercats #3 © WB & Ted Wolf

The Tick #8 © Ben Edlund

	GD 2.0	VG 4.0	FN 6.0	VF 8.0	VF/NM 9.0	NM- 9.2

	GD 2.0	VG 4.0	FN 6.0	VF 8.0	VF/NM 9.0	NM- 9.2

18; c-17. **Wood** a-1-11, 15(w/Ditko-12, 18), (inks-#9, 13, 14, 16, 17), 19i, 20r; c-1-8, 9i, 10-13(#10 w/Williamson(p)), 16.

T.H.U.N.D.E.R. AGENTS (See Blue Ribbon Comics, Hall of Fame Featuring the…, JCP Features & Wally Wood's…)
JC Comics (Archie Publications): May, 1983 - No. 2, Jan, 1984

1,2: 1-New Manna/Blyberg-c/a. 2-Blyberg-c   6.00

THUNDER BIRDS (See Cinema Comics Herald)

THUNDERBOLT (See The Atomic…)

THUNDERBOLT (Peter Cannon…; see Crisis on Infinite Earths & Peter…)
Charlton Comics: Jan, 1966; No. 51, Mar-Apr, 1966 - No. 60, Nov, 1967

1-Origin & 1st app. Thunderbolt	4	8	12	28	44	60
51-(Formerly Son of Vulcan #50)	3	6	9	20	30	40
52-59: 54-Sentinels begin. 59-Last Thunderbolt & Sentinels (back-up story)						
	3	6	9	14	19	24
60-Prankster app.	3	6	9	15	21	26
57,58 ('77)-Modern Comics-r						4.00

NOTE: Aparo a-60. **Morisi** a-1, 51-56, 58; c-1, 51-56, 58, 59.

THUNDERBOLT JAXON (Revival of 1940s British comics character)
DC Comics (WildStorm): Apr, 2006 - No. 5, Sept, 2006 ($2.99, limited series)

1-5-Dave Gibbons-s/John Higgins-a   3.00
TPB (2007, $19.99) r/#1-5; intro. by Gibbons; cover gallery   20.00

THUNDERBOLTS (Also see New Thunderbolts and Incredible Hulk #449)
Marvel Comics: Apr, 1997 - No. 81, Sept, 2003; No. 100, May, 2006 - Present ($1.95-$2.99)

1-($2.99)-Busiek-s/Bagley-c/a	1	2	3	5	7	9
1-2nd printing; new cover colors						2.50
2-4: 2-Two covers. 4-Intro. Jolt						6.00
5-11: 9-Avengers app.						3.50
12-($2.99)-Avengers and Fantastic Four-c/app.						4.00
13-24: 14-Thunderbolts return to Earth. 21-Hawkeye app.						3.00
25-($2.99) Wraparound-c						2.50
26-38: 26-Manco-a						2.50
39-($2.99) 100 Page Monster; Iron Man reprints						3.00
40-49: 40-Begin $2.25-c; Sandman-c/app. 44-Avengers app. 47-Captain Marvel app.						
49-Zircher-a						2.50
50-($2.99) Last Bagley-a; Captain America becomes leader						3.00
51-74,76,77,80,81: 51,52-Zircher-a. 80-Dr. Doom app. 80,81-Spider-Man app.						2.50
75-($3.50) Hawkeye leaves the team; Garcia-a						3.50
78,79-($2.99-c) Velasco-a begins						3.00
(See New Thunderbolts for #82-99)						
100 (5/06, $3.99) resumes from New Thunderbolts #18; back-up origin stories						4.00
101-109: 103-105-Civil War x-over						3.00
110-New team begins including Bullseye, Venom and Norman Osborn; Ellis-s/Deodato-a						5.00
111-116-Ellis-s/Deodato-a. 112-Stan Lee cameo						3.00
Annual '97 ($2.99)-Wraparound-c						3.00
Annual 2000 ($3.50) Breyfogle-a						3.50
… By Warren Ellis Vol. 1 HC (2007, $24.99, dustjacket) r/#150-154, …: Desperate Measures						
and stories from Civil War: Choosing Sides and The Initiative						25.00
Civil War: Thunderbolts TPB (2007, $13.99) r/#101-105						14.00
…: Desperate Measures (9/07, $2.99, one-shot) Jenkins-s/Steve Lieber-a						3.00
…: Distant Rumblings (#-1) (7/97, $1.95) Busiek-s						5.00
First Strikes (1997, $4.99,TPB) r/#1,2						5.00
…: Guardian Protocols (2007, $10.99) r/#106-109						11.00
…: Life Sentences (7/01, $3.50) Adlard-a						3.50
…: Marvel's Most Wanted TPB ('98, $16.99) r/origin stories of original Masters of Evil						17.00
Wizard #0 (bagged with Wizard #89)						2.50

THUNDERBOLTS PRESENTS: ZEMO - BORN BETTER
Marvel Comics: Apr, 2007 - No. 4, July, 2007 ($2.99, limited series)

1-4-History of Baron Zemo; Nicieza-s/Grummett-a/c   3.00
TPB (2007, $10.99) r/#1-4   11.00

THUNDERBUNNY (See Blue Ribbon Comics #13, Charlton Bullseye & Pep Comics #393)
Red Circle Comics: Jan, 1984 (Direct sale only)
WaRP Graphics: Second series No. 1, 1985 - No. 6, 1985
Apple Comics: No. 7, 1986 - No. 12, 1987

1-Humor/parody; origin Thunderbunny; 2 page pin-up by Anderson   5.00
(2nd series) 1,2-Magazine size   3.00
3-12-Comic size   2.50

THUNDERCATS (TV)
Marvel Comics (Star Comics)/Marvel #22 on: Dec, 1985 - No. 24, June, 1988 (75¢)

1-Mooney-c/a begins	2	4	6	8	11	14

2-20: 2-(65¢ & 75¢ cover exists). 12-Begin $1.00-c. 18-20-Williamson-i						
	1	2	3	5	7	9
21-24: 23-Williamson-c(i)	1	3	4	6	8	10

THUNDERCATS (TV)
DC Comics (WildStorm): No. 0, Oct, 2002 - No. 5, Feb, 2003 ($2.50/$2.95, limited series)

0-($2.50) J. Scott Campbell-c/a   3.00
1-5-($2.95) 1-McGuinness-a/c; variant cover by Art Adams; rebirth of Mumm-Ra   3.00
…/ Battle of the Planets (7/03, $4.95) Kaare Andrews-s/a; 2 covers by Campbell & Ross   5.00
…: Origins-Heroes & Villains (2/04, $3.50) short stories by various   3.50
…Reclaiming Thundera TPB (2003, $12.95) r/#0-5   13.00
… Sourcebook (1/03, $2.95) pin-ups and info on characters; art by various; A. Adams-c   3.00

THUNDERCATS: DOGS OF WAR
DC Comics (WildStorm): Aug, 2003 - No. 5, Dec, 2003 ($2.95, limited series)

1-5: 1-Two covers by Booth & Pearson; Booth-a/Layman-s. 2-4-Two covers   3.00
TPB (2004, $14.95) r/#1-5   15.00

THUNDERCATS: ENEMY'S PRIDE
DC Comics (WildStorm): Aug, 2004 - No. 5 ($2.95, limited series)

1-5-Vriens-a/Layman-s   3.00
TPB (2005, $14.99) r/#1-5   15.00

THUNDERCATS: HAMMERHAND'S REVENGE
DC Comics (WildStorm): Dec, 2003 - No. 5, Apr, 2004 ($2.95, limited series)

1-5-Avery-s/D'Anda-a. 2-Variant-c by Warren   3.00
TPB (2004, $14.95) r/#1-5   15.00

THUNDERCATS: THE RETURN
DC Comics (WildStorm): Apr, 2003 - No. 5, Aug, 2003 ($2.95, limited series)

1-5: 1-Two covers by Benes & Cassaday; Gilmore-s   3.00
TPB (2004, $12.95) r/series   13.00

THUNDER MOUNTAIN (See Zane Grey, Four Color #246)

THUNDERSTRIKE (See Thor #459)
Marvel Comics: June, 1993 - No. 24, July, 1995 ($1.25)

1-($2.95, 52 pgs.)-Holo-grafx lightning patterned foil-c; Bloodaxe returns   3.00
2-24: 2-Juggernaut-c/s. 4-Capt. America app. 4-6-Spider-Man app. 8-bound-in trading card
     sheet. 18-Bloodaxe app. 24-Death of Thunderstrike   2.50
Marvel Double Feature…Thunderstrike/Code Blue #13 ($2.50)-Same as
     Thunderstrike #13 w/Code Blue flip book   2.50

TICK, THE (Also see The Chroma-Tick)
New England Comics Press: Jun, 1988 - No. 12, May, 1993
($1.75/$1.95/$2.25; B&W, over-sized)

Special Edition 1-1st comic book app. serially numbered & limited to 5,000 copies						
	5	10	15	35	55	75
Special Edition 1-(5/96, $5.95)-Double-c; foil-c; serially numbered (5,001 thru 14,000)						
& limited to 9,000 copies						6.00
Special Edition 2-Serially numbered and limited to 3000 copies						
	5	10	15	30	48	65
Special Edition 2-(8/96, $5.95)-Double-c; foil-c; serially numbered (5,001 thru 14,000)						
& limited to 9,000 copies	1	2	3	5	6	8
1-Regular Edition 1st printing; reprints Special Ed. 1 w/minor changes						
	4	8	12	24	37	50
1-2nd printing						6.00
1-3rd-5th printing						3.00
2-Reprints Special Ed. 2 w/minor changes	2	4	6	13	18	22
2-8-All reprints						3.00
3-5 ($1.95): 4-1st app. Paul the Samurai	1	3	4	6	8	10
6,8 ($2.25)						5.00
7-1st app. Man-Eating Cow.						6.00
8-Variant with no logo, price, issue number or company logos.						
	2	4	6	10	14	18
9-12 ($2.75)						4.00
12-Special Edition; card-stock, virgin foil-c; numbered edition						
	2	4	6	13	18	22
Pseudo-Tick #13 (11/00, $3.50) Continues story from #12 (1993)						4.00
Promo Sampler-(1990)-Tick-c/story	1	2	3	5	6	8

TICK, THE (One shots)

… Big Back to School Special 1-(10/98, $3.50, B&W) Tick & Arthur undercover in H.S.   3.50
… Big Cruise Ship Vacation Special 1-(9/00, $3.50, B&W)   3.50
… Big Father's Day Special 1-(6/00, $3.50, B&W)   3.50
… Big Halloween Special 1-(10/99, $3.50, B&W)   3.50
… Big Halloween Special 2000 (10/00, $3.50)   3.50
… Big Halloween Special 2001 (9/01, $3.95)   4.00

Tick-Tock Tales #5 © ME

Tiger Girl #1 © GK

Timber Wolf #2 © DC

	GD 2.0	VG 4.0	FN 6.0	VF 8.0	VF/NM 9.0	NM- 9.2

... Big Mother's Day Special 1-(4/00, $3.50, B&W) — 3.50
... Big Red-N-Green Christmas Spectacle 1-(12/01, $3.95) — 4.00
... Big Romantic Adventure 1-(2/98, $2.95, B&W) Candy box-c with candy map on back — 3.50
... Big Summer Annual 1-(7/99, $3.50, B&W) Chainsaw Vigilante vs. Barry — 3.50
... Big Summer Fun Special 1-(8/98, $3.50, B&W) Tick and Arthur at summer camp — 3.50
... Big Tax Time Terror 1-(4/00, $3.50, B&W) — 3.50
... Big Year 2000 Spectacle 1-(3/00, $3.50, B&W) — 3.50
... Incredible Internet Comic 1-(7/01, $3.95, color) r/New England Comics website story — 4.00
Introducing the Tick 1-(4/02, $3.95, color) summary of Tick's life and adventures — 4.00
The Tick's Back #0 -(8/97, $2.95, B&W) — 4.00
The Tick's Comic Con Extravaganza 1-(6/07, $3.95, color) Wang-c — 4.00
The Tick's 20th Anniversary Special Edition #1 (5/07, $5.95) short stories by various;
 history of the character; creator profiles; 2 covers by Suydam & Bisley — 6.00
--MASSIVE SUMMER DOUBLE SPECTACLE
 1,2-(7,8/00, $3.50, B&W) — 3.50
TICK & ARTIE
1-(6/02, $3.50, color) prints strips from Internet comic — 3.50
2-(10/02, $3.95) — 4.00
TICK AND ARTHUR, THE
New England Comics: Feb, 1999 - No. 6 ($3.50, B&W)
 1-6-Sean Wang-s/a — 3.50
TICK BIG BLUE DESTINY, THE
New England Comics: Oct, 1997 - No. 9 ($2.95)
 1-4: 1-"Keen" Ed. 2-Two covers — 3.50
 1-($4.95) "Wicked Keen" Ed. w/die cut-c — 5.00
 5-($3.50) — 3.50
 6-Luny Bin Trilogy Preview #0 (7/98, $1.50) — 3.50
 7-9: 7-Luny Bin Trilogy begins — 3.50
TICK BIG BLUE YULE LOG SPECIAL, THE
New England Comics: Dec, 1997; 1999 ($2.95, B&W)
 1-"Jolly" and "Traditional" covers; flip book w/"Arthur Teaches the Tick About Hanukkah"
 ...1999 ($3.50) — 3.50
 Tick Big Yule Log Special 2001-(12/00, $3.50, B&W) — 3.50
TICK, THE : CIRCUS MAXIMUS
New England Comics: Mar, 2000 - No. 4, Jun, 2000 ($3.50, B&W)
 1-4-Encyclopedia of characters from Tick comics — 3.50
 Giant No. 1 (8/03, $14.95) r/#1-4, Redux — 15.00
 Redux No. 1 (4/01, $3.50) — 3.50
TICK, THE - COLOR
New England Comics: Jan, 2001 - Present ($3.95)
 1-6: 1-Marc Sandroni-a — 4.00
TICK, THE : DAYS OF DRAMA
New England Comics: July, 2005 - No. 6, June, 2006 ($4.95/$3.95, limited series)
 1-($4.95) Dave Garcia-a; has a mini-comic attached to cover — 5.00
 2-6-($3.95) — 4.00
TICK, THE - HEROES OF THE CITY
New England Comics: Feb, 1999 - Present ($3.50, B&W)
 1-6-Short stories by various — 3.50
TICK KARMA TORNADO (The...)
New England Comics Press: Oct, 1993 - No. 9, Mar, 1995 ($2.75, B&W)
 1-($3.25) — 4.00
 2-9: 2-$2.75-c begins — 3.50
TICK'S BIG XMAS TRILOGY, THE
New England Comics: Dec, 2002 - No. 3, Dec, 2002 ($3.95, limited series)
 1-3 — 4.00
TICK'S GOLDEN AGE COMIC, THE
New England Comics: May, 2002 - No. 3, Feb, 2003 ($4.95, Golden Age size)
 1-3-Facsimile 1940s-style Tick issue; 2 covers — 5.00
 Giant Edition TPB (9/03, $12.95) r/#1-3 — 13.00
TICK'S GIANT CIRCUS OF THE MIGHTY, THE
New England Comics: Summer, 1992 - No. 3, Fall, 1993 ($2.75, B&W, magazine size)
 1-(A-O). 2-(P-Z). 3-1993 Update — 4.00
TICKLE COMICS (Also see Gay, Smile, & Whee Comics)
Modern Store Publ.: 1955 (7¢, 5x7-1/4", 52 pgs)

	GD 2.0	VG 4.0	FN 6.0	VF 8.0	VF/NM 9.0	NM- 9.2
1	6	12	18	28	34	40

TICK TOCK TALES
Magazine Enterprises: Jan, 1946 - V3#33, Jan-Feb, 1951

	GD 2.0	VG 4.0	FN 6.0	VF 8.0	VF/NM 9.0	NM- 9.2
1-Koko & Kola begin	15	30	45	86	133	180
2	10	20	30	54	72	90
3-10	9	18	27	50	65	80
11-33: 19-Flag-c. 23-Muggsy Mouse, The Pixies & Tom-Tom the Jungle Boy app.						
24-X-mas-c. 25-The Pixies & Tom-Tom app.	8	16	24	44	57	70

TIGER (Also see Comics Reading Libraries in the Promotional Comics section)
Charlton Press (King Features): Mar, 1970 - No. 6, Jan, 1971 (15¢)

	GD 2.0	VG 4.0	FN 6.0	VF 8.0	VF/NM 9.0	NM- 9.2
1	3	6	9	14	19	24
2-6	2	4	6	8	11	14

TIGER BOY (See Unearthly Spectaculars)
TIGER GIRL
Gold Key: Sept, 1968 (15¢)

	GD 2.0	VG 4.0	FN 6.0	VF 8.0	VF/NM 9.0	NM- 9.2
1(10227-809)-Sparling-c/a; Jerry Siegel scripts. Some issues have a pin-up on back cover instead of advertising	4	8	12	24	37	50

TIGERMAN (Also see Thrilling Adventure Stories)
Seaboard Periodicals (Atlas): Apr, 1975 - No. 3, Sept, 1975 (All 25¢ issues)

	GD 2.0	VG 4.0	FN 6.0	VF 8.0	VF/NM 9.0	NM- 9.2
1-3: 1-Origin; Colan-c. 2,3-Ditko-p in each	2	4	6	8	10	12

TIGER WALKS, A (See Movie Comics)
TIGRA (The Avengers)
Marvel Comics: May, 2002 - No. 4, Aug, 2002 ($2.99, limited series)
 1-4-Christina Z-s/Deodato-c/a — 3.00
TIGRESS, THE
Hero Graphics: Aug, 1992 - No. 6?, June, 1993 ($3.95/$2.95/$3.95, B&W)
 1,6: 1-Tigress vs. Flare. 6-44 pgs. — 4.00
 2-5: 2-$2.95-c begins — 3.00
TILLIE THE TOILER (See Comic Monthly)
Dell Publishing Co.: No. 15, 1941 - No. 237, July, 1949

	GD 2.0	VG 4.0	FN 6.0	VF 8.0	VF/NM 9.0	NM- 9.2
Four Color 15(1941)	45	90	135	275	455	635
Large Feature Comic 30(1941)	34	68	102	195	308	420
Four Color 8(1942)	23	46	69	169	302	435
Four Color 22(1943)	17	34	51	126	223	320
Four Color 55(1944), 89(1945)	13	26	39	97	171	245
Four Color 106('45),132('46): 132-New stories begin	10	20	30	68	119	170
Four Color 150,176,184	9	18	27	63	107	150
Four Color 195,213,232	7	14	21	50	83	115

TIMBER WOLF (See Action Comics #372, & Legion of Super-Heroes)
DC Comics: Nov, 1992 - No. 5, Mar, 1993 ($1.25, limited series)
 1-5 — 2.50
TIME BANDITS
Marvel Comics Group: Feb, 1982 (one-shot, Giant)
 1-Movie adaptation — 4.00
TIME BEAVERS (See First Comics Graphic Novel #2)
TIME BREAKERS
DC Comics (Helix): Jan, 1997 - No. 5, May, 1997 ($2.25, limited series)
 1-5-Pollack-s — 2.50
TIMECOP (Movie)
Dark Horse Comics: Sept, 1994 - No. 2, Nov, 1994 ($2.50, limited series)
 1,2-Adaptation of film — 2.50
TIME FOR LOVE (Formerly Romantic Secrets)
Charlton Comics: V2#53, Oct, 1966; Oct, 1967 - No. 47, May, 1976

	GD 2.0	VG 4.0	FN 6.0	VF 8.0	VF/NM 9.0	NM- 9.2
V2#53(10/66) Herman-s Hermits app.	3	6	9	20	30	40
1(10/67)	4	8	12	22	34	45
2(12/67)-10	3	6	9	15	21	26
11-20	2	4	6	11	16	20
21-29: 28-Shirley Jones poster. 29-Bobby Sherman pin-up	2	4	6	9	13	16
30-(10/72)-David Cassidy full page poster	3	6	9	17	25	32
31-47	2	4	6	8	11	14

TIMELESS TOPIX (See Topix)
TIMELY PRESENTS: ALL WINNERS
Marvel Comics: Dec, 1999 ($3.99)
 1-Reprints All Winners Comics #19 (Fall 1946); new Lago-c — 4.00

The Time Machine FC #1085 © Loews Inc.

Tim Holt #21 © ME

Tiny Tot Comics #3 © EC

	GD 2.0	VG 4.0	FN 6.0	VF 8.0	VF/NM 9.0	NM- 9.2

TIMELY PRESENTS: HUMAN TORCH
Marvel Comics: Feb, 1999 ($3.99)
1-Reprints Human Torch Comics #5 (Fall 1941); new Lago-c ... 4.00

TIME MACHINE, THE
Dell Publishing Co.: No. 1085, Mar, 1960 (H.G. Wells)
Four Color 1085-Movie, Alex Toth-a; Rod Taylor photo-c
14 28 42 100 178 255

TIME MASTERS
DC Comics: Feb, 1990 - No. 8, Sept, 1990 ($1.75, mini-series)
1-8: New Rip Hunter series. 5-Cave Carson, Viking Prince app. 6-Dr. Fate app. ... 2.50

TIMESLIP COLLECTION
Marvel Comics: Nov, 1998 ($2.99, one-shot)
1-Pin-ups reprinted from Marvel Vision magazine ... 3.00

TIMESLIP SPECIAL (The Coming of the Avengers)
Marvel Comics: Oct, 1998 ($5.99, one-shot)
1-Alternate world Avengers vs. Odin ... 6.00

TIME TO RUN (Based on 1973 Billy Graham movie)
Spire Christian Comics (Fleming H. Revell Co.): 1975 (39¢)
nn-By Al Hartley   2 4 6 8 10 12

TIME TUNNEL, THE (TV)
Gold Key: Feb, 1967 - No. 2, July, 1967 (12¢)
1-Photo back-c on both issues   7 14 21 47 76 105
2   5 10 15 35 55 75

TIME TWISTERS
Quality Comics: Sept, 1987 - No. 21, 1989 ($1.25/$1.50)
1-21: Alan Moore scripts in 1-4, 6-9, 14 (2 pg.). 14-Bolland-a (2 pg.). 15,16-Guice-c ... 2.50

TIME 2: THE EPIPHANY (See First Comics Graphic Novel #9)

TIMEWALKER (Also see Archer & Armstrong)
Valiant: Jan, 1994 - No. 15, Oct, 1995 ($2.50)
1-15,0(3/96): 2-"JAN" on-c, February, 1995 in indicia. ... 2.50
Yearbook 1 (5/95, $2.95) ... 3.00

TIME WARP (See The Unexpected #210)
DC Comics, Inc.: Oct-Nov, 1979 - No. 5, June-July, 1980 ($1.00, 68 pgs.)
1   2 4 6 8 11 14
2-5   1 3 4 6 8 10
NOTE: *Aparo* a-1. *Buckler* a-1p. *Chaykin* a-2. *Ditko* a-1-4. *Kaluta* c-1-5. *G. Kane* a-2. *Nasser* a-4. *Newton* a-1-5p. *Orlando* a-1-3.

TIME WARRIORS: THE BEGINNING
Fantasy General Comics: 1986 (Aug) - No. 2, 1986? ($1.50)
1,2-Alpha Track/Skellon Empire ... 2.25

TIM HOLT (Movie star) (Becomes Red Mask #42 on; also see Crack Western #72, & Great Western)
Magazine Enterprises: 1948 - No. 41, April-May, 1954 (All 36 pgs.)
1-(A-1 #14)-Line drawn-c w/Tim Holt photo on-c; Tim Holt, His horse Lightning & sidekick Chito begin   61 122 183 381 616 850
2-(A-1 #17)(9-10/48)-Photo-c begin, end #18   34 68 102 192 296 400
3-(A-1 #19)-Photo back-c   25 50 75 144 222 300
4(1-2/49),5: 5-Photo front/back-c   18 36 54 101 156 210
6-(5/49)-1st app. The Calico Kid (alias Rex Fury), his horse Ebony & Sidekick Sing-Song (begin series); photo back-c   30 60 90 173 267 360
7-10: 7-Calico Kid by Ayers. 8-Calico Kid by Guardineer (r-in/Great Western #10).
9-Map of Tim's Home Range   16 32 48 89 137 185
11-The Calico Kid becomes The Ghost Rider (origin & 1st app.) by Dick Ayers (r-in/Great Western I.W. #8); his horse Spectre & sidekick Sing-Song begin series   46 92 138 281 458 635
12-16,18-Last photo-c   14 28 42 80 115 150
17-Frazetta Ghost Rider-c   40 80 120 243 389 535
19,22,24: 19-Last Tim Holt-c; Bolle line-drawn-c begin; Tim Holt photo on covers #19-28, 30-41. 22-interior photo-c   24 36 69 97 125
20-Tim Holt becomes Redmask (origin); begin series; Redmask-c #20-on
17 34 51 96 148 200
21-Frazetta Ghost Rider/Redmask-c   40 80 120 231 358 485
23-Frazetta Redmask-c   32 64 96 180 278 375
25-1st app. Black Phantom   21 42 63 121 186 250
26-30: 28-Wild Bill Hickok, Bat Masterson team up with Redmask. 29-B&W photo-c
11 22 33 62 86 110
31-33-Ghost Rider ends   10 20 30 58 79 100

34-Tales of the Ghost Rider begins (horror)-Classic "The Flower Women" & "Hard Boiled Harry!"   14 28 42 82 121 160
35-Last Tales of the Ghost Rider   11 22 33 62 86 110
36-The Ghost Rider returns, ends #41; liquid hallucinogenic drug story   13 26 39 74 105 135
37-Ghost Rider classic "To Touch Is to Die!", about Inca treasure   13 26 39 74 105 135
38-The Black Phantom begins (not in #39); classic Ghost Rider "The Phantom Guns of Feather Gap!"   13 26 39 74 105 135
39-41: All 3-D effect c/stories   14 28 42 81 118 155
NOTE: *Dick Ayers* a-7, 9-41. *Bolle* a-1-41; c-19, 20, 22, 24-28, 30-41.

TIM McCOY (Formerly Zoo Funnies; Pictorial Love Stories #22 on)
Charlton Comics: No. 16, Oct, 1948 - No. 21, Aug, 1949 (Western Movie Stories)
16-John Wayne, Montgomery Clift app. in "Red River"; photo back-c   41 82 123 250 400 550
17-21: 17-Allan "Rocky" Lane guest stars. 18-Rod Cameron guest stars. 19-Whip Wilson, Andy Clyde guest stars. 20-Jimmy Wakely guest stars.
21-Johnny Mack Brown guest stars   37 74 111 210 323 435

TIMMY
Dell Publishing Co.: No. 715, Aug, 1956 - No. 1022, Aug-Oct, 1959
Four Color 715 (#1)   5 10 15 30 48 65
Four Color 823 (8/57), 923 (8/58), 1022   3 6 12 26 41 55

TIMMY THE TIMID GHOST (Formerly Win-A-Prize?; see Blue Bird)
Charlton Comics: No. 3, 2/56 - No. 44, 10/64; No. 45, 9/66; 10/67 - No. 23, 7/71; V4#24, 9/85 - No. 26, 1/86
3(1956) (1st Series)   12 24 36 67 94 120
4,5   8 16 24 40 50 60
6-10   3 6 9 19 29 38
11,12(4/58,10/58)-(100 pgs.)   6 12 18 41 66 90
13-20   3 6 9 17 25 32
21-45(1966)   2 4 6 13 18 22
1(10/67, 2nd series)   3 6 9 15 21 26
2-10   2 4 6 10 13 16
11-23: 23 (7/71)   1 3 4 8 10 12
24-26 (1985-86): Fago-r (low print run)   6.00

TIM TYLER (See Harvey Comics Hits #54)

TIM TYLER (Also see Comics Reading Libraries in the Promotional Comics section)
Better Publications: 1942
1   15 30 45 85 130 175

TIM TYLER COWBOY
Standard Comics (King Features Synd.): No. 11, Nov, 1948 - No. 18, 1950
11-By Lyman Young   9 18 27 50 65 80
12-18: 13-15-Full length western adventures   7 14 21 35 43 50

TINKER BELL (Disney, TV)(See Walt Disney Showcase #37)
Dell Publishing Co.: No. 896, Mar, 1958 - No. 982, Apr-June, 1959
Four Color 896 (#1)-The Adventures of...   8 16 24 56 93 130
Four Color 982-The New Advs. of...   8 16 24 52 86 120

TINY FOLKS FUNNIES
Dell Publishing Co.: No. 60, 1944
Four Color 60   15 30 45 111 198 285

TINY TESSIE (Tessie #1-23; Real Experiences #25)
Marvel Comics (20CC): No. 24, Oct, 1949 (52 pgs.)
24   12 24 36 67 94 120

TINY TIM (Also see Super Comics)
Dell Publishing Co.: No. 4, 1941 - No. 235, July, 1949
Large Feature Comic 4('41)   40 80 120 244 392 540
Four Color 20(1941)   37 74 114 213 339 465
Four Color 42(1943)   16 32 48 118 209 300
Four Color 235   6 12 18 37 59 80

TINY TOT COMICS
E. C. Comics: Mar, 1946 - No. 10, Nov-Dec, 1947 (For younger readers)
1(nn)-52 pg. issues begin, end #4   40 80 120 235 368 500
2 (5/46)   22 44 66 128 202 275
3-10: 10-Christmas-c   20 40 60 117 184 250

TINY TOT FUNNIES (Formerly Family Funnies; becomes Junior Funnies)
Harvey Publ. (King Features Synd.): No. 9, June, 1951
9-Flash Gordon, Mandrake, Dagwood, Daisy, etc.   8 16 24 42 54 65

Tip Top Comics #39 © UFS

Titans #25 © DC

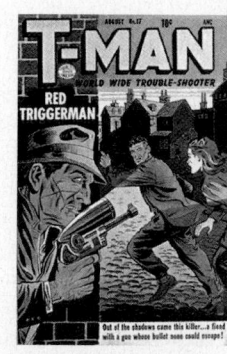

T-Man #17 © QUA

	GD 2.0	VG 4.0	FN 6.0	VF 8.0	VF/NM 9.0	NM- 9.2		GD 2.0	VG 4.0	FN 6.0	VF 8.0	VF/NM 9.0	NM- 9.2

TINY TOTS COMICS
Dell Publishing Co.: 1943 (Not reprints)

	GD	VG	FN	VF	VF/NM	NM-
1-Kelly-a(2); fairy tales	40	80	120	239	380	520

TIPPY & CAP STUBBS (See Popular Comics)
Dell Publishing Co.: No. 210, Jan, 1949 - No. 242, Aug, 1949

Four Color 210 (#1)	5	10	15	32	51	70
Four Color 242	4	8	12	26	41	55

TIPPY'S FRIENDS GO-GO & ANIMAL
Tower Comics: July, 1966 - No. 15, Oct, 1969 (25¢)

1	9	18	27	60	100	140
2-5,7,9-15: 12-15 titled "Tippy's Friend Go-Go"	5	10	15	32	51	70
6-The Monkees photo-c	8	16	24	54	90	125
8-Beatles app. on front/back-c	10	20	30	70	123	175

TIPPY TEEN (See Vicki)
Tower Comics: Nov, 1965 - No. 25, Oct, 1969 (25¢)

1	10	20	30	68	119	170
2-4,6-10	6	12	18	39	62	85
5-1 pg. Beatles pin-up	6	12	18	43	69	95
11-20: 16-Twiggy photo-c	6	12	18	37	59	80
21-25	5	10	15	32	51	70
Special Collectors' Editions nn-(1969, 25¢)	6	12	18	37	59	80

TIPPY TERRY
Super/I. W. Enterprises: 1963

Super Reprint #14('63)-r/Little Groucho #1	2	4	6	8	10	12
I.W. Reprint #1 (nd)-r/Little Groucho #1	2	4	6	8	10	12

TIP TOP COMICS
United Features #1-188/St. John #189-210/Dell Publishing Co. #211 on:
4/36 - No. 210, 1957; No. 211, 11-1/57-58 - No. 225, 5-7/61

1-Tarzan by Hal Foster, Li'l Abner, Broncho Bill, Fritzi Ritz, Ella Cinders, Capt. & The Kids begin; strip-r (1st comic book app. of each)	958	1916	2874	5461	8481	11,500
2	229	458	687	1305	2028	2750
3-Tarzan-c	204	408	612	1163	1807	2450
4	119	238	357	678	1052	1425
5-8,10: 7-Photo & biography of Edgar Rice Burroughs. 8-Christmas-c	83	166	249	473	737	1000
9-Tarzan-c	104	208	312	593	922	1250
11,13,16,18-Tarzan-c: 11-Has Tarzan pin-up	79	158	237	450	700	950
12,14,15,17,19,20: 20-Christmas-c	60	120	180	342	534	725
21,24,27,30-(10/38)-Tarzan-c	63	126	189	359	560	760
22,23,25,26,28,29	43	86	129	245	378	510
31,35,38,40	38	76	114	216	343	470
32,36-Tarzan-c: 32-1st published Jack Davis-a (cartoon). 36-Kurtzman panel (1st published comic work)	54	108	162	338	557	775
33,34,37,39-Tarzan-c	50	100	150	305	503	700
41-Reprints 1st Tarzan Sunday; Tarzan-c	54	108	162	338	557	775
42,44,46,48,49	32	64	96	186	293	400
43,45,47,50,52-Tarzan-c. 43-Mort Walker panel	40	80	120	239	380	520
51,53	31	62	93	178	282	385
54-Origin Mirror Man & Triple Terror, also featured on cover	39	78	117	224	355	485
55,56,58,60: Last Tarzan by Foster	25	50	75	148	232	315
57,59,61,62-Tarzan by Hogarth	32	64	96	186	293	400
63-80: 65,67-70,72-74,77,78-No Tarzan	15	30	45	88	137	185
81-90	14	28	42	80	115	150
91-99	13	26	39	72	101	130
100	14	28	42	76	108	140
101-140: 110-Gordo story. 111-Li'l Abner app. 118, 132-No Tarzan. 137-Sadie Hawkins Day story	10	20	30	54	72	90
141-170: 145,151-Gordo stories. 157-Last Li'l Abner; lingerie panels	8	16	24	44	57	70
171-188-Tarzan reprints by B. Lubbers in all. 173-Peanuts by Schulz begins; no Peanuts in #174-183	9	18	27	47	61	75
189-225-Peanuts (8 pgs.) in most	8	16	24	40	50	60
Bound Volumes (Very Rare) sold at 1939 World's Fair; bound by publisher in pictorial comic boards (also see Comics on Parade)						
Bound issues 1-12	300	600	900	1970	3485	5000
Bound issues 13-24	172	344	516	1075	1788	2500
Bound issues 25-36	152	304	456	950	1575	2200

NOTE: *Tarzan by Foster-#1-40, 44-50; by Rex Maxon-#41-43; by Burne Hogarth-#57, 59, 62.*

TIP TOPPER COMICS

United Features Syndicate: Oct-Nov, 1949 - No. 28, 1954

1-Li'l Abner, Abbie & Slats	12	24	36	67	94	120
2	8	16	24	44	57	70
3-5: 5-Fearless Fosdick app.	8	16	24	40	50	60
6-10: 6-Fearless Fosdick app.	7	14	21	37	46	55
11-16	6	12	18	31	38	45
17(6-7/52) (2nd app. of Peanuts by Schulz in comics?) (see United Comics #22 for 5-6/52 app.)	9	18	27	52	69	85
18-26: 18-24,26-Early Peanuts (2 pgs.). 25-Early Peanuts (3 pgs.) 26-Twin Earths	9	18	27	47	61	75
27,28-Twin Earths	8	16	24	40	50	60

NOTE: *Many lingerie panels in Fritzi Ritz stories.*

TITAN A.E.
Dark Horse Comics: May, 2000 - No. 3, July, 2000 ($2.95, limited series)

1-3-Movie prequel; Al Rio-a	3.00

TITANS (Also see Teen Titans, New Teen Titans and New Titans)
DC Comics: Mar, 1999 - No. 50, Apr, 2003 ($2.50/$2.75)

1-Titans re-form; Grayson-s; 2 covers	3.00
2-11,13-24,26-50: 2-Superman-c/app. 9,10,21,22-Deathstroke app. 24-Titans from "Kingdom Come" app. 32-36-Asamiya-c. 44-Begin $2.75-c	2.75
12-($3.50, 48 pages)	3.50
25-($3.95) Titans from "Kingdom Come" app.; Wolfman & Faerber-s; art by Pérez, Cardy, Grumment, Jimenez, Dodson, Pelletier	4.00
Annual 1 ('00, $3.50) Planet DC; intro Bushido	3.50
...Secret Files 1,2 (3/99, 10/00; $4.95) Profile pages & short stories	5.00

TITANS/ LEGION OF SUPER-HEROES: UNIVERSE ABLAZE
DC Comics: 2000 - No. 4, 2000 ($4.95, prestige format, limited series)

1-4-Jurgens-s/a; P. Jimenez-a; teams battle Universo	5.00

TITAN SPECIAL
Dark Horse Comics: June, 1994 ($3.95, one-shot)

1-($3.95, 52 pgs.)	4.00

TITANS: SCISSORS, PAPER, STONE
DC Comics: 1997 ($4.95, one-shot)

1-Manga style Elseworlds; Adam Warren-s/a(p)	5.00

TITANS SELL-OUT SPECIAL
DC Comics: Nov, 1992 ($3.50, 52 pgs., one-shot)

1-Fold-out Nightwing poster; 1st Teeny Titans	3.50

TITANS/ YOUNG JUSTICE: GRADUATION DAY
DC Comics: Early July, 2003 - No. 3, Aug, 2003 ($2.50, limited series)

1,2-Winick-s/Garza-a; leads into Teen Titans and The Outsiders series. 2-Lilith dies	2.50
3-Death of Donna Troy (Wonder Girl)	2.50
TPB (2003, $6.95) r/#1-3; plus previews of Teen Titans and The Outsiders series	7.00

T-MAN (Also see Police Comics #103)
Quality Comics Group: Sept, 1951 - No. 38, Dec, 1956

1-Pete Trask, T-Man begins; Jack Cole-a	40	80	120	239	380	520
2-Crandall-a	21	42	63	124	195	265
3,7,8: All Crandall-c	19	38	57	112	176	240
4,5-Crandall-c/a each	21	42	63	120	188	255
6-"The Man Who Could Be Hitler" c/story; Crandall-c.	21	42	63	124	195	265
9,10-Crandall-a	16	32	48	94	147	200
11-Used in POP, pg. 95 & color illo.	14	28	42	80	115	150
12,13,15-19,21,22-26: 21- "The Return of Mussolini" c/story. 23-H-Bomb panel. 24-Last pre-code issue (4/55). 25-Not Crandall-a	12	24	36	67	94	120
14-Hitler-c	15	30	45	85	130	175
20-H-Bomb explosion-c/story	15	30	45	84	127	170
27-33,35-38	12	24	36	67	94	120
34-Hitler-c	14	28	42	76	108	140

NOTE: *Anti-communist stories common. Crandall c-2-10. Cuidera c(i)-1-38. Bondage c-15.*

TMNT... (Also see Teenage Mutant Ninja Turtles and related titles)
Mirage Publishing: March 2007 ($3.25/$4.95, B&W, one-shots)

...: Raphael Movie Prequel 1; ...: Michelangelo Movie Prequel 2; ...: Donatello Movie Prequel 3; ...: April Movie Prequel 4; ...: Leonardo Movie Prequel 5; back-story for movie	3.25
...: The Official Movie Adaptation ($4.95) adapts 2007 movie; Munroe-c	5.00

TMNT MUTANT UNIVERSE SOURCEBOOK
Archie Comics: 1992 - No. 3, 1992? ($1.95, 52 pgs.)(Lists characters from A-Z)

1-3: 3-New characters; fold-out poster	2.50

Toka #1 © DELL

Tomahawk #1 © DC

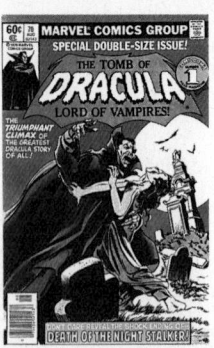

Tomb of Dracula #70 © MAR

	GD 2.0	VG 4.0	FN 6.0	VF 8.0	VF/NM 9.0	NM- 9.2
TNT COMICS **Charles Publishing Co.: Feb, 1946 (36 pgs.)**						
1-Yellowjacket app.	31	62	93	178	282	385
TOBY TYLER (Disney, see Movie Comics) **Dell Publishing Co.: No. 1092, Apr-June, 1960**						
Four Color 1092-Movie, photo-c	6	12	18	43	69	95
TODAY'S BRIDES **Ajax/Farrell Publishing Co.: Nov, 1955; No. 2, Feb, 1956; No. 3, Sept, 1956; No. 4, Nov, 1956**						
1	9	18	27	47	61	75
2-4	6	12	18	31	38	45
TODAY'S ROMANCE **Standard Comics: No. 5, March, 1952 - No. 8, Sept, 1952 (All photo-c?)**						
5-Photo-c	10	20	30	56	76	95
6-Photo-c; Toth-a	10	20	30	58	79	100
7,8	8	16	24	44	57	70
TOE TAGS FEATURING GEORGE A. ROMARO **DC Comics: Dec, 2004 - No. 6, May, 2005 ($2.95-$2.99)**						
1-6-Zombie story by George Romaro; Wrightson-c/Castillo-a						3.00
TOKA (Jungle King) **Dell Publishing Co.: Aug-Oct, 1964 - No. 10, Jan, 1967 (Painted-c #1,2)**						
1	4	8	12	26	41	55
2	3	6	9	16	23	30
3-10	3	6	9	14	19	24
TOKYO STORM WARNING (See Red/Tokyo Storm Warning for TPB) **DC Comics (Cliffhanger): Aug, 2003 - No. 3, Dec, 2003 ($2.95, limited series)**						
1-3-Warren Ellis-s/James Raiz-a						3.00
TOMAHAWK (Son of... on-c of #131-140; see Star Spangled Comics #69 & World's Finest Comics #65) **National Periodical Publications: Sept-Oct, 1950 - No. 140, May-June, 1972**						
1-Tomahawk & boy sidekick Dan Hunter begin by Fred Ray	172	344	516	1075	1788	2500
2-Frazetta/Williamson-a (4 pgs.)	66	132	198	413	687	960
3-5	41	82	123	250	400	550
6-10: 7-Last 52 pg. issue	35	70	105	201	318	435
11-20	24	48	72	139	220	300
21-27,30: 30-Last precode (2/55)	21	42	63	122	191	260
28-1st app. Lord Shilling (arch-foe)	22	44	66	126	198	270
29-Frazetta-r/Jimmy Wakely #3 (3 pgs.)	27	54	81	156	246	335
31-40	17	34	51	98	154	210
41-50	10	20	30	67	116	165
51-56,58-60	8	16	24	58	97	135
57-Frazetta-r/Jimmy Wakely #6 (3 pgs.)	10	20	30	68	119	170
61-77: 77-Last 10¢ issue	8	16	24	52	86	120
78-85: 81-1st app. Miss Liberty. 83-Origin Tomahawk's Rangers	6	12	18	43	69	95
86-99: 96-Origin/1st app. The Hood, alias Lady Shilling	5	10	15	30	48	65
100	5	10	15	32	51	70
101-110: 107-Origin/1st app. Thunder-Man	4	8	12	24	37	50
111-115,120,122: 122-Last 12¢ issue	4	8	12	22	34	45
116-1st Neal Adams cover	5	10	15	35	55	75
117-119,121,123-130-Neal Adams-c	4	8	12	24	37	50
131-Frazetta-r/Jimmy Wakely #7 (3 pgs.); origin Firehair retold	3	6	9	19	29	38
132-135: 135-Last 15¢ issue	3	6	9	15	21	26
136-138,140 (52 pg. Giants)	3	6	9	17	25	32
139-Frazetta-r/Star Spangled #113	3	6	9	14	19	24

NOTE: *Fred Ray* c-1, 2, 8, 11, 30, 34, 35, 40-43, 45, 46, 82. Firehair by *Kubert*-131-134, 136. *Maurer* a-138. *Severin* a-135. *Starr* a-5. *Thorne* a-137, 140.

TOM AND JERRY (See Comic Album #4, 8, 12, Dell Giant #21, Dell Giants, Golden Comics Digest #1, 5, 8, 13, 15, 18, 22, 25, 28, 35, Kite fun Book & March of Comics #21, 46, 61, 70, 88, 103, 119, 128, 145, 154, 173, 190, 207, 224, 281, 295, 305, 321,333, 345, 361, 365, 388, 400, 444, 451, 463, 480)

TOM AND JERRY (...Comics, early issues) (M.G.M.)
(Formerly Our Gang No. 1-59) (See Dell Giants for annuals)
Dell Publishing Co./Gold Key No. 213-327/Whitman No. 328 on: No. 193, 6/48; No. 60, 7/49 - No. 212, 7-9/62; No. 213, 11/62 - No. 291, 2/75; No. 292, 3/77 - No. 342, 5/82 - No. 344, 6/84

	GD 2.0	VG 4.0	FN 6.0	VF 8.0	VF/NM 9.0	NM- 9.2
Four Color 193 (#1)-Titled "M.G.M. Presents..."	22	44	66	165	295	425
60-Barney Bear, Benny Burro cont. from Our Gang; Droopy begins	11	22	33	79	140	200
61	9	18	27	65	113	160
62-70: 66-X-Mas-c	8	16	24	54	90	125
71-80: 77,90-X-Mas-c. 79-Spike & Tyke begin	6	12	18	43	69	95
81-99	6	12	18	39	62	85
100	6	12	18	41	66	90
101-120	5	10	15	32	51	70
121-140: 126-X-Mas-c	5	10	15	30	48	65
141-160	4	8	12	26	41	55
161-200	4	8	12	24	37	50
201-212(7-9/62)(Last Dell issue)	4	8	12	22	34	45
213,214-(84 pgs.)-Titled "...Funhouse"	6	12	18	41	66	90
215-240: 215-Titled "...Funhouse"	3	6	9	17	25	32
241-270	2	4	6	11	16	20
271-300: 286-"Tom & Jerry"	2	4	6	8	11	14
301-327 (Gold Key)	1	3	4	6	8	10
328,329 (Whitman)	2	4	6	8	11	14
330(8/80),331(10/80), 332-(3-pack only)	3	6	9	20	30	40
333-341: 339(2/82), 340(2-3/82), 341(4/82)	2	4	6	8	10	12
342-344 (All #90058, no date, date code, 3-pack): 342(6/83), 343(8/83), 344(6/84)	3	6	9	14	19	24
Mouse From T.R.A.P. 1(7/66)-Giant, G. K.	5	10	15	30	48	65
Summer Fun 1(7/67, 68 pgs.)(Gold Key)-Reprints Barks' Droopy from Summer Fun #1	5	10	15	30	48	65

NOTE: #60-87, 98-121, 268, 277, 289, 302 as 52 pgs.. Reprints #225, 241, 245, 247, 252, 254, 266, 268, 270, 292-327, 329-342, 344.

TOM & JERRY (Formerly Beware)
Harvey Comics: Sept, 1991 - No. 18, Aug, 1994 ($1.25)

	GD 2.0	VG 4.0	FN 6.0	VF 8.0	VF/NM 9.0	NM- 9.2
1-18: 1-Tom & Jerry, Barney Bear-r by Carl Barks						3.00
50th Anniversary Special 1 (10/91, $2.50, 68 pgs.)-Benny the Lonesome Burro-r by Barks (story/a)/Our Gang #9						4.00

TOMB OF DARKNESS (Formerly Beware)
Marvel Comics Group: No. 9, July, 1974 - No. 23, Nov, 1976

	GD 2.0	VG 4.0	FN 6.0	VF 8.0	VF/NM 9.0	NM- 9.2
9	3	6	9	16	22	28
10-23: 11,16,18-21-Kirby-a. 15,19-Ditko-r. 17-Woodbridge-r/Astonishing #62; Powell-r. 20-Everett Venus-r/Venus #19. 22-r/Tales To Astonish #27; 1st Hank Pym. 23-Everett-r	2	4	6	9	12	15
20,21-(30¢-c variants, limited distribution)(5,7/76)	4	8	12	24	37	50

TOMB OF DRACULA (See Giant-Size Dracula, Dracula Lives, Nightstalkers, Power Record Comics & Requiem for Dracula)
Marvel Comics Group: Apr, 1972 - No. 70, Aug, 1979

	GD 2.0	VG 4.0	FN 6.0	VF 8.0	VF/NM 9.0	NM- 9.2
1-1st app. Dracula & Frank Drake; Colan-p in all; Neal Adams-c	14	28	42	102	181	260
2	7	14	21	47	76	105
3-6: 3-Intro. Dr. Rachel Van Helsing & Inspector Chelm. 6-Neal Adams-c	6	12	18	37	59	80
7-9	5	10	15	30	48	65
10-1st app. Blade the Vampire Slayer (who app. in 1998 and 2002 movies)	17	34	51	128	227	325
11,14-16,20:	4	8	12	22	34	45
12-2nd app. Blade; Brunner-c(p)	6	12	18	41	66	90
13-Origin Blade	8	16	24	52	86	120
17,19: 17-Blade bitten by Dracula. 19-Blade discovers he is immune to vampire's bite. 1st mention of Blade having vampire blood in him	5	10	15	30	48	65
18-Two-part x-over cont'd in Werewolf by Night #15	4	8	12	26	41	55
21,24-Blade app.	4	8	12	22	34	45
22,23,26,27,29	3	6	9	16	22	28
25-1st app. & origin Hannibal King	3	6	9	18	27	35
25-2nd printing (1994)	2	4	6	8	10	12
28-Blade app. on-c & inside as an illusion	3	6	9	19	29	38
30,41,42-45-Blade app. 45-Intro. Deacon Frost, the vampire who bit Blade's mother	3	6	9	17	25	32
31-40	3	6	9	14	19	24
43-45-(30¢-c variants, limited distribution)	4	8	12	28	44	60
46,47-(Regular 25¢ editions)(4-8/76)	2	4	6	9	13	16
46,47-(30¢-c variants, limited distribution)	3	6	9	20	30	40
48,49,51-57,59,60: 57,59,60-(30¢-c)	2	4	6	9	13	16
50-Silver Surfer app.	3	6	9	17	25	32
57,59,60-(35¢-c variants)(6-9/77)	4	8	12	24	37	50
58-All Blade issue (Regular 30¢ edition)	3	6	9	20	30	40
58-(35¢-c variant)(7/77)	7	14	21	45	73	100
61-69	2	4	6	9	13	16
70-Double size	3	6	9	17	25	32

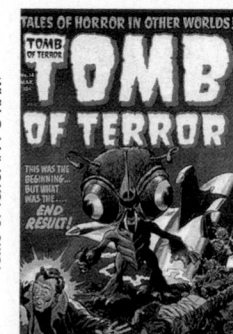

Tomb of Terror #14 © HARV

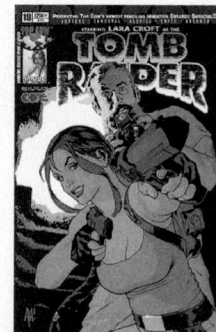

Tomb Raider #18 © Eidos

Tom Mix Western #20 © FAW

	GD 2.0	VG 4.0	FN 6.0	VF 8.0	VF/NM 9.0	NM- 9.2

NOTE: **N. Adams** c-1, 6. **Colan** a-1-70p; c(p)-8, 38-42, 44-56, 58-70. **Wrightson** c-43.

TOMB OF DRACULA, THE (Magazine)
Marvel Comics Group: Oct, 1979 - No. 6, Aug, 1980 (B&W)

1,3: 1-Colan-a; features on movies "Dracula" and "Love at First Bite" w/photos.						
3-Good girl cover-a; Miller-a (2 pg. sketch)	2	4	6	10	14	18
2,6: 2-Ditko-a (36 pgs.). Nosferatu movie feature. 6-Lilith story w/Sienkiewicz-a						
	2	4	6	8	10	12
4,5: Stephen King interview	2	4	6	11	16	20

NOTE: **Buscema** a-4p, 5p. **Chaykin** c-5, 6. **Colan** a(p)-1, 3-6. **Miller** a-3. **Romita** a-2p.

TOMB OF DRACULA
Marvel Comics (Epic Comics): 1991 - No. 4, 1992 ($4.95, 52 pgs., squarebound, mini-series)

Book 1-4: Colan/Williamson-a; Colan painted-c						5.00

TOMB OF DRACULA
Marvel Comics: Dec, 2004 - No. 4, Mar, 2005 ($2.99, limited series)

1-4-Blade app.; Tolagson-a/Sienkiewicz-c						3.00

TOMB OF LEGEIA (See Movie Classics)

TOMB OF TERROR (Thrills of Tomorrow #17 on)
Harvey Publications: June, 1952 - No. 16, July, 1954

1	43	86	129	262	431	600
2	27	54	81	158	249	340
3-Bondage-c; atomic disaster story	28	56	84	162	256	350
4-12: 4-Heart ripped out. 8-12-Nostrand-a	26	52	78	152	239	325
13-Special S/F issue	37	74	111	213	339	465
14-Classic S/F-c; Check-a	46	92	138	281	466	650
15-S/F issue; c-shows face exploding	86	172	258	538	894	1250
16-Special S/F issue; Nostrand-a	34	68	102	197	311	425

NOTE: **Edd Cartier** a-13? **Elias** c-2, 5-16. **Kremer** a-1, 7; c-1. **Nostrand** a-8-12, 15r 16. **Palais** a-2, 3, 5-7. **Powell** a-1, 3, 5, 9-16. **Sparling** a-12, 13, 15.

TOMB RAIDER (one-shots)
Image Comics (Top Cow Prod.)

...: Arabian Nights (8/04, $5.99) Avery-s/Tan-a/c						6.00
... Cover Gallery 2006 (4/06, $2.99) artist galleries and series gallery; pin-ups						3.00
.../The Darkness Special 1 (2001, TopCowStore.com)-Wohl-s/Tan-a						3.00
Epiphany 1 (8/03, $4.99)-Jurgens-s/Banks-a/Haley-c; preview of Witchblade Animated Takeover 1 (1/04, $2.99)-Benefiel-a/Daniel-c						5.00
... Vs. The Wolf-Men: Monster War 2005 (7/05, $2.99) 2nd part of Monster War x-over						3.00
.../Witchblade/Magdalena/Vampirella #1 (8/05, $2.99, B&W) three covers; Chin-a						3.00

TOMB RAIDER: JOURNEYS
Image Comics (Top Cow Prod.): Jan, 2002 - No. 12, May, 2003 ($2.50/$2.99)

1-12: 1-Avery-s/Drew Johnson-a. 1-Two covers by Johnson & Hughes						3.00

TOMB RAIDER: THE GREATEST TREASURE OF ALL
Image Comics (Top Cow Prod.): 2002; Oct, 2005 ($6.99)

Prelude (2002, 16 pgs., no cover price) Jusko-c/a						3.00
1-(10/05, $6.99) Jusko-a/Jurgens-s; sketch pages, reference photos, art in progress						7.00

TOMB RAIDER: THE SERIES (Also see Witchblade/Tomb Raider)(Also see Promotional Comics section for Free Comic Book Day edition)
Image Comics (Top Cow Prod.): Dec, 1999 - No. 50, Mar, 2005 ($2.50/$2.99)

1-Jurgens-s/Park-a; 3 covers by Park, Finch, Turner						4.00
2-24,26-29,31-50: 21-Black-c w/foil. 31-Mhan-a. 37-Flip book preview of Stryke Force						3.00
25-Michael Turner-c/a; Witchblade app.; Endgame x-over with Witchblade #60 & Evo #1						5.00
30-($4.99) Tony Daniel-a						5.00
#0 (2001, $2.50) Avery-s/Ching-a/c						2.50
#1/2 (10/01, $2.95) Early days of Lara Croft; Jurgens-s/Lopez-a						3.00
.... Chasing Shangri-La (2002, $12.95, TPB) r/#11-15						13.00
... Gallery (12/00, $2.95) Pin-ups & previous covers by various						3.00
... Magazine (6/01, $4.95) Hughes-c; r/#1,2; Jurgens interview						5.00
... Mystic Artifacts (2001, $14.95, TPB) r/#5-10						15.00
... Saga of the Medusa Mask (9/00, $9.95, TPB) r/#1-4; new Park-c						10.00
... Vol. 1 Compendium (11/06, $59.99) r/#1-50; variant covers and pin-up art						60.00

TOMB RAIDER/WITCHBLADE SPECIAL (Also see Witchblade/Tomb Raider)
Top Cow Prod.: Dec, 1997 (mail-in offer, one-shot)

1-Turner-s/a(p); green background cover	1	3	4	6	8	10
1-Variant-c with orange sun background	1	3	4	6	8	10
1-Variant-c with black sides	1	3	4	6	8	10
1-Revisited (12/98, $2.95) reprints #1, Turner-c						3.00
...: Trouble Seekers TPB (2002, $7.95) rep. T.R./W & W/T.R. W/T.R. 1/2; new Turner-c						8.00

TOMBSTONE TERRITORY
Dell Publishing Co.: No. 1123, Aug, 1960

Four Color 1123	8	16	24	56	93	130

TOM CAT (Formerly Bo; Atom The Cat #9 on)
Charlton Comics: No. 4, Apr, 1956 - No. 8, July, 1957

4-Al Fago-c/a	8	16	24	44	57	70
5-8	6	12	18	31	38	45

TOM CORBETT, SPACE CADET (TV)
Dell Publishing Co.: No. 378, Jan-Feb, 1952 - No. 11, Sept-Nov, 1954 (All painted covers)

Four Color 378 (#1)-McWilliams-a	16	32	48	118	209	300
Four Color 400,421-McWilliams-a	10	20	30	68	119	170
4(11-1/53) - 11	8	16	24	54	90	125

TOM CORBETT SPACE CADET (See March of Comics #102)

TOM CORBETT SPACE CADET (TV)
Prize Publications: V2#1, May-June, 1955 - V2#3, Sept-Oct, 1955

V2#1-Robot-c	32	64	96	186	293	400
2,3-Meskin-c	24	48	72	139	220	300

TOM, DICK & HARRIET (See Gold Key Spotlight)

TOM JUDGE: END OF DAYS
Image Comics: Jan, 2003 ($3.99)

1-Jenkins-s/Crain-a; flip book wih Evo Preview Edition; Silvestri-c						4.00

TOM LANDRY AND THE DALLAS COWBOYS
Spire Christian Comics/Fleming H. Revell Co.: 1973 (35/49¢)

nn-35¢ edition	2	4	6	13	18	22
nn-49¢ edition	2	4	6	9	12	15

TOM MIX WESTERN (Movie, radio star) (Also see The Comics, Crackajack Funnies, Master Comics, 100 Pages Of Comics, Popular Comics, Real Western Hero, Six Gun Heroes, Western Hero & XMas Comics)
Fawcett Publications: Jan, 1948 - No. 61, May, 1953 (1-17: 52 pgs.)

1 (Photo-c, 52 pgs.)-Tom Mix & his horse Tony begin; Tumbleweed Jr. begins, ends #52,54,55	79	158	237	494	797	1100
2 (Photo-c)	38	76	114	219	340	460
3-5 (Painted/photo-c): 5-Billy the Kid & Oscar app.	27	54	81	155	240	325
6-8: 6,7 (Painted/photo-c). 8-Kinstler tempera-c	23	46	69	132	204	275
9,10 (Painted/photo-c)-Used in SOTI, pgs. 323-325	22	44	66	127	196	265
11-Kinstler oil-c	19	38	57	108	167	225
12 (Painted/photo-c)	17	34	51	96	148	200
13-17 (Painted-c, 52 pgs.)	17	34	51	96	148	200
18,22 (Painted-c, 36 pgs.)	15	30	45	84	127	170
19 (Painted-c, 52 pgs.)	15	30	45	86	133	180
20,21,23 (Painted-c, 52 pgs.)	15	30	45	84	127	170
24,25,27-29 (52 pgs.): 24-Photo-c begin, end #61. 29-Slim Pickens app.	14	28	42	78	112	145
26,30 (36 pgs.)	13	26	39	74	105	135
31-33,35-37,39,40,42 (52 pgs.): 39-Red Eagle app.	13	26	39	72	101	130
34,38 (36 pgs. begin)	12	24	36	67	94	120
41,43-60: 57-(9/52)-Dope smuggling story	9	18	27	52	69	85
61-Last issue	11	22	33	60	83	105

NOTE: Photo-c from 1930s Tom Mix movies (he died in 1940). Many issues contain ads for Tom Mix, Rocky Lane, Space Patrol and other premiums. Captain Tootsie by **C.C. Beck** in #6-11, 20.

TOM MIX WESTERN
AC Comics: 1988 - No. 2, 1989? ($2.95, B&W w/16 pgs. color, 44 pgs.)

1-Tom Mix-r/Master #124,128,131,102 plus Billy the Kid-r by Severin; photo front/back/inside-c						3.50
2-($2.50, B&W)-Gabby Hayes-r; photo covers						3.00
...Holiday Album 1 (1990, $3.50, B&W, one-shot, 44 pgs.)-Contains photos & 1950s Tom Mix-r; photo inside-c						4.00

TOMMY OF THE BIG TOP (Thrilling Circus Adventures)
King Features Synd./Standard Comics: No. 10, Sep, 1948 - No. 12, Mar, 1949

10-By John Lehti	9	18	27	50	65	80
11,12	6	12	18	31	38	45

TOMMYSAURUS REX
Image Comics: Aug, 2004 ($11.95, B&W, graphic novel)

Vol. 1 - Doug TenNapel-s/a						12.00

TOMMY TOMORROW (See Action Comics #127, Real Fact #6, Showcase #41,42,44,46,47 & World's Finest #102)

TOMOE (Also see Shi: The Way of the Warrior #6)
Crusade Comics: July, 1995 - No. 3, June, 1996 ($2.95)

0-3: 2-B&W Dogs o' War preview. 3-B&W Demon Gun preview						3.00

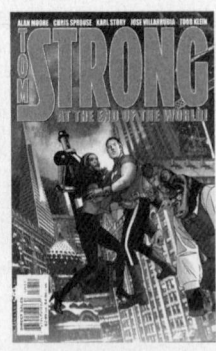

Tom Strong #36 © ABC

Tongue Lash II #1 © Taylor

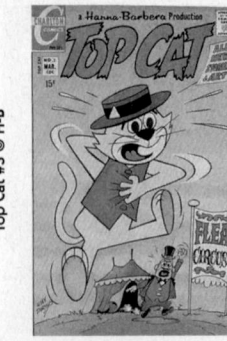

Top Cat #3 © H-B

	GD 2.0	VG 4.0	FN 6.0	VF 8.0	VF/NM 9.0	NM- 9.2
0 (3/96, $2.95)-variant-c.						3.00
0-Commemorative edition (5,000)	2	4	6	8	10	12
1-Commemorative edition (5,000)	2	4	6	9	12	15
1-($2.95)-FAN Appreciation edition						3.00
TPB (1997, $14.95) r/#0-3						15.00

TOMOE: UNFORGETTABLE FIRE
Crusade Comics: June, 1997 ($2.95, one-shot)

	GD 2.0	VG 4.0	FN 6.0	VF 8.0	VF/NM 9.0	NM- 9.2
1-Prequel to Shi: The Series						3.00

TOMOE-WITCHBLADE/FIRE SERMON
Crusade Comics: Sept, 1996 ($3.95, one-shot)

	GD 2.0	VG 4.0	FN 6.0	VF 8.0	VF/NM 9.0	NM- 9.2
1-Tucci-c						5.00
1-($9.95)-Avalon Ed. w/gold foil-c						10.00

TOMOE-WITCHBLADE/MANGA SHI PREVIEW EDITION
Crusade Comics: July, 1996 ($5.00, B&W)

	GD 2.0	VG 4.0	FN 6.0	VF 8.0	VF/NM 9.0	NM- 9.2
nn-San Diego Preview Edition						5.00

TOMORROW KNIGHTS
Marvel Comics (Epic Comics): June, 1990 - No. 6, Mar, 1991 ($1.50)

	GD 2.0	VG 4.0	FN 6.0	VF 8.0	VF/NM 9.0	NM- 9.2
1-6: 1-($1.95, 52 pgs.)						2.50

TOMORROW STORIES
America's Best Comics: Oct, 1999 - No. 12, Aug, 2002 ($3.50/$2.95)

	GD 2.0	VG 4.0	FN 6.0	VF 8.0	VF/NM 9.0	NM- 9.2
1-Two covers by Ross and Nowlan; Moore-s						3.50
2-12-($2.95)						3.00
... Special (1/06, $6.99) Nowlan-c; Moore-s; Greyshirt tribute to Will Eisner						7.00
... Special 2 (5/06, $6.99) Gene Ha-c; Moore-s; Promethea app.						7.00
Book 1 Hardcover (2002, $24.95) r/#1-6						25.00
Book 1 TPB (2003, $17.95) r/#1-6						18.00
Book 2 Hardcover (2004, $24.95) r/#7-12						25.00
Book 2 TPB (2005, $17.99) r/#7-12						18.00

TOM SAWYER (See Adventures of... & Famous Stories)

TOM SKINNER-UP FROM HARLEM (See Up From Harlem)

TOM STRONG (Also see Many Worlds of Tesla Strong)
America's Best Comics: June, 1999 - No. 36, May, 2006 ($3.50/$2.95/$2.99)

	GD 2.0	VG 4.0	FN 6.0	VF 8.0	VF/NM 9.0	NM- 9.2
1-Two covers by Ross and Sprouce; Moore-s/Sprouse-a						4.00
2-36: 4-Art Adams-a (8 pgs.) 13-Fawcett homage w/art by Sprouse, Baker, Heath 20-Origin of Tom Stone. 22-Ordway-a. 31,32-Moorcock-s						3.00
...: Book One HC ('00, $24.95) r/#1-7, cover gallery and sketchbook						25.00
...: Book One TPB ('01, $14.95) r/#1-7, cover gallery and sketchbook						15.00
...: Book Two HC ('02, $24.95) r/#8-14, sketchbook						25.00
...: Book Two TPB ('03, $14.95) r/#8-14, sketchbook						15.00
...: Book Three HC ('04, $24.95) r/#15-19, sketchbook						25.00
...: Book Three TPB ('04, $17.95) r/#15-19, sketchbook						18.00
...: Book Four HC ('04, $24.95) r/#20-25, sketch pages						25.00
...: Book Four TPB ('05, $17.99) r/#20-25, sketch pages						18.00
...: Book Five HC ('05, $24.99) r/#26-30, sketch pages						25.00
...: Book Six HC ('06, $24.99) r/#31-36						25.00

TOM STRONG'S TERRIFIC TALES
America's Best Comics: Jan, 2002 - No. 12 ($3.50/$2.95)

	GD 2.0	VG 4.0	FN 6.0	VF 8.0	VF/NM 9.0	NM- 9.2
1-Short stories; Moore-s; art by Adams, Rivoche, Hernandez, Weiss						3.50
2-12-($2.95) 2-Adams, Ordway, Weiss-a; Adams-c. 4-Rivoche-a. 5-Pearson, Aragonés-a 11-Timm-a						3.00
...: Book One HC ('04, $24.95) r/#1-6, cover gallery and sketch pages						25.00
...: Book One SC ('05, $17.99) r/#1-6, cover gallery and sketch pages						18.00
...: Book Two HC ('05, $24.95) r/#7-12, covers						25.00

TOM TERRIFIC! (TV)(See Mighty Mouse Fun Club Magazine #1)
Pines Comics (Paul Terry): Summer, 1957 - No. 6, Fall, 1958
(See Terry Toons Giant Summer Fun Book)

	GD 2.0	VG 4.0	FN 6.0	VF 8.0	VF/NM 9.0	NM- 9.2
1-1st app.?; CBS Television Presents...	23	46	69	130	205	280
2-6-(scarce)	16	32	48	92	144	195

TOM THUMB
Dell Publishing Co.: No. 972, Jan, 1959

	GD 2.0	VG 4.0	FN 6.0	VF 8.0	VF/NM 9.0	NM- 9.2
Four Color 972-Movie, George Pal	8	16	24	58	97	135

TOM-TOM, THE JUNGLE BOY (See A-1 Comics & Tick Tock Tales)
Magazine Enterprises: 1947 - No. 3, 1947; Nov, 1957 - No. 3, Mar, 1958

	GD 2.0	VG 4.0	FN 6.0	VF 8.0	VF/NM 9.0	NM- 9.2
1-Funny animal	11	22	33	64	90	115
2,3(1947): 3-Christmas issue	9	18	27	47	61	75
Tom-Tom & Itchi the Monk 1(11/57) - 3/3(58)	5	10	15	24	30	35
I.W. Reprint No. 1,2,8,10: 1,2,8-r/Koko & Kola #?	2	4	6	8	10	12

TONGUE LASH
Dark Horse Comics: Aug, 1996 - No. 2, Sept, 1996 ($2.95, lim. series, mature)

	GD 2.0	VG 4.0	FN 6.0	VF 8.0	VF/NM 9.0	NM- 9.2
1,2: Taylor-c/a						3.00

TONGUE LASH II
Dark Horse Comics: Feb, 1999 - No. 2, Mar, 1999 ($2.95, lim. series, mature)

	GD 2.0	VG 4.0	FN 6.0	VF 8.0	VF/NM 9.0	NM- 9.2
1,2: Taylor-c/a						3.00

TONKA (Disney)
Dell Publishing Co.: No. 966, Jan, 1959

	GD 2.0	VG 4.0	FN 6.0	VF 8.0	VF/NM 9.0	NM- 9.2
Four Color 966-Movie (Starring Sal Mineo)-photo-c	8	16	24	58	97	135

TONTO (See The Lone Ranger's Companion...)

TONY TRENT (The Face #1,2)
Big Shot/Columbia Comics Group: No. 3, 1948 - No. 4, 1949

	GD 2.0	VG 4.0	FN 6.0	VF 8.0	VF/NM 9.0	NM- 9.2
3,4: 3-The Face app. by Mart Bailey	18	36	54	105	165	225

TOODLES, THE (The Toodle Twins with #1)
Ziff-Davis (Approved Comics)/Argo: No. 10, June-Aug, 1951; Mar, 1956 (Newspaper-r)

	GD 2.0	VG 4.0	FN 6.0	VF 8.0	VF/NM 9.0	NM- 9.2
10-Painted-c, some newspaper-r by The Baers	12	24	36	67	94	120
...Twins 1(Argo, 3/56)-Reprints by The Baers	8	16	24	42	54	65

TOO MUCH COFFEE MAN
Adhesive Comics: July, 1993 - No. 10, Dec, 2000 ($2.50, B&W)

	GD 2.0	VG 4.0	FN 6.0	VF 8.0	VF/NM 9.0	NM- 9.2
1-Shannon Wheeler story & art	2	4	6	9	12	15
2,3	1	2	3	5	7	9
4,5						6.00
6-10						3.00
Full Color Special-nn($2.95),2-(7/97, $3.95)						4.00

TOO MUCH COFFEE MAN SPECIAL
Dark Horse Comics: July, 1997 ($2.95, B&W)

	GD 2.0	VG 4.0	FN 6.0	VF 8.0	VF/NM 9.0	NM- 9.2
nn-Reprints Dark Horse Presents #92-95						3.00

TOO MUCH HOPELESS SAVAGES
Oni Press: June, 2003 - No. 4, Apr, 2004 ($2.99, B&W, limited series)

	GD 2.0	VG 4.0	FN 6.0	VF 8.0	VF/NM 9.0	NM- 9.2
1-4-Van Meter-s/Norrie-a						3.00
TPB (8/04, $11.95, digest-size) r/series						12.00

TOOTS & CASPER
Dell Publishing Co.: No. 5, 1942

	GD 2.0	VG 4.0	FN 6.0	VF 8.0	VF/NM 9.0	NM- 9.2
Large Feature Comic 5	20	40	60	117	184	250

TOP ADVENTURE COMICS
I. W. Enterprises: 1964 (Reprints)

	GD 2.0	VG 4.0	FN 6.0	VF 8.0	VF/NM 9.0	NM- 9.2
1-r/High Adv. (Explorer Joe #2); Krigstein-r	2	4	6	11	16	20
2-Black Dwarf-r/Red Seal #22; Kinstler-c	2	4	6	13	18	22

TOP CAT (TV) (Hanna-Barbera)(See Kite Fun Book)
Dell Publishing Co./Gold Key No. 4 on: 12-2/61-62 - No. 3, 6-8/62; No. 4, 10/62 - No. 31, 9/70

	GD 2.0	VG 4.0	FN 6.0	VF 8.0	VF/NM 9.0	NM- 9.2
1 (TV show debuted 9/27/61)	14	28	42	100	178	255
2-Augie Doggie back-ups in #1-4	8	16	24	54	90	125
3-5: 3-Last 15¢ issue. 4-Begin 12¢ issues; Yakky Doodle app. in 1 pg. strip. 5-Touché Turtle app.	6	12	18	43	69	95
6-10	5	10	15	32	51	70
11-20	4	8	12	24	37	50
21-31-Reprints	3	6	9	19	29	38

TOP CAT (TV) (Hanna-Barbera)(See TV Stars #4)
Charlton Comics: Nov, 1970 - No. 20, Dec, 1973

	GD 2.0	VG 4.0	FN 6.0	VF 8.0	VF/NM 9.0	NM- 9.2
1	6	12	18	37	59	80
2-10	3	6	9	20	30	40
11-20	3	6	9	17	25	32

NOTE: #8 (1/72) went on sale late in 1972 between #14 and #15 with the 1/73 issues.

TOP COMICS
K. K. Publications/Gold Key: July, 1967 (All reprints)

	GD 2.0	VG 4.0	FN 6.0	VF 8.0	VF/NM 9.0	NM- 9.2
nn-The Gnome-Mobile (Disney-movie)	2	4	6	11	16	20
1-Beagle Boys (#7), Beep Beep the Road Runner (#5), Bugs Bunny, Chip 'n' Dale, Daffy Duck (#50), Flipper, Huey, Dewey & Louie, Junior Woodchucks, Lassie, The Little Monsters (#71), Moby Duck, Porky Pig (has Gold Key label - says Top Comics on inside), Scamp, Super Goof, Tom & Jerry, Top Cat (#21), Tweety & Sylvester (#7), Walt Disney C&S (#322), Woody Woodpecker known issues; each character given own book	2	4	6	11	16	14
1-Donald Duck (not Barks), Mickey Mouse	2	4	6	11	16	20
1-Flintstones	3	6	9	20	30	40
1-Huckleberry Hound, Yogi Bear (#30)	2	4	6	13	18	22

Top Comics #2 © WB

Topix #9 © CG

Top-Notch Comics #12 © AP

	GD 2.0	VG 4.0	FN 6.0	VF 8.0	VF/NM 9.0	NM- 9.2
1-The Jetsons	4	8	12	28	44	60
1-Tarzan of the Apes (#169)	3	6	9	15	21	26
1-Three Stooges (#35)	3	6	9	17	25	32
1-Uncle Scrooge (#70)	3	6	9	16	22	28
1-Zorro (r/G.K. Zorro #7 w/Toth-a; says 2nd printing)	2	4	6	13	18	22
2-Bugs Bunny, Daffy Duck, Mickey Mouse (#114), Porky Pig, Super Goof, Tom & Jerry, Tweety & Sylvester, Walt Disney's C&S (r/#325), Woody Woodpecker	2	4	6	8	11	14
2-Donald Duck (not Barks), Three Stooges, Uncle Scrooge (#71)-Barks-c, Yogi Bear (#30), Zorro (r/#8; Toth-a)	2	4	6	10	14	18
2-Snow White & 7 Dwarfs(6/67)(1944-r)	2	4	6	9	13	16
3-Donald Duck	2	4	6	10	14	18
3-Uncle Scrooge (#72)	2	4	6	11	16	20
3,4-The Flintstones	4	8	12	20	30	40
3,4: 3-Mickey Mouse (r/#115), Tom & Jerry, Woody Woodpecker, Yogi Bear. 4-Mickey Mouse, Woody Woodpecker	2	4	6	8	11	14

NOTE: Each book in this series is identical to its counterpart except for cover, and came out at same time. The number in parentheses is the original issue it contains.

TOP COW (Company one-shots)
Image Comics (Top Cow Productions)

... Book of Revelations (7/03, $3.99)-Pin-ups and info; art by various; Gossett-c	4.00
... Convention Sketchbook 2004 (4/04, $3.00, B&W) art by various	3.00
... Preview Book 2005 (3/05, 99¢) Preview pages of Tomb Raider, Darkness, Rising Stars	2.50
... Productions, Inc./Ballistic Studios Swimsuit Special (5/95, $2.95)	3.00
...'s Best of: Dave Finch Vol. 1 TPB (8/06, $19.99) r/issues of Cybrforce, Aphrodite IX, Ascension and The Darkness; art & cover gallery	20.00
...'s Best of: Michael Turner Vol. 1 TPB (12/05, $24.99) r/Witchblade #1,10,12,18,19,25 & Witchblade/Tomb Raider chapters 1&3; Tomb Raider #25; art & cover gallery	25.00
... Secrets: Special Winter Lingerie Edition 1 (1/96, $2.95) Pin-ups	3.00
... 2001 Preview (no cover price) Preview pages of Tomb Raider; Jusko-a; flip cover & pages of Inferno	2.50

TOP COW CLASSICS IN BLACK AND WHITE
Image Comics (Top Cow): Feb, 2000 - Present ($2.95, B&W reprints)

...: Aphrodite IX #1(9/00) B&W reprint	3.00
...: Ascension #1(4/00) B&W reprint plus time-line of series	3.00
...: Battle of the Planets #1(1/03) B&W reprint plus script and cover gallery	3.00
...: Darkness #1(3/00) B&W reprint plus time-line of series	3.00
...: Fathom #1(5/00) B&W reprint	3.00
...: Magdalena #1(10/02) B&W reprint plus time-line of series	3.00
...: Midnight Nation #1(9/00) B&W preview	3.00
...: Rising Stars #1(7/00) B&W reprint plus cover gallery	3.00
...: Tomb Raider #1 (12/00) B&W reprint plus back-story	3.00
...: Witchblade #1 (2/00) B&W reprint plus back-story	3.00
...: Witchblade #25(5/01) B&W reprint plus interview with Wohl & Haberlin	3.00

TOP DETECTIVE COMICS
I. W. Enterprises: 1964 (Reprints)

	GD 2.0	VG 4.0	FN 6.0	VF 8.0	VF/NM 9.0	NM- 9.2
9-r/Young King Cole #14; Dr. Drew (not Grandenetti)	2	4	6	10	14	18

TOP DOG (See Star Comics Magazine, 75¢)

TOP DOG
Star Comics (Marvel): Apr, 1985 - No. 14, June, 1987 (Children's book)

1-14: 10-Peter Parker & J. Jonah Jameson cameo	4.00

TOP ELIMINATOR (Teenage Hotrodders #1-24; Drag 'n' Wheels #30 on)
Charlton Comics: No. 25, Sept, 1967 - No. 29, July, 1968

	GD 2.0	VG 4.0	FN 6.0	VF 8.0	VF/NM 9.0	NM- 9.2
25-29	3	6	9	16	22	28

TOP FLIGHT COMICS: Four Star Publ.: 1947 (Advertised, not published)

TOP FLIGHT COMICS
St. John Publishing Co.: July, 1949

	GD 2.0	VG 4.0	FN 6.0	VF 8.0	VF/NM 9.0	NM- 9.2
1(7/49, St. John)-Hector the Inspector; funny animal	9	18	27	52	69	85

TOP GUN (See Luke Short, 4-Color #927 & Showcase #72)

TOP GUNS OF THE WEST (See Super DC Giant)

TOPIX (...Comics) (Timeless Topix-early issues) (Also see Men of Battle, Men of Courage & Treasure Chest)(V1-V5#1,V7 on-paper-c)
Catechetical Guild Educational Society: 11/42 - V10#15, 1/28/52
(Weekly - later issues)

	GD 2.0	VG 4.0	FN 6.0	VF 8.0	VF/NM 9.0	NM- 9.2
V1#1(8 pgs.,8x11")	24	48	72	139	220	300
2,3(8 pgs.,8x11")	14	28	42	80	115	150
4-8(8 pgs.,8x11")	11	22	33	64	90	115
V2#1-10(16 pgs.,8x11"): V2#8-Pope Pius XII	10	20	30	56	76	95
V3#1-10(16 pgs.,8x11"): V3#1-(9/44)	10	20	30	54	72	90
V4#1-10: V4#1-(9/45)	9	18	27	47	61	75

	GD 2.0	VG 4.0	FN 6.0	VF 8.0	VF/NM 9.0	NM- 9.2
V5#1(10/46,52 pgs.,2(11/46),no #3),4(1/47)-9(6/47),10(7/47), 14(11/47),15(12/47)	8	16	24	40	50	60
11(8/47),12(9/47)-Life of Christ editions	10	20	30	54	72	90
V6#4(1/48),5(2/48),7(3/48),8(4/48),9(5/48),10(6/48),11(7/48)-14 (no #1-3,6)	7	14	21	35	43	50
V7#1(9/1/48)-20(6/15/49), 36 pgs.	6	12	18	29	36	42
V8#1(9/19/49)-3,5-11,13-30(5/15/50)	6	12	18	28	34	40
4-Dagwood Splits the Atom(10/10/49)-Magazine format	8	16	24	42	54	65
12-Ingels-a	10	20	30	54	72	90
V9#1(9/25/50)-11,13-30(5/14/51)	6	12	18	27	33	38
12-Special 36 pg. Xmas issue, text illos format	6	12	18	28	34	40
V10#1(10/1/51)-15: 14-Hollingsworth-a	6	12	18	27	33	38

TOP JUNGLE COMICS
I. W. Enterprises: 1964 (Reprint)

	GD 2.0	VG 4.0	FN 6.0	VF 8.0	VF/NM 9.0	NM- 9.2
1(nd)-Reprints White Princess of the Jungle #3, minus cover; Kintsler-a	3	6	9	16	23	30

TOP LOVE STORIES (Formerly Gasoline Alley #2)
Star Publications: No. 3, 5/51 - No. 19, 3/54

	GD 2.0	VG 4.0	FN 6.0	VF 8.0	VF/NM 9.0	NM- 9.2
3(#1)	23	46	69	132	209	285
4,5,7-9: 8-Wood story	18	36	54	105	165	225
6-Wood-a	24	48	72	139	220	300
10-16,18,19-Disbrow-a	18	36	54	105	165	225
17-Wood art (Fox-r)	19	38	57	112	176	240

NOTE: All have L. B. Cole covers.

TOP-NOTCH COMICS (...Laugh #28-45; Laugh Comix #46 on)
MLJ Magazines: Dec, 1939 - No. 45, June, 1944

	GD 2.0	VG 4.0	FN 6.0	VF 8.0	VF/NM 9.0	NM- 9.2
1-Origin/1st app. The Wizard; Kardak the Mystic Magician, Swift of the Secret Service (ends #3), Air Patrol, The Westpointer, Manhunters (by J. Cole), Mystic (ends #2) & Scott Rand (ends #3) begin; Wizard covers begin, and #8	571	1142	1713	4000	7000	10,000
2-(1/40)-Dick Storm (ends #8), Stacy Knight M.D. (ends #4) begin; Jack Cole-a; 1st app. Nazis swastika on-c	241	482	723	1506	2503	3500
3-Bob Phantom, Scott Rand on Mars begin; J. Cole-a	169	338	507	1056	1753	2450
4-Origin/1st app. Streak Chandler on Mars; Moore of the Mounted only app.; J. Cole-a	150	300	450	938	1557	2175
5-Flag-c; origin/1st app. Galahad; Shanghai Sheridan begins (ends #8); Shield cameo; Novick-a; classic-c	166	332	498	1038	1719	2400
6-Meskin-a	109	218	327	681	1128	1575
7-The Shield x-over in Wizard; The Wizard dons new costume	134	264	402	838	1394	1950
8-Origin/1st app. The Firefly & Roy, the Super Boy 9/40, 2nd costumed boy hero after Robin?; also see Toro in Human Torch #1 (Fall/40)	152	304	456	950	1575	2200
9-Origin & 1st app. The Black Hood; 1st Black Hood-c & logo (10/40); Fran Frazier begins (Scarce)	554	1108	1662	3878	6789	9700
10-2nd app. Black Hood	193	386	579	1206	2003	2800
11-3rd Black Hood	124	248	372	775	1288	1800
12-15	109	218	327	681	1128	1575
16-18,20	95	190	285	594	985	1375
19-Classic bondage-c	100	200	300	625	1038	1450
21-30: 23-26-Roy app. 24-No Wizard. 25-Last Bob Phantom. 27-Last Firefly. 28-Suzie, Pokey Oakey begin. 29-Last Kardak	67	134	201	419	697	975
31-44: 33-Dotty & Ditto by Woggon begins (2/43, 1st app.). 44-Black Hood series ends	41	82	123	250	400	550
45-Last issue	46	92	138	281	461	640

NOTE: J. Binder a-1-3. Meskin a-2, 3, 6, 15. Bob Montana a-30; c-28-31. Harry Sahle c-42-45. Woggon a-33-40, 42. Bondage c-17, 19. Black Hood also appeared on radio in 1944.Black Hood app. on c-9-34, 41-44. Roy the Super Boy app. on c-8, 9, 11-27. The Wizard app. on c-1-8, 11-13, 15-22, 24, 25, 27. Pokey Oakey app. on c-28-43. Suzie app. on c-44-on.

TOPPER & NEIL (TV)
Dell Publishing Co.: No. 859, Nov, 1957

	GD 2.0	VG 4.0	FN 6.0	VF 8.0	VF/NM 9.0	NM- 9.2
Four Color 859	5	10	15	30	48	65

TOPPS COMICS: Four Star Publications: 1947 (Advertised, not published)

TOPS
July, 1949 - No. 2, Sept, 1949 (25¢, 10-1/4x13-1/4", 68 pgs.)
Tops Magazine, Inc. (Lev Gleason): (Large size-magazine format; for the adult reader)

	GD 2.0	VG 4.0	FN 6.0	VF 8.0	VF/NM 9.0	NM- 9.2
1 (Rare)-Story by Dashiell Hammett; Crandall/Lubbers, Tuska, Dan Barry, Fuje-a; Biro painted-c	124	248	372	775	1288	1800
2 (Rare)-Crandall/Lubbers, Biro, Kida, Fuje, Guardineer-a						

Top 10 #9 © ABC

The Tormented #1 © Sterling

Total Justice #3 © DC

	GD 2.0	VG 4.0	FN 6.0	VF 8.0	VF/NM 9.0	NM- 9.2
	117	234	351	731	1216	1700

TOPS COMICS
Consolidated Book Publishers: 1944 (10¢, 132 pgs.)

2000-(Color-c, inside in red shade & some in full color)-Ace Kelly by Rick Yager, Black Orchid, Don on the Farm, Dinky Dinkerton (Rare)   26   52   78   152   239   325
NOTE: This book is printed in such a way that when the staple is removed, the strips on the left side of the book correspond with the same strips on the right side. Therefore, if strips are removed from the book, each strip can be folded into a complete comic section of its own.

TOPS COMICS (See Tops in Humor)
Consolidated Book (Lev Gleason): 1944 (7-1/4x5", 32 pgs.)

2001-The Jack of Spades (costumed hero)	16	32	48	92	144	195
2002-Rip Raider	10	20	30	56	76	95
2003-Red Birch (gag cartoons)	5	10	15	22	26	30
2004-Gag cartoons	16	32	48	92	144	195

TOP SECRET
Hillman Publ.: Jan, 1952

| 1 | 20 | 40 | 60 | 117 | 184 | 250 |

TOP SECRET ADVENTURES (See Spyman)

TOP SECRETS (...of the F.B.I.)
Street & Smith Publications: Nov, 1947 - No. 10, July-Aug, 1949

1-Powell-c/a	35	70	105	201	318	435
2-Powell-c/a	25	50	75	145	228	310
3-6,8,10-Powell-a	22	44	66	128	202	275
9-Powell-c/a	23	46	69	132	209	285
7-Used in SOTI, pg. 90 & illo. "How to hurt people"; used by N.Y. Legis. Comm.; Powell-a	34	68	102	197	311	425
NOTE: Powell c-1-3, 5-10.

TOPS IN ADVENTURE
Ziff-Davis Publishing Co.: Fall, 1952 (25¢, 132 pgs.)

| 1-Crusader from Mars, The Hawk, Football Thrills, He-Man; Powell-a; painted-c | 46 | 92 | 138 | 281 | 466 | 650 |

TOPS IN HUMOR (See Tops Comics?)
Consolidated Book Publ. (Lev Gleason): 1944 (7-1/4x5")

| 2001(#1)-Origin The Jack of Spades, Ace Kelly by Rick Yager, Black Orchid (female crime fighter) app. | 16 | 32 | 48 | 92 | 144 | 195 |
| 2 | 11 | 22 | 33 | 64 | 90 | 115 |

TOP SPOT COMICS
Top Spot Publ. Co.: 1945

| 1-The Menace, Duke of Darkness app. | 35 | 70 | 105 | 201 | 318 | 435 |

TOPSY-TURVY (Teenage)
R. B. Leffingwell Publ.: Apr, 1945

| 1-1st app. Cookie | 14 | 28 | 42 | 76 | 108 | 140 |

TOP TEN
America's Best Comics: Sept, 1999 - No. 12, Oct, 2001 ($3.50/$2.95)

1-Two covers by Ross and Ha/Cannon; Alan Moore-s/Gene Ha-a						3.50
2-11-($2.95)						3.00
12-($3.50)						3.50
Hardcover ('00, $24.95) Dust jacket with Gene Ha-a; r/#1-7						25.00
Softcover ('00, $14.95) new Gene Ha-c; r/#1-7						15.00
Book 2 HC ('02, $24.95) Dust jacket with Gene Ha-a; r/#8-12						25.00
Book 2 SC ('03, $14.95) new Gene Ha-c; r/#8-12						15.00
...: The Forty-Niners HC (2005, $24.99, dust jacket) prequel set in 1949; Moore-s/Ha-a						25.00

TOP TEN: BEYOND THE FARTHEST PRECINCT
America's Best Comics: Oct, 2005 - No. 5, Feb, 2006 ($2.99, limited series)

| 1-5-Jerry Ordway-a/Paul DiFilippo-s | | | | | | 3.00 |
| TPB (2006, $14.99) r/series; cover sketch pages | | | | | | 15.00 |

TOR (Prehistoric Life on Earth) (Formerly One Million Years Ago)
St. John Publ. Co.: No. 2, Oct, 1953; No. 3, May, 1954 - No. 5, Oct, 1954

3-D 2(10/53)-Kubert-c/a	14	28	42	76	108	140
3-D 2(10/53)-Oversized, otherwise same contents	12	24	36	67	94	120
3-D 2(11/53)-Kubert-c/a; has 3-D cover	12	24	36	67	94	120
3-5-Kubert-c/a: 3-Danny Dreams by Toth; Kubert 1 pg. story (w/self portrait)	14	28	42	76	108	140
NOTE: The two October 3-D's have same contents and Powell art; the October & November issues are titled 3-D Comics. All 3-D issues are 25¢ and came with 3-D glasses.

TOR (See Sojourn)
National Periodical Publications: May-June, 1975 - No. 6, Mar-Apr, 1976

| 1-New origin by Kubert | 2 | 4 | 6 | 8 | 10 | 12 |
| 2-6: 2-Origin-r/St. John #1 | | | | | | 6.00 |
NOTE: Kubert a-1, 2-6r; c-1-6. Toth a(p)-3r.

TOR (3-D)
Eclipse Comics: July, 1986 - No. 2, Aug, 1987 ($2.50)

| 1,2: 1-r/One Million Years Ago. 2-r/Tor 3-D #2 | | | | | | 5.00 |
| ...2-D: 1,2-Limited signed & numbered editions | 1 | 2 | 3 | 4 | 5 | 7 |

TOR
Marvel Comics (Epic Comics/Heavy Hitters): June, 1993 - No. 4, 1993 ($5.95, limited series)

| 1-4: Joe Kubert-c/a/scripts | | | | | | 6.00 |

TOR BY JOE KUBERT
DC Comics: 2001 - 2003 ($49.95, hardcovers with dust jacket)

Volume 1 (2001) r/One Million Years Ago #1 & 3-D Comics #1&2 in flat color; script pages, sketch pages, proposals for TV and newspapers strips; intro. by Roy Thomas						50.00
Volume 2 (2002) r/Tor (St. John) #3-5; Danny Dreams; portfolio section						50.00
Volume 3 (2003) r/Tor (DC '75) #1; (Marvel '93) #1-4; portfolio section						50.00

TORCH OF LIBERTY SPECIAL
Dark Horse Comics (Legend): Jan, 1995 ($2.50, one-shot)

| 1-Byrne scripts | | | | | | 2.50 |

TORCHY (...Blonde Bombshell) (See Dollman, Military, & Modern)
Quality Comics Group: Nov, 1949 - No. 6, Sept, 1950

1-Bill Ward-c, Gil Fox-a	159	318	477	994	1647	2300
2,3-Fox-c/a	68	136	204	425	705	985
4-Fox-c/a(3), Ward-a (9 pgs).	85	170	255	531	878	1225
5,6-Ward-c/a, 9 pgs; Fox-a(3) each	100	200	300	625	1038	1450
Super Reprint #16(1964)-r/#4 with new-c	10	20	30	60	93	125

TO RIVERDALE AND BACK AGAIN (Archie Comics Presents...)
Archie Comics: 1990 ($2.50, 68 pgs.)

| nn-Byrne-c, Colan-a(p); adapts NBC TV movie | | | | | | 5.00 |

TORMENTED, THE (Becomes Surprise Adventures #3 on)
Sterling Comics: July, 1954 - No. 2, Sept, 1954

| 1,2: Weird/horror stories | 26 | 52 | 78 | 152 | 239 | 325 |

TORNADO TOM (See Mighty Midget Comics)

TORSO (See Jinx: Torso)

TOTAL ECLIPSE
Eclipse Comics: May, 1988 - No. 5, Apr, 1989 ($3.95, 52 pgs., deluxe size)

| Book 1-5: 3-Intro/1st app. new Black Terror. 4-Many copies have upside down pages and are mis-cut | | | | | | 4.00 |

TOTAL ECLIPSE
Image Comics: July, 1998 (one-shot)

| 1-McFarlane-c; Eclipse Comics character pin-ups by Image artists | | | | | | 2.50 |

TOTAL ECLIPSE: THE SERAPHIM OBJECTIVE
Eclipse Comics: Nov, 1988 ($1.95, one-shot, Baxter paper)

| 1-Airboy, Valkyrie, The Heap app. | | | | | | 3.00 |

TOTAL JUSTICE
DC Comics: Oct, 1996 - No. 3, Nov, 1996 ($2.25, bi-weekly limited series) (Based on toyline)

| 1-3 | | | | | | 2.50 |

TOTAL RECALL (Movie)
DC Comics: 1990 ($2.95, 68 pgs., movie adaptation, one-shot)

| 1-Arnold Schwarzenegger photo-c | | | | | | 3.00 |

TOTAL WAR (M.A.R.S. Patrol #3 on)
Gold Key: July, 1965 - No. 2, Oct, 1965 (Painted-c)

| 1-Wood-a in both issues | 7 | 14 | 21 | 45 | 73 | 100 |
| 2 | 5 | 10 | 15 | 35 | 55 | 75 |

TOTEMS (Vertigo V2K)
DC Comics (Vertigo): Feb, 2000 ($5.95, one-shot)

| 1-Swamp Thing, Animal Man, Zatanna, Shade app.; Fegredo-c | | | | | | 6.00 |

TO THE HEART OF THE STORM
Kitchen Sink Press: 1991 (B&W, graphic novel)

Softcover-Will Eisner-s/a/c						15.00
Hardcover ($24.95)						25.00
TPB-(DC Comics, 9/00, $14.95) reprints 1991 edition						15.00

TO THE LAST MAN (See Zane Grey Four Color #616)

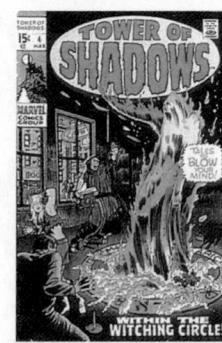

Tower of Shadows #4 © MAR

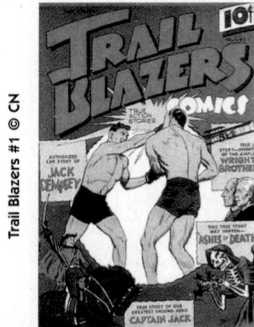

Trail Blazers #1 © CN

Transformers #63 © Hasbro

	GD 2.0	VG 4.0	FN 6.0	VF 8.0	VF/NM 9.0	NM- 9.2

TOUCH OF SILVER, A
Image Comics: Jan, 1997 - No. 6, Nov, 1997 ($2.95, B&W, bi-monthly)

1-6-Valentino-s/a; photo-c: 5-color pgs. w/Round Table		3.00
TPB ($12.95) r/#1-6		13.00

TOUGH KID SQUAD COMICS
Timely Comics (TCI): Mar, 1942

	GD	VG	FN	VF	VF/NM	NM-
1-(Scarce)-Origin & 1st app.The Human Top & The Tough Kid Squad; The Flying Flame app.	954	1908	2862	6678	11,689	16,700

TOWER OF SHADOWS (Creatures on the Loose #10 on)
Marvel Comics Group: Sept, 1969 - No. 9, Jan, 1971

	GD	VG	FN	VF	VF/NM	NM-
1-Romita-c, classic Steranko-a; Craig-a(p)	7	14	21	49	80	110
2,3: 2-Neal Adams-a. 3-Barry Smith, Tuska-a	4	8	12	26	41	55
4,6: 4-Marie Severin-c. 6-Wood-a	4	8	12	22	34	45
5-B. Smith-a(p), Wood-a; Wood draws himself (1st pg., 1st panel)	4	8	12	23	36	48
7-9: 7-B. Smith-a(p), Wood-a. 8-Wood-a/Wrightson-c. 9-Wrightson-c; Roy Thomas app.	4	8	12	26	41	55
Special 1(12/71, 52 pgs.)-Neal Adams-a; Romita-c	4	8	12	22	34	45

NOTE: *J. Buscema a-1p, 2p, Special 1r. Colan a-3p, 6p, Special 1. J. Craig a(r)-1p. Ditko a-6, 8, 9r, Special 1. Everett a-9(i)r; c-5i. Kirby a-5(p)r. Severin c-5p, 6. Steranko a-1p. Tuska a-3. Wood a-5-8. Issues 1-9 contain new stories with some pre-Marvel age reprints in 6-9. H. P. Lovecraft adaptation-9.*

TOXIC AVENGER (Movie)
Marvel Comics: Apr, 1991 - No. 11, Feb, 1992 ($1.50)

1-11: Based on movie character. 3,10-Photo-c		2.50

TOXIC CRUSADERS (TV)
Marvel Comics: May, 1992 - No. 8, Dec, 1992 ($1.25)

1-8: 1-3,8-Sam Kieth-c; based on USA network cartoon		2.50

TOXIC GUMBO
DC Comics (Vertigo): 1998 ($5.95, one-shot, mature)

1-McKeever-a/Lydia Lunch-s		6.00

TOXIN (Son of Carnage)
Marvel Comics: June, 2005 - No. 6, Nov, 2005 ($2.99, limited series)

1-6-Milligan-s/Robertson-a; Spider-Man app.		3.00
....The Devil You Know TPB (2006, $17.99) r/#1-6		18.00

TOYBOY
Continuity Comics: Oct, 1986 - No. 7, Mar, 1989 ($2.00, Baxter paper)

1-7		3.00

NOTE: *N. Adams a-1; c-1, 2,5. Golden a-7p; c-6,7. Nebres a(i)-1,2.*

TOYLAND COMICS
Fiction House Magazines: Jan, 1947 - No. 2, Mar, 1947; No. 3, July, 1947

	GD	VG	FN	VF	VF/NM	NM-
1-Wizard of the Moon begins	30	60	90	174	275	375
2,3-Bob Lubbers-c. 3-Tuska-a	16	32	48	94	147	200

NOTE: *All above contain strips by Al Walker.*

TOY TOWN COMICS
Toytown/Orbit Publ./B. Antin/Swapper Quarterly: 1945 - No. 7, May, 1947

	GD	VG	FN	VF	VF/NM	NM-
1-Mertie Mouse; L. B. Cole-c/a; funny animal	40	80	120	380	380	520
2-L. B. Cole-a	23	46	69	135	213	290
3-7-L. B. Cole-a. 5-Wiggles the Wonderworm-c	20	40	60	117	184	250

TRAGG AND THE SKY GODS (See Gold Key Spotlight, Mystery Comics Digest #3,9 & Spine Tingling Tales)
Gold Key/Whitman No. 9: June, 1975 - No. 8, Feb, 1977; No. 9, May, 1982 (Painted-c #3-8)

	GD	VG	FN	VF	VF/NM	NM-
1-Origin	2	4	6	10	14	18
2-8: 4-Sabre-Fang app. 8-Ostellon app.	1	3	4	6	8	10
9-(Whitman, 5/82) r/#1	1	2	3	5	7	9

NOTE: *Santos a-1, 2, 9r; c-3-7. Spiegel a-3-8.*

TRAIL BLAZERS (Red Dragon #5 on)
Street & Smith Publications: 1941; No. 2, Apr, 1942 - No. 4, Oct, 1942
(True stories of American heroes)

	GD	VG	FN	VF	VF/NM	NM-
1-Life story of Jack Dempsey & Wright Brothers	35	70	105	201	318	435
2-Brooklyn Dodgers-c/story; Ben Franklin story	22	44	66	128	202	275
3,4: 3-Fred Allen, Red Barber, Yankees stories	20	40	60	117	184	250

TRAIL COLT (Also see Extra Comics & Manhunt!)
Magazine Enterprises: 1949 - No. 2, 1949

	GD	VG	FN	VF	VF/NM	NM-
nn(A-1 #24)-7 pg. Frazetta-a r-in Manhunt #13; Undercover Girl app.; The Red Fox by L. B. Cole; Ingels-c; Whitney-a (Scarce)	40	80	120	235	368	500
2(A-1 #26)-Undercover Girl; Ingels-c; L. B. Cole-a (6 pgs.)	31	62	93	178	282	385

TRAKK: MONSTER HUNTER (Stan Winston's...)
Image Comics: Sept, 2003 - Present ($2.95)

1,2-Two covers by Tan & Bisley; Tan-a		3.00

TRANSFORMERS, THE (TV)(See G.I. Joe and...)
Marvel Comics Group: Sept, 1984 - No. 80, July, 1991 (75¢/$1.00)

	GD	VG	FN	VF	VF/NM	NM-
1-Based on Hasbro Toys	2	4	6	11	16	20
2-5: 2-Golden-c. 3-(1/85) Spider-Man (black costume)-c/app. 4-Texeira-c; brief app. of Dinobots	2	4	6	8	10	12
6-10: 6-1st Josie Beller. 8-Dinobots 1st full app. 9-Circuit Breaker 1st full app. 10-Intro Constructicons	1	2	3	5	6	8
11-49: 11-1st app. Jetfire. 14-Jetfire becomes an Autobot; 1st app. of Grapple, Hoist, Smokescreen, Skids, and Tracks. 17-1st app. of Blaster, Powerglide, Cosmos, Seaspray, Warpath, Beachcomber, Preceptor, Straxus, Kickback, Bombshell, Shrapnel, Dirge, and Ramjet. 19-1st Omega Supreme. 21-1st app. of Aerialbots; 1st Slingshot; Circuit Breaker app. 22-Retells origin of Circuit Breaker, 1st Stunticons. 23-Battle at Statue of Liberty. 24-1st app. Protectobots, Combaticons; Optimus Prime killed. 25-1st Predacons. 26-Intro The Mechanic, Prime's Funeral. 27-1st Trypticon app.; Grimlock named new Autobot leader. 28-The Mechanic app. 29-Intro Scraplets, 1st app. of Triple Changers						5.00
50-60: 53-Jim Lee-a. 54-Intro Micromasters. 60-Brief 1st app. of Primus	1	2	3	5	6	8
61-70: 61-Origin of Cybertron and the Transformers, Unicron app.; app. of Primus, creator of the Transformers. 62-66 Matrix Quest 5-part series. 67-Jim Lee-c	2	4	6	8	10	12
71-77: 75-($1.50, 52 pgs.) (Low print run)	3	6	9	14	20	25
78,79 (Low print run)	3	6	9	18	27	35
80-Last issue	4	8	12	22	34	45

NOTE: *Second and third printings of most early issues (1-9?) exist and are worth less than originals. Was originally planned as a four issue mini-series. Wrightson a-64i(4 pgs.).*

TRANSFORMERS
IDW Publishing: No. 0, Oct, 2005 (99¢, one-shot)

0-Prelude to Transformers: Infiltration series; Furman-s/Su-a; 4 covers		2.50

TRANSFORMERS ARMADA (Continues as Transformers Energon with #19)
(Also see Promotional Comics section for FCBD Ed.)
Dreamwave Productions: July, 2002 - No. 18, Dec, 2003 ($2.95)

1-Sarracini-s/Raiz-a; wraparound gatefold-c		3.00
2-18		3.00
Vol. 1 TPB (2003, $13.95) r/#1-5		14.00
Vol. 2 TPB (2003, $15.95) r/#6-11		16.00

TRANSFORMERS ARMADA: MORE THAN MEETS THE EYE
Dreamwave Productions: Mar, 2004 - No. 3, May, 2004 ($4.95, limited series)

1-3-Pin-ups with tech info; art by Pat Lee & various		5.00

TRANSFORMERS, BEAST WARS: THE GATHERING
IDW Publishing: Feb, 2006 - No. 4, May, 2006 ($2.99, limited series)

1-4-Furman-s/Figueroa-a; mulitple covers on all		3.00
TPB (8/06, $17.99) r/series; sketch pages & gallery of covers and variants		18.00

TRANSFORMERS COMICS MAGAZINE (Digest)
Marvel Comics: Jan, 1987 - No. 10, July, 1988

	GD	VG	FN	VF	VF/NM	NM-
1,2-Spider-Man-c/s	2	4	6	9	12	15
3-10	2	4	6	8	10	12

TRANSFORMERS ENERGON (Continued from Transformers Armada #18)
Dreamwave Productions: No. 19, Jan, 2004 - No. 30, Dec, 2004 ($2.95)

19-30-Furman-s		3.00

TRANSFORMERS: ESCALATION
IDW Publishing: Nov, 2006 - No. 6, Apr, 2007 ($3.99, limited series)

1-6-Furman-s/Su-a; multiple covers		4.00

TRANSFORMERS: EVOLUTIONS - HEARTS OF STEEL
IDW Publishing: June, 2006 - No. 4, Sept, 2006 ($2.99, limited series)

1-4-Bumblebee meets John Henry in 1880s railroad times		3.00

TRANSFORMERS: GENERATION 1
Dreamwave Productions: Apr, 2002 - No. 6, Oct, 2002 ($2.95)

Preview- 6 pg. story; robot sketch pages; Pat Lee-a		2.00
1-Pat Lee-a; 2 wraparound covers by Lee		4.00
2-6: 2-Optimus Prime reactivated; 2 covers by Pat Lee		3.00
...Vol. 1 HC (2003, $49.95) r/#1-6; black hardcover with red foil lettering and art		50.00
...Vol. 1 TPB (2002, $17.95) r/#1-6 plus six page preview; 8 pg. preview of future issues		18.00

TRANSFORMERS: GENERATION 1 (Volume 2)
Dreamwave Productions: Apr, 2003 - No. 6, Sept, 2003 ($2.95)

Transformers: Generation 1 #1 © Hasbro

Transmetropolitan #15 © Ellis & Robertson

Trapped! #1 © HARV

	GD 2.0	VG 4.0	FN 6.0	VF 8.0	VF/NM 9.0	NM- 9.2

1-6: 1-Pat Lee-a; 2 wraparound gatefold covers by Lee — 3.00
1-($5.95) Chrome wraparound variant-c — 6.00
...Vol. 2 TPB (IDW Publ., 3/06, $19.99) r/#1-6 plus cover gallery — 20.00

TRANSFORMERS: GENERATION 1 (Volume 3)
Dreamwave Productions: No. 0, Dec, 2003 - Present ($2.95)
0-10: 0-Pat Lee-a. 1-Figueroa-a; wrapaound-c — 3.00

TRANSFORMERS: GENERATION 2
Marvel Comics: Nov, 1993 - No. 12, Oct, 1994 ($1.75)

	GD 2.0	VG 4.0	FN 6.0	VF 8.0	VF/NM 9.0	NM- 9.2
1-($2.95, 68 pgs.)-Collector's ed. w/bi-fold metallic-c	1	3	4	6	8	10

1-11: 1-Newsstand edition (68 pgs.). 2-G.I. Joe app., Snake-Eyes, Scarlett, Cobra
Commander app. 5-Red Alert killed, Optimus Prime gives Grimlock leadership of Autobots.

	GD 2.0	VG 4.0	FN 6.0	VF 8.0	VF/NM 9.0	NM- 9.2
6-G.I. Joe app.	1	2	3	4	5	7
12-($2.25, 52 pgs.)	1	3	4	6	8	10

TRANSFORMERS: GENERATIONS
IDW Publishing: Mar, 2006 - No. 12, Mar, 2007 ($1.99/$2.49/$3.99)
1,2: 1-R/Transformers #7 (1985); preview of Transformers, Beast Wars. 2-R/#13 — 2.50
3-10-($2.49) 3-R/Transformers #14 (1986). 4-6-Reprint #16-18. 7-R/#24 — 2.50
11,12-($3.99) — 4.00
Volume 1 (12/06, $19.99) r/#1-6; cover gallery — 20.00

TRANSFORMERS/G.I. JOE
Dreamwave Productions: Aug, 2003 - No. 6, Mar, 2004 ($2.95/$5.25)
1-Art & gatefold wraparound-c by Jae Lee; Ney Rieber-s; variant-c by Pat Lee — 3.00
1-($5.95) Holofoil wraparound-c by Norton — 6.00
2-6-Jae Lee-a/c — 3.00
TPB (8/04, $17.95) r/#1-6; cover gallery and sketch pages — 18.00

TRANSFORMERS/G.I. JOE: DIVIDED FRONT
Dreamwave Productions: Oct, 2004 ($2.95)
1-Art & gatefold wraparound-c by Pat Lee — 3.00

TRANSFORMERS: HEADMASTERS
Marvel Comics: July, 1987 - No. 4, Jan, 1988 ($1.00, limited series)
1-Springer, Akin, Garvey-a — 5.00
2-4-Springer-c on all — 4.00

TRANSFORMERS: INFILTRATION
IDW Publishing: Jan, 2006 - No. 6, June, 2006 ($2.99, limited series)
1-6-Furman-s/Su-a; multiple covers on all — 3.00
... Cover Gallery (8/06, $5.99) — 6.00

TRANSFORMERS: MEGATRON ORIGIN
IDW Publishing: May, 2007 - Present ($3.99, limited series)
1-Alex Milne-a; 2 covers — 4.00

TRANSFORMERS: MICROMASTERS
Dreamwave Productions: June, 2004 - No. 4 ($2.95, limited series)
1-4-Ruffolo-a; Pat Lee-c — 3.00

TRANSFORMERS: MORE THAN MEETS THE EYE
Dreamwave Productions: Apr, 2003 - No. 8, Nov, 2003 ($5.25)
1-8-Pin-ups with tech info on Autobots and Decepticons; art by Pat Lee & various — 5.25
Vol. 1,2 (2004, $24.95, TPB) 1-r/#1-4. 2-r/#5-8 — 25.00

TRANSFORMERS: MOVIE ADAPTATION (For the 2007 live action movie)
IDW Publishing: Jun, 2007 - No. 4, June, 2007 ($3.99, weekly limited series)
1-4: Wraparound covers on each; Milne-a — 4.00

TRANSFORMERS: MOVIE PREQUEL (For the 2007 live action movie)
IDW Publishing: Feb, 2007 - No. 4, May, 2007 ($3.99, limited series)
1-4: 1-Origin of the Transformers on Cybertron; multiple covers on each — 4.00
TPB (6/07, $19.99) r/series; gallery of covers and variants — 20.00

TRANSFORMERS: SPOTLIGHT
IDW Publishing: Sept, 2006 - Present ($3.99)
... Hot Rod (11/06); ... Kup (4/07); ... Nightbeat (10/06); ... Shockwave (9/06); ... Sixshot
(12/06); ... Soundwave (3/07); ... Ultra Magnus (1/07); multiple covers on each — 4.00

TRANSFORMERS: STORMBRINGER
IDW Publishing: Jul, 2006 - No. 4, Oct, 2006 ($2.99, limited series)
1-4-Furman-s/Figueroa-a; multiple covers on all — 3.00
TPB (2/07, $17.99) r/series; cover gallery and sketch pages — 18.00

TRANSFORMERS SUMMER SPECIAL
Dreamwave Productions: May, 2004 ($4.95)
1-Pat Lee-a; Figueroa-a — 5.00

TRANSFORMERS: TARGET 2006
IDW Publishing: Apr, 2007 - Present ($3.99, limited series)
1-3-Reprints from 1980s series; multiple covers on all — 4.00

TRANSFORMERS: THE ANIMATED MOVIE
IDW Publishing: Oct, 2006 - No. 4, Jan, 2007 ($3.99, limited series)
1-4-Adapts animated movie; Don Figueroa-a — 4.00

TRANSFORMERS, THE MOVIE
Marvel Comics Group: Dec, 1986 - No. 3, Feb, 1987 (75¢, limited series)
1-3-Adapts animated movie — 4.00

TRANSFORMERS: THE WAR WITHIN
Dreamwave Productions: Oct, 2002 - No. 6, Mar, 2003 ($2.95)
1-6-Furman-s/Figueroa-a. 1-Wraparound gatefold-c — 3.00
TPB (2003, $15.95) r/#1-6; plus cover gallery — 16.00

TRANSFORMERS UNIVERSE
Marvel Comics Group: Dec, 1986 - No. 4, Mar, 1987 ($1.25, limited series)
1-4-A guide to all characters — 5.00
TPB-r/#1-4 — 10.00

TRANSFORMERS WAR WITHIN: THE AGE OF WRATH
Dreamwave Productions: Sept, 2004 - No. 6 ($2.95, limited series)
1-3-Furman-s/Ng-a — 3.00

TRANSFORMERS WAR WITHIN: THE DARK AGES
Dreamwave Productions: Oct, 2003 - No. 6 ($2.95)
1-6: 1-Furman-s/Wildman-a; two covers by Pat Lee & Figueroa — 3.00
TPB (2004, $17.95) r/#1-6; plus cover gallery and design sketches — 18.00

TRANSIT
Vortex Publ.: March, 1987 - No. 5, Nov, 1987 (B&W)

	GD 2.0	VG 4.0	FN 6.0	VF 8.0	VF/NM 9.0	NM- 9.2
1-5-Ted McKeever-s/a	1	2	3	5	6	8

TRANSMETROPOLITAN
DC Comics (Vertigo): Sept, 1997 - No. 60, Nov, 2002 ($2.50)

	GD 2.0	VG 4.0	FN 6.0	VF 8.0	VF/NM 9.0	NM- 9.2
1-Warren Ellis-s/Darick Robertson-a(p)	2	4	6	8	10	12
2,3	1	2	3	4	5	7
4-8						4.00
9-60: 15-Jae Lee-c. 25-27-Jim Lee-c. 37-39-Bradstreet-c						2.50

Back on the Street ('97, $7.95) r/#1-3 — 8.00
Dirge ('03, $14.95) r/#43-48 — 15.00
Filth of the City ('01, $5.95) Spider's columns with pin-up art by various — 6.00
Gouge Away ('02, $14.95) r/#31-36 — 15.00
I Hate It Here ('00, $5.95) Spider's columns with pin-up art by various — 6.00
Lonely City ('01, $14.95) r/#25-30; intro. by Patrick Stewart — 15.00
Lust For Life ('98, $14.95) r/#4-12 — 15.00
One More Time ('04, $14.95) r/#55-60 — 15.00
Spider's Thrash ('02, $14.95) r/#37-42; intro. by Darren Aronofsky — 15.00
Tales of Human Waste ('04, $9.95) r/Filth of the City, I Hate It Here & story from Vertigo
Winter's Edge 2 — 10.00
The Cure ('03, $14.95) r/#49-54 — 15.00
The New Scum ('00, $12.95) r/#19-24 & Vertigo: Winter's Edge #3 — 13.00
Year of the Bastard ('99, $12.95) r/#13-18 — 13.00

TRANSMUTATION OF IKE GARUDA, THE
Marvel Comics (Epic Comics): July, 1991 - No. 2, 1991 ($3.95, 52 pgs.)
1,2 — 4.00

TRAPMAN
Phantom Comics: June, 1994 - No. 2, 1994? ($2.95, quarterly, unfinished limited series)
1,2 — 3.00

TRAPPED!
Periodical House Magazines (Ace): Oct, 1954 - No. 4, April, 1955

	GD 2.0	VG 4.0	FN 6.0	VF 8.0	VF/NM 9.0	NM- 9.2
1 (All reprints)	10	20	30	54	72	90
2-4: 4-r/Men Against Crime #4 in its entirety	7	14	21	35	43	50

NOTE: Colan a-1, 4. Sekowsky a-1.

TRASH
Trash Publ. Co.: Mar, 1978 - No. 4, Oct, 1978 (B&W, magazine, 52 pgs.)

	GD 2.0	VG 4.0	FN 6.0	VF 8.0	VF/NM 9.0	NM- 9.2
1,2: 1-Star Wars parody. 2-UFO-c	2	4	6	9	13	16
3-Parodies of KISS, the Beatles, and monsters	2	4	6	13	18	22
4-(84 pgs.)-Parodies of Happy Days, Rocky movies	3	6	9	14	19	24

TRAVELS OF JAIMIE McPHEETERS, THE (TV)
Gold Key: Dec, 1963

Treasure Chest V1 #1 © George A. Pflaum

Treasure Comics #7 © Prize

Treehouse of Horror #6 © Bongo

	GD 2.0	VG 4.0	FN 6.0	VF 8.0	VF/NM 9.0	NM- 9.2
1-Kurt Russell photo on-c plus photo back-c	4	8	12	23	36	48

TREASURE CHEST (Catholic Guild; also see Topix)
George A. Pflaum: 3/12/46 - V27#8, July, 1972 (Educational comics)
(Not published during Summer)

	GD 2.0	VG 4.0	FN 6.0	VF 8.0	VF/NM 9.0	NM- 9.2
V1#1	27	54	81	158	249	340
2-6 (5/21/46): 5-Dr. Styx app. by Baily	14	28	42	80	115	150
V2#1-20 (9/3/46-5/27/47)	11	22	33	60	83	105
V3#1-5,7-20 (1st slick cover)	10	20	30	54	72	90
V3#6-Jules Verne's "Voyage to the Moon"	11	22	33	64	90	115
V4#1-20 (9/9/48-5/31/49)	9	18	27	47	61	75
V5#1-20 (9/6/49-5/31/50)	8	16	24	44	57	70
V6#1-20 (9/14/50-5/31/51)	8	16	24	42	54	65
V7#1-20 (9/13/51-6/5/52)	8	16	24	40	50	60
V8#1-20 (9/11/52-6/4/53)	7	14	21	37	46	55
V9#1-20 ('53-'54), V10#1-20 ('54-'55)	7	14	21	35	43	50
V11('55-'56), V12('56-'57)	6	12	18	29	36	42
V13#1,3-5,7,9-V17#1 ('57-'63)	6	12	18	27	33	38
V13#2,6,8-Ingels-a	6	12	18	41	66	90
V17#2- "This Godless Communism" series begins(not in odd #'d issues); cover shows hammer & sickle over Statue of Liberty; 8 pg. Crandall-a of family life under communism	17	34	51	128	227	325
V17#3,5,7,9,11,13,15,17,19	3	6	9	16	23	30
V17#4,6,14- "This Godless Communism" stories	12	26	39	93	164	235
V17#8-Shows red octopus encompassing Earth, firing squad; 8 pg. Crandall-a	15	30	45	107	191	275
V17#10- "This Godless Communism" - how Stalin came to power, part I; Crandall-a	14	28	42	102	181	260
V17#12-Stalin in WWII, forced labor, death by exhaustion; Crandall-a	14	28	42	102	181	260
V17#17-Kruschev takes over; de-Stalinization	14	28	42	102	181	260
V17#18-Kruschev's control; murder of revolters, brainwash, space race by Crandall	14	28	42	102	181	260
V17#20-End of series; Kruschev-people are puppets, firing squads hammer & sickle over Statue of Liberty, snake around communist manifesto by Crandall	16	32	48	118	209	300
V18#1-20, V19#11-20, V20#1-20(1964-65): V18#11-Crandall draws himself & 13 other artists on cover	3	6	9	16	22	28
V18#5- "What About Red China?" - describes how communists took over China	7	14	21	50	83	115
V19#1-10- "Red Victim" anti-communist series in all	7	14	21	50	83	115
V21-V25(1965-70)-(two V24#5's 11/7/68 & 11/21/68) (no V24#6)	3	6	9	14	19	24
V26, V27#1-8 (V26,27-68 pgs.)	3	6	9	16	22	28
Summer Edition V1#1-6('66), V2#1-6('67)	3	6	9	16	23	30

NOTE: *Anderson* a-V18#13. *Borth* a-V7#10-19 (serial), V8#8-17 (serial), V9#1-10 (serial), V13#2, 6, 11, V14-V25 (except V22#1-3, 11-13), Summer Ed. V1#3-6. *Crandall* a-V16#7, 9, 12, 14, 16-18, 20; V17#1, 2, 4-6, 10, 12, 14, 16-18, 20; V18#1, 2, 3(2 pg.), 7, 9-20; V19#4, 11, 13, 16, 19, 20; V20#1, 2, 4, 6, 8-10, 12, 14-16, 18, 20; V21#1-5, 8-11, 13, 16-18; V22#3, 7, 9-11, 14; V23#3, 6, 9, 16, 18; V24#7, 8, 10, 13, 16; V25#8, 16; V27#1-7r; 8r(2 pg.), Summer Ed. V1#3-5, V2#3; c-V16#7, V18#2(part), 7, 11, V19#4, 19, 20, V20#15, V21#5, 9, V22#3, 7, 9, 11, V23#9, 16, V24#13, 16, V25#8, Summer Ed. V1#2 (back c-V1#2-5). *Powell* a-V10#11. V19#11, 15, V10#13, V13#6, 8 all have wraparound covers.

TREASURE CHEST OF THE WORLD'S BEST COMICS
Superior, Toronto, Canada: 1945 (500 pgs., hard-c)

	GD 2.0	VG 4.0	FN 6.0	VF 8.0	VF/NM 9.0	NM- 9.2
Contains Blue Beetle, Captain Combat, John Wayne, Dynamic Man, Nemo, Li'l Abner; contents can vary - represents random binding of extra books; Capt. America on-c	90	180	270	563	932	1300

TREASURE COMICS
Prize Publications? (no publisher listed): No date (1943) (50¢, 324 pgs., cardboard-c)

	GD 2.0	VG 4.0	FN 6.0	VF 8.0	VF/NM 9.0	NM- 9.2
1-(Rare)-Contains rebound Prize Comics #7-11 from 1942 (blank inside-c)	248	496	744	1550	2575	3600

TREASURE COMICS
Prize Publ. (American Boys' Comics): June-July, 1945 - No. 12, Fall, 1947

	GD 2.0	VG 4.0	FN 6.0	VF 8.0	VF/NM 9.0	NM- 9.2
1-Paul Bunyan & Marco Polo begin; Highwayman & Carrot Topp only app.; Kiefer-a	48	96	144	293	484	675
2-Arabian Knight, Gorilla King, Dr. Styx begin	28	56	84	162	256	350
3,4,9,12: 9-Kiefer-a	22	44	66	128	202	275
5-Marco Polo-c; Krigstein-a	28	56	84	162	256	350
6,11-Krigstein-a; 11-Krigstein-c	27	54	81	156	246	335
7,8-Frazetta-a (5 pgs. each). 7-Capt. Kidd Jr. app.	41	82	123	250	400	550
10-Simon & Kirby-c/a	36	72	108	208	329	450

NOTE: *Barry* a-9-11; c-12. *Kiefer* a-3, 5, 7; c-2, 6, 7. *Roussos* a-11.

TREASURE ISLAND (See Classics Illustrated #64, Doc Savage Comics #1, King Classics, Movie Classics & Movie Comics)

Dell Publishing Co.: No. 624, Apr, 1955 (Disney)

	GD 2.0	VG 4.0	FN 6.0	VF 8.0	VF/NM 9.0	NM- 9.2
Four Color 624-Movie, photo-c	8	16	24	54	90	125

TREASURY OF COMICS
St. John Publishing Co.: 1947: No. 2, July, 1947 - No. 4, Sept, 1947; No. 5, Jan, 1948

	GD 2.0	VG 4.0	FN 6.0	VF 8.0	VF/NM 9.0	NM- 9.2
nn(#1)-Abbie an' Slats (nn on-c, #1 on inside)	14	28	42	80	115	150
2-Jim Hardy Comics; featuring Windy & Paddles	11	22	33	62	86	110
3-Bill Bumlin	10	20	30	54	72	90
4-Abbie an' Slats	11	22	33	62	86	110
5-Jim Hardy Comics #1	11	22	33	62	86	110

TREASURY OF COMICS
St. John Publishing Co.: Mar, 1948 - No. 5, 1948 (Reg. size); 1948-1950
(Over 500 pgs., $1.00)

	GD 2.0	VG 4.0	FN 6.0	VF 8.0	VF/NM 9.0	NM- 9.2
1	19	38	57	112	176	240
2(#2 on-c, #1 on inside)	12	24	36	67	94	120
3-5	10	20	30	56	76	95
1-(1948, 500 pgs., hard-c)-Abbie & Slats, Abbott & Costello, Casper, Little Annie Rooney, Little Audrey, Jim Hardy, Ella Cinders (16 books bound together) (Rare)	121	242	363	756	1253	1750
1(1949, 500 pgs.)-Same format as above	110	220	330	688	1144	1600
1(1950, 500 pgs.)-Same format as above; different-c; (also see Little Audrey Yearbook) (Rare)	110	220	330	688	1144	1600

TREASURY OF DOGS, A (See Dell Giants)

TREASURY OF HORSES, A (See Dell Giants)

TREEHOUSE OF HORROR (Bart Simpson's...)
Bongo Comics: 1995 - Present ($2.95/$2.50/$3.50/$4.50/$4.99, annual)

	NM- 9.2
1-(1995, $2.95)-Groening-c; Allred, Robinson & Smith stories	3.50
2-(1996, $2.50)-Stories by Dini & Bagge; infinity-c by Groening	3.00
3-(1997, $2.50)-Dorkin-s/Groening-c	3.00
4-(1998, $2.50)-Lash & Dixon-s/Groening-c	3.00
5-(1999, $3.50)-Thompson-s; Shaw & Aragonés-s/a; TenNapel-s/a	3.50
6-(2000, $4.50)-Mahfood-s; DeCarlo-a; Morse-s/a; Kuper-s/a	4.50
7-(2001, $4.50)-Hamill-s/Morrison-a; Ennis-s/McCrea-a; Sakai-s/a; Nixey-s/a; Brereton back-c	4.50
8-(2002, $3.50)-Templeton, Shaw, Barta, Simone, Thompson-s/a	3.50
9-(2003, $4.99)-Lord of the Rings-Brereton-a; Dini, Naifeh, Millidge, Boothby, Noto-s/a	5.00
10-(2004, $4.99)-Monsters of Rock w/Alice Cooper, Gene Simmons, Rob Zombie and Pat Boone; art by Rodriguez, Morrison, Morse, Templeton	5.00
11-(2005, $4.99)-EC style w/art by John Severin, Angelo Torres & Al Williamson and flip book with Dracula by Wolfman/Colan and Squish Thing by Wein/Wrightson	5.00
12-(2006, $4.99)-Terry Moore, Kyle Baker, Eric Powell-s/a	5.00
13-(2007, $4.99)-Oswalt, Posehn, Lennon-s; Guerra, Austin, Barta, Rodriguez-a	5.00

TREKKER (See Dark Horse Presents #6)
Dark Horse Comics: May, 1987 - No. 6, Mar,1988 ($1.50, B&W)

	NM- 9.2
1-6: Sci/Fi stories	2.50
Color Special 1 (1989, $2.95, 52 pgs.)	3.00
Collection ($5.95, B&W)	6.00
Special 1 (6/99, $2.95, color)	3.00

TRENCHCOAT BRIGADE, THE
DC Comics (Vertigo): Mar, 1999 - No. 4, Jun, 1999 ($2.50, limited series)

	NM- 9.2
1-4: Hellblazer, Phantom Stranger, Mister E, Dr. Occult app.	2.50

TRENCHER (See Blackball Comics)
Image Comics: May, 1993 - No. 4, Oct, 1993 ($1.95, unfinished limited series)

	NM- 9.2
1-4: Keith Giffen-c/a/scripts. 3-Supreme-c/story	2.50

TRIALS OF SHAZAM!
DC Comics: Oct, 2006 - No. 12 ($2.99)

	NM- 9.2
1-7-Winick-s/Porter-a	3.00
... Volume 1 TPB (2007, $14.99) r/#1-6 and story from DCU Brave New World #1	15.00

TRIB COMIC BOOK, THE
Winnipeg Tribune: Sept. 24, 1977 - Vol. 4, #36, 1980 (8-1/2"x11", 24 pgs., weekly) (155 total issues)

	GD 2.0	VG 4.0	FN 6.0	VF 8.0	VF/NM 9.0	NM- 9.2
V1# 1-Color pages (Sunday strips)-Spiderman, Asterix, Disney's Scamp, Wizard of Id, Doonesbury, Inside Woody Allen, Mary Worth, & others (similar to Spirit sections)	2	4	6	10	14	18
V1#2-15, V2#1-52, V3#1-52, V4#1-33	2	4	6		8	10
V4#34-36 (not distributed)	2	4	6	11	16	20

NOTE: All issues have Spider-Man. Later issues contain Star Trek and Star Wars. 20 strips in ea. The first newspaper to put Sunday pages into a comic book format.

TRIBE (See WildC.A.T.S #4)

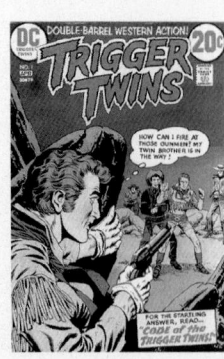

Trigger Twins #1 © DC

Trout #1 © Troy Nixey

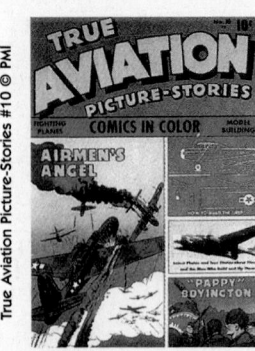

True Aviation Picture-Stories #10 © PMI

	GD 2.0	VG 4.0	FN 6.0	VF 8.0	VF/NM 9.0	NM- 9.2

Image Comics/Axis Comics No. 2 on: Apr, 1993; No. 2, Sept, 1993 - No. 3, 1994 ($2.50/$1.95)

1-By Johnson & Stroman; gold foil & embossed on black-c						2.50
1-($2.50)-Ivory Edition; gold foil & embossed on white-c; available only through the creators						2.50
2,3: 2-1st Axis Comics issue. 3-Savage Dragon app.						2.50

TRIBUTE TO STEVEN HUGHES, A
Chaos! Comics: Sept, 2000 ($6.95)

| 1-Lady Death & Evil Ernie pin-ups by various artists; testimonials | | | | | | 7.00 |

TRIGGER (See Roy Rogers'...)

TRIGGER
DC Comics (Vertigo): Feb, 2005 - No. 8, Sept, 2005 ($2.95/$2.99)

| 1-8-Jason Hall-s/John Watkiss-a/c | | | | | | 3.00 |

TRIGGER TWINS
National Periodical Publications: Mar-Apr, 1973 (20¢, one-shot)

| 1-Trigger Twins & Pow Wow Smith-r/All-Star Western #94,103 & Western Comics #81; Infantino-r(p) | 2 | 4 | 6 | 13 | 18 | 22 |

TRINITY (See DC Universe: Trinity)

TRINITY ANGELS
Acclaim Comics (Valiant Heroes): July, 1997 - No. 12, June, 1998 ($2.50)

| 1-12-Maguire-s/a(p):4-Copycat-c | | | | | | 3.00 |

TRIPLE GIANT COMICS (See Archie All-Star Specials under Archie Comics)

TRIPLE THREAT
Special Action/Holyoke/Gerona Publ.: Winter, 1945

| 1-Duke of Darkness, King O'Leary | 32 | 64 | 96 | 186 | 293 | 400 |

TRIPLE-X
Dark Horse Comics: Dec, 1994 - No. 7, June, 1995 ($3.95, B&W, limited series)

| 1-7 | | | | | | 4.00 |

TRIUMPH (Also see JLA #28-30, Justice League Task Force & Zero Hour)
DC Comics: June, 1995 - No. 4, Sept, 1995 ($1.75, limited series)

| 1-4: 3-Hourman, JLA app. | | | | | | 2.50 |

TRIUMPHANT UNLEASHED
Triumphant Comics: No. 0, Nov, 1993 - No. 1, Nov, 1993 ($2.50, lim. series)

| 0-Serially numbered, 0-Red logo, 0-White logo (no cover price; giveaway), 1-Cover is negative & reverse of #0-c | | | | | | 2.50 |

TROLL (Also see Brigade)
Image Comics (Extreme Studios): Dec, 1993 ($2.50, one-shot, 44 pgs.)

1-1st app. Troll; Liefeld scripts; Matsuda-c/a(p)						2.50
Halloween Special (1994, $2.95)-Maxx app.						3.00
...Once A Hero (8/94, $2.50)						2.50

TROLLORDS
Tru Studios/Comico V2#1 on: 2/86 - No. 15, 1988; V2#1, 11/88 - V2#4, 1989 (1-15: $1.50, B&W)

1-15: 1-Both printings. 6-Christmas issue; silver logo						2.50
V2#1-4 ($1.75, color, Comico)						2.50
Special 1 ($1.75, 2/87, color)-Jerry's Big Fun Bk.						2.50

TROLLORDS
Apple Comics: July, 1989 - No. 6, 1990 ($2.25, B&W, limited series)

| 1-6: 1-"The Big Batman Movie Parody" | | | | | | 2.50 |

TROLL PATROL
Harvey Comics: Jan, 1993 ($1.95, 52 pgs.)

| 1 | | | | | | 2.50 |

TROLL II (Also see Brigade)
Image Comics (Extreme Studios): July, 1994 ($3.95, one-shot)

| 1 | | | | | | 4.00 |

TRON (Based on the video game and film)
Slave Labor Graphics: Apr, 2006 - Present ($3.50)

| 1-4: 1-DeMartinis-a/Walker & Jones-s | | | | | | 3.50 |

TROUBLE
Marvel Comics (Epic): Sept, 2003 - No. 5, Jan, 2004 ($2.99, limited series)

| 1-5-Photo-c; Richard and Ben meet Mary and May; Millar-s/Dodson-a | | | | | | 3.00 |
| 1-2nd printing with variant Frank Cho-c | | | | | | 5.00 |

TROUBLED SOULS

	GD 2.0	VG 4.0	FN 6.0	VF 8.0	VF/NM 9.0	NM- 9.2

Fleetway: 1990 ($9.95, trade paperback)

| nn-Garth Ennis scripts & John McCrea painted-c/a. | | | | | | 10.00 |

TROUBLEMAKERS
Acclaim Comics (Valiant Heroes): Apr, 1997 - No. 19, June, 1998 ($2.50)

| 1-19: Fabian Nicieza scripts in all. 1-1st app. XL, Rebound & Blur; 2 covers. 8-Copycat-c. 12-Shooting of Parker | | | | | | 2.50 |

TROUBLE SHOOTERS, THE (TV)
Dell Publishing Co.: No. 1108, Jun-Aug, 1960

| Four Color 1108-Keenan Wynn photo-c | 5 | 10 | 15 | 35 | 55 | 75 |

TROUBLE WITH GIRLS, THE
Malibu Comics (Eternity Comics) #7-14/Comico V2#1-4/Eternity V2#5 on: 8/87 - #14, 1988; V2#1, 2/89 - V2#23, 1991? ($1.95, B&W/color)

1-14 ($1.95, B&W, Eternity)-Gerard Jones scripts & Tim Hamilton-c/a in all.						2.50
V2#1-23-Jones scripts, Hamilton-c/a.						2.50
Annual 1 (1988, $2.95)						3.00
Christmas Special 1 (12/91, $2.95, B&W, Eternity)-Jones scripts, Hamilton-c/a						3.00
Graphic Novel 1,2 (7/88, B&W)-r/#1-3 & #4-6						8.00

TROUBLE WITH GIRLS, THE: NIGHT OF THE LIZARD
Marvel Comics (Epic Comics/Heavy Hitters): 1993 - No. 4, 1993 ($2.50/$1.95, lim. series)

| 1-Embossed-c; Gerard Jones scripts & Bret Blevins-c/a in all | | | | | | 2.50 |
| 2-4: 2-Begin $1.95-c. | | | | | | 2.50 |

TROUT
Oni Press: Oct, 2001 - No. 2, Feb, 2002 ($2.95, B&W, limited series)

| 1,2-Troy Nixey-s/a | | | | | | 3.00 |

TRUE ADVENTURES (Formerly True Western)(Men's Adventures #4 on)
Marvel Comics (CCC): No. 3, May, 1950 (52 pgs.)

| 3-Powell, Sekowsky-a; Brodsky-c | 16 | 32 | 48 | 94 | 147 | 200 |

TRUE ANIMAL PICTURE STORIES
True Comics Press: Winter, 1947 - No. 2, Spring-Summer, 1947

| 1,2 | 10 | 20 | 30 | 56 | 76 | 95 |

TRUE AVIATION PICTURE STORIES (Becomes Aviation Adventures & Model Building #16 on)
Parents' Mag. Institute: 1942; No. 2, Jan-Feb, 1943 - No. 15, Sept-Oct, 1946

1-(#1 & 2 titled ...Aviation Comics Digest)(not digest size)	15	30	45	85	130	175
2	10	20	30	56	76	95
3-14: 3-10-Plane photos on-c. 11,13-Photo-c	9	18	27	50	65	80
15-(Titled "True Aviation Adventures & Model Building")	9	18	27	47	61	75

TRUE BRIDE'S EXPERIENCES (Formerly Teen-Age Brides)
(True Bride-To-Be Romances No. 17 on)
True Love (Harvey Publications): No. 8, Oct, 1954 - No. 16, Feb, 1956

8	9	18	27	50	65	80
9,10: 10-Last pre-code (2/55)	7	14	21	37	46	55
11-15	6	12	18	31	38	45
16-Last issue	7	14	21	37	46	55

NOTE: Powell a-8-10, 12, 13.

TRUE BRIDE-TO-BE ROMANCES (Formerly True Bride's Experiences)
Home Comics/True Love (Harvey): No. 17, Apr, 1956 - No. 30, Nov, 1958

17-S&K-c; Powell-a	10	20	30	56	76	95
18-20,22,25-28,30	6	12	18	31	38	45
21,23,24,29-Powell-a. 29-Baker-a (1 pg.)	7	14	21	35	43	50

TRUE COMICS (Also see Outstanding American War Heroes)
True Comics/Parents' Magazine Press: April, 1941 - No. 84, Aug, 1950

1-Marathon run story; life story Winston Churchill	31	62	93	178	282	385
2-Red Cross story; Everett-a	15	30	45	85	130	175
3-Baseball Hall of Fame story; Chiang Kai-Shek-c/s	17	34	51	100	158	215
4,5: 4-Story of American flag "Old Glory". 5-Life story of Joe Louis	14	28	42	80	115	150
6-Baseball World Series story	15	30	45	90	140	190
7-10: 7-Buffalo Bill story. 10,11-Teddy Roosevelt	11	22	33	62	86	110
11-14,16,18-20: 11-Thomas Edison, Douglas MacArthur stories. 13-Harry Houdini story. 14-Charlie McCarthy story. 18-Story of America begins, ends #26. 19-Eisenhower-c/s	10	20	30	54	72	90
15-Flag-c; Bob Feller story	10	20	30	58	79	100
17-Brooklyn Dodgers story	11	22	33	64	90	115

True Confidences #2 © FAW

True Crime Comics #5 © Magazine Villa

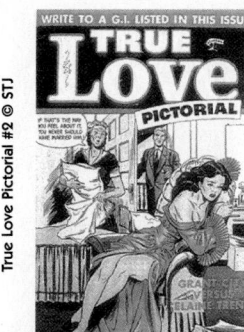

True Love Pictorial #2 © STJ

	GD 2.0	VG 4.0	FN 6.0	VF 8.0	VF/NM 9.0	NM- 9.2

21-30: 24-Marco Polo story. 28-Origin of Uncle Sam. 29-Beethoven story.

30-Cooper Brothers baseball story	9	18	27	47	61	75
31-Red Grange "Galloping Ghost" story	8	16	24	40	50	60

32-46: 33-Origin/1st app. Steve Saunders, Special Agent of the FBI, series begins.

35-Mark Twain story. 38-General Bradley-c/s. 39-FDR story. 44-Truman story.

46-George Gershwin story	7	14	21	37	46	55
47-Atomic bomb issue (c/story, 3/46)	10	20	30	56	76	95

48-54,56-65: 49-1st app. Secret Warriors. 53-Bobby Riggs story. 58-Jim Jeffries (boxer) story; Harry Houdini story. 59-Bob Hope story; pirates-c/s. 60-Speedway Speed Demon-c/story.

	7	14	21	35	43	50
55-(12/46)-1st app. Sad Sack by Baker (1/2 pg.)	9	18	27	47	61	75
66-Will Rogers-c/story	7	14	21	37	46	55

67-1st oversized issue (12/47); Steve Saunders, Special Agent begins

	8	16	24	42	54	65

68-70,74-77,79: 68-70,74-77-Features Steve Sanders True FBI advs.

68-Oversized; Admiral Byrd-c/s. 69-Jack Benny story. 74-Amos 'n' Andy story						
	6	12	18	31	38	45
71-Joe DiMaggio-c/story	9	18	27	47	61	75
72-Jackie Robinson story; True FBI advs.	8	16	24	40	50	60
73-Walt Disney's life story	9	18	27	47	61	75
78-Stan Musial-c/story; True FBI advs.	8	16	24	40	50	60

80-84 (Scarce)-All distr. to subscribers through mail only; paper-c. 80-Rocket trip to the moon

story. 81-Red Grange story	18	36	54	103	162	220

(Prices vary widely on issues 80-84)

NOTE: *Bob Kane* a-7. *Palais* a-80. *Powell* c/a-80. #80-84 have soft covers and combined with Tex Granger, Jack Armstrong, and Calling All Kids. #68-78 featured true FBI adventures.

TRUE COMICS AND ADVENTURE STORIES
Parents' Magazine Institute: 1965 (Giant) (25¢)

1,2: 1-Fighting Hero of Viet Nam; LBJ on-c	3	6	9	18	27	35

TRUE COMPLETE MYSTERY (Formerly Complete Mystery)
Marvel Comics (PrPI): No. 5, Apr, 1949 - No. 8, Oct, 1949

5	26	52	78	152	239	325
6-8: 6-8-Photo-c	20	40	60	117	184	250

TRUE CONFIDENCES
Fawcett Publications: 1949 (Fall) - No. 4, June, 1950 (All photo-c)

1-Has ad for Fawcett Love Adventures #1 but, publ. as Love Memoirs #1 as Marvel published the title first; Swayze-a	18	36	54	103	162	220
2-4: 3-Swayze-a. 4-Powell-a	11	22	33	64	90	115

TRUE CRIME CASES (…From Official Police Files)
St. John Publishing Co.: 1944 (25¢, 100 pg. Giant)

nn-Matt Baker-c	46	92	138	281	466	650

TRUE CRIME COMICS (Also see Complete Book of…)
Magazine Village: No. 2, May, 1947; No. 3, July-Aug, 1948 - No. 6, June-July, 1949; V2#1, Aug-Sept, 1949 (52 pgs.)

2-Jack Cole-c/a; used in SOTI, pgs. 81,82 have illo. "A sample of the injury-to-eye motif" & illo. "Dragging living people to death"; used in POP, pg. 105; "Murder, Morphine and Me" classic drug propaganda story used by N.Y. Legis. Comm.

	159	318	477	994	1647	2300
3-Classic Cole-c/a; drug story with hypo, opium den & with drawing addict	114	228	342	713	1182	1650

4-Jack Cole-c/a; c-taken from a story panel in #3 (r-(2) SOTI & POP stories/#2?)

	98	196	294	613	1019	1425

5-Jack Cole-c, Marijuana racket story (Canadian ed. w/cover similar to #3 exists w/out drug story)

	66	132	198	413	682	950

6-Not a reprint, original story (Canadian ed. reprints #4 w/different coloring on-c)

	53	106	159	323	537	750

V2#1-Used in SOTI, pgs. 81,82 have illo. "Dragging living people to death"; Toth, Wood (3 pgs.), Roussos-a; Cole-r from #2

	90	180	270	563	932	1300

NOTE: V2#1 was reprinted in Canada as V2#9 (12/49); same-c & contents minus Wood-a.

TRUE FAITH
Fleetway: 1990 ($9.95, graphic novel)

nn-Garth Ennis scripts	2	4	6	12	16	20
Reprinted by DC/Vertigo ('97, $12.95)						13.00

TRUE GHOST STORIES (See Ripley's…)

TRUE LIFE ROMANCES (…Romance on cover)
Ajax/Farrell Publications: Dec, 1955 - No. 3, Aug, 1956

1	10	20	30	58	79	100
2	8	16	24	40	50	60
3-Disbrow-a	8	16	24	44	57	70

TRUE LIFE SECRETS

Romantic Love Stories/Charlton: Mar-April, 1951 - No. 28, Sept, 1955; No. 29, Jan, 1956

1-Photo-c begin, end #3?	14	28	42	80	115	150
2	9	18	27	47	61	75
3-19: 12-"I Was An Escort Girl" story	8	16	24	40	50	60
20-29: 25-Last precode(3/55)	7	14	21	35	43	50

TRUE LIFE TALES (Formerly Mitzi's Romances #8?)
Marvel Comics (CCC): No. 8, Oct, 1949 - No. 2, Jan, 1950 (52 pgs.)

8(#1, 10/49), 2-Both have photo-c	11	22	33	62	86	110

TRUE LOVE
Eclipse Comics: Jan, 1986 - No. 2, Jan, 1986 ($2.00, Baxter paper)

1,2-Love stories reprinted from pre-code Standard Comics; Toth-a(p) in both;

1-Dave Stevens-c. 2-Mayo-a						3.00

TRUE LOVE CONFESSIONS
Premier Magazines: May, 1954 - No. 11, Jan, 1956

1-Marijuana story	13	26	39	72	101	130
2	8	16	24	42	54	65
3-11	7	14	21	37	46	55

TRUE LOVE PICTORIAL
St. John Publishing Co.: 1952 - No. 11, Aug, 1954

1-Only photo-c	18	36	54	105	165	225
2-Baker-c/a	26	52	78	152	239	325

3-5(All 25¢, 100 pgs.): 4-Signed story by Estrada. 5-(4/53)-Formerly Teen-Age Temptations; Kubert-a in #3; Baker-a in #3-5

	40	80	120	235	368	500
6,7: Baker-c/a; signed stories by Estrada	24	48	72	139	220	300
8,10,11-Baker-c/a	24	48	72	139	220	300
9-Baker-c	18	36	54	105	165	225

TRUE LOVE PROBLEMS AND ADVICE ILLUSTRATED (Becomes Romance Stories of True Love No. 45 on)
McCombs/Harvey Publ./Home Comics: June, 1949 - No. 6, Apr, 1950; No. 7, Jan, 1951 - No. 44, Mar, 1957

V1#1	15	30	45	86	133	180
2-Elias-c	10	20	30	54	72	90
3-10: 3,4,7-9-Elias-c	8	16	24	42	54	65
11-13,15-23,25-31: 31-Last pre-code (1/55)	7	14	21	35	43	50
14,24-Rape scene	7	14	21	37	46	55
32-37,39-44	6	12	18	29	36	42
38-S&K-c	9	18	27	52	69	85

NOTE: *Powell* a-1, 2, 7-14, 17-25, 28, 29, 33, 40, 41. #3 has *True Love*… on inside.

TRUE MOVIE AND TELEVISION (Part teenage magazine)
Toby Press: Aug, 1950 - No. 3, Nov, 1950; No. 4, Mar, 1951 (52 pgs.)(1-3: 10¢)

1-Elizabeth Taylor photo-c; Gene Autry, Shirley Temple app.						
	55	110	165	344	572	800

2-(9/50)-Janet Leigh/Liz Taylor/Ava Gardner & others photo-c; Frazetta John Wayne illo from J.Wayne Adv. Comics #2 (4/50)

	41	82	123	250	400	550

3-June Allyson photo-c; Montgomery Cliff, Esther Williams, Andrews Sisters app; Li'l Abner featured; Sadie Hawkins' Day

	31	62	93	178	282	385
4-Jane Powell photo-c (15¢)	19	38	57	112	176	240

NOTE: 16 pgs. in color, rest movie material in black & white.

TRUE SECRETS (Formerly Our Love?)
Marvel (IPS)/Atlas Comics (MPI) #4 on: No. 3, Mar, 1950; No. 4, Feb, 1951 - No. 40, Sept, 1956

3 (52 pgs.)(IPS one-shot)	14	28	42	82	121	160
4,5-7-10	9	18	27	52	69	85
6,22-Everett-a	11	22	33	62	86	110
11-20	9	18	27	47	61	75
21,23-28: 24-Colletta-c. 28-Last pre-code (2/55)	8	16	24	42	54	65
29-40: 34,36-Colletta-a	8	16	24	40	50	60

TRUE SPORT PICTURE STORIES (Formerly Sport Comics)
Street & Smith Publications: V1#5, Feb, 1942 - V5#2, July-Aug, 1949

V1#5-Joe DiMaggio-c/story	37	74	111	214	340	465
6-12 (1942-43): 12-Jack Dempsey story	21	42	63	122	191	260

V2#1-12 (1943-45): 7-Stan Musial-c/story; photo story of the New York Yankees

	20	40	60	117	184	250

V3#1-12 (1946-47): 7-Joe DiMaggio, Stan Musial, Bob Feller & others back from the armed service story. 8-Billy Conn vs. Joe Louis-c/story

	19	38	57	109	172	235
V4#1-12 (1948-49) V5#1,2	18	36	54	105	165	225

NOTE: *Powell* a-V3#10, V4#1-4, 6-8, 10-12; V5#1, 2; c-V3#11, 12, V4#3-7, 9-12. *Ravielli* c-V5#2.

TRUE STORIES OF ROMANCE

True-To-Life Romances #12 © QUA

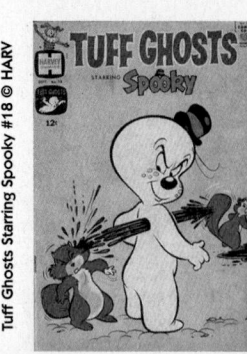
Tuff Ghosts Starring Spooky #18 © HARV

Turok, Dinosaur Hunter #4 © Acclaim

	GD 2.0	VG 4.0	FN 6.0	VF 8.0	VF/NM 9.0	NM- 9.2		GD 2.0	VG 4.0	FN 6.0	VF 8.0	VF/NM 9.0	NM- 9.2
Fawcett Publications: Jan, 1950 - No. 3, May, 1950 (All photo-c)							**TPB** (2004, $17.99) r/series						18.00
1	14	28	42	80	115	150	**TRY-OUT WINNER BOOK**						
2,3: 3-Marcus Swayze-a	10	20	30	58	79	100	**Marvel Comics:** Mar, 1988						
TRUE STORY OF JESSE JAMES, THE (See Jesse James, Four Color 757)							1-Spider-Man vs. Doc Octopus						5.00
TRUE SWEETHEART SECRETS							**TSR WORLD** (...Annual on cover only)						
Fawcett Publications: 5/50; No. 2, 7/50; No. 3, 1951(nd); No. 4, 9/51 - No. 11, 1/53 (All photo-c)							**DC Comics:** 1990 ($3.95, 84 pgs.)						
1-Photo-c; Debbie Reynolds?	15	30	45	88	137	185	1-Advanced D&D, ForgottenRealms, Dragonlance & 1st app. Spelljammer						4.00
2-Wood-a (11 pgs.)	18	36	54	105	165	225	**TSUNAMI GIRL**						
3-11: 4,5-Powell-a. 8-Marcus Swayze-a. 11-Evans-a							**Image Comics:** 1999 - No. 3, 1999 ($2.95)						
	11	22	33	64	90	115	1-3-Sorayama-c/Paniccia-s/a						3.00
TRUE TALES OF LOVE (Formerly Secret Story Romances)							**TUBBY** (See Marge's...)						
Atlas Comics (TCI): No. 22, April, 1956 - No. 31, Sept, 1957							**TUFF GHOSTS STARRING SPOOKY**						
22	10	20	30	54	72	90	**Harvey Publications:** July, 1962 - No. 39, Nov, 1970; No. 40, Sept, 1971 - No. 43, Oct, 1972						
23-24,26-31-Colletta-a in most:	8	16	24	40	50	60	1-12¢ issues begin	12	24	36	82	146	210
25-Everett-a; Colletta-a	8	16	24	44	57	70	2-5	7	14	21	45	73	100
TRUE TALES OF ROMANCE							6-10	5	10	15	32	51	70
Fawcett Publications: No. 4, June, 1950							11-20	4	8	12	24	37	50
4-Photo-c	10	20	30	54	72	90	21-30: 29-Hot Stuff/Spooky team-up story	3	6	9	16	23	30
TRUE 3-D							31-39,43	2	4	6	13	18	22
Harvey Publications: Dec, 1953 - No. 2, Feb, 1954 (25¢)(Both came with 2 pair of glasses)							40-42: 52 pg. Giants	3	6	9	14	20	25
1-Nostrand, Powell-a	5	10	15	35	55	75	**TUFFY**						
2-Powell-a	6	12	18	37	59	80	**Standard Comics:** No. 5, July, 1949 - No. 9, Oct, 1950						
NOTE: Many copies of #1 surfaced in 1984.							5-All by Sid Hoff	7	14	21	35	43	50
TRUE-TO-LIFE ROMANCES (Formerly Guns Against Gangsters)							6-9	5	10	15	23	28	32
Star Publ.: #8, 11-12/49; #9, 1-2/50; #3, 4/50 - #5, 9/50; #6, 1/51 - #23, 10/54							**TUFFY TURTLE**						
8(#1, 1949)	24	48	72	139	220	300	**I. W. Enterprises:** No date						
9(#2),4-10	17	34	51	100	158	215	1-Reprint	2	4	6	8	11	14
3-Janet Leigh/Glenn Ford photo on-c plus true life story of each							**TUG & BUSTER**						
	19	38	57	109	172	235	**Art & Soul Comics:** Nov, 1995 - No. 7, Feb, 1998 ($2.95, B&W, bi-monthly)						
11,22,23	15	30	45	86	133	180	1-7: Marc Hempel-c/a/scripts						3.00
12-14,17-21-Disbrow-a	16	32	48	94	147	200	1-(Image Comics, 8/98, $2.95, B&W)						3.00
15,16-Wood & Disbrow-a in each	19	38	57	109	169	235	**TUROK**						
NOTE: Kamen a-13. Kamen/Feldstein a-14. All have L.B. Cole covers.							**Acclaim Comics:** Mar, 1998 - No. 4, Jun, 1998 ($2.50)						
TRUE WAR EXPERIENCES							1-4-Nicieza-s/Kayanan-a						2.50
Harvey Publications: Aug, 1952 - No. 4, Dec, 1952							..., Child of Blood 1 (1/98, $3.95) Nicieza-s/Kayanan-a						4.00
1	8	16	24	56	93	130	... Evolution 1 (8/02, $2.50) Nicieza-s/Kayanan-a						2.50
2-4	5	10	15	32	51	70	..., Redpath 1 (10/97, $3.95) Nicieza-s/Kayanan-a						4.00
TRUE WAR ROMANCES (Becomes Exotic Romances #22 on)							... / Shadowman 1 (2/99, $3.95) Priest-s/Broome & Jimenez-a						4.00
Quality Comics Group: Sept, 1952 - No. 21, June, 1955							...: Spring Break in the Lost Land 1 (7/97, $3.95) Nicieza-s/Kayanan-a						4.00
1-Photo-c	14	28	42	76	108	140	...: Tales of the Lost Land 1 (4/98, $3.95)						4.00
2	8	16	24	44	57	70	...: The Empty Souls 1 (4/97, $3.95) Nicieza-s/Kayanan-a; variant-c						4.00
3-10: 9-Whitney-a	8	16	24	40	50	60	**TUROK, DINOSAUR HUNTER** (See Magnus Robot Fighter #12 & Archer & Armstrong #2)						
11-21: 20-Last precode (4/55). 14-Whitney-a	7	14	21	35	43	50	**Valiant/Acclaim Comics:** June, 1993 - No. 47, Aug, 1996 ($2.50)						
TRUE WAR STORIES (See Ripley's...)							1-($3.50)-Chromium & foil-c						3.50
TRUE WESTERN (True Adventures #3)							1-Gold foil-c variant						5.00
Marvel Comics (MMC): Dec, 1949 - No. 2, March, 1950							0, 2-47: 4-Andar app. 5-Death of Andar. 7-9-Truman/Glanzman-a. 11-Bound-in trading card.						
1-Photo-c; Billy The Kid story	16	32	48	94	147	200	16-Chaos Effect						2.50
2-Alan Ladd photo-c	20	40	60	115	180	245	Yearbook 1 (1994, $3.95, 52 pgs.)						4.00
TRUMP							**TUROK, SON OF STONE** (See Dan Curtis, Golden Comics Digest #31 & March						
HMH Publishing Co.: Jan, 1957 - No. 2, Mar, 1957 (50¢, magazine)							of Comics #378, 399, 408)						
1-Harvey Kurtzman satire	25	50	75	145	228	310	**Dell Publ. Co. #1-29**(9/62)/**Gold Key #30**(12/62)-85(7/73)/**Gold Key or**						
2-Harvey Kurtzman satire	20	40	60	117	184	250	**Whitman #86**(9/73)-125(1/80)/**Whitman #126**(3/81) on: No. 596, 12/54 - No. 29, 9/62; No. 30,						
NOTE: Davis, Elder, Heath, Jaffee art-#1,2; Wood a-1. Article by Mel Brooks in #2.							12/62 - No. 91, 7/74; No. 92, 9/74 - No. 125, 1/80; No. 126, 3/81 - No. 130, 4/82						
TRUMPETS WEST (See Luke Short, Four Color #875)							Four Color 596 (12/54)(#1)-1st app./origin Turok & Andar; dinosaur-c. Created by						
TRUTH ABOUT CRIME (See Fox Giants)							Matthew H. Murphy; written by Alberto Giolitti	50	100	150	413	757	1100
TRUTH ABOUT MOTHER GOOSE (See Mother Goose, Four Color #862)							Four Color 656 (10/55)(#2)-1st mention of Lanok	30	60	90	225	413	600
TRUTH BEHIND THE TRIAL OF CARDINAL MINDSZENTY, THE (See Cardinal Mindszenty in the Promotional Comics section))							3(3-5/56)-5: 3-Cave men	20	40	60	150	268	385
TRUTHFUL LOVE (Formerly Youthful Love)							6-10: 8-Dinosaur of the deep; Turok enters Lost Valley; series begins.						
Youthful Magazines: No. 2, July, 1950							9-Paul S. Newman-s (most issues thru end)	15	30	45	107	191	275
2-Ingrid Bergman's true life story	11	22	33	64	90	115	11-20: 17-Prehistoric Pygmies	11	22	33	79	140	200
TRUTH RED, WHITE & BLACK							21-29	8	16	24	58	97	135
Marvel Comics: Jan, 2003 - No. 6 ($3.50, limited series)							30-1st Gold Key. 30-33-Painted back-c.	9	18	27	60	100	140
1-Kyle Baker-a/Robert Morales-s; the testing of Captain America's super-soldier serum						3.50	31-Drug use story	8	16	24	58	97	135
2-7: 3-Isaiah Bradley 1st dons the Captain America costume						3.50	32-40	7	14	21	45	73	100
							41-50	6	12	18	37	59	80
							51-57,59,60	5	10	15	32	51	70
							58-Flying Saucer c/story	5	10	15	35	55	75

Turok, Timewalker #2 © Acclaim

Tweety and Sylvester #19 © WB

24: Nightfall #1 © 20th Century Fox

	GD 2.0	VG 4.0	FN 6.0	VF 8.0	VF/NM 9.0	NM- 9.2
61-70: 62-12¢ & 15¢ covers. 63,68-Line drawn-c	4	8	12	26	41	55
71-84: 84-Origin & 1st app. Hutec	4	8	12	22	34	45
85-99: 93-r-c/#19 w/changes. 94-r-c/#28 w/changes. 97-r-c/#31 w/changes.						
98-r/#58 w/o spaceship & spacemen on-c. 99-r-c/#52 w/changes.	3	6	9	18	27	35
100	4	8	12	23	36	48
101-129: 114,115-(52 pgs.). 129(2/82)	3	6	9	20	30	40
130(4/82)-Last issue	5	10	15	32	51	70
Giant 1(30031-611) (11/66)-Slick-c; r/#10-12 & 16 plus cover to #11	10	20	30	68	119	170
Giant 1-Same as above but with paper-c	11	22	33	75	133	190

NOTE: Most painted-c; line-drawn #63 & 130. *Alberto Gioletti* a-24-27, 30-119, 123; painted-c No. 30-129. *Sparling* a-117, 120-130. Reprints-#36, 54, 57, 75, 112, 114(1/3), 115(1/3), 118, 121, 125, 127(1/3), 128, 129(1/3), 130(1/3), Giant 1. Cover r-93, 94, 97-99, 126(all different from original covers.)

TUROK THE HUNTED
Valiant/Acclaim Comics: Mar, 1995 - No. 2, Apr, 1995 ($2.50, limited series)
| 1,2-Mike Deodato-a(p); price omitted on #1 | | | | | | 2.50 |

TUROK THE HUNTED
Acclaim Comics (Valiant): Feb, 1996 - No. 2, Mar, 1996 ($2.50, limited series)
| 1,2-Mike Grell story | | | | | | 2.50 |

TUROK, TIMEWALKER
Acclaim Comics (Valiant): Aug, 1997 - No. 2, Sept, 1997 ($2.50, limited series)
| 1,2-Nicieza story | | | | | | 2.50 |

TUROK 2 (Magazine)
Acclaim Comics: Oct, 1998 ($4.99, magazine size)
| ...Seeds of Evil-Nicieza-s/Broome & Benjamin-a; origin back-up story | | | | | | 5.00 |
| #2 Adon's Curse -Mack painted-c/Broome & Benjamin-a; origin pt. 2 | | | | | | 5.00 |

TUROK 3: SHADOW OF OBLIVION
Acclaim Comics: Sept, 2000 ($4.95, one-shot)
| 1-Includes pin-up gallery | | | | | | 5.00 |

TURTLE SOUP
Mirage Studios: Sept, 1987 ($2.00, 76 pgs., B&W, one-shot)
| 1-Featuring Teenage Mutant Ninja Turtles | | | | | | 5.00 |

TURTLE SOUP
Mirage Studios: Nov, 1991 - No. 4, 1992 ($2.50, limited series, coated paper)
| 1-4: Features the Teenage Mutant Ninja Turtles | | | | | | 2.50 |

TV CASPER & COMPANY
Harvey Publications: June, 1963 - No. 46, April, 1974 (25¢ Giants)
1- 68 pg. Giants begin; Casper, Little Audrey, Baby Huey, Herman & Catnip, Buzzy the Crow begin	12	24	36	82	146	210
2-5	6	12	18	43	69	95
6-10	5	10	15	30	48	65
11-20	4	8	12	24	37	50
21-31: 31-Last 68 pg. issue	3	6	9	18	27	35
32-46: All 52 pgs.	3	6	9	16	23	30

NOTE: Many issues contain reprints.

TV FUNDAY FUNNIES (See Famous TV...)
TV FUNNIES (See New Funnies)
TV FUNTIME (See Little Audrey)
TV LAUGHOUT (See Archie's...)
TV SCREEN CARTOONS (Formerly Real Screen)
National Periodical Publ.: No. 129, July-Aug, 1959 - No. 138, Jan-Feb, 1961
| 129-138 (Scarce) | 6 | 12 | 18 | 43 | 69 | 95 |

TV STARS (TV) (Newsstand sales only)
Marvel Comics Group: Aug, 1978 - No. 4, Feb, 1979 (Hanna-Barbera)
1-Great Grape app.	3	6	9	18	27	35
2,4: 4-Top Cat app.	3	6	9	16	22	28
3-Toth-c/a; Dave Stevens inks	3	6	9	17	25	32

TV TEENS (Formerly Ozzie & Babs; Rock and Rollo #14 on)
Charlton Comics: V1#14, Feb, 1954 - V2#13, July, 1956
V1#14 (#1)-Ozzie & Babs	10	20	30	54	72	90
15 (#2)	6	12	18	33	41	48
V2#3(6/54) - 6-Don Winslow	6	12	18	31	38	45
7-13-Mopsy. 8(7/55). 9-Paper dolls	6	12	18	29	36	42

TWEETY AND SYLVESTER (1st Series) (TV) (Also see Looney Tunes and Merrie Melodies)
Dell Publishing Co.: No. 406, June, 1952 - No. 37, June-Aug, 1962

	GD 2.0	VG 4.0	FN 6.0	VF 8.0	VF/NM 9.0	NM- 9.2
Four Color 406 (#1)	10	20	30	71	126	180
Four Color 489,524	6	12	18	41	66	90
4 (3-5/54) - 20	5	10	15	32	51	70
21-37	4	8	12	28	44	60

(See March of Comics #421, 433, 445, 457, 469, 481)

TWEETY AND SYLVESTER (2nd Series)(See Kite Fun Book)
Gold Key No. 1-102/Whitman No. 103 on: Nov, 1963; No. 2, Nov, 1965 - No. 121, June, 1984
1	4	8	12	28	44	60
2-10	3	6	9	18	27	35
11-30	2	4	6	13	18	22
31-50	2	4	6	9	12	15
51-70	1	3	4	6	8	10
71-102	1	2	3	5	6	8
103,104 (Whitman)	1	3	4	6	8	10
105(9/80),106(10/80),107(12/80) 3-pack only	3	6	9	20	30	40
108-116: 113(2/82),114(2-3/82),115(3/82),116(4/82)	2	4	6	8	10	12
117-121 (All # 90094 on-c; nd, nd code): 117(6/83). 118(7/83). 119(2/84)-r(1/3). 120(5/84).						
121(6/84)	3	6	9	14	19	24
Digest nn (Charlton/Xerox Pub., 1974) (low print run)	2	4	6	11	16	20
Mini Comic No. 1(1976, 3-1-1/4x6-1/2")	1	3	4	6	8	10

12 O'CLOCK HIGH (TV)
Dell Publishing Co.: Jan-Mar, 1965 - No. 2, Apr-June, 1965 (Photo-c)
| 1 | 6 | 12 | 18 | 39 | 62 | 85 |
| 2 | 5 | 10 | 15 | 30 | 48 | 65 |

2099 A.D.
Marvel Comics: May, 1995 ($3.95, one-shot)
| 1-Acetate-c by Quesada & Palmiotti | | | | | | 4.00 |

2099 APOCALYPSE
Marvel Comics: Dec, 1995 ($4.95, one-shot)
| 1-Chromium wraparound-c; Ellis script | | | | | | 5.00 |

2099 GENESIS
Marvel Comics: Jan, 1996 ($4.95, one-shot)
| 1-Chromium wraparound-c; Ellis script | | | | | | 5.00 |

2099 MANIFEST DESTINY
Marvel Comics: Mar, 1998 ($5.99, one-shot)
| 1-Origin of Fantastic Four 2099; intro Moon Knight 2099 | | | | | | 6.00 |

2099 UNLIMITED
Marvel Comics: Sept, 1993 - No. 10, 1996 ($3.95, 68 pgs.)
| 1-10: 1-1st app. Hulk 2099 & begins. 1-3-Spider-Man 2099 app. 9-Joe Kubert-c; Len Wein & Nancy Collins scripts | | | | | | 4.00 |

2099 WORLD OF DOOM SPECIAL
Marvel Comics: May, 1995 ($2.25, one-shot)
| 1-Doom's "Contract w/America" | | | | | | 2.50 |

2099 WORLD OF TOMORROW
Marvel Comics: Sept, 1996 - No. 8, Apr, 1997 ($2.50) (Replaces 2099 titles)
| 1-8: 1-Wraparound-c. 2-w/bound-in card. 4,5-Phalanx | | | | | | 2.50 |

21
Image Comics (Top Cow Productions): Feb, 1996 - No. 3, Apr, 1996 ($2.50)
| 1-3: Len Wein scripts | | | | | | 2.50 |
| 1-Variant-c | | | | | | 2.50 |

21 DOWN
DC Comics (WildStorm): Nov, 2002 - No. 12, Nov, 2003 ($2.95)
| 1-12: 1-Palmiotti & Gray-s/Saiz-a/Jusko-c | | | | | | 3.00 |
| ...: The Conduit (2003, $19.95, TPB) r/#1-7; intro by Garth Ennis | | | | | | 20.00 |

24 (Based on TV series)
IDW Publishing: July, 2004 - Present ($6.99/$7.49, square-bound, one-shots)
...: Midnight Sun (7/05, $7.49) J.C. Vaughn & Mark Haynes-s; Renato Guedes-a						7.50
...: One Shot (7/04, $6.99)-Jack Bauer's first day on the job at CTU; Vaughn & Haynes-s; Guedes-a						7.00
...: Stories (1/05, $7.49) Manny Clark-a; Vaughn & Haynes-s						7.50

24: NIGHTFALL (Based on TV series)
IDW Publishing: Nov, 2006 - No. 6 ($3.99, limited series)
| 1-5-Two years before Season One; Vaughn & Haynes-s; Diaz-a; two covers | | | | | | 4.00 |

2020 VISIONS
DC Comics (Vertigo): May, 1997 - No. 12, Apr, 1998 ($2.25, limited series)

Twilight Experiment #1
© Palmiotti, Gray & Santacruz

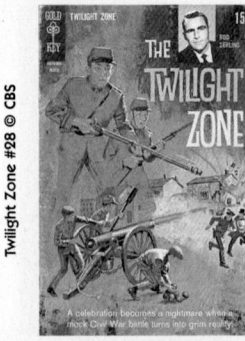

Twilight Zone #28 © CBS

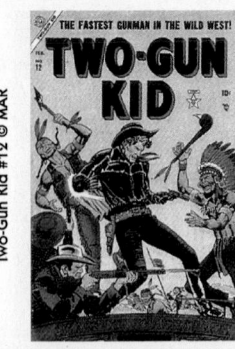

Two-Gun Kid #12 © MAR

	GD 2.0	VG 4.0	FN 6.0	VF 8.0	VF/NM 9.0	NM- 9.2		GD 2.0	VG 4.0	FN 6.0	VF 8.0	VF/NM 9.0	NM- 9.2

1-12-Delano-s: 1-3-Quitely-a. 4-"la tormenta"-Pleece-a 2.50

20,000 LEAGUES UNDER THE SEA (Movie)(See King Classics, Movie Comics & Power Record Comics)
Dell Publishing Co.: No. 614, Feb, 1955 (Disney)

Four Color 614-Movie, painted-c ... 8 16 24 58 97 135

TWICE TOLD TALES (See Movie Classics)

TWILIGHT
DC Comics: 1990 - No. 3, 1991 ($4.95, 52 pgs, lim. series, squarebound, mature)

1-3: Tommy Tomorrow app; Chaykin scripts, Garcia-Lopez-c/a 5.00

TWILIGHT EXPERIMENT
DC Comics (WildStorm): Apr, 2004 - No. 6, Sept, 2005 ($2.95, limited series)

1-6-Gray & Palmiotti/Santacruz-a 3.00

TWILIGHT MAN
First Publishing: June, 1989 - No. 4, Sept, 1989 ($2.75, limited series)

1-4 .... 2.75

TWILIGHT ZONE, THE (TV) (See Dan Curtis & Stories From...)
Dell Publishing Co./Gold Key/Whitman No. 92: No. 1173, 3-5/61 - No. 91, 4/79; No. 92, 5/82

Four Color 1173 (#1)-Crandall-c/a ... 21 42 63 156 278 400
Four Color 1288-Crandall/Evans-c/a ... 12 24 36 87 156 225
01-860-207 (5-7/62-Dell, 15¢) ... 9 18 27 63 107 150
12-860-210 on-c; 01-860-210 on inside(8-10/62-Dell)-Evans-c/a (3 stories)
 ... 9 18 27 63 107 150
1(11/62-Gold Key)-Crandall/Frazetta-a (10 & 11 pgs.); Evans-a
 ... 14 28 42 99 175 250
2 ... 8 16 24 58 97 135
3-11: 3(11 pgs.),4(10 pgs.),9-Toth-a ... 6 12 18 43 69 95
12-15: 12-Williamson-a. 13,15-Crandall-a. 14-Orlando/Crandall/Torres-a
 ... 5 10 15 35 55 75
16-20 ... 4 8 12 26 41 55
21-25: 21-Crandall-a(r). 25-Evans/Crandall(r); Toth-r/#4; last 12¢ issue
 ... 3 6 9 20 30 40
26,27: 26-Flying Saucer-c/story; Crandall, Evans-a(r). 27-Evans-r(2)
 ... 3 6 9 19 29 38
28-32: 32-Evans-a(r) ... 3 6 9 17 25 32
33-51: 43-Celardo-a. 51-Williamson-a ... 2 4 6 13 18 22
52-70 ... 2 4 6 10 14 18
71-82,86-91: 71-Reprint ... 2 4 6 8 11 14
83-(52 pgs.) ... 2 4 6 11 16 20
84-(52 pgs.) Frank Miller's 1st comic book work ... 4 8 12 22 34 45
85-Frank Miller-a (2nd) ... 2 4 6 13 18 22
92-(Whitman, 5/82) Last issue; r/#1. ... 2 4 6 9 13 16
Mini Comic #1 (1976, 3 1/4-3/4-1/2") ... 2 4 6 8 10 12
NOTE: *Bolle* a-13(w/*McWilliams*), 50, 55, 57, 59, 77, 78, 80, 83, 84. *McWilliams* a-59, 78, 80, 82, 84. *Miller* a-84, 85. *Orlando* a-15, 19, 20, 22, 23. *Sekowsky* a-3. *Simonson* a-50, 54, 55, 83r. *Weiss* a-31. *Wood* c/a: see *Mystery Comics Digest* 3, 6, 9, 12, 15, 18, 21, 24). Reprints-26(1/3), 71, 73, 79, 83, 84, 86, 92. Painted c-1-91.

TWILIGHT ZONE, THE (TV)
Now Comics: Nov, 1990 ($2.95); Oct, 1991; V2#1, Nov, 1991 - No. 11, Oct, 1992 ($1.95); V3#1, 1993 - No. 4, 1993 ($2.50)

1-(11/90, $2.95, 52 pgs.)-Direct sale edition; Neal Adams-a, Sienkiewicz-c; Harlan Ellison scripts 3.00
1-(11/90, $1.75)-Newsstand ed. w/N. Adams-c 2.50
1-Prestige Format (10/91, $4.95)-Reprints above with extra Harlan Ellison short story 5.00
1-Collector's Edition (10/91, $2.50)-Non-code approved and polybagged; reprints 11/90 issue; gold logo, 1-Reprint ($2.50)-r/direct sale 11/90 version, 1-Reprint ($2.50)-r/newsstand 11/90 version each... .... 2.50
V2#1-Direct sale & newsstand ed. w/different-c 2.50
V2#2-8,10-11 .... 2.50
V2#9-($2.95)-3-D Special; polybagged w/glasses & hologram on-c 3.00
V2#9-($4.95)-Prestige Edition; contains 2 extra stories & a different hologram on-c; polybagged w/glasses 5.00
V3#1-4, Anniversary Special 1 (1992, $2.50) 2.50
...Science Fiction Special (3/93, $3.50) 3.50

TWINKLE COMICS
Spotlight Publishers: May, 1945

1 ... 24 48 72 137 216 295

TWIST, THE
Dell Publishing Co.: July-Sept, 1962

01-864-209-Painted-c ... 4 8 12 24 37 50

TWISTED TALES (See Eclipse Graphic Album Series #15)
Pacific Comics/Independent Comics Group (Eclipse) #9,10: 11/82 - No. 8, 5/84; No. 9, 11/84; No. 10, 12/84 (Baxter paper)

1-9: 1-B. Jones/Corben-c; Alcala-a; nudity/violence in al. 2-Wrightson-c; Ploog-a 4.00
10-Wrightson painted art; Morrow-c 6.00
NOTE: *Bolton* painted c-4, 6, 7; a-7. *Conrad* a-1, 3, 5; c-1i, 3, 5. *Guice* a-8. *Wildey* a-3.

TWO BIT THE WACKY WOODPECKER (See Wacky...)
Toby Press: 1951 - No. 3, May, 1953

1 ... 10 20 30 54 72 90
2,3 ... 6 12 18 31 38 45

TWO FACES OF TOMORROW, THE
Dark Horse: Aug, 1997 - No. 13, Aug, 1998 ($2.95/$3.95, B&W, lim. series)

1-13: 1-Manga 4.00

TWO-FISTED TALES (Formerly Haunt of Fear #15-17)
(Also see EC Archives • Two-Fisted Tales)
E. C. Comics: No. 18, Nov-Dec, 1950 - No. 41, Feb-Mar, 1955

18(#1)-Kurtzman-c ... 88 176 264 704 1102 1500
19-Kurtzman-c ... 65 130 195 520 810 1100
20-Kurtzman-c ... 41 82 123 328 514 700
21,22-Kurtzman-c ... 34 68 102 272 424 575
23-25-Kurtzman-c ... 26 52 78 208 324 440
26-35: 33- "Atom Bomb" by Wood ... 19 38 57 152 239 325
36-41 ... 15 30 45 120 190 260
Two-Fisted Annual (1952, 25¢, 132 pgs.) ... 97 194 291 728 1064 1400
Two-Fisted Annual (1953, 25¢, 132 pgs.) ... 76 152 228 570 835 1100
NOTE: *Berg* a-29. *Colan* a-39b. *Craig* a-18, 19, 32. *Crandall* a-35, 36. *Davis* a-20-36, 40; c-30, 34, 35, 41, Annual 2. *Evans* a-34, 40, 41; c-40. *Feldstein* a-18. *Krigstein* a-41. *Kubert* a-32, 33. *Kurtzman* a-18-25; c-18-29, 31, Annual 1. *Severin* a-26, 28, 29, 31, 34-41 (No. 37-39 are all-*Severin* issues); c-36-39. *Severin/Elder* a-19-29, 31, 33, 36. *Wood* a-18-28, 30-35; c-31-32, 33. Special issues: #26 (ChanJin Reservoir), 31 (Civil War), 35 (Civil War). Canadian reprints known; see Table of Contents. #25-Davis bio. #27-Wood bio. #28-Kurtzman bio.

TWO-FISTED TALES
Russ Cochran/Gemstone Publishing: Oct, 1992 - No. 24, May, 1998 ($1.50/$2.00/$2.50)

1-24: 1-4r/Two-Fisted Tales #18-21 w/original-c 2.50

TWO-GUN KID (Also see All Western Winners, Best Western, Black Rider, Blaze Carson, Kid Colt, Western Winners, Wild West, & Wild Western)
Marvel/Atlas (MCI No. 1-10/HPC No. 11-59/Marvel No. 60 on): 3/48(No mo.) - No. 10, 11/49; No. 11, 12/53 - No. 59, 4/61; No. 60, 11/62 - No. 92, 3/68; No. 93, 7/70 - No. 136, 4/77

1-Two-Gun Kid & his horse Cyclone begin; The Sheriff begins
 ... 109 218 327 681 1128 1575
2 ... 45 90 135 275 450 625
3,4: 3-Annie Oakley app. ... 36 72 108 208 329 450
5-Pre-Black Rider app. (Wint. 48/49); Anti-Wertham editorial (1st?)
 ... 39 78 117 224 355 485
6-10(11/49): 8-Blaze Carson app. 9-Black Rider app.
 ... 28 56 84 162 256 350
11(12/53)-Black Rider app.; 1st to have Atlas globe on-c; explains how Kid Colt became an outlaw ... 22 44 66 128 202 275
12-Black Rider app. ... 21 42 63 122 191 260
13-20: 14-Opium story ... 15 30 45 90 140 190
21-24,26-29 ... 15 30 45 86 133 180
25,30: 25-Williamson-a (5 pgs.). 30-Williamson/Torres-a (4 pgs.)
 ... 15 30 45 90 140 190
31-33,35,37-40 ... 8 16 24 54 90 125
34-Crandall ... 8 16 24 56 93 130
36,41,42,48-Origin in all ... 8 16 24 56 93 130
43,44,47 ... 7 14 21 45 73 100
45,46-Davis-a ... 7 14 21 49 80 110
49,50,52,53-Severin-a(2/3) in each ... 6 12 18 41 66 90
51-Williamson-a (5 pgs.) ... 7 14 21 49 80 110
54,55,57,59-Severin-a(3) in each. 59-Kirby-a; last 10¢ issue (4/61)
 ... 6 12 18 41 66 90
56 ... 6 12 18 37 59 80
58,60-New origin. 58-Kirby/Ayers-c/a "The Monster of Hidden Valley" cover/story (Kirby monster-c) ... 7 14 21 45 73 100
60-Edition w/handwritten issue number on cover ... 8 16 24 54 90 125
61,62-Kirby-a ... 6 12 18 37 59 80
63-74: 64-Intro. Boom-Boom ... 4 8 12 26 41 55
75-77-Kirby-a ... 5 10 15 30 48 65
78-89 ... 3 6 9 19 29 38
90,95-Kirby-a ... 3 6 9 17 32 42
91,92: 92-Last new story; last 12¢ issue ... 3 6 9 17 25 32

2001: A Space Odyssey #2 © MAR

Ultimate Daredevil and Elektra #2 © MAR

Ultimate Fantastic Four #5 © MAR

	GD 2.0	VG 4.0	FN 6.0	VF 8.0	VF/NM 9.0	NM- 9.2
93,94,96-99	2	4	6	13	18	22
100-Last 15¢-c	3	6	9	14	19	24
101-Origin retold/#58; Kirby-a	3	6	9	14	19	24
102-120-reprints	2	4	6	8	10	12
121-136-reprints. 129-131-(Regular 25¢ editions)	2	4	6	8	10	12
129-131-(30¢-c variants, limited distribution)(4-8/76)	3	6	9	20	30	40

NOTE: Ayers a-26, 27. Davis c-45-47. Drucker a-23. Everett a-82, 91. Fuje a-13. Heath a-3(2), 4(3), 5(2), 7; c-13, 21, 23, 53. Keller a-16, 19, 28. Kirby a-54, 55, 57-62, 75-77, 90, 95, 101, 119, c-10, 52, 54-65, 67-72, 74-76, 116. Maneely a-20; c-11, 12, 16, 19, 20, 25-28, 30, 35, 49. Powell a-38, 102, 104. Severin a-9, 29, 51, 55, 57, 99r(3); c-9, 51. Shores c-1-8, 11. Trimpe c-99. Tuska a-11, 12. Whitney a-87, 89-91, 98-113, 124, 129; c-87, 89, 91, 113. Wildey a-21. Williamson a-110r. Kid Colt in #13, 14, 16-21.

TWO GUN KID: SUNSET RIDERS
Marvel Comics: Nov, 1995 - No. 2, Dec, 1995 ($6.95, squarebound, lim. series)

1,2: Fabian Nicieza scripts in all. 1-painted-c.						7.00

TWO GUN WESTERN (1st Series) (Formerly Casey Crime Photographer #1-4? or My Love #1-4?)
Marvel/Atlas Comics (MPC): No. 5, Nov, 1950 - No. 14, June, 1952

	GD 2.0	VG 4.0	FN 6.0	VF 8.0	VF/NM 9.0	NM- 9.2
5-The Apache Kid (Intro & origin) & his horse Nightwind begin by Buscema	26	52	78	152	239	325
6-10: 8-Kid Colt, The Texas Kid & his horse Thunder begin?	19	38	57	112	176	240
11-14: 13-Black Rider app.	14	28	42	80	115	150

NOTE: Maneely a-6, 7, 9; c-6, 11-13. Morrow a-9. Romita a-8. Wildey a-8.

2-GUN WESTERN (2nd Series) (Formerly Billy Buckskin #1-3; Two-Gun Western #5 on)
Atlas Comics (MgPC): No. 4, May, 1956

	GD	VG	FN	VF	VF/NM	NM-
4-Colan, Ditko, Severin, Sinnott-a; Maneely-c	15	30	45	88	137	185

TWO-GUN WESTERN (Formerly 2-Gun Western)
Atlas Comics (MgPC): No. 5, July, 1956 - No. 12, Sept, 1957

	GD	VG	FN	VF	VF/NM	NM-
5-Return of the Gun-Hawk-c/story; Black Rider app.	15	30	45	85	130	175
6,7	12	24	36	67	94	120
8,10,12-Crandall-a	13	26	39	72	101	130
9,11-Williamson-a in both (5 pgs. each)	14	28	42	76	108	140

NOTE: Ayers a-9. Colan a-5. Everett c-12. Forgione a-5, 6. Kirby a-12; c-5, 6, 8, 11. Maneely a-6, 8, 12; c-5, 6, 8, 11. Morrow a-9, 10. Powell a-7, 11. Severin c-10. Sinnott a-5. Wildey a-9.

TWO MINUTE WARNING
Ultimate Sports Ent.: 2000 - No. 2 ($3.95, cardstock covers)

1,2-NFL players & Teddy Roosevelt battle evil						4.00

TWO MOUSEKETEERS, THE (See 4-Color #475, 603, 642 under M.G.M.'s...;

TWO ON A GUILLOTINE (See Movie Classics)

TWO-STEP
DC Comics (Cliffhanger): Dec, 2003 - No. 3, Jul, 2004 ($2.95, limited series)

1-3-Warren Ellis-s/Amanda Conner-a						3.00

2000 A.D. MONTHLY/PRESENTS (Showcase #25 on)
Eagle Comics/Quality Comics No. 5 on: 4/85 - #6, 9/85; 4/86 - #54, 1991 ($1.25-$1.50, Mando paper)

1-6,1-25:1-4 r/British series featuring Judge Dredd; Alan Moore scripts begin.						
1-25 ($1.25)-Reprints from British 2000 AD						2.50
26,27/28, 29/30, 31-54: 27/28, 29/30,31-Guice-c						2.50

2001, A SPACE ODYSSEY (Movie) (See adaptation in Treasury edition)
Marvel Comics Group: Dec, 1976 - No. 10, Sept, 1977 (30¢)

	GD	VG	FN	VF	VF/NM	NM-
1-Kirby-c/a in all	2	4	6	9	13	16
2-7,9,10	1	2	3	5	6	8
7,9,10-(35¢-c variants, limited distribution)(6-9/77)	3	6	9	16	23	30
8-Origin/1st app. Machine Man (called Mr. Machine)	2	4	6	10	14	18
8-(35¢-c variant, limited distribution)(6,8/77)	4	8	12	28	44	60
...Treasury 1 ('76, 84 pgs.)-All new Kirby-a	3	6	9	15	21	26

2001 NIGHTS
Viz Premiere Comics: 1990 - No. 10, 1991 ($3.75, B&W, lim. series, mature readers, 84 pgs.)

1-10: Japanese sci-fi. 1-Wraparound-c						4.25

2010 (Movie)
Marvel Comics Group: Apr, 1985 - No. 2, May, 1985

1,2-r/Marvel Super Special movie adaptation.						2.50

TYPHOID (Also see Daredevil)
Marvel Comics: Nov, 1995 - No. 4, Feb, 1996 ($3.95, squarebound, lim. series)

1-4: Van Fleet-c/a						4.00

UFO & ALIEN COMIX
Warren Publishing Co.: Jan, 1978 (B&W magazine, 84 pgs., one-shot)

	GD	VG	FN	VF	VF/NM	NM-
nn-Toth-a, J. Severin-a(r); Pie-s	2	4	6	10	14	18

UFO & OUTER SPACE (Formerly UFO Flying Saucers)
Gold Key: No. 14, June, 1978 - No. 25, Feb, 1980 (All painted covers)

	GD 2.0	VG 4.0	FN 6.0	VF 8.0	VF/NM 9.0	NM- 9.2
14-Reprints UFO Flying Saucers #3	1	3	4	6	8	10
15,16-Reprints	1	3	4	6	8	10
17-25: 17-20-New material. 23-McWilliams-a. 24-(3 pg.-r). 25-Reprints UFO Flying Saucers #2 w/cover	1	3	4	6	8	10

UFO ENCOUNTERS
Western Publishing Co.: May, 1978 ($1.95, 228 pgs.)

	GD	VG	FN	VF	VF/NM	NM-
11192-Reprints UFO Flying Saucers	3	6	9	20	30	40
11404-Vol.1 (128 pgs.)-See UFO Mysteries for Vol.2	3	6	9	17	25	32

UFO FLYING SAUCERS (UFO & Outer Space #14 on)
Gold Key: Oct, 1968 - No. 13, Jan, 1977 (No. 2 on, 36 pgs.)

	GD	VG	FN	VF	VF/NM	NM-
1(30035-810) (68 pgs.)	4	8	12	26	41	55
2(11/70), 3(11/72), 4(11/74)	2	4	6	13	18	22
5(2/75)-13: Bolle-a #4 on	2	4	6	9	12	15

UFO MYSTERIES
Western Publishing Co.: 1978 ($1.00, reprints, 96 pgs.)

	GD	VG	FN	VF	VF/NM	NM-
11400-(Vol.2)-Cont'd from UFO Encounters, pgs. 129-224	3	6	9	17	25	32

ULTIMAN GIANT ANNUAL (See Big Bang Comics)
Image Comics: Nov, 2001 ($4.95, B&W, one-shot)

1-Homage to DC Comic's 1960's annuals						5.00

ULTIMATE... (Collects 4-issue alternate titles from X-Men Age of Apocalypse crossovers)
Marvel Comics: May, 1995 ($8.95, trade paperbacks, gold foil covers)

Amazing X-Men, Astonishing X-Men, Factor-X, Gambit & the X-Ternals, Generation Next, X-Calibre, X-Man						9.00
Weapon X						10.00

ULTIMATE ADVENTURES
Marvel Comics: Nov, 2002 - No. 6, Dec, 2003 ($2.25)

1-6: 1-Intro. Hawk-Owl; Zimmerman-s/Fegredo-a. 3-Ultimates app.						2.50
One Tin Soldier TPB (2005, $12.99) r/#1-6						13.00

ULTIMATE ANNUALS
Marvel Comics: 2006; 2007 ($13.99, SC)

Vol. 1 (2006, $13.99) r/Ult. FF Ann. #1, Ult. X-Men Ann. #1, Ult S-M #1, Ultimates Ann #1						14.00
Vol. 2 (2007, $13.99) r/Ult. FF Ann. #2, Ult. X-Men Ann. #2, Ult S-M #2, Ultimates Ann #2						14.00

ULTIMATE CIVIL WAR: SPIDER-HAM (See Civil War and related titles)
Marvel Comics: March, 2007 ($2.99, one-shot)

1-Spoof of Civil War series featuring Spider-Ham; art by various incl. Olivetti, Severin						3.00

ULTIMATE DAREDEVIL AND ELEKTRA
Marvel Comics: Jan, 2003 - No. 4, Mar, 2003 ($2.25, limited series)

1-4-Rucka-s/Larroca-c/a; 1st meeting of Elektra and Matt Murdock						2.50
...Vol.1 TPB (2003, $11.99) r/#1-4, Daredevil Vol. 2 #9; Larroca sketch pages						12.00

ULTIMATE ELEKTRA
Marvel Comics: Oct, 2004 - No. 5, Feb, 2005 ($2.25, limited series)

1-5-Carey-s/Larroca-c/a. 2-Bullseye app.						2.50
... : Devil's Due TPB (2005, $11.99) r/#1-5						12.00

ULTIMATE EXTINCTION (See Ultimate Nightmare and Ultimate Secret limited series)
Marvel Comics: Mar, 2006 - No. 5, July, 2006 ($2.99, limited series)

1-5-The coming of Gah Lak Tus; Ellis-s/Peterson-a						3.00
TPB (2006, $12.99) r/#1-5						13.00

ULTIMATE FANTASTIC FOUR
Marvel Comics: Feb, 2004 - Present ($2.25/$2.50/$2.99)

1-Bendis & Millar-s/Adam Kubert-a/Hitch-c						5.00
2-20: 2-Adam Kubert-a/c; intro. Moleman 7-Ellis-s/Immonen-a begin; Dr. Doom app. 13-18-Kubert-a. 19,20-Jae Lee-a. 20-Begin $2.50-c						3.00
21-Marvel Zombies; begin Greg Land-c/a; Mark Millar-s; variant-c by Land						4.00
22-29,33-46: 24-26-Namor app. 28-President Thor. 33-38-Ferry-a. 42-46-Silver Surfer						3.00
30-32-Marvel Zombies; Millar/Land-a; Dr. Doom app.						4.00
30-32-Zombie variant-c by Suydam						5.00
Annual 1 (10/05, $3.99) The Inhumans app.; Jae Lee-a/Mark Millar-s/Greg Land-c						4.00
Annual 2 (10/06, $3.99) Mole Man app.; Immonen & Irving-a/Carey-s						4.00
.../X-Men 1 (3/06, $2.99) Carey-s/Ferry-a; continued from Ult. X-Men/Fantastic Four #13.00						
... Vol. 1: The Fantastic (2004, $12.99, TPB) r/#1-6; cover gallery						13.00
... Vol. 2: Doom (2004, $12.99, TPB) r/#7-12						13.00
... Vol. 3: N-Zone (2005, $12.99, TPB) r/#13-18						13.00
... Vol. 4: Inhuman (2005, $12.99, TPB) r/#19,20 & Annual #1						13.00

Ultimate Nightmare #1 © MAR

Ultimates 2 #13 © MAR

Ultimate Spider-Man #52 © MAR

	GD 2.0	VG 4.0	FN 6.0	VF 8.0	VF/NM 9.0	NM- 9.2

... Vol. 5: Crossover (2006, $12.99, TPB) r/#21-26 ..... 13.00
... Vol. 6: Frightful (2006, $14.99, TPB) r/#27-32; gallery of cover sketches & variants 15.00
... Vol. 7: God War (2007, $16.99, TPB) r/#33-38 ..... 17.00
... Vol. 8: Devils (2007, $12.99, TPB) r/#39-41 & Annual #2 ..... 13.00
Volume 1 HC (2005, $29.99, 7x11", dust jacket) r/#1-12; introduction, proposals and scripts by Millar and Bendis; character design pages by Hitch 30.00
Volume 2 HC (2006, $29.99, 7x11", dust jacket) r/#13-20; Jae Lee sketch page 30.00
Volume 3 HC (2007, $29.99, 7x11", dust jacket) r/#21-32; Greg Land sketch pages 30.00

ULTIMATE GALACTUS TRILOGY
Marvel Comics: 2007 ($34.99, hardcover, dustjacket)
HC-Oversized reprint of Ultimate Nightmare #1-5, Ultimate Secret #1-4, Ultimate Vision #0, and Ultimate Extinction #1-5; sketch pages and cover galery 35.00

ULTIMATE IRON MAN
Marvel Comics: May, 2005 - No. 5, Feb, 2006 ($2.99, limited series)
1-Origin of Iron Man; Orson Scott Card-s/Andy Kubert-a; two covers 3.00
1-2nd & 3rd printings; each with B&W variant-c 3.00
2-5-Kubert-c 3.00
Volume 1 HC (2006, $19.99, dust jacket) r/#1-5; rough cut of script for #1, cover sketches 20.00
Volume 1 SC (2006, $14.99) r/#1-5; rough cut of script for #1, cover sketches 15.00

ULTIMATE MARVEL FLIP MAGAZINE
Marvel Comics: July, 2005 - Present ($3.99/$4.99)
1-11-Reprints Ultimate Fantastic Four and Ultimate X-Men in flip format 4.00
12-26-($4.99) 5.00

ULTIMATE MARVEL MAGAZINE
Marvel Comics: Feb, 2001 - No. 11, 2002 ($3.99, magazine size)
1-11- Reprints of recent stories from the Ultimate titles plus Marvel news and features.
1-Reprints Ultimate Spider-Man #1&2. 11-Lord of the Rings-c 4.00

ULTIMATE MARVEL TEAM-UP (Spider-Man Team-up)
Marvel Comics: Apr, 2001 - No. 16, July, 2002 ($2.99/$2.25)
1-Spider-Man & Wolverine; Bendis-s in all; Matt Wagner-a/c 5.00
2,3-Hulk; Hester-a 3.50
4,5,9-16: 4,5-Iron Man; Allred-a. 9-Fantastic Four; Mahfood-a. 10-Man-Thing; Totleben-a. 11-X-Men; Clugston-Major-a. 12,13-Dr. Strange; McKeever-a.14-Black Widow; Terry Moore-a. 15,16-Shang-Chi; Mays-a 3.00
6-8-Punisher; Sienkiewicz-a. 7,8-Daredevil app. 4.00
TPB (11/01, $14.95) r/#1-5 ..... 15.00
... Ultimate Collection TPB ('06, $29.99) r/#1-16 & Ult. Spider-Man Spec.; sketch pages 30.00
HC (8/02, $39.99) r/#1-16 & Ult. Spider-Man Special; Bendis afterword 30.00
...: Vol. 2 TPB (2003, $11.99) r/#9-13; Mahfood-c 12.00
...: Vol. 3 TPB (2003, $12.99) r/#14-16 & Ultimate Spider-Man Super Special; Moore-c 13.00

ULTIMATE NIGHTMARE (Leads into Ultimate Secret limited series)
Marvel Comics: Oct, 2004 - No. 5, Feb, 2005 ($2.25, limited series)
1-5: Ellis-s; Ultimates, X-Men, Nick Fury app. 1,2,4,5-Hairsine-a/c. 3-Epting-a 2.50
Ultimate Galactus Book 1: Nightmare TPB (2005, $12.99) r/Ultimate Nightmare #1-5 ..... 13.00

ULTIMATE POWER
Marvel Comics: Dec, 2006 - No. 9 ($2.99, limited series)
1-7: 1-Ultimate FF meets the Squadron Supreme; Bendis-s; Land-a/c. 2-Spider-Man, X-Men and the Ultimates app. 6-Doom app. 3.00
1-Variant sketch-c 5.00
1-Director's Cut (2007, $3.99) r/#1 and B&W pencil and ink pages; covers to #2,3 ..... 4.00

ULTIMATES, THE (Avengers of the Ultimate line)
Marvel Comics: Mar, 2002 - No. 13, Apr, 2004 ($2.25)
1-Intro. Capt. America; Millar-s/Hitch-a & wraparound-c 6.00
2-Intro. Giant-Man and the Wasp 4.00
3-12: 3-1st Capt. America in new costume. 4-Intro. Thor. 5-Ultimates vs. The Hulk. 8-Intro. Hawkeye. 3.00
13-($3.50) 3.50
... Volume 1 HC (2004, $29.99) oversized r/series; commentary pages with Millar & Hitch; cover gallery and character design pages; intro. by Joss Whedon 30.00
... Volume 1: Super-Human TPB (8/02, $12.99) r/#1-6 ..... 13.00
... Volume 2: Homeland Security TPB (2004, $17.99) r/#7-13 ..... 18.00

ULTIMATES 2
Marvel Comics: Feb, 2005 - No. 13, Feb, 2007 ($2.99/$3.99)
1-Millar-s/Hitch-a; Giant-Man becomes Ant-Man 3.00
2-11: 6-Intro. The Defenders. 7-Hawkeye shot. 8-Intro The Liberators 3.00
12,13-($3.99) Wraparound-c; X-Men, Fantastic Four, Spider-Man app. 4.00
13-Variant white cover featuring The Wasp 40.00
Annual 1 (10/05, $3.99) Millar-s/Dillon-a/Hitch-c; Defenders app. 4.00

Annual 2 (10/06, $3.99) Deodato-a; flashback to WWII with Sook-a; Falcon app. 4.00
... Volume 1: Gods & Monsters TPB (2005, $15.99) r/#1-6 ..... 16.00
... Volume 2: Grand Theft America TPB (2007, $19.99) r/#7-13; cover gallery w/sketches 20.00

ULTIMATE SECRET (See Ultimate Nightmare limited series)
Marvel Comics: May, 2005 - No. 4, Dec, 2005 ($2.99, limited series)
1-4-Ellis-s; Captain Marvel app. 1,2-McNiven-a. 2,3-Ultimates & FF app. 3.00
Ultimate Galactus Book 2: Secret TPB (2006, $12.99) r/#1-4 ..... 13.00

ULTIMATE SIX (Reprinted in Ultimate Spider-Man Vol. 5 hardcover)
Marvel Comics: Nov, 2003 - No. 7, June, 2004 ($2.25) (See Ultimate Spider-Man for TPB)
1-The Ultimates & Spider-Man team-up; Bendis-s/Quesada & Hairsine-a; Cassaday-c 5.00
2-7-Hairsine-a; Cassaday-c 2.50

ULTIMATE SPIDER-MAN
Marvel Comics: Oct, 2000 - Present ($2.99/$2.25/$2.99)

	GD 2.0	VG 4.0	FN 6.0	VF 8.0	VF/NM 9.0	NM- 9.2
1-Bendis-s/Bagley & Thibert-a; cardstock-c; introduces revised origin and cast separate from regular Spider-continuity	6	12	18	41	66	90
1-Variant white-c (Retailer incentive)	9	18	27	60	100	140
1-DF Edition	4	8	12	28	44	60
1-Free Comic Book Day giveaway & Kay Bee Toys variant - (See Promotional Comics section)						
2-Cover with Spider-Man on car	3	6	9	18	27	35
2-Cover with Spider-Man swinging past building	3	6	9	18	27	35
4-Uncle Ben killed	3	6	9	16	23	30
5-7: 6,7-Green Goblin app.	3	6	9	18	27	35
8-13: 13-Reveals secret to MJ	1	2	3	5	7	9

14-21: 14-Intro. Gwen Stacy & Dr. Octopus 5.00
22-($3.50) Green Goblin returns 3.50
23-32 ..... 2.50
33-1st Ultimate Venom-c; intro. Eddie Brock 3.00
34-38-Ultimate Venom 2.50
39-49,51-59: 39-Nick Fury app. 43,44-X-Men app. 46-Prelude to Ultimate Six; Sandman app. 51-53-Elektra app. 54-59-Doctor Octopus app. 2.50
50-($2.99) Intro. Black Cat 2.50
60-Intro. Ultimate Carnage on cover 3.00
61-Intro Ben Reilly; Punisher app. 2.50
62-Gwen Stacy killed by Carnage 3.00
63-92: 63,64-Carnage app. 66,67-Wolverine app. 68,69-Johnny Storm app. 78-Begin $2.50-c. 79-Debut Moon Knight. 81-85-Black Cat app. 90-Vulture app. 91-94-Deadpool 2.50
93-99: 93-Begin $2.99-c. 95-Morbius & Blade app. 97-99-Clone Saga 3.00
100-($3.99) Wraparound-c; Clone Saga; re-cap of previous issues 4.00
101-104-Clone Saga continues; Fantastic Four app. 102-Spider-Woman origin 3.00
104-($3.99) Clone Saga concludes; Fantastic Four and Dr. Octopus app. 4.00
105-114: 106-110-Daredevil app. 111-Last Bagley art; Immonen-a (6 pgs.). 112-Immonen-a; Norman Osborn app. 4.00
Annual 1 (10/05, $3.99) Kitty Pryde app.; Bendis-s/Brooks-a/Bagley-c 4.00
Annual 2 (10/06, $3.99) Punisher, Moon Knight and Daredevil app.; Bendis-s/Brooks-a 4.00
Collected Edition (1/01, $3.99) r/#1-3 ..... 4.00
...Special (7/02, $3.50) art by Bagley and various incl. Romita,Sr., Brereton, Cho, Mack, Sienkiewicz, Phillips, Pearson, Oeming, Mahfood, Russell 3.50
Ultimate Spider-Man 100 Project (2007, $10.00, SC, charity book for the HERO Initiative) collection of 100 variant covers by Romita Sr. & Jr., Cho, Bagley, Quesada and more 10.00
...: Venom HC (2007, $19.99) r/#33-39 ..... 20.00
...(Vol. 1): Power and Responsibility TPB (4/01, $14.95) r/#1-7 ..... 15.00
...(Vol. 2): Learning Curve TPB (12/01, $14.95) r/#8-13 ..... 15.00
...(Vol. 3): Double Trouble TPB (6/02, $17.95) r/#14-21 ..... 18.00
Vol. 4: Legacy TPB (2002, $14.99) r/#22-27 ..... 15.00
Vol. 5: Public Scrutiny TPB (2003, $11.99) r/#28-32 ..... 12.00
Vol. 6: Venom TPB (2003, $15.99) r/#33-39 ..... 16.00
Vol. 7: Irresponsible TPB (2003, $12.99) r/#40-45 ..... 13.00
Vol. 8: Cats & Kings TPB (2004, $17.99) r/#46-53 ..... 18.00
Vol. 9: Ultimate Six TPB (2004, $17.99) r/#46 & Ultimate Six #1-7 ..... 18.00
Vol. 10: Hollywood TPB (2004, $12.99) r/#54-59 ..... 13.00
Vol. 11: Carnage TPB (2004, $12.99) r/#60-65 ..... 13.00
Vol. 12: Superstars TPB (2005, $12.99) r/#66-71 ..... 13.00
Vol. 13: Hobgoblin TPB (2005, $15.99) r/#72-78 ..... 16.00
Vol. 14: Warriors TPB (2005, $17.99) r/#79-85 ..... 18.00
Vol. 15: Silver Sable TPB (2006, $15.99) r/#86-90 & Annual #1 ..... 16.00
Vol. 16: Deadpool TPB (2006, $19.99) r/#91-96 & Annual #2 ..... 20.00
Vol. 17: Clone Saga TPB (2006, $24.99) r/#97-105 ..... 25.00
Vol. 17: Ultimate Knights TPB (2007, $15.99) r/#106-111 ..... 18.00
Hardcover (3/02, $34.95, 7x11", dust jacket) r/#1-13 & Amazing Fantasy #15; sketch pages and Bill Jemas' initial plot and character outlines 35.00
Volume 2 HC (2003, $29.99, 7x11", dust jacket) r/#14-27; pin-ups & sketch pages 30.00
Volume 3 HC (2003, $29.99, 7x11", dust jacket) r/#28-39 & #1/2; script pages 30.00

Ultimate Vision #1 © MAR

Ultimate X-Men #78 © MAR

Ultragirl #3 © MAR

	GD	VG	FN	VF	VF/NM	NM-		GD	VG	FN	VF	VF/NM	NM-
	2.0	4.0	6.0	8.0	9.0	9.2		2.0	4.0	6.0	8.0	9.0	9.2

Volume 4 HC (2004, $29.99, 7x11", dust jacket) r/#40-45, 47-53; sketch pages — 30.00
Volume 5 HC (2004, $29.99, 7x11", dust jacket) r/#46,54-59, Ultimate Six #1-7 — 30.00
Volume 6 HC (2005, $29.99, 7x11", dust jacket) r/#60-71; sketch page — 30.00
Volume 7 HC (2006, $29.99, 7x11", dust jacket) r/#72-85; sketch & profile pages — 30.00
Volume 8 HC (2007, $29.99, 7x11", dust jacket) r/#86-96 & Annual #1&2; sketch page — 30.00
Wizard #1/2 — 1 — 3 — 4 — 6 — 8 — 10

ULTIMATE TALES FLIP MAGAZINE
Marvel Comics: July, 2005 - Present ($3.99/$4.99)

1-11-Each reprints 2 issues of Ultimate Spider-Man in flip format — 4.00
12-26-($4.99) — 5.00

ULTIMATE VISION
Marvel Comics: No. 0, Jan, 2007 - No. 5 ($2.99, limited series)

0-Reprints back-up serial from Ultimate Extinction and related series; pin-ups — 3.00
1-4: 1-(2/07) Carey-s/Peterson-a/c — 3.00

ULTIMATE WAR
Marvel Comics: Feb, 2003 - No. 4, Apr, 2003 ($2.25, limited series)

1-4-Millar-s/Bachalo-c/a; The Ultimates vs. Ultimate X-Men — 2.50
Ultimate X-Men Vol. 5: Ultimate War TPB (2003, $10.99) r/#1-4 — 11.00

ULTIMATE WOLVERINE VS. HULK
Marvel Comics: Feb, 2006 - No. 6 ($2.99, limited series)

1,2-Leinil Yu-a/c; Damon Lindelof-s — 3.00

ULTIMATE X-MEN (Also see Promotional Comics section for FCBD Ed.)
Marvel Comics: Feb, 2001 - Present ($2.99/$2.25/$2.50)

1-Millar-s/Adam Kubert & Thibert-a; cardstock-c; introduces revised origin and cast
separate from regular X-Men continuity — 3 — 6 — 9 — 14 — 20 — 25
1-DF Edition — 30.00
1-DF Sketch Cover Edition — 45.00
2 — 2 — 4 — 6 — 11 — 16 — 20
3-6 — 2 — 4 — 6 — 8 — 11 — 14
7-10 — 6.00
11-24,26-33: 13-Intro. Gambit. 18,19-Bachalo-a. 23,24-Andrews-a — 3.00
25-($3.50) leads into the Ultimate War mini-series; Kubert-a — 3.50
34-Spider-Man-c/app.; Bendis-s begin; Finch-a — 4.00
35-74: 35-Spider-Man app. 36,37-Daredevil-c/app. 40-Intro. Angel. 42-Intro. Dazzler.
44-Beast dies. 46-Intro. Mr. Sinister. 50-53-Kubert-a; Gambit app. 54-57,59-63-Immonen-a.
60-Begin $2.50-c. 66-Kirkman-s begin. 69-Begin $2.99-c — 3.00
61-Retailer Edition with variant Coipel B&W sketch-c — 10.00
61-Retailer Edition with variant Coipel B&W sketch-c — 10.00
75-($3.99) Turner-c; intro. Cable; back-up story with Emma Frost's students — 4.00
76-86: 76-Intro. Bishop — 3.00
Annual 1 (10/05, $3.99) Vaughan-s/Raney-a; Gambit & Rogue in Vegas — 4.00
Annual 2 (10/06, $3.99) Kirkman-s/Larroca-a; Nightcrawler & Dazzler — 4.00
...Fantastic Four 1 (2/06, $2.99) Carey-s/Ferry-a; concluded in Ult. Fantastic Four/X-Men — 3.00
...Fantastic Four TPB (2006, $12.99) reprints Ult X-Men/Ult. FF x-over and Official Handbook
of the Ultimate Marvel Universe #1-2 — 13.00
... Ultimate Collection Vol. 1 (2006, $24.99) r/#1-12 & #1/2; unused Bendis script for #1 — 25.00
... Ultimate Collection Vol. 2 (2007, $24.99) r/#13-25; Kubert cover sketch pages — 25.00
...: (Vol. 1) The Tomorrow People TPB (7/01, $14.95) r/#1-6 — 15.00
...: (Vol. 2) Return to Weapon X TPB (4/02, $14.95) r/#7-12 — 15.00
Vol. 3: World Tour TPB (2002, $17.99) r/#13-20 — 18.00
Vol. 4: Hellfire and Brimstone TPB (2003, $12.99) r/#21-25 — 13.00
Vol. 5 (See Ultimate War)
Vol. 6: Return of the King TPB (2003, $16.99) r/#26-33 — 17.00
Vol. 7: Blockbuster TPB (2004, $12.99) r/#34-39 — 13.00
Vol. 8: New Mutants TPB (2004, $12.99) r/#40-45 — 13.00
Vol. 9: The Tempest TPB (2004, $10.99) r/#46-49 — 11.00
Vol. 10: Cry Wolf TPB (2005, $8.99) r/#50-53 — 9.00
Vol. 11: The Most Dangerous Game TPB (2005, $9.99) r/#54-57 — 10.00
Vol. 12: Hard Lessons TPB (2005, $12.99) r/#58-60 & Annual #1 — 13.00
Vol. 13: Magnetic North TPB (2006, $12.99) r/#61-65 — 13.00
Vol. 14: Phoenix? TPB (2006, $14.99) r/#66-71 — 15.00
Vol. 15: Magical TPB (2007, $11.99) r/#72-74 & Annual #2 — 12.00
Vol. 16: Cable TPB (2007, $14.99) r/#75-80; sketch pages — 15.00
Volume 1 HC (8/02, $34.99, 7x11", dust jacket) r/#1-12 & Giant-Size X-Men #1;
sketch pages and Millar and Bendis' initial plot and character outlines — 35.00
Volume 2 HC (2003, $29.99, 7x11", dust jacket) r/#13-25; script for #20 — 30.00
Volume 3 HC (2003, $29.99, 7x11", dust jacket) r/#26-33 & Ultimate War #1-4 — 30.00
Volume 4 HC (2005, $29.99, 7x11", dust jacket) r/#34-45 — 30.00
Volume 5 HC (2006, $29.99, 7x11", dust jacket) r/#46-57; Vaughan intro.; sketch pages — 30.00
Volume 6 HC (2006, $29.99, 7x11", dust jacket) r/#58-65, Annual #1 & Wizard #1/2 — 30.00
Volume 7 HC (2007, $29.99, 7x11", dust jacket) r/#66-74, Annual #2 — 30.00
Wizard #1/2 — 2 — 4 — 6 — 9 — 12 — 15

ULTRA
Image Comics: Aug, 2004 - No. 8, Mar, 2005 ($2.95, limited series)

1-8: 1-Intro. Ultra/Pearl Penalosa; Luna Brothers-s/a — 3.00
Vol. 1: Seven Days TPB (4/05, $17.95) r/#1-8; sketch pages — 18.00

ULTRAFORCE (1st Series) (Also see Avengers/Ultraforce #1)
Malibu Comics (Ultraverse): Aug, 1994 - No. 10, Aug, 1995 ($1.95/$2.50)

0 (9/94, $2.50)-Perez-c/a. — 2.50
1-($2.50, 44 pgs.)-Bound-in trading card; team consisting of Prime, Prototype, Hardcase,
Pixx, Ghoul, Contrary & Topaz; Gerard Jones scripts begin, ends #6; Perez-c/a begins. — 2.50
1-Ultra 5000 Limited Silver Foil Edition — 4.00
1-Holographic-c, no price — 6.00
2-5: Perez-c/a in all. 2 (10/94, $1.95)-Prime quits, Strangers cameo. 3-Origin of Topaz;
Prime rejoins. 5-Pixx dies. — 2.50
2 ($2.50)-Florescent logo; limited edition stamp on-c — 3.00
6-10: 6-Begin $2.50-c, Perez-c/a. 7-Ghoul story, Steve Erwin-a. 8-Marvel's Black Knight
enters the Ultraverse (last seen in Avengers #375); Perez-c/a. 9,10-Black Knight app.;
Perez-c. 10-Leads into Ultraforce/Avengers Prelude — 2.50
Malibu "Ashcan ": Ultraforce #0A (6/94) — 2.50
.../Avengers Prelude 1 (8/95, $2.50)-Perez-c. — 2.50
.../Avengers 1 (8/95, $3.95)-Warren Ellis script; Perez-c/a; foil-c — 4.00

ULTRAFORCE (2nd Series)(Also see Black September)
Malibu Comics (Ultraverse): Infinity, Sept, 1995 - V2#15, Dec, 1996 ($1.50)

Infinity, V2#1-15: Infinity-Team consists of Marvel's Black Knight, Ghoul, Topaz, Prime &
redesigned Prototype; Warren Ellis scripts begin, ends #3; variant-c exists. 1-1st
app.Cromwell, Lament & Wreckage. 2-Contains free encore presentation of Ultraforce #1;
flip book "Phoenix Resurrection" Pt. 7. 7-Darick Robertson, Jeff Johnson & others-a.
8,9-Intro. Future Ultraforce (Prime, Hellblade, Angel of Destruction, Painkiller & Whipslash);
Gary Erskine-c/a. 9-Foxfire app. 10-Len Wein scripts & Deodato Studios-c/a begin.
10-Lament back-up story. 11-Ghoul back-up story by Pander Bros. 12-Ultraforce vs. Maxis
(cont'd in Ultraverse Unlimited #2); Exiles & Iron Clad app. 13-Prime leaves; Hardcase
returns — 2.50
Infinity (2000 signed) — 4.00
.../Spider-Man ($3.95)-Marv Wolfman script; Green Goblin app; 2 covers exist. — 4.00

ULTRAGIRL
Marvel Comics: Nov, 1996 - No. 3 Mar, 1997($1.50, limited series)

1-3: 1-1st app. — 2.50

ULTRA KLUTZ
Onward Comics: 1981; 6/86 - #27, 1/89, #28, 4/90 - #31, 1990? ($1.50/$1.75/$2.00, B&W)

1 (1981)-Re-released after 2nd #1 — 2.50
1-30: 1-(6/86). 27-Photo back-c — 2.50
31-($2.95, 52 pgs.) — 3.00

ULTRAMAN
Nemesis Comics: Mar, 1994 - No. 4, Sept, 1994 ($1.75/$1.95)

1-($2.25)-Collector's edition; foil-c; special 3/4 wraparound-c — 3.00
1-($1.75)-Newsstand edition — 2.50
2-4: 3-$1.95-c begins — 2.50
#(-1) (3/93) — 2.50

ULTRAMAN TIGA
Dark Horse Comics: Aug, 2003 - No. 10, June, 2004 ($3.99)

1-10-Khoo Fuk Lung-a/Tony Wong-s — 4.00

ULTRAVERSE DOUBLE FEATURE
Malibu Comics (Ultraverse): Jan, 1995 ($3.95, one-shot, 68 pgs.)

1-Flip-c featuring Prime & Solitaire. — 4.00

ULTRAVERSE ORIGINS
Malibu Comics (Ultraverse): Jan, 1994 (99c, one-shot)

1-Gatefold-c; 2 pg. origins all characters — 2.50
1-Newsstand edition; different-c, no gatefold — 2.50

ULTRAVERSE PREMIERE
Malibu Comics (Ultraverse): 1994 (one-shot)

0-Ordered thru mail w/coupons — 5.00

ULTRAVERSE UNLIMITED
Malibu Comics (Ultraverse): June, 1996; No. 2, Sept, 1996 ($2.50)

1,2: 1-Adam Warlock returns to the Marvel Universe; Rune-c/app. 2-Black Knight, Reaper &
Sierra Blaze return to the Marvel Universe — 2.50

ULTRAVERSE YEAR ONE
Malibu Comics (Ultraverse): 1994 ($4.95, one-shot)

nn-In-depth synopsis of the first year's titles & stories. — 5.00

Uncanny Origins #6 © MAR

Uncanny Tales #20 © Atlas

Uncle Scrooge #12 © DIS

	GD 2.0	VG 4.0	FN 6.0	VF 8.0	VF/NM 9.0	NM- 9.2

	GD 2.0	VG 4.0	FN 6.0	VF 8.0	VF/NM 9.0	NM- 9.2

ULTRAVERSE YEAR TWO
Malibu Comics (Ultraverse): Aug, 1995 ($4.95, one-shot)

nn-In-depth synopsis of second year's titles & stories						5.00

ULTRAVERSE YEAR ZERO: THE DEATH OF THE SQUAD
Malibu Comics (Ultraverse): Apr, 1995 - No. 4, July, 1995 ($2.95, lim. series)

1-4: 3-Codename: Firearm back-up story.						3.00

UNBIRTHDAY PARTY WITH ALICE IN WONDERLAND (See Alice In Wonderland, Four Color #341)

UNBOUND
Image Comics (Desperado): Jan, 1998 ($2.95, B&W)

1-Pruett-s/Peters-a						3.00

UNCANNY ORIGINS
Marvel Comics: Sept, 1996 - No. 14, Oct, 1997 (99¢)

1-14: 1-Cyclops. 2-Quicksilver. 3-Archangel. 4-Firelord. 5-Hulk. 6-Beast. 7-Venom. 8-Nightcrawler. 9-Storm. 10-Black Cat. 11-Black Knight. 12-Dr. Strange. 13-Daredevil.

14-Iron Fist						2.50

UNCANNY TALES
Atlas Comics (PrPI/PPI): June, 1952 - No. 56, Sept, 1957

	GD	VG	FN	VF	VF/NM	NM-
1-Heath-a; horror/weird stories begin	89	178	267	556	921	1285
2	48	96	144	293	484	675
3-5	41	82	123	256	416	575
6-Wolvertonish-a by Matt Fox	43	86	129	262	431	600
7-10: 8-Atom bomb story; Tothish-a (by Sekowsky?). 9-Crandall-a						
	38	76	114	222	351	480
11-20: 17-Atom bomb panels; anti-communist story; Hitler story. 19-Krenkel-a.						
20-Robert Q. Sale-c	28	56	84	164	260	355
21-25,27: 25-Nostrand-a?	25	50	75	145	228	310
26-Spider-Man prototype c/story	35	70	105	201	318	435
28-Last precode issue (1/55); Kubert-a; #1-28 contain 2-3 sci/fi stories each						
	26	52	78	150	235	320
29-41,43-49,51	18	36	54	103	162	220
42,54,56-Krigstein-a	19	38	57	109	172	235
50,53,55-Torres-a	18	36	54	103	162	220
52-Oldest Iron Man prototype (2/57)	20	40	60	115	180	245

NOTE: **Andru** a-15, 17. **Ayers** a-22. **Bailey** a-51. **Briefer** a-5. **Brodsky** c-1, 3, 4, 6, 8, 12-16, 19. **Brodsky/Everett** c-9. **Cameron** a-47. **Colan** a-11, 16, 17, 52. **Drucker** a-37, 42, 45. **Everett** a-2, 9, 12, 32, 36, 39, 48; c-7, 11, 17, 39, 41, 50, 52, 53. **Fass** a-9, 10, 15, 24. **Forte** a-18, 27, 34, 52, 53. **Heath** a-13, c-5, 10, 18. **Keller** a-3. **Lawrence** a-14, 17, 19, 23, 27, 28, 35. **Maneely** a-4, 8, 10, 16, 29, 35; c-2, 22, 26, 33, 38. **Moldoff** a-23. **Morisi** a-48. **Morrow** a-46, 51. **Orlando** a-49, 50, 53. **Powell** a-12, 18, 34, 36, 38, 43, 50, 56. **Robinson** a-3, 13. **Reinman** a-12. **Romita** a-10. **Roussos** a-8. **Sale** a-47, 53; c-20. **Sekowsky** a-15, 52. **Sinnott** a-15, 52. **Torres** a-53. **Tothish-a** by Andru-27. **Wildey** a-22, 48.

UNCANNY TALES
Marvel Comics Group: Dec, 1973 - No. 12, Oct, 1975

	GD	VG	FN	VF	VF/NM	NM-
1-Crandall-r/Uncanny Tales r/'50s)	3	6	9	16	23	30
2-12: 7,12-Kirby-a	2	4	6	10	14	18

NOTE: Ditko reprints-#4, 6-8, 10-12.

UNCANNY X-MEN, THE (See X-Men, The, 1st series, #142-on)

UNCANNY X-MEN AND THE NEW TEEN TITANS (See Marvel and DC Present...)

UNCENSORED MOUSE, THE
Eternity Comics: Apr, 1989 - No. 2, Apr, 1989 ($1.95, B&W)(Came sealed in plastic bag)(Both contain racial stereotyping & violence)

	GD	VG	FN	VF	VF/NM	NM-
1,2-Early Gottfredson strip-r in each	2	4	6	9	12	15

NOTE: Both issues contain unauthorized reprints. Series was cancelled. Win Smith r-1, 2.

UNCLE CHARLIE'S FABLES
Lev Gleason Publ.: Jan, 1952 - No. 5, Sept, 1952 (All have Biro painted-c)

	GD	VG	FN	VF	VF/NM	NM-
1-Norman Maurer-a; has Biro's picture	15	30	45	88	137	185
2-Fuje-a; Biro photo	10	20	30	54	72	90
3-5	9	18	27	47	61	75

UNCLE DONALD & HIS NEPHEWS DUDE RANCH (See Dell Giant #52)

UNCLE DONALD & HIS NEPHEWS FAMILY FUN (See Dell Giant #38)

UNCLE JOE'S FUNNIES
Centaur Publications: 1938 (B&W)

	GD	VG	FN	VF	VF/NM	NM-
1-Games, puzzles & magic tricks, some interior art; Bill Everett-c						
	57	114	171	356	591	825

UNCLE MILTY (TV)
Victoria Publications/True Cross: Dec, 1950 - No. 4, July, 1951 (52 pgs.)(Early TV comic)

	GD	VG	FN	VF	VF/NM	NM-
1-Milton Berle photo on-c of #1,2	53	106	159	323	537	750
2	35	70	105	201	318	435

	GD	VG	FN	VF	VF/NM	NM-
3,4	29	58	87	167	264	360

UNCLE REMUS & HIS TALES OF BRER RABBIT (See Brer Rabbit, 4-Color #129, 208, 693)

UNCLE SAM
DC Comics (Vertigo): 1997 - No. 2, 1997 ($4.95, limited series)

1,2-Alex Ross painted c/a. Story by Ross and Steve Darnell.						5.00
Hardcover (1998, $17.95)						18.00
Softcover (2000, $9.95)						10.00

UNCLE SAM AND THE FREEDOM FIGHTERS
DC Comics: Sept, 2006 - No. 8, Apr, 2007 ($2.99, limited series)

1-8-Acuña-a/c; Gray & Palmiotti-s. 3-Intro. Black Condor						3.00
TPB (2007, $14.99) r/#1-8 and story from DCU Brave New World #1						15.00

UNCLE SAM QUARTERLY (Blackhawk #9 on)(See Freedom Fighters)
Quality Comics Group: Autumn, 1941 - No. 8, Fall, 1943 (see National Comics)

1-Origin Uncle Sam; Fine/Eisner-c, chapter headings, 2 pgs. by Eisner;
(2 versions: dark cover, no price; light cover with price sticker); Jack Cole-a

	GD	VG	FN	VF	VF/NM	NM-
	376	752	1128	2444	4322	6200
2-Cameos by The Ray, Black Condor, Quicksilver, The Red Bee, Alias the Spider, Hercules						
& Neon the Unknown; Eisner, Fine-c/a	131	262	393	819	1360	1900
3-Tuska-c/a; Eisner-a(2)	97	194	291	606	1003	1400
4	86	172	258	538	894	1250
5,7-Hitler, Mussolini & Tojo-c	110	220	330	688	1144	1600
6,8	67	134	201	419	697	975

NOTE: **Kotzky** (or **Tuska**) a-3-8.

UNCLE SCROOGE (Disney) (Becomes Walt Disney's... #210 on) (See Cartoon Tales, Dell Giants #33, 55, Disney Comic Album, Donald and Scrooge, Dynabrite, Four Color #178, Gladstone Comic Album, Walt Disney's Comics & Stories #98, Walt Disney's ...)
Dell #1-39/Gold Key #40-173/Whitman #174-209: No. 386, 3/52 - No. 39, 8-10/62; No. 40, 12/62 - No. 209, 7/84

Four Color 386(#1)-in "Only a Poor Old Man" by Carl Barks; r-in Uncle Scrooge & Donald Duck #1('65) & The Best of Walt Disney Comics (1974). The very 1st cover app. of Uncle Scrooge

	GD	VG	FN	VF	VF/NM	NM-
	152	304	456	1292	2396	3500
1-(1986)-Reprints F.C. #386; given away with lithograph "Dam Disaster at Money Lake" & as a subscription offer giveaway to Gladstone subscribers						
	3	6	9	15	20	24
Four Color 456(#2)-in "Back to the Klondike" by Carl Barks; r-in Best of U.S. & D.D. #1('66) & Gladstone C.A. #4	78	156	234	663	1232	1800
Four Color 495(#3)-r-in #105	52	104	156	442	821	1200
4(12-2/53-54)-r-in Gladstone Comic Album #11	41	82	123	328	589	850
5-r-in Gladstone Special #2 & Walt Disney Digest #1						
	35	70	105	263	482	700
6-r-in U.S. #106,165,233 & Best of U.S. & D.D. #1('66)						
	29	58	87	212	381	550
7-The Seven Cities of Cibola by Barks; r-in #217 & Best of D.D. & U.S. #2 ('67)						
	25	50	75	184	330	475
8-10: 8-r-in #111,222. 9-r-in #104,214. 10-r-in #67	21	42	63	156	278	400
11-20: 11-r-in #237. 17-r-in #215. 19-r-in Gladstone C.A. #1. 20-r-in #213						
	17	34	51	128	227	325
21-30: 24-X-Mas-c. 26-r-in #211	14	28	42	102	181	260
31-35,37-40: 34-r-in #228. 40-X-Mas-c	12	24	36	87	156	225
36-1st app. Magica De Spell; Number one dime 1st identified by name						
	14	28	42	102	181	260
41-60: 48-Magica De Spell-c/story (3/64). 49-Sci/fi-c. 51-Beagle Boys-c/story (8/64)	10	20	30	73	129	185
61-63,65,66,68-71:71-Last Barks issue w/original story (#71-he only storyboarded the script)						
	9	18	27	65	113	160
64-Barks Vietnam War story "Treasure of Marco Polo" banned for reprints by Disney from 1977-1989 because of its Third World revolutionary war theme. It later appeared in the hardcover Carl Barks Library set (4/89) and Walt Disney's Uncle Scrooge Adventures #42 (1/97)	14	28	42	99	175	250
67,72,73: 67,72,73-Barks-r	9	18	27	63	107	150
74-84: 74-Barks-r(1pg.). 75-81,83-Not by Barks. 82,84-Barks-r begin						
	7	14	21	45	73	100
85-100	6	12	18	39	62	85
101-110	5	10	15	32	51	70
111-120	4	8	12	24	37	50
121-141,143-152,154-157	3	6	9	19	29	38
142-Reprints Four Color #456 with-c	3	6	9	20	30	40
153,158,162-164,166,168-170,178,180: No Barks	2	4	6	13	18	22
159-160,165,167	3	6	9	14	19	24
161(r/#14), 171(r/#11), 177(r/#16),183(r/#6)-Barks-r	3	6	9	14	19	24
172(1/80),173(2/80)-Gold Key. Barks-a	3	6	9	16	23	30

940

Uncle Wiggily FC #276
© Howard Garis

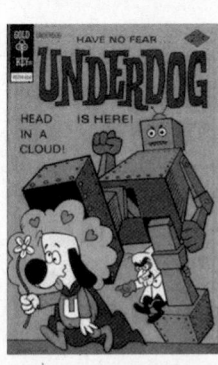

Underdog #6 © Leonardo TTV

Undertaker #5 © Chaos!

	GD 2.0	VG 4.0	FN 6.0	VF 8.0	VF/NM 9.0	NM- 9.2
174(3/80),175(4/80),176(5/80)-Whitman. Barks-a	3	6	9	21	32	42
177(6/80),178(7/80)	4	8	12	22	34	45
179(9/80)(r/#9)-(Very low distribution)	36	72	108	270	498	725
180(11/80),181(12/80, r/4-Color #495) pre-pack?	5	10	15	32	51	70
182-195: 184,185,187,188-Barks-a. 182,186,191-194-No Barks. 189(r/#5),						
190(r/#4), 195(r/4-Color #386)	3	6	9	15	21	26
196(4/82),197(5/82): 196(r/#13)	3	6	9	16	23	30
198-209 (All #90038 on-c; pre-pack; no date or date code): 198(4/83), 199(5/83), 200(6/83),						
201(6/83), 202(7/83), 203(7/83), 204(8/83), 205(8/83), 206(4/84), 207(5/83), 208(6/84),						
209(7/84). 198-202,204-206: No Barks. 203(r/#12), 207(r/#93,92), 208(r/U.S. #18),						
209(r/U.S. #21)-Barks-r	3	6	9	18	27	35
Uncle Scrooge & Money(G.K.)-Barks-r/from WDC&S #130 (3/67)						
	5	10	15	32	51	70
Mini Comic #1(1976)(3-1/4x6-1/2")-r/U.S. #115; Barks-c						
	2	4	6	8	10	12
NOTE: Barks c-Four Color 386, 456, 495, #4-37, 39, 40, 43-71.						

UNCLE SCROOGE & DONALD DUCK
Gold Key: June, 1965 (25¢, paper cover)

1-Reprint of Four Color #386(#1) & lead story from Four Color #29						
	8	16	24	54	90	125

UNCLE SCROOGE COMICS DIGEST
Gladstone Publishing: Dec, 1986 - No. 5, Aug, 1987 ($1.25, Digest-size)

1,3	1	2	3	5	6	8
2,4						6.00
5 (low print run)	1	2	3	5	7	9

UNCLE SCROOGE GOES TO DISNEYLAND (See Dell Giants)
Gladstone Publishing Ltd.: Aug, 1985 ($2.50)

1-Reprints Dell Giant w/new-c by Mel Crawford, based on old cover						
	2	4	6	8	10	12
...Comics Digest 1 ($1.50, digest size)	2	4	6	8	11	14

UNCLE SCROOGE IN COLOR
Gladstone Publishing: 1987 ($29.95, Hardcover, 9-1/4"X12-1/4", 96 pgs.)

nn-Reprints "Christmas on Bear Mountain" from Four Color 178 by Barks; Uncle Scrooge's Christmas Carol (published as Donald Duck & the Christmas Carol, A Little Golden Book), reproduced from the original art as adapted by Norman McGary from pencils by Barks; and Uncle Scrooge the Lemonade King, reproduced from the original art, plus Barks' original pencils						
	4	8	12	24	37	50
nn-Slipcase edition of 750, signed by Barks, issued at $79.95						300.00

UNCLE SCROOGE THE LEMONADE KING
Whitman Publishing Co.: 1960 (A Top Top Tales Book, 6-3/8"x7-5/8", 32 pgs.)

2465-Storybook pencilled by Carl Barks, finished art adapted by Norman McGary						
	36	72	108	270	498	725

UNCLE WIGGILY (See March of Comics #19)
Dell Publishing Co.: No. 179, Dec, 1947 - No. 543, Mar, 1954

Four Color 179 (#1)-Walt Kelly-c	15	30	45	111	198	285
Four Color 221 (3/49)-Walt Kelly-c	9	18	27	63	107	150
Four Color 276 (5/50), 320 (#1, 3/51)	8	16	24	52	86	120
Four Color 349 (9-10/51), 391 (4-5/52)	6	12	18	43	69	95
Four Color 428 (10/52), 503 (10/53), 543	5	10	15	35	55	75

UNDEAD, THE
Chaos! Comics (Black Label): Feb, 2002 ($4.99, B&W)

1-Pulido-s/Denham-a						5.00

UNDERCOVER GIRL (Starr Flagg) (See Extra Comics & Manhunt!)
Magazine Enterprises: No. 5, 1952 - No. 7, 1954

5(#1)(A-1 #62)-Fallon of the F.B.I. in all	38	76	114	222	351	480
6(A-1 #98), 7(A-1 #118)-All have Starr Flagg	36	72	108	208	329	450
NOTE: Powell c-6, 7. Whitney a-5-7.						

UNDERDOG (TV)(See Kite Fun Book, March of Comics #426, 438, 467, 479)
Charlton Comics/Gold Key: July, 1970 - No. 10, Jan, 1972; Mar, 1975 - No. 23, Feb, 1979

1 (1st series, Charlton)-1st app. Underdog	9	18	27	60	100	140
2-10	5	10	15	32	51	70
1 (2nd series, Gold Key)	6	12	18	41	66	90
2-10	4	8	12	22	34	45
11-20: 13-1st app. Shack of Solitude	3	6	9	18	27	35
21-23	3	6	9	19	29	38

UNDERDOG
Spotlight Comics: 1987 - No. 3?, 1987 ($1.50)

1-3						4.00

UNDERDOG (Volume 2)
Harvey Comics: Nov, 1993 - No. 5, July, 1994 ($2.25)

1-5						4.00
Summer Special (10/93, $2.25, 68 pgs.)						4.00

UNDERSEA AGENT
Tower Comics: Jan, 1966 - No. 6, Mar, 1967 (25¢, 68 pgs.)

1-Davy Jones, Undersea Agent begins	8	16	24	58	97	135
2-6: 2-Jones gains magnetic powers. 5-Origin & 1st app. of Merman. 6-Kane/Wood-c(r)	6	12	18	37	59	80
NOTE: Gil Kane a-3-6; c-4, 5. Moldoff a-2i.						

UNDERSEA FIGHTING COMMANDOS (See Fighting Undersea...)
I.W. Enterprises: 1964

I.W. Reprint #1,2('64): 1-r/#? 2-r/#1; Severin-c	2	4	6	9	13	16

UNDERTAKER (World Wrestling Federation)
Chaos! Comics: Feb, 1999 - No. 10, Jan, 2000 ($2.50/$2.95)

Preview (2/99)						2.50
1-10: Reg. and photo covers for each. 1-(4/99)						3.00
1-($6.95) DF Ed.; Brereton painted-c						7.00
...Halloween Special (10/99, $2.95) Reg. & photo-c						3.00
Wizard #0						2.50

UNDERWATER CITY, THE
Dell Publishing Co.: No. 1328, 1961

Four Color 1328-Movie, Evans-a	7	14	21	47	76	105

UNDERWORLD (...True Crime Stories)
D. S. Publishing Co.: Feb-Mar, 1948 - No. 9, June-July, 1949 (52 pgs.)

1-Moldoff (Shelly)-c; excessive violence	45	90	135	275	450	625
2-Moldoff (Shelly)-c; Ma Barker story used in SOTI, pg. 95; female electrocution panel; lingerie art	41	82	123	254	410	565
3-McWilliams-c/a; extreme violence, mutilation	40	80	120	235	368	500
4-Used in Love and Death by Legman; Ingels-a	34	68	102	197	311	425
5-Ingels-a	24	48	72	139	220	300
6-9: 8-Ravielli-a	19	38	57	112	176	240

UNDERWORLD
DC Comics: Dec, 1987 - No. 4, Mar, 1988 ($1.00, limited series, mature)

1-4						2.50

UNDERWORLD (Movie)
IDW Publishing: Sept, 2003; Dec, 2005 ($6.99)

1-Movie adaptation; photo-c						7.00
...Evolution (12/05, $7.49) adaptation of movie sequel; Vazquez-a						7.50
TPB (7/04, $19.99) r/#1 and Underworld:Red in Tooth and Claw #1-3						20.00

UNDERWORLD
Marvel Comics: Apr, 2006 - No. 5, Aug, 2006 ($2.99, limited series)

1-5: Staz Johnson-a. 2-Spider-Man app. 3,4-Punisher app.						3.00

UNDERWORLD CRIME
Fawcett Publications: June, 1952 - No. 9, Oct, 1953

1	34	68	102	197	311	425
2	21	42	63	124	195	265
3-6,8,9 (8,9-exist?)	19	38	57	112	176	240
7-(6/53)-Bondage/torture-c	43	86	129	262	431	600

UNDERWORLD: RED IN TOOTH AND CLAW (Movie)
IDW Publishing: Feb, 2004 - No. 3, Apr, 2004 ($3.99, limited series)

1-3-The early days of the Vampire and Lycan war; Postic & Marinkovich-a						4.00

UNDERWORLD STORY, THE (Movie)
Avon Periodicals: 1950

nn-(Scarce)-Ravielli-c	29	58	87	170	268	365

UNDERWORLD UNLEASHED
DC Comics: Nov, 1995 - No. 3, Jan, 1996 ($2.95, limited series)

1-3: Mark Waid scripts & Howard Porter-c/a(p)						3.50
...: Abyss: Hell's Sentinel 1-($2.95)-Alan Scott, Phantom Stranger, Zatanna app.						3.00
...: Apokolips-Dark Uprising 1 ($1.95)						2.25
...: Batman-Devil's Asylum 1-($2.95)-Batman app.						3.00
...: Patterns of Fear-($2.95)						3.00
TPB (1998, $17.95) r/#1-3 & Abyss-Hell's Sentinel						18.00

UNEARTHLY SPECTACULARS
Harvey Publications: Oct, 1965 - No. 3, Mar, 1967

The Unexpected #202 © DC

Union #4 © WSP

Universe X #9 © MAR

	GD 2.0	VG 4.0	FN 6.0	VF 8.0	VF/NM 9.0	NM- 9.2
1-(12¢)-Tiger Boy; Simon-c	4	8	12	24	37	50
2-(25¢ giants)-Jack Q. Frost, Tiger Boy & Three Rocketeers app.; Williamson, Wood, Kane-a; r-1 story/Thrill-O-Rama #2	4	8	12	28	44	60
3-(25¢ giants)-Jack Q. Frost app.; Williamson/Crandall-a; r-from Alarming Advs. #1,1962	4	8	12	28	44	60

NOTE: Crandall a-3r. G. Kane a-3. Orlando a-3. Simon, Sparling, Wood c-2. Simon/Kirby a-3r. Torres a-1?. Wildey a-1(3). Williamson a-2. Wood a-2(2).

UNEXPECTED, THE (Formerly Tales of the...)
National Per. Publ./DC Comics: No. 105, Feb-Mar, 1968 - No. 222, May, 1982

	GD 2.0	VG 4.0	FN 6.0	VF 8.0	VF/NM 9.0	NM- 9.2
105-Begin 12¢ cover price	6	12	18	37	59	80
106-113: 113-Last 12¢ issue (6-7/69)	4	8	12	26	41	55
114,115,117,118,120-125	3	6	9	19	29	38
116 (36 pgs.)-Wrightson-a?	3	6	9	20	30	40
119-Wrightson-a, 8pgs.(36 pgs.)	4	8	12	28	44	60
126,127,129-136-(52 pgs.)	3	6	9	19	29	38
128(52 pgs.)-Wrightson-a	4	8	12	28	44	60
137-156	2	4	6	11	16	20
157-162-(100 pgs.)	4	8	12	24	37	50
163-188: 187,188-(44 pgs.)	2	4	6	9	12	15
189,190,192-195 ($1.00, 68 pgs.): 189 on are combined with House of Secrets & The Witching Hour	2	4	6	9	13	16
191-Rogers-a(p) ($1.00, 68 pgs.)	2	4	6	10	14	18
196-222: 200-Return of Johnny Peril by Tuska. 205-213-Johnny Peril app. 210-Time Warp story. 222-Giffen-a	1	2	3	5	7	9

NOTE: Neal Adams c-110, 112-115, 118, 121, 124. J. Craig a-195. Ditko a-189, 221p, 222p; c-222. Drucker a-107r, 132r. Giffen a-219, 222. Kaluta c-203, 212. Kirby a-127r, 162. Kubert c-204, 214-216, 219-221. Mayer a-217p, 220, 221p. Moldoff a-136r. Moreira a-133. Mortimer a-212p. Newton a-205, 207p; c-191. Perez a-217p. Redondo a-155, 166, 195. Reese a-145. Sparling a-107, 205-209p, 212p. Spiegle a-217. Starlin c-198. Toth a-126r, 127r. Tuska a-127, 132, 134, 136, 139, 152, 180, 200p. Wildey a-128r, 193. Wood a-122i, 133i, 137i, 138i. Wrightson a-161r(2 pgs.). Johnny Peril a-r/#106-114, 116, 117, 200, 205-213.

UNEXPECTED ANNUAL, THE (See DC Special Series #4)

UNHOLY UNION
Image Comics (Top Cow): July, 2007 ($3.99, one-shot)
1-Witchblade & The Darkness meet Hulk, Ghost Rider & Doctor Strange; Silvestri-c ... 4.00

UNIDENTIFIED FLYING ODDBALL (See Walt Disney Showcase #52)

UNION
Image Comics (WildStorm Productions): June, 1993 - No. 0, July, 1994 ($1.95, lim. series)
0-(7/94, $2.50)	2.50
0-Alternate Portacio-c (See Deathblow #5)	5.00
1-($2.50)-Embossed foil-c; Texeira-c/a in all	2.50
1-($1.95)-Newsstand edition w/o foil-c	2.50
2-4: 4-(7/94)	2.50

UNION
Image Comics (WildStorm Prod.): Feb, 1995 - No. 9, Dec, 1995 ($2.50)
1-3,5-9: 3-Savage Dragon app. 6-Fairchild from Gen 13 app.	2.50
4-($1.95, Newsstand)-WildStorm Rising Pt. 3	2.50
4-($2.50, Direct Market)-WildStorm Rising Pt. 3, bound-in card	2.50

UNION: FINAL VENGEANCE
Image Comics (WildStorm Productions): Oct, 1997 ($2.50)
1-Golden-c/Heisler-s ... 2.50

UNION JACK
Marvel Comics: Dec, 1998 - No. 3, Feb, 1999 ($2.99, limited series)
1-3-Raab-s/Cassaday-s/a ... 3.00

UNION JACK
Marvel Comics: Nov, 2006 - No. 4, Feb, 2007 ($2.99, limited series)
1-4-Gage-s/Perkins-c/a	3.00
...: London Falling TPB (2007, $10.99) r/#1-4; Perkins sketch page	11.00

UNITED COMICS (Formerly Fritzi Ritz #7; has Fritzi Ritz logo)
United Features Syndicate: Aug, 1940; No. 8, 1950 - No. 26, Jan-Feb, 1953

	GD 2.0	VG 4.0	FN 6.0	VF 8.0	VF/NM 9.0	NM- 9.2
1(68 pgs.)-Fritzi Ritz & Phil Fumble	23	46	69	135	213	290
8-Fritzi Ritz, Abbie & Slats	8	16	24	44	57	70
9-21: 20-Strange As It Seems; Russell Patterson Cheesecake-a	8	16	24	40	50	60
22-(5-6/52) 2 pgs. early Peanuts by Schulz (1st in comics?)	11	22	33	60	83	105
23-26: 23-(7-8/52). 24-(9-10/52). 25-(11-12/52). 26-(1-2/53). All have 2 pgs. early Peanuts by Schulz	9	18	27	50	65	80

NOTE: Abbie & Slats reprinted from Tip Top.

UNITED NATIONS, THE (See Classics Illustrated Special Issue)

UNITED STATES AIR FORCE PRESENTS: THE HIDDEN CREW
U.S. Air Force: 1964 (36 pgs.)

	GD 2.0	VG 4.0	FN 6.0	VF 8.0	VF/NM 9.0	NM- 9.2
nn-Schaffenberger-a	2	4	6	10	14	18

UNITED STATES FIGHTING AIR FORCE (Also see U.S. Fighting Air Force)
Superior Comics Ltd.: Sept, 1952 - No. 29, Oct, 1956

	GD 2.0	VG 4.0	FN 6.0	VF 8.0	VF/NM 9.0	NM- 9.2
1	13	26	39	72	101	130
2	8	16	24	42	54	65
3-10	7	14	21	37	46	55
11-29	7	14	21	35	43	50

UNITED STATES MARINES
William H. Wise/Life's Romances Publ. Co./Magazine Ent. #5-8/Toby Press #7-11: 1943 - No. 4, 1944; No. 5, 1952 - No. 8, 1952; No. 7 - No. 11, 1953

	GD 2.0	VG 4.0	FN 6.0	VF 8.0	VF/NM 9.0	NM- 9.2
nn-Mart Bailey-a	20	40	60	117	184	250
2-Bailey-a; Tojo classic-c	43	86	129	262	431	600
3-Tojo-c	40	80	120	235	368	500
4	13	26	39	74	105	135
5(A-1 #55)-Bailey-a, 6(A-1 #60), 7(A-1 #68), 8(A-1 #72)	10	20	30	56	76	95
7-11 (Toby)	9	18	27	47	61	75

NOTE: Powell a-5-7.

UNITY
Valiant: No. 0, Aug, 1992 - No. 1, 1992 (Free comics w/limited dist., 20 pgs.)
0 (Blue)-Prequel to Unity x-overs in all Valiant titles; B. Smith-c/a. (Free to everyone that bought all 8 titles that month.)	2.50
0 (Red)-Same as above, but w/red logo (5,000).	3.00
1-Epilogue to Unity x-overs; B. Smith-c/a. (1 copy available for every 8 Valiant books ordered by dealers.)	2.50
1 (Gold), 1-(Platinum)-Promotional copy.	6.00
...: The Lost Chapter 1 (Yearbook) (2/95, $3.50)-"1994" in indicia	4.00

UNITY 2000 (See preludes in Shadowman #3,4 flipbooks)
Acclaim Comics: Nov, 1999 - No. 3, Jan, 2000 ($2.50, unfinished limited series planned for 6 issues)
Preview -B&W plot preview and cover art; paper cover	2.50
1-3-Starlin-a/Shooter-s	2.50

UNIVERSAL MONSTERS
Dark Horse Comics: 1993 ($4.95/$5.95, 52 pgs.)(All adapt original movies)

	GD 2.0	VG 4.0	FN 6.0	VF 8.0	VF/NM 9.0	NM- 9.2
Creature From the Black Lagoon nn-($4.95)-Art Adams/Austin-c/a, Dracula nn-($4.95), Frankenstein nn-($3.95)-Painted-c/a, The Mummy nn-($4.95)-Painted-c	1	2	3	4	5	7
...: Cavalcade of Horror TPB (1/06, $19.95) r/one-shots; Eric Powell intro. & cover						20.00

UNIVERSAL PRESENTS DRACULA-THE MUMMY & OTHER STORIES
Dell Publishing Co.: Sept-Nov, 1963 (one-shot, 84 pgs.) (Also see Dell Giants)

	GD 2.0	VG 4.0	FN 6.0	VF 8.0	VF/NM 9.0	NM- 9.2
02-530-311-r/Dracula 12-231-212, The Mummy 12-437-211 & part of Ghost Stories No. 1	17	34	51	126	223	320

UNIVERSAL SOLDIER (Movie)
Now Comics: Sept, 1992 - No. 3, Nov, 1992 (Limited series, polybagged, mature)
1-3 ($2.50, Direct Sales) 1-Movie adapatation; hologram on-c (all direct sales editions have painted-c)	2.50
1-3 ($1.95, Newsstand)-Rewritten & redrawn code approved version; all newsstand editions have photo-c	2.50

UNIVERSE
Image Comics (Top Cow): Sept, 2001 - No. 8, July, 2002 ($2.50)
1-7-Jenkins-s	2.50
8-($4.95) extra short-s by Jenkins; pin-up pages	5.00

UNIVERSE X (See Earth X)
Marvel Comics: Sept, 2000 - No. 12, Sept. 2001 ($3.99/$3.50, limited series)
0-Ross-c/Braithwaite-a/Ross & Krueger-s	4.00
1-12: 5-Funeral of Captain America	3.50
... Beasts (6/00, $3.99) Yeates-a/Ross-c	4.00
... Cap (Capt. America) (2/01, $3.99) Yeates & Totleben-a/Ross-c; Cap dies	4.00
... 4 (Fantastic 4) (10/00, $3.99) Brent Anderson-a/Ross-c	4.00
... Iron Men (9/01, $3.99) Anderson-a/Ross-c; leads into #12	4.00
... Omnibus (6/01, $3.99) Ross B&W sketchbook and character bios	4.00
Sketchbook- Wizard supplement; B&W character sketches and bios	2.50
...Spidey (1/01, $3.99) Romita Sr. flashback-a/Guice-a/Ross-c	4.00
...X (11/01, $3.99) Series conclusion; Braithwaith-a/Ross wraparound-c	4.00
Volume 1 TPB (1/02, $24.95) r/#0-7 & Spidey, 4, & Cap; new Ross-c	25.00
Volume 2 TPB (6/02, $24.95) r/#8-12 &X, Beasts, Iron Men and Omnibus	25.00

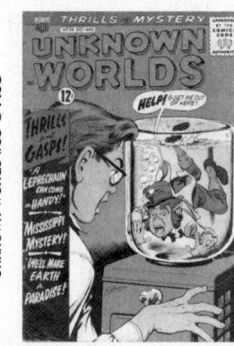

Unknown Worlds #35 © ACG

Untold Tales of Purgatori #1 © Chaos!

Untold Tales of Spider-Man #6 © MAR

	GD 2.0	VG 4.0	FN 6.0	VF 8.0	VF/NM 9.0	NM- 9.2

UNKNOWN MAN, THE (Movie)
Avon Periodicals: 1951

nn-Kinstler-c	28	56	84	162	256	350

UNKNOWN SOLDIER (Formerly Star-Spangled War Stories)
National Periodical Publications/DC Comics: No. 205, Apr-May, 1977 - No. 268, Oct, 1982
(See Our Army at War #168 for 1st app.)

205	2	4	6	13	18	22
206-210,220,221,251: 220,221 (44pgs.). 251-Enemy Ace begins						
	2	4	6	9	13	16
211-218,222-247,250,252-264	2	4	6	8	10	12
219-Miller-a (44 pgs.)	2	4	6	11	16	20
248,249,265-267: 248,249-Enemy Ace. 265-267-Enemy Ace vs. Balloon Buster.						
	2	4	6	8	10	12
268-Death of Unknown Soldier	3	6	9	14	19	24

NOTE: *Chaykin* a-234. *Evans* a-265-267; c-235. *Kubert* c-Most. *Miller* a-219p. *Severin* a-251-253, 260, 261, 265-267. *Simonson* a-254-256. *Spiegle* a-258, 259, 262-264.

UNKNOWN SOLDIER, THE (Also see Brave &the Bold #146)
DC Comics: Winter, 1988-'89 - No. 12, Dec, 1989 ($1.50, maxi-series, mature)

1-12: 8-Begin $1.75-c		3.00

UNKNOWN SOLDIER
DC Comics (Vertigo): Apr, 1997 - No 4, July, 1997 ($2.50, mini-series)

1-Ennis-s/Plunkett-a/Bradstreet-c in all		6.00
2-4		4.00
TPB (1998, $12.95) r/#1-4		13.00

UNKNOWN WORLD (Strange Stories From Another World #2 on)
Fawcett Publications: June, 1952

1-Norman Saunders painted-c	45	90	135	275	450	635

UNKNOWN WORLDS (See Journey Into...)
UNKNOWN WORLDS
American Comics Group/Best Synd. Features: Aug, 1960 - No. 57, Aug, 1967

1-Schaffenberger-c	19	38	57	138	244	350
2-Dinosaur-c/story	11	22	33	79	140	200
3-5	9	18	27	65	113	160
6-11: 9-Dinosaur-c/story. 11-Last 10¢ issue	8	16	24	54	90	125
12-19: 12-Begin 12¢ issues?; ends #57	6	12	18	43	69	95
20-Herbie cameo (12-1/62-63)	7	14	21	45	73	100
21-35: 35-Herbie one pagers thru #39	5	10	15	32	51	70
36- "The People vs. Hendricks" by Craig; most popular ACG story ever						
	5	10	15	35	55	75
37-46	4	8	12	28	44	60
47-Williamson-a r-from Adventures Into the Unknown #96, 3 pgs.; Craig-a						
	5	10	15	30	48	65
48-57: 53-Frankenstein app.	4	8	12	26	41	55

NOTE: *Ditko* a-49, 50p, 54. *Forte* a-3, 6, 11. *Landau* a-56(2). *Reinman* a-3, 9, 13, 20, 22, 23, 36, 38, 54. *Whitney* c/a-most issues. John Force, Magic Agent app.-35, 36, 48, 50, 52, 54, 56.

UNKNOWN WORLDS OF FRANK BRUNNER
Eclipse Comics: Aug, 1985 - No. 2, Aug, 1985 ($1.75)

1,2-B&W-r in color		3.50

UNKNOWN WORLDS OF SCIENCE FICTION
Marvel Comics: Jan, 1975 - No. 6, Nov, 1975; 1976 ($1.00, B&W Magazine)

1-Williamson/Krenkel/Torres/Frazetta-r/Witzend #1, Neal Adams-r/Phase 1; Brunner & Kaluta-r; Freas/Romita-c	3	6	9	14	19	24
2-6: 5-Kaluta text illos	2	4	6	11	16	20
Special 1(1976,100 pgs.)-Newton painted-c	3	6	9	14	19	24

NOTE: *Brunner* a-2; c-4, 6. *Buscema* a-Special 1p. *Chaykin* a-5. *Colan* a(p)-1, 3, 5, 6. *Corben* a-4. *Kaluta* a-2, Special 1(ext illos); c-2. *Morrow* a-3, 5, *Nino* a-3, 6, Special 1. *Perez* a-2, 3. Ray Bradbury interview in #1.

UNLIMITED ACCESS (Also see Marvel Vs. DC)
Marvel Comics: Dec, 1997 - No. 4, Mar, 1998 ($2.99/$1.99, limited series)

1-Spider-Man, Wonder Woman, Green Lantern & Hulk app.		3.50
2,3-($1.99): 2-X-Men, Legion of Super-Heroes app. 3-Original Avengers vs. original Justice League		2.50
4-($2.99) Amalgam Legion vs. Darkseid & Magneto		3.00

UN-MEN, THE
DC Comics (Vertigo): Oct, 2007 - Present ($2.99)

1-Whelan-s/Hawthorne-a/Hanuka-c		3.00

UNSANE (Formerly Mighty Bear #13, 14? or The Outlaws #10-14?)(Satire)
Star Publications: No. 15, June, 1954

15-Disbrow-a(2); L. B. Cole-c	34	68	102	197	311	425

UNSEEN, THE
Visual Editions/Standard Comics: No. 5, 1952 - No. 15, July, 1954

5-Horror stories in all; Toth-a	41	82	123	250	400	550
6,7,9,10-Jack Katz-a	30	60	90	174	275	375
8,11,13,14	23	46	69	132	209	285
12,15-Toth-a. 12-Tuska-a	30	60	90	174	275	375

NOTE: *Nick Cardy* c-12. *Fawcette* a-13, 14. *Sekowsky* a-7, 8(2), 10, 13, 15.

UNTAMED
Marvel Comics (Epic Comics/Heavy Hitters): June, 1993 - No. 3, Aug, 1993 ($1.95, lim. series)

1-($2.50)-Embossed-c		2.75
2,3		2.50

UNTAMED LOVE (Also see Frank Frazetta's Untamed Love)
Quality Comics Group (Comic Magazines): Jan, 1950 - No. 5, Sept, 1950

1-Ward-c, Gustavson-a	26	52	78	152	239	325
2,4: 2-5-Photo-c	16	32	48	94	147	200
3,5-Gustavson-a	17	34	51	100	158	215

UNTOLD LEGEND OF CAPTAIN MARVEL, THE
Marvel Comics: Apr, 1997 - No. 3, June, 1997 ($2.50, limited series)

1-3		2.50

UNTOLD LEGEND OF THE BATMAN, THE (Also see Promotional section)
DC Comics: July, 1980 - No. 3, Sept, 1980 (Limited series)

1-Origin; Joker-c; Byrne's 1st work at DC		6.00
2,3		4.50

NOTE: *Aparo* a-1i, 2, 3. *Byrne* a-1p.

UNTOLD ORIGIN OF THE FEMFORCE, THE (Also see Femforce)
AC Comics: 1989 ($4.95, 68 pgs.)

1-Origin Femforce; Bill Black-a(i) & scripts		6.00

UNTOLD TALES OF CHASTITY
Chaos! Comics: Nov, 2000 ($2.95, one-shot)

1-Origin; Steven Grant-s/Peter Vale-c/a		3.00
1-Premium Edition with glow in the dark cover		13.00

UNTOLD TALES OF LADY DEATH
Chaos! Comics: Nov, 2000 ($2.95, one-shot)

1-Origin of Lady Death; Cremator app.; Kaminski-s		3.00
1-Premium Edition with glow in the dark cover by Steven Hughes		13.00

UNTOLD TALES OF PURGATORI
Chaos! Comics: Nov, 2000 ($2.95, one-shot)

1-Purgatori in 57 B.C.; Rio-a/Grant-s		3.00
1-Premium Edition with glow in the dark cover		13.00

UNTOLD TALES OF SPIDER-MAN (Also see Amazing Fantasy #16-18)
Marvel Comics: Sept, 1995 - No. 25, Sept, 1997 (99¢)

1-Kurt Busiek scripts begin; Pat Olliffe-c/a in all (except #9).		3.00
2-22, -1(7/97), 23-25: 2-1st app. Batwing. 4-1st app. The Spacemen (Gantry, Orbit, Satellite & Vacuum). 8-1st app. The Headsman; The Enforcers (The Big Man, Montana, The Ox & Fancy Dan) app. 9-Ron Frenz-a. 10-1st app. Commanda. 16-Reintro Mary Jane Watson. 21-X-Men-c/app. 25-Green Goblin		2.50
...'96-(1996, $1.95, 64 pgs.)-Kurt Busiek scripts; Mike Allred-c/a; Kurt Busiek & Pat Olliffe app. in back-up story; contains pin-ups		2.50
...'97-(1997, $1.95)-Wraparound-c		2.50
...: Strange Encounters ('98, $5.99) Dr. Strange app.		6.00

UNTOLD TALES OF THE NEW UNIVERSE (Based on Marvel's 1986 New Universe titles)
Marvel Comics: May, 2006 ($2.99, series of one-shots)

...: D. P. 7 - Takes place between issues #4 & 5 of D. P. 7 series; Bright-a/Cebulski-s		3.00
...: Justice - Peter David-s/Carmine Di Giandomenico-a		3.00
...: Nightmask - Takes place between issues #4 & 5 of Nightmask series; The Gnome app.		3.00
...: Psi-Force - Tony Bedard-s/Russ Braun-a		3.00
...: Star Brand - Romita & Romita Jr.-c/Pulido-a		3.00
TPB (2006, $15.99) r/one-shots & stories from Amaz. Fantasy #18,19 & New Avengers #16		16.00

UNTOUCHABLES, THE (TV)
Dell Publishing Co.: No. 1237, 10-12/61 - No. 4, 8-10/62 (All have Robert Stack photo-c)

Four Color 1237(#1)	20	40	60	146	261	375
Four Color 1286	14	28	42	102	181	260
01-879-207, 12-879-210(01879-210 on inside)	9	18	27	63	107	150

UNTOUCHABLES
Caliber Comics: Aug, 1997 - No. 4 ($2.95, B&W)

1-4: 1-Pruett-s; variant covers by Kaluta & Showman		3.00

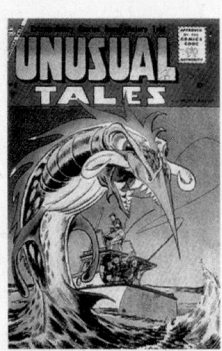

Unusual Tales #6 © CC

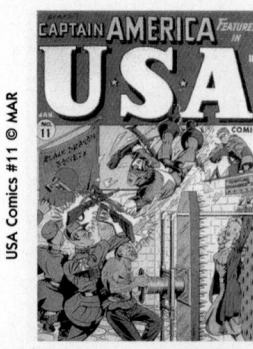

USA Comics #11 © MAR

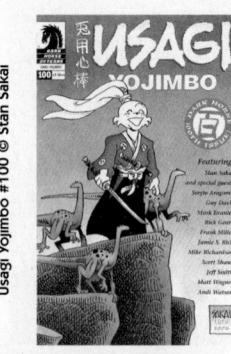

Usagi Yojimbo #100 © Stan Sakai

	GD 2.0	VG 4.0	FN 6.0	VF 8.0	VF/NM 9.0	NM- 9.2

UNUSUAL TALES (Blue Beetle & Shadows From Beyond #50 on)
Charlton Comics: Nov, 1955 - No. 49, Mar-Apr, 1965

	GD 2.0	VG 4.0	FN 6.0	VF 8.0	VF/NM 9.0	NM- 9.2
1	30	60	90	174	275	375
2	15	30	45	86	133	180
3-5	13	26	39	72	101	130
6-Ditko-c only	15	30	45	86	133	180
7,8-Ditko-c/a. 8-Robot-c	27	54	81	156	246	335
9-Ditko-c/a (20 pgs.)	30	60	90	172	271	370
10-Ditko-c/a(4)	31	62	93	180	285	390
11-(3/58, 68 pgs.)-Ditko-a(4)	30	60	90	172	271	370
12,14-Ditko-a	18	36	54	105	165	225
13,16-20	6	12	18	43	69	95
15-Ditko-c/a	23	46	69	130	205	280
21,24,28	5	10	15	35	55	75
22,23,25-27,29-Ditko-a	9	18	27	65	113	160
30-49	4	8	12	26	41	55

NOTE: *Colan* a-11. *Ditko* c-22, 23, 25-27, 31(part).

UP FROM HARLEM (Tom Skinner...)
Spire Christian Comics (Fleming H. Revell Co.): 1973 (35/49¢)

	GD 2.0	VG 4.0	FN 6.0	VF 8.0	VF/NM 9.0	NM- 9.2
nn	2	4	6	8	10	12

UP-TO-DATE COMICS
King Features Syndicate: No date (1938) (36 pgs.; B&W cover) (10¢)

nn-Popeye & Henry cover; The Phantom, Jungle Jim & Flash Gordon by Raymond, The Katzenjammer Kids, Curley Harper & others. Note: Variations in content exist.

	GD 2.0	VG 4.0	FN 6.0	VF 8.0	VF/NM 9.0	NM- 9.2
	25	50	75	145	228	310

UP YOUR NOSE AND OUT YOUR EAR (Satire)
Klevart Enterprises: Apr, 1972 - No. 2, June, 1972 (52 pgs., magazine)

	GD 2.0	VG 4.0	FN 6.0	VF 8.0	VF/NM 9.0	NM- 9.2
V1#1,2	2	4	6	10	14	18

URTH 4 (Also see Earth 4)
Continuity Comics: May, 1989 - No. 4, Dec, 1990 ($2.00, deluxe format)

1-4: Ms. Mystic characters. 2-Neal Adams-c/a   2.50

URZA-MISHRA WAR ON THE WORLD OF MAGIC THE GATHERING
Acclaim Comics (Armada): 1996 - No. 2, 1996 ($5.95, limited series)

1,2   6.00

U.S. (See Uncle Sam)

USA COMICS
Timely Comics (USA): Aug, 1941 - No. 17, Fall, 1945

	GD 2.0	VG 4.0	FN 6.0	VF 8.0	VF/NM 9.0	NM- 9.2
1-Origin Major Liberty (called Mr. Liberty #1); Rockman by Wolverton; 1st app. The Whizzer by Avison; The Defender with sidekick Rusty & Jack Frost begin; The Young Avenger only app.; S&K-c plus 1 pg. art	1150	2300	3450	8500	15,000	22,000
2-Origin Captain Terror & The Vagabond; last Wolverton Rockman; Hitler-c	394	788	1182	2561	4531	6500
3-No Whizzer	300	600	900	1931	3366	4800
4-Last Rockman, Major Liberty, Defender, Jack Frost, & Capt. Terror; Corporal Dix app.	290	580	870	1813	3007	4200
5-Origin American Avenger & Roko the Amazing; The Blue Blade, The Black Widow & Victory Boys, Gypo the Gypsy Giant & Hills of Horror only app.; Sergeant Dix begins; no Whizzer; Hitler, Mussolini & Tojo-c	269	538	807	1681	2791	3900
6-Captain America (ends #17), The Destroyer, Jap Buster Johnson, Jeep Jones begin; Terror Squad only app.	333	666	1000	2165	3833	5500
7-Captain Daring, Disk-Eyes the Detective by Wolverton app.; origin & only app. Marvel Boy (3/43); Secret Stamp begins; no Whizzer; Sergeant Dix; classic Schomburg-c	333	666	1000	2165	3833	5500
8,10: 10-The Thunderbird only app.	248	496	744	1550	2575	3600
9-Last Secret Stamp; Hitler-c; classic-c	276	552	828	1725	2863	4000
11,12: 11-No Jeep Jones	179	358	537	1119	1860	2600
13-17: 13-No Whizzer; Jeep Jones ends. 15-No Destroyer; Jap Buster Johnson ends	134	268	402	838	1394	1950

NOTE: *Brodsky* c-14. *Gabrielle* c-4. *Schomburg* c-6, 7, 10, 12, 13, 15-17. *Shores* a-1, 4; c-9, 11. *Ed Win* a-4. *Cover features:* 1-The Defender; 2, 3-Captain Terror; 4-Major Liberty; 5-Victory Boys; 6-17-Captain America & Bucky.

U.S. AGENT (See Jeff Jordan...)

U.S. AGENT (See Captain America #354)
Marvel Comics: June, 1993 - No. 4, Sept, 1993 ($1.75, limited series)

1-4   2.50

U.S. AGENT
Marvel Comics: Aug, 2001 - No. 3, Oct, 2001 ($2.99, limited series)

1-3: Ordway-s/a(p)/c. 2,3-Captain America app.   3.00

USAGI YOJIMBO (See Albedo, Doomsday Squad #3 & Space Usagi)
Fantagraphics Books: July, 1987 - No. 38 ($2.00/$2.25, B&W)

	GD 2.0	VG 4.0	FN 6.0	VF 8.0	VF/NM 9.0	NM- 9.2
1	1	2	3	5	7	9
1,8,10-2nd printings						2.50
2-9						4.00
10,11: 10-Leonardo app. (TMNT). 11-Aragonés-a						6.00
12-29						3.00
30-38: 30-Begin $2.25-c						3.00
Color Special 1 (11/89, $2.95, 68 pgs.)-new & r						3.50
Color Special 2 (10/91, $3.50)						3.50
Color Special #3 (10/92, $3.50)-Jeff Smith's Bone promo on inside-c						3.50
Summer Special 1 (1986, B&W, $2.75)-r/early Albedo issues						3.00

USAGI YOJIMBO
Mirage Studios: V2#1, Mar, 1993 - No. 16, 1994 ($2.75)

V2#1-16: 1-Teenage Mutant Ninja Turtles app.   3.00

USAGI YOJIMBO
Dark Horse Comics: V3#1, Apr, 1996 - Present ($2.95/$2.99, B&W)

	NM- 9.2
V3#1-99,101-105: Stan Sakai-c/a	3.00
100-(1/07, $3.50) Stan Sakai roast by various incl. Aragonés, Wagner, Miller, Geary	3.50
Color Special #4 (7/97, $2.95) "Green Persimmon"	3.00
Daisho TPB ('98, $14.95) r/Mirage series #7-14	15.00
Demon Mask TPB ('01, $15.95)	16.00
Glimpses of Death TPB (7/06, $15.95) r/#76-82	16.00
Grasscutter TPB ('99, $16.95) r/#13-22	17.00
Gray Shadows TPB ('00, $14.95) r/#23-30	15.00
Seasons TPB ('99, $14.95) r/#7-12	15.00
Shades of Death TPB ('97, $14.95) r/Mirage series #1-6	15.00
The Brink of Life and Death TPB ('98, $14.95) r/Mirage series #13,15,16 & Dark Horse series #1-6	15.00
The Shrouded Moon TPB (1/03, $15.95) r/#46-52	16.00

U.S. AIR FORCE COMICS (Army Attack #38 on)
Charlton Comics: Oct, 1958 - No. 37, Mar-Apr, 1965

	GD 2.0	VG 4.0	FN 6.0	VF 8.0	VF/NM 9.0	NM- 9.2
1	6	12	18	39	62	85
2	3	6	9	21	32	42
3-10	3	6	9	18	27	35
11-20	3	6	9	17	25	32
21-37	3	6	9	16	22	28

NOTE: *Glanzman* c/a-9, 10, 12. *Montes/Bache* a-33.

USA IS READY
Dell Publishing Co.: 1941 (68 pgs.), one-shot

	GD 2.0	VG 4.0	FN 6.0	VF 8.0	VF/NM 9.0	NM- 9.2
1-War propaganda	40	80	120	244	392	540

U.S. BORDER PATROL COMICS (Sgt. Dick Carter of the...) (See Holyoke One Shot)

USER
DC Comics (Vertigo): 2001 - No. 3, 2001 ($5.95, limited series)

1-3-Devin Grayson-s; Sean Phillips & John Bolton-a   6.00

U.S. FIGHTING AIR FORCE (Also see United States Fighting Air Force)
I. W. Enterprises: No date (1960s?)

	GD 2.0	VG 4.0	FN 6.0	VF 8.0	VF/NM 9.0	NM- 9.2
1,9(nd): 1-r/United States Fighting...#?. 9-r/#1	2	4	6	8	11	14

U.S. FIGHTING MEN
Super Comics: 1963 - 1964 (Reprints)

	GD 2.0	VG 4.0	FN 6.0	VF 8.0	VF/NM 9.0	NM- 9.2
10-r/With the U.S. Paratroops #4(Avon)	2	4	6	9	13	16
11,12,15-18: 11-r/Monty Hall #10. 12,16,17,18-r/U.S. Fighting Air Force #10,3,?&? 15-r/Man Comics #11	2	4	6	9	13	16

U.S. JONES (Also see Wonderworld Comics #28)
Fox Features Syndicate: Nov, 1941 - No. 2, Jan, 1942

	GD 2.0	VG 4.0	FN 6.0	VF 8.0	VF/NM 9.0	NM- 9.2
1-U.S. Jones & The Topper begin; Nazi-c	124	248	372	775	1288	1800
2-Nazi-c	83	166	249	519	860	1200

U.S. MARINES
Charlton Comics: Fall, 1964 (12¢, one-shot)

	GD 2.0	VG 4.0	FN 6.0	VF 8.0	VF/NM 9.0	NM- 9.2
1-1st app. Capt. Dude; Glanzman-a	3	6	9	20	30	40

U.S. MARINES IN ACTION
Avon Periodicals: Aug, 1952 - No. 3, Dec, 1952

	GD 2.0	VG 4.0	FN 6.0	VF 8.0	VF/NM 9.0	NM- 9.2
1-Louis Ravielli-c/a	10	20	30	54	72	90
2,3: 3-Kinstler-c	8	16	24	40	50	60

U.S. 1
Marvel Comics Group: May, 1983 - No. 12, Oct, 1984 (7,8: painted-c)

U.S. War Machine V2 #12 © MAR

Valley of the Dinosaurs #1 © CC

Vampirella #14 © WP

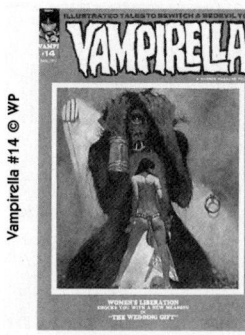

	GD 2.0	VG 4.0	FN 6.0	VF 8.0	VF/NM 9.0	NM- 9.2

1-12: 2-Sienkiewicz-c. 3-12-Michael Golden-c ... 2.50

U.S. PARATROOPS (See With the...)

U.S. PARATROOPS
I. W. Enterprises: 1964?

1,8: 1-r/With the U.S. Paratroops #1; Wood-c. 8-r/With the U.S. Paratroops #6; Kinstler-c	2	4	6	9	13	16

U.S. TANK COMMANDOS
Avon Periodicals: June, 1952 - No. 4, Mar, 1953

1-Kinstler-c	11	22	33	60	83	105
2-4: Kinstler-c	8	16	24	44	57	70
I.W. Reprint #1,8: 1-r/#1. 8-r/#3	2	4	6	9	13	16

NOTE: Kinstler a-l.W. #1; c-1-4, I.W. #1, 8.

U.S. WAR MACHINE (Also see Iron Man and War Machine)
Marvel Comics (MAX): Nov, 2001 - No. 12, Jan, 2002 ($1.50, B&W, weekly limited series)

1-12-Chuck Austen-s/a/c ... 2.50
TPB (12/01, $14.95) r/#1-12 ... 15.00

U.S. WAR MACHINE 2.0
Marvel Comics (MAX): Sept, 2003 - No. 3, Sept, 2003 ($2.99, weekly, limited series)

1-3-Austen-s/Christian Moore-CGI art ... 3.00

"V" (TV)
DC Comics: Feb, 1985 - No. 18, July, 1986

1-Based on TV movie & series (Sci/Fi) ... 3.00
2-18: 17,18-Denys Cowan-a ... 2.50

VACATION COMICS (Also see A-1 Comics)
Magazine Enterprises: No. 16, 1948 (one-shot)

A-1 16-The Pixies, Tom Tom, Flying Fredd & Koko & Kola	6	12	18	31	38	45

VACATION DIGEST
Harvey Comics: Sept, 1987 ($1.25, digest size)

1	1	2	3	5	6	8

VACATION IN DISNEYLAND (Also see Dell Giants)
Dell Publishing Co./Gold Key (1965): Aug-Oct, 1959; May, 1965 (Walt Disney)

Four Color 1025-Barks-a	16	32	48	114	202	290
1(30024-508)(G.K., 5/65, 25c)-r/Dell Giant #30 & cover to #1 ('58); celebrates Disneyland's 10th anniversary	5	10	15	35	55	75

VACATION PARADE (See Dell Giants)

VALERIA THE SHE BAT
Continuity Comics: May, 1993 - No. 5, Nov, 1993

1-Premium; acetate-c; N. Adams-a/scripts; given as gift to retailers	1	2	3	5	6	8

5 (11/93)-Embossed-c; N. Adams-a/scripts ... 3.00
NOTE: Due to lack of continuity, #2-4 do not exist.

VALERIA THE SHE BAT
Acclaim Comics (Windjammer): Sept, 1995 - No.2, Oct, 1995 ($2.50, limited series)

1,2 ... 2.50

VALKYRIE (See Airboy)
Eclipse Comics: May,1987 - No. 3, July, 1987 ($1.75, limited series)

1-3: 2-Holly becomes new Black Angel ... 2.50

VALKYRIE
Marvel Comics: Jan, 1997 ($2.95, one-shot)

1-w/pin-ups ... 3.00

VALKYRIE!
Eclipse Comics: July, 1988 - No. 3, Sept, 1988 ($1.95, limited series)

1-3 ... 2.50

VALLEY OF THE DINOSAURS (TV)
Charlton Comics: Apr, 1975 - No. 11, Dec, 1976 (Hanna-Barbera)

1-W. Howard-i	2	4	6	13	18	22
2,4-11: 2-W. Howard-i	2	4	6	8	10	12
3-Byrne text illos (early work, 7/75)	2	4	6	9	13	16

VALLEY OF THE DINOSAURS (Volume 2)
Harvey Comics: Oct, 1993 ($1.50, giant-sized)

1-Reprints ... 3.00

VALLEY OF GWANGI (See Movie Classics)

VALOR
E. C. Comics: Mar-Apr, 1955 - No. 5, Nov-Dec, 1955

1-Williamson/Torres-a; Wood-c/a	27	54	81	216	333	450
2-Williamson-c/a; Wood-a	21	42	63	168	264	360
3,4: 3-Williamson, Crandall-a. 4-Wood-c	16	32	48	128	202	275
5-Wood-c/a; Williamson/Evans-a	15	30	45	120	185	250

NOTE: Crandall a-3, 4. Ingels a-1, 2, 4, 5. Krigstein a-1-5. Orlando a-3, 4; c-3. Wood a-1, 2, 5; c-1, 4, 5.

VALOR
Gemstone Publishing: Oct, 1998 - No. 5, Feb, 1999 ($2.50)

1-5-Reprints ... 2.50

VALOR (Also see Legion of Super-Heroes & Legionnaires)
DC Comics: Nov, 1992 - No. 23, Sept, 1994 ($1.25/$1.50)

1-22: 1-Eclipso The Darkness Within aftermath. 2-Vs. Supergirl. 4-Vs. Lobo. 12-Lobo cameo. 14-Legionnaires, JLA app. 17-Austin-c(i); death of Valor. 18-22-Build-up to Zero Hour ... 2.50
23-Zero Hour tie-in ... 3.00

VALOR THUNDERSTAR AND HIS FIREFLIES
Now Comics: Dec, 1986 ($1.50)

1-Ordway-c(p) ... 2.50

VAMPI (Vampirella's...)
Harris Publications (Anarchy Studios): Aug, 2000 - No. 25, Feb, 2003 ($2.95/$2.99)

Limited Edition Preview Book (5/00) Preview pages & sketchbook ... 3.00
1-(8/00, $2.95) Lau-a(p)/Conway-s ... 3.00
1-Platinum Edition ... 20.00
2-25: 17-Barberi-a ... 3.00
2-25-Deluxe Edition variants ($9.95): 4-Finch-c. 5-Wieringo-c. 6-Cha-c ... 10.00
...Digital 1 (11/01, $2.95) CGI art; Haberlin-s ... 3.00
...Digital Preview (Anarchy Studios, 7/01, $2.95) preview of CGI art ... 3.00
Switchblade Kiss HC (2001, $24.95) r/#1-6 ... 25.00
Vicious Preview Ed. (Apr, 2003, $1.99) Flip book w/ Xin: Journey of the Monkey King Preview Ed. ... 2.50
Wizard #1/2 (mail order, $9.95) includes sketch pages ... 10.00

VAMPIRE BITES
Brainstorm Comics: May, 1995 - No. 2, Sept, 1996 ($2.95, B&W)

1,2:1-Color pin-up ... 3.00

VAMPIRE LESTAT, THE
Innovation Publishing: Jan, 1990 - No. 12, 1991 ($2.50, painted limited series)

1-Adapts novel; Bolton painted-c on all	2	4	6	10	14	18
1-2nd printing (has UPC code, 1st prints don't)						3.00
1-3rd & 4th printings						2.50
2-1st printing	1	2	3	5	6	8
2-2nd & 3rd printings						2.50
3-5						5.00
3-6,9-2nd printings						2.50
6-12						3.00

VAMPIRELLA (Magazine)(See Warren Presents)
Warren Publishing Co./Harris Publications #113: Sept, 1969 - No. 112, Feb, 1983; No. 113, Jan, 1988? (B&W)

1-Intro. Vampirella in original costume & wings; Frazetta-c/intro. page; Adams-a; Crandall-a	40	80	120	300	550	800
2-1st app. Vampirella's cousin Evily-c/s; 1st/only app. Draculina, Vampirella's blonde twin sister	14	28	42	103	184	265
3 (Low distribution)	36	72	108	270	498	725
4,6	10	20	30	73	129	185
5,7,9: 5,7-Frazetta-c. 9-Barry Smith-a; Boris/Wood-c	11	22	33	75	133	190
8-Vampirella begins by Tom Sutton as serious strip (early issues-gag line)	11	22	33	79	140	200
10-No Vampi story; Brunner, Adams, Wood-a	7	14	21	45	73	100
11-Origin & 1st app. Pendragon; Frazetta-c	7	14	21	50	83	115
12-Vampi by Gonzales begins	7	14	21	50	83	115
13-15: 14-1st Maroto-a; Ploog-a	7	14	21	50	83	115
16,22,25: 16-1st full Dracula-c/app. 22-Color insert preview of Maroto's Dracula. 25-Vampi on cocaine-s	7	14	21	47	76	105
17,18,20,21,23,24: 17-Tomb of the Gods begins by Maroto, ends #22. 18-22-Dracula-a	7	14	21	47	76	100
19 (1973 Annual) Creation of Vampi text bio	8	16	24	54	90	125
26,28,34,35,39,40: All have 8 pg. color inserts. 28-Board game inside covers. 34,35-1st Fleur the Witch Woman. 39,40-Color Dracula-s. 40-Wrightson bio	5	10	15	32	51	70
27 (1974 Annual) New color Vampi-s; mostly-r	6	12	18	37	59	80

Vampirella #71 © WP

Vampirella (Monthly) #11 © Harris

Vampirella: Death and Destruction #2 © Harris

	GD	VG	FN	VF	VF/NM	NM-
	2.0	4.0	6.0	8.0	9.0	9.2

29,38,45: 38-2nd Vampi as Cleopatra/Blood Red Queen of Hearts; 1st Mayo-a.
 5 10 15 32 51 70
30-32: 30-Intro. Pantha; Corben-a(color). 31-Origin Luana, the Beast Girl.
32-Jones-a 5 10 15 32 51 70
33-Wrightson-a; Pantha ends 5 10 15 32 51 70
36,37: 36-1st Vampi as Cleopatra/Blood Red Queen of Hearts; issue has 8 pg. color insert.
37-(1975 Annual) 5 10 15 35 55 75
41-44,47,48: 41-Dracula-s 4 8 12 28 44 60
46-(10/75) Origin-r from Annual 1 5 10 15 30 48 65
49-1st Blind Priestess; The Blood Red Queen of Hearts storyline begins; Poe-s
 4 8 12 28 44 60
50-Spirit cameo by Eisner; 40 pg. Vampi-s; Pantha & Fleur app.; Jones-a
 4 8 12 28 44 60
51-53,56,57,59-62,65,66,68,75,79,80,82-86,88,89: 60-62,65,66-The Blood Red Queen of
 Hearts app. 60-1st Blind Priestess-c 3 6 9 21 32 42
54,55,63,81,87: 54-Vampi-s (42 pgs.); 8 pg. color Corben-a(r). 55-All Gonzales-a(r).
63-10 pgs. Wrightson-a 3 6 9 21 32 42
58,70,72: 58-(92 pgs.) 70-Rook app. 4 8 12 24 37 50
64,73: 64-(100 pg. Giant) All Mayo-a; 70 pg. Vampi-s. 73-69 pg. Vampi-s; Mayo-a
 4 8 12 26 41 55
67,69,71,74,76-78-All Barbara Leigh photo-c 4 8 12 24 37 50
90-99: 90-Toth-a. 91-All-r; Gonzales-a. 93-Cassandra St. Knight begins, ends #103;
new Pantha series begins, ends #108 3 6 9 21 32 42
100 (96 pg. r-special)-Origin reprinted from Ann. 1; mostly reprints; Vampirella appears
topless in new 21 pg. story 8 16 24 52 86 120
101-104,106,107: All lower print run. 101,102-The Blood Red Queen of Hearts app.
107-All Maroto photo-a issue 6 12 18 37 59 80
105,108-110: 108-Torpedo series by Toth begins; Vampi nudity splash page.
110-(100 pg. Summer Spectacular) 6 12 18 37 59 80
111,112: Low print run. 111-Giant Collector's Edition ($2.50) 112-(84 pgs.) last Warren issue
 7 14 21 49 80 110
113 (1988)-1st Harris Issue; very low print run 26 52 78 211 348 485
Annual 1(1972)-New definitive origin of Vampirella by Gonzales; reprints by Neal Adams
(from #1), Wood (from #9) 25 50 75 184 330 475
Special 1 (1977) Softcover (color, large-square bound)-Only available thru mail order
 15 30 45 107 191 275
Special 1 (1977) Hardcover (color, large-square bound)-Only available through mail order
(scarce)(500 produced, signed & #'d) 32 64 96 240 445 650
#1 1969 Commemorative Edition (2001, $4.95) reprints entire #1 5.00
...Crimson Chronicles Vol. 1 (2004, $19.95, TPB) reprints stories from #1-10 20.00
...Crimson Chronicles Vol. 2 (2005, $19.95, TPB) reprints stories from #11-18 20.00
...Crimson Chronicles Vol. 3 (2005, $19.95, TPB) reprints stories from #19-28 20.00
...Crimson Chronicles Vol. 4 (2006, $19.95, TPB) reprints stories from #29-41 20.00
NOTE: **Ackerman** s-1-3. **Neal Adams** a-1, 10p, 19p(r/#10), 44(1 pg.), Annual 1. **Alcala** a-78, 90, 93i. **Bodé/Todd** c-3. **Bodé/Jones** c-4. **Boris/Wood** c-9. **Brunner** a-10, 12(1 pg.). **Corben** a-30, 31, 33, 36, 54; c-30, 31, 33, 54. **Crandall** a-1, 19(r/#1). **Frazetta** c-1, 5, 7, 11, 31. **Heath** a-58, 61, 67, 76-78, 83. **Infantino** a-57-62. **Jones** a-5, 9, 12, 27, 32 (color), 33(2 pg.), 34, 50i, 83+. **Ken Kelly** c-6, 38, 39, 40(back-c), 46, 70, 95. **Nebres** a-84, 88-90, 92-96. **Nino** a-59i, 61i, 67, 76, 85, 90. **Ploog** a-14. **Barry Smith** a-9. **Starlin** a-78. **Sutton** a-1-5, 7-11, Annual 1. **Toth** a-90i, 108, 110. **Wood** a-9, 10. **Wrightson** a-33(w/Jones), 40(Bio cameo) 63r. All reprint issues-19, 74, 83, 91, 105, 107, 109, 111. Annuals from 1973 on are included in regular numbering. Later annuals are same format as regular issues. Color inserts (8 pgs.) in 22, 25-28, 30-35, 39, 40, 45, 46, 49, 54, 55, 67, 72. 16 pg color insert in #36.

VAMPIRELLA (Also see Cain/... & Vengeance of...)
Harris Publications: Nov, 1992 - No. 5, Nov, 1993 ($2.95)
0-Bagged 5.00
0-Gold 3 6 9 16 23 30
1-Jim Balent inks in #1-3; Adam Hughes c-1-3 2 4 6 11 16 20
1-2nd printing 5.00
1-(11/97) Commemorative Edition 3.00
2 2 4 6 9 12 15
3-5: 4-Snyder III-c. 5-Brereton painted-c 1 2 3 5 6 8
Trade paperback nn (10/93, $5.95)-r/#1-4; Jusko-c 1 2 3 4 5 7
NOTE: Issues 1-5 contain certificates for free Dave Stevens Vampirella poster.

VAMPIRELLA (THE NEW MONTHLY)
Harris Publications: Nov, 1997 - No. 26, Apr, 2000 ($2.95)
1-3-"Ascending Evil" -Morrison & Millar-s/Conner & Palmiotti-a. 1-Three covers
by Quesada/Palmiotti, Conner, and Conner/Palmiotti 3.00
1-3-($9.95) Jae Lee variant covers 10.00
1-($24.95) Platinum Ed.w/Quesada-c 25.00
4-6-"Holy War"-Small & Stull-a, 4-Linsner variant-c 3.00
7-9-"Queen's Gambit"-Shi app. 7-Two covers. 8-Pantha-c/app. 3.00
7-($9.95) Conner variant-c 10.00
10-12-"Hell on Earth"; Small-a/Coney-s. 12-New costume 3.00
10-Jae Lee variant-c 1 3 4 6 8 10
13-15-"World's End" Zircher-p; Pantha back-up, Texeira-a 3.00

	GD	VG	FN	VF	VF/NM	NM-
	2.0	4.0	6.0	8.0	9.0	9.2

16,17: 16-Pantha-c;Texeira-a; Vampi back-up story. 17-(Pantha #2) 3.00
18-20-"Rebirth": Jae Lee-c on all. 18-Loeb-s/Sale-a. 19-Alan Davis-a. 20-Bruce Timm-a 3.00
18-20-($9.95) Variant covers: 18-Sale. 19-Davis. 20-Timm 12.00
21-26: 21,22-Dangerous Games; Small-a. 23-Lady Death-c/app.; Cleavenger-a. 24,25-Lau-a.
26-Lady Death & Pantha-c/app.; Cleavenger-a 3.00
0-(1/99) also variant-c with Pantha #0; same contents 3.00
TPB ($7.50) r/#1-3 "Ascending Evil" 8.00
Ascending Evil Ashcan (8/97, $1.00) 2.50
...: Grant Morrison/Mark Millar Collection TPB (2006, $24.95) r/#1-6; interviews 25.00
Hell on Earth Ashcan (7/98, $1.00) 2.50
... Presents: Tales of Pantha TPB (2006, $19.95) r/stories from #13-17 & one-shots 20.00
The End Ashcan (3/00, $6.00) 6.00
...30th Anniversary Celebration Preview (7/99) B&W preview of #18-20 10.00

VAMPIRELLA
Harris Publications: June, 2001 - No. 22, Aug, 2003 ($2.95/$2.99)
1-Four covers (Mayhew w/foil logo, Campbell, Anacleto, Jae Lee) Mayhew-a;
Mark Millar-s 3.00
2-22: 2-Two covers (Mayhew & Chiodo). 3-Timm var-c. 4-Horn var-c. 7-10-Dawn Brown-a;
Pantha back-up w/Texeira-a. 15-22-Conner-c 3.00
Giant-Size Ashcan (5/01, $5.95) B&W preview art and Mayhew interview 6.00
... Halloween Trick & Treat (10/04, $4.95) stories & art by various; three covers 5.00
... : Nowheresville Preview Edition (3/01, $2.95)- previews Mayhew art and photo models 3.00
...Nowheresville TPB (1/02, $12.95) r/#1-3 with cover gallery 13.00
... Summer Special #1 (2005, $5.95) Batman Begins photo-c and 2 variant-c 6.00
.... 2006 Halloween Special (2006, $2.95) Conner-c; Hester-s/Segovia-a; 4 covers 3.00

VAMPIRELLA & PANTHA SHOWCASE
Harris Publications: Jan, 1997 ($1.50, one-shot)
1-Millar-s/Texeira-c/a; flip book w/"Blood Lust"; Robinson-s/Jusko-c/a 3.00

VAMPIRELLA & THE BLOOD RED QUEEN OF HEARTS
Harris Publications: Sept, 1996 ($9.95, 96 pgs., B&W, squarebound, one-shot)
nn-r/Vampirella #49,60-62,65,66,101,102; John Bolton-c; Michael Bair back-c
 1 3 4 6 8 10

VAMPIRELLA: BLOODLUST
Harris Publications: July, 1997 - No. 2, Aug, 1997 ($4.95, limited series)
1,2-Robinson-s/Jusko-painted c/a 5.00

VAMPIRELLA CLASSIC
Harris Publications: Feb, 1995 - No. 5, Nov, 1995 ($2.95, limited series)
1-5: Reprints Archie Goodwin stories. 3.00

VAMPIRELLA COMICS MAGAZINE
Harris Publications: Oct, 2003 - Present ($3.95/$9.95, magazine-sized)
1-9-($3.95) 1-Texiera-c; b&w and color stories, Alan Moore interview; reviews. 2-KISS
interview. 4-Chiodo-c. 6-Brereton-c 4.00
1-9-($9.95) 1-Three covers (Model Photo cover, Palmiotti-c, Wheatley Frankenstein-c) 10.00

VAMPIRELLA: CROSSOVER GALLERY
Harris Publications: Sept, 1997 ($2.95, one-shot)
1-Wraparound-c by Campbell, pinups by Jae Lee, Mack, Allred, Art Adams,
Quesada & Palmiotti and others 3.00

VAMPIRELLA: DEATH & DESTRUCTION
Harris Publications: July, 1996 - No. 3, Sept, 1996 ($2.95, limited series)
1-3: Amanda Conner-a(p) in all. 1-Tucci-c. 2-Hughes-c. 3-Jusko-c 3.00
1-($9.95)-Limited Edition; Beachum-c 10.00

VAMPIRELLA/DRACULA & PANTHA SHOWCASE
Harris Publications: Aug, 1997 ($1.50, one-shot)
1-Ellis, Robinson, and Moore-s; flip book w/"Pantha" 3.00

VAMPIRELLA/DRACULA: THE CENTENNIAL
Harris Publications: Oct, 1997 ($5.95, one-shot)
1-Ellis, Robinson, and Moore-s; Beachum, Frank/Smith, and Mack/Mays-a
Bolton-painted-c 6.00

VAMPIRELLA: INTIMATE VISIONS
Harris Publications: 2006 ($3.95, one-shots)
..., Amanda Conner 1 - r/Vampirella Monthly #1 with commentary; interview; 2 covers 4.00
..., Joe Jusko 1 - r/Vampirella; Blood Lust #1 with commentary; interview; 2 covers 4.00

VAMPIRELLA: JULIE STRAIN SPECIAL
Harris Publications: Sept, 2000 ($3.95, one-shot)
1-Photo-c w/yellow background; interview and photo gallery 4.00
1-Limited Edition ($9.95); cover photo w/black background 10.00

Vampirella Lives #2 © Harris

Vampire Tales #7 © MAR

Vamps: Hollywood and Vein #6 © Lee & Simpson

	GD	VG	FN	VF	VF/NM	NM-
	2.0	4.0	6.0	8.0	9.0	9.2

VAMPIRELLA/LADY DEATH (Also see Lady Death/Vampirella)
Harris Publications: Feb, 1999 ($3.50, one-shot)
1-Small-a/Nelson painted-c — 3.50
1-Valentine Edition ($9.95); pencil-c by Small — 10.00
VAMPIRELLA: LEGENDARY TALES
Harris Publications: May, 2000 - No. 2, June, 2000 ($2.95, B&W)
1,2-Reprints from magazine; Cleavenger painted-c — 3.00
1,2-($9.95) Variant painted-c by Mike Mayhew — 10.00
VAMPIRELLA LIVES
Harris Publications: Dec, 1996 - No. 3, Feb, 1997 ($3.50/$2.95, limited series)
1-Die cut-c; Quesada & Palmiotti-c, Ellis-s/Conner-a — 3.50
1-Deluxe Ed.-photo-c — 3.50
2,3-($2.95)-Two editions (1 photo-c): 3-J. Scott Campbell-c — 3.00
VAMPIRELLA: MORNING IN AMERICA
Harris Publications/Dark Horse Comics: 1991 - No. 4, 1992 ($3.95, B&W, lim. series, 52 pgs.)
1,2-All have Kaluta painted-c — 1 2 3 5 6 8
3,4 — 1 3 4 6 8 10
VAMPIRELLA OF DRAKULON
Harris Publications: Jan, 1996 - No. 5, Sept, 1996 ($2.95)
0-5: All reprints. 0-Jim Silke-c. 3-Polybagged w/card. 4-Texeira-c — 3.00
VAMPIRELLA/PAINKILLER JANE
Harris Publications: May, 1998 ($3.50, one-shot)
1-Waid & Augustyn-s/Leonardi & Palmiotti-a — 3.50
1-($9.95) Variant-c — 10.00
VAMPIRELLA PIN-UP SPECIAL
Harris Publications: Oct, 1995 ($2.95, one-shot)
1-Hughes-c, pin-ups by various — 5.00
1-Variant-c — 5.00
VAMPIRELLA QUARTERLY
Harris Publications: Spring, 2007; Summer 2007 ($4.95)
Spring, 2007,Summer 2007-New stories and re-colored reprints; six covers — 5.00
VAMPIRELLA: RETRO
Harris Publications: Mar, 1998 - No. 3, May, 1998 ($2.50, B&W, limited series)
1-3: Reprints; Silke painted covers — 3.00
VAMPIRELLA: REVELATIONS
Harris Publications: No. 0, Oct, 2005 - No. 3, Feb, 2006 ($2.99, limited series)
0-3-Vampirella's origin retold, Lilith app.; Carey-s/Lilly-a; two covers on each — 4.00
... Book 1 TPB (2006, $12.95) r/series; Carey interview, script for #1, Lilly sketch pages — 13.00
VAMPIRELLA: SAD WINGS OF DESTINY
Harris Publications: Sept, 1996 ($3.95, one-shot)
1-Jusko-c — 4.00
VAMPIRELLA/SHADOWHAWK: CREATURES OF THE NIGHT (Also see Shadowhawk)
Harris Publications: 1995 ($4.95, one-shot)
1 — 5.00
VAMPIRELLA/SHI (See Shi/Vampirella)
Harris Publications: Oct, 1997 ($2.95, one-shot)
1-Ellis-s — 3.00
1-Chromium-c — 6.00
VAMPIRELLA: SILVER ANNIVERSARY COLLECTION
Harris Publications: Jan, 1997 - No. 4 Apr, 1997 ($2.50, limited series)
1-4: Two editions: Bad Girl by Beachum, Good Girl by Silke — 3.00
VAMPIRELLA'S SUMMER NIGHTS
Harris Publications: 1992 (one-shot)
1-Art Adams infinity cover; centerfold by Stelfreeze — 3 7 10 19 27 35
VAMPIRELLA STRIKES
Harris Publications: Sept, 1995 - No. 8, Dec, 1996 ($2.95, limited series)
1-8: 1-Photo-c. 2-Deodato-c; polybagged w/card. 5-Eudaemon-c/app; wraparound-c;
alternate-c exists. 6-(6/96)-Mark Millar script; Texeira-c; alternate-c exists. 7-Flip book — 3.00
1-Newsstand Edition; diff. photo-c, 1-Limited Ed.; diff. photo-c — 3.00
Annual 1-(12/96, $2.95) Delano-s; two covers — 3.00
VAMPIRELLA: 25TH ANNIVERSARY SPECIAL
Harris Publications: Oct, 1996 ($5.95, squarebound, one-shot)
nn-Reintro The Blood Red Queen of Hearts; James Robinson, Grant Morrison & Warren Ellis

scripts; Mark Texeira, Michael Bair & Amanda Conner-a(p); Frank Frazetta-c — 6.00
nn-($6.95)-Silver Edition — 7.00
VAMPIRELLA VS. HEMORRHAGE
Harris Publications: Apr, 1997($3.50)
1 — 3.50
VAMPIRELLA VS. PANTHA
Harris Publications: Mar, 1997 ($3.50)
1-Two covers; Millar-s/Texeira-a — 3.50
VAMPIRELLA/WETWORKS (See Wetworks/Vampirella)
Harris Publications: June, 1997 ($2.95, one-shot)
1 — 3.00
1-($9.95) Alternate Edition; cardstock-c — 10.00
VAMPIRELLA/WITCHBLADE
Harris Publications: 2003; Oct, 2004; Oct, 2005 ($2.99, one-shots)
1-Brian Wood-s/Steve Pugh-a; 3 covers by Texeira, Conner and Pugh — 3.00
....: The Feast (10/05, $2.99) Joyce Chin-a; covers by Chin, Conner, Rodriguez — 3.00
....: Union of the Damned (10/04, $2.99, one-shot) Sharp-a; three covers — 3.00
Trilogy TPB (2006, $12.95) r/one-shots; art gallery and gallery of multiple covers — 13.00
VAMPIRE'S CHRISTMAS, THE
Image Comics: Oct, 2003 ($5.95, over-sized graphic novel)
nn-Linsner-s/a; Dubisch-painted-a — 6.00
VAMPIRE TALES
Marvel Comics Group: Aug, 1973 - No. 11, June, 1975 (75¢, B&W, magazine)
1-Morbius, the Living Vampire begins by Pablo Marcos (1st solo Morbius series
& 5th Morbius app.) — 6 12 18 41 66 90
2-Intro. Satana; Steranko-r — 4 8 12 28 44 60
3,5,6: 3-Satana app. 5-Origin Morbius. 6-1st Lilith app. in this title (see Giant-Size Chillers #1
for debut) — 4 8 12 24 37 50
4,7 — 3 6 9 19 29 38
8-1st solo Blade story (see Tomb of Dracula) — 4 8 12 28 44 60
9-Blade app. — 4 8 12 24 37 50
10,11 — 3 6 9 19 29 38
Annual 1(10/75)-Heath-r/#9 — 3 6 9 19 29 38
NOTE: Alcala a-6, 8, 9i. Boris c-4. Chaykin a-7. Everett a-1r. Gulacy a-7p. Heath a-9. Infantino a-3r.
Gil Kane a-4, 5r.
VAMPIRE VERSES, THE
CFD Productions: Aug, 1995 - No. 4, 1995 ($2.95, B&W, mature)
1-4 — 3.00
VAMPI VICIOUS
Harris Publications (Anarchy Studios): Aug, 2003 - No. 3, Nov, 2003 ($2.99)
1-3: 1-McKeever-s/Dogan-a; 3 covers by Dogan, Lau & Noto. 3-Kau-a — 3.00
VAMPI VICIOUS CIRCLE
Harris Publications (Anarchy Studios): Jun, 2004 - No. 3, Sept, 2004 ($2.99/$9.95)
1-3: B. Clay Moore-s — 3.00
1-3-($9.95) Limited Edition w/variant-c. 1-Noto-c. 2-Norton-c. 3-Lucas-c — 10.00
VAMPI VICIOUS RAMPAGE
Harris Publications (Anarchy Studios): Feb, 2005 - No. 2, Apr, 2005 ($2.99)
1,2: Raab-s/Lau-a; two covers on each — 3.00
VAMPI VS. XIN
Harris Publications (Anarchy Studios): Oct, 2004 - No. 2, Jan, 2005 ($2.99)
1,2-Faerber-s/Lau-a; two covers — 3.00
VAMPS
DC Comics (Vertigo): Aug, 1994 - No. 6, Jan, 1995 ($1.95, lim. series, mature)
1-6-Bolland-c — 3.00
Trade paperback ($9.95)-r/#1-6 — 10.00
VAMPS: HOLLYWOOD & VEIN
DC Comics (Vertigo): Feb, 1996 - No. 6, July, 1996 ($2.25, lim. series, mature)
1-6: Winslade-c — 2.50
VAMPS: PUMPKIN TIME
DC Comics (Vertigo): Dec, 1998 - No. 3, Feb, 1999 ($2.50, lim. series, mature)
1-3: Quitely-c — 2.50
VANGUARD (...Outpost: Earth) (See Megaton)
Megaton Comics: 1987 ($1.50)
1-Erik Larsen-c(p) — 3.00

Vault of Evil #3 © MAR

Vault of Horror #17 © WMG

Vengeance of Vampirella #6 © Harris

	GD 2.0	VG 4.0	FN 6.0	VF 8.0	VF/NM 9.0	NM- 9.2		GD 2.0	VG 4.0	FN 6.0	VF 8.0	VF/NM 9.0	NM- 9.2

VANGUARD (See Savage Dragon #2)
Image Comics (Highbrow Entertainment): Oct, 1993 - No. 6, 1994 ($1.95)

1-6: 1-Wraparound gatefold-c; Erik Larsen back-up-a; Supreme x-over. 3-(12/93)-Indicia says December 1994. 4-Berzerker back-up. 5-Angel Medina-a(p) 3.00

VANGUARD (See Savage Dragon #2)
Image Comics: Aug, 1996 - No. 4, Feb, 1997 ($2.95, B&W, limited series)

1-4 .... 3.00

VANGUARD: ETHEREAL WARRIORS
Image Comics: Aug, 2000 ($5.95, B&W)

1-Fosco & Larsen-a 6.00

VANGUARD ILLUSTRATED
Pacific Comics: Nov, 1983 - No. 11, Oct, 1984 (Baxter paper)(Direct sales only)

1-6,8-11: 1,7-Nudity scenes. 2-1st app. Stargrazers (see Legends of the Stargrazers; Dave Stevens-c 3.00
7-1st app. Mr. Monster (r-in Mr. Monster #1) 5.00
NOTE: Evans a-7. Kaluta c-5, 7p. Perez a-6; c-6. Rude a-1-4; c-4. Williamson c-3.

VANGUARD: STRANGE VISITORS
Image Comics: Oct, 1996 - No.4, Feb, 1997 ($2.95, B&W, limited series)

1-4: 3-Supreme-c/app. 3.00

VAN HELSING: FROM BENEATH THE RUE MORGUE (Based on the 2004 movie)
Dark Horse Comics: Apr, 2004 ($2.99, one-shot)

1-Hugh Jackman photo-c; Dysart-s/Alexander-a 3.00

VANITY (See Pacific Presents #3)
Pacific Comics: Jun, 1984 - No. 2, Aug, 1984 ($1.50, direct sales)

1,2: Origin 2.50

VARIETY COMICS (The Spice of Comics)
Rural Home Publ./Croyden Publ. Co.: 1944 - No. 2, 1945; No. 3, 1946

1-Origin Captain Valiant	21	42	63	124	195	265
2-Captain Valiant	14	28	42	78	112	145
3(1946-Croyden)-Captain Valiant	12	24	36	67	94	120

VARIETY COMICS (See Fox Giants)

VARSITY
Parents' Magazine Institute: 1945

1	8	16	24	44	57	70

VAULT OF EVIL
Marvel Comics Group: Feb, 1973 - No. 23, Nov, 1975

1 (1950s reprints begin)	3	6	9	16	23	30
2-23: 3,4-Brunner-a. 11-Kirby-a	2	4	6	10	14	18

NOTE: Ditko a-14r, 15r, 20-22r. Drucker a-10r(Mystic #52), 13r(Uncanny Tales #42). Everett a-11r(Menace #2), 13r(Menace #4); c-10. Heath a-5r. Gil Kane c-1, 6. Kirby a-11. Krigstein a-20r(Uncanny Tales #54). Reinman r-1. Tuska a-6r.

VAULT OF HORROR (Formerly War Against Crime #1-11)
E. C. Comics: No. 12, Apr-May, 1950 - No. 40, Dec-Jan, 1954-55

12 (Scarce)-ties w/Crypt Of Terror as 1st horror comic	471	942	1413	3768	5884	8000
13-Morphine story	99	198	297	792	1234	1675
14	88	176	264	704	1102	1500
15- "Terror in the Swamp" is same story w/minor changes as "The Thing in the Swamp" from Haunt of Fear #15	75	150	225	600	938	1275
16,	58	116	174	464	725	985
17-Classic werewolf-c	65	130	195	520	811	1100
18,19	46	92	138	368	577	785
20-25: 22-Frankenstein-c & adaptation. 23-Used in POP, pg. 84; Davis-a(2); Ingels bio. 24-Craig bio.	38	76	114	304	477	650
26-B&W & color illos in POP	38	76	114	304	477	650
27-36: 30-Dismemberment-c. 31-Ray Bradbury biog. 32-Censored-c. 35-X-Mas-c. 36- "Pipe Dream" classic opium addict story by Krigstein; "Twin Bill" cited in articles by T.E. Murphy, Wertham	32	64	96	256	398	540
37-1st app. Drusilla, a Vampirella look alike; Williamson-a	32	64	96	256	403	550
38-39: 39-Bondage-c	31	62	93	248	384	520
40-Low distribution	38	76	114	304	477	650

NOTE: Craig art in all but No. 13 & 33; c-12-40. Crandall a-33, 34, 39. Davis a-17-38. Evans a-27, 28, 30, 32, 33. Feldstein a-12-16. Ingels a-13-20, 22-40. Kamen a-15-22, 25, 29. Krigstein a-36, 38-40. Kurtzman a-12, 13. Orlando a-24, 31, 40. Wood a-12-14. #22, 29 & 31 have Ray Bradbury adaptations. #16 & 17 have H. P. Lovecraft adaptations.

VAULT OF HORROR, THE
Gladstone Publ.: Aug, 1990 - No. 6, June, 1991 ($1.95, 68 pgs.)(#4 on: $2.00)

1-Craig-c(r); all contain EC reprints						4.00
2-6: 2,4-6-Craig-c(r). 3-Ingels-c(r)						3.00

VAULT OF HORROR
Russ Cochran/Gemstone Publishing: Sept, 1991 - No. 5, May, 1992 ($2.00); Oct, 1992 - No. 29, Oct, 1999 ($1.50/$2.00/$2.50)

1-29: E.C reprints. 1-4r/VOH #12-15 w/original-c 3.00

V...–COMICS (Morse code for "V" - 3 dots, 1 dash)
Fox Features Syndicate: Jan, 1942 - No. 2, Mar-Apr, 1942

1-Origin V-Man & the boys; The Banshee & The Black Fury, The Queen of Evil, & V-Agents begin; Nazi-c	128	256	384	800	1325	1850
2-Nazi bondage/torture-c	90	180	270	563	932	1300

VECTOR
Now Comics: 1986 - No. 4, 1986? ($1.50, 1st color comic by Now Comics)

1-4: Computer-generated art 2.50

VEILS
DC Comics (Vertigo): 1999 ($24.95, one-shot)

Hardcover-($24.95) Painted art and photography; McGreal-s 25.00
Softcover ($14.95) 15.00

VELOCITY (Also see Cyberforce)
Image Comics (Top Cow Productions): Nov, 1995 - No. 3, Jan, 1996 ($2.50, limited series)

1-3: Kurt Busiek scripts in all. 2-Savage Dragon-c/app. 3.00

VENGEANCE OF VAMPIRELLA (Becomes Vampirella: Death & Destruction)
Harris Comics: Apr, 1994 - No. 25, Apr, 1996 ($2.95)

1-($3.50)-Quesada/Palmiotti "bloodfoil" wraparound cover 6.00
1-2nd printing; blue foil-c 3.00
1-Gold 18.00
2-8: 8-Polybagged w/trading card 4.00
9,25: 10-w/coupon for Hyde -25 poster. 11,19-Polybagged w/ trading card. 25-Quesada & Palmiotti red foil-c 3.00
...: Bloodshed (1995, $6.95) 7.00

VENGEANCE OF VAMPIRELLA: THE MYSTERY WALK
Harris Comics: Nov, 1995 ($2.95, one-shot)

0 .... 3.00

VENGEANCE SQUAD
Charlton Comics: July, 1975 - No. 6, May, 1976 (#1-3 are 25¢ issues)

1-Mike Mauser, Private Eye begins by Staton	2	4	6	8	10	12
2-6: Morisi-a in all	1	2	3	4	5	7
5,6 (Modern Comics-r, 1977)						4.00

VENOM
Marvel Comics: June, 2003 - No. 18, Nov, 2004 ($2.25)

1-7-Herrera-a/Way-s. 6,7-Wolverine app. 2.50
8-18-($2.99): 8-10-Wolverine-c/app.; Kieth-c. 11-Fantastic Four app. 3.00
... Vol. 1: Shiver (2004, $13.99, TPB) r/#1-5 .... 14.00
... Vol. 2: Run (2004, $19.99, TPB) r/#6-13 .... 20.00
... Vol. 3: Twist (2004, $13.99, TPB) r/#14-18 .... 14.00

VENOM: Marvel Comics (Also see Amazing Spider-Man #298-300)

... ALONG CAME A SPIDER, 1/96 - No. 4, 4/96 ($2.95)-Spider-Man & Carnage app. 3.00
... CARNAGE UNLEASHED, 4/95 - No. 4, 7/95 ($2.95) 3.00
... DEATHTRAP: THE VAULT, 3/93 ($6.95) r/Avengers: Deathtrap: The Vault 7.00
... FUNERAL PYRE, 8/93- No. 3, 10/93 ($2.95)-#1-Holo-grafx foil-c; Punisher app. in all 3.00

VENOM: LETHAL PROTECTOR
Marvel Comics: Feb, 1993 - No. 6, July, 1993 ($2.95, limited series)

1-Red holo-grafx foil-c; Bagley-c/a in all						5.00
1-Gold variant sold to retailers						15.00
1-Black-c (at least 58 copies have been authenticated by CGC since 2000)	9	18	27	63	107	150

NOTE: Counterfeit copies of the black-c exist and are valueless

2-6: Spider-Man app. in all 3.00
... LICENSE TO KILL, 6/97 - No. 3, 8/97 ($1.95) 2.50
... NIGHTS OF VENGEANCE, 8/94 - No. 4, 11/94 ($2.95), #1-Red foil-c 3.00
... ON TRIAL, 3/97 - No. 3, 5/97 ($1.95) 2.50
... SEED OF DARKNESS, 7/97 ($1.95) #(-1) Flashback 2.50
... SEPARATION ANXIETY,12/94- No. 4, 3/95 ($2.95) #1-Embossed-c 3.00
... SIGN OF THE BOSS,3/97 - No. 2, 10/97 ($1.99) 2.50

Venom: The Finale #3 © MAR

Veronica #40 © AP

Vertigo Visions: Dr. Occult #1 © DC

	GD 2.0	VG 4.0	FN 6.0	VF 8.0	VF/NM 9.0	NM- 9.2

	GD 2.0	VG 4.0	FN 6.0	VF 8.0	VF/NM 9.0	NM- 9.2

... SINNER TAKES ALL, 8/95 - No. 5, 10/95 ($2.95) — 3.00

... SUPER SPECIAL, 8/95($3.95) #1-Flip book — 4.00

... THE ENEMY WITHIN, 2/94 - No. 3, 4/94 ($2.95)-Demogoblin & Morbius app.
1-Glow-in-the-dark-c — 3.00

... THE FINALE, 11/97 - No. 3, 1/98 ($1.99) — 2.50

... THE HUNGER, 8/96- No. 4, 11/96 ($1.95) — 2.50

... THE HUNTED, 5/96-No. 3, 7/96 ($2.95) — 3.00

... THE MACE, 5/94 - No. 3, 7/94 ($2.95)-#1-Embossed-c — 3.00

... THE MADNESS, 11/93- No. 3, 1/94 ($2.95)-Kelley Jones-c/a(p).
1-Embossed-c; Juggernaut app. — 3.00

... TOOTH AND CLAW, 12/96 - No. 3, 2/97 ($1.95)-Wolverine-c/app. — 2.50

... VS. CARNAGE, 9/04 - No. 4, 12/04 ($2.99)-Milligan-s/Crain-a; Spider-Man app. — 3.00
TPB (2004, $9.99) r/#1-4 — 10.00

VENTURE
AC Comics (Americomics): Aug, 1986 - No. 3, 1986? ($1.75)
1-3: 1-3-Bolt. 1-Astron. 2-Femforce. 3-Fazers — 2.50

VENTURE
Image Comics: Jan, 2003 - No. 4, Sept, 2003 ($2.95)
1-4-Faerber-s/Igle-a — 3.00

VENUS (See Agents of Atlas, Marvel Spotlight #2 & Weird Wonder Tales)
Marvel/Atlas Comics (CMC 1-9/LCC 10-19): Aug, 1948 - No. 19, Apr, 1952 (Also see Marvel
Mystery #91)

1-Venus & Hedy Devine begin; 1st app. Venus; Kurtzman's "Hey Look"	138	276	414	863	1432	2000
2	78	156	234	488	807	1125
3,5	60	120	180	375	625	875
4-Kurtzman's "Hey Look"	61	122	183	381	633	885
6-9: 6-Loki app. 7,8-Painted-c. 9-Begin 52 pgs.; book-length feature "Whom the Gods Destroy!"	53	106	159	330	545	760
10-S/F-horror issues begin (7/50)	74	148	222	463	769	1075
11-S/F end of the world (11/50)	86	172	258	538	894	1250
12-Colan-a	50	100	150	305	503	700
13-16-Venus by Everett, 2-3 stories each; covers-#13,15,16; 14-Everett part cover (Venus).	85	170	255	531	878	1225
17-19-Classic Everett horror & skull covers; Venus app. 17-Bondage-c	114	228	342	713	1182	1650

NOTE: Berg s/f story-13. Everett c-13, 14(part; Venus only), 15-19. Heath s/f story-11. Maneely s/f story 10(3pg.), 16. Morisi a-19. Syd Shores c-6.

VERI BEST SURE FIRE COMICS
Holyoke Publishing Co.: No date (circa 1945) (Reprints Holyoke one-shots)
1-Captain Aero, Alias X, Miss Victory, Commandos of the Devil Dogs, Red Cross,
Hammerhead Hawley, Capt. Aero's Sky Scouts, Flagman app.;

same-c as Veri Best Sure Shot #1	39	78	117	225	355	485

VERI BEST SURE SHOT COMICS
Holyoke Publishing Co.: No date (circa 1945) (Reprints Holyoke one-shots)
1-Capt. Aero, Miss Victory by Quinlan, Alias X, The Red Cross, Flagman, Commandos of the
Devil Dogs, Hammerhead Hawley, Capt. Aero's Sky Scouts;

same-c as Veri Best Sure Fire #1	39	78	117	225	355	485

VERMILLION
DC Comics (Helix): Oct, 1996 - No. 12, Sept, 1997 ($2.25/$2.50)
1-12: 1-4: Lucius Shepard scripts. 4,12-Kaluta-c — 2.50

VERONICA (Also see Archie's Girls, Betty &...)
Archie Comics: Apr, 1989 - Present
1-(75¢-c) — 6.00
2-10: 2-(75¢-c) — 4.00
11-38 — 3.00
39-Love Showdown pt. 4, Cheryl Blossom — 5.00
40-70: 34-Neon ink-c — 3.00
71-186: 134-Begin $2.19-c. 152,155-Cheryl Blossom app. 163-Begin $2.25-c — 2.50

VERONICA'S PASSPORT DIGEST MAGAZINE (Becomes Veronica's Digest Magazine #3 on)
Archie Comics: Nov, 1992 - No. 6 ($1.50/$1.79, digest size)
1 — 5.00
2-6 — 3.00

VERONICA'S SUMMER SPECIAL (See Archie Giant Series Magazine #615, 625)

VERTICAL
DC Comics (Vertigo): 2003 ($4.95, 3-1/4" wide pages, one-shot)

1-Seagle-s/Allred & Bond-a; odd format 1/2 width pages with some 20" long spreads — 5.00

VERTIGO: FIRST OFFENSES
DC Comics (Vertigo): 2005 ($4.99, TPB)
TPB-Reprints first issues of The Invisibles, Preacher, Fables, Sandman Mystery Theater, and
Lucifer — 5.00

VERTIGO: FIRST TASTE
DC Comics (Vertigo): 2005 ($4.99, TPB)
TPB-Reprints first issues of Y: The Last Man, 100 Bullets, Transmetropolitan, Books of Magick:
Life During Wartime, Death: The High Cost of Living, and Saga of the Swamp Thing #21
(Alan Moore's first story on that title) — 5.00

VERTIGO GALLERY, THE: DREAMS AND NIGHTMARES
DC Comics (Vertigo): 1995 ($3.50, one-shot)
1-Pin-ups of Vertigo characters by Sienkiewicz, Toth, Van Fleet & others; McKean-c — 4.00

VERTIGO JAM
DC Comics (Vertigo): Aug, 1993 ($3.95, one-shot, 68 pgs.)(Painted-c by Fabry)
1-Sandman by Neil Gaiman, Hellblazer, Animal Man, Doom Patrol, Swamp Thing,
Kid Eternity & Shade the Changing Man — 5.00

VERTIGO POP! BANGKOK
DC Comics (Vertigo): July, 2003 - No. 4, Oct, 2003 ($2.95, limited series)
1-4-Camuncoli-c/a; Jonathan Vankin-s — 3.00

VERTIGO POP! LONDON
DC Comics (Vertigo): Jan, 2003 - No. 4, Apr, 2003 ($2.95, limited series)
1-4-Philip Bond-c/a; Peter Milligan-s — 3.00

VERTIGO POP! TOKYO
DC Comics (Vertigo): Sept, 2002 - No. 4, Dec, 2002 ($2.95, limited series)
1-4-Seth Fisher-c/a; Jonathan Vankin-s — 3.00

VERTIGO PREVIEW
DC Comics (Vertigo): 1992 (75¢, one-shot, 36 pgs.)
1-Vertigo previews; Sandman story by Neil Gaiman — 2.50

VERTIGO RAVE
DC Comics (Vertigo): Fall, 1994 (99¢, one-shot)
1-Vertigo previews — 2.50

VERTIGO SECRET FILES
DC Comics (Vertigo): Aug, 2000 ($4.95)
...: Hellblazer 1 (8/00, $4.95) Background info and story summaries — 5.00
...: Swamp Thing 1 (11/00, $4.95) Backstories and origins; Hale-c — 5.00

VERTIGO VERITE: THE UNSEEN HAND
DC Comics (Vertigo): Sept, 1996 - No. 4, Dec, 1996 ($2.50, limited series)
1-4: Terry LaBan scripts in all — 2.50

VERTIGO VISIONS
DC Comics (Vertigo): June, 1993 - Present (one-shots)
Dr. Occult 1 (7/94, $3.95) — 4.00
Dr. Thirteen 1 (9/98, $5.95) Howarth-s — 6.00
Prez 1 (7/95, $3.95) — 4.00
The Geek 1 (6/93, $3.95) — 4.00
The Eaters ($4.95, 1995)-Milligan story. — 5.00
The Phantom Stranger 1 (10/93, $3.50) — 3.50
Tomahawk 1 (7/98, $4.95) Pollack-s — 5.00

VERTIGO WINTER'S EDGE
DC Comics (Vertigo): 1998, 1999 ($7.95/$6.95, square-bound, annual)
1-Winter stories by Vertigo creators; Desire story by Gaiman/Bolton; Bolland wraparound-c — 8.00
2,3-($6.95)-Winter stories: 2-Allred-c. 3-Bond-c; Desire by Gaiman/Zulli — 7.00

VERTIGO X ANNIVERSARY PREVIEW
DC Comics (Vertigo): 2003 (99¢, one-shot, 48 pgs.)
1-Previews of upcoming titles and interviews; Endless Nights, Shade, The Originals — 2.25

VERY BEST OF DENNIS THE MENACE, THE
Fawcett Publ.: July, 1979 - No. 2, Apr, 1980 (95¢/$1.00, digest-size, 132 pgs.)

1,2-Reprints	1	3	4	6	8	10

VERY BEST OF DENNIS THE MENACE, THE
Marvel Comics Group: Apr, 1982 - No. 3, Aug, 1982 ($1.25, digest-size)

1-3: Reprints	1	2	3	5	7	9
1,2-Mistakenly printed with DC logo on cover	2	4	6	8	11	14

NOTE: Hank Ketcham c-all. A few thousand of #1 & 2 were printed with DC emblem.

Vic Flint #1 © STJ

Vigilante #4 © DC

Violator #4 © TMP

	GD	VG	FN	VF	VF/NM	NM-
	2.0	4.0	6.0	8.0	9.0	9.2

VERY VICKY
Meet Danny Ocean: 1993? - No. 8, 1995 ($2.50, B&W)

1-8, …: Calling All Hillbillies (1995, $2.50)						2.50

VEXT
DC Comics: Mar, 1999 - No. 6, Aug, 1999 ($2.50, limited series)

1-6-Giffen-s. 1-Superman app.						2.50

V FOR VENDETTA
DC Comics: Sept, 1988 - No. 10, May, 1989 ($2.00, maxi-series)

1-Alan Moore scripts in all; David Lloyd-a						5.00
2-10						4.00
HC (1990) Limited edition						60.00
HC (2005, $29.99, dustjacket) r/series; foreward by Lloyd; promo art and sketches						30.00
Trade paperback (1990, $14.95)						15.00

VIC BRIDGES FAZERS SKETCHBOOK AND FACT FILE
AC Comics: Nov, 1986 ($1.75)

1						3.00

VICE
Image Comics (Top Cow): Nov, 2005 - Present ($2.99)

1-5-Coleite-s/Kirkham-a. 1-Three covers						3.00
1-Code Red Edition; variant Benitez-c						3.00

VIC FLINT(Crime Buster…)(See Authentic Police Cases #10-14 & Fugitives From Justice #2)
St. John Publ. Co.: Aug, 1948 - No. 5, Apr, 1949 (Newspaper reprints; NEA Service)

	GD	VG	FN	VF	VF/NM	NM-
1	14	28	42	76	108	140
2	10	20	30	54	72	90
3-5	9	18	27	47	61	75

VIC FLINT (Crime Buster…)
Argo Publ.: Feb, 1956 - No. 2, May, 1956 (Newspaper reprints)

	GD	VG	FN	VF	VF/NM	NM-
1,2	9	18	27	47	61	75

VIC JORDAN (Also see Big Shot Comics #32)
Civil Service Publ.: April, 1945

	GD	VG	FN	VF	VF/NM	NM-
1-1944 daily newspaper-r	14	28	42	76	108	140

VICKI (Humor)
Atlas/Seaboard Publ.: Feb, 1975 - No. 4, Aug, 1975 (No. 1,2: 68 pgs.)

	GD	VG	FN	VF	VF/NM	NM-
1,2-(68 pgs.)-Reprints Tippy Teen; Good Girl art	3	6	9	20	30	40
3,4 (Low print)	3	6	9	20	30	40

VICKI VALENTINE (…Summer Special #1)
Renegade Press: July, 1985 - No. 4, July, 1986 ($1.70, B&W)

1-4-Woggon, Rausch-a; all have paper dolls. 2-Christmas issue						3.00

VICKY
Ace Magazine: Oct, 1948 - No. 5, June, 1949

	GD	VG	FN	VF	VF/NM	NM-
nn(10/48)-Teenage humor	8	16	24	40	50	60
4(12/48), nn(2/49), 4(4/49), 5(6/49): 5-Dotty app.	7	14	21	35	43	50

VIC TORRY & HIS FLYING SAUCER (Also see Mr. Monster's…#5)
Fawcett Publications: 1950 (one-shot)

	GD	VG	FN	VF	VF/NM	NM-
nn-Book-length saucer story by Powell; photo/painted-c	67	134	201	419	697	975

VICTORY
Topps Comics: June, 1994 ($2.50, unfinished limited series)

1-Kurt Busiek script; Giffen-c/a; Rob Liefeld variant-c exists						2.50

VICTORY
Image Comics: May, 2003 - No. 4, Feb, 2004 ($2.95, limited series)

1-4: 1-Two covers; Francisco-a. 4-Two covers						3.00

VICTORY (Volume 2)
Image Comics: Aug, 2004 - No. 4, Jan, 2005 ($2.95, limited series)

1-4: 1-Three covers; Francisco-a						3.00

VICTORY COMICS
Hillman Periodicals: Aug, 1941 - No. 4, Dec, 1941 (#1 by Funnies, Inc.)

	GD	VG	FN	VF	VF/NM	NM-
1-The Conqueror by Bill Everett, The Crusader, & Bomber Burns begin; Conqueror's origin in text; Everett-c	300	600	900	1894	3197	4500
2-Everett-c/a	128	256	384	800	1325	1850
3,4	83	166	249	519	860	1200

VIC VERITY MAGAZINE
Vic Verity Publ.: 1945; No. 2, Jan?, 1947 - No. 7, Sept, 1946 (A comic book)

	GD	VG	FN	VF	VF/NM	NM-
1-C. C. Beck-c/a	23	46	69	130	205	280
2-Beck-c	14	28	42	80	115	150
3-7: 6-Beck-a. 7-Beck-c	12	24	36	69	97	125

VIDEO JACK
Marvel Comics (Epic Comics): Nov, 1987 - No. 6, Nov, 1988 ($1.25)

1-5						2.50
6-Neal Adams, Keith Giffen, Wrightson, others-a						4.00

VIETNAM JOURNAL
Apple Comics: Nov, 1987 - No. 16, Apr, 1991 ($1.75/$1.95, B&W)

1-16: Don Lomax-c/a/scripts in all, 1-2nd print						3.00
…: Indian Country Vol. 1 (1990, $12.95)-r/#1-4 plus one new story						13.00

VIETNAM JOURNAL: VALLEY OF DEATH
Apple Comics: June, 1994 - No. 2, Aug, 1994 ($2.75, B&W, limited series)

1,2: By Don Lomax						4.00

VIGILANTE, THE (Also see New Teen Titans #23 & Annual V2#2)
DC Comics: Oct, 1983 - No. 50, Feb, 1988 ($1.25, Baxter paper)

1-Origin						3.00
2-16,19-49: 3-Cyborg app. 4-1st app. The Exterminator; Newton(p). 6,7-Origin. 20,21-Nightwing app. 35-Origin Mad Bomber. 47-Batman-c/s						2.50
17,18-Alan Moore scripts						4.00
50-Ken Steacy painted-c						3.00
Annual nn, 2 ('85, '86)						2.50

VIGILANTE
DC Comics: Nov, 2005 - No. 6, Apr, 2006 ($2.99, limited series)

1-6-Bruce Jones-s. 1,2,4-6-Ben Oliver-a						3.00

VIGILANTE: CITY LIGHTS, PRAIRIE JUSTICE (Also see Action Comics #42, Justice League of America #78, Leading Comics & World's Finest #244)
DC Comics: Nov, 1995 - No. 4, Feb, 1996 ($2.50, limited series)

1-4: James Robinson scripts in all						2.50

VIGILANTES, THE
Dell Publishing Co.: No. 839, Sept, 1957

	GD	VG	FN	VF	VF/NM	NM-
Four Color 839-Movie	7	14	21	47	76	105

VIGILANTE 8: SECOND OFFENSE
Chaos! Comics: Dec, 1999 ($2.95, one-shot)

1-Based on video game						3.00

VIKINGS, THE (Movie)
Dell Publishing Co.: No. 910, May, 1958

	GD	VG	FN	VF	VF/NM	NM-
Four Color 910-Buscema-a, Kirk Douglas photo-c	8	16	24	54	90	125

VILLAINS AND VIGILANTES
Eclipse Comics: Dec, 1986 - No. 4, May, 1987 ($1.50/$1.75, limited series, Baxter paper)

1-4: Based on role-playing game. 2-4 ($1.75-c)						2.50

VILLAINS UNITED (Leads into Infinite Crisis)
DC Comics: July, 2005 - No. 6, Dec, 2005 ($2.95/$2.50, limited series)

1-6-Simone-s/JG Jones-c. 1-The Secret Six and the "Society" form						3.00
…: Infinite Crisis Special 1 (6/06, $4.99) Simone-s/Eaglesham-a						5.00
TPB (2005, $12.99) r/#1-6; background info on villains						13.00

VILLAINY OF DOCTOR DOOM, THE
Marvel Comics: 1999 ($17.95, TPB)

nn-Reprints early battle with the Fantastic Four						18.00

VIMANARAMA
DC Comics (Vertigo): Apr, 2005 - No. 3, June, 2005 ($2.95, limited series)

1-3-Grant Morrison-s/Philip Bond-a						3.00
TPB (2005, $12.99) r/#1-3						13.00

VINTAGE MAGNUS (…Robot Fighter)
Valiant: Jan, 1992 - No. 4, Apr, 1992 ($2.25, limited series)

1-4: 1-Layton-c; r/origin from Magnus R.F. #22						2.50

VIOLATOR (Also see Spawn #2)
Image Comics (Todd McFarlane Productions): May, 1994 - No. 3, Aug, 1994 ($1.95, limited series)

1-Alan Moore scripts in all						5.00
2,3: Bart Sears-c(p)/a(p)						4.00

VIOLATOR VS. BADROCK
Image Comics (Extreme Studios): May, 1995 - No. 4, Aug, 1995 ($2.50, limited series)

1-4: Alan Moore scripts in all. 1-1st app Celestine; variant-c (3?)						2.50

Violent Messiahs #7 © Hurricane Ent.

The Vision #2 © MAR

Voodoo Child #1 © Virgin Comics

	GD 2.0	VG 4.0	FN 6.0	VF 8.0	VF/NM 9.0	NM- 9.2

VIOLENT MESSIAHS (...: Lamenting Pain on cover for #9-12, numbered as #1-4)
Image Comics: June, 2000 - Present ($2.95)

1-Two covers by Travis Smith and Medina		4.00
1-Tower Records variant edition		5.00
2-8: 5-Flip book sketchbook		3.00
9-12-Lamenting Pain; 2 covers on each		3.00
...: Genesis (12/01, $5.95) r/'97 B&W issue, Wizard 1/2 prologue		6.00
...: The Book of Job TPB (7/02, $24.95) r/#1-8; Foreward by Gossett		25.00

VIP (TV)
TV Comics: 2000 ($2.95, unfinished series)

1-Based on the Pamela Lee TV show; photo-c	3.00

VIPER (TV)
DC Comics: Aug, 1994 - No. 4, Nov, 1994 ($1.95, limited series)

1-4-Adaptation of television show	2.50

VIRGINIAN, THE (TV)
Gold Key: June, 1963

	GD	VG	FN	VF	VF/NM	NM-
1(10060-306)-Part photo-c of James Drury plus photo back-c		4	8	12	26	41	55

VIRTUA FIGHTER (Video Game)
Marvel Comics: Aug, 1995 (2.95, one-shot)

1-Sega Saturn game	3.00

VIRUS
Dark Horse Comics: 1993 - No. 4, 1993 ($2.50, limited series)

1-4: Ploog-c	2.50

VISION, THE
Marvel Comics: Nov, 1994 - No. 4, Feb, 1995 ($1.75, limited series)

1-4	2.50

VISION, THE (AVENGERS ICONS: ...)
Marvel Comics: Oct, 2002 - No. 4, Jan, 2003 ($2.99, limited series)

1-4-Geoff Johns-s/Ivan Reis-a	3.00
...: Yesterday and Tomorrow TPB (2005, $14.99) r/#1-4 & Avengers #57 (1st app.)	15.00

VISION AND THE SCARLET WITCH, THE (See Marvel Fanfare)
Marvel Comics Group: Nov, 1982 - No. 4, Feb, 1983 (Limited series)

1-4: 2-Nuklo & Future Man app.	3.00

VISION AND THE SCARLET WITCH, THE
Marvel Comics Group: Oct, 1985 - No. 12, Sept, 1986 (Maxi-series)

V2#1-12: 1-Origin; 1st app. in Avengers #57. 2-West Coast Avengers x-over	2.50

VISIONS
Vision Publications: 1979 - No. 5, 1983 (B&W, fanzine)

	GD	VG	FN	VF	VF/NM	NM-
1-Flaming Carrot begins(1st app?); N. Adams-c	3	6	9	21	32	42
2-N. Adams, Rogers-a; Gulacy back-c; signed & numbered to 2000	3	6	9	17	25	32
3-Williamson-c(p); Steranko back-c	2	4	6	11	16	20
4-Flaming Carrot-c & info.	2	4	6	11	16	20
5-1 pg. Flaming Carrot	1	3	4	6	8	10

NOTE: *Eisner* a-4. *Miller* a-4. *Starlin* a-3. *Williamson* a-5. After #4, Visions became an annual publication of The Atlanta Fantasy Fair.

VISITOR, THE
Valiant/Acclaim Comics (Valiant): Apr, 1995 - No. 13, Nov, 1995 ($2.50)

1-13: 8-Harbinger revealed. 13-Visitor revealed to be Sting from Harbinger	2.50

VISITOR VS. THE VALIANT UNIVERSE, THE
Valiant: Feb, 1995 - No. 2, Mar, 1995 ($2.95, limited series)

1,2	3.00

VOGUE (Also see Youngblood)
Image Comics (Extreme Studios): Oct, 1995 - No.3, Jan, 1996 ($2.50, limited series)

1-3: 1-Liefeld-c, 1-Variant-c	2.50

VOID INDIGO (Also see Marvel Graphic Novel)
Marvel Comics (Epic Comics): 11/84 - No. 2, 3/85 ($1.50, direct sales, unfinished series, mature)

1,2: Cont'd from Marvel G.N.; graphic sex & violence	2.50

VOLCANIC REVOLVER
Oni Press: Dec, 1998 - No. 3, Mar, 1999 ($2.95, B&W, limited series)

1-3: Scott Morse-s/a	3.00
TPB (12/99, $9.95, digest size) r/#1-3 and Oni Double Feature #7 prologue	10.00

VOLTRON (TV)
Modern Publishing: 1985 - No. 3, 1985 (75¢, limited series)

1-3: Ayers-a in all	4.00

VOLTRON: DEFENDER OF THE UNIVERSE (TV)
Image Comics: No. 0, May, 2003 - No. 5, Sept, 2003 ($2.50)

0-Jolley-s/Brooks-a; character pin-ups with background info	2.50
1-5-($2.95) 1-Three covers by Norton, Brooks and Andrews; Norton-a	3.00
...: Revelations TPB (2004, $11.95, digest-sized) r/#1-5; cover gallery	12.00

VOLTRON: DEFENDER OF THE UNIVERSE (TV)
Image Comics: Jan, 2004 - No. 11, Dec, 2004 ($2.95)

1-11: 1-Jolley-s; wraparound-c	3.00

VOODA (Jungle Princess) (Formerly Voodoo)
Ajax-Farrell (Four Star Publications): No. 20, April, 1955 - No. 22, Aug, 1955

	GD	VG	FN	VF	VF/NM	NM-
20-Baker-c/a (r/Seven Seas #6)	40	80	120	235	368	500
21,22-Baker-a plus Kamen/Baker story, Kimbo Boy of Jungle, & Baker-c(p) in all.						
22-Censored Jo-Jo-r (name Powaa)	35	70	105	204	322	440

NOTE: #20-22 each contain one heavily censored-r of South Sea Girl by *Baker* from Seven Seas Comics with name changed to Vooda. #20-r/Seven Seas #6; #21-r/#4; #22-r/#3.

VOODOO (Weird Fantastic Tales) (Vooda #20 on)
Ajax-Farrell (Four Star Publ.): May, 1952 - No. 19, Jan-Feb, 1955

	GD	VG	FN	VF	VF/NM	NM-
1-South Sea Girl-r by Baker	59	118	177	369	610	850
2-Rulah story-r plus South Sea Girl from Seven Seas #2 by Baker (name changed from Alani to El'nee)	48	96	144	293	484	675
3-Bakerish-a; man stabbed in face	40	80	120	240	383	525
4,8-Baker-r. 8-Severed head panels	40	80	120	240	383	525
5-7,9,10: 5-Nazi death camp story (flaying alive). 6-Severed head panels	34	68	102	197	311	425
11-18: 14-Zombies take over America. 15-Opium drug story-r/Ellery Queen #3. 16-Post nuclear world story.17-Electric chair panels	30	60	90	174	275	375
19-Bondage-c; Baker-r(2)/Seven Seas #5 w/minor changes & #1, heavily modified; last pre-code; contents & covers change to jungle theme	38	76	114	219	347	475
Annual 1(1952, 25¢, 100 pgs.)-Baker-a (scarce)	124	248	372	775	1288	1800

VOODOO
Image Comics (WildStorm): Nov, 1997 - No. 4, Mar, 1998 ($2.50, lim. series)

1-4:Alan Moore-s in all; Hughes-a. 2-4-Rio-a	2.50
1-Platinum Ed	10.00
Dancing on the Dark TPB ('99, $9.95) r/#1-4	10.00
...-Zealot: Skin Trade (8/95, $4.95)	5.00

VOODOO (See Tales of...)

VOODOO CHILD (Weston Cage & Nicolas Cage's...)
Virgin Comics: July, 2007 - Present ($2.99)

1-3: 1-Mike Carey-s/Dean Hyrapiet-a; covers by Hyrapiet & Templesmith	3.00

VOODOOM
Oni Press: June, 2000 ($4.95, B&W)

1-Scott Morse-s/Jim Mahfood-a	5.00

VORTEX
Vortex Publs.: Nov, 1982 - No. 15, 1988 (No month) ($1.50/$1.75, B&W)

	GD	VG	FN	VF	VF/NM	NM-
1 ($1.95)-Peter Hsu-a; Ken Steacy-c; nudity	1	2	3	5	7	9
2,12: 2-1st app. Mister X (on-c only). 12-Sam Kieth-a						6.00
3-11,13-15						3.00

VORTEX
Comico: 1991 - No. 2? ($2.50, limited series)

1,2: Heroes from The Elementals	2.50

VOYAGE TO THE BOTTOM OF THE SEA (Movie, TV)
Dell Publishing Co./Gold Key: No. 1230, Sept-Nov, 1961; Dec, 1964 - #16, Apr, 1970 (Painted-c)

	GD	VG	FN	VF	VF/NM	NM-
Four Color 1230 (1961)	10	20	30	70	123	175
10133-412(#1, 12/64)(Gold Key)	7	14	21	50	83	115
2(7/65) - 5: Photo back-c, 1-5	5	10	15	35	55	75
6-14	4	8	12	28	44	60
15,16-Reprints	3	6	9	18	27	35

VOYAGE TO THE DEEP
Dell Publishing Co.: Sept-Nov, 1962 - No. 4, Nov-Jan, 1964 (Painted-c)

	GD	VG	FN	VF	VF/NM	NM-
1	5	10	15	35	55	75
2-4	4	8	12	24	37	50

Wagon Train #8 © DELL

Walk In #1 © Virgin Comics

The Walking Dead #40 © Robert Kirkman

	GD 2.0	VG 4.0	FN 6.0	VF 8.0	VF/NM 9.0	NM- 9.2

WACKO
Ideal Publ. Corp.: Sept, 1980 - No. 3, Oct, 1981 (84 pgs., B&W, magazine)

	GD 2.0	VG 4.0	FN 6.0	VF 8.0	VF/NM 9.0	NM- 9.2
1-3	2	4	6	8	10	12

WACKY ADVENTURES OF CRACKY (Also see Gold Key Spotlight)
Gold Key: Dec, 1972 - No. 12, Sept, 1975

1	3	6	9	14	19	24
2	2	4	6	9	12	15
3-12	1	3	4	6	8	10

(See March of Comics #405, 424, 436, 448)

WACKY DUCK (...Comics #3-6; formerly Dopey Duck; Justice Comics #7 on)
(See Film Funnies)
Marvel Comics (NPP): No. 3, Fall, 1946 - No. 6, Summer, 1947; Aug, 1948 - No. 2, Oct, 1948

3	23	46	69	132	209	285
4-Infinity-c	20	40	60	117	184	250
5,6(1947)-Becomes Justice comics	17	34	51	98	154	210
1(1948)	16	32	48	94	147	200
2(1948)	14	28	42	76	108	140
I.W. Reprint #1,2,7('58): 1-r/Wacky Duck #6	2	4	6	9	13	16
Super Reprint #10(I.W. on-c, Super-inside)	2	4	6	9	13	16

WACKY QUACKY (See Wisco)

WACKY RACES (TV)
Gold Key: Aug, 1969 - No. 7, Apr, 1972 (Hanna-Barbera)

1	5	10	15	35	55	75
2-7	4	8	12	22	34	45

WACKY SQUIRREL (Also see Dark Horse Presents)
Dark Horse Comics: Oct, 1987 - No. 4, 1988 ($1.75, B&W)

1-4: 4-Superman parody						2.50
Halloween Adventure Special 1 (1987, $2.00)						2.50
Summer Fun Special 1 (1988, $2.00)						2.50

WACKY WITCH (Also see Gold Key Spotlight)
Gold Key: March, 1971 - No. 21, Dec, 1975

1	4	8	12	23	36	48
2	3	6	9	14	19	24
3-10	2	4	6	9	13	16
11-21	1	3	4	6	8	10

(See March of Comics #374, 398, 410, 422, 434, 446, 458, 470, 482)

WACKY WOODPECKER (See Two Bit the...)
I. W. Enterprises/Super Comics: 1958; 1963

I.W. Reprint #1,2,7 (nd-reprints Two Bit...): 7-r/Two-Bit, the Wacky Woodpecker #1.						
	2	4	6	8	11	14
Super Reprint #10('63): 10-r/Two-Bit, The Wacky Woodpecker #?						
	2	4	6	8	11	14

WAGON TRAIN (1st Series) (TV) (See Western Roundup under Dell Giants)
Dell Publishing Co.: No. 895, Mar, 1958 - No. 13, Apr-June, 1962 (All photo-c)

Four Color 895 (#1)	10	20	30	71	126	180
Four Color 971(#2),1019(#3)	7	14	21	45	73	100
4(1-3/60),6-13	6	12	18	39	62	85
5-Toth-a	6	12	18	43	69	95

WAGON TRAIN (2nd Series)(TV)
Gold Key: Jan, 1964 - No. 4, Oct, 1964 (All front & back photo-c)

1-Tufts-a in all	5	10	15	32	51	70
2-4	4	8	12	24	37	50

WAITING PLACE, THE
Slave Labor Graphics: Apr, 1997 - No. 6, Sept, 1997 ($2.95)

1-6-Sean McKeever-s						3.00
Vol. 2 - 1(11/99), 2-11						3.00
12-($4.95)						5.00

WAITING ROOM WILLIE (See Sad Case of...)

WAKE THE DEAD
IDW Publ.: Sept, 2003 - No. 5, Mar, 2004 (limited series)

1-5-Steve Niles-s/Chee-a						4.00
TPB (6/04, $19.99) r/series; intro. by Michael Dougherty; embossed die cut cover						20.00

WALK IN (Dave Stewart's ...)
Virgin Comics: Dec, 2006 - No. 6, May, 2007 ($2.99)

1-6: 1-5-Parker-s/Padlekar-a. 6-Parker-a						3.00

WALKING DEAD, THE

Image Comics: Oct, 2003 - Present ($2.95/$2.99, B&W)

						GD 2.0 ... NM- 9.2
1-Robert Kirkman-s in all/Tony Moore-a						40.00
2						15.00
3-10: 3-6-Tony Moore-a. 7-Charlie Adlard-a begins						5.00
11-42						3.00
... Book 1 HC (2006, $29.99) r/#1-12; sketch pages, cover gallery; Kirkman afterword						30.00
...Vol. 1: Days Gone Bye (5/04, $9.95, TPB) r/#1-4						10.00
...Vol. 2: Miles Behind Us (10/04, $12.95, TPB) r/#7-12						13.00
...Vol. 3: Safety Behind Bars (2005, $12.95, TPB) r/#13-18						13.00
...Vol. 4: The Heart's Desire (2005, $12.99, TPB) r/#19-24						13.00
...Vol. 5: The Best Defense (2006, $12.99, TPB) r/#25-30						13.00
...Vol. 6: This Sorrowful Life (2007, $12.99, TPB) r/#31-36						13.00
...Vol. 7: The Calm Before (2007, $12.99, TPB) r/#37-42						13.00

WALLY (Teen-age)
Gold Key: Dec, 1962 - No. 4, Sept, 1963

1	3	6	9	21	32	42
2-4	3	6	9	17	25	32

WALLY THE WIZARD
Marvel Comics (Star Comics): Apr, 1985 - No. 12, Mar, 1986 (Children's comic)

1-12: Bob Bolling a-1,3; c-1,9,11,12						4.00
1-Variant with "Star Chase" game on last page and inside back-c						8.00

WALLY WOOD'S T.H.U.N.D.E.R. AGENTS (See Thunder Agents)
Deluxe Comics: Nov, 1984 - No. 5, Oct, 1986 ($2.00, 52 pgs.)

1-5: 5-Jerry Ordway-c/a in Wood style						5.00

NOTE: *Anderson* a-2i, 3i. *Buckler* a-4. *Ditko* a-3, 4. *Giffen* a-1p-4p. *Perez* a-1p, 2, 4; c-1-4.

WALT DISNEY CHRISTMAS PARADE (Also see Christmas Parade)
Whitman Publ. Co. (Golden Press): Wint, 1977 ($1.95, cardboard-c, 224 pgs.)

11191-Barks-r/Christmas in Disneyland #1, Dell Christmas Parade #9 & Dell Giant #53						
	4	8	12	26	41	55

WALT DISNEY COMICS DIGEST
Gold Key: June, 1968 - No. 57, Feb, 1976 (50¢, digest size)

1-Reprints Uncle Scrooge #5; 192 pgs.	7	14	21	50	83	115
2-4-Barks-r	5	10	15	35	55	75
5-Daisy Duck by Barks (8 pgs.); last published story by Barks (art only)						
plus 21 pg. Scrooge-r by Barks	8	16	24	52	86	120
6-13-All Barks-r	4	8	12	22	34	45
14,15	3	6	9	16	23	30
16-Reprints Donald Duck #26 by Barks	3	6	9	21	32	42
17-20-Barks-r	3	6	9	18	27	35
21-31,33,35-37-Barks-r; 24-Toth Zorro	3	6	9	16	23	30
32,41,45,47-49	2	4	6	11	16	20
34,38,39: 34-Reprints 4-Color #318. 38-Reprints Christmas in Disneyland #1.						
39-Two Barks-r/WDC&S #272, 4-Color #1073 plus Toth Zorro-r						
	3	6	9	16	23	30
40-Mickey Mouse-r by Gottfredson	2	4	6	13	18	22
42,43-Barks-r	2	4	6	13	18	22
44-(Has Gold Key emblem, 50¢)-Reprints 1st story of 4-Color #29,256,275,282						
	5	10	15	32	51	70
44-Republished in 1976 by Whitman; not identical to original; a bit smaller, blank back-c, 69¢						
	3	6	9	16	23	30
46,50,52-Barks-r. 52-Barks-r/WDC&S #161,132	2	4	6	11	16	20
51-Reprints 4-Color #71	3	6	9	16	23	30
53-55: 53-Reprints Dell Giant #30. 54-Reprints Donald Duck Beach Party #2.						
55-Reprints Dell Giant #49	2	4	6	10	14	18
56-r/Uncle Scrooge #32 (Barks)	2	4	6	13	18	22
57-r/Mickey Mouse Almanac('57) & two Barks stories	2	4	6	11	16	20

NOTE: *Toth* a-52r. #1-10, 196 pgs.; #11-41, 164 pgs.; #42 on, 132 pgs. Old issues were being reprinted & distributed by Whitman in 1976.

WALT DISNEY GIANT (Disney)
Bruce Hamilton Co. (Gladstone): Sept, 1995 - No. 7, Sept, 1996 ($2.25, bi-monthly, 48 pgs.)

1-7: 1-Scrooge McDuck in the Yukon; Rosa-c/a/scripts plus r/F.C. #218. 2-Uncle Scrooge-r by Barks plus 17 pg. text story. 3-Donald the Mighty Duck; Rosa-c; Barks & Rosa-r. 4-Mickey and Goofy; new-a (story actually stars Goofy. Mickey Mouse by Caesar Ferioli; Donald Duck by Giorgio Cavazzano (1st in U.S.) 6-Uncle Scrooge & the Jr. Woodchucks; new-a and Barks-r. 7-Uncle Scrooge-r by Barks plus new-a						3.00

NOTE: *Series was initially solicited as Uncle Walt's Collectory. Issue #8 was advertised, but later cancelled.*

WALT DISNEY PAINT BOOK SERIES
Whitman Publ. Co.: No dates; circa 1975 (Beware! Has 1930s copyright dates) (79¢-c, 52 pgs. B&W, treasury-sized) (Coloring books, text stories & comics-r)

#2052 (Whitman #886-r) Mickey Mouse & Donald Duck Gag Book

Walt Disney's Comics and Stories #22 © DIS

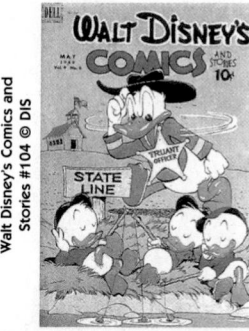

Walt Disney's Comics and Stories #104 © DIS

Walt Disney's Comics and Stories #594 © DIS

	GD 2.0	VG 4.0	FN 6.0	VF 8.0	VF/NM 9.0	NM- 9.2
#2053 (Whitman #677-r)	3	6	9	21	32	42
#2054 (Whitman #670-r) Donald-c	4	8	12	23	36	42
#2055 (Whitman #627-r) Mickey-c	3	6	9	21	32	42
#2056 (Whitman #660-r) Buckey Bug-c	3	6	9	19	29	38
#2057 (Whitman #887-r) Mickey & Donald-c	3	6	9	21	32	42

WALT DISNEY PRESENTS (TV)(Disney)
Dell Publishing Co.: No. 997, 6-8/59 - No. 6, 12-2/1960-61; No. 1181, 4-5/61 (All photo-c)

	GD 2.0	VG 4.0	FN 6.0	VF 8.0	VF/NM 9.0	NM- 9.2
Four Color 997 (#1)	7	14	21	49	80	110
2(12-2/60)-The Swamp Fox(origin), Elfego Baca, Texas John Slaughter (Disney TV series) begin	5	10	15	32	51	70
3-6: 5-Swamp Fox by Warren Tufts	5	10	15	30	48	65
Four Color 1181-Texas John Slaughter	7	14	21	47	76	105

WALT DISNEY'S CHRISTMAS PARADE (Also see Christmas Parade)
Gladstone: Winter, 1988; No. 2, Winter, 1989 ($2.95, 100 pgs.)

	GD 2.0	VG 4.0	FN 6.0	VF 8.0	VF/NM 9.0	NM- 9.2
1-Barks-r/painted-c	2	4	6	8	10	12
2-Barks-r	1	2	3	5	7	9

WALT DISNEY'S CHRISTMAS PARADE
Gemstone Publishing: Dec, 2003; 2004, 2005, 2006 ($8.95, prestige format)

1-4: 1-Reprints and 3 new European holiday stories. 2-All reprints. 3-Reprints and 2 new stories, 4-Reprints and 5 new stories						9.00

WALT DISNEY'S COMICS AND STORIES (Cont. of Mickey Mouse Magazine)
(#1-30 contain Donald Duck newspaper reprints) (Titled "Comics And Stories" #264 to #?; titled "Walt Disney's Comics and Stories" #511 on)
Dell Publishing Co./Gold Key #264-473/Whitman #474-510/Gladstone #511-547/ Disney Comics #548-633/Gemstone Publishing #634 on:
10/40 - #263, 8/62; #264, 10/62 - #510, 7/84; #511, 10/86 - #633, 2/99; #634, 7/03 - Present
NOTE: The whole number can always be found at the bottom of the title page in the lower left-hand and right hand panel.

	GD 2.0	VG 4.0	FN 6.0	VF 8.0	VF/NM 9.0	NM- 9.2
1(V1#1-c; V2#1-indicia)-Donald Duck strip-r by Al Taliaferro & Gottfredson's Mickey Mouse begin	1833	3666	5500	13,000	23,000	33,000
2	714	1428	2142	5000	8750	12,500
3	317	634	951	1981	3291	4600
4-X-Mas-c; 1st Huey, Dewey & Louie-c this title (See Mickey Mouse Magazine V4#2 for 1st-c ever)	214	428	642	1338	2219	3100
4-Special promotional, complimentary issue; cover same used one corner was blanked out & boxed in to identify the giveaway (not a paste-over). This special pressing was probably sent out to former subscribers to Mickey Mouse Mag. whose subscriptions had expired. (Very rare-5 known copies)	300	600	900	1970	3485	5000
5-Goofy-c	172	344	516	1075	1788	2500
6-10: 8-Only Clarabelle Cow-c (1st)	145	290	435	906	1503	2100
11-14: 11-Huey, Dewey & Louie-c/app.	110	220	330	688	1144	1600
15-17: 15-The 3 Little Kittens (17 pgs.). 16-The 3 Little Pigs (29 pgs.); X-Mas-c	97	194	291	606	1003	1400
17-The Ugly Duckling (4 pgs.)	97	194	291	606	1003	1400
18-21	86	172	258	538	894	1250
22-30: 22-Flag-c. 24-The Flying Gauchito (1st original comic book story done for WDC&S)	69	138	207	431	716	1000
27-Jose Carioca by Carl Buettner (2nd original story in WDC&S)						
31-New Donald Duck stories by Carl Barks begin (See F.C. #9 for 1st Barks Donald Duck)	339	678	1017	2244	3902	5600
32-Barks-a	193	386	579	1206	2003	2800
33-Barks-a; infinity-c	131	262	393	819	1360	1900
34-Gremlins by Walt Kelly begin, end #41; Barks-a	103	206	309	644	1072	1500
35,36-Barks-a	97	194	291	606	1003	1400
37-Donald Duck by Jack Hannah	54	108	162	338	557	775
38-40-Barks-a. 39-X-Mas-c. 40,41-Gremlins by Kelly						
	64	128	192	400	663	925
41-50-Barks-a. 43-Seven Dwarfs-c app. (4/44). 45-50-Nazis in Gottfredson's Mickey Mouse Stories	53	106	159	323	537	750
51-60-Barks-a. 51-X-Mas-c. 52-Li'l Bad Wolf begins, ends #203 (not in #55). 58-Kelly flag-c	29	58	87	212	381	550
61-70: Barks-a. 61-Dumbo story. 63,64-Pinocchio app. 63-Cover swipe from New Funnies #94. 64-X-Mas-c. 65-Pluto story. 66-Infinity-c. 67,68-Mickey Mouse Sunday-r by Bill Wright	25	50	75	184	330	475
71-80: Barks-a. 75-77-Brer Rabbit stories, no Mickey Mouse. 76-X-Mas-c	19	38	57	138	244	350
81-87,89,90: Barks-a. 82-Goofy-c. 82-84-Bongo stories. 86-90-Goofy & Agnes app.						
89-Chip 'n' Dale story	16	32	48	118	209	300
88-1st app. Gladstone Gander by Barks (1/48)	20	40	60	150	268	385
91-97,99: Barks-a. 95-1st WDC&S app. 96-No Mickey Mouse; Little Toot begins, ends #97. 99-X-Mas-c	15	30	45	107	191	275

	GD 2.0	VG 4.0	FN 6.0	VF 8.0	VF/NM 9.0	NM- 9.2
98-1st Uncle Scrooge app. in WDC&S (11/48)	26	52	78	195	348	500
100-(1/49)-Barks-a	17	34	51	128	227	325
101-110-Barks-a. 107-Taliaferro-c; Donald acquires super powers						
	13	26	39	95	168	240
111,114,117-All Barks-a	11	22	33	79	140	200
112-Drug (ether) issue (Donald Duck)	11	22	33	79	140	200
113,115,116,118-123: No Barks. 116-Dumbo x-over. 121-Grandma Duck begins, ends #168; not in #135,142,146,155	8	16	24	58	97	135
124,126-130-All Barks-a. 124-X-Mas-c	10	20	30	68	119	170
125-1st app. Junior Woodchucks (2/51); Barks-a	14	28	42	99	175	250
131,133,135-137,139-All Barks-a	9	18	27	65	113	160
132-Barks-a(2) (D. Duck & Grandma Duck)	10	20	30	68	119	170
134-Intro. & 1st app. The Beagle Boys (11/51)	17	34	51	128	227	325
138-Classic Scrooge money story	14	28	42	102	181	260
140-(5/52)-1st app. Gyro Gearloose by Barks; 2nd Barks Uncle Scrooge-c; 3rd Uncle Scrooge cover app.	17	34	51	128	227	325
141-150-All Barks-a. 143-Little Hiawatha begins, ends #151,159						
	8	16	24	54	90	125
151-170-All Barks-a	7	14	21	47	76	105
171-199-All Barks-a	6	12	18	43	69	95
200	7	14	21	47	76	105
201-240: All Barks-a. 204-Chip 'n' Dale & Scamp begin						
	6	12	18	37	59	80
241-283: Barks-a. 241-Dumbo x-over. 247-Gyro Gearloose begins, ends #274.						
256-Ludwig Von Drake begins, ends #274	5	10	15	32	51	70
284,285,287,290,295,296,309-311-Not by Barks	3	6	9	16	23	30
286,288,291-294,297,298,300-308-All Barks stories; 293-Grandma Duck's Farm Friends.						
297-Gyro Gearloose. 298-Daisy Duck's Diary-r	3	6	9	19	29	38
289-Annette-c & back-c & story; Barks-a	4	8	12	22	34	45
299-307-All contain early Barks-r (#43-117). 305-Gyro Gearloose						
	3	6	9	20	30	40
312-Last Barks issue with original story	3	6	9	20	30	40
313-315,317-327,329-334,336-341	3	6	9	14	19	24
316-Last issue published during life of Walt Disney	3	6	9	14	19	24
328,335,342-350-Barks-r	3	6	9	14	19	24
351-360-With posters inside; Barks reprints (2 versions of each with & without posters)						
	4	8	12	23	36	48
351-360-Without posters...	3	6	9	14	19	24
361-400-Barks-r	3	6	9	14	19	24
401-429-Barks-r	2	4	6	13	18	22
430,433,437,438,441,444,445,466-No Barks	2	4	6	8	10	12
431,432,434-436,439,440,442,443-Barks-r	2	4	6	9	13	16
446-465,467-473-Barks-r	2	4	6	8	11	14
474(3/80),475-478 (Whitman)	2	4	6	13	18	22
479(8/80),481(10/80)-484(1/81) pre-pack only	4	8	12	28	44	60
480 (8-12/80)-(Very low distribution)	9	18	27	65	113	160
484 (1/81, 40c-c) Cover price error variant (scarce)	5	10	15	32	51	70
485-499: 494-r/WDC&S #98	2	4	6	10	14	18
500-510 (All #90011 on-c; pre-packs): 500(4/83), 501(5/83), 502&503(7/83), 504-506(all 8/83), 507(4/84), 508(5/84), 509(6/84), 510(7/84). 506-No Barks						
	2	4	6	11	16	20
511-Donald Duck by Daan Jippes (1st in U.S.; in all through #518); Gyro Gearloose Barks-r begins (in most through #547); Wuzzles by Disney Studio (1st by Gladstone)						
	3	6	9	16	23	30
512,513	2	4	6	9	13	16
514-516,520	1	2	3	5	7	9
517-519,521,522,525,527,529,530,532-546: 518-Infinity-c. 522-r/1st app. Huey, Dewey & Louie from D. Duck Sunday. 535-546-Barks-r. 537-1st Donald Duck by William Van Horn in WDC&S. 541-545-52 pgs. 546,547-68 pgs. 546-Kelly-r. 547-Rosa-r						5.00
523,524,526,528,531,547: Rosa-s/a in all. 523-1st Rosa 10 pager						
	2	4	6	8	11	14
548-($1.50, 6/90)-1st Disney issue; new-a; no M. Mouse						6.00
549,551-570,572,573,577-579,581,584 ($1.50): 549-Barks-r begins, ends #585, not in #555, 556, & 564. 551-r/1 story from F.C. #29. 556,578-r/Mickey Mouse Cheerios Premium by Dick Moores. 562,563,568-570, 572, 581-Gottfredson strip-r. 570-Valentine issue; has Mickey/Minnie centerfold. 584-Taliaferro strip-r						4.00
550 ($2.25, 52 pgs.)-Donald Duck by Barks; previously printed only in The Netherlands (1st time in U.S.); r/Chip 'n Dale & Scamp from #204						5.00
571-($2.95, 68 pgs)-r/Donald Duck's Atom Bomb by Barks from 1947 Cheerios premium						6.00
574-576,580,582,583 ($2.95, 68 pgs.): 574-r/1st Pinocchio Sunday strip (1939-40). 575-Gottfredson-r, Pinocchio-r/WDC&S #64. 580-r/Donald Duck's 1st app. from Silly Symphony strip 12/16/34 by Taliaferro; Gottfredson strip-r begin; not in #584 & 600. 582,583-r/Mickey Mouse on Sky Island from WDC&S #1,2						5.00
585 ($2.50, 52 pgs.)-r/#140; Barks-r/WDC&S #140						5.00

	GD	VG	FN	VF	VF/NM	NM-		GD	VG	FN	VF	VF/NM	NM-
	2.0	4.0	6.0	8.0	9.0	9.2		2.0	4.0	6.0	8.0	9.0	9.2

586,587: 586-Gladstone issues begin again; begin $1.50-c; Gottfredson-r begins (not in #600).
587-Donald Duck by William Van Horn begins   4.00
588-597: 588,591-599-Donald Duck by William Van Horn   3.00
598,599 ($1.95, 36 pgs.): 598-1/1st drawings of Mickey Mouse by Ub Iwerks   3.00
600 ($2.95, 48 pgs.).-L.B. Cole-(r)/WDC&S #1; Barks-r/WDC&S #32 plus Rosa, Jippes, Van Horn-r and new Rosa centerspread   4.00
601-611 ($5.95, 64 pgs., squarebound, bi-monthly): 601-Barks-a, r/Mickey Mouse V1#1, Rosa-a/scripts. 602-Rosa-c. 604-Taliaferro strip-r/1st Silly Symphony Sundays from 1932. 604,605-Jippes-a. 605-Walt Kelly-c; Gottfredson "Mickey Mouse Outwits the Phantom Blot" r/F.C. #16   6.00
612-633 ($6.95): 633-(2/99) Last Gladstone issue   7.00
634-675: 634-(7/03) First Gemstone issue; William Van Horn-c. 666-Mickey's Inferno   7.00
676-681: 676-Begin $7.50-c. 677-Bucky Bug's 75th Anniversary   7.50
682-685-($7.99)   8.00
NOTE: (#1-38, 68 pgs.) #39-42, 60 pgs.; #43-57, 61-134, 143-168, 446, 447, 52 pgs.; #58-60, 135-142, 169-540, 36 pgs.)

NOTE: **Barks** art in all issues #31 on, except where noted; c-95, 96, 104, 108, 109, 130-172, 174-178, 183, 198-200, 204, 206-209, 212-216, 218, 220, 226, 228-233, 235-238, 240-243, 247, 250, 253, 256, 260, 261, 276-283, 288-292, 295-298, 301, 303, 304, 306, 307, 309, 310, 313-316, 319, 321, 322, 324, 326, 328, 329, 331, 332, 334, 341, 342, 350, 351, 527r, 530r, 540(never before published), 546r, 557-586r(most), 596p, 601p. **Kelly** a-24p, 34-41, 43; r-522-524, 546, 547, 582, 583; covers(most)-34-118, 531r, 537r, 541r-543r, 562r, 571r, 605r. Walt Disney's Comics & Stories featured Mickey Mouse serials which were in practically every issue from #1 through #394 and #511 to date. The titles of the serials, along with the issues they are in, are listed in previous editions of this price guide. **Floyd Gottfredson** Mickey Mouse serials in issues #1-14, 69-84, 78-100, 128, 566-572, 582, 583, 586-599, 601-603, 605-present, plus "Service with a Smile" in #13; "Mickey Mouse in a Warplant" (3 pgs.), and "Pluto Catches a Nazi Spy" (4 pgs.) in #62; "Mystery Next Door", #93; "Sunken Treasure", #94; "Aunt Marissa", #95 (r in #575); "Gangland", #98 (r in #562); "Thanksgiving Dinner", #99 (r in #567); and "The Talking Dog", #100 (r in #563); "Morty's Escapade", #128. "The Brave Little Tailor", #580; "Introducing Mickey Mouse Movies", #591; Circus Roustabout, #585; "Rumplewatt the Giant", #604. Mickey Mouse by **Paul Murry** #152-547 except 155-57 (Dick Moore), 327-29 (Tony Strobl), 348-50 (Jack Manning), 533 (Bill Wright). **Don Rosa** story-a-523, 524, 528, 526, 531, 547, 601-present. **Al Taliaferro** Silly Symphonies in #5- "Three Little Pigs"; #13- "Birds of a Feather"; #14- "The Boarding School Mystery"; #15- "Cookieland" and "Three Little Kittens"; #16- "The Practical Pig"; #17- "The Ugly Duckling"; "The Wise Little Hen" in #580; and "Ambrose the Robber Kitten"; #19- "Penguin Isle"; and "Bucky Bug" in #20-23, 25, 26, 28 (one continuous story from 1932-34; first 2 pgs. not Taliaferro). Gottfredson strip r-562, 563, 568-572, 581, 585, 586, 590. Taliaferro strip r-584, 580. Van Horn a-537, 545, 561, 574, 587, 588, 591-present.

WALT DISNEY'S COMICS DIGEST
Gladstone: Dec, 1986 - No. 7, Sept, 1987

1		1	2	3	5	6	8
2-7						6.00

WALT DISNEY'S COMICS PENNY PINCHER
Gladstone: May, 1997 - No. 4, Aug, 1997 (99¢, limited series)

1-4   2.50

WALT DISNEY'S DONALD AND MICKEY (Formerly Walt Disney's Mickey and Donald)
Gladstone (Bruce Hamilton Co.): No. 19, Sept, 1993 - No. 30, 1995 ($1.50, 36 & 68 pgs.)

19,21-24,26-30: New & reprints. 19,21,23,24-Barks-r. 19,26-Murry-r. 22-Barks "Omelet" story r/WDC&S #146. 27-Mickey Mouse story by Caesar Ferioli (1st U.S work). 29-Rosa-c; Mickey Mouse story actually starring Goofy (does not include Mickey except on title page.)   4.00
20,25-($2.95, 68 pgs.): 20-Barks, Gottfredson-r   5.00
NOTE: Donald Duck stories were all reprints.

WALT DISNEY'S DONALD DUCK ADVENTURES (D.D. Adv. #1-3)
Gladstone: 11/87- No. 20, 4/90 (1st Series); No. 21,8/93-No. 48, 2/98(3rd Series)

1		1	2	3	4	5	7
2-r/F.C. #308						3.00

3,4,6,7,9-11,13,15-18: 3-r/F.C. #223. 4-r/F.C. #62. 9-r/F.C. #159, "Ghost of the Grotto". 11-r/F.C. #159, "Adventure Down Under." 16-r/F.C. #291; Rosa-c. 18-r/FC #318; Rosa-c   3.00
5,8-Don Rosa-c/a   5.00
12($1.50, 52pgs)-Rosa-c/a w/Barks poster   6.00
14-r/F.C. #29, "Mummy's Ring"   4.00
19($1.95, 68 pgs.)-Barks-r/F.C. #199 (1 pg.)   3.00
20($1.95, 68 pgs.)-Barks-r/F.C. #189 & cover-r; William Van Horn-a   3.00
21,22: 21-r/D.D. #46. 22-r/F.C. #282   3.00
23-25,27,29,31,32-($1.50, 36 pgs.): 21,23,29-Rosa-c. 23-Intro/1st app. Andold Wild Duck by Marco Rota. 24-Van Horn-a. 27-1st Pat Block-a, "Mystery of Widow's Gap." 31,32-Block-c   2.50
26,28($2.95, 68 pgs.): 26-Barks-r/F.C. #108, "Terror of the River". 28-Barks-r/F.C. #199, "Sheriff of Bullet Valley"   4.00
30($2.95, 68 pgs.)-Barks-r/F.C. #367, Barks' "Christmas for Shacktown"   4.00
33($1.95, 68 pgs.)-Barks-r/F.C. #408, Barks' "The Golden Helmet;"Van Horn-c   3.00
34-43: 34-Rosa-c. Name $1.50-c. 34,35,37-Block-a/scripts. 38-Van Horn-c/a   2.50
44-48-($1.95-c)   2.50
NOTE: Barks a-1-22r, 26r, 28r, 33r, 36r; c-3r, 8r, 10r, 14r, 20r. Block a-24, 34, 35, 37; c-27, 30-32, 34, 35, 37. Rosa a-5, 8, 12, 43; c-13, 16, 18, 21, 23, 43.

WALT DISNEY'S DONALD DUCK ADVENTURES (2nd Series)

Disney Comics: June, 1990 - No. 38, July, 1993 ($1.50)

1-Rosa-a & scripts   5.00
2-21,23,25,27-33,35,36,38: 2-Barks-r/WDC&S #35; William Van Horn-a begins, ends #20. 9-Barks-r/F.C. #178. 9,11,14,17-No Van Horn-a. 11-Mad #1 cover parody. 14-Barks-r. 17-Barks-r. 21-r/FC #203 by Barks. 29-r/MOC #20 by Barks   3.00
22,24,26,34,37: 22-Rosa-a (10 pgs.) & scripts. 24-Rosa-a & scripts. 26-r/March of Comics #41 by Barks. 34-Rosa-c/a. 37-Rosa-a; Barks-r   4.00
NOTE: Barks r-2, 4, 9(F.C. #178), 14(D.D #45), 17, 21, 26, 27, 29 , 35, 36(D.D #60)-38. Taliaferro a-34r, 36r.

WALT DISNEY'S DONALD DUCK ADVENTURES (Take-Along Comic)
Gemstone Publishing: July, 2003 - Present ($7.95, 5" x 7-1/2")

1-21-Mickey Mouse & Uncle Scrooge app. 9-Christmas-c   8.00

WALT DISNEY'S DONALD DUCK AND FRIENDS
Gemstone Publishing: No. 308, Oct, 2003 - No. 346, Dec, 2006 ($2.95)

308-346: 308-Numbering resumes from Gladstone Donald Duck series; Halloween-c. 332-Halloween-c; r/#26 by Carl Barks   3.00

WALT DISNEY'S DONALD DUCK AND MICKEY MOUSE (Formerly Walt Disney's Donald and Mickey)
Gladstone (Bruce Hamilton Company): Sept, 1995 - No. 7, Sept, 1996 ($1.50, 32 pgs.)

1-7: 1-Barks-r and new Mickey Mouse stories in all. 5,6-Mickey Mouse stories by Caesar Ferioli. 7-New Donald Duck and Mickey Mouse x-over story; Barks-r/WDC&S #51   2.50
NOTE: Issue #8 was advertised, but cancelled.

WALT DISNEY'S DONALD DUCK AND UNCLE SCROOGE
Gemstone Publishing: Nov, 2005 ($6.95, square-bound one-shot)

nn-New story by John Lustig and Pat Block and r/Uncle Scrooge #59   7.00

WALT DISNEY'S DONALD DUCK IN THE CASE OF THE MISSING MUMMY
Gemstone Publishing: Oct, 2007 ($8.99, square-bound one-shot)

nn-New story by Shelley and Pat Block and r/Donald Duck FC #29   9.00

WALT DISNEY SHOWCASE
Gold Key: Oct, 1970 - No. 54, Jan, 1980 (No. 44-48: 68pgs., 49-54: 52pgs.)

	GD	VG	FN	VF	VF/NM	NM-
1-Boatniks (Movie)-Photo-c	3	6	9	18	27	35
2-Moby Duck	3	6	9	14	19	24
3,4,7: 3-Bongo & Lumpjaw-r. 4,7-Pluto-r	2	4	6	10	14	18
5-$1,000,000 Duck (Movie)-Photo-c	3	6	9	16	22	28
6-Bedknobs & Broomsticks (Movie)	3	6	9	16	22	28
8-Daisy & Donald	2	4	6	11	16	20
9- 101 Dalmatians (cartoon feat.); r/F.C. #1183	3	6	9	17	25	32
10-Napoleon & Samantha (Movie)-Photo-c	3	6	9	16	22	28
11-Moby Duck-r	2	4	6	10	14	18
12-Dumbo-r/Four Color #668	2	4	6	11	16	20
13-Pluto-r	2	4	6	10	14	18
14-World's Greatest Athlete (Movie)-Photo-c	3	6	9	16	22	28
15- 3 Little Pigs-r	2	4	6	11	16	20
16-Aristocats (cartoon feature); r/Aristocats #1	3	6	9	16	22	28
17-Mary Poppins; r/M.P. #10136-501-Photo-c	3	6	9	16	22	28
18-Gyro Gearloose; Barks-r/F.C. #1047,1184	3	6	9	18	27	35
19-That Darn Cat; r/That Darn Cat #10171-602-Hayley Mills photo-c	3	6	9	16	22	28
20,23-Pluto-r	2	4	6	11	16	20
21-Li'l Bad Wolf & The Three Little Pigs	2	4	6	10	14	18
22-Unbirthday Party with Alice in Wonderland; r/Four Color #341	3	6	9	19	24
24-26: 24-Herbie Rides Again (Movie); sequel to "The Love Bug"; photo-c. 25-Old Yeller (Movie); r/F.C. #869; Photo-c. 26-Lt. Robin Crusoe USN (Movie); r/Lt. Robin Crusoe USN #10191-601; photo-c	2	4	6	11	16	20
27-Island at the Top of the World (Movie)-Photo-c	3	6	9	14	19	24
28-Brer Rabbit, Bucky Bug-r/WDC&S #58	2	4	6	11	16	20
29-Escape to Witch Mountain (Movie)-Photo-c	3	6	9	14	19	24
30-Magica De Spell; Barks-r/Uncle Scrooge #36 & WDC&S #258	3	6	9	21	32	42
31-Bambi (cartoon feature); r/Four Color #186	2	4	6	13	18	22
32-Spin & Marty-r/F.C. #1026; Mickey Mouse Club (TV)-Photo-c	3	6	9	19	24
33-40: 33-Pluto-r/F.C. #1143. 34-Paul Revere's Ride with Johnny Tremain (TV); r/F.C. #822. 35-Goofy-r/F.C. #952. 36-Peter Pan-r/F.C. #442. 37-Tinker Bell & Jiminy Cricket-r/F.C. #982,989. 38,39-Mickey & the Sleuth, Parts 1 & 2. 40-The Rescuers (cartoon feature)	2	4	6	9	13	16
41-Herbie Goes to Monte Carlo (Movie); sequel to "Herbie Rides Again"; photo-c	2	4	6	10	14	18
42-Mickey & the Sleuth	2	4	6	9	13	16
43-Pete's Dragon (Movie)-Photo-c	2	4	6	13	18	22

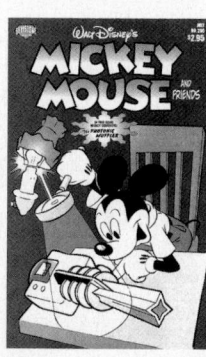

Walt Disney's Mickey Mouse and Friends #290 © DIS

Walt Disney's Uncle Scrooge #346 © DIS

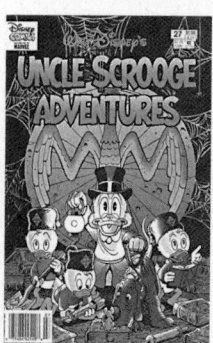

Walt Disney's Uncle Scrooge Adventures #27 © DIS

	GD	VG	FN	VF	VF/NM	NM-
	2.0	4.0	6.0	8.0	9.0	9.2

44-Return From Witch Mountain (new) & In Search of the Castaways-r
(Movies)-Photo-c; 68 pg. giants begin

| | 3 | 6 | 9 | 14 | 19 | 24 |

45-The Jungle Book (Movie); r/#30033-803

| | 3 | 6 | 9 | 17 | 25 | 32 |

46-48: 46-The Cat From Outer Space (Movie)(new), & The Shaggy Dog (Movie)-r/F.C. #985;
photo-c. 47-Mickey Mouse Surprise Party-r. 48-The Wonderful Advs. of Pinocchio-r/F.C.
#1203; last 68 pg. issue

| | 2 | 4 | 6 | 10 | 14 | 18 |

49-54: 49-North Avenue Irregulars (Movie); Zorro-r/Zorro #11; 52 pgs. begin; photo-c.
50-Bednbobs & Broomsticks-r/#6; Mooncussers-r/World of Adv. #1; photo-c.
51-101 Dalmatians-r. 52-Unidentified Flying Oddball (Movie); r/Picnic Party #8; photo-c.
53-The Scarecrow-r (TV). 54-The Black Hole (Movie)-Photo-c (predates Black Hole #1)

| | 2 | 4 | 6 | 9 | 13 | 16 |

WALT DISNEY'S MAGAZINE (TV)(Formerly Walt Disney's Mickey Mouse Club Magazine)
(50¢, bi-monthly)
Western Publishing Co.: V2#4, June, 1957 - V4#6, Oct, 1959

V2#4-Stories & articles on the Mouseketeers, Zorro, & Goofy and other Disney characters
& people

| | 7 | 14 | 21 | 45 | 73 | 100 |

V2#5, V2#6(10/57)

| | 6 | 12 | 18 | 41 | 66 | 90 |

V3#1(12/57), V3#3-5

| | 6 | 12 | 18 | 37 | 59 | 80 |

V3#2-Annette Funicello photo-c

| | 11 | 22 | 33 | 77 | 136 | 195 |

V3#6(10/58)-TV Zorro photo-c

| | 8 | 16 | 24 | 52 | 86 | 120 |

V4#1(12/58) - V4#2-4,6(10/59)

| | 6 | 12 | 18 | 37 | 59 | 80 |

V4#5-Annette Funicello photo-c, w/ 2-photo articles

| | 11 | 22 | 33 | 77 | 136 | 195 |

NOTE: V2#4-V3#6 were 11-1/2x8-1/2", 48 pgs.; V4#1 on were 10x8", 52 pgs. (Peak circulation of 400,000).

WALT DISNEY'S MERRY CHRISTMAS (See Dell Giant #39)

WALT DISNEY'S MICKEY AND DONALD (M & D #1,2)(Becomes Walt Disney's Donald &
Mickey #19 on)
Gladstone: Mar, 1988 - No. 18, May, 1990 (95¢)

1-Don Rosa-a; r/1949 Firestone giveaway 6.00
2-8: 3-Infinity-c. 4-8-Barks-r 3.00
9-15: 9-r/1948 Firestone giveaway; X-Mas-c 3.00
16($1.50, 52 pgs.)-r/FC #157 .... 5.00
17-(68 pgs.) Barks M.M.-r/FC #79 plus Barks D.D.-r; Rosa-a; x-mas-c ... 6.00
18($1.95, 68 pgs.)-Gottfredson-r/WDC&S #13,72-74; Kelly-c(r); Barks-r ... 5.00
NOTE: Barks reprints in 1-15, 17, 18. Kelly c-13r, 14 (r/Walt Disney's C&S #58), 18r.

WALT DISNEY'S MICKEY MOUSE ADVENTURES (Take-Along Comic)
Gemstone Publishing: Aug, 2004 - Present ($7.95, 5" x 7-1/2")

1-12-Goofy, Donald Duck & Uncle Scrooge app. 8.00

WALT DISNEY'S MICKEY MOUSE AND BLOTMAN IN BLOTMAN RETURNS
Gemstone Publishing: Dec, 2006 ($5.99, squarebound, one-shot)

nn-Wraparound-c by Noel Van Horn; Super Goof back-up story 6.00

WALT DISNEY'S MICKEY MOUSE AND FRIENDS
Gemstone Publishing: No. 257, Oct, 2003 - No. 295, Dec, 2006 ($2.95)

257-295: 257-Numbering resumes from Gladstone Mickey Mouse series; Halloween-c.
285-Return of the Phantom Blot 3.00

WALT DISNEY'S MICKEY MOUSE CLUB MAGAZINE (TV)(Becomes Walt Disney's Magazine)
Western Publishing Co.: Winter, 1956 - V2#3, Apr, 1957 (11-1/2x8-1/2", quarterly, 48 pgs.)

V1#1

| | 14 | 28 | 42 | 102 | 181 | 260 |

2-4

| | 8 | 16 | 24 | 56 | 93 | 130 |

V2#1,2

| | 7 | 14 | 21 | 45 | 73 | 100 |

3-Annette photo-c

| | 13 | 26 | 39 | 90 | 160 | 230 |

Annual(1956)-Two different issues; ($1.50-Whitman); 120 pgs., cardboard covers,
11-3/4x8-3/4"; reprints

| | 14 | 28 | 42 | 102 | 181 | 260 |

Annual(1957)-Same as above

| | 12 | 24 | 36 | 82 | 146 | 210 |

WALT DISNEY'S MICKEY MOUSE MEETS BLOTMAN
Gemstone Publishing: Aug, 2005 ($5.99, squarebound, one-shot)

nn-Wraparound-c by Noel Van Horn; Super Goof back-up story 6.00

WALT DISNEY'S PINOCCHIO SPECIAL
Gladstone: Spring, 1990 ($1.00)

1-50th anniversary edition; Kelly-r/F.C. #92 .... 3.00

WALT DISNEY'S SPRING FEVER
Gemstone Publishing: Apr, 2007 ($9.50, squarebound)

1-New stories and reprints incl. "Mystery of the Swamp" by Carl Barks ... 9.50

WALT DISNEY'S THE ADVENTUROUS UNCLE SCROOGE McDUCK
Gladstone: Jan, 1998 - No 2, Mar, 1998 ($1.95)

1,2: 1-Barks-a(r). 2-Rosa-a(r) 2.50

WALT DISNEY'S THE JUNGLE BOOK
W.D. Publications (Disney Comics): 1990 ($5.95, graphic novel, 68 pgs.)

nn-Movie adaptation; movie rereleased in 1990 .... 6.00
nn-($2.95, 68 pgs.)-Comic edition; wraparound-c 3.00

WALT DISNEY'S UNCLE SCROOGE (Formerly Uncle Scrooge #1-209)
Gladstone #210-242/Disney Comics #243-280/Gladstone #281-318/Gemstone #319 on:
No. 210, 10/86 - No. 242, 4/90; No. 243, 6/90 - No. 318, 2/99; No. 319, 7/03 - Present

210-1st Gladstone issue; r/WDC&S #134 (1st Beagle Boys)

| | 2 | 4 | 6 | 9 | 13 | 16 |

211-218: 216-New story ("Go Slowly Sands of Time") plotted and partly scripted by Barks.
217-r/U.S. #7, "Seven Cities of Cibola"

| | 2 | 4 | 6 | 9 | 12 | 15 |

219-"Son Of The Sun" by Rosa (his 1st pro work)

| | 3 | 6 | 9 | 14 | 20 | 25 |

220-Don Rosa-a/scripts

| | 1 | 2 | 3 | 5 | 6 | 8 |

221-223,225,228-234,236-240 .... 4.00
224,226,227,235: 224-Rosa-c/a. 226,227-Rosa-a. 235-Rosa-a/scripts 5.00
241-($1.95, 68 pgs.)-Rosa finishes over Barks-r 6.00
242-($1.95, 68 pgs.)-Barks-r; Rosa-a(1 pg.) 6.00
243-249,251-260,264-275,277-280,282-284-($1.50): 243-1st by Disney Comics. 274-All Barks
issue. 275-Contains centerspread by Rosa. 279-All Barks issue; Rosa-c. 283-r/WDC&S #98 .. 3.00
250-($2.25, 52 pgs.)-Barks-r; wraparound-c 4.00
261-263,276-Don Rosa-c/a 5.00
281-Gladstone issues start again; Rosa-c 6.00
285-The Life and Times of Scrooge McDuck Pt. 1; Rosa-c/a/scripts

| | 1 | 3 | 4 | 6 | 8 | 10 |

286-293: The Life and Times of Scrooge McDuck Pt. 2-8; Rosa-c/a/scripts.
293-($1.95, 36 pgs.)-The Life and Times of Scrooge McDuck Pt. 9 .... 6.00
294-299, 301-308-($1.50, 32 pgs.): 294-296-The Life and Times of Scrooge McDuck Pt. 10-12.
297-The Life and Times of Uncle Scrooge Pt. 0; Rosa-c/a/scripts 3.00
300-($2.25, 48 pgs.)-Rosa-c; Barks-r/WDC&S #104 and U.S. #216; r/U.S. #220;
includes new centerfold 4.00
309-318-($6.95) 318-(2/99) Last Gladstone issue 7.00
319-360: 319-(7/03) First Gemstone issue; The Dutchman's Secret by Don Rosa ... 7.00
361-366: 361-Begin $7.50-c 7.50
367-370-($7.99) 8.00
... Adventures, The Barks/Rosa Collection Vol. 1 (Gemstone, 7/07, $8.50) reprints Pygmy
Indians appearances in U.S. #18 by Barks and WDC&S #633 by Rosa ... 8.50
Land of the Pygmy Indians from US #18
Walt Disney's The Life and Times of Scrooge McDuck by Don Rosa TPB (Gemstone, 2005,
$16.99) Reprints #285-296, with foreword, commentaries & sketch pages by Rosa ... 17.00
Walt Disney's The Life and Times of Scrooge McDuck Companion by Don Rosa TPB
(Gemstone, 2006, $16.99) additional chapters, with foreword & commentaries ... 17.00
NOTE: Barks r-210-218, 220-223, 224(2pg.), 225-234, 236-242, 245, 246, 250-253, 255, 256, 258, 261(2 pg.),
265, 267, 268, 270(2), 272-284, 299-present; c(r)-210, 212, 221, 228, 229, 232, 233, 284. scripts-287, 293. Rosa
a-219, 220, 224, 226, 227, 235, 261-263, 268. c/s-275-270, 285-289; c-219, 224, 231, 261-263, 276, 278-281, 285-
296; scripts-219, 220, 224, 235, 261-263, 268, 276, 285-296.

WALT DISNEY'S UNCLE SCROOGE ADVENTURES (U. Scrooge Advs. #1-3)
Gladstone Publishing: Nov, 1987 - No. 21, May, 1990; No. 22, Sept, 1993 -
No. 54, Feb, 1998

1-Barks-r begin, ends #26

| | 1 | 2 | 3 | 5 | 6 | 8 |

2-4 .... 4.00
5,9,14: 5-Rosa-c/a; no Barks-r. 9,14-Rosa-a 5.00
6-8,10-13,15-19: 10-r/U.S. #18(all Barks) 3.00
20,21 ($1.95, 68 pgs.) 20-Rosa-c/a. 21-Rosa-a 5.00
22 ($1.50)-Rosa-c; r/U.S. #26 .... 5.00
23-($2.95, 68 pgs.)-Vs. The Phantom Blot-r/P.B. #3; Barks-r 4.00
24-26,29,31,32,34-36: 24,25,29,31,32-Rosa-c. 25-r/U.S. #21 .... 2.50
27-Guardians of the Lost Library - Rosa-c/a/story; origin of Junior Woodchuck Guidebook 3.00
28-($2.95, 68 pgs.)-r/U.S. #13 w/restored missing panels 4.00
30-($2.95, 68 pgs.)-r/U.S. #12; Rosa-c 4.00
33-($2.95, 64 pgs.)-New Barks story 3.00
37-54 .... 2.50
NOTE: Barks r-1-4, 6-8, 10-13, 15-21, 23, 24; c(r)-15, 16, 17, 21. Rosa a-5, 9, 14, 20, 21, 27, 51; c-5, 13, 14,
17(finishes), 20, 22, 24, 25, 27, 28, 51; scripts-5, 9, 14, 27.

WALT DISNEY'S UNCLE SCROOGE AND DONALD DUCK
Gladstone: Jan, 1998 - No. 2, Mar, 1998 ($1.95)

1,2: 1-Rosa-a(r) 2.50

WALT DISNEY'S UNCLE SCROOGE ADVENTURES IN COLOR
Gladstone Publ.: Dec, 1995 - Present ($8.95/$9.95, squarebound, 56 issue limited series)
(Polybagged w/card) (Series chronologically reprints all the stories written & drawn by Carl
Barks)

1-56: 1-(12/95) r/FC #386. 15-(12/96)-r/US #15. 16-(12/96)-r/US #16.
18-(1/97)-r/US #18 .... 10.00

WALT DISNEY'S VACATION PARADE

Wambi, Jungle Boy #2 © FH

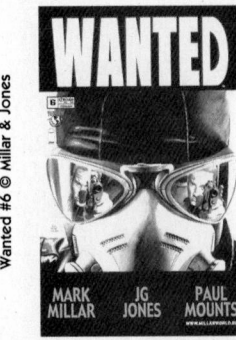

Wanted #6 © Millar & Jones

Wanted #28 © Toytown

	GD 2.0	VG 4.0	FN 6.0	VF 8.0	VF/NM 9.0	NM- 9.2

Gemstone Publishing: 2004 - Present ($8.95/$9.95, squarebound, annual)

1-3: 1-Reprints stories from Dell Giant Comics Vacation Parade 1 (July 1950)						9.00
4-(5/07, $9.95)						10.00

WALT DISNEY'S WHEATIES PREMIUMS (See Wheaties in the Promotional section)

WALT DISNEY'S WORLD OF THE DRAGONLORDS
Gemstone Publishing: 2005 ($12.99, squarebound, graphic novel)

SC-Uncle Scrooge, Donald & nephews app.; Byron Erickson-s/Giorgio Cavazzano-a   13.00

WALT DISNEY TREASURES - DISNEY COMICS: 75 YEARS OF INNOVATION
Gemstone Publishing: 2006 ($12.99, TPB)

SC-Reprints from 1930-2004, including debut of Mickey Mouse newspaper strip   13.00

WALTER LANTZ ANDY PANDA (Also see Andy Panda)
Gold Key: Aug, 1973 - No. 23, Jan, 1978 (Walter Lantz)

	GD	VG	FN	VF	VF/NM	NM-
1-Reprints	3	6	9	14	19	24
2-10-All reprints	2	4	6	9	12	15
11-23: 15,17-19,22-Reprints	1	2	3	5	7	9

WALT KELLY'S...
Eclipse Comics: Dec, 1987; Apr, 1988 ($1.75/$2.50, Baxter paper)

...Christmas Classics 1 (12/87)-Kelly-r/Peter Wheat & Santa Claus Funnies,
...Springtime Tales 1 (4/88, $2.50)-Kelly-r   2.50

WALTONS, THE (See Kite Fun Book)

WALT SCOTT (See Little People)

WALT SCOTT'S CHRISTMAS STORIES (See Christmas Stories, 4-Color #959, 1062)

WAMBI, JUNGLE BOY (See Jungle Comics)
Fiction House Magazines: Spr, 1942; No. 2, Win, 1942-43; No. 3, Spr, 1943; No. 4, Fall, 1948; No. 5, Sum, 1949; No. 6, Spr, 1950; No. 7-10, 1950(nd); No. 11, Spr, 1951 - No. 18, Win, 1952-53 (#1-3: 68 pgs.)

	GD	VG	FN	VF	VF/NM	NM-
1-Wambi, the Jungle Boy begins	93	186	279	581	966	1350
2 (1942)-Kiefer-c	50	100	150	305	503	700
3 (1943)-Kiefer-c/a	40	80	120	235	368	500
4 (1948)-Origin in text	25	50	75	148	232	315
5 (Fall, 1949, 36 pgs.)-Kiefer-c/a	20	40	60	117	184	250
6-10: 7-(52 pgs.)-New logo	18	36	54	105	165	225
11-18	14	28	42	80	115	150
I.W. Reprint #8('64)-r/#12 with new-c	3	6	9	14	20	25

NOTE: Alex Blum c-8. Kiefer c-1-5. Whitman c-11-18.

WANDERERS (See Adventure Comics #375, 376)
DC Comics: June, 1988 - No. 13, Apr, 1989 ($1.25) (Legion of Super-Heroes spin off)

1-13: 1,2-Steacy-c. 3-Legion app.   2.50

WANDERING STAR
Pen & Ink Comics/Sirius Entertainment No. 12 on: 1993 - No. 21, Mar, 1997 ($2.50/$2.75, B&W)

	GD	VG	FN	VF	VF/NM	NM-
1-1st printing; Teri Sue Wood c/a/scripts in all	1	2	3	5	6	8
1-2nd and 3rd printings						2.75
2-1st printing.						4.00
2-21: 2-2nd printing. 12-(1/96)-1st Sirius issue						2.75
Trade paperback ($11.95)-r/1-7; 1st printing of 1000, signed and #'d						18.00
Trade paperback-2nd printing, 2000 signed						15.00
TPB Volume 2,3 (11/98, 12/98, $14.95) 2-r/#8-14, 3-r/#15-21						15.00

WANTED
Image Comics (Top Cow): Dec, 2003 - No. 6, Feb, 2004 ($2.99)

1-Three covers; Mark Millar-s/J.G. Jones-a; intro Wesley Gibson						3.00
1-4-Death Row Edition; r/#1-4 with extra sketch pages and deleted panels						3.00
2-6: 2-Cameos of DC villains. 6-Giordano-a in flashback scenes						3.00
...Dossier (5/04, $2.99) Pin-ups and character info; art by Jones, Romita Jr. & others						3.00
HC (2005, $29.99) r/#1-6 & Dossier; intro by Vaughan, sketch pages & Cover gallery						30.00

WANTED COMICS
Toytown Publications/Patches/Orbit Publ.: No. 9, Sept-Oct, 1947 - No. 53, April, 1953 (#9-33: 52 pgs.)

	GD	VG	FN	VF	VF/NM	NM-
9-True crime cases; radio's Mr. D. A. app.	24	48	72	139	220	300
10,11: 10-Giunta-a; radio's Mr. D. A. app.	15	30	45	84	127	170
12-Used in SOTI, pg. 277	15	30	45	88	137	185
13-Heroin drug propaganda story	14	28	42	82	121	160
14-Marijuana drug mention story (2 pgs.)	14	28	42	78	112	145
15-17,19,20	12	24	36	69	97	125
18-Marijuana story, "Satan's Cigarettes"; r-in #45 & retitled	24	48	72	139	220	300
21,22: 21-Krigstein-a. 22-Extreme violence	13	26	39	72	101	130

	GD	VG	FN	VF	VF/NM	NM-
23,25-34,36-38,40-44,46-48,53	10	20	30	58	79	100
24-Krigstein-a; "The Dope King", marijuana mention story	14	28	42	78	112	145
35-Used in SOTI, pg. 160	14	28	42	76	108	140
39-Drug propaganda story "The Horror Weed"	15	30	45	88	137	185
45-Marijuana story from #18	12	24	36	69	97	125
49-Has unstable pink-c that fades easily; rare in mint condition	11	22	33	64	90	115
50-Has unstable pink-c like #49; surrealist-a by Buscema; horror stories	13	26	39	72	101	130
51- "Holiday of Horror" junkie story; drug-c	14	28	42	80	115	150
52-Classic "Cult of Killers" opium use story	14	28	42	80	115	150

NOTE: Buscema c-50, 51. Lawrence and Leav c/a most issues. Syd Shores c/a-48; c-37. Issues 9-46 have wanted criminals with their descriptions & drawn picture on cover.

WANTED: DEAD OR ALIVE (TV)
Dell Publishing Co.: No. 1102, May-July, 1960 - No. 1164, Mar-May, 1961

	GD	VG	FN	VF	VF/NM	NM-
Four Color 1102 (#1)-Steve McQueen photo-c	12	24	36	87	156	225
Four Color 1164-Steve McQueen photo-c	9	18	27	63	107	150

WANTED, THE WORLD'S MOST DANGEROUS VILLAINS (See DC Special)
National Periodical Publ.: July-Aug, 1972 - No. 9, Aug-Sept, 1973 (All reprints & 20¢ issues)

	GD	VG	FN	VF	VF/NM	NM-
1-Batman, Green Lantern (story r-from G.L. #1), & Green Arrow	3	6	9	20	30	40
2-Batman/Joker/Penguin-c/story r-from Batman #25; plus Flash story (r-from Flash #121)	3	6	9	16	23	30
3-9: 3-Dr. Fate(r/More Fun #65), Hawkman(r/Flash #100), & Vigilante(r/Action #69). 4-Green Lantern(r/All-American #61) & Kid Eternity(r/Kid Eternity #15). 5-Dollman/Green Lantern. 6-Burnley Starman; Wildcat/Sargon. 7-Johnny Quick(r/More Fun #76), Hawkman(r/Flash #90), Hourman by Baily(r/Adv. #72). 8-Dr. Fate/Flash(r/Flash #114).						
9-S&K Sandman/Superman	3	6	9	14	19	24

NOTE: B. Bailey a-7r. Infantino a-2r. Kane r-1, 5. Kubert r-3i, 6, 7. Meskin r-3, 7. Reinman r-4, 5.

WAR (See Fightin' Marines #122)
Charlton Comics: Jul, 1975 - No. 9, Nov, 1976; No. 10, Sept, 1978 - No. 47, 1984

	GD	VG	FN	VF	VF/NM	NM-
1-Boyette painted-c	2	4	6	11	16	20
2-10	1	3	4	6	8	10
11-20	1	2	3	4	5	7
21-40						6.00
41-47 (lower print run): 47-Reprints	1	2	3	4	5	7
7,9 (Modern Comics-r, 1977)						4.00

WAR, THE (See The Draft & The Pitt)
Marvel Comics: 1989 - No. 4, 1990 ($3.50, squarebound, 52 pgs.)

1-4: Characters from New Universe   3.50

WAR ACTION (Korean War)
Atlas Comics (CPS): April, 1952 - No. 14, June, 1953

	GD	VG	FN	VF	VF/NM	NM-
1	20	40	60	117	184	250
2	12	24	36	69	97	125
3-10,14: 7-Pakula-a	10	20	30	54	72	90
11-13-Krigstein-a	10	20	30	58	79	100

NOTE: Brodsky c-1-4. Heath a-1; c-7, 14. Keller a-6. Maneely a-1. Tuska a-2, 8.

WAR ADVENTURES
Atlas Comics (HPC): Jan, 1952 - No. 13, Feb, 1953

	GD	VG	FN	VF	VF/NM	NM-
1-Tuska-a	16	32	48	94	147	200
2	10	20	30	56	76	95
3-7,9-13: 3-Pakula-a. 7-Maneely-c	9	18	27	50	65	80
8-Krigstein-a	10	20	30	56	76	95

NOTE: Brodsky a-3, 6, 8, 11, 12. Heath a-5, 7, 10; c-4, 5, 9, 13. Robinson a-3; c-10.

WAR ADVENTURES ON THE BATTLEFIELD (See Battlefield)

WAR AGAINST CRIME! (Becomes Vault of Horror #12 on)
E. C. Comics: Spring, 1948 - No. 11, Feb-Mar, 1950

	GD	VG	FN	VF	VF/NM	NM-
1-Real Stories From Police Records on-c #1-9	76	152	228	475	788	1100
2,3	45	90	135	275	450	625
4-9	41	82	123	250	400	550
10-1st Vault Keeper app. & 1st Vault of Horror	206	412	618	1648	2574	3500
11-2nd Vault Keeper app.; 1st horror-c	124	248	372	992	1546	2100

NOTE: All have Johnny Craig covers. Feldstein a-4, 7-9. Harrison/Wood a-11. Ingels a-1, 2, 8. Palais a-8. Changes to horror with #10.

WAR AGAINST CRIME
Gemstone Publishing: Apr, 2000 - No. 11, Feb, 2001 ($2.50)

1-11: E.C. reprints   2.50

WAR AND ATTACK (Also see Special War Series #3)

War Birds #2 © FH

Warfront #1 © HARV

Warlands #3 © Dreamwave

	GD 2.0	VG 4.0	FN 6.0	VF 8.0	VF/NM 9.0	NM- 9.2
Charlton Comics: Fall, 1964; V2#54, June, 1966 - V2#63, Dec, 1967						
1-Wood-a (25 pgs.)	4	8	12	28	44	60
V2#54(6/66)-#63 (Formerly Fightin' Air Force)	3	6	9	14	20	25
NOTE: *Montes/Bache a-55, 56, 60, 63.*						
WAR AT SEA (Formerly Space Adventures)						
Charlton Comics: No. 22, Nov, 1957 - No. 42, June, 1961						
22	7	14	21	35	43	50
23-30	5	10	15	24	30	35
31-42	3	6	9	16	23	30
WAR BATTLES						
Harvey Publications: Feb, 1952 - No. 9, Dec, 1953						
1-Powell-a; Elias-c	9	18	27	63	107	150
2-Powell-a	5	10	15	35	55	75
3-5,7-9: 3,7-Powell-a	5	10	15	32	51	70
6-Nostrand-a	6	12	18	39	62	85
WAR BIRDS						
Fiction House Magazines: 1952(nd) - No. 3, Winter, 1952-53						
1	16	32	48	94	147	200
2,3	11	22	33	62	86	110
WARBLADE: ENDANGERED SPECIES (Also see WildC.A.T.S: Covert Action Teams)						
Image Comics (WildStorm Productions): Jan, 1995 - No. 4, Apr, 1995 ($2.50, limited series)						
1-4: 1-Gatefold wraparound-c						2.50
WAR COMBAT (Becomes Combat Casey #6 on)						
Atlas Comics (LBI No. 1/SAI No. 2-5): March, 1952 - No. 5, Nov, 1952						
1	15	30	45	88	137	185
2	10	20	30	56	76	95
3-5	9	18	27	47	61	75
NOTE: *Berg a-2, 4, 5. Brodsky c-1, 2, 4, 5. Henkel a-5. Maneely a-1, 4; c-3.*						
WAR COMICS (War Stories #5 on)(See Key Ring Comics)						
Dell Publishing Co.: May, 1940 (No month given) - No. 4, Sept, 1941						
1-Sikandur the Robot Master, Sky Hawk, Scoop Mason, War Correspondent begin;						
McWilliams-c; 1st war comic	57	114	171	356	591	825
2-Origin Greg Gilday (5/41)	34	68	102	195	308	420
3-Joan becomes Greg Gilday's aide	23	46	69	132	209	285
4-Origin Night Devils	24	48	72	139	220	300
WAR COMICS						
Marvel/Atlas (USA No. 1-41/JPI No. 42-49): Dec, 1950 - No. 49, Sept, 1957						
1	26	52	78	152	239	325
2	14	28	42	82	121	160
3-10	12	24	36	69	97	125
11-Flame thrower w/burning bodies on-c	14	28	42	80	115	150
12-20	10	20	30	58	79	100
21,23-32: 26-Valley Forge story. 32-Last pre-code issue (2/55)	9	18	27	50	65	80
22-Krigstein-a	10	20	30	58	79	100
33-37,39-42,44,45,47,48	9	18	27	50	65	80
38-Kubert/Moskowitz-a	10	20	30	54	72	90
43,49-Torres-a. 43-Severin/Elder E.C. swipe from Two-Fisted Tales #31	10	20	30	54	72	90
46-Crandall-a	10	20	30	54	72	90
NOTE: *Colan a-4, 36, 48, 49. Drucker a-37, 43, 48. Everett a-17. Heath a-7-9, 16, 19, 36; c-11, 16, 19, 23, 25, 26, 29-32, 36. G. Kane a-19. Lawrence a-36. Maneely a-7, 9, 14, 20; c-6, 27, 37. Orlando a-42, 48. Pakula a-26. Ravielli a-27. Reinman a-11, 16, 26. Robinson a-15; c-13. Severin a-26, 27; c-48.*						
WAR DANCER (Also see Charlemagne, Doctor Chaos #2 & Warriors of Plasm)						
Defiant: Feb, 1994 - No. 6, July, 1994 ($2.50)						
1-3,5,6: 1-Intro War Dancer; Weiss-c/a begins. 1-3-Weiss-a(p). 6-Pre-Schism issue						2.50
4-($3.25, 52 pgs.)-Charlemagne app.						3.25
WAR DOGS OF THE U.S. ARMY						
Avon Periodicals: 1952						
1-Kinstler-c/a	15	30	45	83	124	165
WARFRONT						
Harvey Publications: 9/51 - #35, 11/58; #36, 10/65; #39, 2/67						
1-Korean War	10	20	30	70	123	175
2	6	12	18	39	62	85
3-10	5	10	15	32	51	70
11,12,14,16-20	4	8	12	28	44	60
13,15,22-Nostrand-a	6	12	18	39	62	85
21,23-27,31-33,35	4	8	12	28	44	60
28-30,34-Kirby-c	6	12	18	41	66	90
36-(12/66)-Dynamite Joe begins, ends #39; Williamson-a	5	10	15	32	51	70
37-Wood-a (17 pgs.)	5	10	15	32	51	70
38,39-Wood-a, 2-3 pgs.; Lone Tiger app.	4	8	12	28	44	60
NOTE: *Powell a-1-6, 9-11, 14, 17, 20, 23, 25-28, 30, 31, 34, 36. Powell/Nostrand a-12, 13, 15. Simon c-36?, 38.*						
WAR FURY						
Comic Media/Harwell (Allen Hardy Assoc.): Sept, 1952 - No. 4, Mar, 1953						
1-Heck-c/a in all; Palais-a; bullet hole in forehead-c; all issues are very violent; soldier using flame thrower on enemy	28	56	84	162	256	350
2-4: 4-Morisi-a	15	30	45	85	130	175
WAR GODS OF THE DEEP (See Movie Classics)						
WARHAWKS						
TSR, Inc.: 1990 - No. 10, 1991 ($2.95, 44 pgs.)						
1-10-Based on TSR game, Spiegle a-1-6						3.00
WARHEADS						
Marvel Comics UK: June, 1992 - No. 14, Aug, 1993 ($1.75)						
1-Wolverine-c/story; indicia says #2 by mistake						3.00
2-14: 2-Nick Fury app. 3-Iron Man-c/story. 4,5-X-Force. 5-Liger vs. Cable. 6,7-Death's Head II app. (#6 is cameo)						2.50
WAR HEROES (See Marine War Heroes)						
WAR HEROES						
Dell Publishing Co.: 7-9/42 (no month); No. 2, 10-12/42 - No. 11, 3/45 (Published quarterly)						
1-General Douglas MacArthur-c	26	52	78	152	239	325
2	15	30	45	84	127	170
3,5: 3-Pro-Russian back-c	13	26	39	72	101	130
4-Disney's Gremlins app.	18	36	54	105	165	225
6-11: 6-Tothish-a by Discount	10	20	30	56	76	95
NOTE: *No. 1 was to be released in July, but was delayed. Painted c-4, 6-9.*						
WAR HEROES						
Ace Magazines: May, 1952 - No. 8, Apr, 1953						
1	11	22	33	62	86	110
2-Lou Cameron-a	8	16	24	42	54	65
3-8: 6,7-Cameron-a	7	14	21	37	46	55
WAR HEROES (Also see Blue Bird Comics)						
Charlton Comics: Feb, 1963 - No. 27, Nov, 1967						
1,2: 2-John F. Kennedy story	4	8	12	24	37	50
3-10	3	6	9	17	25	32
11-26	3	6	9	14	19	24
27-1st Devils Brigade by Glanzman	3	6	9	17	25	32
NOTE: *Montes/Bache a-3-7, 21, 25, 27; c-3-7.*						
WAR IS HELL						
Marvel Comics Group: Jan, 1973 - No. 15, Oct, 1975						
1-Williamson-a(r), 5 pgs.; Ayers-a	3	6	9	16	22	28
2-8-Reprints. 6-(11/73). 7-(6/74). 7,8-Kirby-a	2	4	6	8	11	14
9-Intro Death	4	8	12	28	44	60
10-15-Death app.	3	6	9	16	22	28
NOTE: *Bolle a-3r. Powell a-1. Woodbridge a-1. Sgt. Fury reprints-7, 8.*						
WARLANDS						
Image Comics: Aug, 1999 - No. 12, Feb, 2001 ($2.50)						
1-9,11,12-Pat Lee(p)/Adrian Tsang-s						2.50
10-($2.95) Flip book w/Shidima preview						3.00
...Chronicles 1,2 (2/00, 7/00; $7.95) 1-r/#1-3. 2-r/#4-6						8.00
...Darklyte TPB (8/01, $14.95) r/#0,1/2,1-6 w/cover gallery; new Lee-c						15.00
...Epilogue: Three Stories (3/01, $5.95) includes r/Wizard #1/2 & AE #0						6.00
Another Universe #0						3.00
Wizard #1/2						5.00
WARLANDS: THE AGE OF ICE (Volume 2)						
Image Comics: July, 2001 - No. 9, Nov, 2002 ($2.95)						
#0-(2/02, $2.25)						2.50
#1/2 (4/02, $2.25)						2.50
1-9: 2-Flip book preview of Banished Knights						3.00
TPB (2003, $15.95) r/#1-9						16.00
WARLANDS: DARK TIDE RISING (Volume 3)						
Image Comics: Dec, 2002 - No. 6, May, 2003 ($2.95)						
1-6: 1-Wraparound gatefold-c						3.00

Warlock #6 © MAR

Warlord #76 © DC

War Machine #8 © MAR

	GD 2.0	VG 4.0	FN 6.0	VF 8.0	VF/NM 9.0	NM- 9.2

WARLOCK (The Power of...)(Also see Avengers Annual #7, Fantastic Four #66, 67, Incredible Hulk #178, Infinity Crusade, Infinity Gauntlet, Infinity War, Marvel Premiere #1, Marvel Two-In-One Annual #2, Silver Surfer V3#46, Strange Tales #178-181 & Thor #165)
Marvel Comics Group: Aug, 1972 - No. 8, Oct, 1973; No. 9, Oct, 1975 - No. 15, Nov, 1976

	GD 2.0	VG 4.0	FN 6.0	VF 8.0	VF/NM 9.0	NM- 9.2
1-Origin by Kane	6	12	18	39	62	85
2,3	3	6	9	20	30	40
4-8: 4-Death of Eddie Roberts	2	4	6	13	18	22
9-Starlin's 2nd Thanos saga begins, ends #15; new costume Warlock; Thanos cameo only; story cont'd from Strange Tales #178-181; Starlin-c/a in #9-15	3	6	9	18	27	35
10-Origin Thanos & Gamora; recaps events from Capt. Marvel #25-34. Thanos vs.The Magus-c/story	3	6	9	21	32	42
11-Thanos app.; Warlock dies	3	6	9	15	21	26
12-14: (Regular 25¢ edition) 14-Origin Star Thief; last 25¢ issue	2	4	6	11	16	20
12-14-(30¢-c, limited distribution)	3	6	9	20	30	40
15-Thanos-c/story	2	4	6	13	18	22

NOTE: *Buscema a-2p; c-8p.* **G. Kane** *a-1p, 3-5p; c-1p, 2, 3, 4p, 5p, 7p.* **Starlin** *a-9-14p; c-9, 10, 11p, 12p, 13-15.* **Sutton** *a-1-8i.*

WARLOCK (...Special Edition on-c)
Marvel Comics Group: Dec, 1982 - No. 6, May, 1983 ($2.00, slick paper, 52 pgs.)

1-Warlock-r/Strange Tales #178-180.						4.00
2-6: 2-r/Str. Tales #180,181 & Warlock #9. 3-r/Warlock #10-12(Thanos origin recap). 4-r/Warlock #12-15. 5-r/Warlock #15, Marvel Team-Up #55 & Avengers Ann. #7. 6-r/2nd half Avengers Annual #7 & Marvel Two-in-One Annual #2						4.00
Special Edition #1(12/83)						4.00

NOTE: *Byrne a-5r.* **Starlin** *a-1-6r; c-1-6(new). Direct sale only.*

WARLOCK
Marvel Comics: V2#1, May, 1992 - No. 6, Oct, 1992 ($2.50, limited series)

V2#1-6: 1-Reprints 1982 reprint series w/Thanos						2.50

WARLOCK
Marvel Comics: Nov, 1998 - No. 4, Feb, 1999 ($2.99, limited series)

1-4-Warlock vs. Drax						3.00

WARLOCK (M-Tech)
Marvel Comics: Oct, 1999 - No. 9, June, 2000 ($1.99/$2.50)

1-5: 1-Quesada-c. 2-Two covers						2.50
6-9: 6-Begin $2.50-c/a. 8-Avengers app.						2.50

WARLOCK
Marvel Comics: Nov, 2004 - No. 4, Feb, 2005 ($2.99, limited series)

1-4-Adlard-a/Williams-c						3.00

WARLOCK AND THE INFINITY WATCH (Also see Infinity Gauntlet)
Marvel Comics: Feb, 1992 - No. 42, July, 1995 ($1.75) (Sequel to Infinity Gauntlet)

1-Starlin-scripts begin; brief origin recap; sequel to Infinity Gauntlet						3.00
2,3: 2-Reintro Moondragon						2.50
4-24,26: 7-Reintro The Magus; Moondragon app.; Thanos cameo on last 2 pgs. 8,9-Thanos battles Gamora-c/story. 8-Magus & Moondragon app. 10-Thanos-c/story; Magus app. 13-Hulk x-over. 21-Drax vs. Thor						2.50
25-($2.95, 52 pgs.)-Die-cut & embossed double-c; Thor & Thanos app.						3.00
28-42: 28-$1.95-c begins						2.50

NOTE: *Austin c/a-1-4i, 7i.* **Leonardi** *a(p)-1, 2, 5; 6, 9, 10, 14, 15, 20.* **Williams** *a(i)-8, 12, 13, 16-19.*

WARLOCK CHRONICLES
Marvel Comics: June, 1993 - No. 8, Feb, 1994 ($2.00, limited series)

1-($2.95)-Holo-grafx foil & embossed-c; origin retold; Starlin scripts begin; Keith Williams-a(i) in all						3.00
2-8: 3-Thanos & Mephisto-c/story. 4-Vs. Magus-c/s. 8-Contains free 16 pg. Razorline insert						2.50

WARLOCK 5
Aircel Pub.: 11/86 - No. 22, 5/89; V2#1, June, 1989 - V2#5, 1989 ($1.70, B&W)

1-5,7-11-Gordon Derry-s/Denis Beauvais-a thru #11. 5-Green Cyborg on-c. 5-Misnumbered as #6 (no #6); Blue Girl on-c.						2.50
12-22-Barry Blair-s/a. 18-$1.95-c begins						3.00
V2#1-5 ($2.00, B&W)-All issues by Barry Blair						2.50
Compilation 1,2: 1-r/#1-5 (1988, $5.95), 2-r/#6-9						6.00

WARLORD (See 1st Issue Special #8)
National Periodical Publications/DC Comics #123 on: 1-2/76; No.2, 3-4/76; No.3, 10-11/76 - No. 133, Win, 1988-89

	GD 2.0	VG 4.0	FN 6.0	VF 8.0	VF/NM 9.0	NM- 9.2
1-Story cont'd from 1st Issue Special #8	3	6	9	18	27	35
2-Intro. Machiste	2	4	6	10	14	18
3-5	2	4	6	8	10	12
6-10: 6-Intro Mariah. 7-Origin Machiste. 9-Dons new costume	1	2	3	5	6	8
11-20: 11-Origin-r. 12-Intro Aton. 15-Tara returns; Warlord has son						5.00
21-36,40,41: 27-New facts about origin. 28-1st app. Wizard World. 32-Intro Shakira. 40-Warlord gets new costume						4.00
22-Whitman variant edition	2	4	6	10	14	18
37-39: 37,38-Origin Omac by Starlin. 38-Intro Jennifer Morgan, Warlord's daughter. 39-Omac ends.						5.00
42-48: 42-47-Omac back-up series. 48-(52 pgs.)-1st app. Arak; contains free 14 pg. Arak Son of Thunder; Claw The Unconquered app.						4.00
49-62,64-99,101-132: 49-Claw The Unconquered app. 50-Death of Aton. 51-Reprints #1. 55-Arion Lord of Atlantis begins, ends #62. 91-Origin w/new facts. 114,115-Legends x-over. 125-Death of Tara. 131-1st DC work by Rob Liefeld (9/88)						3.00
63-The Barren Earth begins; free 16pg. Masters of the Universe preview						4.00
100-($1.25, 52 pgs.)						4.00
133-($1.50, 52 pgs.)						4.00
Remco Toy Giveaway (2-3/4x4")						5.00
Annual 1-6 ('82-'87): 1-Grell-c/a(p). 6-New Gods app.						4.00
The Savage Empire TPB (1991, $19.95) r/#1-10,12 & First Issue Special #8; Grell intro.						25.00

NOTE: *Grell a-1-15, 16-50p, 51r, 52p, 59p, Annual 1p; c-1-70, 100-104, 112, 116, 117, Annual 1, 5.* **Wayne Howard** *a-64i.* **Starlin** *a-37-39p.*

WARLORD
DC Comics: Jan, 1992 - No. 6, June, 1992 ($1.75, limited series)

1-6: Grell-c & scripts in all						2.50

WARLORD
DC Comics: Apr, 2006 - No. 10, Jan, 2007 ($2.99)

1-10: 1-Bruce Jones-s/Bart Sears-a. 10-Winslade-a						3.00

WARLORDS (See DC Graphic Novel #2)

WAR MACHINE (Also see Iron Man #281,282 & Marvel Comics Presents #152)
Marvel Comics: Apr, 1994 - No. 25, Apr, 1996 ($1.50)

"Ashcan" edition (nd, 75¢, B&W, 16 pgs.)						2.50
1-($2.00, 52 pgs.)-Newsstand edition; Cable app.						2.25
1-($2.95, 52 pgs.)-Collectors ed.; embossed foil-c						3.00
2-14, 16-25: 2-Bound-in trading card sheet; Cable app. 2,3-Deathlok app. 8-red logo						2.50
8-($2.95)-Polybagged w/16 pg. Marvel Action Hour preview & acetate print; yellow logo						3.00
15 ($2.50)-Flip book						2.50

WAR MAN
Marvel Comics (Epic Comics): Nov, 1993 - No. 2, Dec, 1993 ($2.50, lim. series)

1,2						2.50

WAR OF THE GODS
DC Comics: Sept, 1991 - No. 4, Dec, 1991 ($1.75, limited series)

1-4: Perez layouts, scripts & covers. 1-Contains free mini posters (Robin, Deathstroke). 2-4-Direct sale versions include 4 pin-ups printed on cover stock plus different-c						2.50

WAR OF THE UNDEAD
IDW Publishing: Jan, 2007 - No. 3, Apr, 2007 ($3.99, limited series)

1-3-Bryan Johnson-s/Walter Flanagan-a						4.00

WAR OF THE WORLDS, THE
Caliber: 1996 - No. 5 ($2.95, B&W, 32 pgs.)(Based on H. G. Wells novel)

1-5: 1-Randy Zimmerman scripts begin						3.00

WARP
First Comics: Mar, 1983 - No. 19, Feb, 1985 ($1.00/$1.25, Mando paper)

1-Sargon-Mistress of War app.; Brunner-c/a thru #9						2.50
2-19: 2-Faceless Ones begin. 10-New Warp advs. & Outrider begin						2.50
Special 1-3: 1(7/83, 36 pgs.)-Origin Chaos-Prince of Madness; origin of Warp Universe begins, ends #3. 2(1/84)-Lord Cumulus vs. Sargon Mistress of War ($1.00). 3(6/84)-Chaos-Prince of Madness						2.50

WARPATH (Indians in the...)
Key Publications/Stanmor: Nov, 1954 - No. 3, Apr, 1955

	GD 2.0	VG 4.0	FN 6.0	VF 8.0	VF/NM 9.0	NM- 9.2
1	11	22	33	62	86	110
2,3	8	16	24	40	50	60

WARPED
Empire Entertainment (Solson): Jun, 1990 - No. 2, Oct-Nov, 1990 (B&W mag)

1,2						2.50

WARP GRAPHICS ANNUAL
WaRP Graphics: Dec, 1985; 1988 ($2.50)

1-Elfquest, Blood of the Innocent, Thunderbunny & Myth Adventures						5.00

Warren Presents #1 © WP

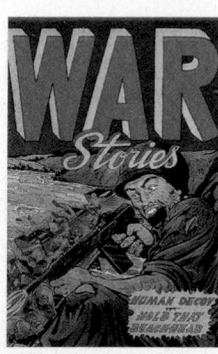

War Stories #2 © AJAX

Washable Jones #1 © TOBY

	GD 2.0	VG 4.0	FN 6.0	VF 8.0	VF/NM 9.0	NM- 9.2

1 (1988) 4.00

WARREN PRESENTS
Warren Publications: Jan, 1979 - No. 14, Nov, 1981(B&W magazine)

	GD	VG	FN	VF	VF/NM	NM-
1-Eerie, Creepy, & Vampirella-r; Ring of the Warlords; Merlin-s; Dax-s; Sanjulian-c			3	6	9	15	21	26
2-6(10/79): 2-The Rook. 3-Alien Invasions Comix. 4-Movie Aliens. 5-Dracula '79.						
6-Strange Stories of Vampires Comix	2	4	6	9	13	16
8(10/80)-r/1st app. Pantha from Vamp. #30	2	4	6	11	16	20
9(11/80) Empire Encounters Comix	2	4	6	10	14	18
13(10/81),14(11/81):13-Sword and Sorcery Comix	3	6	9	14	19	24
(#7,10,11,12 may not exist, or may be a Special below)						
Special-Alien Collectors Edition (1979)	3	6	9	14	19	24
Special-Close Encounters of the Third Kind (1978)	2	4	6	9	13	16
Special-Lord of the Rings (6/79)	3	6	9	19	29	38
Special-Meteor (1/80)	2	4	6	9	13	16
Special-Moonraker/James Bond (10/79)	2	4	6	9	13	16
Special-Star Wars (1977)	3	6	9	19	29	38

WAR REPORT
Ajax/Farrell Publications (Excellent Publ.): Sept, 1952 - No. 5, May, 1953

	GD	VG	FN	VF	VF/NM	NM-
1	14	28	42	76	108	140
2-Flame thrower w/burning bodies on-c	13	26	39	74	105	135
3,5	8	16	24	44	57	70
4-Used in POP, pg. 94	9	18	27	50	65	80

WARRIOR (Wrestling star)
Ultimate Creations: May, 1996 - No. 4, 1997 ($2.95)

1-4: Warrior scripts; Callahan-c/a. 3-Wraparound-c. 4-Warrior #3 in indicia; pin-ups 3.00
1-Variant-c. 5.00
X-Mas (11/96, $3.50) listed as "No. 3" in indicia; pin-ups by various; Quesada-c 3.50

WARRIOR COMICS
H.C. Blackerby: 1945 (1930s DC reprints)

	GD	VG	FN	VF	VF/NM	NM-
1-Wing Brady, The Iron Man, Mark Markon	22	44	66	128	202	275

WARRIOR OF WAVERLY STREET, THE
Dark Horse Comics: Nov, 1996 - No. 2, Dec, 1996 ($2.95, mini-series)

1,2-Darrow-c 3.00

WARRIORS
CFD Productions: 1993 (B&W, one-shot)

	GD	VG	FN	VF	VF/NM	NM-
1-Linsner, Dark One-a	2	4	6	10	14	18

WARRIORS OF PLASM (Also see Plasm)
Defiant: Aug, 1993 - No. 13, Aug, 1995 ($2.95/$2.50)

1-4: Shooter-scripts; Lapham-c/a. 1-1st app. Glory. 4-Bound-in fold-out poster 3.00
5-7,10-13: 5-Begin $2.50-c. 13-Schism issue 2.50
8,9-($2.75, 44 pgs.) 2.75
The Collected Edition (2/94, $9.95)-r/Plasm #0, WOP #1-4 & Splatterball 10.00

WAR ROMANCES (See True...)

WAR SHIPS
Dell Publishing Co.: 1942 (36 pgs.)(Similar to Large Feature Comics)

nn-Cover by McWilliams; contains photos & drawings of U.S. war ships

	GD	VG	FN	VF	VF/NM	NM-
	18	36	54	103	162	220

WARSTONE
Devil's Due Publishing: Apr, 2004 ($4.95, one-shot)

1-Josh Blaylock-s/Matt & Mike Cossin-a 5.00

WAR STORIES (Formerly War Comics)
Dell Publ. Co.: No. 5, 1942(nd); No. 6, Aug-Oct, 1942 - No. 8, Feb-Apr, 1943

	GD	VG	FN	VF	VF/NM	NM-
5-Origin The Whistler	26	52	78	152	239	325
6-8: 6-8-Night Devils app. 8-Painted-c	20	40	60	115	180	245

WAR STORIES (Korea)
Ajax/Farrell Publications (Excellent Publ.): Sept, 1952 - No. 5, May, 1953

	GD	VG	FN	VF	VF/NM	NM-
1	12	24	36	67	94	120
2	8	16	24	40	50	60
3-5	7	14	21	37	46	55

WAR STORIES (See Star Spangled...)

WAR STORY
DC Comics (Vertigo): Nov, 2001 - Present ($4.95, series of World War II one-shots)

...: Archangel (4/03) Ennis-s/Erskine-a 5.00
...: Condors (3/03) Ennis-s/Ezquerra-a 5.00
...: D-Day Dodgers (12/01) Ennis-s/Higgins-a 5.00
...: J For Jenny (2/03) Ennis-s/Lloyd-a 5.00
...: Johann's Tiger (11/01) Ennis-s/Weston-a 5.00
...: Nightingale (2/02) Ennis-s/Lloyd-a 5.00
...: Screaming Eagles (1/02) Ennis-s/Gibbons-a 5.00
...: The Reivers (1/03) Ennis-s/Kennedy-a 5.00
Vol. 1 (2004, $19.95) r/Johann's Tiger, D-Day Dodgers, Screaming Eagles, Nightingale 20.00
Vol. 2 (2006, $19.99) r/J For Jenny, The Reivers, Condors, Archangel; Ennis afterword 20.00

WARSTRIKE
Malibu Comics (Ultraverse): May, 1994 - No. 7, Nov, 1995 ($1.95)

1-7: 1-Simonson-c 2.50
1-Ultra 5000 Limited silver foil 4.00
Giant Size 1 (12/94, 2.50, 44pgs.)-Prelude to Godwheel 2.50

WART AND THE WIZARD (See The Sword & the Stone under Movie Comics)
Gold Key: Feb, 1964 (Walt Disney)(Characters from Sword in the Stone movie)

	GD	VG	FN	VF	VF/NM	NM-
1 (10102-402)	4	8	12	28	44	60

WARTIME ROMANCES
St. John Publishing Co.: July, 1951 - No. 18, Nov, 1953

	GD	VG	FN	VF	VF/NM	NM-
1-All Baker-c/a	40	80	120	235	368	500
2-All Baker-c/a	28	56	84	162	256	350
3,4-All Baker-c/a	26	52	78	152	239	325
5-8-Baker-c/a(2-3) each	24	48	72	139	220	300
9,11,12,16,18: Baker-c/a each. 9-Two signed stories by Estrada	18	36	54	105	165	225
10,13-15,17-Baker-c only	15	30	45	83	124	165

WAR VICTORY ADVENTURES (#1 titled War Victory Comics)
U.S. Treasury Dept./War Victory/Harvey Publ.: Summer, 1942 - No. 3, Winter, 1943-44 (5¢)

1-(Promotion of Savings Bonds)-Featuring America's greatest comic art by top syndicated cartoonists; Blondie, Joe Palooka, Green Hornet, Dick Tracy, Superman, Gumps, etc.; (36 pgs.); all profits were contributed to U.S.O. & Army/Navy relief funds

	GD	VG	FN	VF	VF/NM	NM-
	41	82	123	250	400	550
2-Battle of Stalingrad story; Powell-a (8/43); flag-c	22	44	66	128	202	275
3-Capt. Red Cross-c & text only; Powell-a	20	40	60	117	184	250

WAR WAGON, THE (See Movie Classics)

WAR WINGS
Charlton Comics: Oct, 1968

	GD	VG	FN	VF	VF/NM	NM-
1	3	6	9	14	19	24

WARWORLD!
Dark Horse Comics: Feb, 1989 ($1.75, B&W, one-shot)

1-Gary Davis sci/fi art in Moebius style 2.50

WASHABLE JONES AND THE SHMOO (Also see Al Capp's Shmoo)
Toby Press: June, 1953

	GD	VG	FN	VF	VF/NM	NM-
1- "Super-Shmoo"	19	38	57	109	172	235

WASH TUBBS (See The Comics, Crackajack Funnies)
Dell Publishing Co.: No. 11, 1942 - No. 53, 1944

	GD	VG	FN	VF	VF/NM	NM-
Four Color 11 (#1)	28	56	84	227	384	540
Four Color 28 (1943)	19	38	57	141	251	360
Four Color 53	14	28	42	102	181	260

WASTELAND
DC Comics: Dec, 1987 - No. 18, May, 1989 ($1.75-$2.00 #13 on, mature)

1-5(4/88), 5(5/88), 6(5/88)-18: 13,15-Orlando-a 2.50
NOTE: *Orlando* a-12, 13, 15. *Truman* a-10; c-13.

WATCHMEN
DC Comics: Sept, 1986 - No. 12, Oct, 1987 (maxi-series)

	GD	VG	FN	VF	VF/NM	NM-
1-Alan Moore scripts & Dave Gibbons-c/a in all	1	3	4	6	8	10

2-12 .... 7.00
Hardcover Collection-Slip-cased-r/#1-12 w/new material; produced by Graphitti Designs 80.00
Trade paperback (1987, $14.95)-r/#1-12 .... 20.00

WATER BIRDS AND THE OLYMPIC ELK (Disney)
Dell Publishing Co.: No. 700, Apr, 1956

	GD	VG	FN	VF	VF/NM	NM-
Four Color 700-Movie	5	10	15	35	55	75

WATERWORLD: CHILDREN OF LEVIATHAN
Acclaim Comics: Aug, 1997 - No. 4, Nov, 1997 ($2.50, mini-series)

1-4 .... 2.50

WAY OF THE RAT
CrossGeneration Comics: Jun, 2002 - No. 24, June, 2004 ($2.95)

Weapon Zero #9 © TCOW

Web of Evil #7 © QUA

Web of Spider-Man #2 © MAR

	GD 2.0	VG 4.0	FN 6.0	VF 8.0	VF/NM 9.0	NM- 9.2
1-24: 1-Dixon-s/ Jeff Johnson-a. 5-Whigham-a. 9,14-Luke Ross-a						3.00
Free Comic Book Day Special (6/03) reprints #1 w/features, interviews, CrossGen info						2.25
...: The Walls of Zhumar Vol. 1 (1/03, $15.95) r/#1-6						16.00
Vol. 2: The Dragon's Wake (2003, $15.95) r/#7-12						16.00

WEAPON X
Marvel Comics: Apr, 1994 ($12.95, one-shot)

nn-r/Marvel Comics Presents #72-84						13.00

WEAPON X
Marvel Comics: Mar, 1995 - No. 4, June, 1995 ($1.95)

1-Age of Apocalypse						4.00
2-4						2.50

WEAPON X
Marvel Comics: Nov, 2002 - No. 28, Nov, 2004 ($2.25/$2.99)

1-7: 1-Sabretooth-c/app.; Tieri-s/Jeanty-a						2.50
8-28: 8-Begin $2.99-c. 14-Invaders app. 15-Chamber joins. 16-18,21-25-Wolverine app.						3.00
Vol. 1: The Draft TPB (2003, $21.99) r/#1-5, #1/2 & The Draft one-shots						22.00
Vol. 2: The Underground TPB (2003, $19.99) r/#6-13						20.00
Wizard #1/2 (2002)						5.00

WEAPON X: DAYS OF FUTURE NOW
Marvel Comics: Sept, 2005 - No. 5, Jan, 2006 ($2.99, limited series)

1-5-Tieri-s/Sears-a; Chamber, Sauron & Fantomex app.						3.00
TPB (2006, $13.99) r/#1-5						14.00

WEAPON X: THE DRAFT (Leads into 2002 Weapon X series)
Marvel Comics: Oct, 2002 ($2.25, one-shots)

...Kane 1- JH Williams-c/Raimondi-a						2.50
...Marrow 1- JH Williams-c/Badeaux-a						2.50
...Sauron 1- JH Williams-c/Kerschl-a; Emma Frost app.						2.50
...Wild Child 1- JH Williams-c/Van Sciver-a; Aurora (Alpha Flight) app.						2.50
...Zero 1- JH Williams-c/Plunkett-a; Wolverine app.						2.50

WEAPON ZERO
Image Comics (Top Cow Productions): No. T-4(#1), June, 1995 - No. T-0(#5), Dec, 1995
($2.50, limited series)

T-4(#1): Walt Simonson scripts in all.						5.00
T-3(#2) - T-1(#4)						4.00
T-0(#5)						3.00

WEAPON ZERO
Image Comics (Top Cow Productions): V2#1, Mar, 1996 - No. 15, Dec, 1997 ($2.50)

V2#1-Walt Simonson scripts.						3.00
2-14: 8-Begin Top Cow. 10-Devil's Reign						2.50
15-($3.50) Benitez-a						3.50

WEAPON ZERO/SILVER SURFER
Image Comics/Marvel Comics: Jan, 1997($2.95, one-shot)

1-Devil's Reign Pt. 1						3.00

WEASELGUY: ROAD TRIP
Image Comics: Sept, 1999 - No. 2 ($3.50, limited series)

1,2-Steve Buccellato-s/a						3.50
1-Variant-c by Bachalo						5.00

WEASELGUY/WITCHBLADE
Hyperwerks: July, 1998 ($2.95, one-shot)

1-Steve Buccellato-s/a; covers by Matsuda and Altstaetter						3.00

WEASEL PATROL SPECIAL, THE (Also see Fusion #17)
Eclipse Comics: Apr, 1989 ($2.00, B&W, one-shot)

1-Funny animal						2.50

WEAVEWORLD
Marvel Comics (Epic): Dec, 1991 - No. 3, 1992 ($4.95, lim. series, 68 pgs.)

1-3: Clive Barker adaptation						5.00

WEB, THE (Also see Mighty Comics & Mighty Crusaders)
DC Comics (Impact Comics): Sept, 1991 - No. 14, Oct, 1992 ($1.00)

1-14: 5-The Fly x-over 9-Trading card inside						2.50
Annual 1 (1992, $2.50, 68 pgs.)-With Trading card						3.00

NOTE: *Gil Kane c-5, 9, 10, 12-14. Bill Wray a(i)-1-9, 10(part).*

WEB OF EVIL
Comic Magazines/Quality Comics Group: Nov, 1952 - No. 21, Dec, 1954

	GD 2.0	VG 4.0	FN 6.0	VF 8.0	VF/NM 9.0	NM- 9.2
1-Used in SOTI, pg. 388. Jack Cole-a; morphine use story						
	59	118	177	369	610	850
2-4,6,7: 2,3-Jack Cole-a. 4,6,7-Jack Cole-c/a	41	82	123	252	406	560
5-Electrocution-c/story; Jack Cole-c/a	47	94	141	287	474	660
8-11-Jack Cole-a	40	80	120	235	368	500
12,13,15,16,19-21	25	50	75	145	228	310
14-Part Crandall-c; Old Witch swipe	26	52	78	152	239	325
17-Opium drug propaganda story	26	52	78	150	235	320
18-Acid-in-face story	26	52	78	152	239	325

NOTE: *Jack Cole a(2 each)-2, 6, 8, 9. Cuidera c-1-21i. Ravielli a-13.*

WEB OF HORROR
Major Magazines: Dec, 1969 - No. 3, Apr, 1970 (Magazine)

1-Jeff Jones painted-c; Wrightson-a, Kaluta-a	8	16	24	52	86	120
2-Jones painted-c; Wrightson-a(2), Kaluta-a	7	14	21	45	73	100
3-Wrightson-c/a (1st published-c); Brunner, Kaluta, Bruce Jones-a						
	7	14	21	45	73	100

WEB OF MYSTERY
Ace Magazines (A. A. Wyn): Feb, 1951 - No. 29, Sept, 1955

1	54	108	162	338	562	785
2-Bakerish-a	32	64	96	186	293	400
3-10: 4-Colan-a	28	56	84	162	256	350
11-18,20-26: 12-John Chilly's 1st cover art. 13-Surrealistic-c. 20-r/The Beyond #1						
	24	48	72	139	220	300
19-Reprints Challenge of the Unknown #6 used in N.Y. Legislative Committee						
	24	48	72	139	220	300
27-Bakerish-a(r/The Beyond #2); last pre-code ish	24	44	66	128	202	275
28,29: 28-All-r	17	34	51	98	154	210

NOTE: *This series was to appear as "Creepy Stories", but title was changed before publication. Cameron a-6, 8, 11-13, 17-20, 22, 24, 25, 27; c-8, 13, 17. Palais a-28r. Sekowsky a-1-3, 7, 8, 11, 14, 21, 29. Tothish a-by Bill Discount #16. 29-all-r, 19-28-partial-r.*

WEB OF SCARLET SPIDER
Marvel Comics: Oct, 1995 - No. 4, Jan, 1996 ($1.95, limited series)

1-4: Replaces "Web of Spider-Man"						2.50

WEB OF SPIDER-MAN (Replaces Marvel Team-Up)
Marvel Comics Group: Apr, 1985 - No. 129, Sept, 1995

1-Painted-c (5th app. black costume?)	2	4	6	9	12	15
2,3						5.00
4-8: 7-Hulk x-over; Wolverine splash						4.00
9-13: 10-Dominic Fortune guest stars; painted-c						4.00
14-17,19-28: 19-Intro Humbug & Solo						3.00
18-1st app. Venom (behind the scenes, 9/86)						3.00
29-Wolverine, new Hobgoblin (Macendale) app.	1	2	3	5	6	8
30-Origin recap The Rose & Hobgoblin I (entire book is flashback story); Punisher & Wolverine cameo						4.00
31,32-Six part Kraven storyline begins						5.00
33-37,39-47,49: 36-1st app. Tombstone						3.00
38-Hobgoblin app.; begin $1.00-c						4.00
48-Origin Hobgoblin II(Demogoblin) cont'd from Spectacular Spider-Man #147; Kingpin app.	1	2	3	5	7	9
50-($1.50, 52 pgs.)						3.50
51-58						2.50
59-Cosmic Spidey cont'd from Spect. Spider-Man						3.50
60-89,91-99,101-106: 66,67-Green Goblin (Norman Osborn) app. as a super-hero. 69,70-Hulk x-over. 74-76-Austin-c(i). 76-Fantastic Four x-over. 78-Cloak & Dagger app. 81-Origin/1st app. Bloodshed. 84-Begin 6 part Rose & Hobgoblin II storyline; last $1.00-c. 86-Demon leaves Hobgoblin; 1st app. Demogoblin. 93-Gives brief history of Hobgoblin. 93,94-Hobgoblin (Macendale) Reborn-c/story, parts 1,2; MoonKnight app. 94-Venom cameo. 95-Begin 4 part x-over w/Spirits of Venom w/Ghost Rider/Blaze/Spidey vs. Venom & Demogoblin (cont'd in Ghost Rider/Blaze #5,6). 96-Spirits of Venom part 3; painted-c. 101,103-Maximum Carnage x-over. 103-Venom & Carnage app. 104-106-Nightwatch back-up stories						2.50
90-($2.95, 52 pgs.)-Polybagged w/silver hologram-c, gatefold poster showing Spider-Man & Spider-Man 2099 (Williamson-i)						3.50
90-2nd printing; gold hologram-c						3.00
100-($2.95, 52 pgs.)-Holo-grafx foil-c; intro new Spider-Armor						4.00
107-111: 107-Intro Sandstorm; Sand & Quicksand app.						2.50
112-116, 118, 119, 121-124, 126-128: 112-Begin $1.50-c; Venom app. 113-Regular Ed.; Gambit & Black Cat app. 118-1st solo clone story; Venom app.						2.50
113-($2.95)-Collector's ed. polybagged w/foil-c; 16 pg. preview of Spider-Man cartoon & animation cel						3.00
117-($1.50)-Flip book; Power & Responsibility Pt.1						2.50
117-($2.95)-Collector's edition; foil-c; flip book						3.00
119-($6.45)-Direct market edition; polybagged w/ Marvel Milestone Amazing Spider-Man #150 & coupon for Amazing Spider-Man #396, Spider-Man #53, & Spectacular Spider-Man #219.						

Wedding Bells #2 © QUA

Weird Chills #2 © Key Pub.

Weird Fantasy #16 © WMG

	GD 2.0	VG 4.0	FN 6.0	VF 8.0	VF/NM 9.0	NM- 9.2

120 ($2.25)-Flip book w/ preview of the Ultimate Spider-Man ... 7.00
125 ($3.95)-Holodisk-c; Gwen Stacy clone ... 2.50
125,129: 25 ($2.95)-Newsstand. 129-Last issue ... 4.00 / 3.00
Annual 1 (1985) ... 3.00

Annual 2 (1986)-New Mutants; Art Adams-a	1	2	3	5	6	8

Annual 3-10 ('87-'94, 68 pgs.): 4-Evolutionary War x-over. 5-Atlantis Attacks; Captain Universe by Ditko (p) & Silver Sable stories; F.F. app. 6-Punisher back-up plus Capt. Universe by Ditko; G. Kane-a. 7-Origins of Hobgoblin I, Hobgoblin II, Green Goblin I & II & Venom; Larsen/Austin-c. 9-Bagged w/card ... 3.00
Super Special 1 (1995, $3.95)-flip book ... 4.00
NOTE: *Art Adams* a-Annual 2. *Byrne* c-3-6. *Chaykin* c-10. *Mignola* a-Annual 2. *Vess* c-1, 8, Annual 1, 2. *Zeck* a-6i, 31, 32; c-31, 32.

WEBSPINNERS: TALES OF SPIDER-MAN
Marvel Comics: Jan, 1999 - No. 18, Jun, 2000 ($2.99/$2.50)
1-DeMatteis-s/Zulli-a; back-up story w/Romita Sr. art ... 3.00
1-($6.95) DF Edition ... 7.00
2,3: 2-Two covers ... 2.50
4-11,13-18: 4,5-Giffen-a; Silver Surfer-s/app. 7-9-Kelly-s/Sears and Smith-a.
10,11-Jenkins-s/Sean Phillips-a ... 2.50
12-($3.50) J.G. Jones-c/a; Jenkins-s ... 3.50

WEDDING BELLS
Quality Comics Group: Feb, 1954 - No. 19, Nov, 1956

	GD	VG	FN	VF	VF/NM	NM-
1-Whitney-a	15	30	45	85	130	175
2	10	20	30	56	76	95
3-9: 8-Last precode (4/55)	8	16	24	42	54	65
10-Ward-a (9 pgs.)	14	28	42	80	115	150
11-14,17	7	14	21	37	46	55
15-Baker-c	10	20	30	54	72	90
16-Baker-c/a	12	24	36	69	97	125
18,19-Baker-a each	10	20	30	54	72	90

WEDDING OF DRACULA
Marvel Comics: Jan, 1993 ($2.00, 52 pgs.)
1-Reprints Tomb of Dracula #30,45,46 ... 2.50

WEEKENDER, THE (Illustrated...)
Rucker Pub. Co.: V1#1, Sept, 1945? - V1#4, Nov, 1945; V2#1, Jan, 1946 - V2#3, Aug, 1946 (52 pgs.)

	GD	VG	FN	VF	VF/NM	NM-
V1#1-4: 1-Same-c as Zip Comics #45, inside-c and back-c blank; Steel Sterling, Senor Banana, Red Rube and Ginger. 2-Capt. Victory on-c. 3-Super hero-c; Mr. E, Dan Hastings, Sky Chief and the Echo. 4-Same-c as Punch Comics #10 (9/44); r/Hale the Magician (7 pgs.) & r/Mr. E (8 pgs.-Lou Fine? or Gustavson?) plus 3 humor strips & many B&W photos & r/newspaper articles plus cheesecake photos of Hollywood stars	17	34	51	98	154	210
V2#1-Same-c as Dynamic Comics #11; 36 pgs. comics, 16 in newspaper format with photos; partial Dynamic Comics reprints; 4 pgs. of cels from the Disney film Pinocchio; Little Nemo story by Winsor McCay, Jr.; Jack Cole-a	19	38	57	109	172	235
V2#2,3: 2-Same-c as Dynamic Comics #9 by Raboy; Dan Hastings (Tuska), Rocket Boy, The Echo, Lucky Coyne. 3-Humor-c by Boddington?; Dynamic Man, Ima Slooth, Master Key, Dynamic Boy, Captain Glory	17	34	51	98	154	210

WEIRD
Eerie Publications: V1#10, 1/66 - V8#6, 12/74; V9#1, 1/75 - V14#3, Nov, 1981 (Magazine) (V1-V8: 52 pgs.; V9 on: 68 pgs.)

	GD	VG	FN	VF	VF/NM	NM-
V1#10(#1)-Intro. Morris the Caretaker of Weird (ends V2#10); Burgos-a	7	14	21	49	80	110
11,12	5	10	15	30	48	65
V2#1-4(10/67), V3#1(1/68), V2#6(4/68)-V2#7,9,10(12/68)	5	10	15	30	48	65
V2#8-r/Ditko's 1st story/Fantastic Fears #5	6	12	18	37	59	80
V3#1(2/69)-V3#4	4	8	12	24	41	55

V3#5(12/69)-Rulah reprint; "Rulah" changed to "Pulah"; LSD story reprinted in Horror Tales

	GD	VG	FN	VF	VF/NM	NM-
V4#4, Tales From the Tomb V2#4, & 20	4	8	12	26	41	55
V4#1-6(/70), V5#1-6('71), V6#1-7('72), V7#1-7('73), V8#1-3, V8#4(8/74), V8#4(10/74), (V8#5 does not exist), V8#6('74), V9#1-4(1/75-'76), V10#1-3('77), V11#1-4('78), V12#1(2/79)-V14#3(11/81)	4	8	12	26	41	55

NOTE: There are two V8#4 issues (8/74 & 10/74). V9#4 (12/76) has a cover swipe from Horror Tales V5#1 (2/73). There are two V13#3 issues (6/80 & 9/80).

WEIRD
DC Comics (Paradox Press): Sum, 1997 - Present ($2.99, B&W, magazine)
1-4: 4-Mike Tyson-c ... 3.00

WEIRD, THE
DC Comics: Apr, 1988 - No. 4, July, 1988 ($1.50, limited series)

1-4: Wrightson-c/a in all ... 3.00

WEIRD ADVENTURES
P. L. Publishing Co. (Canada): May-June, 1951 - No. 3, Sept-Oct, 1951

	GD	VG	FN	VF	VF/NM	NM-
1- "The She-Wolf Killer" by Matt Baker (6 pgs.)	57	114	171	356	591	825
2-Bondage/hypodermic panel	45	90	135	275	450	625
3-Male bondage/torture-c; severed head story	40	80	120	235	368	500

WEIRD ADVENTURES
Ziff-Davis Publishing Co.: No. 10, July-Aug, 1951

	GD	VG	FN	VF	VF/NM	NM-
10-Painted-c	40	80	120	235	368	500

WEIRD CHILLS
Key Publications: July, 1954 - No. 3, Nov, 1954

	GD	VG	FN	VF	VF/NM	NM-
1-Wolverton-r/Weird Mysteries No. 4; blood transfusion-c by Baily	86	172	258	538	894	1250
2-Extremely violent injury to eye-c by Baily; Hitler story	103	206	309	644	1072	1500
3-Bondage E.C. swipe-c by Baily	48	96	144	293	484	675

WEIRD COMICS
Fox Features Syndicate: Apr, 1940 - No. 20, Jan, 1942

	GD	VG	FN	VF	VF/NM	NM-
1-The Birdman, Thor, God of Thunder (ends #5), The Sorceress of Zoom, Blast Bennett, Typhon, Voodoo Man, & Dr. Mortal begin; George Tuska bondage-c	469	938	1407	3283	5742	8200
2-Lou Fine-c	231	462	693	1444	2397	3350
3,4: 3-Simon-c. 4-Torture-c	121	242	363	756	1253	1750
5-Intro. Dart & sidekick Ace (8/40) (ends #20); bondage/hypo-c	126	252	378	788	1307	1825
6,7-Dynamite Thor app. in each. 6-Super hero covers begin	93	186	279	581	966	1350
8-Dynamo, the Eagle (11/40, early app.; see Science #1) & sidekick Buddy & Marga, the Panther Woman begin	91	182	273	569	947	1325
9,10: 10-Navy Jones app.	74	148	222	463	769	1075
11-19: 16-Flag-c. 17-Origin The Black Rider.	56	112	168	350	580	810
20-Origin The Rapier; Swoop Curtis app; Churchill & Hitler-c	72	144	216	450	750	1050

NOTE: Cover features: Sorceress of Zoom-4; Dr. Mortal-5; Dart & Ace-6-13, 15; Eagle-14, 16-20.

WEIRD FANTASY (Formerly A Moon, A Girl, Romance; becomes Weird Science-Fantasy #23 on)
E. C. Comics: No. 13, May-June, 1950 - No. 22, Nov-Dec, 1953

	GD	VG	FN	VF	VF/NM	NM-
13(#1) (1950)	197	394	591	1576	2463	3350
14-Necronomicon story; Cosmic Ray Bomb explosion-c/story by Feldstein; Feldstein & Gaines star	91	182	273	728	1139	1550
15,16: 16-Used in SOTI, pg. 144	63	126	189	504	790	1075
17 (1951)	53	106	159	424	662	900
6-10: 6-Robot-c	44	88	132	352	551	750
11-13 (1952): 11-Feldstein bio. 12-E.C. artists cameo; Orlando bio. 13-Anti-Wertham "Cosmic Correspondence"	35	70	105	280	440	600
14-Frazetta/Williamson(1st team-up at E.C.)/Krenkel-a (7 pgs.); Orlando draws E.C. staff	49	98	147	392	609	825
15-Williamson/Evans-a(3), 4,3,&7 pgs.	35	70	105	280	440	600
16-19-Williamson/Krenkel-a in all. 18-Williamson/Feldstein-c. 19-Williamson bio.	33	66	99	264	412	560
20-Frazetta/Williamson-a (7 pgs.)	37	74	111	296	461	625
21-Frazetta/Williamson-c & Williamson/Krenkel-a	49	98	147	392	609	825
22-Bradbury adaptation	26	52	78	208	324	440

NOTE: *Ray Bradbury* adaptations-13, 17-20, 22. *Crandall* a-22. *Elder* a-17. *Feldstein* a-13(#1)-8; c-13(#1)-18 (#18 w/ Williamson), 20. *Harrison/Wood* a-13. *Kamen* a-13(#1)-16, 18-22. *Krigstein* a-22. *Kurtzman* a-13(#1)-17(#5), 6. *Orlando* a-9-22 (2 stories in #16); c-19, 22. *Severin/Elder* a-18-21. *Wood* a-13(#1)-14, 17(2 stories ea. in #10-13). Ray Bradbury adaptations in #17-19, 22. Canadian reprints exist; see Table of Contents.

WEIRD FANTASY
Russ Cochran/Gemstone Publ.: Oct, 1992 - No. 22, Jan, 1998 ($1.50/$2.00/$2.50)
1-22: 1,2: 1,2-r/Weird Fantasy #13,14; Feldstein-c. 3-5-r/Weird Fantasy #15-17 ... 3.00

WEIRD HORRORS (Nightmare #10 on)
St. John Publishing Co.: June, 1952 - No. 9, Oct, 1953

	GD	VG	FN	VF	VF/NM	NM-
1-Tuska-a	57	114	171	356	591	825
2,3: 3-Hashish story	37	74	111	213	337	460
4,5	32	64	96	186	293	400
6-Ekgren-c; atomic bomb story	50	100	150	305	503	700
7-Ekgren-c; Kubert, Cameron-a	52	104	156	317	521	725
8,9-Kubert-c/a	41	82	123	250	400	550

NOTE: *Cameron* a-7, 9. *Finesse* a-1-5. *Forgione* a-6. *Morisi* a-3. Bondage c-8.

WEIRD MYSTERIES
Gillmor Publications: Oct, 1952 - No. 12, Sept, 1954

Weird Romance #1 © ECL

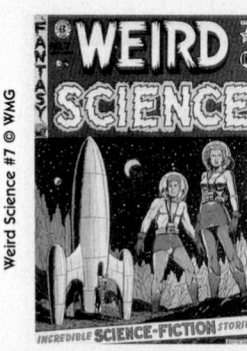
Weird Science #7 © WMG

Weird Tales of the Future #4 © Aragon

	GD	VG	FN	VF	VF/NM	NM-			GD	VG	FN	VF	VF/NM	NM-
	2.0	4.0	6.0	8.0	9.0	9.2			2.0	4.0	6.0	8.0	9.0	9.2

1-Partial Wolverton-c swiped from splash page "Flight to the Future" in Weird Tales of the Future #2; "Eternity" has an Ingels swipe — 93 186 279 581 966 1350
2- "Robot Woman" by Wolverton; Bernard Baily-c reprinted in Mister Mystery #18; acid in face panel — 121 242 363 756 1253 1750
3,6: Both have decapitation-c — 60 120 180 375 625 875
4- "The Man Who Never Smiled" (3 pgs.) by Wolverton; Classic B. Baily skull-c — 112 224 336 700 1163 1625
5-Wolverton story "Swamp Monster" (6 pgs.). Classic exposed brain-c — 124 248 372 775 1288 1800
7-Used in SOTI, illo "Indeed", illo "Sex and blood" — 83 166 249 519 860 1200
8-Wolverton-c panel-r/#5; used in a '54 Readers Digest anti-comics article by T. E. Murphy entitled "For the Kiddies to Read" — 57 114 171 356 591 825
9-Excessive violence, gore & torture — 54 108 162 338 557 775
10-Silhouetted nudity panel — 49 98 147 299 492 685
11,12: 12-r/Mr. Mystery #8(2), Weird Mysteries #3 & Weird Tales of the Future #6 — 45 90 135 275 455 635
NOTE: Baily c-2-12. Anti-Wertham column in #5. #1-12 all have 'The Ghoul Teacher' (host).

WEIRD MYSTERIES (Magazine)
Pastime Publications: Mar-Apr, 1959 (35¢, B&W, 68 pgs.)
1-Torres-a; E. C. swipe from Tales From the Crypt #46 by Tuska "The Ragman" — 10 20 30 56 76 95

WEIRD MYSTERY TALES (See DC 100 Page Super Spectacular)

WEIRD MYSTERY TALES (See Cancelled Comic Cavalcade)
National Periodical Publications: July-Aug, 1972 - No. 24, Nov, 1975
1-Kirby-a; Wrightson splash pg. — 5 10 15 32 51 70
2-Titanic-c/s — 3 6 9 19 29 38
3,21: 21-Wrightson-c — 3 6 9 16 22 28
4-10 — 2 4 6 11 16 20
11-20,22-24 — 2 4 6 9 13 16
NOTE: Alcala a-5, 10, 13, 14. Aparo c-4. Bailey a-8. Bolle a-8?. Howard a-4. Kaluta a-4, 24; c-1. G. Kane a-10. Kirby a-1, 2p, 3p. Nino a-5, 6, 9, 13, 16, 21. Redondo a-9, 17. Sparling c-6. Starlin a-3?, 4. Wood a-23.

WEIRD ROMANCE (Seduction of the Innocent #9)
Eclipse Comics: Feb, 1988 ($2.00, B&W)
1-Pre-code horror-r; Lou Cameron-r(2) — 2.25

WEIRD SCIENCE (Formerly Saddle Romances) (Becomes Weird Science-Fantasy #23 on)
(Also see EC Archives • Weird Science)
E. C. Comics: No. 12, May-June, 1950 - No. 22, Nov-Dec, 1953
12(#1) (1950)-"Lost in the Microcosm" classic-c/story by Kurtzman; "Dream of Doom" stars Gaines & E.C. artists — 197 394 591 1576 2463 3350
13-Flying saucers over Washington-c/story, 2 years before supposed UFO sighting — 91 182 273 728 1139 1550
14-Robot, End of the World-c/story by Feldstein — 85 170 255 680 1065 1450
15-War of Worlds-c/story (1950) — 79 158 237 632 991 1350
5-Atomic explosion-c — 60 120 180 480 753 1025
6-8,10 — 50 100 150 400 625 850
9-Wood's 1st EC-c — 53 106 159 424 662 900
11-14 (1952) 11-Kamen bio. 12-Wood bio — 35 70 105 280 440 600
15-18-Williamson/Krenkel-a in each; 15-Williamson-a. 17-Used in POP, pgs. 81,82.
18-Bill Gaines doll app. in story — 37 74 111 296 469 635
19,20-Williamson/Frazetta-a (7 pgs. each). 19-Used in SOTI, illo "A young girl on her wedding night stabs her sleeping husband to death with a hatpin..." 19-Bradbury bio. — 47 94 141 376 588 800
21-Williamson/Frazetta-a (6 pgs.); Wood draws E.C. staff; Gaines & Feldstein app. in story — 47 94 141 376 588 800
22-Williamson/Frazetta/Krenkel-a (8 pgs.); Wood draws himself in his story (last pg. & panel) — 47 94 141 376 588 800
NOTE: Elder a-14, 19. Evans a-22. Feldstein a-12(#1)-8; c-12(#1)-8, 11. Ingels a-15. Kamen a-12(#1)-13, 15-18, 20, 21. Kurtzman a-12(#1)-7. Orlando a-10-22. Wood a-12(#1), 13(#2), 5-22 (#9, 10, 12, 13 all have 2 Wood stories); c-9, 10, 12-22. Canadian reprints exist; see Table of Contents. Ray Bradbury adaptations in #17-22.

WEIRD SCIENCE
Gladstone Publishing: Sept, 1990 - No. 4, Mar, 1991 ($1.95/$2.00, 68 pgs.)
1-4: Wood-c(r); all reprints in each — 3.00

WEIRD SCIENCE (Also see EC Archives • Weird Science)
Russ Cochran/Gemstone Publishing: Sept, 1992 - No. 22, Dec, 1997 ($1.50/$2.00/$2.50)
1-22: 1,2: r/Weird Science #12,13 w/original-c. ,4-r/#14,15. 5-7-w/original-c — 3.00

WEIRD SCIENCE-FANTASY (Formerly Weird Science & Weird Fantasy)
(Becomes Incredible Science Fiction #30)
E. C. Comics: No. 23 Mar, 1954 - No. 29, May-June, 1955 (#23,24: 15¢)
23-Williamson, Wood-a; Bradbury adaptation — 34 68 102 272 429 585
24-Williamson & Wood-a; Harlan Ellison's 1st professional story, "Upheavall", later adapted into a short story as "Mealtime", and then into a TV episode of Voyage to the Bottom of the Sea as "The Price of Doom" — 34 68 102 272 429 585
25-Williamson-c; Williamson/Torres/Krenkel-a plus Wood-a; Bradbury adaptation; cover price back to 10¢ — 38 76 114 304 472 640
26-Flying Saucer Report; Wood, Crandall-a; A-bomb panels — 35 70 105 280 440 600
27-Adam Link/I Robot series begins? — 34 68 102 272 429 585
28-Williamson/Krenkel/Torres-a; Wood-a — 35 70 105 280 440 600
29-Frazetta-c; Williamson/Krenkel & Wood-a; last pre-code issue; new logo — 82 164 246 656 1028 1400
NOTE: Crandall a-26, 27, 29. Evans a-26. Feldstein c-24, 26, 28. Kamen a-27, 28. Krigstein a-23-25. Orlando a-in all. Wood a-in all; c-23, 27. The cover to #29 was originally intended for Famous Funnies #217 (Buck Rogers), but was rejected for being "too violent."

WEIRD SCIENCE-FANTASY
Russ Cochran/Gemstone Publishing: Nov, 1992 - No. 7, May , 1994 ($1.50/$2.00/$2.50)
1-7: 1,2: r/Weird Science-Fantasy #23,24. 3-7 r/#25-29 — 3.00

WEIRD SCIENCE-FANTASY ANNUAL
E. C. Comics: 1952, 1953 (Sold thru the E. C. office & on the stands in some major cities) (25¢, 132 pgs.)
1952-Feldstein-c — 255 510 765 1913 2807 3700
1953-Feldstein-c — 152 304 456 1140 1670 2200
NOTE: The 1952 annual contains books cover-dated in 1951 & 1952, and the 1953 annual may vary from 1952 & 1953. Contents of each annual may vary in same year.

WEIRD SECRET ORIGINS
DC Comics: Oct, 2004 ($5.95, square-bound, one-shot)
nn-Reprints origins of Dr. Fate, Spectre, Congorilla, Metamorpho, Animal Man & others — 6.00

WEIRD SUSPENSE
Atlas/Seaboard Publ.: Feb, 1975 - No. 3, July, 1975
1-3: 1-Tarantula begins. 3-Freidrich-s — 1 2 3 5 7 9
NOTE: Boyette a-1-3. Buckler c-1, 3.

WEIRD SUSPENSE STORIES (Canadian reprints of Crime SuspenStories #1-3; see Table of Contents)

WEIRD TALES ILLUSTRATED
Millennium Publications: 1992 - No. 2, 1992 ($2.95, high quality paper)
1,2-Bolton painted-c. 1-Adapts E.A. Poe & Harlan Ellison stories. 2-E.A. Poe & H.P. Lovecraft adaptations — 3.50
1-($4.95, 52 pgs.)-Deluxe edition w/Tim Vigil-a not in regular #1; stiff-c; Bolton painted-c — 5.00

WEIRD TALES OF THE FUTURE
S.P.M. Publ. No. 1-4/Aragon Publ. No. 5-8: Mar, 1952 - No. 8, July-Aug, 1953
1-Andru-a(2); Wolverton partial-c — 107 214 321 669 1110 1550
2,3-Wolverton-c/a(3) each. 2- "Jumpin Jupiter" satire by Wolverton begins, ends #5 — 145 290 435 906 1503 2100
4- "Jumpin Jupiter" satire, partial Wolverton-c — 126 252 378 788 1307 1825
5-Wolverton-c/a(2); "Jumpin Jupiter" satire — 145 290 435 906 1503 2100
6-Bernard Baily-c — 55 110 165 344 572 800
7- "The Mind Movers" from the art to Wolverton's "Brain Bats of Venus" from Mr. Mystery #7 which was cut apart, pasted up, partially redrawn, and rewritten by Harry Kantor, the editor; Baily-c — 124 248 372 775 1288 1800
8-Reprints Weird Mysteries #1(10/52) minus cover; gory cover showing heart ripped out, by B. Baily — 79 158 237 494 822 1150

WEIRD TALES OF THE MACABRE (Magazine)
Atlas/Seaboard Publ.: Jan, 1975 - No. 2, Mar, 1975 (75¢, B&W)
1-Jeff Jones painted-c; Boyette-a — 3 6 9 16 23 30
2-Boris Vallejo painted-c; Severin-a — 3 6 9 19 29 38

WEIRD TERROR (Also see Horrific)
Allen Hardy Associates (Comic Media): Sept, 1952 - No. 13, Sept. 1954
1- "Portrait of Death", adapted from Lovecraft's "Pickman's Model"; lingerie panels, Hitler story — 57 114 171 356 591 825
2,3: 2-Text on Marquis DeSade, Torture, Demonology & St. Elmo's Fire. 3-Extreme violence, whipping, torture; article on sin eating, dowsing — 48 96 144 293 484 675
4-Dismemberment, decapitation, article on human flesh for sale, Devil, whipping — 48 96 144 293 484 675
5-Article on body snatching, mutilation; cannibalism story — 41 82 123 256 416 575
6-Dismemberment, decapitation, man hit by lightning — 45 90 135 275 450 625
7-Body burning in fireplace-c — 41 82 123 256 416 575
8,11: 8-Decapitation story; Ambrose Bierce adapt. 11-End of the world story w/atomic blast panels; Toothish-a by Bill Discount — 42 84 123 258 422 585
9,10,13: 13-Severed head panels — 37 74 111 213 337 460
12-Discount-a — 37 74 111 213 337 460

Weird War Tales #11 © DC

Weird Wonder Tales #17 © DC

Welcome Back Kotter #2 © Wolper

	GD 2.0	VG 4.0	FN 6.0	VF 8.0	VF/NM 9.0	NM- 9.2		GD 2.0	VG 4.0	FN 6.0	VF 8.0	VF/NM 9.0	NM- 9.2

NOTE: *Don Heck* a-most issues; c-1-13. *Landau* a-6. *Morisi* a-2-5, 7, 9, 12. *Palais* a-1, 5, 6, 8(2), 10, 12. *Powell* a-10. *Ravielli* a-11, 20.

WEIRD THRILLERS
Ziff-Davis Publ. Co. (Approved Comics): Sept-Oct, 1951 - No. 5, Oct-Nov, 1952 (#2-5: painted-c)

1-Rondo Hatton photo-c	88	176	264	550	913	1275
2-Toth, Anderson, Colan-a	62	124	186	388	644	900
3-Two Powell, Tuska-a; classic-c; Everett-a	86	172	258	538	894	1250
4-Kubert, Tuska-a	59	118	177	369	615	860
5-Powell-a	54	108	162	338	557	775

NOTE: *M. Anderson* a-2, 3. *Roussos* a-4. #2, 3 reprinted in Nightmare #10 & 13; #4, 5 reprinted in Amazing Ghost Stories #16 & #15.

WEIRD VAMPIRE TALES (Comic magazine)
Modern Day Periodical Pub.: V3 #1, Apr, 1979 - V5 #3, Mar, 1982 (B&W)

V3 #1 (4/79) First issue, no V1 or V2	4	8	12	24	37	50
V3 #2-4	3	6	9	18	27	35
V4 #2 (4/80), V4 #3 (7/80) (no V4 #1)	3	6	9	16	23	30
V5 #1 (1/81), V5 #2 (two issues, 4/81 & 8/81)	3	6	9	16	23	30
V5 #3 (3/82) Last issue; low print	3	6	9	20	30	40

WEIRD WAR TALES
National Periodical Publ./DC Comics: Sept-Oct, 1971 - No. 124, June, 1983 (#1-5: 52 pgs.)

1-Kubert-a in #1-4,7; c-1-7	22	44	66	165	295	425
2,3-Drucker-a: 2-Crandall-a. 3-Heath-a	10	20	30	68	119	170
4,5: 5-Toth-a; Heath-a	8	16	24	54	90	125
6,7,9,10: 6,10-Toth-a. 7-Heath-a	5	10	15	35	55	75
8-Neal Adams-c/a(i)	6	12	18	41	66	90
11-20	3	6	9	19	29	38
21-35	3	6	9	14	20	25
36-(68 pgs.)-Crandall & Kubert-r/#2; Heath-r/#3; Kubert-c	3	6	9	16	22	28
37-50: 38,39-Kubert-c	2	4	6	8	11	14
51-63: 58-Hitler-c/app. 60-Hindenburg-c/s	2	4	6	8	10	12
64-Frank Miller-a (1st DC work)	4	8	12	22	34	45
65-67,69-89,91,92: 89-Nazi Apes-c/s.	1	2	3	5	6	8
68-Frank Miller-a (2nd DC work)	3	6	9	16	23	30
90-Hitler app.	1	2	3	5	7	9
93-Intro/origin Creature Commandos	1	3	4	6	8	10
94-Return of War that Time Forgot; dinosaur-c/s	2	4	6	8	10	12
95,96,98,102-123: 98-Sphinx-c. 102-Creature Commandos battle Hitler. 110-Origin/1st app. Medusa. 123-1st app. Captain Spaceman	1	2	3	5	6	8
97,99,100,101,124: 99-War that Time Forgot. 100-Creature Commandos in War that Time Forgot. 101-Intro/origin G.I. Robot	2	4	6	8	10	12

NOTE: *Chaykin* a-76, 82. *Ditko* a-95, 99, 104-106. *Evans* c-73, 74, 83, 85. *Kane* c-116, 118. *Kubert* c-55, 58, 60, 62, 72, 75-81, 87, 88, 90-96, 100, 103, 104, 106, 107. *Newton* a-122. *Starlin* c-89. *Sutton* a-91, 92, 103. *Creature Commandos* - 93, 100-102, 105, 108-112, 114, 116-119, 121, 124. *G.I. Robot* - 101, 108, 111, 113, 116-118, 120, 122. *War That Time Forgot* - 94, 99, 100, 103, 106, 109, 120.

WEIRD WAR TALES
DC Comics (Vertigo): June, 1997 - No. 4, Sept, 1997 ($2.50)

1-4-Anthology by various		3.00

WEIRD WAR TALES
DC Comics (Vertigo): April, 2000 ($4.95, one-shot)

1-Anthology by various; last Biukovic-a		5.00

WEIRD WESTERN TALES (Formerly All-Star Western)
National Per. Publ.: No. 12, June-July, 1972 - No. 70, Aug, 1980

12-(52 pgs.)-3rd appr. Jonah Hex; Bat Lash, Pow Wow Smith reprints; El Diablo by Neal Adams/Wrightson	13	26	39	90	160	230
13-Jonah Hex-c & 4th app.; Neal Adams-a	8	16	24	58	97	135
14-Toth-a	6	12	18	43	69	95
15-Adams-c/a; no Jonah Hex	4	8	12	26	41	55
16,17,19,20	4	8	12	26	41	55
18,29: 18-1st all Jonah Hex issue (7-8/73) & begins. 29-Origin Jonah Hex	6	12	18	37	59	80
21-28,30: Jonah Hex in all	3	6	9	19	29	38
31-38: Jonah Hex in all. 38-Last Jonah Hex	3	6	9	16	23	30
39-Origin/1st app. Scalphunter & begins	2	4	6	10	14	18
40-47,50-69: 64-Bat Lash-c/story	1	2	3	5	6	8
48,49: (44 pgs.)-1st & 2nd app. Cinnamon	1	2	3	5	7	9
70-Last issue	2	4	6	8	10	12

NOTE: *Alcala* a-16, 17. *Evans* inks-39-48; c-39i, 40, 47. *G. Kane* a-15, 20. *Kubert* c-12, 33. *Starlin* c-44, 45. *Wildey* a-26. 48 & 49 are 44 pgs..

WEIRD WESTERN TALES
DC Comics (Vertigo): Apr, 2001 - No. 4, Jul, 2001 ($2.50, limited series)

1-4-Anthology by various		2.50

WEIRD WONDER TALES
Marvel Comics Group: Dec, 1973 - No. 22, May, 1977

1-Wolverton-r/Mystic #6 (Eye of Doom)	3	6	9	17	25	32
2-10	2	4	6	11	16	20
11-22: 16-18-Venus-r by Everett from Venus #19,18 & 17. 19-22-r/Dr. Droom (re-named Dr. Druid) by Kirby. 22-New art by Byrne	2	4	6	10	14	18
15-17-(30¢-c variants, limited distribution)(4-8/76)	3	6	9	15	21	27

NOTE: All 1950s & early 1960s reprints. *Check* r-17. *Colan* r-7. *Ditko* r-4, 5, 10-13, 19-21. *Drucker* r-12, 20. *Everett* r-3(Spellbound #16), 6(Astonishing #10), 9(Adv. Mystery #5). *Heath* a-13r. *Heck* a-14r. *Gil Kane* c-1, 2, 10. *Kirby* r-4, 6, 10, 11, 13, 15-22; c-17, 19, 20. *Krigstein* r-19. *Kubert* r-22. *Maneely* r-8. *Mooney* r-7p. *Powell* r-3, 7. *Torres* r-7. *Wildey* r-2, 7.

WEIRD WORLDS (See Adventures Into...)

WEIRD WORLDS (Magazine)
Eerie Publications: V1#10(12/70), V2#1(2/71) - No. 4, Aug, 1971 (52 pgs.)

V1#10-Sci-fi/horror	4	8	12	26	41	55
V2#1-4	4	8	12	24	34	45

WEIRD WORLDS (Also see Ironwolf: Fires of the Revolution)
National Periodical Publications: Aug-Sept, 1972 - No. 9, Jan-Feb, 1974; No. 10, Oct-Nov, 1974 (20 20¢ issues)

1-Edgar Rice Burrough's John Carter Warlord of Mars & David Innes begin (1st DC app.); Kubert-c	2	4	6	13	18	22
2-4: 2-Infantino/Orlando-c. 3-Murphy Anderson-c. 4-Kaluta-c	2	4	6	8	11	14
5-7: .5-Kaluta-c. 7-Last John Carter.	1	3	4	6	8	10
8-10: 8-Iron Wolf begins by Chaykin (1st app.)	1	2	3	5	7	9

NOTE: *Neal Adams* a-2i, 3i. *John Carter* by *Anderson* #1-3. *Chaykin* c-7, 8. *Kaluta* a-4; c-4-6, 10. *Orlando* a-4i; c-2, 3, 4i. *Wrightson* a-2i, 4i.

WELCOME BACK, KOTTER (TV) (See Limited Collectors' Edition #57 for unpublished #11)
National Periodical Publ./DC Comics: Nov, 1976 - No. 10, Mar-Apr, 1978

1-Sparling-a(p)	3	6	9	16	22	28
2-10: 3-Estrada-a	2	4	6	9	13	16

WELCOME SANTA (See March of Comics #63,183)

WELCOME TO HOLSOM
Gospel Publishing House: 2005 - Present (no cover price)

1-12-Craig Schutt-s/Steven Butler-a		2.50

WELCOME TO THE LITTLE SHOP OF HORRORS
Roger Corman's Cosmic Comics: May, 1995 -No. 3, July, 1995 ($2.50, limited series)

1-3		2.50

WELCOME TO TRANQUILITY
DC Comics (WildStorm): Feb, 2007 - Present ($2.99)

1-9: 1-Simone-s/Googe-a; two covers by Googe and Campbell. 8-Pearson-a		3.00

WELLS FARGO (See Tales of...)

WENDY AND THE NEW KIDS ON THE BLOCK
Harvey Comics: Mar, 1991 - No. 3, July, 1991 ($1.25)

1-3		2.50

WENDY DIGEST
Harvey Comics: Oct, 1990 - No. 5, Mar, 1992 ($1.75, digest size)

1-5		4.00

WENDY PARKER COMICS
Atlas Comics (OMC): July, 1953 - No. 8, July, 1954

1	11	22	33	60	83	105
2	8	16	24	44	57	70
3-8	8	16	24	40	50	60

WENDY, THE GOOD LITTLE WITCH (TV)
Harvey Publ.: 8/60 - #82, 11/73; #83, 8/74 - #93, 4/76; #94, 9/90 - #97, 12/90

1-Wendy & Casper the Friendly Ghost begin	26	52	78	195	348	500
2	13	26	39	93	164	235
3-5	9	18	27	65	113	160
6-10	7	14	21	47	76	105
11-20	5	10	15	35	55	75
21-30	4	8	12	26	41	55
31-50	3	6	9	18	27	35
51-64,66-69	2	4	6	13	18	22
65 (2/71)-Wendy origin.	2	4	6	15	25	32
70-74: All 52 pg. Giants	3	6	9	17	23	30
75-93	2	4	6	9	13	16

	GD 2.0	VG 4.0	FN 6.0	VF 8.0	VF/NM 9.0	NM- 9.2
94-97 (1990, $1.00-c): 94-Has #194 on-c						5.00

(See Casper the Friendly Ghost #20 & Harvey Hits #7, 16, 21, 23, 27, 30, 33)

WENDY THE GOOD LITTLE WITCH (2nd Series)
Harvey Comics: Apr, 1991 - No. 15, Aug, 1994 ($1.00/$1.25 #7-11/$1.50 #12-15)

	GD	VG	FN	VF	VF/NM	NM-
1-15-Reprints Wendy & Casper stories. 12-Bunny app.						3.00

WENDY WITCH WORLD
Harvey Publications: 10/61; No. 2, 9/62 - No. 52, 12/73; No. 53, 9/74

	GD	VG	FN	VF	VF/NM	NM-
1-(25¢, 68 pg. Giants begin)	14	28	42	102	181	260
2-5	8	16	24	52	86	120
6-10	6	12	18	37	59	80
11-20	4	8	12	28	44	60
21-30	4	8	12	22	34	45
31-39: 39-Last 68 pg. issue	3	6	9	17	25	32
40-45: 52 pg. issues	2	4	6	13	18	22
46-53	2	4	6	9	13	16

WEREWOLF (Super Hero) (Also see Dracula & Frankenstein)
Dell Publishing Co.: Dec, 1966 - No. 3, April, 1967

	GD	VG	FN	VF	VF/NM	NM-
1-1st app.	4	8	12	22	34	45
2,3	3	6	9	14	19	24

WEREWOLF BY NIGHT (See Giant-Size..., Marvel Spotlight #2-4 & Power Record Comics)
Marvel Comics Group: Sept, 1972 - No. 43, Mar, 1977

	GD	VG	FN	VF	VF/NM	NM-
1-Ploog-a cont'd. from Marvel Spotlight #4	10	20	30	70	123	175
2	5	10	15	35	55	75
3-5	4	8	12	26	41	55
6-10	3	6	9	20	30	40
11-14,16-20	3	6	9	16	22	28
15-New origin Werewolf; Dracula-c/story cont'd from Tomb of Dracula #18; classic Ploog-c	4	8	12	22	34	45
21-31	2	4	6	10	14	18
32-Origin & 1st app. Moon Knight (8/75)	9	18	27	65	113	160
33-2nd app. Moon Knight	5	10	15	32	51	70
34,36,38-43: 35-Starlin/Wrightson-c	2	4	6	9	13	16
37-Moon Knight app; part Wrightson-a	3	6	9	16	23	30
38,39-(30¢ variants, limited distribution)(5,7/76)	3	6	9	20	30	40

NOTE: *Bolle* a-6i. *G. Kane* a-11p, 12p; c-21, 22, 24-30, 34p. *Mooney* a-7i. *Ploog* a-1-4p, 5, 6p, 7p, 13-16p; c-5-8, 13-16. *Reinman* a-8i. *Sutton* a(i)-9, 11, 16, 35.

WEREWOLF BY NIGHT (Vol. 2, continues in Strange Tales #1 (9/98))
Marvel Comics Group: Feb, 1998 - No. 6, July, 1998 ($2.99)

	GD	VG	FN	VF	VF/NM	NM-
1-6-Manco-a; 2-Two covers. 6-Ghost Rider-c/app.						3.00

WEREWOLVES & VAMPIRES (Magazine)
Charlton Comics: 1962 (One Shot)

	GD	VG	FN	VF	VF/NM	NM-
1	8	16	24	58	97	135

WEST COAST AVENGERS
Marvel Comics Group: Sept, 1984 - No. 4, Dec, 1984 (lim. series, Mando paper)

	GD	VG	FN	VF	VF/NM	NM-
1-Origin & 1st app. W.C. Avengers (Hawkeye, Iron Man, Mockingbird & Tigra)						4.00
2-4						3.00

WEST COAST AVENGERS (Becomes Avengers West Coast #48 on)
Marvel Comics Group: Oct, 1985 - No. 47, Aug, 1989

	GD	VG	FN	VF	VF/NM	NM-
V2#1-41						3.00
42-47: 42-Byrne-a(p)/scripts begin. 46-Byrne-c; 1st app. Great Lakes Avengers						3.00
Annual 1-3 (1986-1988): 3-Evolutionary War app.						3.00
Annual 4 (1989, $2.00)-Atlantis Attacks; Byrne/Austin-a						3.00

WESTERN ACTION
I. W. Enterprises: No. 7, 1964

	GD	VG	FN	VF	VF/NM	NM-
7-Reprints Cow Puncher #? by Avon	2	4	6	8	11	14

WESTERN ACTION
Atlas/Seaboard Publ.: Feb, 1975

	GD	VG	FN	VF	VF/NM	NM-
1-Kid Cody by Wildey & The Comanche Kid stories; intro. The Renegade	1	3	4	6	8	10

WESTERN ACTION THRILLERS
Dell Publishers: Apr, 1937 (10¢, square binding; 100 pgs.)

	GD	VG	FN	VF	VF/NM	NM-
1-Buffalo Bill, The Texas Kid, Laramie Joe, Two-Gun Thompson, & Wild West Bill app.	83	166	249	519	860	1200

WESTERN ADVENTURES COMICS (Western Love Trails #7 on)
Ace Magazines: Oct, 1948 - No. 6, Aug, 1949

	GD	VG	FN	VF	VF/NM	NM-
nn(#1)-Sheriff Sal, The Cross-Draw Kid, Sam Bass begin	21	42	63	124	195	265

	GD 2.0	VG 4.0	FN 6.0	VF 8.0	VF/NM 9.0	NM- 9.2
nn(#2)(12/48)	13	26	39	72	101	130
nn(#3)(2/49)-Used in SOTI, pgs. 30,31	13	26	39	74	105	135
4-6	11	22	33	62	86	110

WESTERN BANDITS
Avon Periodicals: 1952 (Painted-c)

	GD	VG	FN	VF	VF/NM	NM-
1-Butch Cassidy, The Daltons by Larsen; Kinstler-a; c-part-r/paperback Avon Western Novel #1	16	32	48	92	144	195

WESTERN BANDIT TRAILS (See Approved Comics)
St. John Publishing Co.: Jan, 1949 - No. 3, July, 1949

	GD	VG	FN	VF	VF/NM	NM-
1-Tuska-a; Baker-c; Blue Monk, Ventrilo app.	26	52	78	152	239	325
2-Baker-c	20	40	60	117	184	250
3-Baker-c/a; Tuska-a	24	48	72	139	220	300

WESTERN COMICS (See Super DC Giant #15)
National Per. Publ.: Jan-Feb, 1948 - No. 85, Jan-Feb, 1961 (1-27: 52pgs.)

	GD	VG	FN	VF	VF/NM	NM-
1-Wyoming Kid & his horse Racer, The Vigilante in "Jesse James Rides Again" (Meskin-a), Cowboy Marshal, Rodeo Rick begin	76	152	228	475	788	1100
2	37	74	111	214	340	465
3,4-Last Vigilante	33	66	99	192	304	415
5-Nighthawk & his horse Nightwind begin (not in #6); Captain Tootsie by Beck	28	56	84	160	253	345
6,7,9,10	21	42	63	124	195	265
8-Origin Wyoming Kid; 2 pg. pin-ups of rodeo queens	32	64	96	186	293	400
11-20	18	36	54	103	162	220
21-40: 24-Starr-a. 27-Last 52 pgs. 28-Flag-c	14	28	42	82	121	160
41,42,44-49: 49-Last precode issue (2/55)	14	28	42	80	115	150
43-Pow Wow Smith begins, ends #85	14	28	42	81	118	155
50-60	12	24	36	67	94	120
61-85-Last Wyoming Kid. 77-Origin Matt Savage Trail Boss. 82-1st app. Fleetfoot, Pow Wow's girlfriend	10	20	30	56	76	95

NOTE: *G. Kane, Infantino* art in most. *Meskin* a-1-4. *Moreira* a-28-39. *Post* a-3-5.

WESTERN CRIME BUSTERS
Trojan Magazines: Sept, 1950 - No. 10, Mar-Apr, 1952

	GD	VG	FN	VF	VF/NM	NM-
1-Six-Gun Smith, Wilma West, K-Bar-Kate, & Fighting Bob Dale begin; headlight-a	36	72	108	208	329	450
2	19	38	57	109	172	235
3-5: 3-Myron Fass-c	18	36	54	103	162	220
6-Wood-a	32	64	96	186	293	400
7-Six-Gun Smith by Wood	32	64	96	186	293	400
8	18	36	54	103	162	220
9-Tex Gordon & Wilma West by Wood; Lariat Lucy app.	32	64	96	186	293	400
10-Wood-a	29	58	87	170	268	365

WESTERN CRIME CASES (Formerly Indian Warriors #7,8; becomes The Outlaws #10 on)
Star Publications: No. 9, Dec, 1951

	GD	VG	FN	VF	VF/NM	NM-
9-White Rider & Super Horse; L. B. Cole-c	21	42	63	120	188	255

WESTERNER, THE (Wild Bill Pecos)
"Wanted" Comic Group/Toytown/Patches: No. 14, June, 1948 - No. 41, Dec, 1951 (#14-31: 52 pgs.)

	GD	VG	FN	VF	VF/NM	NM-
14	15	30	45	85	130	175
15-17,19-21: 19-Meskin-a	9	18	27	52	69	85
18,22-25-Krigstein-a	11	22	33	60	83	105
26(4/50)-Origin & 1st app. Calamity Kate, series ends #32; Krigstein-a	14	28	42	78	112	145
27-Krigstein-a(2)	13	26	39	74	105	135
28-41: 33-Quest app. 37-Lobo, the Wolf Boy begins	8	16	24	40	50	60

NOTE: *Mort Lawrence* a-20-27, 29, 37, 39; c-19, 22-24, 26, 27. *Leav* c-14-18, 20, 31. *Syd Shores* a-39; c-34, 35, 37-41.

WESTERNER, THE
Super Comics: 1964

	GD	VG	FN	VF	VF/NM	NM-
Super Reprint 15-17: 15-r/Oklahoma Kid #? 16-r/Crack West. #65; Severin-c; Crandall-r. 17-r/Blazing Western #2; Severin-c	2	4	6	8	11	14

WESTERN FIGHTERS
Hillman Periodicals/Star Publ.: Apr-May, 1948 - V4#7, Mar-Apr, 1953 (#1-V3#2: 52 pgs.)

	GD	VG	FN	VF	VF/NM	NM-
V1#1-Simon & Kirby-c	36	72	108	208	329	450
2-Not Kirby-a	14	28	42	78	112	145
3-Fuje-c	11	22	33	64	90	125
4-Krigstein, Ingels, Fuje-a	13	26	39	72	101	130

Western Hearts #3 © STD

Western Love #2 © Prize

Western Outlaws #20 © FOX

	GD 2.0	VG 4.0	FN 6.0	VF 8.0	VF/NM 9.0	NM- 9.2
5,6,8,9,12	9	18	27	52	69	85
7,10-Krigstein-a	11	22	33	60	83	105
11-Williamson/Frazetta-a	30	60	90	174	275	375
V2#1-Krigstein-a	11	22	33	60	83	105
2-12: 4-Berg-a	8	16	24	42	54	65
V3#1-11,V4#1,4-7	8	16	24	40	50	60
12,V4#2,3-Krigstein-a	11	22	33	60	83	105
3-D 1(12/53, 25¢, Star Publ.)-Came w/glasses; L. B. Cole-c	36	72	108	208	329	450

NOTE: *Kinstlerish a*-V2#6, 8, 9, 12; V3#2, 5-7, 11, 12; V4#1(plus cover). *McWilliams a*-11. *Powell a*-V2#2. *Reinman a*-1-12, V4#3. *Rowich c*-5, 6i. *Starr a*-5.

WESTERN FRONTIER
P. L. Publishers: Apr-May, 1951 - No. 7, 1952

	GD 2.0	VG 4.0	FN 6.0	VF 8.0	VF/NM 9.0	NM- 9.2
1	14	28	42	76	108	140
2	8	16	24	44	57	70
3-7	7	14	21	37	46	55

WESTERN GUNFIGHTERS (1st Series) (Apache Kid #11-19)
Atlas Comics (CPS): No. 20, June, 1956 - No. 27, Aug, 1957

	GD 2.0	VG 4.0	FN 6.0	VF 8.0	VF/NM 9.0	NM- 9.2
20	13	26	39	74	105	135
21-Crandall-a	13	26	39	74	105	135
22-Wood & Powell-a	18	36	54	103	162	220
23,24: 23-Williamson-a. 24-Toth-a	13	26	39	74	105	135
25-27	10	20	30	54	72	90

NOTE: *Berg a*-20. *Colan a*-20, 26, 27. *Crandall a*-21. *Heath a*-25. *Maneely a*-24, 25; c-22, 23, 25. *Morisi a*-24. *Morrow a*-26. *Pakula a*-23. *Severin c*-20, 27. *Torres a*-26. *Woodbridge a*-27.

WESTERN GUNFIGHTERS (2nd Series)
Marvel Comics Group: Aug, 1970 - No. 33, Nov, 1975 (#1-6: 25¢, 68 pgs.)

	GD 2.0	VG 4.0	FN 6.0	VF 8.0	VF/NM 9.0	NM- 9.2
1-Ghost Rider begins; Fort Rango, Renegades & Gunhawk app.	5	10	15	30	48	65
2,3,5,6: 2-Origin Nightwind (Apache Kid's horse)	3	6	9	17	25	32
4-Barry Smith-a	3	6	9	21	32	42
7-(52 pgs) Origin Ghost Rider retold	3	6	9	16	23	30
8-13: 10-Origin Black Rider. 12-Origin Matt Slade	2	4	6	11	16	20
14-Steranko-c	2	4	6	11	16	20
15-20	2	4	6	8	11	14
21-33	2	4	6	8	10	12

NOTE: *Baker r*-2, 3. *Colan r*-2. *Drucker r*-3. *Everett a*-6i. *G. Kane c*-29, 31. *Kirby a*-1p(r), 5, 10-12; c-19, 21. *Kubert r*-2. *Maneely r*-2, 10. *Morrow r*-29. *Severin c*-10. *Shores a*-3, 4. *Barry Smith a*-4. *Steranko c*-14. *Sutton a*-1, 2i, 5, 4. *Torres r*-26('57). *Wildey r*-8, 9. *Williamson r*-2, 18. *Woodbridge r*-27('57). Renegades in #4, 5; Ghost Rider in #1-7.

WESTERN HEARTS
Standard Comics: Dec, 1949 - No. 10, Mar, 1952 (All photo-c)

	GD 2.0	VG 4.0	FN 6.0	VF 8.0	VF/NM 9.0	NM- 9.2
1-Severin-a; Whip Wilson & Reno Browne photo-c	23	46	69	130	205	280
2-Beverly Tyler & Jerome Courtland photo-c from movie "Palomino"; Williamson/Frazetta-a (2 pgs.)	23	46	69	130	205	280
3-Rex Allen photo-c	14	28	42	80	115	150
4-7,10: 4-Severin & Elder, Al Carreno-a. 5-Ray Milland & Hedy Lamarr photo-c from movie "Copper Canyon". 6-Fred MacMurray & Irene Dunn photo-c from movie "Never a Dull Moment". 7-Jock Mahoney & Bill Williams & Jane Nigh photo-c	14	28	42	78	112	145
8-Randolph Scott & Janis Carter photo-c from "Santa Fe"; Severin & Elder-a	14	28	42	80	115	150
9-Whip Wilson & Reno Browne photo-c; Severin & Elder-a	15	30	45	83	124	165

WESTERN HERO (Wow Comics #1-69; Real Western Hero #70-75)
Fawcett Publications: No. 76, Mar, 1949 - No. 112, Mar, 1952

	GD 2.0	VG 4.0	FN 6.0	VF 8.0	VF/NM 9.0	NM- 9.2
76(#1, 52 pgs.)-Tom Mix, Hopalong Cassidy, Monte Hale, Gabby Hayes, Young Falcon (ends #78,80), & Big Bow and Little Arrow (ends #78,80); painted-c begin	23	46	69	132	209	285
77 (52 pgs.)	14	28	42	82	121	160
78,80-82 (52 pgs.): 81-Capt. Tootsie by Beck	14	28	42	80	115	150
79,83 (36 pgs.): 83-Last painted-c	13	26	39	72	101	130
84-86,88-90 (52 pgs.): 84-Photo-c begin, end #112. 86-Last Hopalong Cassidy	13	26	39	74	105	135
87,91,95,99 (36 pgs.): 87-Bill Boyd begins, ends #95	11	22	33	64	90	115
92-94,96-98,101 (52 pgs.): 96-Tex Ritter begins. 101-Red Eagle app.	12	24	36	69	97	125
100 (52 pgs.)	13	26	39	74	105	135
102-111: 102-Begin 36 pg. issues	11	22	33	64	90	115
112-Last issue	12	24	36	69	97	125

NOTE: 1/2 to 1 pg. Rocky Lane (Carnation) in 80-83, 86, 88, 97. Photo covers feature Hopalong Cassidy #84, 86, 89; Tom Mix #85, 87, 90, 92, 94, 97; Monte Hale #88, 91, 93, 95, 98, 100, 104, 107, 110; Tex Ritter #96, 99, 101, 105, 108, 111; Gabby Hayes #103.

WESTERN KID (1st Series)
Atlas Comics (CPC): Dec, 1954 - No. 17, Aug, 1957

	GD 2.0	VG 4.0	FN 6.0	VF 8.0	VF/NM 9.0	NM- 9.2
1-Origin; The Western Kid (Tex Dawson), his stallion Whirlwind & dog Lightning begin	18	36	54	107	169	230
2 (2/55)-Last pre-code	11	22	33	62	86	110
3-8	10	20	30	54	72	90
9,10-Williamson-a in both (4 pgs. each)	10	20	30	56	76	95
11-17	8	16	24	44	57	70

NOTE: *Ayers a*-6, 7. *Maneely c*-2-7, 10, 13-15. *Romita a*-1-17; c-1, 12. *Severin c*-16, 17.

WESTERN KID, THE (2nd Series)
Marvel Comics Group: Dec, 1971 - No. 5, Aug, 1972 (All 20¢ issues)

	GD 2.0	VG 4.0	FN 6.0	VF 8.0	VF/NM 9.0	NM- 9.2
1-Reprints; Romita-c/a(3)	3	6	9	16	22	28
2,4,5: 2-Romita-a; Severin-c. 4-Everett-r	2	4	6	9	13	16
3-Williamson-a	2	4	6	11	16	20

WESTERN KILLERS
Fox Features Syndicate: nn, July?, 1948; No. 60, Sept, 1948 - No. 64, May, 1949; No. 6, July, 1949

	GD 2.0	VG 4.0	FN 6.0	VF 8.0	VF/NM 9.0	NM- 9.2
nn(#59?)(nd, F&J Trading Co.)-Range Busters; formerly Blue Beetle #57?	24	48	72	139	220	300
60 (#1, 9/48)-Extreme violence; lingerie panel	26	52	78	152	239	325
61-Jack Cole, Starr-a	21	42	63	122	191	260
62-64, 6 (#6-exist?)	19	38	57	109	172	235

WESTERN LIFE ROMANCES (My Friend Irma #3 on?)
Marvel Comics (IPP): Dec, 1949 - No. 2, Mar, 1950 (52 pgs.)

	GD 2.0	VG 4.0	FN 6.0	VF 8.0	VF/NM 9.0	NM- 9.2
1-Whip Wilson & Reno Browne photo-c	20	40	60	117	184	250
2-Audie Murphy & Gale Storm photo-c	16	32	48	94	147	200

WESTERN LOVE
Prize Publ.: July-Aug, 1949 - No. 5, Mar-Apr, 1950 (All photo-c & 52 pgs.)

	GD 2.0	VG 4.0	FN 6.0	VF 8.0	VF/NM 9.0	NM- 9.2
1-S&K-a; Randolph Scott photo-c from movie "Canadian Pacific" (see Prize Comics #76)	31	62	93	178	282	385
2,5-S&K-a: 2-Whip Wilson & Reno Browne photo-c. 5-Dale Robertson photo-c	23	46	69	132	209	285
3,4: 3-Pat Williams photo-c	15	30	45	85	130	175

NOTE: *Meskin & Severin/Elder a*-2-5.

WESTERN LOVE TRAILS (Formerly Western Adventures)
Ace Magazines (A. A. Wyn): No. 7, Nov, 1949 - No. 9, Mar, 1950

	GD 2.0	VG 4.0	FN 6.0	VF 8.0	VF/NM 9.0	NM- 9.2
7	12	24	36	67	94	120
8,9	10	20	30	54	72	90

WESTERN MARSHAL (See Steve Donovan...)
Dell Publishing Co.: No. 534, 2-4/54 - No. 640, 7/55 (Based on Ernest Haycox's "Trailtown")

	GD 2.0	VG 4.0	FN 6.0	VF 8.0	VF/NM 9.0	NM- 9.2
Four Color 534 (#1)-Kinstler-a	6	12	18	39	62	85
Four Color 591 (10/54), 613 (2/55), 640-All Kinstler-a	5	10	15	35	55	75

WESTERN OUTLAWS (Junior Comics #9-16; My Secret Life #22 on)
Fox Features Syndicate: No. 17, Sept, 1948 - No. 21, May, 1949

	GD 2.0	VG 4.0	FN 6.0	VF 8.0	VF/NM 9.0	NM- 9.2
17-Kamen-a; Iger shop-a in all; 1 pg. "Death and the Devil Pills" r-in Ghostly Weird #122	32	64	96	186	293	400
18-21	18	36	54	105	165	225

WESTERN OUTLAWS
Atlas Comics (ACI No. 1-14/WPI No. 15-21): Feb, 1954 - No. 21, Aug, 1957

	GD 2.0	VG 4.0	FN 6.0	VF 8.0	VF/NM 9.0	NM- 9.2
1-Heath, Powell-a; Maneely hanging-c	21	42	63	120	188	255
2	12	24	36	67	94	120
3-10: 7-Violent-a by R.Q. Sale	10	20	30	54	72	90
11,14-Williamson-a in both (6 pgs. each)	11	22	33	60	83	105
12,18,20,21: Severin covers	9	18	27	50	65	80
13,15: 13-Baker-a. 15-Torres-a	10	20	30	54	72	90
16-Williamson text illo	9	18	27	50	65	80
17,19-Crandall-a. 17-Williamson text illo	10	20	30	54	72	90

NOTE: *Ayers a*-7, 10, 18, 20. *Bolle a*-21. *Colan a*-5, 10, 11, 17. *Drucker a*-11. *Everett a*-9, 10. *Heath a*-1; c-3, 4, 8, 16. *Kubert a*-9p. *Maneely a*-13, 16, 17, 19; c-1, 5, 7, 9, 10, 12, 13. *Morisi a*-18. *Powell a*-3, 16. *Romita a*-7, 13. *Severin a*-8, 16, 19; c-17, 18, 20, 21. *Tuska a*-6, 15.

WESTERN OUTLAWS & SHERIFFS (Formerly Best Western)
Marvel/Atlas Comics (IPC): No. 60, Dec, 1949 - No. 73, June, 1952

	GD 2.0	VG 4.0	FN 6.0	VF 8.0	VF/NM 9.0	NM- 9.2
60 (52 pgs.)	21	42	63	122	191	260
61-65: 61-Photo-c	16	32	48	94	147	200
66-Story contains 5 hangings	16	32	48	94	147	200
66-72	14	28	42	76	108	140
67-Cannibalism story	16	32	48	94	147	200
73-Black Rider story; Everett-c	15	30	45	83	124	165

Western Picture Stories #1 © CM

Wetworks #1 © WSP

What If...? (1st) #31 © MAR

	GD 2.0	VG 4.0	FN 6.0	VF 8.0	VF/NM 9.0	NM- 9.2		GD 2.0	VG 4.0	FN 6.0	VF 8.0	VF/NM 9.0	NM- 9.2

NOTE: *Maneely a-62, 67; c-62, 69-73.* *Robinson a-68.* *Sinnott a-70.* *Tuska a-69-71.*

WESTERN PICTURE STORIES (1st Western comic)
Comics Magazine Company: Feb, 1937 - No. 4, June, 1937

	GD	VG	FN	VF	VF/NM	NM-
1-Will Eisner-a	193	386	579	1206	2003	2800
2-Will Eisner-a	100	200	300	625	1038	1450
3,4: 3-Eisner-a. 4-Caveman Cowboy story	83	166	249	519	860	1200

WESTERN PICTURE STORIES (See Giant Comics Edition #6, 11)
WESTERN ROMANCES (See Target...)
WESTERN ROUGH RIDERS
Gillmor Magazines No. 1,4 (Stanmor Publ.): Nov, 1954 - No. 4, May, 1955

	GD	VG	FN	VF	VF/NM	NM-
1	9	18	27	47	61	75
2-4	7	14	21	35	43	50

WESTERN ROUNDUP (See Dell Giants & Fox Giants)
WESTERN SERENADE
DC Comics: May/June, 1949

nn - Ashcan comic, not distributed to newsstands, only for in-house use   (no known sales)

WESTERN TALES (Formerly Witches...)
Harvey Publications: No. 31, Oct, 1955 - No. 33, July-Sept, 1956

	GD	VG	FN	VF	VF/NM	NM-
31,32-All S&K-a; Davy Crockett app. in each	18	36	54	107	169	230
33-S&K-a; Jim Bowie app.	18	36	54	103	162	220

NOTE: *#32 & 33 contain Boy's Ranch reprints.* *Kirby c-31.*

WESTERN TALES OF BLACK RIDER (Formerly Black Rider; Gunsmoke Western #32 on)
Atlas Comics (CPS): No. 28, May, 1955 - No. 31, Nov, 1955

	GD	VG	FN	VF	VF/NM	NM-
28 (#1): The Spider (a villain) dies	20	40	60	115	180	245
29-31	14	28	42	82	121	160

NOTE: *Lawrence a-30.* *Maneely c-28-30.* *Severin a-28.* *Shores c-31.*

WESTERN TEAM-UP
Marvel Comics Group: Nov, 1973 (20¢)

	GD	VG	FN	VF	VF/NM	NM-
1-Origin & 1st app. The Dakota Kid; Rawhide Kid-r; Gunsmoke Kid-r by Jack Davis	3	6	9	20	30	40

WESTERN THRILLERS (My Past Confessions #7 on)
Fox Features Syndicate/M.S. Distr. No. 52: Aug, 1948 - No. 6, June, 1949; No. 52, 1954?

	GD	VG	FN	VF	VF/NM	NM-
1- "Velvet Rose" (Kamenish-a); "Two-Gun Sal", "Striker Sisters" (all women outlaws issue); Brodsky-c	48	96	144	293	484	675
2	24	48	72	139	220	300
3-6: 4,5-Bakerish-a; 5-Butch Cassidy app.	19	38	57	112	176	240
52-(Reprint, M.S. Dist.)-1954? No date given (becomes My Love Secret #53)	9	18	27	47	61	75

WESTERN THRILLERS (Cowboy Action #5 on)
Atlas Comics (ACI): Nov, 1954 - No. 4, Feb, 1955 (All-r/Western Outlaws & Sheriffs)

	GD	VG	FN	VF	VF/NM	NM-
1	15	30	45	88	137	185
2-4	10	20	30	54	72	90

NOTE: *Heath c-3.* *Maneely a-1; c-2.* *Powell a-4.* *Robinson a-4.* *Romita c-4.* *Tuska a-2.*

WESTERN TRAILS (Ringo Kid Starring in...)
Atlas Comics (SAI): May, 1957 - No. 2, July, 1957

	GD	VG	FN	VF	VF/NM	NM-
1-Ringo Kid app.; Severin-a	14	28	42	76	108	140
2-Severin-c	9	18	27	50	65	80

NOTE: *Bolle a-1, 2.* *Maneely a-1, 2.* *Severin c-1, 2.*

WESTERN TRUE CRIME (Becomes My Confessions)
Fox Features Syndicate: No. 15, Aug, 1948 - No. 4, June, 1949

	GD	VG	FN	VF	VF/NM	NM-
15(#1)-Kamen-a; formerly Zoot #14 (5/48)?	32	64	96	186	293	400
16(#2)-Kamenish-a; headlight panels, violence	23	46	69	132	209	285
3-Kamen-a	25	50	75	145	228	310
4-6: 4-Johnny Craig-a	15	30	45	90	140	190

WESTERN WINNERS (Formerly All-Western Winners; becomes Black Rider #8 on & Romance Tales #7 on?)
Marvel Comics (CDS): No. 5, June, 1949 - No. 7, Dec, 1949

	GD	VG	FN	VF	VF/NM	NM-
5-Two-Gun Kid, Kid Colt, Black Rider; Shores-c	31	62	93	178	282	385
6-Two-Gun Kid, Black Rider, Heath Kid Colt story; Captain Tootsie by C.C. Beck	26	52	78	152	239	325
7-Randolph Scott Photo-c w/true stories about the West	26	52	78	152	239	325

WEST OF THE PECOS (See Zane Grey, 4-Color #222)
WESTWARD HO, THE WAGONS (Disney)
Dell Publishing Co.: No. 738, Sept, 1956 (Movie)

	GD	VG	FN	VF	VF/NM	NM-
Four Color 738-Fess Parker photo-c	9	18	27	63	107	150

WE3
DC Comics (Vertigo): Oct, 2004 - No. 3, May, 2005 ($2.95, limited series)

					NM-
1-3-Domestic animal cyborgs: Grant Morrison-s/Frank Quitely-a					3.00
TPB (2005, $12.99) r/series					13.00

WETWORKS (See WildC.A.T.S: Covert Action Teams #2)
Image Comics (WildStorm): June, 1994 - No. 43, Aug, 1998 ($1.95/$2.50)

					NM-
1- "July" on-c; gatefold wraparound-c; Portacio/Williams-c/a					3.00
1-Chicago Comicon edition					6.00
1-(2/98, $4.95) "3-D Edition" w/glasses					5.00
2-4					2.50
2-Alternate Portacio-c, see Deathblow #5					6.00
5-7,9-24: 5-($2.50). 13-Portacio-c. 16,17-Fire From Heaven Pts. 4 & 11					2.50
8 ($1.95)-Newstand, Wildstorm Rising Pt. 7					2.25
8 ($2.50)-Direct Market, Wildstorm Rising Pt. 7					2.50
25-($3.95)					4.00
26-43: 32-Variant-c by Pat Lee & Charest. 39,40-Stormwatch app. 42-Gen 13 app.					2.50
Sourcebook 1 (10/94, $2.50)-Text & illustrations (no comics)					2.50
Voyager Pack (8/97, $3.50)- #32 w/Phantom Guard preview					3.50

WETWORKS
DC Comics (WildStorm): Nov, 2006 - Present ($2.99)

					NM-
1-12: 1-Carey-s/Portacio-a; two covers by Portacio and Van Sciver. 2-Golden var-c					
3-Pearson var-c. 4-Powell var-c					3.00

WETWORKS/VAMPIRELLA (See Vampirella/Wetworks)
Image Comics (WildStorm Productions): July, 1997 ($2.95, one-shot)

					NM-
1-Gil Kane-c					3.00

WHACK (Satire)
St. John Publishing Co. (Jubilee Publ.): Oct, 1953 - No. 3, May, 1954

	GD	VG	FN	VF	VF/NM	NM-
1-(3-D, 25¢)-Kubert-a; Maurer-c; came w/glasses	27	54	81	158	249	340
2,3-Kubert-a in each. 2-Bing Crosby on-c; Mighty Mouse & Steve Canyon parodies. 3-Li'l Orphan Annie parody; Maurer-c	15	30	45	84	127	170

WHACKY (See Wacky)
WHA...HUH?
Marvel Comics: 2005 ($3.99, one-shot)

					NM-
1-Humor spoofs of Marvel characters; Mahfood-a/c; Bendis, Stan Lee and others-s					4.00

WHAM COMICS (See Super Spy)
Centaur Publications: Nov, 1940 - No. 2, Dec, 1940

	GD	VG	FN	VF	VF/NM	NM-
1-The Sparkler, The Phantom Rider, Craig Carter and his Magic Ring, Detecto, Copper Slug, Speed Silvers by Gustavson, Speed Centaur & Jon Linton (s/f) begin	159	318	477	994	1647	2300
2-Origin Blue Fire & Solarman; The Buzzard app.	103	206	309	644	1072	1500

WHAM-O GIANT COMICS
Wham-O Mfg. Co. : April, 1967 (98¢, newspaper size, one-shot)(Six issue subscription was advertised)

	GD	VG	FN	VF	VF/NM	NM-
1-Radian & Goody Bumpkin by Wood; 1 pg. Stanley-a; Fine, Tufts-a; flying saucer reports; wraparound-c	8	16	24	56	93	130

WHAT IF? (1st Series) (What If? Featuring... #13 & #7-33)
Marvel Comics Group: No. 1, Feb - No. 47, Oct, 1984; June, 1988 (All 52 pgs.)

	GD	VG	FN	VF	VF/NM	NM-
1-Brief origin Spider-Man, Fantastic Four	3	6	9	16	23	30
2-Origin The Hulk retold	2	4	6	8	11	14
3-5: 3-Avengers. 4-Invaders. 5-Capt. America	1	3	4	6	8	10
6-10,13,17: 8-Daredevil; Spidey parody. 9-Origins Venus, Marvel Boy, Human Robot, 3-D Man. 13-Conan app.; John Buscema-c/a(p). 17-Ghost Rider & Son of Satan app.	1	2	3	5	7	9
11,12,14-16: 11-Marvel Bullpen app.						6.00
18-26,29: 18-Dr. Strange. 19-Spider-Man. 22-Origin Dr. Doom retold						5.00
27-X-Men app.; Miller-c	2	4	6	12	16	20
28-Daredevil by Miller; Ghost Rider app.	2	4	6	9	11	14
30- "What If...Spider-Man's Clone Had Lived?"	1	2	3	5	7	9
31-Begin $1.00-c; featuring Wolverine & the Hulk; X-Men app.; death of Hulk, Wolverine & Magneto	2	4	6	14	18	22
32-34,36-46: 32,36-Byrne-a. 34-Marvel crew each draw themselves. 37-Old X-Men & Silver Surfer app. 39-Thor battles Conan						4.00
35-What if Elektra had lived?; Miller/Austin-a.	1	2	3	5	6	8
Special 1 ($1.50, 6/88)-Iron Man, F.F., Thor app.						3.00
... Classic Vol. 1 TPB (2004, $24.99) r/#1-6; checklist						25.00
... Classic Vol. 2 TPB (2005, $24.99) r/#7-12						25.00
... Classic Vol. 3 TPB (2006, $24.99) r/#14,15,17-20						25.00

NOTE: *Austin a-27p, 32i, 34, 35i; c-35i, 36i.* *J. Buscema a-13p, 15p; c-10, 13p, 23p.* *Byrne a-32i, 36; c-36p.* *Colan a-21p; c-17p, 18p, 21p.* *Ditko a-35.* *Golden c-29, 40-42.* *Guice a-40p.* *Gil Kane a-3p, 3-9p, 24p; c(p)-*

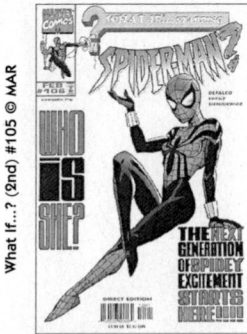

What If...? (2nd) #105 © MAR

What If Jessica Jones...? #1 © MAR

Where Monsters Dwell #2 © MAR

	GD 2.0	VG 4.0	FN 6.0	VF 8.0	VF/NM 9.0	NM- 9.2		GD 2.0	VG 4.0	FN 6.0	VF 8.0	VF/NM 9.0	NM- 9.2

2-4, 7, 8. **Kirby** a-11p; c-9p. 11p. **Layton** a-32i, 33i; c-30, 32p, 33j, 34. **Mignola** c-39i. **Miller** a-28p, 32i, 34(1), 35p; c-27, 28p. **Mooney** a-8i, 30i. **Perez** a-15p. **Robbins** a-4p. **Sienkiewicz** c-43-46. **Simonson** a-15p, 32i. **Starlin** a-32i. **Stevens** a-8, 16i(part). **Sutton** a-21p, 18p, 28. **Tuska** a-5p. **Weiss** a-37p.

WHAT IF...? (2nd Series)
Marvel Comics: V2#1, July, 1989 - No. 114, Nov, 1998 ($1.25/$1.50)

V2#1-...The Avengers Had Lost the Evol. War						4.00
2-5: 2-Daredevil, Punisher app.						3.00
6-X-Men app.						4.00
7-Wolverine app.; Liefeld-c/a(1st on Wolvie?)						5.00
8,10,11,13-15,17-30: 10-Punisher app. 11-Fantastic Four app.; McFarlane-c(i).13-Prof. X; Jim Lee.-c. 14-Capt. Marvel; Lim/Austin-c.15-F.F.; Capullo-c/a(p). 17-Spider-Man/Kraven. 18-F.F. 19-Vision. 20,21-Spider-Man. 22-Silver Surfer by Lim/Austin-c/a 23-X-Men. 24-Wolverine; Punisher app. 25-(52 pgs.)-Wolverine app. 26-Punisher app. 27-Namor/F.F. 28,29-Capt. America. 29-Swipes cover to Avengers #4. 30-(52 pgs.)-F.F.						3.00
9,12-X-Men						3.50
16-Wolverine battles Conan; Red Sonja app.; X-Men cameo						4.00
31-50: 31-Cosmic Spider-Man & Venom app.; Hobgoblin cameo. 32,33-Phoenix; X-Men app. 35-Fantastic Five w/Spidey). 36-Avengers vs. Guardians of the Galaxy. 37-Wolverine; Thibert-c(i). 38-Thor; Rogers-(part). 40-Storm; X-Men app. 41-(52 pgs.)-Avengers vs. Galactus. 42-Spider-Man. 43-Wolverine. 44-Venom/Punisher. 45-Ghost Rider. 46-Cable. 47-Magneto. 49-Infinity Gauntlet w/Silver Surfer & Thanos. 50-(52 pgs.)-Foil embossed-c; "What If Hulk Had Killed Wolverine"						3.00
51-(7/93) "What If the Punisher Became Captain America" (see it happen in 2007's Punisher War Journal #6-10)						6.00
52-104: 52-Dr. Doom. 54-Death's Head. 57-Punisher as Shield. 58-"What if Punisher Had Killed Spider-Man" w/cover similar to Amazing S-M #129. 59-...Wolverine led Alpha Flight. 60-X-Men Wedding Album. 61-Bound-in card sheet. 61,86,88-Spider-Man. 74,77,81,84,85-X-Men. 76-Last app. Watcher in title. 78-Bisley-c. 80-Hulk. 87-Sabretooth. 89-Fantastic Four. 90-Cyclops & Havok. 91-The Hulk. 93-Wolverine. 94-Juggernaut. 95-Ghost Rider. 100-($2.99, double-sized) Gambit and Rogue, Fantastic Four						3.00
105-Spider-Girl debut; Sienkiewicz-a	2	4	6	12	16	20
106-114: 106-Gambit. 108-Avengers. 111-Wolverine. 114-Secret Wars						2.50
#(-1) Flashback (7/97)						3.00

WHAT IF...? (one-shots)
Marvel Comics: Feb, 2005 ($2.99)

... Aunt May Had Died Instead of Uncle Ben? - Brubaker-s/DiVito-a/Brase-c						3.00
... Dr. Doom Had Become The Thing? - Karl Kesel-s/Paul Smith-a/c						3.00
... General Ross Had Become the Hulk? - Peter David-s/Pat Olliffe-a/Gary Frank-c						3.00
... Jessica Jones Had Joined The Avengers? - Bendis-s/Gaydos/McNiven-a						3.00
... Karen Page Had Lived? - Bendis-s/Lark-a/c						3.00
... Magneto and Professor X Had Formed The X-Men Together? - Claremont-s/Raney-a						3.00
What If...: Why Not? TPB (2005, $16.99) r/one-shots						17.00

WHAT IF... (one-shots)
Marvel Comics: Feb, 2006 ($2.99)

... : Captain America - Fought in the Civil War?; Bedard-s/Di Giandomenico-a						3.00
... : Daredevil - The Devil Who Dares; Daredevil in feudal Japan; Veitch-s/Edwards-a						3.00
... : Fantastic Four - Were Cosmonauts?; Marshall Rogers-a/c; Mike Carey-s						3.00
... : Submariner - Grew Up on Land?; Pak-s/Lopez-a						3.00
... : Thor - Was the Herald of Galactus?; Kirkman-s/Oeming-a/c						3.00
... : Wolverine - In the Prohibition Era; Way-s/Proctor-a/Harris-c						3.00
What If: Mirror Mirror TPB (2006, $16.99) r/one-shots; design pages and Rogers sketches						17.00

WHAT IF ?... (one-shots altering recent Marvel "event" series)
Marvel Comics: Jan, 2007 - Feb, 2007 ($3.99)

... Avengers Disassembled; Parker-s/Lopresti-a/c						4.00
... Spider-Man The Other; Peter David-s/Khoi Pham-a; Venom app.						4.00
... Wolverine Enemy of the State; Robinson-s/DiGiandomenico-a/Alexander-c						4.00
... X-Men Age of Apocalypse; Remeder-s/Wilkins-a/Djurdjevic-c						4.00
... X-Men Deadly Genesis; Hine-s/Yardin-a/c						4.00
What If?: Event Horizon TPB (2007, $16.99) r/one-shots; design pages and cover sketches						17.00

'WHAT'S NEW? - THE COLLECTED ADVENTURES OF PHIL & DIXIE'
Palliard Press: Oct, 1991 - No. 2, 1991 ($5.95, mostly color, sq.-bound, 52 pgs.)

1,2-By Phil Foglio						6.00

WHAT THE- -?!
Marvel Comics: Aug, 1988 - No. 26, 1993 ($1.25/$1.50/$2.50, semi-annual #5 on)

1-All contain parodies						3.00
2-24: 3-X-Men parody; Todd McFarlane-a. 5-Punisher/Wolverine parody; Jim Lee-a. 6-Punisher, Wolverine, Alpha Flight. 9-Wolverine. 16-EC back-c parody. 17-Wolverine/Punisher parody. 18-Star Trek parody w/Wolverine. 19-Punisher, Wolverine, Ghost Rider. 21-Weapon X parody. 22-Punisher/Wolverine parody						2.50
25-Summer Special 1 (1993, $2.50)-X-Men parody						2.50
26-Fall Special ($2.50, 68 pgs.)-Spider-Ham 2099-c/story; origin Silver Surfer; Hulk &						

Doomsday parody; indica reads "Winter Special."   2.50
NOTE: **Austin** a-6i. **Byrne** a-2, 6, 10; c-2, 6-8, 10, 12, 13. **Golden** a-22. **Dale Keown** a-8p(8 pgs.). **McFarlane** a-3. **Rogers** c-15i, 16p. **Severin** a-2. **Staton** a-21p. **Williamson** a-2i.

WHEE COMICS (Also see Gay, Smile & Tickle Comics)
Modern Store Publications: 1955 (7¢, 5x7-1/4", 52 pgs.)

	GD	VG	FN	VF	VF/NM	NM-
1-Funny animal	6	12	18	28	34	40

WHEEDIES (See Panic #11 -EC Comics)

WHEELIE AND THE CHOPPER BUNCH (TV)
Charlton Comics: July, 1975 - No. 7, July, 1976 (Hanna-Barbera)

	GD	VG	FN	VF	VF/NM	NM-
1-3: 1-Byrne text illo (see Nightmare for 1st art); Staton-a. 2-Byrne-a.						
2,3-Mike Zeck text illos. 3-Staton-a; Byrne-c/a	3	6	9	16	23	30
4-7-Staton-a	2	4	6	12	16	20

WHEN KNIGHTHOOD WAS IN FLOWER (See The Sword & the Rose, 4-Color #505, 682)

WHEN SCHOOL IS OUT (See Wisco in Promotional Comics section)

WHERE CREATURES ROAM
Marvel Comics Group: July, 1970 - No. 8, Sept, 1971

	GD	VG	FN	VF	VF/NM	NM-
1-Kirby/Ayers-c/a(r)	3	6	9	20	30	40
2-8: 2-5,7,8-Kirby-c/a(r). 6-Kirby-a(r)	3	6	9	16	22	28

NOTE: **Ditko** r-1-6, 7. **Heck** r-2, 5. All contain pre super-hero reprints.

WHERE IN THE WORLD IS CARMEN SANDIEGO (TV)
DC Comics: June, 1996 - No. 4, Dec, 1996 ($1.75)

1-4: Adaptation of TV show						2.50

WHERE MONSTERS DWELL
Marvel Comics Group: Jan, 1970 - No. 38, Oct, 1975

	GD	VG	FN	VF	VF/NM	NM-
1-Kirby/Ditko-r; all contain pre super-hero-r	4	8	12	22	34	45
2-10: 4-Crandall-a(r)	3	6	9	16	22	28
11,13-20: 11-Last 15¢ issue. 18,20-Starlin-c	2	4	6	13	18	22
12-Giant issue (52 pgs.)	3	6	9	18	27	35
21-37: 21-Reprints 1st Fin Fang Foom app.	2	4	6	10	14	18
38-Williamson-r/World of Suspense #3	2	4	6	13	18	22

NOTE: **Colan** r-12. **Ditko** a(r)-4, 6, 8, 10, 12, 17-19, 23-25, 37. **Kirby** r-1-3, 5-16, 18-27, 30-32, 34-36, 38; c-12? **Reinman** a-3r, 4r, 12? **Severin** c-15.

WHERE'S HUDDLES? (TV) (See Fun-In #9)
Gold Key: Jan, 1971 - No. 3, Dec, 1971 (Hanna-Barbera)

	GD	VG	FN	VF	VF/NM	NM-
1	3	6	9	19	29	38
2,3: 3-r/most #1	2	4	6	11	16	20

WHIP WILSON (Movie star) (Formerly Rex Hart; Gunhawk #12 on; see Western Hearts, Western Life Romances, Western Love)
Marvel Comics: No. 9, April, 1950 - No. 11, Sept, 1950 (#9,10: 52 pgs.)

	GD	VG	FN	VF	VF/NM	NM-
9-Photo-c; Whip Wilson & his horse Bullet begin; origin Bullet; issue #23 listed on splash page; cover changed to #9	53	106	159	323	529	735
10,11: Both have photo-c. 11-36 pgs.	30	60	90	174	275	375
I.W. Reprint #1(1964)-Kinstler-c; r-Marvel #11	3	6	9	16	22	28

WHIRLWIND COMICS (Also see Cyclone Comics)
Nita Publication: June, 1940 - No. 3, Sept, 1940

	GD	VG	FN	VF	VF/NM	NM-
1-Origin & 1st app. Cyclone; Cyclone-c	221	442	663	1381	2291	3200
2,3: Cyclone-c	103	206	309	644	1072	1500

WHIRLYBIRDS (TV)
Dell Publishing Co.: No. 1124, Aug, 1960 - No. 1216, Oct-Dec, 1961

	GD	VG	FN	VF	VF/NM	NM-
Four Color 1124 (#1)-Photo-c	8	16	24	56	93	130
Four Color 1216-Photo-c	8	16	24	52	86	120

WHISKEY DICKEL, INTERNATIONAL COWGIRL
Image Comics: Aug, 2003 ($12.95, softcover, B&W)

nn-Mark Ricketts-s/Mike Hawthorne-a; pin-up by various incl. Oeming, Thompson, Mack						13.00

WHISPER (Female Ninja)
Capital Comics: Dec, 1983 - No. 2, 1984 ($1.75, Baxter paper)

1,2: 1-Origin; Golden-c, Special (11/85, $2.50)						2.50

WHISPER (Vol. 2)
First Comics: Jun, 1986 - No. 37, June, 1990 ($1.25/$1.75/$1.95)

1-37						2.50

WHISPER
Boom! Studios: Nov, 2006 ($3.99)

1-Grant-s/Dzialowska-a						4.00

WHITE CHIEF OF THE PAWNEE INDIANS
Avon Periodicals: 1951

White Tiger #5 © MAR

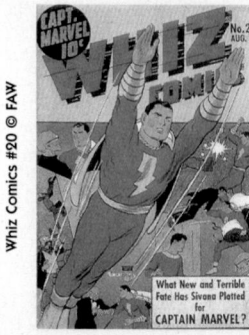

Whiz Comics #20 © FAW

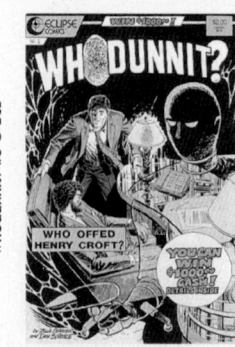

Whodunnit? #3 © ECL

	GD 2.0	VG 4.0	FN 6.0	VF 8.0	VF/NM 9.0	NM- 9.2
nn-Kit West app.; Kinstler-c	16	32	48	92	144	195

WHITE EAGLE INDIAN CHIEF (See Indian Chief)

WHITE FANG
Disney Comics: 1990 ($5.95, 68 pgs.)

nn-Graphic novel adapting new Disney movie						6.00

WHITE INDIAN
Magazine Enterprises: No. 11, July, 1953 - No. 15, 1954

	GD	VG	FN	VF	VF/NM	NM-
11-(A-1 94), 12(A-1 101), 13(A-1 104)-Frazetta-r(Dan Brand) in all from Durango Kid.						
11-Powell-c	23	46	69	130	205	280
14(A-1 117), 15(A-1 135)-Check-a; Torres-a-#15	14	28	42	76	108	140

NOTE: #11 contains reprints from Durango Kid #1-4; #12 from #5, 9, 10, 11; #13 from #7, 12, 13, 16. #14 & 15 contain all new stories.

WHITEOUT (Also see Queen & Country)
Oni Press: July, 1998 - No. 4, Nov, 1998 ($2.95, B&W, limited series)

1-4: 1-Matt Wagner-c. 2-Mignola-c. 3-Gibbons-c						3.00
TPB ($10.95) r/#1-4; Miller-c						11.00

WHITEOUT: MELT
Oni Press: Sept, 1999 - No. 4, Feb, 2000 ($2.95, B&W, limited series)

1-4-Greg Rucka-s/Steve Lieber-a						3.00

WHITE PRINCESS OF THE JUNGLE (Also see Jungle Adventures & Top Jungle Comics)
Avon Periodicals: July, 1951 - No. 5, Nov, 1952

	GD	VG	FN	VF	VF/NM	NM-
1-Origin of White Princess (Taanda) & Capt'n Courage (r); Kinstler-c						
	55	110	165	344	572	800
2-Reprints origin of Malu, Slave Girl Princess from Avon's Slave Girl Comics #1 w/Malu changed to Zora; Kinstler-c/a(2)	40	80	120	244	392	540
3-Origin Blue Gorilla; Kinstler-c/a	37	74	111	215	340	465
4-Jack Barnum, White Hunter app.; r/Sheena #9	32	64	96	186	293	400
5-Blue Gorilla by McCann?; Kinstler inside-c; Fawcette/Alascia-a(3)						
	34	68	102	197	311	425

WHITE RIDER AND SUPER HORSE (Formerly Humdinger V2#1; Indian Warriors #7 on; also see Blue Bolt #1, 4Most & Western Crime Cases)
Novelty-Star Publications/Accepted Publ.: No. 4, 9/50 - No. 6, 3/51

	GD	VG	FN	VF	VF/NM	NM-
4-6-Adapts "The Last of the Mohicans". 4(#1)-(9/50)-Says #11 on inside						
	16	32	48	92	144	195
Accepted Reprint #5(r/#5),6 (nd); L.B. Cole-c	9	18	27	50	65	80

NOTE: All have L. B. Cole covers.

WHITE TIGER
Marvel Comics: Jan, 2007 - No. 6, Nov, 2007 ($2.99, limited series)

1-6: 1-David Mack-c; Pierce & Liebe-s/Briones-a; Spider-Man & Black Widow app.						3.00
...: A Hero's Compulsion SC (2007,$14.99) r/#1-6; re-cap and profile page						15.00

WHITE WILDERNESS (Disney)
Dell Publishing Co.: No. 943, Oct, 1958

	GD	VG	FN	VF	VF/NM	NM-
Four Color 943-Movie	6	12	18	43	69	95

WHITMAN COMIC BOOK, A
Whitman Publishing Co.: Sept., 1962 (136 pgs.; 7-3/4x5-3/4; hardcover) (B&W)

	GD	VG	FN	VF	VF/NM	NM-
1-3,5,7: 1-Yogi Bear. 2-Huckleberry Hound. 3-Mr. Jinks and Pixie & Dixie. 5-Augie Doggie & Loopy de Loop. 7-Bugs Bunny-r from #47,51,53,54 & 55						
	6	12	18	43	69	95
4,6: 4-The Flintstones. 6-Snooper & Blabber Fearless Detectives/Quick Draw McGraw of the Wild West	7	14	21	47	76	105
8-Donald Duck-reprints most of WDC&S #209-213. Includes 5 Barks stories, 1 complete Mickey Mouse serial by Paul Murry & 1 Mickey Mouse serial missing the 1st episode						
	18	24	52	86	120	

NOTE: Hanna-Barbera #1-6(TV), reprints of British tabloid comics. Dell reprints-#7,8.

WHIZ COMICS (Formerly Flash & Thrill Comics #1)(See 5 Cent Comics)
Fawcett Publications: No. 2, Feb, 1940 - No. 155, June, 1953

	GD	VG	FN	VF	VF/NM	NM-
1-(nn on cover. #2 inside)-Origin & 1st newsstand app. Captain Marvel (formerly Captain Thunder) by C. C. Beck (created by Bill Parker), Spy Smasher, Golden Arrow, Ibis the Invincible, Dan Dare, Scoop Smith, Sivana, & Lance O'Casey begin						
	7000	14,000	21,000	40,000	67,500	95,000

(The only Mint copy sold in 1995 for $176,000 cash)

1-Reprint, oversize 13-1/2x10". **WARNING**: This comic is an exact duplicate reprint (except for dropping "Gangway for Captain Marvel" from-c) of the original except for its size. DC published in 1974 with a second cover titling it as a Famous First Edition. There have been many reported cases of the outer cover being removed and the interior sold as the original edition. The reprint with the new outer cover removed is practically worthless. See Famous First Edition for value.

	GD	VG	FN	VF	VF/NM	NM-
2-(3/40, nn on cover, #3 inside); cover to Flash #1 redrawn, pg. 12, panel 4; Spy Smasher reveals I.D. to Eve	457	914	1371	3200	5600	8000

	GD 2.0	VG 4.0	FN 6.0	VF 8.0	VF/NM 9.0	NM- 9.2
3-(4/40, #3 on-c, #4 inside)-1st app. Beautia	327	654	981	2126	3763	5400
4-(5/40, #4 on cover, #5 inside)-Brief origin Capt. Marvel retold						
	297	594	891	1856	3078	4300
5-Captain Marvel wears button-down flap on splash page only						
	248	496	744	1550	2575	3600
6-10: 7-Dr. Voodoo begins (by Raboy-#9-22)	183	366	549	1144	1897	2650
11-14: 12-Capt. Marvel does not wear cape	124	248	372	775	1288	1800
15-Origin Sivana; Dr. Voodoo by Raboy	133	266	399	831	1378	1925
16-18-Spy Smasher battles Captain Marvel	128	256	384	800	1325	1850
19,20	86	172	258	538	894	1250
21-(9/41)-Origin & 1st app. Lt. Marvels, the 1st team in Fawcett comics. In this issue, Capt. Death similar to Ditko's later Dr. Strange	91	182	273	569	947	1325
22-24: 23-Only Dr. Voodoo by Tuska	68	134	204	425	705	985
25-(12/41)-Captain Nazi jumps from Master Comics #21 to take on Capt. Marvel solo after being beaten by Capt. Marvel/Bulletman team, causing the creation of Capt. Marvel Jr.; 1st app./origin of Capt. Marvel Jr. (part II of trilogy origin by CC. Beck & Mac Raboy); Captain Marvel sends Jr. back to Master #22 to aid Bulletman against Capt. Nazi; origin old Shazam in text	543	1086	1629	3800	6650	9500
26-30	60	120	180	375	625	875
31,32: 32-1st app. The Trolls; Hitler/Mussolini satire by Beck						
	53	106	159	323	537	750
33-Spy Smasher, Captain Marvel x-over on cover and inside						
	60	120	180	375	625	875
34,36-40: 37-The Trolls app. by Swayze	40	80	120	240	383	525
35-Captain Marvel & Spy Smasher-c	49	98	147	299	492	685
41-50: 43-Spy Smasher, Ibis, Golden Arrow x-over in Capt. Marvel. 44-Flag-c. 47-Origin recap (1 pg.)	36	72	108	208	329	450
51-60: 52-Capt. Marvel x-over in Ibis. 57-Spy Smasher, Golden Arrow, Ibis cameo						
	29	58	87	170	268	365
61-70	27	54	81	158	249	340
71,77-80	26	52	78	150	235	320
72-76-Two Captain Marvel stories in each; 76-Spy Smasher becomes Crime Smasher						
	26	52	78	152	239	325
81-99: 86-Captain Marvel battles Sivana Family; robot-c. 91-Infinity-c						
	26	52	78	150	235	320
100-(8/48)-Anniversary issue	26	52	78	150	235	320
101-106: 102-Commando Yank app. 106-Bulletman app.						
	29	58	87	170	268	365
107-149: 107-Capitol Building photo-c. 108-Brooklyn Bridge photo-c. 112-Photo-c. 139-Infinity-c. 140-Flag-c. 142-Used in POP, pg. 89						
	25	50	75	145	228	310
150-152-(Low dist.)	25	50	75	145	228	310
153-155-(Scarce):154,155-1st/2nd Dr. Death stories	28	56	84	162	256	350
	37	74	111	213	337	460

NOTE: C.C. Beck Captain Marvel-No. 25(part). Krigstein Golden Arrow-No. 75, 78, 91, 95, 96, 98-100. Mac Raboy Dr. Voodoo-No. 9-22. Captain Marvel-No. 25(part). M.Swayze a-37, 38, 59; c-38. Schaffenberger c-138-155(most). Wolverton 1/2 pg. "Culture Corner"-No. 65-67, 68(2 1/2 pgs), 70-85, 87-96, 98-100, 102-109, 112-121, 123, 125, 126, 128-131, 133, 134, 136, 142, 143, 146.

WHIZ KIDS (Also see Big Bang Comics)
Image Comics: Apr, 2003 ($4.95, B&W, one-shot)

1-Galahad, Cyclone, Thunder Girl and Moray app.; Jeff Austin-a						5.00

WHOA, NELLIE (Also see Love & Rockets)
Fantagraphics Books: July, 1996 - No. 3, Sept, 1996 ($2.95, B&W, lim. series)

1-3: Jamie Hernandez-c/a/scripts						3.00

WHODUNIT
D.S. Publishing Co.: Aug-Sept, 1948 - No. 3, Dec-Jan, 1948-49 (#1,2: 52 pgs.)

	GD	VG	FN	VF	VF/NM	NM-
1-Baker-a (7 pgs.)	24	48	72	139	220	300
2,3-Detective mysteries	13	26	39	74	105	135

WHODUNNIT?
Eclipse Comics: June, 1986 - No. 3, Apr, 1987 ($2.00, limited series)

1-3: Spiegle-a. 2-Gulacy-c						2.50

WHO FRAMED ROGER RABBIT (See Marvel Graphic Novel)

WHO IS NEXT?
Standard Comics: No. 5, Jan, 1953

	GD	VG	FN	VF	VF/NM	NM-
5-Toth, Sekowsky, Andru-c; crime stories	20	40	60	117	184	250

WHO IS THE CROOKED MAN?
Crusade: Sept, 1996 ($3.50, B&W, 40 pgs.)

1-Intro The Martyr, Scarlet 7 & Garrison						3.50

WHO'S MINDING THE MINT? (See Movie Classics)

WHO'S WHO IN STAR TREK
DC Comics: Mar, 1987 - #2, Apr, 1987 ($1.50, limited series)

Wilbur Comics #6 © AP

Wild Boy of the Congo #5 © Z-D

WildC.A.Ts #27 © WSP

	GD 2.0	VG 4.0	FN 6.0	VF 8.0	VF/NM 9.0	NM- 9.2

1,2 .... 6.00
NOTE: *Byrne a-1, 2. Chaykin c-1, 2. Morrow a-1, 2. McFarlane a-2. Perez a-1. Sutton a-1, 2.*

WHO'S WHO IN THE LEGION OF SUPER-HEROES
DC Comics: Apr, 1987 - No. 7, Nov, 1988 ($1.25, limited series)
1-7 .... 4.00

WHO'S WHO: THE DEFINITIVE DIRECTORY OF THE DC UNIVERSE
DC Comics: Mar, 1985 - No. 26, Apr, 1987 (Maxi-series, no ads)
1-DC heroes from A-Z 4.00
2-26: All have 1-2 pgs-a by most DC artists 4.00
NOTE: *Adams a-4, 11, 18, 20. Anderson a-1-5, 7-12, 14, 15, 19, 21, 23-25. Aparo a-2, 3, 9, 10, 12, 13, 14, 15, 17, 18, 21, 23. Byrne a-4, 7, 14, 16, 18i, 19, 22i, 24; c-22. Cowan a-3-5, 8, 10-13, 16-18, 22-25. Ditko a-19-22. Evans a-20. Giffen a-1, 3, 6, 8, 13, 15, 17, 18, 23. Grell a-6, 9, 14, 20, 23, 25, 26. Infantino a-1-10, 12, 15, 17-22, 24, 25. Kaluta a-14, 21. Gil Kane a-1-11, 13, 14, 16, 19, 21-23, 25. Kirby a-2-6, 8-18, 20, 22, 25. Kubert a-2, 3, 7-11, 19, 20, 25. Erik Larsen a-24. McFarlane a-10-12, 17, 19, 20. Morrow a-4, 7, 25, 26. Orlando a-1, 4, 10, 11, 21i. Perez a-1-5, 8-19, 22-26; c-1-4, 13-18. Rogers a-1, 2, 5-7, 11, 12, 15, 24. Starlin a-13, 14, 16. Stevens a-4, 7, 18.*

WHO'S WHO UPDATE '87
DC Comics: Aug, 1987 - No. 5, Dec, 1987 ($1.25, limited series)
1-5: Contains art by most DC artists 3.00
NOTE: *Giffen a-1. McFarlane a-1-4; c-4. Perez a-1-4.*

WHO'S WHO UPDATE '88
DC Comics: Aug, 1988 - No. 4, Nov, 1988 ($1.25, limited series)
1-4: Contains art by most DC artists 3.00
NOTE: *Giffen a-1. Erik Larsen a-1.*

WICKED, THE
Avalon Studios: Dec, 1999 - No. 7, Aug, 2000 ($2.95)
Preview (7/99, $5.00, B&W) 5.00
1-7-Anacleto-c/Martinez-a 3.00
...: Medusa's Tale (11/00, $3.95, one shot) story plus pin-up gallery 4.00
...: Vol. 1: Omnibus (2003, $19.95) #/#0-8; Drew-c 20.00

WICKED WEST, THE
Image Comics: Oct, 2004 - Present ($9.95/$15.99, graphic novel)
1-Neil Vokes-a/Todd Livingston & Robert Tinnell-s; vampires in the Wild West 10.00
Vol. 2: Abomination & Other Tales ($15.99) s/a by various 16.00

WILBUR COMICS (Teen-age) (Also see Laugh Comics, Laugh Comix, Liberty Comics #10 & Zip Comics)
MLJ Magazines/Archie Publ. No. 8, Spring, 1946 on: Sum', 1944 - No. 87, 11/59; No. 88, 9/63; No. 89, 10/64; No. 90, 10/65 (No. 1-46: 52 pgs.) (#11-41 are quarterly)

	GD	VG	FN	VF	VF/NM	NM-
1	53	106	159	323	537	750
2(Fall, 1944)	29	58	87	170	268	365
3,4(Wint, '44-45; Spr, '45)	21	42	63	122	191	260

5-1st app. Katy Keene (Sum, '45) & begin series; Wilbur story same as Archie story in Archie #1 except Wilbur replaces Archie

	100	200	300	625	1038	1450
6-10: 10-(Fall, 1946)	24	48	72	139	220	300
11-20	15	30	45	86	133	180
21-30: 30-(4/50)	11	22	33	62	86	110
31-50	9	18	27	52	69	85
51-70	8	16	24	44	57	70
71-90: 88-Last 10¢ issue (9/63)	4	8	12	26	41	55

NOTE: *Katy Keene in No. 5-56, 58-61, 63-69. Al Fagaly c-6-9, 12-24 at least. Vigoda c-2.*

WILD
Atlas Comics (IPC): Feb, 1954 - No. 5, Aug, 1954

	GD	VG	FN	VF	VF/NM	NM-
1	26	52	78	152	239	325
2	15	30	45	90	140	190
3-5	15	30	45	83	124	165

NOTE: *Berg a-5; c-4. Burgos c-3. Colan a-4. Everett a-1-3. Heath a-2, 3, 5. Maneely a-1-3, 5; c-1, 5. Post a-2, 5. Ed Win a-1, 3.*

WILD (This Magazine Is...) (Satire)
Dell Publishing Co.: Jan, 1968 - No. 3, 1968 (Magazine, 52 pgs.)

	GD	VG	FN	VF	VF/NM	NM-
1-3	3	6	9	14	19	24

WILD ANIMALS
Pacific Comics: Dec, 1982 ($1.00, one-shot, direct sales)
1-Funny animal; Sergio Aragones-a; Shaw-c/a 4.00

WILD BILL ELLIOTT (Also see Western Roundup under Dell Giants)
Dell Publishing Co.: No. 278, 5/50 - No. 643, 7/55 (No #11,12) (All photo-c)
Four Color 278(#1, 52pgs.)-Titled "Bill Elliott"; Bill & his horse Stormy begin;
photo front/back-c begin

	13	26	39	90	160	230
2 (11/50), 3 (52 pgs.)	8	16	24	52	86	120
4-10(10-12/52)	6	12	18	41	66	90

	GD	VG	FN	VF	VF/NM	NM-
Four Color 472(6/53),520(12/53)-Last photo back-c	5	10	15	35	55	75
13(4-6/54) - 17(4-6/55)	5	10	15	32	51	70
Four Color 643 (7/55)	5	10	15	30	48	65

WILD BILL HICKOK (Also see Blazing Sixguns)
Avon Periodicals: Sept-Oct, 1949 - No. 28, May-June, 1956

	GD	VG	FN	VF	VF/NM	NM-
1-Ingels-c	23	46	69	135	213	290
2-Painted-c; Kit West app.	13	26	39	74	105	135
3-5-Painted-c (4-Cover by Howard Winfield)	10	20	30	54	72	90
6-10,12: 8-10-Painted-c. 12-Kinstler-c	10	20	30	54	72	90
11,13,14-Kinstler-c/a (#11-c & inside-f/c art only)	10	20	30	58	79	100
15,17,18,20: 18-Kit West story. 20-Kit West by Larsen						
	9	18	27	47	61	75
16-Kamen-a; r-3 stories/King of the Badmen of Deadwood						
	9	18	27	50	65	80
19-Meskin-a	9	18	27	47	61	75
21-Reprints 2 stories/Chief Crazy Horse	8	16	24	44	57	70
22-McCann-a?; r/Sheriff Bob Dixon's...	8	16	24	44	57	70
23-27: 23-Kinstler-c. 24-27-Kinstler-c/a(r) (24,25-r?)	8	16	24	44	57	70
28-Kinstler-c/a (new); r-/Last of the Comanches	9	18	27	47	61	75
I.W. Reprint #1-r/#2; Kinstler-c	2	4	6	9	13	16
Super Reprint #10-12: r/#10-r/#18. 11-r/#?. 12-r/#8	2	4	6	9	13	16

NOTE: *#23, 25 contain numerous editing deletions in both art and script due to code. Kinstler c-6, 7, 11-14, 17, 18, 20-22, 24-28. Howard Larsen a-1, 2, 4, 5, 6(3), 7-9, 11, 12, 17, 18, 20-24, 26. Meskin a-7. Reinman a-6, 17.*

WILD BILL HICKOK AND JINGLES (TV)(Formerly Cowboy Western) (Also see Blue Bird)
Charlton Comics: No. 68, Aug, 1958 - No. 75, Dec, 1959

	GD	VG	FN	VF	VF/NM	NM-
68,69-Williamson-a (all are 10¢ issues)	11	22	33	60	83	105
70-Two pgs. Williamson-a	8	16	24	42	54	65
71-75 (#76, exist?)	6	12	18	28	34	40

WILD BILL PECOS WESTERN (Also see The Westerner)
AC Comics: 1989 ($3.50, 1/2 color/1/2 B&W, 52 pgs.)
1-Syd Shores-c/a(r)/Westerner; photo back-c 4.00

WILD BOY OF THE CONGO (Also see Approved Comics)
Ziff-Davis No. 10-12,4-8/St. John No. 9,11 on: No. 10, 2-3/51 - No. 12, 8-9/51; No. 4, 10-11/51 - No. 9, 10/53; No. 11-#15,6/55 (No #10, 1953)

10(#1)(2-3/51)-Origin; bondage-c by Saunders (painted); used in SOTI,
pg. 189; painted-c begin, end #9

	23	46	69	135	213	290
11(4-5/51),12(8-9/51)-Norman Saunders painted-c	14	28	42	76	108	140
4(10-11/51)-Saunders painted bondage-c	14	28	42	76	108	140
5(Winter,'51)-Saunders painted-c	12	24	36	67	94	120
6,8,9(10/53): 6-Saunders-c. 6-9-Painted-c	12	24	36	67	94	120
7(8-9/52)-Kinstler-c	14	28	42	76	108	140
11-13-Baker-c. 11-r/#7 w/new Baker-c; Kinstler-a (2 pgs.)						
	14	28	42	82	121	160
14(4/55)-Baker-c; r-#12('51)	14	28	42	82	121	160
15(6/55)	10	20	30	56	76	95

WILDCAT (See Sensation Comics #1)

WILDC.A.T.S ADVENTURES (TV cartoon)
Image Comics (WildStorm): Sept, 1994 - No. 10, June, 1995 ($1.95/$2.50)
1-10 .... 2.50
Sourcebook 1 (1/95, $2.95) 3.00

WILDC.A.T.S: COVERT ACTION TEAMS (Also see Alan Moore's... for TPB reprints)
Image Comics (WildStorm Productions): Aug, 1992 - No. 4, Mar, 1993; No. 5, Nov, 1993 - No. 50, June, 1998 ($1.95/$2.50)
1-1st app; Jim Lee/Williams-c/a & Lee scripts begin; contains 2 trading cards (Two diff versions of cards inside); 1st WildStorm Productions title 4.50
1-All gold foil signed edition 12.00
1-All gold foil unsigned edition 8.00
1-Newsstand edition w/o cards 5.00
1-"3-D Special"(8/97, $4.95) w/3-D glasses; variant-c by Jim Lee. 5.00
2-($2.50)-Prism foil stamped-c; contains coupon for Image Comics #0 & 4 pg. preview to Portacio's Wetworks (back-p) 4.50
2-With coupon missing 2.25
2-Direct sale misprint w/o foil-c 3.00
2-Newsstand ed., no prism or coupon 2.50
3-Lee/Liefeld-c (1/93-c, 12/92 inside) 3.50
4-($2.50)-Polybagged w/Topps trading card; 1st app. Tribe by Johnson & Stroman; Youngblood cameo 3.50
4-Variant w/red card 6.00
5-7-Jim Lee/Williams-c/a; Lee script 3.00
8-X-Men's Jean Grey & Scott Summers cameo 4.00

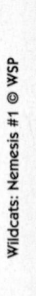

Wildcats V2 #24 © WSP

Wildcats: Nemesis #1 © WSP

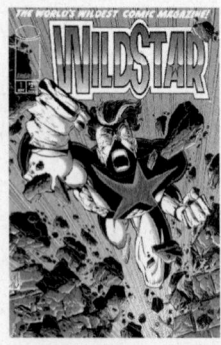

Wildstar #1 © Gordon & Ordway

	GD	VG	FN	VF	VF/NM	NM-
	2.0	4.0	6.0	8.0	9.0	9.2

9-12: 10-1st app. Huntsman & Soldier; Claremont scripts begin, ends #13.
11-1st app. Savant, Tapestry & Mr. Majestic. — 3.00
11-Alternate Portacio-c, see Deathblow #5 — 5.00
13-19,21-24: 15-James Robinson scripts begin, ends #20. 15,16-Black Razor story.
  21-Alan Moore scripts begin, end #34; intro Tao & Ladytron; new WildC.A.T.S team forms
  (Mr. Majestic, Savant, Condition Red (Max Cash), Tao & Ladytron). 22-Maguire-a — 3.00
20-($2.50)-Direct Market, WildStorm Rising Pt. 2 w/bound-in card — 3.00
20-($1.95)-Newsstand, WildStorm Rising Part 2 — 2.50
25-($4.95-Alan Moore script; wraparound foil-c. — 5.00
26-49: 29-(5/96)-Fire From Heaven Pt 7; reads Apr on-c. 30-(6/96)-Fire From Heaven Pt. 13;
  Spartan revealed to have transplanted personality of John Colt (from Team One:
  WildC.A.T.S). 31-(9/96)-Grifter rejoins team; Ladytron dies — 2.50
40-($3.50)Voyager Pack bagged w/Divine Right preview — 6.00
50-($3.50) Stories by Robinson/Lee, Choi & Peterson/Benes, and Moore/Charest; Charest
  sketchbook; Lee wraparound-c — 4.00
50-Chromium cover — 6.00
Annual 1 (2/98, $2.95) Robinson-s — 3.00
Compendium (1993, $9.95)-r/#1-4; bagged w/#0 — 10.00
Sourcebook 1 (9/93, $2.50)-Foil embossed-c — 2.50
Sourcebook 1-($1.95)-Newsstand ed. w/o foil embossed-c — 2.50
Sourcebook 2 (11/94, $2.50)-wraparound-c — 2.50
Special 1 (11/93, $3.50, 52 pgs.)-1st Travis Charest WildC.A.T.S-a — 3.50
...A Gathering of Eagles (5/97, $9.95, TPB) r/#10-12 — 10.00
.../ Cyberforce: Killer Instinct TPB (2004, $14.95) r/#5-7 & Cyberforce V2 #1-3 — 15.00
...Gang War ('98, $16.95, TPB) r/#28-34 — 17.00
...Homecoming (8/98, $19.95, TPB) r/#21-27 — 20.00

WILDCATS
DC Comics (WildStorm): Mar, 1999 - No. 28, Dec, 2001 ($2.50)
1-Charest-a; six covers by Lee, Adams, Bisley, Campbell, Madureira and Ramos;
  Lobdell-s — 3.00
1-($6.95) DF Edition; variant cover by Ramos — 7.00
2-28: 2-Voodoo cover. 3-Bachalo variant-c. 5-Hitch-a/variant-c. 7-Meglia-a. 8-Phillips-c
  begins. 17-J.G. Jones-c. 18,19-Jim Lee-c. 20,21-Dillon-a — 2.50
Annual 2000 (12/00, $3.50) Bermejo-a; Devil's Night x-over — 3.50
...: Battery Park ('03, $17.95, TPB) r/#20-28; Phillips-c — 18.00
... Ladytron (10/00, $5.95) Origin; Casey-s/Canete-a — 6.00
... Mosaic (2/00, $3.95) Tuska-a (10 pg. back-up story) — 4.00
...: Serial Boxes ('01, $14.95) TPB r/#14-19; Phillips-a — 15.00
...: Street Smart ('00, $24.95, HC) r/#1-6; Charest-c — 25.00
...: Street Smart ('02, $14.95, SC) r/#1-6; Charest-c — 15.00
...: Vicious Circles ('00, $14.95, TPB) r/#8-13; Phillips-a — 15.00

WILDCATS (Volume 4)
DC Comics (WildStorm): Dec, 2006 - Present ($2.99)
1-Grant Morrison-s/Jim Lee-a; Jim Lee-c — 3.00
1-Variant-c by Todd McFarlane/Jim Lee — 6.00

WILDC.A.T.S/ ALIENS
Image Comics/Dark Horse: Aug, 1998 ($4.95, one-shot)

	1	2	3	5	6	8
1-Ellis-s/Sprouse-a/c; Aliens invade Skywatch; Stormwatch app.; death of Winter; destruction of Skywatch	1	2	3	5	6	8
1-Variant-c by Gil Kane	1	3	4	6	8	10

WILDCATS: NEMESIS
DC Comics (WildStorm): Nov, 2005 - No. 9, July, 2006 ($2.99, limited series)
1-9: 1-Robbie Morrison-s/Talent Caldwell & Horacio Domingues-a/Caldwell-c — 3.00
TPB (2006, $19.99) r/#1-9; cover gallery — 20.00

WILDC.A.T.S: SAVANT GARDE FAN EDITION
Image Comics/WildStorm Productions: Feb, 1997 - No. 3, Apr, 1997 (Giveaway, 8 pgs.)
(Polybagged w/Overstreet's FAN)
1-3: Barbara Kesel-s/Christian Uche-a(p) — 3.00
1-3: (Gold) All retailer incentives — 10.00

WILDC.A.T.S TRILOGY
Image Comics (WildStorm Productions): June, 1993 - No. 3, Dec, 1993 ($1.95, lim. series)
1-($2.50)-1st app. Gen 13 (Fairchild, Burnout, Grunge, Freefall) Multi-color foil-c;
  Jae Lee-c/a in all — 5.00
1-($1.95)-Newsstand ed. w/o foil-c — 2.50
2,3-($1.95)-Jae Lee-c/a — 2.50

WILDCATS VERSION 3.0
DC Comics (WildStorm): Oct, 2002 - No. 24, Oct, 2004 ($2.95)
1-24: 1-Casey-s/Nguyen-a; two covers by Nguyen and Rian Hughes and Nguyen.
  8-Back-up preview of The Authority: High Stakes pt. 3 — 3.00
...: Brand Building TPB (2003, $14.95) r/#1-6 — 15.00

...: Full Disclosure TPB (2004, $14.95) r/#7-12 — 15.00

WILDC.A.T.S/ X-MEN: THE GOLDEN AGE (See also X-Men/WildC.A.T.S: The Dark Age)
Image Comics (WildStorm Productions): Feb, 1997 ($4.50, one-shot)
1-Lobdell-s/Charest-a; Two covers (Charest, Jim Lee) — 5.00
1-"3-D" Edition ($6.50) w/glasses — 7.00

WILDC.A.T.S/ X-MEN: THE MODERN AGE
Image Comics (WildStorm Productions): Aug, 1997 ($4.50, one-shot)
1-Robinson-s/Hughes-a; Two covers (Hughes, Paul Smith) — 5.00
1-"3-D" Edition ($6.50) w/glasses — 7.00

WILDC.A.T.S/ X-MEN: THE SILVER AGE
Image Comics (WildStorm Productions): June, 1997 ($4.50, one-shot)
1-Lobdell-s/Jim Lee-a; Two covers(Neal Adams, Jim Lee) — 5.00
1-"3-D" Edition ($6.50) w/glasses — 7.00

WILDCORE
Image Comics (WildStorm Prods.): Nov, 1997 - No. 10, Dec, 1998 ($2.50)
1-10: 1-Two covers (Booth/McWeeney, Charest) — 2.50
1-($3.50)-Voyager Pack w/DV8 preview — 3.50
1-Chromium-c — 5.00

WILD DOG
DC Comics: Sept, 1987 - No. 4, Dec, 1987 (75¢, limited series)
1-4 — 2.50
Special 1 (1989, $2.50, 52 pgs.) — 2.50

WILDERNESS TREK (See Zane Grey, Four Color 333)

WILDFIRE (See Zane Grey, FourColor 433)

WILDFLOWER
Sirius Entertainment/Neko Press: 1996 - Present (B&W)
1-5-('96, $2.50) Billy Martinez-s/a — 2.50
... Beginnings TPB (Neko Press, 2003, $14.99) r/#1-5 — 15.00
... Dark Euphoria 1 (2004, $2.99) Kiethan Jones-a/c; Martinez-s — 3.00
... Dark Euphoria 1,2 (2004, $3.99) w/alternate-c by Martinez — 4.00
... Tribal Screams 1-4 (10/00 - 2/03, $2.99) — 3.00
... Tribal Screams 1 ($4.99) w/alternate-c by Dark One — 5.00
... Y2K (16 pgs, edition of 2000) each contains an original Martinez sketch — 10.00

WILD FRONTIER (Cheyenne Kid #8 on)
Charlton Comics: Oct, 1955 - No. 7, Apr, 1957

	GD	VG	FN	VF	VF/NM	NM-
1-Davy Crockett	10	20	30	54	72	90
2-6-Davy Crockett in all	7	14	21	37	46	55
7-Origin & 1st app. Cheyenne Kid	9	18	27	47	61	75

WILD GIRL
DC Comics (WildStorm): Jan, 2005 - No. 6, Jun, 2005 ($2.95/$2.99)
1-6-Leah Moore & John Reppion-s/Shawn McManus-a/c — 3.00

WILDGUARD: CASTING CALL
Image Comics: Sept, 2003 - No. 6, Feb, 2004 ($2.95)
1-6: 1-Nauck-s/a; two covers by Nauck and McGuinness. 2-Wieringo var-c. 6-Noto var-c — 3.00
... Vol. 1: Casting Call (1/05, $17.95, TPB) r/#1-6; cover gallery; Todd Nauck bio — 18.00
Wildguard: Fire Power 1 (12/04, $3.50) Nauck-a; two covers — 3.50

WILDGUARD: FOOL'S GOLD
Image Comics: July, 2005 - No. 2, July, 2005 ($3.50, bi-weekly limited series)
1,2-Todd Nauck-s/a — 3.50

WILDSIDERZ
DC Comics (WildStorm): No. 0, Aug, 2005 - Present ($1.99/$3.50)
0-(8/05, $1.99) Series preview & character profiles; J. Scott Campbell-a — 2.50
1,2: 1-(10/05, $3.50) J. Scott Campbell-s/a; Andy Hartnell-s — 3.50

WILDSTAR (Also see The Dragon & The Savage Dragon)
Image Comics (Highbrow Entertainment): Sept, 1995 - No. 3, Jan, 1996 ($2.50, lim. series)
1-3: Al Gordon scripts; Jerry Ordway-c/a — 2.50

WILDSTAR: SKY ZERO
Image Comics (Highbrow Entertainment): Mar, 1993 - No. 4, Nov, 1993 ($1.95, lim. series)
1-4: 1-($2.50)-Embossed-c w/silver ink; Ordway-c/a in all — 2.50
1-($1.95)-Newsstand ed. w/silver ink-c, not embossed — 2.50
1-Gold variant — 6.00

WILD STARS
Collector's Edition/Little Rocket Productions: Summer, 1984 - Present (B&W)
Vol. 1 #1 (Summer 1984, $1.50) — 5.00

Wild Thing #1 © MAR

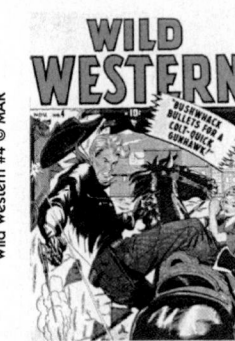

Wild Western #4 © MAR

Wild Wild West #1 © CBS

	GD 2.0	VG 4.0	FN 6.0	VF 8.0	VF/NM 9.0	NM- 9.2

Vol. 2 #1 (Winter 1988, $1.95) Foil-c; die-cut front & back-c — 5.00
Vol. 3: #1-6-Brunner-c; Tierney-s. 1,2-Brewer-a. 3-6-Simons-a — 3.00
   7-($5.95) Simons-a — 6.00
TPB (2004, $17.95) r/Vol. 1-3 — 18.00

WILDSTORM
Image Comics/DC Comics (WildStorm Publishing): 1994-2001 (one-shots)
...Annual 2000 (12/00, $3.50) Devil's Night x-over; Moy-a — 3.50
...Chamber of Horrors (10/95, $3.50)-Bisley-c — 3.50
...Fine Arts: Spotlight on Jim Lee (2/07, $3.50) art and covers by Lee with commentary — 3.50
...Fine Arts: Spotlight on J. Scott Campbell (5/07, $3.50) art and covers with commentary — 3.50
...Fine Arts: The Gallery Collection (12/98, $19.95) Lee-c — 20.00
...Halloween 1 (10/97, $2.50) Warner-c — 2.50
...Rarities 1(12/94, $4.95, 52 pgs.)-r/Gen 13 1/2 & other stories — 5.00
...Summer Special 1 (2001, $5.95) Short stories by various; Hughes-c — 6.00
...Swimsuit Special 1 (12/94, $2.95), ...Swimsuit Special 2 (1995, $2.50) — 3.00
...Swimsuit Special '97 #1 (7/97, $2.50) — 2.50
...Thunderbook 1 (10/00, $6.95) Short stories by various incl. Hughes, Moy — 7.00
...Ultimate Sports 1 (8/97, $2.50) — 2.50
...Universe Sourcebook (5/95, $2.50) — 2.50

WILDSTORM!
Image Comics (WildStorm Publishing): Aug, 1995 - No. 4, Nov, 1995 ($2.50, B&W/color, anthology)
1-4: 1-Simonson-a — 2.50

WILDSTORM RISING
Image Comics (WildStorm Publishing): May, 1995 - No.2, June, 1995 ($1.95/$2.50)
1-($2.50)-Direct Market, WildStorm Rising Pt. 1 w/bound-in card — 2.50
1-($1.95)-Newsstand, WildStorm Rising Pt. 1 — 2.50
2-($2.50)-Direct Market, WildStorm Rising Pt. 10 w/bound-in card; continues in WildC.A.T.S #21. — 2.50
2-($1.95)-Newsstand, WildStorm Rising Pt. 10 — 2.50
Trade paperback (1996, $19.95)-Collects x-over; B. Smith-c — 20.00

WILDSTORM SPOTLIGHT
Image Comics (WildStorm Publishing): Feb, 1997 - No. 4 ($2.50)
1-4: 1-Alan Moore-s — 2.50

WILDSTORM UNIVERSE '97
Image Comics (WildStorm Publishing): Dec, 1996 - No. 3 ($2.50, limited series)
1-3: 1-Wraparound-c. 3-Gary Frank-c — 2.50

WILDTHING
Marvel Comics UK: Apr, 1993 - No. 7 Oct, 1993 ($1.75)
1-($2.50)-Embossed-c; Venom & Carnage cameo — 2.50
2-7: 2-Spider-Man & Venom. 6-Mysterio app. — 2.50

WILD THING (Wolverine's daughter in the M2 universe)
Marvel Comics: Oct, 1999 - No. 5, Feb, 2000 ($1.99)
1-5: 1-Lim-a in all. 2-Two covers — 2.50
Wizard #0 supplement; battles the Hulk — 2.50
Spider-Girl Presents Wild Thing: Crash Course (2007, $7.99, digest) r/#0-5 — 8.00

WILDTIMES
DC Comics (WildStorm Productions): Aug, 1999 ($2.50, one-shots)
...Deathblow #1 -set in 1899; Edwards-a; Jonah Hex app., ...DV8 #1 -set in 1944; Altieri-s/p;
  Sgt. Rock app., ...Gen13 #1 -set in 1969; Casey-s/Johnson-a; Teen Titans app.,
  ...Grifter #1 -set in 1923; Paul Smith-a, ...Wetworks -Waid-s/Lopresti-a; Superman app. — 2.50
...WildC.A.T.s #0 -Wizard supplement; Charest-c — 2.50

WILD WEST (Wild Western #3 on)
Marvel Comics (WFP): Spring, 1948 - No. 2, July, 1948
1-Two-Gun Kid, Arizona Annie, & Tex Taylor begin; Shores-c
| | 34 | 68 | 102 | 197 | 311 | 425 |
2-Captain Tootsie by Beck; Shores-c
| | 23 | 46 | 69 | 130 | 205 | 280 |

WILD WEST (Black Fury #1-57)
Charlton Comics: V2#58, Nov, 1966
V2#58
| | 2 | 4 | 6 | 11 | 16 | 20 |

WILD WEST C.O.W.-BOYS OF MOO MESA (TV)
Archie Comics: Dec, 1992 - No. 3, Feb, 1993 (limited series)
V2#1, Mar, 1993 - No. 3, July, 1993 ($1.25)
1-3,V2#1-3 — 2.50

WILD WESTERN (Formerly Wild West #1,2)
Marvel/Atlas (WFP): No. 3, 9/48 - No. 57, 9/57 (3-11: 52 pgs, 12-on: 36 pgs)

3(#1)-Tex Morgan begins; Two-Gun Kid, Tex Taylor, & Arizona Annie continue from Wild West
| | 27 | 54 | 81 | 158 | 249 | 340 |
4-Last Arizona Annie; Captain Tootsie by Beck; Kid Colt app.
| | 20 | 40 | 60 | 115 | 180 | 245 |
5-2nd app. Black Rider (1/49); Blaze Carson, Captain Tootsie (by Beck) app.
| | 23 | 46 | 69 | 130 | 205 | 280 |
6-8: 6-Blaze Carson app; anti-Wertham editorial | 15 | 30 | 45 | 88 | 137 | 185 |
9-Photo-c; Black Rider begins, ends #19 | 19 | 38 | 57 | 109 | 172 | 235 |
10-Charles Starrett photo-c | 22 | 44 | 66 | 126 | 198 | 270 |
11-(Last 52 pg. issue) | 15 | 30 | 45 | 85 | 130 | 175 |
12-14,16-19: All Black Rider-c/stories. 12-14-The Prairie Kid & his horse Fury app.
| | 15 | 30 | 45 | 83 | 124 | 165 |
15-Red Larabee, Gunhawk (origin), his horse Blaze, & Apache Kid begin, end #22;
  Black Rider-c/story | 15 | 30 | 45 | 84 | 127 | 170 |
20-30: 20-Kid Colt-c begins. 24-Has 2 Kid Colt stories. 26-1st app. The Ringo Kid? (2/53);
  4 pg. story. 30-Katz-a | 12 | 24 | 36 | 69 | 97 | 125 |
31-40 | 10 | 20 | 30 | 54 | 72 | 90 |
41-47,49-51,53,57 | 9 | 18 | 27 | 47 | 61 | 75 |
48-Williamson/Torres-a (4 pgs); Drucker-a | 10 | 20 | 30 | 56 | 76 | 95 |
52-Crandall-a | 10 | 20 | 30 | 56 | 76 | 95 |
54,55-Williamson-a in both (5 & 4 pgs.), #54 with Mayo plus 2 text illos
| | 10 | 20 | 30 | 56 | 76 | 95 |
56-Baker-a? | 9 | 18 | 27 | 47 | 61 | 75 |
NOTE: Annie Oakley in #46, 47. Apache Kid in #15-22, 39. Arizona Kid in #21, 23. Arrowhead in #34-39. Black Rider in #5, 9-19, 33-44. Fighting Texan in #17. Kid Colt in #4-6, 9-11, 20-47, 52, 54-56. Outlaw Kid in #43. Red Hawkins in #13, 14. Ringo Kid in #26, 39, 41, 43, 44, 46, 47, 50, 52-56. Tex Morgan in #3, 4, 6, 9, 11. Tex Taylor in #3-6, 9, 11. Texas Kid in #23-25. Two-Gun Kid in #3-6, 9, 11, 12, 33-39, 41. Wyatt Earp in #47. Ayers a-41, 42, 53, 54. Berg a-26; c-24. Colan a-49. Forte a-28, 30. Al Hartley a-16. Heath a-4, 5, 8; c-34, 44. Keller a-24, 26(2), 29-40, 44-46, 48, 52. Maneely a-10, 12, 15, 16, 28, 35, 38, 40-45; c-18-22, 33, 35, 36, 38, 39, 41, 42, 45, 53, 54, 56. Morisi a-23, 52. Pakula a-42, 52. Powell a-51. Romita a-24(2). Severin a-46, 47; c-48. Shores a-3, 5, 30, 31, 33, 35, 36, 38, 41; c-3-5. Sinnott a-34-39. Wildey a-43. Bondage c-19.

WILD WESTERN ACTION (Also see The Bravados)
Skywald Publ. Corp.: Mar, 1971 - No. 3, June, 1971 (25¢, reprints, 52 pgs.)
1-Durango Kid, Straight Arrow-r; with all references to "Straight" in story relettered to
  "Swift"; Bravados begin; Shores-a (new) | 3 | 6 | 9 | 14 | 19 | 24 |
2,3: 2-Billy Nevada, Durango Kid. 3-Red Mask, Durango Kid
| | 2 | 4 | 6 | 9 | 13 | 16 |

WILD WESTERN ROUNDUP
Red Top/Decker Publications/I. W. Enterprises: Oct, 1957; 1960-'61
1(1957)-Kid Cowboy-r | 5 | 10 | 14 | 20 | 24 | 28 |
I.W. Reprint #1('60-61)-r/#1 by Red Top | 2 | 4 | 8 | 11 | 14 |

WILD WEST RODEO
Star Publications: 1953 (15¢)
1-A comic book coloring book with regular full color cover & B&W inside
| | 8 | 16 | 24 | 44 | 57 | 70 |

WILD WILD WEST, THE (TV)
Gold Key: June, 1966 - No. 7, Oct, 1969 (All have Robert Conrad photo-c)
1-McWilliams-a | 12 | 24 | 36 | 84 | 150 | 215 |
1-Variant edition with photo back-c (scarce) | 13 | 26 | 39 | 95 | 168 | 240 |
2-McWilliams-a | 9 | 18 | 27 | 60 | 110 | 140 |
2-Variant edition with photo back-c (scarce) | 9 | 18 | 27 | 65 | 113 | 160 |
3-7 | 7 | 14 | 21 | 50 | 83 | 115 |

WILD, WILD WEST, THE (TV)
Millennium Publications: Oct, 1990 - No. 4, Jan?, 1991 ($2.95, limited series)
1-4-Based on TV show — 3.00

WILKIN BOY (See That...)

WILL EISNER READER
Kitchen Sink Press: 1991 ($9.95, B&W, 8 1/2" x 11", TPB)
nn-Reprints stories from Will Eisner's Quarterly; Eisner-s/a/c — 10.00
nn-(DC Comics, 10/00, $9.95) — 10.00

WILL EISNER'S JOHN LAW: ANGELS AND ASHES, DEVILS AND DUST
IDW Publ.: Apr, 2006 - No. 4 ($3.99, B&W, limited series)
1-New stories with Will Eisner's characters; Gary Chaloner-s/a — 4.00

WILLIE COMICS (Formerly Ideal #1-4; Crime Cases #24 on; Li'l Willie #20 & 21)
(See Gay Comics, Laugh, Millie The Model & Wisco)
Marvel Comics (MgPC): #5, Fall, 1946 - #19, 4/49; #22, 1/50 - #23, 5/50 (No #20 & 21)
5(#1)-George, Margie, Nellie the Nurse & Willie begin
| | 23 | 46 | 69 | 130 | 205 | 280 |
6,8,9 | 14 | 28 | 42 | 80 | 115 | 150 |
7(1),10,11-Kurtzman's "Hey Look" | 14 | 28 | 42 | 81 | 118 | 155 |

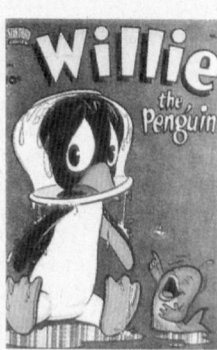

Willie the Penguin #1 © STD

Wings Comics #73 © FH

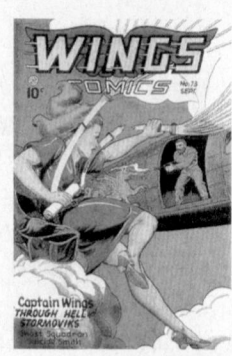

The Winter Men #1 © Lewis & Leon

	GD 2.0	VG 4.0	FN 6.0	VF 8.0	VF/NM 9.0	NM- 9.2
12,14-18,22,23	13	26	39	74	105	135
13,19-Kurtzman's "Hey Look" (#19-last by Kurtzman?)	14	28	42	76	108	140

NOTE: Cindy app. in #17. Jeanie app. in #17. Little Lizzie app. in #22.

WILLIE MAYS (See The Amazing...)

WILLIE THE PENGUIN
Standard Comics: Apr, 1951 - No. 6, Apr, 1952

1-Funny animal	9	18	27	47	61	75
2-6	6	12	18	28	34	40

WILLIE THE WISE-GUY (Also see Cartoon Kids)
Atlas Comics (NPP): Sept, 1957

1-Kida, Maneely-a	9	18	27	50	65	80

WILLOW
Marvel Comics: Aug, 1988 - No. 3, Oct, 1988 ($1.00)

1-3-R/Marvel Graphic Novel #36 (movie adaptation)		3.00

WILL ROGERS WESTERN (Formerly My Great Love #1-4; see Blazing & True Comics #66)
Fox Features Syndicate: No. 5, June, 1950 - No. 2, Aug, 1950

5(#1)	32	64	96	186	293	400
2: Photo-c	27	54	81	156	246	335

WILL TO POWER (Also see Comic's Greatest World)
Dark Horse Comics: June, 1994 - No. 12, Aug, 1994 ($1.00, weekly limited series, 20 pgs.)

1-12: 12-Vortex kills Titan.		2.50

NOTE: Mignola c-10-12. Sears c-1-3.

WILL-YUM!
Dell Publishing Co.: No. 676, Feb, 1956 - No. 902, May, 1958

Four Color 676 (#1), 765 (1/57), 902	4	8	12	26	41	55

WIN A PRIZE COMICS (Timmy The Timid Ghost #3 on?)
Charlton Comics: Feb, 1955 - No. 2, Apr, 1955

V1#1-S&K-a; Poe adapt; E.C. War swipe	67	134	201	419	697	975
2-S&K-a	48	96	144	293	484	675

WINDY & WILLY
National Periodical Publications: May-June, 1969 - No. 4, Nov-Dec, 1969

1- r/Dobie Gillis with some art changes begin	4	8	12	28	44	60
2-4	3	6	9	18	27	35

WINGS COMICS
Fiction House Mag.: 9/40 - No. 109, 9/49; No. 110, Wint, 1949-50; No. 111, Spring, 1950; No. 112, 1950(nd); No. 113 - No. 115, 1950(nd); No. 116, 1952(nd); No. 117, Fall, 1952 - No. 122, Wint, 1953-54; No. 123 - No. 124, 1954(nd)

1-Skull Squad, Clipper Kirk, Suicide Smith, Jane Martin, War Nurse, Phantom Falcons, Greasemonkey Griffin, Parachute Patrol & Powder Burns begin	266	532	798	1663	2757	3850
2	100	200	300	625	1038	1450
3-5	68	136	204	425	705	985
6-10: 8-Indicia shows #7 (#8 on cover)	54	108	162	338	557	775
11-15	49	98	147	299	492	685
16-Origin & 1st app. Captain Wings & begin series	53	106	159	323	537	750
17-20	41	82	123	254	410	565
21-30	40	80	120	237	374	510
31-40	36	72	108	208	329	450
41-50	29	58	87	170	268	365
51-60: 60-Last Skull Squad	27	54	81	158	249	340
61-67: 66-Ghost Patrol begins (becomes Ghost Squadron #71 on), ends #112?	25	50	75	145	228	310
68,69: 68-Clipper Kirk becomes The Phantom Falcon-origin, Part 1; part 2 in #69	25	50	75	145	228	310
70-72: 70-1st app. The Phantom Falcon in costume, origin-Part 3; Capt. Wings battles Col. Kamikaze in all	24	48	72	139	220	300
73-99: 80-Phantom Falcon by Larsen. 99-King of the Congo begins?	24	48	72	139	220	300
100-(12/48)	25	50	75	145	228	310
101-124: 111-Last Jane Martin. 112-Flying Saucer-c/story (1950). 115-Used in POP, pg. 89	19	38	57	109	172	235

NOTE: Bondage covers are common. Captain Wings battles Sky Hag-#75, 76; ...Mr. Atlantis-#85-92; ...Mr. Pupin(Red Agent)-#98-103. Capt. Wings by Elias-#52-64, 68, 69; by Lubbers-#29-32, 70-111; by Renee-#33-46. Evans a-85-106, 108-111(Jane Martin); text illos-72-84. Larsen a-52, 59, 64, 73-77. Jane Martin by Fran Hopper-#68-84; Suicide Smith by John Celardo-#72, 74, 76, 80-104; by Hollingsworth-#68-70, 105-109, 111; Ghost Squadron by Astarita-#67-79; by Maurice Whitman-#80-111. King of the Congo by Moreira-#99, 100. Skull Squad by M. Baker-#52-60; Clipper Kirk by Baker-#60, 61; by Colan-#53; by Ingels-(some issues?). Phantom Falcon by Larsen-#73-84. Elias c-59-72. Fawcette c-3-12, 16, 17, 19, 22-33. Lubbers c-74-109. Tuska a-5. Whitman c-110-124. Zolnerwich c-15, 21.

WINGS OF THE EAGLES, THE
Dell Publishing Co.: No. 790, Apr, 1957 (10¢ & 15¢ editions exist)

Four Color 790-Movie; John Wayne photo-c; Toth-a	14	28	42	100	178	255

WINKY DINK (Adventures of...)
Pines Comics: No. 75, Mar, 1957 (one-shot)

75-Marv Levy-c/a	6	12	18	31	38	45

WINKY DINK (TV)
Dell Publishing Co.: No. 663, Nov, 1955

Four Color 663 (#1)	8	16	24	52	86	120

WINNIE-THE-POOH (Also see Dynabrite Comics)
Gold Key No. 1-17/Whitman No. 18 on: January, 1977 - No. 33, July, 1984 (Walt Disney) (Winnie-The-Pooh began as Edward Bear in 1926 by Milne)

1-New art	3	6	9	16	22	28
2-5: 5-New material	2	4	6	9	13	16
6-17: 12-up-New material	2	4	6	8	10	12
18,19(Whitman)	2	4	6	9	13	16
20,21('80) pre-pack only	3	6	9	20	30	40
22('80) (scarcer) pre-pack only	4	8	12	26	41	55
23-28: 27(2/82), 28(4/82)	2	4	6	9	13	16
29-33 (#90299 on-c, no date or date code; pre-pack): 29(4/82), 30(5/83), 31(8/83), 32(4/84), 33(7/84)	3	6	9	16	22	28

WINNIE WINKLE (See Popular Comics & Super Comics)
Dell Publishing Co.: 1941 - No. 7, Sept-Nov, 1949

Large Feature Comic 2 (1941)	28	56	84	162	256	350
Four Color 94 (1945)	12	24	36	87	156	225
Four Color 174	8	16	24	58	97	135
1(3-5/48)-Contains daily & Sunday newspaper-r from 1939-1941	8	16	24	52	86	120
2 (6-8/48)	6	12	18	37	59	80
3-7	4	8	12	28	44	60

WINTER MEN, THE
DC Comics (WildStorm): Oct, 2005 - No. 5, Nov, 2006 ($2.99, limited series)

1-5-Brett Lewis-s/John Paul Leon-a		3.00

WINTER SOLDIER: WINTER KILLS (See Captain America 2005 series)
Marvel Comics: Feb, 2007 ($3.99, one-shot)

1-Flashback to Christmas Eve 1944; Toro & Sub-Mariner app.; Brubaker-s/Weeks-a		4.00

WINTERWORLD
Eclipse Comics: Sept, 1987 - No. 3, Mar, 1988 ($1.75, limited series)

1-3		2.50

WISDOM
Marvel Comics (MAX): Jan, 2007 - No. 6, July, 2007 ($3.99, limited series)

1-6: 1-Hairsine-a/c; Cornell-s. 3-6-Manuel Garcia-a		4.00
...: Rudiments of Wisdom TPB (2007, $21.99) r/#1-6; series pitch and sketch page		22.00

WISE GUYS (See Harvey...)

WISE LITTLE HEN, THE
David McKay Publ./Whitman: 1934 ,1935(48 pgs.) ; 1937 (Story book)

nn-(1934 edition w/dust jacket)(48 pgs. with color, 8-3/4x9-3/4") -Debut of Donald Duck (see Advs. of Mickey Mouse); Donald app. on cover with Wise Little Hen & Practical Pig; painted cover; same artist as the B&W's from Silly Symphony Cartoon, The Wise Little Hen (1934) (McKay)						
Book w/dust jacket	235	470	705	1469	2435	3400
Dust jacket only	55	110	165	344	572	800
nn-(1935 edition w/dust jacket), same as 1934 ed.	138	276	414	863	1432	2000
888 (1937)(9-1/2x13", 12 pgs.)(Whitman) Donald Duck app.	34	68	102	197	311	425

WISE SON: THE WHITE WOLF
DC Comics (Milestone): Nov, 1996 - No. 4, Feb, 1997 ($2.50, limited series)

1-4: Ho Che Anderson-c/a		2.50

WIT AND WISDOM OF WATERGATE (Humor magazine)
Marvel Comics: 1973, 76 pgs., squarebound

1-Low print run	4	8	12	22	34	45

WITCHBLADE (Also see Cyblade/Shi, Tales Of The..., & Top Cow Classics)
Image Comics (Top Cow Productions): Nov, 1995 - Present ($2.50/$2.99)

0	1	2	3	5	6	8
1/2-Mike Turner/Marc Silvestri-c	3	6	9	20	30	40
1/2 Gold Ed., 1/2 Chromium-c	3	6	9	20	30	40

Witchblade #105 © TCOW

Witchblade/Elektra #1 © TCOW/MAR

Witches Tales #15 © HARV

	GD 2.0	VG 4.0	FN 6.0	VF 8.0	VF/NM 9.0	NM- 9.2
1/2-(Vol. 2, 11/02, $2.99) Wohl-s/Ching-a/c						3.00
1-Mike Turner-a(p)	4	8	12	21	30	40
1,2-American Ent. Encore Ed.	1	2	3	4	5	7
2,3	2	4	6	11	16	20
4,5	2	4	6	9	13	16
6-9: 8-Wraparound-c. 9-Tony Daniel-a(p)	1	2	3	5	7	9
9-Sunset variant-c	2	4	6	8	10	12
9-DF variant-c	2	4	6	11	16	20
10-Flip book w/Darkness #0, 1st app. the Darkness	2	4	6	8	10	12
10-Variant-c	2	4	6	9	12	15
10-Gold logo	3	6	9	16	23	30
10-($3.95) Dynamic Forces alternate-c	1	2	3	5		8
11-15						5.00
16-19: 18,19-"Family Ties" Darkness x-over pt. 1,4						4.00
18-Face to face variant-c, 18-American Ent. Ed., 19-AE Gold Ed.						
	1	2	3	5	6	8
20-25: 24-Pearson, Green-a. 25-($2.95) Turner-a(p)						3.00
25 (Prism variant)						30.00
25 (Special)						15.00
26-39: 26-Green-a begins						2.50
27 (Variant)						10.00
40-49,51-53: 40-Begin Jenkins & Veitch-s/Keu Cha-c. 47-Zulli-c/a						2.50
40-Pittsburgh Convention Preview edition; B&W preview of #40						3.00
41-eWanted Chrome-c edition						5.00
49-Gold logo	1	2	3	5	6	8
50-($4.95) Darkness app.; Ching-a; B&W preview of Universe						5.00
54-59: 54-Black outer-c with gold foil logo; Wohl-s/Manapul-a						2.50
55-Variant Battle of the Planets Convention cover						3.00
60-74,76-91,93-99: 60-($2.99) Endgame x-over with Tomb Raider #25 & Evo #1.						3.00
64,65-Magdalena app. 71-Kirk-a. 77,81-85-Land-c. 80-Four covers. 87-Bachalo-a						3.00
75-($4.99) Manapul-a						5.00
92-($4.99) Origin of the Witchblade; art by various incl. Bachalo, Perez, Linsner, Cooke						5.00
100-($4.99) Five covers incl. Turner, Silvestri, Linsner; art by various; Jake dies						5.00
101-109: 103-Danielle Baptiste gets the Witchblade; Linsner variant-c						3.00
... and Tomb Raider (4/05, $2.99) Jae Lee-c; art by Lee and Texiera						3.00
...: Animated (8/03, $2.99) Magdalena & Darkness app.; Dini-s/Bone, Bullock, Cooke-a/c						3.00
...: Art of the Witchblade (7/06, $2.99) pin-ups by various incl. Turner, Land, Linsner						3.00
...: Bearers of the Blade (7/06, $2.99) pin-up/profiles of bearers of the Witchblade						3.00
...: Blood Oath (8/04, $4.99) Sara teams with Phenix & Sibilla; Roux-a						5.00
...: Blood Relations TPB (2003, $12.99) r/#54-58						13.00
...: Compendium Vol. 1 (2006, $59.99) r/#1-50; gallery of variant covers and art						60.00
...: Compendium Vol. 2 (2007, $59.99) r/#51-100; gallery of variant covers and art						60.00
...: Cover Gallery Vol. 1 (12/05, $2.99) intro. by Stan Lee						3.00
.../Darkchylde (7/00, $2.50) Green-s/a(p)						2.50
.../Dark Minds (6/04, $9.99) new story plus r/Dark Minds/Witchblade #1						10.00
.../Darkness: Family Ties Collected Edition (10/98, $9.95) r/#18,19 and Darkness #9,10						10.00
.../Darkness Special (12/99, $3.95) Green-a						4.00
...: Demon 1 (2003, $6.99) Mark Millar-s/Jae Lee-c/a						7.00
...: Distinctions (See Tales of the Witchblade)						
.../Elektra (3/97, $2.95) Devil's Reign Pt. 6						3.00
... Gallery (11/00, $2.95) Profile pages and pin-ups by various; Turner-c						3.00
Infinity (5/99, $3.50) Lobdell-s/Pollina-c/a						3.50
.../Lady Death (11/01, $4.95) Manapul-c/a						5.00
...: Prevailing TPB (2000, $14.95) r/#20-25; new Turner-c						15.00
...: Revelations TPB (2000, $24.95) r/#9-17; new Turner-c						25.00
.../The Punisher (6/07, $3.99) Marz-s/Melo-a/Linsner-c						4.00
.../Tomb Raider #1/2 (7/00, $2.95) Covers by Turner and Cha						3.00
... vs. Frankenstein: Monster War 2005 (8/05, $2.99) pt. 3 of x-over						3.00
...: Witch Hunt Vol. 1 TPB (2/06, $14.99) r/#80-85; Marz intro.; Choi afterward; cover gallery						15.00
Wizard #500						10.00
.../Wolverine (6/04, $2.99) Basaldua-c/a; Claremont-s						3.00

WITCHBLADE/ALIENS/THE DARKNESS/PREDATOR
Dark Horse Comics/Top Cow Productions: Nov, 2000 ($2.99)

	GD 2.0	VG 4.0	FN 6.0	VF 8.0	VF/NM 9.0	NM- 9.2
1-3-Mel Rubi-a						3.00

WITCHBLADE COLLECTED EDITION
Image Comics (Top Cow Productions): July, 1996 - No. 8 ($4.95/$6.95, squarebound, limited series)

	GD 2.0	VG 4.0	FN 6.0	VF 8.0	VF/NM 9.0	NM- 9.2
1-7-($4.95): Two issues reprinted in each						5.00
8-($6.95) r/#15-17						7.00
...Slipcase (10/96, $10.95)-Packaged w/ Coll. Ed. #1-4						11.00

WITCHBLADE: DESTINY'S CHILD
Image Comics (Top Cow): Jun, 2000 - No. 3, Sept, 2000 ($2.95, lim. series)

	GD 2.0	VG 4.0	FN 6.0	VF 8.0	VF/NM 9.0	NM- 9.2
1-3: 1-Boller-a/Keu Cha-c						3.00

WITCHBLADE: MANGA (Takeru Manga)
Image Comics (Top Cow): Feb, 2007 - Present ($2.99/$3.99)

	GD 2.0	VG 4.0	FN 6.0	VF 8.0	VF/NM 9.0	NM- 9.2
1-4-Colored reprints of Japanese Witchblade manga. 1-Three covers. 2-Two covers						3.00
5-8-($3.99)						4.00

WITCHBLADE: OBAKEMONO
Image Comics (Top Cow Productions): 2002 ($9.95, one-shot graphic novel)

	GD 2.0	VG 4.0	FN 6.0	VF 8.0	VF/NM 9.0	NM- 9.2
1-Fiona Avery-s/Billy Tan-a; forward by Straczynski						10.00

WITCHBLADE: SHADES OF GRAY
Dynamite Ent./Top Cow: 2007 - No. 4, 2007 ($3.50, lim. series)

	GD 2.0	VG 4.0	FN 6.0	VF 8.0	VF/NM 9.0	NM- 9.2
1,2: 1-Sara Pezzini meets Dorian Gray; Segovia-a; multiple covers						3.50

WITCHBLADE/ TOMB RAIDER SPECIAL (Also see Tomb Raider/...)
Image Comics (Top Cow Productions): Dec, 1998 ($2.95)

	GD 2.0	VG 4.0	FN 6.0	VF 8.0	VF/NM 9.0	NM- 9.2
1-Based on video game character; Turner-a(p)						3.00
1-Silvestri variant-c						5.00
1-Turner bikini variant-c						10.00
1-Prism-c						12.00
Wizard 1/2 -Turner-s						10.00

WITCHCRAFT (See Strange Mysteries, Super Reprint #18)
Avon Periodicals: Mar-Apr, 1952 - No. 6, Mar, 1953

	GD 2.0	VG 4.0	FN 6.0	VF 8.0	VF/NM 9.0	NM- 9.2
1-Kubert-a; 1 pg. Check-a	71	142	213	444	735	1025
2-Kubert & Check-a	52	104	156	317	521	725
3,6: 3-Lawrence-a; Kinstler inside-c	41	82	123	256	416	575
4-People cooked alive c/story	47	94	141	287	474	660
5-Kelly Freas painted-c	53	106	159	323	529	735

NOTE: Hollingsworth a-4-6; c-4, 6. McCann a-3?

WITCHCRAFT
DC Comics (Vertigo): June, 1994 - No. 3, Aug, 1994 ($2.95, limited series)

	GD 2.0	VG 4.0	FN 6.0	VF 8.0	VF/NM 9.0	NM- 9.2
1-3: James Robinson scripts & Kaluta-c in all						4.00
1-Platinum Edition						8.00
Trade paperback-(1996, $14.95)-r/#1-3; Kaluta-c						15.00

WITCHCRAFT: LA TERREUR
DC Comics (Vertigo): Apr, 1998 - No. 3, Jun, 1998 ($2.50, limited series)

	GD 2.0	VG 4.0	FN 6.0	VF 8.0	VF/NM 9.0	NM- 9.2
1-3: Robinson-s/Zulli & Locke-a; interlocking cover images						2.50

WITCHES
Marvel Comics: Aug, 2004 - No. 4, Sept, 2004 ($2.99, limited series)

	GD 2.0	VG 4.0	FN 6.0	VF 8.0	VF/NM 9.0	NM- 9.2
1-4: 1,2-Deodato, Jr-a; Dr. Strange app. 3,4-Conrad-a						3.00
... Vol. 1: The Gathering (2004, $9.99) r/series						10.00

WITCHES (Witches Western Tales #29,30)
Witches Tales/Harvey Publications: Jan, 1951 - No. 28, Dec, 1954 (date misprinted as 4/55)

	GD 2.0	VG 4.0	FN 6.0	VF 8.0	VF/NM 9.0	NM- 9.2
1-Powell-a (1 pg.)	55	110	165	344	572	800
2-Eye injury panel	35	70	105	204	322	440
3-7,9,10	26	52	78	154	242	330
8-Eye injury panels	27	54	81	158	249	340
11-13,15,16: 12-Acid in face story	24	48	72	139	220	300
14,17-Powell-a/inside-c 17-Atomic disaster story	26	52	78	150	235	320
18-Nostrand-a; E.C. swipe/Shock S.S.	26	52	78	150	235	320
19-Nostrand-a; E.C. swipe/ "Glutton"; Devil-c	27	54	81	158	249	340
20-24-Nostrand-a. 21-E.C. swipe; rape story. 23-Wood E.C. swipes/Two-Fisted Tales #34						
	26	52	78	150	235	320
25-Nostrand-a; E.C. swipe/Mad Barber; decapitation-c						
	40	80	120	235	368	500
26-28: 27-r/#6 with diff.-c. 28-r/#8 with diff.-c	18	36	54	105	165	225

NOTE: Check a-24. Elias c-8, 10, 16-27. Kremer a-18; c-25. Nostrand a-17-25; 14, 17(w/Powell). Palais a-1, 2, 4(2), 5(2), 7-9, 12, 14, 15, 17. Powell a-3-7, 10, 11, 19-27. Bondage-c 1, 3, 5, 6, 8, 9.

WITCHES TALES (Magazine)
Eerie Publications: V1#7, July, 1969 - V7#1, Feb, 1975 (B&W, 52 pgs.)

	GD 2.0	VG 4.0	FN 6.0	VF 8.0	VF/NM 9.0	NM- 9.2
V1#7(7/69)	6	12	18	39	62	85
V1#8(9/69), 9(11/69)	5	10	15	35	55	75
V2#1-6('70), V3#1-6('71)	4	8	12	26	41	55
V4#1-6('72), V5#1-6('73), V6#1-6('74), V7#1	4	8	12	24	37	50

NOTE: Ajax/Farrell reprints in early issues.

WITCHES' WESTERN TALES (Formerly Witches Tales)(Western Tales #31 on)
Harvey Publications: No. 29, Feb, 1955 - No. 30, Apr, 1955

	GD 2.0	VG 4.0	FN 6.0	VF 8.0	VF/NM 9.0	NM- 9.2
29,30-Featuring Clay Duncan & Boys' Ranch; S&K-r/from Boys' Ranch including-c.						
29-Last pre-code	18	36	54	107	169	230

WITCHFINDER, THE

Witching Hour #83 © DC

Witness #1 © MAR

Wolverine #28 © MAR

	GD 2.0	VG 4.0	FN 6.0	VF 8.0	VF/NM 9.0	NM- 9.2

Image Comics (Liar): Sept, 1999 - No. 3, Jan, 2000 ($2.95)

1-3-Romano-a/Sharon & Matthew Scott-plot 3.00

WITCH HUNTER
Malibu Comics (Ultraverse): Apr, 1996 ($2.50, one-shot)

1 .... 2.50

WITCHING, THE
DC Comics (Vertigo): Aug, 2004 - No. 10, May, 2005 ($2.95/$2.99)

1-10-Vankin-s/Gallagher-a/McPherson-c. 1,2-Lucifer app. 3.00

WITCHING HOUR ("The ..." in later issues)
National Periodical Publ./DC Comics: Feb-Mar, 1969 - No. 85, Oct, 1978

	GD	VG	FN	VF	VF/NM	NM-
1-Toth-a, plus Neal Adams-a (2 pgs.)	12	24	36	82	146	210
2,6: 6-Toth-a	6	12	18	41	66	90
3,5-Wrightson-a; Toth-p. 3-Last 12¢ issue	6	12	18	43	69	95
4,7-12: Toth-a in all. 8-Toth, Neal Adams-a	4	8	12	28	44	60
13-Neal Adams-c/a, 2pgs.	5	10	15	30	48	65
14-Williamson/Garzon, Jones-a; N. Adams-c	5	10	15	32	51	70
15	3	6	9	16	23	30
16-21-(52 pg. Giants)	3	6	9	19	29	38
22-37,39,40	2	4	6	11	16	20
38-(100 pgs.)	5	10	15	30	48	65
41-60	2	4	6	9	12	15
61-83,85	1	3	4	6	8	10
84-(44 pgs.)	2	4	6	8	10	12

NOTE: Combined with The Unexpected with #189. Neal Adams c-7-11, 13, 14. Alcala a-24, 27, 33, 41, 43. Anderson a-9, 38. Cardy c-4, 5. Kaluta a-7. Kane a-12p. Morrow a-10, 13, 15, 16. Nino a-31, 40, 45, 47. Redondo a-20, 23, 24, 34, 65; c-53. Reese a-23. Sparling a-1, 3-12, 38r. Toth a-1, 3-12, 38r. Tuska a-11, 12. Wood a-15.

WITCHING HOUR, THE
DC Comics (Vertigo): 1999 - No. 3, 2000 ($5.95, limited series)

1-3-Bachalo & Thibert-c/a; Loeb & Bachalo-s 6.00
Hardcover (2000, $29.95) r/#1-3; embossed cover 30.00
Softcover (2003, $19.95) r/#1-3 .... 20.00

WITHIN OUR REACH
Star Reach Productions: 1991 ($7.95, 84 pgs.)

nn-Spider-Man, Concrete by Chadwick, Gift of the Magi by Russell; X-mas stories;
    Chadwick-c; Spidey back-c 8.00

WITH THE MARINES ON THE BATTLEFRONTS OF THE WORLD
Toby Press: 1953 (no month) - No. 2, Mar, 1954 (Photo covers)

	GD	VG	FN	VF	VF/NM	NM-
1-John Wayne story	29	58	87	170	268	365
2-Monty Hall in #1,2	10	20	30	56	76	95

WITH THE U.S. PARATROOPS BEHIND ENEMY LINES (Also see U.S. Paratroops...;
#2-6 titled U.S. Paratroops...)
Avon Periodicals: 1951 - No. 6, Dec, 1952

	GD	VG	FN	VF	VF/NM	NM-
1-Wood-c & inside f/c	17	34	51	98	154	210
2-Kinstler-c & inside f/c only	11	22	33	60	83	105
3-6: 6-Kinstler-c & inside f/c only	10	20	30	54	72	90

NOTE: Kinstler c-2, 4-6.

WITNESS, THE (Also see Amazing Mysteries, Captain America #71, Ideal #4, Marvel Mystery #92 & Mystic #7)
Marvel Comics (MjMe): Sept, 1948

	GD	VG	FN	VF	VF/NM	NM-
1(Scarce)-Rico-c?	221	442	663	1381	2291	3200

WITTY COMICS
Irwin H. Rubin Publ./Chicago Nite Life News No. 2: 1945 - No. 2, 1945

	GD	VG	FN	VF	VF/NM	NM-
1-The Pioneer, Junior Patrol; Jap war-c	30	60	90	172	271	370
2-The Pioneer, Junior Patrol	15	30	45	85	130	175

WIZARD OF FOURTH STREET, THE
Dark Horse Comics: Dec, 1987 - No. 2, 1988 ($1.75, B&W, limited series)

1,2; Adapts novel by S/F author Simon Hawke 2.50

WIZARD OF OZ (See Classics Illustrated Jr. 535, Dell Jr. Treasury No. 5, First Comics Graphic Novel, Marvelous..., & Marvel Treasury of Oz)
Dell Publishing Co.: No. 1308, Mar-May, 1962 (TV)

	GD	VG	FN	VF	VF/NM	NM-
Four Color 1308	11	22	33	79	140	200

WIZARD'S TALE, THE
Image Comics (Homage Comics): 1997 ($19.95, squarebound, one-shot)

nn-Kurt Busiek-s/David Wenzel-painted-a/c 20.00

WOLF & RED
Dark Horse Comics: Apr, 1995 - No. 3, June, 1995 ($2.50, limited series)

1-3: Characters created by Tex Avery 2.50

WOLFF & BYRD, COUNSELORS OF THE MACABRE (Becomes Supernatural Law with issue #24)
Exhibit A Press: May, 1994 - No. 23, Aug, 1999 ($2.50, B&W)

1-23-Batton Lash-s/a 2.50

WOLF GAL (See Al Capp's...)

WOLFMAN, THE (See Movie Classics)

WOLFPACK
Marvel Comics: Feb, 1988 ($7.95); Aug, 1988 - No. 12, July, 1989 (Lim. series)

1-1st app./origin (Marvel Graphic Novel #31) 8.00
1-12 .... 2.50

WOLVERINE (See Alpha Flight, Daredevil #196, 249, Ghost Rider; Wolverine; Punisher, Havok &..., Incredible Hulk #180, Incredible Hulk &..., Kitty Pryde And..., Marvel Comics Presents, New Avengers, Power Pack, Punisher and..., Spider-Man vs... & X-Men #94)

WOLVERINE (See Incredible Hulk #180 for 1st app.)
Marvel Comics Group: Sept, 1982 - No. 4, Dec, 1982 (limited series)

	GD	VG	FN	VF	VF/NM	NM-
1-Frank Miller-c/a(p) in all; Claremont-s	5	10	15	32	51	70
2-4	4	8	12	24	37	50
... By Claremont & Miller HC (2006, $19.99) r/#1-4 & Uncanny X-Men #172-173						20.00
TPB 1(7/87, $4.95)-Reprints #1-4 with new Miller-c	2	4	6	10	14	18
TPB nn (2nd printing, $9.95)-r/#1-4	2	4	6	8	10	12

WOLVERINE
Marvel Comics: Nov, 1988 - No. 189, June, 2003 ($1.50/$1.75/$1.95/$1.99/$2.25)

	GD	VG	FN	VF	VF/NM	NM-
1	4	8	12	22	34	45
2	2	4	6	13	18	22
3-5: 4-BWS back-c	2	4	6	9	13	16
6-9: 6-McFarlane back-c. 7,8-Hulk app.	1	3	4	6	8	10
10-1st battle with Sabretooth (before Wolverine had his claws)						
	3	6	9	16	23	30
11-16: 11-New costume	1	2	3	5	6	8
17-20: 17-Byrne-c/a(p) begins, ends #23	1	2	3	4	5	7
21-30: 24,25,27-Jim Lee-c. 26-Begin $1.75-c						5.00
31-40,44,47						4.00
41-Sabretooth claims to be Wolverine's father; Cable cameo						6.00
41-Gold 2nd printing ($1.75)						2.50
42-Sabretooth, Cable & Nick Fury app.; Sabretooth proven not to be Wolverine's father						
	1	2	3	5	6	8
42-Gold ink 2nd printing ($1.75)						2.50
43-Sabretooth cameo (2 panels); saga ends						5.00
45,46-Sabretooth-c/stories						5.00
48-51: 48,49-Sabretooth app. 48-Begin 3 part Weapon X sequel. 50-(64 pgs.)-Die cut-c; Wolverine back to old yellow costume; Forge, Cyclops, Jubilee, Jean Grey & Nick Fury app. 51-Sabretooth-c & app.						4.00
52-74,76-80: 54-Shatterstar (from X-Force) app. 55-Gambit, Jubilee, Sunfire-c/story. 55-57,73-Gambit app. 57-Mariko Yashida dies (Late 7/92). 58,59-Terror, Inc. x-over. 60,62,64-Sabretooth storyline (60,62,64-c)						4.00
75-($3.95, 68 pgs.)-Wolverine hologram on-c						5.00
81-84,86: 81-bound-in card sheet						3.00
85-($2.50)-Newsstand edition						3.00
85-($3.50)-Collectors edition						5.00
87-90 ($1.95)-Deluxe edition						3.00
87-90 ($1.50)-Regular edition						2.50
91-99,101-114: 91-Return from "Age of Apocalypse", 93-Juggernaut app. 94-Gen X app. 101-104-Elektra app. 104-Origin of Onslaught. 105-Onslaught x-over. 110-Shaman-c/app. 114-Alternate-c						3.00
100 ($3.95)-Hologram-c; Wolverine loses humanity	1	2	3	5	7	9
100 ($2.95)-Regular-c						4.00
115-124: 115- Operation Zero Tolerance						2.50
125-($2.99) Wraparound-c; Viper secret						3.00
125-($6.95) Jae Lee variant-c						7.00
126-144: 126,127-Sabretooth-c/app. 128-Sabretooth & Shadowcat app.; Platt-a. 129-Wendigo-c/app. 131-Initial printing contained lettering error. 133-Begin Larsen-s/Matsuda-a. 138-Galactus-c/app. 139-Cable app.; Yu-a. 142,143-Alpha Flight app.						2.50
145-($2.99) 25th Anniversary issue; Hulk and Sabretooth app.						3.00
145-($3.99) Foil enhanced cover (also see Promotional section for Nabisco mail-in ed.)						5.00
146-149: 147-Apocalypse: The Twelve; Angel-c/app. 149-Nova-c/app.						2.50
150-($2.99) Steve Skroce-s/a						3.00
151-174,176-182,184-189: 151-Begin $2.25-c. 154,155-Liefeld-s/a. 156-Churchill-a. 159-Chen-a begins. 160-Sabretooth app. 163-Texeira-a(p). 167-BWS-c. 172,173-Alpha Flight app. 176-Colossus app. 185,186-Punisher app.						2.50
175,183-($3.50) 175-Sabretooth app.						3.50

Wolverine V3 #21 © MAR

Wolverine: Origins #1 © MAR

Wolverine/Punisher #1 © MAR

	GD	VG	FN	VF	VF/NM	NM-			GD	VG	FN	VF	VF/NM	NM-
	2.0	4.0	6.0	8.0	9.0	9.2			2.0	4.0	6.0	8.0	9.0	9.2

#(-1) Flashback (7/97) Logan meets Col. Fury; Nord-a ... 2.50
Annual nn (1990, $4.50, squarebound, 52 pgs.)-The Jungle Adventure; Simonson scripts; Mignola-c/a ... 5.00
Annual 2 (12/90, $4.95, squarebound, 52 pgs.)-Bloodlust ... 5.00
Annual nn (#3, 8/91, $5.95, 68 pgs.)-Rahne of Terror; Cable & The New Mutants app.; Andy Kubert-c/a (2nd print exists) ... 6.00
Annual '95 (1995, $3.95) ... 4.00
Annual '96 (1996, $2.95)- Wraparound-c; Silver Samurai, Yukio, and Red Ronin app. ... 3.00
Annual '97 ($2.99) - Wraparound-c ... 3.00
Annual 1999, 2000 ($3.50) : 1999-Deadpool app. ... 3.50
Annual 2001 ($2.99) - Tieri-s; JH Williams-c ... 3.00
...Battles The Incredible Hulk nn (1989, $4.95, squarebound, 52 pg.) r/Incr. Hulk #180,181 ... 5.00
Best of Wolverine Vol. 1 HC (2004, $29.99) oversized reprints of Hulk #181, mini-series #1-4, Capt. America Ann., #8, Uncanny X-Men #205 & Marvel Comics Presents #72-84 ... 30.00
...Black Rio (11/98, $5.99)-Casey-s/Oscar Jimenez-a ... 6.00
...Blood Debt TPB (7/01, $12.95)-r/#150-153; Skroce-c ... 13.00
...Blood Hungry nn (1993, $6.95, 68 pgs.)-Kieth-r/Marvel Comics Presents #85-92 w/ new Kieth-c ... 7.00
...: Bloody Choices nn (1993, $7.95, 68 pgs.)-r/Graphic Novel; Nick Fury. ... 8.00
... Cable Guts and Glory (10/99, $5.99) Platt-a ... 6.00
... Classic Vol. 1 TPB (2005, $12.99) r/#1-5 ... 13.00
... Classic Vol. 2 TPB (2005, $12.99) r/#6-10 ... 13.00
... Classic Vol. 3 TPB (2006, $14.99) r/#11-16; The Gehenna Stone Affair ... 15.00
... Classic Vol. 4 TPB (2006, $14.99) r/#17-23 ... 15.00
... Classic Vol. 5 TPB (2006, $14.99) r/#24-30 ... 15.00
.../Deadpool: Weapon X TPB (7/02, $21.99)-r/#162-166 & Deadpool #57-60 ... 22.00
... Doombringer (11/97, $5.99)-Silver Samurai-c/app. ... 6.00
... Evilution (9/94, $5.95) ... 6.00
...: Global Jeopardy 1 (12/93, $2.95, one-shot)-Embossed-c; Sub-Mariner, Zabu, Ka-Zar, Shanna app.; produced in cooperation with World Wildlife Fund ... 3.00
...Inner Fury nn (1992, $5.95, 52 pgs.)-Sienkiewicz-c/a ... 6.00
...: Judgment Night (2000, $3.99) Shi app.; Battlebook ... 4.00
... Killing (9/93)-Kent Williams-a ... 6.00
... Knight of Terra (1995, $6.95)-Ostrander script ... 7.00
... Legends Vol. 2: Meltdown (2003, $19.99) r/Havok & Wolverine: Meltdown #1-4 ... 20.00
... Legends Vol. 3 (2003, $12.99) r/#181-186 ... 13.00
... Legends Vol. 4,5: 4-(See Wolverine: Xisle). 5-(See Wolverine: Snikt!) ...
... Legends Vol. 6: Marc Silvestri Book 1 (2004, $19.99) r/#31-34, 41-42, 48-50 ... 20.00
.../ Nick Fury: The Scorpio Connection Hardcover (1989, $16.95) ... 25.00
.../ Nick Fury: The Scorpio Connection Softcover(1990, $12.95) ... 15.00
... Not Dead Yet (12/98, $14.95, TPB)-r/#119-122 ... 15.00
...: Save The Tiger 1 (7/92, $2.95, 84 pgs.)-Reprints Wolverine stories from Marvel Comics Presents #1-10 w/new Kieth-c ... 3.00
...Scorpio Rising ($5.95, prestige format, one-shot) ... 6.00
.../Shi: Dark Night of Judgment (Crusade Comics, 2000, $2.99) Tucci-a ... 3.00
...Triumphs And Tragedies-(1995, $16.95, trade paperback)-r/Uncanny X-Men #109,172,173, Wolverine limited series #4, & Wolverine #41,42,75 ... 17.00
...Typhoid's Kiss (6/94, $6.95)-r/Wolverine stories from Marvel Comics Presents #109-116 ... 7.00
...Vs. Spider-Man 1 (3/95, $2.50) -r/Marvel Comics Presents #48-50 ... 2.50
...Witchblade 1 (3/97, $2.95) Devil's Reign Pt. 5 ...
Wizard #1/2 (1997) Joe Phillips/a(p) ... 10.00
NOTE: Austin c-3i. Bolton c(back)-5. Buscema a-1-16,25,27p; c-1-10. Byrne a-17-22p, 23; c-1(back), 17-22, 23p. Colan a-24. Andy Kubert c/a-51. Jim Lee c-24, 25, 27. Silvestri a(p)-31-43, 45, 46, 48-50, 52, 53, 55-57; c-31-42p, 43, 45p, 46p, 48, 49p, 50p, 52p, 53p, 55-57p. Stroman a-44p; c-60p. Williamson a-1i, 3i; c(i)-1, 3-6.

WOLVERINE (Volume 3)
Marvel Comics: July, 2003 - Present ($2.25/$2.50/$2.99)

1-Rucka-s/Robertson-a ... 4.00
2-19: 6-Nightcrawler app. 13-16-Sabretooth app. ... 3.00
20-Millar-s/Romita, Jr.-a begin, Elektra app. ... 4.00
20-B&W variant-c ... 8.00
21-39: 21-Elektra c/app. 23,24-Daredevil app. 26-28-Land-a. 29-Quesada-c; begin $2.50-c. 33-35-House of M. 36,37-Decimation. 36-Quesada-c. 39-Winter Soldier app. ... 3.00
40,43-48: 40-Begin $2.99-c; Winter Soldier app.; Texeira-a. 43-46-Civil War; Ramos-a. 45-Sub-Mariner app. ... 3.00
41,49-($3.99) 41-C.P. Smith-a/Stuart Moore-s ... 4.00
42-Civil War ... 5.00
50-($3.99) Sabretooth app.; Bianchi-a/c & Loeb-s begin; wraparound-c; McGuinness-a ... 4.00
50-($3.99) Variant Edition; uncolored art and cover; Bianchi pencil art page ... 4.00
51-55-(Regular and variant uncolored editions) Bianchi-a/Loeb-s; Sabretooth app. ... 3.00
55-EC-style variant-c by Greg Land ... 5.00
56-($3.99) Howard Chaykin-a/c ... 4.00
57-Suydam Zombie-c; Chaykin-a ... 3.00
...: Blood & Sorrow TPB (2007, $13.99) r/#41,49, stories from Giant-Size Wolverine #1 and X-Men Unlimited #12 ... 14.00

Civil War: Wolverine TPB (2007, $17.99) r/#42-48; gallery of B&W cover inks ... 18.00
...Enemy of the State HC Vol. 1 (2005, $19.99) r/#20-25; Ennis intro.; variant covers ... 20.00
...Enemy of the State HC Vol. 2 (2005, $19.99) r/#26-32 ... 20.00
...Enemy of the State SC Vol. 1 (2005, $14.99) r/#20-25; Ennis intro.; variant covers ... 15.00
...Enemy of the State SC Vol. 2 (2006, $16.99) r/#26-32 ... 17.00
...Enemy of the State - The Complete Edition (2006, $34.99) r/#20-32; Ennis intro.; sketch pages, variant covers and pin-up art ... 35.00
...Origins & Endings HC (2006, $19.99) r/#36-40 ... 20.00
...Origins & Endings SC (2006, $13.99) r/#36-40 ... 14.00
...Vol. 1: The Brotherhood (2003, $12.99) r/#1-6 ... 13.00
...Vol. 2: Coyote Crossing (2004, $11.99) r/#7-11 ... 12.00

WOLVERINE AND THE PUNISHER: DAMAGING EVIDENCE
Marvel Comics: Oct, 1993 - No. 3, Dec, 1993 ($2.00, limited series)

1-3: 2,3-Indicia says "The Punisher and Wolverine..." ... 3.00

WOLVERINE/CAPTAIN AMERICA
Marvel Comics: Apr, 2004 - No. 4, Apr, 2004 ($2.99, limited series)

1-4-Derenick-a/c ... 3.00

WOLVERINE: DAYS OF FUTURE PAST
Marvel Comics: Dec, 1997 - No. 3, Feb, 1998 ($2.50, limited series)

1-3: J.F. Moore-s/Bennett-a ... 2.50

WOLVERINE/DOOP (Also see X-Force and X-Statix)(Reprinted in X-Statix Vol. 2)
Marvel Comics: July, 2003 - No. 2, July, 2003 ($2.99, limited series)

1,2-Peter Milligan-s/Darwyn Cooke & J. Bone-a ... 3.00

WOLVERINE/GAMBIT: VICTIMS
Marvel Comics: Sept, 1995 - No. 4, Dec, 1995 ($2.95, limited series)

1-4: Jeph Loeb scripts & Tim Sale-a; foil-c ... 4.00

WOLVERINE/HULK
Marvel Comics: Apr, 2002 - No. 4, July, 2002 ($3.50, limited series)

1-4-Sam Kieth-s/a/c ... 3.50
Wolverine Legends Vol. 1: Wolverine/Hulk (2003, $9.99, TPB) r/#1-4 ... 10.00

WOLVERINE: NETSUKE
Marvel Comics: Nov, 2002 - No. 4, Feb, 2003 ($3.99, limited series)

1-4-George Pratt-s/painted-a ... 4.00

WOLVERINE: ORIGINS
Marvel Comics: June, 2006 - Present ($2.99)

1-15,17: 1-Daniel Way-s/Steve Dillon-a/Quesada-c ... 3.00
1-10-Variant covers. 1-Turner. 2-Quesada & Hitch. 3-Bianchi. 4-Dell'Otto. 7-Deodato ... 4.00
16-($3.99) Captain America WW2 app.; preview of Wolverine #56; r/X-Men #268 ... 4.00
16-Variant-c by McGuinness ... 4.00
Annual 1 (9/07, $3.99) Way-s/Andrews-a; flashback to 1932 ... 4.00
... Vol. 1 - Born in Blood HC (2006, $19.99, dustjacket) r/#1-5; variant covers ... 20.00
... Vol. 1 - Born in Blood SC (2007, $13.99) r/#1-5; variant covers ... 14.00
... Vol. 2 - Savior HC (2007, $19.99, dustjacket) r/#6-10; variant covers ... 20.00
... Vol. 2 - Savior SC (2007, $13.99) r/#6-10; variant covers ... 14.00
... Vol. 3 - Swift & Terrible HC (2007, $19.99, dustjacket) r/#11-15 ... 20.00
... Vol. 3 - Swift & Terrible SC (2007, $13.99) r/#11-15 ... 14.00

WOLVERINE/PUNISHER
Marvel Comics: May, 2004 - No. 5, Sept, 2004 ($2.99, limited series)

1-5: Milligan-s/Weeks-a ... 3.00
... Vol. 1 TPB (2004, $13.99) r/series ... 14.00

WOLVERINE/PUNISHER REVELATIONS (Marvel Knights)
Marvel Comics: Jun, 1999 - No. 4, Sept, 1999 ($2.95, limited series)

1-4: Pat Lee-a(p) ... 4.00
...: Revelation (4/00, $14.95, TPB) r/#1-4 ... 15.00

WOLVERINE SAGA
Marvel Comics: Sept, 1989 - No. 4, Mid-Dec, 1989 ($3.95, lim. series, 52 pgs.)

1-Gives history; Liefeld/Austin-c (front & back) ... 5.00
2-4: 2-Romita, Jr./Austin-c. 4-Kaluta-c. ... 5.00

WOLVERINE: SNIKT!
Marvel Comics: July, 2003 - No. 5, Nov, 2003 ($2.99, limited series)

1-5-Manga-style; Tsutomu Nihei-s/a ... 3.00
Wolverine Legends Vol. 5: Snikt! TPB (2003, $13.99) r/#1-5 ... 14.00

WOLVERINE: SOULTAKER
Marvel Comics: May, 2005 - No. 5, Aug, 2005 ($2.99, limited series)

1-5-Yoshida-s/Nagasawa-a/Terada-c; Yukio app. ... 3.00
TPB (2005, $13.99) r/#1-5 ... 14.00

Wolverine: The End #1 © MAR

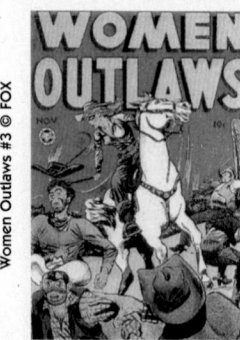

Women Outlaws #3 © FOX

Wonder Comics #11 © BP

	GD 2.0	VG 4.0	FN 6.0	VF 8.0	VF/NM 9.0	NM- 9.2

WOLVERINE: THE END
Marvel Comics: Jan, 2004 - No. 6, Dec, 2004 ($2.99, limited series)
1-5-Jenkins-s/Castellini-a — 3.00
1-Wizard World Texas variant-c — 20.00
TPB (2005, $14.99) r/#1-5 — 15.00

WOLVERINE: THE ORIGIN
Marvel Comics: Nov, 2001 - No. 6, July, 2002 ($3.50, limited series)
1-Origin of Logan; Jenkins-s/Andy Kubert-a; Quesada-c — 40.00
1-DF edition — 60.00
2 — 15.00
3 — 9.00
4-6 — 5.00
HC (3/02, $34.95, 11" x 7-1/2") r/#1-6; dust jacket; sketch pages and treatments — 35.00
HC (2006, $19.99) r/#1-6; dust jacket; sketch pages and treatments — 20.00
SC (2002, $14.95) r/#1-6; afterwords by Jemas and Quesada — 15.00

WOLVERINE: XISLE
Marvel Comics: June, 2003 - No. 5, June, 2003 ($2.50, weekly limited series)
1-5-Bruce Jones-s/Jorge Lucas-a — 2.50
Wolverine Legends Vol. 4 TPB (2003, $13.99) r/ #1-5 — 14.00

WOMEN IN LOVE (A Feature Presentation #5)
Fox Features Synd./Hero Books: Aug, 1949 - No. 4, Feb, 1950
1 — 32 64 96 186 293 400
2-Kamen/Feldstein-c — 26 52 78 154 242 330
3 — 18 36 54 105 165 225
4-Wood-a — 21 42 63 124 195 265

WOMEN IN LOVE (Thrilling Romances for Adults)
Ziff-Davis Publishing Co.: Winter, 1952 (25¢, 100 pgs.)
nn-(Scarce)-Kinstler-a; painted-c — 54 108 162 338 557 775

WOMEN OF MARVEL
Marvel Comics: 2006, 2007 ($24.99, TPB)
SC-Reprints 1st apps. of Dazzler, Ms. Marvel, Shanna, The Cat plus notable stories of other female Marvel characters; Mayhew-c — 25.00
Vol. 2 (2007) More stories of female Marvel characters; Mayhew-c; cover process art — 25.00

WOMEN OUTLAWS (My Love Memories #9 on)(Also see Red Circle)
Fox Features Syndicate: July, 1948 - No. 8, Sept, 1949
1-Used in SOTI, illo "Giving children an image of American womanhood"; negligee panels — 78 156 234 488 807 1125
2,3: 3-Kamenish-a — 59 118 177 369 615 860
4-8 — 47 94 141 287 474 660
nn(nd)-Contains Cody of the Pony Express; same cover as #7 — 32 64 96 186 293 400

WOMEN TO LOVE
Realistic: No date (1953)
nn-(Scarce)-Reprints Complete Romance #1; c-/Avon paperback #165 — 40 80 120 235 368 500

WONDER BOY (Formerly Terrific Comics) (See Blue Bolt, Bomber Comics & Samson)
Ajax/Farrell Publ.: No. 17, May, 1955 - No. 18, July, 1955 (Code approved)
17-Phantom Lady app. Bakerish-c/a — 46 92 138 281 466 650
18-Phantom Lady app. — 40 80 120 235 368 500
NOTE: Phantom Lady not by Matt Baker.

WONDER COMICS (Wonderworld #3 on)
Fox Features Syndicate: May, 1939 - No. 2, June, 1939 (68 pgs.)
1-(Scarce)-Wonder Man only app. by Will Eisner; Dr. Fung (by Powell), K-51 begins;
Bob Kane-a; Eisner-c — 1367 2734 4100 10,300 18,150 26,000
2-(Scarce)-Yarko the Great, Master Magician (see Samson) by Eisner begins; 'Spark' Stevens
by Bob Kane, Patty O'Day, Tex Mason app. Lou Fine's 1st-c; Fine-a (2 pgs.);
Yarko-c (Wonder Man-c #1) — 469 938 1407 3283 5742 8200

WONDER COMICS
Great/Nedor/Better Publications: May, 1944 - No. 20, Oct, 1948
1-The Grim Reaper & Spectro, the Mind Reader begin; Hitler/Hirohito bondage-c — 179 358 537 1119 1860 2600
2-Origin The Grim Reaper; Super Sleuths begin, end #8,17 — 72 144 216 450 750 1050
3-5: 3-Indicia reads "Vol. 1, #2" — 66 132 198 413 682 950
6-10: 6-Flag-c. 8-Last Spectro. 9-Wonderman begins — 53 106 159 323 537 750
11-14: 11-Dick Devens, King of Futuria begins, ends #14. 11,12-Ingels-c & splash pg.

14-Bondage-c — 62 124 186 388 644 900
15-Tara begins (origin), ends #20 — 71 142 213 444 735 1025
16,18: 16-Spectro app.; last Grim Reaper. 18-The Silver Knight begins — 62 124 186 388 644 900
17-Wonderman with Frazetta panels; Jill Trent with all Frazetta inks — 64 128 192 400 663 925
19-Frazetta panels — 62 124 186 388 644 900
20-Most of Silver Knight by Frazetta — 72 144 216 450 750 1050
NOTE: Ingels c-11, 12. Roussos a-19. Schomburg (Xela) c-1-10; (airbrush)-13-20. Bondage c-12, 13, 15. Cover features: Grim Reaper #1-8; Wonder Man #9-15; Tara #16-20.

WONDER DUCK (See Wisco)
Marvel Comics (CDS): Sept, 1949 - No. 3, Mar, 1950
1-Funny animal — 16 32 48 94 147 200
2,3 — 12 24 36 67 94 120

WONDERFUL ADVENTURES OF PINOCCHIO, THE (See Movie Comics & Walt Disney Showcase #48)
Whitman Publishing Co.: April, 1982 (Walt Disney)
nn-(#3 Continuation of Movie Comics?); r/FC #92 — 6.00

WONDERFUL WORLD FOR BOYS AND GIRLS
DC Comics: May, 1964
nn - Ashcan comic, not distributed to newsstands, only for in-house use (no known sales)

WONDERFUL WORLD OF DISNEY, THE (Walt Disney)
Whitman Publishing Co.: 1978 (Digest, 116 pgs.)
1-Barks-a (reprints) — 3 6 9 16 23 30
2 (no date) — 2 4 6 11 16 20

WONDERFUL WORLD OF THE BROTHERS GRIMM (See Movie Comics)

WONDERLAND COMICS
Feature Publications/Prize: Summer, 1945 - No. 9, Feb-Mar, 1947
1-Alex in Wonderland begins; Howard Post-c — 20 40 60 117 184 250
2-Howard Post-c/a(2) — 12 24 36 69 97 125
3-9: 3,4-Post-c — 10 20 30 56 76 95

WONDER MAN (See The Avengers #9, 151)
Marvel Comics Group: Mar, 1986 ($1.25, one-shot, 52 pgs.)
1 — 3.00

WONDER MAN
Marvel Comics Group: Sept, 1991 - No. 29, Jan, 1994 ($1.00)
1-29: 1-Free fold out poster by Johnson/Austin. 1-3-Johnson/Austin-c/a.
2-Avengers West Coast x-over. 4 Austin-c(i) — 2.50
Annual 1 (1992, $2.25)-Immonen-a (10 pgs.) — 3.00
Annual 2 (1993, $2.25)-Bagged w/trading card — 2.50

WONDER MAN
Marvel Comics: Feb, 2007 - No. 5, June, 2007 ($2.99, limited series)
1-5: 1-Peter David-s/Andrew Currie-a; Beast app. 4-Nauck-a — 3.00
...: My Fair Super Hero TPB (2007, $13.99) r/#1-5; Currie sketch page — 14.00

WONDERS OF ALADDIN, THE
Dell Publishing Co.: No. 1255, Feb-Apr, 1962
Four Color 1255-Movie — 6 12 18 43 69 95

WONDER WOMAN (See Adventure Comics #459, All-Star Comics, Brave and the Bold, DC Comics Presents, JLA, Justice League of America, Legend of..., Power Record Comics, Sensation Comics, Super Friends and World's Finest Comics #244)

WONDER WOMAN
DC Comics: Jan 1942
1-Ashcan comic, not distributed to newsstands, only for in-house use. Cover art is Sensation Comics #1 with interior being Sensation Comics #2. A CGC certified 8.5 copy sold for $17,250 in 2002.

WONDER WOMAN
National Periodical Publications/All-American Publ./DC Comics:
Summer, 1942 - No. 329, Feb, 1986
1-Origin Wonder Woman retold (more detailed than All Star #8); H. G. Peter-c/a begins — 2400 4800 7200 18,000 32,500 47,000
1-Reprint, Oversize 13-1/2x10". WARNING: This comic is an exact reprint of the original except for its size. DC published it in 1974 with a second cover titling it as a Famous First Edition. There have been many reported cases of the outer cover being removed and the interior sold as the original edition. The reprint with the new outer cover removed is practically worthless. See Famous First Edition for value.
2-Origin/1st app. Mars; Duke of Deception app. — 423 846 1269 2961 5181 7400
3 — 241 482 723 1506 2503 3500
4,5: 5-1st Dr. Psycho app. — 190 380 570 1188 1969 2750

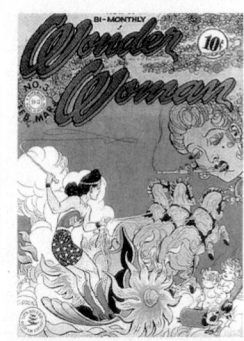

Wonder Woman #3 © DC

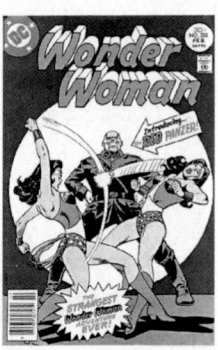

Wonder Woman #928 © DC

Wonder Woman (2nd series) #130 © DC

	GD 2.0	VG 4.0	FN 6.0	VF 8.0	VF/NM 9.0	NM- 9.2
6-9: 6-1st Cheetah app.	145	290	435	906	1503	2100
10-Invasion from Saturn classic sci-fi-c/s	154	308	462	963	1594	2225
11-20	114	228	342	713	1182	1650
21-30: 23-Story from Wonder Woman's childhood	91	182	273	569	947	1325
31-33,35-40: 38-Last H.G. Peter-c	66	132	198	413	687	960
34-Robot-c	69	138	207	431	716	1000
41-44,46-49: 49-Used in SOTI, pgs. 234,236; last 52 pg. issue						
	55	110	165	344	572	800
45-Origin retold	110	220	330	688	1144	1600
50-(44 pgs.)-Used in POP, pg. 97	56	112	168	350	580	810
51-60: 60-New logo	45	90	135	275	450	625
61-72: 62-Origin of W.W. i.d. 64-Story about 3-D movies. 70-1st Angle Man app. 72-Last pre-code (2/55)	41	82	123	250	400	550
73-90: 80-Origin The Invisible Plane. 85-1st S.A. issue. 89-Flying saucer-c/story	39	78	117	225	355	485
91-94,96,97,99: 97-Last H. G. Peter-a	31	62	93	178	282	385
95-A-Bomb-c	34	68	102	195	308	420
98-New origin & new art team (Andru & Esposito) begin (5/58)...W.W. id w/new facts						
	36	72	108	208	329	450
100-(8/58)	39	78	117	225	355	485
101-104,106,108-110	28	56	84	162	256	350
105-(Scarce, 4/59)-W. W.'s secret origin; W. W. appears as girl (no costume yet) (called Wonder Girl - see DC Super-Stars #1)	121	242	363	756	1253	1750
107-1st advs. of Wonder Girl; 1st Merboy; tells how Wonder Woman won her costume						
	40	80	120	235	368	500
111-120	22	44	66	128	202	275
121-126: 121-1st app. Wonder Woman Family. 122-1st app. Wonder Tot. 124-Wonder Woman Family app. 126-Last 10¢ issue	18	36	54	105	165	225
127-130: 128-Origin The Invisible Plane retold. 129-3rd app. Wonder Woman Family (#133 is 4th app.)	10	20	30	70	123	175
131-150: 132-Flying saucer-c	9	18	27	63	107	150
151-155,157,158,160-170 (1967): 151-Wonder Girl solo issue						
	7	14	21	49	80	110
156-(8/65)-Early mention of a comic book shop & comic collecting; mentions DCs selling for $100 a copy	8	16	24	52	86	120
159-Origin retold (1/66); 1st S.A. origin?	9	18	27	63	107	150
171-176	6	12	18	37	59	80
177-W. Woman/Supergirl battle	7	14	21	49	80	110
178-1st new Wonder Woman on-c only; appears in old costume w/powers inside						
	7	14	21	50	83	115
179-Classic-c; wears no costume to issue #203	7	14	21	47	76	105
180-195: 180-Death of Steve Trevor. 195-Wood inks	4	8	12	28	44	60
196 (52 pgs.)-Origin-r/All Star #8 (6 out of 9 pgs.)	5	10	15	30	48	65
197,198 (52 pgs.)-Reprints	5	10	15	30	48	65
199-Jeff Jones painted-c; 52 pgs.	7	14	21	45	73	100
200 (5-6/72)-Jeff Jones-c; 52 pgs.	7	14	21	49	80	110
201,202-Catwoman app. 202-Fafhrd & The Grey Mouser debut.						
	3	6	9	20	30	40
203,205-210,212: 212-The Cavalier app.	3	6	9	16	22	28
204-Return to old costume; death of I Ching.	3	6	9	20	30	40
211,214-(100 pgs.)	6	12	18	43	69	95
213,215,216,218-220: 220-N. Adams assist	3	6	9	14	19	24
217: (68 pgs.)	3	6	9	18	27	35
221,222,224-227,229,230,233-236,238-240	2	4	6	8	11	14
223,228,231,232,237,241,248: 223-Steve Trevor revived as Steve Howard & learns W.W.'s I.D. 228-Both Wonder Women team up & new World War II stories begin, end #243. 231,232: 48A app. 237-Origin retold. 241-Intro Bouncer; Spectre app. 248-Last Steve Trevor Howard dies (44 pgs.)	2	4	6	19	13	16
242-246,252-266,269,270: 243-Both W. Women team-up again. 269-Last Wood a(i) for DC? (7/80)	1	2	3	5	6	8
247,249-251: 247,249 (44 pgs.) 249-Hawkgirl app. 250-Origin/1st app. Orana, the new W. Woman. 251-Orana dies. 271-Huntress & 3rd Life of Steve Trevor begin						
	1	2	3	5	7	9
250-252,255-262,264-(Whitman variants, low print run, no issue # on cover)						
	2	4	6	10	14	18
267,268-Re-intro Animal Man (5/80 & 6/80)	1	3	4	6	8	10
272-280,284-286,289,290,294-299,301-325						5.00
281-283-Joker-c/stories in Huntress back-ups	1	2	3	5	7	9
287,288,291-293: 287-New Teen Titans x-over. 288-New costume & logo.						
291-293-Three part epic with Super-Heroines						6.00
300-($1.50, 76 pgs.)-Anniv. issue; Giffen-a; New Teen Titans, Bronze Age Sandman, JLA & G.A. Wonder Woman app.; 1st app. Lyta Trevor who becomes Fury in All-Star Squadron #25; G.A. Wonder Woman & Steve Trevor revealed as married						6.00
326-328						6.00

	GD 2.0	VG 4.0	FN 6.0	VF 8.0	VF/NM 9.0	NM- 9.2
329 (Double size)-S.A. W.W. & Steve Trevor wed	2	4	6	8	10	12
....: The Greatest Stories Ever Told TPB (2007, $19.99) intro. by Lynda Carter; Ross-c						20.00

NOTE: Andru/Esposito c-66-160(most). Buckler a-300. Colan a-288-305p; c-288-290p. Giffen a-300p. Grell c-217. Kaluta c-297. Gil Kane c-294p, 303-305, 307, 312, 314. Miller c-298p. Morrow c-233. Nasser a-232p; c-231p, 232p. Bob Oskner c(i)-39-65(most). Perez c-283p, 284p. Spiegle a-312. Staton a(p)-241, 271-287, 289, 290, 294-299; c(p)-241, 245, 246. Huntress back-up stories 271-287, 289, 290, 294-299, 301-321.

WONDER WOMAN
DC Comics: Feb, 1987 - No. 226, Apr, 2006 (75¢/$1.00/$1.25/$1.95/$1.99/$2.25/$2.50)

	GD 2.0	VG 4.0	FN 6.0	VF 8.0	VF/NM 9.0	NM- 9.2
0-(10/94) Zero Hour; released between #90 & #91	1	2	3	5	6	8
1-New origin; Perez-c/a begins	1	2	3	4	5	7
2-5						5.00
6-20: 9-Origin Cheetah. 12,13-Millennium x-over. 18,26-Free 16 pg. story						4.00
21-49: 24-Last Perez-a; scripts continue thru #62						3.00
50-($1.50, 52 pgs.)-New Titans, Justice League						4.00
51-62: Perez scripts. 60-Vs. Lobo; last Perez-c. 62-Last $1.00-c						3.00
63-New direction and Bolland-c begin; Deathstroke story continued from W. W. Special #1						2.50
64-84						2.50
85-1st Deodato-a; ends #100	2	4	6	8	10	12
86-88: 88-Superman-c & app.						5.00
89-97: 90-(9/94)-1st Artemis. 91-(11/94). 93-Hawkman app. 96-Joker-c						4.00
98,99						3.00
100 ($2.95, Newsstand)-Death of Artemis; Bolland-c ends.						4.00
100 ($3.95, Direct Market)-Death of Artemis; foil-c.						6.00
101-119, 121-125: 101-Begin $1.95-c; Byrne-c/a/scripts begin. 101-104-Darkseid app. 105-Phantom Stranger cameo. 106-108-Phantom Stranger & Demon app. 107,108-Arion app. 111-1st app. new Wonder Girl. 111,112-Vs. Doomsday. 112-Superman app. 113-Darkseid c/app; Sugar & Spike app.						2.50
120 ($2.95)-Perez-c						3.00
126-149: 128-Hippolyta becomes new W.W. 130-133-Flash (Jay Garrick) & JSA begin. 136-Diana returns to W.W. role; last Byrne issue. 137-Priest-s. 139-Luke-s/Paquette-a begin; Hughes-c thru #146						2.50
150-($2.95) Hughes-c/Clark-a; Zauriel app.						3.00
151-158-Hughes-c. 153-Superboy app.						2.50
159-163: 159-Begin $2.25-c. 160,161-Clayface app. 162,163-Aquaman app.						2.50
164-171: Phil Jimenez-s/a begin; Hughes-c; Batman app. 168,169-Pérez co-plot 169-Wraparound-c.170-Lois Lane-c/app.						2.50
172-Our Worlds at War; Hippolyta killed						3.00
173,174: 173-Our Worlds at War; Darkseid app. 174-Every DC heroine app.						2.50
175-($3.50) Joker: Last Laugh; JLA app.; Jim Lee-c						3.50
176-199: 177-Paradise Island returns. 179-Jimenez-a. 184,185-Hippolyta/c/app.; Hughes-c 186-Cheetah app. 189-Simonson-s/Ordway-a begin. 190-Diana's new look. 195-Rucka-s/Drew Johnson-a begin. 197-Flash-c/app. 198,199-Noto-c						2.50
200-($3.95) back-up stories in 1940s and 1960s styles; pin-up by various						4.00
201-218,220-225: 203,204-Batman-c/app. 204-Matt Wagner-c. 212-JLA app. 214-Flash app. 215-Morales-a begins. 218-Begin $2.50-c. 220-Batman app.						2.75
219-Omac tie-in/Sacrifice pt. 4; Wonder Woman kills Max Lord; Superman app.						3.00
219-(2nd printing) Altered cover with red background						2.50
226-Last issue; flashbacks to meetings with Superman; Rucka-s/Richards-a						3.00
#1,000,000 (11/98) 853rd Century x-over; Deodato-c						3.00
Annual 1,2: 1 ($88, $1.50)-Art Adams-a. 2 ('89, $2.00, 68 pgs.)-All women artists issue; Perez-c(i)/a.						4.00
Annual 3 (1992, $2.50, 68 pgs.)-Quesada-c(p)						3.00
Annual 4 (1995, $3.50)-Year One						3.50
Annual 5 (1996, $2.95)-Legends of the Dead Earth story; Byrne scripts; Cockrum-a						3.00
Annual 6 (1997, $3.95)-Pulp Heroes						4.00
Annual 7,8 ('98,'99, $2.95)-7-Ghosts; Wrightson-c. 8-JLApe, A.Adams-c						3.00
...: Beauty and the Beasts TPB (2005, $19.95) r/#15-19 & Action Comics #600						20.00
...: Bitter Rivals TPB (2004, $13.95) r/#200-205; Jones-c						13.00
...: Challenge of the Gods TPB ('04, $19.95) r/#8-14; Pérez-s/a						20.00
...: Destiny Calling TPB (2006, $19.99) r/#20-24 & Annual #1; Pérez-c & pin-up gallery						20.00
...Donna Troy (6/98, $1.95) Girlfrenzy; Jimenez-a						2.50
... Down To Earth TPB (2004, $14.95) r/#195-200; Greg Land-c						15.00
... 80-Page Giant 1 (2002, $4.95) reprints in format of 1960s' 80-Page Giants						5.00
...: Eyes of the Gorgon TPB ('05, $19.99) r/#206-213						20.00
Gallery (1996, $3.50)-Bolland-c; pin-ups by various						4.00
...: Gods and Mortals TPB ('04, $19.95) r/#1-7; Pérez-a						20.00
...: Gods of Gotham TPB ('01, $5.95) r/#164-167; Jimenez-s/a						6.00
...: Land of the Dead TPB ('06, $12.99) r/#214-217 & Flash #219						13.00
Lifelines TPB ('98, $9.95) r/#106-112; Byrne-c/a						10.00
...: Mission's End TPB ('06, $19.99) r/#218-226; cover gallery						20.00
...: Our Worlds at War (10/01, $2.95) History of the Amazons; Jae Lee-c						3.00
...: Paradise Found TPB ('03, $14.95) r/#171-177, Secret Files #3; Jimenez-s/a						15.00
...: Paradise Lost TPB ('02, $14.95) r/#164-170; Jimenez-s/a						15.00
Plus 1 (1/97, $2.95)-Jesse Quick/c app.						3.00

Wonder Woman (3rd series) #9 © DC

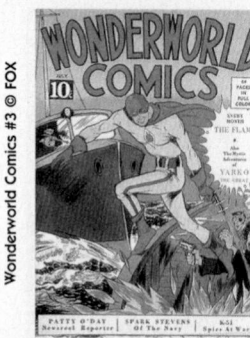

Wonderworld Comics #3 © FOX

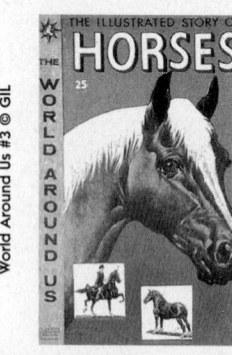

World Around Us #3 © GIL

	GD 2.0	VG 4.0	FN 6.0	VF 8.0	VF/NM 9.0	NM- 9.2
Second Genesis TPB (1997, $9.95)-r/#101-105						10.00
Secret Files 1-3 (3/98, 7/99, 5/02; $4.95)						5.00
Special 1 (1992, $1.75, 52 pgs.)-Deathstroke-c/story continued in Wonder Woman #63						4.00
...: The Blue Amazon (2003, $6.95) Elseworlds; McKeever-a						7.00
The Challenge Of Artemis TPB (1996, $9.95)-r/#94-100; Deodato-c/a						10.00
...: The Once and Future Story (1998, $4.95) Trina Robbins-s/Doran & Guice-a						5.00

NOTE: **Art Adams** a-Annual 1. **Byrne** c/a 101-107. **Bolton** a-Annual 1. **Deodato** a-85-100. **Perez** a-Annual 1; c-Annual 1(i). **Quesada** c(p)-Annual 3.

WONDER WOMAN (Also see Amazons Attack mini-series)
DC Comics: Aug, 2006 - Present ($2.99)

	GD 2.0	VG 4.0	FN 6.0	VF 8.0	VF/NM 9.0	NM- 9.2
1-Donna Troy as Wonder Woman after Infinite Crisis; Heinberg-s/Dodson-a/c						3.00
1-Variant-c by Adam Kubert						4.00
2-12: 2-4-Giganta & Hercules app. 6-Jodi Picoult-s begins. 8-Hippolyta returns. 9-12-Amazons Attack tie-in; JLA app.						3.00

WONDER WOMAN: AMAZONIA
DC Comics: 1997 ($7.95, Graphic Album format, one shot)

	GD 2.0	VG 4.0	FN 6.0	VF 8.0	VF/NM 9.0	NM- 9.2
1-Elseworlds; Messner-Loebs-s/Winslade-a						8.00

WONDER WOMAN SPECTACULAR (See DC Special Series #9)

WONDER WOMAN: SPIRIT OF TRUTH
DC Comics: Nov, 2001 ($9.95, treasury size, one-shot)

	GD 2.0	VG 4.0	FN 6.0	VF 8.0	VF/NM 9.0	NM- 9.2
nn-Painted art by Alex Ross; story by Alex Ross and Paul Dini						10.00

WONDER WOMAN: THE HIKETEIA
DC Comics: 2002 ($24.95, hardcover, one-shot)

	GD 2.0	VG 4.0	FN 6.0	VF 8.0	VF/NM 9.0	NM- 9.2
nn-Wonder Woman battles Batman; Greg Rucka-s/J.G. Jones-a						25.00
Softcover (2003, $17.95)						18.00

WONDERWORLD COMICS (Formerly Wonder Comics)
Fox Features Syndicate: No. 3, July, 1939 - No. 33, Jan, 1942

	GD 2.0	VG 4.0	FN 6.0	VF 8.0	VF/NM 9.0	NM- 9.2
3-Intro The Flame by Fine; Dr. Fung (Powell-a), K-51 (Powell-a?), & Yarko the Great, Master Magician (Eisner-a) continues; Eisner/Fine-c	686	1372	2058	4800	8400	12,000
4-Lou Fine-c	321	642	963	2087	3694	5300
5,6,9,10: Lou Fine-c	186	372	558	1163	1932	2700
7-Classic Lou Fine-c	300	600	900	1970	3485	5000
8-Classic Lou Fine-c	276	552	828	1725	2863	4000
11-Origin The Flame	141	282	423	881	1466	2050
12-15:13-Dr. Fung ends; last Fine-c(p)	114	228	342	713	1182	1650
16-20	85	170	255	531	776	1225
21-Origin The Black Lion & Cub	78	156	234	488	807	1125
22-27: 22,25-Dr. Fung app.	62	124	186	388	644	900
28-Origin & 1st app. U.S. Jones (8/41); Lu-Nar, the Moon Man begins	83	166	249	519	860	1200
29,31,33	50	100	150	305	503	700
30-Intro & Origin Flame Girl	91	182	273	569	947	1325
32-Hitler-c	76	152	228	475	788	1100

NOTE: *Spies at War* by **Eisner** in #13, 17. *Yarko* by **Eisner** in #3-11. **Eisner** text illos-3. **Eisner** text illos-4. **Nordling** a-4-14. **Powell** a-3-12. **Tuska** a-5-9. Bondage-c 14, 15, 28, 31, 32. Cover features: The Flame-#3, 5-31; U.S. Jones-#32, 33.

WONDERWORLDS
Innovation Publishing: 1992 ($3.50, squarebound, 100 pgs.)

	GD 2.0	VG 4.0	FN 6.0	VF 8.0	VF/NM 9.0	NM- 9.2
1-Rebound super-hero comics, contents may vary; Hero Alliance, Terraformers, etc.						3.50

WOODSY OWL (See March of Comics #395)
Gold Key: Nov, 1973 - No. 10, Feb, 1976

	GD 2.0	VG 4.0	FN 6.0	VF 8.0	VF/NM 9.0	NM- 9.2
1	2	4	6	13	18	22
2-10	2	4	6	8	10	12

WOODY WOODPECKER (Walter Lantz... #73 on?)(See Dell Giants for annuals)
(Also see The Funnies, Jolly Jingles, Kite Fun Book, New Funnies)
Dell Publishing Co./Gold Key No. 73-187/Whitman No. 188 on:
No. 169, 10/47 - No. 72, 5-7/62; No. 73, 10/62 - No. 201, 3/84 (nn #192)

	GD 2.0	VG 4.0	FN 6.0	VF 8.0	VF/NM 9.0	NM- 9.2
Four Color 169(#1)-Drug turns Woody into a Mr. Hyde	17	34	51	126	223	320
Four Color 188	11	22	33	79	140	200
Four Color 202,232,249,264,288	8	16	24	58	97	135
Four Color 305,336,350	6	12	18	41	66	90
Four Color 364,374,390,405,416,431('52)	5	10	15	35	55	75
16 (12-1/52-53) - 30('55)	4	8	12	24	44	60
31-50	4	8	12	22	34	45
51-72 (Last Dell)	3	6	9	18	27	35
73-75 (Giants, 84 pgs., Gold Key)	5	10	15	32	51	70
76-80	3	6	9	16	22	28
81-103: 103-Last 12¢ issue	3	6	9	14	19	24

	GD 2.0	VG 4.0	FN 6.0	VF 8.0	VF/NM 9.0	NM- 9.2
104-120	2	4	6	11	16	20
121-140	2	4	6	9	12	15
141-160	1	3	4	6	8	10
161-187	1	2	3	5	7	9
188,189 (Whitman)	2	4	6	8	11	14
190(9/80),191(11/80)-pre-pack only	3	6	9	21	32	42
(No #192)						
193-197: 196(2/82), 197(4/82)	2	4	6	10	14	18
198-201 (All #90062 on-c, no date or date code, pre-pack): 198(6/83), 199(7/83), 200(8/83), 201(3/84)	3	6	9	14	20	25
Christmas Parade 1(11/68-Giant)(G.K.)	4	8	12	26	41	55
Summer Fun 1(6/66-G.K.)(84 pgs.)	5	10	15	30	48	65
nn (1971, 60¢, 100 pgs. digest) B&W one page gags	3	6	9	17	25	32

NOTE: 15¢ Canadian editions of the 12¢ issues exist. Reprints-No. 92, 102, 103, 105, 106, 124, 125, 152, 153, 157, 162, 165, 194(1/3)-200(1/3).

WOODY WOODPECKER (See Comic Album #5,9,13, Dell Giant #24, 40, 54, Dell Giants, The Funnies, Golden Comics Digest #1, 3, 5, 8, 15, 16, 20, 24, 32, 37, 44, March of Comics #16, 34, 85, 93, 109, 124, 139, 158, 177, 184, 203, 222, 239, 249, 261, 420, 454, 466, 478, New Funnies & Super Book #12, 24)

WOODY WOODPECKER
Harvey Comics: Sept, 1991 - No. 15, Aug, 1994 ($1.25)

	GD 2.0	VG 4.0	FN 6.0	VF 8.0	VF/NM 9.0	NM- 9.2
1-15: 1-r/W.W. #53						2.50
50th Anniversary Special 1 (10/91, $2.50, 68 pgs.)						3.00

WOODY WOODPECKER AND FRIENDS
Harvey Comics: Dec, 1991 - No. 4, 1992 ($1.25)

	GD 2.0	VG 4.0	FN 6.0	VF 8.0	VF/NM 9.0	NM- 9.2
1-4						2.50

WORD WARRIORS (Also see Quest for Dreams Lost)
Literacy Volunteers of Chicago: 1987 ($1.50, B&W)(Proceeds donated to help literacy)

	GD 2.0	VG 4.0	FN 6.0	VF 8.0	VF/NM 9.0	NM- 9.2
1-Jon Sable by Grell, Ms. Tree, Streetwolf; Chaykin-c						3.00

WORLD AROUND US, THE (Illustrated Story of...)
Gilberton Publishers (Classics Illustrated): Sep, 1958 -No. 36, Oct, 1961 (25¢)

	GD 2.0	VG 4.0	FN 6.0	VF 8.0	VF/NM 9.0	NM- 9.2
1-Dogs; Evans-a	9	18	27	52	69	85
2-4: 2-Indians; Check-a. 3-Horses; L. B. Cole-c. 4-Railroads; L. B. Cole-a (5 pgs.)	9	18	27	47	61	75
5-Space; Ingels-a	10	20	30	58	76	95
6-The F.B.I.; Disbrow, Evans, Ingels-a	10	20	30	56	76	95
7-Pirates; Disbrow, Ingels, Kinstler-a	9	18	27	52	69	85
8-Flight; Evans, Ingels, Crandall-a	9	18	27	52	69	85
9-Army; Disbrow, Ingels, Orlando-a	9	18	27	47	61	75
10-13: 10-Navy; Disbrow, Evans, Kinstler-a. 11-Marine Corps. 12-Coast Guard; Ingels-a (9 pgs.). 13-Air Force; L.B. Cole-c	9	18	27	47	61	75
14-French Revolution; Crandall, Evans, Kinstler-a	10	20	30	56	76	95
15-Prehistoric Animals; Al Williamson-a, 6 & 10 pgs. plus Morrow-a	10	20	30	58	79	100
16-18: 16-Crusades; Kinstler-a. 17-Festivals; Evans, Crandall-a. 18-Great Scientists; Crandall, Evans, Torres, Williamson, Morrow-a	9	18	27	52	69	85
19-Jungle; Crandall, Williamson, Morrow-a	10	20	30	58	79	100
20-Communications; Crandall, Evans, Torres-a	10	20	30	56	76	95
21-American Presidents; Crandall/Evans, Morrow-a	10	20	30	56	76	95
22-Boating; Crandall, Evans-a	8	16	24	44	57	70
23-Great Explorers; Crandall, Evans-a	9	18	27	52	69	85
24-Ghosts; Morrow, Evans-a	10	20	30	56	76	95
25-Magic; Evans, Morrow-a	10	20	30	56	76	95
26-The Civil War	11	22	33	62	86	110
27-Mountains (High Advs.); Crandall/Evans, Morrow, Torres-a	9	18	27	52	69	85
28-Whaling; Crandall, Evans, Morrow, Torres, Wildey-a; L.B. Cole-c	9	18	27	52	69	85
29-Vikings; Crandall, Evans, Torres, Morrow-a	10	20	30	58	79	100
30-Undersea Adventure; Crandall/Evans, Kirby, Morrow, Torres-a	10	20	30	56	76	95
31-Hunting; Crandall/Evans, Ingels, Kinstler, Kirby-a	9	18	27	52	69	85
32,33: 32-For Gold & Glory; Morrow, Kirby, Crandall, Evans-a. 33-Famous Teens; Torres, Crandall, Evans-a	9	18	27	52	69	85
34-36: 34-Fishing; Crandall/Evans-a. 35-Spies; Kirby, Morrow?, Evans-a. 36-Fight for Life (Medicine); Kirby-a	9	18	27	52	69	85

NOTE: See Classics Illustrated Special Edition. Another *World Around Us* issue entitled *The Sea* had been prepared in 1962 but was never published in the U.S. It was published in the British/European *World Around Us* series. Those series then continued with seven additional WAU titles not in the U.S. series.

WORLD BELOW, THE
Dark Horse Comics: Mar, 1999 - No. 4, Jun, 1999 ($2.50, limited series)

	GD 2.0	VG 4.0	FN 6.0	VF 8.0	VF/NM 9.0	NM- 9.2
1-4-Paul Chadwick-s/c/a						2.50
TPB (1/07, $12.95) r/#1-4; intro. by Chadwick; gallery of sketches and covers						13.00

World of Archie #8 © AP

World of Fantasy #7 © MAR

World's Finest Comics #11 © DC

	GD 2.0	VG 4.0	FN 6.0	VF 8.0	VF/NM 9.0	NM- 9.2

WORLD BELOW, THE: DEEPER AND STRANGER
Dark Horse Comics: Dec, 1999 - No. 4, Mar, 2000 ($2.95, B&W)

1-4-Paul Chadwick-s/c/a						3.00

WORLD FAMOUS HEROES MAGAZINE
Comic Corp. of America (Centaur): Oct, 1941 - No. 4, Apr, 1942 (comic book)

1-Gustavson-c; Lubbers, Glanzman-a; Davy Crockett, Paul Revere, Lewis & Clark, John Paul Jones stories; Flag-c	110	220	330	688	1144	1600
2-Lou Gehrig life story; Lubbers-a	46	92	138	281	466	650
3,4-Lubbers-a. 4-Wild Bill Hickok story; 2 pg. Marlene Dietrich story	43	86	129	262	431	600

WORLD FAMOUS STORIES
Croyden Publishers: 1945

1-Ali Baba, Hansel & Gretel, Rip Van Winkle, Mid-Summer Night's Dream	14	28	42	76	108	140

WORLD IS HIS PARISH, THE
George A. Pflaum: 1953 (15¢)

nn-The story of Pope Pius XII	6	12	18	28	34	40

WORLD OF ADVENTURE (Walt Disney's...)(TV)
Gold Key: Apr, 1963 - No. 3, Oct, 1963 (12¢)

1-Disney TV characters; Savage Sam, Johnny Shiloh, Capt. Nemo, The Mooncussers	3	6	9	21	32	42
2,3	3	6	9	15	21	26

WORLD OF ARCHIE, THE (See Archie Giant Series Mag. #148, 151, 156, 160, 165, 171, 177, 182, 188, 193, 200, 208, 213, 225, 232, 237, 244, 249, 456, 461, 468, 473, 480, 485, 492, 497, 504, 509, 516, 521, 532, 543, 554, 565, 574, 587, 599, 612, 627)

WORLD OF ARCHIE
Archie Comics: Aug, 1992 - No. 22 ($1.25/$1.50)

1						4.00
2-15: 9-Neon ink-c						3.00
16-22						2.50

WORLD OF FANTASY
Atlas Comics (CPC No. 1-15/ZPC No. 16-19): May, 1956 - No. 19, Aug, 1959

1	46	92	138	281	466	650
2-Williamson-a (4 pgs.)	31	62	93	178	282	385
3-Sid Check, Roussos-a	27	54	81	156	246	335
4-7	21	42	63	124	195	265
8-Matt Fox, Orlando, Berg-a	23	46	69	132	209	285
9-Krigstein-a	22	44	66	126	198	270
10-15: 11-Torres-a	18	36	54	103	162	220
16-Williamson-a (4 pgs.); Ditko, Kirby-a	25	50	75	145	228	310
17-19-Ditko, Kirby-a	25	50	75	145	228	310

NOTE: Ayers a-3. B. Baily a-5, 6, 8. Brodsky c-3. Check a-3. Ditko a-17, 19. Everett a-2; c-4-7, 9, 12, 13. Forte a-4. Infantino a-14. Kirby c-15, 17-19. Krigstein a-9. Maneely c-2, 14. Mooney a-14. Morrow a-7. Orlando a-8, 13, 14. Pakula a-9. Powell a-4, 6. R.Q. Sale a-3, 9. Severin c-1.

WORLD OF GIANT COMICS, THE (See Archie All-Star Specials under Archie Comics)

WORLD OF GINGER FOX, THE (Also see Ginger Fox)
Comico: Nov, 1986 ($6.95, 8 1/2 x 11", 68 pgs., mature)

Graphic Novel ($6.95)						7.00
Hardcover ($27.95)						28.00

WORLD OF JUGHEAD, THE (See Archie Giant Series Mag. #9, 14, 19, 24, 30, 136, 143, 149, 152, 157, 161, 166, 172, 178, 183, 189, 194, 202, 209, 215, 227, 233, 239, 245, 251, 457, 463, 469, 475, 481, 487, 493, 499, 505, 511, 517, 523, 531, 542, 553, 564, 577, 590, 602)

WORLD OF KRYPTON, THE (World of...#3) (See Superman #248)
DC Comics, Inc.: 7/79 - No. 3, 9/79; 12/87 - No. 4, 3/88 (Both are lim. series)

1-3 (1979, 40¢; 1st comic book mini-series): 1-Jor-El marries Lara. 3-Baby Superman sent to Earth; Krypton explodes; Mon-el app.						5.00
1-4 (75¢)-Byrne scripts; Byrne/Simonson-c						3.00

WORLD OF METROPOLIS, THE
DC Comics: Aug, 1988 - No. 4, July, 1988 ($1.00, limited series)

1-4: Byrne scripts						3.00

WORLD OF MYSTERY
Atlas Comics (GPI): June, 1956 - No. 7, July, 1957

1-Torres, Orlando-a; Powell-a?	46	92	138	281	466	650
2-Woodish-a	20	40	60	117	184	250
3-Torres, Davis, Ditko-a	24	48	72	139	220	300
4-Pakula, Powell-a	24	48	72	139	220	300
5,7: 5-Orlando-a	19	38	57	112	176	240

6-Williamson/Mayo-a (4 pgs.); Ditko-a; Crandall text illo	24	48	72	139	220	300

NOTE: Brodsky c-2. Colan a-7. Everett c-1, 3. Pakula a-4, 6. Romita a-2. Severin c-7.

WORLD OF SMALLVILLE
DC Comics: Apr, 1988 - No. 4, July, 1988 (75¢, limited series)

1-4: Byrne scripts						3.00

WORLD OF SUSPENSE
Atlas News Co.: Apr, 1956 - No. 8, July, 1957

1	40	80	120	240	383	525
2-Ditko-a (4 pgs.)	24	48	72	139	220	300
3,7-Williamson-a in both (4 pgs.); #7-with Mayo	23	46	69	135	213	290
4-6,8	19	38	57	112	176	240

NOTE: Berg a-6. Cameron a-2. Ditko a-2. Drucker a-1. Everett a-1, 5; c-6. Heck a-5. Maneely a-1; c-1-3. Orlando a-5. Powell a-6. Reinman a-1. Roussos a-4. Shores a-1.

WORLD OF WHEELS (Formerly Dragstrip Hotrodders)
Charlton Comics: No. 17, Oct, 1967 - No. 32, June, 1970

17-20-Features Ken King	3	6	9	18	27	35
21-32-Features Ken King	3	6	9	16	22	28
Modern Comics Reprint 23(1978)						5.00

WORLD OF WOOD
Eclipse Comics: 1986 - No. 4, 1987; No. 5, 2/89 ($1.75, limited series)

1-4:1-Dave Stevens-c. 2-Wood/Stevens-c						4.00
5 ($2.00, B&W)-r/Avon's Flying Saucers						5.00

WORLD'S BEST COMICS
DC Comics: Feb 1940

nn - Ashcan comic, not distributed to newsstands, only for in-house use. Cover art is Action Comics #29 with interior being Action Comics #24 (no known sales)

WORLD'S BEST COMICS (World's Finest Comics #2 on)
National Per. Publications (100 pgs.): Spring, 1941 (Cardboard-c)(DC's 6th annual format comic)

1-The Batman, Superman, Crimson Avenger, Johnny Thunder, The King, Young Dr. Davis, Zatara, Lando, Man of Magic, & Red, White & Blue begin; Superman, Batman & Robin covers begin (inside-c is blank); Fred Ray-c; 15¢ cover price	1412	2824	4236	10,000	17,000	24,000

WORLD'S BEST COMICS: GOLDEN AGE SAMPLER
DC Comics: 2003 (99¢, one-shot, samples from DC Archive editions)

1-Golden Age reprints from Superman #6, Batman #5, Sensation #11, Police #11						2.50

WORLD'S BEST COMICS: SILVER AGE SAMPLER
DC Comics: 2004 (99¢, one-shot, samples from DC Archive editions)

1-Silver Age reprints from Justice League #4, Adventure #247, Our Army at War #81						2.50

WORLDS BEYOND (Stories of Weird Adventure)(Worlds of Fear #2 on)
Fawcett Publications: Nov, 1951

1-Powell, Bailey-a; Moldoff-c	46	92	138	281	466	650

WORLDS COLLIDE
DC Comics: July, 1994 ($2.50, one-shot)

1-($2.50, 52 pgs.)-Milestone & Superman titles x-over						2.50
1-($3.95, 52 pgs.)-Polybagged w/vinyl clings						4.00

WORLD'S FAIR COMICS (See New York...)

WORLD'S FINEST (Also see Legends of The World's Finest)
DC Comics: 1990 - No. 3, 1992 ($3.95, squarebound, limited series, 52 pgs.)

1-3: Batman & Superman team-up against The Joker and Lex Luthor; Dave Gibbons scripts & Steve Rude-c/a. 2,3-Joker/Luthor painted-c by Steve Rude						5.00
TPB-($19.95) r/#1-3						20.00

WORLD'S FINEST COMICS (Formerly World's Best Comics #1)
National Periodical Publ./DC Comics: No. 2, Sum, 1941 - No. 323, Jan, 1986 (#1-17 have cardboard covers) (#2-9 have 100 pgs.)

2 (100 pgs.)-Superman, Batman & Robin covers continue from World's Best; (cover price 15¢ #2-70)	442	884	1326	2873	5087	7300
3-The Sandman begins; last Johnny Thunder; origin & 1st app. The Scarecrow	327	654	981	2126	3763	5400
4-Hop Harrigan app.; last Young Dr. Davis	252	504	756	1575	2613	3650
5-Intro. TNT & Dan the Dyna-Mite; last King & Crimson Avenger	252	504	756	1575	2613	3650
6-Star Spangled Kid begins (Sum/42); Aquaman app.; S&K Sandman with Sandy in new costume begins, ends #7	186	372	558	1163	1932	2700
7-Green Arrow begins (Fall/42); last Lando & Red, White & Blue; S&K art						

World's Finest Comics #41 © DC

World's Finest Comics #174 © DC

Worlds of Fear #7 © FAW

	GD 2.0	VG 4.0	FN 6.0	VF 8.0	VF/NM 9.0	NM- 9.2
	186	372	558	1163	1932	2700
8-Boy Commandos begin (by Simon(p) #12); last The King; includes "Minute Man Answers the Call" promo	176	352	528	1100	1825	2550
9-Batman cameo in Star Spangled Kid; S&K-a; last 100 pg. issue; Hitler, Mussolini, Tojo-c	204	408	612	1275	2113	2950
10-S&K-a; 76 pg. issues begin	166	332	498	1038	1719	2400
11-17: 17-Last cardboard cover issue	134	268	402	838	1394	1950
18-20: 18-Paper covers begin; last Star Spangled Kid. 19-Joker story. 20-Last quarterly issue	128	256	384	800	1325	1850
21-30: 21-Begin bi-monthly. 30-Johnny Everyman app.	88	176	264	550	913	1275
31-40: 33-35-Tomahawk app. 35-Penguin app.	81	162	243	506	841	1175
41-50: 41-Boy Commandos end. 42-The Wyoming Kid begins (9-10/49), ends #63. 43-Full Steam Foley begins, ends #48. 48-Last square binding. 49-Tom Sparks, Boy Inventor begins; robot-c	64	128	192	400	663	925
51-60: 51-Zatara ends. 54-Last 76 pg. issue. 59-Manhunters Around the World begins (7-8/52), ends #62	60	120	180	375	625	875
61-64: 61-Joker story. 63-Capt. Compass app.	59	118	177	369	610	850
65-Origin Superman; Tomahawk begins (7-8/53), ends #101	86	172	258	538	894	1250
66-70-(15¢ issues, scarce)-Last 15¢, 68pg. issue	59	118	177	369	610	850
71-(10¢ issue, scarce)-Superman & Batman begin as team (7-8/54); were in separate stories until now; Superman & Batman exchange identities; 10¢ issues begin	134	268	402	838	1394	1950
72,73-(10¢ issue, scarce)	88	176	264	550	913	1275
74-Last pre-code issue	64	128	192	400	663	925
75-(1st code approved, 3-4/55)	62	124	186	388	644	900
76-80: 77-Superman loses powers & Batman obtains them	50	100	150	305	503	700
81-90: 84-1st S.A. issue. 88-1st Joker/Luthor team-up. 89-2nd Batmen of All Nations (aka Club of Heroes). 90-Batwoman's 1st app. in World's Finest (10/57, 3rd app. anywhere) plus-c app.	27	54	81	203	364	525
91-93,95-99: 96-99-Kirby Green Arrow. 99-Robot-c	20	40	60	150	268	385
94-Origin Superman/Batman team retold	51	102	153	408	742	1075
100 (3/59)	34	68	102	255	465	675
101-110: 102-Tommy Tomorrow begins, ends #124	14	28	42	99	175	250
111-121: 111-1st app. The Clock King. 113-Intro. Miss Arrowette in Green Arrow; 1st Bat-Mite/Mr. Mxyzptlk team-up (11/60). 117-Batwoman-c. 121-Last 10¢ issue	11	23	33	79	140	200
122-128: 123-2nd Bat-Mite/Mr. Mxyzptlk team-up (2/62). 125-Aquaman begins (5/62), ends #139 (Aquaman #1 is dated 1-2/62)	9	18	27	63	107	150
129-Joker/Luthor team-up-c/story	10	20	30	71	126	180
130-142: 135-Last Dick Sprang story. 140-Last Green Arrow. 142-Origin The Composite Superman (villain); Legion app.	8	16	24	52	86	120
143-150: 143-1st Mailbag. 144-Clayface/Brainiac team-up; last Clayface until Action #443	6	12	18	43	69	95
151-153,155,157-160: 157-2nd Super Sons story; last app. Kathy Kane (Bat-Woman) until Batman Family #10; 1st Bat-Mite	5	10	15	35	55	75
154-1st Super Sons story; last Bat-Woman in costume until Batman Family #10.	6	12	18	39	62	85
156-1st Bizarro Batman; Joker-c/story	9	18	27	63	107	150
161,170 (80-Pg. Giants G-28,G-40)	6	12	18	41	66	90
162-165,167,168,171,172: 168,172-Adult Legion app.	4	8	12	28	44	60
166-Aquaman-c/story	5	10	15	32	51	70
169-3rd app. new Batgirl(9/67)(cover and 1 panel cameo); 3rd Bat-Mite/Mr. Mxyzptlk team-up	5	10	15	30	48	65
173-('68)-1st S.A. app. Two-Face as Batman becomes Two-Face in story	8	16	24	56	93	130
174-Adams-c	5	10	15	30	48	65
175,176-Neal Adams-c/a; both reprint J'onn J'onzz origin/Detective #225,226	5	10	15	30	51	70
177-Joker/Luthor team-up-c/story	5	10	15	30	48	65
178-(9/68) Intro. of Super Nova (revived in "52" weekly series); Adams-c	4	8	12	24	37	50
179-(80 Page Giant G-52) -Adams-c; r/#94	6	12	18	37	59	80
180,182,183,185,186: Adams-c on all. 182-Silent Knight-r/Brave & Bold #6. 185-Last 12¢ issue. 186-Johnny Quick-r	4	8	12	22	34	45
181,184,187: 187-Green Arrow origin-r by Kirby (Adv. #256).	3	6	9	20	30	40
188,197:(Giants G-64,G-76; 64 pages)	5	10	15	32	51	70
189-196: 190-193-Robin-r	3	6	9	17	25	32
198,199-3rd Superman/Flash race (see Flash #175 & Superman #199). 199-Adams-c	8	16	24	58	97	135
200-Adams-c	3	6	9	20	30	40
201-203: 203-Last 15¢ issue.	3	6	9	16	22	28
204,205-(52 pgs.) Adams-c: 204-Wonder Woman app. 205-Shining Knight-r (6 pgs.) by Frazetta/Adv. #153; Teen Titans x-over	3	6	9	17	25	32
206 (Giant G-88, 64 pgs.)	4	8	12	28	44	60
207,212-(52 pgs.)	3	6	9	17	25	32
208-211(25¢-c) Adams-c: 208-(52 pgs.) Origin Robotman-r/Det. #138. 209-211-(52 pgs.)	3	6	9	17	25	35
213,214,216-222,229: 217-Metamorpho begins, ends #220; Batman/Superman team-ups resume. 229-r/origin Superman-Batman team	2	4	6	10	14	18
215-Intro. Batman Jr. & Superman Jr.	3	6	9	17	25	32
223-228-(100 pgs.) 223-N. Adams-c. 223-Deadman origin. 226-N. Adams, S&K, Toth-r; Manhunter part origin-r/Det. #225,226. 227-Deadman app.	4	8	12	26	41	55
230-(68 pgs.)	3	6	9	16	23	30
231-243,247,248: 242-Super Sons. 248-Last Vigilante	2	4	6	8	10	12
244-246-Adams-c: 244-$1.00, 84 pg. issues begin; Green Arrow, Black Canary, Wonder Woman, Vigilante begin; 246-Death of Stuff in Vigilante; origin Vigilante retold	2	4	6	11	16	20
249-252 (84 pgs.) Ditko-a: 249-The Creeper begins by Ditko, 84 pgs. 250-The Creeper origin retold by Ditko. 252-Last 84 pg. issue	2	4	6	11	16	20
253-257,259-265: 253-Capt. Marvel begins; 68 pgs. begin, end #265. 255-Last Creeper. 256-Hawkman begins. 257-Black Lightning begins. 263-Super Sons. 264-Clay Face app.	2	4	6	8	10	12
258-Adams-c	2	4	6	8	11	14
266-270,272-282-(52 pgs.) 267-Challengers of the Unknown app.; 3 Lt. Marvels return. 268-Capt. Marvel Jr. origin retold. 274-Zatanna begins. 279, 280-Capt. Marvel Jr. & Kid Eternity learn they are brothers	1	3	4	6	8	10
271-(52pgs.) Origin Superman/Batman team retold	2	4	6	8	10	12
283-299: 284-Legion app.	1	2	3	4	5	7
300-($1.25, 52pgs.).-Justice League of America, New Teen Titans & The Outsiders app.; Perez-a (3 pgs.)	1	2	3	5	6	8
301-322: 304-Origin Null and Void. 309,319-Free 16 pg. story in each (309-Flash Force 2000, 319-Mask preview)						3.00
323-Last issue						6.00

NOTE: Neal Adams a-230ir; c-174-176, 178-180, 182, 183, 185, 186, 199-205, 208-211, 244-246, 258. Austin a-244-246i. Burnley a-8, 10; c-7-9, 11-14, 15p?, 16-18p, 20-31p. Colan a-274p; 297, 299. Ditko a-249-255. Giffen a-322; c-284p. 322. G. Kane a-38, 174r, 282, 283; c-281, 282, 289. Kirby a-187. Kubert Zatara-40-44. Miller c-285p. Mooney c-134. Morrow a-245-248. Mortimer c-16-21, 26-71. Nasser a(p)-244-246, 259, 260. Newton a-253-281p. Orlando a-224r. Perez a-300i; c-271, 276, 277p, 278p. Fred Ray c-1-5. Fred Ray/Robinson c-13-16. Robinson a-5, 6, 9-11, 13?, 14-16; c-6. Rogers a-259p. Roussos a-212r. Simonson c-291. Spiegle a-275-278, 284. Staton a-262p, 273p. Swan/Moldoff c-126. Swan/Mortimer c-79-82. Toth a-228r. Tuska a-230r, 250p, 252p, 254p, 257p, 283p, 284p, 308p. Boy Commandos by Infantino #39-41.

WORLD'S FINEST COMICS DIGEST (See DC Special Series #23)

WORLD'S FINEST: OUR WORLDS AT WAR
DC Comics: Oct, 2001 ($2.95, one-shot)

1-Concludes the Our Worlds at War x-over; Jae Lee-c; art by various						3.00

WORLD'S GREATEST ATHLETE (See Walt Disney Showcase #14)

WORLD'S GREATEST SONGS
Atlas Comics (Male): Sept, 1954

	GD 2.0	VG 4.0	FN 6.0	VF 8.0	VF/NM 9.0	NM- 9.2
1-(Scarce)-Heath & Harry Anderson-a; Eddie Fisher life story plus-c; gives lyrics to Frank Sinatra song "Young at Heart"	40	80	120	235	368	500

WORLD'S GREATEST STORIES
Jubilee Publications: Jan, 1949 - No. 2, May, 1949

	GD 2.0	VG 4.0	FN 6.0	VF 8.0	VF/NM 9.0	NM- 9.2
1-Alice in Wonderland; Lewis Carroll adapt.	32	64	96	186	293	400
2-Pinocchio	30	60	90	174	275	375

WORLDS OF FEAR (Stories of Weird Adventure)(Formerly Worlds Beyond #1)
Fawcett Publications: V1#2, Jan, 1952 - V2#10, June, 1953

	GD 2.0	VG 4.0	FN 6.0	VF 8.0	VF/NM 9.0	NM- 9.2
V1#2	46	92	138	281	466	650
3-Evans-a	40	80	120	244	392	540
4-6(9/52)	38	76	114	219	347	475
V2#7-9	34	68	102	197	311	425
10-Saunders painted-c; man with no eyes surrounded by eyeballs-c plus eyes ripped out story	90	180	270	563	932	1300

NOTE: Moldoff c-2-8. Powell a-2, 4, 5. Sekowsky a-4, 5.

WORLDSTORM
DC Comics (WildStorm): Nov, 2006 (Dec on cover) - Present ($2.99)

1,2-Previews and pin-ups for re-launched WildStorm titles.1-Art Adams-c						3.00

WORLDS UNKNOWN
Marvel Comics Group: May, 1973 - No. 8, Aug, 1974

World War Hulk #2 © MAR

Worst From Mad #12 © EC Publ.

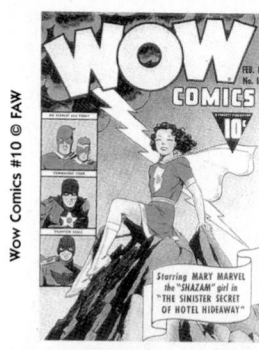

Wow Comics #10 © FAW

	GD 2.0	VG 4.0	FN 6.0	VF 8.0	VF/NM 9.0	NM- 9.2
1-r/from Astonishing #54; Torres, Reese-a	3	6	9	14	19	24
2-8	2	4	6	9	13	16

NOTE: **Adkins/Mooney** a-5. **Buscema** c/a-4p. W. Howard c/a-3i. **Kane** a(p)-1,2; c(p)-5, 6, 8. **Sutton** a-2. **Tuska** a(p)-7, 8; c-7p. No. 7, 8 has Golden Voyage of Sinbad movie adaptation.

WORLD WAR HULK (See Incredible Hulk #106)
Marvel Comics: Aug, 2007 - No. 5 ($3.99, limited series)

1-Hulk returns to Earth; Iron Man and Avengers app.; Romita Jr.-a/Pak-s/Finch-c						4.00
1-Variant cover by Romita Jr.						6.00
2-4: 2-Hulk battles The Avengers and FF; Finch-c. 3,4-Dr. Strange app.						4.00
2-4-Variant cover by Romita Jr.						6.00
...: Gamma Files (2007, $3.99) profile pages of Hulk characters						4.00
...Prologue: World Breaker 1 (7/07, one-shot) Rio, Weeks, Phillips, Miyazawa-a						4.00

WORLD WAR HULK: FRONT LINE (See Incredible Hulk #106)
Marvel Comics: Aug, 2007 - No. 6 ($2.99, limited series)

1-4-Ben Urich & Sally Floyd report World War Hulk; Jenkins-s/Bachs-a						3.00

WORLD WAR HULK: GAMMA CORPS
Marvel Comics: Sept, 2007 - No. 4 ($2.99, limited series)

1-3-Tieri-s/Ferreira-a/Roux-c						3.00

WORLD WAR HULK: X-MEN (See New Avengers: Illuminati and Incredible Hulk #92)
Marvel Comics: Aug, 2007 - No. 3, Oct, 2007 ($2.99, limited series)

1-3-Gage-s/DiVito-a/McGuinness-c; Hulk invades the Xavier Institute						3.00

WORLD WAR STORIES
Dell Publishing Co.: Apr-June, 1965 - No. 3, Dec, 1965

1-Glanzman-a in all	4	8	12	26	41	55
2,3	3	6	9	17	25	32

WORLD WAR II (See Classics Illustrated Special Issue)

WORLD WAR II: 1946
Antarctic Press: Oct, 1998 - No. 2 ($3.95, B&W)

1,2-Nomura-s/a						4.00

WORLD WAR III
Ace Periodicals: Mar, 1953 - No. 2, May, 1953

1-(Scarce)-Atomic bomb blast-c; Cameron-a	90	180	270	563	932	1300
2-Used in **POP**, pg. 78 & B&W & color illos; Cameron-a	57	114	171	356	591	825

WORLDWATCH
Wild and Wooly Press: June, 2004 - No. 3, Dec, 2004 ($2.95)

1-3-Austen-s/Derenick-a. 1-B&W. 2,3-Color						3.00

WORLD WITHOUT END
DC Comics: 1990 - No. 6, 1991 ($2.50, limited series, mature, stiff-c)

1-6: Horror/fantasy; all painted-c/a						2.50

WORLD WRESTLING FEDERATION BATTLEMANIA
Valiant: 1991 - No. 5?, 1991 ($2.50, magazine size, 68 pgs.)

1-5: 5-Includes 2 free pull-out posters						4.00

WORST FROM MAD, THE (Annual)
E. C. Comics: 1958 - No. 12, 1969 (Each annual cover is reprinted from the cover of the Mad issues being reprinted)(Value is 1/2 if bonus is missing)

nn(1958)-Bonus: record labels & travel stickers; 1st Mad annual; r/Mad #29-34	86	129	242	431	600	
2(1959)-Bonus is small 33⅓ rpm record entitled "Meet the Staff of Mad"; r/Mad #35-40	41	82	123	257	419	580
3(1960)-Has 20x30" campaign poster "Alfred E. Neuman for President"; r/Mad #41-46	17	34	51	128	227	325
4(1961)-Sunday comics section; r/Mad #47-54	16	32	48	120	213	305
5(1962)-Has 33-1/3 record; r/Mad #55-62	23	46	69	171	306	440
6(1963)-Has 33-1/3 record; r/Mad #63-70	23	46	69	171	306	440
7(1964)-Mad protest signs; r/Mad #71-76	10	20	30	70	123	175
8(1965)-Build a Mad Zeppelin	11	22	33	79	140	200
9(1966)-33-1/3 rpm record; Beatles on-c	16	32	48	120	213	305
10(1967)-Mad bumper sticker	7	14	21	47	76	105
11(1968)-Mad cover window stickers	6	12	18	43	69	95
12(1969)-Mad picture postcards; Orlando-a	6	12	18	43	69	95

NOTE: Covers: **Bob Clarke**-#8. **Mingo**-#7, 9-12.

WOTALIFE COMICS (Formerly Nutty Life #2; Phantom Lady #13 on)
Fox Features Syndicate/Norlen Mag.: No. 3, Aug-Sept, 1946 - No. 12, July, 1947; 1959

3-Cosmo Cat, Li'l Pan, others begin	11	22	33	60	83	105
4-12-Cosmo Cat, Li'l Pan in all	9	18	27	47	61	75

	GD 2.0	VG 4.0	FN 6.0	VF 8.0	VF/NM 9.0	NM- 9.2
1(1959-Norlen)-Atomic Rabbit, Atomic Mouse; reprints cover to #6; reprints entire book?	8	16	24	40	50	60

WOTALIFE COMICS
Green Publications: 1957 - No. 5, 1957

1	7	14	21	35	43	50
2-5	5	10	15	22	26	30

WOW COMICS ("Wow, What A Magazine!" on cover of first issue)
Henle Publishing Co.: July, 1936 - No. 4, Nov, 1936 (52 pgs., magazine size)

1-Buck Jones in "The Phantom Rider" (1st app. in comics), Fu Manchu; Capt. Scott Dalton begins; Will Eisner-a (1st in comics); Baily-a(1); Briefer-c	300	600	900	1881	3141	4400
2-Ken Maynard, Fu Manchu, Popeye by Segar plus article on Popeye; Eisner-a	204	408	612	1275	2113	2950
3-Eisner-c/a(3); Popeye by Segar, Fu Manchu, Hiram Hick by Bob Kane, Space Limited app.; Jimmy Dempsey talks about Popeye's punch; Bob Ripley Believe it or Not begins; Briefer-a	190	380	570	1188	1969	2750
4-Flash Gordon by Raymond, Mandrake, Popeye by Segar, Tillie The Toiler, Fu Manchu, Hiram Hick by Bob Kane; Eisner-a(3); Briefer-c/a	235	470	705	1469	2435	3400

WOW COMICS (Real Western Hero #70 on)(See XMas Comics)
Fawcett Publ.: Winter, 1940-41; No. 2, Summer, 1941 - No. 69, Fall, 1948

nn(#1)-Origin Mr. Scarlet by S&K; Atom Blake, Boy Wizard, Jim Dolan, & Rick O'Shay begin; Diamond Jack, The White Rajah, & Shipwreck Roberts, only app.; 1st mention of Gotham City in comics; the cover was printed on unstable paper stock and is rarely found in fine or mint condition; blank inside-c; bondage-c by Beck	1300	2600	3900	10,000	18,000	26,000
2 (Scarce)-The Hunchback begins	300	600	900	1931	3366	4800
3 (Fall, 1941)	138	276	414	863	1432	2000
4-Origin & 1st app. Pinky	145	290	435	906	1503	2100
5	83	166	249	519	860	1200
6-Origin & 1st app. The Phantom Eagle (7/15/42); Commando Yank begins	83	166	249	519	860	1200
7,8,10: 10-Swayze-c/a on Mary Marvel	62	124	186	388	644	900
9 (1/6/43)-Capt. Marvel, Capt. Marvel Jr., Shazam app.; Scarlet & Pinky x-over; Mary Marvel-c/stories begin (cameo #9)	155	310	465	969	1610	2250
11-17,19,20: 15-Flag-c	47	94	141	287	474	660
18-1st app. Uncle Marvel (10/43); infinity-c	49	98	147	299	492	685
21-30: 23-Robot-c. 28-Pinky x-over in Mary Marvel	30	60	90	176	278	380
31-40: 32-68-Phantom Eagle by Swayze	22	44	66	126	198	270
41-50	20	40	60	117	184	250
51-58: Last Mary Marvel	19	38	57	109	172	235
59-69: 59-Ozzie (teenage) begins. 62-Flying Saucer gag-c (1/48). 65-69-Tom Mix stories (cont'd in Real Western Hero)	17	34	51	98	154	210

NOTE: Cover features: Mr. Scarlet-#1-5; Commando Yank-#6, 7, (w/Mr. Scarlet-#6), 7, (w/Mr. Scarlet #8); Mary Marvel-#9-56, (w/Commando Yank-#46-50), (w/Mr. Scarlet & Commando Yank-#51), (w/Mr. Scarlet & Pinky #53), (w/Phantom Eagle #54), (w/Commando Yank & Phantom Eagle #58); Ozzie-#59-69.

WRAITHBORN
DC Comics (WildStorm): Nov, 2005 - No. 6, July, 2006 ($2.99, limited series)

1-6-Marcia Chen & Joe Benitez-s/a						3.00
TPB (2007, $19.99) r/series; sketch pages and unused cover sketches						20.00

WRATH (Also see Prototype #4)
Malibu Comics: Jan, 1994 - No. 9, Nov, 1995 ($1.95)

1-9: 2-Mantra x-over. 3-Intro/1st app. Slayer. 4,5-Freex app. 8-Mantra & Warstrike app. 9-Prime app.						2.50
1-Ultra 5000 Limited silver foil						4.00
Giant Size 1 (2.50, 44 pgs.)						2.50

WRATH OF THE SPECTRE, THE
DC Comics: May, 1988 - No. 4, Aug, 1988 ($2.50, limited series)

1-3: Aparo-r/Adventure #431-440						4.00
4-Three scripts intended for Adventure #441-on, but not drawn by Aparo until 1988						5.00
TPB (2005, $19.99) r/series; Peter Sanderson intro.						20.00

WRECK OF GROSVENOR (See Superior Stories #3)

WRETCH, THE
Caliber: 1996 ($2.95, B&W)

1-Phillip Hester-a/scripts						3.00

WRETCH, THE
Amaze Ink: 1997 - No. 4, 1998 ($2.95, B&W)

1-4-Phillip Hester-a/scripts						3.00
... Vol. 1: Everyday Doomsday (4/03, $13.95)						14.00

Wyatt Earp #11 © ATLAS

X-Babies: Murderama #1 © MAR

Xena #1 © Universal Studios

	GD 2.0	VG 4.0	FN 6.0	VF 8.0	VF/NM 9.0	NM- 9.2

WRINGLE WRANGLE (Disney)
Dell Publishing Co.: No. 821, July, 1957

Four Color 821-Based on movie "Westward Ho, the Wagons"; Marsh-a; Fess Parker photo-c

	GD 2.0	VG 4.0	FN 6.0	VF 8.0	VF/NM 9.0	NM- 9.2
	8	16	24	52	86	120

WULF THE BARBARIAN
Atlas/Seaboard Publ.: Feb, 1975 - No. 4, Sept, 1975

	GD 2.0	VG 4.0	FN 6.0	VF 8.0	VF/NM 9.0	NM- 9.2
1,2: 1-Origin; Janson-a. 2-Intro. Berithe the Swordswoman; Janson-a w/Neal Adams, Wood, Reese-a assists	2	4	6	8	10	12
3,4: 3-Skeates-s. 4-Friedrich-s	1	2	3	5	7	9

WYATT EARP
Atlas Comics/Marvel No. 23 on (IPC): Nov, 1955 - #29, June, 1960; #30, Oct, 1972 - #34, June, 1973

	GD 2.0	VG 4.0	FN 6.0	VF 8.0	VF/NM 9.0	NM- 9.2
1	21	42	63	120	188	255
2-Williamson-a (4 pgs.)	14	28	42	76	108	140
3-6,8-11: 3-Black Bart app. 8-Wild Bill Hickok app.	11	22	33	60	83	105
7,12-Williamson-a, 4 pgs. ea.; #12 with Mayo	11	22	33	60	83	105
13-20: 17-1st app. Wyatt's deputy, Grizzly Grant	10	20	30	54	72	90
21-Davis-c	9	18	27	50	65	80
22-24,26-29: 22-Ringo Kid app. 23-Kid From Texas app. 29-Last 10¢ issue	8	16	24	42	54	65
25-Davis-a	8	16	24	44	57	70
30-Williamson-r (1972)	2	4	6	11	16	20
31-34-Reprints. 32-Torres-a(r)	2	4	6	9	13	16

NOTE: **Ayers** a-8, 10(2), 17, 20(4). **Berg** a-9. **Everett** c-6. **Kirby** c-25, 29. **Maneely** a-1; c-1-4, 8, 12, 17, 20. **Maurer** a-2(2), 3(4), 4(4), 8(4). **Severin** a-4, 9(4), 10; c-2, 9, 10, 14. **Wildey** a-5, 17, 24, 28.

WYATT EARP (TV) (Hugh O'Brian Famous Marshal)
Dell Publishing Co.: No. 860, Nov, 1957 - No. 13, Dec-Feb, 1960-61 (Hugh O'Brian photo-c)

	GD 2.0	VG 4.0	FN 6.0	VF 8.0	VF/NM 9.0	NM- 9.2
Four Color 860 (#1)-Manning-a	9	18	27	65	113	160
Four Color 890,921(6/58)-All Manning-a	7	14	21	49	80	110
4 (9-11/58) - 12-Manning-a. 5-Photo back-c	6	12	18	37	59	80
13-Toth-a	6	12	18	39	62	85

WYATT EARP FRONTIER MARSHAL (Formerly Range Busters) (Also see Blue Bird)
Charlton Comics: No. 12, Jan, 1956 - No. 72, Dec, 1967

	GD 2.0	VG 4.0	FN 6.0	VF 8.0	VF/NM 9.0	NM- 9.2
12	9	18	27	47	61	75
13-19	6	12	18	31	38	45
20-(68 pgs.)-Williamson-a(4), 8,5,5,& 7 pgs.	10	20	30	54	72	90
21-(100 pgs.) Mastroserio, Maneely, Severin-a (signed LePoer)	4	8	12	24	37	50
22-30	3	6	9	16	23	30
31-50	2	4	6	12	16	20
51-72 (1967)	2	4	6	9	11	14

WYNONNA EARP
Image Comics (WildStorm Productions): Dec, 1996 - No. 5, Apr, 1997 ($2.50)

1-5-Smith-s/Chin-a	2.50

WYNONNA EARP: HOME ON THE STRANGE
IDW Publishing: Dec, 2003 - No. 3, Feb, 2004 ($3.99)

1-3-Smith-s/Ferreira-a	4.00

WYRMS
Marvel Comics (Dabel Brothers): Feb, 2007 - Present ($2.99)

1-5-Orson Scott Card & Jake Black-s. 1-3-Batista-a	3.00

X (Comics' Greatest World: X #1 only) (Also see Comics' Greatest World & Dark Horse Comics #8)
Dark Horse Comics: Feb, 1994 - No. 25, Apr, 1996 ($2.00/$2.50)

1-25: 3-Pit Bulls x-over. 8 -Ghost-c & app. 18-Miller-c.; Predator app. 19-22-Miller-c.	2.50
Hero Illustrated Special #1,2 (1994, $1.00, 20 pgs.)	2.50
One Shot to the Head (1994, $2.50, 36 pgs.)-Miller-c.	2.50

NOTE: **Miller** c-18-22. **Quesada** a-6. **Russell** a-6.

XANADU COLOR SPECIAL
Eclipse Comics: Dec, 1988 ($2.00, one-shot)

1-Continued from Thoughts & Images	2.50

XAVIER INSTITUTE ALUMNI YEARBOOK (See X-Men titles)
Marvel Comics: Dec, 1996 ($5.95, square-bound, one-shot)

1-Text w/art by various	6.00

X-BABIES
Marvel Comics: (one-shots)

...: Murderama (8/98, $2.95) J.J. Kirby-a	3.50
...: Reborn (1/00, $3.50) J.J. Kirby-a	3.50

X-CALIBRE
Marvel Comics: Mar, 1995 - No. 4, July, 1995 ($1.95, limited series)

1-4-Age of Apocalypse	2.50

XENA (TV)
Dynamite Entertainment: 2006 - Present ($3.50)

1-4-Three covers on each; Neves-a/Layman-s	3.50
Vol. 2 #1-4-(Dark Xena) Four covers; Salonga-a/Layman-s	3.50
Annual 1 (2007, $4.95) Three covers; Salonga-a/Champagne-s	5.00

XENA: WARRIOR PRINCESS (TV)
Topps Comics: Aug, 1997 - No. 0, Oct, 1997 ($2.95)

	GD 2.0	VG 4.0	FN 6.0	VF 8.0	VF/NM 9.0	NM- 9.2
1-Two stories by various; J. Scott Campbell-c	1	3	4	6	8	10
1,2-Photo-c	1	3	4	6	8	10
2-Stevens-c						6.00
0-(10/97)-Lopresti-c, 0-(10/97)-Photo-c	1	2	3	5	6	8
...First Appearance Collection ('97, $9.95) r/Hercules the Legendary Journeys #3-5 and 5-page story from TV Guide						10.00

XENA: WARRIOR PRINCESS (TV)
Dark Horse Comics: Sept, 1999 - No. 14, Oct, 2000 ($2.95/$2.99)

1-14: 1-Mignola-c and photo-c. 2,3-Bradstreet-c & photo-c	3.00

XENA: WARRIOR PRINCESS AND THE ORIGINAL OLYMPICS (TV)
Topps Comics: Jun, 1998 - No. 3, Aug, 1998 ($2.95, limited series)

1-3-Regular and Photo-c; Lim-a/T&M Bierbaum-s	3.00

XENA: WARRIOR PRINCESS-BLOODLINES (TV)
Topps Comics: May, 1998 - No. 2, June, 1998 ($2.95, limited series)

1,2-Lopresti-s/c/a. 2-Reg. and photo-c	3.00
1-Bath photo-c, 1-American Ent. Ed.	4.00

XENA: WARRIOR PRINCESS / JOXER: WARRIOR PRINCE (TV)
Topps Comics: Nov, 1997 - No. 3, Jan, 1998 ($2.95, limited series)

1-3-Regular and Photo-c; Lim-a/T&M Bierbaum-s	3.00

XENA: WARRIOR PRINCESS-THE DRAGON'S TEETH (TV)
Topps Comics: Dec, 1997 - No. 3, Feb, 1998 ($2.95, limited series)

1-3-Regular and Photo-c; Teranishi-a/Thomas-s	3.00

XENA: WARRIOR PRINCESS-THE ORPHEUS TRILOGY (TV)
Topps Comics: Mar, 1998 - No. 3, May, 1998 ($2.95, limited series)

1-3-Regular and Photo-c; Teranishi-a/T&M Bierbaum-s	3.00

XENA: WARRIOR PRINCESS VS. CALLISTO (TV)
Topps Comics: Feb, 1998 - No. 3, Apr, 1998 ($2.95, limited series)

1-3-Regular and Photo-c; Morgan-a/Thomas-s	3.00

XENOBROOD
DC Comics: No. 0, Oct, 1994 - No. 6, Apr, 1995 ($1.50, limited series)

0-6: 0-Indicia says "Xenobroods"	2.50

XENON
Eclipse Comics: Dec, 1987 - No. 23, Nov. 1, 1988 ($1.50, B&W, bi-weekly)

1-23	2.50

XENOTECH
Mirage Studios: Sept, 1993 - No. 3, Dec, 1994 ($2.75)

1-3: Bound with 2 trading cards. 2-(10/94)	2.75

XENOZOIC TALES (Also see Cadillacs & Dinosaurs, Death Rattle #8)
Kitchen Sink Press: Feb, 1986 - No. 14, Oct, 1996

	GD 2.0	VG 4.0	FN 6.0	VF 8.0	VF/NM 9.0	NM- 9.2
1-Mark Schultz-s/a in all	1	3	4	6	8	10
1(2nd printing)(1/89)						3.00
2-14						5.00
Volume 1 ($14.95) r/#1-6 & Death Rattle #8						15.00
Volume 2 (5/03, $14.95, TPB) B&W r/#7-14; intro by Frank Cho						15.00

XENYA
Sanctuary Press: Apr. 1994 - No. 3 ($2.95)

1-3: 1-Hildebrandt-c; intro Xenya	3.00

XERO
DC Comics: May, 1997 - No. 12, Apr, 1998 ($1.75)

1-7	2.50
8-12	2.50

X-FACTOR (Also see The Avengers #263, Fantastic Four #286 and Mutant X)

X-Factor #48 © MAR

X-Factor (3rd series) #5 © MAR

X-Force #127 © MAR

	GD	VG	FN	VF	VF/NM	NM-
	2.0	4.0	6.0	8.0	9.0	9.2

Marvel Comics Group: Feb, 1986 - No. 149, Sept, 1998

1-($1.25, 52 pgs)-Story recaps 1st app. from Avengers #263; story cont'd from F.F. #286; return of original X-Men (now X-Factor); Guice/Layton-a; Baby Nathan app. (2nd after X-Men #201) ... 6.00
2-4 ... 4.00
5-1st brief app. Apocalypse (2 pages) ... 4.00
6-1st full app. Apocalypse ... 1 ... 3 ... 4 ... 6 ... 8 ... 10
7-10: 10-Sabretooth app. (11/86, 3 pgs.) cont'd in X-Men #212; 1st app. in an X-Men comic book ... 4.00
11-22: 13-Baby Nathan app. in flashback. 14-Cyclops vs. The Master Mold. 15-Intro wingless Angel ... 3.00
23-1st brief app. Archangel (2 pages) ... 1 ... 2 ... 3 ... 4 ... 5 ... 7
24-1st full app. Archangel (now in Uncanny X-Men); Fall Of The Mutants begins; origin Apocalypse ... 1 ... 2 ... 3 ... 5 ... 7 ... 9
25,26: Fall Of The Mutants; 26-New outfits ... 3.00
27-39,41-83,87-91,93-99,101: 35-Origin Cyclops. 38,50-(52 pgs.): 50-Liefeld/McFarlane-c. 51-53-Sabretooth app. 52-Liefeld-c(p). 54-Intro Crimson; Silvestri-c/a(i). 60-X-Tinction Agenda x-over; New Mutants (w/Cable) x-over in #60-62; Wolverine in #62. 60-Gold ink 2nd printing. 61,62-X-Tinction Agenda. 62-Jim Lee-c. 63-Portacio/Thibert-c/a(p) begins, ends #69. 65-68-Lee co-plots. 65-The Apocalypse Files begins, ends #68. 66,67-Baby Nathan app. 67-Inhumans app. 68-Baby Nathan is sent into future to save his life. 69,70-X-Men(w/Wolverine) x-over. 71-New team begins (Havok, Polaris, Strong Guy, Wolfsbane & Madrox); Stroman-c/a begins. 71-2nd printing (w/$1.25). 75-(52 pgs.). 77-Cannonball (of X-Force) app. 87-Quesada-c/a(p) in monthly comic begins,ends #92.
88-1st app. Random ... 2.50
40-Rob Liefeld-c/a (4/89, 1st at Marvel?) ... 3.00
84-86 -Jae Lee a(p); 85,86-Jae Lee-c. Polybagged with trading card in each; X-Cutioner's Song x-overs ... 3.00
92-($3.50, 68 pgs.)-Wraparound-c by Quesada w/Havok hologram on-c; begin X-Men 30th anniversary issues; Quesada-a. ... 5.00
92-2nd printing ... 2.50
100-($2.95, 52 pgs.)-Embossed foil-c; Multiple Man dies. ... 5.00
100-($1.75, 52 pgs.)-Regular edition ... 2.50
102-105,107: 102-bound-in card sheet ... 2.50
106-($2.00)-Newsstand edition ... 2.50
106-($2.95)-Collectors edition ... 3.00
108-124,126-148: 112-Return from Age of Apocalypse. 115-card insert. 119-123-Sabretooth app. 123-Hound app. 124-w/Onslaught Update. 126-Onslaught x-over; Beast vs. Dark Beast 128-w/card insert; return of Multiple Man. 130-Assassination of Grayson Creed. 146,148-Moder-a ... 2.50
125-($2.95)-"Onslaught"; Post app.; return of Havok ... 4.00
149-Last issue ... 3.00
#(-1) Flashback (7/97) Matsuda-a ... 2.50
Annual 1-9: 1-(10/86-'94, 68 pgs.) 3-Evolutionary War x-over. 4-Atlantis Attacks; Byrne/Simonson-a;Byrne-c. 5-Fantastic Four, New Mutants x-over; Keown 2 pg. pin-up. 6-New Warriors app.; 5th app. X-Force cont'd from X-Men Annual #15. 7-1st Quesada-a(p) on X-Factor plus-c(p). 8-Bagged w/trading card. 9-Austin-a(i) ... 3.00
...Prisoner of Love (1994, $4.95, 52 pgs.)-Starlin scripts; Guice-a ... 5.00
... Visionaries: Peter David Vol. 1 TPB (2005, $15.99) r/#71-75 ... 16.00
... Visionaries: Peter David Vol. 2 TPB (2007, $15.99) r/#76-78 & Incr. Hulk #390-392 ... 16.00
NOTE: *Art Adams* a-41p, 42p. *Buckler* a-50p. *Liefeld* a-40; c-40, 50p, 52p. *McFarlane* c-50i. *Mignola* c-70. *Brandon Peterson* a-78p(part). *Whilce Portacio* c/a(p)-63-69. *Quesada* a(p)-87-92; Annual 7. c(p)-78, 79, 82, Annual 7. *Simonson* a-11, 13-15, 17-19, 21, 23-31, 33, 34, 36-39; c-12, 16. *Paul Smith* a-44-48; c-43. *Stroman* a-71-75, 77, 78(part), 80, 81; c(p)-71-77, 80, 81, 84. *Zeck* c-2.

X-FACTOR (Volume 2)
Marvel Comics: June, 2002 - No. 4, Oct, 2002 ($2.50)

1-4: Jensen-s/Ranson-a. 1-Phillips-c. 2,3-Edwards-c ... 2.50

X-FACTOR
Marvel Comics: Jan, 2006 - Present ($2.99)

1-23: 1-Peter David-s/Ryan Sook-a. 8,9-Civil War. 21-23-Endangered Species back-up ... 3.00
...: The Longest Night HC (2006, $19.99, dust jacket) r/#1-6; sketch pages by Sook ... 20.00
...: The Longest Night SC (2007, $14.99) r/#1-6; sketch pages by Sook ... 15.00
...: Life and Death Matters HC (2007, $19.99, dust jacket) r/#7-12 ... 20.00
...: Life and Death Matters SC (2007, $14.99) r/#7-12 ... 15.00

X-51 (Machine Man)
Marvel Comics: Sept, 1999 - No. 12, Jul, 2000 ($1.99/$2.50)

1-7: 1-Joe Bennett-a. 2-Two covers ... 2.50
8-12: 8-Begin $2.50-c ... 2.50
Wizard #0 ... 2.50

X-FILES, THE (TV)
Topps Comics: Jan, 1995 - No. 41, July, 1998 ($2.50)

-2(9/96)-Black-c; r/X-Files Magazine #1&2 ... 1 ... 3 ... 4 ... 6 ... 8 ... 10

-1(9/96)-Silver-c; r/Hero Illustrated Giveaway ... 1 ... 3 ... 4 ... 6 ... 8 ... 10
0-($3.95)-Adapts pilot episode ... 4.00
0-"Mulder" variant-c ... 1 ... 2 ... 3 ... 5 ... 6 ... 8
0-"Scully" variant-c ... 1 ... 2 ... 3 ... 5 ... 6 ... 8
1/2-W/certificate ... 3 ... 6 ... 9 ... 14 ... 20 ... 25
1-New stories based on the TV show; direct market & newsstand editions; Miran Kim-c on all ... 9 ... 16 ... 23 ... 30
2 ... 2 ... 4 ... 6 ... 10 ... 14 ... 18
3,4 ... 1 ... 2 ... 3 ... 5 ... 6 ... 8
5-10 ... 4.00
11-41: 11-Begin $2.95-c. 21-W/bound-in card. 40,41-Reg. & photo-c ... 3.00
Annual 1,2 ($3.95) ... 4.00
Afterflight TPB ($5.95) Art by Thompson, Saviuk, Kim ... 6.00
Collection 1 TPB ($19.95)-r/#1-6. ... 20.00
Collection 2 TPB ($19.95)-r/#7-12, Annual #1. ... 20.00
...Fight the Future ('98, $5.95) Movie adaptation ... 6.00
Hero Illustrated Giveaway (3/95) ... 2 ... 4 ... 6 ... 9 ... 12 ... 15
Special Edition 1-5 ($4.95)-r/#1-3, 4-6, 7-9, 10-12, 13, Annual 1 ... 5.00
Star Wars Galaxy Magazine Giveaway (B&W) ... 1 ... 3 ... 4 ... 6 ... 8 ... 10
Trade paperback ($19.95) ... 20.00
Volume 1 TPB (Checker Books, 2005, 19.95) r/#13-17, #0, Season One: Squeeze ... 20.00
Volume 2 TPB (Checker Books, 2005, $19.95) r/#18-24, #1/2, Comics Digest #1 ... 20.00
Volume 3 TPB (Checker Books, 2006, $19.95) r/#23-26, Fire, Ice, Hero III. Giveaway ... 20.00

X-FILES COMICS DIGEST, THE
Topps Comics: Dec, 1995 - No. 3 ($3.50, quarterly, digest-size)

1-3: 3; 1,2: New X-Files stories w/Ray Bradbury Comics-r ... 4.00
NOTE: *Adlard* a-1, 2. *Jack Davis* a-2r. *Russell* a-1r.

X-FILES, THE: GROUND ZERO (TV)
Topps Comics: Nov, 1997 - No. 4, March, 1998 ($2.95, limited series)

1-4-Adaptation of the Kevin J. Anderson novel ... 3.00

X-FILES, THE: SEASON ONE (TV)
Topps Comics: July, 1997 - July, 1998 ($4.95, adaptations of TV episodes)

1,2,Squeeze, Conduit, Ice, Space, Fire, Beyond the Sea, Shadows ... 5.00

X-FORCE (Becomes X-Statix) (Also see The New Mutants #100)
Marvel Comics: Aug, 1991 - No. 129, Aug, 2002 ($2.75/$2.25)

1-($1.50, 52 pgs.)-Polybagged with 1 of 5 diff. Marvel Universe trading cards inside (1 each); 6th app. of X-Force; Liefeld-c/a begins ... 4.00
1-1st printing with Cable trading card inside ... 5.00
1-2nd printing; metallic ink-c (no bag or card) ... 2.50
2-4: 2-Deadpool-c/story. 3-New Brotherhood of Evil Mutants app. 4-Spider-Man x-over; cont'd from Spider-Man #16; reads sideways ... 3.00
5-10: 6-Last $1.00-c. 7-Weapon X back-ups. 8-Intro The Wild Pack (Cable, Kane, Domino, Hammer, G.W. Bridge, & Grizzly); Liefeld-c/a (4); Mignola-a. 10-Weapon X full-length story (part 3). 11-1st Weapon Prime; Deadpool-c/story ... 3.00
11-15,19-24,26-33: 15-Cable leaves X-Force ... 2.50
16-18-Polybagged w/trading card in each; X-Cutioner's Song x-overs ... 3.00
25-($3.50, 52 pgs.)-r/#1 w/Cable hologram on-c; Cable returns ... 4.00
34-37,39-45: 34-bound-in card sheet ... 2.50
38,40-43: 38-($2.00)-Newsstand edition. 40-43 ($1.95)-Deluxe edition ... 2.50
38-($2.95)-Collectors edition (prismatic) ... 5.00
44-49,51-67: 44-Return from Age of Apocalypse. 45-Sabretooth app. 49-Sebastian Shaw app. 52-Blob app., Onslaught cameo. 55-Vs. S.H.I.E.L.D. 56-Deadpool app. 57-Mr. Sinister & X-Man-c/app. 57,58-Onslaught x-over. 59-W/card insert; return of Longshot. 60-Dr. Strange ... 2.50
50 ($3.95)-Gatefold wrap-around foil-c ... 4.00
50 ($3.95)-Liefeld variant-c ... 5.00
68-74: 68-Operation Zero Tolerance ... 2.50
75,100-($2.99): 75-Cannonball-c/app. ... 3.00
76-99,101,102: 81-Pollina poster. 95-Magneto-c. 102-Ellis-s/Portacio-a ... 2.50
103-115: 103-Begin $2.25-c; Portacio-a thru #106. 115-Death of old team ... 2.25
116-New team debuts; Allred-c/a; Milligan-s; no Comics Code stamp on-c ... 4.00
117-129: 117-Intro. Mr. Sensitive. 120-Wolverine-c/app. 123-'Nuff Said issue. 124-Darwyn Cooke-a/c. 128-Death of U-Go Girl. 129-Fegredo-a ... 2.50
#(-1) Flashback (7/97) story of John Proudstar; Pollina-a ... 2.50
Annual 1-3 ('92-'94, $3.50)-1-1st Greg Capullo-a(p) on X-Force. 2-Polybagged w/trading card; intro X-Treme & Neurtag ... 3.00
...And Cable '95 (12/95, $3.95)-Impossible Man app. ... 4.00
...And Cable '96, ...'97 ('96, 7/97) - '96-Wraparound-c ... 3.50
...And Spider-Man: Sabotage nn (11/92, $6.95)-Reprints X-Force #3,4 & Spider-Man #16 ... 7.00
.../ Champions '98 ($3.50) ... 3.50
Annual 99 ($3.50) ... 3.50
...: Famous, Mutant & Mortal HC (2003, $29.99) oversized r/#116-129; foreward by Milligan;

X-Man #49 © MAR

X-Men #7 © MAR

X-Men #120 © MAR

	GD	VG	FN	VF	VF/NM	NM-
	2.0	4.0	6.0	8.0	9.0	9.2

gallery of covers and pin-ups; script for #123 ... 30.00
...New Beginnings TPB (10/01, $14.95) r/#116-120 ... 15.00
...Rough Cut ($2.99) Pencil pages and script for #102 ... 3.00
...Youngblood (8/96, $4.95)-Platt-c ... 5.00
NOTE: *Capullo* a(p)-15-25, Annual 1; c(p)-14-27. **Rob Liefeld** a-1-7, 9p; c-1-9, 11p; plots-1-12. *Mignola* a-8p.

X-FORCE
Marvel Comics: Oct, 2004 - No. 6, Mar, 2005 ($2.99, limited series)

1-6-Liefeld-c/a; Nicieza-s. 5,6-Wolverine & The Thing app. ... 3.00
X-Force & Cable Vol. 1: The Legend Returns (2005, $14.99) r/#1-6 ... 15.00

X-FORCE MEGAZINE
Marvel Comics: Nov, 1996 ($3.95, one-shot)

1-Reprints ... 4.00

X-FORCE: SHATTERSTAR
Marvel Comics: Apr, 2005 - No. 4, July, 2005 ($2.99, limited series)

1-4-Liefeld-c/s; Michaels-a ... 3.00
TPB ($15.99) r/#1-4 & New Mutants #99,100 ... 16.00

XIMOS: VIOLENT PAST
Triumphant Comics: Mar, 1994 - No. 2, Mar, 1994 ($2.50, limited series)

1,2 ... 2.50

XIN: JOURNEY OF THE MONKEY KING
Anarchy Studios: May, 2003 - No. 3, July, 2003 ($2.99)

Preview Edition (Apr, 2003, $1.99) Flip book w/ Vampi Vicious Preview Edition ... 2.50
1-3-Kevin Lau-a. 1-Three covers by Lau, Park and Nauck. 2-Three covers ... 3.00

XIN: LEGEND OF THE MONKEY KING
Anarchy Studios: Nov, 2002 - No. 3, Jan, 2003 ($2.99)

Preview Edition (Summer 2002, Diamond Dateline supplement) ... 2.50
1-3-Kevin Lau-a. 1-Two covers by Lau & Madureira. 2-Two covers by Lau & Oeming ... 3.00
TPB (10/03, $12.95) r/#1-3; cover gallery and sketch pages ... 13.00

X-MAN (Also see X-Men Omega & X-Men Prime)
Marvel Comics: Mar, 1995 - No. 75, May, 2001 ($1.95/$1.99/$2.25)

1-Age of Apocalypse ... 5.00
1-2nd print ... 2.50
2-4,15: 25-($2.99)-Wraparound-c ... 3.00
5-24, 26-28: 5-Post Age of Apocalypse stories begin. 5-7-Madelyne Pryor app.
10-Professor X app. 12-vs. Excalibur. 13-Marauders. 14-Vs. Cable; Onslaught
app. 15-17-Vs. Holocaust. 17-w/Onslaught Update. 18-Onslaught x-over; X-Force-c/app;
Marauders app. 19-Onslaught x-over. 20-Abomination-c/app.; w/card insert. 23-Bishop app.
24-Spider-Man, Morbius-c/app. 27-Re-appearance of Aurora(Alpha Flight) ... 2.50
29-49,51-62: 29-Operation Zero Tolerance. 37,38-Spider-Man-c/app. 56-Spider-Man app. ... 2.50
50-($2.99) Crossover with Generation X ... 3.00
63-74: 63-Ellis & Grant-s/Olivetti-a begins. 64-Begin $2.25-c ... 2.50
75 ($2.99) Final issue; Alcatena-a ... 3.00
#(-1) Flashback (7/97) ... 2.50
...'96, ...'97-($2.95)-Wraparound-c; '96-Age of Apocalypse ... 3.00
...: All Saints' Day ('97, $5.99) Dodson-a ... 6.00
.../Hulk '98 ($2.99) Wraparound-c; Thanos app. ... 3.00

XMAS COMICS
Fawcett Publications: 12?/1941 - No. 2, 12?/1942; (50¢, 324 pgs.)
No. 7, 12?/1947 (25¢, 132 pgs.)(#3-6 do not exist)

1-Contains Whiz #21, Capt. Marvel #2, Bulletman #2, Wow #3, & Master #18; Raboy back-c.
Not rebound, remaindered comics; printed at same time as originals

	394	788	1182	2561	4531	6500

2-Capt. Marvel, Bulletman, Spy Smasher ... 159 318 477 994 1647 2300
7-Funny animals (Hoppy, Billy the Kid & Oscar) ... 66 132 198 413 682 950

XMAS COMICS
Fawcett Publications: No. 4, Dec, 1949 - No. 7, Dec, 1952 (50¢, 196 pgs.)

4-Contains Whiz, Master, Tom Mix, Captain Marvel, Nyoka, Capt. Video, Bob Colt,
Monte Hale, Hot Rod Comics, & Battle Stories. Not rebound, remaindered comics;
printed at the same time as originals. Stocking on cover is made of green or red felt

	71	142	213	444	735	1025

5-7-Same as above. 5- Red felt on-c. 7-Bill Boyd app.; stocking on cover is made of green
felt (novelty cover) ... 55 110 165 344 572 800

X-MEN, THE
(See Adventures of Cyclops and Phoenix, Amazing Adventures, Archangel, Brotherhood, Capt.
America #172, Classic X-Men, Exiles, Further Adventures of Cyclops & Phoenix, Gambit, Giant-Size..., Heroes
For Hope..., Kitty Pryde & Wolverine, Marvel & DC Present, Marvel Collector's Edition:..., Marvel Fanfare, Marvel
Graphic Novel, Marvel Super Heroes, Marvel Team-Up, Marvel Triple Action, The Marvel X-Men Collection, New
Mutants, Official Marvel Index To..., Rogue, Special Edition..., Ultimate..., Uncanny..., Wolverine, X-
Factor, X-Force, X-Terminators)

X-MEN, THE
(1st series)(Becomes Uncanny X-Men at #142)(The X-Men #1-93;

X-Men #94-141) (The Uncanny X-Men on-c only #114-141)
Marvel Comics Group: Sept, 1963 - No. 66, Mar, 1970; No. 67, Dec, 1970 - No. 141, Jan,
1981

1-Origin/1st app. X-Men (Angel, Beast, Cyclops, Iceman & Marvel Girl); 1st app.
Magneto & Professor X ... 700 1400 2100 6500 12,750 19,000
2-1st app. The Vanisher ... 152 304 456 1292 2396 3500
3-1st app. The Blob (1/64) ... 83 166 249 706 1303 1900
4-1st Quicksilver & Scarlet Witch & Brotherhood of the Evil Mutants (3/64);
1st app. Toad; 2nd app. Magneto ... 85 170 255 723 1337 1950
5-Magneto & Evil Mutants-c/story ... 57 114 171 485 893 1300
6,7: 6-Sub-Mariner app. 7-Magneto app. ... 50 100 150 400 725 1050
8,9,11: 8-1st Unus the Untouchable. 9-Early Avengers app. (1/65); 1st Lucifer.
11-1st app. The Stranger. ... 40 80 120 300 550 800
10-1st S.A. app. Ka-Zar & Zabu the sabertooth (3/65) 38 76 114 285 518 750
12-Origin Prof. X; Origin/1st app. Juggernaut ... 44 88 132 352 639 925
13-Juggernaut and Human Torch app. ... 30 60 90 225 413 600
14,15: 14-1st app. Sentinels. 15-Origin Beast ... 31 62 93 233 429 625
16-20: 19-1st app. The Mimic (4/66) ... 18 36 54 132 234 335
21-27,29,30: 27-Re-enter The Mimic (r-in #75); Spider-Man cameo
... 13 26 39 93 164 235
28-1st app. The Banshee (1/67)(r-in #76) ... 19 38 57 138 244 350
28-2nd printing (1994) ... 2 4 6 8 10 12
31-34,36,37,39: 34-Adkins-c/a. 39-New costumes ... 10 20 30 71 126 180
35-Spider-Man x-over (8/67)(r-in #83); 1st app. Changeling
... 22 44 66 165 295 425
38,40: 38-Origins of the X-Men series begins, ends #57. 40-(1/68) 1st app. Frankenstein's
monster at Marvel ... 11 22 33 75 133 190
41-49: 42-Death of Prof. X (Changeling disguised as). 44-1st S.A. app. G.A. Red Raven.
49-Steranko-c; 1st Polaris ... 9 18 27 64 110 155
50,51-Steranko-c/a ... 10 20 30 67 116 165
52 ... 9 18 27 60 100 140
53-Barry Smith-c/a (his 1st comic book work) ... 10 20 30 67 116 165
54,55-B. Smith-c/a. 54-1st app. Alex Summers who later becomes Havok. 55-Summers
discovers he has mutant powers ... 10 20 30 67 116 165
56,57,59-63,65-Neal Adams-a(p). 56-Intro Havok w/o costume. 60-1st Sauron.
65-Return of Professor X. ... 10 20 30 67 116 165
58-1st app. Havok in costume; N. Adams-a(p) ... 12 24 36 82 146 210
62,63-2nd printings (1994) ... 2 4 6 8 10 12
64-1st app. Sunfire ... 9 18 27 65 113 160
66-Last new story w/original X-Men; battles Hulk ... 10 20 30 70 123 175
67-70: 67-Reprints begin, end #93. 67-70: (52 pgs.) ... 8 16 24 54 86 120
71-93: 71-Last 15¢ issue. 72: (52 pgs.) 73-86-r/#25-38 w/new-c. 83-Spider-Man-c/story.
87-93-r/#39-45 with covers ... 7 14 21 47 76 105
94 (8/75)-New X-Men begin (see Giant-Size X-Men for 1st app.); Colossus, Nightcrawler,
Thunderbird, Storm, Wolverine, & Banshee join; Angel, Marvel Girl & Iceman resign
... 65 130 195 520 835 1150
95-Death of Thunderbird ... 15 30 45 107 191 275
96,97 ... 9 18 27 63 107 150
98,99-(Regular 25¢ edition)(4,6/76) ... 9 18 27 61 103 145
98,99-(30¢-c variants, limited distribution) ... 16 32 48 114 202 290
100-Old vs. New X-Men; part origin Phoenix; last 25¢ issue (8/76)
... 10 20 30 70 123 175
100-(30¢-c variant, limited distribution) ... 19 38 57 138 244 350
101-Phoenix origin concludes ... 11 22 33 79 140 200
102-104: 102-Origin Storm. 104-1st brief app. Starjammers; Magneto-c/story
... 7 14 21 49 80 110
105-107-(Regular 30¢ editions). 106-(8/77)Old vs. New X-Men. 107-1st full app. Starjammers;
last 30¢ issue ... 7 14 21 45 73 100
105-107-(35¢-c variants, limited distribution) ... 11 22 33 79 140 200
108-Byrne-a begins (see Marvel Team-Up #53) ... 7 14 21 49 80 110
109-1st app. Weapon Alpha (becomes Vindicator) ... 7 14 21 45 73 100
110,111: 110-Phoenix joins ... 5 10 15 35 55 75
112-116 ... 5 10 15 35 55 75
117-119: 117-Origin Professor X ... 4 8 12 28 44 60
120-1st app. Alpha Flight, story line begins (4/79); 1st app. Vindicator (formerly
Weapon Alpha); last 35¢ issue ... 6 12 18 43 69 95
121-1st full Alpha Flight story ... 6 12 18 41 66 90
122-128: 125-Spider-Man x-over. 124-Colossus becomes Proletarian
... 4 8 12 26 41 55
129-Intro Kitty Pryde (1/80); last Banshee; Dark Phoenix saga begins; intro. Emma Frost
(White Queen) ... 5 10 15 32 51 70
130-1st app. The Dazzler by Byrne (2/80) ... 4 8 12 26 41 55
131-135: 131-Dazzler app.; 1st White Queen-c. 133-Wolverine app. 134-Phoenix becomes
Dark Phoenix ... 4 8 12 26 41 55

Uncanny X-Men #257 © MAR

Uncanny X-Men #353 © MAR

Uncanny X-Men #450 © MAR

	GD	VG	FN	VF	VF/NM	NM-
	2.0	4.0	6.0	8.0	9.0	9.2

136,138: 138-Dazzler app.; Cyclops leaves — 4 8 12 22 34 45
137-Giant; death of Phoenix — 4 8 12 28 44 60
139-Alpha Flight app.; Kitty Pryde joins; new costume for Wolverine — 4 8 12 26 41 55
140-Alpha Flight app. — 4 8 12 26 41 55
141-Intro Future X-Men & The New Brotherhood of Evil Mutants; 1st app. Rachel (Phoenix II); Death of Franklin Richards — 4 8 12 28 44 60

X-MEN: Titled THE UNCANNY X-MEN #142, Feb, 1981 - Present

142-Rachel app.; deaths of alt. future Wolverine, Storm & Colossus — 5 10 15 35 55 75
143-Last Byrne issue — 4 8 12 26 41 55
144-150: 144-Man-Thing app. 145-Old X-Men app. 148-Spider-Woman, Dazzler app. 150-Double size — 2 4 6 9 12 15
151-157,159-161,163,164: 161-Origin Magneto. 163-Origin Binary. 164-1st app. Binary as Carol Danvers — 1 3 4 6 8 10
158-1st app. Rogue in X-Men (6/82, see Avengers Annual #10) — 3 6 9 15 21 26
162-Wolverine solo story — 2 4 6 9 13 16
165-Paul Smith-c/a begins, ends #175 — 2 4 6 8 10 12
166-170: 166-Double size; Paul Smith-a. 167-New Mutants app. (3/83); same date as New Mutants #1; 1st meeting w/X-Men; ties into N.M. #3,4; Starjammers app.; contains skin "Tattooz" decals. 168-1st brief app. Madelyne Pryor (last page) in X-Men (see Avengers Annual #10) — 1 2 3 5 7 9
171-Rogue joins X-Men; Simonson-c/a — 2 4 6 11 16 20
172-174: 172,173-Two part Wolverine solo story. 173-Two cover variations, blue & black. 174-Phoenix cameo — 1 2 3 4 5 7
175-(52 pgs.)-Anniversary issue; Phoenix returns — 1 3 4 6 8 10
176-185,187-192,194-199: 181-Sunfire app. 182-Rogue solo story. 184-1st app. Forge (8/84). 190,191-Spider-Man & Avengers x-over. 195-Power Pack x-over — 1 2 3 4 5 7
186,193: 186-Double-size; Barry Smith/Austin-a. 193-Double size; 100th app. New X-Men; 1st app. Warpath in costume (see New Mutants #16) — 1 2 3 5 6 8
200-(12/85, $1.25, 52 pgs.) — 1 2 3 5 6 8
201-(1/86)-1st app. Cable? (as baby Nathan; see X-Factor #1); 1st Whilce Portacio-c/a(i) on X-Men (guest artist) — 3 6 9 14 20 25
202-204,206-209: 204-Nightcrawler solo story; 2nd Portacio-a(i) on X-Men. 207-Wolverine/Phoenix story — 1 2 3 4 5 7
205-Wolverine solo story by Barry Smith — 2 4 6 8 11 14
210,211-Mutant Massacre begins — 3 6 9 14 19 24
212,213-Wolverine vs. Sabretooth (Mutant Mass.) — 3 6 9 16 22 28
214-221,223,224: 219-Havok joins (7/87); brief app. Sabretooth. 221-1st app. Mr. Sinister — 1 2 3 4 5 7
222-Wolverine battles Sabretooth-c/story — 3 6 9 14 19 24
225-242: 225-227: Fall Of The Mutants. 226-Double size. 240-Sabretooth app. 242-Double size, X-Factor app., Inferno tie-in — 1 2 3 4 5 7
243,245-247: 245-Rob Liefeld-a(p) — 1 2 3 4 5 7
244-1st app. Jubilee — 3 6 9 16 23 30
248-1st Jim Lee art on X-Men (1989) — 2 4 6 13 18 22
248-2nd printing (1992, $1.25) — 3.00
249-252: 252-Lee-c — 1 2 3 4 5 7
253-255: 253-All new X-Men begin. 254-Lee-c — 1 2 3 4 5 7
256,257-Jim Lee-c/a begins — 1 2 3 5 7 9
258-Wolverine solo story; Lee-c/a — 1 2 3 5 7 9
259-Silvestri-c/a — 1 2 3 4 5 7
260-265-No Lee-a. 260,261,264-Lee-c — 1 2 3 4 5 7
266-(8/90) 1st full app. Gambit (see Annual #14)-No Lee-a — 4 8 12 22 34 45
267-Jim Lee-c/a resumes; 2nd full Gambit app. — 2 4 6 9 13 16
268-Capt. America, Black Widow & Wolverine team-up; Lee-a — 2 4 6 10 14 18
268,270: 268-2nd printing. 270-Gold 2nd printing — 3.00
269,273-275: 269-Lee-a. 273-New Mutants (Cable) & X-Factor x-over; Golden, Byrne & Lee part pencils. 275-(52 pgs.)-Tri-fold by Jim Lee (p); Prof. X — 1 2 3 4 5 7
270-X-Tinction Agenda begins — 1 2 3 4 5 8
271-2nd X-Tinction Agenda — 1 2 3 5 6 8
275-Gold 2nd printing — 2.50
276-280: 277-Last Lee-c/a. 280-X-Factor x-over — 6.00
281-(10/91)-New team begins (Storm, Archangel, Colossus, Iceman & Marvel Girl); Whilce Portacio-c/a begins; Byrne scripts begin; wraparound-c (white logo) — 1 2 3 4 5 7
281-2nd printing with red metallic ink logo w/o UPC box ($1.00-c); does not say 2nd printing inside — 3.00

282-1st brief app. Bishop (cover & 1 page) — 2 4 6 8 10 12
282-Gold ink 2nd printing ($1.00-c) — 3.00
283-1st full app. Bishop (12/91) — 2 4 6 8 10 12
284-299: 284-Last $1.00-c. 286,287-Lee plots. 287-Bishop joins team. 288-Lee/Portacio plots. 290-Last Portacio-c/a. 294-Peterson-a(p) begins (#292 is 1st Peterson-c). 294-296 ($1.50)-Bagged w/trading card in each; X-Cutioner's Song x-overs; Peterson/Austin-c/a on all — 4.00
300-($3.95, 68 pgs.)-Holo-grafx foil-c; Magneto app. — 6.00
301-303,305-309,311 — 3.00
303,307-Gold Edition — 1 2 3 5 6 8
304-($3.95, 68 pgs.)-Wraparound-c with Magneto hologram on-c; 30th anniversary issue; Jae Lee-a (4 pgs.) — 6.00
310-($1.95)-Bound-in trading card sheet — 3.00
312-$1.50-c begins; bound-in card sheet; 1st Madureira — 4.00
313-321 — 3.00
316,317-($2.95)-Foil enhanced editions — 4.00
318-321-($1.95)-Deluxe editions — 3.00
322-Onslaught — 5.00
323,324,326-346: 323-Return from Age of Apocalypse. 328-Sabretooth-c. 329,330-Dr. Strange app. 331-White Queen-c/app. 334-Juggernaut app.; w/Onslaught Update. 335-Onslaught, Avengers, Apocalypse, & X-Man app. 336-Onslaught. 338-Archangel's wings return to normal. 339-Havok vs. Cyclops; Spider-Man app. 341-Gladiator/c/app. 342-Deathbird cameo; two covers. 343,344-Phalanx — 3.00
325-($3.95)-Anniversary issue; gatefold-c — 5.00
342-Variant-c — 1 3 4 6 8 10
347-349:347-Begin $1.99-c. 349-"Operation Zero Tolerance" — 3.00
350-($3.99, 48 pgs.) Prismatic etched foil gatefold wraparound-c; Trial of Gambit; Seagle-s begin — 1 2 3 5 6 8
351-359: 353-Bachalo-a begins. 354-Regular-c. 355-Alpha Flight-c/app. 356-Original X-Men-c — 3.00
354-Dark Phoenix variant-c — 5.00
360-($2.99) 35th Anniv. issue; Pacheco-c — 3.00
360-($3.99) Etched Holo-foil enhanced-c — 4.00
360-($6.95) DF Edition with Jae Lee variant-c — 7.00
361-374: 361-Gambit returns; Skroce-a. 362-Hunt for Xavier pt. 1; Bachalo-a. 364-Yu-a. 366-Magneto-c. 369-Juggernaut-c — 3.00
375-($2.99) Autopsy of Wolverine — 4.00
376-379: 376,377-Apocalypse: The Twelve — 3.00
380-($2.99) Polybagged with X-Men Revolution Genesis Edition preview — 4.00
381,382,384-389,391-393: 381-Begin $2.25-c; Claremont-s. 387-Maximum Security — 3.00
383-($2.99) — 3.50
390-Colossus dies to cure the Legacy Virus — 4.00
394-New look X-Men begins; Casey-s/Churchill-c/a — 3.50
395-399-Poptopia. 398-Phillips & Wood-a — 3.00
400-($3.50) Art by Ashley Wood, Eddie Campbell, Hamner, Phillips, Pulido and Matt Smith; wraparound-c by Wood — 4.00
401-415: 401-'Nuff Said issue; Garney-a. 404,405,407-409,413-415-Phillips-a — 3.00
416-421: 416-Asamiya-a begins. 421-Garney-a — 3.00
422-($3.50) Alpha Flight app.; Garney-a — 4.00
423-(25c-c) Holy War pt. 1; Garney-a/Philip Tan-c — 3.00
424-449,452-454: 425,426,429,430-Tan-a. 428-Birth of Nightcrawler. 437-Larroca-a begins. 444-New team, new costumes; Claremont-s/Davis-a begins. 448,449-Coipel-a — 3.00
450,451,455-459-X-23 app.; Davis-a — 3.00
460-471: 460-Begin $2.50-c; Raney-a. 462-465-House of M. 464-468-Bachalo-a — 3.00
472-490: 472-Begin $2.99-c; Bachalo-a. 475-Wraparound-c — 3.00
#(-1) Flashback (7/97) Ladronn-c/Hitch & Neary-a — 3.00
Special 1(12/70)-Kirby-c/a; origin The Stranger — 9 18 27 63 107 150
Special 2(11/71, 52 pgs.) — 7 14 21 47 76 105
Annual 3(1979, 52 pgs.)-New story; Miller/Austin-a; Wolverine still in old yellow costume — 4 8 12 24 37 50
Annual 4(1980, 52 pgs.)-Dr. Strange guest stars — 2 4 6 9 12 15
Annual 5(1981, 52 pgs.) — 1 2 3 5 7 9
Annual 6-8('82-'84 52 pgs.)-6-Dracula app. — 6.00
Annual 9,10('85, '86)-9-New Mutants x-over cont'd from New Mutants Special Ed. #1; Art Adams-a. 10-Art Adams-a — 1 2 3 5 7 9
Annual 11-13:('87-'89, 68 pgs.)- 12-Evolutionary War; A.Adams-a(p). 13-Atlantis Attacks — 4.00
Annual 14(1990, $2.00, 68 pgs.)-1st app. Gambit (minor app., 5 pgs.); Fantastic Four, New Mutants (Cable) & X-Factor x-over; Art Adams-c/a(p) — 3 6 9 14 20 25
Annual 15 (1991, $2.00, 68 pgs.)-4 pg. origin; New Mutants x-over; 4 pg. Wolverine solo back-up story; 4th app. X-Force cont'd from New Warriors Annual #1 — 4.00
Annual 16-18 ('92-'94, 68 pgs.)-16-Jae Lee-c/a(p). 17-Bagged w/card — 3.00
Annual '95-(11/95, $3.95)-Wraparound-c — 4.00
Annual '96,'97-Wraparound-c — 3.00
.../Fantastic Four Annual '98 ($2.99) Casey-s — 3.00

X-Men #72 © MAR

(New) X-Men #114 © MAR

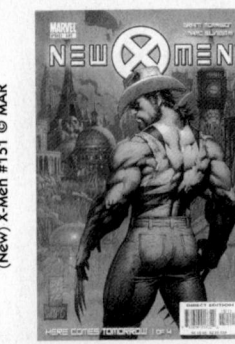

(New) X-Men #151 © MAR

	GD	VG	FN	VF	VF/NM	NM-
	2.0	4.0	6.0	8.0	9.0	9.2

Annual '99 ($3.50) Jubilee app. 3.50
Annual 2000 ($3.50) Cable app.; Ribic-a 3.50
Annual 2001 ($3.50, printed wide-ways) Ashley Wood-c/a; Casey-s 3.50
Annual (Vol. 2) #1 (8/06, $3.99) Storm & Black Panther wedding prelude 4.00
...At The State Fair of Texas (1983, 26 pgs., one-shot); Supplement to the Dallas Times Herald

| | 2 | 4 | 6 | 9 | 12 | 15 |

...: The Dark Phoenix Saga TPB 1st printing (1984, $12.95) 40.00
...: The Dark Phoenix Saga TPB 2nd-5th printings 30.00
...: The Dark Phoenix Saga TPB 6th-10th printings 20.00
... Days of Future Past TPB (2004, $19.99) r/#138-143 & Annual #4 .... 20.00
... Eve of Destruction TPB (2005, $14.99) r/#391-393 & X-Men #111-113; Churchill-c 15.00
...:Dream's End (2004, $17.99)-r/Death of Colossus story arc from Uncanny X-Men #388-390, Cable #87, Bishop #16 and X-Men #108,110; debut pages from Giant-Size X-Men #1 .... 15.00
...From The Ashes TPB (1990, $14.95) r/#168-176 .... 7.00
...God Loves, Man Kills ($6.95)-r/Marvel Graphic Novel #5 .... 14.00
...God Loves, Man Kills - Special Edition (2003, $4.99)-reprint with new Hughes-c 5.00
House of M: Uncanny X-Men TPB (2006, $13.99) r/#462-465 and selections from Secrets Of The House of M one-shot 14.00
...In The Days of Future Past TPB (1989, $3.95, 52 pgs.) 4.00
...Old Soldiers TPB (2004, $19.99) r/#213,215 & Ann. #11; New Mutants Ann. #2&3 .... 20.00
...Poptopia TPB (10/01, $15.95) r/#394-399 .... 16.00
...: Rise & Fall of the Shi'ar Empire HC (2007, $34.99, dustjacket) r/#475-486; bonus art 35.00
Uncanny X-Men Omnibus Vol. 1 HC (2006, $99.99, dust jacket) r/Giant-Size X-Men #1, (Uncanny) X-Men #94-131 & Annual #3; cover gallery, promo and sketch art 100.00
Vignettes (9/01, $17.95) r/Claremont & Bolton Classic X-Men #1-13 .... 18.00
Vignettes Vol. 2 TPB (2005, $17.99) r/Claremont & Bolton Classic X-Men #14-25 .... 18.00
... Vol. 1: Hope TPB (2003, $12.99) r/#410-415; Harris-a 13.00
... Vol. 2: Dominant Species TPB (2003, $11.99) r/#416-420; Asamiya-c 12.00
... Vol. 3: Holy War TPB (2003, $17.99) r/#421-427 .... 18.00
... Vol. 4: The Draco TPB (2004, $15.99) r/#428-434 .... 16.00
... Vol. 5: She Lies with Angels TPB (2004, $11.99) r/#437-441 .... 12.00
... Vol. 6: Bright New Mourning TPB (2004, $14.99) r/#435,436,442,443 & (New) X-Men #155,156; Larroca sketch covers 15.00
... - The New Age Vol. 1: The End of History (2004, $12.99) r/#444-449 .... 13.00
... - The New Age Vol. 2: The Cruelest Cut (2005, $11.99) r/#450-454 .... 12.00
... - The New Age Vol. 3: On Ice (2006, $15.99) r/#455-461 .... 16.00
... - The New Age Vol. 4: End of Greys (2006, $19.99) r/#466-471 .... 20.00
... - The New Age Vol. 5: First Foursaken (2006, $11.99) r/#472-474 & Annual #1 .... 12.00

NOTE: Art Adams a-Annual 9, 10p, 12p, 14p; c-218p. Neal Adams a-56-63p, 65p; c-56-63. Adkins a-34, 35p; c-31, 34, 35. Austin a-108i, 109i, 111-117i, 119-143i, 186i, 204i, 228i, 294-297i. Annual 3i, 7i, 9i, 13; c-109-111i, 114-122i, 123, 124-141i, 142, 143, 196i, 204i, 228i, 294-297i, Annual 3i. J. Buscema c-42, 43, 45. Buscema/Tuska a-45. Byrne a(p)-108, 109, 111-143, 273; c(p)-113-116, 127, 129, 131-141. Capullo c-14. Ditko r-86, 89-91, 93. Everett c-73. Golden a-273, Annual 7p. Guice a-216p, 217p. G. Kane c(p)-33, 74-76, 79, 80, 94, 95. Kirby a(p)-1-17 (#12-17, 67r-layouts); c(p)-1-17, 25, 30 (18, 26-parts). Layton a-105i; c-112i, 113i. Jim Lee a(p)-248, 256-258, 267-277; c(p)-252, 254, 256-261, 264, 267, 270, 275-277, 286. Perez a-Annual 3p; c(p)-112, 128, Annual 3. Peterson a(p)-294-300, 304(part); c(p)-294-299. Whilce Portacio a(p)-281-286, 289, 290; a(i)-267; c-281-285p, 289p, 290; c(i)-267. Romita, Jr. a-300; c-300. Roussos a-84i. Simonson a-171p; c-171, 217. B. Smith a-53, 186p, 198p, 205, 214; c-53-55, 186p, 198, 205, 212, 214, 216. Paul Smith a(p)-165-170, 172-175, 278; c-165-175p, 289p, 290; c(i)-267. Sparling a-78p. Steranko a-50p, 51p; c-49-51. Sutton a-106i. Art Thibert a(i)-281-286; c(i)-281, 282, 284, 285. Toth a-12p, 67p(r). Tuska a-40-42i, 43-46p, 88i(r); c-39-41, 77p, 78p. Williamson a-202i, 203i, 211i; c-202i, 203i, 206i. Wood c-14i.

UNCANNY X-MEN AND THE NEW TEEN TITANS (See Marvel and DC Present...)

X-MEN (2nd Series)
Marvel Comics: Oct, 1991 - Present ($1.00/$1.25/$1.95/$1.99)

1 a-d ($1.50, 52 pgs.)-Jim Lee-c/a begins, ends #11; new team begins (Cyclops, Beast, Wolverine, Gambit, Psylocke & Rogue); new Uncanny X-Men & Magneto app.; four different covers exist 4.00
1 e ($3.95)-Double gate-fold-c consisting of all four covers from a-d by Jim Lee; contains all pin-ups from #1a-d plus inside-c foldout poster; no ads; printed on coated stock 5.00
2-7: 4-Wolverine back to old yellow costume (same date as Wolverine #50); last $1.00-c. 5-Byrne scripts. 6-Sabretooth-c/story 4.00
8-10: 8-Gambit vs. Bishop-c/story; last Lee-a; Ghost Rider cameo cont'd in Ghost Rider #26. 9-Wolverine vs. Ghost Rider; cont'd/G.R. #26. 10-Return of Longshot 5.00
11-13,17-24,26-29,31: 12,13-Art Thibert c/a. 28,29-Sabretooth app. 4.00
11-Silver ink 2nd printing; came with X-Men board game

| | 2 | 4 | 6 | 9 | 12 | 15 |

14-16-($1.50)-Polybagged with trading card in each; X-Cutioner's Song x-overs; 14-Andy Kubert-c/a begins 4.00
25-($3.50, 52 pgs.)-Wraparound-c with Gambit hologram on-c; Professor X erases Magneto's mind

| | 2 | 4 | 6 | 9 | 10 | 12 |

25-30th anniversary issue w/B&W-c with Magneto in color & Magneto hologram & no price on-c

| | 2 | 4 | 6 | 9 | 12 | 15 |

25-Gold 30.00
30-($1.95)-Wedding issue w/bound-in trading card sheet 5.00
32-37: 32-Begin $1.50-c; bound-in card sheet. 33-Gambit & Sabretooth-c/story 3.00

36,37-($2.95)-Collectors editions (foil-c) 5.00
38-44,46-49,51-53, 55-65: 42,43- Paul Smith-a. 46,49,53-56-Onslaught app. 51-Waid scripts begin, end #56. 54-(Reg. edition)-Onslaught revealed as Professor X. 55,56-Onslaught x-over; Avengers, FF & Sentinels app. 56-Dr. Doom app. 57-Xavier taken into custody; Byrne-c/swipe (X-Men,1st Series #138). 59-Hercules-c/app. 61-Juggernaut-app. 62-Re-intro. Shang Chi; two covers. 63-Kingpin cameo. 64- Kingpin app. 3.00
45-($3.95)-Annual issue; gatefold-c 5.00
50-($2.95)-Vs. Onslaught, wraparound-c 4.00
50-($3.95)-Vs. Onslaught, wraparound foil-c 5.00
50-($2.95)-Variant gold-c

| | | | 3 | 6 | 9 | 20 | 30 | 40 |

50-($2.95)-Variant silver-c

| | | | 1 | 2 | 3 | 5 | 6 | 8 |

54-(Limited edition)-Embossed variant-c; Onslaught revealed as Professor X

| | | | 3 | 6 | 9 | 16 | 23 | 30 |

66-69,71-74,76-79: 66-Operation Zero Tolerance. 76-Origin of Maggott 3.00
70-($2.99, 48 pgs.)-Joe Kelly-s begin, new members join 3.50
75-($2.99, 48 pgs.) vs. N'Garai; wraparound-c 3.50
80-($3.99) 35th Anniv. issue; holo-foil-c 5.00
80-($2.99) Regular-c 3.50
80-($6.95) Dynamic Forces Ed.; Quesada-c 7.00
81-93,95: 82-Hunt for Xavier pt. 2. 85-Davis-a. 86-Origin of Joseph. 87-Magneto War ends. 88-Juggernaut app. 3.00
94-($2.99) Contains preview of X-Men: Hidden Years 3.50
96-99: 96,97-Apocalypse: The Twelve 3.00
100-($2.99) Art Adams-c; begin Claremont-s/Yu-a 4.00
100-DF alternate-c

| | | | 3 | 6 | 8 | 10 |

101-105,107,108,110-114: 101-Begin $2.25-c. 107-Maximum Security x-over; Bishop-c/app. 108-Moira MacTaggart dies; Senator Kelly shot. 111-Magneto-c. 112,113-Eve of Destruction 3.00
106-($2.99) X-Men battle Domina 3.50
109-($3.50, 100 pgs.) new and reprinted Christmas-themed stories 4.00
114-Title change to "New X-Men", Morrison-s/Quitely-c/a begins 4.00
115-Two covers (Quitely & BWS) 3.00
116-125,127-149: 116-Emma Frost joins. 117,118-Van Sciver-a. 121,122,135-Quitely-a. 127-Leon & Sienkiewicz-a. 128-Kordey-a. 132,139-141-Jimenez-a. 136-138-Quitely-a. 142-Sabretooth app.; Bachalo-c/a thru #145. 146-Maggott returns; Jimenez-a 3.00
126-($3.25) Quitely-a; defeat of Cassanova 3.50
150-($3.50) Jean Grey dies again; last Jimenez-a 4.00
151-156: 151-154-Silvestri-c/a 3.00
157-169: 157-X-Men Reload begins 3.00
170-184: 171- Begin $2.50-c. 175,176-Crossover with Black Panther #8,9. 181-184-Apocalypse returns 3.00
185-199,201-203: 185-Begin $2.99-c. 188-190,192-194,197-199-Bachalo-a. 195,196,201-203-Ramos-a. 201-203-Endangered Species back-up 3.00
200-($3.99) Two wraparound covers by Bachalo & Finch; Bachalo & Ramos-a 4.00
#(-1) Flashback (7/97); origin of Magneto 3.00
Annual 1-3 ('92-'94, $2.25-$2.95, 68 pgs.) 1-Lee-c & layouts; #2-Bagged w/card 4.00
Special '95 ($3.95) 4.00
... '96,...'97-Wraparound-c 3.00
... Dr. Doom '98 Annual ($2.99) Lopresti-a 3.50
... Annual '99 ($3.50) Adam Kubert-c 3.50
Annual 2000 ($3.50) Art Adams-c/Claremont-s/Eaton-a 3.50
...2001 Annual ($3.50) Morrison-s/Yu-a; issue printed sideways 3.50
...2007 Annual #1 (3/07, $3.99) Casey-s/Brooks-a; Cable and Mystique app. 4.00
Animation Special Graphic Novel (12/90, $10.95) adapts animated series 11.00
Ashcan #1 (1994, 75¢) Introduces new team members 2.25
Ashcan (75¢ Ashcan Edition) (1994) 2.25
... Archives Sketchbook (12/00, $2.99) Early B&W character design sketches by various incl. Lee, Davis, Yu, Pacheco, BWS, Art Adams, Liefeld 3.00
...: Bizarre Love Triangle TPB (2005, $9.99)-r/X-Men #171-174 .... 10.00
... / Black Panther TPB (2006, $11.99)-r/X-Men #175,176 & Black Panther (2005) #8,9 .... 12.00
...: Blood of Apocalypse (2006, $17.99)-r/X-Men #182-187 .... 18.00
...: Day of the Atom (2005, $19.99)-r/X-Men #157-165 .... 20.00
Decimation: X-Men - The Day After TPB (2006, $15.99) r/#177-181 & Decimation: House of M - The Day After 16.00
...: Declassified (10/00, $3.50) Profile pin-ups by various; Jae Lee-c 3.50
...: Endangered Species (8/07, $3.99) prologue to 17-part back-up series in X-Men titles 4.00
...: Fatal Attractions ('94, $17.95)-r/x-Factor #92, X-Force #25, Uncanny X-Men #304, X-Men #25, Wolverine #75, & Excalibur #71 .... 18.00
...: Golgotha (2005, $12.99)-r/X-Men #166-170 .... 13.00
...: Millennial Visions (8/00, $3.99) Various artists interpret future X-Men 4.00
...: Millennial Visions 2 (1/02, $3.50) Various artists interpret future X-Men 3.50
...: Mutant Genesis (2006, $19.99)-r/X-Men #1-7; sketch pages and extra art 20.00
New X-Men: E is for Extinction TPB (11/01, $12.95) r/#114-117 .... 13.00
New X-Men: Imperial TPB (7/02, $19.99) r/#118-126; Quitely-c 20.00

X-Men Adventures #8 © MAR

X-Men: Evolution #1 © MAR

X-Men/Fantastic Four #2 © MAR

	GD	VG	FN	VF	VF/NM	NM-
	2.0	4.0	6.0	8.0	9.0	9.2

New X-Men: New Worlds TPB (2002, $14.99) r/#127-133; Quitely-c ... 15.00
New X-Men: Riot at Xavier's TPB (2003, $11.99) r/#134-138; Quitely-c ... 12.00
New X-Men: Vol. 5: Assault on Weapon Plus TPB (2003, $14.99) r/#139-145 ... 15.00
New X-Men: Vol. 6: Planet X TPB (2004, $12.99) r/#146-150 ... 13.00
New X-Men: Vol. 7: Here Comes Tomorrow TPB (2004, $10.99) r/#151-154 ... 11.00
New X-Men: Volume 1 HC (2002, $29.99) oversized r/#114-126 & 2001 Annual ... 30.00
New X-Men: Volume 2 HC (2003, $29.99) oversized r/#127-141; sketch & script pages ... 30.00
New X-Men: Volume 3 HC (2004, $29.99) oversized r/#142-154; sketch & script pages ... 30.00
New X-Men Omnibus HC (2006, $99.99) oversized r/#114-154 & Annual 2001; Morrison's
    original pitch; sketch & script pages; variant covers & promo art; Carey intro. ... 100.00
... Pizza Hut Mini-comics-(See Marvel Collector's Edition: X-Men in Promotional Comics section)
... Premium Edition #1 (1993)-Cover says "Toys 'R' Us Limited Edition X-Men" ... 2.25
...: Rarities (1995, $5.95)-Reprints ... 6.00
...: Road Trippin' ('99, $24.95, TPB) r/X-Men road trips ... 25.00
...: Supernovas ('07, $34.99, oversized HC w/d.j.) r/X-Men 188-199 & Annual #1 ... 35.00
...: The Coming of Bishop ('95, $12.95)-r/Uncanny X-Men #282-285, 287,288 ... 13.00
...: The Magneto War (3/99, $2.99) Davis-a ... 3.00
...: The Rise of Apocalypse ('98, $16.99)-r/Rise Of Apocalypse #1-4, X-Factor #5,6 ... 17.00
... Visionaries: Chris Claremont ('98, $24.95)-r/Claremont-s; art by Byrne, BWS, Jim Lee ... 25.00
... Visionaries: Jim Lee ('02, $29.99)-r/Jim Lee-a from various issues between Uncanny X-Men
    #248 & 286; r/Classic X-Men #39 and X-Men Annual #1 ... 30.00
...: Visionaries: Joe Madureira (7/00, $17.95)-r/Uncanny X-Men #325,326,329,330,341-343;
    new Madureira-c ... 18.00
...: Zero Tolerance ('00, $24.95, TPB) r/crossover series ... 25.00
NOTE: *Jim Lee* a-1-11p; c-1-6p, 7, 8, 9p, 10, 11p. *Art Thibert* a-6-9i, 12, 13; c-6i, 12, 13.

X-MEN ADVENTURES (TV)
Marvel Comics: Nov, 1992 - No. 15, Jan, 1994 ($1.25)(Based on animated series)

1-Wolverine, Cyclops, Jubilee, Rogue, Gambit ... 3.50
2-15: 3-Magneto-c/story. 6-Sabretooth-c/story. 7-Cable-c/story. 10-Archangel guest star.
    11-Cable-c/story. 15-(1.75, 52 pgs.) ... 3.00

X-MEN ADVENTURES II (TV)
Marvel Comics: Feb, 1994 - No. 13, Feb, 1995 ($1.25/$1.50)(Based on 2nd TV season)

1-13: 4-Bound-in trading card sheet. 5-Alpha Flight app. ... 3.00
...Captive Hearts/Slave Island (TPB, $4.95)-r/X-Men Adventures #5-8 ... 5.00
...The Irresistible Force, The Muir Island Saga (5.95, 10/94, TPB) r/X-Men Advs. #9-12 6.00

X-MEN ADVENTURES III (TV)(See Adventures of the X-Men)
Marvel Comics: Mar, 1995 - No. 13, Mar, 1996 ($1.50) (Based on 3rd TV season)

1-13 ... 3.00

X-MEN: AGE OF APOCALYPSE
Marvel Comics: May, 2005 - No. 6, June, 2005 ($2.99, weekly limited series)

1-6-Bachalo-c/a; Yoshida-s; follows events in the "Age of Apocalypse" storyline ... 3.00
... One Shot (5/05, $3.99) prequel to series; Hitch wraparound-c; pin-ups by various ... 4.00
X-Men: The New Age of Apocalypse TPB (2005, $20.99) r/#1-6 & one-shot ... 21.00

X-MEN ALPHA
Marvel Comics: 1994 ($3.95, one-shot)

nn-Age of Apocalypse; wraparound chromium-c   1   2   3   5   6   8
nn ($49.95)-Gold logo ... 50.00

X-MEN/ALPHA FLIGHT
Marvel Comics Group: Dec, 1985 - No. 2, Dec, 1985 ($1.50, limited series)

1,2: 1-Intro The Berserkers; Paul Smith-a ... 5.00

X-MEN/ALPHA FLIGHT
Marvel Comics: May, 1998 - No. 2, June, 1998 ($2.99, limited series)

1,2-Flashback to early meeting; Raab-s/Cassaday-s/a ... 3.00

X-MEN AND POWER PACK
Marvel Comics: Dec, 2005 - No. 4, Mar, 2006 ($2.99, limited series)

1-3-Sumerak-s/Gurihiru-a. 1-Wolverine & Sabretooth app. ... 3.00
...: The Power of X (2006, $6.99, digest size) r/#1-4 ... 7.00

X-MEN AND THE MICRONAUTS, THE
Marvel Comics Group: Jan, 1984 - No. 4, Apr, 1984 (Limited series)

1-4: Guice-c/a(p) in all ... 4.00

X-MEN: APOCALYPSE/DRACULA
Marvel Comics: Apr, 2006 - No. 4, July, 2006 ($2.99, limited series)

1-4-Tieri-s/Henry-a/Jae Lee-c ... 3.00
TPB (2006, $10.99) r/series; cover gallery ... 11.00

X-MEN ARCHIVES
Marvel Comics: Jan, 1995 - No. 4, Apr, 1995 ($2.25, limited series)

1-4: Reprints Legion stories from New Mutants. 4-Magneto app. ... 3.00

X-MEN ARCHIVES FEATURING CAPTAIN BRITAIN
Marvel Comics: July, 1995 - No. 7, 1996 ($2.95, limited series)

1-7: Reprints early Capt. Britain stories ... 3.00

X-MEN BLACK SUN (See Black Sun:...)

X-MEN BOOKS OF ASKANI
Marvel Comics: 1995 ($2.95, one-shot)

1-Painted pin-ups w/text ... 3.00

X-MEN: CHILDREN OF THE ATOM
Marvel Comics: Nov, 1999 - No. 6 ($2.99, limited series)

1-6-Casey-s; X-Men before issue #1. 1-3-Rude-c/a. 4-Paul Smith-c/Rude-c.
    5,6-Essad Ribic-c/a ... 3.00
TPB (11/01, $16.95) r/series; sketch pages; Casey intro. ... 17.00

X-MEN CHRONICLES
Marvel Comics: Mar, 1995 - No. 2, June, 1995 ($3.95, limited series)

1,2: Age of Apocalypse x-over. 1-wraparound-c ... 5.00

X-MEN: CLANDESTINE
Marvel Comics: Oct, 1996 - No. 2, Nov, 1996 ($2.95, limited series, 48 pgs.)

1,2: Alan Davis-c(p)/a(p)/scripts & Mark Farmer(i)/a(i) in all; wraparound-c ... 3.00

X-MEN CLASSIC (Formerly Classic X-Men)
Marvel Comics: No. 46, Apr, 1990 - No. 110, Aug, 1995 ($1.25/$1.50)

46-110: Reprints from X-Men. 54-(52 pgs.). 57,60-63,65-Russell-c(i); 62-r/X-Men #158(Rogue).
    66-r/#162(Wolverine). 69-Begins-r of Paul Smith issues (#165 on). 70,79,90,97(52 pgs.).
    70-r/X-Men #166. 90-r/#186. 100-(1.50). 104-r/X-Men #200 ... 3.00

X-MEN CLASSICS
Marvel Comics Group: Dec, 1983 - No. 3, Feb, 1984 ($2.00, Baxter paper)

1-3: X-Men-r by Neal Adams ... 6.00
NOTE: *Zeck* c-1-3.

X-MEN: COLOSSUS BLOODLIINE
Marvel Comics: Nov, 2005 - No. 5, Mar, 2006 ($2.99, limited series)

1-5-Colossus returns to Russia; David Hine-s/Jorge Lucas-a; Bachalo-c ... 3.00
TPB (2006, $13.99) r/#1-5 ... 14.00

X-MEN: DEADLY GENESIS (See Uncanny X-Men #475)
Marvel Comics: Jan, 2006 - No. 6, July, 2006 ($3.99/$3.50, limited series)

1-($3.99) Silvestri-c swipe of Giant-Size X-Men #1; Hairsine-a/Brubaker-s ... 4.00
2-6-($3.50) 2-Silvestri-c; Banshee killed. 4-Intro Kid Vulcan ... 3.50
HC (2006, $24.99, dust jacket) ... 25.00
SC (2006, $19.99) r/#1-6 ... 20.00

X-MEN: EARTHFALL
Marvel Comics: Sept, 1996 ($2.95, one-shot)

1-r/Uncanny X-Men #232-234; wraparound-c ... 3.00

X-MEN: EMPEROR VULCAN
Marvel Comics: Nov, 2007 - No. 5 ($2.99, limited series)

1-Starjammers app.; Yost-s/Diaz-a/Tan-c ... 3.00

X-MEN: EVOLUTION (Based on the animated series)
Marvel Comics: Feb, 2002 - No. 9, Sept, 2002 ($2.25)

1-9: 1-8-Grayson-s/Udon-a. 9-Farber-s/J.J.Kirby-a ... 3.00
TPB (7/02, $8.99) r/#1-4 ... 9.00
Vol. 2 TPB (2003, $11.99) r/#5-9; Asamiya-c ... 12.00

X-MEN FAIRY TALES
Marvel Comics: July, 2006 - No. 4, Oct, 2006 ($2.99, limited series)

1-4-Re-imagining of classic stories; Cebulski-s. 2-Baker-a. 3-Sienkiewicz-a. 4-Kobayashi-a ... 3.00
TPB (2006, $10.99) r/#1-4 ... 11.00

X-MEN/ FANTASTIC FOUR
Marvel Comics: Feb, 2005 - No. 5, June, 2005 ($3.50, limited series)

1-5-Pat Lee-a/c; Yoshida-s; the Brood app. ... 3.50
HC (2005, $19.99, 7 1/2" x 11", dustjacket) oversized r/#1-5; cover gallery ... 20.00

X-MEN FIRST CLASS
Marvel Comics: Nov, 2006 - No. 8, Jun, 2007 ($2.99, limited series)

1-8-Xavier's first class of X-Men; Cruz-a/Parker-s. 7-Thor app. 7-Scarlet Witch app. ... 3.00
... Special 1 (7/07, $3.99) Nowlan-c; Nowlan, Paul Smith, Coover, Dragotta & Allred-a ... 4.00
... - Tomorrow's Brightest HC (2007, $24.99, d.j) r/#1-8; cover & character design art ... 25.00

X-MEN FIRST CLASS (2nd series)
Marvel Comics: Aug, 2007 - Present ($2.99)

1-4: 1-Cruz-a/Parker-s; Fantastic Four app. ... 3.00

X-Men: Liberators #1 © MAR

X-Men: Phoenix - Endsong #1 © MAR

X-Men 2: The Movie © MAR & 20th Century Fox

	GD	VG	FN	VF	VF/NM	NM-
	2.0	4.0	6.0	8.0	9.0	9.2

X-MEN FIRSTS
Marvel Comics: Feb, 1996 ($4.95, one-shot)

1-r/Avengers Annual #10, Uncanny X-Men #266, #221; Incredible Hulk #181 ... 5.00

X-MEN FOREVER
Marvel Comics: Jan, 2001 - No. 6, June, 2001 ($3.50, limited series)

1-6-Jean Grey, Iceman, Mystique, Toad, Juggernaut app.; Maguire-a ... 3.50

X-MEN: HELLFIRE CLUB
Marvel Comics: Jan, 2000 - No. 4, Apr, 2000 ($2.50, limited series)

1-4-Origin of the Hellfire Club ... 2.50

X-MEN: HIDDEN YEARS
Marvel Comics: Dec, 1999 - No. 22, Sept. 2001 ($3.50/$2.50)

1-New adventures from pre-#94 era; Byrne-s/a(p) ... 3.50
2-4,6-11,13-22-($2.50): 2-Two covers. 3-Ka-Zar app. 8,9-FF-c/app. ... 3.00
5-($2.75) ... 3.00
12-($3.50) Magneto-c/app. ... 3.50

X-MEN: KITTY PRYDE - SHADOW & FLAME
Marvel Comics: Aug, 2005 - No. 5, Dec, 2005 ($2.99, limited series)

1-5-Akira Yoshida-s/Paul Smith-a/c; Kitty & Lockheed go to Japan ... 3.00
TPB (2006, $14.99) r/#1-5 ... 15.00

X-MEN: LIBERATORS
Marvel Comics: Nov, 1998 - No. 4, Feb, 1999 ($2.99, limited series)

1-4-Wolverine, Nightcrawler & Colossus; P. Jimenez ... 3.00

X-MEN LOST TALES
Marvel Comics: 1997 ($2.99)

1,2-r/Classic X-Men back-up stories ... 3.00

X-MEN OMEGA
Marvel Comics: June, 1995 ($3.95, one-shot)

nn-Age of Apocalypse finale	1	3	4	6	8	10
nn-($49.95)-Gold edition						50.00

X-MEN: PHOENIX
Marvel Comics: Dec, 1999 - No. 3, Mar, 2000 ($2.50, limited series)

1-3: 1-Apocalypse app. ... 3.00

X-MEN: PHOENIX - ENDSONG
Marvel Comics: Mar, 2005 - No. 5, June, 2005 ($2.99, limited series)

1-5-The Phoenix Force returns to Earth; Greg Land-c/a; Greg Pak-s ... 3.00
HC (2005, $19.99, dust jacket) r/#1-5; Land sketch pages ... 20.00
SC (2006, $14.99) ... 15.00

X-MEN: PHOENIX - LEGACY OF FIRE
Marvel Comics: July, 2003 - No. 3, Sep, 2003 ($2.99, limited series)

1-3-Manga-style; Ryan Kinnard-s/a/c; intro page art by Adam Warren ... 3.00

X-MEN: PHOENIX - WARSONG
Marvel Comics: Nov, 2006 - No. 5, Mar, 2007 ($2.99, limited series)

1-5-Tyler Kirkham-a/Greg Pak-s/Marc Silvestri-c ... 3.00
HC (2007, $19.99, dustjacket) r/#1-5; variant cover gallery and Handbook pages ... 20.00

X-MEN PRIME
Marvel Comics: July, 1995 ($4.95, one-shot)

nn-Post Age of Apocalypse begins	1	3	4	6	8	10

X-MEN RARITIES
Marvel Comics: 1995 ($5.95, one-shot)

nn-Reprints hard-to-find stories ... 6.00

X-MEN ROAD TO ONSLAUGHT
Marvel Comics: Oct, 1996 ($2.50, one-shot)

nn-Retells Onslaught Saga ... 3.00

X-MEN RONIN
Marvel Comics: May, 2003 - No. 5, July, 2003 ($2.99, limited series)

1-5-Manga-style X-Men; Torres-s/Nakatsuka-a ... 3.00

X-MEN: SEARCH FOR CYCLOPS
Marvel Comics: Oct, 2000 - No. 4, Mar, 2001 ($2.99, limited series)

1-4-Two covers (Raney, Pollina); Raney-a ... 3.00

X-MEN SPOTLIGHT ON... STARJAMMERS (Also see X-Men #104)
Marvel Comics: 1990 - No. 2, 1990 ($4.50, 52 pgs.)

1,2: Features Starjammers ... 4.50

	GD	VG	FN	VF	VF/NM	NM-
	2.0	4.0	6.0	8.0	9.0	9.2

X-MEN SURVIVAL GUIDE TO THE MANSION
Marvel Comics: Aug, 1993 ($6.95, spiralbound)

1 ... 7.00

X-MEN: THE COMPLETE AGE OF APOCALYPSE EPIC
Marvel Comics: 2005 - Vol. 4, 2006 ($29.99, TPB)

Book 1-4: Chronological reprintings of the crossover ... 30.00

X-MEN: THE EARLY YEARS
Marvel Comics: May, 1994 - No. 17, Sept, 1995 ($1.50/$2.50)

1-16: r/X-Men #1-8 w/new-c ... 3.00
17-$2.50-c; r/X-Men #17,18 ... 3.00

X-MEN: THE END
Marvel Comics: Oct, 2004 - No. 6, Feb, 2005 ($2.99, limited series)

1-6-Claremont-s/Chen-a/Land-c ... 3.00
... Book One: Dreamers and Demons TPB (2005, $14.99) r/#1-6 ... 15.00

X-MEN: THE END - HEROES AND MARTYRS (Volume 2)
Marvel Comics: May, 2005 - No. 6, Oct, 2005 ($2.99, limited series)

1-6-Claremont-s/Chen-a/Land-c; continued from X-Men: The End ... 3.00
... Vol. 2 TPB (2006, $14.99) r/#1-6 ... 15.00

X-MEN: THE END (MEN & X-MEN) (Volume 3)
Marvel Comics: Mar, 2006 - No. 6, Aug, 2006 ($2.99, limited series)

1-6-Claremont-s/Chen-a. 1-Land-c. 2-6-Gene Ha-c ... 3.00
... Vol. 3 TPB (2006, $14.99) r/#1-6 ... 15.00

X-MEN: THE MANGA
Marvel Comics: Mar, 1998 - No. 26, June, 1999 ($2.99, B&W)

1-26-English version of Japanese X-Men comics: 23,24-Randy Green-c ... 3.00

X-MEN: THE MOVIE
Marvel Comics: Aug, 2000; Sept, 2000

Adaptation (9/00, $5.95) Macchio-s/Williams & Lanning-a ... 6.00
Adaptation TPB (9/00, $14.95) Movie adaptation and key issue reprints of main characters;
   four photo covers (movie X, Magneto, Rogue, Wolverine) ... 15.00
Prequel: Magneto (8/00, $5.95) Texeira & Palmiotti-a; art & photo covers ... 6.00
Prequel: Rogue (8/00, $5.95) Evans & Nikolakakis-a; art & photo covers ... 6.00
Prequel: Wolverine (8/00, $5.95) Waller & McKenna-a; art & photo covers ... 6.00
TPB X-Men: Beginnings (8/00, $14.95) reprints 3 prequels w/photo-c ... 15.00

X-MEN 2: THE MOVIE
Marvel Comics: 2003

Adaptation (6/03, $3.50) Movie adaptation; photo-c; Austen-s/Zircher-a ... 3.50
Adaptation TPB (2003, $12.99) Movie adaptation & r/Prequels Nightcrawler & Wolverine ... 13.00
Prequel: Nightcrawler (5/03, $3.50) Kerschl-a; photo cover ... 3.50
Prequel: Wolverine (5/03, $3.50) Mandrake-a; photo cover; Sabretooth app. ... 3.50

X-MEN: THE 198 (See House of M)
Marvel Comics: Mar, 2006 - No. 5, July, 2006 ($2.99, limited series)

1-5-Hine-s/Muniz-a ... 3.00
... Files (2006, $3.99) profiles of the 198 mutants who kept their powers after House of M ... 4.00
Decimation: The 198 (2006, $15.99, TPB) r/#1-5 & X-Men: The 198 Files ... 16.00

X-MEN: THE ULTRA COLLECTION
Marvel Comics: Dec, 1994 - No. 5, Apr, 1995 ($2.95, limited series)

1-5: Pin-ups; no scripts ... 3.00

X-MEN: THE WEDDING ALBUM
Marvel Comics: 1994 ($2.95, magazine size, one-shot)

1-Wedding of Scott Summers & Jean Grey ... 3.00

X-MEN TRUE FRIENDS
Marvel Comics: Sept, 1999 - No. 3, Nov, 1999 ($2.99, limited series)

1-3-Claremont-s/Leonardi-a ... 3.00

X-MEN 2099 (Also see 2099: World of Tomorrow)
Marvel Comics: Oct, 1993 - No. 35, Aug, 1996 ($1.25/$1.50/$1.95)

1-($1.75)-Foil-c; Ron Lim/Adam Kubert-a begins ... 3.50
1-2nd printing ($1.75) ... 3.00
1-Gold edition (15,000 made); sold thru Diamond for $19.40 ... 20.00
2-24,26-35: 3-Death of Tina; Lim-c/a(p) in #1-8. 8-Bound-in trading card sheet. 35-Nostromo
   (from X-Nation) app; storyline cont'd in 2099: World of Tomorrow ... 3.00
25-($2.50)-Double sized ... 3.50
Special 1 ($3.95) ... 4.00
...: Oasis ($5.95, one-shot) -Hildebrandt Bros.-c/a ... 6.00

X-MEN ULTRA III PREVIEW

X-Men Unlimited #1 © MAR

Xombi #0 © Milestone

X-Treme X-Men #7 © MAR

	GD 2.0	VG 4.0	FN 6.0	VF 8.0	VF/NM 9.0	NM- 9.2

Marvel Comics: 1995 ($2.95)

nn-Kubert-a ... 3.00

X-MEN UNIVERSE
Marvel Comics: Dec, 1999 - Present ($4.99/$3.99)

1-8-Reprints stories from recent X-Men titles ... 5.00
9-15-($3.99) ... 4.00

X-MEN UNIVERSE: PAST, PRESENT AND FUTURE
Marvel Comics: Feb, 1999 ($2.99, one-shot)

1-Previews 1999 X-Men events; background info ... 3.00

X-MEN UNLIMITED
Marvel Comics: 1993 - No. 50, Sept, 2003 ($3.95/$2.99, 68 pgs.)

1-Chris Bachalo-c/a; Quesada-a. ... 5.00
2-11: 2-Origin of Magneto script. 3-Sabretooth-c/story. 10-Dark Beast vs. Beast; Mark Waid script. 11-Magneto & Rogue ... 4.00
12-33: 12-Begin $2.99-c; Onslaught x-over; Juggernaut-c/app. 19-Caliafore-a. 20-Generation X app. 27-Origin Thunderbird. 29-Maximum Security x-over; Bishop-c/app. 30-Mahfood-a. 31-Stelfreeze-c/a. 32-Dazzler; Thompson-c/a 33-Kaluta-c ... 3.00
34-37,39,40-42-($3.50) 34-Von Eeden-a. 35-Finch, Conner, Maguire-a. 36-Chiodo-c/a; Larroca, Totleben-a. 39-Bachalo-c; Pearson-a. 41-Bachalo-c; X-Statix app. ... 3.50
38-($2.25) Kitty Pryde; Robertson-a ... 3.00
43-50-($2.50) 43-Sienkiewicz-c/a; Paul Smith-a. 45-Noto-c. 46-Bisley-a. 47-Warren-s/Mays-a. 48-Wolverine story w/Isanove painted-a ... 3.00
X-Men Legends Vol. 4: Hated and Feared TPB (2003, $19.99) r/stories by various ... 20.00
NOTE: *Bachalo* c/a-1. *Quesada* a-1. *Waid* scripts-10

X-MEN UNLIMITED
Marvel Comics: Apr, 2004 - Present ($2.99)

1-14: 1-6-Pat Lee-c; short stories by various. 2-District X preview; Granov-a ... 3.00

X-MEN VS. DRACULA
Marvel Comics: Dec, 1993 ($1.75)

1-r/X-Men Annual #6; Austin-c(i) ... 3.00

X-MEN VS. THE AVENGERS, THE
Marvel Comics Group: Apr, 1987 - No. 4, July, 1987 ($1.50, limited series, Baxter paper)

1 ... 4.00
2-4 ... 3.00

X-MEN VS. THE BROOD, THE
Marvel Comics Group: Sept, 1996 - No. 2, Oct, 1996 ($2.95, limited series)

1,2-Wraparound-c; Ostrander-s/Hitch-a(p) ... 3.00
TPB('97, $16.99) reprints X-Men/Brood: Day of Wrath #1,2 & Uncanny X-Men #232-234 ... 17.00

X-MEN VISIONARIES
Marvel Comics: 1995,1996,2000 (trade paperbacks)

nn-($8.95) Reprints X-Men stories; Adam & Andy Kubert-a ... 9.00
...2: The Neal Adams Collection (1996) r/X-Men #56-63,65 ... 30.00
...2: The Neal Adams Col. (2nd printing, 2000, $24.95) new Adams-c ... 25.00

X-MEN/WILDC.A.T.S.: THE DARK AGE (See also WildC.A.T.S./X-Men...)
Marvel Comics: 1998 ($4.50, one-shot)

1-Two covers (Broome & Golden); Ellis-s ... 4.50

X-NATION 2099
Marvel Comics: Mar, 1996 - No. 6, Aug, 1996 ($1.95)

1-($3.95)-Humberto Ramos-a(p); wraparound, foil-c ... 4.00
2-6: 2,3-Ramos-a. 4-Exodus-c/app. 6-Reed Richards app ... 3.00

X-O MANOWAR (1st Series)
Valiant/Acclaim Comics (Valiant) No. 43 on: Feb, 1992 - No. 68, Sept, 1996 ($1.95/$2.25/$2.50, high quality)

0-(8/93, $3.50)-Wraparound embossed chromium-c by Quesada; Solar app.; origin Aric (X-O Manowar) ... 3.50
0-Gold variant ... 5.00
1-Intro/1st app. & partial origin of Aric (X-O Manowar); Barry Smith/Layton-a

	1	2	3	5	6	8

2-4: 2-B. Smith/Layton-c. 3-Layton-c(i). 4-1st app. Shadowman ... 6.00
5-15: 5-B. Smith-c. 6-Begin $2.25-c; Ditko-a(p). 7,8-Unity x-overs. 7-Miller-c. 8-Simonson-c. 12-1st app. Randy Calder. 14,15-Turok-c/stories ... 3.00
15-Hot pink logo variant; came with Ultra Pro Rigid Comic Sleeves box; no price on cover ... 4.00
16-24,26-43: 20-Serial number contest insert. 27-29-Turok x-over. 28-Bound-in trading card. 30-1st app. new "good skin"; Solar app. 33-Chaos Effect Delta Pt. 3. 42-Shadowman app.; includes X-O Manowar Birthquake! Prequel ... 2.50
25-($3.50)-Has 16 pg. Armorines #0 bound-in w/origin ... 3.50

44-68: 44-Begin $2.50-c. 50-X, 50-O, 51, 52, 63-Bart Sears-c/a/scripts. 68-Revealed that Aric's past stories were premonitions of his future ... 2.50
Trade paperback nn (1993, $9.95)-Polybagged with copy of X-O Database #1 inside ... 10.00
Yearbook 1 (4/95, $2.95) ... 3.00
NOTE: *Layton* a-1i, 2i(part); c-1, 2i, 3i, 6i, 21i. *Reese* a-4i(part); c-26i.

X-O MANOWAR (2nd Series)(Also see Iron Man/X-O Manowar: Heavy Metal)
Acclaim Comics (Valiant Heroes): V2#1, Oct, 1996 - No. 21, Jun, 1998 ($2.50)

V2#1-21: 1-Mark Waid & Brian Augustyn scripts begin; 1st app. Donavon Wylie; Rand Banion dies; painted variant-c exists. 2-Donavon Wylie becomes new X-O Manowar. 7-9-Augustyn-s. 10-Copycat-c ... 2.50

X-O MANOWAR FAN EDITION
Acclaim Comics (Valiant Heroes): Feb, 1997 (Overstreet's FAN giveaway)

1-Reintro the Armorines & the Hard Corps; 1st app. Citadel; Augustyn scripts; McKone-c/a ... 4.00

X-O MANOWAR/IRON MAN: IN HEAVY METAL (See Iron Man/X-O Manowar: Heavy Metal)
Acclaim Comics (Valiant Heroes): Sept, 1996 ($2.50, one-shot)
(1st Marvel/Valiant x-over)

1-Pt 1 of X-O Manowar/Iron Man x-over; Arnim Zola app.; Nicieza scripts; Andy Smith-a ... 2.50

XOMBI
DC Comics (Milestone): Jan, 1994 - No. 21, Feb, 1996 ($1.75/$2.50)

0-($1.95)-Shadow War x-over; Simonson silver ink varnish-c ... 2.50
1-21: 1-John Byrne-c. ... 2.50
1-Platinum ... 8.00

X-PATROL
Marvel Comics (Amalgam): Apr, 1996 ($1.95, one-shot)

1-Cruz-a(p) ... 2.50

XSE
Marvel Comics: Nov, 1996 - No. 4, Feb, 1997 ($1.95, limited series)

1-4: 1-Bishop & Shard app. ... 2.50
1-Variant-c ... 3.00

X-STATIX
Marvel Comics: Sept, 2002 - No. 26, Oct, 2004 ($2.99/$2.25)

1-($2.99)Allred-a/c; intro. Venus Dee Milo; back-up w/Cooke-a ... 3.00
2-9-($2.25) 4-Quitely-a. 5-Pope-c/a ... 2.50
10-26: 10-Begin $2.99-c; Bond-a; U-Go Girl flashback. 13,14-Spider-Man app. 21-25-Avengers app. 26-Team dies ... 3.00
... Vol. 1: Good Omens TPB (2003, $11.99) r/#1-5 ... 12.00
... Vol. 2: Good Guys & Bad Guys TPB (2003, $15.99) r/#6-10 & Wolverine/Doop #1&2 ... 16.00
... Vol. 3: Back From the Dead TPB (2004, $19.99) r/#11-18 ... 20.00
... Vol. 4: X-Statix Vs. the Avengers TPB (2004, $19.99) r/#19-26; pin-ups ... 20.00

X-STATIX PRESENTS: DEAD GIRL
Marvel Comics: Mar, 2006 - No. 5, July, 2006 ($2.99, limited series)

1-5-Dr. Strange, Dead Girl, Miss America, Tike app. Milligan-s/Dragotta & Allred-a ... 3.00
TPB (2006, $13.99) r/series ... 14.00

X-TERMINATORS
Marvel Comics: Oct, 1988 - No. 4, Jan, 1989 ($1.00, limited series)

1-1st app.; X-Men/X-Factor tie-in; Williamson-i ... 3.00
2-4 ... 2.50

X, THE MAN WITH THE X-RAY EYES (See Movie Comics)

X-TREME X-MEN (Also see Mekanix)
Marvel Comics: July, 2001 - No. 46, Jun, 2004 ($2.99/$3.50)

1-Claremont-s/Larroca-c/a ... 4.00
2-24: 2-Two covers (Larroca & Pacheco); Psylocke killed ... 3.00
25-35, 40-46: 25-30-God Loves, Man Kills II; Stryker app.; Kordey-a ... 3.00
36-39-($3.50) ... 3.50
Annual 2001 ($4.95) issue opens longways ... 5.00
... Vol. 1: Destiny TPB (2002, $19.95) r/#1-9 ... 20.00
... Vol. 2: Invasion TPB (2003, $19.99) r/#10-18 ... 20.00
... Vol. 3: Schism TPB (2003, $16.99) r/#19-23; X-Treme X-Posé #1&2 ... 17.00
... Vol. 4: Mekanix TPB (2003, $16.99) r/Mekanix #1-6 ... 17.00
... Vol. 5: God Loves Man Kills TPB (2003, $19.99) r/#25-30 ... 20.00
... Vol. 6: Intifada TPB (2004, $16.99) r/#24,31-35 ... 17.00
... Vol. 7: Storm the Arena TPB (2004, $16.99) r/#36-39 ... 17.00
... Vol. 8: Prisoner of Fire TPB (2004, $19.99) r/#40-46 and Annual 2001 ... 20.00

X-TREME X-MEN: SAVAGE LAND
Marvel Comics: Nov, 2001 - No. 4, Feb, 2002 ($2.99, limited series)

1-4-Claremont-s/Sharpe-c/a; Beast app. ... 3.00

X-23: Target X #2 © MAR

Yankee Comics #2 © CHES

Yeah! #1 © Peter Bagge

	GD 2.0	VG 4.0	FN 6.0	VF 8.0	VF/NM 9.0	NM- 9.2

X-TREME X-POSE
Marvel Comics: Jan, 2003 - No. 2, Feb, 2003 ($2.99, limited series)

1,2-Claremont-s/Ranson-a/Migliari-c						3.00

X-23 (See debut in NYX #3)(See NYX X-23 HC for reprint)
Marvel Comics: Mar, 2005 - No. 6, July, 2005 ($2.99, limited series)

1-Origin of the Wolverine clone girl; Tan-a						4.00
1-Variant Billy Tan-c with red background						5.00
2-6-Origin continues						3.00
2-Variant B&W sketch-c						5.00
...: Innocence Lost TPB (2006, $15.99) r/#1-6						16.00

X-23: TARGET X
Marvel Comics: Feb, 2007 - No. 6, July, 2007 ($2.99, limited series)

1-6-Kyle & Yost-s/Choi & Oback-a. 6-Gallery of variant covers and sketches						3.00
TPB (2007, $15.99) r/#1-6; gallery of variant covers and sketches						16.00

X-UNIVERSE
Marvel Comics: May, 1995 - No. 2, June, 1995 ($3.50, limited series)

1,2: Age of Apocalypse						5.00

X-VENTURE (Super Heroes)
Victory Magazines Corp.: July, 1947 - No. 2, Nov, 1947

	GD	VG	FN	VF	VF/NM	NM-
1-Atom Wizard, Mystery Shadow, Lester Trumble begin	110	220	330	688	1144	1600
2	54	108	162	338	557	775

XYR (See Eclipse Graphic Album Series #21)

YAK YAK
Dell Publishing Co.: No. 1186, May-July, 1961 - No. 1348, Apr-June, 1962
Four Color 1186 (#1)- Jack Davis-c/a; 2 versions, one minus 3 pgs.

	GD	VG	FN	VF	VF/NM	NM-
	8	16	24	58	97	135
Four Color 1348 (#2)-Davis c/a	8	16	24	52	86	120

YAKKY DOODLE & CHOPPER (TV) (See Dell Giant #44)
Gold Key: Dec, 1962 (Hanna-Barbera)

	GD	VG	FN	VF	VF/NM	NM-
1	7	14	21	50	83	115

YANG (See House of Yang)
Charlton Comics: Nov, 1973 - No. 13, May, 1976; V14#5, Sept, 1985 - No. 17, Jan, 1986
(No V14#14, series resumes with #15)

	GD	VG	FN	VF	VF/NM	NM-
1-Origin; Sattler-a begins; slavery-s	2	4	6	11	16	20
2-13(1976)	1	2	3	6	9	10
15-17(1986): 15-Reprints #1 (Low print run)						6.00
3,10,11(Modern Comics-r, 1977)						4.00

YANKEE COMICS
Harry 'A' Chesler: Sept, 1941 - No. 7, 1942?

	GD	VG	FN	VF	VF/NM	NM-
1-Origin The Echo, The Enchanted Dagger, Yankee Doodle Jones, The Firebrand, & The Scarlet Sentry; Black Satan app.; Yankee Doodle Jones app. on all covers	179	358	537	1119	1860	2600
2-Origin Johnny Rebel; Major Victory app.; Barry Kuda begins	80	160	240	500	830	1160
3,4: 4-(3/42)	59	118	177	369	615	860
4 (nd, 1940s; 7-1/4x5", 68 pgs, distr. to the service)-Foxy Grandpa, Tom, Dick & Harry, Impy, Ace & Deuce, Dot & Dash, Ima Slooth by Jack Cole (Remington Morse publ.)	12	24	36	67	94	120
5-7 (nd; 10¢, 7-1/4x5", 68 pgs.)(Remington Morse publ.)-urges readers to send their copies to servicemen	10	20	30	58	79	100

YANKEE DOODLE THE SPIRIT OF LIBERTY
Spire Publications: 1984 (no price, 36 pgs)

	GD	VG	FN	VF	VF/NM	NM-
nn-Al Hartley-s/c/a	2	4	6	8	10	12

YANKS IN BATTLE
Quality Comics Group: Sept, 1956 - No. 4, Dec, 1956; 1963

	GD	VG	FN	VF	VF/NM	NM-
1-Cuidera-c(i)	10	20	30	58	79	100
2-4: Cuidera-c(i)	8	16	24	40	50	60
I.W. Reprint #3(1963)-r/#?; exist?	2	4	6	9	12	15

YARDBIRDS, THE (G. I. Joe's Sidekicks)
Ziff-Davis Publishing Co.: Summer, 1952

	GD	VG	FN	VF	VF/NM	NM-
1-By Bob Oskner	10	20	30	56	76	95

YARN MAN (See Megaton Man)
Kitchen Sink : Oct, 1989 ($2.00, B&W, one-shot)

1-Donald Simpson-c/a/scripts						2.50

YARNS OF YELLOWSTONE
World Color Press: 1972 (50¢, 36 pgs.)

	GD	VG	FN	VF	VF/NM	NM-
nn-Illustrated by Bill Chapman	2	4	6	8	11	14

YEAH!
DC Comics (Homage): Oct, 1999 - No. 9, Jun, 2000 ($2.95)

1-Bagge-s/Hernandez-a						3.00
2-9: 2-Editorial page contains adult language						3.00

YELLOW CLAW (Also see Giant Size Master of Kung Fu)
Atlas Comics (MjMC): Oct, 1956 - No. 4, Apr, 1957

	GD	VG	FN	VF	VF/NM	NM-
1-Origin by Joe Maneely	100	200	300	625	1038	1450
2-Kirby-a	79	158	237	494	822	1150
3,4-Kirby-a; 4-Kirby/Severin-a	76	152	228	475	788	1100

NOTE: Everett c-3. Maneely c-1. Reinman a-2i, 3. Severin c-2, 4.

YELLOWJACKET COMICS (Jack in the Box #11 on)(See TNT Comics)
E. Levy/Frank Comunale/Charlton: Sept, 1944 - No. 10, June, 1946

	GD	VG	FN	VF	VF/NM	NM-
1-Intro & origin Yellowjacket; Diana, the Huntress begins; E.A. Poe's "The Black Cat" adaptation	66	132	198	413	682	950
2-Yellowjacket-c begin, end #10	41	82	123	250	400	550
3,5	40	80	120	240	383	525
4-E.A. Poe's "Fall of the House Of Usher" adaptation; Palais-a	41	82	123	250	400	550
6	48	96	144	293	484	675
7-Classic skull-c; Toth-a (1 pg. gag feature)	97	194	291	606	1003	1400
8-10: 1,3,4,6-10-Have stories narrated by old witch in "Tales of Terror" (1st horror series?)	47	94	141	287	474	660

YELLOWSTONE KELLY (Movie)
Dell Publishing Co.: No. 1056, Nov-Jan, 1959/60

	GD	VG	FN	VF	VF/NM	NM-
Four Color 1056-Clint Walker photo-c	6	12	18	37	59	80

YELLOW SUBMARINE (See Movie Comics)

YEAR ONE: BATMAN/RA'S AL GHUL
DC Comics: 2005 - No. 2, 2005 ($5.99, squarebound, limited series)

1-Devin Grayson-s/Pâul Gulacy-a						6.00
TPB (2006, $9.99) r/#1,2						10.00

YEAR ONE: BATMAN SCARECROW
DC Comics: 2005 - No. 2, 2005 ($5.99, squarebound, limited series)

1-Scarecrow's origin; Bruce Jones-s/Sean Murphy-a						6.00

YIN FEI THE CHINESE NINJA
Leung's Publications: 1988 - No. 8, 1990 ($1.80/$2.00, 52 pgs.)

1-8						2.50

YOGI BEAR (See Dell Giant #41, Golden Comics Digest, Kite Fun Book, March of Comics #253, 265, 279, 291, 309, 319, 337, 344, Movie Comics under "Hey There It's…" & Whitman Comic Books)

YOGI BEAR (TV) (Hanna-Barbera) (See Four Color #990)
Dell Publishing Co./Gold Key No. 10 on: No. 1067, 12-2/59-60 - No. 9, 7-9/62; No. 10, 10/62 - No. 42, 10/70

	GD	VG	FN	VF	VF/NM	NM-
Four Color 1067 (#1)-TV show debuted 1/30/61	10	20	30	71	126	180
Four Color 1104,1162 (5-7/61)	7	14	21	49	80	110
4(8-9/61) - 6(12-1/61-62)	6	12	18	37	59	80
Four Color 1271(11/61)	6	12	18	37	59	80
Four Color 1349(1/62)-Photo-c	8	16	24	58	97	135
7(2-3/62) - 9(7-9/62)-Last Dell	6	12	18	37	59	80
10(10/62-G.K.), 11(1/63)-titled "Yogi Bear Jellystone Jollies" (80 pgs.); 11-X-mas-c	7	14	21	47	76	105
12(4/63), 14-20	5	10	15	30	48	65
13(7/63, 68 pgs.)-Surprise Party	7	14	21	47	76	105
21-30	3	6	9	20	30	40
31-42	3	6	9	17	25	32

YOGI BEAR (TV)
Charlton Comics: Nov, 1970 - No. 35, Jan, 1976 (Hanna-Barbera)

	GD	VG	FN	VF	VF/NM	NM-
1	4	8	12	28	44	60
2-6,8-10	3	6	9	16	23	30
7-Summer Fun (Giant, 52 pgs.)	4	8	12	28	44	60
11-20	3	6	9	16	22	28
21-35: 28-31-partial-r	2	4	6	11	16	20
Digest (nn, 1972, 75¢-c, B&W, 100 pgs.) (scarce)	3	6	9	19	29	38

YOGI BEAR (TV)(See The Flintstones, 3rd series & Spotlight #1)
Marvel Comics Group: Nov, 1977 - No. 9, Mar, 1979 (Hanna-Barbera)

	GD	VG	FN	VF	VF/NM	NM-
1,7-9: 1-Flintstones begin (Newsstand sales only)	3	6	9	16	23	30

Young Allies Comics #6 © MAR

Young Avengers #1 © MAR

Young Brides #2 © PRIZE

	GD	VG	FN	VF	VF/NM	NM-
	2.0	4.0	6.0	8.0	9.0	9.2

2-6 ... 2 4 6 11 16 20

YOGI BEAR (TV)
Harvey Comics: Sept, 1992 - No. 6, Mar, 1994 ($1.25/$1.50) (Hanna-Barbera)

V2#1-6 ... 3.00
...Big Book V2#1,2 ($1.95, 52 pgs): 1-(11/92). 2-(3/93) ... 3.00
...Giant Size V2#1,2 ($2.25, 68 pgs.): 1-(10/92). 2-(4/93) ... 3.00

YOGI BEAR (TV)
Archie Publ.: May, 1997

1 ... 3.00

YOGI BEAR'S EASTER PARADE (See The Funtastic World of Hanna-Barbera #2)

YOGI BERRA (Baseball hero)
Fawcett Publications: 1951 (Yankee catcher)

nn-Photo-c ... 71 142 213 444 735 1025

YOSEMITE SAM (...& Bugs Bunny) (TV)
Gold Key/Whitman: Dec, 1970 - No. 81, Feb, 1984

1	4	8	12	28	44	60
2-10	3	6	9	16	22	28
11-20	2	4	6	10	14	18
21-30	2	4	6	8	11	14
31-50	1	3	4	6	8	10
51-65 (Gold Key)	1	2	3	5	6	8
66,67 (Whitman)	2	4	6	8	10	12
68(9/80), 69(10/80), 70(12/80) 3-pack only	3	6	9	18	27	35
71-78: 76(2/82), 77(3/82), 78(4/82)	2	4	6	8	11	14
79-81 (All #90263 on-c, no date or date code; 3-pack): 79(7/83). 80(8/83). 81(2/84)-(1/3-r)	2	4	6	13	18	22

(See March of Comics #363, 380, 392)

YOUNG ALLIES COMICS (All-Winners #21; see Kid Komics #2)
Timely Comics (USA 1-7/NPI 8,9/YAI 10-20): Sum, 1941 - No. 20, Oct, 1946

1-Origin/1st app. The Young Allies (Bucky, Toro, others); 1st meeting of Captain America & Human Torch; Red Skull-c & app.; S&K-c/splash; Hitler-c; Note: the cover was altered after its preview in Human Torch #5. Stalin was shown with Hitler but was removed due to Russia becoming an ally ... 1367 2734 4100 10,300 17,900 25,500
2-(Winter, 1941)-Captain America & Human Torch app.; Simon & Kirby-c ... 388 776 1164 2522 4461 6400
3-Fathertime, Captain America & Human Torch app.; Remember Pearl Harbor issue (Spring, 1942); Stan Lee scripts; Vs. Japs-c/full-length story ... 300 600 900 1894 3197 4500
4-The Vagabond & Red Skull, Capt. America, Human Torch app. Classic Red Skull-c ... 412 824 1236 2678 4739 6800
5-Captain America & Human Torch app. ... 207 414 621 1294 2147 3000
6,7,10: 10-Origin Tommy Tyme & Clock of Ages; ends #19 ... 152 304 456 950 1575 2200
8-Classic Schomburg WW2 bondage-c ... 159 318 477 994 1647 2300
9-Hitler, Tojo, Mussolini-c. ... 179 358 537 1119 1860 2600
11-20: 12-Classic decapitation story ... 103 206 309 644 1072 1500
NOTE: **Brodsky** c-15. **Gabrielle** a-3; c-3, 4. **S&K** c-1, 2. **Schomburg** c-5-13, 16-19. **Shores** c-20.

YOUNG ALL-STARS
DC Comics: June, 1987 - No. 31, Nov, 1989 ($1.00, deluxe format)

1-31: 1-1st app. Iron Munro & The Flying Fox. 8,9-Millennium tie-ins ... 2.50
Annual 1 (1988, $2.00) ... 2.50

YOUNG AVENGERS
Marvel Comics: Apr, 2005 - Present ($2.99)

1-Intro. Iron Lad, Patriot, Hulkling, Asgardian; Heinberg-s/Cheung-a ... 5.00
1-Director's Cut (2005, $3.99) r/#1 plus character sketches; original script ... 4.00
2-12: 3-6-Kang app. 7-DiVito-a. 9-Skrulls app. ... 3.00
... Special 1 (2/06, $3.99) origins of the heroes; art by various incl. Neal Adams, Jae Lee, Bill Sienkiewicz, Gene Ha, Michael Gaydos and Pasqual Ferry ... 4.00
... Vol. 1: Sidekicks HC (2005, $19.99, dustjacket) r/#1-6; character design sketches ... 20.00
... Vol. 1: Sidekicks TPB (2006, $14.99) r/#1-6; character design sketches ... 15.00
... Vol. 2: Family Matters HC (2006, $22.99, dustjacket) r/#7-12 & YA Special #1 ... 23.00
... Vol. 2: Family Matters SC (2007, $17.99) r/#7-12 & YA Special #1 ... 18.00

YOUNGBLOOD (See Brigade #4, Megaton Explosion & Team Youngblood)
Image Comics (Extreme Studios): Apr, 1992 - No. 4, Feb, 1993 ($2.50, lim. series); No. 6, June, 1994 (No #5) - No. 10, Dec, 1994 ($1.95/$2.50)

1-Leifeld-c/a/scripts in all; flip book format with 2 trading cards; 1st Image/Extreme Studios title. ... 5.00
1,2-2nd printing ... 2.50
2-(JUN-c, July 1992 indicia)-1st app. Shadowhawk in solo back-up story; 2 trading cards

inside; flip book format; 1st app. Prophet, Kirby, Berzerkers, Darkthorn ... 2.50
3,0,4,5: 3-(OCT-c, August 1992 indicia)-Contains 2 trading cards inside (flip book); 1st app. Supreme in back-up story. 0-(12/92, $1.95)-Contains 2 trading cards; 2 cover variations exist, green or beige logo; w/Image #0 coupon. 4-(2/93)-Glow-in-the-dark cover w/2 trading cards; 2nd app. Dale Keown's The Pitt; Bloodstrike app. 5-Flip book w/Brigade #4 ... 2.50
6-($3.50, 52 pgs.)-Wraparound-c ... 3.50
7-10: 7, 8-Liefeld-c(p)/a(p)/story. 8,9-(9/94) 9-Valentino story & art ... 2.50
Battlezone 1 (May-c, 4/93 inside, $1.95)-Arsenal app; Liefeld-c(p) ... 2.50
Battlezone 2 (7/94, $2.95)-Wraparound-c ... 3.00
Yearbook 1 (7/93, $2.50)-Fold out panel; 1st app. Tyrax & Kanan ... 2.50
...Super Special (Winter '97, $2.99) Sprouse -a ... 3.00
TPB (1996, $16.95)-r/Team Youngblood #8-10 & Youngblood #6-8,10 ... 17.00

YOUNGBLOOD
Image Comics (Extreme Studios)/Maximum Press No. 14: V2#1, Sept, 1995 - No. 14, Dec, 1996 ($2.50)

V2#1-10,14: Roger Cruz-a in all. 4-Extreme Destroyer Pt. 4 w/gaming card. 5-Variant-c exists. 6-Angela & Glory. 7-Shadowhunt Pt. 3; Shadowhawk app. 8,10-Thor (from Supreme) app. 10-(7/96). 14-(12/96)-1st Maximum Press issue ... 2.50

YOUNGBLOOD (Volume 3)
Awesome/ Awesome-Hyperwerks #2 on: Feb, 1998 - No. 2, Aug, 1998 ($2.50)

1-Alan Moore-s/Skroce & Stucker-a; 12 diff. covers ... 2.50
1-Gold foil-c; 1+ Alter Ego Gold Foil ... 5.00
1-Blue foil-c Orlando Con Ed. ... 10.00
2-(8/98) Skroce & Liefeld covers ... 2.50
...Imperial 1 (Arcade Comics, 6/04, $2.99) Kirkman-sMychaels-a ... 3.00

YOUNGBLOOD: STRIKEFILE
Image Comics (Extreme Studios): Apr, 1993 - No. 11, Feb, 1995 ($1.95/$2.50/$2.95)

1-10: 1-($1.95)-Flip book w/Jae Lee-c/a & Liefeld-c/a in #1-3; 1st app. The Allies,Giger, & Glory. 3-Thibert-i asisst. 4-Liefeld-c(p); no Lee-a. 5-Liefeld-c(p). 8-Platt-a ... 3.00
NOTE: *Youngblood: Strikefile* began as a four issue limited series.

YOUNGBLOOD/X-FORCE
Image Comics (Extreme Studios): July, 1996 ($4.95, one-shot)

1-Cruz-a(p); two covers exist ... 5.00

YOUNG BRIDES (True Love Secrets)
Feature/Prize Publ.: Sept-Oct, 1952 - No. 30, Nov-Dec, 1956 (Photo-c: 1-4)

V1#1-Simon & Kirby-a	36	72	108	208	329	450
2-S&K-a	19	38	57	109	172	235
3-6-S&K-a	17	34	51	98	154	210
V2#1-7,10 (#7-18)-S&K-a	16	32	48	94	147	200
8,9-No S&K-a	9	18	27	47	61	75
V3#1-3(#19-21)-Last precode (3-4/55)	8	16	24	44	57	70
4,6(#22,24), V4#1,3(#25,27)	8	16	24	40	50	60
V3#5(#23)-Meskin-c	8	16	24	42	54	65
V4#2(#26)-All S&K issue	15	30	45	88	137	185
V4#4(#28)-S&K-a	14	28	42	76	108	140
V4#5,6(#29,30)	8	16	24	44	57	70

YOUNG DR. MASTERS (See The Adventures of Young Dr. Masters)

YOUNG DOCTORS, THE
Charlton Comics: Jan, 1963 - No. 6, Nov, 1963

V1#1	3	6	9	21	32	42
2-6	3	6	9	14	19	24

YOUNG EAGLE
Fawcett Publications/Charlton: 12/50 - No. 10, 6/52; No. 3, 7/56 - No. 5, 4/57 (Photo-c: 1-10)

1-Intro Young Eagle	18	36	54	103	162	220
2-Complete picture novelette "The Mystery of Thunder Canyon"	10	20	30	58	79	100
3-9	9	18	27	50	65	80
10-Origin Thunder, Young Eagle's Horse	8	16	24	44	57	70
3-5(Charlton)-Formerly Sherlock Holmes?	7	14	21	35	43	50

YOUNG GUNS SKETCHBOOK
Marvel Comics: Feb, 2005 ($3.99, one-shot)

1-Sketch pages from 2005 Marvel projects by Coipel, Granov, McNiven, Land & others ... 4.00

YOUNG HEARTS
Marvel Comics (SPC): Nov, 1949 - No. 2, Feb, 1950

1-Photo-c	14	28	42	80	115	150
2-Colleen Townsend photo-c from movie	10	20	30	54	72	90

YOUNG HEARTS IN LOVE

Young Justice #6 © DC

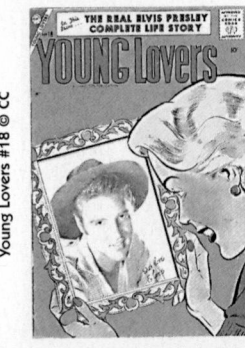

Young Lovers #18 © CC

Young Romance #6 © PRIZE

	GD 2.0	VG 4.0	FN 6.0	VF 8.0	VF/NM 9.0	NM- 9.2
Super Comics: 1964						
17,18: 17-r/Young Love V5#6 (4-5/62)	2	4	6	9	13	16
YOUNG HEROES (Formerly Forbidden Worlds #34)						
American Comics Group (Titan): No. 35, Feb-Mar, 1955 - No. 37, Jun-Jul, 1955						
35-37-Frontier Scout	10	20	30	54	72	90
YOUNG HEROES IN LOVE						
DC Comics: June, 1997 - No. 17; #1,000,000, Nov, 1998 ($1.75/$1.95/$2.50)						
1-1st app. Young Heroes; Madan-a						3.00
2-17: 3-Superman-c/app. 7-Begin $1.95-c						2.50
#1,000,000 (11/98, $2.50) 853 Century x-over						2.50
YOUNG INDIANA JONES CHRONICLES, THE						
Dark Horse Comics: Feb, 1992 - No. 12, Feb, 1993 ($2.50)						
1-12: Dan Barry scripts in all						2.50
NOTE: *Dan Barry a(p)-1, 2, 5, 6, 10; c-1-10. Morrow a-3, 4, 5p, 6p. Springer a-1i, 2i.*						
YOUNG INDIANA JONES CHRONICLES, THE						
Hollywood Comics (Disney): 1992 ($3.95, squarebound, 68 pgs.)						
1-3: 1-r/YIJC #1,2 by D. Horse. 2-r/#3,4. 3-r/#5,6						4.00
YOUNG JUSTICE (Also see Teen Titans and Titans/Young Justice)						
DC Comics: Sept, 1998 - No. 55, May, 2003 ($2.50/$2.75)						
1-Robin, Superboy & Impulse team-up; David-s/Nauck-a						4.00
2,3: 3-Mxyzptlk app.						3.00
4-20: 4-Wonder Girl, Arrowette and the Secret join. 6-JLA app. 13-Supergirl x-over.						
20-Sins of Youth aftermath						3.00
21-49: 25-Empress ID revealed. 28,29-Forever People app. 32-Empress origin. 35,36-Our						
Worlds at War x-over. 38-Joker: Last Laugh. 41-The Ray joins. 42-Spectre-c/app.						
44,45-World Without YJ x-over pt. 1,5; Ramos-c. 48-Begin $2.75-c						2.75
50-($3.95) Wonder Twins,CM3 and other various DC teen heroes app.						4.00
51-55: 53,54-Darkseid app. 55-Last issue; leads into Titans/Young Justice mini-series						2.75
#1,000,000 (11/98) 853 Century x-over						2.50
...: A League of Their Own (2000, $14.95, TPB) r/#1-7, Secret Files #1						15.00
...: 80-Page Giant (5/99, $4.95) Ramos-c; stories and art by various						5.00
...: In No Man's Land (7/99, $3.95) McDaniel-c						4.00
...: Our Worlds at War (8/01, $2.95) Jae Lee-c; Linear Men app.						3.00
...: Secret Files (1/99, $4.95) Origin-s & pin-ups						5.00
...: The Secret (6/98, $1.95) Girlfrenzy; Nauck-a						2.50
YOUNG JUSTICE: SINS OF YOUTH (Also see Sins of Youth x-over issues and Sins of Youth: Secret Files)						
DC Comics: May, 2000 - No. 2, May, 2000 ($3.95, limited series)						
1,2-Young Justice, JLA & JSA swap ages; David-s/Nauck-a						4.00
TPB (2000, $19.95) r/#1,2 & all x-over issues						20.00
YOUNG KING COLE (...Detective Tales)(Becomes Criminals on the Run)						
Premium Group/Novelty Press: Fall, 1945 - V3#12, July, 1948						
V1#1-Toni Gayle begins	32	64	96	186	293	400
2	15	30	45	88	137	185
3-4	15	30	45	83	124	165
V2#1-(7-8/9/46-7/47): 6,7-Certa-c	11	22	33	64	90	115
V3#1,3-6,8,9,12: 3-Certa-c. 5-McWilliams-c/a. 8,9-Harmon-c	11	22	33	62	86	110
2-L.B. Cole-a; Certa-c	15	30	45	90	140	190
7-L.B. Cole-c/a	21	42	63	124	195	265
10,11-L.B. Cole-c	18	36	54	105	165	225
YOUNG LAWYERS, THE (TV)						
Dell Publishing Co.: Jan, 1971 - No. 2, Apr, 1971						
1	3	6	9	16	23	30
2	2	4	6	11	16	20
YOUNG LIFE (Teen Life #3 on)						
New Age Publ./Quality Comics Group: Summer, 1945 - No. 2, Fall, 1945						
1-Skip Homeier, Louis Prima stories	15	30	45	85	130	175
2-Frank Sinatra photo on-c plus story	16	32	48	94	147	200
YOUNG LOVE (Sister title to Young Romance)						
Prize(Feature)Publ.(Crestwood): 2-3/49 - No. 73, 12-1/56-57; V3#5, 2-3/60 - V7#1, 6-7/63						
V1#1-S&K-c/a(2)	47	94	141	287	474	660
2-Photo-c begin; S&K-a	26	52	78	152	239	325
3-S&K-a	18	36	54	107	169	230
4-5-Minor S&K-a	14	28	42	81	118	155
V2#1(#7)-S&K-a(2)	18	36	54	107	169	230
2-5(#8-11)-Minor S&K-a	13	26	39	74	105	135

	GD 2.0	VG 4.0	FN 6.0	VF 8.0	VF/NM 9.0	NM- 9.2
6,8(#12,14)-S&K-c only. 14-S&K 1 pg. art	14	28	42	82	121	160
7,9-12(#13,15-18)-S&K-c/a	18	36	54	107	169	230
V3#1-4(#19-22)-S&K-c/a	17	34	51	98	154	210
5-7,9-12(#23-25,27-30)-Photo-c resume; S&K-a	15	30	45	85	130	175
8(#26)-No S&K-a	9	18	27	47	61	75
V4#1,6(#31,36)-S&K-a	14	28	42	81	118	155
2-5,7-12(#32-35,37-42)-Minor S&K-a	12	24	36	67	94	120
V5#1-12(#43-54), V6#1-9(#55-63)-Last precode; S&K-a in #1,2,4,6,8						
	8	16	24	44	57	70
V6#10-12(#64-66)	4	8	12	26	41	55
V7#1-7(#67-73)	4	8	12	23	36	48
V3#5(2-3/60),6(4-5/60)(Formerly All For Love)	4	8	12	22	34	45
V4#1-6(7-60)-6(4-5/61)	3	6	9	21	32	42
V5#1(6-7/61)-6(4-5/62)	3	6	9	21	32	42
V6#1-6(7-62)-6(4-5/63), V7#1	3	6	9	20	30	40
NOTE: *Meskin a-14(2), 27, 42. Powell a-V4#6. Severin/Elder a-V1#3. S&K art not in #53, 57, 61, 63-65. Photo-c most V3#5-V5#11.*						
YOUNG LOVE						
National Periodical Publ.(Arleigh Publ. Corp #49-61)/DC Comics:						
#39, 9-10/63 - #120, Wint./75-76; #121, 10/76 - #126, 7/77						
39	5	10	15	35	55	75
40-50	4	8	12	24	37	50
51-68,70	4	8	12	22	34	45
69-(80 pg. Giant)(8-9/68)	6	12	18	39	62	85
71,72,74-77,80	3	6	9	18	27	35
73,78,79-Toth-a	3	6	9	19	29	38
81-99: 88-96-(52 pg. Giants)	3	6	9	17	25	32
100	3	6	9	18	27	35
101-106,115-120	3	6	9	15	21	26
107 (100 pgs.)	7	14	21	50	83	115
108-114 (100 pgs.)	7	14	21	45	73	100
121-126 (52 pgs.)	4	8	12	24	37	50
NOTE: *Bolle a-117. Colan a-107r. Nasser a-123, 124. Orlando a-122. Simonson c-125. Toth a-73, 78, 79, 122-125r. Wood a-109r(4 pgs.).*						
YOUNG LOVER ROMANCES (Formerly & becomes Great Lover...)						
Toby Press: No. 4, June, 1952 - No. 5, Aug, 1952						
4,5-Photo-c	8	16	24	44	57	70
YOUNG LOVERS (My Secret Life #19 on)(Formerly Brenda Starr?)						
Charlton Comics: No. 16, July, 1956 - No. 18, May, 1957						
16,17('56): 16-Marcus Swayze-a	9	18	27	52	69	85
18-Elvis Presley picture-c, text story (biography)(Scarce)	60	120	180	375	625	875
YOUNG MARRIAGE						
Fawcett Publications: June, 1950						
1-Powell-a; photo-c	13	26	39	74	105	135
YOUNG MEN (Formerly Cowboy Romances)(...on the Battlefield #12-20(4/53); ...In Action #21)						
Marvel/Atlas Comics (IPC): No. 4, 6/50 - No. 11, 10/51; No. 12, 12/51 - No. 28, 6/54						
4-(52 pgs.)	20	40	60	115	180	245
5-11	14	28	42	78	112	145
12-23: 12-20-War format. 21-23-Hot Rod issues starring Flash Foster	13	26	39	74	105	135
24-(12/53)-Origin Captain America, Human Torch, & Sub-Mariner which are revived thru #28;						
Red Skull app.	300	600	900	1881	3141	4400
25-28: 25-Romita-c/a (see Men's Advs.). 27-Death of Golden Age Red Skull						
	117	234	351	731	1216	1700
25-2nd printing (1994)	2	4	6	8	10	12
NOTE: *Berg a-7, 14, 17, 18, 20; c-17? Brodsky c-4-9, 13, 14, 16, 17, 21-25. Burgos c-26-28. Colan a-14, 15. Everett a-18-20. Heath a-13, 14. Maneely c-10, 12, 15. Robinson c-18. Captain America by Romita-#24?, 25, 26?, 27, 28. Human Torch by Burgos-#25, 27, 28. Sub-Mariner by Everett-#24-28.*						
YOUNG REBELS, THE (TV)						
Dell Publishing Co.: Jan, 1971						
1-Photo-c	3	6	9	14	19	24
YOUNG ROMANCE COMICS (The 1st romance comic)						
Prize/Headline (Feature Publ.) (Crestwood): Sept-Oct, 1947 - V16#4, June-July, 1963 (#1-33: 52 pgs.)						
V1#1-S&K-c/a(2)	50	100	150	305	503	700
2-S&K-c/a(2-3)	32	64	96	186	293	400
3-6-S&K-c/a(2-3) each	28	56	84	162	256	350
V2#1-6(#7-12)-S&K-c/a(2-3) each	26	52	78	150	235	320
V3#1-3(#13-15): V3#1-Photo-c begin; S&K-a	17	34	51	98	154	210
4-12(#16-24)-Photo-c; S&K-a	17	34	51	98	154	210

Youthful Romances #5 © Pix-Parade

Y: The Last Man #38 © Vaughan & Guerra

Zatanna #2 © DC

	GD 2.0	VG 4.0	FN 6.0	VF 8.0	VF/NM 9.0	NM- 9.2
V4#1-11(#25-35)-S&K-a	16	32	48	94	147	200
12(#36)-S&K, Toth-a	18	36	54	105	165	225
V5#1-12(#37-48), V6#4-12(#52-60)-S&K-a	16	32	48	94	147	200
V6#1-3(#49-51)-No S&K-a	9	18	27	52	69	85
V7#1-11(#61-71)-S&K-a in most	14	28	42	81	118	155
V7#12(#72), V8#1-3(#73-75)-Last precode (12-1/54-55)-No S&K-a						
	8	16	24	44	57	70
V8#4(#76, 4-5/55), 5(#77) No S&K-a	8	16	24	40	50	60
V8#6-8(#78-80, 12-1/55-56)-S&K-a	12	24	36	67	94	120
V9#3,5,6(#81, 2-3/56, 83,84)-S&K-a	12	24	36	67	94	120
4, V10#1(#82,85)-All S&K-a	13	26	39	72	101	130
V10#2-6(#86-90, 10-11/57)-S&K-a	8	16	24	52	86	120
V11#1,2,5,6(#91,92,95,96)-S&K-a	8	16	24	52	86	120
3,4(#93,94), V12#2,4,5(#98,100,101)-No S&K	4	8	12	26	41	55
V12#1,3,6(#97,99,102)-S&K-a	8	16	24	52	86	120
V13#1(#103)-Powell-a; S&K's last-a for Crestwood	8	16	24	52	86	120
2,4-6(#104-108)	4	8	12	23	36	48
V13#3(#105, 4-5/60)-Elvis Presley-c app. only	6	12	18	39	62	85
V14#1-6, V15#1-6, V16#1-4(#109-124)	3	6	9	21	32	42

NOTE: Meskin a-16, 24(2), 33, 47, 50. Robinson/Meskin a-6. Leonard Starr a-11. Photo c-13-32, 34-65. Issues 1-3 say "Designed for the More Adult Readers of Comics" on cover.

YOUNG ROMANCE COMICS (Continued from Prize series)
National Periodical Publ.(Arleigh Publ. Corp. No. 127): No. 125, Aug-Sept, 1963 - No. 208, Nov-Dec, 1975

125	7	14	21	45	73	100
126-140	4	8	12	26	41	55
141-153,156-162,165-169	3	6	9	20	30	40
154-Neal Adams-c	4	8	12	28	44	60
155-1st publ. Aragonés-s (no art)	4	8	12	26	41	55
163,164-Toth-a	4	8	12	24	37	50
170-172 (68 pg. Giants): 170-Michell from Young Love ends; Lily Martin, the Swinger begins						
	4	8	12	26	41	55
173-183 (52 pgs.)	4	8	12	22	34	45
184-196	3	6	9	16	22	28
197-204-(100 pgs.)	6	12	18	43	69	95
205-208	3	6	9	14	20	25

YOUNG ZEN: CITY OF DEATH
Entity Comics: Late 1994 ($3.25, B&W)

1						3.25

YOUNG ZEN INTERGALACTIC NINJA (Also see Zen...)
Entity Comics: 1993 - No. 3, 1994 ($3.50/$2.95, B&W)

1-($3.50)-Polybagged w/Sam Kieth chromium trading card; gold foil logo						3.50
2,3-($2.95)-Gold foil logo						3.00

YOUR DREAMS (See Strange World of...)

YOU'RE UNDER ARREST (Manga)
Dark Horse Comics: Dec, 1995 - No. 8, July, 1996 ($2.95, limited series)

1-8						3.00

YOUR UNITED STATES
Lloyd Jacquet Studios: 1946

nn-Used in SOTI, pg. 309,310; Sid Greene-a	23	46	69	135	213	290

YOUTHFUL HEARTS (Daring Confessions #4 on)
Youthful Magazines: May, 1952 - No. 3, Sept, 1952

1- "Monkey on Her Back" swipes E.C. drug story/Shock SuspenStories #12; Frankie Laine photo on-c; Doug Wildey-a in al	29	58	87	170	268	365
2,3: 2-Vic Damone photo on-c. 3-Johnny Raye photo on-c						
	20	40	60	117	184	250

YOUTHFUL LOVE (Truthful Love #2)
Youthful Magazines: May, 1950

1	14	28	42	76	108	140

YOUTHFUL ROMANCES
Pix-Parade #1-14/Ribage #15 on: 8-9/49 - No. 5, 4/50; No. 6, 2/51; No. 7, 5/51 - #14, 10/52; #15, 1/53 - #18, 7/53; No. 5, 9/53 - No. 9, 8/54

1-(1st series)-Titled Youthful Love-Romances	26	52	78	152	239	325
2-Walter Johnson c-1-4	15	30	45	90	140	190
3-5	14	28	42	78	112	145
6,7,9-14(10/52, Pix-Parade); becomes Daring Love #15). 10(1/52)-Mel Torme photo on-c						
12-Tony Bennett photo-c, 8pg. story & text bio.13-Richard Hayes (singer) photo-c/story; Bob & Ray photo/text story.	13	26	39	72	101	130
8-Frank Sinatra photo/text story; Wood-c/a	18	36	54	105	165	225

15-18 (Ribage)-All have photos on-c. 15-Spike Jones photo-c/story. 16-Tony Bavaar photo-c						
	12	24	36	67	94	120
5(9/53, Ribage)-Les Paul & Mary Ford photo-c/story; Charlton Heston photo/text story						
	11	22	33	62	86	110
6-9: 6-Bobby Wayne (singer) photo-c/story; Debbie Reynolds photo/text story. 7(2/54)-Tony Martin photo-c/story; Cyd Charise photo/text story. 8(5/54)-Gordon McCrae photo-c/story. (8/54)-Ralph Flanagan (band leader) photo-c/story; Audrey Hepburn photo/text story						
	10	20	30	56	76	95

Y: THE LAST MAN
DC Comics (Vertigo): Sept, 2002 - Present ($2.95/$2.99)

1-Intro. Yorick Brown; Vaughan-s/Guerra-a/J.G. Jones-c						
	2	4	6	8	10	12
2	1	2	3	5	6	8
3-5						6.00
6-58: 16,17-Chadwick-a. 21,22-Parlov-a. 32,39-41,48,53,54-Sudzuka-a.						3.00
...Double Feature Edition (2002, $5.95) r/#1,2						6.00
... - Cycles TPB (2003, $12.95) r/#6-10; sketch pages by Guerra						13.00
... - Girl on Girl TPB (2005, $12.99) r/#32-36						13.00
... - Kimono Dragons TPB (2006, $14.99) r/#43-48						15.00
... - Motherland TPB (2007, $14.99) r/#49-54						15.00
... - One Small Step TPB (2004, $12.95) r/#11-17						13.00
... - Paper Dolls TPB (2006, $14.99) r/#37-42						15.00
... - Ring of Truth TPB (2005, $14.99) r/#24-31						15.00
... - Safeword TPB (2004, $12.95) r/#18-23						13.00
... - Unmanned TPB (2002, $12.95) r/#1-5						13.00

Y2K: THE COMIC
New England Comics Press: Oct, 1999 ($3.95, one-shot)

1-Y2K scenarios and survival tips						4.00

YUPPIES FROM HELL (Also see Son of...)
Marvel Comics: 1989 ($2.95, B&W, one-shot, direct sales, 52 pgs.)

1-Satire						3.00

ZAGO, JUNGLE PRINCE (My Story #5 on)
Fox Features Syndicate: Sept, 1948 - No. 4, Mar, 1949

1-Blue Beetle app.; partial-r/Atomic #4 (Toni Luck)	62	124	186	388	644	900
2,3-Kamen-a	50	100	150	305	503	700
4-Baker-c	41	82	123	256	416	575

ZANE GREY'S STORIES OF THE WEST
Dell Publishing Co./Gold Key 11/64: No. 197, 9/48 - No. 996, 5-7/59; 11/64 (All painted)

Four Color 197(#1)(9/48)	11	22	33	79	140	200
Four Color 222,230,236('49)	7	14	21	47	76	105
Four Color 246,255,270,301,314,333,346	5	10	15	32	51	70
Four Color 357,372,395,412,433,449,467,484	4	8	12	28	44	60
Four Color 511-Kinstler-a; Kubert-a	5	10	15	32	51	70
Four Color 532,555,583,604,616,632(5/55)	4	8	12	28	44	60
27(9-11/55) - 39(9-11/58)	4	8	12	28	44	60
Four Color 996-5-7/59	4	8	12	28	44	60
10131-411-(11/64-G.K.)-Nevada; r/4-Color #996	3	6	9	20	30	40

ZANY (Magazine)(Satire)(See Frantic & Ratfink)
Candor Publ. Co.: Sept, 1958 - No. 4, May, 1959

1-Bill Everett-c	11	22	33	64	90	115
2-4: 4-Everett-c	7	14	27	47	61	75

ZATANNA (See Adv. Comics #413, JLA #161, Supergirl #1, World's Finest Comics #274)
DC Comics: July, 1993 - No. 4, Oct, 1993 ($1.95, limited series)

1-4						2.50
...: Everyday Magic (2003, $5.95, one-shot) Dini-s/Mays-a/Bolland-c; Constantine app.						6.00
Special 1(1987, $2.00)-Gray Morrow-c/a						3.00

ZAZA, THE MYSTIC (Formerly Charlie Chan; This Magazine Is Haunted V2#12 on)
Charlton Comics: No. 10, Apr, 1956 - No. 11, Sept, 1956

10,11	12	24	36	69	97	125

ZEALOT (Also see WildC.A.T.s: Covert Action Teams)
Image Comics: Aug, 1995 - No. 3, Nov, 1995 ($2.50, limited series)

1-3						2.50

ZEGRA JUNGLE EMPRESS (Formerly Tegra)(My Love Life #6 on)
Fox Features Syndicate: No. 2, Oct, 1948 - No. 5, April, 1949

2	62	124	186	388	644	900
3-5	48	96	144	293	484	675

ZEN (Intergalactic Ninja)

Zero Girl #3 © I Before E Inc.

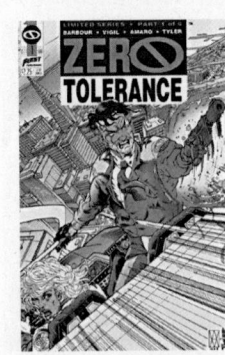

Zero Tolerance #1 © First Comics

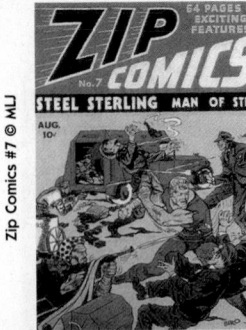

Zip Comics #7 © MLJ

	GD 2.0	VG 4.0	FN 6.0	VF 8.0	VF/NM 9.0	NM- 9.2

Zen Comics Publishing: No. 0, Apr, 2003 - No. 4, Aug, 2003 ($2.95)

0-4-Bill Maus-a/Steve Stern-s. 0-Wraparound-c						3.00

ZEN INTERGALACTIC NINJA
No Publisher: 1987 -1993 ($1.75/$2.00, B&W)

1	2	4	6	10	14	18
2-6: Copyright-Stern & Cote	1	3	4	6	8	10
V2#1-4-($2.00)						3.00
V3#1-5-($2.95)						3.00
... :Christmas Special 1 (1992, $2.95)						3.00
... :Earth Day Special 1 (1993, $2.95)						3.00

ZEN, INTERGALACTIC NINJA (mini-series)
Zen Comics/Archie Comics: Sept, 1992 - No. 3, 1992 ($1.25)(Formerly a B&W comic by Zen Comics)

1-3: 1-Origin Zen; contains mini-poster						3.00

ZEN INTERGALACTIC NINJA
Entity Comics: No. 0, June-July, 1993 - No. 3, 1994 ($2.95, B&W, limited series)

0-Gold foil stamped-c; photo-c of Zen model						3.00
1-3: Gold foil stamped-c; Bill Maus-c/a						3.00
0-(1993, $3.50, color)-Chromium-c by Jae Lee						3.50
...Sourcebook 1-(1993, $3.50)						3.50
...Sourcebook '94-(1994, $3.50)						3.50

ZEN INTERGALACTIC NINJA: APRIL FOOL'S SPECIAL
Parody Press: 1994 ($2.50, B&W)

1-w/flip story of Renn Intergalactic Chihuahua						3.00

ZEN INTERGALACTIC NINJA COLOR
Entity Comics: 1994 - No. 7, 1995 ($2.25)

1-($3.95)-Chromium die cut-c						4.00
1, 0-($2.25)-Newsstand; Jae Lee-c; r/...All New Color Special #0						3.00
2-($2.50)-Flip book						3.00
2-($3.50)-Flip book, polybagged w/chromium trading card						3.50
3-7						3.00
Summer Special (1994, $2.95)						3.00
Yearbook: Hazardous Duty 1 (1995)						3.00
Zen-isms 1 (1995, 2.95)						3.00
Ashcan-Tour of the Universe-(no price) w/flip cover						3.00

ZEN INTERGALACTIC NINJA COMMEMORATIVE EDITION
Zen Comics Publishing: 1997 ($5.95, color)

1-Stern-s/Cote-a						6.00

ZEN INTERGALACTIC NINJA MILESTONE
Entity Comics: 1994 - No. 3, 1994 ($2.95, limited series)

1-3: Gold foil logo; r/Defend the Earth						3.00

ZEN INTERGALATIC NINJA SPRING SPECTACULAR
Entity Comics: 1994 ($2.95, B&W, one-shot)

1-Gold foil logo						3.00

ZEN INTERGALACTIC NINJA STARQUEST
Entity Comics: No. 1 - No. 6, 1995 ($2.95, B&W)

1-6: Gold foil logo						3.00

ZEN, INTERGALACTIC NINJA: THE HUNTED
Entity Comics: 1993 - No. 3, 1994 ($2.95, B&W, limited series)

1-3: Newsstand Edition; foil logo						3.00
1-($3.50)-Polybagged w/chromium card by Kieth; foil logo						3.50

ZERO GIRL
DC Comics (Homage): Feb, 2001 - No. 5, Jun, 2001 ($2.95, limited series)

1-5-Sam Kieth-s/a						3.00
TPB (2001, $14.95) r/#1-5; intro. by Alan Moore						15.00

ZERO GIRL: FULL CIRCLE
DC Comics (Homage): Jan, 2003 - No. 5, May, 2003 ($2.95, limited series)

1-5-Sam Kieth-s/a						3.00
TPB (2003, $17.95) r/#1-5						18.00

ZERO HOUR: CRISIS IN TIME (Also see Showcase '94 #8-10)
DC Comics: No. 4(#1), Sept, 1994 - No. 0(#5), Oct, 1994 ($1.50, limited series)

4(#1)-0(#5)						4.00
"Ashcan"-(1994, free, B&W, 8 pgs.) several versions exist						2.25
TPB ('94, $9.95)						10.00

ZERO KILLER
Dark Horse Comics: Jul, 2007 - Present ($2.99)

1-Arvid Nelson-s/Matt Camp-a						3.00

ZERO PATROL, THE
Continuity Comics: Nov, 1984 - No. 2 ($1.50); 1987 - No. 5, May, 1989 ($2.00)

1,2: Neal Adams-c/a; Megalith begins						4.00
1-5 (#1,2-reprints above, 1987)						3.00

ZERO TOLERANCE
First Comics: Oct, 1990 - No. 4, Jan, 1991 ($2.25, limited series)

1-4: Tim Vigil-c/a(p) (his 1st color limited series)						3.00

ZERO ZERO
Fantagraphics: Mar, 1995 -No. 27 ($3.95/$4.95, B&W, anthology, mature)

1-7,9-15,17-25						5.00
8,16						6.00
26-($4.95) Bagge-c						5.00

ZIGGY PIG-SILLY SEAL COMICS (See Animal Fun, Animated Movie-Tunes, Comic Capers, Krazy Komics, Silly Tunes & Super Rabbit)
Timely Comics (CmPL): Fall, 1944 - No. 6, Fall, 1946

	GD	VG	FN	VF	VF/NM	NM-
1-Vs. the Japs	27	54	81	158	249	340
2	14	28	42	82	121	160
3-5	14	28	42	76	108	140
6-Infinity-c	15	30	45	84	127	170
I.W. Reprint #1(1958)-r/Krazy Komics	2	4	6	9	13	16
I.W. Reprint #2,7,8	2	4	6	9	13	16

ZIP COMICS
MLJ Magazines: Feb, 1940 - No. 47, Summer, 1944 (#1-7?: 68 pgs.)

	GD	VG	FN	VF	VF/NM	NM-
1-Origin Kalathar the Giant Man, The Scarlet Avenger, & Steel Sterling; Mr. Satan (by Edd Ashe), Nevada Jones (masked hero) & Zambini, the Miracle Man, War Eagle, Captain Valor begins	503	1006	1509	3521	6161	8800
2-Nevada Jones adds mask & horse Blaze	241	482	723	1506	2503	3500
3-Biro robot-c	200	400	600	1250	2075	2900
4,5-Biro WW2-c	159	318	477	994	1647	2300
6-8-Biro-c	138	276	414	863	1432	2000
9-Last Kalathar & Mr. Satan; classic-c	157	314	471	981	1628	2275
10-Inferno, the Flame Breather begins, ends #13	148	296	444	925	1538	2150
11,12: 11-Inferno without costume	110	220	330	688	1144	1600
13-Electrocution-c	124	248	372	775	1288	1800
14,16,19	103	206	309	644	1072	1500
15-Classic spider-c	134	264	402	838	1394	1950
17-Last Scarlet Avenger; women in bondage being cooked alive-c by Biro	128	256	384	800	1325	1850
18-Wilbur begins (9/41, 1st app.)	128	256	384	800	1325	1850
20-Origin & 1st app. Black Jack (11/41); Hitler-c	176	352	528	1100	1825	2550
21,23-26: 25-Last Nevada Jones. 26-Black Witch begins; last Captain Valor; "Remember Pearl Harbor!" cover caption	93	186	279	581	966	1350
22-Classic-c	159	318	477	994	1647	2300
27-Intro. Web (7/42) plus-c app.	179	358	537	1119	1860	2600
28-Origin Web	152	304	456	950	1575	2200
29-The Hyena app. (scarce)	76	152	228	475	.788	1100
30	62	124	186	388	644	900
31,33-38: 34-1st Applejack app. 35-Last Zambini, Black Jack. 38-Last Web issue	50	100	150	305	503	700
32-Classic skeleton Nazi WW2-c	76	152	228	475	788	1100
39-Red Rube begins (origin, 8/43)	50	100	150	305	503	700
40-46: 45-Wilbur ends	45	90	135	275	450	625
47-Last issue; scarce	46	92	138	281	466	650

NOTE: *Biro* a-5, 9, 17; c-3-17. *Meskin* a-1-3, 5-7, 9, 10, 12, 13, 15, 16 at least. *Montana* c-29, 30, 32-35. *Novick* c-18-28, 31. *Sahle* c-37, 38, 40-46. *Bondage* c-8, 9, 33, 34. Cover features: Steel Sterling-1-43, 47; (w/Blackjack-20-27 & Web-27-35); 28-39; (w/Red Rube-40-43); Red Rube-44-47.

ZIP-JET (Hero)
St. John Publishing Co.: Feb, 1953 - No. 2, Apr-May, 1953

	GD	VG	FN	VF	VF/NM	NM-
1-Rocketman-r from Punch Comics; #1-c from splash in Punch #10	76	152	228	475	788	1100
2	49	98	147	299	492	685

ZIPPY THE CHIMP (CBS TV Presents...)
Pines (Literary Ent.): No. 50, March, 1957; No. 51, Aug, 1957

	GD	VG	FN	VF	VF/NM	NM-
50,51	8	16	24	40	50	60

ZODY, THE MOD ROB
Gold Key: July, 1970

Zombie World: Eat Your Heart Out #1 © DH

Zoot #9 © FOX

Zorro #5 © Zorro Prods.

	GD 2.0	VG 4.0	FN 6.0	VF 8.0	VF/NM 9.0	NM- 9.2
1	3	6	9	16	23	30

ZOMBIE
Marvel Comics: Nov, 2006 - No. 4, Feb, 2007 ($3.99, limited series)
1-4-Kyle Hotz-a/c; Mike Raicht-s ... 4.00
TPB (2007, $13.99) r/#1-4 ... 14.00

ZOMBIE KING
Image Comics: No. 0, June, 2005 ($2.95, B&W, one-shot)
0-Frank Cho-s/a ... 5.00

ZOMBIE PROOF
Moonstone: 2007 - Present ($3.50)
1-J.C. Vaughn-s/Vincent Spencer-a; two covers by Spencer and Neil Vokes ... 3.50
1-Baltimore Comic-Con variant-c by Vokes ... 5.00

ZOMBIES!: ECLIPSE OF THE UNDEAD
IDW Publ.: Nov, 2006 - No. 4, Feb, 2007 ($3.99, limited series)
1-4-Torres-s/Herrera-a; two covers ... 4.00

ZOMBIES!: FEAST
IDW Publ.: May, 2006 - No. 5, Oct, 2006 ($3.99, limited series)
1-5: 1-Chris Bolton-a/Shane McCarthy-s. 3-Lorenzana-a ... 4.00

ZOMBIE WORLD (one-shots)
Dark Horse Comics
... :Eat Your Heart Out (4/98, $2.95) Kelley Jones-c/s/a ... 3.00
... :Home For The Holidays (12/97, $2.95) ... 3.00

ZOMBIE WORLD: CHAMPION OF THE WORMS
Dark Horse Comics: Sept, 1997 - No. 3, Nov, 1997 ($2.95, limited series)
1-3-Mignola & McEown-c/s/a ... 3.00

ZOMBIE WORLD: DEAD END
Dark Horse Comics: Jan, 1998 - No. 2, Feb, 1998 ($2.95, limited series)
1,2-Stephen Blue-s/a ... 3.00

ZOMBIE WORLD: TREE OF DEATH
Dark Horse Comics: Jun, 1999 - No. 4, Oct, 1999 ($2.95, limited series)
1-4-Mills-s/Deadstock-a ... 3.00

ZOMBIE WORLD: WINTER'S DREGS
Dark Horse Comics: May, 1998 - No. 4, Aug, 1998 ($2.95, limited series)
1-4-Fingerman-s/Edwards-a ... 3.00

ZONE (Also see Dark Horse Presents)
Dark Horse Comics: 1990 ($1.95, B&W)
1-Character from Dark Horse Presents ... 2.50

ZONE CONTINUUM, THE
Caliber Press: 1994 ($2.95, B&W)
1 ... 3.00

ZOO ANIMALS
Star Publications: No. 8, 1954 (15¢, 36 pgs.)

	GD 2.0	VG 4.0	FN 6.0	VF 8.0	VF/NM 9.0	NM- 9.2
8-(B&W for coloring)	7	14	21	37	46	55

ZOO FUNNIES (Tim McCoy #16 on)
Charlton Comics/Children Comics Publ.: Nov, 1945 - No. 15, 1947

	GD 2.0	VG 4.0	FN 6.0	VF 8.0	VF/NM 9.0	NM- 9.2
101(#1)(11/45, 1st Charlton comic book)-Funny animal; Al Fago-c	21	42	63	120	188	255
2(12/45, 52 pgs.) Classic-c	15	30	45	83	124	165
3-5	11	22	33	62	86	110
6-15: 8-Diana the Huntress app.	9	18	27	52	69	85

ZOO FUNNIES (Becomes Nyoka, The Jungle Girl #14 on)
Capitol Stories/Charlton Comics: July, 1953 - No. 13, Sept, 1955; Dec, 1984

	GD 2.0	VG 4.0	FN 6.0	VF 8.0	VF/NM 9.0	NM- 9.2
1-1st app.? Timothy The Ghost; Fago-c/a	11	22	33	64	90	115
2	8	16	24	42	54	65
3-7	7	14	21	37	46	55
8-13-Nyoka app.	9	18	27	52	69	85
1(1984) (Low print run)						6.00

ZOONIVERSE
Eclipse Comics: 8/86 - No. 6, 6/87 ($1.25/$1.75, limited series, Mando paper)
1-6 ... 2.50

ZOO PARADE (TV)
Dell Publishing Co.: #662, 1955 (Marlin Perkins)

	GD 2.0	VG 4.0	FN 6.0	VF 8.0	VF/NM 9.0	NM- 9.2
Four Color 662	5	10	15	32	51	70

ZOOM COMICS
Carlton Publishing Co.: Dec, 1945 (one-shot)
nn-Dr. Mercy, Satannas, from Red Band Comics; Capt. Milksop origin retold

	GD 2.0	VG 4.0	FN 6.0	VF 8.0	VF/NM 9.0	NM- 9.2
	40	80	120	235	368	500

ZOOT (Rulah Jungle Goddess #17 on)
Fox Features Syndicate: nd (1946) - No. 16, July, 1948 (Two #13s & 14s)

	GD 2.0	VG 4.0	FN 6.0	VF 8.0	VF/NM 9.0	NM- 9.2
nn-Funny animal only	21	42	63	122	191	260
2-The Jaguar app.	19	38	57	109	172	235
3(Fall, 1946) - 6-Funny animals & teen-age	12	24	36	69	77	125
7-(6/47)-Rulah, Jungle Goddess (origin/1st app.)	100	200	300	625	1038	1450
8-10	69	138	207	431	716	1000
11-Kamen bondage-c	72	144	216	450	750	1050
12-Injury-to-eye panels, torture scene	52	104	156	317	521	725
13(2/48)	52	104	156	317	521	725
14(3/48)-Used in SOTI, pg. 104, "One picture showing a girl nailed by her wrists to trees with blood flowing from the wounds, might be taken straight from an ill. ed. of the Marquis deSade"	66	132	198	413	682	950
13(4/48),14(5/48)-Western True Crime #15 on?	52	104	156	317	521	725
15,16	52	104	156	317	521	725

ZORRO (Walt Disney with #882)(TV)(See Eclipse Graphic Album)
Dell Publishing Co.: May, 1949 - No. 15, Sept-Nov, 1961 (Photo-c 882 on)
(Zorro first appeared in a pulp story Aug 19, 1919)

	GD 2.0	VG 4.0	FN 6.0	VF 8.0	VF/NM 9.0	NM- 9.2
Four Color 228 (#1)	20	40	60	146	261	375
Four Color 425,617,732	12	24	36	82	146	210
Four Color 497,538,574-Kinstler-a	12	24	36	87	156	225
Four Color 882-Photo-c begin;1st TV Disney; Toth-a	15	30	45	107	191	275
Four Color 920,933,960,976-Toth-a in all	11	22	33	80	143	205
Four Color 1003('59)-Toth-a	11	22	33	80	143	205
Four Color 1037-Annette Funicello photo-c	14	28	42	100	178	255
8(12-2/59-60)	8	16	24	56	93	130
9-Toth-a	9	18	27	60	100	140
10,11,13-15-Last photo-c	8	16	24	54	90	125
12-Toth-a; last 10¢ issue	9	18	27	60	100	140

NOTE: Warren Tufts a-4-Color 1037, 8, 9, 10, 13.

ZORRO (Walt Disney)(TV)
Gold Key: Jan, 1966 - No. 9, Mar, 1968 (All photo-c)

	GD 2.0	VG 4.0	FN 6.0	VF 8.0	VF/NM 9.0	NM- 9.2
1-Toth-a	8	16	24	52	86	120
2,4,5,7-9-Toth-a. 5-r/F.C. 1003 by Toth	5	10	15	30	48	65
3,6-Tufts-a	4	8	12	28	44	60

NOTE: #1-9 are reprinted from Dell issues. Tufts a-3, 4. #1-r/F.C. #882. #2-r/F.C. #960. #3-r/#12-c & #8 inside. #4-r/#9-c & insides. #6-r/#11(all); #7-r/#14-c. #8-r/F.C. #933 inside & back-c & #976-c. #9-r/F.C. #920.

ZORRO (TV)
Marvel Comics: Dec, 1990 - No. 12, Nov, 1991 ($1.00)
1-12: Based on TV show. 12-Toth-c ... 3.00

ZORRO (Also see Mask of Zorro)
Topps Comics: Nov, 1993 - No. 11, Nov, 1994 ($2.50/$2.95)
0-(11/93, $1.00, 20 pgs.)-Painted-c; collector's ed. ... 2.50
1,4,6-9,11: 1-Miller-c. 4-Mike Grell-c. 6-Mignola-c. 7-Lady Rawhide by Gulacy. 8-Perez-c. 9-Julie Bell-c. 11-Lady Rawhide-c ... 3.00
2-Lady Rawhide app. (not in costume) ... 5.00

3-1st app. Lady Rawhide in costume, 3-Lady Rawhide-c by Adam Hughes	1	2	3	5	6	8

5-Lady Rawhide app. ... 4.00
10-($2.95)-Lady Rawhide-c/app. ... 3.00
The Lady Wears Red (12/98, $12.95, TPB) r/#1-3 ... 13.00
Zorro's Renegades (2/99, $14.95, TPB) r/#4-8 ... 15.00

ZOT!
Eclipse Comics: 4/84 - No. 10, 7/85; No. 11, 1/87 - No. 36 7/91 ($1.50, Baxter-p)
1 ... 5.00
2,3 ... 4.00
4-10: 4-Origin. 10-Last color issue ... 3.00
10 1/2 (6/86, 25¢, Not Available Comics) Ashcan; art by Feazell & Scott McCloud ... 4.00
11-14,15-35-($2.00-c) B&W issues ... 3.00
14 1/2 (Adventures of Zot! in Dimension 10 1/2)(7/87) Antisocialman app. ... 3.00
36-($2.95-c) B&W ... 4.00

Z-2 COMICS (Secret Agent...)(See Holyoke One-Shot #7)

ZULU (See Movie Classics)

GUILTY BY ASSOCIATION!

In a guide filled with advertising, how do you make the right decision when it comes to selling your comic books or comic art?

Below is a small list of individuals whom I have represented for the sale of their property the past fifteen years:

Bruce Hamilton (Publisher of Another Rainbow), Jerry Siegel (creator and author of Superman), Bill Gaines (Publisher of *MAD Magazine* and EC Comics), Murphy Anderson, Jack & Roz Kirby, Dick Ayers, Alex Ross, Al Feldstein, Johnny Craig, Carl Barks, Rob Liefeld, Burne Hogarth, The George Herriman Family Estate, Graham Nash, Time Warner for *MAD Magazine*, Jim Lee, Jack Davis, Denis Kitchen for the Kurtzman Estate, Frank & Ellie Frazetta, Michael Whelan, Gil Kane, Russ Heath and Stan Lee

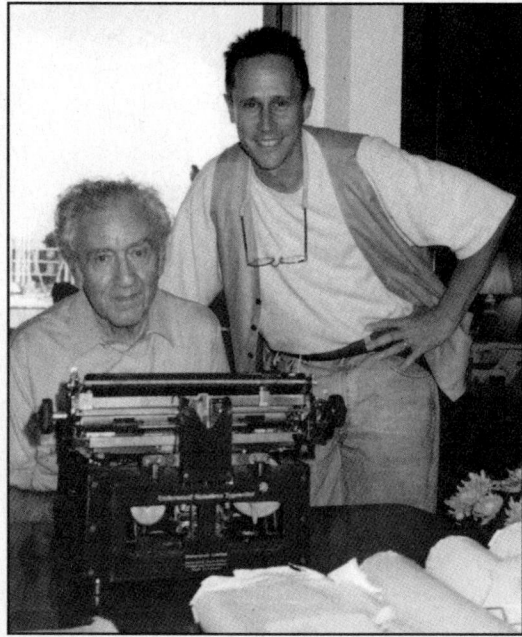

Jerry Weist with Jerry Siegel at Mr. Siegel's home with the original typewriter on which he wrote his original Superman scripts, during an appraisal for Sotheby's auctions.

1.) By inaugarating SOTHEBY'S COMIC BOOK and COMIC ART AUCTIONS in 1991, I changed forever the marketplace, making it easier for owners of rare comics and artwork to realize the highest possible prices for their property.

2.) By authoring *The Comic Art Price Guide* 1st and 2nd editions, I made it possible for common people and family members of artists or collectors to have a clear understanding of the value of their artwork

3.) By creating "event" auctions on eBay, I have become one of the leading Power Sellers in America, and have helped dozens of clients realize the top prices for their collections, while working on a modest commission.

MY PROMISE TO YOU:

My promise to you is simple. I promise to appraise and evaluate your collectible property and sell it for the highest possible price. No one else you deal with will have the experience, the creative will, the years of knowledge, as well as the desire to bring you outstanding results as I will.

This simple promise is backed by my years of experience in the Auction world and by working with some of the most important artists and publishers in the comics field and by having researched comic books and comic art for over 40 years.

*** 1.) Do you will to sell your comic art or comic books privately?
I promise to give you an honest appraisal and the most money for your property.

*** 2.) Do you wish to bring your collection to auction to realize the best possible price?
I promise to represent you for the best possible results at auction, using all my years of Sotheby's and eBay experience to give you an outstanding result.

*** 3.) Do you wish to negotiate a "private sale" of your comic book artwork and have me work on a small commission? I promise to use all my years of experience in the comic art field and my position in the art market as author of *The Comic Art Price Guide* to get you the best possible price for your artwork.

You may contact me at jerryweist@adelphia.net, my home phone (978) 283-1419, or my home office at Jerry Weist, 18 Edgemoor Road, Gloucester, Massachusetts, 10930, USA.

Senior Overstreet Advisor since the 1970s, Charter CGC Member, Sotheby's Comic Art and Comic Book Consultant, eBay seller of the month and Power Seller with over 400 100% positive feedbacks, author of *The Comic Art Price Guide*, with over 40 years experience in the comic field.

GET THE SKINNY ON MICKEY AND MINNIE

At Geppi's Entertainment Museum, you can visit the leader of the band that's made for you and me, not to mention his girlfriend and faithful pooch! Mickey, Minnie, Pluto and the rest of the Disney gang are on display at the museum, starting in the "When Heroes Unite" gallery. Mickey has evolved quite a bit over the years, and at GEM you'll see how changing styles and fashions played a role in making this mouse into the icon he is today.

1009

Business Card Ads

THE OVERSTREET COMIC BOOK PRICE GUIDE BUSINESS CARD ADS are a great way to advertise in the Guide! Simply send us your business card and we'll reduce it and run it as is. Have your ad seen by thousands of serious comic book collectors for an entire year! If you are a comic book or collectible dealer, retail establishment, mail-order house, etc., you can reach potential customers throughout the United States and around the world in our BUSINESS CARDS ADS!

Business Card Ads

We Want Your Help!

The Overstreet Comic Book Price Guide and *Hake's Price Guide To Character Toys* need your contributions!
If you see something we've missed in *The Overstreet Comic Book Price Guide*, or if you have comic character
collectibles not included in *Hake's Price Guide To Character Toys*, we want to know about it!

Conact us at: feedback@gemstonepub.com

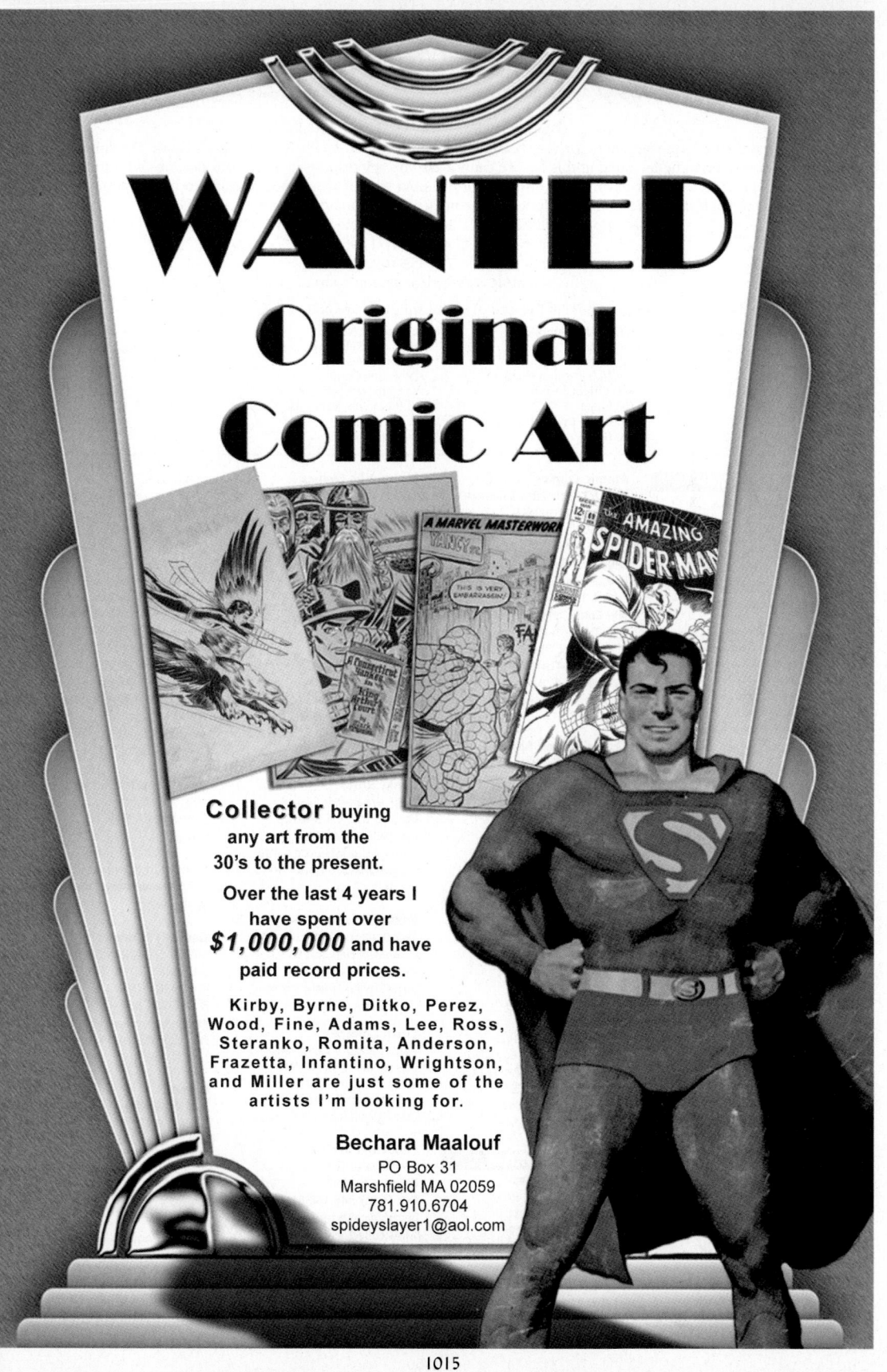

Directory Listings

Items stocked by these shops are noted at the end of each listing and are coded as follows:

(a) Golden Age Comics
(b) Silver Age Comics
(c) Bronze Age Comics
(d) New Comics & Magazines
(e) Back Issue magazines
(f) Comic Supplies
(g) Collectible Card Games
(h) Role Playing Games
(i) Gaming Supplies
(j) Manga
(k) Anime
(l) Underground Comics
(m) Original Comic Art
(n) Pulps
(o) Big Little Books
(p) Books - Used
(q) Books - New
(r) Comic Related Posters
(s) Movie Posters
(t) Trading Cards
(u) Statues/Mini-busts, etc.
(v) Premiums (Rings, Decoders, etc.)
(w) Action Figures
(x) Other Toys
(y) Records/CDs
(z) DVDs/VHS
(1) Doctor Who Items
(2) Simpsons Items
(3) Star Trek Items
(4) Star Wars Items
(5) HeroClix

ALABAMA

Quality Comix
Brent Moeshlin
7956 Vaughn Rd. #374
Montgomery, AL 36116
PH: (334) 300-1106
bmoeshlin@qualitycomix.com
www.qualitycomix.com

ARIZONA

Atomic Comics
3155 West Chandler Blvd.
Chandler, AZ 85226
PH: (480) 940-6061
info@atomiccomics.com
www.atomiccomics.com
(a-k,r,u,1-5)

Stalking Moon Bookstore
5930 W. Greenway Rd. Ste. 23
Glendale, AZ 85306
PH: (602) 896-9992
comics@stalking-moon.com
www.stalking-moon.com
(d-k,r,t,u,w-z,1,5)

Atomic Comics
1120 South Country Club
#105
Mesa, AZ 85210
PH: (480) 649-0807
info@atomiccomics.com
www.atomiccomics.com
(a-k,r,t,u,w,1-5)

All About Books & Comics
5060 N. Central
Phoenix, AZ 85012
PH: (602) 277-0757
FAX: (602) 678-0065
alan@All About Comics.com
www.All About Comics.com
(a-j,l,n,o,r-u,w,x,2-5)

Atomic Comics
4537 East Cactus Road
Phoenix, AZ 85032
PH: (602) 923-0733
info@atomiccomics.com
www.atomiccomics.com
(a-k,r,u,w,1-5)

Atomic Comics
10215 North 28th Drive #A1
Phoenix, AZ 85051
PH: (602) 395-1066
info@atomiccomics.com
www.atomiccomics.com
(a-k,r,t,u,w,1-5)

The Comic Island
21840 North 43rd St.
Phoenix, AZ 85050
PH: (480) 419-1554
FAX: (602) 528-4150
www.thecomicisland.com
(a,b)

Charlie's Comic Books
5445 E. 22nd Street #115
Tucson, AZ 85711-5405
PH: (520) 320-0279
charlie@charliescomics.com
charlie85705@aol.com
www.charliescomics.com
(a-l,r,t,u,w,x,z,2,4,5)

ARKANSAS

The Comic Book Store
9307 Treasure Hill
Little Rock, AR 72227
PH: (501) 227-9777
cbsrock@swbell.net
(a-g,i,j,n,r,t,u,w,x,1-5)

Collector's Edition
3217 John F. Kennedy Blvd.
North Little Rock, AR 72116
PH: (501) 791-4222
cbsrock@swbell.net
(a-g,i,j,n,r,t,u,w,x,1-5)

CALIFORNIA

Beach Ball Comics
3024-G West Ball Road
Anaheim, CA 92804
PH: (714) 826-6127
sales@beachballcomics.com
www.beachballcomics.com
(a-d,f,j,k,l,p-s,u,w,x,z,1-4)

Metropolis Comics
16509 Bellflower Blvd.
Bellflower, CA 90706
PH: (562) 263-0277
FAX: (562) 461-9131
metropolis@metrohero.com
www.metrohero.com
(a-j,l,r,t,u,w,z,1-5)

LA Comic Con
Bruce Schwartz
224 East Orange Grove Ave.
Burbank, CA 91502
PH: (818) 954-8432
info@comicbookscifi.com
www.comicbookscifi.com
(a-h,j-m,s-u,w-z,1-5)

Bunky Brothers
1243 Broadway Ave
Burlingame, CA 94010
PH: (909) 941-6402
bunky@BunkyBrothers.info
www.bunkybrothers.com
(a-c,m,s,x,3,4)

Profiles in History
26901 Agoura Rd. Ste. 150
Calabasas Hills, CA 91301
PH: (800) 942-8856
www.ProfilesinHistory.com
(m,s,3,4)

Crush Comics
2869 Castro Valley Blvd.
Castro Valley, CA 94546
PH: (510) 581-4779
crushcomics@yahoo.com
(b-d,f,g,i,j,r,t,u,3-5)

Collectors Ink
2593 State Hwy. 32
Chico, CA 95973
PH: (530) 345-0958
beverly@collectorsink.com
www.collectorsink.com
(a-g,i,r,t,u,w,x,1-5)

Comic Ink
7980 Amador Valley Blvd.
Dublin, CA 94568
PH: (925) 829-5572
lenstoys@sbcglobal.net
(b-f,r,s,u,w,x,2-4)

HighQualityComics.com
1106 2nd St., #110
Encinitas, CA 92024
PH: (800) 682-3936
FAX: (760) 723-7269
E-Mail: customerservice
@HighQualityComics.com
Web:
www.HighQualityComics.com
(a-f,j-m,p-u,w,x,2-4)

Treasure Island Comics
40819 Fremont Blvd.
Fremont, CA 94538
PH: (510) 770-1168
FAX: (510) 770-1168
a@treasureislandcomics.com
www.treasureislandcomics.com
(b-d,f,q,u,w)

Geoffrey's Comics
15900 Crenshaw Blvd.
Gardena, CA 90249
PH: (310) 538-3198
FAX: (310) 538-1114
geoffreyscomics@yahoo.com
www.geoffreyscomics.com
(a-d,f,l,n,p)

Legacy 1
123 W. Wilson Ave.
Glendale, CA 91203
PH: (818) 247-8803
FAX: (818) 247-2328
Legacycomics@hotmail.com
www.Legacycomics.com
(a-k,r,t,u,w,x,2-5)

Fantasy Books & Games
2247 First St.
Livermore, CA 94550
PH: (925) 449-5233
FAX: (925) 449-3061
FBANDG@aol.com
(a-j,o,r,t,u,w,x,4,5)

The Comic Cellar
505 S. Myrtle Ave.
Monrovia, CA 91016
PH: (626) 358-1808
comiccellar@comiccellar.com
www.comiccellar.com
(a-f,j,l,m,r,w,4)

West Coast Fantasy
23901-B Sunnymead Blvd.
Moreno Valley, CA 92553
PH/FAX: (951) 924-7866
westcoastfantasy@verizon.net
(b-d,f,g,r,t,u,w,x,z,3-5)

Comic Collector Shop
167 E. El Camino Real
Mountain View, CA 94040
PH: (650) 965-8272
FAX: (650) 965-9753
www.comiccollectorshop.com

Lee's Comics
1020-F N. Rengstorff Ave.
Mountain View, CA 94043
PH: (650) 965-1800
Lee@LCOMICS.com
www.LCOMICS.com
(a-j,l,n,o,q,r,t,u,w,x,1-5)

ComicStore.com
212 9th Street Suite 215
Oakland, CA 94607
PH: (510) 821-2431
info@comicstore.com
spideysweb@gmail.com
www.comicstore.com

Dr. Comics & Mr. Games
4014 Piedmont Ave.
Oakland, CA 94611
PH: (510) 601-7800
FAX: (510) 601-1371
drcomics@earthlink.net
(a-d,f-j,l,n,q,r,u,w,2,5)

Terry's Comics
Buying All 10¢ & 12¢
original priced comics
P.O. Box 2065
Orange, CA 92859
PH: (714) 288-8993 or
Hotline: (800) 938-0325
FAX: (714) 288-8992
info@terryscomics.com
www.terryscomics.com
(a,b,d-h,m,n,q)

San Diego Comics
6937 El Cajon Blvd.
San Diego, CA 92115
PH: (619) 698-1177
RockofEasy@aol.com
www.san-diego-comics.com
(a-f,p)

Amazing Adventures
3115 Vicente St.
San Francisco, CA 94116
PH: (415) 661-1344
FAX: (415) 661-1694
orders@
amazing-adventures.com
(a-g,i,l,m,o,q,t-x,2,4,5)

Amazing Fantasy
650 Irving St.
San Francisco, CA 94122
PH: (415) 681-4344
amazingfantasy00@aol.com
www.amazingfantasy.com
(a-g,l-o,r,t,u,w,x,2-5)

Lee's Comics
2222 S. El Camino Real
San Mateo, CA 94403
PH: (650) 571-1489
mark@LCOMICS.com
www.LCOMICS.com
(a-j,l,n,o,q,r,t,u,w,x,1-5)

**Hi De Ho Comics & Books
with Pictures**
1st Floor, Plaza de los Comics
525 Santa Monica Blvd.
Santa Monica, CA 90401-2409
PH: (310) 394-2820
info@hideho.com
www.hideho.com
www.hideho.net
(a-g,j-u,w,x,z,1-4)

Mega City Comics & Toys
1784 Erringer Rd.
Simi Valley, CA 93065
PH: (805) 583-3027
PH: Toll-Free (866) 936-6843
MegaCityComicsAndToys
@yahoo.com
(a-z,1-5)

Ralph's Comic Corner
2379 E. Main St.
Ventura, CA 93003
PH: (805) 653-2732
ralph@ralphscomiccorner.com
www.ralphscomiccorner.com
(a-f,j,l,r,t,w)

Blue Chip Collectibles
P.O. Box 4328
West Hills, CA 91307
PH: (818) 271-8678
email@BlueChipCollectibles.com
www.BlueChipCollectibles.com

Comics Unlimited
16344 Beach Blvd.
Westminster, CA 92683
PH: (714) 841-6646
FAX: (714) 841-2407
comics@comicsunlimited.com
www.comicsunlimited.com
(a-g,i,j,l,r,t,u,w,x,1-5)

Collector's Paradise
7131 Winnetka Ave.
Winnetka, CA 91306
PH/FAX: (888) 999-9455
collectorsparadise@socal.rr.com
http://comicsandcards.net
(b,d,f-j,q,r,t,u,w,x,2-5)

All The Good Stuff
861 Gray Ave. Suite P
Yuba City, CA 95991
PH: (530) 671-5344
FAX: (530) 671-5308
(d-g,i,q,t,2-5)

**Colorado Coins, Cards &
Comics**
6695 Wadsworth Blvd.
Arvada, CO 80003
PH: (303) 425-0924
FAX: (303) 425-4826
tblcollectibles@yahoo.com
www.tblcollectibles.com
(a-j,t,u,w,4,5)

All C's Collectibles
1250 S. Abilene St.
Aurora, CO 80012
PH: (303) 751-6882
FAX: (303) 695-7827
ALLCS@comcast.net
www.AllCsCollectibles.com
(a-g,i,l,r,t,u,w,x,2-5)

Time Warp Comics & Games
3105 28th Street
Boulder, CO 80301
PH: (303) 443-4500
FAX: (303) 443-1379
timewarp1@time-warp.com
www.time-warp.com
(a-k,r-u,w,x,2-5)

RTS Unlimited, Inc.
P. O. Box 150412
Lakewood, CO 80215-0412
PH: (303) 403-1840
FAX: (303) 403-1837
rtsunlimited@earthlink.net
www.RTSUnlimited.com
(a-f)

The Bookie
155 Burnside Avenue
East Hartford, CT 06108
PH: (860) 289-1208
halthebookie@sbcglobal.net
(a-g,j-l,n-r,t,u,w,3,4)

Matt's Sportscards & Comics
169 Elm Street
Enfield, CT 06082
PH: (860) 749-8702
mattssportscardsandcomics
@cox.net
www.myspace.com/
mattscollectibles
(a-g,j,k,m,o,r,t-z,3-5)

Sarge's Comics Etc.
124 State Street
New London, CT 06320
PH: (860) 443-2004
sarge@sargescomics.com
www.sargescomics.com
(a-l,p-r,u,w-z,1-5)

Showcase New England
Dan Greenhalgh
67 Gail Drive
Northford, CT 06472
PH: (203) 484-4579
FAX: (203) 484-4837
comics@showcasene.com

Wonderland Comics
112 Main Street Ste. 15
Putnam, CT 06260
PH: (860) 963-1027
FAX: (860) 935-0000
wonderlandcomics@aol.com
www.wonderlandcomics.com
(a-j,l,q-s,u,w,x,1-5)

DJ's Comics
1171 North Colony Road
Wallingford, CT 06492
PH: (203) 294-1576
djscomics@snet.net
(a-d,f-i,r,u,w,z,2,4,5)

Beav's Comics
124 West Main Streeet
Middletown, DE 19709
PH: (302) 449-5581
FAX: (302) 449-5578
beavs_comics@comcast.net
www.beavs-comics.com
(d,f,g,j,r,u,w,5)

The Comic Book Shop
1711 Marsh Road
Smyrna, DE 19810
PH: (302) 477-1119
FAX: (302) 477-0645
comicshop@
thecomicbookshop.com
www.thecomicbookshop.com
(a-g,l,r,t,u,w,x,1-5)

The Comics Club
714 W. Lumsden Rd.
Brandon, FL 33511
PH: (813) 653-4111
mail@comicsclub.com
www.comicsclub.com
(b-d,f-i,u,w)

Pedigree Comics, Inc.
13678 Plaza Mayor Drive
Delray Beach, FL 33446
PH: (561) 496-7667
FAX: (561) 496-7667
E-Mail: DougSchmell
@pedigreecomics.com
www.pedigreecomics.com

Samuel Frazer
11005 Lakeland Circle
Fort Myers, FL 33913
PH/FAX: (239) 768-0649
sfrazer457@aol.com
(a,b,o)

Collector's Comics
2547 S. Federal Highway
Fort Pierce, FL 34982
PH/FAX: (772) 465-5750
collectorscomics@bellsouth.net
www.collectorscomics.net
(a-i,m-o,q,r,u,w,x,z,3-5)

Paul Dyroff Comics
P.O. Box 953972
Lake Mary, FL 32795
PH: (321) 368-3993
FAX: (407) 688-2768
pdyroff@cfl.rr.com
www.paulscollectibles.com
(a-c,e,l-p,s,t,v,x)

Demolition Comics IV
1404 Seminole Blvd.
Largo, FL 33770
PH: (727) 581-7600
info@demolitioncomics.com
www.demolitioncomics.com
(a-j,r-u,w,x,2-5)

Tate's Comics + Toys
+ Videos + More
4566 North University Drive
Lauderhill, FL 33351
PH: (954) 748-0181
FAX: (954) 578-3949
emailus@tatescomics.com
www.tatescomics.com
(a-m,q-s,u,w-z,1-5)

Phil's Comic Shoppe
6512 West Atlantic Blvd.
Margate, FL 33063
PH: (954) 977-6947
philscomix@worldnet.att.net
(b-f,l,m,u,w,5)

CGC
P.O. Box 4738
Sarasota, FL 34230
PH: (877) NM-Comic
FAX: (941) 360-2558
www.scgccomics.com

David T. Alexander Collectibles
P.O. Box 273086
Tampa, FL 33618
PH: (813) 968-1805
FAX: (813) 264-6226
davidt@cultureandthrills.com
www.dtacollectibles.com
(a-c,e,l-o,r,s)

Demolition Comics I
4049 S. Dale Mabry Hwy
Tampa, FL 33611
PH: (813) 832-2692
FAX: (813) 681-9071
info@demolitioncomics.com
www.demolitioncomics.com
(a-j,l,r-u,w,x,2-5)

Demolition Comics II
4149 West Waters Ave.
Tampa, FL 33614
PH: (813) 885-5171
FAX: (813) 681-9071
info@demolitioncomics.com
www.demolitioncomics.com
(a-j,l,r-u,w,x,2-5)

Demolition Comics III
2564 E. Fowler Ave.
Tampa, FL 33612
PH: (813) 866-1780
info@demolitioncomics.com
www.demolitioncomics.com
(a-j,r-u,w,x,2-5)

GEORGIA
Oxford Comics
2855 Piedmont Rd.
Atlanta, GA 30305
PH: (404) 233-8682
(a-z,1-5)

Tales of Wonder
3037 Summer Oak Place
Buford, GA 30518
PH: (770) 904-2221
service@talesofwonder.com
www.talesofwonder.com
(a-e,j,q,u,3,4)

Odin's
360 Killian Hill Rd.
Suite G-5
Lilburn, GA 30047
PH: (770) 923-0123
www.odinscomics.com
(a-i,r,t,u,w,x,5)

Odin's
2100-C Fountain Square
Snellville, GA 30078
PH: (770) 413-0123
www.odinscomics.com
(a-i,r,t,u,w,x,1-5)

ILLINOIS
Graham Crackers Comics
77 E. Madison St.
Chicago, IL 60622
PH: (312) 629-1810
FAX: (312) 629-1812
patrick@grahamcrackers.com
www.grahamcrackers.com

The Paper Escape
205 West First Street
Dixon, IL 61021
PH: (815) 284-7567
E-Mail: paperescape
@paperescape.com
www.paperescape.com
(d,f-k,p-r,t,u,w,x,z,1,3,4)

GEM Comics
125 W. First St.
Elmhurst, IL 60126
PH: (630) 833-8787
(b-d,f-j,r,u,5)

Stand-Up Comics
3249 Ridge Road
Lansing, IL 60438
PH: (708) 474-6880
E-Mail: standupguys@
stand-upcomics.com
www.stand-upcomics.com
(b-d,f,w,x,4,5)

Dreamland Comics
105 W. Rockland Rd.
Libertyville, IL 60048
PH: (847) 680-0727
info@dreamland-comics.com
www.dreamland-comics.com
(b-d,f-j,r,t,u,w,4,5)

Alien Entertainment
543 E. Roosevelt Road
Lombard, IL 60148
PH: (888) 734-7386
FAX: (630) 261-9888
cs@alienentertainmentstore.com
www.alienentertainmentstore.com

Al N' Ann's Collectibles
3819 W. Main
McHenry, IL 60050
PH: (815) 344-9696
al@alnanns.com
www.alnanns.com
(b-d,f,g,i,r-u,w,x,2,4,5)

Calliope's Realm Comics
133 S. Washington St.
Inside A-1 Antiques
Naperville, IL 60540
PH: (630) 420-7710
calliopescomics@gmail.com
www.calliopes.net
(a-d,f,g,i,j,m,o,t,u,w,1-5)

Graham Crackers Comics
1271 Rickert Drive
Naperville, IL 60540
PH: (630) 355-4310
mikewall@grahamcrackers.com
www.grahamcrackers.com

One Stop Comics
111 South Ridgeland
Oak Park, IL 60302
PH: (708) 524-2287
www.onestopcomics.net

Mellow Blue Planet
2212 5th Ave.
Rock Island, IL 61201
PH/FAX: (309) 788-1653
E-Mail: mellowblueplanet
@hotmail.com
(a-f,i,j,l,o,r-u,w,x,z,2-5)

Dreamland Comics
1415 W. Schaumburg Rd.
Schaumburg, IL 60194
PH: (847) 524-6060
Laurie@dreamlandcomics.com
www.dreamlandcomics.com
(b-j,r,t,u,w,x,1-5)

Comics Galore
1058 Hillgrove Ave.
Western Springs, IL 60558
PH: (708) 784-3300
(b-d,f,g,i,r,t,w,2-5)

INDIANA
The Book Broker
2717 Covert Ave.
Evansville, IN 47714
PH: (812) 479-5647
FAX: (812) 473-8196
BBR1975@aol.com
(a-k,p,t,u,w-z,5)

Comics Ina Flash
P.O. Box 3611
Evansville, IN 47735-3611
PH: (812) 401-6127
comicflash@aol.com
www.comicsinaflash.com

Books, Comics & Things
5936 W. Jefferson Blvd.
Fort Wayne, IN 46804
PH: (260) 431-4999
bct@bctcomics.com
www.bctcomics.com

Books, Comics & Things
2212 Maplecrest Rd.
Fort Wayne, IN 46815
PH: (260) 493-6116
bct@bctcomics.com
www.bctcomics.com

Superherogameland
2212 Maplecrest Rd.
Fort Wayne, IN 46815
PH: (260) 493-6116
support
@superherogameland.com
www.superherogameland.com

Comic Carnival East
9729 East Washington St.
Indianapolis, IN 46229
PH/FAX: (317) 898-5010
ComicCarnivale@aol.com
www.ComicCarnival.com
(a-l,n,q-u,w,x,z,1-5)

Comic Carnival North
7225 N. Keystone Avenue
Indianapolis, IN 46240
PH: (317) 253-8882
FAX: (317) 257-1450
www.ComicCarnival.com
(a-k,p-u,w,z,2,5)

Comic Carnival
Southport Centre
7311 U.S. 31 South
Indianapolis, IN 46227
PH: (317) 889-8899
www.ComicCarnival.com
(a-o,q-u,w-z,1-5)

Comic Carnival West
3837 N. High School Rd.
Suite #7
Indianapolis, IN 46254
PH/FAX: (317) 293-4386
ComicCarnivalw@aol.com
www.ComicCarnival.com
(a-k,r,t,u,w,x,5)

Lightspeed Hobbies
5884 U.S. Hwy 6
In the Portage Commons
Portage, IN 46368
PH/FAX: (219) 764-7314
customerservice
@lightspeedhobbies.com
www.lightspeedhobbies.com
(d,f-i,r,u,w,5)

IOWA
Mayhem Comics and Games
2532 Lincoln Way
Ames, IA 50014
PH/FAX: (515) 292-3510
shop@mayhemcomics.com
www.mayhemcomics.com
(a-l,r-u,w,x,1,4,5)

Majestic Comics, Ltd.
7100 NE 16th Ct.
Ankeny, IA 50021
PH: (515) 480-4451
E-Mail:majcomic@mchsi.com
majcomic.home.mchsi.com
(a-c,e,f,j,k,n,p,s,z)

KANSAS

B•Bop Comics & Games
5336 W. 95th Street
Prairie Village, KS 66217
PH: (913) 383-1777
(a-n,p-u,w,x,z,1-5)

KENTUCKY

The Great Escape
2945 Scottsville Rd.
Bowling Green, KY 42104
PH: (270) 782-8092
TGE@bellsouth.net
www.TheGreatEscapeOnline.com
(a-i,k-p,r-u,w-z,1-5)

Dale Roberts
PO Box 707
Calvert City, KY 42029
PH: (270) 395-9832
buycomics@aol.com

Comic Book World, Inc.
7130 Turfway Rd.
Florence, KY 41042
PH: (859) 371-9562
FAX: (859) 371-6925
comicbw@one.net
www.comicbookworld.com
(a-j,l,n,o,r,t,u,w,1-5)

Comic Book World, Inc.
6905 Shepherdsville Rd.
Louisville, KY 40219
PH: (502) 964-5500
FAX: (502) 964-5500
comicbw@one.net
www.comicbookworld.com
(a-j,l,n,o,r,t,u,w,1-5)

The Great Escape
2433 Bardstown Rd.
Louisville, KY 40205
PH: (502) 456-2216
TGE@bellsouth.net
www.TheGreatEscapeOnline.com
(a-l,p,r-u,w-z,1-5)

Leroy Harper
P.O. Box 212
West Paducah, KY 42086
PH: (270) 748-9364
LHCOMICS@hotmail.com

MAINE

Top Shelf Comics
25 Central St.
Bangor, ME 04401
PH: (207) 947-4939
topshelf@tcomics.com
www.tcomics.com
(a,b,c,d,e,f,u)

Casablanca Comics
151 Middle St.
Portland, ME 04101
PH: (207) 780-1676
FAX: (207) 253-1536
E-Mail: comics@
casablancacomics.com
www.casablancacomics.com
(a-j,l,q,r,u,w,x,5)

Casablanca Comics
778 Roosevelt Trail
Rich Plaza
Windham, ME 04062
PH: (207) 892-0056
FAX: (207) 253-1536
casablancawind@aol.com
www.casablancacomics.com
(b-d,f-j,q,r,w,x,5)

MARYLAND

E. Gerber
1720 Belmont Ave.; Suite C
Baltimore, MD 21244

Esquire Comics.com
Mark S. Zaid, ESQ.
P.O. Box 3422492
Bethesda, MD 20827
PH: (202) 498-0011
esquirecomics@aol.com
www.esquirecomics.com
(b-k,r,u,w,4,5)

Alternate Worlds
72 Cranbrook Road
Yorktowne Plaza
Cockeysville, MD 21030
PH: (410) 666-3290
altworldstore@att.net
(b-j,r,u,w,x,2,4,5)

Comics To Astonish Inc.
9400 Snowden River Pkwy.
Columbia, MD 21045
PH: (410) 381-2732
comics2u@aol.com
www.comicstoastonish.com
(a-k,m,r,t,u,w,z,2,3,5)

Washington Street Books
131 North Washington St.
Havre De Grace, MD 21078
PH: (410) 939-6215
E-Mail: washbks@erols.com
www.washingtonstreetbooks.com

Comic Classics
365 Main Street
Laurel, MD 20707
PH: (301) 490-9811
(a-g,j,l,r-u,w,x,3-5)

**Aardvarks Videos, Comics &
Games**
300 Clubhouse Dr.
Lusby, MD 20657
PH: (410) 394-6366
Theanteater@mac.com
www.theanteater.net
(b-k,t,u,w,x,z,2,4,5)

Aardvarks Comics & Games
29015 Three Notch Road
Mechanicsville, MD 20659
PH: (301) 884-0488
Theanteater@mac.com
www.theanteater.net
(b-k,r,t,u,w,x,z,2,4,5)

Cards, Comics & Collectibles
100-A Chartley Drive
Reisterstown, MD 21136
PH: (410) 526-7410
FAX: (410) 526-4006
E-Mail: cardscomicscollectibles
@yahoo.com
(a-g,j,l,o,r,t,u,w,x,z,2-5)

Diamond Comic Distributors
1966 Greenspring Drive
Timonium, MD 21093
PH: (800) 45-COMIC

Diamond Select Toys
1966 Greenspring Drive
Suite 402
Timonium, MD 21093

Game Trader Magazine
1966 Greenspring Dr.; Ste 300
Timonium, MD 21093
PH: (410) 560-7100
FAX: (410) 560-7589
sandrew@diamondcomics.com
www.gametrademagazine.com

MASSACHUSETTS

New England Comics, Inc.
131 Harvard Avenue
Allston, MA 02134
PH: (617) 783-1848
office@newenglandcomics.com
www.newenglandcomics.com
(b-l,r,t,u,w,x,z,1-5)

New England Comics, Inc.
744 Crescent St.
East Crossing Plaza
Brockton, MA 02302
PH: (508) 559-5068
office@newenglandcomics.com
www.newenglandcomics.com
(b-k,r,t,u,w,x,z,1-5)

New England Comics, Inc.
316 Harvard St.
Coolidge Corner
Brookline, MA 02446
PH: (617) 566-0115
office@newenglandcomics.com
www.newenglandcomics.com
(b-l,r,t,u,w,x,z,1-5)

New England Comics, Inc.
14 A Eliot Street
Cambridge, MA 02138
PH: (617) 354-5352
office@newenglandcomics.com
www.newenglandcomics.com
(b-l,r,t,u,w,x,z,1-5)

Gary Dolgoff
116 Pleasant St.
Easthampton, MA 01027
PH: (413) 529-0326
FAX: (413) 529-9824
gary@garydolgoffcomics.com
www.garydolgoffcomics.com

That's Entertainment II
C. A. P. Plaza
56 John Fitch Highway
Fitchburg, MA 01420
PH: (978) 342-8607
fitch@thatse.com
www.thatse.com
(a-u,w,x,z,1-5)

Jerry Weist
18 Edgemoor Rd.
Gloucester, MA 01930
PH: (978) 283-1419
jerryweist@adelphia.net

New England Comics, Inc.
95 Pleasant St.
Malden, MA 02148
PH: (781) 322-2404
office@newenglandcomics.com
www.newenglandcomics.com
(a-k,r,t,u,w,x,z,1-5)

Harrison's Comics
3850 Mystic Valley Parkway
Medford, MA 02155
PH: (781) 391-6111
harrisonscomics@hotmail.com
www.harrisonscomicsltd.com
(b-j,q,r,t,u,w,x,z,1-4)

New England Comics, Inc.
732 Washington Street
Norwood, MA 02062
PH: (781) 769-4552
office@newenglandcomics.com
www.newenglandcomics.com
(b-k,r,t,u,w,x,z,1-5)

New England Comics, Inc.
1511 Hancock St.
Quincy, MA 02169
PH: (617) 770-1848
office@newenglandcomics.com
www.newenglandcomics.com
(a-k,r,t,u,w,x,z,1-5)

Bill Cole Enterprises Inc.
P.O. Box 60, Dept. 01
Randolph, MA 02368-0060
PH: (781) 986-2653
FAX: (781) 986-2656
bcemylar@cwbusiness.com
www.bcmylar.com

**Harrison's Comics &
Collectibles**
252 Essex St.
Salem, MA 01970
PH: (978) 741-0786
FAX: (978) 741-0737
harrisonscomics@hotmail.com
www.harrisonscomicsltd.com
(a-j,l,m,o,w-z,1-5)

Monkeyhouse Entertainment
28 Elm St. (Rt. 110)
Salisbury, MA 01952
PH: (978) 504-9068
monkeyhouse55@aol.com
monkeyhouseentertainment.com
(a-g,j,k,l,n,w,y)

Web-Head Enterprises
239 North Ave.
Wakefield, MA 01880
PH: (781) 246-1797
emcity@verizon.net
www.webheadenterprises.com
(a-g,i,p,r,t,u,w-z,1-5)

The Outer Limits
463 Moody St.
Waltham, MA 02453
PH: (781) 891-0444
askOuterLimits@aol.com
www.myspace.com/eouterlimits
(a-j,l-x,z,1-5)

SuperWorld Comics.com
Ted Vanliew
P.O. Box 20924
Worcester, MA 01602
PH: (508) 754-0792
lvanliew@aol.com
Superworldcomics.com

That's Entertainment
244 Park Avenue (Rt. 9)
Worcester, MA 01609
PH: (508) 755-4207
ken@thatse.com
www.thatse.com
(a-z,1-5)

Comics North!
425 N. Main Street
Cheboygan, MI 49721-1546
PH: (231) 627-3740
(b-f,h-j,r,s,w,z,1,3)

Motor City Comics
33228 W. 12 Mile Rd.
PMB 286
Farmington Hills, MI 48334
PH: (248) 426-8059
FAX: (248) 426-8064
orders@MotorCityComics.com
www.MotorCityComics.com
(a-c,e,l-o,v,w,x,4)

Detroit Comics
23333 Woodward
Ferndale, MI 48220
PH: (248) 548-COMX(2669)
DetroitComics@excite.com
www.DetroitComics.com

Comix Corner
32004 Utica Road
Fraser, MI 48026
PH: (586) 296-2758
(c,d,f,r,u,w,5)

Tardy's Collector's Corner, Inc.
2009 Eastern Ave. S.E.
Grand Rapids, MI 49507
PH: (616) 247-7828
tccorner@iserv.net
www.tardys.com
(a-f,j-m,p-r,u,w,x,5)

**Fanfare Sports
/Entertainment, Inc.**
4415 S. Westnedge Ave.
Kalamazoo, MI 49008
PH: (269) 349-8866
info@fanfare-se.com
www.fanfare-se.com
(a-k,m,r,t,u,w-z,1-5)

Harley Yee Comics
P.O. Box 51758
Livonia, MI 48151-5758
PH: (800) 731-1029
FAX: (734) 421-7928
HarleyComx@aol.com
www.HarleyYeeComics.com

Comics Archives Inc.
25650 Plymouth Rd.
Redford, MI 48239
PH: (313) 937-8860
FAX: (313) 937-9663
CArchives@twmi.rr.com
www.ComicsArchives.com
(b-d,f,r,t)

Comix Corner
861 E. Auburn Rd.
Rochester Hills, MI 48307
PH: (248) 852-3356
(c,d,f,r,u,w,5)

Bob's Comics
26030 Groesbeck
Warren, MI 48089
PH: (586) 779-4130
bobscomics@sbcglobal.net
(a-g,j-l,r,s,u,w,x,z,1-5)

Nostalgia Zone
3149-1/2 Hennepin Ave. South
Minneapolis, MN 55406
PH: (612) 822-2806
order@nostalgiazone.com
www.nostalgiazone.com
(a-c,e,f,j-t,v,x,2)

Midway Book & Comic
1579 University Ave.
St. Paul, MN 55104
PH: (651) 644-7605
FAX: (651) 644-8786
(a-f,n-p)

Ken Stribling
P.O. Box 16004
Jackson, MS 39236-6004
PH: (601) 977-5254
kenstrib@was.net

B•Bop Comics & Games
3940 Main Street
Kansas City, MO 64111
PH: (816) 753-BBOP(2267)
(a-n,p-u,w,x,z,1-5)

Clint's Comics
3941 Main Street
Kansas City, MO 64111
PH: (816) 561-2848
jimc@clintscomics.com
www.clintscomics.com
(a-g,j-l,n,o,q-s,u,w-z,1-5)

Friendly Frank's Comic Cavern
5404 NW 64th St.
Kansas City, MO 64151
PH: (816) 746-4569
(a-m,p,r,t,u,w,x,z,1-5)

Castle Collectables
3504 S. 22nd St.
St. Joseph, MO 64503
PH: (816) 261-4038
galactus@gimail.af.mil
d,f-i,t,u,w,z,2-5)

**Robert Beerbohm
Comic Art**
P.O. Box 507
Fremont, NE 68026
PH: (402) 727-4071
Robert@BLBComics.com
www.BLBComics
(a,b,c,e,l-o,r)

Ground Zero Hobby
794 Fort Crook Rd. S
Omaha, NE 68005
PH/FAX: (402) 292-3750
gzbellevue@cox.net
www.gzbellevue.com
(b-i,p,w,x,4,5)

Ground Zero Hobby
4601 S. 50th St. #103
Omaha, NE 68117
PH/FAX: (402) 733-7212
gzomaha@cox.net
www.gzomaha.com
(b-i,t,u,w,4,5)

Krypton Comics
2819 S. 125th Ave.
Suite 261
Omaha, NE 68144
PH: (402) 391-4131
dean@kryptoncomicsomaha.com
www.kryptoncomicsomaha.com

Redbeard's Book Den
P.O. Box 217
Crystal Bay, NV 89402
PH: (775) 831-4848
FAX: (775) 831-4483
www.redbeardsbookden.com
(a,b,c,l,o,p)

Rare Books & Comics
James F. Payette
P.O. Box 750
Bethlehem, NH 03574
PH: (603) 869-2097
FAX: (603) 869-3475
JimPayette@msn.com
(a,b,c,e,n,o,p)

Jetpack Comics LLC
112 Portland Street
Rochester, NH 03867
PH: (603) 330-9636
info@jetpackcomics.com
www.jetpackcomics.com

Nathan Rose
34 First Avenue
Denville, NJ 07828
PH: (973) 462-5981
comicart@natesgreat.com

NeatStuffCollectilbes.com
Michael Carbonaro
66 Grand Avenue
Englewood, NJ 07631
PH: (718) 326-2713
E-Mail: neatstuffcollectibles
@yahoo.com
www.NeatStuffCollectibles.com

The Joker's Child
12-23 River Road
Ground Floor
Fair Lawn, NJ 07410
PH: (201) 794-6830
FAX: (201) 794-3379
ost@jokerschild.com
www.jokerschild.com
(a-g,i,j,q,t,u,w,x,1-5)

ZAPP! Comics
3710 Rt. 9 South
Freehold Raceway Mall
Freehold, NJ 07728
PH: (732) 866-6655
zappcomics@aol.com
www.zappcomics.com
(a-g,i,j,r,t,u,w,x,z,2,4,5)

The Comic Book Store
30 N. Main Street
Glassboro, NJ 08028
PH: (856) 442-0402
alex@theComicBookStore.net
www.theComicBookStore.net
(b-d,f-i,l)

Hot Flips
22 E. Lafayette St.
Hackensack, NJ 07601
PH: (800) 922-3547
FAX: (201) 488-5813
hotflipsnj@yahoo.com
www.hotflips.com
(f,i)

Traders of Babylon
265 1st St.
Hoboken, NJ 07030
PH: (201) 659-0802
babylon@pipeline.com
www.romanceart.biz
(a-f,j-m,r,w,5)

Ralph DeLuca
157 Park Ave.
Madison, NJ 07940
PH: (800) 392-4050
PH(outside USA):
(973) 377-1007
FAX: (973) 377-4020
ralph@ralphdeluca.com
www.ralphdeluca.com

Main St. Comics & Toys
74 N. Main St.
Milltown, NJ 08850
PH: (732) 828-7886
mscomics@aol.com
www.myspace.com/mscomics
(a-g,i,l,r,t,u,w,x,4,5)

J&S Comics
168 W. Sylvania Ave.
Neptune, NJ 07753
PH: (732) 988-5717
jandscomics@aol.com

Fat Jack's Comicrypt
521 White Horse Pike
Oaklyn, NJ 08107
PH: (856) 858-3877
FAX: (215) 963-9361
fatjacks@comcast.net
(a-l,r,t,u,w,x,z,5)

J&S Comics
Jim Walsh
98 Madison Avenue
Red Bank, NJ 07701
PH: (732) 988-5717
jandscomics@aol.com
www.jscomics.com

All-Star Auctions
Nadia Mannarino
122 West End Avenue
Ridgewood, NJ 07450
PH: (201) 652-1305
FAX: (501) 325-6504
nadia@allstarauctions.net
www.allstarauctions.net

Commuter Comics
50 West South Orange Ave.
South Orange, NJ 07079
PH: (973) 762-6666
commutercomics@aol.com
www.commutercomics.com
(a-h,j-l,q,r,t,u,w,x,2-5)

ZAPP! Comics
574 Valley Road
Wayne, NJ 07470
PH: (973) 628-4500
FAX: (973) 628-1771
zappcomics@aol.com
www.zappcomics.com
(a-g,i,j,r,t,u,w,x,z,2,4,5)

JHV Associates
(By Appointment Only)
P. O. Box 317
Woodbury Heights, NJ 08097
PH: (856) 845-4010
FAX: (856) 845-3977
JHVassoc@hotmail.com
(a,b,n,s)

NEW MEXICO

**True Believers Comics
& Gallery**
801-B Cerrillos Rd.
Santa Fe, NM 87505
PH: (505) 992-TRUE
kevin@true-believers.com
www.true-believers.com
(a-d,f,g,j-m,r,u,w,x,2,4,5)

NEW YORK

Silver Age Comics
22-55 31 St.
Astoria, NY 11105
PH: (718) 721-9691
PH: (800) 278-9691
FAX: (718) 728-9691
gus@silveragecomics.com
www.silveragecomics.com
(a-g,j-o,r,t,u,w,x,z,2-4)

Excellent Adventures Comics
110 Milton Ave. (Rt. #50)
Ballston Spa, NY 12020
PH: (518) 884-9498
(a-i,m-o,r,u-w,3-5)

Lil' Joe's Comics & Candy
7012 15th Ave.
Brooklyn, NY 11228
PH: (347) 645-9619
DKNY9666@aol.com
(b,d-g,r,t,u,w,2)

Pinocchio Collectibles
1814 McDonald Ave.
(off Ave. P)
Brooklyn, NY 11223
PH: (718) 645-2573
(b-f)

St. Mark's Comics
148 Montague St.
Brooklyn, NY 11201
PH: (718) 935-0911
(a-g,j,l,o,q,r,t,u,w,x,1-5)

Conrad Eschenberg
Route 1, Box 204-A
Cold Spring, NY 10516
PH: (914) 265-2649
comicart@pcrealm.net
www.comicsnart@pcrealm.net

HighGradeComics.com
17 Bethany Drive
Commack, NY 11725
PH: (631) 543-1917
FAX: (631) 864-1921
E-Mail: BobStorms@
HighGradeComics.com
www.HighGradeComics.com
(a,b,c)

Tomorrow's Treasures
P.O. Box 925
Commack, NY 11725
PH/FAX: (631) 543-5737
comics@tomorrowstreasures.com
www.tomorrowstreasures.com.

Fantasy-Comics
P.O. Box 732
Goldens Bridge NY 10526
PH: (914) 301-5252
FAX: (914) 232-3027
buying@fantasy-comics.com
www.Fantasy-Comics.com

Comicollectors.net
Marnin Rosenberg
P.O. Box 2047
Great Neck, NY 11022
PH: (516) 466-8147
www.comiccollectors.net
www.collectorsassemble.com

The Comic Depot, LLC
2538 Route 9N
Stewart's Plaza
Greenfield Center, NY 12833
PH/FAX: (518) 893-2900
comicdep@comicdepotLLC.com
www.comicdepotLLC.com
(a-d,f-i,r,s,u,w,5)

Comics For Collectors, Inc.
207 N. Aurora St.
Ithaca, NY 14850
PH: (607) 272-3007
comics@ComicsForCollectors.com
www.ComicsForCollectors.com

Mahopac Cards & Comics
P.O. Box 444
1000 Miller Road Plaza
Mahopac, NY 10541
PH: (845) 621-2699
FAX: (845) 621-6719
mahopaccards@aol.com
www.mahopaccards.com
(d,f,g,i,t,u,w,2,4,5)

Ravenswood Inc.
8451 Seneca Turnpike
New Hartford, NY 13413
PH: (315) 735-3699
FAX: (315) 735-3204
E-Mail:ravenswoodcomics
@verizon.net
www.ravenswoodcomics.com
(a-j,m,q-u,w,x,1-5)

Best Comics
1300 Jericho Turnpike
New Hyde Park, NY 11040
PH: (516) 328-1900
TommyBest@aol.com
www.bestcomics.com
(a-f,u,w,x,3-5)

Jericho Comics
1300 Jericho Turnpike
New Hyde Park, NY 11040
PH: (516) 328-1900
TommyBest@aol.com
www.bestcomics.com
(a-d,f,u,w,x,3-5)

Cosmic Comics
10 East 23rd Street
New York, NY 10010
PH: (212) 460-5322
FAX: (212) 260-4304
comixink@aol.com
www.cosmiccomics.com
(a-f,j,l,m,o,t,u,w,z,1-5)

Metropolis
873 Broadway
Suite 201
New York, NY 10003
PH: (800) 229-6387
FAX: (212) 260-4304
E-Mail: buying@
metropoliscomics.com
www.metropoliscomics.com

Midtown Comics
459 Lexington Ave.
(Corner of 45th Street)
New York, NY 10017
PH: (212) 302-8192
info@midtowncomics.com
www.midtowncomics.com

Midtown Comics
200 West 40th Street
(Corner of 7th Ave, 2nd floor)
New York, NY 10018
PH: (212) 302-8192
info@midtowncomics.com
www.midtowncomics.com

St. Mark's Comics
11 St. Mark's Place
New York, NY 10003
PH: (212) 598-9439
FAX: (212) 477-1294
(a-g,j,l,o,q,r,t,u,w,x,z,1-5)

**House of Fantasy Comics
& Games**
1709 Pine Ave.
Niagara Falls, NY 14301-2231
PH: (716) 282-8838
HofFantasy@aol.com
(b-l,r-u,w,x)

Bags Unlimited, Inc.
7 Canal St.
Rochester, NY 14608
PH: (800) 767-2247
FAX: (585) 328-8526
info@bagsunlimited.com
www.bagsunlimited.com

Amazing Comics
12 Gillette Ave.
Sayville, NY 11782
PH: (631) 567-8069
info@amazingco.com
www.amazingco.com
(a-g,r,t,u,w)

Alternate Realities
700 Central Park Avenue
Scarsdale, NY 10583
PH: (914) 723-7950
info@alternaterealities.com
www.alternaterealities.com
(b-g,i,j,r,t,u,w,x,4,5)

Four Color Comics
Rob Rogovin
P.O. Box 1399
Scarsdale, NY 10583
PH: (914) 722-4696
keybooks@aol.com

Paragon Comics, LLC
1243 Kings Road
Schenectady, NY 12303
PH: (518) 346-4578
FAX: (480) 393-5720
info@paragoncomics.com
www.paragoncomics.com
(a-d,m,w,1-5)

Fourth World Comics
33 Route 111
Smithtown, NY 11787
PH: (631) 366-4440
fourgle@aol.com
www.fourthworldcomics.com

Long Island Comics
672 Sunrise Hwy.
West Babylon, NY 11704
PH: (631) 321-4822 after 2 PM
Frank@licomics.com
www.licomics.com
(b-f)

NORTH CAROLINA

Ultimate Chapel Hill Comics
1322 Fordham Blvd.
Hwy 15-501
Chapel Hill, NC 27514
PH/FAX: (919) 960-8107
UltimateComicsOnline
@yahoo.com
www.UltimateComicsOnline.com
(a-g,j,l,m,r,u,w,x,4,5)

Ultimate Comics
105 West Hwy 54 #229
Durham, NC 27713
PH: (919) 806-8282
FAX: (919) 960-8107
UltimateComicsOnline
@yahoo.com
www.UltimateComicsOnline.com
(b-d,f,g,j,q,t,u,w,x,2,4,5)

Ultimate Comics Northgate
1058 West Club Blvd.
Durham, NC 27701
PH: (919) 286-4737
FAX: (919) 960-8107
UltimateComicsOnline
@yahoo.com
www.UltimateComicsOnline.com
(d,f,g,j,r,t,u,w,x,4,5)

Acme Comics
2150 Lawndale Dr.
Greensboro, NC 27408
PH: (336) 574-2263
www.AcmeComics.com
(a-d,f,r,u,w,x,5)

Sidekick Comics and Magazines
3210 Springs Rd. NE
Hickory, NC 28601
PH: (828) 256-1030
SidekickComicsAndMagazines
@yahoo.com
www.SidekickComicsAnd
Magazines.com
(d-g,i,q,r,t,u,w)

The Hobby Shop
Wilson Mall
1501 Ward Blvd.
Wilson, NC 27893
PH: (252) 291-3384
FAX: (252) 291-5149
info@thehobbyshopofwilson.com
www.thehobbyshopofwilson.com
(b-d,f-k,p-r,t,u,w,4,5)

NORTH DAKOTA

Barry's Collector Corner
1826 S. Washington St.
Grand Cities Mall
Grand Forks, ND 58201
PH: (701) 795-1386
UNDBKB@aol.com
(a-j,l,m,o,p,s-y,2-5)

OHIO

Up Up & Away!
4016 Harrison Avenue
Cincinnati, OH 45211
PH: (513) 661-6300
FAX: (513) 661-6312
kendall@upupandawaycomics.com
www.upupandawaycomics.com
(a-j,m,r,u,w,2-5)

Fearless Readers Comics
1613 Huffman Ave.
Dayton, OH 45403
PH: (937) 252-3036
FearlessReadersComics
@yahoo.com
(a-f,l,o)

Bookery Fantasy
16 West Main St.
Fairborn, OH 45324
PH: (937) 879-1408
FAX: (937) 879-9327
E-Mail:BookeryFan@aol.com
www.BookeryFantasy.com
(a-l,n-u,w,x,z,1-5)

Parker's Records & Comics
1222 Suite C Rt. 28
Milford, OH 45150
PH: (513) 575-3665
FAX: (513) 575-3665
E-Mail: dkparker39@fuse.net
www.parkersrc.com
(b-i,y)

Monarch Comics
4400 Heatherdowns
Toledo, OH 43614
PH: (419) 382-1451
(b-d,f,g,r,t,u,w,x,5)

OKLAHOMA

All Star Comics
6900 N. May Ave. #10
Oklahoma City, OK 73116
PH/FAX: (405) 842-7800
wgreenewood@cox.net
(a-h,l,n,o,s,w,1-5)

Comic Empire of Tulsa
3122 S. Mingo Road
Tulsa, OK 74146
PH: (918) 664-5808
(a-f,l)

Gardner's Used Books & Comics Inc.
4421 S. Mingo Rd.
Tulsa, OK 74146
PH: (918) 627-7323
FAX: (918) 250-8828
rgardnergtsgub@coxinet.net
(a-f,i-k,n,p,s,t,w-z,2-4)

Mammoth Comics
4616 E. 11 St.
Tulsa, OK 74112
PH: (918) 836-9636
mammothcomics@gmail.com
www.mammothcomics.com
(a-g,i,r,t,u,w,x,5)

Want List Comics
(Appointment Only)
P.O. Box 701932
Tulsa, OK 74170
PH: (918) 299-0440
E-Mail: wlc777@cox.net
(a,b,c,m,n,o,s,t,x,3)

OREGON

Emerald City Comics
770 E 13th
Eugene, OR 97401
PH: (541) 345-2568
(c,d,f-k,r,w,x,z,5)

Nostalgia Collectibles
527 Willamette Street
Eugene, OR 97401
PH: (541) 484-9202
darrell7g@comcast.net
(a-g,i-u,w-y,2-5)

PENNSYLVANIA

Beachead Comics
1601 W. Chew St.
Allentown, PA 18102
PH: (610) 437-6372
BeachCom@aol.com
www.beacheadcomics.com
(a-g,i,j,l,o-u,w,x,1-4)

Dreamscape Comics
302 W. Broad St.
Bethlehem, PA 18018
PH: (610) 867-1178
nyutko@ptd.net
www.DreamscapeComics.com
(b-j,l,n,p,q,t,u,w-z,1,3-5)

New Dimension Comics
Clear View Mall
101 Clear View Circle
Butler, PA 16001
PH: (724) 282-5283
butler@ndcomics.com
(a-z,1-5)

New Dimension Comics
20550 Route 19,
Piazza Plaza
Cranberry Township, PA
16066
PH: (724) 776-0433
cranberry@ndcomics.com
(a-z,1-5)

New Dimension Comics
516 Lawrence Ave.
Ellwood City, PA 16117
PH: (724) 758-2324
ec@ndcomics.com
(a-z,1-5)

Comic Universe
446 MacDade Blvd.
P.O. Box 246
Folsom, PA 19033
PH: (610) 461-7960
chessflink@yahoo.com
www.comicuniverse.net
(a-g,j,k,m,p-r,t,u,w,x,z,1-5)

The Comic Store
28 McGovern Ave.
Lancaster, PA 17602
PH: (717) 397-8737
FAX: (717) 397-8903
comicstore@juno.com
www.comicstorepa.com

Tropic Comics
John Chruscinski
18 Chesapeake St.
Lyndora, PA 16045
PH: (724) 283-7800
Zepp68@bellsouth.net
www.tropiccomics.com
(a-c,e,j,l-t,w-z,2-4)

New Dimension Comics
113 East McMurray Road
McMurray, PA 15317
PH: (724) 941-5445
colin@ndcomics.com
(a-z,1-5)

Comix Connection - Mechanicsburg
6200 Carlisle Pike Suite C
Mechanicsburg, PA 17050
PH: (717) 591-2727
Bill@comixconnection.com
www.comixconnection.com
(b-j,r,t,u,w,5)

Flynn's Comics
212 Chestnut Lane
North Wales, PA 19454
PH: (215) 260-6284
purchasing@FlynnsComics.com
www.FlynnsComics.com

Comics And Paperbacks Plus
201 East Main Street
Palmyra, PA 17078
PH: (717) 838-4854
ralph@
comicsandpaperbacksplus.com
www.comicsandpaperbacksplus.com
(a-f,j,p,r,x,4,5)

Fat Jack's Comicrypt
2006 Sansom St.
Philadelphia, PA 19103
PH: (215) 963-0788
FAX: (215) 963-9361
fatjacks@comcast.net
(a-g,j,l,r,t,u,w,5)

Ontario Street Comics
2235 E. Ontario St.
Philadelphia, PA 19134
PH: (215) 288-7338
wfink27240@aol.com
(b-d,f-h,j,p,r,t,u,v,w,2-5)

Duncan Comics, Books & Accessories
1047 Perry Highway
Pittsburgh, PA 15237
PH: (412) 635-0886
DuncanBooks@aol.com
www.DuncanComics.com
(a-g,n-p,r,t,u,w,x,1-5)

Eide's Entertainment
1121 Penn Ave.
Pittsburgh, PA 15222
PH: (412) 261-0900
FAX: (412) 261-3102
eides@eides.com
www.eides.com
(a-g,i-z,1-5)

Dave's American Comics
Buying All 10¢ & 12¢
original priced comics
P.O. Box 8198
Radnor, PA 19087-8198
PH: (610) 275-8817 or
Hotline: (800) 938-0325
FAX: (714) 288-8992
davesamerican@earthlink.net
www.terryscomics.com
(a,b,d-h,m,n,q)

Village Games, Comics & Books
13 Market Plaza
Reinholds, PA 17569
PH: (717) 484-4314
dbowen@ptd.net
http://stores.ebay.com/
Village-Games
(a-j,n,p,q,x,1-5)

New Dimension Comics
Pittsburgh Century III Mall
3075 Clairton Rd. #940
West Mifflin, PA 15213
PH: (412) 655-8661
ndccentury3@verizon.net
(a-z,1-5)

Comic Store West
2111 Industrial Hwy.
York, PA 17402
PH: (717) 845-9198
Bstoner@comicstorewest.com
www.comicstorewest.com
(d,f,h,t)

Comix Connection - York
West Manchester Mall
1800 Loucks Rd., Suite 688
York, PA 17408
PH: (717) 767-4871
Ned@comixconnection.com
www.comixconnection.com
(b-j,r,t,u,w,5)

Hake's Americana
3679 Concord Rd.
York, PA 17402
PH: (866) 404-9800
www.hakes.com

RHODE ISLAND

The Time Capsule
537 Pontiac Ave.
Cranston, RI 02910
PH: (401) 781-5017
E-Mail: ryeremian@aol.com
(a-z,1-5)

Fantasy Zone Comics
7610 Post Road
North Kingston, RI 02852
PH: (401) 294-6044
FZComics@ids.net
(b-f,p,u)

Shadowland Comics & Collectibles
2025 Smith St.
North Providence, RI 02911
PH/FAX: (401) 349-4611
ShadowlandComics@cox.net
www.ShadowlandComics.com
(b-g,i,r,w,x,5)

SOUTH CAROLINA

Planet Comics
2704 N. Main St.
Anderson, SC 29621
PH: (864) 261-3578
planetcomics@gmail.com
www.planetcomics.net
(a-l,o-u,w,x,z,1-5)

Heroes and Dragons
510 Bush River Rd.
Columbia, SC 29210
PH: (803) 731-4376
chris@HeroesandDragons.com
www.HeroesandDragons.com

Green Dragon, Inc.
7671 Northwoods Blvd.
Ste. 5-T
North Charleston, SC 29406
PH: (843) 797-2052
adrianabc@bellsouth.net
www.greendragoninc.net
(c-l,n,p,r,u,w,y,z,1-5)

TENNESSEE

Dewayne's World - Comics & Games
459 E. Sullivan Street
Kingsport, TN 37660
PH/FAX: (423) 247-8997
dewayne@dewaynes-world.com
(a-d,f-i,r,u,w,x,4,5)

The Great Escape
111B N. Gallatin Rd.
Madison, TN 37115
PH: (615) 865-8052
TGE@bellsouth.net
www.TheGreatEscapeOnline.com
(a-p,r-u,w-z,1-5)

The Great Escape
1925 Broadway
Nashville, TN 37203
PH: (615) 327-0646
TGE@bellsouth.net
www.TheGreatEscapeOnline.com
(a-p,r-u,w-z,1-5)

TEXAS

Lone Star Comics
511 E. Abram St.
Arlington, TX 76010
PH: (817) 860-7827
FAX: (817) 860-2769
lonestar@lonestarcomics.com
www.mycomicshop.com/
overstreet
(a-j,n,q,u-x,1-5)

Capstone Comics
2121 W. Parmer Ln. #107
Austin, TX 78727
PH: (512) 339-4251
FAX: (512) 339-3635
info@capstonecomics.com
www.capstonecomics.com
(a-d,f,g,r,s,u,w,x,2,4,5)

Comic Heaven
P.O. Box 900
Big Sandy, TX 75755
PH: (903) 636-5555

Big World Comics
1104 E. Beltline Rd. #104
Carrollton, TX 75006
PH: (972) 245-0968
bigworld@flash.net
www.BigWorldComics.com
(b-i,l,r,s,u,w,4,5)

Classics Incorporated
Matt Nelson
P.O. Box 600263
Dallas, TX 75360
PH: (214) 459-1866
Spectre52@aol.com

Heritage Auction Galleries
3500 Maple Avenue
17th Floor
Dallas, TX 75219-3941
PH: (800) 872-6467
www.HA.com

Titan Comics
3701 W. Northwest Hwy #125
Dallas, TX 75220
PH: (214) 350-4420
info@titancomics.com
www.titancomics.com

Duncanville Bookstore
101 W. Camp Wisdom Rd.
Suite J
Duncanville, TX 75116
PH: (972) 298-7546
FAX: (972) 298-1777
AndyMac2570@aol.com
www.DuncanvilleBookstore.com
(a-f,p,r,u,w-y,4)

Bill Hughes' Vintage Collectables
P.O. Box 270244
Flower Mound, TX 75027
PH: (972) 539-9190
FAX: (973) 432-4070
Whughes199@yahoo.com
www.vintagecollectables.net

The Comic Asylum
4750 N. Jupiter Rd. #112
Garland, TX 75044
PH: (972) 414-7760
inmates@thecomicasylum.com
www.thecomicasylum.com
(c,d,f-i,l,m,r,5)

Bedrock City Comic Co.
6517 Westheimer
Houston, TX 77057
PH: (713) 780-0675
www.bedrockcity.com
(a-g,j-o,r-x,z,1-5)

Bedrock City Comic Co.
4683 FM1960 West
Houston, TX 77069
PH: (281) 444-9763
www.bedrockcity.com
(a-g,j-o,r-x,z,1-5)

Bedrock City Comic Co.
10910 Old Katy Rd.
Houston, TX 77043
PH: (713) 365-0063
www.bedrockcity.com
(c-g,j-m,r-x,z,1-5)

Third Planet
2718 Southwest Freeway
Houston, TX 77098
PH: (713) 528-1067
TJ@third-planet.com
www.third-planet.com
(a-z,1-5)

M&M Comic Service
3128 Hidden Haven St.
San Antonio, TX 78261
PH: (830) 438-6131
service@mmcomics.com
www.mmcomics.com
(b,c,d,j,k,l,q,u,w,z,1-4)

Ground Zero Comics
1700 SSE Loop 323, Suite 302
Tyler, TX 75701
PH: (903) 566-1185
info@groundzerocomics.com
www.groundzerocomics.com
(b-h,j,r,u,w,3-5)

Bedrock City Comic Co.
106 W. Bay Area Blvd.
Webster, TX 77598
PH: (281) 557-2748
www.bedrockcity.com
(a-g,j-o,r-x,z,1-5)

VIRGINIA

Destination Comics
601 Concord Ave.
Charlottesville, VA 22903
PH: (434) 296-9007
destinationcomics@gmail.com
www.myspace.com/
destinationcomics
(b-d,f-k,r,u,w,x,z,2,5)

Trilogy Shop #2
700 E. Little Creek Rd.
Norfolk, VA 23518
PH: (757) 587-2540
FAX: (757) 587-5637
trilogy2@TrilogyComics.net
www.TrilogyComics.net
(d,f-j,w,5)

B & D Comic Shop
802 Elm Avenue SW
Roanoke, VA 24016
PH: (540) 342-6642
FAX: (540) 342-6694
bdcomics1@verizon.net
www.banddcomics.com
(c,d,f,r,w,5)

NOVA Comics
6324 Springfield Plaza
Springfield, VA 22150
PH: (703) 912-6682
novacomics@verizon.net
www.novacomics.com
(a-d,f,r,t,u,w,2-5)

Trilogy Comics #1
5773 Princess Anne Rd.
Virginia Beach, VA 23462
PH: (757) 490-2205
FAX: (757) 671-7721
trilogy1@TrilogyComics.net
www.TrilogyComics.net
(a-j,n-p,r-u,w,x,4,5)

WASHINGTON
PGC Mint
Mark Wilson
PO Box 340
Castle Rock, WA 98611
PH: (360) 274-9163
FAX: (360) 274-2270
pgcmintsales@aol.com
www.pgcmint.com

Dreamstrands Comics, Inc.
115 N. 85th St.
Seattle, WA 98103
PH: (206) 297-3737
www.dreamstrands.com
(b-d,f,g,i,j,r,t,u,w,x,3-5)

Golden Age Collectables
1501 Pike Place Market
401 Lower Level
Seattle, WA 98101
PH: (206) 622-9799
FAX: (206) 622-9595
GACollect@aol.com
www.GoldenAgeCollectables.com
(a-o,q-x,z,1-5)

Zanadu Comics
1923 3rd Ave.
Seattle, WA 98101-1104
PH: (206) 443-1316
FAX: (206) 443-0652
zanadu@zanaducomics.com
www.zanaducomics.com
(d-f,j-l,q,r,u,w,x,z,1-5)

WEST VIRGINIA
Comic World
1204 - 4th Avenue
Huntington, WV 25701
PH: (304) 522-3923
(a-f,l,r,w,5)

WISCONSIN
1st Appearance Comics
W730 State Road 35
Fountain City, WI 54629
PH: (608) 687-7572
FAX: (608) 687-7573
joe@1stappearance.com
www.1stappearance.com
(a-c,w,x,4)

Capital City Comics
1910 Monroe St.
Madison, WI 53711
PH: (608) 251-8445
(a-f,j-u,w-z,4,5)

Jef Hinds Comics
PO Box 44803
Madison, WI 53744-4803
PH: (800) 791-3037
www.jhcomics.com
(a,b,c,f)

Westfield Comics
8608 University Green
PO Box 620470
Middleton, WI 53562-0470
www.westfieldcomics.com

AUSTRALIA
Gold Coast Comics
8 Longview Court
Nerang, Queensland 4211
PH: 07 5502 0523
kingoil@hotmail.com

CANADA
ALBERTA
Another Dimension
424B - 10 St. NW
Calgary, Alberta T2N 1V9
PH: (403) 283-7078
FAX: (403) 283-7080
E-Mail: comics@
another-dimension.com
www.another-dimension.com
(a-f,j,l,m,q,r,u,w,x,z,2-4)

BRITISH COLUMBIA
Golden Age Collectables
852 Granville St.
Vancouver, B.C., V6Z 1K3
PH: (604) 683-2819
www.gacvan.com
(a-o,q-u,w,x,z,1-5)

MANITOBA
Doug Sulipa's Comic World
Box 21986
Steinbach, MB., R5G 1B5
PH: (204) 346-3674
FAX: (204) 346-1632
E-Mail: cworld@mts.net
www.dougcomicworld.com
(a-c,e,l,n,o,p,r,s,t,y,z,1,3,4)

Raven Toys, Comics & Games
214 St. Mary's Rd.
Winnipeg, MB., R2H 1J3
PH: (204) 231-8354
ravenscomics@mts.net
www.manitobacomiccon.com
(a-m,p-r,t,u,w,x,1-5)

NOVA SCOTIA
Monster Comic Lounge
2091 Gottingen St.
Halifax, Nova Scotia B3K 3B2
PH: (902) 429-2398
mcrossman@ns.sympatico.ca
(b-d,f-j,u,w,3-5)

ONTARIO
Fantasy Realm
227 Pitt St.
Cornwall, ONT. K6J 3P8
PH/FAX: (613) 933-7997
fantasyrlm@glen-net.ca
www.fantasyrealm.ca
(b-e,t,w,3,4)

Big B Comics
1045 Upper James St.
Hamilton, ONT. L9C 3A6
PH: (905) 318-9636
FAX: (905) 318-9055
mailbox@bigbcomics.com
www.bigbcomics.com
(a-g,i,j,q,r,u,w,x,2-5)

B.A.'s Comics
426 Hamilton Road
London, ONT. N5Z 1R9
PH: (519) 439-9636
ba.lm@rogers.com
(a-f,l,n)

L.A. Mood Comics and Games
350 Richmond St.
London, ONT. N6A 3C3
PH: (519) 432-3987
mailbox@lamoodcomics.com
www.lamoodcomics.blogspot.
com
(a-o,r,t,u,w,x,1-5)

Fan Expo Canada
Aman Gupta
38 Riverlea Dr.
Toronto, Ontario M9P 2H4
PH: (416) 241-7827
FAX: (416) 241-6827
agupta@hobbystar.com
www.FanExpoCanada.com

Paradise Comics
Peter Dixon
3278 Yonge St.
Toronto, ONT. M4N 2L6
PH: (416) 487-9807
FAX: (416) 487-9907
paradisecomics@on.aibn.com
www.paradisecomics.com

Pendragon Comics
3759 Lakeshore Boulevard West
Toronto, ONT M8W 1R1
PH: (416) 253-6974
pendragoncomics@rogers.com
www.pendragoncomics.com
(a-l,t,u,w,5)

3RD Quadrant Comics
468 Spadina Rd.
Toronto, ON
PH: (416) 974-9211
idamahn@yahoo.com
www.3rdquadrantcomics.com

QUEBEC
Boite à B.D.
3161B Dagenais Ouest
Laval, QC H7P 1T8
PH: (450) 628-9917
FAX: (450) 628-7126
johnnycomix@arobas.net
(c,d,f-j,l,p-u,w,x,2-5)

Heroes Comics
1116 Cure LaBelle
Laval, QC H7V 2V5
PH: (450) 686-9155
FAX: (450) 686-2097
E-Mail: heroes@dsuper.net

Carsleys Comics
1117 St. Catherine St. West,
Suite #917
Montreal, QC, H3B 1H9
PH: (514) 843-3365
FAX: (514) 289-9332
carsleyscomics@vendio.com
www.carsleyscomics.com
(a-f,j,l,o)

ENGLAND
Silver Acre Comics
P.O. Box 114
Chester CH4 8WQ
England UK
PH: 01244680048
FAX: 01244680686
International phone:
+441244680048
sales@silveracre.com
www.silveracre.com

GERMANY
Fantastic Store
Koelner Str. 64
Kommern, NRW 53894
PH: 0049-2443-911554
FAX: 0049-2443-911966
fantasticstore@t-online.de
(a-d,f-h,j,k,r,u,w,z,2-4)

INTERNET
**ComicLink Auctions &
Exchange**
PH: (718) 246-0300
buysell@ComicLink.com
www.ComicLink.com

John Haines Rare Comics
PH: (216) 390-0129
E-Mail: jhrc@roadrunner.com
eBay Store: John Haines Rare
Comics

Koop's Comics
PH: (301) 752-6857
E-Mail:
dr.koop@koopscomics.com
www.koopscomics.com

M&M Comic Service
PH: (830) 438-6131
service@mmcomics.com
www.previewscatalog.com
www.mmcomics.com
(d,j,k,l,q,t,u,w,x,z,1-5)

a - Story art; a(i) - Story art inks; a(p) - Story art pencils; a(r) - Story art reprint.

ADULT MATERIAL - Contains story and/or art for "mature" readers. Re: sex, violence, strong language.

ADZINE - A magazine primarily devoted to the advertising of comic books and collectibles as its first publishing priority as opposed to written articles.

ALLENTOWN COLLECTION - A collection discovered in 1987-88 just outside Allentown, Pennsylvania. The Allentown collection consisted of 135 Golden Age comics, characterized by high grade and superior paper quality.

ANNUAL - (1) A book that is published yearly; (2) Can also refer to some square bound comics.

ARRIVAL DATE - The date written (often in pencil) or stamped on the cover of comics by either the local wholesaler, newsstand owner, or distributor. The date precedes the cover date by approximately 15 to 75 days, and may vary considerably from one locale to another or from one year to another.

ASHCAN - A publisher's in-house facsimile of a proposed new title. Most ashcans have black and white covers stapled to an existing coverless comic on the inside; other ashcans are totally black and white. In modern parlance, it can also refer to promotional or sold comics, often smaller than standard comic size and usually in black and white, released by publishers to advertise the forthcoming arrival of a new title or story.

ATOM AGE - Comics published from 1946-1956.

B&W - Black and white art.

BACK-UP FEATURE - A story or char-acter that usually appears after the main feature in a comic book; often not featured on the cover.

BAD GIRL ART - A term popularized in the early '90s to describe an attitude as well as a style of art that portrays women in a sexual and often action-oriented way.

BAXTER PAPER - A high quality, heavy, white paper used in the printing of some comics.

BC - Abbreviation for Back Cover.

BI-MONTHLY - Published every two months.

BI-WEEKLY - Published every two weeks.

BONDAGE COVER - Usually denotes a female in bondage.

BOUND COPY - A comic that has been bound into a book. The process requires that the spine be trimmed and sometimes sewn into a book-like binding.

BRITISH ISSUE - A comic printed for distribution in Great Britain; these copies sometimes have the price listed in pence or pounds instead of cents or dollars.

BRITTLENESS - A severe condition of paper deterioration where paper loses its flexibility and thus chips and/or flakes easily.

BRONZE AGE - Comics published from 1970 to 1984.

BROWNING - (1) The aging of paper characterized by the ever-increasing level of oxidation characterized by darkening; (2) The level of paper deterioration one step more severe than tanning and one step before brittleness.

c - Cover art; c(i) - Cover inks; c(p) - Cover pencils; c(r) - Cover reprint.

CAMEO - The brief appearance of one character in the strip of another.

CANADIAN ISSUE - A comic printed for distribution in Canada; these copies sometimes have no advertising.

CCA - Abbreviation for Comics Code Authority.

CCA SEAL - An emblem that was placed on the cover of all CCA approved comics beginning in April-May, 1955.

CENTER CREASE - See Subscription Copy.

CENTERFOLD or **CENTER SPREAD** - The two folded pages in the center of a comic book at the terminal end of the staples.

CERTIFIED GRADING - A process provided by a professional grading service that certifies a given grade for a comic and seals the book in a protective Slab.

CF - Abbreviation for Centerfold.

CFO - Abbreviation for Centerfold Out.

CGC - Abbreviation for the certified comic book grading company, Comics Guaranty, LLC.

CIRCULATION COPY - See Subscription Copy.

CIRCULATION FOLD - See Subscription Fold.

CLASSIC COVER - A cover considered by collectors to be highly desirable because of its subject matter, artwork, historical importance, etc.

CLEANING - A process in which dirt and dust is removed.

COLOR TOUCH - A restoration process by which colored ink is used to hide color flecks, color flakes, and larger areas of missing color. Short for Color Touch-Up.

COLORIST - An artist who paints the color guides for comics. Many modern colorists use computer technology.

COMIC BOOK DEALER - (1) A seller of comic books; (2) One who makes a living buying and selling comic books.

COMIC BOOK REPAIR - When a tear, loose staple or centerfold has been mended without changing or adding to the original finish of the book. Repair may involve tape, glue or nylon gossamer, and is easily detected; it is considered a defect.

COMICS CODE AUTHORITY - A voluntary organization comprised of comic book publishers formed in 1954 to review (and possibly censor) comic books before they were printed and distributed. The emblem of the CCA is a white stamp in the upper right hand corner of comics dated after February 1955. The term "post-Code" refers to the time after this practice started, or approximately 1955 to the present.

COMPLETE RUN - All issues of a given title.

CON - A convention or public gathering of fans.

CONDITION - The state of preservation of a comic book, often inaccurately used interchangeably with Grade.

CONSERVATION - The European Confederation of Conservator-Restorers' Organizations (ECCO) in its professional guidelines, defines conservation as follows: "Conservation consists mainly of direct action carried out on cultural heritage with the aim of stabilizing condition and retarding further deterioration."

COPPER AGE - Comics published from 1984 to 1992.

COSMIC AEROPLANE COLLECTION - A collection from Salt Lake City, Utah discovered by Cosmic Aeroplane Books, characterized by the moderate to high grade copies of 1930s-40s comics with pencil check marks in the margins of inside pages. It is thought that these comics were kept by a commercial illustration school and the check marks were placed beside panels that instructors wanted students to draw.

COSTUMED HERO - A costumed crime fighter with "developed" human powers instead of super powers.

COUPON CUT or COUPON MISSING - A coupon has been neatly removed with scissors or razor blade from the interior or exterior of the comic as opposed to having been ripped out.

COVER GLOSS - The reflective quality of the cover inks.

COVER TRIMMED - Cover has been reduced in size by neatly cutting away rough or damaged edges.

COVERLESS - A comic with no cover attached. There is a niche demand for coverless comics, particularly in the case of hard-to-find key books otherwise impossible to locate intact.

C/P - Abbreviation for Cleaned and Pressed. See Cleaning.

CREASE - A fold which causes ink removal, usually resulting in a white line. See Reading Crease.

CROSSOVER - A story where one character appears prominently in the story of another character. See X-Over.

CVR - Abbreviation for Cover.

DEALER - See Comic Book Dealer.

DEACIDIFICATION - Several different processes that reduce acidity in paper.

DEBUT - The first time that a character appears anywhere.

DEFECT - Any fault or flaw that detracts from perfection.

DENVER COLLECTION - A collection consisting primarily of early 1940s high grade number one issues bought at auction in Pennsylvania by a Denver, Colorado dealer.

DIE-CUT COVER - A comic book cover with areas or edges precut by a printer to a special shape or to create a desired effect.

DISTRIBUTOR STRIPES - Color brushed or sprayed on the edges of comic book stacks by the distributor/wholesaler to code them for expedient exchange at the sales racks. Typical colors are red, orange, yellow, green, blue, and purple. Distributor stripes are not a defect.

DOUBLE - A duplicate copy of the same comic book.

DOUBLE COVER - When two covers are stapled to the comic interior instead of the usual one; the exterior cover often protects the interior cover from wear and damage. This is considered a desirable situation by some collectors and may increase collector value; this is not considered a defect.

DRUG PROPAGANDA STORY - A comic that makes an editorial stand about drug use.

DRUG USE STORY - A comic that shows the actual use of drugs: needle use, tripping, harmful effects, etc.

DRY CLEANING - A process in which dirt and dust is removed.

DUOTONE - Printed with black and one other color of ink. This process was common in comics printed in the 1930s.

DUST SHADOW - Darker, usually linear area at the edge of some comics stored in stacks. Some portion of the cover was not covered by the comic immediately above it and it was exposed to settling dust particles. Also see Oxidation Shadow and Sun Shadow.

EDGAR CHURCH COLLECTION - See Mile High Collection.

EMBOSSED COVER - A comic book cover with a pattern, shape or image pressed into the cover from the inside, creating a raised area.

ENCAPSULATION - Refers to the

process of sealing certified comics in a protective plastic enclosure. Also see Slabbing.

EYE APPEAL - A term which refers to the overall look of a comic book when held at approximately arm's length. A comic may have nice eye appeal yet still possess defects which reduce grade.

FANZINE - An amateur fan publication.

FC - Abbreviation for Front Cover.

FILE COPY - A high grade comic originating from the publisher's file; contrary to what some might believe, not all file copies are in Gem Mint condition. An arrival date on the cover of a comic does not indicate that it is a file copy, though a copyright date may.

FIRST APPEARANCE - See Debut.

FLASHBACK - When a previous story is recalled.

FOIL COVER - A comic book cover that has had a thin metallic foil hot stamped on it. Many of these "gimmick" covers date from the early '90s, and might include chromium, prism and hologram covers as well.

FOUR COLOR - Series of comics produced by Dell, characterized by hundreds of different features; named after the four color process of printing. See One Shot.

FOUR COLOR PROCESS - The process of printing with the three primary colors (red, yellow, and blue) plus black.

FUMETTI - Illustration system in which individual frames of a film are colored and used for individual panels to make a comic book story. The most famous example is DC's *Movie Comics* #1-6 from 1939.

GATEFOLD COVER - A double-width fold-out cover.

GENRE - Categories of comic book subject matter; e.g. Science Fiction, Super-Hero, Romance, Funny Animal, Teenage Humor, Crime, War,

Western, Mystery, Horror, etc.

GIVEAWAY - Type of comic book intended to be given away as a premium or promotional device instead of being sold.

GLASSES ATTACHED - In 3-D comics, the special blue and red cellophane and cardboard glasses are still attached to the comic.

GLASSES DETACHED - In 3-D comics, the special blue and red cellophane and cardboard glasses are not still attached to the comic; obviously less desirable than Glasses Attached.

GOLDEN AGE - Comics published from 1938 (*Action Comics* #1) to 1945.

GOOD GIRL ART - Refers to a style of art, usually from the 1930s-50s, that portrays women in a sexually implicit way.

GREY-TONE COVER - A cover art style in which pencil or charcoal underlies the normal line drawing, used to enhance the effects of light and shadow, thus producing a richer quality. These covers, prized by most collectors, are sometimes referred to as Painted Covers but are not actually painted.

HC - Abbreviation for Hardcover.

HEADLIGHTS - Forward illumation devices installed on all automobiles and many other vehicles... OK, OK, it's a euphemism for a comic book cover prominently featuring a woman's breasts in a provocative way. Also see Bondage Cover for another collecting euphemism that has long since outlived its appropriateness in these politically correct times.

HOT STAMPING - The process of pressing foil, prism paper and/or inks on cover stock.

HRN - Abbreviation for Highest Reorder Number. This refers to a method used by collectors of Gilberton's *Classic Comics* and *Classics Illustrated* series to distin-

guish first editions from later printings.

ILLO - Abbreviation for Illustration.

IMPAINT - Another term for Color Touch.

INDICIA - Publishing and title information usually located at the bottom of the first page or the bottom of the inside front cover. In some pre-1938 comics and many modern comics, it is located on internal pages.

INFINITY COVER - Shows a scene that repeats itself to infinity.

INKER - Artist that does the inking.

INTRO - Same as Debut.

INVESTMENT GRADE COPY - (1) Comic of sufficiently high grade and demand to be viewed by collectors as instantly liquid should the need arise to sell; (2) A comic in VF or better condition; (3) A comic purchased primarily to realize a profit.

ISSUE NUMBER - The actual edition number of a given title.

ISH - Short for Issue.

JLA - Abbreviation for Justice League of America.

JSA - Abbreviations for Justice Society of America.

KEY, KEY BOOK or KEY ISSUE - An issue that contains a first appearance, origin, or other historically or artistically important feature considered especially desirable by collectors.

LAMONT LARSON - Pedigreed collection of high grade 1940s comics with the initials or name of its original owner, Lamont Larson.

LENTICULAR COVERS or "FLICKER" COVERS - A comic book cover overlayed with a ridged plastic sheet such that the special artwork underneath appears to move when the cover is tilted at different angles perpendicular to the ridges.

LETTER COL or LETTER COLUMN - A feature in a comic book that prints and sometimes responds to letters written by its readers.

LINE DRAWN COVER - A cover published in the traditional way where pencil sketches are overdrawn with india ink and then colored. See also Grey-Tone Cover, Photo Cover, and Painted Cover.

LOGO - The title of a strip or comic book as it appears on the cover or title page.

LSH - Abbreviation for Legion of Super-Heroes.

MAGIC LIGHTNING COLLECTION - A collection of high grade 1950s comics from the San Francisco area.

MARVEL CHIPPING - A bindery (trimming/cutting) defect that results in a series of chips and tears at the top, bottom, and right edges of the cover, caused when the cutting blade of an industrial paper trimmer becomes dull. It was dubbed Marvel Chipping because it can be found quite often on Marvel comics from the late '50s and early '60s but can also occur with any company's comic books from the late 1940s through the middle 1960s.

MILE HIGH COLLECTION - High grade collection of over 22,000 comics discovered in Denver, Colorado in 1977, originally owned by Mr. Edgar Church. Comics from this collection are now famous for extremely white pages, fresh smell, and beautiful cover ink reflectivity.

MODERN AGE - A catch-all term applied to comics published since 1992.

MYLAR™ - An inert, very hard, space-age plastic used to make high quality protective bags and sleeves for comic book storage. "Mylar" is a trademark of the DuPont Co.

ND - Abbreviation for No Date.

NN - Abbreviation for No Number.

NO DATE - When there is no date given on the cover or indicia page.

NO NUMBER - No issue number is given on the cover or indicia page; these are usually first issues or one-shots.

N.Y. LEGIS. COMM. - New York Legislative Committee to Study the Publication of Comics (1951).

ONE-SHOT - When only one issue is published of a title, or when a series is published where each issue is a different title (e.g. Dell's Four Color Comics).

ORIGIN - When the story of a character's creation is given.

OVER GUIDE - When a comic book is priced at a value over Guide list.

OXIDATION SHADOW - Darker, usually linear area at the edge of some comics stored in stacks. Some portion of the cover was not covered by the comic immediately above it, and it was exposed to the air. Also see Dust Shadow and Sun Shadow.

p - Art pencils.

PAINTED COVER - (1) Cover taken from an actual painting instead of a line drawing; (2) Inaccurate name for a grey-toned cover.

PANELOLOGIST - One who researches comic books and/or comic strips.

PANNAPICTAGRAPHIST - One possible term for someone who collects comic books; can you figure out why it hasn't exactly taken off in common parlance?

PAPER COVER - Comic book cover made from the same newsprint as the interior pages. These books are extremely rare in high grade.

PARADE OF PLEASURE - A book about the censorship of comics.

PB - Abbreviation for Paperback.

PEDIGREE - A book from a famous and usually high grade collection - e.g. Allentown, Lamont Larson, Edgar Church/Mile High, Denver, San Francisco, Cosmic Aeroplane, etc. Beware of non-pedigree collections being promoted as pedigree books; only outstanding high grade collections similar to those listed qualify.

PENCILER - Artist that does the pencils...you're figuring out some of these definitions without us by now, aren't you?

PERFECT BINDING - Pages are glued to the cover as opposed to being stapled to the cover, resulting in a flat binded side. Also known as Square Back or Square Bound.

PG - Abbreviation for Page.

PHOTO COVER - Comic book cover featuring a photographic image instead of a line drawing or painting.

PIECE REPLACEMENT - A process by which pieces are added to replace areas of missing paper.

PIONEER AGE - Comics published from the 1500s to 1828.

PLATINUM AGE - Comics published from 1883 to 1938.

POLYPROPALENE - A type of plastic used in the manufacture of comic book bags; now considered harmful to paper and not recommended for long term storage of comics.

POP - Abbreviation for the anti-comic book volume, Parade of Pleasure.

POST-CODE - Describes comics published after February 1955 and usually displaying the CCA stamp in the upper right-hand corner.

POUGHKEEPSIE - Refers to a large collection of Dell Comics file copies believed to have originated from the warehouse of Western Publishing in Poughkeepsie, NY.

PP - Abbreviation for Pages.

PRE-CODE - Describes comics published before the Comics Code Authority seal began appearing on covers in 1955.

PRE-HERO DC - A term used to describe More Fun #1-51 (pre-Spectre), Adventure #1-39 (pre-Sandman), and Detective #1-26 (pre-Batman). The term is actually inaccurate because technically there were "heroes" in the above books.

PRE-HERO MARVEL - A term used to describe *Strange Tales* #1-100 (pre-Human Torch), *Journey Into Mystery* #1-82 (pre-Thor), *Tales To Astonish* #1-35 (pre-Ant Man), and *Tales Of Suspense* #1-38 (pre-Iron Man).

PRESERVATION - Another term for Conservation.

PRESSING - A term used to describe a variety of processes or procedures, professional and amateur, under which an issue is pressed to eliminate wrinkles, bends, dimples and/or other perceived defects and thus improve its appearance. Some types of pressing involve disassembling the book and performing other work on it prior to its pressing and reassembly. Some methods are generally easily discerned by professionals and amateurs. Other types of pressing, however, can pose difficulty for even experienced professionals to detect. In all cases, readers are cautioned that unintended damage can occur in some instances. Related defects will diminish an issue's grade correspondingly rather than improve it.

PROVENANCE - When the owner of a book is known and is stated for the purpose of authenticating and documenting the history of the book. Example: A book from the Stan Lee or Forrest Ackerman collection would be an example of a value-adding provenance.

PULP - Cheaply produced magazine made from low grade newsprint. The term comes from the wood pulp that was used in the paper manufacturing process.

QUARTERLY - Published every three months (four times a year).

R - Abbreviation for Reprint.

RARE - 10-20 copies estimated to exist.

RAT CHEW - Damage caused by the gnawing of rats and mice.

RBCC - Abbreviation for Rockets Blast Comic Collector, one of the first and most prominent adzines instrumental in developing the early comic book market.

READING COPY - A comic that is in FAIR to GOOD condition and is often used for research; the condition has been sufficiently reduced to the point where general handling will not degrade it further.

READING CREASE - Book-length, vertical front cover crease at staples, caused by bending the cover over the staples. Square-bounds receive these creases just by opening the cover too far to the left.

REILLY, TOM - A large high grade collection of 1939-1945 comics with 5000+ books.

REINFORCEMENT - A process by which a weak or split page or cover is reinforced with adhesive and reinforcement paper.

REPRINT COMICS - In earlier decades, comic books that contained newspaper strip reprints; modern reprint comics usually contain stories originally featured in older comic books.

RESTORATION - Any attempt, whether professional or amateur, to enhance the appearance of an aging or damaged comic book using additive procedures. These procedures may include any or all of the following techniques: recoloring, adding missing paper, trimming, re-glossing, reinforcement, glue, etc. Amateur work can lower the value of a book, and even professional restoration has now gained a negative aura in the modern marketplace from some quarters. In all cases a restored book can never be worth the same as an unrestored book in the same condi-

tion. There is no consensus on the inclusion of pressing, non-aqueous cleaning, tape removal and in some cases staple replacement in this definition. Until such time as there is consensus, we encourage continued debate and interaction among all interested parties and reflection upon the standards in other hobbies and art forms.

REVIVAL - An issue that begins republishing a comic book character after a period of dormancy.

ROCKFORD - A high grade collection of 1940s comics with 2000+ books from Rockford, IL.

ROLLED SPINE - A condition where the left edge of a comic book curves toward the front or back; a defect caused by folding back each page as the comic was read.

ROUND BOUND - Standard saddle stitch binding typical of most comics.

RUN - A group of comics of one title where most or all of the issues are present. See Complete Run.

S&K - Abbreviation for the legendary creative team of Joe Simon and Jack Kirby, creators of Marvel Comics' Captain America.

SADDLE STITCH - The staple binding of magazines and comic books.

SAN FRANCISCO COLLECTION - (see Reilly, Tom)

SCARCE - 20-100 copies estimated to exist.

SEDUCTION OF THE INNOCENT - An inflammatory book written by Dr. Frederic Wertham and published in 1953; Wertham asserted that comics were responsible for rampant juvenile deliquency in American youth.

SET - (1) A complete run of a given title; (2) A grouping of comics for sale.

SEMI-MONTHLY - Published twice a month, but not necessarily Bi-Weekly.

SEWN SPINE - A comic with many

spine perforations where binders' thread held it into a bound volume. This is considered a defect.

SF - Abbreviation for Science Fiction (the other commonly used term, "sci-fi," is often considered derogatory or indicative of more "low-brow" rather than "literary" science fiction, i.e. "sci-fi television."

SILVER AGE - Comics published from 1956 to 1970.

SILVER PROOF - A black and white actual size print on thick glossy paper hand-painted by an artist to indicate colors to the engraver.

SLAB - Colloquial term for the plastic enclosure used by grading certification companies to seal in certified comics.

SLABBING - Colloquial term for the process of encapsulating certified comics in a plastic enclosure.

SOTI - Abbreviation for Seduction of the Innocent.

SPINE - The left-hand edge of the comic that has been folded and stapled.

SPINE ROLL - A condition where the left edge of the comic book curves toward the front or back, caused by folding back each page as the comic was read.

SPINE SPLIT SEALED - A process by which a spine split is sealed using an adhesive.

SPLASH PAGE - A Splash Panel that takes up the entire page.

SPLASH PANEL - (1) The first panel of a comic book story, usually larger than other panels and usually containing the title and credits of the story; (2) An oversized interior panel.

SQUARE BACK or SQUARE BOUND - See Perfect Binding.

STORE STAMP - Store name (and sometimes address and telephone number) stamped in ink via rubber stamp and stamp pad.

SUBSCRIPTION COPY - A comic sent through the mail directly from the publisher or publisher's agent. Most are folded in half, causing a subscription crease or fold running down the center of the comic from top to bottom; this is considered a defect.

SUBSCRIPTION CREASE - See Subscription Copy.

SUBSCRIPTION FOLD - See Subscription Copy. Differs from a Subscription Crease in that no ink is missing as a result of the fold.

SUN SHADOW - Darker, usually linear area at the edge of some comics stored in stacks. Some portion of the cover was not covered by the comic immediately above it, and it suffered prolonged exposure to light. A serious defect, unlike a Dust Shadow, which can sometimes be removed. Also see Oxidation Shadow.

SUPER-HERO - A costumed crime fighter with powers beyond those of mortal man.

SUPER-VILLAIN - A costumed criminal with powers beyond those of mortal man; the antithesis of Super-Hero.

SWIPE - A panel, sequence, or story obviously borrowed from previously published material.

TEAR SEALS - A process by which a tear is sealed using an adhesive.

TEXT ILLO. - A drawing or small panel in a text story that almost never has a dialogue balloon.

TEXT PAGE - A page with no panels or drawings.

TEXT STORY - A story with few if any illustrations commonly used as filler material during the first three decades of comics.

3-D COMIC - Comic art that is drawn and printed in two color layers, producing a 3-D effect when viewed through special glasses.

3-D EFFECT COMIC - Comic art that is drawn to appear as if in 3-D but isn't.

TITLE - The name of the comic book.

TITLE PAGE - First page of a story showing the title of the story and possibly the creative credits and indicia.

TRIMMED - (1) A bindery process which separates top, right, and bottom of pages and cuts comic books to the proper size; (2) A repair process in which defects along the edges of a comic book are removed with the use of scissors, razor blades, and/or paper cutters. Comic books which have been repaired in this fashion are considered defectives.

TTA - Abbreviation for Tales to Astonish.

UK - Abbreviation for British edition (United Kingdom).

UNDER GUIDE - When a comic book is priced at a value less than Guide list.

UPGRADE - To obtain another copy of the same comic book in a higher grade.

VARIANT COVER - A different cover image used on the same issue.

VERY RARE - 1 to 10 copies estimated to exist.

VICTORIAN AGE - Comics published from 1828 to 1883.

WANT LIST - A listing of comics needed by a collector, or a list of comics that a collector is interested in purchasing.

WAREHOUSE COPY - Originating from a publisher's warehouse; similar to file copy.

WHITE MOUNTAIN COLLECTION - A collection of high grade 1950s and 1960s comics which originated in New England.

X-OVER - Short for Crossover.

ZINE - Short for Fanzine.

Feature Article Index

Over the years, *The Official Overstreet Comic Book Price Guide* has grown into much more than a simple catalog of values. Almost since the very beginning, Bob has worked hard to make sure that the book reflects the latest information about the hobby, and this has resulted in some fascinating in-depth articles about aspects of the industry and the rich history of comics. Sadly, many of you may never have read a lot of these articles, or even knew they existed.

These two pages contain a comprehensive index to every feature article ever published in *The Official Overstreet Comic Book Price Guide*. From interviews with legendary creators to exhaustively researched retrospectives, it's all here. Enjoy this look back at the Overstreet legacy, and remember, many of these editions are still available through Gemstone and your local comic book dealer.

Note: The first three editions of *The Guide* had no feature articles, but from #4 on, a tradition was born that has carried through to the very volume. This index begins with the 4th edition and lists all articles published up to and including last year's 37th edition of the guide.

AUTHOR (S)	TITLE	EDITION	PGS.
	Good Lord! choke...gasp...It's EC!	#09 (1979)	A-43-76
	L. B. Cole: The Man Behind the Mask	#11 (1981)	A-55-72
Borock, Steve	Comic Book Certification: An Overview of Comic Guaranty, LLC.	#35 (2005)	1007-1011
	An Insiders Look at CGC and Comic Book Certification	#36 (2006)	1044-1047
	CGC, The Art and Science of Comic Book Certification	#37 (2007)	1036-1039
Braden, Scott	Strange Adventures - A Conversation with Murphy Anderson	#27 (1997)	A-30-32
	Built to Last (with Scott Braden)	#28 (1998)	89-102
Calhoun, Pat S.	Living on Borrowed Time! A Nostalgic Look at the Early Years of DC's Challengers of the Unknown (with Gary M. Carter)	#24 (1994)	A-157-164
	100 Years - A Century of Comics	#25 (1995)	A-107-123
Carter, Gary M.	DC Before Superman (written with Ken Lane Carter)	#13 (1983)	A-72-86
	The Silver Age... The Beginning: A Comparative Chronology of the First Sliver Age Comic Books	#20 (1990)	A-94-107
	Journey into the Unknown World of Atlas Fantasy (written with Pat S. Calhoun)	#22 (1992)	A-87-103
	Silver Sagas of the Scarlet Speedster: Whirlwind Adventures of the Fastest Man Alive! 1956-1960	#23 (1993)	A-80-86
Chesney, Landon	The Archives of the Comic Book Price Guide	#06 (1976)	44-45
DeFuccio, Jerry	An Interview with Will Eisner, Creator of the Spirit	#06 (1976)	31-37
	Norman Mingo and Alfred: The World's Greatest Facelift	#12 (1982)	A-45-57
	Charles Clarence Beck: The World's Second Mightiest Mortal	#15 (1985)	A-78-88
Dempsey, "Little" Jimmy	Great Old Radio Premiums	#13 (1983)	A-62-63
Disbrow, Jay	Confessions of a Former Comic Book Artist	#08 (1978)	A-31-38
Estrada, Jackie	Friends of Lulu Sound Off on Comics	#28 (1998)	79-81
Fulop, Scoot D.	Archie Comics Publications: The Mirth of a Legend	#21 (1991)	A-77-78
Hamilton, Bruce	The Mystery of the 12 Missing EC's	#25 (1995)	A-99-106
	Special Feature: Grading - The Next Revolution for Comic Books	#29 (1999)	17-21
Hancer, Kevin B.	Edgar Rice Burroughs and the Comics	#05 (1975)	33-38
Hessee, Tim	The Pop Hollinger Story: The First Comic Book Collector/Dealer	#12 (1982)	A-58-66
Huesman, Mark	Legiondary Adventures	#29 (1999)	101-106
Irons, Christopher	The Man Behind the Cover - L. B. Cole	#18 (1988)	A-77
Kronenberg, Michael	Indelible Shadows: The Spectacular Rise of Artist Jim Lee	#36 (2006)	1052-1055
	Patriot Act!!! (Captain America profile)	#37 (2007)	1024-1029
Leavitt, Craig	Katy Keene - The Overstreet Connection	#14 (1984)	A-67-78
Lee, Stan	Twenty-Five Years? I Don't Believe It!	#16 (1986)	A-82-84
Marek, Carl, et al.	Good Girl Art - An Introduction: Why it Was and What it Was (produced by the American Comic Book Co.)	#06 (1976)	38-43
	Esoteric Comics: The Ultimate Collection (produced by the American Comic Book Co. in Consultation with Scott Shaw)	#07 (1977)	A-30-35
	Women in Comics (in collaboration with Art Amsie)	#08 (1978)	A-54-75
	For Those Who Know How to Look	#09 (1979)	A-35-42
Moore, Dale	Comic Book Charites: Lifelines of the Industry	#34 (2004)	964-966
Murray, Will	Marvel's Hammer: The Mighty Thor	#36 (2006)	1028-1039
	The Untold Origin of Daredevil	#37 (2007)	1030-1035
Novinskie, Charles S.	Sixty Years of Wonder Woman	#31 (2001)	26-29

Comic Characters Delivered Weekly

When you log onto

SCOOP

Scoop is the FREE, weekly, e-newsletter from Gemstone Publishing and Diamond International Galleries for collectors and pop culture enthusiasts of all ages. It covers the past, present and future of comic character collectibles, the latest industry news, media happenings and so much more - to get you tuned into those trends that have shaped our history and our development as a society. Read the latest about the characters you love - and get to know other characters both old and new. So don't wait - visit **http://scoop.diamondgalleries.com** to check it all out!

it was an oddly cold day in August 1989. The mist settled in among the Manhattan skyscrapers creating a spooky EC setting as Russ Cochran and I walked over to Bill Gaines' apartment from our hotel. It still seems like only yesterday when Russ called me with the news that Bill Gaines has decided to sell his EC collection. Russ would be handling the sale and I was needed to verify the collection and to arrange the copies of each issue by grade. We both knew that he had put away twelve copies of every EC 35-40 years ago and sealed them away in boxes. Now the time had come to open those packages.

Thoughts were rushing through our heads about the significance of the day. We had many questions to be answered. We wondered what the condition would be like, how white the pages would be, if any issues would be missing, and if something new would be discovered. We finally arrived at the Gaines' apartment at 10:15 AM. After clearing security, we arrived at his doorstep. Bill and his wife Anne cheerfully invited us in. Their apartment was like a curio shop, filled with mementos, souvenirs, and Statues of Liberty which they had collected for many years. Over to the right were bookshelves filled with bound ECs and *MAD*s. But what really caught our eyes was a genuine shrunken head sitting on the shelf (see the *Haunt of Fear* #8 cover). After gasping and choking for a second, we settled down around a large dining room table where the work would be performed.

In the closet were six large cardboard boxes which contained the ECs. The comics were wrapped in brown paper by issue number and sealed in the boxes. Before the comic books were handled, Russ and I put on white cotton film editor's gloves.

The first box was opened and the first package of comics was set on the table. We began with *Vault of Horror* #40 and worked backwards to *War Against Crime* #10. Russ cut open each package, counted the issues and handed them to me for arrangement by grade. Anne placed the ID labels on Mylar bags while Bill supervised.

After each stack was graded, Russ placed them in Mylar sleeves. At this point the copies were divided into two groups, one to be sold and one to be retained by Bill. Depending on shortages, Bill wanted to keep up to four copies for his personal use.

It soon became apparent, after going through just a few packages, that we were seeing something out of the ordinary. The books were dazzling. They were essentially in brand new condition with full cover gloss and extra white pages. The cover colors were brilliant, with only a few exceptions. All of the noticeable defects either occurred during printing or trimming or the way they were wrapped. Some corners were bumped, and some issues were wrinkled.

We were disappointed to find no annuals or Pre-Trend comics, except for *War Against Crime* #10 and 11, and *Crime Patrol* #15 and 16. But we were surprised to find most all of the different versions of M.C. Gaines' books: *Picture Stories from the Bible*, *Science*, *American History* and *World History*. Some carried the All-American seal, some the

OPENED...

by Robert M. Overstreet with Gary M. Carter

DC seal, and others had the familiar EC seal.

After opening a few of the packages and seeing the pristine condition of the books, we just had to check out their smell. The white pages and inks were still so fresh, that opening the books and smelling the insides swept us back to 1950. It was a smell we all remembered. Those of us who can recognize an Edgar Church Collection (Mile High) comic by its smell would have trouble distinguishing between it and the Gaines smell. It soon became obvious that we were looking at probably the best surviving sets of EC comics. As a comparison, many of the Harvey file copies had brown edges due to the way they were stored. Some of the Dell file copies also had minor browning on the edges. Since the Gaines collection was never read, and was wrapped air-

Angie Meyer (left) and Russ Cochran's daughter Sylvia (right) flank legendary EC Publisher Bill Gaines during the evaluation of the Gaines File collection.

tight, the only comparable collection would be the Church collection. In the Dell and Harvey file copies there were issues missing from the runs, and in some cases there were probably as many as 100 copies of each issue.

Bill had remembered that there were twelve copies in each package, but we found that many had been opened, probably before Gaines moved to that apartment in 1961. We found that most issues did have twelve copies, but there were many packages that contained nine, ten, or eleven copies, and a few with only seven copies, and one issue with only one copy (*Vault of Horror* #12).

The work was tedious, the days were long, but they were filled with memories that we shall never forget. As we looked at these books, we traded stories about our memories of seeing each cover for the first time, and stories of how we tracked down that particular issue for our collections. Each day we played Christmas music and sang Christmas carols as we continued processing the mountain of unopened packages. At each day's end we returned to our hotel immersed in EC dust, Christmas Spirit, and childhood memories.

After spending a few days going through these books, Russ and I agreed that it was an experience that any EC fan would have enjoyed — the historic unveiling of the Gaines File collection. It was like opening 300 little time capsules that hadn't seen the light of day for 35-40 years. Being small-town collectors we both felt privileged and honored to be present at

Robert M. Overstreet evaluates a then-freshly opened issue of Frontline Combat #4, documenting the now legendary Gaines File collection.

such a historic occasion. We hope that these notes will in some way make it possible for all other collectors and fans to have been there also.

On Friday, August 11, we processed *Vault of Horror*, *Tales from the Crypt*, *Haunt of Fear*, *Crime SuspenStories* and *Shock SuspenStories*. On Saturday, August 12, we did W*eird Science*, *Weird Fantasy*, *Weird Science-Fantasy*, *Incredible Science-Fiction*, all of the New Direction titles (such as *Valor* and *Impact*), *MAD* and *Panic*. On Sunday we were joined by Russ's daughter, Sylvia, and Angie Meyer, and we did *Two-Fisted Tales*, *Frontline Combat*, the 3-D comics, and the various *Picture Stories* series. The actual sets of books were put together Sunday afternoon, which finished the project.

As interesting footnote, we learned that *Impact* #1 was originally printed by Charlton Press. The printing quality was poor, so Gaines had the entire run destroyed, saving only one copy. It was then printed again and distributed to the stands.

Years later, of course, the Gaines File collection has become one of the most sought-after pedigreed collections of comic books. As has been documented in our Market Reports over the past few editions of this Guide and from the incredible success of Gemstone's *EC Archives* project, the interest in these classics shows no signs of waning now.

This article appeared in different form in Overstreet's Golden Age & Silver Age Quarterly.

Golden Age Comics'

back in the mid-1930s, many pulp magazine publishers were considering entering the new and growing field of comic books. Fantastic stories starring incredible heroes were right up their alley. The fact that the stories

Ashcans – First Editions

by Gary Colabuono & Mark Zaid

were told with words and pictures was probably looked on as a nuisance and an additional cost, but there was no denying the popularity of the Sunday comic strips, and it was hoped that these new comic books just might turn into a profitable venture.

By the late-1930s, some of these established pulp publishers were now full-fledged comics publishers — Martin Goodman (Timely), Ned Pines (Nedor), Captain Billy Fawcett (Fawcett), and Harry Donenfeld (DC). These men, as well as an entire new generation of entrepreneurs, suddenly found themselves involved in a race to create and market new comic-book titles. Titles that they soon discovered were leaping off the newsstand and exciting the imaginations of readers across the country.

Success not only brewed profits but also fierce competition among the publishers. Though there existed an environment of skilled artists and writers at each of the different companies, as well as studios from which entire finished comic books could be purchased, it was still an easy matter to be influenced by, and at times outright copy, your competitors' characters. It soon became apparent to some of the early leaders in the industry that it was as important to protect their characters as it was to create them. That usually translated to pursuing copyright and trademark protection as well as litigation to enforce perceived rights.

Back in the early days of comics publishing the most com-

Action Comics #1 ashcan featured the artwork which was rejected as the cover art for Detective Comics #2. The interior of this ashcan is the historically significant Detective Comics #1

mon procedure to secure a trademark for a potentially valuable title was to create an ashcan edition of the proposed comic book, which differ from the modern-day term, commonly referring to mass-produced promotional booklets. Though the specific origins of the word are unknown, ashcan was a publishing term used to describe a dummy or prototype copy. Over the years some have confused ashcans with efforts to secure copyright protection rather than trademarks. In simplistic terms, a copyright protects the original expression of an idea, but not the actual idea, while a trademark addresses a title or logo.

By using ashcans to secure trademarks, the publishers saved money and, more importantly, time. Instead of going through the lengthy task of writing and drawing, as well as the long arduous production process of color separations, engraving and printing, companies would simply create the title's logo, affix it to a piece of existing cover art, and then shoot a Velox of it. A Velox is a positive photographic print typically used by newspapers as a pre-press proof, which accounts for ashcan covers being black and white rather than color. After the cover was created, it was trimmed to comic-book size and then stapled to the interior of a previously published book, or sometimes just some loose story pages. The ashcan was now complete. For all practical purposes it had the appearance of a legitimate comic book – and since the U.S. Patent & Trademark Office (USPTO) apparently accepted them as authentic comic books for trademark registration, no higher authority in the country existed to dispute this claim. Nor, apparently, did anyone ever seek to try.

During 1937 – 1944, especially, some of the most important and famous titles in American comic book history were seemingly registered and protected using an ashcan copy (titles such as *Superman Comics*, *Wonder Woman* and *Flash Comics*). So too were some titles most collectors have never heard of to this day including *Mystery Trail*, *Superman/Superhombre* and *Red, White & Blue Comics*. Since so few were created, we as collectors can only marvel at the few examples that still exist today (usually only two to six copies were made and one would be provided to the USPTO). These comic book first editions are pop culture artifacts of the highest order and the rarest of collectibles.

But was an ashcan actually a legitimate vehicle for securing trademark protection for a title? All evidence suggests that the publishers of the day thought so. However, until U.S. law was changed in the 1980s, so as to more closely reflect international practice, in order to trademark a title a publisher had to first "use" the title in order to secure his mark. Simple registration would not legally suffice. This meant, as a matter of law, that the sought-after-title had to actually be placed into market use before submission.

Evidence does exist from the 1950s that DC once mailed an ashcan copy out-of-state and requested it be returned under the apparent premise that this could arguably constitute the title entering the stream of commerce. Yet it is clear that

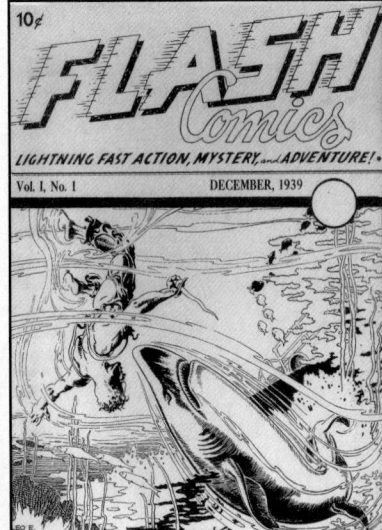

Flash Comics #1 ashcan produced by Fawcett Publications featured the first appearance of Captain Thunder later changed to Captain Marvel. Flash Comics #1 ashcan by DC Comics featured the cover art from Adventure Comics #41 and the interior of All-American Comics #8. While both publishers applied for the title DC Comics acquired the rights causing Fawcett to drop their interest in it.

this was never the case for the majority of known ashcans as many of the titles were never placed into use even once, whether before or after the ashcan's creation. Instead it appears publishers labored under the mistaken impression that the first to the door of the USPTO was the winner. Had they known otherwise, comic history today might well be different for some of the hobby's better-known characters.

Although many early publishers used ashcans, not all utilized them to secure their titles. DC and Fawcett were the largest publishers to use this method of registration and most ashcans that exist today are from these two companies. A very limited number of ashcans from smaller companies have found their way into the hobby but no ashcans have ever been identified that were created by such mainstream publishers of the day as Timely, Centaur, Fox, MLJ, Dell or Fiction House. Why this appears to be the case remains a complete mystery.

Regrettably, very little historical evidence exists to answer the many questions that surround the creation and use of ashcans. Those who utilized the concept have generally passed on, and the only publisher to have created ashcans and still be in existence today, DC, has no institutional memory beyond possessing select copies within their vault. Sadly, apparently the USPTO purged its files and whatever they might have contained in the late 1970s.

DC Ashcans – Sol's Provenance

In 1985 Joe Desris, long-time collector and comics' historian, arranged to interview Sol Harrison for a book he was writing that detailed early comic-book character licensing. Desris flew to Florida where Harrison was living after his retirement. When he arrived at Harrison's home, he was greeted not only by a warm and genteel host, but also by a font of knowledge of the early years of comics' publishing.

Sol Harrison started his career at DC comics in 1941 as art director and production manager. His main responsibility in those days was overseeing color separations and he ultimately designed a quality control process that was unequaled in the industry. His hard work and inventiveness led to his becoming president of the company in 1976, where he remained until his retirement in 1980.

During this first visit, knowing that Desris was a noted collector/dealer of Golden Age comic books, Harrison asked him if he would look at some items he had saved from his long tenure at DC. Together they opened boxes that hadn't been disturbed for decades. In one particular box a few strange-looking comic books caught Desris' attention. When asked what they were, Harrison said they were ashcans – dummy copies that were created to secure trademarks for new DC titles. Before then, this was a term known to only a few in the collecting community. Desris was intrigued and agreed to show them to some collectors to gauge interest and to see if anyone would buy them.

In October 1985, Desris brought 6 ashcans to a Chicago Minicon where many of the top dealers and collectors in the Midwest gathered every month. Desris showed the books around but found little interest – mainly due to the lofty price tag of $10,000 that Harrison was hoping to get. Gary Colabuono, the co-author of this fea-

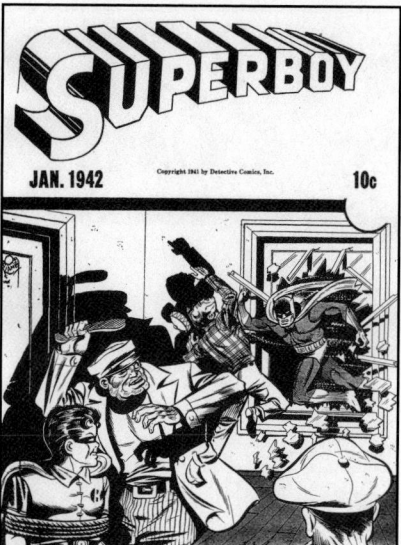

Double Action Comics #2 cover proof is one of two cover proofs that are in existence along with only four copies of the complete book. Superboy ashcan featured the cover art from Detective Comics #57 and the interior of Action Comics #57.

ture, when given a chance to inspect them, immediately fell in love with them and wrote a check on the spot.

"I didn't know what they were," Colabuono said. "But I knew they looked interesting, some of the titles were obviously historically important, and they had an impeccable provenance. I just had to have them. I remember vividly that when I got home my wife asked if I had purchased anything at the show. When I showed her the ashcans and told her how much I had paid for them she thought I was crazy! "

This "love at first sight" encounter would send Colabuono on a 20-year mission to learn all he could about ashcans and continue to build his collection. Over the years, he would subsequently acquire 33 additional complete ashcans and numerous loose covers. This is the largest collection to date that any one collector has ever amassed.

Colabuono's passion to acquire more ashcans led to his scouring ads in the *Comics' Buyer's Guide* and other hobby magazines. It was a rare moment that anyone else was identified as owning an ashcan, much less someone willing to part with it.

Colabuono ran annual full-page ads in *The Official Overstreet Comic Book Price Guide* for 15 years looking to buy authentic Golden Age ashcans. "In all those years I never acquired a single ashcan from any of those ads. I got many calls from people who had common black-and-white comics and even some rare books that weren't listed in the Guide, but never a real ashcan. To me, it's proof of their rarity," he said.

And the final piece of the ashcan

puzzle was finally put into place when the 2006 edition of The Official Overstreet Comic Book Price Guide listed all the known DC ashcans. "Having them listed in the Guide was important to me because it would legitimize them as actual comic books and not just interesting oddities," said Colabuono. "It was a profound moment in my collecting career when they were listed in the Guide."

The Superman Family of Ashcans

DC had hit the jackpot with Superman. By 1942, it was evidently clear that the character was an enormous hit not only in comic books but also in feature cartoons, radio and countless other products. It was critical that DC protect every variation of "Super," and they used ashcans to do it.

The Superwoman, Superboy and Supergirl ashcans demonstrate that DC was taking no chances with their franchise character – and any spin-offs they were contemplating. Although no images of the characters were ever created with the ashcans, the logos all show the same "Super" arching letters. As the ashcans show, it's clear that DC intended to discourage any competitors from breaking up their family of "Super" titles.

The Battle of the Flashes: Fawcett vs. DC

One ashcan in particular soon provided an insight into the battles between two major publishing giants — DC and Fawcett. In late 1939 Fawcett and DC apparently found themselves in a heated race to see who would be the first to secure the

Supergirl ashcan featured the cover art from Boy Commandos #1 and the interior of Action Comics #80. The Boy Commandos #1 artwork was used on a number of ashcan covers including Movie Cartoons, Movie Fables, Movie Gems, Screen Cartoons, Screen Comics, Screen Fables, Screen Funnies, and Screen Gems. The Superman Comics ashcan featured the cover art from Action Comics #7 and the interior of Action Comics #8.

trademark for Flash Comics. DC's ashcan edition dated December 1939 pre-dated Fawcett's ashcan by just one month and Fawcett, likely not wanting to battle litigious-minded DC, which had already sued other publishers for copyright infringement of its best known character, Superman, backed off and changed their title to Thrill Comics. Apparently the Fastest Man Alive was more than a match for the World's Mightiest Mortal — or at least their lawyers may have been. Ironically, Fawcett ended up dumping this second title too (perhaps because it was too easily confused with Nedor's Thrilling Comics published in February 1940) and ultimately published the first Captain Marvel story in Whiz Comics dated February 1940.

With the discovery of the Fawcett ashcans in 1983 by dealers negotiating the purchase of inventory from the publisher's family, the mystery of why the first newsstand issue of Whiz Comics is numbered # 2 was presumably solved. Of course, although Superman and Captain Marvel never confronted each other during their heyday within the pages of a comic book, Fawcett and DC eventually did lock arms in mortal combat. DC sued Fawcett in 1941 citing copyright infringement and spent more than a decade in litigation. The case was eventually settled in 1954.

The Action Ashcans

When Harry Donenfeld was convinced by Sheldon Mayer that maybe this "Superman" character could be a big hit, he decided that Superman would be the lead feature in a new comic book he was about to publish, but he was uncertain about the title of the book. He knew it would include the word ACTION, but was that all? According to Batman film producer and comics historian Michael Uslan, Donenfeld allegedly had ashcans of four titles created: Action Comics, Double Action Comics, Triple Action Comics and Action Funnies.

It's interesting to note that three copies exist today of the Action Comics ashcan, two of which in the hands of collectors with the third copy located in the vaults of DC Comics. Only one copy of Double Action Comics #1 is purported to exist, and was recorded by author Robert M. Overstreet in The Overstreet Comic Book Price Guide. There are at least four complete copies and two loose covers of Double Action Comics #2, which is a color comic thereby distinguishing itself from an ashcan. No copies of Triple Action Comics have ever surfaced, nor does any historical record (including at DC) support its existence. The Action Funnies ashcan — once erroneously thought in collecting circles to be the predecessor to Action Comics — is the most "common" of the group with four known copies.

One copy of the Action Funnies ashcan, now in the collection of co-author Mark S. Zaid, has a particularly interesting folklore history. Apparently during the height of the sociological/political battles launched in the late 1940s by such individuals as Dr. Frederic Wertham, over the educational value, or per-

Superwoman ashcan featured the cover art from Action Comics #3 and the interior of Action Comics #38. The Action Funnies ashcan featured the cover art from Action Comics #3 and the interior of Detective Comics #10.

ceived lack thereof, of comic books, a graduate student authored a dissertation that was utilized by the publishing community to rebut some of the disparaging claims. The leadership of DC was so appreciative that in the mid-1950s it gifted items, including a copy of Action Funnies, to the student. The copy still bears his name more than fifty years later!

Ashcans: Gerber 10's

Interest has grown steadily in the past few years as more and more collectors are exposed to ashcans and their importance within the hobby. A handful of copies, primarily the Fawcett editions, are now listed in the 1989 Gerber Photo-Journal Guide to Comics, and most DC titles are listed in the The Official Overstreet Comic Book Price Guide. Perhaps, in this new electronic age of global communication, new ashcan finds will also emerge.

Those who have had the opportunity to personally examine an ashcan will tell you that it's a remarkable experience. To hold the first-edition of such titles as Action Comics and Superman Comics is nothing less than awe-inspiring.

Gary Colabuono is a long-time collector, dealer, retailer, historian and show promoter. The industry recognized him with the first Will Eisner Spirit of Comics award in 1993.

Mark S. Zaid is an attorney in Washington, D.C. and an avid collector of ashcans. Visit his Web site at www.EsquireComics.com. Both men are advisors to Overstreet's Comic Book Price Guide.

FROM "A LONG TO TODAY'S

Even in the past, comics medium

When film scholars speak of what Star Wars was to film in the 1970s, the terms often used are nearly biblical: Before and After.

The depressing decade of Watergate and stagflation had brought with it dystopic science fiction films, with everything from Silent Running to Soylent Green telling viewers to check their optimism at the door. The world of Logan's Run was a nice place to visit, but if you stayed too long, you'd be zapped by a talking rhinestone.

Star Wars, with its clear-cut message of good over evil, changed all that in 1977 — as well as the way films were produced. What's less known is the extent to which it did the same for comics. It may well have helped save Marvel finan-

TIME AGO" GALAXY

By John Jackson Miller

cially (and, by extension, the industry). But it did more than that. It gave solid reassurance to publishers that the right comics product could be repackaged again and again for new markets, a lesson whose dividends are paying off today in bookstores everywhere.

And for their part, comics have given something back, as well, helping to reinvent what licensed products are. The word "merchandise" might work for a poster or a coffee mug, but a Star Wars comic book today is an integral, contributing part of an ongoing multimedia story!

What Star Wars Did for Comics: Notes from an Intervention

If you thought the movies were depressing, the comics industry of the mid-1970s was in a malaise that Jimmy Carter couldn't have imagined. The distribution system was falling apart. Comic books, which had long been "loss leaders" for retailers, weren't nearly as attractive once they began catching up with inflation; between 1971 and 1977, Marvel and DC prices doubled. And fans were getting less for their money still: story page counts had been cut so that every other page of a 1977 Marvel was an ad. Many newsstands dropped comics altogether. And the comics shop market, which would remedy many of these problems, was still in its infancy.

It was through one of those stores, in fact, that the fuse was lit.

Star Wars #1

Roy Thomas has told the story several times, from the text page of his *Star Wars* #1 to his 30th anniversary essay in *Alter Ego*. George Lucas, who had found mainstream success with *American Graffiti* in 1973, had just embarked upon a monumental film project — but he had also gone in as a silent partner on the comic art gallery section of Ed Summer's Supersnipe Comic Art Emporium in Manhattan. Which is how Lucas and Thomas came to meet — and how Thomas first learned of the film over dinner. That first meeting bore fruit in the summer of 1976, when Lucas's publicist, Charlie Lippincott, approached Thomas to intercede on their behalf with Marvel — after the publisher had already rejected the project once.

But Lucas was insistent on getting Star Wars comics into print, even suggesting Howard Chaykin as artist, according to Thomas. So Thomas met with Stan Lee and won approval for a six-issue adaptation for which Marvel paid essentially nothing in licensing rights — and even then, according to accounts from both Thomas and later editor-in-chief Jim Shooter, the company had to be dragged into it kicking and screaming. Marvel's circulation director complained about the length of the adaptation and the requirement that #1 and #2 precede the release of the film. (The comics were actually advertising, by the studio's lights.) But Thomas stood firm on the original plan, and he and Chaykin both appeared with

Lippincott at the 1976 San Diego Comic-Con at a slideshow jointly promoting the film and the comics, long months before the rest of the world knew what was coming. The result: decent sales on the issues before the film's release, Thomas recalls. But after it?

"If we hadn't done *Star Wars*, we would have gone out of business," Shooter said in a 2000 online interview. "*Star Wars* single-handedly saved Marvel." Marvel did not publish postal statistics for the first two years of the series, but *Star Wars* surely became the #1 comic book in the industry beginning in the summer of 1977 — as it still was in 1979, when Marvel reported average monthly sales of 278,759 copies, just ahead of the TV-show driven *Incredible Hulk*. But the real numbers were for those early adaptation issues — over 1 million copies each, a number not seen in the field since the Carl Barks duck-titles in 1960. And, interestingly, the vast majority wasn't sold on the newsstand or even comics shops…

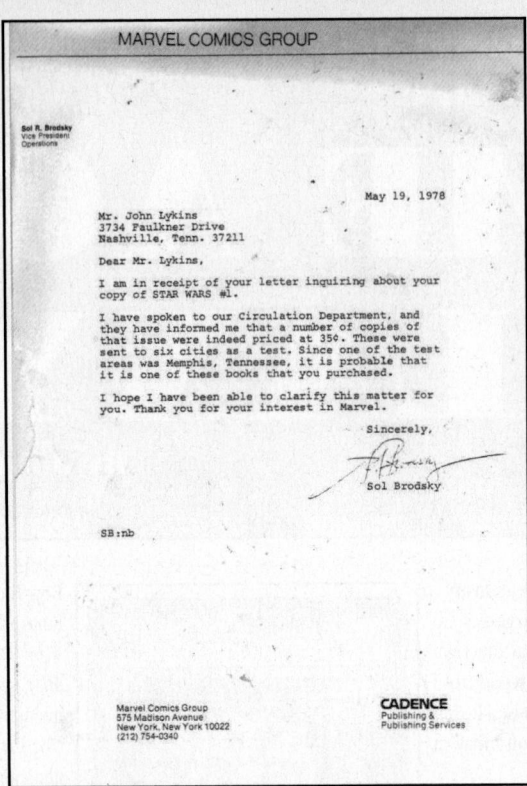

This letter from Marvel's Sol Brodsky confirming the much sought-after Star Wars #1 35¢ Variant as a marketing test. Courtesy: Dan Cusimano.

newsstand distribution, including department, toy, and drug stores. By altering its Top Comics concept, Western found in the early 1970s it could sell random assortments of its Gold Key comics in three-copy bags — albeit with variant Whitman covers to prevent copies from reentering the newsstand system as returns. Marvel and DC contracted with Western to do the same thing with their own titles in late 1976 and 1978 respectively. The first "Marvel Whitmans" (the Whitman name appeared nowhere on them, except sometimes on the bag) were not second, but rather simultaneous printings of February 1977 cover-dated issues. And, as with the Gold Keys, the comics were random assortments from a single month.

Star Wars would change that practice. July-dated *Star Wars* #1 does not appear to have been part of the Whitman simultaneous-print program, but later issues were; the 30¢ Whitman editions of #2 – 4 are all first printings, produced at the same time as the newsstand versions. Soon after the movie was released — and after Marvel had ordered its 35¢ price change — both Whitman and newsstand distributor Curtis Circulation ordered their own waves of reprints of #1 – 4.

So Whitman changed its packaging approach. Finding itself with exclusive merchandise in a market starved for it, Whitman produced special Star Wars-labeled bags just for the reprints. Demand from retailers was so high that Whitman apparently suspended its printings of all Marvel titles for three months in late 1977 to focus exclusively on *Star Wars* reprints. There are large-diamond editions of Amazing Spider-Man #165 – 175, but they do not appear again until #179. It's the same for the whole line for the January to March 1978 cover dates — with the exception of the *Star Wars* title itself. The practice continued, with even new issues of *Star Wars* getting their own packaging. Original Whitman copies of later issues of the series were stockpiled until three could be gathered together and sold in bags with the movie's logo. "All-new

May the Shelf Life Be With You: Another Star Wars Discovery

If the modern trade paperback is built upon the willingness of people to buy reprinted comic books, conveniently packaged, then *Star Wars* provided some heavy early proof-of-concept. No previous comic book had been reprinted so soon, so often, or in such a variety of formats.

The Whitman bagged editions. The Marvel treasury-sized edition. The Del Rey black-and-white mass-market paperback. All provided just what Marvel desperately needed most in the mid-1970s: a way to get comics to the public by sidestepping the flailing newsstand market. But where the developing comics-shop market focused on serving hardcore fans, most of the *Star Wars* reprints went into outlets that had abandoned comics — or that had never had them.

Through the coloring books and puzzles of its Whitman brand, Western Publishing sold into many locations without stories not seen in the movie! Issues 10, 11, 12" screams one bag label. If you weren't near one of the few comics shops in 1978, Whitman was saving copies for you — at least for one title!

Whitman and other jobbers bagging comics tried to repeat the phenomenon over the next few years with titles like Battlestar Galactica and Raiders of the Lost Ark — almost always media or toy properties — but nothing matched the success of Star Wars. But Star Wars had also shown there could be new life for old comics in other formats, too. In August 1977, Marvel put the six-issue film adaptation into two treasury-sized tabloid editions, with versions each for Curtis and Whitman. And in November, the adaptation found its way into bookstores with … a paperback collection. Sort of. Mass-market paperbacks reprinting comics in the 1960s and 1970s largely reprinted comic strips —

Star Wars #107, the last Marvel issue

Trade collections had appeared before — and it was, of course, at the height of the early 1990s boom when lavish editions abounded. But reprints of older comics had never before been seen as that desirable by comics fans — no one bought a Marvel Triple Action if there was a prayer of finding the original Avengers copy somewhere. But Star Wars in the 1970s had shown that conveniently grouped "snap reprints" of high-demand new material could sell — and that knowledge, plus the backing of the direct market, helped make ever more attractive packages possible. So for Star Wars comics fans, 1993 was the year the "DVD" arrived — a decade-plus before the movie DVD actually did!

Galaxy, Interrupted

though there were attempts to adapt comic-book material to the small size. Lancer produced "collector's album" paperbacks for Marvel's marquee titles in 1966, cutting and pasting strips of black-and-white panels sideways on the printed page. By 1977, Marvel was trying again with Pocket Books running its color pages greatly reduced in size. But Del Rey had the book license for Star Wars, so it was under their imprint that the whole comics adaptation finally found print in one place at one time — if in murky black-and-white, shot down drastically from the original size. (It was no Treasury edition — but at least the panels weren't sideways!) By The Empire Strikes Back, Marvel had the book reprint license itself — showing that, even if the eventual format that would make comics palatable to bookstores wasn't there yet, comics publishers must have understood there was some market there to be had.

When it came time for Dark Horse to reprint its initial work, Star Wars: Dark Empire in May 1993, it was apparent just how much value the repurposing of comics had gained in the intervening years. Six issues, just like the movie adaptation — but offered in color at the size of the original printing, along with such extras as sketchbook pages and Tom Veitch's 28-page story treatment. And that's not even getting into the signed hardcover Dark Horse simultaneously offered with its own slipcase and gold-foil embossed faux-leather hardcover.

The game had largely changed by the time Marvel published Archie Goodwin and Al Williamson's adaptation of The Empire Strikes Back. There were many other licensees by then — and while the Del Rey novelization was out before the film, the Marvel version, again six issues, only began as part of the regular series after that, still running in the magazine long after the series back in 1977 had moved on to new stories. Marvel addressed this in 1983 by adapting Return of the Jedi outside the ongoing title as a four-issue limited series, which also allowed it to get the adaptation out quickly as a Marvel Super Special. (Too quickly, as it would turn out: A retailer put copies on sale three weeks before the street date, revealing major plot points — and when none other than Mark Hamill discovered a copy and contacted Lucasfilm, Marvel sent Peter David out to New York shops to try to get the copies off the shelf.)

Regardless, the sales were never to regain their lofty heights, despite quality runs by writers David Michelinie and Jo Duffy, the latter charged with the challenging task of keeping interest going in the series after both the filmgoers and the filmmaker had moved on. By the time Marvel wrapped the ongoing series in 1986 with #107, sales had dropped below 140,000 copies, making that issue a prized collectible in later years. And so, after the kids' comics Droids and Ewoks ended in the summer of 1987, Marvel's decade-long association with

Star Wars came to a close. Blackthorne produced the first of three 3-D Star Wars issues at the end of that year, but that was it for the 1980s.

But things were brewing again at Skywalker Ranch. Lucas had been through a costly divorce — even selling off what would become Pixar to Steve Jobs — and the licensing engine was revved up again. Del Rey released the first new Star Wars novel in years, Heir to the Empire, in June 1991, picking up where events after Return of the Jedi had left off.

Enter Dark Horse Comics, which had been a good steward of the Aliens license and had already done business with Lucasfilm on Indiana Jones. Company founder Mike Richardson made a presentation to Lucasfilm representatives laying out how Dark Horse would approach the series, focusing on stories that would fit and interact with continuity established elsewhere. And with Dark Horse, he suggested, Lucasfilm would have a greater share of the publisher's attention. Dark Horse was growing, but it didn't have the sprawling hundred-plus monthly offerings that Marvel had gotten to in the boom times of early 1990s. Here, Star Wars would be a bigger deal.

And it was. The result of that meeting, Star Wars: Dark Empire, was a six-issue story (just as the first adaptation was) which, like the Del Rey novels that had topped the best-seller charts, tracked Luke Skywalker and company on their post-Jedi travels. Written by Tom Veitch and lavishly illustrated by Cam Kennedy, the story was a grand tour of what comics fans had gone without for several years. It was an immediate hit when released in December 1991, and while it wasn't the #1 comic book of the year, the first issue still came in 19th place for the month, putting Dark Horse solidly in the top ranks of comics publishers.

Star Wars has helped it remain there ever since, even after the "Big Six" had shrunk by two. Dark Horse followed Dark Empire up by plunging into the past, both literally and figuratively — first reprinting classic newspaper strips, and then doing the first explorations of the "thousand generations" in which the Jedi kept order in Tales of the Jedi. In addition to its own original works, Dark Horse also adapted Star Wars novels, such as Splinter of the Mind's Eye, and took part in a coordinated multimedia release under the Shadows of the Empire banner in 1996, a warm-up act for the cinematic return to follow. Dark Horse played an important role in readying fans for the films again, first for the 1997 Special Editions, then for the prequels in 1999, 2002, and 2005.

Two-Way Street: What Comics Have Done for Star Wars

Today, the Dark Horse trade paperback library is robust, with everything from the old Marvel material to current titles like Legacy and Knights of the Old Republic available. They're a required part of any Star Wars fan's ready reference library, whether they're into comics or not. There's a good reason for that: it all counts. With the exception of a handful of imaginary stories since the Dark Horse age began, it all "happened," as far as the licensor is concerned.

It wasn't always that way. Long before the "Expanded Universe" — as the agglomeration of Star Wars fiction in other media has come to be known — the ancillary media tended to go their own way. Luke could swim and Leia couldn't in Splinter of the Mind's Eye; in Archie Goodwin's Star Wars comics, it was the other way around (which made a lot more sense, considering where Luke was from). And the opportunities to actually foreshadow events in the films were minimal. Goodwin got to deal with restoring the bounty on Han Solo only in the last page of the issue before the scheduled start of The Empire Strikes Back. Duffy got to do a plot involving the "Bothan spies" presaging Return of the Jedi, but the movie had long since been out before those comics were released.

Rather, the real occupational hazard for comics creators in the Marvel-era appears to have been a lack of information about what was coming later on. For the very first post-film story, Thomas said he perceived the filmmakers were still trying to piece together what they wanted to do next — the result being that his Magnificent Seven storyline for #7 – 10 drew criticism from Lucas for being too close to the movie and for

> "With graphic novels, and comics in general, finding increasing acceptance in mainstream America, Star Wars has taken its place along side the traditional and long lasting comic franchises and can be found in virtually every retail location in which comics can be found."
>
> *- Mike Richardson*
> *Dark Horse Comics*

including a large bipedal green rabbit. (Fairly or not, the bunny, Jaxxon, would in later years symbolize for many fans the lack of studio-licensee coordination in this period — strangely, nobody seems to have been bothered by the big porcupine in those issues).

Later, there were broad general rules, like no Han Solo rescue or Luke/Vader confrontation between Empire and Jedi — but that didn't stop writers from accidentally guessing what was going to happen in the upcoming films. The Lahsbees, a diminutive bear race invented by Duffy, got new visuals after they were judged to be too close to the Ewoks. And Michelinie famously guessed that there was no reason for the Empire not to build another Death Star (albeit with a screen door nailed over that pesky exhaust port). That had to be changed into The Tarkin, a base that was built just around a big Death Star gun. "They didn't say specifically that they'd be doing a Death Star in the next movie, but we assumed it'd be something similar," Michelinie said.

Contrast that with the situation in the Dark Horse era. "The decision to make the comics part of the continuity was in place by the time we started," said Randy Stradley, Vice President of Publishing and editor and writer of many Star Wars comics. "In fact, by that time, the decision had been made that pretty much every bit of story material produced for Star Wars was continuity, or should be written to fit previous continuity." New comics at every stage — plot, script, pencils, and final product — are not only approved by Lucasfilm representatives, they're vetted by Leland Chee, the corporate keeper of the continuity database known as the "Holocron." But it's not just new comics — it's everything.

That's had three major impacts. First, obviously, there's a consistency in the appearance of characters, the look of locations, and the functioning of objects. There's latitude for different artistic interpretations, but elements identifiable in one medium or issue are generally identifiable in another — lowering a barrier to entry for new readers.

Second, there's a free flow of characters, events, and concepts in all directions. Ki-adi Mundi, the cone-headed hero created for Dark Horse's adjectiveless Star Wars series, later appeared in the prequel films, even getting whacked by the Emperor. Dark Horse's Old Republic comics became the basis for two popular Knights of the Old Republic video games in the 21st century — which themselves energized a new comics title by

Star Wars: Dark Empire #1, the first of many Star Wars comics from Dark Horse Comics.

that name. Unlike Las Vegas, what happens in comics doesn't necessarily stay in comics.

Finally, and perhaps most importantly for the long-term growth of the comics readership, Lucasfilm has helped to foster a sense of parity between the mediums in the public eye, something new and unusual for licensed franchises. Fans trying to reconcile differing levels of "canon" with other properties have had to resort to pecking orders and gyrations — films trump novels, novels trump comics, and games are out there in the ether somewhere. But the 1996 Shadows of the Empire campaign was marked by an effort to spread important story material out across the various media, and that practice has continued. Comics are a place where important things are allowed to happen — like the marriage of Luke Skywalker in Union, or the establishment of the far future of the galaxy in John Ostrander and Jan Duursema's Legacy.

Perhaps that's why Dark Horse's line, relaunched in 2006, has improved on sales even in the absence of more films to foreshadow. They're where the action in the Star Wars universe is — literally. And with new issue in the shop practically every week, fans who want to know what's next in the milieu have figured out where they can find their most frequent fix.

"Star Wars influenced comics and movies both," Thomas said. "Suddenly, everyone in movies (and sometimes TV) all loved the idea of being adapted. They flooded Marvel and DC in a way they hadn't before, when we'd only been previously approached by the people handling Golden Voyage of Sinbad — and another horror movie a bit later, which Gerry Conway and I saw at a screening but didn't pick up. But on the other hand, there were probably no more freebies for the comics companies as the first six issues of Star Wars had been!"

Star Wars influenced comics — and, in a way, comics are now influencing Star Wars in return. Together, they may not rule the galaxy, but they've kept people entertained for a long time — and will do so for a long time to come.

Author of several books and hundreds of articles about comics, archivist John Jackson Miller currently maintains his historical research at The Comics Chronicles (www.comichron.com) website. He has also written comic books including Iron Man, Crimson Dynamo, Bart Simpson — and for Dark Horse, Star Wars: Knights of the Old Republic.

A CGC Primer: *Comic Book*

Comic book certification has made a major impact in the comic book hobby. More than almost anyone ever thought it could! Today, hobbyists trade, buy and sell comic books over the internet with the comfort that the CGC-certified grade accurately represents their condition and that precise descriptions appear on the CGC certification labels. In addition, over 1,000 collectors display their comic book collections online in the Comics Registry, competing for awards for the best collection. Collectors also regularly consult the online CGC Census to see exactly how many copies of a particular issue were graded, and how an individual copy ranks against the existing certified population. All these changes have emerged in the past eight years, since CGC first opened.

How does professional comic book certification work? Here's a firsthand look at the process.

The Formation of CGC

CGC opened in January of 2000 under the umbrella of the Certified Collectibles Group, which also includes the largest rare coin certification company in the world, Numismatic Guaranty Corporation (NGC), and the leading currency certification company, Paper Money Guaranty (PMG). To form CGC, the Collectibles Group sought out talented and ethical individuals to grade comic books. Experts needed necessary skills to verify a comic book's authenticity and to detect restoration that can affect its value. To identify these individ-

uals, many of the most respected individuals in the hobby were consulted, and, based on their recommendations, a core grading team was selected.

The hobby's leaders were again called upon to develop a uniform grading standard. Everyone seemed to agree that the Overstreet reference was the foundation of this standard, but there were a number of subjective interpretations of its published definitions. It was critical to understand how these guidelines were being applied to the everyday buying and selling of comics. To accomplish this, approximately 50 of the hobby's top experts took part in an arduous, if not grueling, grading test. Their grades were averaged and an accurate grading standard reflecting the collective experience of the hobby's most prominent figures was thus developed. CGC now has the best standard and the best team to apply it consistently and impartially.

The next step was to develop a tamper-evident holder for the long-term storage and display of certified comics. This proved to be a significant technical challenge. Exhaustive material tests were conducted to determine that they were archival safe. To create a true first line of defense in a prudent plan for storage, it was determined that the comic books should be sealed in a soft inner well, then sealed again inside a tamper evident hard plastic case with interlocking ridges to enable compact storage. The CGC certified grade appears on a label sealed inside the holder for an additional level of security.

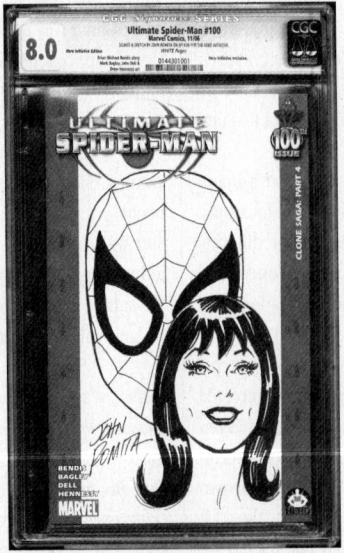

Submitting comics to CGC

Typically, comics received by CGC are submitted through one of our authorized member-dealers each of whom has passed a thorough background check by CGC's Accounting and Customer Service departments. This ensures that a customer's comic is in reliable hands when it's being prepared for shipment to CGC's offices in Florida. The value of such a precaution is self-evident, but it also relieves the collector or investor from having to provide personal and financial informa-

How Professional Certification Works

by Steve Borock, President & Primary Grader, CGC

tion which he or she may wish to keep confidential. Another option for individuals who wish to submit comics directly to CGC is to become a member of the Collectors' Society. Such membership provides for direct submission to any one of the companies comprising the Certified Collectibles Group, as well as offering numerous other benefits.

Pre-printed submission invoices are provided to all of CGC's authorized member-dealers. The member-dealer who handles a customer's submission keeps the bottom copy of each invoice as a record of the comics being sent to CGC. Included on the invoice is the submitter's declaration of each book's value. This is important information to have in the unlikely event of a package being lost while in transit. Comics are typically sent to CGC's offices by registered mail or through an insured express company.

The Comics are Received

CGC's Receiving Department opens the newly arrived packages each morning and immediately verifies that the number of books in each package matches the number shown on the invoice. Once this is done, a more detailed comparison is made to ensure that their invoice descriptions correspond to the actual comics. This information is entered into a computer, and the comics will henceforth be traceable at all stages of

the grading process by their invoice number and their line number within that invoice. Each book is placed within protective mylar that has affixed to it a label bearing the invoice and line item numbers; information which is duplicated on the label in a bar-coded inscription for quick reading by the computer. Before any grading is performed, each book is examined by a CGC

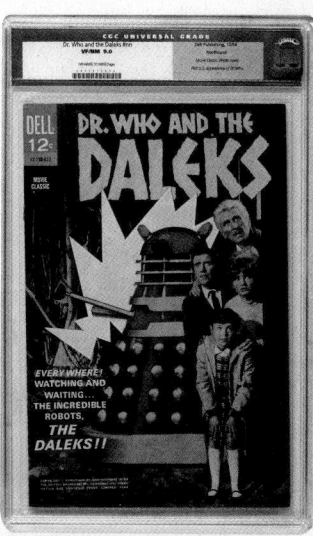

CGC encapsulates a wide variety of comic books ranging from promotional comics to larger magazine size books.

Restoration Detection Expert. If any form of restoration work is detected, this information is entered into the computer so that it will be available to the grading team.

The Grading Process

The members of the CGC grading team come from diverse backgrounds, and many were comic book dealers at some time in their careers. In becoming familiar with market standards for comic book grading, experience in the commercial sector can be an essential ingredient. Once they joined CGC, these individuals immediately cease all commercial trading. All CGC employees are prohibited from commercially buying and selling comic books. In this way CGC can remain completely impartial, having no vested interest other than a devotion to serving clients through accurate and consistent grading.

After being examined by a Restoration Detection Expert, a book then passes to a pre-grader. At this stage the comic books are in barcoded mylar sleeves, and have been separated from their original invoice. This step is taken to ensure that graders do not know whose books they are grading, as a further guarantee of impartiality. The pre-grader begins the grading process by counting the book's pages and entering into the computer any peculiarities or flaws that may affect a book's grade. Some examples of this would be "a tear on third page," "a corner crease – does not break color," "a ?' inch spine split," and so forth. He then enters this information, if necessary, into the "Graders Notes" field and assigns his grading opinion. When the next grader examines the comic, he is not able to see the first person's assigned grade, so as to not influence his own evaluation. After determining his own grade for the comic, he can then view the Graders Notes entered by the previous grader, and he may add to this commentary if he believes more remarks are in order. This same process is repeated as the comic passes to the Grading Finalizer. He makes a final restoration check before determining his own grade, at which time he then reviews the grades and notes entered by the previous graders. If all grades are in agreement or are very close, he will then assign the book's final grade. It then is forwarded to the Encapsulation Department for sealing. If there is disagreement among the graders, a discussion will ensue until a final determination is made and the book forwarded.

Encapsulating the Comics

After each comic has been graded and the necessary numbers and text entered into their respective data fields, all the comics on a particular invoice are taken from the Grading Department into the Encapsulation Department. Here, appropriately color-coded labels are printed out bearing a suitable descriptive text, including each book's grade and identification number. This last item is extremely important, as it serves to make each certified comic unique and is also an important deterrent to counterfeiting CGC's valued product. All of the above information is duplicated in a bar code, which appears underneath the written text on the comic's label.

The newly-printed labels are stacked in the same sequence as the comics to be encapsulated with them, ensuring that each book and its label match one another. The comic is now ready to be fitted inside an archival-quality interior well, which is then sealed within a transparent capsule, along with the book's color-coded label. This is accomplished through a combination of compression and ultrasonic vibration. The result is a newly-encapsulated CGC comic, ready to be shipped to its proud owner.

The Comics are Shipped

After encapsulation, all comics are returned briefly to the Grading Department for a quality control inspection. Here, they are examined to make certain that their labels are correct for both the grade and its accompanying descriptive information. The quality control person also inspects each book for any flaws in its holder, such as scuffs or nicks. While these are quite rare, CGC is careful to make certain that the comics it certifies are not only accurately graded but attractively presented as well.

When all the comics have been inspected, they're either held in CGC's vault for in-person pick-up by the submitter or delivered to our Shipping Department for packaging. The comics are counted and their labels checked against the original hand-written or typed invoice to make certain that no mistakes have occurred. A Shipping Department employee then verifies the method of transport as selected by the submitter on the invoice and prepares the comics for delivery.

Each comic book graded receives a numerical grade ranging from .5 or poor to 10.0 or Gem Mint

No matter whether the US Postal Service or some private carrier is used, the method of packaging is essentially the same.

The encapsulated comics are placed vertically inside boxes made of very sturdy cardboard. These boxes contain a row of dividers so that the capsules don't come into contact with one another. In 2005, CGC developed a custom shipping box to enable the highest level of stability during shipping. A copy of the submitter's invoice is included before the box is sealed and heavy tape is used to prevent accidental or unauthorized opening of the box while it's in transit.

The barcode of every comic book is scanned before it is placed into its shipping box. The status of the book is changed to "shipped" in our tracking system, and we retain an infallible record of what books were shipped in which box. This is the final critical step of our detailed internal tracking system.

The CGC Label

Comic books certified by CGC bear color-coded labels that have different meanings. Whenever purchasing a CGC-certified comic, be certain to note not just the book's grade but also its label category. A Universal label is denoted by the color blue and indicates that a book was not found to have any qualifying defects or signs of restoration. There is one exception to this policy: At CGC's discretion, comics having a very minor amount of glue and/or color touch-up may still qualify for a Universal label provided that they were produced approximately 1950 or earlier and that such restoration is noted underneath the assigned grade.

As its name implies, the Restored label, identified by the color purple, is used for books found to have restoration work performed on them. The grade assigned is based on the book's appearance, with the restoration noted. A distinction is made between Amateur and Professional restoration, this judgment being based on the materials used. Since the degree of work performed is also significant with restored books, there are a total of seven possible descriptions under the Restored label. Each description is prefaced with the word "Apparent," followed by "Slight," "Moderate," or "Extensive" in combination with the final descriptors Amateur or Professional. Examples of Restored labels might read "Apparent Moderate Professional" or "Apparent Slight Amateur," both descriptions then being followed by the book's grade. Finally, comics which have had no restoration other than a trimming of their covers or edges are labeled as simply Apparent, followed by their grade.

The Qualified label is green, and this indicates that one quali-fying defect is present on a book. An example of such a qualifying feature would be a missing Marvel Value Stamp that does not affect the story. While such a book technically may grade 1.5, it may appear to grade 9.6. In such instances, assigning a grade of just 1.5 does not fully represent the value of the comic to a collector. Through use of the green Qualified label, a comic buyer is able to make an informed decision as to what he is purchasing in terms of its overall desirability.

Because of the complexity involved, green labels are assigned quite seldom and then only when considered absolutely necessary. In addition, Comic books that have a signature, that do not fall under the Signature Series label (see below), get the Qualified label. This is the most common use for the Qualified label. This shows what the grade of the book would have been if the signature was not present.

CGC's Signature Series label is yellow, and is used when a comic book has been signed or been sketched on by a creator in the presence of a CGC representative, assuring the signature's or sketch's authenticity. Only books that meet CGC's strict criteria for authenticity are eligible for the Signature Series label. In addition to the certified grade, the yellow label includes who signed it and when it was signed. If appropriate, a Signature Series label may state at which venue a book was signed. In 2007, CGC introduced a Signature Series Restored label. Similar to the CGC Signature Series label in color, it can be differentiated by a purple bar across the type. Restoration is noted in the same fashion as on the purple CGC Restored label, and, as with the regular Signature Series label, restored books must be signed in the presence of CGC representatives in order to be eligible for signature authentication.

In October of 2003, CGC began to certify comic book related magazines. The certification process and label system for magazines is exactly the same as for comic books. Some examples of comic book related magazines CGC certifies are MAD Magazine, Vampirella, Savage Tales, Eerie, and Famous Monsters of Filmland.

Color coded labels found on the CGC holder include Universal, Restored, Qualified, Signature Series, and Signature Series Restored.

For more information on comic book certification and CGC's many services, please visit our website at www.CGCcomics.com

The Overstreet Hall of Fame was conceived to single out individuals who have made great contributions to the comic book arts. This includes writers, artists, editors, publishers and others who have plied their craft in insightful and meaningful ways.

While such evaluations are inherently subjective, they also serve to aid in reflecting upon those who shaped the experience of reading comic books over the years. This year's class of inductees begins on this next page. First, though, we offer a list of the previous inductees:

Class of 2006	Class of 2007
Murphy Anderson	Dave Cockrum
Jim Aparo	Steve Ditko
Jim Lee	Bruce Hamilton
Mac Raboy	Martin Nodell
	George Pérez
	Jim Shooter
	Dave Stevens
	Alex Toth
	Michael Turner

Originally known to fans only as "The Good Duck Artist," in 1935, Carl Barks went to work for the Disney Studios and storyboarded cartoons such as *Donald's Nephews* and *Donald's Cousin Gus*. In 1942, Western Publishing asked him to work on the comic story "Donald Duck Finds Pirate Gold," and then to rewrite and draw a 10-page Donald story for *Walt Disney's Comics and Stories* #31. Soon, he became a regular contributor, lasting 25 years in the position, until his retirement in 1967. After retiring, though, Barks kept active. In 1971 he obtained permission from Disney to produce and sell oil paintings based on the Duck characters. In 1976 Disney withdrew permission, but in 1982 Another Rainbow Publishing, which had just secured a license from Disney to produce lithographs of Barks' paintings, commissioned him to paint two new oils per year. In 1995, Barks finally retired for real. He died on August 25, 2000, just shy of 100 years old.

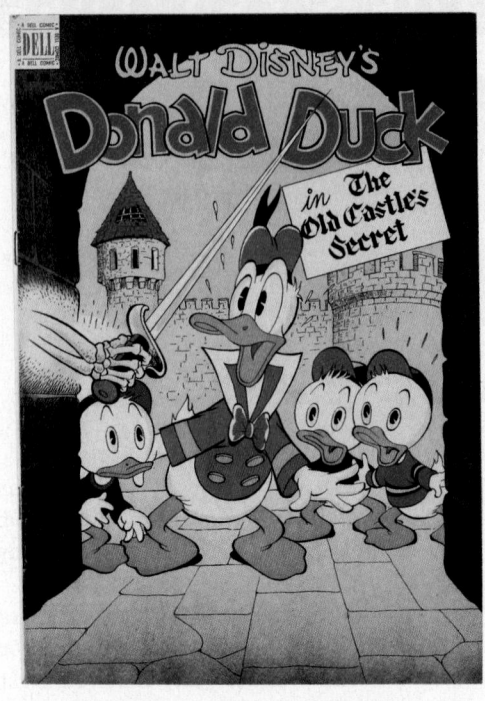

FOUR COLOR COMICS #189
Barks' first cover. June 1948. © DIS

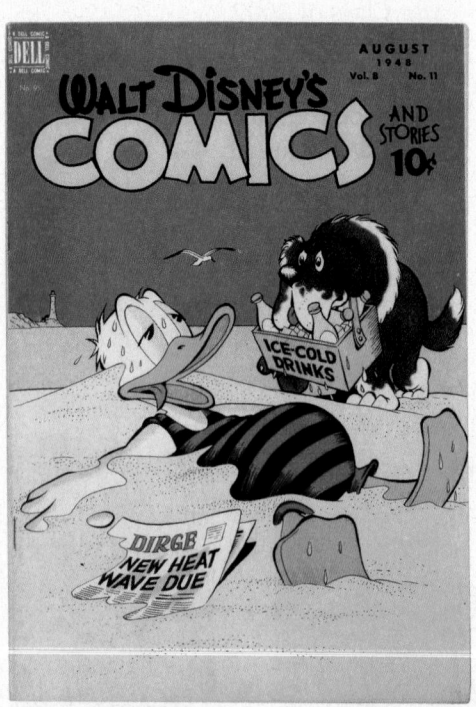

WALT DISNEY'S COMICS AND STORIES #189
Barks' first WDC&S cover. August 1948. © DIS

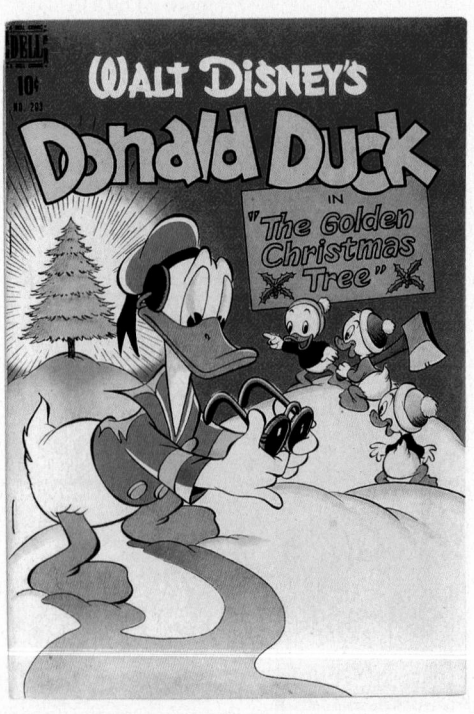

FOUR COLOR COMICS #203
December 1948. © DIS

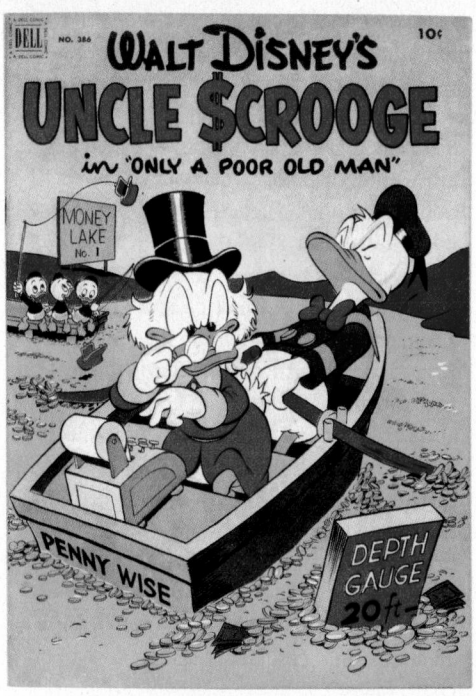

FOUR COLOR COMICS #386
First Scrooge issue. March 1952. © DIS

WALT DISNEY'S COMICS AND STORIES #140
First WDC&S cover with Scrooge. May 1952. © DIS

UNCLE SCROOGE #4
December 1953. © DIS

WALT DISNEY'S COMICS AND STORIES #1047
First Gyro Gearloose cover. November 1959. © DIS

THE SPIRIT NEWSPAPER SECTION
August 25, 1940. © Will Eisner

Considered by many to be the father of the American graphic novel, Will Eisner was a writer, artist, master storyteller, and businessman. In a career that spanned eight decades, he created The Spirit, John Law, Lady Luck, Mr. Mystic, Uncle Sam, Blackhawk and numerous other characters. He co-founded the Eisner – Iger Studios, then created the Spirit sections which were issued weekly in newspapers across America, and developed and packaged *P.S. Magazine* for the U.S. Army. His book *A Contract With God* is arguably the first American graphic novel, and he continued to produce numerous other important works well into his 80s with the quality for which he was known. At one Harvey Awards ceremony, he received honors for works produced 60 years apart (*The Spirit* and *Last Day in Vietnam*). Eisner passed away following heart surgery, but left an almost immeasurable legacy.

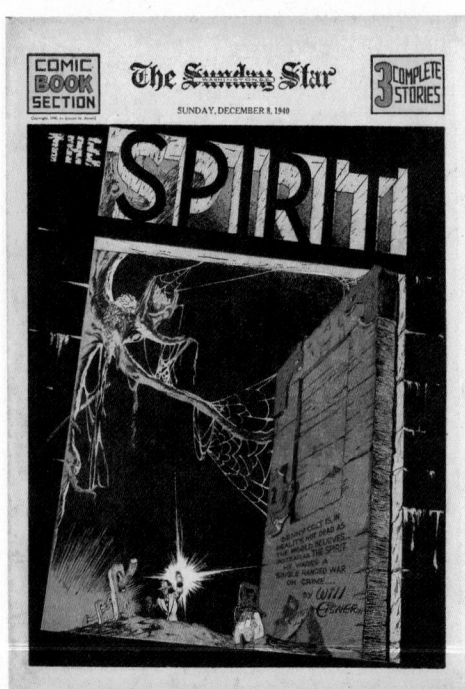

THE SPIRIT NEWSPAPER SECTION
December 8, 1940. © Will Eisner

THE SPIRIT NEWSPAPER SECTION
October 6, 1946. © Will Eisner

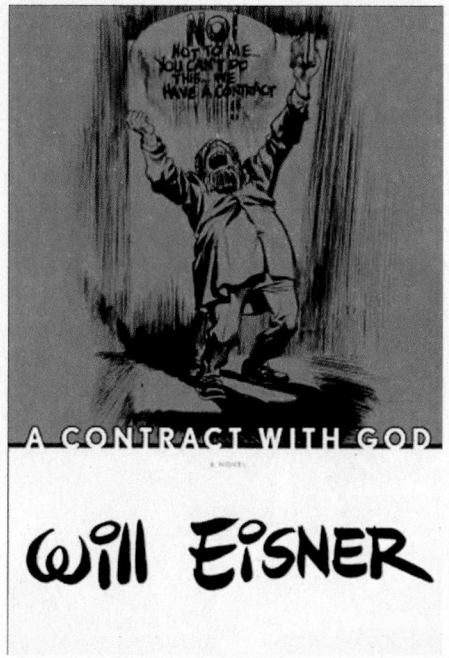

A CONTRACT WITH GOD
1978. © Will Eisner

DROPSIE AVENUE: THE NEIGHBORHOOD
1995. © Will Eisner

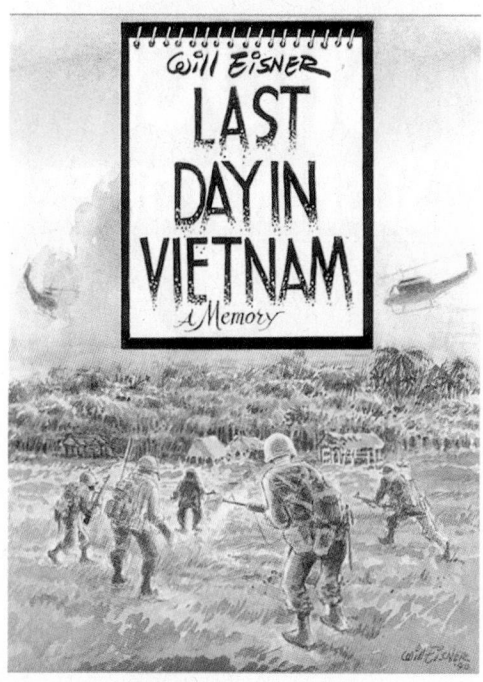

LAST DAY IN VIETNAM
July 2000. © Will Eisner

**WILL EISNER'S THE SPIRIT
ARCHIVES VOLUME 15**
2004. © Will Eisner

As an editor with EC Comics, Al Feldstein created, wrote, illustrated and edited titles in one of the most influential comic book lines in history. With a body of work ranging from horror (*Tales from the Crypt*) to science-fiction to crime and suspense, his contributions have been reprinted numbers of times over the years. They also stood up to the harshest critic: time. In 1955, he became editor of *MAD*, which had started as part of EC's comic book line-up and survived the demise of its sister publications by graduating to magazine format. Under his editorship, the magazine's circulation steadily increased from 375,000 to almost 3 million. Using his own pen name, he christened Alfred E. Neuman, *MAD*'s trademark character, and made short work of many social conventions. In 1984, Feldstein retired from *MAD* to devote his time to painting, something he continues in his Montana home.

THE HAUNT OF FEAR #9
September-October 1951. © WMG

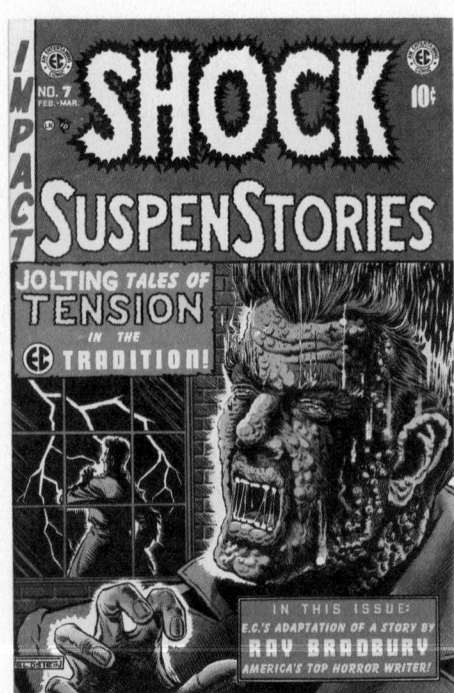

SHOCK SUSPENSTORIES #7
February-March 1953. © WMG

SHOCK SUSPENSTORIES #9
June-July 1953. © WMG

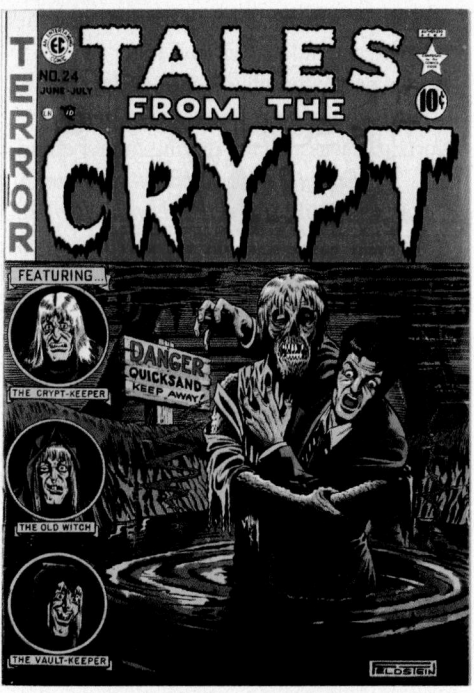

TALES FROM THE CRYPT #24
June-July 1951. © WMG

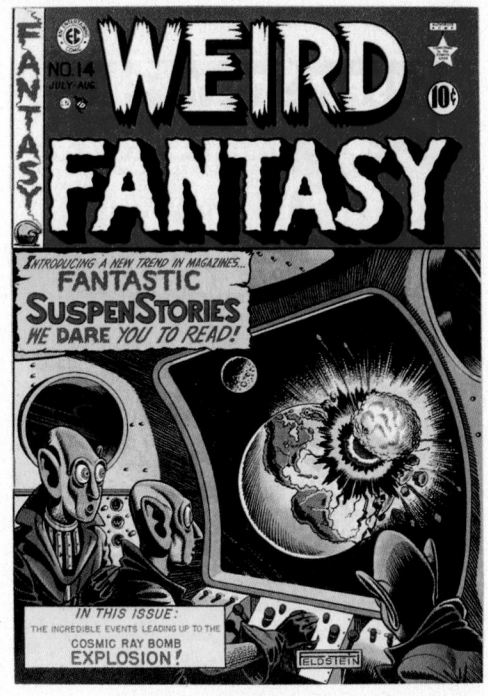

WEIRD FANTASY #14 (#2)
July-August 1950. © WMG

WEIRD SCIENCE #13 (#2)
July-August 1950. © WMG

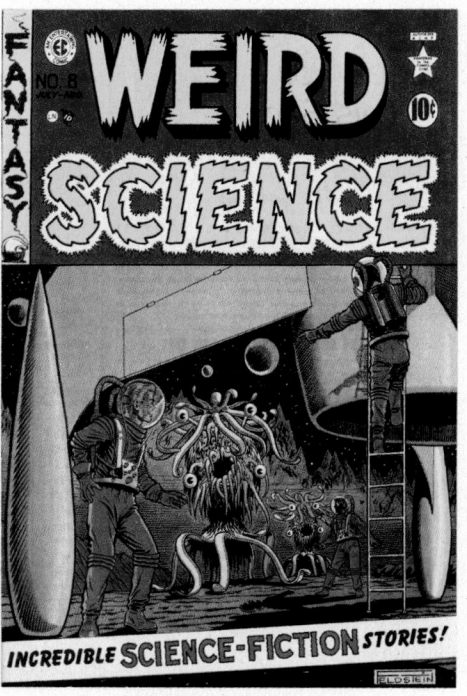

WEIRD SCIENCE #8
July-August 1951. © WMG

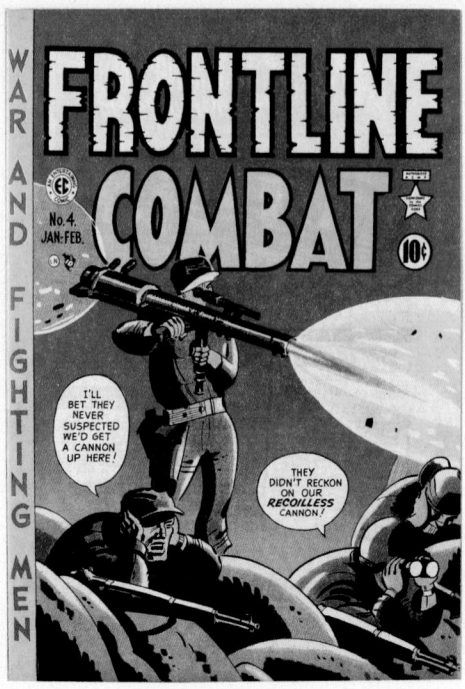

FRONTLINE COMBAT #4
January-February 1952. © WMG

Harvey Kurtzman was a cartoonist, writer, editor, artist and master storyteller. Best known as the founding editor of *MAD* in its original comic book form at EC Comics, Kurtzman was also the driving force behind EC's *Two-Fisted Tales* and *Frontline Combat*. He also created *Hey Look!*, *Trump*, *Help!*, and *Humbug*. Throughout his career, he worked with artists such as Will Elder, Jack Davis, John Severin, Wally Wood, and Russ Heath, among others, but his method of scripting and providing page layouts had the impact of making a Harvey Kurtzman story come out looking like a Harvey Kurtzman story no matter who illustrated it. His war comics are generally considered among the best the genre has ever experienced even though they clearly portray the high cost of war on individuals rather than more typical war stories. The long-running comic book industry Harvey Awards are named in his honor.

FRONTLINE COMBAT #9
November-December 1952. © WMG

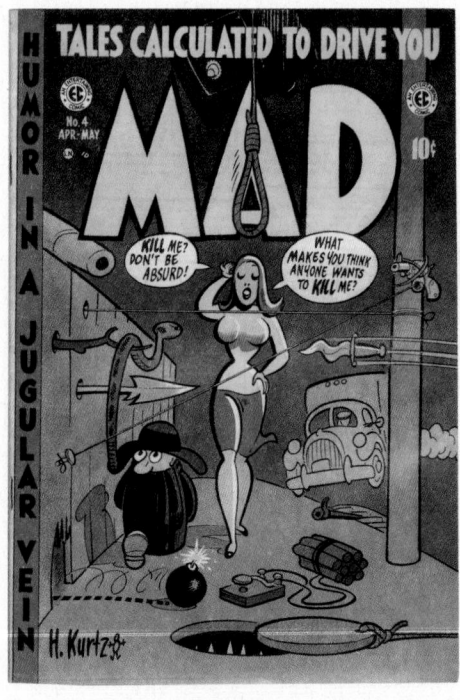

MAD #4
April-May 1953. © WMG

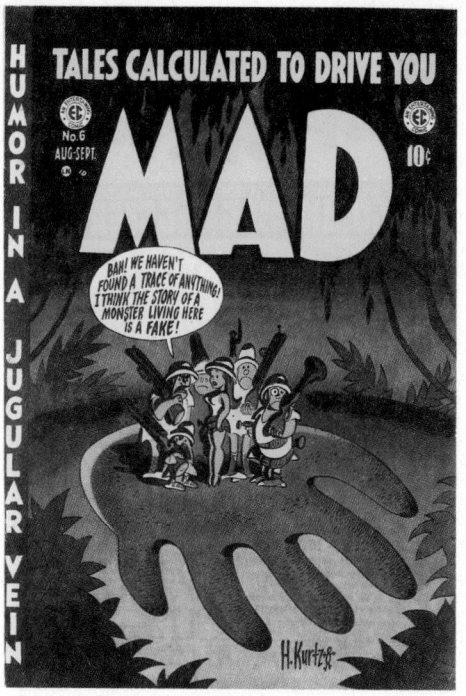

MAD #6
August-September 1953. © WMG

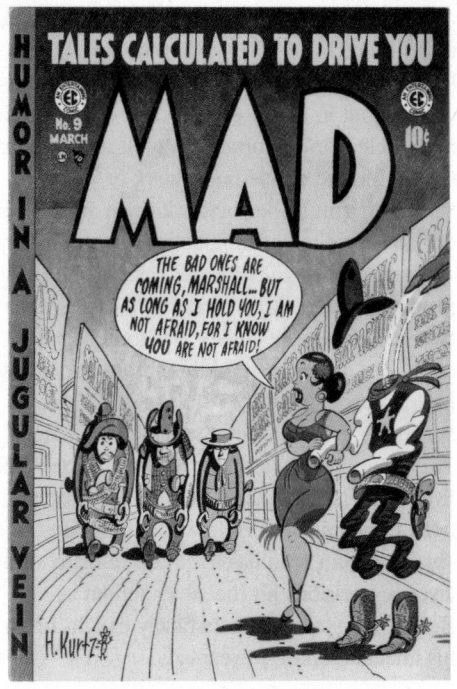

MAD #9
February-March 1954. © WMG

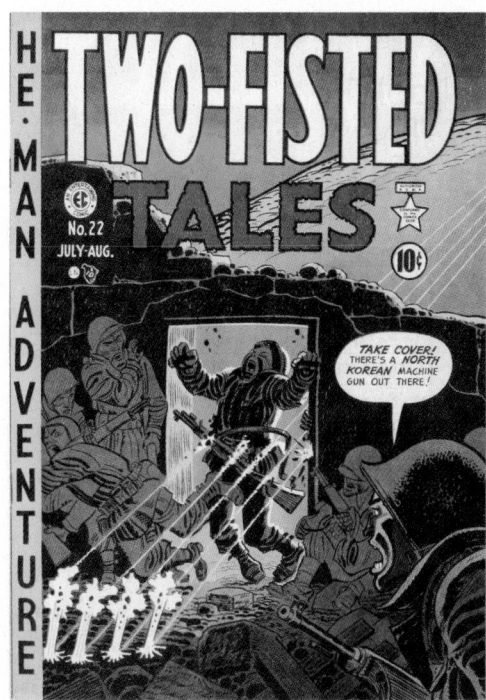

TWO-FISTED TALES #22
July-August 1951. © WMG

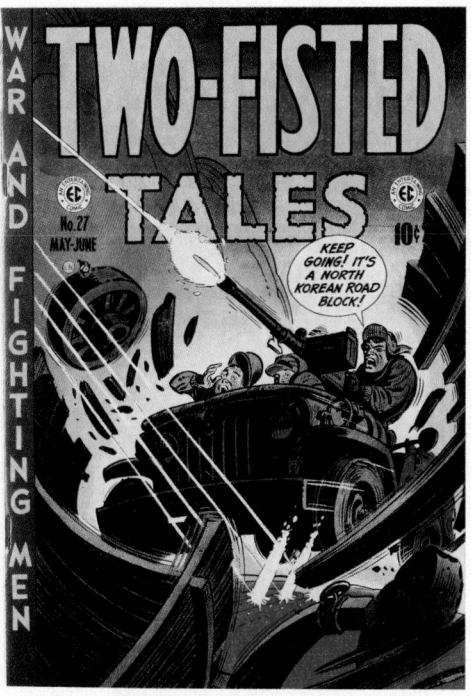

TWO-FISTED TALES #27
May-June 1952. © WMG

"Captain America Foils the Traitor's Revenge," a text piece in *Captain America Comics #3* (May 1941) might not have been the most auspicious debut in the history of the comics, but it is nonetheless an important event. It marked the first published comic book work of young Stanley Martin Lieber, better known as Stan Lee, the writer, editor, creator, co-creator, publisher and pitchman who developed and relentlessly promoted the identity of Marvel Comics. After two decades in which Lee was forced to do comics as others wanted them done, he finally he tried them his way. The Fantastic Four, Spider-Man, Thor, The Avengers, The X-Men, The Incredible Hulk and others were the result. Eventually moving to the west coast to spearhead the company's Hollywood ambitions, this entertainment icon has lived to see many of his favorite creations hit the silver screen as Hollywood special effects finally caught up to his imagination of 40 years ago.

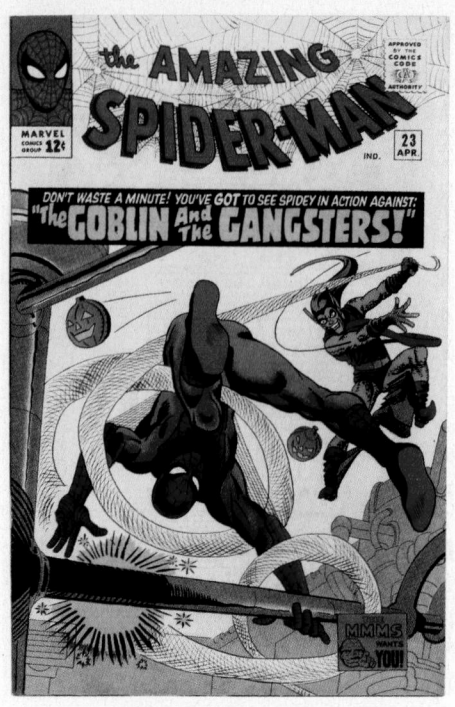

AMAZING SPIDER-MAN #23
April 1965. © MAR

THE AVENGERS #16
May 1965. © MAR

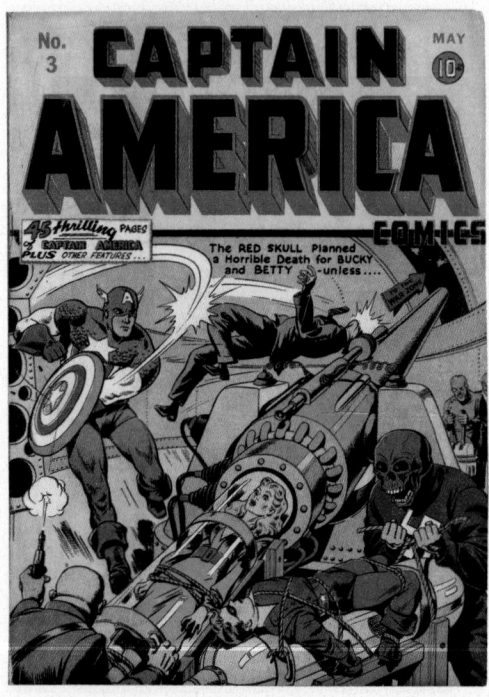

CAPTAIN AMERICA COMICS #3
May 1947. © MAR

FANTASTIC FOUR #51
June 1966. © MAR

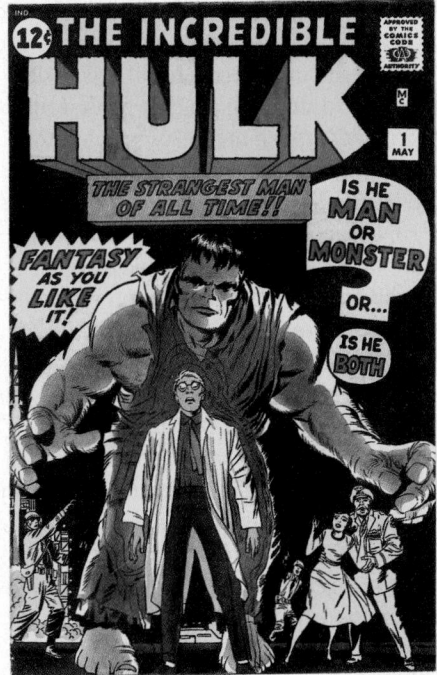

INCREDIBLE HULK #1
May 1962. © MAR

**SGT. FURY AND HIS
HOWLING COMMANDOS #5**
January 1964. © MAR

X-MEN #4
March 1964. © MAR

Marshall Rogers visually defined Batman for a generation of fans. Teamed with writer Steve Englehart and inker Terry Austin, Rogers delivered the lead stories in a highly praised run on *Detective Comics* in the 1970s which introduced mob boss Rupert Thorne, Bruce Wayne's love interest Silver St. Cloud, and the Joker Fish. He simultaneously drew a memorable run of *Mister Miracle*. Rogers also worked with Englehart on *Coyote* in serialized form in the pages of *Eclipse Magazine*, *Madam Xanadu*, *Scorpio Rose*, *Silver Surfer* and later, again with Austin inking, on the mini-series *Batman: Dark Detective*. Rogers also illustrated a run on *Doctor Strange* and teamed with writer Don McGregor on the original *Detectives, Inc.* graphic novel. His work also appeared in *G.I. Joe*, *Howard The Duck*, *Green Lantern: Evil's Might*, *Batman: Legends of the Dark Knight*, and his own creation, *Cap'n Quick and a Foozle*. He passed away unexpectedly at the age of 57.

DETECTIVE COMICS #475
February 1978. © DC

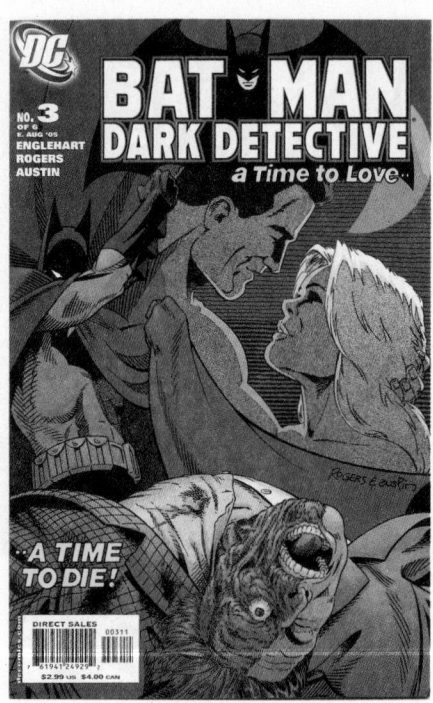

BATMAN: DARK DETECTIVE #3
Early August 2005. © DC

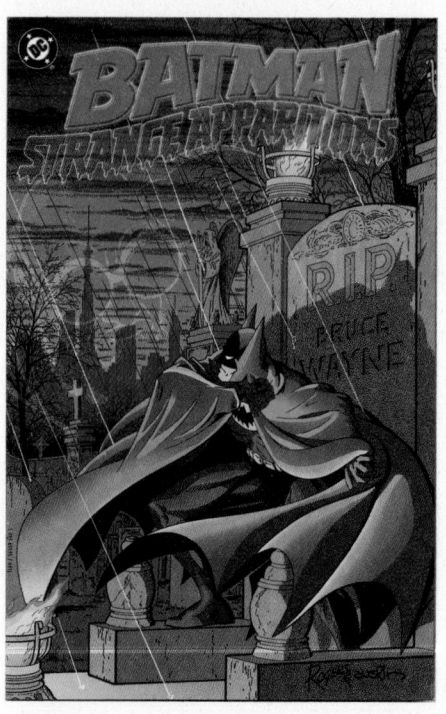

BATMAN: STRANGE APPARITIONS TPB
1999. © DC

DAUGHTERS OF THE DRAGON:
DEADLY HANDS SPECIAL
2006. © MAR

DETECTIVES INC. #1
April 1985. © McGregor & Rogers

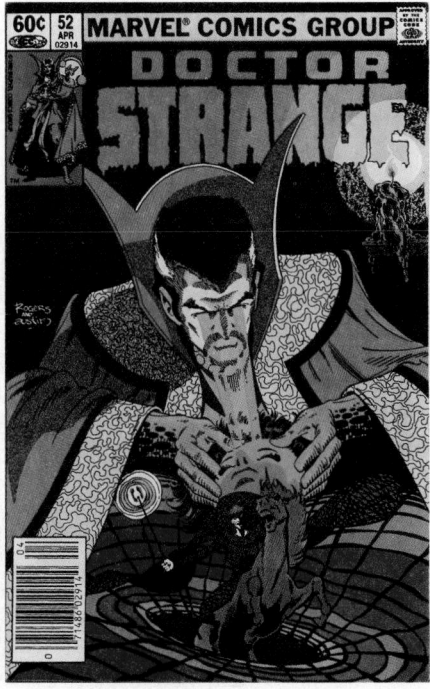

DOCTOR STRANGE #52
April 1982. © MAR

MISTER MIRACLE #20
October 1977. © DC

AMAZING SPIDER-MAN #56
January 1968. © MAR

AMAZING SPIDER-MAN #100
September 1971. © MAR

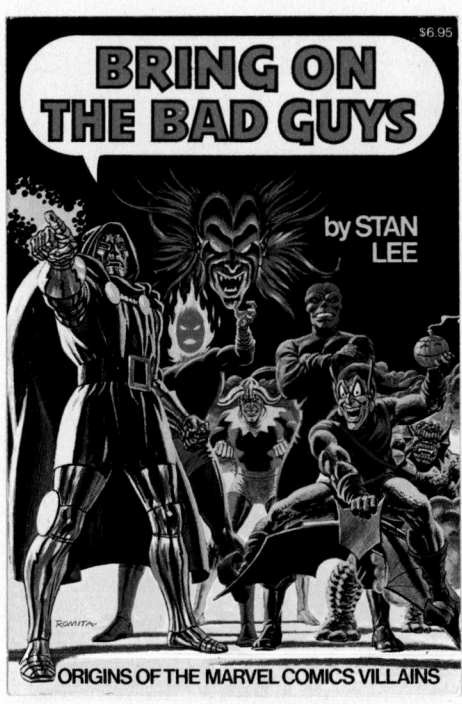

BRING ON THE BAD GUYS
Softcover. Fireside Book Series. 1976. © MAR

CAPTAIN AMERICA COMICS #78
September 1954. © MAR

Even if they have never seen a comic book, anyone who saw the visual imagery in the first two Spider-Man feature films has seen the work of John Romita, Sr. (credited simply as John Romita for a good portion of his career). Imagery based on his strong, distinctive, character-rich comic book work permeated just about every important scene in those movies. He worked in the industry for years before he took over the art duties on *Amazing Spider-Man* from Steve Ditko, but his dynamic style and fluid linework put his stamp on Spidey almost immediately, forever associating him with the character. His influence on successive generations of Marvel Comics artists was foreseen by Stan Lee, who hired him as Art Director for the company. Although he is officially retired, his work still pops up from time to time, always to smiles from his fans and fellow professionals.

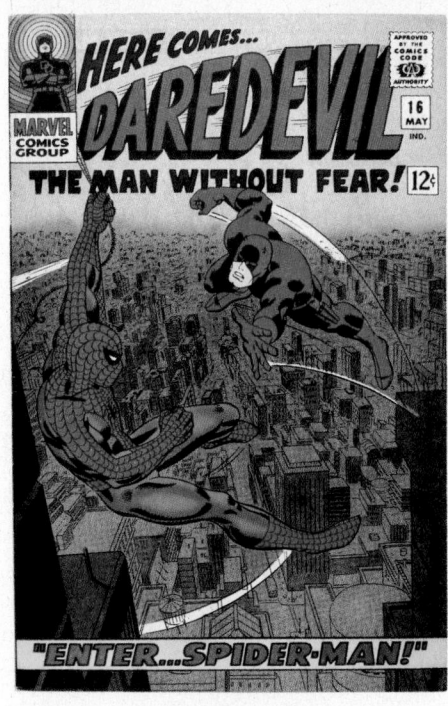

DAREDEVIL #16
May 1966. © MAR

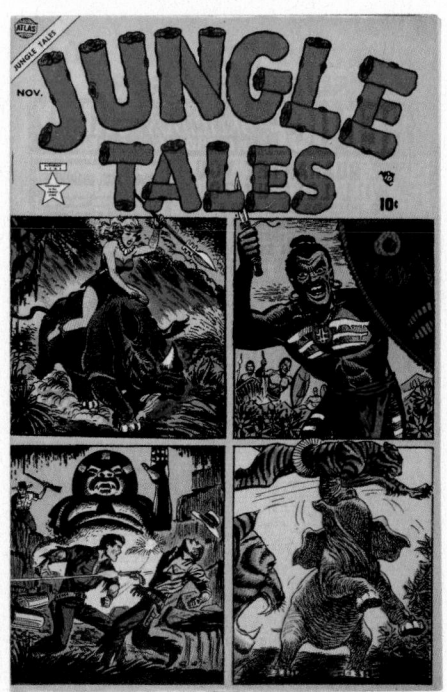

JUNGLE TALES #2
November 1954. © MAR

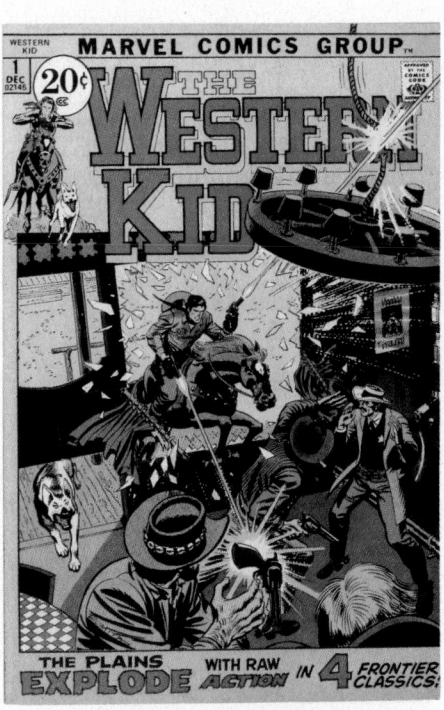

THE WESTERN KID #1
December 1971. © MAR

After making his American comics debut in the pages of *Amazing Spider-Man Annual* #11, John Romita, Jr. quickly established himself as a popular artist with a healthy run on *Iron Man*. He then launched into his first run on *Amazing Spider-Man*, the series that had made his father a fan favorite. He followed this with stints on *Uncanny X-Men*, *Daredevil*, *Daredevil: Man Without Fear*, *Star Brand*, *Punisher War Zone*, *Cable*, *The Mighty Thor*, a second run on *Iron Man*, *Wolverine*, a second run on *Amazing Spider-Man*, *The Black Panther*, *The Sentry*, *The Eternals*, and the "World War Hulk" event. He illustrated the *Punisher-Batman* crossover and his creator-owned *The Gray Area*, which was released by Image Comics. He has worked with John, Sr. on a number of special occasions, always to the delight of the comic-buying public, but has clearly worked to develop his own style, sometimes sharing only a commitment to great storytelling with his father.

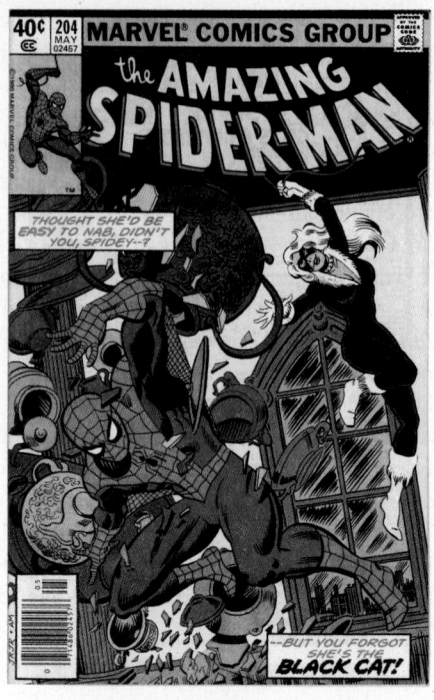

AMAZING SPIDER-MAN #204
May 1980. © MAR

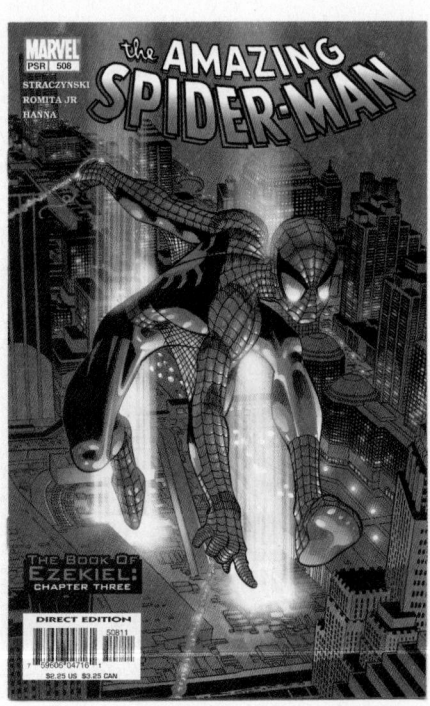

AMAZING SPIDER-MAN #508
July 2004. © MAR

DAREDEVIL #256
July 1988. © MAR

**DAREDEVIL THE MAN
WITHOUT FEAR #3**
December 1993. © MAR

ETERNALS HC
2007. © MAR

THE GRAY AREA #1
June, 2004. © John Romita, Jr. and Glen Brunswick

UNCANNY X-MEN #200
December 1985. © MAR

It's difficult to measure the impact Julius "Julie" Schwartz had on the comic book world. In fact, as we observed at the time of his passing, we would probably need to invent a new unit of measurement just to begin to cover it. He was Ray Bradbury's first agent and an important voice in science fiction before he ever joined All-American Comics in 1944. Working with writers such as John Broome and artists like Gil Kane, Murphy Anderson, Carmine Infantino, and Joe Kubert, he began the underpinnings of what would become the resurgence of superhero comics in the 1950s and '60s. After re-introducing and revamping characters such as Flash and Green Lantern, he helped develop DC's "multiverse" by having the then-current incarnations of characters meet their predecessors, kicking off one of the best-loved eras in the company's history. He was continually a force for reinvention of characters and served as a goodwill ambassador after his retirement.

AMAZING WORLD OF DC COMICS #3
November 1974. © DC

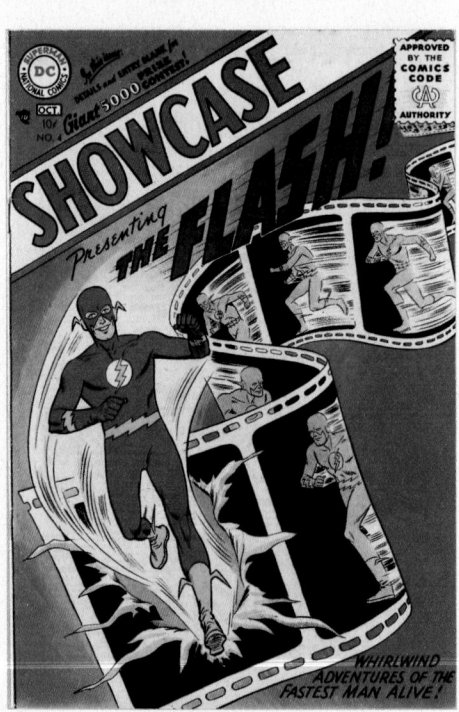

SHOWCASE #4
September-October 1956. © DC

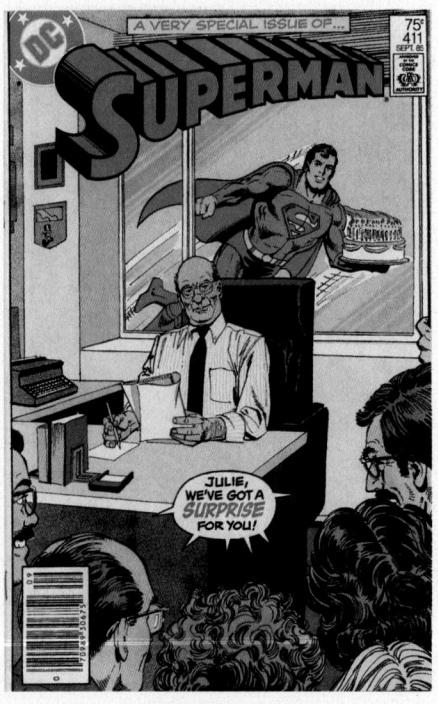

SUPERMAN #411
September 1985. © DC

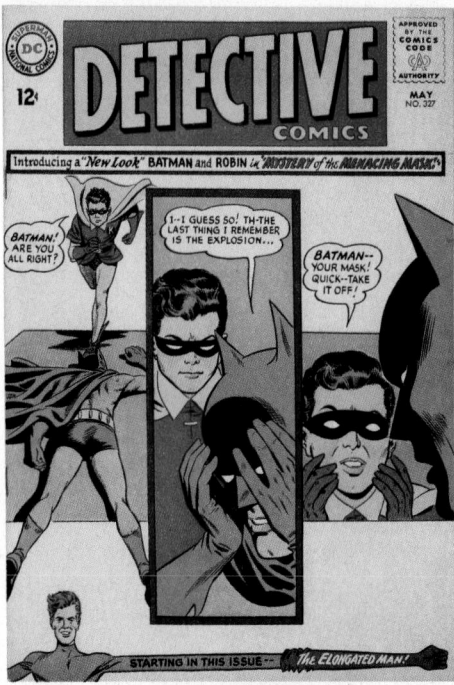

DETECTIVE COMICS #327
May 1964. Debut of the yellow oval Bat-emblem. © DC

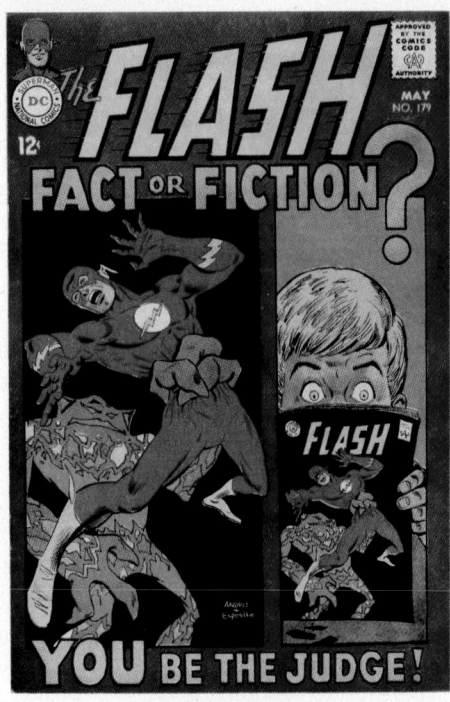

THE FLASH #179
May 1968. The Flash first meets Julius
Schwartz on Earth-Prime. © DC

MYSTERY IN SPACE #59
May 1960. © DC

SUPERMAN #233
January 1971. © DC

Also known as "Ringo," artist Mike Wieringo was best known for his work on DC Comics' *The Flash*, Marvel Comics' *Fantastic Four*, and *Tellos*; the creator-owned fantasy series he developed with friend and writer Todd DeZago. In an era in which many artists rely on shock or over-the-top style, his clean, deceptively simple linework captured the heroism superheroes are supposed to embody and earned the artist a strong fan following.

Born in Venice, Italy in 1963, he joined writer Mark Waid on DC's *The Flash* with issue #80 in 1993; during their run the two co-created the character Impulse. Wieringo also illustrated *Robin* at DC, *Sensational Spider-Man* (with DeZago) at Marvel, and then created *Tellos*. He also illustrated stints on *Adventures of Superman* and (again with Waid) on *Fantastic Four*, and *Spider-Man and the Fantastic Four*, among other projects. Wieringo passed away suddenly on August 12, 2007 at age 44.

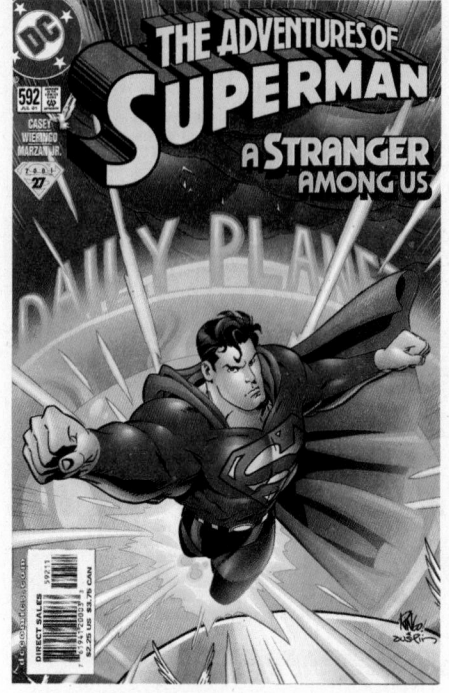

ADVENTURES OF SUPERMAN #592
July 2001. © DC

FANTASTIC FOUR Vol. 3 #60
October 2002. © MAR

THE FLASH #92
July 1994. Debut of Impulse. © DC

JUSTICE LEAGUE QUARTERLY #11
Summer 1993. © DC

ROGUE TPB
1995. © MAR

SENSATIONAL SPIDER-MAN #8
September 1996. © MAR

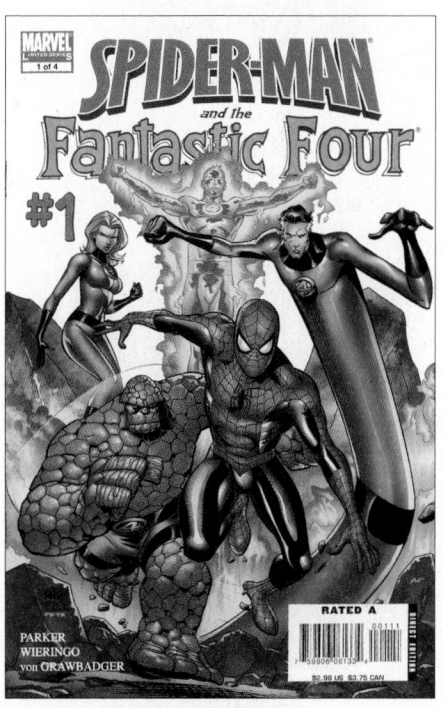

**SPIDER-MAN AND
THE FANTASTIC FOUR #1**
June 2007. © MAR

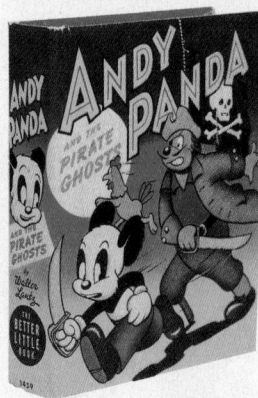

ANDY PANDA AND THE
PIRATE GHOSTS
BLB #1459 · 1949. © WHIT

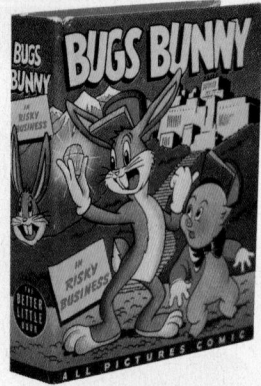

BUGS BUNNY
IN RISKY BUSINESS
BLB #1440 · 1948. © WB

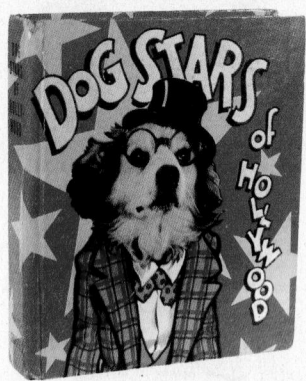

DOG STARS
OF HOLLYWOOD
BLB #1114 · 1936. © Saalfield

G-MAN
BREAKING THE GAMBLING RING
BLB #1493 · 1938. © WHIT

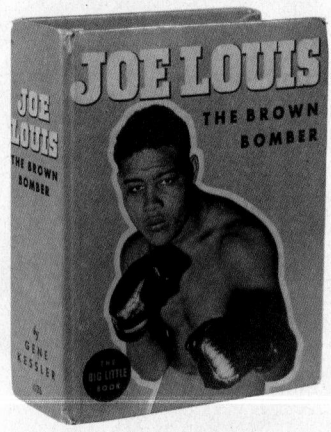

JOE LOUIS
THE BROWN BOMBER
BLB #1105 · 1936. © WHIT

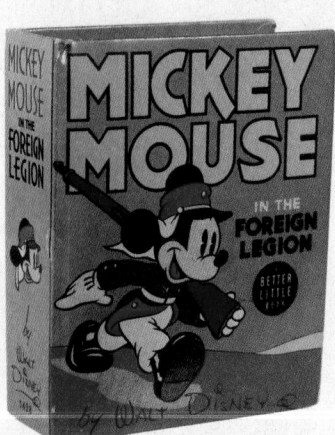

MICKEY MOUSE,
IN THE FOREIGN LEGION
BLB #1428 · 1940. © DIS

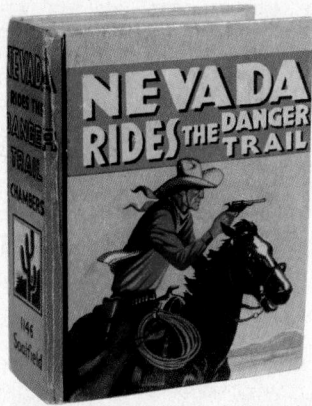

NEVADA RIDES THE DANGER TRAIL
BLB #1146 · 1938. © Saalfield

ROBINSON CRUSOE
BLB #719 · c.1933. © WHIT

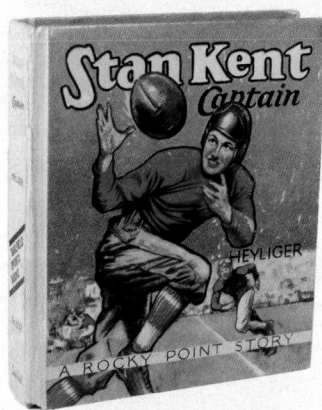

STAN KENT, CAPTAIN
BLB #1132 · 1937. © Saalfield

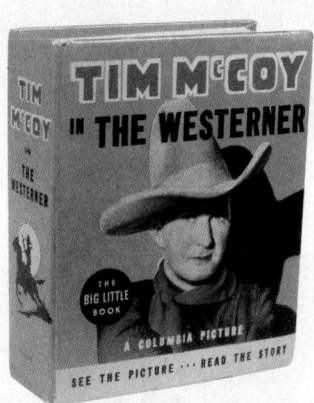

**TIM McCOY IN
THE WESTERNER**
BLB #1193 · 1936. © WHIT

**WALT DISNEY'S CINDERELLA AND
THE MAGIC WAND**
BLB #711-10 · 1950. © DIS

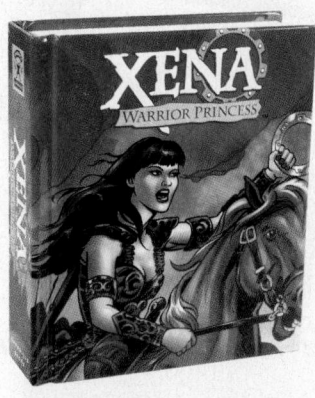

XENA · WARRIOR PRINCESS
Chronicle Books · 1998. © Universal TV

ADVENTURES WITH THE DC SUPER HEROES
2007. Geppi's Entertainment Museum/
Free Comic Book Day edition. © DC

DAN CURTIS GIVEAWAYS #1-3
1974. © Dan Curtis Prods., Paramount
and Cayuga Prods.

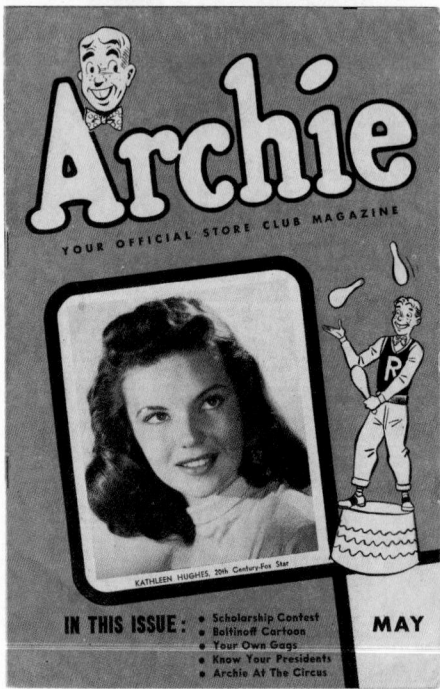

ARCHIE SHOE-STORE GIVEAWAY
May 1949. Kathleen Hughes photo cover. © AP

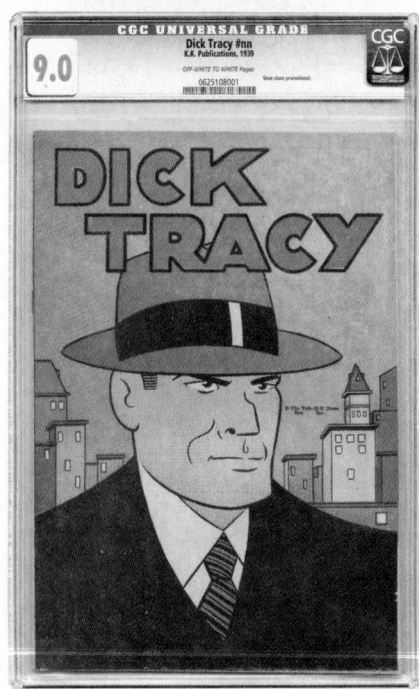

DICK TRACY
1939. Shoe store giveaway © NYNS

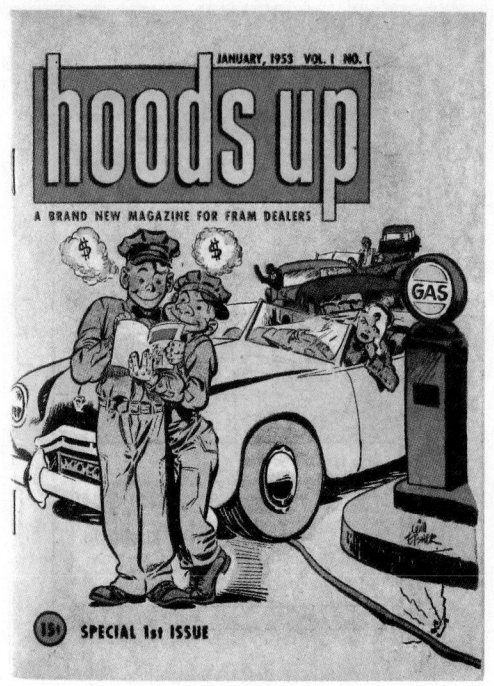

HOODS UP #1
January 1953. © Fram Corp.

MARCH OF COMICS #54
1950. © Gene Autry

TASTEE-FREEZ COMICS #1
1957. © HARV

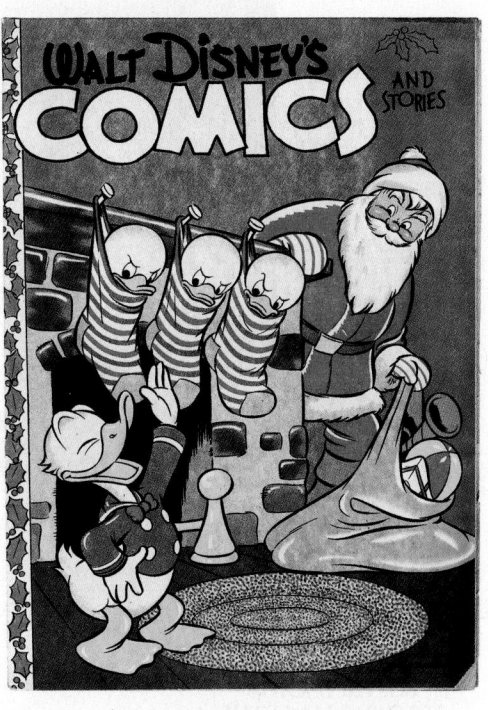

WALT DISNEY'S COMICS AND STORIES nn
1943. Department store giveaway. © DIS

AIN'T IT A GRAND & GLORIOUS FEELING?
1922. © WHIT

ALL THE FUNNY FOLKS
Edition with Dust Jacket. 1926. © World Press Today Inc.

HAPPY HOOLIGAN HOME AGAIN
1907. © Frederick A. Stokes

BUSTER BROWN
STOCKING MAGAZINE
1906. © Buster Brown Stocking Co.

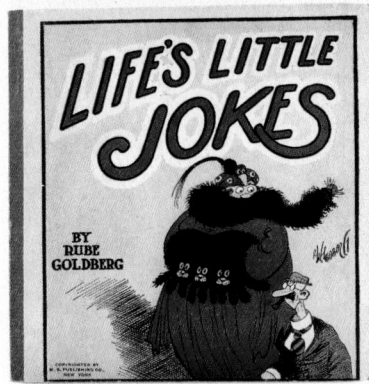

LIFE'S LITTLE JOKES
nd 1924. © M. S. Publication Co.

LITTLE SAMMY SNEEZE
December 1905. © New York Herald Co.

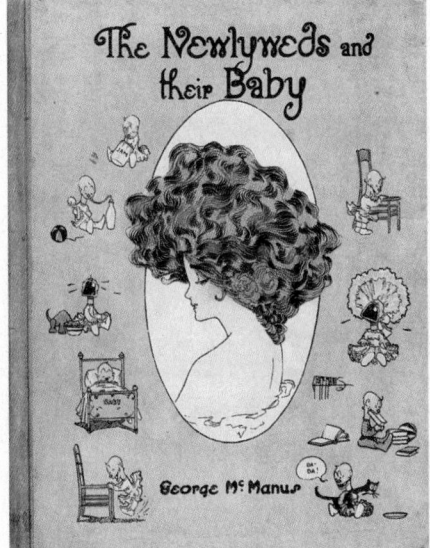

THE NEWLYWEDS AND THEIR BABY
1917. © Saalfield

OH SKIN-NAY!
1913. © P. F. Volland & Co.

ACTION COMICS #137
October 1949. © DC

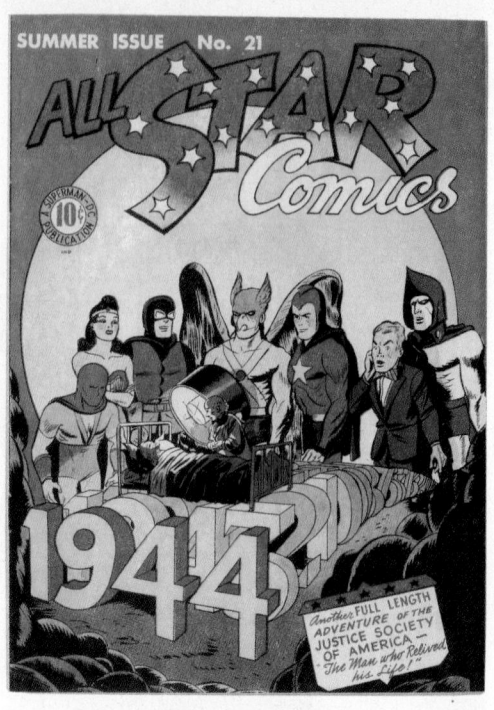

ALL STAR COMICS #21
Summer 1944. © DC

AMAZING-MAN COMICS #7
November 1939. © CEN

ARCHIE'S PAL, JUGHEAD #11
April 1952. © AP

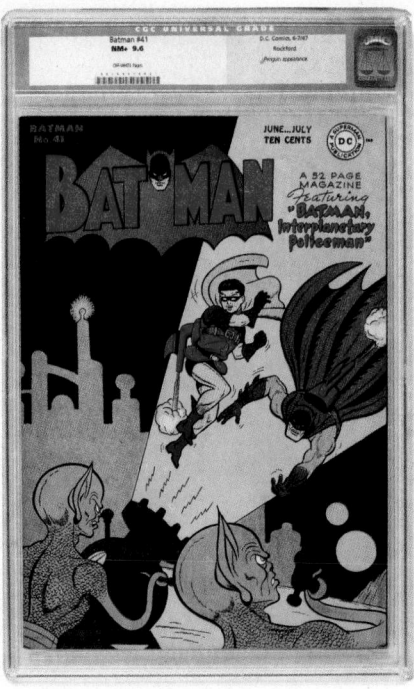

BATMAN #41
June-July 1947. © DC

BLUE RIBBON COMICS #12
May 1941. © MLJ

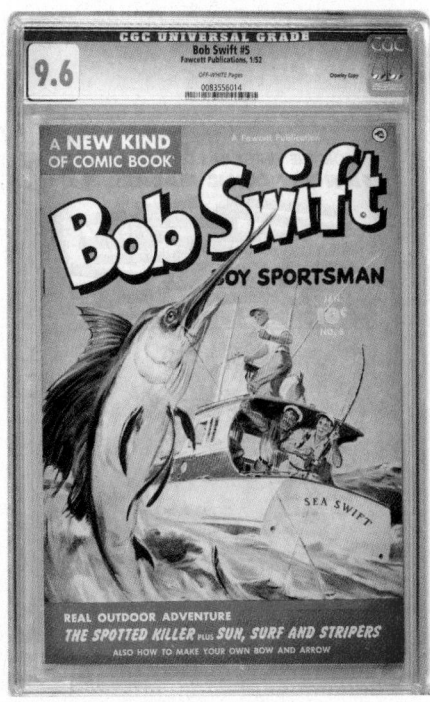

BOB SWIFT #5
January 1952. © FAW

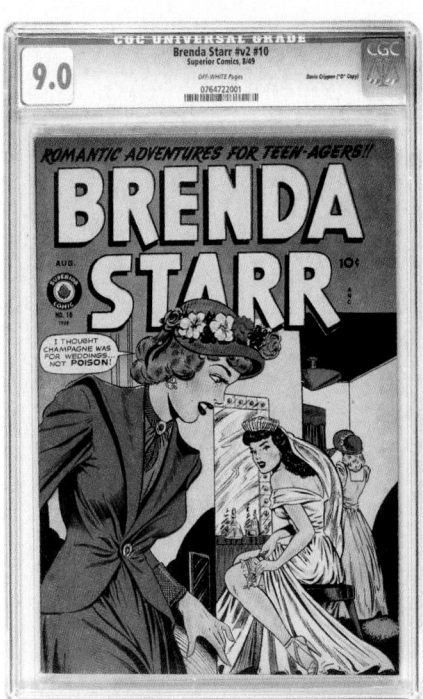

BRENDA STARR Vol. 2 #10
August 1949. © SUPR

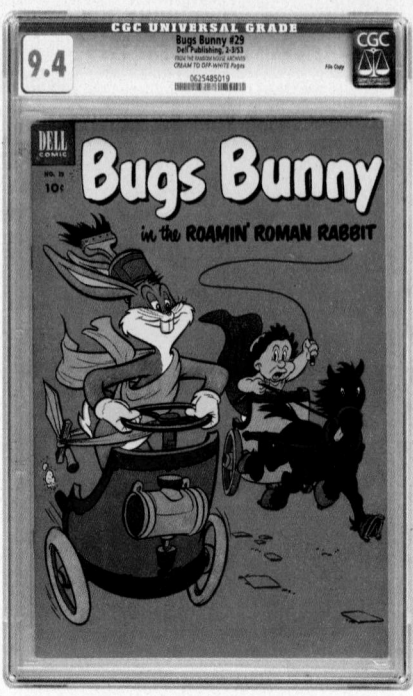

BUGS BUNNY #29
February-March 1953. © WB

CAPTAIN AMERICA COMICS #59
November 1946. © MAR

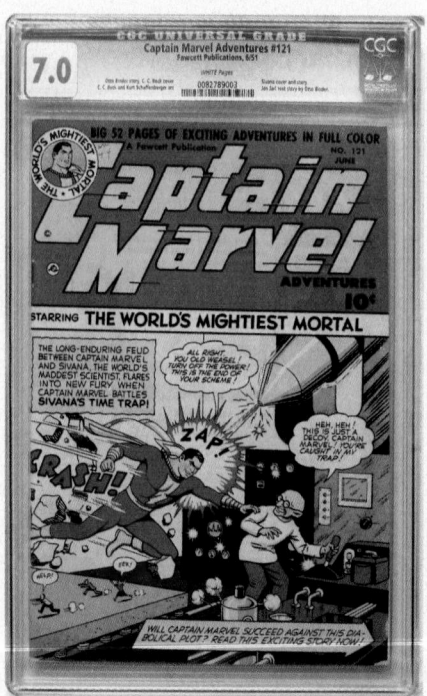

CAPTAIN MARVEL ADVENTURES #121
June 1951. © FAW

COMIC CAVALCADE #16
August-September 1946. © DC

DAREDEVIL COMICS #24
May 1944. © LEV

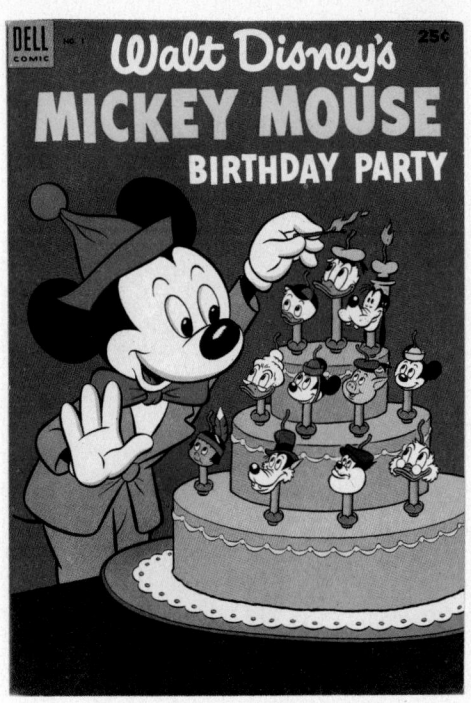

**DELL GIANT - MICKEY MOUSE
BIRTHDAY PARTY #1**
September 1953. © DIS

FIGHTING YANK #18
November 1946. © NEDOR

FIRST LOVE ILLUSTRATED #13
July 1951. © HARV

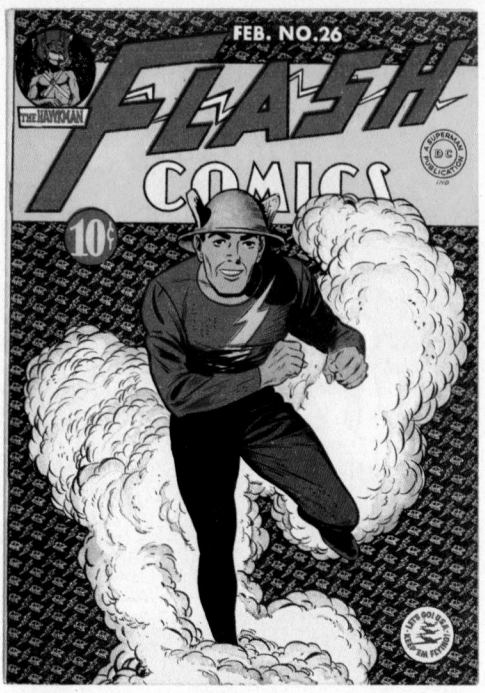

FLASH COMICS #26
February 1942. © DC

GREEN MASK #8
December 1941. © FOX

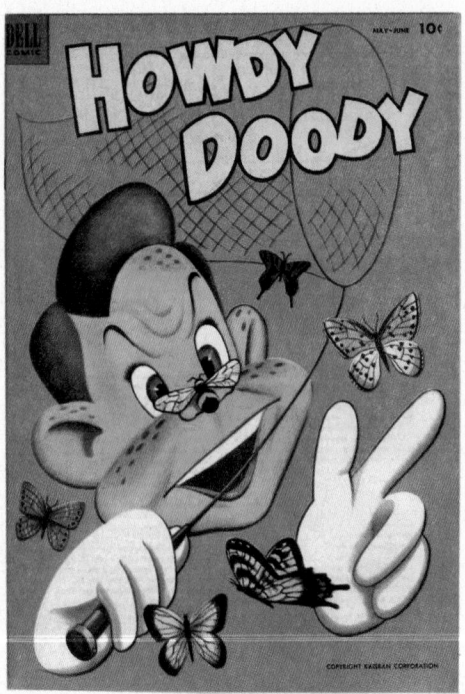

HOWDY DOODY #22
May-June 1953. © Kagran Corp.

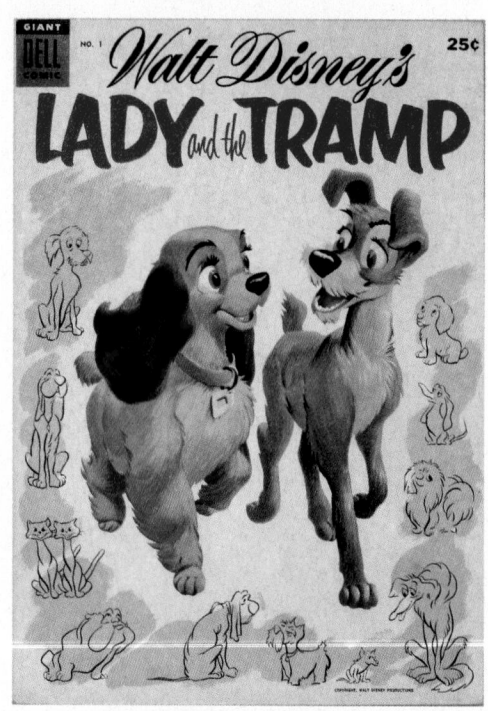

LADY AND THE TRAMP #1
June 1955. © DIS

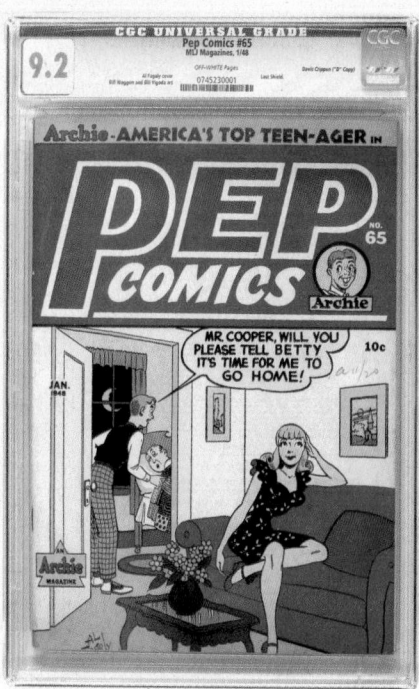

PEP COMICS #65
January 1948. © AP

ROY ROGERS COMICS #88
April 1955. © DELL

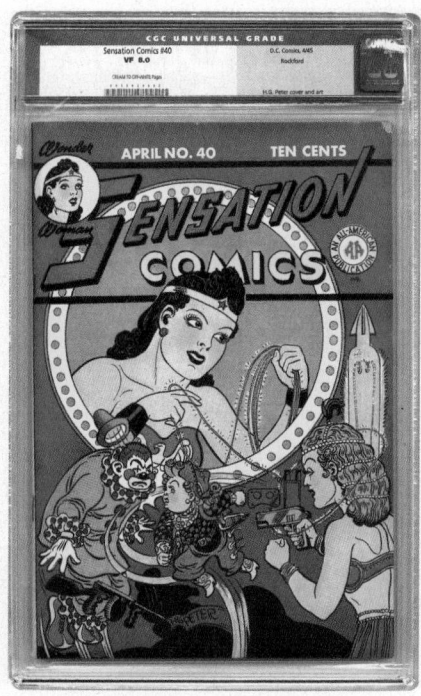

SENSATION COMICS #40
April 1945. © DC

SHEENA, QUEEN OF THE JUNGLE #16
Summer 1952. © FH

SPEED COMICS #9
June 1940. © HARV

SUPERMAN #14
January-February 1942. © DC

TRUE LOVE PICTORIAL #2
February 1953. © STJ

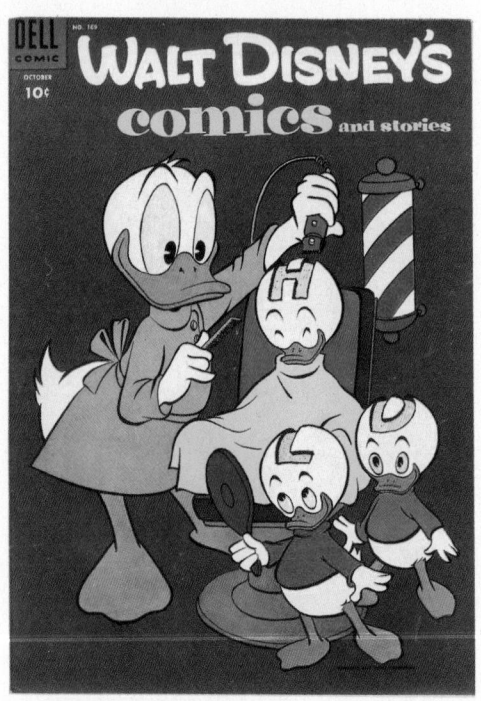

**WALT DISNEY'S COMICS AND
STORIES #169**
October 1954. © DIS

WEIRD COMICS #7
October 1940. © FOX

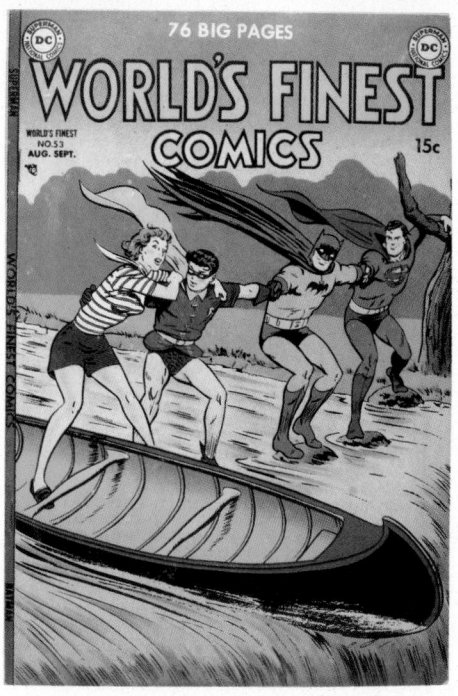

WORLD'S FINEST COMICS #53
August-September 1951. © DC

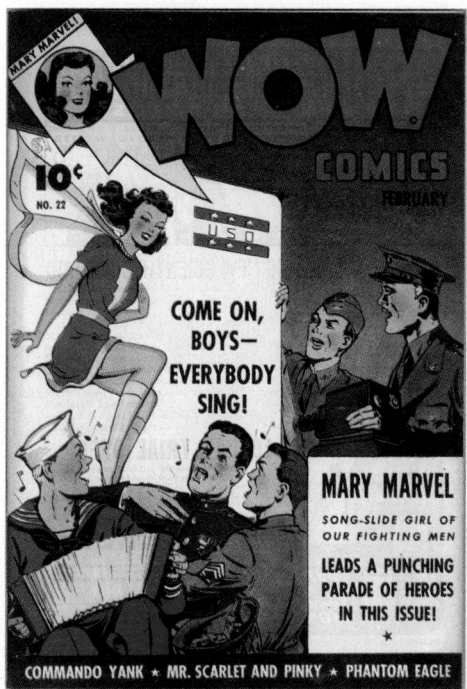

WOW COMICS #22
February 1944. © FAW

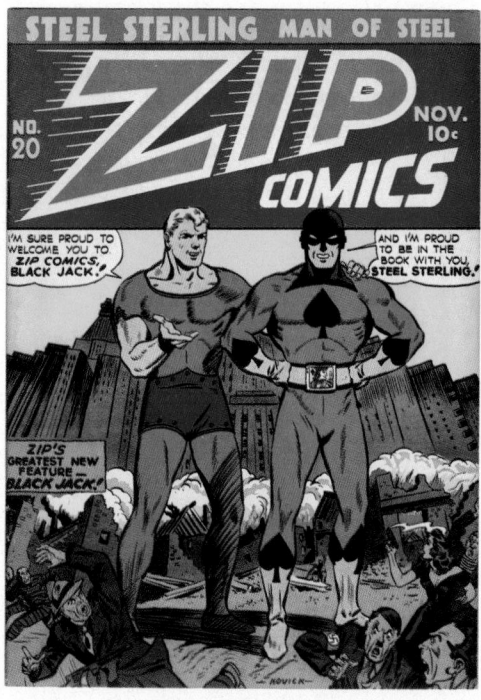

ZIP COMICS #20
November 1941. © MLJ

AMAZING SPIDER-MAN #37
June 1966. © MAR

BATMAN #207
December 1968. © DC

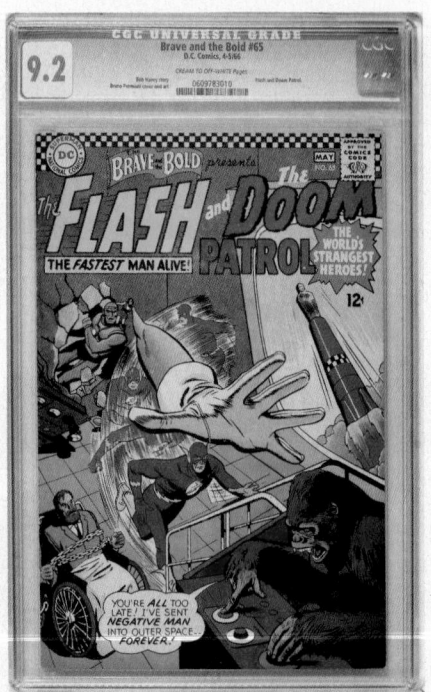

BRAVE AND THE BOLD #65
April-May 1966. © DC

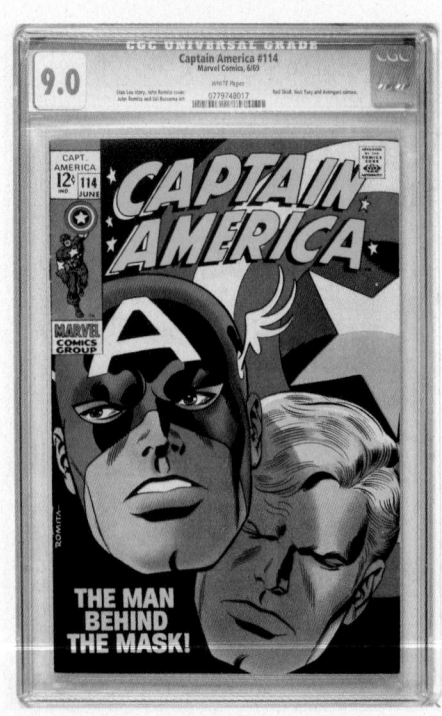

CAPTAIN AMERICA #114
June 1969. © MAR

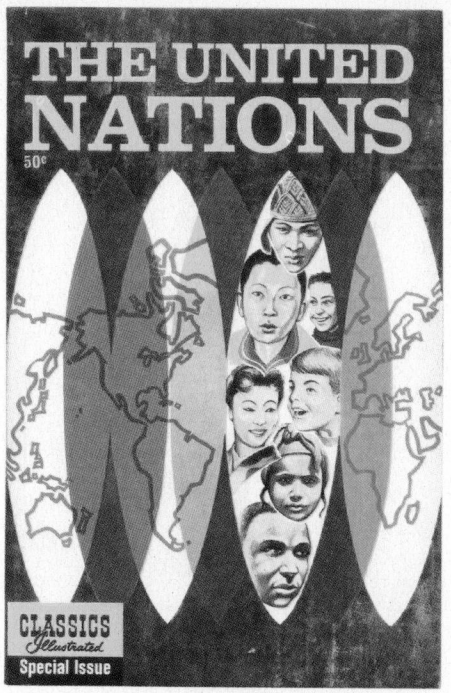

CLASSICS ILLUSTRATED SPECIAL ISSUE
1964. © GIL

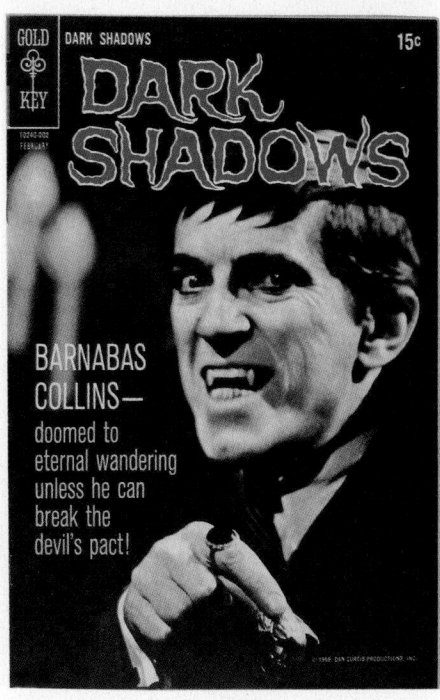

DARK SHADOWS #4
February 1970. © Dan Curtis Prods.

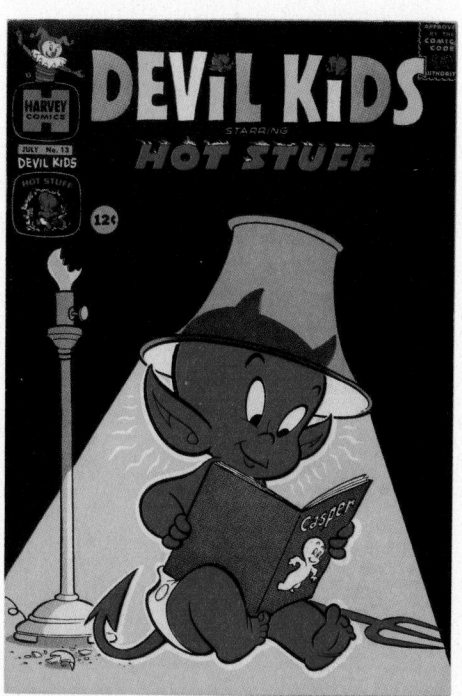

DEVIL KIDS STARRING HOT STUFF #13
July 1964. © Harvey

FANTASTIC FOUR #40
July 1965. © MAR

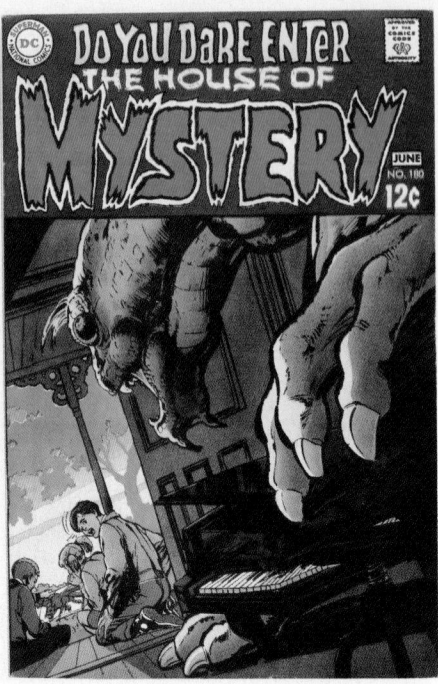

HOUSE OF MYSTERY #180
May-June 1969. © DC

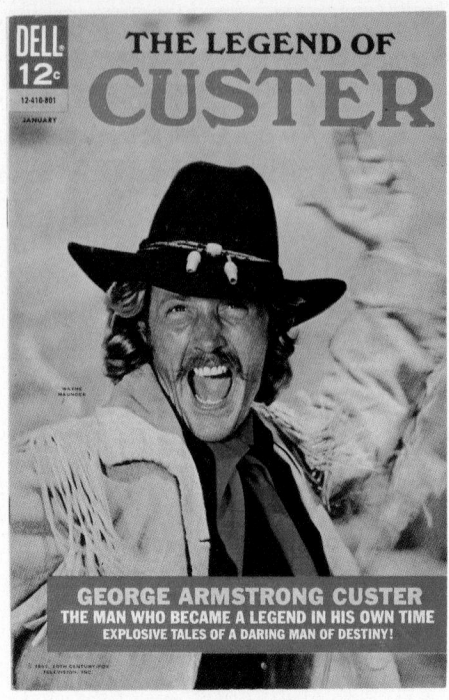

THE LEGEND OF CUSTER #1
January 1968. © 20th Century Fox

METAL MEN #7
April-May 1964. © DC

MOVIE CLASSICS - DIE, MONSTER, DIE!
March 1966. © Alta Vista Film

MY LOVE #2
November 1969. © MAR

**SGT. FURY AND HIS HOWLING
COMMANDOS ANNUAL #1**
1965. © MAR

**SUPERMAN'S PAL
JIMMY OLSEN #76**
April 1964. © DC

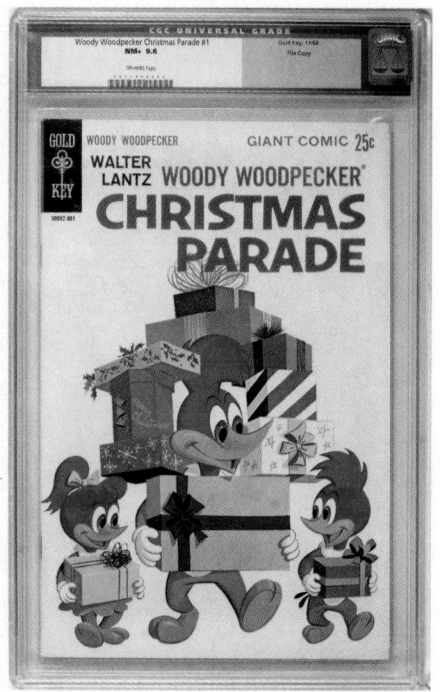

**WOODY WOODPECKER'S
CHRISTMAS PARADE #1**
November 1968. © Walter Lantz

AMAZING SPIDER-MAN #170
July 1977. © MAR

CONAN THE BARBARIAN #100
July 1979. © Conan Properties

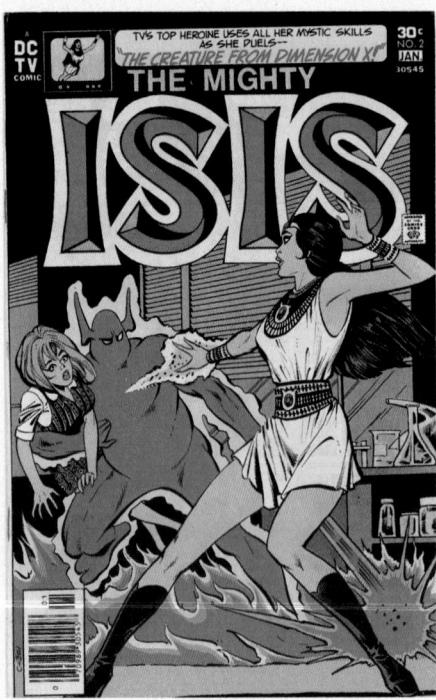

ISIS #2
January 1977. © DC

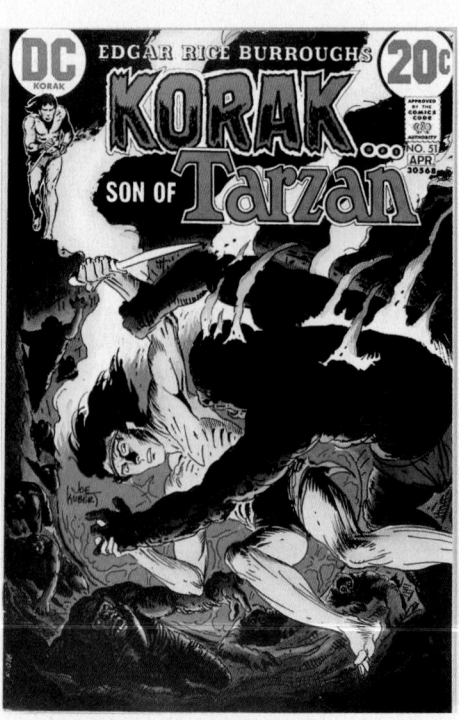

KORAK, SON OF TARZAN #51
March-April 1973. © ERB

STAR WARS #14
August 1978. © Lucasfilm, Ltd.

TOMB OF DRACULA #16
January 1974. © MAR

UNDERDOG #7
June 1976. © Leonardo TTV

WONDER WOMAN #207
August-September 1973. © DC

AMAZING SPIDER-MAN #328
January 1990. © MAR

BATMAN #408
June 1987. © DC

IRON MAN #228
March 1988. © MAR

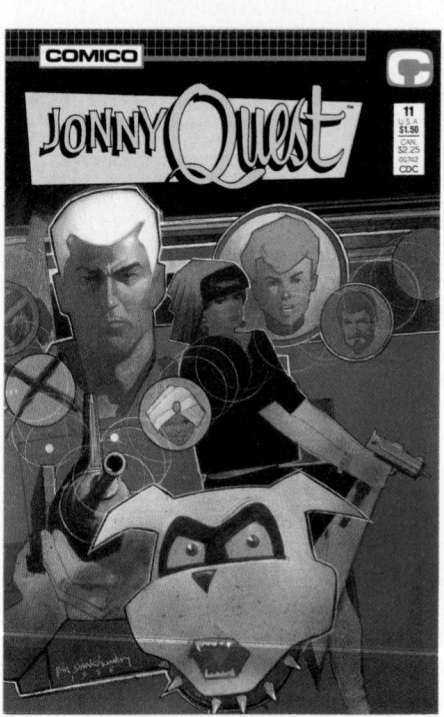

JONNY QUEST #11
April 1987. © H-B

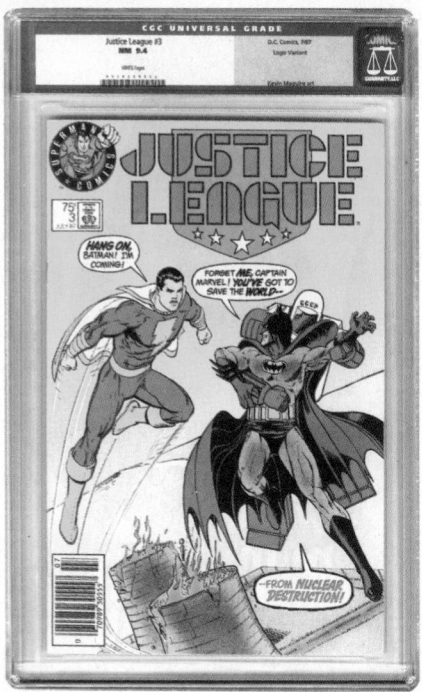

JUSTICE LEAGUE #3
July 1987. © DC

TEENAGE MUTANT NINJA TURTLES #8
1986. © Mirage Studios

**WALT DISNEY'S UNCLE SCROOGE
ADVENTURES #1**
November 1987. © DIS

WOLVERINE #13
October 1989. © MAR

ARCHIE'S LOVE SHOWDOWN SPECIAL #1
1994. © AP

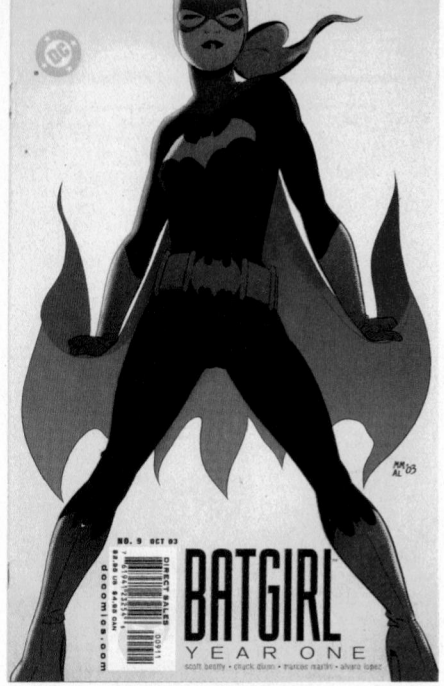

BATGIRL YEAR ONE #9
October 2003. © DC

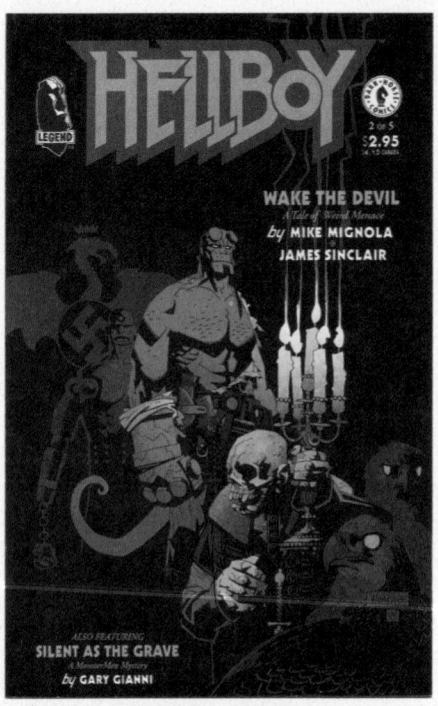

HELLBOY: WAKE THE DEVIL #2
July 1996. © Michael Mignola

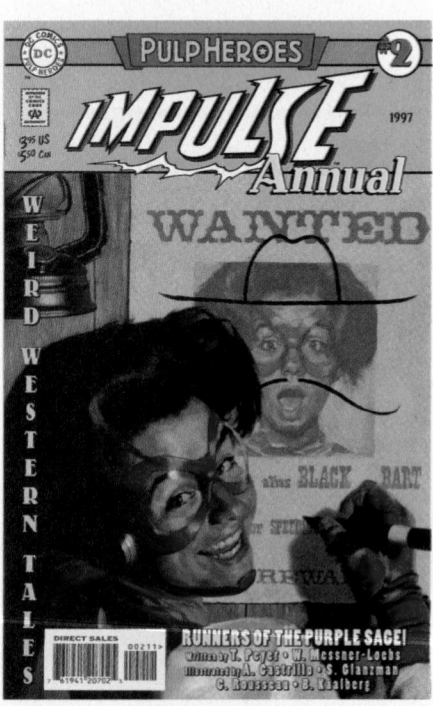

IMPULSE ANNUAL #2
1997. © DC

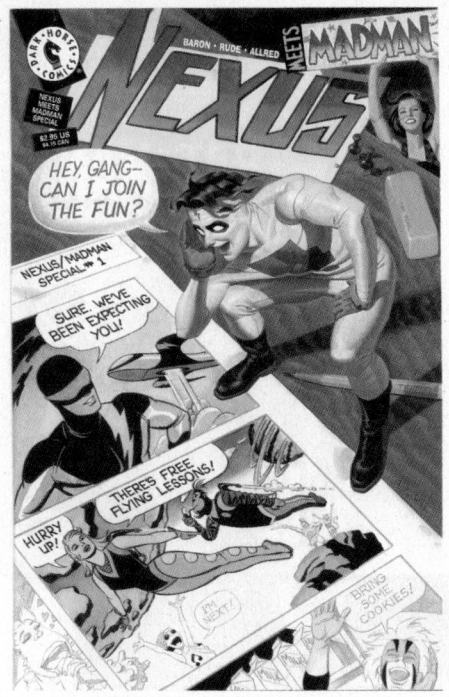

NEXUS MEETS MADMAN
May 1996. © Mike Baron, Steve Rude and Mike Allred

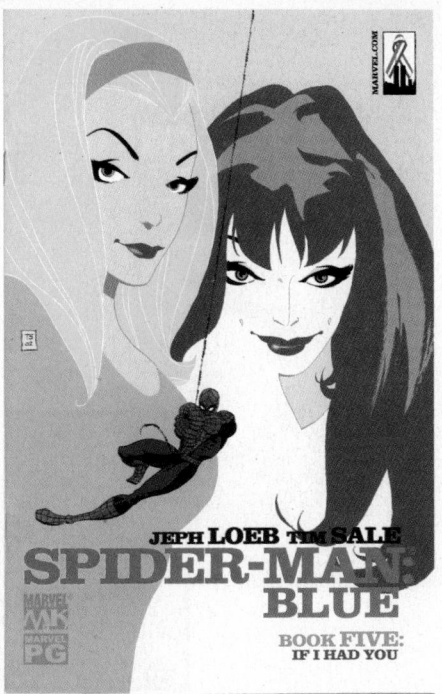

SPIDER-MAN: BLUE #5
November 2002. © MAR

THE WALKING DEAD #1
October 2003. © Robert Kirkman

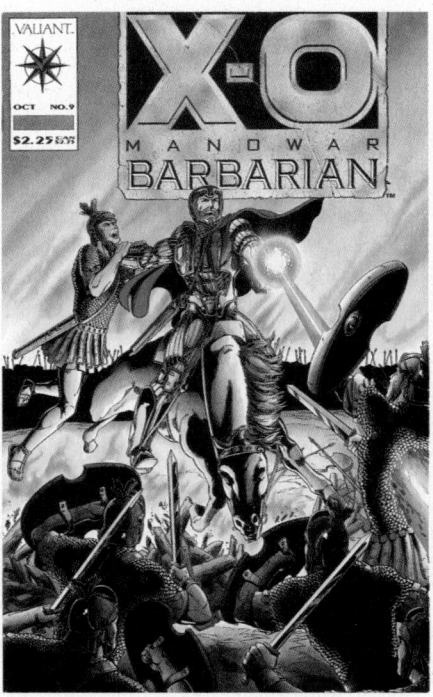

X-O MANOWAR #9
October 1992. © VAL

AMAZING FANTASY #15
August 1962. © MAR
Signed by Stan Lee

BATMAN #368
February 1984. © DC
Signed by Dick Giordano

CAPTAIN AMERICA (5th Series) #14
April 2006. © MAR
Signed by Joe Simon

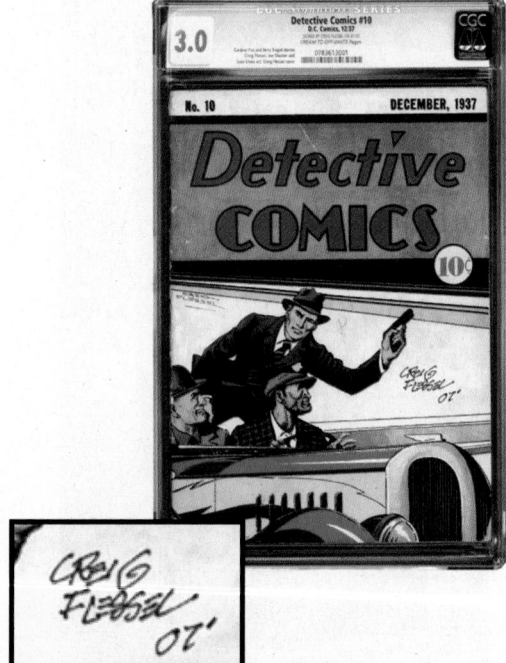

DETECTIVE COMICS #10
December 1937. © DC
Signed by Creig Flessel

DONATELLO, TEENAGE MUTANT NINJA TURTLE #1
August 1986. © Mirage Studios
Signed by Kevin Eastman

300 #1
May 1998. © Frank Miller
Signed by Frank Miller

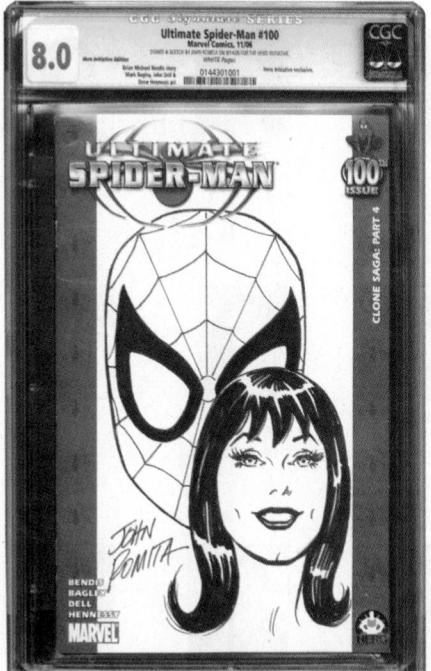

ULTIMATE SPIDER-MAN #100
HERO Initiative Edition. November 2006. © MAR
Signature and sketch by John Romita

X-MEN #40
January 1968. © MAR
Signed by Roy Thomas and George Tuska

Overstreet Advisors

WELDON ADAMS
Comics Historian
Fort Worth, TX

DAVID T. ALEXANDER
David Alexander Comics
Tampa, FL

TYLER ALEXANDER
David Alexander Comics
Tampa, FL

LON ALLEN
Heritage Comics Auctions
Dallas, TX

DAVE ANDERSON
Want List Comics
Tulsa, OK

STEPHEN BARRINGTON
Collector
Chickasaw, AL

LAUREN BECKER
Warp 9 Comics
Clawson, MI

ROBERT BEERBOHM
Robert Beerbohm Comic Art
Fremont, NE

JON BERK
Collector
Hartford, CT

PETER BILELIS, ESQ.
Collector
South Windsor, CT

BRIAN BLOCK
WB Auction Services
Adamstown, PA

DR. ARNOLD T. BLUMBERG
Curator
Geppi's Entertainment Museum

STEVE BOROCK
Primary Grader
Comics Guaranty, LLC

KEVIN BOYD
CGC Signature Series Director
Toronto, ONT Canada

MIKE BRODER
Tropic Comics
Fort Lauderdale, FL

MICHAEL BROWNING
Collector
Danville, WV

MICHAEL CARBONARO
Neatstuffcollectibles.com
Englewood, NJ

GARY CARTER
Collector
Coronado, CA

JOHN CHRUSCINSKI
Tropic Comics
Lyndora, PA

GARY COLABUONO
Dealer/Collector
Elk Grove Village, IL

BILL COLE
Bill Cole Enterprises, Inc.
Randolph, MA

TIM COLLINS
RTS Unlimited, Inc.
Lakewood, CO

JACK COPLEY
Archie Collector
Florida

DAN CUSIMANO
Flying Donut Trading Co.
Reston, VA

PETER DIXON
Paradise Comics
Toronto, ONT Canada

GARY DOLGOFF
Gary Dolgoff Comics
Easthampton, MA

BRUCE ELLSWORTH
Gold Coast Comics
Nerang, QLD, Australia

CONRAD ESCHENBERG
Collector/Dealer
Cold Spring, NY

MICHAEL EURY
Author
Lake Oswego, OR

RICHARD EVANS
Bedrock City Comics
Houston, TX

D'ARCY FARRELL
Pendragon Comics
Toronto, ONT Canada

STEPHEN FISHLER
Metropolis Collectibles, Inc.
New York, NY

DAN FOGEL
Hippy Comix, Inc.
El Sobrante, CA

CHRIS FOSS
Heroes & Dragons
Columbia, SC

STEVEN GENTNER
Golden Age Specialist
Portland, OR

STEVE GEPPI
Diamond Int. Galleries
Timonium, MD

Overstreet Advisors

MICHAEL GOLDMAN
Motor City Comics
Farmington Hills, MI

TOM GORDON III
Gemstone Publishing
Timonium, MD

JAMIE GRAHAM
Graham Crackers
Chicago, IL

DANIEL GREENHALGH
Showcase New England
Northford, CT

ERIC J. GROVES
Dealer/Collector
Oklahoma City, OK

JOHN HAINES
Dealer/Collector
Kirtland, OH

ROBERT HALL
Collector
Harrisburg, PA

JIM HALPERIN
Heritage Comics Auctions
Dallas, TX

MARK HASPEL
Grader
Comics Guaranty, LLC

JOHN HAUSER
Dealer/Collector
New Berlin, WI

GREG HOLLAND
Collector
Alexander, AR

BILL HUGHES
Dealer/Collector
Flower Mound, TX

ROB HUGHES
Arch Angels
Manhattan Beach, CA

WILLIAM INSIGNARES
Demolition Comics
Tampa, FL

ED JASTER
Heritage Comics Auctions
Dallas, TX

BRIAN KETTERER
Collector
Philadelphia, PA

DENNIS KEUM
Fantasy Comics
Goldens Bridge, NY

TIM KUPIN
Koop's Comics
Waldorf, MD

PHIL LEVINE
Dealer/Collector
Three Bridges, NJ

PAUL LITCH
Modern Age Specialist
Comics Guaranty, LLC

LARRY LOWERY
Big Little Books Specialist
Danville, CA

JOE MANNARINO
All Star Auctions
Ridgewood, NJ

NADIA MANNARINO
All Star Auctions
Ridgewood, NJ

HARRY MATETSKY
Collector
Middletown, NJ

DAVE MATTEINI
Collector
New York, NY

JON McCLURE
Dealer/Collector
Durango, CO

TODD MCDEVITT
New Dimension Comics
Cranberry Township, PA

MIKE McKENZIE
Alternate Worlds
Cockeysville, MD

FRED McSURLEY
Dealer/Collector
Holland, Ohio

PETER MEROLO
Collector
Sedona, AZ

JOHN JACKSON MILLER
Comics Historian, Writer
Waupaca, WI

STEVE MORTENSEN
Colossus Comics
Santa Clara, CA

MICHAEL NAIMAN
Silver Age Specialist
San Diego, CA

MARC NATHAN
Cards, Comics & Collectibles
Reisterstown, MD

JOSHUA NATHANSON
ComicLink
Brooklyn, NY

MATT NELSON
Classics Incorporated
Carrolltown, TX

Overstreet Advisors

CHARLIE NOVINSKIE
Silver Age Specialist
Grand Junction, CO

RICHARD OLSON
Collector/Academician
Poplarville, MS

TERRY O'NEILL
Terry's Comics
Orange, CA

GEORGE PANTELA
GPAnalysis for Comics
Hampton, Victoria, Australia

JIM PAYETTE
Golden Age Specialist
Bethlehem, NH

CHRIS PEDRIN
Pedrin Conservatory
Redwood City, CA

JOHN PETTY
Heritage Comics Auctions
Dallas, TX

JIM PITTS
Surf City Comix
Mountain View, CA

BILL PONSETI
Collector
Saucier, MS

RON PUSSELL
Redbeard's Book Den
Crystal Bay, NV

JO ANN REISLER
Collector
Vienna, VA

STEPHEN RITTER
Collector
Beavercreek, OH

DAVE ROBIE
Big Little Books Specialist
Lancaster, PA

ROBERT ROGOVIN
Four Color Comics
Scarsdale, NY

MARNIN ROSENBERG
Collectors Assemble
Great Neck, NY

CHUCK ROZANSKI
Mile High Comics
Denver, CO

MATT SCHIFFMAN
Bronze Age Specialist
Bend, OR

DOUG SCHMELL
Pedigree Comics, Inc.
Wellington, FL

JOHN SNYDER
Diamond Int. Galleries
Timonium, MD

TONY STARKS
Silver Age Specialist
Evansville, IN

WEST STEPHAN
Collector
Bradenton, FL

AL STOLTZ
Basement Comics
Havre de Grace, MD

KEN STRIBLING
Action Island
Jackson, MS

DOUG SULIPA
"Everything 1960-1996"
Manitoba, Canada

MAGGIE THOMPSON
Comics Buyer's Guide
Iola, WI

MICHAEL TIERNEY
The Comic Book Store
Little Rock, AR

TED VAN LIEW
Superworld Comics
Worcester, MA

JOE VERENEAULT
JHV Associates
Woodbury Heights, NJ

BOB WAYNE
DC Comics
New York City, NY

LON WEBB
Dark Adventure Comics
Norcross, GA

JERRY WEIST
Sotheby's
Gloucester, MA

MARK WILSON
PGC Mint
Castle Rock, WA

ALEX WINTER
Hake's Americana
Timonium, MD

HARLEY YEE
Dealer/Collector
Detroit, MI

MARK ZAID
EsquireComics.com
Bethesda, MD

VINCENT ZURZOLO, JR.
Metropolis Collectibles, Inc.
New York, NY

Overstreet Price Guide Back Issues

The Official Overstreet® Comic Book Price Guide has held the record for being the longest running annual comic book publication. We are now celebrating our 38th anniversary, and the demand for the Overstreet® price guides is very strong. Collectors have created a legitimate market for them, and they continue to bring record prices each year. Collectors also have a record of comic book prices going back further than any other source in comic fandom. The prices listed below are for NM condition only, with GD-25% and FN-50% of the NM value. Canadian editions exist for a couple of the early issues. Special thanks to Robert Rogovin of Four Color Comics for his assistance in researching the prices listed in this section.
Abbreviations: SC-softcover, HC-hardcover, L-leather bound.

1970	1970	1972	1973
#1 White SC $1800.00	#1 Blue SC (2nd Printing) $1500.00	#2 SC $650.00 #2 HC $1100.00	#3 SC $300.00 #3 HC $950.00

1974	1975	1976	1977
#4 SC $165.00 #4 HC $475.00	#5 SC $155.00 #5 HC $260.00	#6 SC $105.00 #6 HC $155.00	#7 SC $145.00 #7 HC $230.00

1978	1979	1980	1981
#8 SC $130.00 #8 HC $180.00	#9 SC $130.00 #9 HC $180.00	#10 SC $140.00 #10 HC $190.00	#11 SC $85.00 #11 HC $115.00

1982

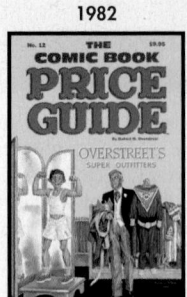

#12 SC $85.00
#12 HC $115.00

1983

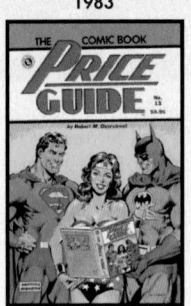

#13 SC $85.00
#13 HC $115.00

1984

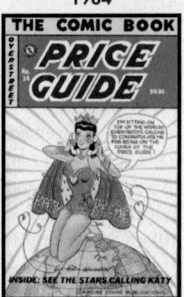

#14 SC $55.00
#14 HC $110.00
#14 L $170.00

1985

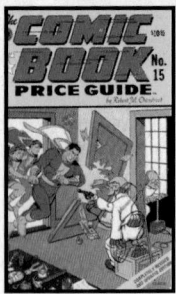

#15 SC $55.00
#15 HC $80.00
#15 L $160.00

1986

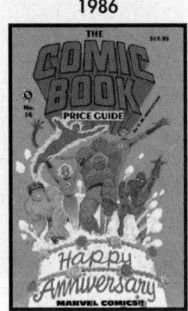

#16 SC $60.00
#16 HC $85.00
#16 L $170.00

1987

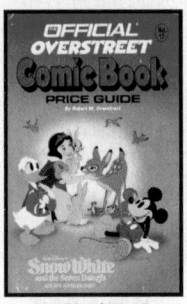

#17 SC $55.00
#17 HC $110.00
#17 L $160.00

1988

#18 SC $45.00
#18 HC $65.00
#18 L $160.00

1989

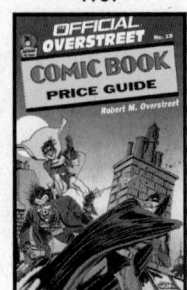

#19 SC $50.00
#19 HC $60.00
#19 L $170.00

1990

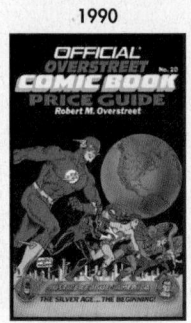

#20 SC $32.00
#20 HC $50.00
#20 L $135.00

1991

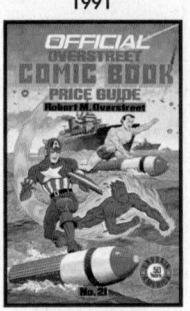

#21 SC $35.00
#21 HC $55.00
#21 L $145.00

1992

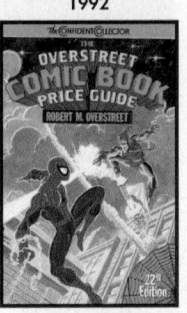

#22 SC $32.00
#22 HC $50.00

1993

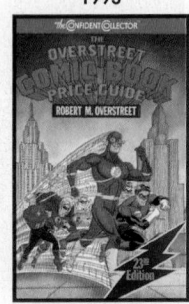

#23 SC $32.00
#23 HC $50.00

1994

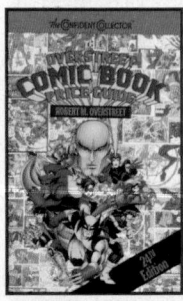

#24 SC $26.00
#24 HC $36.00

1995

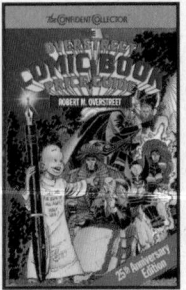

#25 SC $26.00
#25 HC $36.00
#25 L $110.00

1996

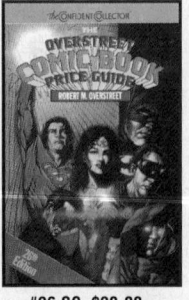

#26 SC $20.00
#26 HC $30.00
#26 L $100.00

1997

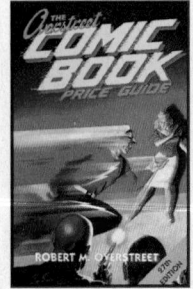

#27 SC $22.00
#27 HC $38.00
#27 L $125.00

1997

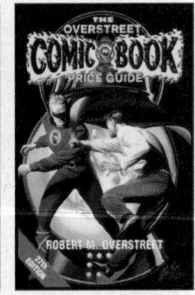

#27 SC $22.00
#27 HC $38.00
#27 L $125.00

1998

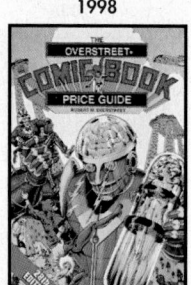

#28 SC $20.00
#28 HC $35.00

1998

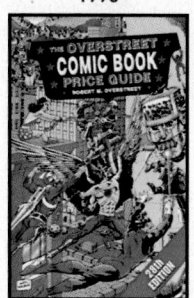

#28 SC $20.00
#28 HC $35.00

1999

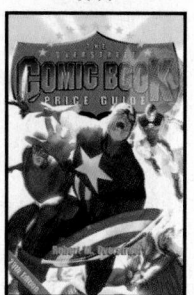

#29 SC $22.00
#29 HC $38.00

1999

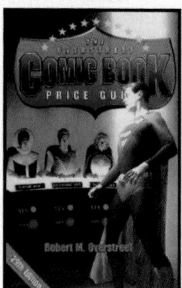

#29 SC $20.00
#29 HC $35.00

2000

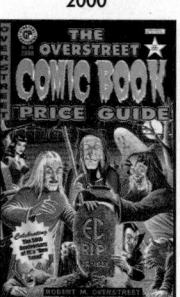

#30 SC $22.00
#30 HC $32.00

2000

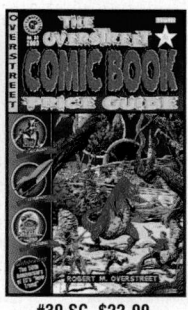

#30 SC $22.00
#30 HC $32.00

2001

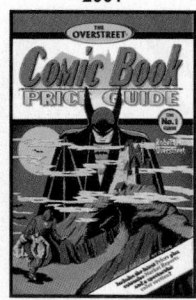

#31 SC $22.00
#31 HC $32.00

2001

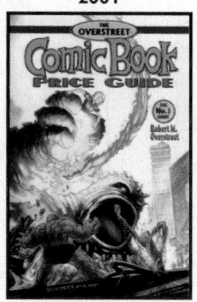

#31 SC $22.00
#31 HC $32.00

2001

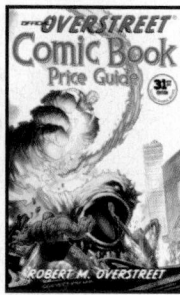

#31 Bookstore Ed.
SC only $22.00

2002

#32 SC $22.00
#32 HC $32.00

2002

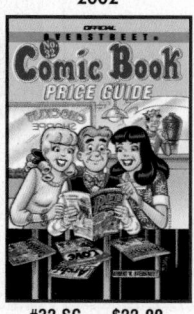

#32 SC $22.00
#32 HC $32.00

2002

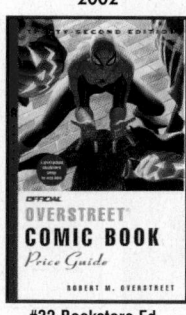

#32 Bookstore Ed.
SC only $22.00

2003

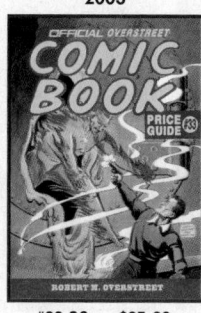

#33 SC $25.00
#33 HC $32.00

2003

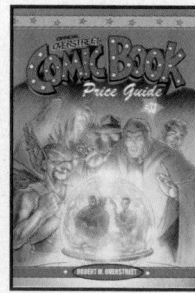

#33 SC $25.00
#33 HC $32.00

2003

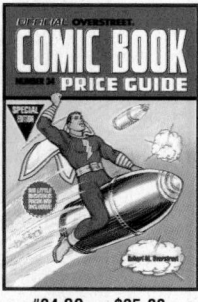

#33 Bookstore Ed.
SC only $25.00

2004

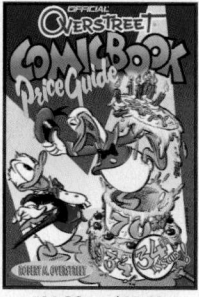

#34 SC $25.00
#34 HC $32.00

2004

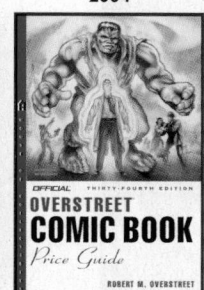

#34 SC $25.00
#34 HC $32.00

2004

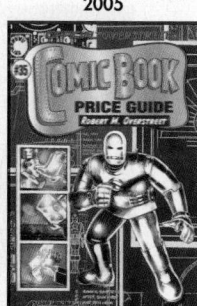

#34 Bookstore Ed.
SC only $25.00

2005

#35 SC $25.00
#35 HC $32.00

2005

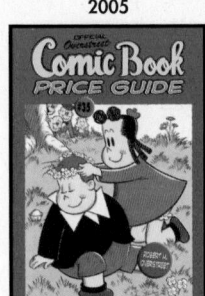

#35 SC $25.00
#35 HC $40.00

2005

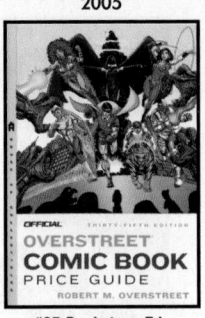

#35 Bookstore Ed.
SC only $25.00

2006

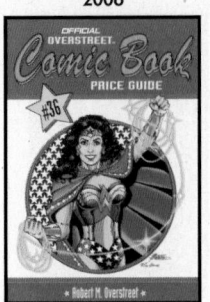

#36 SC $25.00
#36 HC $32.00

2006

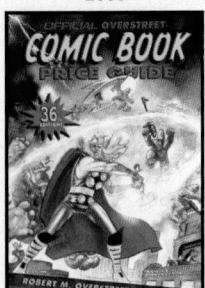

#36 SC $25.00
#36 HC $32.00

2006

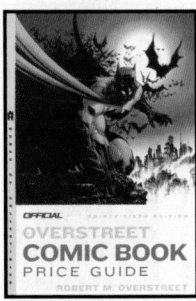

#36 Bookstore Ed.
SC only $25.00

2007

#37 SC $30.00
#37 HC $35.00

2007

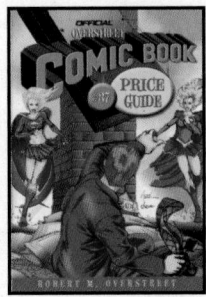

#37 SC $30.00
#37 HC $35.00

2007

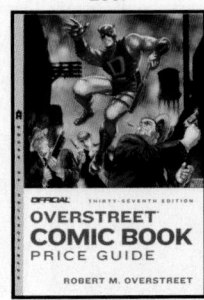

#37 Bookstore Ed.
SC only $30.00

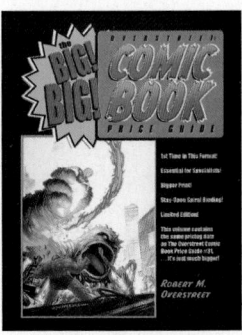

#31 Workbook - 2001
$35.00

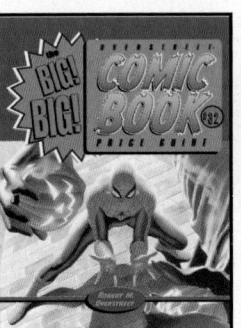

#32 Workbook - 2002
$35.00

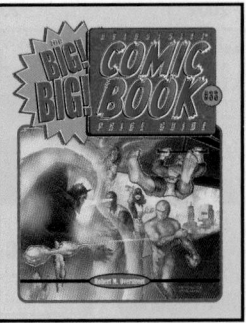

#33 Workbook - 2003
$37.00

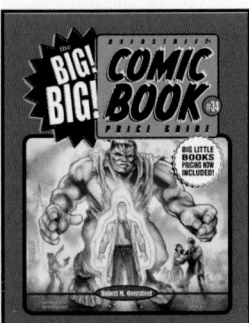

#34 Workbook - 2004
$37.00

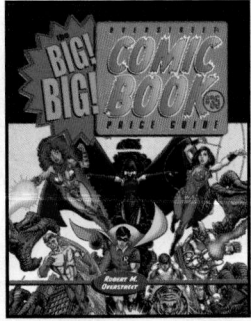

#35 Workbook - 2005
$37.00

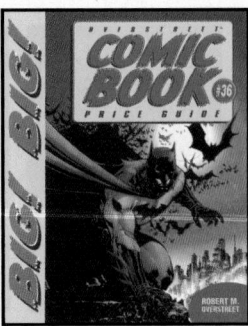

#36 Workbook - 2006
$37.00

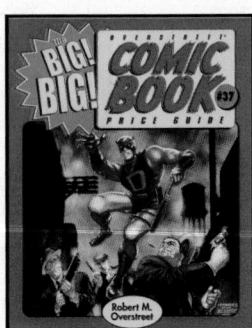

#37 Workbook - 2007
$37.00

Advertisers' Index

STEP BACK IN TIME
TO AN ERA OF SUPERB ARTISTRY AND IMAGINATION